PROPERTY OF
THE CARTER CENTER
RESOURCE ROOM
PLEASE DO NOT REMOVE
D1710078
Greenland
(DENMARK)
Alaska
(U.S.A.)
CANADA
REYKJAVÍK
ICELAND
OTTAWA
St Pierre &
Miquelon
(FRANCE)
UNITED STATES
OF AMERICA
Chicago
New York
WASHINGTON
Atlantic
Ocean
Los Angeles
Bermuda
(U.K.)
MEXICO
BAHAMAS
Turks &
Caicos Is
(U.K.)
Puerto
Rico
(U.S.A.)
British Virgin Is (U.K.)
U.S. Virgin Is (U.S.A.)
Anguilla (U.K.)
ST KITTS & NEVIS
ANTIGUA & BARBUDA
Montserrat (U.K.)
Guadeloupe (FRANCE)
DOMINICA
Martinique (FRANCE)
ST LUCIA
BARBADOS
ST VINCENT & THE GRENADINES
GRENADA
TRINIDAD
& TOBAGO
CAPE
VERDE
Hawaii
(U.S.A.)
Pacific
Ocean
MEXICO
CITY
BELIZE
Cayman Is.
(U.K.)
CUBA
DOM.
REP.
JAMAICA
HAITI
HONDURAS
GUATEMALA
EL SALVADOR
NICARAGUA
COSTA RICA
PANAMA
Aruba
(NETH.)
Neth.
Ant.
(NETH.)
CARACAS
VENEZUELA
GUYANA
SURINAME
French Guiana
(FRANCE)
BOGOTÁ
COLOMBIA
QUITO
ECUADOR
BRAZIL
LIMA
PERU
LA PAZ
BOLIVIA
BRASÍLIA
PARAGUAY
Rio de Janeiro
ASUNCIÓN
São Paulo
CHILE
SANTIAGO
ARGENTINA
URUGUAY
MONTEVIDEO
BUENOS
AIRES
Falkland
Islands
(U.K.)
South Georgia & the
South Sandwich Islands
(U.K.)
MARSHALL
IS
NAURU
KIRIBATI
SOLOMON
ISLANDS
TUVALU
Tokelau
(N.Z.)
Wallis &
Futuna Is
(FRANCE)
SAMOA
American
Samoa
(U.S.A.)
VANUATU
FIJI
TONGA
Niue
(N.Z.)
Cook Is
(N.Z.)
French Polynesia
(FRANCE)
Pitcairn Is
(U.K.)
Norfolk Is.
(AUSTRALIA)
NEW ZEALAND
WELLINGTON
Digital Cartography by: Map Creation Ltd
Woodlands Park Avenue,
Maidenhead, Berks., SL6 3LT

The Far East and Australasia 2003

The Far East and Australasia 2003

34th Edition

LONDON AND NEW YORK

First published 1969

Thirty-Third Edition 2003

11 New Fetter Lane, London, EC4P 4EE, England
(A member of the Taylor & Francis Group)

ISBN 1-85743-133-2
ISSN 0071-3791

Library of Congress Catalog Card Number 74-417170

Editor: Lynn Daniel
Associate Editor (South Asia): Priya Shah
Regional Organizations Editors: Catriona Appeatu Holman, Helen Canton
Statistics Editor: Andrew Thomas
Technology Editor: Ian Preston
Assistant Editors: Camilla Chew, Katie Dawson, Lucy Dean, Driss Fatih, Iain Frame, Anthony Gladman, Elizabeth Kerr, Catriona Marcham, Matthew Milton, Tiara Misquitta, Annamarie Rowe, Yoel Sano, Daniel Ward
Contributing Editors: Simon Chapman, David Lea (Commodities)
Editorial Co-ordinator: Mary Hill
Editorial Clerical Assistants: Zoë Hood, Haydon Lawrence

Typeset by MPG Dataworld and printed by Unwin Brothers Limited
The Gresham Press
Old Woking, Surrey

FOREWORD

The 34th edition of THE FAR EAST AND AUSTRALASIA encompasses a period of important developments in the region. East Timor finally acceded to full independence in May 2002, and in the same month Aung San Suu Kyi, leader of the opposition in Myanmar, was released from house arrest. The Australian Government's policy on asylum-seekers continued to attract much attention, while several of the Pacific Islands experienced political upheaval during 2002, notably Papua New Guinea. In Afghanistan the Taliban regime was removed in late 2001, leading to a period of much uncertainty.

A new article by Rohan Gunaratna examines Current Security Issues in Asia, a subject brought dramatically to the fore in October 2002 by the devastating bomb attack on the Indonesian island of Bali and by renewed international concerns regarding North Korea's nuclear programme. Meanwhile, the Kashmir issue had again brought India and Pakistan to the brink of war, with both countries claiming to have deployed nuclear missiles. In Sri Lanka, however, in a significant development that was largely overshadowed by events elsewhere, the separatist Tamil Tigers renounced their claim for full independence in favour of autonomy proposals, thus giving rise to genuine hopes of a peaceful settlement of the island's long-running conflict.

All essays are updated annually by specialist authors and researchers. The statistical surveys, directories and bibliographies have also been extensively revised. A calendar of the key political events between November 2001 and October 2002 provides a convenient reference guide to the developments of the last 12 months. Extensive coverage of international organizations and their recent activities in the Far East and Australasia is provided, along with a directory of research institutes and a general bibliography. Information on the region's major commodities is also included. This edition contains a completely new section on coffee, reflecting in particular Viet Nam's rapid emergence as a leading world producer.

The editors are once again grateful to all the contributors for their articles and advice and to the numerous governments and organizations that have returned questionnaires and provided statistical and other information.

October 2002

ACKNOWLEDGEMENTS

The editors gratefully acknowledge the co-operation, interest and advice of all the authors who have contributed to this volume. We are also greatly indebted to innumerable organizations connected with the Asia-Pacific region, especially the national statistical and information offices, whose valued co-operation in providing information is greatly appreciated.

We are particularly grateful for the use of material from the following sources: the UN's *Statistical Yearbook, Statistical Yearbook for Asia and the Pacific, Demographic Yearbook, Industrial Commodity Statistics Yearbook, National Accounts Statistics* and *International Trade Statistics Yearbook*; the *UNESCO Statistical Yearbook*; FAO's Statistical Database, *Yearbook of Forest Products* and *Yearbook of Fishery Statistics*; the ILO's *Yearbook of Labour Statistics*; the IMF's *Government Finance Statistics Yearbook* and monthly *International Financial Statistics*; the World Bank's *World Bank Atlas, Global Development Finance, World Development Report* and *World Development Indicators*; the World Tourism Organization's *Yearbook of Tourism Statistics*; and the Asian Development Bank's *Asian Development Outlook* and *Key Indicators of Developing Asian and Pacific Countries*. We are also grateful to the International Institute for Strategic Studies, Arundel House, 13–15 Arundel Street, London, WC2R 3DX, United Kingdom, for the use of defence statistics from *The Military Balance 2001–2002*.

The following publications have been of special value in providing regular coverage of the affairs of the Asian and Pacific region: *The Far Eastern Economic Review*, and its *Asia Yearbook*, Hong Kong; *IMF Survey*, Washington, DC, USA; and *Keesing's Record of World Events*, Cambridge, United Kingdom.

HEALTH AND WELFARE STATISTICS: SOURCES AND DEFINITIONS

Fertility Source: WHO, *The World Health Report* (2001). The number of children that would be born per woman, assuming no female mortality at child-bearing ages and the age-specific fertility rates of a specified country and reference period.

Under-5 mortality rate Source: UNDP, *Human Development Report* (2002). The ratio of registered deaths of children under 5 years to the total number of registered live births over the same period.

HIV/AIDS Source: UNDP, *Human Development Report* (2002). Estimated percentage of adults aged 15 to 49 years living with HIV/AIDS. < indicates 'fewer than'.

Health expenditure Source: WHO, *The World Health Report* (2001).
US $ per head (PPP)
International dollar estimates, derived by dividing local currency units by an estimate of their purchasing-power parity (PPP) compared with the US dollar. PPPs are the rates of currency conversion that equalize the purchasing power of different currencies by eliminating the differences in price levels between countries.
% of GDP
GDP levels for OECD countries follow the most recent UN System of National Accounts. For non-OECD countries a value was estimated by utilizing existing UN, IMF and World Bank data.
Public expenditure
Government health-related outlays plus expenditure by social schemes compulsorily affiliated with a sizeable share of the population, and extrabudgetary funds allocated to health services. Figures include grants or loans provided by international agencies, other national authorities, and sometimes commercial banks.

Access to water and sanitation Source: WHO, *Global Water Supply and Sanitation Assessment* (2000 Report). Defined in terms of the type of technology and levels of service afforded. For water, this includes house connections, public standpipes, boreholes with handpumps, protected dug wells, protected spring and rainwater collection; allowance is also made for other locally defined technologies. 'Access' is broadly defined as the availability of at least 20 litres per person per day from a source within 1 km of the user's dwelling. Sanitation is defined to include connection to a sewer or septic tank system, pour-flush latrine, simple pit or ventilated improved pit latrine, again with allowance for acceptable local technologies. Access to water and sanitation does not imply that the level of service or quality of water is 'adequate' or 'safe'.

Human Development Index (HDI) Source: UNDP, *Human Development Report* (2002). A summary of human development measured by three basic dimensions: prospects for a long and healthy life, measured by life expectancy at birth; knowledge, measured by adult literacy rate (two-thirds' weight) and the combined gross enrolment ratio in primary, secondary and tertiary education (one-third weight); and standard of living, measured by GDP per head (PPP US $). The index value obtained lies between zero and one. A value above 0.8 indicates high human development, between 0.5 and 0.8 medium human development, and below 0.5 low human development. Countries with insufficient data were excluded from the HDI. In total, 173 countries were ranked for 2000.

CONTENTS

CONTENTS

CONTENTS

PART THREE

Regional Information

List of Maps

Index of Territories

THE CONTRIBUTORS

Zachary Abuza. Assistant Professor of Political Science and International Relations, Simmons College, Boston, USA.

Ahmed Mukarram. Former Resident Fellow, Rajiv Gandhi Institute for Contemporary Studies, Rajiv Gandhi Foundation, New Delhi, India.

Rokiah Alavi. Assistant Professor, Department of Economics, International Islamic University, Kuala Lumpur, Malaysia.

Bryant J. Allen. Senior Fellow, Department of Human Geography, Research School of Pacific and Asian Studies, The Australian National University, Canberra, Australia.

Frédéric Angleviel. Senior Lecturer in Contemporary History, University of New Caledonia, New Caledonia.

Robert Ash. Senior Lecturer, Department of Economics, School of Oriental and African Studies, University of London, United Kingdom.

Simon Baker. Formerly of the Demography Program, Research School of Social Sciences, The Australian National University, Canberra, Australia.

Lok Raj Baral. Former Professor, Department of Political Science, Tribhuvan University, Kathmandu, Nepal.

Sanjaya Baru. Editor, The Financial Express, New Delhi, India.

Ian Brown. Reader, South-East Asian Economic History, School of Oriental and African Studies, University of London, United Kingdom.

T. Louise Brown. Lecturer in Asian Studies, The Japan Centre, University of Birmingham, United Kingdom.

Jenny J. Bryant. Former Reader, Geography Department, University of the South Pacific, Suva, Fiji.

Joseph S. Chung. Professor Emeritus of Economics, Stuart School of Business, Illinois Institute of Technology, Chicago, USA.

Lesley Connors. Department of Politics, School of Oriental and African Studies, University of London, United Kingdom.

Robert Cribb. Senior Fellow, Research School of Pacific and Asian Studies, The Australian National University, Canberra, Australia.

Harvey Demaine. Associate Professor of Regional, Rural and Agricultural Development Planning, Asian Institute of Technology, Bangkok, Thailand.

Chris Dixon. Professor, Department of Politics and Modern History, London Guildhall University, London, United Kingdom.

Tilak Doshi. Fellow, Institute of Southeast Asian Studies, Singapore.

Chris Edwards. Former Senior Lecturer, School of Development Studies, University of East Anglia, Norwich, United Kingdom.

B. H. Farmer. Late Former Director, Centre of South Asian Studies, University of Cambridge, United Kingdom.

W. B. Fisher. Late Professor of Geography, University of Durham, United Kingdom.

C. P. Fitzgerald. Late Emeritus Professor, The Australian National University, Canberra, Australia.

Dean Forbes. Pro Vice-Chancellor (International) and Professor, School of Geography, Population and Environmental Management, Flinders University, Adelaide, Australia.

Aidan Foster-Carter. Honorary Senior Research Fellow in Sociology and Modern Korea, University of Leeds, United Kingdom.

Michael Freeberne. Former Lecturer in Geography, School of Oriental and African Studies, University of London, United Kingdom.

Nick Freeman. Associate Senior Fellow, Institute of Southeast Asian Studies, Singapore.

François Gipouloux. Senior Research Fellow, Centre d'études sur la Chine moderne et contemporaine, Ecole des Hautes Etudes en Sciences Sociales, Paris, France.

Jeanine Graham. Senior Lecturer in History, University of Waikato, Hamilton, New Zealand.

Rohan Gunaratna. Senior Research Fellow, Centre for the Study of Terrorism and Political Violence, University of St Andrews, Scotland, United Kingdom.

Sok Hach. Economist, Cambodia Development Resource Institute, Phnom-Penh, Cambodia.

I. R. Hancock. Former Reader in History, The Australian National University, Canberra, Australia.

Hans Hendrischke. Associate Professor and Head, Department of Chinese and Indonesian Studies, The University of New South Wales, Sydney, Australia.

Sarwar O. H. Hobohm. Former Senior Economist/Editor, Asia-Pacific, Country Analysis and Forecasting Division, The Economist Intelligence Unit, London, United Kingdom.

Edith Hodgkinson. Economic journalist specializing in developing countries, London, United Kingdom.

Athar Hussain. Deputy Director, Asia Research Centre, London School of Economics and Political Science, University of London, United Kingdom.

Kenneth E. Jackson. Deputy Head of Department, Economics Department, University of Auckland, New Zealand.

Santosh Jatrana. Asian MetaCentre for Population and Sustainable Development, Asia Research Institute, National University of Singapore, Singapore.

Patrick Jory. Lecturer, School of Asian Studies, The University of Western Australia, Nedlands, Western Australia.

Mushtaq H. Khan. Lecturer, Department of Economics, School of Oriental and African Studies, London, United Kingdom.

Frank H. H. King. Former Professor of Economic History, The University of Hong Kong, Hong Kong.

Bruce Koepke. Research Scholar, Centre for Arab and Islamic Studies (the Middle East and Central Asia), The Australian National University, Canberra, Australia.

Bruce Henry Lambert. Affiliate Professor and Director of Network Development, European Institute of Japanese Studies, Stockholm School of Economics, Stockholm, Sweden.

Philip E. T. Lewis. Director, Centre for Labour Market Research, Murdoch University, Western Australia.

Adam McCarty. Economic Consultant, Hanoi, Viet Nam.

Allister McGregor. Former Lecturer in Development Studies, School of Social Sciences, University of Bath, United Kingdom.

A. E. McQueen. Former Assistant General Manager, New Zealand Government Railways, New Zealand.

Ruth McVey. Emeritus Reader in Politics with reference to South-East Asia, School of Oriental and African Studies, University of London, United Kingdom.

William Maley. Associate Professor of Politics, University College, University of New South Wales, Australian Defence Force Academy, Canberra, Australia.

Peter Marsden. Writer on Afghanistan affairs, London, United Kingdom.

John McGuire. Associate Professor, Department of Social Sciences, Curtin University of Technology, Perth, Australia.

N. J. Miners. Former Reader in Political Science, Department of Politics and Public Administration, The University of Hong Kong, Hong Kong.

Sharif al Mujahid. Former Head, Department of Communication, International Islamic University, Petaling Jaya, Malaysia.

Murni Mohamed. Director, Department of Economic Planning and Development, Ministry of Finance, Bandar Seri Begawan, Brunei.

Andrew C. Nahm. Former Professor Emeritus of History and Consultant to the Office of International Education and Programs, Western Michigan University, USA.

Neville Norman. Professor, Department of Economics, University of Melbourne, Australia.

Geoffrey Parrinder. Emeritus Professor of the Comparative Study of Religions, University of London, United Kingdom.

Gavin Peebles. Former Associate Professor, Department of Economics, The National University of Singapore, Singapore.

G. H. Peiris. Professor, Department of Geography, University of Peradeniya, Sri Lanka.

Sorpong Peou. Associate Professor of Political Science/International Relations, Faculty of Comparative Culture, Sophia University, Tokyo, Japan.

Michael Pinches. Senior Lecturer, Department of Anthropology, The University of Western Australia, Nedlands, Western Australia.

Qazi Masood Ahmed. Associate Professor of the Institute of Business Administration, Technical Adviser, Social Policy and Development Centre, Karachi, Pakistan.

Peter Robb. Professor and Head, Department of History, South Asia, School of Oriental and African Studies, University of London, United Kingdom.

J. W. Rowe. Former Director-General, New Zealand Employers' Federation, New Zealand.

S. W. R. de A. Samarasinghe. Professor, Tulane University of Louisiana, New Orleans, USA, and Director, International Centre for Ethnic Studies, Kandy, Sri Lanka.

Alan J. K. Sanders. Mongolist, Reading, United Kingdom.

John Sargent. Reader in Geography, School of Oriental and African Studies, University of London, United Kingdom.

Asad Sayeed. Research Director, Pakistan Institute of Labour, Education and Research, Karachi, Pakistan.

Brian Shaw. Honorary Research Fellow, Centre of Asian Studies, The University of Hong Kong, Hong Kong.

Kingsley M. de Silva. Executive Director, International Centre for Ethnic Studies, Kandy, Sri Lanka.

Josef Silverstein. Former Professor Emeritus of Political Science, Rutgers University, New Brunswick, USA.

Ralph Smith. Professor of the History of South-East Asia, School of Oriental and African Studies, University of London, United Kingdom.

Ross Steele. Lecturer and Director, Graduate Program in Population and Human Resources, School of Geography, Population and Environmental Management, Flinders University, Adelaide, Australia.

Richard Storry. Late Director of the Far East Centre, Oxford, United Kingdom.

Martin Stuart-Fox. Professor and Head of Department, Department of History, The University of Queensland, Brisbane, Australia.

Laura Summers. Lecturer, Department of Politics and Asian Studies, University of Hull, United Kingdom.

Ian Talbot. Professor, South Asian Studies, School of International Studies and Law, Coventry University, United Kingdom.

James Tang. Associate Professor and Head, Department of Politics and Public Administration, University of Hong Kong, Hong Kong.

David Taylor. Vice-Provost (Academic Development and Special Projects), Aga Khan University, Karachi, Pakistan.

Christopher Torrens. Freelance writer, Shanghai, People's Republic of China.

Hajah Rosni Haji Tungkat. Acting Director, Department of Economic Planning and Development, Ministry of Finance, Bandar Seri Begawan, Brunei.

C. M. Turnbull. Honorary Research Fellow, Centre for Asian Studies, and Former Professor of History, The University of Hong Kong, Hong Kong.

Marika Vicziany. Associate Professor and Interim Director, Monash Asia Institute, Head, Asian Economics Research Unit, Director, National Centre for South Asian Studies, Monash University, Clayton, Victoria, Australia.

Richard Vokes. Former Lecturer in Economics and South-East Asian Studies, Centre of South-East Asian Studies, University of Kent at Canterbury, United Kingdom.

Michael Williams. Reader in Geography and Fellow of Oriel College, University of Oxford, United Kingdom.

Michael Yahuda. Professor, Department of International Relations, London School of Economics and Political Science, University of London, United Kingdom.

Akira Yamazaki. Former Editorial Writer, *Nihon Keizai Shimbun* (Japan Economic Journal), Tokyo, Japan.

Malcolm E. Yapp. Former Professor of the History of West Asia, School of Oriental and African Studies, University of London, United Kingdom.

ABBREVIATIONS

Acad.	Academician; Academy
ACP	African, Caribbean and Pacific (States)
ACT	Australian Capital Territory
AD	Anno Domini
ADB	Asian Development Bank
Adm.	Admiral
Admin.	Administration, Administrative, Administrator
AFTA	ASEAN Free Trade Area
AG	Aktiengesellschaft (limited company)
a.i.	ad interim
AIDS	acquired immunodeficiency syndrome
Alt.	Alternate
AM	Amplitude Modulation
ANZUS	Australia, New Zealand and the United States
Apdo	Apartado (Post Box)
APEC	Asia-Pacific Economic Co-operation
approx.	approximately
Apt	Apartment
AR	Autonomous Region
ARF	ASEAN Regional Forum
ASEAN	Association of South East Asian Nations
Asscn	Association
Assoc.	Associate
Asst	Assistant
Aug.	August
auth.	authorized
Avda	Avenida (Avenue)
Ave	Avenue
BC	Before Christ
Bd	Board
b/d	barrels per day
Bhd	Berhad (public limited company)
BIS	Bank for International Settlements
Bldg(s)	Building(s)
Blk	Block
Blvd	Boulevard
BOT	build-operate-transfer
BP	Boîte Postale (Post Box)
br.(s)	branch(es)
Brig.	Brigadier
C	Centigrade
c.	circa
cap.	capital
Capt.	Captain
CCP	Chinese Communist Party
Cdre	Commodore
Cen.	Central
CEO	Chief Executive Officer
cf.	confer (compare)
CFC	chlorofluorocarbon
CFP	Communauté française du Pacifique
Chair.	Chairman/Chairwoman
CIA	(US) Central Intelligence Agency
Cie	Compagnie
c.i.f.	cost, insurance and freight
C-in-C	Commander-in-Chief
circ.	circulation
CIS	Commonwealth of Independent States
cm	centimetre(s)
CMEA	Council for Mutual Economic Assistance (COMECON)
cnr	corner
c/o	care of
Co	Company
Col	Colonel
Comm.	Commission
Commdr	Commander
Commdt	Commandant
Commr	Commissioner
Conf.	Conference
Confed.	Confederation
Corpn	Corporation
CP	Case Postale, Caixa Postal (Post Box)
CPO	Central Post Office
Cttee	Committee
cu	cubic
cwt	hundredweight
Dec.	December
Dem.	Democratic
Dep.	Deputy
dep.	deposit(s)
Dept	Department
Devt	Development
Dir	Director
Div.	Division
DPRK	Democratic People's Republic of Korea
Dr	Doctor
Dra	Doutora (Doctor)
DRAM	dynamic random access memory
Drs	Doctorandus (Netherlands doctor's degree)
dwt	dead weight tons
E	East, Eastern
EAEC	East Asia Economic Caucus
EAGA	East ASEAN Growth Area
EC	European Community
ECU	European Currency Unit(s)
Ed.(s)	Editor(s)
Edif.	Edifício (Building)
edn	edition
e.g.	exempli gratia (for example)
Eng.	Engineer; Engineering
EPZ	Export Processing Zone
ESCAP	Economic and Social Commission for Asia and the Pacific
est.	established; estimate, estimated
etc.	etcetera
EU	European Union
excl.	excluding
Exec.	Executive
exhbn(s)	exhibition(s)
Ext.	Extension
f.	founded
FAO	Food and Agriculture Organization
FDI	foreign direct investment
Feb.	February
Fed.	Federal, Federation
Flt	Flight
FM	Frequency Modulation
fmr(ly)	former(ly)
f.o.b.	free on board
Fr	Father
Fri.	Friday
ft	foot (feet)
g	gram(s)
GATT	General Agreement on Tariffs and Trade
GDP	Gross Domestic Product
Gen.	General
GNP	Gross National Product
Gov.	Governor
Govt	Government
GPO	General Post Office
grt	gross registered tons
GSP	gross state product
GWh	gigawatt hour(s)
ha	hectare(s)
HDI	human development index
HE	His (or Her) Excellency; His Eminence
HH	His (or Her) Highness; His Holiness
HIV	human immunodeficiency virus
hl	hectolitre(s)
HM	His (or Her) Majesty
HMS	His (or Her) Majesty's Ship
HMSO	Her Majesty's Stationery Office
Hon.	Honorary
hp	horsepower
HQ	Headquarters
hr(s)	hour(s)
HRH	His (or Her) Royal Highness
HYV	high-yielding variety
ibid.	ibidem (from the same source)
IBRD	International Bank for Reconstruction and Development (World Bank)
i.e.	id est (that is to say)
ILO	International Labour Organization
IMF	International Monetary Fund
in	inch(es)
Inc	Incorporated
incl.	including
Inst.	Institute
Int.	International
IPCC	Intergovernmental Panel on Climate Change
Ir	Insinyur (Engineer)

ABBREVIATIONS

IRF	International Road Federation
Is	Islands
ISIC	International Standard Industrial Classification
Jan.	January
Jr	Junior
Jt	Joint
Jtly	Jointly
K	kina (Papua New Guinea currency)
kg	kilogram(s)
kHz	kilohertz
KK	Kaien Kaisha (limited company)
km	kilometre(s)
kW	kilowatt(s)
kWh	kilowatt hour(s)
lb	pound(s)
LDC	less-developed country
LNG	liquefied natural gas
LPG	liquefied petroleum gas
Lt	Lieutenant
Ltd	Limited
m	metre(s)
m.	million
Maj.	Major
Man.	Manager, Managing
MCPO	Manila Central Post Office
mem.	member
mfg	manufacturing
mfr(s)	manufacturer(s)
mg	milligram
Mgr	Monseigneur, Monsignor
MHz	megahertz
MIA	Missing in Action
Mil.	Military
Mlle	Mademoiselle
mm	millimetre(s)
Mme	Madame
Mon.	Monday
MP	Member of Parliament
Mt	Mount
MV	Motor Vessel
MW	megawatt(s)
MWh	megawatt hour(s)
N	North, Northern
n.a.	not available
NAFTA	North American Free Trade Agreement
Nat.	National
NCO	Non-Commissioned Officer
n.e.s.	not elsewhere specified
NGO	non-governmental organization
NIC	newly-industrializing country
NIE	newly-industrializing economy
No.	number
Nov.	November
NR	Nepalese Rupee(s)
nr	near
nrt	net registered tons
NSW	New South Wales
NT	Northern Territory
NV	Naamloze Vennootschap (limited company)
NZ	New Zealand
Oct.	October
OECD	Organisation for Economic Co-operation and Development
OER	official exchange rate
OPEC	Organization of Petroleum Exporting Countries
opp.	opposite
Ord.	ordinary
Org.(s)	Organization(s)
oz	ounce(s)
p(p).	page(s)
p.a.	per annum
Parl.	Parliament(ary)
PB	Private Bag
Perm.	Permanent
PLC	Public Limited Company
PMB	Private Mail Bag
PNG	Papua New Guinea
PO	Post Office
POB	Post Office Box
PPP	purchasing power parity
Pres.	President
Prin.	Principal
Prof.	Professor
Propr	Proprietor
Prov.	Province, Provincial
PT	Perseroan Terbatas (limited company)
Pt	Point
Pte	Private
Pty	Proprietary
p.u.	paid up
publ.(s)	publication(s); published
Publr	Publisher
Pvt	Private
Qld	Queensland
q.v.	quod vide (to which refer)
R(s)	Rupee(s)
R & D	research and development
Rd	Road
regd	registered
Rep.	Representative
Repub.	Republic
res	reserves
retd	retired
Rev.	Reverend
Rm	Room
RM	Ringgit Malaysia
ro-ro	roll-on roll-off
Rp.	Rupiah (Indonesian currency)
Rt	Right
S	South, Southern
SA	South Australia; Société anonyme, Sociedad Anónima (limited company)
SAARC	South Asian Association for Regional Co-operation
SAR	Special Administrative Region
SARL	Sociedade Anônima de Responsibilidade Limitada (limited company)
Sat.	Saturday
Sdn Bhd	Sendirian Berhad (private limited company)
SDR	Special Drawing Right(s)
SEATO	South-East Asia Treaty Organization
Sec.	Secretary; Section
Secr.	Secretariat
Sept.	September
SEZ	Special Economic Zone
SITC	Standard International Trade Classification
Soc.	Society
SOE	State-Owned Enterprise
Sq.	Square
sq	square (in measurements)
Sr	Senior
St	Street; Saint, San, Santo
subs.	subscribed
Sun.	Sunday
Supt	Superintendent
Tas	Tasmania
tech.	technical
tel.	telephone
TEU	20-foot equivalent unit
Thur.	Thursday
trans.	translator, translated
Treas.	Treasurer
Tue.	Tuesday
TV	television
UHF	ultra-high frequency
UK	United Kingdom
UN	United Nations
UNCTAD	United Nations Conference on Trade and Development
UNDP	United Nations Development Programme
UNEP	United Nations Environment Programme
UNESCO	United Nations Educational, Scientific and Cultural Organization
UNFPA	United Nations Population Fund
UNHCR	United Nations High Commissioner for Refugees
UNIDO	United Nations Industrial Development Organization
UNTAC	United Nations Transitional Authority in Cambodia
UNTAET	United Nations Transitional Administration in East Timor
USA	United States of America
USAID	United States Agency for International Development
USSR	Union of Soviet Socialist Republics
VAT	Value-added tax
Ven.	Venerable
VHF	very high frequency
Vic	Victoria
viz.	videlicet (namely)
Vol(s)	Volume(s)
W	West, Western
WA	Western Australia
Wed.	Wednesday
WHO	World Health Organization
WTO	World Trade Organization
yr(s)	year(s)

INTERNATIONAL TELEPHONE CODES

To make international calls to telephone and fax numbers listed in The Far East and Australasia, dial the international code of the country from which you are calling, followed by the appropriate country code for the organization you wish to call (listed below), followed by the area code (if applicable) and telephone or fax number listed in the entry.

	Country code	+ or – GMT*
Afghanistan	93	+4½
Australia	61	+8 to +10
Australian Dependencies in the Indian Ocean		
Christmas Island	61	+7
Cocos (Keeling) Islands	61	+6½
Bangladesh	880	+6
Bhutan	975	+6
Brunei	673	+8
Cambodia	855	+7
China, People's Republic	86	+8
Special Administrative Regions:		
Hong Kong	852	+8
Macao	853	+8
China (Taiwan)	886	+8
East Timor	670	+9
India	91	+5½
Indonesia	62	+7 to +9
Japan	81	+9
Korea, Democratic People's Republic (North Korea)	850	+9
Korea, Republic (South Korea)	82	+9
Laos	856	+7
Malaysia	60	+8
Maldives	960	+5
Mongolia	976	+7 to +9
Myanmar	95	+6½
Nepal	977	+5¾
New Zealand	64	+12
Pakistan	92	+5
The Pacific Islands		
Australian Pacific Territories		
Norfolk Island	672	+11½
British Pacific Territory		
Pitcairn Islands	872	–8
Fiji	679	+12
French Pacific Territories		
French Polynesia	689	–9 to –10
Wallis and Futuna Islands	681	+12
French Pacific Overseas Country		
New Caledonia	687	+11
Kiribati	686	+12 to +13
The Marshall Islands	692	+12
The Federated States of Micronesia	691	+10 to +11
Nauru	674	+12
New Zealand Pacific Territory		
Tokelau	690	–10
New Zealand Pacific: Associated States		
Cook Islands	682	–10
Niue	683	–11
Palau	680	+9
Papua New Guinea	675	+10
Samoa	685	–11
Solomon Islands	677	+11
Tonga	676	+13
Tuvalu	688	+12
USA: State of Hawaii	1	-10
US Commonwealth Territory in the Pacific		
Northern Mariana Islands	1 670	+10
US External Territories in the Pacific		
American Samoa	1 684	–11
Guam	1 671	+10
Vanuatu	678	+11
The Philippines	63	+8
Singapore	65	+8
Sri Lanka	94	+6
Thailand	66	+7
Viet Nam	84	+7

* Time difference in hours + or – Greenwich Mean Time (GMT). The times listed compare the standard (winter) times. Some countries adopt Summer (Daylight Saving) Times—i.e. + 1 hour—for part of the year.

EXPLANATORY NOTE ON THE DIRECTORY SECTION

The Directory section of each chapter is arranged under the following headings, where they apply:

THE CONSTITUTION

THE GOVERNMENT

- HEAD OF STATE
- CABINET/COUNCIL OF MINISTERS
- MINISTRIES

LEGISLATURE

STATE GOVERNMENTS

POLITICAL ORGANIZATIONS

DIPLOMATIC REPRESENTATION

JUDICIAL SYSTEM

RELIGION

THE PRESS

PUBLISHERS

BROADCASTING AND COMMUNICATIONS

- TELECOMMUNICATIONS
- RADIO
- TELEVISION

FINANCE

- CENTRAL BANK
- STATE BANKS
- COMMERCIAL BANKS
- DEVELOPMENT BANKS
- INVESTMENT BANKS
- SAVINGS BANKS
- FOREIGN BANKS
- STOCK EXCHANGE
- INSURANCE

TRADE AND INDUSTRY

- GOVERNMENT AGENCIES
- DEVELOPMENT ORGANIZATIONS
- CHAMBERS OF COMMERCE AND INDUSTRY
- INDUSTRIAL AND TRADE ASSOCIATIONS
- EMPLOYERS' ORGANIZATIONS
- UTILITIES
- MAJOR COMPANIES
- CO-OPERATIVES
- TRADE UNIONS

TRANSPORT

- RAILWAYS
- ROADS
- INLAND WATERWAYS
- SHIPPING
- CIVIL AVIATION

TOURISM

DEFENCE

EDUCATION

CALENDAR OF POLITICAL EVENTS IN THE FAR EAST AND AUSTRALASIA, NOVEMBER 2001–OCTOBER 2002

NOVEMBER 2001

1 **Thailand:** the limitations of the Government's reform efforts were highlighted when a spokesman for the Armed Forces claimed that they were unaware of the whereabouts of Sub-Lt Duangchalerm Yoobamrung; son of Chalerm Yoobamrung (an influential member of the House of Representatives belonging to the New Aspiration Party—NAP), he had allegedly murdered a police officer during a brawl in a nightclub in October and then fled to evade arrest.

3 **Northern Marianas:** legislative elections were conducted, following which the Republican Party held the majority of seats in both the House of Representatives and the Senate; the concurrent gubernatorial election was won by Juan Nekai Babauta, who took office in January 2002.

3 **Singapore:** at legislative elections, the People's Action Party won 82 of 84 elective seats in the Parliament.

4 **Philippines:** the trial of former President Joseph Estrada on charges of economic plunder resumed, having been postponed following its original commencement in October 2001.

5–6 **ASEAN/Brunei:** in Bandar Seri Begawan the Association of South East Asian Nations held its annual summit meeting, which was also attended by representatives from the People's Republic of China, Japan and the Republic of Korea; China signed a free-trade agreement with ASEAN.

5 **Cambodia:** a court in Phnom-Penh sentenced 26 people to prison after they were convicted of participating in an attempted coup in November 2000; a further 30 men had been convicted in June 2001.

8 **Republic of Korea:** President Kim Dae-Jung resigned from the presidency of the ruling Millennium Democratic Party (MDP).

8 **Vanuatu:** former Prime Minister Barak Sope was charged with fraud; he was believed to have forged two government-supported Letters of Guarantee without authority during his time in office.

9 **Afghanistan:** with the assistance of US-led forces, the United Islamic Front for the Salvation of Afghanistan (commonly known as the United Front or Northern Alliance) captured Mazar-i-Sharif from the ruling Taliban.

9–14 **Democratic People's Republic of Korea/ Republic of Korea:** the sixth round of inter-Korean talks were held, but broke down owing to disagreements over the venue of the next round.

9 **Laos:** five European activists, who had been detained in October 2001 after handing out pro-democracy leaflets during a peaceful demonstration in Vientiane, were convicted of attempting to foment unrest and ordered to be deported from the country.

9 **Myanmar:** two senior generals, Lt-Gen. Win Myint and Deputy Prime Minister Tin Hla, were dismissed from the Cabinet, apparently owing to allegations of corruption that had been made against them.

9 **Pakistan:** the Afghan Defence Council, a grouping of more than 30 militant Islamist organizations, called a national strike, which was only partially observed.

10–11 **Afghanistan:** the United Front took control of Herat.

10 **Australia:** at the federal election, the Liberal-National coalition won 82 of the150 seats in the House of Representatives; John Howard was thus returned to office for a third consecutive term as Prime Minister; Kim Beazley, the leader of the opposition Labor Party, subsequently resigned and was replaced by Simon Crean.

11 **Indonesia:** Theys Eluay, the leader of Irian Jaya's pro-independence Presidium Dewan Papua (PDP—Papua Presidium Council), was found dead in his car.

11 **Myanmar:** in a further cabinet reshuffle, the ruling military junta announced the retirement of Deputy Prime Ministers Rear-Adm. Maung Maung Khin and Lt-Gen. Tin Tun, Minister for Culture Win Sein, Minister for Co-operatives Aung San, and Minister for Immigration Saw Tun.

12–13 **Afghanistan:** the United Front captured Kabul and occupied Jalalabad two days later.

12 **Bangladesh:** the Bangladesh Nationalist Party's presidential candidate, Prof. A. Q. M. Badruddoza Chowdhury, was declared elected unopposed by the Jatiya Sangsad as the country's new Head of State.

13 **Nepal:** peace negotiations between the Communist Party of Nepal—CPN (Maoist) and the Government collapsed.

18 **India:** a minor government reorganization was effected.

19 **Malaysia:** the Government appointed a new Attorney-General, Senior Deputy Public Prosecutor Abdul Gani Patail, to replace Ainum Mohamad Said, who had resigned because of ill health.

19 **Philippines:** a faction of the Moro National Liberation Front (MNLF), led by the outgoing Governor, Nur Misuari, staged an uprising in the Autonomous Region of Muslim Mindanao, in contravention of a five-year peace agreement with the Government.

21 **Malaysia:** the country's King, Sultan Salahuddin Abdul Aziz Shah, died at the age of 75, having ruled since September 1999.

21 **Nepal:** the leader of the CPN (Maoist) announced the end of the cease-fire between Maoist insurgents and the Government.

22 **Afghanistan/Pakistan:** the Pakistani Government ordered the closure of the Taliban embassy in Islamabad, marking the end of Pakistan's diplomatic relations with the Taliban regime.

22 **Philippines:** Imelda Marcos, widow of the former President, pleaded not guilty to four charges of corruption related to her activities during the 1970s.

23 **Nepal:** the Maoists established a parallel central government, the 'United People's Revolutionary Government'.

25–28 **Afghanistan:** an estimated 300 Taliban prisoners and 40 United Front troops were killed after US and British special forces assisted the United Front in curbing a Taliban revolt in Qala-i-Jhangi.

25 **Hong Kong:** about 500 protesters marched through Hong Kong to demand that the Chief Executive, Tung Chee-hwa, relinquish power upon the expiry of his current term of office.

26 **Afghanistan:** Taliban forces surrendered to United Front forces, allowing the latter to capture Kunduz.

26 **Nepal:** in response to the escalation of violence, and on the recommendation of the Council of Ministers, King Gyanendra declared a state of emergency, and for the first time authorized the deployment of the army to curb the insurgency; he also promulgated the Terrorist and Disruptive Activities Ordinance 2001, which sanctioned a number of counter-terrorist measures.

26 **Philippines:** Farouk Hussein, whose candidacy had been endorsed by President Gloria Macapagal Arroyo, was elected the new Governor of the Autonomous Region of Muslim Mindanao; a 21-member regional Assembly was also elected.

27 **Afghanistan:** a conference of 28 Afghan leaders representing four factions, including the United Front, hosted by the UN, commenced in Bonn, Germany.

27 **Myanmar:** UN envoy Razali Ismail arrived to hold meetings with military, opposition and ethnic leaders and to attempt to revive discussions between the ruling State Peace and Development Council (SPDC) and Aung San Suu Kyi, leader of the opposition National League for Democracy (NLD).

28 **Afghanistan:** the United Front rejected a UN proposal to deploy an international security force in Afghanistan to support the interim administration; the United Front insisted that domestic security would be its responsibility.

28 **Indonesia:** 'Tommy' Suharto, son of the former President, was arrested on suspicion of having ordered the murder of Justice Syafiuddin Kartasasmita, the judge who had upheld his previous prison sentence for corruption, in July 2001.

28 **Viet Nam:** the National Assembly finally ratified a landmark trade agreement with the USA, marking the complete restoration of normal relations between the former enemies.

29 **Norfolk Island:** a general election was conducted.

30 **Bhutan:** in a traditional ceremony, King Jigme inaugurated the drafting of a new Constitution.

30 **East Timor:** the Constituent Assembly approved the structure of a draft Constitution.

30 **Japan:** following a controversial amendment of the country's Constitution, the House of Councillors approved the dispatch of Japanese Self-Defense Forces (SDF) to the Indian Ocean to support the US-led campaign in Afghanistan.

DECEMBER 2001

1 **Taiwan:** at elections to the Legislative Yuan, the Democratic Progressive Party (DPP) emerged as the biggest single party, securing 87 of the 225 seats in the chamber; the Kuomintang (KMT) won 68 seats.

3 **Philippines:** Imelda Marcos was permitted to take leave from her corruption trial for one month, in order to receive medical treatment in the People's Republic of China.

4 **Thailand:** King Bhumibol Adulyadej publicly criticized Prime Minister Thaksin Shinawatra during a national address, warning that the Government's 'double standards' were leading the country towards 'catastrophe'.

5 **Afghanistan:** the 28 Afghan leaders attending a UN-hosted conference in Bonn signed an agreement to establish a 30-member multi-ethnic interim administration to preside for six months from 22 December; Hamid Karzai was appointed head of the new interim Government.

5 **Solomon Islands:** at elections to the National Parliament, the Solomon Islands Alliance for Change Coalition (SIACC) secured 12 of the available 50 seats; 22 seats were won by independent candidates.

5 **Sri Lanka:** at elections to the Parliament, the United National Party (UNP) won 109 of the 225 seats (45.6% of the vote), the People's Alliance (PA) obtained 77 seats (37.2%), the Janatha Vimukthi Peramuna secured 16 seats (9.1%) and the Tamil National Alliance won 15 seats (3.9%).

6 **Papua New Guinea:** following the conclusion of the Bougainville peace agreement, the process of weapons disposal began.

7 **Afghanistan:** the remaining members of the Taliban surrendered Qandahar, while other members fled the city, marking the end of the Taliban regime.

7 **Cook Islands:** the governing coalition, comprising the Democratic Alliance Party (DAP) of Prime Minister Terepai Maoate and the New Alliance Party (NAP) led by his former deputy, Norman George, collapsed when the latter (who had been dismissed as Deputy Prime Minister in August) withdrew from the coalition; George demanded a general election.

8 **People's Republic of China:** the Mayor of Shanghai, Xu Kuangdi, resigned from office and was succeeded by the Deputy Mayor, Chen Liangyu.

8 **Myanmar:** Nobel Prize winners attending a gathering in Oslo, Norway, urged the military junta to release fellow Nobel laureate Aung San Suu Kyi from house arrest.

9 **Sri Lanka:** Ranil Wickremasinghe was inaugurated as Prime Minister.

11 **Australia/Nauru:** in return for financial aid, Nauru signed an agreement with Australia whereby the former would accommodate as many as 1,200 asylum-seekers (who had attempted to enter Australia illegally) for the duration of the processing of their claims.

11 **East Timor:** the Special Panel for Serious Crimes established by the UN Transitional Administration in East Timor (UNTAET) convicted 10 former pro-Indonesia militiamen of crimes against humanity, the first such convictions to have been handed down in relation to the crimes committed during the aftermath of the 1999 referendum on independence.

11 **Philippines:** the Supreme Court intervened in the trial on charges of plunder of former President Estrada to remove the presiding judge, Justice Anacleto Badoy, in response to Estrada's accusations of bias against him.

12 **Afghanistan:** the United Front deadline for the surrender of members of the Taliban and al-Qa'ida (Base) organization expired without the complete surrender of the remaining forces.

12 **People's Republic of China:** China formally acceded to the World Trade Organization (WTO), having secured membership on 11 November.

12–15 **People's Republic of China/Myanmar:** Chinese President Jiang Zemin held talks with Gen. Than Shwe on a visit to Myanmar, the first Chinese Head of State to visit the country since 1985.

12 **Sri Lanka:** a new coalition Government, the United National Front, was sworn in.

13 **India:** five armed assailants attempted to launch an apparent suicide attack on the union parliament building in New Delhi; although no parliamentary deputies were hurt in the attack, 14 people were killed (including a number of policemen, some security officials, a groundsman and the five assailants) and some 25 were injured in the unsuccessful assault.

13 **Indonesia:** the Supreme Court ruled that 'Tommy' Suharto would have to serve 13 months of an 18-month prison sentence, taking into account the time that he had spent as a fugitive.

13 **Malaysia:** the new King, Tuanku Syed Sirajuddin Ibni Al-Marhum Syed Putra Jamalullail, Raja of Perlis, was sworn in.

13 **Tuvalu:** Koloa Talake was elected Prime Minister by Parliament after the Government of Faimalaga Luka was defeated in a vote of 'no confidence'; an entirely new Cabinet was appointed.

14 **India/Pakistan:** the Indian Government formally held the Pakistan-based militant Islamist Jaish-e-Mohammed and Lashkar-e-Taiba groups responsible for the attack on the union parliament and demanded that Pakistan halt the activities of the two organizations and arrest their leaders; Pakistan had immediately condemned the attack, but now demanded clear evidence to support India's allegations.

14 **Nepal:** following several weeks of violence, including two bomb attacks, Prime Minister Sher Bahadur Deuba declared that he would not resume negotiations with the Maoist insurgents until they surrendered their arms.

16 **India:** a senior police official confirmed that all the assailants of the attack on the union parliament building had been Pakistani nationals; three days later one of the accused admitted his involvement and alleged publicly that Pakistani security and intelligence agencies had provided support to those directly responsible for the attack.

17 **Solomon Islands:** Sir Allan Kemakeza, leader of the People's Alliance Party, was elected as Prime Minister; a new Cabinet was subsequently appointed.

18 **Cambodia:** the Cambodian People's Party (CPP) expelled three senators from the Senate and also from the party for voting to help defeat legislation intended to lengthen the amount of time that the authorities could detain a person without formal charge.

19 **Myanmar:** it was reported that a military reshuffle had taken place.

19 **Sri Lanka:** the Liberation Tigers of Tamil Eelam (LTTE) announced a unilateral one-month cease-fire to commence from midnight on 24 December; two days later the Government responded with the declaration of a cease-fire as a 'gesture of goodwill'; both sides later renewed the truce for a further month.

20 **Afghanistan:** despite suggestions that Osama bin Laden (leader of al-Qa'ida) and the Taliban leader, Mola Mohammad Omar, were in hiding in the Tora Bora hills, there appeared to be no sign of the leaders or their close associates after the capture and search of the cave complex by the United Front and US-led coalition; the UN Security Council adopted a resolution authorizing an International Security Assistance Force (ISAF), led by the United Kingdom, to help maintain security in Kabul over the next six months; deployment began in mid-January; the decision was opposed by various factions in Afghanistan.

20 **Indonesia:** warring Christian and Muslim factions signed a 10-point agreement in Malino, South Sulawesi, intended to end the recurrent conflict that had affected the area around Poso, Central Sulawesi, since December 1998.

21 **Fiji:** the suspension of Fiji's membership of the Commonwealth (imposed in June 2000) was lifted at a meeting of the organization in London; sanctions imposed on the country by the EU, however, remained in place until early 2002.

21 **India/Pakistan:** as tension between India and Pakistan continued to mount, India recalled its high commissioner to Islamabad and announced that overground transport services between the two countries would be suspended from 1 January 2002; in the mean time, positions were being reinforced with troops and weapons on both sides of the Line of Control dividing Indian and Pakistani Kashmir and on both sides of the international border.

22 **Afghanistan:** a 29-member Afghan Interim Authority was inaugurated; Hamid Karzai was sworn in as Chairman.

22 **Japan/Democratic People's Republic of Korea:** Japanese patrol boats sank a suspected North Korean espionage vessel, which had entered Japan's economic exclusion zone.

22 **Pakistan:** the Minister of Local Government, Rural Development, Labour, Manpower and Overseas Pakistanis, Omar Asghar Khan, resigned, announcing his intention to establish a political party, the National Democratic Party.

25 **Viet Nam:** a session of the National Assembly, at which a number of constitutional amendments were adopted, ended.

26 **Afghanistan:** Hamid Karzai appointed Gen. Dostam as Vice-Chairman and Deputy Minister of Defence, thereby increasing the number of positions in the new Government to 30.

27 **Afghanistan:** a new videotape of bin Laden was broadcast by the Qatar-based satellite television company, Al-Jazeera, supporting claims that the Islamist militant was still alive; it was impossible, however, to establish the date of the recording; in the mean time, the US-led coalition continued its search for the leaders of al-Qa'ida and the Taliban.

27 **India/Pakistan:** India announced personnel reductions of both countries' diplomatic missions and a ban on Pakistan Airlines from flying over India, a measure that Pakistan reciprocated.

27 **Malaysia:** a court convicted 19 members of al-Ma'unah, an Islamic cult, of treason for plotting to overthrow the Government; they had been arrested after killing two hostages during a confrontation with security forces in July 2000.

31 **India/Pakistan:** following reports that the Pakistani authorities had detained the two leaders of the groups held responsible for the attack on the Indian parliament building, as well as some 80 suspected militants, the Indian Government demanded that the two leaders be extradited (together with 20 other named militants) to stand trial in India.

JANUARY 2002

1 **Indonesia:** special autonomy laws for the province of Irian Jaya entered into force; henceforth the province was to be officially known as Papua.

1 **Taiwan:** Taiwan formally acceded to the WTO.

2 **Sri Lanka:** the Government announced the reduction of economic sanctions on the northern LTTE-controlled areas.

4 **Malaysia:** the authorities announced the arrest of 13 members of the Islamist Kumpulan Mujahidin Malaysia (KMM), a fundamentalist group believed to be engaged in a long-term plot to overthrow the Government; the group was alleged to have links to terrorist suspect Zacarias Moussaoui, who had been detained following the attacks on the USA on 11 September 2001.

5 **Singapore:** the Government announced that in the previous month it had arrested 15 people (14 Singaporeans and one Malaysian) in connection with suspected planned bomb attacks on various US and Western targets in the country; 13 of the suspects were thought to be members of the Islamist terrorist organization, Jemaah Islamiah.

5–6 **Nepal/SAARC:** the 11th summit meeting of the South Asian Association for Regional Co-operation took place in Kathmandu.

7 **Indonesia:** Akbar Tandjung, President of the Golkar Party and Speaker of the House of Representatives, was charged with the misuse of funds from BULOG, the state logistics agency, to fund the 1999 Golkar election campaign.

7 **Philippines:** the former Governor of the Autonomous Region of Muslim Mindanao, Nur Misuari, was extradited to the Philippines from Malaysia, having been charged with staging a rebellion.

9 **Afghanistan:** the Interim Authority confirmed that seven senior Taliban members, who had surrendered to a local Afghan commander, had been released without the approval of the Interim Authority or US-led forces.

9 **Sri Lanka:** Norwegian diplomats arrived in the capital to resume Norway's mediation in the civil war.

9–15 **Japan:** Prime Minister Junichiro Koizumi visited Indonesia, Malaysia, the Philippines, Singapore and Thailand.

10 **Hong Kong:** the Court of Final Appeal ruled that 5,000 migrants from the Chinese mainland with relatives in Hong Kong had no right of abode in the SAR.

11 **Indonesia:** former President Abdurrahman Wahid was questioned concerning the corruption charges against 'Tommy' Suharto.

12 **Pakistan:** in his address to the nation, President Musharraf announced an indefinite ban on the activities of five predominantly separatist groups, along with plans to reform the country's system of *madrassas* (Islamic religious schools), many of which were accused of promoting extremism and theocracy; he also rejected India's demand to extradite a group of suspected Islamist militants to stand trial in India.

14 **East Timor/Indonesia:** President Megawati approved the appointment of 18 legal experts to a special human rights tribunal intended to try cases arising from the violence that had occurred in East Timor following its referendum on independence in 1999.

14 **Philippines:** the Government announced that some 650 US troops were to be dispatched to the south of the country, where they were to engage in joint counter-terrorism operations with the Philippine armed forces.

15 **Afghanistan:** the UN Security Council authorized a resolution removing the sanctions imposed on Ariana Afghan Airlines.

15 **Cambodia:** according to a report released by the UN, 15 candidates or political activists, all members of the Sam Rainsy Party or FUNCINPEC, had been killed or had died in suspicious circumstances since January 2001.

16 **Afghanistan:** the Interim Authority banned poppy cultivation and drugs-trafficking.

16 **Australia:** amid continuing controversy over the Government's stringent immigration policy, inmates of a remote detention centre in Woomera began a hunger strike in protest at the delays in the processing of their claims for asylum and at their poor living conditions.

16 **Pakistan:** the Government announced that the total number of seats in the new National Assembly would be increased to 350 (from 217) and would include 60 seats reserved for women and 25 seats reserved for technocrats; separate lists for minority candidates and voters were also to be abolished.

16 **Thailand:** the trial of Sub-Lt Duangchalerm Yoobamrung for the alleged murder of a police officer began *in absentia*.

17 **East Timor:** Sérgio Vieira de Mello, head of UNTAET, announced that the territory would hold its first presidential election on 14 April 2002.

19 **Malaysia:** it was announced that seven more members of the Islamist KMM had been arrested.

20 **Malaysia:** at a by-election in the Perlis district of Indera Kayangan, the ruling Barisan Nasional (BN) defeated the opposition Parti Keadilan Nasional.

21 **Cambodia:** as campaigning for the forthcoming local elections commenced, Vat Din, a candidate for the opposition Sam Rainsy Party, was found dead.

21 **East Timor:** a Commission for Reception, Truth and Reconciliation was inaugurated to investigate the alleged atrocities committed by Indonesian forces during the occupation period.

21–23 **Taiwan:** President Chen reorganized the Executive Yuan, appointing Yu Shyi-kun, hitherto his Secretary-General, as the new Premier.

22 **India/Pakistan:** an armed attack by four suspected Islamist militants on a US cultural centre in Kolkata (Calcutta), in which five Indian policemen were killed, placed bilateral relations under renewed strain when the Indian authorities attempted to link the unidentified assailants (who had escaped after the attack) to the Pakistani intelligence services; police also connected a criminal organization in West Bengal with the attack.

22 **Mongolia:** the Civil Courage Party and the Mongolian Republican Party (MRP) agreed to merge into a single party, the Civil Courage Republican Party (CCRP); an inaugural congress was subsequently held on 25 February, and Sanjaasürengiin Oyuun of the CCP was elected Chairman of the new party.

23 **Malaysia:** the Parti Bersatu Sabah (PBS) was readmitted to the ruling coalition, the BN.

23 **Papua New Guinea:** the National Parliament unanimously endorsed the Organic Law enacting the Bougainville peace agreement, along with a bill containing the requisite legislation; following the ratification of the legislation in late March, the

Papua New Guinea Defence Force began its withdrawal from Bougainville.

25 **Afghanistan:** the Interim Authority announced the convening of a Special Independent Commission, known as the Loya Jirga Commission, which, according to the Bonn Agreement, would formulate the rules for the Emergency Loya Jirga.

25 **India:** a 'routine' test of the country's ballistic-missile arsenal was conducted; the navy carried out a missile test five days later.

28 **Afghanistan:** US-led forces raided a hospital in Qandahar and killed six Islamist militants, thereby removing the final members of Taliban resistance.

29 **Japan:** the controversial Minister of Foreign Affairs, Makiko Tanaka, was dismissed; she was replaced by Yoriko Kawaguchi.

29 **Republic of Korea:** President Kim Dae-Jung began a major reorganization of the State Council, replacing nine ministers.

31 **East Timor:** the UN Security Council adopted a resolution extending the mandate of UNTAET until 20 May 2002, the date on which the territory was to accede formally to independence.

31 **Philippines:** joint exercises between Philippine and US troops commenced on the island of Basilan.

FEBRUARY 2002

3 **Cambodia:** local elections were held to determine the leadership of 1,621 *khum* (communes); the elections were the country's first at *khum* level since independence.

4 **Malaysia:** former Deputy Prime Minister Anwar Ibrahim launched his final appeal against his 1999 conviction for corruption; the appeal had already been postponed three times.

8 **Afghanistan:** the former Taliban Minister of Foreign Affairs, Mawlawi Wakil Ahmad Motawakkil, surrendered to the authorities.

8 **Cambodia:** the UN unexpectedly announced that it was abandoning negotiations with the Cambodian Government over a UN role in the establishment of a tribunal to try former leaders of the Khmers Rouges for genocide and crimes against humanity.

8 **Sri Lanka:** the Prime Minister avoided a coalition crisis when he persuaded two government members, both representatives of the Ceylon Workers' Congress, to withdraw their resignations.

9 **East Timor:** the Constituent Assembly voted to approve a draft constitution.

9 **India:** it was reported that the Government of the United Arab Emirates had extradited to India the principal suspect for the attack on the US cultural centre in Kolkata in January.

10 **Malaysia:** police and supporters of the opposition Pan-Malaysian Islamic Party (PAS) clashed in the town of Baling, north of Kuala Lumpur; some 30 people were subsequently arrested.

10–19 **Myanmar:** the UN special rapporteur for human rights, Paulo Sérgio Pinheiro, visited the country, meeting with SPDC members and opposition leader Aung San Suu Kyi during his stay; 11 political prisoners were released, to coincide with his visit.

11 **Cambodia:** the Government stated that it was prepared to readmit the UN to talks on the establishment of a tribunal but that it was prepared to conduct the trials of former Khmer Rouge leaders without UN participation.

12 **Cook Islands:** Prime Minister Terepai Maoate was defeated in a vote of 'no confidence'; he was replaced by the Deputy Prime Minister, Robert Woonton; an extensive ministerial reorganization followed.

12 **Indonesia:** a peace accord was signed between Christian and Muslim leaders in the Maluku (Molucca) islands, with the intention of ending three years of sectarian fighting in the area.

13 **Afghanistan:** Ismail Khan and Taj Mohammad Wardak were appointed Governors of Herat and Paktia provinces, respectively.

13–21 **India:** assembly elections in the states of Manipur, Punjab, Uttaranchal and Uttar Pradesh took place; the Bharatiya Janata Party fared badly in all four elections; Congress achieved victory in Punjab and Uttaranchal; a coalition government was formed in Manipur in early March.

13 **Philippines:** the Government signed an agreement with the USA concerning the terms on which joint exercises between US and Philippine troops on the island of Basilan were to be conducted; the US troops were to train the military in counter-insurgency measures.

14 **Afghanistan:** Abdul Rahman, the Minister of Tourism and Civil Aviation, was assassinated.

14 **Indonesia/New Zealand:** four pro-Indonesia militiamen were charged with the murder in July 2000 of a UN peace-keeping soldier from New Zealand.

15 **Fiji:** an appeal court ruled that the Prime Minister (who in January had rejected opposition demands for his resignation following the revelation of a financial scandal) had violated the Constitution by failing to include any member of the opposition Fiji Labour Party (FLP) in his Cabinet.

15 **Nepal:** two factions of the Communist Party of Nepal, Unified Marxist-Leninist (UML) and Marxist-Leninist (ML), merged.

18 **East Timor/Indonesia:** 17 suspects were indicted by UN prosecutors in Dili for crimes against humanity allegedly committed in April 1999, when the house of independence leader Manuel Carrascalão had been attacked; three days later, in Jakarta, seven senior officials, including the former Governor of East Timor, Abílio Soares, were charged with crimes against humanity arising from the violence that had surrounded the referendum in East Timor in August 1999.

18 **Fiji:** George Speight, who had led the armed coup in May 2000, pleaded guilty to treason on the opening day of his trial; he was sentenced to death on the same day, but the sentence was immediately commuted to life imprisonment by President Iloilo.

18–25 **Myanmar:** officials from the International Labour Organization (ILO) visited the country on a trip intended to ascertain whether the Government had ended forced labour practices in the country; they claimed that they had been denied access to opposition leader Aung San Suu Kyi, in contravention of the terms of their visit, and that the Government had provided little evidence that it was prepared to accept assistance in bringing an end to forced labour.

19 **Taiwan:** a political impasse in the Legislative Yuan ended when the opposition Kuomintang (KMT) failed to secure the majority required to force the Government to accept revised legislation on the allocation of local budgets.

21–22 **People's Republic of China:** US President George W. Bush visited China where a summit meeting was held with President Jiang Zemin; little progress was made on outstanding matters relating to trade and defence issues.

21 **Nepal:** the legislature voted to extend the state of emergency by three months.

22–23 **Nepal:** in order to mark the sixth anniversary of the start of the insurgency and to protest against the state of emergency, Maoist guerrillas organized a two-day nation-wide strike.

22 **Sri Lanka:** the Government and LTTE signed an agreement on an indefinite cease-fire to take effect the following day; a Sri Lankan Monitoring Mission, comprising non-Sri Lankans and led by representatives of Norway, was established to monitor the cease-fire.

23 **Cambodia:** former Khmer Rouge military commander Ta Mok was formally charged with crimes against humanity.

24 **Laos:** elections were held to the 109-member National Assembly, only one of those elected was not a member of the ruling Lao People's Revolutionary Party (LPRP), ensuring that it secured a comprehensive victory.

25 **Cambodia:** the official results of the local elections gave the ruling CPP control of 1,597 of the country's 1,621 *khum*, the SRP control 13 and FUNCINPEC 10; election monitors reported that the elections could not be considered to have been either free or fair.

25 **India:** a senior Vishwa Hindu Parishad (VHP) leader disregarded government pleas to await a ruling by the Supreme Court on the status of the disputed religious site in Ayodhya, and announced that the movement of building material to the site would begin on 15 March.

26 **Australia/East Timor/Indonesia:** officials held the first ever trilateral talks on future co-operation issues in Denpasar, Indonesia.

27 **India:** a cycle of communal violence broke out in Gujarat after a train carrying members of the VHP returning from a visit to the disputed religious site in Ayodhya was attacked by a group of suspected Muslim militants; an estimated 600–700 people had been killed by 12 March, the majority of whom were Muslims.

27 **Thailand:** two reporters from the Hong Kong-based *Far Eastern Economic Review* had their visas revoked after it was alleged that they posed a threat to national security, following the publication of an article deemed critical of the relationship between the King and the Prime Minister.

28 **Cambodia:** 20 people, including a US citizen, were given prison terms, following the third trial of those connected with an attempted coup in November 2000.

28 **Hong Kong:** Tung Chee-hwa secured a second five-year term as Chief Executive, having gained the support of 714 members of the 800-strong election committee.

28 **Nepal:** the House of Representatives approved the Government's anti-terrorism ordinance, promulgated in November; the Government later agreed to limit the duration of the ordinance to two years.

MARCH 2002

3 **Thailand:** at by-elections held in 14 constituencies where the results of the 2001 general election had been declared invalid, Thai Rak Thai lost five seats; nevertheless, the party retained its secure legislative majority.

4 **Thailand:** the Nation Multimedia Group was ordered by the Ministry of Defence to cease its provision of news programmes to a local radio station operated (like all Thai radio frequencies) by the Armed Forces because they were deemed to contain material critical of the Prime Minister.

5 **People's Republic of China:** the fifth session of the Ninth National People's Congress, attended by nearly 3,000 delegates, opened in Beijing; the Government's determination to combat corruption was reiterated.

6 **Thailand:** a minor government reorganization was announced; changes included the appointment to the Cabinet of Suwat Liptapanlop, leader of the Chart Pattana party, which had recently joined the ruling coalition.

6 **Philippines:** Rigoberto Tiglao was appointed to the Cabinet as Press Secretary, replacing Noel Cabrera, who had resigned in the previous week.

6–7 **Tonga:** at a general election, where 52 candidates competed for the nine commoners' seats in the Legislative Assembly, the Human Rights and Democracy Movement won seven seats, compared with five at the previous election.

7 **East Timor:** Yacobus Bere was given a prison sentence after being convicted of the murder of a UN peace-keeping soldier in 1999.

7 **Indonesia:** 'Tommy' Suharto was charged with arranging the murder of Justice Syafiuddin Kartasasmita in July 2001 and with the illegal possession of firearms; Akbar Tandjung, Speaker of the House of Representatives, was detained on corruption charges.

7 **Myanmar:** Aye Zaw Win, son-in-law of U Ne Win, and three of U Ne Win's grandsons (Aye Ne Win, Kyaw Ne Win and Zwe Ne Win) were arrested following the discovery of an alleged coup attempt.

7 **Thailand:** the visas of two foreign journalists for the weekly *Far Eastern Economic Review* were reinstated following their revocation in February; the Nation Media Group alleged that it had received a copy of a letter ordering a special anti-money laundering department to investigate the bank accounts of 18 journalists or publications that were deemed to be critical of the Government.

8 **India:** President Narayan imposed presidential rule on the state of Uttar Pradesh after no party was able to assemble a coalition government following state elections.

9 **Kiribati/Maldives/Tuvalu:** it was reported that the three countries were to take legal action against the USA over its refusal to sign the Kyoto Protocol relating to global warming.

9 **Myanmar:** it was reported that the commander of the Air Force, Maj.-Gen. Myint Swe, and the Chief of Police, Maj.-Gen. Soe Win, had been dismissed for their alleged role in the recently discovered coup attempt.

10 **Myanmar:** Gen. U Ne Win was placed under house arrest by the ruling junta following the discovery of the alleged coup attempt; his daughter, Sandar Win, and several other relatives were also detained.

9–13 **Taiwan:** the Minister of National Defense, Tang Yao-ming, attended a conference on defence and security issues in Florida, USA, where he met senior US officials.

10 **Wallis and Futuna:** at elections to the Territorial Assembly the right-wing Rassemblement pour la République (RPR) retained a majority, winning 13 seats, with the remaining seven being secured by various left-wing candidates and independents.

11 **Nepal:** the Minister of Forest and Soil Conservation, Gopal Man Shrestha, and his deputy, Surendra Hamal, resigned amid allegations of corruption.

13 **Indonesia:** the central bank governor, Sjahril Sabirin, was sentenced to three years in prison fol-

lowing his conviction for stealing bank funds to fund the election campaign of former President B. J. Habibie; he remained in his post pending an appeal.

14 **Nepal:** the House of Representatives approved an item of legislation that gave women equal property rights with their male siblings for the first time.

14–16 **Myanmar:** a mission from the European Union (EU) visited the country on a trip intended to encourage political reconciliation; it held discussions with the ruling junta and met with Aung San Suu Kyi.

14 **Sri Lanka:** Ranil Wickremasinghe visited Jaffna, the first Prime Minister to do so since 1982.

15 **India:** security forces prevented Hindu nationalists from defying a court order and entering the disputed religious site in Ayodhya.

17 **New Zealand/Solomon Islands:** Bridget Nichols, the New Zealand Deputy High Commissioner to Solomon Islands, was discovered dead at her home having been fatally injured with a knife.

18 **Japan:** Koichi Kato, an ally of Prime Minister Koizumi, resigned from the Liberal-Democratic Party (LDP) following a tax-evasion scandal; he relinquished his seat in the Diet on 8 April.

20 **Myanmar:** the SPDC signed an agreement with the ILO to allow the organization to open a permanent liaison office in Yangon.

20 **Sri Lanka:** at local elections held in 247 districts, the United National Party (UNP) secured victory in 240 councils and the People's Alliance (PA) won four councils.

20 **Taiwan:** the Minister of Economic Affairs, Christine Tsung, resigned, citing an adverse political climate, and was replaced by her deputy, Lin Yi-fu.

22 **East Timor:** the first Constitution of the new nation was promulgated.

23 **Myanmar/Thailand:** a clash occurred between Thai troops and the Myanma United Wa State Army (UWSA) in the Thai border province of Chiang Mai; one Thai soldier and 12 UWSA guerrillas were killed.

25 **Indonesia:** the trial on corruption charges of Akbar Tandjung, Speaker of the House of Representatives, began.

25 **Malaysia:** the resumption of the appeal of Anwar Ibrahim, which had been adjourned in February 2002, was delayed by one day owing to a bomb scare.

26 **India:** the controversial Prevention of Terrorism Ordinance was approved by a rare joint session of the Rajya Sabha and Lok Sabha.

26 **New Zealand:** Prime Minister Helen Clark began a series of meetings with the US President, Secretary of State and other officials, the first visit to the USA by a Labour Prime Minister since the deterioration in bilateral relations in the mid-1980s as a result of New Zealand's anti-nuclear stance.

27 **Sri Lanka:** it was announced that peace negotiations between the Government and the LTTE were likely to be held in May in Thailand; the talks were eventually held in September.

28 **Indonesia/Democratic People's Republic of Korea/Republic of Korea:** President Megawati Sukarnoputri of Indonesia arrived in North Korea and held talks with Kim Jong Il; she subsequently travelled to South Korea, as part of a regional tour.

28 **Myanmar/Thailand:** the Thai Ministry of Foreign Affairs lodged an official protest with the Myanma Government over a clash that had occurred in the border area on 23 March.

30 **Solomon Islands:** Laurie Chan was appointed the Minister of Finance, following the dismissal of Michael Maina.

31 **Malaysia:** at a by-election to the Ketari seat in the Pahang State Assembly, Prime Minister Mahathir's BN won a greatly increased majority against the Democratic Action Party (DAP); his victory was largely attributed to increased fears of Islamist militancy.

APRIL 2002

1 **Myanmar:** it was announced that U Ne Win's relatives would be tried for high treason at an open trial following the alleged coup attempt.

1 **Thailand:** the Constitutional Court formally granted a request by the NAP that it be permitted to merge with Thai Rak Thai, following the latter party's vote on the issue on 24 January.

2–9 **Japan/People's Republic of China:** the Chairman of the National People's Congress (NPC), Li Peng, paid a goodwill visit to Japan, to mark the 30th anniversary of the establishment of diplomatic relations.

2 **Singapore:** the former leader of the Workers' Party, J. B. Jeyaretnam, made a public apology in the High Court in order to end the series of defamation suits brought against him by the Government; in return the Government abandoned seven outstanding suits against him.

3 **Indonesia:** the first violence since the signing of a peace agreement in February occurred in eastern Maluku when a bomb exploded in Ambon, causing four deaths.

3–6 **Democratic People's Republic of Korea/Republic of Korea:** President Kim Dae-Jung's special envoy, Lim Dong-Won, visited North Korea and held talks with Kim Jong Il.

3 **Malaysia:** six opposition activists, imprisoned without trial under the Internal Security Act for allegedly plotting to overthrow the Government, began a hunger strike, demanding that the Government allow Anwar Ibrahim, the imprisoned former Deputy Prime Minister, to travel abroad to receive surgery.

4 **Afghanistan:** the Interim Authority claimed to have prevented an assassination attempt on Hamid Karzai.

4 **Nepal:** the Government reduced the controversial restrictions it had imposed on the media and political parties as part of the state of emergency.

7 **Afghanistan:** violent protests against an opium eradication programme began throughout the country.

8 **Afghanistan:** an assassination attempt was made on the Vice-Chairman of the Interim Authority and Minister of Defence, Marshal Mohammed Fahim.

8 **Malaysia:** the Government secured the passage of controversial legislation amending the election law.

10–11 **Indonesia:** there was a further outbreak of violence in Maluku.

10 **Nepal:** it was reported that the ruling Nepali Congress Party (NCP) had expelled the Minister of Information and Communications from the party for a period of two years.

10 **Sri Lanka:** the leader of the LTTE, Velupillai Prabhakaran, addressed an international press conference for the first time in more than 10 years.

13 **Sri Lanka:** the leader of the LTTE signed a pact with the Sri Lanka Muslim Congress, allowing the

largest Muslim party in Sri Lanka to participate in proposed negotiations with the Government.

14 **East Timor:** Xanana Gusmão, veteran leader of the independence movement, and Francisco Xavier do Amaral, Vice-President of the Legislative Assembly, contested the nation's first presidential election; Xanana Gusmão was subsequently declared the winner, having received almost 83% of the votes cast.

15 **Democratic People's Republic of Korea:** massive celebrations were held to commemorate the 90th anniversary of the birth of Kim Il Sung; two days earlier, some 55 generals were promoted, and later in the month Shin Il Nam was appointed Vice-Premier and Chairman of the Commission for Capital Construction.

15 **Republic of Korea:** Jeon Yun-Churl, hitherto Chief Presidential Secretary, was appointed Deputy Prime Minister for Finance and the Economy, replacing Jun Nyum.

15 **Myanmar/Thailand:** a bomb exploded on the so-called 'Friendship Bridge' linking the two countries, killing at least seven people.

16 **Indonesia:** authorities in Ambon arrested Alex Manuputty, leader of the Christian separatist organization the Maluku Sovereignty Front, on charges of treason.

18 **Afghanistan:** former King Zahir Shah returned to Afghanistan from exile in Italy as a 'private citizen'.

18 **Malaysia:** it was announced that a further 14 alleged members of the KMM had been detained under the Internal Security Act, bringing the total being held under the Act to 62.

20 **Niue:** at a general election, all 20 incumbent members of the Niue Assembly retained their seats; however, Premier Sani Lakatani was then defeated in a leadership challenge by his deputy, Young Vivian, who subsequently formed a coalition Government, with Lakatani as Deputy Premier.

20 **Philippines:** the number of US troops deployed in the southern Philippines was increased to 1,000; it was reported that the US military presence might continue for longer than the six months originally envisaged.

21 **Philippines:** in a series of bombings attributed to Islamist militants, 15 people were killed by an explosion in the southern city of General Santos; President Gloria Macapagal Arroyo imposed a state of emergency in the city.

22 **Japan:** Prime Minister Junichiro Koizumi paid an unexpected visit to the controversial Yasukuni Shrine honouring Japan's war dead, his second visit since becoming Prime Minister; the visit was condemned by China and South Korea.

23–26 **Myanmar:** UN envoy Razali Ismail returned with the intention of encouraging the resumption of negotiations between the ruling junta and the opposition NLD; he met twice with Aung San Suu Kyi during his visit.

23–26 **Myanmar/Thailand:** SPDC Vice-Chairman Gen. Maung Aye visited Thailand to hold talks with the Thai Government concerning drug-smuggling and border tensions.

23–27 **Nepal:** after a series of strikes in March, the Maoist insurgents organized a five-day general strike.

24 **Singapore:** the leader of the Singapore Democratic Party (SDP), Chee Soon Juan, stated his intention to defend lawsuits brought against him by Prime Minister Goh Chok Tong and Senior Minister Lee Kuan Yew relating to an allegation made by Chee in October 2001 that the Government had lent public funds to former President Suharto of Indonesia.

25 **Indonesia:** the Maluku Sovereignty Front raised flags in Ambon to commemorate the 52nd anniversary of its foundation, provoking Muslims in the area and causing the leader of Laskar Jihad, Ja'far Umar Thalib, to urge all Muslims in the islands to renew their war against the Christian community.

25 **Malaysia:** the new King officially assumed his duties.

27 **Indonesia:** armed men raided a village near Ambon, capital of Maluku, killing 14 Christians.

27 **Republic of Korea:** the ruling MDP formally inaugurated Roh Moo-Hyun as its candidate for the presidential elections in December.

27 **Sri Lanka:** the Prime Minister rejected the LTTE demand for an independent Tamil state, or eelam.

28 **People's Republic of China:** Vice-President Hu Jintao began his first official visit to the USA, where he met President George W. Bush and other senior officials.

29 **India:** the Minister of Coal and Mines resigned and withdrew his Lok Jan Shakti party from the ruling National Democratic Alliance, in protest against the Government's handling of the situation in Gujarat.

30 **East Timor:** Madalena Brites Boavida was sworn in as the new Minister of Finance, following the resignation of Fernando Borges.

30 **Afghanistan:** it was reported that Abdul Hakim Taniwal and Mawlawi Ali Jalali had been appointed Governors of Khost and Paktika provinces, respectively.

30 **India:** the EU's report on the situation in Gujarat, which corroborated a number of other reports published in April, concluded that the riots and killings had been, contrary to the official account, not in reaction to the attack on a train carrying Hindu activists, but in fact an organized massacre of Muslims, and that the security forces had been under orders not to intervene.

30 **Pakistan:** a national referendum seeking endorsement for Musharraf's term of office as President to be extended by five years, and approval of the Government's political and economic programme, was held, despite widespread criticism; 97.7% of the votes cast supported the proposal.

MAY 2002

1 **Niue:** Young Vivian was elected Prime Minister by the Fono (legislature), with 14 votes to six.

2 **Democratic People's Republic of Korea/Viet Nam:** Vietnamese President Tran Duc Luong arrived in Pyongyang, beginning a four-day visit.

2 **Thailand:** Sub-Lt Duangchalerm Yoobamrung was extradited from Malaysia and charged with the murder of a police officer in October 2001.

2 **Vanuatu:** at legislative elections, the Union of Moderate Parties (UMP) secured 15 of the 52 seats available in Parliament and the Vanuaaku Pati (VP) won 14, enabling them to continue in office as a coalition Government.

3 **India:** a new coalition Government was formed in Uttar Pradesh.

3 **Myanmar:** the trial began of the relatives of Gen. U Ne Win accused of treason in connection with the coup attempt in March.

3 **Viet Nam:** the Russian navy formally transferred the Cam Ranh naval base to the control of Viet Nam.

4 **Indonesia:** the leader of Laskar Jihad, Ja'far Umar Thalib, was arrested for allegedly inciting the violence that had led to a massacre in Maluku in April; a further outbreak of violence in Ambon caused the deaths of at least two people.

6 **Indonesia:** one of 'Tommy' Suharto's lawyers, Elza Syarief, was detained by police in connection with allegations that witnesses had been bribed to lie during the murder trial of the former President's son, which had begun in March.

6 **Republic of Korea:** President Kim Dae-Jung resigned from the MDP, in order to concentrate on state affairs during his final months in office.

6 **Myanmar:** opposition leader Aung San Suu Kyi was unconditionally released from house arrest after nearly 20 months in detention.

6–7 **Philippines:** the Government and the leadership of the Moro Islamic Liberation Front (MILF) signed further peace agreements in Malaysia.

7 **Indonesia/Malaysia/Philippines:** the neighbouring countries signed a trilateral anti-terrorism pact enabling them to exchange intelligence and launch joint police operations in an effort to combat regional terrorist organizations.

8 **People's Republic of China/Japan/Democratic People's Republic of Korea:** as increasing numbers of North Koreans sought refuge in foreign diplomatic missions, a serious dispute between China and Japan arose after the Chinese authorities entered the Japanese consulate in Shenyang, China, and forcibly removed several North Korean asylum-seekers; they were later allowed to travel to South Korea.

8 **Indonesia:** the two men allegedly hired by 'Tommy' Suharto to assassinate Justice Syafiuddin Kartasasmita in July 2001 were found guilty of murder and sentenced to life imprisonment.

8 **Pakistan:** a 'suicide bomb' attack perpetrated by suspected Islamist militants outside a hotel in Karachi killed 16 people, mostly French engineers.

9–10 **Indonesia:** government representatives held talks with the separatist Free Aceh Movement (GAM) in Geneva, Switzerland, and signed an agreement as a basis for future negotiations.

10 **India:** the Lok Sabha elected unopposed Manohar Joshi as its Speaker, replacing Mohan Chandra Balayogi, who had died in March.

11–14 **Democratic People's Republic of Korea/ Republic of Korea:** Park Geun-Hye, daughter of former South Korean President Park Chung-Hee, visited North Korea where she had talks with Kim Jong Il, the North Korean leader; she subsequently established a new political party, the Korean Coalition for the Future (KCTF).

12 **Pakistan:** the Government announced plans to establish a federal anti-terrorism task force, following a rise in the number of Islamist militant and sectarian attacks.

13 **Myanmar:** opposition leader Aung San Suu Kyi called for an immediate start to reconciliation discussions with the ruling junta and stated that her main priority was to secure the release of other NLD members from imprisonment.

13–15 **Malaysia:** Prime Minister Mahathir Mohamed visited Washington, DC, and met with US President George W. Bush, who expressed his gratitude to Malaysia for its continued co-operation in the US-led campaign against terrorism.

14 **India/Pakistan:** tension between the two countries rose again after an army camp in Jammu and Kashmir was attacked by suspected Islamist militants; two days later India identified the gunmen as Pakistani nationals.

17 **Myanmar:** in a significant test of her freedom of movement, Aung San Suu Kyi visited the offices of the NLD in Shwepyitha, near Yangon.

17 **Nepal:** Prime Minister Deuba tabled a parliamentary motion proposing an extension of the state of emergency (which was due to expire on 25 May), prompting strong opposition from within and outside his party.

18 **India/Pakistan:** India requested the withdrawal of Pakistan's high commissioner to India; tensions heightened with the reinforcement of troops by both countries on their respective sides of the border.

18 **Republic of Korea:** President Kim Dae-Jung's youngest son, Kim Hong-Gul, was arrested for alleged involvement in a bribery scandal; another of Kim's sons, Kim Hong-Up, subsequently became involved in a similar scandal.

19 **Viet Nam:** a new 498-member National Assembly was elected; only 51 of the new deputies were not members of the Communist Party.

20 **Cambodia:** Prince Norodom Chakrapong, a son of King Norodom Sihanouk, launched a new political party, the Prince Norodom Chakrapong Khmer Soul party.

20 **East Timor:** the tenure of the UN interim administration in the country ended as the country was formally granted independence; Xanana Gusmão was officially inaugurated as the new country's President, the Government was sworn in and Parliament held its inaugural session, during which the legislature voted to apply for membership of the UN.

20 **Myanmar/Thailand:** fighting began along the border with Thailand between Government troops and their allies in the United Wa State Army (UWSA) and the Shan State Army (SSA); the SPDC accused Thailand of supporting the SSA, and Thai army units engaged in some cross-border artillery fire.

20 **Nepal:** the editor of the pro-Maoist newspaper *Janadisha* was arrested by security forces; it was later reported that he had died while in custody, allegedly under torture.

20 **Sri Lanka:** 19 days after the first major violation of the cease-fire agreement by government forces and the LTTE, the head of the Sri Lanka Monitoring Mission issued a statement conveying concern over increasing harassment of civilians by the LTTE.

20–21 **ASEAN/Malaysia:** ministers responsible for home and security affairs attended a meeting on terrorism in Kuala Lumpur, at the end of which they issued a statement reaffirming ASEAN's commitment to co-operation in combating terrorism in the region.

21 **Afghanistan:** the election of 1,051 delegates by district representatives under the monitoring of the UN and the Loya Jirga Commission began; the selection process ended on 5 June.

21 **East Timor:** Special Representative of the UN Secretary-General, Sérgio Vieira de Mello, left the country and was succeeded by Indian diplomat Kamalesh Sharma; UNTAET was also replaced by a smaller UN presence—the UN Mission of Support in East Timor (UNMISET)—which was to be maintained for two years.

21 **India/Pakistan:** the leader of the All-Party Hurriyat Conference, Abdul Ghani Lone, was assassinated by suspected Islamist extremists.

21 **Sri Lanka:** the first direct talks for seven years between the Government and the LTTE took place on the Jaffna peninsula.

22 **Cambodia:** former Khmer Rouge commander Gen. Sam Bith was finally arrested for the abduction and murder of three Western tourists during a train ambush in 1994; he had been charged with the murders in January 2000.

22 **Myanmar/Thailand:** the Myanma Government closed the shared border owing to the deterioration of bilateral relations.

22 **Nepal:** a rift in the ruling party led King Gyanendra to dissolve unexpectedly the House of Representatives, on the recommendation of the Prime Minister; a general election was scheduled to take place on 13 November, and the incumbent Government was instructed to rule the country in the interim.

22 **Pakistan:** the United Kingdom announced that the number of British diplomatic staff in Pakistan was being reduced, owing to the growing number of Islamist militant attacks against foreigners.

23 **Afghanistan:** the UN Security Council authorized the extension of the ISAF for six months beyond June.

23 **Cambodia:** Gen. Sam Bith was formally charged with terrorism, conspiracy to commit murder, membership of an armed force and destruction of property; You Hockry was forced to stand down as Co-Minister of the Interior by party leader Prince Ranariddh, following accusations of disloyalty from FUNCINPEC members.

23 **Nepal:** Prime Minister Deuba was suspended from the NCP (being expelled three days later for a three-year period); three ministers, including the Minister of Finance, resigned from the Government in protest at the calling of early elections.

24 **Afghanistan:** the provincial government in Khost warned all civilians to cease the traditional firing of weapons at wedding ceremonies after US forces reportedly fired on wedding celebrations, having mistaken the gunfire for Taliban activity.

25–28 **Pakistan:** a series of 'routine' tests of the country's ballistic-missile arsenal was conducted.

27 **Nepal:** the state of emergency was extended for three months by royal decree.

28 **Brunei:** 13 foreigners who had been investigating the Amedeo scandal were finally permitted to leave the country, after it had been reported that they had been refused permission to depart.

28 **Thailand:** the Government survived motions of 'no confidence' brought against 15 ministers in the House of Representatives, including nine members of the Cabinet, by the opposition; the charges had been based on allegations of corruption and conflicts of interest; it was also reported that the opposition had filed impeachment petitions with the National Counter-Corruption Commission against eight ministers.

31 **Cambodia:** four people were sentenced to prison terms after being convicted of terrorist offences following the bombing of two hotels in Phnom-Penh in July 2001.

JUNE 2002

2 **French Polynesia:** Michel Buillard and Béatrice Vernaudon, both candidates of the right-wing RPR, were elected to serve as the Territory's two representatives in the French National Assembly.

3 **Cambodia:** Hang Dara, one of the original founders of FUNCINPEC, defected from the party and announced that he would form his own party, the Hang Dara Movement Democratic Party, to contest the 2003 general election.

3 **Vanuatu:** at the first meeting of Parliament since the general election in May, Edward Natapei was re-elected as Prime Minister and a new Cabinet was appointed.

3–10 **Cambodia:** the UN Secretary-General's Special Representative for Human Rights, Peter Leuprecht, visited the country and intimated that attempts were under way to facilitate the restarting of talks on a joint human rights tribunal.

4 **Myanmar/Thailand:** masked gunmen dressed like members of the Karen National Union (KNU) opened fire on a Thai school bus near the border, killing three children; the KNU denied responsibility for the attack.

4 **New Zealand/Samoa:** on a visit to Apia, Helen Clark, the New Zealand Prime Minister, unexpectedly issued a formal apology for the errors committed by New Zealand during the country's administration of Samoa in 1914–62.

4 **Philippines:** Senator John Osmeña defected to the opposition, thus depriving the ruling People Power Coalition of its narrow majority in the upper house and undermining the Government's control over the legislature.

5 **People's Republic of China:** the authorities announced a three-month campaign to tighten controls over content of the internet.

5 **Indonesia:** four people were killed when a bomb exploded on a bus near Poso, the capital of eastern Sulawesi, in the worst outbreak of violence to have occurred in the region since a peace agreement was signed in December 2001.

5 **Myanmar:** the SPDC announced a military campaign to retake control of outposts and camps in Shan State, on the border with Thailand.

7 **Pakistan:** the Minister of Foreign Affairs, Abdul Sattar, tendered his resignation on health grounds; his replacement, Inamul Haque, was announced 12 days later.

7 **Philippines:** two hostages, who had been held by members of the Islamist separatist Abu Sayyaf group since May 2001, were killed during a rescue operation by government troops; the one remaining US hostage was freed.

10 **Afghanistan:** former King Zahir Shah declared that he would not be a candidate in the forthcoming presidential election, in an attempt to dispel uncertainty.

10 **India/Pakistan:** following international efforts to ease tensions between the two countries, India withdrew five naval ships from patrol off the coast of Pakistan, allowed Pakistani civilian aircraft to enter its airspace and appointed a new high commissioner to Pakistan.

11 **Afghanistan:** the Emergency Loya Jirga convened to select an Afghan Transitional Authority, which was to take over from the Interim Authority for at least 18 months, as envisaged by the Bonn Agreement.

13 **Afghanistan:** Hamid Karzai won the presidential election, receiving 1,295 of the approximately 1,575 votes cast by members of the Loya Jirga.

14 **People's Republic of China/Democratic People's Republic of Korea/Republic of Korea:** a diplomatic confrontation followed the arrival of North Korean asylum seekers at the South Korean

embassy in Beijing; China allowed them to leave the country later in the month.

14 **Malaysia:** it was reported that 13 alleged members of the KMM, detained under the Internal Security Act, had been sentenced to a two-year period of detention.

15 **Papua New Guinea:** voting began in a general election; the poll, which was originally scheduled to last two weeks, became considerably more protracted owing to administrative problems and widespread election-related violence.

16 **Republic of Korea:** the opposition Grand National party (GNP) won a decisive victory in local elections.

16–19 **Nepal:** the NCP formally split during a general convention held by the Deuba faction of the NCP; at the assembly Prime Minister Deuba was unanimously elected as party president and Girija Prasad Koirala was expelled from the party; the Koirala faction had boycotted the convention.

17 **Taiwan:** Premier Yu Shyi-kun appointed Liu Shyh-fang as Secretary-General of the Executive Yuan, replacing Lee Ying-yuan.

19 **Afghanistan:** following the approval of the Loya Jirga delegates, Hamid Karzai appointed his cabinet, retaining most of the incumbent members of the Interim Authority; Karzai was inaugurated as President.

19 **Japan:** Muneo Suzuki, a former legislator belonging to the LDP, was arrested on bribery charges.

19 **Nepal:** the Minister of Agriculture, Mahesh Acharya, resigned.

19 **Pakistan:** it was announced that the Government had approved an ordinance for the registration of *madrassas*, according to which only *madrassas* that were registered by the Madrassa Education Board within the next six months would be allowed to operate.

20 **Afghanistan:** Turkey took over command of the ISAF.

20 **Indonesia:** despite ongoing peace negotiations, GAM guerrillas ambushed a military patrol in northern Sumatra, resulting in six deaths.

20 **Myanmar/Thailand:** Thai troops fired across the border into Myanmar from Chiang Mai province after two Thai soldiers were injured by Myanma shells; Thailand denied that it supported Myanma insurgent ethnic militias but admitted that it had allowed Myanma refugees from the conflict to cross the border.

21 **Bangladesh:** President A. Q. M. Badruddoza Chowdhury resigned from office.

21 **Philippines:** it was reported that Abu Sabaya, a senior leader of the Islamist separatist group, Abu Sayyaf, had been killed during a gunfight at sea.

22 **Indonesia:** GAM guerrillas reportedly killed five workers and abducted a further eight from an oil palm plantation in East Aceh.

22 **Malaysia:** during a speech to the annual congress of the United Malays National Organization (UMNO) Prime Minister Mahathir dramatically announced that he intended to resign immediately; he was, however, persuaded to withdraw his resignation shortly afterwards.

23 **India:** Omar Abdullah was appointed President of the Jammu and Kashmir National Conference.

23 **Malaysia:** Fadzil Noor, President of the opposition PAS, died following heart surgery; Deputy President Abdul Hadi Awang assumed the party leadership on an interim basis.

24 **Afghanistan:** the Afghan Supreme Court dismissed a blasphemy charge against the outgoing Minister of Women's Affairs, Dr Sima Samar.

24 **Bangladesh:** the main opposition party, the Awami League, ended its eight-month boycott of Parliament.

24 **Hong Kong:** Chief Executive Tung Chee-hwa appointed a new, expanded 14-member Executive Council, four members of which were drawn from the private sector; critics warned that the changes would weaken the civil service.

24 **Pakistan:** President Musharraf announced a Chief Executive's Order stipulating that all candidates for future elections to federal and provincial legislatures should hold a university degree.

25 **Indonesia:** it was reported that nine members of the Kopassus special forces regiment would stand trial for the murder of Theys Eluay in November 2001; on the same day Yafet Yelemaken, another member of the PDP, was found dead in suspicious circumstances.

25 **Malaysia:** it was announced that Prime Minister Mahathir would resign in October 2003, when he would be succeeded by Deputy Prime Minister Abdullah Ahmed Badawi; during the transitional period Abdullah would assume increasing responsibility for the administration of the Government.

25 **Pakistan:** Omar Asghar Khan, the founder of the National Democratic Party and former minister, was found dead.

26 **Afghanistan:** President Karzai appointed Habiba Sorabi as the Minister of Women's Affairs, to replace Dr Sima Samar, who had been accused by an Islamist militant party as being unIslamic.

26 **Myanmar:** Aung San Suu Kyi visited Mandalay on her first major political trip since her release from house arrest in May.

26–27 **Pakistan:** President Musharraf publicly announced his radical proposals for constitutional reform.

27 **East Timor/Indonesia:** the trial of the former pro-Indonesia militia leader, Eurico Guterres, began at a human rights tribunal in Jakarta.

28 **Myanmar/Thailand:** the Thai Prime Minister, Thaksin Shinawatra, claimed that bilateral relations had deteriorated to a new low point and could only be improved with an apology from Myanmar.

29 **Indonesia:** GAM rebels were blamed for the abduction of nine crewmen servicing the offshore oil industry and who had been heading for an oil field off North Aceh.

29 **Democratic People's Republic of Korea/Republic of Korea:** a South Korean patrol boat was sunk with the loss of five lives during a gun battle between North and South Korean vessels in the Yellow Sea; some 30 North Korean sailors were also believed to have been killed.

JULY 2002

1–4 **East Timor:** President Xanana Gusmão went to Indonesia on his first official visit, accompanied by six ministers.

1 **India:** a government reorganization was effected.

1 **Thailand:** Sub-Lt Duangchalerm Yoobamrung, son of a senior politician, appeared in court following his extradition from Malaysia to stand trial for murder.

2 **Philippines:** Vice-President Teofisto Guingona announced his resignation as Secretary of Foreign Affairs with effect from 15 July; President Gloria

Macapagal Arroyo assumed the portfolio on an interim basis.

3 **Malaysia:** Prime Minister Mahathir announced his intention to relinquish all his party and government posts upon his resignation and nominated the Minister of Defence, Najib bin Tun Abdul Razak, as the future Deputy Prime Minister.

6 **Afghanistan:** Vice-President and Minister of Reconstruction, Haji Abdul Qadir, was assassinated, raising concern over the new Transitional Authority's stability.

6 **Indonesia:** the separatist GAM released 18 hostages whom it had kidnapped in the previous month, including the nine crewmen who had been servicing the offshore oil industry.

6 **Pakistan:** President Musharraf issued a decree barring former premiers and chief ministers from seeking a third term in office.

8 **Malaysia:** the acting President of PAS, Abdul Hadi Awang, announced the imposition of Islamic law in Terengganu state, of which he was the Chief Minister.

9 **Pakistan:** an Islamist militant group publicly admitted that it had organized the bombing outside a US consulate in Karachi in June.

10 **Republic of Korea:** President Kim Dae-Jung reorganized the State Council and appointed Chang Sang as the country's first ever female Prime Minister; however, her nomination was rejected by the National Assembly on 31 July.

10 **Malaysia:** Anwar Ibrahim, the former Deputy Prime Minister, lost his final appeal against his conviction for corruption.

10 **Pakistan:** President Musharraf announced that elections to the federal and provincial legislatures would be held on 10 October; former premier Benazir Bhutto was sentenced to three years' imprisonment for failing to appear before a court on corruption charges.

15 **India:** A. P. J. Abdul Kalam was elected as the country's President.

15 **Pakistan:** four men were convicted of the kidnapping and murder of US journalist Daniel Pearl; a British-born Islamist militant, Ahmed Omar Saeed Sheikh, was sentenced to death, while his co-defendants were sentenced to life imprisonment.

16 **India:** the Chief Minister of Jammu and Kashmir announced that scientific tests had shown that five men killed by Indian security forces in March 2000 had been local civilians and not, as maintained at the time, militants responsible for the murder of 35 Sikhs.

18 **Malaysia:** at a by-election to the Pendang seat (vacant since the death of Fadzil Noor) in the Dewan Rakyat, the ruling BN secured a narrow victory.

19 **India:** the Chief Minister of Gujarat resigned and recommended the dissolution of the state assembly, following criticisms of his handling of the situation in Gujarat; Narendra Modi was requested to continue as leader of a caretaker government until state elections were held.

19 **Vanuatu:** former Prime Minister Barak Sope was convicted of fraud and sentenced to a three-year prison term.

21 **People's Republic of China/Nauru/Taiwan:** Nauru established diplomatic relations with the People's Republic of China, thereby ending its ties with Taiwan.

21 **Taiwan:** President Chen assumed the chairmanship of the DPP.

23 **Afghanistan:** US authorities in Afghanistan declared that they would provide armed guards for President Hamid Karzai, in response to renewed fears for his safety.

23 **Philippines:** the US troops that had been deployed on the island of Basilan since February began to withdraw as military operations came to an end.

24 **Philippines:** Blas Ople was appointed as the new Secretary of Foreign Affairs.

24 **Viet Nam:** the new National Assembly formally re-elected Tran Duc Luong to the country's presidency for a second term; a reorganization of the Assembly's Standing Committee had been approved on the previous day, with Nguyen Van An returned to the office of Chairman.

25 **People's Republic of China:** senior leaders began gathering at the resort town of Beidaihe to discuss the forthcoming 16th Congress of the Chinese Communist Party (CCP) and the question of political succession.

25 **Tuvalu:** a general election took place at which six incumbent members of the 15-member Parliament (including Prime Minister Koloa Talake) lost their seats.

26 **Indonesia:** 'Tommy' Suharto was convicted of the murder of Justice Syafiuddin Kartasasmita, of the illegal possession of weapons and of fleeing from justice; he was sentenced to a 15-year prison term.

27 **New Zealand:** a general election took place at which the Labour Party secured a second term in office, although it failed to secure an overall majority in the House of Representatives; Prime Minister Helen Clark returned to office at the head of a minority Government, appointing a new Cabinet.

28 **Pakistan:** Benazir Bhutto was re-elected as leader of the Pakistan People's Party (PPP).

29 **ASEAN/Brunei:** ASEAN ministers of foreign affairs, followed by members of the ASEAN Regional Forum (ARF), convened in Bandar Seri Begawan; four days later US Secretary of State Colin Powell and member countries signed a declaration to co-operate in the campaign against terrorism.

29 **Solomon Islands:** a major cabinet reshuffle was effected.

30 **Bangladesh/Pakistan:** during his visit to Bangladesh, Pakistani President Musharraf apologized unreservedly for the atrocities committed by Pakistani troops during Bangladesh's 1971 war of liberation.

30 **Japan:** Prime Minister Koizumi successfully defeated a no-confidence motion sponsored by the Democratic Party.

31 **Malaysia:** all illegal migrant workers were expected to leave the country under the terms of new legislation; those who remained would face penalties of fines, imprisonment and caning.

AUGUST 2002

1 **Indonesia:** the trial of the Islamist militant, Ja'far Umar Thalib, was postponed until 15 August on the orders of the judge, who claimed that the defendant appeared ill, although Thalib had not requested any postponement.

2 **People's Republic of China/Pakistan:** President Jiang Zemin received President Musharraf during the latter's brief visit to Beijing.

2 **Tuvalu:** Saufatu Sopoanga was elected Prime Minister, defeating opposition candidate Amasone Kilei by eight parliamentary votes to seven.

3 **Pakistan:** Shahbaz Sharif was elected leader of the pro-Nawaz Pakistan Muslim League.

3 **Taiwan:** during a televised conference, President Chen Shui-bian stated his support for a referendum to determine the island's future.

4 **Vanuatu:** the police arrested 15 officials, including the newly appointed commissioner of police, Mael Apisai, on charges of seditious conspiracy.

5 **Pakistan:** in order to avoid the possible disqualification of the PPP led by Benazir Bhutto, the Pakistan People's Party Parliamentarians (PPPP) was created to contest the forthcoming general elections.

5 **Papua New Guinea:** Sir Michael Somare was elected Prime Minister unopposed winning 88 parliamentary votes.

7 **Myanmar:** Aung San Suu Kyi challenged the SPDC to order the swift and unconditional release of all political prisoners to demonstrate its commitment towards the achievement of democracy.

7 **Viet Nam:** the National Assembly approved an extensive government reorganization, which included the creation of three new ministries; Phan Van Khai remained in the office of Prime Minister.

8 **New Caledonia:** a reallocation of ministerial portfolios was completed.

8 **Niue:** Prime Minister Young Vivian dismissed his Deputy Prime Minister, Sani Lakatani, after he voted with the opposition to defeat the Government's budget proposals.

9 **Afghanistan:** a car bomb attack in Jalalabad, one of series of explosions in Afghanistan, by suspected Taliban members, killed 25 people and injured 80.

9 **Republic of Korea:** following the heavy defeat of the MDP in by-elections on the previous day, President Kim Dae-Jung appointed Chang Dae-Whan as Prime Minister; however, his nomination was rejected by the National Assembly on 28 August.

9 **Myanmar:** the ruling SPDC released 14 political prisoners, including six members of the opposition NLD.

9 **Pakistan:** suspected Islamist militants attacked a chapel in the grounds of a Christian hospital in Taxila, killing three nurses and wounding nearly 30 others; this incident occurred four days after an attack on a Christian missionary school, in which six people were killed.

11 **Indonesia:** the legislature approved a total of 14 amendments to the 1945 Constitution, including provisions for the direct election of the country's President and Vice-President from 2004 and the abolition of the 38 parliamentary seats reserved for the armed forces; a proposal to introduce Islamic law, however, was rejected.

12 **India:** Bhairon Singh Shekhawat was elected as Vice-President (his predecessor died two weeks before the scheduled election date).

13 **Papua New Guinea:** Prime Minister Sir Michael Somare appointed a new Cabinet dominated by 19 recently elected MPs.

13 **Philippines:** Secretary for Education Raul Roco resigned, protesting against the President's endorsement of a corruption investigation into his use of public funds; Ramon Bacani was later appointed acting Secretary.

14 **Bhutan:** the incumbent Minister of Agriculture, Kinzang Dorji, was inaugurated as Prime Minister.

14 **East Timor/Indonesia:** in Jakarta Abílio Soares, the former governor of East Timor, was sentenced to a three-year prison term by a human rights tribunal after being found guilty of two charges of 'gross rights violations' for failing to prevent violence involving those subordinate to him; the verdict was the first concerning human rights relating to the violence surrounding the referendum on East Timor's independence in 1999.

14-17 **Indonesia/Taiwan:** Taiwanese Vice-President Annette Lu visited Indonesia and met several ministers to discuss investment and labour issues.

15 **East Timor/Indonesia:** the human rights tribunal in Jakarta acquitted the former police chief of East Timor, Timbul Silaen, of charges of failing to control his subordinates during the violence of 1999; five other police and army officers were also acquitted, provoking widespread criticism of the tribunal from human rights organizations and demands for the UN to establish an international tribunal on East Timor.

15 **Hong Kong:** 16 Falun Gong practitioners were convicted and fined for obstructing pedestrians in a public demonstration, the first time members of the religious cult had been prosecuted in the territory.

15 **Indonesia:** the trial of the Laskar Jihad leader, Ja'far Umar Thalib, on charges of inciting hatred and rebellion and defamation of the President and Vice-President, began.

19 **Indonesia:** the trial of the leader of the Christian Maluku Sovereignty Front, Alex Manuputty, for subversion began in Jakarta.

20 **Myanmar/Thailand:** the Thai Minister of Foreign Affairs, Surakiart Sathirathai, stated that the two countries had agreed to hold talks to resolve border disputes.

21 **Australia:** Senator Natasha Stott Despoja, leader of the Australian Democrats (who held the balance of power in the upper house), resigned; she was subsequently replaced by Andrew Bartlett.

21 **Pakistan:** President Musharraf enacted the Legal Framework Order, which introduced a series of amendments to the Constitution and validated all the military decrees approved since the coup in 1999; as a result, the President's powers were enlarged and the military was ensured influence in decision-making beyond the parliamentary elections in October.

22 **Solomon Islands:** Rev. Augustin Geve, the Minister for Youth and Sports and Women's Affairs, was assassinated.

22 **Vanuatu:** Prime Minister Natapei assumed the police and mobile force portfolios from Joe Natuman, Minister of Internal Affairs.

26 **India:** Anant Gangaram Geete was appointed Minister of Power, following Suresh Prabhu's resignation from the post.

27 **Federated States of Micronesia:** a referendum was held on proposed amendments to the Constitution, including issues related to the education and justice systems, dual citizenship and the election of the President; none of the 14 proposals received the necessary 75% support to pass into law.

27 **Vanuatu:** 27 policemen were suspended and charged with mutiny in connection with the arrests of 15 officials earlier in the month.

28 **Nepal:** the state of emergency expired; as a result, the Maoist insurgents intensified their violent campaign.

29 **Indonesia:** the conviction of central bank governor Sjahril Sabirin for corruption was overturned by an appeal court.

29 **Vanuatu:** a new acting police commissioner was appointed.

30 **Mongolia:** it was reported that the Dalai Lama, the exiled spiritual leader of Tibet, had cancelled a visit to Mongolia, owing to the refusal of a South Korean airline to transport him via Seoul.

30 **Pakistan:** election officials in Sindh province rejected Benazir Bhutto's candidacy in the forthcoming National Assembly elections, owing to her criminal conviction.

31 **Indonesia:** two US teachers and an Indonesian citizen were killed following an ambush near the US-owned Freeport mine in Papua; the Free Papua Movement (OPM) was believed to be responsible for the attack.

31 **Philippines:** government negotiators met representatives from the National Democratic Front in Quezon City with the intention of resuming peace talks.

SEPTEMBER 2002

1 **Pakistan:** the former Prime Minister, Nawaz Sharif, withdrew his candidacy for the parliamentary elections, reportedly in solidarity with Benazir Bhutto.

1 **Malaysia:** it was reported that Prime Minister Mahathir had temporarily halted mass deportations of illegal immigrants owing to diplomatic pressure and to protests in Indonesia and the Philippines against the apparently inhumane nature of the expulsions.

1 **Vanuatu:** the Government signed an agreement with rival security forces aimed at ending the police revolt over the controversial appointment of police commissioner Mael Apisai.

2 **Japan:** Yasuo Tanaka was overwhelmingly re-elected to the governorship of Nagano prefecture having been ousted by the prefectural legislature in July; his success was widely seen as a victory for reformist political forces.

4 **Cambodia:** a court rejected the final appeal of former Khmer Rouge leader Nuon Paet against his life sentence for the murder of three Western tourists in 1994.

4 **Indonesia:** Akbar Tandjung was found guilty of the corruption charges against him and sentenced to a three-year prison term; however, he remained in his post as Speaker of the House of Representatives pending an appeal.

4 **Sri Lanka:** the Government removed its official ban on the LTTE, a prerequisite set by the LTTE to negotiations.

5 **Afghanistan:** President Karzai escaped an assassination attempt in Qandahar, hours after a bomb explosion in Kabul killed 30 people and injured at least 160 others; al-Qa'ida was held responsible for both attacks.

6 **APEC:** meeting in Mexico, finance ministers of the Asia-Pacific Economic Co-operation forum announced proposals to combat the illicit funding of international terrorism.

6 **Cambodia:** reversing an earlier acquittal, a court convicted former Khmer Rouge leader Col Chhouk Rin of the murder of three Western tourists in 1994.

7–8 **Nepal:** more than 350 people were reportedly killed during the first two major Maoist offensives since the state of emergency was lifted.

9–11 **Pakistan:** Pakistani authorities arrested 12 alleged members of al-Qa'ida, including the Yemeni-born Ramzi Binalshibh, a principal suspect in the attacks on the USA on 11 September 2001.

11 **India:** the state Minister of Law and Parliamentary Affairs of Jammu and Kashmir was killed during his local election campaign by suspected militant Islamists.

11 **Indonesia:** a British and a US woman were arrested and charged with visa violations in Aceh; it was believed they had made contact with the separatist GAM.

11 **Taiwan:** the Executive Yuan approved the draft legislation for the Political Party Law, which would ban parties from owning or investing in profit-making enterprises; on the same day, for the 10 consecutive year, the General Committee of the UN General Assembly rejected a proposal for Taiwan's participation in the UN.

12 **Nepal:** the Maoist leader's offer of a cease-fire was rejected by political parties for lacking credibility.

12 **Pakistan:** Shahbaz Sharif, the leader of the PML (Nawaz), was disqualified from entering the general elections, for defaulting on a bank loan.

16 **India:** the first of four phases of local assembly elections in Jammu and Kashmir began.

16 **Republic of Korea:** Chung Mong-Joon, an independent legislator and organizer of the recent football World Cup, announced his candidacy for the presidential elections in December, ending months of speculation.

16 **Singapore:** the Government announced that in August a total of 21 terrorist suspects, believed to be members of Jemaah Islamiah, had been arrested on suspicion of planning attacks on US interests in Singapore; some of the detainees were alleged to have received training at al-Qa'ida camps in Afghanistan, while others had reportedly trained at a base in the southern Philippines.

16–18 **Sri Lanka:** at the first round of peace negotiations between the Government and the LTTE in Thailand, the LTTE abandoned their demand for independence and agreed to consider regional autonomy and self-government; both sides also agreed to focus on the reconstruction and rehabilitation of the Tamil-controlled areas in the north and east and to appeal to international donors for assistance; they also discussed the issue of internally displaced people.

17 **Japan/Democratic People's Republic of Korea:** Junichiro Koizumi made the first ever visit by a Japanese Prime Minister to North Korea, where he held talks with Kim Jong Il; the latter admitted that North Korea had kidnapped Japanese citizens during the 1970s and 1980s.

17 **Nepal:** the Election Commission refused to recognize Prime Minister Deuba's breakaway faction as the official NCP; instead, the mainstream Koirala faction retained this title.

18 **Democratic People's Republic of Korea/ Republic of Korea:** ceremonies were held on both sides of the demilitarized zone (DMZ) to mark the beginning of reconstruction work on the inter-Korean rail link.

19 **Sri Lanka:** the Government proposed in Parliament a constitutional amendment that would restrict the right of the President to dissolve Parliament within one year after a general election if the Government held a majority.

22 **India/Maldives:** the Indian Prime Minister, Atal Bihari Vajpayee, arrived in the Maldives at the start of a four-day official visit.

23–24 **ASEM:** at the fourth Asia-Europe meeting in Copenhagen, Denmark, leaders from 10 Asian countries and 25 European nations focused on trade and security issues, adopting a joint declaration on combating international terrorism.

23 **Indonesia:** a grenade explosion near a building used by the US embassy in Jakarta killed one person.

24–25 **India/Pakistan:** suspected Islamist militants forced entry into a Hindu temple in Gujarat and shot about 30 worshippers; the gunmen were shot dead by security forces, ending a night-long siege of the temple; the Indian Government believed that Pakistan was responsible for the attack, an allegation strongly rejected by the Pakistani Government.

24 **Democratic People's Republic of Korea:** in an unprecedented development, the Presidium of the Supreme People's Assembly (SPA) appointed Yang Bin, a Chinese businessman of Dutch citizenship, as the first governor of the newly established Shinuiju Special Administrative Region; however, he was arrested by the Chinese Government soon after the announcement of his appointment.

25 **Indonesia:** a bomb exploded in Aceh shortly before President Megawati was due to arrive on her second visit to the troubled province since assuming office.

26 **Myanmar:** the four relatives of Gen. U Ne Win who had been arrested in March for their involvement in an attempted coup were convicted of treason and sentenced to death.

27 **East Timor:** the country became the 191st member of the UN.

30 **Japan:** Prime Minister Koizumi reorganized the Cabinet, appointing the Minister of Economic and Fiscal Policy, Heizo Takenaka, to serve concurrently as Minister of the Financial Services Agency; four other ministers were also replaced.

OCTOBER 2002

1 **Vanuatu:** public prosecutors withdrew the charges against 18 of the 26 police officers accused of mutiny, leaving eight senior officers to face trial.

2 **Australia/Myanmar:** in Yangon the Australian Minister for Foreign Affairs, Alexander Downer, met government officials and opposition leader Aung Sang Suu Kyi for discussions, during the first visit to Myanmar by an Australian minister for nearly 20 years.

2 **Philippines:** a bomb explosion in the southern city of Zamboanga killed four people, including a US soldier.

3 **Democratic People's Republic of Korea:** the US Assistant Secretary of State for East Asian and Pacific Affairs, James Kelly, began a visit to Pyongyang for discussions with senior officials, the highest level of contact since President George W. Bush's denunciation in January of North Korea as part of an 'axis of evil'.

3 **Nepal:** Prime Minister Deuba requested King Gyanendra to postpone the general election by one year, citing the deteriorating law and order situation.

3 **Thailand:** Prime Minister Thaksin Shinawatra effected a reallocation of cabinet portfolios, which included the appointment of heads to six new ministries created through reforms of the bureaucracy.

4 **Nepal:** King Gyanendra dismissed the Prime Minister and the interim Council of Ministers for reportedly failing to organize the forthcoming general election; he assumed executive power and postponed indefinitely the election that had been scheduled for November.

4 **Solomon Islands:** the Government announced a reduction in the number of ministries from 20 to 10.

5 **Republic of Korea:** the National Assembly overwhelmingly approved Kim Suk-Soo as the new Prime Minister.

8 **India:** the local assembly elections in Jammu and Kashmir ended; no single party had won a majority of the seats, the outgoing Jammu and Kashmir National Conference secured 28 seats, Congress won 20 seats and the regional People's Democratic Party (PDP) won 16 seats; Congress and PDP were invited to form a coalition government.

10 **Pakistan:** elections for the National Assembly and Provincial Assemblies took place; initial results suggested that the pro-Musharraf Pakistan Muslim League Quaid-e-Azam Group had won the largest number of seats in the National Assembly (74), the Pakistan People's Party Parliamentarians secured 63 seats and the coalition of religious parties won 45 seats.

11 **India:** the Chief Minister of Jammu and Kashmir, Dr Farooq Abdullah, resigned after results showed that his Jammu and Kashmir Conference Party had lost the state elections; a few days later Governor's rule was imposed on the state, in order to allow politicians more time to form a new state government.

11 **Nepal:** King Gyanendra appointed a nine-member interim Government, headed by former premier Lokendra Bahadur Chand.

12 **Indonesia:** a bomb exploded in a night-club on the island of Bali, killing almost 200 people, including many tourists, the majority of whom were young Australians; Islamist terrorists were suspected to be responsible for the attack.

14 **Japan/Democratic People's Republic of Korea:** the five surviving Japanese nationals who had been kidnapped by North Korean agents in the 1970s and 1980s finally returned to Japan for a short visit; however, their children were not allowed to accompany them.

15 **Myanmar/Thailand:** the shared border reopened following an improvement in bilateral relations.

16 **Republic of Korea/Macao:** during a visit to Seoul, the Chief Executive of Macao, Edmund Ho, discussed economic and commercial co-operation with South Korean President Kim Dae-Jung.

17 **Democratic People's Republic of Korea:** in a remarkable disclosure, the country confirmed the existence of its nuclear-weapons programme, thus giving rise to renewed international concern.

17 **Philippines:** in Zamboanga two bombs exploded in crowded shopping centres, killing several people and injuring more than 160; the Abu Sayyaf group was believed to be responsible.

18 **People's Republic of China/Democratic People's Republic of Korea:** in Beijing senior officials from the US State Department urged the Chinese Government to assist in diplomatic efforts to stabilize the deteriorating situation on the Korean peninsula.

18 **Indonesia:** as international pressure mounted, President Megawati announced emergency measures providing for the introduction of the death penalty for convicted terrorists.

18 **Philippines:** in Manila a bus bombing killed at least three and injured more than 20.

22 **People's Republic of China:** President Jiang Zemin began an official visit to the USA, his pro-

gramme including a meeting with President George W. Bush.

22 **Philippines:** five men, believed to be members of Abu Sayyaf, were arrested in connection with the recent bomb attacks.

23 **Democratic People's Republic of Korea/ Republic of Korea:** following three days of bilateral discussions in Pyongyang, the two countries agreed to resolve international concerns over the North Korean nuclear programme through the active pursuit of dialogue and joint efforts to maintain peace on the Korean peninsula.

24 **APEC:** representatives of the 21 member countries of the Asia-Pacific Economic Co-operation began convening in Mexico for the forum's 10th annual meeting; attention was expected to focus on security issues.

25 **India/Pakistan:** India announced that it had commenced a withdrawal of troops from its border with Pakistan, where they had been deployed since December 2001; however, Indian troops stationed along the Line of Control, dividing the disputed Kashmir region, were to remain in position.

28 **Myanmar:** UN envoy Paulo Sérgio Pinheiro was scheduled to end a week's visit to the country, during which he had discussions with Aung San Suu Kyi, his first meeting with the pro-democracy leader since her release from house arrest in May.

29 **Japan/Democratic People's Republic of Korea:** bilateral discussions on the restoration of normal relations were scheduled to recommence.

31 **Sri Lanka:** the next round of peace negotiations between the Government and the LTTE was scheduled to begin.

PART ONE
General Survey

CURRENT SECURITY ISSUES IN ASIA

ROHAN GUNARATNA

Since the early 1990s security in Asia (defined, as here, to exclude the Middle East—or West Asia—and Central Asia) has witnessed a series of new threats facilitated by modern technologies and carried out by new perpetrators. Although the old threats persist, these new fears, of which terrorism is the most portent, affect both the security of the region and beyond. The unprecedented acts of terrorism carried out by organizations in Asia: the use of the poisonous gas, sarin, by the religious sect Aum Shinrikyo against Japanese citizens in 1994 and 1995; the manipulation of computer technology by US 'cells' of the Liberation Tigers of Tamil Eelam (LTTE) to co-ordinate simultaneous attacks against Sri Lankan diplomatic missions world-wide in 1996; the airborne 'suicide attacks' on New York and Washington, DC, USA, on 11 September 2001, for which the USA held the Afghan-based Islamist fundamentalist al-Qa'ida (Base) organization responsible; and the bombing of a night-club on the Indonesian island of Bali in October 2002; have sharply raised international insecurity. The attacks marked a transformation in the prevailing tensions within Asia, necessitating a similar change in attitudes towards security issues in the region—a broader, more comprehensive understanding of the many threats to security was required if the consequent responses were to prove effective.

The most immediate threat to communities world-wide in 2001–02 was that posed by al-Qa'ida. Afghanistan had become the ideal base for al-Qa'ida activities after the Islamist militant Taliban regime offered refuge to Osama bin Laden, the Saudi-born leader of al-Qa'ida, in 1997. A close relationship between bin Laden and the Taliban leader ensued, with bin Laden developing considerable influence over the Taliban. Until October 2001 a joint Taliban-al-Qa'ida training infrastructure provided volunteers to fight in conflicts in Afghanistan, Algeria, Bosnia and Herzegovina, the Russian federal subjects of Chechnya and Dagestan, Egypt, Indonesia, Kashmir, the Yugoslav province of Kosovo and Metohija, the Philippines, Tajikistan, and against targets in the West. The founder members of the Taliban and al-Qa'ida were Afghan-trained *mujahidin* who, imbued by their defeat of the Soviet army in 1989, believed that the West was evil. In February 1998 al-Qa'ida and its associates issued a manifesto condemning the USA's alleged anti-Islamic actions and announced a *fatwa* ordering Muslims to kill Americans and their allies under the auspices of 'The International Islamic Front for Jihad Against Jews and Crusaders'. Even after the attacks in September 2001, the front reportedly continued to attack or attempt to destroy non-Islamic targets. The oldest Jewish synagogue in Djerba, Tunisia, was attacked in April 2002, for example, and in May a 'suicide bomber' killed 14 people, mostly French naval technicians, in Karachi, Pakistan. The front also allegedly attempted to destroy the US embassy and the American Cultural Center in Paris, to poison the water supply to the US embassy in Rome, to attack multiple targets in Singapore, and to strike US and British warships in the straits of Gibraltar and Melaka (Malacca). The threat of future al-Qa'ida attacks was prevalent in 2002 and was likely to persist in the foreseeable future. Although membership of al-Qa'ida reached only an estimated 3,000, in mid-2002 there reportedly existed a core of more than 100,000 dispersed Muslims mainly from Asia, the Middle East and North Africa who had participated in the semi-covert multinational and anti-Soviet campaign in Afghanistan in 1979–89 (see the chapter on Afghanistan). By 2002 the centre of gravity of international terrorism had shifted from the Middle East to Asia.

Although the long-standing period of hostility between the USA and the Soviet Union known as the Cold War ended in the early 1990s, the international community did not transform its law enforcement, security and intelligence systems to respond to the post-Cold War threats until after the terrorist attacks on the USA in September 2001. Areas where conflict had been largely neglected by the international community—for example, Afghanistan, Chechnya, Israel/Palestinian Autonomous Areas and Kashmir—became havens for post-Cold War militant groups. These terrorist organizations managed to develop close political, economic and military links with little difficulty. They learned from each other's operational efforts, successes and failures and co-operated in the fields of technology, personnel, finance and intelligence. The international community miscalculated the sophisticated capabilities of these groups. The West, in particular, misunderstood the threat posed by these organizations. The tragic events in the USA of 11 September 2001 exposed the inability of one country single-handedly to protect itself; only a multi-pronged, multi-dimensional, multi-agency and a multinational response against security threats would be effective in stabilizing the international system.

BACKGROUND

The civil war in Lebanon, which began in 1975 and involved Shi'ite and Sunni Muslim, Maronite Christian and Druze militias, created the ideal conditions for foreign terrorist groups to establish a presence. Organizations such as the Japanese Red Army, the Provisional Irish Republican Army, the LTTE, the Armenian Secret Army for the Liberation of Armenia, Partiya Karkeren Kurdistan (Kurdistan Workers' Party, restyled in April 2002 as KADEK—Congress for Freedom and Democracy in Kurdistan), the Red Army Faction, Turkish Left, and Palestinian groups, established bases particularly in the Syrian-controlled Beka'a valley in Lebanon. Even after Israel intervened and the Palestinian Liberation Organization withdrew to Tunis (Tunisia), southern Lebanon remained a perfect training ground for such groups as Hezbollah and alleged state sponsors of militancy, for example Iran. Similarly, the Soviet occupation of Afghanistan in 1979–89 and the subsequent disengagement of the West from the collapsed state provided suitable conditions for the rise in Islamist militancy. The Taliban were profoundly disillusioned by the factional fighting and criminal actions of the *mujahidin* leadership in the early 1990s, and believed that their fundamentalism provided the only way to cleanse the social system. Pakistan gave considerable support to the Taliban and made great efforts to control the regime, mainly for economic and security reasons. Increasingly, the Kashmir issue became the main motive for Pakistan's support of the Taliban. At the same time, the Taliban leaders' unique outlook provided an opportunity for several Islamist radical groups, notably al-Qa'ida, to establish a presence in Afghanistan and to train mercenaries to participate in campaigns world-wide.

The end of the Cold War encouraged these developments. The international arms market became saturated following the end of US- and Soviet-supported surrogate wars in Africa, Asia and South America. Furthermore, the economic decline in the former USSR meant that financial, rather than security, considerations determined the sale of weapons. Consequently, some Asian terrorist organizations gained access to automatic weapons, including stand-off-weapons and explosives, at competitive prices. In 1979–91 the West, particularly the USA, sponsored or shipped to Afghanistan, via Pakistan, some 400,000 AK-47 guns; 700 US-manufactured *Stinger* missiles, Italian-made anti-personnel mines, 40–50 Swiss-designed anti-aircraft guns, Egyptian mortars, British surface-to-air missiles, 100,000 Indian rifles, 60,000 rifles and 8,000 light machine guns from Egypt, and more than 100m. rounds of ammunition. Similarly, access to dual technologies (which can be used for both military and civil purposes)—satellite communications, secure data communications and advanced sea transport—allowed terrorist groups to strike military and civilian land and sea targets. Accessibility to such sophisticated weapons and dual technologies propelled violent political conflicts to low intensity conflicts, and from low intensity conflicts to high intensity conflicts. The number of fatalities and casualties per attack increased as arms became more readily available. In recent times Asian terrorist groups have employed or expressed an interest in acquiring Chemical, Biological, Radiological and Nuclear (CBRN) material or expertise in its production, particularly through criminal organizations. The acquisition of such material by terrorist groups poses the most significant threat to the international system.

The increase in terrorist lethality led to greater internal displacement in target countries. Similarly, heightened fears over human rights abuses and the lack of humanitarian assistance in host countries caused an escalation of migration and unprecedented refugee flows. By infiltrating their diaspora and migrant communities, Asian terrorist groups developed advanced support infrastructures outside Asia to disseminate propaganda, raise funds, train members, procure weapons and obtain sea transport. Using the support networks spanning across Africa, the Balkans, the Caucasus, the Middle East, the USA and Canada and Western Europe, organizations influenced by both secular and pseudo-religious ideologies conducted long-range terrorist operations. The geographical reach of these contemporary groups steadfastly increased, owing to the communications revolution, which intensified in the 1990s. Inexpensive international travel and the proliferation of information and communications technologies—satellite television, facsimile machines, the internet and mobile cellular telephones—improved interaction between members and supporters domestically and world-wide, and allowed leaders to maintain effective command and control of their followers. Middle Eastern groups were able easily to work with their Asian counterparts and to network with migrant populations and organizations with compatible aims and objectives. Similarly, undisciplined terrorist groups based in Asia transformed into sophisticated entities. In order to ensure wider impact, some Asian terrorist groups increased the scope of their activities to include guerrilla warfare, assassination attempts, sabotage, propaganda, electoral politics, trade and investments.

Has terrorism in the post-Cold War era replaced the nuclear threat associated with the Cold War? What is evident is that the number of internal armed conflicts has exponentially increased since the early 1990s. In Asia, as is mostly the case elsewhere in the world, terrorism is largely a derivative of armed conflicts. Ethnic and religious conflicts fuel as many as 80% of armed campaigns in the early 21st century. Unlike the ideologically motivated militant groups of the Cold War era, the majority of contemporary terrorist organizations and political movements benefit from the post-1990 global resurgence of ethnicity and religiosity. These ethno-political and religious conflicts produce the highest level of fatalities and casualties, the largest internal displacements and refugee flows, and reports of the greatest human rights violations. What is certain is that terrorism has emerged as the primary post-Cold War security threat. However, although Islamist terrorism is the most publicized threat, there are other potent forces that endanger the stability of Asia.

CONFLICT ZONES

Geographically, Asia, as defined here, occupied 16% of the world's land area, but included 55.5% of the world's population in mid-2001. Asia's overwhelming feature was its vulnerability to armed conflict. South Asia and parts of South-East Asia were particularly affected by armed conflicts. Apart from the dispute between India and Pakistan over Kashmir, the majority of the South Asian conflicts in the early 21st century are domestic: in India clashes occurred in the states of Assam, Bihar, Jammu and Kashmir, Manipur, Nagaland and Tripura; in Nepal, Maoist insurgents continued a violent campaign to overthrow the monarchy and to establish a 'socialist' state; in Sri Lanka the LTTE had entered negotiations but continued to train and re-arm militants to infiltrate southern Sri Lanka. Some disputes posed a serious threat to other countries: more than 10 Islamist groups in Pakistan were preparing to strike targets in India and the West. In Afghanistan the international community sought to establish a stable civil administration after US-led forces dislodged the Taliban and al-Qa'ida from state control. State sponsorship of militancy (the provision of sanctuary, weapons and training to groups in inimical states, for example) evidently influenced some of the conflicts, particularly between India and Pakistan.

In South-East Asia, guerrilla and terrorist groups motivated by ethno-nationalist aims operated in Cambodia, Indonesia, the Philippines, Myanmar and Xinjiang (the People's Republic of China). Although the number of organizations driven by left-wing ideologies had declined, the New People's Army (the military wing of the Communist Party of the Philippines) continued to pose a significant threat to that South-East Asian state. The Philippine Muslim secessionist groups Abu Sayyaf and the Moro Islamic Liberation Front (MILF—engaged in peace negotiations in mid-2002), Kumpulan Mujahidin Malaysia, and the Indonesian Mujahidin Council (or Majlis Mujahidin Indonesia—MMI) were reportedly associates of al-Qa'ida. Despite attempts in Singapore from December 2001 to uncover and disband Jemaah Islamiah (Islamic Group), the South-East Asian wing of al-Qa'ida remained active in Indonesia, Malaysia, the Philippines and Thailand. The potential for violent conflict between states and between state and armed non-state protagonists remained high, owing to a number of unresolved disputes. At the same time, however, a number of groups, both in South Asia (the Shanthi Bahini Movement in Bangladesh) and in South-East Asia (the Pattani United Liberation Organization in Thailand) had returned to non-violence.

As opposed to internal conflicts, the threat of international conflict receded in the 1990s. None the less, two inter-state disputes in Asia remained unresolved: one between India and Pakistan over Kashmir and the Siachen glacier (the highest battlefield in the world); and the other between the Democratic People's Republic of Korea (North) and the Republic of Korea (South) over their shared border. There is potential for conflict between the People's Republic of China and Taiwan and also between China and several other Asian countries over the Spratly (Nansha) Islands. The lethality and intensity of most conflicts has increased. Compared with the Middle East, Asia is affected more by both domestic and international armed conflict.

THREATS AND POTENTIAL THREATS

Twelve potential and actual security threats can be identified in the Asian conflict spectrum. Although a large number of these threats are not unique to this region, the problems of widespread poverty, corruption and militarization, particularly in South and South-East Asia, add a new dimension to internal tensions in Asia.

Ethno-politics

Since the end of the Cold War, ethnic conflict has emerged as the principal source of destabilization and organized violence, resulting in mass killings, the destruction of whole communities and a rise in the number of refugees. In the absence of a restraining moral code of conduct, ethnic 'entrepreneurs' continue to devise communities by creating or exploiting ethnic differences. Ethnicity, affecting mostly the poorer regions of South and South-East Asia, is employed as an effective tool to politicize, radicalize and mobilize constituencies, transcending state borders. The reconfiguration of geography, history, politics, and religion after decolonization has also complicated security matters in parts of Asia.

Religious Intolerance

Religious intolerance, especially fundamentalism, constitutes a security threat. Traditionally, most communities in the region have lived under the shadow of other faiths, and as a result are tolerant and moderate. However, some Asian leaders are accused of employing virulent religious rhetoric to retain or gain political power. As well as religious intolerance, the region is experiencing a resurgence of Hindu, Islamist and Christian fundamentalism. Extremism in one faith provokes and reinforces fundamentalism in another. The election of the Hindu nationalist Bharatiya Janata Party (BJP) to government in India in early 1998, for example, created an environment conducive for other fundamentalist forces, particularly Islamist militancy, to emerge. The cases of Afghanistan and Kashmir, amongst others, demonstrate that the loss of political and economic privileges renders citizens vulnerable to fundamentalist ideologies. Until 1989 the Kashmiri insurgency was motivated by a secular ideology; from the late 1980s, however, an Islamist ideology originating from Afghanistan began to permeate the disputed territory. The insurgency escalated, causing tension to increase between Hindu and Islamic communities throughout South Asia. The rise of Hindu and Islamist fundamentalism could divide the population along sectarian lines, strategically weakening the overall long-term stability of a secular India. South-East Asia has witnessed a rise in Christian fundamentalism. In the Philippines the Mindanao Christian Unified Command (MCUC—a Christian umbrella movement); the Puluhan Group led by Isaac Gustillo; the Itaman Group headed by 'Commander Jack'; Kusog Kristiano Kamindanawan (KKK) led by Gideon Sagrado; and the Ilaga Movement chaired by Ligaya Buko are attempting to disrupt the peace process in Mindanao. The KKK, together with the Family of the Remnants of God (another Philippine religious group), reportedly planned in 1997 to assassinate the leader of the Moro National Liberation Front (MNLF), Nur Misuari, and Philippine President Fidel Ramos. Christian communities in South and South-East Asia (notably in East Timor and Maluku—Moluccas—in Indonesia) are targets of organized attacks by fundamentalist groups angry at reports of proselytization to Christianity.

Terrorism

Prevalent in the region since the early 1970s, terrorism has assumed a new dimension with the formation of transnational ideological, financial and technological networks. Terrorism became an even more serious threat to regional and international stability owing to these transnational or 'support' networks facilitating the transfer of such technologies as landmines, equipment for 'suicide bombers', and mortars between groups. Therefore, despite attempts by the Japanese Government to contain the militant organization, Aum Shinrikyo maintains an extensive network stretching from East Asia across South-East Asia and South Asia into the West. Similarly, al-Qa'ida established cells world-wide and reportedly receives support from similarly motivated groups in 94 countries. The MILF received, procured and exchanged military and financial assistance from diverse sources, particularly the Gulf region, North African states and individual donors. Occasionally, these support networks transform into operational networks to carry out terrorist attacks on host countries.

Weapons of Mass Destruction

Weapons of mass destruction (WMD) and missile technologies are proliferating in Asia, particularly India, North Korea and Taiwan, despite attempts by the West to curb the growth. Exactly 10 years after China carried out its first nuclear test, India exploded a 15,000 metric ton nuclear device in 1974. Pakistan's nuclear programme began soon after the Indian army intervened in East Pakistan (now Bangladesh), and by 1990 both India and Pakistan were classified by the Western intelligence and security agencies as undeclared nuclear powers. In May 1998 India conducted five underground nuclear explosions; Pakistan responded two weeks later with six tests. The two countries thereby claimed their nuclear power status and overtly entered the nuclear arms race. The UN Security Council condemned the actions and passed a resolution urging the two countries to resume high-level dialogue on all issues, including the disputed area of Kashmir. It was clear that the South Asian arms race could be controlled only by addressing the roots of regional tension over Kashmir and not by regulating proliferation. However, no real steps were taken by the international community to relieve tension, and it was unlikely that India and Pakistan could resolve the dispute over Kashmir without third-party mediation. Until the international community addresses the issue of Kashmir, the potential for the dispute to graduate into a conventional war remains high, and in turn the risk of nuclear war could become a reality. Since states determined to achieve nuclear status are likely to develop a nuclear capability, the threat of proliferation is set to become even harder to control, especially in a world moving towards multi-polarity. Other states in the region reportedly expressed an interest in developing clandestine nuclear and missile programmes. India, Myanmar, North Korea, Pakistan, South Korea Taiwan and Thailand reportedly possess, or are increasingly willing to procure, expertise and biological and chemical material. Furthermore, a few Asian terrorist groups have employed (Aum Shinrikyo and the LTTE) or expressed an interest in acquiring (Barbar Khalsa International in India, Harakat-ul Mujahidin based in Pakistan, and al-Qa'ida) CBRN technology. In this context, both the terrorist-criminal and terrorist-state-sponsorship nexus pose a risk to security. As the capability of intelligence services to monitor these groups is limited, it is not unlikely that some of these organizations will acquire and employ CBRN technology in the future.

Small Arms Transfers

The above also endanger the security of Asia. Asian, Middle Eastern, Eastern European and southern former Soviet states provide conventional weapons to Asian militant groups. Weapons originally intended for use in conflicts that have ended or are in decline are sent to other conflict zones, thus adjusting the threat level. In the early 21st century most Asian governments depended on arms imports from outside the region. However, once Asian states begin to develop their own arms-production capabilities, cases of weapons being intercepted by militant groups en route are likely to increase. In the 1990s it was reported that, world-wide, small arms killed 90% of combatants and non-combatants. Despite determined efforts by the UN Department for Disarmament Affairs, many governments have yet to develop substantial measures towards macro-disarmament. At the same time, although US, Russian and other large intelligence agencies reduced their operations to monitor arms transfers in the region, domestic agencies failed comprehensively to monitor and disrupt arms transfers by militant groups. As a result, sophisticated weapons continue to proliferate among terrorist and criminal groups in Asia.

Unregulated Migration

The illegal transfer of people and migrant-terrorist networks also pose a threat to Asian security. The scale of international unregulated migration, especially economic migrants, since the end of the Cold War, has dramatically increased. Both criminals and terrorists use ships to smuggle people from Asia to Africa and Europe across the Indian Ocean and to the USA and Canada across the Pacific Ocean. The smuggling organizations, extending from China to Hong Kong, Taiwan, Singapore, Thailand, Central America and the USA and Canada, use false and modified travel documents. Since early 2000 the multi-million dollar operation has earned about US $10,000 per person smuggled. Illegal migration has negative effects on the country of origin and of settlement. For example, some migrant communities, seen as resisting integration, are considered an obstacle to the economic development of some host communities. Although economic migrants do not pose a security threat to Asia, refugees who have left conflict-ridden areas to relocate in the West pose a threat to their countries of origin. For instance, Sikh and Kashmiri militant groups and the LTTE draw support from such migrant communities, particularly the more radical among the new arrivals to Australasia, Europe, and the USA and Canada. The development of a Tamil diaspora outside Sri Lanka enabled the LTTE to expand internationally, by establishing offices and cells world-wide to generate funds, procure weapons and operate a fleet of ships for drugs- and arms-trafficking. Substantial segments of the Kashmiri and Sikh diaspora who support militant organizations in their country of origin lobby foreign governments against allocating aid to India and provide direct material assistance to the extremists. Kashmiri and Sikh terrorist organizations operating under the name of other sympathetic or unsuspecting organizations in Europe, the USA and Canada reportedly raise about US $10m.–$20m. annually; the LTTE earn approximately US $40m.–$50m. annually. In the 1990s such funds were transferred from Australian, European (notably British, German, Scandinavian—particularly Swedish—and Swiss), US and Canadian feeder bank accounts to main procurement accounts in Singapore and, thereafter, to Bulgaria and Ukraine. Despite the existence of extradition treaties between India and the United Kingdom and Canada, respectively, some Canadian and British Sikhs are reportedly at the forefront of support for militancy in India. The majority of support for terrorism in Asia is generated in affluent Europe, the USA and Canada. A comprehensive understanding of the flexible and resilient international support networks is vital if any efforts to disrupt them are to be effective. In addition to the 1999 UN International Convention for the Suppression of the Financing of Terrorism, an international organization is required to regulate migrant-terrorist support networks.

The increase in the lethality of conflicts is likely to raise the scale of migration from conflict zones in Asia to the West. It was reported that one person out of every 120 persons in the world had been forced to flee his or her home in the 1990s. According to the office of the UN High Commissioner for Refugees, Asia (including West and Central Asia) continued to account for more refugees than Africa in 2001; furthermore, there were fewer returnees to Asia than to Africa. The flow of refugees from conflict zones has complicated inter-state relations, particularly in South and South-East Asia, and has adversely affected regional security.

Narcotics

The cultivation of opium, a serious problem in Asia, is concentrated in two areas: the 'Golden Crescent' in south-western Asia, comprising large parts of Afghanistan and smaller areas in Pakistan; and the 'Golden Triangle' in South-East Asia, comprising the border areas of Laos, Myanmar and Thailand. The two regions combined are the biggest suppliers of illegal narcotics to the rest of the world. Drugs-traffickers take advantage of major transit routes to Europe and to the USA and Canada. In 2000 80% of the heroin seized in the USA reportedly originated in Myanmar; 20% of the heroin seized originated in Afghanistan—a two-fold increase compared with four years previously. Although Afghanistan superseded Myanmar as the world's leading producer of opium in 1994, the Afghan Transitional Authority's commitment to combat the cultivation, processing and trafficking of illegal drugs (which led to a ban in January 2002) was likely to shift the production of narcotics to neighbouring countries and other regions. Afghan-produced heroin is available at such a low cost in the region (about 10 times less than the price in New York) that consumption has escalated. Heroin is available at a price comparable to that of vodka in Kyrgyzstan, indicating saturated production in Central Asia. The increase in consumption within the region is considered a problem of regional security because of the terrorist-criminal nexus. Drugs-trafficking is a major source of revenue for terrorist and organized crime networks, particularly those with transnational links. As armed ethnic groups in Myanmar control the flow of narcotics from their country, so do armed Islamist groups, by taxing organized crime networks, control the flow of narcotics from Afghanistan. Drugs-traffickers have used a route through Pakistan, Chechnya, Turkey, Albania, Kosovo, Bosnia and Herzegovina to western Europe since 2000. Other routes traverse Iran and Russia. In addition, the Kosovo Liberation Army, the Armed Islamic Group of Algeria and KADEK play a role in the transport of narcotics and the protection of organized criminal networks at the European end of the route. Many terrorist and guerrilla groups also control the territories where the narcotics are cultivated or refined. Until the collapse of their regime in December 2001, the Taliban earned huge sums of money to fund their fight against opposition forces by taxing opium cultivators.

The production and trafficking of illicit drugs pose an increasing threat to the economy, health, and law and order of the region. According to official figures, Pakistan, for example, housed an estimated 1.5m. heroin addicts and 2m. cocaine addicts in the late 1990s. To make matters worse, although one in 15 adults in Pakistan was addicted to heroin, the state had the capacity to rehabilitate only 500 addicts at a time. In Manipur, India, the number of heroin addicts rose from 600 in 1988 to some 30,000–40,000 in 1996; concomitantly, the number of HIV/AIDS cases among drug addicts increased and is continuing to rise. The Joint UN Programme on HIV/AIDS (UNAIDS) Epidemic Update 2001 stated that in Jakarta, Indonesia, HIV infection rates among intravenous drug users under treatment increased from 15% in 2000 to 40% in 2001. It was also reported that seven provinces in China were experiencing local HIV epidemics in 2001, and that as many as 70% of injecting drug users in a number of areas such as Yili Prefecture in Xinjiang had been infected with the virus. Furthermore, more than 50% of intravenous drug users had contracted HIV in Yunnan Province (China), Myanmar, Nepal and Thailand by 2001. The sex industry, connected to the illegal trafficking of women, is another significant factor in the rising epidemic. Although the national prevalence rate of HIV/AIDS in many countries is low (2% in Myanmar, for example, and less than 1% in India) in the cases of populous India, Indonesia and China, a low national prevalence rate has little meaning. The HIV/AIDS epidemic, although fairly new to the area, is escalating at a fast rate and could potentially pose a serious security threat by adversely affecting the demographics and economic development of the region. In 2001 the number of HIV/AIDS cases in Asia and the Pacific increased by 1.07m. to reach an estimated 7.1m. (of which 6.1m. cases were reported in South and South-East Asia). Immediate large-scale prevention programmes are required to prevent a major epidemic affecting more than 55% of the world's population. Programmes in Thailand were successful in preventing HIV infections; nevertheless, by 2001 there were 0.7m. cases of HIV/AIDS in the country, with AIDS having become the leading cause of death.

The abuse of synthetic Amphetamine-Type Stimulants (ATS) has reportedly increased in recent years: in 1998/99 the amount of ATS seized throughout the world increased by an average 16%. According to the UN Office for Drug Control and Crime Prevention, in the late 1990s some 30m. people, or 0.8% of the global population, consumed ATS world-wide. An increasing proportion of drug abusers are the young. Insurgents in Myanmar, particularly on the Myanma–Thai border, are engaged in the high-level production of these drugs. Although the UN General Assembly discussed Asia at a special session in 1988, to mark the UN Convention Against Illicit Traffic in Narcotic Drugs and Psychotropic Substances, international efforts to regulate the threat of narcotics failed. In fact, the annual consumption of illegal drugs by about 3.3%–4.1% of the world's population is rising. The lack of effective state control in Afghanistan and Myanmar has turned Asia into a significant contributor to the world-wide production and consumption of narcotics. The drugs trade, the HIV/AIDS epidemic and illegal trafficking of women by the sex industry combined thus pose a serious threat to the stability of the region.

Border Disputes

Disputes over maritime and territorial borders also affect regional security. The question of sovereignty of the Spratly Islands, for example, claimed by Brunei, China, Malaysia, the Philippines, Taiwan and Viet Nam, remains unresolved. Similarly, border disputes exist between India and several of its neighbours, notably Bangladesh, China and Pakistan. China and Pakistan fought wars with India over disputed borders. Recently, there have been border concerns between India and Sri Lanka over Kachchtivu in Tamil Nadu, India, and between India and the Maldives over the southern islands of Malikku (Minicoy). The existing state of affairs between two countries plays a critical role in either exacerbating or mitigating border conflicts. Although not simply border issues, China's claim to Taiwan and the conflict between the two Koreas cause regional, as well as international, tension.

Water Resources

The necessity to share common resources is another source of tension in the region. A long-lasting solution to the disputes between Bangladesh, India and Nepal over the sharing of water from the River Ganges would only be reached through bilateral or multilateral agreements. However, in the past, water was used for political leverage against Bangladesh, a state vulnerable both to floods and desertification. Ironically, India and Pakistan reached a lasting agreement on the sharing of the Indus waters in 1960, thereby proving that even states disagreeing over political-security issues are able to resolve environmental disputes. There is also potential for water-sharing disputes between Singapore and Malaysia, and between Cambodia, China, Laos, Thailand and Viet Nam over the water resources of the Mekong River. There are numerous other environmental issues that affect the internal and international security of the Asian states. It is clear that if water resources in Asia are not properly managed, they could become a major source of conflict in the future.

Maritime Piracy

The absence of an international organization with effective powers actively to fight piratical violence allowed piracy to increase in the late 1990s. In 1997 there were 229 reported attacks on ships at sea or at anchor. International Maritime

Bureau (IMB) figures showed that pirates carried guns on 68 occasions in 1997, more than double the number of times reported in 1996. The IMB also reported that 51 people were killed in pirate attacks in 1997, compared with 26 in the previous year. Furthermore, more than 400 crew members were taken hostage in 1997, compared with 194 in 1996. Pirates and terrorists continued to attack an increasing number of ships with greater lethality in 2002. Asia, particularly South-East Asia, was more exposed than any other region. The highest risk areas have long been the waters of six countries: Brazil, India, Indonesia, the Philippines, Sri Lanka and Thailand. These areas accounted for more than one-half of the attacks in 1997. Although the number of attacks in Indonesian waters decreased to 47 in 1997 from 57, the waters remained the highest risk area. Furthermore, although the number of attacks in Philippine waters diminished, the serious problem of ship hijackings associated with attacks continued. Significantly, many of the ship hijackings in Asia took place outside Chinese ports, where the cargo had been removed. A number of ships in the Indian Ocean disappeared in the late 1990s, indicating that Asian criminal and terrorist organizations were participating in 'phantom shipping'. Maritime policing is expected to reduce the number of acts of piracy; however, with access to more sophisticated weapons, piratical violence is predicted to become more lethal.

Organized Crime

Since the mid-1990s, organized crime, already prevalent in East and South-East Asia, has established a presence in the cities of South Asia. Organized crime networks in China, Hong Kong and Japan have also spread to the West. It is predicted that as South Asia moves towards the culture of the market economy, organized crime will become firmly established. Increasingly, terrorist and criminal organizations operate together, and, as a result, terrorist groups are becoming less dependent on state sponsors and on their domestic and international supporters. In the 1990s, particularly in the latter part, terrorist groups learned to emulate criminal networks. Through sympathetic or unsuspecting organizations and through terrorist organizations operating under false names in Europe, the USA and Canada, many Asian terrorist groups generated huge revenues from video and compact disc piracy, business in phone cards and credit card fraud. With the decline in state sponsorship of militancy especially after the September 2001 attacks on the USA, terrorist groups are expected to become increasingly dependent on organized crime to survive and fund their operations.

Poverty

Finally, there is the issue of poverty and quality of life. Apart from exceptions such as Hong Kong, Japan and Singapore, Asia comprises mainly low- and middle-income countries. If we compare South Asia's social and economic status to that of other regions, we can see that in 1998 43% of the South Asian population suffered from absolute poverty, compared with 39.1% in sub-Saharan Africa and 23.5% in South America. Although South Asia performed better than sub-Saharan Africa in giving its people education, health and nutrition, the sub-region hosted more than one-half (92.4m.) of the 175m. children under the age of five world-wide who were malnourished, compared with 15% in sub-Saharan Africa. In 1998 some 77% of South Asians had access to health services, compared with 56% in sub-Saharan Africa. As a result, South Asian life expectancy is around 60 years of age, whereas in sub-Saharan Africa it is 52. Similarly, infant mortality in South Asia is 84 deaths per 1,000 live births and 93 deaths in sub-Saharan Africa. Although Asian governments have implemented measures to control population growth (the two most populous countries in the region—and indeed in the world—China and India, account for more than 2,000m. people), it is clear that some Asian countries have failed to deliver adequate economic growth. This shortcoming, if prolonged, could provoke rebellion and conflict.

CONCLUSION

It is evident that the existing and emerging threats after the end of the Cold War transcend the territorial boundaries of the nation-state. Asia is not an exception to this trend. The phenomena of globalization—the increase in permeability of country borders, enhanced communication, the rapid movement and migration of people, unrestricted flow of information and greater access and transfer of lethal technology—have added a new dimension to Asian security, forcing security planners to reconsider strategy on a local, national, regional and global level. By 2002 Asian governments had achieved partial successes at fighting terrorism and organized crime; most other threats remained at manageable levels.

In order to respond to the threats beyond the immediate (one–two years) and medium (five years) term, governments must be aware of the region's numerous opportunities and challenges. In the early 21st century Asia is a paradox of poverty and rapid growth. South Asia is the most culturally diverse, as well as the most densely populated sub-region (comprising more than 1,000m. people—one-fifth of the world's population). The Indian population is projected to exceed China's population by 2025. At the same time, economically, South Asia is the fastest growing region in the world. None the less, the population explosion, poverty, disease, illiteracy and armed conflict make South Asia one of the most insecure regions in the world.

By contrast, South-East Asia has prospered, its economic growth surpassing other regions. Consequently, forces of nationalism and communism have diminished, and proxy wars have virtually ended. Unlike the South Asian Association for Regional Co-operation (SAARC), the Association of South East Asian Nations (ASEAN) has developed a 'corporate culture' of close consultation and co-operation, which had begun to influence and attract other states in the region by the early 21st century. South-East Asia consists of just over 500m. people, and stands between two giants: China and India. South-East Asian states are growing rapidly, militarily and economically, both in competition with each other and against external powers.

Although economic prosperity has increased stability, the threat of terrorism, crime, narcotics, piracy, ethno-nationalism, religious fundamentalism, uncontrolled migration, refugee flows and the proliferation of light arms have all contributed to the region's instability. South-East Asia recorded the highest incidence of piracy, which is not an unusual occurrence in the sub-region. However, the most potent threat facing South-East Asia in 2002 was terrorism, a phenomenon imported from Afghanistan, Pakistan and the Middle East. Islamist militant groups—comprising Egyptians, Algerians, Palestinians, Saudis and Lebanese—have intensified operations in the region. Trained members, particularly those taught by the Taliban and al-Qa'ida, continue to operate both in South and South-East Asia, trying to recruit fresh support and to establish new cells, despite international efforts to curb their activities. The threat of terrorism is perhaps the most difficult and complex problem faced by the international community in the early 21st century, and only a multi-faceted response will be effective in dismantling the organizations involved and in safeguarding the security of citizens in Asia and world-wide.

BIBLIOGRAPHY

Alagappa, Muthiah (Ed.). *Asian Security Practice: Material and Ideational Influences*. Stanford, CA, Stanford University Press, 1998.

Alexander, Yonah, and Swetnam, Michael S. *Usama bin Laden's al-Qaida: Profile of a Terrorist Network*. New York, NY, Transnational Publishers, 2001.

Arquilla, John, and Ronfeldt, David (Eds). *Networks and Netwars: The Future of Terror, Crime and Militancy*. Santa Monica, CA, RAND Corporation, 2001.

Bergen, Peter L. *Holy War, Inc.: Inside the Secret World of Osama bin Laden*. New York, NY, Free Press, 2001.

Bodansky, Yossef. *Bin Laden: The Man Who Declared War on America*. Roseville, CA, Prima Publishing, 2001.

Davids, Douglas J. *Narco-Terrorism: A Unified Strategy to Fight a Growing Terrorist Menace*. New York, NY, Transnational Publishers, 2002.

Esposito, John. *Unholy War, Terror in the Name of Islam*. Oxford University Press, 2002.

Gilmartin, David, and Lawrence, Bruce B. *Beyond Turk and Hindu: Rethinking Religious Identities in Islamicate South Asia*. Gainesville, FL, University Press of Florida, 2000.

Gunaratna, Rohan. *Sri Lanka's Ethnic Crisis and National Security*. Colombo, South Asian Network on Conflict Research, 2000.

Inside Al Qaeda, Global Network of Terror. New York, NY, Columbia University Press, 2002.

Hefner, Robert W., and Horvatich, Patricia (Eds). *Islam in an Era of Nation-States: Politics and Religious Renewal in Muslim Southeast Asia*. Honolulu, HI, University of Hawaii Press, 1997.

Hoffman, Bruce. *Inside Terrorism*. New York, NY, Columbia University Press, 1999.

Laquer, Walter. *The New Terrorism: Fanaticism and the Arms of Mass Destruction*. Oxford University Press, 1999.

Lintner, Bertil. *Crime, Business and Politics in Asia*. Crows Nest, NSW, Allen and Unwin, 2002.

Maley, William (Ed.). *Fundamentalism Reborn? Afghanistan and the Taliban*. New York, NY, New York University Press, 1998.

Man, W. K. *Muslim Separatism: The Moros of Southern Philippines and the Malays of Southern Thailand*. Singapore, Oxford University Press, 1990.

McCoy, Alfred W. *The Politics of Heroin in Southeast Asia*. London, HarperCollins Publishers Ltd, 1972.

Miller, Judith, Engelberg, Stephen, and Broad, William J. *Germs: Biological Weapons and America's Secret War*. New York, NY, Simon & Schuster, 2001.

Perkovich, George. *India's Nuclear Bomb: The Impact on Global Proliferation*. Berkeley and Los Angeles, CA, University of California Press, 2001.

Rabasa, Angel, and Chalk, Peter. *Indonesia's Transformation and the Stability of Southeast Asia*. Santa Monica, CA, RAND Corporation, 2001.

Rashid, Ahmed. *Taliban: The Story of the Afghan Warlords*. London, Pan Macmillan, 2001.

Reeve, Simon. *The New Jackals: Ramzi Yousef, Osama bin Laden and the Future of Terrorism*. Boston, MA, Northeastern University Press, 1999.

Reich, Walter (Ed.). *Origins of Terrorism: Psychologies, Ideologies, Theologies, States of Mind*. Washington, DC, Woodrow Wilson Centre Press, 1998.

Singh Tatla, Darshan. *The Sikh Diaspora: Search for Statehood*. Seattle, WA, University of Washington Press, 1998.

Smith, Martin. *Burma: Insurgency and the Politics of Ethnicity*. Dhaka, University Press, 1999.

Tan, Andrew. *Armed Rebellion in ASEAN States: Persistence and Implications*. Canberra, Strategic and Defence Studies Centre, Australian National University, 2000.

Tan, Andrew, and Boutin, Ken. *Non Traditional Security Issues in Southeast Asia*. Singapore, Institute for Defence and Strategic Studies, 2001.

Wilson, A. J. *Sri Lankan Tamil Nationalism: Its Origins and Development in the Nineteenth and Twentieth Centuries*. Seattle, WA, University of Washington Press, 2000.

POPULATION IN ASIA AND THE PACIFIC

SIMON BAKER

Based on an earlier article by MICHAEL WILLIAMS
Revised for this edition by SANTOSH JATRANA

THE IMPORTANCE OF THE ASIAN-PACIFIC POPULATION

The overwhelming feature of the population of the Asia-Pacific region is its diversity. The countries include the world's largest and smallest nations, and have some of the highest and lowest levels of fertility, mortality and migration existing today. The region includes six of the world's 10 most populous countries: China, India, Indonesia, Pakistan, Bangladesh and Japan. Throughout the Pacific, however, there are some of the world's smallest populations, including those of Pitcairn, Tokelau and Niue. Life expectancy, an indicator of well-being, also varies greatly within the region. In 2002 nine countries or territories, Australia, Guam, Hong Kong, Japan, the Republic of Korea, Macao, New Zealand, Singapore and Taiwan, had a life expectancy of 75 years or more; but Afghanistan, East Timor and Laos, for example, had an average life span of less than 55 years. Furthermore, there is great economic and social disparity within the region. It includes some of the world's richest nations: Japan, Singapore, Australia and New Zealand; and a number of extremely poor nations, such as Afghanistan and Cambodia, which have been devastated by war.

In mid-2002, excluding the Asiatic section of the Russian Federation but including other parts of former Soviet Asia, there were an estimated 3,766m. people living in Asia and 32m. people in the Pacific, totalling 61.1% of the world's population, living in a mere 29.7% of the total area of the world (excluding Antarctica), or only 23.8% if the large but sparsely-populated areas of Australia and New Zealand are excluded. This total includes the population of the former Soviet republics in central Asia (about 57m.) and an estimated 65.6m. people living in Iran (considered to be parts of South-Central Asia) and a further 197m. in western Asia (i.e. the Middle East and the former Soviet republics of Armenia, Azerbaijan and Georgia), areas not covered in this essay.

In mid-2002 the annual natural rate of population increase in the Asia-Pacific region (excluding the Middle East) varied from a mere 0.2% for Japan to 1.8% for South-Central Asia. Some small Pacific countries, such as the Marshall Islands and Solomon Islands, with levels of 3.7% and 3.4% respectively, had very high natural rates of growth. These rates of increase must be seen in perspective against the trends in other continents. When compared with the average annual rate of natural increase of 2.9% for middle Africa, they are not so spectacular; on the other hand, when compared with the rate of –0.5% for Eastern Europe (including Asiatic Russia), they are enormous. The implications of these figures are made clearer if we consider the time that is required to double a population at a constant growth rate. At 0.5% per annum it takes 139 years; at 1% it takes 70 years; at 2% it takes 35 years; and at 3% it takes 23 years.

Nevertheless, it is the large base population from which Asia's annual growth emanates that is the crucial factor. This produced an increment averaging 48.9m. persons annually over the period 1970–80, and it is estimated that this increment remained fairly steady, at about 55.8m. persons annually, during the period 1985–90. Because of this, Asia's share of the world population increased from 55.5% in 1950 to 60.6% in 2002. Largely owing to the recent sharp decline in the growth rate of China's population, this proportion was expected slowly to decrease in the 21st century. Even so, Asia will retain the preponderant share of the world's population for the foreseeable future. Expressed simply, Asia's population in 1980 was greater than that of the world in 1950; in 2000 it almost equalled that of the world in 1970; and by 2025, according to projections by the UN, it is expected to be greater than that of the world in 1984.

From mid-1997 the Asia-Pacific region experienced an economic crisis, which had a particularly detrimental effect on the poorest countries of the region. In these countries there are serious problems of unemployment and underemployment, leading to low productivity and low levels of average income per head. Socially, there are problems of malnutrition, illiteracy, sub-standard housing, inadequate medical care, and poverty. A reduction in the annual increment of people through a decrease in births, supported by a variety of reproductive-health programmes, is regarded as a crucial factor in the planning policies of a number of the countries of the region, for it is generally believed that many of the social and economic problems arise from (or, at least, are linked to) the demographic situation.

Fertility, mortality and migration, combined with the present base population and its composition, will determine the future population of the Asia-Pacific region. It is important, therefore, to examine the total numbers in each country, the relationship of the population to land resources, and the sex and age structures of the populations, and finally the distribution by urban and rural residence.

Table 1. Population in the Asia-Pacific Region and by Major World Region

	Mid-year population (million)			Annual rate of natural increase (%)	Total fertility rate (children per woman)	Life expectancy (years at birth)	Area	Population density (per sq km)
	1980	1990	2002	2002	2002	2002	('000 sq km)	2002
Asia (excl. Asiatic Russia)	2,631	3,164	3,766	1.3	2.6	67	31,764	119
Eastern Asia	1,178	1,350	1,512	0.7	1.7	72	11,762	129
South-Central Asia	982	1,225	1,521	1.8	3.3	63	10,776	141
South-Eastern Asia	358	440	536	1.5	2.7	67	4,495	119
Western Asia	113	149	197	2.0	3.9	68	4,731	42
Oceania (excl. Hawaii)	22.5	26.3	32	1.0	2.5	75	8,537	4
Australia and New Zealand	17.7	20.2	23.6	0.7	1.8	79	7,984	3
Africa	469	619	840	2.4	5.2	53	30,306	28
Northern America (incl. Hawaii)	255	283	319	0.6	2.1	77	21,517	15
Latin America and the Caribbean	361	440	531	1.7	2.7	71	20,533	26
Europe (incl. Asiatic Russia)	693	722	728	–0.1	1.4	74	22,986	32
World (excl. Antarctica)	4,430	5,255	6,215	1.3	2.8	67	135,641	46

Sources: mainly UN, *World Population Prospects: The 2000 Revision*; Population Reference Bureau, Washington, DC, 2002.

CHARACTERISTICS OF THE PRESENT POPULATION

Total Numbers

Asia includes the world's two most populous countries: the People's Republic of China which, including Hong Kong and Macao but excluding Taiwan, had an estimated 1,288m. inhabitants in mid-2002 (an increase of 147m. since mid-1990 and of 202m. since mid-1985); and India, the population of which also surpassed 1,000m. in 2000, reaching 1,049.5m. in mid-2002 (a rise of 214.1m. between 1990 and 2002 and of 290.6m. since 1985). These two countries, which together contain more than one-third of humanity, both far surpass the next two largest entities, the USA (the population of which reached 287.4m. at mid-2002) and Indonesia (population 217.0m. at mid-2002). Recent estimates confirm that Pakistan (143.5m. at mid-2002), Bangladesh (133.6m. at mid-2002) and Japan (127.4m. at mid-2002) exceed other nations of the world except the four above-mentioned, Brazil (173.8m. at mid-2002), Russia (143.5m. at mid-2002) and Nigeria (129.9m. in mid-2002). In addition, there were at mid-2002 five other countries in Asia (excluding Iran and Turkey) with populations exceeding 40m., namely the Philippines (80.0m.), Viet Nam (79.7m.), Thailand (62.6m.), Myanmar (formerly Burma, 49.0m.) and the Republic of Korea (48.4m.), while the populations of the remaining countries of the region are substantially smaller. In some ways the size of the population of a country is not of great significance, but in one respect it is. Administrative efficiency, the co-ordination of economic and social development, and the diffusion of innovations are often more difficult within larger population entities than within small ones.

Population Density

In terms of land area, there is great variation among the countries of the region. China and Australia are among the world's largest countries, with a total of 9.6m. and 7.7m. sq km respectively, whereas Hong Kong and Singapore have about 1,100 and 660 sq km of land respectively. Using the size of the countries and their populations, a concept of population density can be created. A warning must be given, however, on interpreting overall population density as an indicator of 'crowding'. The crudeness of the measure is refined somewhat by relating population to the amount of agricultural land but, even then, the density does not reflect wholly the true position because the quality of the land, the level of technology, the productivity per person, and the patterns of settlement all alter the significance of any given ratio. Having said that, however, if we do relate population to arable land and land under permanent crops, as assessed by the UN Food and Agriculture Organization (FAO), then densities such as 26.0 persons per ha were recorded for Japan in 1999 and 24.5 per ha for the Republic of Korea, while those for China (including Taiwan) were 9.4, Bangladesh 15.0, Indonesia 6.8, India 5.9, and for Thailand only 3.4. The atypical figure of 35,220 per ha for Singapore illustrates the difficulties of assessing the significance of these ratios. On 2000 estimates, after Japan, Hong Kong had the second highest level of GNP per head on the basis of purchasing-power parity (PPP) of countries in the Asia-Pacific region, with Singapore ranked fourth, thus illustrating the importance of services, trade and industry in mitigating the problems inherent in high population densities.

Table 2. Population and Income of Selected Countries of the Asia-Pacific Region

Country	Estimated mid-2002 population (million)	Total fertility rate (children per woman) 2002	Infant mortality (per 1,000 live births) 2002	Annual rate of natural increase (%) 2002	'Doubling time' at current natural increase rate (years)	Life expectancy at birth (years) 2002 Males	Life expectancy at birth (years) 2002 Females	GNP per head (US $) 2000*
Asia:	3,766.0	2.6	53	1.3	54	66	69	4,280
Afghanistan	27.8	6.0	154	2.4	29	46	44	n.a.
Bangladesh	133.6	3.3	66	2.2	32	59	59	1,590
Bhutan	0.9	4.7	61	2.5	28	66	66	1,440
Brunei	0.4	2.7	15	2.0	35	71	76	24,910†
Cambodia	12.3	4.0	95	1.7	41	54	58	1,440
China, People's Republic (excl. Hong Kong and Macao)	1,280.7	1.8	31	0.7	99	69	73	3,920
East Timor	0.8	4.4	135	1.5	47	47	48	n.a.
Hong Kong	6.8	0.9	3.1	0.2	347	77	82	25,590
India	1,049.5	3.2	68	1.7	41	62	64	2,340
Indonesia	217.0	2.6	46	1.6	44	66	70	2,830
Japan	127.4	1.3	3.2	0.2	347	78	85	27,080
Korea, Democratic People's Republic (North)	23.2	2.1	42	0.7	99	62	67	n.a.
Korea, Republic (South)	48.4	1.5	8	0.8	87	72	80	17,300
Laos	5.5	4.9	104	2.3	30	52	55	1,540
Macao	0.4	0.9	4	0.4	174	75	80	18,190
Malaysia	24.4	3.2	8	1.9	37	70	75	8,330
Mongolia	2.4	2.5	37	1.5	47	61	65	1,760
Myanmar (formerly Burma)	49.0	3.1	90	1.3	54	54	59	n.a.
Nepal	23.9	4.1	64	2.1	33	58	57	1,370
Pakistan	143.5	4.8	86	2.1	33	63	63	1,860
Philippines	80.0	3.5	26	2.2	32	65	71	4,220
Singapore	4.2	1.4	2.2	0.8	87	76	80	24,910
Sri Lanka	18.9	2.0	17	1.2	58	70	74	3,460
Taiwan	22.5	1.4	6.1	0.6	116	73	78	14,188‡
Thailand	62.6	1.8	20	0.8	87	70	75	6,320
Viet Nam	79.7	2.3	30	1.4	50	67	70	2,000
Oceania:	32.0	2.5	30	1.0	70	73	77	18,770
Australia	19.7	1.7	5.2	0.6	116	77	82	24,970
Fiji	0.9	3.3	20	1.9	37	65	69	4,480
New Zealand	3.9	2.0	5.3	0.7	99	76	81	18,530
Papua New Guinea	5.0	4.8	77	2.3	30	56	58	2,180
Solomon Islands	0.5	5.7	25	3.4	21	67	68	1,710

* World Bank data, calculated on the basis of purchasing-power parity, rather than at current exchange rates.
† Referring to 1998.
‡ Data in current prices (Source: *Monthly Bulletin of Statistics,* Taipei).
Source (unless otherwise indicated): Population Reference Bureau, Washington, DC, 2002.

However, in more rural countries the ratio has some validity: unless there is the development of more industry and commerce to absorb the ever-increasing number of people, then the pressure on land resources will become greater. The availability of new land is limited, unless it is taken from the tropical rain forests. This practice, however, has obvious dangers. Nepal and the Himalayas generally are especially adversely affected because the clearing of steep slopes results in devastating soil erosion. Some of the world's highest levels of deforestation have occurred in Asia and the Pacific. During 1990–2000, according to the World Bank, Nepal lost an annual average of 1.8% of its forests. The comparable figure for Sri Lanka was 1.6%, for both the Philippines and Myanmar 1.4%, and for Indonesia and Malaysia 1.2%. Land has been engulfed in the expansion of cities (which are usually located on the best land), while the depletion of arable land through soil erosion, exhaustion and other forms of degradation must also be taken into account. In addition, the amount of irrigated land lost through salinization probably reaches millions of hectares. It is likely that land being taken out of production will counteract the amount of land gained through the extension of cultivation, so that not only will the population of Asia increase in the future but the supply of productive land will barely increase. It must be stressed, however, that this problem is a world-wide concern. According to a study by the International Food Policy Research Institute in 2000, nearly 40% of the world's agricultural land is seriously degraded because of problems such as erosion and nutrient depletion. This study suggested that almost 75% of cropland in Central America was seriously degraded, as well as 20%, mostly pasture, in Africa and 11% in Asia.

Sex Composition

Sex, together with age, is one of the two most important controls of future growth, and also, incidentally, of social ranking. In countries that are aiming towards economic and social development, the position and proportion of women and youth in society are important because of their influence on the composition of the work-force, their ability to contribute to national prosperity, and their ability to reproduce and so contribute to future population growth.

Further evidence of demographic diversity, in the Asia-Pacific region, is found in parents' sex preference for children. In some, but not all, Asian countries (in Thailand, for example, there is little or no preference for boys), there is a tendency to favour the care of male babies and children. There is evidence that the implementation in China in 1979 of the one-child policy has encouraged the infanticide of female babies, usually by simple neglect. Furthermore, with the development of medical technology, in particular the increased availability of ultrasound scanning and amniocentesis testing, it has been estimated that as many as 1.7m. female foetuses are aborted annually in China alone. By mid-1995 the Governments of both China and India had, in theory, banned tests to identify the sex of the unborn. In late 2000, furthermore, as the central Government of China attempted to encourage regional authorities to implement stricter local controls, the Government of Anhui Province issued a new directive to prohibit the use of ultrasound equipment for the purposes of gender determination. There have been reports of baby girls being abandoned at railway stations or on the steps of city halls by disappointed parents. In 1993 a study of the sex ratio in five of China's provinces revealed it to be in excess of 120 boys for every 100 girls, with one township in Shandong Province reporting a ratio of 163.8 per 100. In 1995, according to information provided by family-planning departments, China's male–female birth ratio was 131:100. According to the provisional results of the 2000 census, however, the national ratio was 106.74 males per 100.00 females. These unbalanced ratios are inevitably leading to a lack of marriage partners and to social tensions. A Jilin provincial newspaper in 1995 referred to 'a growing army of desperate bachelors the size of an average African state, which is no small threat to the nation's future security . . . It is likely that by the next century the country will have more than 100m. men with few prospects of finding wives'. Indeed, the abduction of Chinese women from poorer regions for the purposes of enforced marriage is an increasing problem, thousands of cases being reported annually.

Usually, the life expectancy of women is greater than that of men by six or seven years. In the poorer countries of the region, however, the difference is much smaller or even reversed. In 2002 Afghanistan and Nepal, for example, had life expectancies greater for males than for females. On average, Afghani men lived until they were 46, two years longer than women, while in Nepal the life expectancies were 58 and 57 years for males and females respectively (see Table 2). The difference in life expectancy between men and women in the richer and poorer nations is partly due to the great diversity of maternal health care in the region. The maternal mortality rate ranges from less than 10 per 100,000 live births in Hong Kong, China and Australia to well over 1,000 per 100,000 live births in Nepal, Bhutan and Afghanistan, a difference of 100 times.

Within a given population, the sex ratio may be expressed as the number of males per 1,000 females. At mid-2000, according to the US Census Bureau website, the estimated ratio for the world's population was 1,013, i.e. close to parity. There was, however, a sharp contrast between more developed regions (with a ratio of 942) and less developed regions (1,031). Within the Asia-Pacific region there was great variation among nations. In south-eastern Asia there was parity between the two sexes, with a ratio of 1,000. The ratio in southern and south-western Asia was 1,060, in northern and central Asia it was 910, while in the Pacific region it was 1,010. The country with the highest proportion of males was Brunei, with a ratio of 1,102.

The situation in India has always remained unfavourable to females. According to the 2001 census, the sex ratio for India's population was 1,072 males per 1,000 females. This ratio was significantly higher than those of neighbouring countries: Pakistan (1,066), China (1,059), and Bangladesh (1,049). For India, however, the 2001 ratio indicated a slight improvement from that observed at the 1991 census (1,079). There are phenomenal differences across states. While Kerala had a sex ratio of 940 males per 1,000 females, Haryana's ratio of 1,160 reflected considerable gender imbalance. Furthermore, it was reported that in the rural region of Dholpur, in Rajasthan, the ratio in 2001 was 1,220 males per 1,000 females. The problem of rising numbers of unmarried youths, meanwhile, was leading to an increase in those sharing the wife of an elder brother. The unbalanced ratio may arise from neglect of females at all stages, which results in their higher mortality at younger ages, high maternal mortality, sex-selective female abortions and female infanticide. All these reasons are indicative of discrimination against girls and women, which may be due to the preference for sons and to the low status of women in India. As indicated above, female predominance is usually a feature of developed economies, where standards of health care are generally high. However, the same phenomenon may also occur in countries affected by war. Russia, which suffered huge losses of men in the Second World War, continues to have a large female majority in the population, with a 2000 sex ratio of only 879 males per 1,000 females. The comparable ratio for Western Europe was 957. The lowest ratios in the Asia-Pacific region in 2000 were those of Cambodia (939), Viet Nam (968) and Laos (982). In war-ravaged Viet Nam, for example, some single women, unable to find a permanent partner, risk social disapproval by having a child out of wedlock, in an attempt to provide security for their old age. Other countries with sub-parity ratios were Japan (959), Myanmar (993) and New Zealand (986). In subsequent decades, according to UN projections, several of these countries will show a trend towards demographic parity of the sexes.

A recent and positive development has been the great gains females have made in many of the education systems of the region. This has particularly been the case in South-East Asia, where girls are now outnumbering boys in some education systems. In Thailand, for example, 54% of post-secondary students in 1992 were females. Since then the proportion of females to males in the education system has increased. Such advances, however, have not been uniform throughout the region, with females still lagging behind males in the education systems of countries such as Bangladesh and Pakistan. Furthermore, gender equity remains a major issue throughout the region. The gains being made, however, have major implications for the demographic dynamics of the region. They have allowed greater exposure of women to 'modernization', which has been crucial for the acceptance of family-planning and hence future population control.

Table 3. Distribution of Population by Dependent Age Groups and by Urban and Rural Residence for Selected Countries (mid-2002)

	% of total population in age group (years)		% of total population residing in urban or rural areas	
	0–14	65+	Urban	Rural
Asia:	30	6	38	62
Afghanistan	43	3	22	78
Bangladesh	40	3	23	77
Bhutan	39	5	16	84
Cambodia	43	4	16	84
China (excl. Hong Kong and Macao)	23	7	38	62
India	36	4	28	72
Indonesia	31	5	39	61
Japan	14	18	78	22
Korea, Democratic People's Republic	27	6	59	41
Korea, Republic	22	7	79	21
Laos	43	4	17	83
Malaysia	33	4	57	43
Mongolia	34	4	57	43
Myanmar (formerly Burma)	33	5	27	73
Nepal	41	4	11	89
Pakistan	42	4	33	67
Philippines	37	4	47	53
Singapore	21	7	100	0
Sri Lanka	27	6	30	70
Taiwan	21	9	77	23
Thailand	24	6	31	69
Viet Nam	31	6	24	76
Oceania:	25	10	69	31
Australia	20	12	85	15
Fiji	35	3	46	54
New Zealand	23	12	77	23
Papua New Guinea	39	4	15	85

Source: Population Reference Bureau, Washington, DC, 2002.

Age Composition

Rapid declines in fertility and mortality have resulted in a changing age composition for most of the countries of the Asia-Pacific region. Dividing the population into broad age groups, we find that children under 15 years of age constituted 30% of the Asian population at mid-2002. The proportion was 22% in eastern Asia, but 32% in south-eastern Asia and 37% in South-Central Asia. In a number of south and south-west Asian countries the ratio was close to 40% (see Table 3), while among the highest rates in the region were those found in Afghanistan, Cambodia and Laos (each with 43%). The comparable ratio for the developed world was 19%.

The recent declines in fertility throughout the Asia-Pacific region will mean that over time the proportion of the population under 15 years of age will decrease. The implications of high, but declining, proportions of young people are manifold. China and Thailand are two countries in which gains are being made as a result of earlier fertility reductions. In 1978 33% of the Chinese population was under 15; by 2002, however, this had declined to 23%. At the same time the proportion of people of working age has increased to 70%. China has therefore enjoyed a rapid decrease in youth dependency, while old-age dependency has not, as yet, become a problem. Although the proportion of retired people is currently rising, the number of elderly people is unlikely to become burdensome until the post-2025 period. China is thus in a fortunate position of having a declining dependency ratio, which will enable easier economic and social development. If Thailand's fertility had not fallen from the levels prevailing in the late 1960s, the number of young people reaching the work-force would today be rising by about 3% annually. This increase would have placed immense pressure on Thailand, especially in a time of economic crisis, as occurred in the late 1990s. Instead, the actual number is declining by about 0.5% per year. Fertility declines in the region will eventually lead to major socio-economic gains. It will, for example, make it easier to provide more and better education facilities. With declining numbers of primary school children, the Thai Government has been able to expand the secondary education system. Between 1988 and 1993 the number of classrooms used for primary education declined by 800. In the same period, the number of classrooms used in secondary education increased by 23,000, many of them in schools that were originally only for primary grades.

In general, members of the youth group (15–24 years of age) are more vocal and critical of their elders than any others and they will apply pressure for more radical solutions to social inequalities, such as inadequate health care, scarce food supplies, sub-standard housing, and particularly unemployment, especially as the concentration of this particular age group is far greater in urban than in rural areas. Expanding secondary and tertiary education has, in a sense, mobilized this feeling in student protest, a potent factor for purposeful change. This was illustrated by the student protests in Indonesia during May 1998, which helped to oust the Suharto regime.

The success of fertility control will inevitably result in the challenge of ageing. Population ageing means an increase in the elderly share of the total population. In the 21st century the number of elderly in the Asia-Pacific region is expected to rise dramatically. This will provide new challenges for individuals, families, and governments in terms of providing care and support for the increasingly elderly population in the future.

A major concern of ageing for the region is that, as rapid as the fertility decline has been in some of the countries, the process of ageing will be equally rapid. The speed of this change can be measured in terms of the number of years needed for the share of aged people (65 years and over) to increase from 7% to 14%. Countries in this region are ageing more rapidly than did those in the West. Sweden took 85 years, while Japan took only 25 years. In the 21st century China is predicted to take 30 years, the Republic of Korea 20 years and Singapore only 18 years.

Given that Western Europe required more than a century to develop the social security systems for the elderly and in view of the speed with which a number of Asian-Pacific populations will age, these countries will have to make fast and intensive efforts to cope with their ageing citizens. Will the traditional family units be able to cope with this increase? Will Asian-Pacific Governments be able to institute and finance adequate workers' pension schemes? Will the old become the new poor? In Singapore, in a bid to support the tradition of filial piety, legislation relating to the maintenance of parents was adopted in 1995. Nursing homes may demand financial assistance from offspring on behalf of their elderly patients. Between June and December 1996 alone the Tribunal for the Maintenance of Parents heard more than 200 cases. By 2000, furthermore, the growing disparity between rich and poor, the latter group comprising mainly elderly people, was leading to much debate in Singapore. In China, meanwhile, the Government hoped increasingly to distribute the burden of caring for the ageing population across the family, the State and the private sector. At the time of the 2000 census, fewer than 7% of Chinese citizens were aged 65 and over. By 2030 it was estimated that the elderly would comprise 22% of China's population. Upon taking office in 2001, the new Japanese Prime Minister, Junichiro Koizumi, declared the rapid ageing of the population, along with the attendant burden on health services, to be a major problem facing the country. With one of the world's fastest-ageing societies, those over 65 years of age already accounted for more than 17% of Japan's population.

Urban-Rural Distribution

The extent of urbanization in the Asia-Pacific region also varies greatly (see Table 3), from Singapore, with 100% of its population, to East Timor, with only 8% of its population estimated to be urban in 2002. The Pacific nations are the most urbanized, with an average level of 69% for this sub-region. The two largest countries of the Pacific, Australia and New Zealand, and a number of small island states are highly urbanized. It is estimated that 100% of Nauru's population lives in an urban area. East and North-East Asia are also highly urbanized, except for the largest country, China, which in 2002 had only 38% of its population in urban areas. Excluding the enclave of Macao, which is estimated to be 99% urban, the Republic of Korea is the most urbanized society in this sub-region, with 79% of its people living in cities. This is followed by Japan, with 78% of its population residing in urban areas.

This is not to say, however, that the characteristically rural, less-developed countries have no urban problems. There has been a continued high rate of rural to urban migration in these countries. According to the Asian Development Bank (ADB), on average rural to urban migration accounted for about 40% of urban growth during the 1970s and 1980s. Urbanization is proceeding at a faster rate than the growth of employment (certainly of manufacturing), and it is straining the economic and social facilities and infrastructures that are available. In this respect, the less well-developed world is reversing the historical experiences of the developed countries, where urbanization was a response to a sharp increase in industrialization, which provided ample employment opportunities for the rapidly-growing labour force.

While many urban dwellers continue to live in slum and squatter settlements, the growth of urban agglomerations is unlikely to diminish as the years progress. According to UN estimates, the urban population of eastern, southern and south-eastern Asia increased from 1,085m. at mid-1995 to 1,254m. in 2000, and was projected to rise to a staggering 2,241m. by 2025. In 2002 the UN reported that the number of urban agglomerations in Asia (including the Middle East) with more than 1m. inhabitants had increased from 104 in 1980 to 195 in 2000. By 2000, according to the same set of estimates, Tokyo remained the largest urban agglomeration, with a population of 26.4m., followed by Mexico City (with 18.1m.), São Paulo (18.0m.), New York (16.7m.) and Mumbai (Bombay), with 16.1m. Elsewhere in Asia by 2000 the population of Kolkata was 13.1m. and that of Shanghai 12.9m. Meanwhile, Dhaka (12.5m.), Delhi (12.4m.), Jakarta (11.0m.), Osaka (also 11.0m.), Beijing (10.8m.) and Karachi (10.0m.) also ranked among the 16 most populous urban agglomerations in the world. By 2015, furthermore, the populations of Metro Manila and Tianjin were also expected to exceed 10m. inhabitants.

Potential for rural–urban migration is immense. The gradual urbanization of the region provides both challenges and opportunities. The already serious problems of inadequate housing and infrastructure, water shortages, traffic congestion, environmental pollution, social alienation and the general accentuation of inequalities in standards of living will become worse. In Thailand, for example, in 1997 the ADB warned that inadequate sewage treatment in Bangkok was leading to the risk of epidemic. On the other hand, the greater concentration of the population in cities could allow easier access to education and health services, creating benefits for the various nations of the region.

THE DYNAMIC ASPECTS OF POPULATION

The size of the Asia-Pacific region's population tends to conceal underlying dynamics of the demographic structure of the various societies that make up the region. Changing numbers arise from fertility, mortality and migration.

Fertility

The Asia-Pacific region, and the developing world as a whole, is undergoing a reproductive revolution. Women from vastly different cultures, political systems, and social and economic status have started to desire smaller families. By 2002 the majority of the countries in the Asia-Pacific region were in a phase of fertility decline. The lowest levels of fertility, as indicated by the total fertility rate (TFR—the average number of children born to a woman during her lifetime), were recorded in East and North-East Asia. All the countries in this area, except for Mongolia, had TFRs at or below replacement level (a TFR of 2.1 is regarded as at replacement level; that is, the number of children women need on average to maintain a constant population). At only 0.9, the lowest TFRs in the region, and indeed in the world, were recorded in Hong Kong and Macao. (The continuing decline in Hong Kong's fertility, however, was expected to be offset by an influx of immigrants from mainland China.) Other countries of East and North-East Asia also had low to very low TFRs. Japan recorded a rate of 1.3, while Taiwan and the Republic of Korea registered rates of 1.4 and 1.5 respectively. China also had a low rate, of 1.8. Within the whole Asia-Pacific region, other countries with TFRs at 2.1 or lower included Australia (1.7), the Democratic People's Republic of Korea (2.1), New Zealand (2.0), Singapore (1.4) and Thailand (1.8). These below-replacement fertility levels have been occurring for a number of years. By 2002 Australia had had below-replacement fertility levels for 25 years, China 11 years, Japan 32 years, New Zealand 25 years, the Republic of Korea 20 years, Singapore 27 years, Thailand 10 years, and Taiwan 14 years.

Between 1965 and 1990 the population of Asia (including the Middle East) increased at an average annual rate of 2%. The past decline in the mortality rate accounted for the growth in population numbers, which continues despite the widespread and dramatic reductions in the fertility rate among most countries of the region. Taking 1970 as a datum point, it is apparent that fertility has declined, not only in those countries that had been experiencing substantial declines in fertility in the 1960s (such as Japan) but also in many other countries where fertility levels had remained virtually unchanged during the 1960s.

Table 4. Percentage of Currently-Married Women (aged 15–49 years) Using any Method of Contraception in Selected Countries

Country	All methods	Modern methods
Bangladesh	54	43
China (excl. Hong Kong and Macao)	84	83
India	48	43
Indonesia	57	55
Japan	56	48
Korea, Republic	81	67
Malaysia*	55	30
Myanmar	33	28
Nepal	39	35
Pakistan	28	20
Philippines	47	32
Sri Lanka*	66	44
Thailand	72	70
Viet Nam	74	61

* Figures relate to situation prior to 1996.
Source: Population Reference Bureau, Washington, DC, 2002.

Examples of the decline from the 1970s include Sri Lanka, where the TFR declined from 4.7 in the 1965–70 period to 2.0 in 2002; and Singapore, from 3.5 to 1.4. It is important to note that the diversity in the Asia-Pacific region also occurs within countries. In Singapore, the ethnic Malay TFR is above replacement level, while the Indian and Chinese TFRs are well below, at 1.8 and 1.5 respectively. Another example of this diversity within countries is the Indian state of Kerala, which has below-replacement fertility, yet the country as a whole has a TFR of 3.2. Other significant examples of fertility decline, during the same period, include Peninsular Malaysia, where the TFR declined from 5.9 to 3.2; and, most significantly of all because of its immense population base, China, where the TFR declined from 6.1 in 1965–70 to only 1.8 in 2002. Furthermore, the TFR in Indonesia decreased from 6.4 children in 1969/70 to 2.6 in 2002; similarly, Thailand (6.5 to 1.8), the Philippines (6.6 to 3.5) and Fiji (6.5 to 3.3).

To a great extent, the success of family planning depends on the status of women, on the dissemination of information and the provision of quality reproductive-health services. As a result, with improvements in the status of women, increasing levels of literacy and greater levels of urbanization, the percentage of currently-married women using any method of contraception has increased (see Table 4).

The contents of Table 2 can now be partly regrouped as in Table 5, according to fertility rates. The highest-ranking countries have managed to achieve and sustain a low level of fertility. Undoubtedly, this success was primarily the result of the relatively high status of females, almost total literacy in the adult population and the availability of a wide range of fertility-regulating techniques, strategies and inducements. The introduction of cheap, efficient and safe abortion in Japan from 1948 (the contraceptive pill becoming widely available there only in 1999) and in Singapore from 1969 was very effective, indeed too effective, some would now argue (see below). In addition, in Singapore a wide range of sophisticated monetary disincentives applied to people having large families. Income tax relief was limited to the first three children, maternity leave was restricted to the first two pregnancies, childbirth costs were increased after the first two deliveries, and priority was given to small families for public housing; in fact, a reversal of all the normally accepted democratic welfare principles. However, in the late 1980s the then Prime Minister of Singapore, Lee Kuan Yew, expressed concern at the rapidly-declining birth rates, particularly among the better-educated women in the community, who either remain unmarried or have only one child. 'Levels of competence will decline', he said. At current rates of reproduction, the population will decline after 2025, and in the 1990s couples were being urged to have at least two, if not three or four, children ('Have three or more if you can afford it'). In August 2000, as Singapore's birth rate continued to decline, the Government announced a new programme of financial incentives to encourage couples to have more children.

Table 5. Fertility and Infant Mortality Rates in Countries of the Asia-Pacific Region Ranked according to Fertility Regulation (2002)

	Total fertility rate (per woman)	Infant mortality rate (per 1,000 live births)
Hong Kong	0.9	3
Macao	0.9	4
Japan	1.3	3
Singapore	1.4	2
Taiwan	1.4	6
Korea, Republic	1.5	8
Australia	1.7	5
China (excl. Hong Kong and Macao)	1.8	31
Thailand	1.8	20
New Zealand	2.0	5
Sri Lanka	2.0	17
Korea, Democratic People's Republic	2.1	42
Viet Nam	2.3	30
Mongolia	2.5	37
Indonesia	2.6	46
Brunei	2.7	15
Myanmar	3.1	90
Malaysia	3.2	8
India	3.2	68
Fiji	3.3	20
Bangladesh	3.3	66
Philippines	3.5	26
Cambodia	4.0	95
Nepal	4.1	64
East Timor	4.4	135
Bhutan	4.7	61
Papua New Guinea	4.8	77
Pakistan	4.8	86
Laos	4.9	104
Solomon Islands	5.7	25
Afghanistan	6.0	154

Source: Population Reference Bureau, Washington, DC, 2002.

In Japan, meanwhile, by the early 21st century serious concern was being expressed with regard to that country's declining fertility rate, which was perceived as a significant threat to productivity, pension schemes and the health service. In 1998/99 expenditure on medical services for Japanese citizens aged 70 and over reached 10,170,000m. yen. Some local authorities were beginning to offer cash payments to Japanese couples who produced a child. In an attempt to improve the rate of marriages and hopefully of births, an even more unusual initiative was implemented by the provincial Government of Saga, in western Japan, where a match-making scheme, financed by tax-payers, was established.

The Republic of Korea has similarly experienced a major decline in fertility. The TFR began to decline steadily in the late 1960s and reached below-replacement level in the 1980s. At least four factors contributed to this rapid decline in fertility: a spectacular rise in the standard of living; an increase in women's age at first marriage; wider use of contraceptives; and greater use of induced abortions. Age at first marriage rose, as young women increasingly spent more time in education and as employment opportunities for unmarried women expanded. Broad socio-economic changes and declines in infant and child mortality, combined with effective nation-wide family-planning programmes, resulted in a norm of small families.

Health services in most of the highest-ranking countries are good, and the infant mortality rates (IMRs) among some of the lowest in the world, at fewer than four infant deaths per 1,000 live births in Japan, Hong Kong and Singapore. Parents know that the probability is high that a calculated number of pregnancies will achieve a calculated desirable family size; therefore people are not reproducing to combat infant mortality. Per caput incomes in these countries are among the highest in the Asia-Pacific region. There are moderate to good social services for the aged, which again removes one of the incentives for having large families. These are the most urbanized and most industrialized countries of the region.

Most of the middle-ranking countries have experienced a noticeable lowering of fertility. The greatest achievement has undoubtedly been that of China, where the TFR of 1.8 in 2002 is below the replacement level. China, with its centralized control of society and economy, has a clear record of success in raising average economic standards and in reducing population growth. After an initial period of regarding population control as anathema under conventional Marxist doctrine, the country began a birth-control programme during the early 1960s. The programme progressed with great impact following the period of political instability and unrest that resulted from the 'Cultural Revolution' and the death of Mao Zedong in 1976. China accepted funds and technical assistance from the UN Population Fund (UNFPA), and institutes of population research were established at Beijing University and elsewhere. A major census was undertaken in July 1982 that settled the question of the size of China's massive population: it totalled 1,008,181,000. The population increased to 1,130,510,638 at the next census in July 1990. The provisional results of the census conducted in November 2000 indicated that the population of China had reached 1,265,830,000. There is a rigorous enforcement of the minimum marriage age at 22 years for men and 20 for women, and Chinese couples are normally permitted to have only one child. New regulations introduced in 1994 aimed to curb 'early marriages and births'. In 1991, in an attempt to curb the rising rate of marriage failures among couples with a daughter, a change in Chinese law prevented the gender of the offspring being cited as grounds for divorce. In 2000, furthermore, legislation to outlaw 'second wives' (and thus second children) was presented to the Chinese legislature. The increasing wealth of men in China's southern provinces, in particular, and the resultant return to traditional concubinage, was perceived by the authorities as a serious threat not only to the one-child policy but to the very institution of marriage. Couples are allowed to have a second only in special circumstances, for example in some inland rural areas, in an effort to halt female infanticide. The one-child policy has also been amended to permit some couples to have a second child if the first is a daughter of at least eight years of age and if the mother is at least 30 years old.

By 1999 the Chinese Government was beginning to indicate that the problem of demographic growth was under control and that the one-child limit had been introduced as 'a policy for one generation'. Greater consideration was thus to be given to the social consequences of the one-child policy. Another exception to the one-child policy is a little-known provision that permits an only child married to another only child to have a second baby, on condition that the two children are born four years apart. During the 1980s and 1990s the provision was rarely applied. In the early 21st century, however, as the first 'one-child' generation reaches marriageable age, this provision may become an issue of some significance. Certain local authorities provide special treatment for families with one child, including priority in entry to kindergarten and schools, health care, jobs, housing and rations. In some places, fines are levied against three-child families. In mid-2002 China's first national family-planning law took effect, with the aim of eliminating the arbitrary nature of policies in different localities. Henceforth, couples producing more than one child were to pay a graded form of compensation. Local governments were to assume financial responsibility for family-planning budgets, rather than depending on the proceeds of fines imposed on parents.

Also in mid-2002 it emerged that China's family-planning policy was being further relaxed. As part of a trial project supported by UNFPA, birth quotas in 32 rural counties were removed, and the central Government planned to extend to an additional 800 rural counties this voluntary approach to family-planning. Another innovation under the UNFPA scheme dispensed with the need for couples to submit an application to the authorities to have their first child. (Previously, an application was sometimes refused if the village quota had already been filled.) City residents remained limited to one child.

In pointing out the success of the one-child policy in China, it has sometimes been overlooked that this was achieved, in part, through coercion and a deliberate lack of sensitivity to the country's cultural traditions, principally the favouring of male babies. Moreover, the single child raised without siblings in an environment that traditionally valued large families may encounter problems of maladjustment. Psychologists have warned, apparently to little avail, of the effects on these 'little emperors' of overindulgence, particularly as families move towards the one-two-four pattern: one child, two parents and four grandparents.

The low-ranking countries listed in Table 5 include India, Pakistan and Bangladesh, which together contain a large percentage of the region's population. Despite the relatively high TFRs, all three countries have experienced declines in fertility. A dramatic decline in birth rates is taking place in India and also Bangladesh. The TFR of India has been falling for three decades, from more than 5.3 children per woman in 1970 to 3.2 children in 2002. The impetus behind this fertility change has been modernization: rising levels of literacy, urbanization, and improvements in the status of women. The Indian Government learned that emphasis on birth-control programmes, particularly on the socially sensitive method of sterilization by vasectomy, was inept. Public reaction against the programme at the 1977 elections was a manifestation of the failure of experts and officials to perceive the cultural psychology of the population which they were administering. Furthermore, reaction to the dictatorial and over-zealous attitudes of local officials in the initial contraception programme provided many lessons for those countries wishing to accelerate their birth-control programmes. A multi-faceted approach, through fiscal as well as medical methods and economic motivation, is the most successful. India, Pakistan and Bangladesh have all introduced oral contraceptives into their national family-planning programmes.

Despite hostility from the Islamic clergy, Bangladesh now considers population control to be an integral part of economic planning. Its TFR in the 1965–70 period was close to 7, but has declined substantially to stand at 3.3 in 2002. Up to 20,000 trained family-planning personnel have been sent into rural areas to advise and to motivate people to accept and act upon the ideal of smaller families. In late 1995 it was announced that a campaign to encourage one-child families was to be initiated. Also, the increasing availability of socially-acceptable employment for unskilled Bangladeshi women, mainly in the new garment factories, is leading to later marriages.

Mortality and Life Expectancy

Mortality is the second aspect of population dynamics. The best indicators of mortality levels within and between societies are the life expectancy and the IMR (infant deaths per 1,000 live births). Throughout the region life expectancy has increased and IMR has decreased, reflecting improved standards of living. Most countries of the Asia-Pacific region have achieved major victories in controlling mortality. The Japanese now have the longest life expectancy of any nationality in the world. Even poor countries in the region, such as Viet Nam, have made great progress. In 1978 the Vietnamese had an average life expectancy of only 48 years and an IMR of 115. By 2002, however, life expectancy had increased to 67 for men and to 70 for women, and the IMR had declined to 30.

Like the European and North American countries before them, the Asian-Pacific countries reduced mortality before fertility. The result is a growing population. This is illustrated by the case of Pakistan. According to estimates, life expectancy increased in Pakistan from an average of 51 years for both sexes in 1978 to 63 for both men and women by 2002. In the same period the IMR declined from 139 to 86. However impressive this is, the TFR remained relatively high and thus the gap between births and deaths initially widened. Over the years 1985–90, according to official estimates, the average increase was 3.4%. By 2002, although still high, the growth rate had declined to 2.1%, thus leading to a doubling of the population within about 33 years. According to the latest UN projections, Pakistan will become the fifth most populous country by 2014 (having overtaken Brazil), with its population rising to 227.8m. in 2020 and to 272.7m. by 2030, following Indonesia (with a projected population of 261.9m. in 2020 and of 282.9m. by 2030).

Although there have been major advances in reducing mortality throughout the Asia-Pacific region, there are still a number of countries with poor mortality levels. The lowest life expectancies and highest IMRs in 2002 were found in South-Central Asia. Life expectancy on average, for this sub-region, was only 62 for men and 63 for women, while the IMR was 69. The country with the poorest level was war-torn Afghanistan, with a life expectancy of only 46 for men and 44 for women, while its IMR was a disturbing 154. This was followed by East Timor, with an IMR of 135. Laos, Cambodia, Myanmar and Pakistan had estimated IMRs of 104, 95, 90 and 86 respectively.

Future reductions in mortality within the Asia-Pacific region are dependent on the socio-economic gains that will be made and on changes in lifestyle. For example, reductions in smoking and motor accidents would increase life expectancy. By the beginning of the 21st century, however, smoking (with the resultant incidence of disease and the increasing burden on health services) had become a particularly serious problem in China where more than 300m. (an estimated one-third of the entire global cigarette market) were smokers.

Increased mortality levels also occur with the spread of old and new diseases such as measles, tuberculosis, malaria, and HIV/AIDS. Taking just one of these diseases, HIV/AIDS, this has had a dramatic effect on demographic patterns. Of the 45 countries classified in 2000 by the Population Division of the UN Department of Economic and Social Affairs as highly affected by HIV/AIDS, only four were in Asia (Cambodia, India, Myanmar and Thailand), but the regional impact has been substantial. By 1999 more than 3m. people in the Asia-Pacific region had died of AIDS-related illnesses, and projections indicated that the infection would continue to spread. UNAIDS estimated that in the Asia-Pacific region by the end of 2001 6.6m. people (including the 1.1m. adults and children newly-infected during that year) were carrying HIV/AIDS. At the end of 2001, in India alone, an estimated 3.97m. people were living with HIV/AIDS (in terms of numbers second only to South Africa). The sharpest increases in rates of infection per head have been found in Cambodia and Myanmar. An estimated 4% of Cambodians were infected by late 1999, although by late 2001 this was estimated to have decreased to 2.7%. In 1999 the Government of Myanmar reported a total of 802 AIDS-related deaths in the country. A UN source, however, estimated Myanmar's death toll from AIDS in 1999 at 48,000. Indonesia, the world's fourth most populous country, has also witnessed a particularly sharp rise in infection rates, particularly among drug-users in Jakarta.

Owing to the populous nature of the country (as in India), China's relatively low rate of infection has nevertheless led to a large number of cases. By 2001 China was beginning to acknowledge the extent of its HIV/AIDS problem. In March of that year official statistics indicated a total of only 23,905 cases in China. The Ministry of Health, however, admitted that the total might be in excess of 600,000, with some observers fearing an increase to as many as 10m. by 2010. UNAIDS estimated that in the first six months of 2001 alone the number of reported infections of HIV had increased by 67% and that by the end of that year a total of 850,000 Chinese were living with HIV/AIDS. In January 2001, in an unprecedented move, the Chinese authorities announced the implementation of legislation in Chengdu, the capital of Sichuan Province, to counter the spread of HIV/AIDS; measures included a ban on those infected with HIV/AIDS from marrying. In Henan Province, meanwhile, in a scandal that emerged only in 2001, as many as 500,000 residents had become infected after selling their blood plasma to commercial companies that had employed unhygienic practices. Similar situations were developing in Anhui and Shanxi Provinces. Meanwhile, serious local epidemics of HIV were reported among injecting drug-users in at least seven Chinese provinces. In mid-2002, furthermore, the Government admitted that the number of HIV cases in China could have reached 1m.

In May 2002 a report published by an Australian aid agency stated that as many as 15,000 of the 4.6m. (adult) population of Papua New Guinea were HIV-positive. AIDS-related diseases had become a major cause of death in Port Moresby, the capital. It was feared that 40% of the adult population might die within 20 years.

Despite the disturbing figures, there have been some positive signs of progress in combating the HIV/AIDS problem. Although Thailand had a total of 755,000 people living with HIV/AIDS by late 1999 and 66,000 deaths were reported in that year alone, during the 1990s the country dramatically decreased the prevalence levels of the disease. Despite the fact that AIDS had become the leading cause of death in Thailand, the number of new HIV infections declined from 143,000 in 1991 to 29,000 in 2001. This success was a result of a massive campaign that was supported by the Government but that allowed the active involvement of communities and NGOs in formulating national policies and strategies. By 2001, however, as the pattern of the spread of HIV/AIDS changed to encompass, for example, increasing numbers of married women infected by their husbands, some Thai campaigners feared that the Government's programme was losing momentum.

Migration

Migration is the third aspect of population dynamics. The movement of people, within and out of the Asia-Pacific region, has grown in importance. These movements have been permanent and temporary, legal and illegal, forced and unforced. Virtually every country in the region has become involved as a significant origin and/or destination of international movements. There are three major types of migration in the region. The first is the emigration of 'settlers' from the Asia-Pacific region to North America, Australia and New Zealand. In the 1990s some 500,000 persons annually emigrated to these destinations from the Philippines, China, India and other Asian countries. The region has become one of the most important sources of this type of migration around the world. In the 1990s nearly 40% of US immigrants were from Asia.

The second type of migration has been the movement of people for humanitarian reasons. Some of the largest forced international migrations in history have occurred in recent times, the number of refugees more than doubling (to reach a peak of 17.8m.) between 1980 and 1992 alone, according to estimates by the office of the UN High Commissioner for Refugees (UNHCR). At December 2001 UNHCR estimated that there were nearly 19.8m. refugees, asylum-seekers and others of concern in the world, of whom the Asia-Pacific region was accommodating almost 1.7m. The massive displacement from Afghanistan to Pakistan and Iran (which was sheltering more than 3.8m. refugees at the end of 2001) has been dominant. Following the return to relative stability in Afghanistan in late 2001, with the assistance of UNHCR by March 2002 more than 1.3m. refugees had chosen to return to their homeland.

The third type of movement has been that of people migrating, both within nations and internationally, in order to work. The major impetus to this came in 1973 with the increase in petroleum prices, which allowed Bahrain, Kuwait, Oman, Qatar, Saudi Arabia and the United Arab Emirates to undertake large infrastructural projects. In 1992 foreign labourers in these countries numbered more than 7m. By the mid-1990s intra-Asian movement had become much more significant, and at least 3m.–4m. Asians were employed outside of their home countries but within Asia, primarily in the region's seven major labour-importing countries: Japan, the Republic of Korea, Hong Kong, Taiwan, Singapore, Malaysia, and Thailand. The principal labour-exporting countries include Bangladesh, China, Indonesia, the Philippines and, again, Malaysia and Thailand. One of the most substantial movements was from Indonesia to Malaysia, involving up to 1m. workers and accounting for more than 10% of the Malaysian work-force. From late 1997, however, with the onset of the economic crisis in East and South-East Asia, large numbers of foreign workers were repatriated to their countries of origin.

Birth Control and Economic Growth

The International Conference on Population and Development, held in Cairo, Egypt, in September 1994, which was attended by representatives of 182 countries, set the agenda for future attempts to control populations. The Conference adopted a Programme of Action, establishing the objectives to be pursued for the next 20 years (despite reservations recorded by the representatives of some predominantly Roman Catholic and Islamic countries, concerning sections which they regarded as endorsing abortion and sexual promiscuity). The Programme emphasized the necessity of empowering and educating women, ensuring reproductive health, advancing equality of the sexes, and encouraging national endeavours and international co-operation. Annual expenditure required for the implementation of the objectives was estimated to amount to US $17,000m. for the year 2000, increasing to US $21,700m. in 2015: of these amounts, the international community or donor countries would need to contribute about one-third. If successfully implemented, the Programme of Action was expected to limit world population growth to a level below the UN's (then) medium projection of a population of 7,154m. in 2015 (compared with 6,055m. in 2000).

Birth control alone is unlikely to achieve any solution unless it is accompanied by economic development. The relationship between low rates of population growth and high rates of economic growth is well illustrated in Japan, the Republic of Korea and Taiwan. Further to reduce fertility in the Asia-Pacific region requires greater financial security. Measures that would be beneficial would be the creation of a fairer world-trading system that would remove the subsidies from European and US farm produce, a reduction or elimination of debt repayments, aid, land reform, social reform, women's education and emancipation, and in general the elimination of the extremes of gross inequalities. In other words, couples are unlikely to plan their families unless they can plan their whole lives in terms of income, employment security, adequate health, shelter and education. Family-planning is the desired aim, however achieved, while birth-control is merely the technological means of achieving it. Finally, birth control can have little immediate effect on the problems of malnutrition, unemployment and poor housing; it is essentially a long-term process, taking from one to two decades to produce a result.

In the final analysis, family-planning is essential for the Asia-Pacific region's future, but the massive population numbers cannot be solved by implementing a programme of birth control without changing aspects of their societies. The lessons learnt, from the changes that have taken place in the region, indicate that improving economic conditions and raising the status of women has a major impact on the society as a whole and the countries' population dynamics. Richer families are in a much better position to control the number of children they have. Also, women who acquire more education are in a better position not only to gain access to family-planning services but also to decide the number of children they want.

FOOD AND AGRICULTURE

Great advances have been made in food production. The world's food supply has expanded faster than the world's population, substantially increasing the amount of food available per person. Between 1961 and 1994 average daily per caput food supplies rose by more than 20%. Importantly, the greatest increases occurred in developing countries where, during the above-mentioned years, daily food calories per person rose from about 1,900 to 2,600, while their populations nearly doubled. Access to food has also expanded, resulting in the decline of the percentage of people who are malnourished. In 1960 59% of the global population consumed less than the minimum required for good health. By 1994 the percentage had decreased to 38%.

Despite the great advances that have been made in producing extra food, huge problems remain. Levels of nutrition are still appallingly low in some countries, people continue to die from the sheer lack of food, while millions of children are growing up seriously debilitated physically and mentally by malnutrition. It was estimated by the World Bank that in 1993–99 47% of the children of South Asia were malnourished. Millions of others consume only the minimum number of calories, but fail to gain the necessary protein, vitamins and minerals to lead a healthy life. Better conditions prevailed in East Asia and the Pacific, where only 12% of children were classified as underweight.

Of major concern from the late 1990s were continued reports of a large-scale famine in the Democratic People's Republic of Korea. By mid-1999 an estimated 1.5m.–3.5m. North Koreans had died of starvation since 1995. In 1998 a nutritional survey conducted by the World Food Programme (WFP), the United Nations Children's Fund (UNICEF) and the European Union (EU) showed that some 16% of North Korean children under the age of seven were suffering from acute malnutrition, while 60% suffered long-term malnutrition. Although food production reportedly increased during 1999, there remained a substantial shortfall. FAO estimated output of rice at 2.3m. tons in 1999 but at less than 1.7m. tons in 2000, maize at 1.2m. tons in 1999 and at 1.0m. tons in 2000 and potatoes at around 1.4m. tons in both 1999 and 2000. Food shortages were exacerbated by drought in 2000–01. In 2001 WFP was providing assistance to some 7.6m. North Koreans. In April 2002, however, WFP was obliged to suspend food assistance to about 1.5m. needy North Koreans, owing to a shortfall in aid.

Table 6. Aspects of Agriculture and Food Production and Nutrition for Selected Countries in the Asia-Pacific Region

	Index of production per person, 2001 (1989–91 = 100)		Daily calorific intake per person, 2000	% of labour force employed in agriculture, etc., 2000
	Agriculture	Food (net)		
Asia:				
Afghanistan	92.8*	93.2*	1,539	67.0
Bangladesh	109.1	110.7	2,103	55.6
Bhutan	93.0	93.0	n.a.	93.8
Cambodia	111.6	112.7	2,070	70.1
China†	155.5	160.8	3,029	66.9
India	105.3	106.1	2,428	59.6
Indonesia	99.3	99.4	2,902	48.4
Japan	88.8	89.4	2,762	4.1
Korea, Democratic People's Republic	78.1	78.5	2,185	30.1
Korea, Republic	117.1	118.3	3,093	10.0
Laos	127.3	130.1	2,266	76.5
Malaysia	103.8	117.0	2,919	18.7
Mongolia	89.4	89.2	1,981	24.3
Myanmar	142.6	143.1	2,842	70.2
Nepal	101.6	101.9	2,436	93.0
Pakistan	103.7	108.7	2,452	47.1
Philippines	105.8	107.8	2,379	39.5
Sri Lanka	109.2	109.8	2,406	45.5
Thailand	105.5	103.5	2,505	56.5
Viet Nam	137.6	129.1	2,583	67.3
Oceania:				
Australia	114.7	126.8	3,176	4.6
Fiji	87.0	87.3	2,861	39.9
New Zealand	109.3	117.6	3,252	9.0
Papua New Guinea	96.0	94.5	2,175	74.1

* 1999 figure.

† Includes Taiwan.

Sources: FAO, *Production Yearbook*, and internet apps.fao.org.

Food Production

Asian food production has to be viewed in a global context because food surpluses elsewhere (the USA, Canada and Australia, along with member countries of the EU) are the source of the imports. Fluctuations in output in these developed countries, owing to the removal of land from production or from poor harvests, can cause hardships in the developing Asian-Pacific countries. Output from the developed nations is geared to the world market prices. During periods of oversupply and low prices land is not farmed. With increasing prices, however, land is brought back into production. Output trends, carry-over stocks and hence prices are vitally important to Asia, and are quickly reflected in nutritional levels.

A summary of the performance of some of the countries in the region with regard to food production and nutrition is given in Table 6. In many countries, food production has continued to rise, most notably in China (including Taiwan), from a per caput production index (1989–91=100) of 90.5 in 1986 to 144.9 in 1997 and reaching 160.8 in 2001. Over the 1991–2000 period Myanmar, in particular, reversed previous trends and also showed substantial increases, rising from 97.7 in 1991 to 118.6 in 1998 and rising to 143.1 in 2001. India, a country that previously suffered food shortages, suddenly became successful by pursuing a variety of small-scale improvements and by intensively using existing labour rather than by importing tractors and machinery. Between 1950 and the end of the 20th century India's grain harvest trebled. Past deficits (in 1987 the index was only 89.7) have been transformed into surpluses (104.9 in 1998 and 106.1 in 2001), the country becoming a modest exporter of grain. Many other countries are also aiding their small farmers, with positive results.

In countries that have experienced social and political upheavals, however, the picture is not so positive. In Cambodia the per caput index of food production declined steadily during the political transformations in the early 1990s, falling to 88.9 in 1994, but subsequently recovered to stand at 107.4 in 1998 and at 112.7 in 2001. In Mongolia the index declined from 102.9 in 1991 to 69.5 in 1994, rising thereafter to reach 76.2 in 1998 and 89.2 in 2001. Ethnic unrest in Sri Lanka has been reflected in fluctuations in the production of food and other agricultural commodities. The food production index decreased from 113.2 in 1995 to 98.8 in 1996, rising to 105.7 in 1998 and 109.8 in 2001.

Social and political changes have led to increased food production in a number of countries. One major innovation that gathered momentum after 1985 was the introduction of private plots and profit motives in the communist nations of Asia, in an effort to stimulate production. In China communes were reorganized, with the family as the basic production unit. Families were assigned quotas by the commune, and private plots were enlarged. Food production increased significantly, and the first 'millionaire' farmer emerged in 1987. Viet Nam has similarly allowed peasants to keep or sell food over and above targets, again leading to substantial increases in production. Indeed, by 1989 Viet Nam had become one of the world's largest exporters of rice.

Increased food production has also occurred because of scientific advances. The much-vaunted success of the higher-yielding varieties (HYV), introduced in the 1960s, provided a respite in the campaign to expand food production sufficiently to maintain nutritional levels as population increased. The penetration of the new varieties into traditional crop programmes was very uneven, however, varying from 10% to 60% between countries. Better varieties have come on to the market occasionally. These can be harvested four times annually on irrigated fields or twice a year on unirrigated fields, but the amount of fertilizer needed to sustain these continuous periods of growth is enormous. In 2000 the International Rice Research Institute (IRRI), based in the Philippines, announced the creation of a new rice strain, which could be introduced within three–five years and increase yields by as much as 35%. New developments in genetically-modified (GM) plants, if socially accepted, could dramatically improve yields. China, India, Indonesia, Thailand and Viet Nam participate in the IRRI's Asian Rice Biotechnology Network, which in the future may develop GM varieties of rice. In early 2001 China remained the only country in Asia to grow a GM crop, namely cotton, while Japan had given approval for three varieties of GM seed. Major exporters of agricultural products, such as Thailand, Viet Nam and India, however, were required to consider whether the overseas marketing advantages of avoiding GM crops would in fact outweigh the increases in yields or the nutritional benefits that GM crops might provide to feed expanding populations.

World output of cereals has increased, although rising production is often accompanied by declining prices which, while excellent for the food-importing countries of Asia, does affect those few countries that are net exporters of grains or other primary produce. The ramifications are far-reaching because North American farmers have reduced the area sown with wheat as a consequence of the low returns, the accumulation of reserve stocks, and drought. If the reduction in planting coincides with another series of harvest failures elsewhere in the world, then a new food shortage will appear. The situation could become critical. Flooding or drought in China, in particular, may reduce output. Under its Ninth Five-Year Plan for the years 1996–2000, China placed greater emphasis on food production, aiming to raise the annual grain harvest to 600m. metric tons by the year 2000. In 1998 a record harvest of 512m. tons of grain (cereals, pulses, soybeans and tubers in 'grain equivalent') was attained. China's grain harvest was recorded at 509m. tons in 1999 but, partly owing to drought, at only 462.51m. tons in 2000, thus falling far short of the target. In 2001 grain output decreased further, to an estimated 450m. tons. This declining trend was attributed to various factors, including a decrease in the agricultural area owing to urban development, ecological disasters and a shift to the more profitable crops of fruits and vegetables. Furthermore, China's entry to the World Trade Organization (WTO) in late 2001 was expected to compound the problem, with the availability of cheaper imports exerting pressure on state grain prices.

At the FAO World Food Summit in November 1996 attention was drawn to the fact that China's gradual shift from consumption of rice to that of grain was jeopardizing world grain stocks, particularly of wheat. Crops need to be diversified, and more emphasis placed on tubers and 'green-leaf' vegetables, which are often despised by urban dwellers and the affluent but are the basis of the peasant diet. Grain yields per ha appeared to level off in the 1990s, in contrast to the large increases that occurred during the period from the early 1950s to the mid-1980s. For example, after reaching almost 5.8 metric tons per ha in 1967, Japanese rice yields declined in subsequent years, before rising to a peak of 6.4 in 1984. Yields continued to fluctuate in the 1990s, standing at 6.4 tons per ha in 1999 and rising to 6.7 tons in 2000. At around 6.2 tons per ha in 2000, China's rice yield was also among the highest in the region, along with that of the Republic of Korea (almost 6.6 tons). This stabilization of yield is partly the result of the attainment of the limits of availability of essential resources such as land and water, and even their actual decline, with soil erosion, salinization, deforestation and flooding. In China, for example, it was estimated in 2000 that desertification affected 27% of the country's territory and that this area was expanding by 2,460 sq km annually. Increasingly, the basis of the environment of food production will need to be given attention in order to sustain the region's population. Nevertheless, in May 1997 FAO reported a considerable improvement in Asian-Pacific food security since the mid-1990s and a continuation in the decline in the number of malnourished people in the region. Cereal consumption remained static, while production rose and imports were increased. At the FAO World Food Summit held in June 2002 (postponed from November 2001 owing to security concerns), the wider use of biotechnology to produce drought-resistant, high-yield GM crops was strongly promoted by the US delegation. Critics claimed, however, that farmers in developing countries would become reliant on US corporations. Meanwhile, FAO estimated that the number of undernourished people in China had declined by 76m. within 10 years.

In late 2001 scientists warned that some agricultural harvests might decrease by more than 30%, owing to the rise in global temperatures. A number of the staple food crops grown in tropical regions were believed to be approaching their thermal limits, encountering difficulties in flowering and setting seed. Harvests of rice, wheat and maize, in particular, appeared likely to decline by 10% for every one degree Celsius increase in temperature.

Nutritional Levels

Table 6 shows the daily calorific intake per person. Only a few of the developing countries of the region have not yet achieved an average nutritional level that comfortably exceeds the minimum health requirements of around 2,250 calories per day. Food supplies, however, are not distributed equally, and probably about half (some would say more than half) of the population receives amounts considerably less than the national average. The poorest income classes are involved in more continuous labour than others, and usually need a greater nutritional intake in order to maintain their physical effort.

Active Engagement in Agriculture

Finally, one other aspect of agriculture and food production deserves examination. A clear indication of an economically-advanced economy is the low proportion of the working population engaged in agriculture, forestry and fishing (see Table 6). In Asia and Oceania there are the examples of Australia (4.6% in 2000) and Japan (4.1%), or even, at a somewhat higher level but still low by the standards of the region, New Zealand (9.0%), the Republic of Korea (10.0%) and Malaysia (18.7%). Many countries have substantially more than half of their labour force engaged in agriculture, the proportion reaching as high as 93.8% in Bhutan and 93.0% in Nepal.

Although the percentage figures for all countries have declined considerably, as a growing proportion of the population increase has been moved into secondary and tertiary activities, this percentage decline conceals the fact that the absolute numbers on the land are increasing rapidly. For example, although 65.3% of the economically-active population in Bangladesh was engaged in agriculture in 1990, decreasing to 55.6% in 2000, the actual number of people in agriculture increased from 33.6m. to more than 38.7m. Similarly, in India the proportion fell from 64.0% in 1990 to 59.6% in 2000, but the actual number rose from 231.1m. to more than 263.7m. In Pakistan the percentage decline was from 51.8% to 47.1%, but the absolute number rose from 22.0m. to 24.5m. China's decrease from 72.2% to 66.9% (including Taiwan) was, in fact, an increase in absolute numbers from 493.1m. to almost 510.8m. The pressure on the productive land, therefore, is not diminishing but increasing. Consequently, landlessness is rising. A considerable percentage of the region's farmers are landless, and the proportion will increase further as natural disasters and environmental degradation reduce the amount of land available.

DEVELOPMENT AND INTERNAL INEQUALITIES

Too often the desire for economic development has been seen purely in monetary terms, and this has been at a cost of environmental degradation and social inequalities. Only recently have attempts been made to extend the concept of development beyond that of economic performance and to see social needs and aspirations as being closely linked to the process of development. Similarly, only relatively recently have attempts been made to analyse in detail the scope and nature of the internal inequalities within nations and among regions of the world. In 1997 a comprehensive report issued by Pakistan's Human Development Centre, with support from The United Nations Development Programme (UNDP), concluded that South Asia had become the poorest, most illiterate and malnourished region in the world (having fallen behind sub-Saharan Africa for the first time), and warned of revolution in India within a decade if the problem of the widening disparity between rich and poor were not addressed. In its 1997 *Human Development Report*, however, UNDP concluded that the division of income and assets such as land and credit was at its most equitable in East and South-East Asia, these countries making substantial investment in education and health services.

Economic growth has often accentuated internal patterns of inequality. There is debate, however, about the importance of this. One side argues that with increasing levels of inequality fewer people will identify the benefits of economic growth with their own personal lives and the result, it is claimed, will be their failure to respond to family planning. Couples are unlikely to plan their families unless they can plan their whole lives (in terms of income, employment, shelter and security) with some degree of assurance. A second opinion argues that poverty is a greater problem than inequality. Thailand, until 1996, was a country that had increasing levels of inequality, but at the same time the level of poverty decreased. During a period of rapid economic growth rich Thais gained a greater share of the country's wealth, but at the same time poor people did become better off. Although there was growing inequality, standards of living were improving and couples were willing to limit their family sizes.

There are many examples of inequalities, that of food supply being perhaps the most obvious and basic. Yet there are others. For example, the per caput income figures in Table 2 do give a reasonably correct view of the relative levels of affluence among countries, but they do not identify the enormous inequalities of income that occur in the least developed of the countries of the region. Estimates of the percentage of the population living at poverty level vary enormously but, whichever measure is taken, the result is disturbing. Within East Asia and the Pacific in 1999 there were an estimated 260m. people living on US $1 or less per day, compared with 452m. in 1990. In South Asia the number of people living on less than US $1 a day stood at 490m. in 1999, compared with 495m. in 1990. On the whole, the tendency is for urban areas to have slightly less inequality than rural areas. Nevertheless, even in the urban areas inequality is increasing rapidly. If poverty is measured not in income but in terms of access to facilities, then urban areas have a clear advantage. For example, according to UNDP, in rural Pakistan in 1985–95, only 35% of the population had reasonable access to health services, compared with 99% in urban areas. Reasonable access to supplies of safe drinking water also varies between town and country, with 90% of the urban population of Nepal having adequate supplies, compared with only 43% in the rural areas in 1990–95.

Within rural areas, land ownership is a crucial measure and criterion of poverty and social well-being, for from it stem status, employment and leisure. The statistics on the distribution of holdings by size groups are endless, but typically the poorest 25% of the rural households possess hardly any land, while the bulk of the land is held by the leading 25% of the households. The landless labourers who are products of this inequality of ownership create problems of precisely unknown but undoubtedly great magnitude, and their ranks are swelled continuously by the small owner-occupiers, tenants, share-croppers and artisans displaced by population growth, and also by the centralization of the means of production.

Unemployment is one measure of poverty in societies without the welfare and social support mechanisms of developed countries. Traditional concepts of what is employed and unemployed have rarely had much meaning in rural or urban Asia, where kinship bonds, much underemployment and the seasonal nature of agriculture are common in rural areas, and concepts of the duration of the working day or week are poorly defined in urban areas. Official surveys totally underplay the extent of unemployment. For example, in rural India in the early 1990s the number of people wholly unemployed stood at 6% of the potential adult male labour force; but if underemployment is taken into account, the figure was 23%. In China, meanwhile, the number of rural unemployed was estimated at 150m. by 2001.

It is clear that a large proportion of the population is not able to contribute to national growth. Their numbers are probably higher in the urban areas than in rural areas, higher for the young than for the old, and for men as compared with women. The Republic of Korea, Singapore, Japan, Hong Kong, Australia, New Zealand, Thailand and Malaysia have experienced shortages of skilled labour, but within these countries and elsewhere there has been an oversupply of unskilled workers. The economic crisis that started in 1997 increased levels of unemployment throughout the region. Countries such as Thailand, which had been importing labour from other countries, subsequently faced a growing unemployment rate.

Although many new jobs have been created in the services sectors since the 1990s, for example in the rapidly-expanding data-processing businesses of India, the numbers of unemployed have also been swelled by technological change. In some countries the rate of industrial growth has been too slow to absorb the increasing population, and the introduction of capital-intensive labour-saving techniques in factory and farm has not absorbed but actually replaced people. To all this must be added the ever-rising aspirations brought about by the expansion of the educational system, and of the type of education given. Young people sometimes feel unsuited to the jobs that are available.

The inter-relationship between economic inequality and social inequality with family size is important. There is an observable inverse relationship between per caput income (and consumption) and family size. It is worth considering, however, whether smaller family sizes produce higher incomes or higher incomes produce smaller families—an argument of cause and effect that has far-reaching ramifications. There is also a clear association between the level of education received and the level of personal earnings, and hence the adoption of contraceptive methods and eventual family size.

THE ROLE OF AID

One way of creating the conditions for further fertility control and continued improvements in mortality levels is through aid. This can be achieved directly through population assistance, or indirectly by raising the standard of living, which allows people to control their fertility. Direct population aid accounted for only 2.3% of official development assistance in 1995. Although a relatively small proportion, this totalled almost US $1,600m. Including development banks' loans, the primary funds exceeded US $2,000m. Of this money, 53% was for family-planning services, 10% for basic reproductive-health services, and 16% for basic research, population data collection and development analysis. The Asia-Pacific region received 26% of the funding. Most went to South Asia, followed by South-East Asia. The Pacific, reflecting its small population base, received a minor percentage.

The USA's decision in July 2002 to withhold financing of US $34m. from UNFPA, on the grounds that funds were being used to promote coercive policies such as abortion and enforced sterilization, was condemned by China, which repudiated the accusations. The EU subsequently agreed to offset the shortfall with aid of €32m. for sexual and reproductive health projects in 22 countries.

The majority of aid, of course, is not directly given for population assistance, but as official development assistance. The largest donors of this type of aid in 2000 were Japan, the USA, Germany, the United Kingdom and France. Despite being the largest donors, none of these nations met the UN's objective of giving 0.7% of gross national product (GNP). In 2000, according to UNDP, only Denmark (1.06% of GNP), the Netherlands (0.84%), Norway (0.80%), Sweden (also 0.80%), and Luxembourg (0.71%) disbursed net official development assistance of more than the target level, while countries like Australia, the United Kingdom and the USA donated only 0.27%, 0.32% and 0.10% respectively. Although its aid was equivalent to only 0.28% of its GNP, Japan remained by far the world's largest donor and the country that provided the most assistance to the Asia-Pacific region. The ability of Japan to assist the region will, however, be tested by the country's own continued economic problems.

It is increasingly felt that aid should not be narrowly focused on purely economic goals, and that the main aim of aid should be to eradicate the complex nexus of socio-economic poverty. The best means of achieving this might be to give money that can be used on the projects that the recipient country needs most, but this remains a distant goal. Furthermore, emphasis should be given to projects that will raise the status of women. As noted above, where the position of women has improved, decreases in mortality and fertility have been achieved.

Past emphasis on infrastructural development and the expansion of industrial production was based on the assumption that industrial growth would promote all sectors of the economy, including agriculture. Too often, however, agriculture was seriously neglected, production actually declined and food imports increased, all against a background of reasonably available food aid. The conventional emphasis on overall growth had consequently been questioned. Moreover, there is the problem of the prevention of the 'leakage' of benefits from the poverty-ridden population at whom the aid is aimed to the more affluent section which is usually far more capable of taking advantage of it. The need is more for a basic 'human-needs' approach directed away from expenditure on grandiose projects that are often technologically inappropriate to the environment and society to which they are applied. A further important problem is that conventional aid does not necessarily promote productive employment. Indeed, it may have the opposite effect because capital-intensive and labour-saving projects may be given priority. What is needed is the creation of efficient labour-intensive technology to absorb the underemployed and unemployed. Thus, the expansion of small family farms (given that all support facilities are provided), the most efficient sector of the economy and the most deserving of aid, may be the way of striking simultaneously at the problems of food supply, social well-being, employment and ultimately, at family size. Therefore, it would be desirable to abandon aims of maximizing efficiency through aid, and to concentrate on employment creation. This would absorb the un- and underemployed, and would lead to the growth of the GNP, rather than to its retardation, as is commonly supposed.

The countries of the developing world still need the investment of private money, but the pursuit by lenders of increased productivity must be seen as secondary to that of increasing employment. Too often investment by large companies is not helpful because they tend to import their own technology and to promote the goods that have been most successful in their own home markets and which, incidentally, will probably appeal to the most affluent section of the community in the recipient country.

According to most authorities, the gap between the developing and the developed economies (or, more bluntly, the poor and the rich countries) is increasing rather than diminishing. The rate of economic growth of the poorer countries is usually less than that of the richer countries, even at their current reduced rates. The closing of the gap seems impossible, and it may, in some cases, even widen. Also, the sharp increase in petroleum prices after 1973 moved wealth away from the developed and developing countries alike, to the members of the Organization of the Petroleum-Exporting Countries (OPEC), undermining the ability of the rich to help the poor, as well as increasing the costs of food production. The Gulf War of early 1991, and the loss of remittances from overseas workers, exacerbated the situation. The regional economic crisis, which first affected Thailand in 1997 and then extended to other countries of the region, increased the divide between the developed and developing nations. It is against this background that aid, with associated trade, must be seen as a means of encouraging socio-economic progress, not being focused narrowly on raising the GNP, but on unfolding the creative potentialities inherent in societies to achieve the total human needs, values and standards of the good life.

Debt

For many developing nations, including those of the Asia-Pacific region, repayment of debt is placing burdens on their societies. Concessionary flows of capital from IMF lending and export credits have been a significant source of project finance for many developing countries, but the loans and the interest payments have to be repaid eventually: burdens which the developing world can scarcely afford. Finally, there are the non-concessionary commercial bank loans (raised on the international money market), the magnitude of which is difficult to quantify accurately. These loans give rise to the 'debt problem' that now exercises the minds and actions of financial institutions and governments throughout the world.

Of a calculated preliminary world total (of developing countries reporting debt to the World Bank) at 31 December 2001 of US $2,442,082m. of external debt (including debt-service payment arrears), US $604,322m. was incurred by East Asia and the Pacific, and US $159,289m. by South Asia. Considering the region's proportion of the world's population and attendant problems, this is relatively low and financially prudent, but an alternative interpretation could be that some countries are so poor that they are not a good lending proposition.

FUTURE POPULATION GROWTH

The Population Division of the UN Department of Economic and Social Affairs regularly works on revising projections of world population growth. Its medium variant is usually adopted as the one most likely to occur.

Taking, first, a global view, according to the UN's *World Population Prospects: The 2000 Revision,* the world's population reached 6,057m. at mid-2000 and (using the medium variant) was projected to increase to 9,322m. by 2050. This revised projection would thus be higher than the 8,909m. anticipated by the UN's 1998 revision. Of that difference of 413m., higher future fertility levels projected for the 16 developing countries (mainly in Africa) where fertility has not yet shown signs of a sustained decline are responsible for 59%. The somewhat higher recent fertility estimated in the 2000 revision for several populous countries (such as Bangladesh, India and Nigeria) accounts for a further 32% of that difference.

Population growth is projected to decelerate in both the more developed and the less developed regions. However, whereas the growth rate is projected to remain positive for the less developed regions until 2050, after 2025 the populations of the more developed regions are expected to decline. By 2045–50, therefore, the population in the more developed regions is projected to be declining at a rate of 0.19% per year, whereas the population of the less developed regions will continue to increase, growing at a rate of 0.57% per year.

The population of the more developed regions (Europe, northern America, Japan, Australia and New Zealand) was 1,191m. at mid-2000, while that of the less developed regions was 4,865m., but by 2050 the comparable totals will be 1,181m. and 8,141m. Thus, while the share of the world's population living in developed regions is expected to decline from 19.7% in 2000 to 12.7% in 2050, the proportion inhabiting less developed regions will, it is forecast, rise steadily from 80.3% in 2000 to 87.3% in 2050.

As far as Asia and Oceania are concerned, the projected increase in population would represent a 47.9% rise within 50 years, with the total growing from 3,703m. in 2000 to 5,475m. in 2050. Patterns of fertility will change, a striking feature of this being (according to the UN Population Division) the estimated reduction in China's average annual rate of growth from 2.21% in 1970–75 to 0.90% in 1995–2000 and to 0.34% by 2020–25, followed by an annual contraction in the population of 0.26% by 2045–50. Japan's rate of annual increase was expected to decline from 1.33% in 1970–75 to 0.26% in 1995–2000. Thereafter, the Japanese population was expected to decrease annually by 0.35% in 2020–25 and by 0.59% in 2045–50.

Despite the declines in average annual rates of growth, the region will still expand. The population of the Indian subcontinent (Bangladesh, India, Pakistan and Sri Lanka) will grow from 1,306.6m. in 2000 to 1,836.1m. in 2025 and to 2,204.7m. in 2050, when India alone will have a projected 1,572.1m. inhabitants. This region will account for about 23.7% of the world's population in 2050. The population of China is expected to increase from 1,275.1m. in 2000 to 1,470.8m. in 2025 and then to decline to 1,462.1m. in 2050, when it will account for almost 16% of the world's population (compared with 21% in 2000). Australia and New Zealand will also have generally falling rates of growth, projected to decline from 2.07% and 1.79% respectively per annum in 1970–75 to 1.15% and 0.94% in 1995–2000 and to 0.67% and 0.37% in 2020–25, and to 0.41% and 0.01% in 2050, leading to a rise in the two countries' population from 22.9m. in 2000 to 27.8m. in 2025 and to a smaller increase, to 30.9m., in 2050. However, the Pacific region (particularly Solomon Islands) was expected to retain high annual birth rates, usually of about 30 per 1,000, at least until the beginning of the 21st century, thus leading to growth rates of about 2% per annum and the consequent rapid doubling of the population within restricted resource bases on already crowded island sites.

Projected trends in mortality suggest that levels will decline globally, but there are significant regional variations. The average annual death rate in industrialized and less developed nations was almost exactly equal in 1985–90, since when the rate has tended to rise in developed regions because of their ageing populations. Average life expectancy at birth in 2020–25 is expected to reach 71.6 years in south-eastern Asia, 78.2 years in eastern Asia and 80.5 years in Australia and New Zealand, but it will be only 70.2 years in south-central Asia. The corresponding figures in 2045–50 are 76.7 for south-eastern Asia, 81.6 years in eastern Asia, 82.5 years in Australia and 75.5 years in south-central Asia. As for the structure of the population, it is expected that the proportion of very young people in the Asian population will decline because of reductions in birth rates, and that the proportion of old persons will increase considerably. In eastern Asia, for example (according to 2000 projections), the number of people over 60 years of age will increase from 11.9% of the population in 2000 to 32.1% by 2050. By custom, the elderly in Asia have been looked after by the next generation down. However, with fewer of these productive people in the population, and with multiple generations in households as each cohort survives, serious problems are looming for the future. Many countries will have to decide if it is the family or the state that looks after the elderly. While the elderly increase as a proportion of the population, those of working age (15–64) will not diminish in absolute terms. Employment needs will multiply and the drift of active and able young people from rural areas to urban areas will continue at an increasing rate, with implications for the cities to which they go and for the elderly people whom they leave behind. According to 1999 forecasts, the proportion of the Asian population resident in urban areas will rise from 17% in 1950 to a projected 53% in the year 2030. By comparison, during the same period the proportion of the population urbanized in Europe will rise from 52% to 83%.

Although the speed of fertility decline in the Asia-Pacific region has been greater than previously projected, there will be a continuing growth in the region's population until well into the 21st century. Population growth in the Asia-Pacific region will depend on how quickly, or how slowly, birth rates decline in the areas where hitherto there has been either no decline or only a moderate decline. In India, for example, much of the decline in the birth rate has taken place in the more literate southern states. Yet in the heavily-populated northern states, where rates of illiteracy and fertility are much higher, birth rates may not decline as rapidly, leading to an unprecedented growth in population. Elsewhere, recent survey data from a number of Asia-Pacific countries, including Bangladesh, indicate that the rates of fertility decline recorded previously have decelerated. Hence, the question of demographic disparity and imbalance will remain a key issue of population growth in the 21st century. This represents a major challenge for the poorer countries of the region, where growth will be concentrated, and in particular, for the populous countries of southern Asia. It will require not only all the ingenuity and effort of the countries concerned to provide adequate social justice and food supplies for their populations, but also all the generosity and sympathy of the more affluent world to assist in this task, a task currently all the more complex and difficult in a world that is trying to cope with intermittent crises in economic stability.

BIBLIOGRAPHY

Abbugao, M. 'Scientist unveils new super rice'. *Bangkok Post*, Bangkok, 30 March 2000.

Arnold, F., Choe, M. K., and Roy, T. K. 'Son preference, the family-building process and child mortality in India'. *Population Studies*, 52, 3, pp. 301–316, 1998.

Arnold, F., and Liu Zhaoxiang. 'Sex Preference, Fertility and Family Planning in China'. *Population and Development Review*, 12, pp. 221–246, 1986.

Atoh, M. 'Countries with Substantially Below-Replacement Fertility: The Case of Japan', International Symposium on Population and Development Policies in Low Fertility Countries in Changing Age Structures. Korea Institute for Health and Social Affairs, Seoul, 1998.

Bangkok Post. 'Food Production up'. Bangkok, 21 June 2000.

Barkat, A., Uddin, M. A. and Hossain, M. 'Bangladesh Country Report: Implementation of ICPD Programme of Action and the Bali Declaration on Population and Sustainable Development', High-level Meeting to Review the Implementation of the Programme of Action of the International Conference on Population and Development and the Bali Declaration on Population and Sustainable Development and to Make Recommendations for Further Action. Bangkok, 1998.

Bongaarts, J. 'Global Trends in AIDS Mortality', *Population and Development Review*, 22, 1, pp. 21–45, 1996.

Brown, Lester R. *Who Will Feed China?* New York, W. W. Norton & Co, 1995.

Brown, Lester R., and Kane, Hal. *Full House: Reassessing the Earth's Population Carrying Capacity*. New York, W. W. Norton & Co, 1994.

Caldwell, J., Caldwell, P., and McDonald, P. 'Consequences of Low Fertility and Policy Responses', International Symposium on Population and Development Policies in Low Fertility Countries in Changing Age Structures. Korea Institute for Health and Social Affairs, Seoul, 1998.

Cannon, T., and Jenkins, A. *The Geography of Contemporary China: The Impact of Deng Xiaoping's Decade*. London, Routledge, 1990.

Carty, W. P., et al. *Success in a Challenging Environment: Fertility Decline in Bangladesh*. Population Reference Bureau, Washington, DC, 1993.

Chern, Wen S., Carter, Colin A., and Shei Shun-Yi (Eds). *Food Security in Asia*. Cheltenham, Edward Elgar, 2000.

Choe, M. K. 'Consequences of Fertility Decline in the Republic of Korea: Policy Responses', International Symposium on Population and Development Policies in Low Fertility Countries in Changing Age Structures. Korea Institute for Health and Social Affairs, Seoul, 1998.

Cohen, Joel E. *How Many People Can The Earth Support?* New York, W. W. Norton & Co, 1996.

Conly, S. R., and Camp, S. L. *China's Family Planning Program: Challenging The Myths*. Population Action International, 1992.

India's Family Planning Challenge: From Rhetoric to Action. Population Action International, 1992.

Conly, S. R., and Speidel, J. J. *Global Population Assistance—A Report Card on the Major Donor Countries*. Population Action International, 1993.

Croll, E. 'Production v. Reproduction: a threat to China's development strategy', *World Development*, Vol. II, 1983, pp. 467–81.

'The Household, Family and Reform' in Benewick, R., and Wingrove, P. (Eds), *Reforming the Revolution*. London, Macmillan, 1988.

Endangered Daughters—Discrimination and Development in Asia. London, Routledge, 2000.

Dyson, T. 'Population Growth and Food Production: Recent Global and Regional Trends', *Population and Development Review*, 20, pp. 397–411, 2 June 1994.

Earthscan. *Tough Choices: Facing the Challenge of Food Security*. London, 1996.

The Economist. *Pocket World in Figures—1994 edition*. The Economist Books Ltd, in association with Hamish Hamilton Ltd, 1993.

ESCAP. *2000 ESCAP Population Data Sheet*. Bangkok, ESCAP.

Food and Agriculture Organization (FAO).

Production Yearbook and *Trade Yearbook*.

'Chronic food supply problems persist in DPR Korea suggesting continued dependence on large-scale food assistance'. Internet www.fao.org/WAICENT/faoinfo/economic/giew/english/alertes/2000/SRDPRK06.htm, 20 June 2000.

Guibert-Lantoine, C., and Monnier, A. 'The demographic situation of Europe and the developed countries overseas: an annual report', *Population: An English Selection*, 9, pp. 243–268, 1997.

Hugo, G. 'Asia on the Move: Research Challenges for Population Geography', *International Journal of Population Geography*, 2, pp. 95–118, 1996.

Hull, T. 'The setting: demographic mosaic of the Asia Pacific region—issues defining the future', *Asia Pacific Viewpoint*, 38, 3, pp. 193–199, 1997.

Jones, G. 'The Bali Declaration and the Programme of Action of the International Conference on Population and Development in the Context of the Population Dynamics of the Asian and Pacific Region', High-level Meeting to Review the Implementation of the Programme of Action of the International Conference on Population and Development and the Bali Declaration on Population and Sustainable Development and to Make Recommendations for Further Action. Bangkok, 1998.

Jowett, J. 'China's Population: 1,133,709,738 and Still Counting', *Geography*, 78, 4, pp. 401–419, 1993.

Lutz, W. 'The Future of World Population', *Population Bulletin*, 49, 1, pp. 1–47, 1994.

Lutz, Wolfgang (Ed.). *The Future Population of the World: What Can We Assume Today?* London, Earthscan, 1996.

Martin, P., and Widgren, J. 'International Migration: A Global Challenge', *Population Bulletin*, 51, 1, pp. 1–48, 1996.

Mitchell, D., Ingco, M., and Duncan, R. *The World Food Outlook*. Cambridge, Cambridge University Press, 1997.

Myers, N. *Deforestation Rates in Tropical Countries and their Climatic Implications*. London, Friends of the Earth, 1989.

Myrdal, Gunnar. *Asian Drama: Inquiry into the Poverty of Nations*, 3 vols, New York, Pantheon Books, 1968.

Panos Institute. *Private Decisions, Public Debate: Women, Reproduction & Population*. London, Panos Publications, 1994.

Peng Xizhe and Guo Zhigang (Eds). *The Changing Population of China*. Oxford, Blackwell Publishers, 2002.

Phillips, David. R. (Ed.). *Ageing in the Asia-Pacific Region—Issues, Policies and Future Trends*. London, Routledge, 2000.

Population Reference Bureau. *Population Today: News, Numbers, and Analysis*. Washington, DC, Vol. 30, No. 4, May/June 2002.

Population Reference Bureau. *World Population Data Sheet*, annually. Washington, DC, and www.prb.org.

Randel, J., and German, T. (Eds). *The Reality of Aid 1994*. ActionAid, 1994.

Registrar General of India, *Census of India 2001*. Provisional Population Totals, Series 1, India, Paper 1 of 2001, Office of the Registrar General of India, New Delhi, 2001; internet www.censusindia.net.

Robey, B., Rubstein, S., and Morris, L. 'The Fertility Decline in Developing Countries', *Scientific American*, pp. 30–37, December, 1993.

Ruffolo, V. P., and Chayovan, N. 'Consequences of Low Fertility and Policy Responses in Thailand', International Symposium on Population and Development Policies in Low Fertility Countries in Changing Age Structures. Korea Institute for Health and Social Affairs, Seoul, 1998.

Scharping, Thomas. *Birth Control in China 1949–1999: Population Policy and Demographic Development*. Richmond, Curzon Press, 2000.

Simon, J. *The Ultimate Resource*. Princeton, NJ, Princeton University Press, 1982.

UNAIDS. *Report on the global HIV/AIDS epidemic*. Internet www.unaids.org/epidemic_update/report/Epi_report.htm.

United Nations. *Demographic Yearbook*.

The Sex and Age Distributions of the World Populations: The 1996 Revision, 1997.

World Population Prospects: The 2000 Revision, 2001.

World Urbanization Prospects: The 2001 Revision, 2002.

United Nations Development Programme (UNDP). *Human Development Report*, annually. Oxford University Press.

United Nations. Economic and Social Commission for Asia and the Pacific and Japanese Organization for International Cooperation in Family Planning. *Population Ageing in Asia and the Pacific*. New York, 1996.

UNFPA. *Global Population Assistance Report 1995*. New York, UNFPA, 1997.

Footprints and Milestones: Population and Environmental Change. The State of World Population 2001. New York, UNFPA.

UNICEF. *Estimates of Maternal Mortality*. Internet www.unicef.org/reseval/mattab.htm. 30 August 2002.

US Bureau of the Census. *Sex ratios*. Internet www.census.gov/cgi-bin/ipc/idbagg. 30 June 2000.

Visaria, L. 'Approaching Replacement Fertility: A Case of India', International Symposium on Population and Development Policies in Low Fertility Countries in Changing Age Structures. Korea Institute for Health and Social Affairs, Seoul, 1998.

Visaria, L., and Visaria, P. 'India's Fertility Declines, But It Still Leads World in Population Growth', *Population Today*, 23, 10, 1–2, 1995.

World Bank. *World Bank Atlas*, annually. Oxford University Press.

World Development Report, annually. Oxford University Press.

World Development Indicators, annually. Oxford University Press.

'Income poverty'. Internet www.worldbank.org/poverty/data/trends/income.htm. 30 June 2000.

World Health Organization. *AIDS Epidemic Update*. Geneva, December 1998.

Yanagishita, M. 'Japan's Foreign Aid Surpasses U.S. As Population Aid Grows', *Population Today*, 23, 11, 1–2, November, 1995.

Yap, M. T. 'Countries with Substantially Below Replacement Fertility: Singapore Status', International Symposium on Population and Development Policies in Low Fertility Countries in Changing Age Structures. Korea Institute for Health and Social Affairs, Seoul, 1998.

ENVIRONMENTAL ISSUES OF ASIA AND THE PACIFIC

ROSS STEELE

POPULATION, DEVELOPMENT AND THE ENVIRONMENT

The Asia-Pacific region illustrates the stark reality that 'environmental' issues cannot be considered independently of issues of human and economic resource development. In mid-2002 this diverse and immense region was home to around 3,478m. people, about 60% of the world's population, whose numbers are growing annually. The region is also home to the industrialized economies of Japan, Australia and New Zealand and to the rapidly-expanding 'tiger economies' of East Asia, which until interrupted by the 1997–99 currency crisis, recorded impressive economic growth rates. The Asia-Pacific region also contains some of the world's poorer nations where development capital is scarce, and large minorities lack the most basic human needs, such as sufficient food, adequate supplies of clean drinking water, minimal shelter, and access to health care and education. Governance in these circumstances is weak and undeveloped, immediate concerns dominate the political agenda, with governments and citizens taking the view that economic growth must be the first priority, even if it means serious environmental damage. In this context, 'environmental' strategies not concerned with the economic and political realities of development and with satisfying legitimate human aspirations will prove to be ineffectual.

Paul Ehrlich, the eminent US population biologist, has advanced the I=PAT model in an attempt to predict the impact on the environment (I) of the three major components of development: population growth (P), increased affluence (A) and technology (T). Given that the Asia-Pacific region's population will continue to grow significantly for the next 20–30 years and that the level of affluence, and therefore consumption, of the rapidly-growing middle classes will rise even more quickly, then total environmental impact must inevitably increase greatly. In order to achieve the increase in affluence demanded by their growing populations, with minimal environmental damage, the developing nations of the region must receive massive transfers of new, ecologically-appropriate technology from the developed nations. Unfortunately, many of the attempts at rapid industrialization over the last 25 years or so have made use of outmoded 'dirty' technology, which has only served to exacerbate environmental damage. This cannot be allowed to continue in the Asia-Pacific region because the environmental challenges that this area will face in the next 20–30 years will be of such magnitude that any failure will have an impact on our global future.

THE REGION'S MAJOR ENVIRONMENTAL ISSUES

The Asia-Pacific region experiences a great variety of environmental problems. This is not unexpected in view of the region's enormous size and extreme diversity of physical and human environments. The problems that are most serious over large geographic areas include deforestation and loss of biodiversity, loss and degradation of agricultural land, ground, water and air pollution, global warming and rising sea-levels. The region is also experiencing rapidly-growing urban environmental problems with polluted air, and difficulties of water supply and waste disposal. The environmental consequences of megaprojects, such as the Three Gorges Dam in China, are attracting much international attention, along with concern about the impact of events such as the forest fires in Indonesia in 1997–98 and subsequently, major flooding in China, Bangladesh and India in 1998 and 1999, and in Jakarta, the Indonesian capital, in 2002, and the environmental impact of the 1997–99 economic crisis in East and South-East Asia. More recently, salinization of water and land in the principal agricultural regions of Australia has become a major cause of concern, along with damage done to coral reefs in South-East Asia and the Pacific, including Australia's Great Barrier Reef, by global warming, coastal development, overfishing and other human activity. An assessment of which of these environmental issues is of most concern is a matter of subjective judgement; however, as the most populous countries of the region still have a majority of their population resident in rural areas, environmental issues that affect rural people will be given most emphasis. Nevertheless, it should be stressed that, although these so-called 'green issues' are currently of greatest concern to informed observers in the developed countries, they will be surpassed in importance by 'brown issues' of the urban environment very shortly, since it is projected that during the first two decades of the 21st century a majority of the region's population will become urban dwellers.

A selection of these major environmental issues will now be discussed. Issues in the most populous developing countries will be emphasized because of their global and life-threatening nature, but this is not to imply that the more industrially-advanced countries in the region do not experience serious difficulties. Because of the immense scale of the environmental problems, detailed case studies are included in preference to general discussions, so that the human dimensions of the problems and their inter-relationships may be better understood.

LOSS AND DEGRADATION OF AGRICULTURAL LAND

The most critical environmental issue facing the Asia-Pacific region today is the continual loss and degradation of its most highly productive arable land which, if allowed to continue at the present rates, will threaten the ability of the region's most populous countries to feed their own people. Land is lost to agricultural production by many processes, such as conversion to non-agricultural uses or by erosion and pollution of the topsoil. These processes can convert hitherto-productive arable land, capable of producing food crops, into unproductive wasteland, which then requires expensive rehabilitation before production can be resumed. More serious than the absolute loss of land to agricultural production is what two observers, Blaikie and Brookfield, have termed the 'quiet crisis', whereby the productivity of agricultural land is gradually, but insidiously, reduced by the dual processes of degradation and pollution. Another analyst, A. Burnett, defines 'degradation' as the term used to refer to the processes that lead to the loss of productivity in soils and to a decline of surface and underground storages and flows of water. Pollution is described as the contamination of air, water and soil by human activity. These two processes have had their most damaging impact on agricultural productivity in the two most populous countries in the region, China and India. However, the ecologically fragile semi-arid environments of Australia, Afghanistan and Mongolia, and the steeply-sloping foothills of Nepal, the uplands of Java, New Guinea and New Zealand have also been seriously eroded and degraded by ecologically unsuited land-management practices driven by economic and population pressures.

Loss and Degradation of Arable Land in China

Faced with the problem of feeding a major portion of the world's population on a disproportionately small share of the earth's arable land, for the last 2,000 years the Chinese people have been exhorted to subjugate nature. From pre-modern times China has converted extensive areas of natural ecosystems to crop fields, but this trend intensified during the 'grain first' policy of the 1960s when the leadership was belatedly forced to give top priority to increased food production after the famine of 1959–61. The environmental consequences soon became apparent, and the early 1960s witnessed a greatly-accelerated degradation of China's farm soils, grasslands, forests and wetlands. Chinese sources put the total losses of arable land for 1957–77 at a conservative 29.3m. ha, equivalent to 26% of the nation's total arable area in 1957. Vaclav Smil, an expert on China's environmental problems, has claimed that about 7m. ha of this arable land was lost through requisitions for construction projects. Desertification, salinization and alkalization claimed another 5m. ha of this loss of farmlands and grasslands between 1957 and 1977, with some 90% blamed on improper land use, involving conversions of semi-arid grasslands to grain fields and to overgrazing. About 10m. ha of sloping grasslands unwisely converted into fields was lost to erosion. During this 20-year period the total area of arable land was boosted by the reclamation of 17.3m. ha of new land coming from the conversion of forests and wetlands, but yields were very often disappointing, with cultivation frequently being abandoned after several years. The remaining 7m. ha of the total 29m. ha was lost when this converted land reverted to non-arable uses. Therefore, the largest single cause of arable land loss would appear to be erosion on grassland or wasteland taken into use since the late 1950s, although as Smil points out, some erosion has a much earlier origin, especially in the Loess Plateau of northern China.

Official estimates of arable land in China seriously underestimate its extent. In the late 1980s and early 1990s official sources estimated the total area at about 96m. ha (Table 1), whereas country-wide sample surveys and satellite images suggest a total of at least 130m. ha. Despite this discrepancy, Chinese experts suggest that the extent of reporting inaccuracies has not changed over the last 30 years, and that the large gross losses of farmland revealed by the official estimates (Table 1) are indeed real. These official figures suggest a cumulative loss of about 40m. ha of arable land since the late 1950s, which Smil has estimated is the equivalent of a loss in food production capacity for at least 350m. people. The mean annual loss of more than 400,000 ha during the 1980s was equal to a loss in food production for about 5m. people every year. The mean annual loss for the first four years of the 1990s was even higher, at about 550,000 ha.

Table 1. Total and Per Caput Availability of Farmland in China and Reported Losses of Farmland, 1949–93

Year	Farmland		
	Total (million ha)	Per caput (ha)	Gross loss of farmland
1949	97.88	0.180	n.a.*
1957	111.83	0.173	n.a.
1965	103.59	0.143	n.a.
1970	101.10	0.122	n.a.
1979	99.50	0.102	n.a.
1985	97.60	0.092	1,000,000
1986	96.85	0.090	640,000
1987	95.89	0.088	470,000
1988	95.72	0.086	510,000
1989	95.65	0.085	198,000
1990	95.67	0.084	733,000
1991	95.65	0.083	580,000
1992	95.60	0.082	243,000
1993	95.50	0.081	620,000

* Note: The farmland loss data are not available for 1949–79; however, the average annual loss for 1957–86 was 526,000 ha.

Source: Smil, V. 'Environmental problems in China: estimates of economic costs', *East-West Center Special Reports,* No. 5, Table 4, p. 34, East-West Center, 1996.

Since 1978 a new household production responsibility system (*baogan*) has provided the incentive for families to intensify crop production and revert to more profitable and environmentally-sustainable forms of land use. Much of the subsequent loss of farmland has been a result of restoration of wetlands, grasslands or slopelands unwisely converted to farmland in the two decades of Maoist campaigns. However, deforestation and accelerated erosion continue, despite strict edicts banning excessive timber-logging and cutting of firewood. Between 1980 and 1985 a total of 2.45m. ha of cropland was lost, about one-quarter to frantic house-building by newly-private farmers. In 1987 a national limit was introduced, which decreed that no more than 200,000 ha of farmland may be used for non-agricultural construction projects in a year, but the rapid pace of economic expansion, especially the uncontrolled development of rural industries and the establishment of special industrial zones, led to increased losses of farmland in the 1990s. Although the current downturn in Asian economic growth rates may temporarily curb the loss, increasing population, rapid industrialization and extension of transport links will make continued losses inevitable in future years. Moreover, these losses will probably include some of the most productive agricultural land on rich alluvial soils close to major towns and cities. Smil estimates that recent losses represent an annual decline of 300,000–750,000 ha of sown farmland when the multi-cropping ratio is considered, with wet rice land accounting for at least one-fifth of the total loss. An extensive programme of creating new agricultural land by labour-intensive practices, such as the terracing of deforested slopes, the hand deposition of alluvial soils behind these embankments and the development of intricate water-control schemes, have added to the area of farmland since the 1950s, but since the mid-1960s losses have surpassed gains. It is now estimated that there are no more than 10m. ha of land in the whole country that can be converted to farmland at an acceptable cost.

To offset the losses of agricultural land, Chinese farming has become much more intensive. Traditional Chinese agriculture has been seen by the West as a model of sustainable agriculture where soil fertility was maintained and increased by complex crop rotations, planting of green manures and the recycling of crop residues, human and animal wastes and other organic matter. More recently, China has become the world's largest producer and consumer of synthetic fertilizers. Despite these efforts, Chinese agriculture is now faced with the serious problem of declining soil quality caused by increased soil erosion and a rapid decrease in traditional organic recycling. Between the early 1950s and 1992 the extent of all lands affected by soil erosion more than doubled, from approximately 150m. ha to 367m. ha, equivalent to more than one-third of China's territory. About 30m. ha of Chinese farm fields are affected and although the regional rates of damage vary considerably, the Loess Plateau (an area half the size of France) has the highest rates in the world, with the equivalent of 2 cm of topsoil being denuded each year. Very high rates were also reported from the provinces of Heilongjiang and Sichuan, and recent Chinese reports suggest that overall China loses some 5,000m. metric tons of topsoil per year from its eroding soils. It is claimed that this loss is equivalent to all macronutrients (nitrogen, phosphorus and potassium) applied in chemical fertilizers. The economic costs of soil erosion include crop-yield losses caused by the removal of the soil's organic matter, fine clay content, water retention capacity and plant nutrients. The actual yield losses have been estimated as negligible in most of China's wet farmlands, at 5% over a century on fields with tolerable erosion rates, and at 25% on the most seriously affected farmland. Other economic costs of soil erosion include the value of soil nutrients lost which, if yields are to be maintained, have to be replaced by chemical fertilizers; lost irrigation and hydroelectricity-generating capacity of reservoirs owing to silting; additional expenses for filtering silted water for urban and industrial uses; capital costs required to counteract the damage caused by increased siltation of river beds, lakes and reservoirs; and damage done by the increased frequency and severity of flooding. One example will illustrate the scale of these problems. Increased siltation along the lower Huanghe (Yellow River), downstream from the Loess region in the north, has raised the height of the river-bed above the adjacent floodplain by about 1 m per decade, increasing dramatically the risks of catastrophic flooding of the North China plain. If a break in a dike south of Jinan occurred today, it would flood up to 33,000 sq km and affect the livelihoods of some 18m. people. A 1994 decision requiring that all cropland used for construction be offset by land reclaimed elsewhere has exacerbated the extent of soil erosion. The fast-growing coastal provinces, such as Guangdong, Shandong and Jiangsu, that have lost much cropland to urban development and industrial construction are now paying other more ecologically fragile regions in the north-west, such as Inner Mongolia, Gansu, Qinghai and Xinjiang, to plough ever more marginal land to offset their own losses. Intensified wind erosion, land abandonment and migration eastward have been the ultimate result. In April 2001 a huge dust storm originating in northern China was reported to have covered parts of western Canada and the USA with a layer of dust.

The advent of the 'grain first' policy in the early 1960s discouraged many traditional crop rotations and reduced the cultivation of green manures, which in turn led to a reduction in soil organic matter. Further reduction occurred with the increased use of stalks and straw for household fuel rather than for recycling and with other changes arising from the economic privatization of agriculture in the late 1970s. The increased availability of chemical fertilizers in the early 1980s, the pressures of privatized farming which encouraged the monocropping of cereals, and the construction of modern sewage treatment plants, all worked to discourage the continuation of traditional organic recycling practices. The loss of organic matter in cultivated soils leads to a breakdown in the soil structure with the soil becoming more compacted and less permeable, which increases soil run-off. It also dramatically reduces the number of soil invertebrates such as earthworms, which play a key role in maintaining soil fertility. By the late 1980s some 13m. ha of China's arable land were contaminated by pesticide residues and another 7m. ha were polluted by industrial wastes. In recent years torn plastic sheeting, originally used to conserve soil moisture and accelerate crop ripening, has become mixed with cropland soils. It is believed to be responsible for reduced yields on at least 1m. ha of cropland.

The cumulative loss of about 40m. ha of farmland in China since the late 1950s and the serious degradation of the fertility and quality of the remaining arable soils, owing to increased soil erosion and the spread of less environmentally-sustainable management practices, pose doubts about the ability of China to feed itself in future decades. Technological advances will further increase the productivity of agriculture in China over the coming decades, but the above discussion reveals that, unless the environmental degradation caused by present and past farming practices is dramatically reduced, major advances in productivity will be required simply to maintain production at existing levels. This raises the question as to who will be able to provide the increased food that will be demanded by China's expanding population and required by even more rapidly-rising living standards.

A report by the environmentalist group, Greenpeace China, delivered in Beijing in August 1999, reiterated these concerns and claimed that China faced 'environmental meltdown' if it waited to get rich before addressing its many serious problems. China's rapid economic growth rates were blamed for most of the damage, which has caused the loss of some of its best farmland to industrial development and urban growth, recurring and worsening floods, the worst dust storms in memory in northern China, acid rain and foul urban water and air. However, the fact that this message could be delivered in Beijing, and the unprecedented candour of reporting on the role of deforestation in the fatal summer floods of 1998, suggest that the authorities are beginning to accept the seriousness of environmental problems. The western interior, which is home to one-quarter of China's 1,300m. people and comprises more than one-half of the country's land area, is the most adversely affected region, with the poorest 10 areas of the west accounting for just 15% of gross domestic product. In March 2000 China's most senior economic planner pledged to reverse the environmental destruction of its western interior by turning steeply-terraced fields into forest and exhausted cropland into pasture. He stated that some 70% of that year's fixed asset investments would be directed to the west, in an attempt to bring the region out of poverty and environmental degradation. Official sources claim that this process has already begun, with 4.05m. ha of afforestation and 5.7m. ha of mountain passes converted into forest in 1999. However, whether the more than 35,000m. trees planted in China since 1981 have received proper care and survived is another matter. An official report in 2001 estimated that every year an average of 2,460 sq km of vegetated land in China deteriorates into desert and another 1m. ha of land suffer from serious erosion.

DEFORESTATION

Over the last two decades deforestation has received far more publicity than any other environmental issue in the Asia-Pacific region. Much of the initial concern was limited to ecologists, but this is no longer the case, with citizens increasingly aware of the importance of natural forests in protecting soil from erosion, maintaining soil productivity, preventing flooding and providing valuable timbers for national revenue. Moreover, the forests of South-East Asia have been inhabited by local people for at least 39,000 years and today are still the home of some 30m. indigenous people; any damage to their habitat has a critical impact on their way of life and survival.

The populous countries of China, India and Bangladesh historically contained substantial areas of forest, but most of this has long been lost and converted to other uses such as agriculture. Much of the forest that has survived in these countries does so only in a seriously-degraded form, with the extent and quality of the forest cover being reduced by indiscriminate logging and the illegal gathering of firewood, inappropriate road-making methods, forest fires and heavy grazing. In China, despite a programme of reafforestation, annual cutting of forest resources surpasses new growth by more than 40%, and approximately 45% of the uplands suffer soil erosion as a result of deforestation. Today, just 12% of the total land area remains in forest. India has a similar proportion of its land under forest cover, but almost half of the recorded forest area is now degraded, with the number of animals grazing in the forests increasing from 25m. cow units in 1951 to 100m. in 1995. In Bangladesh, expansion of agricultural land has reduced forest cover to 16% of the total land area, with no primary rain forest remaining. A similar dramatic decrease in forest cover has also occurred in Nepal, with serious consequences for land degradation and flooding.

Table 2. Loss of Forest Cover in Eight South-East Asian Countries, 1965–90

	According to Map Sources Between 1970 and 1990			According to FAO Sources Between 1965 and 1988		
	Forest cover in 1990	Loss between 1970 and 1990		Forest cover in 1988	Loss between 1965 and 1988	
Major Countries	'000 sq km	'000 sq km	%	'000 sq km	'000 sq km	%
Myanmar	311.8 (46.0)*	128.2	29.1	323.8 (48.0)*	128.9	27.3
Thailand	149.6 (24.0)	106.9	41.7	141.6 (28.0)	99.0	41.2
Cambodia	113.2 (63.0)	22.5	16.6	113.2 (63.0)	20.5	15.3
Laos	124.6 (53.0)	41.3	24.9	129.0 (54.0)	21.0	14.0
Viet Nam	56.7 (17.0)	124.8	68.8	93.1 (28.0)	62.1	40.0
Malaysia	200.4 (61.0)	72.6	26.6	193.4 (59.0)	48.4	20.0
Indonesia	1,179.1 (62.0)	243.8	17.1	1,134.3 (59.0)	103.7	8.4
Philippines	66.0 (22.0)	84.0	56.0	107.5 (36.0)	63.0	37.0
Total	2,201.6	824.1	27.8	2,236.1	546.6	19.6

* Note: The figures in parentheses are the percentage of a nation's total land area under forest cover in 1990 and 1988, according to map sources and to FAO sources.

Source: Adapted from Tables 1, 2, and 3 in Bernard, S., and De Koninck, R. 'The retreat of the forest in Southeast Asia: A cartographic assessment', *Singapore Journal of Tropical Geography,* Vol. 17, No. 1, pp. 1–14, 1996.

It is the deforestation and degradation of the tropical rain forests of South-East Asia, however, that is the current issue of greatest concern to environmentalists. There are a number of reasons for this concern. First, unlike the Indian subcontinent and East Asia, South-East Asia still contains very large areas of primary tropical rain forest. Second, if measured in terms of hectares of forest deforested per hectare of national territory, the rate of deforestation in South-East Asia has probably been the highest in the world since 1980. Third, the forests of this area are the habitat of millions of indigenous people, many of whom still practise traditional lifestyles. Fourth, this region, especially the western part of insular South-East Asia (sometimes termed Malesia and comprising Sumatra, Peninsular Malaysia and the island of Borneo), is renowned for its exceedingly rich biodiversity. There are estimated to be at least 25,000 species of flowering plants in Malesia along with 350 species of the dipterocarp family. The dense, tall forests have recently provided the tropical timber trade with some of its most valuable hardwood species. Borneo, for example, as well as being a centre of diversity of plant species, contains an immense array of animal and insect species with very high rates of endemism. Finally, the forests of South-East Asia have been regarded by local political leaders as one of their last untamed resources and an appropriate site of megaprojects to dam rivers, construct commercial plantations of rubber and oil palm, and as settlement destinations for landless citizens from more densely-populated regions.

Recent research has revealed large variations in estimates of deforestation rates in South-East Asia, but there is little doubt that in the last decade they have at least equalled the highest in the tropical world at well over 1% of the forest cover per year. Table 2 shows discrepancies between the two major data sources in estimates of recent forest cover and of forest loss over the two decades of the 1970s and the 1980s. The percentage of the earlier cover lost is also shown. Both sources estimate that in the late 1960s about 62%–66% of the total land area of South-East Asia was covered in forest, but that by the late 1980s 20%–25% had been lost completely to agriculture or other uses. Definitions of deforestation, however, are inconsistent. The FAO data do not classify as deforestation temporary clearing of forest that was logged and left to regrow, even if it was clearcut, whereas temporary clearing by shifting cultivators is included. Moreover, the data provide no estimates of degraded forest lands as secondary forest is not identified, but they are probably very extensive.

The area of forest lost shows great variation by country and by source, with the largest absolute losses in Myanmar (Burma), Indonesia, Thailand, the Philippines and Viet Nam. Regardless of the source, the three countries with the smallest expanse of remaining forests (Table 2), Viet Nam, the Philippines and Thailand, were also those where deforestation was most rapid. About 48,000 sq km of the forest loss in Viet Nam and Cambodia occurred during the Viet Nam War, but since the mid-1970s there has also been serious deforestation by loggers and farmers. Thailand lost some 40% of its forest cover in the 1970s and 1980s, leading it to impose a ban on logging, as did Viet Nam, but illegal logging remains a problem and the ban has placed greater pressure on the more plentiful forest resources of their poorer neighbours, Myanmar, Laos and Cambodia. In Thailand and Myanmar much of the forest being lost is open broadleaf forest, which contains valuable timber such as teak. The Philippines has probably the worst record of deforestation in South-East Asia, with the small areas of surviving virgin forest confined to the most inaccessible mountainous areas. In 2002 a report entitled *The State of the Forest: Indonesia* by Forest Watch Indonesia and Global Forest Watch concluded that 40% of the forests existing in Indonesia in 1950 had been cleared by 2000, forest cover declining from 162m. ha to 98m. ha. It is of even greater concern that the rate of forest loss appears to be accelerating. During the 1980s the amount of forest lost was about 1m. ha per year (or 1.2m. ha according to Table 2), rising to about 1.7m. ha in the early 1990s, and then increasing to 2m. ha from 1996. Indonesia's lowland tropical forests, the richest in timber resources and biodiversity, are those most at risk. They have almost entirely disappeared in Sulawesi and are predicted to be entirely cleared in Sumatra by 2005 and in Kalimantan by 2010 if current trends continue. Rapid deforestation has also occurred in Myanmar and Malaysia in recent years, with most of the large areas lost being closed broadleaf forests, the most valuable of all forest types in terms of biodiversity.

What has been the environmental impact of this deforestation? Its direct effects are on the forest and its biodiversity (both in terms of its flora and fauna), and on soils and hydrology. Few hard data are available to quantify the species loss rates, as a complete biological inventory of many areas has never been done, but there is little doubt that the forest areas are suffering accelerating and irreversible loss of biodiversity. The Malesian region alone has been a major source of the world's crop plants and fruits, such as sugar cane, bananas and rice on the margins of the region. It has also been the source of some medicinal plants. The house-gardens and plots of shifting cultivators contain a huge variety of plant types, the survival of which is critical to the shrinking crop gene-pools of modern agriculture. The impact of deforestation on wildlife has been acute. In the Republic of Korea, for example, deforestation and the use of pesticides and fertilizers has led to the loss of more than 100 animal species in recent years. In Cambodia deforestation has resulted in the destruction of three-quarters of the country's wildlife habitat, while Bangladesh has very little wildlife habitat left. The tiger, elephant and rhinoceros are now reduced to very small numbers in South-East Asia owing to the loss of their habitat, and the forest fires in East Kalimantan in 1997–98, themselves at least partially a result of logging and deforestation, have dramatically illustrated the dangers posed to the survival of the orangutan, the proboscis monkey and other monkey species.

Once the forest canopy is reduced, the exposed soil is eroded and leached of its nutrients and organic material, which then limits forest regrowth and reduces its quality. It becomes degraded secondary forest. This, in turn, by a series of positive feedback mechanisms, alters the carbon cycle and the radiation balance, reduces transpiration and thereby contributes to climate change and desertification. Logging and conversion to agricultural uses fragment the forest areas that remain and increase the length of the borders of these forests relative to their total areal extent. This fragmentation magnifies the impact of forest-clearing and degradation on biodiversity loss. These exposed and degraded zones are more vulnerable to dry spells than inaccessible heavily-forested areas; they transfer less moisture into the atmosphere, reduce humidity and are more vulnerable to fire. Because secondary growth is easier to clear and cultivate than primary forest, it is attractive to swidden cultivators and is more likely to be completely deforested. The topsoils that remain, once deprived of their biomass cover (their critical nutrient source), lose nutrients after several cropping cycles and are soon abandoned by shifting cultivators. The exposed soils allow more rapid run-off than forest cover and are more easily eroded. Modern mechanical logging practices, requiring roads and using heavy machinery on steep, previously-inaccessible land, have accelerated rates of soil compaction, loss of topsoil, reductions in water percolation and exposure to erosion. Some studies have shown an 18-fold increase in soil loss after logging, which increases siltation, raises river-beds and flooding downstream. For example, in November and December 1999 the central coast of Viet Nam was inundated by the worst floods of the century, which cost more than 700 lives and caused extensive damage to houses and farmland. Widespread illegal logging was blamed for much of this damage.

Although the causes of deforestation vary by country, traditional shifting or swidden cultivation, along with agricultural development, have for many years been held responsible for about 50% of the deforestation; another 25% has been blamed on settlers who move into areas after logging operations, with an additional 10% being due to commercial logging and another 10% due to infrastructure development such as road-building or dam construction. Recent research in Indonesia suggests that at least 67% of the deforestation was due to macro-level programmes deliberately encouraged by the Government, such as commercial logging (including the attendant damage caused by machinery, camps, roads and log yards), agricultural resettlement known locally as transmigration (this programme was stopped in 1999) and smallholder cash-crop schemes emphasizing tree crops such as rubber and oil palm. Forest was also cleared for large-scale plantations of industrial timber and estate crops, but 75% of these proposed timber plantations were never planted. In contrast, traditional shifting cultivation accounted for just 27% of deforestation and in reality probably much less than this, for there are now very few genuine examples of these traditional farmers who practise rotational swidden farming. Those who remain are likely to be limited to inaccessible inner areas of the forest remote from the market economy and population pressures. A study published in 1999 by two analysts, A. Angelsen and D. P. Resosudarmo, of areas of Riau, West and East Kalimantan and Central Sulawesi concluded that the monetary crisis and its associated breakdown of governance created opportunities for better-off farmers, immigrants and urban dwellers with capital to convert forests to highly profitable crops. The situation has been made worse by an excess capacity in the wood-processing industry. Much of the gap between the legal supply of wood and demand is being filled by illegal logging, which accounted for approximately 65% of the total timber supply in 2000. The situation is likely to worsen in the short term as Indonesia moves rapidly towards a system of 'regional autonomy', with the provincial and district governments largely lacking the capacity, the funds and often the will to govern effectively. The ready availability of chain saws and vehicles has increased the impact of illegal logging in recent times.

Some writers explain the causes of deforestation in terms of two contrasting models: the frontier model, which identifies networks of entrepreneurs, companies and small farmers as the chief agents of deforestation using private capital and with assistance from the state and local élites; and the immiserization model, which sees local shifting cultivators and landless peasants as the key protagonists, forced to clear land for subsistence and smallholder cash-cropping under the pressure of growing populations, devalued local currencies and poverty. Research has shown that both models have some validity, with the immiserization model being more relevant in places with small remnant forests and rapidly-growing populations, but the frontier model more relevant where there are large blocks of forests and where frontier conditions prevail. Often the frontier model describes the initial stages of deforestation during periods of rapid economic expansion, whereas the alternative model is more appropriate at a later stage once the forests have been made more accessible and deforestation rises and falls in response to changes in the economic and social conditions of the local rural poor. Economic recession, for example, would be expected to retard frontier deforestation, but promote deforestation in already settled areas. The risks to the forests from modern and traditional sources wax and wane, but generally, as a country becomes more developed, the overall risk of continued deforestation tends to decrease once a threshold level of economic development has been achieved. Development-planners and policy-makers interested in conserving forestry resources and in improving their sustainability must address not only the local pressures that lead to deforestation, but also the macro-development framework that continues to make deforestation profitable to private entrepreneurs and responsible government officials.

WATER AVAILABILITY AND POLLUTION

Obtaining sufficient supplies of unpolluted water is an increasing problem for the rural and urban populations of the region. Much of the contamination of water supplies is caused by the improper disposal of human waste, chemicals and other hazardous materials from both manufacturing and agricultural activities. The quality of surface and groundwater supplies has deteriorated as the pace of industrialization has accelerated and as farmers have attempted to maximize their returns with increased applications of fertilizers and pesticides. Growing populations and improved living standards have at the same time raised the demand for clean water for agricultural, industrial, domestic, and even recreational uses. A brief discussion of the situation in India and China will highlight current and future problems of water availability.

Population increase alone has reduced the availability of per caput renewable fresh water resources in India from 6,000 cu m per year in 1947 to about 2,300 cu m in 1997, and by the year 2017 it is predicted that the figure will be as low as 1,600 cu m. As water resources are unevenly distributed, in some regions of the country (in the east between the Pennar and the Kanyakumari rivers) the water stress is already severe, with annual availability as low as 400 cu m per head. The spread of the 'Green Revolution', with its emphasis on high-yielding varieties of cereal crops, has been accompanied by an extraordinary increase in privately-owned shallow tube-wells. In 12 districts in Punjab and three in Haryana the exploitation of groundwater exceeds its recharge. In Mehsana district in Gujarat and also in Coimbatore district in Tamil Nadu groundwater aquifers have been permanently depleted. The overexploitation of groundwater will lead to increasing costs of extraction in the future, and this will have the most severe impact on small and marginal farms. Falling water tables can also lead to increased salinity, seawater intrusion and contamination of water in the aquifer. Another problem is wastage of surface water, some 45% of water used in irrigation being lost because of seepage from unlined channels and another 15% being wasted owing to over-application. As a result of inadequate water-treatment facilities and high pollution loads, India's water bodies are highly contaminated. In local areas groundwater aquifers have been polluted with heavy metals, chemicals such as fluorides and phenols, and coliform bacteria. The largest cities in India generate around 20,000m. litres of sewage wastewater daily, but treat only about 2,000m. litres. The inadequate drinking water and sanitation water infrastructures lead to high levels of water-related diseases, which account for two-thirds of all diseases in India.

The pressure placed on China's water resources is perhaps even greater than in India. Between 1950 and 1990 the population of China doubled, urban population increased five-fold, industrial output rose about 80-fold and the area of irrigated land tripled. These trends have continued, with China's cities being required to absorb more than 100m. additional residents in the 1990s. The Worldwatch Institute, a research organization based in Washington, DC, has estimated that by the year 2030 China's total water demand will have increased from 483,000m. tons in 1995 to 1,068,000m. tons. The most dramatic increases in demand will be for industrial (417%) and residential (330%) uses, but the demand for agricultural water is also projected to increase by 66%. China's total water resources may be enough to meet these quantitative demands, but they are very unevenly distributed. The humid south with four-fifths of the water and 700m. people is dominated by the vast Changjiang (Yangtze River) which will probably continue to supply an adequate quantity of water, even if industrial pollution may limit its use. Some Chinese experts have warned that certain stretches of even the mighty Changjiang may be dry by the year 2020. The arid north comprising the four basins of the Huanghe (Yellow), Liao, Hai, and Huai Rivers is home to 550m. persons and two-thirds of the nation's cropland. All four of these northern basins currently face acute water shortages, which can only become more desperate as demand increases. In the drought year of 1997 the Huanghe failed to reach Shandong Province, the source of one-fifth of China's corn and one-seventh of its wheat production, much of which is irrigated from the river. As agriculture simply cannot economically compete with industry or residential demands for water, more and more of China's surface water is being diverted to non-farm uses. To survive, farmers are increasingly turning to underground water reserves, many of which are being pumped out more rapidly than the rate at which they can be naturally recharged. The result is that in the North China Plain the water table has fallen by an average of 1.5m annually over the last five years. This is unsustainable in the long term. The eventual outcome will be a cessation of pumping and a reversion to dryland farming with a 50%–66% decline in yields. In 1998 senior Chinese officials estimated that rural villages nation-wide were facing annual water shortages of 30,000m. tons, which had reduced grain production by 20m. tons, enough to feed more than 65m. people. In 1998 two observers, Lester R. Brown and Brian Halweil, predicted that unless China can significantly curtail its projected demand for non-agricultural water, by the year 2030 water shortages will have reduced China's ability to feed itself to such an extent that the country's growing demand for grain imports will pose a threat to the world's food security. Water shortages are already being faced in 300 of China's 617 largest cities, including Beijing and Tianjin, where overexploitation of underground aquifers has caused widespread surface subsidence.

Water pollution in China is as serious as in India and further limits the supply of clean water available for drinking and irrigation. Surveys in the 1980s revealed that more than 20% of the 878 major rivers examined had water so badly polluted that it could not be used for irrigation. In urban areas 80% of China's surface water was contaminated, and only six of the country's 27 largest cities had drinking water within state standards. Municipal wastes are commonly released untreated into local water bodies, and the rapid growth of small and medium-sized factories in rural areas has resulted in industrial wastes contaminating local surface water used for drinking. Phenols, heavy metals and organic wastes are the most common pollutants. Because the local farmers use river mud as a fertilizer, residues of chromium, lead and cadmium are now being found in many staple crops. In the Huanghe basin abnormally high rates of stunting, mental retardation and developmental diseases are linked to high concentrations of arsenic and lead in the water and food. To date, pollution of water with nitrates has not been a problem in China, but the experience of the USA suggests that given China's extremely high usage of nitrogen fertilizers, high nitrate loadings will appear in China's drinking water within the next decade and result in increased risks to human health. Continued growth in energy consumption will involve increased use of coal, which in the case of China is high in sulphur content. This will result in heavier acid deposition on water bodies from acid rain, which will degrade water quality even further and pose threats to aquatic life and humans in both China and Japan.

ENVIRONMENTAL PROBLEMS IN URBAN AREAS

Although, in terms of global impact and the number of people immediately affected, rural environmental problems have hitherto been of most significance, it is now recognized that 'brown' environmental issues in the cities of the Asia-Pacific region will be of greater importance to local residents in the next quarter-century. There are several reasons for this. First, the number and proportion of the region's inhabitants resident in urban areas will increase dramatically over the next 20 years or so. In 1995 the urban population totalled 1,150m., some 33% of the total population; by 2020 it is projected to total at least 2,400m., an increase of some 109% in just 25 years, and to comprise 55% of the region's total inhabitants. Second, by the year 2015, it is expected that there will be 27 megacities worldwide (cities with more than 10m. inhabitants) and that 17 of these will be in the Asia-Pacific region. Probably as much as 80% of the region's economic growth will be generated by that urban population, with the megacities being in the forefront of the challenge of determining if this growth can be sustained environmentally. Third, the majority of the major cities are sited on or near river estuaries, some of the most productive natural ecosystems in the region. Any serious environmental pollution here has the potential to damage fertile agricultural land, surrounding aquaculture and productive marine environments. Fourth, these large cities are characterized by rapidly-growing middle classes who, unlike the environmentalists of the West, are relatively indifferent to deforestation, global warming, wildlife issues and endangered species, but instead are increasingly concerned that their politicians do something about environmental problems that create threats to their health, such as air pollution, traffic accidents, contaminated or insufficient water supplies, and inadequate waste treatment and disposal systems.

Kirk Smith and others have recently developed Abdel Omran's concept of the Epidemiological Transition to help explain the dynamics of environmental health risks in cities in the developing world. This suggests that, as economic development progresses, environmental health risks and the patterns of overall ill health undergo transition. For example, in the early stages of development traditional infectious and parasitic diseases are common, and are associated with rural and urban poverty, poor nutrition and sanitation, and unclean water supplies. These may be termed traditional health risks, which at this stage are considerable and reflected in high infant and child mortality rates. As development progresses, the risks to health decrease as water and sanitation conditions improve, along with better nutrition and higher standards of living. As this occurs, however, modern risks to health arise from new factors such as pesticide run-off, inadequate toxic-waste disposal, air pollution and motor vehicle accidents, which in time increase the risks to health and cause illnesses like cancer and heart disease. The transition point is the level of development at which there is equal risk to health from both modern and traditional environmental and technological factors. In short, there is a risk transition from a condition of less development, when there are many and high risks to health from traditional environmental factors, to a more developed condition where the overall risks to health from environmental factors are few and low, but where the causal factors are modern and post-industrial in nature.

In this article it is argued that the total risks to health (both short-term and long-term) during the transition point may well be greater than the low point predicted in the risk transition model. This is because in the Asia-Pacific region there is a considerable overlap of traditional and modern environmental risk factors and the possibility of synergistic consequences. For example, entirely new kinds of airborne environmental risks are created when crop residues contaminated with modern pesticides are used as traditional cooking fuels inside rudimentary shelters. However, this model provides a useful framework, which will facilitate inter-country comparison of traditional and modern urban environmental risk factors in relation to the level of development. The hypothesis of the environmental risk transition predicts that risks to the health of a city resident may be predicted by the level of economic development of that city. Hence in very poor cities (Category 1) such as Dhaka, Kolkata (Calcutta), Hanoi, Ho Chi Minh City, Vientiane, Yangon (Rangoon), and also in the poorest slum areas of Manila and Jakarta, traditional problems such as inadequate access to clean drinking water, pollution of drinking water by human waste and poor community sanitation, have increased the incidence of water-borne disease. In Manila, untreated or poorly-treated domestic water accounts for 40% of water pollution, followed by industrial waste water (38%) and domestic solid waste (22%). Less than 15% of Metro Manila is served by sewers, and in the past 10 years there has been an increase in water-borne diseases such as diarrhoea, typhoid, paratyphoid and salmonella infections. In Dhaka, Bangladesh, over 80% of hospital admissions are related to water-borne diseases.

In middle-income cities (Category 2) such as Bangkok, Kuala Lumpur, Beijing, Shanghai, New Delhi, Mumbai (Bombay), Jakarta and Surabaya, more modern problems such as air pollution are a major concern. This pollution is caused by a rapid growth of motorized vehicles, combined with antiquated road systems and heavy concentrations of industry. Improved living standards have increased the production of solid waste in these cities, and the safe disposal of domestic and industrial waste is now a major problem. The poorer neighbourhoods of these cities are concurrently exposed to high traditional health risks from water-borne disease, which probably means that the overall risk to their health from this overlap and possible synergism of traditional and modern risk factors may be greater than that faced by inhabitants of Category 1 cities. A study prepared by the United Nations Environment Programme (UNEP) and the World Health Organization (WHO) revealed that all of the 10 cities surveyed in the region (Bangkok, Beijing, Mumbai, Kolkata, Delhi, Jakarta, Karachi, Manila, Seoul and Shanghai) had their air quality seriously affected by suspended particulate matter; Beijing, Seoul and Shanghai have serious to moderate sulphur dioxide pollution; Bangkok, Manila and Jakarta have a moderate lead problem; Jakarta has a moderate carbon monoxide problem; Beijing and Jakarta have a moderate ozone problem; while none of the cities had excessive concentrations of nitrogen dioxide in their air. Virtually all of the major cities of China and India, along with Bangkok and Jakarta, experience more than 100 days annually during which suspended particulate matter concentrations exceed the WHO standard of 230 micrograms/cu m. This compares with major cities in Japan and Australia, which do not suffer any days above the standard. Bangkok's estimated losses in 1989 from particulate matter amounted to 51m. restricted-activity days and 26m. lost workdays, together with 1,400 excess mortalities. In China sulphur dioxide concentrations are believed to be largely responsible for lung cancer mortality rates three to seven times higher in the nation's cities than in the country as a whole. In Mumbai, where there is a large concentration of heavy industry, people living near the congested industrial areas suffered from a much higher incidence of diseases such as chronic bronchitis, tuberculosis, skin allergies, anaemia and eye irritations than residents in a cleaner suburb.

In high-income cities (Category 3) such as Tokyo, Osaka, Sydney and Melbourne, urban environmental health risks are much lower and confined to hazardous wastes (biological and toxic wastes associated with advanced technology), indoor air pollution, and occasional but usually minor problems with localized water contamination. Amenity issues are of more concern to the relatively affluent residents, as they demand high-quality design, landscaping, green space and recreational facilities.

However, an interesting initiative is being attempted in Taiyuan, a grimy industrial city in north-east China, to overcome its problem of air pollution. In a national survey in 1999 and 2000 this city was found to have the nation's worst level of air pollution at nearly nine times the safe level. Most of this was caused by smoke and sulphur dioxide emanating from the city's many coal-fired hearths and industrial boilers. Unlike London and Los Angeles, which adopted classic command-and-control measures to deal with their problems, Taiyuan is letting the market decide. It proposes to use emissions trading, in an attempt to achieve a 50% reduction in sulphur-dioxide output within five years. Agreement was reached with the Asian Development Bank to develop a system whereby permits to pollute will be issued to the city's worst offenders. These permits will be tradable, so that polluters can either retain the right to pollute and pay for this privilege, or restrain their own output of sulphur dioxide and sell the right to another organization. By reducing the total permitted tonnage of gas each year, overall pollution levels can hopefully be reduced in the most economically efficient manner. Nantong, another Chinese city, has already carried out a trial of this approach with the help of a US environmental group. The approach is a good illustration of the mistaken logic of the conventional view that poor cities like Taiyuan cannot afford rich-world environmental standards and that clean air and greenery are luxury goods. Instead, the Chinese leadership appears to be moving towards acceptance of the contrary view that, besides being bad for individuals, pollution is bad for the economy and that improvements in economic growth and welfare will eventually more than compensate for the immediate costs required to reduce it. This change in attitude has been strongly endorsed by the World Bank, which estimated that in the late 1990s China lost between 3.5% and 7.7% of its potential economic output as a result of the detrimental health effects of pollution on the country's workforce.

Most of the above-mentioned urban environmental problems are a result of the failure of governance, which in some cases, but by no means in all, is due to weaknesses in the national economy. Governments fail to control industrial pollution and occupational exposure; to promote environmental health; to ensure that city-dwellers have the basic infrastructure and services essential to health and a decent living environment; and to plan in advance so that sufficient land is made available for low-income housing. These shortcomings are all too often due to the oversight, corruption, vested interests and a lack of commitment to the public good by government officials and politicians. These failures of governance are just as common in the small cities as in the large cities of the region, and they are also emerging even in the cities of the South Pacific. It is obvious from the above discussion that strategies designed to improve environmental conditions in the major urban centres of the region must focus explicitly on the problems of the poor. In particular, they must focus on public health and environmental measures to prevent or limit the transmission of diarrhoeal diseases, typhoid, cholera, and other water-borne, or water-based diseases, or acute respiratory infections and tuberculosis, or vector-borne diseases such as malaria, dengue fever and yellow fever.

GLOBAL WARMING AND RISING SEA-LEVELS

There is now widespread agreement among scientists that the world's climate will warm over the 21st century owing to a more pronounced 'greenhouse' effect caused by the huge amounts of carbon dioxide and other gases, such as methane, being released into the atmosphere as a result of modern human activities. The major contributing activities have been greater energy use, in particular the increased burning of fossil fuels, the expansion of more intensive agricultural land uses, deforestation, and the manufacture of particular chemicals such as the now widely-banned chlorofluorocarbons (CFCs). The Asia-Pacific region already contributes more than one-third of the global emissions of carbon dioxide. The rapid industrial growth predicted for populous countries like China and India over the 21st century, and the fact that at least for the next 30 years this growth will be driven by a huge rise in the use of fossil fuels, will increase this share dramatically. According to the United Nations' Intergovernmental Panel on Climate Change (IPCC), a doubling of carbon dioxide in the atmosphere will make the climate warmer by approximately 3°C. What is not known is how rapidly this doubling will occur and what effect this will have on future temperatures. The World Meteorological Organization suggests that a rise of 3.0°C may occur as early as 2030 if the effects of other greenhouse gases are included, but Mike Hulme, a British climatologist, offers more conservative estimates of temperature change in the range of 1.5°C to 4.5°C by 2100, and a best estimate of transient warming of only 1.2°C by 2050. However, the Third Assessment Report (TAR) of the IPCC released in 2001, has projected globally-averaged surface temperature increases of 1.4°C to 5.8°C over the period 1990 to 2100, greater than those predicted by the Second Assessment Report (SAR) of 1996. Already the earth's average surface temperature has risen by approximately 0.6°C in the last century, with new analyses for the Northern Hemisphere indicating that these temperature increases have been the largest of any century during the past 1,000 years.

The major likely effect of global warming is a potential rise in the mean sea-level owing to the thermal expansion of ocean water and the melting of ice caps. The TAR has projected that mean sea-levels will rise by 0.09 to 0.88 m between 1990 and 2100, slightly less than predicted in the SAR. This will seriously threaten the very existence of low-lying developing countries such as the Maldives, Tuvalu, Tonga, Kiribati, and Vanuatu where 90% of the population lives along the coasts. Flooding during cyclones and king tides will increase, affecting soils and salinizing freshwater supplies. Water tables will rise, coastal farmland will be abandoned forcing inhabitants to cultivate steeper slopes, leading to soil erosion. Tourism, which is the mainstay of many small island economies, will also be adversely affected as beaches and sea walls are destroyed. Coral reefs, which protect tropical islands, will also be severely affected, and there will be fewer fish and shellfish. Coastal vegetation, particularly mangroves, will be lost, along with their protection from wave erosion and their fish-breeding environments. This may well lead to significant local human migration and the loss of cultural heritages.

Natural systems can be particularly vulnerable to climate change in direct relation to the amount and speed of that change because of their limited adaptive capacity. Working Group II of the IPCC (2001) has already observed changes including shrinkage of glaciers, break-up of part of the Antarctic ice shelf, thawing of permafrost, later freezing and earlier break-up of ice on rivers and lakes, lengthening of mid- to high-latitude growing seasons, poleward and altitudinal shifts of plant and animal ranges, declines of some plant and animal populations, and earlier flowering of trees, emergence of insects, and egg-laying in birds. The Working Group warned that natural systems at risk of irreversible damage include glaciers, coral reefs and atolls, mangroves, boreal and tropical forests, polar and alpine ecosystems, prairie wetlands and remnant native grasslands.

Hulme has modelled the likely effects of temperature increases on the vegetation of China and concluded that in the Xinjiang Uygur Autonomous Region of north-west China, the climate would become warmer and drier, rendering sustainable livestock production difficult. In the more arable areas to the east and the north-east a rise in temperatures would increase the diversity of crops that could be grown and may lead to higher production. However, wet rice, the main food crop, requires plentiful water supplies, and Hulme concludes that any rise in temperature would decrease the effectiveness of water available from precipitation and irrigation sources since evapotranspiration rates would increase. The decrease in water availability would tend to depress yields of rice and also wheat.

Temperature increases in India would also be likely to depress yields of rice and wheat, the major food crops, and would exacerbate India's looming water shortages. Model simulations also suggest that the frequency of cyclones would increase as a result of global warming and that this could have catastrophic effects for the rural populations of India and Bangladesh located in coastal low-lying areas. Models to predict the effects of global warming have been developed for other countries, but the results are not consistent and few predictions can be made with certainty. However, the 2001 reports of the IPCC project a number of adverse impacts on human systems from global warming. These include a general reduction in crop yields in most tropical, sub-tropical and mid-latitude regions, decreased water availability for populations in many water-scarce regions, particularly in the subtropics, an increase in the number of people exposed to vector-borne and water-borne diseases and to heat-stress mortality, a widespread increase in the risk of flooding for many human settlements, and an increased energy demand for space cooling owing to higher summer temperatures.

Perhaps one of the most underestimated effects of global warming will be that it will bring about shifts in major climatic zones and in vegetation types. Many animal and plant species may be able to follow these shifts in habitat provided the changes are relatively slow. Rapid changes in habitat, however, combined with artificial barriers such as agricultural land use or urban development, may make it impossible for many species to relocate to more favourable ecological sites, and this may become a major threat to future biodiversity in the most densely-settled countries of the region.

THE IMPACT OF MEGAPROJECTS

Encouraged by economic success and by the immense needs of their burgeoning populations, the countries of the Asia-Pacific region have launched a disproportionately high number of megaprojects over past decades. These have ranged from massive population redistribution schemes, such as the transmigration project of Indonesia, and the Federal Land Development Authority (FELDA) schemes of Malaysia, to projects aimed at hydroelectric power generation and the provision of increased water storage by the building of huge dams such as the Three Gorges Dam in China, the Mekong Basin dams in Thailand and Laos, the Bakun Dam in Sarawak, and the Narmada Valley Project in India.

Three Gorges Project, China

Perhaps the project that emphasizes most clearly the environmental and social issues raised by these enormous schemes is the Three Gorges Project in China. By any measure this is a huge project, which will dam the Changjiang (River Yangtze), China's biggest river and the world's third-longest, with a massive concrete wall 2 km long and 185 m high. This will be the largest concrete structure in the world which, like the Great Wall before it, will be visible from space. The dam will create a reservoir 660 km long, stretching from the dam wall near Yichang to Chongqing, China's largest municipality with more than 30m. inhabitants. When complete, it will be the biggest electricity-generating facility in the world, with an installed capacity of 18,200 MW (equivalent to 11% of China's total consumption). It will include the largest ship-lift in the world and make the Changjiang navigable to ships of up to 10,000 tons for over 1,600 km inland, all the way to Chongqing, which will thus become one of the world's most important seaport cities. Cost estimates range from US $11,000m., when approved in 1992, to as much as US $100,000m. Construction began in 1994, with completion scheduled for 2009. Proponents of the dam claim that it will protect from disastrous floods millions of people living along the middle and lower reaches of the river (which killed some 300,000 people in floods in the 20th century alone); that it will generate up to 18,000 MW of electricity for China's industrial centres and thereby provide a much-awaited economic boost for the long-neglected hinterland; and transform the fast-flowing Changjiang into a smooth, navigable waterway for ocean-going vessels. The dam's power-generation capacity will save the burning of 100m. tons of coal and prevent the emission of 2m. tons of sulphur dioxide into the atmosphere, where it is the major cause of acid rain.

Unfortunately, this massive project is predicted to extract equally huge social, cultural and environmental costs, so much so that its environmental impact has been likened to that of the Soviet draining of the Aral Sea. Because of these fears, international financial support for the project has been withdrawn, and China now has to raise the funds itself. Premier Zhu Rongji, appointed in March 1998, limited the project's access to state funds and, unlike his predecessors, failed publicly to endorse the scheme. The first problem is concern over the ability of China effectively to manage quality control and minimize corruption in such a huge project. These doubts were confirmed with the arrest of the head of the now-defunct Three Gorges Economic Development Corporation for corruption, the scandal also involving other senior officials. Premier Zhu Rongji reinforced these concerns when in 1999 he used the phrase 'tofu dregs' to describe inferior dikes and dams built along the flood-prone Changjiang, and in April 2002 a senior Chinese expert stated that cracks had appeared in the concrete wall of the dam. The second problem is that the three gorges themselves, the site of some of the most scenic and beautiful landscape anywhere in the world, will be partially flooded and devalued as a wilderness area. Third, the reservoir's 47,280 gigalitres of water will flood six counties and some 100,000 ha of cropland, including 46,000 ha of the most fertile land along the river basin, at a time when the loss of agricultural land is threatening China's ability to feed itself. Fourth, by changing the hydrology of the river for thousands of kilometres, the dam will destroy commercial fish stocks and threaten with extinction endangered animal species unique to the region such as the Siberian white crane, the Yangtze River dolphin, the Chinese alligator, the finless porpoise, as well as the rare Chinese sturgeon. Fifth, the rising dam waters will force at least 1.2m. local residents to abandon their ancestral homes and terraced farmland. Officials have planned for these people to be relocated in stages, 500,000 by 2003, and the remainder by 2009, hopefully to other farming areas. Recent reports acknowledge that there is widespread opposition to resettlement, villagers being fearful that they will suffer a fate similar to most of those previously relocated from other dam sites in China, who have been left destitute, without adequate compensation or shelter, forced to eke out an existence on poor farmland in inhospitable locations far from their homeland and resented by the local people. Sixth, there is increasing concern from environmentalists that by slowing the flow of water the dam will lower the Changjiang's ability to dissipate the huge load of human, industrial and mining waste which it currently receives. In the reservoir area alone there are 3,000 factories and mines, which produce 10,000m. tons of waste per year containing 50 different toxins. Some of these chemicals and heavy metals will end up in the reservoir along with the sewage from Chongqing, and result in increased waste content levels. International medical literature has recently highlighted the public health risks posed by the dam, particularly the threat of schistosomiasis, a parasitic disease that is endemic along the Changjiang below the dam.

Geologists are also concerned about a seventh problem, the high degree of sediment carried by the Changjiang, which is presently transported downstream and deposited as fertile silt on the river's floodplain or as sediment at the river's mouth near Shanghai. Construction of the dam will trap much of this silt in the reservoir where it could shorten the life of the dam, perhaps block effluent pipes, and even prevent the opening of sluice gates, thereby threatening the safety of the dam in a major flood. Similar problems occurred at the 'indestructible' Banqiao dam, which drowned up to 230,000 persons when it collapsed after record rains in 1975. Uncertainty over the effectiveness of methods to control the build-up of sediment, combined with China's past history of dam disasters, heightens concerns about the safety of such a huge structure on China's biggest river. An eighth and related concern is that, by reducing sediment supplies to the coastline, the dam will cause increased coastal erosion at the mouth of the Changjiang and lead to the loss of some of China's most productive farmland, an effect that would be compounded by any future sea-level rises. A ninth effect is that river discharge downstream of the dam will be reduced and expose the water supply of Shanghai to salt-water intrusion, which is already a problem. Finally, the dam will submerge some of China's most outstanding historical sites and cultural relics, including Dachang, a town settled 1,500 years ago during the Three Kingdoms period. Unfortunately, the time and money available to save the archaeological relics is insufficient, and in the absence of a major international effort, something still not permitted by the Government, only a fraction of the relics can be saved.

In 1997 officials decided to flood the dam's 660-km reservoir to its upper operating level of 175 m in the sixth year of operation (2009), instead of during the 10th year as originally planned. This, it was hoped, would quickly maximize electricity output and speed up repayment of the capital costs. A reversal of this decision was requested in a petition to China's senior leaders by 53 eminent academics and engineers, on the grounds that rapidly flooding the reservoir would increase sediment build-up (it would begin before erosion in the tributary streams could be controlled), submerge drainage outlets and back up sewerage from Chongqing city, and force an additional 300,000 people to leave their homes. By June 2000 only 227,000 of the 1.2m.–1.5m. residents who were to be displaced by the dam had been resettled.

RECENT DEVELOPMENTS

Of the many recent events that have caused environmental concern in the Asia-Pacific region, four have been selected for brief discussion. The first is that of the forest fires in Indonesia in 1997–98, which sent a cloud of unwelcome haze across the borders of neighbouring Singapore and Malaysia, emphasizing once again that major environmental problems do not respect national borders. The second is the environmental significance of major flooding in China, Bangladesh, India and Indonesia in 1998, 1999 and 2002. Two long-term very difficult environmental problems will then be highlighted. The first is recent evidence that suggests global warming is threatening the very survival of coral reefs in the Asia-Pacific region, and the final topic is the threat of wet and dry land salinization to agricultural land in Australia. Both suggest that the problems facing the region must be robustly addressed by both its developed and less developed countries.

Forest Fires in Indonesia

Between August and November 1997 the Asia-Pacific region experienced its most serious transborder environmental problem when Indonesia, Malaysia, Singapore, Brunei and southern Thailand were smothered by thick smoke haze originating from forest fires in Indonesia. Although geological and historical evidence suggests that similar forest fires have a long history in the region and occurred in recent severe dry seasons in 1982, 1987, 1990 and 1991–95, the smoke generated by the fires of 1997 was more serious. The 1997 haze was so severe that it provoked international consternation and an unprecedented apology from the Indonesian Government. The 1997 forest fires began in July of that year, and by late September were raging out of control in central and South Sumatra, and in central, South and West Kalimantan. Smaller fires were also reported in East Kalimantan, Sulawesi, eastern Indonesia and in the mountain areas of Java and Irian Jaya (West Papua, now Papua). By early December 1997 most of these fires had been doused by north-east monsoon rains. Unfortunately, these rains failed to reach East Kalimantan, and by mid-January 1998 extremely dry conditions had combined with economic crisis and impoverishment to drive people into the forest to clear land by means of fire, thereby creating a wildfire in the whole of the Mahakam basin, west and south of Samarinda, the provincial capital. Kutai National Park, north of Samarinda, one of the island's most significant rainforest and ecological reserves and home to around 2,500 endangered orangutans, had by late March been extensively damaged by fire. By the beginning of May 1998, when rain put out the fires, 5.2m. ha had been burned in East Kalimantan, of which more than 630,000 ha was totally burned out or severely-burned dipterocarp forest (most of which had been selectively logged), while another 590,000 ha was peat-swamp forest, plantation and degraded forest. Serious damage had been done to the habitat of many endangered animals, and a toxic smoke haze was generated over the province causing respiratory problems for some 5,000 people.

In economic terms, the direct fire-related damage to Indonesia has been estimated to total US $7,900m., and the loss of forest resources has been considerable. Valuable timber and rattan have been destroyed, along with the houses, crops and fruit trees of local residents. The total land area burned by the 1997–98 fires was 9.7m. ha, of which 4.8m. ha was forest, and the damage to biodiversity and to the health of forest ecosystems has been profound. The most serious large-scale and intense fires of 1997–98 were in logged-over forest where the canopy had been broken and logging residue on the forest floor had dried out and became ready fuel. Other areas of disturbed forest, particularly areas of secondary forest favoured by swidden cultivators, were severely damaged, and with regular fires the floristically-rich multi-layered forest vegetation can be converted into a single-layer fire-resistant *alang-alang (Imperata cylindrica)* grassland. Damage to the primary forest was less widespread and was concentrated in the more exposed areas near logging roads or other disturbances, and often confined only to the undergrowth. Other serious concerns were expressed about the damage the fires had done to already endangered animal species such as the Sumatran tiger, Asian elephant, Javan rhinoceros, sunbear and the orangutan, particularly when the fires spread into national parks.

Interestingly, the health and economic costs of the smoke haze created by the fires received more attention than the direct damage, probably because of the international implications and the discomfort caused to residents of Singapore and Kuala Lumpur. The immediate dangers of the smoke haze were highlighted on 27 September 1997, when an airbus crashed while attempting to land at Medan, North Sumatra, killing all 234 persons on board, followed about 10 hours later by the collision of two vessels in the Melaka Strait with the loss of 29 sailors. In both accidents, poor visibility caused by the haze was believed to be a contributing factor.

There is little doubt that 'background haze' caused by local air pollution has been getting worse over the last decade in Peninsular Malaysia, where it is particularly serious during the dry season from July to August. In 1997, however, the level of pollution was increased dramatically by the proximity of the fires in Sumatra and the transport of smoke particulates from Kalimantan by a south-easterly wind stream. During September–October 1997 the smoke haze became so dangerous to health that many local populations in Sumatra and Kalimantan had to remain indoors. Analysis of the smoke haze revealed that of the five main haze components, ozone, sulphur dioxide, carbon monoxide, nitrogen dioxide and particulates, it was only the level of particulates that was elevated enough to cause concern in Kuala Lumpur and Singapore, but the high level of particulates in Sarawak quadrupled the incidence of adult asthma and increased significantly the incidence of upper respiratory tract infections and conjunctivitis. An estimated 70m. people in South-East Asia were affected by the haze, of whom 2,000–3,000 may have died as a result of related diseases.

The haze-related damages alone incurred by the 1997 fires have been estimated at US $1,384m. for the whole region, with the greatest burden falling on Indonesia, where estimates exceeded US $1,000m., with more than 90% of the losses attributable to short-term health costs and the remainder owing to lost tourist revenues, airline cancellations and airport closures. Costs to Malaysia exceeded US $300m., mainly from industrial and agricultural production losses and a sharp decline in tourism revenue, while Singapore lost more than US $60m. in tourist receipts. The estimates do not take into account long-term damage to health, which may persist for decades and surpass short-term health costs.

The onset in May 1997 of the second most intense climatic phenomenon of the last 30 years, known as El Niño, exacerbated normal dry-season drought conditions and increased the fire hazard in the months that followed, but almost all of the fires were intentionally lit to assist land-clearing by commercial oil-palm and timber plantations, government-sponsored transmigration projects, 'spontaneous' migrants and local small-scale swidden cultivators. Logging activities, resulting in clearing, road-building, the expansion of secondary forest and increased fragmentation of forest cover, have been the major contributor to an increase in the risk of forest fires over the last decade. Any future attempts to prevent and control the impending risks and hazards of fire must incorporate the enforcement of government regulations, which prohibit the use of fire by large timber and plantation companies and by small farmers. They must also educate swidden cultivators, who have traditionally used small fires to prepare secondary forest for planting, of the increased risks of controlled burns becoming extensive wildfires in times of intense drought and in increasingly-degraded forest environments. Attempts must also be made to encourage the application of fire-breaks and the use of tractors to remove the larger trees before controlled burns clear the rest of the land. In general, what Indonesia and its neighbours need is not more and better fire-fighting, but more effective governance that can enforce a fundamental change in land management. Problems posed by the monetary and political crises currently overwhelming Indonesia, and its excessively rapid move to regional autonomy, suggest that the changes in governance to which its citizens aspire will not occur in the near future.

In August 1999, and again in March 2000, smoke haze from forest fires in the Indonesian islands of Sumatra and Kalimantan once more began to shroud parts of neighbouring Malaysia and Singapore. However, this time the Indonesian Government's publicly-stated intention to summon logging companies and review their licences appeared to pre-empt another crisis like that of 1997–98.

Flooding in China, India, Bangladesh and Indonesia

Across East, South and South-East Asia the summer monsoon months of June to September of 1998 brought major flooding which resulted in the deaths of some 6,700 people. In China the Changjiang basin, home to some 400m. people, bore most of the damage from floods said to be the worst since 1954, with more than 3,000 people being killed, 14m. persons made homeless and 4.4m. ha of cropland destroyed, but streams in the north-west and north-east of the country also reached record levels. Total damage in central China alone was estimated at US $20,000m. In northern and eastern India the worst flooding for many years killed at least 2,500 people, submerged tens of thousands of villages and destroyed more than 3m. ha of crops. In Bangladesh more than 900 people died and many millions were left homeless in the worst flooding in 10 years along the Ganges and Jamuna rivers, when unusually heavy rains continued for nearly a month and a series of higher-than-normal tides were provoked by undersea earthquakes in the Bay of Bengal. The flooding extended to other parts of Asia, hundreds of people being killed in South Korea and Nepal, and in February 1999 southern Mindanao island in the Philippines also experienced death and devastation from severe flooding.

Government officials and meteorologists have placed much of the blame for the floods on heavier-than-usual monsoon rains caused by La Niña, the destructive twin of the weather phenomenon known as El Niño, which caused drought and contributed to forest fires in South-East Asia in 1997–98. Prominent environmentalists, however, while acknowledging the role of La Niña, also point out that, although heavy, rainfall in 1998 was in fact lower than in previous major flood years. Instead, they attribute most of the blame for the record floods to decades of poor land-use management, which has resulted in widespread deforestation, soil erosion, siltation, and more rapid and concentrated run-off. In China the last 20 years have witnessed widespread deforestation from the once heavily-forested Qinghai-Tibet Plateau to the Changjiang basin, which has now lost 85% of its original forest cover. The result is much more rapid runoff and serious erosion, which has pushed massive quantities of silt into the river and raised the river bed and flood levels downstream. Reclamation of more than 13,000 sq km of natural lakes in the middle and lower reaches of the river and the silting up of those that have survived has reduced the capacity of these lakes to act as natural flood reservoirs. The storage capacity lost has been estimated at equivalent to about 5.8 times the capacity of the Three Gorges Dam when it is completed. The spontaneous settlement of landless migrants on embankments in the flood-prone lake areas where they build their own dikes has worsened the flood problem by further reducing the storage capacity of the lakes and exposing more people to the risk of annual flooding. Similar environmental damage caused by inappropriate land-use practices, deforestation and population pressure was largely responsible for the serious flooding in India, Nepal and Bangladesh in 1998 and the Philippine floods were also attributed to past deforestation.

The positive outcome is that the damage caused by the flooding, at least in China, has forced the authorities to take seriously fears expressed by a new generation of ecologists that China's economic growth is environmentally unsustainable if present policies and practices are continued. In an attempt to prevent further deforestation, in August 1998 China's State Council banned the opening up of new lands by the cutting of forests, suspended all forest land construction projects, and directed that occupation of all forest land required cabinet-level approval. These logging bans initially applied mainly to the Changjiang and Huanghe valleys, but in early 1999 they were extended to 18 provinces with 1.2m. sq km of woodlands. China has also initiated plans to grow an additional 6.7m. ha of young quick-growing trees to offset the shortage of timber in its domestic market caused by the logging ban and obviate the need for imports. The lack of basic research prior to the announcement of these decisions has been criticized, but at least the Chinese authorities have taken the problem seriously and made some courageous decisions. Unfortunately, there is little evidence of a similar political commitment in the other countries that experienced the serious floods of 1998.

Events of late 1999 underline the critical need for decisive action to prevent further deforestation. On 29 October a major cyclone, with winds of up to 300 km per hour, came ashore from the Bay of Bengal and ripped through the coastal state of Orissa. The accompanying tidal surge, coupled with torrential rain and burst river banks, flooded the flat coastal region and the delta of the River Mahanadi, causing the deaths of up to 20,000 inhabitants and severe loss of property. The high velocity of the tidal surge appears to have caused most of the damage. Mangrove forests that grew on tidal shorelines between the high and low water marks once covered this entire coastline. They acted as a wind and wave break and trapped sediments in their roots, and gave the sea-bed a shallow shape that in the past would have dissipated the incoming wave energy from the cyclone-prone Bay of Bengal. Unfortunately, over the past 40 years India has lost more than one-half of its mangrove forests. Orissa, in particular, has witnessed large-scale destruction of its mangrove and casuarina forests in the last decade, with much of the area being converted into ponds for raising tiger-prawns, a particularly lucrative form of aquaculture critical to the economy of the state. These shrimp farms provided no protection against the waves and tidal surges created by the cyclone. Local environmentalists have since pointed out that, despite the severity of the cyclone and the battering it inflicted on a 250-km strip of coastline, it was only the heavily-mangrove-denuded patch of about 100 km between Basudevpur and Astarang through which the high tidal surge killed thousands of people in minutes. As a local leader remarked, 'Cyclones are no stranger to Orissa, but we are responsible for the worst devastation this time'. Despite campaigns to stop the deforestation, 2.5 sq km of mangrove forest is still being destroyed each year in the state's coastal region, as local politicians allow more migrants to settle in the area.

In January, February and March 2002 the 16m. residents of Greater Jakarta were reminded of the intimate interrelationship between urban and rural environmental changes and their consequences. At the end of January the city experienced heavy, but not exceptional, rains at the height of the annual wet season. After almost a week of rain to the south of Jakarta in the vicinity of Bogor and Ciawi, in the catchment area of some of the 13 streams that criss-cross the alluvial plain on which Jakarta is sited, residents of the city awoke in the early hours of Saturday 2 February to find major roads in the city and even the grounds of the Presidential Palace under water. In the next three weeks more than 300,000 residents, mostly poor people with houses on low-lying land near the Ciliwung and Pesanggrahan Rivers and their tributaries and many others in North, East and West Jakarta, were evacuated to temporary shelter in public buildings, as their houses were flooded with filthy water to a depth of 2–3m. At least 20 people lost their lives, and subsequent disease caused by polluted drinking water and piles of garbage caused additional deaths. At the height of the floods it was estimated that some 35% of the city was under water, in what officials acknowledge was the most extensive flooding ever experienced by Jakarta.

It should be emphasized that annual flooding is not a new problem for Jakarta; the Dutch colonial administration built an intricate system of canals that minimized, but did not solve, the problem. However, Indonesia's environmentalists claim that the impact of the major recent floods of 1996 and 2002 has been exacerbated by rapid population growth, unplanned and badly planned urban development, rapid deforestation, ineffective governance and a lack of an appreciation that if environmental constraints are ignored then widespread flooding, landslides and expensive disruptions to the city's economic life and increased hardships for the city's poor, will be the inevitable result. In just four years between 1988 and 1992 some 2,800 ha of agricultural land on the city's outskirts were converted into housing and industrial estates, causing massive disruption to the city's natural drainage system and increasing the rate of run-off. In the 1950s there were some 185 small ponds in and around Jakarta with a total area of 1,304 ha, which created a natural catchment for run-off during the wet season. By the late 1980s there were still six natural ponds in Jakarta, but by 1994 these had been reduced to just two. Suburbanization, golf course construction and ill-planned industrial development has also reduced the number of drainage ponds in the neighbouring local government areas of Bogor, Bekasi and Tangerang in West Java. At the same time no significant progress has been made on construction of the East Flood Canal, first planned in the early 1970s, and on public works to clear silt from the West Flood Canal, built by the Dutch in 1924. Development of an exclusive residential complex on a former protected marsh area and mangrove forest in North Jakarta, which was approved by the former Suharto Government, has been blamed by ecologists for worsening flooding of the toll road linking Jakarta to its international airport and for disruption of the ecological balance of the Jakarta Bay coastline. Serious ecological damage has also occurred in the catchment areas south of Jakarta, where past governments have encouraged excessive deforestation of hilly and mountainous terrain that has increased the rapidity and scale of the run-off following torrential wet season downpours. Official sources downplay the role of corrupt and ineffective governance in creating this ecological tragedy, and instead tend to shift the blame to Jakarta's poor, who are held responsible for clogging the city's drainage system with their garbage and squatter housing. Of course, some of the problems can be attributed to the behaviour of the city's poor, but it is the large conglomerates, estate developers and senior government officials that have had the power and the wealth to prevent these cases of ecological negligence. Unless this behaviour changes in the near future, Jakarta will have little choice but to prepare its poorer residents for more serious annual flooding in future years.

Threats to Coral Reefs

In general, coral reefs are found in shallow waters, between the Tropic of Capricorn and the Tropic of Cancer. Their total extent is unknown, although it probably exceeds 600,000 sq km. They represent less than 0.2% of the total area of oceans and cover an area equivalent to 4% of the world's cropland area. Coral reefs resemble tropical rain forests in that they both thrive in nutrient-poor conditions (where nutrients are largely tied up in living matter), yet support rich communities through incredibly efficient recycling processes. Both exhibit very high levels of species diversity. Coral reefs and other marine ecosystems contain more varied life forms than do land habitats, with all but one of the world's 33 phyla (major kinds of organisms) being found in marine environments. The species richness of coral reefs is unparalleled in the marine environment and the most species-rich reefs are found in the Asia-Pacific region in a swath extending throughout South-East Asia to the Great Barrier Reef, off north-eastern Australia. The Great Barrier Reef (GBR), the world's largest system of coral reefs (covering 349,000 sq km), supports more than 700 species of coral, 1,500 species of fish, and more than 4,000 species of molluscs. In addition, 252 species of birds nest and breed on the coral cays, five species of turtles live on the reef, and several species of whales and dolphins are associated with it. Indeed, coral reefs of the Indo-West-Pacific support more than 16% of the world's estimated 19,000 species of freshwater and marine fish. The GBR alone, occupying only 0.1% of the ocean surface, supports nearly 8% of the world's fish species; in comparison the coastal waters of the Mediterranean Sea support less than 25% as many fish species. The level of species endemism is much lower on coral reefs than in tropical rain forests, however, which means that they are less threatened by species extinction. Nevertheless, for many communities in the Asia-Pacific region coral reefs are a vital source of food, an attraction for much-needed tourist dollars and a protective buffer for vulnerable coastlines. The survival of many of their species also depends on other affiliated ecosystems with coral reefs, mangroves, and sea-grass beds being linked physically and biologically.

In the 1990s, however, it became obvious that the coral reefs of the world are in serious trouble, with large-scale degradation occurring in East Africa, South and South-East Asia, parts of the Pacific and across the Caribbean. Nearly all of this degradation has been caused by human activity. In South-East Asia, which has about 30% of the world's reefs, rapid economic growth and increased population pressure have been concentrated in coastal areas, placing heavy reliance on marine resources. This has produced considerable sediment and nutrient pollution, especially from the major coastal cities and numerous coastal resorts on the islands in the region. The result has been the loss of much of the coral cover in reefs near centres of population, followed by a dramatic decline in fish numbers and catches. The damage is exacerbated by roving bands of fishermen who are damaging reefs by using dynamite, cyanide and muro-ami, a fishing method whereby divers (often children) pound on coral reefs to drive fish out into the net. These are the most threatened reefs of any region of the world, with some 80% of their number now at risk of degradation. In contrast, human stresses to Australian reefs are minimal, except on some reefs close to the land because population density is low, the level of economic development is high, and there is low fishing pressure. However, inner shelf reefs in the GBR have suffered degradation from increased sediment and nutrient run-off caused by cattle-grazing and sugar-cane growing.

There were reports of unprecedented widespread bleaching of hard and soft corals in widely separated parts of the world from mid-1997 to the last months of 1998. This bleaching occurred in parallel with big changes in the global climate with a severe El Niño event during late 1997 and early 1998, which switched to a strong La Niña in mid-1998. This has suggested to some researchers that global warming may be posing a much greater danger to the survival of the world's corals than direct human actions. Some bleaching may be a seasonal event in the Pacific, Indian Ocean and the Caribbean. Frequently corals recover from bleaching, but death may result if the stress is prolonged or extreme. Normally fast-growing, branching corals in the Indo-Pacific are more susceptible than slow-growing boulder corals, which, if they are bleached, frequently recover in one to two months. However, in this event, some 700-year-old *Porites* corals on inner reefs of the GBR and Viet Nam were extensively bleached, and some died. Water temperatures over the entire Indian Ocean were exceptionally warm for four to five months in 1998, and corals all the way from Mozambique to Western Australia and Indonesia bleached very heavily, with many dying. Prior to this, localized bleaching had been known to reef scientists for many decades, but only on a small scale as in over-heated tidal pools. Mass instances of coral bleaching, of which six have occurred since 1979, are unrecorded in earlier scientific literature, and it is claimed indigenous peoples with long reliance on reefs, have no words in their languages to describe this phenomenon.

Bleaching occurs when coral organisms are stressed by excessive heat or other factors. When they are stressed they suddenly expel the microscopic plants or algae, known as zooxanthellae, which live in their cells in a normally very successful symbiotic relationship. The coral polyps provide the plants with crucial nutrients such as ammonia and phosphate, while the zooxanthellae deliver to the coral polyps food and essential compounds from photosynthesis. It is the microscopic algae that give the corals their tremendous range of brilliant colours, reds, browns, greens, yellows and blues, so when the corals expel their algae they lose their colour and become bleached. When this happens the coral animal loses much of its food supply and in the nutrient starved waters in which coral thrives they begin to starve and eventually die, unless water temperatures quickly return to normal.

The coral bleaching of 1997–98 was the most geographically widespread ever recorded, and the most important question is whether this was simply a severe isolated occurrence, or whether events like this will happen more frequently as temperatures rise with global warming. It is too soon to answer this question with any certainty. However, sea temperatures in tropical waters, where most corals live, have increased by nearly 1°C in the last 100 years. Being highly temperature-sensitive, many corals are already close to the top of their thermal range and with this in mind Professor Ove Hoegh-Guldberg, the director of the University of Sydney's coral reef research institute, has recently projected that if current rates of warming continue, coral bleaching is set to increase steadily in intensity all over the world until it occurs annually by 2030–70. This would devastate coral reefs globally to such an extent that they would be eliminated from most areas of the world by 2100. Hoegh-Guldberg's projections were regarded by many as unduly pessimistic until late 1998, but have since been taken much more seriously and generally coincide with other major international models of climate change. There is now widespread concern that unless global warming and growth in the emission of greenhouse gases are rapidly curbed, most Caribbean reefs may well be dead by 2020, with southern and central parts of the GBR and many reefs in South-East Asia following by 2030.

Salinization of Water and Land in the Agricultural Regions of Australia

Located in the relatively fertile well-watered south-east of Australia, the Murray-Darling Basin is Australia's largest and economically most significant river system. It covers over 1m. sq km, equivalent to 14% of the country's total area, and is the source of 41% of the nation's agricultural wealth. The basin grows 71% of Australia's total area of irrigated crops and pastures. Although one of the world's major river systems in terms of length and catchment area, its surface run-off is among the smallest in comparison with that of other systems of similar size. Indeed, owing to the semi-arid climate, some 86% of the basin contributes virtually no surface run-off to the river systems except during floods. The basin is a naturally saline environment in terms of its soils, geology, surface water and groundwater, with the low river flows and limited leaching possible in this dry environment concentrating salinity levels. The natural flora and fauna are adapted to these conditions, but human activities have greatly increased salinity levels until they have begun to cause significant problems for all water and land users, agricultural, domestic and industrial.

In terms of surface water and groundwater salinity, the problems are of more concern in the southern parts of the basin. In the Murray, the major stream of the basin, the salinity levels increase markedly downstream owing to natural processes such as increased evaporation, and the inflow from naturally occurring saline groundwater which can have salinities up to 50,000 electrical conductivity units (EC). Water with levels of more than 700 EC is unsuitable for irrigating most horticultural crops, while 800 EC is the accepted maximum level for domestic supplies in large towns and cities. However, the naturally-occurring levels of salinity have been exacerbated by drainage flows of saline water from irrigation areas and from rising groundwater levels, both of which are results of inappropriate forms of land-use management. So far, even in years of very low flow, the Murray and its major tributaries have delivered water of acceptable quality for drinking purposes, although in dry years the lower Murray water is of such high salinity that it may cause crop damage if used for irrigation. Recent research, however, shows an alarming increase in salt loads and salinity in many basin streams even further north in New South Wales, with some predictions estimating that salinity levels may exceed safe maximum levels for human consumption. This finding is of grave concern for irrigators and for residents of Adelaide and other settlements dependent on the Murray and its tributaries for domestic water supplies.

Land salinization occurs naturally in parts of the basin, but the concern here is with secondary or induced salinization resulting from European-style land use practices. In order to maximize the feed for their introduced sheep and to obtain commercial returns from the land, European settlers removed deep-rooted native grasses, shrubs and trees, which were replaced with shallow-rooted annual crops and pastures. This resulted in a major reduction in water use and increased the quantity of water added to groundwaters. The water tables then rose, gradually dissolving naturally-occurring salts that had hitherto been harmlessly held in the soils above the natural water tables. As the water table rose, these newly-dissolved salts were then brought towards the surface, where the salt was concentrated by evaporation. When the water table is within one metre of the surface, waterlogging and salinization frequently occur and, since the concentrated salts are now within the root zone, substantial losses in agricultural production can result. In the basin's irrigation areas (the most extensive in Australia and the basis of the country's rice, horticultural and viticultural industries) the problem of rising water tables owing to removal of the native vegetation has been compounded by the application of large quantities of water, frequently, at least in the early years, without any drainage facilities to remove surplus water. A decade ago it was estimated that 96,000 ha were affected by salinization, while another 560,000 ha had water tables within 2 m of the surface and rising rapidly. This rise in water tables in one irrigation district of southern New South Wales has been at the rate of 27 cm per year, and in another area in Victoria it has been described as an 'underground flood'. High salinity levels reduce irrigation crop yields and can cause loss of orchard trees. In some areas productivity losses of at least 7% are now common, with losses of 30% predicted within 30 years. By the year 2010 it is expected that all irrigation areas in the southern basin will have water tables within 2 m of the surface, casting severe doubts on the sustainability of agricultural production in areas where the groundwaters are saline. Fortunately, the problem is now being slowly recognized, and a range of measures such as surface and subsurface drains, groundwater pumping, use of groundwater for irrigation, water harvesting, tree planting, disposal of saline water into evaporation basins, and more efficient water usage and district-wide action plans supported by public funds are now being implemented. The problem is now so serious, however, that a long-term commitment beyond the tenure of several governments is urgently required.

Although induced salinization was once regarded as a problem only in irrigated lands, it is now known that salinization is a far more extensive problem on the basin's drylands and in other parts of Australia (especially in the south-west of Western Australia where some 443,000 ha of land is affected), with both croplands and pastures being damaged by rising water tables. Nationally, it has recently been estimated that dryland salinity threatens one-fifth of Australia's arable land (an area three times the size of Tasmania), and this process cannot be reversed easily or quickly. Excessive removal of native vegetation has been the major cause of these rising water tables. A 1993 study estimated that at least 200,000 ha of land were seriously affected and that more than 1m. ha were at risk of dryland salinity. A 1995 study greatly increased the area at risk, estimating that in New South Wales alone up to 5m. ha were endangered if present land-management practices continued. The land affected may be lost to agricultural production or experience reduced productivity if it is still capable of use. Local communities have become more aware of the problem in the last few years, and are now growing more trees and perennial pastures and making less use of long fallows, in an attempt to reduce accessions of water to the water tables. The abandonment of land and the introduction of more salt-tolerant crops, however, may be the only alternative in the more badly affected areas. In June 2001 all of the state and territory governments responsible for parts of the Murray-Darling Basin joined the Commonwealth of Australia and a Community Advisory Committee in committing themselves to an integrated catchment management programme to rehabilitate the Basin. This is a critical first step in the process; however, difficult political decisions, such as forgoing current water rights in the interests of enhancing environmental stream flows to safeguard long-term agricultural productivity, have yet to be taken.

Future Concerns

This article has served to emphasize the nexus between environmental issues and the demographic, economic and political realities of development in the Asia-Pacific region. This linkage will become even stronger in the future as the people of the region strive to achieve their legitimate aspirations of a better lifestyle. Looking ahead in this new century, it is clear that environmental issues will increasingly be international, rather than national or local, in their significance. Efforts to minimize the environmental 'footprint' of development must inevitably involve technology transfer, financial support and compensation mechanisms that are at least multinational, if not global in scale, if they are to succeed.

BIBLIOGRAPHY

General

Blaikie, P., and Brookfield, H. (Eds). *Land Degradation and Society*. London, Methuen, 1987.

Brookfield, H., and Byron, Y. (Eds). *South-East Asia's Environmental Future: The Search for Sustainability*. Kuala Lumpur, United Nations University Press and Oxford University Press, 1993.

Burnett, A. *The Western Pacific: Challenge of Sustainable Growth*. Aldershot, England, Edward Elgar, 1992.

Ehrlich, P. R., and Holdren, J. P. 'Impact of population growth', *Science*, Vol. 171, pp. 1212–1217, 1971.

Hardjono, J. (Ed.). *Indonesia: Resources, Ecology, and Environment*. Singapore, Oxford University Press, 1991.

Harrison, P. *The Third Revolution: Population, Environment and A Sustainable World*. London, Penguin Books, 1992.

Howard, M. C. *Asia's Environmental Crisis*. Boulder, CO, Westview Press, 1993.

Meyer, W. B. *Human Impact on the Earth*. Cambridge, Cambridge University Press, 1996.

McDowell, M. A. 'Development and the environment in ASEAN', *Pacific Affairs*, Vol. 62, No. 3, pp. 307–329, 1989.

Parnwell, M. J. G., and Bryant, R. L. (Eds). *Environmental Change in South-East Asia: People, Politics and Sustainable Development*. London, Routledge in association with the ESRC Global Environmental Change Programme, 1996.

Ramphal, S., and Sinding, S. W. (Eds). *Population Growth and Environmental Issues*. Westport, CT, Praeger Publishers, 1996.

World Bank. *World Development Report 1992: Development and the Environment*. New York, Oxford University Press, 1992.

Loss and Degradation of Agricultural Land

Smil, V. 'Land degradation in China: an ancient problem getting worse' in P. Blaikie and H. Brookfield. *Land Degradation and Society*. London, Methuen, pp. 214–222, 1987.

'Environmental problems in China: estimates of economic costs', *East-West Center Special Reports*, No. 5, pp. 1–62, Honolulu, HI, East-West Center, 1996.

Centre for International Earth Science Information Network, Columbia University. Internet www.ciesin.org

Deforestation

Angelsen, A. 'Shifting cultivation and 'deforestation': A study from Indonesia', *World Development*, Vol. 23, No. 10, pp. 1713–1729, 1995.

Angelsen, A., and D. P. Resosudarmo. 'Krismon, Farmers and Forests: the Effects of the Economic Crisis on Farmers' Livelihoods and Forest Use in the Outer Islands of Indonesia', Bogor, Center for International Forest Research, 1999.

Bernard, S., and De Koninck, R. 'The retreat of the forest in Southeast Asia: A cartographic assessment', *Singapore Journal of Tropical Geography*, Vol. 17, No. 1, pp. 1–14, 1996.

Brookfield, H., Potter, L., and Byron, Y. *In Place of the Forest: Environmental and Socio-economic Transformation in Borneo and the Eastern Malay Peninsula*. Tokyo, United Nations University Press, 1995.

Collins, N. M., Sayer, J. A., and Whitmore, T. C. (Eds). *The Conservation Atlas of Tropical Forests: Asia and the Pacific*. London, Macmillan, 1991.

Forest Watch Indonesia and Global Forest Watch. *The State of the Forest: Indonesia*. Washington, DC, Global Forest Watch, 2002. Internet www.wri.org/wripubs.html.

Magdalena, F. V. 'Population growth and the changing ecosystem in Mindanao', *Sojourn*, Vol. 11, No. 1, pp. 105–127, 1996.

Potter, L. 'Environmental and social aspects of timber exploitation in Kalimantan, 1967–1989' in J. Hardjono (Ed.). *Indonesia: Resources, Ecology, and Environment*. Singapore, Oxford University Press, pp. 177–211, 1991.

'The onslaught on the forests in South-East Asia' in H. Brookfield and Y. Byron (Eds). *South-East Asia's Environmental Future: The Search for Sustainability*. Tokyo, United Nations University Press, pp. 103–123, 1993.

Rudel, T., and Roper, J. 'The paths to rainforest destruction: Crossnational patterns of tropical deforestation, 1975–90', *World Development*, Vol. 25, No. 1, pp. 53–65, 1997.

Tole, L. 'Sources of deforestation in tropical developing countries'. *Environmental Management*, Vol. 22, No. 1, pp. 19–33, 1998.

World Bank, Environment and Social Development Unit. *Indonesia: Environment and Natural Resource Management in a Time of Transition*. New York, The World Bank, 2001. Internet www.worldbank.org. Under the Documents and Reports Section search for Indonesia: Environment.

Water Availability and Pollution

Brown, L. R., and Halweil, B. 'China's water shortage could shake world food security', *World-Watch*, pp. 10–21, July/August 1998.

Smil, V. 'Environmental problems in China: estimates of economic costs', *East-West Center Special Reports*, No. 5, pp. 1–62, Honolulu, HI, East-West Center, 1996.

Tata Energy Research Institute. *Looking Back to Think Ahead: Green India 2047*. New Delhi, Tata Energy Research Institute, 1998. Executive summary: internet www.teriin.org/pub/books/green/green.htm.

Environmental Problems in Urban Areas

Bartone, C., Bernstein, J., Leitmann, J., and Eigen, J. *Toward Environmental Strategies for Cities: Policy Considerations for Urban Environmental Management in Developing Countries*. Strategic Options for Managing the Urban Environment, No. 18, Washington, The World Bank, 1994.

Douglass, M. 'Planning for environmental stability in the extended Jakarta metropolitan region', in N. Ginsburg, B. Koppel and T. G. McGee (Eds). *The Extended Metropolis: Settlement Transition in Asia*. Honolulu, HI, University of Hawaii Press, pp. 239–273, 1991.

Firman, T. 'Land conversion and urban development in the Northern Region of West Java, Indonesia', *Urban Studies*, Vol. 34, No. 7, pp. 1027–1046, 1997.

Firman, T., and I. A. I. Dharmapatni, 'The challenges to sustainable development in Jakarta metropolitan development', *Habitat International*, Vol. 18, No. 3, pp. 79–94, 1994.

Hardoy, J. E., Mitlin, D., and Satterthwaite, D. *Environmental Problems in Third World Cities*. London, Earthscan Publications, 1992.

Lohani, B. N., and Whitington, T. P. 'Environmental management: An intersectoral approach' in Stubbs, J., and Clarke, G. (Eds). *Megacity Management in the Asian and Pacific Region: Policy Issues and Innovative Approaches*. Volume One of the Proceedings of the Regional Seminar on Megacities Management in Asia and the Pacific, Manila, Asian Development Bank, pp. 131–174, 1996.

McKee, D. L. *Urban Environments in Emerging Economies*. Westport, CT, Praeger Publishers, 1994.

Parai, A., Benhart, J. E., and Rense, W. C. 'Water Supply in Selected Mega Cities of Asia' in A. K. Dutt, F. J. Costa, S. Aggarwal and A. G. Noble (Eds). *The Asian City: Processes of*

Development, Characteristics and Planning. Dordrecht, Kluwer Academic Publishers, pp. 205–212, 1994.

Serageldin, I., Cohen, M. A., and Sivaramakrishnan, K. C. (Eds). *The Human Face of the Urban Environment*. Proceedings of the Second Annual World Bank Conference on Environmentally Sustainable Development, Environmentally Sustainable Development Proceedings Series No. 6, Washington, The World Bank, 1994.

Smith, K. R., and Lee, Y. F. 'Urbanisation and the Environmental Risk Transition' in J. D. Kasarda and A. M. Parnell (Eds). *Third World Cities: Problems, Policies and Prospects*. London, Sage, pp. 161–179, 1993.

Stubbs, J., and Clarke, G. (Eds). *Megacity Management in the Asian and Pacific Region: Policy Issues and Innovative Approaches*. Volume One of the Proceedings of the Regional Seminar on Megacities Management in Asia and the Pacific, Manila, Asian Development Bank, 1996.

Tata Energy Research Institute. Internet www.teriin.org. *The Weekend Australian,* 'Economic losses provide spur for cleaner air', Melbourne, p.18, 1–2 June 2002. Reprinted from *The Economist.*

Webster, D. 'The Urban Environment in Southeast Asia: Challenges and Opportunities', *Southeast Asian Affairs 1995*. Singapore, Institute of Southeast Asian Studies, 1995.

Global Warming and Rising Sea-Levels

Hulme, M. 'Global warming and the implications for Asia and the Pacific', in *The Far East and Australasia 1998*, London, Europa Publications, pp. 42–49, 1997.

Intergovernmental Panel on Climate Change. *IPCC Third Assessment Report: Contributions of IPCC Working Groups.* Internet www.ipcc.ch/; The Summaries for Policymakers and Technical Summaries.

Watson, R. T., Zinyowera, M. C., and Moss, R. H. *The Regional Impacts of Climate Change: An Assessment of Vulnerability.* New York, Intergovernmental Panel on Climate Change and Cambridge University Press, 1998.

The Impact of Megaprojects

Three Gorges Dam Project, China

Dai Qing. *The River Dragon Has Come*. Edited by J. G. Thibodeau and P. Williams, translated by Ming Yi. Probe International and International Rivers Network, 1998.

International Rivers Network. *IRN's Three Gorges Campaign.* Internet www.irn.org/programs/threeg/.

Probe International, Three Gorges Probe. Internet www.probe international.org/pi/3g/index.cfm.

Transmigration in Indonesia

Donner, W. *Land Use and Environment in Indonesia*. Honolulu, HI, University of Hawaii Press, 1987.

Fearnside, P. M. 'Transmigration in Indonesia: Lessons from its environmental and social impacts', *Environmental Management*, Vol. 21, No. 4, pp. 553–570, 1997.

Secrett, C. 'The environmental impact of transmigration', *The Ecologist*, Vol. 16, No. 2/3, pp. 77–88, 1986.

Recent Developments

Forest Fires in Indonesia, 1997–98

Integrated Forest Fire Management Project and German Agency for Technical Cooperation. Internet www.iffm.org.

Parry, R. L. 'Borneo's forests burn on the bonfire of big business', *The Independent*, London, p. 11, 9 February 1998.

Schindler, L. 'Fire Management in Indonesia—quo vadis?' Internet www.iffm.org/ See under 'Report'.

The Straits Times, Singapore, 22 September–4 October 1997.

Wirawan, N. 'The hazard of fire' in H. Brookfield and Y. Byron (Eds). *South-East Asia's Environmental Future: The Search for Sustainability*. Kuala Lumpur, United Nations University Press and Oxford University Press, pp. 242–266, 1993.

Flooding in China, India, Bangladesh and Indonesia

Becker, J. 'China's struggle to hold back floodwaters, a disaster born of progress', *South China Morning Post*, 15 August 1998.

China Daily, 'China—Logging ban scope expanded', 8 February 1999.

Dwi Iswandono. 'Corruption has contributed to flooding', *The Jakarta Post,* 31 January 2002. Internet ecologyasia.com/News-Archives/Jan_2002/

Eckert, P. 'Forest loss contributes to Asia's flood woes', Reuters, 27 August 1998.

Threats to Coral Reefs

Birkeland, C. *Life and Death of Coral Reefs*. New York, Chapman and Hall, 1997.

Bryant, D., Burke, L., McManus, J., and Spalding, M. *Reefs at Risk: A Map-Based Indicator of Potential Threats to the World's Coral Reefs*. Washington DC, World Resources Institute, 1998. Internet www.wri.org/wri/reefsatrisk/

Wilkinson, C. (Ed.). 'Status of coral reefs of the world: 1998'. Townsville, Global Coral Reef Monitoring Network and Australian Institute of Marine Science, 1998.

Wilkinson, C. 'The 1997–1998 mass bleaching event around the world', Townsville, Global Coral Reef Monitoring Network and Australian Institute of Marine Science, 1998.

Salinization of Water and Land in the Agricultural Regions of Australia

Australia, Department of the Environment, Sport and Territories, State of the Environment Advisory Council. *Australia: State of the Environment 1996*. Collingwood, Melbourne, CSIRO Publishing, 1996.

Crabb, P. *Murray-Darling Basin Resources*. Canberra, Murray-Darling Basin Commission, 1997.

Murray-Darling Basin Ministerial Council. *The Salinity Audit: A 100-year perspective, 1999*. Canberra, Murray-Darling Basin Commission, 1999.

Murray-Darling Basin Ministerial Council. *Integrated Catchment Management in the Murray-Darling Basin 2001–2010: Delivering a sustainable future*. Canberra, Murray-Darling Basin Ministerial Council, 2001. Internet: www.mdbc.gov .au/index.htm; 18 June 2001; follow the links to *The Integrated Catchment Management Policy Statement.*

Walker, G., Gilfedder, M., and Williams, J. *Effectiveness of Current Farming Systems in the Control of Dryland Salinity*. Canberra, CSIRO, 1999.

THE RELIGIONS OF ASIA AND THE PACIFIC

GEOFFREY PARRINDER

Islam

Islam means 'submission' or surrender to God, and a Muslim, from the same root, is a surrendered person. This faith was taught by Muhammad, but Muslims object to being called Muhammadan or Mahometan because they do not worship the founder of their religion. Although a late entrant among the world's great religions, Islam is a universal faith, with an estimated 1,200m. followers in the year 2000.

HISTORICAL BACKGROUND

Muhammad lived from AD 570 to 632 in Arabia, which was largely pagan and polytheistic with small communities of Jews and Christians. The town of Mecca was already a sacred place, and it was part of the religious genius of Muhammad to purge some of its holy sites of idolatrous associations and incorporate them into the new religion, particularly the Ka'ba shrine, a cube-like sanctuary in the middle of Mecca. Jewish and Christian figures were also honoured by Muhammad, especially Abraham, Moses and Jesus, and many of their stories occur in the sacred book, the Koran. Yet the central themes of Muhammad's teaching came in his own experience: the unity of God, his word to man, the judgement of unbelievers and paradise for the righteous. From AD 610 onwards Muhammad received divine visions and messages and preached a monotheistic faith. Most of the leaders of Mecca, however, rejected it, and in AD 622 Muhammad migrated to Medina 320 km to the north. This 'migration' (*Hijra* or *Hegira*) was later taken as the beginning of the Muslim era from which its calendar is dated. In Medina, Muhammad became leader of a community, and after successful battles against the Meccans he eventually ruled over much of Arabia. He returned to Mecca in triumph in AD 630, cleansing the Ka'ba of idols, but going back to Medina where he died two years later.

Muhammad was followed by Caliphs (*Khalifas*, 'successors') who greatly extended the rule of Islam. Under Abu Bakr the Arab armies conquered Babylon, and under 'Umar (Omar) Syria, Palestine and Egypt fell to their rule. Jerusalem and Alexandria surrendered, led by their Christian patriarchs who were glad to be rid of Byzantine Greek overlords. Arab rule was not unduly oppressive, allowing the survival of Christian communities to this day in Syrian, Coptic, Greek and other churches. Arab armies slowly pressed on into North Africa, crossed into Spain in AD 711, and were only repelled from central France in AD 732. To the east the second Persian empire fell to the Arabs, who entered northern India in AD 705 and sent embassies as far as China. As the Arab empire consolidated, it absorbed Eastern and Western cultures and produced its own contributions; Greek philosophy, mathematics and medicine were preserved by the Arabs during the Dark Ages of Europe.

The Arab empire dominated the Near and Middle East, from Spain to central Asia, and the caliphate came to be located in Baghdad until its fall to the Mongols in 1258. After the capture of Constantinople (Istanbul) in 1453 the caliph lived there until his office was abolished by the Turkish Government in 1924. The Turkish empire broke up into independent polities, and Turkey itself became Westernized and secularized, a tendency that has prevailed in varying degrees in other Islamic countries.

BELIEFS AND PRACTICE

There are Five Pillars of practical religion in Islam:

(i) The first is the Witness that 'there is no god but God' (*Allah*) and that 'Muhammad is the Apostle of God'. This confession is called from the minaret or a mosque by a *muezzin* ('crier') at the times of daily prayer. It stresses the unity and omnipotence of God, but it does not necessarily make Muslims into fatalists, an attitude that may derive as much from social as from theological reasons;

(ii) The second Pillar is Prayer, which is to be said five times a day, turning towards the Ka'ba shrine in Mecca. Muslims unroll prayer mats and pray in a *mosque* (a 'place of prostration'), at home, or wherever they are, bowing and prostrating to God and reciting set verses from the Koran in Arabic. On Fridays there is congregational worship in central mosques attended by men but not normally by women, in which worship includes the formal prayers and usually a short sermon;

(iii) No collection of money is made in the mosque, but the third Pillar is Almsgiving, which provides for the sick and poor in lands where there are few social services;

(iv) The fourth Pillar is Fasting from food and drink, which is obligatory on all healthy adults during the hours of daylight for the whole of the ninth month, Ramadan. The sick, pregnant women, travellers and children are exempt, but adults should fast when restored to normal life. Some modern states extend exemption to students, soldiers and factory workers, and it is said that the true fast is from sin. Since the Islamic year is lunar, the date of Ramadan falls a little earlier each year compared with the solar calendar (see section on Calendars, Time Reckoning and Weights and Measures), and in northern countries fasting in summer is a considerable trial. The fast ends with one of the two great Muslim festivals, *Id al Fitr* (festival of breaking the fast) or *Little Bairam*;

(v) The fifth Pillar is Pilgrimage (*hajj*) to Mecca, which is incumbent at least once in a lifetime on every Muslim, who may then take the title *Hajji*. About 1m. pilgrims go every year to Mecca, which is the holy city forbidden to all but Muslims, and some take months or years to perform the ambition of a lifetime, travelling by air, sea, lorry or on foot. The pilgrimage is in the 12th month and must be performed in simple dress donned at a distance of 16 km from Mecca, women's heads covered, faces usually unveiled. The central ritual entails going round the Ka'ba seven times, kissing a Black Stone in its walls, and visiting hills outside Mecca where sheep and other animals are sacrificed. At the same time Muslims all over the world sacrifice sheep, and this constitutes the principal festival, *Id al Kabir*, *Qurban* or *Bairam*. This ceremony unites all Muslims and is popularly linked with Abraham's sacrifice of a sheep in place of his son. *Mouloud* (*Maulid*), the birthday of the Prophet, is another popular modern anniversary.

The Holy War (*Jihad*) was one means of the unparalleled spread of Islam in the first centuries, but despite pressures it has not been elevated into a Pillar of religion. Today theologians interpret the *Jihad* as war against sin in the soul.

The Koran (*Qur'ān*, 'recitation' or 'reading') is regarded as the very Word of God and not to be subjected to criticism. The Koran is about as long as the New Testament, in 114 chapters (*suras*) of uneven length, the longest ones coming first after the opening chapter. The Opening (*Fatiha*) is repeated twice at least at all times of daily prayer, preceded by the ascription 'in the name of God, the Merciful, the Compassionate'. Two short chapters at the end are also used in prayers, and instructed and pious Muslims may repeat other chapters, always in Arabic. Modern translations of the Koran are now allowed for private use and there have always been many commentaries. The chief message of the Koran is the majesty of God, his oneness, demand for human obedience and coming judgement. The later and longer chapters include much family and social legislation, for marriage, divorce, personal and communal behaviour.

The Koran is not the only authority for Muslims, but it is supplemented by numerous Traditions (*Hadith*), which include sayings attributed to the Prophet and his companions. Doctrine and morals are further interpreted by Comparison and Consent. Four law schools arose, which apply Islamic law (*shari'a*) to all activities of life. In Asia the two principal law schools are the *Hanafi* in central Asia and the Indian subcontinent, and the *Shafi'i* in the East Indies. In modern times interpretation of law ranges between conservative rigorism and modernism; many of the Traditions are debated but the Koran remains sacrosanct.

The Islamic community (*umma*) is the basis of the brotherhood of Islam, which from the early centuries aimed at making this religion international and above tribal rivalries. This is still the ideal, though the rise of nationalism has brought divisive interests into the Muslim world.

SECTS AND MYSTICS

The great majority, probably over 80%, of Muslims are *Sunni*, followers of 'the path', custom or tradition. They accept the first four caliphs (Abu Bakr, 'Umar, 'Uthman, 'Ali) as 'rightly guided', receive six authentic books of Traditions, and belong to one of the four schools of law. Other Muslims claim to follow true tradition but differ on its interpretation.

Shi'a Muslims

The major division came early. The Shi'a or 'followers' of 'Ali believed that as cousin and son-in-law of Muhammad, 'Ali should have been his first successor and they reject the first three caliphs of Sunni Islam. When at last his turn came, there was a division and another caliph was set up in Damascus. The Shi'a became linked with patriotism in Iraq, which objected to rule from Syria. Husain, a son of 'Ali, went to found a kingdom in Iraq, but was intercepted by rival troops and slain at Karbala. Husain became the great Shi'a martyr, the anniversary of whose death in Muharram, the first month of the Islamic calendar, is the occasion for days of mourning and long Passion Plays in Shi'a towns. At the climax of the play Husain receives the key of intercession from the Angel Gabriel and promises paradise to all who call upon him.

The basic Shi'a beliefs are the same as those of the Sunni, but 'Ali is added after Muhammad in the confession of faith. Their most distinctive doctrine is that of the *Imam*, spiritual 'leader', which was used in preference to caliph for the head of state. Most Shi'a are 'Twelvers', recognizing 12 Imams, of whom the last disappeared in AD 878, but it is believed that he will return again as the *Mahdi* ('guided one') to put down evil and restore righteousness on earth. In 1502 Shi'ism became the established religion of Iran, and it is strongest there and in Iraq and north India. *Ayatollahs* ('signs of God') are conservative religious leaders in Iran.

Isma'ilis

Some of the Shi'a are Isma'ilis, believing that it was the seventh Imam, Isma'il, who was the last when he disappeared in AD 765, hence they are also called 'Seveners'. There were political as well as religious reasons for the schism. There are mystical beliefs in the 'light' of the Imam, eternal and ever-present, and various grades of initiation into mysteries. There are small groups of Isma'ilis in Afghanistan and Central Asia, and larger ones in Pakistan, Bangladesh and India. Offshoots are most of the Khojas whose leader is the Aga Khan. These Isma'ili Khojas are found in Mumbai (Bombay), Gujarat, Sind, other Indian and neighbouring towns and in East Africa. They number over 200,000, in active and educated communities, noted for social works.

Ahmadiyya Movement

At Qadian in India and Lahore in Pakistan there are centres of a modern movement called Ahmadiyya, after Ghulam Ahmad of the Punjab who, from 1890, was set forth as the expected Mahdi, Messiah and Avatar. After struggles and divisions the Ahmadiyya have published many books in English, sent missionaries to Africa, and propounded teachings, most of which are orthodox Islam but with some modern polemics.

Sufis

Sufi mystics have been found in all branches of Islam from the early days, so called from the woollen (*suf*) robes that they wore, like Christian monks. In the face of orthodox formalism and deism, the Sufis taught the love of God, and sometimes this verged on pantheism or identity with God. The Sufis came to be accepted, partly through the efforts of the Persian philosopher, Ghazali, himself a mystic. Many popular shrines are tombs of holy men or sheikhs.

DISTRIBUTION

Most of the population of Afghanistan are Sunni Muslims. In Pakistan Islam is the state religion, about 97% of the population being Muslim. In Bangladesh by the year 2000 the number of Muslims was estimated at 127m. and, according to estimates from India, the number of Muslims in that country had also reached 127m. Indonesia is predominantly Muslim with over 150m. adherents, and it has a larger number of Muslims than any other country in the Islamic world. Islam is the state religion in Malaysia, followed by most Malays. There are Muslim minorities in Sri Lanka, Myanmar, Thailand and the Philippines. In China there are some large Muslim communities, mainly among the Wei Wuer (Uygur) and Hui minorities.

Hinduism

Hinduism, with an estimated 1,071m. adherents in 2000, is the name given by Europeans to the major religion of India.

HISTORICAL BACKGROUND

The name is derived from India and the River Indus in the north-west. Here flourished an extensive city culture from about 2500 to 1500 BC, contemporary with ancient Mesopotamia and Egypt. These cities were destroyed by invading Aryans, but remains indicate that Indus Valley religion included worship of a Mother Goddess and of a Lord of Yogis and animals, like Shiva, a great god today. A caste system arose from conquest and colour, at the head of which were the Brahmin priests who imposed their religion.

The Brahmins compiled the most ancient religious texts, the *Vedas* ('knowledge'), in four collections. These were not written down for many centuries but passed on orally. The early history of Hinduism is scanty, with no historical founder and no organized church, but development can be traced in religious texts. The Vedas are hymns to many gods of heaven and earth, and they portray a relatively simple religion in some ways like that of the Homeric Greeks, who were also Aryans. The Vedic hymns were probably compiled between 1500 and 800 BC, but their use was restricted to the upper castes. Today they are used only by priests and at marriage and funeral ceremonies. They were followed by the *Upanishads* ('sitting-down-near', teaching sessions), dialogues of which the principal were compiled between 800 and 300 BC. The Upanishads are called *Vedanta* ('end of the Vedas'), although this term is also used for some later philosophies. They discuss philosophical questions: the origins of the world and man, the nature of divinity and the human soul, death and immortality, self-discipline and devotion.

From this time onwards arose masses of religious works, which became the chief inspiration of most Hindus. Two great epic poems, the *Mahabharata*, 'great India' story, and the *Ramayana*, 'the story of Rama', include myth, history, theology and ethics. The personal gods of the Vedas reappear but with many others, no doubt from the Indus Valley and indigenous sources. A creating deity, Brahma, plays a small part, but Shiva, Vishnu and the Goddess come from now on to be the major deities of Hinduism. Vishnu, a minor Vedic god, became important through his *Avatars* ('descents'), visible embodiments on earth in animal and human form. The two chief human Avatars were Rama and Krishna, the latter a dark god of herdsmen, a warrior king, and a lover of the soul. A small section of the Great Epic is the *Bhagavad-Gita*, 'the Song of the Lord' Krishna, the best known of all Indian scriptures, which gives the teachings of the god Krishna on reincarnation, salvation, deity and devotion. Stories of Krishna and other gods continued in the *Puranas*, 'ancient tales', composed down to the Middle Ages. Many medieval Indian poets also produced popular songs in praise of Krishna, Rama, Shiva and the Goddess, and devotional groups flourished, especially in Bengal and southern India.

In modern times external influences and internal pressures brought reforms of Hinduism. Muslim invasions began in the eighth century AD, but became most potent under the rule of the Mughals from the 16th to the 19th centuries. Christian missions and European trade developed especially in the 19th and 20th centuries. Both Islam and Christianity criticized Hinduism for polytheism, idolatry and practices such as *suttee* (*satī*, widow-burning). Modern Hinduism is presented as 'eternal truth', including all that is best from other faiths but with its special emphasis either in pantheism or devotion.

BELIEFS

Belief in the indestructibility of the soul is basic to Hinduism; it is both pre-existence and post-existence. Transmigration from one life to another, or reincarnation, is universally held, but the endless births and deaths are a harsh cycle from which ways of salvation are offered, through knowledge, works or devotion. The next life is conditioned by *Karma*, 'works' or the entail of works. This explains the inequalities and sufferings of life, to those who accept it in faith, but it does not necessarily lead to fatalism. Karma can be improved by good actions, and the next rebirth may be to a higher level. Yet those who do wrong may descend to the animal level or even lower; hence there is a great respect for animal life and many Hindus are vegetarians.

From early times Indians have practised self-discipline, and there are many holy men, sadhus, swamis and the like. *Yoga* is a general name for both discipline and union, related to the English 'yoke'. It may consist in forms of physical exercise and control, in Hatha ('force') Yoga. Some adepts claim supernatural powers, like levitation. Most practitioners engage in breath-control and sit in cross-legged postures. Raja ('royal') Yoga proceeds to mastery of mind, concentration or emptying of thought, and attainment of supreme knowledge or bliss.

The Caste System

The caste system greatly developed over the centuries. There are four basic castes: Brahmin priests, Raja or Kshatriya rulers and warriors, Vaishya artisan merchants and Shudra servants. The first three are 'twice born' through initiation with sacred threads at adolescence. However, the castes have been expanded with many local and occupational castes, said to number over 3,000, with further sub-castes, and below these are millions of outcastes who perform the most menial tasks. Caste distinctions are rigid in theory, and Brahmins in particular are offended by any contact with low castes; eating between castes is prohibited. Many occupational and guild distinctions remain, but modern conditions, liberal laws and closer communications are breaking down exclusiveness. Communal quarrels arise between castes and religions, particularly in anything that touches the sacredness of the cow.

TEMPLES AND WORSHIP

India is a land of magnificent architectural monuments, most of them religious. The temples have small inner sanctuaries surrounded by large open paved courtyards, tanks for ritual washing, and walls with stone gates and towers. Temple worship is performed by priests without much lay assistance, but people visit the courtyards for quiet prayer and meditation.

Modern temples are less impressive, but there are countless little shrines by the wayside or in the middle of streets, at which people stop to place gifts and pray. Hindu homes have rooms or corners for images and devotion, where flowers are placed and incense burns. Worship is performed at home. There is no sabbath or regular obligation to visit temples, but for festivals and annual events great crowds assemble there, when images are carried in procession in chariots or on elephants.

There are countless holy places, from the Himalayas in the north to the extreme southern capes, and pilgrimages are made to seven chief sites. The holiest place of all is Varanasi (Banaras) on the middle Ganges, where steps (*ghats*) lead down from temples into the sacred river in which people wash and pray. 'Burning ghats' are reserved for cremation, the normal lot of the Hindu dead. Varanasi is full of holy men, dressed in yellow robes or smeared with ashes, begging and awaiting death in the sacred city. Great assemblies are held here and at other places every few years, at which millions of people gather to bathe in the river.

There are many Hindu festivals and all deities have sacred days. *Holi* in the spring is an ancient fertility feast when coloured water is sprinkled on participants and the praises of Krishna and his loves are chanted. *Dashara* or *Dassehra* in the autumn is marked by carnival figures of the hero Rama and his demon enemy, Ravana, the latter being packed with crackers which are set alight at the end. *Divali* in November is a feast of lights for the gracious goddess, Lakshmi, consort of Vishnu, when lamps welcome the patroness of wealth, business and learning. In other popular feasts the god of fortune, Ganesha, son of Shiva, is carried in the form of images of pink elephants, or Shiva, the lord both of Yoga and the dance, is depicted as the dancing god within a flaming circle, often represented in bronze images.

ORGANIZATION AND DISTRIBUTION

There is little widespread organization in Hindu religion. The followers of Shiva, Vishnu and the Mother are joined in their own cult sympathy, and sometimes divided between cults in antagonism. There are centres of learning and worship, but many local differences of practice. Monasteries and retreat houses (*ashrams*) cater for cults and societies, but no large-scale monastic organization compares with those of Buddhism and Christianity. Many Hindu holy men are solitaries, and may be seen sitting alone or living in secluded places with a few disciples.

In modern times the Brahmo and Arya Samaj have organized themselves, and also significant is the Ramakrishna Mission. Taking its name from a 19th-century holy man of Bengal, Shri Ramakrishna, and directed by his disciple Swami Vivekananda, the Mission initiated religious, educational and social works and undertakes much literary propaganda. The Vishwa Hindu Parishad (World Hindu Council) takes religious and political action to promote the role of Hinduism as the religion of India, and it inspired action against the Islamic Babri mosque at Ayodhya (see Recent History of India). From Pondicherry, south of Chennai (Madras), the Aurobindo Ashram engages in meditation, education, industrial work and literary propaganda, and there are many smaller similar agencies.

Hinduism is virtually confined to the peoples of the Indian subcontinent, although it is practised also in Bali and by peoples of Indian origin in Sri Lanka. It has commonly been said that a Hindu is one born into a caste and who accepts the Vedic scriptures, and therefore it is an ethnic and not a missionary religion; but in past centuries Hinduism spread as far away as Bali and Cambodia, and today some of its missionaries choose Europe and North America as their fields.

Other Indian Religions

ZOROASTRIANISM

This ancient religion, which in origins was akin to that of the Aryan Indians, was practised by related peoples in Iran, but it survives today mainly in small communities in India. The Parsis (Persians) migrated to India from the ninth century onwards under pressure from Muslim invaders. They settled mainly in the region of Mumbai, although there are groups elsewhere in India and East Africa, numbering in all about 218,000. The prophetic reformer of the religion was Zoroaster (Zarathushtra), generally dated 630–553 BC. He taught faith in one God, Ahura Mazda ('Lord Wisdom'), who was goodness opposed to the spirit of evil, Ahriman. In hymns, *Gathas*, attributed to him, Zoroaster told of visions of the heavenly court to which he was summoned, and received the doctrines and duties that would reform his country's religion. Following set-backs in its first decade, the movement attracted support in Bactria to the east of Persia, and after years of preaching, Zoroaster was killed in a struggle with opposing priests. His religion slowly developed, led by priests called *Magi*, and in the early Christian centuries it became the state religion of Iran until the Muslim conquest in the seventh century AD. There are now some 50,000 Zoroastrians in Iran.

Beliefs and Practice

The basic Parsi scriptures are the *Avesta*, which include hymns and ritual and practical regulations and are still recited in ancient Persian. Belief in the opposition of the good and evil spirits has caused this religion to be called dualistic, but Parsis believe that the dualism is temporary since Ahura Mazda (Ohrmazd) will triumph. There is a strong moral emphasis, and its followers call it the Religion of the Good Life; by virtuous conduct and moderation men help God to overcome evil. Ahura Mazda is the supreme God, but there are other angelic and demonic spirits. Especially important is Mithra or Meher, a god of the old Iranian religion, who now becomes the judge at death. Belief in life after death is strong in Zoroastrianism and probably influenced Judaism and Christianity with its ideas of angels and demons, the end of the world, judgement and eternal life. It is believed that departed souls have their deeds weighed in scales and then cross a narrow bridge to paradise; the evil fall into a purgatory but eventually all are saved.

Parsi temples contain no images, but sacred fire always burns there, fed by sandalwood. Thus, they are called 'fire temples' by other Indians. The dead are disposed of in 'towers of silence' where vultures destroy the flesh, which must not defile the earth or fire. Some of these towers are outside Mumbai, though closed to the public. A decline in vulture numbers owing to disease, however, in 2001 prompted the Parsi community of Mumbai to install a solar reflector at the site in order to accelerate the process of decomposition, pending the implementation of a vulture-breeding programme. Elsewhere Parsi dead are buried in lead coffins. There have been reforms in modern times, and religious instruction is given in new expositions of the faith. Parsi priests wear white robes, while old Parsis have traditional dress with hard hats and robes, but many Parsis wear modern European or Indian dress. As a small ingrown community, the Parsis are highly educated, and in trade and public service they play a disproportionately large role. Women are emancipated, enter temples equally with men, and take part in educational and public affairs.

JAINISM

The Jains are an Indian religious community, numbering an estimated 4.3m. in the year 2000. It is possible that the religion existed in India before the arrival of the Aryan invaders in about 1500 BC, since its beliefs in reincarnation and types of asceticism seem to have been non-Aryan. The Jains say that their religion is eternal and is renewed in successive ages by *Jinas* ('conquerors'), of whom there have been 24 at long intervals in the present world aeon. The last Jina was given the title of Mahavira ('great man') and lived in the sixth century BC, a little before Gautama Buddha, whose life was similar in some ways. After the death of his parents, Mahavira left his wife and family (though one sect says he was celibate) and went about naked begging alms and seeking enlightenment. He achieved this after 13 years, and became a *Jina* and omniscient. He is said to have had great success, with a community of 50,000 monks and nuns and many lay followers. Mahavira died in the lower Ganges valley, entering *Nirvana*, the 'blowing out' of desire and life.

Beliefs and Practice

Jains do not believe in a creator God, since the world is eternal, and they have been called atheistic. The 24 *Jinas*, however, are objects of worship, and some Hindu gods also figure in their temple imagery. Jains believe in the eternity of countless souls, which are immersed in matter and evil, but by renunciation of desire they can rise to Nirvana at the ceiling of the universe. Monks are the nearest to salvation, and sectarian differences divide the 'white-clad' monks in robes from the 'sky-clad' who are naked. The best known Jain doctrine is 'non-violence' or harmlessness (*ahimsa*). All life is sacred; this involves vegetarianism and abstention from taking any life by hunting, farming or fishing. Monks sweep the ground in their path to avoid treading on insects, filter their drink, and wear cloths before their mouths to keep out insects. In modern times Jain stress on non-violence has inspired reformers, like the Hindu Mahatma Gandhi.

Despite ascetic practices and absence of deity, the Jains have built some of the most splendid temples in India through the patronage of rich followers. The main anniversary is at the end of August when wrongs are confessed, fasting practised, and the birthday of Mahavira is celebrated. The Hindu feast of *Divali* is also popular, and the goddess Lakshmi is invoked for success. Being excluded from many occupations that involve taking or endangering life, the Jains have prospered in commerce and are influential in public affairs. Some modern Jains try to adapt asceticism to current conditions, but monks continue on the hard way to Nirvana.

SIKHISM

The Sikhs are one of the largest Indian religious minorities, with the number of followers estimated at 24m. in the year 2000. The men are easily recognizable by turbans and beards. The Sikh religion is relatively modern and developed, like Hindu devotional movements, with some influence from Islam.

Medieval Hindu poets sang the praises of Krishna and Rama, the Avatars of Vishnu, and in the 15th century Kabir concentrated on Rama as the sole deity. Kabir was a Muslim weaver of Varanasi, but was trained by a Hindu teacher. He taught that there is one God behind the many names of Allah, Rama and Krishna. Kabir composed and sang poems denouncing priests and scriptures. He suffered persecution, but at his death both Hindus and Muslims claimed him for their own and established rival shrines. The followers of the path of Kabir, *Kabirpanthis*, number about 1m., chiefly in north-central India.

A little later in the Punjab lived Nanak (1469–1538) who founded the Sikhs. He was a Hindu who also sought the unity of God and had a vision in which he was told to teach faith in God as the True Name. He travelled widely, but was most successful in the Punjab where groups of *Sikhs* ('disciples') followed him. Nanak was the great *Guru* ('teacher'), and though he was followed by nine other Gurus they were regarded as essentially identical to Guru Nanak. The Sikhs suffered persecution from the Muslims. The 10th Guru, Gobind Singh, founded an inner militant society, Khalsa ('the pure'), with initiation by a sword and adding the name Singh ('lion') to all initiates. Members of the Khalsa have five marks: beard and hair uncut (hence the turban), wearing shorts, steel comb in hair, steel bangle on the right wrist, and steel dagger at the side. With this militant force the Sikhs won independence in the Punjab until British rule intervened. At the partition of India in 1947 the line between India and Pakistan ran across the Punjab, and the Sikhs rose to assert their independence. They were subsequently expelled from Pakistan and placed within the Indian state, although constant moves have been made towards fuller autonomy.

Beliefs and Practice

Sikhs believe in one God, with Guru Nanak his perfect teacher, and their temples have no images. Their scriptures, the *Adi Granth* ('first book'), contain poems by Kabir and Hindu and Muslim composers, as well as by Guru Nanak and other Gurus. It is an anthology of lofty religious verse which is chanted daily, in the Punjabi language, by Sikhs in public and private devotion.

Sikh temples are usually white buildings with golden domes, and alongside is a tank or small lake for ritual washing. The Adi Granth scriptures are carried into the temple at dawn and chanted by relays of readers until nightfall, when the book is returned to a treasury. The principal shrine is the Golden Temple at Amritsar, the most sacred Sikh town and centre of administration. Sikhs are found in many Indian cities, as well as in Africa, Europe and North America, but their strength remains in the Punjab.

Buddhism

Buddhism arose in India, although it has almost disappeared there. Its great successes as a missionary religion have been in South-East and East Asia, to which it took Indian thought and culture.

HISTORICAL BACKGROUND

The founder was named Siddhartha, but is more generally known by the family name of Gautama (the Sanskrit form; Gotama in Pali), or from his clan Shakyamuni, 'the sage of the Shakyas'. The dates commonly accepted for Gautama by Western scholars are 563–483 BC, though Chinese Buddhists put them hundreds of years earlier. Primary evidence is scanty, and begins with inscriptions made by the Emperor Ashoka from about 260 BC, some of which still remain.

Gautama was born in Lumbini, in Nepal (the place being marked by a stone), of a local king and into the warrior caste rather than the priestly Brahmin. From many legends it is clear that his parents were married, the birth was not virginal, and the boy grew up in relative seclusion but was married and had a son. Riding outside the palace at the age of 29, Gautama saw four signs: an old man, a sick man, a corpse and an ascetic. These showed him the suffering of the world, and the calm of leaving it, and led to his great renunciation. He left his wife and child by night, and for years tried various teachers and ways towards enlightenment but without success. Finally, near Gaya on a tributary of the Ganges, Gautama sat under a tree called the Bo or Bodhi-tree, the 'tree of enlightenment', and waited for light to come. After a day and a night knowledge came; he understood the rising and passing away of beings, the cause of suffering, the end of rebirth and the way to Nirvana. Now he was a Buddha, an 'enlightened one', and went to preach his doctrine in a park to the north of the holy city of Varanasi.

The Buddha was followed at first by small groups of monks and laymen but soon became successful, especially in middle India, where the town of Rajagriha (modern Rajgir) was a centre for the religion. For some 40 years the Buddha went about teaching. The monastic order (*Sangha*) was the centre of activity, and after some hesitation orders of nuns were formed as well. Finally, the Buddha died after eating tainted food and was cremated, tradition saying that his relics were divided among eight regions.

At the Buddha's death, 500 monks met in a cave, and the chief disciple, Ananda, recited the *Vinaya*, the monkish rules that form the first part of the Buddhist scriptures. The Buddha and his followers came into conflict with Brahmin priests, Jains, Yoga teachers and others, and taught that the way of the Buddha was best. They rejected the Hindu scriptures and were regarded as heretics. There was also some caste rivalry, and possibly Buddhism inherited both some of the communal differences and the religious beliefs of the ancient Indus Valley cultures.

A great impulse to the spread of Buddhism was given by Ashoka in the third century BC, who turned from martial conquests to the peaceful way of Buddhism, inscribing decrees ordering faith and morality, restoring Buddhist sacred sites, and sending missionaries to Sri Lanka and elsewhere. Buddhism became the dominant religion of South-East Asia, despite some remains of ancient animism. In the first century AD Buddhist monks took scriptures, images and relics to China, and in the sixth century to Japan, in both countries mingling with local religions, which retained much of their appeal. In the land of its origin Buddhism flourished for over 1,000 years, but finally almost died out in India under pressure from reviving Hindu devotional cults and destruction of temples and monasteries by invading Muslims. Recently there has been some Buddhist success among the Indian outcastes, claiming 5m. converts.

BELIEFS

The Buddha taught *Dharma* (or *Dhamma*) which is law, virtue, right, religion or truth, and this is expounded as the Middle Way between the extremes of sensuality and asceticism. At his enlightenment Gautama saw the solution of the suffering that had troubled him and enunciated it in the Four Noble Truths. These are: the universal fact of suffering, the cause of suffering which is craving or desire, the cessation of suffering by ending craving, and the method of cessation by the Noble Eightfold Path. This Path is a way of discipline in eight steps, each of which is called Right. They fall into three groups, the first beginning the path in Right View and Resolve. Then come practical activity in Right Speech, Action and Livelihood. Finally, there are higher spiritual states: Right Effort, Concentration and Contemplation.

This is a scheme of moral and spiritual improvement without reference to the Hindu gods. Some of them appear in Buddhist legend but always subservient to the Buddha. The Hindu teaching of the impersonal divine Brahman seems to have been unknown to the Buddha and his system has been called atheistic or agnostic; but in fact the Buddha himself is the supreme and omniscient teacher and object of adoration. A Buddhist does not save himself, but he relies on the teaching of experts and the celestial Buddha.

The Buddha also criticized the Hindu doctrine of the soul, which he declared could not be identified with any of the bodily elements. At death the five constituents of the body dissolved and were not passed on to another life. Yet Buddhism held firmly to the Indian belief in rebirth, and the cycle of existence was caused by desire from which one could escape only by following the path of the Buddha. The link between one life and another was *Karma*, the entail of deeds that determined a higher or lower destiny in the next life. To become free from this round of existence was the supreme goal, the indescribable *Nirvana* (*Nibbana*), the 'blowing out' of desire and life.

Northern Buddhism

The above are the basic beliefs of southern Buddhists, but in the north further doctrines developed in which multitudes of celestial beings offered gracious help to mankind. Southern Buddhists believe that there have been several Buddhas in the past and there will be some in the future, the next one, Maitreya, being a fat jolly figure bringing fortune. In the present long world aeon, however, there is only one Buddha, the supreme Gautama. In northern Buddhism not only are thousands of Buddhas accepted now but there are countless *Bodhisattvas* ('beings of enlightenment'), who have deferred their own salvation until all beings are saved. This led to a universalism and a religion of faith and grace, which was able to absorb many Chinese and other deities in the guise of Bodhisattvas. The Chinese Kwanyin (Japanese Kwannon) is the 'lady of compassion', not a goddess but a Bodhisattva, a kindly giver of children and a saviour who immediately hears the cries of all suppliants. In Tibet (Xizang) the Dalai Lama is the incarnation of this Bodhisattva, not of Gautama.

More abstruse philosophical doctrines were also taught in northern Buddhism: the three bodies of the Buddha, and an idealistic doctrine of the Void in which Buddhas and believers are merged in a neutral monism somewhat like the Hindu Brahman. There were links with Chinese Daoism in this pantheism, and later Zen Buddhism emerged from the fusion of ideas. On the popular level, *Pure Land* Buddhism offered the hope of a Western paradise, presided over by another Buddha, Amida.

SCHOOLS AND ORGANIZATION

The southern Buddhists call themselves *Theravada*, followers of the 'tradition of the elders'. They are concentrated in Sri Lanka, Myanmar (formerly Burma), Thailand, Laos and Cambodia, where their graceful buildings, dagobas, pagodas or wats, decorate towns and countryside. Here relics are enshrined, innumerable Buddha images sit in various postures, and worshippers go to meditate. Traditional education was in the monasteries, which are still strong. Yellow-robed monks go on begging rounds every morning, and scholars study the scriptures, the *Tripitaka* ('three baskets'). There are minor sects but general uniformity of belief and practice.

The northern Buddhists are *Mahayana*, followers of the 'great Vehicle' to salvation, as against the others whom they call *Hinayana*, of the 'small Vehicle'. In Tibet Mahayana Buddhism has traditionally been the state religion, incorporating some beliefs of a primitive Bon religion whose gods are taken as guardians of Buddhism. There are two chief schools of monks, the Yellow Hats being reformed and dominant, and the Red Hats of an earlier tradition. The chief monks are lamas, of whom the head is the Dalai Lama. In 1959 he fled from Tibet to exile in India, where he remained in 2002. Despite Chinese oppression, Buddhism continues to be the religion of the Tibetan people.

Buddhism in China and Japan

Buddhism was at first opposed in China, since it withdrew young men from active life into monasteries and its teaching seemed to be contrary to the popular cults of the ancestors. Yet, despite some fierce persecutions, Buddhism became part of Chinese life and exercised a great influence not only on religion but on culture and the arts. Confucian scholars criticized the use of relics but popular devotion cherished them, and Buddhist monks became particularly active in reciting texts at funerals and memorial services. Chinese Buddhism evolved the popular *Pure Land* sects, the meditative *Chan*, and the scholarly and tolerant *Dian-Dai*. Under communism, Buddhist activity has been severely curtailed, and many monasteries have been closed or converted into schools and barracks; but there has also been extensive restoration of Buddhist centres in the interests of antiquarian study and the preservation of monuments of national culture, in famous cave-temples and grottoes in Shanxi, Henan and Xinjiang. A strictly-controlled Chinese Buddhist Association was founded in 1953. In 1997 a document issued by the Chinese Government claimed that there were 200,000 Buddhist monks and nuns and 13,000 temples. Tibet was said to have 46,000 monks and nuns.

In Japan Buddhism appealed to both leaders and people. In the sixth century AD it came first from Korea and then from China, and it developed writing and Chinese culture. Buddhism soon gained a firm footing in Japan under the regent Prince Shotoku, who was regarded as an incarnation of the Bodhisattva Kwannon. Buddhism came to terms with the ancient Japanese Shinto religion by declaring that the Shinto gods were manifestations of Buddha originals. When the colossal bronze Buddha at Nara was begun, the emperor received the blessing of the chief Shinto deity. A synthesis called Dual (*Ryobu*) Shinto was formed in which Buddhists controlled all but the most important Shinto shrines. This lasted over 1,000 years, until the Shinto revival in 1868 when Ryobu Shinto was abolished. Buddhism came under attack for a time, but it had entered too deeply into Japanese life and its contribution to thought and the arts could not be hidden.

Japanese Buddhism adopted Chinese schools: *Pure Land* as *Jodo*, and *Dian-Dai* as *Tendai*. The school of Nichiren opposed the emotional cults by claiming to return to the original teaching of the Buddha, but he was still the glorified Shakyamuni sitting on a Vulture Peak in the Himalayas. Chinese Chan became known to a wider world through Japanese *Zen* (both based on an Indian word for 'meditation'). It stressed the search for enlightenment in daily work and so encouraged many arts. It also became popular with the military, the Samurai warriors, in Zen teaching of martial arts. Zen teachers are critical of some traditional texts, but they use basic ones in meditation techniques and they have monasteries where Zen is taught. Zen monks are the only ones in Japan who continue the daily begging round.

Japanese Buddhism has developed congregational worship more than other parts of the Buddhist world, and there are great temples with lavish ritual services. There are modern sectarian movements that show the influence of Shinto naturalism and sometimes of Christianity. From Japan Buddhist missions have gone to the Pacific islands, especially Hawaii, and the western coast of the USA.

Organization

The different Buddhist schools have loose organization. Traditionally, monasteries have been the centres of doctrine and discipline, and their chief abbots are the religious authorities; in centralized systems such as Tibet the Dalai Lama and the Panchen Lama disputed the supremacy. Monks and nuns are, of course, celibate, but where there are large numbers of priests, as in Japan, they are usually married. Since the days of Ashoka, laymen have been encouraged to attend the monasteries at weekly or fortnightly special days, and many go there also for meditation during the rainy season.

Other East Asian Religions

CONFUCIANISM

It has been debated whether Confucianism was a religion, but what has been known in the West under this title was a compound of ancient Chinese popular cults, ancestral worship, state ritual and moral precepts. Alongside, and often mingling with this Confucianism, were also indigenous Daoism and imported Buddhism, which together have been called the Three Religions or rather Three Ways of China, since none of them was an exclusive system.

Kongfuzi or Master Kong, latinized as Confucius (551–478 BC), lived in the state of Lu in north China. Of humble rank and largely self-educated, he became a teacher asking questions and giving maxims, like a Chinese Socrates, rather than a systematic philosopher. Some of his pupils came to occupy high office, but although in later life Confucius toured the country looking for a state that would put his ideas into practice, he was unsuccessful. It is said, on dubious grounds, that he then compiled the Chinese Classics, the *Book of History*, the *Book of Odes* and the *Book of Changes*, and also the *Annals of Lu*. Confucius was not a founder of a religion, though he criticized some forms of ritual. His thoughts are found in a small book called *Analects* (*Lun Yu*), and they emphasize the importance of propriety (*li*) in personal and social conduct. Filial piety and correct observance of ancestral cults are commended, and the duties of rulers to subjects as well as servants to masters. His personal religious attitude appears in the sense of Heaven (*Tian*) inspiring him, judging his acts and hearing prayer.

About a century later his most famous follower, Mencius, praised Confucius as the greatest of all sages, and he was more successful in advising rulers to follow just and peaceful ways. The cult of Confucius grew slowly: by the second century BC Chinese emperors adapted his teachings to their purposes, and in AD 59 sacrifice was ordered to Confucius in every school. He was called 'the Teacher of ten thousand generations', but he was not deified and Confucian halls were different from the temples of other religions, with memorial tablets instead of images. The scholars (mandarins) were concerned with the preservation of the teachings of Confucius, and until this century examinations for public service were in the Confucian classics.

The popular religion of China was a worship of nature and hero gods, similar to those of India or ancient Greece. In the villages the gods of earth were the most important for work, and the god of the hearth dominated homes. 'Wall and moat' gods protected towns, and storm and disease spirits were propitiated at need. The local cults were idealized in great state functions when the emperor sacrificed to heaven on the marble terraces of the Temple of Heaven in Beijing, or paid homage to the agricultural gods at a great altar of Land and Grain. The emperor ploughed the first furrow in spring and cut the first corn in summer, as a model for the country.

Cults of the ancestors were highly developed in China, though it has been claimed that they were derived from filial piety and not religious worship. Great expense was made at funerals and incense burnt daily before the tablets of the recently dead. Later the tablets were removed to ancestral halls, with the tablet of the family founder on the highest shelf. At the winter solstice sacrifices were offered and food eaten communally. In the Festival of Hungry Souls lighted paper boats are sent sailing down rivers to help the dead in their journey to the afterworld.

In modern times many of the old temples and images of village and town gods have been destroyed, but ancestral ceremonies are still widely observed. Confucius has been condemned as a feudalist but also honoured as the greatest national teacher. Six years after his tomb was redecorated, it was ransacked by 'Red Guards', although these depredations were made good in 1981. Yet Confucianism has not been classified as a religion, and remains as an invisible force in which some of the old attitudes continue in new guise.

DAOISM

Daoism (Taoism) is China's indigenous nature and personal religion and inspires much of its culture and philosophy. The word Dao is a path or way, regarded as the true principle of life and the universe. There is a Dao of heaven, a Dao of earth and a Dao of man, which is harmony with these. In Confucian writings Dao is moral and practical, but in Daoism it is mystical and universal.

Lao Zi is a legendary figure who is said to have lived just before Confucius and rebuked him, but this reflects later controversy. Lao Zi is said to have written the *Dao De Jing*, the classic of 'the Way and its Power', in 81 chapters. This is a charming and profound work, perhaps written in the third century BC by an anonymous quietist. Dao is here called indefinable and eternal, it cannot be grasped, but by quietness its influence extends over the 10,000 material things. This is a nature mysticism, in which a favourite symbol is water, which passively overcomes everything. Formal morality is opposed by 'actionless activity', and militarism is strongly repudiated.

Two centuries later this quietism was taken further by Zhuang Zi, who taught that men should live according to nature and practise a kind of Yoga or 'sitting in forgetfulness'. The *Yang* and *Yin*, positive and negative principles of nature, are seen in heaven and earth, light and dark, male and female, and are symbolized in the circle with two pear-shaped halves that appears in much oriental decoration. Daoists began the search for supernatural powers which would come by living naturally, controlling breathing, eating uncooked food and walking through fire. Anchorites lived in the country drinking dew, and expeditions set out for the Isles of the Blest whose inhabitants were supposed to be immortal. The unfortunate associations with magic led Daoism into superstition, and the close link of its priests with the people brought many temples of earth and city gods under their care.

When Buddhism arrived in China it was both opposed and imitated by the indigenous religions. Daoist temples and images multiplied, and rituals for helping the living and the dead developed from Buddhist examples. Lao Zi received the title of 'Emperor of Mysterious Origin' and other gods were added to form a pantheon, which had huge and often frightening images, while heavens and hells dazzled the pious. More philosophical was the mingling of Daoism and Buddhism in the Chan (Zen) sect, which sought enlightenment by the way of nature. In the arts Daoism had great influence by applying the principle of 'seeing without looking' to painting and writing.

Nowadays condemnation of superstitions has led to the outward decline of Daoism, except in Hong Kong, Taiwan and Malaysia. In China the association of Daoism with secret societies made it the potent force in revolts like the Boxer Rising in 1900, and the Pervading-Unity Dao society, which was crushed only in the 1950s. A governmental Chinese Daoist Association was established in 1957, later than societies controlling other religions. The spirit of Daoism, however, remains as a pervading influence in Chinese life. According to government figures, there are 25,000 Daoist priests and nuns.

SHINTO

When Buddhist monks arrived in Japan in the sixth century AD they called the religion of the country *Shen-Dao*, the 'Way of the Gods', contrasted with the Way of the Buddha. There was little writing, and the monks recorded the Chronicles of Japan (*Nihongi*), which give Shinto mythology and traditional lore.

It is said that in the beginning heaven and earth were not yet separated into *Yo* and *In*, like the Chinese *Yang* and *Yin*. Then appeared the chief deity, the sun goddess, Amaterasu. Her brother the storm god, Susanowo, made Amaterasu hide in the cave of heaven until she was induced to emerge by other deities, a myth explaining light and dark, summer and winter, and eclipses. Later Amaterasu sent her grandson Ninigi to rule the earth and marry the goddess of Mt Fuji, and they were the ancestors of the first Emperor of Japan, Jimmu Tenno. Thus, the royal family claimed descent from the supreme deity, while other notables took various gods as their ancestors.

There are countless Shinto deities, associated with mountains and earth, rain and wind, sea and harbours, food and fertility. One of the most popular is Inari, the rice god, who is represented by the fox and has many images in this form. Japanese love of nature appears in pilgrimages that are made to sacred mountains, and in the location of their temples. Traditionally, Shinto temples were small wooden buildings, based on ancient patterns which are constantly renewed, situated in large parks with fountains and decorative rocks, but many smaller shrines are found by the wayside or in towns.

When Buddhism came, Dual Shinto was formed and many temples came under Buddhist control, being embellished with images and ritual. After the first contact with Europeans, Japan was closed to the West from the 17th century to 1854, and the country was ruled by feudal dictators (shogun). Yet Shinto revival gathered strength and was associated with the Emperor as the descendant of Amaterasu. In 1868 the Emperor Meiji was restored to effective power and State Shinto was established. Adoration of the Emperor grew and reverence to the imperial portrait was imposed in all public life and in schools, even those of Buddhists and Christians. For a time it was said that Shinto was a world religion, since the Emperor was child of the sun. This Emperor-centred Shinto was not traditional, although it inspired fanatical patriotism, and in 1946 the Emperor repudiated 'the fictitious idea that the Emperor is manifest god'.

The State Shinto shrines were disestablished in 1947 and had to rely on public support. Nevertheless, many great national shrines, like that of Amaterasu at Ise, have remained important and are attended on occasions of national significance. The ordinary Shinto shrines are directed by bodies of priests who perform the rituals, and lay people attend to offer prayers and recite texts. The quietness and beauty of the surroundings add to their attraction, and they are visited by families. In Japanese homes there are shelves for Shinto or Buddhist symbols, at which incense, leaves and water are regularly offered.

Sect Shinto

After the establishment of State Shinto, it was seen that distinctions would have to be made for popular modern movements, which were called Sect Shinto. Some of the new sects are Buddhist, and others centre on mountain pilgrimages, but the most notable are communities in which healing by faith is important. They are like societies or churches, with known founders, and relatively monotheistic. 'The Teaching of Golden Light' (*Konko-kyo*) was founded in the 19th century by Kawade Bunjiro, who said that the god of golden metal possessed him and was the sole deity. Though a Shinto priest, Bunjiro denounced narrow patriotism and taught the need for sincere rather than ritual prayer. At about the same time a woman, Miki Nakayama, founded 'the Teaching of Heavenly Wisdom' (*Tenri-kyo*). She practised healing by faith, and encouraged her followers to work communally at building temples, schools and houses. A new city of Tenri has been built round a sanctuary where it is believed that a new age will soon begin. This is one of the richest and largest religious organizations, with more than 3m. followers and thousands of missionary teachers.

In 1930 the 'Creative-Value Study Society' (*Soka Gakkai*) arose from the militant Nichiren sect of Japanese Buddhism. Suppressed during the Second World War, it has strong support among the working classes, and has been linked with the Komeito, a political party that has members in the Japanese Diet.

Christianity in Asia and the Pacific

Christianity began as an Asian religion and, although its principal expansion was to the West, it has remained in minorities in the Near East and has spread in missions to most Asian countries. The Syrian Orthodox Church in India claims to have been founded by the Apostle Thomas, and there is evidence of its existence at least from the fifth century. The rites and traditions are derived from the Jacobite Church of Syria, which separated from other Orthodox churches after the Council of Chalcedon in AD 451. These Indian churches are divided into Orthodox Syrian and Mar Thoma Syrian, and a further section has been in communion with Rome since the 17th century as one of its Uniate churches. These Syrian Christians are found almost exclusively in Malabar, Travancore and Cochin, and number over 2m. Other Christian communities all over India are the result of modern Western missions and have 45m. adherents, of whom more than half are Roman Catholics. In Pakistan there are 2m. Christians.

Myanmar (formerly Burma) has 4m. Christians and Sri Lanka 1.7m. Christians, the latter being largely Roman Catholic and found in Sinhalese, Tamil and mixed communities. In Indonesia there are over 31m. Christians, mostly Protestant, and both they and Roman Catholics have seen massive increases in recent years. In Viet Nam almost 6m. Christians survive under communist rule, with church leadership being elderly but with young people attracted to house-churches led by lay activists. In Korea churches were closed in the North under communism, and 2m. Christians fled to the South where numbers have risen dramatically, with mass baptisms especially of Protestants. There are now 21m. Christians in the Republic of Korea.

China has witnessed numerous attempts at evangelization, from Nestorian Christians in the seventh century, Roman Catholic orders in the 16th, to modern Catholic and Protestant missions. Anti-imperialist movements brought the formation of a self-governing Chinese Christian Three-Self Patriotic Church for all Protestants in 1958, small denominations being closed and all missionaries expelled. A Chinese Patriotic Catholic Association was also created, and bishops were consecrated without the authority of the Vatican. All outward forms of religion were forbidden during the Cultural Revolution of 1966–76. Some churches, especially in the cities, subsequently reopened, but reconciliation with Rome has not occurred. Official estimates indicate 10m. Chinese Protestants and 4m. Catholics, while an 'underground' Roman Catholic Church, loyal to the Pope, claims a large following.

In Japan there were successful Catholic missions in the 16th century, but Christianity was banned from 1613. Some converts continued to practise religion in secret as Hidden Christians (*Sempuku* or *Kakure Kirishitan*). With the opening of Japan to the West, foreign missions returned in 1859. Most of the Hidden Christians were absorbed into the Roman Catholic Church, but some 30,000 still prefer to remain independent. Under nationalist pressure all Protestant churches were joined in a United Church (*Kyodan*) in 1940. Some refused to join—Anglicans, Adventists and Salvation Army—and although officially they ceased to exist, they revived after 1945. There are many Japanese indigenous Christian denominations, parallel to Buddhist and Shinto sects. A notable Non-church Movement (*Mukyokai*), founded in 1900, has no buildings, priests or organization but is firmly based on the Bible. Christians of all denominations are estimated at more than 5m.

The Philippines is the most predominantly Christian nation in Asia, with over 70m. Roman Catholics and 5m. Protestants, but a Protestant Independent Church of Christ has more members than any mission-founded church. Missions arrived in the 16th century, and mass movement led to the formal Christianization of the whole population within a century, with indigenous culture largely replaced by that of the Spanish missionaries. The Constitution of 1973 separated church and state and guaranteed religious freedom, but it invoked 'the aid of the Divine Providence'. The churches long supported the establishment, but they were divided under the Marcos dictatorship, and most favoured the change to the Aquino Government in early 1986.

In Oceania both Christian missions to indigenous populations and the influx of many Europeans, especially in Australasia, led to the dominance of Christianity. In Hawaii 68% of the people are Christian, and in Papua New Guinea the figure is 96%. The Constitution of Samoa (formerly Western Samoa) makes it a Christian state, but in American Samoa church and state are separated. In Fiji 83% of ethnic Fijians are claimed as Christian but, with 80% of Fijian Indians being Hindus, there have been religious and political clashes leading to a military coup by native Fijians in 1987. Indigenous churches resulted from schisms in Fiji. Similarly, in Tonga Methodists were divided into four denominations, with the monarch as head of the original mission organization, the Free Wesleyan Church. The Evangelical Church is stronger than the Roman Catholic in French Polynesia, but the position is reversed in New Caledonia, which has a large French population.

According to the 1996 census, Roman Catholics are the most numerous in Australia, where 70.9% were counted as Christian (27.0% Catholic, 22.0% Anglican). The Roman Catholic community has increased owing to the immigration of Irish, Italians and Spaniards. The Australian state is secular, but 'the blessing of Almighty God' is invoked in the Constitution. In New Zealand most of the original Maori population is formally Christian, though some Maoris do not state their religion on census returns. Several Maori churches were not founded by whites, the largest being the Ratana Church, named after Takapotiki Ratana following his visions in 1918, and its followers have held Maori seats in the national legislature. There are an estimated 14m. Protestants and 8m. Roman Catholics in Oceania, including Australia and New Zealand.

Other Religions and Sects

There are small numbers of Jews in some Asian and Pacific countries. Tradition claims Jewish settlements at Cochin, in India, from the first century; one branch is now clearly Semitic and the other more typically Indian. There are 17,000 Jews in India, 1,500 in Japan, 5,700 in New Zealand and 100,000 in Australia.

In many countries there are members of the modern missionary Bahá'í faith, founded in Iran by Bahá'u'llah in 1863, with a synthesis of religion claimed as scientific and evolutionary. Bahá'ís number 250,000 in the Philippines, 30,000 in Korea, 16,000 in Japan, 20,000 in Australia, and smaller numbers elsewhere.

Religious beliefs and customs frequently mingle old and new. Although most Australian Aborigines are now claimed as Christian, traditional ideas are still important—supernatural beings and cultural heroes, and Australian versions of the 'totems', an American Indian word used to designate clan emblems. In Polynesia and New Zealand the sacred power of 'mana' has been held to reside especially in priests and chiefs, and the concept of 'taboo' or 'tapu' is used for prohibited or sacred objects or actions. So-called Cargo Cults developed in parts of Oceania when the arrival of western trade brought hopes of vast cargoes of goods by supernatural means. There have been 30 Cargo Cults in Papua and 70 in New Guinea, inspired by charismatic prophets.

Various types of syncretistic religions have flourished. In Java the religion Agama Jawa is a mixture classed officially as Muslim, but containing elements also from animism, Hinduism and Buddhism. It is practised both by peasants and by urbanized classes. In Korea the Chundo Kyo (Ch'ondogyo), the Religion of the Heavenly Way, is a mixture of animism, Buddhism, Confucianism and Christianity, though it is claimed as Eastern Learning in contrast to the Western. Followers of the Unification Church are popularly called Moonies after the founder, the Rev. Sun Myung Moon, a Korean whose teachings merge Christian and Buddhist ideas; they are active in many countries in Asia, North America and Europe. In Viet Nam the Caodai, 'High Tower', founded in 1919, merges Buddhist, Confucian and Christian practices and beliefs, venerates past and present religious figures, and claims some 5m. members. Other movements include the Theosophical Society, founded in 1875, and the more recent Transcendental Meditation and Hare Krishna societies, which mingle Indian and Western ideas and practices.

In China in recent years international attention has focused on the controversial Falun Gong (also known as Falun Dafa), a spiritual movement founded in 1992 by Li Hongzhi, a Chinese citizen who subsequently became resident in the USA. Encompassing Buddhist and Daoist elements, Falun Gong incorporates ancient traditions of physical exercise and meditation and is based on the principles of truth, compassion and tolerance. By 1999 the movement claimed a membership of 70m., including many Chinese government and military officials. In April of that year, in a peaceful protest, 10,000 followers of the sect converged on the walled compound of the communist leadership in Beijing to demand recognition for the movement. In July 1999, however, Falun Gong was officially banned, on the grounds that it constituted a 'threat to society'. Thousands of the movement's supporters were detained for allegedly challenging the authority of the Chinese Communist Party, and an arrest warrant for Li Hongzhi was issued. In October 2000, furthermore, Falun Gong was declared to be a political rival and an enemy of the nation. The suppression of Falun Gong continued, and in September 2001 the group claimed that a total of 278 of its members had died in custody since 1999. The Chinese Government, meanwhile, blamed Falun Gong for the deaths of 1,600 people, including suicides.

BIBLIOGRAPHY

General

Adler, Joseph. *Chinese Religions.* London, Routledge, 2002.

Beckerlegge, Gwilym (Ed.). *The World Religions Reader.* London, Routledge, 2000.

Bowker, John (Ed.). *The Oxford Dictionary of World Religions.* Oxford, Oxford University Press, 1999.

The Cambridge Illustrated History of Religions. Cambridge, Cambridge University Press, 2002.

Brown, A. (Ed.). *Festivals in World Religions.* London and New York, Longman, 1986.

Carr, Brian, and Mahalingam, Indira (Eds). *Companion Encyclopedia of Asian Philosophy.* London, Routledge, 2000.

Fisher, Mary Pat. *Religion in the Twenty-First Century.* London, Routledge, 1999.

Religions Today. London, Routledge, 2001.

Fowler, Jeaneane, et al. *World Religions.* Brighton, Sussex Academic Press, 1997.

Hardy, Friedhelm (Ed.). *The World's Religions: the Religions of Asia.* London, Routledge, 1990.

Hinnells, John R. (Ed.). *The Penguin Dictionary of Religions.* Harmondsworth, Penguin Books, 1997.

The New Penguin Handbook of Living Religions. Harmondsworth, Penguin Books, 2000.

Keene, Michael. *World Religions.* Oxford, Lion Publishing, 2002.

Keyes, Charles F., Kendall, Laurel, and Hardacre, Helen (Eds). *Asian Visions of Authority: Religion and the Modern States of East and Southeast Asia.* Honolulu, HI, University of Hawaii Press, 1994.

King, Ursula (Ed.). *Turning Points in Religious Studies.* Edinburgh, T. & T. Clark, 1990.

Kitagawa, Joseph M. (Ed.). *The Religious Traditions of Asia—Religion, History and Culture.* London, RoutledgeCurzon, 2002.

Palmer, Martin. *'The Times' World Religions.* London, Times Books, 2002.

Parrinder, E. G. *A Dictionary of Non-Christian Religions.* 2nd Edn, London and Philadelphia, Hulton, 1981.

Sexual Morality in the World's Religions. Oxford, Oneworld Publications, 1996.

Rogers, Kirsteen, and Hickman, Clare. *The Usborne Internet-linked Encyclopedia of World Religions.* London, Usborne Publishing, 2001.

Smart, Ninian. *The World's Religions.* Cambridge, Cambridge University Press, 1989.

Reasons and Faiths. London, Routledge, 2000.

World Philosophies. London, Routledge, 2000.

Smith, Jonathan Z. (Ed.) *The HarperCollins Dictionary of Religion.* London, Fount, 1996.

Woodhead, Linda, et al. (Eds). *Religions in the Modern World—Traditions and Transformations.* London, Routledge, 2001.

Yusa, Michiko. *Japanese Religions.* London, Routledge, 2002.

Zaehner, R. C. *The Hutchison Encyclopedia of Living Faiths.* Oxford, Helicon, 1997.

Islam

Ahmed, Akbar S. *Islam Today.* London, I. B. Tauris, 1998.

Armstrong, Karen. *Islam: A Short History.* London, Weidenfeld & Nicolson, 2000.

Bloom, Jonathan, and Blair, Sheila. *Islam—Empire of Faith.* London, BBC Consumer Publishing (Books), 2001.

Cook, Michael. *The Koran: A Very Short Introduction.* Oxford, Oxford Paperbacks, 2000.

Cragg, Kenneth. *Counsels in Contemporary Islam.* Edinburgh and Chicago, Edinburgh University Press, 1965.

The Wisdom of the Sufis. London, Sheldon Press, 1976.

Muhammad and the Christian: A Question of Response. Oxford, Oneworld Publications, 1999.

Jesus and the Muslim: An Exploration. Oxford, Oneworld Publications, 1999.

The Call of the Minaret. Oxford, Oneworld Publications, 2000.

Daniel, Norman. *Islam and the West: The Making of an Image.* Oxford, Oneworld Publications, 1995.

Dawood, N. J. (Trans.). *The Koran.* Harmondsworth, Penguin Books, 1997.

Elias, Jamal J. *Islam.* London, Routledge, 1999.

Esposito, John L. (Ed.) *The Oxford History of Islam.* Oxford, Oxford University Press, 2000.

Fisher, H. J. *Ahmadiyya.* London, Oxford University Press, 1963.

Jones, Alan (Ed.). *The Koran.* London, Phoenix Press, 2001.

Jordan, Michael. *Islam.* London, Carlton Books, 2002.

Khan, M. Z. *Muhammad, Seal of the Prophets.* London, 1980.

Mutalib, Hussin, and Hashmi, Taj ul-Islam (Eds). *Islam, Muslims and the Modern State.* New York, St Martin's Press, 1994.

Nasr, S. H. *Living Sufism.* London, 1972.

Parrinder, E. G. *Jesus in the Qur'ān.* 3rd Edn, Oxford, Oneworld Publications, 1995.

Robinson, Francis (Ed.), and Lapidus, Ira M. *The Cambridge Illustrated History of the Islamic World.* Cambridge, Cambridge University Press, 1999.

Robinson, Neal. *The Sayings of Muhammad.* London, Duckworth, 1991.

Islam: A Concise Introduction. Richmond, Surrey, Curzon Press, 1998.

Ruthven, Malise. *Islam: A Very Short Introduction.* Oxford, Oxford Paperbacks, 2000.

Islam in the World. Harmondsworth, Penguin Books, 2000.

Smith, M. *The Way of the Mystics.* London, Sheldon Press, 1976.

Tayob, Abdulkader. *Islam: A Short Introduction.* Oxford, Oneworld Publications, 1999.

Trimingham, J. S. *The Sufi Orders in Islam.* Oxford, Clarendon Press, 1971.

Watt, W. M. *Muhammad, Prophet and Statesman.* London and New York, Oxford University Press, 1961.

Islamic Fundamentalism and Modernity. London and New York, 1988.

Zebiri, Kate. *Muslims and Christians Face to Face.* Oxford, Oneworld Publications, 1996.

Hinduism

Bhatt, Chetan. *Hindu Nationalism.* Oxford, Berg Publishers, 2001.

Chaudhuri, Nirad C. *Hinduism: A Religion to Live By.* London, Chatto and Windus, 1979.

Cross, Stephen. *Way of Hinduism.* London, HarperCollins, 2002.

De Bary, W. T. (Ed.). *Sources of Indian Tradition.* New York, Columbia University Press, and London, Oxford University Press, 1958.

Deshpande, P. Y. *The Authentic Yoga.* London, 1978.

Flood, Gavin. *An Introduction to Hinduism.* Cambridge, Cambridge University Press, 1996.

Fowler, Jeaneane. *Hinduism—Beliefs and Practices.* Brighton, Sussex Academic Press, 1997.

Gelberg, S. J. (Ed.). *Hare Krishna.* New York, 1983.

Klostermaier, Klaus K. *A Concise Encyclopedia of Hinduism.* Oxford, Oneworld Publications, 1998.

Hinduism: A Short History. Oxford, Oneworld Publications, 2000.

Knott, Kim. *Hinduism: A Very Short Introduction.* Oxford, Oxford Paperbacks, 2000.

Lipner, Julius J. *Hindus—Their Religious Beliefs and Practices.* London, Routledge, 1998.

Michell, George. *The Hindu Temple: An Introduction to its Meaning and Form.* London, 1977.

O'Flaherty, W. D. *Hindu Myths.* Harmondsworth, Penguin Books, 1975.

The Rig Veda, An Anthology. Harmondsworth, Penguin Books, 1981.

Parrinder, E. G. *The Bhagavad Gita, A Verse Translation.* Oxford, Oneworld Publications, 1996.

Avator and Incarnation. Oxford, Oneworld Publications, 1997.

Sen, K. M. *Hinduism.* Harmondsworth, Penguin Books, 1991.

Sharma, Arvind (Ed.). *The Study of Hinduism.* Columbia, University of South Carolina Press, 2002.

Shattuck, Cybelle. *Hinduism.* London, Routledge, 1999.

Singh, K. *Gurus, Godmen and Good People.* Delhi, 1975.

Stutley, Margaret and James. *A Dictionary of Hinduism.* London, Routledge and Kegan Paul, 1977.

Zaehner, R. C. *Hindu Scriptures.* London and New York, Dent, 1965.

Zoroastrianism

Boyce, Mary. *Zoroastrians: Their Religious Beliefs and Practices.* London, Routledge, Revised Edn, 2000.

Clark, Peter. *Zoroastrianism—An Introduction to an Ancient Faith.* Brighton, Sussex Academic Press, 1998.

Hinnells, John. *Persian Mythology.* 2nd Edn, London, Newnes, 1985.

Zoroastrianism and Parsi Studies. Aldershot, Ashgate Publishing, 2000.

Kreyenbroek, Philip G., and Munshi, Shehnaz N. *Living Zoroastrianism.* Richmond, Surrey, Curzon Press, 2000.

Nigosian, S. A. *The Zoroastrian Faith.* Montréal, McGill-Queen's University Press, 1993.

Zaehner, R. C. *The Teachings of the Magi.* London and New York, Dent, 1975.

Dawn and Twilight of Zoroastrianism. London, Phoenix Press, 2002.

Jainism

Jaini, P. S. *The Jaina Path of Perfection.* Berkeley, 1979.

Mookerjee, S. *The Jaina Philosophy of Non-absolutism.* 2nd Edn, Delhi, 1978.

Schubring, W. *The Doctrine of the Jains.* Varanasi, Motilal, 1962.

Shah, Natubhai. *Jainism—The World of Conquerors.* Brighton, Sussex Academic Press, 1998.

Sharma, Arvind. *A Jaina Perspective on the Philosophy of Religion.* Delhi, Motilal Banarsidass Publishers, 2001.

Sinclair Stevenson, M. *Heart of Jainism.* New Delhi, Munshiram Manoharlal Publishers, 1995.

Von Glasenapp, Helmuth, and Shrotri, Shridar B. (Trans.). *Jainism.* Delhi, Motilal Banarsidass Publishers, 1999.

Warren, Herbet, and Gandhi, Virchand R. (Eds). *Jainism.* Crest Publishing House, 1999.

Sikhism

Chranjit, Ajitsingh. *Wisdom of Sikhism.* Oxford, Oneworld Publications, 2001.

Cole, W. Owen, and Singh Sambhi, Piara. *The Sikhs—Their Religious Beliefs and Practices.* Brighton, Sussex Academic Press, 1995.

Cort, John E. *Jains in the World.* New York, NY, Oxford University Press, 2001.

Mardia, K. V. *The Scientific Foundations of Jainism.* Delhi, Motilal Banarsidass Publishers, 2002.

McLeod, W. H. *Gurū Nānak and the Sikh Religion.* Oxford, Clarendon Press, 1968.

Exploring Sikhism. New York, Oxford University Press, 2000.

Shackle, Christopher, Mandair, Arvind-pal, and Singh, Gurharpal (Eds). *Sikh Religion, Culture and Ethnicity.* Richmond, Surrey, Curzon Press, 2001.

Singh, D. *Indian Bhakti Tradition and the Sikh Gurus.* Chandigarh, 1968.

Singh Kalsi, Sewa. *The Simple Guide to Sikhism.* Folkestone, Global Books, 1999.

Singh Mann, Gurinder. *Sikhism.* London, Routledge, 2002.

Singh, Patwant. *The Sikhs.* London, John Murray, 1999.

Singh, T. (Ed.). *Selections from the Sacred Writings of the Sikhs.* London, Allen & Unwin, 1960.

Vaudeville, C. *Kabīr.* Oxford, Clarendon Press, 1974.

Buddhism

Armstrong, Karen. *Buddha.* London, Orion, 2002.

Bechert, Heinz, and Gombrich, Richard. *The World of Buddhism.* London, Thames and Hudson, 1991.

Brannen, N. S. *Sōka Gakkai.* Richmond, VA, John Knox Press, 1968.

Carrithers, Michael. *Buddha: A Very Short Introduction.* Oxford, Oxford Paperbacks, 2001.

Conze, Edward. *A Short History of Buddhism.* Oxford, Oneworld Publications, 1996.

Conze, Edward (Ed.). *Buddhist Texts through the Ages.* Oxford, Oneworld Publications, 1995.

Corless, R. *The Vision of Buddhism.* New York, Paragon House, 1989.

Dumoulin, H. *Zen Enlightenment.* New York and Tokyo, 1979.

Eckel, Malcolm David. *Buddhism: Origins, Beliefs, Practices, Holy Texts, Sacred Places.* Oxford, Oxford University Press, 2002.

Fowler, Merv. *Buddhism—Beliefs and Practices.* Brighton, Sussex Academic Press, 1999.

Gethin, Rupert. *The Foundations of Buddhism.* Oxford, Oxford Paperbacks, 1998.

Gombrich, Richard. *Theravada Buddhism: A Social History from Ancient Benares to Modern Colombo.* London, Routledge, 1988.

Harvey, Peter. *An Introduction to Buddhism.* Cambridge, Cambridge University Press, 1990.

Hawkins, Bradley K. *Buddhism.* London, Routledge, 1999.

Hoffmann, H. *The Religions of Tibet.* London and Munich, Allen & Unwin, 1956.

Humphreys, Christmas. *Buddhism.* Harmondsworth, Penguin Books, 1990.

Keown, Damien. *Buddhism: A Very Short Introduction.* Oxford, Oxford Paperbacks, 2000.

Ling, T. O. *The Buddha: Buddhist Civilization in India and Ceylon.* London, Temple Smith, 1973.

Buddhist Revival in India. 1975.

The Buddha's Philosophy of Man; Early Indian Buddhist Dialogues. London, Dent, 1981.

Parrinder, E. G. *The Sayings of the Buddha.* London, Duckworth, 1991.

Pye, M. *The Buddha.* London, 1979.

Schloegel, I. *The Wisdom of the Zen Masters.* London, Sheldon Press, 1975.

Skilton, Andrew. *A Concise History of Buddhism.* Birmingham, Windhorse Publications, 1997.

Tucci, E. *The Religions of Tibet.* London, 1980.

Williams, Paul. *Buddhist Thought—A Complete Introduction to the Indian Tradition.* London, Routledge, 2000.

Mahayana Buddhism—The Doctrinal Foundations. London, Routledge, 1989.

Zwolf, W. *Heritage of Tibet.* London, 1981.

Confucianism and Daoism

Barrett, Tim, and Zhou Xun. *The Wisdom of the Confucians.* Oxford, Oneworld Publications, 2001.

Berthrong, John, and Berthrong, Evelyn. *Confucianism: A Short Introduction.* Oxford, Oneworld Publications, 2000.

Blofeld, J. *The Secret and Sublime: Taoist Mysteries and Magic.* London, 1973.

Brooks, E. Bruce, and Brooks, A. Taeko. *The Original Analects.* New York, NY, Columbia University Press, 2001.

Christie, A. *Chinese Mythology.* London, Hamlyn, 1968.

Clarke, J. J. *The Tao of the West—Western Transformations of Taoist Thought.* London, Routledge, 2000.

Dawson, Raymond (Trans.). *Confucius—The Analects.* Oxford, Oxford Paperbacks, 2000.

De Bary, W. T. (Ed.). *Sources of Chinese Tradition.* New York and London, Columbia University Press, 1960.

Forstater, Mark. *The Spiritual Teachings of the Tao.* London, Hodder and Stoughton, 2001.

Kaizuka, Shigeki, and Bownas, Geoffrey (Trans.). *Confucius: His Life and Thought.* Mineola, NY, Dover Publications, 2002.

Needham, J., and Ronan, C. A. *The Shorter Science and Civilisation in China, Vol. 1.* Cambridge, Cambridge University Press, 1978.

Nylan, Michael. *The Five 'Confucian' Classics.* Yale University Press, New Haven, CT, 2001.

Oldstone-Moore, Jennifer. *Confucianism: Origins, Beliefs, Practices, Holy Texts, Sacred Places.* Oxford, Oxford University Press, 2002.

Robinet, Isabelle. *Taoism: Growth of a Religion.* Stanford, CA, Stanford University Press, 1997.

Roth, Harold D. *Original Tao.* New York, NY, Columbia University Press, 1999.

Smith, D. H. *Chinese Religions.* London, Weidenfeld & Nicolson, 1968.

Confucius. London, Temple Smith, 1973.

The Wisdom of the Taoist Mystics. London, Sheldon Press, 1980.

Tu Wei-Ming (Ed.). *Confucian Traditions in East Asian Modernity.* Cambridge, MA, Harvard University Press, 1996.

Waley, Arthur (Trans.). *The Analects of Confucius.* New York, NY, Vintage Books, 1989.

The Way and its Power. 3rd Edn, London, Allen & Unwin, 1949.

Watts, Alan, and Watts, Mark (Ed.). *Taoism: Way Beyond Seeking.* Boston, MA, Tuttle Publishing, 2001.

Wildish, Paul. *Principles of Taoism.* London, HarperCollins, 2000.

Wong, Eva. *The Shambhala Guide to Taoism.* Boston, MA, Shambhala Publications, 1997.

Yao Xinzhong. *An Introduction to Confucianism.* Cambridge, Cambridge University Press, 2000.

Shinto

Bocking, Brian. *A Popular Dictionary of Shinto.* Richmond, Surrey, Curzon Press, 1996.

Breen, John, and Teeuwen, Mark (Eds). *Shinto in History: Ways of the Kami.* Richmond, Curzon Press, 2000.

Bunce, W. K. *Religions in Japan.* 2nd Edn, Tokyo, Tuttle, 1973.

Harris, Victor (Ed.). *Shinto.* London, British Museum Press, 2001.

Herbert, J. *Shinto.* London, Allen & Unwin, 1967.

Kidder, E. *Ancient Japan.* Oxford, 1977.

Philippi, Donald. L. (Trans.). *Kojiki.* New York, NY, Columbia University Press, 1977.

Picken, Stuart D. B. *Historical Dictionary of Shinto.* Lanham, MD, Scarecrow Press, 2001.

Reader, Ian. *The Simple Guide to Shinto.* Folkestone, Global Books, 1998.

Satow, E. *Ancient Japanese Rituals & the Revival of Pure Shinto.* London, Kegan Paul International, 2002.

Tsunoda, R. (Ed.). *Sources of Japanese Tradition.* New York and London, Columbia University Press, 1958.

Van Straelen, H. *The Religion of Divine Wisdom.* Tokyo, S.V.D. Research Institute, 1954.

Christianity

Barraclough, G. (Ed.). *The Christian World.* London, 1981.

Barrett, D. B. (Ed.). *World Christian Encyclopedia.* Nairobi, Oxford University Press, 1982.

Chidester, David. *Christianity—A Global History.* London, Allen Lane, 2000.

Cross, F. L. (Ed.). *The Oxford Dictionary of the Christian Church.* 3rd Edn, London, Oxford University Press, 1997.

Drummond, R. H. *A History of Christianity in Japan.* Michigan, 1971.

Hastings, Adrian (Ed.). *A World History of Christianity.* London, Cassell, 1999.

Hastings, Adrian, Mason, Alistair, and Pyper, Hugh (Eds). *The Oxford Companion to Christian Thought.* Oxford, Oxford University Press, 2000.

Neill, S. *A History of Christian Missions.* Harmondsworth, Penguin Books, 1964.

Parrinder, E. G. *A Concise Encyclopedia of Christianity.* Oxford, Oneworld Publications, 1998.

Schimmel, A., and Falaturi, A. *We Believe in One God: The Experience of God in Christianity and Islam.* London, 1979.

Sunquist, Scott W. (Ed.) et al. *A Dictionary of Asian Christianity.* Grand Rapids, MI, Eerdmans, 2001.

Wilson, Brian. *Christianity.* London, Routledge, 1999.

Other Religions

Barker, E. (Ed.). *New Religious Movements.* New York, Mellen Press, 1982.

Becoming a Moonie. Oxford, 1985.

Best, E. *Maori Religion and Mythology.* New York, 1976.

Cohn-Sherbok, Dan. *Judaism and other Faiths.* London, Macmillan, 1994.

A Short History of Judaism. Oxford, Oneworld Publications, 1996.

A Concise Encyclopedia of Judaism. Oxford, Oneworld Publications, 1998.

Eliade, M. *Australian Religions.* Ithaca and London, Cornell University Press, 1973.

Geels, A. *Subud and the Javanese Mystical Tradition.* Richmond, Surrey, Curzon Press, 1997.

Geertz, C. *The Religion of Java.* Chicago, 1976.

Goldberg, D. J., and Rayner, J. D. *The Jewish People.* Harmondsworth, Penguin Books, 1987.

Lindstrom, Lamont. *Cargo Cult: Strange Stories of Desire from Melanesia and Beyond.* Honolulu, HI, University of Hawaii Press, 1993.

Momen, Moojan. *The Bahá'í Faith: A Short Introduction.* Oxford, Oneworld Publications, 1999.

Parratt, J. *Papuan Belief and Ritual.* New York, Vantage Press, 1976.

Perkins, M., and Hainsworth, P. *The Bahá'í Faith.* London, 1980.

Smith, Peter. *The Bahá'í Faith: A Short History.* Oxford, Oneworld Publications, 1999.

A Concise Encyclopedia of the Bahá'í Faith. Oxford, Oneworld Publications, 1999.

Swain, Tony, and Trompf, Garry. *The Religions of Oceania.* London, Routledge, 1995

Whitehouse, Harvey. *Inside the Cult: Religious Innovation and Transmission in Papua New Guinea.* Oxford, Clarendon Press, 1997.

Worsley, P. *The Trumpet Shall Sound: A Study of 'Cargo' Cults in Melanesia.* London, 1968.

THE ASIAN-PACIFIC COMMUNITY IN THE PACIFIC CENTURY

DEAN FORBES

For decades the 21st century was heralded as the 'Pacific century'. Yet Asian-Pacific nations entered the new millennium less certain about their future in a globalizing economy than they were during the last quarter of the 20th century. The huge concentrations of people in Asian nations, the undoubted natural resources and the long history of technological development and science in China and Japan (and India) once encouraged the view that Asian-Pacific nations would dominate the world economy in the new century. However, during the late 1990s progress was interrupted. The Asian economic crisis, political problems within some key nations, enduring tensions between countries and halting progress on the formation of an effective, institutionalized Pacific community cautioned against a straightforward acceptance of the 'Pacific century'. Mounting evidence now suggests that the recent pace of social and economic change in the Asia-Pacific region has recovered following the economic crisis of the late 1990s. Despite the dangers illustrated by the terrorist attacks on the USA on 11 September 2001, optimism about the future of the Asia-Pacific region is returning, bolstered by the global showpiece of the 2002 football World Cup held in Japan and the Republic of Korea.

WHAT IS THE ASIA-PACIFIC REGION?

The Asia-Pacific region has displaced the term 'Asia' in much discourse during the last few decades. The 'Asian region' has been conventionally defined, for more than a century, as the states from the Middle East to, in the east, the Pacific coast of the Asian continent and its adjacent island states. The Ural Mountains have been regarded as the boundary between Europe and Asia. Asia-Pacific, by contrast, refers to the countries of East Asia (China, Taiwan, Japan, the Republic of Korea (South Korea) and the Democratic People's Republic of Korea (North Korea)), and South-East Asia (Indonesia, East Timor, the Philippines, Thailand, Malaysia, Singapore, Brunei, Viet Nam, Cambodia, Laos and Myanmar, formerly Burma). In addition, the eastern territories (previously the Soviet Far East) of the Commonwealth of Independent States (the CIS), Australia and New Zealand are considered to form part of this region. Finally, the numerous microstates of the Pacific make up another component of the region. They are large in number, but small in size. The most populous component is Melanesia, which contains Papua New Guinea and Fiji, the biggest of the Pacific island states. There are also the tiny states of Micronesia in the North-West Pacific, and the small Polynesian states of the South Pacific. Being small, they are not all independent, but have retained a variety of allegiances with countries such as New Zealand, France and the USA. The Pacific Basin is defined as including all the states located in or adjacent to the Pacific Ocean. In addition to the territories of the Asia-Pacific region, this includes the USA, Canada, Mexico and the smaller states of Central America, together with the principal Pacific economies of South America, such as Chile, Peru, Ecuador and Colombia.

ECONOMIC INTEGRATION AND THE NEW SPACE ECONOMY

The second half of the 20th century witnessed some remarkable political and economic changes in the Asia-Pacific region. At the conclusion of the Second World War in 1945 the Japanese were defeated and their economy was in ruins. Many of Japan's neighbours in the region were still colonies, albeit straining to free themselves of their imperial oppressors. China was in turmoil, being in the midst of a bitter civil war. Within a decade the Japanese economy had started a surge of growth, China had stabilized under Mao Zedong, and many of the countries throughout the region had achieved political independence.

Then, in the 1980s and 1990s, the newly-industrializing economies (NIEs), Hong Kong, Singapore, the Republic of Korea and Taiwan, began to experience exceptional economic growth rates. They were followed by a second generation of NIEs, notably Thailand and Malaysia. In fact, a World Bank study published in 1993 argued that eight Asian economies (Japan, Hong Kong, Singapore, the Republic of Korea, Taiwan, Malaysia, Indonesia and Thailand) had performed exceptionally well between 1965 and 1990, growing on average by 5.5% annually. This was a significantly faster rate of growth than that achieved by the United Kingdom during its rapid economic development of the 19th century (1.2% annually) or later by the USA (1.6% annually).

There are three competing explanations of why these countries achieved extraordinary rates of economic growth. One theory argues that judicious public policies and government management strategies primed the NIEs to focus on a successful export-led programme of development. Singapore and Japan are considered the best illustrations of this argument. A second explanation centres on the adoption of free-market strategies. This is sometimes called the 'getting the prices right' approach because of its emphasis on allowing markets to operate unimpeded. Hong Kong and Taiwan are often cited in support of this approach. A third explanation ascribes Asia's success to so-called 'Asian values', a reference to the Confucian values of thrift, communalism and dedication to family which are said to underpin the success of Asian entrepreneurs, particularly the Chinese in the People's Republic and overseas Chinese communities. Most observers acknowledge that each of these explanations has some validity, although no single model provides a complete understanding.

Market Socialism

Some of the socialist and former socialist countries of Asia-Pacific have embarked on economic reforms that have permitted them to participate in the economic growth within the region. China and Viet Nam have led the way in terms of opening up the economy to outside forces, and trying to develop so-called 'market socialism'. Laos has cautiously followed the same path. Despite the UN-sponsored election of May 1993, ongoing violence in Cambodia caused serious concern to other South-East Asian countries, although the defeat of the Khmers Rouges subsequently led to greater stability and Cambodia's outlook has steadily improved. The new problems faced in Cambodia increasingly resemble the difficulties confronting its neighbours, including the incompatibility of more open economies with non-democratic governments. The Democratic People's Republic of Korea has steadfastly refused to be affected by the new style of socialist development. Its recalcitrant approach to nuclear non-proliferation exacerbates regional concerns about the likelihood of its becoming a good neighbour, and the country has experienced serious economic problems and widespread starvation. A North Korean festival in 2002 designed to upstage the southern neighbour's hosting of the football World Cup underlined the country's lack of understanding of world opinion of its plight.

The continued opening of the Chinese economy, in particular, leading to further trade and economic growth, is crucial to the economic development of the region. The brutal suppression of students protesting in support of increased democratic rights in Beijing in June 1989, and the more general ambivalence (not to say confusion) within the Chinese leadership concerning the appropriate combination of economic and political reform, raised serious questions, at least in the short term, about China's contribution. China's conservative leadership, however, withstood the pressure and continues to promote its open economy strategy, resulting in a resurgence of interest by foreign investors and traders. The southern province of Guangdong has been heralded as an emergent NIE. The death of 'paramount' leader Deng Xiaoping in February 1997 did not destabilize

China's ruling élite to the extent anticipated in western countries, nor did it cause China to deviate from the economic direction first charted by Deng. China's pursuit of the capitalist path led it, following protracted negotiations, to join the World Trade Organization (WTO) in late 2001, thus encouraging optimism that China's economy would continue to open.

Viet Nam has pursued a slower but more determined approach to economic liberalization. The reform process commenced in 1979, but the pace quickened after 1986. Although Viet Nam remains steadfast in its rejection of political pluralism, economic reform continues to surge forward. The ending of the US economic embargo on Viet Nam in early 1994 cleared the way for the country's further integration into the global economy. It accelerated the influx of optimistic foreigners into Viet Nam, in search of what many mistakenly anticipated would be an economic bonanza. By 2000 many foreign investors had departed from Viet Nam, disillusioned by the lack of government support and by the unreliability of agreements with local companies. The existence throughout the Pacific Basin of large communities of Vietnamese refugees who are, in general, opposed to the current regime in Viet Nam, is inhibiting the response to changes in that country. The election of Nong Duc Manh as General Secretary of the Communist Party of Viet Nam in early 2001 encouraged the view that Viet Nam's leadership would gradually become less conservative. Many are anticipating an acceleration of the economic integration of the Indo-China region with other Pacific Basin countries over the next few years. Viet Nam's *rapprochement* with the old enemy, China, is an interesting illustration of its altering relationship with its neighbours. The decision by the Association of South East Asian Nations (ASEAN) to admit Viet Nam to full membership in 1995 underlined the importance of the new connections being forged within the region.

Regional Economic Integration

The emergence of significant economies in the Asia-Pacific region has encouraged speculation that the global economy is increasingly clustering around three major poles: a North American pole, in which the USA is the key economy; a European pole centred on the European Union (EU); and an Asia-Pacific pole. These three economic poles dominate the global economy. According to World Bank data, North America produced 28.3% of global GNP in 1995, the EU 29.5% and the Asia-Pacific region 26.6%. In 1997 the USA accounted for 12.3% of world merchandise trade, the EU 37.4%, and the Asia-Pacific region 16.8%. Altogether, therefore, these three major poles of the global economy accounted for 84.4% of global GNP and two-thirds (66.5%) of total trade in merchandise. The emergence of three core global growth poles, combined with the formation of economic unions such as the North American Free Trade Agreement (NAFTA) and the EU, has exacerbated fears that the world economy risks developing three or more major international trade blocs. The danger this poses is that it could slow down, or even halt, the achievements of the WTO and of its predecessor, the General Agreement on Tariffs and Trade (GATT), to open up world trade to all countries no matter where they are located.

One of the remarkable features of the Pacific Basin region is the high and increasing levels of economic integration among countries. In total, 66% of exports of Asia-Pacific Economic Co-operation (APEC) member countries in 1992 were destined for other member countries (compared with 53% in 1981). Intra-regional imports accounted for 67.1% of total imports in 1992, and subsequently grew at a rate of 8.1% per year, considerably faster than imports from outside this region. Trade among APEC members in 1992 accounted for about two-thirds of overall world trade, and the share has been growing steadily. Economic integration among Asian-Pacific economies is a little lower, but on the increase nevertheless. As an illustration, Thailand's exports to Asian NIEs in 1994 for the first time exceeded its exports to the USA, while its exports to ASEAN countries exceeded its exports to Japan. In 1999 the 21 member economies of APEC accounted for 43.85% of total global trade.

Japan is the dominant economic power within the Asia-Pacific region, and shares the economic leadership of the Pacific Basin as a whole with the USA. There is speculation that a 'yen bloc' is beginning to precipitate within the region. At present there is little immediate prospect of any form of monetary union of Asian-Pacific nations, as in the EU. However, the yen is increasingly used for inter-regional trade, though it remains far less important than the US dollar.

Japan's substantial trade surplus with the USA has given rise to some bitterness between the two countries over the years, Japan being accused of unfair trading practices. The tension between the two economic superpowers on either side of the Pacific needs to be resolved if progress is to be made on increased regional integration. Japan's continuing economic stagnation has also been a cause of considerable concern, as a buoyant Japanese economy is important to prosperity throughout the region; signs began to appear in 2002 that the economy was recovering, and this apparent revival was expected to be bolstered by the World Cup. Some tensions over trade imbalances also exist between the USA and Taiwan and the Republic of Korea, although these have not yet been as serious.

The pattern of direct foreign investment within the Pacific Basin has been dominated for many decades by investment from colonial powers to their existing and former colonies. These traditional, capital-exporting countries have also diversified their patterns of investment. The USA has a large (greater than 15%) share of investment in the Republic of Korea, Indonesia, Thailand, Singapore, Hong Kong and Malaysia, while Australia and New Zealand both have substantial stocks in Fiji.

New patterns of capital exports, however, have developed in recent years. Without a doubt, the major area of growth has stemmed from Japan's interest in Pacific Basin countries. Also important is the emergence of Hong Kong and Singapore and, to a smaller extent, of some of the other quickly-developing countries in the region, as capital exporters. Some of this investment is a product of international migration, as Asian business people seek to diversify their holdings in advance of moving residence from places such as Hong Kong to Vancouver, Honolulu or Sydney. The growth of a so-called 'overseas Chinese' business network has become an increasingly powerful economic force in the Asia-Pacific region. It is sometimes argued that if the economic activities of the inhabitants of the 'overseas Chinese' states (Taiwan, Hong Kong and Singapore) were added to the activities of Chinese business communities in Indonesia, Thailand, Malaysia, Australia, Canada and the USA, it would represent a level of overseas economic activity as large as that of the Japanese. Such a comparison underlines the importance of 'overseas Chinese' business networks in enhancing the linkages among the economies of the Pacific Basin.

New Space Economies

There are other emerging, distinctive characteristics of Asian-Pacific economic growth. The large metropolises, such as Seoul, Jakarta, Manila, Taipei and Shanghai, are growing rapidly as a result of the key role they perform in the modern economies of their respective countries. The concentration of economic wealth in the metropolises exacerbates economic inequalities with other domestic regions, especially the rural areas. Tokyo, Singapore and, to a certain extent, Bangkok are acquiring the characteristics of 'world cities', linking with a global network of cities that provide important, high-level services to the regional and global economy. Such is the pace of expansion and development within the megacities of the Asia-Pacific region that some argue that a series of mega-urban regions connecting clusters of large cities are beginning to emerge along the Pacific coast.

Another tendency in the Asia-Pacific region has been the formation of localized trilateral links by countries. These have been labelled 'natural economic territories' or NETS. Singapore is pressing ahead with the development of a 'growth triangle' linking it to the Malaysian state of Johor and the Indonesian province of Riau. Whereas the Singaporeans see it as a way of combining the comparative advantages of each of the regions, for Indonesia it is a means of developing one of its outer island regions. It has already made considerable progress in opening Batam Island as an industrial estate and special economic zone, and future plans will include the extension of the development to Bintan and Bulu islands.

The apparent success of this growth triangle has prompted the development of another area linking Medan (Indonesia), Penang (Malaysia) and Songkhla (Thailand). Another arrangement is the Brunei-Indonesia-Malaysia-Philippines-East

ASEAN Growth Area (BIMP-EAGA). Established in March 1994, it provides a formal link between adjacent regions of the member countries. Its aim is to foster regional advancement through the encouragement of private-sector led, market-driven development. During 1996 the formation of an Australia-Indonesia Development Area was announced, designed to foster economic links between northern Australia and eastern Indonesia. The Asian Development Bank (ADB) is promoting greater links within a Mekong River Zone that would connect Yunnan Province and adjacent parts of China with Thailand, Myanmar and the three states of Indo-China. Meanwhile, China has also been considering restructuring and developing its internal regions to foster international links with neighbouring countries. An example is a gigantic project planned for the development of the Tumen River area in the north-east, which would facilitate economic links with Russia, Japan and the Koreas.

It would be premature to claim that these localized co-operative economic arrangements (or NETS) have yet achieved very much. Nevertheless, they do reflect serious experimentation with new forms of economic linkages among Asian-Pacific countries.

The Asian Economic Crisis

Many countries of the region were affected by the Asian financial and economic crisis. This first came to world attention in mid-1997, as the Thai baht rapidly lost value against the US dollar. Because of the interconnections among Asian economies, the impact rapidly spread to Indonesia, Malaysia, the Philippines, the Republic of Korea and Hong Kong. Many other countries in the region, such as Viet Nam, Japan, Australia and Singapore, were also adversely affected.

Indonesia was worst affected by this economic crisis. According to the ADB, the gross domestic product (GDP) of Indonesia was estimated to have contracted by 13.2% in 1998. In 1999, however, the country's GDP increased by 0.9%, in 2000 by 4.8% and in 2001 by 3.3%, before being forecast to expand by 3.0% in 2002. Meanwhile, President Suharto resigned in May 1998, a victim of the crisis, mismanagement and widespread corruption. His successor, former Vice-President B. J. Habibie, struggled to return Indonesia to a sound economic footing, but was tarnished by his links to the previous regime. Following the legislative elections of June 1999, as a result of which Suharto's ruling Golkar party lost office, Abdurrahman Wahid was elected President of Indonesia in October. An unexpected choice, many considered Wahid to be erratic, fearing that the country's economic outlook remained bleak. Wahid subsequently faced the prospect of impeachment, following allegations of corruption and inept management of the economy, thus compounding Indonesia's difficulties, and in July 2001 he was replaced by Vice-President Megawati Sukarnoputri.

By 1999 the region's economies had begun to recover. In 2000, according to the ADB, Singapore and Malaysia recorded GDP growth rates of 9.9% and 8.5% respectively, while the economy of Thailand expanded by 4.2% and that of the Philippines by 3.9%. In 2001, however, owing to the global economic downturn (particularly in the electronics sector), Singapore's GDP contracted by 2.0%. While that country experienced its worst recession since independence in 1965, rates of growth declined sharply elsewhere in South-East Asia: to 0.4% in Malaysia, to 1.8% in Thailand and to 3.4% in the Philippines. Hong Kong's GDP, meanwhile, expanded by 10.5% in 2000 but by only 0.1% in 2001. Although initially among the most seriously affected, the Republic of Korea was able to recover in the most spectacular manner. With national and local governments emphasizing austerity, shunning non-Korean products, and prioritizing effort on those worst affected, the country managed to reverse its economic fortunes: GDP growth was estimated at 10.9% in 1999, at 9.3% in 2000 and at 3.0% in 2001. The economies of China and Taiwan, both of which maintained positive rates of growth in 1998–99, best withstood the immediate repercussions of the 1997 Asian economic crisis; in 2000 GDP expanded by an estimated 8.0% in China and by 5.9% in Taiwan. In 2001, however, while China's GDP grew by 7.3%, Taiwan entered recession, with its GDP contracting by 1.9%.

COMMUNICATIONS AND INFRASTRUCTURE

Political and economic changes are not the only ones of importance to the region. The transport and communications networks of the Asia-Pacific region are changing along with the increasing integration of the area. Revenue passenger-miles for intra-Asian air routes increased by 12.4% per annum between 1970 and 1990, while Europe-Asia links grew by 17.0% annually, and trans-Pacific traffic by12.2%. For comparison, the global average growth rate was 7.2%, while North Atlantic services grew by 7.4% annually. Similarly, the world's three fastest growing air cargo routes are the intra-Asian routes together with those linking the Asia-Pacific with Europe and North America. A major air corridor links Singapore, Bangkok, Taipei, Seoul and Tokyo, reflecting one of the region's central economic axes. Boeing, the US aerospace company, forecast that between 2000 and 2019 air traffic would expand by 7.0% annually in North Asia, including China, and by 5.4% in South-East Asia (compared with a North American growth rate of 3.3%). Since the 1990s numerous Asian countries have implemented substantial airport-upgrading programmes.

Nevertheless, the global recession of the early 1990s, the Asian economic crisis of the late 1990s and, more recently, the terrorist attacks on the USA in September 2001 have meant that a number of regional airlines are in financial trouble. Further difficulties arise from the rigidities caused by practices such as cabotage, in which foreign carriers are barred from domestic routes. Financial stringencies have accelerated moves towards partial or full privatization of regional airlines (such as Air New Zealand and Qantas), and the cross-ownership of airline shares. By 2002, however, Air New Zealand was in the process of being returned to the state sector.

New technology in the shipping of cargo is also facilitating economic expansion. The growth of 'intermodalism', or a combination of procedures to move goods by container from the factory door to the floor of the salesroom, using a variety of transport modes all supervised by a single company, is of rising importance in Hong Kong, Japan and Taiwan. It meshes with the 'just-in-time' production and distribution methods that are becoming more widespread among the most competitive enterprises in those same countries. The region's major container ports have witnessed huge growth in recent years.

Communications networks throughout the Asia-Pacific region are developing extremely quickly. With a receiver dish it is now possible for residents of the region to receive about 20 different free-to-air television services. Star TV (Satellite Television Asian Region) is the best known of the multi-region broadcasters. Acquired by Rupert Murdoch's News Corporation in 1993, Hong Kong-based Star TV beams its images across a region that includes India, China and most of mainland South-East Asia. Singapore and Malaysia have banned the private ownership of parabolic dishes, hoping to restrict access to satellite broadcasts, a move that has proved ineffective in China.

The overall impact of the increasing quantity of satellite television in the Pacific Basin needs to be considered in greater depth than hitherto. There may be some gains in terms of regional cohesion, or at least greater regional awareness. A television viewer in Hanoi might watch a programme produced in Mumbai (Bombay) and targeted to an Indian audience, followed by Mandarin language advertisements for cognac directed at a Chinese audience, all broadcast from studios in Hong Kong. At the same time, the restricted ownership of such all-pervasive media as satellite television, and the inevitable tendency to focus on low-cost mass entertainment, will certainly have considerable social and cultural ramifications, particularly for the smaller countries of the region.

Communications infrastructure is a vital component of information flows and economic integration. At present the Pacific Ocean is spanned by optical fibre submarine cable linking the USA through Hawaii with, on the one hand, Guam, the Philippines and Taiwan, and on the other, Hong Kong, Japan and the Republic of Korea. A sea-bed optical fibre cable links Australia and New Zealand, a connection between New Zealand and Hawaii was completed in 1993, and the link between Australia and Guam was installed in 1994. A high-grade cable—TPC4—linking Japan and Canada and the USA directly was opened at the end of 1992. The regional network is still far from complete, however, because the ASEAN countries, for instance, are still poorly connected. Moreover, domestic communications arrangements within many Asian-Pacific countries, particularly in the non-metropolitan urban and rural areas, remain woefully inadequate. Growing regional interest in e-commerce became apparent during 1999 and 2000 as investors, particularly in Hong Kong, latched on to the internet 'bubble economy', investing heavily in 'dot.com' companies. Countries such as Singapore, Australia and Japan have made large advances in recent years towards developing the infrastructure required of the so-called new economy; but in Hong Kong interest has surged, and many expect that China will soon follow. By 2000 there were an estimated 115m. internet users in Asia, equivalent to about one-third of the world total.

NATIONALISM, POLITICAL TENSION AND IDENTITY

Growing economic links within the Pacific Basin, together with the expansion of the infrastructure that facilitates them, has been a feature of the turn of the century. However, political tensions over trade and territory continue.

Ironically, the end of the 'Cold War' has made the region a more complicated and fluid place and, it is feared, more unstable. This provides an added incentive for improving the quality and frequency of dialogue among nations of the Pacific Basin. In recent years, contradictory forces within the region have both helped and hindered progress towards increased integration, although, on balance, they would seem to indicate slow, but steady, moves towards greater interdependence.

Economic and political leadership from Japan is important to the long-term stability of the region, yet Japan has consistently faced serious difficulties in the choice of a long-term Prime Minister. The Japanese have for some time accepted a far quicker turnover of their most senior politicians than would be acceptable in many (but certainly not all) western nations. The unexpected election of Junichiro Koizumi as Prime Minister in April 2001 and his stated support for economic reform have been lauded, although most recognize his lack of support from old-style Japanese power-brokers. Leadership instability may have contributed to the deceleration of the Japanese economy in recent years, but the succession of leaders does not seem to have significantly damaged the country's overseas economic interests. This is generally attributed to the strength and continuity of the government bureaucracy. However, as Japan's international economic power revives, so will the nation be expected to play an increasingly important political role within the Pacific Basin and beyond. The greater pressure on leaders that this entails will not be made any easier by the uncertainty which, in the last few years, has unsettled the elected senior ministers of the country.

Among South-East Asian nations, Singapore and Malaysia, supported by a combination of consistent economic growth and political stability, have both steadily increased their regional profiles. The move towards democracy in a number of other countries throughout the region, such as Thailand and the Republic of Korea, is a welcome shift in political directions. While the absence of democratic institutions has not necessarily been a barrier to closer economic links, the long-term sustainability of regional relations will depend on workable democratic institutions with mechanisms that allow for a smooth transfer of power. In Indonesia dissatisfaction with the Suharto regime over high-level corruption and the outrageous wealth of the Suharto family had been mounting for many years. Nevertheless, Suharto was re-elected in March 1998 to another presidential term. Opposition continued to grow, however, particularly from student protesters in Jakarta, who were increasingly concerned by the regime's failure to address the suffering experienced in Indonesia as a result of the economic austerity measures imposed by the IMF, and in May 1998 Suharto was forced to resign (see above).

Territorial Disputes

Various territorial disputes continue to give rise to friction in the region. After some difficulties, the British administration withdrew from Hong Kong, which was reincorporated by China and became a Special Administrative Region (SAR) on 1 July 1997. The impact this will have on the development of southern China, in particular, and on stability in the wider East Asian region, in general, has been the object of much speculation, some of it frenzied. However, the establishment of the SAR of Hong Kong has proved less disruptive than most anticipated, although the underlying tensions may take time to surface. China's more ambitious long-term wish to reabsorb Taiwan, not to mention the long-standing problem of resistance to the incorporation of Tibet (Xizang) into China, will remain sources of continuing friction. The Chinese Government seems determined to raise the tension over Taiwan, causing many Asian countries to fear that the relationship could become the region's most dangerous flashpoint. The repercussions of a collision between a Chinese fighter aircraft and a US reconnaissance aircraft in early 2001 illustrated the strained relations between the two countries. President George W. Bush's affirmation of the USA's support for Taiwan, although a reiteration of the existing US position, further exacerbated bilateral tensions.

North and South Korea from time to time reflect on the prospects of a united Korea. Few, however, expected any serious progress while the regime of Kim Jong Il continued to hold power in the North, showing little indication of wishing to end its isolation. Nevertheless, unprecedented talks in mid-2000 in Pyongyang between the two countries' leaders, Kim Jong Il and Kim Dae-Jung, and the resultant increase in bilateral co-operation, raised hopes once again. During 2000–01 Australia, New Zealand, the Philippines and various EU members were among the countries to establish diplomatic relations with the Democratic People's Republic of Korea. In July 2000 the country was formally admitted to the ASEAN Regional Forum (ARF), and in October of that year the US Secretary of State, Madeleine Albright, paid an historic visit to Pyongyang. The Republic of Korea's closer links to China, and the continued economic failures of the Democratic People's Republic of Korea, have no doubt contributed towards persistent tensions. A serious famine in 1997 and subsequent years devastated the countryside, leading some to speculate that the crisis might eventually bring down the regime of Kim Jong Il.

Ongoing disputes over control of islands in the South China Sea are another potential flashpoint in the region. China makes an 'historic claim' to all of the Paracel and Spratly Islands. Altogether, China claims a massive tongue-shaped region stretching from Hainan Island south as far as Indonesia's Natuna Islands. Viet Nam, the Philippines, Malaysia and Indonesia all vigorously dispute this ambit claim, though do not agree on the merits of one another's claims. Apart from the signs of China's territorial ambitions, there are clearly important resources at stake. As an example, Indonesia's Natuna gas field, with estimated reserves of 45 m. m. cu ft, is one of the world's largest, yet falls within the territory claimed by China. Occasional military skirmishes within the region are an indication that these disputes could easily escalate.

Many countries in the Pacific Basin are still consolidating their internal territories; but regional groups periodically make their desires for separation or enhanced regional autonomy clearly known. The violent suppression by the Indonesian military of a demonstration in Dili, the capital of East Timor, in November 1991 and the resultant high death toll brought widespread international condemnation. East Timor, along with Irian Jaya (now Papua) and Aceh, was for many years a region that resisted centralized Indonesian rule. The decision by the Indonesian Government in 1999 to support a referendum to allow East Timorese to vote for autonomy within Indonesia, or independence, quickly led to violence after most voters favoured separation. The horrific violence perpetrated by the Indonesian military was eventually ended by external forces, following which East Timor was placed under UN control in preparation for full independence. East Timor achieved its formal independence in May 2002 in a ceremony attended by President Megawati of Indonesia, but for the moment the new country's continuing vulnerability is potentially destabilizing for its neighbours.

Another set of incidents involved a group of landowners from the island of Bougainville who were seeking to establish a state of their own, separate from Papua New Guinea. This led in 1989 to the closure of the huge copper mine on Bougainville. The unrest continued politically to destabilize Papua New Guinea, as well as severely weakening the country's economy. The Bougainville People's Congress was established in 1999. Continuing conflict over territory in Solomon Islands is causing unease. In Fiji the coup by George Speight in mid-2000 revived concerns about tensions in Fiji's ethnically mixed population and heightened awareness of the extent of instability in Pacific island nations.

Regional Politics and Identity

Bill Clinton's accession to the Presidency of the USA in 1993 held very important implications for regional unity. His strong support for the APEC meeting in Seattle in 1993 allayed fears, to some extent, about his interest in the region. Nevertheless, the USA under Clinton became involved in major disputes with Japan over trade issues, with China over human rights and with Indonesia over labour matters. Furthermore, numerous small issues remained unresolved. Together, these issues heightened concerns that the Clinton Administration had not formulated a coherent and workable strategy for the Pacific Basin. After his election in late 2000 President George W. Bush moved to appoint officials with sound experience in foreign policy and in Asian affairs, but inclined towards a hard-line approach. He began to shift Clinton's effort on multilateralism, to focus more on bilateral links and to relax US concerns about human rights, while strengthening security obligations. In 2001 the 11 September attacks on the USA changed decisively the pattern of world politics. Countries such as the Philippines, Indonesia and Malaysia were identified as having active groups linked to al-Qa'ida, the Islamist organization held responsible for the terrorist attacks. Malaysia and the Philippines acted quickly to suppress such activities, and demonstrated support for the USA, as did Australia. In the immediate term the 'war on terrorism' has had limited implications for the major Asian-Pacific nations such as Japan and China, but the long-term consequences are far from clear.

Refugee movements through the Asia-Pacific region have been as important as anywhere else in the world. However, the recent significant movements of refugees and economic migrants out of Afghanistan, Iraq, Iran and neighbouring countries has had a relatively small impact on the region. The exception is a continuing flow of Middle Eastern refugees through South-East Asia in the direction of Australia where, amid much controversy, the Government has attempted to curb the flow by diverting potential immigrants into neighbouring countries.

The growth in regional economies, new political links and tensions, and restructuring of the region's economic space have reconfigured the Asia-Pacific region. Yet the economic forces favouring greater integration are counterbalanced by the complex interaction among various social and cultural characteristics. On the one hand, nationalism is of increasing importance, fostered not just by political parties as a means of garnering support, but also by symbolically significant developments encouraged by an expanded middle class. National currencies have long been an important symbol of the territorial and economical integrity of the nation. Literatures in indigenous languages, as well as in the universal medium of English, have helped to shape national identity. Likewise, the emergence of important films and nascent national cinemas throughout the Asia-Pacific region have added further layers of complexity to nationalist sentiments. On the other hand, there is also a greater sense of pan-Asian identity evident throughout the region. For example, the Singapore Government has tried for many years to foster a sense of South-East Asian identity, based around the membership of ASEAN. Sports events are another avenue for supporting a broader sense of the region. Some of these movements highlight the ambiguous place of Australia in the Asia-Pacific region.

TOWARDS AN ASIAN-PACIFIC COMMUNITY

Economic growth and closer economic unity within the Pacific Basin have so far taken place without institutional support of the kind now in existence in Europe, or that which occurred among the Atlantic nations comprising the original members of the Organisation for Economic Co-operation and Development (OECD). However, a number of governments have seen the need for a supportive institutional structure, which could aid economic development and the advent of the 'Pacific century'. Although there have been few active government organizations for the whole of the Pacific Basin, there are many formal intergovernmental agreements and groupings that are intended to foster regional integration of a political, economic or other variety.

The Economic and Social Commission for Asia and the Pacific (ESCAP), the UN institution based in Bangkok, Thailand, is the geographically most comprehensive organization within the region, but it has limited effectiveness as a policy-influencing agency. Much-needed reforms were introduced in 1993, when the leadership of the organization changed. The ADB, based in Manila, the Philippines, functions as a regional bank for channelling development finance from the industrial countries to the developing countries. However, it also provides a limited forum for discussion of broader social and economic issues within the region.

ASEAN is the most important formal grouping of countries within the Pacific Basin (Fig. 1). Its core members until 1995 were Indonesia, Thailand, Malaysia, the Philippines, Singapore and Brunei. Viet Nam joined in July 1995, Myanmar (Burma) and Laos were admitted in mid-1997 and Cambodia in 1998 (see below). The Pacific nations have the Pacific Community (formerly the South Pacific Commission—SPC) and the Pacific Islands Forum (formerly the South Pacific Forum) and Pacific Islands Forum Secretariat, the member countries of which have discussed with ASEAN ways of establishing an associate relationship.

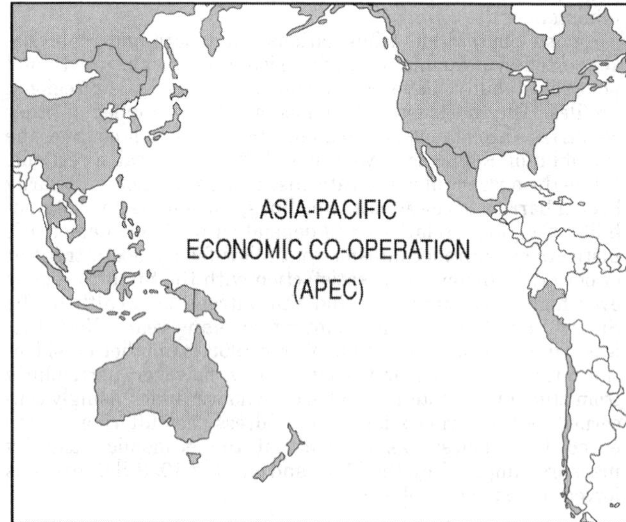

Figure 1. Major Regional Groups.

The ANZUS Security Treaty linking the USA, Australia and New Zealand remains in place. However, New Zealand's refusal to allow nuclear-powered or armed ships into its ports from 1985 strained relations with the USA and prevented ANZUS from functioning as originally intended. In September 1999 President Clinton announced the end of the 14-year ban on New

Zealand's participation in military exercises with the USA. However, New Zealand's decision in 2001 to cut back its armed forces caused heightened concern in Canberra and Washington.

Finally, a series of bilateral links binds countries of the region together. For instance, Australia and New Zealand have a policy of Closer Economic Relations (CER), which has resulted in an integrated labour market and, from mid-1990, free goods trade between the two countries.

ASIA-PACIFIC ECONOMIC CO-OPERATION

The post-war origins of the concept of an economic community spanning a large part of the Pacific first emerged in the 1960s. It reflected concerns about the formation of the European Community (EC—now EU), which, it was believed, could become inward-looking and threaten global market access. Initially, Japan suggested the formation of a Pacific free trade area (PAFTA), linking the Pacific Five industrialized countries: Japan, the USA, Canada, Australia and New Zealand. However, the proposal was not pursued, partly owing to concerns about Japanese hegemony (some recalled Japan's Second World War plans for a Greater East Asia Co-prosperity Sphere) and partly reflecting fears among the smaller industrial nations that they would not receive a fair share of the benefits from such an arrangement.

While government involvement waned following this initiative, economists formed a Pacific Trade and Development Conference, delegates of which have met regularly since the late 1960s. At about the same time, a group of business representatives, bankers and industrialists established a Pacific Basin Economic Council to discuss trade and investment issues.

Government interest in an Organization for Pacific Trade and Development (OPTAD) revived during the late 1970s when the issue was once again seriously discussed in Japan, the USA and Australia. The goals of OPTAD were to provide a safety valve for countries with high levels of economic interdependence, to stimulate regional trade and investment flows, to encourage consultation and discussion of long-term development issues, and to provide an umbrella for the formation of further economic alliances.

Subsequently, a series of Pacific Economic Co-operation Conferences (PECCs), beginning in Canberra in 1980, were held throughout the region to discuss closer economic ties. This fostered discussion on a regional approach to multilateral trade negotiations and trade policy, human resource development issues, and consultative mechanisms for minerals, energy and fisheries. A restricted institutional structure was built to support the initiative, including task forces and a secretariat.

A round of discussions regarding APEC followed a speech given by Australian Prime Minister Bob Hawke in Seoul in January 1989. He argued that the time had come to establish a formal body for inter-government dialogue and consultation on regional economic issues. Unlike the European model, it would require only modest institutional support: there was no intention of establishing a large regional bureaucracy.

Recognizing the growing significance of exports to the countries of the region, one of the emphases of such a body was to promote the round of multilateral trade negotiations under GATT, which was superseded by the WTO. Australia took a leading role in the Cairns Group promoting free trade in agricultural products, and envisaged APEC having a parallel role. It was a strongly-held view that APEC should not be a regional trading bloc.

Considerable discussion of the concept of an APEC took place during and following the annual meeting of the ASEAN countries in Bandar Seri Begawan (Brunei), in July 1989. Interestingly, the EC expressed strong concern about the proposed group, fearing that its large size might give it an excessive role in the world economy that could, eventually, be prejudicial to global free trade. However, the EC (now EU) itself has progressed towards a single market. In the circumstances, it was unlikely that Pacific Basin countries would take European concerns about the size and goals of APEC too seriously.

A meeting of the APEC group was held in Canberra in November 1989, attended by ministers of foreign and economic affairs from 12 nations: the six original members of ASEAN, the USA, Canada, New Zealand, Japan, the Republic of Korea and the host country, Australia. At the second APEC ministerial meeting, held in Singapore in July 1990, discussions focused on mutual concerns about free trade issues and GATT. The ASEAN members were more concerned with textile quotas and EC agricultural subsidies, whereas agriculture was of most concern for the non-ASEAN group. In a united demonstration of intentions, members agreed to reduce barriers to trade in goods and services between participants.

The Third Ministerial Meeting was held in Seoul in November 1991. For the first time the People's Republic of China, Taiwan (officially called Chinese Taipei in the group) and Hong Kong were invited to attend, bringing the total number of members of APEC to 15. Key issues for discussion included the Seoul Declaration, an endorsement by APEC members of the GATT Uruguay Round, free trade within the group—focusing on concerns about restrictions on agricultural imports into Japan and the Republic of Korea—and the establishment of a permanent APEC secretariat.

Some remained concerned that an achievable task for APEC had not been properly defined. Most believed a free-trade area to be Utopian, but recognized the advantages of the so-called 'integrated market of 2 billion people'. Australian Prime Minister Paul Keating had talked of compatible standards for key commodities such as motor vehicles, pharmaceuticals and telecommunication equipment, and mutual recognition of professional and trade qualifications.

One of the most significant demonstrations of APEC's growing importance came with the summit meeting held in Seattle, USA, in November 1993. For the first time it incorporated a heads-of-government meeting, attended by leaders from 12 member countries, including US President Bill Clinton, President Jiang Zemin of China and the Japanese Prime Minister, Morihiro Hosokawa. Prime Minister Mahathir of Malaysia boycotted the meeting, while Taiwan and Hong Kong, in deference to China's wishes, were represented at senior levels, rather than by heads of government.

Assessments of the Seattle meeting were generally favourable. As a meeting of heads of government it generated extensive press coverage and provided a symbol of improving dialogue within the region (this was summarized in the phrase 'the meeting is the message'). The fundamental issues were concerns expressed at the apparent stalling of the Uruguay Round of the GATT negotiations. The 'Blair House' accord on farm trade liberalization was endorsed and a statement released supporting the concept of an 'Asian-Pacific community', although the meaning of this was purposely left vague. Membership of the group was increased to 17, with the addition of Mexico and Papua New Guinea. Chile, which fulfilled membership criteria of an open economic policy and extensive economic links with APEC members, joined in 1994.

The venue for APEC's next heads-of-government meeting in 1994 was the Indonesian resort town of Bogor. The most significant outcome was the Bogor Declaration. Drafted by key Indonesians and agreed to by all the heads (though Malaysia's position was unclear), the Declaration committed APEC's 'industrialized economies' to achieving free trade by 2010 and the 'developing economies' to the same goal by 2020. Trade and investment liberalization, according to the Declaration, would facilitate links between APEC members and between members and non-APEC nations.

APEC's 1995 meeting was held in Osaka, Japan. The prime item for discussion was the 'Action Agenda' for implementing the trade liberalization measures agreed upon at the previous meeting in Bogor. The outcome was less clear than many expected. Whilst there was general agreement that all member states would strive to achieve the goals set out in the Bogor Declaration, there was no compulsion on them to do so, nor to meet the deadlines given.

The 1996 APEC heads-of-government meetings were held in Subic Bay, in the Philippines. Each country submitted plans for tariff cuts to the meetings, but disappointingly these varied substantially in content and detail. The Philippines, as host, offered the most ambitious plan, to reduce tariffs to 5% by 2004. APEC members also agreed to harmonize their tariff categories by the end of 1997 and their customs-clearance procedures by 1998.

The 1997 meeting was held in Vancouver, Canada. It coincided with the start of the Asian financial and economic crisis, and resulted in broad approval by leaders of rescue strategies for the region. There was also agreement on the reduction of trade barriers in nine specific fields, symbolizing the need to press on with reform. The meeting also decided to increase membership to 21 from November 1998, with the inclusion of Russia, Viet Nam and Peru. This was in spite of strong opposition, amid concerns that the inclusion of Russia would weaken the Pacific orientation of the group.

The 1998 meeting of APEC leaders was held in Kuala Lumpur. The focus was the continuing Asian economic crisis, and the widespread disappointment of observers in APEC's response to it. Non-government organizations meeting in Kuala Lumpur made known their overall concerns.

The 1999 APEC meeting, held in Auckland, New Zealand, was dominated by the crisis in East Timor. Nevertheless, leaders considered measures to sustain the economic recovery in Asia. Principles regarding the enhancement of competition and of regulatory reform were endorsed. Also under discussion was the forthcoming round of multilateral trade negotiations scheduled to be initiated by the WTO.

APEC's 2000 meeting was held in Bandar Seri Begawan, Brunei. It was attended by Bill Clinton, in his final days as President. (He travelled afterwards to Viet Nam.) Discussions at the meeting focused on trade liberalization and information technology.

The next APEC meeting was held in Shanghai, China, in October 2001 (after the September terrorist attacks on the USA). China's objection to Taiwan's representation at the meeting led to the departure of the latter's delegation. President George W. Bush attended, embracing Jiang Zemin in a widely noticed symbolic gesture and underlining the importance the USA sees in China's geopolitical position. The meeting agreed to release a statement condemning terrorism, but significantly did not produce a statement on actions to bring this about, nor on targeting al-Qa'ida.

There is some disquiet that progress within APEC is slow, and there are fears that it may stall. The phrase that seems to sum up expectations of APEC is 'open regional co-operation', differentiating it from the more inward-looking view that characterizes European endeavours. While this ambitious agenda for free trade attracts attention, another kind of barrier has equally important implications for trade and economic integration within the region. The existence of a host of country-specific regulations affecting trade, customs and transport, and product specifications concerning safety and health standards, labelling, environmental protection and so on continue to hamper economic transactions. Nor will these prove easy to dismantle. Nevertheless, progress towards removing unnecessary and outdated restrictions of this kind would go a long way towards making intra-regional trade easier and less costly.

The campaign within APEC towards more free trade, however, needs to be kept in perspective. The leading role of Japan (and, to a lesser extent, the USA) in APEC's attempt to achieve more free trade continues to be hindered by its failure to open its own markets to a wider range of imported goods. Despite its economic growth being based on an outward-looking strategy, many in the Republic of Korea are resisting further moves that would bring about an opening of the Korean market. Much the same accusations could be levelled at a number of the other members of the group.

Despite the very great diversity that characterizes the existing 21 members of APEC, and the halting progress being made in institutional terms, there is already a remarkable degree of economic integration. It is estimated that about two-thirds of the trade of APEC members is intra-group. This is much larger than intra-group trade among members of the EU. The 'flying geese' pattern of Asian development, as it is sometimes referred to, is clearly a model which a number of Latin American countries, among others, look upon with considerable interest. However, it seems increasingly possible that bilateral trade negotiations will rise in number and intensity, and may do more to free up trade than the laboured negotiations within APEC.

ASEAN AND OTHER REGIONAL ORGANIZATIONS

Despite progress on APEC, ASEAN has remained the most effective regional grouping up to the present. Some believe it is on the verge of substantially increasing its importance well beyond its symbolic significance. ASEAN celebrated its 30th anniversary in 1997. The organization's decision to expand in 1997 signalled a wish to play a more prominent role within South-East Asia as well as on the world stage. The embracing of Viet Nam and Laos was relatively uncontroversial, although a little ironic given that one of ASEAN's earliest tasks was the containment of socialism, particularly in Viet Nam. The high level of political instability in Cambodia in July 1997 resulted in ASEAN's postponement of its entry. Myanmar and Laos were admitted as planned, however. The decision to include Myanmar in the group precipitated much condemnation owing to its poor human-rights record. Cambodia was eventually accepted by ASEAN in December 1998, bringing the organization's total membership to 10. Politics aside, it is likely that ASEAN membership will severely strain the human resources of the new members, which suggests that they will not participate in the full range of ASEAN meetings for some years to come.

Initiatives within the organization have focused on two issues: trade and security. Moves during 1992 led to agreement to form an ASEAN Free Trade Area (AFTA) over the next 15 years. A start on tariff cuts was made at the beginning of 1993. It will lead eventually to a common 5% tariff for an agreed schedule of processed agricultural and manufactured goods traded within the group. In contrast to the past, the dialogue on regional security in the early 1990s took on a greater prominence at the ASEAN foreign ministers' meetings and in the post-meetings talks with representatives from other nations with interests in the region. Some believe it may eventually lead to a regional security plan. Of course, there remain tensions within the group. Some, for example, fear that Singapore is pressing too hard for ASEAN to develop closer links with China.

In November 1999 the third ASEAN informal summit meeting was held in Manila, the Philippines, attended by the leaders of the 10 member countries, plus China, Japan and the Republic of Korea. The ASEAN + 3 agenda included agreement to meet annually, as well as support for a Japanese proposal to establish an Asian monetary fund. The meeting highlighted the search for more effective links within the Asia-Pacific region, albeit at a time when many business commentators now stress the importance of global over regional interests. ASEAN has resisted requests from Australia to expand the arrangement to an ASEAN + 4 configuration.

The first Asia-Europe Meeting (ASEM) was held in Bangkok in March 1996. The 15 member countries of the EU attended, together with representatives from the seven ASEAN countries and China, Japan and the Republic of Korea. Discussions focused on economic issues, including trade and investment, without any firm agreements being reached. Nevertheless, it marked a maturing of European attitudes towards Asia's growth economies. The second ASEM was held in London in April 1998. Despite their recent accession to ASEAN, Laos and Myanmar were not represented at the meeting, which was dominated by discussion of the Asian financial crisis. The third ASEM, which was convened in Seoul, the South Korean capital, in October 2000, welcomed the recent reconciliation between the two Korean nations, and declared its commitment to the promotion of human rights. The 10 Asian and 15 EU countries endorsed various initiatives relating to economic globalization and information technology (including an Initiative to Address the Digital Divide and the establishment of a Trans-Eurasia Information Network). The meeting also approved an initiative to co-operate on the combating of transnational crime. The fourth ASEM was scheduled to be held in Denmark in 2002.

Public expressions of concern about increasing global trade and economic links in 2000 and 2001 have shifted attention to regional and bilateral arrangements. The first East Asian-Latin American Co-operation Forum was held in Chile in April 2001. A Pacific Five initiative is being discussed by Singapore, Australia, New Zealand, the USA and Chile. A Closer Economic Partnership between Singapore, Australia and New Zealand has been broached, and in April 2001 a New Zealand-Singapore agreement was signed.

Given the apprehension with which NAFTA is viewed in the region, it is rather ironic that the idea was suggested in Washington by former US President George Bush that NAFTA itself might one day be expanded to incorporate Asian-Pacific countries including Australia, Singapore, New Zealand, Hong

Kong and Taiwan. However, it was made clear that this was some distance away. President George W. Bush, who took office in January 2001, subsequently gave support to the idea of a grouping of Free Trade Areas of the Americas.

ASIA-PACIFIC IN THE PACIFIC CENTURY

The Asia-Pacific region has moved to the forefront of world attention, largely owing to the spectacular economic growth that marked most of the last two decades of the 20th century. Nevertheless, the majority of Asian-Pacific countries are far from affluent, with most containing large numbers of poor people living in impoverished urban settlements and rural villages. The Asian-led economic crisis had a devastating impact on Indonesia, in particular, and seriously weakened a number of other regional economies. The high levels of economic integration have, in the past, helped to spread economic growth. With the onset of the 1997 crisis, the same integration meant that most economies suffered.

However, optimism is now growing that most Asian-Pacific economies have recovered from the 1997 crisis and will continue to increase their role in a fluid global economy. Moreover, the reorganization of the space economies of the region is likely to be permanent. Increasing levels of economic integration and radically different economic links between territories, such as the 'natural economic territories', are a reflection of the dynamic regional economies of Asia-Pacific. Yet this is a complex matter, as ongoing political and territorial disputes, not to mention rising nationalism, continue to draw peoples and nations often in opposite directions.

Regional organizations such as APEC and ASEAN have emerged in the Asia-Pacific region and throughout the Pacific Basin more generally. However, the maturing of these organizations has occurred slowly, and they played a disappointingly limited role in addressing the Asian economic crisis of 1997 and other major world events since then. The challenge for both organizations in the 21st century is to justify the faith that many supporters have placed in them to achieve the development of a stronger sense of community in the Asia-Pacific region.

BIBLIOGRAPHY

Aho, C. M. 'America and the Pacific century: trade conflict or cooperation?' *International Affairs*, Vol. 69, No. 1, pp. 19–37, 1993.

Ariff, M., and Hill, H. *Export-orientated Industrialisation: The ASEAN Experience*. London, Allen and Unwin, 1985.

Arndt, H. W., and Hill, H. (Eds). *Southeast Asia's Economic Crisis*. Singapore, Institute of Southeast Asian Studies, 1999.

Asian Development Bank. *Asian Development Outlook*. Manila, annually.

Economic Cooperation in the Greater Mekong Subregion. Manila, 1993.

Subregional Economic Cooperation. Manila, 1993.

Benjamin, R., and Kurdle, R. T. (Eds). *The Industrial Future of the Pacific Basin*. Boulder, CO, Westview Press, 1984.

Bora, B., and Findlay, C. (Eds). *Regional Integration and the Asia-Pacific*. Melbourne, Oxford University Press, 1996.

Borthwick, M. *Pacific Century: The Emergence of Modern Pacific Asia*. Boulder, CO, Westview Press, 1992.

Bowles, P. 'ASEAN, AFTA and the 'new regionalism'.' *Pacific Affairs*, Vol. 70, No. 2, pp. 219–234, 1997.

Burnett, A. *The Western Pacific: Challenge of Sustainable Growth*. Aldershot, Edward Elgar, 1992.

Chan Heng Chee (Ed.). *The New Asia-Pacific Order*. Singapore, Institute of Southeast Asian Studies, 1997.

Chin, K. W. 'The institutional structure of ASEAN: governmental and private sectors', in Thuraisingham, A. (Ed.), *ASEAN: A Bibliography*. Singapore, Institute of Southeast Asian Studies, pp. xv–xxxv, 1988.

Clark, G. L., and Kim Won Bae (Eds). *Asian NIEs & the Global Economy: Industrial Restructuring & Corporate Strategy in the 1990s*. Baltimore, The Johns Hopkins University Press, 1995.

Commonwealth of Australia, Department of Foreign Affairs and Trade. *The APEC Region: Trade and Investment*. Canberra, 1993.

Daly, M. T., and Logan, M. I. *The Brittle Rim: Finance, Business and the Pacific Region*. Ringwood, Penguin, 1989.

Dirlik, A. *What Is In a Rim? Critical Perspectives on the Pacific Region Idea*. Boulder, CO, Westview Press, 1993.

Dixon, C. *South East Asia in the World Economy: A Regional Geography*. Cambridge, Cambridge University Press, 1991.

Donnen, R. L., and Dickson, B. J. (Eds). *The Emerging Pacific Community: A Regional Perspective*. Boulder, CO, Westview Press, 1984.

Drysdale, P. *International Economic Pluralism: Economic Policy in East Asia and the Pacific*. Sydney, Allen and Unwin, in association with the Australia-Japan Research Centre, the Research School of Pacific Studies, The Australian National University, 1988.

Elek, A. 'Pacific economic co-operation: policy choices for the 1990s'. *Asian-Pacific Economic Literature*, Vol. 6, No. 1, pp. 1–15, 1992.

'Trade policy options for the Asia-Pacific region in the 1990's: the potential for open regionalism'. *American Economic Review*, Vol. 82, No. 2, pp. 74–78, 1992.

Eminent Persons Group. *Achieving the APEC Vision: Free and Open Trade in the Asia Pacific*. Singapore, Asia-Pacific Economic Co-operation, 1994.

Findlay, C., and Forsyth, P. 'Air transport in the Asian-Pacific region', *Asian-Pacific Economic Literature*, Vol. 6, No. 2, pp. 1–10, 1992.

Findlay, C., Sien, C. L., and Singh, K. (Eds). *Asia Pacific Air Transport: Challenges and Policy Reforms*. Singapore, Institute of Southeast Asian Studies,1997.

Forbes, D. K. *Asian Metropolis: Urbanisation and the Southeast Asian City*. Melbourne, Oxford University Press, 1996.

'What's in it for us? Images of Pacific Asian development' in C. Dixon and D. Drakakis-Smith (Eds), *Economic and Social Development in Pacific Asia*. London, Routledge, pp. 43–62, 1993.

'Regional integration, internationalisation and the new geographies of the Pacific Rim' in R. Watters and T. G. McGee (Eds), *Asia Pacific: New Geographies of the Pacific Rim*. London, C. Hurst, pp. 13–28, 1997.

'Imaginative geography and the post-colonial spaces of Pacific Asia' in T. C. Wong and M. Singh (Eds), *Development and Challenge: Southeast Asia in the New Millennium*. Singapore, Times Academic Press, pp. 1–22, 1999.

Fuchs, R. J., Jones, G. W., and Pernia, E. M. (Eds). *Urbanization and Urban Policies in Pacific Asia*. Boulder, CO, Westview Press, 1987.

Gallant, N., and Stubbs, R. 'APEC's dilemmas: institution-building around the Pacific rim', *Pacific Affairs*, Vol. 70, No. 2, pp. 203–218, 1997.

Garnaut, R. *Australia and the Northeast Asian Ascendancy*. Australian Government Publishing Service, Canberra, 1989.

Guisinger, S. 'A Pacific Basin Investment Agreement', *ASEAN Economic Bulletin*, Vol. 19, pp. 176–183, 1993.

Harris, S. 'Economic cooperation and institution building in the Asia-Pacific region' in R. Higgott, R. Leaver and J. Ravenhill (Eds), *Pacific Economic Relations in the 1990s: Cooperation or Conflict?* Sydney, Allen and Unwin, pp. 271–289, 1992.

'Policy networks and economic cooperation: policy coordination in the Asia-Pacific region', *Pacific Review*, Vol. 7, No. 4, 1994.

Harris, S., and Klintworth, G. (Eds). *China as a Great Power in the Asia-Pacific Region: Myths, Realities and Challenges*. Melbourne, Longman Cheshire, 1995.

Imada, P., and Naya, S. (Eds). *AFTA: The Way Ahead*. Singapore, Institute of Southeast Asian Studies, 1992.

Keating, P. *Engagement: Australia Faces the Asia-Pacific*. Sydney, Macmillan, 2000.

Kraus, W., and Lutkenhorst, W. *The Economic Development of the Pacific Basin*. New York, St Martin's Press, 1986.

Lambert, J.M. 'Institution-building in the Pacific - Canada in APEC', *Pacific Affairs*, Vol. 70, No. 2, pp. 195–202, 1997.

Lau, T. S., and Suryadinata, L. (Eds). *Moving Into the Pacific Century: The Changing Regional Border in the Asia-Pacific*. Singapore, Heinemann Asia, 1988.

Leinbach, T., and Ulack, R. (Eds). *Southeast Asia: Diversity and Development*. New Jersey, Prentice-Hall, 2000.

Linge, G. J. R., and Forbes, D. K. (Eds). *China's Space Economy: Recent Developments and Reforms*. Hong Kong, Oxford University Press, 1990.

McGee, T. G., and Robinson, I. M. (Eds). *The Mega-urban Regions of Southeast Asia*. Vancouver, UBC Press, 1995.

Manning, R. A., and Stern, P. 'The myth of the Pacific community', *Foreign Affairs*, November/December, 1994.

Montes, M. *The Currency Crisis in Southeast Asia (Updated Edition)*. Singapore, Institute of Southeast Asian Studies, 1998.

Naya, S., and Plummer, M. G. 'ASEAN economic co-operation: the new international economic environment' in K. S. Sandhu et al, *The ASEAN Reader*, Singapore, Institute of Southeast Asian Studies, pp. 191–196, 1992.

Okita, S. 'Developing the Asia-Pacific region' in K. S. Sandhu, S. Siddique, C. Jeshurun, A. Rajah, J. C. H. Tan and P. Thambipillai, *The ASEAN Reader*. Singapore, Institute of Southeast Asian Studies, pp. 500–503, 1992.

Palat, R. A. (Ed.). *Pacific-Asia and the Future of the World-System*. Westport, Greenwood Press, 1993.

Palmer, N. D. *The New Regionalism in Asia and the Pacific*. Massachusetts, Lexington Books, 1991.

Rimmer, P. 'Regional economic integration in Pacific Asia', *Environment and Planning A*, Vol. 26, No. 11, pp. 1731–1760, 1994.

Rimmer, P. (Ed.). *Pacific Rim Development: Integration and Globalisation in the Asia-Pacific Economy*. Sydney, Allen and Unwin, 1997.

Rudner, M. 'APEC: the challenges of Asia Pacific Economic Cooperation', *Modern Asian Studies*, Vol. 29, No. 2, pp. 403–407, 1995.

Savage, V. R., Kong, L., and Neville, W. (Eds.). *The Naga Awakens: Growth and Change in Southeast Asia*. Singapore, Times Academic Press, 1998.

Scalapino, R. A. 'The United States and Asia: future prospects', *Foreign Affairs* Vol. 70, No. 5, pp. 19–40, 1991/92.

Segal, G. *Rethinking the Pacific*. Oxford, Clarendon Press, 1991.

Soesastro, H. (Ed.). *Indonesian Perspectives on APEC and Regional Co-operation in Asia-Pacific*. Jakarta, Centre for Strategic and International Studies, 1994.

Sopiee, N., See, C. L., and Jin, L. S. (Eds). *ASEAN at the Crossroads*. Kuala Lumpur, Institute of Strategic and International Studies, 1987.

Spate, O. H. K. *The Pacific Since Magellan: Vol. I: The Spanish Lake*. Canberra, Australian National University Press, 1979.

The Pacific Since Magellan: Vol. II: Monopolists and Freebooters. Canberra, Australian National University Press, 1983.

The Pacific Since Magellan, Vol. III: Paradise Found and Lost. Sydney, Australian National University Press, 1988.

Tan, G. *ASEAN Economic Development and Cooperation*. Singapore, Times Academic Press, 1996.

Tan, K. Y., Toh, M. H., and Low, L. 'ASEAN and Pacific economic co-operation' in K. S. Sandhu et al, *The ASEAN Reader*, Singapore, Institute of Southeast Asian Studies, pp. 313–320, 1992.

United Nations Development Programme. *Human Development Report*, annually. New York, Oxford University Press.

Ward, R. G. 'Earth's empty quarter? The Pacific islands in a Pacific century'. *Geographical Journal,* Vol. 155, No. 2, pp. 235–246, 1989.

Watters, R., and McGee, T. G. (Eds). *Asia Pacific: New Geographies of the Pacific Rim*. London, C. Hurst, 1997.

Whitlam, E. G. *A Pacific Community*. Cambridge, MA, Harvard University Press, 1981.

Wilson, R., and Dirlik, A. (Eds). *Asia/Pacific as Space of Cultural Production*. Durham, NC, Duke University Press.

World Bank. *The East Asian Miracle: Economic Growth and Public Policy*. New York, Oxford University Press, 1993.

World Development Indicators. New York, Oxford University Press, annually.

Zainuddin, D. *ASEAN Economic Co-operation: Agenda for the 1990s*. Singapore, Institute of Southeast Asian Studies, 1990.

PART TWO
Country Surveys

AFGHANISTAN

Physical and Social Geography

W. B. FISHER

Occupying an area of 652,225 sq km (according to official figures; other estimates are in the range 620,000 sq km–700,000 sq km), Afghanistan has the shape of a very irregular oval, with its major axis running from north-east to south-west and extending over roughly 1,125 km, and the minor axis at right angles to this, covering about 560 km. The country is, in the main, a highland mass lying mostly at an altitude of 1,200 m or more, but it presents a very variable pattern of extremely high and irregular mountain ridges, some of which exceed 6,000 m, ravines and broader valleys, parts of which are very fertile, and an outer expanse of undulating plateau, wide river basins, and lake sumps.

Politically, Afghanistan has two frontiers of major length: one on the north with Turkmenistan, Uzbekistan and Tajikistan, the other on the south and east with Pakistan. The latter frontier follows what was once termed the Durand Line (after the representative of British India, Sir Mortimer Durand, who negotiated it in 1893 with the ruler of Afghanistan). So long as the British occupied India, it was generally accepted as forming the Indo-Afghan frontier, but in 1947, with the recognition of Pakistan as a successor to the British, the Afghan Government recalled that, for much of the 18th century, Peshawar and other parts of the Indus Valley had formed part of a larger Afghan state and were, moreover, occupied largely by Pashtuns, who are of closely similar ethnic character to many Afghans. Accordingly, the Durand Line frontier was denounced by Afghanistan, and claims were made that the territories as far as the line of the Indus, including Chitral, Swat and Peshawar, and continuing as far as the Pashtun areas of the North-West Frontier Province and Balochistan, ought to be recognized as an autonomous state, 'Pashtunistan'. This remains a subject of dispute between Afghanistan and Pakistan.

There are shorter but no less significant frontiers on the west with Iran and on the north-east with the People's Republic of China. This last was fully agreed only in 1963, and the precise location of others in the south and west has not been completely delimited: an indication of the extreme difficulties of terrain, and an explanation of the uncertainty regarding the actual area of Afghanistan. It is noteworthy that, in order to erect a 'buffer' between the then competing empires of Russia and India, under the Durand Treaty of 1893 the Wakhan district, a narrow strip of land 320 km long and under 16 km wide in its narrowest part, was attached to Afghanistan. The allocation of this strip, which controls the Baroghil Pass over the Pamir, avoided the existence of a Soviet-Indian frontier.

PHYSICAL FEATURES

The main topographical feature of Afghanistan is a complex of irregular highlands, which is relatively broad and low in the west and very much higher and narrower towards the east. In this eastern part the mountains form a group of well-defined chains, which are known by the general name of the Hindu Kush ('Hindu destroyer'), and are linked further eastward first to the Pamirs and then to the main Himalayan system. The Eastern Hindu Kush ranges form the southern defining limit of the Wakhan strip while, a short distance to the north and east, a small but high ridge, the Little Pamir, forms the topographic link between the Hindu Kush and the main Pamir. From maximum heights of 6,000 m–7,000 m the peaks decline in altitude westwards, attaining 4,500 m–6,000 m in the zone close to Kabul. Further west still, the ridges are no more than 3,500 m–4,500 m and in the extreme west they open out rather like the digits of a hand, with much lower Parapamisus ridges (proto-Pamir) forming the last member of the mountain complex. The various ridges are distinguished by separate names. The Hindu Kush, which has a general altitude of about 4,500 m, with peaks 2,000 m–3,000 m higher still, is, however, narrow and crossable by quite a number of passes, some of which are indirect and snow-bound for much of the year.

Afghanistan forms a major watershed from which rivers flow outward. The Amu-Dar'ya (Oxus) rises on the north side of the Hindu Kush and flows north-westwards into Turkmenistan. Here, away from the mountains, the presence of small pockets of loess (a yellowish soil of high fertility) offers scope for agriculture. The Hari Rud rises a short distance only from the Amu-Dar'ya, but flows westward through Herat to terminate in a salt, closed basin on the Iranian frontier. From the south and west of the Hindu Kush flow a number of streams that become tributaries of the Indus; and in the extreme south-west the Helmand river flows through arid country to end, like the Hari Rud, in a closed basin that is partly within Iranian territory. The Helmand basin is of interest in that, because of a curious balance in water-level at its lowest part, the river here reverses its flow seasonally, and remains for much of its length non-brackish instead of becoming progressively more saline, as is normal when there is no outlet to the sea. The Helmand basin thus offers distinct potential for agricultural improvement, including the development of irrigation schemes; but political difficulties (part of the lower basin is Iranian territory) and remoteness have been inhibiting factors.

The lower-lying areas, which are in the main more densely peopled, occur either as a series of peripheral zones to north and south, or as a series of interior valleys and basins between the main mountain ridges of the centre. Largest of these areas is the piedmont lying on the northern flanks of the mountains and dropping northwards in altitude to merge into the steppelands of former Soviet Central Asia. This is Bactria (Balkh), a region of, in places, light yellowish, loessic soils. An interior situation, shut off from the sea by mountains, means that rainfall is deficient and falls mainly over the mountains. Streams fed partly by mountain snow-melt straggle across the plain, to lose themselves in the sand, feed salt swamps, or in a few cases, join others to form larger rivers such as the Hari Rud. Much of Bactria thus consists of semi- or full desert with sheets of sand and gravel in many places, with, nearer the mountains, outwash of larger, coarser scree. Given stable political conditions, this area with its areas of highly fertile loess soils and moderate water supplies offers much scope for economic development. For long inhabited by pastoral nomads, and disputed politically by various claimants (Afghanistan, Iran and the former USSR), this northern zone was developed rapidly with irrigated cotton growing as a main element. Links with the former USSR were considerable, and the two chief towns of Herat in the west and Mazar-i-Sharif in the north have grown considerably in size over recent years, mainly for political (rather than economic) reasons.

On the south, towards the east, is the Kabul basin, which is a relatively flat zone hemmed in closely by steep mountain ridges. Some distance away to the north-west, and reachable through two major passes is the narrower Vale of Bamian; whilst south-east of Kabul occurs another fertile lowland zone around Jalalabad. Here lower elevation and southerly situation produce warmer conditions, especially in winter, as compared with most of the rest of Afghanistan.

In the south-west, extending through Ghazni as far as Qandahar, there is another series of cultivated zones; but the extent of this piedmont area is much smaller than the corresponding one described above as Bactria. To the west, aridity, the price of declining altitude, increases, so the lowland passes into the desert areas of Registan and the Dasht-i-Mayo. Registan has seasonal flushes of grass, which support relatively large numbers of pastoral nomads, who, however, are becoming increasingly settled following irrigation development on the Helmand and Arghandab rivers.

Two other regional units may be mentioned. South of the Parapamisus and Kuh-i-Baba mountain ranges are a number of parallel but lower massifs, with narrow valleys between. Here because of altitude there is a relatively abundant rainfall, but owing to topography, the region is one of remoteness and difficulty. This is the Hazarajat, so called from the name of the Hazara inhabitants, and it still remains, despite a central position, one of the least known and visited parts of the country. Another equally remote highland, this time located north-east of Kabul, is Nuristan, again high and mountainous, but well-wooded in places, and supporting a small population of cultivators and pastoralists who use the summer pastures of the high hills and move to lower levels in winter.

CLIMATE

Climatically, Afghanistan demonstrates a very clear relationship with Iran and the Middle East, rather than with Monsoon Asia, in that it has an almost arid summer, a small amount of rainfall, which is largely confined to the winter season, and considerable seasonal variation in temperature. The monsoonal condition of heavy summer rainfall does not occur, despite Afghanistan's proximity to India. Annual rainfall ranges from 100 mm–150 mm in the drier, lower areas of the west and north, to 250 mm–400 mm in the east; on the highest mountains there is more still. Kabul, with an average of 330 mm per annum, is typical of conditions in the east, and Herat with 125 mm typical of the west. Almost all this falls in the period December to April, though there can be a very occasional downpour at other times, even in summer, when a rare damp monsoonal current penetrates from the Indian lowlands. Temperatures are best described as extreme. In July the lowlands experience temperatures of 43°C, with 49°C not uncommon—this is true of Jalalabad on the edge of the Indus lowlands. Yet the effects of altitude are important, and Kabul, at an elevation of 1,800 m, does not often experience temperatures of over 38°C. Winter cold can be bitter, with minima of −22°C to −26°C on the higher plateau areas, and, as a result, there are heavy blizzards in many mountain areas. The January mean in Kabul is −4°C. A further difficulty is the prevalence of strong winds, especially in the west, where a persistent and regular wind blows almost daily from June to September and affects especially the Sistan area of the lower Helmand basin, where it is known as the 'Wind of 120 Days'.

POPULATION

The considerable variation in the types of terrain, and the substantial obstacles imposed by high mountains and deserts, have given rise to marked ethnic and cultural differences, so that heterogeneity in human populations is most characteristic. The Pashtuns live mainly in the centre, south and east of the country, and are probably numerically the largest group. The Ghilzays, also of the areas adjacent to Pakistan, are thought to be of Turkish origin, like the Uzbeks who live in the north, mainly in the Amu-Dar'ya lowlands. Another important element comprises the Tajiks or Parziwans who are of Persian origin, and in the opinion of some represent the earliest inhabitants of the country. Other groups, such as the Hazara (who are reputed to have come in as followers of Genghis Khan) and the Chahar Aimak, may have Mongol ancestry, but they now speak Farsi (Persian) and the Hazara are Shi'a Muslims. In the north-east, the presence of fair-haired groups has suggested historic connections with Europe. Another possibly indigenous group of long standing is the Nuristani or Kafirs, now small in number. Most Afghans (the Hazara and Qizilbash of Kabul excepted) are Muslims of the Sunni sect. Pashto (Pakhto), one of the eastern group of Iranian languages, is spoken by about 30% of the total population (numerous other Pashto-speakers live across the frontier in Pakistan). Since 1936 Pashto and Dari (a dialect of Farsi) have been the official languages of the country, using an augmented Arabic script.

Economic progress has been inhibited by a difficult topography, an extreme climate with a generally deficient rainfall and political instability. Traditionally, small communities lived by cultivation where water and soil were available, and there were relatively numerous pastoralists, mostly nomads, who formed an important section of the community. Even today, it is estimated that about 15% of the population is nomadic, and tribal organization is strong. In 1999, according to FAO estimates, only 12% of Afghanistan's total area was classified as arable land.

History

AHMED MUKARRAM

Based on an earlier article by MALCOLM E. YAPP

Revised by WILLIAM MALEY and BRUCE KOEPKE

EARLY HISTORY

Throughout its history Afghanistan has been influenced by varied combinations of domestic and external factors. A salient religious element combined with distinct tribal identities, either clashing or collaborating, would often converge with external socio-political forces so as to herald new historical dynamics. The situation becomes more comprehensible when taking into account the distinctive terrain and geographical location of this land-locked country. For a very long time Afghanistan's rugged mountain valleys and rather inhospitable deserts have naturally demarcated the boundaries of various tribal or ethno-linguistic communities. Likewise, the country's location as a meeting place of three geographical and cultural regions—the Iranian plateau to the west, the Central Asian republics of the former USSR to the north, and the Indian subcontinent to the south—has allowed it to become a base for various trans-regional incursions into these different areas. Owing to the religious and ethno-linguistic commonalities that it shares with its neighbours, Afghanistan has often played a crucial role in their development. Such trans-regionalism was somehow suited to the long-prevailing situation of dynastic empires with shifting borders and fluctuating authority. With the advent of the nation state throughout the area following decolonization, however, trans-regionality became more subtle and, at the same time, rather volatile, with each country jealously guarding its own territory and geo-political interests.

For centuries Afghanistan has been either the starting-point or the destination of various incursions (both military and socio-political). In ancient times, it was through Afghanistan that the Aryans moved into India and Iran, where they established powerful civilizations. Before becoming a centre of Buddhism under Emperor Ashoka in the third century BC, Afghanistan witnessed the growth and prevalence of Zoroastrianism during the sixth and fifth centuries BC. In the fourth century BC Alexander the Great of Greece invaded Afghanistan with the aim of annihilating the rival Persian empire. The influence of Buddhism was quite far-reaching in Afghanistan, as confirmed by recent archaeological research. The colossal statues of Buddha in the Hazara heartland of Bamian in central Afghanistan, destroyed by the Taliban in early 2001, were not only the largest of their type but also constituted irrefutable proof of the popularization of the Indian religion. The Gandharan civilization, which reached its zenith in the second century AD and which epitomized a fascinating synthesis of various Indian,

Greek and Persian cultures, flourished in eastern Afghanistan, with its epicentre in the northern region of present-day Pakistan. The pluralism of Afghan society can be traced back, to a large extent, to these external influences and invasions. It is not surprising, therefore, that, even after so many centuries, many Afghan tribes (especially the Pashtuns) occasionally seek common ancestry with the Jews—some ethnologists, however, claim that the link is purely mythical. Long before Arab Muslims, led by Mohammad bin Qasim, invaded Sindh in 712 AD, Afghanistan had already become one of the provinces of the Ummayyad Caliphate based in Damascus, Syria. Within a few years, it was through Afghanistan that Islam reached Central Asia and the interior of China. It was also via Afghanistan that the Muslim *ulama* (religious scholars) and *sufis* (mystics) moved into the South Asian subcontinent and led the early mass conversions in northern India. The subsequent rulers of Muslim India, who were known as the Delhi Sultans (although they were actually overwhelmingly Turkish), extended their campaigns into India in the early 13th century AD after conquering and consolidating their hold on power in Afghanistan.

During its ancient and medieval past, Afghanistan was known under a variety of different names, such as Aryana, Khurasan, Badakhshan or Kabul province. The country's history has been a curious mixture of localism and internationalism. Afghanistan played a major role in regional affairs, whilst simultaneously maintaining its introverted localism. The Afghan people usually mounted strong resistance to any invasion from outside, but their local factionalism prevented them from establishing a formidable united front. The Turkic and Mongol invaders from the north invariably used coercion against the Afghan inhabitants, but, after having subjugated them, offered them various incentives to join them in further military expeditions in adjoining territories. The limitations of the rural economy and the rather inclement climate both helped to persuade numerous Afghans to join forces with invading armies. This provides one explanation for the regular migrations from Afghanistan into the Indian subcontinent since ancient times.

It was not simply for material reasons, however, that the Afghans sided with the conquerors; an equal amount of religious enthusiasm in the name of jihad ('holy war') also helped to ensure their participation. Mahmud of Ghazni (988–1031), who was originally a Turk, used Afghanistan as his base, from which he launched 17 invasions into northern India. Under the Delhi Sultans, Afghanistan was politically and economically integrated into the Indian Muslim heartland. During the Mongol invasions led by Genghis Khan in the 13th century, Afghanistan, like its Central Asian, Iranian and Indian neighbours, was severely ravaged and large numbers of people were killed. Many followers of the Mongol warlord settled in Afghanistan, and their eventual acculturation into Islam made them a new source of military strength for various, successive Muslim dynasties. The Hazaras of Afghanistan trace their origins from these Mongol conquerors. Babur, who founded the Indian Mogul dynasty after defeating the last Delhi Sultan in 1526 at Panipat, was himself of Turkic origin and had been expelled from his native Ferghana in Uzbekistan. On his paternal side, Babur was a descendant of the Mongol warlord Timur (Tamerlane), whose dynasty was based in Samarkand in Uzbekistan, while, on his maternal side, Babur traced his ancestry back to Genghis Khan. Prior to invading India, Babur captured Kabul, where, at his request, he was later buried. Afghanistan was an important part of the Mogul empire and survived attempts by the rival Shi'a Safavid dynasty in Persia to wrest control of these areas from the Mogul rulers.

Following the death of Emperor Aurangzeb in 1707, the Mogul empire suffered a rapid decline, with various provinces, especially those in distant areas, seeking independence from Delhi. The invasion of Afghanistan from Iran by Nadir Shah in the 1730s, followed by his headlong assault on Delhi, further weakened the Mogul empire. The true founder of the Afghan state, however, is usually considered to be Ahmad Shah Abdali (reigned 1747–72), who created a tribal empire in Afghanistan and northern India, following his victories over the Marathas of India. The growing clash of interests between an expansive Tsarist Russia and an ambitious British East India Company meant that a sovereign Afghanistan provided a convenient buffer zone between the two rival powers. Once again, local and international factors combined to shape and influence the history and politics of the Afghan people. Abdali, who was based in Kabul, consolidated his rule in Afghanistan by establishing a tribal confederacy. Under his successors, northern India was lost and civil war broke out in Afghanistan, which became divided into a number of separate ethno-tribal principalities. By 1863 Afghanistan had been reunited by the Amir Dost Muhammad Khan Barakzay. During his reign, the first Anglo-Afghan war (1839–42) took place when, because of fears of the spread of Russian influence towards India, British Indian forces occupied Afghanistan. The second Anglo-Afghan war (1878–80) was the consequence of similar British fears and led to the overthrow of Dost Muhammad's eventual successor, Shir Ali (1869–79), and the establishment of a new ruler, Abd ar-Rahman (1880–1901). During the reign of Abd ar-Rahman the boundaries of Afghanistan assumed their present form. The western frontier with Iran had been demarcated in 1872; the northern frontier with Russian-controlled Turkestan (now Turkmenistan) was demarcated in 1885–87 and 1895; and the southern and eastern frontiers with British India and its dependencies were outlined in the Durand Agreement of 1893 and demarcated in 1894–96. In order to avoid a meeting of the Russian and British Indian frontiers, the Wakhan strip, linking north-east Afghanistan with the Chinese frontier, was attached to Afghanistan. Within these limits, Abd ar-Rahman established a strong centralized Government. Although obliged to accept British control of his foreign relations, Abd ar-Rahman preserved Afghanistan's internal independence.

MODERN AFGHANISTAN, 1901–73

Abd ar-Rahman was succeeded as Amir by his son, Habibullah, who maintained the absolutist system of his father. Habibullah introduced educational reforms: the first secondary school was founded in 1904 and the curriculum of the traditional religious schools was broadened. During his reign a modernizing, nationalist movement of Afghan intellectuals developed around the newspaper *Siraj al-Akhbar* (1911–19), edited by Mahmud Tarzi. During the First World War Afghanistan remained neutral.

On 20 February 1919 Habibullah was assassinated and was succeeded by his youngest son, Amanullah, who immediately proclaimed the independence of Afghanistan. War with the United Kingdom broke out when Afghan forces entered British Indian territory. Afghan forces in the Khaibar Pass were quickly repulsed but those in Waziristan achieved some successes before an armistice was signed. Under the Treaty of Rawalpindi signed in August 1919, peace was established, the British subsidy ended and the Durand frontier confirmed. A separate letter effectively recognized Afghanistan's independence. In November 1921 a treaty between the United Kingdom and Afghanistan was signed.

Amanullah, 1919–29

Amanullah confirmed Afghanistan's independence through agreements with other countries. In September 1920 he signed an agreement with Soviet Russia, in March 1921 with Kemalist Turkey, and in June 1921 with Iran. Diplomatic relations were opened with other countries. His hopes of territorial expansion were ended when neighbouring regimes consolidated their power. Amanullah began an extensive programme of modernization. The first Afghan Constitution was promulgated in 1923 and the whole administrative system was reorganized; a system of legislative councils was established; a new system of courts was set up with secular codes of law; major reforms were made in taxation and budgeting (the first government budget was introduced in 1922); and efforts at economic modernization were made. After a visit to Europe in 1927–28 Amanullah became more ambitious and announced a further series of reforms especially directed against traditional social customs, including the wearing of the veil. Amanullah saw himself as a modernizer in the mould of Atatürk in Turkey and Reza Shah in Iran; in retrospect, however, his failings were to be perceived as anti-Islamic in his single-minded pursuit of Westernization and to allow his army to become weak. In the latter half of 1928 tribal risings broke out in eastern Afghanistan, culminating in the occupation of Kabul in January 1929 by a Tajik villager, known as the Baccha-i Saqqaw, who proclaimed himself Habibullah II of Afghanistan. Amanullah fled to India and thence to Europe, where he died in 1960.

Nadir Shah, 1929–33

Leadership of the opposition to Habibullah II fell to a group of brothers, Nadir, Hashim, Aziz, Shah Wali and Shah Mahmud Khan, who were members of the Musahiban family and were descended from a brother of Dost Muhammad Khan. Political disagreements with Amanullah had driven them into self-imposed exile. In 1929 they returned to rally the Pashtun tribes against the Tajik, Habibullah, and in October captured Kabul. Habibullah and some of his followers were executed. Nadir Shah became ruler and initiated a programme of pacification, conciliation and cautious reform, beginning with the reorganization of the army. In 1931 he introduced a new Constitution. In foreign policy he followed the traditional neutralist policy, seeking good relations with the USSR and the United Kingdom, while attempting to win the support of other European countries and the USA.

The replacement of Amanullah by the Musahiban family deeply divided the Afghan élite. In 1933 first Aziz and then Nadir were assassinated. Nadir was succeeded as King by his only son, Zahir Shah, but real power resided with the family as a whole and especially with Hashim, who became Prime Minister.

Afghanistan, 1933–53

The policy of the Musahibans was to preserve national independence, foster nationalist feeling and pursue modernization with circumspection. In foreign affairs they sought correct relations with the United Kingdom and the USSR and close connections with other Muslim countries, especially Turkey, Iran and Iraq, with which Afghanistan had signed the Sa'adabad Pact in 1937. Attempts to form close links with the USA enjoyed little success, but important economic and technical connections were made with Germany. Nevertheless, during the Second World War Afghanistan preserved its neutrality. The growth of nationalism was encouraged by the adoption of Pashto (Pakhto) as the official language in 1937; by the development of education at all levels, leading up to various institutions of higher education which were eventually grouped together in the University of Kabul in 1946; by the improvement of communications; and by the increased circulation of newspapers. Economic modernization concentrated on improving the infrastructure. A national bank was founded in 1932 and roads were developed, including a major new route to northern Afghanistan, which became the scene of important developments in the cotton and textile industries. However, as in previous periods, all modernization projects were hampered by lack of money and during the Second World War the prevailing economic dislocation led to discontent and tribal risings in 1944 and 1945.

Hashim was succeeded as Prime Minister in 1946 by his brother, Shah Mahmud Khan. In 1947 Afghanistan planned a major economic development, centring on the massive Helmand Valley scheme, designed to irrigate a large area of western Afghanistan. The scheme was poorly planned and failed to yield any results commensurate with the cost. Between 1951 and 1953 Afghanistan once again found itself in severe economic trouble. The post-war period also saw Afghanistan's first experiment with parliamentary democracy. In 1947 the 'Awakened Youth' movement began to agitate for social reform and to criticize government policy. In 1949 relatively free elections were permitted and the seventh Afghan Parliament (1949–51) gave voice to criticisms of the Government and traditional institutions, and enacted some liberal reforms, including laws providing for a free press. Outside Parliament, radical groups became stronger, especially among students. The critics, however, belonged to a tiny middle-class group, without real support in the country, and were easily silenced when the Government abandoned conciliation and returned to a policy of strict control in the elections for the eighth Parliament in 1952. Several of the liberal leaders were imprisoned. The seeds of a new type of opposition, however, had been planted in Afghanistan.

In foreign affairs the most notable event was the end of British rule in India and the creation in 1947 of the new states of Pakistan and India. Afghanistan's former balancing role was no longer possible, and the country inevitably inclined more towards the USSR. This new direction was strengthened by the reopening of the question of the tribal lands on Pakistan's north-western frontier. The Afghans contended that the Pashtun tribesmen should be given the choice of joining Pakistan or forming an independent 'Pashtunistan'. The issue led to a deterioration in relations between Afghanistan and Pakistan (which, in contrast to the former, began to align itself more with the Western bloc and the People's Republic of China) and handicapped Afghanistan's transit trade through Pakistan.

Daud Khan, 1953–63

In September 1953 Shah Mahmud was replaced as Prime Minister by his nephew, Lt-Gen. Sardar Mohammad Daud Khan, son of Aziz. Under Daud, Afghanistan returned to the path of autocratic modernization, now pursued with greater determination and ruthlessness. Daud favoured state-directed economic development aimed at improving communications. Large-scale economic aid was obtained from the USSR from 1955 onwards, as well as considerable help from the USA. Afghanistan's first Five-Year Plan was launched in 1956. The Prime Minister also obtained military assistance, arms and training facilities from the USSR and greatly strengthened the army. Daud introduced important social reforms, especially improving the status of women.

In foreign affairs Daud pressed more strongly the case for 'Pashtunistan', particularly after West Pakistan's 'one unit' scheme of 1955 threatened the considerable autonomy that the tribal areas had enjoyed since 1947. Daud denounced the 1921 Anglo-Afghan treaty, which had endorsed the frontier line, and summoned a national assembly to pass a resolution supporting 'Pashtunistan'. Eventually Afghan-Pakistan relations deteriorated to the point where Afghan troops entered Pakistan tribal territory, and in 1961 diplomatic relations were severed and the border closed. Afghanistan's economic development was consequently disrupted.

The Constitutional Period, 1963–73

In March 1963 Daud resigned, and a new Government was formed by Dr Muhammad Yusuf, the first Prime Minister not of royal birth. With Iranian help, relations between Afghanistan and Pakistan were quickly restored, and the border was re-opened. Relations with the USSR remained good, and close economic and other links continued. The new Government's main concern was with a programme of liberal domestic reform, combining Western ideas with Islamic religious and political beliefs, of which the centre-piece was a new Constitution promulgated in October 1964. The Constitution provided for an elected lower house and partially elected upper house of Parliament. Elections were held, on a non-party basis, in September 1965, with women voting for the first time.

In October 1965 riots led to the resignation of Yusuf's Government. Further disturbances took place under the succeeding Government of Muhammad Hashim Maiwandwal, who resigned in November 1967. Student riots continued, and there was even fighting among factions in Parliament. Apart from a reorganization of provincial administration, by which 27 provinces were created, and the introduction of a new liberal press law, which led to a rapid increase in the number of unofficial newspapers, there was little legislative reform. Government and Parliament were usually deadlocked in opposition, with the result that political parties were not legalized and democracy was not extended downwards to provincial and municipal councils. Although numerically insignificant, the radical left was especially vocal and grouped itself around a succession of newspapers (*Khalq, Parcham* and *Shu'la-yi Jawed*).

There was no improvement in the situation under the new Prime Minister, Nur Ahmad Etemadi (November 1967–June 1971). In the 13th Parliament, elected in August 1969, there was a marked change as compared with the 12th. The 1965 Parliament had been elected on a very small turn-out, which had led to the vocal predominance of Kabuli radicals; the 13th Parliament attracted much greater attention from the traditional Afghan élite, the turn-out in the election was much higher, and the radicals were almost extinguished. Nevertheless, although the basis of their opposition was different, the traditional élite were just as vociferous in their denunciations of the Government as the radicals were. In June 1971 Etemadi's Government resigned, and a new Government was formed under

Abd az-Zahir, who remained in office until December 1972. The new Government established better relations with Parliament, and succeeded in obtaining parliamentary approval for some long-delayed legislative proposals.

In the early 1970s Afghanistan was severely afflicted by three successive seasons of drought in central and north-western regions. A very large proportion of the sheep stock was lost, there was starvation (with considerable loss of life in some provinces, especially in Ghor) and substantial emigration to Pakistan and Iran. International aid alleviated, but did not eliminate, the problems, and there was serious criticism of the Government's handling of the crisis. A new Government, led by Muhammad Musa Shafiq, was formed in December 1972.

THE REPUBLIC OF AFGHANISTAN, 1973–78

On 17 July 1973 a virtually bloodless military coup resulted in the deposition of King Zahir Shah and the establishment of a republic, headed by the former Prime Minister, Lt-Gen. Muhammad Daud, who created a dictatorship dominated by his relations and close associates. The 1964 Constitution was abolished and Afghanistan was declared a republic. Daud renounced his royal titles and took office as Head of State, Prime Minister and Minister of Foreign Affairs and Defence.

A Loya Jirga (Grand National Council), appointed from among notable tribal elders by provincial governors, was convened in January 1977 and adopted a new Constitution, providing for presidential government and a one-party state. Daud was elected to continue as President for six years and the Loya Jirga was then dissolved. In March President Daud formed a new civilian Government, nominally ending military rule.

Daud's main objective was rapid economic development, centred on the improvement of communications, including the construction of a railway to develop the extensive mineral resources of central Afghanistan. To finance this work he increased tax yields three-fold and sought foreign aid from traditional suppliers, including the Western and Eastern blocs, and, increasingly, from Iran and the oil-rich Arab states. The President tightened state control over the economy; in 1975 the principal private bank, the Banke Milli Afghan, was nationalized; in 1976 a major Seven-Year Plan was launched; and a modest measure of land reform was announced (but not implemented). In foreign affairs, Daud followed a traditional policy of neutrality, maintaining good relations with the USA and the USSR. In 1975 the Soviet-Afghan Treaty of Neutrality and Non-Aggression was renewed for a further 10 years. Relations with Pakistan, which deteriorated when Daud revived the 'Pashtunistan' dispute, improved after 1976 following Soviet and Iranian mediation.

THE REVOLUTION OF APRIL 1978

During the latter part of 1977 and in 1978 Daud increased his attacks on political opponents of the right and left. Following leftist anti-Government demonstrations in Kabul in April 1978, the President ordered the arrest of seven leaders of the People's Democratic Party of Afghanistan (PDPA, founded 1965, divided into Khalq and Parcham factions in 1967, reunited in 1976) and began a purge of army officers and civil servants. On 27 April 1978 the commanders of military and air force units in the Kabul area staged a coup, which became known as the Great Saur (April) Revolution, and on the following day, after heavy fighting against troops loyal to Daud, the rebels gained the victory. Daud, nearly all his family, the leading ministers and the principal military commanders were killed. The military rebels released the imprisoned PDPA leaders and brought them to power. The revolution appeared to have been a purely internal struggle, although the USSR immediately recognized the new regime. The 1977 Constitution was abolished, the Republic of Afghanistan was renamed the Democratic Republic of Afghanistan, power was vested in a Revolutionary Council, and the PDPA became the only political party. The PDPA leader, Nur Muhammad Taraki, was appointed President of the Revolutionary Council and Prime Minister.

AFGHANISTAN UNDER TARAKI AND AMIN, 1978–79

The PDPA came to power without any previously agreed programme of reform, and its long-term strategy was not fully revealed until the publication of the draft Five-Year Plan in August 1979. This plan envisaged a state socialist system: economic growth at 5% per annum, universal primary education and a major adult literacy programme. The central element in the PDPA policy, land reform, was the subject of three edicts issued between July and November 1978. These edicts provided for the gradual reduction of rural indebtedness, the abolition of dowries, and a major distribution of land holdings in favour of landless peasants. The object was political: to destroy the basis of the political power of the former landlord-backed regimes and to win for the PDPA the allegiance of the peasant masses. In the absence of an industrial proletariat in Afghanistan, PDPA support was drawn from a tiny urban intelligentsia and professional groups. The programme failed in its aim, and the poorly-designed land reform and adult literacy campaigns caused widespread opposition to the Government, leading to armed insurrection in almost all provinces, the flight of thousands of refugees to Pakistan and Iran, and great economic dislocation.

From the start, the PDPA Government was divided by factional disputes. Between July 1978 and March 1979 the Parcham faction was eliminated from the Government and party apparatus. The power of the Minister of Foreign Affairs, Hafizullah Amin, steadily increased. He became Secretary of the PDPA (July 1978), Prime Minister (March 1979) and Minister of Defence (July 1979). In September 1979 Amin overthrew Taraki and assumed the presidency of the Revolutionary Council. Taraki was murdered in early October. Amin now pursued a radical, uncompromising policy. Opponents were imprisoned and executed, a counter-coup was defeated in October, and, after the failure of an amnesty appeal, a new campaign against the opposition in the provinces was launched. In an attempt to legitimize his own position, Amin appointed a committee to draft a new constitution, and he tried to set up a new 'broad front' organization—the National Organization for the Defence of the Revolution. Amin failed either to win over his opponents or to suppress them, and the flight of refugees from Afghanistan increased rapidly. The Government accused Pakistan, Iran, the USA, Egypt, the People's Republic of China and other countries of aiding the opposition. Relations between Afghanistan and the USA had steadily deteriorated; in February 1979 the US ambassador, Adolph Dubs, had been killed in a kidnap attempt, and the USA had reduced its aid. Afghanistan began to depend more heavily on the USSR (with which a treaty of friendship and co-operation had been signed in November 1978) for civil and military advice and equipment, and for financial aid. Amin's relations with the USSR, however, deteriorated, owing to continued Soviet pressure for the adoption of more moderate policies and the formation of a broad-based government in Afghanistan. In December 1979 about 80,000 Soviet combat troops invaded Afghanistan and overthrew Amin, who was executed. The Soviet invasion was defended on the basis of the November 1978 Treaty of Friendship and Article 51 of the UN Charter. It was claimed that Amin, who was accused of plotting with foreign powers to partition Afghanistan, had been overthrown by an internal revolution, and that military support from the USSR had been requested by the new regime. World opinion was sceptical of such claims, and a Soviet withdrawal was demanded by the UN General Assembly, the Organization of the Islamic Conference (OIC), the Association of South East Asian Nations (ASEAN) and the Non-aligned Movement, as well as by Western powers.

Soon after the April Revolution in 1978 many Afghans began seeking asylum in Pakistan. The number of refugees quickly increased due to the rapid and transformative reforms of the new regime in Kabul, which had a particularly radical impact on the local khans, tribal chieftains and religious clerics. Simultaneously, several pockets of resistance were established across Afghanistan. Ruthless retaliatory suppression by the Kabul regime forced thousands more Afghan refugees into neighbouring Pakistan and Iran. Given the tribal and state-level support available to the refugees on their arrival in their country of asylum, they were soon able to regroup themselves into various bodies of resistance. The willing assistance from the Pakistani regime, under Gen. Mohammad Zia ul-Haq, and from several other Muslim countries, combined with support from US intelligence officials, helped these groups to transform themselves into organized bodies, using the ideology of Islamic jihad for recruitment purposes. The international media generally responded sympathetically when faced with images and reports of vast numbers of Afghan refugees struggling across the Hindu Kush into Pakistan and through inhospitable deserts into Iran. The Afghan crisis proved a highly emotive issue and international aid agencies donated substantial relief funds and facilities to the refugees living in tented villages in the border regions of Pakistan and Iran. In certain areas of the media the plight of the refugees was somewhat romanticized, with tales of the humble tribesmen in their heroic struggle against the might of the ruthless communist superpower.

Reflecting their traditions of valour, religiosity and tribal honour, the Afghan refugee camps became training centres for groups of *mujahidin* ('holy warriors'), who were willing to lay down their lives for Islam and their homeland against a foreign onslaught. Thus, the Afghan resistance evolved as, what was considered by many participants, an heroic battle against tyranny, with several external supporters volunteering to help in the struggle for their own respective reasons. Many of the *mujahidin* were genuinely enthused by the spirit of jihad, whilst it was alleged that a number of them were enlisted from various regions of the Muslim world by the US Central Intelligence Agency (CIA) and other such intelligence organizations. However, it should be noted that even before the influx of foreign assistance and weapons, the Afghans had already launched their resistance movement. Iran, however, was not as receptive as Pakistan to foreign assistance, given the turmoil arising from its own revolution in 1979, and usually kept the refugees confined to their camps. In contrast, in Pakistan, although the majority of Afghan refugees remained in the North-West Frontier Province (NWFP) and Balochistan, they were permitted to travel throughout the country and were even allowed to establish restaurants and small vending businesses. While Iran vehemently denounced the Soviet incursion into Afghanistan, it simultaneously attempted to distance itself somewhat from the USA. Throughout the 1980s Iran encouraged Pakistan to continue indirect talks with officials of the communist-supported regime in Kabul, which were held in Geneva, Switzerland, under the auspices of the UN. While Pakistan promoted greater co-operation among the predominantly Sunni Afghan resistance groups based in Peshawar in the NWFP, Iran supported the coalition of Shi'ite resistance groups based in Tehran. Such divergences between Iran and Pakistan became more apparent in the late 1990s following the seizure of Kabul by the extremist Taliban.

THE KARMAL REGIME, 1980–86

Amin was replaced as Head of State by Babrak Karmal, leader of the Parcham faction and a former Deputy Prime Minister under Taraki, having been flown into Kabul by a Soviet aircraft from virtual exile in Eastern Europe. The Karmal regime encountered serious problems, notably party disunity, the weakness of the economy, and the inadequacies of the bureaucracy and the army. Purges, desertions and mutinies reduced the strength of the army from about 90,000 in 1978 to an estimated 35,000 in 1981. Despite repeated efforts to rebuild the army, it remained weak, and there was extensive reliance on other services, including the police, revolutionary guards, 'social order brigades', local defence groups, border and tribal militias, and civil defence units. Dependence upon Soviet military forces steadily increased.

President Karmal initiated a policy, known as the second ('developmental') stage of the revolution, involving a stated commitment to conciliation, respect for tribal and religious customs and the creation of a broadly based national government. In June 1981 the regime launched the National Fatherland Front (NFF), incorporating the PDPA and other organizations, with the aim of promoting national unity. The policy of conciliation made slow progress. In January 1984 the land reform programme was drastically modified: the upper limit on land holdings was raised to reconcile middle-income peasants, and exemptions were allowed for supporters of the regime. The literacy programme was continued, but concessions were made to women. In 1985 the conciliation policy was given a new impetus with the summoning of a Loya Jirga in April, followed by a high Jirga of tribes in September.

The major problem for the Karmal regime was the continuing civil war in Afghanistan. The conflict brought economic dislocation to large parts of the country, and there was a mass movement of population from the countryside to Kabul, and of refugees to Pakistan (more than 3m.) and Iran (more than 2m.). Soviet forces mounted aerial attacks, which destroyed villages, agricultural production and irrigation systems. The anti-Government guerrilla forces (*mujahidin*), fragmented among local groups and many organizations operating from Afghan refugee communities in Pakistan and Iran, damaged bridges, power stations and transmission lines, destroyed public buildings, interrupted communications, deprived the Government of authority over large areas of the countryside, mounted attacks in towns and killed many sympathizers of the regime. The popular resistance was initially poorly armed, but in 1984–85 it began to receive greater support from external sources (particularly from the USA and China), including more effective weapons and training. In May 1985 the seven principal Peshawar-based guerrilla organizations formed an alliance, called the Ittehad-i-Islami Afghan Mujahidin (the Islamic Union of Afghan Mujahidin—IUAM) to co-ordinate their political and military operations. In 1987 an eight-party alliance was formed, called the Hizb-i Wahadat-i Islami (Islamic Unity Party), comprising Shi'ite Afghan resistance groups based in Iran. The Karmal regime sought to retain control of the principal towns and main roads and to attack major guerrilla concentrations, and employed retaliatory terror-bombing against villages that were believed to be sheltering rebels. In September 1985 a policy of sealing the Pakistan border was announced. Throughout 1985 and 1986, however, there were many violations of the Afghanistan/Pakistan border, involving shelling, bombing and incursions into neighbouring airspace.

In May 1985 the NFF was given a non-PDPA Chairman, Abd ar-Rahim Hatif. In 1985–86 elections were held for new local government organs, in accordance with a scheme that had been approved in February 1984. It was claimed that 60% of those who were elected were non-party members. In November 1985 the regime announced a new policy of national compromise, known as 'broadening the social pillars of the revolution', as a result of which several non-party personalities, including representatives of tribes and nationalities, were appointed to government posts. A commission was also established to draft a new Constitution, to replace the provisional 'basic principles' that had been approved in April 1980.

THE NAJIBULLAH REGIME AND NATIONAL RECONCILIATION, 1986–88

In May 1986 Dr Najibullah, formerly the head of the state intelligence bureau (KHAD), was appointed General Secretary of the PDPA, in place of Karmal. In November Karmal also resigned from the Politburo and from his post as President of the Revolutionary Council. Haji Muhammad Chamkani, formerly First Vice-President (and a non-PDPA member), became acting President of the Revolutionary Council, pending the introduction of a new constitution and the establishment of a permanent legislature. There was no change in the direction of government policy, although Najibullah pursued the policy of national compromise with greater vigour, under pressure from the new General Secretary of the Communist Party of the Soviet Union, Mikhail Gorbachev. In late December an extraordinary plenum of the Central Committee of the PDPA approved a policy of 'national reconciliation', involving negotiations with opposition groups, and the proposed formation of a government of national unity. In January 1987 a Supreme Extraordinary Commission for National Reconciliation, led by Abd ar-Rahim Hatif (the Chairman of the National Committee of the NFF), was formed to conduct the negotiations. The NFF was renamed the National Front (NF), was given a much-enlarged Central Committee and was made organizationally separate from the PDPA. There were also important modifications of policy, including the accordance of greater prominence to Islamic precepts and a major relaxation of the land reform programme, which left little of the original concept. In July, as part of the process of national reconciliation, several developments occurred: a law permitting the formation of other political parties (according to certain provisions) was introduced; and Najibullah announced that the PDPA would be prepared to share power with representatives of opposition groups in the event of the formation of a coalition government of national unity. In September Najibullah was unanimously elected as President of the Revolutionary Council, and Chamkani resumed his former post as First Vice-President. In order to strengthen his position, Najibullah ousted all the remaining supporters of Karmal from the Central Committee and Politburo of the PDPA in October. In November a Loya Jirga unanimously elected Najibullah as President of the State and ratified a new Constitution. The main innovations incorporated in this Constitution were: the formation of a multi-party political system, under the auspices of the NF; the formation of a bicameral legislature, called the Meli Shura (National Assembly), composed of a Sena (Senate) and a Wolasi Jirga (House of Representatives); the granting of a permanent constitutional status to the PDPA; the bestowal of extensive powers on the President, who was to hold office for seven years; and the reversion of the name of the country from the Democratic Republic to the Republic of Afghanistan.

In April 1988 elections were held to both houses of the new Meli Shura, which replaced the Revolutionary Council. Of the total 192 seats in the Sena, 115 were contested, while the majority of the remaining seats were filled by senators appointed by President Najibullah. According to government figures, about 1.6m. people participated in the elections, despite the fact that they were boycotted by the *mujahidin*, who denounced them as fraudulent. The Government, however, left vacant 50 of the 234 seats in the Wolasi Jirga, and a small number of seats in the Sena, in the hope that the guerrillas would abandon their armed struggle and present their own representatives to participate in the new Government. The PDPA, itself, won only 46 seats in the Wolasi Jirga, but was guaranteed support from the NF, which gained 45, and from the various newly-recognized left-wing parties, which won a combined total of 24 seats. In May Dr Muhammad Hasan Sharq (a non-PDPA member and a Deputy Prime Minister since June 1987) assumed the premiership in place of Sultan Ali Keshtmand (who had held the position since June 1981), and in June 1988 a new Council of Ministers was appointed. The Government's much-vaunted policy of national reconciliation won limited support from small, local resistance groups, but was rejected outright by major *mujahidin* parties.

Indirect negotiations between the Afghan and Pakistani Ministers of Foreign Affairs concerning the situation in Afghanistan began in 1981, under UN auspices, and were continued in Geneva between 1982 and 1988. In October 1986 the USSR made a token withdrawal of six regiments (6,000–8,000 men) from Afghanistan. An agreement on a complete Soviet withdrawal was eventually signed on 14 April 1988. The Geneva accords comprised five documents: detailed undertakings by Pakistan and Afghanistan, relating to non-intervention and non-interference in each other's affairs; international guarantees of Afghan independence (with the USA and the USSR as the principal guarantors); arrangements for the voluntary and safe return of Afghan refugees; a document linking the preceding documents with a timetable for a Soviet withdrawal; and the establishment of a 50-man UN monitoring force, which was to maintain surveillance of the Soviet troop departures and to oversee the return of the refugees. The withdrawal of Soviet troops (who numbered 100,000, according to Soviet figures, or 115,000, according to Western sources) commenced on 15 May 1988. It was agreed that one-half of the Soviet troops were to withdraw by 15 August and the remainder by 15 February 1989.

Neither the *mujahidin* nor Iran played any part in the formulation of the Geneva accords, and, despite initial protests by Pakistan, no agreement was incorporated regarding the composition of an interim coalition government in Afghanistan, or the 'symmetrical' cessation of Soviet aid to the Government in Kabul and US aid to the *mujahidin*. Accordingly, despite the commencement of the departure of Soviet forces in mid-1988, the supply of arms to both sides was not halted and the violent conflict continued. Pakistan repeatedly denied accusations, made by the Afghan and Soviet Governments, that it had violated the Geneva accords by continuing to harbour Afghan guerrillas and by acting as a conduit for arms supplies to the latter from various sympathizers (notably the USA).

THE CIVIL WAR: 1988–2001

It was widely anticipated that the Kabul Government would quickly fall following the withdrawal of direct Soviet military support. In mid-1988 the *mujahidin* increased their military activities, attacking small provincial centres and launching missiles against major cities, several of which were besieged. However, the guerrillas, disadvantaged by their lack of organization and limited experience of modern strategic warfare, failed to achieve a significant military success. They also failed to make any notable advances on the political front. Talks between the IUAM and the Islamic Unity Party repeatedly failed to produce any agreement regarding the composition of a broadly based interim government. The IUAM, therefore, summoned its own shura (assembly) in Rawalpindi, Pakistan, in February 1989, during which a new interim government-in-exile (known as the Afghan Interim Government, AIG) was elected. Prof. Sibghatullah Mojaddedi was appointed President of the AIG, while Abd ar-Rasul Sayef, the leader of one of the fundamentalist groups, was appointed acting Prime Minister. In the following month the AIG received a form of recognition when it was granted membership of the OIC. It was, however, officially recognized by only four countries. In June, none the less, the US Government appointed a special envoy to the *mujahidin*, with the rank of personal ambassador. The AIG failed to gain any substantial support or recognition from the guerrilla commanders, who were beginning to establish their own unofficial alliances within Afghanistan itself. In mid-1989 the unity of the *mujahidin* forces was seriously weakened by an increase in internecine violence among the various guerrilla groups, while the AIG was riven by disputes between the moderates and the fundamentalists. The USA, Saudi Arabia and Pakistan began to reduce financial aid and military supplies to the IUAM in Peshawar, and to undertake the difficult task of delivering arms and money directly to guerrilla commanders and tribal leaders inside Afghanistan.

On 18 February 1989, following the completion of the withdrawal of Soviet troops from Afghanistan, Najibullah carried out a reshuffle of the Council of Ministers, which involved the replacement of non-communist ministers with loyal PDPA members. On the same day, Prime Minister Sharq, who had been the figurehead of the policy of national reconciliation, resigned from his post and was replaced by the former Prime Minister, Sultan Ali Keshtmand. Following the declaration of a state of emergency by Najibullah (citing allegations of repeated violations of the Geneva accords by Pakistan and the USA) and the suspension of sections of the Constitution on 19 February, a PDPA-dominated 20-member Supreme Council for the Defence of the Homeland was established. The Council, which was led by President Najibullah and was composed of ministers, members of the PDPA Politburo and high-ranking military figures, assumed full responsibility for the country's economic, political and military policies (although the Council of Ministers continued to function).

In March 1989, only one month after the withdrawal of its remaining troops, the USSR resumed an intensive series of airlifts of supplies to Kabul. In addition, the Afghan Government constructed a new road from Kabul to Bagram in an effort to break the blockade of access by road to the USSR that had been created by the obstructive activities of the *mujahidin*. At the same time, Najibullah's Government maintained its attempts, through the policy of national reconciliation, to negotiate cease-fire agreements with local *mujahidin* commanders in Afghanistan, offering them aid and local autonomy in the areas that they controlled. These attempts at reconciliation, however, achieved only limited success.

The success of the army in repelling *mujahidin* attacks and in maintaining supplies of goods to provincial towns led to a feeling among certain military and PDPA leaders that the regime in Kabul could win a military victory and that it was unnecessary to seek a political solution through the process of national reconciliation, which could involve a loss of power on the part of the ruling party. From June 1989 onwards there were widespread fears of a *coup d'état*. In December a conspiracy, implicating PDPA and army leaders and Gulbuddin Hekmatyar's faction of the guerrilla group, Hizb-i Islami (Islamic Party), was uncovered, and about 100 arrests were made in Kabul. On 6 March 1990 the Minister of Defence, Lt-Gen. Shahnawaz

Tanay (with the alleged support of the air force, some divisions of the army and Hekmatyar), led an unsuccessful coup attempt against Najibullah's Government. The Afghan Government accused Pakistani military intelligence of having played a leading role in the coup attempt—an accusation that was strenuously denied by the Pakistani Government. Following the defeat of the conspirators, Najibullah carried out extensive purges of PDPA and army leaders and made the decision to move rapidly back towards some form of constitutional civilian government. On 20 May the state of emergency was lifted; the Supreme Council for the Defence of the Homeland was disbanded; a new Council of Ministers (in which PDPA members retained the key posts), under the premiership of Fazel Haq Khalikyar, the Governor of the western province of Herat, was appointed; and a special commission was established to draft amendments to the Constitution. On 28–29 May a Loya Jirga, convened in Kabul, considered and ratified the constitutional changes, greatly reducing Afghanistan's socialist orientation; ending the PDPA's and the NF's monopoly over executive power and preparing for democratic elections acceptable to all parties in Afghanistan; introducing greater political and press freedom; encouraging the development of the private sector and increased foreign investment; lessening the role of the State and giving greater prominence to Islam. The extensive powers of the presidency were, however, retained. At the end of June the second and final party congress of the PDPA was held, at which the party's name was changed to the Homeland Party (HP) (Hizb-i Watan), the Politburo and the Central Committee were replaced by an Executive Board and a Central Council respectively, and a new party programme was adopted, of which the hallmark was hostility to ideology. A new and balanced foreign policy, inclining towards the Islamic and non-aligned movements, was announced and, for the first time in an official context, the Soviet intervention in Afghanistan's internal affairs in 1979 was described as a mistake. Najibullah remained as Chairman of the ruling party. In October the informal alliance between the country's various left-wing parties was terminated, and in the following month the HP agreed to co-operate with the Islamist Hezbollah-e Afghanistan. At the same time, the NF was disbanded and its erstwhile members joined the new Afghanistan Peace Front.

The search for a political solution was conducted both at international and at local level. The Afghan Government's policy of persuading states to reopen their diplomatic missions in Kabul met with some success in mid-1990, when France and Italy did so. The USSR, preoccupied with domestic problems and anxious to reduce the continuing Afghan burden, and the USA, increasingly disillusioned with the factious and unsuccessful *mujahidin*, frequently held discussions about the situation in Afghanistan. It was agreed at these meetings that the UN should adopt the leading role in mediations and, following extensive consultations with the regional powers involved in the crisis, the UN Secretary-General made a declaration on 21 May 1991, based on the UN General Assembly resolution of 7 November 1990, setting out five principles for a settlement, the main points of which were as follows: recognition of the national sovereignty of Afghanistan; the right of the Afghan people to choose their own government and political system; the creation, for an interim period, of an 'independent, credible and authorized mechanism' to oversee free and fair elections to a broadly based government; a UN-monitored cease-fire; and the donation of sufficient financial aid to facilitate the return of the refugees and economic and social reconstruction. The declaration was welcomed by the Governments of Afghanistan and Pakistan, but was rejected by the AIG.

With help from the CIA and from the Pakistani Inter-Services Intelligence Directorate (ISI), new military campaigns were launched by the *mujahidin* in the latter half of 1980, in an attempt to impress their international supporters, disrupt the return of refugees and hinder contacts between the Government and moderate guerrillas. In late March 1991, following more than two weeks of heavy fighting, the south-eastern city of Khost was captured by the *mujahidin*. The loss of Khost was the most severe reversal sustained by Najibullah's Government since the Soviet withdrawal and caused a decline in the regime's morale and a corresponding surge in confidence for the *mujahidin*. Guerrilla attacks on Gardez, Ghazni, Qandahar, Jalalabad and Herat were also carried out in 1991, and communications between cities and with the Soviet border were severed. In Kabul, however, the beleaguered regime held fast. Reflecting its growing disenchantment with the guerrilla cause, the US Government substantially reduced its aid to the *mujahidin* in 1991. However, the balance of power shifted decisively from 1 January 1992 when, following US-Soviet discussions in the wake of the failed coup attempt in Moscow in August 1991, all Soviet aid to Najibullah's regime was discontinued.

In February 1992 Pakistan made it clear that, rather than continuing actively to encourage the *mujahidin* through arms supplies and training, it was urging all the guerrilla factions, including the fundamentalist Hizb-i Islami, to support the five-point UN peace plan (see above). In doing so, Pakistan was effectively abandoning its insistence on the installation of a fundamentalist government in Kabul. The Pakistani Government now believed that it was in its best interests to stabilize Afghanistan, particularly in view of the prospective valuable trading links offered by the newly independent Central Asian republics situated to the north of Afghanistan (many of the leaders of these new states were wary of Islamist fundamentalism). The presence of more than 3m. Afghan refugees in the NWFP was also becoming an increasingly heavy financial burden for the Pakistani Government.

In late March 1992, following a series of meetings with the UN special representative for Afghanistan, Benon Sevan, Najibullah announced that he and his Government would immediately step down in the event of the formation of an interim neutral government in Afghanistan, as envisaged in the UN peace plan. This important concession appeared to remove the oft-repeated objection to participating in peace talks expressed by the *mujahidin*. In the same month there were growing fears that the peace process might be threatened by an increase in ethnic divisions, within both the army and a number of *mujahidin* groups, between the majority Pashtuns and minority ethnic groups such as the Uzbeks and the Tajiks. As a result of a mutiny staged by Uzbek government militia forces, under the command of Gen. Abdul Rashid Dostam, the northern city of Mazar-i-Sharif was captured by the *mujahidin* in March. In mid-April Najibullah accepted a UN proposal to hand over power to a 15-member neutral council (which was to include *mujahidin* representatives), which was to precede the establishment of an interim government, which was, in turn, to supervise the holding of elections. A few days later, however, on 16 April, events took an unexpected turn when Najibullah was forced to resign by his own ruling party, following the capture of the strategically important Bagram air base and the nearby town of Charikar, only 50 km north of the capital, by the Jamiat-i Islami (Islamic Society) guerrilla group under the leadership of the Tajik commander, Ahmad Shah Masoud. Abd ar-Rahim Hatif, one of the Vice-Presidents, assumed the post of acting President. It was later learned that, following an unsuccessful escape attempt, Najibullah was in hiding in Kabul, under UN protection. Meanwhile, Masoud was establishing an informal alliance of guerrillas and disaffected government militia, including Gen. Dostam's Uzbek forces, and attempting to form a workable coalition among the drastically divided *mujahidin*. Within a few days of Najibullah's downfall, every major town in Afghanistan was under the control of different coalitions of *mujahidin* groups co-operating with disaffected local army commanders. Masoud was appointed head of a security committee by *mujahidin* leaders in Peshawar and given orders to secure Kabul. On 25 April the forces of both Masoud and rival leader Hekmatyar entered the capital, the army willingly surrendering its key positions, and immediately the city was riven by *mujahidin* faction-fighting. The four-member military council that had, a few days earlier, replaced the Government relinquished power to the *mujahidin*.

The Establishment of a Mujahidin Government

Having discarded the UN's proposal to form a neutral council, the guerrilla leaders in Peshawar agreed to establish a 51-member interim Islamic Jihad Council, composed of military and religious heads, which was to assume power in Kabul. The leader of the small, moderate Jebha-i-Nejat-i-Melli (National Liberation Front), Prof. Sibghatullah Mojaddedi, was to chair the Islamic Jihad Council for two months, after which period a

10-member Leadership Council, comprising *mujahidin* chiefs and presided over by the head of the Jamiat-i Islami, Prof. Burhanuddin Rabbani, would be set up for a period of four months. Within the six months a Loya Jirga was to meet to designate an interim administration that was to hold power for up to a year, pending elections. Mojaddedi arrived in Kabul on 28 April 1992 as the President of the new interim Afghan administration. The Islamic Jihad Council was not, however, supported by Hekmatyar, whose radical beliefs differed substantially from Mojaddedi's more tolerant outlook. At the end of the month, however, Hekmatyar's forces lost control of their last stronghold in the centre of Kabul. On 29 April the Prime Minister of Pakistan, Mohammad Nawaz Sharif, became the first foreign statesman officially to visit the newly proclaimed Islamic State of Afghanistan. Within a few weeks the new Government had won almost universal diplomatic recognition. By early May about one-half of the Islamic Jihad Council had arrived in Kabul. On 5 May President Mojaddedi announced the formation of an acting Council of Ministers. Masoud was given the post of Minister of Defence, and the premiership was set aside for Ustad Abdol Sabur Farid, a Tajik commander from the Hizb-i Islami (Hekmatyar declined to accept the post). One of Mojaddedi's first acts as President was to declare a general amnesty and to urge Hekmatyar and his followers to lay down their arms. Hekmatyar, however, who claimed to be particularly angered at the presence of Gen. Dostam's Uzbek forces in the capital, continued to bombard Kabul with artillery and indiscriminate rocket launches from his various strongholds around the city, killing and wounding scores of citizens. In an attempt to retain a degree of order, President Mojaddedi made urgent appeals to senior officials of the former communist regime to remain at their posts. Mojaddedi's authority was jeopardized when Rabbani prematurely established the Leadership Council (which was, under the terms of the Peshawar Agreement—see above—to succeed the Islamic Jihad Council after two months) on his arrival in Kabul in early May. As part of the process of Islamization in Afghanistan, alcohol and narcotics were banned and the wearing of strict Islamic dress by all women was proposed.

The Islamic State of Afghanistan under President Burhanuddin Rabbani

On 28 June 1992 Mojaddedi surrendered power to the Leadership Council, which immediately offered Burhanuddin Rabbani the presidency of the country and the concomitant responsibility for the interim Council of Ministers for four months, as set forth in the Peshawar Agreement. On 6 July Farid arrived in Kabul to assume the premiership, which had been held open for him since late April. On taking charge of the presidency, Rabbani announced the adoption of a new Islamic national flag, the establishment of an economic council, which was to address Afghanistan's serious economic problems, and the appointment of a commission to draw up a new constitution. In early August the withdrawal of the members of the Hizb-i Islami faction led by Maulvi Muhammad Yunus Khalis from the Leadership Council revealed serious rifts within the Government. A further problem for the long-suffering country was the continuing inter-*mujahidin* violence in Kabul. Within days, the violence had escalated into a full-scale ground offensive, launched by Hekmatyar's forces against the capital. The airport was closed down, hundreds of people were killed or wounded, and tens of thousands of civilians fled Kabul in fear of their lives. In response, President Rabbani expelled Hekmatyar from the Leadership Council and dismissed Prime Minister Farid. The fighting was so fierce that it forced even the staff of the UN and of its High Commissioner for Refugees (UNHCR) to withdraw from Kabul. Although the clashes were mainly between the forces of Hekmatyar and the Government, they also involved the militia of the Shi'ite Hizb-i Wahadat against the Sunni Ittehad-i-Islami (Islamic Union). Furthermore, the fighting was not confined to Kabul, but extended to other provinces as well.

In September 1992 President Rabbani paid official visits to Pakistan and Iran, seeking political and economic aid. The policy of these two strategically important neighbouring countries regarding the situation in Afghanistan had been to avoid anything that would undermine the authority of the central Afghan Government and hamper the establishment of peace. A major factor in convincing Pakistan and Iran of the beneficial nature of this conciliatory policy was the continued presence of about 6m. Afghan refugees whom the Pakistani and Iranian Governments were desperate to repatriate. A successful repatriation programme depended mainly upon a speedy restoration of order and peace in Kabul and the rest of Afghanistan. To this end, both Pakistan and Iran supported Afghanistan's entry into the regional Economic Co-operation Organization (ECO) in November. President Rabbani attended an ECO meeting in Istanbul in July 1993, and returned with promises of economic co-operation from major participant countries.

In September 1992 President Rabbani announced that an advisory council, to be known as the Resolution and Settlement Council (Shura-e Ahl-e Hal wa Aqd), was to be convened by the end of his presidential term, i.e. by the end of October. The council, the members of which were to be nominated by the Leadership Council, local commanders, religious scholars and elders, was to represent all the provinces and *mujahidin* groups. The mandate of the advisory council was to act as a constituent assembly, to legislate for the country, and to elect the future President. Towards the end of October the Leadership Council agreed to extend Rabbani's tenure of the presidency by 45 days. The advisory council was not convened until late December. Hekmatyar, Mojaddedi, and the Shi'ite Hizb-i Wahadat denounced the 1,335-member council as stage-managed by President Rabbani; they regarded it as illegitimate, demanded its dissolution, and called for the President's resignation. Hekmatyar demanded the formation of a new interim government and the holding of a general election within six months. On 30 December the advisory council elected Rabbani, who was the sole candidate, as President of Afghanistan for a further two years. The appointment met with the approval of Pakistan, Iran and Saudi Arabia. In early January 1993, 200 members of the advisory council were selected to constitute the future membership of the country's legislature.

The establishment of the advisory council and the re-election of President Rabbani provoked yet further heavy fighting, loss of life, and internal dislocation of the population in Kabul and other provinces in early 1993. Owing to the worsening violence, all Western diplomats had left Kabul by the end of January. Following mediation efforts by Pakistan, Iran and Saudi Arabia, a peace accord was signed by President Rabbani, Hekmatyar, Mojaddedi and leaders of other major *mujahidin* factions in Islamabad, Pakistan, on 7 March, in which the signatories agreed on the formation of an interim government, which was to hold power for a period of 18 months. President Rabbani was to remain as Head of State, and Hekmatyar (or his nominee) was to assume the premiership of the acting Council of Ministers. The signatories also agreed on an immediate cease-fire, the holding of legislative elections within six months, the establishment of a 16-member defence commission, which was to be responsible for the formation of a national army, and the seizure of heavy weapons from warring factions in an attempt to restore peace and order. The peace accord was officially approved and signed by the Governments of Pakistan, Saudi Arabia and Iran.

Hekmatyar was not able to present a new Council of Ministers until late May 1993 (it was sworn in the following month). Each *mujahidin* group was eventually allocated two ministerial posts with further positions left vacant for other representatives (representatives from Gen. Dostam's group of predominantly Uzbek militiamen—known collectively as the National Islamic Movement (NIM) (Jonbesh-i Melli-i Islami)—were offered two posts in July). One of Hekmatyar's most noteworthy decisions in the formation of the new Council of Ministers was to remove one of his most powerful rivals, Masoud, from the crucial post of Minister of Defence. The new Prime Minister promised to hold a general election by October. The temporary headquarters of the Government were situated in Charasiab, Hekmatyar's military base, about 25 km south of Kabul. In September it was reported that a new draft Constitution (known as the Basic Law) had been drawn up and approved by a special commission, in preparation for the holding of a general election.

The powers of the offices of President and Prime Minister were not clearly demarcated by the Islamabad agreement and, given the personal differences between the incumbents (Rabbani and Hekmatyar, respectively), it was very much expected that the two officials would find themselves at cross purposes. In addition, Hekmatyar believed the advisory council to be a constraint on his authority. These factors seriously hampered the working of a Government that was supposed to represent the interests of a number of groups whose allegiances were divided along ethnic, linguistic, sectarian and regional lines. In effect, the new Government was faced with a stupendous task: it had to restore the authority of central government; establish law and order and peace; provide security and the very basic necessities of life to an impoverished population; and rebuild and repair the basic infrastructure of the country. No less daunting was the undertaking of rehabilitating about 6m. Afghan refugees living in Pakistan and Iran who had begun to return to Afghanistan in large numbers. Such an immense task required a strong central authority. However, the question of centralism was in itself a serious issue of contention in Afghanistan. Given the ethnic and sectarian diversity of Afghan people, pressures for a federal structure were great. The ethnic minorities, such as the Uzbeks and Tajiks in the northern provinces, and the religious minority of Shi'ites in the west, would strongly have resisted any authoritarian centre dominated by the Sunni Pashtuns unless their own interests were taken into account. Certain provinces already existed almost independently of the authorities in Kabul. In addition, some socio-political groups did not share the strict religious tenets of Prime Minister Hekmatyar. The task of the new Government then, in essence, was to restore the authority and power of the centre without making it appear too centralized.

Throughout 1993 the socio-political differences between various groups resulted in continued fighting in and around Kabul and in other provinces. In addition to the violence on the domestic front, trouble had been developing, since early 1993, on the Afghan-Tajik border. The Tajik Islamist groups who were opposed to the former communist elements in the Government of Tajikistan were compelled by the government forces (which were supported by units of the Russian CIS troops) to take refuge across the border in Afghanistan and launch their armed attacks from there. The Tajik Islamists were actively supported by a considerable number of Afghan sympathizers. This involvement elicited armed retaliation as well as political protests from the Tajik and Russian Governments. It was widely believed that the main source of weapons to the Tajik rebels was Hekmatyar, who was also reported to have established training camps in Afghanistan for Islamist Tajik fighters.

President Rabbani was sensitive to such matters as the troubles on the Afghan-Tajik border, and had been attempting to adopt a reconciliatory approach towards the neighbouring countries of Afghanistan. His policy, in contrast to that of Hekmatyar, avoided any ideologically based attitude at regional or international level. Rather, the President tried to concentrate on the socio-economic reconstruction of Afghanistan, an approach that required an improvement in relations with the world community in general and neighbouring countries in particular. In pursuance of this goal, Rabbani avoided interference in the internal affairs of other nations. In August 1993 the Afghan and Tajik Governments issued a joint communiqué underlining their commitment to respect the inviolability of their respective borders. Representatives of the UNHCR were also involved in the negotiations as large numbers of people had been displaced on both sides of the border as a result of the fighting; in mid-1993 there were an estimated 90,000 Tajik refugees living in Afghanistan (although, according to UN data, this figure had decreased to an estimated 30,000 by the end of 1994). In December 1993 the Afghan government forces attempted to clear the Afghan and Tajik militias from the border area. (By mid-November 1997, according to the Tajik authorities, all of the Tajik refugees had been repatriated, and rebel Tajik forces were being incorporated into government troops.)

Prime Minister Hekmatyar's domestic and international policy, on the other hand, was less inhibited by such practical considerations and was more orientated by ideology. On the Tajik-Afghan issue, for example, he exhibited his customary dislike for Russian forces and demanded their withdrawal from the Afghan border, so that the problem could be solved bilaterally between the countries involved. Hekmatyar's main objection remained Rabbani's continuing tenure of the presidency. Hekmatyar offered to step down from his own post if Rabbani did likewise and if a neutral government were appointed to oversee the holding of a general election in order to elect a new leadership. Rabbani, however, favoured firstly the appointment of a new leader to whom he could transfer the presidency. This remained the principal issue of contention between the two main protagonists in the Afghan imbroglio, and ensured the continuation of the civil war despite the repeatedly pronounced desire of the two leaders to reconcile their differences for the sake of the country.

The fighting intensified from the beginning of 1994 when, in one of the most significant shifts of alliance, Gen. Dostam transferred his allegiance to his hitherto arch-enemy, Hekmatyar, and the supporters of the two combined to confront the forces of Rabbani and Masoud. The militia of groups such as the Shi'ite Hizb-i Wahadat and the Sunni Ittehad-i-Islami also joined the fray. Fighting spread throughout the provinces, resulting in large numbers of military and civilian casualties and the internal displacement of thousands of people. In February 1994 there were 200,000 displaced Afghans (the majority from Kabul) in Jalalabad alone. It was a measure of the frustration caused by the ongoing situation that the warring factions within Afghanistan as well as neighbouring countries and international organizations, such as the UN and the OIC, made several serious (but ultimately unsuccessful) attempts in the first half of 1994 to end the civil war and restore peace to Afghanistan. In May the special envoy of the UN Secretary-General met the former King of Afghanistan, Zahir Shah, in Rome, Italy, to discuss the Afghan situation. At this meeting it was proposed that the former King could return to Afghanistan and attempt to form a government of national reconciliation; this proposal, however, attracted very little support within Afghanistan itself. In June the Supreme Court ruled that Rabbani could retain the presidency for a further six months, but failed to grant a similar extension to Hekmatyar's premiership. The UN generally enjoyed the reputation of being neutral and trustworthy among the Afghan warring factions. However, in the absence of any neutral social, legal or political body among the Afghans themselves, a breakthrough in the two-year impasse eluded all concerned. None the less, the continued efforts and negotiations indicated a widespread desire for peace among the Afghan people and all the parties involved in the crisis.

The Emergence of the Taliban

It was in the midst of this pervasive mood of war-weariness, frustration and longing for peace that there suddenly emerged a new phenomenon, which caught every party unawares and which dramatically changed the political situation in Afghanistan. This was the rise of a new military force known as the Taliban (the plural form of 'Talib', meaning 'seeker of religious knowledge'), which appeared on the political scene completely unexpectedly. The new grouping's military campaign began in southern Afghanistan near the border with Pakistan and was first reported around August–September 1994. Initially, the emergence of the Taliban was not taken into serious consideration, Afghanistan being a country where armed skirmishes were daily occurrences. Consequently, a part of Afghanistan had already passed under the control of the Taliban by the time the new group had achieved prominence in Afghan political affairs. The members of the Taliban, who were led by Mola Mohammad Omar, were reported to have been former students of Islamic sciences in *madrassas* (Islamic religious schools) established by Afghan refugees in Pakistan. The Taliban were predominantly young Pashtun men, who were highly motivated by and dedicated to religious teachings and visions. A number of the group's senior members had gained military experience through combat against Soviet troops during the 1980s. Various sources claimed that the Pakistani ISI was instrumental in the creation of the Taliban, but the Government of Pakistan denied any involvement. Initially, the Taliban numbered a mere few hundred men, but their ranks very rapidly swelled (to an estimated 25,000) as their swift military campaign advanced virtually unchecked. The Taliban won a major victory in October 1994 when they captured the city of Qandahar. In February 1995 the Taliban routed Hekmatyar's men from their headquarters in Charasiab, and within a month they controlled 10 provinces, mostly in southern and south-eastern Afghanistan.

The principal reason for the success of the Taliban appeared to be, above all, their religious zeal as well as their frustration with the Afghan civil war, which, over the previous two years, had claimed more than 15,000 lives (mostly civilians), left hundreds of thousands homeless, and devastated vast areas of Kabul and its environs. (The misery of the common Afghan people was exacerbated by the fact that this destruction compounded the extensive suffering they had endured during their struggle against the Soviet occupation.) With a moral and religious slant to its military campaign, the group attempted to restore law and order based on *Shari'a* (Islamic law). The Taliban disarmed local militia and suppressed highway banditry, thus facilitating the safe and regular supply of basic requirements to the population. The group's professed ultimate goal was the demobilization of all armed forces and the establishment of peace and an Islamic system of government throughout the country. In the Qandahar area, after years of suffering and hardship, people generally welcomed the new group with enthusiasm; in other areas, the Taliban encountered significant opposition, which they overcame with superior supplies of personnel and equipment.

By mid-March 1995, however, the Taliban had begun to suffer their first serious reversals. It seemed that the group's military strength had been overestimated and had not been tested by any concerted resistance until it threatened to capture Kabul. Although they defeated Hekmatyar's forces both within and around the capital, the Taliban were unable to retain the captured positions when President Rabbani's supporters staged a massive counter-offensive. The Taliban militia's subsequent retreat from Kabul was as rapid as its advances towards the city had been.

Ironically, the person who appeared to have gained optimum benefit from the rise of the Taliban was not their leader, but President Rabbani. Since 1992 Rabbani had been involved in a serious confrontation with his arch-rival, Hekmatyar, but had been unable to drive his forces away from Kabul. The Taliban, however, did exactly this, thus achieving in a matter of months what Rabbani had been unable to effect in years. Having been disburdened of Hekmatyar's forces in this fortuitous manner and having put all the other militia groups, including the Taliban and Gen. Dostam's forces, on the defensive for the first time in three years, the President's supporters controlled the capital city and its surrounding areas and were able to make advances into neighbouring provinces. Rabbani's determination not to relinquish office until a credible alternative could be found resulted in an acrimonious exchange of accusations between him and the Head of the UN Special Mission to Afghanistan, Mahmoud Mestiri. Rabbani claimed that he was prepared to relinquish power, but would only do so when a transitional council representing all the provinces and major *mujahidin* factions was agreed upon by all the parties concerned. The Taliban, however, refused to participate in any transitional process.

In mid-1995 Rabbani's forces, which were enjoying an unprecedented level of authority and confidence, controlled 10 provinces, 10 others were held by the Taliban and the remainder were under the control of various other groups. Kabul had become relatively peaceful, and normal civilian life had begun to resume. An indication of the improving situation was the fact that a growing number of countries were considering reopening their embassies in the capital. The President's authority was so buoyant in mid-1995 that even the Taliban, despite certain dissenting voices among their ranks, felt compelled to negotiate with him. In spite of the talks, however, relations between the two parties remained far from amicable.

Afghan-Pakistani relations reached a new nadir in early September 1995 when the Taliban achieved a major victory against President Rabbani's forces, capturing the Shindand air base, the key north-western city of Herat and the surrounding province, overthrowing the local ruler, Ismail Khan. This constituted a serious set-back for the Government and a substantial boost for the Taliban. Rabbani openly accused Pakistan of arming and supporting the student militia—Pakistan, in turn, denied any involvement. The day following the fall of Herat, hundreds of demonstrators ransacked and set fire to the Pakistani embassy in Kabul. The building was destroyed, one employee was killed and a number were wounded (including the ambassador himself). In retaliation, Pakistan expelled the Afghan ambassador and a number of other Afghan diplomats from Islamabad, but refrained from totally severing diplomatic relations. The Iranian authorities were ostensibly uneasy regarding the possibility of the installation of a Taliban-backed ruler in Afghanistan; they demonstrated their displeasure over alleged Pakistani aid to the Taliban and reaffirmed their support for President Rabbani. The Afghan Government presented a formal complaint against Pakistan's suspected involvement to the UN Secretary-General, requesting an official condemnation and an end to foreign interference in the internal affairs of Afghanistan. In October the Taliban launched a massive ground and air assault on Kabul, but by early January 1996 had failed to breach the capital's defences. The constant bombardment of the besieged city, however, resulted in hundreds more civilian deaths, and the road blockades around the capital caused serious shortages of vital supplies. It was amidst this tense situation that the Rabbani Government launched a concerted effort to hold peace talks with the major Afghan opposition groups and leaders, notably the Taliban, Gen. Dostam and Hekmatyar. At the same time, the President also made conciliatory overtures to Pakistan. The Afghan Government subsequently achieved the first small, though symbolically significant, diplomatic breakthrough when it signed a peace agreement with the Shi'ite Hizb-i Wahadat in mid-January 1996. Despite the conduct of exploratory talks with other major opposition parties throughout the first quarter of the year, the fighting in and around Kabul intensified. However, in late May, in a critical development (known as the Mahipar Agreement), President Rabbani persuaded his arch-rival, Hekmatyar, to rejoin the Government. The President offered Hekmatyar's Hizb-i Islami the strategic posts of Prime Minister, Minister of Defence and Minister of Finance. This was, indeed, a significant concession to Hekmatyar, since the removal (once more) of Masoud, Rabbani's trusted aide, from the defence portfolio had long been one of Hekmatyar's main demands and an issue of contention between him and the Government. Hekmatyar's forces arrived in Kabul during May to defend the capital against the Taliban—this move was no doubt viewed by some of the protagonists as revenge against the student militia who had, in the previous year, dislodged Hekmatyar's men from their key strongholds around Kabul. Hekmatyar himself resumed the post of Prime Minister in late June, and President Rabbani appointed a new Council of Ministers in early July, which was to hold power for a period of 6–12 months pending the staging of a general election. In addition, under the terms of the Mahipar Agreement, a Constitution to cover the interim period was drawn up and published.

The Rabbani Government in Exile and the 'Islamic Emirate of Afghanistan'

The political situation was radically altered in late September 1996 when, as a culmination of two weeks of sweeping military advances (including the capture of the crucial eastern city of Jalalabad), the Taliban seized control of Kabul following fierce clashes with government troops, who fled northwards together with the deposed Government. One of the first acts of the Taliban in the captured capital was the summary execution of former President Najibullah and his brother. On assuming power, the Taliban declared Afghanistan a 'complete' Islamic state and appointed an interim Council of Ministers, led by Mola Mohammad Rabbani, to administer the country (of which they now controlled about two-thirds). The Taliban imposed an extremist Islamic code—women were not permitted to enter employment or be formally educated beyond the age of eight; non-religious cultural and artistic practices (for example, music, dance and sport), as well as television, gambling and alcohol were all banned; amputations and public stonings were enforced as forms of punishment; compulsory attendance at mosques by all men was introduced; and women were ordered into purdah.

In mid-October 1996 the former Minister of Defence, Masoud, and his troops repulsed the Taliban forces and regained some lost territory in the Panjshir Valley to the north of Kabul. Taliban hopes that the opposition would remain divided were thwarted following the formation in that month of a powerful military and logistical alliance by Gen. Dostam, Masoud and the leader of Hizb-i Wahadat, Abdol Karim Khalili. Gen.

Dostam, who controlled six northern provinces, apparently decided to establish this unlikely alliance after cease-fire talks between himself and the Taliban broke down. By late October the anti-Taliban forces, whose leaders were now collectively known as the Supreme Council for the Defence of Afghanistan (the headquarters of which were situated in Gen. Dostam's stronghold of Mazar-i-Sharif), had launched a concerted offensive against Kabul in the hope of ousting the Islamist militia. Despite repeated calls for a cease-fire from various foreign governments and the UN, and despite complaints by Amnesty International regarding civilian casualties and abuses of human rights, the fighting between the Taliban and the allied opposition continued into January 1997. In mid-January, following the rapid collapse of UN-sponsored talks in Islamabad, the Taliban launched an unexpected offensive, advancing north and capturing Bagram air base and the provincial capital of Charikar. By late January the Taliban had made significant military gains and had pushed the front line to about 100 km north of Kabul. In an attempt to halt the Taliban advance northwards, Gen. Dostam's forces used explosives to block the vital Salang Highway, the main link between northern and southern Afghanistan. In response, the Taliban moved westwards, but were stopped at the Shibar Pass by Hizb-i Wahadat forces. The situation underwent a dramatic development in mid-May when, following the defection of the Uzbek Gen. Abdul Malik and his men to the Taliban, the latter were able to capture the strategically important northern town of Mazar-i-Sharif with relatively little bloodshed. Gen. Dostam was reported to have fled to Turkey, and his position as leader of the NIM was assumed by Gen. Malik.

The Taliban now controlled about 80% of the country, including all of the major towns and cities. Their position was also strengthened around this time by Pakistan's decision to be the first country to accord formal recognition to the Taliban Government (closely followed by Saudi Arabia and the United Arab Emirates). Taliban control of Mazar-i-Sharif, however, was extremely short-lived, and within only three days of entering the town they were in full retreat. It appeared that Gen. Malik's tenuous alliance with the Taliban had collapsed almost immediately and his troops, together with Shi'ite militia, forced the newcomers out after ferocious fighting. The Taliban were soundly routed, and by early June 1997 their forces had retreated almost 200 km south of Mazar-i-Sharif. Taliban officials later alleged that, following the recapture of Mazar-i-Sharif, about 3,000 Taliban prisoners-of-war were summarily executed by their captors. The regional aspect of the Afghan conflict was highlighted at the beginning of June, when the Taliban decided to close down the Iranian embassy in Kabul; the Iranian Government was widely suspected of actively aiding the anti-Taliban northern alliance. The alliance was reported to have been expanded and strengthened in early June by the inclusion of the forces of Hekmatyar and of the Mahaz-i-Melli-i-Islami (National Islamic Front), led by Pir Sayed Ahmad Gailani. This new coalition, which superseded the Supreme Council for the Defence of Afghanistan, was known as the United Islamic Front for the Salvation of Afghanistan, commonly known as the United Front, and frequently referred to as the Northern Alliance. Despite the arrival of thousands of reinforcements from training camps in Pakistan (many of whom were, however, inexperienced teenagers), the Taliban suffered a series of military defeats in northern Afghanistan, and by late July United Front forces were within firing range of Kabul, having recaptured Charikar and the air base at Bagram. In mid-August it was reported that the United Front had appointed a new Government, based in Mazar-i-Sharif, with Rabbani continuing as President, Abdorrahim Ghafurzai as Prime Minister, Masoud as Minister of Defence and Gen. Malik as Minister of Foreign Affairs. The former Prime Minister in the anti-Taliban administration, Hekmatyar, refused to recognize the new Government. Within a few days of its appointment, however, seven members of the new Government, including Prime Minister Ghafurzai, were killed in an aeroplane crash. In September Gen. Dostam was reported to have returned to Mazar-i-Sharif from Turkey, and in the following month the member parties of the United Front re-elected him as commander of the forces of the alliance and appointed him as Vice-President of the anti-Taliban administration. However, there were reports of a bitter rivalry between Gen. Dostam and Gen. Malik and skirmishes between their respective forces. Gen. Dostam's battle for supremacy with his rival led him to make overtures to the Taliban, including offers of exchanges of prisoners-of-war. Gen. Dostam also accused Gen. Malik of having massacred about 3,000 Taliban prisoners earlier in the year (see above). By late November Gen. Dostam had resumed the leadership of the NIM, ousting Gen. Malik. In late October the Taliban unilaterally decided to change the country's name to the Islamic Emirate of Afghanistan and altered the state flag, moves that were condemned by the opposition alliance and all of Afghanistan's neighbours (with the exception of Pakistan). In late 1997 the World Food Programme (WFP) launched an emergency operation to help people facing starvation in the impoverished central region of Hazarajat (held by the Shi'ite Hizb-i Wahadat), which had been blockaded by the Taliban since August. In January 1998, however, the UN was forced to suspend its airlifts of emergency supplies when Taliban aircraft bombed the area. Meanwhile, in mid-December 1997 the UN Security Council issued a communiqué expressing its concern at the alleged massacres of civilians and prisoners-of-war being perpetrated by various factions in Afghanistan. In May 1998 a UN exploratory mission visited the sites of alleged atrocities to assess the feasibility of a full-scale war-crimes investigation being carried out.

In February and May 1998 the political crisis in Afghanistan was temporarily overshadowed by two devastating earthquakes in the northern provinces of Takhar and Badakhshan, which resulted in the deaths of more than 8,500 people and left about 47,000 homeless. The international relief campaigns were hampered by poor weather conditions, difficult access as a result of inhospitable terrain and continuing fighting.

In March 1998 the UN ceased operating aid programmes in the southern province of Qandahar (where the political headquarters of the Taliban were located) following attacks on staff and constant harassment by the Taliban. In the same month there were reports of factional fighting between rival members of the United Front in and around Mazar-i-Sharif, highlighting the fragile nature of the anti-Taliban alliance. In April, following the launch of a major diplomatic initiative by the USA, the Taliban and the United Front held talks, sponsored by the UN and the OIC, in Islamabad, the first formal peace negotiations between the two opposing sides for more than a year. The USA's re-entry into the troubled arena of the Afghan crisis was interpreted in various ways: the result of public pressure on the US administration by women's rights lobbies; the need for a prompt end to the violence to enable US companies to construct oil and gas pipelines from Central Asia across Afghanistan to markets in South Asia; and a desire to improve relations with Iran. The following month, however, the talks broke down and were postponed indefinitely, and fighting resumed to the north of Kabul. One of the main reasons cited for the failure of the negotiations was the refusal of the Taliban to lift the blockade on the central Hazarajat region, where thousands of people were reported to be at risk of imminent starvation.

Relations between the Taliban Government and the UN deteriorated in June 1998, as a result of the former's decision to close more than 100 private schools and numerous small, home-based vocational courses in Kabul, many of which were educating girls. On 1 August the Taliban captured the northern city of Shiberghan, Gen. Dostam's new headquarters, after a number of his Uzbek commanders allegedly accepted bribes from the Taliban and switched allegiance. Gen. Dostam was reported to have fled to the Uzbek border and thence to Turkey. Following the recapture of Mazar-i-Sharif by the Taliban (amongst whose ranks were now alleged to be considerable numbers of extremist volunteers from a number of other Islamic countries, including Pakistan, Saudi Arabia, Algeria and Egypt) in early August, nine Iranian consular officials and one Iranian journalist who were based in the city were reported to have been captured and killed by Taliban militia. In early September Afghanistan and Iran appeared to be on the verge of open warfare, as 70,000 Iranian troops were deployed on the mutual border. The situation became more serious when it emerged that nine of the missing Iranian nationals had, in fact, been murdered by members of the Taliban as they stormed Mazar-i-Sharif (it was later reported that 2,000 Shi'ite Hazara civilians had been systematically massacred by the guerrillas after recapturing the city). Both Iran and Afghanistan massed more troops on the border; by mid-September 500,000 Iranian troops had reportedly been placed on full military alert in readiness for conflict with their neighbour. In mid-October, in an attempt to defuse the tension, the Taliban agreed to free all Iranian prisoners being held in Afghanistan and to punish those responsible for the killing of the nine Iranian consular staff. By the end of the year the situation appeared much calmer, with the Taliban having expressed regret for the deaths of the Iranian nationals and Iran having scaled down its border forces and announced that it had no intention of invading Afghanistan.

Meanwhile, on 20 August 1998 the USA launched simultaneous air-strikes against alleged terrorist bases in eastern Afghanistan and Sudan, reportedly operated by an exiled Saudi-born militant leader, Osama bin Laden, in retaliation for the bombing of two US embassies in East Africa earlier that month. Bin Laden had served as a *mujahid* against the Soviet-backed Government in the 1980s, during which time he reportedly received financial and logistic support from the Pakistani ISI, which was principally responsible for channelling CIA-supplied arms to *mujahidin* groups and Arab volunteers. Bin Laden reportedly also received Saudi donations and used his own wealth to support the *mujahidin* cause. In 1996 bin Laden settled in Afghanistan, and from 1997 resided in Qandahar, enjoying the hospitality of the Taliban militia. Following the US military action, which resulted in the deaths of 21 people, many aid agencies (including UN agencies) withdrew their remaining expatriate staff from Afghanistan, fearing terrorist acts of vengeance. In September 1998 the Taliban suffered a considerable set-back when Saudi Arabia (one of only three countries officially to recognize the regime) withdrew its funding and political support and recalled its envoy from Kabul. The decision by the Saudi Government substantially to downgrade its relations with the Taliban appeared to have been prompted by its opposition to the reported brutality of the guerrilla authorities and to their sheltering of bin Laden, the leader of the militant and Wahabbi-influenced al-Qa'ida al-Sulbah (Solid Base) terrorist organization. Relations were aggravated when the Saudi Government, in response to US pressure, sent Prince Turki to Qandahar to persuade the Taliban to extradite bin Laden—the Taliban leader refused to hand over bin Laden and, at the same time, insulted the royal family. In the following month the Taliban stated that, although they were not willing to extradite the Saudi dissident, in the event of a lawsuit being filed against him, they would be prepared to place him on trial in Afghanistan. The Taliban also insisted that bin Laden was under close supervision, with his activities and media access suitably restricted. In late November evidence submitted by the US Government to the Taliban 'Supreme Court' was deemed by the latter as inadequate grounds for bin Laden's arrest.

In mid-September 1998 the Taliban captured the capital of Bamian Province, a Shi'ite stronghold; this victory meant that any substantial anti-Taliban opposition was effectively restricted to Masoud's stronghold in north-eastern Afghanistan. The Taliban's advances in the north alarmed Russia and the Central Asian states, which feared the unsettling potential of an extremist Islamic army along their southern borders. In December the UN Security Council threatened the Taliban with the imposition of sanctions and called on the regime to commence negotiations with the opposition. Pakistan, on the other hand, demonstrated its diplomatic isolation with regard to the Afghan situation, by defending the Taliban and urging the other members of the UN to recognize its government. The destabilizing influence of the fundamentalist administration was illustrated in the same month by the decision made by the international consortium (led by the US company, UNOCAL) to abandon plans to construct a trans-Afghanistan natural gas and oil pipeline. (UNOCAL left the consortium in December.) In December 1998–January 1999, despite threats from local Taliban commanders, WFP delivered emergency food aid to more than 120,000 people in the beleaguered region of Hazarajat.

In January 1999 it was reported that the United Front had established a multi-ethnic Supreme Military Council, or Shura-i-Nazar, under the command of Masoud, the aim of which was to give fresh impetus to the anti-Taliban movement and to co-ordinate manoeuvres against the Taliban forces in northern Afghanistan. Despite a certain degree of optimism being raised by the holding of UN-monitored direct peace talks between representatives of the Taliban and the United Front in Ashgabat, Turkmenistan, in February and March, and in Tashkent, Uzbekistan, in July, ultimately very little was actually achieved as a result of the negotiations. On a more positive note, in March the first UN personnel returned to Afghanistan since their evacuation in August 1998 (following the murder of three UN employees); this represented the beginning of a phased return of UN international staff to Afghanistan.

In early July 1999, following reports that bin Laden was being sheltered in eastern Afghanistan, the USA imposed financial and economic sanctions on the Taliban regime in a further attempt to persuade it to hand over the terrorist leader (who the US authorities suspected of planning more atrocities) to stand trial in the USA. In response, the Taliban claimed that the sanctions would have very little impact, since the volume of direct trade between Afghanistan and the USA was minimal, and again refused to extradite bin Laden. Nevertheless, the USA's position towards the Taliban seemed to prompt the Taliban movement to adopt a more radical stance.

On 28 July 1999, following the closure of the peace talks in Tashkent, the Taliban forces launched a multi-pronged attack against their opponents. Within three days the Taliban had seized Bagram air base to the north of Kabul, and the capital of Parvan province, Charikar. These gains proved short-lived; a counter-attack by forces loyal to Masoud enabled them to retake both targets by 6 August. However, during the period of the Taliban 'scorched-earth' response to Masoud's offensive (i.e. the policy in warfare of removing or destroying everything that might be useful to an invading enemy, especially by fire), large numbers of civilians were displaced. At least 65,000 people fled north to the Panjshir Valley, while a further 60,000 headed south to Kabul. Some 12,450 of the displaced persons (including 8,000 children) were accommodated in the compound of the former Soviet embassy in the capital, while others were moved to the old Sar Shahi refugee camp outside Jalalabad. The fugitives claimed that their houses and crops had been destroyed by the Taliban, as had boundary markers and irrigation systems. On a more positive note, around the same time some 87,000 persons who had been displaced from Bamian by the Taliban during March–May managed to return to their homes. While the ground activities of the Taliban offered them no decisive advantages, their air force mounted raids on areas outside Taliban control. During September Taloqan, the capital of the north-eastern province of Takhar, was bombed by the Taliban on a number of occasions, resulting in the deaths of both Afghan civilians and a French journalist; in May 2000 a further Taliban bombing raid on Taloqan killed an Afghan UN field worker and six of his seven children.

A number of blows were struck against Taliban targets during 1999 and the first half of 2000, although exactly by whom remained unclear. In late August 1999 a major bomb explosion near Mola Mohammad Omar's residence in Qandahar reportedly claimed the lives of 40 people, including some members of the Taliban leader's family. In November a bomb exploded outside the Wazir Akbar Khan mosque in Kabul, and in June 2000 there was a bomb explosion in the capital's Zarnigar Park. The Taliban blamed their 'enemies' for these explosions, but their opponents attributed the blasts to factional divisions within the Taliban movement and, in particular, to increasing opposition to Omar's perceived autocracy. The opponents of the Taliban were also afflicted by internecine discord, and in November 1999 Najmuddin Khan, the leading commander in Burhanuddin Rabbani's native province of Badakhshan, and an important member of Masoud's Shura-i-Nazar, was killed in an ambush. The morale of the anti-Taliban forces was lifted in late March 2000, however, with the sensational escape from Qandahar of Ismail Khan, the celebrated former resistance leader and governor of Herat province, who had been handed over to the Taliban in May 1997 during Gen. Malik's brief affiliation with the latter. In the following month the Commander of the Taliban Air Force, Akhtar Mohammad Mansuri, was dismissed from his post for his alleged involvement in Khan's escape. In interviews following his escape, Khan spoke warmly of the United Front leaders Masoud and Dostam, but bitterly attacked Malik, thus complicating Masoud's task of drawing Dostam and Malik, both of whom had returned to Afghanistan in December 1999, into a unified front.

On 15 October 1999 the UN Security Council adopted Resolution 1267, which imposed mandatory sanctions against the Taliban from 14 November. These sanctions (namely, an embargo on all Taliban-controlled overseas assets and a ban on the international flights of the national airline, Ariana Afghan Airlines), which complemented those unilaterally introduced by the US administration from 6 July, were specifically linked to the continuing presence in Afghanistan under Taliban protection of bin Laden and to the Afghan regime's persistent refusal to hand over the suspected terrorist leader to stand trial in the USA or in a third (possibly Islamic) country. Following the imposition of the sanctions (which, although limited and largely irrelevant in economic terms, were, none the less, deeply demoralizing for the already beleaguered Afghan people), there were reports of large-scale demonstrations throughout Afghanistan, and international aid organizations once again came under attack. Demonstrations were mounted against UN offices in Qandahar and Kabul; in Farah province, a UN office was destroyed in an arson attack. The impact of the sanctions was expected to be alleviated, however, by the reopening of key trade routes along the Afghan-Iranian border (which had been closed for 18 months) in late November. Yet economic circumstances in Kabul became increasingly dire, and in January 2000 the Taliban were faced with the embarrassment of a major robbery in the retail district of Kabul's money market. This incident appeared to belie the Taliban claim to have brought security to areas under their control.

During its 1999 session, which was held in September–November, the UN General Assembly again declined to accept the credentials of the Taliban nominee, leaving control of Afghanistan's UN seat with President Burhanuddin Rabbani's 'Islamic State of Afghanistan' rather than with the 'Islamic Emirate' of the Taliban. In late October Mola Mohammad Omar announced an extensive reorganization of key Taliban civilian, military and diplomatic posts, including changes in the Council of Ministers. Of especial note was the appointment of an English-speaking moderate, Wakil Ahmad Motawakkil (the Taliban leader's erstwhile spokesman), to the post of Minister of Foreign Affairs, in an apparent attempt to improve the international image of the Taliban.

The Taliban offensive of July 1999 came only nine days after a UN-sponsored meeting in Tashkent had concluded with a declaration signed by Pakistan, Iran, China, Russia, the USA and Uzbekistan asserting that the Afghan conflict should be resolved through peaceful means. That the new offensive was launched (seemingly regardless of international opinion) almost immediately after this request was presented was undoubtedly one of the contributing factors to the announcement in October by the UN Secretary-General's Special Envoy to Afghanistan, Lakhdar Brahimi, that he was suspending his mediation efforts in the Afghan conflict on the grounds that the Taliban and Afghanistan's neighbouring states were not co-operating in his mission. In February 2000 the UN Secretary-General announced the appointment of Francesc Vendrell as Head of the UN Special Mission to Afghanistan, and as Personal Representative of the Secretary-General, with the rank of Assistant Secretary-General. However, relations between the UN and the Taliban remained tense, and in late March the former temporarily withdrew its expatriate staff from Qandahar in protest at the invasion of UN offices by members of the Taliban in the wake of the escape from custody of Ismail Khan (see above); the UN employees returned to work the following month.

The Taliban movement continued to come under criticism from the international community for numerous reasons. Pakistan's staunch support for the Taliban, however, which had appeared to be wavering under US pressure in the weeks preceding the overthrow of Mohammad Nawaz Sharif's Government in Islamabad by a military coup in October 1999, was reasserted by the leadership of the new military regime partially in response to demands made by Pakistan's right-wing religious parties. Alleged human rights violations under the Taliban were strongly condemned in two reports presented to the 56th Session of the UN Commission on Human Rights, which took place in Geneva in March/April 2000. One report also criticized UN personnel in Afghanistan, accusing them of 'missing the wood for the trees' and being overimpressed by 'paltry, incremental changes'.

During 1999 and the first half of 2000 fresh political and diplomatic initiatives were taken by former King Zahir Shah. In September 1999 Zahir Shah's office in Rome released a taped broadcast by the former monarch in which he foreshadowed the idea of an 'emergency Loya Jirga' (representing the interests of all sectors of the Afghan population) to address the Afghanistan problem. This step was followed by the convening in Rome in November of a meeting of Afghan dignitaries to facilitate and expand on the proposal. One of the most active participants in this process was a former Deputy Minister of Foreign Affairs under President Burhanuddin Rabbani, Hamid Karzai. (Hamid Karzai had joined the Taliban briefly in 1994, but soon after emerged as one of their strong critics and an advocate of the monarchic 'Rome Group'.)

In May 2000 delegations were dispatched by Zahir Shah to Washington, DC, and New York, USA, to discuss with US and UN officials how the Loya Jirga proposition (known as the 'Rome Process') might be expedited. However, while Masoud was prepared to offer support to the process—recognizing its potential to split the Taliban—the Taliban themselves treated the proposals with the greatest caution. At the end of May former King Zahir Shah distanced himself even further from the Taliban than ever when he issued a strongly critical statement in response to remarks made at a press conference a few days earlier by Pakistan's Chief Executive, Gen. Pervez Musharraf, which had sought to justify Pakistan's support for the Taliban on the grounds of their Pashtun ethnicity.

From early 2000 humanitarian agencies working in Afghanistan became increasingly concerned at the onset of a severe drought, the worst the country had suffered since the famine of 1971–72. Qandahar, Helmand, Zabul, Uruzgan and Nimroz were particularly badly affected, but the centre and north of the country were also not spared. Widespread deaths were reported amongst the livestock of Afghanistan's nomads. In Qandahar the fall in the level of the water table led to the drying up of shallow wells, on which 90% of the city depended. The urgency of the humanitarian situation prompted a *démarche* in mid-May 2000 to the Afghan authorities—both the Taliban and representatives of the Islamic State of Afghanistan—from the constituent states of the Afghanistan Support Group, in which they voiced their alarm that considerable human, material and financial resources were being devoted to the war effort, while a severe drought affected a large part of the country. Renewed Taliban assaults in the vicinity of the Salang Tunnel at the end of May suggested that this protest had gone unheeded.

From mid-2000 tension between the Taliban and humanitarian agencies intensified. In mid-August the Taliban temporarily closed down bakeries in Kabul run by WFP. In June 2001 WFP threatened to cease its operations at the 130 bakeries unless the Taliban withdrew a restriction on the hiring of Afghan women (the employment of females being forbidden) to conduct a survey of food requirements in the capital. A compromise was reached to allow the bakeries to continue operating. Meanwhile, UN officials spoke with increasing candour of the threat to their operations posed by non-Afghan extremists, who supported the Taliban and overtly displayed a strong dislike of Western aid workers. This became further evident when the Taliban Department of the Promotion of Virtue and Prevention of Vice (commonly referred to as the 'religious police') raided an Italian-funded hospital in early May 2001 on the grounds that both sexes had been working in the same building. In the following month the Taliban officially announced that all foreigners had to comply with *Shari'a*. Opium cultivation remained a matter of major concern for the international community. On 28 July 2000 Mola Mohammad Omar announced a complete ban on opium poppy cultivation. Reports in April 2001 confirmed that the previously abundant opium crop had been virtually eliminated. The Taliban, however, received little credit for their action against poppy cultivation, partly because of the suspicion that it had been prompted by an unmanageable accumulation of heroin stocks, and by the impact of drought. Yet the relatively successful implementation of their ban led to some of the United Front-controlled territories becoming Afghanistan's major opium-growing areas. As a result of the scaling down of its activities, the financially-constrained UN International Drug Control Programme (UNDCP) was unable to implement crop-substitution programmes designed to assist those who had complied with the Taliban, thus creating tension between local Taliban activists and Pashtun farmers.

Drought was one of the main factors contributing to external and internal population displacement in Afghanistan; continued fighting was another. In early September 2000 Taloqan, the seat of President Rabbani's Government (and headquarters of the United Front), was captured by the Taliban in a major military operation, forcing Rabbani to re-establish his position in Faizabad. Heavy conflict also took place in Hazarajat. In early January 2001 the Taliban reportedly carried out the massacre of 300 civilians in the central town of Yakaolang; evidence of the killings was uncovered when the town was recaptured by the United Front, prompting a formal allegation by the UN Secretary-General, Kofi Annan. The Taliban was the focus of international attention, following their announcement of a decree on 26 February, which, citing idolatry as anti-Islamic, ordered the destruction of all statuary in Afghanistan depicting living creatures, including the world's tallest standing Buddhas in Bamian. Despite intense international protests, the destruction of the country's pre-Islamic cultural heritage took place in March. Hindu and Sikh statues were recognized as elemental to the respective religious practices and thus were not demolished. Given that Mola Mohammad Omar had ordered the preservation of all ancient relics in 1999, this decree prompted extensive speculation about the reasons for the new approach. Theories ranged from antagonism towards the people of Bamian, to an inept plan to force the international community to re-engage with the Taliban as Afghanistan's government. With evidence that emerged from the beginning of US-led military operations in Afghanistan in October 2001, it appeared that allies of bin Laden had taken control of the Taliban, pushing aside moderate activists in a power struggle.

In late April 2001 the Chairman of the Taliban Interim Council of Ministers, Mola Mohammad Rabbani, died. In the following month the Taliban ordered all non-Muslim minorities to wear a distinctive yellow badge or cloth to identify them while outdoors. Members of the Hindu community were instructed to hang strips of yellow cloth outside their homes and Hindu women were to wear veils. Sikhs were not required to identify themselves, as they were clearly distinguished by their turbans. This decision provoked international outrage; the Taliban defended the action, claiming that their aim was to prevent the unnecessary detention of non-Muslims for not complying with Muslim practices.

It was also speculated that the destruction of the statues at Bamian was an emotional reaction to the increasing isolation of the Taliban, which was furthered by their refusal to extradite bin Laden. Following the attack on the *USS Cole* in the Yemeni port of Aden by a terrorist group suspected of connections with bin Laden in October 2000, Russia and the USA proposed a UN Security Council Resolution urging sanctions against the Taliban. The resolution, passed in mid-December, stated that unless the Taliban surrendered bin Laden and closed down military training camps by 19 January 2001, the international community would impose an arms embargo on the Taliban, tighten an existing flight embargo and the 'freeze' on Taliban assets abroad and close Ariana Afghan Airlines offices abroad. The weapons embargo would not affect the anti-Taliban forces. The Taliban refused to concede to the demands, and the sanctions entered into force in mid-January. The imposition of further sanctions led to the breakdown of efforts by the Head of the UN Special Mission to Afghanistan, Francesc Vendrell, to persuade the Taliban and their opponents to participate in open-ended negotiations. In May the Taliban ordered the closure of all offices of the UN Mission, in retaliation for the UN's closure of the Taliban UN office in the USA, an action in compliance with the sanctions. In late July the UN Security Council approved a further resolution urging states to tighten the monitoring and enforcement of sanctions. Not only did tension exist between the UN Mission and the Security Council, but also between the UN's political and humanitarian wings, and between the UN and Pakistan. This became evident as the conditions in the Jalozai refugee camp in Pakistan deteriorated. A large number of the refugees escaping drought and fighting were Tajiks (in contrast to earlier waves of displaced people), who were unlikely to sympathize with the overwhelmingly Pashtun Taliban. Pakistani officials claimed that the occupants of Jalozai were not refugees but 'economic migrants'; the UN strongly disagreed. The Pakistani military prevented the UN from providing necessary food, shelter and sanitation; in March the UN Secretary-General, Kofi Annan, was barred from visiting the camp during a tour of the region. Furthermore, despite repeated requests, Pakistan refused to grant the UN a new site to shelter the constant influx of refugees. The position of internally displaced people was equally dismal. In early 2001 up to 15,000 refugees were stranded on the marshy islands on the River Pyanj near the Afghan-Tajik Border, as a result of heavy fighting in the area. Tajikistan refused to accept the displaced persons, alleging that armed militants were among the refugees.

The assumption of power by the Taliban in Kabul in 1996 had serious repercussions on regional politics involving the neighbouring Central Asian states, China, India, Iran, Pakistan, Russia and the USA. With the end of the 'Cold War' and the collapse of the former USSR in the late 1980s, the region of Central Asia has acquired immense strategic importance owing to its proximity to Russia and China and to its possession of huge energy and mineral resources. Since the Central Asian countries are land-locked, the significance of countries such as Iran, Afghanistan and Pakistan as conduits to transport energy resources and goods has also increased. Countries like Iran, Pakistan, India and the Central Asian states have been advocating the preservation of the territorial integrity of Afghanistan, and have been anxious to witness the instalment of a stable and strong government in Kabul to restore peace in the country, thus facilitating their economic interests in the region. It was widely believed that the Taliban were supported by Pakistan and Saudi Arabia; on the opposing side, to various degrees, were Iran, India, the Central Asian states and Russia. The Russian authorities were particularly aggrieved by the Taliban recognition of the separatist Islamic republic of Chechnya. In May 2000 the Russian Government threatened the Taliban with the possibility of long-range air-strikes against suspected terrorist bases in Afghanistan which were allegedly sheltering and supporting Chechen rebels and Islamist militants from the Central Asian states. In 1998–99 the Taliban regime cultivated relations with China; a defence co-operation agreement was signed by the two parties and oil and gas contracts in Afghanistan (previously given to Turkmenistan) were awarded to China. China's investment in Afghanistan over this period (including the proposed construction of a new cement factory in Qandahar) was the highest among the country's limited foreign investors.

The US attitude towards the Afghan crisis was ambiguous at best, partly because the USA did not thereby face any direct threat to its national interests, and viewed Afghanistan through the prism of its hostility to the hospitality extended by the Taliban to bin Laden. The USA's primary concern was to secure influence over the exploration and exploitation of the vast energy resources of Central Asia, while containing Iranian and Russian involvement in the area.

The Radical Taliban against the Strengthened United Front

The return of two formerly powerful leaders to the United Front—the Uzbek military commander Gen. Dostam from exile in Turkey to north-western Afghanistan in April 2001, and Ismail Khan, Herat's former Governor, to the western provinces in mid-May—provided an important psychological boost for the main anti-Taliban offensives in mid-2001. In an effort to garner support from the international community and to urge it to pressure Pakistan to halt its support for the Taliban, United Front leader Masoud travelled to Europe in April and held successful discussions with a number of European leaders. Meanwhile, in Afghanistan the United Front retained firm control over Badakhshan province, the headquarters of President Rabbani's Islamic State of Afghanistan and, hosting the opposition's only functioning airport and overland supply link with Tajikistan, a vital logistical base for the anti-Taliban resistance. Masoud, therefore, managed to establish an important military base in Khwaja Bahauddin near the Takhar/

Badakhshan border. Control over these north-eastern territories once again guaranteed the Rabbani Government's claim to the UN seat.

In May–July 2001 sporadic clashes between the Taliban and the United Front persisted primarily in the provinces of Takhar and Kunduz. Two bomb explosions in Kabul during this period, however, were clear reminders that the Taliban regime's control of the capital was tenuous. Nevertheless, with massive troop enforcements of up to 20,000 soldiers, the Taliban were determined to capture the remaining United Front-held territories. In early June serious human rights abuses were again committed by the Taliban in the predominantly Shi'ite populated Hazarajat region. In mid-June the Taliban set fire to more than 4,500 houses and 500 shops and buildings in the town of Yakaolang, killing many Hazaras, after recapturing the area.

Meanwhile, in June 2001, the Taliban announced that bin Laden was their guest and that they would not allow him to use Afghan soil as a base to commit attacks against other countries. At the end of the month the Taliban yielded to international pressure and withdrew its controversial decree imposed in May forcing Hindus to wear and use marks of identification. Another set of contentious edicts was issued in July: the use of the internet was outlawed in an attempt to prevent access to anti-Islamic material; and women were banned from visiting picnic areas. In addition to the extant censorship of non-religious cultural practices, items such as tape recorders, telephone sets, juicers, video equipment, musical instruments, fashion catalogues, lipstick and neckties were added to the list of non-Islamic goods. After the destruction of the Buddha statues in Bamian in March, the Taliban again were the subject of international scrutiny following the arrest of eight foreign and 16 Afghan humanitarian workers of the German-based Christian non-governmental organization 'Shelter Now International' in early August on charges of Christian proselytization. In early September the Taliban closed down two other Christian aid organizations on similar grounds. Shortly afterwards the Taliban offered to release the detained humanitarian workers—who had been brought to trial in an Islamic court—in exchange for the release of Sheikh Omar Abdul Rahman, an Egyptian militant Islamist sentenced to life imprisonment in the USA; however, the offer was rejected. On 6 October, one day before US-led military strikes in Afghanistan began, the Taliban proposed the release of the foreign aid workers in exchange for the withdrawal of the US-led military threats; a request which was promptly dismissed. The eight foreign aid workers were eventually rescued in mid-November by a military operation.

In June and July 2001 the United Front, under the command of Ismail Khan, succeeded in capturing a number of districts in Ghowr province, especially those around the provincial capital of Chagcharan. By the end of July reports emerged supporting the long-suspected claims that foreign fighters were substantially assisting the Taliban. Thousands of foreign militant Islamists, many belonging to the Uzbek-based Islamist Movement of Uzbekistan (IMU) under the leadership of Jumaboy Khojiyev (known as Juma Namangoniy), and also Pakistanis, Arabs, and Chechens, were believed to have been fighting alongside the Taliban. Although the focus of the conflict remained largely unchanged throughout August, the Taliban continued to suffer losses in Ghowr. Fighting also intensified in Kapisa, Parwan and Takhar provinces. In early September United Front forces, comprising at least 12,000 troops under the command of Masoud, pushed forward their southern front line to the Bagram air base, approximately 50 km north of Kabul. The explosion of a bomb near the Taliban Ministry of Internal Affairs appeared to reflect the United Front's increased confidence caused by its proximity to the capital, combined with its strengthened military capacity and a possible fragmentation of the Taliban. However, on 9 September the United Front was to suffer a profound set-back. Masoud was seriously injured in a 'suicide bomb' attack at his military base in Khwaja Bahauddin carried out by two Arabs travelling with Belgian passports and posing as journalists. Masoud died some six days later. Evidence that has emerged from abandoned al-Qa'ida camps since the fall of Kabul to anti-Taliban forces in mid-November seems to indicate clearly that these Arab 'suicide bombers' were linked to bin Laden.

THE REPERCUSSIONS OF 11 SEPTEMBER 2001 AND THE FALL OF THE TALIBAN

The USA's approach to Afghanistan and the Taliban regime drastically changed on 11 September 2001 when it became a direct target of terrorism allegedly organized by bin Laden and his al-Qa'ida organization. The terrorist attacks on New York and Washington, DC, USA, provoked international outrage. Although bin Laden denied his involvement in the attacks, the USA soon declared that it had enough information to prove bin Laden's guilt and his involvement as the mastermind of the attacks. The UN imposed diplomatic sanctions and an arms embargo on the Taliban. Meanwhile, the USA swiftly began to form a broad anti-terrorist coalition. Even Pakistan, despite being threatened with military action by the Taliban, under considerable pressure reversed its policy and agreed to co-operate with the US-led coalition. Some six days after the attacks a Pakistani delegation visited Afghanistan to present Taliban leaders with an ultimatum to surrender bin Laden or face US-led retaliatory attacks. A few days later, amidst mounting speculation of an imminent US-led military strike, a *shura* (council) of 1,000 Afghan religious leaders under the leadership of Mola Mohammad Omar issued a *fatwa* concluding that bin Laden should leave voluntarily and in his own time. In addition, the *shura* demanded that the UN and OIC should hold independent investigations into the events, and threatened to initiate a jihad if the USA attacked Afghanistan. The Taliban had earlier declared that they would expel bin Laden if their regime gained international recognition, but the offer was immediately repudiated by the USA. It remained highly unlikely that Taliban leaders would surrender bin Laden, even though they reportedly asked to see evidence of his involvement in the attacks, a request rejected by the USA. Al-Qa'ida had become increasingly involved in Taliban affairs: in late August bin Laden reportedly had been appointed Commander-in-Chief of the Taliban forces. Meanwhile, the leader of Hizb-i Islami and 'spoiler extraordinaire' Hekmatyar, alarmed by the imminent US military engagement, announced in late September that he would join the Taliban if the USA were to attack Afghanistan.

Immediately after the September 2001 terrorist attacks, the USA announced that it would assist a broad-based resistance to the Taliban. By the end of September, US forces were covertly supporting the United Front. India, Iran and Russia had also publicly declared their support for the United Front. Following the suicide attacks on the USA, heavy fighting took place in Takhar, Balkh and Samangan provinces. Rather than imploding after the assassination of Masoud, the United Front was, in fact, more motivated than ever to eliminate the Taliban. The anti-Taliban forces' ongoing military effectiveness was initially not due to increased US support, but was largely due to Masoud's implementation of the Shura-i-Nazar in January 1999. Importantly, this military council was not based on patrimonial rule, but, rather, on institutional effort. The loss of districts in Badghis province in western Afghanistan at the end of September 2001 indicated that the Taliban militia was beginning to falter. In early October, however, the Taliban staged a surprise offensive by dropping cluster bombs on Charikar, the provincial capital of Parwan province near Kabul; the action had little effect. In anticipation of US retaliation, the Taliban reportedly announced the mobilization of 300,000 men; in reality the figure would have been closer to around 45,000 troops.

In September 2001 the United Arab Emirates and Saudi Arabia severed diplomatic links with the Taliban. Pakistan, by now a very close US ally, closed its embassy, but maintained diplomatic relations. In an attempt to persuade the Taliban to extradite bin Laden to the USA, Pakistani President Pervez Musharraf ordered the Director-General of the ISI, Lt-Gen. Mahmood Ahmed, to visit the Taliban leader in Qandahar in late September. As this visit yielded no results, Musharraf removed him from his position on his return and appointed a more moderate replacement, Ehsanul Haq. This move was part of a wider radical reorganization of the military high command and the intelligence service, replacing a number of senior personnel with known sympathies for the country's militant Islamist cause. In the mean time, the USA deployed aircraft around Afghanistan, in preparation for a military attack. Pakistan and Uzbekistan agreed to grant US forces access to their air bases for emergency operations; the latter also allowing search-and-rescue operations to be conducted from its bases. Tajikistan consented to its bases being used for humanitarian operations. At the end of September 2001 US and British military officials confirmed that special military forces had entered Afghanistan to prepare for a planned offensive against al-Qa'ida and the Taliban.

By early August 2001 it had appeared that the humanitarian crisis in Afghan refugee camps in north-western Pakistan was beginning to improve; however, threats of a retaliatory attack on al-Qa'ida and Taliban bases led to fears of a large-scale humanitarian catastrophe. A two-year long drought and ongoing civil war had already left Afghanistan with more than 1m. internally displaced people. The removal by the UN and other aid organizations of foreign staff, owing to security fears; the immediate closure of borders with all six neighbouring countries; and remaining food sources in Afghanistan expected to last only two–three weeks, meant that Afghanistan's impoverished population faced starvation. UNHCR announced that 5m. Afghans required immediate humanitarian assistance in order to survive. In late September communications were restored with Afghan aid workers and the delivery of emergency humanitarian assistance was resumed. Some two months later WFP recommenced delivering food packages by air to Afghanistan. Efforts to provide humanitarian and medical aid were occasionally thwarted by the theft of supplies, allegedly by the Taliban. By December 2001 approximately 3m. people in Afghanistan were still reported to be facing severe hunger; however, the food crisis was largely contained during the cold months of December 2001–March 2002 as a result of the extensive relief efforts of the international community.

'Operation Enduring Freedom'

After the Taliban failed to extradite bin Laden to the USA, on the evening of 7 October 2001 US-led forces began the aerial bombardment of suspected al-Qa'ida camps and strategic Taliban positions. A few days later the Taliban lifted communication restrictions on bin Laden, enabling him to carry out a 'war' against the USA. The US-led military campaign, named 'Operation Enduring Freedom', proved to be so highly effective that US President George W. Bush announced on 17 October that the Taliban regime's air force and defence systems had been destroyed.

Soon after the military operation began, discussions involving the USA, the United Kingdom, other UN Security Council members and countries bordering Afghanistan for a broad-based transitional government were under way. More than 1,000 exiled Afghan commanders and tribal elders at a meeting in late October 2001 pledged to create a broad-based government to be led by the former King, Zahir Shah; however, deep divisions between rival opposition groups also emerged. Some warned against the inclusion of United Front members, who were mainly Uzbeks, Tajiks and Hazara, in a government that was to represent a majority Pashtun population. Western Governments and the UN were concerned by the outcome of the meeting. Furthermore, the USA initially envisaged the participation of moderate Taliban members in the Government and had requested Pakistan to encourage a bloc of such fighters to join the proposed transitional administration; however, Pakistan had not enjoyed any success in dividing the Taliban. Plans to establish an alternative transitional council were hampered further by the capture and assassination of the anti-Taliban opposition leader Abdul Haq, a moderate ethnic Pashtun and member of the Rome Group, who had entered Afghanistan from Pakistan in mid-October accompanied by 50 anti-Taliban fighters in an attempt to galvanize an uprising among moderate Taliban members in Nangarhar province. Hamid Karzai, another moderate Pashtun member of the Rome Group, returned to Afghanistan with US assistance in mid-October, also with the intention of organizing an anti-Taliban rebellion around Uruzgan province. By mid-October reports emerged that the Taliban Minister of Foreign Affairs, Wakil Ahmad Motawakkil, had defected.

In late October 2001 the US Commander-in-Chief, Tommy Franks, met Gen. Muhammad Qassim Fahim, Masoud's military successor in the United Front, in Dushanbe, Tajikistan. This meeting led to significantly improved co-ordination between the US-led coalition and United Front military offensives. In anticipation of the imminent defeat of the Taliban in major regions, US Secretary of State, Colin Powell, announced on 9 November that the United Front should refrain from entering Kabul until a leadership council was formed. Nevertheless, within one week, the United Front rapidly seized control of most of Afghanistan's northern provinces, which were largely inhabited by non-Pashtun ethnic groups. United Front forces, under the control of the Uzbek leader Gen. Dostam, the Shi'ite commander of Hizb-i Wahadat, Haji Mohammad Mohaqqeq, and the Tajik commander of the Jamiat-i Islami, Gen. Mohammad Atta, captured the first major city, Mazar-i-Sharif, on 9 November. Some two days later, the United Front had taken control of Samangan, Sar-e Pol, Faryab, Jawzjan, Baghlan, Takhar and Bamian provinces. On 13 November, despite the explicit wishes of the USA, the Panjshiri faction of the United Front entered Kabul unopposed; anti-Taliban forces also captured Herat. A day later Jalalabad was the first major Pashtun city to fall to United Front forces. At the end of November, a violent uprising of Taliban and al-Qa'ida prisoners in Mazar-i-Sharif had to be quashed with tremendous force after a CIA agent was killed—the first US fatality in Afghanistan. Juma Namangoniy, bin Laden's alleged deputy, leader of the IMU and Chief of the Taliban northern forces, was reportedly killed near Mazar-i-Sharif. There were reports of defections by large groups of Taliban fighters, as their morale declined. At the same time, many conservative Taliban and militant foreign fighters had retreated and sought refuge in Kunduz, an area with a high concentration of Pashtuns. However, after a two-week battle, Kunduz was captured by anti-Taliban forces in late November and more than 5,000 Taliban and allied fighters surrendered as a result of extensive US-led bombing. The non-Afghans who surrendered—mainly Pakistanis, Chechens and Arabs—were treated brutally by United Front fighters.

In early December 2001 the United Front and US-led forces defeated the remaining members of the Taliban in Qandahar; the entrance of Hamid Karzai into Qandahar with an unarmed convoy marking the end of the Taliban regime. One week later Colin Powell announced that the al-Qa'ida network had been destroyed in Afghanistan and that the country was no longer a haven for terrorist activity. Small- to medium-sized concentrations of al-Qa'ida fighters, however, reportedly still existed in Paktia, Paktika, Khost, Ghazni, Zabul, Qandahar and Uruzgan provinces. The highly successful US-led 'Operation Enduring Freedom' in conjunction with the United Front managed to rout the Taliban in two months. There were no exact figures of civilian casualties available, although estimates ranged between 1,000 and 2,000.

Following the defeat of the final Taliban strongholds, US-led forces intensified efforts to locate bin Laden and other senior al-Qa'ida members. The United Front issued a deadline to Taliban and al-Qa'ida fighters to surrender by 12 December 2001. Taliban forces reportedly agreed to surrender, but in the end retreated. Consequently, US-led bombing of targets in the Tora Bora mountains and associated cave complexes in eastern Afghanistan, in which the Taliban and al-Qa'ida were thought to be hiding, resumed. Relying heavily on local commanders for intelligence and ground assistance, this operation, resulting in high civilian casualties as well as the escape of enemy forces, proved to be only marginally successful. By mid-June 2002 there remained approximately 11,000 troops from 17 countries in Afghanistan. The USA and its allies continue to search for remnants of the Taliban and al-Qa'ida, and it seemed likely that coalition forces would remain in Afghanistan for some time yet.

THE PATH TO DEMOCRACY: 2001–

The Bonn Agreement and the Interim Authority

One of the preliminary discussions regarding the establishment of an alternative authority in Afghanistan took place in late September 2001 in Rome between a United Front delegation led by Younis Qanooni and the former King, Zahir Shah. As a result of the discussion, an agreement was reached to establish a 'Supreme Council of National Unity', a *de facto* government to be in place until the convening of a Loya Jirga which would select a new multi-ethnic government. In early October UN Secretary-General Kofi Annan reappointed Lakhdar Brahimi as his Special Representative to Afghanistan and endowed him with the broad role of co-ordinator of UN humanitarian and diplomatic efforts. In mid-October Brahimi presented a five-point formula to the UN Security Council. At an important meeting of Afghanistan's neighbours (China, Iran, Pakistan, Tajikistan, Turkmenistan and Uzbekistan) plus the USA and Russia (the 'Six Plus Two' group) in mid-November in New York delegates stressed the need for a broad-based government in post-Taliban Afghanistan. The Taliban regime's only remaining official contact with the outside world ended in late November when its former main ally, Pakistan, severed all diplomatic links with the Taliban and closed their last embassy.

In late November and early December 2001 Germany hosted and provided considerable support for a UN-brokered conference in Petersberg, near Bonn. The conference was attended by 28 Afghan leaders representing the United Front, the Rome Group led by Zahir Shah, the pro-Iranian Cyprus Process connected with Homayoun Jareer, and the Peshawar process headed by the moderate religious leader Pir Sayed Gailani, in addition to other leading figures. The Taliban were not invited to these discussions. Alongside the talks in Petersberg, a parallel civil society conference was organized by the Swiss Peace Foundation in nearby Bad Honnef, in which 80 representatives participated, allowing delegates of both meetings to interact. In early December the leaders signed the Agreement on Provisional Arrangements in Afghanistan Pending the Re-establishment of Permanent Government Institutions, also known as the Bonn Agreement. The UN Security Council endorsed the agreement immediately in a resolution. Under the general provisions a 30-member multi-ethnic Interim Authority was to be established and to preside for six months from 22 December. The Interim Authority would also include a Special Independent Commission for the Convening of an Emergency Loya Jirga and a Supreme Court in addition to other courts as deemed necessary. It was also agreed that at the end of this transitional period an Emergency Loya Jirga chaired by former King Zahir Shah would appoint a Transitional Authority, which would govern Afghanistan until a fully representative government could be elected no later than two years from the date of the convening of the Emergency Loya Jirga. During the tenure of the Interim Authority Afghanistan would revert to the relatively liberal Constitution of 1964, which had been approved by former King Zahir Shah and which blended *Shari'a* with Western concepts of justice. Hamid Karzai was named Chairman of the administration, which was to comprise 11 Pashtuns, eight Tajiks, five Hazaras, three Uzbeks and three members of smaller tribal and religious groups. Tajik members of the Panjshiri faction of Masoud's Shura-i-Nazar (the first group to enter Kabul)—Younis Qanooni, Gen. Fahim (self-promoted to Marshal in April) and Dr Abdullah Abdullah—were appointed to the three most important portfolios of interior, defence and foreign affairs, respectively. It appeared that the Rome Group and the United Front had come to an agreement about the role of the former monarch Zahir Shah whose return was granted under this deal. Two delegates at the Petersberg conference, the Pashtun governor of Nangarhar, Haji Abdul Qadir, and the Hazara Karim Khalili, however, stormed out of the 'Bonn Talks' declaring inadequate representation of their interests. The Uzbek military commander, Gen. Dostam, the former Governor of Herat, Ismail Khan, and the former Tajik President, Burhanuddin Rabbani, who were not in Germany, also felt marginalized.

In December 2001 the Interim Authority was inaugurated in Kabul; Karzai was sworn in as Chairman. Security during the ceremony was provided by British forces. Immediately after the administration was established Karzai appointed Gen. Dostam as Deputy Minister of Defence. Another important figure, Ismail Khan, was offered the post of Governor of Herat; his son, Mirwais Sadiq, was allocated the labour and social affairs portfolio. Following the distribution of ministerial posts, it became apparent that a number of former *mujahidin* and military commanders had resumed considerable command over regions they had controlled in the past. Afghanistan's reconstruction process, already outlined during the Bonn Talks, was sealed financially at a conference in Tokyo, Japan, in January 2002. The international community pledged US $4,500m. over an indefinite period; US $1,800m. was to be made available for 2002. Also in January, a 21-member Special Independent Commission for the Convening of the Emergency Loya Jirga was established. The Commission, commonly known as the Loya Jirga Commission, was responsible for creating the rules for the selection process and conduct of the Emergency Loya Jirga.

Military and Security Operations during the Interim Authority

The adoption of UN Security Council Resolution 1386 in late December 2001 authorized, as envisaged in the Bonn Agreement, the establishment for six months of an International Security Assistance Force (ISAF) to help maintain security in Kabul (with enforcement, if necessary) until a national army was operational. Some 19 countries were authorized to form a security force, led by the United Kingdom. Deployment of the ISAF began in mid-January 2002. A UN Security Council resolution approved in May authorized the extension of the ISAF for six months beyond June. The security force's mandate would remain restricted to Kabul, however, despite requests by the Interim Authority for the security operations to cover the entire country. In June Turkey took over command of the ISAF. The security force was also responsible for the training of Afghan security forces. In early April the first 600-man battalion for an 'Afghan National Guard' was inducted to serve as the Presidential Guard from mid-2002. At the same time, the USA agreed to lead a US $235m. effort to rebuild an 80,000 strong Afghan multi-ethnic military force that would also include the training of border guards. The first 2,000–3,000 US-trained soldiers were envisaged to be ready by the end of 2002. Some 20 Afghan foreign ministry officials were also receiving training in Ankara, Turkey. Meanwhile, however, commanders of the erstwhile United Front continued to reorganize their own armies, preventing scarce resources from being sent to the Afghan National Army and making the task of creating a multi-ethnic national army even more difficult.

In March 2002 'Operation Anaconda' was launched predominantly by Afghan, Australian, Canadian and US forces against alleged Taliban and al-Qa'ida strongholds in the Shah-i Kot valley in Paktia province. The operation, which was planned as a three-day mission, was met with heavy resistance and developed into a 17-day conflict resulting in the deaths of coalition soldiers. The month of April became one of the most volatile and conflict-riven months under the interim administration; US-led and Afghan forces were faced with considerable security threats. The distribution of leaflets offering rewards for the assassination of westerners and US personnel was discovered in eastern Afghanistan, for example. In mid-April British troops launched their first major military operation in Afghanistan, joining US and Afghan soldiers in Paktia. In May–June a number of smaller operations were conducted by US-led forces with the support of Afghan ground troops to search for Taliban and al-Qa'ida remnants in eastern Afghanistan, under the code name 'Operation Mountain Lion'.

The Emergency Loya Jirga

As envisaged in the Bonn Agreement, Afghanistan's Emergency Loya Jirga took place in Kabul on 11–19 June 2002. Under the monitoring of the UN and the Loya Jirga Commission, district representatives elected 1,051 delegates, the majority of the estimated 1,650 participants. International aid groups, universities and other organizations designated by the Commission, appointed an additional 600 members in order to ensure that gender, geographic, ethnic and political balance was achieved. Although the UN reported incidents of vote-rigging and intimidation of candidates, these activities did not appear significantly to hinder the selection of candidates. Karzai won the presidential election, with 1,295 of the approximately 1,575 votes cast. Massouda Jalal, a medical doctor and the first woman in Afghanistan's history to stand as a candidate, came second with 171 votes, and Mahfouz Nedaei received 109 votes. Some 83 people abstained from voting. This traditional grand council served as an important milestone in Afghanistan's process of democratization. Unthinkable only one year previously, the appointment of a broad-based, gender-sensitive and multi-ethnic Transitional Authority was the first step towards stability and the reconciliation of interests of Afghanistan's diverse and factionalized communities, bringing together a large representation of Afghanistan's population and providing an initial platform to vent grievances.

However, the 36-hour delay to the start of the Loya Jirga signalled the mounting tensions among the major protagonists—the former King Zahir Shah, Hamid Karzai, members of the United Front and independent regional leaders. Shortly before the opening of the assembly, serious tensions regarding Zahir Shah's candidature for the presidency had emerged. Even though most Afghans were generally pleased that the former monarch had returned to Kabul, there was resistance to his political engagement, particularly from Islamist groups. Only after the USA reportedly applied pressure did the former monarch in early June 2002 clarify his position and officially withdraw his candidature. Shortly afterwards, another candidate, the former President and important representative of the United Front, Burhanuddin Rabbani, also renounced his candidature. The Loya Jirga concluded with the ceremonial inauguration of President Karzai. Following approval from the Loya Jirga delegates, earlier that day Karzai had appointed his cabinet, retaining most of the incumbent members of the Interim Authority. The main change in the Transitional Authority's cabinet was the appointment of the Pashtun Taj Mohammad Wardak, the former Governor of Paktia, to the interior ministry. Wardak replaced the Tajik Younis Qanooni who had resigned from his post at the beginning of the Loya Jirga. As a result, the incoming cabinet comprised a more equal ethnic distribution of ministerial portfolios. Qanooni, nevertheless, was assigned the education portfolio. Two other Panjshiri Tajiks from the United Front also retained their positions: Minister of Defence Marshal Fahim and Minister of Foreign Affairs Dr Abdullah Abdullah. Marshal Fahim was also appointed Vice-President. The Hazara Karim Khalili and the Pashtun Haji Abdul Qadir, two influential regional military commanders, were also appointed Vice-Presidents. The Pashtun Ashraf Ghani, Karzai's adviser, was selected as Minister of Economy and Finance. Karzai confirmed his plans to establish a Wolasi Jirga (House of Representatives). The assembly, however, failed to come to an agreement over the structure and powers of the Wolasi Jirga. Karzai proposed to create commissions to deal with this and other important issues. It was envisaged that the election procedure for the parliament would take into account geographic and demographic representation. A constitutional commission was also proposed to draft a new Constitution. The incoming Transitional Authority also had the challenging tasks of convening a Constitutional Loya Jirga within 18 months and implementing free and fair elections within two years.

Domestic and Foreign Affairs under the Interim Authority

The withdrawal of more than 5,000 United Front soldiers from Kabul in early January 2002 was the first sign that the Bonn Agreement was taking effect. In addition to numerous foreign visits by Karzai and some of his senior cabinet members, visits to Kabul early in the year by several leaders of the over 60 nations supportive of the campaign against terrorism bolstered the new-found commitment towards reconstruction and peace-building. The British Prime Minister Tony Blair, as well as some US senators, briefly visited Kabul in early January; Colin Powell paid a visit in mid-January; and in early April a momentous meeting between Pakistan's President Pervez Musharraf and Karzai took place in the capital—the first visit to Afghanistan by a Pakistani leader in 10 years, even more significant owing to the fact that Pakistan had previously been the main ally of the Taliban. In May German Chancellor Gerhard Schroeder arrived for talks with Karzai. The early re-establishment of several foreign missions by such countries as China, Germany, Iran, Saudi Arabia and the USA, as well as the European Union (EU) reinforced the growing stability and security in Kabul. In mid-February the Interim Authority readopted the national flag approved in the 1964 constitution. A national anthem, however, had not been selected for the nascent Government, causing some upheaval during the opening of the Loya Jirga in June.

In March 2002 Afghans were again able to celebrate Nowruz, the Persian New Year—an event previously banned by the Taliban regime. The festivities included the expression of artistic and cultural practices. Immediately after these celebrations, a new academic year commenced for more than 1.5m. children, including girls. On a domestic level, one of the most significant events in the first half of 2002 was the return of the former monarch Zahir Shah to Afghanistan after 29 years of exile. His return in mid-April had been delayed by one month for security reasons. In early May US President Bush lifted US trade restrictions that had been imposed 16 years before by former President Ronald Reagan. The USA remained the principal protagonist in both military intervention and reconstruction in Afghanistan.

After being closed for nearly 10 years, the Salang Pass, Afghanistan's main route connecting Kabul with the north, reopened in mid-January 2002, following a clearance operation by Russian and French teams. On the same day two-year-old UN sanctions were lifted, allowing Ariana Afghan Airlines to operate again as an international carrier. Six of the airline's aeroplanes had been destroyed, however, during the recent military operation, leaving the Interim Authority with only two aircraft. In order to assist Afghanistan's national carrier, India announced in early May that it would provide it with three Airbus A-300. By June Ariana Afghan Airlines was providing direct services to India, Iran, Pakistan, Tajikistan and the United Arab Emirates. At the end of March Tajikistan Airlines began flight operations to Kabul, followed, in early April, by Iran's Mahan Airlines and, in mid-May, by Pakistan International Airways. At the end of May, the leaders of Afghanistan, Pakistan and Turkmenistan signed a memorandum of understanding, agreeing to construct a gas pipeline extending from Central Asia, through Afghanistan to the Pakistani port city of Gwadar. The project would ensure significant financial revenue for the Afghan Government.

Nahrin, in Baghlan province, was hit by a devastating earthquake in late March 2002; violent aftershocks persisted for several days thereafter. More than 800 people were estimated to have died and several thousand families were left homeless. Owing to the presence of coalition troops and international aid agencies, the victims were able to receive aid much more quickly than during previous devastating earthquakes in 1998. The repatriation of Afghan refugees since the defeat of the Taliban had proved highly successful. In early April UNHCR reported that more than 50,000 Afghan refugees were returning from Pakistan every week. One week later a joint voluntary repatriation programme between UNHCR and the Iranian Government was launched to facilitate the repatriation of more than 400,000 Afghans from Iran. In mid-June UNHCR announced that more than 1m. Afghans had returned with a further million expected by the end of the year. This rapid return of refugees alone, however, might lead to another humanitarian disaster, especially if the repatriation projects do not receive urgently needed funds.

Factional Fighting and the Re-emergence of Regional Leaders

Despite the numerous positive developments since the inauguration of the Interim Authority, a number of serious security concerns beleaguered Kabul and regional centres. The murder of Abdul Rahman, the Minister of Civil Aviation and Tourism, in Kabul in February 2002 was followed by numerous dangerous incidents, especially in April. The assassination attempt on Marshal Fahim, in Jalalabad; the arrest of some 300 supporters of Hekmatyar's Hizb-i Islami who were alleged to have plotted against the Interim Authority; the firing on British peacekeepers in Kabul; and a bomb explosion in Khost, were clear signs that not everyone was satisfied with the Interim Authority and that major security concerns existed for Karzai's administration. Moreover, the murders of eight Loya Jirga delegates, the arrest of a number of candidates, and an attack on a Loya Jirga Commission vehicle during the selection process were apparent indications that politics in post-Taliban Afghanistan remained volatile. In May–June several important Pashtun areas in eastern and southern Afghanistan became the centres of violent unrest. Jalalabad airport was attacked in early May and almost a fortnight later two missiles were fired at a base for British marines near Gardez, the provincial capital of Paktia. At the end of the month a bomb exploded outside the office of Gul Agha Sherzai (the provincial governor of Qandahar) and, in early June, rockets were launched at Qandahar airfield by unknown attackers. In mid-June, during the Emergency Loya Jirga, the UN special envoy Brahimi notified Karzai and held a meeting with three factional leaders of Balkh province about several serious incidents of lawlessness and violence by armed men in northern Afghanistan. These security violations could potentially lead to the withdrawal of the UN and international humanitarian organizations from northern Afghanistan. Another major threat to Afghanistan's national security (as discussed earlier) was posed by followers of the extremist Islamist Hekmatyar who was alleged to have been involved with militant activities against the Interim Authority as well as against the USA and allied troops. Hekmatyar had returned to Afghanistan from exile in Iran by the end of February. In May the CIA unsuccessfully attempted to assassinate Hekmatyar in Kunar province by firing a missile from an unmanned drone. The assassination of Abdul Qadir, a leading moderate Pashtun and important supporter of Karzai, in early July represented a damaging set-back for the new Government, particularly in its attempts to reconcile ethnic divides. Karzai immediately commanded a five-member delegation to investigate the murder. Fears for Karzai's safety led the President to request US troops to replace his Afghan bodyguards.

The volatile political situation in Afghanistan was further compounded by the USA's policy of hiring and arming soldiers of local—but at times renegade—commanders in former Taliban strongholds, in the hope of capturing Taliban and al-Qa'ida members. The US-supported and former Karzai-appointed Governor of Paktia province, Padshah Khan Zadran, for example, was a supporter of the former King, Zahir Shah, but strongly opposed the Karzai administration. On the day of the inauguration of the Interim Authority in December 2001, US aircraft mistakenly bombed a convoy of tribal leaders travelling to Kabul to attend the ceremonial procedures for the interim administration; up to 60 people were killed. Intelligence used to plan this attack was allegedly supplied to the USA by Zadran. The US anti-terrorist strategy was brought into question when a wedding party in Uruzgan province was bombed by mistake by US forces in early July, as a result of which some 54 people died. It appeared that the US forces mistook the traditional celebratory firing of a rifle at an Afghan wedding for hostile anti-aircraft gunfire. The US military had earlier received information that senior Taliban leaders were hiding in a village in Uruzgan province.

After Karzai appointed Taj Mohammad Wardak to replace Zadran as Governor of Paktia in March 2002, troops loyal to Zadran provoked violent clashes in the region, which occasionally resulted in civilian deaths. The situation became more tense when Karzai appointed Abdul Hakim Taniwal as Governor of Khost in May. Zadran's forces continued to maintain command of Khost and Zadran initially refused to step down to let Taniwal take control. By the end of April Karzai had announced that he would send government troops to Gardez to stop the fighting and asked for the arrest of Zadran. If this were to happen, it would be the first time that such action has been taken by a post-Taliban authority. Despite repeated warnings from the Afghan administration, Zadran and his followers continued to hold rallies demanding that Zadran be appointed leader of 'Great Paktia' (a single province before 1978, comprising Khost, Paktia and Paktika provinces).

The re-emergence of virtually autonomous fiefdoms under the control of powerful regional leaders was a typical pattern in Afghanistan during the 23 years of civil war. In mid-2002 both Gen. Dostam and Ismail Khan continued to claim considerable authority in Afghanistan's north-western and western provinces, while supporting the Afghan government. Gen. Dostam wielded considerable power in Samangan, Sar-e Pol and parts of Mazar-i-Sharif and was believed to be in command of more than 7,000 troops. Ismail Khan, in turn, controlled most of the western provinces and, from his base in Herat, reportedly instructed some 30,000 soldiers. The Minister of Defence and Masoud's former deputy, Marshal Fahim, exerted strong influence in Kabul and the Tajik-inhabited north-eastern provinces. In the Hazarajat region, Karim Khalili of the Hizb-i Wahadat with allegedly 10,000 fighters remained undoubtedly the most influential commander in central Afghanistan. A number of powerful Pashtun leaders established themselves in southern and south-eastern Afghanistan. Gul Agha Sherzai held considerable influence in Qandahar.

In mid-February 2002 a UN employee was murdered in Mazar-i-Sharif, the centre of reprisal attacks against Pashtuns in March and other armed attacks on humanitarian organizations and staff, including the rape of a UN staff member in mid-June. This northern city was largely under the control of the Tajik commander Gen. Atta, but two other commanders also wielded significant influence in this region: Gen. Dostam and Mohammad Mohaqqeq. In an attempt to unify these three oft-feuding ethnic factions in Sar-e Pol and near Mazar-i-Sharif in north-western Afghanistan, the UN brokered an agreement in early February, according to which a 600-strong security force was to be established in the region representing all three factions. As a result, weapons and armed personnel were withdrawn to the factions' respective bases. In July British and US special forces brokered a deal between Gen. Dostam and Gen. Atta, whereby the two commanders agreed to establish a joint anti-terrorism unit, comprising troops from both of their factions. In mid-February, in response to the ethnically motivated violence against Pashtuns in northern Afghanistan, the Karzai administration authorized an independent commission to investigate the reports of violence and the findings of the international human rights organization, Human Rights Watch (HRW).

In early October 2001 HRW had already named a number of military figures in Afghanistan who had committed serious human rights abuses, such as Gen. Dostam and Mohaqqeq. Yet, both of these commanders, formerly aligned with the United Front, served as senior cabinet members in the Interim Authority. Fully aware of the importance of these powerful regional leaders, Karzai chose Herat as his first internal visit as Chairman of the Interim Authority in early February in order to pay his tributes to Ismail Khan, whom he later appointed to the previously held title of Governor of Herat. This further highlights the continuing influence of regional leaders, a fact confirmed by the visit by the US Secretary of Defense, Donald Rumsfeld, to Ismail Khan during his brief trip to Afghanistan in late April. Rumsfeld's visit also reflected US concerns about possible Iranian foreign influence on powerful leaders in Afghanistan. In addition to these regional actors, disputes between local rival leaders and/or commanders, often politically motivated by inter- and extra-party, as well as ethnic, differences, were also destabilizing factors in Nangarhar, Nimroz, Wardak, Zabul, and Kunduz provinces.

Economy

KEVIN RAFFERTY

Revised by PETER MARSDEN

BACKGROUND AND PROBLEMS OF DEVELOPMENT

The Afghan economy is essentially based on subsistence agriculture, with levels of productivity varying from one river valley to the next and from one part of the country to another. Trade links with Afghanistan's many neighbours have influenced the nature of each micro-economy, and the complexities of more than 20 years of conflict have led the economic fortunes of these micro-economies to rise and fall. Thus, for example, the areas targeted by Soviet forces suffered particular economic damage, while, until recently, the important entrepôt functions served by Kabul and Mazar-i-Sharif had been lost by the effective closure of the trade route to Uzbekistan as a direct consequence of the ongoing conflict. The desert terrain and high altitude of much of the country have made it particularly vulnerable to climatic changes, and the devastating droughts in 2000 and 2001 negated the improvements in agricultural production achieved through painstaking efforts over the previous few years. It has never been easy to present an accurate profile of Afghanistan's economy. The problem of data collection was compounded by the 1978 coup and the Soviet invasion of December 1979, which removed most of the rural areas from government control. The collapse of the Soviet-supported Government in April 1992 and the subsequent anarchy led to an accelerating deterioration in the infrastructure of government ministries. Record-keeping effectively ceased at this point, leaving those seeking to identify economic trends dependent on extrapolations produced by the UN from statistics collected at the local level by non-governmental organizations (NGOs) and UN consultants. Even the World Bank, the Asian Development Bank (ADB) and the UN's Economic and Social Commission for Asia and the Pacific (ESCAP) subsequently stopped publishing data on Afghanistan in their annual reports.

During the 1980s more than 3m. refugees fled to Pakistan, while a similar number crossed into Iran and yet others escaped to the West. In all, according to the office of the United Nations High Commissioner for Refugees (UNHCR) estimates, the number of Afghan refugees totalled 5.5m. by 1988 (3.15m. in Pakistan and 2.35m. in Iran), equivalent to 25%–30% of the country's total population. Afghanistan's economic difficulties were compounded in mid-1992 when, following the downfall of the Soviet-supported Government in Kabul and the installation of a *mujahidin* administration, thousands of refugees began to return to their devastated homeland. By March 1993 it was estimated that about 2m. Afghan refugees had returned to their homeland—approximately 200,000 from Iran and 1.8m. from Pakistan. However, the pace of return decelerated after 1993 as refugees responded with caution to the continuing instability in Afghanistan arising from the failure of the various *mujahidin* parties to agree on a power-sharing arrangement. Periodic intensifications of the conflict subsequently resulted in the arrival of new refugees in Pakistan and Iran, as well as the displacement of people to other parts of Afghanistan. The emergence of the Taliban and their capture of Qandahar in October 1994 had only a marginal impact on the rate of return of refugees, in spite of the significant improvement in stability in southern Afghanistan. Conversely, the capture of Herat by the Taliban in September 1995 resulted in an outflow of professionals to Iran, and the seizure of Kabul in September 1996 led to a rapid depletion in the remaining professional classes as large numbers of them fled to Pakistan. The capture of Taloqan, in north-eastern Afghanistan, by the Taliban in September 2000, and the ensuing fighting, led more than 170,000 people to flee to Pakistan. In mid-2001 Iran was hosting 1.4m. Afghan refugees, while Pakistan was accommodating more than 1.2m. The number of refugees returning to Afghanistan was insignificant, owing to the serious drought and the escalating conflict. In addition to the refugees living abroad, it was estimated that at least 1m. people were internally displaced within Afghanistan itself. The level of internal displacement was compounded by the US-led military intervention, which began in October 2001, and the consequent constraints on NGO access to drought-affected areas. It gradually eased as greater access was gained; however, considerable strains were placed on the economy by the return of more than 1.3m. refugees from Pakistan and more than 124,000 from Iran by early August 2002, following the December 2001 Agreement on Provisional Arrangements in Afghanistan Pending the Re-establishment of Permanent Government Institutions, also known as the Bonn Agreement.

The effectiveness of the Government in Kabul was always tested by the rugged terrain of steep mountains, high desert plateaux and narrow valleys and by tribal and feudal laws. Official statistics relating to Afghanistan were often vague or unreliable. Figures for the size of the population provide an appropriate example. The first national census, conducted in June 1979, gave a total of 15,551,358, of whom an estimated 2.5m. were nomads. However, the Kabul regime ignored the subsequent mass exodus of refugees in its compilation of statistics, which continued to show a steady rise in the population. According to the US Central Intelligence Agency (CIA), the population of Afghanistan at mid-2001 (including nomads) was estimated at 26,813,057. The age distribution of the population was: 42% 0–14 years, 55% 15–64 years and 3% 65 years and over. The population growth rate was estimated at 3.48% (adjusted for the return of refugees from Iran). This figure was based on a birth rate of 41.42 per 1,000 population, a death rate of 17.72 per 1,000, and a net migration rate of 11.11 migrants per 1,000. The sex ratio was 1.05 males per female at birth. Other vital statistics included an infant mortality rate of 147.02 deaths per 1,000 live births (Asia's highest). According to WHO, life expectancy at birth in 2000 was 44.2 years for males and 45.1 years for females—by far the lowest in all Asia—and the total fertility rate was 6.9 infants born per woman.

Although adherence to Islam is a major unifying factor, Afghan society is characterized by a marked sectarian, ethnic and linguistic heterogeneity. The majority of the population are Sunni Muslims, constituting 84% of the total, 15% are Shi'ite Muslims and a small fraction of the remaining 1% of the population adhere to other beliefs. A breakdown by ethnicity reveals that Pashtuns constitute 38% of the population, Tajiks 25%, Uzbeks 6%, Hazaras 19% and the remainder belong to minor ethnic groups (Aimaks, Turkmen, Baloch and others). The numerous different languages spoken by the Afghan people include Pashto (Pakhto) (by 38%), Dari (a dialect of Farsi or Iranian) (47%), Turkic languages (mainly Uzbek and Turkmen) (11%) and 30 minor languages (primarily Balochi and Pashai) (4%). Many people are bilingual.

By 2001 the 23 years of conflict had tested the Afghan population and its traditions to their limits. Although the traditional tribal and other community-based structures have largely remained intact, the power of the elders has, in many areas, been challenged by young military commanders and by entrepreneurs engaged in the illegal economy. The religious certainties offered by the Taliban were initially welcomed as a respite from the prevailing sense of chaos, but their appeal had all but evaporated by the time of the US-led military campaign. Conversely, the initial optimism created by the Bonn Agreement was soon replaced by apprehension that the peace process could unravel. The position of women in society was central to the political movements of the 20th century in Afghanistan, including that of the Taliban. Traditionally, women and men have had complementary economic roles in the agricultural sector, with women, for example, carrying out sowing, weeding and livestock care, while men ploughed and took the major share of harvesting. Women have been heavily burdened by early marriage and multiple pregnancies, which have taken a considerable toll on their health. Efforts to improve their situation by King Amanullah in 1929 provoked conservative reprisals, and it was not until the introduction of the 1964 Constitution that any significant legislative changes were implemented. These benefited the urban population primarily and resulted in significant numbers of girls receiving education up to tertiary level and entering professions such as teaching, medicine and office work. The exodus of professionals that followed the assumption of power by the *mujahidin* in 1992 and the series of Taliban conquests during 1994–2001 represented a serious loss, for which the provision of alternative employment by NGOs and UN agencies could not adequately compensate. Neither the *mujahidin* nor the Taliban were willing to move beyond a highly conservative interpretation of women's role in society and the interim administrations established under the Bonn Agreement will need to conduct with sensitivity the mission to improve female access to education, employment and health care in order not to provoke a conservative counter-attack. The primary hope for any significant improvement lies in changing attitudes within the rural population, with female education and employment gradually becoming both acceptable and desirable. NGOs and UN agencies also need to respond with caution to this emerging flexibility in the face of varying levels of resistance at the local level. The growing power of militants within the Taliban, in response to the US air-strikes of August 1998 and the imposition of UN sanctions in November 1999 and December 2000, left a legacy of radical conservatism amongst some elements in Afghan society which could be easily encouraged by insensitive actions by US and other coalition forces operating in Afghanistan.

Afghanistan has one of the highest levels of adult illiteracy in Asia—64% in 1999, according to UNESCO estimates—but it is likely to be even higher as a consequence of the large-scale exodus of professionals. According to UNESCO estimates, 36% of children in the relevant age-groups (males 49%; females 22%) were enrolled in primary and secondary schools in 1995. These figures were dramatically affected, however, by the enforced closure of girls' schools by the Taliban from September of that year and the simultaneous ban on female employment outside the health sector. With so many boys' schools dependent on female teachers, access to education for boys was also reduced by these Taliban measures. The involvement of NGOs in education ensured a minimal level of provision, but they were heavily constrained by the sensitivities of the *mujahidin* and the Taliban to foreign participation in Afghan education, both in terms of the curriculum and the degree of access to the population. Both political movements felt more comfortable with the Islamic education provided by *madrassas* (mosque schools), and the Taliban drew heavily on these institutions for recruits to assist them in their military campaigns. After the defeat of the Taliban regime, the Interim Authority (December 2001–June 2002), established in accordance with the Bonn Agreement, supported the reopening of schools for both girls and boys from late March 2002. The UN Children's Fund (UNICEF) in conjunction with the Afghan Ministry of Education predicted that 1.7m. children would return to school; however, in July almost 1.25m. children were confirmed to be attending school in 20 out of 32 provinces, indicating that the total number of children might have exceeded initial expectations. About 30% of the pupils in those 20 provinces were girls; similarly, of the 27,000 teachers, 36% were women.

With regard to higher education, in 1991 there were six institutions of higher learning: the University of Kabul, Nangarhar University, the Polytechnic Institute, the Islamic University, Balkh University, the State Medical Institute, and the Institute of Pedagogy. In that year there were a total of 17,000 students enrolled in these institutions. Higher education has suffered as a result of the conflict, along with primary and secondary education. Kabul University, which was established in 1932, remained closed for three years after the *mujahidin* took control of the capital in 1992. A large number of professors had already fled during the Soviet occupation (1979–89). The University was reopened in March 1995. When the Taliban captured Kabul in September 1996, the University was temporarily closed; on its reopening, female staff and students were no longer allowed to attend. The new Transitional Authority (which took over in June 2002) was devising a policy framework for tertiary education.

Health services available to the people of Afghanistan were scarce even before the 1978 coup. Since then, they have been affected by varying levels of provision, dependent on the ability of the Soviet-supported Government to invest in the health sector between 1978 and 1992, the effective collapse of the government health infrastructure from 1992 onwards, the restrictions placed by the Taliban on female access to health care and employment, and a mixed array of services operated by UN agencies, by the International Committee of the Red Cross (ICRC) and by various NGOs since 1989. The ability of humanitarian agencies to provide health care has been largely determined by the willingness of the major donors to maintain funding levels. There are indications that the health status of at least part of the population has shown some improvement as a consequence of the greater access of NGOs to the population in the refugee camps in Pakistan and in remote rural areas. The health service provided by the Iranian Government has also benefited those Afghans who sought refuge in Iran. However, infant and maternal mortality rates remain extremely high throughout Afghanistan, as do the levels of diarrhoeal diseases, malaria, tuberculosis, measles and leishmaniasis. Landmine injuries are also at an alarming level and would have an even more damaging impact if it were not for the surgical and prosthetic services provided by the ICRC and a number of NGOs. The restrictions imposed by the Taliban on female access to health care represented a major constraint. The failure of much of the 2000 and 2001 harvests as a result of drought is expected to have lowered significantly the resistance of the population to disease, and the shortage of water will also have exposed the Afghan people to greater public health hazards. The work undertaken by NGOs and UN agencies over the years to improve wells, piped water systems, sanitation and drainage will hopefully mitigate the effect of the drought, but further urgent work is needed in response to the crisis. Cholera preparedness is a major priority for humanitarian agencies each summer. The government hospitals in the main urban centres, including regional hospitals in Kabul, Herat, Mazar-i-Sharif and Jalalabad, depend heavily on UN agencies, the ICRC and NGOs for supplies, maintenance and clinical support. Various studies undertaken by the World Food Programme (WFP) and other international organizations indicate high levels of malnutrition in many areas, with a large proportion of the population having steadily sold off their assets over the years in their efforts to survive.

According to CIA figures on Afghanistan, GDP has fallen substantially over the past 20 years or so, primarily owing to the loss of labour and capital and the disruption in the trade and transport sectors. It was estimated that in 1999 GDP in terms of purchasing power parity totalled US $21,000m. (equivalent to US $800 per head). It was probable that this substantially declined in 2000–01 owing to the drought.

The Start of Economic Planning

Only in 1932, when the Banke Milli Afghan (National Bank) was established, did modern economic development begin. Before that, the only modern features were the Government's workshops in Kabul, chiefly providing for the needs of the army, and one small hydroelectric station. The formation of the bank gave an impetus to the foundation of private companies. These were mainly concerned with trading in the skins and wool of karakul (a breed of sheep) and lambs, but textile and sugar companies were also established. However, progress was slow and, even at the end of the Second World War, internal trade was carried by caravan and inter-city roads were not paved. Only about 20,000 kW of power was installed, and few consumer goods were made locally.

In 1946 the new Prime Minister, Shah Mahmud Khan, began an ambitious economic development programme, using Afghanistan's agricultural exports as its base. The scheme failed, however, for lack of finance. The next attempt to start economic planning occurred when Muhammad Daud assumed the premiership in 1953. Again, he encountered problems in finding foreign finance, and the US Government refused to lend general support to the first Five-Year Plan, which was launched in 1957. The USA was prepared to provide money only for individual projects. However, the Prime Minister neatly avoided that problem by improving relations with the Soviet Union and delicately playing off the USSR and the USA so that the latter closely followed, and almost matched, Soviet aid to Afghanistan. The USSR was prepared to underwrite a general five-year economic exercise. In all, between 1957 and 1972 the USSR offered more than US $900m. to support these plans (i.e. nearly 60% of foreign aid, although some Western experts claim that the promised sums were larger than those actually handed over). The USA provided the second largest amount of aid, but it usually offered better terms.

The first three Plans (for 1957–61, 1962–67 and 1968–72, respectively) cannot be portrayed as an attempt to control the whole economy, although the Government described its policy as one for a 'guided economy' and later a 'mixed, guided economy'. The Plans offered a series of projects basically to improve the infrastructure.

The first Plan set the pattern by putting great emphasis on communications, particularly road building and the establishment of air links, both national and international. In addition, 32 industrial projects were due to begin, although not all were started. The achievements of the first Plan were variable. Its great merits were the attempts to establish the development of a planned economy, to exploit external sources of finance, and at the same time to realize the need for internal finance. The great drawback was that this boldness in planning was not matched by much success in implementation.

By the time of the second Plan, the difficulties of the planning were beginning to be apparent, at least to outsiders. Proper cost-benefit studies were neglected, and the impact of projects on income and job opportunities was virtually ignored. The second Plan also attempted to expand the role of the public sector because private industry was not big enough to undertake developments in power, gas supply and making of cement, chemicals, and other important capital-intensive industry. One problem that was not properly examined beforehand was where to find competent operators and managers to run the plants. At the start of the third Plan the Government reviewed the achievements and the lessons of the first two Plans and emphasized the need to turn to more quickly yielding projects. However, in practice, this proved more difficult.

For all this, 16 years of planning and public investment of Afs 53,000m. produced an impressive list of achievements. Before planning started there were no paved roads in Afghanistan, few permanent bridges and air transport was almost non-existent. By the end of the third Plan, in 1972, the country had 2,780 km of paved roads and two international and 29 local airports. Dams and bridges had been constructed. Registration of motor vehicles in Kabul increased from 16,000 in 1962 to 52,000 in 1971. In industry, production of cotton cloth quadrupled to 62m. m, cement making and shoe manufacturing began, and the output of the soap, sugar and coal industries increased by between 100% and 300%. Electricity production rose almost ninefold to 442.6m. kWh. Natural gas production was started and reached 2,635m. cu m annually, much of which was exported to the USSR. There were major achievements in education, with the number of schools increasing from 804 to nearly 4,000, teachers from 4,000 to 20,000, and pupils from 125,000 to 700,000. Industrial employment rose from 18,000 in 1962 to nearly 27,000 in 1971. More than 60 private enterprise industries were established, employing nearly 5,000 people.

The fourth Plan was published in 1973. As with previous plans, the proposed programme of development depended on assistance from the USSR for its chief support. However, the planning procedure was disrupted by the coup in July, and actual planning was on an annual basis. In 1976 an ambitious Seven-Year Plan was announced. Before it had time to take effect, however, President Daud was overthrown in the April 1978 coup, and the Plan was abandoned.

Between the 1930s and the 1980s successive governments in Kabul tried hard to lay the foundation of a modern state. The much-abused Daud introduced the notion of planning and was instrumental in securing Moscow's help. Some 3,000 km of properly metalled roads were built and air links were established. Of course, many questions can be asked about the efficiency of Plan expenditure. For example, more than 30% of expenditure from the first three Plans went on building the giant highways which opened up the country—some of them truly magnificent works of engineering, like the Salang tunnel—but what use were they in helping local people living in scattered villages to get their crops to market? Although 85% of Afghans live in rural areas, although agriculture contributes more than 50% of GNP and although 80% of export earnings have traditionally come from agricultural products, a much smaller proportion of Plan expenditure went to help agriculture or livestock, and little of the money went to the smaller farmers. Of the Afs 12,500m. spent on the agricultural sector, one-half went on two huge irrigation projects. More attention to feeder roads to get crops to market, to small irrigation schemes and to agricultural extension work might have helped to increase agricultural production and to bring the ordinary Afghans into the market economy.

In addition, much financing was allocated to grandiose schemes that were unsuitable for a poor and sparsely-populated country. Qandahar airport, a US-aided project, never had enough traffic even when tourists and others could move about freely. Other schemes, such as the French-assisted Balkh textile mill, exceeded their original budget. Sometimes this was because the Kabul planners were working in an ideal world and tended to ignore reality and the country's slow pace. Yet other ventures were based on out-of-date technology, including the Soviet-built Mazar-i-Sharif fertilizer factory.

Nevertheless, by the end of the Daud era, there was hope of building a modern country with the prospect of prosperity ahead of it. There was scope for greatly increased agricultural yields and export earnings. Tree and field crops and livestock all had potential that had not been realized. Cotton proved competitive in world markets, fresh fruit from the orchards of Afghanistan was, at one time, in demand around the Gulf, while dried fruits, such as raisins, could be marketed world-wide. Mineral reserves had yet to be opened up. Industry, especially that devoted to the processing of agricultural products, would offer increased value-added as well as employment in the modern sector.

THE SEVEN-YEAR PLAN AND SUBSEQUENT TRENDS

In 1976 President Daud inaugurated an ambitious Seven-Year Economic and Social Development Plan intended to make major advances towards solving the problems of poverty and underdevelopment. The Plan became academic, however, because of the change of government. In view of the political set-backs to the economy, its targets—to increase the GNP by more than 50% by 1983, with annual growth rates of 6.3% or double those of the past—were hopelessly unrealistic.

Two aspects of the Plan are still worth noting. One was that Daud saw the principal thrust of development effort coming from the public sector and the main assistance from the USSR. Second, the Plan aimed, through a US $2,000m. project, to build a 1,800-km railway system linking with Iran in the west and Pakistan, at Spin Boldak, in the east. Economically, it was a doubtful venture and, although occasional statements are still made to indicate the desirability of a rail network, the National Development Framework drawn up by the Afghan Interim Authority did not mention rail transport.

Following the Saur Revolution in which Daud was overthrown in April 1978, the new ruler, Nur Muhammad Taraki, invited numerous advisers from Moscow as he tried to remodel the economy. The Taraki Government quickly formulated plans to address the problems of those people so far unaffected by economic change. A Five-Year Plan started in 1979. This proposed a total investment of Afs 105,000m., 25% of which was to be allocated to agriculture in order to triple output. Investment in industry (in 1979 employing only 12% of the working population) and mining was to amount to Afs 43,654m. in order to increase the contribution of industry to GNP from 23% to 41%. The Plan envisaged the comprehensive development of both heavy and light industry based on the effective utilization of natural resources. Towards the end of 1978 it decreed important new measures: a major land reform limiting families to 15 irrigated acres each (this unpopular reform, however, had been greatly amended and practically invalidated by 1987); a decree remit-ting debts of peasants; and dowry rules outlawing payment of more than Afs 300 (about US $8) in dowries and raising the minimum age for marriage to 16 years for women and 18 years for men. These measures caused a confrontation with the powers of the old village and tribal order. The wisdom of such a direct attack could clearly be doubted. Given the distrust of officialdom it was not surprising that the reforms were ignored or circumvented. However, the Government claimed at the beginning of 1980 that there were already almost 1,200 agricultural co-operatives in the country. The Five-Year Plan aimed for a total of 4,500, involving more than 1m. people. By early 1990, however, the alleged number of agricultural co-operatives had fallen to about 663.

The room for manoeuvre economically was reduced with the return of large numbers of Afghan workers from Iran in 1979 and the early 1980s. The remittances from the workers had allowed the country to support a growing trade deficit. Without this inflow of about US $100m. each year, Afghanistan was forced to rely even more on foreign help to pursue its economic plans. Western protests over the presence of Soviet troops in the country affected the amount of aid coming into Afghanistan. The 1979/80 budget envisaged a 15% decrease in development spending, which seemed to indicate that previously pledged aid would not necessarily be forthcoming. In January 1980 the World Bank stopped disbursing funds for development projects in Afghanistan, as Bank representatives had been unable to supervise the projects. This decision affected the payment of US $115m., out of a total US $227m. that had been approved. Socialist countries were expected to contribute 66% of the foreign aid needed for basic projects in the 1979–84 Plan.

By 1981 links with the West had been almost completely severed. Able Afghan students, who would in the past have gone to universities in the West, now went to Soviet universities. The whole education system had been remoulded to fit an Eastern European system, with much emphasis on the virtues of communism. The judicial system was also reformed. Even Western planners and technical advisers, attached to the UN, were replaced by East Europeans or Indians. Reports appeared daily in 1980 and 1981 of new co-operation agreements signed between Kabul and Moscow. By 1983 the nexus between Afghanistan and the USSR and other communist countries was almost complete.

Nevertheless, the extent of the control exercised by the capital was limited. The rebels opposed to the Kabul-Moscow axis had a free run of the countryside, and even towns like Qandahar, the second largest city, had their 'no go' areas as far as the Kabul regime was concerned. The traditional economy, however, did suffer, a fact that was marked by the outflow of refugees. Furthermore, by early 1981 it was clear that the Soviet leaders were trying to use the issue of food supplies as a weapon against the rebellion. Food shortages became acute as the regime destroyed grain stores, cattle and crops, in an attempt to bring dissidents under control. By mid-1981 this had begun to cause a significant migration from the countryside to the towns and also to neighbouring Pakistan and Iran, bringing new social upheaval. In April 1982 Kabul pleaded for a resumption of aid. Fazle Haq Khalikyar, First Deputy Minister of Finance, said: 'We find it regrettable and unfair that the flow of aid to our country should remain suspended even by international financial institutions because of political considerations and pressures.' He spoke of 'Democratic Afghanistan's righteous cause'. However, the President of the ADB declared that aid to Afghanistan would have to wait until the situation was 'more conducive'.

Total aid from the West and from the Organization of the Petroleum Exporting Countries (OPEC) decreased from about US $100m. per year in the late 1970s to US $23.2m. in 1981, with the prospect of further falls as new commitments dwindled to US $13.9m. in 1981, compared with a peak of more than US $200m. in the mid-1970s. In 1977, before Daud was killed, Afghanistan received more than US $20m. from OPEC; by 1980, such aid was only US $1.5m. (In 1997, however, according to UN figures, Afghanistan received US $123.6m. in bilateral official development assistance and US $155.3m. in multilateral official development assistance.)

The various pressures on the economy were becoming evident. Khalikyar claimed that there had been a 1.6% increase in GNP in the Afghan year 1359 (1980/81). He said, however, that in that year agriculture had declined by about 1% and industry had been 'relatively stagnant', so his optimism may not have been justified. In 1360 (1981/82) he promised greater growth, with a rise of 9.5% in industry and 3.5% in agriculture. He mentioned the support that the Government had given, including provision of inputs, setting of remunerative prices and ensuring of bank credit. Yet he conceded that, because of recession, the targets represented a difficult challenge.

The impact of these developments did not show in the statistics that Kabul supplied to the ADB and other international bodies. The annual report of the ADB presented Afghanistan as having a trade surplus of US $120m. (exports US $707m. and imports US $587m.) in 1982. After surpluses in 1979, 1980 and 1981 (citing the IMF *Direction of Trade Yearbook* of 1982), the ADB claimed that non-communist countries still accounted for most of Afghanistan's trade in 1981. Based on statistics, only 21.5% of exports went to the USSR and Eastern Europe, while only 30.6% of imports came from the Soviet bloc. According to FAO, Afghanistan's wheat output continued to increase, to 3.1m. metric tons in 1982. Somewhat unaccountably, if the picture was so favourable, Afghanistan's international reserves were estimated to have declined by US $120m. to US $394.5m. in 1982.

The fall in reserves was nearer the truth. Afghan officials admitted that, by late 1982, the country depended on the USSR for 84% of its machinery, 65% of its cotton fabrics, 96% of petroleum products and all of its sugar imports. In 1981 the two countries had concluded a mutual trade agreement for the period 1981–85, whereby Afghanistan was to supply the USSR with raw materials, natural gas and food products in return for industrial equipment and machinery. (During this period, Soviet trade with Afghanistan was reported to have increased by almost 300%.) According to government figures, in 1986/87 Eastern bloc countries accounted for 68% (USSR 60%) of the total trade turnover (imports and exports). In 1986/87 the largest importer from Afghanistan was the USSR, which purchased goods to the value of US $382m. The USSR was moving in to supply aid, offsetting the reductions in assistance from the West and OPEC. Soviet non-military assistance increased from US $34m. in 1979 to US $284m. in 1981.

According to President Karmal, other imports from the USSR included up to 200,000 metric tons of wheat per year, 30,000 tons of rice and 17,000 tons of edible oils, plus dairy products. Cynical commentators thought that these figures were underestimates. An indication of the plight of the country and the limited writ of the Kabul Government came in the 1982–83 Development Plan, in which transport was allocated 27.4% of resources and agriculture only 10.4%, in spite of the great dependence of the people on agriculture. The largest share of the Plan, 37.6%, was given to the mining and power industries, which also suited Soviet needs. Soviet engineers were moving to help extract Afghanistan's minerals for export to the USSR.

In 1982, according to some Afghan officials, more than 60% of exports and imports were arranged under barter agreements with Soviet bloc countries. By 1983, according to IMF data, Afghanistan's reserves of foreign exchange had declined to less than US $190m., forcing the Government to ask the USSR to buy more goods on its behalf. Not all of this was to the USSR's disadvantage, as the country was reportedly making a profit by reselling fruit, imported from Afghanistan, to Eastern Europe. Economists claimed that the USSR was paying only US $12 per 1,000 cu m for Afghanistan's gas, lower than the world price and lower than the price that the USSR charged for its gas exported to Western Europe. In any case, the USSR did not pay cash for the gas, but offset it against Afghanistan's obligations for imports and loans. In 1984 it was estimated that the USSR had spent US $12,000m. altogether in Afghanistan since its troops entered the country, and most of this sum was subject to repayment. In addition, perhaps US $2,000m. per year had been provided in military assistance, and even this—unlike Soviet aid to Viet Nam and Cuba—was not free. A further five-year trade agreement between Afghanistan and the USSR, under which bilateral trade was to expand by 30%, was signed in 1986. In 1987 the Government estimated that financial contributions from the USSR constituted 40% of the country's civilian budget. The USSR and member-countries of the Council for Mutual Economic Assistance (CMEA) were to contribute 97%

(USSR 81%) of foreign aid to Afghanistan for 1988/89, which totalled an estimated US $223.3m., an increase of 14.5% compared with 1987/88. In June 1988 the UN launched an appeal to raise US $1,160m. towards the implementation of a large-scale, 18-month programme for reconstruction and rehabilitation in Afghanistan. In October the USSR pledged to contribute US $600m. in humanitarian aid. The world-wide response, however, was rather poor. In January 1991 the Soviet Government announced that aid from the USSR to Afghanistan in 1991 would total US $714m., of which US $500m. would be in grant aid (compared with US $214m. in grant aid in 1990).

In the 1980s life was grim for the residents of Kabul and other major towns. As the population of Afghanistan as a whole declined, the population of Kabul increased from about 600,000 to considerably more than 1m. (1,420,000, according to a Kabul Radio report in February 1989). Prices soared, with a doubling, and even tripling, of the cost of some essential supplies, such as food and accommodation. Wheat and other basic foodstuffs had to be imported into the cities and towns from the USSR. Power cuts were frequent, even without the disruptive exploits of guerrillas. During 1981–85 the annual rate of inflation remained at about 20%.

Sultan Ali Keshtmand, the Prime Minister under Babrak Karmal's regime, admitted in April 1983 that rebel activity was having a disruptive effect. He stated that guerrillas had destroyed more than one-half of Afghanistan's schools and hospitals, as well as 75% of communication lines. The rebels had also damaged water and power stations. In all, he said, the attacks since December 1979 had cost about Afs 24,000m. 'This is equivalent to the amount spent on development in the 20 years prior to our revolution', he declared, admitting the dire situation to which the Soviet invasion had brought one of the most backward countries in the world.

It was reported in May 1984 that, despite the relentless Soviet pressure, bazaars in Kabul were still flourishing, and that there were plenty of Japanese goods available in the city. Smuggling was rife, with the tacit acceptance of the authorities; 'black' (illegal) money was freely 'laundered'; and US dollars changed hands at twice the official rate of exchange.

In January 1986 the Government announced a Five-Year Economic and Social Development Plan (March 1986–March 1991), involving proposed expenditure of Afs 115,000m. (US $2,300m.). The Government admitted that spending on such a scale would necessitate a large amount of external assistance. The main emphasis of the Plan was on improving the infrastructure and on increasing investment in industry. The Plan objectives included: the extraction of gas condensate to rise to 6,000 tons annually; coal output to double to 370,000 tons per year by 1991; a new petroleum refinery to be constructed in Jawzjan Province; new irrigation systems to be constructed (at the cost of Afs 5,200m.) throughout the country; a Soviet-assisted project to connect Kabul and adjacent provinces to the Soviet power grid by 1991; the Industrial Development Bank to provide Afs 2,660m. to promote the handicraft industry; a unified banking system was to be established, and private businessmen and local merchants to be encouraged under a government-sponsored system of 'state capitalism'. (Traders accounted for 45% of foreign trade and 80% of domestic business in Afghanistan.) The economy, which, according to government figures, had expanded by less than 2% annually since 1980, was projected to grow by 25% over the Plan period. Gross industrial production was scheduled to increase by 28% between 1986 and 1991, agricultural production by 14%–16%, domestic trade by 150% and foreign trade by 17%. Despite the Government's policy of national reconciliation, which was inaugurated in December 1986, and the Soviet withdrawal, which was completed in February 1989, the economy, as a whole, showed no real signs of improvement, and the above ambitious targets were, as expected, not attained. Dr Najibullah, who became party leader in May 1986 and Head of State in November 1987, continued the basic economic policies of his predecessor, including maintaining and augmenting links with the USSR and other Eastern bloc countries through increased bilateral trade and joint projects, and encouraging the development of the private sector in industry.

Agriculture

Agriculture, including animal husbandry, is the primary occupation of the majority of Afghan households—about 85% of the total population are estimated to be supported by the agricultural sector. Landholding arrangements in Afghanistan are very complicated and intricate. In a large number of cases, the people who actually cultivate the land have no formal title to it. No uniform measurement of land exists throughout the country and different areas have singular methods of measuring the land. There are a number of systems of land tenure in Afghanistan, including freehold, sharecropping, lease and mortgage. The country's major crops are wheat, maize, barley, potatoes, fodder, fruit and opium poppy.

Of the total land area of about 85.2m. ha, an estimated 7.91m. ha are considered to be arable. However, only about one-half of the arable land is cultivated every year. Experts estimate that a mere 2.6m. ha of irrigated land provide 85% of the crops. The impact of lack of water was demonstrated in 1971, when there was severe drought, as a result of which the production of wheat, the country's principal crop, declined from nearly 2.5m. metric tons to below 2m. tons, and millions of livestock were slaughtered. The output of crops did not recover to pre-drought levels until two years later. Afghanistan is capable of achieving an annual production of more than 3m. tons of wheat, 160,000 tons of seed (unginned) cotton, 500,000 tons of paddy rice, 800,000 tons of maize, up to 400,000 tons of barley, about 1m. tons of fruit, 100,000 tons of sugar beet and 700,000 tons of sugar cane.

The severe drought of 1970 and 1971 was estimated to have led to the deaths of between 30% and 50% of Afghanistan's livestock, which in 1970 were estimated at 6.5m. karakul sheep, 15m. ordinary sheep, 3.7m. cattle, 3.2m. goats and 500,000 horses. By 1975 it was estimated that the herds had recovered to their 1970 levels. By 1979, however, the number of livestock had, once more, declined considerably, and it was estimated that it would require four or five years to restore the cattle herds to an adequate level. Following the Soviet invasion and the exodus of refugees, regular agricultural production was severely disrupted: fertilizers and new seed became scarce, about one-third of total farms were abandoned, large areas of arable land were destroyed and many irrigation systems were badly damaged. Nevertheless, the Government continued to publish production figures as if the situation were normal. The Government claimed that the volume of agricultural products had increased by 0.7% in 1987/88. An external source, however, estimated that, by 1988, total food production had declined to around 45% of the level prevailing before the Soviet invasion, the number of livestock had fallen drastically, and Afghanistan had to import 500,000 metric tons of wheat annually from the USSR. According to the UN Development Programme (UNDP), cereal imports totalled 156,000 tons in 1992, compared with 322,000 tons in 1990. The value of food aid reached US $5.1m. in 1992. According to UN estimates, the agricultural sector provided 64.4% of GDP in 1993, while the value of agricultural output in that year decreased by 8.6%, compared with the previous year. By the mid-1990s agricultural production was beginning to show signs of definite recovery (albeit with significant regional variations), benefiting from the work undertaken by returning refugees from 1992 onwards, with the support of humanitarian agencies, and the improved stability in southern Afghanistan deriving from the emergence of the Taliban. The Crop and Food Supply Assessment carried out by an FAO/WFP mission in 1997 and 1998 estimated that cereal production in those two years was the highest in several years. Total cereal production in 1998 was estimated to be 3.85m. metric tons, which was 5% higher than in 1997 and perhaps the largest output since 1978. The farmers' response to the high cereal prices of the year before (US $300 per ton), favourable precipitation during winter and spring, and enhanced security were cited as the main factors for the increase in production. In the north of the country, surplus cereal could not be transferred to Kabul, Bamian or Badakhshan provinces, where food scarcity and high prices for grain prevailed owing to the blockage of the supply routes. This led to a reduction in the price of wheat and other major cereals in the northern provinces. The Afghan population, however, still depends on food imported from abroad or that distributed by the aid community. Total cereal production in

1999 was an estimated 3.24m. tons. The increased production of recent years has been more than offset by a serious drought in 2000–01. The drought was caused by a combination of low rainfall and mild winter conditions. As a consequence, the rain-fed wheat effectively failed, and the areas that have normally been dependent on snow melt from the mountains to feed the *karezes* (hillside tunnels) and springs that facilitate irrigation have suffered significant losses in production. Irrigation from tube-wells has been less affected.

An FAO/WFP Assessment Mission in 2000 estimated that, owing to the drought, 2.3m. metric tons of cereal would have to be imported to supplement the dramatically reduced food production, in spite of a tripling of WFP food aid. Concerns were expressed, however, that, because a significant proportion of the population had been obliged to sell their assets over a long period in order to survive and because there were insufficient employment opportunities, there might not be sufficient cash in the economy to enable people to purchase this quantity of imported wheat. Total cereal production decreased to an estimated 1.9m. tons in 2000, similar to the level reached during the 1971 drought. In June 2001 the FAO/WFP Crop and Food Supply Assessment Mission to Afghanistan reported that cereal output for that year was projected to be around 2m. tons, and the cereal deficit was expected to reach 2.2m. tons, marginally less than the level in 2000. However, the significant decrease in average wage levels for daily labourers in 2000–01, in response to declining employment opportunities, placed the population in an even weaker financial position to purchase imported wheat. The ban on opium production introduced by the Taliban in 2001 was another factor in the reduction of income, both for the landowners concerned and for the large number of people who had worked as daily labourers in the opium harvest. The bulk of the imported food originates from Pakistan, but supplies also come in from Iran and Central Asia. Late winter rains eased fears that the drought would continue into 2002 and enabled irrigated areas to aim at reasonable levels of cultivation. However, food vulnerability remains a very serious problem in the rain-fed areas of central and northern Afghanistan, owing to shortages of appropriate seed varieties for high altitude conditions.

The years of warfare have resulted in great losses of livestock and have proved a huge set-back in terms of the generation of income from both food and non-food sources. In Afghanistan livestock is an important source of food, cash income, household manure, wool, traction, transport, and a way of storing capital. Many households rely on the sale of milk, meat and live animals. Not only agricultural households engage in animal husbandry; it is also a major source of income for the nomadic groups, which constitute an estimated 15% of the total population. Livestock is the only means of subsistence for the majority of these people, who move from place to place looking for greener pastures. The most important livestock types in Afghanistan are sheep, goats and cattle. Animal husbandry in Afghanistan is vulnerable to drought, short summer season, failure of fodder crop, disease, decreases in the price of livestock, and increase in the price of cereals (this last point is of particular note, owing to the dependence of nomadic groups on the exchange of animals for grain). The droughts of 2000 and 2001 have had a devastating effect on livestock numbers, with some parts of the country suffering an almost complete loss of their livestock populations. The overall reduction in livestock herds as a result of the drought is estimated at 40%.

Industry

On assuming the premiership in 1953 Sardar Mohammad Daud Khan introduced a number of socio-political as well as economic reforms. From the mid-1950s onwards followed a decade of rapid industrialization. Both the USA and the USSR provided important development assistance; the latter benefactor was crucial in providing support for the expansion and upgrading of Afghanistan's established industries. Other socialist countries, such as the German Democratic Republic and Czechoslovakia, also extended co-operation to help develop the industrial sector in Afghanistan. Large-scale investments were in the infrastructure. The process of industrialization continued at a steady pace, and by the late 1980s there was a significant and diversified industrial sector in Afghanistan, with most of the consumer goods being produced domestically.

However, the contribution of industry to GDP remained relatively small. Handicrafts, especially carpet-making and weaving, still contributed more to GDP than modern industry. In 1972, owing to the Government's concern to expand new industries, an Industrial Development Bank was established. However, industrial employment hardly increased at all in the ensuing years from the 1971 level, when it was estimated that 27,000 people had paid jobs among a total working population of about 4m. Even the oldest established and largest industry, cotton textiles, did not achieve the capacity to produce enough cloth—output was 32.1m. m in 1988/89—to satisfy domestic demand. Exports of cotton declined by about 80% between 1979 and 1985, from US $47m. to US $9.5m. In 1987 the Government introduced a number of incentives for cotton farmers, including tax exemption and transport allowances. According to the IMF, however, revenue from cotton exports fell by 52.8% from US $5.3m. in 1989/90 to US $2.5m. in 1990/91. Production of cement reached 128,000 tons in 1985/86, but declined to a record low of 70,000 tons in 1988/89; output was estimated to have increased, however, to 115,000 in 1995/96. Changes in construction activity were responsible for these fluctuations. After the Soviet invasion in 1979, Afghanistan became increasingly dependent for its industrial progress upon the USSR and other Eastern bloc countries. Two new cement factories (including a second factory at Ghowri, which was being built with Czechoslovak assistance) were due to be completed by 1990, and were expected to have a combined annual production capacity of 510,000 tons. Official sources claimed that the volume of industrial output increased by 3.5% in 1987. According to government figures, income from industrial production totalled Afs 37,000m. in 1986/87 (equivalent to 23.8% of GDP), with the handicraft sector accounting for Afs 15,000m. (1.3% more than in 1985/86). Following the overthrow of President Daud in 1978, successive governments were anxious to encourage private enterprise, but subject to government surveillance. According to official sources, the private sector contributed Afs 4,370m. (11.8%) towards the total income from industry in 1986/87. According to UN estimates, the industrial sector (including mining, manufacturing, power and construction) provided 20% of GDP in 1993, while the value of industrial output in that year decreased by 11.4%, compared with the previous year.

The manufacturing industry of Afghanistan was traditionally dominated by small-scale enterprises relying on the production of agricultural commodities. Many such industries were engaged in the processing of food products, such as flour, sugar and vegetable oil. Other branches of the manufacturing industry included textiles, carpets, leather products and handicrafts. There were some large-scale industries in the public sector, such as cotton mills and cement plants, one fertilizer plant (in Mazar-i-Sharif), an engineering plant and a metal workshop. Most of the state-owned plants are no longer functioning, and the few that remain in operation are producing at a very low capacity. This situation is the result of the physical damage caused by the war and of the shortage of raw materials for industrial production. Only one type of industry seems to have survived the devastating effects of war and that is the traditional handicraft sector. Carpets, leather, embroidery and fur products are still being manufactured. Moreover, woodwork shops, motor workshops and construction-related activity all continue to operate. The National Development Framework drawn up by the Interim Authority in 2002 places a strong focus on the creation of an environment that will support a central role for the private sector in developing the economy.

Mining and Energy

Afghanistan has extensive resources of coal, salt, chromium, iron ore, silver, gold, fluorite, talc, mica, copper and lapis lazuli, but the country's problems of access and transport have caused doubts about the commercial viability of mining them. The most successful find has been of natural gas. In 1980 a new complex for the extraction and purification of gas became operational at Jarquduq, with an annual capacity of 2,000m. cu m. During the 1980s and early 1990s natural gas was Afghanistan's major export commodity, and, according to figures from the IMF, it accounted for about 24% of the total income from exports in

1988/89. Up until 1991 most (more than 90%) of the natural gas being produced in Afghanistan was piped to the USSR as payment for imports and debts. Military action did not stop the flow of gas. Government sources reported that about 2,600m. cu m of gas were exported to the USSR in 1985/86, but Western sources claimed that four times that amount flowed to the USSR in the late 1980s. It was difficult to be accurate because the meters measuring the flow were on the Soviet side of the border and *mujahidin* repeatedly blew up the pipeline. The USSR needed the gas to help to develop its Central Asian republics and to compensate for gas that it exported to Western Europe. Gas production in northern Afghanistan was discontinued for an extended period; however, it is unclear whether its production ceased immediately after the collapse of the Soviet-supported Government in April 1992 or continued until the first Taliban attack on the production area in May 1997 set in motion a period of instability. Gas reserves were estimated at 150,000m. cu m in 2002, whereas petroleum reserves from six oilfields were thought to amount to only 12m. metric tons. The Transitional Authority was in mid-2002 considering the best means by which both gas and oil resources could be used in support of the National Development Framework. Gas production had recommenced by mid-2002, but at a minimal level. Hard coal production, centred at Pol-e-Khomri, reached 167,000 tons in 1987, aided by considerable investment in coal-mining equipment, supplied by Czechoslovakia. In the same year a Czechoslovak company signed a contract to supply equipment for the reconstruction of the hard-coal mines in the north of the country. The aim was to increase annual production of hard coal to 180,000 tons. In 1988, however, hard coal production decreased by 17.4% to 138,000 tons, and by 1996 estimated annual production had plummeted to only 4,000 tons.

Iron ore reserves at Hajigak in Bamian province, with 1,700m. metric tons of high-grade ore (62%), are the most promising discoveries of recent decades. However, although the ore would fetch a good price, much of it is located at heights of 3,500m. or more. Moreover, there would be high costs involved in exporting it from remote Afghanistan, which has no seaport of its own, nor even any railways. Other minerals were developed under the Soviet-supported regime. A copper-mining and smelter project was initiated at Ainak, near Kabul, which was projected to give Afghanistan 2% of world copper production. The country's total reserves of copper ore may be 4.7m. tons. Another mineral that may become important is uranium. According to an employee of the Afghan Ministry of Mines and Industries who defected to the West, Soviet workers had begun to mine the metal from newly discovered fields. The communist regime's energy plans included the development of two small oilfields in the north of the country. Further prospecting for petroleum and gas was being carried out, under Soviet supervision, in the same area in 1988. Petroleum products were imported at privileged low prices from Iran and the USSR. In 1987 the USSR agreed to supply Afghanistan with 547,000 tons of petroleum products (10% more than in 1986). The Afghan Government, however, planned to increase internal sources of energy by establishing hydro- and thermal electric power stations. Hydroelectricity constitutes about 80% of energy resources. The first hydroelectric power station to be built since 1978 began operating in 1983 at Asadabad. The construction of the large Sarobi II hydroelectric dam on the Kabul River was still under way in 1991 when the USSR collapsed. It has since provided the primary source of power for Kabul, albeit on the basis of an extremely curtailed and erratic supply compounded by war damage and heavily constrained access to spare parts. Afghanistan's first steel smelter (built with Soviet technical and financial assistance) started functioning at the Jangalak factory complex in 1987.

The emergence of the newly independent Central Asian republics in 1991 provided the opportunity for major gas- and petroleum-producing countries to seek an alternative market to Moscow as the primary purchaser of their mineral products. Turkmenistan, with its large natural gas reserves, was therefore interested in proposals put forward by an Argentine company, Bridas, to construct a pipeline across Afghanistan to transport gas from Turkmenistan to Pakistan and beyond. Pakistan was also enthusiastic about the project, which promised to respond to its own energy requirements and additionally to provide substantial income from the transit of the gas through Pakistan to a new port on the Arabian Sea. The US company, UNOCAL, also expressed a keen interest in the project, and the Argentine and US companies competed fiercely with each other to secure agreements with Turkmenistan, Pakistan and the Taliban. The capture of Kabul by the Taliban in September 1996 gave initial hope to the two companies that the Taliban might soon control the whole country and provide the necessary stability for the project to proceed. However, the opposition forces enjoyed some initial success in resisting the northbound offensives launched by the Taliban, and it was not until August 1998 that the northern town of Mazar-i-Sharif was taken. Even then, the Taliban hold on the parts of the country that they controlled did not offer sufficient stability, and the US air-strikes against Afghanistan later in August, in response to the continued asylum given by the Taliban to the exiled Saudi-born militant leader, Osama bin Laden, who was suspected of significant involvement in the bombing of two US embassies in East Africa earlier that month, made it difficult for UNOCAL to continue its engagement with the Taliban. In December UNOCAL announced that it was withdrawing from the consortium of international oil companies engaged in the proposed pipeline project (UNOCAL had established the consortium in October 1997). The project was subsequently suspended, but Pakistan, Turkmenistan and the Taliban continued their discussions, in the hope of finding opportunities to revive the scheme. More recently, in late May 2002, formal agreement was reached between the Afghan Interim Authority and the Governments of Turkmenistan and Pakistan to facilitate the construction of one or more pipelines from Turkmenistan to Pakistan. In early August the ADB formally announced that it was willing to take part in the feasibility study; Japan had already shown interest in participating in the project. The future of the project was not only dependent on the security situation in Afghanistan, but was also linked with complex options relating to the extraction and transport of Central Asian gas and petroleum reserves. The USA's stance on the desirability of a pipeline through Afghanistan was influenced by whether it could continue to rely on the existence of a friendly regime in another resource-rich country, Saudi Arabia.

In November 1998 the Taliban announced their intention to resume operating ruby mines in Nangarhar province. Earlier in the year the Taliban regime had claimed that monthly revenue from the allegedly renascent mining sector in Afghanistan totalled US $3.5m. (including revenue from the recently revived steel-smelting plant in Baghlan province). The new National Development Framework envisaged that the Transitional Authority would launch a full geological survey of Afghanistan to provide information on the use and development of precious stones.

Trade, Balance of Payments and Finance

Afghanistan's trade is small and in the 1980s it became increasingly dependent on the USSR, its northern neighbour. This was partly because of the mounting difficulties of using land routes to Pakistan and India, Afghanistan's principal trade outlets, both for fresh fruit going to the subcontinent and for other goods going beyond. In addition, turmoil in Iran rendered trade via the west difficult.

Throughout the 1970s, the balance of payments showed a surplus, owing to tourism, which raised revenue of up to US $10m. annually, and remittances from Afghans working abroad. The main export items at that time were fresh fruit and vegetables to Pakistan and India, natural gas to the territories constituting the former USSR, karakul skins and wool to the fur markets of Europe, and carpets and rugs (more than 1m. sq m per year), raw cotton and dried fruits and nuts, which were the country's major export items after gas. Imports included machinery, petroleum, pharmaceuticals, textiles and other consumer goods.

The USSR was Afghanistan's main trading partner before the invasion of 1979, and in 1977/78 provided 26% of imports and took 37% of the country's exports. Total trade turnover (imports plus exports) between the two countries increased by 44% in 1979, compared with the previous year. According to official figures, total trade with the USSR rose from US $708.4m. in 1980 to an estimated US $1,615.5m. in 1991. This dependence on the USSR increased as other countries were either unable or unwilling to export their products to Afghanistan, and as foreign aid from the West began to disappear. Over the five-year period 1986–91, the total value of trade between Afghanistan and other countries was estimated to amount to only US $5,000m., compared with US $43,000m. in the period 1981–85.

In 1978–79 the Afghan Chamber of Commerce and Industry acted as the sole agent for the 22 importers' associations and controlled all import business. However, in order to encourage the private sector, the Government returned these exclusive export rights to the private merchants in 1980.

By the end of 1992, following the disintegration of the USSR in December 1991, Afghanistan had three separate economic systems based on support from Iran in the west, Pakistan in the east and the former Soviet Central Asian republics to the north, in addition to numerous sub-economies based on drug and weapon sales or smuggling.

The general negative trend in trade was apparent throughout the 1990s. The sharpest declines in both exports and imports occurred in 1992 and 1993. During these two years the total value of exports declined to US $60m. and US $62m., respectively, compared with US $284m. in 1991. Similarly, the cost of imports decreased from US $765m. in 1991 to US $237m. in 1992 and US $200m. in 1993. In 1996, following the accession to power of the Taliban, trade showed signs of a degree of revival. In 1996/97, according to UN figures, total exports were estimated at US $125m. and the major export commodities included fruits and nuts, hand-woven carpets, wool, cotton, hides and pelts, and precious and semi-precious gems. The most important export markets in 1997 were Pakistan, Western Europe and the USA. In 1996/97, according to UN figures, total imports were estimated at US $496m. and consisted mainly of food, petroleum products and other consumer goods. The principal sources of imports in 1997 were Singapore, Japan and Western Europe. These official statistics do not, however, include illegal trade and smuggling. The trade deficit would be much lower if the illegal revenue from the export of opium were included.

The slow growth of the economy created difficulties in raising the Government's internal revenues and the budget deficit rose steadily. About one-half of the ordinary revenues was derived from indirect taxes. The next largest contributor was revenue from natural gas, providing 21% of the total in 1979 and 34% in 1980. Only 10% of the revenues came from direct taxes. In 1979/80 domestic revenues were estimated at Afs 15,788m. The greatest expenditure was on defence, accounting for almost 40% of the total. Social services were allocated 20% of expenditure. Domestic revenues rose by 48.7% to an estimated Afs 23,478m. in 1980/81. In 1984/85, according to UN figures, current revenue increased by 8.3%, compared with the previous year, to Afs 37,615m. (taxes 17,081m., non-tax 20,534m.) and total expenditure rose by 18.5% to Afs 51,177m. (current 43,177m., capital 8,000m.), thus producing a budgetary deficit of Afs 13,562m.

In 1975 the Government decreed that all banks in Afghanistan had been nationalized in an attempt to establish a more organized banking system. The move was directed at the Banke Milli Afghan, as the other banks were already under government control. The banking system ceased to function effectively following the collapse of the Soviet-backed Government in April 1992. Since then, financial transfers have been largely effected through the 'hawala' system, using informal networks, and through the informal money market for foreign exchange transfers.

The Taliban introduced a formal taxation system through which taxes were levied on agricultural production, landholdings and imported goods, among other sources. In addition, an Islamic tax (*zakat*) was charged on each family. The imposition of these taxes aroused some hostility at the local level, and there were indications that the Taliban had eased the tax burden in response to the drought in 2000.

The National Development Framework provides for the re-establishment of a functioning central bank, a competitive commercial banking sector and non-banking financial services including micro-finance, credit unions, insurance and pensions. The Afghan Interim Authority, and later the Transitional Authority, raised revenue through overflight rights and customs dues levied on goods passing through Kabul. In mid-July 2002 the Transitional Authority finally managed to convince provincial governors to transfer customs duties levied at Afghanistan's border crossing points and elsewhere within the country to the central government. It was expected that customs duties would raise US $83m. of the US $460.3m. budget for 2002/03; the Government hoped that the rest of budget would be provided by foreign assistance.

THE ILLEGAL ECONOMY

The massive supply of weapons to the *mujahidin* by the US Government during the period of Soviet occupation and direct support for the Afghan regime (1979–92) had, it could reasonably be argued, a destabilizing effect on both Afghanistan and Pakistan and may have fuelled the illicit arms trade in the region. It may also have created the conditions for the rapid expansion of the illegal economy over the past few years, with smuggling and drugs as key components. The smuggling trade has as its foundation the Afghan Transit Trade Agreement, through which Afghanistan is permitted to transport goods across Pakistan from Karachi duty-free for use in Afghanistan. This agreement has been abused so that goods have been smuggled back into Pakistan, having barely entered Afghanistan, and are then sold in what are termed *bara* markets near the border and elsewhere in Pakistan, thus benefiting from the absence of duty. The Government of Pakistan estimated in 1991 that cross-border smuggling was resulting in an annual loss of more than US $5,000m. to its economy. Following his assumption of power in late 1999, Pakistan's new leader, Gen. Pervez Musharraf, attempted to clamp down on this smuggling through a combination of measures, including further restrictions on the goods that could be imported duty-free, the imposition of a sales tax on goods sold in the *bara* markets and the introduction of greater border controls. However, he faced fierce resistance as he sought to overcome the endemic corruption sustaining the smuggling trade. This illegal trade was, until prohibited by the UN sanctions of December 2000, facilitated by the transport by air of duty-free goods from Dubai, United Arab Emirates, to Jalalabad, from where they were smuggled into Pakistan. In addition, goods were brought in from Iran, benefiting from significant state subsidies. A further important component is the large-scale illegal export of Afghanistan's scarce timber reserves. The National Development Framework seeks to address the conditions that have facilitated the illegal economy, but the many vested interests involved will inevitably hinder progress.

Opium production in Afghanistan reached its highest ever level in 1999, surpassing output in Myanmar (formerly Burma), with 4,600 metric tons. However, production declined by 29%, to an estimated 3,275 tons, in 2000, largely owing to the prevailing drought. In 2001 the ban on opium production, announced by the Taliban in July 2000, took effect in Taliban-controlled areas. Although this decision might have been taken on religious grounds and out of concern over possible opium and heroin addiction within Afghanistan, the international community responded with caution to the visible evidence that production had ceased. In part, this development could be seen as a response to the very strong financial arguments for the imposition of a ban, including the fact that high production in previous years risked leading to a saturation of the market and thus creating a substantial decline in opium prices. The international community was also mindful of the fact that significant stockpiles, sufficient to meet global demand for many years to come, reportedly remained in Afghanistan. This scepticism largely arose from reports that the ban had resulted in a tenfold increase in the price of opium in Afghanistan over the previous year. However, the international community was perceived to have failed to react positively to the ban. This weak response contributed to a deteriorating relationship between the Taliban and the humanitarian agencies. The UN International Drug Control Programme (UNDCP), meanwhile, estimated that opium production in the opposition-controlled area of north-eastern Afghanistan would be in the region of 500 tons in 2001. There are clear indications that opium cultivation in the traditional production areas has resumed since the collapse of the Taliban regime. Although the Afghan Interim Authority introduced a formal ban on opium production and embarked on enforcement operations to destroy poppy crops in some areas, the UNDCP estimated that production in 2002 was likely to be in the region of 2,000 tons.

Statistical Survey

Source (unless otherwise stated): Central Statistics Authority, Block 4, Macroraion, Kabul; tel. (93) 24883.

Area and Population

AREA, POPULATION AND DENSITY

Area (sq km)	652,225*
Population (census results)	
23 June 1979†	
Males	6,712,377
Females	6,338,981
Total	13,051,358
Population (official estimates at mid-year)‡	
1984	17,672,000
1985	18,136,000
1986	18,614,000
Density (per sq km) at mid-1986	28.5

* 251,773 sq miles.

† Figures exclude nomadic population, estimated to total 2,500,000. The census data also exclude an adjustment for underenumeration, estimated to have been 5% for the urban population and 10% for the rural population.

‡ These data include estimates for nomadic population (2,734,000 in 1983), but take no account of emigration by refugees. Assuming an average net outflow of 703,000 persons per year in 1980–85, the UN Population Division has estimated Afghanistan's total mid-year population (in '000) as: 14,519 in 1985; 14,529 in 1986; 14,709 in 1987 (Source: UN, *World Population Prospects: 1988*). In late 1999 it was estimated that the total Afghan refugee population numbered 2.6m., of whom 1.2m. were living in Pakistan and 1.4m. in Iran.

Population (UN estimates, including nomads, at mid-year): 19,073,000 in 1995; 19,816,000 in 1996; 20,349,000 in 1997; 20,764,000 in 1998; 21,202,000 in 1999; 21,765,000 in 2000; 22,474,000 in 2001 (Source: UN, *World Population Prospects: The 2000 Revision*).

PROVINCES (estimates, 2000)

	Area (sq km)	Population	Density (per sq km)	Capital
Kabul	4,462	2,766,800	620.1	Kabul
Kapisa	1,842	429,600	233.2	Mahmud-e-Iraqi
Parvan	9,584	748,200	78.1	Charikar
Wardak‡	8,938	347,100	38.8	Maidanshahr
Loghar‡	3,880	306,100	78.9	Pul-i-Alam
Ghazni	22,915	1,023,700	44.7	Ghazni
Paktia	6,432	741,100	115.2	Gardez
Nangarhar	7,727	1,370,700	177.4	Jalalabad
Laghman	3,843	631,100	164.2	Mehter Lam
Kunar	4,942	537,500	108.8	Asadabad
Badakhshan	44,059	938,500	21.3	Faizabad
Takhar	12,333	735,000	59.6	Taloqan
Baghlan‡	21,118	805,800	38.2	Baghlan
Kunduz	8,040	715,600	89.0	Kunduz
Samangan	11,262	520,400	46.2	Aybak
Balkh	17,249	1,432,100	83.1	Mazar-i-Sharif
Jawzjan	11,798	676,000	57,3	Shiberghan
Faryab	20,293	868,500	42.8	Meymaneh
Badghis	20,591	626,800	30.4	Qaleh-ye-Now
Herat	54,778	1,273,100	23.2	Herat
Farah	48,471	421,900	8.7	Farah
Nimroz	41,005	203,800	5.0	Zaranj
Helmand	58,584	852,500	14.6	Lashgar Gah
Qandahar	54,022	1,367,600	25.3	Qandahar
Zabul	17,343	378,700	21.8	Qalat
Uruzgan	30,784	281,100	9.1	Terin Kowt
Ghor	36,479	592,400	16.2	Chaghcharan
Bamian	14,175	445,300	31.4	Bamian
Paktika	19,482	430,300	22.1	Sharan
Nuristan†	9,225	n.a.	n.a.	Nuristan
Sar-e Pol*	15,999	626,100	39.1	Sar-e Pol
Khost†	4,152	n.a.	n.a.	Khost
Total	645,807	23,093,400	35.8	

* Sar-e Pol province (formerly part of Balkh, Jawzjan and Samangan provinces) had been created by 1990.

† Nuristan province (formerly part of Kunar and Laghman provinces) and Khost province (formerly part of Paktia province) had been created by 1991 and 1995, respectively. Competing factions reportedly disagreed about whether they were legally created.

‡ By 1996 the capital of Loghar province had changed to Pul-i-Alam from Baraki Barak and the capital of Wardak province had moved to Maidanshahr from Kowt-i-Ashrow; it was reported that the capital of Baghlan province had moved to Pol-e-Khomri: this was yet to be confirmed.

Source: Gwillim Law, *Administrative Subdivisions of Countries*.

PRINCIPAL TOWNS (estimated population at March 1982)

Kabul (capital)	1,036,407	Kunduz	57,112
Qandahar	191,345	Baghlan	41,240
Herat	150,497	Maymana	40,212
Mazar-i-Sharif	110,367	Pul-i-Khomri	32,695
Jalalabad	57,824	Ghazni	31,985

Estimated population at July 1988: Kabul 1,424,400; Qandahar 225,500; Herat 177,300; Mazar-i-Sharif 130,600 (Source: UN, *Demographic Yearbook 1997*).

BIRTHS AND DEATHS (UN estimates, annual averages)

	1985–90	1990–95	1995–2000
Birth rate (per 1,000)	49.0	48.0	47.6
Death rate (per 1,000)	23.8	22.5	22.0

Source: UN, *World Population Prospects: The 2000 Revision*.

Expectation of life (WHO estimates, years at birth, 2000): Males 44.2; females 45.1 (Source: WHO, *World Health Report*).

ECONOMICALLY ACTIVE POPULATION*
(ISIC Major Divisions, persons aged 8 years and over, 1979 census)

	Males	Females	Total
Agriculture, hunting, forestry and fishing	2,358,821	10,660	2,369,481
Mining and quarrying	57,492	1,847	59,339
Manufacturing	170,908	252,465	423,373
Electricity, gas and water	11,078	276	11,354
Construction	50,670	416	51,086
Wholesale and retail trade	135,242	2,618	137,860
Transport, storage and communications	65,376	867	66,243
Other services	716,511	32,834	749,345
Total	3,566,098	301,983	3,868,081

* Figures refer to settled population only and exclude 77,510 persons seeking work for the first time (66,057 males; 11,453 females).

Mid-2000 (estimates in '000): Agriculture, etc. 5,942; Total labour force 8,872. (Source: FAO).

Health and Welfare

KEY INDICATORS

Fertility (births per woman, 2000)	6.9
Under-5 mortality rate (per 1,000 live births, 1999)	257
HIV/AIDS (% of persons aged 15–49, 1994)	<0.01
Physicians (per 1,000 head, 1997)	0.11
Hospital beds (per 1,000 head, 1990)	0.25
Health expenditure (1998): US $ per head (PPP)	11
% of GDP	1.6
public (% of total)	57.7
Access to water (% of persons, 2000)	13
Access to sanitation (% of persons, 2000)	12

For sources and definitions, see explanatory note on p. vi.

Agriculture

PRINCIPAL CROPS ('000 metric tons)

	1997	1998	1999
Wheat	2,711	2,834	2,499
Rice (paddy)	400	450	280
Barley	250	240	216
Maize	300	330	240
Millet*	22	22	22
Potatoes*	235	235	235
Pulses*	50	50	50
Sesame seed*	24	24	24
Cottonseed	66†	66*	66*
Cotton (lint)*	22	22	22
Vegetables*	612	632	652
Watermelons*	90	90	90
Cantaloupes and other melons*	22	22	22
Grapes	330†	330†	330*
Sugar cane*	38	38	38
Sugar beets*	1	1	1
Apples*	18	18	18
Peaches and nectarines*	14	14	14
Plums*	35	35	35
Oranges*	12	12	12
Apricots*	38	38	38
Other fruit*	230	230	230

* FAO estimate(s). † Unofficial figure.

Source: FAO.

LIVESTOCK ('000 head, year ending 30 September)

	1997	1998	1999
Horses	100	100	104
Mules*	26	28	30
Asses	805	860	920
Cattle	2,895	3,008	2,600
Camels	242	265	290
Sheep	15,110	16,252	14,000
Goats	5,530	6,599	6,000
Chickens (million)	7	8	7

* FAO estimate(s).

Source: FAO.

LIVESTOCK PRODUCTS ('000 metric tons)

	1997	1998	1999
Beef and veal*	156	171	149
Mutton and lamb*	123	128	112
Goat meat	33	39	35
Poultry meat	14	15	14
Other meat*	12	12	12
Cows' milk*	1,593	1,825	1,560
Sheep's milk	227	246	210
Goats' milk*	100	120	135
Cheese	23	26	25
Butter and ghee	37	42	36
Hen eggs*	18	18	18
Honey*	3	3	3
Wool:			
greasy*	20	20	20
scoured*	12	13	13
Cattle hides	17	19	17
Sheepskins	19	20	18
Goatskins	6	8	7

* FAO estimate(s).

Source: FAO.

Forestry

ROUNDWOOD REMOVALS
('000 cubic metres, excl. bark)

	1997	1998	1999
Sawlogs, veneer logs and logs for sleepers*	856	856	856
Other industrial wood	862	881	904
Fuel wood	6,217	6,354	6,523
Total	7,935	8,091	8,283

* Assumed to be unchanged from 1976.

2000: Annual production as in 1999 (FAO estimates).

Source: FAO, *Yearbook of Forest Products*.

SAWNWOOD PRODUCTION
(FAO estimates, '000 cubic metres, incl. railway sleepers)

	1974	1975	1976
Coniferous (softwood)	360	310	380
Broadleaved (hardwood)	50	20	20
Total	410	330	400

1977–2000: Annual production as in 1976 (FAO estimates).

Source: FAO, *Yearbook of Forest Products*.

Fishing

(FAO estimates, metric tons, live weight)

	1997	1998	1999
Total catch (freshwater fishes)	1,250	1,200	1,200

Source: FAO, *Yearbook of Fishery Statistics.*

Mining

(estimates, '000 metric tons, unless otherwise indicated)

	1998	1999	2000
Hard coal	190	200	200
Natural gas (million cubic metres)*	2,600	3,000	3,000
Copper ore†	5	5	5
Salt (unrefined)	13	13	13
Gypsum (crude)	3	3	3

* Figures refer to gross output. Marketed production (estimates, million cubic metres) was: 2,200 in 1998; 2,500 in 1999; 2,500 in 2000.

† Figures refer to metal content.

Source: US Geological Survey.

Industry

SELECTED PRODUCTS

(year ending 20 March, '000 metric tons, unless otherwise indicated)

	1986/87	1987/88	1988/89
Margarine	3.5	3.3	1.8
Vegetable oil	4	n.a.	n.a.
Wheat flour*	187	203	166
Wine ('000 hectolitres)*	289	304	194
Soft drinks ('000 hectolitres)	8,500	10,300	4,700
Woven cotton fabrics (million sq metres)	58.1	52.6	32.1
Woven woollen fabrics (million sq metres)	0.4	0.3	0.3
Footwear—excl. rubber ('000 pairs)*	613	701	607
Rubber footwear ('000 pairs)*	2,200	3,200	2,200
Nitrogenous fertilizers†	56	57	55
Cement	103	104	70
Electric energy (million kWh)*‡	1,171	1,257	1,109

* Production in calendar years 1986, 1987 and 1988.

† Production in year ending 30 June.

‡ Provisional.

Wheat flour ('000 metric tons): 1,832 in 1994; 2,029 in 1995; 2,145 in 1996.

Nitrogenous fertilizers (provisional, year ending 30 June, '000 metric tons): 14 in 1994/95; 10 in 1995/96; 5 in 1996/97; 5 in 1998/99; 5 in 1999/2000.

Cement (provisional, '000 metric tons): 116 in 1998; 120 in 1999; 120 in 2000.

Electric energy (provisional, year ending 20 March, million kWh): 565 in 1996/97; 505 in 1997/98; 485 in 1998/99.

Sources: UN, *Industrial Commodity Statistics Yearbook* and *Statistical Yearbook for Asia and the Pacific*, FAO (Rome) and US Geological Survey.

Finance

CURRENCY AND EXCHANGE RATES

Monetary Units

100 puls (puli) = 2 krans = 1 afghani (Af).

Sterling, Dollar and Euro Equivalents (31 May 2002)

£1 sterling = 4,400.1 afghanis;
US $1 = 3,000.0 afghanis;
€1 = 2,816.1 afghanis;
10,000 afghanis = £2.272 = $3.333 = €3.551.

Exchange Rate

The foregoing information refers to the official exchange rate. The official rate was maintained at US $1 = 1,000 afghanis between 1 May 1995 and 30 April 1996. From 1 May 1996 a rate of US $1 = 3,000 afghanis has been in operation. However, this rate is applicable to only a limited range of transactions. There is also a market-determined rate, which was US $1 = 34,000 afghanis in March 2002.

BUDGET (million afghanis, year ending 20 March)

	1983/84	1984/85
Current revenue	34,744	37,615
Taxes	13,952	17,081
Non-taxes	20,792	20,534
Current expenditure	37,760	43,177
Capital expenditure	5,433	8,000

Source: UN, *Statistical Yearbook for Asia and the Pacific.*

BANK OF AFGHANISTAN RESERVES (US $ million at December)*

	1989	1990	1991
IMF special drawing rights	10.63	9.02	6.67
Reserve position in IMF	6.41	6.97	7.01
Foreign exchange	226.65	250.41	221.22
Total	243.69	266.40	234.89

* Figures exclude gold reserves, totalling 965,000 troy ounces since 1980. Assuming a gold price of 12,850 afghanis per ounce, these reserves were officially valued at US $245.06 million in December of each year 1985–91.

IMF special drawing rights (US $ million at December): 4.37 in 1992; 2.76 in 1993; 1.40 in 1994.

Reserve position in IMF (US $ million at December): 6.78 in 1992; 6.77 in 1993; 7.19 in 1994; 7.33 in 1995; 7.09 in 1996; 6.65 in 1997; 6.94 in 1998; 6.77 in 1999; 6.42 in 2000; 6.20 in 2001.

Source: IMF, *International Financial Statistics.*

MONEY SUPPLY (million afghanis at 21 December)

	1989	1990	1991
Currency outside banks	222,720	311,929	454,750
Private-sector deposits at Bank of Afghanistan	12,838	13,928	19,368
Demand deposits at commercial banks	11,699	18,217	n.a.

Source: IMF, *International Financial Statistics.*

COST OF LIVING

(retail price index, excluding rent; base: 1990 = 100)

	1989	1990	1991
All items	67.9	100.0	143.8

Source: UN, *Statistical Yearbook for Asia and the Pacific.*

NATIONAL ACCOUNTS

('000 million afghanis at constant 1978 prices)

Gross Domestic Product by Economic Activity

	1991	1992	1993
Agriculture, hunting, forestry and fishing	59.9	62.7	57.3
Mining and quarrying Manufacturing Electricity, gas and water	29.2	14.3	12.3
Construction	7.0	5.8	5.5
Wholesale and retail trade, restaurants and hotels	11.1	10.5	10.1
Transport, storage and communications	4.8	4.5	2.0
Finance, insurance, real estate and business services	2.1	2.0	1.8
GDP in purchasers' values	114.1	99.8	89.0

Source: UN, *Statistical Yearbook for Asia and the Pacific*.

BALANCE OF PAYMENTS (US $ million)

	1987	1988	1989
Exports of goods f.o.b.	538.7	453.8	252.3
Imports of goods f.o.b.	-904.5	-731.8	-623.5
Trade balance	-365.8	-278.0	-371.2
Exports of services	35.6	69.6	8.2
Imports of services	-156.3	-120.0	-103.4
Balance on goods and services	-486.5	-328.4	-466.4
Other income received	19.2	23.3	20.1
Other income paid	-11.3	-11.5	-7.9
Balance on goods, services and income	-478.6	-316.6	-454.2
Current transfers received	311.7	342.8	312.1
Current transfers paid	—	—	-1.2
Current balance	-166.9	26.2	-143.3
Investment liabilities	-33.9	-4.1	-59.6
Net errors and omissions	211.6	-47.7	182.8
Overall balance	10.8	-25.6	-20.1

Source: IMF, *International Financial Statistics*.

OFFICIAL DEVELOPMENT ASSISTANCE (US $ million)

	1996	1997	1998
Bilateral	84.3	123.6	88.2
Multilateral	98.7	106.5	65.7
Total	183.0	230.1	153.9
Grants	183.1	230.1	154.1
Loans	-0.1	0.0	-0.2
Per caput assistance (US $)	9.0	11.0	7.2

Source: UN, *Statistical Yearbook for Asia and the Pacific*.

External Trade

PRINCIPAL COMMODITIES (US $ '000, year ending 20 March)

Imports c.i.f.	1980/81	1981/82	1983/84*
Wheat	798	18,100	38,251
Sugar	40,833	50,328	25,200
Tea	28,369	n.a.	23,855
Cigarettes	5,114	7,219	12,755
Vegetable oil	17,320	26,332	30,481
Drugs	4,497	4,195	3,768
Soaps	9,991	17,256	8,039
Tyres and tubes	16,766	12,764	28,823
Textile yarn and thread	16,800	24,586	n.a.
Cotton fabrics	873	6,319	n.a.
Rayon fabrics	6,879	9,498	n.a.
Other textile goods	52,546	49,036	n.a.
Vehicles and spare parts	89,852	141,062	n.a.
Petroleum products	124,000	112,093	n.a.
Footwear (new)	2,058	5,275	5,317
Bicycles	2,042	488	1,952
Matches	1,171	1,542	1,793
Sewing machines	140	285	266
Electric and non-electric machines	2,333	765	n.a.
Chemical materials	7,464	6,636	n.a.
Agricultural tractors	1	8,280	n.a.
Fertilizers	8,325	3,300	3,904
Used clothes	2,523	1,875	5,334
Television receivers	5,391	3,241	10,139
Other items	106,662	92,307	n.a.
Total	551,748	622,416	846,022

* Figures for 1982/83 are not available.

Total imports c.i.f. (US $ million, year ending 20 March): 347 in 1994/95; 359 in 1995/96; 621 in 1996/97; 570 in 1997/98; 498 in 1998/99; 600 in 1999/2000. Source: UN, *Statistical Yearbook for Asia and the Pacific*.

Exports f.o.b.	1988/89	1989/90	1990/91
Fruit and nuts	103,400	110,200	93,300
Karakul fur skins	6,100	3,600	3,000
Natural gas	93,200	n.a.	n.a.
Wool	30,900	5,500	9,600
Carpets	39,100	38,000	44,000
Cotton	8,000	5,300	2,500
Total (incl. others)	394,700	235,900	235,100

Source: IMF, *International Financial Statistics*.

1991/92 (million afghanis, year ending 20 March): Dried fruit and nuts 165,770; Karakul skins 4,303; Wool 19,953; Carpets and rugs 52,887.

1992/93 (million afghanis, year ending 20 March): Dried fruit and nuts 33,259; Wool 7,585; Carpets and rugs 21,920.

1995/96 (million afghanis, year ending 20 March): Dried fruit and nuts 19,282; Karakul skins 27; Wool 122; Carpets and rugs 67,083.

Total exports f.o.b. (US $ million, year ending 20 March): 102 in 1994/95; 166 in 1995/96; 127 in 1996/97; 146 in 1997/98; 142 in 1998/99; 150 in 1999/2000.

Source: UN, *Statistical Yearbook for Asia and the Pacific*.

PRINCIPAL TRADING PARTNERS (estimates, US $ million)

Imports	1997	1998	1999
ASEAN members	149	51	41
Indonesia	20	19	12
Malaysia	10	11	7
Singapore	101	14	14
Thailand	18	7	8
SAARC members	58	81	121
Bangladesh	10	10	1
India	25	26	27
Pakistan	21	42	90
Central Asian republics	39	46	41
Kazakhstan	9	13	8
Kyrgyzstan	4	3	3
Tajikistan	3	4	2
Turkmenistan	23	26	28
Other Asian countries			
China, People's Republic	36	27	18
Hong Kong	11	7	5
Japan	97	67	73
Turkey	7	24	n.a.
Western Europe	67	64	40
Russia	21	15	15
USA	13	8	20
Total (incl. others)	561	495	468

Exports	1997	1998	1999
ASEAN members	8	1	2
Singapore	7	—	1
SAARC members	35	34	46
India	3	8	9
Pakistan	30	25	36
Central Asian republics	6	9	4
Tajikistan	4	6	—
Turkmenistan	2	3	3
Other Asian countries			
China, People's Republic	1	n.a.	3
Japan	9	1	1
Western Europe	45	56	25
Russia	7	7	6
USA	10	16	8
Total (incl. others)	147	143	111

Source: UN, *Statistical Yearbook for Asia and the Pacific.*

Transport

ROAD TRAFFIC (estimates, '000 motor vehicles in use)

	1994	1995	1996
Passenger cars	31.0	31.0	31.0
Commercial vehicles	25.0	25.0	25.0

Source: International Road Federation, *World Road Statistics.*

CIVIL AVIATION ('000)

	1996	1997	1998
Kilometres flown	6,000	6,000	3,000
Passengers carried	256	90	53
Passenger-km	286,000	158,000	88,000
Freight ton-km	40,000	50,000	24,000

Source: UN, *Statistical Yearbook.*

Tourism

	1996	1997	1998
Tourist arrivals ('000)	4	4	4
Tourism receipts (US $ million)	1	1	1

Source: World Tourism Organization, *Yearbook of Tourism Statistics.*

Communications Media

	1995	1996	1997
Radio receivers ('000 in use)	2,400	2,550	2,750
Television receivers ('000 in use)	200	250	270
Main telephone lines ('000 in use)*†	29	29	29
Daily newspapers:			
Number	15*	12	n.a.
Average circulation ('000 copies)	200*	113	n.a.

* Estimate(s).

† **1998–2000:** Main telephone lines in use assumed unchanged.

Source: mainly UNESCO, *Statistical Yearbook.*

Education

(1995/96)

	Institutions	Teachers	Pupils
Pre-primary	88	2,110	n.a.
Primary	2,146	21,869	1,312,200
Secondary*	n.a.	19,085	512,900
Higher	n.a.	n.a.	12,800

* Figures refer to general secondary education only, excluding vocational and teacher training.

Source: UN, *Statistical Yearbook for Asia and the Pacific.*

Adult literacy rate (UNESCO estimates): 36% in 1999 (Source: UN Development Programme, *Human Development Report*).

Directory

The Constitution

Immediately after the coup of 27 April 1978 (the Saur Revolution), the 1977 Constitution was abolished. Both Nur Mohammad Taraki (Head of State from April 1978 to September 1979) and his successor, Hafizullah Amin (September–December 1979), promised to introduce new constitutions, but these leaders were removed from power before any drafts had been prepared by special commissions which they had appointed. On 21 April 1980 the Revolutionary Council ratified the Basic Principles of the Democratic Republic of Afghanistan. These were superseded by a new Constitution ratified in April 1985. Another new Constitution was ratified during a meeting of a Loya Jirga (Grand National Council), held on 29–30 November 1987. This Constitution was amended in May 1990. The following is a summary of the Constitution as it stood in May 1990.

GENERAL PROVISIONS

The fundamental duty of the State is to defend the independence, national sovereignty and territorial integrity of the Republic of Afghanistan. National sovereignty belongs to the people. The people exercise national sovereignty through the Loya Jirga and the Meli Shura.

Foreign policy is based on the principle of peaceful co-existence and active and positive non-alignment. Friendship and co-operation are to be strengthened with all countries, particularly neighbouring and Islamic ones. Afghanistan abides by the UN Charter and the Universal Declaration of Human Rights and supports the struggle against colonialism, imperialism, Zionism, racism and fascism. Afghanistan favours disarmament and the prevention of the proliferation of nuclear and chemical weapons. War propaganda is prohibited.

Islam is the religion of Afghanistan and no law shall run counter to the principles of Islam.

Political parties are allowed to be formed, providing that their policies and activities are in accordance with the provisions of the Constitution and the laws of the country. A party that is legally formed cannot be dissolved without legal grounds. Judges and prosecutors cannot be members of a political party during their term of office.

Pashtu and Dari are the official languages.

The capital is Kabul.

The State shall follow the policy of understanding and co-operation between all nationalities, clans and tribes within the country to ensure equality and the rapid development of backward regions.

The family constitutes the basic unit of society. The State shall adopt necessary measures to ensure the health of mothers and children.

The State protects all forms of legal property, including private property. The hereditary right to property shall be guaranteed according to Islamic law.

For the growth of the national economy, the State encourages foreign investment in the Republic of Afghanistan and regulates it in accordance with the law.

RIGHTS AND DUTIES OF THE PEOPLE

All subjects of Afghanistan are equal before the law. The following rights are guaranteed: the right to life and security, to complain to the appropriate government organs, to participate in the political sphere, to freedom of speech and thought, to hold peaceful demonstrations and strikes, to work, to free education, to protection of health and social welfare, to scientific, technical and cultural activities, to freedom of movement both within Afghanistan and abroad, to observe the religious rites of Islam and of other religions, to security of residence and privacy of communication and correspondence, and to liberty and human dignity.

In criminal cases, an accused person is considered innocent until guilt is recognized by the court. Nobody may be arrested, detained or punished except in accordance with the law.

Every citizen is bound to observe the Constitution and the laws of the Republic of Afghanistan, to pay taxes and duties to the State in accordance with the provisions of the law, and to undertake military service, when and as required.

LOYA JIRGA

This is the highest manifestation of the will of the people of Afghanistan. It is composed of: the President and Vice-Presidents, members of the Meli Shura (National Assembly), the General Prosecutor, the Council of Ministers, the Attorney-General, his deputies and members of the Attorney-General's Office, the chairman of the Constitution Council, the heads of the provincial councils, representatives from each province, according to the number of their representatives in the Wolasi Jirga (House of Representatives), elected by the people by a general secret ballot, and a minimum of 50 people, from among prominent political, scientific, social and religious figures, appointed by the President.

The Loya Jirga is empowered: to approve and amend the Constitution; to elect the President and to accept the resignation of the President; to consent to the declaration of war and armistice; and to adopt decisions on major questions regarding the destiny of the country. The Loya Jirga shall be summoned, opened and chaired by the President. Sessions of the Loya Jirga require a minimum attendance of two-thirds of the members. Decisions shall be adopted by a majority vote. In the event of the dissolution of the Wolasi Jirga (House of Representatives), its members shall retain their membership of the Loya Jirga until a new Wolasi Jirga is elected. Elections to the Loya Jirga shall be regulated by law and the procedure laid down by the Loya Jirga itself.

THE PRESIDENT

The President is the Head of State and shall be elected by a majority vote of the Loya Jirga for a term of seven years. No person can be elected as President for more than two terms. The President is accountable, and shall report, to the Loya Jirga. The Loya Jirga shall be convened to elect a new President 30 days before the end of the term of office of the outgoing President. Any Muslim citizen of the Republic of Afghanistan who is more than 40 years of age can be elected as President.

The President shall exercise the following executive powers: the supreme command of the armed forces; the ratification of the resolutions of the Meli Shura; the appointment of the Prime Minister; the approval of the appointment of ministers, judges and army officials; the granting of citizenship and the commuting of punishment; the power to call a referendum, to proclaim a state of emergency, and to declare war (with the consent of the Loya Jirga). Should a state of emergency continue for more than three months, the consent of the Loya Jirga is imperative for its extension.

In the event of the President being unable to perform his duties, the presidential functions and powers shall be entrusted to the first Vice-President. In the event of the death or resignation of the President, the first Vice-President shall ask the Loya Jirga to elect a new President within one month. In the event of resignation, the President shall submit his resignation directly to the Loya Jirga.

MELI SHURA

The Meli Shura (National Assembly) is the highest legislative organ of the Republic of Afghanistan. It consists of two houses: the Wolasi Jirga (House of Representatives) and the Sena (Senate). Members of the Wolasi Jirga (representatives) are elected by general secret ballot for a legislative term of five years. Members of the Sena (senators) are elected and appointed in the following manner: two people from each province are elected for a period of five years; two people from each provincial council are elected by the council for a period of three years; and the remaining one-third of senators are appointed by the President for a period of four years.

The Meli Shura is vested with the authority: to approve, amend and repeal laws and legislative decrees, and to present them to the President for his signature; to interpret laws; to ratify and annul international treaties; to approve socio-economic development plans and to endorse the Government's reports on their execution; to approve the state budget and to evaluate the Government's report on its execution; to establish and make changes to administrative units; to establish and abolish ministries; to appoint and remove Vice-Presidents, on the recommendation of the President; and to endorse the establishment of relations with foreign countries and international organizations. The Wolasi Jirga also has the power to approve a vote of confidence or no confidence in the Council of Ministers or one of its members.

At its first session, the Wolasi Jirga elects, from among its members, an executive committee, composed of a chairman, two deputy chairmen and two secretaries, for the whole term of the legislature. The Sena elects, from among its members, an executive committee, composed of a chairman for a term of five years, and two deputy chairmen and two secretaries for a term of one year.

Ordinary sessions of the Meli Shura are held twice a year and do not normally last longer than three months. An extraordinary session can be held at the request of the President, the chairman of either house, or one-fifth of the members of each house. The houses of the Meli Shura can hold separate or joint sessions. Sessions require a minimum attendance of two-thirds of the members of each house and decisions shall be adopted by a majority vote. Sessions are open, unless the houses decide to meet in closed sessions.

The following authorities have the right to propose the introduction, amendment or repeal of a law in either house of the Meli Shura: the President, the standing commissions of the Meli Shura, at least one-tenth of the membership of each house, the Council of Ministers, the Supreme Court, and the office of the Attorney-General.

If the decision of one house is rejected by the other, a joint committee, consisting of an equal number of members from both houses, shall be formed. A decision by the joint committee, which will be agreed by a two-thirds majority, will be considered valid after approval by the President. If the joint committee fails to resolve differences, the matter shall be discussed in a joint session of the Meli Shura, and a decision reached by a majority vote. The decisions that are made by the Meli Shura are enforced after being signed by the President.

After consulting the chairman of the Wolasi Jirga, the chairman of the Sena, the Prime Minister, the Attorney-General and the chairman of the Constitution Council, the President can declare the dissolution of the Wolasi Jirga, stating his justification for doing so. Re-elections shall be held within 3 months of the dissolution.

COUNCIL OF MINISTERS

The Council of Ministers is composed of: a Prime Minister, deputy Prime Ministers and Ministers. The Council of Ministers is appointed by the Prime Minister. It is empowered: to formulate and implement domestic and foreign policies; to formulate economic development plans and state budgets; and to ensure public order.

The Council of Ministers is dissolved under the following conditions: the resignation of the Prime Minister, chronic illness of the Prime Minister, the withdrawal of confidence in the Council of Ministers by the Meli Shura, the end of the legislative term, or the dissolution of the Wolasi Jirga or the Meli Shura.

THE JUDICIARY

(See section on the Judicial System.)

THE CONSTITUTION COUNCIL

The responsibilities of this body are: to evaluate and ensure the conformity of laws, legislative decrees and international treaties with the Constitution; and to give legal advice to the President on constitutional matters. The Constitution Council is composed of a chairman, a vice-chairman and eight members, who are appointed by the President.

LOCAL ADMINISTRATIVE ORGANS

For the purposes of local administration, the Republic of Afghanistan is divided into provinces, districts, cities and wards. These administrative units are led, respectively, by governors, district administrators, mayors and heads of wards. In each province a provincial council and district councils are formed in accordance with the law. Provincial councils and district councils each elect a chairman and a secretary from among their members. The term of office of a provincial council and a district council is three years.

FINAL PROVISIONS

Amendments to the Constitution shall be made by the Loya Jirga. Any amendment shall be on the proposal of the President, or on the proposal of one-third and the approval of two-thirds of the members of the Meli Shura. Amendment to the Constitution during a state of emergency is not allowed.

Note: Following the downfall of Najibullah's regime in April 1992, a provisional *mujahidin* Government assumed power in Kabul. In July an acting executive body, known as the Leadership Council, appointed a special commission to draw up a new and more strictly Islamic Constitution. In September 1993 it was reported that a draft Constitution had been approved by the commission, in preparation for the holding of a general election.

In May 1996, following the signing of the Mahipar Agreement between President Burhanuddin Rabbani and Gulbuddin Hekmatyar, a Constitution to cover the interim period pending the holding of a general election was drawn up and published. The main provisions of the **Constitution of the Interim Period** were as follows:

General provision: Afghanistan is an Islamic country where all aspects of the life of the people shall be conducted according to the tenets of Shari'a.

President: The President is the Head of State and exercises the highest executive power; the President is the supreme commander of the armed forces and his approval is required for the appointment of all civil and military officials; the President is authorized to declare war or peace (on the advice of the Council of Ministers or an Islamic Shura), to approve death sentences or grant pardons, to summon and dismiss a Shura, and to sign international treaties. In the event of the President's death, the presidential functions and powers shall be entrusted to the President of the Supreme Court until a new Head of State can be appointed.

Council of Ministers: The Council of Ministers, under the leadership of the Prime Minister, shall discuss and make decisions regarding government policy (both internal and external), the annual budget and administrative regulations, all of which shall be referred to the President for his assent.

According to the Agreement on Provisional Arrangements in Afghanistan Pending the Re-establishment of Permanent Government Institutions (also known as the Bonn Agreement) signed in December 2001, following the overthrow of the Taliban regime, Afghanistan reverted to the Constitution of 1964. (As long as the provisions were not inconsistent with those included in the Bonn Agreement; provisions relating to the monarchy, the executive body and legislature were excluded. In addition, existing laws could remain as long as they were consistent with the Bonn Agreement and the 1964 Constitution.) The Transitional Authority, with the assistance of the UN, was to establish a Constitutional Commission to draft a new Constitution before the Constitutional Loya Jirga convened in December 2003.

The Government

On 11–19 June 2002 an Emergency Loya Jirga, comprising approximately 1,650 delegates, 1,051 of whom were elected by tribal representatives, and the remainder selected by aid organizations, universities and other civil society bodies to ensure diverse representation, convened. The Loya Jirga appointed a broad-based, gender-sensitive Transitional Authority and a Head of State. At least 18 months later a Constitutional Loya Jirga, in the form of a constituent assembly, was scheduled to adopt a new constitution and prepare the country for democratic elections.

TRANSITIONAL AUTHORITY
(July 2002)

President: HAMID KARZAI.

Vice-Presidents: Marshal MUHAMMAD QASSIM FAHIM, ABDUL KARIM KHALILI, HEDAYAT AMIN ARSALA, NAMATULLAH SHAHRANI.

Special Adviser on Security: YOUNIS QANOONI.

Cabinet:

Minister of Defence: Marshal MUHAMMAD QASSIM FAHIM.

Minister of Foreign Affairs: Dr ABDULLAH ABDULLAH.

Minister of Finance: ASHRAF GHANI.

Minister of Interior Affairs: TAJ MOHAMMAD WARDAK.

Minister of Planning: Haji MOHAMMAD MOHAQQEQ.

Minister of Communications: MASOOM STANAKZAI.

Minister of Border Affairs: ARIF NURZAI.

Minister of Refugees: INTAYATULLAH NAZERI.

Minister of Mines: JUMA M. MUHAMMADI.

Minister of Light Industries: MOHAMMAD ALIM RAZM.

Minister of Public Health: Dr SOHAILA SIDDIQI.

Minister of Commerce: SAYED MUSTAFA KASEMI.

Minister of Agriculture: SAYED HUSSAIN ANWARI.

Minister of Justice: ABBAS KARIMI.

Minister of Information and Culture: SAYED MAKHDOOM RAHIM.

Minister of Reconstruction: MOHAMMAD FAHIM FARHANG.

Minister of Haj and Mosques: MOHAMMAD AMIN NAZIRYAR.

Minister of Urban Affairs: YUSUF PASHTUN.

Minister of Public Works: ABDUL ALI.

Minister of Social Affairs: NOOR MOHAMMAD KARKIN.

Minister of Water and Power: AHMAD SHAKAR KARKAR.

Minister of Irrigation and the Environment: AHMAD YUSUF.

Minister of Martyrs and Disabled People: ABDULLAH WARDAK.

Minister of Higher Education: SHARIF FAIZ.

Minister of Civil Aviation and Tourism: Mir WAIS SADDIQ.

Minister of Transport: SAYED MOHAMMAD ALI JAWAD.

Minister of Education: YOUNIS QANOONI.

Minister of Rural Development: HANIF ASMAR.

Minister of Women's Affairs: HABIBA SORABI.

MINISTRIES

Office of the Council of Ministers: Shar Rahi Sedarat, Kabul; tel. (93) 26926.

Office of the Prime Minister: Shar Rahi Sedarat, Kabul; tel. (93) 26926.

Ministry of Agriculture: Jamal Mina, Kabul; tel. (93) 41151.

Ministry of Border Affairs: Shah Mahmud Ghazi Ave, Kabul; tel. (93) 21793.

Ministry of Civil Aviation and Tourism: POB 165, Ansari Wat, Kabul; tel. (93) 21015.

Ministry of Commerce: Darulaman Wat, Kabul; tel. (93) 2290090; fax (93) 2290089.

Ministry of Communications: Mohammad Jan Khan Wat, Kabul; fax (20) 290022; e-mail admin@af-com-ministry.org; internet www.af-com-ministry.org.

Ministry of Defence: Darulaman Wat, Kabul; tel. (93) 41232.

Ministry of Education: Mohammad Jan Khan Wat, Kabul; tel. and fax (93) 020200000.

Ministry of Finance: Shar Rahi Pashtunistan, Kabul; tel. (93) 26041.

Ministry of Foreign Affairs: Shah Mahmud Ghazi St, Shar-i-Nau, Kabul; tel. (93) 25441.

Ministry of Haj and Mosques: Kabul.

Ministry of Higher Education: Jamal Mina, Kabul; tel. (93) 40041; f. 1978.

Ministry of Information and Culture: Mohammad Jan Khan Wat, Kabul; tel. and fax (93) 020200000.

Ministry of Interior Affairs: Shar-i-Nau, Kabul; tel. (93) 32441.

Ministry of Irrigation and Environment: Kabul.

Ministry of Justice: Shar Rahi Pashtunistan, Kabul; tel. (93) 23404.

Ministry of Light Industries: Ansari Wat, Kabul; tel. (93) 41551.

Ministry of Martyrs and Disabled People: Kabul.

Ministry of Mines: Shar Rahi Pashtunistan, Kabul; tel. (93) 25841.

Ministry of Planning: Shar-i-Nau, Kabul; tel. (93) 21273.

Ministry of Public Health: Micro-Rayon, Kabul; tel. (93) 40851.

Ministry of Public Works: Kabul.

Ministry of Reconstruction: Micro-Rayon, Kabul; tel. (93) 63701.

Ministry of Refugees: Kabul.

Ministry of Rural Development: Kabul.

Ministry of Social Affairs: Kabul.

Ministry of Transport: Ansari Wat, Kabul; tel. (93) 25541.

Ministry of Water Resources Development and Irrigation: Darulaman Wat, Kabul; tel. (93) 40743.

Ministry of Urban Affairs: Kabul.

Ministry of Water and Power: Kabul.

Ministry of Women's Affairs: Kabul.

Legislature

A Meli Shura (National Assembly) was established in 1987 to replace the Revolutionary Council. It was composed of two houses: the Wolasi Jirga (House of Representatives) and the Sena (Senate). However, following the downfall of Najibullah's regime in April 1992, an interim *mujahidin* Government took power in Kabul and both houses were dissolved. A High State Council was formed under the chairmanship of the President. In September 1996 the Taliban took over Kabul and closed down the council. On assuming power, the regime adopted an Interim Council of Ministers to administer the country. After the Taliban regime collapsed in late 2001, an Interim Authority was installed. Owing to the failure of the Emergency Loya Jirga in June 2002 to agree on a future National Assembly, President Karzai announced that a National Assembly Commission would be established to address the composition and powers of a new legislature.

Political Organizations

Afghan Mellat Party (Afghan Social Democratic Party): e-mail ajmal.mirranay@afghanmellat.com; internet www.afghanmellat .com; Pres. Dr Anwar-ul-Haq Ahady.

Harakat-i Islami i Afghanistan (Islamic Movement of Afghanistan): Kabul; Leader Ayatollah Muhammed Asif Munshi.

Hizb-i Islami Gulbuddin (Islamic Party Gulbuddin): e-mail info@hezb-e-islami.org; internet www.hezb-e-islami.org; Pashtun/ Turkmen/Tajik; Leader Gulbuddin Hekmatyar; c. 50,000 supporters (estimate); based in Iran in 1998–99.

Hizb-i Islami Khalis (Islamic Party Khalis): Pashtun; Leader Maulvi Muhammad Yunus Khalis; c. 40,000 supporters (estimate).

Hizb-i Wahadat i Islami (Islamic Unity Party): Kabul; coalition of Hazara groups; Leaders Karim Khalili, Mohaqiq.

Ittihad-i-Islami Bara i Azadi Afghanistan (Islamic Union for the Liberation of Afghanistan): Pashtun; Leader Prof. Abdul Rasul Sayef; Dep. Leader Ahmad Shah Ahmadzay; c. 18,000 supporters (estimate).

Jamiat-i Islami (Islamic Society): internet www.jamiat .com; Turkmen/Uzbek/Tajik; Leaders Prof. Burhanuddin Rabbani, Gen. Muhammed Fahim; Sec.-Gen. Enayatollah Shadab; c. 60,000 supporters (estimate).

Jebha-i-Nejat-i-Melli (National Liberation Front): Pashtun; Leader Prof. Hazrat Sibghatullah Mojaddedi; Sec.-Gen. Zabihollah Mojaddedi; c. 15,000 supporters (estimate).

Jonbesh-i Melli-i Islami (National Islamic Movement): f. 1992; formed mainly from troops of former Northern Command of the Afghan army; predominantly Uzbek/Tajik/Turkmen/Ismaili and Hazara Shi'ite; Leader Gen. Abdul Rashid Dostam; 65,000–150,000 supporters.

Khudamul Furqan Jamiat (Association of Servants of the Koran Society): Kabul; Pashtun; former mems of the Taliban; revived Dec. 2001; Chief: Ahmad Amin Mujaddedi.

Mahaz-i-Melli-i-Islami (National Islamic Front): Pashtun; Leader Pir Sayed Ahmad Gailani; Dep. Leader Hamed Gailani; c. 15,000 supporters (estimate).

Nizat-i-Milli: Kabul; f. 2002; Leader Younis Qanooni.

Taliban: internet www.taleban.com; emerged in 1994; Islamist fundamentalist; mainly Sunni Pashtuns; in power 1996–2001; largely disbanded; Leader Mola Mohammad Omar.

Diplomatic Representation

EMBASSIES IN AFGHANISTAN

Austria: POB 24, Zarghouna Wat, Kabul; tel. (93) 32720.

Bangladesh: Kabul; tel. (93) 25783.

Bulgaria: Wazir Akbar Khan Mena, Kabul; tel. (93) 20683; Ambassador: Angel Urbetsov.

China, People's Republic: Sardar Shah Mahmoud Ghazi Wai, Kabul; tel. (93) 20446; Ambassador: Sun Yuxi.

Cuba: Shar Rahi Haji Yaqub, opp. Shar-i-Nau Park, Kabul; tel. (93) 30863.

France: POB 62, Shar-i-Nau, Kabul; tel. (93) 23631; Chargé d'affaires a.i.: Jean-Marin Schuh.

Germany: Wazir Akbar Khan Mena, POB 83, Kabul; tel. (93) 22432; Ambassador: Rainer Eberle.

Hungary: POB 830, Sin 306–308, Wazir Akbar Khan Mena, Kabul; tel. (93) 24281.

India: Malalai Wat, Shar-i-Nau, Kabul; tel. (93) 30556; Ambassador: Vivek Katju.

Indonesia: POB 532, Wazir Akbar Khan Mena, District 10, Zone 14, Road Mark Jeem House 93, Kabul; tel. (93) 20586.

Iran: Shar-i-Nau, Kabul; tel. (93) 26255; Ambassador: Mohammad Ibrahim Taherian.

Iraq: POB 523, Wazir Akbar Khan Mena, Kabul; tel. (93) 24797.

Italy: POB 606, Khoja Abdullah Ansari Wat, Kabul; tel. (93) 24624; Ambassador: Domenico Giorgi.

Japan: POB 80, Wazir Akbar Khan Mena, Kabul; tel. (93) 26844; Ambassador: Kinichi Komano.

Korea, Democratic People's Republic: Wazir Akbar Khan Mena, House 28, Sarak 'H' House 103, Kabul; tel. (93) 22161.

Kuwait: Kabul; Chargé d'affaires: Naseer Ahmed Noor.

Libya: 103 Wazir Akbar Khan, Kabul; tel. (20) 25948; fax (20) 290160.

Mongolia: Wazir Akbar Khan Mena, Sarak 'T' House 8714, Kabul; tel. (93) 22138.

Pakistan: Kabul; tel. (91) 287464; fax (91) 287460; Ambassador: Rustam Shah Mohmand.

Poland: Gozargah St, POB 78, Kabul; tel. (93) 42461.

Russia: Darulaman Wat, Kabul; tel. (93) 41541; Ambassador: Mikhail Konarovskii.

Saudi Arabia: Kabul; Chargé d'affaires: Fahd al-Qahtani.

Slovakia: Taimani Wat, Kala-i-Fatullah, Kabul; tel. (93) 32082.

Sudan: Kabul.

Sweden: Kabul; Ambassador: Peter Teijer.

Tajikistan: Kabul; Ambassador: FARHOD MAHKAMOV.

Turkey: Shar-i-Nau, Kabul; tel. (93) 20072; Ambassador: MUFIT OZDES.

Turkmenistan: Kabul; Ambassador: AMANMAMMET YARANOW.

United Arab Emirates: Kabul; Ambassador: ALI MUHAMMAD AL-SHAMSI.

United Kingdom: Karte Parwan, Kabul; tel. (93) 30512; Ambassador: RONALD NASH.

USA: Wazir Akbar Khan Mena, Kabul; tel. (93) 62230; Ambassador: ROBERT FINN.

Uzbekistan: Kabul; Ambassador: ALISHER AHMADJONOV.

Viet Nam: 3 Nijat St, Wazir Akbar Khan Mena, Kabul; tel. (93) 26596.

Judicial System

After 23 years of civil war, which ended in December 2001 with the defeat of the Taliban, there no longer existed a functioning national judicial system. In accordance with the Bonn Agreement, Afghanistan reverted to the Constitution of 1964, which combined *Shari'a* with Western concepts of justice. A new constitution was expected to be introduced in December 2003. In the mean time, a judicial commission was established in June 2002 to address the issues of judicial and legislative reform.

Chief Justice: FAZUL HADI SHINWARI.

Religion

The official religion of Afghanistan is Islam. Muslims comprise 99% of the population, approximately 84% of them of the Sunni and the remainder of the Shi'ite sect. There are small minority groups of Hindus, Sikhs and Jews.

ISLAM

The High Council of Ulema and Clergy of Afghanistan: Kabul; f. 1980; 7,000 mems; Chair. Mawlawi ABDOL GHAFUR SENANI.

The Press

Many newspapers and periodicals stopped appearing on a regular basis or, in a large number of cases, ceased publication during the civil war. Following the defeat of the Taliban in late 2001, a number of newspapers and periodicals resumed publication or were established for the first time.

PRINCIPAL DAILIES

Anis: (Friendship): Ministry of Information and Culture, Mohammad Jan Khan Wat, Kabul; f. 1927; evening; independent; Dari, Uzbek and Pashto; state-owned; news and literary articles; Chief Editor MOHAMMAD S. KHARNIKASH; circ. 25,000.

Hewad (Homeland): Kabul; tel. (93) 26851; f. 1959; revived by the Taliban in 1998; Pashto; state-owned.

Kabul Times: POB 983, Ansari Wat, Kabul; tel. (93) 61847; f. 1962 as Kabul Times, renamed Kabul New Times in 1980; ceased publication in 2001; revived in 2002 under new management; English; state-owned.

Shari'at: Kabul.

PERIODICALS

Aamu: Aria Press, Kabul; quarterly; research; circ. 1,000.

Ambastagi: Aria Press, Kabul; weekly; circ. 1,000.

Kabul Weekly: Kabul; f. 1993, banned in 1997, revived in 2002; Dari, Pashto, English and French; weekly; independent; Editor-in-Chief FAHIM DASHTY; circ. c. 4,000.

Malalai: Kabul; f. 2002; monthly; women's; Chief Editor JAMILA MUJAHID.

Payam-e-Mujahid: Panjshir; internet www.payamemujahid.com; weekly; Dari and Pashto; controlled by Burhanuddin Rabbani.

Roz (The Day): Kabul; f. 2002; monthly; women's; Dari, Pashto, French and English; Editor-in-Chief LAILOMA AHMADI.

Seerat (Character): Kabul; f. 2002; weekly; women's; circ. 1,000; Deputy Editor NAJIBA MURAM.

Women's Mirror: Kabul; f. 2002; weekly; independent; women's.

Zanbil e Gham: Kabul; monthly; satirical.

NEWS AGENCIES

Afghan Islamic Press: Peshawar, North-West Frontier Province, Pakistan.

Aria Press: Kabul; f. 1987 in Dushanbe, Tajikistan; independent; publishes three newsletters.

Bakhtar Information Agency (BIA): Ministry of Information and Culture, Mohammad Jan Khan Wat, Kabul; tel. (93) 24089; f. 1939; Head Sultan AHMAD BAHEEN.

Reuters: POB 1069, Islamabad, Pakistan; tel. (51) 2274757; e-mail simon.denyer@reuters.com; Bureau Chief: SIMON DENYER.

PRESS ASSOCIATIONS

Plans were under way in mid-2002 to create an independent journalists' union in Kabul.

Afghanistan Women in Media Network: Kabul; f. 2002; association of female media staff; Pres. JAMILA MUJAHID.

Publishers

Some of the following publishers were forced to close down during the Taliban regime. Since the fall of the Taliban, publishers have been slowly reopening, with the help of the UN and other international aid agencies and foreign publishing houses.

Afghan Book: POB 206, Kabul; f. 1969; books on various subjects, translations of foreign works on Afghanistan, books in English on Afghanistan and Dari language textbooks for foreigners; Man. Dir JAMILA AHANG.

Afghanistan Today Publishers: POB 983, c/o The Kabul Times, Ansari Wat, Kabul; tel. (93) 61847; publicity materials; answers enquiries about Afghanistan.

Balhaqi Book Publishing and Importing Institute: POB 2025, Kabul; tel. (93) 26818; f. 1971 by co-operation of the Government Printing House, Bakhtar News Agency and leading newspapers; publishers and importers of books; Pres. MUHAMMAD ANWAR NUMYALAI.

Book Publishing Institute: Herat; f. 1970 by co-operation of Government Printing House and citizens of Herat; books on literature, history and religion.

Book Publishing Institute: Qandahar; f. 1970; supervised by Government Printing House; mainly books in Pashto language.

Educational Publications: Ministry of Education and Training, Mohd Jan Khan Wat, Kabul; tel. (93) 21716; textbooks for primary and secondary schools in the Pashto and Dari languages; also three monthly magazines in Pashto and in Dari.

Franklin Book Programs Inc: POB 332, Kabul.

Historical Society of Afghanistan: Kabul; tel. (93) 30370; f. 1931; mainly historical and cultural works and two quarterly magazines: *Afghanistan* (English and French), *Aryana* (Dari and Pashto); Pres. AHMAD ALI MOTAMEDI.

Institute of Geography: Kabul University, Kabul; geographical and related works.

International Center for Pashto Studies: Kabul; f. 1975 by the Afghan Govt with the assistance of UNESCO; research work on the Pashto language and literature and on the history and culture of the Pashto people; Pres. and Assoc. Chief Researcher J. K. HEKMATY; publs *Pashto* (quarterly).

Kabul University Press: Kabul; tel. (93) 42433; f. 1950; textbooks; two quarterly scientific journals in Dari and in English, etc.

Research Center for Linguistics and Literary Studies: Afghanistan Academy of Sciences, Akbar Khan Mena, Kabul; tel. (93) 26912; f. 1978; research on Afghan languages (incl. Pashto, Dari, Balochi and Uzbek) and Afghan folklore; Pres. Prof. MOHAMMED R. ELHAM; publs *Kabul* (Pashto), *Zeray* (Pashto weekly) and *Khurasan* (Dari).

Government Publishing House

Government Printing House: Kabul; tel. (93) 26851; f. 1870 under supervision of the Ministry of Information and Culture; Dir SAID AHMAD RAHAA.

Broadcasting and Communications

TELECOMMUNICATIONS

Afghan Wireless Communication Company (AWCC): Ministry of Communications Bldg, Mohammad Jan Khan Wat, Kabul; tel. and fax (93) 200000; e-mail; info@afghanwireless.com; internet www.afghanwireless.com; f. 1999; jt venture between the Afghan Government and Telephone Systems International, Inc of the USA; reconstruction of Afghanistan's national and international telecommunications network; by June 2002 mobile and fixed-line telecommunications services covered Herat, Jalalabad, Kabul, Mazar-i-Sharif and Qandahar; the first centre providing internet services was opened in Kabul in July; CEO EHSAN BAYAT.

BROADCASTING

The media were severely restricted by the militant Taliban regime (1996–2001): television was banned and Radio Afghanistan was renamed Radio Voice of Shari'a. The overthrow of the Taliban in November–December 2001 led to the liberation of the media. On 13 November Radio Afghanistan was revived in Kabul; music was broadcast for the first time in five years. A few days later Kabul TV was resurrected, and a woman was employed as its newsreader.

Radio-Television Afghanistan: POB 544, Ansari Wat, Kabul; tel. (93) 20355; revived in 2001; programmes in Dari, Pashto, Turkmen and Uzbek; Gen. Dir MOHAMMAD ISAQ.

Radio Herat: Herat.

Radio Kabul: Kabul.

Voice of Freedom: Kabul; f. 2002; broadcasts one hour a day in Dari and Pashto; German-funded.

Kabul TV: Kabul; revived in 2001; broadcasts four hrs daily; Dir HUMAYUN RAWI.

TV Badakshan: Faizabad; f. 1987 as Faizabad TV, name changed in 2000; Pashto and Dari.

Balkh Radio and TV: Mazar-i-Sharif; Pashto and Dari; Chair. ABDORRAB JAHED.

Finance

(cap. = capital; auth. = authorized; p.u. = paid up; res = reserves; m. = million; brs = branches; amounts in afghanis unless otherwise stated)

BANKING

In June 1975 all banks were nationalized. There are no foreign banks operating in Afghanistan. The banking sector was under reconstruction in 2002, following the collapse of the Taliban regime.

Da Afghanistan Bank (Central Bank of Afghanistan): Ibne Sina Wat, Kabul; tel. (93) 24075; f. 1939; main functions: banknote issue, modernize the banking system, re-establish banking relations with international banks, create a financial market system, foreign exchange regulation, govt and private depository, govt fiscal agency; Gov. Dr ANWAR-UL-HAQ AHADY; 84 brs.

Agricultural Development Bank of Afghanistan: POB 414, Cineme Pamir Bldg, Jade Maiwand, Kabul; tel. (93) 24459; f. 1959; makes available credits for farmers, co-operatives and agro-business; aid provided by IBRD and UNDP; Chair. Dr M. KABIAR; Pres. Dr ABDULLAH NAQSHBANDI.

Banke Milli Afghan (Afghan National Bank): Jana Ibn Sina, Kabul; tel. (93) 25451; f. 1932; Chair. ABDUL WAHAB ASSEFI; Pres. ELHAMUDDIN QIAM; 16 brs.

Export Promotion Bank of Afghanistan: 24 Mohd Jan Khan Wat, Kabul; tel. (93) 24447; f. 1976; provides financing for exports and export-orientated investments; Pres. MOHAMMAD YAQUB NEDA; Vice-Pres. BURHANUDDIN SHAHIM.

Industrial Development Bank of Afghanistan: POB 14, Shar-i-Nau, Kabul; tel. (93) 33336; f. 1973; provides financing for industrial development; cap. 10,500m. (1996); Pres. Haji RAHMATULLAH.

Pashtany Tejaraty Bank (Afghan Commercial Bank): Mohd Jan Khan Wat, Kabul; tel. (93) 26551; f. 1954 to provide short-term credits, forwarding facilities, opening letters of credit, purchase and sale of foreign exchange; Chair. Dr BASIR RANJBAR; Pres. and CEO ZIR GUL WARDAK; 14 brs.

INSURANCE

There is one national insurance company:

Afghan National Insurance Co: National Insurance Bldg, Park, Shar-i-Nau, POB 329, Kabul; tel. (93) 33531; fax (762) 523846; f. 1964; mem. of Asian Reinsurance Corpn; marine, aviation, fire, motor and accident insurance; Pres. M. ABDULLAH MUDASIR; Claims Man. MEHRABUDDIN MATEEN.

No foreign insurance companies are permitted to operate in Afghanistan.

Trade and Industry

GOVERNMENT AGENCIES

Board for the Promotion of Private Investment: Kabul.

Export Promotion Department: Ministry of Commerce, Darulaman Wat, Kabul; fax (93) 2290089; f. 1969; provides guidance for traders, collects and disseminates trade information, markets and performs quality control of export products.

High Commission for Combating Drugs: Kabul.

CHAMBERS OF COMMERCE AND INDUSTRY

Afghan Chamber of Commerce and Industry: Mohd Jan Khan Wat, Kabul; tel. (93) 26796; fax (93) 2290089; Head Mola MOHAMMAD DAUD ABED.

Federation of Afghan Chambers of Commerce and Industry: Darulaman Wat, Kabul; f. 1923; includes chambers of commerce and industry in Ghazni, Qandahar, Kabul, Herat, Mazar-i-Sharif, Fariab, Jawzjan, Kunduz, Jalalabad and Andkhoy.

INDUSTRIAL AND TRADE ASSOCIATIONS

Afghan Carpet Exporters' Guild: POB 3159, Darulaman Wat, Kabul; tel. (93) 41765; f. 1967; a non-profit-making, independent organization of carpet manufacturers and exporters; Pres. ZIAUDDIN ZIA; c. 1,000 mems.

Afghan Cart Company: POB 61, Zerghona Maidan, Kabul; tel. (20) 2201309; fax (20) 290238; f. 1988; the largest export/import company in Afghanistan; imports electrical goods, machinery, metal, cars, etc.; exports raisins, medical herbs, wood, animal hides, etc; Pres. KABIR IMAQ.

Afghan Fruit Processing Co: POB 261, Industrial Estate, Puli Charkhi, Kabul; tel. (93) 65186; f. 1960; exports raisins, other dried fruits and nuts.

Afghan Raisin and Other Dried Fruits Institute: POB 3034, Sharara Wat, Kabul; tel. (93) 30463; exporters of dried fruits and nuts; Pres. NAJMUDDIN MUSLEH.

Afghan Wool Enterprises: Shar-i-Nau, Kabul; tel. (93) 31963.

Afghanistan Karakul Institute: POB 506, Puli Charkhi, Kabul; tel. (93) 61852; f. 1967; exporters of furs; Pres. G. M. BAHEER.

Afghanistan Plants Enterprise: POB 122, Puli Charkhi, Kabul; tel. (93) 31962; exports medicines, plants and spices.

Handicraft Promotion and Export Centre: POB 3089, Sharara Wat, Kabul; tel. (93) 32935; MOMENA RANJBAR.

Parapamizad Co Ltd: Jadai Nader Pashtoon, Sidiq Omar Market, POB 1911, Kabul; tel. (93) 22116; export/import co; Propr PADSHAH SARBAZ.

TRADE UNION

National Union of Afghanistan Employees (NUAE): POB 756, Kabul; tel. (93) 23040; f. 1978, as Central Council of Afghanistan Trade Unions, to establish and develop the trade union movement, including the formation of councils and organizational cttees in the provinces; name changed in 1990; composed of seven vocational unions; 300,000 mems; Pres. A. HABIB HARDAMSHAID; Vice-Pres. ASAD KHAN NACEIRY.

Transport

RAILWAYS

There is no railway system currently operating in Afghanistan.

ROADS

In 2001 there were an estimated 23,500 km of roads, of which more than 18,000 km were unpaved. All-weather highways link Kabul with Qandahar and Herat in the south and west, Jalalabad in the east and Mazar-i-Sharif and the Amu-Dar'ya river in the north. A massive reconstruction programme of the road system in Afghanistan began in early 2002. The Salang Highway was rehabilitated, thus reconnecting Kabul with the north.

Afghan International Transport Company: Kabul.

Afghan Container Transport Company Ltd: House No. 43, St No. 2, Left West of Charahe-Haji Yaqub, Shar-e-Naw, Kabul; tel. and fax (20) 2201392.

Afghan Transit Company: POB 530, Ghousy Market, Mohammad Jan Khan Wat, Kabul; tel. (93) 22654.

AFSOTR: Kabul; resumed operations in 1998; transport co; 90 vehicles.

Land Transport Company: Khoshal Mena, Kabul; tel. (93) 20345; f. 1943; commercial transport within Afghanistan.

The Milli Bus Enterprise: Ministry of Transport, Ansari Wat, Kabul; tel. (93) 25541; state-owned and -administered; 721 buses; Pres. Eng. AZIZ NAGHABAN.

Salang-Europe International Transport and Transit: Kabul; f. 1991 as joint Afghan/Soviet co; 500 vehicles.

INLAND WATERWAYS

There are 1,200 km of navigable inland waterways, including the Amu-Dar'ya (Oxus) river, which is capable of handling vessels of up to about 500 dwt. River ports on the Amu-Dar'ya are linked by road to Kabul.

CIVIL AVIATION

In early 2002 there were international airports at Kabul and Qandahar, and almost 50 local airports were located throughout the country.

Ministry of Civil Aviation and Tourism: POB 165, Ansari Wat, Kabul; tel. (93) 21015.

Ariana Afghan Airlines: POB 76, Afghan Air Authority Bldg, Ansari Wat, Kabul; tel. (93) 2554145; fax (93) 761280785; f. 1950; merged with Bakhtar Afghan Airlines Co Ltd in 1985; govt-owned; flights suspended in Nov. 1999–Jan. 2002, owing to UN sanctions; flights to India and United Arab Emirates resumed in March 2002; Pres. Capt. JAHED AZIMI.

Tourism

Afghanistan's potential tourism attractions include: Bamian, with its thousands of painted caves; Bandi Amir, with its suspended lakes; the Blue Mosque of Mazar; Herat, with its Grand Mosque and minarets; the towns of Qandahar and Girishk; Balkh (ancient Bactria), 'Mother of Cities', in the north; Bagram, Hadda and Surkh Kotal (of interest to archaeologists); and the high mountains of the Hindu Kush. Furthermore, ruins of a Buddhist city dating from the second century were discovered in July 2002 in southern Afghanistan. The restoration of cultural heritage, sponsored by UNESCO, was under way in mid-2002; however, it was decided that the two largest standing Buddha statues that had been destroyed by the Taliban in March 2001 should not be reconstructed. In 1998 an estimated 4,000 tourists visited Afghanistan and receipts from tourism amounted to around US $1m.

Afghan Tourist Organization (ATO): Ansari Wat, Shar-i-Nau, Kabul; tel. (93) 30323; f. 1958; Pres. MOHD KAZIM WARDAK (acting).

Defence

Following the defeat of the Taliban in late 2001, an International Security Assistance Force (ISAF) was deployed in Kabul to help maintain security in the capital. The 4,500–5,000-strong ISAF, led by the United Kingdom until Turkey took over command in June 2002, was also responsible for the training of the Afghan National Guard. In April the first 600-man multi-ethnic battalion of the Afghan National Guard was inducted to guard the presidential palace and ministries. It was envisaged that the Afghan National Guard would form the basis of a new Afghan National Army (ANA). US Special Forces began training an initial set of recruits for the ANA in May; the first battalion graduated in June. It was intended that the ANA would eventually be a force of some 60,000, supported by a border guard of 12,000 and an air force of 8,000. By the end of 2002 Afghans were expected to commence a gradual process of taking over training responsibilities, with the support of an academy with its own Afghan commandant and logistical support staff.

Education

The prolonged war resulted in a large-scale exodus of teachers, and some 3,600 school buildings were damaged or destroyed.

Before the Taliban rose to power, primary education began at seven years of age and lasted for six years. Secondary education, beginning at 13 years of age, lasted for a further six years. As a proportion of the school-age population, the total enrolment at primary and secondary schools was equivalent to 36% (males 49%; females 22%) in 1995. Primary enrolment in that year was equivalent to an estimated 49% of children in the relevant age-group (boys 64%; girls 32%), while the enrolment ratio at general secondary schools in 1996 was equivalent to 22% (boys 32%; girls 11%).

Following their seizure of power in late September 1996, the Taliban banned education for girls over the age of eight, closed all the women's institutes of higher education and drew up a new Islamic curriculum for boys' schools. Education in areas under the control of the United Front continued to operate. In Panjshir, for example, 49 schools were open, but had to close in late 1999 to allow internally displaced people to live in school buildings. The co-educational university in Bamian functioned until the Taliban captured the province. Aid agencies in eastern Afghanistan supported primary schools. Even in areas controlled by the Taliban, Afghans attempted to continue to educate girls. In mid-1998 the UN was angered by the Taliban's decision to close more than 100 private schools and numerous small, home-based vocational courses in Kabul, many of which were educating girls. UNICEF reported that by December 1998 about 90% of girls and 66% of boys were not enrolled in school. According to Taliban figures, in September 1999 1,586,026 pupils were being educated by 59,792 teachers in 3,836 *madrassas* (mosque schools).

After the Taliban regime was defeated in late 2001, the Afghan Interim Administration, with the help of foreign governments, UNICEF and humanitarian organizations, began to rehabilitate the education system. In late March 2002 more than 1.5m. boys and girls commenced a new academic year at more than 4,500 schools around the country. The World Food Programme (WFP) embarked on a food-for-education programme; organizations world-wide supplied educational material and tents were provided as temporary classrooms. According to UNICEF, in July almost 1.25m. children were confirmed to be attending some 2,744 schools in 20 out of 32 provinces. Of these children, 1.1m. were enrolled in grades one to six (primary education, see above) and 30% were girls. It was estimated that enrolment in the whole country had increased by 60% compared with the previous academic year; the enrolment of girls had increased by an estimated 90%. More than 27,000 teachers were involved in education in 20 provinces in July, 36% of whom were women. UNICEF and other aid agencies began the reconstruction of 100 damaged schools; by July 48 had been completed or were near completion. Several hundred other schools were also being rehabilitated.

Kabul University opened for men and women in March 2002. Foreign universities as well as governments and non-governmental organizations donated books and teaching materials. Universities in at least five other provinces were being rehabilitated.

Bibliography

GENERAL

Anderson, Ewan W., and Dupree, Nancy H. (Eds). *The Cultural Basis of Afghan Nationalism.* London and New York, Pinter Publishers Ltd, 1990.

Caroe, Olaf. *The Pathans: 550 BC–AD 1957.* Oxford, Oxford University Press, 1976.

Centlivres, Pierre. *Les Bouddhas d'Afghanistan.* Lausanne, Editions Favre, 2001.

Doubleday, Veronica. *Three Women of Herat.* London, Jonathan Cape, 1988.

Dupree, Louis. *Afghanistan.* Princeton, NJ, Princeton University Press, 1973.

Gall, Sandy. *Afghanistan: Agony of a Nation.* London, The Bodley Head, 1988.

Grassmuck, George, and Adamec, Ludwig (Eds). *Afghanistan: Some new approaches.* Ann Arbor, MI, Center for Near Eastern and North African Studies, University of Michigan, 1969.

Griffiths, John C. *Afghanistan.* London, Pall Mall Press, 1967.

King, Peter. *Afghanistan, Cockpit in Asia.* London, Bles, 1966, Taplinger, NY, 1967.

Klimburg, M. *Afghanistan.* Vienna, Austrian UNESCO Commission, 1966.

Latifa, and Hachemi, Shekeba. *My Forbidden Face: Growing Up Under the Taliban: A Young Woman's Story.* Talk Miramax Books, 2002.

Lessing, Doris. *The Wind Blows Away Our Words.* London, Picador, 1988.

Mousavi, Sayed Askar. *The Hazaras of Afghanistan: An Historical, Cultural, Economic and Political Study.* New York, NY, St Martin's Press, 1997.

Orywal, Erwin (Ed.). *Die ethnischen Gruppen Afghanistans: Fallstudien zu Gruppenidentität und Intergruppenbeziehungen.* Wiesbaden, Dr Ludwig Reichert Verlag, 1986.

Singer, André. *Lords of the Khyber.* London, Faber, 1984.

Skaine, Rosemarie. *The Women of Afghanistan Under the Taliban.* Jefferson, NC, McFarland & Company, Inc, 2001.

Szabo, Albert, and Borfield, Thomas J. *Afghanistan: An Atlas of Indigenous Domestic Architecture.* Austin, University of Texas Press, 1991.

Tapper, Nancy. *Bartered Brides: Politics, Gender and Marriage in an Afghan Tribal Society.* Cambridge, Cambridge University Press, 1991.

Van Dyk, Jere. *In Afghanistan. An American Odyssey.* New York, NY, Coward-McCann, 1983.

Vogelsang, Willem. *The Afghans (People of Asia).* Oxford, Blackwell Publishers, 2001.

Wilber, Donald N. *Afghanistan.* New Haven, CT, 1956.

Annotated Bibliography of Afghanistan. New Haven, CT, 1962.

GEOGRAPHY AND TRAVELS

Burnes, Sir Alexander. *Cabool.* London, John Murray, 1842, reprinted Lahore 1961.

Byron, Robert. *Road to Oxiana.* London, Jonathan Cape, 1937.

Elliot, Jason. *An Unexpected Light—Travels in Afghanistan.* London, Picador, 1999.

Elphinstone, M. *An Account of the Kingdom of Caubul and its Dependencies in Persia, Tartary and India.* London, John Murray, 1815, reprinted Oxford University Press, 1972.

Hahn, H. *Die Stadt Kabul und ihr Umland.* 2 vols. Bonn, 1964–65.

Hamilton, Angus. *Afghanistan.* London, Heinemann, 1966.

Hodson, Peregrine, *Under a Sickle Moon: A Journey through Afghanistan.* London, Hutchinson, 1986.

Humlum, J. *La Géographie de l'Afghanistan.* Copenhagen, Gyldendal, 1959.

Levi, Peter. *Journeys in Afghanistan.* London, Penguin, 1984.

Wolfe, N. H. *Herat.* Kabul, Afghan Tourist Organization, 1966.

Wood, John. *A Personal Narrative of a Journey to the Source of the River Oxus by the Route of Indus, Kabul and Badakshan.* London, John Murray, 1841, reprinted Oxford University Press, 1976.

HISTORY AND POLITICS

Adamec, Ludwig W. *Afghanistan 1900–1923.* Berkeley, University of California, 1967.

Afghanistan's Foreign Affairs to the Mid-Twentieth Century. Tucson, AZ, University of Arizona Press, 1974.

Historical Dictionary of Afghanistan. London, Scarecrow Press Inc, 1991.

Akhramovich, R. T. *Outline History of Afghanistan after the Second World War.* Moscow, 1966.

Akram, Assem. *Histoire de la guerre d'Afghanistan.* Paris, Editions Balland, 1996.

Alder, G. J. *British India's Northern Frontier, 1865–1895.* London, Longman, 1963.

Alexander, Yonah, and Swetnam, Michael. *Usama bin Laden's Al-Qaida: Profile of a Terrorist Network.* New York, NY, Transnational Publishing, 2001.

Alexievich, Svetlana. *The Zinky Boys.* London, Chatto and Windus, 1991.

Anwar, Raja. *The Tragedy of Afghanistan: A First-hand Account.* London, Verso, 1988.

Arney, George. *Afghanistan.* London, Mandarin Books, 1990.

Arnold, Anthony. *Afghanistan's Two-Party Communism: Parcham and Khalq.* Stanford University, CA, Hoover Institution Press, 1984.

Bergen, Peter L. *Holy War, Inc.: Inside the Secret World of Osama bin Laden.* London, George Weidenfeld and Nicolson, 2001.

Blanc, Florent. *Ben Laden et l'Amérique.* Paris, Bayard Editions, 2001.

Bocharov, Gennady. *Russian Roulette: The Afghanistan War through Russian Eyes.* London, Hamish Hamilton, 1991.

Borer, Douglas A. *Superpowers Defeated: Vietnam and Afghanistan Compared.* London, Frank Cass, 1999.

Borovik, Artyom. *The Hidden War: A Russian Journalist's Account of the Soviet War in Afghanistan.* New York, NY, Atlantic Monthly Press, 1991.

Bosworth, C. E. *The Ghaznavids.* Edinburgh University Press, 1963.

Bradsher, Henry S. *Afghan Communism and Soviet Intervention.* Karachi, Oxford University Press, 1999.

Cambridge History of India. Vols I, III, IV, V, VI.

Carew, Tom. *Jihad: The Secret War in Afghanistan.* Edinburgh, Mainstream Publishing Co, 2001.

Cooley, John K. *Unholy Wars: Afghanistan, America and International Terrorism.* London, Pluto Publishing Ltd, 1999.

Córdovez, Diego, and Harrison, Selig. *Out of Afghanistan: The Inside Story of the Soviet Withdrawal.* Oxford, Oxford University Press, 1995.

Dollot, René. *Afghanistan.* Paris, Payot, 1937.

Dorronsoro, Gilles. *La Révolution Afghane, des Communistes aux Tâlêban.* Paris, Karthala Editions, 2000.

Dupree, Louis, and Linnet, Albert (Eds). *Afghanistan in the 1970s.* New York, Praeger, 1974, and London, Pall Mall Press.

Edwards, David B. *Heroes of the Age: Moral Fault Lines on the Afghan Frontier.* Berkeley and Los Angeles, CA, University of California Press, 1996.

Before Taliban: Genealogies of the Afghan Jihad. Berkeley and Los Angeles, CA, University of California Press, 2002.

Ellis, Deborah. *Women of the Afghan War.* London, Greenwood Publishing Group, 2000.

Emadi, Hafizullah. *State, Revolution and Superpowers in Afghanistan.* New York, NY, Praeger Publishers, 1990.

Esposito, John L. (Ed.). *Political Islam: Revolution, Radicalism or Reforms?* London, Lynne Rienner Publishers, 1997.

Ewans, Martin. *Afghanistan—A New History.* London, Routledge Curzon, 2002, 2nd edn.

Fletcher, Arnold. *Afghanistan, Highway of Conquest.* Cornell and Oxford University Presses, 1965.

Fraser-Tytler, Sir W. Kerr. *Afghanistan.* Oxford University Press, 1950, 3rd edn., 1967.

Fullerton, John. *The Soviet Occupation of Afghanistan.* London, Methuen, 1984.

Ghaus, Abdul Samad. *The Fall of Afghanistan: An Insider's Account.* Oxford, Pergamon Press, 1988.

Girardet, Edward R. *Afghanistan: The Soviet War.* London, Croom Helm, 1985.

Giustozzi, Antonio. *War, Politics and Society in Afghanistan, 1978–1992.* London, C. Hurst & Co, (Publishers) Ltd, 2000.

Gohari, M. J. *Taliban: Ascent to Power.* Oxford, Oxford University Press, 2001.

Goodson, Larry P. *Afghanistan's Endless War: State Failure, Regional Politics, and the Rise of the Taliban.* Washington, DC, University of Washington Press, 2001.

Gregorian, Vartan. *The Emergence of Modern Afghanistan.* Stanford, CA, Stanford University Press, 1969.

Griffin, Michael. *Reaping the Whirlwind: The Taliban Movement in Afghanistan.* London, Pluto Publishing Ltd, 2001.

Griffiths, John C. *Afghanistan: A History of Conflict.* London, André Deutsch, 2001.

Halliday, Fred. *Islam and the Myth of Confrontation.* London, I. B. Tauris & Co, 1995.

Hopkirk, Peter. *The Great Game.* London, John Murray Publishers Ltd, 1990.

Hyman, Anthony. *Afghanistan under Soviet Domination: 1964–81.* New York, NY, St Martin's Press.

Johnson, Chris. *Afghanistan: A Land in Shadow.* Oxford, Oxfam, 1998.

Kakar, Hasan, *Afghanistan, 1880–1896.* Karachi, 1971.

Government and Society in Afghanistan. Tucson, AZ, University of Arizona Press, 1979.

Khan, M. M. S. M. (Ed.). *The Life of Abdur Rahman, Amir of Afghanistan.* London, John Murray, 1900.

Khan, Riaz M. *Untying the Afghan Knot: Negotiating Soviet Withdrawal.* Durham, North Carolina, Duke University Press, 1991.

Klass, Rosanne (Ed.). *Afghanistan: The Great Game Revisited.* New York, NY, Freedom House, 1988.

Lee, Jonathan L. *The 'Ancient Supremacy': Bukhara, Afghanistan and the Battle for Balkh, 1731–1901.* Leiden, E. J. Brill, 1996.

Macrory, Patrick. *Signal Catastrophe.* London, Hodder and Stoughton, 1966.

Magnus, Ralph. H., and Naby, Eden. *Afghanistan: Marx, Mullah and Mujahid.* Boulder, CO, Westview Press, 1997.

Maley, William (Ed.). *The Foreign Policy of the Taliban.* New York, NY, Council on Foreign Relations, 2000.

Fundamentalism Reborn? Afghanistan and the Taliban. London, C. Hurst & Co (Publishers) Ltd, 2001.

Maley, William, and Saikal, Fazel Haq. *Political Order in Post-Communist Afghanistan.* London, Lynne Rienner Publishers, 1992.

Marsden, Peter. *The Taliban: War, Religion and the New Order in Afghanistan.* London, Zed Books Ltd, 1998.

Masson, V. M., and Romodin, V. A. *Istoriya Afghanistana.* Moscow, Academy of Sciences of the USSR, 1964–65.

Matinuddin, Kamal. *The Taliban Phenomenon: Afghanistan 1994–97*. Karachi, Oxford University Press, 2000.

McChesney, Robert D. *Kabul Under Siege: Fayz Muhammad's Account of the 1929 Uprising*. Princeton, NJ, Markus Wiener Publishers, 1999.

Mohun Lal. *Life of the Amir Dost Mohammed Khan of Kabul*. London, Longman, 1846, reprinted Oxford University Press, 1978.

Nojumi, Neamotollah. *The Rise of the Taliban in Afghanistan: Mass Mobilization, Civil War and the Future of the Region*. London, Palgrave Macmillan, 2002.

Newell, Richard S. *The Politics of Afghanistan*. Ithaca, NY, Cornell University Press, 1972.

Noelle, Christine. *State and Tribe in Nineteenth-Century Afghanistan: The Reign of Amir Dost Muhammad Khan (1826–1863)*. Richmond, Curzon Press, 1998.

Olsen, Asta. *Islam and Politics in Afghanistan*. Scandinavian Institute of Asian Studies—Monograph Series, No. 67, 1996.

Poullada, Leon B. *Reform and Rebellion in Afghanistan, 1919–1929*. Ithaca, NY, Cornell University Press, 1972.

Rahman, Fatuhur, and Bashir, A. Qureshi. *Afghans Meet Soviet Challenge*. Peshawar, Institute of Regional Studies, 1981.

Rashid, Ahmed. *The Resurgence of Central Asia: Islam or Nationalism?* London, Zed Books Ltd, 1994.

Taliban: The Story of the Afghan Warlords. London, Pan Macmillan, 2001.

Reeve, Simon. *The New Jackals: Ramzi Yousef, Osama bin Laden and the Future of Terrorism*. Boston, MA, Northeastern University Press, 1999.

Roy, Olivier. *L'Afghanistan: Islam et modernité politique*. Paris, Seuil, 1985.

Islam and Resistance in Afghanistan. Cambridge University Press, 1987.

Rubin, Barnett. *The Fragmentation of Afghanistan: State Formation and Collapse in the International System*. London, Yale University Press, 1995.

Saikal, Amin, and Maley, William. *Regime Change in Afghanistan: Foreign Intervention and the Politics of Legitimacy*. Boulder, CO, Westview Press, 1991.

Sykes, Sir Percy. *A History of Afghanistan*. London, Macmillan, 1940.

Urban, Mark. *War in Afghanistan*. London, Macmillan Press, 1988.

Victor, Jean-Christophe. *La cité des murmures: L'enjeu afghan*. Paris, Editions J. C. Lattès, 1985.

Waller, John H. *Beyond the Khyber Pass: Road to British Disaster in the First Afghan War*. New York, NY, Random House, 1990.

Yousaf, Mohammed. *Silent Soldier: The Man behind the Afghan Jihad*. Lahore, Jhang Publishers, 1991.

Yousaf, Mohammed, and Adkin, Mark. *The Bear Trap: Afghanistan's Untold Story*. London, Leo Cooper, 1992.

ECONOMY

Fry, Maxwell J. *The Afghan Economy*. Leiden, 1974.

Malekyar, Abdul Wahed. *Die Verkehrsentwicklung in Afghanistan*. Cologne, 1966.

Nägler, Horst. *Privatinitiative beim Industrieaufbau in Afghanistan*. Düsseldorf, Bertelsmann Universitätsverlag, 1971.

Rhein, E. and Ghaussy, A. Ghanie. *Die wirtschaftliche Entwicklung Afghanistans, 1880–1965*. Hamburg, C. W. Leske Verlag, 1966.

AUSTRALIA

Physical and Social Geography

A. E. McQUEEN

With revisions by the editorial staff

The Commonwealth of Australia covers an area of 7,692,030 sq km (2,969,909 sq miles). Nearly 39% of its land mass lies within the tropics; Cape York, the northernmost point, is only 10° S of the Equator. At the other extreme, the southern limit of the mainland lies at 39° S or, if Tasmania is included, at 43° S, a distance on the mainland alone of 3,134 km from north to south. From east to west, Australia spans a distance of 3,782 km.

CLIMATE AND VEGETATION

The wide latitudinal range as well as the size and compact shape of Australia produce a climate with widely varying effects in different parts of the country. The climatic differences can be assigned generally to latitude, and therefore to its liability to influence rainfall either from tropical rain-bearing air masses or from the westerly wind belt which affects the southern areas of Australia. It is important to note, too, that the average elevation of the land surface is only about 275 m; nearly three-quarters of Australia is a great central plain, almost all of it at 185 m–460 m above sea-level, with few high mountains. The Dividing Range, running parallel to most of the east coast, is the most notable; the highest peak, Mt Kosciusko, reaches 2,228 m. This general lack of mountains, coupled with the moderating effects of the surrounding oceans, means that there are fewer abrupt regional climatic changes than would be found on land masses in comparable latitudes elsewhere.

The northern part of the continent, except the Queensland coast, comes under the influence of summer tropical monsoons. This produces a wet summer as the moist air flows in from the north-west; but winter is dry, with the prevailing wind coming from the south-east across the dry interior. Both the north-east and north-west coasts are liable to experience tropical cyclones between December and April, and these storms, with accompanying heavy rain, will occasionally continue some distance inland.

The southern half of Australia lies in the mid-latitude westerly wind belt for the winter half of the year; consequently winter is the wet season. Winter rainfall in the south-east and south-west corners of Australia and Tasmania is particularly high—at least by Australian levels—with maximum falls occurring on the windward sides of the mountains in each area. Rainfall decreases rapidly inland with distance from the coast, with the result that parts of central Australia record some very low annual average rainfall figures; the area of lowest average annual rainfall is the 460,000 sq km around Lake Eyre in South Australia, which receives an average of some 100 mm per year. At the other extreme lies Tully (17° 55′ S), on the east coast of Queensland, with an annual average of 4,048 mm. Overall, few parts of Australia enjoy abundant rainfall; and even where occasional heavy falls are recorded, the unreliability of its seasonal distribution may well lessen its value in terms of pasture growth. Only south-west Western Australia, western Tasmania and Victoria south of the divide can be classed as areas of reliable precipitation; elsewhere reliability decreases away from the coast, with wide variations being recorded at stations such as Whim Creek (20° 52′ S, 117° 51′ E) where 745 mm once fell in a single day, but only 4.3 mm was recorded in all of 1924.

Very high temperatures, sometimes exceeding 50°C (122°F), are experienced during the summer months over the central parts of the country and for some distance to the south, as well as during the pre-monsoon months in the north. Australia's insular nature and other features tend to hold temperatures at a rather lower general level than other southern hemisphere land areas in the same latitudes, but temperatures are high enough to produce an evaporation rate, especially in inland areas, which in turn is high enough to exert a marked influence on soil and vegetation patterns. In much of the interior, xerophytic plant species, such as spinifex, salt bush, blue bush and dwarf eucalyptus, adapted to very dry and variable conditions, are capable of supporting a limited cattle population. Between these arid areas and the zones of higher rainfall lie the semi-arid plains on which the main vegetation is mulga (*Acacia*) and mallee scrub (*Eucalyptus* spp.) in which several stems rise from a common woody base. It is this type of land that carries most of the sheep in New South Wales and Western Australia; it is also here, as well as in the still drier interior, that the major effects of drought are seen—and drought occurs with sufficient regularity to have a limiting effect upon the long-term stock population. Since the 1860s Australia has suffered from 10 major droughts affecting most of the country (most recently in 1991–95), as well as several others causing severe losses in particular areas.

In the colder south-eastern areas the length of the growing season is mainly dependent upon temperatures, but elsewhere the availability of soil moisture is the major variable. The growing season lasts for nine months or more along the east coast and in south-western Australia; elsewhere, and especially in the interior, there are wide variations according to both the intensity and seasonal distribution of rainfall. Underground water supplies are fairly widespread in the semi-arid parts of Australia, including the resources of the Great Artesian Basin, fed from inland slopes of the mountain range to make one of the largest such catchments in the world. In some areas, notably the Barkly Tableland, stock-raising is largely dependent upon bore water.

SOILS AND LAND USE

Soils are very diverse in both type and origin, and are of low natural fertility over large areas, owing to the great geological age of Australia and the subsequent poor qualities of the parent materials. Climate has a marked effect on soil type, with seasonal desiccation and surface erosion coinciding with the extreme dry and wet seasons which affect much of the continent. Salinity and alkalinity are also problems, especially in arid southern Australia.

The generalized pattern of land use falls into three broad zones. The first comprises some 70% of the land area, and covers all central Australia, reaching the coast along the shores of the Bight and in north-west Australia. About one-third of the area is desert, useless for farming; the rest is of only marginal value for pastoral activities, and then only in the areas close to the rather more favourable conditions of the second zone. This second zone covers only some 17% of Australia, and contains a wide variety of climate and soil types; it is included within a broad belt over 300 km wide extending from the Eyre peninsula paralleling the east coast, and across the northern part of Australia to the Kimberleys. In this zone most farming is practised in the temperate part of the area, including the growing of more than 90% of all wheat sown; the zone also supports some 40% of the nation's sheep, 30% of the beef cattle and 20% of the dairy cattle.

The third general zone comprises a belt of land along the east coast from Cairns southward and then westward to south-east South Australia, all of Tasmania, south-west Western Australia and a small part of the Northern Territory around Darwin. Much of this zone (which covers some 13% of the continent) is of broken relief; in the remaining areas the pattern of land use is quite complex. In the northern parts beef grazing dominates, but in the remainder most forms of cropping and livestock production are found. Nearly all Australia's forests are within this zone, as are almost all of the dairying, sugar, fat-lamb, horticulture and high-producing beef cattle areas. The potential for pasture improvement, especially in the southern areas, is considerable.

POPULATION

Although there has been much immigration from Asia, particularly Viet Nam, in recent years, the majority of Australia's population is still of European stock. At the 1991 census 238,950 people were enumerated as Aboriginal people and 26,902 as Torres Strait Islanders. The total population at the census of August 1996 was 17,892,423 (of whom 386,049 were enumerated as Aboriginal and Torres Strait Islanders), giving a density of only 2.3 inhabitants per sq km, one of the lowest national figures in the world. At the census of August 2001 the population was estimated at 18,972,350. In terms of population, as well as land use, Australia can be divided into three broad zones, corresponding, in many respects, to those outlined in the last section: one part almost unpopulated, another sparsely populated and the final part containing the great majority of the people. This distribution pattern means that any discussion of 'averages', in terms of population densities, is of only limited value; this is specially so when the proportion of each state's population living in the respective state capitals is revealed (see Statistical Survey). The concentration of population within each state is matched by a concentration, on a national scale, in the south-east of Australia. New South Wales and Victoria contained almost 59% of the nation's population in 1995; if that of Tasmania is added, the figure exceeds 61%. Over the country as a whole, settlement is closely related to the areas of moderate rainfall and less extreme temperatures, a pattern initiated by the early growth of towns and cities based on a predominantly pastoral farming community dependent upon farm exports for a livelihood. The result has been the rapid growth of settlement around major ports on which state railway systems were centred, and a subsequent development of manufacturing industry at these port centres where imported raw materials were available, where a skilled labour force could be found and where distribution facilities to all parts of the respective states were readily available. Only in Queensland and Tasmania did this basic pattern vary to any extent; in Queensland because of the widespread distribution of intensive farming (especially the cultivation of sugar cane) along a coast well serviced with ports, and in Tasmania because the more dispersed distribution of agricultural and other resources called into being a number of moderate-sized towns and commercial centres.

History

I. R. HANCOCK

COLONIZATION

European colonization of Australia began on 26 January 1788, when a British settlement was established at Port Jackson (now Sydney) under the first Governor of New South Wales (NSW), a colony founded in 1786. Indigenous Australians, the dark-skinned Aboriginal people whose forebears had inhabited the continent for more than 60,000 years, do not celebrate anniversaries of that date (now styled Australia Day) because it recalls the beginnings of land dispossession, massacres and disease, and two centuries of treatment as non-citizens in their own land. White Australians observe the date principally because it provides a holiday weekend; few rejoice in their origins. After all, NSW (which originally included present-day Victoria and Queensland) was founded as a penal colony; it was governed in the early days by undistinguished naval and army officers, policed by the dissolute soldiers of the notorious 'Rum Corps' and populated mostly by the worst elements from British prisons. The subsequent arrival of free settlers, the establishment of the wool industry and the exploration of lands beyond Sydney Cove did not immediately transform the penal settlement into a progressive colony. In 1830 more than 90% of the population of NSW and Van Diemen's Land (the other major penal colony, renamed Tasmania in 1856) were either convicts, former convicts or relatives of convicts.

Yet, by 1840, when the transportation of convicts to NSW was abolished, and the total population had risen to 190,000, it was evident that pockets of permanent, free settlement were forming the basis of new and thriving European communities. Colonization had extended more than 300 km from Sydney, smaller communities had been established in what have become the states of Queensland, Victoria and Western Australia, and contemporary British concepts of systematic colonization were being implanted in South Australia. The prominent members of the colonies were the 'squatters', large-scale sheep-farmers who had taken over grazing-land, and the merchants and small professional class in the towns. The bulk of the free white population consisted of skilled Protestant artisans from England and Scotland, who worked alongside ex-convicts and Irish labourers. They were not refugees from intolerance, or ideologues in pursuit of a different social order. The objective of the settlers was material self-improvement; their concerns were worldly, rather than spiritual; and, if the majority disliked the pretensions of the 'squatter aristocracy', they were all intent on attaining a better standard of living.

The history of white Australia from the 1840s to the 1890s is dominated by three themes. The first of these was a dramatic growth of economic activity, resulting from the expansion of the pastoral and mining industries and of the urban centres. The 'gold rushes' of the 1850s provided some stimulus, especially in Victoria, but the important factors behind the sustained economic boom of 1860–90 were migration, British capital investment and active colonial participation in the development of public works, pastoral farming, mining, small-scale manufacturing and urban land transactions. One effect of the boom was the rapid urbanization of Australian society. By 1891, when the population had risen to 4m., nearly one-third of Australia's inhabitants resided in the colonial capital cities, and almost two-thirds in cities and towns. Australia had become the most urbanized country in the world. A further by-product of the boom was the formation of a social structure which remains in place today; of a substantial urban bourgeoisie (both divided within itself and opposed, in the 19th century, to the pastoral families), and a substantial, although not then permanent, labour force which was becoming highly unionized and which was determined to maintain and improve its standard of living. Finally, the boom created an ambivalent relationship with the British economic system. On the one hand, the Australian colonies were dependencies: they supplied raw materials, bought British manufactures and returned dividends to British investors. On the other hand, economic growth was largely determined by local entrepreneurs who manipulated imported capital in their own interests until the boom faltered in the late 1880s and the London market intervened to assert control over wayward colonial speculators.

The second theme was the expansion of responsible and democratic government. Several communities wanted to separate formally from NSW; all the colonies sought to govern their affairs independently from British government supervision; and urban elements attempted to curb the powers and influence of the established pastoral and mercantile interests. The result was that, by the end of the 1850s, NSW, Queensland, South Australia, Tasmania and Victoria had separate Constitutions, the essential features of responsible government, and a form of parliamentary democracy which included the secret ballot and a wide adult male franchise.

These changes were approved by a British Government that had come to recognize from its North American experience that a devolution of powers was a relatively inexpensive and trouble-free way of manipulating white colonists. Moreover, the Constitutions of the 1850s did not create radical or anti-imperial democracies. Power in colonial politics passed to the urban middle class, to liberals who continued their attack on the bastions of privilege, such as the upper houses of state legislatures, and who used their majorities in the lower houses to regulate wages and working conditions, to release some of the squatters' lands for small farmers, to establish free, compulsory and secular education, and to develop redistributive systems of taxation. However, like their conservative opponents, most colonial liberals remained steadfastly loyal to the British Empire. The bonds of kinship, sentiment, trade and investment, and fears about the physical vulnerability of this outpost of British civilization, were much too strong for most colonial politicians to contemplate republicanism or total separation.

There was, however, a perceptible interest in the concept of an Australian identity. This attempt to invent and popularize a distinctive nationalism formed the third theme dominating Australia's history in the conservative latter part of the 19th century. The origins of this attempt are complex. A critical factor was that, by the time of the 1891 census, more than two-thirds of the population had been born in Australia; another was that Irish-born Australians and others of Irish descent together constituted about 20% of the total population. There was a firm basis upon which to build a separate Australian identity, and a sizeable proportion who had cause to regard Britain as the fountainhead of exploitation and privilege. Not surprisingly, the more vociferous nationalists were found among the Irish and the labouring classes, and their fusion of political radicalism and nationalism was cemented through the growth of the trade union movement in the 1880s and of the colonial Labor parties in the 1890s. Urbanized Australia would find its 'inner self' in legends about the bush (the wild, uncultivated regions of the Australian interior, where men were supposedly egalitarians and rugged individualists). The conservatives, who were empire loyalists, excluded themselves from true nationalism. Non-whites were deliberately left out. Asians (of whom the Chinese, in the 19th century, and the Japanese, in the early 20th century, were the most feared) were regarded as a threat both to Australia's security and (as cheap labour) to the living standards of the European working class.

ECONOMIC DEPRESSION AND POLITICAL FEDERATION

The immediate threat to living standards, however, was posed by the great depression of the 1890s. The unemployment rate rose to 30% of the labour force, there was serious industrial unrest and widespread rural distress, and banks and financial institutions collapsed or suspended business. The causes were both international and domestic, and also, to some extent (because of a prolonged drought), environmental. Significantly, as in 1929, the depression was particularly severe because of extravagant investment policies and because of a tendency among Australians to live beyond their material means. Yet the 1890s were not a period of unrelieved gloom. The nascent Labor parties combined with middle-class liberals to implement more social and political reforms, and the concept of Australia as a 'working man's paradise' began to acquire some credibility. Hesitant moves towards federation also gathered pace, prompted by an increasing concern about defence, a lively propagation of nationalist sentiments and the desire to improve economic co-operation. The economic motive was central. Apart from the obvious advantages of pooling resources, the diverging tariff policies of NSW and Victoria (the one favoured free trade while the other was strongly protectionist) were creating artificial and damaging barriers. Despite set-backs, one of which was that Western Australia almost did not participate, the Federal Constitution received the royal assent in 1900. A decade which had begun so disastrously, and from which, in economic terms, the country did not recover until the Second World War, had ended on a note of some optimism.

The Commonwealth of Australia was formally established on 1 January 1901. White Australians must have felt more conscious of their country's potential than those hapless individuals who had landed at Sydney Cove in 1788. One reason for confidence was that, despite the recent depression and drought, the white population had established a strong export-orientated economy and had implanted and extended the institutions and values of British civilization to all the fertile parts of the continent. Another cause for pride was that Australia had established an advanced social democracy, to such an extent that women were entitled to vote for, and be members of, the Commonwealth Parliament, although convention still decreed that they should see themselves primarily as wives and mothers. The Aboriginal population was not so fortunate. Blacks were not even recorded in official censuses, and it was assumed that they would soon be extinct or become fully assimilated. Asians were not to be admitted. One of the early acts of the Commonwealth was to introduce the 'White Australia' policy (i.e. restricting the right of settlement to Europeans), which was supported by all the factions and parties within the political spectrum. Other policies also emanated from a broadly-based consensus: the principle of a basic minimum wage to provide a reasonable standard of living for a working man, his wife and three children; the regulating of industrial relations through arbitration courts; and the establishment of a local defence force, which included an Australian navy.

The formative years between 1901 and 1914 were important for the development of the modern party system. Colonial political divisions had extended beyond 1901. The tariff issue continued to divide conservatives and liberals, and to foster different state loyalties. However, in 1908–09 the Labor Party abandoned its electoral and parliamentary alliance with the largely middle-class liberal protectionists, grouped around Alfred Deakin from Victoria. Threatened with electoral annihilation, suspicious of Labor's strict caucus system and demands for solidarity from its supporters, and worried that Labor was becoming an avowedly class party, the Deakinites joined the other two non-Labor (and more conservative) parties in federal politics and formed the Fusion. This action established the present division of Australian politics. It also forged a coalition of rural and urban interests which, with the addition of the Country (now National) Party and after undergoing several changes of name, has governed Australia for most of the country's federal history.

The Fusion itself remained in office only briefly in 1909–10. The Labor Party achieved majorities in both the House of Representatives and the Senate (the two chambers of the Federal Parliament) when it won a decisive victory at a general election in 1910. Having formed short-lived minority governments in 1904 and again in 1908–09, Labor could now enact its own programme. Yet, although the conservatives worried about the predatory 'socialist tiger', Labor in office did not, and could not, radically alter the established system. The new Government founded the Commonwealth Bank, formed the Australian navy, introduced a maternity allowance and imposed a mild land tax. Andrew Fisher, the Prime Minister, was neither an ideologue nor a radical. Socialist elements inside and outside the party, and especially in Victoria (where the tradition of extremism still survives), might criticize the parliamentary leadership for sacrificing principles and opportunities, but Fisher could always reply that the Constitution had limited the powers of the Commonwealth Government, had created a conservative High Court which sought to protect private enterprise and states' rights, and had made it very difficult to obtain support for constitutional amendments by means of referenda. More importantly, Fisher knew that his parliamentary party was composed of reformers and nationalists, rather than revolutionaries and socialists, and, in any case, was becoming much more concerned about the menace of Germany than about the operations of capitalism.

THE FIRST WORLD WAR

Labor lost office, briefly, in 1913. The subsequent Liberal Government was forced to call a general election on the eve of the First World War. During his victorious election campaign, Fisher pledged that, in the event of war, Australia would stand by the empire to 'our last man and our last shilling'. In August 1914, when the United Kingdom (UK) entered the war, the prospect of having to honour the pledge seemed to be remote, and most Australians endorsed his sentiment. Young men from all backgrounds rushed to join the Australian Imperial Force

(AIF). A mere handful of socialists, pacifists and feminists questioned the 'obligation' to fight Europe's war, or wondered why conservative empire loyalists and radical nationalists were fighting together for 'King and Country'. This remarkable consensus soon fractured because the conflict became protracted, with Australian forces involved in bloody campaigns at Gallipoli (in Turkey) and in Flanders (Belgium); because the working class felt that it was bearing the brunt of high prices, low wages and unemployment; and because the Labor Government (led, after 1915, by W. M. (Billy) Hughes) had abandoned all interest in social reform in its bid to win the war before dealing with any other issue.

The consensus was irreparably shattered in late 1916, when the Government proposed to conscript young men for overseas service. The decision exposed deep ethnic, religious and class divisions in Australian society, which had been momentarily submerged beneath the effusions of loyalty to the empire and the universal pride in the achievements of the 'diggers' at Anzac Cove during the Gallipoli campaign. The Irish Roman Catholics, in particular, had lost much of their enthusiasm for the imperial cause, following the executions of Irish nationalists after the anti-British Easter rising in Dublin in 1916. They opposed conscription, along with the bulk of organized labour. The conscription issue, in fact, split the Labor Party, which Hughes left after narrowly losing a national plebiscite on the question in October 1916. He joined, and led his former conservative and liberal opponents in, the new Nationalist Party, and left a bitter legacy among his former Labor colleagues. By the time of the second plebiscite on conscription in December 1917 (which was also lost, by a slightly greater margin), the consensus of 1914 was a distant memory.

Nearly 60,000 Australians died in the First World War, and two-thirds of those who embarked with the AIF became casualties. There were few glorious victories, and one notable defeat. The AIF had fought well at Gallipoli, but the campaign had ended in a humiliating withdrawal. Nevertheless, many historians regard Gallipoli and the war itself as instruments in Australia's progression from a federation to a nation. Perhaps there has been less emphasis in recent years on the nation-building characteristics of the AIF, although, in the longer perspective, it remains true that the character of Australian nationalism was affected by the experiences of the First World War. Nationalism became associated with political conservatism, a change which was signified by the non-Labor group's adoption of the title 'Nationalist', by its strong support for (and from) the soldiers who had returned from the war, and by its assumption of Labor's role as the party most committed to national defence. 'Nationalism' remained an exclusive property, although it had temporarily changed hands, and it could now be used by any section of Australian society to promote and legitimize its cause.

THE INTER-WAR PERIOD

Like the rest of the Western world in 1918, when the First World War ended, Australians set out to enjoy the peace. There was prosperity for some, but for most Australians the 1920s were years of contradiction. Unemployment never fell below 6.5%, there was considerable turmoil in the power and transport industries, the discord stirred by the conscription debates spilled over into class antagonism, and some disillusioned ex-servicemen were attracted to right-wing extremism. The Nationalists, who had replaced Hughes by Stanley (later Lord) Bruce in 1923 and had formed a coalition Government with the new Country Party, wanted to pursue a policy of national development based upon a migration programme, capital investment, expanding trade, industrialization and closer rural settlement. The slogan of the 1920s—'Men, Money, Markets'—neatly encapsulated their objectives. The omission of any reference to social experimentation was significant. Labor Governments in some Australian states introduced additional welfare programmes, but the prevailing orthodoxy had abandoned the social laboratory and the 'working man's paradise'. Development, rather than redistribution, was considered to be the correct path to a better standard of living. To this end, trade union demands for higher wages and shorter working hours had to be resisted; employers reduced their costs simply by shutting down uneconomic enterprises, and Bruce became preoccupied with the regulation of industrial relations. His long-term solutions were to rely on the market, and to give the states responsibility for industrial arbitration, rather than the Commonwealth Government. This latter decision led to his defeat by a revived Labor Party at the 1929 general election.

James Scullin, the Labor leader, became Prime Minister of Australia just one month before the 'crash' on the New York stock market sent the Western world into a devastating economic depression. Although Australia could not have escaped the disaster, the effects were exacerbated by the policies that had been adopted during the 1920s. Both the Commonwealth and State Governments had borrowed heavily from the British capital market to finance rural development, urban construction and transport programmes. Much of this investment was either unproductive or likely to be productive only in the long term. The extent of borrowing can be measured by the fact that in 1928 the annual payments on public loans accounted for 28% of Australia's export income. When that income collapsed between 1928 and 1930, and when the London market refused to provide further loans and massive repayments on short-term borrowing became due, the Australian economy experienced a deeper depression than most other Western countries. Unemployment rose to nearly 30% in 1932. According to the 1933 census, one-half of unemployed males had been out of work for at least two years, and one-tenth had been unemployed for four years or more. Recovery was eventually assisted by the developing manufacturing sector, which had sheltered behind high tariff barriers since 1921. It was completed only with the outbreak of war in September 1939.

The depression of the 1930s had a major impact on Australian politics. The Governments that were in power in late 1929 were defeated in subsequent elections. Meanwhile, the Labor Party experienced another split. The right-wing members departed, and their leader, Joseph Lyons, a former Premier of Tasmania, became Prime Minister of a non-Labor coalition. The immediate cause of the split was an argument about policies for dealing with the depression. Essentially, it was a debate about whether to balance budgets or to increase expenditure. Orthodox economists, the Bank of England and the major financial institutions in Australia adopted the conservative approach and, through the majority of non-Labor groups in the Senate and their control of the Commonwealth Bank, were able to impose their will on the Labor Government. Lyons favoured reductions in wage rates and the honouring of overseas debts; J. T. Lang, the contentious Labor Premier of NSW, advocated the repudiation of such debts; Lang's rivals in the party concentrated on a programme of expanding public works to solve unemployment and to increase demand. Labor, in fact, split several ways, and Scullin was unable to control the factions. After Lyons had left the party, Labor was defeated at the 1931 general election; Lang, who was dismissed by the Governor of NSW, continued to quarrel with the official Labor Party in his state; and Labor remained out of federal office until John Curtin became Prime Minister in 1941, replacing Robert (later Sir Robert) Menzies, who had succeeded Lyons on his death in 1939.

WAR AND ITS AFTERMATH

The Second World War, which Australia entered in September 1939 (when Britain declared war on Germany), marked a shift from dependence upon the UK to dependence upon the USA. The fall of Singapore to Japanese forces and the subsequent defeat of Britain's Royal Navy in Asian waters in early 1942 forced the Curtin Government to seek US assistance to contain the Japanese advance. Now, more than 50 years later, Australian Governments still play the same junior (and generally supportive) role in US strategy. The ANZUS treaty, which was signed by Australia, New Zealand and the USA in 1951, during the Korean War, enshrined the relationship which had been developed during the wartime alliance, and has continued to be regarded by Australians as the guarantee of their security, even after New Zealand was effectively excluded by the USA in 1984 for banning vessels believed to be powered by nuclear energy or to be carrying nuclear weapons.

A second development after 1945, when the Second World War ended, saw Australians become more closely involved in their immediate region and in the wider world. Improved communications, the expansion of private travel, business, sport, diplomacy and educational exchanges all contributed to a greater awareness of non-British societies. The campaign against Japan during the Second World War also contributed to this process by forcing Australians to acknowledge that Asia, rather than Europe, would determine their future. For some Australians, the war also compounded the historic fear of the 'yellow peril', and, for that reason, its role in ending isolation was double-edged: the acceptance of Australia's location on the perimeter of Asia was accompanied by a tendency to regard the region as a potential battleground, to identify Asian nationalists as 'communists' and to rely upon defensive alliances with 'safe' Asian regimes.

A third development was the decision to launch a migration programme. Previous arguments about the need to 'populate or perish' were reinforced by Japanese wartime successes in the Pacific Ocean. Traditionally suspicious of migration schemes for their effect on employment prospects, Labor in government in the 1940s argued that migrants were needed to develop Australia's post-war economy. The motives were almost entirely utilitarian: Australia needed skilled and unskilled labour, it needed to raise consumer demand and it sought to populate the empty spaces. The only real 'human' concern was whether 'British' Australians would, in the absence of sufficient migrants from the UK, accept tens of thousands of displaced persons from war-devastated Europe.

The post-war migration programme changed the face of Australian society. By the early 1980s a population of nearly 16m. people included fewer than 70% of British stock, and more than 100 nationalities (the latter swelled in number by the admission of immigrants from the Middle East in the 1960s, and from Asia in the 1970s). The vast majority of 'British' Australians managed to ignore the 'New Australians' for 20 years, but they could not do so indefinitely. Successive Australian Governments recognized that migrants did not automatically assimilate, and that a high proportion of them were exploited and lived in poverty. Official policy now promotes the theme of 'multi-culturalism', while implementing schemes of migrant-support and language-training. Meanwhile, the former 'White Australia' policy and the exclusively utilitarian approaches have been replaced by policies that accept migrants who are refugees, who possess needed skills or who qualify under a family reunion scheme. It is not clear how far 'British' Australians have accepted these changes. Tensions, exacerbated by economic recession, are apparent in those working-class suburbs where the non-white migrants have congregated. On the other hand, the older non-British immigrants, particularly Greeks and Italians, now wield considerable political influence and are making an impact on Australian cultural development.

Another by-product of the Second World War was that thousands of women were introduced into the labour market, and into jobs that hitherto had been regarded as 'men's work'. Enlistments for service in the armed forces, Australia's role of supplying raw materials for the armed assault on the Japanese, and fear of invasion were the key factors in breaking down the barriers. A significant outcome was the demand by women that they should enjoy parity of wages for this work and not the 54% of a man's wage which they had been receiving for 'women's work'. This demand was resisted by employers, who regarded women as a reserve of cheap labour; by moralists, who worried about women's attitudes to their primary roles as wives and mothers; and by some of the unions, who feared that women would eventually replace men in some jobs. Although the Government decided that women should receive at least 90% of the male wage for the duration of the war, the principle of equal pay was not formally conceded until 30 years later. Nor did the entry of large numbers of women into the work-force mean that they remained there: the end of the war brought a mass return to domestic pursuits. Nevertheless, thousands of young women had experienced a different life, and many of them, from choice or necessity, returned to work during the 1950s. By the late 1970s the next generation was demanding, and sometimes achieving, a wider and more profound form of recognition.

Finally, the war marked a turning-point for the Labor Party. Labor regarded the war, and its own return to power, as an opportunity to reconstruct society and to ensure its place as the 'natural' Government of Australia. A decisive electoral victory in 1943 gave Curtin—and, after Curtin's death in 1945, Joseph Chifley—sufficient parliamentary strength for the Government to survive any immediate popular hostility to social engineering. The Governments of the 1940s intended to nationalize the banking system, to expand social services, to implement schemes of national development and to ensure full employment. By the 1949 general election, however, a majority of the electorate had become discontented with 'socialist' controls, consumer restraint and trade-union militancy. Menzies, leading the new Liberal Party, returned to power on promises of combating communism and liberating the economy. The Liberals (in coalition with the Country Party) espoused the popular policies for the age of affluence and the 'Cold War', while Labor retained policies and rhetoric that were more suited to the era of depression, and the party remained in federal opposition for the next 23 years.

LIBERAL DOMINANCE, 1949–72

There are several reasons why the Liberals held power for so long. First, there was the world economic boom which, in Australia, was characterized and promoted by massive inflows of capital, by immigration and by industrialization. Most Australians enjoyed a vastly improved standard of living in the 1950s and 1960s, and the maintenance of this prosperity, together with the capacity to meet rising expectations, depended upon the continued expansion of the economy. Expansion was therefore crucial to the Liberal hegemony: significantly, the two occasions on which Menzies came close to electoral defeat—in 1954 and 1961—coincided with periods of economic contraction. For the most part, and despite the fact that Australia's economic performance did not match that of comparable countries, Menzies and his successors reaped the benefits of sustained growth and rising living standards.

A second reason for the longevity of Liberal rule was another split in the Labor Party. The issue was communism, complicated by sectarianism. From the mid-1940s, so-called 'industrial groups' had been successfully challenging communist influence in the trade union movement. Official Labor policy supported these groups but there was growing disquiet: Protestants regarded the Roman Catholic influence over the groups with suspicion; secularists denounced religious pressure; and the radical left-wing elements regarded intense anti-communism as an excuse to stifle their militancy. Dr Herbert Evatt, a former High Court judge who had succeeded Chifley as Labor leader in 1951, brought the dispute to a head in late 1954. The avowedly anti-communist (and predominantly Roman Catholic) wing of the Labor Party broke away in 1955, and used its voting power, through the preference system, to keep Labor out of federal office, and out of power in Queensland and Victoria. Apart from breaking the traditional links between working-class Roman Catholics and the Labor Party (a process which was assisted by the arrival of non-Irish Roman Catholic migrants), the Roman Catholic factions were now openly opposing each other. The principal beneficiaries were the non-Labor parties.

A third, and closely related, factor behind the Liberals' long reign was their ability to exploit the 'Cold War' and the historic fears of invasion from the north. Communism was now viewed as the most significant threat, and Asia was seen as a region of potential danger. Australia's Communist Party wielded little influence, even though Menzies attempted to ban it in 1951, but he skilfully elevated fears of communism into the central issue at successive national elections. Moreover, he was always able to make the damaging charge that the Labor Party, after its split, was sympathetic to communism. In this sense, the Viet Nam war was a bonus: the Government could enter the war, in an attempt to stem the 'red tide', by offering token military support to the USA (in the form of a small task force), thereby ensuring continued US support for the ANZUS pact. Additionally, the opponents of Australia's involvement in Viet Nam could be accused of undermining the country's long-term security. Ironically, at a general election in 1966 (50 years after Hughes had failed to carry the first conscription plebiscite in what had been a war supported by consensus), the Australian electorate gave the non-Labor parties their largest-ever parliamentary majority to that date, on the issues of fighting in Viet Nam and sending conscripts.

LABOR ASCENDANCY, 1972–96

Menzies retired from politics in 1966. No subsequent leader achieved his command of the federal parliamentary Liberal Party which, for the next two decades, was afflicted by personal feuds, power struggles, ideological disputes and disagreements with the Country (renamed National) Party. Apart from Malcolm Fraser, a grazier from Victoria, who led the Liberals between 1975 and 1983, Menzies' successors were mostly amiable but often second-rate, and were surrounded by mediocre personalities.

The Labor Party benefited from the domestic problems of the coalition. Led by Gough Whitlam, an able lawyer and charismatic leader, following the electoral disaster of 1966, Labor shed its image as the party of the 1930s and abandoned its policies of nationalization. Seeking, instead, to represent the grievances and idealism of educated urban radicals, Labor set out to improve the quality of life for all Australians, while emphasizing its concern for such disadvantaged groups as women, Aborigines, migrants and the poor. After achieving a big swing in the 1969 elections, Labor entered the 1972 campaign with a persuasive theme: 'It's time for a change'. Labor was now modern and respectable, and the electorate voted to end 23 years of coalition rule.

Labor's misfortune was to regain power just at the end of the long economic boom. A reforming government was bound to increase public spending, thereby fuelling inflation without reducing unemployment. The world recession was partly to blame, and the troubles of this inexperienced Labor Government were magnified by the ruthless tactics of the non-Labor parties in the Senate, where Labor did not have a majority. The Government, however, was also to blame for its early demise in 1975. Whitlam and his ministers tried to do too much too soon: they spent unwisely, behaved arrogantly and harboured too many financial and moral scandals. An unusual action brought them down. The non-Labor parties used the Senate to hold up the budget, and the Governor-General dismissed the Prime Minister on 11 November 1975 and dissolved the Parliament. There was talk of revolution in the streets, and Whitlam called on the people 'to maintain their rage'. In fact 'Whitlamism' and not the dismissal was the issue. Malcolm Fraser, the fourth Liberal leader since Menzies, won the largest parliamentary majority in federal history. Two years later, with Whitlam still leading the Labor Party, Fraser again won decisively.

Although the coalition held federal office from 1975 to March 1983, Labor's long-term future was much brighter than the setbacks of 1975 and 1977 indicated. Firstly, the party, under William Hayden, who succeeded Whitlam, converted the heady idealism of the late 1960s into practical goals, a transition more readily achieved in the states where Labor won several victories from the mid-1970s. Secondly, the federal coalition was undermined or thwarted by its own ministerial scandals and resignations, by a lack of nerve in translating rhetoric into action, by the newly-formed Australian Democrats who took the balance of power in the Senate and, most important of all, by its failure to solve the twin problems of inflation and unemployment (both reached 10% by 1983). Fraser was narrowly returned to power in 1980 but, after calling an early election in March 1983, lost to a confident Labor Party now led by Robert (Bob) Hawke, a former President of the Australian Council of Trade Unions (ACTU).

By late 1990 Labor held power in five of the six states, had won three more federal elections (1984, 1987 and 1990) and Hawke had entered an unprecedented fourth term as Labor Prime Minister. The Federal Government had drastically cut back government expenditure in trying to balance the budget, and it had opened up the financial markets, invited foreign banks to operate in the country, floated the Australian dollar, reduced company and income tax, cut back the protective tariff and adopted the 'user pays' philosophy. The party of Ben Chifley was now applauded by corporate managers, millionaire investors and media magnates, while the ACTU leadership formed a congenial relationship with business and government and was committing itself to enterprise bargaining.

Despite community discontent, and the hardships arising from the collapse of commodity prices in 1986 and of the international share markets in 1987, the main opposition parties failed to combat the new Labor ascendancy. The opposition promised huge tax cuts, lower mortgage rates and greater deregulation and privatization of the economy. The coalition, however, lacked direction, appeared improbable as the defender of the underprivileged, could offer nothing to the environmentalists (who, throughout the late 1980s, steadily built a strong electoral base), and was weakened by the electoral decline of the National Party in Queensland and northern NSW, amidst accusations of corruption and neglect.

Nevertheless, by early 1993, the Labor Government seemed destined for defeat. In the Labor heartland the Federal Government's policies had intensified the effects of the world recession, and the rate of unemployment had risen to 10%. The business community was concerned by the rising level of international debt, rural areas were depressed by recurrent drought and poor commodity prices, and small businesses and financial conglomerates were collapsing. The environmentalists, meanwhile, were questioning the Federal Government's commitment. Furthermore, two State Labor governments—in Victoria and Western Australia—had been defeated following revelations of financial mismanagement. Paul Keating, the Treasurer, had become Prime Minister at the end of 1991 following a bitter power struggle with Hawke. Although regarded as a first-rate parliamentary performer, Keating's arrogance irritated many voters. Moreover, the Liberal-National coalition, now led by John Hewson, a presentable economics professor of working-class origins, appealed to the development-conscious and recession-weary with a comprehensive 'Fightback!' programme, which promised radical income tax cuts to offset a goods and services tax.

Yet, in March 1993, Labor actually doubled its small majority in an election where the unemployment figures alone would have been expected to bring down a government. Keating had effectively depicted the coalition's comprehensive programmes for deregulating education, health, and industrial relations as socially divisive, and especially harmful to the poor, ethnic groups and women. Labor presented itself as the saviour of an Australia destined for a heartless and tax-burdened future, while Hewson openly confronted a cautious electorate with destabilizing and costly remedies.

Keating, however, misinterpreted the election result of 1993, believing that he had a mandate to implement his own agenda: the 'Mabo' legislation (approved by Parliament in December of that year and named after the claimant, Eddie Mabo, whereby Aboriginal people were granted the right to claim title to their traditional lands) to effect an historic reconciliation with Aboriginal people; a closer economic and political association with Asia; more funding for the arts; and the transformation of Australia into a republic. In fact, the electorate disliked Keating's Government, but could not accept the Hewson alternative. After three further years of Keating's perceived arrogance, of lectures extolling a 'big picture' (which most Australians neither understood nor cared for), of unfulfilled promises, and of handouts to allegedly 'privileged' minorities and favoured interest groups, at the election of 2 March 1996 the voters turned in their thousands to the coalition parties. John Howard, a revived leader from the post-Fraser era (who had replaced Alexander Downer, Hewson's successor as leader of the Liberal Party, in January 1995), won such an overwhelming victory that Labor's federal heartland contracted to parts of the south-east corner of the country.

A CONSERVATIVE AUSTRALIA

The Howard approach, replicated to some extent in the states, combined a post-Keynesian economic liberalism with a formidable moral and social conservatism. Thus, the Government pared back or 'outsourced' services and sought to reform workplace relations in order to reduce the role of arbitration and the power of the trade unions, and to eliminate inefficiencies and uncompetitive practices. It was more concerned with tax reform than welfare, less interested in Aboriginal reconciliation than in attempting to thwart the High Court decision that allowed native title to co-exist with pastoral and mining leases. A cost-cutting Government, which by 1999 had successfully created a substantial budget surplus and which wanted to recreate the relaxed and prosperous Menzies years when family values were more firmly implanted, was finding it difficult, however, to reduce unemployment, boost small business, effect full workplace reform, improve the prospects for those in 'the bush' and secure the implementation of its tax programme.

Several factors rendered the Government's task more difficult. First, the Asian economic crisis caused general uncertainty from mid-1997, and specifically affected the tourist and export industries (although the latter did benefit from the declining value of the Australian dollar). Nevertheless, the economic policies pursued by the Howard Government enabled Australia to withstand the worst of the Asian crisis. Second, the Government committed a number of political blunders—most notably, in imposing higher charges on those entering homes for the aged, in proceeding too zealously with dockside reform (leading to an acrimonious dispute over trade unionists' rights), and in failing to maintain consistent standards with regard to the pecuniary interests of its ministers. Third, the Government, and especially the National Party, lost support because of the emergence of the One Nation Party. Pauline Hanson, a former Liberal candidate and fish-and-chip shop owner, exploited a racial prejudice that is almost as long-standing as the European history of Australia. Formed in early 1997, the new grouping attracted clamorous support from among the hitherto silent or silenced voters who objected to Asian immigration and to special treatment for Aboriginal people. Above all, One Nation benefited from hostility towards government intervention in the economy, high unemployment, the established political parties and politicians in general. In 1998 One Nation preferences helped to defeat the Liberal-National Coalition Government in Queensland and, in October of that year, polled nearly 1m. votes in a federal election, which Howard had called to obtain a mandate for the introduction of a goods and services tax (GST) and the full privatization of the telecommunications sector. Although Hanson herself was defeated, One Nation made some inroads into the coalition's vote and it won a Senate seat, while anger about Howard's refusal to advance reconciliation and his early willingness to tolerate Hansonism certainly reduced support for the coalition.

The election of October 1998 revealed one of the paradoxes of modern Australian politics. An avowedly conservative Government had challenged Australians to accept radical reform, and the electorate responded by nearly electing an historically more radical Labor Party, in order to conserve the past. One effect of the election was to encumber the Liberal-National Government with an even more hostile Senate. No Government has controlled the Senate since July 1981 because the electoral system of proportional representation (introduced in 1949) has allowed independents and minor parties to hold the balance of power. Between 1996 and June 1999 that balance was shared by two independents who were formerly members of the Labor Party. A key figure was Brian Harradine, an independent from Tasmania and an old-style, right-wing trade unionist and devout Catholic, who represented the smallest Australian state and was elected with fewer than 25,000 primary votes. In May 1999 he effectively defeated the Government's plan to introduce its original GST. From July (when the Senators elected in October 1998 took their seats) a majority of the Australian Democrats, who now held the balance of power in the upper house, forced the Government to revise the GST in order to exclude some food items and to ensure greater protection for the environment. The outcome was a tax regime so complex that few could understand it, and so unwieldy that even its supporters were having doubts about its value.

Meanwhile, John Howard, the most socially-conservative Prime Minister since Menzies, continued to resist demands that he grant a formal apology on behalf of the Australian people to the 'stolen generation'; that is, to part-Aboriginal children who had been forcibly removed from their homes to be fully assimilated into 'White Australia'. The Prime Minister refused to involve himself fully in the campaign for reconciliation between White and Aboriginal Australia, and ruled out any notion of a treaty. The Government also repudiated the findings of two UN reports, released in March and July 2000, which were highly critical of Australia's treatment of the Aboriginal population. The reports focused upon the mandatory prison sentences for minor property offences in force in the Northern Territory and Western Australia, which appeared to target juvenile Aborigines. In August 2000, at the conclusion of a test case brought in the Northern Territory by two members of the 'stolen generation', who hoped to win compensation for the trauma occasioned by their removal from their families, the Federal Court ruled that the Government was not obliged to pay punitive damages to the two Aboriginal claimants, on the grounds of insufficient evidence. As many as 30,000 similar cases had been pending. To some extent encouraged by this decision, the Government continued in 2000–02 to resist demands for an apology and for compensation and instead, drawing some support from significant figures within the Aboriginal communities, declared itself committed to solving the basic problems of education, health and housing. Derided by Aboriginal leaders and by left-wing liberals as reactionary, Howard sensed that the silent majority accepted his agenda. Moreover, he knew how to exploit division. He successfully campaigned for the retention of the monarchy in the referendum of November 1999 on the question of the introduction of a republican system of government. Pro-republicans voted against the proposed republic as they objected to the particular 'politicians' model' (largely Howard's creation) being offered. (Opinion polls had indicated that more than two-thirds of Australians would support the introduction of a republican system if the head of state were to be directly elected.)

It is becoming very difficult to discern the lasting trends in Australian politics. Assuming that there is no sudden and fundamental reversal, the traditional certainties—a high tariff barrier, 'White Australia' (despite the emergence of One Nation), a benign welfare state and a centralized arbitration system—have been the casualties of the last 20 to 30 years. It is unclear, however, just what the Australian electorate wants in their place. By the late 1990s Australian voters, never enamoured of politicians, were even more likely to oust a government without regard for its subsequent replacement. By 2002 the non-Labor Governments of Victoria, Western Australia and South Australia, and of the Northern Territory and of the Australian Capital Territory, had all been defeated. Labor administrations thus governed in all the states and the territories but, with the exception of the NSW and Queensland Labor Governments (which were re-elected in 1999 and 2001 respectively), Labor's overall primary vote continued to decline in state elections. The party had to rely on electoral dissatisfaction with the incumbent governments and in some cases, somewhat to its embarrassment, on the preference votes of One Nation supporters.

By March 2001 it seemed that the Howard Government would suffer the same fate as the State and Territory non-Labor administrations. Its traditional supporters—small businesses, self-funded retirees and residents of the 'bush'—were angry about the GST and what they saw as a decline in benefits and services. Opinion polls were pointing to a landslide victory for Labor at the forthcoming federal election, due by the end of the year. The Government succeeded, however, in minimizing the effects of the world recession upon the economy and, in a period of growth, appealed to those defined as 'aspirational' voters, principally the residents of the outer metropolitan area of Sydney and Melbourne who were primarily interested in improving their standard of living. Labor's level of popularity was already rising in the opinion polls when, from August 2001, the Government unexpectedly found itself able to exploit the issues of immigration, adopting an uncompromising policy on asylum-seekers, and of international terrorism.

Although Australia had been accepting some 12,000 refugees annually, the Government was not prepared to accept those claiming to be asylum-seekers who tried to enter the country illegally. Since 2000 a number had arrived on overcrowded and often unseaworthy boats at the Australian dependency of Christmas Island or on the Western Australian coast, whereupon they were placed in remote detention centres while their applications for admission were slowly processed. The Government, which described them as 'queue jumpers' and illegal immigrants, believed that most of those coming from Afghanistan, Iran and Iraq did not in fact qualify for refugee status. Matters came to a head at the end of August 2001 when a Norwegian container ship, the *Tampa*, rescued 433 people from a sinking boat off Christmas Island and the Government refused the vessel permission to enter Australian waters. The subsequent week-long dispute ended only when the Government agreed to ferry the asylum-seekers on board the *Tampa* to New Zealand and Nauru (and promised to reimburse the latter's costs) where their applications for admission to Australia as refugees would be processed. Shortly afterwards the Government adopted the so-called 'Pacific Solution', whereby neighbouring South Pacific nations agreed to accept asylum-seekers while their claims were being processed in exchange for financial aid. The whole issue of asylum-seekers assumed greater significance following the terrorist attacks on the USA on 11 September 2001. Majority public opinion, already supportive of the Government's stand over 'illegal immigrants', moved even more strongly in its favour when Howard aligned Australia with President George W. Bush's 'war against terrorism' and resisted demands to release asylum-seekers from mandatory detention. The popularity of the once-beleaguered Howard Government thus soared. Responding to the popular mood, the Labor Party, led since 1996 by Kim Beazley, the son of a Whitlam Government minister, agreed to support Howard's position on asylum-seekers and the 'war on terrorism'. As a result, Labor managed to restrict the swing towards the Government to just 2% at the federal election held on 10 November, promising to 'roll back' parts of the GST. Nevertheless, Labor lost votes to the Greens and to the Australian Democrats, who had been critical of the Government's stand on the refugee issue, while former Labor strongholds, especially around Sydney, were won, convincingly, by Liberal candidates. The Liberal-National coalition therefore won 82 of the 150 seats in the House of Representatives, thus narrowly securing a third consecutive term of office. Labor took two fewer seats than at the previous federal election, winning 65. The One Nation Party won no seats in either the House of Representatives or the Senate. (In December Pauline Hanson resigned as leader of the One Nation Party to concentrate on contesting charges of electoral fraud brought against her in July 2001.)

Having lost the election it expected to win, the Labor Party, now led by Simon Crean, a former President of the ACTU and the son of another minister of the Whitlam Government, entered a period of introspection and recrimination. It made little headway against the Government despite rising interest rates and a budget in May 2002 that reduced disability allowances and raised pharmaceutical costs. Furthermore, as controversy over the 'Pacific Solution' continued, grants of up to $A10,000 for each family were offered as an incentive for asylum-seekers to leave the region. For its part, the Government attempted to seal Australia's borders by eliminating all areas beyond the mainland where potential immigrants might make an initial application for admission. Bolstered by a UN finding in June 2002 that most of the asylum-seekers on *Tampa* were not genuine refugees, the Government continued to exploit the issues of border security and the 'war on terrorism', as well as the strength of the economy, to maintain its hold on public opinion. John Howard, so often dismissed by the media and in radical circles as a mere suburban solicitor, had become one of only five Australian Prime Ministers to have won three or more successive federal elections. As had happened to many of his predecessors, on both sides of politics, war had drawn him closer to the USA. His challenge in 2002, however, was to use Australia's commitment to the 'war on terrorism' to win concessions from the USA over its trade tariffs, which had affected the Australian economy and the Liberal-National coalition's rural constituency in particular. In the mean time, Howard was obliged to deal with the leadership ambitions of Peter Costello, his Treasurer, a situation reminiscent of that preceding the disintegration of the Hawke-Keating relationship in 1991.

Arguably, under Howard, Australia has become a harder, meaner place. Although the Anglo-Celt hegemony is slowly giving way to a multi-cultural society, the question now is whether Australia will remain tolerant and free of ethnic tensions. It faced other problems in 2001–02. There was the growing division between rich and poor, the increasing resentment against globalization, and the repercussions of the spectacular collapses of an insurance conglomerate, of a major telecommunications company and of the country's second airline. Furthermore, authority was to some extent under siege because of the accusations levelled against Australia's Governor-General, a former Anglican Archbishop, and also a Catholic Archbishop that they, along with their respective churches, had supported members of the clergy guilty of child sexual abuse and disregarded the perpetrators' victims.

Perhaps the one enduring feature is that White Australians still assume that life and politics are about delivering a better standard of living. The better-off and the employed will continue to support the political party or the system that enhances, or at least preserves, their level of disposable income, keeps inflation and interest rates under control, and provides their children with a decent education and their families with a satisfactory health service.

AUSTRALIA AND ASIA

In the late 1990s the One Nation phenomenon and events in East Timor threatened attempts, in progress since the 1960s, to place Australia more firmly within the Asian environment. Historically, White Australians regarded Asia with apprehension. They saw their country as a European offshoot, geographically isolated and ever in danger from the 'yellow peril': from invasion, 'swamping', cheap goods, inexpensive labour and alien cultures. First, it was the Chinese on the gold-fields in the 1850s; then, in the 20th century, it was the Japanese. Australians could never quite resolve whether they despised the supposedly inferior or feared the possibly superior. Either way, the Immigration Restriction Act of 1901 would save Australia from 'Asianization'. Subsequently, the Second World War and concerns about communism ensured that contacts with Asia emphasized military alliances (notably the South-East Asia Treaty Organization—SEATO), identifying real and potential Asian enemies. Even so, aid programmes, expanding trade, closer diplomatic and educational links and two-way tourism fostered official and informal relations. The Whitlam Government recognized the communist People's Republic of China (diplomatic relations being established in December 1972), Hawke successfully sought the formation of the Asia-Pacific Economic Co-operation forum (APEC, the inaugural conference of which took place in Canberra in November 1989), and all Governments since the 1960s have striven for a closer association with Asia.

Inevitably, successive Australian Governments and the business community have been obliged to compromise principles for the sake of friendship and trade. Shocked by the massacre in Tiananmen Square in Beijing in 1989, all Governments since then have proceeded carefully with regard to issues of human rights in China, although it was worth noting that by 2002 the conservative John Howard had held meetings with President Jiang Zemin more often than he had met any other world leader. Closer to home, East Timorese support groups, along with critics of corruption and authoritarianism in Indonesia, failed to persuade successive Australian Governments that their strong support for President Suharto was unacceptable. Pragmatism thus triumphed over a concern for democracy and human rights, in a sense suggesting that historic fears of Asia had merely been supplemented by a recognition of economic opportunities. In defence of these opportunities, Australia willingly joined attempts to support the ailing Asian economies following the crisis of 1997. Furthermore, to signal gratitude and support for an old ally, the Howard Government was one of the last to acknowledge that Suharto could not remain in power. Equally, the Government refused to demand strong action by his successor, President B. J. Habibie, when in 1999 it became clear that Indonesia's armed forces were aiding local Timorese militias that were attacking outspoken supporters of full independence for East Timor. Nevertheless, the Australian Government did support the referendum in East Timor held in August 1999, provided unarmed police officers to protect the process, and then sought UN intervention when the territory's overwhelming vote for independence led to the destruction of life and property by pro-Jakarta militias and elements of the Indonesian army (see chapter on East Timor). Australia also contributed the commander and (in its biggest operation since the Viet Nam War) the largest single contingent (4,500 personnel) to the International Force for East Timor (Interfet) and, subsequently, some 2,000 personnel to the UN Transitional Administration in East Timor (UNTAET). Thus, after decades of fostering friendly relations, Australia's relationship with Indonesia was now severely strained; in response, in mid-2000 President Abdurrahman Wahid of Indonesia, who replaced Habibie, postponed his visit to Australia. Furthermore, it hardly helped the overall relationship with Asia when John Howard appeared to suggest that Australia would act as the USA's 'deputy sheriff' in the region.

After several postponements, Howard and Wahid finally met in Canberra in June 2001, but a month later Wahid was removed from office and replaced by Megawati Sukarnoputri. Although tensions did ease during the latter part of 2001 and in the period prior to the formal declaration of East Timorese independence in May 2002, the Australian Government continued to argue that Indonesian-supported militia leaders and Indonesian generals should be tried for the atrocities committed in 1999–2000. There also remained concerns that Indonesia might experience a military coup and that separatist and religious movements might cause the distintegration of Indonesia itself. In either event, the whole region would become more volatile. The issue of people-smuggling also threatened the Australia-Indonesia relationship because Canberra believed that the Indonesian Government was not doing enough to control the use of its own waters. Nevertheless, Howard visited Indonesia in early 2002 and, despite being ignored by some Indonesian leaders, was able to secure an agreement whereby the two countries would co-operate in the 'war against terrorism'. The saving factor, as ever, was the recognition by both Governments that the two countries had more to gain through co-operation rather than hostility. Business, education contacts and tourism were too important.

Economy

NEVILLE NORMAN

Despite the restraints on economic activity arising from the Asian financial crisis that began in 1997 and from the terrorist attacks on the USA in September 2001, the Australian economy was exhibiting a leading position of economic growth by mid-2002. Indeed, in 2002 it recorded its 10th year of consecutive positive economic growth, accompanied by a low rate of inflation. No period in Australia's history from 1901, or of its colonies before that, displayed such a sustained span of recession-free economic activity. Few Western-style economies could boast the 4% growth rate that Australia had achieved in the fiscal year 2001/02 (July 2001 to June 2002). This is not to imply that there were not pressures, difficulties, risks, uncertainties and corporate failures. The year 2001 witnessed the demise of large companies in the airline, telephony and insurance sectors. There were also concerns arising from Australia's external dependence, some ongoing tax tensions, major contentious domestic policy reviews and the risk of higher inflation rates. This brief statement of the economic condition suggests the need for a fuller and deeper appreciation of the structure and functioning of the Australian economy.

In the year to March 2002 the national income of Australia, in current prices, totalled $A702,000m. Within this aggregate figure, household income was $A610,000m., from which persons paid $A81,000m. in income tax, consumed $A420,000m. and saved $A16,000m. Spending on exports and on imports was each about $A150,000m. in the year to March 2002. Real gross domestic product (GDP), after allowing for price movements, rose by 4.2% in the year to March 2002. This rate of economic growth was lower than the average Australia achieved in the 1960s, but higher than the trend established from 1970. It remained above the growth performance of most other Western economies in the period 2000–02. In the 1950s and 1960s the average annual rate of economic growth was 5.8%. The 1970s in Australia witnessed a slowdown in both population growth and productivity growth, resulting in an historically-low average annual rate of economic growth of just 1.2%. The country's economic growth rate recovered to an annual average of 2.7% in the 1980s and further to 3.7% in the 1990s. Australia did not experience the extent of growth of equity values when the US stock markets surged upwards in the 1990s, nor the degree of downturn that took place in mid–2002.

The trends in some overall ratios give a useful impression of the Australian economy. The share of government spending at all levels in national income rose from just under 20% in 1948 to more than 30% in 1984. Since then the government share has stabilized or slightly fallen. The ratio of imports to domestic product sales has increased from 17% in 1948 to 27% in 1990 and then markedly to 41% in 2002. This can be taken as confirmation of a substantially open Australian economy. Meanwhile, the ratio of household savings to household income after tax has decreased from just over 20% to 8% in 1990 and to 2.8% in 2002. In the half-century from 1950 Australia became less dependent on agricultural exports; it developed an advanced industrial and technological base with world-standard transport and communications networks, despite the low population density.

PERCEPTIONS, REALITY AND POLICY

So often the external perception of Australia is through its tradition of primary-product exports, its films and its contemporary sporting achievements. These visions of Australia can easily depart from the reality of a modern economy, where the majority of its people reside in cities, use computers actively and exhibit one of the highest comparative standards of educational and training achievement in the world.

This is not to say that Australia has not sought to gain advantage from its image as a primary-product exporter. After the Havana Conference of 1947 that established the General Agreement on Tariffs and Trade (GATT), which was subsequently superseded by the World Trade Organization (WTO), there was much pressure from the contracting parties, as they were known, to reduce tariffs and other trade barriers multilaterally. Australia sought dispensation from this process on the grounds that it was a 'midway' country. By this it was meant that Australia was in many ways similar to a developed country, in terms of national income per caput (indeed in the later 19th century it led the world on this test). However, in relation to the structure of its exports and its exposure to large inherited fluctuations in economic activity arising from significant dependence on the global economy, it was more akin to the developing world. Images of outback Australia in films and tourism promotions appear to have spread this perception. Yet from the earliest days of Western-style settlement the majority of the population lived in cities relatively close to the coast. Even in the early 21st century nearly 30% of the national population resided in just two cities—Sydney and Melbourne.

In the high-technology area, it is true that relatively little of the 'innovation' aspect of scientific advancement is performed in Australia, notwithstanding that several major inventions in electronic technology, aircraft navigation, agricultural chemicals, agricultural harvesting, materials processing and logistics have been made in Australia. This is because large companies find it to their comparative advantage to focus the development side of these inventions in huge research establishments in North America and Europe in particular. Yet Australian consumers, businesses and governments remain advanced users of high-technology products. Research and development policy continues to be a major focus of attention in Australia.

Australia has moved a considerable distance from the 'quarry and farm' image it had acquired and which still figures prominently in some international perceptions. However, Australia remained in the leading 20 countries in the world on the basis of gross national product (GNP) per head of population. Australia's rate of economic growth in real terms, at 4.2% in 2001/02, exceeded that of any Western economy.

Economics and International Diplomacy

There is a complex connection between Australia's international political stance and material developments in trade and economic activity. For example, Australian merchandise export trade became prominent with Japan, Korea and Viet Nam relatively soon after Australia ceased hostilities against these countries in the 1940s, 1950s and 1960s, respectively. In 1973 Australia became one of the first countries to recognize the sovereignty of China and to establish formal diplomatic links with the People's Republic. Very considerable trade and educational links then followed between the two countries. There was some lapse in this connection when Australia became a prominent official critic of the massacre in Tiananmen Square in 1989. The economic and cultural links, however, were little affected and had again become extremely strong by mid–2002, when a huge long-term contract for supplies of natural gas to China was won by the Australian north-west shelf energy supplier, Woodside. Illustrating this theme with a different example, Australia took a lead in international criticism of the Iraqi leadership during mid-2002, causing retaliation from that country which threatened to cancel significant orders of Australian wheat. The shipments were refused entry to Iraqi ports for some weeks. These examples serve to illustrate the ongoing close relationships between international strategic policy and economic conditions. They also bring to prominence the way in which international images of a country may serve to enhance or limit its commercial progress.

Planning or the Market?

As regards the philosophy of economic policy, Australia maintains a commitment to national budgets that are balanced or in surplus, to significant growth in living standards and to low inflation. The Australian Government as such does not make or accept formal plans or targets for the population size and structure and for the main national economic variables. There are frequently calls from within Australia for formal population targets and economic planning agencies to be given official status. During 2002 conferences convened by state governments and industrial bodies took place, at which many delegates supported population size, structure and growth targets. The matters were discussed and debated by a wide range of representative groups. However, Australian Governments have not embraced these proposals.

From 1996 to 2002 a target zone was announced for consumer price inflation rates in the range of 2% to 3 % per annum; but this target zone was proposed and maintained by the central bank, the Reserve Bank of Australia, based in Sydney. That authority also has, since its creation in 1959, carried formal responsibility for stability of the currency and overall supervision of the financial system. In 1965 a Committee for Economic Inquiry (Vernon Committee) proposed a more formal economic planning mechanism, a Council of Economic Planning. That notion was roundly condemned by the Government of the day, and an aversion to central planning concepts has been part of the written and unwritten Australian political ethos ever since. During the tenure of the Hawke Government (1983–91) an Economic Planning and Advisory Council did operate, until its functions were absorbed into other bodies; it had effectively disappeared by 1996 when the Howard Government took office.

In relation to industrial policy, the Australian approach has been for decades to follow a monitored market course. That is, there are regulations to oversee the workings of the market in relation to mergers, corporate affairs, trade practices, construction proposals, consumer protection, the environment, foreign investment, financial transactions, insurance and banking. In the 1980s and 1990s some of these regulations were eased, especially in relation to the labour market and to international and financial transactions. The traditional Australian approach was to limit transactions at the point of entry into Australia: substantial barrier protection, mainly in the form of tariff duties, was erected against foreign supplies of goods; foreign investment was examined and restricted; immigration was strictly controlled. Through a series of reductions in tariffs and the elimination of most non-tariff means of border protection, Australia has liberalized its trading policy. It has been prominent in the international arena in securing and pressing for the removal of agricultural trade barriers multilaterally. Banking regulations that in the 1950s limited the deposit structure, entity ownership and asset allocation of the main banks and financial institutions have been liberalized. Prudential supervision and control of the financial sector has since 1998 been predominantly the responsibility of a newly created Australian Prudential Regulation Authority (APRA). Competition policy generally prohibits few transactions absolutely. Practices of firms that mislead consumers or are deemed unfair are illegal, as are a number of trade practices, arrangements and mergers that substantially lessen competition.

TRENDS IN POPULATION AND VITAL STATISTICS

In June 2002 the population of Australia was almost exactly 19.7m. persons, rising at the rate of 1.29 % per year. At June 2002 births occurred on average at just over one birth every two minutes, and deaths on average at just less than one death every four minutes. The natural increase was supplemented by long-term overseas migration equivalent in 2002 to almost exactly one-half of the population increase itself. The equal contribution of long-term migration and natural increase to population growth represented a return to conditions of the 1960s when natural increase and migration were each relatively higher than they were in 2002. During the 1980s the share of population growth attributed to international migration was just less than 30%. The resumption of approximately equal contributions from both migration and natural increase has more to do with Australian fertility declines affecting the latter than with any acceleration of inward international migration. The overseas-born component of the Australian population in March 2002 was 24.2%.

As in most Western-style economies, the rates of marriage and childbirth have been falling significantly, while the average age at marriage has been rising, as has the ratio of aged dependants to the total working population. The median age of the Australian resident population was 35.7 years in 2001, having risen from 31.2 in 1986 and 34.2 years in 1996. Reflecting Australia's position as a favoured and rapidly growing tourist destination, some 4.5m. persons arrived and left Australia as short-term visitors in the year 2001/02. With an average stay of 1.5 months, these temporary residents comprised an average of 3% of the Australian population during early 2002.

The proportion of the Australian population aged 65 years and over at census night on 7 August 2001 increased to 12.6%, as compared with 12.1% in 1996 and 10.2% in 1986. A total of 50.7% of the population in 2001 was female, and 28.2% of the Australian population was born overseas. English was the only language spoken in 79.1% of the homes in August 1991, Italian being the most common other language. Some 47.0% of the homes contained families without children, a proportion that despite the image of increasing incidence of childless couples has remained stable since the early 1990s. There is an increasing proportion of adult persons living alone in Australian homes, including 7.4% of the population in 2001 being divorced (and not remarried), compared with 1.9% of this status in 1971. Lone persons living in an Australian dwelling overall accounted for 22.9% of the population, compared with 18.1% in 1971.

Statistical projections indicate that the proportion of adults who will never marry is rising, being 29% for men and 23% for women, as seen at 1999, compared with equivalent demographic conditions at 1986 with 21% and 14% never-marry rates, respectively for males and females. Using the same methodology, the likelihood of marriages ending in divorce was 32%. The crude divorce rate at 2001 was 2.6 per 1,000 of population, compared with 4.3 for the USA, 2.9 for the United Kingdom and 2.5 for Canada. The crude marriage rate in Australia in 2001 was 5.9 per 1,000 population, compared with 8.9 in the USA and 5.4 in the United Kingdom.

Life expectancy at December 2001 was 77 years at birth for males and 82 years for females. These figures are higher than in the USA (74 and 79 years) and the United Kingdom (74 and 80 years), and similar to those of Japan, Switzerland and Sweden. The main causes of death in Australia at December 2001 were cancer (27.8%), heart disease (20.7%) and stroke (9.6%). At the rates of childbirth prevailing at October 2001, 24% of Australian women would remain childless at the end of their reproductive lives. During the 1990s the proportion of the Australian population aged 25–64 years with a professional, vocational or higher educational qualification rose from 46.5% to 51.0%.

AGRICULTURE, MINING AND MANUFACTURING

Agriculture

Agriculture remains an important source of export earnings for Australia. While farming activities may have accounted for just 3% of Australia's GDP in 2002, and only 2% of its employment, the agricultural sector nevertheless contributed 16% of export earnings in the year to March 2002. The share of Australian export earnings arising from agriculture has declined from a range of 35%–29% during the 1980s to 12%–16 % in the years 2000–02. This farm product share of Australia's exports compared with 24.4% in 1990 and 49.0% in 1970. The proportion of the Australian total employment base engaged in agriculture was 2.1% in 2000/01, having decreased from 3.8% in 1980 and 7.8% in 1960. There were 110,500 agricultural establishments in Australia in 2000/01, declining from 202,800 in 1960/61.

Agricultural activities occupy a high proportion of the arable land in Australia, although they offer relatively little employment. This is due to the rapid productivity growth achieved in its production processes, and declining relative demand for agricultural products. Within the aggregate value of gross farm production in the year to March 2002, the most prominent contributors were beef (15%), wheat (14%), fruit and nuts (10%), milk (10%), wool (8%), and vegetables (6%). In the first half of the 20th century wool alone dominated Australian export earnings, leaving aside some periods of intense gold-mining activity. Beef, lamb and wheat have also been traditionally the main export-earners. The erosion of preferential entry into the United Kingdom in the 1970s, the emergence of mineral and, more recently, manufacturing exports, and competition from new international suppliers, have diminished the relative position of these traditional exports.

From the mid-1990s wool suffered the further specific difficulties of competition from synthetic products, declining demand and prices, compounded by the Asian financial crisis of the late 1990s and the aftermath of an unsuccessful attempt of policy intervention in Australia to maintain wool prices. A huge stockpile of wool had emerged by 1996. It had been completely sold before 2002. A privatized Australian Wheat Board carries out the marketing of Australian-grown wheat. The direct role of government in marketing agricultural products in general is very limited. The traditional exports now appear as a stable and efficient, if smaller, component of the economy.

Intensive production of fruit and vegetables is conducted in Australia around urban settlement areas in every state and on land areas that are relatively close to the coastline. However, the major broad-acre developments are found further inland. For example, the sheep-wheat belt is located in an ellipse on the eastern and southern part of the Australian land mass some 150–1,300 km from the coast. Dairy production has moved further from the cities with the development of irrigation and water storage facilities. Wine-producing areas are found, in some cases, close to Adelaide, Melbourne and Perth, but also in low-rainfall zones in every state. About two-thirds of the continent is classified as low-rainfall desert, being the central, northern and western zones. Little economic activity, except for mining operations and large-scale grazing activities, are carried on in these inland zones, with some tourism locations interspersed.

On a value basis, crops and livestock each contributed substantially and similarly to Australian national production, with the gross value of crops being $A18,092m., and livestock $A16,322m. in 2000/01. The gross value of agricultural production overall was $A33,600m., an 11% increase on the previous year. Some 5.54 m. ha of coarse grains (mainly corn) were planted in 2000/01, with production volume reaching 11.39m. tons, of which 40.3% was exported. Within this domestic production figure for coarse grains, corn accounts for 68% of the tonnage produced and barley for 17%. Australia produced 1.06m. tons of cotton, 10.56m. litres of milk, 0.16m. tons of butter and 0.36m. tons of cheese in 2000/01.

In 2000 there were 27.59m. head of cattle and 118.6m. sheep (mostly in New South Wales and Victoria), yielding production of some 3.11m. tons of red meat, of which 1.745m. tons were exported, a figure that increased markedly in 2001 as a result of meat production difficulties and health problems in Europe. Australia produces 5% of the world's pulses and 3% of the world's sugar. There were 12.08m. ha of wheat planted in 2000/01, yielding 21.17m. tons, of which 16.26m. tons (77%) were exported. The rapid productivity growth of wheat farming is reflected in the fact that in 1980 production was almost exactly one-half of this figure. The crop was planted on approximately the same land area allocated to wheat in each period. In 2000/01, Australia exported 15% of the world's internationally traded wheat. The country's wool production totalled 652,000 tons in 2000/01, some 28% of the world aggregate greasy wool clip. In 2000 Australia produced a turnover of $A51,100m. in food-processing and beverage products, of which $A14,900m. represented value added by the food-products processing function.

Some individual agricultural industries face specific difficulties. The dairy industry by mid-2002 was confronting adverse conditions owing to water shortages, long-term competition from margarine, and greatly increased competition from New Zealand, in cheese production especially, since freer market access was granted in the early 1990s. Aggressive competition in wheat markets since 1999 has caused difficulty when Australia, as in its response to falling sugar prices in the 1970s, failed to follow market prices fully downwards. There are also some notable successes, including greatly increased penetration of Australian beef and rice in Japan and other Asian outlets. Australia had also reached considerable prominence as a premium exporter of table wines. By 2002 some 37% of Australian wine production was exported, mainly to Europe, as compared with 12% in 1980. Some 1.85m. tons of grapes were crushed in 2000/01, making 1.42m. tons of wine, with 384.1m. litres sold domestically. Some 339.8m. litres were exported, 165m. litres to the United Kingdom and 67.7m. litres to the USA. Imports of wines in that year reached just 12.8m. litres.

Australia reaps the benefit from its providential endowment of agricultural resources and a reputation for high-quality in processing. These benefits are tempered by the long-term trend of declining relative prices of agricultural staples in world markets. Australia has been prominent in seeking freer access for primary products in protected world markets, using overt and other forms of diplomatic pressure to make its position known. In June 2002 Australian Prime Minister John Howard addressed the US Congress, combining unequivocal endorsement for the USA's position on international terrorism with firm disagreement on the protectionist aspects of that country's trade policy.

Mining

Some 4.9% of the Australian GDP arose directly from mining activities in 2000/01. A high proportion of all major minerals (other than brown coal) was exported. In the case of uranium oxide, the entire mineral output was exported because of domestic consumption prohibitions. About 27% of Australian export earnings was derived from mineral exports in 2000/01. There was considerable environmental attention to the conditions of mineral exploration, production and handling. Legal issues arising from land rights claims with traditional landowners remain controversial in some areas of the industry.

There is a considerable disparity between the location of the major valuable mineral deposits and the areas desired for habitation. Coal and valuable mineral deposits occur mainly inland and in low-rainfall areas. This potential problem has been addressed in three ways. First, some considerable settlements have developed at mine sites, such as Broken Hill, — about 800 km west of Sydney; Newcastle, 160 km north of Sydney; Wollongong, 130 km south of Sydney, and Ballarat and Bendigo, both around 160 km north-west of Melbourne on slightly different arcs. Second, the development of high-productivity extraction techniques and the availability of concentrate ores and their transport that has limited the need for workers to be at the location of the major deposits or agricultural areas. Third, there is a well-developed system of moving workers to mine sites. There is also the capacity to take workers into temporary locations, for instance in the agricultural areas during harvesting and shearing times. Quite commonly, workers will be engaged for periods of two–three weeks working intensively, followed by two weeks off-site.

Historically, Australia has experienced pronounced booms associated with specific mineral products, especially gold. Since the late 1960s, commencing with iron ore, bituminous coal and bauxite, a long-sustained phase of mineral development has been evident. Both Australian and foreign-owned companies have developed huge resources of natural gas, coal, uranium, copper, lead, zinc and petroleum. There was no sign in the early 21st century that this long phase of mineral development had ended. Government financial support for mining development through state and federal budgets has been reduced significantly since 1990. Industrial relations conditions have generally improved, although the 80% reduction in working days lost per employee between 1984 and 2001 conceals continuing tensions over pay and conditions that cause international buyers of coal, particularly, to be ready to substitute alternative suppliers if Australian sources prove unreliable.

Australia has impressive endowments of the world's proven mineral reserves, with over 80% of the world's rutile and beach sands, 27% of the uranium oxide; around 40% of brown coal (lignite) and 22% of black/bituminous coal. While Australia has substantial petroleum resources, mostly beyond its south-east and north-west coastlines, it still needs to import about one-third of its domestic oil and petroleum needs. The main production data recorded that in the year to June 2001 oil and gas exploration accounted for 38% of mining value added in Australia, followed by coal (26%), iron ore (12%) and gold ore (8%).

In 2000 Australia mined 53.8m. tons of bauxite, processing this into 15.68m. tons of alumina, of which 79% was exported; primary aluminium production reached 1.77m. tons of which 1.402m. tons were exported, mostly to Japan and the Republic of Korea. This export trade represented 10% of the world trade in aluminium. In 2000/01 322m. tons of black coal were produced, mostly from Queensland (54%) and New South Wales (43%). After washing the coal, this figure was reduced to a net 257.84m. tons, of which 193.5m. tons (77%) were exported. Australia produced 513,000 tons of refined copper and 301 tons of gold in 2000/01. In the same year Australian output of crude petroleum and condensate reached 43,264m. litres, of which 44% was exported, together with 2,785m. litres of liquefied petroleum gas (LPG), while the country produced 33,800m. cu m of natural gas. Australian rutile production was just over one-half of the world's supply. In 2000/01 Australia produced 7.58m. tons of uranium, some 28.5% of the world's aggregate uranium production (Canada being the leader with 9.92m. tons). Output of zinc in 2000 reached 1.38m. tons, some 15.9% of the world's total supply.

Rationalization and consolidation in Australia's mineral industries was substantial in the 1990s. This was partly caused by the ending of income tax exemption for gold-mining operations that had prevailed for decades, and by the mergers of larger operators. Mergers and take-overs are still closely monitored and are often prevented. In late 2001 the (Royal Dutch) Shell company was blocked by a Treasurer decree on 'public interest' grounds from taking over the operations of the Australian north-west shelf gas producer, Woodside, although it retained significant interests therein. Seldom are gold producers out of the news concerning financial reconstruction and policy agitation. Some of the policy guidelines remain unclear or inconsistent as viewed by investors, explorers and producers.

Manufacturing

As in many Western-style economies, there has been a declining trend in the relative position of the manufacturing sector since the early 1970s. This decrease has resulted from a combination of reduced import-duty protection, the emergence of low-cost foreign suppliers in textile, clothing, footwear and metal manufactures, especially from Asia, and declining household budget shares devoted to manufactured goods. A considerable proportion of manufacturing activity is geared to serving the needs of mining and agricultural sectors, which are relatively larger than in countries with a similar degree of economic development. In the financial year 2000/01 manufacturing value added totalled $A74,640m., a growth rate of 5.0% on the previous year and representing 11.2% of the national GDP. Food, beverages and tobacco provided some 20% of employment and added value within the manufacturing sector. The contribution of machinery and equipment sectors was similar. A further 15% of manufacturing added value was contributed by metal product manufacturing, and also by petroleum and chemical products (10%), printing and publishing (9%), wood products (7.2%), and textiles, clothing and footwear (6.5%).

In the year to June 2002 Australian manufacturing establishments produced 1,744m. litres of beer, 18,367 tons of tobacco and cigarette products, 398,000 tons of newsprint, 847,000 tons of wood pulp, 17,652m. litres of automotive gasoline, 1,515m. clay bricks and 6.29m. tons of basic iron,

There are several areas of policy uncertainty that impinge especially on the goods-producing sectors of the Australian economy, notably the large variations in the approach to research and development, export promotion and certain taxation issues. However, the manufacturing sector has arguably gained in relation to other sectors of the Australian economy from the introduction of the New Tax System on1 July 2000. This is because that tax initiative involved the elimination of wholesale sales taxation, which applied only to manufactured goods, and its replacement at the substantially lower rate of 10% by the goods and services tax (GST—see below).

Within the manufacturing sector there is considerable interest in the motor vehicle industry, in which major international vehicle builders have long been represented. Vehicle registrations were rising at an average annual rate of 2.4% in the period 1999–2002. The average age of cars on the road in Australia was 10.5 years in 2001, having risen from 6.1 years in 1971. Public policy support for this sector has been reduced. However, in April 1998 the Howard Government announced a pause in the programmed reduction of motor vehicle import duties, based on agreement with the leading vehicle builders that cost-reducing plant and equipment investment would take place. Considerable modernization and extension of facilities subsequently followed.

INFRASTRUCTURE, ENERGY AND COMMUNICATIONS

Transport

There are clearly difficulties in covering a land area similar to that of the USA with advanced transport networks, given Australia's small population. Yet through significant government involvement and an active private sector there has been substantial coverage by road, rail, air and shipping facilities. From the late 1980s the domestic and international airline operations controlled by the Commonwealth Government were combined into Qantas, which was then sold to the private sector, a significant share being acquired by British Airways. In addition, the main airport infrastructure was divided into lots for sale by auction. Similarly, port and rail systems were exposed to greater competition by the removal of legislation requiring carriage of selected goods by designated modes, by privatization of some of these operations, and the introduction of corporatization principles into management and performance procedures. In the period 1999–2002, negotiations and disputes concerning the access arrangements and pricing of these facilities occasioned much activity in competition law.

Since the mid-1990s Australia has followed a more 'open-skies' policy in permitting a wider range of international airline operators to participate in the Australian market. In domestic operations the traditional concept was for a 'two-airline policy' to operate. This involved one carrier being government-owned and one (Ansett) being privately-owned, with entry by any other potential provider being made impossible through bans on aircraft imports. Heavily-monitored 'rationalization agreements' ensured that the two carriers had equal traffic, timetables, aircraft, facilities and profits. From the late 1970s the scope for competition and differential outcomes was markedly increased. The liberalization proceeded rapidly in the 1980s and early 1990s. The entry of third carriers and their failure in the 1990s provided warnings that competition might have become 'excessive'. Just three days after 11 September 2001 the main always-private airline carrier, with its origins in the 1930s, suddenly and completely collapsed. Ansett had previously been sold to international trucking and news operators TNT and News Corp and then was acquired by Air New Zealand. Two further attempts at entry were more successful, the sustaining entrant, Virgin Blue, occupying a significant role alongside Qantas by mid-2002. The transport sector accounts for 6% of Australia's GDP.

Communications

As in the transport sector, the traditional dominant role in the communications sector was played by a government-owned and -controlled enterprise that has since been privatized. With responsibilities once for both post and telephony, these operations were divided in the 1970s, and in 1993 Telecom was renamed Telstra and partly privatized. Again, as in transport, new entrants have appeared, the main operator being Cable & Wireless Optus. Many smaller operators exist in specialist areas. During 2002 a government review of the five-year process of telecommunications deregulation was carried out. Australia Post is the corporatized principal supplier of postal services. It is also exposed to competition and in turn has widened its functions to provide stationery sales and bill-paying services. The communications sector accounts for 5% of Australia's GDP.

Information Technology (IT)

During the world-wide 'technology boom' of 1995–2001 in particular, Australia was commonly classified as an old-technology economy. The country's continuing substantial dependence on agricultural and mineral exports may encourage this perception. Such an image is not supported by facts relating directly to information technology in Australia. There is almost complete coverage of basic telephony and the adoption and use of advanced IT. There were over 600 internet service providers (ISPs) in Australia at June 2001, this number having declined by 4% over the previous year owing to the difficulties the technology industries were experiencing world-wide in 2001. The proportion of Australian businesses with a web presence had risen from 6% in 1997/98 to 22% in 2000/01. The percentage of businesses with internet access increased from 29% in 1997/98 to 56% in 2000/01. Some 37% of Australian households had internet access in November 2000. The incidence of internet usage increased significantly with household income and where children under 18 were in the household complement (48% compared with 32%); internet usage was greater in metropolitan areas than in rural areas (40% compared with 32%).

Energy Supply and Distribution

Energy and gas supplies have until recently been provided by state-owned and -operated monopolies with considerable fiscal support. Privatization of most of these services has been accompanied by debate and efficiency drives, increased accountability of the enterprises concerned and generally reduced or restrained consumer prices. Each of the energy-sector enterprises is subject to new 'access' regulations relating both to the conditions on which supplies are made available and to the prices charged. The dominant source of energy is electricity, which in turn is generated from (black and brown) coal and natural gas. Including the domestic energy component of coal and natural gas, the energy sector accounted for 4.5% of Australia's GDP in the year to March 2002.

The responsibility for energy provision and distribution has traditionally rested with state governments. Each tended to permit gas and electricity boards to assume quasi-monopoly positions in the entire production chain from energy extraction, to production and distribution to consumers. For legal and logistical reasons, there was no possibility of trade or exchange of energy products between the separate Australian states until recent times. The emergence of gas pipelines that crossed state boundaries in the 1970s and the 1991 facilitation of electricity sales between the states typify the liberalization that has taken place. In addition, the main electricity and gas providers have been split up, the common arrangement being for distribution systems in each state to be divided into some three to six regional areas sold to private interests that were by 2002 free to compete with each other. Even where government maintained ownership, as in New South Wales, the component businesses were subject to stringent profit-making requirements combined with consumer service monitoring.

OTHER SERVICES

Despite the image of rural and mining production being associated traditionally with the Australian economic and cultural landscape, the majority of residents since British occupation over the last two centuries have lived in towns and cities and engaged in service activities. Australia has an advanced network of personal and business service industries, including legal, finance, education, medical, health and community services, leisure and sporting service activities. Banking, insurance and accounting services are predominantly controlled by large companies with international operations. Retail distribution activities involve both large and small operators. After correction for price movements, the value of retail sales in Australia has remained particularly constant on a per caput basis since 1980. Within the aggregate there has been substitution against some food groups (meat and sugars) and an increasing trend towards processed food not prepared in the home. Shopping hours are very liberal, and internet purchasing of services, especially travel services, is rising rapidly.

The tertiary sector can be usefully divided into the wholesaling, storage and retailing of products; community and charitable services; health and medical services; education; tourism and leisure activities; legal, accounting and business services; and financial services. The retail sector features two prominent chain-store entities: Coles Myer, established in 1985 by a merger of two successful family companies that were involved in over 40% of the retail transactions of Australia, the market now being shared more evenly with Woolworths-Safeway, along with thousands of smaller establishments. The health sector features a hospital system shared between government and private ownership, supported by national and private insurance arrangements; independent medical practitioners and a large network of pharmaceutical retailers supplied by production and importing companies featuring most of the world's leading pharmaceutical manufacturers.

Education

An advanced internationally-focused education sector exists in Australia. Private (mostly church-based) primary and secondary schools and government (taxpayer-funded) schools operate in competition with each other. Universities and tertiary technical training institutes are mainly government-owned. There are some private tertiary institutions. From the mid-1990s full fee-paying tertiary students, many of them from other countries, became an increasing part of the educational intake. Australian universities began to market their services by website, promotional visits to other (mainly Asian) countries and in some cases by setting up establishments in other countries. For example, Monash University (Melbourne) established a campus in Malaysia in the mid-1990s.

Legal, Accounting and Business Services

Legal firms went through a process of merger in the 1990s to establish some large firms, mainly serving government and major companies, not least with the work required in association with the privatization of the power and telephony sectors. Small-scale service providers are found in every main town offering legal, accounting or financial services. In the accounting area, all major international firms are prominent in Australia. However, during 2001/02 the firm of Arthur Andersen was merged into other operators, as it was in most parts of the world. In banking there are four major banks, each private or privatized. An unlegislated 'four pillars' policy operates to ensure that the 'big four' cannot merge further, although it is rumoured that moves have been made to test this policy through the courts. Insurance services are provided by major international underwriters, supported by affiliated agents and independent brokers, each subject to increasingly onerous regulations. In every one of these service areas, large and small firms co-exist, serving different parts of the market.

Tourism and Leisure Industries

The number of international visitors to Australia totalled 4.43m. in 2001/02, a decrease of 5% on the previous year. This temporary decline reflected the global pause in international tourism in late 2001 and was an uncharacteristic interruption in a period of rapid growth, from 1.1m. international tourist arrivals in 1984 to 2.1m. arrivals in 1988 and an average annual compound growth of 6.3 % between 1988 and 2001. The main source of international tourists is New Zealand (15.6% of the total in the year to May 2002), followed by Japan (13.8%), the United Kingdom (8.7%) and the USA (5.9%). Tourism services comprised $A26,300m. value added in 2001, or some 4.7% of the economy, having risen from 3.0% in 1990. Some 24% of this activity is attributed to serving international tourists. There were 227m. visitor nights occasioned by domestic travellers in 2000/01. The occupancy rate for hotels and serviced apartments in March 2002 was 63%, while that for motels and guesthouses was 54%. There were 551,000 persons engaged in tourism-generating employment in 2000/01, or 6.3% of national employment. Findings by the Bureau of Tourism Research show that some 55% of international tourist arrivals land initially in Sydney, although only about 34% of visitor nights are spent by them in New South Wales, Sydney's state. Considerable statistical information is available on the events and theme parks tourists attend and satisfaction surveys derived therefrom.

In 2002 there were many contentious issues and pressures within the tertiary or services sector, including debates about education funding, retrenchments in the finance and accounting sector, and pressures in support and opposition to an informal 'four pillars' policy to prevent mergers among the leading banks. In addition, since July 2000 the services sector has sustained significantly increased tax burdens with the introduction of the the New Tax System (see below). Arguably, the tertiary sector was relatively untaxed under the previous arrangements, whence the tax burden has become more uniformly spread.

FOREIGN TRADE AND THE BALANCE OF PAYMENTS

Since December 1983 Australia has operated a freely floating currency regime with little interference either directly or indirectly from Parliament or the monetary authorities. This means that all overseas monetary inflows will match the overseas outflows in aggregate, although at various stopping points in the external accounts imbalances can be, and are, evident. Through Australia's history the gap between exports and imports by value, the merchandise trade balance, has swung significantly from surplus to deficit. However, the overall external accounts exhibit a pronounced and permanent strong long-term capital inflow, alongside persistent current-account outflows of freight payments and interest and debt-servicing payments. Undoubtedly this situation reflects the combination of huge natural resources and development potential with the limited population and savings base within Australia. It also means that Australia is significantly influenced by world interest rates. It has therefore gained from the epoch of relatively low interest rates since the mid-1990s. In principle the adjustments that once took place through movements in Australia's level of international reserves have in the years since 1983, or even since 1977, been absorbed through exchange rate changes. Because of its diminished reliance on primary export staples and greater economic flexibility, not least through the exchange rate mechanism described here, the Australian economy is now less likely to suffer from the cyclical behaviour of world markets that once took it quickly from boom to slump.

Merchandise Trade

In the year 2000/01 overall exports of goods and services totalled $A153,100m., with imports reaching $A152,400 m., implying a small surplus on trade in goods and services of $A700m. Exports and imports of goods alone were both almost exactly $A120,000m.

The main export destinations in 2000/01 were Japan (which purchased 19.7%), the USA (9.9%), the Republic of Korea (7.4%), China (6.3%), New Zealand (5.8%) and Taiwan (4.4%). Among the range of prominent manufactured exports are road vehicles (14% of the total), medicines and pharmaceuticals (8%), beverages (7%) and electrical machinery and automatic data-processing equipment (each 6%). Overall, the rural component of exported goods had declined from 30% in 1981 to less than 20% in 2001. By type of product, metal ores accounted for 12.4% of the total in 2001 (largely exported to Japan, China and the Republic of Korea), coal for 10.4%, non-ferrous metals and petroleum each 7.7%, meat 5.3%, cereals 4.4% and road vehicles 3.5%

The trade pattern is changing rapidly with substantial growth in exports to India (up by 30% in 2000/01) and of motor vehicle exports to the Middle East, especially Saudi Arabia. In 2000/01 some 59% of exports were manufactures, particularly non-ferrous metals and meat products; the mining sector provided 27% of exports by value. By product type, coal represented 9% of the total value of exports in 2000/01, oil 6%, gold, iron ore, aluminium and aluminium ores and wheat each 4%, beef and wool each 3%. The dominant product category in imports is machinery, accounting for 43.5% of total import values in the year to March 2002. In the same period the main sources of imports were the USA (which supplied 17.9%), Japan (13.8%) and China (9.4%).

Invisibles and Internationally Traded Services

Despite the movement to a net surplus in relation to international tourism activity since 1994, the non-merchandise current account between Australia and other countries remained significantly in deficit. This category is dominated by a small number of net deficit items, especially freight and insurance outgoings and the repatriation of interest payments and dividends abroad. In 2000/01 the main destinations for exports of services were the USA (which purchased 16.2%), Japan (11.8%) the United Kingdom (11.0%) and New Zealand (7.2%). Travel and tourism services comprised 47% of the total, with transport and freight services 25% and communications 5%.

Taking trade and other current international financial flows into consideration, the current-account deficit stood at $A18,565m. in the year to March 2002. That deficit had been as high as $A33,258m. in the year to June 2000. At 31 March 2002 Australia's net external debt stood at $A332,010m., equivalent to 47.3% of the GDP for that period. The fact that some 80% of this debt was privately incurred and was secured on prime, often export-orientated, assets caused independent international assessments by analysts and credit-rating agencies to offer a confident view of Australia's financial future. Any significant increase in world interest rates, however, would immediately raise the invisible debit component of the balance of payments. This is perhaps a more relevant risk factor than the traditional concerns about primary product export dependence, which are largely confined to history.

Exchange Rates

Given the structural changes in relation to trade and other international economic dealings and the enhanced role for the exchange rate mechanism, it is not surprising that significant movements in exchange rates involving the Australian dollar have taken place. Mostly the tendency has been for a long-term decline of the Australian dollar in the cross rates associated with almost every major currency. In the period from 31 May 1980 to 31 May 2002, the Australian dollar decreased in value by 36.9% on a trade-weighted basis against other currencies, including a depreciation of 51.3% against the US dollar, 72.6% against the Japanese yen and 20.9% against the pound sterling. In September 2001 the Australian dollar reached a low of just over 48 US cents, from which it had recovered to 57 cents by June 2002.

From 1949 to 1967 the Australian dollar was fixed to the pound sterling and followed the IMF practice of maintaining fixed rates in the absence of a 'fundamental disequilibrium' in the balance of payments. That rule was tested many times, in both directions, including a strong surplus position in 1972 that moved quickly into deficit in 1974. From 1977 a managed float achieved some flexibility, until the Hawke Government in December 1983 adopted the free float. Significant currency depreciation took place from January 1985. It is not credible to argue that the floating dollar has 'caused' the pronounced long-term fall in the value of the Australian dollar. It is arguable that the adjustments would have taken place under any exchange rate system, and that under the free-float arrangements they have been smoother and form part of a much better managed Australian economy.

ECONOMIC DEVELOPMENT AND GOVERNMENT POLICY

Labour Market Trends

At June 2002 the Australian labour force totalled 9,311,000 persons, of whom about 624,000 remained unemployed (6.3% of the workforce). The labour force comprised 64% of the total population. This workforce participation rate has, as in many countries, grown markedly since the 1960s, especially with the increasing propensity of women, particularly married women, to work outside the home. The unemployment rate had in the late 1990s been in the range of 7%–9%, although in the 1960s it was seldom above 2%. In late 1992 the unemployment rate reached a post-war peak of 10.7%. In June 2002 the number of employed males was 5.21m., of whom 4.44m. were employed full time. The employment data for females were 4.11m. and 2.22m., respectively. The proportion of the Australian workforce engaged in part-time work is thus far greater in the case of females, and it has been rising significantly in recent years.

Economic Management

The Australian experience provides a useful case study for debates about the merits of short-term policy intervention to manage the economy. Its history contains some classic mistakes of policy where demand management was moving to intensify cyclical fluctuations, as in 1961 when boom-curbing tax increases and monetary restraints deepened the recession that was already in train. More recently, problems in reading the movements in the economy and the effects of monetary policy already initiated caused cyclical intensification at the end of the 1980s. Since that time, the demand management record has tended to support the view that active short-term policy intervention can be beneficial.

By 2002 annual economic growth since 1992 had averaged 3.6%. During that time quarterly growth rates had been negative on only two occasions: September 1993 and December 2000. Adopting the convention of two successive quarters of negative GDP growth to indicate 'recession', Australia has thus been recession-free for over a decade. No period of its history boasts this record. By mid-2002, however, there remained pressures and tensions for both the economy and policy-makers.

Australia incurred high inflation rates in the 1970s, both relative to its own past and in comparison with most other Western-style economies. Wage surges, sensitivity to world oil prices and currency depreciation can be cited as the main causative factors. Between 1990 and the March quarter of 2002, the general index of consumer prices (CPI) rose from 100 to 137. The prices of individual products subject to technological change, such as household appliances (119) and communications (106), rose less quickly, while areas subject to tax and public policy intervention on pricing rose most rapidly, such as alcohol and tobacco products (204) and education (205). Taking into account these latter categories, in which microeconomic policy dictates caused substantial price increases, the general rise in consumer prices from 1990 reflected centrally on overall economic management. The compound average 2.63% annual CPI increase was the result. These data also incorporated the exceptional 6.1% annual inflation rate of 2000/01 with the switch to indirect taxes under the New Tax System. In the year to the March quarter of 2002 the overall CPI rose by 2.9%, with food prices going up by 4.8% and clothing by 1.4%, while transport prices remained stationary.

Average weekly earnings for all employees were estimated at $A839 in March 2002, compared with $A781 in March 2000. At March 2002 the average rate of increase in earnings was 3.6%. The growth in rates of pay for males and females has been similar in recent years, following the move to more equal pay in the 1970s. The contained and regular growth in these data compared with spates of wage acceleration in the early 1970s, with earnings rising by more than 35% in 1973/74, and again in 1981/82 when wages rose by 18%. Considerable policy effort has been made by both major political parties in office to prevent the recurrence of these sharp increases.

Lying behind the lower inflation regime is a commitment in policy manifesto and action to budgetary restraint that avoids the excesses of government in the 1970s. Formal budgetary targets were tried and removed in the 1970s and early 1980s. However, the commitment to fiscal discipline is reflected in policy pledges, speeches by the Treasurer and budget documents. When the Labor Government of Bob Hawke assumed office in 1984 it demonstrated a commitment to economic deregulation and financial liberalization, freer trade and budgetary responsibility. That tradition was continued by both political parties: the Labor administration until March 1996 and the Liberal-National coalition subsequently. The Howard Government had since March 1996 turned the headline (federal) budget deficit of $A5,001m. in 1995/96 into a surplus of $A22,100m. in 1999/2000. However, the net operating balances of all levels of government in Australia declined from $A14,365m. in 1999/2000 to $A3,264m. in 2000/01. The federal Government remained a net lender in 2000/01, allocating $A5,459m., while the states were new borrowers of $A2,350m. Although the annual budget surpluses were reduced, their positive sign implies ongoing debt reduction from the public authorities and a tribute to good economic management.

Competition Policy Reform

By mid-2002 Australia had completed significant changes to its personal and company tax system. However, major amendments were proposed for the Trade Practices Act (TPA), the principal organ of competition policy. The existing form of the TPA had been in operation since 1974 and was modelled more on the US approach of court-based litigation than on the British system of investigation and examination in a more neutral setting. There are limited exemptions for any specific entity or trade practice, although immunity through authorization is available for potentially illegal agreements between corporations on the grounds of public interest justification. The central provisions are subject to an economic-based test of 'substantial lessening for competition in a market for goods and services', and this is the principal test for assessing proposed mergers and horizontal and vertical arrangements. Among the per se offences not subject to a test of competition as such, the Act contains strictures against misleading consumers and price fixing. These provisions have been clarified by case law and by clear legal drafting. One further area of per se offence concerns corporations that abuse their 'market power' by taking advantage thereof for the purpose of damaging competitors, preventing entry or deterring competitive behaviour. It is this section of the TPA that has generated most controversy and prompted some agitation for it to be strengthened.

Tax Reform and Tax Trends

There are distinctive features of both the Australian taxation system and the process that has led to its current structure and administration. The Australian Taxation Office administers the system, collects the dominating federal taxes and handles rulings, objections and appeals. Massive legislation and case law supports the system, especially in relation to income and deductions definitions applying to persons and companies. Controversial areas also included international company transfer pricing, fringe benefits (for which a special tax exists) and anti-avoidance provisions.

With overall (federal, state and local) taxes comprising just under 30% of its GDP, Australia is one of the least taxed countries among the members of the Paris-based Organisation for Economic Co-operation and Development (OECD). With nearly 60% of the federal taxes collected coming from taxes on personal income alone, few other countries have tax jurisdictions that rely so prominently on any one tax type or tax base. This is despite the introduction in July 2000 of a value-added tax, the goods and services tax (GST), at the general rate of 10%. The personal income tax rate schedule is also steeply progressive with high marginal tax rates applying at relatively low taxable incomes. The highest marginal tax rate is just under 50%. For the tax year 2002/03 it applied at taxable incomes at or above $A60,000 (or around US$33,000, using exchange rates as at July 2002). High excise taxes are levied on alcoholic drinks (with wine treated more lightly), petroleum products and tobacco and cigarettes. The GST applies widely to all purchases, with zero-rating ('GST-free') treatment of food and exports and exemption ('input-taxed' is the Australian word) for financial transactions and rent. Companies are taxed as from July 2002 at a standard rate on company profits of 30.0%, with allowances in dividend distributions to tax-paying persons for tax already paid by companies. State governments rely on transfers from federal authorities for at least one-half of their revenues. Thus, there exists considerable vertical fiscal imbalance: the federal government raising far more revenue than it requires for its own expenditures, the states being dependent on the intergovernmental transfers, supplementing them with taxes on share and land transactions and on gambling. Local authorities levy rates geared to property values.

This description of the Australian tax system as at mid-2002 does not reveal the controversies and dynamic aspects of tax reform that lay behind the system. Some seven separate rounds of tax reform debates and proposals commenced in 1972. They predated the introduction of the New Tax System (NTS), which involved as its centre-piece the GST. The NTS was implemented by the federal Government of John Howard as from July 2000. It was accompanied by significant 'price exploitation provisions' to limit price increases, despite which Australia's annual inflation rate increased sharply, from an underlying rate of 2.3% in June 2000 to 6.1% in the year following its introduction. The price exploitation provisions involved price monitoring, heavy fines and public exposure for companies breaching the guidelines. The provisions ended in June 2002.

Prominent politicians of each major political party had previously promoted the structural shift towards GST or its equivalent, in all cases without success until the Howard initiative put the issue to the federal electorate in October 1998. Economists generally supported the reform proposals. Lying behind them was a wartime initiative in 1942 to pass control of income tax 'as a temporary measure' from the states to the Commonwealth. These powers have not since been returned. In the mean time, the steeply progressive personal tax structure adopted and developed in the high inflation years of the 1950s meant that by the 1970s relatively low-income persons were incurring marginal tax rates designed many years previously for high-income persons. Opponents in each round of reform proposals objected to the administrative burdens resulting from any change on businesses, to the adverse effects of GST-type taxes on low-income households (despite proposals of generous compensation measures at each stage), and to the repercussions for inflation levels and for industry. Even when the Howard Government was returned to office at the 1998 election, with the issue of GST dominating the debates and differences between the parties, political difficulties required it to make many concessions and in several ways to increase the administrative complexity of the system. At the November 2001 federal election, the opposition Labor Party did not succeed with proposals to 'roll back' the GST. While the post-11 September environment favoured the incumbent Government, it was safe to conclude that the GST had become an entrenched part of the Australian tax system.

The NTS involved repealing other indirect taxes, notably a wholesale sales tax that applied at rates of up to 30% on manufactured goods alone. The NTS thus caused prices in general, but especially of services, to rise, while some manufactured goods experienced price reductions, for example motor vehicles and jewellery. The short-term dynamics of effecting these changes caused disruption, especially in housing and vehicle sales. One curiosity of the NTS is that the federal Government that created it does not classify any GST revenue as its own. Instead, it collects GST as an 'agency function', passing the proceeds to the states in compensation for their loss of some of their fiscal transfer supports. Students of tax and government trends in Australia thus need to be careful in drawing inferences from the downward trend in the ratio of federal taxes and outlays to GDP from the fiscal year 2000/01 onwards.

In addition to the struggle to change the longer-term shape of the tax system, there remain short-term economic management tensions reflected in annual budgets and other fiscal policies. The date for the delivery of the federal budget and most state budgets has settled on May, the convention until the mid-1990s having been for budgets to be announced in August. After the experience of fiscal neglect in the mid-1970s, during which government outlays rose by 46% in one year alone (1974/75), Australian governments have shown disciplined commitment to fiscal responsibility.

FUTURE CHALLENGES

The challenges for the main decision-makers in the Australian economy are a combination of issues that face most advanced economies and some that are specific to the Australian economic structures and legal and political environment. Foremost is the need to continue economic growth, avoiding any recurrence of recession or unacceptable inflationary pressures. In some ways, the real economy moves disparately from the financial sector, although profit expectations, which drive financial values, cannot for long be separated from the position and prospects in real terms of underlying economic activity. As in the USA, share price indices rose spectacularly in the late 1990s at a time when the real economy grew only moderately. Between 31 December 1996 and 31 December 1999 the USA's Dow Jones industrial share price index rose by 78.3%. The ASX200, the Australian stock market price index, rose substantially but by the much more modest rate of 29.9%. Subsequently, and until 31 May 2002, the US index fell by 15%, while the Australian index rose slightly. A challenge is for markets to see that these are equilibrium corrections in financial markets and that the Australian index did not need to undergo the same degree of correction. Meanwhile, some domestic markets were booming, notably that of housing. In the year to May 2002 the number of dwelling approvals rose by 23%. In part, this activity reflected some fiscal incentives to overcome timing difficulties with the introduction of the GST; it also reflected the low interest rates that had prevailed from about 1996 and which declined further in 2001. There is a medium-term challenge for Australia to maintain the trend of national productivity growth above 2% a year and closer to 3%. Policy reversals in relation to science and technology have not assisted this objective.

Australia can claim to have exhibited an excellent record of economic management between 1984 and mid-2002. The country has achieved a calmer industrial scene, a more open and flexible economy and much less reliance on exports of primary products. Australia has a modern economy that has embraced advanced IT. It is arguably underpopulated from an economic viewpoint. Some of the images of Australia as a primary-product exporter, with huge fluctuations in the external payments balances limiting its growth potential, are long outdated.

Statistical Survey

Source (unless otherwise stated): Australian Bureau of Statistics, POB 10, Belconnen, ACT 2616; tel. (2) 6252-7911; fax (2) 6251-6009; internet www.abs.gov.au.

Area and Population

AREA, POPULATION AND DENSITY

Area (sq km)	7,692,030*
Population (census results)†	
6 August 1996	17,892,423
7 August 2001	
Males	9,362,021
Females	9,610,329
Total	18,972,350
Population (official estimates at mid-year)†	
1999	18,937,200
2000	19,157,100
2001	19,386,700
Density (per sq km) at mid-2001	2.5

* 2,969,909 sq miles.

† Census results exclude, and estimates include, an adjustment for under-enumeration, estimated to have been 1.9% in 1991. Estimates also exclude overseas visitors in Australia and include Australian residents temporarily overseas. The estimates shown above have not been revised to take account of the August 2001 census result. The adjusted estimate for mid-2001 is 19,485,278 (density 2.5 per sq km).

STATES AND TERRITORIES (30 June 2001)

	Area (sq km)	Estimated Population	Density (per sq km)
New South Wales (NSW)	800,640	6,609,304	8.3
Victoria	227,420	4,822,663	21.2
Queensland	1,730,650	3,635,121	2.1
South Australia	983,480	1,514,854	1.5
Western Australia	2,529,880	1,906,114	0.8
Tasmania	68,400	472,931	6.9
Northern Territory	1,349,130	200,019	0.1
Australian Capital Territory (ACT)	2,360	321,680	136.3
Jervis Bay Territory	70	n.a.	n.a.
Total	7,692,030	19,485,278*	2.5

* Includes populations of Jervis Bay Territory, Christmas Island and the Cocos (Keeling) Islands.

PRINCIPAL TOWNS (estimated population at 30 June 2000)*

Canberra (national capital)	310,500
Sydney (capital of NSW)	4,085,600
Melbourne (capital of Victoria)	3,466,000
Brisbane (capital of Queensland)	1,626,900
Perth (capital of W Australia)	1,381,100
Adelaide (capital of S Australia)	1,096,100
Newcastle	483,300
Gold Coast-Tweed	404,300
Wollongong	264,400
Hobart (capital of Tasmania)	194,200
Sunshine Coast	178,000
Geelong	157,900
Townsville	130,000
Cairns	115,600

* Figures refer to metropolitan areas, each of which normally comprises a municipality and contiguous urban areas.

BIRTHS, MARRIAGES AND DEATHS*

	Registered live births		Registered marriages		Registered deaths	
	Number	Rate (per 1,000)	Number	Rate (per 1,000)	Number	Rate (per 1,000)
1993	260,229	14.7	113,255	6.4	121,599	6.9
1994	258,051	14.5	111,174	6.2	126,692	7.1
1995	256,190	14.2	109,386	6.1	125,133	6.9
1996	253,834	13.9	106,103	5.8	128,719	7.0
1997	251,842	13.5	106,735	5.8	129,350	6.9
1998	249,616	13.3	110,598	5.9	127,202	6.8
1999	248,870	13.1	114,316	6.0	128,102	6.8
2000	249,636	13.0	113,400†	5.9	128,300†	6.7

* Data are tabulated by year of registration rather than by year of occurrence.

† Figures are rounded.

Expectation of life (WHO estimates, years at birth, 2000): Males 76.6, Females 82.1 (Source: WHO, *World Health Report*).

ECONOMICALLY ACTIVE POPULATION (annual averages, '000 persons aged 15 years and over, excluding armed forces)

	1999	2000*	2001*
Agriculture, forestry and fishing	431.9	437.5	428.8
Mining	76.4	78.2	78.3
Manufacturing	1,073.0	1,113.1	1,129.8
Electricity, gas and water supply	64.6	64.5	65.7
Construction	663.1	695.4	681.3
Wholesale trade	522.1	494.9	438.7
Retail trade	1,322.5	1,324.6	1,331.2
Accommodation, cafés and restaurants	417.6	432.8	469.0
Transport and storage	414.3	407.3	421.2
Communication services	154.6	169.3	182.6
Finance and insurance	315.3	327.5	337.3
Property and business services	961.5	988.7	1,081.0
Government administration and defence	349.5	345.8	365.8
Education	612.2	609.3	621.1
Health and community services	814.5	828.1	874.8
Cultural and recreational services	212.5	217.1	225.2
Personal and other services	341.9	352.3	342.5
Total employed	8,747.4	8,886.5	9,074.3
Unemployed	684.4	661.4	625.5
Total labour force (incl. others)	9,467.1	9,577.9	9,755.4
Males	5,359.6	5,398.6	5,471.8
Females	4,107.5	4,179.3	4,283.6

* Year ending June.

Source: *ABS Labour Force Australia*.

Health and Welfare

KEY INDICATORS

Fertility (births per woman, 2000)	1.8
Under-5 mortality rate (per 1,000 live births, 2000)	6
HIV/AIDS (% of persons aged 15–49, 2001)	0.07
Physicians (per 1,000 head, 1998)	2.40
Hospital beds (per 1,000 head, 1996)	8.5
Health expenditure (1998): US $ per head (PPP)	2,080
% of GDP	8.6
public (% of total)	69.9
Access to water (% of persons, 2000)	100
Access to sanitation (% of persons, 2000)	100
Human Development Index (2000): ranking	5
value	0.939

For sources and definitions, see explanatory note on p. vi.

Agriculture

PRINCIPAL CROPS ('000 metric tons)

	1999	2000	2001
Wheat	25,012	24,757	20,000
Rice (paddy)	1,101	1,753	1,239*
Barley	5,043	5,596	5,893*
Maize	338	406	420†
Oats	1,092	1,292	1,300†
Millet	43†	57	60†
Sorghum	1,891	2,116	1,423
Triticale (wheat-rye hybrid)	521	764	800†
Potatoes	1,327	1,200	1,250†
Sugar cane	38,534	38,165	31,039*
Dry broad beans	166	188	200†
Dry peas	357	401	410†
Chick-peas	187	230	240†
Lentils	103	163	180†
Vetches	53	24	24†
Lupins	1,968	800	1,500†
Soybeans (Soya beans)	105	104	105†
Sunflower seed	147	170	180†
Rapeseed	2,427	1,661	1,900†
Cottonseed	983	1,251	1,010†
Cabbages†	58	58	60
Lettuce	131	152	145†
Tomatoes	394	414	425†
Cauliflower	113	115†	120†
Pumpkins, squash and gourds	107	110†	115†
Chillies and green peppers	41	45†	50†
Dry onions	224	247	250†
Green peas	66	67	65†
Carrots	257	283	265†
Green corn	57	55†	55†
Watermelons	66	85	86†
Cantaloupes and other melons	101	115†	125†
Grapes	1,266	1,343	1,425†
Apples	334	320	310†
Pears	157	156	160†
Peaches and nectarines	93	86	90†
Oranges	446	509	470†
Tangerines, mandarins, clementines and satsumas	78	85	87†
Pineapples	131	139	140†
Bananas	225	257	275†
Cotton (lint)	634	698	755†

* Unofficial figure.
† FAO estimate(s).
Source: FAO.

LIVESTOCK ('000 head at 31 March)

	1999	2000	2001
Horses*	220	220	220
Cattle	26,578	27,588	27,588*
Pigs	2,626	2,433	2,433*
Sheep	115,456	118,552	120,000*
Goats*	200	200	200
Chickens	91,472	96,000*	96,000*
Ducks*	400	400	400
Turkeys*	1,300	1,300	1,300

* FAO estimate(s).
Source: FAO.

LIVESTOCK PRODUCTS ('000 metric tons)

	1999	2000	2001
Beef and veal	2,010.5	1,987.9	2,040.0*
Mutton and lamb	628.7	680.5	663.0*
Goat meat	8.1	8.1	8.1
Pig meat	362.2	362.4	389.0*
Horse meat	21.3	21.3	21.3
Chicken meat	611.3	613.4	662.0*
Duck meat	7.7	8.0	8.2†
Turkey meat†	22.8	22.8	22.8
Cows' milk*	10,483	11,172	11,398
Butter*	176	179	166
Cheese	335.4	369.2	444.0*
Hen eggs	147.7*	148.0†	149.0†
Honey	18.9	18.9†	18.9†
Wool:			
greasy	673	685	700†
clean	437*	437†	437†
Cattle hides (fresh)†	230	230	230
Sheepskins (fresh)	139.8	150.4	150.4

* Unofficial figure(s).
† FAO estimate(s).

Note: Figures for meat and milk refer to the 12 months ending 30 June of the year stated.

Source: FAO.

Forestry

ROUNDWOOD REMOVALS ('000 cubic metres, excl. bark)

	1998	1999	2000
Sawlogs, veneer logs and logs for sleepers	10,073	10,043	11,036
Pulpwood	10,502	9,840	12,310
Other industrial wood	609	704	814
Fuel wood	2,700	5,974	5,974
Total	23,884	26,561	30,134

Source: FAO.

SAWNWOOD PRODUCTION
('000 cubic metres, incl. railway sleepers)

	1998	1999	2000
Coniferous (softwood)	2,327	2,338	2,593
Broadleaved (hardwood)	1,384	1,335	1,384
Total	3,711	3,673	3,977

Source: FAO.

Fishing

('000 metric tons, live weight, year ending 30 June)

	1996/97	1997/98	1998/99
Capture	198.0	205.4	216.3
Skipjack tuna	5.6	3.5	9.8
Sharks, rays, skates, etc.	12.6	10.5	10.2
Australian spiny lobster	9.9	10.4	16.1
Penaeus shrimps	23.9	24.7	23.4
Scallops	8.6	9.9	11.6
Aquaculture	26.6	28.1	33.7
Atlantic salmon	7.6	7.1	9.2
Total catch	224.6	233.5	250.1

Note: Figures exclude aquatic plants ('000 metric tons, capture only): 21.2 in 1997; 20.8 in 1998; 20.8 in 1999. Also excluded are crocodiles, recorded by number rather than by weight. The number of Estuarine crocodiles caught was: 8,777 in 1997; 9,896 in 1998; 8,185 in 1999. The number of Australian crocodiles caught was: 194 in 1997; 309 in 1998. Also excluded are pearl oyster shells (FAO estimates, metric tons): 250 in 1997; 250 in 1998; 250 in 1999.

Source: FAO, *Yearbook of Fishery Statistics*.

Mining

('000 metric tons, unless otherwise indicated)

	1998	1999	2000
Hard coal	285,000	293,000	301,000
Lignite	63,900	66,000	65,000
Crude petroleum ('000 barrels)	225,935	226,665	208,472
Natural gas (million cu metres)	30,364	30,743	30,794
Iron ore: gross weight	155,731	151,558	170,999
metal content	99,418	93,807	106,232
Copper ore*	607	739	830
Nickel ore (metric tons)*	143,513	127,000	168,300
Bauxite	44,553	48,416	53,802
Lead ore*	619	681	678
Zinc ore*	1,066	1,163	1,410
Tin ore (metric tons)*	10,174	10,011	9,146
Manganese ore (metallurgical):			
gross weight	1,500	1,900	1,613
metal content	729	929	787
Chromite	80	70	90
Ilmenite	2,425	1,989	2,156
Leucoxene	31	31	27
Rutile	243	190	237
Tantalum and niobium (columbium) concentrates (metric tons)‡	1,150	1,230	1,600
Zirconium concentrates	369	359	373
Antimony ore (metric tons)*	1,800†	1,679	1,511
Cobalt ore (metric tons)*†	4,000	7,000	5,100
Silver (metric tons)*	1,474	1,720	2,060
Uranium (metric tons)*§	4,885	5,979	7,578
Gold (kilograms)*	310,070	301,070	296,410
Limestone†	12,000	12,000	12,000
Bertonite and bentonitic clay†	104	180	180
Kaolin and ball clay†	180	200	220
Brick clay and shale†	8,000	8,000	8,000
Magnesite (metric tons)	360,115	280,505	349,783
Phosphate rock‖	1†	1†	805
Barite (Barytes)†	13	18	20
Salt (unrefined)	9,033	10,022	8,798
Gypsum (crude)†	1,900	2,500	3,800
Talc (metric tons)¶	199,315	190,037	178,545
Pyrophyllite (metric tons)¶	702	347	1,727
Diamonds ('000 carats):			
gem	18,379	16,381	14,656
industrial	22,464	13,403	11,992

* Figures refer to the metal content of ores and concentrates.

† Estimated production.

‡ The estimated metal content (in metric tons) was: Niobium (Columbium) 140 in 1998, 140 in 1999, 160 in 2000; Tantalum 330 in 1998, 350 in 1999, 485 in 2000.

§ Data from the World Nuclear Association (London, United Kingdom).

‖ The estimated phosphoric acid content (in '000 metric tons) was 28% in 2000.

¶ Production during 12 months ending 30 June of the year stated.

Source (unless otherwise indicated): US Geological Survey.

Industry

SELECTED PRODUCTS

(year ending 30 June, '000 metric tons, unless otherwise indicated)

	1997/98	1998/99	1999/2000
Pig-iron	7,928	7,453	6,489
Blooms and slabs from continuous casting	8,356	7,698	6,742
Aluminium—unwrought*	1,589	1,686	1,742
Copper—unwrought	286	313	477
Lead—unwrought*	185	199	233
Zinc—unwrought*	304	323	405
Tin—unwrought (metric tons)*	650	595	600
Motor spirit (petrol—million litres)	18,592	18,705	18,652
Fuel oil (million litres)	1,673	1,634	1,839
Diesel-automotive oil (million litres)	13,183	12,968	12,737
Aviation turbine fuel (million litres)	5,423	5,219	5,538
Clay bricks (million)	1,532	1,594	1,735
Woven cotton fabrics (incl. towelling, '000 sq metres)†	62,000	56,000	n.a.
Woven woollen fabrics (incl. blanketing, '000 sq metres)†	6,600	6,300	n.a.
Electricity (million kWh)	176,212	179,630	184,790
Cement	7,236	7,704	7,937
Concrete—ready-mixed ('000 cu m)	17,412	18,601	20,597
Newsprint	402	400	381
Wheat flour†	1,762	1,857	n.a.
Beer (million litres)	1,757	1,729	1,768
Tobacco and cigarettes (metric tons)	21,257	21,045	20,688

* Primary refined metal only.

† Source: UN, *Industrial Commodity Statistics Yearbook*.

2000/01: Wine (million litres) 1,035. Source: Australian Wine and Brandy Corporation.

Finance

CURRENCY AND EXCHANGE RATES

Monetary Units

100 cents = 1 Australian dollar ($A).

Sterling, US Dollar and Euro Equivalents (31 May 2002)

£1 sterling = $A2.5849;
US $1 = $A1.7624;
€1 = $A1.6544;
$A100 = £38.69 = US $56.74 = €60.45.

Average Exchange Rate (US $ per Australian dollar)

1999 0.6453
2000 0.5823
2001 0.5176

COMMONWEALTH GOVERNMENT BUDGET

($A million, year ending 30 June)

Revenue	1998/99	1999/2000	2000/01
Tax revenue	141,104	152,457	151,156
Direct taxes	103,017	113,687	120,861
Individuals	76,729	83,161	76,599
Companies	20,734	23,982	35,136
Indirect taxes, etc.	32,415	33,534	25,601
Non-tax revenue	5,341	17,465	10,369
Total	146,444	169,921	161,526

Expenditure	1998/99	1999/2000	2000/01
Defence	11,202	9,956	11,360
Education	9,736	10,587	10,966
Health	23,343	23,540	25,242
Social security and welfare	52,779	57,129	66,898
Economic services	7,666	7,924	9,940
General public services	8,142	19,131	11,923
Public-debt interest	7,508	9,493	5,836
Total (incl. others)	140,814	160,408	156,783

Source: Reserve Bank of Australia, *Bulletin*.

OFFICIAL RESERVES (US $ million at 31 December)

	1999	2000	2001
Gold*	743	699	709
IMF special drawing rights	72	94	109
Reserve position in IMF	1,633	1,243	1,412
Foreign exchange	19,507	16,782	16,434
Total	21,956	18,817	18,664

* Valued at market-related prices.

Source: IMF, *International Financial Statistics.*

MONEY SUPPLY ($A million at 31 December)

	1999	2000	2001
Currency outside banks	24,604	26,928	28,471
Demand deposits at trading and savings banks	101,179	110,660	138,456
Total money (incl. others)	125,945	137,720	167,035

Source: IMF, *International Financial Statistics.*

COST OF LIVING (Consumer Price Index*; base: 1990 = 100)

	1998	1999	2000
Food	122.3	126.4	129.5
Electricity, gas and other fuels†	120.1	120.0	126.2
Clothing	104.8	103.7	106.8
Rent‡	91.7	94.7	101.2
All items (incl. others)	117.3	119.1	124.4

* Weighted average of eight capital cities.

† From September 1998 including water and sewerage.

‡ Including expenditure on maintenance and repairs of dwellings; from September 1998 excluding mortgage interest charges and including house purchase and utilities.

Source: ILO, *Yearbook of Labour Statistics.*

2001: Food 138.0; All items 129.8 (Source: UN, *Monthly Bulletin of Statistics*).

NATIONAL ACCOUNTS ($A million, year ending 30 June)

National Income and Product (at current prices)

	1997/98	1998/99	1999/2000
Compensation of employees	270,267	286,761	303,134
Operating surplus	143,093	146,791	159,384
Domestic factor incomes	413,360	433,552	462,518
Consumption of fixed capital	87,621	91,509	97,531
Gross domestic product (GDP) at factor cost	500,981	525,061	560,049
Indirect taxes *Less* Subsidies	64,900	70,356	72,093
GDP in purchasers' values	565,881	595,417	632,141
Net factor income from abroad	−17,955	−18,328	−18,591
Gross national product	547,926	577,089	613,550
Less Consumption of fixed capital	87,621	91,509	97,531
National income in market prices	460,305	485,580	516,019

Expenditure on the Gross Domestic Product (at current prices)

	1997/98	1998/99	1999/2000
Government final consumption expenditure	103,045	108,733	117,773
Private final consumption expenditure	333,407	353,757	373,313
Increase in stocks	960	5,307	2,062
Gross fixed capital formation	133,215	142,230	151,103
Statistical discrepancy	—	—	2,739
Total domestic expenditure	570,627	610,027	644,251
Exports of goods and services	113,829	111,843	125,774
Less Imports of goods and services	118,575	126,453	140,954
GDP in purchasers' values	565,881	595,417	631,810

Gross Domestic Product by Economic Activity
(provisional, at constant prices)

	1997/98*	1998/99†	1999/2000‡
Agriculture, hunting, forestry and fishing	16,668	19,044	19,005
Mining and quarrying	23,769	23,873	26,183
Manufacturing	65,878	73,800	75,560
Electricity, gas and water	14,292	13,496	11,314
Construction	30,003	34,334	34,434
Wholesale and retail trade	61,519	62,366	66,679
Transport, storage and communications	49,129	50,317	54,049
Finance, insurance, real estate and business services	92,060	97,243	114,389
Ownership of dwellings	49,169	52,961	55,603
Public administration and defence	23,185	22,906	22,702
Other community, recreational and personal services (incl. restaurants and hotels)	88,849	96,419	95,079
Sub-total	514,522	546,759	574,997
Taxes on products *Less* subsidies on products	42,734	42,680	48,303
Statistical discrepancy	−333	2,107	−2,347
GDP in purchasers' values	556,923	591,546	620,963

* At constant 1996/97 prices.

† At constant 1997/98 prices.

‡ At constant 1998/99 prices.

BALANCE OF PAYMENTS (US $ million)

	1999	2000	2001
Exports of goods f.o.b.	56,096	64,041	63,667
Imports of goods f.o.b.	−65,826	−68,752	−61,644
Trade balance	−9,730	−4,711	2,023
Exports of services	17,354	18,390	16,123
Imports of services	−18,304	−18,075	−16,692
Balance on goods and services	−10,681	−4,396	1,455
Other income received	6,909	8,586	7,720
Other income paid	−19,211	−19,533	−18,389
Balance on goods, services and income	−22,983	−15,344	−9,215
Current transfers received	3,003	2,622	2,242
Current transfers paid	−3,032	−2,669	−2,221
Current balance	−23,012	−15,391	−9,194
Capital account (net)	819	615	590
Direct investment abroad	2,989	−5,133	−11,126
Direct investment from abroad	5,699	11,512	4,067
Portfolio investment assets	−6,443	−4,714	−6,838
Portfolio investment liabilities	17,224	14,484	16,828
Financial derivatives assets	247	−966	327
Financial derivatives liabilities	1,054	387	−141
Other investment assets	−2,906	−4,210	314
Other investment liabilities	10,105	2,954	5,701
Net errors and omissions	929	−902	569
Overall balance	6,705	−1,365	1,096

Source: IMF, *International Financial Statistics.*

External Trade

PRINCIPAL COMMODITIES ($A million, year ending 30 June)

Imports f.o.b.	1998/99	1999/2000	2000/01
Food and live animals	3,760	3,954	4,236
Mineral fuels, lubricants, etc.	4,621	7,680	10,473
Petroleum, petroleum products, etc.	4,524	7,516	10,295
Chemicals and related products	11,435	12,497	14,200
Medicinal and pharmaceutical products	3,041	3,520	4,371
Basic manufactures	12,855	13,654	14,055
Machinery and transport equipment	45,418	51,442	53,492
Machinery specialized for particular industries	4,234	4,153	3,835
General industrial machinery, equipment and parts	5,770	5,398	5,729
Office machines and automatic data-processing machines	7,104	7,589	8,317
Telecommunications and sound-recording and reproducing apparatus and equipment	4,926	6,773	7,938
Other electrical machinery, apparatus, appliances and parts	5,870	6,213	6,782
Road vehicles (incl. air-cushion vehicles) and parts*	11,904	12,784	14,346
Other transport equipment and parts*	2,848	5,432	3,409
Miscellaneous manufactured articles	14,463	15,479	16,804
Total (incl. others)	97,611	110,078	118,264

* Data on parts exclude tyres, engines and electrical parts.

Exports f.o.b.	1998/99	1999/2000	2000/01
Food and live animals	15,453	16,892	20,115
Meat and meat preparations	4,000	4,467	5,772
Cereals and cereal preparations	5,041	4,940	5,405
Crude materials (inedible) except fuels	17,219	18,381	23,592
Textile fibres and waste*	4,070	4,299	5,590
Metalliferous ores and metal scrap	10,665	11,314	14,761
Mineral fuels, lubricants, etc.	14,162	18,083	25,211
Coal, coke and briquettes	9,302	8,337	10,840
Petroleum, petroleum products, etc.	3,133	7,145	10,868
Chemicals and related products	3,575	4,195	5,146
Basic manufactures	10,117	12,328	14,011
Non-ferrous metals	5,399	7,395	9,398
Machinery and transport equipment	10,324	11,619	13,408
Road vehicles (incl. air-cushion vehicles) and parts†	2,091	2,808	3,833
Miscellaneous manufactured articles	3,447	3,826	4,455
Non-monetary gold (excl. gold ores and concentrates)	6,335	5,031	5,110
Total (incl. others)	85,991	97,286	119,602

* Excluding wool tops.
† Data on parts exclude tyres, engines and electrical parts.

PRINCIPAL TRADING PARTNERS ($A million, year ending 30 June)

Imports f.o.b.	1998/99	1999/2000	2000/01
Canada	1,547	1,848	1,866
China, People's Republic	6,106	7,515	9,881
France	2,202	2,228	2,478
Germany	6,082	5,791	6,174
Hong Kong	1,228	1,280	1,367
Indonesia	3,275	2,701	3,277
Ireland	1,000	937	1,140
Italy	2,916	3,043	3,259
Japan	13,587	14,110	15,371
Korea, Republic	3,894	4,311	4,710
Malaysia	2,845	3,765	4,177
New Zealand	3,950	4,372	4,565
Papua New Guinea	781	1,353	1,457
Saudi Arabia	532	1,002	1,613
Singapore	2,944	4,359	3,898
Sweden	1,575	1,646	1,624
Switzerland	1,092	1,279	1,171
Taiwan	2,978	3,244	3,327
Thailand	1,902	2,422	2,780
United Kingdom	5,545	6,350	6,321
USA	20,893	22,135	22,356
Viet Nam	972	1,726	2,431
Total (incl. others)	97,611	110,078	118,264

Exports f.o.b.	1998/99	1999/2000	2000/01
Belgium-Luxembourg	1,085	1,089	1,003
Canada	1,274	1,175	1,768
China, People's Republic	3,748	4,959	6,846
France	914	871	1,079
Germany	1,409	1,245	1,490
Hong Kong	3,071	3,211	3,904
India	1,837	1,588	2,086
Indonesia	2,199	2,408	3,119
Italy	1,564	1,575	2,100
Japan	16,566	18,822	23,479
Korea, Republic	6,320	7,615	9,209
Malaysia	1,859	2,141	2,506
Netherlands	866	1,378	1,738
New Zealand	5,838	6,739	6,872
Papua New Guinea	1,014	927	1,050
Philippines	1,208	1,304	1,495
Saudi Arabia	1,060	1,334	2,196
Singapore	3,417	4,855	5,997
South Africa	943	1,039	1,296
Taiwan	4,202	4,696	5,871
Thailand	1,306	1,703	2,219
United Kingdom	4,473	4,158	4,639
USA	7,983	9,602	11,654
Total (incl. others)	85,991	97,286	119,602

Transport

RAILWAYS (traffic)

	1997/98	1998/99	1999/2000
Passengers carried (million)	587.7	595.2	629.2
Freight carried (millon metric tons)	487.5	492.0	508.0
Freight ton-km ('000 million)	125.2	127.4	134.2

* Traffic on government railways only.

ROAD TRAFFIC ('000 vehicles registered at 31 October)

	1997	1998	1999
Passenger vehicles	9,206.2	9,526.7	9,719.9
Light commercial vehicles	1,632.2	1,686.4	1,721.2
Trucks	418.4	426.9	427.8
Buses	61.1	64.0	65.9
Motor cycles	313.1	328.8	333.8

SHIPPING

Merchant Fleet (registered at 31 December)

	1999	2000	2001
Number of vessels	621	631	622
Total displacement ('000 grt)	2,084.2	1,912.1	1,887.8

Source: Lloyd's Register-Fairplay, *World Fleet Statistics*.

INTERNATIONAL SEA-BORNE TRAFFIC

('000 metric tons, year ending 30 June)

	1997/98	1998/99	1999/2000
Goods loaded	427,968	438,816	487,500
Goods unloaded	52,032	57,612	54,180

Source: UN, *Monthly Bulletin of Statistics*.

CIVIL AVIATION (traffic)*

	1997	1998	1999
International services:			
Passenger arrivals	7,090,979	7,153,514	7,540,535
Passenger departures	7,010,931	7,084,655	7,442,226
Freight carried (metric tons)	649,371	631,908	680,458
Mail carried (metric tons)	21,975	23,437	25,316
Domestic services†:			
Passengers carried	23,375,317	23,574,788	24,375,906
Passenger-km ('000)	26,357,069	26,774,140	27,842,795
Freight and mail carried (metric tons)	190,680	192,770	192,326

* Includes Christmas Island and Norfolk Island.

† Year ending 30 June.

Tourism

VISITOR ARRIVALS BY COUNTRY OF ORIGIN*

	1999	2000†	2001†
Canada	78,393	89,100	93,100
China, People's Republic	97,996	124,400	162,700
Germany	144,509	144,600	147,300
Hong Kong	134,158	n.a.	n.a.
Indonesia	90,992	102,900	97,800
Japan	707,463	720,300	676,900
Korea, Republic	108,634	160,100	176,000
Malaysia	139,793	153,500	154,400
New Zealand	728,798	821,100	799,800
Singapore	266,966	276,100	293,200
Taiwan	147,495	135,000	111,400
Thailand	61,849	74,200	79,200
United Kingdom	528,431	578,000	621,200
USA	417,046	482,100	443,200
Total (incl. others)	4,459,503	4,946,200	4,871,000

* Visitors intending to stay for less than one year.

† Preliminary figures.

Receipts from tourism ($A million): 17,000 in 1999; 19,800 in 2000.

Source: Australian Tourist Commission, Sydney.

Communications Media

	1999	2000	2001
Television receivers ('000 in use)	13,400	14,129	n.a.
Telephones ('000 main lines in use)	9,760	10,050	10,060
Mobile cellular telephones ('000 subscribers)	6,315	8,562	11,169
Personal computers ('000 in use)	7,900	8,900	10,000
Internet users ('000)	5,600	6,600	7,200

Source: International Telecommunication Union.

Radio receivers ('000 in use, 1997): 25,500.

Facsimile machines ('000 in use, 1997): 900.

Book production (1994): 10,835 titles.

Newspapers (1996): 65 dailies (estimated combined circulation 5,370,000); 98 non-dailies (circulation 383,000).

Source: mainly UNESCO, *Statistical Yearbook*.

Education

(August 2001)

	Institutions	Teaching staff	Students ('000)
Government schools	6,942	152,138*	2,248.2†
Non-government schools	2,654	69,789*	1,019.9
Higher educational institutions	47‡	78,228	726.4

* Full-time teaching staff and full-time equivalent of part-time teaching staff.

† Comprising 1,384,866 primary and 863,353 secondary students.

‡ Public institutions only.

Directory

The Constitution

The Federal Constitution was adopted on 9 July 1900 and came into force on 1 January 1901. Its main provisions are summarized below:

PARLIAMENT

The legislative power of the Commonwealth of Australia is vested in a Federal Parliament, consisting of HM the Queen (represented by the Governor-General), a Senate, and a House of Representatives. The Governor-General may appoint such times for holding the sessions of the Parliament as he or she thinks fit, and may also from time to time, by proclamation or otherwise, prorogue the Parliament, and may in like manner dissolve the House of Representatives. By convention, these powers are exercised on the advice of the Prime Minister. After any general election Parliament must be summoned to meet not later than 30 days after the day appointed for the return of the writs.

THE SENATE

The Senate is composed of 12 senators from each state, two senators representing the Australian Capital Territory and two representing the Northern Territory. The senators are directly chosen by the people of the state or territory, voting in each case as one electorate, and are elected by proportional representation. Senators representing a state have a six-year term and retire by rotation, one-half from each state on 30 June of each third year. The term of a senator representing a territory is limited to three years. In the case of a state, if a senator vacates his or her seat before the expiration of the term of service, the houses of parliament of the state for which the senator was chosen shall, in joint session, choose a person to hold the place until the expiration of the term or until the election of a successor. If the state parliament is not in session, the Governor of the state, acting on the advice of the state's executive council, may appoint a senator to hold office until parliament reassembles, or until a new senator is elected.

The Senate may proceed to the dispatch of business notwithstanding the failure of any state to provide for its representation in the Senate.

THE HOUSE OF REPRESENTATIVES

In accordance with the Australian Constitution, the total number of members of the House of Representatives must be as nearly as practicable double that of the Senate. The number in each state is in proportion to population, but under the Constitution must be at least five. The House of Representatives is composed of 150 members, including two members for the Australian Capital Territory and two members for the Northern Territory.

Members are elected by universal adult suffrage and voting is compulsory. Only Australian citizens are eligible to vote in Australian elections. British subjects, if they are not Australian citizens or already on the rolls, have to take out Australian citizenship before thay can enrol and before they can vote.

Members are chosen by the electors of their respective electorates by the preferential voting system.

The duration of the Parliament is limited to three years.

To be nominated for election to the House of Representatives, a candidate must be 18 years of age or over, an Australian citizen, and entitled to vote at the election or qualified to become an elector.

THE EXECUTIVE GOVERNMENT

The executive power of the Federal Government is vested in the Queen, and is exercisable by the Governor-General, advised by an Executive Council of Ministers of State, known as the Federal Executive Council. These ministers are, or must become within three months, members of the Federal Parliament.

The Australian Constitution is construed as subject to the principles of responsible government and the Governor-General acts on the advice of the ministers in relation to most matters.

THE JUDICIAL POWER

See Judicial System, below.

THE STATES

The Australian Constitution safeguards the Constitution of each state by providing that it shall continue as at the establishment of the Commonwealth, except as altered in accordance with its own provisions. The legislative power of the Federal Parliament is limited in the main to those matters that are listed in section 51 of the Constitution, while the states possess, as well as concurrent powers in those matters, residual legislative powers enabling them to legislate in any way for 'the peace, order and good Government' of their respective territories. When a state law is inconsistent with a law of the Commonwealth, the latter prevails, and the former is invalid to the extent of the inconsistency.

The states may not, without the consent of the Commonwealth, raise or maintain naval or military forces, or impose taxes on any property belonging to the Commonwealth of Australia, nor may the Commonwealth tax state property. The states may not coin money.

The Federal Parliament may not enact any law for establishing any religion or for prohibiting the exercise of any religion, and no religious test may be imposed as a qualification for any office under the Commonwealth.

The Commonwealth of Australia is charged with protecting every state against invasion, and, on the application of a state executive government, against domestic violence.

Provision is made under the Constitution for the admission of new states and for the establishment of new states within the Commonwealth of Australia.

ALTERATION OF THE CONSTITUTION

Proposed laws for the amendment of the Constitution must be passed by an absolute majority in both Houses of the Federal Parliament, and not less than two or more than six months after its passage through both Houses the proposed law must be submitted in each state to the qualified electors.

In the event of one House twice refusing to pass a proposed amendment that has already received an absolute majority in the other House, the Governor-General may, notwithstanding such refusal, submit the proposed amendment to the electors. By convention, the Governor-General acts on the advice of the Prime Minister. If in a majority of the states a majority of the electors voting approve the proposed law and if a majority of all the electors voting also approve, it shall be presented to the Governor-General for Royal Assent.

No alteration diminishing the proportionate representation of any state in either House of the Federal Parliament, or the minimum number of representatives of a state in the House of Representatives, or increasing, diminishing or altering the limits of the state, or in any way affecting the provisions of the Constitution in relation thereto, shall become law unless the majority of the electors voting in that state approve the proposed law.

STATES AND TERRITORIES

New South Wales

The state's executive power is vested in the Governor, appointed by the Crown, who is assisted by an Executive Council composed of cabinet ministers.

The state's legislative power is vested in a bicameral Parliament, composed of the Legislative Council and the Legislative Assembly. The Legislative Council consists of 42 members directly elected for the duration of two parliaments (i.e. eight years), 21 members retiring every four years. The Legislative Assembly consists of 93 members and sits for four years.

Victoria

The state's legislative power is vested in a bicameral Parliament: the Upper House, or Legislative Council, of 44 members, elected for two terms of the Legislative Assembly; and the Lower House, or Legislative Assembly, of 88 members, elected for a minimum of three and maximum of four years. One-half of the members of the Council retires every three–four years.

In the exercise of the executive power the Governor is assisted by a cabinet of responsible ministers. Not more than six members of the Council and not more than 17 members of the Assembly may occupy salaried office at any one time.

The state has 88 electoral districts, each returning one member, and 22 electoral provinces, each returning two Council members.

Queensland

The state's executive power is vested in the Governor, appointed by the Crown, who is assisted by an Executive Council composed of Ministers. The state's legislative power is vested in the Parliament comprising the Legislative Assembly (composed of 89 members who are elected at least every three years to represent 89 electoral districts) and the Governor, who assents to bills passed by the Assembly. The state's Constitution anticipates that Ministers are also members of the Legislative Assembly and provides that up to 18 members of the Assembly can be appointed Ministers.

South Australia

The state's Constitution vests the legislative power in a Parliament elected by the people and consisting of a Legislative Council and a House of Assembly. The Council is composed of 22 members, one-half of whom retires every three years. Their places are filled by new members elected under a system of proportional representation, with the whole state as a single electorate. The executive has no authority to dissolve this body, except in circumstances warranting a double dissolution.

The 47 members of the House of Assembly are elected for four years from 45 electoral districts.

The executive power is vested in a Governor, appointed by the Crown, and an Executive Council consisting of 10 responsible ministers.

Western Australia

The state's administration is vested in the Governor, a Legislative Council and a Legislative Assembly.

The Legislative Council consists of 34 members, two of the six electoral regions returning seven members on a proportional representation basis, and four regions returning five members. Election is for a term of four years.

The Legislative Assembly consists of 57 members, elected for four years, each representing one electorate.

Tasmania

The state's executive authority is vested in a Governor, appointed by the Crown, who acts upon the advice of his premier and ministers, who are elected members of either the Legislative Council or the House of Assembly. The Council consists of 15 members who sit for six years, retiring in rotation. The House of Assembly has 25 members elected for four years.

Northern Territory

On 1 July 1978, the Northern Territory was established as a body politic with executive authority for specified functions of government. Most functions of the Federal Government were transferred to the Territory Government in 1978 and 1979, major exceptions being Aboriginal affairs and uranium mining.

The Territory Parliament consists of a single house, the Legislative Assembly, with 25 members. The first Parliament stayed in office for three years. As from the election held in August 1980, members are elected for a term of four years.

The office of Administrator continues. The Northern Territory (Self-Government) Act provides for the appointment of an Administrator by the Governor-General charged with the duty of administering the Territory. In respect of matters transferred to the Territory Government, the Administrator acts with the advice of the Territory Executive Council; in respect of matters retained by the Commonwealth, the Administrator acts on Commonwealth advice.

Australian Capital Territory

On 29 November 1988 the Australian Capital Territory (ACT) was established as a body politic. The ACT Government has executive authority for specified functions, although a number of these were to be retained by the Federal Government for a brief period during which transfer arrangements were to be finalized.

The ACT Parliament consists of a single house, the Legislative Assembly, with 17 members. The first election was held in March 1989. Members are elected for a term of three years.

The Federal Government retains control of some of the land in the ACT for the purpose of maintaining the Seat of Government and the national capital plan.

Jervis Bay Territory

Following the attainment of self-government by the ACT (see above), the Jervis Bay Territory, which had formed part of the ACT since 1915, remained a separate Commonwealth Territory, administered by the then Department of the Arts, Sport, the Environment and Territories. The area is governed in accordance with the Jervis Bay Territory Administration Ordinance, issued by the Governor-General on 17 December 1990.

The Government

Head of State: HM Queen ELIZABETH II (succeeded to the throne 6 February 1952).

Governor-General: Dr PETER J. HOLLINGWORTH (assumed office 29 June 2001).

THE MINISTRY
(August 2002)

Cabinet Ministers

Prime Minister: JOHN HOWARD.

Deputy Prime Minister and Minister for Transport and Regional Services: JOHN ANDERSON.

Minister for Foreign Affairs: ALEXANDER DOWNER.

Treasurer: PETER COSTELLO.

Minister for Trade: MARK VAILE.

Minister for Defence and Leader of the Government in the Senate: Senator ROBERT HILL.

Minister for Communications, Information Technology and the Arts: Senator RICHARD ALSTON.

Minister for Employment and Workplace Relations: TONY ABBOTT.

Minister for Education, Science and Training: Dr BRENDAN NELSON.

Minister for Health and Ageing: Senator KAY PATTERSON.

Minister for Industry, Tourism and Resources: IAN MACFARLANE.

Minister for the Environment and Heritage: Dr DAVID KEMP.

Minister for Finance and Administration: Senator NICHOLAS MINCHIN.

Minister for Family and Community Services: AMANDA VANSTONE.

Minister for Agriculture, Fisheries and Forestry: WARREN TRUSS.

Minister for Immigration and Multicultural and Indigenous Affairs: PHILLIP RUDDOCK.

Attorney-General: DARYL WILLIAMS.

Other Ministers

Minister for Regional Services, Territories and Local Government: WILSON TUCKEY.

Minister for Revenue and Assistant Treasurer: Senator HELEN COONAN.

Minister for Small Business and Tourism: JOE HOCKEY.

Minister for Forestry and Conservation: Senator IAN MACDONALD.

Minister for Science: PETER MCGAURAN.

Minister for Employment Services: MAL BROUGH.

Minister for Children and Youth Affairs: LAWRENCE ANTHONY.

Minister Assisting the Minister for Defence and Minister for Veterans' Affairs: Senator DANNA VALE.

Minister for Ageing: KEVIN ANDREWS.

Special Minister of State: Senator ERIC ABETZ.

Minister for Justice and Customs: Senator CHRISTOPHER ELLISON.

Minister for the Arts and Sport: Senator ROD KEMP

Minister for Citizenship and Multicultural Affairs: GARY HARDGRAVE.

DEPARTMENTS

Department of the Prime Minister and Cabinet: 3–5 National Circuit, Barton, ACT 2600; tel. (2) 6271-5111; fax (2) 6271-5414; internet www.dpmc.gov.au.

Aboriginal and Torres Strait Islander Commission: Lovett Tower, Woden Town Centre, Phillip, ACT 2606; tel. (2) 6121-4000; fax (2) 6121-4621; internet www.atsic.gov.au.

Department of Agriculture, Fisheries and Forestry: GPOB 858, Canberra, ACT 2601; tel. (2) 6272-3933; fax (2) 6272-3008; internet www.affa.gov.au.

Attorney-General's Department: Robert Garran Offices, Barton, ACT 2600; tel. (2) 6250-6666; fax (2) 6250-5900; internet www.law.gov.au.

Department of Communications, Information Technology and the Arts: GPOB 2154, Canberra, ACT 2601; tel. (2) 6271-1000; fax (2) 6271-1901; internet www.dcita.gov.au.

Department of Defence: Russell Offices, Russell Drive, Campbell, Canberra, ACT 2600; tel. (2) 6265-9111; e-mail webmaster@cbr.defence.gov.au; internet www.defence.gov.au.

Department of Education, Science and Training: GPOB 9880, Canberra, ACT 2601; tel. (2) 6240-8111; fax (2) 6240-8571; e-mail library@detya.gov.au; internet www.detya.gov.au.

Department of Employment and Workplace Relations: GPOB 9879, Canberra, ACT 2601; tel. (2) 6121-6000; fax (2) 6121-7542; e-mail webmaster@dewrsb.gov.au; internet www.dewrsb.gov.au.

Department of the Environment and Heritage: GPOB 787, Canberra, ACT 2601; tel. (2) 6274-1111; fax (2) 6274-1123; internet www.ea.gov.au.

Department of Family and Community Services: Box 7788, Canberra Mail Centre, ACT 2610; tel. (2) 6244-7788; fax (2) 6244-5540; e-mail facs.internet@facs.gov.au; internet www.facs.gov.au.

Department of Finance and Administration: John Gorton Bldg, King Edward Tce, Parkes, ACT 2600; tel. (2) 6263-2222; fax (2) 6273-3021; internet www.dofa.gov.au.

Department of Foreign Affairs and Trade: GPOB 12, Canberra City, ACT 2601; tel. (2) 6261-1111; fax (2) 6261-3959; internet www.dfat.gov.au.

Department of Health and Ageing: GPOB 9848, Canberra, ACT 2601; tel. (2) 6289-1555; fax (2) 6281-6946; internet www.health.gov.au.

Department of Immigration and Multicultural and Indigenous Affairs: Benjamin Offices, Chan St, Belconnen, ACT 2617; tel. (2) 6264-1111; fax (2) 6264-2670; internet www.immi.gov.au.

Department of Industry, Tourism and Resources: GPOB 9839, Canberra, ACT 2601; tel. (2) 6213-6000; fax (2) 6213-7000; e-mail distpubs@isr.gov.au; internet www.industry.gov.au.

Department of Transport and Regional Services: GPOB 594, Canberra, ACT 2601; tel. (2) 6274-7111; fax (2) 6257-2505; e-mail publicaffairs@dotrs.gov.au; internet www.dotrs.gov.au.

Department of the Treasury: Langton Crescent, Parkes, ACT 2600; tel. (2) 6263-2111; fax (2) 6273-2614; internet www.treasury.gov.au.

Department of Veterans' Affairs: POB 21, Woden, ACT 2606; tel. (2) 6289-1111; fax (2) 6289-6025; internet www.dva.gov.au.

Legislature

FEDERAL PARLIAMENT

Senate

President: Senator MARGARET REID.

Election, 10 November 2001

Party	Seats*
Liberal Party of Australia	31
Australian Labor Party	28
Australian Democrats Party	8
National Party of Australia	3
Greens	2
Independents	3
One Nation	1
Total	76

* The election was for 36 of the 72 seats held by state senators and for all four senators representing the Northern Territory and the Australian Capital Territory (See The Constitution). The figures for seats refer to the totals held from 1 July 2002.

House of Representatives

Speaker: NEIL ANDREW.

Election, 10 November 2001

Party	Seats
Liberal Party of Australia	69
Australian Labor Party	65
National Party of Australia	13
Independents	3
Total	150

State and Territory Governments

(July 2002)

NEW SOUTH WALES

Governor: MARIE BASHIR, Level 3, Chief Secretary's Bldg, 121 Macquarie St, Sydney, NSW 2000; tel. (2) 9242-4200; fax (2) 9242-4266; internet www.nsw.gov.au.

Premier: ROBERT (BOB) J. CARR (Labor), Level 40, Governor Macquarie Tower, 1 Farrer Place, Sydney, NSW 2000; tel. (2) 9228-5239; fax (2) 9228-3935; e-mail bob.carr@ nsw.gov.au.

VICTORIA

Governor: JOHN LANDY, Government House, Melbourne, Vic 3004; tel. (3) 9655-4211; fax (3) 9654-8430; internet www.governor.vic.gov.au.

Premier: STEPHEN P. BRACKS (Labor); 1 Treasury Place, Vic 3000; internet www.premier.vic.gov.au.

QUEENSLAND

Governor: Maj.-Gen. PETER M. ARNISON, Government House, Brisbane, Qld 4001; tel. (7) 3858-5700; fax (7) 3858-5701; e-mail govhouse@govhouse.qld.gov.au; internet www.govhouse.qld.gov.au.

Premier: PETER D. BEATTIE (Labor), Executive Bldg, 100 George St, Brisbane, Qld 4002; tel. (7) 3224-2111; fax (7) 3229-2990; internet www.premiers.qld.gov.au.

SOUTH AUSTRALIA

Governor: MARJORIE JACKSON-NELSON, Government House, North Terrace, Adelaide, SA 5000; tel. (8) 8203-9800; fax (8) 8203-9899; e-mail govthsesa@saugov.sa.gov.au; internet www.sa.gov.au.

Premier: MICHAEL (MIKE) RANN (Labor), 200 Victoria Square, Adelaide, SA 5001; tel. (8) 8463-3166; fax (8) 8463-3168; e-mail premier@saugov.sa.gov.au; internet www.ministers.sa.gov.au.

WESTERN AUSTRALIA

Governor: Lt-Gen. JOHN MURRAY SANDERSON, Government House, Perth, WA 6000; tel. (8) 9429-9199; fax (8) 9325-4476; e-mail enquiries@govhouse.wa.gov.au; internet www.wa.gov.au.

Premier: GEOFFREY GALLOP (Labor), 24th Floor, 197 St George's Terrace, Perth, WA 6000; tel. (8) 9222-9888; fax (8) 9322-1213; e-mail wa-government@mpc.wa.gov.au; internet www.premier.wa.gov.au.

TASMANIA

Governor: Sir GUY STEPHEN MONTAGUE GREEN, Government House, Hobart, Tas 7000; tel. (3) 6234-2611; fax (3) 6234-2556; internet www.tas.gov.au.

Premier: JAMES A. BACON (Labor), GPOB 123B, Hobart, Tas 7001; tel. (3) 6233-3464; fax (3) 6234-1572; e-mail premier@dpac.tas.gov.au; internet www.premier.tas.gov.au.

NORTHERN TERRITORY

Administrator: JOHN ANICTOMATIS, GPOB 497, Darwin, NT 0801; tel. (8) 8999-7103; fax (8) 8981-5521; internet www.nt.gov.au/administrator.

Chief Minister: CLARE MARTIN (Labor); GPOB 3146, Darwin, NT 0801; tel. (8) 8901-4000; fax (8) 8901-4099; e-mail chiefminister.nt@nt.gov.au; internet www.nt.gov.au/ministers.

AUSTRALIAN CAPITAL TERRITORY

Chief Minister: JONATHAN STANHOPE (Labor); Legislative Assembly Bldg, Civic Square, London Circuit, Canberra, ACT 2601; tel. (2) 6205-0104; fax (2) 6205-0399; e-mail canberraconnect@.act.gov.au; internet www.act.gov.au.

Political Organizations

Australians for Constitutional Monarchy (ACM): GPOB 9841, Sydney, NSW 2001; tel. (2) 9231-2200; fax (2) 9231-2359; e-mail acmhq@norepublic.com.au; internet www.norepublic.com.au; f. 1992; also known as No Republic; Exec. Dir KERRY JONES.

Australian Democrats Party: Victorian Division, G1/Eastbourne House, 62 Wellington Pde, East Melbourne, Vic 3002; tel. (3) 9419-5808; fax (3) 9419-5697; e-mail senator.bartlett@democrats.org.au; internet www.democrats.org.au; f. 1971; comprises the fmr Liberal Movement and the Australia Party; Leader Senator ANDREW BARTLETT.

Australian Greens: GPOB 1108, Canberra, ACT 2601; e-mail frontdesk@greens.org.au; internet www.greens.org.au; f. 1992; Leader Senator BOB BROWN.

Australian Labor Party (ALP): Centenary House, 19 National Circuit, Barton, ACT 2600; tel. (2) 6120-0800; fax (2) 6120-0801; e-mail natsect@alp.org.au; internet www.alp.org.au/; f. 1891; advocates social democracy; trade unions form part of its structure; Fed. Parl. Leader SIMON CREAN; Nat. Pres. GREG SWORD; Nat. Sec. GEOFF WALSH.

Australian Republican Movement (ARM): POB A870, Sydney South, NSW 1235; tel. (2) 9267-8022; fax (2) 9267-8155; e-mail republic@ozemail.com.au; internet www.republic.org.au; Chair. GREG BARNS; Nat. Dir JAMES TERRIE.

Communist Party of Australia: 65 Campbell St, Surry Hills, NSW 2010; tel. (2) 9212-6855; fax (2) 9281-5795; e-mail cpa@cpa.org.au; internet www.cpa.org.au; f. 1971; fmrly Socialist Party; advocates public ownership of the means of production, working-class political power; Pres. Dr H. MIDDLETON; Gen. Sec. P. SYMON.

Liberal Party of Australia: Federal Secretariat, Cnr Blackall and Macquarie Sts, Barton, ACT 2600; tel. (2) 6273-2564; fax (2) 6273-1534; e-mail libadm@liberal.org.au; internet www.liberal.org.au; f. 1944; advocates private enterprise, social justice, individual liberty and initiative; committed to national development, prosperity and security; Fed. Dir LYNTON CROSBY; Fed. Parl. Leader JOHN HOWARD.

National Party of Australia: John McEwen House, National Circuit, Barton, ACT 2600; tel. (2) 6273-3822; fax (2) 6273-1745; e-mail federal@nationalparty.org; internet www.nationalparty.org; f. 1916 as the Country Party of Australia; adopted present name in 1982; advocates balanced national development based on free enterprise, with special emphasis on the needs of people outside the major metropolitan areas; Fed. Pres. HELEN DICKIE; Fed. Parl. Leader JOHN ANDERSON; Fed. Dir ANDREW HALL.

One Nation Party: GPOB 812, Ipswich, Qld 4304; e-mail pauline@onenation.com.au; internet www.onenation.com.au; f. 1997; opposes globalization, high immigration and special funding for Aboriginal people, advocates public ownership of major services; Pres. (vacant); Vice-Pres. JOHN FISHER.

Diplomatic Representation

EMBASSIES AND HIGH COMMISSIONS IN AUSTRALIA

Argentina: POB 4835, Kingston, ACT 2604; tel. (2) 6273-9111; fax (2) 6273-0500; e-mail eaust@canberra.teknet.net.au; internet www.argentina.org.au; Ambassador: NÉSTOR E. STANCANELLI.

Austria: POB 3375, Manuka, ACT 2603; tel. (2) 6295-1533; fax (2) 6239-6751; e-mail austria@bigpond.net.au; internet www.austriaemb.org.au/; Ambassador: Dr OTMAR KOLER.

Bangladesh: POB 5, Red Hill, ACT 2603; tel. (2) 6295-3328; fax (2) 6295-3351; e-mail bdoot.canberra@cyberone.com.au; High Commissioner: MIRZA SHAMSUZZAMAN.

Belgium: 19 Arkana St, Yarralumla, ACT 2600; tel. (2) 6273-2501; fax (2) 6273-3392; e-mail canberra@diplobel.org; Ambassador: LUK DARRAS.

Bosnia and Herzegovina: 5 Beale Crescent, Deakin, ACT 2600; tel. (2) 6232-4646; fax (2) 6232-5554; e-mail embaucbr@webone.com.au; internet www.bosnia.webone.com.au; Ambassador: Dr RADOMIR DAVIDOVIĆ.

Brazil: GPOB 1540, Canberra, ACT 2601; tel. (2) 6273-2372; fax (2) 6273-2375; e-mail brazil@connect.net.au; internet brazil.org.au; Ambassador: ANTÔNIO AUGUSTO DAYRELL DE LIMA.

Brunei: 10 Beale Crescent, Deakin, ACT 2603; tel. (2) 6285 4500; fax (2) 6285-4545; High Commissioner: Haji ZAKARIA Haji AHMAD (acting).

Cambodia: 5 Canterbury Crescent, Deakin, ACT 2600; tel. (2) 6273-1259; fax (2) 6273-1053; e-mail cambodianembassy@ozemail.net.au; internet www.embassyofcambodia.org.nz/au; Ambassador: HOR NAMBORA.

Canada: Commonwealth Ave, Canberra, ACT 2600; tel. (2) 6270-4000; fax (2) 6273-3285; internet www.canada.org.au; High Commissioner: JEAN T. FOURNIER.

Chile: POB 69, Red Hill, ACT 2603; tel. (2) 6286-2430; fax (2) 6286-1289; e-mail chilemb@embachile-australia.com; internet www.embachile-australia.com; Ambassador: CRISTÓBAL VALDÉS.

China, People's Republic: 15 Coronation Drive, Yarralumla, ACT 2600; tel. (2) 6273-4780; fax (2) 6273-4878; Ambassador: WU TAO.

Colombia: GPOB 2892, Canberra City, ACT 2601; tel. (2) 6257-2027; fax (2) 6257-1448; e-mail emaustralia@iprimus.com.au; internet www.embacol.org.au; Ambassador: JUAN SANTIAGO URIBE.

Croatia: 14 Jindalee Crescent, O'Malley, ACT 2606; tel. (2) 6286-6988; fax (2) 6286-3544; e-mail croemb@bigpond.com; Ambassador: Dr MLADEN IBLER.

Cyprus: 30 Beale Crescent, Deakin, ACT 2600; tel. (2) 6281-0832; fax (2) 6281-0860; e-mail cyphicom@iprimus.com.au; High Commissioner: SOTOS LIASSIDES.

Czech Republic: 8 Culgoa Circuit, O'Malley, ACT 2606; tel. (2) 6290-1386; fax (2) 6290-0006; e-mail canberra@embassy.mzv.cz; Ambassador: JOSEF SLÁDEK.

Denmark: 15 Hunter St, Yarralumla, ACT 2600; tel. (2) 6273-2196; fax (2) 6273-3864; e-mail dkembact@dynamite.com.au; Ambassador: JENS OSTENFELD.

Ecuador: 1st Floor, Law Society Bldg of Canberra, 11 London Circuit, ACT 2601; tel. (2) 6262-5282; fax (2) 6262-5285; e-mail embecu@hotkey.net.au; Ambassador: Dr ABELARDO POSSO-SERRANO.

Egypt: 1 Darwin Ave, Yarralumla, ACT 2600; tel. (2) 6273-4437; fax (2) 6273-4279; Ambassador: ASSEM AHMED MEGAHED.

Fiji: POB 159, Deakin West, ACT 2600; tel. (2) 6260-5115; fax (2) 6260-5105; e-mail fhc@cyberone.com.au; High Commissioner: JIOJI KONROTE.

Finland: 12 Darwin Ave, Yarralumla, ACT 2600; tel. (2) 6273-3800; fax (2) 6273-3603; e-mail finland@austarmetro.com.au; internet www.finland.org.au; Ambassador: ANNELI PUURA-MÄRKÄLÄ.

France: 6 Perth Ave, Yarralumla, ACT 2600; tel. (2) 6216-0100; fax (2) 6216-0127; e-mail embassy@france.net.au; internet www.embafrance-au.org; Ambassador: PIERRE VIAUX.

Germany: 119 Empire Circuit, Yarralumla, ACT 2600; tel. (2) 6270-1911; fax (2) 6270-1951; e-mail embgerma@bigpond.net.au; internet www.germanembassy-canberra.com; Ambassador: Dr HORST BÄCHMANN.

Greece: 9 Turrana St, Yarralumla, ACT 2600; tel. (2) 6273-3011; fax (2) 6273-2620; e-mail greekemb@greekembassy-au.org; Ambassador: FOTIOS-JEAN XYDAS.

Holy See: POB 3633, Manuka, ACT 2603 (Apostolic Nunciature); tel. (2) 6295-3876; Apostolic Nuncio: Most Rev. FRANCESCO CANALINI, Titular Archbishop of Valeria.

Hungary: 17 Beale Crescent, Deakin, ACT 2600; tel. (2) 6282-3226; fax (2) 6285-3012; e-mail hungcbr@ozemail.com.au; Ambassador: Dr ISTVÁN GYÜRK.

India: 3–5 Moonah Place, Yarralumla, ACT 2600; tel. (2) 6273-3999; fax (2) 6273-1308; e-mail hciisi@cyberone.com.au; High Commissioner: C. P. RAVINDRANATHAN.

Indonesia: 8 Darwin Ave, Yarralumla, ACT 2600; tel. (2) 6273-8600; fax (2) 6250-6017; e-mail embindo@cyberone.com.au; Ambassador: SUDJADNAN PARNOHADININGRAT.

Iran: POB 3219, Manuka, ACT 2603; tel. (2) 6290-2427; fax (2) 6290-2431; internet www.embassyiran.org.au; Ambassador: Dr GHOLAMALI KHOSHROO.

Iraq: 48 Culgoa Circuit, O'Malley, ACT 2606; tel. (2) 6286-1333; fax (2) 6290-1788; Chargé d'affaires: NATIK A. RADHI.

Ireland: 20 Arkana St, Yarralumla, ACT 2600; tel. (2) 6273-3022; fax (2) 6273-3741; e-mail irishemb@cyberone.com.au; Ambassador: DECLAN M. KELLY.

Israel: 6 Turrana St, Yarralumla, ACT 2600; tel. (2) 6273-1309; telex 62224; fax (2) 6273-4273; e-mail israelembassy@israemb.org; internet www.mfa.gov.il; Ambassador: GABBY LEVY.

Italy: 12 Grey St, Deakin, ACT 2600; tel. (2) 6273-3333; fax (2) 6273-4223; e-mail embassy@ambitalia.org.au; internet www.ambitalia.org.au; Ambassador: DINO VOLPICELLI.

Japan: 112 Empire Circuit, Yarralumla, ACT 2600; tel. (2) 6273-3244; fax (2) 6273-1848; e-mail embofjpn@ozemail.com.au; internet www.japan.org.au; Ambassador: ATSUSHI HATAKANAKA.

Jordan: 20 Roebuck St, Red Hill, ACT 2603; tel. (2) 6295-9951; fax (2) 6239-7236; Ambassador: Dr KHALDOUN THARWAT TALHOUNI.

Kenya: GPOB 1990, Canberra, ACT 2601; tel. (2) 6247-4788; fax (2) 6257-6613; e-mail kenrep@dynamite.com.au; High Commissioner: STEVEN A. LOYATUM.

Korea, Republic: 113 Empire Circuit, Yarralumla, ACT 2600; tel. (2) 6270-4100; fax (2) 6273-4839; e-mail embassy-au@mofat.go.kr; internet www.mofat.go.kr; Ambassador: SONG YOUNG-SHIK.

Laos: 1 Dalman Crescent, O'Malley, ACT 2606; tel. (2) 6286-4595; fax (2) 6290-1910; e-mail clao@cyberone.com.au; Ambassador: VICHIT XINDAVONG.

Lebanon: 27 Endeavour St, Red Hill, ACT 2603; tel. (2) 6295-7378; fax (2) 6239-7024; Ambassador: MICHEL BITAR.

Malaysia: 7 Perth Ave, Yarralumla, ACT 2600; tel. (2) 6273-1544; fax (2) 6273-2496; e-mail malcnbera@kln.gov.my; High Commissioner: M. H. ARSHAD.

Malta: 38 Culgoa Circuit, O'Malley, ACT 2606; tel. (2) 6290-1724; fax (2) 6290-2453; e-mail maltahc@bigpond.com; High Commissioner: IVES DE BARRO.

Mauritius: 2 Beale Crescent, Deakin, ACT 2600; tel. (2) 6281-1203; fax (2) 6282-3235; e-mail mhccan@cyberone.com.au; High Commissioner: PATRICE CURÉ.

Mexico: 14 Perth Ave, Yarralumla, ACT 2600; tel. (2) 6273-3905; fax (2) 6273-1190; e-mail embamex@mexico.org.au; internet www.embassyofmexicoinaustralia.org; Ambassador: RAPHAEL STEGER-CATAÑO.

Myanmar: 22 Arkana St, Yarralumla, ACT 2600; tel. (2) 6273-3811; fax (2) 6273-4357; Ambassador: Mr AYE.

Netherlands: 120 Empire Circuit, Yarralumla, ACT 2600; tel. (2) 6220-9400; fax (2) 6273-3206; e-mail can@minbuza.nl; internet www.Netherlands.org.au; Ambassador: H. H. M. SONDAAL.

New Zealand: Commonwealth Ave, Canberra, ACT 2600; tel. (2) 6270-4211; fax (2) 6273-3194; e-mail nzhccba@austarmetro.com.au; High Commissioner: SIMON MURDOCH.

Nigeria: POB 241, Civic Square, ACT 2608; tel. (2) 6282-7411; fax (2) 6282-8471; e-mail chancery@nigeria-can.org.au; internet www.nigeria-can.org.au; High Commissioner: Dr RUFAI A. O. SOULE.

Norway: 17 Hunter St, Yarralumla, ACT 2600; tel. (2) 6273-3444; fax (2) 6273-3669; e-mail emb.canberra@mfa.no; Ambassador: OVE THORSHEIM.

Pakistan: POB 684, Mawson, ACT 2607; tel. (2) 6290-1676; fax (2) 6290-1073; e-mail parepcanberra@actonline.com.au; High Commissioner: KHIZAR HAYAT KHAN NIAZI.

Papua New Guinea: POB E432, Queen Victoria Terrace, Kingston, ACT 2604; tel. (2) 6273-3322; fax (2) 6273-3732; High Commissioner: RENAGI R. LOHIA.

Peru: POB 106, Red Hill, ACT 2603; tel. (2) 6273-8752; fax (2) 6273-8754; e-mail embassy@embaperu.org.au; internet www.embaperu.org.au; Ambassador: JOSÉ LUIS GARAYCOCHEA.

Philippines: 1 Moonah Place, Yarralumla, Canberra, ACT 2600; tel. (2) 6273-2535; fax (2) 6273-3984; e-mail cbrpe@philembassy.au.com; internet www.philembassy.au.com; Ambassador: DELIA DOMINGO-ALBERT.

Poland: 7 Turrana St, Yarralumla, ACT 2600; tel. (2) 6273-1208; fax (2) 6273-3184; e-mail ambpol@clover.com.au; Ambassador: Dr TADEUSZ SZUMOWSKI.

Portugal: 23 Culgoa Circuit, O'Malley, ACT 2606; tel. (2) 6290-1733; fax (2) 6290-1957; e-mail sab@mail2me.com.au; Ambassador: Dr JOSÉ VIEIRA BRANCO.

Romania: 4 Dalman Crescent, O'Malley, ACT 2606; tel. (2) 6286-2343; fax (2) 6286-2433; e-mail roembcbr@cyberone.com.au; internet www.roembau.org.au; Ambassador: MANUELA VULPE.

Russia: 78 Canberra Ave, Griffith, ACT 2603; tel. (2) 6295-9033; fax (2) 6295-1847; e-mail rusembassy@lightningpl.net.au; Ambassador: LEONID MOISEEV.

Samoa: POB 3274, Manuka, ACT 2603; tel. (2) 6286-5505; fax (2) 6286-5678; e-mail samoahcaussi@netspeed.com.au; High Commissioner: Leiataua Dr KILIFOTI S. ETEUATI.

Saudi Arabia: POB 63, Garran, ACT 2605; tel. (2) 6282-6999; fax (2) 6282-8911; e-mail saudiemb@hotmail.com; Ambassador: MOHAMAD I. AL-HEJAILAN.

Singapore: 17 Forster Crescent, Yarralumla, ACT 2600; tel. (2) 6273-3944; fax (2) 6273-9823; e-mail shc.cbr@u030.aone.net.au; internet www.mfa.gov.sg/canberra; High Commissioner: ASHOK KUMAR MIRPURI.

Slovakia: 47 Culgoa Circuit, O'Malley, ACT 2606; tel. (2) 6290-1516; fax (2) 6290-1755; e-mail slovak@cyberone.com.au; internet www.slovakemb-aust.org: Ambassador: Dr ANNA TURENIČOVÁ.

Slovenia: POB 284, Civic Square, Canberra, ACT 2608; tel. (2) 6243-4830; fax (2) 6243-4827; e-mail vca@mzz-dkp. gov.si; internet slovenia.webone.com.au; Chargé d'affaires: BOJAN BERTONCELJ.

Solomon Islands: POB 256, Deakin West, ACT 2600; tel. (2) 6282-7030; fax (2) 6282-7040; e-mail info@solomon.emb.gov.au; High Commissioner: MILNER TOZAKA.

South Africa: cnr State Circle and Rhodes Place, Yarralumla, ACT 2600; tel. (2) 6273-2424; fax (2) 6273-3543; e-mail info@rsa.emb.gov.au; internet www.rsa.emb.gov.au; High Commissioner: ZOLILE MAGUGU.

Spain: POB 9076, Deakin, ACT 2600; tel. (2) 6273-3555; fax (2) 6273-3918; e-mail embespau@mail.mae.es; internet www.embaspain.com; Ambassador: JOSÉ RAMÓN BARANAÑO.

Sri Lanka: 35 Empire Circuit, Forrest, ACT 2603; tel. (2) 6239-7041; fax (2) 6239-6166; e-mail slhc@atrax.net.au; internet slhccanberra.webjump.com; High Commissioner: JANAKA PERERA.

Sweden: 5 Turrana St, Yarralumla, ACT 2600; tel. (2) 6270-2700; fax (2) 6270-2755; e-mail sweden@austarmetro.com.au; Ambassador: LARS-ERIK WINGREN.

Switzerland: 7 Melbourne Ave, Forrest, ACT 2603; tel. (2) 6273-3977; fax (2) 6273-3428; e-mail vertretung@can.rep.admin.ch; Ambassador: ANDRÉ FAIVET.

Thailand: 111 Empire Circuit, Yarralumla, ACT 2600; tel. (2) 6273-1149; fax (2) 6273-1518; e-mail rtecanberra@mfa.go.th; Ambassador: SAWANIT KONGSIRI.

Turkey: 60 Mugga Way, Red Hill, ACT 2603; tel. (2) 6295-0227; fax (2) 6239-6592; e-mail turkembs@bigpond.net.au; internet www.turkishembassy.org.au; Ambassador: TANSU OKANDAN.

United Arab Emirates: 36 Culgoa Circuit, O'Malley, ACT 2606; tel. (2) 6286-8802; fax (2) 6286-8804; e-mail uaeembassy@bigpond.com; internet www.users.bigpond.com/uaeembassy; Ambassador: KHALIFA MOHAMMED BAKHIT AL-FALASI.

United Kingdom: Commonwealth Ave, Canberra, ACT 2600; tel. (2) 6270-6666; fax (2) 6273-3236; e-mail BHC.Canberra@uk.emb.gov.au; internet www.uk.emb.gov.au; High Commissioner: Sir ALASTAIR GOODLAD.

USA: Moonah Place, Yarralumla, ACT 2600; tel. (2) 6214-5600; fax (2) 6214-5970; Ambassador: EDWARD W. GNEHM.

Uruguay: POB 5058, Kingston, ACT 2604; tel. (2) 6273-9100; fax (2) 6273-9099; e-mail urucan@austarmetro.com.au; Ambassador: PABLO SADER.

Venezuela: 5 Culgoa Circuit, O'Malley, ACT 2606; tel. (2) 6290-2968; fax (2) 6290-2911; e-mail embaustralia@venezuela-emb-org.au; internet www.venezuela-emb.org.au; Ambassador: LIONEL VIVAS

Viet Nam: 6 Timbarra Crescent, O'Malley, ACT 2606; tel. (2) 6286-6059; fax (2) 6286-4534; e-mail vnembassy@webone.com.au; internet www.au.vnembassy.org; Ambassador: VU CHI CONG.

Yugoslavia: POB 728, Mawson, ACT 2607; tel. (2) 6290-2630; fax (2) 6290-2631; Ambassador: RADOMIR JERGIĆ.

Zimbabwe: 11 Culgoa Circuit, O'Malley, ACT 2606; tel. (2) 6286-2700; fax (2) 6290-1680; e-mail zimbabwe1@austarmetro.com.au; High Commissioner: FLORENCE L. CHITAURO.

Judicial System

The judicial power of the Commonwealth of Australia is vested in the High Court of Australia, in such other Federal Courts as the Federal Parliament creates, and in such other courts as it invests with Federal jurisdiction.

The High Court consists of a Chief Justice and six other Justices, each of whom is appointed by the Governor-General in Council, and has both original and appellate jurisdiction.

The High Court's original jurisdiction extends to all matters arising under any treaty, affecting representatives of other countries, in which the Commonwealth of Australia or its representative is a party, between states or between residents of different states or between a state and a resident of another state, and in which a writ of mandamus, or prohibition, or an injunction is sought against an officer of the Commonwealth of Australia. It also extends to matters arising under the Australian Constitution or involving its interpretation, and to many matters arising under Commonwealth laws.

The High Court's appellate jurisdiction has, since June 1984, been discretionary. Appeals from the Federal Court, the Family Court and the Supreme Courts of the states and of the territories may now be brought only if special leave is granted, in the event of a legal question that is of general public importance being involved, or of there being differences of opinion between intermediate appellate courts as to the state of the law.

Legislation enacted by the Federal Parliament in 1976 substantially changed the exercise of Federal and Territory judicial power, and, by creating the Federal Court of Australia in February 1977, enabled the High Court of Australia to give greater attention to its primary function as interpreter of the Australian Constitution. The Federal Court of Australia has assumed, in two divisions, the jurisdiction previously exercised by the Australian Industrial Court and the Federal Court of Bankruptcy and was additionally given jurisdiction in trade practices and in the developing field of administrative law. In 1987 the Federal Court of Australia acquired jurisdiction in federal taxation matters and certain intellectual property matters. In 1991 the Court's jurisdiction was expanded to include civil proceedings arising under Corporations Law. Jurisdiction has also been conferred on the Federal Court of Australia, subject to a number of exceptions, in matters in which a writ of mandamus, or prohibition, or an injunction is sought against an officer of the Commonwealth of Australia. The Court also hears appeals from the Court constituted by a single Judge, from the Supreme Courts of the territories, and in certain specific matters from State Courts, other than a Full Court of the Supreme Court of a state, exercising Federal jurisdiction.

In March 1986 all remaining categories of appeal from Australian courts to the Queen's Privy Council in the UK were abolished by the Australia Act.

FEDERAL COURTS

High Court of Australia

POB E435, Kingston, Canberra, ACT 2604; tel. (2) 6270-6811; fax (2) 6270-6868; internet www.hcourt.gov.au.

Chief Justice: ANTHONY MURRAY GLEESON.

Justices: MARY GAUDRON, MICHAEL MCHUGH, WILLIAM GUMMOW, MICHAEL DONALD KIRBY, KENNETH MADISON HAYNE, IAN DAVID FRANCIS CALLINAN.

Federal Court of Australia

Chief Justice: MICHAEL ERIC JOHN BLACK.

In 2002 there were 47 other judges.

Family Court of Australia

Chief Justice: ALISTAIR BOTHWICK NICHOLSON.

In 2002 there were 50 other judges.

NEW SOUTH WALES

Supreme Court

Chief Justice: JAMES JACOB SPIGELMAN.

President: KEITH MASON.

Chief Judge in Equity: PETER WOLSTENHOME YOUNG.

Chief Judge at Common Law: JAMES ROLAND TOMSON WOOD.

VICTORIA

Supreme Court

Chief Justice: JOHN HARBER PHILLIPS.

President of the Court of Appeal: JOHN SPENCE WINNEKE.

QUEENSLAND

Supreme Court

Chief Justice: PAUL DE JERSEY.

President of the Court of Appeal: MARGARET MCMURDO.

Senior Judge Administrator, Trial Division: MARTIN PATRICK MOYNIHAN.

Central District (Rockhampton)

Resident Judge: PETER RICHARD DUTNEY.

Northern District (Townsville)

Resident Judge: KEIRAN ANTHONY CULLINANE.

Far Northern District (Cairns)

Resident Judge: STANLEY GRAHAM JONES.

SOUTH AUSTRALIA

Supreme Court

Chief Justice: JOHN JEREMY DOYLE.

WESTERN AUSTRALIA

Supreme Court

Chief Justice: DAVID KINGSLEY MALCOLM.

TASMANIA

Supreme Court

Chief Justice: WILLIAM JOHN ELLIS COX.

AUSTRALIAN CAPITAL TERRITORY

Supreme Court

Chief Justice: JEFFREY ALLAN MILES.

NORTHERN TERRITORY

Supreme Court

Chief Justice: BRIAN FRANK MARTIN.

Religion

CHRISTIANITY

According to the provisional results of the population census of August 2001, Christians numbered 12,764,342.

National Council of Churches in Australia: Locked Bag 199, QVB PO, Sydney, NSW 1230; tel. (2) 9299-2215; fax (2) 9262-4514; e-mail christianworldservice@ncca.org.au; internet www.ncca.org.au; f. 1946; 14 mem. churches; Pres. Archbishop JOHN BATHERSBY; Gen. Sec. Rev. DAVID GILL.

The Anglican Communion

The constitution of the Church of England in Australia, which rendered the church an autonomous member of the Anglican Communion, came into force in January 1962. The body was renamed the Anglican Church of Australia in August 1981. The Church comprises five provinces (together containing 22 dioceses) and the extra-provincial diocese of Tasmania. At the 2001 population census there were an estimated 3,881,162 adherents.

National Office of the Anglican Church: General Synod Office, Box Q190, QVB PO, Sydney, NSW 1230; tel. (2) 9265-1525; fax (2) 9264-6552; e-mail gsoffice@anglican.org.au; internet www.anglican.org.au; Gen. Sec. Rev. Dr B. N. KAYE.

Archbishop of Adelaide and Metropolitan of South Australia: Most Rev. IAN G. C. GEORGE, Bishop's Court, 45 Palmer Place, North Adelaide, SA 5006; fax (8) 8305-9399; e-mail Igeorge.churchoffice@anglicare-sa.org.au.

Archbishop of Brisbane and Metropolitan of Queensland: Dr PHILLIP JOHN ASPINALL, Bishopsbourne, GPOB421, Brisbane, Qld 4001; tel. (7) 3835-2218; fax (7) 3832-5030; e-mail relliott@anglicanbrisbane.org.au; internet www.anglicanbrisbane.gil.com.au.

Archbishop of Melbourne and Metropolitan of Victoria: Most Rev. PETER R. WATSON, Bishopscourt, 120 Clarendon St, East Melbourne, Vic 3002; tel. (3) 9653-4220; fax (3) 9650-2184; e-mail archbishop@melbourne.anglican.com.au.

Archbishop of Perth and Metropolitan of Western Australia, Primate of Australia: Most Rev. Dr PETER F. CARNLEY, GPOB W2067, Perth, WA 6846; tel. (8) 9325-7455; fax (8) 9325-6741; e-mail abcsuite@perth.anglican.org; internet www.perth.anglican.org; also has jurisdiction over Christmas Island and the Cocos (Keeling) Islands.

Archbishop of Sydney and Metropolitan of New South Wales: Most Rev. PETER F. JENSEN, POB Q190, QVB Post Office, Sydney, NSW 1230; tel. (2) 9265-1521; fax (2) 9265-1504; e-mail archbishop@sydney.anglican.asn.au; internet www.anglicanmediasydney.asn.au.

The Roman Catholic Church

Australia comprises five metropolitan archdioceses, two archdioceses directly responsible to the Holy See and 25 dioceses, including one diocese each for Catholics of the Maronite, Melkite and Ukrainian rites, and one military ordinariate. At the census of 1996 there were 4.8m. adherents in the country.

Australian Catholic Bishops' Conference: GPOB 368, Canberra, ACT 2601; tel. (2) 6201-9845; fax (2) 6247-6083; e-mail gensec@catholic.org.au; internet www.catholic.org.au; f. 1979; Pres. Most Rev. FRANCIS PATRICK CARROLL, Archbishop of Canberra and Goulburn; Sec. Very Rev. BRIAN V. FINNIGAN.

Archbishop of Adelaide: Most Rev. PHILIP WILSON, GPOB 1364, Adelaide, South Australia 5001; tel. (8) 8210-8108; fax (8) 8223-2307.

Archbishop of Brisbane: Most Rev. JOHN A. BATHERSBY, Archbishop's House, 790 Brunswick St, New Farm, Brisbane, Qld 4005; tel. (7) 3224-3364; fax (7) 3358-1357; e-mail archbishop@bne.catholic.net.au.

Archbishop of Canberra and Goulburn: Most Rev. FRANCIS PATRICK CARROLL, GPOB 89, Canberra, ACT 2601; tel. (2) 6248-6411; fax (2) 6247-9636.

Archbishop of Hobart: Most Rev. ADRIAN DOYLE, GPOB 62, Hobart, Tas 7001; tel. (3) 6225-1920; fax (3) 6225-3865; e-mail archbishop.hobart@cdftas.com; internet www.hobart.catholic.org.au.

Archbishop of Melbourne: Most Rev. DENIS HART, GPOB 146, East Melbourne, Vic 3002; tel. (3) 9926-5677; fax (3) 9926-5613.

Archbishop of Perth: Most Rev. BARRY J. HICKEY, St Mary's Cathedral, 17 Victoria Sq., Perth, WA 6000; tel. (8) 9223-1350; fax (8) 9221-1716; e-mail archsec@perth.catholic.org.au; internet www.perth.catholic.org.au.

Archbishop of Sydney: Most Rev. GEORGE PELL, St Mary's Cathedral, Sydney, NSW 2000; tel. (2) 9390-5100; fax (2) 9261-8312.

Orthodox Churches

Greek Orthodox Archdiocese of Australia: 242 Cleveland St, Redfern, Sydney, NSW 2016; tel. (2) 9698-5066; fax (2) 9698-5368; f. 1924; 700,000 mems; Primate His Eminence Archbishop STYLIANOS.

The Antiochian, Coptic, Romanian, Serbian and Syrian Orthodox Churches are also represented.

Other Christian Churches

Baptist Union of Australia: POB 377, Hawthorn, Vic 3122; tel. (3) 9818-0341; fax (3) 9818-1041; e-mail bua@baptistvic-asn.au; f. 1926; 64,159 mems; 883 churches; Nat. Pres. Rev. TIM COSTELLO; Nat. Sec. C. K. MOSS.

Churches of Christ in Australia: POB 55, Helensburgh, NSW 2508; tel. (2) 4294-1913; fax (2) 4294-1914; e-mail bobsmith@ozemail.com.au; internet www.churchesofchrist.org.au; 36,000 mems; Pres. Rev. PETER OVERTON; Co-ordinator Rev. ROBERT SMITH.

Lutheran Church of Australia: National Office, 197 Archer St, North Adelaide, SA 5006; tel. (8) 8267-7300; fax (8) 8267-7310; e-mail president@lca.org.au; internet www.lca.org.au; f. 1966; 98,191 mems; Pres. Rev. M. P. SEMMLER.

United Pentecostal Church of Australia: GPOB 1434, Springwood, Qld, 4127; tel. (7) 3806-1817; fax (7) 3806-0029; e-mail homemissions@powerup.com.au; internet www.upca.org.au; 174,720 adherents in 1996.

Uniting Church in Australia: POB A2266, Sydney South, NSW 1235; tel. (2) 8267-4428; fax (2) 8267-4222; e-mail assysec@nat.uca.org.au; internet nat.uca.org.au; f. 1977 with the union of Methodist, Presbyterian and Congregational Churches; 1.4m. mems; Pres. Rev. Prof. JAMES HAIRE; Gen. Sec. Rev. TERENCE CORKIN.

Other active denominations include the Armenian Apostolic Church, the Assyrian Church of the East and the Society of Friends (Quakers).

JUDAISM

The Jewish community numbered an estimated 83,993 at the census of August 2001.

Great Synagogue: 166 Castlereagh St, Sydney, NSW; tel. (2) 9267-2477; fax (2) 9264-8871; e-mail admin@greatsynagogue.org.au; internet www.greatsynagogue.org.au; f. 1828; Sr Minister Rabbi RAYMOND APPLE.

OTHER FAITHS

According to the August 2001 census, Muslims numbered an estimated 281,578, Buddhists 357,813 and Hindus 95,473.

The Press

The total circulation of Australia's daily newspapers is very high, but in the remoter parts of the country weekly papers are even more popular. Most of Australia's newspapers are published in sparsely populated rural areas where the demand for local news is strong. The only newspapers that may fairly claim a national circulation are the dailies *The Australian* and *Australian Financial Review*, and the weekly magazines *The Bulletin, Time Australia* and *Business Review Weekly*, the circulation of most newspapers being almost entirely confined to the state in which each is produced.

ACP Publishing Pty Ltd: 54–58 Park St, Sydney, NSW 2000; tel. (2) 9282-8000; fax (2) 9267-4371; fmrly Australian Consolidated Press Ltd; publishes *Australian Women's Weekly, The Bulletin with Newsweek, Cleo, Cosmopolitan, Woman's Day, Dolly, Belle, Street Machine* and more than 70 other magazines.

APN News and Media Ltd: 10th Floor, 300 Ann St, Brisbane, Qld 4000; tel. (7) 3307-0300; fax (7) 3307-0307; Chair. L. P. HEALY; Chief Exec. VINCENT CROWLEY.

John Fairfax Holdings Ltd: POB 506, Sydney, NSW 2001; tel. (2) 9282-2833; fax (2) 9282-3133; internet www.fairfax.com.au; f. 1987; Chair. BRIAN POWERS; Chief Exec. FREDERICK G. HILMER; publs include *The Sydney Morning Herald, The Australian Financial Review* and *Sun-Herald* (Sydney), *The Age* and BRW Publications (Melbourne); also provides online and interactive services.

The Herald and Weekly Times Ltd: POB 14999, Melbourne MC, Vic 8001; tel. (3) 9292-2000; fax (3) 9292-2002; e-mail newspapers@hwt.newsltd.com.au internet www.heraldsun.com.au; acquired by News Ltd in 1987; Chair. JANET CALVERT-JONES; Man. Dir JULIAN CLARKE; publs include *Herald Sun, Sunday Herald Sun, The Weekly Times, MX*.

The News Corporation: 2 Holt St, Surry Hills, Sydney, NSW 2010; tel. (2) 9288-3000; fax (2) 9288-2300; internet www.newscorp.com; Chair. and CEO K. RUPERT MURDOCH; controls *The Australian* and *The Weekend Australian* (national), *Daily Telegraph, Sunday Telegraph* (Sydney), *The Herald Sun* and *Sunday Herald Sun* (Victoria), *Northern Territory News* (Darwin), *Sunday Times* (Perth), *Townsville Bulletin, Courier Mail, Sunday Mail* (Queensland), *The Mercury* (Tasmania), *The Advertiser, Sunday Mail* (South Australia).

Rural Press Ltd: 159 Bells Line of Road, North Richmond, NSW 2754; tel. (2) 4570-4444; fax (2) 4570-4663; e-mail cosec@rpl.com.au; internet www.rpl.com.au; Chair. JOHN B. FAIRFAX; Man. Dir B. K. MCCARTHY.

West Australian Newspapers Holdings Ltd: Newspaper House, 50 Hasler Rd, Osborne Park, WA 6017; tel. (8) 9482-3111; fax (8) 9482-9080; Chair. T. R. EASTWOOD; Man. Dir D. W. THOMPSON.

Other newspaper publishers include Federal Capital Press (K. Stokes).

NEWSPAPERS

Australian Capital Territory

The Canberra Times: 9 Pirie St, Fyshwick, ACT 2609; POB 7155, Canberra Mail Centre, ACT 2610; tel. (2) 6280-2122; fax (2) 6280-2282; internet www.canberratimes.com f. 1926; daily and Sun.; morning; Editor-in-Chief JACK WATERFORD; circ. 38,694 (Mon.–Fri.), 72,080 (Sat.), 39,075 (Sun.).

New South Wales

Dailies

The Australian: News Ltd, 2 Holt St, Surry Hills, NSW 2010, POB 4245; tel. (2) 9288-3000; fax (2) 9288-3077; f. 1964; edited in Sydney, simultaneous edns in Sydney, Melbourne, Perth, Townsville, Adelaide and Brisbane; Editor-in-Chief DAVID ARMSTRONG; Editor CAMPBELL REID; circ. 122,500 (Mon.–Fri.); *The Weekend Australian* (Sat.) 311,000.

Australian Financial Review: 201 Sussex St, GPOB 506, Sydney, NSW 2000; tel. (2) 9282-2512; fax (2) 9282-3137; f. 1951; Mon.–Fri.; distributed nationally; Publr/Editor-in-Chief MICHAEL GILL; Editor GLEN BURGE; circ. 92,500 (Mon.–Fri.), 92,000 (Sat.).

The Daily Telegraph: 2 Holt St, Surry Hills, NSW 2010; tel. (2) 9288-3000; fax (2) 9288-2300; f. 1879, merged in 1990 with Daily Mirror (f. 1941); 24-hour tabloid; CEO LACHLAN MURDOCH; circ. 442,000.

The Manly Daily: 26 Sydney Rd, Manly, NSW 2095; tel. (2) 9977-3333; fax (2) 9977-2831; e-mail manlydailynews@cng.newsltd.com.au; f. 1906; Tue.–Sat.; Editor STEVE STICKNEY; circ. 89,326.

The Newcastle Herald: 28–30 Bolton St, Newcastle, NSW 2300; tel. (2) 4979-5000; fax (2) 4979-5888; f. 1858; morning; 6 a week; Editor-in-Chief ALAN OAKLEY; circ. 53,456.

The Sydney Morning Herald: 201 Sussex St, GPOB 506, Sydney, NSW 2001; tel. (2) 9282-2822; fax (2) 9282-3253; internet www.smh.com.au; f. 1831; morning; Editor-in-Chief and Publr ALAN REVELL; circ. 231,508 (Mon.–Fri.), 400,000 (Sat.).

Weeklies

Bankstown Canterbury Torch: Nabberly House, Cnr Marion St and Airport Ave, Bankstown, NSW 2200; tel. (2) 9795-0000; fax (2) 9795-0096; f. 1920; Wed.; Editor CHARLES ELIAS; circ. 86,577.

Northern District Times: 79 Rowe St, Eastwood, NSW 2122; tel. (2) 9858-1766; fax (2) 9804-6901; f. 1921; Wed.; Editor D. BARTOK; circ. 55,302.

The Parramatta Advertiser: 142 Macquarie St, Parramatta, NSW 2150; tel. (2) 9689-5370; fax (2) 9689-5353; Wed.; Editor LES POBJIE; circ. 96,809.

St George and Sutherland Shire Leader: 182 Forest Rd, Hurstville, NSW 2220; tel. (2) 9598-3999; fax (2) 9598-3987; f. 1960; Tue. and Thur.; Editor PETER ALLEN; circ. 143,595.

Sun-Herald: Level 24, 201 Sussex St, GPOB 506, Sydney, NSW 2001; tel. (2) 9282-2822; fax (2) 9282-2151; e-mail shnews@mail.fairfax.com.au; internet www. sunherald.com.au; f. 1953; Sun.; Editor PHILIP MCLEAN; circ. 580,000.

Sunday Telegraph: 2 Holt St, Surry Hills, NSW 2010; tel. (2) 9288-3000; fax (2) 9288-3311; f. 1938; Editor JENI COOPER; circ. 720,000.

Northern Territory

Daily

Northern Territory News: Printers Place, POB 1300, Darwin, NT 0801; tel. (8) 8944-9900; fax (8) 8981-6045; f. 1952; Mon.–Sat.; Gen. Man. D. KENNEDY; circ. 24,470.

Weekly

Sunday Territorian: Printers Place, GPOB 1300, Darwin, NT 0801; tel. (8) 8944-9900; fax (8) 8981-6045; Sun.; Editor DAVID COREN; circ. 26,437.

Queensland

Daily

Courier-Mail: 41 Campbell St, Bowen Hills, Brisbane, Qld 4006; tel. (7) 3252-6011; fax (7) 3252-6696; f. 1933; morning; Editor-in-Chief C. MITCHELL; circ. 250,875.

Weekly

Sunday Mail: 9th floor, 41 Campbell St, Bowen Hills, Brisbane, Qld 4006; tel. (7) 3666-8000; fax (7) 3666-6692; e-mail porterk@qnp.newsltd.com.au; f. 1953; Editor KAREN PORTER; circ. 590,423.

South Australia

Daily

The Advertiser: 121 King William St, Adelaide, SA 5001; tel. (8) 8206-2220; fax (8) 8206-3669; e-mail tiser@adv.newsltd.com.au; f. 1858; morning; Editor Melvin Mansell; circ. 203,440 (Mon.–Fri.), 274,045 (Sat.).

Weekly

Sunday Mail: 9th Floor, 121 King William St, Adelaide, SA 5000; tel. (8) 8206-2000; fax (8) 8206-3646; e-mail sullivank@adv.newsltd.com.au; f. 1912; Editor Kerry Sullivan; circ. 345,200.

Tasmania

Dailies

The Advocate: POB 63, Burnie 7320; tel. (3) 6440-7405; fax (3) 6440-7461; e-mail letters.advocate@harrisgroup.com.au; f. 1890; morning; Editor Peter Dwyer; circ. 25,623.

Examiner: 71–75 Paterson St, POB 99A, Launceston, Tas 7250; tel. (3) 6336-7111; fax (3) 6334-7328; e-mail mail@examiner.com.au; internet www.examiner.com.au/examiner/; f. 1842; morning; independent; Editor R. J. Scott; circ. 38,721.

Mercury: 91–93 Macquarie St, Hobart, Tas 7000; tel. (3) 6230-0622; fax (3) 6230-0711; e-mail mercuryedletter@dbl.newsltd.com.au; internet www.news.com.au; f. 1854; morning; Man. Dir Rex Gardner; Editor I. McCausland; circ. 52,815.

Weeklies

Sunday Examiner: 71–75 Paterson St, Launceston, Tas 7250; tel. (3) 6336-7111; fax (3) 6334-7328; e-mail mail@examiner.com.au; f. 1924; Editor R. J. Scott; circ. 42,000.

Sunday Tasmanian: 91–93 Macquarie St, Hobart, Tas 7000; tel. (3) 6230-0622; fax (3) 6230-0711; e-mailsuntas.news@dbl.newsltd.com.au; f. 1984; morning; Man. Dir Rex Gardner; Editor Ian McCausland; circ. 58,325.

Victoria

Dailies

The Age: 250 Spencer St (cnr Lonsdale St), Melbourne, Vic 3000; tel. (3) 9600-4211; fax (3) 9601-2598; e-mail newsdesk@theage.fairfax.com.au; internet www.theage.com.au; f. 1854; independent; morning, incl. Sun.; Publr and Editor-in-Chief Greg Hywood; Associate Publisher and Editor Michael Gawenda; circ. 196,000 (Mon.–Fri.), 330,000 (Sat.), 197,000 (Sun.).

Herald Sun: HWT Tower, 40 City Rd, Southbank, Vic 3006; tel. (3) 9292-2000; fax (3) 9292-2112; e-mail news@heraldsun.com.au; internet www.heraldsun.com.au; f. 1840; 24-hour tabloid; Editor-in-Chief Peter Blunden; circ. 556,027.

Weeklies

Progress Press: 360 Burwood Rd, Hawthorn, Vic 3122; tel. (3) 9818-0555; fax (3) 9818-0029; e-mail editor@ldr.newsltd.com.au; f. 1960; Tue.; Editor Lynne Kinsey; circ. 74,829.

Sunday Herald Sun: HWT Tower, 40 City Rd, Southbank, Vic 3006; tel. (3) 9292-2000; fax (3) 9292-2080; e-mail sundayhs@heraldsun.com.au; f. 1991; Editor Alan Howe; circ. 550,000.

Western Australia

Daily

The West Australian: POB D162, Perth, WA 6001; tel. (8) 9482-3111; fax (8) 9482-3399; e-mail editor@wanews.com.au; f. 1833; morning; Editor Brian Rogers; circ. 214,000 (Mon.–Fri.), 386,000 (Sat.).

Weekly

Sunday Times: 34–42 Stirling St, Perth, WA 6000; tel. (8) 9326-8326; fax (8) 9326-8316; e-mail editorial@sundaytimes.newsltd.com.au; f. 1897; Man. Dir David Maguire; Editor Brett McCarthy; circ. 346,014.

PRINCIPAL PERIODICALS

Weeklies and Fortnightlies

Aussie Post: 35-51 Mitchell St, McMahon's Point, NSW 2060; tel. (2) 9464-3129; fax (2) 9464-3169; e-mail aussiepost@pacpubs.com.au; f. 1864; factual, general interest, Australiana; Mon.; Editor Gill Chalmers; circ. 24,500.

The Bulletin: 54 Park St, Sydney, NSW 2000; tel. (2) 9282-8227; fax (2) 9267-4359; e-mail cclegg@acp.com.au; f. 1880; Wed.; Editor-in-Chief Paul Bailey; circ. 70,000.

Business Review Weekly: Level 2, 469 La Trobe St, Melbourne, Vic 3000; tel. (3) 9603-3888; fax (3) 9670-4328; f. 1981; Chair. and Editorial Dir Robert Gottliebsen; Editor Ross Greenwood; circ. 75,166.

The Countryman: 219 St George's Terrace, Perth, WA 6000; GPOB D162, Perth 6001; tel. (8) 9482-3322; fax (8) 9482-3324; e-mail countryman@wanews.com.au; f. 1885; Thur.; farming; Editor Gary McGay; circ. 13,444.

The Medical Journal of Australia: Locked Bag 3030, Strawberry Hills, NSW 2012; tel. (2) 9954-8666; fax (2) 9954-8699; e-mail mja@ampco.com.au; internet www.mja.com.au; f. 1914; fortnightly; Editor Dr Martin van der Weyden; circ. 27,318.

New Idea: 35–51 Mitchell St, McMahons Point, NSW 2060; tel. (2) 9464-3200; fax (2) 9464-3203; e-mail newidea@pacpubs.com.au; weekly; women's; Editorial Dir Bunty Avieson; circ. 471,000.

News Weekly: POB 186, North Melbourne, Vic 3051; tel. (3) 9326-5757; fax (3) 9328-2877; e-mail freedom@connexus.net.au; f. 1943; publ. by National Civic Council; fortnightly; Sat.; political, social, educational and trade union affairs; Editor Peter Westmore; circ. 12,000.

People: 54 Park St, Sydney, NSW 2000; tel. (2) 9282-8743; fax (2) 9267-4365; e-mail sbutler-white@acp.com.au; weekly; Editor Simon Butler-White; circ. 70,000.

Picture: GPOB 5201, Sydney, NSW 2001; tel. (2) 9288-9686; fax (2) 9267-4372; e-mail picture@acp.com.au; weekly; men's; Editor Tom Foster; circ. 110,000.

Queensland Country Life: POB 586, Cleveland, Qld 4163; tel. (7) 3826-8200; fax (7) 3821-1236; f. 1935; Thur.; Editor Mark Phelps; circ. 33,900.

Stock and Land: 10 Sydenham St, Moonee Ponds, Vic 3039; tel. (3) 9287-0900; fax (3) 9370-5622; e-mail stockland@ruralpress.com; internet www.stockandland.com; f. 1914; weekly; agricultural and rural news; Editor John Carson; circ. 16,000.

That's Life!: 35–51 Mitchell St, McMahons Point, NSW 2060; tel. (2) 9464-3300; fax (2) 9464-3480; e-mail thatslife@pacpubs.com.au; f. 1994; weekly; features; Editor Bev Hadgraft; circ. 465,500 (incl. New Zealand).

Time Australia Magazine: GPOB 3873, Sydney, NSW 2001; tel. (2) 9925-2646; fax (2) 9954-0828; e-mail time.letters@time.com.au; internet www.time.com.au; Editor Steve Waterson; circ. 111,000.

TV Week: 54 Park St, Sydney, NSW 2000; tel. (2) 9288-9611; fax (2) 9283-4849; e-mail tvweek@acp.com.au; internet www.tvweek.ninemsn.com.au; f. 1957; Wed.; colour national; Editor Emma Nolan; circ. 364,044.

The Weekly Times: POB 14999, Melbourne City MC, Vic 8001; tel. (3) 9292-2000; fax (3) 9292-2697; e-mail wtimes@hwt.newsltd.com.au; internet www.news.com.au; f. 1869; farming, regional issues, country life; Wed.; Editor Peter Flaherty; circ. 78,900.

Woman's Day: 54–58 Park St, POB 5245, Sydney, NSW 1028; tel. (2) 9282-8000; fax (2) 9267-4360; e-mail Womansday@acp.com.au; weekly; circulates throughout Australia and NZ; Editor-in-Chief Philip Barker; circ. 765,170.

Monthlies and Others

Architectural Product News: Architecture Media Pty Ltd, Level 3, 4 Princes St, Port Melbourne, Vic 3207; tel. (3) 9646-4760; fax (3) 9646-4918; e-mail apn@archmedia.com.au; internet www.arhmedia.com.au; 6 a year; Editor Sue Harris; circ. 24,871.

Architecture Australia: Architecture Media Pty Ltd, Level 3, 4 Princes St, Port Melbourne, Vic 3207; tel. (3) 9646-4760; fax (3) 9646-4918; e-mail aa@archmedia.com.au; internet www.archmedia.com.au; f. 1904; 6 a year; Editor Ian Close; circ. 14,266.

Australian Hi-Fi: POB 5555, St Leonards, NSW 1590; tel. (2) 9901-6100; fax (2) 9901-6198; e-mail hifi@horwitz.com.au; f. 1970; every 2 months; consumer tests on hi-fi and home theatre equipment; Editor Greg Borrowman; circ. 11,800.

Australian Home Beautiful: 35–51 Mitchell St, McMahons Point, NSW 2060; tel. (2) 9464-3218; fax (2) 9464-3263; e-mail homebeaut@pacpubs.com.au; internet www.homebeautiful.com.au; f. 1925; monthly; Editor Andrea Jones; circ. 83,808.

Australian House and Garden: 54 Park St, Sydney, NSW 2000; tel. (2) 9282-8456; fax (2) 9267-4912; e-mail h&g@acp.com.au; f. 1948; monthly; design, decorating, renovating, gardens, food and travel; Editor Anny Friis; circ. 110,000.

Australian Journal of Mining: Informa Australia Pty Ltd, Level 2, 120 Sussex St, Sydney, NSW 2000; e-mail charles.macdonald@informa.com.au; f. 1986; monthly; mining and exploration throughout Australia and South Pacific; Editor Charles McDonald; circ. 6,771.

Australian Journal of Pharmacy: 100 Harris St, Pyrmont, NSW 2009; tel. (2) 8587-7000; fax (2) 8587-7100; f. 1886; monthly; journal of the associated pharmaceutical orgs; Man. Editor DAVID WESTON; circ. 6,443.

Australian Law Journal: 100 Harris St, Pyrmont, NSW 2009; tel. (2) 8587-7000; fax (2) 8587-7104; f. 1927; monthly; Editor Justice P. W. YOUNG; circ 4,500.

Australian Photography: POB 606, Sydney, NSW 2001; tel. (2) 9281-2333; fax (2) 9281-2750; e-mail robertkeeley@yaffa.com.au; monthly; Editor ROBERT KEELEY; circ. 9,010.

The Australian Women's Weekly: 54–56 Park St, Sydney, NSW 2000; tel. (2) 9282-8000; fax (2) 9267-4459; e-mail FDaniele@acp.com.au; f. 1933; monthly; Editor DEBORAH THOMAS; circ. 718,198.

Belle: 54 Park St, Sydney, NSW 2000; tel. (2) 9282-8000; fax (2) 9267-8037; e-mail belle@acp.com.au; f. 1975; every 2 months; Editor ERIC MATTHEWS; circ. 44,663.

Better Homes and Gardens: 45 Jones St, Ultimo, NSW 2007; tel. (2) 9692-2000; fax (2) 9692-2264; e-mail philippah@mm.com.au; f. 1978; 13 a year; Editor TONI EATTS; circ. 340,133.

Cleo: 54 Park St, Sydney, NSW 2000; POB 4088, Sydney, NSW 2001; tel. (2) 9282-8617; fax (2) 9267-4368; f. 1972; women's monthly; Editor DEBORAH THOMAS; circ. 263,353.

Commercial Photography: GPOB 606, Sydney, NSW 1041; tel. (2) 9281-2333; fax (2) 9281-2750; e-mail yaffa@flex.com.au; every 2 months; journal of the Professional Photographers Asscn of Australia and Photographic Industry Marketing Asscn of Australia; Editor SAIMA MOREL; circ. 3,835.

Cosmopolitan: 54 Park St, Sydney, NSW 2000; tel. (2) 9282-8039; fax (2) 9267-4457; e-mail cosmo@acp.com.au; f. 1973; www.cosmopolitan.com.au; monthly; Editor MIA FREEDMAN; circ. 203,058.

Dolly: 54–58 Park St, Sydney, NSW 1028; tel. (2) 9282-8437; fax (2) 9267-4911; e-mail dolly@ninemsn.com.au; internet www.ninemsn.com.au/dolly; f. 1970; monthly; for young women; Editor VIRGINIA KNIGHT; circ. 177,268.

Ecos: CSIRO, POB 1139, Collingwood, Vic 3066; tel. (3) 9662-7500; fax (3) 9662-7555; internet www.publish.csiro.au; f. 1974; quarterly; reports of CSIRO environmental research findings for the non-specialist reader; Editor BRYONY BENNETT; circ. 8,000.

Electronics Australia: POB 199, Alexandria, NSW 1435; tel. (2) 9353-0620; fax (2) 9353-0613; e-mail electaus@fpc.com.au; internet www.electronicsaustralia.com.au; f. 1922; monthly; technical, radio, television, microcomputers, hi-fi and electronics; Editor GRAHAM CATTLEY; circ. 20,900.

Elle: 54 Park St, Sydney, NSW 2000; tel. (2) 9282-8790; fax (2) 9267-4375; f. 1990; monthly; Editor MARINA GO; circ. 68,154.

Family Circle: Pier 8/9, 23 Hickson Rd, Millers Point, NSW 2000; tel. (2) 8220-2000; fax (2) 8220-2111; e-mail family_circle@mm.com.au; 13 a year; circ. 235,860.

Gardening Australia: POB 199, Alexandria, NSW 1435; tel. (2) 9353-6666; fax (2) 9317-4615; f. 1991; monthly; Editor BRODIE MYERS-COOKE; circ. 87,000.

Houses: Architecture Media Pty Ltd, Level 3, 4 Princes St, Port Melbourne, Vic 3207; tel. (3) 9646-4760; fax (3) 9646-4918; e-mail houses@archmedia.com.au; internet www.archmedia.com.au; f. 1989; 4 a year; Editor SUE HARRIS; circ. 23,768.

HQ: 54 Park St, Sydney, NSW 1028; tel. (2) 9282-8260; fax (2) 9267-3616; e-mail hq@publishing.acp.com.au; internet www.hq.ninemsn.com.au; f. 1989; every 2 months; Publr JOHN ALEXANDER; Editor KATHY BAIL; circ. 32,837.

Manufacturers' Monthly: Level 1/28 Riddell Parade, Elsternwick, Vic 3185; tel. (3) 9245-7777; fax (3) 9245-7750; f. 1961; Editor GREG VIDEON; circ. 15,188.

Modern Boating: The Federal Publishing Co Pty Ltd, 180 Bourke Rd, Alexandria, NSW 2015; tel. (2) 9353-6666; fax (2) 9353-0935; e-mail imacrae@fpc.com.au; internet www.modernboating.com.au; f. 1965; every 2 months; Editor IAN MACRAE; circ. 11,000.

Motor: Locked Bag 12, Oakleigh, Vic 3166; tel (3) 9567-4200; fax (3) 9563-4554; e-mail motor@acpaction.com.au; f. 1954; monthly; Editor GED BULMER; circ. 41,414.

New Woman: Murdoch Magazines, 45 Jones St, Ultimo, NSW 2007; tel. (2) 9692-2000; fax (2) 9692-2488; monthly; Editor-in-Chief GAY BRYANT; circ. 108,444.

The Open Road: L27, 388 George St, Sydney, NSW 2000; tel. (2) 9292-9275; fax (2) 9292-9069; f. 1927; every 2 months; journal of National Roads and Motorists' Asscn (NRMA); Editor STEVE FRASER; circ. 1,555,917.

Personal Investor: Level 2, 469 La Trobe St, Melbourne, Vic 3000; tel. (3) 9603-3888; fax (3) 9670-4328; e-mail pieditor@brw.fairfax.com.au; internet www.personalinvestor.com.au; monthly; Editor ROBIN BOWERMAN; circ. 61,016.

Reader's Digest: 26–32 Waterloo St, Surry Hills, NSW 2010; tel. (2) 9690-6111; fax (2) 9690-6211; monthly; Editor-in-Chief BRUCE HEILBUTH; circ. 508,142.

Street Machine: Locked Bag 756, Epping, NSW 2121; tel. (2) 9868-4832; fax (2) 9869-7390; e-mail streetmachine@acpaction.com.au; Editor MARK OASTLER; circ. 55,000.

TV Hits: Private Bag 9900, North Sydney, NSW 2059; tel. (2) 9464-3300; fax (2) 9464-3508; f. 1988; monthly; circ. 114,509.

TV Soap: 55 Chandos St, St Leonards, NSW 2065; tel. (2) 9901-6100; fax (2) 9901-6166; f. 1983; monthly; Editor BEN MITCHELL; circ. 103,000.

Vogue Australia: Level 2, 170 Pacific Highway, Greenwich, NSW 2065; tel. (2) 9964-3888; fax (2) 9964-3879; f. 1959; monthly; fashion; Editor JULIET ASHWORTH; circ. 54,705.

Wheels: GPOB 4088, Sydney, NSW 2001; tel. (2) 9263-9700; fax (2) 9263-9702; internet www.carpoint.com.au; f. 1953; monthly; international motoring magazine; circ. 60,286.

Wildlife Research: CSIRO Publishing, 150 Oxford St, POB 1139, Collingwood, Vic 3066; tel. (3) 9662-7622; fax (3) 9662-7611; e-mail publishing.wr@_csiro.au; internet www.publish.csiro.au/journals/wr; f. 1974; 6 a year; Man. Editor D. W. MORTON; circ. 1,000.

Your Garden: 35–51 Mitchell St, McMahons Point, NSW 2060; tel. (2) 9464-3586; fax (2) 9464-3487; e-mail yg@pacpubs.com.au; internet www.yourgarden.com.au; monthly; Editor MAREE TREDINNICK; circ. 60,246.

NEWS AGENCIES

AAP Information Services: Locked Bag 21, Grosvenor Place, Sydney, NSW 2000; tel. (2) 9322-8000; fax (2) 9322-8888; f. 1983; owned by major daily newspapers of Australia; Chair. and CEO C. L. CASEY.

Foreign Bureaux

Agence France-Presse (AFP): 7th Floor, 259 George St, Sydney, NSW 2000; tel. (2) 9251-1544; fax (2) 9251-5230; e-mail afpsyd@afp.com; internet www.afp.com; Bureau Chief DAVID MILLIKIN.

Agenzia Nazionale Stampa Associata (ANSA) (Italy): Suite 4, 2 Grosvenor St, Bondi Junction, NSW 2022; tel. (2) 9369-1427; fax (2) 9369-4351; e-mail ansasyd@ozemail.com.au; Bureau Chief CLAUDIO MARCELLO.

Deutsche Presse-Agentur (dpa) (Germany): 36 Heath St, Mona Vale, NSW 2103; tel. (2) 9979-8253; fax (2) 9997-3154; e-mail hofman@zip.com.au; Correspondent ALEXANDER HOFMAN.

Jiji Press (Australia) Pty Ltd (Japan): GPOB 2584, Sydney, NSW 2001; tel. (2) 9230-0020; fax (2) 9230-0024; e-mail jijiaust@bigpond.com; Bureau Chief NOBOTUSHI KOBAYASHI.

Kyodo News Service (Japan): Level 7, 9 Lang St, Sydney, NSW 2000; tel. (2) 9251-5240; fax (2) 9251-4980; e-mail jumper8@attglobal.net; Bureau Chief MASATO ISHII.

Reuters Australia Pty Ltd: Level 30, 60 Margaret St, Sydney, NSW 2031; e-mail Sydney.newsroom@reuters.com; internet www.reuters.com; Bureau Chief PHIL SMITH.

Xinhua (New China) News Agency (People's Republic of China): 50 Russell St, Hackett, Canberra, ACT 2602; tel. (2) 6248-6369; fax (2) 6257-4706; Chief Correspondent LIN ZHENXI.

The Central News Agency (Taiwan) and the New Zealand Press Association are represented in Sydney, and Antara (Indonesia) is represented in Canberra.

PRESS ASSOCIATIONS

Australian Press Council: Suite 303, 149 Castlereagh St, Sydney, NSW 2000; tel. (2) 9261-1930; fax (2) 9267-6826; e-mail info@presscouncil.org.au; internet www.presscouncil.org.au; Chair. Prof. KEN MCKINNON.

Australian Suburban Newspapers Association: POB Q1527, QVB, NSW 1230; tel. (2) 9248-7300; fax (2) 9299-0087; e-mail robyn@printnet.com.au; Sec. ROBYN BAKER.

Country Press Association of SA Incorporated: 198 Greenhill Rd, Eastwood, SA 5063; tel. (8) 8373-6533; fax (8) 8373-6544; f. 1912; represents South Australian country newspapers; Pres. B. PRICE; Exec. Dir M. R. TOWNSEND.

Country Press Australia: POB Q182, Queen Victoria Bldg, Sydney, NSW 2000; tel. (2) 9299-4658; fax (2) 9299-1892; f. 1906; Exec. Dir D. J. SOMMERLAD; 420 mems.

Queensland Country Press Association: POB 103, Paddington, Qld 4064; tel. (7) 3356-0033; Pres. M. HODGSON; Sec. N. D. MCLARY.

Tasmanian Press Association Pty Ltd: 71–75 Paterson St, Launceston, Tas 7250; tel. (3) 6320-255; Sec. L. WHISH-WILSON.

Victorian Country Press Association Ltd: 33 Rathdowne St, Carlton, Vic 3053; tel. (3) 9662-3244; fax (3) 9663-7433; e-mail vcpa@vcpa.com.au; f. 1910; Pres. G. KELLY; Exec. Dir J. E. RAY; 114 mems.

Publishers

Allen and Unwin Pty Ltd: 83 Alexander St, Crows Nest, NSW 2065; tel. (2) 8425-0100; fax (2) 9906-2218; e-mail info@allenandun win.com.au; internet www.allen-unwin.com.au; fiction, trade, academic, children's; Man. Dir PATRICK A. GALLAGHER.

Australasian Medical Publishing Co Pty Ltd: Level 2, 26-32 Pyrmont Bridge Road, Pyrmont, NSW 2009; tel. (2) 9562-6666; fax (2) 9562-6600; e-mail ampco@ampco.com.au; internet www.ampco .com.au; f. 1913; scientific, medical and educational; CEO Dr MARTIN VAN DER WEYDEN.

Britannica.com.au: Locked Bag 927, North Sydney, NSW 2060; tel. (2) 9923-5600; fax (2) 9929-3753; e-mail sales@britannica .com.au; internet www.britannica.com.au; reference, education, art, science and commerce; Man. Dir DAVID CAMPBELL.

Butterworths: Tower 2, 475 Victoria Ave, Chatswood, NSW 2067; tel. (2) 9422-2222; fax (2) 9422-2444; internet www.lexisnexis .com.au; f. 1910; div. of Reed International Books Australia Pty Ltd; legal and commercial; Man. Dir MAX PIPER.

Cambridge University Press (Australia): 10 Stamford Road, Oakleigh, Melbourne, Vic 3166; tel. (3) 9568-0322; fax (3) 9569-9292; e-mail info@cup.edu.au; internet www.cup.edu.au; scholarly and educational; Dir SANDRA MCCOMB.

Commonwealth Scientific and Industrial Research Organisation (CSIRO PUBLISHING): 150 Oxford St, POB 1139, Collingwood, Vic 3066; tel. (3) 9662-7500; fax (3) 9662-7555; e-mail publishing@csiro.au; internet www.publish.csiro.au; f. 1926; scientific and technical journals, books, magazines, videos, CD-ROMs; Gen. Man. P. W. REEKIE.

Doubleday Australia Pty Ltd: 91 Mars Rd, Lane Cove, NSW 2066; tel. (2) 9427-0377; fax (2) 9427-6973; educational, trade, non-fiction, Australiana; Man. Dir BARRY MACMULLEN.

Elsevier (Australia) Pty Ltd: 30–52 Smidmore St, Marrickville, NSW 2204; tel. (2) 9517-8999; fax (2) 9517-2249; e-mail service@ harcourt.com.au; internet www.harcourt.com.au; health sciences, science and medicine; Man. Dir FERGUS HALL.

Gordon and Gotch Ltd: 25–37 Huntingdale Rd, Private Bag 290, Burwood, Vic 3125; tel. (3) 9805-1700; fax (3) 9808-0714; e-mail mavis.thomas@gordongotch.com.au; general; Chair. and Man. Dir I. D. GOLDING.

Harcourt Education Australia: POB 460, Port Melbourne, Vic 3207; tel. (3) 9245-7111; fax (3) 9245-7333; e-mail admin@harcourt education.com.au; internet www.hi.com.au; primary, secondary and tertiary educational; division of Reed International; Man. Dir DAVID O'BRIEN.

Harlequin Enterprises (Australia) Pty Ltd: Unit 2, 3 Gibbes St, Chatswood, NSW 2067; tel. (2) 9415-9200; fax (2) 9415-9292; internet www.eHarlequin.com.au; Man. Dir MICHELLE LAFOREST.

Hodder Headline Australia Pty Ltd: Level 22, 201 Kent, Sydney, NSW 2000; tel. (2) 8248-0800; fax (2) 8248-0810; e-mail auspub@ hha.com.au; internet www.hha.com.au; fiction, general, technical, children's; Man. Dir MALCOLM EDWARDS.

Hyland House Publishing Pty Ltd: POB 122, Flemington, Vic 3031; tel. and fax (3) 9376-4461; e-mail hyland3@netspace.net.au; f. 1976; trade, general, gardening, pet care, Aboriginal, Asian-Pacific public policy, fiction; Rep. MICHAEL SCHOO.

Lansdowne Publishing: Level 1, 18 Argyle St, The Rocks, NSW 2000; tel. (2) 9240-9222; fax (2) 9241-4818; e-mail valerie@ lanspub.com.au; cookery, gardening, health, history, pet care; Chief Exec. STEVEN MORRIS.

LBC Information Services: 100 Harris St, Pyrmont, NSW 2009; tel. (2) 8587-7000; fax (2) 8587-7100; e-mail lbccustomer@thomson .com.au; legal and professional; Man. Dir E. J. COSTIGAN.

Lothian Books: Level 5, 132 Albert Rd, South Melbourne, Vic 3205; tel. (3) 9694 4900; fax (3) 9645-0705; e-mail books@lothian.com.au; internet www.lothian.com.au; f. 1888; gardening, health, craft, business, New Age, self-help, general non-fiction, young adult fiction and children's picture books; Man. Dir PETER LOTHIAN.

McGraw-Hill Australia Pty Ltd: 4 Barcoo St, Roseville, Sydney, NSW 2069; tel. (2) 9415-9899; fax (2) 9417-8872; e-mail cservice_sydney@mcgraw-hill.com; internet www.mcgraw-hill .com.au; educational, professional and technical; Man. Dir FIRGAL ADAMS.

Melbourne University Press: 268 Drummond St, Carlton South, Vic 3053; tel. (3) 9347-0300; fax (3) 9342-0399; e-mail info@ mup.unimelb.edu.au; internet www.mup.com.au; f. 1922; scholarly non-fiction, Australian history and biography; Chair. Prof. BARRY SHEEHAN; Dir JOHN MECKAN.

Murdoch Books: GPOB 1203, Sydney, NSW 2001; tel. (2) 8220-2000; fax (2) 8220-2558; e-mail georginad@mm.com.au; cooking, gardening, DIY, children's; CEO JULIET ROGERS; Publr KAY SCARLETT.

National Library of Australia: Parkes Place, Canberra, ACT 2600; tel. (2) 6262-1111; fax (2) 6273-4493; e-mail phetheri@nla.gov.au; internet www.nla.gov.au; f. 1960; national bibliographic service, etc.; Publications Dir PAUL HETHERINGTON.

Nelson Thomson Learning: 102 Dodds St, South Melbourne, Vic 3205; tel. (3) 9685-4111; fax (3) 9685-4199; e-mail customerservice @nelson.com.au; internet www.nelsonitp.com; educational; Man. Dir G. J. BROWNE.

Oxford University Press: 253 Normanby Rd, South Melbourne, Vic 3205; tel. (3) 9934-9123; fax (3) 9934-9100; f. 1908; general non-fiction and educational; Man. Dir MAREK PALKA.

Pan Macmillan Australia Pty Ltd: Level 18, St Martin's Tower, 31 Market St, Sydney, NSW 2000; tel. (2) 9285-9100; fax (2) 9285-9190; e-mail pansyd@macmillan.com.au; general, reference, children's, fiction, non-fiction; Chair. R. GIBB.

Pearson Education Australia Pty Ltd: 95 Coventry St, South Melbourne, Vic 3205; tel. (3) 9697-0666; fax (3) 9699-2041; e-mail longman.sales@pearsoned.com.au.; internet www.pearsoned.com .au; f. 1957; mainly educational, academic, computer, some general; Man. Dir PAT EVANS.

Penguin Books Australia Ltd: POB 701, Hawthorn, Vic 3122; tel. (3) 9811-2400; fax (3) 9811-2620; internet www.penguin.com.au; f. 1946; general; Man. Dir PETER FIELD; Publishing Dir ROBERT SESSIONS.

Random House Australia Pty Ltd: 20 Alfred St, Milsons Point, NSW 2061; tel. (2) 9954-9966; fax (2) 9954-4562; e-mail random@ randomhouse.com.au; internet www.randomhouse.com.au; fiction, non-fiction, children's and illustrated; Man. Dir MARGARET SEALE.

Reader's Digest (Australia) Pty Ltd: POB 4353, Sydney, NSW 2000; tel. (2) 9690-6111; fax (2) 9699-8165; general; Man. Dir WILLIAM B. TOOHEY.

Scholastic Australia Pty Ltd: Railway Crescent, Lisarow, POB 579, Gosford, NSW 2250; tel. (2) 4328-3555; fax (2) 4323-3827; internet www.scholastic.com.au; f. 1968; educational and children's; Man. Dir KEN JOLLY.

Schwartz Publishing (Victoria) Pty Ltd: 45 Flinders Lane, Melbourne, Vic 3000; tel. (3) 9654-2000; fax (3) 9650-5418; fiction, non-fiction; Dir MORRY SCHWARTZ.

Simon and Schuster Australia: 20 Barcoo St, POB 507, East Roseville, NSW 2069; tel. (2) 9415-9900; fax (2) 9417-4292; general fiction, non-fiction, cooking, gardening, craft, parenting, health, history, travel and biography; Man. Dir JON ATTENBOROUGH.

Thames and Hudson (Australia) Pty Ltd: 11 Central Boulevard, Portside Business Park, Fishermans Bend, Vic 3207; tel. (3) 9646-7788; fax (3) 9646-8790; e-mail thaust@thaust.com.au; art, history, archaeology, architecture, photography, design, fashion, textiles, lifestyle; Man. Dir PETER SHAW.

D. W. Thorpe: 18 Salmon St, Locked Bag 20, Port Melbourne, Vic 3207; tel. (3) 9245-7370; fax (3) 9245-7395; e-mail customer.service@ thorpe.com.au; bibliographic, library and book trade reference; Publishing Man. PAULENE MOREY.

Time Life Australia Pty Ltd: Level 12, 33 Berry St, North Sydney, NSW 2060; tel. (2) 8925-3800; fax (2) 9957-4227; general and educational; Man. Dir ROBERT HARDY.

UNSW Press Ltd: UNSW, Sydney, NSW 2052; tel. (2) 9664-0999; fax (2) 9664-5420; e-mail info.press@unsw.edu.au; f. 1961; scholarly, general and tertiary texts; Man. Dir Dr ROBIN DERRICOURT.

University of Queensland Press: POB 6042, St Lucia, Qld 4067; tel. (7) 3365-2127; fax (7) 3365-7579; e-mail uqp@uqp.uq.edu.au; internet www.uqp.uq.edu.au; f. 1948; scholarly and general cultural interest, incl. Black Australian writers, adult and children's fiction; Gen. Man. LAURIE MULLER.

University of Western Australia Press: c/o University of Western Australia, WA 6009; tel. (8) 9380-3670; fax (8) 9380-1027; e-mail uwap@cyllene.uwa.edu.au; internet www.uwapress.uwa .edu.au; f. 1954; natural history, history, literary studies, Australiana, children's, general non-fiction; Dir Dr JENNY GREGORY.

John Wiley & Sons Australia, Ltd: POB 1226, Milton, Qld 4064; tel. (7) 3859-9755; fax (7) 3859-9715; e-mail brisbane@johnwiley .com.au; internet www.johnwiley.com.au; f. 1954; educational, reference and trade; Man. Dir PETER DONOUGHUE.

Government Publishing House

AusInfo: GPOB 1920, Canberra, ACT 2601; tel. (2) 6275-3442; fax (2) 6275-3682; internet www.ausinfo.gov.au; f. 1970; fmrly Australian Govt Publishing Service; Assistant Sec. MICHELLE KINNANE.

PUBLISHERS' ASSOCIATION

Australian Publishers Association Ltd: 89 Jones St, Ultimo, NSW 2007; tel. (2) 9281-9788; fax (2) 9281-1073; e-mail apa@publishers.asn.au; internet www.publishers.asn.au; f. 1948; c. 130 mems; Pres. SANDY GRANT; Chief Exec. SUSAN BRIDGE.

Broadcasting and Communications

TELECOMMUNICATIONS

By August 2002, more than 100 licensed telecommunication carriers were in operation.

AAPT Ltd: AAPT Centre, 9 Lang St, Sydney, NSW 2000; tel. (2) 9377-7000; fax (2) 9377-7133; internet www.aapt.com.au; f. 1991; long-distance telecommunications carrier; Chair C. L. CASEY; CEO and Man. Dir L. WILLIAMS.

Cable & Wireless Optus Ltd: POB 1, North Sydney, NSW 2059; tel. (2) 9342-7800; fax (2) 9342-7100; internet www.cwo.com.au; f. 1991; general and mobile telecommunications, data and internet services, pay-TV; Chair. Sir RALPH ROBINS; Chief Exec. CHRIS ANDERSON.

Matrix Telecommunications Services: 1st Floor, 24 Artamon Rd, Willoughby, NSW 2068; tel. (2) 9290-4111; fax (2) 9262-2574; f. 1985; mobile communication services; Chair. MARK CARNEGIE; Pres. and CEO JOSEPH YANG.

One.Tel Ltd: Level 28, 9 Castlereagh St, Sydney, NSW 2000; tel. (2) 9777-8111; fax (2) 9777-8199; internet www.onetel.com.au; telecommunication services; Chair. JOHN GREAVES.

Telstra Corpn Ltd: Level 14, 231 Elizabeth St, Sydney, NSW 2000; tel. (2) 9287-4677; fax (2) 9287-5869; internet www.telstra.com.au; general and mobile telecommunication services; Man. Dir and Chief Exec. ZIGGY SWITKOWSKI.

Vodafone Pacific Pty Ltd: Tower A, 799 Pacific Highway, Chatswood, NSW 2067; tel. (2) 9878-7000; fax (2) 9878-7788; internet www.vodafone.com.au; mobile telecommunication services.

Regulatory Authority

Australian Communications Authority (ACA): POB 78, Belconnen, ACT 2616; tel. (3) 9963-6800; fax (3) 9963-6899; e-mail candinfo@aca.gov.au; internet www.aca.gov.au; f. 1997; Commonwealth regulator for telecommunications and radiocommunications; Chair. TONY SHAW.

BROADCASTING

Many programmes are provided by the non-commercial statutory corporation, the Australian Broadcasting Corporation (ABC). Commercial radio and television services are provided by stations operated by companies under licences granted and renewed by the Australian Broadcasting Authority (ABA). They rely for their income on the broadcasting of advertisements. In mid-1993 there were 166 commercial radio stations in operation, and 44 commercial television stations.

In 1997 there were an estimated 25.5m. radio receivers. The number of television receivers in use totalled 14,129 in 2000.

Australian Broadcasting Corporation (ABC): 700 Harris St, Ultimo, POB 9994, Sydney, NSW 2001; tel. (2) 9333-1500 (radio); fax (2) 9333-2603 (radio), (2) 9950-3050 (television); e-mail comments@your.abc.net.au; internet www.abc.net.au; f. 1932 as Australian Broadcasting Commission; became corporation in 1983; one national television network operating on about 700 transmitters and six radio networks operating on more than 6,000 transmitters; Chair. DONALD MCDONALD; Man. Dir RUSSELL BALDING.

Radio Australia: international service broadcast by short wave and satellite in English, Indonesian, Standard Chinese, Khmer, Tok Pisin and Vietnamese.

Radio

Federation of Australian Radio Broadcasters Ltd: Level 5, 88 Foveaux street, Surry Hills, NSW 2010; tel. (2) 9281-6577; fax (2) 9281-6599; e-mail mail@commercialradio.com.au; internet www.commercialradio.com; asscn of privately-owned Australian commercial stations; CEO JOAN WARNER.

Major Commercial Broadcasting Station Licensees

5AD Broadcasting Co Pty Ltd: 201 Tynte St, Nth Adelaide, SA 5006; tel. (8) 8300-1000; fax (8) 8300-1020; internet www.5adfm.com.au; also operates 5DN and Mix102.3; Gen. Man. GRAEME TUCKER.

Associated Communications Enterprises (ACE) Radio Broadcasters Pty Ltd: POB 7515, Melbourne, Vic 3004; tel. (3) 9645-9877; fax (3) 9645-9886; operates six stations; Man. Dir S. EVERETT.

Austereo Pty Ltd: Ground Level, 180 St Kilda Rd, St Kilda, Vic 3182; tel. (3) 9230-1051; fax (3) 9593-9007; e-mail pharvie@austereo.com.au; internet www.austereo.com.au; operates 14 stations; Exec. Chair. PETER HARVIE.

Australian Radio Network Pty Ltd: Level 8, 99 Mount St, North Sydney, NSW 2060; tel. (2) 9464-1000; fax (2) 9464-1010; operates nine stations; CEO NEIL MOUNT.

Australian Regional Broadcasters: 1 June Rd, Gooseberry Hill, WA 6076; tel. (8) 9472-8900; fax (8) 9472-8911; operates three stations; Man. Dir NICK RINGROSE.

Bass Radio: 109 York St, Launceston, Tas 7250; tel. (3) 6331-4844; fax (3) 6334-5858; operates five radio stations and part of RG Capital Radio; Man. DAVE HILL.

Capital Radio: 28 Sharp St, Cooma, NSW 2630; tel. (2) 6452-1521; fax (2) 6452-1006; operates four stations; Man. Dir KEVIN BLYTON.

DMG Regional Radio Pty Ltd: Level 5, 33 Saunders St, Pyrmont, NSW 2009; tel. (2) 9564 9888; fax (2) 9564 9867; e-mail sydoff@dmgradio.com.au; internet www.dmgradio.com.au; operates 59 stations; Gen. Mans KEN GANNAWAY (Western Group), DAVID SCOPELLITI (Northern Group); GARRY LEDDIN (Southern Group); Chair. PAUL THOMPSON.

Grant Broadcasting: 63 Minimbah Rd, Northbridge, NSW 2063; tel. (2) 9958-7301; fax (2) 9958-6906; operates seven stations; Gen. Man. JANET CAMERON.

Greater Cairns Radio Ltd: Virginia House, Abbott St, Cairns, Qld 4870; tel. (7) 4050-0800; fax (7) 4051-8060; e-mail cnssales@dmgradio.com.au; Gen. Man. J. ELLER.

Macquarie Radio Network Pty Ltd: POB 4290, Sydney, NSW 2001; tel. (2) 9269-0646; fax (2) 9287-2772; operates 2GB and 2CH; CEO GEORGE BUSCHMAN.

Moree Broadcasting and Development Company Ltd: 87–89 Balo St, Moree, NSW 2400; tel. (2) 6752-1155; fax (2) 6752-2601; operates two stations; Man. KEN BIRCH.

Radio 2SM Gold 1269: 186 Blues Point Rd, North Sydney, NSW 2060; tel. (2) 9922-1269; fax (2) 9954-3117; f. 1931; CEO and Chair. C. M. MURPHY.

RadioWest Hot FM: POB 10067, Kalgoorlie, WA 6430; tel. (8) 9021-2666; fax (8) 9091-2209; e-mail radio6KG@gold.net.au; f. 1931.

Regional Broadcasters (Australia) Pty: McDowal St, Roma, Qld 4455; tel. (7) 4622-1800; fax (7) 4622-3697; Chair. G. MCVEAN.

RG Capital Radio Pty Ltd: Level 2, Seabank Bldg, 12–14 Marine Parade, Southport, Qld 4215; tel. (7) 5591-5000; fax (7) 5591-2869; operates 34 stations; Man. Dir RHYS HOLLERAN.

Rural Press Ltd: Cnr Pine Mt Rd and Hill St, Raymonds Hill, Qld 4305; tel. (7) 3201-6000; fax (7) 3812-3060; internet www.rpl.com.au; f. 1911; operates five stations; Gen. Man. RICHARD BURNS.

SEA FM Pty Ltd: POB 5910, Gold Coast Mail Centre, Bundall, Qld 4217; tel. (7) 5591-5000; fax (7) 5591-6080; operates 28 stations; Man. Dir RHYS HOLLERAN.

Southern Cross Broadcasting (Australia) Ltd: see under Television.

Supernetwork Radio Pty Ltd: POB 97, Coolangatta, Qld 4225; tel. (7) 5524-4497; fax (7) 5554-3970; operates 15 stations; Chair. W. CARALIS.

Tamworth Radio Development Company Pty Ltd: POB 497, Tamworth, NSW 2340; tel. (2) 6765-7055; fax (2) 6765-2762; operates five stations; Man. W. A. MORRISON.

Tasmanian Broadcasting Network (TBN): POB 665G, Launceston, Tas 7250; tel. (3) 6431-2555; fax (3) 6431-3188; operates three stations; Chair. K. FINDLAY.

Wesgo Ltd: POB 234, Seven Hills, NSW 2147; tel. (2) 9831-7611; fax (2) 9831-2001; operates eight stations; CEO G. W. RICE.

Television

Federation of Australian Commercial Television Stations (FACTS): 44 Avenue Rd, Mosman, NSW 2088; tel. (2) 9960-2622; fax (2) 9969-3520; internet www.facts.org.au; f. 1960; represents all commercial television stations; Chair. JUDITH STACK; CEO JULIE FLYNN.

Commercial Television Station Licensees

Amalgamated Television Services Pty Ltd: Mobbs Lane, Epping, NSW 2121; tel. (2) 9877-7777; fax (2) 9877-7888; f. 1956; originating station for Seven Network TV programming; Exec. Chair. KERRY STOKES.

Australian Capital Television Pty Ltd (Ten Capital): Private Bag 10, Dickson, ACT 2602; tel. (2) 6242-2400; fax (2) 6241-7230; f. 1962; Gen. Man. ERIC PASCOE.

Broken Hill Television Ltd: POB 472, Rocky Hill, Broken Hill, NSW 2880; tel. (8) 8087-6013; fax (8) 8087-8492; internet www.centralonline.com.au; f. 1968; operates one station; Chair. PETER STORROCK; Chief Exec. D. WESTON.

Channel 9 South Australia Pty Ltd: 202 Tynte St, North Adelaide 5006; tel. (8) 8267-0111; fax (8) 8267-3996; f. 1959; Gen. Man. M. COLSON.

Channel Seven Adelaide Pty Ltd: 45–49 Park Terrace, Gilberton, SA 5081; tel. (8) 8342-7777; fax (8) 8342-7717; f. 1965; operates SAS Channel 7; mem. of Seven Network; Man. Dir MAX WALTERS.

Channel Seven Brisbane Pty Ltd: GPOB 604, Brisbane, Qld 4001; tel. (7) 3369-7777; fax (7) 3368-2970; f. 1959; operates one station; mem. of Seven Network; Man. Dir L. M. RILEY.

Channel Seven Melbourne Pty Ltd: 119 Wells St, Southbank, Vic 3006; tel. (3) 9697-7777; fax (3) 9697-7888; e-mail daspinall@seven.com.auf. 1956; operates one station; Chair. KERRY STOKES; Man. Dir DAVID ASPINALL.

Channel Seven Perth Pty Ltd: POB 77, Tuart Hill, WA 6939; tel. (8) 9344-0777; fax (8) 9344-0670; f. 1959; Chair. C. S. WHARTON.

General Television Corporation Pty Ltd: 22–46 Bendigo St, POB 100, Richmond, Vic 3121; tel. (3) 9429-0201; fax (3) 9429-3670; internet www.nine.msn.com.au; f. 1957; operates one station; Man. Dir GRAEME YARWOOD.

Golden West Network: POB 5090, Geraldton, WA 6531; tel. (8) 9921-4422; fax (8) 9921-8096.

Golden West Network Pty Ltd: POB 1062, West Perth, WA 6872; tel. (8) 9481-0050; fax (8) 9321-2470; f. 1967; operates three stations (SSW10, VEW and WAW); Gen. Man. W. FENWICK.

Imparja Television Pty Ltd: POB 52, Alice Springs, NT 0871; tel. (8) 8950-1411; fax (8) 8953-0322; e-mail imparja@ozemailimparja.com.au; internet www.imparja.com.au; CEO CORALLIE FERGUSON.

Independent Broadcasters of Australia Pty Ltd: POB 285, Sydney, NSW 2001; tel. (2) 9264-9144; fax (2) 9264-6334; fmrly Regional Television Australia Pty Ltd; Chair. GRAEME J. GILBERTSON; Sec. JEFF EATHER.

Mt Isa Television Pty Ltd: 110 Canooweal St, Mt Isa, Qld 4825; tel. (7) 4743-8888; fax (7) 4743-9803; f. 1971; operates one station; Station Man. LYALL GREY.

NBN Ltd: Mosbri Crescent, POB 750L, Newcastle, NSW 2300; tel. (2) 4929-2933; fax (2) 4926-2936; f. 1962; operates one station; Man. Dir DENIS LEDBURY.

Network Ten Ltd: GPOB 10, Sydney, NSW 2001; tel. (2) 9650-1010; fax (2) 9650-1170; operates Australian TV network and commercial stations in Sydney, Melbourne, Brisbane, Perth and Adelaide; CEO JOHN MCALPINE.

Nine Network Australia Pty Ltd: POB 27, Willoughby, NSW 2068; tel. (2) 9906-9999; fax (2) 9958-2279; internet www.ninemsn.com.au; f. 1956; division of Publishing and Broadcasting Ltd; operates three stations: TCN Channel Nine Pty Ltd (Sydney), Queensland Television Ltd (Brisbane) and General Television Corporation Ltd (Melbourne); CEO DAVID LECKIE.

Northern Rivers Television Pty Ltd: Peterson Rd, Locked Bag 1000, Coffs Harbour, NSW 2450; tel. (2) 6652-2777; fax (2) 6652-3034; f. 1965; CEO GARRY DRAFFIN.

Prime Television Group: Level 6, 1 Pacific Highway, North Sydney, NSW 2060; tel. (2) 9965-7700; fax (2) 9965-7729; e-mail primetv@primetv.com.au; internet www.primetv.com.au; Chair. PAUL RAMSAY; CEO BRENT HARMAN.

Prime Television (Northern) Pty Ltd: POB 2077, Elermore Vale, NSW 2287; tel. (2) 4952-0500; fax (2) 4952-0502; internet www.primetv.com.au; Gen. Man. BRAD JONES.

Prime Television (Southern) Pty Ltd: POB 465, Orange, NSW 2800; tel. (2) 6361-6888; fax (2) 6363-1889; Gen. Man. D. THISTLETHWAITE.

Prime Television (Victoria) Pty Ltd: Sunraysia Highway, Ballarat, Vic 3350; tel. (3) 5337-1777; fax (3) 5337-1700; e-mail primetv.ballarat@primetv.com.au; Gen. Man. CRAIG WHITFIELD.

Queensland Television Ltd: POB 72, GPO Brisbane, Qld 4001; tel. (7) 3214-9999; fax (7) 3369-3512; f. 1959; operates one station; Gen. Man. IAN R. MÜLLER.

Seven Network Ltd: Level 13, 1 Pacific Highway, North Sydney, NSW 2060; tel. (2) 9967-7903; fax (2) 9967-7972; internet www.seven.com.au; owns Amalgamated Television Services Pty Ltd (Sydney), Brisbane TV Ltd (Brisbane), HSV Channel 7 Pty Ltd (Melbourne), South Australian Telecasters Ltd (Adelaide) and TVW Enterprises Ltd (Perth); Exec. Chair. KERRY STOKES.

Australia Television: international satellite service; broadcasts to more than 30 countries and territories in Asia and the Pacific.

Seven Queensland: 140–142 Horton Parade, Maroochydore, Qld 4558; tel. (7) 5430-1777; fax (7) 5430-1767; f. 1965; fmrly Sunshine Television Network Ltd.

Southern Cross Broadcasting (Australia) Ltd: 41–49 Bank St, South Melbourne, Vic 3205; tel. (3) 9243-2100; fax (3) 9690-0937; internet www.scbnetwork.com.au; f. 1932; operates four TV and four radio stations; Man. Dir A. E. BELL.

Southern Cross Television (TNT9) Pty Ltd: Watchorn St, Launceston, Tas 7250; tel. (3) 6344-0202; fax (3) 6343-0340; f. 1962; operates one station; Gen. Man. BRUCE ABRAHAM.

Special Broadcasting Service (SBS): Locked Bag 028, Crows Nest, NSW 1585; tel. (2) 9430-2828; fax (2) 9430-3700; e-mail sbs.com.au; internet www.sbs.com.au; f. 1980; national multi-cultural broadcaster of TV and radio; Man. Dir NIGEL MILAN.

Spencer Gulf Telecasters Ltd: POB 305, Port Pirie, SA 5540; tel. (8) 8632-2555; fax (8) 8633-0984; e-mail dweston@centralonline.com.au; internet www.centralonline.com.au; f. 1968; operates two stations; Chair. P. M. STURROCK; Chief Exec. D. WESTON.

Swan Television & Radio Broadcasters Pty Ltd: POB 99, Tuart Hill, WA 6939; tel. (8) 9449-9999; fax (8) 9449-9900; Gen. Man. P. BOWEN.

Telecasters Australia Ltd: Level 8, 1 Elizabeth Plaza, North Sydney, NSW 2060; tel. (2) 9922-1011; fax (2) 9922-1033; internet www.telecasters.com.au; operates commercial TV services of TEN Queensland, TEN Northern NSW, Seven Central and Seven Darwin.

Territory Television Pty Ltd: POB 1764, Darwin, NT 0801; tel. (8) 8981-8888; fax (8) 8981-6802; f. 1971; operates one station; Gen. Man. A. G. BRUYN.

WIN Television Griffith Pty Ltd: 161 Remembrance Driveway, Griffith, NSW 2680; tel. (2) 6962-4500; fax (2) 6962-0979; e-mail mtntv@ozemail.com.au; fmrly MTN Television; Man. Dir RAY GAMBLE.

WIN Television Loxton SA Pty Ltd: Murray Bridge Rd, POB 471, Loxton, SA 5333; tel. (8) 8584-6891; fax (8) 8584-5062; f. 1976; operates one station; Exec. Chair. E. H. URLWIN; Gen. Man. W. L. MUDGE.

WIN Television Mildura Pty Ltd: 18 Deakin Ave, Mildura, Vic 3500; tel. (3) 5023-0204; fax (3) 5022-1179; f. 1965; Chair. JOHN RUSHTON; Man. NOEL W. HISCOCK.

WIN Television NSW Network: Television Ave, Mt St Thomas, Locked Bag 8800, South Coast Mail Centre, NSW 2521; tel. (2) 4223-4199; fax (2) 4227-3682; internet www.wintv.com.au; f. 1962; Man. Dir K. KINGSTON; CEO JOHN RUSHTON.

WIN Television Qld Pty Ltd: POB 568 Rockhampton, Qld 4700; tel. (7) 4930-4499; fax (7) 4930-4490; Station Man. R. HOCKEY.

WIN Television Tas Pty Ltd: 52 New Town Rd, Hobart, Tas 7008; tel. (3) 6228-8999; fax (3) 6228-8991; e-mail wintas.com.au; internet www.wintv.com.au; f. 1959; Gen. Man. GREG RAYMENT.

WIN Television Vic Pty Ltd: POB 464, Ballarat, Vic 3353; tel. (3) 5320-1366; fax (3) 5333-1598; internet www.winnet.com.au; f. 1961; operates five stations; Gen. Man. DAVID LANGSFORD.

Satellite, Cable and Digital Television

Digital television became available in metropolitan areas in January 2001 and was to be available in all major regional areas by 2004.

Austar United Communications: Level 29, AAP Centre, 259 George St, Sydney, NSW 2000; tel. (2) 9251-6999; fax (2) 9251-61361812; e-mail austar@austarunited.com.au; internet www.austarunited.com.au; began operations in 1995; 42.7m. subscribers (Sept. 2001); CEO JOHN C. PORTER.

Foxtel: Foxtel Television Centre, Pyrmont, Sydney; internet www.foxtel.com.au; owned by the News Corpn, Telstra Corpn and PBL; 800,100 subscribers (Aug. 2002).

Optus Vision: Tower B, Level 15, 16 Zenith Centre, 821–841 Pacific Highway, Chatswood, NSW 2067; commenced cable services on 11 channels in 1995; 210,000 subscribers (March 1999).

Regulatory Authority

Australian Broadcasting Authority: POB Q500, QVB Post Office, NSW 1230; tel. (2) 9334-7700; fax (2) 9334-7799; e-mail info@aba.gov.au; internet www.aba.gov.au; regulates radio and TV broadcasting, and internet content; Chair. Prof. DAVID FLINT.

Finance

Radical reforms of the financial sector, were introduced in 1998. The banking system was opened up to greater competition. The licensing and regulation of deposit-taking institutions was supervised by the new Australian Prudential Regulation Authority, while consumer protection was the responsibility of the Australian Corporations and Financial Services Commission.

(cap. = capital; p.u. = paid up; res = reserves; dep. = deposits; m. = million; brs = branches; amounts in Australian dollars)

Australian Prudential Regulation Authority (APRA): GPOB 9836, Sydney, NSW 2000; tel. (2) 9210-3000; fax (2) 9210-3411; e-mail APRAinfo@apra.gov.au; internet www.apra.gov.au; responsible for regulation of banks, insurance cos, superannuation funds, credit unions, building societies and friendly societies; CEO GRAEME THOMPSON.

BANKING

Central Bank

Reserve Bank of Australia: GPOB 3947, Sydney, NSW 2001; tel. (2) 9551-8111; fax (2) 9551-8000; e-mail rbainfo.@rba.gov.au; internet www.rba.gov.au; f. 1911; responsible for monetary policy, financial system stability, payment system development; cap. 40m. and res 8,926m., dep. 15,486m., total assets 55,694m., notes on issue 25,434m. (June 2000); Gov. IAN MACFARLANE.

Development Bank

Primary Industry Bank of Australia Ltd: GPOB 4577, Sydney, NSW 1042; tel. (2) 9234-4200; fax (2) 9221-6218; internet www.piba .com.au; f. 1978; cap. 123.2m., res 2.5m.; Chair. H. G. GENTIS; 21 brs.

Trading Banks

ABN AMRO Australia Ltd: Level 29, ABN AMRO Tower, 88 Phillip St, Sydney, NSW 2000; tel. (2) 8259-5000; fax (2) 8259-5444; www.abnamro.com.au; f. 1971; cap. 70m., res 590,000 (Dec. 2000); CEO STEVE CRANE.

Arab Bank Australia Ltd: GPOB N645, Grosvenor Place, 200 George St, Sydney, NSW 2000; tel. (2) 9377-8900; fax (2) 9221-5428; internet www.arabbank.com.au; cap. 55.0m., dep. 464.9m. (Dec. 2000); Chair. KHALID SHOMAN; Man. Dir JACK BEIGHTON.

Australia and New Zealand Banking Group Ltd: GPOB 537E 100 Queen St, Melbourne, Vic 3000; POB 537 E, Melbourne, Vic 3001; tel. (3) 9273-5555; fax (3) 9658-2484; internet www.anz.com; f. 1835; present name adopted in 1970; cap. 5,402.0m., res 786.0m., dep. 112,849.0m. (2000); 871 brs; Chair. C. B. GOODE; CEO JOHN MCFARLANE.

Bank of America Australia Ltd: Level 63, MLC Centre, 19–29 Martin Place, Sydney, NSW 2000; tel. (2) 9931-4200; fax (2) 9221-1023; f. 1964; cap. 150.3m. (Dec. 1998); Man. Dir JOHN LILES.

Bank of Melbourne: 360 Collins St, Melbourne, Vic 3000; tel. (3) 9608-3222; fax (3) 9608-3700; division of Westpac Banking Corpn; f. 1989; cap. 752m., dep. 8,706m. (1997); Chair. CHRIS STEWART; CEO MATTHEW SLATTER; 129 brs.

Bank of Queensland Ltd: 229 Elizabeth St, POB 898, Brisbane, Qld 4001; tel. (7) 3212-3333; fax (7) 3212-3399; internet www.boq.com.au; f. 1874; cap. 189.9m., res 1.0m., dep. 3,699.0m. (Aug. 2001); Chair. NEIL ROBERTS; Man Dir. DAVID P. LIDDY; 97 brs.

Bank of Tokyo-Mitsubishi (Australia) Ltd: Level 26, Gateway, 1 Macquarie Place, Sydney, NSW 2000; tel. (2) 9296-1111; fax (2) 9247-4266; e-mail btmacorp@btma.com.au; cap. 152.9m., res 33,000m., dep. 1,910.8m. (Dec. 2000); f. 1985; Chair. R. NICOLSON; Man. Dir H. KOJIMA.

Bank of Western Australia Ltd (BankWest): Level 7, BankWest Tower, 108 St George's Terrace, POB E237, Perth, WA 6001; tel. (8) 9449-7000; fax (8) 9449-7050; e-mail finmkts@bankwest.com.au.; internet www.bankwest.com.au; f. 1895 as Agricultural Bank of Western Australia, 1945 as Rural and Industries Bank of Western Australia; present name adopted in 1994; cap. 715.9m., res 6m., dep. 12,753.2m. (Feb. 2001); Chair. IAN C. R. MACKENZIE; Man. Dir TERRY C. BUDGE; 109 brs.

Bankers' Trust Australia Ltd: GPOB H4, Australia Sq., Sydney, NSW 2000; tel. (2) 9259-3555; fax (2) 9259-9800; internet www.btal .com.au; f. 1986; cap. 273.3m., dep. 6,266.8m. (Dec. 1997); Man. Dir R. A. FERGUSON; 5 brs.

The Chase Manhattan Bank: GPOB 9816, NSW 2001; tel. (2) 9250-4111; fax (2) 9250-4554; internet www.chase.com; Man. Dir W. SCOTT REID.

Citibank Ltd: GPOB 40, Sydney, NSW 1027; tel. (2) 9239-9100; fax (2) 9239-9110; internet www.citibank.com.au; f. 1954; cap. 457m., res 1m., dep. 5,619m. (Dec. 1998); Country Corporate Officer WILLIAM W. FERGUSON; Chair. THOMAS MCKEAN.

Commonwealth Bank of Australia: Level 1, 48 Martin Place, Sydney, NSW 1155; tel. (2) 9378-2000; fax (2) 9378-3317; internet www.commbank.com.au; f. 1912; cap. 12,521.0m., res 3,265.0m., dep. 142,509.0m. (June 2000); Chair. J. T. RALPH; CEO and Man. Dir D. V. MURRAY; more than 1,500 brs world-wide; merged with Colonial Ltd in 2000.

HSBC Bank Australia Ltd: Level 10, 1 O'Connell Street, Sydney, NSW 2000; tel. (2) 9255-2888; fax (2) 9255-2332; internet www.hsbc.com.au; f. 1985; fmrly HongkongBank of Australia; cap. 560.0m., res 100,000., dep. 5,052.8m. (Dec. 2000); Chair D. J. SAY; CEO CHRIS CROOK; 18 brs.

IBJ Australia Bank Ltd: Level 21, Colonial Centre, 52 Martin Place, Sydney, NSW 2000; tel. (2) 9377-8888; fax (2) 9377-8884; internet www.ibj.com.au; f. 1985; subsidiary of Mizuho Holdings Inc; cap. 104.0m., res 40.0m., dep. 1,336.0m. (Dec. 2000); Chair. M. J. PHILLIPS; Man. Dir YOSHIMICHI KAWASAKI.

ING Bank (Australia) Ltd: Level 13, 140 Sussex St, Sydney, NSW 2000; tel. (2) 9028-4000; fax (2) 9028-4708; f. 1994; cap. 60m., res 1.3m., dep. 1,015.4m. (Dec. 1998); Gen. Man. JULIE BROWN.

Macquarie Bank Ltd: 1 Martin Place, Sydney, NSW 2000; tel. (2) 8232-3333; fax (2) 8232-3350; internet www.macquarie .com.au; f. 1969 as Hill Samuel Australia Ltd; present name adopted in 1985; cap. 391.6m., res 391.3m., dep. 15,111.3m. (March 2001); Chair. DAVID S. CLARKE; Man. Dir ALLAN E. MOSS; 5 brs.

National Australia Bank Ltd: 500 Bourke St, Melbourne, Vic 3000; tel. (3) 8641-3500; fax (3) 8641-4912; internet www .national.com.au/; f. 1858; cap. 9,855m., res 2,006m., dep. 244,661m. (Sept. 2000); Chair. MARK RAYNER; Exec. Dir FRANK CICUTTO; 2,349 brs.

N. M. Rothschild & Sons (Australia) Ltd: Level 16, 1 O'Connell St, Sydney, NSW 2000; tel. (2) 9323-2000; fax (2) 9323-2323; internet www.rothschild.com.au; f. 1967 as International Pacific Corpn; cap. 130.0m., dep. 978.1m. (March 1999); Chair. PHILIP BRASS; Chief Exec. RICHARD LEE.

SG Australia Ltd: Level 21, 400 George St, Sydney, NSW 2000; tel. (2) 9210-8000; fax (2) 9235 3941; internet www.au.sg-ib.com; f. 1981; fmrly Société Générale Australia Ltd; cap. 21.5m., res 208m., dep. 5,656m. (Dec. 1999); CEO MICHEL L. MACAGNO.

St George Bank Ltd: Locked Bag 1, PO, Kogarah, NSW 2217; tel. (2) 9952-1311; fax (2) 9952-1000; e-mail stgeorge@stgeorge.com.au; internet www.stgeorge.com.au; f. 1937 as building society; cap. 3,174m., res 130m., dep. 35,047m. (Sept. 2000); Chair. F. J. CONROY; CEO and Man. Dir GAIL KELLY; 421 brs.

Standard Chartered Bank Australia Ltd: Level 11, 345 George St, Sydney, NSW 2000; tel. (2) 9232-9333; fax (2) 9232-9345; f. 1986; cap. 226.2m., dep. 667.8m. (Dec. 1999); Chair. RICHARD NETTLETON; CEO EUGENE ELLIS.

Toronto Dominion Australia Ltd: Level 34, Rialto South Tower, 525 Collins St, Melbourne, Vic 3000; tel. (3) 9993-1344; fax (3) 9614-0083; internet www.tdbank.ca; f. 1970; cap. 191.5m., res 6.0m., dep. 3,435.4m. (Oct. 1997); Man. Dir STEVE FRYER.

Westpac Banking Corporation: 60 Martin Place, Sydney, NSW 2000; tel. (2) 9226-3311; fax (2) 9226-4128; e-mail westpac@westpac .com.au; internet www.westpac.com.au; f. 1817; cap. 2,258m., res 4,892m., dep. 113,169m. (Sept. 2000); Chair. L. A. DAVIS; Man. Dir DAVID MORGAN.

Foreign Banks

Bank of China (People's Republic of China): 39–41 York St, Sydney, NSW 2000; tel. (2) 9267-5188; fax (2) 9262-1794; e-mail bocsyd@ bigpond.com.au; Gen. Man. GAO JI LU.

Bank of New Zealand: 9th Floor, BNZ House, 333–339 George St, Sydney, NSW 2000; tel. (2) 9290-6666; fax (2) 9290-3414; Chief Operating Officer G. ARMBRUSTER.

BNP Paribas (France): 60 Castlereagh St, Sydney, NSW 2000; POB 269, Sydney, NSW 2001; tel. (2) 9232-8733; fax (2) 9221-3026; e-mail bnp@bnp.com.au; internet www.bnp.com.au; CEO JEAN-FRANÇOIS VARLET; 4 brs.

Deutsche Bank AG (Germany): GPOB 7033, Sydney, NSW 2001; tel. (2) 9258-1234; fax (2) 9241-2565; Man. Dir KENNETH C. BORDA.

STOCK EXCHANGE

Australian Stock Exchange Ltd (ASX): Level 9, 20 Bridge St, Sydney, NSW 2000; tel. (2) 9227-0000; fax (2) 9227-0885; e-mail info@asx.com.au; internet www.asx.com.au; f. 1987 by merger of the stock exchanges in Sydney, Adelaide, Brisbane, Hobart, Melbourne and Perth, to replace the fmr Australian Associated Stock Exchanges; demutualized and listed Oct. 1998; Chair. MAURICE NEWMAN; Man. Dir and CEO RICHARD HUMPHRY.

Supervisory Body

Australian Securities and Investments Commission (ASIC): GPOB 4866, Sydney, NSW 1042; tel. (2) 9911-2000; fax (2) 9911-2030; e-mail infoline@asic.gov.au; internet www.asic.gov.au; f. 1990; corporations and financial products regulator; Chair. DAVID KNOTT.

PRINCIPAL INSURANCE COMPANIES

Allianz Australia Ltd: 2 Market St, Sydney, NSW 2000; tel. (2) 9390-6222; fax (2) 9390-6425; internet www.allianz.com.au; f. 1914; workers' compensation; fire, general accident, motor and marine; Chair. J. S. CURTIS; Man. Dir T. TOWELL.

AMP Ltd: AMP Bldg, 33 Alfred St, Sydney, NSW 2000; tel. (2) 9257-5000; fax (2) 9257-7886; internet www.amplimited.com.au; f. 1849; fmrly Australian Mutual Provident Society; life insurance; Chair. STAN WALLIS; Man. Dir (vacant).

AMP General Insurance Ltd: 10 Loftus St, Sydney Cove, NSW 2000; tel. (2) 9257-2500; fax (2) 9257-2199; internet www.amp.com.au; f. 1958; Chair. GREG COX; Man. Dir GAVIN PEACE.

Australian Guarantee Corpn Ltd: 130 Phillip St, Sydney, NSW 2000; tel. (2) 9234-1122; fax (2) 9234-1225; f. 1925; Chair. J. A. UHRIG; Man. Dir R. THOMAS.

Australian Unity General Insurance Ltd: 114 Albert Rd, South Melbourne, Vic 3205; tel. (3) 9697-0219; fax (3) 9690-5556; e-mail webmaster@austunity.com.au; internet www.austunity.com.au; f. 1948; Chair. LEON HICKEY; Chief Exec. M. W. SIBREE.

Catholic Church Insurances Ltd: 324 St Kilda Rd, Melbourne, Vic 3004; tel. (3) 9934-3000; fax (3) 9934-3460; f. 1911; Chair. Most Rev. KEVIN MANNING, Bishop of Parramatta; Gen. Man. PETER RUSH.

CGU Insurance Ltd: CGU Centre, 485 La Trobe St, Melbourne, Vic 3000; tel. (3) 9601-8222; fax (3) 9601-8366; f. 1960; fire, accident, marine; Chair. HUGH FLETCHER; Man. Dir I. M. BALFE.

The Copenhagen Reinsurance Co Ltd: 60 Margaret St, Sydney, NSW 2000; tel. (2) 9247-7266; fax (2) 9235-3320; internet www.copre.com; reinsurance; Gen. Man. ANDREW ALLISON.

FAI Insurances Ltd: FAI Insurance Group, 333 Kent St, Sydney, NSW 1026; tel. (2) 9274-9000; fax (2) 9274-9900; internet www.fai.com.au; f. 1953; Chair. JOHN LANDERER; CEO RODNEY ADLER.

Fortis Australia Ltd: 464 St Kilda Rd, Melbourne, Vic 3004; tel. (3) 9869-0300; fax (3) 9820-8537; CEO R. B. WILLING.

GeneralCologne Re Australia Ltd: Level 13, 225 George St, Sydney, NSW 2000; tel. (2) 9336-8100; fax (2) 9251-1665; f. 1961; reinsurance, fire, accident, marine; Chair. F. A. McDONALD; Man. Dir G. C. BARNUM.

GIO Australia Holdings Ltd: Level 39, Governor Phillip Tower, 1 Farrer Place, Sydney, NSW 2000; tel. (2) 9255-8090; fax (2) 9251-2079; e-mail emailus@gio.com.au; internet www.gio.com.au; f. 1926; CEO PETER CORRIGAN.

Guild Insurance Ltd: Guild House, 40 Burwood Rd, Hawthorn, Vic 3122; tel. (3) 9810-9820; fax (3) 9819-5670; f. 1963; Man. Dir W. K. BASTIAN.

HIH Insurance Ltd: AMP Centre, 50 Bridge St, Sydney, NSW 2000; tel. (2) 9650-2000; fax (2) 9650-2030; internet www.hih.com.au; f. 1968; Chair. G. A. COHEN; CEO R. R. WILLIAMS.

Lumley General Insurance Ltd: Lumley House, 309 Kent St, Sydney, NSW 1230; tel. (2) 9248-1111; fax (2) 9248-1122; e-mail general@lumley.com.au; Man. Dir D. M. MATCHAM.

Mercantile Mutual Holdings Ltd: 347 Kent St, Sydney, NSW; tel. (2) 9234-8111; fax (2) 9299-3979; internet www.mercantile mutual.com.au; f. 1878; Chair. A. R. BERG; Man. Dir R. J. ATFIELD.

The National Mutual Life Association of Australasia Ltd: 447 Collins St, Melbourne, Vic 3000; tel. (3) 9618-4920; fax (3) 9616-3445; e-mail investor.relations@axa.com.au; internet www.axa.com.au; f. 1869; life insurance, superannuation, income protection; Chair. R. H. ALLERT; Group CEO A. L. OWEN.

NRMA Insurance Ltd: 151 Clarence St, Sydney, NSW 2000; tel. (2) 9292-9222; fax (2) 9292-8472; f. 1926; CEO IAN BROWN (acting).

NZI Insurance Australia Ltd: 9th Floor, 10 Spring St, Sydney, NSW 2000; tel. (2) 9551-5000; fax (2) 9551-5865; Man. Dir H. D. SMITH.

QBE Insurance Group Ltd: 82 Pitt St, Sydney, NSW 2000; tel. (2) 9375-4444; fax (2) 9235-3166; internet www.qbe.com; f. 1886; general insurance; Chair. E. J. CLONEY; Man. Dir F. M. O'HALLORAN.

RAC Insurance Pty Ltd: 228 Adelaide Terrace, Perth, WA 6000; tel. (8) 9421-4444; fax (8) 9421-4593; f. 1947; Gen. Man. TONY CARTER.

RACQ Insurance: POB 4, Springwood, Qld 4127; tel. (7) 3361-2444; fax (7) 3361-2199; e-mail inorris@gio.com.au; internet www.racqinsurance.com.au; f. 1971; CEO I. W. NORRIS.

RACV: 550 Princes Highway, Noble Park, Vic 3174; tel. (3) 9790-2211; fax (3) 9790-3091.

RSA Insurance Australia Ltd: 465 Victoria Ave, Chatswood, NSW 2067; tel. (2) 9978-9000; fax (2) 9978-9807; fire, accident and marine insurance; Gen. Man. E. KULK.

Suncorp Metway: Level 18, 36 Wickham Tce, Brisbane, Qld 4000; tel. (7) 3835-5355; fax (7) 3836-1190; e-mail direct@suncorp.co.au; internet www.suncorp.com.au; f. 1996; Man. Dir STEVE JONES.

Swiss Re Australia Ltd: 363 George St, Sydney, NSW 2000; tel. (2) 8295-9500; fax (2) 8295-9804; f. 1962; Man. Dir R. G. WATTS.

Transport Industries Insurance Co Ltd: 310 Queen St, Melbourne, Vic 3000; tel. (3) 9623-3355; fax (3) 9623-2624; f. 1960; Chair. R. H. Y. SYME; Man. Dir R. G. WATTS.

Wesfarmers Federation Insurance Ltd: 184 Railway Parade, Bassendean, WA 6054; tel. (8) 9273-5333; fax (8) 9273-5290; e-mail mel.rom@wfi.wesfarmers.com.au; internet www.wfi.com.au; Gen. Man. R. J. BUCKLEY.

Westpac Life Ltd: 35 Pitt St, Sydney, NSW 2000; tel. (2) 9220-4768; f. 1986; CEO DAVID WHITE.

World Marine & General Insurances Ltd: 600 Bourke St, Melbourne, Vic 3000; tel. (3) 9609-3333; fax (3) 9609-3634; f. 1961; Chair. G. W. McGREGOR; Man. Dir A. E. REYNOLDS.

Zurich Financial Services Australia Ltd: 5 Blue St, North Sydney, NSW 2060; tel. (2) 9391-1111; fax (2) 9922-4630; CEO MALCOLM M. JONES.

Insurance Associations

Australian Insurance Association: GPOB 369, Canberra, ACT 2601; tel. (2) 6274-0609; fax (2) 6274-0666; f. 1968; Pres. RAYMOND JONES; Exec. Sec. P. M. MURPHY.

Australian and New Zealand Institute of Insurance and Finance: Level 17, 31 Queen St, Melbourne, Vic 3000; tel. (3) 9629-4021; fax (3) 9629-4024; e-mail ceo@theinstitute.com.au; internet www.theinstitute.com.au; f. 1919; Pres. JOHN RICHARDSON; CEO JOAN FITZPATRICK; 11,984 mems.

Insurance Council of Australia Ltd: Level 3, 56 Pitt St, Sydney, NSW 2000; tel. (2) 9253-5100; fax (2) 9253-5111; internet www.ica.com.au; f. 1975; CEO ALAN MASON.

Investment and Financial Services Association (IFSA): Suite 1, Level 24, 44 Market St, Sydney, NSW 2000; tel. (2) 9299-3022; fax (2) 9299-3198; e-mail ifsa@ifsa.com.au; f. 1996; fmrly Life, Investment and Superannuation Asscn of Australia Inc; Chair. ANDREW MOHL; CEO RICHARD GILBERT.

Trade and Industry

GOVERNMENT AGENCY

Austrade: GPOB 5301, Sydney, NSW 2001; e-mail managing.director@austrade.gov.au. internet www.austrade.gov.au; trade and investment facilitation agency; Chair. ROSS ADLER; Man. Dir CHARLES JAMIESON.

CHAMBERS OF COMMERCE

Australian Chamber of Commerce and Industry (ACCI): POB E14, Kingston, ACT 2604; tel. (2) 6273-2311; fax (2) 6273-3286; e-mail acci@acci.asn.au; internet www.acci.asn.au; Pres. Dr JOHN KENIRY; CEO MARK PATERSON.

Chamber of Commerce and Industry of Western Australia (CCIWA): POB 6209, East Perth, WA 6892; tel. (8) 9365-7555; fax (8) 9365-76167550; e-mail whitakerinfo@cciwa.com; internet www.cciwa.com; f. 1890; 6,000 mems; Chief Exec. LYNDON ROWE; Pres. TONY HOWARTH.

Commerce Queensland: Industry House, 375 Wickham Terrace, Brisbane, Qld 4000; tel. (7) 3842-2244; fax (7) 3832-3195; e-mail info@commerceqld.com.au; internet www.commerceqld.com.au; f. 1868; operates World Trade Centre, Brisbane; 5,500 mems; CEO ANDREW CRAIG.

South Australian Employers' Chamber of Commerce and Industry Inc: Enterprise House, 136 Greenhill Road, Unley, SA 5061; tel. (8) 8300-0000; fax (8) 8300-0001; e-mail enquiries@business-sa.com; internet www.business-sa.com; f. 1839; 4,700 mems; CEO P. VAUGHAN.

State Chamber of Commerce (New South Wales): Level 12, 83 Clarence St, GPO 4280, Sydney, NSW 2001; tel. (2) 9350-8100; fax (2) 9350-8199; e-mail worldtradecentre@thechamber.com.au; www.thechamber.com.au; operates World Trade Centre, Sydney; Man. Trade Development JANETTE SHOMAR.

Tasmanian Chamber of Commerce and Industry: GPOB 793H, Hobart, Tas 7001; tel. (3) 6234-5933; fax (3) 6231-1278; CEO TIM ABEY.

Victorian Employers' Chamber of Commerce and Industry: Employers' House, 50 Burwood Rd, Hawthorn, Vic 3122; tel. (3) 9251-4333; fax (3) 9819-3826; e-mail itd@vecci.org.au; f. 1885; CEO N. FEELY.

AGRICULTURAL, INDUSTRIAL AND TRADE ASSOCIATIONS

The Agriculture and Resource Management Council of Australia and New Zealand: Dept of Agriculture, Fisheries and Forestry—Australia, Barton, Canberra, ACT 2600; tel. (2) 6272-5216; fax (2) 6272-4772; e-mail armcanz.contact@affa.gov.au; internet www.affa.gov.au/armcanz; f. 1992 to develop integrated and sustainable agricultural and land and water management policies, strategies and practices; mems comprising the Commonwealth/state/territory and New Zealand ministers responsible for agriculture, soil conservation, water resources and rural adjustment matters; Sec. J. W. GRAHAM.

Standing Committee on Agriculture and Resource Management: f. 1992; an advisory body to the Agriculture and Resource Management Council of Australia and New Zealand; comprises the heads of Commonwealth/state/territory and New Zealand agencies responsible for agriculture, soil conservation and water resources and representatives from CSIRO, Bureau of Meteorology and rural adjustment authorities; Sec. J. W. GRAHAM.

Australian Business Ltd: Private Bag 938, North Sydney, NSW 2059; tel. (2) 9458-7500; fax (2) 9923-1166; e-mail member.services@australianbusiness.com.au; internet www.australianbusiness.com.au; f. 1885; fmrly Chamber of Manufactures of NSW; CEO MARK BETHWAITE.

Australian Dairy Corporation: Locked Bag 104, Flinders Lane, Vic 8009; tel. (3) 9694-3777; fax (3) 9694-3888; e-mail adcenquiries@adc.aust.com; internet www.dairycorp.com.au; provides services to industry in areas of trade policy and market access, domestic and export market devt, and export agency national marketing, international trade development, regulatory activity, industry relations; Chair. DES NICHOLL; Man. Dir ALEXANDER MURDOCH.

Australian Manufacturers' Export Council: POB E14, Queen Victoria Terrace, ACT 2600; tel. (2) 6273-2311; fax (2) 6273-3196; f. 1955; Exec. Dir G. CHALKER.

Australian Wool Services Ltd: Wool House, 369 Royal Parade, Parkville, Vic 3052; tel. (3) 9341-9111; fax (3) 9341-9273; internet www.wool.com.au; f. 2001 following the privatization of the Australian Wool Research and Promotion Organisation; operates two subsidiaries, Australian Wool Innovation which manages wool levy funds and invests in research and development, and The Woolmark Company responsible for commercial development; Chair. RODNEY PRICE.

AWB Ltd: Ceres House, 528 Lonsdale St, Melbourne, Vic 3000; tel. (3) 9209-2000; fax (3) 9670-2782; e-mail awb@awb.com.au; internet www.awb.com.au; f. 1939; fmrly Australian Wheat Board; national and international marketing of grain, financing and marketing of wheat and other grains for growers; 12 mems; Chair. TREVOR FLUGGE; CEO ANDREW LINDBERG.

Business Council of Australia: 15th Floor, 10 Queens Rd, Melbourne, Vic 3004; tel. (3) 9274-7777; fax (3) 9274-7744; public policy research and advocacy; governing council comprises chief execs of Australia's major cos; Pres. STAN WALLIS; Exec. Dir DAVID BUCKINGHAM.

Cotton Australia: Level 2, 490 Crown St, Surry Hills, NSW 2010; tel. (2) 9360-8500; fax (2) 9360-8555; e-mail talktous@cottonaustralia.com.au; internet www.cottonaustralia.com.au; Chair. CHARLES WILSON.

Meat and Livestock Australia: Level 1, 165 Walker St, North Sydney, NSW 2060; tel. 1800-023-100; fax (2) 9463-9393; internet www.mla.com.au; producer-owned co; represents, promotes, protects and furthers interests of industry in both the marketing of meat and livestock and industry-based research and devt activities; Chair. DAVID CROMBIE.

National Farmers' Federation: POB E10, Kingston, ACT 2604; tel. (2) 6273-3855; fax (2) 6273-2331; e-mail nff@nff.org.au; internet www.nff.org.au; Pres. PETER CORISH; CEO ANNA CRONIN.

Trade Policy Advisory Council (TPAC): c/o Dept of Foreign Affairs and Trade, R. G. Casey Bldg, John McEwen Cres., Barton, ACT 2600; tel. (2) 6262-2125; fax (2) 6261-2465; e-mail diane.johnstone@dfat.gov.au; advises the Minister for Trade on policy issues; Chair. GEOFF ALLEN.

WoolProducers: POB E10, Kingston, Canberra, ACT 2604; tel. (2) 6273-2531; fax (2) 6273-1120; e-mail woolproducers@nff.org.au; internet www.woolproducers.com; fmrly Wool Council Australia; comprises 20 mems; represents wool-growers in dealings with the Federal Govt and industry; Pres. SIMON CAMPBELL.

EMPLOYERS' ORGANIZATIONS

Australian Co-operative Foods Ltd: Level 12, 168 Walker St, North Sydney, NSW 2060; tel. (2) 9903-5222; fax (2) 9957-3530; e-mail exports@dairyfarmers.com.au; f. 1900; Man. Dir A. R. TOOTH.

Australian Industry Group: 51 Walker St, North Sydney, NSW 2060; tel. (2) 9466-5566; fax (2) 9466-5599; e-mail louisep@aignsw.aigroup.asn.au; internet www.aigroup.asn.au; f. 1998 through merger of MTIA and ACM; 11,500 mems; Nat. Pres. G. J. ASHTON; CEO ROBERT N. HERBERT; 11,500 mems.

National Meat Association: 25–27 Albany St, Crows Nest, NSW 2065; POB 1208, Crows Nest, NSW 1585; tel. (2) 9906-7767; fax (2) 9906-8022; e-mail lmigachov@nmaa.org.au; internet www.nmaa.org.au; f. 1928; Pres. GARY HARDWICK; CEO KEVIN COTTRILL (acting).

NSW Farmers' Association: GPOB 1068, Sydney, NSW 1041; tel. (2) 92518251-1700; fax (2) 92318251-52491750; e-mail emailus@nswfarmers.org.au; internet www.nswfarmers.org.au; f. 1978; CEO JONATHAN MCKEOWN.

UTILITIES

Australian Gas Association (AGA): GPOB 323, Canberra, ACT 2601; tel. (2) 6272-1555; fax (2) 6272-1566; e-mail canberra@gas.asn.au; internet www.gas.asn.au; 1,000 mems, incl. more than 300 corporate mems; Chair. OLLIE CLARK; Chief Exec. BILL NAGLE.

Australian Institute of Energy: POB 268, Toukley, NSW 2263; tel. 1800-629-945; fax (2) 4393-1114; e-mail aie@tpgi.com.au; internet www.aie.org.au.

Electricity Supply Association of Australia: POB A2492, Sydney South, NSW 1235; tel. (2) 9261-0141; fax (2) 9261-3153 internet www.esaa.com.au; Man. Dir KEITH ORCHISON.

Electricity Companies

Actew AGL: GPOB 366, Canberra City, ACT 2601; tel. (2) 6248-3111; e-mail webmaster@actewagl.com.au; internet www.actewagl.com.au; f. 2000 by amalgamation of ACTEW Corpn Ltd and AGL; supplier of electricity, gas, water and wastewater services; Chief Exec. PAUL PERKINS.

Delta Electricity: POB Q863, QVB, NSW 1230; tel. (2) 9285-2700; fax (2) 9285-2777; internet www.de.com.au; f. 1996; Chief Exec. JIM HENNESS.

ENERGEX: GPOB 1461, Brisbane, Qld 4001; tel. (7) 3407-4000; fax (7) 3407-4609; e-mail enquiries@energex.com.au; internet www.energex.com.au; spans Queensland and New South Wales; CEO GREG MADDOCK.

EnergyAustralia: 145 Newcastle Rd, Wallsend, NSW 2287; tel. (2) 4951-9346; fax (2) 4951-9351; e-mail energy@energy.com.au; internet www.energy.com.au; supplies customers in NSW; CEO PETER HEADLEY; Man. Dir PAUL BROAD.

Ergon Energy: POB 107, Albert St, Brisbane, Qld 4002; tel. (7) 3228-8222; fax (7) 3228-8118; internet www.ergon.com.au; national retailer of electricity.

Generation Victoria Corpn—Ecogen Energy: 5th Floor, 416 Collins St, Melbourne, Vic 3000; tel. (3) 9679-4600; fax (3) 9679-4619; internet www.ecogen-energy.com.au/; f. 1994; CEO GERRY BASTEN.

Great Southern Energy: Level 1, Citilink Plaza, Morriset St, Queanbeyan, NSW 2620; tel. (2) 6214-9600; fax (2) 6214-9860; e-mail mail@gsenergy.com.au; internet www.gsenergy.com.au; state-owned electricity and gas distributor; Chair. BRUCE RODELY.

Powercor Australia Ltd: 40 Market St, Melbourne, Vic 3000; tel. (3) 9683-4444; fax (3) 9683-4499; e-mail info@powercor.com.au; internet www.powercor.com.au; Chair. WILLIAM SHURNIAK; CEO C. T. WAN.

Snowy Mountains Hydro-electric Authority: POB 332, Cooma, NSW 2630; tel. (2) 6452-1777; fax (2) 6452-3794; e-mail info@snowyhydro.com.au; internet www.snowyhydro.com.au.

United Energy Ltd: Level 13, 101 Collins St, Melbourne, Vic 3000; fax (3) 9222-8588; e-mail info@mail.ue.com.au; internet www.ue.com.au; f. 1994, following division of State Electricity Commission of Victoria; transferred to private sector; distributor of electricity and gas.

Western Power Corpn: GPOB L921, Perth, WA 6842; tel. (8) 9326-4911; fax (8) 9326-4595; e-mail info@wpcorp.com.au; internet www.wpcorp.com.au; f. 1995; principal supplier of electricity in WA; Chair. HECTOR STEBBINS (acting); Man. Dir DAVID EISZELE.

Gas Companies

AlintaGas: GPOB W2030, Perth, WA 6846; internet www.alintagas.com.au; f. 1995; CEO ROBERT BROWNING.

Allgas Energy Ltd: 150 Charlotte St, Brisbane, Qld 4000; tel. (7) 3404-1822; fax (7) 3404-1821; e-mail corporate@allgas.com.au; internet www.allgas.com.au; f. 1885; Chief Exec. TOM BLOXSOM.

Australian Gas Light Co: AGL Centre, Corner Pacific Highway and Walker St, North Sydney, NSW 2060; tel. (2) 9922-0101; fax (2) 9957-3671; e-mail aglmail@agl.com.au; internet www.agl.com.au; f. 1837; Chair. M. J. PHILLIPS; Man. Dir. GREG MARTIN.

Envestra: 10th Floor, 81 Flinders St, Adelaide, SA 5000; tel. (8) 8227-1500; fax (8) 8277-1511; e-mail des.petherick@envestra.com.au; internet www.envestra.com.au; f. 1997 by merger of South Australian Gas Co, Gas Corpn of Queensland and Centre Gas Pty Ltd; purchased Victorian Gas Network in 1999; Chair. J. G. ALLPASS; Man. Dir O. G. CLARK.

Epic Energy: GPOB 657, Brisbane, Qld 4001; tel. (2) 6200-1600; fax (7) 3218-1650; internet www.epicenergy.com.au; f. 1996; privately-owned gas transmission co; CEO Sue Ortenstone.

Origin Energy: GPOB 5376, Sydney, NSW 2001; tel. (2) 9220-6400; fax (2) 9235-1661; internet www.origin.energy@originenergy.com.au; Man. Dir Grant King.

TXU: Level 19, East Tower, 40 City Road, Southbank, Vic 3006; tel. (3) 9299-2666; fax (3) 9299-2777; e-mail enq@txu.com.au; internet www.txu.com.au.

MAJOR COMPANIES

Mining and Metals

Alcoa World Alumina Australia: POB 252, Applecross, WA 6153; tel. (8) 9316-5111; fax (8) 9316-5228; f. 1961; internet www.alcoa.com.au; cap. and res $A1,765.3m., sales $A2,670m. (1999); producer of aluminium, bauxite, etc.; Chair. G. John Pizzey; Man. Dir M. Baltzell; 5,274 employees.

BHP Billiton Ltd: 48th Floor, BHP Tower-Bourke Place, 600 Bourke St, Melbourne, Vic 3000; tel. (3) 9609-3333; fax (3) 9609-3015; internet www.bhpbilliton.com.au; f. 2001 by merger of BHP (f. 1885) and Billiton (UK); cap. and res $A9,423m., sales $A21,506m. (2000/01); mining of iron ore, coal, copper, silver and diamonds; iron and steelmaking; oil and natural gas production; operates in every state, the NT and in many foreign countries; has 165 subsidiaries and nine major associated cos; Chair. Don Argus; CEO Paul Anderson; 35,000 employees.

Comalco Ltd: Level 25, Comalco Place, 12 Creek St, Brisbane, Qld 4000; tel. (7) 3867-1711; fax (3) 3867-1775; internet www.comalco.com.au; f. 1960; cap. and res $A1,896m., sales $A2,404m. (1999); aluminium production; Chair. John P. Morschel; Chief Exec. W. Terry Palmer; 4,747 employees.

Goldfields Ltd: Level 16, 1 Castlereagh St, Sydney, NSW 2000; tel. (2) 8223-2400; fax (2) 8223-2444; f. 1995; fmrly Goldfields Kalgoorlie; cap. and res $A89.3m., sales $301.7m. (1999/2000); mining; Chair. R. F. E. Waburton; Man. Dir P. W. Cassidy; 405 employees.

MIM Holdings Ltd: 410 Ann St, Brisbane, Qld 4000; tel. (7) 3833-8000; fax (7) 3832-2426; e-mail corpaff@mimholdings.com.au; internet www.mimholdings.com.au; f. 1970; cap. and res $A2,548m., sales $A4,011m. (2001/02); exploration for precious and base metals; mining, processing and marketing of copper, gold, zinc, lead and silver; mining and marketing of coal; recycling of metals; Chair. L. E. Tutt; Man Dir. V. P. Gauci; 8,434 employees.

Newcrest Mining Ltd: Level 9, 600 St Kilda Rd, Melbourne, Vic 3004; tel. (3) 9522-5333; fax (3) 9525-2996; internet www.newcrest.com.au; f. 1990; mining of gold and other minerals; Chair. Ian R. Johnson.

Normandy Mining Ltd: 100 Hutt St, Adelaide, SA 5000; tel. (8) 8303-1700; fax (8) 8303-1900; internet www.normandy.com.au; f. 1991; cap. and res $A461m., sales $A1,324m. (1999/2000); mining of gold, diamonds and base metals; Chair. and CEO Robert J. Champion de Crespigny.

North Ltd: GPOB 1903R, Melbourne, Vic 3004; tel. (3) 9207-5111; fax (3) 9867-4351; internet www.north.com.au; f. 1976, present name since 1994; cap. and res $A1,329.1m., sales $A2,026.6m. (1998/99); iron ore, gold, copper, zinc, uranium, wood fibre and pump manufacturing; Chair. Dr Michael Deeley; Man. Dir Michael Broomhead; 260 employees.

Pasminco Ltd: Level 15, 380 St Kilda Rd, Melbourne, Vic 3004; tel. (3) 9288-0333; fax (3) 9288-0406; e-mail pasminco@pasminco.com.au; internet www.pasminco.com.au; f. 1988; cap. and res $A1,453m., sales $A1,878m. (1999/2000); mining and smelting; Chair. Mark R. Rayner; CEO David M. Stewart; 4,449 employees.

Placer Dome Asia Pacific Ltd: Level 16, Gold Fields House, 1 Alfred St, Sydney Cove, NSW 2000; tel. (2) 9256-3800; fax (2) 9233-6326; mineral exploration, mining of gold, silver and copper ores; Chair. J. M. Willson; Man. Dir D. W. Zandee.

Rio Tinto Ltd: 33rd Floor, 55 Collins St, Melbourne, Vic 3001; tel. (3) 9283-3333; fax (3) 9283-3707; internet www.riotinto.com.au; f. 1962; fmrly CRA; cap. and res $A11,115m., sales $A13,593m. (2000); exploration and mining group, principally iron ore, aluminium, coal, salt, gold, silver and diamonds; Chair. Robert P. Wilson; Chief Exec. Leigh Clifford; 33,786 employees.

Santos Ltd: Santos House, 91 King William St, Adelaide, SA 5000; tel. (8) 8218-5111; fax (8) 8218-5274; e-mail investor.relations@santos.com.au; cap. and res $A2,310m., sales $A1497m. (2000); gas and petroleum exploration and production; Chair. Stephen Gerlach; Man. Dir J. C. Ellice-Flint; 1,650 employees.

Tubemakers of Australia Ltd: 1 York St, Sydney, NSW 2000; tel. (2) 9239-6666; fax (2) 9251-3042; f. 1946; cap. $A141.4m., sales $A1,400m. (1999); mfrs of steel pipes and tubes; merchandiser of steel and aluminium products; wholly-owned subsidiary of BHP Steel; 4,000 employees.

WMC Ltd: Level 16, IBM Centre, 60 City Road, Southbank, Vic 3006; tel. (3) 9685-6000; fax (3) 9670-3569; internet www.wmc.com.au; f. 1933; fmrly Western Mining Corpn Holdings Ltd; cap. and res $A4,575m., sales $A3,092m. (2000); mining and processing of nickel, gold, copper, uranium, talc and petroleum; exploration for and development of mineral resources; investment in alumina and alumina chemicals; Chair. Ian Burgess; CEO H. M. Morgan; 3,408 employees.

Motor Vehicles

Ford Motor Company of Australia Ltd: 1735 Sydney Rd, Campbellfield, Vic; tel. (3) 9359-8211; fax (3) 9357-1824; internet www.ford.com.au; f. 1925; total assets $A1.3m., sales $A2,921m. (1998); mfrs of passenger and commercial motor vehicles and parts and accessories; Pres. Geoff Polites; 5,200 employees.

Holden Ltd: 241 Salmon St, Port Melbourne, Vic 3207; tel. (3) 9647-1111; fax (3) 9647-2550; internet www.holden.com.au; f. 1986; subsidiary of General Motors Corpn; sales $A4,100m. (1999); mfrs of passenger and commercial vehicles; Chair. and Man. Dir Peter H. Hanenberger; 8,156 employees.

Iveco Trucks Australia Ltd: Princes Hwy, Dandenong, Vic 3175; POB 117, Dandenong, Vic 3175; tel. (3) 9238-2200; fax (3) 9238-2387; e-mail iveco@iveco.com.au; internet www.iveco.com.au; f. 1912; cap. and res $A81.3m., sales $A283.5m. (2001); designers, mfrs and marketers of trucks; Man. Dir Alain Gajnik; 800 employees.

Mitsubishi Motors Australia Ltd: 1284 South Rd, Clovelly Park, SA 5042; tel. (8) 8275-7111; fax (8) 8275-6841; internet www.mitsubishi-motors.com.au; issued cap. $A279.3m., sales $A2,694m. (2001); mfrs of cars, service parts, accessories, automotive components, engines; Pres. and CEO T. R. Phillips; 4,100 employees.

Toyota Motor Corpn Australia Ltd: 155 Bertie St, Port Melbourne, Vic 3207; tel. (3) 9647-4444; fax (3) 9645-1311; cap. and res $A1,830m., sales $A5,660m. (2001); internet www.toyota.com.au; Pres. K. Asano; 4,200 employees.

Petroleum

BP Australia Holdings Ltd: Level 30, The Tower, Melbourne Central, 360 Elizabeth St, Melbourne, Vic 3000; tel. (3) 9268-4111; fax (3) 9268-3321; f. 1952; cap. $A370m.; refining, marketing, exploration, transportation of petroleum products; 30 subsidiaries; Chair. B. K. Sanderson; Man. Dir R. McGimpsey; 2,471 employees.

Chevron Australia Pty Ltd: L 24, 250 St George's, GPOB S1580, Perth, WA 6845; tel. (8) 9216-4000; fax (8) 9216-4444; e-mail gorgon.info@chevron.com; fmrly West Australian Petroleum; exploration and production of petroleum and natural gas; Man. Dir Rhonda Zygoda.

Esso Australia Ltd: 12 Riverside Quay, Southbank, Vic 3000; tel. (3) 9270-3333; fax (3) 9270-3995; internet www.exxon.com; revenue $A1.5m. (1998); subsidiary of Exxon Corpn; active in the upstream oil and gas business; Chair. and Man. Dir Robert C. Olsen; 1,002 employees.

Mobil Exploration & Producing Australia Pty Ltd: Level 29, QV1, 250 St George's Terrace, Perth, WA 6000; tel. (8) 9424-9200; fax (8) 9424-9357; internet www.mobil.com.au; f. 1996 through acquisition of Ampolex Ltd; upstream exploration activities and producing activities in Australia and Papua New Guinea; Man. Dir D. P. Haworth.

Shell Australia Ltd: POB 872K, GPO, Melbourne, Vic 3001; tel. (3) 9666-5444; fax (3) 9666-5008; inc. 1958; cap. $A171m., sales $A8,036m. (1999); group manufactures and markets petroleum and petroleum products; exploration and production of oil, gas and coal; 50 group cos; Chair. and CEO P. Duncan.

Woodside Energy Ltd: 1 Adelaide Terrace, Perth, WA 6000; tel. (8) 9348-4000; fax (8) 9325-8178; internet www.woodside.com.au; cap. and res $A2,108.3m.; sales $A2,395.2m. (2000); exploration and production of petroleum and natural gas; Chair. Charles Goode; Man. Dir J. H. Akehurst.

Rubber and Textiles

Pacific Dunlop Ltd: Level 41, 101 Collins St, Melbourne, Vic 3000; tel. (3) 9270-7270; fax (3) 9270-7300; internet www.pacdun.com; cap. and res $A855m., sales $A5,726m. (1999/2000); marketing, manufacturing and importing of batteries, tyres, plastic and industrial rubber products; latex rubber products; surgical gloves; household gloves; sports equipment; foams and bedding; industrial and thermal insulation; textiles and clothing; footwear; electrical products and telecommunications cables; Chair. John Ralph; Man. Dir Rod Chadwick: 37,836 employees.

Paper and Pulp

Amcor Ltd: 679 Victoria St, Abbotsford, Vic 3067; tel (3) 9226-9000; fax (3) 9226-9050; internet www.amcor.com.au; f. 1926 as Australian Paper Manufacturers (APM) Ltd; cap. and res $A1,345m., sales $A5,737m. (1999/2000); afforestation; production of woodpulp, paper and paperboard and associated goods; manufacture and sale of metal, paper, plastic and corrugated packaging products; trading of industrial and consumer products; 300 locations worldwide, operating in 25 countries; Chair. CHRIS ROBERTS; Man. Dir RUSSELL H. JONES; 17,517 employees.

Food and Drink, etc.

Arnotts Ltd: 11 George St, Homebush, NSW 2160; tel. (2) 9394-3555; fax (2) 9394-3500; e-mail croberts@arnotts.com; internet www.arnotts.com.au; cap. and res $A330.6m., sales $A723.5m. (1996/97); manufacture of biscuits and snacks; Chair. D. M. MCDONALD; Man. Dir and CEO C. I. ROBERTS; 4,900 employees.

Burns Philp & Co Ltd: Level 2, 51–57 Pitt St, Sydney, NSW 2000; tel. (2) 9259-1111; fax (2) 9257-8391; e-mail info@burnsphilp.com; internet www.burnsphilp.com; f. 1883; cap. and res $A272m., sales $A1,286m. (1999/00); global food ingredients mfr, mainly yeast, herbs and spices; Chair. ALAN MCGREGOR; Man. Dir and Chief Exec. TOM DEGNAN; 4,100 employees.

Cadbury Schweppes Australia Ltd: 636 St Kilda Rd, Melbourne, Vic 3004; tel. (3) 9520-7444; fax (3) 9520-7400; internet www.cadbury.com.au; f. 1971; cap. $A170m., sales $A1,226m. (2000); mfrs and distributors of chocolate and sugar confectionery, jams, soft drinks, post mix syrups, fruit juices; Chief Exec., Asia-Pacific, G. M. CASSAGNE.

Coca-Cola Amatil Ltd: GPOB 145, GPO Sydney, NSW 2001; tel. (2) 9259-6666; fax (2) 9259-6623; internet www.ccamatil.com; f. 1904; sales $A4,124.3m. (2000); manufacturing and distribution of beverages in Asia-Pacific; 24 plants, of which 18 are overseas; Chair. DAVID M. GONSKI; 17,165 employees.

Foster's Brewing Group: 77 Southbank Boulevard, Southbank, Vic 3006; tel. (3) 9633-2000; fax (3) 9633-2002; internet www.fosters.com.au; cap. and res $A938m., sales $A3,170m. (1999/2000); production and distribution of beer and wine; operates in Australia, Asia-Pacific and the UK; Chair. FRANK SWAN; CEO E. T. KUNKEL; 8,500 employees.

Goodman Fielder Ltd: 225 George St, Sydney, NSW 2000; tel. (2) 8874-6000; fax (2) 8874-6099; e-mail corporate.affairs@goodmanfielder.com.au; internet www.goodmanfielder.com.au; cap. and res $A632m., sales $A3,136m. (1999/2000); manufacture, sale and export of foods; Chair. JON PETERSON; CEO DAVID HEARN; 14,248 employees.

National Foods Ltd: Level 10, 5 Queens Rd, Melbourne, Vic 3004; tel. (3) 9234-4000; fax (3) 9234-4100; internet www.natfoods.com.au; cap. and res. $A236.3m., sales $A1,096.9.m. (1999/2000); Chair. W. B. CAPP; Man. Dir M. G. OULD; 1,881 employees.

Philip Morris Ltd: 252 Chesterville Rd, POB 1093, Moorabbin, Vic 3189; tel. (3) 8531-1000; fax (3) 8531-1900; mfrs of tobacco products; Man. Dir KATE WRIGHT; 1,000 employees.

Rothmans Holdings Ltd: Level 42, Northpoint, 100 Miller St, North Sydney, NSW 2060; tel. (2) 9956-0666; fax (2) 9956-7442; internet www.rothmans.com.au; cap. and res $A195.0m., sales $A2,466.6m. (1997/98); tobacco production and sale; Chair J. W. UTZ; CEO G. KRELLE.

Southcorp Ltd: 403 Pacific Highway, Artarmon, NSW 2064; tel. (2) 9465-1000; fax (2) 9465-1000; internet www.southcorp.com.au; cap. and res $A1,207.4m., sales $A2,619.9m. (1999/2000); wine; Chair. RICHARD H. ALLERT; Man. Dir and Chief Exec. KEITH LAMBERT; 9,351 employees.

Unilever Australia Export: Private Bag 2, Epping, NSW 2121; tel. (2) 9869-6450; fax (2) 9869-6480; e-mail mike.a.newman@unilever.com; internet www.uae.com.au; sales $A1,288.3m. (2000); marketing ice cream, food, edible oils, toiletries, soap and detergents; Chair. ENZO ALLARA.

George Weston Foods Ltd: Level 20, Tower A, Zenith Centre, 821 Pacific Highway, Chatswood, NSW 2067; tel. (2) 9415-1411; fax (2) 9419-2907; cap. and res $A653.7m., sales $A1,556.2m. (1999/2000); Chair. JOHN HENRY PASCOE; CEO MARVIN WEINMAN; 7,578 employees.

Miscellaneous

Amcor Containers Packaging Australasia: 971 Burke Rd, Camberwell, Vic 3124; tel. (3) 9811-7444; fax (3) 9811-7474; f. 1950; mfrs of aluminium, steel and aerosol cans for food, beverage and other consumer goods, metal and plastic caps and closures, flexible, foil and film packaging, rigid plastic containers, composite cans for food and industrial products, multi-wall paper sacks, and packaging machinery; Man. Dir D. GOLDTHORP; 3,600 employees.

Boral Ltd: AMP Centre, Level 39, 50 Bridge St, Sydney, NSW 2000; tel. (2) 9220-6300; fax (2) 9233-6605; cap. and res $A3,112.1m., sales $A4,898.6m. (1999); quarrying, sand extraction, premixed concrete, fly ash, lightweight aggregate producer, clay and concrete products, road surfacing, road transport, marketing and distribution of cements and industrial lime, windows, doors, timber, plasterboard, bricks, etc.; Chair. Dr KENNETH J. MOSS; Man. Dir ROD T. PEARSE; 15,500 employees.

Brambles Industries Ltd: Level 40, Gateway, 1 Macquarie Place, Sydney, NSW 2000; tel. (2) 9256-5222; fax (2) 9256-5299; internet www.brambles.com.au; f. 1875; cap. and res $A1,485m., sales $A3,192m. (1999/2000); materials movement and distribution, including industrial plant hire, equipment pools, scheduled freight forwarding by road, rail, sea and air, heavy haulage, logistical support programmes for major projects, marine towage and transportation, pollution control services, security services, records management, shipping and travel agencies; Chair. D. R. ARGUS; CEO Sir C. K. CHOW; 14,546 employees.

CSR Ltd: Level 1, 9 Help St, Chatswood, NSW 2057; tel. (2) 9235-8000; fax (2) 9235-8044; internet www.csr.com.au; f. 1855; cap. and res $A2,322m., sales $A6,424m. (2000/01); manufacture of building materials, sugar milling, and investments in aluminium; Chair. I. G. BURGESS; 17,100 employees.

Email Ltd: Joynton Ave, Waterloo, NSW 2017; tel. (2) 9690-7333; fax (2) 9699-3190; internet www.email.com.au; cap. and res $A167m., sales $A2,102m. (1999/2000); manufacture and distribution of consumer, industrial, commercial and home products; Chair. P COTTRELL; Man. Dir R. G. WATERS.

Futuris Corpn Ltd: 26/27 Currie St, Adelaide, SA 5000; tel. (8) 8425-4999; fax (8) 8410-1597; e-mail information@futuris.com.au; internet www.futuris.com.au; cap. and res $A384.3m., sales $A6,776.1m. (2001/02); provision of services to rural sector, automotive components, etc.; Chair. WILLIAM BEISCHER; Man. Dir ALAN NEWMAN.

James Hardie Industries Ltd: 9th Floor, James Hardie House, 65 York St, Sydney, NSW 2000; tel. (2) 9290-5333; fax (2) 9262-4394; internet www.jameshardie.com; cap. and res $A510m., sales $A1,549m. (2000/01); mfrs of fibre cement building products and building systems, supply and installation of insulated panel systems; Chair. A. G. MCGREGOR; CEO Dr R. K. BARTON; 3,729 employees.

Kodak (Australasia) Pty Ltd: 173 Elizabeth St, Coburg, Vic 3058; tel. (3) 9350-1222; fax (3) 9350-2416; internet www.kodak.com.au; cap. and res $A289.5m., sales $A1059.6m. (1999); mfrs of sensitized photographic materials, photographic chemicals and equipment; distributors and retailers; Chair. and Man. Dir JOHN ALLEN; 1,500 employees.

Leighton Holdings Ltd: 472 Pacific Highway, St Leonards, NSW 2065; tel. (2) 9925-6666; fax (2) 9925-6005; internet www.leighton.com.au; cap. and res $A610.5m., sales $A3,445.3m. (1999/2000); construction, infrastructure development, contract mining, property development, telecommunications, waste management; Chair. TIM BESLEY; CEO W. M. KING; 12,688 employees.

Lend Lease Corpn Ltd: Level 46, Tower Bldg, Australia Square, George St, Sydney, NSW 2000; tel. (2) 9236-6111; fax (2) 9252-2192; internet www.lendlease.com.au; cap. and res. $A4,580m. (2000/01); property management, etc.; Chair. JILL CONWAY; Man. Dir DAVID HIGGINS; 4,627 employees.

Mayne Group Ltd: Level 21, 390 St Kilda Rd, Melbourne, Vic 3004; tel. (3) 9868-0700; fax (3) 9867-1179; e-mail webrequests@maynegroup.com; internet www.maynegroup.com.au; sales $A3,158.7m. (2000/2001); transport, security and health-care services; Chair. M. R. RAYNER; Man. Dir P SMEDLEY; 29,000 employees.

Orica Ltd: 1 Nicholson St, Melbourne, Vic 3000; tel. (3) 9665-7111; fax (3) 9665-7937; e-mail companyinfo@orica.com; internet www.orica.com; cap. and res $A1,218m., sales $A3,670m. (1999/2000); mfrs of fertilizers, chemicals, plastics, etc.; Chair DON MERCER; Man. Dir MALCOLM BROOMHEAD.

Wesfarmers Ltd: 11th Floor, Wesfarmers House, 40 The Esplanade, Perth, WA 6000; tel. (8) 9327-4211; fax (8) 9327-4216; internet www.wesfarmers.com.au; cap. and res $A1,085.9m., sales $A3,358.5m. (1999/2000); mfrs of fertilizers and chemicals; gas-processing and distribution; coal mining; building materials, hardware and forest products; rural merchandise and services; transport; insurance; Chair. C. H. PERKINS; Man. Dir and Chief Exec. M. A. CHANEY; 14,000 employees.

TRADE UNIONS

Australian Council of Trade Unions (ACTU): Level 2, 393 Swanston St, Melbourne, Vic 3000; tel. (3) 9663-5266; fax (3) 9663-4051; e-mail mailbox@actu.asn.au; internet www.actu.asn.au; f. 1927; br. in each state, generally known as a Trades and Labour Council; 46 affiliated trade unions; Pres. SHARAN BURROW; Sec. GREGORY COMBET.

Principal Affiliated Unions

Ansett Pilots Association (APA): 19 Napier St, Essendon, Vic 3040; tel. (3) 9375-1941; fax (3) 9375-7405; Pres. HENRY OTTO; Sec. JOHN DOGGETT.

Association of Professional Engineers, Scientists & Managers, Australia (APESMA): POB 1272L, Melbourne, Vic 3001; tel. (3) 9695-8800; fax (3) 9696-9312; e-mail info@apesma.asn.au; internet www.apesma.asn.au; Pres. ROB J. ALLEN; Sec. GREG SUTHERLAND; 24,000 mems.

Australasian Meat Industry Employees' Union (AMIEU): 377 Sussex St, Sydney, NSW 2000; tel. (2) 9264-2279; fax (2) 9261-1970; e-mail amieu_fed@bigpond.com; Fed. Pres. JOHN PYSING; Fed. Sec. T. R. HANNAN; 23,100 mems.

Australian Airline Flight Engineers Association (AAEA): Aspect House, 3/87 Buckley St, Essendon, Vic 3040; tel. (3) 9375-7590; fax (3) 9375-7590; e-mail aeu@aeufederal.org.au; internet www.aeufederal.org.au; f. 1984; Fed. Pres. JEFF SEABURN; Fed. Sec. RON HARE.

Australian Collieries Staff Association (ACSA): POB 21, Merewether, NSW 2291; tel. (02) 4963-5656; fax. (02) 4963-3425; e-mail acsa@acsa.org.au; internet www.acsa.org.au; Gen. Pres. MICK BURGESS; Gen. Sec. WENDY CLEWS.

Australian Education Union (AEU): 120 Clarendon St, Southbank, Vic 3006; tel. (3) 9693-1800; fax (3) 9254-1805; e-mail aeu@aeufederal.org.au; internet www.aeufederal.org.au; f. 1984; Fed. Pres. DENIS FITZGERALD; Fed. Sec. ROBERT DURBRIDGE; 155,000 mems.

Australian Manufacturing Workers' Union/AMWU: POB 160, Granville, NSW 2142; tel. (2) 9897-9133; fax (2) 9897-9274; e-mail amwu2@amwu.asn.au; internet www.amwu.asn.au; Nat. Pres. JULIUS ROE; Nat. Sec. DOUG CAMERON; 170,000 mems.

Australian Services Union (ASU): Ground Floor, 116 Queensberry St, Carlton South, Vic 3053; tel. (3) 9342-1400; fax (3) 9342-1499; e-mail asunatm@asu.asn.au; internet www.asu.asn.au; f. 1885 amalgamated, in present form in 1993; Nat. Sec. PAUL SLAPE; 140,000 mems.

Australian Workers' Union (AWU): 685 Spencer St, West Melbourne, Vic 3003; tel. (2) 9329-8733; fax (2) 9329-2871; e-mail awu@alphalink.net.au; internet www.awu.net.au; f. 1886; Nat. Pres. GRAHAM ROBERTS; Nat. Sec. BILL SHORTEN; 130,000 mems.

Communications, Electrical, Electronic, Energy, Information, Postal, Plumbing and Allied Services Union of Australia (CEPU): POB 812, Rockdale, NSW 2216; tel. (2) 9597-4499; fax (2) 9597-6354; e-mail edno@nat.cepu.asn.au; internet www.cepu.asn.au; Nat Pres. BRIAN BAULK; Nat. Sec. PETER TIGHE; 180,000 mems.

Community and Public Sector Union (CPSU): Level 5, 191–199 Thomas St, Haymarket, NSW 2000; tel. (2) 9334-9200; fax (2) 8204-6902; e-mail cpsu@cpsu.org; internet www.cpsu.org; Nat. Pres. MATTHEW REYNOLDS; Nat. Sec. WENDY CAIRD; 200,000 mems.

Construction, Forestry, Mining and Energy Union (CFMEU): Box Q235, Queen Victoria Bldg, Sydney, NSW 1230; tel. (2) 9267-3393; fax (2) 9267-2460; internet www.cfmeu.asn.au; f. 1992 by amalgamation; Pres. TREVOR SMITH; Sec. JOHN MAITLAND; 120,000 mems.

Finance Sector Union of Australia (FSU): GPOB 2829AA, 341 Queen St, Melbourne, Vic 3001; tel. (3) 9261-5300; fax (3) 9670-2950; e-mail fsuinfo@fsunion.org.au; internet www.fsunion.org.au; f. 1991; Nat. Pres. JOY BUCKLAND; Nat. Sec. TONY BECK; 61,000 mems.

Health Services Union of Australia (HSUA): 171 Drummond St, Carlton, Vic 3053; tel. (3) 9376-8242; fax (3) 9376-8243; e-mail union@hsua.asn.au; internet www.hsua.asn.au; Nat. Pres. MICHAEL WILLIAMSON; Nat. Sec. ROBERT ELLIOTT; 90,000 mems.

Independent Education Union of Australia (IEU): POB 1301, South Melbourne, Vic 3205; tel. (3) 9254-1830; fax (3) 9254-1835; e-mail ieu@ieu.org.au; internet www.ieu.org.au; Fed. Sec. LYNNE ROLLEY; Fed. Pres. RICHARD SHEARMAN; 45,000 mems.

Liquor, Hospitality and Miscellaneous Workers Union (LHMU): Locked Bag 9, Haymarket, NSW 1240; tel. (2) 8204-7200; fax (2) 9281-4480; e-mail lhmu@lhmu.org.au; internet www.lhmu.org.au; f. 1992; Nat. Pres. HELEN CREED; Nat. Sec. JEFF LAWRENCE; 143,800 mems.

Maritime Union of Australia (MUA): 2nd floor, 365 Sussex St, Sydney, NSW 2000; tel. (2) 9267-9134; fax (2) 9261-3481; e-mail muano@mua.org.au; internet www.mua.org.au; f. 1993; Nat. Sec. PADDY CRUMLIN; 10,012 mems.

Media, Entertainment & Arts Alliance (MEAA): POB 723, Strawberry Hills, NSW 2012; tel. (2) 9333-0999; fax (2) 9333-0933; e-mail mail@alliance.org.au; internet www.alliance.org.au; Fed. Sec. CHRISTOPHER WARREN; 30,000 mems.

National Union of Workers (NUW): POB 343, North Melbourne, Vic 3051; tel. (3) 9287-1850; fax (3) 9287-1818; e-mail nuwnat@nuw.org.au; internet www.nuw.org.au; Gen. Sec. GREG SWORD; Gen. Pres. LLOYD FREEBURN; 100,000 mems.

Rail, Tram and Bus Union (RTBU): 83–89 Renwick St, Redfern, NSW 2016; tel. (2) 9310-3966; fax (2) 9319-2096; e-mail rtbu@magna.com.au; internet www.rtbu-nat.com.au; Nat. Pres. R. PLAIN; Nat. Sec. ROGER JOWETT; 35,000 mems.

Shop, Distributive & Allied Employees Association (SDA): 5th Floor, 53 Queen St, Melbourne, Vic 3000; tel. (3) 9629-2299; fax (3) 9629-2646; e-mail sdanat@c031.aone.net.au; internet www.sda.org.au; f. 1908; Nat. Pres. DON FARRELL; Nat. Sec. JOE DE BRUYN; 209,708 mems.

Textile, Clothing and Footwear Union of Australia (TCFUA): Ground Floor, 28 Anglo Rd, Campsie, NSW 2194; tel. (2) 9789-4188; fax (2) 9789-6510; e-mail tcfua@tcfua.org.au; f. 1919; Pres. BARRY TUBNER; Nat. Sec. TONY WOOLGAR; 21,354 mems.

Transport Workers' Union of Australia (TWU): POB 211, Carlton South, Vic 3053; tel. (3) 9347-0099; fax (3) 9347-2502; e-mail twu@twu.com.au; internet www.twu.com.au; Fed. Pres. HUGHIE WILLIAMS; Fed. Sec. JOHN ALLAN; 82,000 mems.

Transport

Australian Transport Council: POB 594, Canberra, ACT 2601; tel. (2) 6274-7851; fax (2) 6274-7703; e-mail atc@dotrs.gov.au; internet www.atcouncil.gov.au; f. 1993; mems include: Federal Minister for Transport and Regional Services, State, Territory and New Zealand Ministers responsible for transport; Sec. D. JONES.

State Transit Authority of New South Wales: 100 Miller St, North Sydney, NSW 2060; tel. (2) 9245-5777; fax (2) 9245-5710; internet www.sta.nsw.gov.au; operates government buses and ferries in Sydney and Newcastle metropolitan areas; Chair. DAVID HERLIHY; CEO JOHN STOTT.

TransAdelaide (South Australia): GPOB 2351, Adelaide, SA 5001; tel. (8) 8218-2200; fax (8) 8218-4399; e-mail info@transadelaide.sa.gov.au; internet www.transadelaide.com.au; f. 1994; fmrly State Transport Authority; operates metropolitan train, bus, tram and Busway services; Gen. Man. SUE FILBY.

RAILWAYS

In June 2001 there were 39,844 km of railways in Australia (including tram and light rail track).

National Rail Corporation Ltd: POB 1419, Parramatta, NSW 2124; tel. (2) 9685-2555; fax (2) 9687-1804; e-mail information@nrc.com.au; internet www.nationalrail.com.au; freight; Chair. P. YOUNG; Man. Dir V. J. GRAHAM.

Public Transport Corporation (Victoria): Level 15, 589 Collins St, Melbourne, Vic 3000; tel. (3) 9619-4222; fax (3) 9619-4911; e-mail j.barry@ptc.vic.gov.au; f. 1989; Exec. Dir JOHN R. BARRY.

QR (Queensland Rail): POB 1429, Brisbane, Qld 4001; tel. (7) 3235-2222; fax (7) 3235-1799; internet www.qr.com.au; Chief Exec. BOB SCHEUBER.

State Rail Authority of New South Wales: POB K349, Haymarket, NSW 1238; tel. (2) 9379-3000; fax (2) 9379-2090; internet www.staterail.nsw.gov.au; f. 1980; responsible for passenger rail and associated coach services in NSW; Chief Exec. LUCIO DE BARTOLOMEO (acting).

Western Australian Government Railways (Westrail): POB 8125, Perth 6849, WA; tel. (8) 9326-2000; fax (8) 9326-2500; internet www.wagr.wa.gov.au; statutory authority competing in the freight, passenger and related transport markets in southern WA; operates 1,029 main line route-km of track; Commr REECE WALDOCK (acting).

ROADS

In June 2001 there were 808,294 km of roads open for general traffic. In 1996 this included 1,000 km of freeways, a further 103 km of toll roads, 45,889 km of highways, 77,045 km of arterial and major roads and 30,596 of secondary tourist and other roads. Local roads in urban areas account for 93,677 km of the network and those in rural localities for 537,278 km.

Austroads Inc: POB K659, Haymarket, NSW 2000; tel. (2) 9264-7088; fax (2) 9264-1657; e-mail austroads@austroads.com.au; internet www.austroads.com.au; f. 1989; asscn of road transport and traffic authorities.

SHIPPING

In December 2001 the Australian merchant fleet comprised 622 vessels, with a total displacement of 1,887,808 grt.

Adsteam Marine Ltd: Level 22, 6 O'Connell St, Sydney, NSW 2000; tel. (2) 9232-3955; fax (2) 9232-3988; e-mail info@adsteam.com.au; f. 1875; fmrly Adelaide Steamship Co; Man. Dir DAVID RYAN; Chief Exec. CLAY FREDERICK.

ANL Ltd (Australian National Line): GPOB 2238T, Melbourne, Vic 3004; tel. (3) 9257-0613; fax (3) 9257-0517; e-mail anl@anl.com.au; f. 1956; shipping agents; coastal and overseas container shipping and coastal bulk shipping; container management services; overseas container services to Hong Kong, Taiwan, the Philippines, Korea, Singapore, Malaysia, Thailand, Indonesia and Japan; extensive transhipment services; Chair. E. G. ANSON; Man. Dir MALCOLM TURNBULL.

BHP Transport Pty Ltd: 27th Level, 600 Bourke St, POB 86A, Melbourne, Vic 3001; tel. (3) 9609-3333; fax (3) 9609-2400; Chair. D. ARGUS; Man. Dir P. ANDERSEN.

William Holyman and Sons Pty Ltd: No. 3 Berth, Bell Bay, Tas 7253; tel. (3) 6382-2383; fax (3) 6382-3391; coastal services; Chair. R. J. HOY.

Howard Smith Ltd: POB N364, Grosvenor Place, Sydney, NSW 2000; tel. (2) 9230-1777; fax (2) 9251-1190; e-mail info@hst.com.au; internet www.howardsmith.com.au; harbour towage and other services; Chair. FRANCIS JOHN CONROY; CEO KENNETH JOHN MOSS.

CIVIL AVIATION

Eastern Australia Airlines: POB 538, Mascot, Sydney, NSW 2020; tel. (2) 9691-2333; fax (2) 9693-2715; internet www.qantas.com.au; subsidiary of Qantas; domestic flights; Gen. Man. ASHLEY KILROY.

Impulse Airlines: Eleventh St, Sydney Kingsford-Smith Airport, Mascot, NSW 2020; tel. (2) 9317-5400; fax (2) 9317-3440; e-mail info@ImpulseAirlines.com.au; internet www.impulseairlines.com.au; f. 1992; domestic services; Chief Exec./Chair. GERRY McGOWAN; Exec. Dir SUE McGOWAN.

National Jet Systems: Adelaide Airport, 28 James Schofield Drive SA 5000; tel. (8) 8238-7200; fax (8) 8238-7238; internet www.nationaljet.com.au; f. 1989; domestic services; Man. Dir DANIELA MARSILLI; Group Gen. Man. Commdr ROBERT BIRKS.

Qantas Airways Ltd: Qantas Centre, 203 Coward St, Mascot, NSW 2020; tel. (2) 9691-3636; fax (2) 9691-3339; internet www.qantas.com.au; f. 1920 as Queensland and Northern Territory Aerial Services; Australian Govt became sole owner in 1947; merged with Australian Airlines in Sept. 1992; British Airways purchased 25% in March 1993; remaining 75% transferred to private sector in 1995; services throughout Australia and to 34 countries, including destinations in Europe, Africa, the USA, Canada, South America, Asia, the Pacific and New Zealand; Chair. MARGARET JACKSON; CEO GEOFF DIXON.

Spirit Airlines: Level 9, 580 St Kilda Rd, Melbourne, Vic 3004; fax (3) 9510-4095; e-mail info@spiritairlines.com.au; internet www.spiritairlines.com.au/; f. 1998; domestic services; CEO MIKE DIXON.

Sunstate Airlines: Lobby 3, Level 2, 153 Campbell St, Bowen Hills, Qld 4006; tel. (7) 3308-9022; fax (7) 3308-9088; e-mail akilroy@qantas.com.au; f. 1982; wholly owned by Qantas; operates passenger services within Queensland and to Newcastle (NSW) and Lord Howe Island; Gen. Man. ASHLEY KILROY.

Virgin Blue: Centenary Place, Level 7, 100 Wickham St, Brisbane, Qld; tel. (7) 3295-3000; e-mail customercare@virginblue.com.au; internet www.virginblue.com.au; domestic services; CEO BRETT GODFREY.

Tourism

The main attractions are the cosmopolitan cities, the Great Barrier Reef, the Blue Mountains, water sports and also winter sports in the Australian Alps, notably the Snowy Mountains. The town of Alice Springs, the Aboriginal culture and the sandstone monolith of Ayers Rock (Uluru) are among the attractions of the desert interior. Much of Australia's wildlife is unique to the country. Australia received 4,871,000 foreign visitors in 2001. The majority of visitors came from New Zealand, Japan, the United Kingdom and the USA. Receipts totalled $A19,800m. in 2000. The 2000 Olympic Games were held in Sydney in September.

Australian Tourist Commission: GPOB 2721, Sydney, NSW 1006; Level 4, 80 William St, Woolloomooloo, Sydney, NSW 2011; tel. (2) 9360-1111; fax (2) 9331-6469; internet www.atc.australia.com; f. 1967 for promotion of international inbound tourism; 13 offices overseas; Chair. NICK EVERS; Man. Dir KEN BOUNDY.

Defence

In August 2001 Australia's armed forces numbered 50,700: army 24,150, navy 12,500, air force 14,050. Military service is voluntary. Australia's defence policy is based on collective security and it is a member of the ANZUS Security Treaty (with New Zealand and the USA), and of the Five Power Defence Arrangements (with Singapore, Malaysia, the UK and New Zealand).

Defence Expenditure: Budgeted at $A12,700m. for 2001.

Chief of the Defence Force: Lt-Gen. PETER J. COSGROVE.

Chief of Navy: Vice-Adm. CHRISTOPHER RITCHIE.

Chief of Army: Lt-Gen. PETER LEAHY.

Chief of Air Force: Air Marshal ALAN GRANT HOUSTON.

Education

Under the federal system of government in Australia, the six states and two territories are responsible for providing education services for their own residents. The Australian Constitution, however, empowers the Federal Government to make special-purpose financial grants to the states for education in both government and non-government schools. Expenditure on education by all levels of government in 1999/2000 was $A34,036m. Responsibility for educational policy rests with the Minister for Education, Training and Youth Affairs, and an education department headed by a Director-General deals with all aspects of education within each state. A small proportion of Australia's school-age children live in remote districts, thus requiring distance education. School attendance in Australia is compulsory and free between the ages of six and 15 years (16 in Tasmania) for all children except those exempted on account of distance, for whom a special form of education is provided. The Federal Government is the most important source of funding for universities.

GOVERNMENT SCHOOLS

In 2001 there were 6,942 government primary and secondary schools, with a total enrolment of 2,248,219 full-time pupils (1,384,866 primary and 863,353 secondary) and 152,138 teachers. Schooling is not compulsory in Australia until the age of six but most children start earlier. Primary schools are generally mixed and cater for children up to the age of 11 or 12.

The co-educational high school offers a wide range of subjects. Most have modern facilities for teaching sciences, information technology and general technology, including woodwork and metal fabrication. Many schools are beginning to focus on vocational education, which prepares students for work. Some states also have separate high schools and colleges specializing in the agricultural, commercial and vocational/technical fields. Some agricultural high schools are residential. The curriculum in these specialist schools consists of general academic subjects and training in the particular area of focus.

INDEPENDENT SCHOOLS

A total of 1,019,922 full-time students were enrolled in the 2,654 non-government or independent schools in 2001. Almost 66% of primary and secondary students at independent schools attended Roman Catholic schools. Most other independent schools are under the auspices of, or are actually administered by, other religious denominations. The teaching staff at independent schools in 2001 totalled 69,789.

The organization of Roman Catholic primary schools is largely through a diocesan Education Office. Many secondary schools are administered by religious orders; however, a growing number now come within general administrative structures in a similar way to primary schools.

EDUCATION FOR CHILDREN IN ISOLATED AREAS

Some children in Australia live in remote areas, which are geographically isolated and do not allow access to the resources usually offered by schools. Australia has developed some innovative approaches to delivering education to overcome these disadvantages. A long-standing example is that of the Schools of the Air, which have been broadcasting lessons for remote primary and secondary school children, using two-way radio equipment, since 1950. Rapid changes in technology have improved the type of educational support offered for remote students. Schools can make use of satellite and television broadcasting and use computer networks to provide an up-to-date curriculum for their students.

EDUCATION NETWORK AUSTRALIA (EdNA)

One Australian initiative that aims to facilitate the provision of cost-effective education to all parts of the community is Education Network Australia (EdNA). EdNA is a multi-faceted process of co-operation and consultation between representatives of all sectors of the education community, including Federal, State and Territory governments, non-government schools, the vocational education and training sector, the higher education sector and the adult and community education sectors. Its aim is to maximize the benefits of information technology for all sectors in Australian education and to avoid duplication between the various sectors and systems. The most visible part of the EdNA initiative is the directory of services, which is available on the Internet. Each sector of the education community is developing its part to meet the needs of its particular client group. The directory is highly innovative and flexible. EdNA is available free of charge on the Internet. Its address is: www .edna.edu.au.

HIGHER EDUCATION

There are 47 public universities and several additional public institutions of higher education, which enrolled a total of 726,418 students in 2001. There are also two small private universities. Most courses last from three to six years. The majority of higher education institutions offer courses to both internal and external students and have postgraduate research facilities.

Most Australian students contribute to the cost of their courses under the Higher Education Contribution Scheme (HECS). Students commencing a new course of study are subject to a three-tiered contribution based on the cost of the course undertaken and its likely future benefits to the individual. Some postgraduate courses are offered on a fee-paying rather than on an HECS-liable basis. From 1998 Australian undergraduate students may also choose to enrol on a fee-paying basis. Financial assistance is available to certain students subject to a means test. In addition, there are a limited number of equity and merit scholarships, which exempt students from the HECS charge.

VOCATIONAL EDUCATION AND TRAINING

Vocational education and training is aimed at assisting people seeking to upgrade their skills, join the work-force or change career paths. Off-the-job training for apprentices and trainees is provided by this sector. In 1999 a total of 1,647,200 students participated in vocational education and training, provided by organizations such as Technical and Further Education (TAFE) institutes, Skills Centres, business colleges, registered private training providers, computer-training colleges and Adult and Community Education centres, which offer a wide range of courses and subjects.

TAFE

Technical and Further Education (TAFE) is the major provider of post-secondary vocational education and training. There are more than 7,000 courses (including non-vocational courses) available at more than 1,000 locations throughout Australia. Most TAFE courses are developed in consultation with the industry concerned. TAFE award courses can be studied both full time and part time, by internal study at campuses, by external studies and also through flexible delivery (open learning).

SKILLS CENTRES

Skills Centres are industry- and enterprise-based training facilities that offer a wide range of accredited training to enterprise employees, industry groups and individuals. Some Skills Centres are located in-plant, some are 'stand alone' and others are linked to a TAFE college. There are approximately 100 Skill Centres around Australia.

REGISTERED PRIVATE TRAINING PROVIDERS

There are many private training institutions, including business colleges, secretarial colleges, computer-training centres and industry-based training centres. They provide training in a wide range of fields such as beauty therapy, hospitality, travel, business, computing, music, aviation, child care, art and design, naturopathy and languages.

ADULT AND COMMUNITY EDUCATION

Adult and Community Education (ACE) centres include neighbourhood centres, non-government adult education providers, community centres and SkillShare centres. They provide recreational, pre-vocational and vocational training to local communities focusing particularly on mature students and long-term unemployed people. Much of the training is in subjects such as arts and humanities, health and community services, office administration and English as a second language. SkillShare centres provide access to training courses and employment-related services to disadvantaged job-seekers. There are more than 1,500 ACE centres around Australia.

Bibliography

GENERAL

Aitken, J. *Land of Fortune: A Study of the New Australia.* London, Secker and Warburg, 1976.

Australian Bureau of Statistics. *Year Book Australia.* Canberra.

Berndt, R. M. and C. H. *The World of the First Australian.* Sydney, Ure Smith, 1964.

Davies, A. F. (Ed.). *Australian Society: A Sociological Introduction.* 2nd Edn, Melbourne, Cheshire, 1970.

Encel, S. *Equality and Authority: A Study of Class, Status and Power.* Melbourne, Cheshire, 1970.

Horne, D. *The Australian People: Biography of a Nation.* Sydney, Angus and Robertson, 1976.

Inglis, K. *Sacred Places: War Memorials in the Australian Landscape.* Carlton, Vic, Melbourne University Press, 1998.

Jeans, D. N. (Ed.). *Australia: A Geography.* Sydney University Press, 1977.

Kewley, T. *Social Security in Australia.* Sydney University Press, 1972.

Maddock, K. J. *The Australian Aborigines.* London, Penguin, 1973.

Pilger, J. *A Secret Country.* London, Jonathan Cape, 1989.

Simpson, C. *The New Australia.* Sydney, Angus and Robertson, 1971.

Spate, O. H. K. *Australia.* Nations of the Modern World Series, London, Benn, 1968.

Stone, Sharman. *Aborigines in White Australia.* Adelaide, Heinemann Educational Books, 1974.

Venturini, V. G. (Ed.). *Australia: A Survey.* Wiesbaden, Otto Harrassowitz, 1970.

HISTORY AND POLITICS

Aitkin, D. *Stability and Change in Australian Politics.* Canberra, 1977.

Alexander, F. *From Curtin to Menzies and After.* Melbourne, Nelson, 1973.

Atkins, B. *Governing Australia.* Sydney, Wiley, 1972.

Attwood, Bain, and Markus, Andrew (Eds). *The Struggle for Aboriginal Rights: A Documentary History.* Sydney, Allen and Unwin, 2000.

Australian Dictionary of Biography (12 vols). Melbourne University Press, 1966–90.

Bennett, S. C. *The Making of the Commonwealth.* Melbourne, Cassell, 1971.

Blainey, Geoffrey. *The Tyranny of Distance.* 2nd Edn, Melbourne, Sun Books, 1976.

Broome, R. *Aboriginal Australians—the Black Response to White Dominance, 1788–1980.* Sydney, 1982.

Clark, M. *A History of Australia (6 vols).* Melbourne University Press, 1962–87. (Abridgement by Michael Cathcart, 1994.)

A Short History of Australia. Melbourne, Macmillan, 1986.

Crisp, L. F. *Australian National Government.* Melbourne, Longman, 1975.

Crowley, F. K. (Ed.). *A New History of Australia.* Melbourne, Heinemann, 1974.

Davies, S. R. (Ed.). *The Government of the Australian States.* London, Longman, 1960.

Davison, Graeme et al. (Eds). *The Oxford Companion to Australian History.* Oxford, Oxford University Press, 2002.

Day, David. *Claiming a Continent: A History of Australia.* Pymble, NSW, Angus & Robertson, 1996.

Edwards, John. *Keating: The Inside Story.* Ringwood, Vic, Penguin Books, 1997.

FitzGerald, Stephen. *Is Australia an Asian Country?* St Leonards, NSW, Allen and Unwin, 1997.

Goot, Murray, and Rowse, Tim (Eds). *Make a Better Offer: The Politics of Mabo.* Leichhardt, NSW, Plato Press, 1994.

Gordon, Michael. *Paul Keating: True Believer.* St Lucia, Qld, University of Queensland Press, 1997.

Hawke, Bob. *The Hawke Memoirs.* Port Melbourne, William Heinemann Australia, 1994.

Headon, D., Warden, J., and Gammadge, B. (Eds). *The Traditions of Australian Republicanism.* St Leonards, NSW, Allen and Unwin, 1994.

Hearn, Mark, and Knowles, Harry. *One Big Union: A History of the Australian Workers' Union, 1886–1994.* Cambridge University Press, 1997.

Hough, Richard. *Captain James Cook: A Biography.* London, Hodder and Stoughton, 1994.

Hughes, C. A. *A Handbook of Australian Government and Politics, 1965–74.*

Hughes, R. *The Fatal Shore.* London, Collins Harvill, 1987.

Irving, Helen. *To Constitute A Nation: A Cultural History of Australia's Constitution.* Cambridge, Cambridge University Press, 1997.

Jack, Ian (Ed.). *Australia, the New New World.* London, Granta Books, 2000.

Keating, Paul. *Advancing Australia: The Speeches of Paul Keating, Prime Minister.* Cremorne Pt, NSW, Big Picture Publications, 1996.

Engagement: Australia Faces the Asia-Pacific. Sydney, Pan MacMillan, 2000.

Kelly, Paul. *The End of Certainty: The Story of the 1980s.* Sydney, Allen and Unwin, 1993.

One Hundred Years. Sydney, Allen and Unwin, 2001.

Knightley, Phillip. *Australia—A Biography of a Nation.* London, Jonathan Cape, 2000.

Lacour-Gayet, R. *A Concise History of Australia.* London, Penguin, 1976.

La Nauze, J. *The Making of the Australian Constitution.* Melbourne University Press, 1972.

Loveday, P., Martin, A. W., and Parker, R. S. *The Emergence of the Australian Party System.* Sydney, 1977.

McGillivray, Mark, and Smith, Gary (Eds). *Australia and Asia.* Oxford, Oxford University Press, 1998.

McIntyre, K. G. *The Secret Discovery of Australia.* London, Souvenir Press, 1977.

MacIntyre, Stuart. *A Concise History of Australia.* Cambridge, Cambridge University Press, 2000.

McKenna, Mark. *The Captive Republic: A History of Republicanism in Australia 1788–1996.* Cambridge, Cambridge University Press, 1997.

Meyer, H. *Australian Politics.* Melbourne, Cheshire, 1971.

Miller, J. D. B. *Australian Government and Politics.* London, Duckworth, 1971.

Oxford History of Australia (5 vols). Melbourne, Oxford University Press, 1986–91.

Reid, G. *Australia's Commonwealth Parliament.* Canberra, Australian Government Publishing Service, 1988.

Richardson, Graham. *Whatever It Takes.* Neutral Bay Junction, NSW, Bantam Books, 1994.

Sawer, G. *The Australian Constitution.* Canberra, Australian Government Publishing Service, 1975.

Sharp, C. A. *The Discovery of Australia.* London, Oxford University Press, 1963.

Shaw, A. G. L. *The Story of Australia.* 5th Edn, London, Faber and Faber, 1983.

Shaw, A. G. L., and Nicolson, H. D. *Australia in the Twentieth Century.* Sydney, Angus and Robertson, 1967.

Sheridan, Greg. *Living with Dragons: Australia Confronts its Asian Destiny.* St Leonards, NSW, Allen and Unwin, 1995.

Solomon, D. *The People's Palace: Parliament in Modern Australia.* Canberra, Australian Government Publishing Service, 1986.

Souter, G. *Acts of Parliament.* Canberra, Australian Government Publishing Service, 1988.

Theophanous, Andrew. *Australian Democracy in Crisis: A New Theoretical Introduction to Australian Politics.* Oxford University Press, 1980.

Ward, R. *A History of Australia: The Twentieth Century 1901–1975.* London, Heinemann, 1978.

Watt, A. *The Evolution of Australian Foreign Policy.* Cambridge University Press, 1967.

Whitington, B. L. *The Menzies Era and After.* Melbourne, Cheshire, 1972.

ECONOMY

Andrews, J. A. *Australia's Resources and their Utilisation.* Sydney, University Press, 1970.

Bell, Stephen, and Head, Brian (Eds). *State Economy and Public Policy in Australia.* Oxford University Press, 1994.

Byrnes, Michael. *Australia and the Asia Game.* St Leonards, NSW, Allen and Unwin, 1994.

Bryan, Dick, and Rafferty, Michael. *The Global Economy in Australia: Global Integration and National Economic Policy.* Allen and Unwin, 1999.

Catley, Bob. *Globalising Australian Capitalism.* Cambridge, Cambridge University Press, 1997.

Caves, R., and Kraus, L. (Eds). *The Australian Economy.* Sydney, George Allen and Unwin, 1983.

Chapman, B., Isaacs, J. E., and Niland, J. R. *Australian Labour Economics Readings.* 3rd Edn, Melbourne, Macmillan, 1985.

Coghill, I. G. *Australia's Mineral Wealth.* Melbourne, Sorrett Publishing, 1971.

Crawford, J. G., and others. *Study Group on Structural Adjustment, March 1979.* Canberra, Australian Government Publishing Service, 1979.

Crawford, J. G., and Okita, S. (Eds). *Raw Materials and Pacific Economic Integration.* London, Croom Helm, 1978.

Downing, R. I. *National Income and Social Accounts: An Australian Study.* 12th Edn, Melbourne University Press, 1971.

Fenna, Alan. *Introduction to Australian Public Policy.* Melbourne, Longman, 1998.

Fitzpatrick, B. C. *British Imperialism and Australia 1783–1833: An Economic History of Australasia.* Sydney University Press, 1971.

The British Empire in Australia: An Economic History, 1834–1939. Melbourne, Macmillan, 1969.

INDECS ECONOMICS. *State of Play 6.* Sydney, George Allen and Unwin, 1990.

Isaac, J. E., and Ford, G., *Australian Labour Relations: Readings.* 2nd Edn, Melbourne, Sun Books, 1971.

Kenwood, George, and Kenwood, A. G. *Australian Economic Institutions Since Federation : An Introduction.* Oxford University Press, 1996

Kreisler, Peter (Ed.). *The Australian Economy.* Allen and Unwin, 1999.

Lewis, M. K., and Wallace, R. H. *Australia's Financial Institution and Markets.* Melbourne, Longman Cheshire, 1985.

Marginson, Simon *Educating Australia: Government, Economy and Citizenship since 1960.* Cambridge, Cambridge University Press, 1997.

Meredith, David, and Dyster, Barrie, *Australia in the Global Economy: Continuity and Change.* Cambridge, Cambridge University Press, 2000.

Painter, Martin. *Collaborative Federalism: Economic Reform in Australia in the 1990s.* Cambridge, Cambridge University Press, 1998.

Pinkstone, Brian, and Meredith, David. *Global Connections: A History of Exports and the Australian Economy.* International Specialized Book Services, 1997.

Shaw, A. G. L. *The Economic Development of Australia.* 7th Edn, Melbourne, 1980.

Sheehan, Peter, et al. *Dialogues on Australia's Future.* Melbourne, Victoria University of Technology, 1996.

Sinclair, W. A. *The Process of Economic Development in Australia.* Melbourne, Cheshire, 1976.

Sinden, J. A. (Ed.). *The Natural Resources of Australia: Prospects and Problems for Development.* Sydney, Angus and Robertson, 1972.

Singh, Anoop, *et al. Australia: Benefiting from Economic Reform.* Washington, DC, IMF, 1998.

Sykes, Trevor. The Bold Riders: Behind Australia's Corporate Collapses. St Leonards, NSW, Allen and Unwin, 1994.

AUSTRALIAN DEPENDENCIES IN THE INDIAN OCEAN

Ashmore and Cartier Islands

The Ashmore Islands (known as West, Middle and East Islands) and Cartier Island are situated in the Timor Sea, about 850 km and 790 km west of Darwin respectively. The Ashmore Islands cover some 93 ha of land and Cartier Island covers 0.4 ha. The islands are small and uninhabited, consisting of sand and coral, surrounded by shoals and reefs. Grass is the main vegetation. Maximum elevation is about 2.5 m above sea-level. The islands abound in birdlife, sea-cucumbers (*bêches-de-mer*) and, seasonally, turtles.

The United Kingdom took formal possession of the Ashmore Islands in 1878, and Cartier Island was annexed in 1909. The islands were placed under the authority of the Commonwealth of Australia in 1931. They were annexed to, and deemed to form part of, the Northern Territory of Australia in 1938. On 1 July 1978 the Australian Government assumed direct responsibility for the administration of the islands, which rests with a parliamentary secretary appointed by the Minister for Regional Services, Territories and Local Government. Periodic visits are made to the islands by the Royal Australian Navy and aircraft of the Royal Australian Air Force, and the Civil Coastal Surveillance Service makes aerial surveys of the islands and neighbouring waters. The oilfields of Jabiru and Challis are located in waters adjacent to the Territory.

In August 1983 Ashmore Reef was declared a national nature reserve. An agreement between Australia and Indonesia permits Indonesian traditional fishermen to continue fishing in the territorial waters and to land on West Island to obtain supplies of fresh water. In 1985 the Australian Government extended the laws of the Northern Territory to apply in Ashmore and Cartier, and decided to contract a vessel to be stationed at Ashmore Reef during the Indonesian fishing season (March–November) to monitor the fishermen.

During 2000–01 increasing numbers of refugees and asylum-seekers attempted to land at Ashmore Reef, hoping to gain residency in Australia. The majority had travelled from the Middle East via Indonesia, where the illegal transport of people was widespread. Consequently, in late 2000 a vessel with the capacity to transport up to 150 people was chartered to ferry unauthorized arrivals to the Australian mainland. In September 2001 the Australian Government introduced an item of legislation to Parliament excising Ashmore Reef and other outlying territories from Australia's migration zone.

Christmas Island

Christmas Island covers an area of about 135 sq km (52 sq miles) and lies 360 km south of Java Head (Indonesia) in the Indian Ocean. The nearest point on the Australian coast is North West Cape, 1,408 km to the south-east. The island forms a rocky peak with a central plateau, and rises to a maximum elevation of 360m above sea-level. The climate is tropical, with a rainy season from December to April. Christmas Island has no indigenous population. The population was 1,906 at the 1996 census (compared with 1,275 in 1991), comprising mainly ethnic Chinese (some 70%), but there were minorities of Malays (about 10%) and Europeans (about 20%). A variety of languages are spoken, but English is the official language. The predominant religious affiliation is Buddhist (55% in 1991). The principal settlement and only anchorage is Flying Fish Cove.

Following annexation by the United Kingdom in 1888, Christmas Island was incorporated for administrative purposes with the Straits Settlements (now Singapore and part of Malaysia) in 1900. Japanese forces occupied the island from March 1942 until the end of the Second World War, and in 1946 Christmas Island became a dependency of Singapore. Administration was transferred to the United Kingdom on 1 January 1958, pending final transfer to Australia, effected on 1 October 1958. The Australian Government appointed Official Representatives to the Territory until 1968, when new legislation provided for an Administrator, appointed by the Governor-General. Responsibility for administration lies with the Minister for Regional Services, Territories and Local Government. In 1980 the Advisory Council was established for the Administrator to consult. In 1984 the Christmas Island Services Corporation was created to perform those functions that are normally the responsibility of municipal government. This body was placed under the direction of the Christmas Island Assembly, the first elections to which took place in September 1985. Nine members were elected for one-year terms. In November 1987 the Assembly was dissolved, and the Administrator empowered to perform its functions. The Corporation was superseded by the Christmas Island Shire Council in 1992.

In May 1994 an unofficial referendum on the island's status was held concurrently with local government elections. At the poll, sponsored by the Union of Christmas Island Workers, the islanders rejected an option to secede from Australia, but more than 85% of voters favoured increased local government control. The referendum was prompted, in part, by the Australian Government's plans to abolish the island's duty-free status (which had become a considerable source of revenue).

Since 1981 all residents of the island have been eligible to acquire Australian citizenship. In 1984 the Australian Government extended social security, health and education benefits to the island, and enfranchised Australian citizens resident there. Full income-tax liability was introduced in the late 1980s.

During the late 1990s an increasing number of illegal immigrants travelling to Australia landed on Christmas Island. In January 2001 Australian government officials denied claims by Christmas Islanders that some 86 illegal immigrants who had arrived at the island from the Middle East via Indonesia were being detained in inhumane conditions. Local people claimed that the detainees were sleeping on concrete floors and were being denied adequate food and medical care.

International attention was focused on Christmas Island in August 2001 when the *MV Tampa*, a Norwegian container ship carrying 433 refugees whom it had rescued from a sinking Indonesian fishing boat, was refused permission to land on the island. As the humanitarian crisis escalated, the Australian Government's steadfast refusal to admit the mostly Afghan refugees prompted international condemnation and led to a serious diplomatic dispute between Australia and Norway. The office of the United Nations High Commissioner for Refugees (UNHCR) and the International Organization for Migration (IOM) expressed grave concern at the situation. Hundreds of Christmas Island residents attended a rally urging the Australian Government to reconsider its uncompromising stance. In September the refugees were transferred (via Papua New Guinea and New Zealand) to Nauru, where their applications for asylum were to be processed. In the same month the Senate in Canberra approved new legislation, which excised Christmas Island and other outlying territories from Australia's official migration zone. The new legislation also imposed stricter criteria for the processing of asylum-seekers and the removal of their right to recourse to the Australian court system. Meanwhile, increasing numbers of asylum-seekers continued to attempt to reach Christmas Island via Indonesia. Among the many controversial incidents that occurred in the waters of Christmas Island in September–December 2001 was that of 186 Iraqis who jumped into the sea when ordered to leave Australian waters in October. They were temporarily housed on Christmas Island before being transferred to Nauru. According to Australian Immigration Department figures, 146 asylum-seekers were turned away from Christmas Island and Ashmore Reef in December 2001. In January 2002 211 asylum-seekers remained on Christmas Island awaiting transferral. In March the Government announced plans to establish a permanent detention centre on the island, the construction of which was expected to cost more than $A150m. The Government was thus preparing to accommodate an anticipated total of 18,000 illegal immigrants who were expected to arrive at Christmas Island during 2002–06.

The economy has been based on the recovery of phosphates. During the year ending 30 June 1984 about 463,000 metric tons were exported to Australia, 332,000 tons to New Zealand and 341,000 tons to other countries. In November 1987 the Australian Government announced the closure of the phosphate mine, owing to industrial unrest, and mining activity ceased in December. In 1990, however, the Government allowed private operators to recommence phosphate extraction, subject to certain conditions such as the preservation of the rainforest. In 2001 the mine employed some 180 workers. The owner of the mine, Phosphate Resources Ltd (trading as Christmas Island Phosphates), was thus the island's largest employer. A total of 570,000 metric tons of phosphate dust were exported in 2001/02, and phosphate exports were worth

$A43.8m. in 1997/98. A 21-year lease, drawn up by the Government and Phosphate Resources Ltd, took effect in February 1998 and, subject to the negotiation of further leases, there were sufficient phosphate deposits for the industry to remain productive until around 2015. The agreement incorporated environmental safeguards and provided for a conservation levy, based on the tonnage of phosphate shipped, which was to finance a programme of rainforest rehabilitation.

Efforts have been made to develop the island's considerable potential for tourism. In 1989, in an attempt to protect the natural environment and many rare species of flora and fauna (including the Abbott's Booby and the Christmas frigate bird), the National Park was extended to cover some 70% of the island. A hotel and casino complex, covering 47 ha of land, was opened in November 1993. In 1994 revenue from the development totalled $A500m., and a 50-room extension to the complex was constructed in 1995. In September 1997, however, Ansett Australia discontinued its twice-weekly air service to the island. Despite the subsequent commencement of a weekly flight from Perth, Western Australia, operated by National Jet Systems, the complex was closed down in April 1998 and some 350 employees were made redundant. In July the resort's casino licence was cancelled and a liquidator was appointed to realize the complex's assets. The closure of the resort had serious economic and social repercussions for the island. An audit of tourist accommodation, conducted in May 2000, counted approximately 140 beds on the island.

Between 1992 and 1999 the Australian Government invested an estimated $A110m. in the development of Christmas Island's infrastructure as part of the Christmas Island Rebuilding Programme. The main areas of expenditure under this programme were a new hospital, the upgrading of ports facilities, school extensions, the construction of housing, power, water supply and sewerage, and the repair and construction of roads. In 2000 further improvements to marine facilities and water supply were carried out, in addition to the construction of new housing to relocate islanders away from a major rockfall risk area. In mid-2001 the Australian Government pledged a net total of over $A50m. for further developments including improvements to the airport and road networks, and an alternative port. The cost of the island's imports from Australia increased from $A13m. in 1998/99 to $A17m. in 1999/2000 and declined to $A16m. in 2000/01 when the Territory's exports to that country earned $A7m. The cost of imports from New Zealand decreased from $NZ9m. in 1998/99 to nil in 2000/01. Although Christmas Island purchased no imports from New Zealand in 2000/01, exports to that country were worth $NZ4m. An estimated 7.5% of the island's population were unemployed in 1996.

Proposals for the development of a communications satellite launching facility on the island were under consideration in 1998. An assessment of the environmental impact was subsequently undertaken, and the scheme received government approval in May 2000. Following an agreement between the Governments of Australia and Russia in May 2001, preparations for the establishment of a space control centre on Christmas Island commenced. Australia and Russia were to contribute up to US $100m. towards the project, the total cost of which was expected to be US $425m. The Christmas Island site was to be developed by the Asia Pacific Space Centre, an Australian company. Construction began in November 2001, with the first rocket launch being planned for 2004. The space centre was expected to become the world's first wholly privately-owned land-based launch facility, with an operational lifespan of 15–20 years. Asia Pacific planned to launch 10–12 satellites annually by 2005. Although the project would create many employment opportunities on the island (an estimated 400 new jobs during construction and 550 during operation) and lead to substantial infrastructural improvements, environmentalists continued to express concern.

Statistical Survey

AREA AND POPULATION

Area: 135 sq km (52 sq miles).

Population: 1,906 (males 1,023, females 883) at census of 30 June 1996; 1,508 (males 850, females 658) at census of 7 August 2001; 1,506 (official estimate) at August 2002. *Ethnic Groups* (census of 30 June 1981): Chinese 1,587; Malay 693; European 336; Total (incl. others) 2,871. Source: mainly UN, *Demographic Yearbook*.

Density (2002): 11.2 per sq km.

Births and Deaths (1985): Registered live births 36 (birth rate 15.8 per 1,000); Registered deaths 2.

Labour Force (1996): 971 (employed 898, unemployed 73).

MINING

Natural Phosphates (official estimates, '000 metric tons): 285 in 1994; 220 in 1995.

FINANCE

Currency and Exchange Rates: Australian currency is used (see p. 118).

EXTERNAL TRADE

Principal Trading Partners (phosphate exports, '000 metric tons, year ending 30 June 1984): Australia 463; New Zealand 332; Total (incl. others) 1,136.

2000/01 ($A million): *Imports:* Australia 16. *Exports:* Australia 7. Source: Australian Bureau of Statistics, *Year Book Australia*.

2000/01 ($NZ million): *Exports:* New Zealand 4. Source: Ministry of Foreign Affairs and Trade, New Zealand.

TRANSPORT

International Sea-borne Shipping (estimated freight traffic, '000 metric tons, 1990): Goods loaded 1,290; Goods unloaded 68. Source: UN, *Monthly Bulletin of Statistics*.

TOURISM

Visitor Arrivals and Departures by Air: 14,513 in 1996; 3,895 in 1997; 2,712 in 1998. Source: *Year Book Australia*.

COMMUNICATIONS MEDIA

Radio Receivers (1997): 1,000 in use.

Television Receivers (1997): 600 in use.

Personal computers (home users, 2001): 506.

Internet users (2001): 1,450.

EDUCATION

Pre-primary (2002): 37 pupils.
Primary (2002): 217 pupils.
Secondary (2002): 124 pupils.

Source: Education Department of Western Australia.

Directory

THE GOVERNMENT

The Administrator, appointed by the Governor-General of Australia and responsible to the Minister for Regional Services, Territories and Local Government, is the senior government representative on the island.

Administrator: WILLIAM TAYLOR.

Administration Headquarters: POB 863, Christmas Island 6798, Indian Ocean; tel. (8) 9164-7901; fax (8) 9164-8524.

Shire of Christmas Island: George Fam Centre, POB 863, Christmas Island 6798, Indian Ocean; tel. (8) 9164-8300; fax (8) 9164-8304; e-mail soci@pulau.cx.

JUDICIAL SYSTEM

The judicial system comprises the Supreme Court, District Court, Magistrate's Court and Children's Court.

Supreme Court: c/o Govt Offices, Christmas Island 6798, Indian Ocean; tel. (8) 9164-7911; fax (8) 9164-8530; Judges (non-resident): ROBERT SHERATON FRENCH, MALCOLM CAMERON LEE.

Managing Registrar: JEFFERY LOW, Govt Offices, Christmas Island 6798, Indian Ocean; tel. (8) 9164-7911; fax (8) 9164-8530.

RELIGION

According to the census of 1991, of the 1,275 residents of Christmas Island, some 55% were Buddhists, 10% were Muslims, and 15% were Christians. Within the Christian churches, Christmas Island lies in the jurisdiction of both the Anglican and Roman Catholic Archbishops of Perth, in Western Australia.

THE PRESS

The Islander: Shire of Christmas Island, George Fam Centre, POB 863, Christmas Island 6798, Indian Ocean; tel. (8) 9164-8300; fax (8) 9164-8304; newsletter; fortnightly; Editor TENG BOON EIANG.

BROADCASTING AND COMMUNICATIONS

Telecommunications

Indian Ocean Communications: Christmas Island; tel (8) 9164-8505; provides stand-alone mobile cellular telephone network; e-mail mobiles@pulau.cx; .

Broadcasting

Radio

Christmas Island Community Radio Service: POB AAA, Christmas Island 6798, Indian Ocean; tel. (8) 9164-8316; fax (8) 9164-8315; f. 1967; operated by the Administration since 1991; daily broadcasting service by Radio VLU-2 on 1422 KHz and 102 MHz FM, in English, Malay, Cantonese and Mandarin; Station Man. The Administrator.

Christmas Island Tropical Radio VLU2: POB AAA, Christmas Island 6798, Indian Ocean; tel. (8) 9164-8316; fax (8) 9164-8315; Chair. DAVID MASTERS; Station Man. The Administrator.

Television

Christmas Island Television: POB AAA, Christmas Island 6798, Indian Ocean.

FINANCE

Banking

Commercial Bank

Westpac Banking Corpn (Australia): Flying Fish Cove, Christmas Island, Indian Ocean; tel. (8) 9164-8221; fax (8) 9164-8241.

TRADE AND INDUSTRY

In April 2001 there were 67 small businesses in operation.

Administration of Christmas Island: POB 868, Christmas Island 6798, Indian Ocean; tel. (8) 9164-7901; fax (8) 9164-8524; operates power, airport, seaport, health services, public housing, local courts; Director of Finance JEFFERY TAN.

Christmas Island Chamber of Commerce: Christmas Island 6798, Indian Ocean; tel. (8) 9164-8249; Pres. DON O'DONNELL; Vice Pres. PHILLIP OAKLEY.

Shire of Christmas Island: George Fam Centre, POB 863, Christmas Island 6798, Indian Ocean; tel. (8) 9164-8300; fax (8) 9164-8304; e-mail soci@iocomm.com.au; f. 1992 by Territories Law Reform Act to replace Christmas Island Services Corpn; provides local govt services; manages tourism and economic development; Pres. DAVID MCLANE; CEO DAVID PRICE.

Union of Christmas Island Workers—UCIW: Poon Saan Rd, POB 84, Christmas Island 6798, Indian Ocean; tel. (8) 9164-8471; fax (8) 9164-8470; e-mail uciw@pulau.cx; fmrly represented phosphate workers; Pres. FOO KEE HENG; Gen. Sec. GORDON THOMSON; 800 mems.

TRANSPORT

There are good roads in the developed areas. National Jet Systems operate a twice-weekly flight from Perth, via the Cocos (Keeling) Islands, and a private Christmas Island-based charter company operates services to Jakarta, Indonesia. In 1998 arrivals and departures by air in Christmas Island totalled 2,712 (compared with 3,895 in the previous year). The Australian National Line (ANL) operates ships to the Australian mainland. Cargo vessels from Fremantle deliver supplies to the island every four to six weeks. The Joint Island Supply System, established in 1989, provides a shipping service for Christmas Island and the Cocos Islands. The only anchorage is at Flying Fish Cove.

TOURISM

Tourism is a growing sector of the island's economy. Visitors are attracted by the unique flora and fauna, as well as the excellent conditions for scuba-diving and game-fishing. In 2000 there were approximately 90 hotel rooms on the island.

Christmas Island Tourism Association/Christmas Island Visitor Information Centre: POB 63, Christmas Island 6798, Indian Ocean; tel. (8) 9164-8382; fax (8) 9164-8080; e-mail cita@christmas.net.au; internet www.christmas.net.au; Tourism Co-ordinator TERESA HENDREN.

Christmas Island Tours and Travel: Christmas Island 6798, Indian Ocean; tel. (8) 9164-7168; fax (8) 9164-7169; e-mail xch@citravel.com.au; Dir TAN SIM KIAT.

Island Bound Travel: tel. (8) 9381-3644; fax (8) 9381 2030; e-mail info@islandbound.com.au.

Parks Australia: Christmas Island 6798, Indian Ocean; tel. (8) 9164-8700; fax (8) 9164-8755.

EDUCATION

The Christmas Island District High School, operated by the Western Australia Ministry of Education, provides education from pre-school level up to Australian 'year 10'. In 2001 enrolment totalled 24 pre-primary, 241 primary and 123 secondary pupils.

Cocos (Keeling) Islands

The Cocos (Keeling) Islands are 27 in number and lie 2,768 km north-west of Perth, in the Indian Ocean. The islands have an area of 14 sq km (5.4 sq miles) and form two low-lying coral atolls, densely covered with coconut palms. The climate is equable, with temperatures varying from 21°C (70°F) to 32°C (90°F), and rainfall of 2,000 mm per year. In 1981 some 58% of the population were of the Cocos Malay community, and 26% were Europeans. The Cocos Malays are descendants of the people brought to the islands by Alexander Hare and of labourers who were subsequently introduced by the Clunies-Ross family (see below). English is the official language, but Cocos Malay and Malay are also widely spoken. Most of the inhabitants are Muslims (56.8% in 1981). Home Island, which had a population of 446 in mid-1992, is where the Cocos Malay community is based. The only other inhabited island is West Island, with a population of 147 in mid-1992, and where most of the European community lives, the administration is based and the airport is located. The total population of the islands was 621 at both the 1998 and 2001 censuses, although official estimates had registered slight increases in the intervening years.

The islands were uninhabited when discovered by Capt. William Keeling, of the British East India Company, in 1609, and the first settlement was not established until 1826, by Alexander Hare. The islands were declared a British possession in 1857 and came successively under the authority of the Governors of Ceylon (now Sri Lanka), from 1878, and the Straits Settlements (now Singapore and part of Malaysia), from 1886. Also in 1886 the British Crown granted all land on the islands above the high-water mark to John Clunies-Ross and his heirs and successors in perpetuity. In 1946, when the islands became a dependency of the Colony of Singapore, a resident administrator, responsible to the Governor of Singapore, was appointed. Administration of the islands was transferred to the Commonwealth of Australia on 23 November 1955. The agent of the Australian Government was known as the Official Representative until 1975, when an Administrator was appointed. The Minister for Regional Services, Territories and Local Government is responsible for the governance of the islands. The Territory is part of the Northern Territory Electoral District.

In June 1977 the Australian Government announced new policies concerning the islands, which resulted in its purchase from John Clunies-Ross of the whole of his interests in the islands, with the exception of his residence and associated buildings. The purchase for $A6.5m. took effect on 1 September 1978. An attempt by the Australian Government to acquire Clunies-Ross' remaining property was deemed by the Australian High Court in October 1984 to be unconstitutional.

In July 1979 the Cocos (Keeling) Islands Council was established, with a wide range of functions in the Home Island village area (which the Government transferred to the Council on trust for the benefit of the Cocos Malay community) and, from September 1984, in the greater part of the rest of the Territory.

On 6 April 1984 a referendum to decide the future political status of the islands was held by the Australian Government, with UN observers present. A large majority voted in favour of integration with Australia. As a result, the islanders were to acquire the rights, privileges and obligations of all Australian citizens. In July 1992 the Cocos (Keeling) Islands Council was replaced by the Cocos (Keeling) Islands Shire Council, modelled on the local government and state law of Western Australia. The Clunies-Ross family was declared bankrupt in mid-1993, following unsuccessful investment in a shipping venture, and the Australian Government took possession of its property.

In September 2001, following an increase in the numbers of illegal immigrants reaching Australian waters (see the chapter on Christmas Island), legislation was passed removing the Cocos Islands and other territories from Australia's official migration zone. In October of that year the Australian Government sent contingency supplies to the islands as a precaution, should it be necessary to accommodate more asylum-seekers. This development provoked concern among many Cocos residents that the former quarantine station used as a detention centre might become a permanent asylum-processing facility under the order of the Australian Government. In December 123 Sri Lankan and Vietnamese asylum-seekers were housed at the station, which was built to accommodate only 40. They were transferred to Christmas Island in February 2002.

The Government admitted that the establishment of an asylum-processing facility on Cocos might become necessary.

Although local fishing is good, some livestock is kept and domestic gardens provide vegetables, bananas and papayas (pawpaws), the islands are not self-sufficient, and other foodstuffs, fuels and consumer items are imported from mainland Australia. A Cocos postal service (including a philatelic bureau) came into operation in September 1979, and revenue from the service is used for the benefit of the community. In early 2000 the islands' internet domain name suffix, '.cc' was sold to Clear Channel, a US radio group, thus providing additional revenue. The conversion of a disused quarantine station into a business centre was under consideration in 2001.

The cost of the islands' imports from Australia increased from $A5m. in 1999/2000 to $A11m. in 2000/01. Exports to Australia totalled $A2m. in 1996/97, but by 2002 the Cocos Islands no longer exported any goods or produce. A clam farm had been established in 2000 but had not progressed sufficiently to yield any export revenue. Coconuts, grown throughout the islands, are the sole cash crop: total output was an estimated 6,100 metric tons in 2000. In 2001/02 the Administration and the Shire provided the support for a study investigating the potential economic benefits of various coconut products, including the production of high-quality carbon from coconut kernels, and the manufacture of furniture from coconut palm wood. The Grants Commission estimated that the Australian Government's net funding of the territory was some $A18m. in 1999. In 2000/01 the Cocos Administration expended approximately $A9m. An estimated 19% of the total labour force was unemployed in 2001, 60% of whom were under the age of 30.

Statistical Survey

AREA AND POPULATION

Area: 14.2 sq km (5.5 sq miles).

Population: 655 (males 338, females 317) at census of 30 June 1996; 621 (males 334, females 287) at census of 7 August 2001. *Ethnic Groups* (census of 30 June 1981): Cocos Malay 320; European 143; Total (incl. others) 555. Source: mainly UN, *Demographic Yearbook*.

Density (2001): 43.7 per sq km.

Births and Deaths (1986): Registered live births 12 (birth rate 19.8 per 1,000); Registered deaths 2.

Labour Force (2001): 270 (employed 218, unemployed 52).

Source: Indian Ocean Group Training.

AGRICULTURE

Production (FAO estimates, metric tons, 2000): Coconuts 6,100; Copra 1,000. Source: FAO.

FINANCE

Currency and Exchange Rates: Australian currency is used (see p. 118).

EXTERNAL TRADE

Principal Commodities (metric tons, year ending 30 June 1985): *Exports*: Coconuts 202. *Imports*: Most requirements come from Australia. The trade deficit is offset by philatelic sales and Australian federal grants and subsidies.

2000/01 ($A '000): *Imports:* Australia 11,000.
Source: *Year Book Australia*.

COMMUNICATIONS MEDIA

Radio Receivers (1992): 300 in use.

Personal computers (home users, 2001): 142.

Internet users (2001): 618.

EDUCATION

Pre-primary (2002): 23 pupils.

Primary (2002): 84 pupils.

Secondary (2002): 31 pupils.

Teaching staff (2002): 18.

Source: Education Department of Western Australia.

Directory

THE GOVERNMENT

The Administrator, appointed by the Governor-General of Australia and responsible to the Minister for Regional Services, Territories and Local Government, is the senior government representative in the islands.

Administrator: WILLIAM TAYLOR (non-resident).

Administrative Offices: POB 1093, West Island, Cocos (Keeling) Islands 6799, Indian Ocean; tel. (8) 9162-6615; fax (8) 9162-6697.

Cocos (Keeling) Islands Shire Council: POB 94, Home Island, Cocos (Keeling) Islands 6799, Indian Ocean; tel. (8) 9162-6649; fax (8) 9162-6668; e-mail info@shire.cc; f. 1992 by Territories Law Reform Act; Pres. MOHAMMED SAID CHONGKIN; CEO BOB JARVIS.

JUDICIAL SYSTEM

Supreme Court, Cocos (Keeling) Islands: West Island Police Station, Cocos (Keeling) Islands 6799, Indian Ocean; tel. (8) 9162-6615; fax (8) 9162-6697; Judge: ROBERT SHERATON FRENCH; Additional Judge: MALCOLM CAMERON LEE.

Magistrates' Court, Cocos (Keeling) Islands: Special Magistrate: (vacant).

Managing Registrar: MARGARET BUCKHOUSE; Cocos (Keeling) Islands 6799, Indian Ocean; tel. (8) 9162-6615; fax (8) 9162-6697.

RELIGION

According to the census of 1981, of the 555 residents, 314 (some 57%) were Muslims and 124 (22%) Christians. The majority of Muslims live on Home Island, while most Christians are West Island residents. The Cocos Islands lie within both the Anglican and the Roman Catholic archdioceses of Perth (Western Australia).

BROADCASTING

Radio

Radio VKW Cocos: POB 33, Cocos (Keeling) Islands 6799, Indian Ocean; tel. (8) 9162-6666; e-mail vkw@kampong.cc; non-commercial; daily broadcasting service in Cocos Malay and English; 200 listeners; Station Man. CATHERINE CLUNIES-ROSS.

Television

A television service, broadcasting Indonesian, Malaysian and Australian satellite television programmes and videotapes of Australian television programmes, began operating on an intermittent basis in September 1992.

INDUSTRY

Cocos (Keeling) Islands Co-operative Society Ltd: Home Island, Cocos (Keeling) Islands 6799, Indian Ocean; tel. (8) 9162-6702; fax (8) 9162-6764; f. 1979; conducts the business enterprises of the Cocos Islanders; activities include boat construction and repairs, copra and coconut production, sail-making, stevedoring and airport operation; owns and operates a supermarket and tourist accommodation; Chair. MOHAMMED SAID BIN CHONGKIN; Gen. Man. RONALD TAYLOR.

TRANSPORT

National Jet Systems operate a twice-weekly service from Perth, via Christmas Island, for passengers, supplies and mail to and from the airport on West Island. Cargo vessels from Singapore and Perth deliver supplies, at intervals of four to six weeks.

Cocos Trader: Cocos (Keeling) Islands 6799, Indian Ocean; tel. (8) 9162-6612; fax (8) 9162-6568; e-mail manpower@kampong.cc; shipping agent.

TOURISM

Cocos Island Tourism Association: POB 30, Cocos (Keeling) Islands 6799, Indian Ocean; tel. (8) 9162-6790; fax (8) 9162-6696; e-mail info@cocos-tourism.cc.

EDUCATION

Primary education is provided at the schools on Home and West Islands. Secondary education is provided to the age of 16 years on West Island. A bursary scheme enables Cocos Malay children to continue their education on the Australian mainland.

Heard Island and the McDonald Islands

These islands are situated about 4,000 km (2,500 miles) south-west of Perth, Western Australia. The Territory, consisting of Heard Island, Shag Island (8 km north of Heard) and the McDonald Islands, is almost entirely covered in ice and has a total area of 369 sq km (142 sq miles). Sovereignty was transferred from the United Kingdom to the Commonwealth of Australia on 26 December 1947, following the establishment by Australia of a scientific research station on Heard Island (which functioned until March 1955). The islands are administered by the Antarctic Division of the Australian Department of the Environment and Heritage. There are no permanent inhabitants. However, in 1991 evidence emerged of a Polynesian community on Heard Island some 700 years before the territory's discovery by European explorers. The island is of considerable scientific interest, as it is believed to be one of the few Antarctic habitats uncontaminated by introduced organisms. Heard Island is about 44 km long and 20 km wide and possesses an active volcano, named Big Ben. In January 1991 an international team of scientists travelled to Heard Island to conduct research involving the transmission of sound waves, beneath the surface of the ocean, in order to monitor any evidence of the 'greenhouse effect' (melting of polar ice and the rise in sea-level as a consequence of pollution). The pulses of sound, which travel at a speed largely influenced by temperature, were to be received at various places around the world, with international co-operation. Heard Island was chosen for the experiment because of its unique location, from which direct paths to the five principal oceans extend. The McDonald Islands, with an area of about 1 sq km (0.4 sq miles), lie some 42 km west of Heard Island. In late 1997 Heard Island and the McDonald Islands were accorded World Heritage status by UNESCO in recognition of their outstanding universal significance as a natural landmark. In 1999 concern was expressed that stocks of the Patagonian toothfish in the waters around the islands were becoming depleted as a result of over-exploitation, mainly by illegal operators. In 2001 the Australian Government's Antarctic Division conducted a five-month scientific expedition to Heard Island. It claimed that glacial cover had retreated by 12% since 1947 as a result of global warming.

BANGLADESH

Physical and Social Geography

B. H. FARMER

With additions by the editorial staff

The People's Republic of Bangladesh covers an area of 147,570 sq km (56,977 sq miles). It straddles the Tropic of Cancer, extending between 20° 30′ and 26° 45′ N, and between 88° 0′ and 92° 40′ E. It is wholly enclosed by Indian territory, except for a short south-eastern frontier with Myanmar (formerly Burma) and a southern, deltaic coast fronting the Bay of Bengal. From the conclusion of British rule in August 1947 until the end of the Indo-Pakistan war of December 1971, Bangladesh constituted the eastern wing of Pakistan: that is, East Pakistan or East Bengal. Bangladesh became formally independent following the capitulation of Pakistani military and civilian authorities on 16 December 1971. The capital is Dhaka.

PHYSICAL FEATURES AND SOILS

Most of Bangladesh consists of an alluvial plain, largely made up of the still-growing, annually-flooded Ganges-Brahmaputra delta, together with a tongue of similar wet plain running up the Surma river between the Assam plateau and the Lushai hills (both in India; though Bangladesh includes a very small portion of lower foothills country, on the Assam boundary, which contains some tea plantations). As in West Bengal (India), belts of older and less fertile deposits lend some little diversity to the plains: notably in the regions known as Barind and the Madhupur jungle tract. To the east of the delta lie the Chittagong Hill Tracts, an area of steep, roughly parallel ranges largely covered with jungle, much of it bamboo.

For the most part, however, Bangladesh is deltaic, and its rural people have evolved a remarkable semi-aquatic life style adapted to deep flooding in the monsoon: for instance, by constructing earthen plinths 4 m or more high to raise their houses above flood-level (or so they hope) and by sowing varieties of rice that will grow in deep water.

Much of Bangladesh has relatively fertile alluvial soils, many of them benefiting from renewal by flooding. There is considerable local variation: for example, areas of sandy soils on the one hand, and of swamp soils on the other (alluvium varying with the rivers that brought it), in addition to Barind and the Madhupur jungle tract. The Chittagong hills have poor skeletal soils.

CLIMATE

The climate of Bangladesh is tropical and is dominated by the seasonally-reversing monsoons. There is no real cool season. In the capital, Dhaka, for example, the average January temperature is 19°C, and the average July temperature 29°C. The 'summer', if it can be called such, is remarkably equable: the average monthly temperature is 29°C from May right through to September. The 'winter' is dry, and crops (in the absence of irrigation or of water-holding depressions, where winter rice can be grown) have to depend on moisture remaining in the soil from the monsoon. There are pre-monsoon rains in April and May, but it is the south-west monsoon that brings heavy rain in earnest: 75% of Dhaka's annual average total of 1,880 mm falls between June and September. Bangladesh has, in fact, a typical humid tropical monsoon climate; but it is a climate subject to violence from time to time, for example when a tropical cyclone, charged with energy and with water vapour and accompanied by high winds, sweeps in and devastates low-lying areas in the coastal parts of the delta. Such 'extreme natural events' tend also to bring high seas and flooding with salt water, so that there is damage to the soil as well as severe loss of life and of crops.

NATURAL RESOURCES

Bangladesh has small reserves of petroleum and coal, and potentially vast resources of natural gas. Gas production began in 1960, and a significant breakthrough occurred in 1995 with the discovery of Sangu, Bangladesh's first offshore field. In 1999/2000 there were approximately 20 gas fields, of which one-half were active. Natural gas provides 70% of Bangladesh's commercial energy. In mid-2002 the country's proven natural gas reserves were estimated at between 12,000,000m. and 15,500,000m. cu ft. Bangladesh has the potential to become a major gas producer and supplier to domestic and external markets. However, many Bangladeshis believe that gas resources should be used for domestic purposes first; both major political parties will consider gas exports only if Bangladesh has sufficient proven reserves to meet 50 years of domestic demand. Bangladesh's petroleum reserves amount to an estimated 56.9m. barrels, with production at about 1,600 barrels per day.

POPULATION

According to the provisional results of the census of March 2001, Bangladesh had a population of 123,151,246, giving an average density of 834.5 per sq km. Apart from territories comprising less than 1,200 sq km in area, Bangladesh is the most densely populated country in the world, despite its overwhelmingly rural and agricultural nature. Even then, average densities are misleading: the density of population is lower than the average in such areas as Barind and the Madhupur jungle tract, and higher than the very high average in other areas, notably those along the lower Padma and Meghna rivers. Bangladesh has one rapidly-growing conurbation, that around the capital, Dhaka, with a population of 3,637,892 (including suburbs) at the March 1991 census. Chittagong, the principal seaport, had a population of 1,566,070 in 1991.

Bangla (Bengali) is the principal language in Bangladesh (as it is in Indian West Bengal), but English is widely used. Some tribal peoples retain their own languages.

History

DAVID TAYLOR

Based on an earlier article by PETER ROBB

Bangladesh has roots in the medieval past, with the consolidation of regional differences between Bengal and other parts of South Asia, and in the distinctions between Bengali Muslims and Hindus, which probably date from the activities of Muslim saints in the 13th century and from subsequent non-Bengali Muslim rulers. By the 20th century Muslims constituted just over one-half of the population of the region, being more heavily concentrated in the eastern districts which are now Bangladesh. The majority were poor, rural and, in many ways, still strongly influenced by the Hinduism from which they had converted. They had initially been relatively little affected by British rule after 1765, which had most impact on the service and landed élites of the region, but in the late 19th century and in the present century the distinctions between ordinary Hindus and Muslims were seen to have been strengthened and made politically relevant by legal, administrative and economic changes. Even so, Indian Muslim support for the political partition of the subcontinent was drawn particularly not from Bengal but from areas where Muslims were in the minority, and as late as 1937 the Muslim League (ML) was electorally ineffective in Bengal in comparison with the local Krishak Proja Samiti of Fazlul Huq.

Nevertheless, Bengali Muslims, too, were drawn into electoral politics and agitation by religious motivation, and many of them came to be persuaded in the 1940s of the advantages to them of the Pakistan idea. In 1943 an ML ministry was formed in Bengal, marking the advance of its propaganda and its alliance with prominent Bengalis.*

EAST PAKISTAN, 1947–71

East Bengal duly became part of Pakistan in 1947, but its people soon came to distrust their partners in the West. East Bengal experienced an influx of officials and merchants, and was at a disadvantage nationally because of the establishment of Urdu as the national language and because of low representation in the army, which was to be the major organ of the Pakistani state. A rising Bengali middle class fostered agitation, which led to concessions that were mainly too few and too late, or undermined by the hard line that was adopted by some of Pakistan's military rulers.

The malcontents came to be led by Sheikh Mujibur Rahman (Mujib) and his Awami League (AL), which advocated the limitation of the central authority to defence and foreign affairs and the retention by each wing of its own economic resources. Mujib was imprisoned in 1966, but released in 1969 with the fall of the President, Field-Marshal Muhammad Ayub Khan. Elections were held in December 1970. The AL was assisted in its campaign by the devastation of the East by flooding, the West being blamed for negligence in sending relief; the AL won all but two of the East's seats in both provincial and national assemblies. President Yahya Khan refused to allow Mujib to become Prime Minister on the basis of the AL's manifesto of complete regional autonomy for East Pakistan, and insisted that he share power with Zulfikar Ali Bhutto, whose party had won the majority of the seats in West Pakistan. Subsequent talks regarding the impasse proved fruitless. The deadlock was broken by a general strike, the AL's seizure of power (10 March 1971), and its declaration of Bangladeshi independence (26 March). This last event was in direct response to a fierce army crackdown the previous day. Large numbers of Bengalis were massacred. Mujib himself was arrested and taken to West Pakistan, but many of his colleagues fled to India where they established a government-in-exile. Millions of refugees also flooded into India, which, on 4 December, invaded in support of the Mukti Bahini ('freedom fighters') and other irregular Bengali groups operating inside East Pakistan. The campaign was brief and successful, and Pakistan's military and civilian authorities capitulated on 16 December. Bangladesh's independence thus became a reality. While the Indian army had played the decisive role at the end of the civil war, the Bengali guerrilla groups and those Bengali troops based in East Pakistan who had deserted *en masse* to join the liberation struggle had also been instrumental in harassing and hindering the Pakistani forces.

INDEPENDENT BANGLADESH

The new country gained prompt international recognition, but was beset by enormous difficulties. There were delicate diplomatic issues to be resolved, and a pressing need for international aid. The loss of professionals through the murder of Bengalis and the removal of Punjabis and other West Pakistanis led to serious staffing problems in commerce and the public services. A problem of order was exacerbated by the failure of the so-called guerrilla groups to disband completely, and by campaigns against the Bihari Muslim minority, who had been arriving in East Pakistan since 1947: as Urdu-speakers, the Biharis' loyalty was held to be suspect. The change of regime made no contribution to the region's economic problems, and the participation of India raised the spectre of another colonialism to replace those of the past.

Sheikh Mujib, released from prison in Pakistan following the end of the civil war, returned to Bangladesh as its first President and was popularly acclaimed as *Bangabandhu* ('Friend of Bengal'). A new, secular and parliamentary Constitution was rapidly promulgated (under which Mujib became Prime Minister) and fresh legislative elections were held in March 1973; these gave the AL a massive majority of 292 out of a total of 300 seats. On 22 February 1974 Pakistan formally recognized Bangladesh's existence and diplomatic relations were established between the two countries. Domestic political stability was not easily maintained, however. Opposition groups of both extremes resorted to terrorism, including Islamist fundamentalists opposed to secession and secularism, and Maoist groups co-operating with Indian Naxalites. In October 1973 the AL formed an alliance with the Communist Party and the pro-Soviet wing of the National Awami Party with a joint policy of suppressing terrorism. A militia, the Rakkhi Bahini, was formed to assist the police. Economic problems also mounted. In July and August 1974 disastrous floods exacerbated an already desperate situation and led to widespread famine. In some areas prices rose by 400%, and there was talk of official corruption, even close to the still-popular Mujib. At the end of December the Government declared a state of emergency and all fundamental rights guaranteed by the Constitution were suspended. Four weeks later the Jatiya Sangsad (Parliament) adopted a Constitution Bill, which replaced the parliamentary with a presidential form of government and provided for the introduction of a one-party system. Mujib became President, assuming absolute powers, and created the Bangladesh Krishak-Sramik (Peasants and Workers) Awami League, excluding all other parties from government.

Coup and Counter-Coup

If nothing else, Bangladesh's independence struggle had created a local military power-base, elements of which were bound to play a political role. They began to do so on 15 August 1975, when a group of discontented young army officers staged a military coup, assassinated Mujib and almost all of his family, and installed Khandakar Mushtaq Ahmed, the former Minister of Commerce, in power. The coup was interpreted by many as the work of pro-West elements disturbed by Mujib's policies, but the young officers who carried out the murders were also

* For earlier history, see also the chapter on India.

driven by personal grievances. The new regime was patently weak, and on 3 November the expected counter-coup took place. In a period of confusion Brig. Khalid Musharaf, a pro-Mujib figure, came briefly to power, and the leaders of the August coup were exiled. However, a former Prime Minister, Tajuddin Ahmed, and other former associates of Mujib, who had been imprisoned after the August coup, were murdered in gaol in Dhaka. On 6 November serious fighting broke out in the Dhaka cantonment between Brig. Musharaf's supporters and left-wing soldiers who suspected his alleged pro-India leanings, in which Musharaf and many others were killed.

Musharaf had forced Mushtaq Ahmed to resign as President in favour of the Chief Justice, Abu Sadat Mohammad Sayem, who was sworn in on 6 November 1975 itself. On the next day, following Musharaf's death, President Sayem became Chief Martial Law Administrator, but real power was exercised by the Chief of Army Staff, Maj.-Gen. Ziaur Rahman (Gen. Zia). One of the most famous of the protagonists in the liberation struggle, Gen. Zia had been imprisoned by Brig. Musharaf, but had been freed by the left-wing soldiers on 6 November. Once in power, however, he moved swiftly to consolidate his position. One of the most important of the left-wing radicals, Lt-Col (retd) Abu Taher, was put on trial and subsequently executed.

The Zia Regime

Gen. Zia initially promised an early return to representative government. From August 1976 political parties were permitted to operate, providing that their manifesto had been approved by the Government. District council elections were held in February 1977, but the general election foreseen for that date was postponed indefinitely in November 1976. The major political change was the supremacy of the army and the end of AL rule. This change was consolidated by the arrest of Mushtaq Ahmed and other possible opponents in November 1976, and by Gen. Zia's assumption first of the powers of Chief Martial Law Administrator, and then of the presidency in April 1977, following the resignation of President Sayem.

In May 1977 a national referendum resulted in a 99% vote in favour of the President and his martial rule policies. A presidential election in June 1978 confirmed this position, and in July the Council of Advisers was replaced by a 28-member Council of Ministers. In September the President formed a new party, the Bangladesh Jatiyatabadi Dal (Bangladesh Nationalist Party—BNP), after a failed attempt to create a 'grand coalition'. In December the President's 'undemocratic' powers were abolished, and in January 1979 a number of political prisoners were released. In February the delayed elections to the Jatiya Sangsad were finally held. Major opposition parties had agreed to take part, after prolonged manoeuvring. A 40% poll produced a two-thirds' majority for the President's allies. In March Azizur Rahman took over as Prime Minister. A new Government was formed, and at the beginning of April martial law was lifted.

Zia's political position was strengthened by the inability of the opposition to present a united front. Several groups broke away from the AL, and an attempt by the opposition to boycott the Jatiya Sangsad in 1980 failed. (However, the BNP itself was not immune to such factional quarrels.) Zia also benefited from his efforts to give the country a more specifically Islamic tone, in contrast to the secular approach of the AL. In April 1977 the Constitution had been amended so as to make the country officially an Islamic republic, although there were few immediate consequences. As part both of his political and of his economic strategies, Zia gave considerable attention to rural development. He made a number of highly publicized visits to rural areas to take part in local development projects. In an effort to galvanize the rural areas, where the pre-1947 system of government remained in place with few alterations, he introduced a new system of local self-government based on *gram sarkars* or village governments. Despite these initiatives, which reflected considerable dynamism and vision, Zia failed to change the culture of Bangladesh politics. Indeed, with his largely personal and non-ideological style of rule he remained very much part of it. The most serious problem he faced was that of asserting his power over the army, which had been his initial vehicle of power. He had quickly distanced himself from the radical left in the army (see above), but he had had to deal with at least six mutinies in the armed forces, and showed no hesitation in suppressing them with considerable force. In the end, however, personal rivalries among the senior officers led to the murder of Gen. Zia in Chittagong on 30 May 1981. The details are uncertain: if a coup was planned, it was poorly carried out, and its leader, Maj.-Gen. Mohammad Abdul Manzur (an army divisional commander only recently sent to Chittagong), was soon captured and then killed in confused circumstances. The country drew back from civil war and waited 180 days for a new president. Once again, a president had been removed by a disappointed former ally, who would fail to succeed to power.

Zia's Vice-President, Abdus Sattar, became acting Head of State pending a presidential election, which he won in November 1981. He was elected mainly in the interests of continuity and for the memory of Zia, but he was elderly and in poor health, and was soon embroiled in a struggle with the military under the Chief of Army Staff, Lt-Gen. Hossain Mohammad Ershad. Ershad denied personal ambition, but in January 1982 persuaded Sattar to establish a National Security Council, formally involving the military chiefs in the Government. The civilians were divided among themselves, and Sattar was beginning to lose control, when, on 24 March 1982, the expected coup took place. As a result, Gen. Ershad succeeded to supreme power as Chief Martial Law Administrator (in December 1983 he also proclaimed himself President), while Sattar himself blamed the take-over on the deterioration of law and order.

Consolidation of Gen. Ershad's Rule

Ershad enjoyed less immediate support than had Zia, but his strategies of political rule were quite similar. The rural areas were seen as the key to his survival, and a new system of local government was introduced to replace the *gram sarkars*. This system was based on the introduction of elected councils at the *upazilla* or sub-district level. The hope was that the distribution of development funds through this mechanism would create a class of political intermediaries tied to the regime through patronage. Regular elections were indeed held, and attracted ambitious local politicians. Ershad also attempted, unsuccessfully, to give the army an institutional role in politics. At the national level, however, and on the streets of Dhaka and the other major cities it proved harder for Ershad to consolidate his position, even though he eventually created his own party, the Jatiya Dal (National Party), to attract those keen to advance towards power. Resentment of Ershad's blatant seizure of power and his subsequent corrupt behaviour meant that the existing opposition parties mostly sank their differences to present a united front. Political unrest in the form of strikes and demonstrations became endemic from an early stage, and Ershad's attempts to hold elections were blocked. In 1985 he responded by holding a referendum on his position as President, which allegedly produced a 94% vote in his favour. The year 1987 witnessed particularly widespread protests organized jointly by almost all the opposition parties, and on 27 November a state of emergency was declared. Demonstrations continued, however, and many people were killed or injured in clashes with the police. A fresh general election was held in March 1988, but the opposition boycott was largely successful. The state of emergency was repealed in the following month. The March 1988 elections produced, in effect, a political stalemate. The opposition continued its agitation, but could not dislodge Ershad from power. In April 1990 Ershad declared that he would present himself as a candidate in the presidential election scheduled to be held in mid-1991. Demonstrations against the Government began again in October 1990. As often before, the epicentre of the unrest was the campus of Dhaka University. To maintain their popular credibility, both Sheikh Hasina Wajed (daughter of Sheikh Mujib and leader of an alliance of eight parties around the AL) and Begum Khaleda Zia (Zia's widow and the leader of another opposition group, of seven parties, headed by the BNP) lent their support to the students. In late November Ershad was forced to impose a new state of emergency, but this action did not succeed in preventing a massive wave of strikes and violent demonstrations throughout the country. Consequently, Ershad resigned, a few days later, on 4 December and the state of emergency was lifted. The Chief Justice, Shahabuddin Ahmed, assumed the post of acting President (in his capacity as Vice-President) and was put at the head of a neutral caretaker

Government pending fresh parliamentary elections. Ershad was placed under house arrest (he was later sentenced to 20 years' imprisonment for illegal possession of firearms and other offences). Apart from the unity and determination of the opposition, notably amongst the students, the key factor in Ershad's downfall was the attitude of the army. Lt-Gen. Muhammad Atiqur Rahman, who held the post of Chief of Army Staff from the time that Ershad relinquished the position in 1986 until his retirement in August 1990, was an Ershad loyalist. His successor, Lt-Gen. Nooruddin Khan, by contrast, adopted a detached stance and refused to allow the army to be used for political purposes. Yet for 10 years Ershad, himself a professional soldier, had been able to retain the support of the army and, in return, had ensured that its material interests were catered to. No civilian regime, of whatever political hue, could hope to survive in Bangladesh if the army were not in some way accommodated.

Democracy Restored

With the new acting President installed, moves were quickly implemented to hold fresh parliamentary elections. The two main participants were the AL alliance and the BNP alliance. After a vigorous campaign, the elections were held on 27 February 1991. Slightly counter to pre-election estimates, the BNP won 138 of the 294 seats for which results were declared. A few days after the election, the BNP was ensured a small working majority in the Jatiya Sangsad, following discussions with the Jamaat-e-Islami, and was, thus, enabled to appoint deputies to 28 of the 30 parliamentary seats reserved for women. Begum Khaleda Zia assumed office as Prime Minister on 19 March at the head of a new Government, which included many of her late husband's colleagues, as well as several senior bureaucrats. On 1 May, only two months after its accession to power, the Government had to contend with the immense difficulties resulting from a devastating cyclone, which killed up to 250,000 people and caused huge economic damage. Criticism of the apparent lack of alacrity with which the administrative machinery responded to the crisis was widespread.

In August 1991 the Jatiya Sangsad approved a constitutional amendment ending 16 years of presidential rule and restoring the Prime Minister as executive leader (under the previous system, both the Prime Minister and the Council of Ministers had been answerable to the President). The amendment, which was formally enforced when it was approved by national referendum in the following month, reduced the role of President, who was now to be elected by the Jatiya Sangsad for a five-year term, to that of a titular Head of State. Accordingly, a new President was elected by the Jatiya Sangsad on 8 October. The successful candidate was the BNP nominee, the erstwhile Speaker of the Jatiya Sangsad, Abdur Rahman Biswas, who received 172 of the 264 votes cast. In September the BNP had gained an absolute majority in the Jatiya Sangsad, following the party's victory in five of the 11 by-elections.

As elsewhere in South Asia, the new Government decided to pursue a policy of economic restructuring, with the help of aid donors, in an attempt to achieve more sustained growth. This entailed the transfer to private ownership of public-sector industries and the imposition of curbs on labour unrest. The Government also moved to dismantle a number of the institutions established under Ershad's regime, in particular the *upazilla* system of local administration, which had been introduced in 1982. These measures evoked some resistance from those immediately affected, but this alone does not explain the fierce and sustained opposition campaign, which was launched by the AL and other parties almost as soon as the new Government had been installed. Deep personal antipathy between Sheikh Hasina Wajed and Begum Khaleda Zia, which had only barely been concealed during the anti-Ershad movement, was one factor, while no political party appeared willing to trust the democratic credentials of its opponents. In April 1992, in an apparent attempt to destabilize the Government, accusations were made against the leader of the Jamaat-e-Islami, Golam Azam, of complicity in Pakistani war crimes in 1971 and of having remained a Pakistani citizen while participating in Bangladesh politics. The AL MPs boycotted the Jatiya Sangsad over the issue and demanded that Azam be put on trial immediately before a special tribunal; in late June, however, the matter was resolved when a compromise was reached.

In the latter half of 1992 the opposition parties launched a series of campaigns against the Government in the hope of rekindling the spirit of the anti-Ershad movements. In mid-August the Government survived a parliamentary motion of 'no confidence', introduced by the AL, by 168 votes to 122. The opposition accused the Government of failing to curb the increasing lawlessness in the country, notably amongst university students. The stringent anti-terrorism measures introduced by the Government in November, however, were widely criticized as being excessively harsh and undemocratic. Subsequently, the opposition parties sank their differences in pursuit of a common demand that the general election due in 1996 be held under the auspices of a neutral, caretaker government. This requisition was based on claims that the Government would misuse its powers in order to engage in electoral malpractice (the AL persistently accused the Government of vote-rigging in the 1991 general election and subsequent by-elections). Many large-scale demonstrations and strikes were organized by the opposition from November 1993 onwards, including, for example, a two-week-long agitation in the second half of March 1995. Some of these events primarily affected the capital, Dhaka, but others were nation-wide. Force had to be used to quell the disturbances, and there were regular fatalities. At the end of 1994 all the opposition members of the Jatiya Sangsad, who had for the preceding nine months boycotted parliamentary sessions, submitted their resignations in an attempt to precipitate a constitutional crisis, but without success. A couple of months earlier, an envoy sent by the Commonwealth Secretariat, Sir Ninian Stephen, had attempted to mediate a solution by which an all-party government under BNP leadership would assume power to oversee the forthcoming elections. However, this proposal was rejected by the opposition parties.

Despite the strength and extent of the street protests, the occasional tests of electoral opinion produced mixed results. In January 1994 the AL won the mayoralties of Dhaka and Chittagong, the country's two largest cities, but in March a by-election success revealed the continuing strength of the BNP elsewhere. Begum Khaleda Zia seemed able during the protests to maintain control of her own party. Wherever possible, however, she took steps to appease sections of the opposition. In September 1994 she cancelled a visit to the UN-sponsored International Conference on Population and Development in Cairo as a gesture to Islamic elements. In response to a severe shortage of fertilizer in late 1994, a situation that threatened to embarrass the Government, the Prime Minister dismissed the minister immediately responsible. In June 1995 former President Ershad was acquitted of illegally possessing arms; his sentence was thus reduced to 10 years. In the following month, however, Ershad was sentenced to a further three years' imprisonment for criminal misconduct.

A significant development in 1993 and 1994 demonstrated that there were forces beyond the immediate control of the Government—namely, the campaign against the feminist writer and publicist, Taslima Nasreen. The campaign was launched in September 1993, following the publication of Nasreen's novel dealing with the hostility to the Hindu minority in Bangladesh, which had manifested itself after the demolition in December 1992 of the mosque at Ayodhya in Uttar Pradesh, India (see chapter on India). The campaign was renewed in May 1994 after the controversial author had given an interview to an Indian newspaper in which she was reported as having said that the Koran needed to be revised to take account of women's issues. Despite her claim that she had been misquoted, there were outraged demands from Islamic bodies in Bangladesh that Nasreen should be executed. The Government issued a warrant for her arrest on blasphemy-related charges, although she had gone into hiding before it could be implemented. Islamist fundamentalists were also accused of instigating attacks on women who were considered to have broken traditional norms of behaviour, and of attempting to obstruct the work of non-governmental organizations (NGOs) involved in areas such as female literacy. In August, with the apparent help of government officials, Nasreen secretly fled Bangladesh and was granted refuge in Sweden. In response, the fundamentalists, led by the Jamaat-e-Islami (which had now abandoned its parliamentary support for the BNP), vowed to attack the Government for seemingly permitting the author's departure.

Despite an escalation in opposition agitation, which frequently brought the country's economy to a near halt, the Government refused to make concessions regarding the key issue of allowing the forthcoming general election to be held under neutral auspices; consequently, all of the main opposition parties boycotted the election, which was held on 15 February 1996. Independent monitors estimated the turn-out at only about 10%–15% of the electorate. The BNP, as virtually the only serious participant in the polls, won an overwhelming victory and claimed that it had, thus, achieved a mandate for a further term in power. Of the 207 legislative seats declared by the end of February, the BNP had won 205 (a partial repoll had been ordered in most of the 93 remaining constituencies where violence had disrupted the electoral process). The opposition refused to recognize the legitimacy of the polls and announced the launch of a 'non-co-operation' movement against the Government. Renewed street protest made the country practically ungovernable and, ultimately, pressure from the army and other sources forced Begum Khaleda Zia to agree to the holding of fresh elections under neutral auspices, as the opposition had demanded all along. The Prime Minister and her Government duly resigned from their posts on 30 March and the Jatiya Sangsad was dissolved. President Biswas appointed the former Chief Justice, Muhammad Habibur Rahman, as acting Prime Minister and asked that a fresh general election be held, under the auspices of an interim neutral government, within three months. A new election commissioner was also appointed who was considered to be both effective and impartial.

The general election was held on 12 June 1996, with the participation of all of the country's major political parties. The turn-out was high, at an estimated 73%, and three separate teams of international observers reported that, in their view, the polls had been free and fair. There existed only minor differences between the main parties, and those were over issues of economic policy; consequently, the electoral contest centred on general perceptions of the parties and their leaders. In the event, the AL won 146 of the 300 elective seats in the Jatiya Sangsad, the BNP 116, the Jatiya Dal 32 and the Jamaat-e-Islami three. An understanding was quickly reached between the AL and the Jatiya Dal, whose main interest was the release of Ershad, who had gained a legislative seat from within prison. Sheikh Hasina Wajed was sworn in as the new Prime Minister on 23 June. Her Council of Ministers incorporated one member from the Jatiya Dal; it also included a number of retired officials and army officers.

During the electoral campaign an abortive military coup attempt took place, which indicated the continuing fragility of the country's institutions. The Chief of Army Staff, Lt-Gen. Abu Saleh Mohammed Nasim, who had objected to the action of the President (who retained direct control of the armed forces during the caretaker period prior to the general election) in dismissing some senior officers for political activity, endeavoured to seize power, but was unable to mobilize sufficient support to achieve his aim. Lt-Gen. Nasim was immediately dismissed, and a new Chief of Army Staff was appointed. The fact that the attempted coup was rapidly and bloodlessly suppressed indicated the reluctance of the majority to return to military rule.

The AL was quickly able to establish a reasonably firm political base for itself. On 23 July 1996 the AL's presidential nominee, retired Chief Justice and former acting President, Shahabuddin Ahmed, was elected unopposed as Bangladesh's new Head of State. Of the 30 parliamentary seats reserved for women, the AL won 27 and the Jatiya Dal three, thus giving the AL an absolute majority in the Jatiya Sangsad. Ershad was released from prison at the beginning of 1997, thereby fulfilling the terms of the AL's election agreement with the Jatiya Dal. The AL Government continued to pursue the policies of economic restructuring adopted by its predecessor, although a great deal of effort was also invested in reopening the case against the assassins of Sheikh Mujib. In November 1996 the Jatiya Sangsad voted unanimously to repeal the indemnity law that had been enacted in 1975 to protect the perpetrators of the military coup in that year; the BNP and the Jamaat-e-Islami, however, boycotted the vote. In November 1998 a Dhaka court sentenced to death 15 of the 19 people accused of Mujib's assassination; four of the defendants were acquitted. Efforts to complete the judicial process were, however, hindered by the reluctance of judges to hear appeals in what was inevitably seen as a politically motivated case. Only four of those convicted were actually in custody in Bangladesh; the 11 others remained fugitives abroad. In April 2000 the Chief Justice established a two-judge bench to review the sentences. By April 2001 the High Court had upheld 12 of the sentences and acquitted three of those originally convicted. In May Bangladesh signed an extradition treaty with the USA, to increase the prospects of the transfer of three defendants, reportedly living in the USA, to the Bangladeshi authorities. In mid-June a defendant in hiding in Zimbabwe died.

The opposition parties, the BNP in particular, viewed agitational politics as the optimum mode of effecting the downfall of the Government. Claims were made that the AL was rigging by-elections, and from mid-November 1996 these assertions were used by the BNP as a reason to boycott parliamentary proceedings. From 1997 the opposition organized a continuous programme of strikes and demonstrations, citing grievances such as tax and price increases and general shortages, as well as claims that the Government was betraying national interests over issues such as the water-sharing agreement with India and the Chittagong Hill Tracts (see below). On occasion, these demonstrations turned violent and resulted in substantial loss of life (as in February and April 1999). The BNP's foremost demand was for the holding of fresh elections, echoing the AL's earlier campaign. The AL, however, strengthened its electoral and parliamentary position through a series of by-election victories. The departure, therefore, of the Jatiya Dal from the coalition in March 1998 had little effect on the ruling party's hold on power. In June and August Begum Khaleda Zia, along with others associated with her Government, was indicted on charges of corruption and abuse of power, allegedly perpetrated during her tenure of the premiership. In December 1998 the opposition was strengthened by a decision by the BNP and the Jamaat-e-Islami to accept Ershad and the Jatiya Dal in the anti-Government movement without any conditions. In August 2000 Ershad received a reduced sentence of five years' imprisonment and was ordered to pay 54m. taka for misappropriating funds during his tenure of power between 1983 and 1990. He began his term of imprisonment, which was reduced to three years and seven months following an appeal, in November. In April 2001 he was released on bail, owing to illness.

In September 1998 Taslima Nasreen, was reported to have secretly returned to Bangladesh after four years in self-imposed exile. On her return, a fresh arrest warrant on charges of blasphemy was issued by a Dhaka court, and the police launched a hunt for her. Islamist extremists reiterated their demand for Nasreen's immediate arrest and execution, and organized street protests. In late November Nasreen voluntarily came out of hiding and surrendered herself before the High Court in Dhaka, where she was granted bail. In January 1999 the author left Bangladesh for Sweden, following renewed death threats from Islamist fundamentalists. In August her second book was banned. Her third novel was allowed to be sold in Bangladesh in 2001; however, her fourth book was banned in August 2002.

In early 1999 political instability and violence escalated. The pace of agitation increased, and in mid-1999 the BNP and other opposition parties began a boycott of parliamentary proceedings. Opposition-led strikes took place in October and December, leading to substantial economic disruption. Following a further strike at the beginning of January 2000, prominent business leaders attempted to negotiate a deal between the Prime Minister and the opposition parties. The leader of the BNP, Begum Khaleda Zia, however, declined to take part. Strikes continued to disrupt the economy. In June the opposition parties returned to the Jatiya Sangsad in order to avoid disqualification (which occurs after an absence of 90 working days from the legislature without the Speaker's approval). However, following accusations that the Government was conspiring to change the Constitution, the opposition members promptly resumed the boycott, claiming that they were not allowed to address the legislature, an allegation denied by the chamber's Speaker. In August three contempt of court petitions were filed against the Prime Minister by members of the Supreme Court Bar Association and opposition leaders, following her criticism of the judiciary and legal profession.

Discontent with the Government continued to increase. In early July 2000 an attempt to assassinate Sheikh Hasina Wajed was foiled. Bomb explosions also became a regular occurrence; the worst incident took place in mid-June 2001 when 22 people were killed at a local office of the AL. No one claimed responsibility, although it was alleged by some that militant Islamist groups were involved. Also in June 2001 the trial began of 15 people accused of involvement in the alleged attempt to assassinate the Prime Minister one year previously. In the same month the Jatiya Sangsad approved a new law under which Sheikh Hasina Wajed and her sister would receive lifelong state security.

At the end of June 2001 the Prime Minister announced that national elections would be held, as scheduled, in September. In mid-July Sheikh Hasina Wajed and her Government duly resigned from their posts, and the Jatiya Sangsad was dissolved. The former Chief Justice, Latifur Rehman, was appointed as acting Prime Minister, heading an interim neutral government, which was responsible for the holding of elections within three months. The general election proceeded on 1 October, although voting was postponed in several constituencies owing to violence. On 9 October elections were held in 15 of those constituencies where voting had been delayed. Despite the considerable violence during the election period, international monitors declared the poll to be free and fair. The BNP-led alliance won a convincing majority (214 of the 300 seats), the AL secured 62 seats and the Jatiya Dal won 14 seats. Begum Khaleda Zia of the BNP was appointed Prime Minister. One notable feature of the parliamentary election had been a renewed alliance between the BNP and the Jamaat-e-Islami. The latter won only 16 seats (of the alliance's 214), but as a result of the partnership and the Jamaat-e-Islami's subsequent participation in the new Government, a series of attacks took place on members of the country's Hindu minority, generally considered to be supporters of the AL. Subsequently, many Bangladeshi Hindus fled as refugees to India. In November the BNP Minister of Foreign Affairs, A. Q. M. Badruddoza Chowdhury, was declared elected unopposed as the country's largely ceremonial President.

The AL's immediate response to its election defeat was to launch a campaign of boycott and agitation. Newly elected members of the legislature effectively refused to take part in parliamentary proceedings until June 2002, and the party as a whole boycotted civic elections in Dhaka and elsewhere in April; a series of strikes was organized to protest against popular grievances, for example the state of law and order in major cities. Begum Khaleda Zia reacted to the disruption by filing major corruption charges against Sheikh Hasina Wajed and other AL members in December 2001, with regard to an arms contract with Russia signed in 1999.

A series of retirements and resignations took place in mid-2002. The most high profile were the early retirement of the Chief of Army Staff and the resignation of the President, both in June. The President's departure was immediately attributed to BNP claims that he had failed to attend a ceremony in honour of the anniversary of Gen. Zia's assassination, but it was alleged that his removal might also be a prelude to constitutional changes. In turn, it was asserted by some that Begum Khaleda Zia was preparing her son, Tarique Rahman (who was appointed joint Secretary-General of the BNP two days after the President's resignation), to take over from her in due course. In early September the BNP candidate, Prof. Iajuddin Ahmed, was declared President by the Election Commission after it was determined that his were the only valid nomination papers for the post.

To a limited extent, the BNP continued with policies of economic restructuring and liberalization in line with international donor advice and support. However, there was considerable resistance to its measures, as demonstrated, for example, by a major strike at Chittagong port.

The Chittagong Hill Tracts

Apart from the difficulties of maintaining political control of the country, successive leaders of Bangladesh from Sheikh Mujib onwards have had to confront an insurgency in the Chittagong Hill Tracts. Minority tribal groups, mostly Buddhist Chakmas, have long demanded autonomy in this region, and have attempted to prevent the continuing settlement in the area of Bengali peasants from the plains, a process which has, in fact, been going on since the 19th century (when Bengalis were settled in the Hill Tracts as plantation workers and clerks by the British administration). Initially, guerrilla activity by the Shanti Bahini ('Peace Force'), which had been waging guerrilla warfare against the Bangladeshi security forces and the Bengali settlers since the early 1970s, was met by retaliatory army action. In 1989, however, the Government took measures to achieve a political solution in the Chittagong Hill Tracts, by introducing concessions providing limited autonomy to the region in the form of three new semi-autonomous hill districts—Rangamati, Bandarban and Khagrachari. In June polls to elect councils for these new districts took place reasonably peacefully, despite attempts at disruption by the Shanti Bahini, who continued to demand total autonomy for the Chakma tribals. The powers vested in the councils were designed to give the tribals sufficient authority to regulate any further influx of Bengali settlers to the districts. By mid-1990, however, it had become increasingly apparent that the Government's peace scheme had failed. The violence had not abated and Buddhist Chakma refugees continued to flood across the border into India (the number of refugees living in camps in Tripura reached about 56,000). A series of efforts was made from 1992 to achieve a lasting solution. India became involved in the negotiations, as it was anxious to be relieved of the burden of caring for the refugees, but this also meant that the problem became embroiled in the broader issue of Indo-Bangladeshi relations. An initial agreement in 1992 failed to generate confidence among the refugees that it would be implemented; they feared persecution by the Bangladesh security forces. A fresh effort in 1994 led to only a very limited number of refugees returning. In December 1996, however, the settlement of the Farakka issue between Bangladesh and India (see below) opened the way to a new initiative. In December 1997 the Bangladeshi Government signed a peace agreement with the political wing of the Shanti Bahini ending the insurgency in the Chittagong Hill Tracts. The treaty offered the rebels a general amnesty in return for the surrender of their arms and gave the tribal people greater powers of self-governance through the establishment of three new elected district councils (to control the area's land management and policing) and a regional council (the chairman of which was to enjoy the rank of a state minister). The peace agreement, which was strongly criticized by the opposition for representing a 'sell-out' of the area to India and a threat to Bangladesh's sovereignty, was expected to accelerate the process of repatriating the remaining refugees from Tripura (who totalled about 31,000 at the end of December 1997). According to official Indian sources, only about 5,500 refugees remained in Tripura by early February 1998. By the end of 2000 most of the Chakma refugees had been repatriated, district and regional councils were in operation and a land commission had been established. The transitional period, following the signing of the treaty, was to end with the withdrawal of the Bangladesh Army from the region by the beginning of 2001, when the army was to be replaced by the Bangladesh Rifles. More than 50,000 Chakma refugees had fled to Arunachal Pradesh, in India, since 1964. In early 2001 a tribal group in the Indian state threatened to force out the refugees if India failed to deport them to Bangladesh. Strikes and protests also took place in the region.

In mid-February 2001 gunmen abducted three engineers, two Danes and one Briton, working on a road-building project in the Chittagong Hill Tracts. The kidnappers demanded a ransom from the Bangladeshi Government in return for the hostages' release. It was believed that the kidnappers belonged to the separatist United People's Democratic Front, which opposed the 1997 peace agreement. In mid-March 2001 the hostages were released. The Government claimed that the army had rescued the men; other sources reported that the Government had agreed to a secret financial arrangement with the kidnappers.

International Relations

Bangladesh's most important bilateral relationship is with India. Despite (although some might say because of) India's role in Bangladesh's liberation struggle, there has always been the fear that it would use its vastly superior strength to intimidate

Bangladesh, especially over economic matters. While relations between the two countries have never been overtly hostile, they have been marked by suspicion and ambiguity. The most troublesome issue to resolve has been the allocation of the Ganges waters, following India's construction of the Farakka barrage, which was completed in 1975. This major civil engineering project was undertaken in order to divert some of the river's flow through the Hooghly river and thus to alleviate the siltation problem at Calcutta. However, this inevitably resulted in a lesser flow of water through the part of the Ganges delta that is situated in Bangladesh, and it has been claimed that this has led to serious consequences for agricultural production owing to greater salination in the coastal areas. Bilateral negotiations began soon after 1971, but produced only limited results and in effect India was able to impose its own solution. However, in December 1996 there appeared to be a breakthrough. The then Indian Minister of External Affairs (shortly to be Prime Minister) I. K. Gujral had, as soon as he assumed office, made a point of trying to improve relations with India's neighbours, and with the help of the Chief Minister of West Bengal, whose approval was vital to the political acceptability of the plan in India, presented a formula for the division of the water. The agreement also allowed for India to have transit rights over Bangladesh territory in order to reach parts of its remote north-eastern states more easily. In addition, negotiations began with regard to Bangladesh selling surplus power to neighbouring parts of India.

Unresolved issues remained, however. In 1992 the demolition of the mosque at Ayodhya (see chapter on India) led to widespread protests on the streets of Bangladesh and to attacks on Hindu temples. On the Indian side, right-wing parties have made a major issue of the alleged presence of large numbers of illegal Bangladeshi migrants in Delhi and elsewhere, while the long-term movement of Bengali settlers across the border into Assam, which has been going on since before 1947, is an important factor in that state's internal politics. In January 1997 the Indian Prime Minister, H. D. Deve Gowda, paid an official visit to Bangladesh, the first Indian Premier to do so for 20 years. In June 1999, during a visit to Dhaka by the Indian Prime Minister, Atal Bihari Vajpayee, to celebrate the inauguration of the first direct passenger bus service between Bangladesh and India, Vajpayee promised Bangladesh greater access to Indian markets and announced that India would give its neighbour US $50m. in credits over three years to help develop its transport and industrial infrastructure. In August the Bangladeshi Government was criticized by the opposition for its approval of proposals to permit the transhipment of Indian goods through Bangladesh to the north-eastern states of India by Bangladeshi transport companies. There were further opposition protests, including a general strike in November 2001, against potential plans, strongly supported by donor agencies such as the World Bank, for the sale of natural gas to India. Despite an agreement in 1992 to settle a border-related problem, outstanding bilateral issues included the dispute over territorial rights to pockets of land or enclaves along the irregular border. Although intermittent efforts were made to resolve this problem, occasional clashes between border guards occurred. The worst fighting since 1976 took place in April 2001 on the Bangladeshi border with the Indian state of Meghalaya. Some 16 Indian border troops and three members of the Bangladesh Rifles were killed. Indian sentiments were outraged by the alleged maltreatment of Indian soldiers by Bangladeshi troops. The situation was brought under control, and both sides agreed to enter negotiations, which were under way in June and July. As a result, two joint working groups were created to review the undemarcated section of the border and the exchange of enclaves. The return to power of the BNP, traditionally seen as anti-India, further delayed the movement.

The question of settlers has also been the major issue in Bangladesh's relations with its eastern neighbour Myanmar (formerly Burma). While the border itself was finally demarcated in 1985, in accordance with a 1979 agreement, during 1991 more than 50,000 Rohingya Muslims, a Myanma ethnic minority who live in the western Arakan region, crossed into Bangladesh claiming persecution by the Myanma authorities. By the end of June 1992 it was officially estimated that the number of Rohingya refugees in Bangladesh had risen to about 270,000. In 1992 an agreement was signed between the Governments of Bangladesh and Myanmar to allow for repatriation, but many of the Rohingyas refused to return. By early September 1994 about 65,000 refugees had reportedly been voluntarily repatriated. Meanwhile, in December 1993 Bangladesh and Myanmar had signed an agreement to instigate border trade between the two countries. By the end of May 1995, according to government figures, more than 216,000 Rohingyas had been repatriated. In July 1999, however, about 20,000 Rohingya refugees remained in camps in Bangladesh, despite the expiry of the official deadline for their repatriation in August 1997. By the end of September 2000 approximately 231,000 refugees had returned to Myanmar. In January 2002 the World Food Programme launched an appeal for financial assistance for 21,500 refugees who remained in two camps in south-eastern Bangladesh. Tension along the border between Bangladesh and Myanmar increased in November, following reports that Myanmar was laying landmines and that Myanma troops had been deployed in the border area. The Bangladeshi security forces were placed on alert. In January 2001 border guards exchanged fire, amid rising tension over a controversial dam project on the River Naaf, which Bangladesh claimed would cause flooding on its territory. The shooting took place after work began in Myanmar on the construction of an embankment. The Myanma authorities agreed to suspend the project to allow further discussions to resolve the problem. Relations were further strained when Myanmar claimed that Bangladesh had violated the border agreement by cultivating shrimps in the area, an allegation denied by the Bangladeshi Government. Border negotiations took place but collapsed following the Myanma Government's refusal to sign the minutes. Finally, in early February Myanmar agreed permanently to cease construction of the dam.

Bangladesh's relations with Pakistan have been surprisingly cordial, given the circumstances of the 1971 war. Diplomatic relations between the two countries were resumed in 1974. One outstanding issue is the position of the so-called Biharis, the Urdu-speaking group who came to what was then East Pakistan in the wake of partition in 1947. Perceived as collaborators by the rest of the Bangladeshi population, many of them have languished in refugee camps ever since, waiting for repatriation. However, successive Pakistan governments have been reluctant to accept them for fear of exacerbating the ethnic crisis in Karachi (see chapter on Pakistan). In 1991 an agreement was reached between Bangladesh and Pakistan which provided for a phased repatriation of the Bihari refugees, but implementation has been very slow. At the end of 2000 a diplomatic dispute between the two countries over claims and counter-claims on responsibility for the events of 1971 indicated that sensitivities remained. At the end of July 2002 Pakistani President Musharraf paid a successful visit to Bangladesh, during which he expressed regret for what had occurred during the 1971 war. No progress was made on the Bihari issue, however.

As part of its policy to attain a stable position within South Asia, Bangladesh took the initiative in establishing the South Asian Association for Regional Co-operation (SAARC). First mooted by Gen. Zia in 1980, SAARC was formally created in 1985, with a Bangladeshi official as its first Secretary-General. The first and seventh summit meetings of the organization were held in Dhaka. Included in SAARC's charter are pledges of non-interference by members in each other's internal affairs and a joint effort to avoid 'contentious' issues whenever the association meets. The SAARC Preferential Trading Arrangement (SAPTA) was signed in April 1993 and came into effect in December 1995. It was also agreed that members should work towards the objective of establishing a South Asian Free Trade Area (SAFTA) by 2005. SAARC, however, encountered difficulties following the imposition of military rule in Pakistan and India's refusal to attend the summit meeting in Kathmandu, Nepal, in November 1999. The summit meeting eventually took place in January 2002, although it was again overshadowed by tension between India and Pakistan.

Although South Asia has been Bangladesh's main area of concern with regard to foreign affairs, its relations with the major world powers have been good. It remains heavily dependent on bilateral and multilateral aid, and holds annual meetings with a consortium of its major donors to discuss development issues. In March 2000 the US President, Bill

Clinton, visited Bangladesh as part of a tour of South Asia. This momentous state visit was the first ever by a US President to Bangladesh. As a result of discussions between the two countries' leaders, who focused on development issues, Clinton announced several aid programmes. In October Sheikh Hasina Wajed visited the USA, where the two leaders focused on environmental matters and investment issues. Domestically, many groups feel that Bangladesh should not be so dependent on the West, the USA in particular, but, as yet, no government has attempted to find an alternative path. In June 1997, however, eight of the world's major Muslim states, including Bangladesh, established a new group, known as the Developing Eight, or D-8, to further economic and political co-operation among the member countries. The 1999 summit meeting was held in Dhaka. D-8, which represents 65% of the world's Muslim population, was widely viewed as an Islamic counterweight to the G-7 group of industrialized nations. In September 2001 the interim administration agreed, with the support of the AL and BNP, to offer the USA use of Bangladeshi airspace and ports in the event of military action against Afghanistan, where the Taliban regime was believed to be harbouring Osama bin Laden and the al-Qa'ida (Base) organization—held principally responsible by the USA for that month's suicide attacks against New York and Washington, DC.

Developmental and Environmental Issues

Over many years East Bengal has been one of the poorest parts of South Asia. The colonial period was one of neglect and stagnation, and during 1947–71 East Pakistan's resources were diverted to the development of West Pakistan. While Bangladesh still lags behind many other parts of the subcontinent, it has made some progress since independence (see the Economy). In fact, it has taken a number of initiatives that have been admired and copied elsewhere. Under Zia, for example, a new pharmaceuticals policy was introduced which restricted the use of expensive proprietary formulations in favour of generic and locally produced drugs. The Grameen Bank, which was established in 1976, pioneered innovative approaches to rural credit provision, and is only one example of the massive role played in Bangladesh by NGOs. These operate very often as partnerships between local organizations and local aid donors. The best of the NGOs allow for local initiatives to express themselves unfettered by government bureaucracy, although others have been criticized for the comparatively lavish lifestyles enjoyed by their employees and for too rigid a following of outside models.

One of the most serious recurrent problems in Bangladesh, and one which often has political and international implications, has been the official handling of natural disasters such as cyclones and floods. The two most serious natural disasters in recent years have been the cyclone in 1991 (see above), which exceeded in intensity even the 1970 cyclone, and the monsoon floods of September 1988. These floods were the most severe in the region's recorded history, and during them three-quarters of the country, including large parts of the capital, were flooded, vast areas of arable land were submerged and as many as 30m. people were left homeless. Famine was avoided by the prompt action of the Government, but, nevertheless, the adverse impact on the economy was substantial. Such economic problems undoubtedly compound the political unrest in Bangladesh. In late 1988 the Government established a National Disaster Prevention Council and urged the use of regional co-operation (specifically with India and possibly with Nepal) to evolve a comprehensive solution to the problem of flooding. In August 1998 the Government appealed for international aid following devastating floods (the worst since 1988), which had caused more than 500 deaths (this figure later rose to more than 1,000) and infrastructural damage estimated at about US $220m. By late August more than 60% of the country was submerged, including large parts of the capital, and the flooding lasted an unprecedented 11 weeks. In August–October 2000 devastating floods caused several hundred deaths and the displacement of more than 1m. people. In the long term, Bangladesh is likely to be one of the countries worst affected by any rise in sea-levels owing to global warming. In such an event, nothing less than a world-wide effort could be of any help.

Economy

MUSHTAQ H. KHAN

Based on an earlier article by ALLISTER McGREGOR

RECENT TRENDS

Bangladesh, classified by the World Bank as one of the successful globalizing economies in the developing world, was affected more severely by the global economic slowdown in the latter half of 2001 than many other countries. Its remarkable success in export growth, especially in the garments sector, made it more vulnerable to global demand, particularly consumer demand from the USA. In July–December 2001 around 1,200 garment factories (approximately one-third of the total) were closed down and some 350,000 workers were made redundant. Similar declines occurred in other sectors; however, the garment industry was one of the worst affected, partly as a result of growing competition from other developing countries as the Multi-Fibre Arrangement (MFA) quotas that had favoured Bangladesh were being phased out. Nevertheless, Bangladesh remains a relatively successful country in the developing world, with one of the highest growth rates of exports in the 1990s. It was classified by the World Bank as one of the 18 most rapidly integrating developing countries in terms of global trade in that decade. It has also been fairly successful in terms of progress in improving health and education, population control and food security, by allocating a major part of the budget to the social sector. Its challenge is to maintain and even increase its growth rate by attracting more investment and by developing the capacity of the state to discipline and regulate the corporate sector. Like many other developing countries, Bangladesh faces serious challenges with regard to enhancing the state's capacity. The state's declining capacity to co-ordinate and regulate the corporate sector and to promote development is repeatedly identified in opinion polls as a serious problem by both ordinary citizens and investors; the issues raised range from such basic areas as maintaining law and order to regulating markets and assisting in technology acquisition.

Economic growth in Bangladesh is still high in comparative terms but has been on a declining trend since 1999. Gross domestic product (GDP) increased by 5.9% in 1999/2000. In 2000/01 GDP grew by 5.2%, driven by a 7.2% growth in industry and a bumper crop in the agricultural sector. In 2001/02 GDP growth was projected to decline to as low as 4.5%, as the effects of the global slowdown began adversely to affect Bangladesh's export and industrial sectors. The global slowdown also caused agricultural growth rates in 2001/02 to decrease significantly compared with the previous year. The decline by 11.5% in exports between July and December 2001 would have had an even more unfavourable effect had remittances from Bangladeshis working abroad decreased as sharply. In fact, however, remittances allowed some domestic investment to continue over 2001/02. The national savings rate was unchanged at 22% of GDP, and national investment remained at 23% of GDP.

Bangladesh remains among the poorest of countries, with per caput GDP of only US $362 in 2002. Despite this, Bangladesh has made remarkable progress in human development, with increases in life expectancy, reductions in population growth and in infant mortality rates, and improved access to essential drugs, sanitation and safe water. Continued improvements require sustained or greater economic growth rates, and this requires more savings and investment. Savings rates are low because of inadequate financial institutions and political instability. Tax revenues increased by a record amount in 2000/01: the National Board of Revenue collected almost 25% more than in the previous year. However, government revenue remained at around 9% of GDP, much lower than in other countries in the region. The commercial banking sector is not utilizing private savings sufficiently; savings through bank deposits amount to less than 2% of GDP. It is hoped that substantial progress can be made on both fronts in the medium term. The financial sector remains vulnerable owing to the bad debts of the commercial banks. The non-performing loans of the banking sector in 2000/01 amounted to 38% of the total loan portfolio. Past and present Bangladesh governments have been officially committed to taking loan defaulters to court, but the sheer scale of the issue suggests that this approach alone is not going to solve the liquidity problem of the banks. The previous government passed the Financial Loan Court Act, which empowered courts to enforce the recovery of debts. The political complexities of taking pre-eminent industrialists to court, however, has prevented any effective action being taken against the major defaulters. Instead, cases have been brought against smaller industrialists lacking political protection. The only feasible long-term solution may be to cancel a substantial part of the bad debt and recapitalize the banking sector using public funds, a prospect many Asian governments will be required to face in the years ahead.

Controlling population growth has been one of the success stories in Bangladesh. From an annual growth rate of around 3.1% in 1971, the rate has fallen to its current level of 1.6%. The fertility rate has declined from an average of seven children per mother to about 3.3. The present population of around 123m., however, is not projected to stabilize until the second half of the 21st century, at about 250m. Average life expectancy for both men and women is approximately 60 years. The rate of literacy has improved from around 26% in 1974 to 41% today. In recent years, the role of the non-governmental sector has proved important, with 40% of new schools since 1990 being established by non-governmental organizations (NGOs), usually with external assistance. However, further improvements in literacy are likely to require a substantial increase in the capacity of the state sector, which remains the basic provider of primary education. This, in turn, depends on the ability of the State to raise tax revenues. The role of foreign aid has been declining and is likely to decrease further in years to come. In 1999, in a break with the past, the World Bank announced that figures for aid would not be pledged at the forthcoming meeting of the Bangladesh Development Forum in Paris. Total aid, which includes grants and low-interest loans, has continued to decline sharply: a total of US $1,700m. of aid commitments were made in 2000/01, but aid disbursements decreased by 13% compared with the previous year. The Government has increasingly been forced to borrow from domestic sources, which in turn has increased the interest component of budgetary expenditure. Administrative and political problems account for a large part of the country's economic difficulties. Interest groups such as politically connected businessmen, trade unions and public-sector employees have extracted resource allocations, which has led to a deterioration in economic efficiency.

AGRICULTURE

Agriculture contributed 26% of GDP and employed 63% of the labour force in the late 1990s. The climate allows for three crops per year. Recent agricultural growth has been based on the increase in area under the third (winter) crop and the substitution of traditional varieties by high-yielding varieties (HYV). The average annual growth rate in agricultural output was a vigorous 3% during 1986–90, but thereafter the rate of growth decelerated, averaging less than 0.5% per year over the period 1990–95. In 1998/99 agricultural growth suffered as a result of the most severe flooding in recent history; 68% of the country was flooded, affecting 30m. people. While the flood waters destroyed the summer crops, they led to bumper winter crops. The net effect was that agricultural production increased by 3.9% in 1998/99. This was comparable to growth in the previous year but much lower than the exceptional rise of 6.4% in 1996/97. In 1999/2000, however, the sector recovered, led by an unusually good monsoon (or *aman*) rice crop. The floods of the previous year appeared to have improved the fertility of the soil by bringing fresh silt downstream. This, together with very favourable weather conditions, contributed to a bumper crop. In 2000/01 Bangladesh produced 27m. metric tons of food grains, around 2m. tons more than domestic requirements. Despite the floods in September 2000, rice production was good enough to make Bangladesh self-sufficient in food for the first time. Conditions in agriculture were favourable owing to good weather, the Government's provision of credit for farmers, the expansion of HYV, and the availability of subsidized fuels, fertilizers and electricity. The 3.1% growth in foodgrain production achieved in 2000/01 was not sustained in 2001/02; instead, output stagnated; none the less, self-sufficiency in food grains was maintained. Widespread flooding in Bangladesh and eastern India in July–August 2002 could have an adverse impact on agricultural output in 2002/03.

If high growth rates in agriculture can be sustained, Bangladesh will make good progress in combating poverty. The land-ownership pattern is characterized by considerable inequality in landholding and also by a high degree of fragmentation of individual farms. The top 10% of landowners hold 49% of the total land area, while the bottom 10% own a mere 2%. One-half of the rural population is effectively landless. The average farm size is small, about 0.8 ha, with over 70% of all farms classified as small (below 1 ha) and only 5% as large (above 3 ha), while agricultural census figures suggest that the majority of farms consist of at least six, and often considerably more, separate plots of land. Several authors have argued that it is this agrarian structure that has represented the major obstacle to the launching of the 'green revolution' in Bangladesh. The fact that individual farms are highly fragmented imposes extra costs on the implementation of some of the new technology, such as irrigation and tractors, making their introduction that much more difficult. Problems of under-utilization of irrigation equipment are also common because of the pattern of land ownership and because of water distribution difficulties. There are frequent complaints about water shortages during critical periods in the crop cycle, which, because HYV yields are relatively sensitive to the timing of irrigation, can be highly costly for small-scale farmers. These disruptions can usually be attributed either to political factors in the management of the distribution of water at a local level, or to wider difficulties with the maintenance of equipment or the supply of diesel fuel or electricity. It is estimated that currently only 32% of net cultivated area is under irrigation, although a recent survey suggests that this could be expanded to around 60% of the cultivable area. Such an expansion could result in almost a doubling of foodgrain production in Bangladesh. Most of the existing irrigation (around 75%) is based on small-scale tube-wells and lift pumps operated by individual farmers or collectives. The lifting of huge quantities of ground water has, in recent years, resulted in concentrations of natural arsenic and widespread arsenic poisoning in rural Bangladesh. Attention to this problem raises an immediate challenge for the Government.

Another factor constraining further growth in the agricultural sector is that risk aversion prevents small-scale farmers increasing fertilizer use at the same rate as larger-scale farmers. Consequently, the growth in fertilizer use has been slowing down. The Government has been attempting to encourage fertilizer use by subsidizing its price, but this strategy has resulted in more exports to neighbouring countries rather than an increase in domestic utilization.

Much of the growth in agricultural output in the early 1980s was due to an expansion of the land area under the third (winter) rice crop (known as the *boro* crop) and under wheat. During 1975–80 80% of foodgrain production was provided by the rain-fed *aus* and *aman* rice crops (the two main summer/monsoon crops), 16% by the *boro* crop, and around 3% by wheat. By the period covering 1985–88, the contribution made by the *aus* and *aman* crops to foodgrain output had fallen to 67%, whereas the contribution made by the winter crop, *boro*, had increased to 26% and wheat to 7%. The expansion of land area under both the *boro* rice crop and wheat depended on the extension of irrigation, and these two crops largely accounted for the growth in foodgrain output in the late 1980s. The area under wheat continues to grow rapidly. In 1996/97 the acreage under wheat cultivation increased by a further 26% and wheat output rose by 29%, contributing significantly to the impressive overall performance of the agricultural sector. At present, 40% of the total land area is double-cropped (i.e. *aus* and *aman* crops) and only 10% is triple-cropped (*aus, aman* and *boro* crops). Increasing the crop yields from land already under cultivation is an alternative, and this too has been happening, at a lower rate, through the introduction of HYV varieties of rice. Yields from HYV varieties are about twice those from traditional varieties of rice. However, in this field too, investment in water systems is essential for future growth. Although optimists believe that HYV varieties can be extended to the flood plains growing *aus* and *aman*, HYV varieties at present account for only 20% of the *aus* and *aman* crops. It is likely that the introduction of HYV crops in the flood plains is too risky and their extension in these areas will only happen on a large scale if flood waters can be controlled. Investment in flood control is not only likely to be beyond the limited means of Bangladesh's hard-pressed economy, it would also probably require the involvement of neighbouring countries. The utilization of HYV varieties has been most dramatic for the *boro* crop. However, the deceleration in the rate of growth of rice production in the first half of the 1990s was largely due to a significant decline in the rate of expansion of the area under *boro* HYV.

The severity of the floods in 1987 and 1988, following a number of serious floods earlier in the decade, prompted much discussion between international donors and the Government of Bangladesh, regarding the quest for long-term solutions to the country's flood problem. The UN Development Programme, USAID (the US development assistance agency), France and Japan all embarked upon pre-feasibility studies for major flood-control programmes and each raised different proposals as to what course of action should be taken. Of the four, all, except that of USAID, envisaged the erection of flood-control embankments, both on the rivers and as protection around major towns. The USAID proposal did not involve an embankment solution, because of prior experiences in the USA and in the People's Republic of China, and, instead, raised the possibility of a regional solution to the problem based on co-operation with both India and Nepal. In mid-1989, in order to avoid the difficulty of having to carry out four separate sets of negotiation, the Government of Bangladesh approached the World Bank and asked it to assume the role of co-ordinator of all donor efforts with respect to flood control. It has been envisaged that a comprehensive flood-control programme might require up to US $10,000m. of assistance over a 20-year period. Of more immediate relevance is the agreement signed by Bangladesh and India in December 1996 regarding the sharing of the Ganges waters during the lean season from March to May. India's controversial construction of the Farakka barrage in 1975 had adversely affected the livelihood of 30m. farmers in Bangladesh. The new agreement gives each country a guaranteed flow of 34,000 cu ft per second of water in alternating 10-day periods during the entire lean season. The implementation of this agreement is expected to bring tremendous potential benefits to farmers in north-western Bangladesh.

For the most part, the 1990s were a period of agrarian success for Bangladesh. Total agricultural output increased by 33% in 1990–2000. Foodgrains was not the only area to experience gains: between 1991/92 and 2000 per caput consumption of fish increased by 9%, potatoes by 25%, meat by 48%, poultry by 120% and milk by 55%. At the same time, per caput consumption of wheat and rice declined marginally and consumption of pulses declined by 13%, reflecting a shift towards higher-value sources of protein. These changes were associated with better nutritional standards experienced by the population, such as improvements in life expectancy, a decline in infant mortality, and lower instances of stunting and wasting in children.

Jute

Jute has traditionally occupied a pivotal position in the Bangladesh economy, in that it represents the major linkage between agriculture and industry. Despite being the country's major cash crop, the area under jute cultivation is very sensitive to relative prices, ranging, for instance, from more than 1m. ha in 1985/86 to around 500,000 ha in 1990/91. Annual jute production varies from 4m.–4.5m. bales, of which 3m.–3.5m. bales are used to manufacture jute goods, mainly for export; the remaining 1m. bales are exported as raw jute. More than one-half of the capacity in jute-manufacturing remains within the public sector, despite very substantial denationalization (particularly of small units). The jute industry, however, has recently been in decline. In 1981/82 exports of jute (both raw and manufactured) accounted for around 65% of Bangladesh's total export earnings, but by 2001 its share of export earnings had fallen to around 4.6%, with the new export leaders, ready-made garments and knitwear, accounting for 75% of export revenue. This decline can be traced to instability on both the demand and supply sides of the market for jute, which has resulted in volatile prices, but with a general downward trend.

Since 1982 the Government has denationalized about one-half of the country's jute mills, amounting to around one-third of production capacity. Privatization, however, does not appear to have directly increased efficiency measured by profitability, and the jute mill sector is the country's largest loss-maker. Despite the fact that the number of employees working in the privatized jute mills has been reduced, profitability does not appear to have improved. By 2001 all but six of the 35 private mills had suspended production, as their failure to service debt on time led to banks withholding vital credit lines. The industry requires new investment and a small but predetermined subsidy to remain viable. Such a subsidy could be justified on the grounds that the jute sector directly and indirectly employs millions of people whose next best employment option may be very unfavourable in the medium term. The World Bank offered Bangladesh a Jute Sector Adjustment Credit worth US $250m. and simultaneously insisted that nine public-sector mills be closed down or privatized by June 1997. The adjustment proposed by the World Bank was not satisfactory, however, to either the public or the private sector, and the adjustment credit was, in the end, not fully taken up. The private-sector jute mills protested strongly at the way in which the World Bank implemented the adjustment, as it led to a number of private mills having to close down while the public sector continued to receive subsidies. In the long term, with growing investment in the production of new types of 'environmentally friendly' jute-based packaging and products, the industry may well prove profitable without a subsidy. The present system of hidden subsidies to the public-sector mills and non-performing loans in the private sector appears to be the poorest solution. Some progress towards restructuring took place when the Government finally closed down the biggest loss-making jute mill in the public sector in June 2002. The huge Adamjee Jute Mills was the world's largest jute mill employing some 17,000 workers, but it had accumulated losses of more than US $200m. since it was nationalized in 1972.

There are potential alternative uses of jute which could be promising. A US company, Proteraa Capital, is carrying out a feasibility study for establishing composite jute plants to make compressed jute blocks, which can be used as building insulation material in Europe and North America. The long-term future of jute as a cash crop in Bangladesh will depend on such ventures.

MANUFACTURING AND MINING

Approximately 70% of manufacturing output is provided by large-scale manufacturing industries. The manufacturing sector employs about 14% of Bangladesh's labour force, but more than 80% of these workers are employed in the small-scale manufacturing sector where wage rates are lower and labour demand is often seasonal. Small-scale industries include hand-loom weaving, bamboo-working and metal-working. Industry accounted for 25.9% of GDP in 2000/01 and employed around 9.5% of the workforce in the late 1990s. The old industrial sector was dominated by the jute industry and other large-scale industries. In contrast, in the 1980s and 1990s, the bulk of the growth in the industrial sector has been led by ready-made garments, knitwear and other small-scale export-based industries. Traditional heavy industries fared badly: the jute industry had particular problems (see above) but even the cotton textiles sector experienced difficulties. Most of the cotton textile units were closed down or operating at a fraction of their capacity. Power cuts and unfair competition from smuggled products, which avoided the payment of customs duties and excise taxes, were blamed. Nevertheless, largely owing to the newer industries, industrial output in general increased by a substantial 86% in 1990–2000, ensuring Bangladesh's emergence as one of the relatively rapidly growing and globalizing economies in the developing world. Industrial growth was particularly rapid in 2000/01, reaching 7.2%. The global economic slowdown, which began in the second half of 2001, combined with the effects of the suicide attacks on the USA in September 2001, meant that industrial growth in Bangladesh in 2001/02 was likely to be much lower. Exports were expected to decline by 8% over the same period. The closing down of around one-third of the garment factories in the latter half of 2001 was likely to be a temporary set-back, but with growing competition in the garments industry, the early 21st century was set to be a period of uncertainty for Bangladesh.

A number of successes in large-scale industry also need to be acknowledged. Increased production of domestic gas has been successfully substituted for oil in the production of electricity, and as the primary source of energy in industry. Gas-based fertilizer production has also increased. At present the country's five urea-fertilizer factories produce about 1.5m. metric tons per year, and there is one factory which produces triple superphosphate (TSP) fertilizer. Domestic demand for fertilizer grew dramatically from 210,000 tons in 1969/70, to 2.3m. tons in 1993/94. Two new fertilizer plants, at Jamuna and Karnaphuli, have recently commenced operating. The gas-fired Karnaphuli plant, Kafco—a US $510m. joint venture between the Government and an international consortium of companies—became operational in December 1994, and Bangladesh began to export liquid ammonia for the first time. The company is to have 4% of its shares floated on the Dhaka stock market. Savings in foreign exchange have also resulted from import-substitution in steel (mainly through ship-breaking) and in pharmaceuticals.

In the 1980s the policy emphasis shifted to encourage a greater export orientation and also the increased participation of the private sector. Measures were introduced in an attempt to reduce bureaucratic obstacles both to private investment and to trade. The Industrial Policy of 1991 identified a further 42 large enterprises for denationalization.

The 1980s and first half of the 1990s witnessed the dramatic growth of the ready-made garments industry, with garments becoming the foremost source of export revenue. By the end of the 1990s the industry employed about 1.5m. skilled workers (most of them women). Exports of ready-made garments in 2000/01 reached an estimated US $3,364m., amounting to 52% of total export earnings. Although some domestic fabric and yarn production has commenced in Bangladesh, the majority of fabric and yarns required by the ready-made garment sector is imported. This means the net export earnings of the sector are considerably lower. There are obviously great opportunities for developing domestic fabric and yarn production, but foreign investments or partnerships are required to transfer the requisite technology. The incentives to develop these industries are even stronger because of the tax exemptions for exports to the European Union (EU) of garments that are manufactured within Bangladesh using Bangladeshi yarn and fabrics. In mid-2000 the EU changed its rules to allow tax-free imports from Bangladesh of garments made with yarn or fabrics from any of the member countries of the South Asian Association for Regional Co-operation (SAARC). This move is likely to help Bangladesh's garments industry, but will damage the country's newly developing yarn and fabric industry which is likely to lose orders to the more advanced industries of India and Pakistan. Paradoxically, Bangladesh is a beneficiary of the MFA quotas, which limit exports of garments to developed countries, since the arrangement favours very poor countries. Under the regulations of the World Trade Organization, the MFA is due to be phased out in 2005. Bangladesh has argued that this does not allow it sufficient time to develop the necessary yarn and fabric industries that it will require to compete with more advanced developing countries, such as the People's Republic of China and India, which already have established domestic yarn and fabric industries. The Government is, therefore, attempting to negotiate an extension of the 2005 deadline and, in the meantime, a 30% increase in quotas for Bangladesh. These developments have further increased the urgency of establishing domestic yarn and fabric industries as rapidly as possible.

Further growth of the industrial sector requires a major commitment by the State to improve the infrastructure and to provide the political stability essential for the consideration of long-term investments by the private sector. The constraints imposed by the budget on public investment have discouraged private-sector investment, despite government commitments made during the 1980s to liberalize the economy, improve incentives and pursue large-scale privatizations. Private-sector investment in manufacturing subsequently experienced a boom, but this was not really linked to the Government's denationalization programme. Rather, it was led by small enterprises in niche export markets which did not require government assistance in technology acquisition. These enterprises included garments, shrimps and leather-product exporters. The Privatization Board was established in 1993 to sell off the 270 remaining state-owned enterprises. By mid-2001 the Privatization Board had succeeded in transferring to the private sector only 28 enterprises, of which 12 were privatized during 1993–96, and a further 16 during 1996–2001. The Privatization Board has proposed the introduction of a law to protect bureaucrats involved in privatization from retrospective prosecution by future governments. Nevertheless, the role of the private sector is increasing owing to new investments in areas previously reserved for the public sector; these include power generation and telecommunications. The Government is also currently considering selling 49% of its shares in the national airline, Biman Bangladesh Airlines, to a foreign airline. Foreign direct investments have been disappointingly low. According to World Bank estimates, foreign investments amounted to only US $400m. in 1998/99, but were projected to rise to US $800m. per year over the next five years. Between 1996 and 2000 total foreign investments amounted to more than US $2,000m., but they were mostly in power and gas sectors where foreign investors were protected by sovereign guarantees, at the cost of increasing the contingent liabilities of the Bangladeshi Government. Projects under discussion include the construction of a US $240m. cement factory at Sunamganj by the French company, La Farge, the building of private container terminals at Dhaka and Chittagong at a combined cost of US $550m., and a US $600m. Canadian project to construct a commuter train link between Tongi and Islampur in Dhaka.

The most exciting recent development in Bangladesh has been the discovery of vast reserves of natural gas. By 1989 14 gas fields, with a total of 22 gas production wells, had been discovered (including one offshore field). The breakthrough occurred in 1995 when the UK company, Cairn Energy, discovered the Sangu field, which is situated 50 km off the coast of southern Bangladesh in the Bay of Bengal. The official estimate of reserves in Sangu is 1,030,000m. cu ft, but Cairn Energy executives believe that the field could hold up to 2,000,000m. cu ft. Other large gas fields include Titas (4,100,000m. cu ft), Kailashtila (3,650,000m. cu ft), Rashidpur (2,240,000m. cu ft), Habiganj (3,670,000m. cu ft) and Jalalabad (1,500,000m. cu ft). The Bibiyana gas field could have reserves of around 5,000,000m. cu ft or more. In 2001/02 annual production of natural gas was an estimated 387,630m. cu ft, providing 70% of the country's commercial energy. There is thus the potential for the gas discoveries to transform Bangladesh into a middle-income country early in the 21st century. On the other hand, large-scale political conflicts may arise if the benefits are not widely and fairly distributed. Government policies have done little to inspire international confidence so far. Many observers have been perplexed by the award of exploration licences to small companies such as Tullow of Ireland rather than to established international companies like Shell and Mobil. This has raised widespread fears of corruption. In June 1999 Mobil withdrew its bid for exploration licences, apparently in protest at the lack of transparency in allocation procedures. In the following month US Occidental, one of the first in the field, sold its exploration rights to Unocal and withdrew from Bangladesh, ostensibly for cash-flow reasons. Without rapid improvements in government transparency and accountability, the gas sector may serve solely to benefit a few at the expense of overall development. An additional problem has been political opposition to allowing gas exports to India, the most obvious large market for the product. The Asian Development Bank offered Bangladesh a US $250m. loan for constructing a gas pipeline should Bangladesh agree to export gas to India. In the mean time, however, a national committee established to report on gas reserves concluded in June 2002 that proven reserves of gas range from 12,000,000m. to 15,500,000m. cu ft, suggesting that proven reserves are lower than previously envisaged. Ultimately, the decision to export gas would have little to do with the size of the reserves and more to do with the price of the gas abroad compared with its value in domestic use. The reluctance of many economists in Bangladesh to countenance major gas exports is probably based on fears that the revenue would be wasted by the Government. If this is the case, it may be rational to leave the gas unexplored. In other words, the political acceptance of gas exports may be contingent on the state improving its capacity to promote development.

TRADE

Bangladesh's trade balance improved during the 1980s. The trade deficit decreased from an average of more than 10% of GDP in the early 1980s to under 5% in 1997. This was assisted by a significant increase in exports, from 7% of GDP in 1990/91 to 15% of GDP in 1999/2000. In 1997/98, however, the trade deficit rose to 7% of GDP, and widened further in 1998/99, owing to the effects of the flooding. The trade deficit remained high in 2000/01 owing to a surge in imports, caused by fiscal expansion. Imports increased by more than 20%, while exports increased by 12.4%. The increased level of remittances during the 1980s permitted Bangladesh to develop a secondary market for foreign exchange, with the exchange rate determined as a result of bidding by importers in an auction market for receipts from Wage Earner's and Export Performance Licensing Schemes (WES). This WES market, intended to finance the expansion of imports, promotes remittances by providing a premium over the official exchange rate. High levels of remittances in 1997/98 meant that, at the equivalent of only 1.1% of GDP, the current-account deficit was a much lesser cause for concern than the large trade deficit. A 9% increase in remittances in 1998/99 was expected to offset the adverse effect of the floods on the trade balance, leaving the current-account deficit more or less unchanged. In 2000/01 remittances declined by around 3% compared with the previous year, as a result of declining demand for Bangladeshi labour overseas owing to the global slowdown. This adversely affected the balance of payments, which was already weakened by a growing trade deficit. In contrast, in 2001/02 the level of remittances fared better than exports; consequently, the current-account deficit was expected to increase to only 2.5% of GDP.

The Government has sought to promote exports by establishing a series of export processing zones (EPZs). Companies establishing operations in these zones are exempt from taxes for a period of 10 years. In addition, imports for re-export are exempt from all import duties and indirect taxes, and trade-union activities are restricted. The combined exports of the Chittagong, Dhaka and Mongla EPZs exceeded US $1,000m. for the first time in 2000/01 to reach US $1,065m. By 2001/02 the EPZs had a total of 172 industrial units in operation, employing 117,000 workers altogether. Total investment reached more than US $500m.

The Government has recently sought to liberalize its regulations concerning imports, by means of the simplification and standardization of import procedures and the cancellation of quantitative restrictions on industrial raw materials. Companies now enjoy unlimited access to imported raw materials through the WES market, enabling them to adjust production to demand. In addition, under the Trade and Industrial Policy Reform Programme, which was introduced in 1983, there have been attempts made to standardize the structure of tariffs and to reduce their level in an effort to improve the potential for export growth. The most radical change has been to free most imports that had, hitherto, been restricted by an import policy order limited to specific items. The unweighted average tariff was reduced from 89% in 1990/91 to 20% in 1998/99. It had stabilized at around 17% in 2000/01. In recent years India has come under pressure from Bangladesh to allow tariff-free access to Bangladeshi exports, particularly jute products. In 2001/02 the trade imbalance with India amounted to US $1,600m. Prior to 1999 India had agreed to a tariff-free status for a list of products that Bangladesh did not really benefit from. In 1999, however, India consented to let Bangladesh itself suggest a list of 25 specific items. Bangladesh was expected to benefit substantially from such a scheme, should it be implemented.

External debt is mostly limited to the public sector and amounted to US $15,070 in June 2001. As a share of GDP this would make Bangladesh a severely indebted country, but because most of the debt is in the form of soft loans from multilateral agencies such as the World Bank, the debt does not constitute a serious problem. By 2001 the debt service was equivalent to around 10% of total export earnings.

FISCAL AND MONETARY POLICIES

Bangladesh enjoys a relatively stable fiscal and monetary regime, although there are concerns that the budget deficit may be worsening. In 2000/01 the overall budgetary deficit was equivalent to approximately 6% of GDP, but the consolidated fiscal deficit, which includes the heavy losses incurred by state-owned enterprises, was 7.9% of GDP. The cost of the budgetary deficit has been increasing, owing to the decline in cheap foreign credit in the form of development aid. This has forced the Government to seek domestic assistance to finance the deficit at a much higher cost. In mid-2001 domestic borrowing financed 56% of the fiscal deficit. The revenue demands on the Government have been increasing owing to a rapidly expanding civil service, which is growing at roughly twice the rate of growth of the population. Pay awards have to be implemented rapidly, as a political necessity, but reorganization of the administration as a whole is subject to delay and obstruction. Large pay increases were awarded to civil servants in 1998/99.

Public-sector losses in jute and power alone were equivalent to the total budget deficit in 1991. The losses incurred by state-owned enterprises have continued to rise, increasing substantially by 50% in 2000/01 compared with the previous year. The sudden deterioration in public-sector performance is partly explained by electoral politics and by the provision of subsidies to some consumers through state-owned trading corporations. These losses affect the budget deficit by reducing revenue and increasing expenditure via subsidies. Nevertheless, the success in revenue generation, combined with some pressure on current expenditure, has meant that resources available for capital expenditure in the annual development plan have risen marginally. Conversely, Bangladesh has been very successful in allocating a relatively high portion of the budget to the social sector: almost 35% of its total budgetary expenditure was spent on education, health, social security and disaster management in the late 1990s. Defence expenditure in 1998 was only 1.4% of GDP, compared with 2.3% in India and 4.3% in Pakistan. This has meant that, despite relatively low budgetary expenditures in aggregate, Bangladesh has been able to make progress in health and education.

The non-performing loans of the financial sector are currently one of the most pressing problems facing the Government and the Bangladesh Bank. In 1997 nine banks in the public and private sectors were declared insolvent because of bad debts. They comprised four nationalized commercial banks, two de-nationalized banks, two specialized banks and one private bank. The scale of the crisis, with one-third to two-thirds of the banks' loan portfolio in the non-performing category, ruled out large-scale loan recovery through litigation as a feasible option. More drastic solutions, including debt cancellations, will have to be considered if the banking sector is to be restructured.

DEVELOPMENT OUTLOOK

In recent years Bangladesh has improved its developmental performance by encouraging the growth of small export-orientated industries. At the same time, various credit programmes are being operated by the Government and NGOs, specifically to support income-generating activities undertaken by the poorest social groups, as well as special programmes for women. The inaccessibility of the banking system for the majority of the people, particularly the poor, has, if anything, increased since the early 1980s and is a major obstacle to development. This can only be partially offset by the success of the micro-credit programmes of NGOs, such as the Grameen Bank, BRAC and Proshika. The lending programmes of these organizations have been targeted at the landless and, in many cases, have focused particularly on women. In sharp contrast to the poor performances in the formal banking sector (especially regarding urban-industrial lending), the recovery rate in the credit programmes of the NGOs has been excellent. However, the small-scale lending activities of the NGOs are no substitute for a reform of the mainstream banking sector.

The resilience of the Bangladesh economy is demonstrated by its ability to grow steadily despite the disruptive impact of mighty floods and cyclones. Even though the Flood Action Plan based on embankment construction (see Agriculture) has its critics, the way forward for Bangladesh must be to discover appropriate flood-control strategies and to invest in the infrastructure. The country's largest infrastructural project, the construction of the 4.8-km, US $700m. Jamuna Bridge, was approved by the World Bank in early 1992, and completed in June 1998. Financed largely by Japan and the World Bank, the bridge is a sterling example of an economically viable large-scale infrastructure project. It is the longest bridge in South Asia, and is almost certain to transform the economy of northern Bangladesh. Already in 1999 the daily traffic across the bridge, of 2,480 vehicles, was greater than the expected 1,750 vehicles per day, and the daily toll collection was 2% higher than projected.

Ultimately, sustained development in Bangladesh will depend primarily on improvements in political stability and on the capacity of the State to boost development by effectively regulating markets, collecting taxes, investing in infrastructure and assisting in technology acquisition by the private sector. This is particularly important given the low technological base of much of Bangladesh's current exports and the need rapidly to advance technologically in the face of growing competition from other developing countries. In addition, Bangladesh needs to make substantial investments in irrigation and flood control, which requires regional co-operation and international support.

Statistical Survey

Source (unless otherwise stated): Bangladesh Bureau of Statistics, Statistics Division, Ministry of Planning, E- 27/A, Agargaon, Sher-e-banglanagar, Dhaka 1207; tel. (2) 9118045; fax (2) 9111064; e-mail ndbp@bangla.net; internet www.bbstats.org.

Area and Population

AREA, POPULATION AND DENSITY

Area (sq km)	147,570*
Population (census results)	
11 March 1991†	111,455,185
23 January 2001†‡	
Males	62,735,988
Females	60,415,258
Total	123,151,246
Population (official estimates at mid-year)§	
1999	128,100,000
2000	129,800,000
2001	131,500,000
Density (per sq km) at January 2001	834.5

* 56,977 sq miles.

† Including adjustment for underenumeration, estimated to have been 3.08% at 1991 census.

‡ Provisional results.

§ Not adjusted to take account of the 2001 census results.

ADMINISTRATIVE DIVISIONS (1991 census)*

Division	Area (sq km)	Population ('000)†	Density (per sq km)
Barisal	13,297	7,757	583.4
Chittagong	33,771	21,865	647.4
Dhaka	31,119	33,940	1,090.7
Khulna	22,274	13,243	594.5
Rajshahi	34,513	27,500	796.8
Sylhet	12,596	7,150	567.6
Total	147,570	111,455	755.3

* Data refer to the local government structure resulting from reorganizations subsequent to the census date, whereby the divisions of Barisal (formerly part of Khulna) and Sylhet (formerly part of Chittagong) were created.

† Including adjustments for net underenumeration.

PRINCIPAL TOWNS (population at 1991 census)*

Dhaka (capital)	3,612,850	Comilla	135,313
Chittagong	1,392,860	Nawabganj	130,577
Khulna	663,340	Dinajpur	127,815
Rajshahi	294,056	Bogra	120,170
Narayanganj	276,549	Sylhet	114,300
Sitakunda	274,903	Brahmanbaria	109,032
Rangpur	191,398	Tangail	106,004
Mymensingh (Nasirabad)	188,713	Jamalpur	103,556
Barisal (Bakerganj)	170,232	Pabna	103,277
Tongi (Tungi)	168,702	Naogaon	101,266
Jessore	139,710	Sirajganj	99,669

* Figures in each case refer to the city proper. The population of the largest urban agglomerations at the 1991 census was: Dhaka 6,487,459 (including Narayanganj and Tongi); Chittagong 2,079,968 (including Sitakunda); Khulna 921,365; Rajshahi 507,435; Mymensingh 273,350; Sylhet 225,541; Comilla 225,259; Rangpur 208,294; Barisal 202,746; Jessore 169,349; Bogra 161,155.

BIRTHS AND DEATHS*

	Registered live births	Registered deaths
	Rate (per 1,000)	Rate (per 1,000)
1990	32.8	11.4
1991	31.6	11.2
1992	30.8	11.0
1993	28.8	10.0
1994	27.8	9.0
1995	26.5	8.4
1996	25.6	8.1

* Registration is incomplete. According to UN estimates, the average annual rates per 1,000 were: Births 35.1 in 1990–95, 31.4 in 1995–2000; Deaths 11.4 in 1990–95, 9.8 in 1995–2000 (Source: UN, *World Population Prospects: The 2000 Revision*).

1997 (provisional): Registered live births 3,057,000 (birth rate 24.6 per 1,000); Registered deaths 958,000 (death rate 7.7 per 1,000) (Source: UN, *Population and Vital Statistics Report*).

Expectation of life (WHO estimates, years at birth, 2000): Males 60.4; Females 60.8. (Source: WHO, *World Health Report*).

ECONOMICALLY ACTIVE POPULATION*
(sample survey, '000 persons aged 10 years and over, year ending June 1996)

	Males	Females	Total
Agriculture, hunting, forestry and fishing	18,382	16,148	34,530
Mining and quarrying	22	1	23
Manufacturing	2,586	1,499	4,085
Electricity, gas and water	90	13	103
Construction	936	80	1,015
Trade, restaurants and hotels	5,573	488	6,060
Transport, storage and communications	2,263	45	2,308
Financing, insurance, real estate and business services	197	16	213
Community, social and personal services	3,343	1,748	5,092
Activities not adequately defined	373	795	1,168
Total employed	33,765	20,832	54,597
Unemployed	933	484	1,417
Total labour force	34,698	21,317	56,014

* Figures exclude members of the armed forces.

Source: ILO, *Yearbook of Labour Statistics*.

Mid-2000 (estimates in '000): Agriculture, etc. 38,732; Total labour force 69,611 (Source: FAO).

Health and Welfare

KEY INDICATORS

Fertility (births per woman, 2000)	3.7
Under-five mortality rate (per 1,000 live births, 2000)	82
HIV/AIDS (% of persons aged 15–49, 2001)	<0.10
Physicians (per 1,000 head, 1997)	0.20
Hospital beds (per 1,000 head, 1994)	0.3
Health expenditure (1998): US $ per head (PPP)	42
% of GDP	3.8
public (% of total)	36.5
Access to water (% of persons, 2000)	97
Access to sanitation (% of persons, 2000)	53
Human Development Index (2000): ranking	145
value	0.478

For sources and definitions, see explanatory note on p. vi.

Agriculture

PRINCIPAL CROPS
('000 metric tons, year ending 30 June)

	1997/98	1998/99	1999/2000
Wheat	1,803	1,988	1,840
Rice (paddy)	29,709	34,427	35,821*
Millet	55	57†	57†
Potatoes	1,553	2,762	2,933
Sweet potatoes	398	383	378
Beans (dry)	83	54	57
Chick-peas	60	12	12
Lentils	163	165	128
Other pulses	213	183	186†
Groundnuts (in shell)	40	42	40*
Areca nuts (betel)	28	28†	28†
Rapeseed	254	253	249
Sesame seed	49	49*	49*
Linseed	50	46	48*
Cottonseed*	40	24	30
Coconuts	89	89	89*
Cabbages	113	115	112
Lettuce	51	52	53
Spinach	25	25	26
Tomatoes	94	98	100
Cauliflower	79	80	80
Pumpkins, squash and gourds	187	187	198
Dry onions	138	131	134
Garlic	40	38	40
Beans (green)	49	49	49
Other vegetables	700	913	931
Cantaloupes and other melons	96	97	79
Sugar cane	7,379	6,951	6,910
Other sugar crops	323	332	332†
Mangoes	187	187	187
Pineapples	149	146	146†
Bananas	625	562	572
Papayas	41	40	40†
Other fruits and berries	404	405	413
Tea (made)	51	56†	56†
Tobacco (leaves)	37	29	35
Pimento and allspice	53	54†	54†
Ginger	39	38	38†
Other spices	47	46	51
Jute	812	711	711†

* Unofficial figure(s). † FAO estimate(s).

Source: FAO.

LIVESTOCK ('000 head, year ending September)

	1998	1999*	2000*
Cattle	23,400	23,652	23,652
Buffaloes	820	828	828
Sheep	1,110	1,121	1,121
Goats	33,500	33,800	33,800
Chickens	138,200	139,300	139,300
Ducks	13,000*	13,000	13,000

* FAO estimate(s).

Source: FAO.

LIVESTOCK PRODUCTS ('000 metric tons)

	1998	1999	2000
Beef and veal	161	170*	170*
Buffalo meat	3.5	3.5*	3.5*
Mutton and lamb	2.6	2.6*	2.6*
Goat meat	126	127	127*
Chicken meat	96.7	98.5	98.5
Duck meat	13	13	13
Cows' milk*	751	755	755
Buffalo milk*	22.4	22.4	22.4
Sheeps' milk	21.8	22.4	22.4
Goats' milk	1,280	1,296	1,296
Ghee*	16.4	16.4	16.6
Hen eggs	130.1	131.5*	131.5*
Other poultry eggs*	26	26	26
Cattle and buffalo hides	31.5	31.8	31.8*
Goatskins	37.6	38.0	38.0*

* FAO estimate(s).

Source: FAO.

Forestry

ROUNDWOOD REMOVALS
(FAO estimates, '000 cubic metres, excl. bark)

	1997	1998	1999
Sawlogs, veneer logs and logs for sleepers	174	174	174
Pulpwood*	69	69	69
Other industrial wood	367	374	380
Fuel wood	31,888	32,441	33,006
Total	32,498	33,058	33,629

2000: Production as in 1999 (FAO estimates).

* Annual output assumed to be unchanged since 1986.

Source: FAO.

SAWNWOOD PRODUCTION (FAO estimates, '000 cubic metres, incl. railway sleepers)

	1993	1994	1995
Total (all broadleaved)	79	79	70

1996–2000: Annual production as in 1995 (FAO estimates).

Source: FAO.

Fishing

('000 metric tons, live weight)

	1997	1998	1999
Capture	829.4	839.1	924.1
Freshwater fishes	451.1	457.1	508.7
Hilsa shad	214.4	205.7	214.6
Marine fishes	135.9	145.3	169.0
Aquaculture	432.1	514.8	620.1
Roho labeo	82.0	95.0	112.0
Catla	66.0	77.0	91.0
Silver carp	82.0	95.0	112.0
Penaeus shrimps	56.5	66.1	81.1
Total catch	1,261.5	1,353.9	1,544.2

Source: FAO, *Yearbook of Fishery Statistics*.

Mining

(million cubic feet, year ending 30 June)

	1999/2000	2000/01	2001/02*
Natural gas	331,247	372,690	387,630

* Estimate.

Source: IMF, *Bangladesh: Selected Issues and Statistical Appendix* (June 2002).

Industry

SELECTED PRODUCTS ('000 metric tons, unless otherwise indicated; year ending 30 June)

	1997/98	1998/99	1999/2000
Refined sugar	163.8	152.6	123.4
Cigarettes (million)	19,889	19,558	19,589*
Cotton yarn ('000 bales)†	294	304	319*
Woven cotton fabrics ('000 metres)	10,255	11,155	11,882*
Jute fabrics‡	381.1	365.3	335.2
Newsprint	7.7	21.6	17.9
Other paper	38.2	38.3	37.0
Fertilizers	2,030.7	1,799.4	1,904.0

* Provisional figure.

† 1 bale = 180 kg.

‡ Production of jute mills.

Source: Bangladesh Bank.

2000/01 ('000 metric tons): Refined sugar 98; Fertilizers 2,073 (Source: Asian Development Bank, *Key Indicators of Developing Asian and Pacific Countries)*.

Finance

CURRENCY AND EXCHANGE RATES

Monetary Units
100 poisha = 1 taka.

Sterling, Dollar and Euro Equivalents (31 May 2002)
£1 sterling = 84.92 taka;
US $1 = 57.90 taka;
€1 = 54.35 taka;
1,000 taka = £11.78 = $17.27 = €18.40.

Average Exchange Rate (taka per US $)
1999 49.085
2000 52.142
2001 55.807

BUDGET (million taka, year ending 30 June)

Revenue	1999/2000*	2000/01†	2001/02‡
Taxation	158,400	191,100	220,200
Customs duties	41,600	48,300	53,500
Income and profit taxes	23,300	30,700	41,000
Excise duties	—	—	3,000
Value-added tax	81,600	96,800	108,300
Other revenue	45,300	37,000	54,300
Total	203,700	228,100	274,600

Expenditure	1999/2000*	2000/01†	2001/02‡
Goods and services	92,500	97,200	94,000
Pay and allowances	56,000	63,100	61,400
Operations and maintenance	7,900	8,900	9,500
Works	2,700	2,700	3,000
Interest payments	37,600	40,500	45,600
Domestic	30,800	31,900	35,900
Foreign	6,900	8,600	9,700
Subsidies and current transfers	46,700	49,300	63,100
Unallocated	7,500	10,200	19,900
Gross current expenditure	184,300	197,200	222,600

* Revised figures.

† Estimates.

‡ Forecasts.

Source: IMF, *Bangladesh: Selected Issues and Statistical Appendix* (June 2002).

PUBLIC-SECTOR DEVELOPMENT EXPENDITURE
(estimates, million taka, year ending 30 June)

	1997/98	1998/99‡	1999/2000§
Agriculture	6,000	6,100	8,400
Rural development	9,000	12,700	16,000
Water and flood control	10,400	8,800	10,200
Industry	1,200	1,000	2,000
Power, scientific research and natural resources	18,800	21,000	26,100
Transport*	22,600	22,500	24,700
Communications	3,900	3,900	5,000
Physical planning and housing	6,000	6,700	10,200
Education	14,900	16,900	19,600
Health	5,300	10,200	15,300
Family planning	6,300		
Social welfare†	1,600	1,700	2,200
Other sectoral	200	—	400
Total sectoral allocations	106,400	111,400	140,100
Block allocations	10,900	8,700	9,200
Food for Work	5,700	5,300	2,400
Technical assistance	3,000	3,200	3,200
Domestic self-financing	1,700	1,800	2,500
Total development expenditure	122,000	125,100	155,000

* Includes Jamuna Bridge.
† Includes employment.
‡ Revised figures.
§ Estimates.

Source: Ministry of Planning (Implementation, Monitoring and Evaluation Division).

INTERNATIONAL RESERVES (US $ million at 31 December)

	1999	2000	2001
Gold*	19.6	29.6	30.6
IMF special drawing rights	0.9	0.4	1.2
Reserve position in IMF	0.3	0.2	0.2
Foreign exchange	1,602.5	1,485.3	1,273.6
Total	1,623.2	1,515.6	1,305.6

* Valued at market-related prices.

Source: IMF, *International Financial Statistics*.

MONEY SUPPLY (million taka at 31 December)

	1999	2000	2001
Currency outside banks	93,870	116,877	127,863
Demand deposits at deposit money banks*	91,055	102,074	114,572
Total money (incl. others)	184,925	218,951	242,437

* Comprises the scheduled banks plus the agricultural and industrial development banks.

Source: IMF, *International Financial Statistics*.

COST OF LIVING (Consumer Price Index, year ending 30 June; base: 1985/86 = 100)

	1998/99	1999/2000	2000/01
Food, beverages and tobacco	229.7	239.1	241.4
Rent, fuel and lighting	231.0	235.9	241.1
Household requisites	199.7	204.7	209.2
Clothing and footwear	171.5	178.6	183.8
Miscellaneous	214.1	220.9	226.1
All items	227.3	236.2	239.9

Source: Bangladesh Bank.

NATIONAL ACCOUNTS
(rounded figures, million taka at current prices, year ending 30 June)

Expenditure on the Gross Domestic Product

	1998/99	1999/2000	2000/01*
Government final consumption expenditure	100,830	108,390	116,540
Private final consumption expenditure	1,707,130	1,838,530	1,979,930
Gross capital formation	487,580	545,870	609,700
Statistical discrepancy	21,500	2,470	−32,640
Total domestic expenditure	2,317,040	2,495,260	2,673,530
Exports of goods and services	289,860	331,450	377,430
Less Imports of goods and services	409,930	455,850	518,420
GDP in purchasers' values	2,196,970	2,370,860	2,532,540
GDP at constant 1995/96 prices	1,934,290	2,049,270	2,155,060

* Source: mainly IMF, *International Financial Statistics*.

Gross Domestic Product by Economic Activity

	1998/99	1999/2000*	2000/01*
Agriculture and forestry	429,900	446,920	456,310
Fishing	124,850	136,740	134,060
Mining and quarrying	20,660	23,110	26,400
Manufacturing	327,830	348,370	379,420
Electricity, gas and water	28,380	30,720	33,460
Construction	156,250	176,220	193,340
Trade, hotels and restaurants	285,490	306,670	340,690
Transport, storage and communications	180,410	197,430	221,290
Financial, real estate and business services	229,350	247,870	262,760
Public administration and defence	55,520	62,340	66,950
Other services	280,570	311,220	332,390
Sub-total	2,119,210	2,287,610	2,447,070
Import duties	77,760	83,250	85,470
GDP in purchasers' values	2,196,970	2,370,860	2,532,540

* Provisional figures.

Source: Bangladesh Bank.

BALANCE OF PAYMENTS (US $ million)

	1998	1999	2000
Exports of goods f.o.b.	5,141.4	5,458.3	6,399.2
Imports of goods f.o.b.	−6,715.7	−7,535.5	−8,052.9
Trade balance	−1,574.3	−2,077.2	−1,653.7
Exports of services	723.9	777.7	815.1
Imports of services	−1,237.1	−1,396.7	−1,620.2
Balance on goods and services	−2,087.4	−2,696.3	−2,458.9
Other income received	91.5	94.3	78.4
Other income paid	−206.1	258.5	−344.8
Balance on goods, services and income	−2,202.1	−2,860.4	−2,725.3
Current transfers received	2,172.9	2,501.4	2,426.5
Current transfers paid	−5.9	−5.3	−7.0
Current balance	−35.2	−364.4	−305.8
Capital account (net)	238.7	364.1	248.7
Direct investment abroad	−3.0	−0.1	—
Direct investment from abroad	190.1	179.7	280.4
Portfolio investment assets	—	−0.2	—
Portfolio investment liabilities	−4.1	−1.1	1.3
Other investment assets	−859.7	−1,143.7	−1,246.8
Other investment liabilities	560.7	518.4	709.1
Net errors and omissions	201.0	258.0	282.4
Overall balance	288.5	−189.2	−30.7

Source: IMF, *International Financial Statistics*.

FOREIGN AID DISBURSEMENTS (US $ million, year ending 30 June)

	1998/99	1999/2000	2000/01
Bilateral donors	638	785	706
Canada	27	28	19
China, People's Republic	—	18	26
Denmark	33	29	5
Germany	37	21	43
India	7	4	20
Japan	235	390	316
Kuwait	6	8	36
Netherlands	43	28	19
Norway	10	19	17
Sweden	22	20	16
United Kingdom	52	61	53
USA	69	92	39
Multilateral donors	898	790	663
Asian Development Bank	218	283	236
International Development Association	477	354	299
European Union	39	5	32
International Fund for Agricultural Development	11	15	—
UN Development Programme	37	7	17
World Food Programme	81	68	1
UNICEF	19	27	49
Islamic Development Bank	12	16	16
Total aid disbursements	1,536	1,575	1,369

Source: Ministry of Finance (Economic Relations Division).

External Trade

PRINCIPAL COMMODITIES (US $ million, year ending 30 June)

Imports	1998/99	1999/2000	2000/01
Rice	680	115	172
Wheat	317	266	177
Edible oil	287	256	218
Petroleum products	270	406	566
Crude petroleum	118	232	273
Chemicals	n.a.	278	339
Cotton	233	277	360
Yarn	283	300	322
Fertilizer	120	140	129
Cement	105	80	44
Textiles	1,109	1,153	1,291
Iron and steel	n.a.	393	464
Capital goods	1,969	2,133	2,515
Total (incl. others)	8,018	8,403	9,363

Exports	1998/99	1999/2000	2000/01
Raw jute	71.8	72.0	67.0
Jute goods (excl. carpets)	301.9	263.0	229.0
Leather and leather products	168.2	195.0	254.0
Frozen shrimp and fish	274.3	344.0	363.0
Ready-made garments	2,984.7	3,083.0	3,364.0
Knitwear and hosiery products	1,035.4	1,270.0	1,496.0
Chemical fertilizers	58.7	60.0	68.0
Total (incl. others)	5,324.0	5,762.0	6,476.0

Source: Bangladesh Bank.

PRINCIPAL TRADING PARTNERS (US $ million)

Imports c.i.f.	1999	2000	2001
Australia	213	175	194
China, People's Republic	534	667	882
Hong Kong	441	470	493
India	1,024	945	1,186
Indonesia	159	193	201
Japan	559	850	581
Korea, Republic	291	348	625
Singapore	659	761	901
United Kingdom	280	239	173
USA	446	214	297
Total (incl. others)	8,352	8,993	9,959

Exports f.o.b.	1999	2000	2001
Belgium	146	175	182
Canada	77	97	100
France	263	289	301
Germany	450	608	624
Hong Kong	62	87	98
Italy	200	228	263
Japan	71	67	64
Netherlands	187	234	253
United Kingdom	364	440	500
USA	1,411	1,779	1,754
Total (incl. others)	4,520	5,590	5,908

Source: Asian Development Bank, *Key Indicators of Developing Asian and Pacific Countries*.

Transport

RAILWAYS (traffic, year ending 30 June)

	1994/95	1995/96	1996/97
Passenger-kilometres (million)	4,037	3,333	3,754
Freight ton-kilometres (million)	760	689	782

Source: Bangladesh Railway.

ROAD TRAFFIC (motor vehicles in use at 31 December)

	1997*	1998*	1999†
Passenger cars	54,784	57,068	60,846
Buses and coaches	29,310	30,361	32,371
Lorries and vans	40,084	42,425	45,234
Road tractors	2,769	2,813	2,999
Motor cycles and mopeds	125,259	145,259	147,205
Total	252,206	277,926	288,655

* Revised figures.

† Estimates.

Source: International Road Federation, *World Road Statistics*.

SHIPPING

Merchant Fleet (registered at 31 December)

	1999	2000	2001
Number of vessels	306	310	317
Total displacement ('000 grt)	377.8	370.1	387.6

Source: Lloyd's Register-Fairplay, *World Fleet Statistics*.

International Sea-borne Freight Traffic
('000 metric tons)

	1999	2000	2001
Total goods loaded	528	n.a.	868
Total goods unloaded	3,612	n.a.	13,631

Source: UN, *Monthly Bulletin of Statistics*.

CIVIL AVIATION

(traffic on scheduled Biman Bangladesh services)

	1996	1997	1998
Kilometres flown (million)	19	20	20
Passengers carried ('000)	1,252	1,315	1,162
Passenger-km (million)	2,995	3,233	3,422
Total ton-km (million)	406	494	524

Source: UN, *Statistical Yearbook*.

Tourism

TOURIST ARRIVALS BY COUNTRY OF NATIONALITY

	1998	1999	2000
China, People's Republic	4,379	5,208	5,901
India	57,937	62,935	74,268
Japan	7,808	7,055	8,006
Korea, Republic	6,154	6,596	6,746
Malaysia	2,857	2,890	3,827
Nepal	4,799	4,733	4,481
Pakistan	12,087	7,894	10,637
United Kingdom	19,605	22,510	29,106
USA	11,358	9,557	11,924
Total (incl. others)	171,961	172,781	199,211

Tourism receipts (US $ million): 51 in 1998; 50 in 1999; 59 in 2000 (estimate).

Source: World Tourism Organization, *Yearbook of Tourism Statistics*.

Hotel rooms*: 4,166 in 1996; 4,249 in 1997; 4,461 in 1998.
Hotel beds: 8,386 in 1996; 8,552 in 1997; 9,407 in 1998.

* Including rooms of similar establishments.

Source: UN, *Statistical Yearbook for Asia and the Pacific*.

Communications Media

	1998	1999	2000
Television receivers ('000 in use)	920	940	960
Telephones ('000 main lines in use)	412.7	433.0	491.3
Facsimile machines (number in use)*†	75,000	n.a.	n.a.
Daily newspapers:			
Number of titles	221	n.a.	n.a.
Average circulation ('000)	2,539	n.a.	n.a.
Non-daily newspapers and other periodicals:			
Number of titles	257	n.a.	n.a.
Average circulation ('000)	1,304	n.a.	n.a.
Books published (number of titles)	483	n.a.	n.a.
Mobile cellular telephones ('000 subscribers)*	75	149	205
Personal computers ('000 in use)	120	130	200
Internet users ('000)	5	50	100

Radio receivers ('000 in use): 6,150 in 1997.

* Twelve months ending 30 June of year stated.

† Provisional figures.

2001: Telephones ('000 main lines in use) 514.0; Mobile cellular telephones ('000 subscribers) 520; Personal computers ('000 in use) 250; Internet users ('000) 150.

Sources: UNESCO, *Statistical Yearbook*; UN, *Statistical Yearbook*; International Telecommunication Union; Bangladesh Bureau of Statistics.

Education

(1997/98*)

	Institutions	Teachers	Students
Primary schools	66,235	250,990	17,627,000
Secondary schools	13,419	161,141	6,289,000
Universities (government)	11	4,334	105,598,000

Technical colleges and institutes (government, 1990/91)†: 141 institutions, 23,722 students.

* Provisional figures.

† In addition to government-owned and managed institutes, there are many privately administered vocational training centres.

Adult literacy rate (UNESCO estimates): 41.3% (males 52.3%; females 29.9%) in 2000. (Source: UN Development Programme, *Human Development Report*).

Directory

The Constitution

The members who were returned from East Pakistan (now Bangladesh) for the Pakistan National Assembly and the Provincial Assembly in the December 1970 elections formed the Bangladesh Constituent Assembly. A new Constitution for the People's Republic of Bangladesh was approved by this Assembly on 4 November 1972 and came into effect on 16 December 1972. Following the military coup of 24 March 1982, the Constitution was suspended, and the country was placed under martial law. On 10 November 1986 martial law was repealed and the suspended Constitution was revived. The main provisions of the Constitution, including amendments, are listed below.

SUMMARY

Fundamental Principles of State Policy

The Constitution was initially based on the fundamental principles of nationalism, socialism, democracy and secularism, but in 1977 an amendment replaced secularism with Islam. The amendment states that the country shall be guided by 'the principles of absolute trust and faith in the Almighty Allah, nationalism, democracy and socialism'. A further amendment in 1988 established Islam as the state religion. The Constitution aims to establish a society free from exploitation in which the rule of law, fundamental human rights and freedoms, justice and equality are to be secured for all citizens. A socialist economic system is to be established to ensure the attainment of a just and egalitarian society through state and co-operative ownership as well as private ownership within limits prescribed by law. A universal, free and compulsory system of education shall be established. In foreign policy the State shall endeavour to consolidate, preserve, and strengthen fraternal relations among Muslim countries based on Islamic solidarity.

Fundamental Rights

All citizens are equal before the law and have a right to its protection. Arbitrary arrest or detention, discrimination based on race, age, sex, birth, caste or religion, and forced labour are prohibited. Subject to law, public order and morality, every citizen has freedom of movement, of assembly and of association. Freedom of conscience, of speech, of the press and of religious worship are guaranteed.

GOVERNMENT

The President

The President is the constitutional Head of State and is elected by Parliament (Jatiya Sangsad) for a term of five years. He is eligible for re-election. The supreme control of the armed forces is vested in the President. He appoints the Prime Minister and other Ministers as well as the Chief Justice and other judges.

The Executive

Executive authority shall rest in the Prime Minister and shall be exercised by him either directly or through officers subordinate to him in accordance with the Constitution.

There shall be a Council of Ministers to aid and advise the Prime Minister.

The Legislature

Parliament (Jatiya Sangsad) is a unicameral legislature. It comprises 300 members and an additional 30 women members elected by the other members. Members of Parliament, other than the 30 women members, are directly elected on the basis of universal adult franchise from single territorial constituencies. Persons aged 18 and over are entitled to vote. The parliamentary term lasts for five years. War can be declared only with the assent of Parliament. In the case of actual or imminent invasion, the President may take whatever action he may consider appropriate.

THE JUDICIARY

The Judiciary comprises a Supreme Court with High Court and an Appellate Division. The Supreme Court consists of a Chief Justice and such other judges as may be appointed by the President. The High Court division has such original appellate and other jurisdiction and powers as are conferred on it by the Constitution and by other law. The Appellate Division has jurisdiction to determine appeals from decisions of the High Court division. Subordinate courts, in addition to the Supreme Court, have been established by law.

ELECTIONS

An Election Commission supervises elections, delimits constituencies and prepares electoral rolls. It consists of a Chief Election Commissioner and other Commissioners as may be appointed by the President. The Election Commission is independent in the exercise of its functions. Subject to the Constitution, Parliament may make provision as to elections where necessary.

The Government

HEAD OF STATE

President: Prof. IAJUDDIN AHMED (took office 6 September 2002).

COUNCIL OF MINISTERS
(August 2002)

Prime Minister and Minister of the Armed Forces Division, of Defence, of the Cabinet Division, of Power, Energy and Mineral Resources, of Chittagong Hill Tracts Affairs, of the Primary and Mass Education Division, and of the Establishment: Begum KHALEDA ZIA.

Minister of Foreign Affairs: M. MORSHED KHAN.

Minister of Home Affairs: ALTAF HUSSAIN CHOWDHURY.

Minister of Local Government, Rural Development and Co-operatives: ABDUL MANNAN BHUIYAN.

Minister of Finance and of Planning: M. SAIFUR RAHMAN.

Minister of Education: Dr OSMAN FARUQUE.

Minister of Labour and Employment: LUTFAR RAHMAN KHAN AZAD.

Minister of Water Resources: Eng. L. K. SIDDIQI.

Minister of Commerce: AMIR KHASRU MAHMUD CHOWDHURY.

Minister of Industry: M. K. ANWAR.

Minister of Post and Telecommunications: MOHAMMAD AMINUL HAQUE.

Minister of Information: TARIQUL ISLAM.

Minister of Jute: Maj. (retd) HAFIZUDDIN AHMED

Minister of Agriculture: MATIUR RAHMAN NIZAMI.

Minister of Food: ABDULLAH AL-NOMAN.

Minister of Housing and Public Works: MIRZA ABBAS.

Minister of Law, Justice and Parliamentary Affairs: MOUDUD AHMED.

Minister of Communications: NAZMUL HUDA.

Minister of Women's and Children's Affairs: KHURSHID JAHAN HAQ.

Minister of Health and Family Welfare: Dr KHANDAKER M. HOSSAIN.

Minister of Social Welfare: ALI AHSAN MUHAMMAD MUJAHID.

Minister of the Environment and Forests: SHAHJAHAN SIRAJ.

Minister for Fisheries and Livestock: SADEQ HOSSAIN KHOKA.

Minister of Textiles: ABDUL MATIN CHOWDHURY.

Minister of Land: M. SHAMSUL ISLAM.

Minister of Disaster Management and Relief: KAMAL IBNE YUSUF.

Minister of Shipping: Lt-Col (retd) AKBAR HOSSAIN.

Minister of Science and Technology: Dr ABDUL MOYEEN KHAN.

Minister without Portfolio: HARUNUR RASHID KHAN MUNNU.

There are also 29 Ministers of State and three Deputy Ministers.

MINISTRIES

Prime Minister's Office: Old Sangsad Bhaban, Tejgaon, Dhaka; tel. (2) 815100; fax (2) 813244; e-mail pm@pmo.bdonline.com; internet www.bangladeshgov.org/pmo.

Ministry of Agriculture: Bangladesh Secretariat, Bhaban 4, 2nd 9-Storey Bldg, Dhaka; tel. (2) 832137; internet www.bangladeshgov.org/moa.

Ministry of Chittagong Hill Tracts Affairs: Dhaka; internet www.bangladeshgov.org/mochta.

Ministry of Civil Aviation and Tourism: Bangladesh Secretariat, Bhaban 6, 19th Floor, Dhaka 1000; tel. (2) 866485.

Ministry of Commerce: Bangladesh Secretariat, Bhaban 3, Dhaka 1000; tel. (2) 862826; fax (2) 865741.

Ministry of Communications: Bangladesh Secretariat, Bhaban 7, 1st 9-Storey Bldg, 8th Floor, Dhaka 1000; tel. (2) 868752; fax (2) 866636.

Ministry of Cultural Affairs: Dhaka; tel. (2) 402133.

Ministry of Defence: Old High Court Bldg, Dhaka; tel. (2) 259082.

Ministry of Disaster Management and Relief: Dhaka; tel. (2) 866262.

Ministry of Education: Bangladesh Secretariat, Bhaban 7, 2nd 9-Storey Bldg, 6th Floor, Dhaka; tel. (2) 404162.

Ministry of Energy and Mineral Resources: Bangladesh Secretariat, Bhaban 6, First Floor, Dhaka 1000; tel. (2) 865918; fax (2) 861110.

Ministry of Finance: Bangladesh Secretariat, Bhaban 7, 1st 9-Storey Bldg, 3rd Floor, Dhaka 1000; tel. (2) 8690202; fax (2) 865581.

Ministry of Fisheries and Livestock: Dhaka; tel. (2) 862430.

Ministry of Food: Dhaka; internet www.bangladeshgov.org/mof.

Ministry of Foreign Affairs: Segunbagicha, Dhaka 1000; tel. (2) 9569129; fax (2) 9562163; e-mail pspmo@bangla.net; internet www.bangladeshonline.com/gob/mofa.

Ministry of Health and Family Welfare: Bangladesh Secretariat, Main Bldg, 3rd Floor, Dhaka; tel. (2) 832079.

Ministry of Home Affairs: Bangladesh Secretariat, School Bldg, 2nd and 3rd Floors, Dhaka; tel. (2) 404142.

Ministry of Housing and Public Works: Bangladesh Secretariat, Bhaban 5, Dhaka; tel. (2) 834494; fax (2) 861290.

Ministry of Industry: Shilpa Bhaban, 91 Motijheel C/A, Dhaka 1000; tel. (2) 9564250; fax (2) 860588.

Ministry of Information: Bangladesh Secretariat, 2nd 9-Storey Bldg, 8th Floor, Dhaka; tel. (2) 235111; fax (2) 834535.

Ministry of Labour and Employment: Bangladesh Secretariat, 1st 9-Storey Bldg, 4th Floor, Dhaka; tel. (2) 404106; fax (2) 813420.

Ministry of Land: Bangladesh Secretariat, Bhaban 4, 2nd 9-Storey Bldg, 3rd Floor, Dhaka.

Ministry of Local Government, Rural Development and Co-operatives: Bangladesh Secretariat, Bhaban 7, 1st 9-Storey Bldg, 6th Floor, Dhaka.

Ministry of Planning: Block No. 7, Sher-e-Bangla Nagar, Dhaka; tel. (2) 815142; fax (2) 822210.

Ministry of Post and Telecommunications: Bangladesh Secretariat, Bhaban 7, 6th Floor, Dhaka 1000; tel. (2) 864800; fax (2) 865775.

Ministry of Religious Affairs: Dhaka; tel. (2) 404346.

Ministry of Science and Technology: Bangladesh Secretariat, Bhaban 6, Dhaka; tel. (2) 8616144; fax (2) 8619606; e-mail most@bangla.net; internet www.most-bd.org.

Ministry of Shipping: Bangladesh Secretariat, Bhaban 6, 8th Floor, Dhaka 1000; tel. (2) 861275.

Ministry of Social Welfare and Women's Affairs: Bangladesh Secretariat, Bhaban 6, New Bldg, Dhaka; tel. (2) 402076.

Ministry of Textiles: Bangladesh Secretariat, Bhaban 6, 11th Floor, Dhaka 1000; tel. (2) 862051; fax (2) 860600.

Ministry of Youth and Sports: Dhaka; tel. (2) 407670.

President and Legislature

PRESIDENT

On 5 September 2002 the Bangladesh Nationalist Party's presidential candidate, Prof. IAJUDDIN AHMED, was declared elected unopposed by the Election Commission as Bangladesh's new Head of State.

JATIYA SANGSAD

(Parliament)

Speaker: JAMIRUDDIN SIRCAR.

General Election, 1 and 9 October 2001

	Seats
Bangladesh Jatiyatabadi Dal (Bangladesh Nationalist Party—BNP)	199*
Awami League (AL)	62
Jamaat-e-Islami Bangladesh	17
Jatiya Dal	14†
Jatiya Dal (Manju)	1
Bangladesh Krishak Sramik Party	1
Independents	6
Total	300

In addition to the 300 directly-elected members, a further 30 seats are reserved for women members.

* Includes six seats won by the Jatiya Dal (Naziur-Firoz) and the Islami Jatiya Oikya Jote.

† Includes several seats won by the Islami Jatiya Oikya Front.

Political Organizations

Awami League (AL): 23 Bangabandhu Ave, Dhaka; f. 1949; supports parliamentary democracy; advocates socialist economy, but with a private sector, and a secular state; pro-Indian; 28-member central executive committee, 15-member central advisory committee and a 13-member presidium; Pres. Sheikh HASINA WAJED; Gen.-Sec. ZILLUR RAHMAN; c. 1,025,000 mems.

Bangladesh Jatiya League: 500A Dhanmandi R/A, Rd 7, Dhaka; f. 1970 as Pakistan National League, renamed in 1972; supports parliamentary democracy; Leader ATAUR RAHMAN KHAN; c. 50,000 mems.

Bangladesh Jatiyatabadi Dal (Bangladesh Nationalist Party—BNP): 29 Minto Rd, Dhaka; f. 1978 by merger of groups supporting Ziaur Rahman, including Jatiyatabadi Gonotantrik Dal (Jagodal—Nationalist Democratic Party); right of centre; favours multi-party democracy and parliamentary system of govt; Chair. Begum KHALEDA ZIA; Sec.-Gen. ABDUL MANNAN BHUIYAN, TARIQUE RAHMAN.

Bangladesh Khelafat Andolon: 314/2 Lalbagh Kellar Morr, Dhaka 1211; tel. (2) 8612465; fax (2) 9881436; e-mail khelafat@cimabd.com; Supreme Leader SHAH AHMADULLAH ASHRAF IBN HAFEZZEE; Sec.-Gen. Maulana MUHAMMAD ZAFRULLAH KHAN.

Bangladesh Krishak Sramik Party (Peasants' and Workers' Party): Sonargaon Bhavan, 99 South Kamalapur, Dhaka 1217; tel. (2) 834512; f. 1914, renamed 1953; supports parliamentary democracy, non-aligned foreign policy, welfare state, guarantee of fundamental rights for all religions and races, free market economy and non-proliferation of nuclear weapons; 15-mem. exec. council; Pres. A. S. M. SULAIMAN; Sec.-Gen. RASHEED KHAN MEMON; c. 125,000 mems.

Bangladesh Muslim League: Dhaka; Sec.-Gen. Alhaj MOHAMMAD ZAMIR ALI.

Bangladesh People's League: Dhaka; f. 1976; supports parliamentary democracy; Leader KHANDAKER SABBIR AHMED; c. 75,000 mems.

Communist Party of Bangladesh: 21/1 Purana Paltan, Dhaka 1000; tel. (2) 9558612; fax (2) 837464; e-mail manzur@bangla.net; f. 1948; Pres. SHAHIDULLAH CHOWDHURY; Gen. Sec. MUJAHIDUL ISLAM SELIM; c. 22,000 mems.

Democratic League: 68 Jigatola, Dhaka 9; tel. (2) 507994; f. 1976; conservative; Leader ABDUR RAZZAK.

Freedom Party: f. 1987; Islamic; Co-Chair. Lt-Col (retd) SAID FARUQ RAHMAN, Lt-Col (retd) KHANDAKAR ABDUR RASHID.

Gonoazadi League: 30 Banagran Lane, Dhaka.

Islami Jatiya Oikya Front: Dhaka.

Islami Jatiya Oikya Jote: Dhaka; mem. of the BNP-led alliance; Chair. Maulana AZIZUL HAQ; Sec.-Gen. Mufti FAZLUL HAQ AMINI.

Islamic Solidarity Movement: 84 East Tejturi Bazar, Tejgaon, Dhaka 1215; tel. (2) 325886; fmrly known as Islamic Democratic League; renamed as above in 1984; Chair. HAFIZ MUHAMMAD HABIBUR RAHMAN.

Jamaat-e-Islami Bangladesh: 505 Elephant Rd, Bara Maghbazar, Dhaka 1217; tel. (2) 401581; f. 1941; Islamic fundamentalist; mem. of the BNP-led alliance; Chair. Prof. GHULAM AZAM; Sec.-Gen. ALI AHSAN MUHAMMAD MUJAHID; Asst Sec.-Gen. MUHAMMAD QUAMARUZZAMAN.

Jatiya Dal (National Party): c/o Jatiya Sangsad, Dhaka; f. 1983 as Jana Dal; reorg. 1986, when the National Front (f. 1985), a five-party alliance of the Jana Dal, the United People's Party, the Gonotantrik Dal, the Bangladesh Muslim League and a breakaway section of the Bangladesh Nationalist Party, formally converted itself into a single pro-Ershad grouping; advocates nationalism, democracy, Islamic ideals and progress; Chair. Lt-Gen. HOSSAIN MOHAMMAD ERSHAD; Sec.-Gen. NAZIUR RAHMAN MONZUR; in April 1999 a group of dissidents, led by MIZANUR RAHMAN CHOWDHURY and ANWAR HUSSAIN MANJU, formed a rival faction; rival faction, led by Kazi FIROZ RASHID, was also formed.

Jatiya Samajtantrik Dal (Rab): breakaway faction of JSD; Pres. A. S. M. ABDUR RAB; Gen. Sec. HASANUL HAQUE INU.

Jatiya Samajtantrik Dal (JSD—(S)) (National Socialist Party): 23 DIT Ave, Malibagh Choudhury Para, Dhaka; f. 1972; left-wing; Leader SHAJAHAN SIRAJ; c. 5,000 mems.

Jatiyo Gonotantrik Party (JAGPA): Purana Paltan, Dhaka; Jt Gen. Secs AZIZUR RAHMAN, SARDAR SHAHJAHAN.

Jatiyo Janata Party: Janata Bhaban, 47A Toyenbee Circular Rd, Dhaka 1000; tel. (2) 9667923; f. 1976; social democratic; Chair. NURUL ISLAM KHAN; Gen. Sec. MUJIBUR RAHMAN HERO; c. 35,000 mems.

National Awami Party—Bhashani (NAP): Dhaka; f. 1957; Maoist; Leader NAZRUL ISLAM; Gen. Sec. ABDUS SUBHANI.

National Awami Party—Muzaffar (NAP—M): 21 Dhanmandi Hawkers' Market, 1st Floor, Dhaka 5; f. 1957, reorg. 1967; c. 500,000 mems; Pres. MUZAFFAR AHMED; Sec.-Gen. PANKAJ BHATTACHARYA.

Parbattya Chattagram Jana Sanghati Samity: f. 1972; political wing of the Shanti Bahini; represents interests of Buddhist tribals in Chittagong Hill Tracts; Leader JATINDRA BODDHIPRIYA ('SHANTU') LARMA.

Samyabadi Dal: Dhaka; Maoist; Leader MOHAMMAD TOAHA.

Zaker Party: f. 1989; supports sovereignty and the introduction of an Islamic state system; Leader SYED HASMATULLAH; Mem. of the Presidium MUSTAFA AMIR FAISAL.

Diplomatic Representation

EMBASSIES AND HIGH COMMISSIONS IN BANGLADESH

Afghanistan: House CWN(C) 2A Gulshan Ave, Gulshan Model Town, Dhaka 1212; tel. (2) 603232.

Australia: 184 Gulshan Ave, Gulshan Model Town, Dhaka 1212; tel. (2) 8813105; fax (2) 8811125; internet www.aushighcomdhaka.org; High Commissioner: ROBERT FLYNN.

Bhutan: House No. SE(N) 12, 107 Gulshan Ave, Dhaka 1212; tel. (2) 8827160; fax (2) 8823939; e-mail kutshab@bdmail.net; Ambassador: LHATU WANGCHUK.

Canada: House 16A, Rd 48, Gulshan Model Town, POB 569, Dhaka 1212; tel. (2) 607071; fax (2) 883043; High Commissioner: JON SCOTT.

China, People's Republic: Plot NE(L) 6, Rd 83, Gulshan Model Town, Dhaka 1212; tel. (2) 884862; Ambassador: HU QIANWEN.

Czech Republic: Dhaka; tel. (2) 601673.

Denmark: House NW(H) 1, Rd 51, Gulshan Model Town, POB 2056, Dhaka 1212; tel. (2) 8821799; fax (2) 8823638; e-mail dandhaka@mail.citechco.net; internet www.citechco.net/dandhaka; Ambassador: NIELS SEVERIN MUNK.

Egypt: House NE(N) 9, Rd 90, Gulshan Model Town, Dhaka 1212; tel. (2) 882766; fax (2) 884883; Ambassador: OSSAMA MOHAMED TAWFIK.

France: House 18, Rd 108, Gulshan Model Town, POB 22, Dhaka 1212; tel. (2) 8813812; Ambassador: MICHEL LUMMAUX.

Germany: 178 Gulshan Ave, Gulshan Model Town, POB 108, Dhaka 1212; tel. (2) 8824735; fax (2) 8823141; e-mail aadhaka@citecho.net; Ambassador: DIETRICH ANDREAS.

Holy See: Lake Rd 2, Diplomatic Enclave, Baridhara Model Town, POB 6003, Dhaka 1212; tel. (2) 8822018; fax (2) 8823574; e-mail ve@bdonline.com; Apostolic Nuncio: Most Rev. EDWARD JOSEPH ADAMS, Titular Archbishop of Scala.

Hungary: 80 Gulshan Ave, Dhaka; tel. (2) 608101; fax (2) 883117; Chargé d'affaires a.i.: I. B. BUDAY.

India: House 120, Rd 2, Dhanmandi R/A, Dhaka 1205; tel. (2) 8615373; fax (2) 8613662; internet www.hcidhaka.org; High Commissioner: MANI LAL TRIPATHI.

Indonesia: CWS(A) 10, 75 Gulshan Ave, Gulshan Model Town, Dhaka 1212; tel. (2) 600131; fax (2) 885391; Ambassador: HADI A. WAYARABI ALHADAR.

Iran: CWN(A) 12 Kamal Ataturk Ave, Gulshan Model Town, Dhaka 1212; tel. (2) 601432; Ambassador: MOHAMMAD SADEQ FAYAZ.

Iraq: House 8, Rd 59, Gulshan 2, Dhaka 1212; tel. (2) 600298; fax (2) 8823277; Ambassador: NAHED ALI AJAJ.

Italy: Plot No. 2 & 3, Rd 74/79, Gulshan Model Town, POB 6062, Dhaka 1212; tel. (2) 882781; fax (2) 882578; e-mail ambdhaka@citechco.net; internet www.citechco.net/italydhaka; Ambassador: MARIO FILIPPO PINI.

Japan: 5 & 7, Dutabash Rd, Baridhara, Dhaka; tel. (2) 870087; fax (2) 886737; Ambassador: YOSHIKAZU KANEKO.

Korea, Democratic People's Republic: House 6, Rd 7, Baridhara Model Town, Dhaka; tel. (2) 601250; Ambassador: RI SANG IL.

Korea, Republic: 4 Madani Ave, Diplomatic Enclave, Baridhara, Dhaka; tel. (2) 872088; fax (2) 883871; e-mail rokdhaka@bangla.net; Ambassador: LEE KYU-HUNG.

Kuwait: Plot 39, Rd 23, Block J, Banani, Dhaka 13; tel. (2) 600233; Ambassador: AHMAD MURSHED AL-SULIMAN.

Libya: NE(D) 3A, Gulshan Ave (N), Gulshan Model Town, Dhaka 1212; tel. (2) 600141; Secretary of People's Committee: MUSBAH ALI A. MAIMOON (acting).

Malaysia: House 4, Rd 118, Gulshan Model Town, Dhaka 1212; tel. (2) 887759; fax (2) 883115; High Commissioner: Dato' ZULKIFLY IBRAHIM BIN ABDUR RAHMAN.

Myanmar: NE(L) 3, Rd 84, Gulshan, Dhaka 1212; tel. (2) 601915; fax (2) 8823740; Ambassador: U OHN THWIN.

Nepal: United Nations Rd, Rd 2, Diplomatic Enclave, Baridhara, Dhaka; tel. (2) 601790; fax (2) 8826401; e-mail rnedhaka@bdmail.net; Ambassador: MADHU RAMAN ACHARYA.

Netherlands: House 49, Rd 90, Gulshan Model Town, POB 166, Dhaka 1212; tel. (2) 882715; fax (2) 883326; e-mail nlgovdha@citechco.net; internet www.citechco.net/Netherlands; Ambassador: J. L. IJZERMANS.

Pakistan: House NE(C) 2, Rd 71, Gulshan Model Town, Dhaka 1212; tel. (2) 885388; High Commissioner: KARAM ELAHI.

Philippines: House NE(L) 5, Rd 83, Gulshan Model Town, Dhaka 1212; tel. (2) 605945; Ambassador: CESAR C. PASTORES.

Poland: House 12A, Rd 86, Gulshan 2, POB 6089, Dhaka 1212; tel. (2) 608503; fax (2) 8827568; e-mail pl_dhaka@citechco.net; Chargé d'affaires a.i.: ZBIGNIEW SMUGA.

Qatar: House 23, Rd 108, Gulshan Model Town, Dhaka 1212; tel. (2) 604477; Chargé d'affaires a.i.: ABDULLAH AL-MUTAWA.

Romania: House 33, Rd 74, Gulshan Model Town, Dhaka 1212; tel. (2) 601467; Chargé d'affaires a.i.: ALEXANDRU VOINEA.

Russia: NE(J) 9, Rd 79, Gulshan Model Town, Dhaka 1212; tel. (2) 8828147; fax (2) 8823735; e-mail rusemb@citechco.net; Ambassador: NIKOLAI G. SHEVCHENKO.

Saudi Arabia: House 12, Rd 92, Gulshan (North), Dhaka 1212; tel. (2) 889124; fax (2) 883616; Ambassador: ABDULLAH OMAR BARRY.

Sri Lanka: House NW 15, Rd 50, Gulshan 2, Dhaka; tel. (2) 882790; fax (2) 883971; e-mail slhc@citechco.net; High Commissioner: S. B. ATUGODA.

Sweden: House 1, Rd 51, Gulshan, Dhaka 1212; tel. (2) 884761; fax (2) 883948; Ambassador: ANDERS JOHNSON.

Thailand: House NW(D) 4, Rd 58–62, Gulshan Model Town, Dhaka 1212; tel. (2) 8812795; fax (2) 8823588; Ambassador: PITHAYA POOKAMAN.

Turkey: House 7, Rd 62, Gulshan Model Town, Dhaka 1212; tel. (2) 8823536; fax (2) 8823873; e-mail dakkabe@citechco.net; Ambassador: (vacant).

United Arab Emirates: House 41, Rd 113, Gulshan Model Town, Dhaka 1212; tel. (2) 9882244; fax (2) 8823225; e-mail info@uaeembassydhaka.com; internet www.uaeembassydhaka.com; Chargé d'affaires a.i.: ABDUL RAZAK HADI.

United Kingdom: United Nations Rd, Baridhara, POB 6079, Dhaka 1212; tel. (2) 8822705; fax (2) 8826181; e-mail ukcomsec@bolonline.com; internet www.ukinbangladesh.org; High Commissioner: Dr DAVID CARTER.

USA: Diplomatic Enclave, Madani Ave, Baridhara, POB 323, Dhaka 1212; tel. (2) 8824700; fax (2) 8823744; e-mail ustc@bangla.net; internet www.usembassy-dhaka.org; Ambassador: MARY ANN PETERS.

Judicial System

A judiciary, comprising a Supreme Court with High Court and Appellate Divisions, is in operation (see under Constitution).

Supreme Court: Dhaka 2; tel. (2) 433585.

Chief Justice: MUSTAFA KAMAL.

Attorney-General: MAHMUDUL ISLAM.

Deputy Attorney-General: A. M. FAROOQ.

Religion

The results of the 1991 census classified 88.3% of the population as Muslims, 10.5% as caste Hindus and scheduled castes, and the remainder as Buddhists, Christians and tribals.

Freedom of religious worship is guaranteed under the Constitution but, under the 1977 amendment to the Constitution, Islam was declared to be one of the nation's guiding principles and, under the 1988 amendment, Islam was established as the state religion.

BUDDHISM

World Federation of Buddhists Regional Centre: Buddhist Monastery, Kamalapur, Dhaka 14; Leader Ven. VISUDDHANANDA MAHATHERO.

CHRISTIANITY

Jatiyo Church Parishad (National Council of Churches): 395 New Eskaton Rd, Moghbazar, Dhaka 2; tel. (2) 402869; f. 1949 as East Pakistan Christian Council; four mem. churches; Pres. Dr SAJAL DEWAN; Gen. Sec. M. R. BISWAS.

Church of Bangladesh—United Church

After Bangladesh achieved independence, the Diocese of Dacca (Dhaka) of the Church of Pakistan (f. 1970 by the union of Anglicans, Methodists, Presbyterians and Lutherans) became the autonomous Church of Bangladesh. In 1986 the Church had an estimated 12,000 members. In 1990 a second diocese, the Diocese of Kushtia, was established.

Bishop of Dhaka: Rt Rev. BARNABAS DWIJEN MONDAL, St Thomas's Church, 54 Johnson Rd, Dhaka 1100; tel. (2) 7116546; fax (2) 7118218; e-mail cbdacdio@bangla.net.

Bishop of Kushtia: Rt Rev. MICHAEL BAROI, Church of Bangladesh, 94 N.S. Rd, Thanapara, Kushtia; tel. (71) 3603.

The Roman Catholic Church

For ecclesiastical purposes, Bangladesh comprises one archdiocese and five dioceses. At 31 December 2000 there were an estimated 263,595 adherents in the country.

Catholic Bishops' Conference: Archbishop's House, 1 Kakrail Rd, Ramna, POB 3, Dhaka 1000; tel. (2) 9358247; fax (2) 8314993; e-mail secabdac@aitlbd.net; f. 1978; Pres. Most Rev. MICHAEL ROZARIO, Archbishop of Dhaka.

Secretariat: CBCB Centre, 24C Asad Ave, Mohammadpur, Dhaka 1207; tel. and fax (2) 9127339; e-mail cbcbsec@bdcom.com; Sec.-Gen. Rt Rev. THEOTONIUS GOMES, Titular Bishop of Zucchabar.

Archbishop of Dhaka: Most Rev. MICHAEL ROZARIO, Archbishop's House, 1 Kakrail Rd, Ramna, POB 3, Dhaka 1000; tel. (2) 9358247; e-mail secabdac@aitlbd.net.

Other Christian Churches

Bangladesh Baptist Sangha: 33 Senpara, Parbatta, Mirpur 10, Dhaka 1216; tel. (2) 8012967; fax (2) 9005842; e-mail bbsangha @bdmail.net; f. 1922; 33,232 mems (2000); Pres. SUSANTA ADHIKARI; Gen. Sec. Rev. ROBERT SARKAR.

In early 2000 there were about 48 denominational churches active in the country, including the Bogra Christian Church, the Evangelical Christian Church, the Garo Baptist Union, the Reformed Church of Bangladesh and the Sylhet Presbyterian Synod. The Baptist Sangha was the largest Protestant Church.

The Press

PRINCIPAL DAILIES

Bengali

Ajker Kagoj: Dhaka; tel. (2) 9138245; fax (2) 9139859; e-mail ajkkagoj@hotmail.com; internet www.ajkerkagoj.com; circ. 9,139,848.

Azadi: 9 C.D.A. C/A, Momin Rd, Chittagong; tel. (31) 224341; f. 1960; Editor Prof. MOHAMMAD KHALED; circ. 13,000.

Banglar Bani: 81 Motijheel C/A, Dhaka 1000; tel. (2) 237548; e-mail bani@bangla.net; f. 1972; Editor Sheikh FAZLUL KARIM SALIM; circ. 20,000.

Dainik Bangla: Dhaka; f. 1964; Editor AHMED HUMAYUN; circ. 65,000.

Dainik Bhorer Kagoj: 8 Link Rd, Banglamotor, Dhaka; tel (2) 868802; fax (2) 868801; e-mail bkagoj@bangla.net; Editor MATIUR RAHMAN; circ. 50,000.

Dainik Birol: 26 R. K. Mission Rd, Motijheel C/A, Dhaka 1203; tel. (2) 7121620; fax (2) 8013721; Chair. of Editorial Bd ABDULLAH AL-NASER.

Dainik Inqilab: 2/1 Ramkrishna Mission Rd, Dhaka 1203; tel. (2) 9563162; fax (2) 9552881; e-mail inqilab@bttb.net; internet www.dailyinqilab.com; Editor A. M. M. BAHAUDDIN; circ. 180,025.

Dainik Ittefaq: 1 Ramkrishna Rd, Dhaka 1203; tel. (2) 256075; e-mail ittefaqnews@bangla.net; internet www.ittefaq.com; f. 1953; Propr/Editor ANWAR HUSSAIN MANJU; circ. 200,000.

Dainik Jahan: 3/B Shehra Rd, Mymensingh; tel. (91) 5677; f. 1980; Editor MUHAMMAD HABIBUR RAHMAN SHEIKH; circ. 4,000.

Dainik Janakantha (Daily People's Voice): Globe Janakantha Shilpa Paribar, Janakantha Bhaban, Dhaka 1000; tel. (2) 9347780; fax (2) 9351317; e-mail janakantha@citechco.net; internet www.janakantha.net; f. 1993; Man. Editor TOAB KHAN; Exec. Editor BORHAN AHMED; circ. 100,000.

Dainik Janata: 24 Aminbagh, Shanti Nagar, Dhaka 1217; tel. (2) 400498; Editor Dr M. ASADUR RAHMAN.

Dainik Janmobhumi: 110/1 Islampur Rd, Khulna; tel. (41) 721280; fax (41) 724324; f. 1982; Editor HUMAYUN KABIR; circ. 30,000.

Dainik Karatoa: Chalkjadu Rd, Bogra; tel. (51) 3660; fax (51) 5898; f. 1976; Editor MOZAMMEL HAQUE LALU; circ. 40,000.

Dainik Khabar: 137 Shanti Nagar, Dhaka 1217; tel. (2) 406601; f. 1985; Editor MIZANUR RAHMAN MIZAN; circ. 18,000.

Dainik Millat: Dhaka; tel. (2) 242351; Editor CHOWDHURY MOHAMMAD FAROOQ.

Dainik Nava Avijan: Lalkuthi, North Brook Hall Rd, Dhaka; tel. (2) 257516; Editor A. S. M. REZAUL HAQUE; circ. 15,000.

Dainik Patrika: 85 Elephant Rd, Maghbazar, Dhaka 1217; tel. (2) 415057; fax (2) 841575; e-mail patrika@citechco.net; Publr and Chief Editor MIA MUSA HOSSAIN; Editor M. FAISAL HASSAN (acting).

Dainik Probaha: 3 KDA Ave, Khulna; tel. (41) 722552; f. 1977; Editor ASHRAF-UL-HAQUE; circ. 11,400.

Dainik Purbanchal: 38 Iqbal Nagar Mosque Lane, Khulna 9100; tel. (41) 22251; fax (41) 21432; f. 1974; Editor LIAQUAT ALI; circ. 42,000.

Dainik Rupashi Bangla: Abdur Rashid Rd, Natun Chowdhury Para, Bagicha Gaon, Comilla 3500; tel. (81) 76689; f. 1972 (a weekly until 1979); Editor Prof. ABDUL WAHAB; circ. 10,000.

Dainik Sangram: 423 Elephant Rd, Baramaghbazar, Dhaka 1217; tel. (2) 9330579; fax (2) 8315094; e-mail dsangram@bttb.net; f. 1970; Chair. ALI AHSAN MUJAHID; Editor ABUL ASAD; circ. 45,000.

Dainik Sphulinga: Amin Villa, P-5 Housing Estate, Jessore 7401; tel. (421) 6433; f. 1971; Editor Mian ABDUS SATTAR; circ. 14,000.

Dainik Uttara: Bahadur Bazar, Dinajpur Town, Dinajpur; tel. (531) 4326; f. 1974; Editor Prof. MUHAMMAD MOHSIN; circ. 8,500.

Ganakantha: Dhaka; f. 1979; morning; Editor JAHANGIR KABIR CHOWDHURY; Exec. Editor SAIYED RABIUL KARIM; circ. 15,000.

Janabarta: 5 Babu Khan Rd, Khulna; tel. (41) 21075; f. 1974; Editor SYED SOHRAB ALI; circ. 4,000.

Jugabheri: Sylhet; tel. (821) 5461; f. 1931; Editor FAHMEEDA RASHEED CHOWDHURY; circ. 6,000.

Manav Jomeen (Human Land): Dhaka; f. 1998; tabloid.

Naya Bangla: 101 Momin Rd, Chittagong; tel. (31) 206247; f. 1978; Editor ABDULLAH AL-SAGIR; circ. 12,000.

Protidin: Ganeshtola, Dinajpur; tel. (531) 4555; f. 1980; Editor KHAIRUL ANAM; circ. 3,000.

Runner: Pyari Mohan Das Rd, Bejpara, Jessore; tel. (421) 6943; f. 1980; circ. 2,000.

Sangbad: 36 Purana Paltan, Dhaka 1000; tel. (2) 9558147; fax (2) 9562882; e-mail sangbad@bangla.net; f. 1952; Editor AHMADUL KABIR; circ. 71,050.

Swadhinata: Chittagong; tel. (31) 209644; f. 1972; Editor ABDULLAH AL-HARUN; circ. 4,000.

English

Bangladesh Observer: Observer House, 33 Toyenbee Circular Rd, Motijheel C/A, Dhaka 1000; tel. (2) 235105; e-mail observer@shapla.net; internet www.thebangladeshobserver.com; f. 1949; morning; Editor S. M. ALI; circ. 75,000.

The Bangladesh Times: Dhaka; tel. (2) 233195; f. 1975; morning; Editor MAHBUB ANAM; circ. 35,000.

Daily Evening News: 26 R. K. Mission Rd, Motijheel C/A, Dhaka 1203; tel. (2) 7121619; fax (2) 8013721; Chair. of Editorial Bd ABDULLAH AL-NASER.

Daily Rupali: 28/A/3 Toyenbee Circular Rd, Dhaka 1000; tel. (2) 235542; fax (2) 9565558; e-mail network@bangla.net; Editor MAFUZUR RAHMAN MITA.

Daily Star: 19 Karwan Bazar, Dhaka 1215; tel. (2) 8124944; fax (2) 8125155; e-mail dseditor@gononet.com; internet www.dailystarnews.com; f. 1991; Publr and Editor MAHFUZ ANAM; circ. 30,000.

Daily Tribune: 38 Iqbal Nagar Mosque Lane, Khulna 9100; tel. (41) 21944; fax (41) 22251; f. 1978; morning; Editor FERDOUSI ALI; circ. 22,000.

Financial Express: 28/1 Toyenbee Circular Rd, 2nd Floor, POB 2526, Dhaka 1000; tel. (2) 9568154; fax (2) 9567049; e-mail tfe@bangla.net; internet www.financial-express.com; f. 1994; Editor-in-Chief REAZUDDIN AHMED.

The Independent: Beximco Media Complex, 32 Kazi Nazrul Islam Ave, Karwan Bazar, Dhaka 1215; tel. (2) 9129938; fax (2) 9127722; e-mail ind@gononet.com; internet www.independent-bangladesh.com; f. 1995; Editor MAHBUBUL ALAM.

New Nation: 1 Ramkrishna Mission Rd, Dhaka 1203; tel. (2) 256071; fax (2) 245536; e-mail newnation@nation-online.com; internet www.nation-online.com; f. 1981; Editor ALAMGIR MOHIUDDIN; circ. 15,000.

People's View: 102 Siraj-ud-Daulla Rd, Chittagong; tel. (31) 227403; f. 1969; Editor SABBIR ISLAM; circ. 3,000.

PERIODICALS

Bengali

Aachal: Dhaka; weekly; Editor FERDOUSI BEGUM.

Adhuna: 1/3 Block F, Lalmatia, Dhaka 1207; tel. (2) 812353; fax (2) 813095; e-mail adab@bdonline.com; f. 1974; quarterly; publ. by the Asscn of Devt Agencies in Bangladesh (ADAB); Exec. Editor MINAR MONSUR; circ. 10,000.

Ahmadi: 4 Bakshi Bazar Rd, Dhaka 1211; tel. (2) 7300808; fax (2) 7300925; e-mail amgb@bol-online.com; f. 1925; fortnightly; Editor-in-Chief M. A. S. MAHMOOD; Exec. Editor MOHAMMAD M. RAHMAN.

Alokpat: 166 Arambagh, Dhaka 1000; tel. (2) 413361; fax (2) 863060; fortnightly; Editor RABBANI JABBAR.

Amod: Chowdhury Para, Comilla 3500; tel. (81) 5193; f. 1955; weekly; Editor SHAMSUN NAHAR RABBI; circ. 6,000.

Ananda Bichitra: Dhaka; tel. (2) 241639, f. 1986; fortnightly; Editor SHAHADAT CHOWDHURY; circ. 32,000.

Begum: 66 Loyal St, Dhaka 1; tel. (2) 233789; f. 1947; women's illustrated weekly; Editor NURJAHAN BEGUM; circ. 25,000.

Bichitra: Dhaka; tel. (2) 232086; e-mail bchitra@bangla.net; f. 1972; weekly; Editor SHAHADAT CHOWDHURY; circ. 42,000.

Chakra: 242A Nakhalpara, POB 2682, Dhaka 1215; tel. (2) 604568; social welfare weekly; Editor HUSNEARA AZIZ.

Chitra Desh: 24 Ramkrishna Mission Rd, Dhaka 1203; weekly; Editor HENA AKHTAR CHOWDHURY.

Chitrali: Observer House, 33 Toyenbee Circular Rd, Motijheel C/A, Dhaka 1000; tel. (2) 9550938; fax (2) 9562243; f. 1953; film weekly; Editor PRODIP KUMAR DEY; circ. 25,000.

Ekota: 15 Larmini St, Wari, Dhaka; tel. (2) 257854; f. 1970; weekly; Editor MATIUR RAHMAN; circ. 25,000.

Fashal: 28J Toyenbee Circular Rd, Motijheel C/A, Dhaka 1000; tel. (2) 233099; f. 1965; agricultural weekly; Chief Editor ERSHAD MAZUMDAR; circ. 8,000.

Ispat: Majampur, Kushtia; tel. (71) 3676; f. 1976; weekly; Editor WALIUR BARI CHOUDHURY; circ. 3,000.

Jaijaidin: 15 New Bailey Rd, Dhaka 1000; tel. (2) 8316448; fax (2) 9568598; e-mail jajadi@aitlbd.net; internet www.jaijaidin.com; f. 1984; weekly; Editor SHAFIK REHMAN; circ. 100,000.

Jhorna: 4/13 Block A, Lalmatia, Dhaka; tel. (2) 415239; Editor MUHAMMAD JAMIR ALI.

Kalantar: 87 Khanjahan Ali Rd, Khulna; tel. (41) 61424; f. 1971; weekly; Editor NOOR MOHAMMAD; circ. 12,000.

Kankan: Nawab Bari Rd, Bogra; tel. (51) 6424; f. 1974; weekly; Editor Mrs SUFIA KHATUN; circ. 6,000.

Kirajagat: National Sports Control Board, 62/63 Purana Paltan, Dhaka; f. 1977; weekly; Editor ALI MUZZAMAN CHOWDHURY; circ. 7,000.

Kishore Bangla: Observer House, Motijheel C/A, Dhaka 1000; juvenile weekly; f. 1976; Editor RAFIQUL HAQUE; circ. 5,000.

Moha Nagar: 4 Dilkusha C/A, Dhaka 1000; tel. (2) 255282; Editor SYED MOTIUR RAHMAN.

Moshal: 4 Dilkusha C/A, Dhaka 1000; tel. (2) 231092; Editor MUHAMMAD ABUL HASNAT; circ. 3,000

Muktibani: Toyenbee Circular Rd, Motijheel C/A, Dhaka 1000; tel. (2) 253712; f. 1972; weekly; Editor NIZAM UDDIN AHMED; circ. 35,000.

Natun Bangla: 44/2 Free School St Bylane, Hatirpool, Dhaka 1205; tel. (2) 866121; fax (2) 863794; e-mail mujib@bangla.net; f. 1971; weekly; Editor MUJIBUR RAHMAN.

Natun Katha: 31E Topkhana Rd, Dhaka; weekly; Editor HAJERA SULTANA; circ. 4,000.

Nipun: 520 Peyarabag, Magbazar, Dhaka 11007; tel. (2) 312156; monthly; Editor SHAJAHAN CHOWDHURY.

Parikrama: 65 Shanti Nagar, Dhaka; tel. (2) 415640; Editor MOMTAZ SULTANA.

Prohar: 35 Siddeswari Rd, Dhaka 1217; tel. (2) 404206; Editor MUJIBUL HUQ.

Protirodh: Dept of Answar and V.D.P. Khilgoan, Ministry of Home Affairs, School Bldg, 2nd and 3rd Floors, Bangladesh Secretariat, Dhaka; tel. (2) 405971; f. 1977; fortnightly; Editor ZAHANGIR HABIBULLAH; circ. 20,000.

Purbani: 1 Ramkrishna Mission Rd, Dhaka 1203; tel. (2) 256503; f. 1951; film weekly; Editor KHONDKER SHAHADAT HOSSAIN; circ. 22,000.

Robbar: 1 Ramkrishna Mission Rd, Dhaka; tel. (2) 256071; e-mail robbar@nation-online.com; internet www.robbar.com; f. 1978; weekly; Editor ABDUL HAFIZ; circ. 20,000.

Rokshena: 13B Avoy Das Lane, Tiktuli, Dhaka; tel. (2) 255117; Editor SYEDA AFSANA.

Sachitra Bangladesh: 112 Circuit House Rd, Dhaka 1000; tel. (2) 402129; f. 1979; fortnightly; Editor A. B. M. ABDUL MATIN; circ. 8,000.

Sachitra Sandhani: 68/2 Purana Paltan, Dhaka; tel. (2) 409680; f. 1978; weekly; Editor GAZI SHAHABUDDIN MAHMUD; circ. 13,000.

Sandip Bhabhan: 28/A/3 Toyenbee Circular Rd, Dhaka; tel. (2) 235542; fax (2) 9565558; e-mail network@bangla.net; weekly; Editor MAFUZUR RAHMAN MITA.

Shishu: Bangladesh Shishu Academy, Old High Court Compound, Dhaka 1000; tel. (2) 230317; f. 1977; children's monthly; Editor GOLAM KIBRIA; circ. 5,000.

Sonar Bangla: 423 Elephant Rd, Mogh Bazar, Dhaka 1217; tel. (2) 400637; f. 1961; Editor MUHAMMED QAMARUZZAMAN; circ. 25,000.

Swadesh: 19 B.B. Ave, Dhaka; tel. (2) 256946; weekly; Editor ZAKIUDDIN AHMED; circ. 8,000.

Tarokalok: Tarokalok Complex, 25/3 Green Rd, Dhaka 1205; tel. (2) 506583; fax (2) 864330; weekly; Editor AREFIN BADAL.

Tide: 56/57 Motijheel C/A, Dhaka 1000; tel. (2) 259421; Editor ENAYET KARIM.

Tilotwoma: 14 Bangla Bazar, Dhaka; Editor ABDUL MANNAN.

English

ADAB News: 1/3, Block F, Lalmatia, Dhaka 1207; tel. (2) 327424; f. 1974; 6 a year; publ. by the Asscn of Devt Agencies in Bangladesh (ADAB); Editor-in-Chief AZFAR HUSSAIN; circ. 10,000.

Bangladesh: 112 Circuit House Rd, Dhaka 1000; tel. (2) 402013; fortnightly; Editor A. B. M. ABDUL MATIN.

Bangladesh Gazette: Bangladesh Government Press, Tejgaon, Dhaka; f. 1947, name changed 1972; weekly; official notices; Editor M. HUDA.

Bangladesh Illustrated Weekly: Dhaka; tel. (2) 23358; Editor ATIQUZZAMAN KHAN; circ. 3,000.

Cinema: 81 Motijheel C/A, Dhaka 1000; Editor SHEIKH FAZLUR RAHMAN MARUF; circ. 11,000.

Detective: Polwell Bhaban, Naya Paltan, Dhaka 2; tel. (2) 402757; f. 1960; weekly; also publ. in Bengali; Editor SYED AMJAD HOSSAIN; circ. 3,000.

Dhaka Courier: Cosmos Centre, 69/1 New Circular Rd, Malibagh, Dhaka 1217; tel. (2) 408420; fax (2) 831942; e-mail cosmos@citecho.net; internet www.dhakacourier.com; weekly; Editor ENAYETULLAH KHAN; circ. 18,000.

Holiday: Holiday Bldg, 30 Tejgaon Industrial Area, Dhaka 1208; tel. (2) 9122950; fax (2) 9127927; e-mail holiday@bangla.net; internet www.weekly-holiday.net; f. 1965; weekly; independent; Editor-in-Chief ENAYETULLAH KHAN; circ. 18,000.

Motherland: Khanjahan Ali Rd, Khulna; tel. (41) 61685; f. 1974; weekly; Editor M. N. KHAN.

Tide: 56/57 Motijheel C/A, Dhaka; tel. (2) 259421; Editor ENAYET KARIM.

Voice From the North: Dinajpur Town, Dinajpur; tel. (531) 3256; f. 1981; weekly; Editor Prof. MUHAMMAD MOHSIN; circ. 5,000.

NEWS AGENCIES

Bangladesh Sangbad Sangstha (BSS) (Bangladesh News Agency): 68/2 Purana Paltan, Dhaka 1000; tel. (2) 235036; Man. Dir and Chief Editor MAHBUBUL ALAM; Gen. Man. D. P. BARUA.

Eastern News Agency (ENA): Dhaka; tel. (2) 234206; f. 1970; Man. Dir and Chief Editor GOLAM RASUL MALLICK.

Islamic News Society (INS): 24 RK Mission Rd, Motijheel C/A, Dhaka 1203; tel. (2) 7121619; fax (2) 8013721; Editor ABDULLAH AL-NASER.

United News of Bangladesh: Dhaka.

Foreign Bureaux

Agence France-Presse (AFP): Shilpa Bank Bldg, 5th Floor, 8 DIT Ave, nr Dhaka Stadium, Dhaka 1000; tel. (2) 242234; Bureau Chief GOLAM TAHABOOR.

Associated Press (AP) (USA): 69/1 New Circular Rd, Dhaka 1217; tel. (2) 833717; Representative HASAN SAEED FARID HOSSAIN.

Inter Press Service (IPS) (Italy): c/o Bangladesh Sangbad Sangstha, 68/2 Purana Paltan, Dhaka 1000; tel. (2) 235036; Correspondent A. K. M. TABIBUL ISLAM.

Reuters Ltd (UK): POB 3993, Dhaka; tel. (2) 864088; fax (2) 832976; Bureau Chief ATIQUL ALAM.

United Press International (UPI) (USA): Dhaka; tel. (2) 233132.

PRESS ASSOCIATIONS

Bangladesh Council of Newspapers and News Agencies: Dhaka; tel. (2) 413256; Pres. Kazi SHAHED AHMED; Sec.-Gen. HABIBUL BASHAR.

Bangladesh Federal Union of Journalists: National Press Club Bldg, 18 Topkhana Rd, Dhaka 1000; tel. (2) 254777; f. 1973; Pres. REAZUDDIN AHMED; Sec.-Gen. SYED ZAFAR AHMED.

Bangladesh Sangbadpatra Karmachari Federation (Newspaper Employees' Fed.): Dhaka; tel. (2) 235065; f. 1972; Pres. RAFIQUL ISLAM; Sec.-Gen. MIR MOZAMMEL HOSSAIN.

Bangladesh Sangbadpatra Press Sramik Federation (Newspaper Press Workers' Federation): 1 Ramkrishna Mission Rd, Dhaka 1203; f. 1960; Pres. M. ABDUL KARIM; Sec.-Gen. BOZLUR RAHMAN MILON.

Dhaka Union of Journalists: National Press Club, Dhaka; f. 1947; Pres. ABEL KHAIR; Gen.-Sec. ABDUL KALAM AZAD.

Overseas Correspondents' Association of Bangladesh (OCAB): 18 Topkhana Rd, Dhaka 1000; e-mail naweed@bdonline.com; f. 1979; Pres. ZAGLUL A. CHOWDHURY; Gen. Sec. NADEEM QADIR; 60 mems.

Publishers

Academic Publishers: 2/7 Nawab-Habibullah Rd, Dhaka 1000; tel. (2) 507355; fax (2) 863060; f. 1982; social sciences and sociology; Jt Man. Dir HABIBUR RAHMAN.

Agamee Prakashani: 36 Bangla Bazar, Dhaka 1100; tel. (2) 7111332; fax (2) 7123945; e-mail agamee@bdonline.com; internet www.agameeprakashani-bd.com; f. 1986; fiction and academic; Chief Exec. OSMAN GANI.

Ahmed Publishing House: 7 Zindabahar 1st Lane, Dhaka 1; tel. (2) 36492; f. 1942; literature, history, science, religion, children's, maps and charts; Man. Dir KAMALUDDIN AHMED; Man. MESBAHUDDIN AHMED.

Ankur Prakashani: 38/4 Bangla Bazar, Dhaka 1100; tel. (2) 9564799; e-mail ankur@bangla.net; f. 1986; academic and general.

Ashrafia Library: 4 Hakim Habibur Rahman Rd, Chawk Bazar, Dhaka 1000; Islamic religious books, texts, and reference works of Islamic institutions.

Asiatic Society of Bangladesh: 5 Old Secretariat Rd, Ramna, Dhaka; tel. (2) 9560500; f. 1952; periodicals on science, Bangla and humanities; Pres. Prof. WAKIL AHMED; Admin. Officer MD ABDUL AWAL MIAH.

Bangla Academy (National Academy of Arts and Letters): Burdwan House, 3 Kazi Nazrul Islam Ave, Dhaka 1000; tel. (2) 869577; f. 1955; higher education textbooks in Bengali, research works in language, literature and culture, language planning, popular science, drama, encyclopaedias, translations of world classics, dictionaries; Dir-Gen. Prof. MONSUR MUSA.

Bangladesh Books International Ltd: Ittefaq Bhaban, 1 Ramkrishna Mission Rd, POB 377, Dhaka 3; tel. (2) 256071; f. 1975; reference, academic, research, literary, children's in Bengali and English; Chair. MOINUL HOSSEIN; Man. Dir ABDUL HAFIZ.

Bangladesh Publishers: 45 Patuatully Rd, Dhaka 1100; tel. (2) 233135; f. 1952; textbooks for schools, colleges and universities, cultural books, journals, etc.; Dir MAYA RANI GHOSAL.

Gatidhara: 38/2-Ka Bangla Bazar, Dhaka 1100; tel. (2) 247515; fax (2) 956600; f. 1988; academic, general and fiction.

Gono Prakashani: House 14/E, Rd 6, Dhanmondhi R/A, Dhaka 1205; tel. (2) 8617208; fax (2) 8613567; e-mail gk@citechco.net; f. 1978; science and medicine; Man. Dir SHAFIQ KHAN; Editor BAZLUR RAHIM.

International Publications: 8 Baitul Mukarram, 1st Floor, GPO Box 45, Dhaka 1000.

Muktadhara: 74 Farashganj, Dhaka 1100; tel. (2) 231374; e-mail muktadhara1971@yahoo.com; f. 1971; educational, literary and general; Bengali and English; Dir J. L. SAHA; Man. Dir C. R. SAHA.

Mullick Brothers: 3/1 Bangla Bazar, Dhaka 1100; tel. (2) 232088; fax (2) 833983; educational.

Osmania Book Depot: 30/32 North Brook Hall Rd, Dhaka 1100.

Puthighar Ltd: 74 Farashganj, Dhaka 1100; tel. (2) 7111374; e-mail muktadhara1971@yahoo.com; f. 1951; educational; Bengali and English; Dir J. L. SAHA; Man. Dir C. R. SAHA.

Rahman Brothers: 5/1 Gopinath Datta, Kabiraj St, Babu Bazar, Dhaka; tel. (2) 282633; educational.

Royal Library: Ispahani Bldg, 31/32 P. K. Roy Rd, Bangla Bazar, Dhaka 1; tel. (2) 250863.

Shahitya Prakash: 51 Purana Paltan, Dhaka 1000; tel. (2) 9560485; fax (2) 9565506; f. 1970; Prin. Officer MOFIDUL HOQUE.

University Press Ltd: Red Crescent Bldg, 114 Motijheel C/A, POB 2611, Dhaka 1000; tel. (2) 9565441; fax (2) 9565443; e-mail upl@bangla.net; internet www.uplbooks.com; f. 1975; educational, academic and general; Man. Dir MOHIUDDIN AHMED.

Government Publishing Houses

Bangladesh Bureau of Statistics: Bldg 8, Room 14, Bangladesh Secretariat, Dhaka 1000; tel. (2) 8612833; f. 1971; statistical year book and pocket book, censuses, surveys, agricultural year book and special reports; Jt Dir S. M. TAJUL ISLAM; Sec. ANIL CHANDRA SINGHA.

Bangladesh Government Press: Tejgaon, Dhaka 1209; tel. (2) 606316; f. 1972.

Department of Films and Publications: 112 Circuit House Rd, Dhaka 1000; tel. (2) 402263.

Press Information Department: Bhaban 6, Bangladesh Secretariat, Dhaka 1000; tel. (2) 400958.

PUBLISHERS' ASSOCIATIONS

Bangladesh Publishers' and Booksellers' Association: 3rd Floor, 3 Liaquat Ave, Dhaka 1; f. 1972; Pres. JANAB JAHANGIR MOHAMMED ADEL; 2,500 mems.

National Book Centre of Bangladesh: 67A Purana Paltan, Dhaka 1000; f. 1963 to promote the cause of 'more, better and cheaper books'; organizes book fairs, publs a monthly journal; Dir FAZLE RABBI.

Broadcasting and Communications

TELECOMMUNICATIONS

Bangladesh Telegraph and Telephone Board: Central Office, Telejogajog Bhaban, 37/E Eskaton Garden, Dhaka 1000; tel. (2) 831500; fax (2) 832577; Chair. M.A. MANNAN CHOWDHURY; Dir (International) MD HASSANUZZAMAN.

Grameen Telecom: Dhaka; f. 1996 by Grameen Bank to expand cellular telephone service in rural areas; Head NAJMUL HUDA.

BROADCASTING

Radio

Bangladesh Betar: NBA House, 121 Kazi Nazrul Islam Ave, Shahabag, Dhaka 1000; tel. (2) 865294; fax (2) 862021; e-mail dgradio@drik.bgd.toolnet.org; f. 1971; govt-controlled; regional stations at Dhaka, Chittagong, Khulna, Rajshahi, Rangpur, Sylhet, Rangamati and Thakurgaon broadcast a total of approximately 160 hours daily; transmitting centres at Lalmai and Rangamati; external service broadcasts 8 transmissions daily in Arabic, Bengali, English, Hindi, Nepalese and Urdu; Dir-Gen. M.I. CHOWDHURY; Dep. Dir-Gen. (Programmes) ASHFAQUR RAHMAN KHAN.

Television

Bangladesh Television (BTV): Television House, Rampura, Dhaka 1219; tel. (2) 866606; fax (2) 832927; f. 1964; govt-controlled; daily broadcasts on one channel from Dhaka station for 10 hours; transmissions also from nationwide network of 14 relay stations; Dir-Gen. SAYED SALAHUDDIN ZAKI; Gen. Man. NAWAZISH ALI KHAN.

Finance

(cap. = capital; res = reserves; dep. = deposits; m. = million; brs = branches; amounts in taka)

BANKING

Central Bank

Bangladesh Bank: Motijheel C/A, POB 325, Dhaka 1000; tel. (2) 9555000; fax (2) 9566212; e-mail banglabank@bangla.net; internet www.bangladesh-bank.org; f. 1971; cap. 30m., res 9,117.9m., dep. 85,313.0m. (June 2000); Gov. Dr MOHAMMED FARASHUDDIN; 9 brs.

Nationalized Commercial Banks

Agrani Bank: Agrani Bank Bhaban, Motijheel C/A, POB 531, Dhaka 1000; tel. (2) 9566160; fax (2) 9563662; f. 1972; 100% state-owned; cap. 2,484m., res 324m., dep. 101,795m. (Dec. 1999); Chair. Dr MOHAMMAD SOHRAB UDDIN; Man. Dir M. A.YOUSOOF; 903 brs.

Janata Bank: 110 Motijheel C/A, POB 468, Dhaka 1000; tel. (2) 9565041; fax (2) 9564644; e-mail id-obd@janatabank-bd.com; internet www.janatabank-bd.com; f. 1972; 100% state-owned; cap. 2,594m., res 540m., dep. 103,846m. (Dec. 2000); Chair. M. AYUBUR RAHMAN; Man. Dir MURSHID KULI KHAN; 894 brs in Bangladesh, 4 brs in the UAE.

Rupali Bank Ltd: Rupali Bhaban, 34 Dilkusha C/A, POB 719, Dhaka 1000; tel. (2) 9564122; fax (2) 9564148; e-mail rblhocom@bdcom.com; f. 1972; 94% state-owned, 6% by public; cap. 1,250m., res 2,862.5m., dep. 39,637.8m. (Dec. 1999); Chair. Dr MOMTAZ UDDIN AHMED; Man. Dir MOHAMMAD YEASIN ALI; 513 brs in Bangladesh, 1 br. in Pakistan.

Sonali Bank: 35–44 Motijheel C/A, POB 3130, Dhaka 1000; tel. (2) 9550426; fax (2) 9561410; f. 1972; 100% state-owned; cap. 3,272.2m., res 2,036.0m., dep. 170,960.7m. (Dec. 1999); Chair. MUHAMMED ALI; Man. Dir M. ENAMUL HAQ CHOWDHURY; 1,313 brs in Bangladesh, 6 brs in United Kingdom and 1 br. in India.

Private Commercial Banks

Al-Arafah Islami Bank Ltd: Rahman Mansion, 161 Motijheel C/A, Dhaka; tel. (2) 9560198; f. 1995; 100% owned by 23 sponsors; cap. 101.2m., res 10m., dep. 534.4m. (Aug. 1996); Chair. A. Z. M. SHAMSUL ALAM; Man. Dir M. M. NURUL HAQUE.

Al-Baraka Bank Bangladesh Ltd: Kashfia Plaza, 35C Naya Paltan (VIP Rd), POB 3467, Dhaka 1000; tel. (2) 410050; fax (2) 834943; f. 1987 on Islamic banking principles; 34.68% owned by Al-Baraka Group, Saudi Arabia, 5.78% by Islamic Development Bank, Jeddah, 45.91% by local sponsors, 5.75% by Bangladesh Govt, 7.8% by general public; cap. 259.6m., res 14.9m., dep. 4,898.1m. (June 1996); Chair. Dr SALEH J. MALAIKAH; Man. Dir ANOWAR AHMED; 33 brs.

Arab Bangladesh Bank Ltd: BCIC Bhaban, 30–31 Dilkusha C/A, POB 3522, Dhaka 1000; tel. (2) 9560312; fax (2) 9564122; e-mail abbank@citecho.net; f. 1981; 95% owned by Bangladesh nationals and 5% by Bangladesh Govt; cap. 409.9m., res 354.8m., dep. 13,899.7m. (Dec. 1999); Chair. M. MORSHED KHAN; Pres. and Man. Dir C. M. KOYES SAMI; 62 brs, 1 br. in India.

City Bank Ltd: Jiban Bima Tower, 10 Dilkusha C/A, POB 3381, Dhaka 1000; tel. (2) 9565925; fax (2) 9562347; e-mail cbl@citechco.net; internet www.thecitybank.com; f. 1983; 50% owned by sponsors and 50% by public; cap. 160.0m., res 263.1m., dep. 17,184.0m. (Dec. 2001); Chair. DEEN MOHAMMAD; Man. Dir ABBAS UDDIN AHMED; 76 brs.

Dhaka Bank Ltd: 1st Floor, Biman Bhaban, 100 Motijheel C/A, Dhaka 1000; tel. (2) 9554514; fax (2) 9556584; e-mail dhakabnk@bdonline.com; internet www.dhakabankltd.com; f. 1995; cap. 303.5m., res 202.2m., dep. 15,085.8m. (Dec. 2001); Chair. A. T. M. HAYATUZZAMAN KHAN; Man. Dir MOHAMMAD MOKHLESUR RAHMAN; 11 brs.

Eastern Bank Ltd: Jiban Bima Bhaban, 2nd Floor, 10 Dilkusha C/A, POB 896, Dhaka 1000; tel. (2) 9556360; fax (2) 9562364; e-mail ebank@bdcom.com; f. 1992; appropriated assets and liabilities of fmr Bank of Credit and Commerce International (Overseas) Ltd; 83% owned by public, 17% owned by government and private commercial banks; cap. 720m., res 2,322m., dep. 13,277m. (Dec. 2001); Chair. M. GHAZIUL HAQUE; Man. Dir K. MAHMOOD SATTAR; 22 brs.

International Finance Investment and Commerce Bank Ltd (IFICB): BSB Bldg, 17th–19th Floors, 8 Rajuk Ave, POB 2229, Dhaka 1000; tel. (2) 9563020; fax (2) 9562015; e-mail ificmd@citechco.net; f. 1983; 40% state-owned; cap. 279.4m., res 311.1m., dep. 17,229.5m. (Dec. 1998); Chair. MANZURUL ISLAM; Man. Dir ATAUL HAQ; 52 brs in Bangladesh, 2 brs in Pakistan.

Islami Bank Bangladesh Ltd (IBBL): Head Office, Islami Bank Tower, 40 Dilkusha C/A, POB 233, Dhaka 1000; tel. (2) 9563046; fax (2) 9564532; e-mail ibbl@ncll.com; internet www.islamibankbd.com; f. 1983 on Islamic banking principles; cap. 640.0m., res 2,097.6m., dep. 47,555.5m. (Jun. 2002); Chair. SHAH ABDUL HANNAN; Exec. Pres. and CEO ABDUR RAQUIB; 122 brs.

National Bank Ltd: 18 Dilkusha C/A, POB 3424, Dhaka 1000; tel. (2) 9557045; fax (2) 9563953; e-mail nblid@bdonline.com; internet www.nblbd.com; f. 1983; 50% owned by sponsors, 45% by general public and 5% by Govt; cap. 430.3m., res 1,142.5m., dep. 24,896.6m. (Dec. 2001); Chair. ABU TAHER MIAH; Man. Dir RAFIQUL ISLAM KHAN; 76 brs.

National Credit and Commerce Bank Ltd: 7–8 Motijheel C/A, POB 2920, Dhaka 1000; tel. (2) 9561902; fax (2) 9566290; e-mail nccbl@bdmail.net; internet www.nccbank-bd.com; f. 1993; 50% owned by sponsors, 50% by general public; cap. 429m., res 375m., dep. 12,500m. (Dec. 2001); Chair. NURUL ISLAM; Man. Dir ANWAR AHMED; 30 brs.

Prime Bank Ltd: Adamjee Court Annex Bldg No. 2, 119–20 Motijheel C/A, Dhaka 1000; tel. (2) 9567265; fax (2) 9567230; e-mail primebnk@bangla.net; internet www.prime-bank.com; f. 1995; cap. 500m., res 366.1m., dep. 13,259.9m. (Dec. 2001); Chair. MOHAMMAD AMINUL HAQUE; Man. Dir M. SHAHJAHAN BHUIYAN; 26 brs.

Pubali Bank Ltd: Pubali Bank Bhaban, 26 Dilkusha C/A, POB 853, Dhaka 1000; tel. (2) 9551614; fax (2) 9564009; e-mail pubali@bdmail.net; f. 1959 as Eastern Mercantile Bank Ltd; name changed to Pubali Bank in 1972; 95% privately-owned, 5% state-owned; cap. 160m., res 644.2m., dep. 25,200.6m. (Dec. 1999); Chair. EMADUDDIN AHMED CHAUDHURY; Man. Dir MOHAMMAD QAMRUL HUDA; 350 brs.

Social Investment Bank: 15 Dilkusha C/A, Dhaka 1000; tel. (2) 9554855; fax (2) 9559013; e-mail sibl@bdonline.com; internet www.siblbd.com; f. 1995; cap. 200.0m., res 16.8m., dep. 3,899.7m. (Dec. 1999); Chair. AHMED AKBAR SOBHAN; Man. Dir GOLAM MUSTAFA; 5 brs.

Southeast Bank Ltd: 3rd Floor, 1 Dilkusha C/A, Dhaka 1000; tel. (2) 9550081; fax (2) 9563102; e-mail seastbk@citechco.net; www.southeastbank-bangladesh.com; f. 1995; cap. 300m., res 261.5m., dep. 8,569.7m. (Dec. 2000); Chair. YUSSUF ABDULLAH HAROON; Pres. and Man. Dir SHAH MOHAMMAD NURUL ALAM; 12 brs.

United Commercial Bank Ltd: Federation Bhaban, 60 Motijheel C/A, POB 2653, Dhaka 1000; tel. (2) 9560585; fax (2) 9560587; f. 1983; 50% owned by sponsors, 45% by general public and 5% by Govt; cap. 230.2m., res 334.8m., dep. 10,102.0m. (Dec. 1999); Chair. ZAFAR AHMED CHOWDHURY; 79 brs.

Uttara Bank Ltd: 90 Motijheel C/A, POB 818, Dhaka 1000; tel. (2) 9560021; fax (2) 8613529; e-mail ublmis@citecho.net; f. 1965 as Eastern Banking Corpn Ltd; name changed to Uttara Bank in 1972 and to Uttara Bank Ltd in 1983; 5% state-owned; cap. 99.8m., res 702.4m., dep. 26,375.1m. (Dec. 2000); Chair. AZHARUL ISLAM; Man. Dir and CEO M. AMINUZAMMAN; 198 brs.

Foreign Commercial Banks

American Express Bank Ltd (USA): ALICO Bldg, 18–20 Motijheel C/A, POB 420, Dhaka 1000; tel. (2) 9561751; fax (2) 9561722; e-mail amexbd@gononet.com; res 537.5m., dep. 6,236.5m. (Dec. 1995); Chair. RICHARD HOLMES; Gen. Man. JOHN A. SMETANKA; 8 brs.

ANZ Grindlays Bank Ltd (UK): 2 Dilkusha C/A, POB 502, Dhaka 1000; tel. (2) 9550181; fax (2) 9562332; e-mail choudhun@anz.com; res 60.5m., dep. 20,060m. (1999); Gen. Man. MUHAMMAD A. ALI; 9 brs.

Citibank, NA (USA): 122–124 Motijheel C/A, POB 1000, Dhaka 1000; tel. (2) 9550060; fax (2) 642611; f. 1995; cap. 209.5m., res 5.5m., dep. 648.8m. (July 1996); Chair. JOHN S. REED; Man. Dir S. SRIDHAR; 1 br.

Crédit Agricole Indosuez (France): 47 Motijheel C/A, POB 3490, Dhaka 1000; tel. (2) 9566566; fax (2) 9465707; res 591m., dep. 5,302m. (Dec. 1997); Country Man. FRANCIS DUBUS; Chief Operating Officer S. R. VATOVEY; 2 brs.

Habib Bank Ltd (Pakistan): 53 Motijheel C/A, POB 201, Dhaka 1000; tel. (2) 9563043; fax (2) 9561784; e-mail hbldhaka@bdonline.com; cap. 80.5m., res 14.3m., dep. 578.6m. (Dec. 1996); Country Man. GHAZANFAR ALI; 2 brs.

The Hongkong and Shanghai Banking Corpn Ltd (Hong Kong): 5th Floor, Anchor Tower, 1/1B Sonargaon Rd, Dhaka, 1205; tel. (2) 9660536; fax (2) 9660554; CEO for Bangladesh DAVID HUMPHREYS.

Muslim Commercial Bank Ltd (Pakistan): 4 Dilkusha C/A, POB 7213, Dhaka 1000; tel. (2) 9568871; fax (2) 860671; cap. 100m., res 4m., dep. 650.3m. (July 1996); Gen. Man. AHMED KARIM; 2 brs.

Standard Chartered Bank (UK): ALICO Bldg, 18–20 Motijheel C/A, POB 536, Dhaka 1000; tel. (2) 9561465; fax (2) 9561758; internet www.standardchartered.com; cap. 215m., dep. 5,850m. (Dec. 1995); Chief Exec. (Bangladesh) GEOFF WILLIAMS; 3 brs.

State Bank of India: 24–25 Dilkusha C/A, POB 981, Dhaka 1000; tel. (2) 9559935; fax (2) 9563991; e-mail sbibd@bangla.net; cap. 190.4m., dep. 557.1m. (March 1997); CEO ASHITAVA GHOSH; 1 br.

Development Finance Organizations

Bangladesh House Building Finance Corpn (BHBFC): HBFC Bldg, 22 Purana Paltan, POB 2167, Dhaka 1000; tel. (2) 9562767; f. 1952; provides low-interest credit for residential house-building; 100% state-owned; cap. 972.9m., total investment 23,255.3m. (Dec. 1999); Chair. S. M. Atiur Rahman; Man. Dir S. M. Moniam Hossein; 9 zonal offices, 13 regional offices and 6 camp offices.

Bangladesh Krishi Bank (BKB): 83–85 Motijheel C/A, POB 357, Dhaka 1000; tel. (2) 9560031; fax (2) 9561211; e-mail bkb@citechco.net; f. 1961 as the Agricultural Development Bank, name changed as above in 1973; provides credit for agricultural and rural devt; also performs all kinds of banking; 100% state-owned; cap. 1,000m., res 820.4m., dep. 38,953m. (June 2001); Chair. Dr A. T. M. Shamsul Huda; Man. Dir A. K. M. Sajedur Rahman; 920 brs.

Bangladesh Samabaya Bank Ltd (BSBL): 'Samabaya Sadan', 9D Motijheel C/A, POB 505, Dhaka 1000; tel. (2) 9564628; f. 1948; provides credit for agricultural co-operatives; cap. 31.6m., res 558m., dep. 22m. (June 1996); Chair. Dr Abdul Moyeen Khan; Gen. Man. Md Abdul Wahed.

Bangladesh Shilpa Bank (BSB) (Industrial Development Bank): 8 Rajuk Ave, POB 975, Dhaka; tel. (2) 9555151; fax (2) 9562061; e-mail bsblink@citechco-net; f. 1972; fmrly Industrial Devt Bank; provides long- and short-term financing for industrial devt in the private and public sectors; also provides underwriting facilities and equity support; 51% state-owned; cap. 1,320.0m., res 778.3m., dep. 571.0m. (June 2000); Chair. Dr Ahsraf Uddin Chowdhury; 15 brs.

Bangladesh Shilpa Rin Sangstha (BSRS) (Industrial Loan Agency): BIWTA Bhaban, 5th Floor, 141-143 Motijheel C/A, POB 473, Dhaka 1000; tel. (2) 9565046; fax (2) 9567057; f. 1972; 100% state-owned; cap. 700m., res 462.8m. (June 1996); Chair. Dr M. Farashuddin; Man. Dir Al-Ameen Chaudhury; 4 brs.

Bank of Small Industries and Commerce Bangladesh Ltd (BASIC): Suite 601/602, Sena Kalyan Bhaban, 6th Floor, 195 Motijheel C/A, Dhaka 1000; tel. (2) 956430; fax (2) 9564829; f. 1988; 100% state-owned; cap. 80m., res 106m., dep. 2,738m. (Dec. 1995); Chair. A. M. Akhter; Man. Dir Alauddin A. Majid; 19 brs.

Grameen Bank: Head Office, Mirpur-2, POB 1216, Dhaka 1216; tel. (2) 801138; fax (2) 803559; e-mail grameen.bank@grameen.net; internet www.grameen.com; f. 1976; provides credit for the landless rural poor; 6.97% owned by Govt; cap. 258.1m., res 188.2m., dep. 6,063.2m. (Dec. 1998); Chair. Rehman Sobhan; Man. Dir Dr Muhammad Yunus; 1,140 brs.

Infrastructure Development Co Ltd (IDCOL): Dhaka; f. 1999; state-owned.

Investment Corpn of Bangladesh (ICB): BSB Bldg, 12th–14th Floor, 8 Rajuk Ave, POB 2058, Dhaka 1000; tel. (2) 9563455; fax (2) 865684; f. 1976; provides devt financing; 27% owned by Govt; cap. 200.0m., res 315.2m. (June 1996); Chair. Hedayat Ahmed; Man. Dir Khairul Huda; 5 brs.

Rajshahi Krishi Unnayan Bank: Sadharan Bima Bhaban, Kazihata, Greater Rd, Rajshahi 6000; tel. (721) 775759; fax (721) 775947; f. 1987; 100% state-owned; cap. 980m., res 208.4m., dep. 2,622.7m. (June 1996); Chair. Md Emran Ali Sarkar; Man. Dir Shahidul Haq Khan.

STOCK EXCHANGES

Chittagong Stock Exchange: CSE Bldg, 1080 Sk Mujib Rd, Agrabad, Chittagong; tel. (31) 714100; fax (31) 714101; e-mail maroof@csebd.com; internet www.csebd.com; CEO Wali-ul-Maroof Matin.

Dhaka Stock Exchange Ltd: 9F Motijheel C/A, Dhaka 1000; tel. (2) 9564601; fax (2) 9564727; email dse@bol-online.com; internet www.dsebd.org; f. 1960; 196 listed cos; Chair. Rakibur Rahman.

Regulatory Authority

Bangladesh Securities and Exchange Commission: Jiban Bima Tower, 15th–16th Floor, 10 Dilkusha C/A, Dhaka 1000; tel. (2) 9568101; fax (2) 9563721; CEO M. Abu Sayeed.

INSURANCE

Bangladesh Insurance Association: Hadi Mansion, 7th Floor, 2 Dilkusha C/A, Dhaka; tel. (2) 237330; Chair. Mayeedul Islam.

Department of Insurance: 74 Motijheel C/A, Dhaka 1000; attached to Ministry of Commerce; supervises activities of domestic and foreign insurers; Controller of Insurance Shamsuddin Ahmad.

In 1973 the two corporations below were formed, one for life insurance and the other for general insurance:

Jiban Bima Corpn: 24 Motijheel C/A, POB 346, Dhaka 1000; tel. (2) 9552047; fax (2) 868112; state-owned; comprises 37 national life insurance cos; life insurance; Man. Dir A. K. M. Mostafizur Rahman.

Sadharan Bima Corpn: 33 Dilkusha C/A, POB 607, Dhaka 1000; tel. (2) 9566108; state-owned; general insurance; Man. Dir M. Lutfar Rahman.

Trade and Industry

GOVERNMENT AGENCIES

Board of Investment: Jiban Bima Tower, 19th Floor, 10 Dilkusha C/A, Dhaka 1000; tel. (2) 9563570; fax (2) 9562312; e-mail ec@boi.bdmail.net; Exec. Chair. Farooq Sobhan; Dep. Dir Lutfur Rahman Bhuiya.

Export Promotion Bureau: 122–124 Motijheel C/A, Dhaka 1000; tel. (2) 9552245; fax (2) 9568000; e-mail epb.tic@pradeshta.net; internet www.epbbd.com; f. 1972; attached to Ministry of Commerce; regional offices in Chittagong, Khulna and Rajshahi; brs in Comilla, Sylhet, Barisal and Bogra; Dir-Gen. Mohammad Abu Zafar; Vice-Chair. Shafiqul Islam.

Petrobangla, Bangladesh Oil, Gas and Mineral Corporation: Petrocenter Bhaban, 3 Kawran Bazar C/A, POB 849, Dhaka 1205; tel. (2) 814936; fax (2) 811613; explores and develops gas, petroleum and mineral resources, manages Bangladesh Petroleum Exploration Co Ltd and Sylhet Gas Fields Ltd; Chair. S. K. Mohammad Abdullah.

Planning Commission: Planning Commission Secretariat, G.O. Hostel, Sher-e-Bangla Nagar, Dhaka; f. 1972; govt agency responsible for all aspects of economic planning and development including the preparation of the five-year plans and annual development programmes (in conjunction with appropriate govt ministries), promotion of savings and investment, compilation of statistics and evaluation of development schemes and projects.

Privatization Board: Jiban Bima Tower, 14th Floor, 10 Dilkusha C/A, Dhaka 1000; tel. (2) 9563723; fax (2) 9563766; e-mail pb@bdonline.com; internet www.bangladeshonline.com/pb; f. 1993; Chair. Kazi Zafrullah; Sec. A. M. M. Nasir Uddin.

Trading Corpn of Bangladesh: 1–2 Kawranbazar, Dhaka 1215; tel. (2) 8111515; fax (2) 8113582; e-mail tcb@bdonline.com; f. 1972; imports, exports and markets goods through appointed dealers and agents; Chair. A. K. M. A. B. Siddique; Sec. Mohammad Shahjahan Miah.

DEVELOPMENT ORGANIZATIONS

Bangladesh Chemical Industries Corpn: BCIC Bhaban, 30–31 Dilkusha C/A, Dhaka; tel. (2) 955280; fax (2) 9564120; e-mail bciccomp@bangla.net; internet www.bangla.net/bcic; Chair. A. K. M. Mosharraf Hossain.

Bangladesh Export Processing Zones Authority: 222 New Eskaton Rd, Dhaka 1000; tel. (2) 8312553; fax (2) 8314967; e-mail bepza@bdmail.net; internet www.bangladesh-epz.com; f. 1983 to plan, develop, operate and manage export processing zones (EPZs) in Bangladesh; in mid-2000 two state-owned EPZs (one in Chittagong and the other in Dhaka) were in operation, and another four EPZs were at the implementation stage; Exec. Chair. Brig M. A. B. Siddique Talukder.

Bangladesh Fisheries Development Corpn: 24–25 Dilkusha C/A, Dhaka 1000; tel. (2) 9552689; fax (2) 9563990; e-mail bfdc@citecho.net; f. 1964; under Ministry of Fisheries and Livestock; development and commercial activities; Chair. Mohammed Musa; Sec. A. K. M. Shahidul Islam.

Bangladesh Forest Industries Development Corpn: Dhaka; Chair. M. Atikullah.

Bangladesh Jute Mills Corpn: Adamjee Court (Annexe), 115–120 Motijheel C/A, Dhaka 1000; tel. (2) 861980; fax (2) 863329; f. 1972; operates 35 jute mills, incl. 2 carpet mills; world's largest manufacturer and exporter of jute goods; bags, carpet backing cloth, yarn, twine, tape, felt, floor covering, etc.; Chair. Maniruddin Ahmad; Man. (Marketing) Md Jahirul Islam.

Bangladesh Small and Cottage Industries Corpn (BSCIC): 137/138 Motijheel C/A, Dhaka 1000; tel. (2) 233202; f. 1957; Chair. Muhammad Sirajuddin.

Bangladesh Steel and Engineering Corpn (BSEC): BSEC Bhaban, 102 Kazi Nazrul Islam Ave, Dhaka 1215; tel. (2) 814616; fax (2) 812846; 16 industrial units; sales US $83m. (1994); cap. US $52m.; Chair. A. I. M. Nazmul Alam; Gen. Man. (Marketing) Ashraful Haq; 8,015 employees.

Bangladesh Sugar and Food Industries Corpn: Shilpa Bhaban, Motijheel C/A, Dhaka 1000; tel. (2) 258084; f. 1972; Chair. M. Nefaur Rahman.

Bangladesh Textile Mills Corpn: Dhaka; tel. (2) 252504; f. 1972; Chair. M. Nurunnabi Chowdhury.

CHAMBERS OF COMMERCE

Federation of Bangladesh Chambers of Commerce and Industry (FBCCI): Federation Bhaban, 60 Motijheel C/A, 4th Floor,

POB 2079, Dhaka 1000; tel. (2) 9560102; fax (2) 863213; f. 1973; comprises 135 trade asscns and 58 chambers of commerce and industry; Pres. YUSUF ABDULLAH HAROON.

Barisal Chamber of Commerce and Industry: Asad Mansion, 1st Floor, Sadar Rd, Barisal; tel. (431) 3984; Pres. Qazi ISRAIL HOSSAIN.

Bogra Chamber of Commerce and Industry: Chamber Bhaban, 2nd Floor, Kabi Nazrul Islam Rd, Jhawtola, Bogra 5800; tel. (51) 4138; fax (51) 6257; f. 1963; Pres. AMJAD HOSSAIN TAJMA; Sr Vice-Pres. Alhaj ABUL KALAM AZAD.

Chittagong Chamber of Commerce and Industry: Chamber House, Agrabad C/A, POB 481, Chittagong; tel. (31) 713366; fax (31) 710183; e-mail ccci@globalctg.net; f. 1959; 4,000 mems; Pres. FARID AHMED CHOWDHURY: Sec. O. G. CHOWDHURY.

Comilla Chamber of Commerce and Industry: Rammala Rd, Ranir Bazar, Comilla; tel. (81) 5444; Pres. AFZAL KHAN.

Dhaka Chamber of Commerce and Industry: Dhaka Chamber Bldg, 1st Floor, 65–66 Motijheel C/A, POB 2641, Dhaka 1000; tel. (2) 9552562; fax (2) 9560830; e-mail dcci@bangla.net; f. 1958; 5,000 mems; Pres. AFTAB UL ISLAM; Sr Vice-Pres. AM MUBASH-SHAR.

Dinajpur Chamber of Commerce and Industry: Chamber Bhaban, Maldhapatty, Dinajpur 5200; tel. (531) 3189; Pres. KHAIRUL ANAM.

Faridpur Chamber of Commerce and Industry: Chamber House, Niltuly, Faridpur; tel. 3530; Pres. KHANDOKER MOHSIN ALI.

Foreign Investors' Chamber of Commerce and Industry: 'Mahbub Castle', 4th Floor, 35-1 Purana Paltan Line, Inner Circular Rd, GPO Box 4086, Dhaka 1000; tel. (2) 8319448; fax (2) 8319449; e-mail ficci@bangla.net; f. 1963 as Agrabad Chamber of Commerce and Industry, name changed as above in 1987; Pres. WALI R. BHUIYAN; Sec. JAHANGIR BIN ALAM.

Khulna Chamber of Commerce and Industry: 5, KDA C/A, Khulna; tel. (41) 24135; e-mail kcci@bttb.net.bd; f. 1934; Pres. S. M. NAZRUL ISLAM.

Khustia Chamber of Commerce and Industry: 15, S Rd, Kushtia; tel. (71) 54068; e-mail kushcham@kushtia.com; Pres. MOHAMMAD MOZIBAR RAHMAN.

Metropolitan Chamber of Commerce and Industry: Chamber Bldg, 4th Floor, 122–124 Motijheel C/A, Dhaka 1000; tel. (2) 9565208; fax (2) 9565212; e-mail sg@citechco.net; internet www.mccibd.org; f. 1904; 310 mems; Sec.-Gen. C. K. HYDER.

Noakhali Chamber of Commerce and Industry: Noakhali Pourshara Bhaban, 2nd Floor, Maiydee Court, Noakhali; tel. 5229; Pres. MOHAMMAD NAZIBUR RAHMAN.

Rajshahi Chamber of Commerce and Industry: Chamber Bhaban, Station Rd, P.O. Ghoramara, Rajshahi 6100; tel. (721) 772115; fax (721) 772412; f. 1960; 800 mems; Pres. OMAR FARUK CHOWDHURY.

Sylhet Chamber of Commerce and Industry: Chamber Bldg, Jail Rd, POB 97, Sylhet 3100; tel. (821) 714403; fax (821) 715210; e-mail scci@btsnet.net; Pres. MOHD SAFWAN CHOUDHURY.

INDUSTRIAL AND TRADE ASSOCIATIONS

Bangladesh Frozen Foods Exporters Association: Dhaka; tel. and fax (2) 837531; e-mail bffea@drik.dgd.toolnet.org; Pres. SALAHUDDIN AHMED.

Bangladesh Garment Manufacturers and Exporters Association: 7–9 Karwanbazar, BTMC Bhaban, Dhaka 1215; tel. (2) 815597; fax (2) 813951; e-mail bgmea@bgmea.agni.co; Pres. KUTUBUDDIN AHMED; Vice-Pres. NURUL HAQ SIKDAR.

Bangladesh Jute Association: BJA Bldg, 77 Motijheel C/A, Dhaka; tel. (2) 9552916; fax (2) 9560137; Chair. M.A. MANNAN; Sec. S. H. PRODHAN.

Bangladesh Jute Exporters Association: Nahar Mansion, 2nd Floor, 150 Motijheel C/A, Dhaka 1000; tel. (2) 9561102.

Bangladesh Jute Goods Association: 2nd Floor, Nahar Mansion, 150 Motijheel C/A, Dhaka 1000; tel. (2) 253640; f. 1979; 17 mems; Chair. M. A. KASHEM, Haji MOHAMMAD ALI.

Bangladesh Jute Mills Association: Adamjee Court, 4th Floor, 115–120 Motijheel C/A, Dhaka 1000; tel. (2) 9560071; fax (2) 9566472; Chair. A. M. ZAHIRUDDIN KHAN.

Bangladesh Jute Spinners Association: 55 Purana Paltan, 3rd Floor, Dhaka 1000; tel. (2) 9551317; fax (2) 9562772; f. 1979; 50 mems; Chair. AHMED HOSSAIN; Sec. SHAHIDUL KARIM.

Bangladesh Tea Board: 171–172 Baizid Bostami Rd, Nasirabad, Chittagong; tel. (31) 682903; fax (31) 682863; e-mail btb@spnetctg.com; internet bdteaboard.com; f. 1951; regulates, controls and promotes the cultivation and marketing of tea, both in Bangladesh and abroad; Contact ALI OHIDUZ ZAMAN.

Bangladesh Textile Mills Association: Moon Mansion, 6th Floor, Block M, 12 Dilkusha C/A, Dhaka 1000; tel. (2) 9552799; fax 9563320; e-mail btma@citechco.net.

Bangladeshiyo Cha Sangsad (Tea Association of Bangladesh): 'Dar-e-Shahidi', 3rd Floor, 69 Agrabad C/A, POB 287, Chittagong 4100; tel. (31) 501009; f. 1952; Chair. QUAMRUL CHOWDHURY; Sec. G. S. DHAR.

UTILITIES

Electricity

Bangladesh Atomic Energy Commission (BAEC): 4 Kazi Nazrul Islam Ave, POB 158, Dhaka 1000; tel. (2) 502600; fax (2) 863051; f. 1964 as Atomic Energy Centre of the fmr Pakistan Atomic Energy Comm. in East Pakistan; reorg. 1973; operates an atomic energy research establishment and a 3-MW research nuclear reactor (inaugurated in January 1987) at Savar, an atomic energy centre at Dhaka, etc.; Chair. M. A. QUAIYUM; Sec. RAFIQUL ALAM.

Bangladesh Power Development Board: Dhaka; e-mail webmaster@bd-pdb.org; internet www.bd-pdb.org; f. 1972; under Ministry of Energy and Mineral Resources; installed capacity 3,603 MW (1999); Chair. QUAMRUL ISLAM SIDDIQUE.

Dhaka Electric Supply Authority: Dhaka; under Ministry of Energy and Mineral Resources.

Powergrid Company of Bangladesh: Dhaka; f. 1996; responsible for power transmission throughout Bangladesh.

Rural Electrification Board: Dhaka; under Ministry of Energy and Mineral Resources.

Water

Chittagong Water Supply and Sewerage Authority: Dampara, Chittagong; tel. (31) 621606; fax (31) 610465; f. 1963; govt corpn; Chair. SULTAN MAHMUD CHOWDHURY.

Dhaka Water Supply and Sewerage Authority: 98 Kazi Nazrul Islam Ave, Kawran Bazar, Dhaka 1215; tel. (2) 8116792; fax (2) 8112109; e-mail mddwasa@bangla.net; f. 1963; govt corpn; Man. Dir K. AZHARUL HAQ.

MAJOR COMPANIES

Automobile Industry

Navana Ltd/Aftab Automobiles Ltd: 125A Motijheel C/A, Dhaka 1000; tel. (2) 9552212; fax (2) 9566324; f. 1963; distributor of vehicles and tyres; Vice-Chair. SHAFIUL ISLAM; Dir AZIZ U. AHAMED.

Chemicals

Beximco Pharmaceuticals: House 19, Rd 7, Dhanmondi R/A, Dhaka 1205; tel. (2) 861891; fax (2) 863470; e-mail bpl@bangla.net; internet www.beximcorp.com; f. 1976; producer of drugs and medicines; Chair. A. S. F. RAHMAN; 926 employees.

Fisons Ltd: Fisons House, 6/2/A Segun Bagicha, Dhaka 1000; tel. (2) 9550020; fax (2) 9562149; internet www.rp-rorer.com.; f. 1964; mfr of pharmaceuticals; cap. and res 400m. taka, sales 783m. taka (1997); Chair. BENOIT GIRETTE; Man. Dir A. K. M. SHAMSUDDIN; 1,000 employees.

Karnaphuli Fertilizer Co Ltd (KAFCO): Head Office, 90–91 Motijheel C/A, Uttara Bank Bhaban, 15th Floor, Dhaka 1000; tel. (2) 9565054; fax (2) 9565063; e-mail kafcodac@dhaka.agni.com; f. 1981; cap. and res 4,415.8m. taka; sales 5,077.4m. taka (1996/97); Bangladesh's largest multinational joint-venture project; 100% export-orientated fully integrated fertilizer complex in Chittagong; annual exports of 575,000 metric tons of granular urea and 165,000 tons of ammonia; Man. Dir Dr M. TOWHIDI; Chair M. AKHTER ALI; 569 employees.

Karnaphuli Rayon and Chemicals Ltd: 92 Sadarghat Rd, Chittagong.

Pharmadesh Laboratories Ltd: 334 Segunbagicha, Dhaka; tel. (2) 408267; fax (2) 833212; f. 1961; pharmaceuticals; cap. 100m. taka; Chair. AZIZUR RAHMAN; Man. Dir HABIBUR RAHMAN; 400 employees.

Zia Fertilizer Co Ltd: Ashuganj, Brahmanbaria 3403; tel. 9352015; fax (2) 9351847; f. 1974; urea and ammonia fertilizer producers; sales 393,612m. taka (2000/01); Man. Dir MOSTAFIZUR RAHMAN; 1,200 employees.

Cotton Textiles, Jute, Man-Made Fibres

Abir International: 2nd Floor, Nirala Bhaban, 9/A Toyenbee Circular Rd, Motijheel C/A, Dhaka 1000; tel. (2) 7111824; fax (2) 7115514; e-mail abirint@bdcom.com; f. 1990; exporter of jute goods, ready-made garments, leather goods and household textiles; Pres. ASLAM HOSSAIN.

Ahad Jute Mills Ltd: 3rd Floor, 55 Purana Paltam Azad Centre, Dhaka 1000; tel. (2) 9567533; fax (2) 9553439.

Amin Brothers Textile Mills Ltd: 3rd Floor, 108 Islampur Rd, Dhaka 1000; tel. (2) 852842; fax (2) 9564676; mfr and wholesaler of fabrics; Man. Dir Mr. AMIN.

Apex Spinning and Knitting Mills Ltd: Biman Bhaban, 5th Floor, 100 Motijheel C/A, Dhaka 1000; tel. (2) 9562383; fax (2) 9562213; e-mail zahur@apexknitting.com; internet www-.apexknitting.com; f. 1990; mfr and exporter of garments; cap. and res 191m. taka, sales 577m. taka (2000/01); Chair. ZAFAR AHMED; Vice-Chair. Dr ZAHUR AHMED; 2,400 employees.

Bangladesh Jute Mills Corporation (BJMC): Adamjee Court (Annexe), 115–120 Motijheel C/A, Dhaka 1000; tel. (2) 9558182; fax (2) 9567508; e-mail bjmc@bttb.net.bd; f. 1972; operates 35 jute mills (incl. two carpet mills); world's largest manufacturer and exporter of jute goods; Chair. Lt-Gen. (retd) ABU OSMAN CHOWDHURY; Gen. Man. B. K. SARKER.

Bangladesh Textile Mills Corporation (BTMC): Bastra Bhaban, 7–9 Kawran Bazar C/A, Dhaka 1215; tel. (2) 9115051; fax (2) 814600; f. 1972; mfr of cotton and wool items; Chair A. F. M. S. ZAMAN.

Dacca Dyeing and Manufacturing Co Ltd: Sharif Mansion, 6th Floor, 56–57 Motijheel C/A, Dhaka 1000; tel. (2) 9558131; fax (2) 9560666; f. 1963; mfr and exporter of household linen and garment fabrics; cap. and res 323.5m. taka, sales 65.5m. taka (2000); Chair. SALAUDDIN QUADER CHOWDHURY; 350 employees.

Islam Jute Mills Ltd: 727 Satmasjid Rd, Dhanmondi R/A, Dhaka 1209; tel. (2) 9119540; fax (2) 813228; Man. Dir SAIFUL ISLAM KHAN.

Karim Jute Mills Ltd: Karim Chambers, 99 Motijheel C/A, Dhaka 1000; tel. (2) 9555729; f. 1957; mfr of jute products; Dir ABDUL GHANI AHMED; 3,200 employees.

Prime Textile Spinning Mills Ltd: Sena Kalyan Bhaban, 8th Floor, 195 Motijheel C/A, Dhaka 1000; tel. (2) 9564851; fax (2) 9564857; e-mail prime@bangla.net; f. 1989; producer of export-quality yarn; cap. and res 1,027.2m. taka, sales 707.0m. taka (1998/99); Chair. and Man. Dir M. A. AWAL; 1,497 employees.

Reaz Garments Ltd: 7–9 Btmc Bhaban, 3rd Floor, Kawran Bazar C/A, Dhaka 1215; tel. (2) 9124634; fax (2) 9123010; e-mail rgl@bdmail.net; ready-made garments.

Gas and Petroleum

Bangladesh Petroleum Corporation (BPC): 1/D Agrabad C/A, Chittagong; tel. (2) 235046; f. 1976; state-owned; producer, importer and exporter of petroleum products, manages Jamuna Oil Co Ltd and Padma Oil Co Ltd; Operations and Planning Dir M. WALIUZ-ZAMAN.

Bangladesh Petroleum Exploration Co Ltd: BAPEX House Building, Finance Corporation, Bhaban, Dhaka 1000; explores and develops gas, petroleum and mineral resources; Man. Dir M. ISMAILI.

Padma Oil Co Ltd: Padma Bhaban, Strand Rd, POB 4, Chittagong 4000; tel. (31) 614235; fax (31) 618312; e-mail padma@spnetctg.com; f. 1965; produces pesticides and markets petroleum products; cap. and res 335.8m. taka, sales 16,204m. taka (1996/97); Chair. A. K. M. SHAMSUDDIN; 1,056 employees.

Petrobangla, Bangladesh Oil, Gas and Mineral Corporation: Petrocenter Bhaban, 3 Kawran Bazar C/A, POB 849, Dhaka 1205; tel. (2) 814936; fax (2) 811613; state-owned; explores and develops gas, petroleum and mineral resources, manages Bangladesh Petroleum Exploration Co Ltd and Sylhet Gas Fields Ltd; Chair S. K. MOHAMMAD ABDULLAH.

Paper

Bangladesh Monospool Paper Manufacturing Co Ltd: 3rd Floor, BCIC Bhabhan, 30–31 Dillkusha C/A, Dhaka 1000; tel. (2) 9560600; fax (2) 9564192.

Bangladesh Paper Products Ltd: 12 Abedin Colony, Love Lane, Chittagong; tel. (31) 206327; fax (31) 223172; f. 1963; cap. US $1.5m., sales $1.1m. (1991); Chair. and Man. Dir MOHAMMED SHAFIQUR RAHAMAN; Exec. Dir M. S. ISLAM; 362 employees.

Eagle Box and Carton Group: Postagola, Dhaka 1204; tel. (2) 7411119; fax (2) 7410641; e-mail eaglebox@bol-online.com; f. 1961; mfr of packaging goods; Man. Dir SHAMSUL ARAFIN.

Khulna Newsprint Mills Ltd: Kalishpur, Khulna.

Sylhet Pulp & Paper Mills: Chhatak, Sunamgonj 3082; tel. (821) 4312.

Miscellaneous

Apex Foods Ltd: Biman Bhaban, 5th Floor, 100 Motijheel C/A, Dhaka 1000; tel. (2) 9562383; fax (2) 9562213; e-mail zafar@apex-foods.com; internet www.apexfoods.com; f. 1980; mfr and exporter of frozen shrimp; cap. and res 360.8m. taka, sales 837.1m. taka (2000/01); Man. Dir ZAFAR AHMED; 1,000 employees.

Bata Shoe Co: Tongi Industrial Area, Tongi, Gazipur; (2) 9800501; fax (2) 9800511; e-mail bata518@batabd.com; internet www.bata.com; f. 1962; mfr of footwear and leather; Man. Dir STEPHEN J. DAVIES.

Meher Industries (Bangladesh) Ltd: Airport Rd, Dhaka 1000; electronics.

People's Ceramic Industries Ltd: Amin Court, 4th Floor, 62–63 Motijheel C/A, Dhaka 1000; tel. (2) 9561947; fax (2) 9561946; e-mail pepcer@bol-online.com; internet www.pcisci.com; mfr of ceramic goods.

Poly Tube Industries: 46 Chawk Circular Rd, Dhaka.

Rahimafrooz Batteries Ltd: 74 Motijheel C/A, Dhaka 1000; tel. (2) 9565221; fax (2) 9568134; e-mail rabl@bangla.net; f. 1960; mfr of batteries; cap. and res 215m. taka, sales 400m. taka; Chair. AFROZ RAHIM; 504 employees.

TRADE UNIONS

In 2001 only 4.3% of the non-agricultural labour force was unionized. There were about 4,200 registered unions, organized mainly on a sectoral or occupational basis. There were 23 national trade unions to represent workers at the national level.

Bangladesh Free Trade Union Congress (BFTUC): 6-A 1–19 Mirpur, Dhaka 1216; tel. (2) 8017001; fax (2) 8015919; e-mail bftuc@agni.com; Gen. Sec. M. R. CHOWDHURY; 98,000 mems.

Bangladesh Jatio Sramik League (BJSL): POB 2730, Dhaka; tel. (2) 282063; fax (2) 863470; 62,000 mems.

Transport

RAILWAYS

In July 2000 Bangladesh Railway and the Indian Railway Board signed an agreement to resume rail services on the Benapole–Petrapole route. The service opened fully in January 2001. In December regular rail services between Bangabandhu and Kolkata (India) resumed.

Bangladesh Railway: Rail Bhaban, Abdul Ghani Rd, Dhaka 1000; tel. (2) 9561200; fax (2) 9563413; e-mail systcan@citechco.net; f. 1862; supervised by the Railway and Road Transport Division of the Ministry of Communications; divided into East and West zones, with HQ at Chittagong (tel. (31) 711294) and Rajshahi (tel. (721) 761576; fax (721) 761982); total length of 2,734 route km (June 1999); 451 stations; Dir-Gen. M. A. RAHIM; Gen. Man. (East Zone) A. Z. M. SAZZADUR RAHMAN; Gen. Man. (West Zone) MD NURUL AMIN-KHAN.

ROADS

In 1999 the total length of roads in use was 207,486 km (19,775 km of highways, 17,297 km of secondary roads and 170,413 km of other roads), of which 9.5% were paved. In 1992 the World Bank approved Bangladesh's US $700m. Jamuna Bridge Project. The construction of the 4.8-km bridge, which was, for the first time, to link the east and the west of the country with a railway and road network, was begun in early 1994. The bridge, which was renamed the Bangabandhu Jamuna Multipurpose Bridge, was officially opened in June 1998.

In June 1999 the first direct passenger bus service between Bangladesh (Dhaka) and India (Kolkata) was inaugurated.

Bangladesh Road Transport Corpn: Paribhaban, DIT Ave, Dhaka; f. 1961; state-owned; operates transport services, incl. truck division; transports govt foodgrain; Chair. AZMAN HOSSAIN CHOWDHURY.

INLAND WATERWAYS

In Bangladesh there are some 8,433 km of navigable waterways, which transport 70% of total domestic and foreign cargo traffic and on which are located the main river ports of Dhaka, Narayanganj, Chandpur, Barisal and Khulna. A river steamer service connects these ports several times a week. Vessels of up to 175-m overall length can be navigated on the Karnaphuli river.

Bangladesh Inland Water Transport Corpn: 5 Dilkusha C/A, Dhaka 1000; tel. (2) 257092; f. 1972; 273 vessels (1986).

SHIPPING

The chief ports are Chittagong, where the construction of a second dry-dock is planned, and Chalna. A modern seaport is being developed at Mongla.

Atlas Shipping Lines Ltd: Atlas House, 7 Sk. Mujib Rd, Agrabad C/A, Chittagong 2; tel. (31) 504287; fax (31) 225520; Man. Dir S. U. CHOWDHURY; Gen. Man. M. KAMAL HAYAT.

Bangladesh Shipping Corpn: BSC Bhaban, Saltgola Rd, POB 641, Chittagong 4100; tel. (31) 713277; fax (31) 710506; e-mail bsc–ctg@spnetctg.com; f. 1972; maritime shipping; 15 vessels, 210,672 dwt capacity (1999); Chair. MOFAZZAL HOSSAIN CHOWDHURY MAYA; Man. Dir ZULFIQAR HAIDAR CHAUDHURY.

Bengal Shipping Line Ltd: Palm View, 100A Agrabad C/A, Chittagong 4100; tel. (31) 714800; fax (31) 710362; e-mail bsl@mkrgroup.com; Chair. MOHAMMED ABDUL AWWAL; Man. Dir MOHAMMED ABDUL MALEK.

Blue Ocean Lines Ltd: 1st Floor, H.B.F.C. Bldg, 1D Agrabad C/A, Agrabad, Chittagong; tel. (31) 501567; fax (31) 225415.

Broadway Shipping Line: Hafiz Estate, 65 Shiddeswari Rd, Dhaka; tel. (2) 404598; fax (2) 412254.

Chittagong Port Authority: POB 2013, Chittagong 4100; tel. (31) 505041; f. 1887; provides bunkering, ship repair, towage and lighterage facilities as well as provisions and drinking water supplies; Chair. MD SHAHADAT HUSSAIN.

Continental Liner Agencies: 3rd Floor, Facy Bldg, 87 Agrabad C/A, Chittagong; tel. (31) 721572; fax (31) 710965; Man. SAIFUL AHMED; Dir (Technical and Operations) Capt. MAHFUZUL ISLAM.

Nishan Shipping Lines Ltd: 1st Floor, Monzoor Bldg, 67 Agrabad C/A, Chittagong; tel. (31) 710855; fax (31) 710044; Dir Capt. A. K. M. ALAMGIR.

CIVIL AVIATION

There is an international airport at Dhaka (Zia International Airport) situated at Kurmitola, with the capacity to handle 5m. passengers annually. There are also airports at all major towns. In 1997 the civil aviation industry was deregulated to permit domestic competition to Biman Bangladesh Airlines. Plans were under way in 2002 to privatize 49% of the national airline.

Biman Bangladesh Airlines: Head Office, Balaka, Kurmitola, Dhaka 1229; tel. (2) 8917400; fax (2) 8913005; internet www.bimanair.com/; f. 1972; 100% state-owned; domestic services to seven major towns; international services to the Middle East, the Far East, Europe, and North America; Chair. Minister of Civil Aviation and Tourism; Man. Dir Air Cmmdre M. KHUSRUL ALAM.

GMG Airlines: ABC House, 9th Floor, 8 Kamal Ataturk Ave, Banani, Dhaka 1213; tel. (2) 8825845; fax (2) 8826115; e-mail gmgairlines@gmggroup.com; internet www.gmgairlines.com; f. 1997; private, domestic airline; Dir (Flight Operations) Capt. HABIBUR RAHMAN; Man. Dir SHAHAB SATTAR.

Tourism

Tourist attractions include the cities of Dhaka and Chittagong, Cox's Bazar—which has the world's longest beach (120 km)—on the Bay of Bengal, and Teknaf, at the southernmost point of Bangladesh. Tourist arrivals totalled 199,211 in 2000. Earnings from tourism in 2000 reached an estimated US $59m. in the same year. The majority of visitors are from India, Japan, Pakistan, the United Kingdom and the USA.

Bangladesh Parjatan Corpn (National Tourism Organization): 233 Airport Rd, Tejgaon, Dhaka 1215; tel. (2) 8117855; fax (2) 8117235; internet www.parjatan.org; there are four tourist information centres in Dhaka, and one each in Bogra, Chittagong, Cox's Bazar, Dinajpur, Khulna, Kuakata, Rangamati, Rangpur, Rajshahi and Sylhet; Chair. MD ABU SALEH; Man. (Public Relations Division) MOHAMMAD AHSAN ULLAH.

Defence

In August 2001 the total active armed forces numbered 137,000: the army had a total strength of 120,000, the navy 10,500 and the air force 6,500. The paramilitary forces, which totalled 63,200, comprised an armed police reserve of 5,000, a 20,000-strong security guard and the Bangladesh Rifles (border guard), numbering 38,000. Military service is voluntary.

Defence Budget: Estimated at 37,400m. taka for 2001.

Chief of Army Staff: Lt-Gen. HASSAN MASHHUD CHOWDHURY.

Chief of Naval Staff: Rear-Adm. IQBAL MUJTABA.

Chief of Air Staff: Air Vice-Marshal FAKHRUL AZAM.

Dir-Gen. of Bangladesh Rifles: Maj.-Gen. A. L. M. FAZLUR RAHMAN.

Education

The Government provides free schooling for children of both sexes for eight years. Primary education, which is compulsory, begins at six years of age and lasts for five years. Secondary education, beginning at the age of 11, lasts for up to seven years, comprising a first cycle of five years and a second cycle of two further years. In 1990 an estimated 62% of children (66% of boys; 58% of girls) in the relevant age-group attended primary schools, while the comparable enrolment ratio at secondary schools was 20% (26% of boys, 14% of girls). In the late 1980s the Government laid great emphasis on the improvement of the primary education system in an attempt to raise the rate of literacy. A scheme was, therefore, undertaken to establish one primary school for every 2,000 people in Bangladesh. Secondary schools and colleges in the private sector vastly outnumber government institutions. There are 11 state universities, including one for agriculture and one for engineering and technology, and an Islamic university. The Government launched an Open University Project in 1992 at an estimated cost of US $34.3m. In 1997/98 there were an estimated 66,235 primary schools and 13,419 secondary schools. In 1999 the indigenous people's association, representing the Santal minority, opened Bangladesh's first school teaching the national curriculum in the Santal language. The school is funded by the Grameen Trust. In 1990/91 there were 141 state-operated technical colleges and vocational institutes and more than 800 colleges offering general education. Educational reform is designed to assist in satisfying the manpower needs of the country, and the greatest importance is given to primary, technical and vocational education. The 2000/01 budget allocated 33,440m. taka to education (equivalent to 17.0% of total government expenditure.

Bibliography

See also India and Pakistan

HISTORY AND GENERAL

Ahamed, Emajuddin. *Military Rule and the Myth of Democracy.* Dhaka, University Press, 1988.

Ahmad, Aziz. *Studies in Islamic Culture in the Indian Environment.* Oxford University Press, 1964.

Islamic Modernism in India and Pakistan 1857–1964. London and New York, Oxford University Press, 1967.

Ahmed, Moudud. *Bangladesh: Constitutional Quest for Autonomy.* Germany, 1976, later Dhaka.

Bangladesh: Era of Sheikh Mujibur Rahman. Dhaka, University Press Ltd, 1983.

Democracy and the Challenge of Development: A Study of Politics and Military Interventions in Bangladesh. Dhaka, University Press Ltd, 1995.

Ahmed, Rafiuddin. *The Bengal Muslims 1871–1906.* Delhi, Oxford University Press, 1981.

Religion, Nationalism and Politics in Bangladesh. New Delhi, South Asia Publishers, 1990.

Ahmed, Sufia. *Muslim Community in Bengal 1884–1912.* Dhaka, 1974.

Alam, M. M., et al. *Development through Decentralization.* Dhaka, University Press, 1994.

Alauddin, Mohammad,et al. *Development, Governance and the Environment in South Asia; The Case of Bangladesh.* New York, St Martin's Press, 1999.

Ali, S. Mahmud. *The Fearful State: Power, People, and Internal War in South Asia.* London, Zed Books, 1993.

Aminul Islam, A. K. M. *A Bangladesh Village.* Prospect Heights, IL, Waveland Press, 1987 (2nd edn).

Baxter, Craig. *Bangladesh: A New Nation in an Old Setting.* Boulder, CO, Westview Press, 1984.

Bhattacharjee, G. P. *Renaissance and Freedom Movement in Bangladesh.* Kolkata, 1973.

Brauns, Claus-Dieter, and Loeffler, Lorenz G. *Mru: Hill People on the Border of Bangladesh.* Basel, Birkhauser Verlag, 1990.

Chakravarty, S. R. *Bangladesh under Mujib, Zia and Ershad.* New Delhi, Har-Anand Publications, 1995.

Chatterji, Joya. *Bengal Divided: Hindu Communalism and Partition, 1932–1947.* Cambridge, Cambridge University Press, 1994.

Chittagong Hill Tracts Commission. *Life is Not Ours: Land and Human Rights in the Chittagong Hill Tracts.* Copenhagen and Amsterdam, 1991.

Choudhury, G. W. *The Last Days of United Pakistan.* London, C. Hurst, 1974.

Gardner, Katy. *Songs at the River's Edge: Stories from a Bangladeshi Village.* London, Virago Press, 1991.

Gordon, Leonard A. *Bengal: the Nationalist Movement.* Delhi, 1974.

Harun-or-Rashid. *The Foreshadowing of Bangladesh: Bengal Muslim League and Muslim Politics 1936–47.* Dhaka, Asiatic Society of Bangladesh, 1987.

Hashmi, Taj-ul-Islam. *Pakistan as a Peasant Utopia: The Communalization of Class Politics in East Bengal, 1920–1947.* Boulder, CO, Westview Press, 1992.

Women and Islam in Bangladesh: Beyond Subjection and Tyranny. New York, St Martin's Press.

Hussain, T. *Land Rights in Bangladesh: Problems of Management.* Dhaka, University Press, 1995.

Islam, Sirajul (Ed.). *History of Bangladesh.* 3 vols, Dhaka, Asiatic Society of Bangladesh, 1992.

Jahan, Rounaq. *Pakistan: Failure in National Integration.* New York, Columbia University Press, 1972.

Bangladesh Politics: Problems and Issues. Dhaka, 1980.

Jacques, Kathryn. *Bangladesh, India and Pakistan: International Relations and Regional Tensions in South Asia.* New York, St Martin's Press, 2000.

Kabir, Bhuian Mohammad Monoar. *Politics of Military Rule and the Dilemmas of Democratization in Bangladesh.* New Delhi, South Asian Publishers, 1999.

Karim, Abdul. *Social History of the Muslims in Bengal.* Dhaka, 1959.

Khan, Mohammad Mohabbat, and Thorp, John (Eds). *Bangladesh: Society, Politics and Bureaucracy.* Dhaka, 1984.

Khan, Muin-Ud-Din Ahmad. *History of the Fara'idi Movement in Bengal 1818–1906.* Karachi, 1965.

Khan, Zillur Rahman. *Leadership in the Least Developed Nations: Bangladesh.* Syracuse, New York, 1983.

Kochanek, Stanley. *Patron-Client Politics and Business in Bangladesh.* New Delhi, Sage Publications, 1993.

Lifschultz, Lawrence. *Bangladesh: The Unfinished Revolution.* London, Zed Press, 1979.

Majumdar, R. C., and Sarkar, Sir Jadunath (Eds). *The History of Bengal.* University of Dhaka, 2 vols, 1942 and 1948.

Maniruzzaman, Talukder. *The Bangladesh Revolution and its Aftermath.* Dhaka, Bangladesh Books International, 1980.

Marshall, P. J. *East Indian Fortunes.* Oxford University Press, 1976.

Mascarenhas, Anthony. *Bangladesh: A Legacy of Blood.* London, Hodder and Stoughton, 1986.

Mujeeb, M. *The Indian Muslims.* London, Allen and Unwin, 1967.

Mukherjee, Ramkrishna. *Six Villages of Bengal.* Bombay, 1971.

Murshid, Tazeen. *The Sacred and the Secular: Bengal Muslim Discourses, 1871-1977.* Calcutta, Oxford University Press, 1995.

Novak, James J. *Bangladesh: Reflections on the Water.* Bloomington and Indianapolis, Indiana University Press, 1993.

Rahman, Mujibur. *Bangladesh, My Bangladesh.* New Delhi and Dhaka, 1972.

Rolt, Francis. *On the Brink in Bengal.* London, John Murray, 1991.

Sarkar, Sumit. *The Swadeshi Movement in Bengal 1903–1908.* New Delhi, 1973.

Sharma, S. *US-Bangladesh Relations: a Critique.* London, Sangam Books, 2002.

Shelley, Mizanur Rahman (Ed.). *The Chittagong Hill Tracts of Bangladesh: The Untold Story.* Dhaka, Centre for Development Research, 1993.

Siddiqui, Kalim. *Conflict, Crisis and War in Pakistan.* London, Macmillan, 1972.

Siddiqui, Khaleda Akter. *Urban Working Women in the Formal Sector in Bangladesh.* Frankfurt, Peter Lang, 2000.

Sisson, Richard, and Rose, Leo E. *War and Secession: Pakistan, India and the Creation of Bangladesh.* Berkeley, University of California Press, 1990.

Timm, R. W. *The Adivasis of Bangladesh.* London, Minority Rights Group, 1991.

Wilcox, W. *The Emergence of Bangladesh: Problems and Opportunities for a redefined American Policy in South Asia.* A Foreign Affairs Study, 1973.

Wright, Denis. *Bangladesh: Origins and Indian Ocean Relations (1971–1975).* New Delhi, Sterling Publishers, 1988.

Zafarullah, Habib (Ed.). *The Zia Episode in Bangladesh Politics.* New Delhi, South Asian Publications, 1996.

Zaheer, Hasan. *The Separation of East Pakistan: The Rise and Realisation of Bengali Muslim Nationalism.* Karachi, Oxford University Press, 1994.

Zene, Cosimo. *The Rishi of Bangladesh.* London, Routledge Curzon, 2002.

Ziring, Lawrence. *Bangladesh from Mujib to Ershad: An Interpretive Study.* Karachi, Oxford University Press, 1992.

ECONOMY

Abdullah, Abu (Ed.). *Modernisation at Bay: Structure and Change in Bangladesh.* Dhaka, University Press Ltd, 1991.

Ahmad, N. A. *New Economic Geography of Bangladesh.* New Delhi, 1976.

Ahmed, M. Farid. *Capital Markets and Institutions in Bangladesh.* Burlington, VT, Ashgate Publishing, 1997.

Alamgir, Mohiuddin. *Bangladesh: A Case of Below Poverty Level Equilibrium Trap.* Dhaka, Bangladesh Institute of Development Studies, 1978.

Arens, J., and Beurden, J. V. *Jhagrapur: Poor Peasants and Women in a Village in Bangladesh.* Birmingham, Third World Publications, 1977.

Bornstein, David. *The Story of the Grameen Bank.* Chicago, Il, University of Chicago Press, 1996.

Boyce, James. *Agrarian Impasse in Bengal.* Oxford University Press, 1987.

Chen, L. C. *Disaster in Bangladesh.* London, Oxford University Press, 1973.

Crow, Ben. *Sharing the Ganges: The Politics and Technology of River Development.* New Delhi, Sage Publications, 1995.

Datta, Anjan Kumar. *Land and Labor Relations in South-West Bangladesh: Resources, Power and Conflict.* New York, St Martin's Press, 1998.

Faaland, J., and Parkinson, J. R. *Bangladesh, The Test Case for Development.* London, Hurst, 1976.

Faaland, J. (Ed.). *Aid and Influence: The Case of Bangladesh.* London, Macmillan, 1981.

Grieve, Roy H., and Huq, M. Mozammel (Eds). *Bangladesh: Strategies for Development.* Dhaka, University Press Ltd, 1995.

Hartmann, Betsy, and Boyce, James. *A Quiet Violence: View from a Bangladesh Village.* London, Zed Press, 1983.

Humphrey, C. E. *Privatization in Bangladesh: Economic Transition in a Poor Country.* Dhaka, University Press Ltd, 1992.

Islam, N. *Development Planning in Bangladesh; Study in Political Economy.* London, 1977.

Development Strategy of Bangladesh. Oxford, Pergamon Press, 1978.

Islam, Nazrul (Ed.). *Addressing the Urban Poverty Agenda in Bangladesh: Critical Issues and the 1995 Survey Findings.* Manila, Asian Development Bank Publications, 1997.

Islam, Rizwanul, and Muqtada, M. *Bangladesh: Selected Issues in Employment and Development.* New Delhi, ILO, 1986.

Jannuzi, F. T., and Peach, J. T. *The Agrarian Structure of Bangladesh.* Boulder, CO, Westview Press, 1980.

Jansen, Eirik G. *Rural Bangladesh: Competition for Scarce Resources.* Oxford University Press, 1986.

Johnson, B. L. C. *Bangladesh.* London, Heinemann, 1975.

Kabeer, Naila. *Power to Choose: Bangladeshi Women and Labor Market Decisions in London and Dhaka.* London, Verso, 2000.

Khan, Azizur Rahman, and Hossain, Mahabub. *The Strategy of Development in Bangladesh.* London, Macmillan, 1990.

Khan, Shakeeb Adnan. *The State and Village Society.* Dhaka, University Press Ltd, 1989.

Kochanek, S. A. *Patron-Client Politics and Business in Bangladesh.* New Delhi, Sage Publications, 1993.

Norbye, O. D. K. (Ed.). *Bangladesh Faces the Future.* Dhaka, University Press Ltd, 1990.

Rahman, Atiur. *Peasants and Classes: A Study in Differentiation in Bangladesh.* London, Zed Press, 1986.

Rashid, S. (Ed.). *Bangladesh Economy: Evaluation and a Research Agenda.* Dhaka, University Press Ltd, 1995.

Robinson, E. A., and Griffin, K. *The Economic Development of Bangladesh within a Socialist Framework: Proceedings of a Conference held by the IEA at Dhaka.* 1974.

Singh, Inderjit. *The Great Ascent: The Rural Poor in South Asia.* London, Johns Hopkins University Press, 1990.

Sobhan, Rehman. *Public Enterprise and the Nature of the State in South Asia.* Dhaka, 1983.

(Ed.). *The Decade of Stagnation: The State of the Bangladesh Economy in the 1980s.* Dhaka, University Press Ltd, 1991.

(Ed.). *Debt Default to the Development Finance Institutions: The Crisis of State Sponsored Entrepreneurship in Bangladesh.* Dhaka, University Press Ltd, 1991.

Stepanek, J. F. *Bangladesh: Equitable Growth.* Oxford, Pergamon Press, 1979.

Stevens, R., et al. *Rural Development in Bangladesh and Pakistan.* Honolulu, University of Hawaii Press, 1976.

Westergaard, K. *State and Rural Society in Bangladesh.* London, Curzon Press, 1985.

Wood, Geoff D. *Bangladesh: Whose Ideas, Whose Interests?* London, Intermediate Technology Publications, 1994.

BHUTAN

Physical and Social Geography

BRIAN SHAW

The Kingdom of Bhutan is a small, land-locked country. To the north and north-west, it adjoins Tibet (the Xizang Autonomous Region) in China. To the south, Bhutan is bordered (west to east) by the present-day Indian states of Sikkim, West Bengal, Assam and Arunachal Pradesh. The country's total area is some 46,500 sq km (17,954 sq miles). It extends approximately from 26° 45′ to 28° 20′ N, and from 88° 50′ to 92° 05′ E. The borders are mostly natural ones; that with Tibet is traditional, following the watershed of the Chumbi valley in the north-west, and the crest of the Himalaya mountain range in the north. The border with India was established by treaty with the United Kingdom in the 19th century. However, it was not until many years later, between 1973 and 1984, that the border's detailed delineation and demarcation were agreed in principle and completed, apart from some portions in southern Bhutan and the area of the Sino-Indian-Bhutanese border in eastern Bhutan, which generally follows the line separating the foothills from the plains.

PHYSICAL FEATURES

Bhutan is almost entirely mountainous, and its terrain is among the most rugged in the world. The elevation above sea-level may increase from 160 m to more than 7,000 m in less than 100 km of distance. Bhutan's physiography is similar to that of Nepal, with the Churia belt being known here, as in nearby Bengal and Assam, as the Duars. From the level plains areas of the Duars in the south, the hills rise steadily to the Great Himalayas. Flat land is limited to the lower reaches of the broader (generally north–south) river valleys, and in small sections of the Duars. Bhutan's highest peak is Gangar Punsum, whose summit is 7,561 m above sea-level. Chomo Lhari, overlooking the Chumbi valley, is 7,352 m high, Jitchu Drake is 6,789 m, and there are many other peaks over 5,000 m. The country's relatively remote location and the terrain acted as strong barriers between Bhutan and its neighbours, and between the peoples of different valleys within the country.

CLIMATE

The country can be divided vertically into three distinct climatic zones, corresponding broadly to the three main geographical divisions (southern foothills, rising from the plains of India; 'inner' Himalayas; and high Himalayas). The southern belt, rising to about 1,500 m above sea-level, has a hot, humid climate, with temperatures remaining fairly even throughout the year (between 15° and 30°C) and with annual rainfall ranging between 2,500 mm and 5,000 mm in some areas. The middle inner Himalayas, from 1,500 m up to about 3,000 m, have a cool, temperate climate, with annual precipitation averaging some 1,000 mm but with more rain in the west. The high northern region, above 3,000 m, has a severe alpine climate, with annual precipitation of around 400 mm. Much of the rain is concentrated in the summer months (from mid-June to September), with the south-west monsoon accounting for 60%–90% of the total annual rainfall. The monsoon is particularly strong in the west. Within these broad ranges, however, there is substantial variation. The climate and rainfall characteristics change dramatically from one valley to the next, with consequent sharp changes in the possibilities for agricultural and pastoral production.

SOILS AND NATURAL RESOURCES

There is little reliable information on soils. In general, the more fertile soils are confined to the valley floors and the Duars. The Geological Survey of Bhutan was established in 1982 to develop preliminary work carried out by the Geological Survey of India, which has shown that Bhutan is comparatively well endowed with natural resources. Deposits of limestone, dolomite, coal, gypsum, tungsten, graphite, copper, lead, zinc, marble, slate and talc have been indicated. Limestone (processed into cement) and dolomite are the principal minerals currently being exploited. Coal reserves are of moderate size and quality. Slate quarrying is operating on a small scale: in 1975 the Bonsegoema deposit, near Wangdiphodrang, was described by feasibility consultants as 'one of the best slate deposits so far known in the world'.

The deep gorges of fast-flowing rivers, fed by the snow-melt of the Himalayas, provide enormous hydroelectric power potential, although the cost of harnessing this energy is also enormous. Forests, covering 74% of the land area, are another major natural resource, although exploitation is at present unbalanced: remote forests are over-mature, while accessible areas (especially in the south) are becoming degraded.

POPULATION AND ETHNIC GROUPS

The 'official overall' population of Bhutan in late 1996 was 600,000. This figure was first given public endorsement in 1990, and was to remain an approximation pending the long-delayed completion of a nation-wide census. Bhutan's first census, held in 1969, reported a total population of 931,514. A 1980 census reported a total of 1,165,000, and the mid-1988 projection, based on this, was for a total of 1,375,400. According to official figures, the present annual growth rate of the population is 2.55%, which, on the basis of an estimated population of 638,000 in 2000, suggests a total of about 670,953 in 2002. These latest revised figures remain approximate, as is also acknowledged to be true for the (unpublished) data acquired from the annual household censuses conducted in each district. Whereas the notional population density at mid-1988 was therefore more than 29 per sq km, that for 2002 (adjusted for the smaller population estimate) was 14.4 per sq km. The population is unevenly distributed: the southern Duar valleys and the eastern region, around Trashigang, are the most heavily populated areas. According to an address made by Bhutan's Minister of Planning at a World Population Day function in July 1997, the then very high rate of population growth of 3.1% would—if unchecked—double the population in 24 years, with major economic and social consequences. At the same time, the Secretary for Health reported that it was hoped, through education, to lower the annual growth rate of the population to 2.56% by 2002. He stated that of Bhutan's 20 districts, population growth was already lower than 2% in 10 and stood at 2% in six; only four districts currently showed a growth rate of more than 2%. A formal population policy was to be finalized before the end of the Eighth Plan period (1997–2002). The 2000 edition of the five-yearly *National Health Survey* (published in early 2001) reported that the growth rate within a sample section of the population had declined from 3.1% in 1994 to 2.5% in 2000, while the average (sample) household size was reported to be 5.42 persons.

The main western valleys are peopled by Ngalong (showing some similarities with Central Tibetans). The Sharchops of the east are most numerous, and are considered by some to be among the earliest (although not aboriginal) inhabitants. The people of central Bhutan, around Bumthang, speak an old and separate language. Nepalese settlers came to work in the southern foothills of Bhutan in the early 20th century, and others migrated until such movement was banned by Bhutan in 1959. Unofficial migration of Nepalese settlers continued, both from Nepal and Assam (following their expulsion from the Indian state in the 1970s), until the 1988–89 southern district censuses, when the recently known illegal migrants were obliged to leave the country. The descendants of these settlers, mostly Hindus, dominate southern Bhutan, and are today referred to as southern Bhutanese. They are thought to comprise

20%–35% of the country's total population, although no reliable figures are available. The Government encourages social integration, and the major religious festivals of Hindus, as well as those of Buddhists, are celebrated. Intermarriage between northern and southern Bhutanese was until 1990 encouraged with gifts of land and money.

History

BRIAN SHAW

EARLY HISTORY

Little is known of the pre-history of Bhutan, although stone artefacts and some remaining megaliths suggest that it was already inhabited by about 2000–1500 BC. No comprehensive archaeological survey has yet been carried out within Bhutan. Buddhism was introduced in the seventh century AD by the Tibetan Buddhist King Srongtsen Gampo, who is recorded as having ordered the building of the first lhakhangs (temples) in old Bhutan: Jampe, in Bumthang (central Bhutan), and Kyichu, in the Paro valley. Since this time, Buddhism has played a large part in shaping the country's institutions, in developing a native artistic spirit and in moulding a national sentiment transcending the localism of particular valleys or regions.

At the end of the eighth century, the Indian Buddhist Saint Padmasambhava (revered in Bhutan as Guru Rimpoche, protector-saint of the kingdom) came from Tibet to Bumthang, and arranged for the construction of rock monasteries in various places, including Taktsang (Tiger's Nest) lhakhang in Paro valley, thus founding the Nyingmapa school of Mahayana Buddhism. The subsequent history of Bhutan is obscure until the end of the 11th century, but by the end of the 12th century a Lhapa school of the Kagyupa sect was established at Paro.

The Drukpa sub-sect was introduced in the first decades of the 13th century by the Tibetan Phajo Drugom Shigpo. He confronted, and finally prevailed over, the Lhapa school, which nevertheless continued to propagate its rival teachings until the 17th century. Phajo Drugom Shigpo founded the first Drukpa monasteries at Phajoding and Tango, in Thimphu valley.

Other sages of various sects came south to Bhutan from Tibet between the 12th and 17th centuries, and constructed other monasteries. In the 15th century the 'divine madman', Drukpa Kinley, came to western Bhutan, and the accounts of his itinerant and Rabelaisian lifestyle continue to be recited with great sympathy and affection by all Bhutanese. Also at this time, the scholar Pema Lingpa was born in Bumthang; he later founded temples there, and created religious and secular dances, based on his vision of Zandog Pelri (the 'copper-coloured mountain'), the heavenly abode of Guru Rimpoche.

The independent theocracy of Druk-yul ('land of the thunder-dragon'), and thus of historical Bhutan, emerges from the early 17th century. A prominent Tibetan lama of the Drukpa sub-sect, Ngawang Namgyal, fled from Tibet to Bhutan in 1616, after the Gelugpa sect, headed by the Dalai Lama, had come to achieve an intolerant dominance at Lhasa, the Tibetan capital. In due course, he took the title Shabdrung ('at whose feet one submits'), and it is as the first Shabdrung that he is widely venerated today, as unifier of the disparate powerful families, as promulgator of a code of law, and as builder of most of the remarkable administrative-temple-fortress complexes known as dzongs (the first of which was started at Simtokha in 1629). After his arrival, successive armies from Tibet, variously at the invitation of opponents of the Shabdrung and at the instigation of the Mongols (who by the late 1630s had overrun the Tsang province of Tibet), attacked western Bhutan, but were always successfully repelled.

The Shabdrung established himself as both temporal and religious ruler of Bhutan, and he created an administrative structure which still finds echoes in present-day arrangements. He founded a state monastic body under an elected spiritual leader, the Je Khenpo (head abbot), and a theocracy under the Desi, or Deb. The Desi was to deal with civil matters, although the Shabdrung retained ultimate authority. A State Council (Lhengye Tshokdu) was also created, and was the forerunner of today's organs of government.

The first Shabdrung's death, some time after 1651, was kept secret for half a century in a successful attempt to prevent the disintegration of the newly unified state. During the first decades of the 18th century, a theory of triple reincarnations of the Shabdrung was established. These were said to take the form of physical, oral and mental aspects, and the persons manifesting the latter were to be considered as successors to the Shabdrung as head of state. Between the recognition of successive Shabdrungs (only six 'mental incarnations' were recognized in the period up to the founding of the monarchy), the Je Khenpo and the Desi sought to maintain a dual system of government: but the membership of the State Council became increasingly secular in orientation. This was true also for the successive Desi and the leaders of the regional administrations. The latter were called dzongpöns, and the three most important—at Daga, Tongsa and Paro—were styled penlops. In due course, rivalry between penlops led to continuing internal disorder; this, together with the developing British hegemony in Assam, brought new challenges to the Bhutanese state from the late 18th century.

BRITISH INTERVENTION

The British had no relations with Bhutan prior to 1772. Bhutan had developed political influence over Cooch Bihar, in 1730 and succeeding years, but, by an agreement made in 1773 between one of the claimants to the throne of this principality and the East India Co, Cooch Bihar became virtually a company dependency. A British expeditionary force drove a Bhutanese garrison from Cooch Bihar and, in hot pursuit, captured the Bhutanese forts of Pasakha and Damimkot. The then Desi thereupon appealed for assistance to the Panchen Lama at Lhasa, acting as regent; the latter responded with an appeasing letter to Warren Hastings (then Governor-General of India). Hastings grasped this opportunity to seek trading relations with both Tibet and Bhutan. Following a peace treaty between the British and the Bhutanese (25 April 1774), in which both sides agreed, in effect, to restore the status quo, he dispatched George Bogle on a political mission to Lhasa, via Thimphu. Further missions by Hamilton (1776, 1777), and by Turner and Davis (1783), were also well received in Bhutan. In the 19th century, however, southern boundary disputes became increasingly troublesome, leading to further British missions, led by Bose in 1815 and by Pemberton and Griffiths in 1838. A draft treaty which was presented by the latter mission, primarily designed to establish commercial intercourse between British India and Bhutan, was rejected by the Bhutanese.

At this time, Bhutan fell into increasing civil disorder; further Bhutanese incursions into the Assam Duars were made, and in 1841 the Assam Duars were annexed, with compensation of Rs 10,000 annually to be paid by the British to Bhutan. Continuing Bhutanese raids into Sikkim and Cooch Bihar in 1862 led to the mission of Ashley Eden (1863–64), which was disastrous in its manner and execution. Following Eden's return, a proclamation of war was issued against Bhutan in November 1864. The south-eastern area of Bhutan, around Dewangiri (present-day Samdrup Jongkhar), was lost to the British forces, and the Duar War came to an end with the signing of the treaty of Sinchula in November 1865. By this instrument, Bhutan ceded the seven Assam Duars and the 11 Bengal Duars to the United Kingdom, and also lost hill territory on the left bank of the river Teesta (including Kalimpong and Pedong), in return for an annual compensation of Rs 50,000.

Towards the end of the 19th century, the weakening of the powers of the central Government in Bhutan was paralleled by the emergence to power of provincial governors, especially the penlops of Paro and of Trongsa (who, in practice, controlled western and central Bhutan respectively), who were fiercely competitive, and who sought to increase their powers. The external situation of Bhutan came to play a part in the settlement of these tendencies. By this time, Bhutan had enjoyed a millennium of trade and religious ties with northern Tibet. While the United Kingdom and Tibet remained on amicable terms, Bhutan could maintain good relations with both neighbours. However, the extension of British power to the south of Bhutan, together with Tibetan border violations against Sikkim and the subsequent growing tension between the British and Tibetans, led Bhutanese leaders to recognize that they should choose which authority of their neighbours they would prefer.

A British mission, led by Younghusband, to Lhasa in 1903–04, ostensibly to open Tibet to trade and to forestall Russian dominance at Lhasa, gave the then Trongsa penlop, Ugyen Wangchuck, his opportunity. Advised by Kazi Ugyen Dorji, and in opposition to the Paro penlop (who preferred to side with the Tibetans), Ugyen Wangchuck accompanied the expedition and was a valuable intermediary between the British and the authorities at Lhasa. He was knighted by the British, and emerged with enhanced prestige within Bhutan.

Although British imperial policy came to repudiate the treaty with Lhasa and to recognize Chinese claims to suzerainty over Tibet, the Younghusband expedition alarmed the Chinese Government into attempting, once again, to assert the long-desired *de facto* political authority over Tibet. In 1910 the Dalai Lama fled to the refuge of India when Chinese forces occupied Lhasa, and the Chinese Government laid claim to Bhutan, Nepal and Sikkim. British and Bhutanese interests coincided at this point. The last Shabdrung had died in 1903, and the Desi had died in 1904. No reincarnation of the Shabdrung had appeared by 1906. The management of Bhutan's civil affairs had come into the hands of Sir Ugyen Wangchuck, and in November 1907 an assembly of the leading members of the clergy, officials and important families agreed to create a hereditary monarchy. Sir Ugyen Wangchuck was unanimously elected first King of Bhutan, thereby ending the dual system of government that had lasted for nearly 300 years.

In 1910 Bhutan signed the treaty of Punakha with the United Kingdom, amending two articles of the Sinchula treaty to increase the allowance payable to Rs 100,000 per year, and to provide a British undertaking 'to exercise no interference in the internal administration of Bhutan' in return for a Bhutanese agreement 'to be guided by the advice of the British Government in regard to its external relations'. These agreements provided the defence that was desired by both parties against Chinese imperial claims. Successive Chinese Governments, up to the present time, seem to have accepted that, by this treaty, Bhutan came within the Indian sphere of influence, whatever the theoretical options may have been prior to 1910. British India seemed to be content to have declared a northern interest where Chinese interests should not encroach.

For a further half-century, Bhutan remained isolated from the outside world. British India maintained sporadic contact with the Bhutanese Government through its political agent at Gangtok, in Sikkim, and the Bhutan trade agent at Kalimpong. In 1949 independent India renewed the provisions of the 1910 treaty with Bhutan, increased the annual payment to Rs 500,000, and restored Dewangiri.

MODERN BHUTAN

The era of the contemporary Bhutanese state dates from 1907. Acceptance of the principle of an hereditary monarchy has been the base from which has evolved the present modified form of what might be described as a proto-constitutional monarchy. Sir Ugyen Wangchuck ruled as Druk Gyalpo ('Precious Ruler of the Druk People') until 1926, when he was succeeded by his son, Jigme Wangchuck, who ruled until 1952. The third monarch, Jigme Dorji Wangchuck, ruled until his early death in 1972, at the age of 43. Major developments occurred during his reign, including the decision to modernize Bhutan, and he is today venerated as the 'father of modern Bhutan'. His son, the present King Jigme Singye Wangchuck, had been appointed Trongsa penlop in May 1972, at the age of 16; he became King in July 1972, on the demise of his father, and formally accepted the Raven Crown, on the Golden Throne of Bhutan, in June 1974.

During his first visit to Bhutan in 1958, the Indian Prime Minister, Jawaharlal Nehru, had stated clearly that 'our only wish is that you remain an independent country, choosing your own way of life and taking the path of progress according to your will'. This premise has been acted upon by successive Indian Prime Ministers. In the wake of events in Tibet from 1959, Bhutan aligned itself with India, closed its borders with Tibet in 1960, and began a massive process of modernization (mostly funded by India) to escape Tibet's fate of subjugation. The first, enormous task was to build roads from the Indian plains to central Bhutan, and from west to east; Indian engineers laboured from 1959 to 1962 to complete the all-weather road between Phuentsholing and Thimphu, with Bhutanese providing the labour as national service, and subsequent development efforts have evolved from this.

Bhutan joined the Colombo Plan in 1962, the UN in 1971, the UN Economic and Social Commission for Asia and the Pacific in 1972, the IMF and the World Bank in 1981 and the Asian Development Bank in 1982. Bhutan is also a committed member of the Non-aligned Movement. Regionally, Bhutan was an enthusiastic founder member of the South Asian Regional Co-operation (SARC) organization (inaugurated in August 1983), consisting of Bangladesh, Bhutan, India, Maldives, Nepal, Pakistan and Sri Lanka. In May 1985 Bhutan was host to the first meeting of Ministers of Foreign Affairs from SARC member countries, which later agreed to give their grouping the formal title of South Asian Association for Regional Co-operation (SAARC).

After 1959 Bhutan accepted more than 6,000 refugees from Tibet. The involvement of some of these in the domestic affairs of Bhutan (in 1964 and again in 1974), and an unwillingness by many to accept proffered Bhutan citizenship, forced the Bhutanese Government by 1979 to decide to expel those who declined to accept its authority. India initially refused to accept any further refugees, but in January 1980 it was agreed that India would absorb some 1,500 of them. By September 1985 some 1,633 refugees had been accepted by India, and 4,206 had requested and received Bhutanese citizenship, while 1,461 had not yet accepted the offer. A revised Citizenship Act, adopted by the Tshogdu Chenmo (National Assembly) in 1985, confirmed residence in Bhutan in 1958 as a fundamental basis for automatic citizenship (as provided for by the 1958 Nationality Act), but this was to be flexibly interpreted. Provision was also made for citizenship by registration for Nepalese immigrants who had resided in the country for at least 20 years (15 years if employed by the Government) and who could meet linguistic and other tests of commitment to the Bhutanese community.

The violent ethnic Nepalese agitation in India for a 'Gurkha homeland' in the Darjeeling-Kalimpong region during the late 1980s and the populist movement in Nepal in 1988–90 (see the chapters on India and Nepal, respectively) spilled over into Bhutan in 1990. Ethnic unrest became apparent in that year when a campaign of intimidation and violence, directed by militant Nepalese against the authority of the Government in Thimphu, was initiated. In September thousands of southern Bhutanese villagers, and Nepalese who marched in from across the Indian border, demonstrated in at least nine border towns in southern Bhutan to protest against domination by the indigenous Buddhist Drukpa. The 'anti-nationals' or 'terrorists', as they are called by the Bhutanese authorities, demand a greater role in the country's political and economic life and are bitterly opposed to official attempts to strengthen the Bhutanese sense of national identity through an increased emphasis on Tibetan-derived, rather than Nepalese, culture and religion (including a formal dress code, Dzongkha as the sole official language, etc.). Bhutanese officials, on the other hand, view the southerners as recent arrivals who abuse the hospitality of their hosts through acts of violence and the destruction of development infrastructure.

Most southern villagers are relatively recent arrivals from Nepal and many of them have made substantial contributions to the development of the southern hills. The provision of free education and health care by the Bhutanese Government acted for many years as a magnet for Nepalese who were struggling to survive in their own country and who came to settle illegally in Bhutan. This population movement was largely ignored by local administrative officials, many of whom accepted incentives to disregard the illegal nature of the influx. The Government's policy of encouraging a sense of national identity, together with rigorous new procedures (introduced in 1988) to check citizenship registration, revealed thousands of illegal residents in southern Bhutan, many of whom had lived there for a decade or more, married local people and raised families. During the ethnic unrest in September 1990, the majority of southern villagers were coerced into participating in the demonstrations by groups of armed and uniformed young men (including many of Nepalese origin who were born in Bhutan). Many of these dissidents, including a large number of secondary school students and former members of the Royal Bhutan Army and of the police force, had fled Bhutan in 1989 and early 1990. In 1988–90 a large number of the dissidents resided in the tea gardens and villages adjoining southern Bhutan. Following the demonstrations that took place in Bhutan in September–October 1990, other ethnic Nepalese left Bhutan. In January 1991 some 234 persons, who claimed to be Bhutanese refugees, reportedly arrived in Maidhar and Tinmai in the Jhapa district of eastern Nepal. In September, at the request of the Nepalese Government, the office of the UN High Commissioner for Refugees (UNHCR) inaugurated a relief programme providing food and shelter for more than 300 people in the *ad hoc* camps. By December the number of people staying in the camps had risen to about 6,000.

The sizes of these camps have been substantially augmented by landless and unemployed Nepalese, who have been expelled from Assam and other eastern states of India. The small and faction-ridden ethnic Nepalese Bhutan People's Party (BPP), which was founded in Kathmandu in 1990 (as a successor to the People's Forum on Democratic Rights, an organization established in 1989), purports to lead the agitation for 'democracy', but has, as yet, presented no clear or convincing set of objectives and has attracted no significant support from within Bhutan itself. Schools and bridges became principal targets for arson and looting during 1990–92, and families known to be loyal to the Bhutanese Government were robbed of their valuables. Most of the schools in southern Bhutan were closed indefinitely from the end of September 1990, in response to threats to the lives of teachers and students' families, but the majority of pupils affected by these closures were provided with temporary places in schools in northern Bhutan. By mid-1995, despite the continuing security problems, some 74 schools and 89 health facilities had been reopened in the five southern districts.

Since 1988 King Jigme has personally authorized the release of over 1,700 militants captured by the authorities. He has stated that, while he has an open mind regarding the question of the pace and extent of political reform (including a willingness to hold discussions with any minority group that has grievances), his Government cannot tolerate pressures for change that are based on intimidation and violence. Although several important leaders of the dissident movement remain in custody, the King has said that they will be released when conditions of law and order return to normal. Some leaders of the BPP have stated that they have no quarrel with the King, but with 'corrupt officials'; on the other hand, certain militants strongly condemn the King as their 'main enemy'. A number of southern Bhutanese officials (including the then Director-General of Power, Bhim Subba, and the Managing Director of the State Trading Corporation, R. B. Basnet) absconded in June 1991 (on the eve of the publication of departmental audits) and went directly to Nepal, where they reportedly sought political asylum on the grounds of repression and atrocities against southern Bhutanese. These accusations were refuted in detail by the Government in Thimphu. The former Secretary-General of the BPP, D. K. Rai, was tried by the High Court in Thimphu in May 1992 and was sentenced to life imprisonment for terrorist acts; a further 35 defendants received lesser sentences and five were acquitted. The alleged master-mind behind the ethnic unrest, Teknath Rizal, came to trial, and was sentenced to life imprisonment in November 1993 after having been found guilty on four of nine charges of offences against the Tsawa Sum ('the country, the King, and the people'); one decision was deferred in the absence of key witnesses. King Jigme subsequently decreed that Rizal would be released from prison 'once the Governments of Bhutan and Nepal resolve the problems of the people living in the refugee camps in eastern Nepal'. About 130 detainees, who were accused of criminal and terrorist acts, were tried during 1995.

Violence continued in the disturbed areas of Samtse, Chhukha, Tsirang, Sarpang and Gelephu throughout 1991–97, and companies of trained militia volunteers were posted to these areas to relieve the forces of the regular army. The state government of West Bengal in India, the territory of which abuts much of southern Bhutan, reaffirmed in 1991 and 1992 that its land would not be used as a base for any agitation against Bhutan.

In late 1991 and throughout 1992 several thousand legally settled villagers left southern Bhutan for the newly established refugee camps in eastern Nepal. The Bhutanese Government alleged that the villagers were being enticed or threatened to leave their homes by militants based outside Bhutan, in order to augment the population of the camps and gain international attention; the dissidents, on the other hand, claimed that the Bhutanese Government was forcing the villagers to leave. The formation of the Bhutan National Democratic Party (BNDP), including members drawn from supporters of the BPP and with the leading dissident, R. B. Basnet, as its President, was announced in Kathmandu in February 1992. Incidents of ethnic violence, almost all of which involved infiltration from across the border by ethnic Nepalese who had been trained and dispatched from the camps in Nepal, reportedly diminished substantially in the first half of 1993 as talks continued between Bhutanese and Nepalese government officials regarding proposals to resolve the issues at stake. The Nepalese Government steadfastly refused to consider any solution that did not include the resettlement in Bhutan of all ethnic Nepalese 'refugees' living in the camps (by November 1993 the number of alleged ethnic Nepalese refugees from Bhutan totalled about 85,000). This proposal was rejected by the Bhutanese Government, which claimed that the majority of the camp population merely professed to be from Bhutan, had absconded from Bhutan (and thus forfeited their citizenship, according to Bhutan's citizenship laws), or had voluntarily departed after selling their properties and surrendering their citizenship papers and rights.

The apparent deadlock was broken, however, when a joint statement was signed by the Ministers of Home Affairs of Bhutan and Nepal on 18 July 1993, which committed each side to establishing a 'high-level committee' to work towards a settlement and, in particular, to fulfilling the following mandate prior to undertaking any other related activity: to determine the different categories of people claiming to have come from Bhutan in the refugee camps in eastern Nepal (which now numbered eight); and to specify the positions of the two Governments on each of these categories, which would provide the basis for the resolution of the problem. The two countries held their first ministerial-level meeting regarding the issue in Kathmandu in October, at which it was agreed that four categories would be established among the people in the refugee camps—'(i) bona fide Bhutanese who have been evicted forcefully; (ii) Bhutanese who emigrated; (iii) non-Bhutanese; and (iv) Bhutanese who have committed criminal acts.' (These categories are henceforth referred to as Category I, II, III and IV.) Further meetings were held in 1994. Following the election of a new Government in Nepal in November of that year, however, little progress was made at joint ministerial meetings held in the first half of 1995. Nepal's communist Government demanded that all persons in the camps be accepted by Bhutan; the Bhutanese authorities, on the other hand, were prepared to accept only the unconditional return of any bona fide Bhutanese citizens who had left the country involuntarily. The Nepalese Government seemed reluctant to inquire too closely into the national status of the ethnic Nepalis in the camps. Nevertheless, diplomatic exchanges continued in the latter half of the year, despite serious political instability in Nepal.

In January 1996 the new Nepalese Prime Minister, Sher Bahadur Deuba, proposed a resumption of intergovernmental talks, this time at foreign minister level. King Jigme welcomed this proposal, but the seventh round of talks, which was held in early April, resulted in demands by Nepal that went beyond the mandate drawn up by the joint ministerial committee in mid-1993. It was widely understood that the Nepalese Government had again reverted to a requisition that all persons in the camps be accepted by Bhutan, regardless of status. This demand remained unacceptable to the Bhutanese Government, which stated that the problem of the people in the camps would not have arisen in the first place, if conditions (such as prospects of free food, shelter, health and education, and 'moral support' by the Nepalese authorities for all persons claiming to be Bhutanese refugees) had not been created when there were only 234 persons in Jhapa making such claims. In addition, the Bhutanese Government stated that even with such conditions attracting people to the refugee camps, a well-organized screening process would have prevented the sheer scale of ethnic Nepalese claiming to be Bhutanese refugees. It added that those responsible for creating the refugee problem in eastern Nepal wanted it to be resolved without receiving any blame. (Until June 1993 no screening of claimants to refugee status had been enforced on the Indo-Nepalese border.) In August 1996 a UNHCR delegation visited Bhutan at the invitation of the authorities and received detailed information from the Bhutanese Government regarding the issue of the camps. Talks at official level were held in March and July 1997 without any public communiqué. Following informal meetings during the SAARC summit in Colombo, Sri Lanka, in late July 1998, the new Chairman of the Council of Ministers and Head of Government in Bhutan, Lyonpo Jigmi Y. Thinley, held talks with the Nepalese Prime Minister, G. P. Koirala; both leaders stated that their meeting had been 'very positive'. Thinley and Koirala agreed that bilateral negotiations would continue through their respective Foreign Ministers on the issue of persons claiming refugee status in Nepal (who now numbered about 100,000); talks were held in Kathmandu in September 1999. The 77th National Assembly session, which took place in June–August 1999, unanimously reiterated that the Bhutanese Government accepted full responsibility for any Bhutanese found to have been forcefully evicted (Category I—see above): such persons would be recognized and accepted as genuine refugees, while those responsible for their eviction would be punished. Category II people who had voluntarily emigrated from the country would be dealt with according to the respective immigration and citizenship laws of Bhutan and Nepal; Category III people 'must return to their own country'; and the repatriation of those in Category IV was to be conducted in accordance with the laws of the two countries.

According to the Bhutanese authorities, following the expulsion of illegal ethnic Nepalese from 1988, the goal of ethnic Nepalese dissidents has been clear and is supported by various political leaders in Kathmandu. In this view, the dissidents wish to obstruct, and if possible reverse, Bhutan's determination to control and restrict the illegal entry of aliens into the country. Ethnic Nepalese view this restriction as 'unfair' and 'against their human rights', especially in the context of continuing unrestricted access into India for Nepalese persons. The Bhutanese Government counters that immigration controls, based on national legislation, are a precondition of Bhutan's sovereignty and security, and also of its cultural survival.

While senior Nepalese government officials now better understand the concerns of the Bhutanese Government, the media of Kathmandu continue to make statements that at best uncritically reflect the viewpoint of the anti-Thimphu organizations. During 1994–98 the US State Department and a prominent human rights organization, Amnesty International, issued reports on human rights in Bhutan which were based on acceptance of the claims of persons in the camps, but which did not appear to balance such assertions against the realities of sanctioned policy and practice within Bhutan.

Following an initial invitation by the Government (in 1991) and subsequent formal agreements between the parties (in 1993, renewed in 1998), representatives of the International Committee of the Red Cross (ICRC) make regular visits to Bhutan to speak with detainees and to inspect prison facilities (most recently, the 18th visit, in December 2001). After several visits (the first of which took place in January 1992), an ICRC delegation leader stated in May 1994 that the ICRC had 'an excellent working relationship' with the Government and in 1997 relations between the two parties were described as 'very fruitful'. The 1993 memorandum of understanding between the ICRC and the Government was renewed in 1998, and in October 1999 the ICRC stated that it had benefited from the 'good co-operation' of the authorities. In July 1994 the newly appointed UN Commissioner for Human Rights was invited to Thimphu and on departure claimed that he had received 'very important information' on the matter of refugees in Nepal. In October the UN Commission on Human Rights (UNCHR) working group on arbitrary detention visited Bhutan at the invitation of the authorities. In March 1995 the working group reported to the UNCHR plenum that the arrest and detention of Teknath Rizal (see above) had been 'not arbitrary', and—at the request of the Bhutanese Government—made 15 recommendations concerning problems in the administration of justice. The Government subsequently invited the working group to return to verify the implementation of these recommendations, which it did in April–May 1996. In its report to the UNCHR, the working group concluded that the recommendations had generally been implemented, and urged the speedy adoption of a revised Code of Criminal Procedure (then being drafted). In addition, the group proposed that technical training for judges and jabmis (publicly certificated advocates or defenders) should be augmented with assistance, as already agreed between Bhutan and the UNCHR. In May 1997 Bhutan was re-elected, for a second three-year term, as one of the six Asian representatives on the UNCHR. An Amnesty International delegation visited eastern Bhutan and Sarpang on invitation for 12 days in late November 1998. On 17 December 1999 (Bhutan's National Day) King Jigme announced the pardon of 200 common-law and other prisoners, including 40 who had been convicted for 'anti-national' acts since 1988. Teknath Rizal was among those pardoned. King Jigme noted that Rizal had already served 10 years in prison, but that he 'had not physically carried out acts of violence and terrorism'. The BPP, however, claimed that the Government had released Rizal only to discredit him, and that he was effectively prohibited from participating in political activity.

In southern Bhutan in 1994 pro-Government southern villagers seized a number of armed terrorists who had allegedly attacked their villages. Those arrested in 1993 and 1994 confirmed that the majority of them were absconders from Bhutan who had been induced by dissident leaders to go to the refugee camps in Nepal, where they subsequently received rudimentary military training before reportedly being ordered to return to Bhutan to commit robbery, arson and other terrorist activities. From December 1995, however, terrorist incidents were fewer, coinciding with the adoption of the 'peace march' tactic by persons claiming to be Bhutanese and seeking to travel from Nepal into Bhutan. These marches continued throughout 1996; a small group of marchers actually reached Phuentsholing in mid-August and again in December before being forced to return to India. The Bhutanese Minister of Home Affairs asserted that those participating in the marches were not Bhutanese, but were non-nationals and emigrants who were attempting to enter the country illegally. A number of isolated bombing incidents occurred throughout Bhutan during 1998 and 1999, most notably in Thimphu's main stadium in early November 1998. In June 1999 it was reported that the Bhutanese police had arrested 80 alleged Bhutanese refugees who were conducting a peaceful demonstration (organized by the Bhutan Gurkha National Liberation Front) in Phuentsholing; the demonstrators claimed to be genuine Bhutanese citizens who were seeking to travel from the camps in Nepal back into Bhutan.

In 1991 'Rongthong' Kinley Dorji (also styled Kuenley or Kunley), a former Bhutanese businessman accused of unpaid loans and of acts against the State, had absconded to Nepal and joined the anti-Government movement. In 1992 he established and became President of a 'Druk National Congress' claiming human-rights violations in Bhutan. The Bhutanese Government's 74th Assembly held in July 1996 discussed Kinley Dorji's case at length, and unanimously demanded his extradition from Nepal in conjunction with the Bhutan-Nepal talks. Following the signing of an extradition treaty between India and Bhutan in December, Kinley was arrested by the Indian authorities during a visit to Delhi in April 1997, and remained in detention until June 1998, when he was released on bail while his case was being examined by the Indian courts; the bail remained in force in August 1999. The extradition treaty was read to the 75th Assembly in July 1997, when Kinley Dorji's case was again discussed at length and demands for his return to Bhutan for trial were unanimously supported (as they were also at the 76th Assembly in mid-1998 and the 77th Assembly in 1999). At the same time the Assembly unanimously resolved that all relatives of 'ngolops' (anti-national militants) in government service should 'be compulsorily retired with post-service benefits', and that the Royal Civil Service Commission should implement this decision 'without undue delay'. By the end of January 1998 some 219 civil servants had been compulsorily retired with full post-service benefits. In July the Minister of Home Affairs reported that the main civil service still retained 2,900 Lhotshampas (Bhutanese of Nepalese origin), constituting some 24% of the total civil service, excluding those in the armed forces and corporations. The 75th Assembly also discussed the intrusions into Bhutan's south-eastern border forests by Bodo and Maoist extremists from the neighbouring Indian state of Assam. The Bhutanese people (especially those from the east of the country) have traditionally enjoyed good relations with the Bodos of Assam.

During 1997 anti-Government activities (culminating in rallies in south-eastern Bhutan in October) were alleged to have been organized in eastern Bhutan by several lay-preacher (Gomchen) students of Lam Dodrup in Sikkim; a number of arrests were subsequently made. Part of the famous historic retreat of Taktsang Monastery, which was visited by Prince Charles of the United Kingdom in February 1998, was badly damaged by fire under suspicious circumstances in April. Reconstruction work, which had cost some Nu 65.2m. by late 2001, was expected to be completed in 2002.

Important institutional changes were introduced in mid-1998, whereby King Jigme relinquished his role as Head of Government (while remaining Head of State) in favour of a smaller elected Council of Ministers (Lhengye Shungtshog), which was to consist of six ministers and all nine members of the Royal Advisory Council (Lodoi Tsokde) and which was to enjoy full executive power under the leadership of a Chairman (elected by ministers, on a rotational basis, for a one-year term in office) who would be Head of Government. On 16 June the King informed the members of the existing Council of Ministers that it was to be dissolved on 26 June, and stated that he had issued a kasho (royal decree) to the Speaker of the National Assembly, which was to be discussed at the pending 76th session. In the decree the King stressed the necessity to promote greater popular participation in the decision-making process, to strengthen the Government's mandate from the people, and to enhance the administration's transparency and efficiency with integral checks and balances 'to safeguard our national interest and security'. He said that the Council of Ministers should now be restructured as an elected body 'vested with full executive powers', and he put forward three key points—(i) All government ministers should henceforth be elected by the National Assembly, with the first election to take place during the 76th session; (ii) a decision should be taken on the exact role and responsibilities of the Council of Ministers; and (iii) the National Assembly should have a mechanism to move a vote of confidence in the King. In elaboration, King Jigme advised that the Council of Ministers should henceforth consist of elected ministers and the members of the Royal Advisory Council, ministers should be elected by secret ballot, candidates should be selected from those who have held senior government posts at the rank of Secretary or above, and a candidate must secure a majority of the votes cast to be considered elected. The portfolios for the elected ministers were to be awarded by the King. A minister's term in office was to be five years, after which he would undergo a vote of confidence in the National Assembly (previously there was no time limit on the tenure of ministerial posts). All decisions adopted by the Council of Ministers were to be based on consensus, and, while the Council 'shall govern Bhutan with full executive powers', it must also keep the King fully informed 'on all matters that concern the security and sovereignty' of the country. The procedures of the Council of Ministers were to be supervised by a Cabinet Secretary appointed by the Council. The 76th session of the National Assembly voted by secret ballot on six new ministerial nominees; all were successful, but all received some negative votes.

An act to regulate the Council of Ministers, which was framed by a committee comprising members of the Government, clergy and people's representatives of the 20 districts, was presented to the 77th session of the National Assembly in mid-1999 and was subjected to extensive discussion and amendment. The rules as finally endorsed explicitly specified that the King had full power to dissolve the Council of Ministers, although King Jigme observed that this meant that the monarch could exercise this mandate for purely personal reasons, even if the Council was discharging its duties in a responsible manner. Procedures for a confidence vote (with regard to the King) were also drafted by the aforementioned committee and presented to the 77th session of the National Assembly, where members unanimously expressed regret over (and opposition to) the draft and repeatedly requested that King Jigme withdraw the proposal. Following a further earnest plea by the King, however, a key draft provision that a confidence vote regarding the monarch should only be placed on the agenda of an assembly session if a minimum of 50% of the districts requested it, was amended to allow the initiative if supported by at least one-third of the assembly members. The 77th session also agreed that ministers should serve a maximum of two consecutive five-year terms.

King Jigme told the Council of Ministers at a special sitting in mid-August 1999 (held for the formal change of Chairman) that it should streamline the Government and create mobility in the higher levels of the civil service when staffing ministries and other organizations, and that it must be responsive to the needs of the people. He also stressed that while governance was the responsibility of the Council of Ministers, the Royal Advisory Council was empowered to ensure that all the policies, laws and resolutions passed by the National Assembly were implemented by the Government. The outgoing Chairman of the Council, Lyonpo Jigmi Yozer Thinley, stated that all the elements were now in place for a democratic system of decision-making, while government was being institutionalized and made more accountable and transparent. At the ceremony held for the formal rotation of Chairman of the Council of Ministers in August 2001, King Jigme expressed satisfaction at the progress of political reform since July 1998, and advised that changes in the fields of national security, the development of the Ninth Plan, and youth employment should be the Council's priorities. At the 11th SAARC summit, held in Kathmandu in January 2002, the incumbent Chairman of the Council, Lyonpo Khandu Wangchuk, was referred to as 'Prime Minister' of Bhutan, a title that subsequently became accepted usage. In accordance with a decree issued by King Jigme in September 2001, a committee to draft a written constitution for Bhutan was inaugurated in late November and began functioning at the end of the year. The 39-member committee was chaired by the Chief Justice and included the Chairman and members of the Royal Advisory Council, five government representatives, the Speaker of the National Assembly, representatives from each of the 20 districts, and two lawyers from the High Court. It was agreed that the first draft, to be completed by October 2002, would be subjected to extensive public comment and review before being presented to the Assembly for formal approval. Further evolution of the role of the National Assembly and the Royal Advisory Council was expected to continue alongside constitutional discussions. At the ceremony held for the formal rotation of Chairman of the Council of Ministers in August 2002, King Jigme reiterated his satisfaction at the achievements of the previous year, but emphasized the importance of closely guiding the process of devolution of authority at the district and geog level. The Government was also responsible for strengthening the private sector in order to accommodate the growing number of school-leavers. The King also recommended that investigations into a site for a second international airport be reviewed.

The activities of the militant 'anti-nationals' were unanimously condemned at the 76th session of the National Assembly in July 1998, but the most pressing security issue was judged to be the perceived threat from the presence of Assamese tribal (Bodo) and communist (United Liberation Front of Assam—ULFA) militants, who had established military training bases in the jungle border regions of south-eastern Bhutan. Particular concern was expressed regarding the Indian military incursions into Bhutanese territory in an attempt to drive the militants out. A serious incident that had taken place in May in Sarpang, reportedly involving 165 armed Indian soldiers, was discussed during the session, and was to be investigated by the Bhutanese and Indian authorities. The Indian authorities subsequently apologized for the incident. In mid-1999 the Minister of Home Affairs, addressing the 77th session of the National Assembly, reported that talks with ULFA second-tier and senior leadership (in November 1998 and May 1999, respectively) had elicited the response that members of the ULFA had been forced to enter Bhutanese territory in 1992, but that they were not ready to leave Bhutanese territory for at least another 18 months. They asserted that they were determined to fight until independence for Assam was achieved, but offered to reduce their military presence in Bhutan. The Bhutanese Government reiterated to the ULFA leaders that its concern was at the very presence of any number of armed militants on Bhutanese soil. After detailed discussion, assembly members decided that all supplies of food and other essentials to the ULFA and Bodo militants must be stopped, that any Bhutanese who assisted the militants should be punished according to the National Security Act, and that discussions should continue with the ULFA to seek a peaceful withdrawal of these foreign forces from Bhutan. The ULFA agreed to be represented at 'the highest level' at future talks.

The 78th session of the National Assembly, held in June–July 2000, thoroughly reviewed the problem of the presence of the armed ULFA and Bodo militants. It was eventually decided that negotiations with the militants' leaders should be further pursued, but that if talks were not successful, Bhutan's armed forces should be used to expel the tribal insurgents from Bhutanese territory. Following two rounds of negotiations, held in November 1998 and May 1999, the ULFA subsequently failed to respond to a proposed third session of talks. In April 2000 the ULFA's Commander-in-Chief, Paresh Barua, expressed disappointment that details of the previous negotiations had been announced to the National Assembly in 1999, and stated that he and the ULFA Chairman now had to consider the 'very serious security risks' involved in entering Bhutan. He suggested sending one of the ULFA's senior advisers and the organization's financial secretary instead, but this level of involvement was not acceptable to the Bhutanese Government, which again insisted that the highest leadership should attend by 15 June 2000 (i.e. immediately prior to the Assembly's 78th session). Barua later confirmed the inability of the senior leadership to attend. The Bodo militants, specifically the National Democratic Front of Bodoland (NDFB), were to be engaged in parallel talks by 15 June, but in early June Ranjan Daimary, the Chairman of the NDFB, advised that he was unable to visit Bhutan for security reasons.

In mid-2001 the Minister of Home Affairs, addressing the 79th session of the National Assembly, reported that negotiations had been held with leaders of the NDFB in October 2000 and May 2001. During the talks, NDFB leaders had responded to a demand for the removal of their camps by declaring their intention to leave Bhutan but would not commit themselves to a deadline. Following three days of discussions in June, representatives of the ULFA agreed to seven points, including the removal of four of the nine military camps in Bhutan by December 2001, and the reduction in strength of the cadres in the remaining camps. Further meetings were planned in order to find a solution to the issue of the remaining five camps. Members of the National Assembly were informed of the Government's preparations in the event of armed conflict with the militants: security had been strengthened, funds had been reserved for fuel supplies and medical support services, and contingency plans had been made to ensure the continued operation of the communications and transport systems. In addition, essential food supplies, such as grains, sufficient to last for three to six months, were stored in towns throughout Bhutan. Disappointment and concern were expressed at the low level of volunteer recruitment; of the 880 men recruited to the army in 2000/01, 27 had deserted and 131 had requested special leave. Districts were asked to send lists of volunteers to army headquarters immediately after the Assembly session. It was subsequently reported at the 80th session of the National Assembly in mid-2002 that of the 2,581 men who volunteered for militia training, only 1,410 reported for training, and of those 380 were medically unfit and 198 sought to leave because of domestic problems. The remaining 808 volunteers wished to join the army permanently as soldiers. Only 24 volunteers from the 20 districts wished to join as militia. The training of volunteers for the militia, therefore, was rendered unviable.

On 31 December 2001 the army visited the four designated ULFA training camps and, confirming that these had been abandoned, began to disable and destroy the training and accommodation facilities. Initially, the whereabouts of the ULFA militants was unknown. It was not possible immediately to ascertain whether the ULFA units had managed to leave Bhutan and, evading Indian military forces in Assam, reach their presumed goals of Bangladesh and Myanmar. At the same time there were concerns that the militants had relocated their camps elsewhere in Bhutan. At the 80th session of the National Assembly in mid-2002 the Minister of Home Affairs confirmed that the ULFA had closed down its military training centre in Martshala geog and camps at Gobarkonda, Nangri and Deori. The ULFA, however, had opened a new camp on a mountain ridge above the main Samdrup Jongkhar–Trashigang highway, raising the total number of camps remaining in Bhutan to six. In the mean time, the NDFB had three main camps and four mobile camps between Lhamoizingkha and Daifam. The Minister of Home Affairs also reported that the Government had only recently become aware that the Indian militant Kamtapur Liberation Organization (KLO) had established camps in Bhangtar dungkhag and near Piping in Lhamoizingkha dungkhag. The KLO armed militants were Rajbansi tribals of North Bengal, bordering Chhukha and Samtse dzongkhags, who were campaigning for separate statehood for the Kamtapuris.

The Minister of Home Affairs stressed that the presence of armed militants in Bhutan remained a grave threat. It appeared that no more negotiations could be held with the NDFB. The issue was further complicated by the presence of KLO militants in Bhutan. Assembly members vigorously debated the developments; some questioned how such events could have arisen, suggesting that Bhutan could not depend on India and should instead look to 'our neighbour in the north'. The Minister of Foreign Affairs countered these views by asserting that there was 'only one path' for India and Bhutan—'the path of goodwill and friendship'. The Assembly endorsed three decisions proposed by the Council of Ministers: first, to hold joint negotiations with the Chairman and the military commander of the ULFA, since in previous meetings no decisions could be taken on the pretext of the absence of one of these leaders; second, the Government would not agree to participate in any more meetings on the reduction of ULFA camps but was only prepared to discuss the closure of the militants' main training camp and headquarters: 'the headquarters of the ULFA must be moved out of Bhutan'. Finally, if ULFA leaders refused to relocate their headquarters, there would be no option but to evict them physically. King Jigme informed the National Assembly that it was important to hold talks with ULFA and NDFB separately. Although the KLO was a new, relatively unknown group—the Government did not even know the identity of its leaders—the King warned that if the authorities had to resort to military action, they would have to deal with all three organizations.

The 78th and 79th sessions of the National Assembly also reviewed the progress of negotiations with the Government of Nepal concerning people in camps in Nepal. Two meetings, in November 1999 and in March 2000, resulted in an agreement on measures to strengthen the mechanism for verifying the national status of these people; although 'much progress' had been made, there was still 'no conclusive agreement' on a number of issues. The verification process could not yet begin, owing to disagreement over one issue: the Bhutanese Government wanted verification of all adults aged 18 years and above, whereas Nepal required verification only on the basis of head of family. According to the Minister of Foreign Affairs at the 78th session, Bhutan found the latter proposal unacceptable, because the head of a family would include as members of the family those who were not legally members; the problem in conducting a census in southern Bhutan was created by (among other factors) the inclusion of non-family members into the registered families. Although many Assembly members argued strongly that no persons who had left Bhutan should be allowed to return, the Minister of Home Affairs reiterated that the Bhutanese Government would take full responsibility for any Bhutanese national found to have been forcibly expelled from Bhutan, while those found to have evicted any genuine Bhutanese would be liable for punishment under Bhutanese law.

Nepal and Bhutan finally achieved a breakthrough at the 10th round of joint ministerial negotiations in December 2000. Both countries agreed that nationality would be verified on the basis of the head of the refugee family for those over 25 years of age. Refugees under 25 years of age would be verified on an individual basis. By the end of January 2001 a Joint Verification Team (JVT), consisting of five officials each from the Nepalese and Bhutanese Governments, had concluded the inspection of the refugee camps. Verification of the nationality of 98,897 people (including 13,000 children born in the camps) claiming refugee status began at the end of March 2001, commencing with the Khudanabari camp. The Minister of Foreign Affairs informed the National Assembly of the progress of the JVT, which had, by early July verified the status of 4,128 individuals. Despite criticisms in the Nepalese press that the pace was too slow, the Minister argued that it was essential for both parties to maintain a credible verification process. He planned to meet his Nepalese counterpart immediately after the Assembly to review how harmonization could conclude simultaneously with verification, as anticipated in the December 2000 bilateral agreement. The Assembly endorsed the ongoing verification process, and decided that any ensuing problems should be resolved first at the secretary level of the two Governments, or, if necessary, at the ministerial level. At a meeting in early November the Ministers of Foreign Affairs of Bhutan and Nepal were unable to harmonize the positions of their respective governments with regard to the four categories for the people in the camps. The Nepalese Minister of Foreign Affairs proposed the reduction of the categories to two—Bhutanese and non-Bhutanese—a suggestion rejected by his Bhutanese counterpart. The Nepalese Minister of Foreign Affairs requested a meeting at the ministerial level (the 12th of its kind) to be convened in early 2002. In late 2001 the verification of individuals in the Khudanabari camp was completed; however, with the recent disagreements over harmonization, the process reached a standstill. Although unofficial discussions with various parties (including the former Nepalese Minister of Foreign Affairs, Bastola, and the leader of the opposition party, Madhav Kumar Nepal) took place in early 2002, the Bhutanese Minister of Foreign Affairs, at the 80th National Assembly, warned that 'the unstable political situation in Nepal might affect the ongoing dialogue and delay a solution'. King Jigme further informed the Assembly that the Government of Nepal's refusal to abide by the agreements reached and signed by previous ministerial joint committees was hindering progress in resolving the problems and delaying the convening of the 12th ministerial level meeting. King Jigme emphasized the importance of holding the next meeting as soon as possible. The Assembly agreed that the Government should continue discussions with the Nepalese Government to seek a lasting solution to the problem.

Reflecting the increasing complexities of contemporary administration, the 77th Assembly passed an unprecedented number of acts in mid-1999 to enhance the prevailing legal framework relating to telecommunications (providing for the creation of a state-owned public corporation, Bhutan Telecom, from the existing Telecommunications Division), the postal sector (enabling Bhutan Post to become an autonomous public-sector corporation), bankruptcy (giving a contemporary context for the rights and duties of borrowers and lenders), movable and immovable property (setting a legal framework for the management of loans, mortgages and related securities and financial services), legal deposit (copies of all 'documentary material' published in Bhutan 'or related to Bhutan' are to be deposited with the National Library in Thimphu), municipalities (establishing legal authority for municipalities to enforce rules relating to urban development), and road safety (strengthening the legal basis for administration of passenger safety and vehicle management). Further indications of the modernization of Bhutan were the inauguration of (limited) television and internet services in June and July, respectively, and the election of nine women to attend the 1999 session of the National Assembly (this number had increased to 11 and 16 by 2000 and 2001, respectively). In the mid-2001 Assembly session, a female councillor was for the first time elected to the Royal Advisory Council. At the end of 1999 a government-endorsed report proposed the rationalization of government under 10 ministries; the proposals were to be fully implemented by 2002. In addition, two new government agencies—the Department of Legal Affairs and the National Employment Board—were established, and a new Department of Aid and Debt Management was created. The 79th session of the National Assembly reviewed and adopted eight draft laws (six of which had been circulated at the previous session), notably a Copyright Act, a Personal Income Tax Act, and a revised Civil and Criminal Procedure Code. Rules for the establishment of a standing legislative committee to draft, review, amend, and ratify national legislation were also submitted. In mid-2001 the Council of Ministers decided to reduce the number of skilled expatriate (principally Indian) workers from 50,000 to 25,000 with immediate effect, and aimed further to decrease the foreign workforce to 12,500 by the end of 2002. The Bhutan Chamber of Commerce and Industries protested against the decision, regarding it as too hasty and arguing that Bhutan's labour force was seasonal owing to rural harvesting and that the Bhutanese generally disparage manual labour. In October 2001 the Council of Ministers permitted the mining industry more time to reduce imported labour, but insisted that all firms and industries would have similar obligations from 2004. Revised rules for geog (village block) and district development committees to create a legal basis for local autonomy in development matters (a fundamental issue under the Ninth Plan) were widely discussed from late 2001, and were approved by the National Assembly at its 80th session in mid-2002. This was considered an important development in the devolution of political authority. New elections for gups (heads of geogs) were scheduled to take place in October. It was envisaged that an Election Act would be adopted to support the proposed constitution. In accordance with the 1999 Municipal Act, residents of Thimphu elected members of the municipal council in late December 2001.

Following the relaxation of many policies in the People's Republic of China since 1978, and looking forward to improved relations between India and China, Bhutan has moved cautiously to assert positions on regional and world affairs that take account of those of India but are not necessarily identical to them. Discussions with China for the formal delineation and demarcation of the northern border were begun in April 1984, and substantive negotiations began in April 1986. The 12th round of talks was held in Beijing in December 1998. Following negotiations, Bhutan and China signed an official interim agreement (the first agreement ever to be signed between the two countries), based on the five principles of peaceful coexistence, to maintain peace and tranquillity in the Bhutan–China border area and, importantly, to observe the status quo of the border as it was prior to May 1959, pending a formal agreement on the border alignment. The disputed area, which was 1,128 sq km during the early rounds of bilateral talks, has since been reduced to 269 sq km in three areas in the north-west of Bhutan. Demarcation of the southern border has been agreed with India, except for small sectors in the middle zone (between Sarpang and Gelephu) and in the eastern zone of Arunachal Pradesh and the *de facto* Sino-Indian border. Following further bilateral discussions in Thimphu in September 1999, the 14th round of negotiations took place in Beijing in November 2000, at which Bhutan extended the area of its claim beyond the boundary offered by the Chinese Government, somewhat to the surprise of the latter. The four sectors under discussion were in the Doklam (a disputed area of about 89 sq km), Sinchulumba, Gieu (an area of about 180 sq km) and Dramana areas. The negotiations continued in Thimphu in November 2001, following which the Chinese Deputy Minister of Foreign Affairs stated that the boundary question generally had been resolved, although relatively minor issues remained outstanding. Bhutan's Minister of Home Affairs led a delegation of experts to Beijing in mid-June 2002 to assert Bhutan's area of claim, where it was agreed that the boundaries claimed by both sides would, henceforth, be depicted on one map to facilitate negotiations. The 80th session of the National Assembly determined that the issue of the northern boundary should be resolved as soon as possible. The 16th round of bilateral talks was scheduled to take place in Beijing in October 2002. In 2001 two delegations from Bhutan (a cultural group, led by the Dorji Lopon, and an officials group, led by the Foreign Secretary) also visited China, in April and July, respectively. The Minister of Foreign Affairs visited Thailand in mid-May, observing that 'Bhutan considered Thailand as the most suitable point' for the conduct of its diplomacy in the region.

In July 1989 a four-day state visit to India by King Jigme Singye Wangchuck reaffirmed the good relations (both political and economic) that exist between Bhutan and India. During a visit to Bhutan in August 1993, the Indian Prime Minister, P. V. Narasimha Rao, stated that he was 'absolutely certain' that these relations would grow stronger. Bhutan's Crown Prince, Dasho Jigme Khesar Namgyal Wangchuck, made his first official visit to India in early 2002.

Although Bhutan continues to have few resident diplomatic representatives (namely, in Bangladesh, India, Kuwait and Thailand), it has established formal relations with 17 countries and with the European Union (EU). It also maintains missions to the UN in New York, USA, and Geneva, Switzerland, and several honorary consulates.

In late October 2001 Bhutan was elected to the UN Economic and Social Council for a three-year term in 2002–04. Despite earlier expectations, it appeared unlikely in mid-2002 that Bhutan would be host to the SAARC annual meeting for several years to come. With a significant part of the economic infrastructure now in place, Bhutan's administration is able to focus in more detail on the relatively neglected areas of domestic politics (e.g. further development of popular participation and representation), and of institutional and social issues (e.g. the consequences of urbanization). Important exhibitions of Bhutan's religious and cultural traditions were held at Hannover, Germany, in 2000 and in New Delhi and Kolkata (Calcutta), India, in late 2001.

Economy

BRIAN SHAW

Until recently, the pattern of economic activity in Bhutan was determined by the country's natural and self-imposed isolation. Subsistence agriculture was supplemented by livestock rearing and by cottage industries based on traditional handicrafts. In the northern region, migrant pasturing of yak and sheep was virtually the sole economic activity. There were few marketable surpluses, limited to what could be carried on a man's back or on a pack-horse, and disposed of by means of barter, mainly in Tibet. Bhutan traded rice in return for wool, salt, tea and precious metals.

In terms of average income, Bhutan is one of the poorest countries in the world, although the statistics should be considered in the context of a self-sufficient, barter economy. According to estimates by the World Bank, Bhutan's gross national product (GNP) per head averaged US $80 in 1980, US $90 in 1983 and US $140 in 1984. In 2000, according to estimates by the same source, the kingdom's GNP, measured at average 1998–2000 prices, was US $479m., equivalent to about US $590 per head (or to US $1,440 on an international purchasing-power parity basis). In 1990–98 GNP per head increased, in real terms, at an average annual rate of 2.1%. During 1990–2000, it was estimated, gross domestic product (GDP) increased, in real terms, by an annual average of 6.3%. Over the same period, according to the World Bank, GDP per head rose at an average annual rate of 3.4%. Total GDP was projected to increase from Nu 18,760.8m. in 1999 to Nu 21,261.3m. in 2000. According to the Asian Development Bank (ADB), compared with the previous year real GDP growth was estimated at 5.7% in 2000 and at 6.5% in 2001. It must be noted, however, that, in the absence of definitive population data, all of these figures are purely notional. On the basis of the current smaller population estimate, GNP per head in the late 1990s was reckoned to be much higher. During 1990–2000 the average annual rate of inflation was 9.5%. The rise in consumer prices reached 12.1% in 1998, before declining to 4.5%, 4.4% and 3.3% in 1999, 2000 and 2001 respectively. According to the Central Statistical Office, the inflation rate stood at 3.6% in June 2001.

AGRICULTURE

The economy of Bhutan is essentially agrarian, with an estimated 94% of the economically active population engaged in agriculture and livestock raising, with 9% of the land under cultivation or permanent pasture, and with agriculture contributing an estimated 35.9% of GDP in 2001.

Under the Fifth Plan (1981–87), only a small expansion of cropped area was proposed, with increases in the output of paddy rice, maize, wheat, barley, buckwheat and millet to come mainly from an increase in yields. Total cereal production was about 196,900 metric tons in 1988. The total land area under paddy cultivation in that year was 34,000 ha; total production of rice was 33,800 tons, and the shortfall in requirements was imported. Maize, the staple diet in eastern and south-central Bhutan, is grown on about 59,000 ha and yielded 86,100 tons in 1988. Output of wheat and barley, cultivated on 16,000 ha, totalled 17,800 tons in 1988. Buck wheat and millet occupy approximately 20,800 ha, cultivated mostly by the swidden (shifting) method, with an annual output of some 16,600 tons. According to the FAO, Bhutan's rice crop reached 50,000 metric tons in 2000. Output of maize totalled 70,000 tons and that of wheat reached 20,000 tons. Emphasis continues to be placed on improving stock, soil fertility, plant protection and farm mechanization.

In early 1988 the newly established Bhutan Development Finance Corporation (BDFC) took over the administration of rural credit schemes, which had been operated by the Royal Monetary Authority of Bhutan since 1982, for loans of up to Nu 20,000 for land improvements and livestock, and for smaller loans of up to Nu 5,000 for seasonal requirements. The BDFC also extends longer-term development loans. In December 1988 the ADB granted a US $2.5m. concessional loan to the BDFC, to aid the expansion of small- and medium-scale industrial enterprises in the private sector. By early 1989, about Nu 20m. had been disbursed by the BDFC to more than 20,000 beneficiaries. The Bank of Bhutan finances larger loans. Major irrigation schemes were inaugurated in south-central Bhutan, where shortage of water and insanitary sources are major problems. By mid-1996, however, it had become generally accepted that the size of the national economy was too limited for domestic demand-based industries and that small-scale industries (particularly in the service sector) better suited the local market. Therefore, the Government's main industrial development strategy in the future needs to be export-orientated. According to the Ministry of Agriculture, its objective of achieving food security by balancing import costs with earnings from exports of cash crops had been achieved by 1999. Increased self-sufficiency remained its aim.

Forests represent one of the most important potential sources of wealth in Bhutan, and it was recognized early that preservation of the forest cover was essential in order to conserve the ecological balance. In the Fifth Plan, detailed surveying, demarcation and management plans for harvesting the forests, and for conservation, were drawn up and implemented. The Forestry Services Division (under the Ministry of Agriculture) has responsibility for maintaining the mature forest, with good tree cover at a minimum of 60% of total land area. In early 1996 a major forest industry complex, the Gedu Wood Manufacturing Corporation, was closed down and all of the failed enterprise's debts were taken up by a Danish aid organization. However, the Bhutan Board Products Ltd factory at nearby Tala continued to operate successfully. Wildlife sanctuaries have been maintained and extended. Since late 1990 many plantations in southern Bhutan (especially of teak and Sal), which were planted in the 1950s and 1960s, have been indiscriminately felled or destroyed by anti-Government militants and by opportunistic smugglers.

INDUSTRY AND COMMUNICATIONS

The proposed expenditure on trade and industry in the Seventh Plan (1992–97) was Nu 1,402.4m. (9% of the total), and was based on exploitation of mineral and forest resources, agricultural produce, and inexpensive power. Private enterprise is mainly small-scale industries, partly reflecting the limited development of entrepreneurial skills in Bhutan. In the Seventh Plan, however, considerable emphasis was to be placed on the formulation of a strategy for the rapid expansion of export-orientated industries. The production of low-cost electricity by the Chhukha hydroelectric (HEP) project (see below) was expected to help to stimulate growth in the industrial sector. The Penden cement factory in southern Bhutan began operating in 1981, and in 2000 produced 263,234 metric tons of cement and 246,140 tons of clinker, earning after-tax profits of Nu 170m. A second cement plant, at Nanglam, with a potential output of 1,500–2,500 tons per day, was to be completed by 1991. Initial access tracks to the site were constructed, but in November 1989 the National Assembly confirmed the Council of Ministers' decision to postpone further development because of doubts concerning the venture's economic viability; work was resumed, however, in 1992. In March 1996 Bhutan signed an agreement with India regarding the construction of a cement plant (which was to have an annual capacity of 500,000 tons) at Dungsam. The project, which was due to be completed by 2002, was estimated to cost Nu 3,000m. (as a grant from India), with an additional Nu 1,000m. required to complete the necessary infrastructure (roads, power lines, railway siding, etc.). It was decided in late 1999 that, because of the security situation on the Bhutan–Assam border, the Dungsam project would once again be suspended, and in November 2001 it was formally closed; however, it was agreed that the project would be re-established as soon as the security situation improved. Vast limestone deposits in Nganglam and a favourable potential market in north-east India rendered the project economically viable. Yangsom Cement Industries (a private undertaking) produces about 30 tons per day. In 2001 Bhutan Fruit Products Ltd produced goods (mainly canned fruits and juices) valued at Nu 111.6m. In May 1985 the World Bank announced a 50-year interest-free loan of US $9m. to assist in the establishment of a plant to produce calcium carbide at Pasakha, near Phuentsholing. Commercial production began in June 1988, and output reached about 10,000 tons (valued at around Nu 85m.) in the six months to January 1989. By 2000 annual production was 19,827 tons, with a value of Nu 474.6m; sales in 2001 increased to Nu 675.9m. Bhutan Ferro Alloys Ltd, which is also based in Pasakha, commenced production in April 1995 and has an installed annual capacity of 15,000 tons of ferro-silicon and micro-silicon; sales in 1999 (exported wholly to India) totalled Nu 534.73m. The production of both these facilities, however, decreased in 2000 compared with 1999, owing to heavy floods in August–October 2000. Sales increased in 2001 to reach Nu 579.0m. In addition, small industrial estates have been established at Phuentsholing, Gelephu and Samdrup Jongkhar, producing a variety of raw materials for consumer goods and industrial products.

In 1984 the Indian Government financed the Indo-Bhutan microwave link, connecting Thimphu with Hashimara. At present the link provides 60 channels out of a total capacity of 300. Thimphu subscribers can now communicate directly, through operator trunk dialling, with Kolkata (Calcutta) and New Delhi and thence to third countries. A Thimphu–Kolkata teleprinter circuit was incorporated in the link. The international service began operating in January 1987, with the Delhi 'gateway' exchange being used for access to third countries. A Japanese company was awarded a contract in 1988 to construct a satellite earth station at Thimphu. This facility, which was inaugurated at the end of March 1990, provides direct high-quality telecommunications access (e.g. by fax) to third countries via London. Agreements have been reached with many countries for two-way access. In July 1991 a public high-speed fax facility for domestic and international services was commissioned at the new GPO building in Thimphu, with technical assistance from India's Department of Telecommunications. Similar facilities are now available in all major towns in Bhutan. Since 1991 the Government of Japan has funded a domestic fully-digital telecommunications network linking all districts with Thimphu. The four-phase plan, using microwave repeaters, was completed in May 1999 at a cost of more than 5,800m. yen, and has the capability to transmit video signals. With the establishment of an internet service, DrukNet, in July, three 'points of presence' have been set up in Thimphu, Trashigang and Phuentsholing to enable direct-dial access from any part of the country. Mobile satellite telephones were made available to the public by Bhutan Telecom from August 2001.

TRADE

Free trade between India and Bhutan was traditional, but mainly by those in the southern region of Bhutan, and the total amount was small compared with the trade between Tibet and Bhutan. From 1960 trade ties were completely reorientated towards India, which in 2000/01 accounted for an estimated 94.3% of Bhutan's exports and 74.0% of imports. A 10-year agreement on trade and transit arrangements between Bhutan and India, signed in 1972, provided for the continuation of free trade. This pact was revised by a 1983 agreement (operative from April 1984), with terms substantially more favourable to Bhutan. In March 1990 the two countries signed a third agreement, which provided for the continuation of Bhutan's free trade with India. India remains Bhutan's largest trading partner, and transit procedures for 13 transhipment points were made simpler. In 1987 Bhutan earned US $500,000 from trade with third countries, but by 1989 the annual total had risen to US $6m. The main exports from Bhutan to India are electricity, wood and wood products, cement and agricultural products; liquor and canned fruits are also exported. An agreement on trade was also signed with Bangladesh in 1980, and renewed for a further 10 years in 1990. After the inauguration of the postal system in 1972, Bhutan's postage stamps became, for a while, the country's main source of foreign-exchange earnings. Since 1976, however, tourism has become an important source of convertible currency (US $9.2m. in 2001).

DEVELOPMENT PLANNING

Planning for economic development began in 1961. The formation of capital had to be achieved almost entirely through external grants, and, to begin with, little revenue could be generated internally. Rising expectations among the people have come to provide a strong impetus to further expansion of development activity. Both the First Plan (1961–66) and the Second Plan (1966–71) were largely financial budgeting exercises. A development secretariat was formed, and sectoral directorates were established. The highest priority was given to ending Bhutan's isolation through constructing transportation links, and 66% of the total outlay in the First Plan was for roads, mainly the Phuentsholing–Thimphu and Samdrup Jongkhar–Trashigang sectors. In the Second Plan, the outlay on roads dropped to 42% of total allocations, while education received 18%. In the Third Plan (1971–76) 20% of expenditure was allocated to roads, and 19% to education. District planning committees (Dzongkhag Yargay Tshochungs, or DYT) were established in the Fourth Plan (1976–81), and were asked to submit development proposals of direct concern to their respective districts. Total expenditure under the provisions of the first four Plans were Nu 107.2m., 202.2m., 475.2m. and 1,106.2m. respectively; the contribution from India was 100%, 98.9%, 89.9%, and 77.1% respectively. Domestic resources provided 1%, 7% and 5.5% for the Second, Third and Fourth Plans respectively. Assistance from the UN system was received for the first time under the Third Plan, providing 3% of total outlay; this increased to 17.5% in the Fourth Plan.

The Fifth Plan (1981–87) was generally regarded as a crucial phase in Bhutan's socio-economic development. The first four Plans had established a minimal infrastructure, and the Fifth Plan provided the occasion for an intensive and continuing review of actual and desired achievements. In outline, this Plan envisaged an outlay of Nu 4,338m. (the actual total of Nu 4,711m., excluding separate provision for the Chhukha hydroelectric project of Nu 1,800m., reflected the imposition of stringent fiscal controls by the Government), of which 30.9% was to be financed by India, and 21.7% from internal revenue.

The average annual increase of GDP, in real terms, was estimated at 6.4% during the Fifth Plan period.

In addition to international aid under UN auspices, Helvetas (the Swiss Association for Technical Assistance), a non-profit organization, has maintained a formal and important presence in Bhutan since 1975. Working with Bhutanese counterparts, its experts have advised on a wide range of projects, involving an actual expenditure (1975–83) of 11,335m. Swiss francs, funded both by the voluntary contributions of its members and by the Swiss Development Corporation of the Swiss Federal Department of Political (Foreign) Affairs. Since 1985, Helvetas has been the co-ordinator for all of the Swiss Government's multilateral assistance to Bhutan.

King Jigme Singye Wangchuck had already, in his 1974 coronation speech, stressed the need to avoid excessive dependence on external assistance, and, instead, to seek to achieve economic self-reliance. To achieve these goals, he proposed five major strategies, to be pursued in the Fifth Plan: self-reliance in each of the country's dzongkhags (districts); decentralization of development administration; increasing popular participation in development decisions; control of maintenance expenditure; and optimum mobilization of internal resources.

Decentralization is a principal current goal, partly to counter a tendency towards a lack of realism that had begun to appear in the central planning process. It is intended to relate policy to the locally perceived needs of the districts, although at present only 30% of projects are implemented at that level. During the first four Plans, there developed a habit of reliance on the central Government's provision of new services; the traditional contribution of free labour was much reduced. The King has clearly expressed the view, during his extensive travels throughout the country, that central assistance towards local projects will depend very much on the willingness of the local people to make their own contributions, especially of labour, to public works.

During an important meeting of officials at the end of 1984, in preparation for drafting the Sixth Plan, the strategies for the Fifth Plan were critically reviewed. In general, it was considered that the concept of dzongkhag self-reliance had been introduced prematurely, and that it needed refinement; that decentralization had come to mean the transfer, rather than the devolution, of power; and that people's participation had been encouraging but needed further strengthening. On the other hand, internal revenue had been increased to the equivalent of 85% of total government maintenance expenditure.

The Sixth Plan (1987–92), which was finally approved by the Tshogdu in July 1987 (but was revised in late 1989), envisaged a total outlay of Nu 9,559.2m., which represented an increase of more than 100%, compared with total expenditure (excluding expenditure on the Chhukha hydroelectric project) in the Fifth Plan. Nine major policy objectives were declared in the Sixth Plan: the strengthening of government administration (including the continued campaign against corruption and nepotism), the preservation and promotion of national identity (particularly through the strengthening of the newly formed Special (now National) Commission for Cultural Affairs and of traditional institutions), the mobilization of internal resources, the enhancement of rural incomes, the improvement of rural housing and resettlement, the consolidation and improvement of services, the development of human resources, the promotion of popular participation in the formulation and execution of development plans and strategies, and the promotion of national self-reliance. The Plan also took into account the increasing international debt burden that would develop as a result of loan repayments due in the early 1990s, and some capital-intensive projects were postponed until the next Plan. By the end of the Plan period (June 1992), total outlay had reached Nu 9,559.2m., but resources were under considerable strain as a result of the destruction of much of the social services infrastructure in southern Bhutan combined with a commitment by the Government to continue development work in the disturbed areas.

The Seventh Plan (1992–97) asserted seven main objectives: self-reliance, with emphasis on internal resource mobilization; sustainability, with emphasis on environmental protection; private-sector development; decentralization and popular participation; human resources' development; balanced development in all districts; and national security. The proposed outlay was Nu 15,590.7m., principally within the Ministry of Social Services, the Ministry of Communications, and the Ministry of Agriculture. By mid-1997 expenditure on the Seventh Plan was already estimated at Nu 21,603.6m.

The Eighth Plan (1997–2002) further refined the seven objectives of the Seventh Plan and explicitly added another: 'the preservation and promotion of cultural and traditional values', relating to literature, art, architecture and religious institutions. During these five years, GDP was forecast to expand at an average annual rate of 6.7%, while the population growth rate was projected to decline to 2.56%. The agriculture sector was projected to grow by 2.5% per year over the plan period through productivity gains and horticultural development. Exports to India and third countries were expected to increase by 15% and 10%, respectively, by 2002. The guiding goal was declared as the establishment of sustainability in development, while balancing achievements with the popular sense of contentment. Core areas were to be the further development of HEP (long-term potential was assessed at 20,000 MW) and further industrialization (including project reports on the Mangdechhu and Punatsangchhu power sites, and the implementation of a silicon carbide project). The Dungsam cement project and the Basochhu and Kurichhu HEP projects were to be completed during the Plan period, as was 50% of the Tala project. The reconstruction work on the damaged Taktsang Monastery, which commenced in May 2000, was expected to cost Nu 45.88m. The Plan also provided for further development of the infrastructure and social services, human resources' development, and renewable natural resources. Development partners meeting in Geneva in January 1997 pledged US $450m. (about 50% of the projected plan outlay). By 2000 the Government had made satisfactory progress in reaching its targets. The mid-term review of the Eighth Plan, carried out in February 2000, showed fund utilization was around 40% of the original planned outlay of Nu 30,000m. This review served as the basis for the Ninth Plan (2002–07). In June 2002 the Minister of Finance reported that actual expenditure on the Eighth Plan was around Nu 40,000m., some 33% more than the original planned outlay, with equal increases in both current and capital expenditure. Nevertheless, the overall resource deficit was limited to Nu 307.8m., owing to a significant increase of Nu 7,580m. in domestic revenues to Nu 20,580m. International concessional loans financed about 5% of the plan.

The Ninth Plan (2002–07), presented to and approved by the National Assembly in June 2002, consists (unlike previous plans) of separate programmes and budget allocations for individual sectors and dzongkhags. The main priorities include the development of rural infrastructure, qualitative improvement in health and education services, greater decentralization and private-sector development. The Plan has five overall goals: improving quality of life and income (especially of the poor); ensuring good governance; promoting private-sector growth and employment generation; preserving and promoting cultural heritage and environment conservation; and achieving rapid economic growth and transformation. GDP was forecast to grow at a higher average annual rate of 7%–8% in 2002–07; this level was deemed necessary in order to maintain momentum in development and to create jobs for new school-leavers. A dynamic private sector was also required for the latter. The major HEP projects at Tala, Kurichhu and Basochu (see below) were scheduled for completion during the Plan period (although outside the Plan's financial framework). It was hoped that the projects would earn sufficient revenue for Bhutan to achieve economic self-reliance. Expenditure during the Plan was expected to reach Nu 70,000m., of which Nu 31,700m. was allocated to current expenditures, Nu 34,900m. was directed to capital investment, and Nu 3,400m. was for debt servicing. Domestic revenue, which was forecast to reach Nu 32,000m., and external resources, amounting to an estimated Nu 35,000m., were expected to cover the proposed outlay (the former covering current expenditure). India would continue to be Bhutan's largest development partner, contributing about 30% of the total plan outlay. Inflation was forecast to grow at an average annual rate of 7% in 2002–07. The dzongkhag plans were geog-based with special focus on the potential, needs and priorities of the individual geogs or lowest level of administrative units.

In his comments on the 2002/03 budget, the Minister of Finance noted that tax revenues would surpass non-tax revenues for the first time. He also reported that GDP grew by more than 6% and average inflation rose by 3.5% in 2001/02. Bhutan's total outstanding convertible-currency foreign debt was about US $120.7m., while outstanding Indian rupee loans stood at Rs 6,696.1m.—in total about Nu 12,611m., or 53% of GDP. The debt-service ratio was less than 4% of the value of exports of goods and services. In 2001 Chhukha power sales to India brought receipts of Nu 2,034.9m. India's agreement to double the Chhukha power tariff (to Nu 1 per unit) from April 1997 earned an extra Nu 124m. in the last quarter of 1996/97. King Jigme announced in June 1999, during ceremonies celebrating his 25 years as monarch, that India had agreed to pay an additional tariff on electricity purchased from Bhutan of 50 chetrum per unit (to Nu 1.50 per unit, compared with Nu 1 previously), thereby making it feasible temporarily to postpone the introduction of personal income tax (PIT). The tariff increase generated additional revenue of Nu 669.5m., which, for the most part, counterbalanced the increases in salary and travel allowances for civil servants implemented in July 1999. Revised PIT, which was due to be levied from July 1999 and which was to include rental income (previously exempt), was deferred, due to widespread misunderstanding and opposition by the business community, in addition to the absence of the requisite legislation. At the 78th session of the National Assembly, however, a draft PIT act was circulated, for further public discussion; this was debated and adopted at the 79th session. Consequently, Bhutanese earning more than Nu 100,000 annually were to pay tax from January 2002 at rates commencing at 10%. (In 2000, meanwhile, taxes paid by the rural population (85% of citizens) remained at less than 1% of the Government's total revenue.) In addition, new legislation regarding a sales, customs and excise tax was passed; about Nu 110m. was expected to be raised from PIT in 2002 alone, with a 9% annual increase thereafter. A national pension plan (National Pension and Providend Fund Plan, and the Armed Force Pension and Provident Fund Scheme) was implemented in 2000; monthly payment of pension entitlements commenced in July 2002.

A second aircraft for the national airline, Druk-Air Corporation, was delivered in December 1992, and the entire cost of US $25m. was paid directly from Bhutan's foreign-currency reserves. None the less, the Minister of Finance reported to the National Assembly in July 1993 that the country's hard-currency reserves stood at US $90m., which exceeded the existing cumulative foreign-debt obligation. The reserves had increased to about US $300m. by mid-2002, and were estimated to be sufficient to finance around 17 months of imports. Two new aircraft for Druk-Air Corporation were scheduled to be delivered during 2002; one of the planes was to be domestically financed, and the other was to be funded by external financing. However, in early 2002 the manufacturers announced the decision to cease production of the type of aircraft contracted by Bhutan. The selection of an alternative aircraft model and a review of purchase arrangements were still being investigated in mid-2002. For 2000/01, grants from the Government of India provided an estimated 17.1% of total budgetary revenue, and direct grants from international agencies amounted to 17.0%. Following the terrorist attacks on the USA in September 2001, several hundred foreign tourists cancelled their visits to Bhutan.

In June 1999 the Minister of Finance told the National Assembly that Bhutan needed to promote exports and narrow the current-account deficit. During 1999/2000 the current-account deficit grew marginally, but the overall balance of payments was positive, owing to large inflows of aid and concessional loans. Non-performing assets decreased in 1998/99 to about 10% (compared with 20% in 1994/95), but increased to less than 15% in 2001/02. Efforts were under way in 2002/03 to reduce this to less than 10%. A major domestic problem in 2000 was rising unemployment (up to 50,000 school-leavers were expected to join the workforce over the next five years; this figure was, however, expected to rise to 70,000 over 2002–07).

The Minister of Finance announced several tax initiatives in June 2002, notably tax holidays (ranging from three to seven years for new industries and institutes, particularly those established in the interior dzongkhags), abolition of export tax on oranges, apples and cardamom, a reinvestment allowance of 20% for incorporated companies as an incentive to expand, and education and life insurance premium deductions for PIT. The Minister reiterated that the Government would consider military action if peaceful means to persuade ULFA and Bodo militants to leave Bhutan failed, despite the fact that armed conflict would seriously hinder the country's development.

The National Technical Training Authority was established to co-ordinate vocational and technical education, and thereby increase employment prospects and promote traditional arts and crafts; private-sector participation in education was also being explored. Bhutan National Bank extended loans totalling Nu 738.8m. in 1998 and declared a 50% dividend on post-tax profits of Nu 47.8m. in that year. However, the excess liquidity that had accumulated in Bhutan's banks was another problem in 2000, requiring prudent fiscal management.

The innovative Bhutan Trust Fund for Environmental Conservation (BTF), which was formally established in 1992 with the help of major contributions from donor countries and agencies, totalled an estimated US $31.2m. at the end of June 2001. By mid-2001 some 40 similar trust funds had been established throughout the world, modelled on the BTF. Income from the Fund will be used to finance projects that are deemed to be productively useful for Bhutan's environment. Management of the Fund was passed to Bhutan in March 2001. Following efforts to mobilize finance for the Health Trust Fund, contributions (including interest) totalled US $10.6m. by May 2002. Bhutan also established a Cultural Trust Fund and a Youth Development Fund. In April 2000 the Bhutanese Government, the World Bank and a Dutch international development organization initiated the Rural Access Project, designed to provide financial and technical assistance for the construction of roads without damaging the environment. The 78th session of the National Assembly approved new legislation regarding environmental protection.

Guidelines for the participation of foreign investors in Bhutan's further development were under review in 2000, while the Bhutanese stock exchange remained closed to external investors. Approval was granted in 2001 for two Singapore-based foreign hotel operators, one of which was to work in partnership with the Bhutan Tourism Corporation, to invest in hotel infrastructure catering to high-income visitors to Bhutan. A third Indian-based hotel chain was granted approval in September 2001 to construct a joint-venture luxury resort in Thimphu from 2002. In 2001 the Bhutan Government continued to divest its shares in state-owned corporations, to encourage further private-sector participation: 20% of government shares in the Royal Insurance Corporation of Bhutan were sold, reducing government shareholding to less than 40%. In September 2001 the Council of Ministers approved the establishment of a soft drinks bottling and preform manufacturing industry at Pasakha, near Phuentsholing.

In mid-2001 the Government was formulating a Memorandum on Foreign Trade Regime in preparation for membership of the World Trade Organization, with which Bhutan held observer status.

ENERGY

The Chhukha HEP project was launched in 1975 and the first turbine was test-turned in April 1986 and synchronized to the neighbouring Indian grid in September. The additional turbines came into operation by mid-1988, and the project was formally inaugurated by the President of India in October 1988. Most of western Bhutan, up to Punakha, is now able to receive electricity from this source. Under the existing arrangements, India bore 60% of all costs of the Chhukha project, with the remaining 40% of costs constituting a long-term, low-interest loan to Bhutan; and the Government of India purchases, at a low price, all power not consumed by Bhutan. Bhutan reimports some power through the Indian grid at the same low price (plus costs for transmission) to serve several southern districts. In 2001 the Chhukha project provided Bhutan with a gross income of Nu 2,175.1m. (Nu 2,034.9m. in power sales to India; Nu 140.2m. in domestic power sales). It is hoped that this relatively cheap power will give a substantial impetus to industrial development in the private sector. By the end of June 1998 39 of the principal towns of Bhutan and 363 villages had electricity, and in mid-1996 total installed capacity under the Department of Power (including the Chhukha project) was 342 MW (of which the Chhukha project provided 325 MW and diesel plants 12 MW), with maximum generation potential of 1,632.9m. units. Maximum domestic demand, however, remained low at 20 MW. Total domestic energy requirement rose from 186.7m. units in 1991/92 to 195.3m. units in 1992/93. The installed capacity of generators within Bhutan includes 35 diesel stations (12 at industrial sites), eight HEP stations and 14 micro-hydroelectric stations.

In November 1990 India and Bhutan signed a memorandum of understanding to permit the execution of detailed reports on the proposed Tala HEP project and the Wangchu reservoir scheme (Chhukha II and Chhukha III, respectively). In March 1996 Bhutan and India agreed to proceed with the Tala project, at an estimated cost of Nu 14,080m. (of which 60% was to be in grants from India and 40% was to be in the form of a loan repayable over 12 years). The water diversion channel was completed in May 1999 and the supply of generating plant contracts (worth Nu 4,210m.) was awarded in October of that year. In 2002 the project continued to proceed ahead of the revised completion date of March 2005. In late 2001 the total cost of the project was expected to reach some Nu 36,000m. When completed, the Tala project will have an installed capacity of 1,020 MW. India and Bhutan also agreed in late 1992 to co-operate to examine the power potential of the Sunkosh river in south-central Bhutan. The detailed Sunkosh Multipurpose Project report presented at the end of 1996, which the Government is still considering, foresees power capacity of 4,060 MW and a construction cost of Nu 77,930m. The project would be based at Kerabari village (Kalikhola); it would take a decade to complete, and could supply power to India's northern and eastern grids. In February 1994 Bhutan and India signed an agreement regarding the construction of the 45-MW Kurichhu HEP project at Gyelpoishing, near Mongar in eastern Bhutan. The first turbine was commissioned in early 2001; a fourth 15-MW unit will bring total capacity to 60 MW on completion. Costs had reached Nu 5,685m. by mid-2001. The first two units of Kurichhu power were connected to the Indian grid in Salakati (Assam) in August 2001, and by mid-2002 three generating units were fully commissioned, with the fourth nearing completion. The project was expected to supply consistent and sufficient electricity to the 10 districts of eastern and central Bhutan, which would eventually lead to social and economic benefits. A 198-km, 132-KV feeder power line from Kurichhu to Geylegphug (via Pemagatshel, Nganglam, Panbang and Tingtibi) was completed in less than one year. In November 2001 Samdrup Jongkhar received power from Kurichhu for the first time via a substation at Deothang. The Basochhu project (66 MW) is being implemented at a revised cost of Nu 1,659m., and is scheduled for completion by 2005; the first (upper) 25 MW phase was inaugurated in mid-January 2002, thereby boosting national electricity output to 440 MW, and work on the second (lower) 40 MW phase started at the end of 2001. Power will initially be distributed to the five western districts, and, on completion of the project, will be extended to the southern districts of Dagana, Tsirang and Sarpang. Eventually the Basochhu project will be linked with the Kurichhu project at Gelephu to form an integrated national power transmission grid. The Bunakha project (180 MW) is currently being assessed; and the Rangjung project (2.2 MW), which was commissioned in April 1996, supplies electricity to more than 3,000 households in the districts of Trashigang and Trashi Yangtse. Bilateral aid donated by the Austrian Government has also assisted the energy sector (including rural electrification) and the provision of renewable natural resources.

HEALTH SERVICES

Modern medical facilities were established in 1962, at a time when low nutritional intake and poor sanitation, along with a high level of parasitic infections and contagious diseases, continued to debilitate the population. By 2001 services provided by the Department of Health covered about 90% of the total population. Life expectancy at birth reached about 66 years in 2001. The infant mortality rate stood at about 8.7% in 1997. Health institutions were, at first, concentrated in the urban areas, but by the beginning of the 21st century the emphasis had shifted to rural areas. National, regional and district hospitals serve as referral centres; basic health units (BHUs), the core of Bhutan's public health system, serve remote communities.

Health assistants, auxiliary-nurse midwives and basic health workers who are employed by the BHUs are given paramedical training at Thimphu's Royal Institute of Health Sciences. In addition, during the Fifth Plan (1981–87), 193 village volunteer health workers were trained in basic health care. At the end of 2000 there were 29 hospitals (as well as 18 indigenous and five leprosy hospitals, providing general health services also), 160 BHUs, 32 dispensaries, 447 outreach clinics, 19 malaria centres and three training institutes. The total number of hospital beds was 1,023 (one for every 665 inhabitants, on the basis of the estimated 2000 population figure), and there were 109 doctors (one for every 6,220 inhabitants) and 1,327 village health workers. The Government has placed considerable importance on the development of indigenous medicine, along with the development of modern medical practices. Indigenous medical units are attached to district hospitals (13 in 2000), each attended by a *drungtsho* (physician) and a *menpa* (compounder) trained by the National Institute of Traditional Medicinal Services (NITMS). In addition to this training, the NITMS provides alternative medical services for outpatients, and researches, collects and manufactures indigenous medicines. In 2000 there were 31 physicians and 17 compounders working in indigenous medical service units.

The Government's principal health care objective was to eliminate, by the year 2000, the most common diseases—waterborne parasites, diarrhoea and dysentery, malaria, tuberculosis, pneumonia and goitre. Extensive publicity is being given, in the rural areas, to the preparation of oral rehydration fluid. Access to safe drinking water increased from 31% of the population in 1987 to 77.8% in 2000. In the same year, 89.0% of villages had access to health services within three hours of walking. An immunization programme against six diseases, for children aged up to 10 months, has been operating since 1979. In 2000 12,686 children were vaccinated against tuberculosis, 10,757 against measles, and 12,228 against both diphtheria and poliomyelitis. In 1990 WHO declared that universal child immunization had been achieved in Bhutan. The number of leprosy patients is decreasing each year (28 at the end of 2000, compared with 3,764 in 1979), and the leprosy hospitals, which were previously operated by the Norwegian Mission, have been nationalized (although the Mission retains a presence in Bhutan). An iodizing plant came into operation in 1984, and all sales of non-iodized salt are now banned. This constitutes a major step towards the eventual elimination of hypothyroidism and cretinism. Malaria is still an endemic disease in southern Bhutan; in 1999 51% of 79,589 blood tests for malaria were positive. A 41-bed hospital (integrated with an indigenous medical facility) was inaugurated in Bumthang in April 1990. By August 1997 eight HIV-positive cases had been reported in Thimphu alone. The budget for the financial year 1998/99 allocated an estimated Nu 883m. (12.5% of total projected expenditure) to health.

Statistical Survey

Source (unless otherwise stated): Royal Government of Bhutan, Thimphu.

Area and Population

AREA, POPULATION AND DENSITY

Area (sq km)	46,500*
Population (official estimates)†	
2000	638,000
2001	654,269
2002	670,953
Density (per sq km) in 2002	14.4

* 17,954 sq miles.

† These figures are much lower than former estimates. The figures for 2001 and 2002 are based on the 2000 estimate and assume an annual population growth rate of 2.55%. It was previously reported that a census in 1969 enumerated a population of 931,514, and a 1980 census recorded a total of 1,165,000. On the basis of the latter figure, a mid-1988 population of 1,375,400 was projected. Other figures in this Survey are derived from the earlier, higher estimates of Bhutan's population.

Capital: Thimphu (estimated population 45,000 at 1 January 2002).

POPULATION OF DISTRICTS*
(mid-1985 estimates, based on 1980 census)

Bumthang	23,842
Dagana	28,352
Gasa†	16,907
Gelephu	111,283
Ha	16,715
Lhuentse	39,635
Mongar	73,239
Paro	46,615
Pemagatshel	37,141
Punakha†	16,700
Samdrup Jongkhar	73,044
Samtse	172,109
Zhemgang	44,516
Thimphu	58,660
Trashigang	177,718
Trongsa	26,017
Tsirang	108,807
Wangdue Phodrang	47,152
Total rural population	1,119,452
Total urban population	167,823
Total	1,286,275

* The above figures are approximate, and predate the creation of a new district, Chhukha, in 1987. Chhukha has an estimated total population of about 13,372 (based on the figure of 3,343 households, with an estimated average of four persons per household), who were formerly included in Samtse, Paro or Thimphu districts. The above figures also predate the creation of a further two new districts, Gasa (previously within Punakha) and Trashi Yangtse (previously within Trashigang), in 1992.

† Gasa and Punakha were merged into a single district, which was to be known as Punakha, in 1987.

BIRTHS AND DEATHS (UN estimates, annual averages)

	1985–90	1990–95	1995–2000
Birth rate (per 1,000)	40.9	38.6	36.2
Death rate (per 1,000)	14.4	11.4	9.8

Source: UN, *World Population Prospects: The 2000 Revision*.

Expectation of life (WHO estimates, years at birth, 2000): Males 60.4; Females 62.5 (Source: WHO, *World Health Report*).

ECONOMICALLY ACTIVE POPULATION
(estimates, '000 persons, 1981/82)

Agriculture, etc.	613
Industry	6
Trade	9
Public services	22
Total	650

Mid-2000 (estimates in '000): Agriculture, etc. 942; Total labour force 1,005 (Source: FAO).

Health and Welfare

KEY INDICATORS

Fertility (births per woman, 2000)	5.3
Under-5 mortality rate (per 1,000 live births, 2000)	100
HIV/AIDS (% of persons aged 15–49, 2001)	<0.10
Physicians (per 1,000 head, 1995)	0.16
Hospital beds (per 1,000 head, 1994)	1.61
Health expenditure (1998): US $ per head (PPP)	71
% of GDP	3.8
public (% of total)	90.3
Access to water (% of persons, 2000)	62
Access to sanitation (% of persons, 2000)	69
Human Development Index (2000): ranking	140
value	0.494

For sources and definitions, see explanatory note on p. vi.

Agriculture

PRINCIPAL CROPS (FAO estimates, '000 metric tons)

	1998	1999	2000
Wheat	20*	20*	20
Rice (paddy)	50	50	50
Barley	5*	5*	5
Maize	85*	70*	70
Millet	7	7	7
Other cereals	7.3	7.3	7.3
Potatoes	34.1	34.1	34.1
Other roots and tubers	21.8	21.8	21.8
Sugar cane	12.8	12.8	12.8
Chillies and green peppers	8.5	8.5	8.5
Oranges	58	58	58
Other fruits (excl. melons)	6.3	6.3	6.3
Nutmeg, mace and cardamon	5.8	5.8	5.8
Other spices	8.1	8.1	8.1

* Unofficial figure.

Source: FAO.

LIVESTOCK (FAO estimates, '000 head, year ending September)

	1998	1999	2000
Horses	30	30	30
Mules	10	10	10
Asses	18	18	18
Cattle	435	435	435
Buffaloes	4	4	4
Pigs	75	75	75
Sheep	59	59	59
Goats	42	42	42
Poultry	310	310	310

Source: FAO.

Yaks ('000 head): 35 in 1993; 39 (provisional) in 1994; 40 (estimate) in 1995 (Source: IMF, *Bhutan—Selected Issues* (February 1997)).

LIVESTOCK PRODUCTS ('000 metric tons)

	1998	1999	2000
Beef and veal	5.8	5.8	5.8
Buffalo meat	0.1	0.1	0.1
Mutton and lamb	0.2	0.2	0.2
Goat meat	0.2	0.2	0.2
Pig meat	1.2	1.2	1.2
Poultry meat	0.3	0.3	0.3
Cows' milk	29.0	29.0	29.0
Buffaloes' milk	2.7	2.7	2.7
Goats' milk	0.2	0.2	0.2
Hen eggs	0.4	0.4	0.4
Cattle hides (fresh)	1.2	1.2	1.2
Sheepskins (fresh)	0.1	0.1	0.1

Source: FAO.

Forestry

ROUNDWOOD REMOVALS (FAO estimates, '000 cubic metres, excl. bark)

	1998	1999	2000
Sawlogs, veneer logs and logs for sleepers*	18	18	18
Other industrial wood*	27	27	27
Fuel wood	4,066	4,142	4,221
Total	4,111	4,187	4,266

* Output assumed to be unchanged since 1995.

Source: FAO.

SAWNWOOD PRODUCTION ('000 cubic metres, incl. railway sleepers)

	1991	1992	1993
Coniferous (softwood)	0	13	12
Broadleaved (hardwood)	35	8	6
Total	35	21	18

1994–2000: Annual production as in 1993 (FAO estimates).
Source: FAO.

Fishing

(FAO estimates, metric tons, live weight)

	1997	1998	1999
Capture			
Freshwater fishes	300	300	300
Aquaculture			
Freshwater fishes	30	30	30
Total catch	330	330	330

Source: FAO, *Yearbook of Fishery Statistics*.

Mining

(metric tons, unless otherwise indicated, year ending 30 June)

	1995/96	1996/97	1997/98
Dolomite	249,253	276,700	240,300
Limestone	266,591	297,900	376,700
Gypsum	52,102	66,600	62,300
Coal	67,994	63,900	53,200
Marble chips (sq ft)	12,841	35,400	n.a.
Slate (sq ft)	92,148	44,100	48,400
Quartzite	50,226	98,100	39,500
Talc	9,158	9,200	11,400
Iron ore	5,516	4,000	5,000
Pink shale/quartzite	5,112	1,400	2,700

Source: Geology and Mines Division, Ministry of Trade and Industry, Royal Government of Bhutan.

Industry

GROSS SALES AND OUTPUT OF SELECTED INDUSTRIES (million ngultrum)

	1999	2000	2001
Penden Cement Authority	684.5	696.7	n.a.
Bhutan Ferro Alloys	534.7	428.4	579.0
Bhutan Fruit Products	124.9	108.5	111.6
Army Welfare Project*	234.9	255.0	283.8
Bhutan Carbide and Chemicals	569.3	474.6	675.9
Bhutan Board Products	257.1	228.6	294.1
Eastern Bhutan Coal Company	97.1	126.5	132.7
Druk Satair Corporation Ltd	77.4	94.0	98.3

* Manufacturer of alcoholic beverages.

Source: Royal Monetary Authority.

Electric energy (million kWh, year ending 30 June): 1,972.2 in 1995/96; 1,838.4 in 1996/97; 1,800.0 in 1997/98.

Revenue from the Chhukha Hydroelectric Project (million ngultrum): 2,141.7 (Internal consumption 122.5, Exports 2,019.1) in 1999; 2,307.4 (Internal consumption 117.8, Exports 2,189.6) in 2000; 2,175.1 (Internal consumption 140.2; Exports 2,034.9) in 2001.

Source: Department of Power, Royal Government of Bhutan.

Finance

CURRENCY AND EXCHANGE RATES

Monetary Units

100 chetrum (Ch) = 1 ngultrum (Nu).

Sterling, Dollar and Euro Equivalents (31 May 2002)

£1 sterling = 71.91 ngultrum;
US $1 = 49.03 ngultrum;
€1 = 46.02 ngultrum;
1,000 ngultrum = £13.91 = $20.40 = €21.73.

Average Exchange Rate (ngultrum per US $)

1999 43.055
2000 44.942
2001 47.186

Note: The ngultrum is at par with the Indian rupee, which also circulates freely within Bhutan. The foregoing figures relate to the official rate of exchange, which is applicable to government-related transactions alone. Since April 1992 there has also been a market rate of exchange, which values foreign currencies approximately 20% higher than the official rate of exchange.

BUDGET (estimates, million ngultrum, year ending 30 June)

Revenue	1996/97	1997/98*	1998/99†
Domestic revenue	2,425	3,079	3,094
Tax	869	1,246	1,285
Non-tax	1,556	1,832	1,809
Grants from Government of India	948	1,335	2,271
Grants from UN and other international agencies	1,284	820	1,479
Total	4,657	5,234	6,844

Expenditure	1996/97	1997/98*	1998/99†
General public services	1,427	1,562	1,985
Economic services	2,205	1,834	3,187
Agriculture and irrigation	430	199	320
Animal husbandry	135	78	149
Forestry	122	132	190
Industries, mining, trade and commerce	36	34	74
Public works, roads and housing	668	502	626
Transport and communication	252	250	161
Power	562	639	1,667
Social services	999	1,119	1,827
Education	517	543	912
Health	469	558	883
Urban development and municipal corporations	13	17	32
Net lending	327	231	45
Total expenditure and net lending	4,958	4,745	7,044

* Provisional figures. † Projected figures.

Source: IMF, *Bhutan—Statistical Annex* (July 1999).

1999/2000 (million ngultrum, revised figures): *Revenue:* Domestic revenue 3,869.8; Other receipts 268.8; Grants 3,616.3; Total 7,754.9. *Expenditure:* Current expenditure 3,743.7; Capital expenditure 4,514.6; Net lending 54.2; Repayment 209.3; Total 8,521.8.

2000/01 (million ngultrum, revised figures): *Revenue:* Domestic revenue 4,492.8; Other receipts 604.8; Grants 3,310.7; Total 8,408.3. *Expenditure:* Current expenditure 4,397.6; Capital expenditure 5,023.4; Net lending 68.5; Repayment 215.5; Total 9,704.9.

2001/02 (million ngultrum, revised figures): *Revenue:* Domestic revenue 4,943.8; Other receipts 527.3; Grants 3,316.9; Total 8,788.0. *Expenditure:* Current expenditure 4,664.3; Capital expenditure 5,447.1; Net lending 72.5; Repayment 231.4; Total 10,415.4.

2002/03 (million ngultrum, forecast): *Revenue*: Domestic revenue 5,100.2; Other receipts 18.3; Grants 4,413.7; Total 9,532.2. *Expenditure*: Current expenditure 4,597.3; Capital expenditure 6,318.8; Net lending 28.3; Repayment 240.3; Total 11,184.6.

Source: Royal Government of Bhutan.

FOREIGN EXCHANGE RESERVES (at 30 June)

	1999	2000	2001
Indian rupee reserves (million Indian rupees)	2,542.3	3,165.0	3,617.3
Royal Monetary Authority	95.3	102.0	89.4
Bank of Bhutan	1,863.7	1,819.5	2,149.7
Bhutan National Bank	583.3	1,191.9	1,328.3
Royal Insurance Corporation of Bhutan	—	51.5	50.0
Convertible currency reserves (US $ million)	200.1	221.8	217.3
Royal Monetary Authority*	193.5	197.7	186.1
Bank of Bhutan	3.0	11.4	16.3
Bhutan National Bank	3.6	12.6	14.8
Royal Insurance Corporation of Bhutan	0.1	—	—

* Includes tranche position in the International Monetary Fund.

Source: Royal Monetary Authority of Bhutan.

MONEY SUPPLY (million ngultrum at 31 December)

	1999	2000	2001
Currency outside banks*	969.2	1,269.6	1,609.9
Demand deposits at the Bank of Bhutan	2,754.9	2,669.5	3,238.2
Total money†	12,665.8	15,661.0	16,312.7

* Including an estimate for Indian rupees.

† Including non-monetary deposits with the Royal Monetary Authority by financial institutions.

Source: Royal Monetary Authority of Bhutan.

COST OF LIVING
(Consumer Price Index at 31 December; base: 1979 = 100)

	1999	2000	2001
All items (excl. rent)	587.0	612.9	632.8

Source: Central Statistical Office of the Planning Commission, Royal Government of Bhutan.

NATIONAL ACCOUNTS (million ngultrum at current prices)

Expenditure on the Gross Domestic Product

	1998	1999	2000
Government final consumption expenditure	3,308	4,271	4,422
Private final consumption expenditure	9,322	10,067	11,329
Increase in stocks	45	108	49
Gross fixed capital formation	6,200	8,127	9,447
Total domestic expenditure	18,875	22,573	25,247
Exports of goods and services	5,148	5,714	6,456
Less Imports of goods and services	7,686	9,164	10,004
GDP in purchasers' values	16,337	19,122	21,698

Source: IMF, *International Financial Statistics*.

Gross Domestic Product by Economic Activity

	1998*	1999*	2000†
Agriculture, forestry and livestock	6,057.5	6,640.8	7,769.1
Mining and quarrying	262.3	325.9	341.0
Manufacturing	1,621.8	1,761.8	1,734.7
Electricity	1,937.1	2,317.9	2,519.8
Construction	1,687.0	2,113.1	2,717.3
Trade, restaurants and hotels	1,159.7	1,281.6	1,465.3
Transport, storage and communications	1,369.5	1,636.7	1,863.2
Finance, insurance and real estate	1,004.0	1,042.0	1,324.1
Community, social and personal services	1,436.9	1,835.9	1,920.0
Sub-total	16,535.8	18,955.7	21,654.5
Less Imputed bank service charges	458.3	441.6	528.0
GDP at factor cost	16,077.5	18,514.1	21,126.5
GDP at constant 1980 factor cost	3,514.3	3,773.4	3,989.5

* Revised figures. † Projected figures.

Source: Royal Monetary Authority of Bhutan.

BALANCE OF PAYMENTS (US $ million, year ending 30 June)

	1998/99	1999/2000	2000/01
Merchandise exports f.o.b.	103.6	111.0	110.3
Merchandise imports c.i.f.	−160.6	−179.7	−211.6
Trade balance	−57.0	−68.7	−101.3
Services and transfers	−39.9	−57.4	−22.0
Current balance	−96.9	−126.1	−123.3
Grants and loans	145.2	167.9	155.1
Foreign direct investment	1.1	—	—
Net errors and omissions	−5.7	−6.4	−8.0
Overall balance	43.7	35.4	23.8

Source: Asian Development Bank, *Key Indicators of Developing Asian and Pacific Countries*.

OFFICIAL DEVELOPMENT ASSISTANCE (US $ million)

	1996	1997	1998
Bilateral donors	42.1	44.6	39.7
Multilateral donors	15.8	21.2	16.0
Total	57.9	65.8	55.7
Grants	54.0	55.6	48.0
Loans	3.9	10.2	7.7
Per caput assistance (US $)	32.0	35.4	27.8

Source: UN, *Statistical Yearbook for Asia and the Pacific*.

SELECTED COMMODITIES (million ngultrum, provisional)

Imports c.i.f.	1995	1996	1997
Wood charcoal	n.a.	122.3	139.6
Telecommunications equipment	n.a.	302.0	491.0
Beer	n.a.	66.0	86.3
Coal	n.a.	44.6	103.3
Diesel oil	136.1	138.8	163.2
Petroleum	64.0	67.4	73.0
Rice	217.3	209.1	215.3
Wheat	39.3	89.0	100.0
Vegetable fats and oils	134.7	134.4	121.1
Cotton fabric	41.9	38.2	n.a.
Industrial machinery	142.0	77.5	54.3
Tyres for buses and trucks	37.5	34.5	n.a.
Iron and steel	115.4	109.6	117.0
Electricity	10.7	7.6	n.a.
Total (incl. others)	3,802.3	4,250.0	4,980.0

Exports f.o.b.	1995	1996	1997
Electricity	721.9	747.6	1,290.0
Calcium carbide	497.9	533.0	546.3
Cement	278.4	253.0	371.4
Particle board	329.1	286.0	329.0
Non-coniferous plywood	32.8	2.2	n.a.
Sawn logs (hard)	71.8	79.1	78.1
Sawn timber (soft)	60.7	27.1	76.5
Cardamom	73.8	68.2	36.9
Wheat and flour	23.8	58.0	n.a.
Mixed fruit/vegetable juice	119.5	86.7	7.8
Coal (bituminous)	n.a.	19.9	25.6
Rum	n.a.	65.0	58.8
Total (incl. others)	3,349.1	3,553.8	4,270.0

1998 (million ngultrum): Electricity 1,338.7; Calcium carbide 583.6; Cement 547.3; Particle board 285.8.

1999 (million ngultrum): Electricity 2,019.1; Calcium carbide 546.8; Cement 433.7; Particle board 247.6.

2000 (estimate, million ngultrum): Calcium carbide 145.4. Source: Asian Development Bank, *Key Indicators of Developing Asian and Pacific Countries*.

PRINCIPAL TRADING PARTNERS
(estimates, US $ million, year ending 30 June)

Imports c.i.f.	1998/99*	1999/2000	2000/01†
India	115.5	139.0	159.3
Other countries	46.8	46.0	56.0
Total	162.3	185.0	215.3

Exports f.o.b.	1998/99	1999/2000	2000/01†
India	98.2	108.0	106.0
Other countries	6.6	6.3	6.3
Total	104.8	114.3	112.3

* Revised figures.

† Preliminary estimates.

Source: Royal Monetary Authority of Bhutan.

Transport

ROAD TRAFFIC

In 2000 there were 19,463 registered, roadworthy vehicles—7,438 light four-wheeled vehicles, 7,793 two-wheeled vehicles (motor cycles and scooters), 2,062 heavy vehicles (trucks, buses, bulldozers, etc.) and 770 taxis. Source: Central Statistical Office, Ministry of Planning.

CIVIL AVIATION (traffic, year ending 30 June)

	1985	1986	1987
Kilometres flown ('000)	152	201	n.a.
Passengers	5,928	7,776	8,700
Passenger-km ('000)	3,349	4,381	n.a.

Paying passengers: 19,608 in 1993, 21,115 in 1994, 22,286 in 1995; 26,806 in 1996; 30,108 in 1997; 31,799 in 1998; 35,500 in 1999; 19,233 in 2000.
Revenue (million ngultrum, year ending 30 June): 241.5 in 1992/93, 188.3 in 1993/94, 213.8 in 1994/95; 252.9 in 1995/96; 280.6 in 1996/97; 326.7 in 1997/98; 157.3 in 1999/2000.

Source: Central Statistical Office, Ministry of Planning, Royal Government of Bhutan.

Tourism

FOREIGN VISITORS BY COUNTRY OF ORIGIN*

	1998	1999	2000
Australia	64	131	179
Austria	270	197	131
France	366	236	399
Germany	520	574	662
Italy	218	276	156
Japan	1,032	1,102	875
Netherlands	370	362	359
Switzerland	170	296	137
Taiwan	135	179	175
United Kingdom	686	646	595
USA	1,471	2,122	2,754
Total (incl. others)	6,203	7,158	7,559

* Figures relate to tourists paying in convertible currency.

Foreign visitor arrivals: 6,393 in 2001.

Receipts (US $ million): 7.84 in 1998; 8.65 in 1999; 9.87 in 2000; 9.20 in 2001.

Sources: Tourism Authority of Bhutan; World Tourism Organization, *Yearbook of Tourism Statistics*.

Government hotel rooms: 560 in 1996; 560 in 1997; 560 (provisional) in 1998 (Source: IMF, *Bhutan—Statistical Annex* (July 1999)).

Communications Media

	1998	1999	2000
Television receivers ('000 in use)	12.5	13.0	13.5
Telephone ('000 main lines in use)	10.4	11.8	13.3
Facsimile machines ('000 in use)	1.5	n.a.	n.a.
Personal computers ('000 in use)	2.5	3.0	3.5
Internet users ('000)	—	0.5	1.5

Radio receivers ('000 in use): 37 in 1997.

Sources: International Telecommunications Union; UNESCO, *Statistical Yearbook.*

Education

	Institutions at 1 April 1999	Students at 15 July 2001		
		Males	Females	Total
Community schools	254	10,165	8,596	18,761
Primary schools		16,621	14,089	30,710
Junior high schools	51	22,666	20,394	43,060
High schools	21	11,816	9,628	21,444
Degree college*	1	451	172	623
Other post-secondary institutions	9	1,348	712	2,060
Private schools	7	1,534	1,393	2,927
Non-formal education (NFE) centres	81	2,210	5,278	7,488

* Affiliated with University of Delhi.

15 July 2001: Total teachers 3,972 (of whom 3,640 at schools, 176 at higher institutes). Total students at higher institutes 2,683.

Source: Ministry of Health and Education, Thimphu.

Adult literacy rate (UNESCO estimates): 42.2% (males 56.3%; females 28.2%) in 1995 (Source: UNESCO, *Statistical Yearbook*).

Directory

The Constitution

The Kingdom of Bhutan has no formal constitution. However, the state system is a modified form of constitutional monarchy. Written rules, which are changed periodically, govern procedures for the election of members of the Council of Ministers, the Royal Advisory Council and the Legislature, and define the duties and powers of those bodies. A special committee was convened in late 2001 to prepare a draft written constitution. The draft was expected to be subjected to public review before being submitted to the National Assembly for formal approval.

The Government

Head of State: HM Druk Gyalpo ('Dragon King') JIGME SINGYE WANGCHUCK (succeeded to the throne in July 1972).

LODOI TSOKDE
(Royal Advisory Council)

(September 2002)

The Royal Advisory Council (Lodoi Tsokde), established in 1965, comprises nine members: two monks representing the Central and District Monastic Bodies (Rabdeys), six people's representatives and a Chairman (Kalyon), nominated by the King. Each geog (group of villages, known also as a block) within a dzongkhag (district) selects one representative, from whom the respective Dzongkhag Yargye Tshogchungs (DYTs—District Development Committees) each agree on one nomination to be forwarded to the National Assembly (Tshogdu Chenmo). From these 20 nominees, the National Assembly, in turn, elects six persons to serve on the Royal Advisory Council as people's representatives for the whole country. The Council's principal task is to advise the Chairman of the Council of Ministers (Lhengye Zhungtshog), as head of government, and to supervise all aspects of administration. The Council is in permanent session, virtually as a government department, and acts, on a daily basis, as the *de facto* Standing Committee of the National Assembly. Representatives of the monastic bodies serve for one year, representatives of the people for three years, and the duration of the Chairman's term of office is at the discretion of the King. Representatives may be re-elected, but not for consecutive terms; they are all full members of the Council of Ministers.

Chairman: Dasho RINZIN GYELTSHEN.

Councillors: Dasho ADAP PASANG*, Dasho LEKI PEMA*, Dasho JAMYANG*, Dasho CHADOR WANGDI*, Dasho (Aum) SONAM WANGCHUK*, Dasho GYELTSHEN*, Lopon UGYEN NAMGYAL†, Lopon GYEMBO DORJI†.

* From November 2001 to November 2004.

† From November 2001 to November 2002.

LHENGYE ZHUNGTSHOG
(Council of Ministers)

(September 2002)

Prime Minister and Chairman (August 2002–July 2003) **and Minister of Agriculture:** Lyonpo KINZANG DORJI.

Minister of Trade and Industry: Lyonpo KHANDU WANGCHUK.

Minister of Finance: Lyonpo YESHEY ZIMBA.

Minister of Foreign Affairs: Lyonpo JIGMI YOZER THINLEY.

Minister of Health and Education: Lyonpo SANGYE NGEDUP DORJI.

Minister of Home Affairs: Lyonpo THINLEY GYAMTSHO.

Cabinet Secretary: Aum NETEN ZANGMO.

All members of the Royal Advisory Council are also members of the Council of Ministers.

MINISTRIES AND OTHER MAJOR GOVERNMENT BODIES

Ministry of Agriculture: POB 252, Thimphu; tel. 322129; fax 323153; internet www.moa.gov.bt.

Ministry of Communications: Division of Information Technology, Old Banquet Hall, Conference Centre, Thimphu; tel. 323215; fax 322184; e-mail dit@druknet.net.bt; internet www.dit.gov.bt.

Ministry of Finance: Tashichhodzong, POB 117, Thimphu; tel. 322223; fax 323154.

Ministry of Foreign Affairs: Convention Centre, POB 103, Thimphu; tel. 323297; fax 323240.

Ministry of Health and Education: Tashichhodzong, POB 726, Thimphu; tel. 322351; fax 324649 (Health Services division); tel. 325146; fax 324823; internet www.education.gov.bt (Education Division).

Ministry of Home Affairs: Tashichhodzong, POB 133, Thimphu; tel. 322301; fax 322214.

Ministry of Trade and Industry: Tashichhodzong, POB 141, Thimphu; tel. 322211; fax 323617; internet www.cdb.gov.bt.

National Commission for Cultural Affairs: Thimphu; tel. 322001; fax 323040; e-mail dorwang@druknet.bt; fmrly Special Commission for Cultural Affairs; Chair. Lyonpo THINLEY GYAMTSHO; Sec. Dasho SANGAY WANGCHUG.

National Environment Commission: Thimphu, POB 466; tel. 323384; fax 323385; Hon. Dep. Minister Dasho NADO RINCHEN.

Office of the Royal Advisory Council: Tashichhodzong, POB 200, Thimphu; tel. 312339; fax 325343.

Royal Audit Authority: Thimphu; tel. 322111; internet www.raa.gov.bt; Auditor-Gen. Dasho KUNZANG WANGDI.

Cabinet Secretariat: Thimphu; tel. 321437; fax 321438.

Legislature

TSHOGDU CHENMO

A National Assembly (Tshogdu Chenmo) was established in 1953. The Assembly has a three-year term and meets (in recent years) at least once a year (usually in June–July). The size of the membership is based, in part, on the population of the districts; although the size is, in principle, subject to periodic revision, in practice the basis for popular representation has remained unchanged since 1953. In 2000 the Assembly had 152 members, including the Speaker and Deputy Speaker. Of this number, 99 were elected by direct popular consensus in the districts (formal voting is used, however, in the event of a deadlock); 10 of the 20 districts elected new public members (chimis) in November 2001, to replace those whose term of office had expired. (Not all of the chimis are elected simultaneously; there are, therefore, overlaps in tenure.) Six were members of the Royal Advisory Council (RAC), elected by secret ballot; the Chairman (Kalyon) of the RAC also sits in the Assembly. Ten seats were reserved for representatives of the Central and District Monk Bodies (of whom two sit as members of the RAC), one was reserved for a representative of industry (elected by the Bhutan Chamber of Commerce and Industry), and the remainder (35) were occupied by officials (including the 20 Dzongdas) selected by the King in conjunction with the National Assembly Secretariat. The Assembly elects its own Speaker from among its members, for a three-year (renewable) term. It enacts laws, advises on constitutional and political matters and debates all important issues. There is provision for a secret ballot on controversial issues, but, in practice, decisions are reached by consensus. Ministers and the six public members of the RAC are chosen by the entire Assembly in a secret ballot. Both the RAC and the Council of Ministers are responsible to the Assembly.

Speaker: Dasho UGYEN DORJI.

Political Organizations

Political parties are banned in Bhutan, in accordance with long-standing legislation. There are, however, a small number of anti-Government organizations, composed principally of Nepali-speaking former residents of Bhutan, which are based in Kathmandu, Nepal.

Bhutan Gurkha National Liberation Front (BGNLF): Nepal; f. 1994; Sec.-Gen. R. P. SUBBA.

Bhutan National Democratic Party (BNDP): POB 3334, Kathmandu, Nepal; tel. 525682; f. 1992; also has offices in Delhi and Varanasi, India, and in Thapa, Nepal; Pres. R. B. BASNET; Gen. Secs HARI P. ADHIKARI (Organization), Dr D. N. S. DHAKAL (Planning and External Affairs).

Bhutan People's Party (BPP): f. 1990 as a successor to the People's Forum on Democratic Rights (f. 1989); advocates unconditional release of all political prisoners, judicial reform, freedom of religious practices, linguistic freedom, freedom of press, speech and expression, and equal rights for all ethnic groups; Pres. (vacant); Gen. Sec. R. K. CHETTRI.

Druk National Congress (DNC): Maharagunj, Chakrapath, Kathmandu, Nepal; f. 1992; claims to represent 'all the oppressed people of Bhutan'; Pres. 'RONGTHONG' KINLEY DORJI.

Human Rights Organization of Bhutan (HUROB): POB 172, Patan Dhoka, Lalitpur, Kathmandu, Nepal; tel. 525046; fax 526038; f. 1991; documents alleged human rights violations in Bhutan and co-ordinates welfare activities in eight refugee camps in Nepal for ethnic Nepalese claiming to be from Bhutan; Chair. S. B. SUBBA; Gen. Sec. OM DHUNGEL.

United Liberation People's Front: f. 1990; Leader BALARAM POUDYAL.

Diplomatic Representation

EMBASSIES IN BHUTAN

Bangladesh: POB 178, Upper Choubachu, Thimphu; tel. 322362; fax 322629; e-mail bdoot@druknet.net.bt; Ambassador: AHMED RAHIM.

India: India House, Lungtenzampa, Thimphu; tel. 322100; fax 323195; Ambassador: K. J. JASROTIA.

Judicial System

Bhutan has Civil and Criminal Codes, which are based on those laid down by the Shabdrung Ngawang Namgyal in the 17th century. An independent judicial authority was established in 1961, but law was mostly administered at the district level until 1968, when the High Court was set up. Existing laws were consolidated in 1982, although annual or biennial conferences of Thrimpons are held to keep abreast of changing circumstances and to recommend (in the first instance, to the King) amendments to existing laws. Most legislation is sent by the Council of Ministers to the National Assembly for approval and enactment. A substantially-revised Civil and Criminal Procedure Code was endorsed by the 79th National Assembly session in July 2001.

Appeal Court: The Supreme Court of Appeal is the King.

High Court (Thrimkhang Gongma): Thimphu; tel. 322344; fax 322921; established 1968 to review appeals from Lower Courts, although some cases are heard at the first instance. The Full Bench is presided over by the Chief Justice. There are normally seven other judges, who are appointed by the King on the recommendation of the Chief Justice and who serve until their superannuation. Three judges form a quorum. The judges are assisted by senior rabjams/ramjans (judges in training). Assistance to defendants is available through jabmis (certificated pleaders). The operation of the legal system and proposed amendments are considered by regular meetings of all the judges and Thrimpons (usually annually, or at least once every two years). Under the mid-1998 grant of governance to an elected Council of Ministers and pending the adoption of detailed regulations, proposed amendments are expected to be submitted to the Council of Ministers for consideration. Major changes to structure, administration and personnel were implemented from mid-2001.

Chief Justice: Lyonpo SONAM TOBGYE.

Judges of the High Court: Dasho THINLEY YOEZER, Dasho PASANG TOBGYE, Dasho KARMA D. SHERPA, Dasho K. B. GHALEY*, Dasho PHUB DORJI.

* Originally nominated as public representative.

Magistrates' Courts (Dzongkhag Thrimkhang): Each district has a court, headed by the thrimpon (magistrate) and aided by a junior rabjam/ramjam, which tries most cases. Appeals are made to the High Court, and less serious civil disputes may be settled by a gup or mandal (village headman) through written undertakings by the parties concerned.

All citizens have the right to make informal appeal for redress of grievances directly to the King, through the office of the gyalpoi zimpon (court chamberlain).

Department of Legal Affairs: tel. 326889; fax 324606; f. 2000; to consist of a prosecution division, with civil and criminal sections, to indict offenders on behalf of the Government; and a legal services division, to assist in the drafting of laws and acts, advance Bhutan's interest internationally in accordance with public international laws, develop the legal profession, and create public awareness of laws and acts; Dir Dasho KINLEY TSHERING.

Religion

The state religion is Mahayana Buddhism, but the southern Bhutanese are predominantly followers of Hinduism. Buddhism was introduced into Bhutan in the eighth century AD by the Indian saint Padmasambhava, known in Bhutan as Guru Rimpoche. In the 13th century Phajo Drugom Shigpo made the Drukpa school of Kagyupa Buddhism pre-eminent in Bhutan, and this sect is still supported by the dominant ethnic group, the Drukpas. The main monastic group, the Central Monastic Body (comprising 1,160 monks), is led by an elected Head Abbot (Je Khenpo), is directly supported by the State and spends six months of the year at Tashichhodzong and at Punakha respectively. A further 2,120 monks, who are members of the District Monastic Bodies, are sustained by the lay population. The Council for Ecclesiastical Affairs oversees all religious bodies. Monasteries (Gompas) and shrines (Lhakhangs) are numerous. Religious proselytizing, in any form, is illegal.

Council for Ecclesiastical Affairs (Dratshang Lhentshog): POB 254, Thimphu; tel. 322754; fax 323867; e-mail dratsang@druknet.net; f. 1984, replacing the Central Board for Monastic Studies, to oversee all Buddhist meditational centres and schools of Buddhist studies, as well as the Central and District Monastic Bodies; daily affairs of the Council are run by the Central Monastic Secretariat; Chair. His Holiness the 70th Je-Khenpo Trulku JIGME CHOEDRA; Sec. SANGAY WANGCHUG; Dep. Sec. NGAWANG PHUNTSHO.

The Press

The Bhutan Review: POB 172, Patan Dhoka, Lalitpur, Kathmandu, Nepal; tel. 525046; fax 523819; f. 1993; monthly organ of the Human Rights Organization of Bhutan (HUROB); opposed to existing government policies.

Kuensel Corporation: POB 204, Thimphu; tel. 322483; fax 322975; internet www.kuenselonline.com; f. 1965 as a weekly govt bulletin;

reorg. as a national weekly newspaper in 1986; became autonomous corporation in 1992 (previously under Dept of Information), incorporating former Royal Government Press; in English, Dzongkha and Nepali; Man. Dir and Editor-in-Chief KINLEY DORJI; Editors (vacant) (Nepali), TENZIN RIGDEN (English), MINDU DORJI (Dzongkha); circ. 280 (Nepali), 12,875 (English), 4,280 (Dzongkha).

Broadcasting and Communications

TELECOMMUNICATIONS

Bhutan Telecom Corporation: POB 134, Thimphu; tel. 322678; fax 324312; e-mail info@telecom.net.bt; internet www.telecom.net.bt; f. 2000; state-owned public corpn; regulation authority; agency for satellite phones; Dir SANGEY TENZING.

DrukNet: Bhutan Telecom, 2/28 Drophen Lam, POB 134, Thimphu; tel. 326998; fax 328160; e-mail info@druknet.bt; internet www.druknet.bt; f. 1999; internet service provider; Head GANGA SHARMA.

BROADCASTING

Radio

In 1994 there were 52 radio stations for administrative communications. Of these, 34 were for internal communications (to which the public had access), and three were external stations serving Bhutan House at Kalimpong and the Bhutanese diplomatic missions in India and Bangladesh.

BBS Corporation (Bhutan Broadcasting Service): POB 101, Thimphu; tel. 323071; fax 323073; e-mail bbs@bbs.com.bt; www.bbs.com.bt; f. 1973 as Radio National Youth Association of Bhutan (NYAB); became autonomous corporation in 1992 (previously under Dept of Information); short-wave radio station broadcasting daily in Dzongkha, Sharchopkha, Nepali (Lhotsamkha) and English; a daily FM programme (for Thimphu only) began in 1987; simultaneous broadcasting in FM for western Bhutan and parts of central and southern Bhutan began in 2000; a one-hour daily television service for Thimphu was introduced in mid-1999 and later increased to two hours daily; Chair. Dasho LEKI DORJI; Exec. Dir KINGA SINGYE.

Television

In June 1999 the BBS Corporation started operating a television service (in Dzongkha and English) in Thimphu; the service was gradually to be expanded throughout the country. Broadcasts were to be limited to a few hours a day and were to consist entirely of national news and documentaries about the Bhutanese. By March 2000, according to the Ministry of Communications, each of the two cable television operators was providing 25 channels.

Finance

(cap. = capital; auth. = authorized; p.u. = paid up; res = reserves; dep. = deposits; m. = million; brs = branches; amounts in ngultrum)

BANKING

Central Bank

Royal Monetary Authority (RMA): POB 154, Thimphu; tel. 323111; fax 322847; e-mail rma-rsd@druknet.net.bt; f. 1982; bank of issue; frames and implements official monetary policy, co-ordinates the activities of financial institutions and holds foreign-exchange deposits on behalf of the Govt; cap. 1.5m.; Chair. Lyonpo YESHEY ZIMBA; Man. Dir SONAM WANGCHUK.

Commercial Banks

Bank of Bhutan: POB 75, Phuentsholing; tel. 252983; fax 252641; e-mail bobhol@druknet.net.bt; f. 1968; 20% owned by the State Bank of India and 80% by the Govt of Bhutan; wholly managed by Govt of Bhutan from 1997; cap. p.u. 100m., res 548.2m., dep. 6,979.7m. (Dec. 2001); Dirs nominated by the Bhutan Govt: Chair. Lyonpo YESHEY ZIMBA; Dirs KARMA DORJI, Dasho YESHI TSHERING; Dirs nominated by the State Bank of India: C. RAMNATH, M. HANUMANTHA RAO; Man. Dir TSHERING DORJI; 26 brs and 2 extension counters.

Bhutan National Bank (BNB): POB 439, Thimphu; tel. 252198; fax 252647; e-mail bnbpling@druknet.net.bt; Bhutan's second commercial bank, in 1996; partially privatized in 1998; 27% owned by Govt, 20.1% by Asian Development Bank and 19.9% by Citibank; auth. cap. 200m., cap. p.u. 59.5m., res 122.3m., dep. 2,489.9m. (1999); Chair. Lyonpo KHANDU WANGCHUK; Man. Dir KIPCHU TSHERING; 4 brs.

Development Bank

Bhutan Development Finance Corporation (BDFC): POB 256, Thimphu; tel. 322579; fax 323428; e-mail bdfc@druknet.net.bt; f. 1988; provides industrial loans and short- and medium-term agricultural loans; cap. p.u. 100m., loans 500m. (2000); Chair. Dasho WANGDI NORBU; Man. Dir KARMA RANGDOL.

STOCK EXCHANGE

Royal Securities Exchange of Bhutan Ltd (RSEB): POB 742, Thimphu; tel. 323995; fax 323849; e-mail rseb@druknet.net.bt; f. 1993; supervised by the Royal Monetary Authority; open to Bhutanese nationals only; 13 listed cos (1998); Chair. SONAM WANGCHUK; CEO TASHI YEZER.

INSURANCE

Royal Insurance Corporation of Bhutan: POB 77, Phuentsholing; tel. 252869; fax 252640; e-mail ricb@druknet.net.bt; f. 1975; provides general and life insurance and credit investment services; Chair. Lyonpo YESHEY ZIMBA; Man. Dir LAMKEY TSHERING; 10 brs and development centres.

Trade and Industry

GOVERNMENT AGENCIES

Food Corporation of Bhutan (FCB): POB 80, Phuentsholing; tel. 252241; fax 252289; e-mail drukfood@druknet.net.bt; f. 1974; activities include procurement and distribution of food grains and other essential commodities through appointed Fair Price Shop Agents; marketing of surplus agricultural and horticultural produce through FCB-regulated market outlets; logistics concerning World Food Programme food aid; maintenance of buffer stocks to offset any emergency food shortages; maintenance of SAARC Food Security Reserve Stock; exporting certain fruits; Man. Dir SHERUB GYALTSHEN; 18 outlets and 100 Fair Price Shops.

Forestry Development Corporation: tel. 323834; fax 325585; Man. Dir NAMGAY WANGCHUK.

Planning Commission: Gyalong Tshokhang, POB 127, Thimphu; tel. 326786; fax 322928; e-mail pcs@pcs.gov.bt; internet www.pcs.gov.bt; headed by the King until 1991, formally reconstituted 1999; consists of 21 officials; proposes socio-economic policy guidelines, issues directives for the formulation of development plans, ensures efficient and judicious allocation of resources, directs socio-economic research, studies and surveys, and appraises the Government on the progress of development plans and programmes; Chair. Lyonpo KINZANG DORJI; Sec. DAW TENZIN.

State Trading Corpn of Bhutan Ltd (STCB): POB 76, Phuentsholing; tel. 252286; fax 252619; e-mail stcbl@druknet.net.bt; manages imports and exports on behalf of the Govt; Chair. Dasho KARMA DORJEE; Man. Dir Dasho DORJI NAMGAY; brs in Thimphu (POB 272; tel. 322953; fax 323781; e-mail stcbthim@druknet.net.bt) and Kolkata (Calcutta), India.

CHAMBER OF COMMERCE

Bhutan Chamber of Commerce and Industry (BCCI): POB 147, Thimphu; tel. 322742; fax 323936; e-mail bcci@druknet.bt; f. 1980; reorg. 1988; promotion of trade and industry and privatization, information dissemination, private-sector human resource development; 434 registered mems; 12-mem. technical advisory committee; 21-mem. district executive committee; Pres. Dasho UGYEN DORJI; Sec.-Gen. Dasho TSHERING DORJI.

UTILITIES

Electricity

Department of Energy: c/o Ministry of Trade and Industry, Tashichhodzong, POB 141, Thimpu; tel. 22159; fax 223507.

Bhutan Electricity Authority (BEA): Thimphu; f. 2001; regulates the electricity supply industry.

Bhutan Power Corporation: Thimphu; f. 2002; responsible for ensuring electricity supply for the whole country at an affordable cost by 2020 and for providing uninterrupted transmission access for export of surplus power; Man. Dir SONAM TSHERING.

Chhukha Hydropower Corporation: Phuentsholing; tel. 252575; fax 252582; f. 1991; state-owned; Chair. Lyonpo YESHEY ZIMBA; Man. Dir YESHEY WANGDI.

Kurichhu Hydropower Corporation: Mongar; tel. 744113; fax 744130; e-mail kpa@druknet.bt; operates and maintains a 60 MW-hydroelectric power-generating facility at Gyelpozhing; Chair. Lyonpo KHANDU WANGCHUK; Man. Dir. CHHEWANG RINZIN.

Tala Hydroelectric Project Authority: POB 908, Tala; tel. 324985; fax 325499; e-mail mdthpa@druknet.net.bt; co-ordinates construction of dam and hydroelectric power-generating facilities; Man. Dir R. N. KHAZANCHI.

Water

Thimphu City Corporation (Water Supply Unit): POB 215, Thimphu; tel. 324710; fax 24315; f. 1982; responsible for water supply of Thimphu municipality (population 32,000); Head BHIMLAL DHUNGEL.

MAJOR COMPANIES

Bhutan Agro Industries Ltd: POB 329, Thimphu; govt undertaking; mfr of natural food products and natural spring water.

Bhutan Board Products Ltd (BBPL): Tala, POB 91, Phuentsholing; tel. 252130; fax 252676; f. 1983; e-mail bbplmd@druknet.net.bt; internet www.bbplelbhutanel.com; jt govt and private-sector venture; mfr of plain and prelaminated graded wood-particle board and ready-to-assemble furniture; Chair. Dasho LEKI DORJI; Man. Dir NAMGEY NIDUP.

Bhutan Carbide and Chemicals Ltd: 1st Floor, TCC Complex Bldg, POB 103, Phuentsholing; tel. 252415; fax 252112; e-mail bcci@druknet.net.bt; f. 1987; 52% owned by Tashi Group and 48% by financial institutions and public shareholders; production of calcium carbide and charcoal; mines chemical-grade limestone; provides reafforestation; located at Pasakha; Chair. Dasho U. DORJI; Man. Dir. P. K. RAO.

Bhutan Dairy Ltd: POB 196, Phuentsholing; tel. 252351; f. 1990 by Ministry of Agriculture; transferred to private ownership in 1994; milk-processing plant at Phuentsholing; produces pasteurized milk, butter, ghee and yoghurt; auth. cap. Nu 30m., cap. p.u. Nu 5.10m.; Man. Dir UGEN WANGDI.

Bhutan Engineering Co (Pvt) Ltd: Tenzin and Wangmo Bldg, Chubachu, POB 378, Thimphu; tel. 324524; fax 323475; e-mail becplth@druknet.net.bt; civil engineering and architectural consultants, major road and bridge construction works, sewerage works and hydropower project works; Man. Dir Dasho DORJI NORBU.

Bhutan Ferro Alloys Ltd: TCC Complex Bldg, 1st Floor, POB 211, Phuentsholing; tel. 252246; fax 252282; e-mail bfal@druknet.net.bt; 25% owned by Govt, 28.5% by Tashi Commercial Corpn, 14% by financial institutions and corporate bodies, 12.5% by private shareholders, 12% by Marubeni Corpn and 8% by Japan International Development Organization Ltd; manufactures and sells ferro-silicon, micro-silica and magnesium ferro-silicon; Chair. Lyonpo KHANDU WANGCHUK; Man. Dir Dasho TOPGYAL DORJI.

Bhutan Fruit Products Ltd: Samtse; tel. 365294; fax 365287; e-mail bfpl@druknet.net.bt; processes canned fruits and vegetables.

Bhutan Logging Corpn: Thimphu; tel. 322615; transferred to private ownership in 1991; Chair. Lyonpo YESHEY ZIMBA; Man. Dir TARA GIRI.

Bhutan Marble and Minerals Ltd: Hotel Taktsang, RICB Bldg, Doibom Lam, POB 199, Thimphu; tel. and fax 323131; Man. Dir T. S. GIRIJAPATHY.

Bhutan Polythene Co Ltd: POB 152, Phuentsholing; tel. 252407; fax 252653; e-mail drukpipe@druknet.net.bt; f. 1989; 100%-owned by private investors; mfrs of high- and medium-density polyethylene pipes; Man. Dir/CEO K. S. DHENDUP.

Chhundu Enterprises: POB 131, Phuentsholing; tel. 371104; fax 252786; operates Bhutan Dolomite Mine, Pugli, and Khagrakhola Dolomite Mine, Gomtu; Propr/Chair. Dasho LHENDUP DORJI; Gen. Man. P. THOMAS OOMMEN.

Dechen Construction Ltd: POB 231, Thimphu; tel. 322976.

Dhendup Group: POB 188, Phuentsholing; tel. 252802; fax 252440; e-mail ajaybtn@druknet.net.bt, conglomerate consisting of:

Dhendup Enterprises: POB 182, Thimphu; tel. 323133; fax 323779; e-mail dilinfo@druknet.net.bt.

Dhendup Construction.

Dhendup Home Industries: Phuentsholing; tel. 252621; mfrs and suppliers of RCC spun pipes and electrical poles.

Dhendup Travel Service: Phuentsholing; tel. 252437; deluxe minibus service between Thimphu and Phuentsholing.

Dhendup Tshongkhang: Phuentsholing; tel. 252580; general order suppliers, hardware, electrical goods, paint, office equipment, pipe fittings, etc.

Dragon Wood Products: Thimphu; tel. 323051; fax 323130; plywood, block boards, flush doors, door/window frames; Chair. Gup LHENKEY GYALTSHEN.

Dralha Group of Industries: POB 105, Phuentsholing; tel. 252284; conglomerate consisting of: Bhutan Biscuits, Drahla Flour Mill and Druk Wood Industries; Man. Dir HRH Ashi Pema C. WANGCHUK.

Druk Penden Enterprise: Head Office, POB 226, Phuentsholing; tel. and fax 252607; e-mail drukpen@druknet.net.bt, conglomerate consisting of Druk Penden Cement Agency, Druk Penden Transport Corporation and Druk Penden Engineering.

Druk Petroleum Corpn Ltd: Phuentsholing; tel. 252861; Man. Dir SANGAY DORJI.

Druk Satair Corpn Ltd: POB 129, Samdrup Jongkhar; tel. 251106; fax 251226; e-mail dsatair@druknet.net.bt; f. 1993; mining and sale of gypsum; auth. cap. Nu 100m.; annual capacity of 90,000 metric tons; Man. Dir SANGEY WANGDI.

Dungsam Cement Authority: Nganglam; tel. 324638; fax 325496; f. 1988 as Dungsum Cement Project, postponed Nov. 1989, revived July 1992 (as part of Seventh and Eighth Five-Year Plans); govt-sponsored; Gen. Man. P. SHEORAN.

Eastern Bhutan Coal Co: POB 107, Samdrup Jongkhar; tel. 251016; fax 251159; e-mail ebcc@druknet.net.bt; mining and supplier of non-coking coal to cement plants and heavy industries.

Handicrafts Development Corpn: Thimphu; tel. 322670; fax 323732; f. 1971 as Handicrafts Emporium; taken over by Bhutan Women's Assen in 1991; Man. Dir LUNGTEN WANGDE.

Karma Group Organisation: POB 57, Phuentsholing; tel. 252304; fax 252391; incorporates Karma Feeds (tel. 252602), Karma Steel Furniture Factory (tel. 252303), Karma Steel Works (Gomtu), Karma Tshongkhang (tel. 253761), Druk Carpets (tel. 252004), Druk Dolomite Corpn (Gomtu) and Slates and Granite Mines (tel. 252890); exports boulders, dolomite and woollen carpets; contractors for road and building construction; contractors for supply of charcoal; mfrs of animal feed and steel furniture; Man. Dir KARMA DORJI.

Lhaki Group Organisation: POB 179, Thimpu; tel. 322570; fax 323916; trading conglomerate with following associates: Lhaki General Stores, Lhaki Construction Co, Lhaki Zokhang, Lhaki Medical Stores, Lhaki Cement Pvt Ltd (Gomtu; tel. 371042; fax 371020; e-mail st@druknet.net.bt), Lhaki Hardware Stores (Phuentsholing; tel. 2451) and Bhutan Mining Enterprises (Pagli; dolomite powder factory); Chair. Gup UGYEN DORJI.

Peljorkhang Enterprise: 11 Chang Lam, POB 187, Thimphu; tel. 323386; fax 322716; computer services; Man. Dir KARMA SINGAY.

Rabten Wood Industries: POB 72, Industrial Estate, Phuentsholing; tel. 252213; fax 252908; f. 1988; manufactures and exports (to Europe) wood products; Man. Dir Lt YENZING DHENDUP.

Singye Group of Companies: Singye Agencies, POB 336, Phuentsholing; tel. 252188; fax 253002; e-mail sagencies@druknet.net.bt; incorporates Singye Industries Pvt Ltd (POB 289, Thimphu; tel. 322585; fax 324152); authorized dealers for motor vehicles and lubricants; engineering.

Tashi Group of Companies: TCC Complex Bldg, POB 78, Phuentsholing; tel. 252246; fax 252110; e-mail tashi@druknet.net.bt; f. 1959; Bhutan's major privately owned commercial group active in wholesale and retail trade, insurance, real estate, tourism, agriculture, hotels, mining, construction and manufacturing; turnover: Nu 3,000m. (1997); Chair. Dasho UGEN DORJI; Man. Dir P. K. RAO.

Ugen Trading House: POB 231, Thimphu; tel. 321019; fax 321071; e-mail ugen@druknet.net.bt; supplier of automobiles, computer software, telecom consumer goods, electrical goods and consultancy.

Yangzom Cement Industry Ltd: POB 331, Tashi Jong, Samtse; tel. 365291; producer of portland cement.

TRADE UNIONS

Under long-standing legislation, trade union activity is illegal in Bhutan.

Transport

ROADS AND TRACKS

In June 1999 there were 3,690.5 km of roads in Bhutan, of which 2,228.9 km were black-topped. Surfaced roads link the important border towns of Phuentsholing, Gelephu, Sarpang and Samdrup Jongkhar in southern Bhutan to towns in West Bengal and Assam in India. There is a shortage of road transport. Yaks, ponies and mules are still the chief means of transport on the rough mountain tracks. By 1990 most of the previously government-operated transport facilities (mainly buses and minibuses) on major and subsidiary routes had been transferred to private operators on the basis of seven-year contracts.

Road Safety and Transport Authority: Thimphu; tel. 321282; fax 322538; under Ministry of Communications; regulates condition of goods and passenger transport services; Dir YESHI TSHERING.

Transport Corpn of Bhutan: Phuentsholing; tel. 252476; f. 1982; subsidiary of Royal Insurance Corpn of Bhutan; operates direct coach service between Phuentsholing and Kolkata via Siliguri.

Other operators are Barma Travels (f. 1990), Dawa Transport (Propr SHERUB WANGCHUCK), Dhendup Travel Service (Phuentsholing; tel. 252437), Gyamtsho Transport, Gurung Transport Service, Namgay Transport, Nima Travels (Phuentsholing; tel. 252384), and Rimpung Travels (Phuentsholing; tel. 252354).

Lorries for transporting goods are operated by the private sector.

CIVIL AVIATION

There is an international airport at Paro. There are also some 30 helicopter landing pads, which are used, by arrangement with the Indian military and aviation authorities, solely by government officials. The Council of Ministers approved the operation of a domestic helicopter service to improve mobility and to promote tourism, to be operated by Bhutan Airways Pvt Ltd. An ambulance helicopter, donated by a Swiss company, was to become available at the end of 2002.

Department of Civil Aviation: c/o Ministry of Communications, Woochu, Paro; tel. 271347; fax 271909; e-mail aviation@druknet.bt; Dir PHALA DORJI.

Druk-Air Corpn Ltd (Royal Bhutan Airlines): Head Office, Nemizampa, PO Paro; tel. 271856; fax 271861; e-mail drukair@druknet.net.bt; internet www.drukair.com; national airline; f. 1981; became fully operational in 1983; services from Paro to Bangladesh, India, Myanmar (from October 2002), Nepal and Thailand; charter services also undertaken; Chair. Dasho Lyonpo JIGMI Y. THINLEY; Man. Dir SANGAY KHANDU.

Tourism

Bhutan was opened to tourism in 1975. In 2001 the total number of foreign visitors was 6,462. Receipts from tourism in 2000 totalled US $9.87m. Tourists travel in organized 'package', cultural or trekking tours, or individually, accompanied by trained guides. Hotels have been constructed at Phuentsholing, Paro, Bumthang, Wangduephodrang and Thimphu, with lodges at Trongsa, Trashigang and Mongar. In addition, there are many small privately operated hotels and guest-houses. Plans for three foreign-managed commercial hotels, in the style of resorts, were under way in early 2002. The Government exercises close control over the development of tourism. In 1987 the National Assembly resolved that all monasteries, mountains and other holy places should be inaccessible to tourists from 1988 (this resolution is flexibly interpreted, however—e.g. Japanese Buddhist tour groups are permitted to visit 'closed' monasteries). In 1991 the Government began transferring the tourism industry to the private sector and licences were issued to new private tourism operators. Rules were introduced in 1995, asserting more stringent controls over private operators, through the Tourism Authority of Bhutan (TAB). In 1998 the Government's tourism policy was liberalized further; by the end of 2001 94 private travel agencies were operating in Bhutan. In 2001 the TAB was reorganized as the Department of Tourism, under the Ministry of Trade and Industry. The Government had identified the industry's potential to grow and to provide significant employment opportunities.

Department of Tourism: POB 126, Thimphu; tel. 323252; fax 323695; e-mail tab@druknet.net.bt; f. 1991; under regulatory authority of Ministry of Trade and Industry; exercises overall authority over tourism policy, pricing, hotel, restaurant and travel agency licensing, visa approvals, etc.; Dir TSHERING YONTEN; Dir SANGAY WANGDI.

Bhutan Tourism Corporation Ltd: POB 159, Thimphu; tel. 322854; fax 323392; e-mail btcl@druknet.bt; internet www.kingdomofbhutan.com.

Association of Bhutan Travel Operators: POB 938, Thimphu; tel. 322862; fax 325286; e-mail abto@net.druknet.net.bt; f. 1998 to provide forum for members' views and to unite, supervise and co-ordinate activities of members; Chair. Dasho UGEN TSECHUP DORJI.

Defence

The strength of the Royal Bhutan Army, which is under the direct command of the King, is officially said to number just over 6,000 and is based on voluntary recruitment augmented by a form of conscription. Part-time militia training for senior school pupils, graduates and civil servants was in operation in 1989–91; subsequently, this training was held in abeyance (although refresher courses are held for those previously trained). Regular army training facilities are provided, on a functional basis, by an Indian military training team (IMTRAT), whose main personnel are stationed at Ha. In addition, the Royal Bhutan Army's Wing 5 is stationed at the Shaba training facility, and a number of militia training camps have been established throughout the country. Militia courses, lasting up to two years, have been provided since late 1990 with the aim of establishing a 'home guard' corps to protect public and government installations and facilities. The Royal Bhutan Army, the Royal Bhutan Guards and the Royal Bhutan Police were significantly strengthened in 2000–01 owing to the growing numbers of armed Indian militants occupying military camps on Bhutanese territory.

No reference is made in the Indo-Bhutan Treaty to any aid by India for the defence of Bhutan. In November 1958, however, the Prime Minister of India declared that any act of aggression against Bhutan would be regarded as an act of aggression against India.

Chief of Operations, Royal Bhutan Army: Lt-Gen. LAM DORJI.

Education

Traditionally, education in Bhutan was purely monastic, and the establishment of the contemporary state education system, with English as the medium of instruction, was the result of the reforming zeal of the third King, Jigme Dorji Wangchuck. The proposed outlay on education under the Eighth Plan (1997–2002) was about 9.4% of total expenditure. The 1998/99 budget allocated an estimated Nu 912m. (12.9% of total projected expenditure) to education. Education is not compulsory, but virtually free education (nominal fees are demanded), including degree courses, is provided by the State. There are no mission schools in Bhutan. Since 1988 seven privately-operated schools have been established (the majority in Thimphu); these schools are under the supervision of the Department of Education.

The total number of enrolled students in Bhutan was 14,000 in 1974. By July 2001, however, the total had risen to 127,073. In the mid-1980s several hundred primary students had to be denied admission to schools in Thimphu because of a lack of places. In order to accommodate additional children, community schools (established in 1989 as 'extended classrooms'—ECRs, but renamed, as above, in 1991) were set up as essentially one-teacher schools for basic primary classes, whence children were to be 'streamed' to other schools.

Pre-primary education usually lasts for one year. Primary education begins at six years of age and lasts for seven years. Secondary education, beginning at the age of 13, lasts for a further four years, comprising two cycles of two years each. In 1988 the total enrolment at primary and secondary schools was equivalent to 18% of the school-age population (males 22%; females 13%). In that year primary enrolment was equivalent to 26% of the relevant age-group (31% of boys; 20% of girls), while the comparable ratio for secondary enrolment was only 5% (boys 7%; girls 2%).

Enrolment at primary schools increased from 9,039 (including only 456 girls) in 1970 to 51,776 (including 22,862 girls) in 1997. Between 1970 and 1997, enrolment at secondary schools increased from 714 (boys 690; girls 24) to 26,435 (boys 14,460; girls 11,975). The latter total included 405 students (boys 224; girls 181) in teacher-training and 1,889 (boys 1,417; girls 472) receiving vocational instruction. In 2001 there were 18,761 pupils in community schools—10,165 boys (54%) and 8,596 girls (46%). In the separate (non-community school) primary classes (including those at junior high schools), of the 73,770 pupils, 39,287 (53%) were boys and 34,483 (47%) were girls. In the senior classes at high and junior high schools in 1997, of the 14,740 students, 8,392 (57%) were boys and 6,348 (43%) were girls. In the two post-secondary classes country-wide (including Sherubtse college), there were 939 students, of whom 590 (63%) were boys and 349 (37%) were girls.

The total number of teachers in Bhutan increased from 461 in 1970 to 2,715 in 1997; of these, 293 were employed in tertiary and special institutions, 250 in community schools and 71 in private schools. However, also of this total, 516 (19%) were non-nationals, reflecting the acute, and growing, shortage of qualified teachers. To compensate, in part, for this deficiency, teaching is provided by contract teachers from India (mainly Kerala) and by young volunteers from New Zealand and the UK, as well as through the UN Volunteers scheme. In July 2001 the total number of teachers working in Bhutan was 3,972 of whom 3,640 were employed at primary and secondary schools and 176 at higher institutes. All of the schools are co-educational and, in general, follow a syllabus reflecting British and Indian practices. English is the medium of instruction, and Dzongkha is a compulsory subject. In 1999 there were more than 320 educational institutions under the supervision of the Department of Education, including 254 primary schools (including community schools), 51 junior high schools, 21 high schools, one degree college and nine other post-secondary institutions. A National Board of Secondary Education and Training was established in 1984, with the aim of revising existing curricula to give a stronger national content. In the same year, the existing teacher-training college at Samtse was upgraded to a National Institute of Education (NIE) for secondary teachers. Primary teachers are also trained at the NIE as well as at the Paro teacher-training college. A second teacher-training college is to be built at Kanglung. In 1986 a Royal Institute of Management (RIM) was established in

Thimphu, incorporating two existing commercial schools. In the same year, a revised curriculum, called the 'New Approach to Primary Education' (NAPE), was implemented in 12 schools. NAPE emphasizes practical studies and learning from, and understanding, the local environment. NAPE was extended to all primary and junior high schools in 1991.

In addition to the schools and training institutes in Bhutan, regular courses are organized by different government departments in agriculture, computer programming, health, secretarial work, etc. A number of students are receiving higher education and training in various technical fields in India, Australia, Bangladesh, Japan, New Zealand, Singapore, the UK, Switzerland and the USA. Returning graduates must complete a one-year induction course, during which they must perform practical work, arranged by the RIM, before becoming eligible to sit the competitive examination for entrance into the civil service. Students from one part of the country are encouraged by the Government to seek admission to schools and educational institutions in other regions, as part of its policy to increase integration of people throughout the country.

There are five main linguistic groups in Bhutan but Dzongkha, spoken in western Bhutan, has been designated the official language. According to estimates by UNESCO, the rate of adult illiteracy averaged 57.8% (males 43.7%; females 71.8%) in 1995.

Indo-Bhutan Treaty

The Treaty of Friendship with India was signed on 8 August 1949.

Treaty of Friendship between the Government of India and the Government of Bhutan

Article 1. There shall be perpetual peace and friendship between the Government of India and the Government of Bhutan.

Article 2. The Government of India undertakes to exercise no interference in the internal administration of Bhutan. On its part the Government of Bhutan agrees to be guided by the advice of the Government of India in regard to its external relations.

Article 3. In place of the compensation granted to the Government of Bhutan under Article 4 of the Treaty of Sinchula and enhanced by the treaty of the eighth day of January 1910 and the temporary subsidy of Rupees one lakh per annum granted in 1942, the Government of India agrees to make an annual payment of Rupees five lakhs to the Government of Bhutan. And it is further hereby agreed that the said annual payment shall be made on the 10th day of January every year, the first payment being made on the 10th day of January 1950. This payment shall continue so long as this treaty remains in force and its terms are duly observed.

Article 4. Further to mark the friendship existing and continuing between the said governments, the Government of India shall, within one year from the date of signature of this treaty, return to the Government of Bhutan about 32 square miles of territory in the area known as Dewangiri. The Government of India shall appoint a competent officer or officers to mark out the area so returned to the Government of Bhutan.

Article 5. There shall, as heretofore, be free trade and commerce between the territories of the Government of India and of the Government of Bhutan; and the Government of India agrees to grant to the Government of Bhutan every facility for the carriage, by land and water, of its produce throughout the territory of the Government of India, including the right to use such forest roads as may be specified by mutual agreement from time to time.

Article 6. The Government of India agrees that the Government of Bhutan shall be free to import with the assistance and approval of the Government of India, from or through India into Bhutan, whatever arms, ammunition, machinery, warlike materials or stores may be required or desired for the strength and welfare of Bhutan and that this arrangement shall hold good for all time as long as the Government of India is satisfied that the intentions of the Government of Bhutan are friendly and that there is no danger to India from such importations. The Government of Bhutan, on the other hand, agrees that there shall be no export of such arms, ammunition, etc., across the frontier of Bhutan either by the Government of Bhutan or by private individuals.

Article 7. The Government of India and the Government of Bhutan agree that Bhutanese subjects residing in Indian territories shall have equal justice with Indian subjects, and that Indian subjects residing in Bhutan shall have equal justice with the subjects of the Government of Bhutan.

Article 8. (1) The Government of India shall, on demand being duly made in writing by the Government of Bhutan, take proceedings in accordance with the provisions of Indian Extradition Act, 1903 (of which a copy shall be furnished to the Government of Bhutan), for the surrender of all Bhutanese subjects accused of any of the crimes specified in the first schedule of the said Act who may take refuge in Indian territory.

(2) The Government of Bhutan shall, on requisition being duly made by the Government of India, or by any officer authorized by the Government of India in this behalf, surrender any Indian subjects, or subjects of a foreign power, whose extradition may be required in pursuance of any agreement or arrangements made by the Government of India with the said power, accused of any of the crimes specified in the first schedule of Act XV of 1903, who may take refuge in the territory under the jurisdiction of the Government of Bhutan and also any Bhutanese subjects who, after committing any of the crimes referred to in Indian territory shall flee into Bhutan, on such evidence of their guilt being produced as that satisfy the local court of the district in which the offence may have been committed.

Article 9. Any differences and disputes arising in the application or interpretation of this treaty shall in the first instance be settled by negotiation. If within three months of the start of negotiations no settlement is arrived at, then the matter shall be referred to the Arbitration of three arbitrators, who shall be nationals of either India or Bhutan, chosen on the following basis:

(i) one person nominated by the Government of India;

(ii) one person nominated by the Government of Bhutan; and

(iii) a Judge of the Federal court or of a High Court of India, to be chosen by the Government of Bhutan, who shall be Chairman.

The judgment of this tribunal shall be final and executed without delay by either party.

Article 10. This treaty shall continue in force in perpetuity unless terminated or modified by mutual consent.

Bibliography

Aris, Michael. *Bhutan: The Early History of a Himalayan Kingdom.* Warminster, Aris and Phillips, 1979.

The Raven Crown: the origins of Buddhist monarchy in Bhutan. London, Serindia Publications, 1994.

Aris, Michael, and Hutt, Michael (Eds). *Bhutan: Aspects of Culture and Development.* Gartmore, Kiscadale, 1994.

Armington, Stan. *Lonely Planet Bhutan.* Hawthorn, Vic, Lonely Planet Publications, 1998.

Aung San Suu Kyi. *Let's Visit Bhutan.* London, Burke Publishing Co. Ltd, 1985.

Basu, Gautam Kumar. *Bhutan: The Political Economy of Development.* Denver, CO, Academic Books, 2000.

Chakravarti, P. C. *India's China Policy.* Bloomington, Indiana University Press, 1962.

Choden, Kunzang. *Bhutanese Tales of the Yeti.* Bangkok, White Lotus Press, 1997.

Collister, Peter. *Bhutan and the British.* London, Serindia Publications, 1987.

Cooper, Robert. *Bhutan.* New York, Marshall Cavendish, 2001.

Crossette, Barbara. *So Close to Heaven: The Vanishing Buddhist Kingdoms of the Himalayas.* New York, Alfred A. Knopf, Inc, 1995.

Dago Tshering (Ed.). *Bhutan: Himalayan Kingdom.* New York, Royal Government of the Kingdom of Bhutan, 1979.

Dhakal, D. N. S., and Strawn, Christopher. *Bhutan: A Movement in Exile.* New Delhi, Nirala Publications, 1994.

Dogra, Ramesh C. (compiler). *Bhutan* (bibliography). London, Clio, 1991.

Dompnier, Robert. *Bhutan: Kingdom of the Dragon*. Boston, Shambala Publications, 1999.

Dorji Wangmo Wangchuk (HM Ashi). *Of Rainbows and Clouds: The life of Yab Ugyen Dorji as told to his Daughter*. London, Serindia Publications, 1999.

Dowman, Keith (Trans.). *The Divine Madman: The Sublime Life and Songs of Drukpa Kinley*. London, Rider, 1980.

Edmunds, Tom Owen. *Bhutan: Land of the Thunder Dragon*. London, Elm Tree Books, 1989.

Gregson, Jonathan. *Kingdoms Beyond the Clouds: Journeys in Search of the Himalayan Kings*. London, Pan Macmillan, 2001.

Grover, Verinder (Ed.). *Encyclopaedia of SAARC Nations: Vol. 6, Bhutan*. New Delhi, Deep and Deep Publications, 1997.

Gupta, Bhabani Sen. *Bhutan: Towards a Grass-root Participatory Polity*. Delhi, Konark Publishers Pvt Ltd, 1999.

Hickman, Katie. *Dreams of the Peaceful Dragon: A Journey through Bhutan*. London, Gollancz, 1987.

Hutt, Michael (Ed.). *Bhutan: Perspectives on Conflict and Dissent*. Gartmore, Kiscadale, 1994.

International Bank for Reconstruction and Development (World Bank). *Bhutan: Development Planning in a Unique Environment*. Washington, DC, World Bank, 1989.

Karan, P. P. *Bhutan: A Physical and Cultural Geography*. Lexington, University of Kentucky Press, 1967.

Bhutan: Development amid Environmental and Cultural Preservation. Tokyo, Institute for the Study of Languages and Cultures of Asia and Africa, 1987.

Karma Ura. *The Hero with a Thousand Eyes: A Historical Novel*. Thimphu, 1995.

The Ballad of Pemi Tshewang Tashi: A Wind-borne Feather. Thimphu, 1996.

Kuhn, Delia, and Kuhn, Ferdinand. *Borderlands*. New York, Knopf, 1962.

Lamb, Alastair. *The China-India Border: The Origins of the Disputed Boundaries*. London, Chatham House Essays, Oxford University Press, 1964.

Asian Frontiers: Studies in a Continuing Problem. London, Pall Mall Press, 1968.

Leifer, M. *Himalaya: Mountains of Destiny*. London, Galley Press, 1962.

Lumley, Joanna. *Joanna Lumley in the Kingdom of the Thunder Dragon*. London, BBC Books, 1997.

Mathew, Joseph C. *Ethnic Conflict in Bhutan*. New Delhi, Nirala Publications, 1999.

Mehra, G. N. *Bhutan: Land of the Peaceful Dragon*. New Delhi, Vikas, 1974.

Mehra, Parshotam. *The Younghusband Expedition. An Interpretation*. Asia Publishing House, 1968.

Misra, H. N. *Bhutan: Problems and Policies*. New Delhi, Heritage Publishers, 1988.

Misra, R. C. *Emergence of Bhutan*. Jaipur, Sandarbh Prakashan, 1989.

Olschak, Blanche C. *Ancient Bhutan: A Study on Early Buddhism in the Himalayas*. Zürich, Swiss Foundation for Alpine Research, 1979.

Olsen, Gunnar (Ed.). *The Case of Bhutan: Development in a Himalayan Kingdom*. Copenhagen, Danish UN Asscn, 1985.

Parmanand. *The Politics of Bhutan: Retrospect and Prospect*. Delhi, Pragati Publications, 1992.

Pommaret, Françoise. *Bhutan*. Hong Kong, Odyssey Passport, 1998.

Punja, Shobita. *Great Monuments of India, Bhutan, Nepal, Pakistan and Shri Lanka*. Hong Kong, The Guidebook Company, 1994.

Rahul, Ram. *Royal Bhutan*. Delhi, ABC Publishing House, 1983.

Ramakant, and Misra, R. C. (Eds). *Bhutan: Society and Polity*. New Delhi, Indus Publishing Co, 1996.

Robinson, Francis (Ed.). *The Cambridge Encyclopaedia of India, Pakistan, Bangladesh, Sri Lanka, Nepal, Bhutan and the Maldives*. Cambridge, Cambridge University Press, 1989.

Rose, Leo E. *The Politics of Bhutan*. Ithaca, NY, Cornell University Press, 1977.

Rustomji, N. K. *Enchanted Frontiers: Sikkim, Bhutan and India's North-Eastern Borderlands*. Calcutta, Oxford University Press, 1973.

Bhutan: The Dragon Kingdom in Crisis. New Delhi, Oxford University Press, 1978.

Savada, Andrea Matles (Ed.). *Nepal and Bhutan: Country Studies*. Washington, DC, Library of Congress for the Department of the Army, 1993.

Schicklgruber, Christian, and Pommaret, Françoise (Eds). *Bhutan: Mountain Fortress of the Gods*. London, Serindia Publications, 1997.

Sharma, S. K., and Sharma, Usha (Eds). *Encyclopaedia of Sikkim and Bhutan* (3 vols). New Delhi, Anmol Publications Pvt Ltd, 1997.

Singh, Amar Kaur Jasbir. *Himalayan Triangle*. London, British Library, 1988.

Singh, Nagendra. *Bhutan, a Kingdom in the Himalayas*. New Delhi, Thomson Press, 1980 (revised edn 1985).

Sinha, A. C. *Bhutan: ethnic identity and national dilemma*. New Delhi, Reliance Publishing House, 1991.

Slocum, Thomas. *In His Majesty's Civil Service: and other contemporary tales of the kingdom of Bhutan*. New York, Rivercross Publications, 1998.

Snellgrove, David L. *Himalayan Pilgrimage*. Oxford, Bruno Cassirer, 1961.

Solverson, Howard. *The Jesuit and the Dragon: The Life of Father William Mackey in the Himalayan Kingdom of Bhutan*. Montréal, Robert Davies Publishing, 1995.

Upadhyay, B. N. *From Mountain Kingdom to Public Sector*. New Delhi, Devika Publications, 2000.

Vas, E. A. *The Dragon Kingdom: Journeys through Bhutan*. New Delhi, Lancer International, 1986.

Verma, Ravi. *India's Role in the Emergence of Contemporary Bhutan*. Delhi, Capital Publishing House, 1988.

van Strydonck, Guy, Pommaret-Imaeda, F., and Imaeda, Yoshiro. *Bhutan: A Kingdom of the Eastern Himalayas*. London, Serindia, 1984.

von Nebesky-Wojkowitz, René. *Where the Mountains are Gods*. London, Weidenfeld and Nicolson, 1956.

White, John Claude. *Sikkim and Bhutan: Twenty-One Years on the North-East Frontier, 1887–1908*. London, Arnold, 1909.

Williamson, Margaret D. *Memoirs of a Political Officer's Wife in Tibet, Sikkim and Bhutan*. London, Wisdom Publications, 1988.

Woodman, Dorothy. *Himalayan Frontiers: a political review of British, Chinese, Indian and Russian rivalries*. London, Barrie and Jenkins, 1969.

Zeppa, Jamie. *Beyond the Earth and Sky: A Journey into Bhutan*. New York, Riverhead Books, 1999.

BRUNEI

Physical and Social Geography

HARVEY DEMAINE

PHYSICAL FEATURES AND CLIMATE

The Sultanate of Brunei (Negara Brunei Darussalam) covers an area of 5,765 sq km (2,226 sq miles) and faces the South China Sea along the north-west coast of the island of Borneo, most of which comprises the Indonesian territory of Kalimantan. On its landward side, Brunei is both surrounded and split into two separate units by Sarawak, part of Malaysia. Brunei is divided into four districts: Brunei/Muara, Tutong and Seria/Belait, in the western section of Brunei, and Temburong, forming the eastern section.

The greater part of Brunei's small territory consists of a low coastal plain, and only on its southern margins does it attain heights of more than 300 m above sea-level. Brunei's highest point is Bukit Pagon, in the east of the country, which reaches 1,841 m above sea-level. Situated only 4°–5° N of the Equator, Brunei has a consistently hot and humid climate, with mean monthly temperatures of around 27°C and a heavy annual rainfall, well distributed throughout the year, of more than 2,500 mm. Except for those areas that have been cleared for permanent cultivation in the coastal zone, about three-quarters of the country is covered by dense equatorial forest, although this has deteriorated in places as a result of shifting cultivation.

POPULATION AND RESOURCES

At the census of August 2001 the population of Brunei was 332,844, compared with 260,482 at the August 1991 census. In 2001 66.7% of the population were Malay and 11.1% Chinese. Indigenous races, which comprised 3.5% of the population, are mainly Muruts, Kedayans and Dusuns. More than 50% of the population were less than 20 years of age in 2000. The Chinese reside mainly in Bandar Seri Begawan (formerly Brunei Town), the capital, and Seria. Bandar Seri Begawan, which occupies an impressive site overlooking the large natural inlet of Brunei Bay, had an estimated population of 27,285 in 2001.

Brunei's natural resources consist almost exclusively of petroleum and natural gas. In the 1980s new petroleum reserves were discovered at Seria, the first significant onshore oilfield in Brunei. Further reserves were discovered in new and existing offshore fields in the early 1990s. At the end of 2000 proven petroleum reserves amounted to 1,400m. barrels, sufficient to maintain output at that year's levels (averaging 195,000 barrels per day) for less than 20 years.

The major source of future development is expected to be natural gas, of which Brunei had proven reserves of 390,000m. cu m at the end of 2000. Natural gas reserves in 2000 were estimated to be sufficient to maintain output until at least 2033, assuming current rates of production. Production of natural gas, which in 2001 totalled 11,751m. cu m, is mostly destined for export to Japan under long-term contracts.

History

C. M. TURNBULL

EARLY HISTORY

One of the world's smallest states, Brunei was once the centre of a great maritime empire. Its origins are obscure, but it was probably founded in the late seventh century by a refugee prince fleeing from the Khmer conquest of Funan. From that time until the 16th century it was the centre of three successive empires, which at their height held sway over much of coastal Borneo and the Philippines. Known to the Chinese as Po-ni, the port lay on the main trading route between China, the western part of the Indonesian archipelago and the Indian Ocean. There was extensive trade between the area and China during the period of the Tang and Song dynasties.

About the middle of the 15th century Brunei became an independent sultanate. The first Sultan married a Malay princess from the powerful Muslim sultanate of Melaka (Malacca), adopted Islam as the court religion and introduced an efficient administration, modelled on Melaka. Brunei profited from trade with Melaka but achieved even greater prosperity after the great Malay port was conquered by the Portuguese in 1511, when many Muslim traders diverted their custom to Brunei. The first European visitors were members of the Spanish expedition which had been led by the Portuguese navigator, Fernão de Magalhães (Magellan). They arrived in 1521, during the reign of Bolkiah, the most illustrious of Brunei's sultans, and described the capital as a large and wealthy city of some 25,000 households, with an impressive and cultivated royal court. Brunei established friendly relations with Portugal. In 1526 the two countries concluded a commercial arrangement, and the Portuguese established a trading post at Brunei. As Portuguese trade with China and Japan expanded, Brunei became a regular port of call on the route between Melaka and Macao, and the Chinese community expanded greatly. Brunei already had quite a large Chinese community, and a 15th-century Chinese trader had married into the royal family and become Sultan himself.

The first half of the 16th century was Brunei's 'golden age', when it claimed suzerainty over the whole coast of Borneo, the Sulu archipelago and Mindanao, and forced Manila to pay tribute. The empire was not a centralized polity but comprised a group of individual river states ruled by vassals, who paid obeisance to the Sultan and secured a revenue through river tolls and poll taxes. The empire depended almost entirely on its ability to control regional trade.

Brunei came into conflict with the Spaniards, who established themselves in the northern Philippines in the latter part of the 16th century. The rivals clashed over trade and religion, and in 1578 the Spaniards seized Brunei for a short period and attempted unsuccessfully to impose Christianity. Eventually the Spaniards abandoned attempts to subdue the southern Philippines, but they raided Brunei periodically, and vassal chiefs in Mindanao and the Sulu archipelago took advantage of Brunei's weakness to break away and establish their own independence. Sulu was an aggressive state, the home of the infamous Balanini pirates, who ravaged the Borneo coasts and even ventured as far as the Straits of Melaka. As recompense for its intervention in a civil war, which racked Brunei for 12 years in the mid-17th century, Sulu claimed the whole of North Borneo (present-day Sabah), a claim that remains unresolved.

Brunei continued to decline, and by the early 19th century the Sultan could lay claim only to the district centring on Brunei Town itself, the Sarawak River and the western coast of northern Borneo. Even here he exerted only weak control along the coastal strip and the lower reaches of the main rivers.

Pirates operated along the coast of North Borneo, and Brunei Town became little more than a trading centre for their plunder and slaves. The stability of the sultanate was also threatened by disputed successions and rebellious chiefs. When antimony was discovered in the Sarawak valley in 1824, Brunei officials were sent to organize local Dayaks to mine the ore. In 1835 the corruption of the Brunei Governor drove the local chiefs and Dayaks to revolt. The province was still in a state of armed rebellion when an English gentleman adventurer, James (later Sir James) Brooke, arrived four years later. In 1841, in return for his help in settling the revolt, Brooke was granted the Sarawak River district and the title of Raja, which was confirmed by the Sultan the following year when Brooke paid the customary tribute at the Brunei court.

BRITISH INTERVENTION

The British connection was to lead to the dissolution of most of Brunei's empire, but was arguably responsible for the continued existence of the sultanate. When Brooke's position at the Brunei court was threatened, the British Navy intervened, and the Sultan was compelled to confirm Brooke's tenure at Sarawak for himself and his successors in perpetuity, to give the island of Labuan to the United Kingdom, and to sign a treaty, in 1847, undertaking not to cede any further territory without British approval. In 1853, as a result of conflict with pirates, the Sultan ceded to Brooke the troublesome Saribas and Skarang districts, which later constituted the Second Division of Sarawak. Eight years later, further piracy, which threatened the profitable sago trade of the Mukah and Oya valleys, compelled the Sultan to cede to Brooke the vast Rejang River basin, which became the Third Division of Sarawak.

James Brooke's successor, his nephew Charles (later Sir Charles) Brooke, wished to extend Sarawak's rule over the lawless upper Baram area, the scene of recurrent friction between the people of Sarawak and Brunei, but for many years the British Government opposed this. In 1874 the British Government rejected Charles Brooke's proposal to place Brunei under the protection of either the United Kingdom or Sarawak. In 1877, however, the Sultan granted the northern part of Borneo (present-day Sabah) to a Hong Kong-based company owned by a British businessman, Alfred Dent, and the Austrian Consul, Von Overbeck. Four years later, Dent purchased the Austrian share, and in that same year the British Government granted him a royal charter to form the British North Borneo Company.

Fears of rival foreign ambitions in the region, inspired by Sultan Abdul Mumin's advancing years and uncertainty concerning the succession, prompted the United Kingdom to give approval in 1882 for Charles Brooke to obtain cession of the Baram basin, which became the Fourth Division of Sarawak. In 1884 he also acquired the Trusan valley. Now only the heartland of Brunei remained, under growing pressure from both Sarawak and the British North Borneo Company. In 1885 the new Sultan, Hashim, promised the Brunei chiefs that he would not alienate any further territory, and in 1888 the United Kingdom made Brunei, Sarawak and North Borneo protectorates, thus assuming paramountcy over the whole of North-West Borneo. The Governor of the Straits Settlements was appointed High Commissioner for Brunei, but the British Government did not appoint a Resident at the Brunei court, and Sarawak continued to present a threat to the sultanate. In 1890 the chiefs of Limbang, which had been in a state of rebellion for some years, asked Raja Brooke to take over their district, which was then joined with Trusan to form the Fifth Division of Sarawak. This deprived Brunei of a valuable food-producing area and divided it into two parts. The British Government offered to pay compensation to the Sultan but the offer was never formally accepted, so that this came to be regarded as a cession by default. In 1916 the United Kingdom formally recognized Limbang as part of Sarawak, but the Sultans of Brunei never acknowledged the cession, and the status of Limbang remained controversial.

By the early 20th century the Tutong and Belait districts were in revolt, many people were migrating into adjoining Sarawak, and the sultanate had contracted to little more than 2,000 sq miles. The United Kingdom considered dividing what remained of Brunei between Sarawak and the British North Borneo Company, but decided against this after considering a detailed report by Stewart McArthur, an officer of the Malayan civil service, who spent six months investigating the situation in Brunei in 1904. In the following year the British Government signed an agreement with the Sultan and senior chiefs, establishing Brunei as a full protectorate, where all matters relating to administration, legislation and taxation were to be conducted on the advice of a British Resident. McArthur was appointed as first incumbent of this post in 1906, and, apart from the period of Japanese occupation, the British Resident remained the effective ruler of Brunei until 1959. The administration was modelled on that of the (British) Federated Malay States, and the Resident was always an official of the Malayan civil service seconded from the peninsula. A modern civil service was created, a land code introduced, and the state revenues organized. The traditional State Council was formalized, with the Sultan presiding but with the Resident as the dominant influence. Despite some dissatisfaction, quasi-colonial rule brought peace and stability to the country and guaranteed Brunei's survival. Brunei's future economic prosperity was also foreshadowed in this period, when petroleum was first discovered in 1903, and a major oilfield was eventually located at Seria in 1929. By the 1930s Brunei's debts had been discharged, and revenues from petroleum exports helped to finance modest programmes in education and social services.

THE POST-WAR PERIOD

Brunei was occupied by Japanese forces from December 1941, shortly after Japan entered the Second World War, until it was liberated by Australian troops in July 1945. The immediate post-war years were devoted to rehabilitation and the resumption of petroleum production, which had been interrupted by the war.

The United Kingdom envisaged an eventual self-governing confederation embracing all the British dependencies in South-East Asia, namely the Malay Peninsula, Singapore and Borneo. As a first step, it planned to abolish protectorate status, bringing all the territories under the direct rule of the British crown. Sarawak and British North Borneo did become crown colonies, but the transition in Brunei was deferred, following difficulties encountered in abrogating the Malay States' treaties. In 1948 the Governor of Sarawak was appointed High Commissioner for Brunei, in place of the Governor of the now defunct Straits Settlements, but this did not alter the protectorate's status or the Resident's powers. Nevertheless, political changes in the region and the prospect of ultimate British withdrawal presented new threats to Brunei's security. These problems dominated Brunei politics for the next 20 years, producing two rival forms of nationalism: an enlightened paternalism, propounded by the Sultan and his supporters, and a form of popular democracy.

In 1953 Sultan Omar Ali Saifuddin III established a commission to help to formulate a written constitution for Brunei. District Councils, nominated by the Sultan, were created in 1954, but little progress was made in devising a constitution. Meanwhile, Brunei's first political party, the Parti Rakyat Brunei (PRB—Brunei People's Party), was formed in 1956, modelled on the left-wing Malayan Parti Rakyat. Its charismatic President, Sheikh Ahmad Azahari (born in Labuan of Arab-Malay parentage), had studied in Java during the Japanese occupation and taken part in the Indonesian struggle for independence against the Dutch. He spent some time in Singapore in the early 1950s, and was imprisoned briefly for organizing the first political demonstration in Brunei. While remaining loyal to the sultanate, the party advocated democratic self-government for Brunei as part of a federation of the three Borneo states. The PRB attracted considerable popular support and in 1957 petitioned the Sultan and the Colonial Office for independence. Leaders of the PRB were angered by their exclusion from the delegation that the Sultan led to London in 1958 for constitutional talks. Under the Brunei Constitution, which was promulgated in 1959, the United Kingdom retained responsibility for Brunei's defence and foreign relations but transferred internal government to the Sultan, who was to preside over an Executive Council and rule with the help of a Legislative Council and District Councils, the latter being elected by universal adult suffrage. The PRB pressed for immediate elections, for independence in Brunei by 1963 and for a merger with the other Borneo states. The Sultan preferred a closer association with the Federation of Malaya, which had gained its independence in 1957. He welcomed the proposal made by Tunku Abdul Rahman, the Malayan Prime Minister, in May 1961, mooting a Malaysian federation to include Malaya, Singapore and the three Borneo territories. This led to heated confrontation between the Sultan's supporters and the PRB.

At district council elections, which were eventually held in August 1962 after many delays, the PRB won all but one of the 55 seats, which also gave its candidates all the indirectly elective legislative council seats. The PRB's campaign had advocated internal democratic reform and rejection of the Malaysia proposal, in favour of a Borneo federation. In September the party united with politicians in Sarawak and North Borneo to form an Anti-Malaysia Alliance, for which Azahari tried to rouse international support. In December 1962, after failing in an attempt to present to the Legislative Council a proposal in favour of independence, separate from Malaysia, Azahari resorted to force and staged a rebellion through the North Borneo Liberation Army, which had strong links with the Indonesian Communist Party and with left-wing extremists in Singapore. The rebels proclaimed a Revolutionary State of North Kalimantan, with Azahari as Prime Minister. The Sultan quickly suppressed the revolt, however, with the aid of British forces from Singapore, and most of Azahari's former supporters in Sarawak and North Borneo disowned his use of force. A state of emergency was declared, the PRB was banned, Azahari went into exile in Malaya, and his supporters fled or were imprisoned. From that time the Sultan ruled by decree, and the emergency laws have been renewed every two years.

The rebellion initially strengthened Sultan Omar's resolve to join Malaysia, as a means of ensuring Brunei's permanent security. In June 1963, however, negotiations collapsed, owing mainly to disputes concerning petroleum revenues, but also to disagreement regarding the Sultan's precedence among Malay rulers. Two meetings between the Tunku and Sultan Omar failed to resolve the issue, and Brunei withdrew from the final negotiations which led to the establishment of Malaysia in September 1963. Brunei's decision not to join Malaysia soured its relations with Kuala Lumpur, and allegations about Indonesia's involvement in the December 1962 revolt strained relations with Jakarta. Brunei was isolated, more than ever dependent on the United Kingdom, and its autocratic Government and semi-colonial status exposed it to international criticism.

Following the 1962 revolt, the ban on the PRB had removed the most articulate opposition, and most other parties united to form a Brunei Alliance Party (BAP), which supported entry to Malaysia. The Sultan ignored the BAP's demand for a fully elected legislature, although he agreed to elections in 1965 for some legislative council seats and replaced the Executive Council with a Council of Ministers. The British Government exerted pressure on Sultan Omar to quicken the pace of constitutional reform, but he insisted on an appointed cabinet. In August 1966 all existing political groups united to form a Brunei People's Independence Party (BPIP), which demanded responsible government, a full ministerial system and a fully elected legislature. The British Government was impatient at the slow progress of constitutional reform, at a time when it was preparing to withdraw most of its forces 'east of Suez'. In 1967 Sultan Omar abdicated in favour of his 21-year-old son, Hassanal Bolkiah, but the ex-Sultan retained effective power. The BPIP failed to gain support at district council elections held in 1968, which were overshadowed by the young Sultan's forthcoming talks in London about the future defence of Brunei. Under a new treaty, which was signed with the United Kingdom in 1971, the 1959 Constitution was amended to give the Sultan full control of all internal matters, with the United Kingdom retaining responsibility for foreign affairs. A separate agreement provided for the stationing of a British battalion of Gurkhas in Brunei.

Brunei developed close ties with Singapore, after the latter's secession from the Federation of Malaysia in 1965, but relations with Malaysia continued to be strained for many years. Malaysia offered political asylum to PRB leaders, permitted the illegal party to open an office in Kuala Lumpur, and in 1975 sponsored a PRB delegation which presented a case for independence to the UN Committee on Decolonization. Brunei recalled all its students from Malaysia for fear that they might become a focus for dissidence, and it officially revived the Limbang claim, with former Sultan Omar crossing the border to incite Limbang villagers against Malaysia.

In 1977 the UN General Assembly adopted a Malaysian-sponsored resolution proposing free elections in Brunei, the end of the ban on political parties and the return of all political exiles to Brunei. While the British Labour Government (whose representative abstained from voting on the UN resolution) was prepared to sever its links with Brunei, the Sultan regarded the association as a protection against the possible encroachment of neighbouring governments, secessionists and political opponents within Brunei itself. The sultanate was reluctant to revise the terms of its 1971 treaty with the United Kingdom until it received assurances that Malaysia and Indonesia would respect Brunei's independence. In June 1978 Sultan Sir Hassanal Bolkiah and his father visited London in an unsuccessful attempt to resist separation from the United Kingdom. In 1979, however, they were compelled to sign an agreement whereby Brunei became a sovereign independent state on 1 January 1984. In September 1983 Brunei concluded a new defence agreement with the United Kingdom, whereby Brunei would continue, at its own expense, to employ the battalion of Gurkhas under British command.

AFTER INDEPENDENCE

When Brunei became independent the Council of Ministers was abolished in favour of a seven-member Cabinet, headed by the Sultan and including his father and two brothers. *Melayu Islam Beraja* (MIB—Malay Islamic Monarchy) was proclaimed as the state ideology promoting Islamic values, an emphasis on the unique nature of Brunei-Malay culture and the importance of the role of the monarchy.

In the 1980s new laws were adopted to increase the share of petroleum revenue accruing to the State. While the demarcation between state revenue and the Sultan's personal wealth was not clearly defined and much was spent on royal prestige projects, all citizens enjoyed free medical care and education, and government housing loans. Indigenous, mainly Malay, inhabitants, *bumiputras* (sons of the soil), received preferential treatment. Even Brunei-born non-*bumiputras* were subject to stringent requirements with respect to residence and language when applications for citizenship were considered. In 1985 90% of the ethnic Chinese, who at that time constituted about one-third of the population, were classified as non-citizens excluded from state benefits. Although they still dominated the private sector, many Chinese began to emigrate.

Increasingly, Brunei's modernization and exposure to the rest of the world were regarded as a potential threat to its moral, cultural and religious traditions. At the same time rising unemployment and, more particularly, a shortage of non-manual jobs (menial work was generally undertaken by immigrant labourers) led to the emergence in the early 1990s of social problems, including drug and alcohol abuse. There was concern at the prospect of the situation deteriorating since more than one-half of the Bruneian population were aged under 20, and educational standards and employment expectations were rising. Partly in response to these incipient problems, from 1990, the state ideology (MIB) was promoted more vigorously. Muslims were encouraged to adhere more closely to the tenets of Islam, with greater emphasis on Islamic holiday celebrations, and in January 1991 the import of alcohol was banned. In December of that year the public celebration of Christmas, the Christian festival, was forbidden. The state Mufti was brought under the direct control of the Sultan rather than the Ministry of Religious Affairs and in that same year the first Islamic bank was established. Under the Seventh National Development Plan (1996–2000) more resources were devoted to building mosques, religious schools and an Islamic college. An Islamic radio station began broadcasting in 1997.

After the former Sultan's death in 1986, the Cabinet was enlarged to 11 ministers, incorporating members of the educated élite. The royal family, however, remained the dominant force in the Government, with the Sultan as Prime Minister and Minister of Defence, and his brothers, Mohamed and Jefri, responsible for foreign affairs and finance respectively. In 1985 the Sultan considered permitting the introduction of a party political system and agreed to the formation of the Parti Kebangsaan Demokratik Brunei (PKDB—Brunei National Democratic Party). The PKDB advocated greater participation in the administration of the Government, democratization and a more equitable distribution of wealth. It attracted a membership of some 3,000, comprising mainly Malay professionals and business executives, but it aroused little public support. Within a year a breakaway faction formed a new party, the Parti Perpaduan Kebangsaan Brunei (PPKB—Brunei National Solidarity Party), which emphasized greater co-operation with the Government. In 1988, however, the President and the Secretary-General of the PKDB, Abdul Latif Hamid and Abdul Latif Chuchu, were arrested and detained for two years under the provisions of the Internal Security Act. The party was dissolved after it had demanded the Sultan's resignation as Head of Government (although not as Head of State), the holding of democratic elections and the ending of the 26-year state of emergency. Meanwhile, at the beginning of 1988 a number of political detainees of the former PRB were released in a general amnesty. In 1990 all political prisoners were released, and in 1996 the few remaining PRB members were permitted to return from exile, providing that they refrained from political activity. In any event, radical politicians found it difficult to attract popular support while most Bruneians continued to enjoy a high standard of living.

In October 1992 Brunei celebrated Sultan Hassanal's Silver Jubilee, but hopes of liberal political concessions were dispelled when the Sultan marked the occasion by reaffirming the central role of the monarchy in a Malay Islamic nation. He assumed a more paternal stance, distancing himself from the extravagant lifestyle of earlier days to stress diligence and mutual responsibility to Brunei as a country with 'its own firm identity and image among the non-secular nations of the world'. District and village councils were established in 1993 and held their first general assembly in May 1996. In 1994 a constitutional committee, chaired by Prince Mohamed, which had been appointed by the Sultan to review the 1959 constitutional arrangements, submitted a new draft constitution to the Sultan for consideration. In February 1995 the PPKB was permitted to hold its first national assembly, at which its newly elected President, Abdul Latif Chuchu, reaffirmed support for the monarchy and the national ideology. However, he also called for democratic elections, and was soon forced to resign by the Government, which renewed the emergency laws. Following an inactive period of three years, in May 1998 the PPKB held an annual general meeting, at which a business executive, Hatta Zainal Abidin, was elected President. The party briefly voiced concern at allegations of official corruption during the Amedeo court case in May 2000 (see below), but soon lapsed into infighting in attempts to oust its President.

The anachronistic political system remained firmly entrenched, and the dominance of the monarchy was reaffirmed in August 1998 when the Sultan's eldest son, Al-Muhtadee Billah Bolkiah, was formally installed as the heir to the throne in a lavish ceremony. The royal family enjoyed a monopoly of power, but maintained its popularity by enabling all citizens to share to some extent in the wealth of the State. There was no income tax, while housing, fuel and other essentials were subsidized and until 1995, when nominal charges were introduced for medical and dental treatment, both health services and education were free for citizens. The populace, as well as foreign dignitaries, were involved in extravagant royal festivities, and at his birthday celebrations in August 1998 the Sultan pledged salary increases for lower-paid civil servants and greater state support for pensioners and the destitute. He frequently exhorted the wealthy to contribute generously to the less privileged, and warned of the dangers of putting economic progress ahead of social development.

The economic crisis that beset South-East Asia from late 1997, together with scandals in Brunei itself, provided the catalyst for economic and, potentially, political change. Initially, Brunei provided assistance to other parts of the region; the sultanate contributed to an IMF emergency programme for Thailand, the state-owned Brunei Investment Agency (BIA) helped to stabilize currencies by buying Singapore dollars and Malaysian ringgit, and Brunei promised to invest in Malaysia to assist its recovery. Brunei itself, however, was adversely affected by a sharp decline in the international price of petroleum and by haze pollution from forest fires in Indonesia and Malaysia in 1997 and 1998, which threatened the development of tourism. The downturn was compounded in July 1998 with the collapse of the Amedeo Development Corporation, Brunei's largest investment and construction firm, which Prince Jefri controlled through his son and which had benefited from numerous lucrative government contracts.

Relations between the Sultan and his younger brother, Jefri, were already severely strained. Lawsuits were brought against Prince Jefri in the USA in 1997 and 1998 by US and British beauty queens alleging sexual misconduct, and in February 1998 two former business associates sued the prince for £80m. in London, claiming that he had reneged on property agreements. The first case was withdrawn when Prince Jefri was granted diplomatic immunity, and the other two lawsuits were settled out of court for undisclosed sums. The cases were unreported in Brunei but attracted wide international publicity and brought Prince Jefri's extravagant and profligate lifestyle into disrepute. In February 1998 the Sultan removed the finance portfolio from Prince Jefri, assuming responsibility for it himself, in the first major cabinet change for 10 years. In the following month the Minister of Health was dismissed, reportedly owing to his inadequate response to the haze over Brunei caused by forest fires in Indonesia and Malaysia, and in June the Sultan accepted the resignation of the Attorney-General and of the Solicitor-General. In July 1998 the Sultan appointed international accountants as executive managers of Amedeo, removed Prince Jefri from the boards of seven telecommunications companies and dismissed him as Chairman of the BIA, which controlled much of Brunei's overseas investment.

For a long time the Brunei Government made no official comment about the collapse of the Amedeo group, the misappropriation of BIA funds, or the role played by Prince Jefri. In August 1999, however, Abdul Aziz Umar, the Minister of Education, who was Chairman of the government task force appointed to investigate the missing BIA funds, admitted that there had been mismanagement. After the failure of private negotiations, the Government and the BIA began civil proceedings against Prince Jefri in Brunei and England, alleging improper withdrawal and use of more than US $28,000m. while he was Minister of Finance and Chairman of the BIA. A total of 71 others were named in the action, including Prince Jefri's eldest son, Prince Muda Abdul Hakeem, along with his private secretary, and more than 60 overseas companies believed to be controlled by Prince Jefri. In April the Brunei court dismissed an appeal against disclosure of his assets, which were 'frozen' worldwide, and rejected his plea for an independent judge from outside Brunei. The court case, which opened in May, dominated the local press, but Prince Jefri and his son reached confidential out-of-court settlements, in which the case against them was abandoned when they agreed to return all assets purchased with BIA funds. In October 2000, however, Haji Awang Kassim, Jefri's former confidential secretary, who had virtually run Amedeo and was deputy managing director of the BIA, was arrested after being extradited from Manila. The State and the BIA also began civil proceedings to recover funds from six other former associates of Prince Jefri, including the former managing directors of two state-owned corporations. Meanwhile, there were angry scenes at meetings of Amedeo creditors in November 2000, when they refused the BIA's settlement terms, and in May 2001 the liquidators sued a former senior official.

In September 1998 the Brunei Darussalam Economic Council (BDEC), chaired by Prince Mohamed, was established to seek ways of improving the economy. The Sultan approved the BDEC's report, released in February 2000, which warned that Brunei's economy was becoming increasingly unsustainable, and appointed Prince Mohamed to oversee the recommended economic recovery plan. There were no proposals to match economic modernization with political reform. The aim was to create a corporate system of government presided over by a traditional monarchy and to transform the bureaucracy into a 'technocracy'. In mid-1999 Prince Mohamed announced that the report on the Constitution had been completed, and in March 2000 seminars on modern management were organized for village headmen, but the Sultan, in his capacity as Prime

Minister and Minister of Defence and of Finance, continued to rule by decree under the state of emergency. Modernization was led by the Sultan, who carried out random checks on government departments. At the same time he continued to play the role of a good Muslim ruler, visiting rural kampongs and making himself accessible to his people, holding open days every year during the three-day Hari Raya festivities, when thousands of people would visit the palace. Crown Prince Al-Muhtadee Billah played an increasing role in public life at home and also visited China and Japan in March 2002. In a speech celebrating his 54th birthday in July 2000 the Sultan, while calling for a new mindset to counter antiquated regulations, with a view to making Brunei a financial hub for the region, also insisted that the economy must be strengthened in line with Islamic teaching in order to preserve social and moral values; repeatedly he urged Muslim devotion, especially at a time of economic difficulty. In September Brunei declared its aim to be a safe haven for 'halal' international financial services in the region. In the following month the Sultan, as Chancellor of the University of Brunei Darussalam, called for Islamic Studies to be upheld as the most important field of education, and in November he officially launched the Islamic Development Bank of Brunei, seven years after the opening of the country's first Islamic bank. In opening the first International Islamic Exposition, which was held in Brunei in August 2001 with participants from 25 countries, Sultan Hassanal urged all Muslims to unite in order to regain the glory of Islam. Brunei reacted with horror to the suicide attacks on the USA on 11 September 2001, repudiating any link between religion and terrorism. While Brunei itself was not threatened, the country aligned itself with the other member states of the Association of South East Asian Nations (ASEAN) and Asia-Pacific Economic Co-operation (APEC), closing ranks against terrorism. The Sultan continued to exhort young people to follow the teachings of the Koran, and he himself went once more on pilgrimage to Mecca in December 2001. Meanwhile, the State was determined to eradicate so-called deviant or extremist teachings among Muslims. In 2000 a Malay martial arts group, which planned armed attacks on what it held to be un-Islamic institutions, was uncovered, and in December three men, including one retired senior police officer and two Malay businessmen, were arrested for allegedly supporting subversive Christian practices, with close links to groups in Sabah and Sarawak.

The broadcast media and the press remained closely controlled. Legislation passed in 1997 required all journalists to register and prohibited undesirable foreign broadcasts, criticism of the royal family, and objectionable religious or cultural material. Until 1999 television was state-owned, but the first commercial television channel was introduced in that year. The Government began to adopt a slightly more relaxed attitude to the press, however, paying heed to mildly critical letters about administrative shortcomings, which began to appear from 1999 in the correspondence pages of the English-language newspaper *Borneo Bulletin*, which was owned by Prince Mohamed. A second English-language newspaper, *News Express*, which was partly owned by the former Attorney-General, was established in August, and was later permitted to publish Brunei's first Chinese-language newspaper and a Malay daily. While official willingness to accept restrained criticism marked a substantial advance, the press exerted self-censorship, avoiding any questioning of the sultanate or national philosophy, and in March 2000 the Government warned newspapers to focus on national development, social well-being and character-building, instead of 'negative news'. In October 2001 a Local Newspapers (Amendment) Order introduced more stringent measures, requiring newspapers to obtain an annual permit, increasing deposit fees and fines and permitting the authorities to suspend any local newspaper without appeal and to ban foreign newspapers from entering the country. *News Express* had to suspend publication temporarily in order to meet the new financial requirements.

The Eighth National Development Plan, encompassing the years 2001–05, repeated aims for diversification, although the discovery of a substantial new oil and gas field by Brunei Shell Petroleum in November 2001 raised the prospect of a renewal of intense activity in the sector. Petroleum prices continued to recover, despite experiencing a sharp decline in the aftermath of the terrorist attacks of September 2001, but Brunei was affected by the continuing regional economic malaise, which brought considerable hardship to many sectors of the population. Unemployment remained a pressing problem, particularly among young university graduates and school-leavers, who constituted 90% of the 6,812 people unemployed in February 2002. The Government wanted to extend corporatization of government departments and agencies, to divert employees from public service into the private sector, and to make the bureaucracy more efficient. However, in view of deeply entrenched practices and prejudices, in November 2000 the Government abandoned plans to substitute performance-related bonuses for the system of automatic salary increments in the civil service.

Meanwhile, Brunei's main problem was the ongoing Amedeo crisis, the continuation of which threatened to impede the nation's recovery and deter the external investment that was vital to the success of the Eighth National Development Plan. In September 2001 about 300 creditors remained unpaid, with no settlement in prospect. The Government was engaged in disputes with Prince Jefri concerning the assets covered by the out-of-court settlement that he had made, and it appeared that the B $9m. raised by a massive auction of the Prince's belongings in Brunei in August 2001 would be subsumed in expenses. Meanwhile, the case was generating huge costs in fee payments to foreign liquidators, lawyers and accountants. In October 2001 the Government intervened and launched Global Evergreen Sdn Bhd—a government-owned corporation under the chairmanship of the Minister of Education, the former Chairman of BIA. Within two months Global Evergreen had settled 97% of all claims and dispensed with the services of overseas consultants. However, in May 2002 it emerged that several of the overseas consultants employed by Global Evergreen had allegedly been prevented from leaving Brunei owing to visa irregularities. The consultants had been investigating the reported embezzlement of an estimated B $10,000m. from Sultan Hassanal and had made inquiries into the conduct of the Minister of Home Affairs, Isa Ibrahim, following which the immigration authorities had raided the company's offices and uncovered the alleged visa errors. The Government denied that it had prevented the consultants from leaving the country, claiming that they had been subjected only to normal immigration procedures, and those involved were finally permitted to leave Brunei. Consequently, by mid-2002 the repercussions of the crisis continued to jeopardize further foreign investment in the country.

Economic change, rising expectations of accountability and transparency, the exposure to outside influences through the internet and satellite television, and the expansion of education in information technology must eventually bring changed attitudes to government.

Recent Foreign Relations

After independence, Brunei began to develop extensive international links. It became a member of the UN, ASEAN, the Commonwealth and the Organization of the Islamic Conference. In 1992 it joined the Non-aligned Movement and established diplomatic ties with Russia and the People's Republic of China. In the same year diplomatic links were formally established with Viet Nam, and in 1993 with Myanmar. In 1995 Brunei entered the World Bank and the IMF. Brunei remained heavily dependent on the United Kingdom and Singapore for defence but the sultanate also forged defence links with Australia and the USA. In 1994 a US-Brunei joint working committee on defence was established, and in July 2001 the USA and Brunei held a large-scale joint naval exercise in the sultanate.

The most immediate foreign policy objective was to establish cordial relations with ASEAN partners. Brunei was closest to Singapore, which remains an important trading partner, a major source of skilled labour and a repository of Brunei's petroleum revenues, with the two currencies 'pegged' under an interchangeability agreement dating from 1967. As small states, Brunei and Singapore share a concern to promote peace and stability in the region, working closely together in bodies such as the ASEAN Regional Forum (ARF—established to address security issues) and APEC. They co-operate in offering training facilities for their armed forces, and in March 2002 conducted an eight-day joint military exercise in Brunei. Ministers and officials exchange regular visits, including a visit by Singapore's Senior Minister, Lee Kuan Yew, in November 2000. In the same month the Port of Singapore Authority Corporation and Brunei Archipelago Development Corporation signed a joint-venture contract to manage and develop Muara Container Terminal for the next 25 years.

From the late 1980s Brunei provided generous aid and investment to promote economic development in Indonesia and the Philippines, and in 1994 the ministers responsible for foreign affairs of Brunei, Indonesia, Malaysia and the Philippines agreed to establish an East ASEAN Growth Area (EAGA). Relations with Malaysia showed the most dramatic improvement. In 1993 the Malaysian Prime Minister, Dato' Seri Dr Mahathir Mohamad, headed a delegation to Brunei, and the two countries agreed to resolve all border disputes, including the Limbang question, through bilateral negotiations. In 1994 Brunei signed an agreement with Malaysia establishing a joint commission to promote co-operation in trade, industry, finance, education, culture and religion. Despite occasional friction, relations remained cordial. Senior officials exchanged frequent visits, and Sultan Hassanal held annual consultations with Prime Minister Mahathir in Brunei or Kuala Lumpur. From the mid-1990s Brunei became more assertive in the region, urging economic co-operation and trade liberalization; the sultanate expressed support for free trade within APEC by the year 2020 and wished to accelerate implementation of the ASEAN Free Trade Area (AFTA). Brunei also hosted a meeting of ASEAN ministers responsible for foreign affairs in July 1995, at which Viet Nam was admitted as the Association's seventh member. (Laos and Myanmar were granted full membership of ASEAN in July 1997 and Cambodia was admitted in April 1999.)

In August 1999 Brunei hosted the South-East Asian Games. At the third unofficial ASEAN summit meeting, held in Manila in November, the Sultan urged greater openness to achieve economic integration, strengthen economies and attract foreign investment. At the same time he argued for closer but more gradual co-operation with Japan, China and the Republic of Korea. In February 2000 Brunei hosted its first APEC Senior Officials' Meeting, with 3,000 delegates from 21 countries, and ASEAN ministers responsible for finance met in Brunei in the following month to discuss a proposal for an Asian monetary fund. In November 2000 Brunei played host to the annual APEC meeting, the largest international event ever staged in Brunei: 6,000 delegates attended, including Presidents Clinton of the USA, Jiang Zemin of China and Putin of Russia. Brunei lobbied intensively for APEC unity, but its hopes of achieving a major breakthrough in obtaining consensus for a new round of World Trade Organization (WTO) talks encountered resistance from some delegates, notably Malaysia, and a compromise was reached.

Brunei staged the seventh ASEAN summit meeting in November 2001, with representatives from China, Japan and the Republic of Korea also in attendance. This first 'working summit' followed an agreement at the previous meeting in Singapore to dispense with ceremony and concentrate on action. At the meeting of the so-called 'ASEAN + 3' the national leaders declared war on terrorism and agreed to form an ASEAN + 3 secretariat. The Sultan envisaged that this would lead to the creation of the largest free trade area in the world. In July 2002 Brunei was host to a meeting of ASEAN ministers responsible for foreign affairs and was also the venue for the ninth meeting of the ARF, which was attended by delegates from the 10 member nations, together with representatives of 13 dialogue partners. Brunei was also to host the ASEAN meeting of ministers of foreign affairs scheduled for November 2002. Meanwhile, Brunei continued to strengthen relations with its individual neighbours. Three ASEAN heads of state visited Brunei in swift succession in August 2001—the Prime Minister of Thailand, the President of the Philippines, and the new President of Indonesia, Megawati Sukarnoputri, who arrived with a large delegation. In the same month Brunei and the Philippines agreed to establish a Bilateral Commission for Co-operation, to be convened in 2002. In October 2001 Sultan Hassanal visited Kuala Lumpur for his annual consultation with the Malaysian Prime Minister. The President of Viet Nam paid a three-day state visit to Brunei in November 2001, and in April 2002 the Sultan received the new Supreme Commander of the Thai Armed Forces.

In view of its ambitions to promote tourism, Brunei was particularly concerned to improve regional co-operation to protect the environment. The sultanate celebrated World Forestry Day in 2000, introduced a total ban on open burning and illegal logging as agreed by ASEAN, and inaugurated ASEAN Environment Year 2000. In January 2001 the Sultan launched both 'Visit Brunei Year 2001' and 'Visit ASEAN Year 2002', but the events of 11 September 2001 caused a depression in the tourism sector after what had been a promising start.

Maintaining harmonious relations with its ASEAN neighbours and with other countries with interests in the region, and trying to balance the needs of modernization and tradition remain the priorities of this wealthy and stable, but potentially vulnerable, small state.

Economy

MURNI MOHAMED

Revised by HAJAH ROSNI HAJI TUNGKAT and the editorial staff

INTRODUCTION

Brunei Darussalam—the Abode of Peace—acceded to full independence in January 1984, following nearly 80 years as a British protectorate. The country's inhabitants (totalling 332,844 in 2001) enjoy one of the world's highest levels of national income per head and rank highly on most social indicators. Malays form the largest ethnic group and comprised an estimated 67.8% of the population at end 2000. Chinese and indigenous tribes people accounted for 14.8% and 5.9% of the populace respectively in that year. The Brunei/Muara district is densely populated (393 people per sq km in 2000), while the Tutong and Belait districts (33 and 29 people respectively), and especially the Temburong district (10), are sparsely inhabited. During 1991–2001 the population of Brunei increased at an average annual rate of 2.5%.

Over the period 1980–93 real gross domestic product (GDP) declined at an average annual rate of 0.2%, while GDP per head declined by 3.0% annually. In 2000 GDP per head, measured at current prices, was B $23,627. A trend of decline was reversed in 1990–2000 when GDP increased by an annual average of 1.5%. The decline in the GDP per caput since the early 1980s, largely owing to the reduction in world oil prices and Brunei's heavy dependence on petroleum exports, has not affected the standard of living of the population, but the Government's fiscal position has deteriorated significantly since the mid-1980s. Brunei's economic growth has been hampered by the small size of its population and by its dependence on foreign workers. Brunei citizens, however, still receive education and healthcare facilities at nominal charges, benefit from a virtually tax-free welfare state, and are eligible for interest-free loans for the construction of houses and purchase of motor cars. Moreover, Brunei has no personal income tax, sales or export tax, though there is a flat-rate corporate levy of 30%, from which the bulk of government revenue is derived.

In September 1998 the Sultan established the Brunei Darussalam Economic Council (BDEC), comprising government officials and business executives and chaired by the Sultan's brother, the Minister of Foreign Affairs, Prince Mohamed Bolkiah. The BDEC devised specific recommendations to restructure the economy, which had suffered from the effects of the regional economic crisis and a severe decline in the international price for petroleum between mid-1997 and the end of 1998. The adverse economic climate was compounded by the huge financial losses incurred by the former Minister of Finance and Chairman of the Brunei Investment Agency (BIA), Prince Jefri Bolkiah, as well as the collapse of the largest domestic company, controlled by Jefri, the Amedeo Development Corporation (see History). In a birthday address in July 1999 the Sultan announced a Business Facilitation Scheme and promised to increase efforts to improve local and foreign business confidence, make bureaucracy more efficient, and encourage private-sector involvement. The economic downturn brought considerable hardship, although the Government tried to ease the burden on the poor. Housing allowances for ministers and senior civil servants were abolished, but pensions and social welfare payments were increased. Nearly three-quarters of the many foreign unskilled labourers were repatriated. Development spending was reduced by almost one-half in 1999 and 2000, and by the end of 2000 unemployment stood at a record level of almost 7,000, mainly young persons.

The unexpectedly candid report from the BDEC, which was released in early 2000, stressed the need for a long-term plan to correct fundamental economic problems, warning that Brunei's economy was 'increasingly unsustainable'. It pointed out that since 1984 GDP had grown at less than one-half the rate of population expansion, leading to a chronic budget deficit and rising unemployment. Between the 1981 and 1991 censuses the population increased by 35%, and by the end of the century 70% of the population was under 30 years old, with 50% below the age of 20. Between the 1991 and 2001 censuses the population increased by 28%. A steady decline in the rate of population increase between successive censuses, however, prompted concerns that Brunei's population was not multiplying at a rapid enough rate to sustain high levels of economic growth. Consequently, the prosperity enjoyed for most of the second half of the 20th century could no longer be taken for granted, and radical reforms were needed. The Sultan approved the report in principle, and in January 2000 Prince Mohamed was appointed to direct Brunei's economic recovery plan. The Government promised to introduce banking and financial reforms, speed up privatization or corporatization of public services, curb waste, and revise land laws to allow foreign ownership. The Civil Service Institute introduced training programmes for officials. Although prospects for future growth had been favourable at the end of 2000, by the end of 2001 Brunei's economic outlook was more uncertain, owing to both a global economic downturn and the effects of the terrorist attacks on the USA in September of that year, which contributed to an international decline in petroleum prices. While the disputes arising from the collapse of the Amedeo Development Corporation had been resolved to a large extent by the Sultan's formation of Global Evergreen Sdn Bhd in 2001, the repercussions of the scandal continued to deter potential foreign investors in 2002.

In the 1970s and 1980s a growing number of eligible Bruneians were sent abroad on scholarships for training in order to obtain the qualifications necessary to take a leading part in future economic development and to reduce the country's dependence on foreign workers. The University of Brunei Darussalam (UBD), founded in 1985, provides primary degree courses in education, arts and social sciences, management studies, natural science and Islamic studies. The first students graduated in 1989, and the student intake has been expanded to about 3,000, compared with 1,138 in 1994. A new campus at Rimba, Gadong, close to the capital, was officially opened in September 1995. Students pursuing more specialized courses, however, continue to be sent abroad. On relocation to Rimba, courses in applied sciences, technology and engineering were introduced. Technical and vocational education was also expanded; in 1998 the country had three technical colleges and five vocational schools. By 1999 the Islamic Institute of Education had merged with the UBD.

The private sector is encouraged to participate in the provision of educational and training facilities. In 2000 there were 65 kindergartens, primary, preparatory, secondary and high schools, as well as one institute managed by the private sector with a total of 29,626 students. The number of private firms handling training and skills management has also increased in recent years, including Kemuda Resource Agency, Further Education Management, Micronet and Infonet.

In 2001 Brunei's GDP, at current prices, decreased to B $7,619.2m. from B $7,995.5m. in 2000. The economy is based largely on wealth from natural gas and petroleum and from the managed funds of the BIA. The proportion of GDP contributed by the petroleum sector, however, declined steadily from 83.7% in 1980 to 35.3% in 1999, but increased to 39.3% in 2001. Brunei is the fourth largest petroleum producer in South-East Asia, after Indonesia, Malaysia and Viet Nam, and is the fourth largest producer of liquefied natural gas (LNG) in the world. Japan and the Republic of Korea have become the major customers for Brunei's natural gas and crude petroleum exports. Based on the current rate of production, the country's petroleum and natural gas reserves are expected to last until 2018 and 2033 respectively. The diversification of the economy into non-petroleum-related activities, which is expected to reduce income disparity (with wealth concentrated hitherto in the petroleum sector), remains a major challenge, although one the Government has proved itself willing to address. The proportion of GDP contributed by the non-oil sector increased annually from 1986 onwards: between 1990 and 1999 the GDP of the non-oil sector grew on average at 4.4% per annum. In 1998 growth declined to 3.8%, in response to the effects of the Asian crisis, the collapse of the Amedeo Development Corporation, lower government capital expenditures and the related decline in consumption.

The petroleum sector was adversely affected by depressed prices on the world oil market in the 1980s. Export earnings from petroleum and natural gas declined from about B $9,700m. in 1980 to B $6,028.7m. in 2000, although the latter figure still constituted 89.7% of Brunei's total export revenue. The petroleum sector did, however, benefit from the effects of the Iraqi invasion of Kuwait in August 1990, with production lost in both those countries. In the mid- and late 1990s the decline in the price of crude petroleum directly affected revenue. However, the appreciation of the US dollar, as well as the improved performance in the non-oil sector, compensated for the decline and helped sustain the recovery of the overall economy, with growth in GDP rising from −1.1% in 1992 to 2.5% in 1999 and 3.0% in 2000. The favourable world crude price and a slight increase in petroleum production boosted the oil sector's growth by 3.2% in 2000, compared with a negative rate of 11.8% in 1998. Similarly, the government sector also improved, expanding by 2.5% in 2000, compared with 1.4% in 1999, while the private sector recorded growth of 3.0% in 2000, compared with 1.7% in 1999. The growth in the non-oil sector derived principally from service-related activities as Brunei hosted various regional summit meetings, most recently the ninth annual Association of South East Asian Nations (ASEAN) Regional Forum (ARF) in July 2002.

Brunei's dependence on imports renders it susceptible to external inflationary conditions. Subsidies on essential foodstuffs and motor spirit (petrol), however, play a part in controlling inflationary pressure. The average annual rate of inflation, as measured by the consumer price index (CPI), was 4.0% during 1980–90 and 2.4% during 1990–94. The index increased by 6.0% in 1995, owing largely to the high import tariff announced by the Government early in the year, although this rise was mitigated somewhat by a tariff reduction on some 700 items during the year. In 1997 inflation was 1.7%, compared with the 2.0% recorded in 1996, when the Government implemented further cuts in the tariffs on imported consumer items, some to zero per cent. In October 1997 the Government began a year-long Household Expenditure Survey that would provide a new base year for the CPI. In 1999 inflation was at a negative rate of 0.1%, a slight increase from the negative rate of 0.4% in 1998, owing to a decline in the price of food items, housing, transport and communications, computer parts and miscellaneous items. However, inflation stood at 1.2% in 2000.

Brunei joined ASEAN on the attainment of independence in 1984. Most of Brunei's trade is conducted with the other members of ASEAN, Singapore being Brunei's leading trading partner within the grouping, as well as a major source of skilled labour, advice and imports. Participation in ASEAN projects has also given Brunei an interest in the economic development of the region, and has enabled the country, through regional projects, to benefit from the economies of scale, whereby the average cost of production is reduced as the volume of output increases. In October 1991 the member states of ASEAN formally announced the establishment of the ASEAN Free Trade Area (AFTA), of which Brunei was one of the principal proponents. The original target for the reduction of tariffs to between 0% and 5% was 2008, but this was subsequently advanced to 2003 and then 2002, when AFTA was formally implemented. In November 1999 the target date for zero tariffs in ASEAN was brought forward from 2015 to 2010. Brunei is also a member of the Asia-Pacific Economic Co-operation (APEC) and of the Organization of the Islamic Conference (OIC). In October 1993 the idea of a 'growth quadrangle', encompassing Mindanao and Palawan (Philippines), Sarawak, Labuan and Sabah (Malaysia), East and West Kalimantan and Sulawesi (Indonesia) and Brunei was mooted, aiming to emulate the Singapore-Johore-Riau 'growth triangle'. At a meeting in Mindanao in November 1994, it was agreed to establish the 'growth quadrangle' as the Brunei-Indonesia-Malaysia-Philippines-East ASEAN Growth Area (BIMP-EAGA). The area has since been expanded with the announcement of the incorporation of additional provinces in Indonesia, including North and South Kalimantan, the Maluku Islands and Irian Jaya (also known as West Papua), in July 1996. It was also decided to locate the secretariat of the East ASEAN Business Council (EABC) in Brunei. The provision of an office and the pledge to fund one-half of the secretariat's operating expenses on a three-year renewable basis are seen as part of Brunei's commitment towards the development of BIMP-EAGA.

Since the formation of BIMP-EAGA, a number of successful working groups have been established through which various projects have been implemented: a construction consortium and a Pan-EAGA Multi-Capital Transportation Network System were formed; the first phase of a programme to reduce telephone tariffs for the four countries comprising the BIMP-EAGA was implemented and a BIMP-EAGA website created; two projects have been launched by the working group, Air Linkages, namely, the Visit Cycle of BIMP-EAGA and the Visit BIMP-EAGA Year 2001; a shipping agreement was established between Brunei and Mindanao; while in the areas of development and tourism, Brunei, Sabah and Sarawak launched a 'Borneo Package' in 1997 as one destination for European tourists. A number of joint ventures have also been formed and memorandums of understanding signed that involved private-sector participation, including the establishment of a Regional Ship Operator Association in BIMP-EAGA, a bark medium processing plant, and co-operation and exchange in education and training.

In August 2001 representatives from BIMP-EAGA and the ASEAN Centre for Energy (ACE) met for the first time to discuss the development of several trans-Borneo power grid interconnection projects, one of which would link Brunei's grid with those of Sarawak and Sabah. In 2002 the feasibility of a Trans-Borneo railway connecting Brunei with several destinations within BIMP-EAGA was also being considered; it was to constitute part of the Pan-EAGA Multi-Capital Transportation Network. In July 2002 the first BIMP-EAGA Customs, Immigration, Quarantine and Security (CIQS) conference took place, as a result of which the member nations agreed to adopt common CIQS policies in an attempt to accelerate regional integration and growth. BIMP-EAGA had been subjected to criticism for its failure to establish adequate institutional mechanisms to facilitate its development, particularly following the formal implementation of AFTA in January 2002. Brunei was to host the third BIMP-EAGA Expo in 2003.

DEVELOPMENT PLANS

There have been seven National Development Plans, covering the periods 1953–58, 1962–66, 1975–79, 1980–84, 1986–90, 1991–95 and 1996–2000, respectively, with the Eighth National Development Plan encompassing the period 2001–05. These Plans, although far from comprehensive, have delineated proposals for government investment in infrastructure, services and incentives, all aimed at diversifying the economy and at increasing private-sector participation. In 1995 the Brunei Industrial Development Plan (IDP) was commissioned to reactivate the non-oil sector; the IDP encompassed several policy recommendations, including the development of a 'niche strategy' for industrial activities and the creation of an environment more conducive to investment promotion. In 1996 a statement was issued by the Government, through the Ministry of Communications, detailing the plan to develop Brunei as a Service Hub for Trade and Tourism (SHuTT) by the year 2003 (see below).

During the Seventh Plan about 5,000 houses were constructed under the Housing Development Programme and Landless Indigenous Housing Scheme, in addition to a number of other institutional and private housing developments. Several new main road projects were completed and opened for traffic. Similarly, a total of 247.1 km of minor roads in densely populated and rural areas were upgraded. Of the total 1,501 development programmes and projects approved for implementation in the Seventh Plan, 53% were completed, 12% were approaching completion and 12% were being implemented by the end of the Plan period, whilst the remainder were either still at preliminary stages, suspended or cancelled for various reasons. In terms of actual expenditure, of the total amount approved (B \$5,057m.), about B \$3,237m. (or 64%) was actually spent. The Seventh National Development Plan formed the third stage in the implementation of the 20-year long-term Development Plan started in 1985, just a year after the country gained independence. This Plan aspired further to improve the quality of life of the people, while at the same time seeking to widen and further enhance the country's economic base. Its overall aims included: the achievement of balanced and sustained socio-economic development through a more outward-looking economic diversification strategy; the continued development of physical infrastructure and public facilities; the implementation of effective human resource development; the implementation of social development projects; the utilization of appropriate technologies; and the continuous protection of the environment. The Government approved a sum of B \$7,200m. under the Seventh Plan for various sectors of the economy: industry was to receive 12.6%, increased from 10% in the previous Plan; transport and communications, 19.5%; social services, 27.5%; public utilities, 21.9%; public building, 8.8%; security (civilian projects for the police and army), 7.3%; and miscellaneous items, which included feasibility studies and local plans, 2.4%.

In September 2001 the Eighth National Development Plan (2001–05) was announced. Under the Plan the economy was expected to experience annual growth of 4%–5%. Total expenditure of B \$7,300m. was approved for its implementation, of which the Government intended to provide only B \$2,900m. For the first time, foreign and local investors were to supply the remaining funding. In November 2001 the Sultan announced that an additional B \$1,000m. would be allocated specifically to economic development projects in 2002. Of this, B \$492m. was to be used to finance completed projects and those carried over from 2001, while B \$504m. was to be allocated to new projects. The Plan continued to emphasize the importance of diversification to Brunei's long-term economic prospects, and to encourage industrial expansion. Private sector and human resources development was, however, accorded priority, particularly in service industries such as finance, tourism, and information and communications technology. In June 2002 the Department of Economic Planning and Development reported that, of the allocated budget of B \$1,000m. for development in 2002, only B \$190m. (19% of the total), had been utilized. It was calculated that, if spending continued at the same rate, only B \$650m. would have been expended by the end of the year. Fears were expressed by some members of the business community that the Government would not succeed in stimulating economic development if it failed to spend the entire budgetary allocation.

Service Hub for Trade and Tourism (SHuTT)

In 1996 the Government announced plans to develop Brunei as a 'Service Hub for Trade and Tourism' (or SHuTT) by the year 2003. Brunei wants to see itself as a bridge for the EAGA member countries to the regional and global markets. At the same time, it aspires to be the gateway to EAGA markets for the rest of the world. Ports, airport facilities and tourism services are being upgraded as part of the move to build on Brunei's telecommunication network both regionally and internationally. Tourism is considered to be a key element of the SHuTT plan: the year 2001 was designated 'Visit Brunei Year' by the Government; the 20th ASEAN Tourism Forum was held in January

2001 in Brunei; and Brunei also hosted the first International Islamic Exposition in August 2001. The year 2002 was designated 'Visit ASEAN Year'. A new tourism unit was established in 1995 under the Ministry of Industry and Primary Resources. Visa requirements were relaxed and border check-points were upgraded. The SHuTT plan aims to exploit and maximize the economic potential of Brunei as a centre for trade and tourism, and forms part of the Government's overall scheme to develop the non-petroleum-based sector of the economy.

Under the SHuTT 2003 plan, Brunei International Airport was to become an airline hub through its promotion as an International Aviation Centre, an Air Freight Services Centre and an Airport City. The widening of the airport's operation area (apron) to accommodate up to eight Boeing-767 aircraft was completed in March 1999. The Postal Services Department introduced a number of programmes as part of the SHuTT 2003 plans, including the establishment of a Premium Services Centre in 1998. The programme has also promoted developments in the telecommunications sector. Under the Seventh Plan, a progamme was established known as the 21st Century Global Multimedia Channel Network (*Ragam 21*) to meet the requirements of various media such as electronic businesses, government on-line, long distance education, telemedicine and various other media. It would also combine computer, broadcasting and telecommunications technology to form a multimedia network. The SHuTT 2003 programme also identified Muara Port as a gateway for international trade. The Ports Department has developed extensive plans for the improvement of infrastructure and operational equipment.

The Brunei Darussalam Economic Council

The Brunei Darussalam Economic Council (BDEC) was established in September 1998 under the chairmanship of Prince Mohamed Bolkiah to examine the situation in Brunei in the light of the regional economic crisis and to recommend measures to revitalize the economy.

In its report, published in February 2000, the BDEC warned that the Bruneian economy was unsustainable, citing the inability of income growth to keep pace with the rise in the population (since 1984 real GDP had increased at less than half the rate of population growth), a persistent budget deficit and rising unemployment. More than 75% of Brunei nationals in the labour force were employed by the Government, and government contracts accounted for most of domestic economic activity. As a result of reduced revenues from petroleum and gas, owing to a significant decline in international prices from mid-1997, and the depletion of Brunei's foreign reserves through the alleged financial mismanagement of Prince Jefri Bolkiah, the Government's capacity to provide employment and to supply the impetus for economic development was impaired. However, the private sector was too small and too dependent on government expenditure to create much-needed employment opportunities.

The BDEC recommended a two-phase strategy, comprising the short-term Action Plan for Recovery (which was to be implemented over a six-month period), and a plan for long-term development called the Strategy for Sustainable Growth. The Action Plan for Recovery included a stimulus package to inject liquidity into the economy to prevent the collapse of large sections of the non-oil and -gas private sector. Projects approved under the Action Plan benefited from the introduction of a fast-track scheme for government payment, the award of tenders and bank credit; government expenditure increased in strategic areas, including the acceleration of government housing projects and the extension of information technology infrastructure into schools and public services; 3,000 unemployed Bruneians were trained in hospitality skills during APEC 2000 in November; and corporate sponsors were found to fund a basic national information technology training scheme for schools, government departments and small- and medium-scale enterprises.

The BDEC also recommended the appointment of a senior minister to oversee the implementation of the recovery plan with the help of an international business advisory panel, an independent public think-tank and a permanent business council comprising members of the local private sector.

The implementation of the Strategy for Sustainable Growth commenced within one year, following the receipt of detailed expert advice to develop the policies. Under the strategy, government finances were to be improved by prioritizing government expenditure and eliminating waste, by reducing the size of the public sector through privatization and by expanding government revenue through the broadening of the tax base and the gradual removal of subsidies. The private sector was to be encouraged to expand in order to reduce the country's dependence on government expenditure. This expansion was to be achieved through privatization, the promotion of local and foreign investment through the simplification of bureaucratic procedures and the encouragement of local business creation through easier access to financing. The restrictions on ownership and development of land were to be reviewed to facilitate investment, and private sector liquidity was to be improved by ensuring prompt government payment. In addition to these measures, the regulatory and legal framework of the country was to be modernized, the transparency of government policies and regulations was to be improved, and an emphasis was to be laid on the development of a superior communications and information technology infrastructure. The competitiveness of the petroleum and gas industry was to be improved and local small- and medium-scale enterprises were to be encouraged through the expansion of existing financial assistance programmes.

PETROLEUM AND NATURAL GAS

Petroleum prospectors arrived in Brunei in the early 1900s, but by 1918 all except the Shell Co had abandoned operations. In 1929 Shell discovered an onshore petroleum deposit in Seria, from which production was gradually expanded to 17,000 barrels per day (b/d) by 1940. The Seria oilfield was extensively damaged during the Second World War, but production was resumed in 1945 and had reached 114,700 b/d by 1956.

The Brunei Shell Petroleum Co (Brunei Shell) began offshore exploration in 1954, and started exploratory drilling on the continental shelf in 1956. In 1963 the South West Ampa field was found to contain large quantities of both petroleum and natural gas. Since 1964 numerous new oilfields, including Fairley, Fairley-Baram, Champion, Magpie, Iron Duke, Jurajan, Perdana, Gannet and, most recently, Egret, have been discovered, in addition to further onshore reserves at Seria and Rasau. Production declined, however, from a record 254,000 b/d in 1979 to 150,000 b/d in 1988 and 1989, in an effort to ensure that extraction rates were suited to economic needs. Production increased in 1990 by an extra 12,000 b/d to meet the unexpected increase in international demand resulting from the Gulf crisis. Contrary to expectation, however, increased production was maintained, with an average production rate of 162,000 b/d in 1991. The Government's equal joint venture with Shell was allowed to maintain the higher flows that it attained during the Gulf crisis, owing to its success in proving substantial new reserves through drillings at very deep levels. The venture's new finds ensured that output could continue until at least the year 2018 at a rate of 150,000–160,000 b/d. Following an increase to its highest levels in more than a decade, 182,000 b/d in 1992, production declined to 158,000 b/d in 1998, but increased again to 215,000 b/d in 2000, before declining to 173,000 b/d in 2001, largely as a result of a decline in global petroleum prices. In 1998 the average price for crude petroleum was US $13.46 per barrel, its lowest level since 1984. Although partially offset by reduced operating costs and a weaker exchange rate, the decline in prices had an adverse effect on Brunei's financial position, prompting the Government to place emphasis upon maximizing production and reducing production costs. Prices subsequently recovered, reaching US $18.48 per barrel in 1999 and US $27.24 per barrel in 2000. Following the terrorist attacks on the USA in September 2001, prices declined to only US $18.55 per barrel. However, by June 2002 prices had recovered to US $25.35 per barrel.

In 1999 Brunei exported 48.8% of its petroleum and natural gas to Japan, 15.2% to the USA, 13.7% to the Republic of Korea, 13.6% to Thailand and 3.0% to Singapore. In 1998 the value of petroleum exports decreased by about 30%, owing principally to the decline in world oil and gas prices as a result of excess supply, as well as a reduction in hydrocarbon demand. However, the rise in the international oil price from July 1999 led to increased petroleum exports, which rose by 58.3% in 1999 and by 77.6% in 2000, before declining in 2001 owing to the decrease in international prices.

Similarly, LNG exports declined by 16.3% during 1998 but recovered slowly, increasing by 4.8% in 1999 and by 55.1% in 2000. Brunei itself uses only about 5% of its oil for domestic purposes; the Seria refinery (capacity 100,000 b/d) produces 5,000–6,000 b/d for domestic consumption. In 2000 exports of petroleum and gas were worth B $6,028.7m., compared with earnings of B $3,601.5m. in 1999.

Brunei is the world's fifth largest exporter of LNG, after Indonesia, Algeria, Malaysia and Australia. Japan and the Republic of Korea are the only major buyers of Brunei's LNG. A 20-year LNG contract with Japan expired in 1993 and was replaced by a new 20-year contract, under which the volume of LNG exported increased to 5.54m. tons (from 5.14m. previously) and the price of gas increased by about 4%. In 1994 Brunei signed a contract with the Republic of Korea to sell up to 0.7m. tons of LNG annually in 1995 and 1996. A sales and purchase agreement was signed in October 1997 between Brunei LNG and Korea Gas Corporation (KOGAS). Under the agreement, Brunei LNG was to supply KOGAS with 0.7m. metric tons per annum of LNG from 1997 to 2013, a period of 16 years. The new agreement confirmed KOGAS as the fourth long-term customer of Brunei LNG, as well as the three Japanese companies (Tokyo Electric Power, Tokyo Gas and Osaka Gas). Brunei LNG will supply the four customers with a total of 6.24m. tons until the year 2013. The regional economic crisis and a surplus of petroleum and gas on world markets resulted in a reduction of gas sales volumes to Japan and the Republic of Korea amounting to 10 B-Class cargoes in 1998. LNG sales increased to 186 B-Class cargoes in 1999 and to 200 B-Class cargoes in 2000, with a further increase to 207 B-Class cargoes expected in 2004.

Brunei Shell's operations are conducted in accordance with the Government's political objectives. New legislation was introduced in the early 1980s to ensure that Brunei would derive maximum benefit from any petroleum exploration by foreign companies. The State was to be an equal partner in all petroleum ventures with foreign interests. Any company wishing to apply for a concession was required to offer the Government a percentage of its annual net profit from petroleum or gas production, at a rate to be fixed before contracts were signed. The aim was to increase competition among prospective concession-holders. A state-controlled petroleum company, similar to those in Malaysia and Indonesia, however, was not envisaged at that point. In January 1993 the Brunei Oil and Gas Authority (BOGA) was formed, its main function being to advise and recommend on policies in all matters pertaining to oil and gas production and implementation. In September 1998 the BOGA and Brunei Shell Petroleum were restructured. The country is not a member of the Organization of the Petroleum Exporting Countries (OPEC).

There are four principal companies involved in the petroleum and natural gas sector, of which Brunei Shell, jointly owned by the Government and the international Shell group, is the largest. In 1969 Brunei LNG was established by the Government, Shell and the Mitsubishi Corporation of Japan, to purchase gas brought on shore by Brunei Shell. In 1987 Brunei Coldgas was owned by these three partners, and shipped gas, after it had been cooled and liquefied by Brunei LNG, to Japan. In 1995, however, Brunei Coldgas merged with Brunei LNG under the name of Brunei LNG. Brunei Shell Marketing Co, jointly owned by the Government and Shell, was established to service the domestic market. Brunei Shell Tankers is the fifth company of the group. However, Brunei Shell did not have a monopoly. A few other companies, namely Jasra-Elf (or Jasra International), a joint venture formed in 1986 between Elf Aquitaine and the locally-owned (i.e. controlled by the royal family) Jasra Jackson, were given concessions, mainly on shore. The Gannet offshore field came into production in 1987. Between 1991 and 1993 there were a number of discoveries of new petroleum and gas reservoirs and fields, including discoveries of gas at the Merpati and Bugan fields. In 1991 exploration by Brunei Shell revealed new petroleum and gas reserves beneath two existing fields, Champion and Iron Duke. Brunei Shell reported that its Enggang-1 exploration well, located 3.5 km off the Seria coast near the Seria-Tali oilfield, tested petroleum at a combined flow of 2,250 b/d and gas at 18.4m. cu ft per day. This was the first exploration success in shallow waters since the 1970s. No information is available, however, on the quantity of recoverable reserves at the Enggang discovery. In addition, Jasra-Elf announced the discovery of two new offshore fields, Juragan and Perdana, which were believed to contain a potential 150m.–200m. barrels. Jaspet Fletcher Challenge also reported a new discovery, the Perdana Deep-1 exploration well. During 1995 exploration activities also confirmed a gas and condensate discovery in the Selangkir-1 field, which tested nearly 500,000 cu m of gas per day. In 1997 Brunei Shell discovered estimated recoverable reserves of 44m. barrels of petroleum at the exploration well, Mampak-1, which was expected to generate production of 7,550 b/d for the first three years before gradually decreasing over the next 15 years. The development of Mampak-1, Selangkir and Bugan began in 2000. The joint venture Jasra-Elf began to produce petroleum and natural gas in March 1999 from the Maharaja Lela Jamalulam discovery made in 1990. Jasra-Elf-Fletcher, a joint venture of three companies (Jasra Jackson, Elf Aquitaine and Jaspet Fletcher Challenge), began to produce petroleum and natural gas in April 1999. Exploration activities continued, and in 1999 a new seismic survey called the Seria High Resolution 3D Seismic Survey was initiated. Early studies have revealed great potential. In November 2001 Brunei Shell announced that it intended to develop a new offshore oil and gas field at Egret, north-east of the Fairley field. The first phase of the development would produce natural gas by August 2003. Also in November 2001 the Government announced that two international consortia had advanced bids for two deep-sea areas in Brunei's offshore exclusive economic zone (EEZ)—Block J (with a total area of 5,020 sq km) and Block K (4,944 sq km). In February 2002 the French company TotalFinaElf, in partnership with BHP Billiton of Australia and Amerada Hess of the USA, won exploration rights to Block J, while a consortium comprising Brunei Shell, Japan's Mitsubishi Corporation and Conoco Brunei Ltd won the right to explore for natural gas in Block K.

In November 2001 a national oil company, wholly owned by the Government, was created—Brunei National Petroleum Company Sdn Bhd (PetroleumBrunei). BOGA was dissolved following the incorporation of the new company in early 2002. PetroleumBrunei intended to initiate the usage of the Production Sharing Contract (PSC) as a new model for the future exploration and production of petroleum and natural gas in Brunei. The PSC would replace the granting of concession rights to companies operative in the region, allowing the Government to exercise greater control over national resources; production-sharing arrangements were not subject to the tax and royalty payments required by concession contracts. The PSC was to be used for the first time for the new areas to which rights had been offered in the EEZ. TotalFinaElf was due to complete the final draft of a production-sharing arrangement with PetroleumBrunei for Block J in mid-2002. As two of Brunei Shell's concessions were due to expire in 2003, it was also hoped that the existence of PetroleumBrunei would reduce Brunei Shell's dominance in the industry and facilitate the development of a domestic industrial base.

Discoveries of petroleum and gas in the 1990s resulted in the continuous upward revision of estimates of the country's hydrocarbons base. Brunei Shell increased its reserves estimates substantially, especially for natural gas. In 1993 it was estimated that current rates of gas production could be maintained for another 40 years. In 2001 proven recoverable reserves of natural gas were estimated to be 390,772m. cu m. LNG exports to Japan have become as important to Brunei's trade account as exports of crude petroleum: in 1999 Brunei exported to Japan crude petroleum to the value of B $343.8m., compared with B $1,435.1m. of LNG exports. In 1999 Brunei also exported casing head petroleum spirit valued at B $93.1m., mainly to the Republic of Korea (which purchased 61.5% of the total). The value of gas exports increased from B $1,557.1m. in 1998 to B $1,632.6m. in 1999.

The BDEC report released in early 2000 (see above) recommended that the competitiveness of the petroleum and gas industry be improved through the maximization of production within the limits prescribed by Brunei's Oil Conservation Policy and through investment in the expansion of LNG production.

In 1987 a co-generation power plant (a joint project involving the Government, Brunei Shell and Brunei LNG) was completed at a cost of B $327m. The plant provides power for industrial and domestic use. In 1999 a gas-processing facility, the Tungku Gas Plant, was completed. Its purpose was to centralize fuel gas treatment for the Brunei East area to ensure a reliable supply of conditioned gas for power plants in Brunei. In the early 1990s the Brunei LNG Plant at Lumut underwent a refurbishment programme costing almost B $500m. The refurbishment and upgrading of facilities at Lumut was required to support the new 20-year contract to supply Japanese customers. In 2001 production of LNG from the Lumut plant was estimated to have reached 6m. metric tons. In early 1998 a new company, Brunei Gas Carriers Sdn Bhd, was formed to build and manage the new LNG vessel with a capacity of 135,000 cu m, which had become operational by July 2002. The shareholders were the Brunei Government (which controlled 80% of the company), Shell International Gas (10%) and the Mitsubishi Corporation (10%). In May 2002 Brunei hosted the GASEX 2002 international natural gas conference, which was attended by representatives of the gas industry from 15 nations.

The Government is also actively promoting the downstream petrochemical industry. Two memorandums of understanding were signed in 1997: the first, with IAB Ingenieur und Anlagenbau GmbH of Germany and Gommann Oil and Gas (Malaysia) Sdn Bhd, provided for the companies to conduct a feasibility study on a proposed 120,000 b/d petroleum refinery; the second, with the Kanematsu Corporation of Japan and the Chinese Petroleum Corporation of Taiwan, provided for the companies to draft a development plan for a proposed 60,000 b/d refinery and petrochemical complex. Both studies were completed in early 2000. The Government also signed an agreement in June 2000 with the Dover Consultant Consortium of Australia, under which a two-part study would be conducted into the development potential of the petrochemical industry. The Consortium submitted a report in June 2001 for consideration by BOGA. In 2002 the Government announced that work had begun on the Pulau Muara Besar project, an integrated petrochemical industrial complex to be situated at the mouth of Brunei Bay. The development constituted part of a programme of schemes announced for further economic diversification in the Eighth National Development Plan. Sungai Liang Industrial site, a site reserved for downstream industry, was also to be developed.

INDUSTRY AND INVESTMENT

In each of its Development Plans, the Government of Brunei has emphasized the need to diversify the economy, through the expansion of agriculture and industry and the development of financial services and tourism. In the 1980s, however, agriculture accounted for only a minor proportion of development expenditure, and industrial development was also slow because of poor infrastructure and a small domestic market. Between 1980 and 1994 the number of private industrial establishments rose from 2,000 to 4,100; while employment in that sector tripled to about 80,000 jobs, however, it failed to absorb the total increase in the labour force. The non-oil private sector contributed 41.3% of GDP in 1999, compared with 38.0% in 1996. In 2000 this contribution declined slightly to 40.5%, owing to less favourable economic conditions.

The Brunei Economic Development Board (EDB) was formed in 1976 with the main objective of promoting and encouraging industries, commerce and other developments in the private sector. It was granted extensive powers, enabling it to purchase, exchange, lease and own land, buildings and other immovable properties; to enter into contracts with other persons to work on its behalf; to underwrite the issue of equity shares, bonds or debentures by industrial enterprises; and to grant loans or advances, or subscribe to stocks, shares, bonds or debentures of industrial enterprises. For many years, one major activity undertaken by the EDB was that of the consideration and approval of applications from local and foreign companies to establish industrial and other projects in Brunei. Under the Investment Incentives Act of 1975, only limited companies that had been granted pioneer status were exempted from the 30% corporate tax and taxes on imported goods, as well as from taxes on imported raw materials not available or produced in Brunei. While approximately 20 industrial activities were declared as pioneer industries and products, the EDB would also consider other activities not mentioned in the list, provided that such industry had not been previously carried out in the country on a commercial scale, had favourable prospects to be developed for exports or if it was in the public interest to encourage the development of the new industry in the country. The Act also covered incentives for the expansion of established enterprises, as well as incentives for foreign loans.

The Government strongly encourages local participation in both the ownership and management of Brunei companies. Under the Investment Incentives Act of 1975, equity participation by Brunei citizens was made compulsory. Although there is no specific restriction on foreign participation in equity, local participation can be of considerable assistance with regard to operating in Brunei, especially when tendering for contracts with either the Government or Brunei Shell. A scheme for financing small and medium-sized business enterprises started in 1978, with the objective of helping local entrepreneurs. With the establishment of the Ministry of Industry and Primary Resources and the Financial Institutional Division of the Ministry of Finance, some of the EDB's activities, such as tourism and insurance, were transferred to both institutions respectively. In March 1995 the management of the scheme was transferred to the Development Bank of Brunei. The EDB itself was merged with the Economic Planning Unit in January 1998, to become the Department of Economic Planning and Development.

In July 2001 the Government enacted the Investment Incentives Order 2001, together with Pioneer Status and Income Tax Relief regulations. These issued guidelines under which certain industries could achieve pioneer status and tax relief could be granted for foreign and local investment, as well as extending the existing period of tax relief. The investment incentives offered included a five-year period of tax relief for companies that chose to invest between US $294,000 and US $1.5m. in approved ventures, an eight-year 'break' for those companies investing more than US $1.5m., and 11 years of relief for ventures located in a high-tech industrial park. Pioneer service companies were specifically designated as any engaged in the provision of engineering, technical, educational, medical or agricultural technology services. Companies engaged in the manufacture of goods for export were also eligible for pioneer status. The Government hoped that the new law and regulations would encourage the development of priority industries within the private sector.

In January 1989 the Ministry of Industry and Primary Resources (MIPR) was established in Bandar Seri Begawan to facilitate foreign investment and to enhance the diversification process. The Ministry functions as a 'one-stop' agency for foreign investors and is responsible for co-ordinating the licensing and approval process. It acts as a focal point for all industrial development. The Ministry's procedures consist of four stages: approval of the concept; the proposal; physical plans; and approval to operate. The Ministry also adopts the EDB's Investment Act and the subsequent Order and regulations and allows pioneer status to be given to any venture company involved in the type of industry listed and declared under them.

Twelve industrial sites, in all four districts, are available to investors. The Brunei Industrial Development Authority (BINA) is the leading agency responsible for providing, designating or allocating industrial sites and complexes. BINA was formed in April 1996, integrating the former Industrial Unit (of the MIPR) and the Co-operative Development department (of the Ministry of Home Affairs). The Technical Committee, which comprises the Ministries of Finance, Development and Industry and Primary Resources and BINA, functions as a co-ordinating forum for accelerating applications, resolving issues concerning land acquisition and manpower requirements and acting as the principal conduit for foreign investors. Strategies employed to develop an industrial base include: resiting existing small industries on an industrial estate, in order to allow them to expand and restructure; creating new industries; providing the industrial sites with adequate infrastructure such as roads, water supply, power and telecommunication facilities, made available at very low rental for periods of up to 20 years; and promoting enterprise by encouraging local business managers to upgrade their skills and technological knowledge. To achieve the latter objective, a Resource Centre was formally established in January 1997, although the Centre had in fact offered training activities since 1964.

By the late 1990s most of Brunei's industrial development was in the hydrocarbons sector: the Seria refinery, the Brunei LNG plant, the propane-bottling plant at Lumut and the co-generation plant. The small non-hydrocarbon manufacturing sector included textile and garment companies, roofing, mineral-water bottling, light food-processing, switchboard electricity, printing and a cement plant project (a joint venture with an Indonesian company). The MIPR, through the Technical Committee, had approved several activities on industrial sites, including coconut-oil processing and the production of digital video discs, stainless steel water storage tanks, stainless steel kitchen equipment, glass fibre reinforced concrete and glass fibre reinforced plastic. In 2001 Summons Holdings Sdn Bhd commenced construction of a silica-processing plant. Equipment imported from Sweden would be used to manufacture high-technology products such as silica plate. The plant would utilize domestic resources of silica sand for the first time. Between 1989 and 2001 nine textile manufacturing companies from Malaysia, Singapore and Indonesia established operations in Brunei. Garment manufacturing is now the second largest contributor to export earnings, after oil and gas: the total value of garments exported in 2000 was B $302m., compared with B $159.8m. in 1999 and B $10m. in 1989. The increase was due to the establishment of new factories and the expansion of existing ones. A total of 99% of the ready-made garments were exported to the USA, Canada and the European Union (EU). The manufacture of traditional handicrafts has also been encouraged by the Government, though on a very small scale.

Structural constraints remain, however, in trying to develop and widen the industrial base. Firms face high labour costs, a very small domestic market, a narrow resource base and a lack of indigenous skilled labour and entrepreneurs; in addition, long-term titles to land ownership are difficult to acquire, and the government bureaucracy has a reputation for being slow-moving although benevolent. These combined factors have hindered significant foreign investment. The sound oil sector (and the fact that the currency is tied to the Singapore dollar) maintains the exchange rate at a high level, thus hampering export possibilities further. In 1995 the Government commissioned a consultancy study to examine ways and means by which to develop the non-oil sector, culminating in the first Brunei Industrial Development Plan. The Government also established a trading and investment division under the MIPR, called Semaun Holdings, to help accelerate industrial development through direct investment. The main sphere of operation is in trading and commercial ventures, particularly in the food, manufacturing and service sectors. Semaun Holdings has since established its own subsidiaries, namely Semaun Seafood and Semaun Prim, and has signed several agreements relating to joint-venture projects. The MIPR also arranges consultative meetings with representatives from the textile industries and industrial complexes, as well as from co-operative societies.

Under the Seventh Plan, the Government allocated B $504.3m. for industrial development (of which B $132m. was reserved for the fund for the development of industries). Major activities were to be orientated towards the opening up of new industrial sites, as well as the improvement of infrastructure for these sites. In 1999 the MIPR was negotiating an agreement with two banks to provide competitive loans to small and medium-sized enterprises for approved projects. Under the Eighth Plan the Government also intended to expand its short-term economic recovery scheme for such enterprises.

The main objectives of the Government's Industrial Development Plan (IDP) were: to promote the growth of the private sector for a wider economic base and to render the nation less dependent on the hydrocarbon sector; to provide employment opportunities for Bruneians in the industrial sector; and to encourage foreign direct investment. The scope of the IDP covered four groupings: the oil and gas downstream activities; physical infrastructure and social services; primary industries and manufacturing; and trade and services. In pursuing the development, a 'niche' role would be adopted, that is, with emphasis on the need to produce 'niche' items or services that have a high value-added, capital-intensive and high-technology content and that are export-orientated. To achieve this strategy, a number of issues still needed to be addressed: administrative and organizational reform; the removal of impediments to growth; the enhancement of the system of incentives to attract more foreign direct investment; and the upgrading of the entrepreneurial skills of the locals. It was intended that the growth of the capital-intensive industries would be promoted through joint ventures and foreign direct investments, while some functions and activities of the Government would be actively considered for corporatization or privatization. Partial privatization has been achieved in several areas, including power generation, telecommunications (equipment and mobile cellular telephone system), transport (taxi and bus services), domestic waste collection outside municipal areas, meat and poultry processing, some trading activities (Muara Port Zone) and selected government services. The Department of Telecommunications was to be fully corporatized by April 2003, together with the Employees Trust Fund. A further 440 ha of land were to be developed in addition to the existing industrial sites in each of four districts. Also, the Muara Export Zone was to be further expanded and transformed into a regional transhipment centre to focus on export activities. In 2002 the Pulau Muara Besar project, an integrated petrochemical industrial complex, was initiated, and plans for the development of Sungai Liang Industrial site were announced under the Eighth National Development Plan.

Construction is one of the most important economic activities, after the oil and gas and public sectors, but remains heavily dependent on government projects. In recent years, however, the pace of construction activities in the private sector has increased, resulting in a high growth rate of 8% per annum on average. Many development projects were undertaken in the late 1980s and 1990s. However, the construction sector was very much affected by the Government's decision in late 1997 to cut the development budget for 1998. The slowdown was evident during the first six months of the year when a number of new projects had to be delayed. However, in June 1998 the Government announced an additional fund totalling B $352m. to promote the sector and reactivate some of the delayed projects. In 1999 and 2000 the Government continued to pursue a prudent fiscal policy and B $605m. and B $550m. respectively were allocated to development.

AGRICULTURE, FORESTRY AND FISHING

Agriculture and forestry were the principal branches of Brunei's economic activity before the discovery of petroleum in the late 1920s. In 1947 more than 50% of the population was employed in the primary sector; by 1971 this had been reduced to 10%. The development of the petroleum and natural gas industries, and that of urban areas, resulted in a migration of the rural population to towns, with a consequent shortage of labour in the agricultural sector. Although the area under cultivation increased from 10% of all land in the mid-1980s to about 15% in 1990, much potential agricultural land remained undeveloped. Farming had become very much a part-time business for most rural families, owing to the availability of more lucrative forms of paid employment.

Agriculture accounted for 2.0% of GDP in 2000. Brunei imports more than 80% of its food requirements. In 2000 food, beverages and tobacco imports amounted to B $394.1 m. (15.0% of the total), while animal and vegetable oils and fats cost a further B $13m. Government policy, however, is to reduce Brunei's dependence on food imports and to aim to achieve self-sufficiency in agriculture. From the early 1980s the Government began a series of measures intended to contribute towards the development of Brunei's agricultural industry. There were still no larger-scale agricultural enterprises in the early 1990s, and commercial agriculture was controlled largely by the Chinese community, producing mainly quick-growing vegetables in urban areas. By 1987 poultry enterprises were able to satisfy local needs, but were dependent on imported feeds. To encourage the rearing of local livestock, an animal-feeds industry was being developed in order to reduce production costs.

The enhancement of long-term food security constituted the overall agricultural objective of the Seventh Plan. The aims of the 1996–2000 agricultural development policy were, therefore:

to enhance activities related to national food security; to develop agro-industrial activity; to produce high value-added products using high-technology farming methods; and to conserve and protect plant biodiversity. For this purpose, attention was focused on the development of basic infrastructure, materials inputs, marketing and regulatory service, with the aims of, firstly, meeting domestic demand and, secondly, developing export potential. The Seventh Plan allocated B $173m., or 2.4% of the overall allocation and triple that of the previous Plan, to the development of agriculture.

Under the plan for enhancing national food security, the essential product groups were poultry and livestock, vegetables and ornamentals, fruits and plantation crops, rice and root crops. The plan for the development of the poultry industry (including the production of eggs and chickens) had two aspects: the first was the encouragement of integrated medium-sized enterprises; the other was the development of the small-scale farm producers linked to processing and marketing centres, such as the Mulaut Abattoir. Such centres act as market outlets for the small-scale poultry producers. The programme emphasized the participation of private enterprise in the development of the industry, government involvement being limited to the provision of basic infrastructure and production-support services. In 1998 egg production reached self-sufficiency through an increase to 77.3m. eggs, compared with 68.0m. eggs in 1997; production increased further to 87.0m. eggs in 2000. However, in 2001 egg production declined by 8%. For chicken-meat production, the Department of Agriculture reported an increase in the self-sufficiency level to 86.6% in 2000, compared with 79.2% in 1999.

The programme for vegetable production was orientated towards the development of high-value products and high-technology farming, such as protected cultivation and hydroponics. At the same time, the technical assistance required by small-scale local farmers was to continue to be provided. The production target for vegetables was 8,500 metric tons, or 75% of local requirements. Keen to ensure quality and to minimize the inflow of pesticides and toxic material into the country, the Government also opened a wholesale centre, necessitating the labelling of imported vegetables. The import of these vegetables affected local production, which declined from 60% of local requirements in 1997 to 53% in 1998. However, in 1999 and 2000 local production increased to 7,007 and 8,863 metric tons respectively. In 2001 vegetable production increased by an estimated 7%. The Plan also envisaged the collection of specimens of local fruit trees as the basis for developing small plantations and for the production of seedlings. It was hoped that this would support the development of large-scale fruit plantations in the future, and also encourage the planting of more local fruit trees. The aim was to increase the level of self-sufficiency from 10% to 70% by the end of the Seventh Plan period. In 1997 the achievement was only 12%. In 2001 fruit production increased by approximately 42% from 2000 levels. With regard to the production of rice, the intention was to develop a production capacity equivalent to 7% of local needs. In 2000, however, the achievement was only 1%. The Eighth National Development Plan set a target to increase rice production to 1,300 metric tons, or 3% of total requirements, by 2005. Rice production was 538.5 metric tons in 2001, an increase of 20% from 2000. The Government encouraged the planting of paddy through various schemes such as price support and the provision of improved infrastructure, irrigation and drainage facilities. Live cattle are imported from Australia, mainly from the government-owned ranches in the Northern Territory; there were also plans to develop goat and deer farming, and to increase the supply (and variety) of red meat in the country from 20 metric tons to 50 tons during the Seventh Plan. In April 1998 the self-sufficiency level for the goat industry was recorded at 11%, while in May 1998 the self-sufficiency level for the buffalo and cattle industry was 6%. Production of cattle rose by 13% in 2001, while that of goats increased by 37%. In June 1997 the Government bought the Brunei Meat Export Company to ensure that consumers in Brunei would continue to obtain reasonably priced genuine halal products. It also bought shares in a halal abattoir in Tennant Creek, owned by the Meat Processing Company in Australia. The Eighth National Development Plan identified halal food processing for export as a prospective growth industry.

The Government, in its effort to encourage greater private-sector participation, has also identified a number of projects for possible private involvement. These include rice production, meat-processing, day-old chick production, supply of fruit-planting materials and ornamental potted plants and tissue-cultured planting materials. The vast BIMP-EAGA market, indeed, promises better prospects for the agricultural development of Brunei, particularly its potential as a reliable source of halal food products.

There is a long tradition of fishing in Brunei, with activity moving away from the rivers and sheltered inshore waters and more towards sea-fishing, owing to the greater use of outboard motors and equipment made of synthetic materials. In 1990 Brunei's total catch of 2,307 metric tons supplied only 35% of domestic demand, compared with almost 70% in 1988. In 2001 Brunei's total commercial catch had increased to 3,839.4 metric tons, compared with 2,860 tons in 2000. To increase fish production, the Government encouraged the establishment of a small, modern offshore fishing industry to meet projected demand and, under the Seventh Plan, B $72.9m. was allocated for the continued development of the country's fisheries sector. The Government emphasizes the sustainable exploitation of the fishery resources. The current permitted exploitation level is self-imposed at the maximum economic yield, and is managed through the number of fishing licences issued for each fishing method. The Brunei Fisheries Limits Act (1982) delimits a maritime area of about 57,000 sq km extending to about 200 nautical miles (370 km) from the coast.

Brunei's relatively clean environment and freedom from extreme natural phenomena, such as typhoons, is conducive to the development of aquaculture. Once identified, potential areas are prepared with the required basic infrastructure such as access roads, water and power supplies. In line with the policy of sustainability, a buffer zone of 50 m is imposed in all aquaculture areas from other land use.

The potential yield, in accordance with the current maximum economic yield level, is about 20,000 metric tons, valued at B $200m. With the present level of exploitation being about 30%, however, there is considerable potential for the expansion of fisheries. In addition, Brunei's marine area is also known to be in the migration path of tuna. In 2001 overall aquaculture production decreased, although production of prawns experienced a substantial increase. With regard to the processing industry, owing to highly selective consumer preferences, only about 60% of the trawlers' catch is marketable. Although the remainder is usually thrown back overboard, it has the potential to be processed, and could then contribute significantly towards import substitution and also towards exports.

Forestry is not economically significant in Brunei, but is important in the conservation of soils, water, wildlife and the environment. Primary (60%) and secondary (20%) rain forest cover about 80% of total land area in Brunei. Forests in Brunei comprise about 5,000 species of plants, including some 2,000 species of trees. These forests are of five main types: mangrove swamps, heath forests, peat swamp forests, mixed dipterocarp forests and montane forests. The Forestry Act of Brunei (1934, and revised in 1984) provides the legal framework for the protection and conservation of forestry resources of the country. In addition, the National Forestry Policy (NFP), issued in 1989, guides and governs all future forestry activities throughout Brunei. The NFP emphasizes the need to protect and conserve the forest resources of the country for both socio-economic and environmental purposes, and institutes sound and sustainable management of the national forest resources. Accordingly, these forests have been functionally categorized into protection forest, conservation forest, production forest, forest recreational areas and National Park, which covers a total area of 50,000 ha.

Logging in Brunei is very limited and is being monitored closely. The Reduced Cut Policy, introduced in 1990, has restricted the total log production of the country. This restriction ensures the sustainable production of local timbers for domestic use. In line with the strong conservation policy, the Forestry Department proposed to incorporate an additional area of 86,411 ha in the forest reserves in an effort to increase reserves from 39% to 55% of existing forest and unallocated state lands.

In accordance with the NFP, many areas have been developed and promoted as 'eco-tourism' attractions. Under the Sixth Plan, for example, the Forestry Department embarked on several environment-related projects, which included the 'regreening' or reafforestation programme, and the establishment of National Park and forest recreational areas. By 1998, 11 forest recreation parks (FRP) had been developed, namely Sg. Liang, Luangan Lalak, Bukit Shahbandart, Berakas, Peradayan, Selirong, Bukit Subok, Sungai Basong, Kuala Belalong, Batang Duri and Ulu Temburong; these have become very popular, particularly among domestic tourists. Under the Seventh National Development Plan, various programmes were introduced for the conservation and protection of forests for both environmental and economic reasons. The forestry sector contributed B $22.3m. to the GDP in 1996, which increased to B $27m. in 2000, or 3.0% of total GDP. This contribution might have been higher, were it not for the Reduced Cut Policy, which limited logging to 100,000 cu m per annum, accounting for only 30% of domestic demand, while the rest had to be imported. Within the framework of the forest conservation policy, B $104m. was allocated to develop the forestry sector, with plantation activity, sustainable timber production, the creation of National Park and forestry recreation areas, the rehabilitation of wasteland and rattan production for the furniture industry all being areas to receive particular emphasis.

The theme of conservation is expected to continue to form the basis of the forestry policy. The long-term plantation programme will ensure that the country becomes self-sufficient in sawn timber and will therefore minimize unnecessary pressures on the forest reserves. It is hoped that this strategy will help maintain the 80% forest cover, and also preserve the rich diversity of the tropical rain forest, making Brunei an ideal centre for eco-tourism and also providing an 'international laboratory' in which scientists can conduct research and studies. With this in mind, a new national herbarium complex in Sungai Liang was completed in 1998. This complex serves as an important referral institution for plant collection in the country. An Andulau Forest Reserve has also been developed as a centre for the conservation of plant bio-diversity.

ENVIRONMENTAL ISSUES

Environmental protection and conservation continue to be integral components of the country's process of ensuring sustainable development in line with the long-term objective of maintaining 'a clean and healthy environment'. A number of environment-related projects, such as beach protection and the control of beach erosion, the rehabilitation of wastelands, the development of social waste collection and disposal schemes, dumping areas, and the aforementioned 're-greening' programme provided evidence of government concern regarding the state of the environment in the country. To facilitate the implementation of these projects the Government established the National Committee on the Environment (NCE) in 1993. The Environment Unit, placed under the Ministry of Development, was also established to serve as the secretariat to the NCE, and co-ordinate and monitor environment-related activities. The National Environment Strategy as envisioned in the Seventh Plan included maintaining sustainable utilization of natural resources, minimizing the negative impact on the environment arising from population growth and human activities and balancing the goals of socio-economic development with the need to sustain environmental quality. In May 2002 the Government upgraded the Environment Unit to the Department of Environment, Parks and Recreation as a reflection of its continuing commitment to the protection of the environment. In June Brunei was a signatory to an ASEAN convention intended to bring an end to the seasonal hazes common to the region, which have an adverse impact upon both agriculture and tourism, as well as the environment. The signatories pledged to strengthen their fire-fighting forces, enforce controls on open burning and establish early warning systems to prevent the spread of smoke pollution.

FOREIGN TRADE

Brunei had large surpluses on its balance of trade from 1972, owing to the country's exports of petroleum and natural gas. Its trade surplus reached a peak of B $8,622.3m. in 1980, but subsequently declined to B $1,939.1m. in 1988. While the decline in revenue from petroleum and gas exports was the principal reason for decreasing trade surpluses, an increase in import levels, owing to a rising standard of living, also contributed to the narrowing of trade gains. In 1990 and 1991 the trade surplus expanded to B $2,197m. and B $2,344.6m. respectively, owing largely to increases in crude petroleum prices. In the following years the trade surplus declined, to a low of B $153.3m. in 1996 before increasing to B $2,191.8m. and B $4,812.8m. in 1999 and 2000 respectively. The latter was mainly due to the substantial increase in the international price of petroleum, which peaked in November 2000. In addition to export revenue, the income accruing from the investment of Brunei's reserves will ensure that the current account of the balance of payments remains in surplus for the foreseeable future. In 1999, of the total export earnings of B $4,325.1m., crude petroleum and casing head petroleum spirit provided B $1,968.9m. (45.5%) and natural gas contributed B $1,632.6m. (37.7%). In 2001 exports totalled B $6,521.8m. In the same year imports cost B $2,076.4m. and included machinery and transport equipment, food, chemicals and other manufactured articles.

In 2001 Japan continued to be Brunei's major trading partner, accounting for 46.0% of total exports. Other major export markets included the Republic of Korea (11.9%), Thailand (11.8%) and Singapore (8.4%). Singapore was the principal source of imports in 2001, accounting for 23.4% of the total. Trade with Malaysia increased rapidly during the mid-1990s, accounting for 22.0% of total trade in 2001. In July 1988 the USA removed Brunei from its Generalized System of Preferences, mainly because Brunei's average annual income of about US $17,000 per head far exceeded the US $8,500 limit for eligibility. Exports were barely affected, as Brunei had never taken full advantage of the trade privileges offered under the system. Brunei adheres to a free-trade system, with an unweighted average tariff rate of 5%.

FINANCE AND BANKING

The investment of the surplus revenue accrued during the 1970s and early 1980s is managed jointly by the government-controlled BIA and a consortium of US, British and Japanese financial institutions. The BIA, formed in July 1983, was initially entrusted with the management of B $12,000m. (about US $6,000m.), transferred from the direct management of the British Crown Agents. The BIA established offices in London, Paris, Brussels, Boston, Tokyo, Hong Kong, Singapore, Kuala Lumpur, Bali and Yangon, managing its foreign reserves in European, North American and Asian markets. The Asian markets, which have attracted increasing interest by Bruneian investors, are also covered by the BIA's headquarters in Brunei. The reserves are invested in government bonds, equities, properties, precious metals and short-term deposits. BIA funds were seriously depleted in the 1990s by the effects of the regional economic crisis, compounded by the huge financial losses incurred under the chairmanship of Prince Jefri and a significant decline in the price of petroleum from mid-1997. There is no external public debt.

There is no central bank in Brunei, with most of the central banking functions being performed by the Financial Institution Division and the Brunei Currency Board, both under the Ministry of Finance. The Brunei dollar is also issued by the Brunei Currency Board. Although there was some speculation that Brunei might sever links with the Singapore dollar following independence in 1984, this did not, in fact, take place. Since Brunei's exports of petroleum and natural gas were priced in terms of the US dollar, a closer link with that unit, rather than with the Singapore dollar, seemed more appropriate.

There are no restrictions on the import of capital from any country, nor are there restrictions on overseas remittances of capital or profits. Non-resident accounts can be maintained, and there is no restriction on borrowing by non-residents. Interest rates tend to move in line with those of Singapore.

In 2000 the financial sector comprised 12 banks, of which nine were branches of foreign institutions, and three finance houses. In November 1986 the National Bank of Brunei was closed by the Government after allegations of the misuse of funds worth B $1,300m. New and more effective banking legislation was subsequently introduced, and a new locally owned bank, the International Bank of Brunei, was created from the former Island Development Bank. In January 1993 the Islamic Bank of Brunei (IBB) was established, replacing the International Bank of Brunei. The potential of foreign banks in Brunei, however, is limited by the small domestic market and an insufficient demand for traditional banking services, owing to the Government's provision of loans for the purchase of housing and cars. In 1991 the Brunei Islamic Trust Fund (Tabung Amanah Islam Brunei—TAIB) was established to promote trade and industry and to further the country's economic development. TAIB became the corner-stone of Brunei's financial direction, geared towards the Islamic principle, and by July 1999 the Trust Fund had a total of 54,723 depositors. In early 1995 the Development Bank of Brunei (DBB) was established. In July 2000 the DBB was transformed into the Islamic Development Bank of Brunei (IDBB). The IDBB became the third Islamic Bank in Brunei and was to provide financial assistance to small and medium enterprises, as the Economic Development Board had done in the past, in line with the teachings of Islam.

By 1999 there were 125 insurance companies registered to operate in Brunei, of which 23 were active. Most of these are branches of foreign companies but some are locally incorporated, namely, the Takaful IBB Bhd and Syarikat Insurans Islam TAIB Sdn Bhd. The insurance companies currently in operation are predominantly small-sized companies. All insurance companies transacting business in Brunei can join the General Insurance Association of Brunei, formed in 1985. In 1998 the gross premium of the general insurance companies decreased to B $67.9m., compared with B $92.4m. in 1997, as a result of the effects of the regional economic crisis.

In July 2000 the Brunei International Financial Centre (BIFC) was established with the specific aim of diversifying and stimulating the value-added service sector of the economy of Brunei and of the Asia-Pacific region, and also to attract overseas professionals and qualified and trained Bruneians to the international business sector. Many observers are sceptical of Brunei's prospects for development as a financial centre for the region, owing to a lack of relevant expertise and a consequent inability to compete with highly-sophisticated centres in the same time zone, such as Tokyo, Hong Kong and Singapore. Moreover, the adjacent Malaysian island of Labuan has similar plans, which have incorporated the establishment of many international merchant banks and which have proved quite successful. However, officials stated that BIFC would complement, rather than compete with, existing Asian financial centres. In July 2002 the Sultan remarked upon the success of the BIFC, noting that the number of international firms registered with it was steadily increasing. The Eighth National Development Plan included plans for the establishment of a Brunei International Offshore Financial Centre (BIOFC), in an attempt to encourage economic diversification and the development of Brunei's technological and service sectors. In March 2002 an amendment to the existing Bank Act was enforced in an attempt to eliminate illegal deposit taking and discourage Bruneians from becoming involved in 'get rich quick' schemes. In 2002 the Government also issued a licence to the International Brunei Exchange Ltd, enabling it to operate an International Securities Exchange in Brunei. It was hoped that the opening of Brunei's first exchange would enlarge the country's role within the global financial market.

In October 1995 Brunei joined the IMF and the World Bank, which qualifies the country for technical assistance and consultative advice from the array of experts from both established institutions, particularly with regard to the diversification of the economy.

In May 2000 attempts to establish a regional framework for financial co-operation, in order to prevent a recurrence of the regional financial crisis of 1997, advanced with an agreement among member nations of ASEAN and Japan, the Republic of Korea and the People's Republic of China (the Chiang Mai initiative) to swap foreign-exchange reserves to avert potential crises.

LABOUR FORCE AND EMPLOYMENT

The labour force in 2000 totalled 145,880, with about 41% comprising foreign workers. Women play a significant role in both the government and private sectors, having taken advantage of the equal educational opportunities in Brunei. The participation rate of women aged 15 years and above was 55% in 2000, compared with 86% for men. The number of female workers increased from 29.5% of the total labour force in 1986 to 47% in 2000.

The establishment of a Government Workers' Provident Fund in 1993, which organized a pension system for non-pensionable government employees and subsequently for employees in the private sector, also helped make the latter more attractive to Bruneians by giving private-sector employees new financial security. Under the scheme, the employee contributed 5% of his or her salary, the employer another 5%, and the State provided the remainder.

The private-sector work-force was estimated at 70,262 in 1998, compared with 63,452 in 1995. In 1995 the construction sector employed 31.0% of private-sector workers, being the most important private industry as regards employment. Brunei Shell Petroleum Co (Brunei Shell), in which the Government has a 50% holding, was the largest private employer in 1991, with some 3,500 staff. The employment capacity of the hydrocarbon sector is limited, however, owing to the highly capital-intensive nature of the industry.

According to the 1995 labour force survey, only 5.4% of the labour force was employed in the manufacturing sector. The private sector is strongly dependent on immigrant labour, primarily from the ASEAN countries, but also from countries such as India, Bangladesh and Pakistan. Professional staff, including doctors, medical specialists and teachers, are mostly recruited from ASEAN, the Indian subcontinent and the United Kingdom. In 2000 there were about 60,000 foreign workers in Brunei. Union activity is low and of very limited scope; collective agreements exist only in the oil sector. In 1998 there was an exodus of foreign workers, including about 16,000 Thais working in the construction sector, reflecting cost-cutting measures in local companies facing increased competition from countries affected by the regional economic crisis, the completion of major government projects, the slowing of public-sector construction and the collapse of the Amedeo Development Corporation.

Despite the perennial shortage of manual labourers and of skilled labour, unemployment among indigenous citizens began to rise in the late 1980s. The 1991 census estimated the rate of unemployment at 4.8% of the labour force, although this estimate was probably lower than the real figure. In 2001 the unemployment rate was estimated at 4.7%. Forecasts of employment prospects for school-leavers between 1992 and 2001 indicated that up to 25% might be unable to secure a job. These fears were compounded by the fact that in February 2002, of 6,812 local people registered as unemployed, 90% were school-leavers. Increasing youth unemployment is a matter of particular concern, since it is believed to be a major reason for nascent social problems in Brunei. The more general employment issue is, however, a crucial one for the long-term viability of the economy: the strong preference for public-sector jobs among Brunei Malays is a major problem; also, there are only a relatively small number of non-manual jobs in the private sector for increasingly well-educated, but not necessarily vocationally and technically skilled, Bruneians. In response, the Government has enforced stricter implementation of the 'Bruneianization' employment policy, whereby Malays receive positive discrimination, and has invested heavily in vocational and technical education. The proportion of Bruneians working for Brunei Shell was over 50% in 1990, up from 37% in 1980. In Brunei LNG, Bruneians accounted for 75% of total manpower. Furthermore, as a result of the Bruneianization programme, an increasing number of senior, supervisory and specialist positions are filled by Brunei nationals. In 1998 85% of the total work-force were local staff; at senior levels, five of six department heads and 11 of 20 division head positions were occupied by local staff. The Competency Assurance System, which was fully implemented at the end of 1998, defined the required knowledge and skills for positions and attempted objectively to measure staff competence. This tool further facilitated the Bruneianization programme.

The Government's Bruneianization policy has caused resentment in the Chinese community, which dominates the private sector: although accounting for 14.9% of the population in 1999, some Chinese are not entitled to Bruneian citizenship, and therefore do not, in the area of employment, benefit from the positive discrimination received by Brunei Malays under the policy. Nevertheless, the future development of the private sector is likely to continue to depend heavily upon Chinese and other foreign participation and labour skills. However, with little hope of acquiring Bruneian citizenship or career advancement, many Chinese choose to emigrate to Australia or Canada.

INFRASTRUCTURE

Under the Eighth National Development Plan, the sum of B $30.3m. was allocated to the improvement of the civil aviation sector. In 2000 Brunei International Airport handled 971,355 passengers and 25,549,196 kg of cargo, compared with 120,000 passengers and negligible levels of air cargo in 1973. The airport is used by five airlines, including the state-owned Royal Brunei Airlines (RBA), which was established in November 1974. In 1997 RBA carried 1.1m. passengers, and passenger volume was expected to increase further by 2003, the year by which it was intended that Brunei would have become established as a 'service hub for trade and tourism' (SHuTT). In 2000 the company operated scheduled services to 30 regional and international destinations. Following an expansion of services, a number of destinations had to be suspended, owing to low passenger demand (Bahrain, Zurich and Cairo in 1996 and Bintulu and Yangon in 1998). RBA is studying the possibility of services to new destinations within the BIMP-EAGA catchment area, as well as other international routes, as part of the national carrier expansion programme. In June 2002 a Brunei International Air Cargo Centre was launched at Brunei International Airport. It was hoped that the centre would enable Brunei to gain access to the competitive air cargo industry, a lucrative source of revenue.

In BIMP-EAGA, the Working Group on Expansion of Air Linkages (in which Brunei is a leading country) has proposed the adoption of an 'open sky' policy, with the signing of memorandums of understanding by member countries. In the wider regional context, the ASEAN meeting for ministers responsible for economic affairs, held in Bandar Seri Begawan in September 1995, proposed a Plan of Action in Transport and Communication, which was to include the development of an 'open sky' policy for ASEAN, with a view to promoting greater co-operation in transport and communication, in support of the AFTA process.

Brunei's principal deep-water port at Muara opened in 1973, and was subsequently expanded. The Muara Port, which covers a total area of 24 ha, contains the transit warehouse, the container marshalling yard and the freight station. The main commercial berth is 611 m in length, with a maximum draught of 10 m. The traditional berth of 87 m with maximum draught of 5.2 m is also available for smaller craft. The port also provides the facilities for the discharge of bulk cement and bulk bitumen. The port operates a 24-hour service, parts of which have been privatized. In 1995 work started on the B $44m. Muara Port expansion, which was to include the deepening of the channel and harbour up to 13.0 m, thereby enabling the port to handle the third generation of vessels with a capacity of 3,000 20-foot equivalent units. A project to extend the berth by a further 250 m was completed in September 1999. Other developments include concessions on port tariffs for direct shipping services and transhipment activities and the inauguration of a new container terminal. In 1999 the Government signed a contract with the Port of Singapore Authority to secure its assistance with Brunei's port development programme.

The other major port is at Kuala Belait, which handles shallow-draught vessels. In December 1997 a B $20m. project was launched to deepen the Kuala Belait river mouth. It was hoped that this initiative would revitalize the maritime industry. The deepening project would provide ships and boats with unhindered access to piers along the river. The Bandar Seri Begawan harbour is used mainly for passenger vessels to the Temburong district and neighbouring Malaysian ports, but passengers travelling to Labuan now need only to board a boat at Serasa, with the journey time being thus reduced to about 30 minutes. Regular freight services are operated to Singapore, Malaysia, Hong Kong, Thailand, Japan, Taiwan, the Philippines and the western seaboard of the USA. There are two loading points near Seria for crude petroleum and natural gas. Rivers are still important transport routes for local shipments.

Between 1992 and 1996 the number of cargo vessels calling at Muara Port increased from 918 to 1,443. Registered seaborne cargo handled by the Ports Department, which totalled 2.4m. 20-foot equivalent units (TEUs) in 1996, declined significantly to 0.06m. TEUs in 2000.

In the late 1980s and early 1990s major changes were made to the road system, resulting in an estimated increase in the total length of road from 1,993.8 km in 1987 to 3,115.3 km in 1999. The main national highway connects Bandar Seri Begawan, Tutong and Kuala Belait. A new highway linking Brunei with Sarawak, in Malaysia, was completed in 1994. Under the Eighth National Development Plan B $433.1m. was allocated to the development of the road system. A Pan-Borneo highway from Sarawak to Sabah, via Brunei, is under construction, but has been delayed by border ambiguities. In April 2002 it was reported that the Malaysian Government was considering implementing the highway project but bypassing Brunei completely. There are no public railways, and rivers form the principal means of communication in the interior. In June 2002 a German company—Project Development Management South East Asia (PDMSEA)—announced that it had allocated US $7m. to a study of the feasibility of constructing a Trans-Borneo Railway. The Trans-Borneo Project aimed to connect Brunei with Kalimantan, Sabah and Sarawak by means of a railway system and was scheduled for completion in 2006. The project formed part of the Pan-EAGA Multi-Capital Transportation Network approved by BIMP-EAGA in 2000.

From the 1980s there was a dramatic increase in the number of road-users. The number of private registered vehicles had increased from 62,047 in 1981 to 186,612 in 2001. Although the price of petrol is relatively low, the costs of vehicle purchase and maintenance are not, particularly following the introduction in early 1995 of new import duties on cars, which ranged from 20% to 200% depending on the engine capacity of the car. The short-term effect was a greater number of smaller cars on the road and increased use of the public transport system.

In the area of telecommunications, Brunei had a ratio of 24 telephones per 100 people in 2000, compared with 15 telephones per 100 people in 1991. To complement the cable telephone system, mobile telephone services were introduced. The number of registered mobile telephone users increased from 36,163 in April 1996 to 95,000 at the end of 2000. Various new services and products have been offered by taking full advantage of the available enhanced capabilities of the digital exchanges. The Department of Telecommunications provides international direct dialling to more than 150 countries through two international gateways, two satellite systems and a network of optical fibre submarine cables. The Government has also moved to liberalize the licensing of satellite television dishes. Under the BIMP-EAGA initiatives, in February 1995 the Government of Brunei and the East Malaysian States of Sabah and Sarawak were exploring arrangements to have a direct telecommunications link between Brunei and both Sabah and Sarawak, as an initial step towards establishing the BIMP-EAGA network, which should also cover Kalimantan, Sulawesi and the southern Philippines. In August 1995 BruNet, the first cyberspace information network, was created, and in September of that year the Ministry of Communications introduced a new pager service, cheaper telephone calls and electronic real-time information systems. BruNet has gained enormous popularity and became over-subscribed in its first year of service, increasing its users from about 900 initial subscribers to an estimated 22,000 by the end of 2000. Pager subscribers also increased from 5,200 in 1991 to about 10,000 in 1996. In January 1998 the Telecommunications Department launched Video Phone Services, and in November 1999 it introduced Business Centres in selected locations. In March 1998 the Postal Services Department introduced the Premium Services Centre for corporate customers. Brunei's strong position in the area of telecommunications is expected to provide the country with an advantage within the BIMP-EAGA. Under the Seventh National Development Plan, the Department of Telecommunications prepared for the two-stage development of Brunei Information Infrastructure. The first step was to transform the Department into a business-orientated organization, which would provide a high level of service to customers. The second stage included the provision of a full range of telecommunications services, including multi-media services. Under the Seventh Plan, the telecommunications sector recorded an encouraging level of growth.

In January 2001 the Brunei Information Technology (BIT) Council was established, following the implementation of the country's first IT Strategic Plan (ISP)—'IT 2000 and beyond'. The ISP's goals included: raising IT literacy within society; promoting its application in both the public and private sector; and ensuring that the sector was provided with adequate IT-skilled personnel to facilitate growth within it. Under the Eighth National Development Plan, B $526m. was allocated specifically to national IT development for the first time. The Department of Telecommunications was to be corporatized and transformed into a government-administered private company by April 2003 as part of an ongoing programme to corporatize many government services. Syarikat Telekom Brunei Bhd (TelBru) was registered in May 2002. The corporatization programme was intended to reduce the Government's direct involvement in the provision of public services and enable it to become a more effective regulator and facilitator. Brunei was to host the International Infocommunications Technology (Infocomtech) Expo in May 2003, emphasizing its commitment to the advancement of IT under the Eighth Plan.

Statistical Survey

Source (unless otherwise stated): Department of Economic Planning and Development, Ministry of Finance, Bandar Seri Begawan 2012; tel. (2) 241991; fax (2) 226132; internet www.depd.gov.bn.

AREA AND POPULATION

Area: 5,765 sq km (2,226 sq miles); *by district:* Brunei/Muara 570 sq km (220 sq miles), Seria/Belait 2,725 sq km (1,052 sq miles), Tutong 1,165 sq km (450 sq miles), Temburong 1,305 sq km (504 sq miles).

Population (excluding transients afloat): 260,482 at census of 7 August 1991; 332,844 (males 168,925, females 163,919) at census of 21 August 2001. *By district* (2001 census): Brunei/Muara 230,030; Seria/Belait 55,602; Tutong 38,649; Temburong 8,563.

Density (2001 census): 57.7 per sq km.

Ethnic Groups (2001 census): Malay 222,145, Chinese 37,039, Other indigenous 11,658, Others 62,002, Total 332,844.

Principal Town: Bandar Seri Begawan (capital), population 27,285 at 2001 census.

Births, Marriages and Deaths (registrations, 2000): Live births 7,481 (birth rate 22.1 per 1,000); Deaths 965 (death rate 2.9 per 1,000); Marriages (1999) 2,089 (marriage rate 6.3 per 1,000).

2001: Birth rate 21.9 per 1,000; Death rate 2.9 per 1,000; Registered marriages 2,091.

Expectation of Life (WHO estimates, years at birth, 2000): Males 73.4; Females 78.7. Source: WHO, *World Health Report*.

Economically Active Population (persons aged 15 years and over, 1991 census): Agriculture, hunting, forestry and fishing 2,162; Mining and quarrying 5,327; Manufacturing 4,070; Electricity, gas and water 2,223; Construction 14,145; Trade, restaurants and hotels 15,404; Transport, storage and communications 5,392; Financing, insurance, real estate and business services 5,807; Community, social and personal services 52,121; Activities not adequately defined 95; *Total employed* 106,746 (males 72,338; females 34,408); Unemployed 5,209 (males 2,745; females 2,464); *Total labour force* 111,955 (males 75,083; females 36,872).

Mid-2001 (estimate): Total labour force 157,000.

HEALTH AND WELFARE

Key Indicators

Fertility (births per woman, 2001): 2.2.

Under-5 Mortality Rate (per 1,000 live births, 2000): 6.

HIV/AIDS (% of persons aged 15–49, 1999): 0.2.

Physicians (per 1,000 head, 1995): 0.85.

Health Expenditure (1998): US $ per head (PPP): 985.
% of GDP: 5.7.
public (% of total): 43.5.

Human Development Index (2000): ranking: 32.
value: 0.856.

For sources and definitions, see explanatory note on p. vi.

AGRICULTURE, ETC.

Principal Crops (estimates, '000 metric tons, 2001): Rice (paddy) 0.4, Vegetables 8.8, Fruit and arable crops 4.1.

Livestock ('000 head, 2001): Cattle 1.6, Buffaloes 5.7, Goats 2.4, Poultry 10,540.

Livestock Products ('000 metric tons, 2001): Beef and veal 16.2; Poultry meat 5.3; Poultry eggs 4.3 (FAO estimate); Cattle hides (fresh) 2.7. Source: FAO.

Forestry ('000 cubic metres, 2001): Round timber 107.2; Sawn timber 39.7; Firewood 0.1; Poles ('000 pieces) 67.3.

Fishing (metric tons, live weight, 2001): Capture 3,500; Aquaculture 339; Total catch 3,839.

MINING

Production (2001, estimates): Crude petroleum ('000 barrels, incl. condensate) 71,000; Natural gas (million cu m, gross) 11,000. Source: US Geological Survey.

INDUSTRY

Production ('000 barrels, unless otherwise indicated, 2001, estimates): Motor spirit (petrol) 1,600; Distillate fuel oils 1,100; Residual fuel oil 500; Cement ('000 metric tons) 227; Electric energy (million kWh, 2000) 2,579. Source: mainly US Geological Survey.

FINANCE

Currency and Exchange Rates: 100 sen (cents) = 1 Brunei dollar (B $). *Sterling, US Dollar and Euro Equivalents* (31 May 2002): £1 sterling = B $2.6188; US $1 = B $1.7855; €1 = B $1.6760; B $100 = £38.19 = US $56.01 = €59.66. *Average Exchange Rate* (Brunei dollars per US $): 1.6950 in 1999; 1.7240 in 2000; 1.7917 in 2001. Note: The Brunei dollar is at par with the Singapore dollar.

Budget (B $ million, 1997): *Revenue:* Tax revenue 1,561 (Import duty 224, Corporate income tax 1,333); Non-tax revenue 1,282 (Commercial receipts 303, Property income 957); Transfers from Brunei Investment Agency 1,146; Total 3,989. *Expenditure:* Ordinary expenditure 2,564 (Prime Minister's Office 183, Defence 548, Foreign Affairs 116, Finance 502, Home Affairs 94, Education 347, Industry and Primary Resources 43, Religious Affairs 113, Development 286, Health 178); Other current expenditure 36; Capital expenditure 1,350; Investment in public enterprises by Brunei Investment Agency 67; Total 4,016.

(B $ million, 1998, estimates): *Revenue:* 2,775 (excl. transfers from Brunei Investment Agency); *Expenditure:* 4,295 (excl. investment by Brunei Investment Agency).

Source: IMF, *Brunei Darussalam: Recent Economic Developments* (April 1999).

Money Supply (B $ million, 2001): Currency outside banks 648.3; Demand deposits at banks 1,724.7; Total money 2,373.0.

Cost of Living (Consumer Price Index; base: 1990 = 100): All items 120.2 in 1999; 121.7 in 2000 (Food 117.8; Clothing and footwear 135.7; Housing 107.2; Transport and communication 137.8; Miscellaneous 122.2); 122.4 in 2001 (Food 118.4; Clothing and footwear 134.5; Housing 107.4; Transport and communication 139.6; Miscellaneous 123.3).

Gross Domestic Product by Economic Activity (B $ million in current prices, 2001): Agriculture, hunting, forestry and fishing 210.0; Mining, quarrying and manufacturing 3,140.9; Electricity, gas and water 65.2; Construction 425.2; Trade, restaurants and hotels 705.0; Transport, storage and communications 434.4; Finance, insurance, real estate and business services 701.0; Community, social and personal services 2,138.7; *Sub-total* 7,820.4; *Less* Imputed bank service charge 201.2; *GDP in purchasers' values* 7,619.2.

Balance of Payments (B $ million, 2001): Exports of goods 6,521.8; Imports of goods –1,968.2; *Trade balance* 4,553.6; Exports of services

863.6; Imports of services −1,887.5; *Balance on goods and services* 3,529.7; Other income received 3,764.7; Other income paid −329.9; *Balance on goods, services and income* 6,964.5; Current transfers received 0; Current transfers paid −175.4; *Current balance* 6,789.1; Foreign investment (net) 448.6; Long-term capital (net) −3,605.9; Short-term capital (net) 330.

EXTERNAL TRADE

Principal Commodities: (B $ million, 2001): *Imports c.i.f.:* Food and live animals 341.27; Chemicals 157.83 Basic manufactures 636.80; Machinery and transport equipment 630.17; Miscellaneous manufactured articles 228.95; Total (incl. others) 2,076.39. *Exports f.o.b.:* Mineral fuels, lubricants, etc. 5,826.72; Machinery and transport equipment 260.72; Miscellaneous manufactured articles 295.65; Total (incl. others) 6,521.76.

Principal Trading Partners (B $ million, 2001): *Imports:* Australia 72.2; People's Republic of China 67.6; France 35.1; Germany 70.8; Hong Kong 104.6; Indonesia 47.8; Italy 93.0; Japan 133.2; Republic of Korea 30.8; Malaysia 456.3; Netherlands 18.1; Singapore 486.9; United Kingdom 82.9; USA 190.0; Total (incl. others) 2,076.4. *Exports:* Japan 2,999.0; Republic of Korea 773.4; Malaysia 42.9; Singapore 549.6; Thailand 770.6; USA 491.7; Total (incl. others) 6,521.8.

TRANSPORT

Road Traffic (registered vehicles, 2001): Private cars 188,720, Goods vehicles 17,828, Motorcycles and scooters 7,162, Buses and taxis 2,267, Others 4,470.

Merchant Fleet (displacement, '000 grt at 31 December): 362.0 in 1999; 361.7 in 2000; 362.7 in 2001. Source: Lloyd's Register-Fairplay, *World Fleet Statistics*.

International Sea-borne Shipping (freight traffic, freight tons, 2001): Goods loaded 103,082; Goods unloaded 891,976. Note: One freight ton equals 40 cubic feet (1.133 cubic metres) of cargo.

Civil Aviation (2001): Passenger arrivals 530,552, passenger departures 522,576; freight loaded 9,699 metric tons, freight unloaded 14,610 metric tons; mail loaded 37 metric tons, mail unloaded 223 metric tons.

TOURISM

Visitor Arrivals by Nationality (incl. excursionists, 2000): Indonesia 68,527; Malaysia 974,132; Philippines 65,842; Singapore 27,995; United Kingdom 43,865; Total (incl. others) 1,306,764.

Tourism Receipts (US $ million): 38 in 1996; 39 in 1997; 37 in 1998. Source: World Bank.

COMMUNICATIONS MEDIA

Radio Receivers (2000, estimate): 362,712 in use.

Television Receivers (2000, estimate): 216,223 in use.

Telephones (2000): 82,600 direct exchange lines in use.

Facsimile Machines (1996, estimate): 2,000 in use. Source: UN, *Statistical Yearbook*.

Mobile Cellular Telephones (2001): 131,246 subscribers.

Personal computers ('000 in use, 2001 estimate): 25. Source: International Telecommunication Union.

Internet users ('000, 2001): 35.0. Source: International Telecommunication Union.

Book Production (1992): 45 titles. (1990): 25 titles; 56,000 copies. Source: UNESCO, *Statistical Yearbook*.

Newspapers (2001): Daily 4; Non-daily 3 (English 2, with circulation of 22,000 copies; Malay 3, with circulation of 39,500 copies; Malay and English 1, with circulation of 9,000 copies).

Other Periodicals (1998): 15 (estimated combined circulation 132,000 copies per issue).

EDUCATION

(2001)

Pre-primary and Primary: 186 schools; 3,806 teachers; 59,369 pupils.

General Secondary: 40 schools; 2,891 teachers; 34,809 pupils.

Teacher Training: 1 college; 51 teachers; 247 pupils.

Vocational: 6 colleges; 505 teachers; 2,509 pupils.

Higher Education: 3 institutes (incl. 1 university); 403 teachers; 3,885 students.

Adult literacy rate (UNESCO estimates): 91.5% (males 94.6%; females 88.1%) in 2000. Source: UN Development Programme, *Human Development Report*.

Directory

The Constitution

Note: Certain sections of the Constitution relating to elections and the Legislative Council have been in abeyance since 1962.

A new Constitution was promulgated on 29 September 1959 (and amended significantly in 1971 and 1984). Under its provisions, sovereign authority is vested in the Sultan and Yang Di-Pertuan, who is assisted and advised by five Councils: the Religious Council, the Privy Council, the Council of Cabinet Ministers, the (inactive) Legislative Council and the Council of Succession. Power of appointment to the Councils is exercised by the Sultan.

The 1959 Constitution established the Chief Minister as the most senior official, with the British High Commissioner as adviser to the Government on all matters except those relating to Muslim and Malay customs.

In 1971 amendments were introduced reducing the power of the British Government, which retained responsibility for foreign affairs, while defence became the joint responsibility of both countries.

In 1984 further amendments were adopted as Brunei acceded to full independence and assumed responsibility for defence and foreign affairs.

THE RELIGIOUS COUNCIL

In his capacity as head of the Islamic faith in Brunei, the Sultan and Yang Di-Pertuan is advised on all Islamic matters by the Religious Council, whose members are appointed by the Sultan and Yang Di-Pertuan.

THE PRIVY COUNCIL

This Council, presided over by the Sultan and Yang Di-Pertuan, is to advise the Sultan on matters concerning the Royal prerogative of mercy, the amendment of the Constitution and the conferment of ranks, titles and honours.

THE COUNCIL OF MINISTERS

Presided over by the Sultan and Yang Di-Pertuan, the Council of Cabinet Ministers considers all executive matters.

THE LEGISLATIVE COUNCIL

The role of the Legislative Council is to scrutinize legislation. However, following political unrest in 1962, provisions of the Constitution relating, *inter alia*, to the Legislative Council were amended, and the Legislative Council has not met since 1984. In the absence of the Legislative Council, legislation is enacted by royal proclamation.

THE COUNCIL OF SUCCESSION

Subject to the Constitution, this Council is to determine the succession to the throne, should the need arise.

The State is divided into four administrative districts, in each of which is a District Officer responsible to the Prime Minister and Minister of Home Affairs.

The Government

HEAD OF STATE

Sultan and Yang Di-Pertuan: HM Sultan Haji HASSANAL BOLKIAH (succeeded 4 October 1967; crowned 1 August 1968).

COUNCIL OF CABINET MINISTERS

(September 2002)

Prime Minister, Minister of Defence and of Finance: HM Sultan Haji HASSANAL BOLKIAH.

Minister of Foreign Affairs: HRH Prince MOHAMED BOLKIAH.

Minister of Home Affairs and Special Adviser to the Prime Minister: Pehin Dato' Haji ISA BIN Pehin Haji IBRAHIM.

Minister of Education: Pehin Dato' Haji ABDUL AZIZ BIN Pehin Haji UMAR.

Minister of Industry and Primary Resources: Dato' Haji ABDUL RAHMAN TAIB.

Minister of Religious Affairs: Pehin Dato' Dr Haji MOHAMAD ZAIN BIN Haji SERUDIN.

Minister of Development: Dato' Seri Paduka Dr Haji AHMAD BIN Haji JUMAT.

Minister of Health: Pehin Dato' Haji ABU BAKAR BIN Haji APONG

Minister of Culture, Youth and Sports: Pehin Dato' Haji HUSSEIN BIN Pehin Haji MOHAMAD YOSOF.

Minister of Communications: Pehin Dato' Haji ZAKARIA BIN Haji SULEIMAN.

There are, in addition, eight deputy ministers.

MINISTRIES

Office of the Prime Minister (Jabatan Perdana Menteri): Istana Nurul Iman, Bandar Seri Begawan BA 1000; tel. (2) 229988; fax (2) 241717; e-mail PRO@jpm.gov.bn; internet www.pmo.gov.bn.

Ministry of Communications (Kementerian Perhubungan): Jalan Menteri Besar, Bandar Seri Begawan BB 3910; tel. (2) 383838; fax (2) 380127; e-mail info@mincom.gov.bn; internet www.mincom.gov.bn.

Ministry of Culture, Youth and Sports (Kementerian Kebudayaan, Belia dan Sukan): Simpang 336, Jalan Kebangsaan, Bandar Seri Begawan BC 4415; tel. (2) 380911; fax (2) 380653; e-mail info@kkbs.gov.bn; internet www.kkbs.gov.bn.

Ministry of Defence (Kementerian Pertahanan): Bolkiah Garrison, Bandar Seri Begawan BB 3510; tel. (2) 386000; fax (2) 331615; e-mail info@mindef.gov.bn; internet www.mindef.gov.bn.

Ministry of Development (Kementerian Pembangunan): Old Airport, Jalan Berakas, Bandar Seri Begawan BB 3510; tel. (2) 241911; e-mail info@mod.gov.bn; internet www.mod.gov.bn.

Ministry of Education (Kementerian Pendidikan): Old Airport, Jalan Berakas, Bandar Seri Begawan BB 3510; tel. (2) 382233; fax (2) 380050; e-mail sutmoe@brunet.bn; internet www.moe.gov.bn.

Ministry of Finance (Kementerian Kewangan): Bandar Seri Begawan 1130; tel. (2) 241991; fax (2) 226132; e-mail info@finance.gov.bn; internet www.finance.gov.bn.

Ministry of Foreign Affairs (Kementerian Hal Ehwal Luar Negeri): Jalan Subok, Bandar Seri Begawan BD 2710; tel. (2) 261177; fax (2) 262904; e-mail info@mfa.gov.bn; internet www.mfa.gov.bn.

Ministry of Health (Kementerian Kesihatan): Jalan Menteri Besar, Bandar Seri Begawan BB 3910; tel. (2) 226640; fax (2) 240980; e-mail moh2@brunet.bn; internet www.moh.gov.bn.

Ministry of Home Affairs (Kementerian Hal Ehwal Dalam Negeri): Jalan Menteri Besar, Bandar Seri Begawan BB 3910; tel. (2) 223225; e-mail info@home-affairs.gov.bn; internet www.home-affairs.gov.bn.

Ministry of Industry and Primary Resources (Kementerian Perindustrian dan Sumber-sumber Utama): Jalan Menteri Besar, Bandar Seri Begawan BB 3910; tel. (2) 382822; fax (2) 382807; e-mail MIPRS2@brunet.bn; internet www.industry.gov.bn.

Ministry of Religious Affairs (Kementerian Hal Ehwal Ugama): Jalan Menteri Besar, Jalan Berakas, Bandar Seri Begawan BB 3910; tel. (2) 382525; fax (2) 382330; e-mail info@religious-affairs.gov.bn; internet www.religious-affairs.gov.bn.

Political Organizations

Parti Perpaduan Kebangsaan Brunei—PPKB (Brunei National Solidarity Party—BNSP): Bandar Seri Begawan; f. 1986, after split in PKDB (see below); ceased political activity in 1988, but re-emerged in 1995; Pres. HATTA ZAINAL ABIDIN.

Former political organizations included: **Parti Rakyat Brunei—PRB** (Brunei People's Party), banned in 1962, leaders are all in exile; **Barisan Kemerdeka'an Rakyat—BAKER** (People's Independence Front), f. 1966 but no longer active; **Parti Perpaduan Kebangsaan Rakyat Brunei—PERKARA** (Brunei People's National United Party), f. 1968 but no longer active; and **Parti Kebangsaan Demokratik Brunei—PKDB** (Brunei National Democratic Party—BNDP), f. 1985 and dissolved by government order in 1988.

Diplomatic Representation

EMBASSIES AND HIGH COMMISSIONS IN BRUNEI

Australia: Teck Guan Plaza, 4th Floor, Jalan Sultan, Bandar Seri Begawan BS 8811; tel. (2) 229435; fax (2) 221652; e-mail ozcombrn@pso.brunet.bn; High Commissioner: ALLASTER COX.

Bangladesh: AAR Villa, 5 Simpang 308, Kampong Lambak Kanan, Jalan Berakas, Bandar Seri Begawan BB 1714; tel. (2) 394716; fax (2) 394715; High Commissioner: Maj.-Gen. ABU ISHAQ IBRAHIM.

Cambodia: 8 Simpang 845, Kampong Tasek, Meradun, Jalan Tutong, Bandar Seri Begawan BF 1520; tel. (2) 654046; fax (2) 650646; Ambassador: ITH DETTOLA.

Canada: 5th Floor, Jalan McArthur Bldg, 1 Jalan McArthur, Bandar Seri Begawan BS 8711; tel. (2) 220043; fax (2) 220040; e-mail hicomcda@brunet.bn; internet www.dfait-maeci.gc.ca/Brunei/; High Commissioner: NEIL REEDER.

China, People's Republic: 1, 3 & 5 Simpang 462, Kampong Sungai Hanching, Jalan Muara, Bandar Seri Begawan BC 2115; tel. (2) 334163; fax (2) 335710; e-mail embproc@brunet.bn; Ambassador: QU WEN MING.

France: Kompleks Jalan Sultan, Units 301–306, 3rd Floor, 51–55 Jalan Sultan, Bandar Seri Begawan BS 8811; tel. (2) 220960; fax (2) 243373; e-mail france@brunet.bn; internet www.france.org.bn; Ambassador: THIERRY BORJA DE MOZOTA.

Germany: Kompleks Bangunan Yayasan Sultan Haji Hassanal Bolkiah, Unit 2.01, Block A, 2nd Floor, Jalan Pretty, Bandar Seri Begawan BS 8711; tel. (2) 225547; fax (2) 240634; e-mail prgerman@brunet.bn; Ambassador: ADALBERT RITTMÜLLER.

India: 'Baitussyifaa', Simpang 40–22, Jalan Sungai Akar, Bandar Seri Begawan BC 3915; tel. (2) 339947; fax (2) 339783; e-mail hicomind@brunet.bn; internet www.brunet.bn/gov/emb/india; High Commissioner: AJAI CHOUDRY.

Indonesia: Simpang 528, Lot 4498, Kampong Sungai Hanching Baru, Jalan Muara, Bandar Seri Begawan BC 2115; tel. (2) 330180; fax (2) 330646; e-mail kbribsb@brunet.bn; internet www.indonesia.org.bn; Ambassador: YUSBAR DJAMIL.

Iran: 19 Simpang 477, Kampong Sungai Hanching, Jalan Muara, BC Bandar Seri Begawan BC 2115; tel. (2) 330021; fax (2) 331744; Ambassador: ABD AL-FAZL MUHAMMAD ALIKHANI.

Japan: 1 and 3 Jalan Jawatan Dalam, 33 Simpang 122, Kampong Kiulap, Bandar Seri Begawan BE 1518; tel. (2) 229265; fax (2) 229481; e-mail embassy@japan.com.bn; Ambassador: SATOSHI HARA.

Korea, Republic: POB 2169, Bandar Seri Begawan BS 8674; tel. (2) 426038; fax (2) 426041; e-mail koreaemb@brunet.bn; Ambassador: KIM HO-TAI.

Laos: Lot 19824, 11 Simpang 480, Jalan Kebangsaan Lama, off Jalan Muara, Bandar Seri Begawan BC 4115; tel. (2) 345666; fax (2) 345888; Ambassador: BOUNTHONG VONGSALY.

Malaysia: 27–29 Simpang 396–39, Lot 9075, Kampong Sungai Akar, Mukim Berakas B, Jalan Kebangsaan, POB 2826, Bandar Seri Begawan BC 4115; tel. (2) 345652; fax (2) 345654; e-mail mwbrunei@brunet.bn; High Commissioner: SALMAN AHMAD.

Myanmar: 14 Lot 2185/46292, Simpang 212, Jalan Kampong Rimba, Gadong, Bandar Seri Begawan BE 3119; tel. (2) 450506; fax (2) 451008; e-mail myanmar@brunet.bn; Ambassador: U THET WIN.

Oman: 35 Simpang 100, Kampong Pengkalan, Jalan Tungku Link, Gadong, Bandar Seri Begawan BE 3719; tel. (2) 446953; fax (2) 449646; e-mail omnembsb@brunet.bn; Ambassador: AHMAD BIN MOHAMMED AL-RIYAMI.

Pakistan: 6 Simpang 23, Kampong Serusop, Jalan Muara, POB 3026, Bandar Seri Begawan BB 2313; tel. (2) 339797; fax (2) 334990; e-mail hcpak@brunet.bn; internet www.brunet.bn/gov/emb/pakistan; High Commissioner: BADR-UD-DEEN.

Philippines: Room 1, 4th and 6th Floors, Badiah Bldg, Mile 1, Jalan Tutong, Bandar Seri Begawan BNA 2111; tel. (2) 241465; fax (2) 237707; e-mail bruneipe@brunet.bn; Ambassador: VIRGINIA H. BENDAVIDEZ.

Saudi Arabia: 1 Simpang 570, Kampong Salar, Jalan Muara, Bandar Seri Begawan BT 2528; tel. (2) 792821; fax (2) 792826; e-mail bnemb@mofa.gov.sa; Ambassador: USTAZ IBRAHIM MUHAMMAD M. USILI.

Singapore: 8 Simpang 74, Jalan Subok, Bandar Seri Begawan; tel. (2) 262741; fax (2) 262743; e-mail singa@brunet.bn; internet www.gov.sg/mfa/brunei/; High Commissioner: V. P. HIRUBALAN.

Thailand: 2 Simpang 682, Jalan Tutong, Kampong Bunut, Bandar Seri Begawan BF 1320; tel. (2) 653108; fax (2) 653032; e-mail thaiemb@brunet.bn; Ambassador: THINAKORN KANASUTA.

United Kingdom: POB 2197, Bandar Seri Begawan BS 8674; tel. (2) 222231; fax (2) 234315; e-mail brithc@brunet.bn; internet www.britain-brunei.org; High Commissioner: ANDREW CAIE.

USA: Teck Guan Plaza, 3rd Floor, Jalan Sultan, Bandar Seri Begawan BS 8811; tel. (2) 229670; fax (2) 225293; e-mail amembbsb@brunet.bn; Ambassador: SYLVIA G. STANFIELD.

Viet Nam: 7 Simpang 538-37-19, Jalan (Duong) Kebangsaan Lama, Bandar Seri Begawan BC 2115; tel. (2) 343167; fax (2) 343169; e-mail vnembassy@hotmail.com; Ambassador: TRAN TIEN VINH.

Judicial System

SUPREME COURT

The Supreme Court consists of the Court of Appeal and the High Court. Syariah (*Shari'a*) courts coexist with the Supreme Court and deal with Islamic laws.

Supreme Court: Km 11/2, Jalan Tutong, Bandar Seri Begawan BA 1910; tel. (2) 225853; fax (2) 241984; e-mail judiciarybn@hotmail.com; internet www.judicial.gov.bn/supr_court.htm.

Chief Registrar: HAIROLARNI Haji ABD MAJID.

The Court of Appeal: composed of the President and two Commissioners appointed by the Sultan. The Court of Appeal considers criminal and civil appeals against the decisions of the High Court and the Intermediate Court. The Court of Appeal is the highest appellate court for criminal cases. In civil cases an appeal may be referred to the Judicial Committee of Her Majesty's Privy Council in London if all parties agree to do so before the hearing of the appeal in the Brunei Court of Appeal.

President: Sir ALLAN ARMSTRONG HUGGINS.

The High Court: composed of the Chief Justice and judges sworn in by the Sultan as Commissioners of the Supreme Court. In its appellate jurisdiction, the High Court considers appeals in criminal and civil matters against the decisions of the Subordinate Courts. The High Court has unlimited original jurisdiction in criminal and civil matters.

Chief Justice: Dato' Seri Paduka MOHAMMED SAIED.

OTHER COURTS

Intermediate Courts: have jurisdiction to try all offences other than those punishable by the death sentence and civil jurisdiction to try all actions and suits of a civil nature where the amount in dispute or value of the subject/matter does not exceed B $100,000.

The Subordinate Courts: presided over by the Chief Magistrate and magistrates, with limited original jurisdiction in civil and criminal matters and civil jurisdiction to try all actions and suits of a civil nature where the amount in dispute does not exceed B $50,000 (for Chief Magistrate) and B $30,000 (for magistrates).

Chief Magistrate: ROSTAINA BINTI Pengiran Haji DURAMAN (acting).

The Courts of Kathis: deal solely with questions concerning Islamic religion, marriage and divorce. Appeals lie from these courts to the Sultan in the Religious Council.

Chief Kathi: Dato' Seri Setia Haji SALIM BIN Haji BESAR.

Attorney-General: Dato' Paduka Haji KIFRAWI BIN Pehin Dato' Haji KIFLI; Attorney-General's Chambers, The Law Bldg, Km 1, Jalan Tutong, Bandar Seri Begawan BA 1910; tel. (2) 244872; fax (2) 223100; e-mail info@agc.gov.bn; internet www.agc.gov.bn.

Solicitor-General: Datin MAGDELENE CHONG.

Religion

The official religion of Brunei is Islam, and the Sultan is head of the Islamic community. The majority of the Malay population are Muslims of the Shafi'is school of the Sunni sect; at the 1991 census Muslims accounted for 67.2% of the total population. The Chinese population is either Buddhist (accounting for 12.8% of the total population at the 1991 census), Confucianist, Daoist or Christian. Large numbers of the indigenous ethnic groups practise traditional animist forms of religion. The remainder of the population are mostly Christians, generally Roman Catholics, Anglicans or members of the American Methodist Church of Southern Asia. At the 1991 census Christians accounted for 10.0% of the total population.

ISLAM

Supreme Head of Islam: Sultan and Yang Di-Pertuan.

CHRISTIANITY

The Anglican Communion

Within the Church of the Province of South East Asia, Brunei forms part of the diocese of Kuching (Malaysia).

The Roman Catholic Church

Brunei comprises a single apostolic prefecture. At December 2000 an estimated 7.6% of the population were adherents.

Prefect Apostolic: Rev. CORNELIUS SIM, St John's Church, POB 53, Kuala Belait KA 1131; tel. (3) 334207; fax (3) 342817; e-mail frcsim@brunet.bn.

The Press

NEWSPAPERS

Borneo Bulletin: Locked Bag No. 2, MPC (Old Airport, Berakas), Bandar Seri Begawan 3799; tel. (2) 451468; fax (2) 451461; e-mail borneobulletin2@brunet.bn; internet www.brunet.bn/news/bb; f. 1953; daily; English; independent; owned by QAF Group; Editor CHARLES REX DE SILVA; circ. 25,000.

Brunei Darussalam Newsletter: Dept of Information, Prime Minister's Office, Istana Nurul Iman, Bandar Seri Begawan BA 1000; tel. (2) 229988; fortnightly; English; govt newspaper; distributed free; circ. 14,000.

Daily News Digest: Dept of Information, Prime Minister's Office, Istana Nurul Iman, Bandar Seri Begawan BA 1000; internet www.brunet.bn/news/dndbd/digest.htm; English; govt newspaper.

Media Permata: Locked Bag No. 2, MPC (Old Airport, Berakas), Bandar Seri Begawan BB 3510; tel. (2) 451468; fax (2) 451461; e-mail mediapermata@brunet.bn; internet www.brunei-online.com/mp; f. 1995; daily (not Sun.); Malay; owned by QAF Group; Editor ABDUL LATIF; circ. 10,000.

News Express: Bandar Seri Begawan; f. 1999; daily; English; Propr PETER WONG; Editor-in-Chief R. NADESWARAN.

Pelita Brunei: Dept of Information, Prime Minister's Office, Old Airport, Berakas BB 3510; tel. (2) 383941; fax (2) 381004; e-mail pelita@brunet.bn; internet www.brunet.bn/news/pelita/pelita1.htm; f. 1956; weekly (Wed.); Malay; govt newspaper; distributed free; Editor TIMBANG BIN BAKAR; circ. 27,500.

Salam: c/o Brunei Shell Petroleum Co Sdn Bhd, Seria 7082; tel. (3) 4184; fax (3) 4189; internet www.shell.com.bn/salam; f. 1953; monthly; Malay and English; distributed free to employees of the Brunei Shell Petroleum Co Sdn Bhd; circ. 46,000.

Publishers

Avesta Printing & Trading Sdn Bhd: 31–35, Block D, Bangunan Pg Anak Siti Rafeah, Jalan Gadong, Bandar Seri Begawan 3180; tel. (2) 445220; fax (2) 441372; Man. PETER WONG.

Borneo Printers & Trading Sdn Bhd: POB 2211, Bandar Seri Begawan BS 8674; tel. (2) 651387; fax (2) 654342; e-mail bptl@brunet.bn.

Brunei Press Sdn Bhd: Lots 8 and 11, Perindustrian Beribi II, Jalan Gadong, Bandar Seri Begawan BE 1118; tel. (2) 451468; fax (2) 451462; e-mail brupress@brunet.bn; internet www.bruneipress.com.bn; f. 1953; Gen. Man. REGGIE SEE.

Capital Trading & Printing Pte Ltd: POB 1089, Bandar Seri Begawan; tel. (2) 244541.

Leong Bros: 52 Jalan Bunga Kuning, POB 164, Seria; tel. (3) 22381.

Offset Printing House: POB 1111, Bandar Seri Begawan; tel. (2) 224477.

The Star Press: Bandar Seri Begawan; f. 1963; Man. F. W. ZIMMERMAN.

Government Publishing House

Government Printer: Government Printing Department, Office of the Prime Minister, Bandar Seri Begawan BB 3510; tel. (2) 382541; fax (2) 381141; e-mail info@printing.gov.bn; internet www.printing.gov.bn; Dir Dato' Paduka WAHID Haji SALLEH.

Broadcasting and Communications

TELECOMMUNICATIONS

DST Communications Sdn Bhd: Block D, Yayasan Sultan Haji Hassanal Bolkiah Kompleks, Bandar Seri Begawan; tel. (2) 232323; e-mail dst-group@simpur.net.bn; internet www.dst-group.com; mobile service provider.

Jabatan Telecom Brunei (Department of Telecommunications of Brunei): Ministry of Communications, Jalan Berakas, Bandar Seri Begawan BB 3510; tel. (2) 382382; fax (2) 382445; e-mail info@telecom.gov.bn; internet www.telecom.gov.bn; scheduled to become Govt-owned company in April 2003; Dir of Telecommunications Awang BUNTAR BIN OSMAN.

BROADCASTING

Radio

Radio Televisyen Brunei (RTB): Prime Minister's Office, Jalan Elizabeth II, Bandar Seri Begawan BS 8610; tel. (2) 243111; fax (2) 241882; e-mail rtbpits@brunet.bn; internet www.rtb.gov.bn; f. 1957;

five radio networks: four broadcasting in Malay, the other in English, Chinese (Mandarin) and Gurkhali; Dir Pengiran Dato' Paduka Haji ISMAIL BIN Pengiran Haji MOHAMED.

The British Forces Broadcasting Service (Military) broadcasts a 24-hour radio service to a limited area.

Television

Radio Televisyen Brunei (RTB): Prime Minister's Office, Jalan Elizabeth II, Bandar Seri Begawan BS 8610; tel. (2) 243111; fax (2) 241882; e-mail rtbpits@brunet.bn; internet www.rtb.gov.bn; f. 1957; programmes in Malay and English; a satellite service relays RTB television programmes to the South-East Asian region for nine hours per day; Dir Pengiran Dato' Paduka Haji ISMAIL BIN Pengiran Haji MOHAMED.

Finance

(cap. = capital; res = reserves; dep. = deposits; brs = branches; amounts in Brunei dollars unless otherwise stated)

BANKING

The Department of Financial Services (Treasury), the Brunei Currency Board and the Brunei Investment Agency (see Government Agencies, below), under the Ministry of Finance, perform most of the functions of a central bank.

Commercial Banks

Baiduri Bank Bhd: Block A, Units 1-4, Kiarong Complex, Lebuhraya Sultan Hassanal Bolkiah, Bandar Seri Begawan BE 1318; tel (2) 455111; fax (2) 455599; e-mail bank@baiduri.com; internet www.baiduri.com; cap. 30m., res 20.1m., dep. 968.9m. (Aug. 2002); Gen. Man. LUC ROUSSELET; 9 brs.

Islamic Bank of Brunei Bhd: Lot 159, Bangunan IBB, Jalan Pemancha, POB 2725, Bandar Seri Begawan BS 8711; tel. (2) 235686; fax (2) 235722; e-mail ibb@brunet.bn; internet www.ibb.com.bn; f. 1981 as Island Development Bank; name changed from International Bank of Brunei Bhd to present name in January 1993; practises Islamic banking principles; Chair. Haji ABDUL RAHMAN BIN Haji ABDUL KARIM; Man. Dir Haji ZAINASALLEHEN BIN Haji MOHAMED TAHIR; 13 brs.

Islamic Development Bank of Brunei Bhd: Ground–4th Floor, Kompleks Setia Kenangan, Kampong Kiulap, Jalan Gadong, Bandar Seri Begawan BE 1518; tel. (2) 232547; fax (2) 233540; e-mail hrdadmin@dbb-bank.com; internet www.idbb-bank.com.bn; f. 1995 as Development Bank of Brunei Bhd; name changed to present in July 2000; practises Islamic banking principles; Man. Dir Pengiran Datin Paduka Hajah URAI Pengiran ALI; 3 brs.

Foreign Banks

Citibank NA (USA): Darussalam Complex, 12–15 Jalan Sultan, Bandar Seri Begawan BS 8811; tel. (2) 243983; fax (2) 237344; e-mail glen.rase@citicorp.com; Vice-Pres. and Country Head PAGE STOCKWELL; 2 brs.

The Hongkong and Shanghai Banking Corpn Ltd (Hong Kong): Jalan Sultan, cnr Jalan Pemancha, Bandar Seri Begawan BS 8811; POB 59, Bandar Seri Begawan BS 8670; tel. (2) 242305; fax (2) 241316; e-mail hsbc@hsbc.com.bn; internet www.hsbc.com.bn; f. 1947; acquired assets of National Bank of Brunei in 1986; CEO WARNER G. N. MANNING; 10 brs.

Maybank (Malaysia): 1 Jalan McArthur, Bandar Seri Begawan BS 8711; tel. (2) 226462; fax (2) 226404; e-mail maybank@brunet.bn; f. 1960; Country Man. AZIZUL ABDUL RASHID; 3 brs.

RHB Bank Bhd (Malaysia): Unit G. 02, Block D, Bangunan Yayasan Sultan Haji Hassanal Bolkiah, Ground Floor, Jalan Pretty, Bandar Seri Begawan BS 8711; tel. (2) 222515; fax (2) 237487; fmrly Sime Bank Bhd; Branch Man. SHAFIK YUSSOF; 1 br.

Standard Chartered Bank (United Kingdom): 1st Floor, 51–55 Jalan Sultan, POB 186, Bandar Seri Begawan BS 8811; tel. (2) 242386; fax (2) 242390; internet www.standardchartered.com/bn; f. 1958; CEO SIMON MORRIS; 8 brs.

United Overseas Bank Ltd (Singapore): Unit G5, RBA Plaza, Jalan Sultan, Bandar Seri Begawan BS 8811; POB 2218, Bandar Seri Begawan BS 8674; tel. (2) 225477; fax (2) 240792; f. 1973; Gen. Man. SIA KEE HENG; 2 brs.

STOCK EXCHANGE

In May 2002 the International Brunei Exchange Ltd (IBX) was granted an exclusive licence to establish an international securities exchange in Brunei.

International Brunei Exchange Ltd (IBX): The Empire, Muara-Tutong Highway, Jerudong BG 3122; e-mail info@ibx.com.bn; internet www.ibx.com.bn; f. 2001; CEO B. C. YONG.

INSURANCE

In 1998 there were 18 general, three life and two composite (takaful) insurance companies operating in Brunei, including:

General Companies

AGF Insurance (Singapore) Pte Ltd: c/o A&S Associates Sdn Bhd, Bangunan Gadong Properties, 03-01, Jalan Gadong, Bandar Seri Begawan BE 4119; tel. (2) 420766; fax (2) 440279; Gen. Man. JEAN NOEL ROUSSELLE.

The Asia Insurance Co Ltd: Unit A1 & A2, 1st Floor, Block A, Bangunan Hau Man Yong Complex, Simpang 88, Kg. Kiulap BE 1518, POB 2226, Bandar Seri Begawan BS 8674; tel. (2) 236100; fax (2) 236102; Man. DAVID WONG KOK MIN.

BALGI Insurance (B) Sdn Bhd: Unit 13, Kompleks Haji Tahir II, 2nd Floor, 3180 Jalan Gadong, Bandar Seri Begawan BE 4119; tel. (2) 422726; fax (2) 445204; Man. Dir PATRICK SIM SONG JUAY.

Borneo Insurance Sdn Bhd: Unit 103, Bangunan Kambang Pasang, Km 2, Jalan Gadong, Bandar Seri Begawan BE 4119; tel. (2) 420550; fax (2) 428550; Man. LIM TECK LEE.

CGU Insurance Bhd: Unit 311, 3rd Floor, Mohamad Yussof Complex, 1.5 Mile, Jalan Tutong, Bandar Seri Begawan BA 1712; tel. (2) 223632; fax (2) 220965; e-mail cgu@brunet.bn; Man. PETER SHACK.

Commercial Union Assurance (M) Sdn Bhd: c/o Jasra Harrisons Sdn Bhd, Jalan McArthur, cnr Jalan Kianggeh, Bandar Seri Begawan BS 8711; tel. (2) 242361; fax (2) 226203; Man. WHITTY LIM.

Cosmic Insurance Corpn Sdn Bhd: Block J, Unit 11, Abdul Razak Complex, 1st Floor, Jalan Gadong, Bandar Seri Begawan BE 3919; tel. (2) 427112; fax (2) 427114; Man. RONNIE WONG.

GRE Insurance (B) Sdn Bhd: Unit 608, 6th Floor, Jalan Sultan Complex, 51-55 Jalan Sultan, Bandar Seri Begawan BS 8811; tel. (2) 226138; fax (2) 243474; Man. MOK HAI TONG.

ING General Insurance International NV: Shop Lot 86, 2nd Floor, Jalan Bunga Raya, Kuala Belait KA 1131; tel. (3) 335338; fax (3) 335338; Man. SHERRY SOON PECK ENG.

Liberty Citystate Insurance Pte Ltd: 1st Floor, Unit 25, Block C, Bangunan Hau Man Yong Complex, Simpang 88, Kampong Kiulap BE 1518, POB 1323, Bandar Seri Begawan BS 8672; tel. (2) 238282; fax (2) 236848; Man. ROBERT LAI CHIN YIN.

Malaysia National Insurance Bhd: 9 Bangunan Haji Mohd Salleh Simpang 103, 1st Floor, Jalan Gadong, Bandar Seri Begawan BE 4119; tel. (2) 443393; fax (2) 427451; Man. ANDREW AK NYAGORN.

MBA Insurance Sdn Bhd: 7 Bangunan Hasbullah I, 1st Floor, Km 4, Jalan Gadong, Bandar Seri Begawan BE 3519; tel. (2) 441535; fax (2) 441534; e-mail cheahmbabrunei@brunet.bn; Man. CHEAH LYE CHONG.

Motor and General Insurance Sdn Bhd: 6 Bangunan Hasbullah II, Km 4, Jalan Gadong, Bandar Seri Begawan BE 3919; tel. (2) 440797; fax (2) 445342; Man. Dir Haji ABDUL AZIZ BIN ABDUL LATIF.

National Insurance Co Bhd: 3rd Floor, Scouts' Headquarters Bldg, Jalan Gadong, Bandar Seri Begawan BE 1118; tel. (2) 426888; fax (2) 429888; e-mail nicb@brunet.bn; internet www.national.com.bn; Gen. Man. CHAN LEK WAI.

Royal and Sun Alliance Insurance (Global) Ltd: Unit 7, 1st Floor, Block B, Kiarong Complex, Lebuhraya Sultan Hassanal Bolkiah, Bandar Seri Begawan BE 1318; tel. (2) 423233; fax (2) 423325; Gen. Man. TOMMY LEONG TONG KAW.

South East Asia Insurance (B) Sdn Bhd: Unit 2, Block A, Abdul Razak Complex, 1st Floor, Jalan Gadong, Bandar Seri Begawan BE 3919; tel. (2) 443842; fax (2) 420860; Gen. Man. JOSEPH WONG SIONG LION.

Standard Insurance (B) Sdn Bhd: 2 Bangunan Hasbullah I, Ground Floor, Bandar Seri Begawan BE 3919; tel. (2) 450077; fax (2) 450076; e-mail feedback@standard-ins.com; internet www.standard-ins.com; Man. PAUL KONG.

Winterthur Insurance (Far East) Pte Ltd: c/o Borneo Co (B) Sdn Bhd, Lot 9771, Km 3½, Jalan Gadong, Bandar Seri Begawan BE 4119; tel. (2) 422561; fax (2) 424352; Gen. Man. ANNA CHONG.

Life Companies

American International Assurance Co Ltd: Unit 509A, Wisma Jaya Building, 5th Floor, No 85/94, Jalan Pemancha, Bandar Seri Begawan BS 8511; tel. (2) 239112; fax (2) 221667; Man. PHILIP TAN.

The Asia Life Assurance Society Ltd: Unit 2, 1st Floor, Block D, Abdul Razak Complex, Jalan Gadong, Bandar Seri Begawan BE

4119; tel. (2) 423755; fax (2) 423754; e-mail asialife@simpur.net.bn; Exec. Officer PATRICIA CHIN YUNG YIN.

The Great Eastern Life Assurance Co Ltd: Suite 1, Badi'ah Complex, 2nd Floor, Jalan Tutong, Bandar Seri Begawan BA 2111; tel. (2) 243792; fax (2) 225754; Man. HELEN YEO.

Takaful (Composite Insurance) Companies

Syarikat Insurans Islam TAIB Sdn Bhd: Bangunan Pusat Komersil dan Perdagangan Bumiputera, Ground Floor, Jalan Cator, Bandar Seri Begawan BS 8811; tel. (2) 237724; fax (2) 237729; e-mail insuranstaib@brunet.bn; internet www.insuranstaib.com.bn; f. 1993; provides Islamic insurance products and services; Man. Dir Haji MOHAMED ROSELAN BIN Haji MOHAMED DAUD.

Takaful IBB Bhd: Unit 5, Block A, Kiarong Complex, Lebuhraya Sultan Hassanal Bolkiah, Bandar Seri Begawan BE 1318; tel. (2) 451804; fax (2) 451808; e-mail takaful@brunet.bn; f. 1993; Man. Dir Awang Haji MOHD ROSELAN BIN Haji MOHD DAUD (acting).

Trade and Industry

GOVERNMENT AGENCIES

Brunei Currency Board: Ministry of Finance Complex, Simpang 295, Jalan Kebansaan, Bandar Seri Begawan BB 3910; tel. (2) 383999; fax (2) 382232; e-mail bcb@brunet.bn; internet www.finance.gov.bn/bcb/bcb_index.htm; f. 1967; maintains control of currency circulation; Sec. Haji MAHADI Haji IBRAHIM; Chair. Minister of Finance.

Brunei Darussalam Economic Council (BDEC): Bandar Seri Begawan; internet www.brudirect.com/BruneiInfo/info/BD_EconomicCouncil.htm; f. 1998; convened to examine the economic situation in Brunei and to recommend short- and long-term measures designed to revitalize the economy; Chair. HRH Prince MOHAMED BOLKIAH.

Brunei Investment Agency: Ministry of Finance, Bandar Seri Begawan 1130; f. 1973; Chair. YAHYA BAKAR.

DEVELOPMENT ORGANIZATIONS

Brunei Industrial Development Authority (BINA): Ministry of Industry and Primary Resources, Km 8, Jalan Gadong, Bandar Seri Begawan BE 1118; tel. (2) 444100; fax (2) 423300; e-mail bruneibina@brunet.bn; internet www.bina.gov.bn; f. 1996: Dir Haji RAZALI MOHD YUSSOF.

Brunei Islamic Trust Fund (Tabung Amanah Islam Brunei): Block A, Unit 2, Ground Floor, Kiarong Complex, Lebuhraya Sultan Hj Hassanal Bolkiah, Bandar Seri Begawan BE 1318; tel. (2) 452666; fax (2) 450877; f. 1991; promotes trade and industry; Chair. Haji AWANG YAHYA BIN Haji IBRAHIM.

Industrial and Trade Development Council: Bandar Seri Begawan; facilitates the industrialization of Brunei; Chair. Minister of Industry and Primary Resources.

Semaun Holdings Sdn Bhd: Unit 2.02, Block D, 2nd Floor, Yayasan Sultan Haji Hassanal Bolkiah Complex, Jalan Pretty, Bandar Seri Begawan BS 8711; tel. (2) 232950; e-mail semaun@brunet.bn; internet www.semaun.gov.bn; promotes industrial and commercial development through direct investment in key industrial sectors; 100% govt-owned; the board of directors is composed of ministers and senior govt officials; Chair. Minister of Industry and Primary Resources; Man. Dir Haji MOHD ZAIN BIN Haji GHAFAR (acting).

CHAMBERS OF COMMERCE

Brunei Darussalam International Chamber of Commerce and Industry: Unit 402-403A, 4th Floor, Wisma Jaya, Jalan Pemancha, Bandar Seri Begawan 8811; tel. (2) 228382; fax (2) 228389; Chair. SULAIMAN Haji AHAI; Sec. Haji SHAZALI BIN Dato' Haji SULAIMAN; 108 mems.

Brunei Malay Chamber of Commerce and Industry: Unit 15, First Floor, Bangunan Halimadul Saadiah, Jalan Gadong, Bandar Seri Begawan BE 3519; POB 1099, Bandar Seri Begawan BS 8672; tel. (2) 422752; fax (2) 422753; f. 1964; Pres. Dato' A. A. HAPIDZ; 160 mems.

Chinese Chamber of Commerce: Chinese Chamber of Commerce Bldg, 72 Jalan Roberts, Bandar Seri Begawan; POB 281, Bandar Seri Begawan BS 8670; tel. (2) 235494; fax (2) 235492; Chair. LIM ENG MING.

National Chamber of Commerce and Industry of Brunei Darussalam: 2nd Floor, 144 Jalan Pemancha, Bandar Seri Begawan BS 8711; tel. (2) 243321; fax (2) 228737; e-mail abas@nccibd.com; internet www.bruneichamber.com; Pres. Sheikh ABAS BIN Sheikh MOHAMED.

STATE HYDROCARBON COMPANIES

Brunei Gas Carriers Sdn Bhd (BGC): Bandar Seri Begawan; f. 1998; LNG shipping co; owned jointly by Brunei Govt, Shell International Gas and Mitsubishi Corpn.

Brunei LNG Sdn Bhd: Lumut KC 2935, Seria; tel. (3) 378125; fax (3) 236919; e-mail hamdillah.b.wahab@shell.com.bn; f. 1969; natural gas liquefaction; owned jointly by the Brunei Govt, Shell and Mitsubishi Corpn; operates LNG plant at Lumut, which has a capacity of 7.2m. tons per year; merged with Brunei Coldgas Sdn Bhd in 1995; Exec. Dir H. A. W. HAMDILLAH.

Brunei National Petroleum Co Sdn Bhd (PetroleumBrunei): 5th Floor, Bangunan Bahirah, Jalan Menteri Besar, Bandar Seri Begawan BB 3910; tel. (2) 387126; fax (2) 383004; e-mail brupet@brunet.bn; f. 2001; wholly Govt-owned; CEO Dato' Paduka Haji MOHD BIN Haji ABDUL WAHAB.

Brunei Shell Marketing Co Bhd: Maya Puri Bldg, 36/37 Jalan Sultan, POB 385, Bandar Seri Begawan; tel. (2) 25739; fax (2) 240470; internet www.bsm.com.bn; f. 1978 (from the Shell Marketing Co of Brunei Ltd), when the Govt became equal partner with Shell; markets petroleum and chemical products throughout Brunei; Man. Dir MAT SUNY Haji MOHD HUSSEIN.

Brunei Shell Petroleum Co Sdn Bhd: Jalan Utara, Panagia, Seria KB 3534; tel. (3) 373999; fax (3) 372040; internet www.shell.com.bn; f. 1957; the largest industrial concern in the country; 50% state holding; Man. Dir JOHN J. C. DARLEY.

Jasra International Petroleum Sdn Bhd: RBA Plaza, 2nd Floor, Jalan Sultan, Bandar Seri Begawan; tel. (2) 228968; fax (2) 228929; petroleum exploration and production; Man. Dir ROBERT A. HARRISON.

MAJOR COMPANIES

Ath-Garments Sdn Bhd: POB 377, Pekan Tutong TA 1141; tel. (4) 261383; fax (4) 261390; e-mail athgmt@brunet.bn; mfr of textiles and garments; Man. Dir Hajah SAADATENA ABDULLAH; 500 employees.

BHP Steel Lysaght (B) Sdn Bhd: Industrial Complex, Beribi, Phase 1, 6 Km, Jalan Gadong, Bandar Seri Begawan BE 1118; tel. (2) 447155; fax (2) 447154; e-mail bhpsteel@brunet.bn; f. 1993; supplier of steel building solutions; Pres. D. MARAN.

Brunei Oxygen Sdn Bhd: Lot 5761, Tapak Perindustrian, Pekan Belait, Kuala Belait KA 1931; tel. (3) 332861; fax (3) 333466; owned by QAF Brunei Sdn Bhd; mfr of industrial gases; Gen. Man. JOHN MUGRIDGE.

Brusteel Sdn Bhd: Lim Eng Ming Bldg, Km 2.5, Jalan Gadong, Bandar Seri Begawan 3188; tel. (2) 445297.

Butra Heidelberger Zement Sdn Bhd (Brunei Cement): Lot 3, Serasa Industrial Area, POB 153, Muara BT 1128; tel. (2) 771395; fax (2) 771404; e-mail bhz@bruneicement.com; internet www.bruneicement.com; f. 1993; mfr and distributor of cement; Man. Dir YAVUZ ERMIS; 115 employees.

Fraser and Neave (B) Bhd: 80 Jalan Perusahaan, Kampong Serasa, Muara; tel. (2) 770839; fax (2) 770151; f. 1981; production and bottling of soft drinks, incl. Coca-Cola; Chair. Dato' Haji ALI BIN Haji MOHD DAUD; 35 employees.

Hunt Concrete Industries Sdn Bhd: Room 302, 1st Floor, Block C, Chandrawaseh Complex, Mile 1, Jalan Tutong, Bandar Seri Begawan; tel. (2) 229249; fax (2) 226596; e-mail hunt@brunet.bn; f. 1983; Chair LIM MING SIONG; Man. Dir KOH MING SHAM; 180 employees.

Jati Freedom Textile Sdn Bhd: Jalan Perusahaan, Simpang 15, Pekan Muara 4080; tel. (2) 770824; fax (2) 770822; mfr of garments; Station Man. ALICE LEE; 420 employees.

Mulaut Abattoir Sdn Bhd: POB 28, Sengkurong 2788; tel. (2) 670289; fax (2) 670800; supply and marketing of livestock and meat products; Dep. Gen. Man. ABD HALIM BIN Haji SAIM; 800 employees.

O'Connor's (B) Sdn Bhd: Sufri Complex, Block D, Km 1, Jalan Tutong, Bandar Seri Begawan; tel. (2) 223109; fax (2) 220391; mfr of telecommunication and electrical equipment.

QAF Brunei Sdn Bhd: QAF Centre, Lot 65-66, Perindustrial Beribi II, Bandar Seri Begawan BE 1118; tel. (2) 453388; fax (2) 452152; e-mail qaf@brunet.bn; internet www.qaf.com; f. 1982; investment holding co with interests in wholesale and retail trade, investment, engineering, offshore services and publishing; subsidiary of Baiduri Holdings Bhd; Chair. HRH Prince MOHAMED BOLKIAH; Man. Dir CHAN THUAN CHAI; 600 employees.

VSL Systems (N) Sdn Bhd: POB 291, MPC-Old Airport, Bandar Seri Begawan BB 3577; tel. (2) 380153; fax (2) 381954; f. 1984; mfr of ready-mixed concrete and concrete products; Man. Dir CHUAH MENG HU; 60 employees.

TRADE UNIONS

Brunei Government Junior Officers' Union: Bandar Seri Begawan; tel. (2) 241911; Pres. Haji ALI BIN Haji NASAR; Gen. Sec. Haji OMARALI BIN Haji MOHIDDIN.

Brunei Government Medical and Health Workers' Union: Bandar Seri Begawan; Pres. Pengiran Haji MOHIDDIN BIN Pengiran TAJUDDIN; Gen. Sec. HANAFI BIN ANAI.

Brunei Oilfield Workers' Union: XDR/11, BSP Co Sdn Bhd, Seria KB 3534; f. 1964; 470 mems; Pres. SUHAINI Haji OTHMAN; Sec.-Gen. ABU TALIB BIN Haji MOHAMAD.

Royal Brunei Custom Department Staff Union: Badan Sukan dan Kebajikan Kastam, Royal Brunei Customs and Excise, Kuala Belait KA 1131; tel. (3) 334248; fax (3) 334626; Chair. Haji MOHD DELI BAKAR; Sec. HAMZAH Haji ABD. HAMID.

Transport

RAILWAYS

There are no public railways in Brunei. The Brunei Shell Petroleum Co Sdn Bhd maintains a 19.3-km section of light railway between Seria and Badas.

ROADS

In 1999 there were 1,150 km of roads in Brunei, of which almost 400 km were paved. The main highway connects Bandar Seri Begawan, Tutong and Kuala Belait. A 59-km coastal road links Muara and Tutong. The Eighth National Development Plan (2001–05) prioritized the development of Brunei's roads and, in particular, the construction of a network of main roads that would connect Brunei Muara, Tutong, Kuala Belait and Temburong. In September 2001 work commenced on the construction of the 15-km Jalan Lumut Bypass. It was scheduled for completion in September 2002.

Land Transport Department: 451979 Km 6, Jalan Gadong, Beribi, Bandar Seri Begawan BE 1110; tel. (2) 451979; fax (2) 424775; e-mail latis@brunet.bn; internet www.land-transport.gov.bn; Dir Awang Haji OTHMAN BIN Haji MOMIN.

SHIPPING

Most sea traffic is handled by a deep-water port at Muara, 28 km from the capital, which has a 611-m wharf and a draught of 8 m. The port has a container terminal, warehousing, freezer facilities and cement silos. In October 2000 a plan to deepen the port to enable its accommodation of larger vessels was announced. The original, smaller port at Bandar Seri Begawan itself is mainly used for local river-going vessels, for vessels to Malaysian ports in Sabah and Sarawak and for vessels under 30 m in length. There is a port at Kuala Belait, which takes shallow-draught vessels and serves mainly the Shell petroleum field and Seria. Owing to the shallow waters at Seria, tankers are unable to come up to the shore to load, and crude petroleum from the oil terminal is pumped through an underwater loading line to a single buoy mooring, to which the tankers are moored. At Lumut there is a 4.5-km jetty for liquefied natural gas (LNG) carriers.

Four main rivers, with numerous tributaries, are an important means of communication in the interior, and boats or water taxis are the main form of transport for most residents of the water villages. Larger water taxis operate daily to the Temburong district.

Bee Seng Shipping Co: 7 Block D, Sufri Complex, Km 2, Jalan Tutong, POB 92, Bandar Seri Begawan; tel. (2) 220033; fax (2) 224495; e-mail beeseng@brunet.bn.

Belait Shipping Co (B) Sdn Bhd: B1, 2nd Floor, 94 Jalan McKerron, Kuala Belait 6081; POB 632, Kuala Belait; tel. (3) 335418; fax (3) 330239; f. 1977; Man. Dir Haji FATIMAH BINTE Haji ABDUL AZIZ.

Brunei Shell Tankers Sdn Bhd: Seria KB 3534; tel. (3) 373999; f. 1986; vessels operated by Shell International Trading and Shipping Co Ltd; Man. Dir CHRIS FINLAYSON.

Harper Wira Sdn Bhd: B2 Bangunan Haji Mohd Yussof, Jalan Gadong, Bandar Seri Begawan 3188; tel. (2) 448529; fax (2) 448529.

Inchcape Borneo: Bangunan Inchcape Borneo, Km 4, Jalan Gadong, Bandar Seri Begawan; tel. (2) 422561; fax (2) 424352; f. 1856; Gen. Man. LO FAN KEE.

New Island Shipping: Unit 5, 1st Floor, Block C, Kiarong Complex, Jalan Kiarong, Bandar Seri Begawan 3186; POB 850, Bandar Seri Begawan 1908; tel. (2) 451800; fax (2) 451480; f. 1975; Chair. TAN KOK VOON; Man. JIMMY VOON.

Pansar Co Sdn Bhd: Muara Port; tel. (2) 445246; fax (2) 445247.

Seatrade Shipping Co: Muara Port; tel. (2) 421457; fax (2) 421453.

Silver Line (B) Sdn Bhd: Muara Port; tel. (2) 445069; fax (2) 430276.

Wei Tat Shipping and Trading Co: Mile 41, Jalan Tutong, POB 103, Bandar Seri Begawan; tel. (2) 65215.

CIVIL AVIATION

There is an international airport near Bandar Seri Begawan, which can handle up to 1.5m. passengers and 50,000 metric tons of cargo per year. The Brunei Shell Petroleum Co Sdn Bhd operates a private airfield at Anduki for helicopter services.

Department of Civil Aviation: Brunei International Airport, Bandar Seri Begawan BB 2513; tel. (2) 330142; fax (2) 331706; e-mail dca@brunet.bn; internet www.civil-aviation.gov.bn; Dir Haji KASIM BIN Haji LATIP.

Royal Brunei Airlines Ltd: RBA Plaza, Jalan Sultan, POB 737, Bandar Seri Begawan BS 8671; tel. (2) 240500; fax (2) 244737; internet www.bruneiair.com; f. 1974; operates services within the Far East and to the Middle East, Australia and Europe; Chair. Dato' Paduka Awang Haji ALIMIN WAHAB; CEO PETER WILLIAM FOSTER.

Tourism

Tourist attractions in Brunei include the flora and fauna of the rainforest and the national parks, as well as mosques and water villages. There were 964,080 foreign visitor arrivals (including same-day visitors) in 1998. Foreign visitor arrivals increased to 1,306,764 in 2000. In 1998 international tourist receipts totalled US $37m. The year 2001 was designated 'Visit Brunei Year'.

Brunei Tourism: c/o Ministry of Industry and Primary Resources, Jalan Menteri Besar, Bandar Seri Begawan BB 3910; tel. (2) 382822; fax (2) 382824; e-mail info@industry.gov.bn; internet www.tourismbrunei.com; Dir-Gen. Sheikh JAMALUDDIN BIN Sheikh MOHAMED.

Defence

At August 2001 the total strength of the Royal Brunei Malay Regiment was 5,900 (including 700 women): army 3,900 (including 250 women); navy 900; air force 1,100 (including 75 women). Military service (for which only ethnic Malays are eligible) is voluntary. Paramilitary forces comprise an estimated 3,750, of which 1,750 are members of the Royal Brunei Police. Since 1971 national defence has been the responsibility of the Brunei Government. A Gurkha battalion of the British army, comprising about 1,070 men in 2001, has been stationed in Brunei since 1971, but is not responsible for internal security (its duty now being to guard the petroleum and gas fields). About 500 Singapore troops, operating a training school, are also stationed in Brunei.

Defence Expenditure: B $610m. in 2001.

Commander of the Royal Brunei Armed Forces: Maj.-Gen. Dato' Paduka Seri Haji MOHD JAAFAR Haji ABD AZIZ.

Education

There are three official languages of instruction, Malay, English and Chinese, and schools are divided accordingly. There are also religious schools. Education is free and is compulsory for 12 years between the ages of five and 16.

All Malay schools are state-administered and are, in general, co-educational. Pre-primary education begins at the age of five years. Primary education in the Malay schools lasts for six years from the age of six years; it is divided into two cycles of three years, lower primary and upper primary. At lower primary level all instruction is in Malay but at upper primary certain subjects, e.g. maths, geography and science, are taught in English. Pupils sit for the Primary Certificate of Education (PCE) examination at the end of primary education.

Secondary education lasts for seven years. The first five years are divided into lower secondary, lasting for three years at the end of which pupils sit the Penilaian Menengah Bawah (PMB—Lower Secondary Assessment) examination, and upper secondary which lasts for two or three years. After the PMB some pupils enrol in vocational schools where courses last for 18 months leading to the National Trade Certificate. Other pupils proceed to upper secondary level where abler students follow a two-year course leading to the Brunei-Cambridge General Certificate of Education Ordinary Level (BC-GCE 'O' Level) examinations and others follow a two-year course leading to the BC-GCE 'N' Level (which was introduced in 1997). At 'N' Level those gaining enough credits follow a further one-year course to 'O' Level. The technical colleges then offer two-year courses to those with adequate 'O' Level passes. Students with the requisite 'O' Level results proceed to the pre-university level to pursue a two-year course leading to the BC-GCE Advanced Level ('A' Level) examination. Students with adequate 'A' Level passes may be eligible for entry to the Universiti Brunei Darussalam or other tertiary institutions or be awarded scholarships to study abroad. The Institut Teknologi Brunei provides courses leading to a Higher National certificate (part-time) or a National Diploma (full-time).

Chinese schools are privately run and not assisted by the Government. They cater for pupils at both primary and secondary levels.

In 1994 enrolment at primary level included 91% of those in the relevant age-group (males 90%; females 91%) and enrolment at secondary level included 68% of pupils (males 64%; females 71%). Enrolment at tertiary level in 1996 was equivalent to 6.6% of the relevant age-group (males 5.3%; females 8.0%).

Public expenditure on education totalled an estimated B $347m. in 1997 (8.6% of total expenditure). Under the Eighth National Development Plan (2001–05) the education sector was allocated B $300m. of the total development budget (4.19%).

Bibliography

See also Malaysia bibliography.

Asian Development Bank Technical Assistance Study. *Brunei Darussalam-Indonesia-Malaysia-Philippines East ASEAN Growth Area (BIMP-EAGA), Final Report Volume 1A, The Overall Integrative Report,* 1996.

Asian Development Bank Technical Assistance Study. *Brunei Darussalam-Indonesia-Malaysia-Philippines East ASEAN Growth Area (BIMP-EAGA), Final Report Volume 2A, Brunei Darussalam Country Profile,* 1996.

Badan Kemajuan Industri Brunei (BINA), Kementerian Perindustrian dan Sumber-Sumber Utama. *Peranan BINA Dalam Mengembangkan Perusahaan Kecil dan Sederhana,* 1997.

Bartholomew, James. *The Richest Man in the World: The Sultan of Brunei.* London, Viking, 1989.

Blomqvist, Hans C. 'Brunei's Strategic Dilemmas'. *The Pacific Review,* Vol. 6, No 2, 1993.

Bolkiah, Prince Mohamed. *Time and the River.* 2000.

Borneo Bulletin. *Brunei Yearbook Key Information on Brunei.* Bandar Seri Begawan.

Braighlinn, G. *Ideological Innovation under Monarchy: Aspects of Legitimisation Activity in Contemporary Brunei.* Amsterdam, V U University Press, 1992.

Brown, D. E. *Brunei, The Structure and History of a Bornean Malay Sultanate.* Brunei, Brunei Museum, 1970.

Brunei Currency Board. *Brunei Darussalam Financial Structure, Functions and Policies.* Bandar Seri Begawan, 1996.

Chalfont, Lord. *By God's Will: A Portrait of the Sultan of Brunei.* London, Weidenfeld and Nicolson, 1989.

Cleary, Mark, and Shuang Yann Wong. *Oil, Economic Development and Diversification in Brunei Darussalam.* London and New York, Macmillan and St Martin's Press, 1994.

Department of Agriculture. *Investment Opportunities in Agro Industry.* Bandar Seri Begawan, 1997.

Department of Telecommunications. *Corporate Mission and Vision.* Bandar Seri Begawan, 1997.

Doshi, Tilak. 'Brunei: the Steady State'. *Southeast Asian Affairs 1991.* Singapore, Institute of Southeast Asian Studies/Heinemann, 1991.

Economic Development Board, Ministry of Finance. *Incentives for Investment in Brunei Darussalam,* Fifth Edn. Bandar Seri Begawan, 1996.

Economic Planning Unit, Ministry of Finance. *Sixth National Development Plan, 1991–1995.* Bandar Seri Begawan.

Economic Planning Unit, Ministry of Finance. *Seventh National Development Plan, 1996–2000.* Bandar Seri Begawan.

Economist Intelligence Unit. *Country Profile: Malaysia, Brunei.* London, 1995–96.

Government of Brunei Darussalam. *Brunei Darussalam in Profile.* London, Shandwick, 1988.

Horton, A. V. M. *The British Residency in Brunei, 1906–1959.* Hull, Centre for South-East Asian Studies, 1984.

Hussainmiya, B. A. *Sultan Omar Ali Saifuddin III and Britain.* Oxford, Oxford University Press, 1995.

Information Department, Prime Minister's Office. *Brunei Darussalam In Brief 1995,* Sixth Edn. Bandar Seri Begawan.

Krausse, Sylvia C. Engelen and Gerald H. *Brunei* (An annotated bibliography.) Oxford, Clio Press, 1988.

Leake, David, Jr. *Brunei: The Modern Southeast Asian Islamic Sultanate.* Jefferson, McFarland and Co, 1990.

McArthur, M. H. S. *Report on Brunei in 1904.* Athens, Ohio, 1987.

Mani, A. 'Negara Brunei Darussalam in 1992. Celebrating the Silver Jubilee'. *Southeast Asian Affairs 1993.* Singapore, Institute of Southeast Asian Studies, 1993.

Metra Consulting. *Handbook of National Development Plans.* London, Graham and Trotman, 1986.

Ministry of Communications. *Brunei Darussalam: Service Hub for Trade and Tourism (SHuTT) 2000 and Beyond.* Bandar Seri Begawan.

Ministry of Industry and Primary Resources. *Brunei Darussalam Investment Guide.* Bandar Seri Begawan.

Ports Department. *Your Regional Business Base, Investors' Handbook.* Bandar Seri Begawan.

Muara Port. Bandar Seri Begawan, 1997.

Ranjit Singh, D. S. *Brunei, 1839-1983, The Problems of Political Survival.* Singapore, Oxford University Press, 1984.

Saunders, Graham. *Bishops and Brookes.* Singapore, Oxford University Press, 1992.

Brunei: A Vision for the Future? Southeast Asian Affairs, 1997. Singapore, Institute of Southeast Asian Studies/Heinemann, 1997.

A History of Brunei. Second Edn. London, RoutledgeCurzon, 2002.

Siddique, Sharon. 'Brunei Darussalam 1991: the Non-secular State'. *Southeast Asian Affairs 1992.* Singapore, Institute of Southeast Asian Studies/Heinemann, 1992.

Statistics Division, Economic Planning Unit, Ministry of Finance. *Brunei Darussalam Statistical Yearbook.* Bandar Seri Begawan.

Tarling, Nicholas. *Britain, the Brookes and Brunei.* Kuala Lumpur, Oxford University Press, 1971.

Tourism Development Division, Ministry of Industry and Primary Resources. *Explore Brunei: A Visitor's Guide.* Third Edn. Bandar Seri Begawan, 1997.

Turnbull, C. M. *A History of Malaysia, Singapore and Brunei.* Sydney, Allen and Unwin, 1989.

Zaini Haji Ahmad, Haji. *The People's Party of Brunei, Selected Documents.* Kuala Lumpur, Insan, 1988.

CAMBODIA

Physical and Social Geography

HARVEY DEMAINE

Cambodia comprises a relatively small and compact territory on the Indo-Chinese peninsula and covers an area of 181,035 sq km (69,898 sq miles), bordered by Thailand to the west, by Laos to the north, and by Viet Nam to the east.

PHYSICAL FEATURES

Apart from the Cardamom and related mountains in the south, which divide the country's interior from its short southern coastline, the greater part of Cambodia consists of a shallow lacustrine basin, centred on Tonlé Sap ('the Great Lake') which was historically of far greater extent than it is today. This lowland drains eastwards, via the Tonlé Sap River, to the Mekong, which flows through the eastern part of the lowlands from north to south before turning eastwards into Viet Nam and to the South China Sea.

Throughout its course across Cambodia, the Mekong River averages about 2 km in width, but it is interrupted by precipitous rapids at Kratié, and by falls at Khone along the Laotian border. Moreover, its flow fluctuates widely from season to season, and during the period of greatest volume between June and October, a substantial portion of its flood-waters is diverted up the Tonlé Sap River (the flow of which is thus reversed) into the Great Lake itself, which comes to occupy an area at least twice as great as it does during the dry season in the early months of the year. The temperature is generally between 20°C and 36°C (68°F to 97°F), and the annual average in Phnom-Penh is 27°C (81°F).

RESOURCES AND POPULATION

With some good alluvial soils, abundant water for irrigation, and a tropical monsoon climate without excessive rainfall, Cambodia has considerable agricultural potential and could undoubtedly support both a wider area and a greater intensity of cultivation than it does at present.

In 1975 Cambodia had an estimated 7.1m. inhabitants and an average population density of 39 per sq km. By 1981, according to a census, the country's population had fallen to 6.7m., owing to warfare, famine and migration, giving a density of only 36.9 per sq km. At the census of 3 March 1998 the population was 11.44 m., and density had increased to 63.18 per sq km. In mid-2001 the population was officially estimated at 13.31m. The capital city, Phnom-Penh, had an estimated population of only 20,000 in 1978. However, in 1998, with the resurgence of internal trade, the city's population was estimated to have risen to 999,804.

History

LAURA SUMMERS

Revised by SORPONG PEOU

Early Khmer civilization, owing to its situation on major Chinese and Indian trade routes, was greatly affected by foreign cultural influences. The assimilation of Indian Brahmans into Khmer society encouraged the adoption of Hindu cults, including the recognition of the supremacy of the god Siva (Shiva) in the 'Funan' period (which extended from the first to the sixth century AD). Archaeological discoveries indicate the existence, at that time, of a highly pluralistic, peninsular political system containing a number of Khmer princely families, each of which supported and promoted family cults. Religious syncretism in the sixth century signalled the beginning of military competition for ascendancy in the Mekong delta. The ensuing wars between the cult-based principalities eventually gave rise to the highly centralized Angkorian empires during the ninth–14th centuries. The rejection of established religious cults and the rise of a moral tradition which united images of royalty, divinity and fertility corresponded to a massive intensification of rice production in the area surrounding the modern city of Siem Reap. A complex system of hydraulics, which diverted the water of highland streams and retained flood waters from the Tonlé Sap (a natural reservoir of the Mekong), permitted year-round agriculture and hitherto unthinkable concentrations of population. Much of the labour required for the building of the irrigation system and its associated, extraordinary temple complexes was provided by slaves, most of whom were prisoners of war or captured tribespeople from the highlands. With each succeeding century, the political influence of Angkor expanded, as did its agrarian economy and artistic achievements. At its greatest extent in the 12th century, during the reign of Jayavarman VII (1181–1218), the Angkorian empire embraced the Chao Phraya plain and parts of the Malay peninsula as well as all principalities and populations south of the Annamite chain in present-day Viet Nam, including the powerful Cham state of Champa. Jayavarman VII was also the first Buddhist King of Angkor. By the late 13th century, the Angkorian civilization displayed unmistakable signs of decadence. In 1431 the declining economic and military capacity of Cambodia were further eroded when the ascendant Thai civilization, based at Sukothai, sacked Angkor and its surrounding sites. Succeeding monarchs abandoned all efforts to continue state-controlled rice cultivation, permanently renounced Hindu cults and shifted their capitals southward to Lovek and Oudong, to the north of the riparian crossroads of Phnom-Penh.

PRE-COLONIAL CAMBODIA

Historians differ significantly in their assessment of society and politics from the 16th to the 19th century. Most French historians, focusing on the dramatic decrease in royal military power after the collapse of the empire, argue that Khmer civilization went into decline. By contrast, US scholars, reacting critically to the socially oppressive features of Angkorian centralization and the construction of monuments (especially since the failed socialist revolution in the 1970s), have argued that the 16th century gave rise to a pluralistic, dispersed, village-centred political order, in which communities, organized around Buddhist temples (*wat*), were able to avoid some of the earlier tyrannical excesses. Nevertheless, it is recognized that these communities were under the control of royally appointed governors who collected taxes and demanded labour service (*corvée*) in the name of the still revered monarch.

By the end of the 18th century, the Khmer kingdom had contracted in geographical size to approximately two-thirds of its present area. The rise of the powerful Chakri dynasty, to the west, and the southward expansion of the demographically buoyant Vietnamese nation resulted in the need to pay tribute to both foreign courts so as to solicit royal respect and paternalist protection. This period of dual Siamese-Vietnamese suzerainty came to an abrupt end after an aborted Vietnamese attempt to annex Cambodia. An indigenous, Buddhist-led rebellion, encouraged (although discreetly) by the monarch and supported by timely military intervention from Siam (Thailand), ultimately defeated the Vietnamese plan, but inevitably led to near-total subordination to the Siamese court. Although, unlike the Vietnamese, the Siamese did not insist on cultural assimilation or commence settling on Khmer land, King Ang Duang approached the French in the hope of signing a treaty of protection. The treaty, signed in 1863 by his son King Norodom, gave France complete control over Cambodia's foreign policy and required the royal court to accept a permanent Resident-General. France proceeded almost immediately to assume colonial control.

COLONIAL CAMBODIA

Inevitably, colonialism had a profound impact on the development of the Cambodian state and its politics. By 1884 a second, far-reaching treaty, imposed on Norodom, established French control over the royal administration, royal treasury and foreign trading. Cambodia was incorporated into the Indo-Chinese Union in 1887, and Union budgetary resources were used to reinforce the prestige and near-sacred regard for the Khmer monarch, as a shield against popular or élite discontent (following the successful suppression of a national uprising in 1884–86).

The colonial order was undermined only by the war in the Pacific. Vichy French collaboration with Japan after 1940, combined with Thailand's alliance with the Japanese, resulted in the Japanese-approved Thai annexation of Battambang province in 1941. King Monivong died and was replaced soon afterwards by King Norodom Sihanouk, who was only 18 years of age. King Sihanouk initially displayed sympathy for the emergent nationalist sentiments forcefully articulated by Son Ngoc Thanh and Buddhist monks, among others. (Thanh was appointed Prime Minister in an 'independent' Cabinet hastily established by the Japanese in 1945.) Sihanouk, however, alarmed by the increasingly anti-royalist tendencies of the nationalist movement, subsequently initiated secret discussions with France, arranging the arrest and exile of Thanh, the resumption of French colonial rule in 1946 and the promulgation of a new Constitution in 1947. The post-war Constitution permitted the formation of political parties and provided for the holding of legislative elections. These reforms satisfied the aspirations of some of the élite nationalists. France, meanwhile, used Cambodia as a rear military staging-area in its war against the Viet Minh (see the chapter on Viet Nam), a strategic manoeuvre which was also attempted by the USA after 1970. The resumption of colonial rule and the exile of Thanh divided the nascent nationalist movement. Some nationalists, responding partly to Viet Minh urgings, formed resistance groups seeking to overthrow both colonialism and monarchy, which was finally seen as a French instrument of repression. These *Issaraks*, or freedom fighters, displayed little internal unity. The mainstream of the nationalist movement (represented by the Democrat Party of Prince Yutevong), although anti-royalist, eschewed violence and opted to remain in Phnom-Penh, seeking to gain power through Parliament. The Democrats were highly successful in the legislative elections, but encountered strong opposition from the powerful Liberal Party, which represented royalist and land-owning families, and the smaller, ultra-conservative Khmer Renovation Party, a movement led by Lt-Gen. (later Marshal) Lon Nol and other high-ranking state functionaries and their families. The nationalist threat prompted Sihanouk to suspend the Constitution in June 1952 and to assume governmental powers. Fearing French defeat in Viet Nam and Democrat and *Issarak* ascendency, Sihanouk undertook a diplomatic mission to France and the USA, pleading for his country's right to independence. This 'Royal Crusade for Independence', as it was later called, succeeded. France conceded independence on 9 November 1953, and thus indirectly awarded to Sihanouk the title of 'father' of independence. Cambodia's independence was ratified by the Geneva Conference on Indo-China in July 1954.

THE SIHANOUK, LON NOL AND POL POT YEARS

The Sihanouk years of 1954–70 brought the restoration of limited constitutional rights to Cambodians, but were also characterized by Sihanouk's efforts to achieve stability, while being faced by renewed challenges from the socialist left, the liberal democratic and reformist centre and extreme right-wing parties and interests. In foreign policy, Sihanouk constantly renewed his nationalist credentials by steadily opposing US imperialism in Viet Nam. In 1955 he abdicated in favour of his father, Norodom Suramarit, to avoid the limitations of his role as constitutional monarch and thus to play a more direct role in politics and government. He founded the Sangkum Reastr Niyum (Popular Socialist Community), which decisively defeated the Democrats at the polls. Prince Sihanouk also created a biannual National Congress, effectively a mass meeting at which the public was invited to present its complaints. Thus, the power of the elected National Assembly was steadily eroded, and the mass media were also increasingly subject to state control and repression. Confronted by severe economic problems after 1966, Sihanouk resorted to arbitrary arrests and to some public executions, especially of 'pro-American' Thanists, who were known in this period as *Khmer Serei*. The political repression and economic disorder that marred the late 1960s affected nearly every well-placed family. The appointment of an emergency Government of National Salvation in 1969, under the leadership of Lon Nol, resulted in a carefully orchestrated *coup d'état* in March 1970. The ostensible motive for the coup was Sihanouk's alleged collaboration with the Vietnamese communist revolutionaries who used Cambodian territory for sanctuary and who seemingly presented a new threat to Cambodia's independence. The organizers of the coup comprised remnants of the old Democrat and Khmer Renovation Parties. In October 1970 Lon Nol proclaimed the Khmer Republic, of which he was elected President in 1972. Thanh became Prime Minister once again briefly in 1972. The Khmer Republic administration was, however, rapidly overwhelmed by the corruption attendant upon a war economy.

Informed of the coup while on a diplomatic mission and convinced of the involvement of the US Central Intelligence Agency, Sihanouk formed an alliance with North Viet Nam and with an underground Marxist insurgency group, the Khmers Rouges, led by Saloth Sar, who later became known as Pol Pot. The Khmers Rouges had initiated an armed struggle against Sihanouk in 1968 and already had a guerrilla force of 3,000 by the time of the coup. Following organized mass demonstrations opposing the coup, there were fears in Saigon and Washington that Lon Nol's administration might rapidly be overthrown. A joint US-South Vietnamese invasion of some 50,000 troops, officially for the purpose of clearing communist Vietnamese forces out of their Cambodian sanctuaries, served only to drive an estimated 30,000 Vietnamese revolutionary troops deeper into the country, where they systematically assisted the Khmers Rouges in raising support and troops for their new, Sihanouk-led United National Front of Cambodia—FUNC. Despite massive US military and economic assistance, the armed forces of Lon Nol were effectively defeated by the end of 1972, perhaps partly because of the unpopularity of the South Vietnamese occupation of parts of eastern Cambodia until 1973. In a desperate attempt to redress the military balance in favour of Lon Nol, the US Air Force engaged in nine months of round-the-clock saturation bombings in 1973 until the US Congress terminated funding. Between 1973 and 1975, confident of victory, the Khmers Rouges gradually assumed control of ministerial portfolios in Sihanouk's Royal Government of National Union of Cambodia (in exile) and put pressure on Vietnamese armed forces and advisers to leave Cambodia. Party cadres who were judged to be too loyal to the Vietnamese or to their revolutionary traditions and ideology were secretly purged; many were killed rather than demoted. By early 1975 Phnom-Penh was completely isolated from all overland and river communications and was dependent on US airlifts. Lon Nol was flown to Hawaii on 1 April 1975, just in advance of a revolutionary occupation of the capital on 17 April. In the following weeks, the entire populations of Phnom-Penh and other refugee-swollen cities were evacuated and resettled in rural areas in agricultural collectives under Khmer Rouge control. Over the next three years an estimated 1.7m. people died as a result of hard labour, inadequate food and medical supplies, harsh treatment and executions. The Khmers Rouges' campaign to transform Cambodia so rapidly was partly stimulated by fears that Viet Nam and the USA would not respect Cambodia's right to independence, especially its right to an 'independent' socialist revolution.

Although he returned to Phnom-Penh, Sihanouk was rapidly eclipsed in the post-war revolutionary turmoil. A new Constitution renamed the state 'Democratic Kampuchea' (DK). National elections were held in March 1976 for a legislative body, the People's Representative Assembly, with the franchise restricted to full member-supporters of the state collectives (approximately one-half of the adult population). In a typical gesture, calculated to initiate bargaining over terms and conditions, Sihanouk declined to serve as Head of State in April. The Assembly, however, elected Khieu Samphan to the Chairmanship of the State Presidium, while the relatively unknown Pol Pot was named Prime Minister. In September 1977, as border conflicts with Viet Nam increased, Pol Pot revealed that the ruling organization was the Communist Party of Kampuchea (CPK). His revised version of party history eliminated all reference to early Vietnamese involvement in the Cambodian communist movement, a clear indication that international solidarity had been permanently ruptured. Social tensions, arising from catastrophic shortfalls in production and the outbreak of full-scale border war with Viet Nam at the end of 1977, provoked extensive purges inside the CPK and emergency attempts to reorganize rural collectives, in an attempt to support the armed forces. Diplomatic relations with Viet Nam were severed on 31 December 1977, after an aborted invasion attempt appeared to confirm CPK fears that Viet Nam intended to incorporate the Kampuchean revolution into a Vietnamese-dominated, communist federation of Indo-China. During the following year relations between the two countries continued to deteriorate. Viet Nam feared that the harsh conditions and instability in Cambodia would make the fiercely independent but increasingly beleaguered CPK dependent upon and vulnerable to the will of the People's Republic of China. On 25 December 1978 Viet Nam invaded Democratic Kampuchea, with a force estimated at more than 200,000 men, supported by the newly-formed Kampuchean National United Front for National Salvation (KNUFNS, now UFCDKF) led by Heng Samrin and comprising CPK dissidents. The rebel forces occupied Phnom-Penh on 7 January 1979. By the beginning of 1980, the defeated Democratic Kampuchean army, which numbered 70,000 on the eve of the assault, had been forced to retreat into remote mountain redoubts along the frontier, with troops estimated at fewer than 30,000.

ESTABLISHMENT OF THE PEOPLE'S REPUBLIC OF KAMPUCHEA

The Vietnamese-supported People's Republic of Kampuchea (PRK) failed to secure widespread international recognition, despite its efforts to portray its installation as the result of an indigenously supported revolutionary uprising against the horrendous violations of human rights by the Democratic Kampuchean Government. The People's Republic of China and members of the Association of South East Asian Nations (ASEAN) viewed Viet Nam's intervention in Kampuchea as another manifestation of traditional Vietnamese expansionism, which constituted a threat to their own security. The USA responded to the invasion by strengthening its economic embargoes on aid and trade with Indo-China, persuading Japan and most member countries of the European Community (now European Union—EU) to join the embargo. Between 1979 and 1981 the dislodged Pol Pot Government continued to be recognized by the UN in view of Viet Nam's open violation of the UN Charter. From 1982 the Government of Democratic Kampuchea had taken the form of a coalition Government-in-exile comprising the Party of Democratic Kampuchea (PDK — the CPK was officially disbanded in 1981), a royalist movement known as FUNCINPEC (a French acronym for United National Front for an Independent, Neutral, Peaceful and Co-operative Cambodia), led by Sihanouk, and the Khmer People's National Liberation Front (KPNLF), led by a former Prime Minister under Sihanouk, Son Sann. An anti-communist republican movement, the KPNLF embraced many important personalities from the Khmer Republic regime and the old Democrat Party. Sihanouk agreed to serve as President in the new Coalition Government of Democratic Kampuchea (CGDK). Although united by their opposition to the Vietnamese occupation of Cambodia and to the communist Government headed by Heng Samrin, which had been installed in Phnom-Penh, the parties that formed the CGDK were unable to function as a political alliance in view of their mutually hostile political visions and aspirations. Each of the three parties fielded its own army, and periodic attempts by the foreign supporters of the CGDK to encourage more than sporadic military co-operation were largely unsuccessful. China supplied nearly all of the weapons required by each of the three armies, while smaller amounts of military, humanitarian and 'non-lethal' aid were supplied to the non-communist FUNCINPEC and the KPNLF by the ASEAN countries, the USA, France and the United Kingdom. The USSR, its allies in Eastern Europe and Cuba supplied and financed the PRK.

By 1988 fighting between the CGDK and the PRK armed forces was of low intensity. The stalemate extended to the political arena. Although Viet Nam formally ignored UN resolutions appealing for a full and unconditional withdrawal and steadfastly rejected appeals from the CGDK and ASEAN for a negotiated end to the occupation, it tacitly responded to international criticism after 1983 by reducing its troop levels during annual rotations. Viet Nam's determination to 'rescue' the revolution in Cambodia and forcibly to restore solidarity between the Cambodian and Vietnamese revolutions was disrupted only by developments in other parts of the communist world. Following reductions in military and economic aid from the USSR in 1987, rapid Sino-Soviet *rapprochement* in 1988 and insistent Soviet pressure to seek a settlement in Cambodia based on 'national reconciliation' and the restoration of the monarchy, Viet Nam made increasingly firm unilateral pledges to withdraw all of its forces from Cambodia by the end of September 1989. Initially, the pledges were made conditional upon Thailand, China and other powers agreeing to withhold their military aid to the Cambodian resistance armies (for Viet Nam refused to accept that it had any unique responsibility to withdraw). Adding its terms to the effort to obtain a 'partial' or 'external' solution, as it was known, the leadership of the ruling Kampuchean People's Revolutionary Party (KPRP) in Phnom-Penh issued an appeal for 'national reconciliation', calling for the formation of a broad coalition government embracing all nationalist forces. The appeal made clear that the envisaged coalition would be guided by the KPRP communists and be based on the legal and administrative framework that had been established in Phnom-Penh in 1979. The KPRP also proposed to offer a senior position in the PRK to Sihanouk, with whom informal talks were arranged. Both Viet Nam and the KPRP continued to oppose any political role for the PDK, and to reject the involvement of the UN in the monitoring of the Vietnamese troop withdrawal.

Mindful of the need to widen its social base, the KPRP announced in 1988 that it would reform its state-controlled economy and proceeded to award managerial autonomy to nationalized industries. In 1989 peasants were informed that traditional usufruct titles to land would be reintroduced and tenants in state-supplied housing were promised property deeds, an act which simultaneously dispossessed pre-1975 owners of urban housing stock. In April 1989 the KPRP-controlled National Assembly voted to change the official name of the PRK to the State of Cambodia (SOC), thus removing the communist designation for a democratic republic. Sihanouk, who had requested the change as a concessionary gesture, refused nevertheless to join the reformed SOC, and continued to urge the creation of an interim, quadripartite coalition government to replace both the CGDK and SOC governmental frameworks, UN supervision of the Vietnamese troop withdrawal, a ceasefire and UN-supervised, national elections. In spite of SOC reluctance to form a coalition, the collapse of communist power elsewhere in the world encouraged Sihanouk as well as France to believe that the situation in Cambodia was evolving towards a settlement. Thus France, aided by Indonesia (acting on behalf of the ASEAN countries), convened an international conference on Cambodia in Paris on 30 July. By this time, the USSR had lent its approval to proposals for an interim, quadripartite coalition government to be led by Sihanouk, but in Paris the delegations representing Viet Nam, Laos and the KPRP continued to oppose an all-party interim government, advocating instead a coalition of 'national reconciliation' excluding the PDK, which was denounced as 'genocidal' and 'anti-national'. They also rejected all proposals for UN intervention in Cambodia, accusing the UN of being politically biased. The communist states also insisted that the SOC deserved legal recognition because it controlled most of the population and administered most of Cambodia's territory. It was further asserted that the SOC alone possessed the sovereign rights to negotiate a solution to Cambodia's internal conflict and to organize national elections.

It rapidly became clear that the allied Indo-Chinese communist parties sought a 'partial' solution focusing on the cessation of external weapons supplies to Cambodia and the establishment of a coalition government that would further weaken and divide the resistance coalition while enhancing the nationalist appeal and legitimacy of the KPRP. Such proposals failed to address the security concerns of China or of the ASEAN countries. The regional supporters of the CGDK sought, if possible, to eradicate Vietnamese influence in Cambodia or, at least, to ensure the restoration of a neutral, Sihanoukist government in which the PDK exercised a clear role as a form of insurance against renewed Vietnamese intervention. Unable to bridge such enormous differences, the Paris Conference deliberations were suspended after one month. One obstacle to the success of the Conference was the failure of the major powers to present a unified view to the Cambodian parties. US delegates reinforced the tendency of each of the two Cambodian sides to resist compromise, for while the USA accepted that peace required awarding political roles to all four parties, its diplomats made no secret of their personal preference for a solution excluding the PDK, as demanded by the SOC. The US Secretary of State, James Baker, stressed that US economic assistance would be greater if a PDK role were minimized. Despite the diplomatic stalemate and encouraged by the open US hostility towards the PDK, Viet Nam proceeded unilaterally to withdraw its regular armed forces from the country at the end of September. Its appeals for reciprocal withdrawals of foreign military support for other Cambodian parties were discounted by foreign intelligence reports noting that hundreds and perhaps thousands of Vietnamese cadres remained in Cambodia in advisory roles and that as many as 3,000 rapid-intervention troops were reintroduced to Cambodian battlefields within a matter of weeks, when fighting between the two Cambodian sides intensified.

As anticipated by Viet Nam, international concern to resolve the Cambodian crisis intensified following the withdrawal of its regular forces. The retreat also prompted a dramatic increase in fighting in several parts of Cambodia, but especially in the west, with the National Army of Democratic Kampuchea (NADK), the army of the PDK, making the most significant advances. This raised the spectre of a military outcome, which no one other than the PDK wanted. Responding to the Cambodian failure to agree on how to form an interim coalition government, a US Congressman, Stephen Solarz, proposed the establishment of an interim UN administration in Cambodia, an idea that circumvented debate about which Government, the SOC or the CGDK, should form the basis for an interim state authority. Solarz also favoured a UN role as a means of promoting human rights education in Cambodia. The Australian Government, acting on Solarz's proposals, undertook the difficult task of persuading Viet Nam, as well as the KPRP, that support for a UN administrative role, UN monitoring of a cease-fire and UN-supervised elections were not incompatible with KPRP desires to retain power and were perhaps the best options for the SOC and Viet Nam to bring an end to their international isolation, which was increasing as a result of the loss of Soviet support. Cautiously, Viet Nam in January 1990 and the KPRP in February agreed to a 'limited' UN role. Concurrently, at the initiative of the USA, the five permanent members of the UN Security Council began monthly meetings to establish a mutually acceptable and practical framework for a settlement which could then be recommended to the Cambodian parties. Since the USA and the USSR had already agreed on the desirability of a non-communist, neutral administration led by Sihanouk, the concern in the first half of 1990 was to persuade China to abandon its continuing diplomatic and military support for the PDK, which remained the principal obstacle to a settlement of the conflict.

The comprehensive political settlement negotiated by the permanent members of the Security Council, which was finally presented in September 1990, envisaged: free and fair elections to be conducted under direct UN administration; the verified withdrawal of foreign forces; the cessation of all military assistance to Cambodia; the repatriation of refugees and displaced persons from Thailand under the auspices of the office of the UN High Commissioner for Refugees (UNHCR); the rehabilitation and reconstruction of Cambodia's economy; the formation of a Supreme National Council (SNC) by the four Cambodian parties (none is treated as a government); and the creation of a UN Transitional Authority in Cambodia (UNTAC), which would have special powers of administration and supervision during a transitional period and which would be headed by a Special Representative of the UN Secretary-General. The SNC would represent Cambodian sovereignty externally during a transitional period and would occupy Cambodia's seat in the UN General Assembly; UNTAC was to have powers of control or supervision over wide areas of national government (especially all agencies responsible for defence, internal security, finance and public information), primarily for the purpose of creating a neutral political environment for the holding of free elections. The UN plan envisaged a substantial reduction in the power wielded by the existing administrative structures, especially the SOC ministries in Phnom-Penh. Sihanouk, the President of the resistance coalition, and Hun Sen, the Chairman of the Council of Ministers of the SOC had informally agreed in June to an equal division of the SNC seats between the two rival Governments (rather than among the four parties). Although this was initially unacceptable to the PDK, which preferred equal representation for each party, as was in fact proposed by the UN, the four parties agreed in September to a 12-member SNC comprising six representatives from the KPRP, two from FUNCINPEC, two from the KPNLF and two from the PDK. It was further agreed that SNC decisions would be taken by consensus, a procedure that awarded each party the power of veto. These compromises were influenced by Chinese diplomats, who quietly informed the PDK, the KPNLF and FUNCINPEC that all military aid to their armies would be gradually reduced and then cease altogether perhaps from the beginning of 1991, and by Soviet diplomats, who reciprocated by advising Viet Nam and Phnom-Penh, to which aid had effectively ceased, to abandon demands for the exclusion of the PDK from a settlement.

With each side none the less fiercely determined to secure the political advantages of holding office, the first meeting of the SNC in September 1990 in the Cambodian embassy in Bangkok finished acrimoniously with no agreement on who should assume the chairmanship of the SNC or who would represent it in the UN General Assembly. The permanent members of the UN Security Council intervened by proposing that Sihanouk head the SNC, a proposal initially unacceptable to the SOC side, which had been seeking joint chairmanship, rotating chairmanship or the compensatory appointment of Hun Sun, as Sihanouk's deputy together with an additional, compensatory seat for the SOC to rebalance the numbers at seven members each. The SOC also raised objections to proposals for the full disarmament of all four Cambodian armies, insisting upon the need to have access to weapons both during and after the proposed transitional period as a guarantee against attempts by the PDK (whose troops and weapons caches might escape UN monitoring) to seize power. Still seeking to portray the UN role as indirect diplomatic recognition, the KPRP also objected to UN plans to exercise control over its ministries. Neither the SOC nor the resistance coalition was reassured when in December the UN Secretary-General's Special Representative for Cambodia explained that the UN's draft agreement for a settlement was based on 'full respect' for Cambodia's existing administrative structures and that the UN accepted that there would be 'three categories of entities exercising powers' during the transitional period: the SNC; UNTAC, which would assume control of all administrative agencies concerned with foreign affairs, national defence, finance, public security and information; and the existing administrative structures in the zones controlled by the four parties, which would continue to function either under UNTAC control or supervision or with no control or supervision. With each side seeking to promote its claim for leadership of the SNC and both anxious (for opposed reasons) about the administrative influence of the KPRP state apparatus on the population, diplomatic progress ceased in early 1991. Military activity intensified during the dry season, rapidly increasing the number of refugees housed in holding centres in Thailand. The UN Secretary-General, Javier Pérez de Cuéllar, appealed in April for a cease-fire.

The diplomatic impasse was broken by Sihanouk, who was irritated by the unproductive informal talks that had resumed in Jakarta; fearful that neglect of the UN plan and pleas for a cease-fire would result in the abandonment of efforts to find a solution to the Cambodian problem, he was also prompted by 'rumours' that China would terminate all supplies of weapons to the PDK, KPNLF and FUNCINPEC armies as early as September 1991. In June Sihanouk announced the resignation of one of the FUNCINPEC representatives in the newly formed, but inoperative, SNC, and appointed himself to the empty seat as a 'simple member'. He then convened and presided, unappointed, over a meeting of the SNC held in Pattaya, Thailand—an effective and logical act of usurpation when it is recalled that each side sought prestige from association with the monarchy and could ill afford to oppose the Prince. At the June SNC meeting in Pattaya, and two others subsequently held in Beijing (in July) and in Pattaya (in August), delegates representing the four Cambodian parties finally agreed that Sihanouk would assume the chairmanship of the SNC, that the SNC would be based in Phnom-Penh and that it would commence functioning in November. The accession of the Prince to the chairmanship of the SNC was achieved without compensation to the SOC because China, in a clear change of foreign policy, concurrently ceased to extend diplomatic recognition to the resistance Government and began to accord equal recognition to all Cambodian parties, and their representatives, specifically to Hun Sen, head of the SOC delegation in the SNC. Adding to the momentum, China also reportedly conceded secretly to Viet Nam that military demobilization, fixed at 100% in the UN draft plan, did not have to be total. The Cambodian parties then agreed at their second meeting in Pattaya to a mutual reduction of 70% in their force levels and weapons stocks, a compromise forced on the PDK by Thailand. The guerrilla-based PDK favoured 100% disarmament, as originally recommended in the UN draft, for this would have effectively destroyed the mechanized SOC army; the NADK would not be so radically affected and remobilization of their forces posed comparatively fewer problems. Whatever PDK intentions were, the Thai Premier informed Khieu Samphan, the leader of the PDK and a PDK member of the SNC, that Thailand might cease selling and transporting food and other supplies to guerrilla bases if there were no compromise. The final significant dispute among the parties involved the modalities of the free and fair elections envisaged by the UN. Under a compromise negotiated within the SNC in September, the SOC abandoned its demands for single-member constituencies with simple plurality elections, a formula favouring the largest, nationally-organized parties, and agreed to a system of proportional representation for each of 21 constituencies, these being the existing SOC provinces (19) and municipalities (two). These issues having been resolved and the UN draft amended accordingly, comprehensive political agreements and treaties were formally signed by the UN Secretary-General, the four Cambodian parties, Viet Nam and 17 other states at a reconvened Paris Conference on 23 October. Although no announcements were made, China halted weapons shipments to its three former allies; Viet Nam, equally, recalled its advisers and ceased to intervene militarily in Cambodia.

IMPLEMENTATION OF THE 1991 PEACE ACCORDS

UN intervention in Phnom-Penh accelerated the liberalizing trends which the KPRP had set in motion in 1988, but also exposed, albeit inadvertently, the profoundly illiberal and authoritarian character of Cambodian politics. Anticipating the arrival of the UN, at an extraordinary party congress the KPRP formally abandoned its one-party state on 18 October 1991, while announcing its support for the creation of a multi-party democracy as the means for securing national reconciliation. The need for an electoral vehicle, rather than a vanguard party, was met by two additional significant developments: the Congress changed the name of the KPRP to the Cambodian People's Party (CPP) and abandoned its Marxist-Leninist ideology. The veteran leader of the KPRP, Heng Samrin, was retired to an honorary role in the party, and replaced as Chairman of the Central Committee by the lesser-known Chea Sim, who named the youthful Hun Sen as his deputy and principal party spokesman. Revitalizing the party's invitation to Sihanouk, Hun Sen declared his support for Sihanouk as an elected President in a new constitutional order to be elaborated following the planned national elections. Sihanouk returned to Phnom-Penh in November to establish the SNC in its national headquarters and negotiated a plan for co-operation between the CPP and FUNCINPEC with Prince Norodom Ranariddh, Sihanouk's son and the leader of FUNCINPEC. The vaguely worded agreement was immediately widely criticized as the basis for a power-sharing arrangement following the elections, and was therefore renounced in December. The friendly approach to FUNCINPEC from the CPP served to emphasize its continuing opposition to a political role for the PDK. Khieu Samphan's return to Phnom-Penh in November provoked a violent demonstration (widely believed to have been orchestrated by the CPP). The villa that housed the PDK delegation to the SNC was besieged and forcibly entered by the demonstrators, and Khieu Samphan and Son Sen were forced to flee to Thailand. A third SNC meeting in Pattaya, at which security arrangements for the PDK were discussed, finally permitted the SNC to begin functioning in Phnom-Penh at the end of December.

In the meantime, civic order in Phnom-Penh had collapsed. Former state employees, dispossessed of their jobs as a result of SOC 'privatizations', began to picket their former workplaces; people dispossessed of their assigned, cheaply leased housing as the result of the now lawful, but often corrupt, sale of state-owned buildings, or evicted from squatter settlements, demonstrated, demanding compensation and new homes. Students demonstrated against corruption amongst senior officials. Public order was only slowly restored by the imposition of a curfew, the assassination of one prominent critic, the use of armed police and security services and the arrest and detention of a large number of demonstrators.

Cambodian expectations of help and protection from the UN could not be satisfied by UNTAC. For its time, UNTAC was the largest multi-functional mission ever attempted, involving 16,000 troops, 3,600 civilian police, 2,400 civilian administrators and approximately 5,000 local employees, giving rise to delays linked to fund-raising (US $1,800m., excluding the costs of repatriation, which were raised separately by the UNHCR) and the recruitment of appropriate personnel. Yasushi Akashi, the most senior Japanese diplomat at the UN, was named Special Representative of the UN Secretary-General in Cambodia and Head of UNTAC, partly to encourage important financial and personnel contributions from Japan. Maj.-Gen. John Sanderson, an Australian, was chosen to head UNTAC's crucially important military component. Unfortunately, UNTAC was not formally established in Phnom-Penh until mid-March 1992, and then with only limited staff. By this time the cease-fire agreed in October had collapsed, for several reasons. Realizing that the arrival of the UN troops would be delayed, the four factions were determined to secure further territorial gains. The PDK refused to comply with the peace process, and in April the UN condemned the party for its failure to co-operate and particularly for its refusal to allow UNTAC officials free access to PDK-controlled territory. The PDK army, the NADK, engaged the CPP army in Kompong Thom, accusing the 'Vietnamese' forces of initiating the offensive. Concurrently, PDK spokesmen accused UNTAC of ignoring its responsibilities under the Paris agreement to control and supervise the withdrawal of all 'foreign forces', claiming the existence of thousands of concealed Vietnamese troops in Cambodia. By early June the PDK announced that its army would not regroup or disarm, in compliance with the demands of the incomplete military contingent of UNTAC. The PDK campaigned for more powers of government, supervision and control to be given to the SNC. Sihanouk, Akashi and all other members of the SNC opposed the PDK proposals on the grounds that the Paris agreement could not be renegotiated. The PDK strongly criticized provisions of the election law introduced by Akashi, which permitted Vietnamese residents to vote providing that the intending voter was born in Cambodia with at least one parent who was also born in Cambodia, or, wherever born, able to prove that at least one parent was a Cambodian person by the place of birth principle.

As the election campaign advanced, a total of 20 parties met UNTAC requirements for a place on the ballot paper. Most of the parties were poorly organized; the majority were vehicles for prominent individuals who in some cases had returned from long periods of exile in the USA, France or Switzerland. Excluding the parties forged during the 1978–91 war, namely the CPP, FUNCINPEC (which altered its title to the FUNCINPEC Party when adopting political status in February 1992) and the political party formed by the KPNLF, the Buddhist Liberal Democratic Party (BLDP) led by Son Sann, the parties lacked the organizational capacity as well as the material means essential for campaigning effectively in every province. Difficulties of access to voters were further compounded by the SOC's obstruction of physical displacement, including private air flights, and SOC refusal to allow access to state-controlled radio and television stations or printing facilities to any party but the CPP, in clear violation of the Paris agreement. UNTAC quickly installed its own radio station in order to educate the Cambodian public about free elections.

The election campaign focused increasingly on issues of war, peace and national survival. The CPP leader, Hun Sen, questioned whether any other party had sufficient 'forces' to govern the country or to oppose Pol Pot. He pledged that the CPP would outlaw the PDK and defeat its forces militarily. The BLDP, together with the majority of parties formed on the basis of bonds of personal loyalty, judged the major issues to be the need to defend Cambodia from Vietnamese immigration and annexation and from parties who worked with and, allegedly, for the Vietnamese, specifically the CPP. To achieve this, it was argued, unity rather than conflict among Cambodians was essential. With their claims to office under open challenge, provincial CPP leaders systematically bullied and threatened anti-CPP party workers and candidates, discouraging many from campaigning; among those who persisted, a large number were murdered. The climate of fear and violence was neutralized in more populous provinces and cities by greater security and transparency in the campaigning and a rising sense of anticipation. Even though they were not competing for votes, the PDK brutally encouraged the rising tides of anti-Vietnamese nationalism by massacring Vietnamese civilians in long-established fishing communities on the Tonlé Sap, provoking a mass exodus of more than 20,000 Cambodian Vietnamese to Viet Nam in April–May 1993. Ranariddh, leading the FUNCINPEC Party's campaign, warned that a CPP election victory would result in renewed civil war between the CPP and the PDK. A FUNCINPEC victory, he stressed, would not return the PDK to power, but would end the war, since a government chosen by the Cambodian people and comprised entirely of Cambodians would eliminate the PDK pretext for continuing to fight the Vietnamese. Ranariddh also promised that his father, Sihanouk, would deal with the problem of Vietnamese immigration; the FUNCINPEC Party's policy on immigration was described summarily as 'non-racist'.

Despite an increase in fighting between Phnom-Penh forces and the PDK, UNTAC's voter registration campaign was extremely successful; by the end of the process in February 1993 4.7m. Cambodians (constituting 97% of the estimated eligible electorate) had been registered. The repatriation of refugees from camps on the Thai border also proceeded on schedule; all 360,000 had been returned to Cambodia by the end of April. Despite fears of PDK assaults against polling stations, 89.6% of all eligible registered voters participated in the elections, which took place on 23–28 May. The PDK, which apparently lacked the capability to disrupt the polls systematically, instead offered its support to the FUNCINPEC Party in the hope of securing a role in government following the election. Early indications of a FUNCINPEC victory in the election prompted allegations of electoral malpractice from the CPP, which protested to Akashi that broadcasts on UNTAC's radio station lacked 'neutrality' and lodged formal complaints about 'irregularities' in the handling of ballot-boxes and partisan management of polling stations in some localities. UNTAC, however, rejected CPP requests for fresh elections in at least four provinces. Hun Sen indicated that the CPP might not recognize the results of the elections, and SOC National Security Ministry officials allegedly prepared a putsch. Sihanouk, supposedly advised of the imminent coup as troops surrounded the Royal Palace, agreed to an interim FUNCINPEC-CPP coalition Government in talks with the CPP Chairman, Chea Sim. The proposal was vetoed, unexpectedly, by Ranariddh who was out of the country. On 5 June the official results of the election were released; the FUNCINPEC Party secured 58 seats with 45.5% of the votes; and the CPP 51 seats with 38.2% of the votes. The CPP carried 11 of the 21 constituencies, with most of its votes coming from the smaller, rural provinces in which many opposition parties had failed to campaign. In Battambang and Kompong Cham (Hun Sen's constituency), where violence, nepotism and corruption were major features of intense party political contests, the CPP won only 31% of the votes cast. In the Phnom-Penh municipality and the capital city province of Kandal, where intimidation and organizational control on the part of the CPP was least effective, the FUNCINPEC Party received 58% of the votes and the CPP only 28%. The BLDP finished a distant third in the national elections, securing 10 seats, while the only other party to gain representation in the Constituent Assembly was MOLINAKA (National Liberation Movement of Cambodia, a breakaway faction from FUNCINPEC), which secured one seat. In June CPP militants in several eastern provinces bordering Viet Nam announced the creation of an 'autonomous' zone. The secessionists, who were nominally led by Prince Norodom Chakkrapong, a son of Sihanouk's and a Vice-Chairman of the Council of Ministers in the SOC administration, expelled UNTAC officials and FUNCINPEC supporters from three provinces in their zone, a partition which Hun Sen and other CPP officials in Phnom-Penh publicly opposed, but secretly endorsed as a means to force Sihanouk and Ranariddh into a power-sharing coalition. Hun Sen arranged for the Constituent Assembly to vote special powers to Sihanouk at its inaugural meeting on 14 July 1993, prefiguring the award of a senior position to the Prince at a later date or, as the FUNCINPEC Party desired, the restoration of the monarchy. Sihanouk's spokesmen announced in July 1993 that Ranariddh and Hun Sen would be co-chairmen of the Provisional National Government of Cambodia, pending a new constitution. The secessionist movement collapsed on 17 July. Although the formation of an interim government and the resumption of powers by Sihanouk were outside the terms of the Paris agreement, UNTAC was powerless to intervene in these developments. In July and August, as Sihanouk attempted to arrange 'round-table' talks with the PDK, so as to end the partition of Cambodia and to complete the process of national reconciliation as understood in royalist terms, the USA continued to object to a role, advisory or otherwise, for the PDK in the coalition. US objections to any involvement of the PDK lent support to the CPP, which wished, not only to exclude the PDK from the coalition, but to secure international support for a resumption of war.

While Sihanouk's attempts to arrange a settlement between the PDK and CPP at meetings in 1993 and 1994 failed, the Prince exerted considerable influence in determining his role—and the role of future kings—in the new constitutional order. On 21 September 1993, the FUNCINPEC-CPP-controlled Constituent Assembly adopted a new Constitution with 139 articles. It was signed and promulgated by Sihanouk on 24 September (in his newly resumed, extra-legal role of 'Head of State' and as Chairman of the SNC, a legal but non-functioning entity). Under the provisions of the Paris peace agreement the Constituent Assembly became the National Assembly, and on the same day Sihanouk acceded to the throne of the new Kingdom of Cambodia. Articles 1–30 of the Constitution proclaimed the country a Kingdom and a 'multi-party liberal democracy'. The duties and responsibilities awarded to the King were those of a constitutional monarch, but Article 9 also specified that the King should serve in the role of 'referee to guarantee the normal functioning of public authorities'. The reigning King, according to the Constitution, should 'not have the power to appoint his successor' who was to be elected by a Royal Council of the Throne. The members of this Council were fixed by the Constitution; they were the Chairman of the National Assembly, the Prime Minister, the Supreme Patriarchs of the Mohanikay and Thammayut Buddhist sects and the First and Second Vice-Chairmen of the National Assembly. The promulgation of the

Constitution coincided with the first public acknowledgements that Sihanouk was seriously ill with cancer. Following his enthronement, Sihanouk underwent two major courses of chemotherapy. Although prevented by law from identifying a crown prince, Sihanouk awarded royal titles to three sons, a half-brother and one relative from the Sisowath line, which indicated his preference in 1994 for Ranariddh to succeed him. Ranariddh's ability to do so remained dependent upon support from the CPP, and specifically from Chea Sim, who was re-elected Chairman of the National Assembly.

THE ROYAL GOVERNMENT OF CAMBODIA

At the end of October 1993 the National Assembly approved the composition of the new Royal Government of Cambodia (RGC), which had been endorsed by Sihanouk. Ranariddh was named First Prime Minister and Hun Sen Second Prime Minister. Paradoxically, the restoration of constitutional government to Cambodia in September 1993, which brought an end to UNTAC's mission, unleashed serious factional disputes within the ruling CPP and FUNCINPEC Party. One reason for this, as indicated above, was that the restoration of Sihanouk to the throne placed the King's personal agenda for the future in confrontation with the predominantly bureaucratic and militarist impulses within the CPP as well as anti-communist, technocratic tendencies within the royalist movement. After 25 years of political turmoil, Cambodia was no longer self-sufficient in cereal production, had little modern infrastructure, and supported excessively large and ill-disciplined security forces. The use of patronage to secure political support during the PRK era had also led to an oversized bureaucracy staffed by a highly politicized corps of civil servants. The parlous state of the national budget (which was supported by international aid donations amounting to approximately US $10m. a month in 1993) lent separate momentum to disagreements both within and between the two ruling parties over their response to the international donor community.

Disputes relating to policy and supremacy within the CPP revolved around Chea Sim, who represented the deeply authoritarian and traditional element of the party. Hun Sen, by contrast, spoke for a younger generation of cadres who had been recruited to the revolutionary cause during the 1970s. This younger generation was widely regarded as more pragmatic, liberal and at greater ease with market-led economic development.

In September 1993 Chea Sim indicated a desire to remove Hun Sen from the Government in advance of the promulgation of the new Constitution by criticizing him for not having made 'sacrifices' for the party. With FUNCINPEC support, Chea Sim succeeded in being elected Chairman of the National Assembly, thereby dislodging the BLDP leader, Son Sann, who had held the post during the period of provisional national government (which extended from June to October 1993). In this new role Chea Sim ignored Sihanouk's initiatives, defended the corporate interests of the army and of the state administration (which were broadly indistinguishable from the organizational interests of the CPP) and urged uncompromising policies towards the PDK. The most significant such policy was the adoption in July 1994 of a law that declared the PDK to be 'an illegal and criminal group', thereby proscribing the party.

Despite its impressive electoral success, the FUNCINPEC Party, in contrast to the CPP, lacked a nation-wide organization of disciplined cadres and supporters. At a ministerial level, however, FUNCINPEC was stronger, and during 1993–94 displayed a pronounced technocratic orientation. Serious differences of opinion on how best to resolve the PDK issue continued to divide party intellectuals; with the PDK being in control of 5–10% of the population and around 10% of national territory, the issue had become one of partitioning the country. The conciliatory position of Sihanouk towards the PDK commanded most support, and there was a belief that if he failed to persuade the PDK to surrender, they could be ignored, on the assumption that they posed no military threat to the cities or to the RGC. The Minister of Finance, Sam Rainsy, a FUNCINPEC member of the National Assembly, judged the traditional, incorporative position of the King as desirable if not essential, but regarded economic growth, rather than political unity, as the key to the Government's stability. As a former banker and advocate of free-market development, Rainsy believed in co-operation with foreign donors in the drafting of reconstruction and stabilization plans. Rainsy attempted to review business contracts negotiated previously by SOC officials. He also tried, unsuccessfully, to introduce an independent system of assessing customs duties on goods. In March 1994 Ranariddh and Hun Sen jointly proposed that Sihanouk remove Rainsy from the Ministry of Finance. The two were drawn together through their common interest in protecting party patronage from the challenges posed by Rainsy. Sihanouk withheld his consent, however, due to Rainsy's evident national popularity (corruption, against which he campaigned, had become a major public issue) and his success in gaining the confidence of donor countries and multilateral agencies upon whom the country depended. The second session of the National Assembly, which convened shortly thereafter, was quickly suspended following disputes over vacancies in the Assembly caused by requests from leaders of the 1993 secessionist movement, and because certain pieces of draft legislation were unfinished.

In June 1994 the two Prime Ministers transferred control of timber exports (then legally proscribed) to the Ministry of National Defence in order to supplement its 1994 budget allocation. The decision, which was undertaken without consultation, undermined IMF attempts to restore fiscal rationality to the budget (see Economy). By this time Ranariddh had begun openly to support the CPP election promise to ban the PDK. Hun Sen publicly challenged Sihanouk's renewed willingness to accommodate PDK demands for a role in government, and his stated desire to assume power if the political system collapsed, by asking him not to denigrate the Constitution. Once introduced in the National Assembly, the law to ban the PDK was initially opposed by a group of approximately 15 legislators, led by Rainsy, on the grounds that it would engender more civil strife and threaten civil liberties. Most members of the National Assembly, including Rainsy, subsequently voted for the law, however, after amendments were agreed safeguarding citizens from possibly false accusations and intimidation. In spite of Sihanouk's indication that he would not sign the measure, as it amounted to a rebuff to his hopes for a government of national unity (he was undergoing chemotherapy in China during the vote), the proposed legislation was quickly signed into law, eventually with Sihanouk's assent, by the acting Head of State, Chea Sim.

Political co-operation between Ranariddh and Hun Sen grew considerably from July 1994, following a coup attempt allegedly instigated by Chakkrapong, in collaboration with Gen. Sin Song, the former SOC Minister of National Security and other military and security elements inside the CPP. With the support of ex-FUNCINPEC army generals and units loyal to Ranariddh, Hun Sen succeeded in arresting Chakkrapong, who protested his innocence and appealed successfully to his father, Sihanouk, to be allowed to go into exile. Sihanouk announced that he would no longer intervene in the affairs of the RGC, adding that he believed reconciliation between the Government and the outlawed PDK (which he had been attempting to promote) had become impossible. Sin Song was also arrested, but escaped to Thailand in September before he could be brought to trial. The Government used the incident to stifle criticism in the national press, suspending publication of the *Morning News* and briefly imprisoning its editor for having published articles implicating many senior CPP officials, including Sar Kheng, in activities surrounding the failed coup. A new press law, adopted by the National Assembly in July 1995, made defamation a criminal offence and codified governmental rights to suspend publication of newspapers that carried articles deemed disruptive of 'national security' and 'political stability'.

The adoption of the law proscribing the PDK, the political eclipse of Sihanouk, and the clamp-down on the press signalled an end to the era of political transition and realignment promoted by the UN in 1992 and 1993. Having neutralized the role of Sihanouk, the two Prime Ministers finally succeeded in removing Rainsy from the Ministry of Finance and from the Cabinet during a government reshuffle in October 1994. However, Rainsy continued to criticize government policies from the floor of the Assembly, demanding in particular, along with other opposition representatives, that the Government permit the Assembly to scrutinize major construction and forestry contracts it had awarded, often with no apparent reference to sector plans or long-term developmental implications. In retaliation, Rainsy was expelled from the FUNCINPEC Party in May 1995 and excluded from his FUNCINPEC seat in the National Assembly in June. Ranariddh, who had made a point of refraining from public disagreements with his CPP and BLDP coalition partners throughout 1994, claimed that it was 'discipline' rather than democracy that was lacking in Cambodia.

The fissiparous and fractious tendencies within the two major parties were reflected in the demise of most other political parties in 1995, the direct consequence of the centralizing, undemocratic consolidation of power in the hands of the leaders of the CPP-FUNCINPEC coalition. In July 1995 Son Sann, the President of the BLDP, and Ieng Muli, the party's Secretary-General and the Minister of Information and the Press in the coalition Government (and a long-standing rival of Son Sann), convened an extraordinary, unofficial congress of the party. Although the two leaders were ostensibly in dispute over the allocation of public appointments offered to the party (one list prepared by Son Sann had been disregarded by the Government and a shorter list prepared by Muli had been accepted), Muli claimed at the special congress that his strategic concern was party political: to determine decisively whether the BLDP was part of the RGC of which he was a member, or whether, as Son Sann believed, the party was part of the parliamentary opposition. The congress elected Muli's candidates as new party officers and passed a vote of 'no confidence' in four of the BLDP members of the National Assembly, including Son Sann. Contrary to expectation, the four were not immediately expelled from the Assembly, and retained their seats as of mid-1996, but a rival congress convened by Son Sann in September 1995 was initially banned and then disrupted by grenade attacks. Hun Sen insisted in September 1995 that the coalition Government would remain in office until 1998, the year of constitutionally mandated elections, and afterwards until the year 2010.

The formation in November 1995 of the Khmer Nation Party (KNP) by Rainsy, who renewed appeals for peace, social justice and the protection of national land and forests, was highly significant, most of all for challenging the organizational viability of Rainsy's former party. In rapid succession a planned FUNCINPEC party congress was postponed until March 1996, Prince Norodom Sirivudh, the party's General Secretary and a personal friend of Rainsy's, was arrested for allegedly expressing a wish to assassinate Hun Sen, and in December 1995, following international and domestic protests over political abuse of the legal system, another intervention from Sihanouk secured Sirivudh's release from prison and exile to France. The violent turn of events clearly alarmed the general public.

The arrest of Sirivudh, organized by Hun Sen, which ultimately deprived FUNCINPEC of its leading organizational personality at the same moment that it faced major defections to the KNP, disrupted the CPP-FUNCINPEC alliance, decisively, if not permanently. However, although the Second Prime Minister appeared to emerge from these events as accountable to no-one, his dominance and the leading role of the CPP did not remain unchallenged. In January 1996 Hun Sen insisted on the reintroduction of 7 January as a public holiday in commemoration of the Vietnamese 'liberation' of 1979. For supporters of the former non-communist resistance of 1979–91, which included FUNCINPEC, this holiday was an affront, representing a denial of Khmer rights to dignity, independence and autonomy, even though the regime installed by the Vietnamese in Phnom-Penh on 7 January 1979 replaced that of Pol Pot. Ranariddh retaliated in January 1996 by denouncing Vietnamese encroachments on Cambodian border territory as a 'full invasion'. The CPP-controlled judiciary proceeded in February with the trial *in absentia* of Sirivudh who was found guilty of criminal conspiracy and of possession of unlicensed firearms and sentenced to 10 years' imprisonment. Recriminations were openly aired in March when Ranariddh accused the CPP of reneging on power-sharing agreements at district (*srok*) level. He also threatened to force early elections by leaving the ruling coalition if the CPP failed to hand over promised positions, which amounted to at least one-half of the headships and one-half of the first deputy headships. Hun Sen demanded a public apology from Ranariddh and in June 1996 instructed CPP provincial governors to ignore normal protocols and not to facilitate visits of the First Prime Minister to their provinces.

The dispute between the two Prime Ministers was communicated through the ranks of their parties, paralysing public administration, obstructing decisions relating to foreign investment and making it impossible to set an agenda for meetings of the National Assembly. Political and ideological tensions were exacerbated by an economic downturn, and especially by the suspension by the IMF of aid to the budget, the devaluation of the national currency in dollar exchanges and labour unrest (see Economy). Being heavily dependent upon informally secured revenues, the two leaders agreed upon a division of spoils in Pailin in anticipation of a government victory in an offensive against the PDK base there. The offensive failed, the morale of poorly paid government soldiers being sapped by the absence of unity and purpose in Phnom-Penh. Military reverses, together with the stalemate over the sharing out of district headships, heightened fears within FUNCINPEC about its prospects for success in both the approaching *khum* (sub-district or commune) headship elections and the legislative elections, the latter scheduled by the Constitution to be held no later than November 1998.

International consultants recommended that both elections be held concurrently in 1998 and that a National Election Commission to include NGOs be established. Confident of their administrative control at the basic level, CPP spokesmen were steadily seeking to limit international expectations of involvement in the elections, beyond that of supplying funding, technical assistance and a modest number of observers. CPP officials and local CPP-controlled security forces also forced the closure of many provincial party offices opened by the KNP in the second half of 1996, and refused KNP requests for permission to establish a radio station. Police harassment, and the assassination of several party officials signalled a refusal to allow opposition parties or leaders to challenge the existing political configuration and balance of forces. Sam Rainsy, with tacit support from FUNCINPEC, emphasized the need for the widest possible international involvement in the forthcoming elections. In June Hun Sen protested his support for political pluralism and the formation of new parties, while denying that the CPP had any aspirations to integrate all parties into one and thereby restore the one-party state of the 1980s. From mid-1996 it was the official policy of the CPP to co-operate with other parties, including FUNCINPEC, on a 'no power-sharing' basis. While conflict between the CPP and FUNCINPEC increased, and the repression of the KNP continued, the CPP lent support to small or newly formed parties and also encouraged defections from the KNP and FUNCINPEC.

In the wake of military set-backs in 1995 and the substantial losses suffered as a result of defections and self-demobilizations in 1995–96, the PDK leadership was shaken by the near-loss of its economic capital at Pailin in April–May 1996. Deprived of Chinese military assistance in 1991, the Khmers Rouges had financed their armed struggle by selling logging and gem concessions to entrepreneurs in neighbouring Thailand and by purchasing weapons and ammunition in private markets. Inadequate or poor agricultural land in zones under the movement's control pushed many communities in the interior to compensate for revenue shortfalls by resorting to banditry, extortion and theft. The appropriation of goods and wealth and the coercive treatment of civilians undermined the historically good social relations between the PDK/NADK and the peasantry. War-weariness was compounded by Phnom-Penh's adoption of the law proscribing the movement in 1994; by January 1995 more than 7,000 fighters had taken advantage of an offer of amnesty made by the RGC. The PDK formed a Provisional Government of National Union and National Salvation of Cambodia (PGNUNSC) in July 1994 and, in early 1995, launched an assault on villages in the north-west, leaving more than 40,000 civilians temporarily displaced. Evidence from defectors and captured archives, however, revealed schisms within the movement arising from policy disputes focusing on various issues, including the Paris peace process in 1991–92, the movement's decision not to participate in the UNTAC election process, its desire to resume armed struggle for the purpose of restoring Democratic Kampuchea, and its decision to promote family production, reliance on free markets and regional autonomy in economic life. Appeals broadcast to the Government to engage in political talks received no public acknowledgement, but negotiators from FUNCINPEC, led by royalist Gen. Nhek Bun Chhay and assisted by Thai authorities, are known to have initiated secret contacts with several DK commanders based near the border with Thailand by no later than mid-1996.

Independent of the FUNCINPEC initiative, policy disputes within the PDK led younger military leaders in the movement's commercial regions of Pailin and Phnom Malai into open confrontation with senior civilian leaders in Anlong Veng. In early August 1996 the Pol Pot-controlled, clandestine radio denounced several field commanders and Ieng Sary, the former DK Minister of Foreign Affairs, as 'traitors' and ordered their immediate arrest. Rejecting the charges, Commanders Y Chhien at Pailin and Sok Pheap at Phnom Malai revealed that they had been unwilling to carry out instructions to recollectivize the economy, starting with the confiscations of means of transport. Once effectively expelled from the movement, the dissident Khmers Rouges indicated their willingness to recognize the authority of the Royal Government and their respect for the Constitution, but made clear their refusal either to surrender or to defect to Phnom-Penh. The Democratic National Union Movement (DNUM), founded by Ieng Sary, was quickly established as a vehicle for negotiating a union with the Government while resisting integration by either side and carefully asserting the political and territorial autonomy of the breakaway region. Subsequently, the DNUM and generals from FUNCINPEC and the CPP competed for brokering opportunities and political influence. Together, they ultimately garnered support from 11 other DK divisions and fronts during late 1996. At the joint request of the two Prime Ministers, a royal amnesty was granted to Ieng Sary for the death sentence given *in absentia* by a PRK tribunal in 1979 and also for criminal penalties arising from the 1994 law that outlawed the DK group. Breakaway troops associated with the DNUM were formally inducted into the command structure of the RCAF in November, although most refused reassignment. In official appointments and commissions announced in January 1997, Y Chhien was appointed Governor of Pailin. Control of the lucrative gem and logging activities, the principal source of income for the DK movement after 1991, was retained by Y Chhien. Although the CPP initially welcomed the dissolution of the DK movement, and acquired the political loyalty of some breakaway DK military commanders, the rekindling of resistance era comradeship among many dissident Khmers Rouges and pro-BLDP and FUNCINPEC military leaders, together with military confrontations between pro-FUNCINPEC and pro-CPP forces in Battambang, unleashed suspicions that FUNCINPEC was aiming for a new political alliance and was even planning to seize control of the provinces of Battambang, Fanteay Meanchey and Siem Reap by military force.

The competition for forces, land rights, and positions quickly renewed power struggles between the two Prime Ministers and their parties, and also fuelled constitutional tensions dividing Hun Sen from the King, whose desire to pardon Chakkrapong, Sirivudh and other civil criminals was rebuffed. The fatal shooting of Hun Sen's brother-in-law in November 1996 resulted in the imprisonment of the security chief of the KNP on seemingly manufactured evidence. In a further repressive move, FUNCINPEC leaders and the KNP President, Sam Rainsy, were accused of personally collaborating with DK criminal elements by a group of self-confessed, defecting Khmer Rouge spies presented to the press for this purpose by Hun Sen. Stopping short of full repudiation of the coalition, senior CPP officials announced that the governing alliance with FUNCINPEC existed in theory only, and asserted that their party was in full control and would win most or all of the approaching 1,453 *khum* headship elections. In an attempt further to marginalize their royalist allies and opponents, many of whom, like Ranariddh and Sam Rainsy, held dual French and Cambodian nationality, the quinquennial congress of the CPP proposed to require candidates for all public offices in Cambodia, including *khum* headships, to hold Cambodian nationality only. FUNCINPEC officials responded by accusing the CPP of attempting to arrange a coup. FUNCINPEC also criticized the predominantly CPP-controlled media and the Ministry of Information for giving greater broadcast coverage to Hun Sen than to Prince Ranariddh. Royalist officials began overtly to supply military protection and political assistance to the KNP at the opening of its party offices in Battambang, and to seek negotiations with the last of the insurgent, Pol Pot-led PDK forces in Anlong Veng.

Alongside the KNP, a new electoral National United Front (NUF) was established in February 1997, to which the BLDP-Son Sann faction and the small Khmer Neutral Party quickly rallied. This revitalization of the historic nationalist front, which had propelled the royalists to power in the 1993 elections, coincided with the publication of an interview with King Sihanouk, in which he revealed his unhappiness with the way in which the governing parties had restored some respectability to the Khmers Rouges, his concerns about the country's future in view of the suspension of IMF assistance, and about deforestation. He also suggested that he might abdicate the throne, as he had done in 1955. Clearly alarmed by the prospect of the King usurping CPP state power, Hun Sen announced that he would cancel local and national elections if Sihanouk should abdicate. He added that if the King did not refrain from interfering in politics, he would seek to amend the Constitution to prohibit all members of the Royal family from participating in politics, thereby ensuring the neutrality of the constitutional monarchy. Prince Ranariddh, in response, stressed that the Constitution allowed no-one to cancel elections, reserving to the National Assembly alone the right to postpone or prolong electoral mandates by a two-thirds majority; he also mildly rebuked his father for the role he had already played in 1993 in conceiving and forging the FUNCINPEC-CPP coalition. The King, though silenced, had successfully exposed the gradual realignment of the royalist movement as well as the authoritarian orientations of the Second Prime Minister. The FUNCINPEC-CPP talks of March 1997 produced little reconciliation and resulted in no renewal of their alliance. In March a grenade attack on a peaceful demonstration outside the National Assembly in Phnom-Penh left 19 dead. The rally was led by Sam Rainsy, the leader of the KNP, and the attack was believed to have been an attempt to assassinate him.

The decline in public order in the second quarter of 1997 was rapid and seemingly irreversible, despite attempts made by a bipartisan FUNCINPEC-CPP Commission for Abnormal Conflict Resolution to uphold the neutrality of national policing and of the army. As the CPP began in earnest to form a new ruling alliance along Malaysian-style lines, it secured support from Ieng Muli of the BLDP, the Democrat Party (In Tam), the Free Development Republican Party (Ted Ngoy), the Khmer Citizens' Party (Nguon Soeur), and the LDP (Chhim Om Yon), and abandoned its demand for electoral candidates to be Cambodian nationals. Despite attempts to negotiate with FUNCINPEC over dates for the forthcoming elections, no agreement was reached. Discussion of the draft election law was disrupted when officials from the Ministry of Interior clashed over the proposed arrest for marijuana smuggling of Mong Rethy, managing director of the rubber-processing and timber firm, Rethy Mecco Company, and senior adviser to the Second Prime Minister in charge of his private 'Hun Sen School' building programme (which had an estimated budget of US $45m.). Ranariddh openly accused Hun Sen of accepting drugs-related money for his lavish personal development projects, while Hun Sen warned against the arrest of Rethy. Hun Sen also lent support to a rebellion against Ranariddh's leadership of the FUNCINPEC party promoted by eight FUNCINPEC members of the National Assembly, thus beginning the process of the accumulation of the necessary parliamentary votes for the deposition of the First Prime Minister on a constitutional basis. A party congress organized by the rebels in June resulted in the formation of FUNCINPEC II and the election of Toan Chhay, a former resistance commander and the FUNCINPEC Governor of Siem Reap, as Chairman. At the same time, the attempt by the exiled Prince Sirivudh (still a seated FUNCINPEC legislator) to return to Phnom-Penh was blocked in Hong Kong, where he was prevented from boarding flights to Cambodia. Equally concerned about political realignments and the possible disintegration of FUNCINPEC, PDK-Anlong Veng radio broadcasts urged public support for the Ranariddh-led NUF, even though the movement continued to detain 15 FUNCINPEC party negotiators who had been taken hostage in mid-February. DNUM leaders expressed fears that inter-party disputes were undermining aspirations for national reconciliation and peace: their former leader, Pol

Pot, was held responsible. While indicating sympathy towards the NUF, however, DNUM leaders declined to join, reiterating their intentions to remain neutral (and autonomous). Ieng Sary nevertheless promised that his party would respect the outcome of future elections, saying that he would employ his forces to make peace if, as in 1993, violence should follow.

The Removal of Prince Ranariddh

One final attempt at reconciling the personal and political disputes dividing the two Prime Ministers occurred in May 1997; within 24 hours, however, Prince Ranariddh had accused Hun Sen of planning to restore a communist dictatorship if the CPP won the elections. The Prince urged the dissolution of the Assembly and the holding of early elections but, as a means of delaying a confrontation in the Assembly, the FUNCINPEC party General Secretary and Acting Chairman of the National Assembly, Loy Simchheang, postponed conflict on the issue of the FUNCINPEC-Ranariddh proposal to expel renegade FUNCINPEC deputies from the Assembly via the procedural device of suspending steering committee meetings. Polarization of party politics was further accentuated at the end of May, when containers of weapons, destined for the First Prime Minister's 1,500-strong bodyguard unit, were seized by CPP officials, and when Ranariddh revealed that Khieu Samphan, the nominal leader of the PDK, had communicated to him a desire to return to mainstream Cambodian politics. Hun Sen sternly warned the Prince against entering into any alliance that would allow the return of the genocidal regime. Controversy over the treatment to be accorded to Pol Pot and the last of his close associates accelerated in early June, when speculation that the FUNCINPEC Party was on the verge of reaching an agreement with Khieu Samphan intensified. FUNCINPEC's senior military adviser, Gen. Nhek Bun Chhay, announced on 2 June that Pol Pot, Ta Mok (Pol Pot's Chief of Staff) and Son Sen (the former DK Commander-in-Chief) would go into voluntary exile in exchange for immunity from prosecution; it was indicated by FUNCINPEC that the exile of these individuals would constitute acceptable grounds for the return to the mainstream political arena of Khieu Samphan, with reports suggesting that there were plans for him to form a new political alliance with FUNCINPEC and Sam Rainsy's KNP. Within days, however, the likelihood of any such arrangement being made disappeared: Pol Pot—who, according to reports, had initially supported the deal with FUNCINPEC—apparently vetoed the agreement at the last moment, and then reportedly ordered the assassination of Son Sen, his wife and nine relatives in retaliation for Son Sen's suspected secret dealings with Hun Sen and a CPP spy network. The news of Son Sen's death was later confirmed by Ranariddh. Pol Pot then reportedly fled in a 10-vehicle convoy, which included Khieu Samphan. The convoy, however, was intercepted by troops wanting to defect to the Government, led by Ta Mok. The surrounding of Pol Pot by mutinous NADK soldiers gave rise to international, and some national, appeals for him to be handed over to the Cambodian Government and brought to justice. These appeals were supported by the two Prime Ministers, but produced no lessening of strife between the two coalition parties. Ranariddh reaffirmed his willingness, in principle, to accept the defection of nearly all Anlong Veng guerrillas, barring only Pol Pot and Ta Mok, and to welcome Khieu Samphan and his National Solidarity Party into the NUF provided that he received the necessary royal amnesty. Hun Sen, however, disregarding his previous negotiations with Ieng Sary, began insisting, *inter alia*, that negotiations with the DK were illegal.

In mid-June 1997, after denouncing the fleeing Pol Pot for acts of treason in an extraordinary public criticism of the former leader, a radio broadcast made on Anlong Veng radio in Khieu Samphan's name pledged the loyalty of the latter's National Solidarity Party to the FUNCINPEC-led NUF and urged all national forces to unite in a struggle against Hun Sen, stigmatized as a 'lackey' of Viet Nam. Within hours, the military bodyguard units of the two Prime Ministers and other high officials clashed on the streets of Phnom-Penh. Characterizing a personal meeting between Ranariddh and Khieu Samphan as an intolerable betrayal, Hun Sen then issued an ultimatum to the Prince giving him a few days in which to decide whether he wished to work with the coalition Government or with Khieu Samphan. The US State Department released a statement at this point, warning that it would be gravely concerned if senior PDK leaders were to be awarded roles in national politics or allowed to retain effective control over any territorial domain, but diplomatically avoided reference to the situation in Pailin. On 20 June Anlong Veng radio announced triumphantly that Pol Pot had surrendered. As the Consultative Group on Cambodia (CGC) met in Paris on 1–2 July, Hun Nheng, the CPP Governor of Kampong Thom province and a brother of Hun Sen, forcibly disarmed 70 of Prince Ranariddh's security guards as the Prince completed a tour of the province. As the DK defector Keo Pong, allegedly acting upon orders from the Second Prime Minister, positioned his troops for an assault on Gen. Nhek Bun Chhay's garrison, the Prince boarded a flight to France.

The airport and large parts of Phnom-Penh were subsequently cordoned off and looted by marauding troops during 4–6 July 1997, and the FUNCINPEC and KNP party offices were ransacked. Hun Sen denied that he was staging a coup or aiming to govern on his own; he insisted, however, that the First Prime Minister had to be replaced. He blamed the outbreak of violence in the capital on a criminal conspiracy mounted by Ranariddh together with the outlawed Khmers Rouges and accused Ranariddh of having broken the law by negotiating with the DK, by unlawfully smuggling ex-DK troops into Phnom-Penh to strengthen his own forces and by secretly importing weapons to arm those forces. Denouncing Ranariddh's real and alleged actions as criminal and unacceptable, Hun Sen ordered the two factions in FUNCINPEC to replace the Prince, and thereby to restore stability to the ruling FUNCINPEC-CPP coalition, protecting the 1993 Constitution and laying the basis for democratic elections in May 1998. Furthermore, Hun Sen revealed that he had already asked both the Co-Defence Minister, Tie Chamrath, and the leader of FUNCINPEC II, Toan Chhay, if they would serve as First Prime Minister, but each had declined. Only three FUNCINPEC leaders—Nhek Bun Chhay, Chau Sambath and Serey Kosal—were unacceptable to Hun Sen. Troops loyal to the CPP and Keo Pong were ordered to locate and eliminate these three; other leading FUNCINPEC figures were also similarly named as targets, including Ho Sok, a FUNCINPEC Ministry of Interior official linked to failed attempts to press criminal charges against associates of the Second Prime Minister. In total, approximately 40 people, including Sambath and Sok, were murdered or assassinated during the week beginning 4 July; tens of thousands of civilians associated with the royalist, democratic or human-rights movements and parties fled into temporary hiding, and approximately one-half of the FUNCINPEC party members in the legislature fled overseas, fearing for their lives. Hun Sen pledged that all FUNCINPEC ministers, legislators and cabinet officials who agreed to withdraw their support from Ranariddh as party leader and Prime Minister would be allowed to retain their positions; he also promised to amend the Constitution to create more positions, allowing individuals belonging to parties not represented in the National Assembly to hold government portfolios.

From France, Prince Ranariddh announced his intention to resist his expulsion from the Government, vowing to employ military force if necessary. Although five FUNCINPEC generals had been killed, Gen. Nhek Bun Chhay and others escaped, and proceeded to establish resistance bases in the north-west. At the UN and in Washington, Ranariddh continued to be recognized as Prime Minister. The US Government expressed strong opposition to the use of force to change the results of the 1993 election and effectively to rupture the Paris accords of 1991. Sam Rainsy, leader of the KNP but acting on behalf of the NUF, issued an appeal to the international community to suspend economic assistance to Cambodia, excluding essential humanitarian aid; Germany and the USA obliged, while Australia suspended military assistance. Both Sam Rainsy and Prince Ranariddh rushed to the Thai-Cambodian border to make contact with the more than 20,000 people fleeing the country, many of whom were their supporters, and quickly agreed with more than 20 temporarily exiled BLDP and FUNCINPEC legislators to establish a Union of Cambodian Democrats (UCD) for the purpose of restoring the legitimate Royal Cambodian Government by peaceful means. ASEAN members agreed at a ministerial conference on 10 July to postpone indefinitely Cambodia's accession to the organization, originally scheduled for 24 July, and formally requested Cambodia to take steps to preserve until the forthcoming elections the power-sharing arrangement agreed following the elections of 1993. ASEAN also agreed to send mediators to Beijing, Bangkok and Phnom-Penh in an attempt to facilitate a peaceful solution to the governmental and political crisis, despite Hun Sen's initial rejection of previous offers of mediation. Hun Sen's decision in mid-July to ask the FUNCINPEC Minister of Foreign Affairs, Ung Huot, to serve concurrently as First Prime Minister provoked international criticism and was widely rejected. In the first DNUM comment on the events of 5–6 July, and as concern grew over the impact of sustained civil strife on the RCAF, Gen. Y Chhien of Pailin stated that his party opposed the ousting of Ranariddh and regarded the nomination of Ung Huot as inappropriate. He appealed for the return of the UN to Cambodia to ensure the restoration of peace and the holding of elections.

In August 1997 the National Assembly voted on the nomination of Ung Huot as First Prime Minister, replacing Prince Norodom Ranariddh: 86 members of the 120-seat National Assembly voted in favour of his appointment. Ung Huot was formally elected when acting Head of State Chea Sim signed a royal decree approving the appointment after King Norodom Sihanouk reportedly gave his authorization; Ung Huot and Hun Sen agreed that a legislative election would be held in May 1998 as planned, and that the winner of that election would become Cambodia's sole Prime Minister. Meanwhile, Hun Sen gave National Assembly members who had left the country three months in which to return before being replaced. Hun Sen insisted that, should Prince Norodom Ranariddh return, however, he would face trial for attempting to negotiate an alliance with remaining Khmer Rouge rebels.

A further significant development in Cambodia in July 1997, meanwhile, was the denunciation and trial of former Khmer Rouge leader, Pol Pot, by his own comrades: an announcement broadcast on the PDK radio station stated that Pol Pot had been sentenced to life imprisonment at the Anlong Veng guerrilla base in north-west Cambodia for 'betraying the Khmer Rouge movement'. It was thought unlikely, however, that Pol Pot would be handed over to the Cambodian Government or to the international authorities to be tried for genocide.

The events of 5–6 July 1997 resulted, in the first instance, in the removal of Prince Ranariddh as First Prime Minister. Yet, more fundamentally, it was an attempt by Hun Sen to re-establish CPP control of the State and to put an end to the parallel FUNCINPEC structure in the armed forces, police and bureaucracy which had been developed since 1993. The killing of several of Ranariddh's senior army and police commanders (a sixth general, Thach Kim Sang, was assassinated in March 1998) and the sentencing *in absentia* of two others (Nhek Bun Chhay and Serey Kosal) to long prison terms, severely weakened Ranariddh's capacity to mount a military challenge. In the immediate aftermath of the fighting, FUNCINPEC forces either agreed to be disarmed or retreated rapidly to their pre-1993 bases on the Thai border, from where they sought to link up with the remaining Khmer Rouge insurgents. Within a month, Nhek Bun Chhay's forces retained only one stronghold, the border village of O Smach in Oddor Meanchey province. Total military control of the country evaded Hun Sen, owing to the failure of repeated government offensives against O Smach and the persistence of FUNCINPEC and PDK activity in other remote areas of the north and west; an internationally sponsored cease-fire was implemented on 27 February 1998.

Achieving total control of the state apparatus proved less difficult. Ung Huot, Ranariddh's replacement as First Prime Minister, served Hun Sen's purposes faithfully: the principle of 'consensus' and equality between the two parties, on which the coalition Government had been founded, was retained in form but not in substance. Except for Ranariddh, Hun Sen left almost all FUNCINPEC appointees in place: his priority was to retain international legitimacy by preserving an unchanged façade of the Royal Government, and it proved as easy for the CPP to work around FUNCINPEC officials as to dismiss them. Hun Sen thus invited FUNCINPEC and BLDP ministers and members of the National Assembly to return from exile to their former positions, and even permitted a small UN team to monitor their safety. Hun Sen did attempt to reorganize the Cabinet in September 1997, with a view to rewarding Ieng Muli, Toan Chhay and others, but this initiative was unexpectedly obstructed by internal disagreements within the remnants of FUNCINPEC and by opposition from the Chea Sim faction of the CPP, whose suspicion of Hun Sen's intentions reached new heights in the period immediately following the events of 5–6 July.

Hun Sen did successfully exploit his newly obtained parliamentary majority to ensure that the CPP would control the preparations for the elections due in 1998 and would retain judicial, as well as bureaucratic and military power, during and after the polls. The National Election Committee, the Supreme Council of Magistracy and the Constitutional Council (the bodies mandated under the Constitution to organize elections, to appoint and supervise judges, and to monitor the constitutionality of laws and judge electoral disputes) were finally established with clear CPP majorities in each. The elections thus took place in a framework determined and managed by Hun Sen.

None the less, matters did not proceed completely as planned. The main obstacle Hun Sen faced was that of international opposition: in particular, ASEAN's refusal to admit Cambodia in July 1997 and the decision of a committee of the UN General Assembly in September to leave Cambodia's seat in the UN vacant until the elections. This latter decision was effectively taken by the USA, Hun Sen's principal critic, and Washington was also responsible for the IMF's decision to suspend aid. Cambodia, meanwhile, suffered from a collapse in investment following fighting in Phnom-Penh and the disastrous decline in the regional economy. Whilst Hun Sen consistently rejected offers from ASEAN, Thailand, the USA and King Sihanouk to mediate between him and Ranariddh, insisting that this was an internal criminal affair to be dealt with by Cambodia's Government and courts, Hun Sen's need for international recognition and aid ultimately proved too great. In February 1998 a 'four-pillar' peace plan, proposed by Japan and strongly supported by the 'Friends of Cambodia', was accepted by both sides. The 'four pillars' were: a cease-fire, to be followed by the reintegration of Ranariddh's forces into the RCAF; the end of ties between the Prince's forces and the PDK; a prompt trial and pardoning of Ranariddh; and his participation in the elections. A cease-fire was declared and was largely adhered to, but reintegration failed to take place and both sides continued to exchange accusations of links with the Khmers Rouges. Two 'show' trials were held (in March) at which Ranariddh was found guilty *in absentia* of smuggling weapons, causing instability, disobeying the orders of superiors and complicity with the Khmers Rouges. He was sentenced to a total of 35 years' imprisonment and ordered, together with his senior military commanders, to pay compensation of more than US $54m. to cover the damages caused in the fighting. After a tense battle of wills and faced with the real prospect of Japan, ASEAN and the EU withdrawing support for the elections, Hun Sen wrote to the King requesting a full pardon for Ranariddh.

The National Election of 1998

Ranariddh thus returned to Cambodia on 30 March 1998, the last of the opposition politicians to do so. None the less, the opposition's ability to compete in the elections (which had been delayed from 23 May to 26 July to allow sufficient time for the National Election Committee to carry out preparations) had been severely weakened. As well as losing equipment, money and their headquarters during the events of July 1997, the opposition had lost all access to the electronic media: the FUNCINPEC-aligned television and radio station and the radio station run by the BLDP had been taken over by the Government. Opposition and UN demands that past political violence be investigated and punished went unheeded. Both the KNP and the BLDP were forced to change their names (to the Sam Rainsy Party (SRP) and Son Sann Party, respectively) owing to ongoing court disputes. The uncertainty over Ranariddh's participation also exacerbated the split within FUNCINPEC: three breakaway parties with quite close ties with the CPP registered for the elections—they were led by Toan Chhay, Ung Huot and Loy Simchheang. Meanwhile, the opposition was adversely affected by internal tensions within the UCD (particularly between Ranariddh and Rainsy), which put an end to the possibility of contesting the election as a coalition. None the less, under strong international pressure and despite grave reservations about the entire electoral process, the opposition did compete.

The election proceeded unexpectedly smoothly. In spite of widespread low-level intimidation and an estimated 12 killings of their members, the FUNCINPEC Party and the SRP managed to attract significant crowds to their campaign rallies. Officially, 93.7% of the 5,395,024 registered went to vote on 26 July 1998, and on the next day the UN-co-ordinated Joint International Observation Group expressed its confidence that the elections had been 'free and fair'. Unsurprisingly, however, the situation soon deteriorated. Official preliminary results awarded the CPP 64 seats, the FUNCINPEC Party 43 and the SRP 15, under a complicated system of proportional representation, although combined support for the FUNCINPEC Party and the SRP, which had gained 31.7% and 14.3% of the vote, respectively, represented a majority of the popular vote; the CPP secured 41.4% of the vote. The 36 other parties failed to obtain a single seat. The results gave the CPP a parliamentary majority but not the two-thirds majority needed to form a government; Hun Sen thus offered to form a 60:40 coalition government with FUNCINPEC, with the provision that he be premier and that the CPP retain all the key ministries. He also suggested the formation of a tripartite coalition, with the SRP being given 10% of ministerial positions and the FUNCINPEC Party 30%. These offers were rejected as premature by FUNCINPEC and the SRP, which alleged massive election irregularities (in the voting, counting and seat allocation process). Both parties' leaders refused to recognize the election results until their complaints were investigated by the National Election Committee. They also announced their intention to boycott the new National Assembly, which was scheduled to convene in September. FUNCINPEC and the SRP lodged nearly 900 complaints of election irregularities. In mid-August the Constitutional Council rejected all but one of the complaints lodged by the SRP and this concerned a vote recount. In October the National Election Committee issued a report, which concluded that there were no discrepancies in the vote count and that the results would stand.

Coalition Government and Democratic Stagnation

In August 1998 King Norodom Sihanouk urged the convening of an informal meeting in Siem Reap of all parties concerned to end the political impasse. His call came amidst steadily rising politically motivated violence. Following another assassination attempt, Rainsy encouraged opposition supporters to occupy an area near the National Assembly, which soon became known as 'Democracy Square'. After a series of speeches containing anti-Vietnamese rhetoric, some of the demonstrators vandalized the Cambodian-Viet Nam Friendship Monument. On the same day the Constitutional Council summarily rejected all opposition complaints.

King Sihanouk convened unsuccessful talks in Siem Reap, involving representatives from the CPP, FUNCINPEC, the SRP and the Constitutional Council in September 1998. While these discussions were in progress two grenades were thrown into the residence of Hun Sen. Hun Sen promptly returned to Phnom-Penh and ordered that Democracy Square be cleared and that the leaders of the demonstrators be arrested. Sam Rainsy, whom Hun Sen accused of responsibility for the grenade attack, immediately sought refuge in a nearby UN office. The police subsequently cleared Democracy Square, precipitating street violence in the capital as groups loyal to Sam Rainsy clashed with supporters of the CPP. Two monks were shot dead, and the Hun Sen Government banned members of the National Assembly from leaving the country. In mid-September Thomas Hammarberg, the UN Secretary-General's Special Representative for Human Rights in Cambodia, announced that, since the police action, 16 bodies (including those of the two monks) had been found. This figure was later revised to 26.

It was in this context that external diplomatic pressures resulted in the resumption of political talks. Ranariddh announced that he was calling off street demonstrations and would meet with the King. He also stated that FUNCINPEC would attend the first session of the National Assembly on 24 September 1998. Sam Rainsy made a similar public announcement. The King convened a summit in Siem Reap involving Chea Sim, Hun Sen, Ranariddh, and Sam Rainsy. An unknown attacker fired two rockets at a convoy of cars carrying members of the legislature and senior officials to the inaugural ceremony of the National Assembly at Angkor Wat. Hun Sen claimed that he was the intended victim of the attack. The ban on foreign travel was lifted. None the less, the tripartite talks broke down in late September, and Ranariddh and Rainsy fled abroad in October.

In early October 1998 the King travelled to Phnom-Penh to renew his efforts to break the political impasse. In November the King hosted discussions involving Hun Sen, Chea Sim and Ranariddh, which resulted in a protocol on power-sharing. Under the terms of this agreement, Hun Sen would remain in office as Prime Minister, while Ranariddh would become the President of the National Assembly, replacing Chea Sim. A full amnesty was granted to Princes Norodom Sirivuth and Norodom Chakrapong and Generals Nhek Bun Chhay, Serey Kosal and Sin Song. A second parliamentary chamber, a senate, was to be created under the chairmanship of Chea Sim, who would also serve as acting Head of State when the King was out of the country. Sam Rainsy, who had not been present at these discussions, was highly critical of them. He nevertheless returned to Cambodia from Paris; Prince Sirivuth also returned to Cambodia in early 1999.

On 4 March 1999 the National Assembly finally voted by 106 to five to amend the Constitution and create a Senate with the power to scrutinize and amend bills before sending them back to the National Assembly for affirmation and final royal assent. Chea Sim was duly elected Chairman of the Senate. Prince Sisowat, Chivoun Monirak and Nhek Bun Chhay were chosen as Deputy Chairmen. Representation in the 61-member Senate was proportional to party strength in the lower house: 31 seats were allocated to the CPP; 21 seats to FUNCINPEC; seven seats to the SRP; and two members were nominated by the King. The inaugural session of the Senate was held on 25 March.

On 30 November 1998 Hun Sen was approved as Prime Minister by a vote of 99 to 13 in the National Assembly. Of the 29 cabinet posts, 15 were accorded to the CPP and the remainder to FUNCINPEC. Both parties shared control of the Ministry of Interior and the Ministry of Defence. The new Government began drafting legislation for the conduct of 'free and fair' elections in Cambodia's *khum*, which were not held until February 2002.

As a result of the November protocol on power-sharing, Hun Sen and Ranariddh agreed to rationalize and reform the RCAF. Cambodia's military was widely viewed as overstaffed, underpaid, unruly and heavily engaged in illegal logging. The exact size of the armed forces was unknown, owing to the large numbers of 'ghost soldiers' on the payroll (soldiers who had either been killed or had returned to their villages but whose pay continued to be collected by senior officers). In late 1999 it was estimated that these soldiers constituted at least one-third of the military's approximately 155,000 personnel. The military was regularly implicated in armed robberies, kidnapping for ransom and drugs-trafficking. In late January 1999, as agreed, Hun Sen resigned as Commander-in-Chief of the RCAF; Gen. Ke Kimyan, the former Chief of the General Staff, was elevated to this position. Of 26 senior positions within the armed forces, FUNCINPEC representatives were given only three posts, including one (of four) deputy commander positions. At the change of command ceremony Hun Sen urged that the armed forces be reduced by 55,000 (from an estimated 148,000) and the police by 24,000 over the next few years. Germany and the Asian Development Bank (ADB) pledged financial assistance for this programme.

By 2000 there were signs that Cambodia was progressing towards the development of a more mature political situation and was beginning to experience greater stability. Within the CPP, Hun Sen's power base appeared to have been consolidated, despite rumours of intra-party struggles. Hun Sen, however, remained guarded against any potential political challengers. Deputy Prime Mininster and Co-Minister of the Interior, Sar Kheng, was perceived by observers to represent the greatest threat to Hun Sen's leadership; it was also alleged that a rift existed between Sar Kheng and Hun Sen's closest ally, Sok An, Minister in charge of the Council of Ministers and perceived by many as the CPP's alternative potential successor to Hun Sen. FUNCINPEC, meanwhile, remained under the leadership of

Ranariddh. At the Party Congress held in March 2000 it was acknowledged that the Party would need to regroup if it were to become an effective political force at the forthcoming *khum* headship elections and beyond. Ranariddh was subject to criticism for his ambivalence regarding the return to FUNCINPEC of former party members who were alleged to have abandoned the Party after the unrest of July 1997. Hun Sen, while retaining FUNCINPEC as his coalition partner in the Government, sought to improve domestic security by adopting severe measures to control weapons and by seeking to reform the armed forces. By late 1999 the Government had reportedly destroyed some 60,000 illegal weapons; however, an estimated 450,000 guns remained in the country, many in the hands of the police and military, some members of which, it was alleged, were heavily implicated in armed robberies and kidnappings.

In 1999/2000 opposition parties received better treatment from the Government. Repressive violence against members of the SRP by elements allied with the Government appeared to have declined in comparison with 1997 and 1998. Rainsy continued to challenge the Government, however, voicing the concerns of groups such as protesting garment workers and the landless. In October 1999 a member of the legislature belonging to the SRP was abducted. Rainsy himself considered this incident to have been politically motivated and asserted that Cambodia continued to be ruled by dictatorial leaders, whom he described as 'crooks, criminals and clowns'. His comments resulted in the issue of a series of threats (apparently from the CPP) against Rainsy and members of his party.

Relations between the two coalition partners in the incumbent Government in 2000–02 remained officially cordial. Ranariddh, as leader of FUNCINPEC and Chairman of the National Assembly, did not want his ministers and members of the legislature to be in conflict with the Hun Sen-dominated CPP; he thus assumed a secondary role in the Government. During its annual congress in March 2001, which marked the party's 20th anniversary, FUNCINPEC reaffirmed its commitment to working closely with the CPP in the interests of peace and reconciliation. After he had taken up the position as FUNCINPEC Secretary-General in July, Prince Norodom Sirivudh also advocated the politics of non-confrontation. This accommodating tone was motivated more by practical considerations than by goodwill: the royalists could no longer afford to risk another violent confrontation with Hun Sen, who had exiled Sirivudh after the latter had been accused of plotting a coup against him and who had also ousted Ranariddh in 1997. Positive relations between the two leaders were based on a mutual understanding that each required the presence of the other for their own political interests. However, preparations for *khum* headship elections, scheduled to take place in February 2002, appeared to prompt the royalists to think strategically about competing with the CPP.

Although the *khum* headship elections that took place on 3 February 2002 appeared to advance the democratization process, it was uncertain whether they brought the country closer to the attainment of what some people referred to as 'grassroots' democracy. While the opposition political parties did participate, they failed to make serious inroads into gaining control of the 1,621 *khum*. The CPP retained approximately 98% of *khum* seats, leaving only 11 for the SRP and 10 for FUNCINPEC. Although the monopoly of power exercised by the CPP over the *khum* was broken, the participation of the SRP and FUNCINPEC appeared to contribute to the legitimacy of elections that were regarded by many as being far from 'free and fair', contrary to the testimony of the EU Election Observation Mission. Moreover, about 1.75m. of the 6.2m. eligible voters did not turn out to vote. Although the cause of the lower than expected turn-out was unclear, the campaign period had been characterized by political intimidation and violence directed at members of the opposition parties. At least 22 *khum* candidates and political activists belonging to FUNCINPEC and the SRP were reported to have been murdered. The Election Monitoring Organizations—comprised of non-governmental groups—issued a joint statement on 12 February rejecting claims that the elections had been 'free and fair'. Their findings included: 128 cases of illegal activities; 105 incidences of intimidation and threats towards voters; 560 occurrences of technical irregularities; 320 cases of obstructions of voters' rights; 20 incidences of explosives and guns being taken into ballot-counting stations; and 57 cases of fraud and biased vote-counting. Overall, the elections allowed the two major opposition parties to claim some victory without weakening the CPP, which had now become more dominant than ever.

Before and after the *khum* elections took place, relations between the CPP and FUNCINPEC remained stable, as the CPP continued to consolidate its control over the country. Political stability was promoted both by FUNCINPEC's new commitment to a non-confrontational style of politics and the weakened ability of the royalists to challenge the CPP. Their party was beleaguered by rifts and new internal frictions. Internal conflicts intensified when the royalists were forced to take sides between those who supported the Deputy Commander-in-Chief of the RCAF, Khan Savoeun (a FUNCINPEC member), and supporters of the Co-Minister of the Interior, You Hockry (another FUNCINPEC member), who was accused of nepotism and corruption. Under growing pressure from the party to resign from his cabinet post, You Hockry finally announced on 23 May 2002 that he would accept the party's decision. At the same time Hang Dara, a senior member of FUNCINPEC, announced that he intended to create a new party. On 27 May he registered the Hang Dara Movement Democratic Party with the Ministry of the Interior, citing his dissatisfaction with FUNCINPEC's performance as his motivation. Another set-back to FUNCINPEC came when Prince Chakrapong (the half-brother of Prince Ranariddh) chose to create a new royalist party, the Prince Norodom Chakrapong Khmer Soul Party, which he registered on 17 May 2002. Its members included Toan Chhay. Chakrapong sought permission to contest the next general election, scheduled for 2003, and offered to form a political alliance with the SRP. With the royalist camp fragmenting, the CPP gained strength. Prince Ranariddh seemed disheartened by these developments; he warned that political divisions within FUNCINPEC would only work to Hun Sen's advantage.

In recent years the overall security environment has improved significantly. In July 2001 Cambodia destroyed more than 6,500 small arms, as part of a world-wide campaign to eliminate illicit light weapons. Between 1999 and 2001 Cambodia destroyed approximately 50,604 weapons. On 24 November 2000, however, a group of Cambodian Freedom Fighters (CFF) staged an unsuccessful coup attempt with an armed attack on government buildings in Phnom-Penh, leaving eight people dead. In total, 47 people, including three US citizens, were charged in connection with the coup attempt. Also in July, two bombs exploded in separate hotels in Phnom-Penh, leaving three people dead. A Cambodian man later admitted to the bombings, claiming that he had acted to extort money. In August two explosions in the main offices of FUNCINPEC in Phnom-Penh injured three people. By mid-2002 the security situation had become somewhat precarious, as politically motivated violence against members of the opposition parties increased and an average of two 'mob' killings a month were reported. Hun Sen also closed down nightclubs in an attempt to prevent the rise of nocturnal crime.

Increasing political stability in Cambodia, however, was still being gained at the expense of genuine democracy. Hun Sen acted as a temporary stabilizing force within the Government, although the death of the Minister of Agriculture, Forestry, Hunting and Fisheries, Chhea Song, in April 2001 precipitated the need for a cabinet reshuffle. Hun Sen continued to describe the inspiration he received from two anti-democratic leaders: the late Prime Minister of Laos, Kaysone Phomvihane, and the anti-Western Prime Minister of Malaysia, Mahathir Mohamad. Although Hun Sen referred to South Korea's President Kim Dae-Jung as a third role model for his treatment of domestic enemies, he did little to accelerate democratic reform at his party's expense.

Major symptoms of the democratic stagnation included the Government's willingness to suppress and pre-empt domestic challenges to its political authority. The New York-based organization, Human Rights Watch, reported that during 2000 the most serious incidents of violence since 1997 had occurred in Phnom-Penh, including numerous attacks against *khum* leaders, mostly directed at members of the SRP. In June 2001 a Cambodian court tried 32 coup plotters arrested after the failed coup attempt in November 2000. Twelve of the 15 defence lawyers walked out of the courtroom after the start of the trial because the court was perceived to be subject to government pressure. Hundreds of armed soldiers and police officers with dogs surrounded the court building. In March 2002 a further 18 men were sentenced to prison terms of between seven and 18 years. Amongst those convicted were members of FUNCINPEC. The judiciary remained subject to criticism.

Cambodia's record on human rights remained questionable. In June 1998 Cambodia established a Human Rights Committee to respond to concerns expressed by the Office of the UN High Commissioner for Human Rights regarding 80 unresolved deaths following the events of July 1997. More than one year after its formation the committee had yet to acknowledge that any politically motivated killings had taken place. There had been no arrests or prosecutions in connection with these murders. Allegations of human rights violations continued. In early 2002 Human Rights Watch issued a review of developments in Cambodia. The report criticized the rise of political violence prior to the *khum* elections, the lack of improvement in prison conditions and the continuation of torture by police and prison officials, who continued to act with impunity. Human Rights Watch also accused the Government of violating the fundamental principle of Non-Refoulment (under which refugees are protected from returning to any country where they might be subjected to inhumane treatment) when deporting more than 100 asylum-seekers (who complained of persecution and repression by Hanoi) back to Viet Nam. In March a senior UN official stated that Cambodia had violated international law by deporting 63 Vietnamese refugees against their will. In June 2002 a UN human rights agency claimed that Cambodians had lost faith in the judiciary, citing 'mob' killings and the failure of the police to intervene, as well as their role in instigating the attacks.

Meanwhile, the CPP seemed confident and even more willing to silence any members who did not adhere to the party line. In December 2001 it tightened its control over its members when it decided to expel three of its senators from the party—two Cambodian-Americans (Chhang Song and Siphan Phay) and one Cambodian-Australian (Savath Pou)—and, shortly afterwards, to expel them from the Senate. The senators claimed to have spoken out on human rights issues and expressed their concerns about corruption amongst government officials.

Despite the holding of elections, socio-economic conditions continued to obstruct the process of democratic consolidation. Cambodia remained one of the poorest countries in the world. Corruption continued to be a serious issue, further weakening the Government's political legitimacy; even Hun Sen admitted the seriousness of corruption within the military and security apparatus. In recent years the economy performed better than in the immediate post-coup period, but the gap between rich and poor continued to widen. Ordinary people still suffered from a lack of health care and could not afford to live comfortably in Phnom-Penh, where the average monthly cost of living was about US $250. The problem of landlessness remained largely unresolved, and was so serious an issue that the UN Secretary-General's Special Representative for Human Rights in Cambodia, Peter Leuprecht (who replaced Thomas Hammarberg in 2000), declared it to be a threat to social stability.

The Demise of the Khmers Rouges and the Issue of Their Trial

The dissolution of the Khmers Rouges entered its final stage in late March 1998, when five divisions rebelled against the leadership of Ta Mok and defected to Hun Sen. Within weeks Anlong Veng was in government possession, and the ever-dwindling Khmer Rouge forces had been almost entirely forced into Thailand. Although Hun Sen embraced Keo Pok (a 68-year-old former DK zonal secretary during the Pol Pot period) as the leader of the rebels, in fact some were Pol Pot and Son Sen loyalists, others were resentful that Ta Mok had reneged on his promises of liberalization, while almost all were weary of the war and realized that defeat was inevitable. Pol Pot himself died on 14 April, only a day after a desperate Ta Mok had offered to hand Pol Pot over to the international community. Pol Pot's death (which was later reliably reported to have been suicide, following a radio broadcast describing Ta Mok's plans) deprived the PDK of its last opportunity to negotiate.

Throughout the last quarter of 1998 the remaining Khmer Rouge leaders negotiated an end to their armed resistance and their re-entry into Cambodian society. A ceremony was held in February 1999, at which time more than 1,500 troops were reintegrated into the ranks of the RCAF. The Khmer Rouge officials, Nuon Chea (the former Chairman of the National Assembly and the second most senior member of the PDK) and Khieu Samphan, left the jungle in December 1998 under an agreement with the Government. They were received warmly by Hun Sen in Phnom-Penh. In March 1999 Ta Mok was captured along the Thai border and placed in detention. In the following month Duch (Kang Khek Ieu), the former director of Tuol Sleng prison (where at least 17,000 prisoners were tortured and executed), was discovered working in Battambang province; he was arrested in May and charged with violating a 1994 law outlawing the Khmers Rouges. The presence of senior Khmer Rouge leaders in Cambodian society prompted calls from within Cambodia, and especially from the international community, for their trial and punishment for crimes committed under the PDK regime. Pressure from Australia and the United Kingdom resulted in the arrest of Gen. Nuon Paet in August 1998. Paet was implicated in the abduction and murder of three tourists in July 1994. In June 1999 he was convicted and sentenced to life imprisonment. Ten other Khmer Rouge leaders, including two former commanders and eight subordinates, were charged and in mid-1999 were awaiting trial. In July 2000 Col Chhouk Rin, one of the former commanders charged with the abduction and murder of the three tourists, was freed after it was decreed that he was covered by the amnesty granted to Khmer Rouge cadres who surrendered to the Cambodian Government. (Chhouk Rin had been appointed a colonel in the Cambodian army after his surrender; however, following strong formal protests at the acquittal from the British, French and Australian Governments, the Cambodian Government subsequently announced that it was to appeal against the court's decision, and in September 2002 Chhouk Rin received a sentence of life imprisonment.) Hun Sen resisted external pressures to try high-level Khmer Rouge leaders, arguing that such action would undermine his attempts to reach national reconciliation with the Khmer Rouge rank and file and prompt a renewal of insurgency. Khmer Rouge leaders, who had been granted a degree of autonomy in their strongholds at Pailin-Phnom Malai, might revert to armed resistance. In January the DNUM, headed by Ieng Sary, held its second national congress and passed a resolution rejecting the prosecution of Khmer Rouge leaders.

None the less, momentum continued towards some sort of international accounting. A US-drafted UN Security Council resolution to extend the mandate of the Hague tribunal on Yugoslavia and Rwanda to cover 'senior Khmer Rouge leaders' made little progress, but a Commission of Experts, appointed by the UN Secretary-General, was established in August 1998 to examine the issue. This team visited Cambodia in November to determine the feasibility of bringing Khmer Rouge leaders to justice. In March 1999 a team of three legal experts commissioned by the UN recommended that 20–30 Khmer Rouge leaders be brought to trial and reparations be made to their victims. The international community and international observers remained consistently sceptical of Cambodia's ability to establish an independent tribunal.

Hun Sen was reported to have considered the idea of a 'truth and reconciliation commission' modelled on that of South Africa. The UN Secretary-General, Kofi Annan, however, argued in a letter to Hun Sen in March 1999 that a tribunal for the Khmers Rouges should be international in character. After several leaders were captured, Hun Sen announced they would be tried under the jurisdiction of the Kingdom of Cambodia. Hun Sen strenuously argued that Cambodian sovereignty should be respected. Both the People's Republic of China and Thailand endorsed his stance. In May, however, when Hun Sen met Thomas Hammarberg he accepted the UN envoy's offer of assistance in refining draft legislation to create a domestic tribunal using international norms and standards, prior to its submission to the National Assembly. This tribunal would include both Cambodian and foreign judges and prosecutors. However, in August, it was clear that Hun Sen was still resisting pressures to form a tribunal for this purpose. The National Assembly approved a law extending the period of detention without trial for those who were accused of 'genocide, crimes against humanity or war crimes' from six months to three years. The effect of this law was to postpone the trials of Ta Mok and Duch, who were both, however, charged with genocide (under a 1979 decree) in early September.

International concern over the culture of judicial impunity that pervaded the country's legal system remained high in 2000. More than 20 years after the collapse of the PDK regime, none of the leaders of the Khmers Rouges had been brought to trial for the atrocities committed under the regime, and several principal Khmer Rouge figures continued to live openly in Pailin. At mid-2000 Ta Mok and Duch remained in government custody, awaiting trial. Although, in the late 1990s, the CPP was believed to have largely opposed any compromise with the UN on the issue of a Khmer Rouge trial, external pressure eventually forced the Government to take action. In April 2000 Hun Sen agreed to co-operate with the UN over a US proposal for the establishment of a UN-sponsored court, which would include both Cambodian and foreign judges and would uphold international standards of justice, as well as maintain Cambodia's national sovereignty. This decision followed a series of visits to Cambodia by foreign dignitaries, including senior US Envoy Ralph Boyce, US Senator John Kerry and Australian Minister of Foreign Affairs, Alexander Downer. It remained unclear, however, how many Khmer Rouge leaders would stand trial before such a court. The extent to which the country's new-found stability might be threatened by the opening of such trials was also uncertain. In July the Cambodian Government and the UN finalized the details of a draft accord on the establishment of a special tribunal to try former Khmer Rouge leaders implicated in atrocities carried out during the regime's rule. It was hoped by the UN that a formal agreement might be signed later the same year.

Until July 2001 Hun Sen continued to appear reluctant to bring Khmer Rouge leaders to justice. He repeatedly warned that any attempt to indict Ieng Sary, the former Minister of Foreign Affairs, would return the country to war. Furthermore, King Sihanouk, who had pardoned Ieng Sary in 1996, expressed similar fears. The legislative process to bring Khmer Rouge leaders to trial thus remained slow.

Legislation to establish a tribunal to try the Khmer Rouge leaders—unanimously passed on 2 January 2001 by the National Assembly and on 15 January by the Senate—gave rise to serious controversy, domestically and internationally. The draft law allegedly failed to meet international standards of justice. The UN Under-Secretary-General for Legal Affairs, Hans Corell, criticized the draft law and urged the Cambodian authorities to prosecute Ieng Sary. In June 2001, however, Hun Sen accused the UN of violating Cambodia's sovereignty, reaffirming his desire to conduct a trial without UN participation. His attack on the UN followed the departure of Peter Leuprecht, the UN Special Representative, who expressed misgivings about the way in which the tribunal law had been formulated and stated that the legislation would benefit from further scrutiny. Reiterating the views of Hun Sen, Ranariddh declared that he was no longer prepared to conform to UN stipulations.

Progress on issues related to the trials of the Khmers Rouges remained indeterminate. On 11 July 2001 86 of the 88 members of the National Assembly who supported the idea of bringing Khmer Rouge leaders to justice passed the legislation. It specified that life imprisonment would be the heaviest penalty that the tribunal could mete out to convicted Khmer Rouge leaders. A general desire for peace and stability, rather than justice, still seemed to have served as the guiding principle for the formulation of the tribunal law. In August King Sihanouk finally endorsed the legislation. (Meanwhile, Hun Sen said that he expected only about 10 former Khmer Rouge commanders to stand trial and reassured the others that they should have nothing to fear.) However Cambodia still failed to satisfy the UN. In February 2002 the UN Secretary-General decided to terminate negotiations with the Cambodian Government, having failed to gain support from the latter for the establishment of a court that would conform to international standards of independence, impartiality and objectivity. The Hun Sen Government responded by stating that it would proceed with the planned trials with or without UN support, blaming the UN for creating obstacles, while defending the position that it had done everything possible to co-operate. It justified its decision by stating that it had not invited the UN to dictate terms to Cambodia. In May Gen. Sam Bith, a former Khmer Rouge commander, was arrested, ostensibly for his participation in a train ambush in 1994 in which 16 people, including three Westerners, died. However, by mid-2002 neither Ta Mok nor Duch had been put on trial. The other Khmer Rouge leaders remained at large.

Foreign Relations Restored and Strengthened

Cambodia's relations with multilateral organizations have generally been strengthened. As a result of the formation of a second coalition Government in November 1998, Cambodia regained its seat at the UN General Assembly in December, following an absence of 15 months. However, relations between Cambodia and the UN were somewhat strained from 1999. In December of that year the office of the UN Secretary-General's special envoy to Cambodia was closed at the request of the Cambodian Government, despite UN pleas for it to remain open for a further year. The Cambodian Government had, however, agreed in August to extend the mandate of the UN Special Representative for Human Rights in Cambodia, Thomas Hammarberg. Hun Sen, meanwhile, contended that the UN should focus more on providing assistance in areas such as the drafting of laws and judicial reform. Relations continued to be uneasy in 2001 and 2002, largely because the Hun Sen Government felt that the UN had forced the country to yield to its demands regarding a Khmer Rouge war crimes tribunal. Relations deteriorated further when the United Nations Drug Control Programme (UNDCP) concluded in February 2001 that the country was fast becoming the most attractive in South-East Asia for transnational criminals. The issue of the Khmer Rouge trial constituted a persistent source of tension in the relationship, as the UN continued to urge Hun Sen's Government to bring Khmer Rouge leaders to justice (see above).

Since the coup in 1997 Cambodia's relations with the international donor community have been generally positive, as the latter continued to pledge financial support. In January 1999 Japan announced the resumption of aid by pledging to fund an electricity project in Phnom-Penh. The CGC agreed in February to provide Cambodia with US $470m. in assistance in the following year, conditional upon the implementation of constitutional reforms and a quarterly review. In June the CGC carried out its first review, identifying as priority areas, the end of illegal logging, and the reform of the armed forces, the civil service and the financial sector. In late 1999 the IMF (which had provided $85m. in budgetary support to Cambodia since 1994 but had suspended its assistance after the political events of July 1997) reached an agreement with Cambodia on a new three-year $81m. loan. In early 2000 the World Bank, which had previously cancelled a three-year $120m. loan arrangement, also agreed to grant Cambodia a new $30m. structural adjustment credit facility. At a meeting of the CGC in Paris in May, donors pledged to provide the country with $548m. in 2001; this aid, however, was to be dependent upon the Cambodian Government's honouring of its commitments to reduce military spending, suppress trafficking in illegal drugs and trim the civil-service payroll. In June 2001 14 donor nations met in Tokyo for a World Bank-sponsored conference on funding for Cambodia. The country had requested $500m. The donors, however, pledged a total of $615m., although with the conditions that Cambodia would take appropriate measures to combat corruption, adopt the tribunal law and promote human rights. Despite the fact that relations between Cambodia and the UN had deteriorated, the IMF remained optimistic regarding Cambodia. In February 2002 it released a $10.4m. credit under the Poverty Reduction and Growth Facility, bringing disbursements under the facility to a total of $52m. In March it issued a report praising Cambodia for the significant progress that it had made on reform; taxation and customs administration had been improved and the Ministry of Economy and Finance had exerted more stringent control over financial management. In June 2002 donors from 22 countries and seven international organizations pledged an annual donation of $635m. to Cambodia; the sum exceeded that pledged in the previous year and was approximately $116m. more than the Government had requested. However, the donor community adopted a more severe policy towards Cambodia by insisting that its support depended upon the country making substantive progress in policy reforms, particularly efforts to combat corruption and to improve the country's legal and judicial institutions.

Meanwhile, Cambodia's relations with ASEAN and individual states in South-East Asia remained positive. The improvement in political stability and domestic security prompted ASEAN officials to agree at their informal summit meeting in Hanoi in late 1998 to admit Cambodia as their 10th member; Cambodia formally acceded to the organization on 30 April 1999. The prospect of ASEAN membership effectively ended Cambodia's diplomatic isolation, and normal foreign relations were restored. In July 1999 Cambodia attended a meeting of the ASEAN Ministers of Foreign Affairs, its first attendance as a full member of the association. The Cambodian Minister of Foreign Affairs, Hor Nam Hong, pledged the Government's commitment to political and economic reforms as Cambodia sought to integrate itself with its South-East Asian neighbours. Hun Sen, meanwhile, maintained that the main reasons for his Government's decision to join ASEAN in 1999 were related to Cambodia's interest in regional security and stability, the ASEAN norm of consensus and the principle of non-interference, the economic growth experienced by ASEAN states over the previous 30 years, and the possibility of ASEAN serving as a gateway for trading relations with the outside world. As a new member of ASEAN, Cambodia was perceived to present a challenge to the unity of the regional group. In October 1999, for instance, Cambodia and the other two most recent entrants to ASEAN—Laos and Viet Nam—held their first unofficial Indo-China 'summit' meeting, which prompted concern across the region. At the meeting, Hun Sen and his Laotian and Vietnamese counterparts expressed their joint opposition to outside intervention in the newly-independent territory of East Timor, hitherto part of Indonesia. Cambodia was perceived by some observers to be part of the 'Indo-China enclave' aligned against some other ASEAN members (particularly Thailand and the Philippines) which had contributed troops to the international peace-keeping force in East Timor.

Cambodia's relations with Viet Nam were periodically strained. In February 1999 a high-level public security delegation led by Gen. Le Van Kham visited Phnom-Penh for talks with Sar Kheng, Deputy Prime Minister and Minister of the Interior. In the following month Cambodia formally established a Cambodia-Viet Nam border joint committee, the first meeting of which was held in March. In May Prince Ranariddh, in his capacity as Chairman of the National Assembly, met his Vietnamese counterpart, Nong Duc Manh, to draw up a programme of co-operation between the two legislatures. Furthermore, Cambodia sought and secured Viet Nam's support for membership of ASEAN's Inter-Parliamentary Organization. Discussions also encompassed the problems along Cambodia's border with Viet Nam. In July Chea Sim, the new Chairman of the Senate, also visited Viet Nam. Meanwhile, in June 1999 Viet Nam's party Secretary-General, Le Kha Phieu, made an official visit to Phnom-Penh. He met King Sihanouk, and held discussions with Hun Sen, Ranariddh and Chea Sim. Although this visit provoked anti-Vietnamese demonstrations, the leaders of the two countries consolidated bilateral relations, agreeing to resolve outstanding border demarcation issues before the end of 2000, and signing co-operation agreements for education and energy. In February 2000 the Chairman of the Vietnamese National Assembly visited Cambodia; the Vietnamese Minister of Foreign Affairs, Nguyen Dy Nien, visited the country in the following month. In May 2000 Cambodia and Viet Nam signed an agreement allowing the latter to search for the remains of Vietnamese soldiers listed as missing in action during the Viet Nam War. While bilateral ties improved, elements of tension remained. Disputes over border issues and illegal migration featured prominently in the relationship. The Cambodian Government's decision to allow a number of Montagnard refugees from Viet Nam to enter Cambodia caused strain, and border demarcation issues also remained a major obstacle to cordial relations. It was reported in August 2000 that Prince Ranariddh had urged Hun Sen to negotiate with Viet Nam owing to the latter's violation of a border agreement signed in 1995. Va Kim Hong, Chairman of Cambodia's Border Dispute Commission, described border agreements with Viet Nam as 'meaningless'. In September 2000 there was a tense confrontation between some 20 Cambodian soldiers and about 40 of their Vietnamese counterparts in a border area in the Cambodian province of Kampong Cham. In June 2001 King Sihanouk urged Hun Sen to 'save the sovereignty' of Cambodia. This was in response to Buth Rasmei Kongkea, the director of the Khmer Border Protection Organization, who accused both Viet Nam and Thailand of having violated all 15 Cambodian provinces that border the two neighbouring countries. In May 2002 a group of Cambodian protesters travelled to Phnom-Penh to complain about land encroachment by Vietnamese authorities. Cambodian leaders, including the Governor of Svay Rieng (the brother of Hun Sen), as well as officials and lawmakers from FUNCINPECC and the SRP, voiced their concerns regarding the problem. In late May the King requested again that the Government investigate this matter and employ harsher measures to prevent border encroachment by neighbouring countries. Overall, however, Cambodia's relations with Viet Nam remained manageable, even though the border issues had yet to be resolved.

Cambodia also continued to maintain stable relations with Thailand. In February 1999 the Supreme Commander of the Royal Thai Armed Forces visited Phnom-Penh to discuss co-operation on the repatriation of 30,000 refugees from Thailand to Cambodia, which constituted the major issue in bilateral relations between the two countries. Gen. Mongkol went to Cambodia to attend the regular meeting of the Cambodian-Thai Committee for Border Peace Maintenance. Later that month the Deputy Minister of Foreign Affairs, Sukhumbhand Paribatra, visited Phnom-Penh to attend the tripartite meeting of Cambodia, Thailand and the UNHCR concerning the final repatriation of Cambodian refugees. In his meeting with Hun Sen, Sukhumbhand also discussed border issues and Cambodia's impending membership of ASEAN. These same issues were raised in July during the visit of the Thai Deputy Prime Minister, Korn Dabbaransi, to Cambodia. In June the Prime Minister of Thailand, Chuan Leekpai, visited Phnom-Penh, where representatives of the Thai and Cambodian Governments pledged to resolve the territorial disputes between their respective countries 'in the spirit of friendship and neighbourliness'. In March a senatorial delegation from Thailand visited Cambodia, seeking ways to settle land- and sea-border disputes between the two countries. In June 2001 the Thai Prime Minister, Thaksin Shinawatra, also visited Cambodia. However, in mid-2002 border issues between the two countries remained unresolved.

Cambodia appeared to enjoy better relations with the other members of ASEAN. After the ASEAN summit meeting in Hanoi in December 1998, the Government made a concerted attempt to improve relations with Cambodia's regional neighbours. Malaysia was an advocate of Cambodia's membership of ASEAN long before the country was formally admitted to the association. Hun Sen paid an official three-day visit to Kuala Lumpur in February 1999 when he discussed Cambodia's proposed new Senate with the Malaysian Prime Minister, Dato' Seri Dr Mahathir Mohamad. At the conclusion of the visit both countries signed an agreement further to expand trade, economic and industrial ties. Cambodia and Indonesia also improved their bilateral ties. In March 2001 Hun Sen paid an official visit to Indonesia, where he held discussions with the President, B. J. Habibie. At the end of the visit an agreement on the protection of investments, trade and tourism was signed. Indonesia also agreed to provide training assistance to the Cambodian police. In August 2001 Indonesia's new President, Megawati Sukarnoputri, arrived in Phnom-Penh for an official visit. Cambodia also sought to improve ties with Singapore. In June 1999 Hun Sen visited Singapore, where he asserted that peace and political stability had returned to his country, which would strive to catch up with other ASEAN members and fulfil its commitments to achieving ASEAN's 2020 vision and Hanoi's Plan of Action. Cambodia-Laos relations were generally positive. The Prime Minister of Laos, Sisavat Keobounphan, visited Cambodia in April 2000 and the new Prime Minister, Boungnang Volachit, also visited in August 2001.

Bilateral ties between Cambodia and other extra-regional states have also been strengthened. During the period from July 1997 until April 1999 Cambodia's relations with most external states were strained. The USA, Germany and Japan suspended all but humanitarian assistance. Hun Sen's Government was repeatedly criticized for refusing to take steps to identify and punish those responsible for politically motivated killings and human rights abuses in 1997–98. In October 1998 the US House of Representatives passed a resolution accusing Hun Sen of genocide and other crimes. In March 1999 it was indicated that a resumption of US assistance was dependent on democratic reforms and Cambodia's agreement to the establishment of an international tribunal to try Khmer Rouge leaders. In July a US official paid a brief visit to Phnom-Penh for discussions with Hun Sen and Ranariddh regarding the trial of Khmer Rouge leaders, democratic reforms and human rights. While little progress was made on these matters, Cambodia had earlier agreed to host a regional conference on the issue of US soldiers listed as missing-in-action during the Viet Nam War. Hun Sen continued to welcome US officials to his country, despite lingering resentment. In November 2000 US Senator John Kerry visited Cambodia, where he indicated that US aid might be resumed if a tribunal to try Khmer Rouge leaders were to meet international standards. Subsequent visits by US officials included those in January 2001 by David Scheffer (the US ambassador-at-large for war crimes issues), Adm. Dennis Blair (the Commander-in-Chief of the US Pacific Command), and a 10-member US congressional delegation led by Richard Gephardt, a senior Democrat politician. At the CGC meeting in Tokyo in June 2001, the USA finally announced that it would resume direct aid to Cambodia. At the donor conference in June 2002 the USA pledged US $45m. Overall, the US strategy of combining pressure with reward was aimed at prompting Cambodia to accelerate the process of bringing Khmer Rouge leaders to justice and at curbing growing Chinese influence in Cambodia. However, there was no significant improvement in bilateral relations in the first half of 2002. In June the US State Department released its second annual Trafficking in Persons Report, which described Cambodia as a 'Tier 3' country (owing to its failure to comply fully with the minimum standards for the elimination of trafficking and to make sufficient efforts to do so) and warned that it could be subjected to aid sanctions by the USA.

In the mean time the People's Republic of China continued to provide political and financial support to the Hun Sen Government and vehemently criticized what it perceived as outside attempts to interfere in Cambodia's internal affairs. In January 1999 it was announced that China would supply agricultural equipment to Cambodia and construct a building to house the new Senate. Hun Sen visited Beijing in February, when he held discussions with the Chinese Premier, Zhu Rongji, and met President Jiang Zemin. Two months later the Cambodian Co-Ministers of Defence, Tea Banh and Prince Sisowath Sireirath, travelled to Beijing for discussions with their counterpart, Gen. Chi Haotian. Cambodia, which had been the recipient of US $3m. of military vehicles from China, secured additional funding of $1.5m. for its armed forces reform programme. In June the Cambodian Minister of Foreign Affairs, Hor Nam Hong, also visited Beijing to enhance bilateral relations. Following Hun Sen's reiteration of an earlier pledge by the Cambodian Government that Cambodia would not engage in political relations with Taiwan, Cambodia's 'one-China' policy was further reaffirmed in March 2000 during Hun Sen's meeting with a visiting Chinese government delegation. In November 2000 President Jiang Zemin visited Cambodia (the first visit by a Chinese head of state since 1966). China offered Cambodia commercial credit worth $200m., including an allocation of $2.7m. for military training.

Relations between Cambodia and Japan remained excellent. In January 2000 the Prime Minister of Japan, Keizo Obuchi, made an official visit to Cambodia, the first by a Japanese head of government in over 40 years. During his visit, Obuchi met with King Norodom Sihanouk and Hun Sen. Obuchi declared the Japanese Government's intention to assist Cambodia's development over the forthcoming decade, having pledged US $140m. in assistance to Cambodia; the Japanese leader also expressed his readiness to send Japanese financial experts to Cambodia to assist in the areas of taxation and debt management, and was reported to be considering providing the Cambodian Government with non-project grants valued at 2,000m. yen. In return, Hun Sen pledged his Government's support for Japan's bid for permanent membership of the UN Security Council. In June 2001 Tokyo pledged to provide annual aid of $118m., thus maintaining its position as Cambodia's largest donor. During the same month Japan's Prince Akishino and his wife, Princess Kiko, made the first visit to Cambodia by members of the Japanese royal family. In early November 2001 the Japanese Government was reported to have planned to nominate a university professor of law as a judge for the Khmer Rouge trials, illustrating its continued interest in Cambodia.

Cambodia also continued to strengthen its bilateral ties with India. In April 2002 Atal Bihari Vajpayee paid a three-day visit to Cambodia—the first visit by an Indian Prime Minister since Jawaharlal Nehru's visit in 1954. Vajpayee reportedly supported Cambodia's apparent intention to proceed with the Khmer Rouge trials without any UN involvement and indicated that his Government would be willing to send an Indian judge to assist in the Cambodian judicial process.

Economy

LAURA SUMMERS

Revised by SOK HACH

ECONOMIC CONDITIONS PRIOR TO 1979

At the time of independence from France the prospects for economic development were promising, not least because King Sihanouk's 'Royal Crusade for Independence' averted the economic devastation of war. Equally important, and in contrast to Viet Nam or Laos, Cambodia possessed ample food supplies and a satisfactory balance of trade, with most foreign exchange being derived from exported agricultural surpluses such as rice, freshwater fish or rubber latex. Nevertheless, the French were frequently criticized for leaving the country with inadequate infrastructure, little industry and high rates of illiteracy. The many formidable constraints on agriculture included low national yields (on average one ton or less of paddy rice per ha), mediocre soils, unreliable rain-fed irrigation systems, low mechanization and productivity, inadequate rural credit mechanisms, and inheritance traditions that resulted in the steady division of land holdings. Population growth rates as high as 3%–4% a year further contributed to pressure on the available arable land. Budget revenues, which came primarily from taxation of external trade, augmented by aid from the USA and France, were increasingly threatened during the 1960s.

Public investment in economic development, and specifically in import-substitution industrialization, began in 1960 in response to the rising costs of imports and the receipt of state-sector aid from the People's Republic of China and (from 1964) Czechoslovakia. State-owned industries producing plywood, cement, textiles, rubber tyres, paper, sugar, glass and tractors (assembled from parts supplied by Czechoslovakia) were established and created competition for private sector importers and retailers; many of the state-sector industries also benefited from US-financed commodity import programmes. Although alarmed by Cambodia's close relations with China, and the combining of East-West aid programmes, the USA continued to be Cambodia's principal aid donor until 1963. Despite the prohibition of defence alliances under the Geneva Agreements of 1954, the USA also supplied 'defence support' aid to the royal constabulary, and granted riel revenues from the commodity imports counterpart fund, directly to the Ministry of Defence, for the payment of army salaries. From Sihanouk's nationalist perspective, which many shared, US aid was meagre, amounting to less than the budget required and less than that awarded to neighbouring states; neither did it respond to Cambodia's mounting deficit nor to its developmental needs as perceived by the Government. Excessively conservative controls on monetary policies, supported by a belief in the need for a 'strong' riel (i.e. an overvalued rate of foreign exchange), discouraged both state and private-sector investment, especially in the faltering agricultural sector. In November 1963, following veiled moves to encourage the USA to increase its aid, the Cambodian Government requested an end to US aid programmes. When this decision, accompanied by sharp denunciations of US policies in southern Viet Nam, failed to secure the expected massive aid increases, Sihanouk proceeded with the nationalization of the financial sector (banking and insurance) and of international trade in January 1964. A state monopoly was also imposed on the production, sale and import of alcohol. (Hitherto informal trading and local brewing had lost the State valuable tax revenues.) Nine private banks, including five foreign banks, were closed and their accounts taken over by the National Bank and two hastily established subsidiaries.

The *étatist* reforms, however, failed significantly to ease the crisis caused by agricultural stagnation and population growth. Neither did the reforms succeed in solving investment and credit problems, despite the imposition of state controls on the import of non-essential luxuries and encouragement of the import of capital goods such as fertilizers. The army and the private sector opposed the reforms, which had become associated with a general foreign policy shift towards the Eastern Bloc and created their own, informal 'black' markets in trade with neighbouring Thailand and Viet Nam. The state industries, already troubled by inefficiencies arising from poor equipment, shortages of spare parts and ineffective and often corrupt management, were unable to compete for local market shares. The eclipse of the formal market by the informal and the deceleration in agricultural production were represented by a decline in annual rates of economic growth, which averaged 7% per annum in 1953–63, but decreased to around 3% in 1963–70, thus barely keeping pace with the official rate of population growth. A state casino, established in Phnom-Penh in 1969 in a desperate attempt to increase budget revenue, failed to generate sufficient income and greatly alienated Sihanouk from important urban political groups. The group of officers led by Gen. Lon Nol, which instigated the military coup and which was supported by important technocrats and business groups, subsequently restored free-market policies, US aid and links to the IMF, the World Bank and the Asian Development Bank (ADB). Expectations of a rapid economic recovery following political realignment with the West, however, were unrealistic. The mobilization of an army numbering 200,000 (in place of a peacetime force of 35,000), intensive US bombing of the countryside, and the flow of rural dwellers into urban areas, exacerbated the already acute economic problems.

In retrospect, the material destruction and human displacements arising from the 1970–75 war can be seen to have prepared the way for the subsequent economic radicalism. Capitalizing on widespread sympathy amongst the Cambodian peasantry for the deposed Sihanouk and, as normal subsistence patterns were disrupted, their alienation from the Phnom-Penh Government, the clandestine Communist Party of Kampuchea (CPK, later known as the Khmers Rouges) began introducing collective forms of rice production in 1973. Initially achieving important economies of scale and gains in productivity, the collectives pooled family land, made use of large-scale irrigation systems and introduced high-yield seed varieties, reportedly imported from China. By 1974 the revolutionary movement had secured control of much of the country's dwindling rice output as well as foreign-owned rubber plantations where reduced operations were taxed. Although the work regime was harsh and food rations minimal, the system was perceived by those it served as a means of survival during the wartime emergency. In total the 1970–75 war reduced the labour force by an estimated 500,000 to 1m., including the departure for overseas exile of tens of thousands of professional people; around 3m. other Cambodians (nearly half the estimated population of about 7m.) became internal refugees, most of whom were located in Phnom-Penh. In the final months of the fighting US food airlifts supplied the capital city, which was finally occupied on 17 April 1975.

The National United Front of Cambodia (NUFC) ordered the inhabitants of Phnom-Penh and other urban centres to leave the cities for the countryside, where they were gradually incorporated into co-operative production units. In economic terms, the NUFC portrayed the evacuation as the only alternative to the massive suffering caused by malnutrition and starvation and the threat of US bombardments. In May 1975 the USA imposed an embargo on aid and trade. Economic realities and the US hostility heightened revolutionary communist suspicions of urban 'feudalists' and the middle classes, both groups being portrayed as exploiters and oppressors of the poor, unproductive 'parasites' on the economy, and allies of US capitalism. The revolutionary aim was to establish a new and classless society in which the unproductive 'new people' would work together with wartime 'base' (or 'old') people in large-scale agricultural co-operatives. Both markets and money were viewed as mechanisms of exploitation, rather than of production, and were abolished. Each co-operative was to be a self-reliant, autonomously managed and mixed production unit. A few state industries, producing goods essential for the modernization of agriculture, were created. New workers, consisting mainly of demobilized soldiers of peasant origin, were ordered to produce necessities such as clothing and blankets, farm machinery (including planters and threshers), boats for river transport, medicines, tyres and printed materials, often using inadequate machinery and materials. Most water pumps for agricultural use were donated by the Democratic People's Republic of Korea, while the People's Republic of China supplied technical assistance (and from 1978, significant amounts of military aid).

The leaders of Democratic Kampuchea, as the country became known, planned to reconstruct and to modernize Cambodia's backward agricultural sector over a period of 10–20 years and to promote industrialization, based primarily on the use of accumulated national capital, over 15–20 years. A five-year plan, introduced in 1976, set overly ambitious annual targets of three tons per ha for paddy, or six or seven tons per ha in regions where a second, dry-season crop was possible. The plan gave priority to rural infrastructure, particularly the construction of dams and industrial-scale irrigation systems. Labour teams, often numbering tens of thousands of manual workers, completed dozens of major projects, but, because engineering skills were denigrated and peasant revolutionary cadres worked to formulas (such as the construction of perfectly square canals regardless of topography), many of the new irrigation systems were technically flawed; some collapsed, disrupting production over wide areas. Output was also affected by a shortage of draught animals or tractors, inadequate seed supplies and high-yield seed stocks, shortages of fertilizers and pesticides, war-damaged (impacted) paddy-fields, soil erosion and the rapid exhaustion of newly cleared land. As the labour force became increasingly demoralized and exhausted, production targets were rarely attained. Although rice output in 1976 may have satisfied national needs, there were acute food shortages in 1977 and in 1978, when adverse weather compounded the profound disorder. With popular hostility growing, the country's leaders blamed foreign powers and their allegedly concealed 'agents' for sabotaging the revolution. More than 20,000 party and administration cadres were secretly detained and executed by the state security service, while, in addition, tens of thousands of alleged enemies, often, but not exclusively 'new people', were detained and then executed by local authorities. In total, some 1.7m. people were believed to have died as a result of malnutrition, disease, exhaustion or execution. A border war with Viet Nam is estimated to have resulted in the deaths of thousands of others.

ECONOMIC DEVELOPMENT FROM 1979 TO 1991

The Vietnamese invasion of Cambodia at the end of 1978 brought most production to an abrupt halt. Vietnamese forces advanced through the countryside, pursuing remnants of the retreating army towards the western and northern frontiers and causing massive population displacement. Many people fled to avoid the fighting or to escape from the oppressive collectives and returned to their home villages in search of relatives or lost property. Following the looting of food stocks and the abandoning of agricultural production, only an international relief effort that cost more than US $300m. prevented a major famine from ensuing. With the inauguration of the People's Republic of Kampuchea (PRK) in 1979, peasant farmers were encouraged to form small production groups known as *krom samaki* ('solidarity groups'), each consisting of approximately 10–15 families. Land remained public property, to be farmed on a collective basis, but each family was also allotted a small private plot. These efforts to reorganize agricultural production were hampered by armed opposition to the new communist regime and by the refusal of most states to recognize a government imposed by Vietnamese invasion forces. Existing embargoes on aid, trade and investment in Cambodia were joined by the European Community (EC—later European Union—EU), Japan and other states in an effort to oblige Viet Nam to withdraw its military forces. Although generous economic assistance to other sectors of the economy was supplied by the USSR and its allies in the Council for Mutual Economic Assistance (CMEA), little aid was available for agriculture.

Another factor that constrained agrarian reconstruction and development was popular resistance to renewed attempts to promote socialism or any collective form of ownership and production. In most rural regions peasants initially agreed to form *krom samaki* and to work rice paddies on a collective basis for as long as shortages of land, draught animals, hand tools, water pumps and petrol made this necessary. Where possible, however, villagers persuaded local party and government officials to distribute farming land and equipment to individual families, who managed them as they chose and who marketed their own produce after paying taxes and collective, village dues owed to local schoolteachers, disabled people or war veterans and the unsupported elderly. Local cadres sometimes continued to organize work such as ploughing and harvesting on a mutual aid basis and as a labour-saving device. *Krom samaki* engaging in fully-collectivized production with no family management of rice paddies or inputs were classified as Level One collectives; those *krom samaki* engaging in only limited collective work, with families retaining effective managerial control over inputs, were known as Level Two administrative units. Level Three units comprised those in which families engaged wholly in private production on land claimed as family property. By 1989 almost 90% of all organized solidarity groups were classified as Level Three. The new administration proved too weak to reimpose socialist forms of agriculture. The promotion of production in any way possible, securing tax revenues, military conscription and political support from the peasantry became the administration's primary concerns.

Between 1981 and 1984 the PRK permitted or recognized three economic sectors: the state sector, which comprised 57 state industries in 1984; a co-operative sector, composed of rural production groups; and a family sector, consisting of rural or urban families engaged in the production of handicrafts or garden crops for exchange in state-controlled markets. Capital for family enterprises was usually derived from hoarded or retrieved savings, or was accumulated in 'black market' trading in refugee camps along the border with Thailand. By 1985 the ruling party had recognized the existence of widespread street vending and petty marketing, and legalized a fourth, private, sector to promote the manufacture of light consumer goods. Small factories, producing everyday necessities such as household utensils or containers, were quickly established. In 1988 a fifth, mixed state and private, sector was created which allowed the establishment of joint ventures with the participation of foreign as well as national entrepreneurs. In the late 1980s the Ministry of Planning acknowledged the existence of about 2,000 private businesses. Concern, however, for the survival of state enterprises, following the reduction in supplies of raw materials from the USSR, prompted their leasing to national and foreign investors.

The pace of economic reform accelerated from 1989 as the Vietnamese army withdrew from Cambodia. Traditional usufruct rights to land and rights to inherit inhabitable property were restored in order to encourage more investment in agriculture and in construction. Transport, health care and education were also partly privatized, as were most state markets. The relaxation of many of the remaining controls on the economy dramatically boosted economic activity, especially in the capital, Phnom-Penh, where, by mid-1989, there were an estimated 13,000 small businesses. The value of private-sector output quickly exceeded that of the State, but with most private investment concentrated in service industries, and in particular import-export services, and with the state sector in decline, real growth for 1989 was only 2.4% compared with the previous year. In 1990, measured at constant 1989 prices, economic growth was negligible.

Economic growth was also constrained by an intensification of the civil war in 1990, resulting in a significant decline in state revenue. Sharp increases in budget expenditure for defence, arising from the expansion of the armed forces and the first ever purchases of military equipment, led to rapid increases in the money supply and in the rate of inflation, which stood at around 200% in 1990 and again in 1991. Foreign aid, excluding military assistance, averaged around US $150m. a year during the five-year plan period (1986–90), most of which the USSR provided. Soviet aid ceased in 1991, and from January of that year the State of Cambodia (SOC), the name of the administration in Phnom-Penh between 1989 and 1993, paid for all its imports from the USSR at international prices and in convertible currency. This represented a double crisis for the budget. Previously, commodities imported from the USSR, on a free or cheap, long-term credit basis, had been sold to finance the budget, and had represented as much as 40% of revenue in some years. From 1991, however, the same commodities, and in particular petroleum and its products, had to be paid for with foreign-currency earnings from Cambodian exports, principally timber. In 1991 30% of the budget was deficit-financed by the printing of new bank notes.

THE ECONOMIC EFFECTS OF THE IMPLEMENTATION OF THE UN PEACE AGREEMENT (1991–93)

Following the signing of the Paris Agreements on a Comprehensive Political Settlement of the Cambodian Conflict in October 1991, international embargoes on aid and trade were removed. The signatories to the Agreements, led by Japan and France, also pledged to assist the Cambodian people in the rehabilitation and reconstruction of the national economy. The first pledge of US $880m., made at the inaugural conference of the International Committee on the Reconstruction of Cambodia (ICORC) held in Tokyo, Japan, in 1992, was committed to reconstruction projects extending over several years, and was to commence after 1993 once a lawfully elected and internationally recognized government had been installed. In 1992 the urban-based, private-sector economy continued to thrive, and activity in housing construction and repair barely kept pace with the demand from the UN Transitional Authority in Cambodia (UNTAC), whose personnel numbered about 21,000. Inflation also increased rapidly as the influx of affluent employees added to existing pressures on the economy. By October 1992 UN contributions to the SOC budget, mostly for the payment of civil servants, had helped to ease overall inflationary pressure, decreasing the annual rate of increase in the consumer price index to around 175% by the end of 1992. In total, UN funds and spending accounted for an estimated one-tenth of Cambodia's GDP in 1992, and for much of the growth in GDP, which was estimated at 7% by the IMF in that year.

The economic recovery was largely confined to urban centres, however, and specifically to import-consuming, property-owning or retailing families. Little trickled down to rural areas, and poor urban consumers complained of price rises for food. Some earnings were repatriated to Viet Nam by the tens of thousands of migrant Vietnamese workers who, encouraged by the UN presence, took most construction jobs. Uncertainty about the economy and about who would be in government after 1993 undermined efforts to collect taxes or customs duties. Senior government officials were witnessed selling off state assets for personal gain, which led to protests from students, workers or the families who found themselves evicted following the auction of government housing. The signing of timber agreements between Thai companies and the political parties also spurred some of the national growth in 1992, but, with hardwoods being irreplaceable and with no reafforestation programme, the rapacious expansion in timber-logging served to undermine confidence in the country's economic future.

Foreign investors and Cambodians returning from abroad after 1991 were wary of investing large sums in an economy that lacked both the legal infrastructure and the tax base essential for stability. The economy's vulnerability to political events was clearly demonstrated in 1993 when growth in GDP slumped to 3.9% because of the civil disorder surrounding the UN-organized elections held in May. Output also declined in agriculture, having been disrupted by continuing, low-intensity warfare, and by sharp fluctuations in the value of the riel, which halved when the inflation rate reached 450%–500% (in yearly terms); this was followed by a recessionary loop in the latter half of 1993. (The annual rate of inflation was finally estimated at 55%.) A measure of stability and confidence in the economy was restored following the successful completion of the elections, the prevention of a coup attempt in June and the formation of a coalition Government.

ECONOMIC DEVELOPMENTS UNDER THE ROYAL GOVERNMENT OF CAMBODIA (1993–)

The withdrawal of UNTAC in the final quarter of 1993 did not provoke the collapse in economic confidence that many, primarily in the expanding service sector, feared. Economic growth reached 5.7% in 1994, 7.6% in 1995 and 7.0% in 1996. The emergency rehabilitation, stabilization and structural adjustment agreements concluded with the World Bank, IMF and ADB helped stabilize the riel. Contrary to public expectations, the riel, in fact, appreciated against a falling US dollar, making the prices of many imports cheaper and allowing structural improvements in the organization of the national budget.

At the end of December 1993 the National Assembly approved new financial laws and a national budget for 1994, which met with widespread approval within the international donor community. Just over one-half (52%) of the proposed budget of US $342.2m. was to have been funded by domestically generated revenue, with the remaining expenditure ($165.2m.)—mostly for capital outlays ($120m.)—being covered by international assistance. In common with previous policy, most domestically generated income was to come from customs duties and consumption taxes levied by the customs authorities. In a significant departure, however, the budget was centralized and placed under the control of the Ministry of Finance, thus depriving individual ministries, state agencies and provincial authorities of their previous financial autonomy, and, specifically, their right to dispose of central budget allocations without accounting, to raise local tax revenues and even to accumulate foreign-exchange earnings. Central control over all revenue collection theoretically permitted government officials to restrain expenditure in some areas (such as defence), to monitor the use of aid more effectively and to direct investment into areas identified as of national importance (for example, production for export and agriculture). A centralized budget also represented a countermeasure to inflation, for which annual benchmarks of 5%–10% are required by donor agencies.

In 1993–94 important progress was made in the area of tax collection, which was a sector that traditionally yielded less than 5% of national output and which was constrained by inadequate revenue laws and corrupt practice. With a combination of new controls and political pressure from the Ministry of Trade, revenue from taxes increased from around US $5m. per month in June 1993 to $10m. per month by the end of the year. As the Government's fiscal position noticeably improved, the Ministry of Finance drafted new legislation designed to attract foreign capital investment, especially long-term inflows, which would encourage the introduction of new technology, export-based industry and tourism, agro-industry and rural development. The new Law on Investment in Cambodia, approved by the National Assembly in August 1994, provided for a low corporate taxation rate of 9%, tax exemptions of up to eight years, five-year loss carried forward, no taxation of reinvested profits, the free repatriation of profits, the leasing of land for up to 70 years and tariff exemptions on imported capital goods destined for use in export-orientated production. In 1994 investments worth $465m. (of which $285m. were domestic) were approved by a newly-created Cambodian Development Council (CDC), more than one-half of which was for tourism and other service industries.

Cambodia's attempts to secure foreign investment in the following years were hindered by investor anxiety about political and budgetary stability; a lack of banking regulations and legal guarantees; the slow implementation of projects as a result of ministerial or local government agencies demanding bribes; and expanding criminal activity linked to poverty, unemployment and other social grievances. The CDC approved investments totalling about US $2,250m. in 1995, and more than $1,000m. in 1996. According to the IMF, however, actual investments remained substantially lower; net foreign investment was estimated at $151m. in 1995 and at $294m. in 1996. Investor confidence was reinforced by other developments: the USA granted Most Favoured Nation (MFN—now Normal Trade Relations) trading status in September 1996, and admitted Cambodia to its Generalized System of Preferences (GSP) in August 1997; Cambodia also joined the International Finance Corporation (IFC) of the World Bank in December 1996, thereby gaining access to multilateral sources of finance for private-sector interests. However, following domestic political unrest in July 1997, which resulted in the removal of Prince Ranariddh as First Prime Minister, and the onset of the regional economic crisis in the same year, foreign direct investment decelerated, and new commitments declined to $759m. for the year. Although the domestic political situation improved following the formation of a potentially stable coalition Government in November 1998 and the cessation of any effective armed resistance in the country, with the surrender or capture of many of the remaining Khmer Rouge leaders, investment approved by the CDC continued to decline sharply during 1999–2001. Such investment reached only $218m. in 2001. One effect of the low level of investment on the country's economy is that it has become increasingly difficult for new entrants into the labour market (numbering about 200,000 people per year) to be absorbed into the labour force.

A major factor governing future prospects for budgetary control of the economy concerned the decision in June 1994 to transfer control of timber extraction and export to the Ministry of National Defence, which had insisted on higher budgetary allocations. To the dismay of environmentalists and international donors, revisions to the 1994 budget in September of that year allocated the security forces a total of 48.3% of recorded, current expenditure; revenues from logging, theoretically controlled and originally set at US $2.2m., rose to $33.2m. Since the transfer of rights of revenue collection to a ministry was in contravention of agreements concluded with international donors, the IMF withheld a disbursement of aid funds at the end of 1994, and resumed payments only in 1995. Although donors publicly renewed their pledges of support, these were conditional upon private government assurances related to budgetary procedures and corruption. The 1995 budget aimed to reduce current expenditure by about 10%, (mainly through reductions in defence and salary outlays) and to increase capital or developmental expenditure. These objectives were to be achieved without resort to environmentally destructive, windfall forestry revenues (set at only $1.5m. for the fiscal year 1995). A planned deficit equal to around 6% of GDP was to be covered by concessional financing, thereby providing a measure of continuing stability for the currency. In the second half of the year the 1995 budget was revised upwards by 20%, owing to higher than expected revenue collections, mostly from timber royalties and exports (recorded at $34m.). Reports of new logging deals in January 1996 (see Forestry, below) prompted the IMF, as well as the World Bank, to withhold a total of $47m. in aid, in support of reserves and agriculture respectively. The Government secured $501m. in new aid pledges at the annual meeting of the Consultative Group for Cambodia (CGC) in July 1996, but was advised by donors of the need for 'prior actions' before structural adjustment projects could proceed. In particular, the Government was expected to honour 1994 pledges to reduce the size of the civil service by 20% (from an October 1994 level of 143,855 employees) and to proceed with military demobilization (reducing the armed forces from 130,000 to 90,000); public expenditure was also to accord higher priority to health, education, agriculture and rural development. Donor advice was taken seriously in parts of the Ministry of Finance, but disorder in the budgetary process worsened: up to 20,000 defecting Khmer Rouge soldiers were inducted into the Royal Cambodian Armed Forces (RCAF); ministries continued to provide jobs as a means of securing political support; and the value of the riel declined sharply against the US dollar in local exchanges, as the effects of the increase in the money supply and pressures on the country's limited reserves were felt.

The violence and political unrest of July 1997 rendered prospects for the future of Cambodia's economic development uncertain. Following Prince Ranariddh's removal from office, several international lenders and donors (including the USA, the IMF and the World Bank) withheld approximately US $100m. in aid for 1997, and made resumption of aid dependent on the successful completion of free and fair national elections. The withdrawal of aid and investment resulted in the estimated loss of 40,000 jobs, mostly in the service sector, and damage in Phnom-Penh from the fighting and ensuing looting was estimated at $100m. The regional economic crisis also affected Cambodia's development, leading to a decrease in investment from the region and to a decline in demand for Cambodian exports. Economic growth thus decelerated in 1997 to about 1%, down from 7% in 1996. Government revenue collection fell by 6% for 1997 compared with the planned budget, owing to decreased revenue from customs duties (caused by a decline in imports) and income taxes. Threatened with a large budget deficit, the Government attempted to reduce spending, but the continued fighting in the north-west and the need to incorporate defecting Khmer Rouge soldiers into the RCAF necessitated increased military spending, and the reductions were thus made in other areas. Inflation increased in 1997, owing to large-scale purchasing prompted by public anxiety in the wake of shortages of certain goods following the political turmoil.

There was no discernible GDP growth in 1998, owing to a poor agricultural performance following a drought, the continued effects of the regional financial crisis, reduced aid levels, and the political uncertainty surrounding the election in July 1998 and its aftermath. Per caput GDP actually declined in real terms by 1.8%. Consumer spending remained depressed following the election. The riel depreciated against the US dollar and some regional currencies, causing an increase in inflation to 12% in 1998. However, the economy recovered in 1999–2001, with growth rates estimated at an annual average of approximately 6.0%, as a result of improved consumer confidence and renewed aid pledges. The CGC pledged US $470m. in February 1999, $548m. in May 2000 and $615m. in June 2001 in aid for those years, although it remained dependent on the fulfilment of commitments to demobilize a large proportion of the armed forces, reform the civil service, halt rampant deforestation and continue financial reforms. To accelerate the pace of reform, the CGC in June 2002 pledged a further $635m. in aid, conditionally linked to the implementation by the Cambodian Government of economic and institutional reforms, mostly in combating corruption and reforming the judicial system.

Cambodia's long-term development requires major investment in infrastructural improvements to attract substantial foreign investments. The country also needs significant resources to be allocated to education, to provide skilled personnel in order to improve its administrative, legal, educational and medical institutions, and also to the health sector in order to improve general health care and to avert an impending HIV/AIDS crisis.

AGRICULTURE

After many years of political instability and the neglect of economic development, agriculture (including forestry and fishing) continued to provide employment for approximately 70% of the population, representing an estimated labour force of 3.9m. in 2000. The declining contribution of agriculture to GDP, from about 60% in 1988 to less than 40% in 2001, is indicative of the continuing poverty in rural areas. Agricultural GDP averaged 0.7% growth per annum, in real terms, during 1995–2001, about two percentage points lower than the rate of growth of the population during the same period. To the perennial problems of poor soils, uncertain rainfall and irregular flooding, inadequate fertilization (by silt or appropriate chemicals) or use of pesticides, may be added shortages of male labour power. As a result of war losses, and the greater political vulnerability of men during the period of Democratic Kampuchea, in the mid-1990s women constituted 54% of the adult population over 15, headed 20% of rural households and held title to substantial paddy land. Widowed women who received land after 1989 experienced difficulty working it, with hired help or the assistance of relatives, and without labour support from *krom samaki*. Many women were forced to sell land or to neglect agriculture in pursuit of other means of income generation. An additional, and serious, problem is the presence of land mines over an estimated 300,000 ha, including 55,000 ha of prime rice-growing land in Siem Reap, Banteay Meanchey and Battambang Provinces, the country's traditional grain basket. In 1997 total cultivated area increased to 2.1m. ha, from 1.8m. ha in 1994, as some land previously laid with land-mines was reclaimed. Following the establishment of a new coalition Government in November 1998, however, plans were announced to improve the agricultural sector through the further clearance of land-mines to augment cultivable land and to consolidate the implementation of the land ownership law to guarantee the safe occupation of land, thus encouraging investment and long-term development.

The retreat from commercial production to subsistence rice production, which characterized the 1980s, can be attributed to the lack of price incentives offered by the successive PRK and SOC Governments. Official purchasing prices for the state markets were low, and only slowly increased when procurement difficulties created food problems in urban areas. As informal or free markets for rice expanded in 1989, prices reportedly reached 40 riels per kg, compared with the state purchasing price of 15 riels. Compulsory deliveries of rice—either in the form of taxation, which was slowly reintroduced in 1983 as voluntary 'patriotic contributions', and later, in the form of levies on output (measured at around 10% of output above 1 ton per ha)—were abandoned in 1989 when progressive rates of taxation were introduced (e.g. 25 kg per ha on land yielding less than 1 ton per ha, up to 60 kg per ha on land yielding more than 2.5 tons per ha). These rates were abandoned in 1992 when the authorities, seeking peasant support in the 1993 elections, declared a 15-year moratorium on the taxation of agriculture. In the early 1990s the introduction of other protectionist policies, including a ban on the export of paddy (which was rescinded in 1995) and exemptions from duties on rice imports, were designed to keep rice prices as low as possible, although, ultimately, they served to undermine producer incentives.

Draught animal stocks were severely depleted during the conflicts of the 1970s, and by 1979 there were only about 1.5m. head of cattle and buffaloes, compared with 3.1m. in 1970. Herds have subsequently recovered and by early 1991 there were 2.9m. head of cattle, including 1.5m. draught animals representing a sufficient number to plough 2.1m. ha of paddy by traditional, manual means. During the 1990s livestock numbers increased further, owing to a rising consumption of meat rather than expansion of cereal production. The UN Food and Agriculture Organization (FAO) estimated total cattle head at 3.0m. in 2000. The livestock sector's contribution to GDP increased by about 4% per annum during the latter half of the 1990s.

Despite the obstacles and constraints, agricultural production improved significantly between the early 1980s and the early 1990s. According to official figures, the annual harvest of paddy rice increased from 565,000 metric tons in 1979 to about 2.55m. tons in 1991, representing the highest level achieved since 1967. Paddy production attained self-sufficiency levels in 1995, rising to 3.5m. tons. This increase was due both to the expansion of the area under cultivation and to improvements in productivity. Paddy production continued to increase steadily thereafter, reaching 4m. tons in 1999. About 300,000 tons of milled rice were exported in that year. Productivity rose from 1.3 tons per ha in the early 1980s to 1.8 tons per ha in 1995, and then to 2.0 tons per ha in 1999, although yields remained among the lowest in Asia. Despite efforts to improve farming techniques and promote new varieties of seeds and fertilizers, no perceptible progress has been made since 1999, owing to successive floods and droughts, and to a lack of development in the irrigation system. In 2001 less than 10% of rice fields were irrigated and irregular rainfall and serious flooding in the Mekong River basin damaged approximately 250,000 ha of rice crops. Extension of irrigation systems, better distribution of new land brought into cultivation and improvement in marketing systems would significantly increase crop production in Cambodia.

Many problems face the agricultural sector, apart from the inability of peasants to bring available land back into production. Among the most important are problems of water control, which have worsened as a direct result of deforestation. Of the 841 irrigation systems surveyed in 1994 by the United Nations Development Programme (UNDP), some 80% had malfunctioned since 1991 owing to damage from recent environmental changes. In 1999 the Government announced plans to expand irrigation networks from 16.6% of cultivable land to 20%. A flat topography prohibits the construction of large dams, except on the Mekong River, while smaller systems were designed for flood patterns that no longer exist in the Mekong-Tonlé Sap basin in Cambodia.

Vegetables and other secondary food crops feature prominently in household consumption and income generation in Cambodia. Vegetables are grown largely on homestead lands and are considered to constitute small-scale production practices. The size of the area under cultivation and levels of production have fluctuated from year to year owing to pest and disease attacks, natural disasters and price fluctuations. Daily per caput vegetable consumption in Cambodia averages about one-half of the standard 200g recommended by FAO. It is estimated that the total annual consumption of vegetables is about 600,000 metric tons. Forestry and lakes are the source of about 25% of all vegetables consumed, while local cultivation accounts for another 25%. The remaining 50% is imported from neighbouring countries. There are more than 40 local and international NGOs who work to improve food security for rural people through the promotion of vegetable growing for both self-consumption and income generation. As a consequence of these activities, the productivity of some areas increased significantly, especially in 2001. Moreover, the horticulture and livestock sectors should benefit from the increased demands of the tourism sector (hotels and restaurants). However, poor infrastructure in rural areas and the inability of local products to compete with imported vegetables in terms of either quality or price cause problems for the growers. In addition, improved distribution of land resources, and the definition of rights and responsibilities over them, are of fundamental importance to Cambodia's development. The country's lack of clear land tenure rights has inhibited business people from investing in the agricultural sector. Nevertheless, the passage of a new Land Law in August 2001 marked a watershed in creating a legal framework for the management of land in Cambodia.

Exports of rubber were once an important source of foreign exchange. Output is generally lower than in the 1960s, however, owing to the neglect of the six old plantations (comprising 52,439 ha in 1969) and their slow rehabilitation during the 1980s. Rubber production was adversely affected by the ageing of trees. While rubber trees began to be replanted in the early 1980s, they took time to mature. Rubber production increased during the mid-1990s, reaching 46,000 tons in 1996, thus approaching the annual outputs achieved in the 1960s when the plantations were mature and routinely restocked. Production declined to 38,600 tons in 1997 and 1998, but significantly recovered to about 47,000 tons annually in 1999–2001, thus reaching the 1996 level. In 1996, meanwhile, world production of rubber began to exceed demand, causing a decline in international prices of 27%. In an attempt to remain competitive, the Government suspended a 10% export tax on rubber in October 1997. This did not, however, halt illegal exports to Viet Nam, which had become prevalent in the early 1990s. Owing to a sharp fall in international rubber prices following the onset of the Asian economic crisis in mid-1997, Cambodia's unit value declined from US $1,108 per metric ton in 1995 to $450 in 2001, resulting in export values of $45m. in 1995 and an estimated $21m. in 2001. Plans for the eventual privatization of the six state-owned plantations (five in Kompong Cham Province and one in Kratié Province) were agreed with the Caisse Française de Développement (now Agence Française de Développement) in January 1995, and involved the introduction of foreign managerial control. By the end of 2001 the six plantations were still in the process of being transformed into 'public enterprises' in preparation for privatization.

FORESTRY

In 1969 the area under forest cover was 13.2m. ha, which accounted for 73% of the national land area. By 1997, however, forest cover had been reduced to about 10.6m. ha, representing only 58% of total land area. Provincial authorities were engaged in widespread illegal logging activities, despite bans on felling and efforts to centralize revenue collection. Much of the exploitation of Cambodia's forests was carried out by Thai companies following the granting of concessionary areas, with rights of exploitation, either directly by the Phnom-Penh authorities, or indirectly by local provincial authorities or opposition party leaders and military officials. Timber concessions incorporating transport across disputed zones often involved payments to more than one party.

On the advice of international environmental agencies, UNTAC imposed a moratorium on round timber exports at the end of 1992. The ban was suspended by the Royal Government in October 1993, ostensibly to permit the export of old timber felled before the UN moratorium and to prevent it from rotting. A system requiring certificates of origin was established, which facilitated taxation and generated immediate revenues for the budget. The suspension was abused, however, and, when evidence of fresh logging activity emerged, the Government re-imposed a ban in March 1994. This ban remained in force until June, when the two Prime Ministers decided independently to revise central government controls and transferred major responsibilities for decisions concerning export licences, concessions and revenue gathering to the Ministry of National Defence. Protests against the resumption of ministerial 'tax farming' in August and September 1994 coincided with severe drought and then flooding in rural areas, thus renewing awareness of the ecological damage arising from deforestation. By November Prince Ranariddh was obliged to pledge the restoration of the ban on logging and to resume attempts to impose fiscal responsibility on national ministries. The new ban on logging came into effect in April 1995, but a timber concession granted to Malaysia's Samling Corporation in August 1994, which awarded rights to exploit 805,509 ha (about 12% of the remaining forest area) over a 60-year period, was not rescinded. Thai companies received renewed authorization to remove previously felled logs from May 1995, but this concession was rapidly and openly abused. In March 1996 it was revealed that the two Prime Ministers had personally authorized 20 Thai companies to remove up to 1,079,300 cu m of logs, when accounts showed that felled, lying timber inside Cambodia following the ban on cutting amounted to only 330,648 cu m. The revelations precipitated the suspension of IMF loans and protests from the co-premiers that the contracts were being misinterpreted.

Seeking to avert criticism at the July 1996 donors' meeting in Tokyo, the Government informed the Thai authorities that the rights of Thai firms to remove felled timber would expire, definitively, on 31 December 1996. By June 1997 environmentalist groups revealed that illegal logging continued without disruption, with companies often securing protection and labour from regional military commanders. Official revenue yields, however, were appallingly low: approximately US $20m. in 1995, $10m. in 1996 and $12.7m. in 1997. Reafforestation projects were being implemented, but would not immediately affect disruptions to seasonal rainfall patterns and falling water levels in the Tonlé Sap.

An intensified campaign against illegal logging was ordered in January 1999 prior to the meeting of multilateral and bilateral aid donors in February. The donors reiterated their stance that aid was to be dependent, amongst other conditions, on Cambodia's implementation of a sustainable forestry management programme to halt the rapid environmental degradation caused by deforestation. By mid-1999 the Government had revoked logging concessions totalling 2,173,041 ha and made this area into forest reserves. In mid-1999, according to official sources, 4,739,153 ha of land was being worked by 14 companies. The World Bank estimated that 4.2m. cu m of commercial timber were illegally felled in 1997 (costing the Government US $100m. in lost revenue), compared with an estimated sustainable yield of 1.5 cu m, and that at this rate Cambodia's timber resources would be depleted within five years. To protect the forests from further deterioration, reforms have been initiated with the support of donors, and remedial measures have been implemented. As a result, production of logs has declined steeply since 2000. To ease access to the country's common property, and as part of the reforms, the Government has allowed local populations access to some forest land (about 5% of the total forest land). Assisted by NGOs, about 200 community forests were established in over 16 provinces at the end of 2001. However, the role played by the village communities in the management of forestry remained in need of enhancement.

FISHING

Fish is the primary source of protein in the national diet. Historically, freshwater catches from the Mekong-Tonlé Sap basin satisfied most of the national requirement, with marine products accounting for less than 20%. Throughout the 1980s total recorded catches increased steadily, reaching 117,800 tons (including 36,400 tons of marine products) in 1991, compared with only 20,000 tons during the famine year of 1980. However, the total catch declined to 111,150 tons in 1992 and 108,900 tons in 1993. Fish farming, introduced by foreign aid agencies and the Vietnamese, supplied about 10% of the freshwater catch in 1990. Ecological changes, such as falling water levels, heavy and rapid flooding, and loss of the forested regions once completely inundated by flooding in the Tonlé Sap, have disrupted fish migrations, breeding and feeding patterns. The forested area around the Tonlé Sap was the main breeding ground for the lake's fish. By 1998 only 39% of the original 10,000 sq km of flooded forest remained under natural vegetation. Moreover, substantial shares of the marine catch are lost to the economy as a result of illegal, offshore fishing by Thai companies which receive unofficial licences, and protection from the coastal marine and rivers police and provincial authorities, to continue their activities. The officially recorded freshwater catch in 1995 was 72,500 tons, an increase of 7,500 tons on the 1994 catch of 65,000 tons. The appearance of improvement is misleading, concealing the over-harvesting of baby *pra kchao* fish which fetch higher prices than mature fish, reductions in the catch of other varieties, owing to ecological changes disrupting breeding and migration patterns, and illegal fishing. Laws prohibiting grenade and electric-shock fishing are enforced in some regions, with aid from the army, but these illegal techniques, and others, are still in common use. Deforestation presents the most serious challenge to inland fishing: according to an Institute of Technology study, the Tonlé Sap will be silted over by the year 2023 if logging continues at the pace set in the early 1990s. The mean depth of the lake declined by 0.5 m to 1 m over the 15 years between January 1979 and January 1994.

Fishing was transferred to the private sector in late 1993, following the creation of the coalition Government. Leases, or 'concessions' as they were called in colonial times, to lots on the Tonlé Sap and inland rivers are sold on a two-yearly basis to the highest bidders. Sales, however, are organized by provincial governors, with arrangements being open to manipulation and abuse at several stages and levels. Successful bidders for one or more of the 280 leases available must pay 40% of their bid as a deposit for exploitation rights, the balance falling due at the end of the lease period. Public revenues from sales of leases increased sharply to US $3.7m. in 1995, from $1.2m. in 1993 and $1.9m. in 1994, but subsequently declined steadily to $2.6m. in 2000, owing to high levels of corruption within the sector. In 2001 the commercial freshwater catch was estimated at 120,000 tons, and the sector contributed about 3% of total GDP.

INDUSTRY

Following the installation of the socialist PRK regime in 1979, many state industries were rehabilitated. In contrast to the patterns of industrial concentration in earlier periods, however, the PRK revival plan involved substantial promotion of industrial activity at the provincial level and significant encouragement of small-scale, family-based handicraft activity.

Without heavy industry in Cambodia, until the mid-1990s the industrial sector was dominated by rice mills (of which there were approximately 1,500) and by 80–100 state industries or factories, including the latex-processing plant in Kompong Cham, which remains wholly state-owned. However, in subsequent years there was significant industrial growth in such areas as textiles, garments, beer and soft drinks, food-processing and construction materials, and in early 1998 a consumer electronics plant started production. Many factories have operated at low levels of efficiency in recent years, being constrained by outdated and virtually unserviceable equipment, frequent interruptions to the power supply and difficulties in securing supplies. The total contribution of industry to GDP was estimated at 15% in 1994, around the same level as the estimated contribution to GDP of the sector in the 1960s. However, owing to the rapid expansion of the garment industry in the latter half of the 1990s, the contribution to GDP of the industrial sector as a whole increased to 24% in 2000.

Many difficulties in privatizing, encouraging and reorganizing industry can be attributed to policies introduced in the socialist era of the 1980s when state companies were overstaffed and depended upon the command economy for administrative support and subsidies. After 1988 managers were awarded local autonomy: they could retain profits earned from the disposal of products surplus to plan targets; they could reinvest such profits in new product lines; and they could pay piece-rates, or bonuses, to productive workers. Many state enterprises received full financial autonomy from the budget after June 1990, which meant that managers had to procure all their supplies from the private sector, to keep accurate accounts and to finance deficits on operations through acquiring loans. As a result many industries were unable to record profits, and by July 1991 about 25 state factories, in economic difficulty, had been leased to private entrepreneurs. Part or all of the labour force were dismissed in some enterprises creating political disruptions and drawing attention, *inter alia*, to the absence of labour laws. At the end of 1998 the Government had privatized 73 industrial enterprises, of which 68 were leased to the private sector and five were joint ventures. There remained only two enterprises to be privatized, whilst one company was to be retained in public ownership.

In the early 1990s the largest industries were engaged in agro-food processing or in the production of construction materials. Between 1995 and 1998, because Cambodia was not yet subject to international quotas, considerable foreign direct investment from Malaysia, Hong Kong, Taiwan, the Republic of Korea, the People's Republic of China and Singapore resulted in the rapid development of the garment sector. By the end of 2000 there were about 220 garment factories, employing 160,000 workers, in operation in Cambodia, compared with 13 in 1995. The garment sector was characterized by poor working conditions and low wages, a situation that provoked labour unrest in the late 1990s. About 70% of the garments were exported to the USA, which granted Cambodia MFN status (now styled Normal Trade Relations) in 1997, and the rest to Europe. Garment exports, which were negligible in 1994, increased to US $378m. in 1998. In January 1999 the USA introduced quantitative restrictions on imports of 12 categories of garment products from Cambodia, necessitating an increased focus on European markets. Nevertheless, in 1999 garment exports increased by 85%, and were valued at $598m. Despite the US quota and global economic slowdown, expansion of the sector remained robust in 2000, and in 2001 exports reached a record level of $1,100m.

Investment in industry decelerated following the events of July 1997. Some factories were damaged or looted during the fighting, and many expatriate staff left the country. The Government pledged to settle claims with companies that suffered damage, but owing to a lack of funds it hoped to achieve this through tax rebates. The industrial sector was also adversely affected by the regional financial crisis, which caused a decline in investment from countries in the region and increased competition in the domestic market in some industries, as the weakening of the baht led to an influx of cheap Thai imports. The Royal Government announced plans in December 1998 to promote the establishment of agro-industrial enterprises (for products like palm oil, rubber and tapioca) and to encourage the development of industrial zones, especially in coastal areas, to prepare goods for export.

Industrial GDP increased by 17.9% in 1996, but the growth rate decelerated to 2.4% in 1997 before registering a strong recovery to about 15% per year during 1998–2001. The GDP of the construction sector followed the same pattern until 1998, increasing by 8.6% and 20.9% in 1995 and 1996 respectively, but then, owing to the loss of external funding in 1997, declining by 8.9% in that year, before growing by 13.4% in 1998. Construction activity remained depressed in 1999, with the sector registering a GDP growth rate of only 1.5%, and then sharply declined in 2000 and 2001, owing to a lack of new investment during that period.

Mining

Mining contributed an estimated 0.2% of GDP in 2001. The sector expanded by 20.1% in 1996 but declined by 1.0% in 1998, before recovering by an estimated 14.4% in 1999. Cambodia possesses few commercially exploitable mineral reserves. Phosphate deposits are processed for use as fertilizer, but the exploitation of deposits of iron ore, silver, bauxite, tin, silicon and manganese is judged unviable. The commercial mining of sapphires and rubies in the Pailin district of Battambang increased dramatically after 1991 when the Khmers Rouges used revenues from this source to offset lost aid from China. In common with the timber trade, Thai companies profited the most. Although the Khmers Rouges were effectively defunct by 1999, many of the gem-mining areas remained under the control of former Khmer Rouge leaders, and exploitation of these resources was largely uncontrolled by the central Government. Use of the Bavel River for the industrial sifting of excavated soil for gems has contaminated water supplies in Battambang Province. There is some gold mining—at a household level—in the eastern provinces. A number of Australian, Canadian and Malaysian companies have signed agreements to prospect in this region, but by 1999 the Government had yet to pass a draft mining law.

In late 1991 international oil companies began offshore exploration for deposits of petroleum and natural gas. Although initial seismic surveys were promising, and Thai geological assessments suggested reserves worth as much as US $15,000m. in disputed parts of the Pattani trough, the extent and accessibility of the reserves have yet to be determined. The most successful tests in 1994 produced flows of 4.7m. cu ft of gas (Enterprise Oil consortium) or 224 barrels of oil per day (Campex). The area of overlapping claims is estimated at 5,570 sq km; Thailand awarded concessions in the area in the 1970s. Proposals for a joint development zone have come to nothing so far, but a memorandum of understanding, issued in June 1996 following talks at prime ministerial level, indicated that negotiations concerning the competing claims would continue. Enterprise Oil halted all exploration in December 1996, but expressed an interest in securing new claims in Cambodian waters. Cambodia signed agreements in November 1997 with five foreign oil companies (two from Japan, and others from the USA, the United Kingdom, and Australia) allowing them to explore in four offshore concessions in the disputed area for an initial payment of $9.6m., followed by an additional $36.6m. over the next 10 years.

Energy

All commercial energy used in Cambodia is imported. Domestic energy is principally derived from timber (6m. cu m of logs were felled in 1997 for domestic consumption). The country has an installed capacity of 28.7 MW, of which 15 MW is accounted for by an oil-fired thermal power plant and the rest by diesel generating units. Only a small proportion of the generating capacity can be utilized, however, owing to a lack of spare parts and a shortage of fuel. Installed generating capacity was 51.97 MW in 1984. Cambodia has considerable hydropower potential. Two hydroelectric plants were under construction in the late 1990s, with numerous other projects under discussion, owing to the potential importance of revenue from sales of electricity to Thailand and Viet Nam. In 1999 the German company Siemens AG proposed a US $500m. project to build two power plants within two years, one with an installed capacity of 320 MW in Sihanoukville and the other of 180 MW in Kompong Speu Province. According to a preliminary strategy drafted by Electricité du Cambodge (ECD), with assistance from the World Bank, almost all of Cambodia was to be electrified by 2015.

FINANCE

Total state revenue in 1989 amounted to only 5.5% of estimated gross national output, with revenue from taxation equal to only 2%. As budget support from the USSR was also falling, the SOC had to seek alternative sources of revenue and to reduce expenditure wherever possible. Steps were immediately taken in 1989–90 to reduce the number of state employees—both civil servants and other workers—and to bring an end to state subsidies in accordance with practices already adopted in Viet Nam and in Laos. As noted above, state factories in deficit were leased to private entrepreneurs, a commercial banking system was introduced and attempts were made to secure improved revenues from taxation. The continued military expenditure, however, (see above) was funded mostly by timber sales and by budget deficit financing.

Until 1989 the new riel, introduced in March 1980, had been relatively stable. However, in preparation for the new terms of trade being arranged with the USSR and the CMEA, in October 1988 a policy of floating rates of exchange was adopted, which closely shadowed changes in 'black market' rates fixed to the value of gold in the Hong Kong market and to the value of the US dollar. The rate of inflation increased throughout 1989, and reached very high levels in 1990–92 in response to the lack of foreign exchange and the heavy government reliance on the printing of new currency. When it appeared that gold and other currencies might replace the national currency in urban market exchanges, in September 1991 the Government banned the use of gold and other currencies and devalued the Cambodian currency to 750 riels per US $1. By the second quarter of 1993, when the rising inflation rate affecting the riel had reached its peak, more than 4,000 riels were required to purchase one dollar. Following the elections, and with stabilization programmes in place, the riel recovered and maintained its position on foreign exchanges at 2,200–2,600 riels to US $1. Since early 1994 official market exchange rates have been kept in line with free market exchanges and adjustments have been made on a daily basis. The Law on Investment, introduced in August 1994, removed all foreign-exchange restrictions that had previously applied to investors. New bank notes, in larger denominations and with portraits of King Sihanouk replacing the socialist images favoured by the PRK/SOC Government, were issued in April 1995.

Macroeconomic indicators were generally positive in 1995, in spite of the failure of new taxes to yield expected revenues. GDP grew by 7.6%, inflation was restricted to 7.7%, and the exchange rate of the riel in relation to the US dollar was stable, at an average of 2,451. Although the disbursement and absorption of aid were decelerating, sectoral growth showed a steady advance. However, an economic deceleration, and pressure on the riel, became evident in 1996. A principal problem for Cambodia is its failure to improve revenue generation; fiscal revenue has remained at equivalent to about 9.5% of GDP since 1994. Meanwhile, budget revenue declined in 1998, reaching only 8.6% of GDP, reflecting the acceleration of problems caused by weak governance and lack of a clear fiscal policy. The implementation of a very generous investment law and various *ad hoc* tax exemptions cost the country millions of US dollars per year in revenue. Following the formation of a second coalition Government, some additional fiscal measures were implemented. The introduction of a valued-added tax (VAT) and competitive bidding for garment export quotas in 1999 sharply boosted government revenue (a 40% increase compared with the previous year). Although significantly lower than forecast, revenue collection in 2001 continued to improve slightly, largely as a result of the enforcement of VAT regulations and non-tax revenue collection. Gross official reserves increased from the equivalent of 2.2 months of imports in 1996 to 3.5 months at the end of 2001, owing to the release by the Bank for International Settlements of gold reserves which had been 'frozen' since the 1970s. This increase in reserves would permit the authorities greater flexibility in exchange-rate management. A new foreign-exchange law had been approved in 1997, which formalized the liberal exchange structure.

The riel depreciated less than other regional currencies in the initial period of the financial crisis beginning in mid-1997, owing to the widespread use of the US dollar in the Cambodian economy. This dependence on the US dollar also mitigated the impact of the depreciation by 27% against the US dollar and the appreciation by 4% against the Thai baht in 1998, which, despite the use of dollars, resulted in an increase in inflation to 12.6% in that year, from 9.1% in 1997. However, inflation slowed from mid-1998, reaching zero in 1999, despite the introduction of the 10% VAT and a 30% increase in the salaries of public-sector workers in that year. Inflation in Phnom-Penh was slightly negative in the 12 months ending December 2001, mainly as a result of the weakness of rice prices. In the provinces, however, living costs rose more rapidly (by about 3% year on year), reflecting an increase in transport costs caused by high fuel prices.

BANKING

The banking sector currently plays only a very modest role in public or private finance. A Law on the Management of Foreign Exchange adopted in August 1991 and a Law on the State Bank of Cambodia adopted in March 1992 gave the former socialist State Bank the powers of a central bank, including the authority to issue money. The ability of the National Bank of Cambodia (NBC, as it was restyled in 1992) to implement monetary policy is severely limited by the widespread use of the US dollar. Although the riel is not convertible in international exchanges, it is freely exchanged. Figures for the end of 1999 showed that total liquidity recorded by the NBC was about 12% of GDP, a slight increase from the end of the previous year (about 11%). This rise was due to a rapid increase in foreign currency deposits, as a result of the significant improvement in the business environment and the regional economic recovery. Liquidity in riels declined to about 4% of GDP in 1999 (from 5% at the end of 1998), while the amount of US dollars circulating through the banking system rose to about 8% of GDP (from 6% at the end of 1998). Foreign currencies circulating outside the banking system are estimated to be at least four times higher than the total liquidity recorded by the NBC. The use of riels is confined to small transactions and low-wage payments, while larger transactions are conducted in foreign currencies such as the US dollar and the Thai baht. Despite this improvement, Cambodian bankers still appear to have little confidence in domestic developments. According to a monetary survey at the end of 2001, net domestic credit remains largely negative, suggesting that Cambodian bankers prefer to place money outside the country rather than to lend it to local investors. Most of the population, meanwhile, make no use of banking services, preferring to keep their limited savings in the form of hoarded gold or US dollars. While the credit services provided by banks are competitive, small-scale business people prefer to borrow from relatives, and small amounts of credit are routinely raised via the organization of tontines. Peasants also rely on relatives for loans, or on shopkeepers and mill-owners who advance cash or goods at exorbitant rates of interest. By the end of 2000 there were about 30 commercial banks, most of them small, private ventures, many of which were alleged to be engaged in the 'laundering' of regional profits from drugs-trafficking. The NBC increased reserve requirements for banks from 5% to 8% and the capital guarantee deposit from 5% to 10% with effect from 1 January 1998, to ensure liquidity and solvency in the banking system. In order further to strengthen the credibility of the sector, the NBC also requested in May 2000 that all commercial banks apply for a new licence. As a result, 11 non-viable banks have shut down, having been unable to comply with the required increase of registered capital to US $13m. from $5m.

TOURISM

Tourism is regarded as one of the most important immediate and long-term sources of foreign exchange. Attempts were made to increase tourism from 1986 as the economy began to experience substantial deficits on its balance of trade with socialist countries (approximately 90m. roubles per annum on average for 1987–90); in 1990 the deficit incurred in trading in the convertible-currency zone exceeded US $20m. Apart from the creation of tourism services, with technical assistance from Viet Nam, in 1988 the Government authorized the establishment of free-trading zones with Thailand and Singapore in the two coastal provinces of Kampot and Koh Kong. Their subsequent success led to the expansion and legalization of cross-border trade with Thailand along the western frontier, with Cambodia exporting rubber, timber and agricultural produce and importing petroleum, machinery and consumer goods, including textiles.

Although tours of Phnom-Penh and Angkor Wat, via Ho Chi Minh City, were made available from 1986, Cambodia attracted fewer than 1,000 visitors in 1987. However, foreign visitor arrivals increased from 118,200 in 1993 to 260,500 in 1996. Visitor arrivals declined substantially following the events of mid-1997, and the year ended with a total of 255,124 arrivals. In December the 131-room Grand Hotel d'Angkor in Siem Reap, which had been refurbished by Raffles Holdings of Singapore at a cost of US $30m., was opened, but vacancy rates in hotels remained high. The Government hoped for an increase in visitors in 1998, and developed a plan for the tourism industry that focused on the Angkor temples, the beaches of Sihanoukville, and 'eco-tourism' in Ratanakiri. However, arrivals (by air) declined to 186,333 in 1998, owing largely to the continued political instability and the violence surrounding the election in July, combined with the effect of the regional financial crisis. The tourism sector recovered significantly following the establishment of a potentially stable coalition Government in November 1998, with the number of total visitors reaching 367,743 in 1999, of whom 262,907 had arrived by air. The significant decline in the number of visitors to Cambodia in 1997 prompted the Government to initiate an 'open-skies' policy, in accordance with which direct flights from overseas would be permitted to land in Siem Reap. Many tour and hotel operators in Phnom-Penh opposed this policy, arguing that it would directly affect their business and other enterprises in the capital. The number of foreign visitors arriving on direct flights to Siem Reap almost tripled in 1999 relative to 1998, and continued to increase significantly during 2000 and 2001, representing 30% of the total number of arrivals by air to Cambodia in 2001. Total arrivals rose to 466,365 in 2000, when tourist receipts totalled $228m.; arrivals were estimated at 463,000 in 2001, when tourist receipts reached about $250m. Despite this increase, however, the tourists tend to stay only for short periods, usually no more than two days, and it remained unclear whether the 'open-skies' policy would benefit the entire economy in the longer term.

Since 1994 the tourism sector has attracted a very high proportion of foreign capital investment. However, the rate of implementation of approved projects is very poor. In 1995 approvals totalled US $1,572m., of which $1,350m. was accounted for by an approved tourism centre project proposed by Ariston of Malaysia: at mid-2002 this project was yet to be realized.

TRADE

From 1997 traditional exports like logs, sawn timber and rubber were superseded by garments, which accounted for 44% of domestic exports (excluding re-exports) in that year and for almost 90% in 2001. Logs and sawn timber accounted for only an estimated 3%, and rubber for 2%, of domestic exports (including estimates for illegal exports) in 2000. Imports were dominated by investment-related products, durable consumer goods and petroleum products. Re-exports—which represented a significant feature of external trade (prompted by the differences in import tariffs between Cambodia and its neighbours) and which included cigarettes, motorcycles, beer and electric equipment (which were re-exported to Viet Nam) and gold (which was principally re-exported to Thailand)—declined sharply in the late 1990s. Re-exports accounted for 62% of total exports in 1995, but declined to an estimated 18% of total exports in 2001.

Despite the slowdown in garment and timber exports, the volume of Cambodia's external trade continued to grow steadily, reaching US $3,343m. in 2001, exceeding the nominal GDP for the first time in Cambodia's history. Exports of goods increased by about 8% in 2001, in contrast to an expansion of 33% in 2000; similarly, imports of goods rose by 7% in 2001, compared with a 14% increase in 2000. In terms of the balance of trade, reduced prices for rubber exports and a sharp decrease in timber exports accounted for the decline of the trade surplus in agricultural products. The trade surplus in the garment sector continued to improve. However, the trade deficit in the energy and non-garment manufacturing sectors increased slightly owing to the expansion in economic activity. As a result, the total trade deficit deteriorated slightly in 2001, reaching $339m., representing 10.5% of the nominal GDP. The balance in the service sector improved significantly in 2001 (by 19%), owing to the expansion in tourism. The outflow of income owed by expatriates (including salaries and profits generated by foreign direct investment) was broadly balanced by the inflow of money repatriated by Cambodians residing overseas. Overall, Cambodia's current-account deficit improved slightly, declining to the equivalent of 6.7% of GDP in 2001, compared with 7.2% in 2000.

Cambodia's relations with the Association of South East Asian Nations (ASEAN) improved significantly following the 1993 elections. In December 1995 Cambodian representatives with observer status attended an ASEAN summit meeting for the first time, and in July 1996 Cambodia's application to become a member of ASEAN was accepted. Formal admission to the association, which had been scheduled for July 1997, was postponed by ASEAN ministers responsible for foreign affairs following the removal of the First Prime Minister, Prince Ranariddh. ASEAN subsequently agreed to reconsider Cambodia's admission following the successful completion of free and fair national elections in July 1998. ASEAN officials agreed in December 1998 to admit Cambodia as its 10th member, following the formation of a coalition Government in November; the formal admission took place on 30 April 1999, following the establishment of a Senate as specified under the coalition agreement. ASEAN membership requires the implementation of the Common Effective Preferential Tariff (CEPT), a system of reciprocal tariff reductions. Cambodia, however, will find it difficult to reduce tariffs for customs duties, which provide a substantial proportion of non-aid revenues to the national budget. The Cambodian Government expected to increase domestic taxes, principally excise duties, to offset the decline in customs duties.

FOREIGN AID

The exact level of Cambodia's outstanding external debt remained unclear at mid-2002, although World Bank documents showed that at the end of 2000 Cambodia's overall foreign debt totalled more than US $2,000m., most of which was owed to Russia. These debts were contracted during four different periods: at the end of the 1960s Cambodia's outstanding external debt amounted to about $50m., all of which was already rescheduled or partly cancelled in 1995, according to the procedure of the 'Paris Club' of creditor nations, and which by mid-2002 had been reduced to about $30m.; however, it appears that Cambodia also owed about $300m. to the USA during 1970–75, and about $800m. of convertible rouble (equivalent to $1,400m.) to Russia during 1980–91. (By mid-2001 the incumbent Cambodian Government had not yet recognized these two debts, although discussions with the USA and Russia on the issue were under way.) After 1993 the Cambodian Government began to borrow again from the World Bank and ADB in order to finance the rehabilitation of the country's public infrastructure; this debt is estimated to amount to $500m. In sum, the total outstanding external debt recognized by the Cambodian Government at the end of 2000 amounted to $530m., while pending debt was estimated at $1,700m. At a conference in Tokyo in June 1992 aid for economic rehabilitation and infrastructural development amounting to $880m. was pledged by approximately 30 donors, including ASEAN. At subsequent donor meetings between 1992 and 2000, pledges rose to more than $3,000m. Disbursements for the repatriation and resettlement of refugees, community development, agriculture, health and sanitation, education and training, public utilities, industry and public administration were spread over several years, and by 1996 were behind schedule, owing to problems of absorption. However, the removal of the first Prime Minister in July 1997 prompted several lenders and donors to cut their aid programmes. The USA, Germany, the IMF and the World Bank suspended all non-humanitarian aid. Other donors made more modest reductions, or continued providing assistance—Australia only ceased providing military assistance, and Japan briefly delayed the release of some funds, while the People's Republic of China made no cuts in aid. Nevertheless, the aid cuts forced the Government to reduce its budget, and to take measures to increase revenue collection, steps that have mitigated but not prevented a growth in the budget deficit. In 1998 foreign assistance was provided for the elections held in July; the EU donated $11.5m., Japan $3m. and the USA an additional $2.3m. (the latter to be administered by NGOs). Donors also helped fund a national census conducted in March 1998, the first since 1962.

In the past donors have regularly requested that budgetary procedures and transparency be improved, and that greater priority be given to basic needs via the expansion of health and education services and the promotion of rural development (the latter of which necessarily requires protection of the environment by means of effective regulation of logging and reafforestation). Among the most important elements of structural reform is the planned reduction in the number of state employees, both civil and military. The fiscal gains have been undermined to some extent by approximately 35,000 patronage appointments offered to parties in the ruling coalition, the obstruction of the privatization of state-owned enterprises, continuing problems with the collection of tax and customs revenues and recourse to parallel budgets or sources of revenue. In pursuing their reform agenda, lending institutions and countries have increasingly attempted to make aid conditional upon improved performance and accountability from the Government, and to transfer aid directly to local areas, thereby circumventing central ministries. A significant number of functions normally assumed by central government, such as the organization and management of credit associations, have been assumed by NGOs. (In June 2002 there were about 1,000 national and international NGOs operating in Cambodia.)

Following the successful formation of a coalition Government in November 1998, the CGC, which comprises 16 countries and six international financial institutions, pledged an assistance grant and loan of US $470m. for Cambodia, at a meeting held in Tokyo in February 1999. The CGC promised a further $548m. in May 2000 in Paris and another $615m. in June 2001 in Tokyo. In June 2002 in Phnom-Penh it pledged further assistance of $635m., as had been expected. The funds were dependent on the Cambodian Government's commitment to implement reforms, including: military demobilization; administrative and fiscal reforms; the reduction of corruption; and the elimination of illegal logging, in order to prevent further environmental damage. The first quarterly review of Cambodia's progress took place in June 1999, when the donors expressed approval of the country's advancement. Also in 1999, following Cambodia's achievement of political progress, Japan (Cambodia's leading aid donor) resumed yen-denominated loans for the first time in 30 years. The IMF resumed assistance to Cambodia in late 1999, following its approval in October of a three-year arrangement under the enhanced structural adjustment facility (ESAF) for Cambodia to support the Government's economic programme for 1999–2000; however, the organization remained critical of Cambodia's fiscal performance. Relative political stability in Cambodia, and the cessation of any formal armed resistance with the collapse of the Khmers Rouges, augurs well for Cambodia to achieve rapid economic development in the coming years. Donors hoped that the importance of aid in the Government's budget would provide impetus for political and financial reform.

Statistical Survey

Source (unless otherwise stated): National Institute of Statistics, Ministry of Planning, Sangkat Boeung Keng Kong 2, blvd Preh Monivong, Phnom-Penh; tel. (23) 216538; fax (23) 213650; e-mail census@camnet.wm.kh; internet www.nis.gov.kh.

Note: Some of the statistics below represent only sectors of the economy controlled by the Government of the former Khmer Republic. During the years 1970–75 no figures were available for areas controlled by the Khmers Rouges.

Area and Population

AREA, POPULATION AND DENSITY

Area (sq km)	181,035*
Population (census results)†	
17 April 1962	5,728,771
Prior to elections of 1 May 1981	6,682,000
3 March 1998	
Males	5,511,408
Females	5,926,248
Total	11,437,656
Population (official estimates at mid-year)	
1999	12,660,000
2000	12,990,000
2001	13,311,000
Density (per sq km) at mid-2001	73.5

* 69,898 sq miles.

† Excluding adjustments for underenumeration.

PROVINCES (1998 census)

	Area (sq km)*	Population	Density (per sq km)
Banteay Mean Chey	6,679	577,772	86.5
Bat Dambang	11,702	793,129	67.8
Kampong Cham	9,799	1,608,914	164.2
Kampong Chhnang	5,521	417,693	75.7
Kampong Spueu	7,017	598,882	85.3
Kampong Thum	13,814	569,060	41.2
Kampot	4,873	528,405	108.4
Kandal	3,568	1,075,125	301.3
Kaoh Kong	11,160	132,106	11.8
Kracheh	11,094	263,175	23.7
Mondol Kiri	14,288	32,407	2.3
Phnom Penh	290	999,804	3,447.6
Preah Vihear	13,788	119,261	8.6
Prey Veaeng	4,883	946,042	193.7
Pousat	12,692	360,445	28.4
Rotanak Kiri	10,782	94,243	8.7
Siem Reab	10,299	696,164	67.6
Krong Preah Sihanouk	868	155,690	179.4
Stueng Traeng	11,092	81,074	7.3
Svay Rieng	2,966	478,252	161.2
Takaev	3,563	790,168	221.8
Otdar Mean Chey	6,158	68,279	11.1
Krong Kaeb	336	28,660	85.3
Krong Pailin	803	22,906	28.5
Total	178,035	11,437,656	64.2

* Excluding Tonlé Sap lake (3,000 sq km).

Principal Towns: Phnom-Penh (capital), population 900,000 in 1991 (estimate); Sihanoukville (Kompong-Som), population 75,000 in 1990 (estimate).

BIRTHS AND DEATHS (annual averages)

	1985–90	1990–95	1995–2000*
Birth rate (per 1,000)	44.2	38.2	38.1
Death rate (per 1,000)	16.5	14.1	10.8

* UN estimates (Source: UN, *World Population Prospects: The 2000 Revision*).

Source (unless otherwise indicated): Ministry of Economy and Finance, Phnom-Penh.

1997: Death rate (per 1,000) 12.0.
1998: Birth rate (per 1,000) 38.0.

(Source: World Health Organization).

Expectation of life (WHO estimates, years at birth, 2000): Males 53.4; Females 58.5 (Source: WHO, *World Health Report*).

EMPLOYMENT

	1998*	1999†	2000‡
Agriculture, forestry and fishing	3,770,982	4,213,620	3,889,048
Mining and quarrying	6,385	5,508	3,328
Manufacturing	158,969	258,876	367,286
Electricity, gas and water	3,278	5,508	3,799
Construction	47,716	82,620	69,773
Wholesale and retail trade	341,351	402,084	436,308
Restaurants and hotels	15,281	27,540	18,794
Transport and communications	118,001	121,176	119,596
Financial intermediation, real estate and renting	4,416	16,524	16,636
Public administration	221,966	187,272	146,986
Education	81,073	88,128	87,385
Health and social work	26,219	27,540	30,235
Other social services	68,311	38,556	40,098
Other services	45,270	44,064	45,905
Total employed	4,909,218	5,519,016	5,275,177

* Based on the results of the 1998 Population Census.

† Based on the results of the Socioeconomic Survey of Cambodia.

‡ Based on the results of the Labour Force Survey of Cambodia.

Source: IMF, *Cambodia: Statistical Appendix* (February 2002).

Health and Welfare

KEY INDICATORS

Fertility (births per woman, 2000)	5.0
Under-5 mortality rate (per 1,000 live births, 2000)	135
HIV/AIDS (% of persons aged 15–49, 2001)	2.70
Physicians (per 1,000 head, 1998)	0.30
Hospital beds (per 1,000 head, 1990)	2.07
Health expenditure (1998): US $ per head (PPP)	54
% of GDP	7.2
public (% of total)	8.4
Access to water (% of persons, 2000)	30
Access to sanitation (% of persons, 2000)	18
Human Development Index (2000): ranking	130
value	0.543

For sources and definitions, see explanatory note on p. vi.

Agriculture

PRINCIPAL CROPS ('000 metric tons)

	1998	1999	2000
Rice (paddy)	3,509.8	4,040.9	4,026.1
Maize	48.5	95.3	157.0
Sweet potatoes	30.5	32.5	28.2
Cassava (Manioc)	66.5	228.5	147.8
Other roots and tubers*	18.5	18.5	18.5
Dry beans	9.2	15.9	15.1
Soybeans (Soya beans)	27.7	35.1	28.1
Groundnuts (in shell)	6.6	9.2	7.5
Sesame seed	5.1	7.4	9.9
Coconuts*	56.0	50.0	45.0
Sugar cane	133.1	159.9	164.2
Tobacco (leaves)	10.1	6.4	7.7
Natural rubber	40.8	45.2	42.4
Vegetables*	465.0	470.0	470.0
Oranges*	63.0	63.0	63.0
Mangoes*	34.0	35.0	35.0
Pineapples*	16.0	16.0	16.0
Bananas*	146.0	147.0	146.0
Other fruits and berries*	58.0	59.2	59.2

* FAO estimates.

Source: FAO.

LIVESTOCK ('000 head, year ending September)

	1998	1999	2000
Horses*	23	25	25
Cattle	2,680	2,826	2,993
Buffaloes	694	654	694
Pigs	239	2,189	1,934
Chickens	13,117	15,249	15,249
Ducks*	4,500	4,600	4,600

* FAO estimates.

Source: FAO.

LIVESTOCK PRODUCTS ('000 metric tons)

	1998	1999	2000
Beef and veal	41.8	42.1	56.7
Buffalo meat	13.1	13.1	13.1
Pig meat	100.0	102.5	105.0
Poultry meat	24.1	25.0	25.1
Cows' milk	20.1	20.4	20.4
Hen eggs*	11.5	11.7	11.7
Other poultry eggs	3.2	3.3	3.3
Cattle hides (fresh)	10.4	10.5	14.2
Buffalo hides (fresh)	2.7	2.7	2.7

* FAO estimates.

Source: FAO.

Forestry

ROUNDWOOD REMOVALS ('000 cubic metres, excl. bark)

	1997	1998	1999
Sawlogs, veneer logs and logs for sleepers	410	410	410
Other industrial wood	630	630	630
Fuel wood	6,813	6,968	7,117
Total	7,853	8,008	8,157

2000: Production as in 1999 (FAO estimates).

Source: FAO, *Yearbook of Forest Products*.

SAWNWOOD PRODUCTION
('000 cubic metres, incl. railway sleepers)

	1997	1998	1999
Total (all broadleaved)	71	40	10

2000: Production as in 1999 (FAO estimates).

Source: FAO, *Yearbook of Forest Products.*

Fishing

('000 metric tons, live weight)

	1997	1998	1999
Capture	102.8	107.9	109.0
Freshwater fishes	73.0	75.7	71.0
Marine fishes	29.8	32.2	38.0
Aquaculture	11.5	14.1	15.0
Total catch	114.3	122.0	124.0

Source: Ministry of Economy and Finance, Phnom-Penh.

Note: Figures exclude crocodiles, recorded by number rather than by weight. The total of estuarine crocodiles caught was: 17,000 in 1997; 40,700 in 1998; 25,380 in 1999 (Source: FAO, *Yearbook of Fishery Statistics*).

Mining

(estimates, '000 metric tons)

	1999	2000	2001
Salt (unrefined)	40	40	40

Source: US Geological Survey.

Industry

SELECTED PRODUCTS ('000 metric tons, unless otherwise indicated)

	1971	1972	1973
Distilled alcoholic beverages ('000 hectolitres)	45	55	36
Beer ('000 hectolitres)	26	23	18
Soft drinks ('000 hectolitres)	25	25*	25*
Cigarettes (million)	3,413	2,510	2,622
Cotton yarn—pure and mixed (metric tons)	1,068	1,094	415
Bicycle tyres and tubes ('000)	208	200*	200*
Rubber footwear ('000 pairs)	1,292	1,000*	1,000*
Soap (metric tons)	469	400*	400*
Motor spirit (petrol)	2	—	—
Distillate fuel oils	11	—	—
Residual fuel oils	14	—	—
Cement	44	53	78
Electric energy (million kWh)†	148	166	150

Cigarettes (million): 4,175 in 1987; 4,200 annually in 1988–92 (estimates by US Department of Agriculture).
Cement ('000 metric tons): 50 in 2001 (estimate by the US Geological Survey).
Electric energy (million kWh)*: 194 in 1995; 201 in 1996; 208 in 1997.
Plywood ('000 cu m): 16 in 1998; 15 in 1999; 27 in 2000 (Source: FAO).

* Estimate. † Production by public utilities only.

(Source: partly UN, *Industrial Commodity Statistics Yearbook*.)

Finance

CURRENCY AND EXCHANGE RATES

Monetary Units

100 sen = 1 riel.

Sterling, Dollar and Euro Equivalents (31 May 2002)

£1 sterling = 5,727.5 riels;
US $1 = 3,905.0 riels;
€1 = 3,665.6 riels;
10,000 riels = £1.746 = $2.561 = €2.728.

Average Exchange Rate (riels per US $)

1999 3,807.8
2000 3,840.8
2001 3,916.3

BUDGET ('000 million riels)

Revenue*	1998	1999	2000
Tax revenue	679.4	947.7	1,026.0
Direct taxes	55.5	82.7	135.6
Profit tax	42.1	63.8	100.9
Indirect taxes	247.5	431.6	500.0
Turnover tax	65.9	21.8	12.6
Value-added tax	90.1	314.9	371.6
Excise duties	76.1	91.8	112.6
Taxes on international trade	376.3	433.4	390.4
Import duties	372.5	415.3	372.8
Other current revenue	230.1	354.8	353.3
Forestry	22.8	36.3	41.0
Receipts from public enterprises	55.5	30.5	51.4
Posts and telecommunications	87.2	108.9	91.9
Public services	17.5	141.9	101.4
Capital revenue	33.2	13.7	29.3
Total	942.7	1,316.2	1,408.6

Expenditure†	1998	1999	2000
Council of Ministers	57	54	85
Ministry of Defence	312	336	309
Ministry of the Interior	173	147	142
Ministry of Economy and Finance	109	134	96
Ministry of Public Works and Transport	13	29	20
Ministry of Agriculture, Forestry, Hunting and Fisheries	18	21	23
Ministry of Education, Youth and Sport	102	156	166
Ministry of Industry, Mines and Energy	3	4	5
Ministry of Health	44	126	102
Ministry of Posts and Telecommunications	54	114	29
Ministry of Social Affairs, Labour, Professional Training and Youth Rehabilitation	48	19	26
Total (incl. others)	1,571	1,825	2,083
Current expenditure	941	1,097	1,189
Capital expenditure	630	728	896

* Excluding grants received.

† Figures for individual ministries exclude externally financed capital expenditure ('000 million riels): 510 in 1998; 504 in 1999; 593 in 2000.

Source: IMF, *Cambodia: Statistical Appendix* (February 2002).

INTERNATIONAL RESERVES (US $ million at 31 December)

	1999	2000	2001
IMF special drawing rights	5.19	0.18	0.51
Foreign exchange	388.00	501.50	586.30
Total	393.19	501.68	586.81

Source: IMF, *International Financial Statistics*.

MONEY SUPPLY (million riels at 31 December)

	1999	2000	2001
Currency outside banks	489,862	494,600	577,780
Demand deposits at deposit money banks	42,092	45,041	31,940
Total money	531,954	539,641	609,720

Sources: Ministry of Economy and Finance, Phnom-Penh, and IMF, *International Financial Statistics*.

COST OF LIVING

(Consumer Price Index for Phnom-Penh; base: 1995 = 100)

	1998	1999	2000
Food, beverages and tobacco	130.9	140.8	136.1
All items	132.8	138.1	137.0

Source: UN, *Monthly Bulletin of Statistics*.

2001 (base: 2000 = 100): All items 99.4 (Source: IMF, *International Financial Statistics*).

NATIONAL ACCOUNTS ('000 million riels at current prices)

Expenditure on the Gross Domestic Product

	1999	2000	2001
Government final consumption expenditure	661.2	736.9	803.9
Private final consumption expenditure	11,082.5	10,925.5	11,032.6
Increase in stocks	181.5	–213.9	265.4
Gross fixed capital formation	1,814.4	1,957.1	2,125.7
Statistical discrepancy	–138.9	–196.9	–482.6
Total domestic expenditure	13,600.7	13,208.7	13,745.0
Exports of goods and services	4,783.8	6,372.8	6,768.6
Less Imports of goods and services	5,797.4	6,649.9	7,148.6
GDP in purchasers' values	12,587.1	12,931.5	13,364.9
GDP at constant 1993 prices	8,889.1	9,569.7	10,176.2

Source: Asian Development Bank, *Key Indicators of Developing Asian and Pacific Countries*.

Gross Domestic Product by Economic Activity

	1999	2000	2001
Agriculture, hunting, forestry and fishing	5,384.8	4,935.3	4,930.0
Mining and quarrying	17.2	18.6	23.8
Manufacturing	1,485.0	1,996.3	2,100.6
Electricity, gas and water	43.5	43.3	56.8
Construction	606.2	631.4	742.9
Trade, restaurants and hotels	1,798.4	1,812.4	1,867.0
Transport, storage and communications	778.9	875.5	940.9
Financing, real estate and business services	893.0	1,000.9	990.5
Public administration	388.6	376.6	369.4
Other services	483.6	525.9	551.1
Sub-total	11,879.2	12,216.1	12,573.0
Less Imputed bank service charge	157.4	154.8	128.0
GDP at factor cost	11,721.8	12,061.3	12,445.0
Indirect taxes, *less* subsidies	865.3	870.2	920.0
GDP in purchasers' values	12,587.1	12,931.5	13,364.9

Source: Asian Development Bank, *Key Indicators of Developing Asian and Pacific Countries*.

BALANCE OF PAYMENTS (US $ million)

	1998	1999	2000
Exports of goods f.o.b.	899.9	979.9	1,327.1
Imports of goods f.o.b.	−1,073.2	−1,211.5	−1,525.1
Trade balance	−173.3	−231.6	−198.0
Exports of services	109.2	130.8	169.9
Imports of services	−175.1	−204.7	−243.5
Balance on goods and services	−239.2	−305.5	−271.6
Other income received	17.8	20.4	31.8
Other income paid	−51.3	−61.9	−84.0
Balance on goods, services and income	−272.7	−346.9	−323.8
Current transfers received	224.0	235.9	304.8
Current transfers paid	−0.6	−1.6	−0.3
Current balance	−49.3	−112.6	−19.3
Capital account (net)	42.0	44.1	38.1
Direct investment from abroad	120.7	143.6	125.7
Other investment assets	−21.0	−61.0	−80.5
Other investment liabilities	54.8	43.7	62.0
Net errors and omissions	−116.5	−7.9	−40.0
Overall balance	30.7	49.9	85.9

Source: IMF, *International Financial Statistics.*

External Trade

PRINCIPAL COMMODITIES (US $ million)

Imports c.i.f.	1998	1999	2000*
Cigarettes	144	119	70
Petroleum products	111	131	175
Motorcycles	44	36	31
Total (incl. others)	1,189	1,337	1,885

Exports f.o.b.	1998	1999	2000*
Crude rubber†	27	28	30
Logs and sawn timber†	178	111	49
Clothing	392	564	1,012
Total (incl. others)‡	867	971	1,399

* Estimates.

† Including estimates for illegal exports.

‡ Including re-exports (US $ million): 263 in 1998; 261 in 1999; 296 (estimate) in 2000.

Sources: IMF, *Cambodia: Statistical Appendix* (February 2002).

PRINCIPAL TRADING PARTNERS (US $ million)

Imports c.i.f.	1999	2000	2001
China, People's Republic	85.9	112.9	169.7
France	41.9	39.3	52.5
Hong Kong	185.7	254.3	288.5
Indonesia	50.9	68.4	73.8
Japan	73.9	58.4	52.4
Korea, Republic	79.9	76.9	111.7
Malaysia	49.9	64.2	66.5
Singapore	99.1	106.0	406.9
Thailand	195.2	221.8	513.2
Viet Nam	85.6	91.5	100.7
Total (incl. others)	1,240.9	1,417.6	2,183.4

Exports f.o.b.	1999	2000	2001
China, People's Republic	8.9	23.8	33.5
France	20.7	27.7	38.5
Germany	40.4	66.0	121.1
Japan	9.3	10.7	55.9
Hong Kong	38.3	262.2	67.7
Singapore	181.7	18.0	49.6
Thailand	18.5	22.9	11.2
United Kingdom	53.4	81.6	105.4
USA	235.8	739.7	898.1
Viet Nam	391.8	19.5	21.5
Total (incl. others)	1,322.8	1,357.6	1,550.5

Source: Asian Development Bank, *Key Indicators of Developing Asian and Pacific Countries.*

Transport

RAILWAYS (traffic)

	1997	1998	1999
Freight carried ('000 metric tons)	16	294	259
Freight ton-km ('000)	36,514	75,721	76,171
Passengers ('000)	553	438	431
Passenger-km ('000)	50,992	43,847	49,894

Source: Ministry of Economy and Finance, Phnom-Penh.

ROAD TRAFFIC (motor vehicles in use at 31 December)

	1998	1999	2000
Passenger cars	208,452	257,711	312,303
Buses and coaches	10,335	14,241	18,918
Lorries and vans	17,494	36,768	49,036
Road tractors	52,021	64,080	77,139
Motorcycles and mopeds	1,138,705	1,361,874	1,609,839

Source: International Road Federation, *World Road Statistics.*

SHIPPING

Merchant Fleet (registered at 31 December)

	1999	2000	2001
Number of vessels	300	405	564
Displacement ('000 grt)	998.7	1,447.5	1,996.7

Source: Lloyd's Register-Fairplay, *World Fleet Statistics.*

International Sea-borne Freight Traffic (estimates, '000 metric tons)

	1988	1989	1990
Goods loaded	10	10	11
Goods unloaded	100	100	95

Source: UN, *Monthly Bulletin of Statistics.*

CIVIL AVIATION (traffic on scheduled services)

	1975	1976	1977
Passenger-kilometres (million)	42	42	42
Freight ton-kilometres ('000)	400	400	400

Source: Statistisches Bundesamt, Wiesbaden, Germany.

Tourism

FOREIGN TOURIST ARRIVALS (by air)*

Country of residence	1998	1999	2000
Australia	6,777	9,471	11,350
Canada	3,298	5,415	5,646
China, People's Repub.	18,035	26,805	30,586
France	18,616	23,754	24,883
Germany	4,199	6,490	7,298
Japan	13,386	17,885	19,906
Korea, Repub.	4,467	6,377	7,536
Malaysia	11,019	12,541	14,701
Singapore	9,123	10,634	10,734
Taiwan	18,239	20,607	21,626
Thailand	10,983	15,272	16,550
United Kingdom	11,156	13,843	15,912
USA	17,945	30,301	35,814
Viet Nam	3,044	5,217	8,333
Total (incl. others†)	186,333	262,907	351,661

* Figures for individual countries refer to arrivals at Pochentong (Phnom-Penh) airport only.

† Including arrivals at Siem Reap airport (10,423 in 1998; 28,525 in 1999; 87,012 in 2000).

Total arrivals (incl. arrivals by land and sea): 367,743 in 1999; 466,365 in 2000 (Source: IMF, *Cambodia: Statistical Appendix*, February 2002).

Source: Ministry of Tourism, Phnom-Penh.

Tourism receipts (US $ million): 166 in 1998; 190 in 1999; 228 in 2000 (Source: World Bank).

Communications Media

	1999	2000	2001
Television receivers ('000 in use)	98	99	n.a.
Telephones ('000 main lines in use)	27.7	30.9	33.5
Mobile cellular telephones ('000 subscribers)	89.1	130.5	223.5
Personal computers ('000 in use)	13	15	20
Internet users ('000)	4.0	6.0	10.0

Facsimile machines (number in use): 884 in 1995; 1,470 in 1996; 2,995 in 1997.

Source: International Telecommunication Union.

Radio receivers ('000 in use): 1,120 in 1995; 1,300 in 1996; 1,340 in 1997 (Source: UNESCO, *Statistical Yearbook*).

Education*

(2000/01)

	Institutions	Teachers	Students
Primary	5,468	52,168	2,408,109
Secondary	662	23,952	388,664
Junior high school	511	18,952	283,578
Senior high school	151	5,000	105,086

* Excluding technical and vocational education and higher education.

Source: IMF, *Cambodia: Statistical Appendix* (February 2002).

Adult literacy rate (UNESCO estimates): 67.8% (males 79.8%; females 57.1%) in 2000 (Source: UN Development Programme, *Human Development Report*).

Directory

The Constitution

The Constitution was promulgated on 21 September 1993; a number of amendments were passed on 4 March 1999. The main provisions are summarized below:

GENERAL PROVISIONS

The Kingdom of Cambodia is a unitary state in which the King abides by the Constitution and multi-party liberal democracy. Cambodian citizens have full right of freedom of belief; Buddhism is the state religion. The Kingdom of Cambodia has a market economy system.

THE KING

The King is Head of State and the Supreme Commander of the Khmer Royal Armed Forces. The monarchist regime is based on a system of selection: within seven days of the King's death the Royal Council of the Throne (comprising the Chairman of the Senate, the Chairman of the National Assembly, the Prime Minister, the Supreme Patriarchs of the Mohanikay and Thoammayutikanikay sects, the First and Second Vice-Chairmen of the Senate and the First and Second Vice-Chairmen of the National Assembly) must select a King. The King must be at least 30 years of age and be a descendant of King Ang Duong, King Norodom or King Sisowath. The King appoints the Prime Minister and the Cabinet. In the absence of the King, the Chairman of the Senate assumes the duty of acting Head of State.

THE LEGISLATURE

Legislative power is vested in the National Assembly (the lower chamber) and the Senate (the upper chamber). The National Assembly has 122 members who are elected by universal adult suffrage. A member of the National Assembly must be a Cambodian citizen by birth over the age of 25 years and has a term of office of five years, the term of the National Assembly. The National Assembly may not be dissolved except in the case where the Royal Government (Cabinet) has been dismissed twice in 12 months. The National Assembly may dismiss cabinet members or remove the Royal Government from office by passing a censure motion through a two-thirds majority vote of all the representatives in the National Assembly. The Senate comprises nominated members, the number of which does not exceed one-half of all of the members of the National Assembly; two are nominated by the King, two are elected by the National Assembly and the remainder are elected by universal adult suffrage. A member of the Senate has a term of office of six years. The Senate reviews legislation passed by the National Assembly and acts as a co-ordinator between the National Assembly and the Royal Government. In special cases, the National Assembly and the Senate can assemble as the Congress to resolve issues of national importance.

CABINET

The Cabinet is the Royal Government of the Kingdom of Cambodia, which is led by a Prime Minister, assisted by Deputy Prime Ministers, with state ministers, ministers and state secretaries as members. The Prime Minister is designated by the King at the recommendation of the Chairman of the National Assembly from among the representatives of the winning party. The Prime Minister appoints the members of the Cabinet, who must be representatives in the National Assembly or members of parties represented in the National Assembly.

THE CONSTITUTIONAL COUNCIL

The Constitutional Council's competence is to interpret the Constitution and laws passed by the National Assembly and reviewed completely by the Senate. It has the right to examine and settle disputes relating to the election of members of the National Assembly and the Senate. The Constitutional Council consists of nine members with a nine-year mandate. One-third of the members are replaced every three years. Three members are appointed by the King, three elected by the National Assembly and three appointed by the Supreme Council of the Magistracy.

The Government

HEAD OF STATE

HM King NORODOM SIHANOUK; acceded to the throne on 24 September 1993.

ROYAL GOVERNMENT OF CAMBODIA
(August 2002)

A coalition of the Cambodian People's Party (CPP) and the FUNCINPEC Party.

Prime Minister: HUN SEN (CPP).

Deputy Prime Minister and Co-Minister of the Interior: SAR KHENG (CPP).

Deputy Prime Minister and Minister of Education, Youth and Sport: TOL LAH (FUNCINPEC).

Senior Ministers: TEA BANH (CPP), KEAT CHHON (CPP), SOK AN (CPP), HOR NAM HONG (CPP), LU LAY SRENG (FUNCINPEC), CHHIM SEAK LENG (FUNCINPEC), HONG SUN HUOT (FUNCINPEC), YOU HOCKRY (FUNCINPEC).

Minister in charge of the Council of Ministers: SOK AN (CPP).

Co-Ministers of Defence: TEA BANH (CPP), Prince SISOWATH SIREIRATH (FUNCINPEC).

Co-Minister of the Interior: YOU HOCKRY (FUNCINPEC).

Minister of Relations with the National Assembly and Inspection: KHUN HAING (FUNCINPEC).

Minister of Foreign Affairs and International Co-operation: HOR NAM HONG (CPP).

Minister of Economy and Finance: KEAT CHHON (CPP).

Minister of Information: LU LAY SRENG (FUNCINPEC).

Minister of Health: HONG SUN HUOT (FUNCINPEC).

Minister of Industry, Mines and Energy: SUY SEM (CPP).

Minister of Planning: CHHAY THAN (CPP).

Minister of Commerce: CHAM PRASIDH (CPP).

Minister of Agriculture, Forestry, Hunting and Fisheries: CHAN SARUN (CPP).

Minister of Culture and Fine Arts: Princess NORODOM BOPHA DEVI (FUNCINPEC).

Minister of Environment: Dr MOK MARETH (CPP).

Minister of Rural Development: LY THUCH (FUNCINPEC).

Minister of Social Affairs, Labour, Professional Training and Youth Rehabilitation: ITH SAM HENG (CPP).

Minister of Posts and Telecommunications: SO KHUN (CPP).

Minister of Cults and Religions: CHEA SAVOEURN (FUNCINPEC).

Minister of Women's Affairs and Veterans: MOU SOK HUOR (FUNCINPEC).

Minister of Public Works and Transport: KHY TAING LIM (FUNCINPEC).

Minister of Justice: NIEV SITHONG (FUNCINPEC).

Minister of Tourism: VENG SEREIVUTH (FUNCINPEC).

Minister of Territorial Organization and Urbanization: IM CHHUN LIM (CPP).

Minister of Water Resources and Meteorology: LIM KEAN HOR (CPP).

Secretary of State for Public Civil Servants: PICH BUN THIN (CPP).

Secretary of State for Civil Aviation: POK SAM EL (FUNCINPEC).

There are also 52 further Secretaries of State.

MINISTRIES

Ministry of Agriculture, Forestry and Fisheries: 200 blvd Norodom, Phnom-Penh; tel. (23) 211351; fax (23) 217320; e-mail ranyvireak@hotmail.com; internet www.fadinap.org/cambodia.

Ministry of Commerce: 20 blvd Norodom, Phnom-Penh; tel. (23) 723775; fax (23) 426396; e-mail sekimoto@bigpond.com.kh; internet www.moc.gov.kh.

Ministry of Cults and Religions: Preah Sisowath Quay, rue 240, Phnom-Penh; tel. (23) 723172; fax (23) 725699; e-mail sophearin@camnet.com.kh.

Ministry of Culture and Fine Arts: 274 blvd Monivong, cnr rue Red Cross, Phnom-Penh; tel. (23) 362647.

Ministry of Defence: blvd Pochentong, Phnom-Penh; tel. (23) 366170; fax (23) 366169.

Ministry of Economy and Finance: 60 rue 92, Phnom-Penh; tel. (23) 722863; fax (23) 427798.

Ministry of Education, Youth and Sport: 80 blvd Norodom, Phnom-Penh; tel. (23) 217253; fax (23) 217250; e-mail crsmeys@camnet.com.kh; internet www.moeys.gov.kh.

Ministry of Environment: 48 blvd Sihanouk Tonle Bassac, Chamkar Morn, Phnom-Penh; tel. (23) 724901; fax (23) 427844; e-mail minenvlb@forum.org.kh; internet www.camnet.com.kh/moe-library/.

Ministry of Foreign Affairs and International Co-operation: 161 Preah Sisowath Quay, Phnom-Penh; tel. (23) 216141; fax (23) 216144; e-mail mfaicasean@bigpond.com.kh; internet www.mfaic.gov.kh.

Ministry of Health: 128 blvd Kampuchea Krom, Phnom-Penh; tel. (23) 366553; fax (23) 426841.

Ministry of Industry, Mines and Energy: 45 blvd Preah Norodom, Phnom-Penh; tel. and fax (23) 428263.

Ministry of Information: Department of International Co-operation and ASEAN Affairs, 62 blvd Monivong, Phnom-Penh; tel. (16) 815237; fax (23) 722618; e-mail coci@camnet.com.kh; internet www.moi-coci.gov.kh.

Ministry of the Interior: 275 blvd Norodom, Phnom-Penh; tel. (23) 363653; fax (23) 212708.

Ministry of Justice: blvd Sothearos, cnr rue 240, Phnom-Penh; tel. (23) 360320; fax (23) 360327.

Ministry of Planning: blvd Monivong, Sangkat Boeung Keng Kong 2, Phnom-Penh; tel. (23) 362307.

Ministry of Posts and Telecommunications: cnr rue Preah Ang Eng and rue Ang Non, Phnom-Penh; tel. (23) 426510; fax (23) 426011; e-mail koyks@camnet.com.kh; internet www.mptc.gov.kh.

Ministry of Public Works and Transport: 200 blvd Norodom, Phnom-Penh; tel. and fax (23) 427862; e-mail mpwt@mpwt.gov.kh; internet www.mpwt.gov.kh.

Ministry of Rural Development: blvd Czechoslovakia/blvd Pochentong, Phnom-Penh; tel. (23) 722425; fax (23) 722425.

Ministry of Social Affairs, Labour, Professional Training and Youth Rehabilitation: 68 blvd Norodom, Phnom-Penh; tel. (23) 725191; fax (23) 427322.

Ministry of Tourism: 3 blvd Monivong, Phnom-Penh 12258; tel. (23) 212837; fax (23) 426877; e-mail info@mot.gov.kh; internet www.mot.gov.kh.

Ministry of Water Resources and Meteorology: Phnom-Penh; internet www.domc.com.kh.

Ministry of Women's Affairs and Veterans: Toultum Poung II, Khan Chamcarmon, Phnom-Penh; tel. (23) 366412; fax (23) 428084.

Legislature

NATIONAL ASSEMBLY

National Assembly, blvd Samdech Sothearos, cnr rue 240, Phnom-Penh; tel. (23) 214136; fax (23) 217769; e-mail kimhenglong@cambodian-parliament.org; internet www.cambodian-parliament.org.

Chairman: Prince NORODOM RANARIDDH (FUNCINPEC).

Election, 26 July 1998

	% of Votes	Seats
Cambodian People's Party	41.4	64
FUNCINPEC Party	31.7	43
Sam Rainsy Party	14.3	15
Others	12.6	—
Total	100.0	122

SENATE

Senate, Chamcarmon Palace, blvd Norodom, Phnom-Penh; tel. (23) 211446; fax (23) 211441; e-mail oum_sarith@camnet.com.kh; internet www.khmersenate.org.

Chairman: CHEA SIM (CPP).

First Vice-Chairman: CHIVAN MONIRAK (FUNCINPEC).

Second Vice-Chairman: NHIEK BUNCHHAY (FUNCINPEC).

Inauguration, 25 March 1999

	Seats
Cambodian People's Party	31
FUNCINPEC Party	21
Sam Rainsy Party	7
King's appointees	2
Total	61

Political Organizations

Buddhist Liberal Party (Kanakpak Serei Niyum Preah Put Sasna): Phnom-Penh; internet www.blp.org; f. 1998; Chair. IENG MULI; Gen. Sec. SIENG LAPRESSE.

Cambodian Freedom Fighters: 2728 E 10th Street, Long Beach, CA 90804, USA; tel. (562) 433-9930; fax (562) 7490; internet www.cffighters.org; f. 1998 in opposition to Hun Sen's leadership; Leader CHHUN YASITH; Sec.-Gen. RICHARD KIRI KIM.

Cambodian People's Party (CPP) (Kanakpak Pracheachon Kampuchea): Chamcarmon, 203 blvd Norodom, Phnom-Penh; tel. and fax (23) 2158801; e-mail cpp@thecpp.org; internet www.thecpp.org; (known as the Kampuchean People's Revolutionary Party 1979–91); 21-mem. Standing Cttee of the Cen. Cttee; Cen. Cttee of 153 full mems; Hon. Chair. of Cen. Cttee HENG SAMRIN; Chair. of Cen. Cttee CHEA SIM; Vice-Chair. HUN SEN; Chair. of Permanent Cttee SAY CHHUM.

Democratic National United Movement (DNUM): Pailin; f. 1996 by IENG SARY, following his defection from the PDK; not a national political party, did not contest 1998 election; DNUM members are also free to join other political parties.

FUNCINPEC Party (United National Front for an Independent, Neutral, Peaceful and Co-operative Cambodia Party): 11 blvd Monivong (93), Sangkat Sras Chak, Khan Daun Penh, Phnom Penh; tel. (23) 428864; fax (23) 426521; e-mail funcinpec@funcinpec.org; internet www.funcinpec.org; FUNCINPEC altered its title to the FUNCINPEC Party when it adopted political status in 1992; the party's military wing was the National Army of Independent Cambodia (fmrly the Armée Nationale Sihanoukiste—ANS); merged with the Son Sann Party in Jan. 1999; Pres. Prince NORODOM RANARIDDH; Sec.-Gen. Prince NORODOM SIRIVUDH.

Hang Dara Movement Democratic Party: c/o National Assembly, blvd Samdech Sothearos, cnr rue 240, Phnom-Penh; f. 2002 by HANG DARA to contest 2003 general election; breakaway faction of the FUNCINPEC Party.

Khmer Citizens' Party (Kanakpak Pulroat Khmer): Phnom-Penh; f. 1996; breakaway faction of Khmer Nation Party (now Sam Rainsy Party); Chair. NGUON SOEUR; Sec.-Gen. IEM RA.

Khmer Democracy Party (Kanakpak Pracheathippatei Khmer): Phnom-Penh; Pres. UK PHURI.

Khmer Neutral Party (Kanakpak Kampuchea Appyeakroet): 14A rue Keo Chea, Phnom-Penh; tel. (23) 62365; fax (23) 27340; e-mail Masavang@datagraphic.fr; internet www.datagraphic.fr/knp/;Pres. BUO HEL.

Khmer Republican Democratic Party (KRDP): Phnom-Penh; f. 1997; supports CPP; Chair. NHUNG SEAP.

Liberal Democratic Party: Phnom-Penh; f. 1993; receives support from members of the armed forces; pro-Government; Chair. Gen. CHHIM OM YON.

MOLINAKA (National Liberation Movement of Cambodia): c/o National Assembly, blvd Samdech Sothearos, cnr rue 240, Phnom-Penh; a breakaway faction of FUNCINPEC; Pres. PRUM NEAKAREACH.

National Union Party (Kanakpak Ruop Ruom Cheat): Phnom-Penh; established by rebel mems of FUNCINPEC Party; Chair. TOAN CHHAY; Sec.-Gen. UNG PHAN.

New Society Party: see Sangkum Thmei Party.

Norodom Chakrapong Khmer Soul Party: c/o National Assembly, blvd Samdech Sothearos, cnr rue 240, Phnom-Penh; f. 2002 by Prince NORODOM CHAKRAPONG; breakaway faction of FUNCINPEC Party.

Reastr Niyum (Nationalist Party): blvd Norodom, Phnom-Penh; tel. (23) 215659; fax (23) 215279; f. 1998; breakaway faction of the FUNCINPEC Party; Pres. UNG HUOT; Sec.-Gen. PU SOTHIRAK.

Sam Rainsy Party (SRP): 71 blvd Sothearos, Phnom-Penh; tel. and fax (23) 217452; e-mail samrainsy@everyday.com.kh; internet www.samrainsyparty.org; f. 1995 as the Khmer Nation Party; name changed as above in 1998; 441,159 mems (Aug. 2001); Pres. SAM RAINSY; Sec.-Gen. MENG RITA (acting).

Sangkum Thmei Party (New Society Party): 4 rue 310, Phnom-Penh; f. 1997 by Loy Simchheang, formerly the Gen. Sec. of FUNCINPEC.

United Front for the Construction and Defence of the Kampuchean Fatherland (UFCDKF): Phnom-Penh; f. 1978 as the Kampuchean National United Front for National Salvation (KNUFNS), renamed Kampuchean United Front for National Construction and Defence (KUFNCD) in 1981, present name adopted in 1989; mass organization supporting policies of the CPP; an 89-mem. Nat. Council and a seven-mem. hon. Presidium; Chair. of Nat. Council CHEA SIM; Sec.-Gen. ROS CHHUN.

Uphold the Cambodian Nation Party: Phnom-Penh; f. 1997 by Pen Sovan, fmr Sec.-Gen. of the Cen. Cttee of the CPP, to contest the 1998 legislative elections; Chair. PEN SOVAN.

Diplomatic Representation

EMBASSIES IN CAMBODIA

Australia: Villa 11 R. V., Senei Vinnavaut Oum (rue 254), Chartaumuk, Khan Daun Penh, Phnom-Penh; tel. (23) 213470; fax (23) 213413; e-mail australian.embassy.cambodia@dfat.gov.au; Ambassador: LOUISE HAND.

Brunei: 237 rue Pasteur 51, Sangkat Boeung Keng Kang 1, Khan Chamcarmon, Phnom-Penh; tel. (23) 211457; fax (23) 211455; e-mail brunei@bigpond.com.kh; Ambassador: (vacant).

Bulgaria: 227/229 blvd Norodom, Phnom-Penh; tel. (23) 217504; fax (23) 212792; e-mail bulgembpnp@camnet.com.kh; Chargé d'affaires a.i.: ROUMEN DONTCHEV.

Canada: Villa 9, R.V. Senei Vinnavaut Oum, Sangkat Chartaumuk, Khan Daun Penh, Phnom-Penh; tel. (23) 213470; fax (23) 211389; e-mail cdnemb@bigpond.com.kh; internet www.dfait-maeci.gc.ca/cambodia; Ambassador: STEFANIE BECK.

China, People's Republic: 156 blvd Mao Tse Toung, Phnom-Penh; tel. (12) 810928; fax (23) 364738; Ambassador: NING FUKUI.

Cuba: 96/98 rue 214, Sangkat Veal Vong, Khan 7 Makara, Phnom-Penh; tel. (23) 213965; fax (23) 217428; e-mail embacuba@camnet.com.kh; Ambassador: NIVSIA CASTRO GUEVARA.

France: 1 blvd Monivong, Phnom-Penh; tel. (23) 430020; fax (23) 430041; e-mail ambafrance@bigpond.com.kh; internet www.ambafrance.gov.kh; Ambassador: ANDRÉ-JEAN LIBOUREL.

Germany: 76–78 rue Yougoslavie, BP 60, Phnom-Penh; tel. (23) 216381; fax (23) 427746; e-mail germanembassy@everyday.com.kh; Ambassador: Dr HELMUT OHLRAUN.

India: Villa 777, blvd Monivong, Phnom-Penh; tel. (23) 210912; fax (23) 213640; e-mail embindia@bigpond.com.kh; Ambassador: PRADEEP KUMAR KAPUR.

Indonesia: 179 rue Pasteur, Khan Daun Penh, Phnom-Penh; tel. (23) 216148; fax (23) 216571; Ambassador: NAZARUDDIN NASUTION.

Japan: 194 blvd Norodom, Sangkat Tonle Bassac, Khan Chamkarmon, Phnom-Penh; tel. (23) 217161; fax (23) 216162; e-mail eojc@bigpond.com.kh; internet www.bigpond.com.kh/users/eojc/index-e.htm; Ambassador: GOTARO OGAWA.

Korea, Democratic People's Republic: 39 rue 268, Phnom-Penh; tel. (15) 912567; fax (23) 426230; Ambassador: KIM JONG NAM.

Korea, Republic: 64 rue 214, Sangkar Beung Rain, Khan Daun Penh, Phnom-Penh; tel. (23) 211901; fax (23) 211903; e-mail koreanemb@bigpond.com.kh; Ambassador: LEE WUN-HYUNG.

Laos: 15–17 blvd Mao Tse Toung, POB 19, Phnom-Penh; tel. (23) 982632; fax (23) 720907; Ambassador: LY SOUTHAVILAY.

Malaysia: Villa 11, 5 rue 254, Sangkat Chaktomouk, Khan Daun Penh, Phnom-Penh; tel. (23) 216176; fax (23) 216004; e-mail mwppenh@bigpond.com.kh; Ambassador: Dato' AHMAD ANUAR ABDUL HAMID.

Myanmar: 181 blvd Norodom, Phnom-Penh; tel. (23) 213664; fax (23) 213665; e-mail M.E.PHNOMPENH@bigpond.com.kh; Ambassador: U TINT LWIN.

Philippines: 33 rue 294, Khan Chamcarmon, Sangkat Tonle Bassac, Phnom-Penh; tel. (23) 215145; fax (23) 215143; e-mail phnompenhpe@bigpond.com.kh; Ambassador: VOLTAIRE T. GAZMIN.

Poland: 767 blvd Monivong, POB 58, Phnom-Penh; tel. (23) 217782; fax (23) 217781; e-mail emb.pol.pp@bigpond.com.kh; Ambassador: KAZIMIERZ A. DUCHOWSKI.

Russia: 213 blvd Sothearos, Phnom-Penh; tel. (23) 210931; fax (23) 216776; e-mail russemba@bigpond.com.kh; Ambassador: VICTOR V. SAMOILENKO.

Singapore: 92 blvd Norodom, Phnom-Penh; tel. (23) 360855; fax (23) 360850; e-mail singemb@bigpond.com.kh; Ambassador: VERGHESE MATHEWS.

Thailand: 196 blvd Norodom, Sangkat Tonle Bassac, Khan Chamkarmon, Phnom-Penh; tel. (23) 363869; fax (18) 810860; e-mail thaipnp@mfa.go.th; Ambassador: CHATCHAWED CHARTSUWAN.

United Kingdom: 27–29 Sras Chak, Khan Daun Penh, Phnom-Penh; tel. (23) 427124; fax (23) 427125; e-mail BRITEMB@bigpond.com.kh; Ambassador: STEPHEN BRIDGES.

USA: 16 rue 228, Phnom-Penh; tel. (23) 216436; fax (23) 216437; internet www.usembassy.state.gov/cambodia/; Ambassador: CHARLES AARON RAY (designate).

Viet Nam: 436 blvd Monivong, Phnom-Penh; tel. (23) 362741; fax (23) 427385; e-mail embbvnpp@camnet.com.kh; Ambassador: NGUYEN DU HONG.

Judicial System

An independent judiciary was established under the 1993 Constitution.

Supreme Court: rue 134, cnr rue 63, Phnom-Penh; tel. 17816663; Chair. DID MONTY.

Religion

BUDDHISM

The principal religion of Cambodia is Theravada Buddhism (Buddhism of the 'Tradition of the Elders'), the sacred language of which is Pali. A ban was imposed on all religious activity in 1975. By a constitutional amendment, which was adopted in April 1989, Buddhism was reinstated as the national religion and was retained as such under the 1993 Constitution. By 1992 2,800 monasteries (of a total of 3,369) had been restored and there were 21,800 Buddhist monks. In 1992 about 90% of the population were Buddhists.

Supreme Patriarchs: Ven. Patriarch TEP VONG, Ven. Patriarch BOU KRI.

Patriotic Kampuchean Buddhists' Association: Phnom-Penh; mem. of UFCDKF; Pres. LONG SIM.

CHRISTIANITY

The Roman Catholic Church

Cambodia comprises the Apostolic Vicariate of Phnom-Penh and the Apostolic Prefectures of Battambang and Kompong-Cham. At 31 December 2000 there were an estimated 19,959 adherents in the country, equivalent to about 0.2% of the population. An Episcopal Conference of Laos and Kampuchea was established in 1971. In 1975 the Government of Democratic Kampuchea banned all religious practice in Cambodia, and the right of Christians to meet to worship was not restored until 1990.

Vicar Apostolic of Phnom-Penh: Rt Rev. EMILE DESTOMBES (Titular Bishop of Altava), 787 blvd Monivong (rue 93), BP 123, Phnom-Penh; tel. and fax (23) 212462; e-mail evecam@camnet.com.kh.

ISLAM

Islam is practised by a minority in Cambodia. Islamic worship was also banned in 1975, but it was legalized in 1979, following the defeat of the Democratic Kampuchean regime.

The Press

NEWSPAPERS

Newspapers are not widely available outside Phnom-Penh.

Areyathor (Civilization): 52 rue Lyuk Lay, Sangkat Chey, Chummneah, Phnom-Penh; tel. (23) 913662; Editor CHIN CHAN MONTY.

Bayon Pearnik: 3 rue 174, POB 2279, Phnom-Penh; tel. (12) 803968; fax (23) 211921; e-mail bp@forum.org.kh; internet www.bayonpearnik.com; f. 1995; English; monthly; Publr and Editor ADAM PARKER; circ. 10,000.

Cambodia Daily: 50B rue 240, Phnom-Penh; tel. (23) 426602; fax (23) 426573; e-mail aafc@forum.org.kh; internet www.cambodiadaily.com; f. 1993; in English and Khmer; Mon.–Sat.; Editor CHRIS DECHERD; Publr BERNARD KRISHER; circ. 3,500.

Cambodia New Vision: POB 158, Phnom-Penh; tel. (23) 219898; fax (23) 360666; e-mail cabinet1b@camnet.com.kh; internet www.cnv.org.kh; f. 1998; official newsletter of the Cambodian Govt.

Cambodia Times: 236 blvd Mao Tse Toung, Phnom-Penh; tel. (23) 721274; fax (23) 426647; f. 1992 (in Kuala Lumpur, Malaysia); English; weekly; Editor KAMARAI ZAMANTABY.

Chakraval: 3 rue 181, Sangkat Tumnop Teuk, Khan Chamkar Mon, Phnom-Penh; tel. (23) 913667; fax (23) 720141; Khmer; daily; Publr KEO SOPHORN; Editor SO SOVAN RITH.

Commercial News: 394 blvd Preah Sihanouk, Phnom-Penh; tel. (23) 721665; fax (23) 721709; e-mail tcnews@camnet.com.kh; f. 1993; Chinese; Chief Editor LIU XIAO GUANG; circ. 6,000.

Construction (Kasang): 126 rue 336, Sangkat Phsar Deum Kor, Khan Tuol Kok, Phnom-Penh; tel. 18818292; Khmer; Editor CHHEA VARY.

Equality Voice: 470 rue 163, Sangkat Boeung Keng Kang, Khan Chamka Mon, Phnom-Penh; tel. 12842471; Khmer; Publr HUON MARA.

Intervention: 56 rue 234, Sangkat Phsar Deum Kor, Khan Toul Kok, Phnom-Penh; tel. 12843285; Khmer; Editor NGUON THAI DAY.

Kampuchea: 158 blvd Norodom, Phnom-Penh; tel. (23) 725559; f. 1979; weekly; Chief Editor KEO PRASAT; circ. 55,000.

Khmer Wisdom: 1588 Khan Russei Keo, Phnom-Penh; tel. 12841377; Khmer; Publr CHEA CHAN THON.

Khmer Youth Voice: 240 rue 374, Sangkat Toul Prey 2, Khan Chamkar Mon, Phnom-Penh; tel. (23) 211336; fax (23) 210137; e-mail sovann@camnet.com.kh; Khmer; twice weekly; Editor UO SOVANN.

Koh Santepheap (Island of Peace): 165 rue 199, East of Sport City, Phnom-Penh; tel. (23) 880052; fax (23) 364515; e-mail kohsantepheap@camnet.com.kh; Khmer; Publr THONG UY PANG.

Moneaksekar Khmer: 27 rue 318, Sangkat Toul Svay Prey 1, Khan Chamkar Mon, Phnom-Penh; tel. (23) 990777; Editor DAM SITHIK.

Neak Chea: 1 rue 158, Daun Penh, Phnom-Penh; tel. (23) 428653; fax (23) 427229; e-mail adhoc@forum.org.kh.

Phnom Penh Daily: 5 rue 84, Corner 61, Sangkat Srah Chak, Khan Daun Penh, Phnom-Penh; tel. 15917682; e-mail ppenhdaily@camnet.com.kn; internet www.phnompenhdaily.com.kh; Khmer; available online in English; Editor VA DANE.

Phnom Penh Post: 10A rue 264, Phnom-Penh; tel. (23) 210309; fax (23) 426568; e-mail michael.pppost@bigpond.com.kh; internet www.phnompenhpost.com; f. 1992; English; fortnightly; Editor-in-Chief MICHAEL HAYES; Publrs MICHAEL HAYES, KATHLEEN HAYES.

Pracheachon (The People): 101 blvd Norodom, Phnom-Penh; tel. (23) 723665; f. 1985; 2 a week; organ of the CPP; Editor-in-Chief SOM KIMSUOR; circ. 50,000.

Rasmei Kampuchea: 476 blvd Monivong, Phnom-Penh; tel. (23) 362881; fax (23) 362472; e-mail rasmei.kampuchea@bigpond.com.kh; daily; local newspaper in northern Cambodia; Editor PEN SAMITHY.

Samleng Thmei (New Voice): 91 rue 139, Sangkat Veal Vong, Khan 7, Phnom-Penh; tel. 15920589; Khmer; Editor KHUN NGOR.

NEWS AGENCIES

Agence Kampuchia de Presse (AKP): 62 blvd Monivong, Phnom-Penh; tel. (23) 430564; e-mail akp@camnet.com.kh; internet www.camnet.com.kh/akp; f. 1978; Dir-Gen. KIT-KIM HUON.

Foreign Bureaux

Agence France-Presse (AFP) (France): 8 rue 214, POB 822, Phnom-Penh; tel. (23) 426227; fax (23) 426226; Correspondent STEFAN SMITH.

Associated Press (AP) (USA): 18C rue 19, BP 870, Phnom-Penh; tel. (23) 426607; e-mail ap@bigpond.com.kh; Correspondent CHRIS FONTAINE.

Deutsche Presse-Agentur (dpa): 5E rue 178, Phnom-Penh; tel. (23) 427846; fax (23) 427846; Correspondent JOE COCHRANE.

Reuters (UK): 15 rue 246, Phnom-Penh; tel. (23) 360334; fax (23) 723405; Bureau Chief ROBERT BIRSEL.

Xinhua (New China) News Agency (People's Republic of China): 19 rue 294, Phnom-Penh; tel. (23) 211608; fax (23) 426613; Correspondent LEI BOSONG.

ASSOCIATIONS

Cambodian Association for the Protection of Journalists (CAPJ): POB 816, Phnom-Penh; tel. (15) 997004; fax (23) 215834; e-mail umsarin@hotmail.com; Pres. UM SARIN.

Khmer Journalists' Association: 101 blvd Preah Norodom, Phnom-Penh; tel. (23) 725459; f. 1979; mem. of UFCDKF; Pres. PIN SAMKHON.

League of Cambodian Journalists (LCJ): 74 rue 205, Sangkat Toulsvayprey, Khan Chamkamon, Phnom-Penh; tel. and fax (23) 360612; Pres. OM CHANDARA.

Broadcasting and Communications

TELECOMMUNICATIONS

Cambodian Samart Communication: 33 blvd Samdech Sothearos, Phnom-Penh; tel. (15) 910022; fax (15) 911703; e-mail somchai.an@hello016-gsm.com; internet www.hello016-gsm.com; operates a national mobile telephone network; CEO SOMCHAI AN.

Camintel: 1 quai Sisowath, Phnom-Penh; tel. (23) 981234; fax (23) 981277; e-mail support@camintel.com; internet www.camintel.com; a jt venture between the Ministry of Posts and Telecommunications and the Indonesian co, Indosat; operates domestic telephone network; Chair. STEVE YANUAN.

Camshin Corporation: 26 rue Preah Monivong, Phnom-Penh; tel. (23) 60001; fax (23) 61234; a jt venture between the Ministry of Posts and Telecommunications and the Thai co, Shinawatra International Co Ltd; telephone communications co.

Telstra Corpn: 58 blvd Norodom, Phnom-Penh; tel. (23) 426022; fax (23) 426023; e-mail Paul.Blanche-Horgan@team.telstra.com;

Australian corpn contracted to manage the international calls system until Oct. 2001; Man. PAUL BLANCHE-HORGAN.

BROADCASTING

Radio

Apsara: 69 rue 57, Sangkat Boeung Keng Kang 1, Khan Chamkarmorn, Phnom-Penh; tel. (23) 303002; fax (23) 214302; internet www.apsaratv.com.kh; Head of Admin. KEO SOPHEAP; News Editor SIN SO CHEAT.

Bayon: c/o Bayon Media Group, 954 rue 2, Takhmau, Kandal Province; tel. (23) 363695; fax (23) 363795; e-mail bayontv@camnet.com.kh; internet www.bayontv.com.kh; Dir-Gen. KEM KUNNAVATH.

Bee Hive Radio: 41 rue 214, Phnom-Penh; tel. (23) 720401; Dir-Gen. MAM SONANDO.

FM 90 MHZ: 65 rue 178, Phnom-Penh; tel. (23) 363699; fax (23) 368623; Dir-Gen. NHIM BUN THON; Dep. Dir-Gen. TUM VANN DET.

FM 99 MHZ: 41 rue 360, Phnom-Penh; tel. (23) 426794; Gen. Man. SOM CHHAYA.

FM 107 MHZ: 81 rue 562, Phnom-Penh; tel. (23) 428047; fax (23) 368212; Dir-Gen. KHUN HANG.

Phnom-Penh Municipality Radio: 131–132 blvd Pochentong, Phnom-Penh; tel. (23) 725205; fax (23) 360800; Gen. Man. KHAMPUN KEOMONY.

RCAF Radio: c/o Borei Keila, rue 169, Phnom-Penh; tel. (23) 366061; fax (23) 366063; f. 1994; Royal Cambodian Armed Forces radio station; Dir THA TANA; News Editor SENG KATEKA.

Vithyu Cheat Kampuchea (National Radio of Cambodia): rue Preah Kossamak, Phnom-Penh; tel. (23) 368140; fax (23) 427319; f. 1978; fmrly Vithyu Samleng Pracheachon Kampuchea (Voice of the Cambodian People); controlled by the Ministry of Information and the Press; home service in Khmer; daily external services in English, French, Lao, Vietnamese and Thai; Dir-Gen. VANN SENG LY; Dep. Dir-Gen. TAN YAN.

Voice of Cambodia: Phnom Penh; e-mail vocri@vocri.org; internet www.vocri.org; Cambodia's first international internet radio station.

There are also eight private local radio stations based in Phnom-Penh, Battambang Province, Sihanoukville, and Stung Treng Province.

Television

Apsara Television (TV11): 69 rue 57, Sangkat Boeung Keng Kang 1, Khan Chamkamorn, Phnom-Penh; tel. (23) 303002; fax (23) 214302; internet www.apsaratv.com.kh; Dir-Gen. SOK EISAN.

Bayon Television (TV27): 954 rue 2, Takhmau, Kandal Province; tel. (23) 363695; fax (23) 363795; e-mail bayontv@camnet.com.kh; internet www.bayontv.com.kh; Dir-Gen. KEM KUNNAVATH.

National Television of Cambodia (Channel 7): 26 blvd Preah Monivong, Phnom-Penh 12201; tel. (23) 722943; fax (23) 426407; e-mail tvk@camnet.gov.kh; internet www.tvk.gov.kh; opened 1983; broadcasts for 10 hours per day in Khmer; Dir-Gen. (Head of Television) MAO AYUTH.

Phnom-Penh Television (TV3): 2 blvd Russia, Phnom-Penh; tel. (12) 814323; fax (23) 360800; e-mail tv3@camnet.com.kh; internet www.tv3.com.kh; Dir-Gen. KHAMPHUN KEOMONY.

RCAF Television (TV5): 165 rue 169, Borei Keila, Phnom-Penh; tel. (23) 366061; fax (23) 366063; e-mail mica.t.v.5@bigpond.com.kh; Editor-in-Chief PRUM KIM.

TV Khmer (TV9): 81 rue 562, Phnom-Penh; tel. (23) 428047; fax (23) 368212; Dir-Gen. KHOUN ELYNA; News Editor PHAN TITH.

Finance

BANKING

The National Bank of Cambodia, which was established as the sole authorized bank in 1980 (following the abolition of the monetary system by the Government of Democratic Kampuchea in 1975), is the central bank, and assumed its present name in February 1992. The adoption of a market economy led to the licensing of privately owned and joint-venture banks from July 1991. At June 1999 there were a further 32 banks operating in Cambodia, including two state-owned banks, 22 locally incorporated private banks and eight branches of foreign banks. Rural financing was often provided by a decentralized system of non-governmental organizations. Plans were confirmed in early 1998 to establish a Rural Development Bank. These institutions are under the supervision of the National Bank of Cambodia.

Central Bank

National Bank of Cambodia: 22–24 blvd Norodom, BP 25, Phnom-Penh; tel. (23) 722563; fax (23) 426117; e-mail nbc2@bigpond.com.kh; f. 1980; cap. 100,000m., res 752,036m., dep. 979,083m. riels (Dec. 2000); Gov. CHEA CHANTO; Dep. Gov. ENG THAYSAN.

State Banks

Foreign Trade Bank: 3 rue 53-114, Sangkat Phsar Thmey I, Khan Daun Penh, Phnom-Penh; tel. (23) 724466; fax (23) 426108; scheduled for privatization; Man. TIM BO PHOL.

Rural Development Bank: 5 rue Preah Ang Eng & rue Preah Ang No, Sangkat Watt Phnom Khan Daun Penh, Phnom-Penh; tel. (23) 982434.

Private Banks

Advanced Bank of Asia Ltd: 97–99 blvd Preah Norodom, Sangkat Boeung Raing, Khan Daun Penh, Phnom-Penh; tel. (23) 720434; fax (23) 720435; Dir CHAE WAN CHO.

Agriculture and Commercial Bank of Cambodia (ACBC) Ltd: 49 rue 214, Samdach Pann, Phnom-Penh; tel. (23) 722272; fax (23) 426683; e-mail 012812428@mobitel.com.kh; Man. THAI SOVANA.

Cambodia Agriculture, Industrial and Merchant Bank: 87 blvd Preah Norodom, Sangkat Phsar Thmey III, Khan Daun Penh, Phnom-Penh; tel. (23) 218667; fax (23) 217751; e-mail kien@bigpond.com.kh; Man. CHHOR SANG.

Cambodia Asia Bank Ltd: 252 blvd Preah Monivong, Sangkat Phsar Thmey II, Khan Daun Penh, Phnom-Penh; tel. (23) 722105; fax (23) 426628; e-mail cab@camnet.com.kh; Man. WONG TOW FOCK.

Cambodia Farmers Bank: 45 rue Kampuchea Viet Nam, Phnom-Penh; tel. (23) 426183; fax (23) 426801; f. 1992; joint venture by Thai business executives and the National Bank of Cambodia; Man. PHOT PUNYARATABANDHU; Dep. Man. NORODOM ARUNRASMY; 2 brs.

Cambodia International Bank Ltd: 21 rue 128, 107 S. Monorom, Khan 7 Makara, Phnom-Penh; tel. (23) 725920; Man. CHIEE YOON CHENG.

Cambodia Mekong Bank: 1 rue Kramoun Sar, Sangkat Phsar Thmey I, Khan Daun Penh, Phnom-Penh; tel. (23) 217114; fax (23) 217122; e-mail ho.mailbox@mekongbank.com; cap. US \$13m, dep. US \$4.4m. (Dec. 2001); Chair. MICHAEL C. STEPHEN; Pres. and CEO KHOV BOUN CHHAY.

Cambodian Commercial Bank Ltd: 26 blvd Preah Monivong, Sangkat Phsar Thmey II, Khan Daun Penh, Phnom-Penh; tel. (23) 426145; fax (23) 426116; e-mail CCBPP@bigpond.com.kh; f. 1991; cap. US \$10m., res US \$0.2m., dep. US \$44.7m. (Dec. 2000); Chair MALEERATNA PLUMCHITCHOM; Dir and Gen. Man. SAHASIN YUTTARAT; 4 brs.

Cambodian Public Bank (Campu Bank): Villa 23, rue Kramoun Sar, Sangkat Phsar Thmey II, Khan Daun Penh, Phnom-Penh; tel. (23) 214111; fax (23) 217655; e-mail campu@bigpond.com.kh; cap. US \$15m., dep. US \$40.6m. (Dec. 2001); Man. CHAN KOK CHOY.

Canadia Bank Ltd: 265–269 rue Preah Ang Duong, Sangkat Wat Phnom, Khan Daun Penh, Phnom-Penh; tel. (23) 215286; fax (23) 427064; e-mail canadia@camnet.com.kh; internet www.canadiabank.com; f. 1991; cap. 50.6m. riels; res 32.3m. riels; dep. 411.6m. riels (2001); Man. PUNG KHEAV SE; 8 brs.

Chansavangwong Bank: 145A–145B rue 154–51, Khan Daun Penh, Phnom-Penh; tel. (23) 427464; fax (23) 427461; Man. TAING LI PHENG.

Emperor International Bank Ltd: 230–232 blvd Preah Monivong, Sangkat Phsar Thmey II, Khan Daun Penh, Phnom-Penh; tel. (23) 426254; fax (23) 428585; e-mail eib@bigpond.com.kh; Man. VAN SOU IENG.

First Overseas Bank Ltd: 20 rue Kramoun Sar, Sangkat Phsar Thmey II, Khan Daun Penh, Phnom-Penh; tel. (23) 213023; fax (23) 427439; e-mail firstoverseas@worldmail.com.kh; Man. CHOY SOOK KUEN; 3 brs.

Global Commercial Bank Ltd: 337 blvd Monivong, Sangkat Orassey 4, Khan 7 Makara, Phnom-Penh; tel. (23) 364258; fax (23) 426612; e-mail gcb@camnet.com.kh; Man. WELLSON HSIEH.

Great International Bank Ltd: 320A–320B blvd Monivong, Khan Daun Penh, Phnom-Penh; tel. (23) 427282; Man. LY TAK BOUALAY.

Khmer Bank (Thaneakar Khmer): 116 rue Sihanouk, Phnom-Penh; tel. (23) 724853; Man. HÉNG KIM Y.

Pacific Commercial Bank Ltd: 350 rue 217, Sangkat Orassey 2, Khan 7 Makara, Phnom-Penh; tel. (23) 426896; Man. TENG DANNY.

Phnom-Penh City Bank Ltd: 101 blvd Norodom, rue 214, Phnom-Penh; tel. (23) 427354; fax (23) 427353; Man. THEERAYUT SEANG AROON.

Rich Nation Bank Ltd: 272–278 Charles de Gaulle, Sangkat Orassey 2, Khan 7 Makara, Phnom-Penh; tel. (23) 720100; fax (23) 720118; e-mail richbank@bigpond.com.kh; Man. HENRY SHI CALLE; Dep. Man. DANIEL CHAN.

Singapore Banking Corporation Ltd: 68 rue Samdech Pan, BP Sangkat Boeung Reang, Khan Daun Penh, Phnom-Penh; tel. (23) 217772; fax (23) 212121; e-mail info@sbc-bank.com; internet www.sbc-bank.com; f. 1993; cap. US $5.5m., dep. US $6.8m. (Dec. 2000); Pres. ANDY KUN; Chair. KAY HONG KUN.

Singapore Commercial Bank Ltd: 316 blvd Preah Monivong, Sangkat Chaktomuk, Khan Daun Penh, BP 1199, Phnom-Penh; tel. and fax (23) 427471; cap. US $5m.; Pres. KONG LOOK SEN; Gen. Man. TEOH SAM MING; 1 br.

Union Commercial Bank Ltd: UCB Building, 61 rue 130, Sangkat Phsar Chas, Khan Daun Penh, Phnom-Penh; tel. (23) 427995; fax (23) 427997; e-mail ucb@bigpond.com.kh; internet www.cambodia-web.net/banking/ucb; f. 1994; cap. US $13m., res US $4m., dep. US $28m. (2001); CEO YUM SUI SANG; 3 brs.

Foreign Banks

Bangkok Bank Ltd (Thailand): 26 M.V. Preah Norodom, POB. 106, Phnom-Penh; tel. (23) 723598; fax (23) 426593; Man. THEWAKUN CHANAKUN.

Crédit Agricole Indosuez (France): 70 blvd Preah Norodom, POB 923, Sangkat Boeung Raing, Khan Daun Penh, Phnom-Penh; tel. (23) 427233; fax (23) 214481; Man. BERNARD PARDIGON.

Krung Thai Bank PLC (Thailand): 149 rue 215 Jawaharlal Nehru, Depot Market 1, Khan Tuolkok Division, Phnom-Penh; tel. (23) 366005; fax (23) 428737; e-mail ktbpmp@camnet.com.kh; Man. NAKROB U-SETTHASAKDI.

Lippo Bank (Indonesia): 273 Preah Andoung, S.K. Wat Phnom, Khan Daun Penh, Phnom-Penh; Man. MARKUS PARMADI.

Maybank Bhd (Malaysia): 4 rue Kramoun Sar, Sangkat Boeung Raing, Khan Daun Penh, Phnom-Penh; tel. (23) 210123; fax (23) 210099;e-mail mbb@camnet.com.kh; internet www.maybank2u.com.my; Man. ABDUL MALEK MOHD KHAIR.

Standard Chartered Bank (UK): 89 blvd Preah Norodom, POB 46, Sangkat Boeung Raing, Khan Daun Penh, Phnom-Penh; tel. (23) 212732; fax (23) 216687; CEO ONG TENG HOON; 1 br.

INSURANCE

Commercial Union: 28 rue 47, Phnom-Penh; tel. (23) 426694; fax (23) 427171; general insurance; Gen. Man. PAUL CABLE.

Indochine Insurance Ltd: 55 rue 178, BP 808, Phnom-Penh; tel. (23) 210701; fax (23) 210501; e-mail insurance@indochine.com.kh; internet www.indochine.net; Dir PHILIPPE LENAIN.

Trade and Industry

DEVELOPMENT ORGANIZATIONS

Council for the Development of Cambodia (CDC): Government Palace, quai Sisowath, Wat Phnom, Phnom-Penh; tel. (23) 981156; fax (23) 428426; f. 1993; Chair. HUN SEN; Sec.-Gen. SOK CHENDA.

Cambodian Investment Board (CIB): Government Palace, quai Sisowath, Wat Phnom, Phnom-Penh; tel. (23) 981156; fax (23) 428426; f. 1993; e-mail CDC.CIB@bigpond.com.kh; internet www.cambodiainvestment.gov.kh; part of CDC; sole body responsible for approving foreign investment in Cambodia, also grants exemptions from customs duties and other taxes, and provides other facilities for investors; Chair. HUN SEN; Sec.-Gen. SOK CHENDA.

CHAMBER OF COMMERCE

Phnom-Penh Chamber of Commerce: 22 rue Kramuon Sar, Sangkat Phsar Thmei 2, Khan Daun Penh, Phnom-Penh; tel. (23) 212265; fax (23) 212270; f. 1995; Pres. SOK KONG.

INDUSTRIAL AND TRADE ASSOCIATIONS

Cambodian Garment Factory Association (CGFA): Phnom-Penh; tel. (12) 888222; fax (23) 427983; Pres. VAN SOU IENG; Sec. ROGER TAN.

Export Promotion Department: Ministry of Commerce, 20A blvd Norodom, Phnom-Penh; tel. (23) 210365; fax (23) 217353; e-mail ogawa@bigpond.com.kh; internet www.moc.gov.kh/depts/epd/general.htm; f. 1997; Dir PRAK NORK.

UTILITIES

Electricity

Electricité du Cambodge: rue 19, Wat Phnom, Khan Daun Penh, Phnom-Penh; tel. (23) 724771; fax (23) 426938; e-mail yim_nolson@bigpond.com.kh; state-owned; Man. Gen. TAN KIM VIN.

Water

Phnom-Penh Water Supply Authority: rue 108, 12201 Phnom-Penh; tel. (23) 724046; fax (23) 428969; e-mail ppwsa@bigpond.com.kh; f. 1996 as an autonomous public enterprise; Dir-Gen. EK SON CHAN.

MAJOR COMPANIES

Cambodia Beverage Co: 287 Phum Mittapheap, District Russey Keo, Phnom-Penh; tel. (18) 810401; fax (18) 810402; mfr of soft drinks.

Cambodia Cement Co: 3 rue 598, Khum Tuk Thla, District Russey Keo, Phnom-Penh; tel. (23) 27540; fax (23) 27815; production of cement.

Continental Indochine Import/Export Co Ltd: 139 blvd Monivong, Phnom-Penh; tel. (23) 366602; fax (23) 366604; e-mail cil@bigpond.com.kh; f. 1992; aviation fuel supply and bulk fuel distribution; mfr of knitwear and woven garments; bar, restaurant and hotel management; Group Chair. CLIVE MCLEOD FAIRFIELD.

Hung Hiep (Cambodia) Co Ltd: 159 rue Pasteur, Phnom-Penh; tel. (23) 213527; fax (23) 216659; dealers in passenger and commercial vehicles.

Muhibbahh Engineering (Cambodia) Ltd: 315 Mao Tse Toung Blvd, Sangkat Phsar Dept III, Khan Toul Kork, Phnom-Penh; tel. and fax (23) 366888; civil engineering, general contracting, real estate development, architectural services.

Total Cambodia: 121 blvd Norodom, Phnom-Penh; tel. (23) 427995; fax (23) 217662; e-mail total.cambodge@camnet.com.kh; international petroleum co.

TRADE UNIONS

Association of Independent Cambodian Teachers: 33 rue 432, Sangkat Boeng Trabaek, Khan Chamka Morn, Phnom Penh; Pres. RUNG CHHUN; Gen.-Sec. CHEA MUNI.

Cambodian Federation of Independent Trade Unions (CFITU): Phnom-Penh; e-mail CFITU@bigpond.com.kh; f. 1979 as Cambodian Federation of Trade Unions; changed name as above in 1999; Chair. ROS SOK; Vice-Chair. TEP KIM VANNARY, KIENG THISOTHA.

Cambodian Union Federation: f. 1997 with the support of the CPP in response to the formation of the FTUWKC.

Free Trade Union of Workers of the Kingdom of Cambodia (FTUWKC): e-mail ftuwkc@forum.org.kh; fmrly Free Trade Union of Khmer Workers, f. 1996 by Mary Ou with the assistance of Sam Rainsy; Leader CHEA VICHEA; Gen. Sec. SUM SAMNEANG.

Transport

RAILWAYS

Royal Railway of Cambodia: Central Railway Station, Railway Square, Sangkat Srach Chak, Khan Daun Penh, Phnom-Penh; tel. 12994168; fax (23) 430815; e-mail RRCcambodia@mobitel.mibitel.com.kh; comprises two 1,000 mm-gauge single-track main lines with a total length of 650 km: the 385-km Phnom-Penh to Poipet line (of which the 48-km Sisophon to Poipet link is awaiting restoration), the 264-km Phnom-Penh to Sihanoukville line and branch lines and special purpose sidings 100 km; the condition of the lines is very poor, with many temporary repairs, owing to mine damage, and the service also suffers from other operational difficulties, such as a shortage of rolling stock; there are 14 'Gares' (main stations), 19 stations and 38 halts; Dir SOKHOM PHEAKAVANMONY.

ROADS

In 1997 the total road network was 35,769 km in length, of which 4,165 km were highways and 3,604 km were secondary roads. In the same year about 7.5% of the road network was paved, but this figure rose to an estimated 11.6% in 1999. West and East Cambodia were linked by road for the first time in December 2001, with the opening of a bridge across the Mekong River.

INLAND WATERWAYS

The major routes are along the Mekong river, and up the Tonlé Sap river into the Tonlé Sap (Great Lake), covering, in all, about 2,400 km. The inland ports of Neak Luong, Kompong Cham and Prek Kdam have been supplied with motor ferries, and the ferry crossings have been improved.

SHIPPING

The main port is Sihanoukville, on the Gulf of Thailand, which has 11 berths and can accommodate vessels of 10,000–15,000 tons. Phnom-Penh port lies some distance inland. Steamers of up to 4,000 tons can be accommodated.

CIVIL AVIATION

There is an international airport at Pochentong, near Phnom-Penh. Prince Norodom Chakkrapong established a new airline named Phnom-Penh Airlines in 1999.

State Secretariat of Civil Aviation (SSCA): 62 blvd Norodom, Phnom-Penh; tel. (16) 855373; fax (23) 426169; e-mail ksaphal-ssca@camnet.com.kh; Dir-Gen. KEO SAPHAL.

Mekong Airlines: Phnom-Penh; f. 2002; joint venture between Hun Kim Leng Investment (51%) and Australian co Via Aviation (49%); domestic and international flights to eight destinations.

President Airlines: 50 blvd Norodom, Phnom-Penh; tel. (23) 427402; fax (23) 212992; f. 1998; domestic and, from August 2002, international passenger services.

Royal Khmer Airlines: 19 Unit 12, rue Preah Kossomak, Phnom-Penh; tel. (23) 216899; fax (23) 428279; f. 2000; domestic and international services.

Royal Phnom-Penh Airways: 209 rue 19, Zingkat Chey Chumneah, Khan Daun Penh, Phnom-Penh; tel. (23) 217419; fax (23) 217420; internet www.rippairways.com; f. 1999; scheduled and charter passenger flights to domestic and regional destinations; Chair. NORODOM CHAKRAPONG.

Siem Reap Airways International: 61A rue 214, Sangkat Beoung Rang, Khan Daun Penh, Phnom-Penh; tel. (23) 720022; fax (23) 720522; internet www.siemreapairways.com; f. 2000; scheduled international and domestic passenger services; CEO PRASERT PRASARTTONG-OSOTH.

Tourism

Tourist arrivals increased to 367,743 in 1999, owing to the improvement in the security situation, and rose to an estimated 466,365 in 2000, in which year tourist receipts reached US $178m. In the first half of 2001 tourist arrivals increased by 33% in comparison with the corresponding period of the previous year, reaching 297,500. In late 2001, however, Cambodia's tourism sector was badly affected by the repercussions of the terrorist attacks on the USA in September. During the first half of 2002 visitor arrivals reached 363,026, an increase of 48.1% in comparison with the corresponding period in 2001.

General Directorate for Tourism: 3 blvd Monivong, Phnom-Penh; tel. (23) 427130; fax (23) 426107; e-mail tourism@camnet.com.kh; f. 1988; Dir SO MARA.

Defence

In August 2001 the total strength of the Royal Cambodian Armed Forces was estimated to be 140,000 (including provincial forces): army 90,000, navy 3,000, air force 2,000 and provincial forces about 45,000. There was a system of conscription in force, for those aged between 18 and 35, for five years, although this had not been implemented since 1993. Paramilitary forces are organized at village level. The defence budget for 2001 was estimated at 500,000m. riels.

Supreme Commander of the Royal Cambodian Armed Forces: King NORODOM SIHANOUK.

Commander-in-Chief: Gen. KE KIMYAN.

Education

Primary education is compulsory for six years between the ages of six and 12. In 1997 enrolment in primary schools was equivalent to 113% of school-age children (males 123%; females 104%). Secondary education comprises two cycles, each lasting three years. In 1996 enrolment at secondary level was equivalent to 24% of those in the relevant age-group (males 31%; females 17%).

In 1996 enrolment at tertiary level was equivalent to 1.0% of those in the relevant age-group (males 2.0%; females 0.5%). Institutions of higher education included Phnom-Penh University, an arts college, a technical college, a teacher-training college, a number of secondary vocational schools and an agricultural college. In 1993, according to a sample survey, the average rate of adult illiteracy was 34.7% (males 20.3%, females 46.6%). Rates varied between urban and rural areas; adult illiteracy in Phnom-Penh was 18.0% (males 8.1%; females 36.7%), whereas in rural areas it was 36.5% (males 21.4%; females 49.0%).

Bibliography

See also Laos and Viet Nam

Acharya, A., Lizée, P., and Peou, S. (Eds). *Cambodia—The 1989 Paris Peace Conference.* New York, Kraus International, 1991.

Ann, Porn Moniroth. *Democracy in Cambodia: Theories and Realities.* Translated by Khieu Mealy and edited by Sok Siphana, Phnom-Penh, Cambodian Institute for Co-operation and Peace, 1996.

Ayres, David M. *Anatomy of a Crisis. Education, Development and the State in Cambodia, 1953–1998.* University of Hawai'i Press, 2001.

Barron, John, and Paul, Anthony. *Peace with Horror: The Untold Story of Communist Genocide in Cambodia.* London, Hodder and Stoughton, 1977.

Becker, Elizabeth. *When the War was Over.* New York, Simon and Schuster, 1987.

Bekaert, Jacques. *Kampuchea Diary 1983–1986: Selected Articles by Jacques Bekaert.* Bangkok, DD Books, 1987.

Briggs, L. P. *The Ancient Khmer Empire.* Philadelphia, Transactions of the American Philosophical Society, 1951.

Brown, Frederick Z., and Timberman, David G. *Cambodia and the International Community: The Quest for Peace, Development and Democracy.* Singapore, Institute of Southeast Asian Studies, 1998.

Carney, Timothy, and Tan Lian Choo. *Whither Cambodia? Beyond the Election.* Singapore, Institute of Southeast Asian Studies, 1993.

Chanda, Nayan. *Brother Enemy. The War after the War.* San Diego, CA, Harcourt Brace Jovanovich, 1986.

Chandler, David P. *A History of Cambodia.* Boulder, CO, Westview Press, 2nd Edn, 1991.

The Tragedy of Cambodian History: Politics, War and Revolution since 1945. New Haven, CT, Yale University Press, 1992.

Brother Number One: A Political Biography of Pol Pot. Boulder, CO, Westview Press, 1992.

Voices from S-21: Terror and History in Pol Pot's Secret Prison. Berkeley, CA, University of California Press, 2000.

Chandler, David P., and Kiernan, B. *Revolution and its Aftermath in Kampuchea.* New Haven, CT, Yale University Press, 1983.

Chandler, David P., Kiernan, B., and Boua, C. *Pol Pot Plans the Future: Confidential Leadership Documents from Democratic Kampuchea.* New Haven, CT, Yale University Press, 1988.

Chang Pao-min. *Kampuchea between China and Vietnam.* Singapore, Singapore University Press, 1985.

Coedes, G. *Les Etats hindouisés d'Indochine et d'Indonésie.* Paris, F. de Boccard, 1948.

Corfield, Justin J. *The Royal Family of Cambodia.* Melbourne, Khmer Language and Culture Centre, 2nd revised Edn, 1993.

Khmers Stand Up! Clayton, Vic, Monash University Centre for Southeast Asian Studies, 1994.

Cour, Claude-Gilles. *Institutions Constitutionelles et Politiques du Cambodge.* Paris, 1965.

Deedrick, Tami. *Khmer Empires (Ancient Civilisations).* London, Raintree Steck-Vaughn, 2001.

Delvert, J. *Le Paysan Cambodgien.* Paris and The Hague, 1961.

DePaul, Kim (Ed.). *Children of Cambodia's Killing Fields: Memoirs by Survivors.* New Haven, CT, Yale University Southeast Asia Studies, 1997.

Doyle, Michael W. *UN Peacekeeping in Cambodia: UNTAC's Civilian Mandate.* Boulder, CO, Lynne Rienner Publishers, 1995.

Ebihara, May M., Mortland, Carol, and Ledgerwood, Judy (Eds). *Cambodian Culture Since 1975.* London, Cornell, 1994.

Engelbert, Thomas, and Goscha, Christopher. *Falling Out of Touch: A Study on Vietnamese Policy Towards an Emerging Cambodian Communist Movement, 1930–1975.* Clayton, Vic, Monash University Asia Institute, 1995.

Etcheson, Craig. *The Rise and Demise of Democratic Kampuchea.* Boulder, CO, Westview Press, 1984.

Evans, Grant, and Rowley, Kelvin. *Red Brotherhood at War.* London, Verso, 1984, revised Edn 1990.

Findlay, Trevor. *Cambodia: The Legacy and Lessons of Untac.* Oxford, Oxford University Press, 1995.

Fitzsimmons, T. (Ed.). *Cambodia, its People, its Society, its Culture.* New Haven, CT, HRAF Press, 2nd Edn, 1959.

Gaillard, Maurice. *Démocratie Cambodgienne: La Constitution du 24 Septembre 1993.* Paris, L'Harmattan, 1944.

Gottesman, Evan R. *Cambodia After the Khmer Rouge: Inside the Politics of Nation Building.* New Haven, CT, Yale University Press, 2002.

Groslier B. *Angkor et le Cambodge au XVIe siècle*. Paris, 1958.

Guy, John. *Sanctuary: the Temples of Angkor*. London, Phaidon Press, 2002.

Hamel, Bernard. *Sihanouk et le Drame Cambodgien*. Paris, L'Harmattan, 1993.

Heder, Steve, and Ledgerwood, Judy (Eds). *Propaganda, Politics and Violence in Cambodia*. London, M. E. Sharpe, 1996.

Hertz, M. F. *A Short History of Cambodia from the days of Angkor to the Present*. London, Stevens and Sons, 1958.

Higham, Charles. *The Civilisation of Angkor*. Weidenfeld, 2001.

Hughes, Caroline. *Untac in Cambodia: The Impact on Human Rights*. Singapore, Institute of Southeast Asian Studies, 1996.

Human Rights Watch/Asia. *Cambodia at War*. London, Human Rights Watch, 1995.

Isaacs, A. R. *Without Honour: Defeat in Vietnam and Cambodia*. Baltimore, MD, Johns Hopkins University Press, 1983.

Jackson, Karl (Ed.). *Cambodia, 1975–1978: Rendezvous with Death*. Princeton, NJ, Princeton University Press, 1990.

Jennar, Raoul M. (Ed.). *The Cambodian Constitutions (1953–1993)*. Bangkok, White Lotus Co, 1995.

Kamm, Henry. *Cambodia: Report from a Stricken Land*. London/New York, Arcade, 1998.

Kèn, Khun. *De la Dictature des Khmers Rouges à l'Occupation Vietnamienne: Cambodge, 1975–1979*. Paris, L'Harmattan, 1994.

Kiernan, Ben. *How Pol Pot Came to Power*. London, Verso/New Left Books, 1985.

(Ed.). *Genocide and Democracy in Cambodia*. New Haven, CT, Yale University Southeast Asia Studies, 1993.

The Pol Pot Regime: Race, Power and Genocide in Cambodia under the Khmer Rouge, 1975–1979. New Haven, CT, Yale University Press, 1996.

Kiernan, B., and Boua, C. (Eds). *Peasants and Politics in Kampuchea 1942–1981*. London, Zed Press, 1982.

Kiljuen, Kimmo (Ed.). *Kampuchea—Decade of the Genocide*. London, Zed Press, 1984.

Kirk, Donald. *Wider War: The Struggle for Cambodia, Thailand and Laos*. New York, Praeger, 1971.

Lafreniere, Bree. *Music Through The Dark: A Tale of Survival in Cambodia*. Honolulu, HI, University of Hawaii Press, 2000.

Leifer, Michael. *Cambodia—The Search for Security*. London, Pall Mall Press, 1967.

Conflict and Regional Order in South-East Asia. London, International Institute for Strategic Studies, Adelphi Papers No. 162, 1980.

Mabbett, I.W., and Chandler, D. *The Khmers*. Oxford, Blackwell, 1995.

Macdonald, M. *Angkor*. London, Jonathan Cape, 1958. Reissued by Oxford University Press, 1987.

Mannika, E. *Angkor Wat: Time, Space and Kingship*. Honolulu, University of Hawaii Press, 1996.

Martin, Marie A. *Le Mal Cambodgien*. Paris, Hachette, 1989.

Cambodia: A Shattered Society. London, University of California, 1994.

May, Someth. *Cambodian Witness*. London, Faber and Faber, 1986.

Mehta, Harish, and Mehta, Julie. *Hun Sen—Strongman of Cambodia*. Singapore, Graham Brash, 2000.

Morris, Stephen J. *Why Vietnam Invaded Cambodia*. London, Cambridge University Press, 2001.

Népote, Jacques. *Parenté et organisation sociale dans le Cambodge moderne et contemporain*. Geneva, Ouzane, 1992.

Népote, Jacques, and Vienne, Marie-Sybille. *Cambodge, Laboratoire d'une Crise*. Paris, Centre des Hautes Etudes sur l'Afrique et l'Asie Modernes, 1993.

Norodom Sihanouk. *War and Hope: the Case for Cambodia*. London, Sidgwick and Jackson, 1980.

Norodom Sihanouk, and Krisher, Bernard. *Sihanouk Reminisces: World Leaders I Have Known*. Bangkok, Editions Duang Kamol, 1990.

Osborne, M. E. *The French Presence in Cochinchina and Cambodia: Rule and Response, 1859–1905*. Ithaca, NY, 1969.

Politics and Power in Cambodia. Victoria, Camberwell, 1973.

Before Kampuchea, Preludes to Tragedy. London, Allen and Unwin, 1979.

Sihanouk: Prince of Light, Prince of Darkness. St Leonards, NSW, Allen and Unwin, 1994.

Ovesen, Jan; Trankell, Ing-Britt, and Öjendal, Joakim. *When Every Household is an Island: Social Organization and Power Structures in Rural Cambodia*. Uppsala, Uppsala Research Reports in Cultural Anthropology, No. 15, 1996.

Peou, Sorpong. *Conflict Neutralization in the Cambodia War: From Battlefield to Ballot-Box*. Kuala Lumpur, New York & Singapore, Oxford University Press, 1997.

Intervention and Change in Cambodia: Towards Democracy? Singapore, Institute of Southeast Asian Studies, 2000.

(Ed.). *Cambodia*. Aldershot, Hampshire, Ashgate Publishing Ltd, 2001.

Picq, Laurence. *Beyond the Horizon: Five Years with the Khmer Rouge*. New York, St Martin's Press, 1989.

Ponchaud, François. *Cambodge; Année Zéro*. Paris, Julliard, 1977; trans. as *Cambodia Year Zero*. Harmondsworth, Penguin, 1978.

Pradham, P. C. *Foreign Policy of Kampuchea*. London, Sangam Books, 1988.

Pradhan, M., and Prescott, N. *A Poverty Profile of Cambodia*. World Bank Discussion Papers, No 373, Washington, DC, World Bank, 1997.

Pran, D. (Ed.). *Children of Cambodia's Killing Fields: Memoirs by Survivors*. New Haven, CT, Yale University Press, 1997.

Preschez, Philippe. *Essai sur la Démocratie au Cambodge*. Paris, 1961.

Quigley, John, and Robinson, Kenneth. (Eds). *Documents from the Trial of Pol Pot and Ieng Sary*. Philadelphia, PA, University of Pennsylvania Press, 2000.

Roberts, David. *Political Transition in Cambodia 1991–1999: Power, Elitism and Democracy*. Richmond, Surrey, Curzon Press, 2001.

Ros, Chantrabot. *La République Khmère*. Paris, L'Harmattan, 1993.

Samphan, Khieu. *Cambodia's Economy and Industrial Development*. Translated and with an introduction by Laura Summers. Ithaca, NY, Cornell University Southeast Asia Program Data Paper III, 1979.

Shawcross, William. *Sideshow: Kissinger, Nixon and the Destruction of Cambodia*. London, André Deutsch, 1979.

The Quality of Mercy: Cambodia, Holocaust and Modern Conscience. London, André Deutsch, 1984.

Cambodia's New Deal. Washington, Carnegie Endowment for International Peace, 1994.

Smith, Roger M. 'Cambodia', in *Governments and Politics of Southeast Asia*, Kahin, G. (Ed.). Ithaca, NY, 1964.

Cambodia's Foreign Policy. Ithaca, NY, 1965.

Sola, Richard. *Le Cambodge de Sihanouk: Espoir, Désillusions et Amertume, 1982–1993*. Paris, Sudestasie, 1994.

Stuart-Fox, Martin, and Ung, Bunhaeng. *The Murderous Revolution*. Bangkok, Tamarind Press, 1986.

Szymusiak, N. *The Stones Cry Out: A Cambodian Childhood 1975–81*. London, Jonathan Cape, 1987.

Thion, Serge. *Watching Cambodia*. Bangkok, White Lotus Co, 1993.

United Nations. *The United Nations and Cambodia, 1991–1995*. New York, United Nations, 1995.

Utting, Peter (Ed.). *Between Hope and Insecurity: The Social Consequences of the Cambodian Peace Process*. Geneva, UNRISD, 1994.

Vandy, Kaonn. *Cambodge; 1940–1991 ou la Politique sans les Cambodgiens*. Paris, L'Harmattan, 1993.

Vickery, Michael. *Cambodia: 1975–1982*. Sydney, Allen and Unwin, 1984.

Kampuchea: Politics, Economics and Society. Sydney, Allen and Unwin, 1987.

Willmott, William E. *The Chinese in Cambodia*. Vancouver, 1967.

Yathay, Pin. *Stay Alive, My Son*. London, Bloomsbury, 1987.

Zhou Mei. *Radio UNTAC of Cambodia: Winning Ears, Hearts and Minds*. Bangkok, White Lotus Co, 1994.

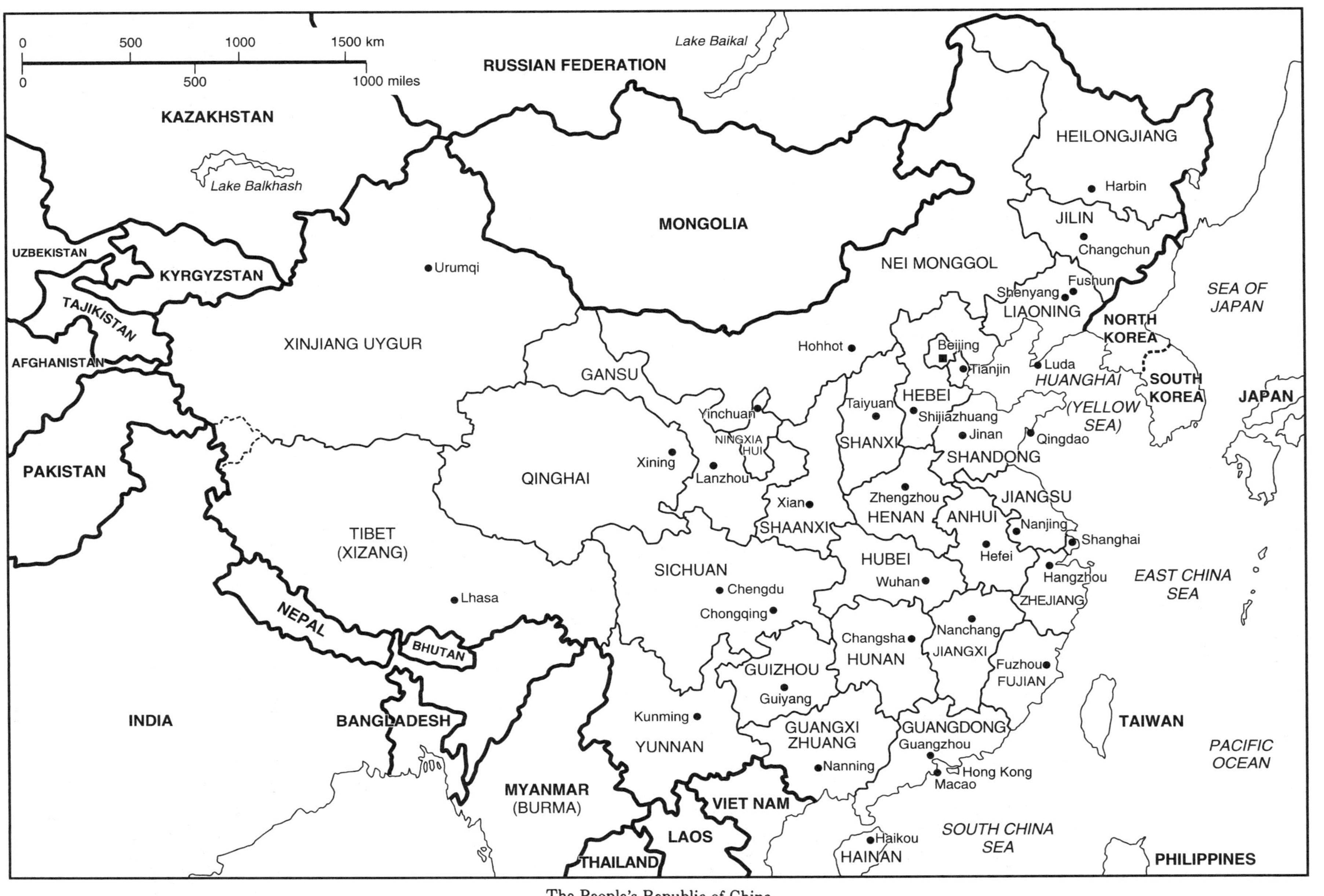

The People's Republic of China

THE PEOPLE'S REPUBLIC OF CHINA

Physical and Social Geography

MICHAEL FREEBERNE

With additions by the editorial staff

The People's Republic of China covers an area of 9,571,300 sq km (almost 3.7m. sq miles) and extends about 4,000 km from north to south and 4,800 km from east to west. Owing to China's mountainous relief and the comparatively undeveloped state of transport, distance creates major economic and political problems. For example, not only is it costly and technically difficult to build a dense communications network, but also repeated attempts to move industry inland and away from the established centres in the east have been seriously hindered by such factors as the long haul for raw materials and markets. Similarly, the vastness of China has made it very hard to provide strong central government from Beijing.

China's land frontiers extend for a total of 20,000 km, and have been the source of some tension. China shares frontiers with the Democratic People's Republic of Korea (North Korea), Mongolia, Russia, Kazakhstan, Kyrgyzstan, Tajikistan, Afghanistan, Pakistan, India, Nepal, Bhutan, Myanmar (formerly Burma), Laos and Viet Nam. The dispute over the boundary between China and India resulted in the border war of 1962. Negotiations regarding the settlement of the dispute by peaceful means continue. The two sections of the Sino-Russian border (in the north-east and the north-west of China) total more than 4,300 km. Various boundary incidents occurred after 1960, but subsequent negotiations resulted in the demarcation of large parts of both sections in the mid-1990s. The delimitation of the eastern section (some 4,200 km) was finally concluded in November 1997. Discussions concerning the shorter western section and the status of two islands continue. China's eastern seaboard is 14,000 km in length. Its territorial waters are dotted with some 5,000 islands, ranging from provincial-sized Hainan down to minute atolls, which include the strategically significant but disputed Xisha (Paracel) and Nansha (Spratly) Islands. Rich in fish (and also petroleum reserves), these waters make a significant contribution to the output of marine and fresh water aquatic products. China lacks an important seafaring tradition, however, partly because the relatively smooth coastline is largely without good natural harbours.

Administratively, the People's Republic of China is divided into 22 provinces, five autonomous regions, and four municipalities, all of which are directly under the central Government. There are more than 2,000 counties, which until the early 1980s were subdivided into more than 50,000 people's communes. As the communes underwent striking changes after their introduction in 1958, much of the effective economic and political organization in China was at production brigade and production team level, which frequently coincided with the natural village. The communes have been superseded by the household contract responsibility system, commonly centred upon the family unit. Other organizational structures, such as macroeconomic and military regions, may embrace various provinces, whilst, as part of Deng Xiaoping's economic reforms and the 'open door' policy, several Special Economic Zones have been established (including Shenzhen, Zhuhai, Shantou, Xiamen and Hainan). In the urban areas, tiny neighbourhood street committees keep a watchful eye on day-to-day activities.

PHYSICAL FEATURES

Physical size alone cannot automatically raise China to the rank of a first-class world power. The West regarded China as a land of fabulous wealth at the height of the Qing empire, but in fact the geographical environment presents considerable obstacles to modernization. According to official figures, in the late 1990s more than 13% of China's surface was cultivated, less than 17% was forest and almost 42% was grassland. Less than 33% of the area was classified as usable. In practice, China must feed more than 20% of the world's population on just 7% of its arable land and with only 8% of its fresh water, and each year farming land is lost while the population continues to expand. Between 1990 and 1994 a total of 1.5m. ha, or 1% of the area sown to grain crops, was lost, not only through increasing urbanization and industrial development, but also through drought and flooding. In May 1997 the Director of the State Land Administration announced the enforcement of stricter curbs on the use of land for non-agricultural development. In 2000 it was calculated that 2.62m. ha of China's territory (or 27% of the total land area) was affected by desertification, with this area expanding by 2,460 sq km annually. The total area affected by soil erosion, meanwhile, was estimated at 3.7m. sq km in 1997. The felling of trees in the remote north-western region of Xinjiang, China's driest area, was banned in mid-1997, in an attempt to halt the process of desertification.

Relief, configuration and climate are critical in suggesting possible settlement areas and zones suitable for economic development. For the most part high in the west and relatively low in the east, China has been compared to a three-section staircase. The Qinghai-Tibet (Xizang) plateau, at over 4,000 m, is the highest flight; next is an arc of plateaux and basins lying at 1,000 m–2,000 m, extending eastwards from the Tarim Basin, across Nei Monggol and the loess lands, then turning south to include the immensely fertile Sichuan Basin and the Yunnan-Guizhou plateau; much of the land that constitutes the lowest flight lies below 500 m and covers the most densely-settled areas, such as the middle and lower Changjiang (Yangtze) basin, the North China plain and the north-eastern plain. About 33% of China's total area comprises mountains; 26% is plateau land; 10% is hill country; 19% is occupied by basins; but only 12% of the surface is composed of plains.

Watering these plains are rivers which in some years bring rich harvests, while in other years they may cause flooding, or dry up altogether with resulting drought famines, which were frequent before 1949. Indeed, China has been characterized as a land that suffers from having either too much water or not enough water, both in terms of regional and seasonal distribution. In the north, the Huanghe (Yellow River) is 5,464 km in length and has a drainage basin of 752,443 sq km. In central China, the Changjiang is 6,300 km long with an annual flow of 9,513,000m. cu m, and a massive drainage basin of 1.8m. sq km, covering one-fifth of the country. The Zhujiang (2,214 km) flows through southern China. Water conservation is actively pursued, and flood control, irrigation, navigation and power generation are all emphasized in numerous multi-purpose projects.

China experienced exceptionally severe flooding of the Changjiang in mid-1998: more than 240m. people were affected, some 14m. people were forced to leave their homes, more than 3,000 people lost their lives and damage costing in excess of US $20,000m. was caused by the worst floods since 1954 (when 30,000 were killed). The authorities conceded that soil erosion, resulting from extensive deforestation, was largely responsible, and acknowledged the need for an accelerated tree-planting programme. The floods of mid-1999 led to over 1,000 deaths and the evacuation of 5.5m. citizens from their homes.

Hydroelectric power provided 7.8% of total energy output in 1999. In 1994 work commenced on the Three Gorges project in Hubei Province. To comprise a 1,983-m dam across the Changjiang and scheduled for completion in 2009, the plant will have an annual generating capacity of 84,700m. kWh of electricity, but involves the submerging of 17,000 ha of farmland

and the displacement of more than 1m. people (see Environmental Issues of Asia and the Pacific). The project will incorporate a massive water-conservancy programme. In November 1997 the damming of the Changjiang, and the diversion of the river into a man-made channel, marked the completion of the first phase of the project. The Xiaolangdi dam, part of a major water-conservancy project on the Huanghe, was completed in October 1997; power generation was to commence by the year 2001, annual capacity reaching 5,100m. kWh.

Increasingly, many Chinese cities, including Beijing and Tianjin, are suffering from acute water shortages. In 1997 it was estimated that some 200 cities were threatened with water deficiency, and scientists have warned of a serious shortage of drinking water by the early 21st century. Furthermore, the rapid degradation of the quality of water supplies through industrial pollution has become a cause of grave concern, leading the Government to implement stricter regulations. In mid-2001 the most severe drought for more than a decade was reported to have left millions of Chinese citizens without adequate drinking water, the most seriously affected areas being Shandong and Liaoning Provinces. In March 2001, meanwhile, the Government announced details of a major project to transport water, via three channels, from the south of the country to the drier northern regions. Construction was scheduled to commence in 2002.

CLIMATE

Climatically, China is dominated by a monsoonal regime. Cold air masses build up over the Asian land mass in winter, and the prevailing winds are offshore and dry. In summer there is a reversal of this pattern, and the rainy season is concentrated in the summer months over the most densely-settled parts of the country in the east and the south. Running from south to north there are six broad temperature zones: tropical and subtropical, warm-temperate and temperate, cold-temperate and the Qinghai-Tibet plateau area, which has its own characteristic regime. January is generally the coldest month and July the hottest. There is a great range in winter temperatures—as much as 15°C between the average for Guangzhou in the south and Harbin in the north. South of the Nanling mountains January temperatures average around 8°C, but they drop to between -8°C and -15°C over much of the north-east, Nei Monggol and the north-west. In summer the temperature difference between Guangzhou and Harbin narrows to 12°C and summer temperatures over much of the country average above 20°C.

The summer monsoon brings abundant rain to coastal China, especially in the south and east, but amounts decrease drastically to the north and west. A humid zone covers much of south-eastern China and the average annual rainfall is above 750 mm. In the semi-humid zone, extending across the north-east, the North China plain and the south-eastern region of the Qinghai-Tibet plateau, the average falls to less than 500 mm. The remainder of the Qinghai-Tibet, the loess, and the Nei Monggol plateaux receive only about 300 mm, while western Nei Monggol and Xinjiang, where there are extensive deserts, get less than 250 mm.

About 80% of the precipitation falls between May and October, with July and August the wettest months. Not infrequently the rain turns the rivers into raging torrents and disastrous floods occur; alternatively, not enough rain falls. To flood and drought can be added other calamities: typhoons, earthquakes, frosts, hailstorms, plant and animal pests, and diseases. The Chinese attributed the grave economic difficulties of the early 1960s, when millions died from starvation, to three factors: the withdrawal of Soviet aid, policy mistakes and natural calamities.

VEGETATION AND NATURAL RESOURCES

Over hundreds of years a great deal of China's natural vegetation has been stripped. The basic contrast is between the forests and woodlands of the eastern half of the country and the grassland-desert complex of the western half. Tree types vary from the tropical rain forests in the south, through evergreen broadleaved forests, mixed mesophytic forests, temperate deciduous broadleaved forests, and mixed northern hardwood and boreal coniferous forests in the north. The eastern Mongolian plateau, the Xiao Hinggan Ling and Da Hinggan Ling (the Lesser and Greater Khingan mountains), and the Changbaishan massif contain 60% of China's forest reserves. Other natural forests are located in Yunnan, Jiangxi, Fujian, Guizhou, Sichuan, Hainan and in the Qinling mountains and along the eastern edge of the Qinghai-Tibet plateau. Most of China's forests are largely inaccessible, however, and there is a serious shortage of workable timber. In 1987 there was a major ecological disaster when a forest fire laid waste vast stretches near to the north-eastern border with the USSR.

Owing to the widespread destruction of natural vegetation, soil erosion is a major problem. Sheet and gully erosion are common; water and wind erosion do great damage in the north, while water erosion is the chief enemy in the south; also, farming malpractices, such as deep ploughing, have aggravated the situation. It has been estimated that about 40% of the total cultivated area comprises 'poor' soils: red loams, saline-alkaline soil and some of the rice paddy soils.

China's total petroleum reserves are estimated at around 140,000m. metric tons and natural gas reserves at more than 33,000,000m. cu m. The Daqing oilfield, China's largest, has provided 47% of China's petroleum output since 1960. The largest reserves are believed to lie in the Tarim Basin, in Xinjiang. China is extremely rich in coal and iron ore. There are abundant reserves of manganese, tungsten and molybdenum, but China is relatively poor in copper, lead and zinc, and nickel supplies are meagre. China has rich resources of salt, moderate reserves of sulphur, while phosphates require development; supplies of gold, tin, fluorite-graphite, magnesite, talc, asbestos and barytes are also comparatively good.

POPULATION

China's fifth national census of 1 November 2000 revealed that the population had grown to an estimated 1,265,830,000, compared with 1,130,510,638 at the time of the fourth census in 1990, 1,008,180,738 at the third census in 1982 and with 582,603,417 at the first census in 1953. These figures, which represent more than one-fifth of the world's population, are formidable in view of both the pressures that population growth has exerted historically and the contemporary problems in the physical environment already outlined. There is, for instance, a striking imbalance in the distribution of population, which is heavily concentrated in the plain and riverine lands of the south-eastern half of the country, while most of the north-western half is, by comparison, thinly populated. This results in very high densities of population in the richest areas for settlement, such as the Changjiang Delta or the Red Basin of Sichuan. Indeed, 90% of the population inhabit little more than 15% of the country's surface area.

Some 91.59% of the population are Han Chinese. The remaining 8.41% belong to one of the national minority groups. Altogether there are over 106m. non-Chinese living within China, chiefly in the peripheral areas beyond the Great Wall, in the north, the north-west and the south-west. There are 55 different minorities scattered throughout 60% of the country. According to the 1990 census, 18 minorities numbered more than 1m. each (see p. 292). Between 1982 and 1990, whilst the Han Chinese population increased by 102m., or 10.80% (1.29% annually), the national minorities grew by 24m., or 35.52% (3.87% per year). However, between 1990 and 2000 the Han Chinese population increased by 116.92m, or 11.22% (1.07% annually), while the national minorities grew by 15.23m., or 16.7% (1.56% annually), the latter thus recording a faster rate of growth than the Han, but significantly slower than in the previous decade.

Although so-called autonomous regions (and also districts and counties) have been established, the larger minority groups have presented the central Government with serious administrative difficulties. Racial, religious and linguistic problems, as in Muslim Xinjiang and Buddhist Tibet, have resulted in several anti-Chinese uprisings since 1949; these have been forcibly suppressed.

Linguistic differences among the seven main Chinese dialects, as well as between Chinese and minority languages, have proved an intractable issue, despite the adoption of Mandarin (Putonghua in Chinese) as the national language, despite attempts at the simplification of the written language by reducing the number of strokes in individual characters and by romanization, and despite campaigns to increase literacy.

In 2000 455.94m. people in China lived in cities or towns, but this is still predominantly a rural country, with almost 64% of the population living in the countryside (compared with almost 88% in 1952). The inequalities in living standards between urban and rural areas present the Chinese with some of their most urgent ideological and practical problems.

In 1999 China recorded a birth rate of 15.23 per thousand, a death rate of 6.46 per thousand and a natural growth rate of 8.77 per thousand. (This was the second successive year that the natural growth rate had declined to below 10 per thousand.) Family-planning programmes from the mid-1950s failed to make any pronounced inroads in the increase in Chinese numbers, and in 1979 the Government issued further directives favouring couples with only one child and penalizing those who practise 'anarchism in parenthood'. In 1988 the Government conceded that it was unlikely to achieve its declared goal of limiting China's population to 1,200m. by the year 2000. In 1998 the State Family Planning Commission announced the family-planning policy for the end of the 20th century and the first half of the next century. It aimed to limit the population to 1,300m. by the year 2000, and to keep the population below 1,400m. in 2010. It estimated that the population would reach a peak of 1,600m. in the mid-21st century, before declining gradually. Peasants are now allowed to have two children, and larger families still are more and more common. Internal migration offers no solution to the population problem. (See also Population in Asia and the Pacific.)

Despite improved grain harvests in the 1970s and the 1980s, with a harvest of 462.5m. metric tons being recorded in 2000, and because the agricultural sector has to provide not only food for a large population but also investment for industrial growth, population pressure must remain central to all domestic and external issues within the foreseeable future.

History up to 1966

C. P. FITZGERALD

PREHISTORY AND CLASSICAL PERIOD

The earliest Chinese written records, recovered by archaeological excavation at the site of what was the capital of the Shang kingdom in Henan Province, date from approximately 1500 BC. Legendary history, for which there is as yet no archaeological evidence, records a previous kingdom, Xia, and a golden age of the rule of Sages, for at least 1,000 years earlier. The agreement between the king list of Shang, as found on the oracle bones discovered at Anyang, and the list preserved in Chinese official history, which are wholly independent of each other, shows that the official history must be treated with some respect. Shang culture included the making of bronze vessels of great beauty, some of which are briefly inscribed. The succeeding period, the Zhou dynasty, from 1100 to 221 BC, continued the Shang culture, but a more elaborate literature appeared, and in the second part of the Zhou rule, from about 800 BC onwards, the feudal system instituted at the foundation broke down. China became a land of contending kingdoms. At the same time there arose the various schools of philosophy (Confucian, Daoist, Moist and Legalist), whose contention matched the military conflict between the kingdoms.

UNIFICATION OF CHINA

From about the date of the death of Confucius (479 BC) until 221 BC China was constantly subjected to the wars of the contending kingdoms, of which the western state of Qin and the southern state of Chu, in the Yangtze (Changjiang) valley, were the chief protagonists. The history of Chu provides all that is known of south China in the earlier period. The struggle was won by Qin in 221 BC. The ruler of that kingdom then assumed the new title of *Huang Di*, translated as 'emperor', and imposed on his new dominions the harsh Legalist code of laws and administration, which had been in force in his country. Qin law despised art and literature, glorifying war and promoting agriculture as the foundation of military power. To suppress the opposition of the literate class in the new empire, the emperor ordered the burning of all books on history and philosophy not included in his own library. Although much was hidden and preserved, this policy did great damage to the recorded literature of China. A few years after his death, a general revolt overthrew the Qin and they were replaced by the Han dynasty, which ruled from 206 BC to AD 221.

THE FIRST EMPIRE AND PERIOD OF PARTITION

The Han dynasty consolidated the new empire, but ruled with moderation. A civil service, filled with educated men recommended by patrons, replaced the feudal system. Free tenure of land created both a landlord and a tenant system, which endured until recent times. Confucianism became the established orthodoxy. The empire was expanded to include the Guangzhou (Canton) region, and later in central Asia as far as the Caspian Sea. Contact with the Roman empire, although slight, is recorded. In art the Han developed mural painting and bas-reliefs, and in literature history was highly esteemed and developed in a systematic and accurate form. Paper and ink replaced bamboo strips and the stylus for writing. After 400 years the Han empire fell in confusion. Contending states were briefly suppressed by a reunion under the Jin dynasty, which itself soon lost North China to the invading Tartar tribes. China was divided from AD 316 to 589. Tartar rulers held the north, and Chinese dynasties the south (Yangtze valley). Both in north and south the dynasties were brief, and internal conflict frequent. Yet the period, although an 'Age of Confusion', was not a 'Dark Age'. Literature flourished in both north and south. Buddhism was introduced and spread widely. The majority of the population being Chinese, the Tartar invaders were soon absorbed, both ethnically and culturally.

THE SECOND EMPIRE, TANG AND SONG DYNASTIES

The Tang dynasty, founded in AD 618, reunited the empire on a lasting basis. The aristocratic military class gave way to a bureaucracy recruited by public examination open to all literates. The administration of government was developed to a degree unknown elsewhere for several centuries to come. Art and literature, especially poetry, flourished. The population recorded by an accurate census in AD 754 was 52,880,488. Archaeological discovery of a census return shows that this figure included women and children. The Song dynasty, which succeeded the Tang after a brief interval, continued the civil service system which now controlled the Government. The Song were unassertive, and failed to recover north-eastern territory lost to nomad invasion at the fall of Tang. In AD 1127 the Song lost North China to an invasion of the Jin Tartars. A century later the Song were conquered, after a long war, by the Mongols. The new Confucian philosophy was the main development in literature; in art Song painting is still the most esteemed. Technical developments include printing, porcelain, the maritime compass, gunpowder and primitive cannon, advances in silk spinning and the development of maritime trade with South and West Asia.

THE LATE EMPIRE AND SUBSEQUENT DYNASTIES

The Mongol conquest of China (1280) was most destructive, especially in the northern half of the country. Huge depopulation occurred, and great areas of fertile land became wilderness. Song culture, though damaged, survived. Mongol rule was oppressive and largely exercised through foreign officials from West Asia and even Europe (Marco Polo). It was also brief. After barely a century the Chinese revolt ended in the foundation of the Ming dynasty and the expulsion of the Mongols (1368). The development of drama, written by unemployed Chinese scholars, is the significant cultural development of the Mongol period.

The Ming dynasty, however, not only restored Chinese rule, but expanded the limits of the empire. South Manzhou (Manchuria) was settled and incorporated, as was Yunnan, at the opposite extremity of the empire. The Ming aimed to restore the style of Tang and Song government, but their rule was much more autocratic. In early Ming (1405–33) expeditions were sent by sea to South-East Asia, the Indian coast, Persian Gulf, Red Sea and East Africa, but this naval activity was abandoned only a few years before the Portuguese first appeared in Far Eastern waters. In late Ming contact with Europeans increased, and the first Roman Catholic missionaries reached China.

From the middle of the 15th century China was threatened, to an increasing extent, by the growth of a new power in what is called Manzhou (Manchuria), or the Three Eastern Provinces. The Manzu tribes, kindred of the Jin Tartars who had ruled northern China in the late Song period, were at first tributary to the Ming. From China, through this contact, they acquired a knowledge of governing techniques, literacy and organization. Late in the 16th century they coalesced into a new kingdom, which threw off allegiance to the Ming, and before long began to encroach on the Ming territory of South Manzhou, or modern Liaoning Province. By the middle of the 17th century they had seized this region and were raiding the Great Wall frontier of China proper. The Ming fell in 1644 to an internal rebellion, which gave the Manzhous (Manchus) the opportunity to enter China and, after nearly 40 years, control the whole empire.

The Qing (Manzhou) dynasty ruled until 1912. The first 150 years, under the three very competent emperors Kang Xi, Yong Zheng and Qian Long, were prosperous and peaceful. At the end of the 18th century the dynasty began to decline. The growth of trade with Europe was at first very profitable to China, but the Manzhous distrusted the foreign traders and imposed restrictions on their activities. The discovery of opium smuggling by British traders brought about the Opium War of 1842; China, unable to match the strength of the British fleet, was defeated. The Treaty of Nanjing, the first of the 'Unequal Treaties' as they came to be called, which followed this defeat, established the system of Treaty Ports, concession areas and the right of extraterritorial jurisdiction. Shanghai was claimed as a British Treaty Port, and by the end of the century had become an International Settlement, guarded by its own multinational troops.

The unsuccessful war, and the internal rebellions that swept the country in the 1850s, weakened the authority of a dynasty always considered alien in the south. Moreover, in the 1870s China began to suffer the encroachment of the European powers. Russia took advantage of the rebellions in China to obtain territory in the north, while in the 1880s France seized Indo-China and forced Beijing to renounce its suzerainty. The United Kingdom and France together waged war with China in 1858 and actually occupied Beijing, exacting a further 'Unequal Treaty'. Towards the end of the century Japan became involved, and in the war of 1894–95 drove the Chinese out of Korea. At home the young intellectuals, inspired by Western education and thinking, adopted revolutionary ideas under the leadership of Dr Sun Yat-sen. In 1911, three years after the death of the empress dowager Ci Xi (who had ruled from 1862), a revolt of the army at Wuhan led to the fall of the dynasty and the abolition of the monarchy.

REPUBLICAN CHINA

Sun Yat-sen was a native of Guangzhou, who had been educated from childhood in Hawaii and then taken a degree at the medical school of Hong Kong. His formation was thus largely foreign and Western. Finding that radical reform was unacceptable to the official world of China, he turned revolutionary and republican, and for more than 10 years maintained an unceasing effort to stir up rebellion in China. He was for long unsuccessful; but his influence grew steadily among the young Chinese studying abroad, particularly in Japan, where the majority of them went. He built up a nationalist party and a secret organization, obtained funds from the overseas Chinese of South-East Asia, and finally his followers were able to infiltrate the army—the new model army whose officers had also studied abroad.

Thus, when the revolution broke out in 1911, it was from the first dominated by the army, a servitude from which it was not to escape for many years. The court had lost further prestige in 1900 by supporting the peasant anti-foreign movement known as the Boxer Rebellion, which for a time threatened to massacre the diplomatic corps in Beijing; the Rebellion was finally crushed by an international expedition, which took Beijing and drove the court to retreat to the west of China. The southern provinces under their great viceroys refused to follow court policy over the Boxers, and virtually concluded a separate peace with the foreign powers. This was a sign of coming disruption. After signing a further humiliating peace, the court returned to Beijing, and in its last years attempted to put through reforms which might have saved it 50 years earlier. It was too late. When Ci Xi died in 1908, there was no competent successor to continue the regency in the name of the next infant emperor, Xuan Tong or Pu Yi. Within three years the revolution had broken out and the dynasty was doomed.

In its last extremity, the imperial regime appealed to the former commander-in-chief of the imperial army, Yuan Shikai, who was out of favour with the new regent, to save it. The northern troops would obey only their old commander; the southern army had transferred its allegiance to the revolution. Yuan took command, but he did not intend to save the dynasty; he hoped to establish his own. First he showed by a brief campaign that he was a serious contender, then began to negotiate with the republicans. A plan was soon arranged. Yuan would bring about the peaceful abdication of the dynasty, which would, in return, be granted very favourable terms, and the republic would elect Yuan to be president. When the first parliament was convened (under conditions of flagrant corruption), Yuan had some of the more able members assassinated, and soon, having obtained a loan from the foreign powers without the assent of parliament, dissolved that body and ruled by decree. Futile and ineffective resistance in the south was speedily crushed. In 1914 Yuan moved to obtain support for a new dynasty with himself as emperor.

The outbreak of the First World War was a factor that worked against this programme. It divided the foreign powers, and left Japan a comparatively free hand in Asia. Japan bribed and armed Yuan's secret opponents, his own generals, who resented his pretensions to the throne. On 25 December 1915 a revolt broke out, and within a few months it was evident that the generals had turned against him, and the projected monarchy was impossible. He renounced his plans, tried to cling to the presidency, but died in June 1916. His death was soon followed by the contests among his former generals who controlled the provinces. The 'war-lord era' from 1917 to 1927 was marked by a series of short civil wars fought entirely between rival militarists to gain control of revenues, and above all of the impotent Government in Beijing, which could dispense the custom revenue collected under foreign supervision to service the external loans, but which still left a valuable revenue for whichever general could dominate Beijing. Within the country there was an increasing breakdown of law and order, banditry, and rural distress.

Nationalism and Communism

In May 1919 the students of Beijing had rioted against the Government's acceptance of the secret arrangement whereby Japan was to acquire the former German-leased port of Qingdao in Shandong. It was generally known that the corrupt politicians and their militarist master had received large sums from Japan for this virtually treasonable decision. The 'May Fourth Movement', as it became known, spread widely; it was the first sign of a new phase of the revolution, a revolt against Western dictation of China's affairs and fate, the first overt reaction of the generation who had grown up since the fall of the empire. Today the Communist Government commemorates it as the opening of a new era.

In May 1925 another violent outbreak followed upon the shooting by International Settlement police of student demonstrators in Shanghai. This time the wave of anger, directed against the United Kingdom and Japan, was nation-wide. There was a total boycott of British and Japanese trade and enterprise.

Hong Kong's labour was withdrawn and its life all but paralysed. Further riots and shootings occurred in Guangzhou, and missionaries were compelled to leave the interior of China. Boycott pickets were established in the Treaty Ports and became an extra-legal militia.

Dr Sun Yat-sen, having failed to obtain any help from the Western powers to reinstate his Government—which he and his followers regarded as the only legal one—had turned to the USSR, which gave him the necessary support in arms, advisers and possibly finance. He regained control of Guangzhou in 1923 and swiftly set about the organization of an efficient government and a new model army. In 1921 the Chinese Communist Party (CCP) had been formally established at a meeting attended by 11 members, one of whom was Mao Zedong. At almost the same time a CCP had been formed in France by students living in Paris. One of its founders was Zhou Enlai. The two parties in China, the CCP still very small, and the Nationalists (Kuomintang—KMT) already gaining wide support, co-operated on the basis that members of the CCP might join the KMT as individuals, but there was no affiliation of the two parties. Aided by the repercussions of May 1925, revolutionary agitation increased rapidly.

After Dr Sun's death in 1925, all hope of peaceful reunion ended, and the KMT Government in Guangzhou prepared for war, which was launched in 1926 against the southern war-lords. Success was rapid, and by early 1927 the whole of the middle Changjiang region had fallen to the KMT, whose armies, commanded by Jiang Jieshi (Chiang Kai-shek), were approaching Shanghai. Alarmed, the Treaty Powers sent troops to defend the International Settlement. The Shanghai workers and boycott pickets, organized by the Communists, rose and seized the Chinese-governed part of Shanghai, expelling the war-lord army. When Jiang's forces arrived, they found Chinese Shanghai already in the hands of the revolutionaries, and facing the acute danger of war with the foreign powers. Jiang had close connections with Chinese big business and finance in Shanghai. These people, good Nationalists, and no friends of the plundering war-lords, were equally very frightened of social revolution and the Communist-controlled workers. Jiang, knowing he had their support, carried out a sudden coup and massacre of the Communists (from which Zhou Enlai narrowly escaped) and broke with the CCP. For several months the situation was confused. Jiang formed a right-wing KMT Government at Nanjing; the former Guangzhou Government was now established at Wuhan, further up the Changjiang, and did not at first break with the CCP. In much of South China, particularly Hunan Province, social revolution, inspired by rural agitators led by Mao Zedong, was sweeping the country.

Before long the two Nationalist Governments coalesced at Nanjing, and Jiang could turn his attention to combating the Communists. From 1929 to 1935 Jiang launched successive extermination campaigns against the Communists, who had now, under the leadership of Mao Zedong and Zhu De, established a Soviet area in the hill country on the Hunan-Jiangxi border. Jiang's campaigns failed until he devised, on the advice of his German staff officers, the plan of blockading the Jiangxi Soviet and thus forcing the Communists to break out or be starved into submission.

In 1935 the Communists set out on what came to be known as the 'Long March', with about 100,000 men and many of their dependants. A year later they reached Yanan, in north Shaanxi, after marching and counter-marching for more than 9,500 km, with 30,000 fighting men. However, they had not been defeated and, during that epic march, Mao Zedong had emerged as the unquestioned leader of the CCP, a position he retained until his death in 1976. The CCP, also, was fully emancipated from long-distance control by Moscow, which had proved uniformly disastrous for several years. Yanan, in the far north-west, was difficult to attack, almost impossible to blockade, and close to the areas soon to be threatened by the impending Japanese invasion.

The Japanese Invasion

In China it was widely recognized that the Japanese had embarked upon an all-out effort to conquer the country. Japan feared that, if it waited, China would grow strong, and it also feared the rise of Communist influence. However, the Nanjing Government was still determined to destroy the CCP before resisting the Japanese. It was not until December 1936, when Jiang's own army, facing the Communists at Xian in Shaanxi, mutinied and held him prisoner until he agreed to cease the civil war, that he was forced to concede to the slogans 'Chinese do not fight Chinese' and 'unite to resist Japanese aggression'. The Japanese did not wait: in July 1937 they struck near Beijing, and the fighting soon escalated into a large-scale, but still undeclared, war.

In the early stages KMT resistance, as at Shanghai and the battle of Taierzhuang in Shandong, had been, at times, effective. The weight of Japanese armament, however, was far superior and they had almost unchallenged air power and complete control of the sea. The KMT forces were driven back from the coast to the mountainous interior of western China, losing nearly two-thirds of the provinces. The difficulties of forcing the Changjiang gorges halted the Japanese at that point, and the added challenge of holding vast conquered territories prevented any further advance. In those conquered territories, particularly North China, the CCP was organizing the guerrilla resistance, which was soon to shake Japanese authority.

The hope of a Chinese military collapse had faded; by early 1942 Japan was involved in the Second World War in the Pacific, and here, too, early victories were proving inconclusive and presaging Japan's eventual defeat. The CCP steadily expanded its guerrilla war until large areas were liberated, in which the CCP set up its own administration, gaining essential experience in social, economic and political reform, including the major problems of land reform. Japanese retaliation was brutal and ruthless, forcing the Chinese peasantry to rely on guerrilla groups for their protection. It roused the national consciousness of an indifferent apolitical peasantry, and was the main factor in building the power of the CCP to national level.

COMMUNIST CHINA

The war was ended neither by the still-passive resistance of the KMT in western China, nor by the activity of the guerrillas, but by the Japanese surrender in August 1945. The termination of the Japanese occupation left China deeply divided. The KMT took over from the Japanese in the southern and eastern provinces. The CCP controlled the rural north, and cut the communications when the KMT flew in men to take over the Japanese-held cities. Civil war loomed close. The USA sent Gen. George C. Marshall to mediate, and to build, if possible, a coalition government. He failed; neither side trusted the other, and the demands made by the KMT would have been a death warrant for the CCP. Early in 1946 the foreshadowed civil war began, but was neither as long nor as destructive as most Chinese had feared it would be. It soon became evident that the CCP was going to win. Its troops fought well under firm discipline; the KMT forces had no will to war, and plundered wherever they went. Gross inflation was ruining the economy and alienating those to whom the KMT looked for support; corruption was rife in the KMT Government and army, and business was almost paralysed. There was nothing that the KMT could offer to enlist the support of any social class, not even the capitalists of Shanghai.

Therefore, despite massive US arms supplies, full control of the air, and vastly superior numbers, the KMT armies were wholly routed in less than three years. Vast numbers surrendered; relatively few were killed in battle. By the end of 1948 the Communists already held all northern China, including the north-eastern provinces that formed Manzhou; they were on the banks of the Changjiang opposite Nanjing. The KMT was no longer united. A large group which favoured peace and negotiation compelled Jiang to renounce his presidency, but was unable to shake his covert control over many units of the army. The Nanjing Government tried to secure peace, and nearly did so, but this effort was sabotaged by the agents of Jiang at the last moment, and the acting President, Li Zongren (Li Tsung-jen), was forced into exile. The war resumed, the Communists crossed the Changjiang, took Nanjing, then Shanghai, and swept on into the south and west. By the middle of 1949, when the People's Republic of China was proclaimed on 1 October in Beijing, the Communists were the masters of China, and Jiang and his remnant forces retreated to Taiwan, where they and their successors have since remained (see the chapter on Taiwan for subsequent history of the island and reunification initiatives).

Yet the failure to end the war by negotiation did China, and the Communists, one serious piece of harm. It destroyed the continuity of the legitimate internationally-recognized Government. If the Nanjing regime had made peace—any sort of peace—it would have remained the legal Government, even if it were now run by the CCP. By failing to win this diplomatic victory, the Communists found their new regime subject to recognition, or non-recognition, at the will of foreign states, and their claim to China's seat at the UN disputed by the KMT protégés of the USA.

This situation continued to be one of the main causes of friction between the People's Republic and the Western powers, who, in their attitudes to the new China, were also deeply divided. To many of the Western, in particular the European, countries the fate of China was settled; the KMT on Taiwan was no longer significant. To the USA, on the other hand, its regime was the 'real China' and the CCP considered to be Soviet 'puppets'. Thus, the CCP regime started out with the open ill will of the USA, the doubtful and wary acceptance of the United Kingdom and other smaller Western powers, and the half-hearted and cautious approval of the USSR. Only two years earlier Stalin had assured the USA that he recognized only Jiang Jieshi as the legitimate ruler of China.

The leading figure in China's political affairs was now Mao Zedong, who was Chairman of the CCP from 1935 until his death in 1976. Chairman Mao, as he was known, also became Head of State in October 1949 but he relinquished this post in December 1958. His successor was Liu Shaoqi, First Vice-Chairman of the CCP, who was elected Head of State in April 1959. The first Premier (head of government) was Zhou Enlai, who held this office from October 1949 until his death in 1976. Zhou was also Minister of Foreign Affairs from 1949 to 1958.

Economic and Social Reform

The early policy of the new regime in Beijing was necessarily one of national renewal. The economy was at a standstill, communications almost wholly interrupted, inflation rampant, public utilities run down by years of neglect. Even foreign trade was deflected into the supply of quick-selling consumer goods, largely useless to the economy, while valuable exports could not be moved and necessary imports could not be paid for. Nevertheless, the new regime, headed by men who had had no experience of urban life for more than 25 years, tackled these tasks with skill and expedition. Within weeks, the railways were running, and supplying coal to Shanghai in place of the normal seaborne supplies which were under a KMT naval blockade. Inflation was brought under steady control and ended, with a new currency, in the following year. Thereafter, the Chinese currency, subjected to violent fluctuations for longer than living memory, remained stable. Foreign trade began to revive, cautiously, being limited to imports of essential goods, and to exports that would earn foreign exchange. The restoration of the cities, some of which were still in partial ruins from wartime bombing, and all neglected, insanitary and decaying, was made a high priority. This improvement brought widespread popular support for the CCP regime, and served to offset other policies that were less immediately appealing to many people. Land reform was the first major socialist, or communist, policy implemented. It was at first a simple redistribution of land in equal lots to all cultivators, including the families of former landlords.

The CCP did not intend to leave the matter at the level of peasant proprietorship of tiny plots. From the first, mutual aid teams were organized to manage the busy agricultural period. Later these were developed into the two stages of co-operative farming, and still later the co-operatives were grouped together into communes. In this way, private ownership of agricultural land was abolished and replaced by the communal system under which each former owner had a share of the commune's revenue allotted by 'work points', based on hours worked. State-owned collective farms were confined to newly-opened lands or reclaimed land not previously privately owned. Whatever other defects and difficulties the new land system encountered, owing to bad weather or administrative over-centralization, it can be said with certainty to have made two major advances: the constant threat of starvation in bad times receded; and water control and supply were made more possible by the new institutional units that replaced the smallholdings. These factors helped the commune system to withstand the great drought years 1960–62 without large-scale famine, although not without stern rationing and some malnutrition. In earlier, less severe, droughts the victims were often numbered by the million.

The Korean War and Relations with the USSR

The Korean War (1950–53) has given rise to a large literature, and its origin and the responsibility for its outbreak are still in dispute. Chinese intervention, after UN forces began to move northwards into the Democratic People's Republic of Korea (DPRK), was forewarned, but the warnings were not heeded. To the Chinese this movement was a direct threat to their vital industrial area of south Manzhou (Liaoning Province), bordering on the DPRK. It was also widely feared in China to be the preliminary move to an invasion of China itself. The extent to which the Chinese intervention was intended to reassert Chinese authority, rather than Soviet influence, in Manzhou and in Korea, remains conjectural. Later developments seem to indicate that this consideration was important. It was certainly a consequence of the war, because, after the cease-fire, the USSR soon renounced the special position that the Chinese had conceded to it in the port of Dalian and over the railways across Manzhou.

In China the effect of the war was to strengthen the prestige of the Government which had, for the first time for more than a century (if ever), shown itself able to meet and match a large-scale Western army. In the years since the truce ending the war was signed at Panmunjom, Chinese relations with the DPRK have not always been smooth. The pretensions of President Kim Il Sung to be a major ideological leader were not appreciated in Beijing. The DPRK's attitude of neutrality in the Sino-Soviet dispute, although undoubtedly very wise, cooled relations with China. On the other hand, foreign observers drew the conclusion that China exercised a restraining influence on the adventurism of President Kim in respect of the Republic of Korea. However, the DPRK was certainly not a Chinese satellite.

In 1957, in the 'Hundred Flowers' movement, the Government permitted open criticism of its methods, if not its basic policies. The extent of the resulting criticisms was probably disconcerting to the authorities, yet much of what was said made its mark and led to some change of style in the CCP. The 'Hundred Flowers' movement was almost contemporary with the first phase of the Sino-Soviet dispute, which grew over the years until the two countries became completely estranged. The original quarrel over ideology developed into a dispute more concerned with national interests, especially after the USSR withdrew its technical aid and experts from China in 1960. This was a severe blow to the developing Chinese industrialization, but the set-back was overcome. After a series of border clashes in 1969, negotiations for a settlement of Sino-Soviet differences concerning the border regions opened in Beijing in October 1969. Subsequent relations between the two countries long remained under strain. The fear of a possible Soviet attack, either using conventional or nuclear weapons, strongly influenced China's military and diplomatic planning. The expectation entertained by the Soviet leaders that, after the death of Mao Zedong, China would prove willing to renew the former friendship, or at least to modify its criticisms of the USSR, was not realized until mid-1989, when relations between the two countries were officially normalized.

The Tibet Issue and Relations with India

All Chinese Governments since the fall of the Qing dynasty have continued to assert rights of sovereignty over Tibet (Xizang), although the western two-thirds of the territory had been, in practice, independent since 1912. Tibet was occupied in 1950 by Chinese Communist forces. In March 1959 there was an unsuccessful armed uprising by Tibetans opposed to Chinese rule. As a result, the Dalai Lama, the head of Tibet's Buddhist clergy and thus the region's spiritual leader, fled with some 100,000 supporters to northern India, where a government-in-exile was established. The Chinese ended the former dominance of the lamas (Buddhist monks) and destroyed many monasteries. Tibet became an 'Autonomous Region' of China in September 1965, but the majority of Tibetans have continued to regard the Dalai Lama as their 'god-king', and to resent the Chinese presence, leading to intermittent unrest.

In 1962 the establishment of Chinese forces on the Indian border with Tibet led to disputes about the position of the undefined and unmarked boundary. China proposed negotiations, but the Indian side rejected them, asserting that the frontier had been established by the United Kingdom before Indian independence. The tension escalated into a border war when Indian forces attempted to expel Chinese troops from some disputed positions. The clash resulted in a Chinese victory, which could have led to an invasion of Indian Assam. China unilaterally terminated the operations and withdrew to the positions already established before the clash. Soviet verbal support for the Indian claim considerably embittered relations between China and the USSR. The frontier dispute remains unsettled (see History of India), with the Chinese holding what they claim to be the correct frontier line.

Recent History

MICHAEL YAHUDA

THE 'CULTURAL REVOLUTION'

Political Background

There is much about the 'Cultural Revolution' that still awaits historical evaluation, but its origins may be traced to political developments that began in the late 1950s. The upheavals in Eastern Europe in 1956, and Mao's growing doubts about the Soviet leadership, led him to the view that, even after the revolution and the establishment of a socialist society on the Leninist model, it was possible that a restoration of capitalism could take place. By 1965 he had convinced himself that this had indeed happened in the USSR, and that, unless action were taken, it could occur in China too. His theory stressed the importance of leadership and of the values that were espoused and institutionalized by those leaders, rather than the character of economic development as such. In Marxist terms, he emphasized the significance of the superstructure rather than the materialistic economic base. Mao's tendency to eulogize the significance of inspired leadership allied to mass activism, as against an institutionalized functional division of labour through orderly bureaucracies, underlay many of the political conflicts in the Chinese leadership from the 'Hundred Flowers' movement onwards. That campaign, in the spring of 1957, called on professionals and intellectuals to criticize the closed-door autocracy of the Chinese Communist Party (CCP), but it was resisted by some of the other, more orthodox, Leninist leaders. It was soon followed by an anti-rightist movement which was to plunge hundreds of thousands of non-CCP intellectuals into a disgrace from which they were not to be rehabilitated for another 20 years.

The 'Great Leap Forward' of 1958 may be seen as illustrative of Mao's preferred approach to economic development. The intention was to unleash the enthusiasm of the masses, under the leadership of politically-inspired CCP cadres, rather than to follow the heavily-bureaucratized system associated with the Soviet model. It turned out to be an economic disaster, which led to the death of 23m. (or possibly as many as 37m.) people through famine. As 70m. peasants laboured to produce worthless steel from back-yard furnaces, the fields remained ill-attended. The cadres vied with each other to provide falsely-inflated production figures, so that the scale of the débâcle did not become apparent to the leadership until well into the following year. Although most of the leaders had initially supported the 'Great Leap' programme, the leadership that met to review the situation in August 1959 was divided. The Minister of Defence, Marshal Peng Dehuai, severely criticized the 'Great Leap', and, at Mao's insistence, he was dismissed. Mao had construed the criticism as a personal attack upon himself. The episode may be seen as a break with those norms of CCP procedure that allowed for open debate (at the highest levels at least), and as the beginning of the elevation of Mao to a higher authority than the collective wisdom of the CCP, as expressed through its organization. Peng was replaced by Marshal Lin Biao, who soon ingratiated himself with Mao by elevating the study of 'Mao Zedong thought' in the armed forces and by emphasizing the army's role as a 'people's army', rather than fulfilling the more professionalist role inspired by the Soviet example.

Much of this was not immediately apparent, as Mao retreated from the daily management of domestic affairs, relinquishing responsibility for this to senior leaders such as Liu Shaoqi, Deng Xiaoping (who had become Secretary-General of the CCP Central Committee in 1954) and Zhou Enlai. While these men directed China's recovery from the three difficult years of 1959–61, Mao apparently confined himself to foreign affairs and ostensibly ideological questions related to the Sino-Soviet conflict.

The Initial Phase, 1966–69

Concerned by what he saw as the decline of the revolutionary ethos in China, and thwarted in his attempts to reassert a more dominant role, Mao launched the 'Great Proletarian Cultural Revolution' in 1966. The movement was directed against those 'party leaders in authority taking the capitalist road'. Mao's shock troops were to be the Red Guards, principally middle-school and university students who were to draw inspiration from Mao himself—now the supreme authority in all matters. They were to be guided by the newly-established 'Cultural Revolution Group' of the Central Committee, a prominent member of which was Mao's wife, Jiang Qing. Having been denied a political role for more than 25 years, she sought to gain revenge against those who had slighted her, and at the same time she imposed a highly limited orthodoxy on culture and the arts. The Red Guards initially focused their attacks on teachers and CCP leaders in schools and universities. However, at the often clandestine instigation of members of the 'Cultural Revolution Group', they soon toppled government ministers and even members of the CCP's Politburo. Mao himself had singled out Liu Shaoqi (the man whom he had once described as his eventual successor) as the leading 'capitalist-roader' (he was dismissed as Head of State in October 1968 and died in prison in 1969), but Deng Xiaoping was also forced to undergo self-criticism and disgrace (in 1966) and few of the other senior leaders survived unscathed. Moreover, by the end of 1966 the CCP itself had virtually ceased to operate as a national organization, and the state administration was barely functioning. The one truly national organization, with an effective chain of command from the centre down to the localities, was the army.

Chinese politics became highly polarized and factionalized. This was to be its predominant character for the ensuing 10 years. The 'Cultural Revolution' itself lacked coherence. Mao's theory of how to avoid what he regarded as a counter-revolution was seriously flawed, as he had not articulated a clear vision of the political system to replace the one that was seen to have gone wrong. All groups and factions in China claimed to be the true followers of 'Mao Zedong thought', and each one stigmatized its opponents as revisionists. When the two radicals, Yao Wenyuan and Zhang Qunqiao (who had been so useful to Mao in launching the 'Revolution' and who were later to be condemned as members of the notorious 'Gang of Four'), reported to Mao in January 1967 about the establishment of a Shanghai Commune, modelled on the Paris Commune of 1871, Mao turned on them, dismissing the new institution as anarchist and insisting on the need for leaders. Meanwhile, the army had been called in to restore order, and it soon began to play a greater role in public life. Rejecting the Commune, Mao turned to the so-called 'three-way revolutionary committees' as the answer to China's absence of organization. These were largely dominated by the army, and included also representatives of surviving older cadres and of the 'revolutionary masses'.

By 1968 Red Guard factions, reduced to their hard-core members, were engaged in internecine armed struggles. Finally, on Mao's insistence, the organizations were disbanded, and, alongside millions of educated young Chinese, their members were sent to the countryside. Mao called for a reconstruction of the CCP. In early 1969, as fighting took place on the riverine border with the USSR, the Ninth Party Congress was convened. The newly-elected Central Committee was dominated by men in military uniform, but it also included people who had been promoted during the 'Cultural Revolution', as well as a small proportion of surviving senior leaders. A new Constitution was proclaimed, in which Lin Biao was designated as Mao's successor—an unusual and irregular constitutional provision. The congress also reviewed the 'Cultural Revolution'.

Factional Conflicts, 1969–76

Many in the West took the congress to signal the end of the 'Cultural Revolution'. The events of mid-1968 certainly brought its end in the streets. Henceforth the 'Cultural Revolution' took the form of increasingly ruthless power struggles at the highest level of the leadership, and clashes between those, on the one side, who tried to institutionalize the so-called 'new-born things' of the 'Revolution' (principally in education and culture, but also in resisting allegedly revisionist economic practices) and those, on the other, who stressed the need for modernization. Underlying all these disputes were the questions of the succession to Mao and the future direction of China.

After the 1969 congress, two main struggles developed. The first centred on Lin Biao and the second was between the 'Cultural Revolutionaries' (led by Jiang Qing), on the one side, and the modernizers (headed by Zhou Enlai and, from 1973, by the rehabilitated Deng Xiaoping), on the other. The official account of the episode leading to Lin Biao's death describes him as plotting the assassination of Mao after having been denied the position of Head of State. Having failed to kill Mao in August–September 1971, Lin allegedly escaped in a requisitioned aircraft, but died as it crashed in neighbouring Mongolia. Whatever the facts may have been, the episode reflected badly on the Chinese political system.

Following Lin's death, many of the leaders who had been disgraced earlier in the 'Cultural Revolution' were brought back to office. The most notable of these was the man who had been reviled in 1966 as China's 'No. 2 capitalist-roader', Deng Xiaoping, in April 1973. Unbeknown to the outside world, Premier Zhou Enlai was terminally ill, and Deng Xiaoping rapidly assumed many of Zhou's responsibilities. This brought about the second major series of political struggles. Lin Biao, who had been reviled as an 'ultra-leftist' in 1972, was now labelled an 'ultra-rightist'—the point being that the previous designation hampered the radical 'Cultural Revolutionaries'. They initiated a highly confusing 'Criticize Lin Biao, criticize Confucius' campaign, which took the form of debates on abstruse historical allegories, and was aimed at discrediting Zhou Enlai. This was followed by equally confusing and inconclusive campaigns on the importance of 'the dictatorship of the proletariat' and on the lessons to be drawn from a medieval novel, *The Water Margin*. For his part, Deng Xiaoping presided over the preparation of three blueprints to modernize education, science and the economy.

Matters reached a climax when Zhou Enlai died in January 1976. Deng Xiaoping, who had re-emerged in the previous year as First Vice-Premier and Chief of the General Staff of the Armed Forces, delivered the funeral address and promptly disappeared from public view. At the Cheng Ming Festival—the traditional time for honouring the dead—in April, public demonstrations in memory of Zhou took place in the major cities. These were the first truly spontaneous demonstrations to have taken place in the history of the People's Republic. The principal demonstration was in Beijing, where hundreds of thousands of people laid wreaths which pointedly eulogized the late Premier, and some went so far as to attack Jiang Qing and to criticize Mao's rule. On 5 April this escalated into a serious public disturbance, known as the 'Tiananmen incident', which led to hundreds of arrests. The episode was condemned as counter-revolutionary by a tense meeting of the CCP's Central Committee. Deng Xiaoping was condemned as the instigator, and was stripped of his official posts, but he was allowed to retain Party membership. The little-known Hua Guofeng, hitherto the Minister of Public Security, was appointed Premier and First Vice-Chairman of the CCP. Although Deng had lost the contest for power (and was dismissed from his posts), the 'Cultural Revolutionary' radicals had not won either. As Mao was becoming increasingly incapacitated, the radicals frantically sought to bolster their position in a final bid to denigrate Deng and his supporters. The country was in a chaotic state, and was later said to have been on the verge of civil war.

Mao died, aged 82, on 9 September 1976. Jiang Qing, her three associates and others of their faction were arrested in October, after manoeuvring to oust Hua Guofeng. They were quickly pilloried as the 'Gang of Four', and the 'Cultural Revolution' was declared to be at an end.

TOWARDS A NEW POLITICAL ORDER

Hua Guofeng and Deng Xiaoping

Hua Guofeng, as Mao's chosen successor and as the man who instigated the arrest of the 'Gang of Four', nevertheless had certain weaknesses, particularly against the challenge of a determined Deng Xiaoping. In October 1976 Hua assumed the post of Chairman of the CCP, alongside his premiership of the State Council (cabinet) (thus notionally succeeding both Mao Zedong and Zhou Enlai), but he was, in truth, a newcomer to the central political stage. He and a few undistinguished members of the Politburo were beneficiaries of the 'Cultural Revolution'. They had not the prestige, the seniority, the experience and the wide range of contacts of the pre-'Cultural Revolution' senior leaders who had either survived as leaders or had been rehabilitated. Moreover, neither Hua nor his fellow beneficiaries could fully negate the 'Cultural Revolution' or reverse the verdict of the 'Tiananmen incident' without undermining their own position. They were committed to modernizing China, yet the programme was not theirs. Having been initiated by Zhou Enlai, the modernization strategy had taken shape under Deng Xiaoping and his group.

By 1977 Deng had returned to prominence again, and in August he was restored to his former posts. Hua and his fellow beneficiaries from the 'Cultural Revolution' sought in vain to retain power by clinging to Mao's fading prestige. They advanced the slogan of following whatever Mao said and whatever he did, and became known as the 'whateverist faction'. In early 1978 Hua Guofeng announced a grandiose plan to modernize the country by 1985 (an extension from the 10-Year Plan advocated by Deng in 1975). The economy, already seriously out of balance, was soon dangerously overextended. The situation culminated at the third plenary session of the 11th CCP Central Committee in December 1978. The plenum criticized the 'whateverist' policy, abandoned the lingering theoretical influences from the 'Cultural Revolution' and adopted policies of 'emancipating the mind' on the basis that 'practice is the sole criterion of truth'. It recognized that the sectors of the economy were badly out of balance and declared that a period of at least three years would be required to adjust these deficiencies. Meanwhile, a start was to be made by raising the official prices paid for a variety of agricultural products.

Deng and his associates, often known as the 'practice group', were constrained by a number of factors which may be regarded as external, including, for example, resistance by groups in the bureaucracy and the CCP whose positions were put under threat by the new emphasis on professionalism. Other senior leaders had misgivings about the pace, and even about some of the directions, of the reforms. There were also internal restraints: Deng Xiaoping should not be regarded as a pragmatist who was only constrained by others from revealing himself fundamentally as un-Marxist or un-Leninist. Deng joined the CCP in the early 1920s, and nothing that he said, even after 1978, suggested that he was other than a Leninist who believed that the CCP should retain its monopoly of political power. He was no social democrat, nor can he be viewed as one who favoured the transformation of China into a capitalist state.

The Significance of the Third Plenum

The third plenum of late 1978 is rightly regarded as one of the major turning-points in the history of the People's Republic. It set in motion a series of reforms that brought about a fundamentally new political and economic order. It also brought new people into the Politburo, notably Hu Yaobang, hitherto director of the CCP's organization department. Above all, it set the stage for a soundly-based programme of economic reforms which could take place against a background of greater institutional regularity, legality and a freedom from the fear of chaotic political campaigns. This also entailed a re-examination of CCP history, a rehabilitation of past leaders and, indeed, a reconsideration of hundreds of thousands of unjust verdicts on people of humbler status.

Leading up to the third plenum, and carrying on into the early months of 1979, there took place a movement for democracy, sometimes known as the 5 April Movement (after the 'Tiananmen incident' in 1976). Groups of young people, many of whom were former Red Guards, displayed wall posters in the centre of Beijing and circulated their own unofficial magazines, demanding the restitution of wrongs by officials and, more defiantly, calling for the establishment of democracy and legality along Western lines. The movement had proved useful to Deng and his reformers in the period prior to the third plenum. Thereafter it became an embarrassment, to be crushed in the name of order. Deng issued a statement which declared that the limits of tolerance were to be judged according to four basic principles. These were the primacy of the socialist road, the dictatorship of the proletariat, the leadership of the CCP and Marxism-Leninism, and 'Mao Zedong thought'. The third was obviously the most crucial. At the fourth plenary session of the 11th Central Committee, held in September 1979, Zhao Ziyang was promoted from an alternate to a full member of the Politburo.

By 1981 the new leadership had produced its own verdict on the history of the CCP. Granted that the 'history' was a product of political compromises and that it had to serve current political aims, it contained far fewer factual distortions than had been the case with such 'histories' during Mao's lifetime. Not surprisingly, the 'history' made a positive assessment of Mao, but it blamed him for assuming excessive personal power and for being too leftist in his last 20 years. The 'Cultural Revolution' was condemned as an unmitigated disaster, based on a theory by Mao that bore no relation to reality. However, the terrible excesses of the 'Cultural Revolution' were blamed on alleged schemers such as the 'Lin Biao' and 'Gang of Four' groups, members of which had been put on trial in the previous year, and sentenced to long periods of imprisonment. Jiang Qing and Zhang Qunqiao had been sentenced to death, unless they repented within two years. Although no evidence was presented suggesting their repentance, their sentences were, in the end, commuted to life imprisonment. Meanwhile, some of those of lesser rank who had been found responsible for the persecution and, indeed, for the deaths of fewer people during the 'Cultural Revolution' were executed.

In December 1982 a new Constitution was promulgated, containing more detailed provisions than ever before on citizens' rights and the specific functions of organizations. In 1980, meanwhile, when Hu Yaobang, newly appointed to the restored post of General Secretary, and Zhao Ziyang, who replaced Hua Guofeng as Premier of the State Council, were elected to the Standing Committee of the Politburo, the old Party Secretariat was revived. By the 12th CCP Congress in September 1982, Deng had been able to bring to an end the practice of life-long tenure of senior CCP positions. A new Central Advisory Commission was established for people of at least 40 years' standing as CCP members. Much emphasis was put on the need to promote more professional, young and middle-aged party members to positions of high responsibility.

In short, the third plenum ushered in a period of political change aimed at promoting China's economic development without sacrificing the Party's monopoly of power. Despite the continual tension between the ensuing economic transformations and the unyielding political dominance by the Party, the system that was begun by the plenary session in December 1978 was to endure for longer than any previous period in the history of the People's Republic.

Modernization Under Deng Xiaoping: Aims and Achievements

The purpose of the economic modernization of the new order was defined as the development of the productive forces in order to raise the standard of living of the Chinese people; and to ensure the long-term security of China in accordance with its status as a world power. The ultimate purpose of the reforms was to transform the country into a 'modern socialist state with Chinese characteristics'. The process of reform, described by Deng Xiaoping in 1979 as China's 'second revolution', lacked any coherent theoretical framework. It proceeded in fits and starts in a pragmatic accommodation to changing circumstances. Nevertheless, the economic achievements were remarkable, with an average annual growth rate from 1978 of nearly 10%. Foreign trade expanded rapidly, as did China's engagement with the international economy. This success, however, has been uneven. The state-owned enterprises that employ the bulk of the urban labour force have stagnated, while the rural-based industries and the foreign-orientated sectors have shown strong growth.

The reforms began in the agricultural sector, as peasants were allowed to revert to family farming at the expense of the collective. Starting in the poorer areas, peasant households were permitted to contract for the use of land for 15 years or more. After fulfilling certain production quotas for the State, they were allowed to cultivate almost any crop they wished, and to sell them either to state agencies at above-quota prices or to market the produce themselves. Up to one-fifth of peasant households have specialized in single commodities or in providing various services or indeed developing local industries. Prominent among them have been the households of CCP members. These reforms led to a phenomenal growth in agricultural output. As the ratio of land to population will necessarily deteriorate, however, there is a need to combine greater efficiency in farming with the provision of employment prospects for the millions of unemployed or underemployed peasants in the countryside.

Reform of the industrial urban sector has proved more difficult by far. Following a three-year period of readjusting structural imbalances between the different sectors of the economy, in October 1984 the Government announced an ambitious programme to revitalize the planning system and the state-run industries. With the exception of a few strategic economic categories, mandatory planning was to be replaced for the bulk of industry by 'guidance planning' or by the macro-economic controls of market forces. The state-owned enterprises were to be responsible for marketing their products and for their profitability. Accordingly, the programme envisaged that enterprise managers would have greater authority to reward and, if necessary, to dismiss workers. It also anticipated that loss-making enterprises could even face bankruptcy. Managers were given the right to sell above-quota production at higher prices. Unlike other parts of the economy, however, the state-owned enterprises proved very difficult to reform; they were as much social as economic units, providing life-long employment, social services and housing.

These economic and political developments have been accompanied by social changes with far-reaching implications. In 1979 Deng Xiaoping finally removed the stigma attendant upon intellectuals for the previous 30 years, by declaring them to be members of the working class. Former business executives and industrialists, and even former landlords and rich peasants, have also, in the main, been redefined as members of the working populace. Positive encouragement has been extended to overseas Chinese communities to contribute to China's modernization. The 'compatriots' of Hong Kong have been the most active element in the development of the various Special Economic Zones (SEZs) located on the southern coast, accounting for up to 80% of the joint ventures and other forms of economic co-operation. The adjoining province of Guangdong has also benefited from the association with Hong Kong. Indeed, the 'open door' policy has been deemed so successful that, beginning with the seventh Five-Year Plan (1986–92), China's economic strategy is being orientated to give priority to the development of its southern and eastern coastal regions. At the same time, laws have been enacted to render the SEZs attractive to foreign investors. In April 1988 it was announced that Hainan

Island would be developed into China's largest SEZ, with the status of a separate province. Although the 1992–96 Five Year Plan reflected a more conservative approach, seeking to 'confine' growth to 6% a year, this was soon challenged by Deng Xiaoping in early 1992, when he called for accelerated economic expansion and emphasized still further a pattern of growth modelled upon that of Hong Kong.

Thus, rural society has been transformed, as the family unit has gained at the expense of collectivism and as the significance of the market and rural-based industries has increased sharply. The political role of the CCP has declined, but many Party members have drawn on the administrative experience and extensive personal networks to establish themselves as 'specialized households', so as to generate sizeable incomes. At the same time rural unemployment, or underemployment, has become more evident while the long-standing provisions against the mobility of the population remain. In the cities tension has grown between the traditionally-favoured state enterprises and the numerous bureaucracies on the one hand, and the newer collective and private operators on the other. The impetus for money-making and consumerism has replaced Maoist orthodoxy, while corruption, nepotism and official racketeering have become more visible and widespread. Most urban dwellers and a growing number of rural people have access to the 'global village' of international television and radio transmissions. Traditional pre-Communist beliefs and customs re-emerged, particularly in the countryside. Official injunctions, designed to inculcate the values of 'socialist spiritual civilization', have been less than successful. The more conservative, veteran leaders have initiated short-lived campaigns against the more reformist CCP leaders and intellectuals. The first, against 'spiritual pollution' in 1983–84, rapidly went to excess and was brought to a premature end. The others, against 'bourgeois liberalization' in early 1987 and mid-1989, involved the dismissals of the General Secretaries of the CCP, Hu Yaobang and his replacement, Zhao Ziyang. These may all be seen as related to the social tensions engendered by the reforms, as they involve the problem of upholding the identity of China as a socialist country under CCP rule, while simultaneously reforming the economy along quasi-capitalist lines and opening it up to foreign influence.

PROBLEMS OF POLITICAL REFORM

By the mid-1980s there was evidence of major divisions within the Chinese élite about the direction and pace of economic reform and, above all, about the extent to which political reform should be a necessary component of economic change. Traditional Communist values no longer held sway. Indeed, the lack of belief in socialism and in the CCP itself, which was a legacy of the 'Cultural Revolution', became a crisis for the system. This crisis was intensified by the corruption and nepotism that was prevalent in the Party at all levels. Intellectuals who had hitherto been relatively quiescent under Party rule became increasingly critical and independent in their thinking.

Although it was not immediately apparent, the sixth plenary session of the 12th CCP Central Committee, held in September 1986, signalled the onset of an ideological struggle between contending factions within the Chinese leadership, which continued until mid-1987 and which finally culminated in the Beijing massacre of 4 June 1989. On the one side were those who favoured greater ideological diversity, democratization and structural reform as necessary for long-term economic modernization. On the other was a more conservative group supported by many of the long-serving revolutionary veterans, who held a more doctrinaire concept of the political role of the CCP, and who feared the potentially disruptive effects of some of the proposed reforms. Underlying the struggle was the question of electing a successor to Deng Xiaoping, and, indeed, successors to the generation of revolutionary veterans in their eighties.

In December 1986 demonstrations by students, demanding a greater measure of democracy, took place in Hefei, and then in Shanghai, Beijing and other major cities. By January 1987 the CCP had condemned these demonstrations as a threat to public order, and new municipal laws were enacted to prohibit them. Conservative leaders of the CCP and the army initiated a campaign against 'bourgeois liberalization' (defined, at the sixth plenary session of the 12th CCP Central Committee, as 'the negation of the socialist system in favour of capitalism'). On 16 January it was announced that Hu Yaobang had submitted his resignation as General Secretary of the CCP, having been compelled to undergo 'self-criticism', following accusations of allowing 'bourgeois liberalization' to spread. Following the departure of Hu Yaobang, Premier Zhao Ziyang assumed the additional duties of acting General Secretary of the CCP. Although he, too, had been a protégé of Deng Xiaoping and was a leading reformer, Zhao had not taken a public stand in the ideological quarrel, and enjoyed wide respect as an effective administrator and economic manager.

The 13th National Congress of the CCP, held in the period 25 October–1 November 1987, provided a major platform for Zhao, who still enjoyed the support of Deng. His report, which had undergone some drafting and redrafting within the Party, put forward the idea that China was at 'the initial stage of socialism'. Accordingly, there was no problem in abandoning the command economy (which by implication had been introduced prematurely) in favour of the market and of co-operation with Western countries provided, of course, that the Party's leading role remained in place. The slogan was that the State would regulate the market and the market would regulate the enterprises. Zhao went on to argue that the Party and state functions should be separated. That is, the Party should withdraw from the direct administration of the State and from the direct administration of enterprises, leaving those tasks to professional civil servants and trained managers respectively.

A new, younger and better-educated Central Committee was chosen. The 175 full and 110 alternate members had an average age of 55 years, and more than two-thirds had received university-level education. Many of the aged revolutionaries formally retired, although Deng Xiaoping retained the chairmanship of the Central Military Commission. The trend towards reform was confirmed at the 7th National People's Congress (NPC), which took place in March–April 1988. The long-standing Chairman of the NPC Standing Committee, Peng Zhen (who had presided over the delay of crucial legislation on enterprises), was replaced by the more reform-minded Wan Li.

In early 1988 Premier Zhao, with the public support of Deng Xiaoping, pursued a policy of rapid price reform, which had immediate inflationary consequences. The official annual inflation rate (considered to be a gross underestimate) rose from 7% in 1987 to more than 13% in the first quarter of 1988 (in urban areas 22%, including 44% for fresh vegetables). By June the rate had risen to 19%, and by July it had reached 24%. After highly contentious meetings of the senior leaders throughout mid-1988, the State Council announced its decision to defer any further reform of prices until 1990. Meanwhile, social tensions had been aggravated, and the economy was showing alarming signs of 'overheating'. A policy of retrenchment was announced.

The Tiananmen Massacre

The political struggle between the reformist and conservative factions in the higher reaches of the Party continued. On 15 April 1989 the former Party General Secretary, Hu Yaobang, died. As he was regarded as a symbol of political reform, student demonstrations erupted once again. Initially, the students were restrained, congregating around the memorial for revolutionary martyrs in Tiananmen Square in Beijing. Although their demand for Hu's posthumous rehabilitation over his forced resignation in January 1987 embarrassed the Party elders, they were nevertheless tolerant of the students. As protests persisted beyond Hu's funeral, Deng Xiaoping's patience expired, and at the instigation of Li Peng he authorized the issuing of a condemnatory *People's Daily* editorial. Unlike the student demonstrations of 1986/87, these protests were relatively restrained in demanding only a dialogue with state leaders and the ending of Party corruption. However, they also demanded a retraction of the editorial and the truthful reporting of their demonstrations. They were soon joined by the ordinary citizens of the capital, by workers, intellectuals, teachers and even civil servants, journalists, members of ministries and the security forces. At one stage, more than 1m. people congregated in the Square and its main approaches. Similar demonstrations took place in 81 other cities in China. The official visit of the Soviet President, Mikhail Gorbachev, from 15 to 18 May, was disrupted and upstaged. Two days earlier, some 3,000 students began a hunger strike to give further impetus to their demands. The

General Secretary of the Party, Zhao Ziyang, appeared to show a degree of sympathy to the demonstrators. After political struggles behind the scenes, which Zhao lost, martial law was declared on 20 May by Premier Li Peng and President Yang Shangkun. However, the soldiers sent to the centre of Beijing were stopped in their tracks by crowds of people. The demonstrators raised their demands by calling for the resignations of Li Peng, Yang Shangkun and Deng Xiaoping. On 30 May they erected a 30-m replica of the Statue of Liberty, called the Goddess of Democracy. On the night of 3–4 June 1989 heavily-armed troops, accompanied by tanks and armoured personnel carriers, shot their way into the main square, killing (according to eye-witness accounts) more than 1,000 students, workers and innocent bystanders. Some of the troops were massacred by the crowd. Both the demonstrations and the killings were witnessed by a world-wide television audience.

A conservative backlash ensued. It was alleged that a counter-revolutionary rebellion had been taking place and that the main victims had been soldiers. The principal decision-makers were the revolutionary veterans, now in their eighties and late seventies. On 23–24 June 1989 a plenary session of the CCP's Central Committee was held. It dismissed Zhao Ziyang from all his Party posts, as well as other prominent reformers, and it established an inquiry to examine his case further. The plenary confirmed Deng's version of events but, at the same time, it asserted its continued commitment to economic reform and the policies of the 'open door'. The Party Secretary from Shanghai, Jiang Zemin, was chosen as the new General Secretary of the CCP, and the Standing Committee of the Politburo was enlarged to six members. However, it was clear from the official accounts of the proceedings, and of the enlarged Politburo meeting that preceded it, that the effective rulers of China were the old revolutionary leaders.

The fifth plenary session of the CCP's Central Committee was held from 30 October to 3 November 1989. An attempt was made to prepare for the impending political succession with the resignation of Deng Xiaoping from the chairmanship of the Party's Central Military Commission in favour of Jiang Zemin. Although this meant that Deng no longer held any official posts, he was more than simply the ordinary retired citizen and CCP member that he claimed to be. He remained the country's effective paramount leader.

Deng Xiaoping's Final Years

In his twilight years Deng carried out two major endeavours of lasting significance for the development of China. He arranged for his succession in such a way as to provide for a smooth transition and to strengthen the institutionalization of Chinese political life. Secondly, he propelled China fully down the road of 'marketization' and rapid economic growth so as to break the hold that the remnant command sector had over the economy.

In the absence of an effective legal system, let alone one that can constrain the senior political leaders, China may still be characterized by what is called there 'rule by men instead of rule by law', but one of the striking legacies of Deng Xiaoping has been the attempt to institutionalize key areas of political life. Thus, the functions of the main central political organizations have been more clearly specified, and meetings are now held at regular intervals according to proper procedures. More importantly, Deng established a system by which office holders must retire once they reach particular ages. Even the senior leaders are technically not allowed to put their names forward for re-election at national congresses once they have reached the age of 70. This development has been strengthened by the transition of leadership from the old guard of the revolutionary veterans to the bureaucratic technocrats who were trained in the Soviet-influenced era of the 1950s. If the former drew their authority from their personal stature as founding fathers who had achieved so much, the latter's standing stemmed from their institutional positions. The link between the two sources of authority was that the technocrats had been selected by the founders as their successors. Although political succession might be seen as a fundamental weakness in the Chinese political system, the actual transition from Deng to Jiang proceeded remarkably smoothly. Jiang Zemin emerged as a political leader in his own right, who, none the less, was constrained by the need to compromise with other major leaders and to cultivate powerful constituencies such as the military.

Deng Xiaoping had technically retired in 1989, yet he continued to dominate Chinese politics until, in late 1994, he declined into inactivity, eventually dying on 19 February 1997, at the age of 92. By living to such an age, he succeeded in surviving most of the other revolutionary veterans, many of whom were less enthusiastic about his reforms and who may well have been able to upstage the younger Jiang Zemin. Notable among these was the austere Chen Yun, the most important of the conservative reformers, who died in April 1995. By the time of Deng's death, his successors, the seven-member Standing Committee of the Politburo headed by Jiang Zemin, whom Deng had designated the 'core leader', had been in charge of daily affairs for a considerable time, so that Deng's passing was marked by a singular calmness.

Deng Xiaoping left behind him a country that had largely recovered from the traumas of the Tiananmen killings, the collapse of the European Communist regimes in 1989, and the demise of the USSR, 'the motherland of socialism', two years later. His response to these critical events, which deepened the crisis of Communism in China, was to emphasize rapid economic growth, in order to increase prosperity and elicit popular support for the stability provided by Communist rule. Influenced by the example of Singapore, Deng saw no contradiction between maintaining authoritarian rule and encouraging rapid economic expansion and the attendant socio-economic changes. The alternative to Communist rule, according to Deng, was the chaos evident in the former USSR. Thus, he strengthened the forces of order while simultaneously stimulating economic reforms and the opening-up of China to the outside world.

In early 1992, in the course of an imperial-like tour of southern China, Deng challenged the prevailing conservative, or 'leftist', drift, by calling for a dramatic increase in the rate of economic growth and for the intensification of the policies of economic reform and openness. He urged Guangdong Province to catch up with the newly-industrialized economies of East Asia, so as to be a model for the rest of China. He promoted the cause of the market, overcoming resistance from Beijing, by denying the significance in this regard of the distinction between capitalist and socialist practices. The 14th Congress of the CCP, held in October 1992, formally endorsed his concept of the 'socialist market economy.' At the Congress Deng oversaw the succession of a younger generation, with the average age of the Politburo being reduced from 69 to under 63, and the 'election' of a Central Committee with more professionally-qualified younger members, 61% of whom were under 55. Just as Deng found that he had to use his personal authority to overcome resistance to economic advance from those institutions whose authority he was trying to enhance, so he realized that he had to carry out a purge of a leading member of the Central Military Commission in the traditional secretive way, rather than in the more modern style he avowedly espoused. Moreover, the only exception to the rejuvenation of the central leaders was in the military, whose two leading figures were 76 and 78 years old. Clearly, Deng had trouble in finding younger men whom both he and the military could trust.

Jiang Zemin as the Core Leader

At the time of his nomination in 1989 many observers inside and outside China regarded Jiang Zemin as a political 'lightweight' and as something of an interim appointment. In the event, Jiang had more than seven years to ease himself into the most senior post. By the time that Deng died in 1997, Jiang Zemin had cleverly manoeuvred some members of his so-called Shanghai faction into leading positions in both the state and party organizations. Perhaps even more significantly, he also made extensive new appointments to the senior military positions. Although some of these were no more than reshuffles of regional leaders, it meant that key military members owed their appointment to Jiang, who has been able to retain the loyalty of the army, despite becoming its first civilian leader without any experience of military service. Thus, by the time of the 15th Party Congress in September 1997, Jiang Zemin was well placed to consolidate his position as the 'core leader'. He successfully removed troublesome opponents, Qiao Shi, the former minister and Chairman of the NPC, who had challenged some of Jiang's positions from an apparently more liberal perspective, and the 81-year-old Gen. Liu Huaqing. Although Jiang did not entirely succeed in determining the new appointments to the Politburo and its Standing Committee, he emerged from the Congress with his personal authority considerably enhanced. The new Central Committee of 193 full and 151 alternate members could be said to reflect Jiang's experience and outlook. Only 43% of the previous Central Committee's members were re-elected, with most of the remainder being excluded owing to their age. Yet the new Committee's average age of 55.9 years was not even six months lower than the previous average at the time of selection. Similarly, the membership remained largely technocratic, with more than 90% educated to college standard, and the vast majority having bureaucratic experience. These developments were taken a stage further at the Ninth NPC, which convened in March 1998, when Li Peng displaced Qiao Shi as Chairman of the NPC Standing Committee and Zhu Rongji, the former Mayor of Shanghai, became the new Premier of the State Council. He announced that the ministries of the State Council would be reduced in number from 40 to 29, with about one-half of these to be headed by ministers aged in their fifties.

Unfortunately, Jiang and Zhu inherited an economy that was already decelerating after the phenomenal rates of double-digit growth achieved in 1993–95. Indeed, Zhu Rongji had been widely praised for having engineered a successful 'soft landing' for the economy. At this stage it became possible for the senior leadership to encourage village democracy as a means to constrain corrupt local officials. The idea was that villagers would hardly choose those who had cheated them. The results were mixed as far as democratic accountability was concerned, since the election results needed confirmation by authorities at the next higher level. Nevertheless, this was a sign of progress in itself, and it attracted much interest in the West. The broader difficulty was that, by the time Jiang and Zhu took office, economic deceleration was becoming a problem, partly because of the impact of the Asian economic crisis that began in July 1997. China lost the Asian market that accounted for nearly one-fifth of the value of its exports, and the amount of foreign direct investment coming into the country began to decline sharply. Furthermore, the long-standing difficulties of the state-owned enterprises (SOEs) suddenly became more acute, leading to a precipitate fall in central government revenues. The post-Deng leadership decided to address the situation by undertaking a fundamental restructuring of the SOEs, despite the rapid rise in unemployment that would ensue. Economically, the SOEs received huge subsidies that in one form or another accounted for one-third of central budgetary expenditure. Yet they were also massively in debt to each other and to the banking sector, which meant that reform of the latter had to be postponed. Accordingly, it was announced at the 15th Party Congress that apart from some 500–1,000 large strategic SOEs, the remaining 150,000 would be restructured by means of amalgamations, share flotations and even bankruptcies. The decision was reaffirmed at the following NPC in March 1998, when the new Premier, Zhu Rongji, also announced that the number of civil servants in the central bureaucracies would be reduced by one-half.

Zhu promised to complete the reforms within three years, thereby suggesting that he did not fully appreciate the severity of the deceleration of domestic demand, which continued to decline during the following two years. Official figures claiming growth rates of 7%–8% took no account of the vast unsold inventories accumulated by SOEs, in particular. The growth of exports declined, as did that of foreign direct investment. Consequently, the pace of reform slowed as the Government attempted to promote expansion through massive state investment in infrastructure (principally transport, communications, energy and water conservation). Nevertheless, the authorities continued to press SOEs to restructure in order to reduce losses; this inevitably entailed laying off workers. In 1999, for example, according to official figures, 11.74m. SOE employees were made redundant, some 40% of whom reportedly found new jobs.

It was against this background of failure to stimulate domestic demand that Zhu Rongji visited Washington in April 1999, prepared to make unprecedented concessions in the hope of gaining US approval for China's bid to enter the World Trade Organization (WTO). The calculation was that the immediate effect of accession would be to stimulate the economy by a rapid inflow of new foreign direct investment and by overcoming obstacles to increasing Chinese exports. However, against the advice of his executive officers, President Clinton refused to endorse the bid for reasons pertaining to US domestic politics. Although Clinton soon changed his mind, the damage was done, and the unfortunate Premier returned home to a storm of criticism from China's telecommunications, finance and agricultural sectors for his readiness to make concessions at their expense. The wave of anti-US feeling provoked by the bombing of the Chinese embassy in Belgrade, Yugoslavia, on 7 May made Zhu's position even worse. Jiang Zemin, who supposedly represented the mainstream approach, continued to call for reform of the SOEs, but qualified this by conveying opposition to privatization. No support was expressed for the Premier's original offer to the USA, and by the end of June the normally assertive and autocratic Zhu seemed in danger of being marginalized. However, in the absence of any alternative economic programme, Zhu survived. As the sentiments aroused by the bombing began to dissipate, in November the USA finally negotiated an agreement on substantially the same terms. The EU followed suit in May 2000, and the way was finally clear for China to join the WTO in late 2001—a development that will not only significantly open China still further to international commerce, but that will also result in the transformation of many features of the Chinese economy. When the second session of the Ninth NPC convened in March 1999 it was evident that the position of the reformers had strengthened, as the Constitution was amended to allow greater scope to private enterprise. Meanwhile, the authorities took steps to strengthen their control of access to the internet within China, and Jiang Zemin encouraged the CCP to establish party cells in private companies.

As far as the President was concerned, a new and entirely unexpected challenge to the status quo emerged with a demonstration in April 1999 by an ostensibly quietist sect encompassing Buddhist and Daoist elements and composed largely of the middle-aged: the Falun Gong. Shocked to find that the sect had adherents in the highest circles of the élite, Jiang hastily had it condemned as a 'cult' and prosecuted it with the full coercive force of the regime. These alleged subversives continued their quiet demonstrations, and they appeared not to be intimidated by harassment and the arrest of thousands of practitioners, including government and party officials. The President's inability to control the spiritual movement entirely was indicative of how much authority, as opposed to power, the CCP had lost. Perhaps with this in mind, Jiang Zemin personally launched a campaign in February 2000 to revitalize the Party, by urging it to stand for the 'three representations', stressing that it would 'always represent the development needs of China's advanced social productive forces, always represent the onward direction of China's advanced culture, and always represent the fundamental interests of the largest number of Chinese people'. It was not until mid-2001 that the Chinese authorities began to overcome the challenge of the Falun Gong, at least to the extent that its followers were no longer able to mount public demonstrations. Yet adherents continually were reported by human rights organizations to be subject to horrendous treatment in prisons and detention camps, which sometimes resulted in mass suicides. During early 2002 members of the Falun Gong were able to intercept television broadcasts in several cities, and broadcast short messages contradicting the Government's anti-cult propaganda. The incidents raised new questions regarding the authorities' ability to control the activities of Falun Gong.

Meanwhile, during 1999–2001 the Chinese authorities were especially active in suppressing open dissent. Religious groups, indigenous human rights campaigners and democracy activists were subject to direct attacks by the security organs. Better-known activists were among those imprisoned without regard to due process, even by the limited terms of Chinese judicial procedures. The regime was particularly alert to the alleged threat posed by Muslim Uygur groups to Chinese rule in the region of Xinjiang. In the course of these three years there were a number of highly-publicized violent incidents associated with them. The regime used these threats as an opportunity to target other religious groups who had not registered with the authorities, thereby resisting their control. Yet during this period of egregious infringements of basic human rights, the Government signed the two main UN Conventions on Human Rights and even ratified the one concerned with economic and social rights. The regime, however, was remorseless when it came to dealing with matters it judged to threaten its ability to control order and social stability. By 2001 the regime had detained a number of mainly US scholars of Chinese origin and thereby received massive adverse publicity. Yet such was the enhanced prestige of China arising, for example, from its new standing in the world as a major trading nation (with its total trade reaching US $475,000m. in 2000, it now ranked as eighth), that Beijing was awarded the Olympic Games for 2008. Many in the West claimed that this would have the effect of encouraging political reform and liberalization. A more likely cause of change would be membership of the WTO, which would require greater adherence to the rule of law and greater respect for the autonomy of professions such as the law, accountancy, banking, etc.

Jiang's attempt to transform the CCP from a proletarian party to one that represented the people as a whole did not command full support within the party. Objections were raised to the idea that business people who had hitherto been regarded as exploiting capitalists could now become party members. Nevertheless, in mid-2001 a plenary session of the Central Committee agreed to admit them. By this stage party leaders had become reconciled to the implications of the fact that the once all-dominant state-owned enterprises contributed less than 30% of the value of industrial production.

The attention of party leaders was increasingly focused on the issue of political succession to be determined at the 16th Party Congress, which was scheduled to commence on 8 November 2002. Under the convention introduced by Deng Xiaoping, the leading triumvirate of President Jiang Zemin, Premier Zhu Rongji and NPC Standing Committee Chairman Li Peng (all having passed the age of 70) were due to retire from all their posts in favour of the next (fourth) generation led by Hu Jintao. It became apparent, however, that Jiang wanted to stay on in at least one of his positions or, failing that, to have his authority enhanced beyond retirement by amending the Party's constitution to incorporate his theory of the 'three represents' and to have his close associates appointed to leading posts. Not surprisingly, many saw this as a bid to retain power at the expense of Hu Jintao, who had been singled out by Deng as 'the core of the fourth generation'. At issue was power and its privileges as no major policy questions seemed to be at stake.

The Social Impact of the Reforms

Chinese society has undergone massive changes since the reforms began more than 20 years ago and, if anything, the pace of change has accelerated in the last decade. Average incomes have more than doubled in real terms, and the number of those classified in dire poverty has declined from over 300m. to under 60m. The Chinese people may be said to have experienced a revolution even more profound than that accompanying the Communist triumph in 1949. The beginnings of a middle class are evident in the prosperous coastal belt, but much of the interior is still held back by the legacy of the Stalinist economic system and by a sense of having fallen behind. Unemployment is increasing, and China's cities are filled with 100m.–150m. migrants from the countryside. After an initial rise, peasant real income has fallen in the last few years. There are many sources for social unrest. Corruption is widespread, and leaders worry that it could lead to the downfall of the Party. Although the regime has strengthened its powers of repression since the Tiananmen killings, and despite its undoubted effectiveness in eliminating all overt forms of political opposition, its actual control over the daily lives of its people has diminished. Communist ideology has few adherents, and Chinese society is pervaded by what the official press describes as 'money worship'. The determinant of schooling, work, type of housing, nature of consumer goods purchased, material quality of life and even place of residence has become money and not the dictates of CCP officials. In May 1994 the authorities finally announced the disbandment of the housing registration system (which had traditionally been the means of tying people to one place and subjecting them to easy control by their local or work units), because it had become unsustainable. In the late 1990s the main sentiment holding the Chinese people together was state-inspired 'patriotism'. Yet this, combined with looser forms of social control, also contributed to greater ethnic unrest in Xinjiang and Tibet where the local peoples found themselves in danger of being displaced by ethnic Chinese who were the principal beneficiaries of the economic reforms. Significantly, a report released in May 2001 under the auspices of the CCP's Organization Department gave a grim impression of an unsettled and sharply-divided society, which was seething with discontent about official corruption, economic inequalities and the failure of existing social safety nets. It detailed widespread riots and disturbances. As seen by the leadership, the answer lay in ensuring that the economy would be able to absorb most of the unemployed by growing at an annual rate of at least 7%. From a longer-term perspective, the key question was whether the political changes that had taken place would give the Government sufficient confidence and the necessary support to survive the social changes that lay ahead. Ominously for the Government, in March 2002 there were large protests in the north-eastern cities of Daqing and Liaoyang by tens of thousands of workers made redundant by the restructuring of state companies, demanding a better social security system. The possibility of further such demonstrations in the future was a source of constant anxiety as the CCP prepared for the transfer of power to the fourth generation leadership.

CHINA AND THE WORLD

During the 'Cultural Revolution', China chose the policy of exclusion—a policy of revolutionary isolationism. In 1965, when the USA first bombed North Viet Nam and then introduced combat troops in the South, Mao decided, after much debate among his colleagues, that China would not join in united action with the USSR to help North Viet Nam, but that it would continue to aid North Viet Nam independently. Meanwhile, he also urged the Vietnamese communists to adopt a low-key guerrilla strategy in the South. His advice was not followed. By 1966 China had suffered several reverses in the developing world, and, having presumably calculated that the USA would neither invade North Viet Nam nor bomb China, Mao was able to focus on the 'Cultural Revolution'. The underlying strategic view, that the USA was the main enemy and that the USSR sought to collude with it (at the expense of China, the developing countries and revolution in general), was shattered in 1968. The USA was seen to have reached the limits of its Viet Nam adventure as a result of the communist offensive during the Tet (lunar new year) festival of that year, while the USSR was regarded as a potential threat because of its invasion of Czechoslovakia (in August 1968) and its major military deployments to the north of China. Beijing promptly abandoned its diplomatic isolation and sought to restore relations with countries bordering the USSR and even with 'heretic' Yugoslavia. This expansion of outside contacts was soon extended to developing countries and to the small and medium-sized capitalist powers.

The military tension with the USSR led to clashes on the Ussuri river border in March 1969. These conflicts were not resolved until a Soviet armoured column penetrated into Xinjiang, and Aleksei Kosygin, the Chairman of the USSR Council of Ministers, held a meeting with Zhou and Mao at Beijing airport in September. Following fears of a Soviet nuclear strike, the US President, Richard Nixon, and his national security adviser, Dr Henry Kissinger, began moves that culminated in the latter's surprise visit to Beijing in July 1971. It was then announced that Nixon would visit China in the early part of the following year. In October the UN General Assembly expelled representatives of Taiwan and invited the People's Republic to take up China's seat. In February 1972 Nixon duly visited China, to be received by Mao and later to sign the famous Shanghai communiqué with Zhou Enlai. In effect, China had helped to change the central balance between the two superpowers by its shift from alliance with the USSR in the 1950s to alignment with the USA in the 1970s.

For the remainder of the 1970s China sought to build an anti-Soviet coalition against what it regarded as the major expansionist power in the world. During this time the closer relations that China forged with the USA were tempered by concern that, in the era of *détente*, the USA was insufficiently vigilant in confronting the alleged Soviet threat, and by anxiety that the US Government was too dilatory over the Taiwan issue.

China's new Western-orientated foreign policy included the normalization of relations with Japan; moreover, in sharp contrast with the earlier period of the 'Cultural Revolution', not only did trade rapidly expand, but, in the period up to Mao's death and the official end of the 'Cultural Revolution' in October 1976, China imported complete industrial plants to the value of more than US $3,000m.

In the aftermath of the final victory of the revolutionary forces in Indo-China in 1975, Chinese fears of Soviet encirclement, following the US withdrawal, increased. These fears were exacerbated by what were perceived as Soviet advances in Africa and in the People's Democratic Republic of Yemen. Events in Indo-China brought matters to a culmination. The rapid deterioration of Sino-Vietnamese relations, accompanied by the emotionally-charged exodus of Hoa Chinese from Viet Nam, was centred mainly on the issue of Cambodia, where China was aligned with the infamous Pol Pot as part of a long-standing policy to deny to Viet Nam dominance over the whole of Indo-China. As Viet Nam consolidated its ties with the USSR in 1978, China signed a treaty of peace and friendship with Japan and, in December (during the course of the vital third plenum), normalized relations with the USA. Towards the end of December Viet Nam duly invaded Cambodia and, within a fortnight, had occupied most of the country and established a subservient regime in Phnom-Penh. In February–March 1979 China attacked Viet Nam in an exercise that was announced in advance to be of limited duration and penetration. The campaign did not go well for China's forces. Nevertheless, after the capture of the provincial capital of Long Son, the Chinese army withdrew. Perhaps both China and Viet Nam had been taught a lesson, but, importantly from the Chinese point of view, the USSR did not directly intervene.

For the next 10 years the result was deadlock in Indo-China, which left Viet Nam in a parlous economic condition, politically isolated and dependent upon the USSR. China, meanwhile, acted along parallel lines with the USA, forged an alliance with Thailand and a diplomatic partnership with the countries of the Association of South East Asian Nations (ASEAN), despite misgivings by at least two of its members. The collapse of the USSR left Viet Nam economically bereft and totally incapable of sustaining its occupation of Cambodia. China, therefore, was able to impose its terms for an accommodation with Viet Nam that was achieved in 1991, and at the same time to co-sponsor a UN Security Council Resolution for settling the Cambodian problem. Accordingly, China was able to attain its main objectives in Indo-China through the UN. In this way Chinese leaders could portray themselves as important and responsible members of the international community—a significant consideration in view of the international disapprobation still attached to China after the Tiananmen killings.

Since embarking upon the policies of reform and opening-up in 1978, economic considerations have become an increasingly important component of China's foreign relations. As China's leaders put it, they sought a tranquil international environment in which to concentrate on domestic economic tasks. To this end, they were quick to seize upon the perceived decline of the Soviet threat, and in 1982, at the 12th Congress of the CCP, Hu Yaobang announced that China was to pursue a foreign policy of independence, which would chart a more balanced path between the two superpowers. Indeed, China still tilted towards the USA, but Chinese leaders sought to manoeuvre more freely. China's problems with the USSR were epitomized by the reiterated demands that it remove the so-called 'three obstacles' (withdraw from Afghanistan, reduce the military threat from the north, and end the support to Viet Nam that enabled it to occupy Cambodia). Following the accession of Mikhail Gorbachev to the Soviet presidency, the USSR developed new approaches to foreign policy which met Chinese demands and paved the way for a summit meeting between Gorbachev and Deng Xiaoping in May 1989. The meeting was overshadowed by the student-led demonstrations in Beijing. Hopes that the two reforming Communist powers might build new relations were dashed in part because of the Tiananmen bloodshed, but in the main because of the collapse of Communism in Eastern Europe, for which the Chinese leadership privately held Gorbachev responsible to a considerable degree. The failure of the Soviet coup of August 1991 disappointed China's leaders. Yet they reacted with unusual aplomb to the collapse of the USSR itself. They very rapidly moved to establish correct relations with the successor states, including those of Central Asia.

China's relations with the West in general, and the USA in particular, have been marked by a curious ambivalence. On the one hand, China's leaders recognize the importance of the West for China's modernization as a supplier of technology, managerial expertise, capital, etc.; and on the other, they fear the possibility of Westernization and the erosion of the Chinese Communist system that may follow. These concerns have focused especially upon relations with the USA. For much of the 1980s China's leaders were able to manoeuvre within the so-called strategic triangle involving both the USSR and the USA. As a result, they were able to reap many of the benefits of a quasi-alignment with the USA without paying what they would have regarded as excessive costs in terms of dependency and loss of independence. Thus, China and the USA pursued parallel policies regarding the Cambodian and Afghan conflicts. They were separately allied with Thailand and Pakistan, and they both gave material and diplomatic support to the armed resistance to the Vietnamese and Russian invaders respectively. The Chinese were also able to gain access to advanced technology of military significance. At the same time the existence of the USSR as a counterweight to the USA enabled China's leaders to pursue in principle an independent foreign policy. Despite the continuation of the Taiwan issue as a problem between the two sides, China won favour within the USA because of its economic reforms and its open-door policies. Its poor record on human rights proved to be no obstacle to gaining US support for accession to international economic organizations, such as the World Bank and the IMF, from which China gained greatly. Unlike the USSR, China was also allowed entry into the domestic US market on the basis of Most Favoured Nation (MFN) trading status (now Normal Trade Relations—NTR).

Much of this changed with the end of the Cold War and the ramifications of the Tiananmen killings. At a stroke, the perhaps unduly favourable image of China's leaders in the West changed fundamentally. Moreover, the ending of the Cold War also brought to a close a period in world history in which China was regarded as an important player in global strategy. Thus marginalized strategically and despised politically because of the Tiananmen massacre, China's leaders found themselves subject to a series of Western sanctions. Sanctions began to be withdrawn within about 18 months, and China's international prestige started to recover. Through skilful diplomacy and by virtue of its size and weight in international affairs, as symbolized by its position as one of the five permanent members of the UN Security Council, China has shown that it cannot be ignored.

Owing to its rapid rate of economic growth, China has come to be regarded as the next rising world power. That view contributed to the US-led insistence that China conform better to what were presented as universal norms of state conduct. In particular, the USA emphasized observance of human rights, agreements about the non-proliferation of weapons of mass destruction and medium-range missiles, greater transparency in military matters and various trade practices, including intellectual property rights (IPR). In 1994 the US President, Bill Clinton, gave way on the MFN issue by dissociating it from human rights. In February 1995, after tense negotiations, the Chinese eventually acceded to US demands on IPR. By this stage, however, Chinese strategists had come to the conclusion that the USA was imposing various constraints upon China in a concerted attempt to maintain its weakness. Matters came to a head when President Lee Teng-hui of Taiwan was granted a visa to visit the USA in a private capacity in April 1995. The USA was then accused of seeking to divide China. Beijing denounced President Lee in the most virulent terms for allegedly seeking independence, and in late 1995 initiated a series of intimidatory military manoeuvres. These culminated in March 1996 with the firing of missiles into the sea within less than 100 km of Taiwan's two major ports. If anything, these tactics produced the opposite of the effect intended, as Lee was overwhelmingly returned to office in the island's first direct presidential election. Moreover, the USA responded by sending two aircraft carrier battle groups. The crisis of March 1996 ironically paved the way for an improvement in Sino-US relations, as both sides sought to avoid similar confrontations in the future. Meanwhile, the USA upgraded its strategic alliance with Japan by agreeing new guidelines that widened the scope of the support that Japan might give to US forces engaged in a conflict in the region. A closer Sino-US dialogue developed, in part to assuage Chinese concerns about the possible implications of those guidelines for the Taiwan Strait. These developments culminated in an important exchange of presidential visits, by Jiang Zemin to the USA, in late October–early November 1997, and by Bill Clinton to China, in late June–early July 1998. The two Presidents agreed to establish a 'strategic partnership', and Clinton's visit was notable for his address to the Chinese people, broadcast live on television and radio, in which he denounced the Tiananmen killings and called for greater democracy. However, Clinton also praised Jiang's personal qualities and the 'moral' worth of China's reform programmes.

This improvement in relations was tested by the election of George W. Bush to the US presidency. After his assumption of office in January 2001, there was no more talk of strategic partnerships; instead China was viewed as a potential 'strategic competitor' in some respects and as a country with which the USA had important economic links in other respects. In practice, relations were strained initially by an accident on 1 April between a US surveillance aircraft and a Chinese jet that was monitoring it. The collision, which killed the pilot of the Chinese aircraft and forced the US aeroplane to make an emergency landing on Hainan Island, led to a crisis that was not resolved until the 24 US crew members had been released 12 days later. Meanwhile, the atmosphere had not been improved by a decision by the new US administration to accede to requests from Taiwan for most of the modern weaponry required by the island. However, both Beijing and Washington recognized that it was not in their interests to allow their relationship to deteriorate unduly and thus ensured that their economic ties were unaffected. The Chinese leadership, nevertheless, objected to what it saw as US hegemonic attempts to prevent China's rise and favoured the development of multi-polarity among the world's great powers as a means to constrain the unilateralism of the single superpower. The Chinese objected especially to aspects of the anti-ballistic-missile systems supported by the Bush administration, as they feared that these would undermine the Chinese deterrent force and promote Taiwanese independence by providing protection for Taiwan against China.

The terrorist attacks on the USA on 11 September 2001 led to a certain improvement in the all-important relationship with that country. China was quick to join the US-led coalition against international terrorism. Although the Chinese leadership did not contribute directly to the campaign against al-Qa'ida and the Taliban of Afghanistan, it did begin to share intelligence and undertook to deny financial assets and service to international terrorists. Although China did not elicit formal US support against alleged Uygur terrorists in Xinjiang, the administration of George W. Bush reduced its criticism of Chinese human rights violations. Jiang was pleased by the fact that President Bush visited China twice within six months (in October 2001 and again in February 2002). Although outstanding differences remained, neither pressed the other hard on any particular issue. From a Chinese perspective this meant having to tolerate a new and potentially prolonged US military presence in Central Asia as well as a revival of the USA's strategic interest in South and South-East Asia.

Nevertheless, the end of the Cold War was strategically beneficial to China, as it ensured that for the first time since its establishment in 1949 the People's Republic was no longer subject to military threat from a superior power. Consequently, the requirements of economic modernization have become even more important in the country's foreign policy. Better relations have been forged with China's neighbours, including the newly-established states of Central Asia and Russia itself. Indeed, relations between Moscow and Beijing have been described by both sets of leaders as better than ever before. In the absence of the Soviet factor, its former allies, Viet Nam and India, have accommodated themselves more to Chinese interests.

The Democratic People's Republic of Korea (North Korea) too found itself more dependent upon China and, under Chinese pressure, along with the Republic of Korea (South Korea) it joined the UN in 1991. Yet it did not follow the Chinese in reforming its troubled economy and in opening up to the outside world, and the North Korean leaders were greatly angered by China's formal recognition of the South in 1992. North Korea then began to use its perceived nuclear potential in a desperate diplomatic bid to ensure its survival. China skilfully manoeuvred between its own conflicting interests of seeking to avoid the collapse of the North, while at the same time striving to prevent the proliferation of nuclear weapons in North-East Asia. The US Government, which eventually reached an agreement with the North in 1994, acknowledged that China had played an important role behind the scenes. In July 1997 it was agreed that China would formally participate in negotiations with North and South Korea and the USA, within the framework of the so-called '2+2' formula. The first round of talks was held in Geneva, in December, and a second round, held in March 1998, was chaired by the Chinese Deputy Minister of Foreign Affairs. Further rounds took place in New York during 1999. Although the talks subsequently stalled, China was pleased with the first North-South summit meeting, which was held in Pyongyang in mid-2000. Chinese interests were best served by the establishment of a kind of co-existence between the two Koreas, as that would allow the North to remain as an unofficial buffer state. Hence, the George W. Bush administration, like its predecessor, had come to realize the advantage of using China as an interlocutor with the North. The North Korean leader, Kim Jong Il himself, who rarely travelled abroad, visited China twice in eight months—in May 2000 and in January 2001—and Jiang Zemin visited North Korea in September 2001, emphasizing the close relationship between the two countries. However, one potential source of disagreement between the two countries was the fate of hundreds of thousands of North Korean refugees living in China. A number of these sought asylum in several foreign embassies in Beijing in early 2002, embarrassing the Chinese authorities.

Elsewhere in the Asia-Pacific region China has made significant gains, amid uncertainties as to whether the country is a stabilizing or a destabilizing influence. On the positive side, despite the Asian financial crisis of the late 1990s, China is acknowledged to have assumed a significant role in enhancing the economy of the region as a whole. It has forged closer ties with Japan, which has become a major trading partner, and economic relations have deepened with the Republic of Korea, Taiwan and the ASEAN countries. China's adjacent provinces of Fujian and Guangdong have become increasingly integrated with the economies of Taiwan and Hong Kong; collectively they are recognized as 'Greater China', which represents one of the USA's largest trading partners. On the more negative side, China has territorial claims involving nearly all of its maritime neighbours. No means have been found of settling the competing claims, and China is torn between the nationalist urge to assert control over these islands and disputed territorial seas, on the one hand, and the economic necessity of establishing stable peaceable relations with the same disputants on the other. Meanwhile, China's leaders are also troubled by what they regard as US hegemonic attempts to constrain China's progress, especially by preventing it from recovering Taiwan. Consequently, China's leaders have put pressure on the South-East Asian nations to disavow the US system of alliances as relics from the Cold War. Yet from the viewpoint of the governments of these countries, the US military presence in the Western Pacific provides reassurance about the stability of the region and indeed it is precisely because of these alliances that they feel able to engage China in constructive ways. The problem is even more evident in the case of Japan. The Chinese authorities still complain that, as the Japanese have not come to terms with their aggression in the recent past (demonstrated by their failure to make a full apology for atrocities committed during 1937–45), the tendency toward militarism is not far below the surface. Consequently, they quietly appreciate that the US security alliance keeps the Japanese from returning to the military path. However, they are concerned that perhaps the USA is preparing Japan to play a more active military role in the region. The visits in 2001 and 2002 by Japanese Prime Minister Junichiro Koizumi to a controversial war memorial honouring Japan's war dead angered China, which feared a resurgence of nationalist feeling in Japan.

In April 1996 an unprecedented multilateral treaty was signed with Russia and the three Central Asian Republics of Kazakhstan, Kyrgyzstan and Tajikistan, the countries becoming known as the Shanghai Five. This went beyond agreement about the demarcation of the long-disputed borders to include commitments to engage in military confidence-building measures and a pledge to refrain from exacerbating ethnic or religious tensions in each other's countries. In June 2001 these links were reaffirmed with the establishment of the Shanghai Co-operation Organization, and the number of participating states was increased to six with the accession of Uzbekistan. However, the importance of this grouping seemed to diminish after September 2001, when the USA began establishing a military presence in the region in connection with its war against the ruling Taliban in Afghanistan. Meanwhile, China's leaders had continued a series of exchanges with their Russian counterparts, culminating in the signing of a new treaty of partnership and friendship in July 2001. The new multilateral character of Chinese diplomacy was also evident in dealings with the regional organizations of South-East Asia where it was becoming an ever more important factor in the regional economy, and in February 2002 China reached a landmark agreement with the 10 member states of ASEAN to work towards a free trade agreement within 10 years.

In 1997 the Chinese Government formally signed the Comprehensive Test Ban Treaty, which prohibits nuclear testing. China's integration with the international community was indeed gathering pace. China's membership of international organizations increased from 71 in 1977 to 677 in 1989, including the World Bank and the IMF. Fifteen years after first applying to rejoin the General Agreement on Tariffs and Trade (GATT), China entered the successor WTO in December 2001. China is a member of the main Asia-Pacific regional organizations, such as APEC and the ASEAN Regional Forum (ARF), but these are mainly of a consultative nature. It remains to be seen whether its neighbours' attempts to engage China in diverse patterns of co-operation will succeed in defusing the incipient conflicts over the sovereignty of groups of islands in adjoining seas (see History of Taiwan) and whether an increasingly-powerful China will be prepared to address the concerns of neighbouring states.

On 1 July 1997 Hong Kong was returned to China under the terms of the Sino-British Joint Declaration that was agreed in September 1984. The Chinese Government undertook to allow Hong Kong to enjoy a high degree of autonomy as a Special Administrative Region (SAR), so as to maintain its economic system and way of life for a further 50 years. This unique arrangement of 'one country, two systems' is regarded in China as a potential model for the eventual reunion of Taiwan with the mainland. The negotiations between the United Kingdom and China were often acrimonious, and the Chinese were particularly displeased with the last British Governor, Christopher Patten, whom they vilified for his attempts to broaden democracy in the territory without first securing their consent. Consequently, in 1997 they replaced the legislature elected in 1995 with a provisional body. Elections to a new legislative body were held in May 1998, under a mixed system of voting, in which the number of people eligible to vote was severely reduced. Yet, despite apprehensions on all sides, the transition to Chinese sovereignty went smoothly. There was little evidence that the Chinese had broken their undertaking not to interfere in the affairs of the SAR. The principal possible exception was in mid-1999 when Beijing issued a reinterpretation of the Basic Law, having been invited to do so by Hong Kong's Chief Executive, Tung Chee-hwa, after his disagreement with a ruling of the Court of Final Appeal. Indeed it has been argued that the problem is less one of China's willingness to interfere, and more related to the perception that Tung may be too eager to anticipate Beijing's wishes. The major problem to affect Hong Kong was the unexpected effect of the Asian economic crisis that began shortly after the territory's transfer in mid-1997. On 19 December 1999 Macao, the first and last Western possession in Asia, returned to Chinese sovereignty on a similar basis to that of Hong Kong.

Although China's leaders are reconciled to the global predominance of the USA as the world's sole superpower, they still seek to encourage movement towards a more multi-polar world that would enable China better to balance US power. In practice, however, China wishes to maintain good relations with the USA largely because it is a major export market and because it is a guarantor of security in the Asia-Pacific region. The conditions of US predominance have served Chinese interests well by providing a peaceful environment in which, since the late 1970s, China has been able to develop its economy so well. The US strategic presence has ensured the absence of war in Korea and the containment of possible Japanese militarism. The main practical issue is the question of Taiwan. Beyond that, the Chinese appear to have learned how to balance their practical need to work with the USA against their principled opposition to much of what the USA stands for. However, with the 16th National Congress of the CCP rescheduled to commence in November 2002, the more immediate problem for China's leaders is how to manage the forthcoming succession against a background of sharpening social contradictions.

Economy

HANS HENDRISCHKE

INTRODUCTION

For China's economic decision-makers, the year 2002 started amidst both enthusiasm and trepidation. In 2001 China had joined the World Trade Organization (WTO) and experienced another year of strong growth in its international trade. At the same time, the domestic economy was suffering from deflation and weak domestic demand. The prospects for 2002 appeared better, with first half-year gross domestic product (GDP) growth of 7.5%, driven by stronger domestic consumer demand and investment in a weak global economic environment. According to official figures, China's GDP in 2001 grew by 7.3%, exports and foreign direct investment (FDI) rose by 6.8% and 14.6% respectively, and profits of large enterprises increased by 8.1%. These positive domestic results were achieved mainly on the basis of a proactive fiscal policy with large-scale deficit spending on infrastructure projects and state-owned enterprises (SOEs). A less well-documented growth element was the regionally-based expansion of the private sector of the economy. The year 2002 witnessed an international debate about the reliability and accuracy of Chinese statistics, in particular regarding the annual GDP growth rate and the volume of bank debt. This debate brought into focus some inherent weaknesses of the Chinese economy. These included the sustainability of state debt and the ability of the State to raise tax revenue, the high indebtedness of the banking sector (with a rate of non-performing loans that, according to different accounts, varied between 25% and 50%), and the interrelated reforms of the SOE sector and social services that were crucial for social stability.

From 1998 China faced a difficult economic environment, as the Asian economic crisis started to affect China's major sources of foreign investment and its regional export markets. The flow of Overseas Chinese capital through Hong Kong, which had returned to Chinese sovereignty in July 1997, into the People's Republic began to decline. Moreover, a radical retrenchment programme for SOE workers and civil servants started to affect all sections of society, and the privatization of social services and housing imposed new burdens on the population. From 1999 to 2001 the major concern was the deceleration of the domestic economy. The Government relied on fiscal policies, with spending on infrastructure investment schemes, and on export expansion to achieve the growth rates of some 7% deemed necessary to ensure social stability. The regional crisis of the late 1990s affected China much less than its neighbours, primarily owing to the restricted convertibility of the yuan, China's reliance on FDI, rather than on short-term capital inflows, and an underlying strong economic performance over several years, with continuous growth in industrial and agricultural output.

In 2001 global recession and the future of the economy of the USA (a major export market) became the major concerns. Government spending on infrastructure and heavy industry continued amid increasing doubts over the sustainability of this policy. In 2002 and 2003 respectively the 16th National Congress of the Chinese Communist Party (CCP) and the 10th National People's Congress (NPC) would bring a new generation of officials to China's leadership. Their agenda would encompass political and economic reforms, including the incorporation of business people into the CCP, taxation and banking reform, privatization and the implementation of WTO-related reforms.

The future development of the Chinese economy is of regional and global importance. Domestically, the reliance of the economy on fiscal spending and social stability in the face of large-scale retrenchments remains a major problem. The over-reliance on government spending for industrial growth in the state sector could affect long-term financial stability, if not counterbalanced by better financial support for the private sector. Internationally, China's economy depends increasingly on trade with and investment from the developed countries, including Japan. As the Asian crisis demonstrated the interdependence of the regional economies, the People's Republic was able to present itself as a responsible power and as a force for stability. Its potential to destabilize neighbouring economies, either through competitive pressure or through political pressure, as in the case of Taiwan, has also become apparent. China's leadership remains committed to economic internationalization and expects WTO membership to enforce market reforms for the domestic economy. After more than two decades of rapid growth, China's economy is now one of the largest in the world, second only to the USA in terms of purchasing-power parity. China is one of the largest markets for investment goods with good potential for growth in new markets, such as telecommunications and financial services, it is a leading supplier of cheap consumer items and, increasingly, it is a global economic power, the decisions of which influence other countries. China's accession to the WTO will gradually integrate its domestic markets further into the international economy, although the full impact of WTO membership on the domestic economy remains to be seen.

HISTORICAL BACKGROUND

Until 1978 the Chinese economy was under the influence of the Maoist egalitarian political ideology. During the 1950s and early 1960s a programme of industrialization, which focused on heavy industries under Soviet-style economic planning, achieved the rapid development of a basic industrial infrastructure. Its development strategy was based on an extremely high savings ratio and on low remuneration of agricultural producers. However, during the latter part of the 1960s and the 1970s isolationist policies restricted China's access to international exchange and technological development. The change in policy came in 1978, two years after the death of Mao Zedong, with the political victory of a group of pragmatic leaders centred around Deng Xiaoping. Their first reform measures were the decollectivization of agricultural production and the raising of state purchase prices for agricultural products. In addition, foreign investment was permitted in Special Economic Zones (SEZs) in China's southern provinces. The immediate success of these policies laid the foundation for a gradual transformation of China's planned economy during the following two decades.

Price reform was the first stage of macroeconomic reform. Initially, price reform addressed an irrational pricing system that disadvantaged agricultural and primary producers and favoured industrial producers. Moreover, retail prices did not reflect costs or purchase prices. In the first stage of price reform, from 1979 onwards, purchase prices for agricultural and rural sideline products were raised to increase incentives for farmers and to create markets for light industrial goods. The price differential between the mining and processing industries was also reduced. In 1985 a dual pricing system was introduced, which allowed planned prices and market prices to coexist, in order to bring the former up to the level of market prices, thus eventually abolishing mandatory pricing. This gave rise to corruption, since officials could make windfall profits by selling goods received under lower planned prices at the higher market prices. More importantly, however, it was an incentive for enterprises to adapt their production to market demand. The overall aim of deregulating the prices of most consumer goods, as well as capital goods, had been achieved by the late 1980s. By 1998 more than 90% of retail prices and some 80% of prices for raw materials and agricultural produce had been liberalized. Price controls still apply in strategic areas, such as electricity and other energy. A further reduction in government control over prices and tariffs was expected to result from China's WTO membership from 2001.

China's dual-track transition strategy meant that the planned economy coexisted with an increasing number of unregulated sectors, such as rural collective enterprises, which guaranteed continued economic growth, while the scope of price controls and general economic planning was gradually reduced. Owing to the faster development of the private and non-state sector of the economy, China was literally 'growing out of the Plan'. However, there was no specific model for the transition to a market economy, and conflicting policies led to frequent macroeconomic crises, with high inflation and social unrest. The gradual nature of China's economic reforms was the result of the continuing influential role of the CCP and a long tradition of state interference in the economy. Unlike the Soviet Communist Party in the late 1980s and early 1990s, which lost most of its influence under the political and economic reforms being effected in the USSR, the CCP maintained its control over macroeconomic policies and reform ideology. The Party preserved a measure of social stability by avoiding the abrupt dismantling of the institutions of the command economy, particularly of the dominant state-enterprise sector, which afforded substantial social service benefits to its work-force. As a result, these inefficient sectors continued to require huge state subsidies. The protection of political structures and the state bureaucracy also led to widespread corruption, and stifled public debate. The gap between actual economic changes and obsolete political structures was a contributory factor in the tragic mishandling of the Tiananmen Square incident, in June 1989, which damaged both the domestic and the international standing of the Chinese leadership. The incident was preceded by high inflation and an impending financial crisis, while, from 1988, economic growth was curtailed by administrative restrictions. The main economic achievements of the 1980s were high growth rates, rising living standards for the rural and urban population, and growing participation in international exchange through trade and the influx of FDI. Macroeconomic policies started to replace administrative control, prices and markets were liberalized and a strongly performing non-state-enterprise sector emerged.

The breakthrough for the transition towards a market economy came in 1992, with an artificially-induced economic boom, the result of a leadership struggle for power over the direction of economic policy. The collapse of the USSR in 1991 had come as a shock to the Chinese leadership and forced it to reconsider its economic strategy. The more conservative route, maintaining administrative and Party control over the economy, was proposed by Chen Yun, one of the architects of economic construction in the 1950s and 1960s. This was rejected by Deng Xiaoping in favour of a market economy with a strong private sector under macroeconomic control, in which the role of the CCP would be restricted to political and social control. In a manoeuvre typical of traditional Chinese politics, Deng Xiaoping rallied support from provincial leaders during a visit to southern China. Later in 1992 the National Congress of the CCP approved Deng Xiaoping's programme of further market reforms and economic liberalization.

Deng Xiaoping's call for increased economic activity led to the establishment of many SEZs for foreign investment, numerous new investment and real estate development projects throughout the country and a revitalization of domestic and border trade. Extra-budgetary finance and uncontrolled monetary expansion contributed to an economic boom, which raised the GDP growth rate to 13.5% in 1993, and increased the rate of inflation to 21.7% in 1994. From mid-1993 Zhu Rongji, as Vice-Premier in charge of economic affairs, was responsible for restraining the uncontrolled economic expansion. His success in effecting a 'soft landing' for the economy in 1996 qualified him for the position of Premier, to which he was elevated in 1998. Economic growth continued to slow down from 1993, recording a GDP growth rate of 8.8% and consumer price inflation of 2.8% in 1997. The 15th CCP Congress in 1997 and the Ninth NPC in 1998 set a new programme for the corporatization of government functions, reform of the state-owned sector of the economy, and accompanying reforms of the social security system and the financial system. The positive international climate up to 1997, huge foreign-exchange reserves and a strong export performance provided the basis for these decisions. Faced with the impact of the Asian financial crisis and declining domestic demand after 1998, the original timetable for these reforms had to be extended. There was concern that the economy might grow too slowly. Economic growth declined to 7.1% in 1999, a figure that was high in international comparison, but considered low by the Chinese leadership concerned about rising unemployment, as official growth figures were likely to overstate actual growth by at least some two percentage points. The targeted GDP growth during the Tenth Five-Year Plan from 2001 to 2005 was 7% per annum.

China still has a mixed economy. Economic issues are closely linked to political developments and power struggles within a system that is hardly transparent to outside observers. However, there is a broad consensus on economic policies, and the transition to the post-Deng era has been smoother than many analysts expected. The leadership has technocratic credentials and seems to be less influenced by the experiences of the previous generation. Nevertheless, the Chinese economy remains politically influenced, and its transition towards a fully-fledged market system is far from complete. Since the institutional and legal framework is still weak, new protagonists emerge as influential forces, including bureaucratic and entrepreneurial élites at central and provincial level. The latter have both protectionist and expansionist interests, as command over industries and enterprises is devolved from the central to the local authorities. The central Government has asserted its authority through several campaigns directed against corruption by local officials. In a move that is indicative of a more sophisticated attitude towards control and distribution of information, Beijing has actively embraced internet-based technology to disseminate information for domestic and foreign consumption with an extensive range of government-sponsored websites.

China's economic achievements since the early 1980s have been considerable: rural and urban incomes have risen continuously; agricultural and industrial production have been deregulated; central planning has been abolished for all but a few industrial sectors; internationalization of the economy has been achieved to a remarkable degree; and a general commitment to further market liberalization and privatization is the hallmark of the ongoing reform process. The most radical change was the establishment of the 'non-state' sector of the economy. This sector comprises private enterprises as well as enterprises of various intermediate ownership forms. Its size and characteristics vary locally. While the exact size of this sector is impossible to quantify, mainly owing to unclear ownership categories and the persistence of administrative links between local authorities and enterprises, it has overtaken the SOE sector in terms of industrial output value, although not in employment and investment in fixed assets. The non-state sector is playing an important role in creating a private market economy and in absorbing excess labour from the agricultural sector and from urban areas. Predictably, the shape of China's future market economy will be characterized by locally varying forms of coexistence of an expanding private sector and a reformed SOE sector.

Since 1999 the focus of government policy has shifted from curbing the unrestrained growth of the economy to preventing a recession. Government spending has been primarily directed towards infrastructure and building construction. Under the 2001–05 Five-Year Plan, a large proportion of state investment has been channelled towards infrastructure projects in the western regions of China. This policy of the 'Great Opening of the West' aims to reduce the economic backwardness of 12 provincial economies, stretching from Nei Mongol (Inner Mongolia) in the north-west to Guangxi Zhuang in the south-west, that have failed to benefit from the rapid economic development of the coastal region. From an economic perspective, there is criticism that this type of expenditure was not achieving the desired multiplier effect and should be directed towards consumer-orientated industries instead. As a result, the economy in 2002 still carried the institutional burdens of the state-owned industrial sector, with loss-making state enterprises dependent on state investment, and the highly-indebted banking and finance sector, on to which the burden of financing the SOEs had been shifted. These are major economic challenges for the 'Fourth Generation' party and state leadership to be installed in 2002–03. The incoming technocratic leadership was expected to institute new policies in support of domestic and foreign private enterprises, including access to CCP membership for Chinese private entrepreneurs and the opening of hitherto closed industries to foreign participation and international competition under the WTO. Domestically, the biggest challenge is the co-ordination and the completion of enterprise, financial and social reforms begun in the 1980s. Comprehensive reform of the SOEs is linked to reform of the financial sector, which is burdened with the accumulated debt of SOEs. Without reform of the banking and financial sector, China will face an economic crisis. Social reform, on the other hand, is a precondition for the reform of the SOEs, because alternative providers have to be created for most of the urban social services, including health care and accommodation, which were formerly provided by the state enterprise sector.

POLITICAL AND ECONOMIC REFORMS

Contrary to the perception that China has undergone economic reforms without reforming its political system, China's economic developments have been accompanied by major political changes. The influence of the CCP has not waned as radically in the process of economic reform, as happened with the Soviet and other Communist Parties. The CCP still defines the public political agenda, but, as an active participant in the gradualist and experimental approach to economic reform in China, is overseeing a shift away from communist ideology to economic and social policies more akin to social democracy. In the transition from administrative interference to macro-economic control by the central Government, the Party has relinquished much of its former influence over the economy. What remains of the orthodox tradition of the Party is its opposition to open public debate, individual rights and a democratic, parliamentary system, as well as its control over public security and strategic sectors of the economy and the State. As electronic media, such as the internet, are threatening the state monopoly on information, the official response has been actively to embrace the new technologies and make government institutions the leading providers of web-based information, while taking selective action against the new media. On the other hand, in its campaign against widespread systemic corruption, the Party and the Government have to rely on public media to maintain a degree of credibility. The tension between pluralistic tendencies engendered by the market economy and the Party's tradition of ideological control of all political discourse remains unresolved. Economic reforms were introduced against a background of political opposition, both from within the CCP and from other sectors of society with interests in a strong role for the central State, such as the military, the state bureaucracies, large SOEs and some provincial governments. The experimental nature of the economic reform process also results from the fact that at every stage the reformers within the CCP had to convince their conservative opponents of the merits of specific reforms, reach compromises or retract reform measures when opposition became too strong. Ideological compromises produced formulations such as 'primary stage of socialism' or 'socialist market economy'. The core issue was the extent to which the State would relax its control over the economy and society. The major macroeconomic reform projects, such as the abolition of central planning, price reform, tax reform, enterprise reform, finance reform and administrative reform, all began in the early 1980s, but were not resolved for nearly two decades, owing to the opposition put forward by the proponents of a strong interventionist state.

The new leaders installed in 1997 and 1998 after the death of Deng Xiaoping gained their economic experience during the recession that followed the Tiananmen Square incident, which demonstrated the inadequacy of administrative controls to manage the economy. They were shocked at the collapse of the USSR and witnessed how Deng Xiaoping, in a final display of strength, created an economic boom that forced a breakthrough for the market economy in 1992 and 1993. They subsequently learned to use macroeconomic policies, as well as administrative means, to lead the overheating economy to a more stable path of development, achieving a successful 'soft landing' in 1996. The State (and through it the CCP) maintained a degree of administrative and corporate control over the economy through corporatization of state institutions and state-owned enterprises, including the listing of majority state-owned corporations on domestic and international share markets. In 1998 China's economic leaders, headed by Premier Zhu Rongji, a trained economist, abolished the central ministries that had been in charge of whole industries and replaced them with state-controlled corporate structures. At present and in the foreseeable future, the State will maintain a strong role in preserving social stability and public confidence in the economy.

Legal and Administrative Reform

The introduction of the rule of law has been another area of reform that has transformed the Chinese economy, as well as social and political life. Legal reform was driven by the economic demand for stable procedures as well as the political and social necessity to create predictability in relation to actions of the state. Economic activity is now regulated by a vast body of economic legislation, although the role of the State remains strong and China's legal system is better described as 'rule by law' than 'rule of law'. One of the first pieces of economic legislation in the reform period was the Joint Venture Law, which created the legal basis for foreign investment in China and was later used to develop corresponding domestic legislation. The development of a regulatory framework for foreign investors coincided with legislation for the domestic market economy. Major steps in the development of economic legislation were the introduction of the Contract Law and, in 1994, the Company Law, which introduced limited liability and share-issuing companies. There is now a large body of codified commercial law regulating the activities of domestic and foreign-invested enterprises. Protection of intellectual property rights has made progress in legislative terms, while there remain weaknesses in implementation. Procedural law has also been established, and litigation is becoming an acceptable means of conflict resolution, in addition to the still important methods of arbitration or informal conflict resolution.

Reform of the central ministries and commissions is changing government administration, particularly since early 1998. Under the Government of Zhu Rongji, the number of central ministries was decreased from 40 to 29 and the personnel of some ministries was reduced by more than one-half. Industries such as coal, power, metallurgy, machine-building, electronics and chemicals were removed from the control of central bureaucracies and overseen by more general supervisory organs, with their operative sections administered by newly-corporatized structures. This was the most radical government change since the beginning of the reform period. In theory, this reform will help to reduce remaining government monopolies and introduce industries to competition. The same restructuring is planned for provincial and sub-provincial governments, but progress has been slower at provincial and local level as a result of strong local autonomy and wide regional differences.

Regionalism

The People's Republic has a unitary system of government that coexists with strong and mostly informal federalist features. Under the central Government, there are a further four levels of government. These include 31 provincial level units (22 provinces, five autonomous regions and four municipalities), 331 prefectural level units, 2,109 county-level units and 44,741 township-level units. They are structured in the form of a 'nested' hierarchy in the sense that higher levels of government deal only with the directly subordinate level and that units at each of these levels have their own independent budget authority. Provincial autonomy and regional differentiation have grown continuously during the reform period, as the coastal provinces, in particular Guangdong Province adjacent to Hong Kong, and later the provinces in the Changjiang (Yangtze) Delta, benefited from their better industrial infrastructure and access to markets. The GDP of the developed and highly industrialized provinces along the coast is much higher than that of the central or western provinces. The four largest provincial economies of Guangdong, Jiangsu, Shandong and Zhejiang account for one-third of the national GDP, with Guangdong alone contributing one-tenth. Their contribution to China's foreign trade volume is even more distinct. Provinces not only differ in terms of comparative and competitive advantages, they also pursue different privatization policies that lead to different regulatory and business environments. For example, provinces such as Guangdong and Zhejiang have a much higher proportion of private enterprises than neighbouring provinces. Provinces also actively compete for foreign investment. Economic exchange between provinces is still hampered by formal and informal trade barriers. One of the expected consequences of China's WTO membership will be the reduction of internal trade restrictions and an increase in domestic trade and competition.

The growing social and economic disparity between China's coastal regions and inland areas is of particular political concern to the central Government, because it could affect political stability. Economically, the central Government has only limited means to its avail, as it has not been able to enforce inter-regional revenue transfers upon the richer provinces that would have an equalizing effect. The Ninth Five-Year Plan, encompassing the period 1996–2000, promoted voluntary partnership schemes, such as capital transfer and cross-regional co-operation, between the relatively well-off coastal provinces and the poorer inland provinces. However, it soon became evident that the coastal region, with its geographical advantages and superior infrastructure, would continue to grow faster, thus widening the gap between inland and coastal China. The Tenth Five-Year Plan (2001–05) specifically focused on the 'Great Opening of the West' in an attempt to strengthen the strategic integration of the Western region, improve its ecological environment and lift its economic standards. The support for the 12 western provinces included in this plan provides large-scale central infrastructure funding for strategic projects, such as highways, rail connections, natural gas pipelines and communication links between China's less-developed western half and the prosperous coastal region. A further focus is on funding for environmental projects, such as large-scale afforestation and water diversion projects that will also help to reduce the looming water shortage in North China. Finally, the Plan includes spending on education and economic infrastructure. The Government has used long-term government bonds to fund these projects.

Fiscal Reform

Fiscal reform, like price reform, was necessary to introduce market incentives into the enterprise sector. Until the first tax reform in 1983, government revenue consisted primarily of the financial surplus of the SOEs, which had to be remitted in full to the State. Tax reform in 1983, under the slogan 'tax for profit', introduced enterprise taxation and allowed enterprises to retain part of their profits as an economic incentive. In a major reform in 1984 value-added tax (VAT) was introduced in an attempt to simplify the tax regime. Taxation was, however, not unified, and different tax rates applied to SOEs, collective enterprises and foreign-funded enterprises. Lower tax rates were used as an incentive to attract foreign investment in the 1980s. A further series of tax reforms in 1994 introduced personal income tax and a uniform corporate taxation rate of 33% for all enterprises, including foreign-invested enterprises. Tax incentives already granted to foreign investors were, however, excluded and foreign-invested enterprises continue to benefit from tax incentives. VAT, at a rate of 17%, was also extended to cover all foreign and domestic enterprises. This tax reform was a response to the decline in total state income and a shift of income from central to local governments. Government revenue had declined from 31% of GDP in 1978 to some 11% in 1995. Subsequently, in the latter part of the 1990s, government revenue as a percentage of GDP increased again, to a level of some 16% from 2000. The 1994 tax reforms also addressed the decline in the central share in tax revenue, which in 1993 had reached its lowest point at 22%. Under a new method of revenue division between central and local governments with two separate tax administrations for the collection of central and local taxes, the share of central revenue increased to more than 56% in 2000. Under the tax-sharing system, the central Government's main sources of revenue in 1999 were, in order of importance, a 75% share of VAT revenue, central consumption tax, tariffs, custom tariffs and VAT on import goods and corporate income tax. Local governments were entitled to local personal and corporate income tax, 25% of VAT revenue, tax on urban land and several other taxes, with the majority of their revenue derived from extrabudgetary items and administrative charges that were not part of regular government revenue. The tax-sharing system is complicated by rebate schemes from the central Government to local governments and by inter-governmental transfer mechanisms. A report by the World Bank in 2002 noted that the heavy expenditure responsibilities of local governments in China were out of line with international practice, as its fiscal system was highly decentralized with sub-national governments accounting for more than 70% of total budgetary expenditure and more than two-thirds of extra-budgetary funds. Erosion of state revenues, the limited ability of the central Government to exercise control over the economy through budgetary means and unequalizing effects of inter-regional transfers remain unsolved problems of financial reform. Increasingly, fiscal policies are used to increase domestic demand and exports in order to stimulate the economy. From 1999 such measures included reduced tax rates on capital and real-estate investments, tax exemptions for investment in western China, increased tax reimbursement for exports, and higher taxation of private savings deposits to encourage consumption. This deficit spending continued into 2002.

Government liabilities have reached a level that has led to warnings about a potential budgetary crisis. In 2001 the budget deficit stood at 3% of GDP, down from 3.2% in 2000. By 2002 estimates of government debts ranged from 100% to 150% of GDP, roughly comparable to Japan. Internationally, a debt-to-GDP ratio of 60% is generally seen as a crisis indicator. These debts included bonds issued by the Treasury, the policy banks, asset management corporations and costs for refinancing the heavily indebted state banks (see below). In addition, the Government will have to fund pensions in increasing volume.

Social Services Reform

Reform of the social security system has three main components: an old-age insurance system, a medical insurance system and an unemployment insurance system, which are established nationwide, but based and managed at provincial level. The transfer of former central industry-based pension funds and responsibilities to provinces has been completed, but the coverage of the system is still very limited. The basic health-care system had 43.3m. participants in the early 21st century. A medical care system, with a basic medical insurance, an enterprise-based supplementary medical insurance and a commercial medical insurance, was expected to become operational by 2002–04. More than 50% of health care expenditure is carried by local governments at county or township level, which are insufficiently funded. The unemployment insurance is still dependent on enterprises, with preparations under way eventually to share the financial burden between companies and employees. The state-based social security system is still rudimentary and underfunded. At the end of 2001 104m. employees and workers had participated in unemployment insurance programmes. The official unemployment rate for 2001 stood at 3.6% (unofficial estimates, however, suggested that the rate of urban unemployment was 8.5% or higher).

The state-based retirement system also had about 100m. participants among employees and workers and 31.7m. among retirees. This has to be seen against the background of an urban employed population of 212.7m. people and the number of 6.6m. people made redundant from SOEs by the end of 2000.

Privatization of urban housing is part of social reforms, as housing under the planned economy was provided by SOEs at minimal cost. Provincial governments have been given enhanced authority to determine specific policies, such as provincial or local mortgage schemes.

Banking and Finance Reform

China's financial and banking system is still dominated by the State. From 1949 to 1983 the People's Bank of China was China's only bank, covering all banking activities, from the issue of currency to account settlement and foreign-currency transactions. In 1984 it became the central bank and its commercial functions were taken over by four new banks: the Industrial and Commercial Bank of China, the Agricultural Bank of China, the People's Construction Bank of China (subsequently China Construction Bank) and the Bank of China. Under the supervision of the People's Bank of China, these four banks with their nation-wide networks of branches dominate the banking sector and hold approximately 60% of total financial assets. The China International Trust and Investment Corporation (CITIC) was established in 1979, with the original aim of attracting Overseas Chinese capital, and later expanded to offer a range of financial services, including leasing and overseas investment. Most provinces have since established their own International Trust and Investment Corporations (ITICs). During the 1980s smaller banks, non-banking financial institutions, and urban and rural credit co-operatives were also established. Urban credit co-operatives have been merged into 80 urban commercial banks to provide services for local medium-sized and small enterprises. The private banking sector is as yet irrelevant. Foreign banks are allowed to provide financial services to foreign-invested enterprises and in foreign currency; however, their operations in local currency are restricted to small enclaves in some SEZs and are only gradually being expanded in preparation for the expansion of their business scope to domestic currency lending under WTO.

When, in the early 1990s in the course of SOE reform, enterprise debt of the SOE sector was transferred from government ministries and their state budget to the banking system, the large commercial banks were forced to convert this debt into loans to the SOEs without, however, being able to cancel bad debts at the required level. Under the existing regulatory framework, banks had to expand their loans to SOEs irrespective of their financial situation. In 2002, according to unofficial sources, the proportion of non-performing loans on the banks' balance sheets was estimated to be as much as 50%, or even higher. Under these conditions, the banking sector cannot be fully commercialized, particularly since the SOEs still interact with the commercial sector operating for non-state enterprises, by issuing guarantees, or through other forms of co-operation.

One response to this dilemma was the establishment of three new policy banks in 1994: the State Development Bank, Export and Import Bank of China and Agricultural Development Bank of China. The original concept of policy banks was for them to assume the burden of financing loss-making SOEs and allow the commercial banks to concentrate on their commercial operations. However, restrictive regulations and political interference prevented the transfer of non-performing loans to the policy banks. With the savings rate increasing (savings deposits by urban and rural residents grew from less than 10% of GDP in 1980 to 67% in 1998), the need to commercialize the banking sector became more urgent. In order to reduce the large volume of non-performing loans burdening the banking sector, a programme of debt-for-equity swaps for the SOE sector was initiated by newly established asset management corporations (AMCs) under the four big commercial banks. The first was Cinda AMC under China Construction Bank, founded in 1998. In 1999 China Orient AMC, China Great Wall AMC and Huarong AMC were set up under the Bank of China, China Construction Bank and the Industrial and Commercial Bank of China. During the second half of 2001, all four AMCs recovered some US $3,000m. from the sale of non-performing loans or physical assets originally valued at $15,000m.

China's stock market, established in 1990 in Shanghai and Shenzhen, has shown spectacular growth, but remains tainted by regulatory problems and by the fact that over 90% of shares traded are issued by government-controlled corporations. The share market is still at an experimental stage. In early 2001 the value of tradeable shares amounted to 18% of GDP, which is still very low in international comparison. By the end of 2001 more than 1,100 enterprises were listed with an overall market capitalization of close to US $500m. More than 100 of China's 500 largest companies, including China Telecom, Anshan Iron and Steel Company and Handan Iron and Steel Company, have been publicly listed. State institutions still hold approximately 60% of shares in these enterprises. China's big state corporations are increasingly listing their shares in international markets. US sources have estimated that between 1993 and 2000 Chinese firms raised $41,000m. through initial public offerings and placements. While half of this sum was raised in 2000 alone, 2001 showed a significant decline. In 2002 a planned large-scale sale of government shares had to be cancelled, as its announcement had led to a collapse in share values in late 2001. This sale of state shares was originally intended to fund social security expenditure. A Code of Corporate Governance for Listed Companies was enacted by China Securities Regulatory Commission in January 2002 as part of a move to improve the reporting of inflated profits and the delisting of loss-making companies. Listed companies are required to undergo supplementary audits by the major international auditing firms.

Domestically, the People's Bank of China reasserted its control over credit allocation by reducing the influence of local governments through the closure of its provincial branches. Instead, nine supra-provincial branches were opened in the cities of Shanghai, Guangzhou, Shenyang, Wuhan, Chengdu, Tianjin, Jinan, Xian and Nanjing. As part of the greater commercialization and diversification of the financial sector, the supervision and management of the securities and insurance industries have been transferred from the People's Bank of China to the China Securities Regulatory Commission and the newly established China Insurance Regulatory Commission. Corporate governance of the banking sector is being strengthened through the appointment of supervisory boards and the placement of independent directors.

China's banking and finance sector will diversify under WTO, although it is not clear what market share foreign financial institutions will eventually secure. There is large pent-up demand for diversified financial services in China's corporate sector, in particular in the private sector, and among private investors. The operating scope of foreign financial institutions is gradually being expanded, but it is too early to predict what impact they will eventually be allowed to have in this so far highly protected market.

Enterprise Reform and Privatization

China has two enterprise sectors: the SOEs and the non-state sector, which comprises rural and urban collective enterprises, private enterprises and foreign-funded enterprises. Non-state enterprises operate in a market environment, while SOEs are still protected by the State through their access to bank loans, irrespective of their economic performance. SOEs are the main cause of the high level of non-performing loans in China's banking sector. The dividing line between the SOE and the non-state sectors has become blurred, as the local governments have been transforming and selling off enterprises under their control without necessarily changing their administrative categorisation. In 1998 the Government initiated a three-year programme to reform the then 986,000 SOEs, which once formed the mainstay of China's economy. Two-thirds of the SOEs reported losses in 1997. They are concentrated in heavy industry and those sectors over which the State wishes to retain control for strategic reasons, or in areas that are not served by the growing non-state enterprise sector. Experimental reforms in the SOE sector have been undertaken since the early 1980s, when economic incentives for workers and management were introduced. From the mid-1980s a bankruptcy law was used on a trial basis, but never fully enforced. Reform of the SOEs has been delayed not only for strategic and ideological reasons, but also because of their role in providing employment and preserving social stability. SOEs employ one-half of the urban work force and provide essential services such as housing, health care and pensions for the majority of the urban population. They cannot be closed down in large numbers until these services can be provided independently. A whole range of reforms, including privatization of housing sector, education and social welfare in general, is therefore linked to SOE reform.

'Grasping the big and enlivening the small' is the slogan under which state control is being confined to a limited number of large corporations concentrated in industrial sectors of strategic importance. In 1999 enterprise reform focused on 6,600 large- and medium-sized SOEs, of which 70% had either become profitable or been restructured by 2000. Improvements were reported for 2001, as a result of the large-scale government-funded infrastructure and construction projects that provided temporary relief for SOEs. Eventually some 1,000 large enterprises will be managed on a commercial basis, but will remain under state control, organized in enterprise groups modelled on the Korean *chaebol*. Enterprises selected for inclusion in these groups will receive state support in settling their debt with the banking sector, if necessary through equity swaps, which started in 1999. Those enterprises fulfilling the financial and organizational requirements will prepare to list their shares on the stock market. By 1998 several hundred large SOEs had been granted pilot status and had begun restructuring.

Medium-sized and small SOEs have been privatized or converted in large numbers, in order to end the State's responsibility for their economic performance and their employees. This is carried out through sale, conversion to joint ownership with employees receiving shares in the enterprises, leasing and other methods, depending on local circumstances. Their number was more than halved to some 34,000 in 2001. Local authorities were given greater authority to conduct experimental and decentralized reforms with these enterprises in 1997, when the number of cities with the right to conduct 'pilot projects' was increased from 58 to 111. Apart from these officially sanctioned experiments, local authorities in some provinces are privatizing enterprises under their control at a faster rate than indicated by official statistics, while there are also indications that not all provinces are following the central Government's time schedule in divesting themselves of these enterprises. A three-year programme extending from 1998 to 2001 to turn around the deficit situation of the SOE sector as a whole has reportedly resulted in several industrial sectors achieving profitability for the first time in several years; these include textiles, building materials and non-ferrous metals.

Development of the non-state enterprise sector, which expanded throughout the 1980s and 1990s, has resulted in the creation of an alternative enterprise sector alongside the state-owned sector. By 2002 its share in China's GDP had reached 33%. The non-state sector includes very different types of enterprises, ranging from small private rural enterprises to collectives and de jure state controlled corporations.

In the 1980s urban collective enterprises had been a means for both local government institutions, as well as private entrepreneurs, to engage in commercial business activity. Under the label of collective enterprises, SOEs could combine some of their assets with other enterprises or operate profitable sections as independent enterprises. This afforded them tax benefits and commercial flexibility, without endangering their SOE structure and related benefits. Private entrepreneurs used collective enterprises to minimize the political risks associated with the operation of private enterprises. In rural areas more than 23m. township and village enterprises had been established since 1979. In 1998 they employed a work force of 125m. (equivalent to 28% of the rural labour force). From 1980 to 1995 their output value increased at an average annual rate of 36%. On a per caput basis, they contributed 30% to rural income in 1996. These enterprises, which are usually organized on a collective basis by local governments and other local participants, are undergoing structural changes, as their unsophisticated products meet increasing competition from the growing urban consumer industries.

The 1994 Company Law has provided the legal basis for incorporation of these enterprises across the urban–rural divide. This new enterprise sector combines private shareholding with involvement by official stakeholders, which makes it possible to overcome the problems posed by weak institutional support and a still rudimentary commercial legal system. According to a 1999 report by the Chinese Academy of Social Sciences, the collective and private sectors together accounted for three-quarters of industrial output value in 1997 and for a growing share in 1998 and 1999. In 1998 the collective sector accounted for 38% and the private sector, which includes foreign-invested enterprises, for 39% of the value of gross industrial output. The non-state sector shows an uneven geographical distribution, as its growth has depended on provincial policies. In several of the wealthy provinces on the east coast, such as Jiangsu, Zhejiang and Guangdong, the value of gross industrial output of the collective sector is several times that of the state sector. The non-state sector has been able to absorb surplus urban and rural labour and has helped to prepare the conditions for further 'downsizing' of the state sector. According to official figures, the 1.76m. registered private enterprises employed more than 200m. workers in 2000. These non-state enterprises, together with some 28,000 foreign-funded businesses, form the basis of China's market economy. The status of the private sector has been continually enhanced, not least because of its ability to absorb labour. In 1999 a constitutional amendment strengthened the legal status of private enterprises by giving them equal rights with other businesses in their commercial access to capital and funding, ahead of further improvements in their constitutional and legal rights in 2002 and 2003.

AGRICULTURE

China's rural economy has changed radically since 1978, when the first series of reform measures released farmers from a rigid planning regime. Until then People's Communes regulated agricultural output and provided no incentives to individual producers. The reforms were in response to local difficulties and a general perception of imminent crisis, as grain consumption was falling below the level of the 1950s. Decollectivization of agricultural production was achieved through the introduction of a contract responsibility system, whereby producers delivered quotas to the State and sold their surplus to the market. Peasant households were able to raise their income by growing cash crops or providing for consumer markets. They also gained rights over the land they cultivated. These institutional changes and increases in state purchase prices laid the foundation for a buoyant period from 1979 to 1983, during which agricultural output increased by more than 5% annually. When the initial effect of these measures started to wane in the mid-1980s, agricultural production continued to grow at slightly lower, but still spectacular, rates. Total production of grain (cereals, pulses, soybeans and tubers in 'grain equivalents'), which was 305m. metric tons in 1978, rose to an all-time peak of 508m. tons in 1999. Since then, government emphasis has shifted from growth to a better products mix. This enabled the Government to encourage further diversification of agriculture, including reafforestation and programmes to reduce environmental damage. Of the sown area for farm crops, 30% was used for cash crops. In 2000 agriculture (including forestry and fishing) contributed 15.9% of GDP, down from 20.4% in 1996 and 30.0% in 1980. In 2000 53.3% of the total national labour force was still employed in the rural sector. Small-scale township and village enterprises provided employment for 128m. workers in rural areas in 2000.

The initial success of agricultural reforms provided the justification for the subsequent broader economic reforms. State procurement prices for agricultural products were raised, both for quota and above-quota purchases by the State. An increase in price of 25% for quota sales and of up to 50% for above-quota sales occurred in 1979, and further rises followed in 1989/90, 1994/95 and 1996. Rural producers, who had long been disadvantaged by unfavourable terms of trade, were the beneficiaries of these measures, while urban consumers received state subsidies to reduce the negative effect of the rising prices. Private local and interregional markets for vegetables and other produce opened. The prices of many products, which had either been rationed or under state control, such as meat and fish, were liberalized. Rice was beginning to be marketized at a regional level in 2000.

Agricultural production in 2001 showed mixed results, with increases in some areas and decreases in others, largely as a result of the Government's decision to lower guaranteed purchasing prices for grain and to reduce over-capacities in other sectors. Grain output in 2001 was 452.6m. metric tons. After several years of decline, cotton output in 2000 and 2001 increased strongly by 13.6% and 20.4 % respectively to reach 5.32m. tons. Output of oil-bearing crops fluctuated, down to 28.72m. tons in 2001. Sugar output, after years of decline, showed a strong 15.1 % increase to 87.9m. tons in 2001. Output of meat and aquatic products continued to grow in 2001 respectively, to 63.4m. tons and 43,75m. tons. China is becoming a net exporter of processed foods and other agricultural products. Its strong comparative advantage in labour-intensive products is reflected in an established record as an exporter of meat, fish, vegetables and fruit. The domestic market is, however, under threat from international competitors that will gain access to Chinese markets under WTO.

Good grain harvests in the 1990s meant that grain handling and management received more attention than increases in production, which are required in the long term to support a growing population. Any major decline in grain production would have serious consequences for the livelihood of millions of people. In recent years the question of whether China will be able to feed its population in the 21st century has captured public attention both inside and outside the country. The Government aims to reach 95% self-sufficiency in grain but, if trends persist, China will increasingly have to resort to imported grain beyond the present level of 10m. metric tons annually. Long-term estimates of required grain imports for the year 2010 range between 15m. tons and an OECD estimate of 136m. tons, with reputable Australian analysts anticipating a figure in the middle of this range. According to official statistics, grain imports peaked in 1995 at 20m. tons, and continued to decline from 10.8m. tons in 1996 to 3.4m. tons in 1999. The Chinese Government maintains that increases in productivity and improved handling and management, will enable domestic agriculture to produce sufficient grain to avoid a crisis in international grain markets when the population reaches its estimated peak in 2030. Since 1994, under the 'governor responsibility system', the responsibility for grain procurement and price subsidies has been devolved to the provincial level. Reform of the grain market in 1999 and 2000 aimed at separating government administration from enterprise functions in the areas of grain production, buying, selling, and storage, and reducing the losses of grain-handling enterprises in a process of gradual commercialization.

INDUSTRY

China's industrialization originated along the coast under the influence of the colonial powers. From the end of the 19th century mainly light industries were founded in the Treaty Ports, notably in Shanghai and Tianjin. One-third of the total output of China's manufacturers was produced by foreign-owned factories, but the economic role of modern industry was limited. Before the outbreak of war in 1937, modern industries produced less than 4% of net domestic product and employed fewer than 2m. workers. Two-thirds of the gross value of national industrial output was produced by handicraft industries and only one-third by industries that relied on machinery for their main production. Heavy industry on a larger scale developed in Manzhou (Manchuria) during the Japanese occupation. However, only 5% of all factories employed more than 500 people when the CCP came to power in 1949. This weak industrial base was concentrated in a few coastal centres, away from the interior regions where the Party had won the civil war. This low starting point helped the economy to achieve high growth rates during the decades of peaceful development that followed. With the aid of the USSR, after 1953 China embarked on a large-scale programme of industrialization. Its focus was on investment projects in China's interior regions. The new industrial infrastructure comprised mainly heavy industries, mining, chemical and metallurgical industries. Inland industrialization continued, though at a lesser pace, after China's break with the USSR in 1960, when the USSR withdrew its experts and advisers. The shift away from the coast intensified during the 1970s, when, for military and strategic reasons, industrial production capacities were established in inaccessible inland areas in order to make China less vulnerable in the event of a Soviet nuclear strike. As a result of isolationist policies during the 1960s and 1970s, China's industrial infrastructure by the end of the 1970s had become technically obsolete and was unable to meet domestic consumer demand. With its closed economy and autarkic regime, China's centrally-managed planned economy was not able to participate in the growth and diversification that other Asian economies experienced during the 1970s. Industrial reform required an opening of China's economy, technical modernization, the relocation of industries closer to markets, reorientation towards consumer demand and reform of enterprise structures and macroeconomic policies.

Inspired by the success of other Asian economies, the first step in industrial reform in 1979 was to attract overseas—mainly Overseas Chinese—investors to establish joint ventures in China. This adoption of the export-orientated development strategies of other Asian countries brought China back into the international economy. The Joint Venture Law of 1979 and a range of additional laws created the basis for foreign direct investment, primarily in Special Economic Zones. The first four SEZs were set up in the vicinity of Hong Kong, with the largest at Shenzhen, close to the border. Overseas direct investment proved to be one of the driving forces behind industrial reform. By 1998 China had become the second-largest recipient of FDI after the USA (see below). Foreign-invested enterprises contributed one-half of China's export and imports in 2001. Foreign investment has brought advanced production technologies and management expertise into China and has introduced competition into hitherto-protected domestic markets. Foreign investment has also helped to relocate China's industrial focus back to the coastal regions and to the centres of consumer demand. In addition joint-venture legislation has provided guidelines for the drafting of domestic economic legislation.

Another element of China's industrial reform strategy was the establishment of market segments amongst the state-owned industry monopolies. One way to achieve this was to stimulate the growth and diversification of consumer-orientated industries, which had to compete for markets. This development of light and consumer industries during the 1980s required less investment than heavy industries and led to lower entry barriers for small-scale collective enterprises. Starting from a regional basis, these new forms of non-state enterprises were able to compete for raw materials and force existing SOEs out of whole industries.

Even after two decades of reform, China's sectoral structure is still dominated by heavy industry. This reflects the earlier policies of Soviet-style industrialization. In 1952 industry (including construction) accounted for no more than 21% of gross national product (GNP), compared with 50% for agriculture and 29% for tertiary activities. In subsequent years heavy industry grew at twice the rate of light industry. Continuing rapid industrialization raised industry's share of GNP to some 50%, while the share of agriculture declined to around 30%. By 1978 heavy industry accounted for 57% of the value of gross industrial output and light industry for 43%.

'Pillar Industries'

China's planning has traditionally been based on 'pillar industries', such as machine-building, electronics, petrochemicals, automobiles, and construction and building materials, which received major investment. Recently, however, information technology and the electronics sector have become the fastest-growing industries and are now considered the first pillar, replacing the traditionally emphasized heavy industries.

The gross output value of China's electronics industry showed the highest growth rate of all industries in 2000, the sector expanding by more than 40%. Electronics, particularly the computer industry, with it high turnover of qualified personnel, is seen as a difficult environment for SOEs. Foreign manufacturers of electronic components are encouraged to compensate for the lack of domestic technical expertise. More than 90.5% of US components are brought into China through Hong Kong. By 2001 China had become the world's fourth largest producer of personal computers (PCs). US products dominate the software market for word-processing, spreadsheets and graphical user interfaces. China's own software industry has been most successful in localizing software written in English. In 2001 there were more than 10,000 software companies and an estimated 400,000 people engaged in software development. Turnover of the Chinese software industry amounted to US $4,000m. in 2001, equivalent to 1.2% of the global software market. Pirated software is a major problem for the development of the market.

Machine-building accounts for one-quarter of the total value of industrial output, with growth figures in 1996 falling below 10% for the first time in five years. Growth has been strongest in agricultural machinery, in particular combine harvesters and tractors. Other growth areas are numerically-controlled machine tools and hydroelectric equipment. The aim was to increase the share of domestic components in these products. By the year 2000 China planned to be able to manufacture heavy-duty generators, 80% of its processing machinery and 50% of equipment for the automobile industry.

China's state-owned petroleum industry has been restructured in recent years into two competing, vertically integrated corporations. The China National Petroleum Corporation (CNPC), originally specialized in petroleum and gas exploration and production, and the China Petrochemical Corporation (Sinopec), originally engaged in refining and distribution, have now expanded their scope and been transformed into regionally-based oil companies. CNPC operates mainly in the north and west, and Sinopec in the south. The other major oil companies are China National Offshore Oil Corporation (CNOOC), responsible for China's offshore exploration and production, and China National Star Petroleum, a new company created in 1997. The petroleum industry was one of the profitable state-owned industries in 2001 as a result of high world oil prices. China's domestic market is set to change under WTO, as international oil companies will be able to enter the market. China's oil companies are expanding their cooperation with foreign partners.

China's automobile industry, originally a 'pillar industry', was downgraded after 1996, but is now being encouraged again. The industry had average annual growth rates of 20% during the 1980s, but the rate of expansion had decreased to under 2% by the mid-1990s. Since 1999 annual domestic production, which then stood at 1.83m. vehicles, has increased at a higher rate, to reach a level of 23.3m. vehicles in 2001. Sales to government institutions have been declining, while corporate clients and private households have raised their share to more than 50% of total sales. Traffic control, urban congestion and pollution, however, will restrict the expansion of car ownership. Government macroeconomic policies appear to favour the channelling of private savings into other sectors, particularly into home ownership. Foreign investment in the industry is strong, and further investment is encouraged. Competition in the vehicle industry is expected to increase, as automobile tariffs will decline from the present average level of 90% to 25% in the years following China's entry into the WTO.

The construction industry has benefited from state spending and from the government policy to privatize residential housing. The value added by the industry grew again strongly, by 7.45%, in 2001. At the end of 2001 a total of 1,787.6m. sq m of housing was under construction and 825.4m. sq m had been completed. At the same time demand for new office space has been low, owing to oversupply in the major cities, and demand for new commercial residential housing remains weak, as consumers concentrate their spending on refurbishing their existing housing. Many transnational corporations have established advanced technology enterprises in China, producing cement, glass, ceramics and wall materials.

ENVIRONMENT

China's rapid industrialization in recent decades has led to serious environmental degradation. Ongoing concerns of China's Ministry of Environment are air pollution, acid rainfall, worsening water quality, and land degradation. China's pollution is mainly energy-related. Emissions of greenhouse gases, sulphur dioxide and particulate matter are very high owing to the widespread use of unwashed coal. Conversion from coal to natural gas for domestic fuel is one of the major measures of the Government to improve urban pollution. North China suffers from a chronic water shortage and desertification. By 2002 China had not agreed to binding targets for the reduction of carbon dioxide emissions under the Kyoto Protocol.

In 2000 36.5% of the more than 300 cities with air quality monitoring stations met national standards for air quality, while another 33% recorded moderate or heavy pollution. This was partly due to the ban on leaded petrol (gasoline) in mid-2000. While the overall count in suspended particles was down, there was no change in the spread of acid rain, which was recorded in 62% of the cities. Water quality remains a concern, as domestic waste water now exceeds industrial waste as a source of pollution. Water quality in rivers and lakes had improved, but remained a serious concern. Red algae tides caused losses to fisheries along the coast. Grasslands in China's western regions are severely affected by desertification and salination. These areas are expanding by 2m. ha each year and are feared to be causing climatic changes in northern China.

Public disclosure of environmental issues has greatly improved. Market-based anti-pollution measures such as emissions charges, 'cap and trade' systems and higher water prices are being introduced. Environmental protection expenditure was expected to amount to 1.4% of GDP during the Tenth Five-Year Plan.

ENERGY

China's energy sector remains one of the weak areas of industrial development. China is the world's third-largest producer and consumer of energy, but energy supply has not kept pace with industrial growth since 1979. Inadequate energy supply remains a constraint on further industrial development, since some 10%–15% of demand cannot be met, although there is regional oversupply of electric power. The centres of energy production and consumption are situated more than 1,000 km apart. Long-distance shipments of coal take up 40% of railway freight capacity. The situation was not expected to improve in the short term. Energy demand was predicted to quadruple between 2000 and 2020, with most of the increase occurring in the coastal provinces of Shandong, Jiangsu, Zhejiang, Shanghai, Fujian and Guangdong, which are far from the centres of coal production in the north-west of China. China's dependence on coal will continue into the foreseeable future; since the long-term availability of supply is guaranteed, it is still regarded as cheaper than other forms of primary energy. This dependence on coal is maintained at huge environmental costs to China.

For many years the dependence on coal has been one of the specific features of China's energy industry. The share of coal in total energy production reached its peak in 1995, at 75.3%, and was gradually reduced, to 67.2% in 2000. The share of crude petroleum was 21.48% and that of natural gas 3.4% in 2000. The contribution of hydroelectricity continued to increase steadily, while that of nuclear energy remained negligible. Alternative and sustainable forms of energy are rarely used.

Electricity Supply

China's installed capacity in 2000 was 294,000 MW, while actual generation was 1,308,000m. kWh. The Tenth Five-Year Plan aimed to raise capacity to 370,000 MW by 2005. Long-term targets for 2010 are 500,000 MW–550,000 MW in capacity and 2,500,000m. kWh of output.

Small-scale power plants with a capacity of 125 MW or less account for 50% of installed capacity of coal-fired stations. These plants are relatively cheap to build, but they incur significant transport costs for coal and emit high levels of carbon dioxide, sulphur dioxide and particles. Where possible, the use of larger and more efficient plants is now being encouraged. Local governments can force factories to use the electricity they produce, even though it might cost more than that generated by the larger stations funded by the central Government. The development of larger grids was expected to facilitate the long-distance transport of electricity, to reduce the need for coal.

The structure of the power sector was altered in 1997, when the operation of the State's power plants was transferred from the former Ministry of Power Industry to the State Power Corporation, with the aim of clearly separating power production and distribution, and also of introducing competition into the industry. The new corporation is responsible for the funding of energy development, as state subsidies to the power industry were to be discontinued in favour of commercial funding from domestic and foreign sources. Power distribution is the task of the State Power Corporation, which has been put in charge of the national electricity grids. Pricing of electricity was formerly the responsibility of provincial governments and prices could vary from one province to another. Under the new arrangements, the State Power Corporation buys electricity from the suppliers to the grid and markets it to consumers.

Coal

Coal is China's major energy source, with approximately one-third of output used for electricity, one-third for industrial boilers and one-third is used for domestic heating and cooking. Cities have started to prohibit the burning of coal for heating and cooking, owing to increasing levels of pollution. Problems arising from the use of coal include greenhouse-gas emissions, air pollution and acid rain.

Coal deposits are concentrated in the north-west of China, in the provinces of Shanxi, Shaanxi, and the Autonomous Region of Nei Monggol. Hardly any coal is produced south of the Changjiang. Coal has to be transported mainly by rail to the eastern coastal areas and the southern provinces. Limited rail capacity has added to the energy shortages along the Changjiang valley and in southern regions. The municipality of Beijing obtains its coal supplies by means of hundreds of trucks making daily journeys from the coalfields of Shanxi Province.

The problems related to coal supply have led to the growth of small, decentralized coal mines, managed either by provincial or by local authorities. Of the total coal output of 1,330m. metric tons in 1996, 43.6% was contributed by small mines organized at township and village level, with the remainder supplied by some 100 national-level coal producers and provincial coal mines. As with power generation, the Government encourages the development of larger, more efficient facilities and has been substantially reducing output by small mines since 1996. In 1999 31,000 small coal mines were closed, and overall output was reduced by 250m. tons to 1,045m. tons, before declining to an estimated 880m. tons in 2000. Another improvement, as a result of technical advances, is to make coal cleaner and easier to transport through liquefaction or gasification.

Petroleum and Natural Gas

With a consumption of 4.9m. barrels per day (b/d) in 2001, China was the world's third largest oil consuming country behind the USA and Japan. China has proven petroleum reserves of 24,000m. barrels. In 2001 production of petroleum amounted to 3.3m. b/d and net petroleum imports to 1.6m. b/d. China became a net importer of petroleum in 1993, although it continues to export small volumes of crude petroleum, mainly to Japan. China's annual petroleum production is not expected to increase significantly in the near future. Of total production, approximately three-quarters are extracted from older oilfields in eastern and north-eastern China. Daqing in north-eastern China is the country's's largest oilfield, accounting for approximately one-third of total output. It began production in 1963 and shows signs of declining output. The second largest oilfield, Liaohe, is also located in north-eastern China. It is improving recovery rates to stabilize production. Expansion of production is expected from new oilfields in Xinjiang, with forecasts that these could reach an output of 1m. b/d by 2008. This will require large-scale infrastructure improvements.

Offshore petroleum contributes 10% to Chinese production of the commodity. Exploitation and new exploration are centred in the Bohai Gulf near Tianjin and the Zhujiang (Pearl River) mouth area in South China. China has also reached an agreement with Viet Nam that prepared the way for joint petroleum and gas production in the Beibu Gulf. Most of the offshore exploration is based on international consortia with Chinese and international partners. Production has started in the South China Sea oil fields, and new fields will go into production during the coming years in the Bohai Gulf fields, where reserves are estimated at 1,500m. barrels.

China has also participated in international petroleum and gas prospecting and exploitation, including petroleum projects in Peru, Canada, Sudan, Thailand, Venezuela and Kazakhstan. Pipeline projects were under discussion with Russia and Kazakhstan in 2001. The economic feasibility of these projects has yet to be established. The China National Petroleum Corporation has invested in Kazakhstan and in Sudan, from where oil exports to China started in 1999.

Gas consumption remains at a relatively low level, amounting to only 3% of total primary energy consumption. Estimates of China's proven reserves of natural gas range between 1,200,000m. and 5,300,000m. cu m. Consumption of natural gas exceeded 25,000m. cu m in 2000 and is planned to double to 50,000m. cu m by 2005 and again to 100,000m. cu m by 2010. In larger cities, gas has already replaced coal as a household fuel. Further discoveries of natural gas reserves are expected as a result of increased petroleum exploration. Natural gas features significantly in national energy planning, as it provides a clean and efficient energy source. According to Chinese estimates, an increase in annual output of up to 100,000m. cu m in the short term could save as much as 400m. tons of coal. A new gas pipeline from Xinjiang to Shanghai is one of the core projects for the development of western China, based on the expectation that it will create a development corridor along its path. Guangdong Province and Shanghai have been targeted as the first trial areas for conversion from coal to natural gas as their main energy supply. Initially, most of the natural gas supply is to come from Australia, under a 25-year, US $ 12,000m. contract signed in 2002.

Hydroelectricity

Hydroelectric power is relatively abundant in China's southern provinces, but the sources are often located in remote areas. In 2000 it accounted for 8.0% of total energy production. By December 1999 the People's Republic's largest hydroelectric power station, at Ertan, was fully functioning. The largest and most controversial hydroelectric project is the Three Gorges Dam, which will add approximately 18,200 MW when construction is completed in 2009, at a total cost of 200,000m. yuan. Another large-scale hydroelectric scheme is planned for the Huanghe (Yellow River) under the newly established Yellow River Hydroelectric Development Corporation, which plans to reach an installed capacity of 15.8 GW. In 2002 seven of 25 planned stations were under construction in provinces along the Huanghe.

Nuclear Power Industry

In 2000 nuclear power supplied less than 1% of total energy. China National Nuclear Corporation plans to raise this level to 5% by the year 2020. In 1998 China had three operational nuclear plants: a Chinese-designed 300-MW pressurized water reactor at Qinshan, in Zhejiang Province, and two 900-MW pressurized water reactors from a French company at Daya Bay, in Guangdong Province. In 2002 the first generation unit of a nuclear power plant in Guangdong Province began operation with a further 1 GW generating unit planned to be operational in 2003. In Zhejiang Province two 600 MW generating units were set to begin operations in 2002. Plans for four French reactors for a 3,600-MW project near Daya Bay, and two Russian 1,000-MW reactors at Liangyungang, in Jiangsu Province, are under way. China is dependent on finance from the supplying countries and therefore has had to acquire a range of different technologies. During the Tenth Five-Year Plan period (2001–05), China is planning to reduce reliance on nuclear industry and not to construct new nuclear power plants, while existing facilities might be expanded and upgraded.

TRANSPORT AND COMMUNICATIONS

Energy supply, transport and telecommunications are weaknesses in China's infrastructure. Transport was designated a priority area under the Tenth Five-Year Plan (2001–05). Projects included the Beijing–Shanghai Express rail project, the Shanghai International Shipping Center, and major transport infrastructure projects in China's western regions. Freight volume rose to 4,365,900m. freight ton-km in 2000; 31.2% thereof was carried by rail, 13.7% by road and 52.8% by water. Passenger volume increased by 7.9%. Of the total volume, 36.8% were carried by rail, 54.2% by road, 8.2% by air and 0.9% by water.

The railway system plays a strategic role in China's infrastructure, since it transports coal from the north-western provinces to the eastern seaboard and the southern provinces where demand is concentrated. New railway corridors were expected to invigorate the economies of adjoining regions, such as the provinces along a new line linking Kowloon (Hong Kong) to Beijing and the south-western line connecting Guangxi Zhuang Autonomous Region and Yunnan Province. The main trunk lines of Beijing–Guangzhou, Harbin–Dalian, Beijing–Shenyang and Lianyungang–Lanzhou carry a freight volume three times their official capacity. A new five-year target was set for the railway system in 1998, which aimed to increase its length from 66,000 km to 70,000 km by the year 2002, with 21,000 km of double-track lines and 15,000 km of electrified lines. Total investment in railway construction was expected to amount to some 350,000m. yuan over the five-year period. High-speed trains, capable of speeds of up to 140 km per hour, have been introduced on routes between Beijing, Shanghai, Harbin and Guangzhou. This is a considerable improvement over the average speed of 60 km per hour on long-distance routes. The railway system is administered by a state monopoly.

Since the 1980s highway construction has helped to create a long-distance network that allows interregional road transport. Prior to this, road networks extended around provincial centres. Between 1990 and 1995 China completed 130,000 km of highways, including 1,619 km of expressways and 9,328 km of wider and dual-carriage roads. The total length of China's highways in 1999 was 1.35m. km, the total length of expressways amounted to 19,000 km in 2001. However, since the 1980s the number of vehicles has increased 10 times faster than the expansion of the road system. The main scheme of the long-term planning for the highway sector is a programme to build a 35,000-km network of 12 national highways linking Beijing to all provincial capitals and larger cities.

China has 13 major ocean shipping ports, each with an annual capacity of more than 5m. metric tons. The volume of freight handled by all ocean ports in 2000 amounted to 1,280m. tons, including 520m. tons of foreign-trade merchandise. The four largest ports were Shanghai, Ningbo, Dalian and Tianjin. At the technical level, Chinese ports do not match international standards; only 20% of trade is containerized, compared with a world average of 50%. Turnover times in Chinese ports are another major concern. The China Ocean Shipping Group is one of the world's largest shipping companies. In 1997 foreign businesses operated 900 of the 2,300 liners departing from Chinese ports. BOT contracts are being encouraged for public terminal berths.

The length of inland shipping waterways reached 119,325 km in 2000. In 1998 some 6,000 km were navigable for vessels with a displacement of 1,000 gross tons. Inland river navigation is particularly developed in southern and south-west China. In 1997 facilities on the Xijiang were upgraded to accommodate 1,000-ton vessels to give Nanning, the capital of Guangxi Zhuang Autonomous Region, access to Hong Kong and Macao. River navigation networks are being set up and expanded in the Zhujiang delta, along the Changjiang and on the Beijing–Hangzhou Grand Canal. Inland river navigation is managed by diverse operators, including household enterprises.

China's aviation industry grew at an annual rate of 20% during the 1990s and continues to expand and upgrade its fleet of aircraft. In 2001, however, 90% of China's 143 airports operated at a loss. Some 95% of passenger traffic is handled by 40 airports, of which only the larger airports, such as Beijing, Shanghai and Guangzhou, are believed to be profitable. This sector has been slow to absorb foreign investment. The first projects started in 1998 with Hong Kong and German investors in Wuhan and Pudong, Shanghai. In 2002 foreign investment was actively sought as part of a restructuring of the industry that will merge China's 10 major airlines into three groups, Air China, China Eastern Airlines and China Southern Airlines. Beijing-based Air China will absorb Chengdu-based China Southwest Airlines and Beijing's China National Aviation Corporation, which hold major shares in Hong Kong's Dragonair and Air Macau. Shanghai-based China Eastern Airlines is to merge with China Northwest Airlines and Yunnan Airlines. Guangzhou-based China Southern Airlines will merge with China Northern Airlines and Xinjiang Airlines; their combined assets will amount to US $6,000m. This group will be the largest, with 512 domestic and 94 international routes. In this process of corporatization, the government-based General Administration of Civil Aviation of China will shed further enterprise functions by establishing the three service groups China Civil Aviation Information (Group), China Aviation Supplies Import and Export (Group) and China Aviation Fuel Group.

China's telecommunications industry experienced a boom during the 1990s, fuelled by huge demand for new technology, and forcing the Ministry of Posts and Telecommunications (MPT) to accelerate the introduction and expansion of a digital network, fibre-optic cables and satellite systems, and mobile communication facilities. In 2000 the volume of its transactions grew by 42%. In 1999 China had 239,735 km of long-distance fibre-optic cable and 65,228 km of long-distance microwave lines. The total number of telephone exchange gates amounted to 179m. Since the introduction of China's mobile telephone network, the number of subscribers has almost doubled every year, and reached 120m. in 2001. Access to data communication is still restricted by high fees and government attempts to control contents. In 1998, however, government institutions and corporations, including SOEs, on a large scale and in co-operation with US software companies, started to provide their own information sites on the internet and allowed experiments in electronic commerce. By early 2002 China had an estimated 56m. internet users, double the figure of the previous year. Internet use is concentrated in major urban centres, mainly in Beijing, Guangzhou and Shanghai. By the end of 2000 China had 620 internet service providers (ISPs) and 1,600 internet content providers (ICPs). Of China's 48,000 registered domain names in mid-2000, three-quarters were commercial. The volume of e-commerce was estimated to be between US $20m. and US $40m. in 2000. The major services are internet-based software and development of internet-based information.

The structure of the whole industry changed in March 1998 when, in a major reform, a new Ministry of Information Technology and Telecommunications Industries was formed by a merger of the MPT, the Ministry of Electronics Industry and parts of the Ministry of Radio, Film and Television, China Aerospace Industry Corporation and China Aviation Industry Corporation. China has two competing carriers, China Telecom and China Unicom. Until 1998 China's telecommunications industry had closed the service operations sector to foreign investment, but opened the equipment and network market construction market. As part of entry terms to the WTO, China will open its telecommunications sector to foreign investment and allow up to 49% foreign ownership in Chinese telecommunications service firms, and a 51% foreign ownership stake in telecommunications value-added and wireless paging service providers within four years after China's admission to the WTO.

FOREIGN TRADE AND INVESTMENT

China's foreign trade and its absorption of foreign investment have played an important part in the reform of its domestic economy and in strengthening its status as a regional and international economic power. China's increased international standing became evident in the course of the Asian economic crisis of 1997/98, with China coming under international pressure not to devalue its currency. In 2001 China's foreign trade performance improved again.

Foreign trade and the participation of the Chinese economy in international competition had long been controversial, for ideological and historical reasons. China's reluctance to participate in international exchange manifested itself in a foreign trade regime that was modelled on the USSR and existed well into the 1980s. Under this structure, some 10 large foreign trade corporations owned by the Ministry of Foreign Economic Relations and Trade (later the Ministry of Foreign Trade and Economic Co-operation), and some technical ministries, monopolized all foreign trade. By acting as an independent intermediary between foreign clients and domestic producers or buyers, they isolated the domestic economy from competition, but also from technical innovation. The foreign trade policy at the beginning of the reform period was still influenced by the former striving for autarky and the concept of import substitution. In the early 1980s the export-led growth of the Asian economies was gradually adopted as a model. In subsequent years foreign trade monopolies were gradually reduced and more than 5,000 Chinese corporations, as well as Sino-foreign joint-venture companies, received foreign trade rights. Since 1999 more than 1,000 private enterprises have also received foreign trading rights. In 2000 foreign-invested enterprises accounted for 52.1% of Chinese imports and 49.9% of total exports. A currency policy favourable to foreign trade also contributed to China's participation in global trade. At the beginning of the reform period the yuan was overvalued to exploit tourism; a dual exchange rate was then introduced, with a lower exchange rate for commercial transactions. From 1994 a much-devalued official rate replaced the split rates and has ever since been kept in a managed float at a level of around 8.3 yuan to one US dollar. In 1996 the yuan was made fully convertible for current-account transactions.

As a result, the volume of China's foreign trade increased from US $20,000m. in 1978 to US $165,500m. in 1992 and to US $474,300m. in 2001. The increase in volume in 2001 amounted to 31.5%. After recording predominantly negative trade balances in the second half of the 1980s, China achieved an overall positive trade balance in the 1990s, except for 1993, when the domestic economic boom restrained the growth in exports. Since then China has maintained an export surplus and has been able to accumulate foreign-currency reserves, which totalled US $212.2m. at the end of 2001. Export performance fluctuated in the late 1990s, with a peak in 1997, a decline in growth in 1998 and substantial improvement from the second half of 1999, which continued into 2000 and 2001, as the other Asian economies recovered from the regional crisis. Export growth in 2001 was 6.8%. In particular, China further improved its trade surplus with the USA, which, according to US figures, rose from US $83,800m. in 2000 to US $87,700m. in 2001. Chinese customs statistics, traditionally much lower, showed a slight decline to US $24,000 in 2001.

In line with its comparative advantage in the sector, China's exports were traditionally dominated by labour-intensive light industrial products, such as textile products (including electrical appliances, telecommunication equipment and toys) in addition to mineral fuels, heavy manufactures and agricultural goods. Government policy is to diversify from the previous dependence on raw materials and primary goods, in favour of more sophisticated industrial goods. In 2000 manufactured goods accounted for 90% of total exports; machinery and electrical equipment alone constituted 42.3%, while the share of garments and fibres had declined to 20.9%. Manufactured products, especially investment goods, are also major components of China's imports, with a share of 45.7% for machinery and electric equipment, and 23.3% for advanced technology products. This trade composition also reflects the requirements of foreign-invested enterprises in China, which in 2000 accounted for 47.9% of total foreign trade. Imports of agricultural products and energy were expected to increase in the short term, with the changing consumption patterns brought about by further industrialization. Trade in services is also growing. From a nearly negligible share in 1989, services exports rose to US $29,700m. in 2000, placing China in 12th position internationally.

Japan has consistently been China's major trading partner since the 1980s, accounting for some 17.5% of total Chinese exports and imports in 2000. The USA has been the second major trading partner, with a share of 15.7% in 2000, slightly higher than that of the European Union (14.6%), and that of Hong Kong (11.4%), the relative importance of which continued to decline. Trade with South-East Asian countries continued to grow strongly, to 8.3% of total foreign trade turnover. Among China's leading 10 trading partners were Taiwan (6.4%), Australia (1.8%), Russia (1.7%) and Canada (1.5%).

From its early beginnings in 1979, foreign investment was intended to help raise China's technical and managerial standards to the level of the major Western economies and, in the first instance, to that of China's Asian neighbours. Foreign investors faced considerable obstacles and resistance, which overseas Chinese investors, including those from Hong Kong and Taiwan, with their more flexible modes of operation were more readily able to overcome. Although the importance of technology transfer was highly publicized in the 1980s, investment in joint-venture enterprises, as the only vehicles for foreign investment, was concentrated in tourism and the service industries. Only in the early 1990s did large-scale Western FDI flow into China. From the mid-1980s to the mid-1990s Asian investors contributed 80% of FDI in China, with Hong Kong alone holding a share of 60%. Hong Kong served as a conduit for Overseas Chinese and Taiwanese investment, and also for Chinese capital that had been transferred overseas and then redirected as foreign investment back into China. Other major investors were the USA, Japan and Western European countries. Their investments were increasingly directed at major 'pillar industries', such as the automobile and telecommunications industries, with the aim of securing a significant market share, if not dominance, in growth industries. This was made possible by the opening of domestic markets for the products of foreign-funded enterprises. As foreign investors were allowed to establish wholly-owned subsidiaries in China, so they were able to bring in more expertise and to compete directly with Chinese enterprises.

Annual inflow of actual FDI into China exceeded US $11,000m. in 1992 and reached US $46,800m. in 2001. In response to fluctuations in foreign investment, the Chinese Government was making efforts to attract more investment from Japan, the USA and Europe and to open new areas of investment, such as infrastructure, telecommunications and services to offset the shortfall at least partially. In 2001, the Chinese economy continued to enjoy investor confidence. China's foreign debt situation is extremely favourable, since its record in repaying foreign debt is sound.

The Effects of WTO Membership

China's major economic challenge in the coming years, apart from its macroeconomic problems, will be its accession to the WTO. China has committed itself to major market access concessions, in particular, a general reduction of tariff levels, opening up of its services sectors, such as insurance, banking, telecommunications, and operation of wholesale and retail distribution networks. Domestic effects will include a short-term increase in unemployment, followed by an expected growth in employment, which is to result from a projected additional GDP growth of 2%–3%. Internal markets will undergo restructuring as provincial protectionism and trade barriers will have to be abolished or reduced. This will increase competition among domestic enterprises. Foreign competition through tariff reduction and increased rivalry by foreign-invested enterprises will place additional competitive pressure on domestic producers. The full impact of these changes will only come to bear during 2005–07, when all non-tariff measures protecting Chinese industries will have to be phased out. Foreign businesses will face an improved business environment with less state protectionism and restrictions and will gain, among others, the rights to import to and export directly to Chinese customers, to engage in distribution and wholesale operations and to invest without trade-distorting requirements. The main domestic Chinese sectors affected by this increased competition will be aerospace, agriculture, the automobile industry, electronics and information technology, entertainment and communications, financial services and steel. The main beneficiaries will be the textiles sector and machine-building, both major export industries for China. From the Government's perspective, the benefits to be found in a globally integrated Chinese market outweigh the disadvantages that individual industries might have to suffer. Beijing's successful bid for the 2008 Olympic Games will have a positive impact on China's international economic integration, quite apart from the estimated investment volume of US $23,000m. in the period preceding the Games, which will attract international tendering and bidding.

Statistical Survey

Source (unless otherwise stated): State Statistical Bureau, 38 Yuetan Nan Jie, Sanlihe, Beijing 100826; tel. (10) 68515074; fax (10) 68515078; e-mail service@stats.gov.cn; internet www.stats.gov.cn.

Note: Wherever possible, figures in this Survey exclude Taiwan. In the case of unofficial estimates for China, it is not always clear if Taiwan is included or excluded. Where a Taiwan component is known, either it has been deducted from the all-China figure or its inclusion is noted. Figures for the Hong Kong Special Administrative Region (SAR — incorporated into the People's Republic of China on 1 July 1997) and for the Macao SAR (incorporated on 20 December 1999) are listed separately (pp. 342–346 and pp. 372–373 respectively). Transactions between the SARs and the rest of the People's Republic continue to be treated as external transactions.

Area and Population

AREA, POPULATION AND DENSITY

Area (sq km)	9,572,900*
Population (census results)	
1 July 1990	1,130,510,638
1 November 2000 (provisional)	
Males	653,550,000
Females	612,280,000
Total	1,265,830,000
Population (official estimates at 31 December)	
1997	1,236,260,000
1998	1,248,100,000
1999	1,259,090,000
Density (per sq km) at 1 November 2000	132.3

* 3,696,100 sq miles.

PRINCIPAL ETHNIC GROUPS (at census of 1 July 1990)

	Number	%
Han (Chinese)	1,039,187,548	91.92
Zhuang	15,555,820	1.38
Manchu	9,846,776	0.87
Hui	8,612,001	0.76
Miao	7,383,622	0.65
Uygur (Uigur)	7,207,024	0.64
Yi	6,578,524	0.58
Tujia	5,725,049	0.51
Mongolian	4,802,407	0.42
Tibetan	4,593,072	0.41
Bouyei	2,548,294	0.23
Dong	2,508,624	0.22
Yao	2,137,033	0.19
Korean	1,923,361	0.17
Bai	1,598,052	0.14
Hani	1,254,800	0.11
Li	1,112,498	0.10
Kazakh	1,110,758	0.10
Dai	1,025,402	0.09
She	634,700	0.06
Lisu	574,589	0.05
Others	3,838,337	0.34
Unknown	752,347	0.07
Total	1,130,510,638	100.00

2000 census (provisional): Han (Chinese) 1,159.4 million (91.59% of total).

BIRTHS AND DEATHS (sample surveys)

	1997	1998	1999
Birth rate (per 1,000)	16.57	16.03	15.23
Death rate (per 1,000)	6.51	6.50	6.46

Marriages (number registered): 8,866,593 in 1998; 8,799,079 in 1999; 8,420,044 in 2000.

Expectation of life (WHO estimates, years at birth, 2000): Males 68.9; Females 73.0 (Source: WHO, *World Health Report*).

PRINCIPAL TOWNS
(Wade-Giles or other spellings in brackets)

Population at 31 December 1998 (official estimates in '000)

Shanghai (Shang-hai)	9,537
Beijing (Pei-ching or Peking, the capital)	7,336
Chongqing (Ch'ung-ch'ing or Chungking)	6,140
Tianjin (T'ien-chin or Tientsin)	5,214
Wuhan (Wu-han or Hankow)	4,284
Harbin (Ha-erh-pin)	4,266
Shenyang (Shen-yang or Mukden)	4,242
Guangzhou (Kuang-chou or Canton)	4,174
Chengdu (Ch'eng-tu)	3,273
Changchun (Ch'ang-ch'un)	2,767
Nanjing (Nan-ching or Nanking)	2,762
Xian (Hsi-an or Sian)	2,718
Dalian (Ta-lien or Dairen)	2,656
Qingdao (Ch'ing-tao or Tsingtao)	2,543
Jinan (Chi-nan or Tsinan)	2,258
Hangzhou (Hang-chou or Hangchow)	2,105
Zhengzhou (Cheng-chou or Chengchow)	2,035
Shijiazhuang (Shih-chia-chuang or Shihkiachwang)	1,983
Taiyuan (T'ai-yüan)	1,937
Changsha (Chang-sha)	1,737
Kunming (K'un-ming)	1,685
Nanchang (Nan-ch'ang)	1,650
Fuzhou (Fu-chou or Foochow)	1,546
Lanzhou (Lan-chou or Lanchow)	1,538

EMPLOYMENT*
(official estimates, '000 persons at 31 December)

	1998	1999	2000
Agriculture, forestry and fishing	332,320	334,930	333,550
Mining	7,210	6,670	5,970
Manufacturing	83,190	81,090	80,430
Electricity, gas and water	2,830	2,850	2,840
Construction	33,270	34,120	35,520
Transport, storage and communications	20,000	20,220	20,290
Wholesale and retail trade and catering	46,450	47,510	46,860
Banking and insurance	3,140	3,280	3,270
Social services	8,680	9,230	9,210
Health care, sports and social welfare	4,780	4,820	4,880
Education, culture, art, radio, film and television broadcasting	15,730	15,680	15,650
Government agencies, etc.	10,970	11,020	11,040
Others	55,060	53,490	56,430
Total	623,630	624,910	625,940

* In addition to employment statistics, sample surveys of the economically active population are conducted. On the basis of these surveys, the total labour force ('000 persons at 31 December) was: 714,070 in 1998; 719,830 in 1999. Of these totals, the number of employed persons ('000 at 31 December) was: 699,570 (agriculture, etc. 348,380; industry 164,400; services 186,790) in 1998; 705,860 (agriculture, etc. 353,640; industry 162,350; services 189,870) in 1999; 711,500 (agriculture, etc. 355,750; industry 160,090; services 195,660) in 2000.

Health and Welfare

KEY INDICATORS

Fertility (births per woman, 2000)	1.8
Under-5 mortality rate (per 1,000 live births, 2000)	40
HIV/AIDS (% of persons aged 15–49, 2001)	0.11
Physicians (per 1,000 head, 1998)	1.62
Hospital beds (per 1,000 head, 1998)	2.91
Health expenditure (1998): US $ per head (PPP)	143
% of GDP	4.5
public (% of total)	39.9
Access to water (% of persons, 2000)	75
Access to sanitation (% of persons, 2000)	38
Human Development Index (2000): ranking	96
value	0.726

For sources and definitions, see explanatory note on p. vi.

ADMINISTRATIVE DIVISIONS (previous or other spelling given in brackets)

	Area ('000 sq km)	Population at 1 November 2000: Total ('000)	Population at 1 November 2000: Density (per sq km)	Capital of province or region	Estimated population ('000) at 31 Dec. 1998*
Provinces					
Sichuan (Szechwan)	487.0	83,290	171	Chengdu (Chengtu)	3,273
Henan (Honan)	167.0	92,560	554	Zhengzhou (Chengchow)	2,035
Shandong (Shantung)	153.3	90,790	592	Jinan (Tsinan)	2,258
Jiangsu (Kiangsu)	102.6	74,380	724	Nanjing (Nanking)	2,762
Guangdong (Kwangtung)	197.1	86,420	438	Guangzhou (Canton)	4,174
Hebei (Hopei)	202.7	67,440	333	Shijiazhuang (Shihkiachwang)	1,983
Hunan (Hunan)	210.5	64,400	306	Changsha (Changsha)	1,734
Anhui (Anhwei)	139.9	59,860	429	Hefei (Hofei)	1,330
Hubei (Hupeh)	187.5	60,280	321	Wuhan (Wuhan)	4,284
Zhejiang (Chekiang)	101.8	46,770	459	Hangzhou (Hangchow)	2,105
Liaoning (Liaoning)	151.0	42,380	281	Shenyang (Shenyang)	4,242
Jiangxi (Kiangsi)	164.8	41,400	251	Nanchang (Nanchang)	1,650
Yunnan (Yunnan)	436.2	42,880	98	Kunming (Kunming)	1,685
Heilongjiang (Heilungkiang)	463.6	36,890	80	Harbin (Harbin)	4,266
Guizhou (Kweichow)	174.0	35,250	203	Guiyang (Kweiyang)	1,421
Shaanxi (Shensi)	195.8	36,050	184	Xian (Sian)	2,718
Fujian (Fukien)	123.1	34,710†	282	Fuzhou (Foochow)	1,546
Shanxi (Shansi)	157.1	32,970	210	Taiyuan (Taiyuan)	1,937
Jilin (Kirin)	187.0	27,280	146	Changchun (Changchun)	2,767
Gansu (Kansu)	366.5	25,620	70	Lanzhou (Lanchow)	1,538
Hainan	34.3	7,870	229	Haikou	438
Qinghai (Tsinghai)	721.0	5,180	7	Xining (Hsining)	691
Autonomous regions					
Guangxi Zhuang (Kwangsi Chuang)	220.4	44,890	204	Nanning (Nanning)	1,143
Nei Mongol (Inner Mongolia)	1,177.5	23,760	20	Hohhot (Huhehot)	886
Xinjiang Uygur (Sinkiang Uighur)	1,646.9	19,250	12	Urumuqi (Urumchi)	1,281
Ningxia Hui (Ninghsia Hui)	66.4	5,620	85	Yinchuan (Yinchuen)	530
Tibet (Xizang)	1,221.6	2,620	2	Lhasa (Lhasa)	105‡
Municipalities					
Shanghai	6.2	16,740	2,700	—	9,537
Beijing (Peking)	16.8	13,820	823	—	7,336
Tianjin (Tientsin)	11.3	10,010	886	—	5,214
Chongqing (Chungking)	82.0	30,900	377	—	6,140
Total	9,572.9	1,262,280§	132		

* Excluding population in counties under cities' administration.

† Excluding islands administered by Taiwan, mainly Jinmen (Quemoy) and Mazu (Matsu), with 49,050 inhabitants according to figures released by the Taiwan authorities at the end of March 1990.

‡ 1982 figure.

§ Excluding 2,500,000 military personnel and 1,050,000 persons with unregistered households.

Agriculture

PRINCIPAL CROPS
('000 metric tons)

	1998	1999	2000
Wheat	109,726	113,880	99,640
Rice (paddy)	198,712	198,487	187,910
Barley	3,400†	3,300†	3,340*
Maize	132,954	128,086	106,000
Rye†	700	628	650
Oats†	756	600	650
Millet	3,113	2,318	2,125*
Sorghum	4,087	3,241	2,582*
Buckwheat†	1,400	1,300	1,327
Triticale (wheat-rye hybrid)†	1,400	1,200	1,000
Potatoes	64,579	56,105	63,000*
Sweet potatoes	115,451	125,925	121,250*
Cassava (Manioc)†	3,700	3,750	3,750
Taro (Coco yam)†	1,425	1,425	1,425
Sugar cane	83,438	74,703	68,280
Sugar beet	14,466	8,639	8,073
Dry beans*	1,567	1,350	1,500
Dry broad beans*	1,827	1,500	1,600
Dry peas*	1,207	940	1,070
Other pulses*	254	245	230
Soybeans (Soya beans)	15,152	14,245	15,300*
Groundnuts (in shell)	11,886	12,639	14,437*
Oil palm fruit†	622	630	640
Castor beans*	230	260	300
Sunflower seed	1,465	1,765	1,950
Rapeseed	8,301	10,132	11,381

— continued	1998	1999	2000
Tung nuts	432	448	453
Sesame seed	656	743	811
Tallowtree seeds†	800	800	820
Linseed	523	404	540*
Cottonseed	9,002	7,658	8,834
Other oilseeds†	975	1,025	1,109
Cabbages†	17,200	18,000	19,450
Asparagus†	3,000	3,150	3,400
Lettuce†	5,650	5,800	6,250
Spinach†	5,600	5,550	6,000
Tomatoes†	17,000	17,800	19,200
Cauliflower†	4,600	4,550	4,900
Pumpkins, squash and gourds†	3,150	3,250	3,500
Cucumbers and gherkins†	15,000	15,850	17,100
Aubergines (Eggplants)†	10,500	11,000	11,880
Green chillies and peppers†	7,250	7,480	8,100
Green onions and shallots†	225	222	240
Dry onions†	10,800	11,250	12,150
Garlic†	5,750	5,900	6,380
Green beans†	1,250	1,350	1,450
Green peas†	1,085	1,150	1,250
Carrots†	4,400	4,500	4,850
Mushrooms†	586	650	700
Other vegetables†	95,090	96,601	104,109
Watermelons	35,485	37,000†	38,000†
Cantaloupes and other melons	4,867	5,650†	6,250†

— continued	1998	1999	2000
Grapes	2,358	2,708	3,282
Apples	19,481	20,802	20,431
Pears	7,275	7,742	8,783
Peaches and nectarines	3,210*	3,960*	4,100†
Plums	3,125*	3,880*	4,150†
Oranges*	2,148	3,090	3,400
Tangerines, mandarins, clementines and satsumas*	5,669	6,720	7,400
Lemons and limes*	189	242	266
Grapefruit and pomelos*	155	195	215
Other citrus fruit*	430	540	594
Mangoes	2,375*	2,920*	3,100†
Pineapples	645	883	970*
Persimmons	1,314	1,481	1,630*
Bananas	3,518	4,194	4,941
Other fruits and berries†	2,637	3,030	3,199
Walnuts	269	274	300*
Other treenuts†	223	225	225
Tea (made)	665	676	683
Pimento and allspice†	205	215	212
Other spices†	256	264	264
Tobacco (leaves)	2,364	2,469	2,552
Jute and jute-like fibres*	248	165	126
Cotton (lint)	4,501	3,829	4,417
Other fibre crops	276	291†	324†
Natural rubber	462	490	500†

* Unofficial figure(s). † FAO estimate(s).

Source: mainly FAO.

LIVESTOCK ('000 head at 31 December)

	1998	1999	2000
Horses	8,981	8,914	8,766
Mules	4,739	4,673	4,530
Asses	9,558	9,348	9,227
Cattle	101,689	104,396	128,663 (Cattle and Buffaloes)
Buffaloes	22,665	22,587	
Camels	335	330	326
Pigs	422,563	431,442	446,815
Sheep	127,352	131,095	133,160
Goats	141,683	148,163	157,159
Rabbits*	175,000	185,000	n.a.
Chickens*	3,300,000	3,500,000	n.a.
Ducks*	550,000	600,000	n.a.
Geese*	185,000	200,000	n.a.

* FAO estimates.

Source: partly FAO.

LIVESTOCK PRODUCTS
('000 metric tons)

	1998	1999	2000
Beef and veal*	4,461	4,688	4,968
Buffalo meat*	338	366	360
Mutton and lamb*	1,239	1,335	1,440
Goat meat*	1,107	1,178	1,300
Pig meat	38,837	38,907	40,314
Horse meat	151	163	166
Rabbit meat	308	310	315†
Poultry meat*	10,563	11,155	11,710
Other meat	361*	357*	362†
Cows' milk	6,621	7,176	7,500†
Buffaloes' milk†	2,450	2,450	2,450
Sheep's milk	824	893	925†
Goats' milk†	185	190	200
Butter	79	79	81
Cheese	174	185	196
Hen eggs	17,172	18,145	18,870*
Other poultry eggs	3,030	3,202	3,330*
Honey	207	230	250†
Raw silk (incl. waste)	68	70	76
Wool: greasy	277	283	290†
scoured	141	144	148†
Cattle hides (fresh)	1,105	1,156	1,156†
Buffalo hides (fresh)	101	110	108
Sheepskins (fresh)	243	257	257†
Goatskins (fresh)	232	261	261†

* Unofficial figure(s). † FAO estimate(s).

Source: FAO.

Forestry

ROUNDWOOD REMOVALS
('000 cubic metres, excl. bark)

	1997	1998	1999
Sawlogs, veneer logs and logs for sleepers*	58,688	59,136	55,160
Pulpwood*	6,673	6,312	5,910
Other industrial wood*	39,824	40,128	37,430
Fuel wood*	203,935	190,883	190,883
Total	309,120	296,459	289,383

* FAO estimates.

2000: Production as in 1999 (FAO estimates).

Source: FAO.

Timber production (official figures, '000 cubic metres): 63,948 in 1997; 59,662 in 1998; 52,368 in 1999; 47,240 in 2000.

SAWNWOOD PRODUCTION
('000 cubic metres, incl. railway sleepers)

	1997	1998*	1999*
Coniferous (softwood)	12,074	10,725	9,515
Broadleaved (hardwood)	8,050	7,150	6,344
Total	20,124	17,875	15,859

* FAO estimates.

2000: Production as in 1999 (FAO estimates).

Source: FAO.

Fishing

('000 metric tons, live weight)

	1997	1998	1999
Capture	15,722.3	17,229.9	17,240.0
Freshwater fishes	1,032.9	1,218.2	1,394.6
Japanese anchovy	1,202.0	1,373.3	1,096.9
Largehead hairtail	1,041.6	1,223.4	1,222.5
Aquaculture	19,315.6	20,795.4	22,789.9
Common carp	1,761.3	1,928.0	2,050.8
Crucian carp	858.5	1,032.0	1,235.7
Bighead carp	1,535.2	1,566.5	1,590.1
Grass carp (White amur)	2,632.4	2,807.5	3,062.4
Silver carp	3,070.5	3,133.0	3,180.2
Pacific cupped oyster	2,328.6	2,833.2	2,988.6
Japanese carpet shell	1,257.5	1,404.4	1,797.2
Total catch	35,038.0	38,025.3	40,029.9

Note: Figures exclude aquatic plants ('000 metric tons, wet weight): 4,899.0 (Capture 184.3, Aquaculture 4,714.7) in 1997; 6,447.1 (Capture 170.5, Aquaculture 6,276.6) in 1998; 7,469.9 (Capture 215.6, Aquaculture 7,254.3) in 1999.

Source: FAO, *Yearbook of Fishery Statistics*.

Aquatic products (official figures, '000 metric tons): 36,017.8 (marine 21,764.2, freshwater 14,253.5) in 1997; 39,065.1 (marine 23,567.2, freshwater 15,497.9) in 1998; 41,224.1 (marine 24,719.2, freshwater 16,504.9) in 1999; 42,784.8 (marine 25,387.4, freshwater 17,397.5) in 2000. The totals include artificially cultured products ('000 metric tons): 20,277.5 (marine 7,910.4 freshwater 12,367.1) in 1997; 21,814.7 (marine 8,600.4, freshwater 13,214.3) in 1998; 23,970.1 (marine 9,743.0, freshwater 14,227.1) in 1999; 25,746.7 (marine 10,612.9, freshwater 15,133.8) in 2000. Figures include aquatic plants on a dry-weight basis ('000 metric tons): 979.8 in 1997; 1,041.2 in 1998; 1,194.4 in 1999; 1,222.0 in 2000. Freshwater plants are not included.

Mining

(estimates, '000 metric tons, unless otherwise indicated)

	1998	1999	2000
Coal*	1,250,000	1,045,000	998,000
Crude petroleum*	161,000	160,000	163,000
Natural gas (million cu m)*	23,279	25,198	27,200
Iron ore: gross weight	246,900	237,000	224,000
metal content	74,500	71,000	67,200
Copper ore†	486	520	590
Nickel ore (metric tons)†	48,700	49,500	51,100
Bauxite	8,200	8,500	9,000
Lead ore†	581	549	570
Zinc ore†	1,273	1,476	1,710
Tin concentrates (metric tons)†	70,100	80,100	97,000
Manganese ore: gross weight	5,300	3,190	4,000
metal content	1,060	630	800
Tungsten concentrates (metric tons)†	30,000	31,100	37,000
Ilmenite	175	180	185
Molybdenum ore (metric tons)†	30,000	29,700	28,900
Vanadium (metric tons)†	15,500	26,000	30,000
Zirconium concentrates (metric tons)	15,000	15,000	15,000
Antimony ore (metric tons)†	97,400	89,600	98,700
Cobalt ore (metric tons)†	40	250	200
Mercury (metric tons)†	230	200	200
Silver (metric tons)†	1,300	1,320	1,600
Uranium (metric tons)†‡	500	500	500
Gold (metric tons)†	178	173	180
Magnesite	2,400	2,450	2,500
Phosphate rock and apatite§	25,000	20,000	19,400
Potash‖	120	150	250
Native sulphur	210	250	250
Fluorspar	2,350	2,400	2,450
Barite (Barytes)	3,300	2,800	3,500
Arsenic trioxide (metric tons)	15,500	16,000	16,000
Salt (unrefined)*	22,425	28,124	31,280
Gypsum (crude)	6,800	6,700	6,800
Graphite (natural)	224	300	400
Asbestos	314	247	370
Talc and related materials	3,800	3,900	3,500
Diamonds ('000 carats)			
Gem	230	230	230
Industrial	900	920	920

* Official figures. Figures for coal include brown coal and waste. Figures for petroleum include oil from shale and coal. Figures for natural gas refer to gross volume of output.

† Figures refer to the metal content of ores, concentrates or (in the case of vanadium) slag.

‡ Data from the World Nuclear Association (London, United Kingdom).

§ Figures refer to gross weight. The estimated phosphoric acid content was 30%.

‖ Potassium oxide (K_2O) content of potash salts mined.

Source: mainly US Geological Survey.

Industry

SELECTED PRODUCTS

Unofficial Figures ('000 metric tons, unless otherwise indicated)

	1997	1998	1999
Rayon and acetate continuous filaments*	72.0	n.a.	n.a.
Rayon and acetate discontinuous fibres*	378.0	n.a.	n.a.
Non-cellulosic continuous filaments*	1,446.7	n.a.	n.a.
Plywood ('000 cu m)†‡	8,098	4,979	7,790
Mechanical wood pulp†‡	440	450	450
Chemical wood pulp†‡	1,755	1,775	2,140
Other fibre pulp†‡	15,986	15,986	16,432
Sulphur§‖¶ (a)	1,400	1,450	1,580
(b)	6,040	4,490	3,860
Kerosene	6,129	6,161¶	n.a.
Residual fuel oil	23,112	21,004¶	n.a.
Lubricating oils¶	4,100	4,200	n.a.
Paraffin wax¶	850	900	n.a.
Petroleum coke	1,470	1,500	n.a.
Petroleum bitumen (asphalt)	2,900	3,000	n.a.
Liquefied petroleum gas	6,679	7,474¶	n.a.
Aluminium (unwrought)	2,180.1	2,361.6	2,808.9
Refined copper (unwrought)	1,152.9	1,109.4	1,210.0§¶
Lead (unwrought)	707.5	758.5	945.1
Tin (unwrought)	67.7	79.3	90.5
Zinc (unwrought)	1,434.4	1,491.9	1,669.8

* Data from the Fiber Economics Bureau, Inc, USA.

† Data from the FAO.

‡ Including Taiwan.

§ Data from the US Geological Survey.

‖ Figures refer to (a) sulphur recovered as a by-product in the purification of coal-gas, in petroleum refineries, gas plants and from copper, lead and zinc sulphide ores; and (b) the sulphur content of iron and copper pyrites, including pyrite concentrates obtained from copper, lead and zinc ores.

¶ Provisional or estimated figure(s).

Source: UN, *Industrial Commodity Statistics Yearbook.*

Official Figures ('000 metric tons, unless otherwise indicated)

	1998	1999	2000
Edible vegetable oils	6,024.8	7,337.9	8,353.2
Raw sugar	8,260	8,610	7,000
Beer	19,876.7	20,987.7	22,313.2
Cigarettes ('000 cases)	33,740	33,400	33,970
Cotton yarn (pure and mixed)	5,420	5,670	6,570
Woven cotton fabrics—pure and mixed (million metres)	24,100	25,000	27,700
Woollen fabrics ('000 metres)	267,767.2	273,173.9	278,323.7
Silk fabrics (metric tons)	67,700	70,200	73,300
Chemical fibres	5,100	6,000	6,940
Paper and paperboard	21,256.3	21,593.0	24,869.4
Rubber tyres ('000)	95,134.6	109,698.4	121,578.7
Sulphuric acid	21,710	23,560	24,270
Caustic soda (Sodium hydroxide)	5,393.7	5,801.4	6,678.8
Soda ash (Sodium carbonate)	7,440	7,660	8,340
Insecticides	559	625	607
Nitrogenous fertilizers (a)*	22,256.7	24,719.6	23,981.1
Phosphate fertilizers (b)*	6,667.9	6,360.7	6,630.3
Potash fertilizers (c)*	1,175.4	1,429.7	1,248.6
Synthetic rubber	589.0	732.8	865.2
Plastics	6,925.8	8,711.0	10,875.1
Motor spirit (gasoline)	34,654.0	37,412.7	41,346.7
Distillate fuel oil (diesel oil)	48,841.1	63,026.8	70,796.2
Coke	128,059.9	120,737.4	121,840.2
Cement	536,000	573,000	597,000
Pig-iron	118,636.7	125,392.4	131,014.8
Crude steel	115,590	124,260	128,500
Internal combustion engines ('000 horse-power)†	160,343.0	178,016.2	188,573.0
Tractors—over 20 horse-power (number)	67,800	65,400	41,000
Railway freight wagons (number)	23,500	18,600	27,300
Road motor vehicles ('000)	1,630	1,832	2,070
Bicycles ('000)	23,124.9	23,975.7	29,067.9
Electric fans ('000)	67,244.9	61,581.4	76,616.1
Mobile communication equipment ('000 units)	22,152	7,266	15,050
Floppy disks ('000)	404,000	460,000	473,000
Microcomputers ('000)	2,914	4,050	6,720
Large semiconductor integrated circuits ('000)	556,000	1,400,000	2,392,000
Colour television receivers ('000)	34,970	42,620	39,360
Cameras ('000)	55,218.7	48,322.9	55,145.2
Electric energy (million kWh)	1,167,000	1,239,300	1,355,600

* Production in terms of (a) nitrogen; (b) phosphoric acid; or (c) potassium oxide.

† Sales.

Finance

CURRENCY AND EXCHANGE RATES

Monetary Units

100 fen (cents) = 10 jiao (chiao) = 1 renminbiao (People's Bank Dollar), usually called a yuan.

Sterling, Dollar and Euro Equivalents (31 May 2002)

£1 sterling = 12.139 yuan;
US $1 = 8.277 yuan;
€1 = 7.769 yuan;
1,000 yuan = £82.38 = $120.82 = €128.71.

Average Exchange Rate (yuan per US $)

1999 8.2783
2000 8.2785
2001 8.2771

Note: Since 1 January 1994 the official rate has been based on the prevailing rate in the interbank market for foreign exchange.

STATE BUDGET (million yuan)*

Revenue	1998	1999	2000
Taxes	926,280	1,068,258	1,258,151
Industrial and commercial taxes	762,542	888,544	1,036,609
Tariffs	31,304	56,223	75,048
Agricultural and animal husbandry taxes	39,880	42,350	46,531
Taxes on income of state-owned enterprises	74,393	63,900	82,741
Taxes on income of collectively-owned enterprises	18,161	17,241	17,222
Other receipts	94,664	105,153	109,250
Sub-total	1,020,944	1,173,411	1,367,401
Less Subsidies for losses by enterprises	33,349	29,003	27,878
Total	987,595	1,144,408	1,339,523
Central Government	489,200	584,921	698,917
Local authorities	498,395	559,487	640,606

Expenditure†	1998	1999	2000
Capital construction	138,774	211,657	209,489
Agriculture, forestry and water conservancy	62,602	67,746	76,689
Culture, education, science and health care‡	215,438	240,806	273,688
National defence	93,470	107,640	120,754
Administration	132,677	152,568	178,758
Pensions and social welfare	17,126	17,988	21,303
Subsidies to compensate price increases	71,212	69,764	104,228
Development of enterprises	64,118	76,605	86,524
Other purposes	284,401	373,993	517,217
Total	1,079,818	1,318,767	1,588,650
Central Government	312,560	415,233	551,985
Local authorities	767,258	903,534	1,036,665

* Figures represent a consolidation of the regular (current) and construction (capital) budgets of the central Government and local administrative organs. The data exclude extrabudgetary transactions, totalling (in million yuan): Revenue 308,229 (central 16,415, local 291,814) in 1998, 338,517 (central 23,045, local 315,472) in 1999; Expenditure 291,831 (central 13,974, local 277,857) in 1998, 313,914 (central 16,482, local 297,432) in 1999.

† Excluding payments of debt interest.

‡ Current expenditure only.

INTERNATIONAL RESERVES (US $ million at 31 December)

	1999	2000	2001
Gold*	608	578	3,093
IMF special drawing rights	741	798	851
Reserve position in IMF	2,312	1,905	2,590
Foreign exchange†	154,675	165,574	212,165
Total†	158,336	168,856	218,698

* Valued at SDR 35 per troy ounce.

† Excluding the Bank of China's holdings of foreign exchange.

Source: IMF, *International Financial Statistics.*

MONEY SUPPLY (million yuan at 31 December)*

	1999	2000	2001
Currency outside banking institutions	1,345,210	1,464,990	1,568,730
Demand deposits at banking institutions	3,235,620	3,846,880	4,414,010
Total money (incl. others)	4,697,640	5,454,100	6,168,850

* Figures are rounded to the nearest 10 million yuan.

Source: IMF, *International Financial Statistics.*

COST OF LIVING
(General Consumer Price Index; base: previous year = 100)

	1998	1999	2000
Food	96.8	95.8	97.4
Clothing	99.2	97.3	99.1
Housing*	101.7	101.7	104.8
All items (incl. others)	99.2	98.6	100.4

* Including water, electricity and fuels.

NATIONAL ACCOUNTS
(million yuan at current prices)

Expenditure on the Gross Domestic Product*

	1998	1999	2000
Government final consumption expenditure	948,480	1,038,830	1,170,530
Private final consumption expenditure	3,692,110	3,933,440	4,291,190
Increase in stocks	191,510	122,610	−36,880
Gross fixed capital formation	2,763,080	2,947,550	3,262,380
Total domestic expenditure	7,595,180	8,042,430	8,687,220
Exports of goods and services / *Less* Imports of goods and services	305,150	224,880	224,030
Sub-total	7,900,330	8,267,310	8,911,250
Statistical discrepancy†	−65,810	−60,560	29,110
GDP in purchasers' values	7,834,520	8,206,750	8,940,360

* Figures are rounded to the nearest 10 million yuan.

† Referring to the difference between the sum of the expenditure components and official estimates of GDP, compiled from the production approach.

Gross Domestic Product by Economic Activity*

	1998	1999	2000
Agriculture, forestry and fishing	1,455,240	1,447,200	1,421,200
Industry†	3,338,790	3,508,720	3,957,030
Construction	523,140	547,060	591,750
Transport, storage and communications	412,130	446,030	491,860
Wholesale and retail trade and catering	675,910	691,030	730,690
Other services	1,429,310	1,566,710	1,747,830
Total	7,834,520	8,206,750	8,940,360

* Figures are rounded to the nearest 10 million yuan.

† Includes mining, manufacturing, electricity, gas and water.

BALANCE OF PAYMENTS (US $ million)

	1998	1999	2000
Exports of goods f.o.b.	183,529	194,716	249,131
Imports of goods f.o.b.	−136,915	−158,734	−214,657
Trade balance	46,614	35,982	34,474
Exports of services	23,895	26,248	30,430
Imports of services	−26,672	−31,589	−36,031
Balance on goods and services	43,837	30,641	28,874
Other income received	5,584	8,330	12,550
Other income paid	−22,228	−22,800	−27,216
Balance on goods, services and income	27,193	16,171	14,207
Current transfers received	4,661	5,368	6,861
Current transfers paid	−382	−424	−550
Current balance	31,472	21,115	20,518
Capital account (net)	−47	−26	−35
Direct investment abroad	−2,634	−1,775	−916
Direct investment from abroad	43,751	38,753	38,399
Portfolio investment assets	−3,830	−10,535	−11,307
Portfolio investment liabilities	98	−699	7,317
Other investment assets	−35,041	−24,394	−43,864
Other investment liabilities	−8,619	3,854	12,329
Net errors and omissions	−18,902	−17,641	−11,748
Overall balance	6,248	8,652	10,693

Source: IMF, *International Financial Statistics.*

External Trade

PRINCIPAL COMMODITIES (distribution by SITC, US $ million)

Imports c.i.f.	1997	1998	1999
Food and live animals	4,288.2	3,763.2	3,590.4
Crude materials (inedible) except fuels	11,727.5	10,536.1	12,526.9
Mineral fuels, lubricants, etc.	10,364.2	6,834.6	8,994.7
Petroleum, petroleum products, etc.	9,389.0	5,941.4	7,713.7
Crude petroleum oils, etc.	5,456.2	3,274.5	4,641.2
Chemicals and related products	19,046.7	19,907.2	23,693.3
Organic chemicals	3,013.5	3,512.3	5,418.4
Artificial resins, plastic materials, etc.	9,210.3	9,504.2	10,442.3
Products of polymerization, etc.	7,648.1	7,798.8	8,315.9
Basic manufactures	32,909.0	31,616.2	34,876.5
Textile yarn, fabrics, etc.	12,527.5	11,248.6	11,261.3
Iron and steel	6,737.8	6,563.1	7,586.8
Machinery and transport equipment	52,722.9	56,774.7	69,404.1
Machinery specialized for particular industries	9,704.9	8,152.4	8,146.1
General industrial machinery, equipment and parts	6,798.2	6,062.6	7,271.4
Office machines and automatic data-processing equipment	4,475.3	5,892.5	7,734.5
Telecommunications and sound equipment	5,966.8	7,817.9	9,363.7
Other electrical machinery, apparatus, etc.	14,056.9	16,670.9	23,866.0
Thermionic valves, tubes, etc.	6,253.9	8,331.6	13,391.0
Electronic microcircuits	3,482.1	4,602.7	7,533.0
Transport equipment and parts*	5,528.4	5,566.1	5,949.3
Miscellaneous manufactured articles	8,352.3	8,348.6	9,632.8
Total (incl. others)	142,370.4	140,236.8	165,699.1

* Data on parts exclude tyres, engines and electrical parts.

Source: UN, *International Trade Statistics Yearbook*.

2000 (US $ million): Food and live animals 4,758; Crude materials (inedible) except fuels 20,004; Mineral fuels, lubricants, etc. 20,637; Chemicals and related products 30,212; Basic manufactures 41,806; Machinery and transport equipment 91,934; Miscellaneous manufactured articles 12,750; Total (incl. others) 225,094.

2001 (US $ million): Food and live animals 4,976; Crude materials (inedible) except fuels 22,128; Mineral fuels, lubricants, etc. 17,495; Chemicals and related products 32,106; Basic manufactures 41,939; Machinery and transport equipment 107,042; Miscellaneous manufactured articles 15,076; Total (incl. others) 243,610.

(Source: Asian Development Bank, *Key Indicators of Developing Asian and Pacific Countries*.)

Exports f.o.b.	1997	1998	1999
Food and live animals	11,050.8	10,599.5	10,447.0
Mineral fuels, lubricants, etc.	6,992.4	5,178.7	4,662.4
Chemicals and related products	10,102.4	10,205.9	10,230.0
Basic manufactures	35,158.4	33,067.6	33,858.9
Textile yarn, fabrics, etc.	14,028.9	12,967.7	13,193.0
Machinery and transport equipment	43,614.4	50,143.0	58,748.6
Office machines and automatic data-processing equipment	9,243.8	11,846.3	13,368.5
Automatic data-processing machines and units	5,361.8	7,066.6	7,922.0
Telecommunications and sound equipment	10,303.8	11,111.0	13,060.9
Other electrical machinery, apparatus, etc.	13,016.4	14,599.2	18,490.0
Transport equipment and parts*	5,528.4	5,566.1	6,259.8
Miscellaneous manufactured articles	69,636.3	69,585.8	72,000.7
Clothing and accessories (excl. footwear)	31,875.5	30,121.2	30,146.4
Footwear	8,149.4	8,054.9	8,355.8
Baby carriages, toys, games and sporting goods	8,045.1	8,412.5	8,511.0
Children's toys, indoor games, etc.	6,983.9	7,258.4	7,324.1
Total (incl. others)	182,791.7	183,809.1	194,930.9

* Data on parts exclude tyres, engines and electrical parts.

Source: UN, *International Trade Statistics Yearbook*.

2000 (US $ million): Food and live animals 12,281; Mineral fuels, lubricants, etc. 7,851; Chemicals and related products 12,098; Basic manufactures 42,549; Machinery and transport equipment 82,602; Miscellaneous manufactured articles 86,282; Total (incl. others) 249,203.

2001 (US $ million): Food and live animals 12,778; Mineral fuels, lubricants, etc. 8,416; Chemicals and related products 13,354; Basic manufactures 43,823; Machinery and transport equipment 94,918; Miscellaneous manufactured articles 87,123;; Total (incl. others) 266,160.

(Source: Asian Development Bank, *Key Indicators of Developing Asian and Pacific Countries*.)

PRINCIPAL TRADING PARTNERS (US $ million)*

Imports c.i.f.	1998	1999	2000
Australia	2,682.5	3,607.2	5,024.0
Brazil	1,133.1	968.6	1,621.4
Canada	2,237.2	2,433.0	3,751.1
Finland	1,260.0	1,831.9	2,353.1
France	3,204.9	3,784.8	3,949.8
Germany	7,020.7	8,335.4	10,408.7
Hong Kong	6,658.0	6,891.9	9,429.0
Indonesia	2,460.9	3,050.9	4,402.0
Italy	2,279.0	2,679.9	3,078.4
Japan	28,275.1	33,763.4	41,509.7
Korea, Republic	15,014.4	17,226.2	23,207.4
Malaysia	2,673.9	3,605.6	5,480.0
Oman	706.5	635.4	3,261.8
Russia	3,640.0	4,222.6	5,769.9
Singapore	4,235.4	4,061.1	5,059.6
Sweden	2,046.4	2,151.8	2,674.7
Taiwan	16,631.1	19,526.8	25,493.6
Thailand	2,414.0	2,780.4	4,380.8
United Kingdom	1,952.6	2,994.8	3,592.5
USA	16,883.2	19,478.3	22,363.2
Total (incl. others)	140,236.8	165,699.1	225,093.7

Exports f.o.b.	1998	1999	2000
Australia	2,365.0	2,704.4	3,428.9
Canada	2,126.9	2,433.0	3,157.8
France	2,822.8	2,921.1	3,705.2
Germany	7,354.3	7,779.6	9,277.8
Hong Kong†	38,741.8	36,862.8	44,518.3
Indonesia	1,170.2	1.779.1	3,061.8
Italy	2,577.4	2,929.5	3,802.0
Japan	29,660.1	32,410.6	41,654.3
Korea, Republic	6,251.5	7,807.6	11,292.4
Malaysia	1,596.4	1,673.8	2,564.9
Netherlands	5,161.8	5,413.0	6,687.2
Russia	1,839.9	1,497.3	2,233.4
Singapore	3,943.9	4,502.2	5,761.0
Taiwan	3,868.9	3,949.9	5,039.0
United Kingdom	4,631.8	4,880.0	6,310.1
USA	37,947.7	41,946.9	52,099.2
Total (incl. others)	183,809.1	194,930.9	249,202.6

* Imports by country of origin; exports by country of consumption.
† The majority of China's exports to Hong Kong are re-exported.

Transport

	1998	1999	2000
Freight (million ton-km):			
Railways	1,251,707	1,283,840	1,390,210
Roads	548,338	572,430	612,940
Waterways	1,940,580	2,126,300	2,373,420
Air	3,345	4,230	5,027
Passenger-km (million):			
Railways	377,342	413,593	453,260
Roads	594,281	619,920	665,740
Waterways	12,027	10,730	10,050
Air	80,024	85,730	97,050

ROAD TRAFFIC ('000 motor vehicles in use)*

	1998	1999	2000
Passenger cars and buses	6,548.3	7,402.3	8,537.3
Goods vehicles	6,278.9	6,769.5	7,163.2
Total (incl. others)	13,193.0	14,529.4	16,089.1

* Excluding military vehicles.

SHIPPING

Merchant Fleet (registered at 31 December)

	1999	2000	2001
Number of vessels	3,285	3,319	3,280
Total displacement ('000 grt)	16,314.5	16,498.8	16,646.1

Source: Lloyd's Register-Fairplay, *World Fleet Statistics*.

Sea-borne Shipping (freight traffic, '000 metric tons)

	1998	1999	2000
Goods loaded and unloaded	922,370	1,051,620	1,256,030

Tourism

FOREIGN VISITORS (arrivals, '000)

Country of origin	1998	1999	2000
Hong Kong and Macao	54,075.4	61,670.6	70,099.4
Taiwan	2,174.6	2,584.6	3,108.6
Australia	186.4	203.5	234.1
Canada	196.0	213.7	236.5
France	138.0	155.6	185.0
Germany	191.9	217.6	239.1
Indonesia	104.6	182.9	220.6
Japan	1,572.1	1,855.2	2,201.5
Korea, Republic	632.8	992.0	1,344.7
Malaysia	300.1	372.9	441.0
Mongolia	264.8	354.5	399.1
Philippines	256.5	298.3	363.9
Russia	692.0	833.0	1,080.2
Singapore	316.4	352.5	399.4
Thailand	144.3	206.4	241.1
United Kingdom	242.9	258.9	283.9
USA	224.8	736.4	896.2
Total (incl. others)	63,478.4	72,795.6	83,443.9

Total tourism receipts (US $ million): 12,602 in 1998; 14,099 in 1999; 16,224 in 2000.

Communications Media

	1998	1999	2000
Television receivers ('000 in use)*	360,000	370,000	380,000
Telephones ('000 main lines in use)	87,420.9	108,715.8	144,829*
Mobile cellular telephones ('000 subscribers)	23,863	43,296	85,260
Personal computers ('000 in use)*	11,200	15,500	20,600
Internet users ('000)*	2,100	8,900	22,500
Book production:			
Titles	130,613	141,831	143,376
Copies (million)	7,238.6	7,316.3	6,270.0
Newspapers:			
Number	2,053	2,038	2,007
Average circulation ('000 copies)	182,110	186,320	179,140
Magazines:			
Number	7,999	8,187	8,725
Average circulation ('000 copies)	209,280	218,450	215,440

* Source: International Telecommunication Union.

1997 ('000 in use): Radio receivers 417,000; Facsimile machines 2,000 (Sources: UNESCO, *Statistical Yearbook*, and UN, *Statistical Yearbook*).

2001: Telepohnes ('000 main lines in use) 179,034; Mobile cellular telephones ('000 subscribers) 144,812; Personal computers ('000 in use) 25,000; Internet users ('000) 33,700 (Source: International Telecommunication Union).

Education

(2000)

	Institutions	Full-time teachers ('000)	Students ('000)
Kindergartens	175,836	856	22,442
Primary schools	553,622	5,860	130,133
General secondary schools	77,268	4,005	73,689
Secondary technical schools	2,963	204	4,125
Teacher-training schools	683	53	770
Agricultural and vocational schools	8,849	320	5,032
Special schools	1,539	32	378
Higher education	1,041	463	5,561

Adult literacy rate (UNESCO estimates): 84.1% (males 91.7%; females 76.3%) in 2000 (Source: UN Development Programme, *Human Development Report*).

Directory

The Constitution

A new Constitution was adopted on 4 December 1982 by the Fifth Session of the Fifth National People's Congress. Its principal provisions, including amendments made in 1993 and 1999, are detailed below. The Preamble, which is not included here, states that 'Taiwan is part of the sacred territory of the People's Republic of China'.

GENERAL PRINCIPLES

Article 1: The People's Republic of China is a socialist state under the people's democratic dictatorship led by the working class and based on the alliance of workers and peasants.

The socialist system is the basic system of the People's Republic of China. Sabotage of the socialist system by any organization or individual is prohibited.

Article 2: All power in the People's Republic of China belongs to the people.

The organs through which the people exercise state power are the National People's Congress and the local people's congresses at different levels.

The people administer state affairs and manage economic, cultural and social affairs through various channels and in various ways in accordance with the law.

Article 3: The state organs of the People's Republic of China apply the principle of democratic centralism.

The National People's Congress and the local people's congresses at different levels are instituted through democratic election. They are responsible to the people and subject to their supervision.

All administrative, judicial and procuratorial organs of the State are created by the people's congresses to which they are responsible and under whose supervision they operate.

The division of functions and powers between the central and local state organs is guided by the principle of giving full play to the initiative and enthusiasm of the local authorities under the unified leadership of the central authorities.

Article 4: All nationalities in the People's Republic of China are equal. The State protects the lawful rights and interests of the minority nationalities and upholds and develops the relationship of equality, unity and mutual assistance among all of China's nationalities. Discrimination against and oppression of any nationality are prohibited; any acts that undermine the unity of the nationalities or instigate their secession are prohibited.

The State helps the areas inhabited by minority nationalities speed up their economic and cultural development in accordance with the peculiarities and needs of the different minority nationalities.

Regional autonomy is practised in areas where people of minority nationalities live in compact communities; in these areas organs of self-government are established for the exercise of the right of autonomy. All the national autonomous areas are inalienable parts of the People's Republic of China.

The people of all nationalities have the freedom to use and develop their own spoken and written languages, and to preserve or reform their own ways and customs.

Article 5: The People's Republic of China shall be governed according to law and shall be built into a socialist country based on the rule of law.

The State upholds the uniformity and dignity of the socialist legal system.

No law or administrative or local rules and regulations shall contravene the Constitution.

All state organs, the armed forces, all political parties and public organizations and all enterprises and undertakings must abide by the Constitution and the law. All acts in violation of the Constitution and the law must be looked into.

No organization or individual may enjoy the privilege of being above the Constitution and the law.

Article 6: The basis of the socialist economic system of the People's Republic of China is socialist public ownership of the means of production, namely, ownership by the whole people and collective ownership by the working people.

The system of socialist public ownership supersedes the system of exploitation of man by man; it applies the principle of 'from each according to his ability, to each according to his work.'

In the initial stage of socialism, the country shall uphold the basic economic system in which the public ownership is dominant and diverse forms of ownership develop side by side, and it shall uphold the distribution system with distribution according to work remaining dominant and a variety of modes of distribution coexisting.

Article 7: The state-owned economy, namely the socialist economy under the ownership of the whole people, is the leading force in the national economy. The State ensures the consolidation and growth of the state-owned economy.

Article 8: The rural collective economic organizations shall implement a two-tier operations system that combines unified operations with independent operations on the basis of household contract operations and different co-operative economic forms in the rural areas—the producers', supply and marketing, credit, and consumers' co-operatives—are part of the socialist economy collectively owned by the working people. Working people who are all members of rural economic collectives have the right, within the limits prescribed by law, to farm plots of cropland and hilly land allotted for their private use, engage in household sideline production and raise privately-owned livestock.

The various forms of co-operative economy in the cities and towns, such as those in the handicraft, industrial, building, transport, commercial and service trades, all belong to the sector of socialist economy under collective ownership by the working people.

The State protects the lawful rights and interests of the urban and rural economic collectives and encourages, guides and helps the growth of the collective economy.

Article 9: Mineral resources, waters, forests, mountains, grassland, unreclaimed land, beaches and other natural resources are owned by the State, that is, by the whole people, with the exception of the forests, mountains, grassland, unreclaimed land and beaches that are owned by collectives in accordance with the law.

The State ensures the rational use of natural resources and protects rare animals and plants. The appropriation or damage of natural resources by any organization or individual by whatever means is prohibited.

Article 10: Land in the cities is owned by the State.

Land in the rural and suburban areas is owned by collectives except for those portions which belong to the State in accordance with the law; house sites and private plots of cropland and hilly land are also owned by collectives.

The State may in the public interest take over land for its use in accordance with the law.

No organization or individual may appropriate, buy, sell or lease land, or unlawfully transfer land in other ways.

All organizations and individuals who use land must make rational use of the land.

Article 11: The non-public sector of the economy comprising the individual and private sectors, operating within the limits prescribed by law, is an important component of the socialist market economy.

The State protects the lawful rights and interests of the non-public sector comprising the individual and private sectors. The State exercises guidance, supervision, and control over the individual and private sectors of the economy.

Article 12: Socialist public property is sacred and inviolable.

The State protects socialist public property. Appropriation or damage of state or collective property by any organization or individual by whatever means is prohibited.

Article 13: The State protects the right of citizens to own lawfully earned income, savings, houses and other lawful property.

The State protects by law the right of citizens to inherit private property.

Article 14: The State continuously raises labour productivity, improves economic results and develops the productive forces by enhancing the enthusiasm of the working people, raising the level of their technical skill, disseminating advanced science and technology, improving the systems of economic administration and enterprise operation and management, instituting the socialist system of responsibility in various forms and improving organization of work.

The State practises strict economy and combats waste.

The State properly apportions accumulation and consumption, pays attention to the interests of the collective and the individual as well as of the State and, on the basis of expanded production, gradually improves the material and cultural life of the people.

Article 15: The State practises a socialist market economy. The State strengthens economic legislation and perfects macro-control. The State prohibits, according to the law, disturbance of society's economic order by any organization or individual.

Article 16: State-owned enterprises have decision-making power in operations within the limits prescribed by law.

State-owned enterprises practise democratic management through congresses of workers and staff and in other ways in accordance with the law.

Article 17: Collective economic organizations have decision-making power in conducting economic activities on the condition that they abide by the relevant laws. Collective economic organizations practise democratic management, elect and remove managerial personnel, and decide on major issues in accordance with the law.

Article 18: The People's Republic of China permits foreign enterprises, other foreign economic organizations and individual foreigners to invest in China and to enter into various forms of economic co-operation with Chinese enterprises and other economic organizations in accordance with the law of the People's Republic of China.

All foreign enterprises and other foreign economic organizations in China, as well as joint ventures with Chinese and foreign investment located in China, shall abide by the law of the People's Republic of China. Their lawful rights and interests are protected by the law of the People's Republic of China.

Article 19: The State develops socialist educational undertakings and works to raise the scientific and cultural level of the whole nation.

The State runs schools of various types, makes primary education compulsory and universal, develops secondary, vocational and higher education and promotes pre-school education.

The State develops educational facilities of various types in order to wipe out illiteracy and provide political, cultural, scientific, technical and professional education for workers, peasants, state functionaries and other working people. It encourages people to become educated through self-study.

The State encourages the collective economic organizations, state enterprises and undertakings and other social forces to set up educational institutions of various types in accordance with the law.

The State promotes the nation-wide use of Putonghua (common speech based on Beijing pronunciation).

Article 20: The State promotes the development of the natural and social sciences, disseminates scientific and technical knowledge, and commends and rewards achievements in scientific research as well as technological discoveries and inventions.

Article 21: The State develops medical and health services, promotes modern medicine and traditional Chinese medicine, encourages and supports the setting up of various medical and health facilities by the rural economic collectives, state enterprises and undertakings and neighbourhood organizations, and promotes sanitation activities of a mass character, all to protect the people's health.

The State develops physical culture and promotes mass sports activities to build up the people's physique.

Article 22: The State promotes the development of literature and art, the press, broadcasting and television undertakings, publishing and distribution services, libraries, museums, cultural centres and other cultural undertakings, that serve the people and socialism, and sponsors mass cultural activities.

The State protects places of scenic and historical interest, valuable cultural monuments and relics and other important items of China's historical and cultural heritage.

Article 23: The State trains specialized personnel in all fields who serve socialism, increases the number of intellectuals and creates conditions to give full scope to their role in socialist modernization.

Article 24: The State strengthens the building of socialist spiritual civilization through spreading education in high ideals and morality, general education and education in discipline and the legal system, and through promoting the formulation and observance of rules of conduct and common pledges by different sections of the people in urban and rural areas.

The State advocates the civic virtues of love for the motherland, for the people, for labour, for science and for socialism; it educates the people in patriotism, collectivism, internationalism and communism and in dialectical and historical materialism; it combats capitalist, feudalist and other decadent ideas.

Article 25: The State promotes family planning so that population growth may fit the plans for economic and social development.

Article 26: The State protects and improves the living environment and the ecological environment, and prevents and remedies pollution and other public hazards.

The State organizes and encourages afforestation and the protection of forests.

Article 27: All state organs carry out the principle of simple and efficient administration, the system of responsibility for work and the system of training functionaries and appraising their work in order constantly to improve quality of work and efficiency and combat bureaucratism.

All state organs and functionaries must rely on the support of the people, keep in close touch with them, heed their opinions and suggestions, accept their supervision and work hard to serve them.

Article 28: The State maintains public order and suppresses treasonable and other criminal activities that endanger national security; it penalizes activities that endanger public security and disrupt the socialist economy as well as other criminal activities; and it punishes and reforms criminals.

Article 29: The armed forces of the People's Republic of China belong to the people. Their tasks are to strengthen national defence, resist aggression, defend the motherland, safeguard the people's peaceful labour, participate in national reconstruction, and work hard to serve the people.

The State strengthens the revolutionization, modernization and regularization of the armed forces in order to increase the national defence capability.

Article 30: The administrative division of the People's Republic of China is as follows:

(1) The country is divided into provinces, autonomous regions and municipalities directly under the central government;

(2) Provinces and autonomous regions are divided into autonomous prefectures, counties, autonomous counties and cities;

(3) Counties and autonomous counties are divided into townships, nationality townships and towns.

Municipalities directly under the central government and other large cities are divided into districts and counties. Autonomous prefectures are divided into counties, autonomous counties, and cities.

All autonomous regions, autonomous prefectures and autonomous counties are national autonomous areas.

Article 31: The State may establish special administrative regions when necessary. The systems to be instituted in special administrative regions shall be prescribed by law enacted by the National People's Congress in the light of the specific conditions.

Article 32: The People's Republic of China protects the lawful rights and interests of foreigners within Chinese territory, and while on Chinese territory foreigners must abide by the law of the People's Republic of China.

The People's Republic of China may grant asylum to foreigners who request it for political reasons.

FUNDAMENTAL RIGHTS AND DUTIES OF CITIZENS

Article 33: All persons holding the nationality of the People's Republic of China are citizens of the People's Republic of China.

All citizens of the People's Republic of China are equal before the law.

Every citizen enjoys the rights and at the same time must perform the duties prescribed by the Constitution and the law.

Article 34: All citizens of the People's Republic of China who have reached the age of 18 have the right to vote and stand for election, regardless of nationality, race, sex, occupation, family background, religious belief, education, property status, or length of residence, except persons deprived of political rights according to law.

Article 35: Citizens of the People's Republic of China enjoy freedom of speech, of the press, of assembly, of association, of procession and of demonstration.

Article 36: Citizens of the People's Republic of China enjoy freedom of religious belief.

No state organ, public organization or individual may compel citizens to believe in, or not to believe in, any religion; nor may they discriminate against citizens who believe in, or do not believe in, any religion.

The State protects normal religious activities. No one may make use of religion to engage in activities that disrupt public order, impair the health of citizens or interfere with the educational system of the state.

Religious bodies and religious affairs are not subject to any foreign domination.

Article 37: The freedom of person of citizens of the People's Republic of China is inviolable.

No citizen may be arrested except with the approval or by decision of a people's procuratorate or by decision of a people's court, and arrests must be made by a public security organ.

Unlawful deprivation or restriction of citizens' freedom of person by detention or other means is prohibited; and unlawful search of the person of citizens is prohibited.

Article 38: The personal dignity of citizens of the People's Republic of China is inviolable. Insult, libel, false charge or frame-up directed against citizens by any means is prohibited.

Article 39: The home of citizens of the People's Republic of China is inviolable. Unlawful search of, or intrusion into, a citizen's home is prohibited.

Article 40: The freedom and privacy of correspondence of citizens of the People's Republic of China are protected by law. No organization or individual may, on any ground, infringe upon the freedom and privacy of citizens' correspondence except in cases where, to meet the needs of state security or of investigation into criminal offences, public security or procuratorial organs are permitted to censor correspondence in accordance with procedures prescribed by law.

Article 41: Citizens of the People's Republic of China have the right to criticize and make suggestions to any state organ or functionary. Citizens have the right to make to relevant state organs complaints and charges against, or exposures of, violation of the law or dereliction of duty by any state organ or functionary; but fabrication or distortion of facts with the intention of libel or frame-up is prohibited.

In case of complaints, charges or exposures made by citizens, the state organ concerned must deal with them in a responsible manner after ascertaining the facts. No one may suppress such complaints, charges and exposures, or retaliate against the citizen making them.

Citizens who have suffered losses through infringement of their civic rights by any state organ or functionary have the right to compensation in accordance with the law.

Article 42: Citizens of the People's Republic of China have the right as well as the duty to work.

Using various channels, the State creates conditions for employment, strengthens labour protection, improves working conditions and, on the basis of expanded production, increases remuneration for work and social benefits.

Work is the glorious duty of every able-bodied citizen. All working people in state-owned enterprises and in urban and rural economic collectives should perform their tasks with an attitude consonant with their status as masters of the country. The State promotes socialist labour emulation, and commends and rewards model and advanced workers. The State encourages citizens to take part in voluntary labour.

The State provides necessary vocational training to citizens before they are employed.

Article 43: Working people in the People's Republic of China have the right to rest.

The State expands facilities for rest and recuperation of working people, and prescribes working hours and vacations for workers and staff.

Article 44: The State prescribes by law the system of retirement for workers and staff in enterprises and undertakings and for functionaries of organs of state. The livelihood of retired personnel is ensured by the State and society.

Article 45: Citizens of the People's Republic of China have the right to material assistance from the State and society when they are old, ill or disabled. The State develops the social insurance, social relief and medical and health services that are required to enable citizens to enjoy this right.

The State and society ensure the livelihood of disabled members of the armed forces, provide pensions to the families of martyrs and give preferential treatment to the families of military personnel.

The State and society help make arrangements for the work, livelihood and education of the blind, deaf-mute and other handicapped citizens.

Article 46: Citizens of the People's Republic of China have the duty as well as the right to receive education.

The State promotes the all-round moral, intellectual and physical development of children and young people.

Article 47: Citizens of the People's Republic of China have the freedom to engage in scientific research, literary and artistic creation and other cultural pursuits. The State encourages and assists creative endeavours conducive to the interests of the people that are made by citizens engaged in education, science, technology, literature, art and other cultural work.

Article 48: Women in the People's Republic of China enjoy equal rights with men in all spheres of life, political, economic, cultural and social, including family life.

The State protects the rights and interests of women, applies the principle of equal pay for equal work for men and women alike and trains and selects cadres from among women.

Article 49: Marriage, the family and mother and child are protected by the State.

Both husband and wife have the duty to practise family planning.

Parents have the duty to rear and educate their minor children, and children who have come of age have the duty to support and assist their parents.

Violation of the freedom of marriage is prohibited. Maltreatment of old people, women and children is prohibited.

Article 50: The People's Republic of China protects the legitimate rights and interests of Chinese nationals residing abroad and protects the lawful rights and interests of returned overseas Chinese and of the family members of Chinese nationals residing abroad.

Article 51: The exercise by citizens of the People's Republic of China of their freedoms and rights may not infringe upon the interests of the State, of society and of the collective, or upon the lawful freedoms and rights of other citizens.

Article 52: It is the duty of citizens of the People's Republic of China to safeguard the unity of the country and the unity of all its nationalities.

Article 53: Citizens of the People's Republic of China must abide by the Constitution and the law, keep state secrets, protect public property and observe labour discipline and public order and respect social ethics.

Article 54: It is the duty of citizens of the People's Republic of China to safeguard the security, honour and interests of the motherland; they must not commit acts detrimental to the security, honour and interests of the motherland.

Article 55: It is the sacred obligation of every citizen of the People's Republic of China to defend the motherland and resist aggression.

It is the honourable duty of citizens of the People's Republic of China to perform military service and join the militia in accordance with the law.

Article 56: It is the duty of citizens of the People's Republic of China to pay taxes in accordance with the law.

STRUCTURE OF THE STATE

The National People's Congress

Article 57: The National People's Congress of the People's Republic of China is the highest organ of state power. Its permanent body is the Standing Committee of the National People's Congress.

Article 58: The National People's Congress and its Standing Committee exercise the legislative power of the State.

Article 59: The National People's Congress is composed of deputies elected by the provinces, autonomous regions and municipalities directly under the Central Government, and by the armed forces. All the minority nationalities are entitled to appropriate representation.

Election of deputies to the National People's Congress is conducted by the Standing Committee of the National People's Congress.

The number of deputies to the National People's Congress and the manner of their election are prescribed by law.

Article 60: The National People's Congress is elected for a term of five years.

Two months before the expiration of the term of office of a National People's Congress, its Standing Committee must ensure that the election of deputies to the succeeding National People's Congress is completed. Should exceptional circumstances prevent such an election, it may be postponed by decision of a majority vote of more than two-thirds of all those on the Standing Committee of the incumbent National People's Congress, and the term of office of the incumbent National People's Congress may be extended. The election of deputies to the succeeding National People's Congress must be completed within one year after the termination of such exceptional circumstances.

Article 61: The National People's Congress meets in session once a year and is convened by its Standing Committee. A session of the National People's Congress may be convened at any time the Standing Committee deems this necessary, or when more than one-fifth of the deputies to the National People's Congress so propose.

When the National People's Congress meets, it elects a presidium to conduct its session.

Article 62: The National People's Congress exercises the following functions and powers:

(1) to amend the Constitution;

(2) to supervise the enforcement of the Constitution;

(3) to enact and amend basic statutes concerning criminal offences, civil affairs, the state organs and other matters;

(4) to elect the President and the Vice-President of the People's Republic of China;

(5) to decide on the choice of the Premier of the State Council upon nomination by the President of the People's Republic of China, and to decide on the choice of the Vice-Premiers, State Councillors, Ministers in charge of Ministries or Commissions and the Auditor-General and the Secretary-General of the State Council upon nomination by the Premier;

(6) to elect the Chairman of the Central Military Commission and, upon his nomination, to decide on the choice of all the others on the Central Military Commission;

(7) to elect the President of the Supreme People's Court;

(8) to elect the Procurator-General of the Supreme People's Procuratorate;

(9) to examine and approve the plan for national economic and social development and the reports on its implementation;

(10) to examine and approve the state budget and the report on its implementation;

(11) to alter or annul inappropriate decisions of the Standing Committee of the National People's Congress;

(12) to approve the establishment of provinces, autonomous regions, and municipalities directly under the Central Government;

(13) to decide on the establishment of special administrative regions and the systems to be instituted there;

(14) to decide on questions of war and peace; and

(15) to exercise such other functions and powers as the highest organ of state power should exercise.

Article 63: The National People's Congress has the power to recall or remove from office the following persons:

(1) the President and the Vice-President of the People's Republic of China;

(2) the Premier, Vice-Premiers, State Councillors, Ministers in charge of Ministries or Commissions and the Auditor-General and the Secretary-General of the State Council;

(3) the Chairman of the Central Military Commission and others on the Commission;

(4) the President of the Supreme People's Court; and

(5) the Procurator-General of the Supreme People's Procuratorate.

Article 64: Amendments to the Constitution are to be proposed by the Standing Committee of the National People's Congress or by more than one-fifth of the deputies to the National People's Congress and adopted by a majority vote of more than two-thirds of all the deputies to the Congress.

Statutes and resolutions are adopted by a majority vote of more than one-half of all the deputies to the National People's Congress.

Article 65: The Standing Committee of the National People's Congress is composed of the following:

the Chairman;
the Vice-Chairmen;
the Secretary-General; and
members.

Minority nationalities are entitled to appropriate representation on the Standing Committee of the National People's Congress.

The National People's Congress elects, and has the power to recall, all those on its Standing Committee.

No one on the Standing Committee of the National People's Congress shall hold any post in any of the administrative, judicial or procuratorial organs of the State.

Article 66: The Standing Committee of the National People's Congress is elected for the same term as the National People's Congress; it exercises its functions and powers until a new Standing Committee is elected by the succeeding National People's Congress.

The Chairman and Vice-Chairmen of the Standing Committee shall serve no more than two consecutive terms.

Article 67: The Standing Committee of the National People's Congress exercises the following functions and powers:

(1) to interpret the Constitution and supervise its enforcement;

(2) to enact and amend statutes with the exception of those which should be enacted by the National People's Congress;

(3) to enact, when the National People's Congress is not in session, partial supplements and amendments to statutes enacted by the National People's Congress provided that they do not contravene the basic principles of these statutes;

(4) to interpret statutes;

(5) to examine and approve, when the National People's Congress is not in session, partial adjustments to the plan for national economic and social development and to the state budget that prove necessary in the course of their implementation;

(6) to supervise the work of the State Council, the Central Military Commission, the Supreme People's Court and the Supreme People's Procuratorate;

(7) to annul those administrative rules and regulations, decisions or orders of the State Council that contravene the Constitution or the statutes;

(8) to annul those local regulations or decisions of the organs of state power of provinces, autonomous regions and municipalities directly under the Central Government that contravene the Constitution, the statutes or the administrative rules and regulations;

(9) to decide, when the National People's Congress is not in session, on the choice of Ministers in charge of Ministries or Commissions or the Auditor-General and the Secretary-General of the State Council upon nomination by the Premier of the State Council;

(10) to decide, upon nomination by the Chairman of the Central Military Commission, on the choice of others on the Commission, when the National People's Congress is not in session.

(11) to appoint and remove the Vice-Presidents and judges of the Supreme People's Court, members of its Judicial Committee and the President of the Military Court at the suggestion of the President of the Supreme People's Court;

(12) to appoint and remove the Deputy Procurators-General and Procurators of the Supreme People's Procuratorate, members of its Procuratorial Committee and the Chief Procurator of the Military Procuratorate at the request of the Procurator-General of the Supreme People's Procuratorate, and to approve the appointment and removal of the Chief Procurators of the People's Procuratorates of provinces, autonomous regions and municipalities directly under the Central Government;

(13) to decide on the appointment and recall of plenipotentiary representatives abroad;

(14) to decide on the ratification and abrogation of treaties and important agreements concluded with foreign states;

(15) to institute systems of titles and ranks for military and diplomatic personnel and of other specific titles and ranks;

(16) to institute state medals and titles of honour and decide on their conferment;

(17) to decide on the granting of special pardons;

(18) to decide, when the National People's Congress is not in session, on the proclamation of a state of war in the event of an armed attack on the country or in fulfilment of international treaty obligations concerning common defence against aggression;

(19) to decide on general mobilization or partial mobilization;

(20) to decide on the enforcement of martial law throughout the country or in particular provinces, autonomous regions or municipalities directly under the Central Government; and

(21) to exercise such other functions and powers as the National People's Congress may assign to it.

Article 68: The Chairman of the Standing Committee of the National People's Congress presides over the work of the Standing Committee and convenes its meetings. The Vice-Chairmen and the Secretary-General assist the Chairman in his work.

Chairmanship meetings with the participation of the Chairman, Vice-Chairmen and Secretary-General handle the important day-to-day work of the Standing Committee of the National People's Congress.

Article 69: The Standing Committee of the National People's Congress is responsible to the National People's Congress and reports on its work to the Congress.

Article 70: The National People's Congress establishes a Nationalities Committee, a Law Committee, a Finance and Economic Committee, an Education, Science, Culture and Public Health Committee, a Foreign Affairs Committee, an Overseas Chinese Committee and such other special committees as are necessary. These special committees work under the direction of the Standing Committee of the National People's Congress when the Congress is not in session.

The special committees examine, discuss and draw up relevant bills and draft resolutions under the direction of the National People's Congress and its Standing Committee.

Article 71: The National People's Congress and its Standing Committee may, when they deem it necessary, appoint committees of inquiry into specific questions and adopt relevant resolutions in the light of their reports.

All organs of State, public organizations and citizens concerned are obliged to supply the necessary information to those committees of inquiry when they conduct investigations.

Article 72: Deputies to the National People's Congress and all those on its Standing Committee have the right, in accordance with procedures prescribed by law, to submit bills and proposals within the scope of the respective functions and powers of the National People's Congress and its Standing Committee.

Article 73: Deputies to the National People's Congress during its sessions, and all those on its Standing Committee during its meetings, have the right to address questions, in accordance with procedures prescribed by law, to the State Council or the Ministries and Commissions under the State Council, which must answer the questions in a responsible manner.

Article 74: No deputy to the National People's Congress may be arrested or placed on criminal trial without the consent of the presidium of the current session of the National People's Congress or, when the National People's Congress is not in session, without the consent of its Standing Committee.

Article 75: Deputies to the National People's Congress may not be called to legal account for their speeches or votes at its meetings.

Article 76: Deputies to the National People's Congress must play an exemplary role in abiding by the Constitution and the law and keeping state secrets and, in production and other work and their public activities, assist in the enforcement of the Constitution and the law.

Deputies to the National People's Congress should maintain close contact with the units which elected them and with the people, listen to and convey the opinions and demands of the people and work hard to serve them.

Article 77: Deputies to the National People's Congress are subject to the supervision of the units which elected them. The electoral units have the power, through procedures prescribed by law, to recall the deputies whom they elected.

Article 78: The organization and working procedures of the National People's Congress and its Standing Committee are prescribed by law.

The President of the People's Republic of China

Article 79: The President and Vice-President of the People's Republic of China are elected by the National People's Congress.

Citizens of the People's Republic of China who have the right to vote and to stand for election and who have reached the age of 45 are eligible for election as President or Vice-President of the People's Republic of China.

The term of office of the President and Vice-President of the People's Republic of China is the same as that of the National People's Congress, and they shall serve no more than two consecutive terms.

Article 80: The President of the People's Republic of China, in pursuance of decisions of the National People's Congress and its Standing Committee, promulgates statutes; appoints and removes the Premier, Vice-Premiers, State Councillors, Ministers in charge of Ministries or Commissions, and the Auditor-General and the Secretary-General of the State Council; confers state medals and titles of honour; issues orders of special pardons; proclaims martial law; proclaims a state of war; and issues mobilization orders.

Article 81: The President of the People's Republic of China receives foreign diplomatic representatives on behalf of the People's Republic of China and, in pursuance of decisions of the Standing Committee of the National People's Congress, appoints and recalls plenipotentiary representatives abroad, and ratifies and abrogates treaties and important agreements concluded with foreign states.

Article 82: The Vice-President of the People's Republic of China assists the President in his work.

The Vice-President of the People's Republic of China may exercise such parts of the functions and powers of the President as the President may entrust to him.

Article 83: The President and Vice-President of the People's Republic of China exercise their functions and powers until the new President and Vice-President elected by the succeeding National People's Congress assume office.

Article 84: In case the office of the President of the People's Republic of China falls vacant, the Vice-President succeeds to the office of President.

In case the office of the Vice-President of the People's Republic of China falls vacant, the National People's Congress shall elect a new Vice-President to fill the vacancy.

In the event that the offices of both the President and the Vice-President of the People's Republic of China fall vacant, the National People's Congress shall elect a new President and a new Vice-President. Prior to such election, the Chairman of the Standing Committee of the National People's Congress shall temporarily act as the President of the People's Republic of China.

The State Council

Article 85: The State Council, that is, the Central People's Government, of the People's Republic of China is the executive body of the highest organ of state power; it is the highest organ of state administration.

Article 86: The State Council is composed of the following: the Premier; the Vice-Premiers; the State Councillors; the Ministers in charge of ministries; the Ministers in charge of commissions; the Auditor-General; and the Secretary-General.

The Premier has overall responsibility for the State Council. The Ministers have overall responsibility for the respective ministries or commissions under their charge.

The organization of the State Council is prescribed by law.

Article 87: The term of office of the State Council is the same as that of the National People's Congress.

The Premier, Vice-Premiers and State Councillors shall serve no more than two consecutive terms.

Article 88: The Premier directs the work of the State Council. The Vice-Premiers and State Councillors assist the Premier in his work.

Executive meetings of the State Council are composed of the Premier, the Vice-Premiers, the State Councillors and the Secretary-General of the State Council.

The Premier convenes and presides over the executive meetings and plenary meetings of the State Council.

Article 89: The State Council exercises the following functions and powers:

(1) to adopt administrative measures, enact administrative rules and regulations and issue decisions and orders in accordance with the Constitution and the statutes;

(2) to submit proposals to the National People's Congress or its Standing Committee;

(3) to lay down the tasks and responsibilities of the ministries and commissions of the State Council, to exercise unified leadership over the work of the ministries and commissions and to direct all other administrative work of a national character that does not fall within the jurisdiction of the ministries and commissions;

(4) to exercise unified leadership over the work of local organs of state administration at different levels throughout the country, and to lay down the detailed division of functions and powers between the Central Government and the organs of state administration of provinces, autonomous regions and municipalities directly under the Central Government;

(5) to draw up and implement the plan for national economic and social development and the state budget;

(6) to direct and administer economic work and urban and rural development;

(7) to direct and administer the work concerning education, science, culture, public health, physical culture and family planning;

(8) to direct and administer the work concerning civil affairs, public security, judicial administration, supervision and other related matters;

(9) to conduct foreign affairs and conclude treaties and agreements with foreign states;

(10) to direct and administer the building of national defence;

(11) to direct and administer affairs concerning the nationalities, and to safeguard the equal rights of minority nationalities and the right of autonomy of the national autonomous areas;

(12) to protect the legitimate rights and interests of Chinese nationals residing abroad and protect the lawful rights and interests of returned overseas Chinese and of the family members of Chinese nationals residing abroad;

(13) to alter or annul inappropriate orders, directives and regulations issued by the ministries or commissions;

(14) to alter or annul inappropriate decisions and orders issued by local organs of state administration at different levels;

(15) to approve the geographic division of provinces, autonomous regions and municipalities directly under the Central Government, and to approve the establishment and geographic division of autonomous prefectures, counties, autonomous counties and cities;

(16) to decide on the enforcement of martial law in parts of provinces, autonomous regions and municipalities directly under the Central Government;

(17) to examine and decide on the size of administrative organs and, in accordance with the law, to appoint, remove and train administrative officers, appraise their work and reward or punish them; and

(18) to exercise such other functions and powers as the National People's Congress or its Standing Committee may assign it.

Article 90: The Ministers in charge of ministries or commissions of the State Council are responsible for the work of their respective departments and convene and preside over their ministerial meetings or commission meetings that discuss and decide on major issues in the work of their respective departments.

The ministries and commissions issue orders, directives and regulations within the jurisdiction of their respective departments and in accordance with the statutes and the administrative rules and regulations, decisions and orders issued by the State Council.

Article 91: The State Council establishes an auditing body to supervise through auditing the revenue and expenditure of all departments under the State Council and of the local government at different levels, and those of the state financial and monetary organizations and of enterprises and undertakings.

Under the direction of the Premier of the State Council, the auditing body independently exercises its power to supervise through auditing in accordance with the law, subject to no interference by any other administrative organ or any public organization or individual.

Article 92: The State Council is responsible, and reports on its work, to the National People's Congress or, when the National People's Congress is not in session, to its Standing Committee.

The Central Military Commission

Article 93: The Central Military Commission of the People's Republic of China directs the armed forces of the country.

The Central Military Commission is composed of the following: the Chairman; the Vice-Chairmen; and members.

The Chairman of the Central Military Commission has overall responsibility for the Commission.

The term of office of the Central Military Commission is the same as that of the National People's Congress.

Article 94: The Chairman of the Central Military Commission is responsible to the National People's Congress and its Standing Committee.

(Two further sections, not included here, deal with the Local People's Congresses and Government and with the Organs of Self-Government of National Autonomous Areas, respectively.)

The People's Courts and the People's Procuratorates

Article 123: The people's courts in the People's Republic of China are the judicial organs of the State.

Article 124: The People's Republic of China establishes the Supreme People's Court and the local people's courts at different levels, military courts and other special people's courts.

The term of office of the President of the Supreme People's Court is the same as that of the National People's Congress; he shall serve no more than two consecutive terms.

The organization of people's courts is prescribed by law.

Article 125: All cases handled by the people's courts, except for those involving special circumstances as specified by law, shall be heard in public. The accused has the right of defence.

Article 126: The people's courts shall, in accordance with the law, exercise judicial power independently and are not subject to interference by administrative organs, public organizations or individuals.

Article 127: The Supreme People's Court is the highest judicial organ.

The Supreme People's Court supervises the administration of justice by the local people's courts at different levels and by the special people's courts; people's courts at higher levels supervise the administration of justice by those at lower levels.

Article 128: The Supreme People's Court is responsible to the National People's Congress and its Standing Committee. Local people's courts at different levels are responsible to the organs of state power which created them.

Article 129: The people's procuratorates of the People's Republic of China are state organs for legal supervision.

Article 130: The People's Republic of China establishes the Supreme People's Procuratorate and the local people's procuratorates at different levels, military procuratorates and other special people's procuratorates.

The term of office of the Procurator-General of the Supreme People's Procuratorate is the same as that of the National People's Congress; he shall serve no more than two consecutive terms.

The organization of people's procuratorates is prescribed by law.

Article 131: People's procuratorates shall, in accordance with the law, exercise procuratorial power independently and are not subject to interference by administrative organs, public organizations or individuals.

Article 132: The Supreme People's Procuratorate is the highest procuratorial organ.

The Supreme People's Procuratorate directs the work of the local people's procuratorates at different levels and of the special people's procuratorates; people's procuratorates at higher levels direct the work of those at lower levels.

Article 133: The Supreme People's Procuratorate is responsible to the National People's Congress and its Standing Committee. Local people's procuratorates at different levels are responsible to the organs of state power at the corresponding levels which created them and to the people's procuratorates at the higher level.

Article 134: Citizens of all nationalities have the right to use the spoken and written languages of their own nationalities in court proceedings. The people's courts and people's procuratorates should provide translation for any party to the court proceedings who is not familiar with the spoken or written languages in common use in the locality.

In an area where people of a minority nationality live in a compact community or where a number of nationalities live together, hearings should be conducted in the language or languages in common use in the locality; indictments, judgments, notices and other documents should be written, according to actual needs, in the language or languages in common use in the locality.

Article 135: The people's courts, people's procuratorates and public security organs shall, in handling criminal cases, divide their functions, each taking responsibility for its own work, and they shall co-ordinate their efforts and check each other to ensure correct and effective enforcement of law.

THE NATIONAL FLAG, THE NATIONAL EMBLEM AND THE CAPITAL

Article 136: The national flag of the People's Republic of China is a red flag with five stars.

Article 137: The national emblem of the People's Republic of China is the Tiananmen (Gate of Heavenly Peace) in the centre, illuminated by five stars and encircled by ears of grain and a cogwheel.

Article 138: The capital of the People's Republic of China is Beijing (Peking).

The Government

HEAD OF STATE

President: JIANG ZEMIN (elected by the Eighth National People's Congress on 27 March 1993; re-elected by the Ninth National People's Congress on 16 March 1998).

Vice-President: HU JINTAO.

STATE COUNCIL
(September 2002)

Premier: ZHU RONGJI.

Vice-Premiers: LI LANQING, QIAN QICHEN, WU BANGGUO, WEN JIABAO.

State Councillors: Gen. CHI HAOTIAN, LUO GAN, WU YI, ISMAIL AMAT, WANG ZHONGYU.

Secretary-General: WANG ZHONGYU.

Minister of Foreign Affairs: TANG JIAXUAN.

Minister of National Defence: Gen. CHI HAOTIAN.

Minister of State Economic and Trade Commission: LI RONGRONG.

Minister of State Development and Planning Commission: ZENG PEIYAN.

Minister of Education: CHEN ZHILI.

Minister of Science and Technology: XU GUANHUA.

Minister of State Commission of Science, Technology and Industry for National Defence: LIU JIBIN.

Minister of State Nationalities Affairs Commission: LI DEZHU.

Minister of Public Security: JIA CHUNWANG.

Minister of State Security: XU YONGYUE.

Minister of Civil Affairs: DOJI CERING.

Minister of Justice: ZHANG FUSEN.

Minister of Supervision: HE YONG.

Minister of Finance: XIANG HUAICHENG.

Minister of Foreign Trade and Economic Co-operation: SHI GUANGSHENG.

Minister of Agriculture: DU QINGLIN.

Minister of Water Resources: WANG SHUCHENG.

Minister of Construction: WANG GUANGTAO.

Minister of Land and Natural Resources: TIAN FENGSHAN.

Minister of Railways: FU ZHIHUAN.

Minister of Communications: HUANG ZHENDONG.

Minister of Information Industry: WU JICHUAN.

Minister of Personnel: ZHANG XUEZHONG.

Minister of Labour and Social Security: ZHANG ZUOJI.

Minister of Culture: SUN JIAZHENG.

Minister of Public Health: ZHANG WENKANG.

Minister of State Family Planning Commission: ZHANG WEIQING.

Governor of the People's Bank of China: DAI XIANGLONG.

Auditor-General of Auditing Administration: LI JINHUA.

MINISTRIES

Ministry of Agriculture: 11 Nongzhanguan Nanli, Chao Yang Qu, Beijing 100026; tel. (10) 64192293; fax (10) 64192468; e-mail webmaster@agri.gov.cn; internet www.agri.gov.cn.

Ministry of Civil Affairs: 147 Beiheyan Dajie, Dongcheng Qu, Beijing 100721; tel. (10) 65135333; fax (10) 65135332.

Ministry of Communications: 11 Jianguomennei Dajie, Dongcheng Qu. Beijing 100736; tel. (10) 65292114; fax (10) 65292345; internet www.moc.gov.cn.

Ministry of Construction: 9 Sanlihe Dajie, Xicheng Qu, Beijing 100835; tel. (10) 68394215; fax (10) 68393333; e-mail webmaster@mail.cin.gov.cn; internet www.cin.gov.cn.

Ministry of Culture: 10 Chaoyangmen Bei Jie, Dongcheng Qu, Beijing 100020; tel. (10) 65551432; fax (10) 65551433; e-mail webmaster@whb1.ccnt.com.cn; internet www.ccnt.com.cn.

Ministry of Education: 37 Damucang Hutong, Xicheng Qu, Beijing 100816; tel. (10) 66096114; fax (10) 66011049; e-mail webmaster@moe.edu.cn; internet www.moe.edu.cn.

Ministry of Finance: 3 Nansanxiang, Sanlihe, Xicheng Qu, Beijing 100820; tel. (10) 68551888; fax (10) 68533635; e-mail webmaster@mof.gov.cn; internet www.mof.gov.cn.

Ministry of Foreign Affairs: 225 Chaoyangmennei Dajie, Dongsi, Beijing 100701; tel. (10) 65961114; fax (10) 65962146; e-mail webmaster@fmprc.gov.cn; internet www.fmprc.gov.cn.

Ministry of Foreign Trade and Economic Co-operation: 2 Dongchangan Jie, Dongcheng Qu, Beijing 100731; tel. (10) 67081526; fax (10) 67081513; e-mail webmaster@moftec.gov.cn; internet www.moftec.gov.cn.

Ministry of Information Industry: 13 Xichangan Jie, Beijing 100804; tel. (10) 66014249; fax (10) 66034248; e-mail webmaster@mii.gov.cn; internet www.mii.gov.cn.

Ministry of Justice: 10 Chaoyangmennan Dajie, Chao Yang Qu, Beijing 100020; tel. (10) 65205114; fax (10) 65205316.

Ministry of Labour and Social Security: 12 Hepinglizhong Jie, Dongcheng Qu, Beijing 100716; tel. (10) 84201235; fax (10) 64218350.

Ministry of Land and Natural Resources: 3 Guanyingyuanxiqu, Xicheng Qu, Beijing 100035; tel. (10) 66127001; fax (10) 66175348; internet www.mlr.gov.cn.

Ministry of National Defence: 20 Jingshanqian Jie, Beijing 100009; tel. (10) 66730000; fax (10) 65962146.

Ministry of Personnel: 12 Hepinglizhong Jie, Dongcheng Qu, Beijing 100716; tel. (10) 84223240; fax (10) 64211417.

Ministry of Public Health: 1 Xizhinenwai Bei Lu, Xicheng Qu, Beijing 100044; tel. (10) 68792114; fax (10) 64012369; e-mail zhou@chsi.moh.gov.cn; internet www.moh.gov.cn.

Ministry of Public Security: 14 Dongchangan Jie, Dongcheng Qu, Beijing 100741; tel. (10) 65122831; fax (10) 65136577.

Ministry of Railways: 10 Fuxing Lu, Haidian Qu, Beijing 100844; tel. (10) 63244150; fax (10) 63242150; e-mail webmaster@ns.chinamor.cn.net; internet www.chinamor.cn.net.

Ministry of Science and Technology: 15B Fuxing Lu, Haidian Qu, Beijing 100862; tel. (10) 68515050; fax (10) 68515006; e-mail officemail@mail.most.gov.cn; internet www.most.gov.cn.

Ministry of State Security: 14 Dongchangan Jie, Dongcheng Qu, Beijing 100741; tel. (10) 65244702.

Ministry of Supervision: 4 Zaojunmiao, Haidian Qu, Beijing 100081; tel. (10) 62256677; fax (10) 62254181.

Ministry of Water Resources: 2 Baiguang Lu, Ertiao, Xuanwu Qu, Beijing 100053; tel. (10) 63203069; fax (10) 63202650.

STATE COMMISSIONS

State Commission of Science, Technology and Industry for National Defence: 2a Guang'anmennan Jie, Xuanwu Qu, Beijing 100053; tel. (10) 63571397; fax (10) 63571398; internet www.costind.gov.cn.

State Development and Planning Commission: 38 Yuetannan Jie, Xicheng Qu, Beijing 100824; tel. (10) 68504409; fax (10) 68512929; e-mail news@sdpc.gov.cn; internet www.sdpc.gov.cn.

State Economic and Trade Commission: 26 Xuanwumenxi Dajie, Xuanwumen Qu, Beijing 100053; tel. (10) 63192334; fax (10) 63192348; e-mail webmaster@setc.gov.cn; internet www.setc.gov.cn.

State Family Planning Commission: 14 Zhichun Lu, Haidian Qu, Beijing 100088; tel. (10) 62046622; fax (10) 62051865; e-mail sfpcdfa@public.bta.net.cn; internet www.sfpc.gov.cn.

State Nationalities Affairs Commission: 252 Taipingqiao Dajie, Xicheng Qu, Beijing 100800; tel. and fax (10) 66017375.

Legislature

QUANGUO RENMIN DAIBIAO DAHUI

(National People's Congress)

The National People's Congress (NPC) is the highest organ of state power, and is indirectly elected for a five-year term. The first plenary session of the Ninth NPC was convened in Beijing in March 1998, and was attended by 2,979 deputies. The first session of the Ninth National Committee of the Chinese People's Political Consultative Conference (CPPCC, Chair. Li Ruihuan), a revolutionary united front organization led by the Communist Party, took place simultaneously. The CPPCC holds discussions and consultations on the important affairs in the nation's political life. Members of the CPPCC National Committee or of its Standing Committee may be invited to attend the NPC or its Standing Committee as observers.

Standing Committee

In March 1998 134 members were elected to the Standing Committee, in addition to the following:

Chairman: Li Peng.

Vice-Chairmen: Tian Jiyun, Jiang Chunyun, Zou Jiahua, Pagbalha Geleg Namgyai, Wang Guangying, Cheng Siyuan, Buhe, Tomur Dawamat, Wu Jieping, Peng Peiyun, He Luli, Zhou Guangzhao, Cao Zhi, Ding Shishun, Cheng Siwei, Xu Jialu, Jiang Zhenghua.

Secretary-General: He Chunlin.

Provincial People's Congresses

Chairmen of Standing Committees of People's Congresses:

Provinces

Meng Fulin (Anhui), Yuan Qitong (Fujian), Lu Kejian (Gansu), Zhang Guoying (Guangdong), Liu Fangren (Guizhou), Bai Keming (Hainan), Cheng Weigao (Hebei), Xu Youfang (Heilongjiang), Ren Keli (Henan), Yu Zhengsheng (Hubei), Yang Zhengwu (Hunan), Chen Huanyou (Jiangsu), Meng Jianzhu (Jiangxi), Wang Yunkun (Jilin), Wang Huaiyuan (Liaoning), Bai Enpei (Qinghai), Li Jianguo (Shaanxi), Zhao Zhihao (Shandong), Lu Gongxun (Shanxi), Xie Shijie (Sichuan), Yin Jun (Yunnan), Li Zemin (Zhejiang).

Special Municipalities

Yu Junbo (Beijing), Wang Yunlong (Chongqing), Chen Tiedi (Shanghai), Zhang Lichang (Tianjin).

Autonomous Regions

Zhao Fulin (Guangxi Zhuang), Liu Mingzu (Nei Monggol), Mao Rubai (Ningxia Hui), Raidi (Tibet—Xizang), Amudun Niyaz (Xinjiang Uygur).

People's Governments

Provinces

Governors:

Xu Zhonglin (Anhui), Xi Jinping (Fujian), Lu Hao (Gansu), Lu Ruihua (Guangdong), Shi Xiushi (acting—Guizhou), Wang Xiaofeng (Hainan), Niu Maosheng (Hebei), Song Fatang (Heilongjiang), Li Keqiang (Henan), Zhang Guoguang (Hubei), Zhang Yunchuan (acting—Hunan), Ji Yunshi (Jiangsu), Huang Zhiquan (Jiangxi), Hong Hu (Jilin), Bo Xilai (Liaoning), Zhao Leji (Qinghai), Cheng Andong (Shaanxi), Zhang Gaoli (Shandong), Liu Zhenua (Shanxi), Zhang Zhongwei (Sichuan), Xu Rongkai (acting—Yunnan), Chai Songyue (Zhejiang).

Special Municipalities

Mayors:

Liu Qi (Beijing), Bao Xuding (Chongqing), Chen Liangyu (Shanghai), Li Shenglin (Tianjin).

Autonomous Regions

Chairmen:

Li Zhaozhuo (Guangxi Zhuang), Uyunqimg (acting—Nei Monggol), Ma Qizhi (Ningxia Hui), Legqog (Tibet—Xizang), Abdulahat Abdurixit (Xinjiang Uygur).

Political Organizations

COMMUNIST PARTY

Zhongguo Gongchan Dang (Chinese Communist Party—CCP): Beijing; f. 1921; 61m. mems in Dec. 1998; at the 15th Nat. Congress of the CCP, in September 1997, a new Cen. Cttee of 193 full mems and 151 alternate mems was elected; at its first plenary session the 15th Cen. Cttee appointed a new Politburo. (16th Nat. Congress scheduled for Nov. 2002.)

Fifteenth Central Committee

General Secretary: Jiang Zemin.

Politburo

Members of the Standing Committee: Jiang Zemin, Li Peng, Zhu Rongji, Li Ruihuan, Hu Jintao, Wei Jianxing, Li Lanqing.

Other Full Members: Ding Guangen, Tian Jiyun, Li Changchun, Li Tieying, Wu Bangguo, Wu Guanzheng, Gen. Chi Haotian, Gen. Zhang Wannian, Luo Gan, Jiang Chunyun, Jia Qinglin, Qian Qichen, Huang Ju, Wen Jiabao.

Alternate Members: Zeng Qinghong, Wu Yi.

Secretariat: Hu Jintao, Wei Jianxing, Ding Guangen, Gen. Zhang Wannian, Luo Gan, Wen Jiabao, Zeng Qinghong.

OTHER POLITICAL ORGANIZATIONS

China Association for Promoting Democracy: 98 Xinanli Guloufangzhuangchang, Beijing 100009; tel. (10) 64033452; f. 1945; mems drawn mainly from literary, cultural and educational circles; Chair. Xu Jialu; Sec.-Gen. Chen Yiqun.

China Democratic League: 1 Beixing Dongchang Hutong, Beijing 100006; tel. (10) 65137983; fax (10) 65125090; f. 1941; formed from reorganization of League of Democratic Parties and Organizations of China; 131,300 mems, mainly intellectuals active in education, science and culture; Chair. Ding Shisun; Sec.-Gen. Zhang Baowen.

China National Democratic Construction Association: 208 Jixiangli, Chaowai Lu, Beijing 100020; tel. (10) 65523229; fax (10) 65523518; internet www.cndca.org.cn; f. 1945; 85,105 mems, mainly industrialists and business executives; Chair. Cheng Siwei; Sec.-Gen. Chen Mingde.

China Zhi Gong Dang (Party for Public Interests): Beijing; e-mail zhigong@public2.east.net.cn; f. 1925; reorg. 1947; mems are mainly returned overseas Chinese and scholars; Chair. LUO HAOCAI; Sec.-Gen. QIU GUOYI.

Chinese Communist Youth League: 10 Qianmen Dongdajie, Beijing 100051; tel. (10) 67018132; fax (10) 67018131; e-mail guoji3 acyt@yahoo.com; f. 1922; 68.5m. mems; First Sec. of Cen. Cttee ZHOU QIANG.

Chinese Peasants' and Workers' Democratic Party: f. 1930 as the Provisional Action Cttee of the Kuomintang; took present name in 1947; more than 65,000 mems, active mainly in public health and medicine; Chair. JIANG ZHENGHUA; Sec.-Gen. YU SHENLONG.

Jiu San (3 September) Society: f. 1946; fmrly Democratic and Science Soc.; 68,400 mems, mainly scientists and technologists; Chair. WU JIEPING; Sec.-Gen. LIU RONGHAN.

Revolutionary Committee of the Chinese Kuomintang: tel. (10) 6550388; f. 1948; mainly fmr Kuomintang mems, and those in cultural, educational, health and financial fields; Chair. HE LULI; Sec.-Gen. LIU MINFU.

Taiwan Democratic Self-Government League: f. 1947; recruits Taiwanese living on the mainland; Chair. ZHANG KEHUI; Sec.-Gen. ZHANG HUAJUN.

During 1998 there were repeated failed attempts by pro-democracy activists to register an opposition party, the Chinese Democratic Party. The leaders of the party (WANG YOUCAI, XU WENLI and QIN YONGMIN) were sentenced to lengthy terms of imprisonment, and many other members of the party were detained.

Diplomatic Representation

EMBASSIES IN THE PEOPLE'S REPUBLIC OF CHINA

Afghanistan: 8 Dong Zhi Men Wai Dajie, Chao Yang Qu, Beijing 100600; tel. (10) 65321582; fax (10) 65321710; Chargé d'affaires: ABDOLBASIR HOTEK.

Albania: 28 Guang Hua Lu, Jian Guo Men Wai, Beijing 100600; tel. (10) 65321120; fax (10) 65325451; Ambassador: KUJTIM XHANI.

Algeria: 2 Dong Zhi Men Wai Dajie, Chao Yang Qu, Beijing 100600; tel. (10) 65321231; fax (10) 65321648; Ambassador: MADJID BOUGUERRA.

Angola: 1-13-1 Tayuan Diplomatic Office Bldg, Beijing 100600; tel. (10) 65326968; Ambassador: MANUEL BERNARDO DE SOUSA.

Argentina: Bldg 11, 5 Dong Wu Jie, San Li Tun, Beijing 100600; tel. (10) 65322090; fax (10) 65322319; e-mail echin@public.bta.net.cn; Ambassador: JUAN CARLOS MORELLI (designate).

Australia: 21 Dong Zhi Men Wai Dajie, San Li Tun, Beijing 100600; tel. (10) 65322331; fax (10) 65326718; e-mail webmaster@austemb.org.cn; Ambassador: DAVID IRVINE.

Austria: 5 Xiu Shui Nan Jie, Jian Guo Men Wai, Beijing 100600; tel. (10) 65322726; fax (10) 65321505; e-mail oebpekin@public.bta.net.cn; Ambassador: ERICH BUTTENHAUSER.

Azerbaijan: 3-2-31 San Li Tun Diplomatic Compound, Beijing 100600; tel. (10) 65324614; fax (10) 65324615; e-mail safirprc@public.fhnet.cn.net; Ambassador: TAMERLAN GARAYEV.

Bahrain: 2-9-1 Tayuan Diplomatic Office Bldg, Beijing 100600; tel. (10) 65325025; fax (10) 65325016; Ambassador: KARIM EBRAHIM AL-SHAKAR.

Bangladesh: 42 Guang Hua Lu, Beijing 100600; tel. (10) 65321819; fax (10) 65324346; e-mail embbd@public.intercom.com.cn; Ambassador: HUMAYUN A. KAMAL.

Belarus: 2-10-1 Tayuan Diplomatic Office Bldg, Xin Dong Lu, Chao Yang Qu, Beijing 100600; tel. (10) 65326426; fax (10) 65326417; Ambassador: ULADZIMIR RUSAKEVICH.

Belgium: 6 San Li Tun Lu, Beijing 100600; tel. (10) 65321736; fax (10) 65325097; e-mail Beijing@diplobel.org; Ambassador: JOHAN MARICOU.

Benin: 38 Guang Hua Lu, Jian Guo Men Wai, Beijing 100600; tel. (10) 65323054; fax (10) 65325103; Ambassador: PIERRE AGO DOSSOU.

Bolivia: 2-3-2 Tayuan Diplomatic Office Bldg, Beijing 100600; tel. (10) 65323074; fax (10) 65324686; e-mail embolch@public3.bta.net.cn; Ambassador: OSCAR D. Z. MEDINACELI.

Botswana: 1-8-1/2 Tayuan Diplomatic Office Bldg, Beijing 100600; tel. (10) 65325751; fax (10) 65325713; Ambassador: ALFRED UYAPO MAJAYE DUBE.

Brazil: 27 Guang Hua Lu, Jian Guo Men Wai, Beijing 100600; tel. (10) 65322881; fax (10) 65322751; e-mail empequim@public.bta.net.cn; Ambassador: AFFONSO CELSO DE OURO-PRETO.

Brunei: Villa No. 3, Qijiayuan Diplomatic Compound, Jian Guo Men Wai Dajie, Chao Yang Qu, Beijing 100600; tel. (10) 65324094; fax (10) 65324097; Ambassador: Pengiran Paduka ASMALEE AHMAD.

Bulgaria: 4 Xiu Shui Bei Jie, Jian Guo Men Wai, Beijing 100600; tel. (10) 65321946; fax (10) 65324502; Ambassador: DIMITAR TZANEV.

Burundi: 25 Guang Hua Lu, Jian Guo Men Wai, Beijing 100600; tel. (10) 65321801; fax (10) 65322381; e-mail ambbubei@yahoo.fr; Ambassador: ALFRED NKURUNZIZA.

Cambodia: 9 Dong Zhi Men Wai Dajie, Beijing 100600; tel. (10) 65321889; fax (10) 65323507; Ambassador: KHEK SYSODA.

Cameroon: 7 San Li Tun, Dong Wu Jie, Beijing 100600; tel. (10) 65321771; fax (10) 65321761; Ambassador: ELEIH-ELLE ETIAN.

Canada: 19 Dong Zhi Men Wai Dajie, Chao Yang Qu, Beijing 100600; tel. (10) 65323536; fax (10) 65324311; Ambassador: JOSEPH CARON.

Cape Verde: Beijing.

Chile: 1 Dong Si Jie, San Li Tun, Beijing 100600; tel. (10) 65321591; fax (10) 65323170; e-mail echilecn@public3.bta.net.cn; Ambassador: BENNY POLLACK ESKENAZI.

Colombia: 34 Guang Hua Lu, Jian Guo Men Wai, Beijing 100600; tel. (10) 65321713; fax (10) 65321969; Ambassador: RODRIGO QUERUBIN LONDOÑO.

Congo, Democratic Republic: 6 Dong Wu Jie, San Li Tun, Beijing 100600; tel. (10) 65321995; fax (10) 65321360; Ambassador: LOMBO LO MANGAMANGA.

Congo, Republic: 7 Dong Si Jie, San Li Tun, Beijing 100600; tel. (10) 65321658; Ambassador: PIERRE PASSI.

Côte d'Ivoire: 9 San Li Tun, Bei Xiao Jie, Beijing 100600; tel. (10) 65321223; fax (10) 65322407; Ambassador: KONAN KRAMO.

Croatia: 2-72 San Li Tun Diplomatic Office Bldg, Beijing 100600; tel. (10) 65326241; fax (10) 65326257; e-mail vrhpek@public.bta.net.cn; Ambassador: ZELJKO KIRINČIĆ.

Cuba: 1 Xiu Shui Nan Jie, Jian Guo Men Wai, Beijing 100600; tel. (10) 65321714; fax (10) 65322870; Ambassador: ALBERTO RODRÍGUEZ ARUFE.

Cyprus: 2-13-2 Tayuan Diplomatic Office Bldg, Liang Ma He Nan Lu, Chao Yang Qu, Beijing 100600; tel. (10) 65325057; fax (10) 65324244; e-mail cyembpek@mail.sparkice.com.cn; Ambassador: PETROS KESTORAS.

Czech Republic: Ri Tan Lu, Jian Guo Men Wai, Beijing 100600; tel. (10) 65326902; fax (10) 65325653; Ambassador: TOMAS SMETANKA.

Denmark: 1 Dong Wu Jie, San Li Tun, Beijing 100600; tel. (10) 65322431; fax (10) 65322439; e-mail bjsamb@um.dk; internet www.dk-embassy-cn.org/; Ambassador: OLE LOENSMANN POULSEN.

Ecuador: 11-2-1 Diplomatic Apartments, Jian Guo Men Wai, Beijing 100600; tel. (10) 65322264; fax (10) 65323158; Ambassador: JOSÉ RAFAEL SERRANO HERRERA.

Egypt: 2 Ri Tan Dong Lu, Jian Guo Men Wai, Beijing 100600; tel. (10) 65321825; fax (10) 65325365; Ambassador: ALI HOUSSAM EL DIN MAHMOUD ELHEFNY.

Equatorial Guinea: 2 Dong Si Jie, San Li Tun, Beijing; tel. (10) 65323709; fax (10) 65323805; Ambassador: MANUEL MOTO TOMO.

Eritrea: Tayuan Diplomatic Office Bldg, Beijing 100600; tel. (10) 56326534; fax (10) 65326532; Ambassador: MOHAMMED NUR AHMED.

Ethiopia: 3 Xiu Shui Nan Jie, Jian Guo Men Wai, Beijing 100600; tel. (10) 65325258; fax (10) 65325591; e-mail ethembcn@public.bta.net.cn; Ambassador: ADDIS ALEM BALEMA.

Fiji: Beijing; Ambassador: LUKE VIDIRI RATUVUKI.

Finland: Beijing Kerry Centre, 26/F South Tower, 1 Guanghua Lu, Beijing 100020; tel. (10) 85298541; fax (10) 85298547; e-mail sanomat.pek@formin.fi; internet www.finland-in-china.com; Ambassador: PASI RUTANEN.

France: 3 Dong San Jie, San Li Tun, Chao Yang Qu, Beijing 100600; tel. (10) 65321331; fax (10) 65324841; e-mail ambafra@public3.bta.net.cn; internet www.lotus.ia.ac.cn/ambafra; Ambassador: PIERRE MOREL.

Gabon: 36 Guang Hua Lu, Jian Guo Men Wai, Beijing 100600; tel. (10) 65322810; fax (10) 65322621; Ambassador: M. OBIANG-NDOUDUM.

Germany: 17 Dong Zhi Men Wai Dajie, San Li Tun, Beijing 100600; tel. (10) 65322161; fax (10) 65325336; Ambassador: JOACHIM BROUDRÉ-GRÖGER.

Ghana: 8 San Li Tun Lu, Beijing 100600; tel. (10) 65321319; fax (10) 65323602; Ambassador: EMMANUEL OSCAR AMEYEDOWO.

Greece: 19 Guang Hua Lu, Jian Guo Men Wai, Beijing 100600; tel. (10) 65321588; fax (10) 65321277; Ambassador: IOANNIS THEOPHANOPOULOS.

Guinea: 2 Xi Liu Jie, San Li Tun, Beijing 100600; tel. (10) 65323649; fax (10) 65324957; Ambassador: EL HADJI DJIGUI CAMARA.

Guinea-Bissau: Diplomatic relations re-established April 1998; Ambassador: NICOLAU DOS SANTOS.

Guyana: 1 Xiu Shui Dong Jie, Jian Guo Men Wai, Beijing 100600; tel. (10) 65321601; fax (10) 65325741; Ambassador: RONALD MORTIMER AUSTIN.

Hungary: 10 Dong Zhi Men Wai Dajie, San Li Tun, Beijing 100600; tel. (10) 65321431; fax (10) 65325053; Ambassador: OTTO JUHASZ.

Iceland: Landmark Tower 1, 802, 8 North Dongsanhuan Lu, Beijing 100004; tel. (10) 65907795; fax (10) 65907801; e-mail icemb.beijing @utn.stjr.is; internet www.iceland.org/cn; Ambassador: OLAFUR EGILSSON.

India: 1 Ri Tan Dong Lu, Jian Guo Men Wai, Beijing 100600; tel. (10) 65321927; fax (10) 65324684; Ambassador: SHIVSHANKAR MENON.

Indonesia: Diplomatic Office Bldg B, San Li Tun, Beijing 100600; tel. (10) 65325486; fax (10) 65325368; e-mail kombei@public3.bta .net.cn; Ambassador: AA KUSTIA.

Iran: 13 Dong Liu Jie, San Li Tun, Beijing 100600; tel. (10) 65322040; fax (10) 65321403; Ambassador: MOHAMMAD HOSSEIN MALAEK.

Iraq: 25 Xiu Shui Bei Jie, Jian Guo Men Wai, Beijing 100600; tel. (10) 65321950; fax (10) 65321596; Ambassador: OSAMA B. MAHMOUD.

Ireland: 3 Ri Tan Dong Lu, Jian Guo Men Wai, Beijing 100600; tel. (10) 65322691; fax (10) 65322168; Ambassador: DECLAN CONNOLLY.

Israel: Room 405, West Wing Office, 1 Jian Guo Men Wai Dajie, Beijing 100004; tel. (10) 65052970; fax (10) 65050328; e-mail israemb@public.bta.net.cn; Ambassador: ITZHAK SHELEF.

Italy: 2 Dong Er Jie, San Li Tun, Beijing 100600; tel. (10) 65322131; fax (10) 65324676; Ambassador: PAOLO BRUNI.

Japan: 7 Ri Tan Lu, Jian Guo Men Wai, Beijing 100600; tel. (10) 65322361; fax (10) 65324625; Ambassador: KORESHIGE ANAMI.

Jordan: 5 Dong Liu Jie, San Li Tun, Beijing 100600; tel. (10) 65323906; fax (10) 65323283; Ambassador: SAMIR I. AL-NAOURI.

Kazakhstan: 9 Dong Liu Jie, San Li Tun, Beijing 100600; tel. (10) 65326182; fax (10) 65326183; e-mail kazconscan@on.aibn.com; Ambassador: KUANYSH SULTANOVICH SULTANOV.

Kenya: 4 Xi Liu Jie, San Li Tun, Beijing 100600; tel. (10) 65323381; fax (10) 65321770; Ambassador: MATTHEW KATHURIMA M'ITHIRI.

Korea, Democratic People's Republic: Ri Tan Bei Lu, Jian Guo Men Wai, Beijing 100600; tel. (10) 65321186; fax (10) 65326056; Ambassador: CHOE JIN SU.

Korea, Republic: 3rd–4th Floors, China World Trade Centre, 1 Jian Guo Men Wai Dajie, Beijing 100600; tel. (10) 65053171; fax (10) 65053458; Ambassador: KIM HA-JOONG.

Kuwait: 23 Guang Hua Lu, Jian Guo Men Wai, Beijing 100600; tel. (10) 65322216; fax (10) 65321607; Ambassador: ABDUL-MUHSEN NASIR A. GEAN.

Kyrgyzstan: 2-4-1 Tayuan Diplomatic Office Bldg, Beijing 100600; tel. (10) 65326458; fax (10) 65326459; e-mail kyrgyzch@public2 .east.net.cn; Ambassador: ERLAN ABDYLDAEV.

Laos: 11 Dong Si Jie, San Li Tun, Chao Yang Qu, Beijing 100600; tel. (10) 65321224; fax (10) 65326748; e-mail laoemcn@public .east.cn.net; Ambassador: SOUKTHAVONE KEOLA.

Latvia: Unit 71, Green Land Garden, No. 1A Green Land Road, Chao Yang Qu, Beijing 100016; tel. (10) 64333863; fax (10) 64333810; e-mail kinas@163bj.com; Ambassador: Dr EINARS SEMANIS.

Lebanon: 51 Dong Liu Jie, San Li Tun, Beijing; tel. (10) 65322197; fax (10) 65322770; Ambassador: ZEIDAN AL-SAGHIR.

Lesotho: 2-3-13 San Li Tun Diplomatic Apartment, Beijing 100600; tel. (10) 65326842; fax (10) 65326845; e-mail doemli@public.bta .net.cn; Ambassador: LEBOHANG K. MOLEKO.

Libya: 3 Dong Liu Jie, San Li Tun, Beijing 100600; tel. (10) 65323666; fax (10) 65323391; Secretary of the People's Bureau: MUFTAH OTMAN MADI.

Lithuania: 8-2-12 Tayuan Diplomatic Office Bldg, Beijing 100600; tel. (10) 65324421; fax (10) 65324451; Ambassador: DAINIUS VOVERIS.

Luxembourg: 21 Nei Wu Bu Jie, Beijing 100600; tel. (10) 65135937; fax (10) 65137268; e-mail ambluxcn@public.bta.net.cn; Ambassador: MARC UNGEHEUER.

Madagascar: 3 Dong Jie, San Li Tun, Beijing 100600; tel. (10) 65321353; fax (10) 65322102; e-mail ambpek@public2.bta.net.cn; Ambassador: ROYAL MICHSELISSON RAOELFILS.

Malaysia: 13 Dong Zhi Men Wai Dajie, San Li Tun, Beijing; tel. (10) 65322531; fax (10) 65325032; Ambassador: Dato' ABDUL MAJID.

Mali: 8 Dong Si Jie, San Li Tun, Beijing 100600; tel. (10) 65321704; fax (10) 65321618; Ambassador: MODIBO TIEMOKO TRAORE.

Malta: 1-52 San Li Tun Diplomatic Compound, Beijing 100600; tel. (10) 65323114; fax (10) 65326125; e-mail savfborg@public3.bta .net.cn; Ambassador: SAVIOUR F. BORG.

Mauritania: 9 Dong San Jie, San Li Tun, Beijing 100600; tel. (10) 65321346; fax (10) 65321685; Ambassador: ABDELLAHI OULD ABDI.

Mexico: 5 Dong Wu Jie, San Li Tun, Beijing 100600; tel. (10) 65321717; fax (10) 65323744; e-mail embmxchn@public.bta.net.cn; Ambassador: SERGIO LEY-LÓPEZ.

Moldova: 3-1-152 Tayuan Diplomatic Office Bldg, Beijing 100600; tel. (10) 65325379; Ambassador: VICTOR BORSEVICI.

Mongolia: 2 Xiu Shui Bei Jie, Jian Guo Men Wai, Beijing 100600; tel. (10) 65321203; fax (10) 65325045; e-mail monembbj@public3 .bta.net.cn; Ambassador: L. AMARSANAA.

Morocco: 16 San Li Tun Lu, Beijing 100600; tel. (10) 65321489; fax (10) 65321453; e-mail embmor@public.bta.net.cn; Ambassador: MIMOUN MEHDI.

Mozambique: 1-7-2 Tayuan Diplomatic Office Bldg, Beijing 100600; tel. (10) 65323664; fax (10) 65325189; e-mail embamoc@public.bta .net.cn; Ambassador: JOSÉ MARIA DA SILVA DE MORAIS.

Myanmar: 6 Dong Zhi Men Wai Dajie, Chao Yang Qu, Beijing 100600; tel. (10) 65321584; fax (10) 65321344; Ambassador: U BA HTAY CHIT.

Namibia: 2-9-2 Tayuan Diplomatic Office Bldg, Beijing 100600; tel. (10) 65324810; fax (10) 65324549; e-mail namemb@eastnet.com.cn; Ambassador: H. U. IPINGE

Nepal: 1 Xi Liu Jie, San Li Tun Lu, Beijing 100600; tel. (10) 65322739; fax (10) 65323251; Ambassador: RAJESHWAR ACHARYA.

Netherlands: 4 Liang Ma He Nan Lu, Beijing 100600; tel. (10) 65321131; fax (10) 65324689; Ambassador: PHILIP DE HEER.

New Zealand: 1 Ri Tan, Dong Er Jie, Chao Yang Qu, Beijing 100600; tel. (10) 65322731; fax (10) 65324317; e-mail nzemb@ eastnet.com.cn; Ambassador: JOHN MCKINNON.

Niger: 3-2-12 San Li Tun, Beijing 100600; tel. (10) 65324279; e-mail nigerbj@public.bta.net.cn; Ambassador: BOZARI SEYDOU.

Nigeria: 2 Dong Wu Jie, San Li Tun, Beijing; tel. (10) 65323631; fax (10) 65321650; Ambassador: OLAGUNJU ADESAKIN.

Norway: 1 Dong Yi Jie, San Li Tun, Beijing 100600; tel. (10) 65322261; fax (10) 65322392; e-mail emb.beijing@mfa.no; Ambassador: HAAKON B. HJELDE.

Oman: 6 Liang Ma He Nan Lu, San Li Tun, Beijing 100600; tel. (10) 65323956; fax (10) 65325030; Ambassador: ABDULLAH HOSNY.

Pakistan: 1 Dong Zhi Men Wai Dajie, San Li Tun, Beijing 100600; tel. (10) 65322504; fax (10) 65322715; e-mail pak@public.bta.net.cn; Ambassador: RIAZ KHOKHAR.

Papua New Guinea: 2-11-2 Tayuan Diplomatic Office Bldg, Beijing 100600; tel. (10) 65324312; fax (10) 65325483; Ambassador: BARNEY RONGAP.

Peru: 1-91 San Li Tun, Bangonglou, Beijing 100600; tel. (10) 65323477; fax (10) 65322178; e-mail embperu@public.bta.net.cn; internet www.embperu.cn.net; Ambassador: MARTHA TOLEDO-OCAMPO UREÑA.

Philippines: 23 Xiu Shui Bei Jie, Jian Guo Men Wai, Beijing 100600; tel. (10) 65321872; fax (10) 65323761; e-mail beijingpe@ cinet.com.cn; internet www.philembassy-china.org; Ambassador: JOSUE L. VILLA.

Poland: 1 Ri Tan Lu, Jian Guo Men Wai, Beijing 100600; tel. (10) 65321235; fax (10) 65321745; Ambassador: KSAWERY BURSKI.

Portugal: 8 San Li Tun Dong Wu Jie, Beijing 100600; tel. (10) 65323497; fax (10) 65324637; Ambassador: PEDRO CATARINO.

Qatar: 2-9-2 Tayuan Diplomatic Office Bldg, 14 Liang Ma He Nan Lu, Beijing 100600; tel. (10) 65322231; fax (10) 65325274; Ambassador: SALEH ABDULLA AL-BOUANIN.

Romania: Ri Tan Lu, Dong Er Jie, Beijing 100600; tel. (10) 65323442; fax (10) 65325728; e-mail roamb@ht.rol.cn.net; Ambassador: IOAN DONCA.

Russia: 4 Dong Zhi Men Nei, Bei Zhong Jie, Beijing 100600; tel. (10) 65321291; fax (10) 65324853; e-mail rusemb@public3.bta.net.cn; Ambassador: IGOR ROGACHEV.

Rwanda: 30 Xiu Shui Bei Jie, Jian Guo Men Wai, Beijing 100600; tel. (10) 65322193; fax (10) 65322006; e-mail ambarwda@public3 .bta.net.cn; internet www.embarwanda-china.com; Ambassador: JOSEPH BONESHA.

Saudi Arabia: 1 Bei Xiao Jie, San Li Tun, Beijing 100600; tel. (10) 65324825; fax (10) 65325324; Ambassador: MOHAMMED A. AL-BESHIR.

Sierra Leone: 7 Dong Zhi Men Wai Dajie, Beijing 100600; tel. (10) 65321222; fax (10) 65323752; Ambassador: ALHUSIN DEEN.

Singapore: 1 Xiu Shui Bei Jie, Jian Guo Men Wai, Beijing 100600; tel. (10) 65323926; fax (10) 65322215; Ambassador: CHIN SIAT YOON.

Slovakia: Ri Tan Lu, Jian Guo Men Wai, Beijing 100600; tel. (10) 65321531; fax (10) 65324814; Ambassador: PETER PAULEN.

Slovenia: Block F, 57 Ya Qu Yuan, King's Garden Villas, 18 Xiao Yun Lu, Chao Yang Qu, Beijing 100016; tel. (10) 64681030; fax (10) 64681040; Ambassador: VLADIMIR GASPARIĆ.

Somalia: 2 San Li Tun Lu, Beijing 100600; tel. (10) 65321752; Ambassador: MOHAMED HASSAN SAID.

South Africa: 5 Dongzhimen Wai Dajie, Chao Yang Qu, Beijing 100016; tel. (10) 65320171; fax (10) 65327319; e-mail safrican@163bj.com; Ambassador: THEMBA M. N. KUBHEKA.

Spain: 9 San Li Tun Lu, Beijing 100600; tel. (10) 65321986; fax (10) 65323401; Ambassador: EUGENIO BREGOLATY OBIOLS.

Sri Lanka: 3 Jian Hua Lu, Jian Guo Men Wai, Beijing 100600; tel. (10) 65321861; fax (10) 65325426; e-mail lkembj@public.east.cn.net; Ambassador: B. A. B. GOONETILLEKE.

Sudan: Bldg 27, San Li Tun, Beijing 100600; tel. (10) 65323715; fax (10) 65321280; e-mail mission.sudan@itu.cn; Ambassador: ABDELHAMEED ABDEEN MOHAMMED.

Sweden: 3 Dong Zhi Men Wai Dajie, San Li Tun, Beijing 100600; tel. (10) 65323331; fax (10) 65325008; e-mail ambassaden.peking@foreign.ministry.se; internet www.swedemb-cn.org.cn; Ambassador: KJELL ANNELING.

Switzerland: 3 Dong Wu Jie, San Li Tun, Beijing 100600; tel. (10) 65322736; fax (10) 65324353; Ambassador: DOMINIQUE DREYER.

Syria: 6 Dong Si Jie, San Li Tun, Beijing 100600; tel. (10) 65321563; fax (10) 65321575; Ambassador: MOHAMMED KHEIR AL-WADI.

Tanzania: 8 Liang Ma He Nan Lu, San Li Tun, Beijing 100600; tel. (10) 65321408; fax (10) 65324985; Ambassador: CHARLES ASILIA SANGA.

Thailand: 40 Guang Hua Lu, Jian Guo Men Wai, Beijing 100600; tel. (10) 65321903; fax (10) 65321748; Ambassador: DON PRAMUDWINAI.

Togo: 11 Dong Zhi Men Wai Dajie, Beijing 100600; tel. (10) 65322202; fax (10) 65325884; Ambassador: NOLANA TA-AMA.

Tunisia: 1 Dong Jie, San Li Tun, Beijing 100600; tel. (10) 65322435; fax (10) 65325818; e-mail ambtun@public.netchina.com.cn; Ambassador: SALAH HAMDI.

Turkey: 9 Dong Wu Jie, San Li Tun, Beijing 100600; tel. (10) 65322490; fax (10) 65325480; e-mail trkelcn@public.bta.net.cn; Ambassador: RAFET AKGUNAY.

Turkmenistan: 5-2-131/5-2-132 Tayuan Diplomatic Compound, Beijing 100600; tel. (10) 65326975; fax (10) 65326976; Ambassador: GURBANMUKHAMMET KASYMOV.

Uganda: 5 Dong Jie, San Li Tun, Beijing 100600; tel. (10) 65322370; fax (10) 65322242; e-mail ugembssy@public.bta.net.cn; internetwww.uganda.cn777.com.cn; Ambassador: PHILIP IDRO.

Ukraine: 11 Dong Liu Jie, San Li Tun, Beijing 100600; tel. (10) 65324013; fax (10) 65326359; e-mail ukrembcn@public3.bta.net.cn; internet www.ukrembcn.org; Ambassador: MYKHAYLO REZNYK.

United Arab Emirates: C801 Lufthansa Center, Office Building 50, Liangmaqiao Lu, Chao Yang Qu, Beijing 100016; tel. (10) 84514416; fax (10) 84514451; Ambassador: JUMA RASHED JASSIM.

United Kingdom: 11 Guang Hua Lu, Jian Guo Men Wai, Beijing 100600; tel. (10) 65321961; fax (10) 65321937; internet www.britishembassy.org.cn; Ambassador: Sir CHRISTOPHER HUM.

USA: 3 Xiu Shui Bei Jie, Beijing 100600; tel. (10) 65323831; fax (10) 65323178; internet www.usembassy-china.org.cn; Ambassador: CLARK T. RANDT.

Uruguay: 1-11-2 Tayuan Diplomatic Office Bldg, Beijing 100600; tel. (10) 65324445; fax (10) 65327375; e-mail urubei@public.bta.net.cn; Ambassador: PELAYO DÍAZ MUGUERZA.

Uzbekistan: 11 Bei Xiao Jie, San Li Tun, Beijing 100600; tel. (10) 65326305; fax (10) 65326304; Ambassador: IZMATILLA R. IRGASHEV.

Venezuela: 14 San Li Tun Lu, Beijing 100600; tel. (10) 65321295; fax (10) 65323817; e-mail embvenez@public.bta.net.cn; Ambassador: JUAN DE JESÚS MONTILLA SALDIVIA.

Viet Nam: 32 Guang Hua Lu, Jian Guo Men Wai, Beijing 100600; tel. (10) 65321155; fax (10) 65325720; Ambassador: BUI HONG PHUC.

Yemen: 5 Dong San Jie, San Li Tun, Beijing 100600; tel. (10) 65321558; fax (10) 65324305; Ambassador: ABDULWAHAB MOHAMED AL-SHAWKANI.

Yugoslavia: 1 Dong Liu Jie, San Li Tun, Beijing 100600; tel. (10) 65323516; fax (10) 65321207; e-mail ambyug@netchina.com.cn; Ambassador: ILIJA DJUKIĆ.

Zambia: 5 Dong Si Jie, San Li Tun, Beijing 100600; tel. (10) 65321554; fax (10) 65321891; Ambassador: MWENYA LWATULA.

Zimbabwe: 7 Dong San Jie, San Li Tun, Beijing 100600; tel. (10) 65323795; fax (10) 65325383; Ambassador: LUCAS PANDE TAVAYA.

Judicial System

The general principles of the Chinese judicial system are laid down in Articles 123–135 of the December 1982 Constitution (q.v.).

PEOPLE'S COURTS

Supreme People's Court: 27 Dongjiaomin Xiang, Beijing 100745; tel. (10) 65136195; f. 1949; the highest judicial organ of the State; handles first instance cases of national importance; handles cases of appeals and protests lodged against judgments and orders of higher people's courts and special people's courts, and cases of protests lodged by the Supreme People's Procuratorate in accordance with the procedures of judicial supervision; reviews death sentences meted out by local courts, supervises the administration of justice by local people's courts; interprets issues concerning specific applications of laws in judicial proceedings; its judgments and rulings are final; Pres. XIAO YANG (five-year term of office coincides with that of National People's Congress, by which the President is elected).

Local People's Courts: comprise higher courts, intermediate courts and basic courts.

Special People's Courts: include military courts, maritime courts and railway transport courts.

PEOPLE'S PROCURATORATES

Supreme People's Procuratorate: 147 Beiheyan Dajie, Beijing 100726; tel. (10) 65126655; acts for the National People's Congress in examining govt depts, civil servants and citizens, to ensure observance of the law; prosecutes in criminal cases. Procurator-Gen. HAN ZHUBIN (elected by the National People's Congress for five years).

Local People's Procuratorates: undertake the same duties at the local level. Ensure that the judicial activities of the people's courts, the execution of sentences in criminal cases and the activities of departments in charge of reform through labour conform to the law; institute, or intervene in, important civil cases that affect the interest of the State and the people.

Religion

During the 'Cultural Revolution' places of worship were closed. After 1977 the Government adopted a policy of religious tolerance, and the 1982 Constitution states that citizens enjoy freedom of religious belief and that legitimate religious activities are protected. Many temples, churches and mosques subsequently reopened. Since 1994 all religious organizations have been required to register with the Bureau of Religious Affairs.

Bureau of Religious Affairs: Beijing; tel. (10) 652625; Dir YE XIAOWEN.

ANCESTOR WORSHIP

Ancestor worship is believed to have originated with the deification and worship of all important natural phenomena. The divine and human were not clearly defined; all the dead became gods and were worshipped by their descendants. The practice has no code or dogma and the ritual is limited to sacrifices made during festivals and on birth and death anniversaries.

BUDDHISM

Buddhism was introduced into China from India in AD 67, and flourished during the Sui and Tang dynasties (6th–8th century), when eight sects were established. The Chan and Pure Land sects are the most popular. According to official sources, in 1998 there were 9,500 Buddhist temples in China. There were 100m. believers in 1997.

Buddhist Association of China (BAC): f. 1953; Pres. (vacant); Sec.-Gen. DAO SHUREN.

Tibetan Institute of Lamaism: Pres. BUMI JANGBALUOZHU; Vice-Pres. CEMOLIN DANZENGCHILIE.

14th Dalai Lama: His Holiness the Dalai Lama TENZIN GYATSO, Thekchen Choeling, McLeod Ganj, Dharamsala 176 219, Himachal Pradesh, India; tel. (91) 1892-21343; fax (91) 1892-21813; e-mail ohhdl@cta.unv.ernet.ind; spiritual and temporal leader of Tibet; fled to India after failure of Tibetan national uprising in 1959.

CHRISTIANITY

During the 19th century and the first half of the 20th century large numbers of foreign Christian missionaries worked in China. According to official sources, there were 10m. Protestants and more than 4m. Catholics in China in 2000, although unofficial sources estimate that the Christian total could be as high as 90m. The Catholic Church in China operates independently of the Vatican.

Three-Self Patriotic Movement Committee of Protestant Churches of China: Chair. LUO GUANZONG; Sec.-Gen. DENG FUCUN.

China Christian Council: 169 Yuan Ming Yuan Lu, Shanghai 200002; tel. (21) 63210806; fax (21) 63232605; e-mail tspmccc@

online.sh.cn; f. 1980; comprises provincial Christian councils; Pres. and acting Sec.-Gen. Rev. CAO SHENGJIE.

The Roman Catholic Church: Catholic Mission, Si-She-Ku, Beijing; Bishop of Beijing MICHAEL FU TIESHAN (not recognized by the Vatican).

Chinese Patriotic Catholic Association: Pres. MICHAEL FU TIESHAN; Sec.-Gen. LIU BAINIAN; c. 3m. mems (1988).

CONFUCIANISM

Confucianism is a philosophy and a system of ethics, without ritual or priesthood. The respects that adherents accord to Confucius are not bestowed on a prophet or god, but on a great sage whose teachings promote peace and good order in society and whose philosophy encourages moral living.

DAOISM

Daoism was founded by Zhang Daoling during the Eastern Han dynasty (AD 125–144). Lao Zi, a philosopher of the Zhou dynasty (born 604 BC), is its principal inspiration, and is honoured as Lord the Most High by Daoists. According to official sources, there were 600 Daoist temples in China in 1998.

China Daoist Association: Temple of the White Cloud, Xi Bian Men, Beijing 100045; tel. (10) 6367179; f. 1957; Pres. MIN ZHITING; Sec.-Gen. YUAN BINGDONG.

ISLAM

According to Muslim history, Islam was introduced into China in AD 651. There were some 18m. adherents in China in 1997, chiefly among the Wei Wuer (Uygur) and Hui people, although unofficial sources estimate that the total is far higher, in the tens of millions.

Beijing Islamic Association: Dongsi Mosque, Beijing; f. 1979; Chair. Imam Al-Hadji SALAH AN SHIWEI.

China Islamic Association: Beijing 100053; tel. (10) 63546384; fax (10) 63529483; f. 1953; Chair. Imam Al-Hadji SALAH AN SHIWEI; Sec.-Gen. YU ZHENGUI.

The Press

In December 2000 China had 2,007 newspaper titles (including those below provincial level) and 8,187 periodicals. Each province publishes its own daily. Only the major newspapers and periodicals are listed below. In late 1999 the Government announced its intention to merge or close down a number of newspapers, leaving a single publication in each province.

PRINCIPAL NEWSPAPERS

Anhui Ribao (Anhui Daily): 206 Jinzhai Lu, Hefei, Anhui 230061; tel. (551) 2827842; fax (551) 2847302; Editor-in-Chief ZHANG YUXUAN.

Beijing Ribao (Beijing Daily): 34 Xi Biaobei Hutong, Dongdan, Beijing 100743; tel. (10) 65131071; fax (10) 65136522; f. 1952; organ of the Beijing municipal cttee of the CCP; Dir WAN YUNLAI; Editor-in-Chief LIU ZONGMING; circ. 700,000.

Beijing Wanbao (Beijing Evening News): 34 Xi Biaobei Hutong, Dongdan, Beijing 100743; tel. (10) 65132233; fax (10) 65126581; f. 1958; Editor XIAO PEI; circ. 800,000.

Beijing Youth Daily: Beijing; national and local news; promotes ethics and social service; circ. 3m.–4m.

Changsha Wanbao (Changsha Evening News): 161 Caie Zhong Lu, Changsha, Hunan 410005; tel. (731) 4424457; fax (731) 4445167.

Chengdu Wanbao (Chengdu Evening News): Qingyun Nan Jie, Chengdu 610017; tel. (28) 664501; fax (28) 666597; circ. 700,000.

China Business Times: Beijing; f. 1989; Editor HUANG WENFU; circ. 500,000.

Chongqing Ribao (Chongqing Daily): Chongqing; Dir and Editor-in-Chief LI HUANIAN.

Chungcheng Wanbao (Chungcheng Evening News): 51 Xinwen Lu, Kunming, Yunnan 650032; tel. (871) 4144642; fax (871) 4154192.

Dazhong Ribao (Dazhong Daily): 46 Jinshi Lu, Jinan, Shandong 250014; tel. (531) 2968989; fax (531) 2962450; internet www.dzdaily.com.cn; f. 1939; Dir XU XIYU; Editor-in-Chief LIU GUANGDONG; circ. 2,100,000.

Economic News: Editor-in-Chief DU ZULIANG.

Fujian Ribao (Fujian Daily): Hualin Lu, Fuzhou, Fujian; tel. (591) 57756; daily; Dir HUANG SHIYUN; Editor-in-Chief HUANG ZHONGSHENG.

Gongren Ribao (Workers' Daily): Liupukang, Andingmen Wai, Beijing 100718; tel. (10) 64211561; fax (10) 64214890; f. 1949; trade union activities and workers' lives; also major home and overseas news; Dir LIU YUMING; Editor-in-Chief SHENG MINGFU; circ. 2.5m.

Guangming Ribao (Guangming Daily): 106 Yongan Lu, Beijing 100050; tel. (10) 63017788; fax (10) 63039387; f. 1949; literature, art, science, education, history, economics, philosophy; Editor-in-Chief YUAN ZHIFA; circ. 920,000.

Guangxi Ribao (Guangxi Daily): Guangxi Region; Dir and Editor-in-Chief CHENG ZHENSHENG.

Guangzhou Ribao (Canton Daily): 10 Dongle Lu, Renmin Zhonglu, Guangzhou, Guangdong; tel. (20) 81887294; fax (20) 81862022; f. 1952; daily; social, economic and current affairs; Editor-in-Chief LI YUANJIANG; circ. 600,000.

Guizhou Ribao (Guizhou Daily): Guiyang, Guizhou; tel. (851) 627779; f. 1949; Dir GAO ZONGWEN; Editor-in-Chief GAN ZHENGSHU; circ. 300,000.

Hainan Ribao (Hainan Daily): 7 Xinhua Nan Lu, Haikou, Hainan 570001; tel. (898) 6222021; Dir ZHOU WENZHANG; Editor-in-Chief CHANG FUTANG.

Hebei Ribao (Hebei Daily): 210 Yuhuazhong Lu, Shijiazhuang, Hebei 050013; tel. (311) 6048901; fax (311) 6046969; f. 1949; Dir GUO ZENGPEI; Editor-in-Chief PAN GUILIANG; circ. 500,000.

Heilongjiang Ribao (Heilongjiang Daily): Heilongjiang Province; Dir JIA HONGTU; Editor-in-Chief AI HE.

Henan Ribao (Henan Daily): 1 Weiyi Lu, Zhengzhou, Henan; tel. (371) 5958319; fax (371) 5955636; f. 1949; Dir YANG YONGDE; Editor-in-Chief GUO ZHENGLING; circ. 390,000.

Huadong Xinwen (Eastern China News): f. 1995; published by Renmin Ribao.

Huanan Xinwen (South China News): Guangzhou; f. 1997; published by Renmin Ribao.

Hubei Ribao (Hubei Daily): 65 Huangli Lu, Wuhan, Hubei 430077; tel. (27) 6833522; fax (27) 6813989; f. 1949; Dir ZHOU NIANFENG; Editor-in-Chief SONG HANYAN; circ. 800,000.

Hunan Ribao (Hunan Daily): 18 Furong Zhong Lu, Changsha, Hunan 410071; tel. (731) 4312999; fax (731) 4314029; Dir JIANG XIANLI; Editor-in-Chief WAN MAOHUA.

Jiangxi Ribao (Jiangxi Daily): 175 Yangming Jie, Nanchang, Jiangxi; tel. (791) 6849888; fax (791) 6772590; f. 1949; Dir ZHOU JINGUANG; circ. 300,000.

Jiefang Ribao (Liberation Daily): 300 Han Kou Lu, Shanghai 200001; tel. (21) 63521111; fax (21) 63516517; f. 1949; Editor-in-Chief JIA SHUMEI; circ. 1m.

Jiefangjun Bao (Liberation Army Daily): Beijing; f. 1956; official organ of the Central Military Comm.; Editor-in-Chief Maj.-Gen. ZHANG ZONGYIN; circ. 800,000.

Jilin Ribao (Jilin Daily): Jilin Province; Dir and Editor-in-Chief YI HONGBIN.

Jingji Ribao (Economic Daily): 2 Bai Zhi Fang Dong Jie, Beijing 100054; tel. (10) 63559988; fax (10) 63539408; f. 1983; financial affairs, domestic and foreign trade; administered by the State Council; Editor-in-Chief WU CHUNHE; circ. 1.2m.

Jinrong Shibao (Financial News): 44 Taipingqiao Fengtaiqu, Beijing 100073; tel. (10) 63269233; fax (10) 68424931.

Liaoning Ribao (Liaoning Daily): Liaoning Province; Dir XIE ZHENGQIAN.

Nanfang Ribao (Nanfang Daily): 289 Guangzhou Da Lu, Guangzhou, Guangdong 510601; tel. (20) 87373998; fax (20) 87375203; f. 1949; Dir LI MENGYU; Editor-in-Chief FAN YIJIN; circ. 1m.

Nanjing Ribao (Nanjing Daily): 53 Jiefang Lu, Nanjing, Jiangsu 210016; tel. (25) 4496564; fax (25) 4496544.

Nongmin Ribao (Peasants' Daily): Shilipu Beili, Chao Yang Qu, Beijing 100025; tel. (10) 65005522; fax (10) 65071154; f. 1980; 6 a week; circulates in rural areas nation-wide; Dir and Editor-in-Chief ZHANG DEXIU; circ. 1m.

Renmin Ribao (People's Daily): 2 Jin Tai Xi Lu, Chao Yang Men Wai, Beijing 100733; tel. (10) 65092121; fax (10) 65091982; f. 1948; organ of the CCP; also publishes overseas edn; Dir XU ZHONGTIAN; Editor-in-Chief WANG CHEN; circ. 2.15m.

Shaanxi Ribao (Shaanxi Daily): Shaanxi Province; Dir LI DONGSHENG; Editor-in-Chief DU YAOFENG.

Shanxi Ribao (Shanxi Daily): 24 Shuangtasi Jie, Taiyuan, Shanxi; tel. (351) 446561; fax (351) 441771; Dir ZHAO WENBIN; Editor-in-Chief LI DONGXI; circ. 300,000.

Shenzhen Commercial Press: Shenzhen; Editor-in-Chief GAO XINGLIE.

Shenzhen Tequ Bao (Shenzhen Special Economic Zone Daily): 4 Shennan Zhonglu, Shenzhen 518009; tel. (755) 3902688; fax (755) 3906900; f. 1982; reports on special economic zones, as well as mainland, Hong Kong and Macao; Dir CHEN XITIAN.

Sichuan Ribao (Sichuan Daily): Sichuan Daily Press Group, 70 Hongxing Zhong Lu, Erduan, Chengdu, Sichuan 610012; tel. and fax (28) 86968000; internet www.sconline.com.cn; f. 1952; Chair. of Bd LI ZHIXIA; Editor-in-Chief TANG XIAOQIANG; circ. 8m.

Tianjin Ribao (Tianjin Daily): 873 Dagu Nan Lu, Heri Qu, Tianjin 300211; tel. (22) 7301024; fax (22) 7305803; f. 1949; Dir and Editor-in-Chief ZHANG JIANXING; circ. 600,000.

Wenhui Bao (Wenhui Daily): 50 Huqiu Lu, Shanghai 200002; tel. (21) 63211410; fax (21) 63230198; f. 1938; Editor-in-Chief SHI JUNSHENG; circ. 500,000.

Xin Min Wan Bao (Xin Min Evening News): 839 Yan An Zhong Lu, Shanghai 200040; tel. (21) 62791234; fax (21) 62473220; f. 1929; specializes in public policy, education and social affairs; Editor-in-Chief JIN FUAN; circ. 1.8m.

Xinhua Ribao (New China Daily): 55 Zhongshan Lu, Nanjing, Jiangsu 210005; tel. (21) 741757; fax (21) 741023; Editor-in-Chief ZHOU ZHENGRONG; circ. 900,000.

Xinjiang Ribao (Xinjiang Daily): Xinjiang Region; Editor-in-Chief HUANG YANCAI.

Xizang Ribao (Tibet Daily): Tibet; Editor-in-Chief LI ERLIANG.

Yangcheng Wanbao (Yangcheng Evening News): 733 Dongfeng Dong Lu, Guangzhou, Guangdong 510085; tel. (20) 87776211; fax (20) 87765103; e-mail ycwbic@ycwb.com.cn; internet www.ycwb.com.cn; f. 1957; Editor-in-Chief PAN WEI WEN; circ. 1.3m.

Yunnan Ribao (Yunnan Daily): Yunnan Province; Editor-in-Chief SUN GUANSHENG.

Zhejiang Ribao (Zhejiang Daily): Zhejiang Province; Dir CHEN MINER; Editor-in-Chief YANG DAJIN.

Zhongguo Qingnian Bao (China Youth News): 2 Haiyuncang, Dong Zhi Men Nei, Beijing 100702; tel. (10) 64032233; fax (10) 64033792; f. 1951; daily; aimed at 14–40 age-group; Dir XU ZHUQING; Editor-in-Chief LI XUEQIAN; circ. 1.0m.

Zhongguo Ribao (China Daily): 15 Huixin Dongjie, Chao Yang Qu, Beijing 100029; tel. (10) 64918633; fax (10) 64918377; internet www.chinadaily.com.cn; f. 1981; English; China's political, economic and cultural developments; world, financial and sports news; also publishes *Business Weekly* (f. 1985), *Beijing Weekend* (f. 1991), *Shanghai Star* (f. 1992), *Reports from China* (f. 1992), *21st Century* (f. 1993); Editor-in-Chief ZHU YINGHUANG; circ. 300,000.

Zhongguo Xinwen (China News): 12 Baiwanzhuang Nanjie, Beijing; tel. (10) 68315012; f. 1952; daily; Editor-in-Chief WANG XIJIN; current affairs.

SELECTED PERIODICALS

Ban Yue Tan (China Comment): Beijing; tel. (10) 6668521; f. 1980; in Chinese and Wei Wuer (Uygur); Editor-in-Chief WANG QIXING; circ. 6m.

Beijing Review: 24 Baiwanzhuang Lu, Beijing 100037; tel. (10) 68326085; fax (10) 68326628; e-mail bjreview@public3.bta.net.cn; internet www.bjreview.com.cn; f. 1958; weekly; edns in English, French, Spanish, Japanese and German; also **Chinafrica** (monthly in English and French); Publr and Editor-in-Chief LIN LIANGQI; Man. Editor LI HAIBO.

BJ TV Weekly: 2 Fu Xing Men Wai Zhenwumiao Jie, Beijing 100045; tel. (10) 6366036; fax (10) 63262388; circ. 1m.

China TV Weekly: 15 Huixin Dong Jie, Chao Yang Qu, Beijing 100013; tel. (10) 64214197; circ. 1.7m.

Chinese Literature Press: 24 Baiwanzhuang Lu, Beijing 100037; tel. (10) 68326010; fax (10) 68326678; e-mail chinalit@public.east.cn.net; f. 1951; monthly (bilingual in English); quarterly (bilingual in French); contemporary and classical writing, poetry, literary criticism and arts; Exec. Editor LING YUAN.

Dianying Xinzuo (New Films): 796 Huaihai Zhong Lu, Shanghai; tel. (21) 64379710; f. 1979; bi-monthly; introduces new films.

Dianzi yu Diannao (Electronics and Computers): Beijing; f. 1985; popularized information on computers and microcomputers.

Elle (China): 14 Lane 955, Yan'an Zhong Lu, Shanghai; tel. (21) 62790974; fax (21) 62479056; f. 1988; monthly; fashion; Pres. YANG XINCI; Chief Editor WU YING; circ. 300,000.

Family Magazine: 14 Siheng Lu, Xinhepu, Dongshan Qu, Guangzhou 510080; tel. (20) 7777718; fax (20) 7185670; monthly; circ. 2.5m.

Feitian (Fly Skywards): 50 Donggan Xilu, Lanzhou, Gansu; tel. (931) 25803; f. 1961; monthly.

Guoji Xin Jishu (New International Technology): Zhanwang Publishing House, Beijing; f. 1984; also publ. in Hong Kong; international technology, scientific and technical information.

Guowai Keji Dongtai (Recent Developments in Science and Technology Abroad): Institute of Scientific and Technical Information of China, 54 San Li He Lu, Beijing 100045; tel. (10) 68570713; fax (10) 68511839; e-mail baiyr@istic.ac.cn; internet www.wanfang.com.cn; f. 1962; monthly; scientific journal; Editor-in-Chief GUO YUEHUA; circ. 40,000.

Hai Xia (The Strait): 27 De Gui Xiang, Fuzhou, Fujian; tel. (10) 33656; f. 1981; quarterly; literary journal; CEOs YANG YU, JWO JONG LIN.

Huasheng Monthly (Voice for Overseas Chinese): 12 Bai Wan Zhuang Nan Jie, Beijing 100037; tel. (10) 68311578; fax (10) 68315039; f. 1995; monthly; intended mainly for overseas Chinese and Chinese nationals resident abroad; Editor-in-Chief FAN DONGSHENG.

Jianzhu (Construction): Baiwanzhuang, Beijing; tel. (10) 68992849; f. 1956; monthly; Editor FANG YUEGUANG; circ. 500,000.

Jinri Zhongguo (China Today): 24 Baiwanzhuang Lu, Beijing 100037; tel. (10) 68326037; fax (10) 68328338; internet www.chinatoday.com.cn; f. 1952; fmrly *China Reconstructs*; monthly; edns in English, Spanish, French, Arabic, German, and Chinese; economic, social and cultural affairs; illustrated; Pres. and Editor-in-Chief HUANG ZU'AN.

Liaowang (Outlook): 57 Xuanwumen Xijie, Beijing; tel. (10) 63073049; f. 1981; weekly; current affairs; Gen. Man. ZHOU YICHANG; Editor-in-Chief JI BIN; circ. 500,000.

Luxingjia (Traveller): Beijing; tel. (10) 6552631; f. 1955; monthly; Chinese scenery, customs, culture.

Meishu Zhi You (Chinese Art Digest): 32 Beizongbu Hutong, East City Region, Beijing; tel. (10) 65591404; f. 1982; every 2 months; art review journal, also providing information on fine arts publs in China and abroad; Editors ZONGYUAN GAO, PEI CHENG.

Nianqingren (Young People): 169 Mayuanlin, Changsha, Hunan; tel. (731) 23610; f. 1981; monthly; general interest for young people.

Nongye Zhishi (Agricultural Knowledge): 21 Ming Zi Qian Lu, Jinan, Shandong 250100; tel. (531) 8932238; e-mail sdnyzs@jn-public.sd.cninfo.net; internet www.sdny.com.cn; f. 1950; fortnightly; popular agricultural science; Dir YANG LIJIAN; circ. 410,000.

Qiushi (Seeking Truth): 2 Shatan Beijie, Beijing 100727; tel. (10) 64037005; fax (10) 64018174; f. 1988 to succeed *Hong Qi* (Red Flag); 2 a month; theoretical journal of the CCP; Editor-in-Chief WANG TIANXI; circ. 1.83m.

Renmin Huabao (China Pictorial): Huayuancun, West Suburbs, Beijing 100044; tel. (10) 68411144; fax (10) 68413023; f. 1950; monthly; edns: two in Chinese, one in Tibetan and 12 in foreign languages; Dir and Editor-in-Chief ZHANG JIAHUA.

Shichang Zhoubao (Market Weekly): 2 Duan, Sanhao Jie, Heping Qu, Shenyang, Liaoning; tel. (24) 482983; f. 1979; weekly in Chinese; trade, commodities, and financial and economic affairs; circ. 1m.

Shufa (Calligraphy): 81 Qingzhou Nan Lu, Shanghai 200233; tel. (21) 64519008; fax (21) 64519015; f. 1977; every 2 months; journal on ancient and modern calligraphy; Chief Editor LU FUSHENG.

Tiyu Kexue (Sports Science): 8 Tiyuguan Lu, Beijing 100763; tel. (10) 67112233. 1981; sponsored by the China Sports Science Soc.; every 2 months; summary in English; Chief Officer YUAN WEIMIN; in Chinese; circ. 20,000.

Wenxue Qingnian (Youth Literature Journal): 27 Mu Tse Fang, Wenzhou, Zhejiang; tel. (577) 3578; f. 1981; monthly; Editor-in-Chief CHEN YUSHEN; circ. 80,000.

Women of China English Monthly: 15 Jian Guo Men Dajie, Beijing 100730; tel. (10) 65134616; fax (10) 65225380; e-mail geo@womenofchina.com.cn; internet www.womenofchina.com.cn; f. 1956; monthly; in English; administered by All-China Women's Federation; women's rights and status, views and lifestyle, education and arts, etc.; Editor-in-Chief YUN PENGJU.

Xian Dai Faxue (Modern Law Science): Southwest University of Political Science and Law, Chongqing, Sichuan 400031; tel. (23) 65382527; e-mail MLS@swupl.edu.cn; f. 1979; bi-monthly; with summaries in English; Dirs CAO MINGDE, LI YUPING.

Yinyue Aihaozhe (Music Lovers): 74 Shaoxing Lu, Shanghai 200020; tel. (21) 64372608; fax (21) 64332019; f. 1979; every two months; music knowledge; illustrated; Editor-in-Chief CHEN XUEYA; circ. 50,000.

Zhongguo Duiwai Maoyi Ming Lu (Directory of China's Foreign Trade): CCPIT Bldg, 1 Fuxingmen Wai Da Jie, Beijing 100860; tel. (10) 68022948; fax (10) 68510201; e-mail inform@press-media.com; f. 1974; monthly; edns in Chinese and English; information on Chinese imports and exports, foreign trade and economic policies; Editor-in-Chief YANG HAIQING.

Zhongguo Ertong (Chinese Children): 21 Xiang 12, Dongsi, Beijing; tel. (10) 6444761; f. 1980; monthly; illustrated journal for elementary school pupils.

Zhongguo Guangbo Dianshi (China Radio and Television): 12 Fucheng Lu, Beijing; tel. (10) 6896217; f. 1982; monthly; reports and comments.

Zhongguo Jin Rong Xin Xi: Beijing; f. 1991; monthly; economic news.

Zhongguo Sheying (Chinese Photography): 61 Hongxing Hutong, Dongdan, Beijing 100005; tel. (10) 65252277; fax (10) 65253197; e-mail cphoto@public.bta.net.cn; internet www.cphoto.com.cn; f. 1957; monthly; photographs and comments; Editor LIU BANG.

Zhongguo Zhenjiu (Chinese Acupuncture and Moxibustion): China Academy of Traditional Chinese Medicine, Dongzhimen Nei, Beijing 100700; tel. (10) 84014607; fax (10) 64013968; e-mail weihongliu@263.net; f. 1981; monthly; publ. by Chinese Soc. of Acupuncture and Moxibustion; abstract in English; Editor-in-Chief Prof. DENG LIANGYUE.

Zijing (Bauhinia): Pres. and Editor-in-Chief CHEN HONG.

Other popular magazines include **Gongchandang Yuan** (Communists, circ. 1.63m.) and **Nongmin Wenzhai** (Peasants' Digest, circ. 3.54m.).

NEWS AGENCIES

Xinhua (New China) News Agency: 57 Xuanwumen Xidajie, Beijing 100803; tel. (10) 63071114; fax (10) 63071210; internet www.xinhuanet.com; f. 1931; offices in all Chinese provincial capitals, and about 100 overseas bureaux; news service in Chinese, English, French, Spanish, Portuguese, Arabic and Russian, feature and photographic services; Pres. TIAN CONGMING; Editor-in-Chief NAN ZHENZHONG.

Zhongguo Xinwen She (China News Agency): POB 1114, Beijing; f. 1952; office in Hong Kong; supplies news features, special articles and photographs for newspapers and magazines in Chinese printed overseas; services in Chinese; Dir WANG SHIGU.

Foreign Bureaux

Agence France-Presse (AFP) (France): 11-11 Jian Guo Men Wai, Diplomatic Apts, Beijing 100600; tel. (10) 65321409; fax (10) 65322371; e-mail afppek@afp.com; Bureau Chief ELIZABETH ZINGO.

Agencia EFE (Spain): 2-2-132 Jian Guo Men Wai, Beijing 100600; tel. (10) 65323449; fax (10) 65323688; Rep. CARLOS REDONDO.

Agenzia Nazionale Stampa Associata (ANSA) (Italy): 1-11 Ban Gong Lu, San Li Tun, Beijing 100600; tel. (10) 65323651; fax (10) 65321954; e-mail barbara@public3.bta.net.cn; Bureau Chief BARBARA ALIGHIERO.

Allgemeiner Deutscher Nachrichtendienst (ADN) (Germany): 7-2-61, Jian Guo Men Wai, Qi Jia Yuan Gong Yu, Beijing 100600; tel. and fax (10) 65321115; Correspondent Dr LUTZ POHLE.

Associated Press (AP) (USA): 6-2-22 Jian Guo Men Wai, Diplomatic Quarters, Beijing 100600; tel. (10) 65326650; fax (10) 65323419; Bureau Chief ELAINE KURTENBACH.

Deutsche Presse-Agentur (dpa) (Germany): Ban Gong Lou, Apt 1-31, San Li Tun, Beijing 100600; tel. (10) 65321473; fax (10) 65321615; e-mail dpa@public3.bta.net.cn; Bureau Chief ANDREAS LANDWEHR.

Informatsionnoye Telegrafnoye Agentstvo Rossii (ITAR—TASS) (Russia): 6-1-41 Tayuan Diplomatic Office Bldg, Beijing 100600; tel. (10) 65324821; fax (10) 65324820; e-mail tassbj@public.bta.net.cn; Bureau Chief ANDREY KIRILLOV.

Inter Press Service (TIPS) (Italy): 15 Fuxing Lu, POB 3811, Beijing 100038; tel. (10) 68514046; fax (10) 68518210; e-mail tipscn@istic.ac.cn; internet www.tips.org.cn; Dir WANG XIAOYING.

Jiji Tsushin (Japan): 9-1-13 Jian Guo Men Wai, Waijiao, Beijing; tel. (10) 65322924; fax (10) 65323413; Correspondents YOSHIHISA MURAYAMA, TETSUYA NISHIMURA.

Korean Central News Agency (Democratic People's Republic of Korea): Beijing; Bureau Chief SONG YONG SONG.

Kyodo News Service (Japan): 3-91 Jian Guo Men Wai, Beijing; tel. (10) 6532680; fax (10) 65322273; e-mail kyodob@ccnet.cn.net; Bureau Chief YASUHIRO MORI.

Magyar Távirati Iroda (MTI) (Hungary): 1-42 Ban Gong Lu, San Li Tun, Beijing 100600; tel. (10) 65321744; Correspondent GYÖRGY BARTA.

Prensa Latina (Cuba): 4-1-23 Jianguomenwai, Beijing 100600; tel. and fax (10) 65321914; e-mail prelatin@public.bta.net.cn; Correspondent ILSA RODRÍGUEZ SANTANA.

Press Trust of India: 5-131 Diplomatic Apts, Jian Guo Men Wai, Beijing 100600; tel. and fax (10) 65322221.

Reuters (UK): Hilton Beijing, 1 Dong Fang Lu/Bei Dong Sanhuan Lu, Chao Yang Qu, Beijing; tel. (10) 64662288; fax (10) 64653052; e-mail hilton@hiltonbeijing.com.cn; internet www.hilton.com; Bureau Man. RICHARD PASCOE.

Tanjug News Agency (Yugoslavia): Qijayuan Diplomatic Apt, Beijing 100600; tel. (10) 65324821.

United Press International (UPI) (USA): 7-1-11 Qi Jia Yuan, Beijing; tel. (10) 65323271; Bureau Chief CHRISTIAAN VIRANT.

The following are also represented: Rompres (Romania) and VNA (Viet Nam).

PRESS ORGANIZATIONS

All China Journalists' Association: Xijiaominxiang, Beijing 100031; tel. (10) 66023981; fax (10) 66014658; Chair. SHAO HUAZE.

China Newspapers Association: Beijing; Chair. XU ZHONGTIAN.

The Press and Publication Administration of the People's Republic of China: 85 Dongsi Nan Dajie, East District, Beijing 100703; tel. (10) 65124433; fax (10) 65127875; Dir YU YOUXIAN.

Publishers

In 2000 there were 565 publishing houses in China. A total of 143,376 titles (and 6,270m. copies) were published in that year.

Beijing Chubanshe Chuban Jituan (Beijing Publishing House Group): 6 Bei Sanhuan Zhong Lu, Beijing 100011; tel. (10) 62016699; fax (10) 62012339; e-mail geo@bph.com.cn; internet www.bph.com.cn; f. 1956; politics, history, law, economics, geography, science, literature, art, etc.; Dir ZHU SHUXIN; Editor-in-Chief TAO XINCHENG.

Beijing Daxue Chubanshe (Beijing University Press): 205 Chengfu Lu, Zhongguancun, Haidian Qu, Beijing 100871; tel. (10) 62752024; fax (10) 62556201; f. 1979; academic and general.

China International Book Trading Corpn: POB 399, 35 Chegongzhuang Xilu, Beijing 100044; tel. (10) 68433113; fax (10) 68420340; e-mail bk@mail.cibtc.co.cn; internet www.cibtc.com.cn; f. 1949; foreign trade org. specializing in publs, including books, periodicals, art and crafts, microfilms, etc.; import and export distributors; Pres. LIU ZHIBIN.

CITIC Publishing House: Capital Mansion, 9/F, 6 Xinyuannan Lu, Chao Yang Qu, Beijing 100004; tel. (10) 64661093; fax (10) 64661098; e-mail citicph@mx.cei.gov.cn; internet www.citicpublish.com.cn; f. 1988; finance, investment, economics and business; Pres. LUO WEIYAO.

Dianzi Gongye Chubanshe (Publishing House of the Electronics Industry—PHEI): POB 173, Wan Shou Lu, Beijing 100036; tel. (10) 68159028; fax (10) 68159025; f. 1982; electronic sciences and technology; Pres. LIANG XIANGFENG; Vice-Pres. WANG MINGJUN.

Dolphin Books: 24 Baiwanzhuang Lu, Beijing 100037; tel. (10) 68326332; fax (10) 68326642; f. 1986; children's books in Chinese and foreign languages; Dir WANG YANRONG.

Falü Chubanshe (Law Publishing House): POB 111, Beijing 100036; tel. (10) 6815325; f. 1980; current laws and decrees, legal textbooks, translations of important foreign legal works; Dir LAN MINGLIANG.

Foreign Languages Press: 19 Chegongzhuang Xi Lu, Fu Xing Men Wai, Beijing 100044; tel. (10) 68413344; fax (10) 68424931; e-mail info@flp.com.cn; internet www.flp.com.cn; f. 1952; books in 20 foreign languages reflecting political and economic developments in People's Republic of China and features of Chinese culture; Dir GUO JIEXIN; Editor-in-Chief XU MINGQIANG.

Gaodeng Jiaoyu Chubanshe (Higher Education Press): 55 Shatan Houjie, Beijing 100009; tel. (10) 64014043; fax (10) 64054602; e-mail linm@public.bta.net.cn; internet www.hep.edu.cn; f. 1954; academic, textbooks; Pres. LIU ZHIPENG; Editor-in-Chief ZHANG ZENGSHUN.

Gongren Chubanshe (Workers' Publishing House): Liupukeng, Andingmen Wai, Beijing; tel. (10) 64215278; f. 1949; labour movement, trade unions, science and technology related to industrial production.

Guangdong Keji Chubanshe (Guangdong Science and Technology Press): 11 Shuiyin Lu, Huanshidong Lu, Guangzhou, Guangdong 510075; tel. (20) 87618770; fax (20) 87769412; e-mail gdkjzbb@zlcn.com; internet www.gdstp.com.cn; f. 1978; natural sciences, technology, agriculture, medicine, computing, English language teaching; Dir HUANG DAQUAN.

Heilongjiang Kexue Jishu Chubanshe (Heilongjiang Science and Technology Press): 41 Jianshe Jie, Nangang Qu, Harbin 150001, Heilongjiang; tel. and fax (451) 3642127; f. 1979; industrial and agricultural technology, natural sciences, economics and management, popular science, children's and general.

Huashan Wenyi Chubanshe (Huashan Literature and Art Publishing House): 45 Bei Malu, Shijiazhuang, Hebei; tel. 22501; f. 1982; novels, poetry, drama, etc.

Kexue Chubanshe (Science Press): 16 Donghuangchenggen Beijie, Beijing 100717; tel. (10) 64034313; fax (10) 64020094; e-mail icd@cspg.net; f. 1954; books and journals on science and technology.

Lingnan Meishu Chubanshe (Lingnan Art Publishing House): 11 Shuiyin Lu, Guangzhou, Guangdong 510075; tel. (20) 87771044; fax (20) 87771049; f. 1981; works on classical and modern painting, picture albums, photographic, painting techniques; Pres. CAO LIXIANG.

Minzu Chubanshe (Nationalities Publishing House): 14 Hepingli Beijie, Beijing 100013; tel. (10) 64211261; f. 1953; books and periodicals in minority languages, e.g. Mongolian, Tibetan, Uygur, Korean, Kazakh, etc.; Editor-in-Chief ZHU YINGWU.

Qunzhong Chubanshe (Masses Publishing House): Bldg 15, Part 3, Fangxingyuan, Fangzhuan Lu, Beijing 100078; tel. (10) 67633344; f. 1956; politics, law, judicial affairs, criminology, public security, etc.

Renmin Chubanshe (People's Publishing House): 8 Hepinglidongjie, Andingmenwai, Beijing; tel. (10) 4213713; managed by the Ministry of Communications; science and technology, textbooks, laws and specifications of communications; Dir and Editor-in-Chief XUE DEZHEN.

Renmin Jiaoyu Chubanshe (People's Education Press): 55 Sha Tan Hou Jie, Beijing 100009; tel. (10) 64035745; fax (10) 64010370; f. 1950; school textbooks, guidebooks, teaching materials, etc.

Renmin Meishu Chubanshe (People's Fine Arts Publishing House): Beijing; tel. (10) 65122371; fax (10) 65122370; f. 1951; works by Chinese and foreign painters, sculptors and other artists, picture albums, photographic, painting techniques; Dir GAO ZONGYUAN; Editor-in-Chief CHENG DALI.

Renmin Weisheng Chubanshe (People's Medical Publishing House): Beijing; tel. (10) 67617283; fax (10) 645143; f. 1953; medicine (Western and traditional Chinese), pharmacology, dentistry, public health; Pres. LIU YIQING.

Renmin Wenxue Chubanshe (People's Literature Publishing House): 166 Chaoyangmen Nei Dajie, Beijing 100705; tel. and fax (10) 65138394; e-mail rwzbs@sina.com; internet www.rw-cn.com; f. 1951; largest publr of literary works and translations into Chinese; Dir and Editor-in-Chief NIE ZHENNING.

Shanghai Guji Chubanshe (Shanghai Classics Publishing House): 272 Ruijin Erlu, Shanghai 200020; tel. (21) 64370011; fax (21) 64339287; f. 1956; classical Chinese literature, history, philosophy, geography, linguistics, science and technology.

Shanghai Jiaoyu Chubanshe (Shanghai Educational Publishing House): 123 Yongfu Lu, Shanghai 200031; tel. (21) 64377165; fax (21) 64339995; f. 1958; academic; Dir and Editor-in-Chief CHEN HE.

Shanghai Yiwen Chubanshe (Shanghai Translation Publishing House): 14 Xiang 955, Yanan Zhonglu, Shanghai 200040; tel. (21) 62472890; fax (21) 62475100; e-mail cpbq@bj.cal.com.cn; internet www.cp.com.cn; f. 1978; translations of foreign classic and modern literature; philosophy, social sciences, dictionaries, etc.

Shangwu Yinshuguan (The Commercial Press): 36 Wangfujing Dajie, Beijing; tel. (10) 65252026; fax (10) 65135899; e-mail comprs@public.gb.com.cn; internet www.cp.com.cn; f. 1897; dictionaries and reference books in Chinese and foreign languages, translations of foreign works on social sciences; Pres. YANG DEYAN.

Shaonian Ertong Chubanshe (Juvenile and Children's Publishing House): 1538 Yan An Xi Lu, Shanghai 200052; tel. (21) 62823025; fax (21) 62821726; e-mail forwardz@public4.sta.net.cn; f. 1952; children's educational and literary works, teaching aids and periodicals; Gen. Man. ZHOU SHUNPEI.

Shijie Wenhua Chubanshe (World Culture Publishing House): Dir ZHU LIE.

Wenwu Chubanshe (Cultural Relics Publishing House): 29 Wusi Dajie, Beijing 100009; tel. (10) 64048057; fax (10) 64010698; e-mail web@wenwu.com; internet www.wenwu.com; f. 1956; books and catalogues of Chinese relics in museums and those recently discovered; Dir SU SHISHU.

Wuhan Daxue Chubanshe (Wuhan University Press): Suojia Hill, Wuhan, Hubei; tel. (27) 7820651; fax (27) 7812661; f. 1981; reference books, academic works, etc.; Pres. and Editor-in-Chief Prof. NIU TAICHEN.

Xiandai Chubanshe (Modern Press): 504 Anhua Li, Andingmenwai, Beijing 100011; tel. (10) 64263515; fax (10) 64214540; f. 1981; directories, reference books, etc.; Dir ZHOU HONGLI.

Xinhua Chubanshe (Xinhua Publishing House): 57 Xuanwumen Xidajie, Beijing 100803; tel. (10) 63074022; fax (10) 63073880; e-mail xhpub@xinhua.org; f. 1979; social sciences, economy, politics, history, geography, directories, dictionaries, etc.; Dir WANG CHUNRONG Editor-in-Chief ZHANG SHOUDI.

Xuelin Chubanshe (Scholar Books Publishing House): 120 Wenmiao Lu, Shanghai 200010; tel. and fax (21) 63768540; f. 1981; academic, including personal academic works at authors' own expense; Dir LEI QUNMING.

Zhongguo Caizheng Jingji Chubanshe (China Financial and Economic Publishing House): 8 Dafosi Dongjie, Dongcheng Qu, Beijing; tel. (10) 64011805; f. 1961; finance, economics, commerce and accounting.

Zhongguo Dabaike Quanshu Chubanshe (Encyclopaedia of China Publishing House): 17 Fu Cheng Men Bei Dajie, Beijing 100037; tel. (10) 68315610; fax (10) 68316510; e-mail ygh@bj.col.com.cn; f. 1978; specializes in encyclopaedias; Dir SHAN JIFU.

Zhongguo Ditu Chubanshe (China Cartographic Publishing House): 3 Baizhifang Xijie, Beijing 100054; tel. (10) 63530808; fax (10) 63531961; e-mail infa@chinamap.com; internet www.chinamap.com; f. 1954; cartographic publr; Dir WANG JIXIAN.

Zhongguo Funü Chubanshe (China Women Publishing House): 24A Shijia Hutong, 100010 Beijing; tel. (10) 65126986; f. 1981; women's movement, marriage and family, child-care, etc.; Dir LI ZHONGXIU.

Zhongguo Qingnian Chubanshe (China Youth Press): 21 Dongsi Shiertiao, Beijing 100708; tel. (10) 84015396; fax (10) 64031803; e-mail cyph@eastnet.com.cn; internet www.cyp.com.cn; f. 1950; literature, social and natural sciences, youth work, autobiography; also periodicals; Dir HU SHOUWEN; Editor-in-Chief XU WENXIN.

Zhongguo Shehui Kexue Chubanshe (China Social Sciences Publishing House): 158A Gulou Xidajie, Beijing 100720; tel. (10) 64073837; fax (10) 64074509; f. 1978; Dir ZHENG WENLIN.

Zhongguo Xiju Chubanshe (China Theatrical Publishing House): 52 Dongsi Batiao Hutong, Beijing; tel. (10) 64015815. 1957; traditional and modern Chinese drama.

Zhongguo Youyi Chuban Gongsi (China Friendship Publishing Corpn): e-mail tmdoxu@public.east.cn.net; Dir YANG WEI.

Zhonghua Shuju (Zhonghua Book Co): 38 Taipingqiao Xili, Fenglai Qu, Beijing; tel. (10) 63458226; f. 1912; general; Pres. SONG YIFU.

PUBLISHERS' ASSOCIATION

Publishers' Association of China: Beijing; f. 1979; arranges academic exchanges with foreign publrs; Hon. Chair. SONG MUWEN; Chair. YU YOUXIAN.

Broadcasting and Communications

TELECOMMUNICATIONS

Ministry of Information Industry: 13 Xichangan Jie, Beijing 100804; tel. (10) 66014249; fax (10) 66034248; e-mail webmaster@mii.gov.cn; internet www.mii.gov.cn; regulates all issues concerning the telecommunications sector.

China Mobile (Hong Kong) Ltd: 60th Floor, The Center, 99 Queen's Rd, Central, Hong Kong; tel. (852) 31218888; fax (852) 25119092; e-mail ca@chinamobilehk.com; internet www.chinamobilehk.com; f. 1997; provides mobile telecommunications services in 13 provinces, municipalities, and autonomous regions of China; world's biggest cellular carrier (2002); Chair. and CEO WANG XIAOCHU.

China Netcom Corpn: Beijing 100032; 9–15/F, Building A, 15/F, Building C, Corporate Square, No.35 Financial St, Xicheng District; tel. (10) 8809-3588; fax (10) 8809-1446; e-mail cnc@china-netcom.com; internet www.cnc.net.cn; f. 1999; internet telephone service provider; merged with China Telecom northern operations (10 provinces) in May 2002; CEO EDWARD TIAN.

China Telecom: 5th Floor, North Wing, Xibianmennei Jie, Xuanwu Qu, Beijing 100053; e-mail info@chinatelecom.com.cn; internet www.chinatelecom.com.cn; f. 1997 as a vehicle for foreign investment in telecommunications sector; operates 'Xiao Ling Tong' mobile phone services; restructured in May 2002 with responsibility for fixed-line network in 21 southern and western provinces; Pres. ZHOU DEQIANG.

China Telecommunications Satellite Group Corpn: Beijing; f. 2001, to provide internet, telephone and related services; Gen. Man. ZHOU ZEHE.

China United Telecommunications Corpn (UNICOM): 1/F, Hongji Centre Office Bldg, 18 Jianguomenei Dajie, Beijing; tel. (10) 65181800; fax (10) 65183405; e-mail webmaster@chinaunicom.com.cn; internet www.chinaunicom.com.cn; f. 1994; cellular telecommunications; Chair. and Pres. YANG XIANZU.

BROADCASTING

In 2000 there were 304 radio broadcasting stations, 737 radio transmitting and relay stations (covering 92.47% of the population), 354 television stations and 51,436 television transmitting and relay stations (covering 93.65% of the population).

Regulatory Authorities

State Administration of Radio, Film and Television (SARFT): 2 Fu Xing Men Wai Dajie, POB 4501, Beijing 100866; tel. (10) 68513409; fax (10) 68512174; internet www.dns.incmrft.gov.cn; controls the Central People's Broadcasting Station, the Central TV Station, Radio Beijing, China Record Co, Beijing Broadcasting Institute, Broadcasting Research Institute, the China Broadcasting Art Troupe, etc.; Chair. TIAN CONGMING.

State Radio Regulatory Authority: Beijing; operates under the State Council; Chair. ZOU JIAHUA.

Radio

China National Radio (CNR): 2 Fu Xing Men Wai Dajie, Beijing 100866; tel. (10) 68045630; fax (10) 68045631; internet www.cnradio.com; f. 1945; domestic service in Chinese, Zang Wen (Tibetan), Min Nan Hua (Amoy), Ke Jia (Hakka), Hasaka (Kazakh), Wei Wuer (Uygur), Menggu Hua (Mongolian) and Chaoxian (Korean); Dir-Gen. YANG BO.

Zhongguo Guoji Guangbo Diantai (China Radio International): 16A Shijingshan Lu, Beijing 100039; tel. (10) 68891001; fax (10) 68891582; e-mail crieng@public.bta.net.cn; internet www.cri.com.cn; f. 1941; fmrly Radio Beijing; foreign service in 38 languages incl. Arabic, Burmese, Czech, English, Esperanto, French, German, Indonesian, Italian, Japanese, Lao, Polish, Portuguese, Russian, Spanish, Turkish and Vietnamese; Dir ZHANG ZHENHUA.

Television

China Central Television (CCTV): 11 Fuxing Lu, Haidian, Beijing 100859; tel. (10) 8500000; fax (10) 8513025; internet www.wtdb.com/CCTV/about.htm; operates under Bureau of Broadcasting Affairs of the State Council, Beijing; f. 1958; operates eight networks; 24-hour global satellite service commenced in 1996; Pres. YANG WEIGWANG.

In April 1994 foreign companies were prohibited from establishing or operating cable TV stations in China. By mid-1996 there were more than 3,000 cable television stations in operation, with networks covering 45m. households. The largest subscriber service is Beijing Cable TV (Dir GUO JUNJIN). Satellite services are available in some areas: millions of satellite receivers are in use. In October 1993 the Government approved new regulations, attempting to restrict access to foreign satellite broadcasts. In September 2001, the Government signed a deal that would allow News Corpn and AOL Time Warner to become the first foreign broadcasters to have direct access to China's markets, although broadcasts would be restricted to Guangdong Province.

Finance

(cap. = capital; auth. = authorized; p.u. = paid up; res = reserves; dep. = deposits; m. = million; amounts in yuan unless otherwise stated)

BANKING

Radical economic reforms, introduced in 1994, included the strengthening of the role of the central bank and the establishment of new commercial banks. The Commercial Bank Law took effect in July 1995. The establishment of private banks was to be permitted.

Regulatory Authority

China Bank Regulatory Commission: Beijing; plans were under way in December 2001 to establish a supervisory and regulatory commission.

Central Bank

People's Bank of China: 32 Chengfang Jie, Xicheng Qu, Beijing 100800; tel. (10) 66194114; fax (10) 66015346; e-mail master@pbc.gov.cn; internet www.pbc.gov.cn; f. 1948; bank of issue; decides and implements China's monetary policies; Gov. DAI XIANGLONG; 2,204 brs.

Other Banks

Agricultural Bank of China: 23A Fuxing Lu, Haidian Qu, Beijing 100036; tel. (10) 68424501; fax (10) 68424493; e-mail webmaster@intl.abocn.com; internet www.abocn.com; f. 1951; serves mainly China's rural financial operations, providing services for agriculture, industry, commerce, transport, etc. in rural areas; cap. 132,011m., res 3,175m., dep. 1,898,957m. (Dec. 2000); Pres. SHANG FULIN; 2,500 brs.

Agricultural Development Bank of China: 2A Yuetanbei Jie, Xicheng Qu, Beijing 100045; tel. (10) 68081557; fax (10) 68081773; f. 1994; cap. 20,000m.; Pres. HE LINXIANG.

Bank of China: 1 Fu Xing Men Nei Dajie, Beijing 100818; tel. (10) 66016688; fax (10) 66016869; e-mail webmaster@bank-of-china.com; internet www.bank-of-china.com; f. 1912; handles foreign exchange and international settlements; operates Orient AMC (asset management corporation) since 1999; cap. 104,500m., res 54,382m., dep. 2,618,477m. (Dec. 2000); Chair. and Pres. LIU MINGKANG; 121 brs.

Bank of Communications Ltd: 18 Xian Xia Lu, Shanghai 200335; tel. (21) 62751234; fax (21) 62752191; internet www.bankcomm.com; f. 1908; commercial bank; cap. 15,302.6m., res 13,267.0m., dep. 391,933.4m. (Dec. 2000); Chair. YIN JIEYAN; Pres. FANG CHENGGUO; 90 brs.

Bank of Shanghai Co Ltd: 585 Zhongshan Lu (E2), Shanghai 200010; tel. (21) 63370888; fax (21) 63370777; e-mail shenjie@bankofshanghai.com.cn; internet www.bankofshanghai.com.cn; f. 1995, as Shanghai City United Bank, assumed present name in 1998; cap. 2,000m., res 2,435m., dep 88,157m. (Dec. 2000); Chair. JIN ZENGDE; Pres. FU JIANHUA.

Beijing City Commercial Bank Corpn Ltd: 2nd Floor, Tower B, Beijing International Financial Bldg, 156 Fuxingmennei Jie, Beijing 100031; tel. (10) 66426928; fax (10) 66426691; e-mail bccbibd@sina.com; internet www.bccb.com.cn; f. 1996, as Beijing City United Bank Corpn, assumed present name in 1998; cap 1,504m., res 1,692m., dep 70,327m. (Dec. 2000); Chair. YAN BINGZHU.

Beijing City Co-op Bank: 65 You An Men Nei Lu, Xuanwu Qu, Beijing 100054; tel. and fax (10) 63520159; f. 1996; cap. 1,000m., res 3,466m., dep. 26,660m. (Dec. 1996); 90 brs.

Bengbu House Saving Bank: 85 Zhong Rong Jie, Bengbu 233000; tel. (552) 2042069.

China and South Sea Bank Ltd: 410 Fu Cheng Men Nei Dajie, Beijing; internet www.cssb.com; f. 1921; cap. 1,200.0m., res 3,735.1m., dep. 38,850.2m. (Dec. 1999); Chair. HUA QINGSHAN.

China Construction Bank (CCB): 25 Jinrong Jie, Beijing 100032; tel. (10) 67598628; fax (10) 67598544; e-mail ccb@bj.china.com; internet www.ccb.com.cn; f. 1954; fmrly People's Construction Bank of China; makes payments for capital construction projects in accordance with state plans and budgets; issues medium- and long-term loans to enterprises and short-term loans to construction enterprises and others; also handles foreign-exchange business; housing loans; operates Cinda AMC (asset management corporation) since 1998 and China Great Wall AMC since 1999; cap. 85,115m., res 20,729m., dep. 2,267,903m. (Dec. 2000); 49 brs.

China Everbright Bank: Everbright Tower, 6 Fu Xing Men Wai Lu, Beijing 100045; tel. (10) 68565577; fax (10) 68561260; e-mail eb@cebbank.com; internet www.cebbank.com; f. 1992 as Everbright Bank of China; acquired China Investment Bank and assumed present name in 1999; cap. 2,800m., res 2,179.6m., dep. 65,343.8m. (Dec. 1998); Pres. WANG CHUAN; Chair. XU BIN; 10 brs.

China International Capital Corporation (CICC): 23rd Floor, Everbright Bldg, 6 Fu Xing Men Wai Dajie, Beijing 100045; tel. (10) 68561166; fax (10) 68561145; f. 1995; international investment bank; 42.5% owned by China Construction Bank; registered cap. US $100m.; CEO EDWIN LIM.

China International Trust and Investment Corporation (CITIC): Capital Mansion, 6 Xianyuannan Lu, Chao Yang Qu, Beijing 100004; tel. (10) 64661105; fax (10) 64662137; f. 1979; economic and technological co-operation; finance, banking, investment and trade; registered cap. 3,000m.; sales US $3,462.7m. (1999/2000); Chair. WANG JUN; Pres. KONG DAN.

China Merchants Bank: News Centre Bldg, 2 Shennan Lu, Shenzhen 518001; tel. (755) 3198888; fax (755) 2090666; e-mail 00430@oa.cmbchina.com; internet www.cmbchina.com; f. 1987; cap. 4,207m., res 5,077m., dep. 197,834m. (Dec. 2000); Chair. QIN XIAO; Pres. MA WEIHUA; 19 brs.

China Minsheng Banking Corporation: 4 Zhengyi Lu, Dongcheng Qu, Beijing 100006; tel. (10) 65269578; fax (10) 65269593; e-mail msbgs@cmbc.com.cn; internet www.cmbc.com.cn; first non-state national commercial bank, opened Jan. 1996; registered cap. 1,380m., res 161.2m., dep. 33,648m. (Dec. 1999); Chair. JING SHUPING; Pres. DONG WENBIAO; 5 brs.

Chinese Mercantile Bank: Ground and 23rd Floors, Dongfeng Bldg, 2 Yannan Lu, Futian Qu, Shenzhen 518031; tel. (755) 3257880; fax (755) 3257801; e-mail szcmbank@public.szptt.net.cn; f. 1993; cap. US $85.3m., res US $3.3m., dep. US $183.8m. (Dec. 1999); Pres. HUANG MINGXIANG.

CITIC Industrial Bank: Block C, Fuhua Bldg, 8 Chao Yang Men Bei Dajie, Dongcheng Qu, Beijing 100027; f. 1987; tel. (10) 65541658; fax (10) 65541671; e-mail webmaster@citicb.com.cn; internet www.citicib.com.cn; f. 1987; cap. 6,809m., res 830m., dep. 187,886m. (Dec. 2000); Chair. WANG JUN; Pres. DOU JIANZHONG; 17 brs.

Export and Import Bank of China: 1 Dingandongli, Yongdingmenwai, Beijing; tel. (10) 67626688; fax (10) 67638940; f. 1994; provides trade credits for export of large machinery, electronics, ships, etc.; Chair. and Pres. YANG ZILIN.

Fujian Asia Bank Ltd: 2nd Floor, Yuan Hong Bldg, 32 Wuyi Lu, Fuzhou, Fujian 350005; tel. (591) 3330788; fax (591) 3330843; f. 1993; cap. US $27.0m., res US $1.8m., dep. US $1.5m. (Dec. 2000); Chair. MA HONG; Gen. Man. SONG JIANXIN.

Fujian Industrial Bank: Zhong Shang Bldg, 154 Hudong Lu, Hualin, Fuzhou, Fujian 350003; tel. (591) 7839338; fax (591) 7841932; internet www.fib.com.cn; f. 1982; cap. 2,000m., res 1,347m., dep. 78,620m. (Dec. 2000); Pres. GAO JIANPING; 16 brs.

Guangdong Development Bank: 83 Nonglinxia Lu, Dongshan Qu, Guangzhou, Guangdong 510080; tel. (20) 87310888; fax (20) 87310779; internet www.gdb.com.cn; f. 1988; cap. 2,688.5m., res 1,471.1m., dep. 141,477.0m. (Dec. 2000); Pres. LIU ZHIQIANG; Chair. LI RUOHONG; 32 brs.

Hua Xia Bank: 9th–12th Floors, Xidan International Mansion, 111 Xidan Bei Dajie, Beijing 100032; tel. (10) 66151199; fax (10) 66188484; e-mail hxbk@public.bta.net.cn; internet www.hxb.cc; f. 1992 as part of Shougang Corpn; registered cap. 2,500m., res 440m., dep. 80,238m. (Dec. 2000); Chair. LU YUCHENG; Pres. WU JIAN.

Industrial and Commercial Bank of China: 55 Fuxingmennai Dajie, Xicheng Qu, Beijing 100031; tel. (10) 66106114; fax (10) 66106053; e-mail webmaster@icbc.com.cn; internet www.icbc .com.cn; f. 1984; handles industrial and commercial credits and international business; operates Huarong AMC (asset management corporation) since 1999; cap. 167,417m., res 14,716m., dep. 3,618,418m. (Dec. 2000); Chair. and Pres. LIU TINGHUAN.

International Bank of Paris and Shanghai: 13th Floor, North Tower, Shanghai Stock Exchange Bldg, 528 Pudong Nan Lu, Shanghai 200120; tel. (21) 58405500; fax (21) 58889232; f. 1992; cap. US $33.6m., res US $1,337,000, dep. US $124.9m. (Dec. 2000); Chair. and Dir JI XIAOHUI.

Kincheng Banking Corporation: 410 Fu Cheng Men Nei Dajie, Beijing; internet kincheng.bocgroup.com; f. 1917; cap. 2,200.0m., res 6,768.8m., dep. 51,873.2m. (Dec. 2000); Chair. SUNG HUNGKAY.

Kwangtung (Gwangdong) Provincial Bank: 410 Fu Cheng Men Nei Dajie, Beijing 100818; internet www.kpb-hk.com; f. 1924; cap. 1,500.0m., res 6,240.0m., dep. 71,535.2m. (Dec. 2000).

National Commercial Bank Ltd: 410 Fu Cheng Men Nei Dajie, Beijing; e-mail hkbrmain@natcombank.bocgroup.com; internet www.natcombank.bocgroup.com; f. 1907; cap. 1,200.0m., res 4,927.6m., dep. 45,291.5m. (Dec. 2000); 26 brs.

Nantong City Commercial Bank Co Ltd: 300 Nanda Lu, Nantong, Jiangsu 226006; tel. (513) 5123040; fax (513) 5123039; e-mail ntccb.id@pub.nt.jsinfo.net; internet www.ntccb.com; f. 1997, as Nantong City United Bank; assumed present name in 1998; cap. 186m., res 18.4m., dep. 4,229.1m., (Dec. 2001); Chair. and Pres. LIU CHANGJI.

Qingdao International Bank: Full Hope Mansion C, 12 Hong Kong Middle Rd, Qingdao, Shandong 266071; tel. (532) 5026230; fax (532) 5026222; e-mail qibankc@public.qd.sd.cn; f. 1996; joint venture between Industrial and Commercial Bank of China and Korea First Bank; cap. 166m., res 8.3m., dep. 78.7m. (Dec. 2000); Pres. DUCK SUNGYUN.

Shanghai Pudong Development Bank: 12 Zhongshan Lu, Shanghai 200002; tel. (21) 63296188; fax (21) 63232036; internet www.spdb.com.cn; f. 1993; cap. 2,410.0m., res 4,538.2m., dep. 119,594.4m. (Dec. 2000); Chair. ZHANG GUANGSHENG; Pres. JIN YUN.

Shenzhen Commercial Bank: Shenzhen Commercial Bank Building, 1099 Shennan Lu, Central, Shenzhen 518031; tel. (755) 5878186; fax (755) 5878189; e-mail ibd@bankofshenzhen.com; internet www.18ebank.com; cap. 1,600m., res 145m., dep. 22,841m. (Dec 2000); Chair. SUN FENG.

Shenzhen Development Bank Co Ltd: 5047 Shen Nan Dong Lu, Shenzhen 518001; tel. (755) 2088888; fax (755) 2081018; e-mail shudi@sdb.com.cn; internet www.sdb.com.cn; f. 1987; cap. 1,945.8m., res 2,793.1m., dep. 59,424.6m. (Dec. 2000); Chair. CHEN ZHAOMIN; Pres. ZHOU LIN.

Sin Hua Bank Ltd: 17 Xi Jiao Min Xiang, Beijing 100031; subsidiary of Bank of China; cap. 2,200.0m., res 7,723.2m., dep. 90,021.3m. (Dec. 1998); Chair. JIANG ZUQI.

State Development Bank (SDB): 29 Fuchengmenwai Lu, Xicheng Qu, Beijing 100037; tel. (10) 68306557; fax (10) 68306541; f. 1994; merged with China Investment Bank 1998; handles low-interest loans for infrastructural projects and basic industries; Gov. CHEN YUAN.

Xiamen International Bank: 10 Hu Bin Bei Lu, Xiamen, Fujian 361012; tel. (592) 5310686; fax (592) 5310685; e-mail xib @public.xm.fj.cn; f. 1985; cap. HK $620m., res HK $473.9m., dep. HK $7,148.3m. (Dec. 2000); Chair. LI LIHUI; 3 brs.

Yantai House Saving Bank: 248 Nan Da Jie, Yantai 264001; tel. (535) 6207047.

Yien Yieh Commercial Bank Ltd: 17 Xi Jiao Min Xiang, Beijing 100031; f. 1915; cap. 800m., res 4,425m., dep. 39,218m. (Dec. 2000); Chair. ZHAO ANGE; Gen. Man. WU GUORUI; 27 brs.

Zhejiang Commercial Bank Ltd: 88 Xi Zhongshan Lu, Ningbo 315010; tel. (574) 87252668; fax (574) 87245409; e-mail zcbho@ mail.nbptt.zj.cn; f. 1993; cap. US $40m., dep. US $86m. (Dec. 1997); Pres. and Chair. DUAN YONGKUAN.

Zhongxin Shiye Bank is a nation-wide commercial bank. Other commercial banks include the Fujian Commercial Bank and Zhaoshang Bank.

Foreign Banks

Before mid-1995 foreign banks were permitted only to open representative offices in China. The first foreign bank established a full branch in Beijing in mid-1995, and by March 1998 there were 51 foreign banks in China. In March 1997 foreign banks were allowed for the first time to conduct business in yuan. However, they are only entitled to accept yuan deposits from joint-venture companies. Representative offices totalled 519 in December 1996. In March 1999 the Government announced that foreign banks, hitherto restricted to 23 cities and Hainan Province, were to be permitted to open branches in all major cities.

STOCK EXCHANGES

Several stock exchanges were in the process of development in the mid-1990s, and by early 1995 the number of shareholders had reached 38m. By 1995 a total of 15 futures exchanges were in operation, dealing in various commodities, building materials and currencies. By the end of 1997 the number of companies listed on the Shanghai and Shenzhen Stock Exchanges had reached 745. In August 1997, in response to unruly conditions, the Government ordered the China Securities Regulatory Commission (see below) to assume direct control of the Shanghai and Shenzhen exchanges.

Stock Exchange Executive Council (SEEC): Beijing; tel. (10) 64935210; f. 1989 to oversee the development of financial markets in China; mems comprise leading non-bank financial institutions authorized to handle securities; Vice-Pres. WANG BOMING.

Securities Association of China (SAC): Olympic Hotel, 52 Baishiqiao Lu, Beijing 100081; tel. (10) 68316688; fax (10) 68318390; f. 1991; non-governmental organization comprising 122 mems (stock exchanges and securities cos) and 35 individual mems; Pres. GUO ZHENQIAN.

Beijing Securities Exchange: 5 Anding Lu, Chao Yang Qu, Beijing 100029; tel. (10) 64939366; fax (10) 64936233.

Shanghai Stock Exchange: 528 Pudong Nan Lu, Shanghai 200120; f. 1990; tel. (21) 68808888; fax (21) 68807813; e-mail webmaster@sse.com.cn; internet www.sse.com.cn; Chair. MAO YINGLIANG; Pres. TU GUANGSHAO.

Shenzhen Stock Exchange: 5045 Shennan Dong Lu, Shenzhen, Guangdong 518010; tel. (755) 20833333; fax (755) 2083117; internet www.sse.org.cn; f. 1991; Chair. ZHENG KELIN; Pres. GUI MINJIE.

Regulatory Authorities

Operations are regulated by the State Council Securities Policy Committee and by the following:

China Securities Regulatory Commission (CSRC): Bldg 3, Area 3, Fangqunyuan, Fangzhuang, Beijing 100078; tel. (10) 67617343; fax (10) 67653117; f. 1993; Chair. ZHOU XIAOCHUAN; Sec.-Gen. WANG YI.

INSURANCE

A new Insurance Law, formulated to standardize activities and to strengthen the supervision and administration of the industry, took effect in October 1995. Changes included the separation of life insurance and property insurance businesses. By late 1998 the number of insurance companies totalled 25. Total premiums rose from 44,000m. yuan in 1994 to some 159,600m. yuan in December 2000. Of the latter figure, property insurance accounted for 58,000m. yuan, life insurance for 85,100m. yuan and health and accident insurance for 14,600m. yuan.

AXA-Minmetals Assurance Co: f. 1999; joint venture by Groupe AXA (France) and China Minmetals Group; Gen. Man. JOSEPH SIN.

China Insurance Co Ltd: 22 Xi Jiao Min Xiang, POB 20, Beijing 100032; tel. (10) 6654231; fax (10) 66011869; f. 1931; cargo, hull, freight, fire, life, personal accident, industrial injury, motor insurance, reinsurance, etc.; Chair. YANG CHAO; Pres. WANG XIANGZHANG.

China Insurance Group: 410 Fu Cheng Men Nei Dajie, Beijing; tel. (10) 66016688; fax (10) 66011869; f. 1996 (fmrly People's Insurance Co of China (PICC), f. 1949); hull, marine cargo, aviation, motor, life, fire, accident, liability and reinsurance, etc.; in process of division into three subsidiaries (life insurance (China Life Insurance

Co—CLIC), property-casualty insurance and reinsurance) by mid-1996, in preparation for transformation into joint-stock cos; 300m. policy-holders (1996); Chair. and Pres. MA YONGWEI.

China Pacific Insurance Co Ltd (CPIC): 12 Zhongshan Lu (Dong 1), Shanghai 200001; tel. (21) 63232488; fax (21) 63218398; internet www.cpic.com.cn.; f. 1991; joint-stock co; Chair. WANG MINGQUAN; Pres. WANG GUOLIANG.

China Ping An Insurance Co: Ping An Bldg, Bagua San Lu, Bagualing, Shenzhen 518029; tel. (755) 82262888; fax (755) 82431019; internet www.pa18.com; f. 1988; Chair. and CEO PETER M. Z. MA.

Hua Tai Insurance Co of China Ltd: Beijing; tel. (10) 68565588; fax (10) 68561750; f. 1996 by 63 industrial cos.

Pacific-Aetna Life Insurance Co: Shanghai; f. 1998 by CPIC and Aetna Life Insurance Co.; China's first Sino-US insurance co.

Tai Ping Insurance Co Ltd: 410 Fu Cheng Men Nei Dajie, Beijing 100034; tel. (10) 66016688; fax (10) 66011869; marine freight, hull, cargo, fire, personal accident, industrial injury, motor insurance, reinsurance, etc.; Pres. SUN XIYUE.

Taikang Life Insurance Co Ltd: Beijing; f. 1996; Chair. CHEN DONGSHENG.

Joint-stock companies include the Xinhua (New China) Life Insurance Co Ltd (Gen. Man. SUN BING). By April 1998 a total of 84 foreign insurance companies had established some 150 offices in China, being permitted to operate in Shanghai and Guangzhou only.

Regulatory Authority

China Insurance Regulatory Commission (CIRC): 410 Fu Cheng Men Nei Dajie, Beijing 100034; tel. (10) 66016688; fax (10) 66018871; internet www.circ.gov.cn; f. 1998; under direct authority of the State Council; Chair. MA YONGWEI.

Trade and Industry

GOVERNMENT AGENCIES

China Council for the Promotion of International Trade (CCPIT): 1 Fuxingmenwai Dajie, Beijing 100860; tel. (10) 68013344; fax (10) 68011370; e-mail ccpitweb@public.bta.net.cn; internet www.ccpit.org; f. 1952; encourages foreign trade and economic co-operation; sponsors and arranges Chinese exhbns abroad and foreign exhbns in China; helps foreigners to apply for patent rights and trade-mark registration in China; promotes foreign investment and organizes tech. exchanges with other countries; provides legal services; publishes trade periodicals; Chair. YU XIAOSONG; Sec.-Gen. ZHONG MIN.

Chinese General Association of Light Industry: 22B Fuwai Dajie, Beijing 100833; tel. (10) 68396114; under supervision of State Council; Chair. YU CHEN.

Chinese General Association of Textile Industry: 12 Dong Chang An Jie, Beijing 100742; tel. (10) 65129545; under supervision of State Council; Chair. SHI WANPENG.

Ministry of Foreign Trade and Economic Co-operation: (see under Ministries).

National Administration of State Property: Dir ZHANG YOUCAI.

State Administration for Industry and Commerce: 8 San Li He Dong Lu, Xicheng Qu, Beijing 100820; tel. (10) 68010463; fax (10) 68020848; responsible for market supervision and administrative execution of industrial and commercial laws; functions under the direct supervision of the State Council; Dir WANG ZHONGFU.

Takeover Office for Military, Armed Police, Government and Judiciary Businesses: Beijing; f. 1998 to assume control of enterprises formerly operated by the People's Liberation Army.

CHAMBERS OF COMMERCE

All-China Federation of Industry and Commerce: 93 Beiheyan Dajie, Beijing 100006; tel. (10) 65136677; fax (10) 65122631; f. 1953; promotes overseas trade relations; Chair. JING SHUPING; Sec.-Gen. CHENG LU.

China Chamber of International Commerce—Shanghai: Jinling Mansions, 28 Jinling Lu, Shanghai 200021; tel. (21) 53060228; fax (21) 63869915; e-mail ccpitllb@online.sh.cn; Chair. YANG ZHIHUA.

China Chamber of International Commerce—Zhuhai: 127 Xinguangli, Zhuhai, Guangdong 519000; tel. (756) 2218954; fax (756) 2228640.

TRADE AND INDUSTRIAL ORGANIZATIONS

Anshan Iron and Steel Co: Huangang Lu, Tiexi Qu, Anshan 114021; tel. and fax (412) 6723090; Pres. LIU JIE.

Baotou Iron and Steel Co: Gangtie Dajie, Kundulun Qu, Baotou 014010, Inner Mongolia; tel. (472) 2125619; fax (472) 2183708; Pres. ZENG GUOAN.

Beijing Urban Construction Group Co Ltd: 62 Xueyuannan Lu, Haidian, Beijing 100081; tel. (10) 62255511; fax (10) 62256027; e-mail cjp@mail.bucg.com; internet www.bucg.com; construction of civil and industrial buildings and infrastructure.

China Aviation Industry Corporation II: 67 Jiao Nan Street, Beijing 100712; tel. (10) 64094013; fax (10) 64032109; e-mail avic@public3.bta.net.cn; Pres. ZHANG YANZHONG.

China Aviation Supplies Corpn: 155 Xi Dongsi Jie, Beijing 100013; tel. (10) 64012233; fax (10) 64016392; f. 1980; Pres. LIU YUANFAN.

China Civil Engineering Construction Corpn (CCECC): 4 Beifeng Wo, Haidian Qu, Beijing 100038; tel. (10) 63263392; fax (10) 63263864; e-mail zongban@ccecc.com.cn; f. 1953; general contracting, provision of technical and labour services, consulting and design, etc.; Pres. QIAN WUYUN.

China Construction International Inc: 9 Sanlihe Lu, Haidian Qu, Beijing; tel. (10) 68394086; fax (10) 68394097; Pres. FU RENZHANG.

China Electronics Corpn: 27 Wanshou Lu, Haidian Qu, Beijing 100846; tel. (10) 68218529; fax (10) 68213745; e-mail cec@public.gb.com.cn; internet www.cec.com.cn; Pres. WANG JINCHENG.

China Garment Industry Corpn: 9A Taiyanggong Beisanhuandong Lu, Chao Yang Qu, Beijing 100028; tel. (10) 64216660; fax (10) 64239134; Pres. DONG BINGGEN.

China General Technology (Group) Holding Ltd: f. 1998 through merger of China National Technical Import and Export Corpn, China National Machinery Import and Export Corpn, China National Instruments Import and Export Corpn and China National Corpn for Overseas Economic Co-operation; total assets 16,000m. yuan; Chair. and Pres. TONG CHANGYIN.

China Gold Co: 1 Bei Jie, Qingnianhu, Andingmenwai, Beijing; tel. (10) 64214831; Pres. CUI LAN.

China Great Wall Computer Group: 38A Xueyuan Lu, Haidian Qu, Beijing 100083; tel. (10) 68342714; fax (10) 62011240; f. 1988; internet www.gwssi.com.cn; Chair. ZHANG ZHIKAI; Gen. Man. GAO KEQIN.

China Great Wall Industry Corpn: Hangtian Changcheng Bldg, 30 Haidian Nanlu, Haidian Qu, Beijing 100080; tel. (10) 68748737; fax (10) 68748865; e-mail cgwic@cgwic.com; internet www.cgwic.com.cn; registered cap. 200m. yuan; Pres. ZHANG XINXIA.

China International Book Trading Corpn: (see under Publishers).

China International Contractors Association: 28 Donghouxiang, Andingmenwai, Beijing 100710; tel. (10) 64211159; fax (10) 64213959; Chair. LI RONGMIN.

China International Futures Trading Corpn: 24th Floor, Capital Mansion, 6 Xinyuan Nan Lu, Chao Yang Qu, Beijing 100004; tel. (10) 64665388; fax (10) 64665140; Chair. TIAN YUAN; Pres. LU JIAN.

China International Telecommunications Construction Corpn (CITCC): 22 Yuyou Lane, Xicheng Qu, Beijing 100035; tel. (10) 66012244; fax (10) 66024103; Pres. QI FUSHENG.

China International Water and Electric Corpn: 3 Liupukang Yiqu Zhongjie, Xicheng Qu, Beijing 100011; tel. (10) 64015511; fax (10) 64014075; e-mail cwe@mx.cei.go.cn; f. 1956 as China Water and Electric International Corpn, name changed 1983; imports and exports equipment for projects in the field of water and electrical engineering; undertakes such projects; provides technical and labour services; Pres. WANG SHUOHAO.

China Iron and Steel Industry and Trade Group Corpn: 17B Xichangan Jie, Beijing 100031; tel. (10) 66067733; fax (10) 66078450; e-mail support@sinosteel.com.cn; internet www.sinosteel.com; f. 1999 by merger of China National Metallurgical Import and Export Corpn, China Metallurgical Raw Materials Corpn and China Metallurgical Steel Products Processing Corpn; Pres. BAI BAOHUA.

China National Aerotechnology Import and Export Corpn: 5 Liangguochang, Dongcheng Qu, Beijing 100010; tel. (10) 64017722; fax (10) 64015381; f.1952; exports signal flares, electric detonators, tachometers, parachutes, general purpose aircraft, etc.; Pres. YANG CHUNSHU; Gen. Man. LIU GUOMIN.

China National Animal Breeding Stock Import and Export Corpn (CABS): 10 Yangyi Hutong Jia, Dongdan, Beijing 100005; tel. (10) 65131107; fax (10) 65128694; sole agency for import and export of stud animals including cattle, sheep, goats, swine, horses, donkeys, camels, rabbits, poultry, etc., as well as pasture and turf grass seeds, feed additives, medicines, etc.; Pres. YANG CHENGSHAN.

China National Arts and Crafts Import and Export Corpn: Arts and Crafts Bldg, 103 Jixiangli, Chao Yang Men Wai, Chao

Yang Qu, Beijing 100020; tel. (10) 65931075; fax (10) 65931036; e-mail po@mbox.cnart.com.cn; internet www.cnart-group.com; deals in jewellery, ceramics, handicrafts, embroidery, pottery, wicker, bamboo, etc.; Pres. CHEN KUN.

China National Automotive Industry Corpn (CNAIC): 46 Fucheng Lu, Haidian Qu, Beijing 100036; tel. (10) 88123968; fax (10) 68125556; Pres. GU YAOTIAN.

China National Automotive Industry Import and Export Corpn (CAIEC): 5 Beisihuan Xi Lu, Beijing 100083; tel. (10) 62310650; fax (10) 62310688; e-mail info@chinacaiec.com; internet www.chinacaiec.com; sales US $540m. (1995); Pres. ZHANG FUSHENG; 1,100 employees.

China National Cereals, Oils and Foodstuffs Import and Export Corpn (COFCO): 7th–13th Floors, Tower A, COFCO Plaza, Jian Guo Men Nei Dajie, Beijing 100005; tel. (10) 65268888; fax (10) 65278612; e-mail minnie@cofco.com.cn; internet www.cofco.com.cn; f. 1952; imports, exports and processes grains, oils, foodstuffs, etc.; also hotel management and property development; sales US $12,099.2m. (1999/2000); Pres. ZHOU MINGCHEN.

China National Chartering Corpn (SINOCHART): Rm 1601/1602, 1607/1608, Jiu Ling Bldg, 21 Xisanhuan Bei Lu, Beijing 100081; tel. (10) 68405601; fax (10) 68405628; e-mail sinochrt@public.intercom.co.cn; f. 1950; functions under Ministry of Foreign Trade and Economic Co-operation; subsidiary of SINOTRANS (see below); arranges chartering of ships, reservation of space, managing and operating chartered vessels; Pres. LIU SHUNLONG; Gen. Man. ZHANG JIANWEI.

China National Chemical Construction Corpn: Bldg No. 15, Songu, Anzhenxili, Chao Yang Qu, Beijing 100029; tel. (10) 64429966; fax (10) 64419698; e-mail cnccc@cnccc.com.cn; internet www.cnccc.com.cn; registered cap. 50m.; Pres. CHEN LIHUA.

China National Chemicals Import and Export Corporation (SINOCHEM): SINOCHEM Tower, A2 Fuxingmenwai Dajie, Beijing 100045; tel. (10) 68568888; fax (10) 68568890; internet www.sinochem.com; f. 1950; import and export, domestic trade and entrepôt trade of oil, fertilizer, rubber, plastics and chemicals; it has made notable development in other areas like industry, finance, insurance, transportation and warehousing; sales US $15,066.2m. (1999/2000); Pres. LIU DESHU.

China National Coal Industry Import and Export Corpn (CNCIEC): 88B Andingmenwai, Dongcheng Qu, Beijing 100011; tel. (10) 64287188; fax (10) 64287166; e-mail cnciec@chinacoal.com; internet www.chinacoal.com; f. 1982; sales US $800m. (1992); imports and exports coal and tech. equipment for coal industry, joint coal development and compensation trade; Chair. and Pres. WANG CHANGCHUN.

China National Coal Mine Corpn: 21 Bei Jie, Heipingli, Beijing 100013; tel. (10) 64217766; Pres. WANG SENHAO.

China National Complete Plant Import and Export Corpn (Group): 9 Xi Bin He Lu, An Ding Men, Beijing; tel. (10) 64253388; fax (10) 64211382; Chair. HU ZHAOQING; Pres. LI ZHIMIN.

China National Electronics Import and Export Corpn: 8th Floor, Electronics Bldg, 23A Fuxing Lu, Beijing 100036; tel. (10) 68219550; fax (10) 68212352; e-mail ceiec@ceiec.com.cn; internet www.ceiec.com.cn; imports and exports electronics equipment, light industrial products, ferrous and non-ferrous metals; advertising; consultancy; Chair. and Pres. QIAN BENYUAN.

China National Export Bases Development Corpn: Bldg 16–17, District 3, Fang Xing Yuan, Fang Zhuang Xiaoqu, Fengtai Qu, Beijing 100078; tel. (10) 67628899; fax (10) 67628803; Pres. XUE ZHAO.

China National Foreign Trade Transportation Corpn (Group) (SINOTRANS): Sinotrans Plaza, A43, Xizhimen Beidajie, Beijing 100044; tel. (10) 62295900; fax (10) 62295901; e-mail office@sinotrans.com; internet www.sinotrans.com; f. 1950; agents for Ministry's import and export corpns; arranges customs clearance, deliveries, forwarding and insurance for sea, land and air transportation; registered cap. 150m. yuan; Chair. and Pres. LUO KAIFU.

China National Import and Export Commodities Inspection Corpn: 15 Fanghuadi Xi Jie, Chao Yang Qu, Beijing 100020; tel. (10) 65013951; fax (10) 65004625; internet www.ccic.com; inspects, tests and surveys import and export commodities for overseas trade, transport, insurance and manufacturing firms; Pres. ZHOU WENHUI.

China National Instruments Import and Export Corpn (Instrimpex): Instrimpex Bldg, 6 Xizhimenwai Jie, Beijing 100044; tel. (10) 68330618; fax (10) 68330528; e-mail zcb@instrimpex.com.cn; internet www.instrimpex.com.cn; f. 1955; imports and exports; technical service, real estate, manufacturing, information service, etc.; Pres. ZHANG RUEN.

China National Light Industrial Products Import and Export Corpn: 910, 9th Section, Jin Song, Chao Yang Qu, Beijing 100021; tel. (10) 67766688; fax (10) 67747246; e-mail info@chinalight.com.cn; internet www.chinalight.com.cn; imports and exports household electrical appliances, audio equipment, photographic equipment, films, paper goods, building materials, bicycles, sewing machines, enamelware, glassware, stainless steel goods, footwear, leather goods, watches and clocks, cosmetics, stationery, sporting goods, etc.; Pres. XU LIEJUN.

China National Machine Tool Corpn: 19 Fang Jia Xiaoxiang, An Nei, Beijing 100007; tel. (10) 64033767; fax (10) 64015657; f. 1979; imports and exports machine tools and tool products, components and equipment; supplies apparatus for machine-building industry; Pres. QUAN YILU.

China National Machinery and Equipment Import and Export Corpn (Group): 6 Xisanhuannan Lu, Liuliqiao, Beijing 100073; tel. (10) 63271392; fax (10) 63261865; f. 1978; imports and exports machine tools, all kinds of machinery, automobiles, hoisting and transport equipment, electric motors, photographic equipment, etc.; Pres. HU GUIXIANG.

China National Machinery Import and Export Corpn: Sichuan Mansion, West Wing, 1 Fu Xing Men Wai Jie, Xicheng Qu, Beijing 100037; tel. (10) 68991188; fax (10) 68991000; e-mail cmc@cmc.com.cn; internet www.cmc.com.cn; f. 1950; imports and exports machine tools, diesel engines and boilers and all kinds of machinery; imports aeroplanes, ships, etc.; Chair. and Pres. CHEN WEIGUN.

China National Medicine and Health Products Import and Export Corpn: Meheco Plaza, 18 Guangming Zhong Jie, Chongwen Qu, Beijing 100061; tel. (10) 67116688; fax (10) 67021579; e-mail webmaster@meheco.com.cn; internet www.meheco.com.cn; Pres. LIU GUOSHENG.

China National Metals and Minerals Import and Export Corpn: Bldg 15, Block 4, Anhuili, Chao Yang Qu, Beijing 100101; tel. (10) 64916666; fax (10) 64916421; e-mail support@minmetals.com.cn; internet www.minmetals.com.cn; f. 1950; principal imports and exports include steel, antimony, tungsten concentrates and ferrotungsten, zinc ingots, tin, mercury, pig-iron, cement, etc.; Pres. MIAO GENGSHU.

China National Native Produce and Animal By-Products Import and Export Corpn (TUHSU): Sanli Bldg, 208 Andingmenwai Jie, Beijing 100011; tel. (10) 64248899; fax (10) 64204099; e-mail info@china-tuhsu.com; internet www.china-tuhsu.com; f. 1949; imports and exports include tea, coffee, cocoa, fibres, etc.; 23 subsidiary enterprises; 9 tea brs; 23 overseas subsidiaries; Pres. ZHANG ZHENMING.

China National Non-Ferrous Metals Import and Export Corpn (CNIEC): 12B Fuxing Lu, Beijing 100814; tel. (10) 63975588; fax (10) 63964424; Chair. WU JIANCHANG; Pres. XIAO JUNQING.

China National Nuclear Corpn: 1 Nansanxiang, Sanlihe, Beijing; tel. (10) 68512211; fax (10) 68533989; internet www.cnnc.com.cn; Pres. LI DINGFAN.

China National Offshore Oil Corpn (CNOOC): PO Box 4705, No. 6 Dongzhimenwai, Xiaojie, Beijing 100027; tel. (10) 84521010; fax (10) 84521044; e-mail webmaster@cnooc.com.cn; internet www.cnooc.com.cn; f. 1982; operates offshore exploration and production of petroleum; sales US $1,341.5m. (1999/2000); Pres. WEN LIUCHENG.

China National Oil Development Corpn: Liupukang, Beijing 100006; tel. (10) 6444313; Pres. CHENG SHOULI.

China National Packaging Import and Export Corpn: Xinfu Bldg B, 3 Dong San Huan Bei Lu, Chao Yang Qu, Beijing 100027; tel. (10) 64611166; fax (10) 64616437; e-mail info@chinapack.net; internet www.chinapack.net; handles import and export of packaging materials, containers, machines and tools; contracts for the processing and converting of packaging machines and materials supplied by foreign customers; registered cap. US $30m.; Pres. ZHENG CHONGXIANG.

China National Petroleum Corpn (CNPC): 6 Liupukang Jie, Xicheng Qu, Beijing 100724; tel. (10) 62094538; fax (10) 62094806; e-mail admin@hq.cnpc.com.cn; internet www.cnpc.com.cn; restructured mid-1998; responsible for petroleum extraction and refining in northern and western China, and for setting retail prices of petroleum products; Pres. MA FUCAI.

China National Publications Import and Export Corpn: 16 Gongrentiyuguandong Lu, Chao Yang Qu, Beijing; tel. (10) 65066688; fax (10) 65063101; e-mail cnpiec@cnpiec.com.cn; internet www.cnpiec.com.cn; imports and exports books, newspapers and periodicals, records, CD-ROMs, etc.; Pres. SONG XIAOHONG.

China National Publishing Industry Trading Corpn: POB 782, 504 An Hua Li, Andingmenwai, Beijing 100011; tel. (10) 64215031; fax (10) 64214540; f. 1981; imports and exports publications, printing equipment technology; holds book fairs abroad; undertakes joint publication; Pres. ZHOU HONGLI.

China National Seed Group Corpn: 16A Xibahe, Chao Yang Qu, Beijing 100028; tel. (10) 64201817; fax (10) 64201820; imports and exports crop seeds, including cereals, cotton, oil-bearing crops, teas, flowers and vegetables; seed production for foreign seed companies etc.; Pres. HE ZHONGHUA.

China National Silk Import and Export Corpn: 105 Bei He Yan Jie, Dongcheng Qu, Beijing 100006; tel. (10) 65123338; fax (10) 65125125; e-mail cnsiec@public.bta.net.cn; internet www.chinasilk.com; Pres. XU HONGXIN.

China National Star Petroleum Corpn: 1 Bei Si Huan Xi Lu, Beijing; e-mail jf@mail.cnspc.com.cn; internet www.cnspc.com.cn; f. 1997; petroleum and gas exploration, development and production; Pres. ZHU JIAZHEN.

China National Technical Import and Export Corpn: Jiuling Bldg, 21 Xisanhuan Beilu, Beijing 100081; tel. (10) 68404000; fax (10) 68414877; e-mail info@cntic.com.cn; internet www.cntic.com.cn; f. 1952; imports all kinds of complete plant and equipment, acquires modern technology and expertise from abroad, undertakes co-production and jt ventures, and technical consultation and updating of existing enterprises; registered cap. 200m.; Pres. WANG HUIHENG.

China National Textiles Import and Export Corpn: 82 Donganmen Jie, Beijing 100747; tel. (10) 65123844; fax (10) 65124711; e-mail webmaster@chinatex.com; internet www.chinatex-group.com; imports synthetic fibres, raw cotton, wool, garment accessories, etc.; exports cotton yarn, cotton fabric, knitwear, woven garments, etc.; Pres. ZHAO BOYA.

China National Tobacco Import and Export Corpn: 11 Hufang Lu, Xuanwu Qu, Beijing 100052; tel. (10) 63533399; fax (10) 63015331; Pres. XUN XINGHUA.

China National United Oil Corpn: 57 Wangfujing Jie, Dongcheng Qu, Beijing 100006; tel. (10) 65223828; fax (10) 65223817; Chair. ZHANG JIAREN; Pres. ZHU YAOBIN.

China No. 1 Automobile Group: 63 Dongfeng Jie, Chao Yang Qu, Changchun, Jilin; tel. (431) 5003030; fax (431) 5001309; f. 1953; mfr of passenger cars; Gen. Man. GENG ZHAOJIE.

China North Industries Group: 46 Sanlihe Lu, Beijing 100821; tel. (10) 68594210; fax (10) 68594232; internet www.corincogroup.com.cn; exports vehicles and mechanical products, light industrial products, chemical products, opto-electronic products, building materials, military products, etc.; Pres. MA ZHIGENG.

China Nuclear Energy Industry Corpn (CNEIC): 1A Yuetan Bei Jie, Xicheng Qu, Beijing 100037; tel. (10) 68013395; fax (10) 68512393; internet www.cnnc.com.cn; exports air filters, vacuum valves, dosimeters, radioactive detection elements and optical instruments; Pres. ZHANG ZHIFENG.

China Road and Bridge Corpn: Zhonglu Bldg, 88C, An Ding Men Wai Dajie, Beijing 100011; tel. (10) 64285616; fax (10) 64285686; e-mail crbc@crbc.com; internet www.crbc.com; overseas and domestic building of highways, urban roads, bridges, tunnels, industrial and residential buildings, airport runways and parking areas; contracts to do surveying, designing, pipe-laying, water supply and sewerage, building, etc., and/or to provide technical or labour services; Chair. ZHOU JICHANG.

China Shipbuilding Trading Corpn Ltd: 10 Yue Tan Bei Xiao Jie, Beijing 100861; tel. (10) 68032560; fax (10) 68033380; e-mail webmaster@cstc.com.cn; internet www.ctsc.com.cn; Pres. LI ZHUSHI.

China State Construction Engineering Corpn: Baiwanzhuang, Xicheng Qu, Beijing 100835; tel. (10) 68347766; fax (10) 68314326; e-mail cscec-us@worldnet.att.net; internet www.cscec.com; sales US $4,726.8m. (1999/2000); Pres. MA TINGGUI.

China State Shipbuilding Corpn: 5 Yuetan Beijie, Beijing; tel. (10) 68030208; fax (10) 68031579; Pres. CHEN XIAOJIN; Gen. Man. XU PENGHANG.

China Tea Import and Export Corpn: Zhongtuchu Bldg, 208 Andingmenwai Jie, Beijing 100011; tel. (10) 64204123; fax (10) 64204101; e-mail info@teachina.com; internet www.chinatea.com.cn; Pres. LI JIAZHI.

China Xinshidai (New Era) Corpn: 40 Xie Zuo Hu Tong, Dongcheng Qu, Beijing 100007; tel. (10) 64017384; fax (10) 64032935; Pres. QIN ZHONGXING.

China Xinxing Corpn (Group): 17 Xisanhuan Zhong Lu, Beijing 100036; tel. (10) 685166688; fax (10) 68514669; e-mail black-lily@nihao.com; internet www.black-lily.com; Pres. FAN YINGJUN.

Chinese General Co of Astronautics Industry (State Aerospace Bureau): 8 Fucheng Lu, Haidian Qu, Beijing 100712; tel. (10) 68586047; fax (10) 68370080; Pres. LIU JIYUAN.

Daqing Petroleum Administration Bureau: Sartu Qu, Daqing, Heilongjiang; tel. (459) 814649; fax (459) 322845; Gen. Man. WANG ZHIWU.

Ma'anshan Iron and Steel Co: 8 Hongqibei Lu, Maanshan 243003, Anhui; tel. (555) 2883492; fax (555) 2324350; Chair. HANG YONGYI; Pres. LI ZONGBI.

Shanghai Automotive Industry Sales Corpn: 548 Caoyang Lu, Shanghai 200063; tel. and fax (21) 62443223; Gen. Man. XU JIANYU.

Shanghai Baosteel Group Corpn: Baosteel Tower, 370 Pudian Lu, Pudong New District, Shanghai; tel. (21) 58358888; fax (21) 68404832; e-mail webman@baosteel.com; internet www.bstl.sh.cn; f. 1998; incorporating Baoshan Iron and Steel Corpn, and absorption of Shanghai Metallurgical Holding Group Corpn, and Shanghai Meishan Group Corpn Ltd; produces steel and steel products; sales US $8,266.0m. (1999/2000); Pres. XIE QIHUA; Chair. of Bd XU DAQUA.

Shanghai Foreign Trade Corpn: 27 Zhongshan Dong Yi Lu, Shanghai 200002; tel. (21) 63217350; fax (21) 63290044; f. 1988; handles import-export trade, foreign trade transportation, chartering, export commodity packaging, storage and advertising for Shanghai municipality; Gen. Man. WANG MEIJUN.

Shanghai International Trust Trading Corpn: 201 Zhaojiabang Lu, Shanghai 200032; tel. (21) 64033866; fax (21) 64034722; f. 1979, present name adopted 1988; handles import and export business, international mail orders, processing, assembling, compensation trade etc.

Shougang Group: Shijingshan, Beijing 100041; tel. (10) 88294166; fax (10) 88295578; e-mail sgjtglb01@shougang.com.cn; internet www.shougang.com.cn; f. 1919; produces iron and steel; sales US $4,396.8m. (1999/2000); Chair. BI QUN; Gen. Man. LUO BINGSHENG.

State Bureau of Non-Ferrous Metals Industry: 12B Fuxing Lu, Beijing 100814; tel. (10) 68514477; fax (10) 68515360; under supervision of State Economic and Trade Commission; Dir ZHANG WULE.

Wuhan Iron and Steel (Group) Co: Qingshan Qu, Wuhan, Hubei Province; tel. (27) 6892004; fax (27) 6862325; proposals for merger with two other steel producers in Hubei announced late 1997; Pres. LIU BENREN.

Xinxing Oil Co (XOC): Beijing; f. 1997; exploration, development and production of domestic and overseas petroleum and gas resources; Gen. Man. ZHU JIAZHEN.

Yuxi Cigarette Factory: Yujiang Lu, Yuxi, Yunnan Province; tel. and fax (877) 2052343; Gen. Man. CHU SHIJIAN.

Zhongjiang Group: Nanjing, Jiansu; f. 1998; multi-national operation mainly in imports and exports, contract projects and real estate; group consists of 126 subsidiaries incl. 25 foreign ventures.

UTILITIES

Electricity

Beijing Power Supply Co: Qianmen Xidajie, Beijing 100031; tel. (10) 63129201.

Beijing Datang Power Generation: 33 Nanbinhe Lu, Xuanwu Qu, Beijing; one of China's largest independent power producers; Chair. JIAO YIAN.

Central China Electric Power Group Co: 47 Xudong Lu, Wuchang, Wuhan 430077; tel. (27) 6813398.

Changsha Electric Power Bureau: 162 Jiefang Sicun, Changsha 410002; tel. (731) 5912121; fax (731) 5523240.

China Atomic Energy Authority: Chair. ZHANG HUAZHU.

China Northwest Electric Power Group Co: 57 Shangde Lu, Xian 710004; tel. (29) 7275061; fax (29) 7212451; Chair. LIU HONG.

China Power Grid Development (CPG): f. to manage transmission and transformation lines for the Three Gorges hydroelectric scheme; Pres. ZHOU XIAOQIAN.

China Yangtze Three Gorges Project Development Corpn: 1 Jianshe Dajie, Yichang, Hubei Province; tel. (717) 6762212; fax (717) 6731787; Pres. LU YOUMEI.

Dalian Power Supply Co: 102 Zhongshan Lu, Dalian 116001; tel. (411) 2637560; fax (411) 2634430; Chief Gen. Man. LIU ZONGXIANG.

Fujian Electric Industry Bureau: 4 Xingang Dao, Taijrang Qu, Fuzhou 350009; tel. and fax (591) 3268514; Dir WANG CHAOXU.

Gansu Bureau of Electric Power: 306 Xijin Dong Lu, Qilihe Qu, Lanzhou 730050; tel. (931) 2334311; fax (93) 2331042; Dir ZHANG MINGXI.

Guangdong Electric Power Bureau: 757 Dongfeng Dong Lu, Guangzhou 510600; tel. (20) 87767888; fax (20) 87770307.

Guangdong Shantou Electric Power Bureau: Jinsha Zhong Lu, Shantou 515041; tel. (754) 8257606.

Guangxi Electric Power Bureau: 6 Minzhu Lu, Nanning 530023; tel. (771) 2801123; fax (771) 2803414.

Guangzhou Electric Power Co: 9th Floor, Huale Bldg, 53 Huale Lu, Guangzhou 510060; tel. (20) 83821111; fax (20) 83808559.

Hainan Electric Power Industry Bureau: 34 Haifu Dadao, Haikou 570203; tel. (898) 5334777; fax (898) 5333230.

Heilongjiang Electric Power Co: B12Fl High Tech Development Zone, Harbin 150001; tel. (451) 2308810; fax (451) 2525878; Chair. XUE YANG.

Huadong Electric Power Group Corpn: 201 Nanjing Dong Lu, Shanghai; tel. (21) 63290000; fax (21) 63290727; power supply.

Huaneng Power International: West Wing, Building C, Tianyin Mansion, 2C Fuxingmennan Lu, Xicheng, Beijing; tel. (10) 66491999; fax (10) 66491888; e-mail ir@hpi.com.cn; internet www.hpi.com.cn; f. 1998; Chair. and Pres. LI XIAOPENG.

Huazhong Electric Power Group Corpn: Liyuan, Donghu, Wuhan, Hubei Province; tel. (27) 6813398; fax (27) 6813143; electrical engineering; Gen. Man. LIN KONGXING.

Inner Mongolia Electric Power Co: 28 Xilin Nan Lu, Huhehaose 010021; tel. (471) 6942222; fax (471) 6924863.

Jiangmen Electric Power Supply Bureau: 87 Gangkou Lu, Jiangmen 529030; tel. and fax (750) 3360133.

Jiangxi Electric Power Bureau: 13 Yongwai Zheng Jie, Nanchang 330006; tel. (791) 6224701; fax (791) 6224830.

National Grid Construction Co: established to oversee completion of the National Grid by 2009.

North China Electric Power Group Corpn: 32 Zulinqianjie, Xuanwu Qu, Beijing 100053; tel. and fax (10) 63263377; Pres. JIAO YIAN.

Northeast China Electric Power Group: 11 Shiyiwei Lu, Heping Qu, Shenyang 110003; tel. (24) 3114382; fax (24)3872665.

Shandong Electric Power Group Corpn: 150 Jinger Lu, Jinan 250001; tel. (531) 6911919.

Shandong International Power Development Co Ltd: 14 Jingsan Lu, Jinan, Shandong 250001; tel. (531) 6929898; fax (531) 6035469; e-mail sipd@sipd.com; internet www.sipd.com.cn; f. 1994; Chair. DA HONGXING.

Shandong Rizhao Power Co Ltd: 1st Floor, Bldg 29, 30 Northern Section, Shunyu Xiaoqu, Jinan 250002; tel. (531) 2952462; fax (531) 2942561.

Shanghai Electric Power Co: 181 Nanjing Dong Lu, Huangpu Qu, Shanghai 200002; tel. (21) 63291010; fax (21) 63248586; Dir GU YINZHANG.

Shenzhen Power Supply Co: 2 Yanhe Xi Lu, Luohu Qu, Shenzhen 518000; tel. (755) 5561920.

Sichuan Electric Power Co: Room 1, Waishi Bldg, Dongfeng Lu, Chengdu 610061; tel. (28) 444321; fax (28) 6661888.

State Power Corpn of China: No. 1 Lane 2, Baiguang Lu, Beijing 100761; tel. (10) 63416475; fax (10) 63548152; e-mail webmaster @sp.com.cn; internet www.cep.gov.cn; f. 1997, from holdings of Ministry of Electric Power; plans to split into three or four regional generating companies and two regional (North and South) grid companies announced in April 2002; Pres. GAO YAN.

Tianjin Electric Power Industry Bureau: 29 Jinbu Dao, Hebei Qu, Tianjin 300010; tel. (22) 24406326; fax (22) 22346965.

Wenergy Co Ltd: 81 Wuhu Lu, Hefei 230001; tel. (551) 2626906; fax (551) 2648061.

Wuhan Power Supply Bureau: 981 Jiefang Dadao, Hankou, Wuhan 430013; tel. (27) 2426455; fax (27) 2415605.

Wuxi Power Supply Bureau: 8 Houxixi, Wuxi 214001; tel. (510) 2717678; fax (510) 2719182.

Xiamen Power Transformation and Transmission Engineering Co: 67 Wenyuan Lu, Xiamen 361004; tel. (592) 2046763.

Xian Power Supply Bureau: Huancheng Dong Lu, Xian 710032; tel. (29) 7271483.

Gas

Beijing Gas Co: 30 Dongsanhuan Zhong Lu, Beijing 100020; tel. (10) 65024131; fax (10) 65023815; Dir LIU BINGIUN.

Beijing Natural Gas Co: Bldg 5, Dixingju, An Ding Men Wai, Beijing 100011; tel. (10) 64262244.

Changchun Gas Co: 30 Tongzhi Jie, Changchun 130021; tel. (431) 8926479.

Changsha Gas Co: 18 Shoshan Lu, Changsha 410011; tel. (731) 4427246.

Qingdao Gas Co: 399A Renmin Lu, Qingdao 266032; tel. (532) 4851461; fax (532) 4858653.

Shanghai Gas Supply Co: 656 Xizang Zhong Lu, Shanghai 200003; tel. (21) 63222333; fax (21) 63528600; Gen. Man. LI LONGLING.

Wuhan Gas Co: Qingnian Lu, Hankou, Wuhan 430015; tel. (27) 5866223.

Xiamen Gas Corpn: Ming Gong Bldg, Douxi Lukou, Hubin Nan Lu, Xiamen 361004; tel. (592) 2025937; fax (592) 2033290.

Water

Beijing District Heating Co: 1 Xidawang Lu, Hongmiao, Chao Yang Qu, Beijing 100026; tel. (10) 65060066; fax (10) 65678891.

Beijing Municipal Water Works Co: 19 Yangrou Hutong, Xicheng Qu, Beijing 100034; tel. (10) 66167744; fax (10) 66168028.

Changchun Water Co: 53 Dajing Lu, Changchun 130000; tel. (431) 8968366.

Chengdu Water Co: 16 Shierqiao Jie, Shudu Dadao, Chengdu 610072; tel. (28) 77663122; fax (28) 7776876.

The China Water Company: f. to develop investment opportunities for water projects.

Guangzhou Water Supply Co: 5 Huanshi Xi Lu, Guangzhou 510010; tel. (20) 81816951.

Haikou Water Co: 31 Datong Lu, Haikou 570001; tel. (898) 6774412.

Harbin Water Co: 49 Xi Shidao Jie, Daoli Qu, Harbin 150010; tel. (451) 4610522; fax (451) 4611726.

Jiangmen Water Co: 44 Jianshe Lu, Jiangmen 529000; tel. (750) 3300138; fax (750) 3353704.

Qinhuangdao Pacific Water Co: Hebei; Sino-US water supply project; f. 1998.

Shanghai Municipal Waterworks Co: 484 Jiangxi Zhong Lu, Shanghai 200002; tel. (21) 63215577; fax (21) 63231346; service provider for municipality of Shanghai.

Shenzhen Water Supply Group Co: Water Bldg, 1019 Shennan Zhong Lu, Shenzhen 518031; tel. (755) 2137836; fax (755) 2137888, e-mail webmaster@waterchina.com; internet www.waterchina.com.

Tianjin Waterworks Group: 54 Jianshe Lu, Heping Qu, Tianjin 300040; tel. (22) 3393887; fax (22) 3306720.

Xian Water Co: Huancheng Xi Lu, Xian 710082; tel. (29) 4244881.

Zhanjiang Water Co: 20 Renmin Dadaonan, Zhanjiang 524001; tel. (759) 2286394.

Zhongshan Water Supply Co: 23 Yinzhu Jie, Zhuyuan Lu, Zhongshan 528403; tel. (760) 8312969; fax (760) 6326429.

Zhuhai Water Supply General Corpn: Yuehai Zhong Lu, Gongbei, Zhuhai 519020; tel. (756) 8881160; fax (756) 8884405

MAJOR COMPANIES

(cap. = capital; res = reserves; m. = million; amounts in yuan, unless otherwise stated)

Anshan Yaxing Group Co Ltd: 15 Zhonghua Lu, Lishan Qu, Anshan, Liaoning 114031; tel. (412) 636761; f. 1987; cap. and res 30m., sales 48m. (1995); 4 corporate mems; iron and steel, real estate; Pres. YU XITING; 320 employees.

Beijing Changning Group: Changping County, Beijing 102206; tel. (10) 69732708; fax (10) 69732587; f. 1985; cap. and res 280m., sales 448m. (1995); 18 corporate mems; machinery, electronics, foods, light industry, building, trade; Pres. SHI SHANLIN; 3,000 employees.

Beijing Time Group: 68 Xisanhuan Beilu, Haidian Qu, Beijing 100044; tel. (10) 68473246; fax (10) 68472343; f. 1984; cap. and res 22m., sales 180m. (1995); 30 corporate mems; testing instruments, welding machinery; Pres. PENG WEIMIN; 300 employees.

Beijing Users Friend Electronic Financial Technology Co Ltd: 48 Baishiqiao Lu, Haidian Qu, Beijing 100081; tel. (10) 68315639; fax (10) 68340691; f. 1988; cap. and res 12m., sales 14m. (1995); 6 corporate mems; software and accounting equipment, electronic office equipment; Pres. WANG WENJING; 150 employees.

Bengang Steel Plates Co Ltd: 16 Renmin Lu, Pingshan Qu, Beixi, Liaoning 117000; tel. (414) 7827344; fax (414) 7827004; f. 1997; revenue US $844.8m. (2000); ferrous metals processing.

Changchai Co Ltd: 123 Huaide Jie, Changzhou, Jiangsu 213002; tel. (519) 6600341; fax (519) 6670765; f. 1913; production of diesel engines and agricultural product-processing machinery; cap. and res 1,324.7m., sales 2,730.3m. (1997); Chair. SHENG TIEPING.

Changchun Fushoude Food Co Ltd: Bldg 8, Beian Xiaoqu, Qingming Jie, Changchun, Jilin 130041; tel. (431) 8918575; fax (431) 8918574; f. 1988; cap. and res 35m., sales 3m. (1995); food; Pres. YIN XIURONG; 370 employees.

Chengdu Huaxi Institute of Chemical Industry: 11 Chadianzi Xijie, Chengdu, Sichuan 610036; tel. (28) 7784460; fax (28) 7760145; f. 1987; cap. and res 9m., sales 28m. (1995); 5 corporate mems; chemical-processing controls; Pres. LI DONGLIN; 160 employees.

China Harbour Engineering Company: 9 Chunxiu Lu, Dong Zhi Men Wai, Beijing 100027; tel. (10) 64154455; fax (10) 64168276; e-mail chechw@homeway.com.cn; civil engineering; sales US $1,333.8m. (1999/2000); Pres. LI HUAIYUAN.

China Petroleum and Chemical Corporation (SINOPEC): No. A6 Huixin East Jie, Chao Yang Qu, Beijing 100029; tel. (10) 64225533; fax (10) 64212429; e-mail webmaster@sinopec.com.cn; internet www.sinopec.com.cn; f. 2000; exploration, development, production, refining, transport and marketing of petroleum and natural gas, production and sales of petrochemicals, chemical fibres, chemical fertilizers, and other chemicals, research and development and application of technology and information; sales US $29m. (1999/2000); Pres. WANG JIMING; Chair. of Bd LI YIZHONG.

SINOPEC Shanghai Petrochemical Co Ltd: Wei Er Lu, Jinshanwei, Shanghai 200540; tel. (21) 57943143; fax (21) 57940050; e-mail spc@spc.com.cn; internet www.spc.com.cn; processing of crude petroleum into synthetic fibres, resins and plastics, and other petroleum products; cap. and res 12,294.8m. (1997), sales US $1,695.6m. (1999/2000); Chair. LU YIPING.

SINOPEC Yizheng Chemical Fibre Co Ltd: Zhenzhou, Yizheng, Jiangsu 211900; tel. (514) 3232235; fax (514) 3233880; internet www.sinopec.com.cn; f. 1993; chemical products; China's largest manufacturer of chemical fibre and world's fifth-largest polyester maker (2001); revenue US $1,088.9m. (2000); Dir. and Gen. Man. XU ZHENGNING.

Chongqing Chang'an Automobile Co Ltd: 260 Jianxin Dong Lu, Jiangbei Qu, Chongqing 400023; tel. (23) 67591249; fax (23) 67866055; internet www.changan.com.cn; revenue US $823.3m. (2000); manufacturers and exports road vehicles and vehicle components.

Chongqing Iron and Steel Co Ltd: 30 Gangtie Jie, Dadukou Qu, Chongqing 400081; tel. (811) 8875551; manufacture and sale of iron and steel products; cap. and res 1,740.6m., sales 2,811.7m. (1998); Chair. GUO DAIYI.

Dong Fang Electrical Machinery Co Ltd: 13 Huanghe Xi Jie, Deyang, Sichuan 618000; tel. (838) 2412144; fax (838) 2203305; info@dfem.com.cn; internet www.dfem.com.cn; production and sale of power-generating equipment; cap. and res 1,204.2m., sales 814.4m. (1998); Chair. YUAN CHANGHE; 7,804 employees.

Dongfeng Motor Corpn: 1 Checheng Lu, Zhangwan Qu, Shiyan 442001; tel. (719) 226987; fax (719) 226815; f. 1969; sales 11,200m. (1998); trucks and automobiles; Gen. Man. MIAO WEI; 90,000 employees.

First Tractor Co Ltd: 154 Jian She Jie, Luoyang City, Henan; tel. (379) 4970038; fax (379) 4978838; production and sale of agricultural tractors; cap. and res 2,358.9m., sales 2,703.6m. (1998); Sec. JIANG GUOLIANG.

Fuzhou Chia Tai-Zhen Hua 851 Biological Products Co Ltd: Bldg 851, 58 Wenqianzhilu, Fuzhou, Fujian 35001; f. 1986; cap. and res 22m., sales 88m. (1995); 5 corporate mems; pharmaceutical products, healthcare; Pres. YANG ZHENHUA; 500 employees.

Gree Group Corp: Beijing Industrial Zone, Zhuhai, Guangdong 519020; tel. (756) 8131888; fax (756) 8885701; e-mail info@gree.com; internet www.gree.com; f. 1985; revenue US $761.8m. (2000); manufactures electronic and electrical goods and machinery; property and transport.

Guangdong Kelon Electrical Appliance Co: 8 Ronggang Lu, Ronggi, Shunde 528303; tel. (765) 6621911; fax (765) 6621260; e-mail kelon@gdkelon.com.hk; internet www.gdkelon.com.hk; f. 1993; domestic electrical appliances, incl. refrigerators; cap. and res 3,319m., sales 3,813m. (1998); Chair. XU TEIFENG; 10,210 employees.

Guangdong Wanli Architectural Machinery Equipment Group Co: 102 He Nan Lu, Chikan Qu, Kai Ping, Guangdong; tel. (750) 2618888; fax (750) 2613288; internet www.moftec.gov.cn /moftec/company/guangdongwanli/indexc.html; construction machinery.

Guangxi Penshibao Co Ltd: Dong Beibuwan Lu, Beihai, Guangxi 536007; tel. (779) 2061699; fax (779) 2050999; e-mail psb@ppp.nn.gx.cn; f. 1985; cap. and res 100m., sales 70m. (1996); foliage fertilizer, plant growth regulator, feed additives, products for agricultural purposes; Pres. WANG XIANGLIN; 500 employees.

Guizhou Elixir of Longevity Group Co: Zhenzhu Lu, Zhenyi, Guizhou 563000; tel. (852) 225273; fax (852) 221988; f. 1985; cap. and res 45m., sales 82m. (1995); 17 corporate mems; pharmaceutical products, healthcare; Pres. ZENG CHAOWEN; 500 employees.

Haci Group Co Ltd: 169 Tongxiang Jie, Harbin, Heilongjiang 150046; tel. (451) 2688688; fax (451) 2686244; f. 1992; cap. and res 28m., sales 110m. (1995); 12 corporate mems; magnetic healthcare products, food engineering; Pres. GE LIWEN; 480 employees.

Haier Group: Inside Haier Garden, Haier Industrial Park, Haier Lu, Qingdao 266101; tel. (532) 8938888; fax (532) 8938666; e-mail info@haier.com; internet www.haier.com; f. 1991; sales US $3,244.0m. (1999/2000); household appliances, pharmaceuticals, air conditioners, refrigerators; Pres. ZHANG RUIMIN; Vice-Pres. SHAO MINGJIN; 18,901 employees.

Hainan Zhongfei (Group) Industry Co Ltd: 2 Zhongfei Bldg, 13 Jichang Dong Lu, Haikou, Hainan; tel. (898) 6796656; fax (898) 6796659; f. 1987; cap. and res 280m., sales 540m. (1995); 27 corporate mems; import and export, real estate, travel and hotels, development of ports, trade; Pres. XIE FEI; 1,200 employees.

Harbin Pharmaceutical Group Co Ltd: 94 Gongchang Lu, Harbin, Heilongjiang 150018; tel. and fax (451) 4604688; f. 1991; revenue US $778.4m. (2000); China's biggest pharmaceuticals company (2000).

Hebei Kangda Fine Chemicals Co: 18 Hongqi Lu, Baoding, Hebei 071000; tel. (312) 231180; fax (312) 233502; f. 1989; cap. and res 16m., sales 24m. (1995); chemicals, pesticides; Pres. ZUO YULONG; 500 employees.

Heibei Qifa Textiles Co Ltd: Xinxingzhen, Lixian County, Hebei 071400; tel. (312) 6561178; f. 1988; cap. and res 30m., sales 120m. (1995); pure knitting wool, chemical fibres, worsted woollen products; Pres. WANG QIFA; 1,100 employees.

Henan Huayu Science and Technology Enterprise Co: 27 South Section, Dongming Lu, Zhengzhou, Henan 450004; tel. (371) 6229005; fax (371) 6229030; f. 1990; cap. and res 25m., sales 18m. (1995); healthcare products; Pres. MENG RUI; 180 employees.

Henan Star Science and Technology (Group) Co Ltd: 31 Nongye Lu, Zhengzhou, Henan 450053; tel. (371) 3812266; fax (371) 3810075; f. 1988; cap. and res 46m., sales 29m. (1995); 24 corporate mems; electric measurement equipment, telecommunication systems, biotech-related healthcare products, chemical building materials; Pres. WANG YUANSI; 510 employees.

Huaibei Chemical Industry Group Co Ltd: Xiangyang Lu, Xiangshan Qu, Huaibei, Anhui 235000; tel. (561) 3021985; fax (561) 3035567; f. 1992; cap. and res 32m., sales 90m. (1995); 5 corporate mems; chemicals, plastic tubes; Pres. WANG PING; 400 employees.

Hubei Tianlong Real Estate Development Co Ltd: 106 Yanjiang Dajie, Hankou, Wuhan, Hubei 430014; tel. (27) 2821597; fax (27) 2848335; f. 1988; cap. and res 65m., sales 128m. (1995); real estate, building materials, machinery and electric products, auto parts, chemicals, garments, furniture, textiles, trade; Pres. ZHONG SHIJIE; 380 employees.

Hunan Tianli Science and Technology Development Co Ltd: Nanhua South Lu, Nanxian County, Hunan 413200; tel. (737) 5223821; fax (737) 5223189; f. 1986; cap. and res 24m., sales 48m. (1995); 11 corporate mems; synthetic liquid fuel, liquid fuel pile sprayer, trade; Pres. WU YONG; 430 employees.

Jiangsu Yinshan Industry Co Ltd: Qilin Town, Zhongshanmenwai, Nanjing, Jiangsu 211135; tel. (25) 2298699; f. 1988; cap. and res 128m., sales 150m. (1995); 5 corporate mems; shutters, decorating materials, auto parts; Pres. BAO BIUYUAN; 4,000 employees.

Jiangxi Binhua Cement Co Ltd: Chengdong Development Zone, Xinyu, Jiangxi 336512; tel. (790) 442364; f. 1988; cap. and res 14m., sales 24m. (1995); cement; Pres. LIAO BINHUA; 800 employees.

Jilin Batong Economic and Trade Co Ltd: 1 Qianjin Dajie, Changchun, Jilin 130012; tel. and fax (431) 5956790; f. 1989; cap. and res. 21m., sales 670m. (1995); 3 corporate mems; electronics, hotels, fisheries, trading; Pres. LI XUYOU; 300 employees.

Jilin Chemical Industrial Co Ltd: 31 Zunyi Dong Jie, Jilin 132021; tel. (432) 3976445; fax (432) 3028146; e-mail webmaster@jcic.com.cn; internet www.jcic.com; production and sale of petroleum and chemical products; revenue US $1,618m. (2000); Chair. JIAO HAIKUN; 6,500 employees.

Jingwei Textile Machinery Co Ltd: 150 Jingwei Jie, Yuci, Shanxi; tel. (354) 2422878; fax (354) 2425428; manufacture and sale of textile machinery; distribution of computers; cap. and res 658.5m., sales 81.1m. (1998); Chair. YIN JUNDE; 5,505 employees.

Jinzhou Petrochemical: 2 Chongqing Lu, Guta, Jinzhou, Liaoning 121001; tel. and fax (416) 4159024; f. 1997; petroleum processing and coking; revenue US $1,094.8m. (2000).

Konka Group Co Ltd: internet www.konka.com; consumer electronics; revenue US $1,089.1m. (2000).

Kunming Machine Tool Co Ltd: 23 Ciba Jie, Kunming, Yunnan 650203; tel. (871) 5212411; fax (871) 5150317; design, development and production of machine tools, precision-measuring equipment, etc.; cap. and res 521.4m., sales 47.3m. (1998); Chair. YE XIANGYU; 3,077 employees.

Legend Group Corpn: 10 Kexueyuan Nan Lu, Haidian Qu, Beijing 100080; tel. (10) 62572181; fax (10) 62570209; e-mail ccd @.legendgrp.com; internet www.legend.com.cn; f. 1984; mfr of personal computers; sales US $2,237.1m. (1999/2000); Chair. and CEO LIU CHUANZHI; 5,000 employees.

New Hope Group Co Ltd: No. 45, Sec. 4, Ren Ming Nan Lu, Chengdu, Sichuan 610041; tel. (28) 5225052; fax (28) 5233678; e-mail nhg@mail.sc.cninfo.net; internet www.newhopegroup.com;

f. 1983; cap. and res 2,500m., sales 6,200m. (1997); 100 corporate mems; animal feed, food, trade; Pres. LIU YONGHAO; 15,000 employees.

Panzhihua New Steel and Vanadium Co Ltd: Nongnong Ping, Panzhihua, Sichuan 617067; tel. (812) 2226008; fax (812) 2226014; f. 1993; metal (incl. high vanadium steel) manufacturing and exports; Rep. HONG JIBI.

Petrochina Co. Ltd: 16 Andelu Xicheng District, Beijing; tel. (10) 84886034; fax (10) 84886039; e-mail webmaster@petrochina.com.cn; internet www.petrochina.com.cn; exploration, development, and production of crude oil and natural gas, and refining, transport, storage, and trade of crude petroleum and its products; sales US $21,256.7m. (1999/2000); Chair. MA FUCAI.

Qingdao Guotai Group Co: 171 Shandong Lu, Sifang Qu, Qingdao, Shandong 266033; tel. (532) 3826502; f. 1987; cap. and res 22m., sales 56m. (1995); 16 corporate mems; mfrs of hardware, electrical goods, chemicals, building materials, garments, footwear, carpets, textiles, trade; Pres. CHEN SHOUGUO; 800 employees.

Qingqi Motorcycle: 34 Heping Lu, Jinan; tel. (531) 6953325; fax (531) 6954219; e-mail jnqqxx@public.jn.sd.cn; internet www .china-qingqi.com/; China's largest producer of motor cycles; Pres. ZHANG JIALING.

Shaanxi Zhenxing Industrial Development Co Ltd: Beichitoucun, Qujiang Township, Xian, Shaanxi 710061; tel. and fax (29) 7279122; f. 1989; cap. and res 15m., sales 46m. (1995); 4 corporate mems; transport, machinery, building materials, trade; Pres. GE ZHENXING; 400 employees.

Shandong Tongda Economic & Technology Corporation: Science and Technology Bldg, 198 Heping Lu, Weifang, Shandong 261021; tel. (536) 321181; fax (536) 321185; f. 1985; cap. and res 460m., sales 130m. (1995); 12 corporate mems; real estate, education, finance, trade, hotels; Pres. LU ZHIQIANG; 480 employees.

Shandong Xinhua Pharmaceutical Co Ltd: 14 Dongyi Jie, Zhangdian Qu, Zibo, Shandong 255005; tel. (533) 2184223; fax (533) 2184991; f. 1943; manufacture and sale of pharmaceuticals; cap. and res 863.8m., sales 973.9m. (1998); Chair. HE DUANSHI; 6,500 employees.

Shanggong Co Ltd: 61 Zhong Hua Jie, Shanghai 200010; manufacture and sale of sewing machines; cap. and res 430.4m., sales 481.1m. (1997); Chair. NI YONGGANG.

Shanghai Automation Instrumentation Co Ltd: 1421 Beijing Jie, Shanghai 200040; tel. (21) 62471057; fax (21) 62791199; f. 1993; manufacture of control systems and meters for industrial use; cap. and res 547.9m., sales 960.8m. (1998); Chair. ZHOU YONGQING; 14,167 employees.

Shanghai Chlor-Alkali Chemical Co Ltd: 47 Longwu Jie, Shanghai 200241; tel. (21) 64340000; fax (21) 64341341; e-mail public@styc.com; internet www.scacc.com; f. 1992; production of industrial chemicals; cap. and res 2,739.4m., sales 2,406.6m. (1997); Chair. XU RONGYI; 9,759 employees.

Shanghai Dajiang (Group) Stock Co Ltd: 26 Guyang Nan Lu, Songjiang, Shanghai 201600; tel. (21) 57822480; fax (21) 57820072; f. 1985; production and sale of animal feed and feed machinery; cap. and res 840.2m., sales 2,354.5m. (1996); Chair. DU SHUGU; 1,300 employees.

Shanghai Erfangji Co Ltd: 265 Chang Zhong Jie, Shanghai 200434; tel. (21) 65318888; fax (21) 65421963; f. 1944; manufacture and sale of textile machinery; cap. and res 746.8m., sales 428.2m. (1997); Chair. ZHENG KEQIN; 5,000 employees.

Shanghai Forever Bicycle Co Ltd: 1357 Zhou Jiazui Jie, Shanghai 200082; tel. (21) 65461514; fax (21) 65458657; design, manufacture and distribution of bicycles; cap. and res 502.0m., sales 729.4m. (1997); Chair. TAO GUOQIANG.

Shanghai Haixin Group Co Ltd; Dongjing Town, Song Jian, Shanghai 201601; tel. (21) 57680168; fax (21) 57610180; f. 1931; manufacture and sale of plush and flannel materials; cap. and res 683.4m., sales 887.6m. (1997); Chair. CHEN JUNMIN; 700 employees.

Shanghai Hongyuan Lighting Equipment Co Ltd: 2 Dehua Lu, Nanxiang Town, Jiading Qu, Shanghai 201802; tel. (21) 59121949; fax (21) 59124464; f. 1987; cap. and res 8m., sales 12m. (1995); 3 corporate mems; high-voltage sodium lamps, lighting equipment and components; Pres. LI WEIDE; 390 employees.

Shanghai Huili Building Materials Co Ltd: 4131 Changma Jie, Zhoupu, Pudong, Shanghai 201318; tel. (21) 58113390; fax (21) 58113449; development, production and sale of wall coatings and PVC flooring; cap. and res 208.5m., sales 196.7m. (1997); Chair. ZHANG YONGDING.

Shanghai Tyre and Rubber Co Ltd: 97 Ji Mo Jie, Pudong New Area, Shanghai 200120; tel. (21) 63290433; fax (21) 63299609; tyres and machinery for production of rubber products; cap. and res 1,827.4m., sales 4,396.3m. (1997); Chair. JIANG YINGSHI; 12,000 employees.

Shanghai Volkswagen Automotive Company Ltd: 63 Antingluopu Lu, Shanghai 201805; tel. (21) 59561888; fax (21) 59572815; jt venture between Volkswagen (Germany) and Shanghai Automotive Industry Corpn to manufacture cars; sales US $3,230.2m. (1999/2000); Chair. LU JIAN.

Shanxi Zhongshan Co Ltd: Shanxi 030002; tel. (351) 2029148; fax (351) 2029984; f. 1986; cap. and res 35m., sales 180m. (1995); coal, mechanical and electric products, auto parts, chemicals, metals, minerals, decorating materials, farm produce, garments, shoes, caps; Pres. HE ZHONG; 1,650 employees.

Shenyang Qiangfeng Group Co: 130-1 Huanghe N. Dajie, Huanggu Qu, Shenyang, Liaoning 110034; tel. (24) 6802626; fax (24) 6801699; f. 1985; cap and res 30m., sales 148m. (1995); 12 corporate mems; building materials, food processing; Pres. KANG BAOXUN; 300 employees.

Shenyang Xiehe Group Co: A8, 19 Sanhaojie, Heping, Shenyang, Liaoning 110003; tel. and fax (24) 3896916; f. 1988; cap. and res 12m., sales 31m. (1995); 3 corporate mems; pharmaceutical products, healthcare, software; Pres. CHEN JUYU; 350 employees.

Shenzhen Mingya Industry Co Ltd: 29th Floor, Tower 2, Nanguo Bldg, Yuanlin Garden, Shenzhen, Guangdong 518028; tel. (755) 5599500; fax (755) 8838478; f. 1989; cap. and res 80m., sales 148m. (1995); 8 corporate mems; real estate, hotels, computers, building materials, trade; Pres. YANG XIAOMING; 120 employees.

Shenzhen Textile (Holdings) Co Ltd: 6th Floor, Shen Fang Bldg, 3 Hua Qiang North Jie, Shenzhen; tel. (755) 3217039; fax (755) 3360139; manufacture of textiles, garments and related products; cap. and res 342.9m., sales 208.6m. (1997); Chair. ZHANG YINGXUE; 1,000 employees.

Sichuan Changhong Electric Co Ltd: 4 Yuejin Lu, Mianyang 621000; tel. (816) 2411114; fax (816) 2337518; f. 1988; manufacture of electrical appliances, electronic components and computers; sales US $1,401.6m. (1999/2000); Chair. NI FUNRENG; 6,500 employees.

Tangshan Iron and Steel Co Ltd: 9 Binhe Lu, Tangshan, Hebei 063016; tel. (315) 2702941; fax (315) 2702198; f. 1995; revenue US $839.1m. (2000); manufacturing of ferrous metals.

Tian Jin Da Heng (Group) Co: 588 Jintang Lu, Tianjin 300300; tel. (22) 24993988; fax (22) 24993986; internet www.daheng.com.cn; f. 1988; cap. and res 50m., sales 300m. (1995); 8 corporate mems; foods and beverages; Pres. WU ZHENGHAI; 1,800 employees.

Wuhan Steel Processing Co Ltd: 3 Yangang Lu, Qingshan Qu, Wuhan Hubei 430080; tel. (27) 86306023; fax (27) 86807873; internet www.wisco.com.cn; f. 1997; revenue US $836.5m. (2000); metals manufacturing; Chair. LIU BENREN.

Wuxi Little Swan Co Ltd: 67 Huiqian Jie, Wuxi 214035; tel. (510) 3704003; fax (510) 3704031; f. 1979; design, development, manufacture and sale of domestic washing machines; cap. and res 1,004.9m. (1996), sales 1,839m. (1997); Chair. ZHU DEKUN.

Xiamen Lianyou Auto Transport Co: 6th Floor, Jindao Hotel, Lianyue Zhonglu, Xiamen, Fujian 361012; tel. (592) 5081698; f. 1987; cap. and res 45m., sales 24m. (1995); 2 corporate mems; transport, auto maintenance, trade, travel; Pres. ZHENG HUISHAN; 300 employees.

Xiangyang-Anti-Aging Institute of Shaanxi: 3 Leyou Bei Lu, Xiangyang, Shaanxi 712000; tel. (910) 3218328; fax (910) 3218606; f. 1988; cap. and res 180m., sales 110m. (1995); 6 corporate mems; pharmaceutical products, healthcare; Pres. LAI HUIWU; 460 employees.

Yunnan Roada High Tech Group Co Ltd: 179 Beijing Lu, Kunming, Yunnan 650051; tel. (871) 5157550; fax (871) 5157551; f. 1988; cap. and res 13m., sales 55m. (1995); 13 corporate mems; minerals, machinery and electric products, real estate, travel, flowers, pharmaceutical products, healthcare, trade; Pres. LUO ZHIHUI; 460 employees.

Zhejiang Huaji Industry and Trade Corporation: Chengguan, Tiantai County, Zhejiang 317200; tel. (576) 3881778; fax (576) 3884988; f. 1988; cap. and res 12m., sales 220m. (1995); 11 corporate mems; chemicals, plastics, tourism, hotels, trading; Pres. ZHAO SHENGHUA; 1,000 employees.

Zhejiang Zhongda Group Co Ltd: 21/F, Tower A, Zhongda Plaza, Hangzhou 310003; tel. (571) 85155000; fax (571) 85777050; internet zhongda.zj-zhongda.com; revenue US $787.8m. (2000); garments and textiles; diversifying into other consumer industries, etc.

Zhenhai Refining and Chemical Co Ltd: Zhenhai Qu, Ningbo, Zhejiang; tel. (574) 6456425; fax (574) 6456155; f. 1974; petroleum refining and production of related chemicals; sales US $1,330.6m. (1999/2000); Chair. ZHANG JIAREN.

Zhengzhou Dahua Furnace Charge Development Co Ltd: 1 Gongnong Lu, Zhengzhou, Henan 450007; tel. (371) 7972805; f. 1984; cap. and res 38m., sales 48m. (1995); fire-proof materials, real estate, building materials, hotel and tourism, trade; Pres. ZHAO HONGJIANG; 600 employees.

TRADE UNIONS

All-China Federation of Trade Unions (ACFTU): 10 Fu Xing Men Wai Jie, Beijing 100865; tel. (10) 68592114; fax (10) 68562030; f. 1925; organized on an industrial basis; 15 affiliated national industrial unions, 30 affiliated local trade union councils; membership is voluntary; trade unionists enjoy extensive benefits; 103,996,000 mems (1995); Chair. WEI JIANXING; First Sec. ZHANG JUNJIU.

Principal affiliated unions:

All-China Federation of Railway Workers' Unions: Chair. HUANG SICHUAN.

Architectural Workers' Trade Union: Sec. SONG ANRU.

China Self-Employed Workers' Association: Pres. REN ZHONGLIN.

Educational Workers' Trade Union: Chair. JIANG WENLIANG.

Light Industrial Workers' Trade Union: Chair. LI SHUYING.

Machinery Metallurgical Workers' Union: Chair. ZHANG CUNEN.

National Defence Workers' Union: Chair. GUAN HENGCAI.

Postal and Telecommunications Workers' Trade Union of China: Chair. LUO SHUZHEN.

Seamen's Trade Union of China: Chair. ZHANG SHIHUI.

Water Resources and Electric Power Workers' Trade Union: Chair. DONG YUNQI.

Workers' Autonomous Federation (WAF): f. 1989; aims to create new trade union movement in China, independent of the All-China Federation of Trade Unions.

Transport

RAILWAYS

Ministry of Railways: 10 Fuxing Lu, Haidian Qu, Beijing 100844; tel. (10) 63244150; fax (10) 63242150; e-mail webmaster@ns .chinamor.cn.net; internet www.chinamor.cn.net; controls all railways through regional divisions. The railway network has been extended to all provinces and regions except Tibet (Xizang), where construction is in progress. Total length in operation in December 2000 was 58,656 km, of which 14,864 km were electrified. The major routes include Beijing–Guangzhou, Tianjin–Shanghai, Manzhouli–Vladivostok, Jiaozuo–Zhicheng and Lanzhou–Badou. In addition, special railways serve factories and mines. A new 2,536-km line from Beijing to Kowloon (Hong Kong) was completed in late 1995. Plans for a 1,450-km high-speed link between Beijing and Shanghai were announced in 1994, and construction was scheduled to begin by 2005. A high-speed link between Beijing and Guangzhou was also planned. China's first high-speed service, linking Guangzhou and Shenzhen, commenced in December 1994. A direct service between Shanghai and Hong Kong commenced in 1997. A new magnetic-levitation ('maglev') railway linking Shanghai to Pudong International airport was being built in co-operation with a German consortium in 2002.

An extensive programme to develop the rail network was announced in early 1998, which aimed to increase the total network to 68,000 km by the year 2000, and to more than 75,000 km by 2005. Railways were to be constructed along the Changjiang valley, starting at Sichuan, and along China's east coast, originating at Harbin. In December 1999 plans were announced for a railway to Kazakhstan. In June 2001 construction began on a new 1,118-km railway linking Tibet with the rest of China, to be completed after 10 years.

City Underground Railways

Beijing Metro Corpn: 2 Beiheyan Lu, Xicheng, Beijing 100044; tel. (10) 68024566; f. 1969; total length 54 km, with 98 km of further lines to be built by the year 2010; Gen. Man. FENG SHUANGSHENG.

Guangzhou Metro: 204 Huanshi Lu, Guangzhou 510010; tel. (20) 6665287; fax (20) 6678232; opened June 1997; total length of 18.5 km, with a further 133 km planned; Gen. Man. CHEN QINGQUAN.

Shanghai Metro Corpn: 12 Heng Shan Lu, Shanghai 200031; tel. (21) 64312460; fax (21) 64339598; f. 1995; 65.8 km open, with at least a further 181.5 km under construction or planned; Pres. SHI LIAN.

Tianjin Metro: 97 Jiefangbei Lu, Heping, Tianjin 300041; tel. (22) 23395410; fax (22) 23396194; f. 1984; total planned network 154 km; Gen. Man. WANG YUJI.

Underground systems were under construction in Chongqing, Nanjing, and Shenzhen, and planned for Chengdu and Qingdao.

ROADS

At the end of 2000 China had 1,402,698 km of highways (of which at least 90% were paved). Four major highways link Lhasa (Tibet) with Sichuan, Xinjiang, Qinghai Hu and Kathmandu (Nepal). A programme of expressway construction began in the mid-1980s. By 2000 there were 16,314 km of expressways (1,313 km of which were constructed in 1997), routes including the following: Shenyang–Dalian, Beijing–Tanggu, Shanghai–Jiading, Guangzhou–Foshan and Xian–Lintong. Expressway construction was to continue, linking all main cities and totalling 55,000 km by 2020. A new 123-km highway linking Shenzhen (near the border with Hong Kong) to Guangzhou opened in 1994. A 58-km road between Guangzhou and Zhongshan connects with Zhuhai, near the border with Macao. Construction of a bridge, linking Zhuhai with Macao, began in June 1998 and was completed in late 1999. A bridge connecting the mainland with Hong Kong was to be built, with completion scheduled for the year 2004. In 1997 some 20% of villages in China were not connected to the road infrastructure.

INLAND WATERWAYS

At the end of 2000 there were some 119,325 km of navigable inland waterways in China. The main navigable rivers are the Changjiang (Yangtze River), the Zhujiang (Pearl River), the Heilongjiang, the Grand Canal and the Xiangjiang. The Changjiang is navigable by vessels of 10,000 tons as far as Wuhan, more than 1,000 km from the coast. Vessels of 1,000 tons can continue to Chongqing upstream.

There were 5,142 river ports at the end of 1996. In 1997 there were some 5,100 companies involved in inland waterway shipping.

SHIPPING

China has a network of more than 2,000 ports, of which more than 130 are open to foreign vessels. In May 2001 plans were announced for the biggest container port in the world to be built on the Yangshan Islands, off shore from Shanghai. The main ports include Dalian, Qinhuangdao, Tianjin, Yantai, Qingdao, Rizhao, Lianyungang, Shanghai, Ningbo, Guangzhou and Zhanjiang. In 2000 the main coastal ports handled 1,219m. metric tons of cargo. In December 2001 China's merchant fleet comprised 3,280 ships, totalling 16.6m. grt.

Bureau of Water Transportation: Beijing; controls rivers and coastal traffic.

China International Marine Containers Group Co Ltd: 5/F, Finance Centre, Shekou, Shenzhen 518067; tel. (755) 26691130; fax (755) 26692707; internet www.cimc.com; f. 1980; container-manufacturing, supply and storage; revenue US $1,081.6m. (2000); Chair. and Dir. LI JIANHONG.

China National Chartering Corpn (SINOCHART): see Trade and Industrial Organizations.

China Ocean Shipping (Group) Co (COSCO): 11th and 12th Floors, Ocean Plaza, 158 Fu Xing Men Nei, Xi Cheng Qu Chao Yang Qu, Beijing 100031; tel. (10) 66493388; fax (10) 66492288; internet www.cosco.com.cn; reorg. 1993, re-established 1997; head office transferred to Tianjin late 1997; br. offices: Shanghai, Guangzhou, Tianjin, Qingdao, Dalian; 200 subsidiaries (incl. China Ocean Shipping Agency—PENAVIC) and joint ventures in China and abroad, engaged in ship-repair, container-manufacturing, warehousing, insurance, etc.; merchant fleet of 600 vessels; 47 routes; Pres. WEI JIAFU.

China Shipping (Group) Co: Shanghai; f. 1997; Pres. LI KELIN.

China Shipping Container Lines Co Ltd: 5th Floor, Shipping Tower, 700 Dong Da Ming Lu, Shanghai 200080; tel. (21) 65966978; fax (21) 65966498; Chair. LI SHAODE.

China Shipping Development Co Ltd Tanker Co: 168 Yuanshen Lu, Pudong New Area, Shanghai 200120; tel. (21) 68757170; fax (21) 68757929.

Fujian Shipping Co: 151 Zhong Ping Lu, Fuzhou 350009; tel. (591) 3259900; fax (591) 3259716; e-mail fusco@pub2.fz.fj.cn; internet www.fusco-cn.com; f. 1950; transport of bulk cargo, crude petroleum products, container and related services; Gen. Man. LIU QIMIN.

Guangzhou Maritime Transport (Group) Co: 22 Shamian Nan Jie, Guangzhou; tel. (20) 84104673; fax (20) 84103074.

CIVIL AVIATION

Air travel is expanding very rapidly. In 2000 a total of 139 civil airports were in operation. Chinese airlines carried a total of 67.2m. passengers in 2000. In 1998 there were 34 airlines, including numerous private companies, operating in China. During 2001–02 a number of regional airlines were in the process of forming alliances and mergers. The Government planned to merge the 10 CAAC (see below) airlines into three large groups, based in Guangzhou, Shanghai and Beijing. **Air China** was planned to incorporate **China National Aviation Corpn** and **China Southwest Airlines**; **China Eastern Airlines** was to incorporate **China Northwest Airlines, Great Wall**, and **Yunnan Airlines**; and **China Southern Airlines** was to incorporate **Air Xinjiang** and **China Northern Airlines**.

General Administration of Civil Aviation of China (CAAC): POB 644, 155 Dongsixi Jie, Beijing 100710; tel. (10) 64014104; fax (10) 64016918; f. 1949 as Civil Aviation Administration of China; restructured in 1988 as a purely supervisory agency, its operational functions being transferred to new, semi-autonomous airlines (see below; also China United Airlines (division of the Air Force) and China Capital Helicopter Service); domestic flights throughout China; external services are mostly operated by **Air China, China Eastern** and **China Southern Airlines**; Dir Liu Jianfeng.

Air China: Beijing International Airport, POB 644, Beijing 100621; tel. (10) 64599068; fax (10) 64599064; e-mail webmaster@mail.airchina.com.cn; internet www.airchina.com.cn; international and domestic scheduled passenger and cargo services; Pres. Wang Kaiyuan.

China Eastern Airlines: 2550 Hongqiao Rd, Hongqiao Airport, Shanghai 200335; tel. (21) 62686268; fax (21) 62686116; e-mail webmaster@cea.online.sh.cn; internet www.cea.online.sh.cn; f. 1987; domestic services; overseas destinations include USA, Europe, Japan, Sydney, Singapore, Seoul and Bangkok; Pres. Liu Shaoyong.

China Northern Airlines: 3-1 Xiaoheyan Lu, Dadong Qu, Shenyang, Liaoning 110043; tel. (24) 88294432; fax (24) 88294037; e-mail northern_air@163.net; internet www.cna.com.cn; f. 1990; scheduled flights to the Republic of Korea, Russia, Hong Kong, Macao and Japan; Pres. Jiang Lianying.

China Northwest Airlines: Laodong Nan Lu, Xian, Shaanxi 710082; tel. (29) 7298000; fax (29) 8624068; e-mail cnwadzz@pub.xa-online.sn.cn; internet www.cnwa.com; f. 1992; domestic services and flights to Macao, Singapore and Japan; Pres. Gao Junqui.

China Southwest Airlines: Shuangliu Airport, Chengdu, Sichuan 610202; tel. (28) 5814466; fax (28) 5582630; e-mail szmaster@cswa.com; internet www.cswa.com; f. 1987; 70 domestic routes; international services to Singapore, Bangkok, Japan, the Republic of Korea and Kathmandu (Nepal); Pres. Zhou Zhengquan.

Changan Airlines: 16/F, Jierui Bldg, 5 South Er Huan Rd, Xian, Shaanxi 710068; tel. (29) 8707412; fax (29) 8707911; e-mail liulei@hnair.com; internet www.changanair.com; f. 1992; local passenger and cargo services; Pres. She Yining.

China General Aviation Corpn: Wusu Airport, Taiyuan, Shanxi 030031; tel. (351) 7040600; fax (351) 7040094; f. 1989; 34 domestic routes; Pres. Zhang Changjing.

China Southern Airlines: Baiyuan International Airport, Guangzhou, Guangdong 510406; tel. (20) 86128473; fax (20) 86658989; e-mail webmaster@cs-air.com; internet www.cs-air.com; f. 1991; merged with Zhong Yuan Airlines, 2000; domestic services; overseas destinations include Bangkok, Fukuoka, Hanoi, Ho Chi Minh City, Kuala Lumpur, Penang, Singapore, Manila, Vientiane, Jakarta and Surabaya; Chair. Liang Huanfu; Pres. Wang Changshun.

China Xinhua Airlines: 1 Jinsong Nan Lu, Chao Yang Qu, Beijing 100021; tel. (10) 67740116; fax (10) 67740126; e-mail infocxh@homeway.com.cn; internet www.chinaxinhuaair.com; f. 1992; Pres. Zhao Zhongying.

China Xinjiang Airlines: Diwopu International Airport, Urumqi 830016; tel. (991) 3801703; fax (991) 3711084; f. 1985; 30 domestic routes; international services to Kazakhstan, Russia, Pakistan, and Uzbekistan; Pres. Zhang Ruifu.

Hainan Airlines: Haihang Devt Bldg, 29 Haixiu Lu, Haikou, Hainan 570206; tel. (898) 6711524; fax (898) 6798976; e-mail webmaster@hnair.com; internet www.hnair.com; f. 1989; undergoing major expansion in 2001–02; 300 domestic services; international services to Korea; Chair. Feng Chen.

Shandong Airlines: Jinan International Airport, Jinan, Shandong 250107; tel. (531) 8734625; fax (531) 8734616; e-mail webmaster@shandongair.com.cn; internet www.shandongair.com f. 1994; domestic services; Pres. Sun Dehan.

Shanghai Air Lines: 212 Jiangming Lu, Shanghai 200040; tel. (21) 62558888; fax (21) 62558885; e-mail liw@shanghai-air.com; internet www.shanghai-air.com; f. 1985; domestic services; also serves Phnom-Penh (Cambodia); Pres. Zhou Chi.

Shenzhen Airlines: Lingtian Tian, Lingxiao Garden, Shenzhen Airport, Shenzhen, Guangdong 518128; tel. (755) 7771999; fax (755) 7777242; internet www.shenzhenair.com; f. 1993; domestic services; Pres. Duan Dayang.

Sichuan Airlines: Chengdu Shuangliu International Airport, Chengdu, Sichuan 610202; tel. (28) 5393001; fax (28) 5393888; e-mail scaloi@public.cd.sc.cn; internet www.hpis.com/sichuan/sichuan.htm; f. 1986; domestic services; Pres. Lan Xingguo.

Wuhan Air Lines: 435 Jianshe Dajie, Wuhan 430030; tel. (87) 63603888; fax (87) 83625693; e-mail wuhanair@public.wh.hb.cn; f. 1986; domestic services; Pres. Cheng Yaokun.

Xiamen Airlines: Gaoqi International Airport, Xiamen, Fujian 361009; tel. (592) 5739888; fax (592) 5739777; internet www.xiamenair.com.cn; f. 1992; domestic services; also serves Bangkok (Thailand); Pres. Wu Rongnan.

Yunnan Airlines: Wujaba Airport, Kunming 650200; tel. (871) 7112999; fax (871) 7151509; internet www.chinayunnanair.com; f. 1992; 49 domestic services; also serves Bangkok, Singapore, and Vientiane (Laos); Pres. Xue Xiaoming.

Zhejiang Airlines: Jian Qiao Airport, 78 Shiqiao Lu, Hangzhou, Zhejiang 310021; tel. (571) 8082490; fax (571) 5173015; e-mail zjair@public.hz.zj.cn; internet www.zjair.com; f. 1990; domestic services; Pres. Luo Qiang.

Tourism

China has enormous potential for tourism, and the sector is developing rapidly. Attractions include dramatic scenery and places of historical interest such as the Temple of Heaven and the Forbidden City in Beijing, the Great Wall, the Ming Tombs, and also the terracotta warriors at Xian. Tibet (Xizang), with its monasteries and temples, has also been opened to tourists. Tours of China are organized for groups of visitors, and Western-style hotels have been built as joint ventures in many areas. By 2000 10,481 tourist hotels were in operation. A total of 83.44m. tourists visited China in 2000. In that year receipts from tourism totalled US $16,224m.

China International Travel Service (CITS): 103 Fu Xing Men Nei Dajie, Beijing 100800; tel. (10) 66011122; fax (10) 66039331; e-mail mktng@cits.com.cn; internet www.cits.net; f. 1954; makes travel arrangements for foreign tourists; subsidiary overseas companies in 10 countries and regions; Pres. Li Luan.

China National Tourism Administration (CNTA): 9A Jian Guo Men Nei Dajie, Beijing 100740; tel. (10) 65138866; fax (10) 65122096; Dir He Guangwei.

Chinese People's Association for Friendship with Foreign Countries: 1 Tai Ji Chang Dajie, Beijing 100740; tel. (10) 65122474; fax (10) 65128354; f. 1954; Pres. Qi Huaiyuan; Sec.-Gen. Bian Qingzu.

State Bureau of Tourism: Jie 3, Jian Guo Men Nei Dajie, Beijing 100740; tel. (10) 65122847; fax (10) 65122095; Dir Liu Yi.

Defence

China is divided into seven major military administrative units. All armed services are grouped in the People's Liberation Army (PLA). In August 2001 total forces were estimated at 2,310,000 (of whom 1,000,000 were conscripts): army 1,600,000, navy 250,000 (including a coastal defence force, a naval air force of 26,000 and a marine force of 5,000), air force 420,000 (including 220,000 air defence personnel). In addition, the forces of the strategic rocket units totalled 100,000. Reserves numbered some 500,000–600,000. Paramilitary forces totalled an estimated 1.5m. Military service is usually by selective conscription, and is for two years in all services.

Defence Expenditure: Budgeted at 120,500m. yuan for 2000.

Chairman of the CCP Central Military Commission (Commander-in-Chief): Jiang Zemin.

Vice-Chairmen: Hu Jintao, Gen. Chi Haotian, Gen. Zhang Wannian.

Director of the General Political Department (Chief Political Commissar): Gen. Yu Yongbo.

Chief of General Staff: Gen. Fu Quanyou.

Commander, PLA Navy: Adm. Shi Yunsheng.

Commander, PLA Air Force: Gen. Qiao Qingchen.

Director, General Logistics Department: Gen. Wang Ke.

Commanders of Military Regions: Lt-Gen. Zhu Qi (Beijing), Gen. Liao Xilong (Chengdu), Gen. Tao Bojun (Guangzhou), Gen. Chen Bingde (Jinan), Lt-Gen. Li Qianyuan (Lanzhou), Gen. Liang Guanglie (Nanjing), Gen. Qian Guoliang (Shenyang).

Education

In May 1985 the CCP Central Committee adopted a decision to reform the country's whole educational structure. This stipulated that nine-year compulsory education was to be implemented in stages, with the date of attaining that goal varying according to regional disparities in development. By the year 2000 it was envisaged that nine-year education would be compulsory for 85% of the population. Fees are payable at all levels of education. The 1997 budget allocated an estimated 118,907m. yuan to education. Private education is expanding rapidly, the number of private schools being estimated at 2,000 in early 1995.

According to the census of July 1990, there were 182,246,000 illiterates and semi-illiterates among the population aged 15 years and over, representing 22.3% of the population. In 2000 a total of 2.58m. adults completed basic literacy courses.

Pre-School Education

Kindergartens are regarded as important in introducing children to ideas that will shape their thought in later life; the education takes the form of games, sports and music. The kindergartens also have economic significance in releasing women for productive work. In 2000 a total of 22.4m. children were enrolled in the 175,836 kindergartens.

Primary Education

Most primary schools have adopted a five- or six-year course. The curriculum includes Chinese language, mathematics, natural science, geography, history, music and art. Senior pupils are required to spend some time engaged in manual labour. In 2000 there were 130.1m. primary school pupils enrolled in 553,622 schools.

Secondary Education

Junior secondary education (in which the enrolment rate was 82.4% in 1996) lasts for three years, followed by upper secondary education for two to three years. The curriculum includes Chinese, mathematics, foreign languages, politics, history, geography, science, music and art. There are also specialized secondary schools which offer subjects such as engineering, medicine, agriculture, business administration and law. Four weeks are set aside for physical labour and technical training, although in rural areas many schools allow pupils to spend time instead engaged in agricultural work, while some schools run their own factories. In 2000 there were 73.7m. students at 77,268 general secondary schools and 4.1m. students at 4,125 secondary technical schools.

Higher Education

University courses last for four or five years, but, in line with the general reform of the whole system, emphasis is being shifted to the establishment of shorter vocational courses (lasting for two to three years), while the proportion of students in the fields of finance and economics, political science and law, management and liberal arts is being increased. Entrance to most courses is by state examination. College graduates may be required to spend some time engaged in factory or farm work. College and university students compete for scholarships, which are awarded according to academic ability. Prior to entering college, however, students are required to complete one year of political education. Since 1981 three types of degree have been awarded: bachelor, master and doctoral. In November 1989 it was announced that post-graduate students were to be selected on the basis of assessments of moral and physical fitness, as well as academic ability. At the end of 2000 a total of 5.56m. undergraduate students were enrolled at the 1,041 general universities, while 3.54m. students were enrolled at the 772 institutes of higher education. In recent years exchanges with foreign universities have been encouraged. In February 2000 a new higher education reform project was launched, with the aim of creating a series of modernized courses, textbooks and software, establishing several education demonstration bases and training a group of able teachers.

Teacher Training

The rapid expansion of primary and secondary school education produced a serious shortage of qualified teachers. Teacher training is mostly undertaken in specialist establishments. Graduates of junior secondary schools may enrol for three years to train as primary school teachers, while teachers for secondary schools must have an educational level equivalent to that of a university graduate. Efforts are also being made to raise the standards of teachers, through the use of short training courses and correspondence courses. In 2000 there were 683 teacher-training establishments, with 770,000 students.

Other Institutions

Much of China's educational effort is devoted to part-time and spare-time systems, both for vocational training and ideological dissemination. The education of peasants and cadres in rural areas takes the form of literacy classes, part-farming and part-study classes, and spare-time study classes. Elementary classes are conducted by factories and workshops, while regular colleges provide tuition by means of correspondence courses and night universities. The inauguration in 1979 of a central radio and television university, which offers basic general courses in a variety of subjects, was followed by the establishment of numerous provincial centres. By 1999 the radio and television universities totalled 45, full-time teachers numbering 25,700. In the same year they had an enrolment of some 48,680 students, who would eventually receive a qualification equivalent to that of a regular higher education.

Bibliography

Adshead, S. A. M. *China in World History*. 3rd Edn, Basingstoke, Macmillan Press, 1999.

Alexandroff, Alan S., Ostry, Sylvia, and Gomez, Rafael (Eds). *China and the Long March to Global Trade—The Accession of China to the World Trade Organization*. London, Routledge, 2000.

Amnesty International. *Death in Beijing*. London, 1989.

An Chen. *Restructuring Political Power in China: Alliances and Opposition, 1978–1998*. Boulder, CO, Lynne Rienner, 1999.

Ash, Robert, Howe, Christopher, and Kueh, Y. Y. (Eds). *China's Economic Reform—A Study with Documents*. London, RoutledgeCurzon, 2002.

Barnett, Robert, and Akiner, Shirin (Eds). *Resistance and Reform in Tibet*. London, Hurst and Co, 1995.

Baum, Richard. *Burying Mao: Chinese Politics in the Age of Deng Xiaoping*. Princeton, NJ, Princeton University Press, 1995.

Becker, Jasper. *Hungry Ghosts: China's Secret Famine*. London, John Murray, 1996.

The Chinese. London, John Murray, 2000.

Benewick, Robert, and Wingrove, Paul (Eds). *China in the 1990s*. Basingstoke, Macmillan, 1995.

Bernstein, Richard, and Munro, Ross H. *The Coming Conflict with China*. New York, Alfred A. Knopf, 1997.

Blackman, Carolyn. *Negotiating China: Case Studies and Strategies*. St Leonards, NSW, Allen and Unwin, 1998.

Bonavia, David. *The Chinese: A Portrait*. London, Allen Lane, 1980.

Deng. Harlow, Longman, 1990.

Bowring, Philip, with Blaisdell, David, and Parry, Jane. *The China Investor*. AsiaPacific Financial Publishing, 1993.

Brahm, Laurence J. *China's Century: The Awakening of the Next Economic Powerhouse*. New York, John Wiley and Sons, 2001.

Breslin, Shaun. *China in the 1980s: Centre-Province Relations in a Reforming Socialist State*. Basingstoke, Macmillan, 1996.

Brodsgaard, Kjeld Erik, and Heurlin, Bertel (Eds). *China's Place in Global Geopolitics*. Richmond, Surrey, Curzon Press, 2001.

Brodsgaard, Kjeld Erik, and Strand, David (Eds). *Reconstructing Twentieth Century China*. Oxford, Oxford University Press, 1998.

Brown, Lester R. *Who Will Feed China?* New York, W. W. Norton, 1995.

Buckley Ebrey, Patricia. *The Cambridge Illustrated History of China*. Cambridge, Cambridge University Press, 1997.

Burstein, Daniel, and de Keijzer, Arne. *Big Dragon: China's Future*. New York, Simon and Schuster, 1998.

Buruma, Ian. *Bad Elements: Chinese Rebels from Los Angeles to Beijing*. London, Random House, 2002.

Chai, Joseph C. H. (Ed.) *The Economic Development of Modern China*. Cheltenham, Edward Elgar, 2000.

Chang, Gordon G. *The Coming Collapse of China*. London, Random House, 2001.

Chang, Iris. *The Rape of Nanking*. New York, Basic Books, 1998.

Chang Jung. *Wild Swans*. London, HarperCollins, 1992.

Chang, Parris H. *Power and Policy in China*. University Park, PA, Pennsylvania State University Press, 1978.

Cheek, Timothy, and Saich, Tony. *New Perspectives on State Socialism in China*. Armonk, NY, M. E. Sharpe, 1999.

Cheng Li. *Rediscovering China: Dynamics and Dilemmas of Reform*. Lanham, MD, Rowman & Littlefield, 1997.

China Publications Centre. *Resolution on CPC History (1949–1981)*. Beijing, Guoji Shudian, 1981.

Ching, Frank (Ed.). *China in Transition*. Hong Kong, Review Publishing Co, 1994.

Ching, Julia. *Probing China's Soul: Religion, Politics and Protest in the People's Republic*. San Francisco, Harper and Row, 1990.

Conboy, Kenneth, and Morrison, James. *The CIA's Secret War in Tibet*. Lawrence, University of Kansas Press, 2002.

Cook, Ian G., and Murray, Geoffrey. *China's Third Revolution: Tensions in the Transition Towards a Post-Communist China*. Richmond, Surrey, Curzon Press, 2001.

Cook, Sarah, Shuje Yao and Juzhong Zhuang (Eds). *The Chinese Economy under Transition*. Basingstoke, Macmillan Press, 2000.

Dai Qing. *The Three Gorges Dam and the Fate of China's Yangtze River and Its People*. Armonk, NY, M. E. Sharpe, 1997.

Dassu, M., and Saich, T. (Eds). *The Reform Decade in China: From Hope to Dismay*. Kegan Paul International, 1993.

Davis, Deborah, and Vogel, Ezra (Eds). *Chinese Society on the Eve of Tiananmen*. Cambridge, MA, Harvard/East Asia, 1991.

Deng Maomao. *Deng Xiaoping, My Father*. New York, Basic Books, 1995.

Department of Foreign Affairs and Trade, Canberra, Australia. *China Embraces the Market: Achievements, Constraints and Opportunities*. 1997.

Dickson, Bruce, and Chao Chien-min. *Remaking the Chinese State: Strategies, Society, and Security*. London, Routledge, 2001.

Ding Yijiang. *Chinese Democracy After Tiananmen*. New York, Columbia University Press, 2002.

Dirlik, Arif. *The Origins of Chinese Communism*. New York, Oxford University Press, 1990.

Donnet, Pierre-Antoine. *Tibet: Survival in Question*. London, Zed Books, 1994.

Dooling, Amy D., and Torgeson, Kristina M. (Eds). *Writing Women in Modern China: An Anthology of Women's Literature from the Early Twentieth-Century*. New York, Columbia University Press, 1998.

Drysdale, Peter, and Song Liang (Eds). *China's Entry into the World Trade Organization*. London, Routledge, 2000.

Edmonds, Richard Louis (Ed). *The People's Republic of China After 50 Years*. Oxford, Oxford University Press, 2000.

Managing the Chinese Environment. Oxford, Oxford University Press, 2000.

Edmonds, Richard Louis, and Wakeman Jr, Frederic (Eds). *Reappraising Republican China*. Oxford, Oxford University Press, 2000.

Ethridge, James M. *Changing China: The New Revolution's First Decade, 1979–88*. Beijing, New World Press, 1989.

Evans, Richard. *Deng Xiaoping and the Making of Modern China*. London, Hamish Hamilton, 1993.

Fairbank, John K., et al. (Eds). *The Cambridge History of China*. 15 vols. Cambridge, Cambridge University Press, 1987–92.

Fairbank, John K. *The Great Chinese Revolution: 1800–1985*. New York, Harper and Row, 1986.

China: A New History. Cambridge, MA, Harvard University Press, 1992.

Faust, John R., and Kornberg, Judith F. *China in World Politics*. Boulder, CO, Lynne Rienner, 1995.

Feuchtwang, Stephan, and Hussain, A. *The Chinese Economic Reforms*. London, Croom Helm, 1983.

Fewsmith, Joseph. *Elite Politics in Contemporary China*. Armonk, NY, M. E. Sharpe, 2000.

FitzGerald, C. P. *Revolution in China*. London, Cresset Press, 1952.

Foreign Languages Press. *Birth of Communist China*. London, Penguin Books, 1964.

Mao Tse-Tung and China. London, Hodder and Stoughton, 1976.

Friedman, Edward, and McCormick, Barrett L. *What if China Doesn't Democratize? Implications for War and Peace*. Armonk, NY, M. E. Sharpe, 2000.

Gao Shangquan. *China's Economic Reform*. Basingstoke, Macmillan, 1996.

Gargan, Edward A. *China's Fate: A People's Turbulent Struggle with Reform and Repression, 1980–1990*. New York, Doubleday, 1991.

Garnaut, Ross G., Guo Shutian and Ma Guonan (Eds). *The Third Revolution in the Chinese Countryside*. Cambridge, Cambridge University Press, 1996.

Garnaut, Ross G., and Yiping Huang (Eds). *Growth Without Miracles: Readings on the Chinese Economy in the Era of Reform*. Oxford, Oxford University Press, 2000.

Garside, Roger. *Coming Alive: China after Mao*. London, André Deutsch, 1981.

Gilley, Bruce. *Tiger on the Brink: Jiang Zemin and China's New Elite*. Berkeley, CA, University of California Press, 1998.

Gittings, John. *China Changes Face: The Road from Revolution 1949–1989*. Oxford, Oxford University Press, 1989.

Real China: From Cannibalism to Karaoke. London, Simon and Schuster, 1996.

Goldman, Merle. *Sowing the Seeds of Democracy in China: Political Reform in the Deng Xiaoping Era*. Cambridge, MA, Harvard University Press, 1994.

Goldstein, Melvyn C., and Beall, Cynthia M. *Nomads of Western Tibet: The Survival of a Way of Life*. Hong Kong, Odyssey Productions, 1990.

Goldstein, Melvyn, Siebenschuh, William, and Tsering, Tashi. *The Struggle for Modern Tibet: The Autobiography of Tashi Tsering*. Armonk, NY, M. E. Sharpe, 1998.

Goodman, David S. G. *Deng Xiaoping and the Chinese Revolution: A Political Biography*. London, Routledge, 1995.

China's Provinces in Reform: Class, Community and Political Culture. London, Routledge, 1997.

Goodman, David S. G. (Ed.). *China's Regional Development*. London, Routledge, 1989.

Goodman, David S. G., and Segal, Gerald. *China in the Nineties: Crisis Management and Beyond*. Oxford, Oxford University Press, 1991.

Goodman, David S. G., and Segal, Gerald (Eds). *China Rising: Nationalism and Interdependence*. London, Routledge, 1997.

Gray, Jack. *Rebellions and Revolutions*. Oxford, Oxford University Press, 1990.

Han Suyin. *Eldest Son: Zhou Enlai and the Making of Modern China, 1898–1976*. London, Jonathan Cape, 1994.

Hannan, Kate. *Industrial Change in China*. London, Routledge, 1998.

Harding, H. (Ed.). *China's Foreign Relations in the 1980s*. New Haven, CT, Yale University Press, 1986.

He Baogang. *The Democratic Implications of Civil Society in China*. Basingstoke, Macmillan, 1997.

Hendrischke, Hans, and Feng Chongyi (Eds). *The Political Economy of China's Provinces: Competitive and Comparative Advantage*. London, Routledge, 1999.

Hicks, George (Ed.). *The Broken Mirror: China After Tiananmen*. Harlow, Longman, 1990.

Hoa, Tran Van. *China's Trade and Investment After the Asia Crisis*. Cheltenham, Edward Elgar, 2000.

Hodder, Rupert. *In China's Image: Chinese Self-perception in Western Thought*. Basingstoke, Macmillan Press, 2000.

Holbig, Heike, and Ash, Robert (Eds). China's *Accession to the World Trade Organization—National and International Perspectives*. London, RoutledgeCurzon, 2002.

Hollingworth, Clare. *Mao and the Men Against Him*. London, Jonathan Cape, 1985.

Hook, Brian (Ed.). *The Cambridge Encyclopedia of China*. Cambridge University Press.

Hsü, Immanuel C. Y. *The Rise of Modern China*. 6th Edn, Oxford University Press, 2000.

Hu Yebi. *China's Capital Market*. Hong Kong, Chinese University Press, 1993.

Hughes, Neil. C. *China's Economic Challenge: Smashing the Iron Rice Bowl*. Armonk, NY, M. E. Sharpe, 2002.

Hutchings, Graham. *Modern China: A Guide to a Century of Change*. Cambridge, MA, Harvard University Press, 2001.

International Food Policy Research Institute (IFPRI). *China's Food Economy to the 21st Century*. Washington, DC, 1997.

Jae Ho Chung. *Central Control and Local Discretion in China: Leadership and Implementation during Post-Mao Decollectivization*. Oxford, Oxford University Press, 2000.

Jefferson, Gary H., and Singh, Inderjit (Eds). *Enterprise Reform in China: Ownership, Transition and Performance*. Oxford, Oxford University Press, 1999.

Jenner, W. J. F. *The Tyranny of History: The Roots of China's Crisis*. London, Allen Lane, 1992.

Joffe, E. *The Chinese Army After Mao*. London, Weidenfeld and Nicolson, 1987.

Johnston, Alastair Iain, and Ross, Robert S. (Eds). *Engaging China—The Management of an Emerging Power*. London, Routledge, 1999.

Joint Economic Committee (Congress of the United States). *China under the Four Modernizations*. Parts 1 and 2. Washington, DC, US Government Printing Office, 1981, 1982.

China's Economic Future: Challenges to US Policy. Armonk, NY, M. E. Sharpe, 1997.

Kaplan, Frederic M., Sobin, Julian M., and Andors, Stephen. *Encyclopaedia of China Today*. New York, Eurasia Press/Harper and Row, 1979.

Karl, Rebecca E. *Staging the World: Chinese Nationalism at the Turn of the Twentieth Century*. Durham, NC, Duke University Press, 2002.

Karmel, Solomon M. *China and and the People's Liberation Army: Great Power or Struggling Developing State?* Basingstoke, Macmillan Press, 2000.

Kim, Samuel S. *China and the World: Chinese Foreign Policy Faces the New Millennium.* Boulder, CO, Westview Press, 1998.

Kraus, Willy. *Private Business in China.* London, Hurst and Co, 1992.

Kristof, Nicholas D., and Wu Dunn, Sheryl. *China Wakes: The Struggle for the Soul of a Rising Power.* New York, Times Books, 1994.

Kwong, Julia. *The Political Economy of Corruption in China.* Armonk, NY, M. E. Sharpe, 1997.

Lam, Willy Wo-Lap. *The Era of Zhao Ziyang: Power Struggle in China, 1986–88.* Hong Kong, A. B. Books and Stationery (International) Ltd, 1989.

China after Deng Xiaoping: The Power Struggle in Beijing since Tiananmen. Singapore, John Wiley, 1995.

The Era of Jiang Zemin. Singapore, Prentice Hall, 1999.

Lampton, David M. *The Making of Chinese Foreign and Security Policy in the Era of Reform.* Stanford, CA, Stanford University Press, 2001.

Lardy, Nicholas R. *China in the World Economy.* Washington, DC, Institute for International Economics, 1994.

China's Unfinished Economic Revolution. Washington, DC, Brookings Institution Press, 1998.

Integrating China into the Global Economy. Washington, DC, Brookings Institution Press, 2002.

Lattimore, Owen. *China Memoirs: Chiang Kai-shek and the War Against Japan.* Tokyo, University of Tokyo Press, 1991.

Lawrance, Alan. *China Under Communism.* London, Routledge, 1998.

Lee, Hong Yung. *The Politics of the Chinese Cultural Revolution.* Berkeley, CA, University of California Press, 1980.

Lee, Ngok. *China's Defence Modernization and Military Leadership.* Sydney, Australian National University Press, 1991.

Lees, Francis A. *China Superpower: Requisites for High Growth.* Basingstoke, Macmillan, 1996.

Li Jun. *Financing China's Rural Enterprises.* London, Routledge Curzon, 2002.

Li Shaomin and Tse, David K. *China Markets Yearbook, 1999.* Armonk, NY, M. E. Sharpe, 2000.

Li Si-ming and Tang Wing-shing (Eds). *China's Regions, Polity and Economy.* Hong Kong, Chinese University Press, 2000.

Li Xueqin (trans. Chang, K. C.) *Eastern Zhou and Qin Civilizations.* New Haven, CT, Yale University Press, 1986.

Lieberthal, Kenneth. *Governing China: From Revolution Through Reform.* New York, W. W. Norton, 1995.

Lin Chong-pin. *China's Nuclear Weapons Strategy: Tradition within Evolution.* London, Lexington Books, 1989.

Liu Guoguang, Wang Luolin, Li Jingwen, Liu Shucheng, and Wang Tongsan (Eds). *Economics Blue Book of the People's Republic of China, 1999.* Armonk, NY, M. E. Sharpe, 2000.

Lloyd, P. J., and Zhang Xiao-guang (Eds). *China in the Global Economy.* Cheltenham, Edward Elgar, 2000.

Lo, Dic. *Market and Institutional Regulation in Chinese Industrialization, 1978–94.* Basingstoke, Macmillan, 1997.

Logan, Pamela. *Among Warriors: A Martial Artist in Tibet.* New York, Overlook Press, 1997.

Ma Bo. *Blood Red Sunset: A Memoir of the Chinese Cultural Revolution.* New York, Penguin Books, 1995.

MacFarquhar, Roderick. *The Origins of the Cultural Revolution.* 2 vols. London, Oxford University Press, 1983, and New York, Columbia University Press, 1984.

MacFarquhar, Roderick (Ed.). *The Politics of China: The Eras of Mao and Deng.* Cambridge, Cambridge University Press, 1997.

Mackerras, Colin. *Modern China: A Chronology.* London, Thames and Hudson, 1983.

Western Images of China. Hong Kong, Oxford University Press, 1989.

Mackerras, Colin, McMillen, Donald H., and Watson, Andrew (Eds). *Dictionary of the Politics of the People's Republic of China.* London, Routledge, 1998.

Marton, Andrew M. *China's Spatial Economic Development—Regional Transformation in the Lower Yangzi Delta.* London, Routledge, 2000.

Mastel, Greg. *The Rise of the Chinese Economy: The Middle Kingdom Emerges.* Armonk, NY, M. E. Sharpe, 1997.

Miles, James. *The Legacy of Tiananmen: China in Disarray.* Ann Arbor, University of Michigan Press, 1996.

Mulvenon, James C. *Soldiers of Fortune: The Rise and Fall of the Chinese Military-Business Complex.* Armonk, NY, M. E. Sharpe, 2000.

Nathan, Andrew J. *China's Crisis.* New York, Columbia University Press, 1990.

China's Transition. New York, Columbia University Press, 1998.

Nathan, Andrew J., Hong Zhaohui and Smith, Steven R. (Eds). *Dilemmas of Reform in Jiang Zemin's China.* Boulder, CO, Lynne Rienner, 1999.

Nathan, Andrew J., and Link, Perry (Eds). *The Tiananmen Papers: The Chinese Leadership's Decision to Use Force Against Their Own People—In Their Own Words.* New York, Public Affairs, 2001.

Nathan, Andrew J., and Ross, Robert S. *The Great Wall and the Empty Fortress: China's Search for Security.* New York, W. W. Norton, 1997.

Naughton, Barry. *Growing Out of the Plan: Chinese Economic Reform 1978–1993.* Cambridge, Cambridge University Press, 1995.

Nolan, Peter. *China's Rise; Russia's Fall.* New York, St Martin's Press, 1995.

OECD, Publications Service. *China in the 21st Century: Long-Term Global Implications.* Paris, 1996.

Ogden, Suzanne. *Inklings of Democracy in China.* Cambridge, MA, Harvard University Press, 2002.

Ogilvy, James A., Schwartz, Peter, and Flower, Joe. *China's Futures: Scenarios for the World's Fastest Growing Economy, Ecology, and Society.* San Francisco, CA, Jossey-Bass, 2000.

Ong, Russell. *China's Security Interests in the Post-Cold War Era.* Richmond, Surrey, Curzon Press, 2001.

Overholt, William H. *China: The Next Economic Superpower.* London, Weidenfeld and Nicolson, 1993.

Panitchpakdi, S, and Clifford, Mark. L. *China and the WTO: Changing China, Changing World Trade.* New York, John Wiley and Sons, 2002.

Perkins, D. W., and Yusuf, S. *Rural Development in China.* World Bank/Johns Hopkins, 1986.

Perry, Elizabeth J. and Selden, Mark (Eds). *Chinese Society: Change, Conflict, and Resistance.* London, Routledge, 1999.

Preston, Peter, and Haacke, Jürgen. *Contemporary China—The Dynamics of Change at the Start of the New Millennium.* London, RoutledgeCurzon, 2002.

Pomfret, Richard. *Investing in China.* London and New York, Harvester Wheatsheaf, 1991.

Rawski, Thomas G. *China's Transition to Industrialization: Producer Goods and Economic Development in the Twentieth Century.* Ann Arbor, MI, University of Michigan Press, 1980.

Economic Growth and Development in China. New York, for World Bank, Oxford University Press, 1980.

Renard, Mary-Françoise. *China and its Regions: Economic Growth and Reform in the Chinese Provinces.* Cheltenham, Edward Elgar, 2001.

Riskin, Carl, Zhao Renwei, and Li Shih. *China's Retreat From Equality: Income Distribution and Economic Transition.* Armonk, NY, M. E. Sharpe, 2000.

Roberts J. A. G. *A History of China.* London, Macmillan, 1999.

Saich, Tony (Ed.). *The Chinese People's Movement.* Armonk, NY, M. E. Sharpe, 1991.

Salisbury, Harrison E. *The Long March: The Untold Story.* New York and London, Macmillan, 1985.

Tiananmen Diary: Thirteen Days in June. Boston, MA, Little, Brown and Co, 1989.

The New Emperors—Mao and Deng. London, HarperCollins, 1992.

Schechter, Danny. *Falun Gong's Challenge to China: Spiritual Practice or 'Evil Cult'?* Askashic Books, 2001.

Schell, Orville, and Shambaugh, David (Eds). *The China Reader: The Reform Era.* New York, NY, Vintage Books, 1999.

Schoenfels, Michael (Ed.). *China's Cultural Revolution.* Armonk, NY, M. E. Sharpe, 1997.

Schwartz, Ronald D. *Circle of Protest: Political Ritual in the Tibetan Uprising.* London, Hurst and Co, 1995.

Segal, Gerald. *Defending China.* Oxford University Press, 1985.

Segal, Gerald, and Yang, Richard. *Chinese Economic Reform: The Impact on Security.* London, Routledge, 1996.

Seligman, Scott D. *Dealing with the Chinese.* New York, Warner Books, 1989.

Seymour, James, and Anderson, Richard. *New Ghosts, Old Ghosts: Prisons and Labor Reform Camps in China.* Armonk, NY, M. E. Sharpe, 1998.

Shakya, Tsering. *The Dragon in the Land of Snows: A History of Modern Tibet Since 1947*. London, Pimlico, 1999.

Shambaugh, David. *Is China Unstable? Assessing the Factors*. Armonk, NY, M. E. Sharpe, 2000.

The Modern Chinese State. Cambridge University Press, 2000.

Shambaugh, David, and Lilley, James. *China's Military Faces the Future*. Armonk, NY, M. E. Sharpe, 1999.

Shao Kuo-Kang. *Zhou Enlai and the Foundations of Chinese Foreign Policy*. Basingstoke, Macmillan, 1996.

Shapiro, James E., et al. *Direct Investment and Joint Ventures in China: A Handbook for Corporate Negotiators*. New York, Quorum Books, 1992.

Shapiro, Judith. *Mao's War Against Nature: Politics and the Environment in Revolutionary China*. New York, Cambridge University Press, 2001.

Sheel, Kamal. *Peasant Society and Marxist Intellectuals in China: Fang Zhimin and the Origin of a Revolutionary Movement in the Xinjiang Region*. Princeton, NJ, Princeton University Press, 1990.

Sheng Lijun. *China's Dilemma: The Taiwan Issue*. Singapore, Institute of Southeast Asian Studies, 2001.

Shirk, Susan. *How China Opened its Door*. Washington, DC, Brookings Institute, 1994.

Short, Philip. *Mao: A Life*. Henry Holt and Co, 2000.

Simmie, Scott and Nixon, Bob. *Tiananmen Square*. Vancouver, Douglas and McIntyre, 1989.

Smil, Vaclav. *China's Environmental Crisis: An Inquiry into the Limits of National Development*. Armonk, NY, M. E. Sharpe, 1993.

Spence, Jonathan. *The Gate of Heavenly Peace: The Chinese and Their Revolution, 1895–1980*. Harmondsworth, Penguin Books, 1982.

The Search for Modern China. London, Century, 2nd Edn, 2000.

God's Chinese Son: The Taiping Heavenly Kingdom of Hong Xiuquan. New York, W. W. Norton, 1996.

The Chan's Great Continent: China in Western Minds. New York, W. W. Norton, 1998.

Starr, John Bryan. *Understanding China: A Guide to China's Economy, History, and Political Structure*. New York, NY, Hill and Wang, 1997.

Steinfeld, Edward S. *Forging Reform in China: The Fate of State-Owned Industry*. Cambridge, Cambridge University Press, 1998.

Stockman, Norman. *Understanding Chinese Society*. Polity, 2002.

Strange, Roger, Slater, Jim, and Wang Limin (Eds). *Trade and Investment in China—The European Experience*. London, Routledge, 1998.

Studwell, Joe. *The China Dream: The Elusive Quest for the Greatest Untapped Market on Earth*. New York, Atlantic Monthly Press, 2002.

Stuttard, John. B. *The New Silk Road: Secrets of Doing Business in China Today*. New York, NY, John Wiley & Sons, 2000.

Sullivan, Lawrence R., with Hearst, Nancy R. *Historical Dictionary of the People's Republic of China, 1949–1997*. Lanham, MD, Scarecrow Press, 1997.

Sulter, Robert G. *Shaping China's Future in World Affairs: The Role of the United States*. Boulder, CO, Westview Press, 1998.

Swaine, Michael D., and Tellis, Ashley J. *Interpreting China's Grand Strategy: Past, Present, and Future*. Santa Monica, CA, Rand, 2000.

Tam On Kit. *The Development of Corporate Governance in China*. Cheltenham, Edward Elgar, 2000.

Teiwes, Frederick C., and Sun, Warren. *The Tragedy of Lin Biao: Riding the Tiger during the Cultural Revolution*. Honolulu, HI, University of Hawaii Press, 1996.

Terrill, Ross. *Mao: A Biography*. Cambridge, Cambridge University Press, 1998.

Teufel Dreyer, June. *China's Political System: Modernization and Tradition*. Basingstoke, Macmillan, 1996.

Tien Hung-mao and Chu Yun-han (Eds). *China under Jiang Zemin*. Boulder, CO, Lynne Rienner, 1999.

Tregear, T. R. *A Geography of China*. University of London Press, 1965.

China: A Geographical Survey. London, Hodder and Stoughton, 1980.

Unger, Jonathan. *Chinese Nationalism*. Armonk, NY, M. E. Sharpe, 1996.

Unger, Jonathan (Ed.). *The Pro-Democracy Protests in China*. Armonk, NY, M. E. Sharpe, 1992.

Vogel, Ezra F. *One Step Ahead in China: Guangdong Under Reform*. Cambridge, MA, Harvard University Press, 1989.

Vogel, Ezra (Ed.). *Living with China: US-China Relations in the Twenty-First Century*. New York, W. W. Norton, 1997.

Waldron, Arthur. *The Great Wall of China: From History to Myth*. Cambridge, Cambridge University Press, 1991.

Wang Gungwu. *The Chinese Way: China's Position in International Relations*. Oslo, Scandinavian University Press, 1995.

Wang Ke-wen (Ed.) *Modern China—An Encyclopedia of History, Culture and Nationalism*. New York, Garland Publishing, 1997.

Wang Shaoguang. *The Chinese Economy in Crisis: State Capacity and Tax Reform*. Armonk, NY, M. E. Sharpe, 2001.

Wasserstrom, Jeffrey, and Perry, Elizabeth. *Popular Protest and Political Culture in Modern China*. Boulder, CO, Westview Press, 1992.

Wei, C. X. George, and Liu Xiaoyuan (Eds). *Chinese Nationalism in Perspective*. Westport, CT, Greenwood Press, 2001.

Wei Jingsheng. *The Courage To Stand Alone: Letters from Prison and Other Writings*. London, Viking, 1997.

Wei, Yehua Dennis. *Regional Develpment in China—State, Globalization and Inequality*. London, Routledge, 2000.

White, Lynn T. *Politics of Chaos: The Organizational Causes of Violence in China's Cultural Revolution*. Princeton, NJ, Princeton University Press, 1989.

Wilson, Dick. *China, The Big Tiger: A Nation Awakes*. London, Little, Brown and Co, 1996.

Wood, Frances. *Did Marco Polo Go to China?* London, Secker and Warburg, 1996.

World Bank. *China: Long-term Development Issues and Options*. Washington, DC, 1985.

China 2020: Development Challenges in the New Century. Washington, DC, 1997.

China's Management of Enterprise Assets: The State as a Shareholder. Washington, DC, 1997.

The Chinese Economy: Fighting Inflation, Deepening Reforms. Washington, DC, 1996.

Wortzel, Larry M. (Ed.) *The Chinese Armed Forces in the 21st Century*. Carlisle, PA, Strategic Studies Institute, 2000.

Wu, Hongda Harry. *Laogai: The Chinese Gulag*. Boulder, CO, Westview Press, 1993.

Wu, Harry. *Troublemaker: One Man's Crusade Against China's Cruelty*. London, Chatto and Windus, 1996.

Wu, Harry, and Wakeman, Carolyn. *Bitter Winds: A Memoir of My Years in China's Gulag*. London, John Wiley and Sons, 1994.

Wu Yanrui. *China's Consumer Revolution—The Emerging Patterns of Wealth and Expenditure*. Cheltenham, Edward Elgar, 1999.

Wu Yanrui (Ed.) *Foreign Direct Investment and Economic Growth in China*. Cheltenham, Edward Elgar, 1999.

China's Economic Growth. London, RoutledgeCurzon, 2002.

Yabuki, Susumu. *China's New Political Economy: The Giant Awakes*. Boulder, CO, Westview Press, 1995.

Yahuda, Michael B. *China's Role in World Affairs*. London, Croom Helm, 1979.

Hong Kong—China's Challenge. London, Routledge, 1996.

Yak-yeow Kueh, Chai, Joseph C. H. and Gang Fan (Eds). *Industrial Reforms and Macroeconomic Instability In China*. Oxford, Oxford University Press, 1999.

Yan Jiaqi, and Gao Gao. *Turbulent Decade: A History of the Cultural Revolution*. Honolulu, HI, University of Hawaii Press, 1996.

Yang, Dali L. *Calamity and Reform in China: State, Rural Society, and Institutional Change since the Great Leap Famine*. Stanford, CA, Stanford University Press, 1996.

Yang, Rae. *Spider Eaters*. Berkeley, CA, University of California Press, 1997.

Yee, Herbert, and Storey, Ian (Eds). *The China Threat: Perceptions, Myths, and Reality*. London, RoutledgeCurzon, 2002.

Zhang Kaiyuan. *Eyewitness Accounts of the Nanjing Massacre*. Armonk, NY, M. E. Sharpe, 2000.

Zhang Xiao-guang. *China's Trade Patterns and International Comparative Advantage*. Basingstoke, Macmillan Press, 1999.

Zhang Zhongxiang. *The Economics of Energy Policy in China—Implications for Global Climate Change*. Cheltenham, Edward Elgar, 1998.

Zheng Shiping. *Party vs. State in Post-1949 China: The Institutional Dilemma*. Cambridge, Cambridge University Press, 1997.

Zhou, Kate Xiao. *How Farmers Changed China*. Boulder, CO, Westview Press, 1996.

Zweig, David. *Internationalizing China: Domestic Interests and Global Linkages*. Cornell University Press, 2002.

CHINESE SPECIAL ADMINISTRATIVE REGIONS

HONG KONG

Physical and Social Geography

MICHAEL FREEBERNE

With additions by the editorial staff

The population of the Special Administrative Region (SAR) of Hong Kong occupies a total land area of only 1,098 sq km (423.9 sq miles). The territory, which reverted to Chinese sovereignty in July 1997, is situated off the south-east coast of Guangdong Province of the People's Republic of China, to the east of the mouth of the Zhujiang (Pearl River), between latitudes 22° 9′ and 22° 37′ N and longitudes 113° 52′ and 114° 30′ E. The SAR comprises the island of Hong Kong, ceded to the United Kingdom by China in 1842, the Kowloon peninsula, ceded in 1860, and the New Territories, which are part of the mainland and were leased to the United Kingdom between 1898 and 1997, together with Deep Bay and Mirs Bay and some 236 outlying islands and islets. The fine anchorages between the capital of Victoria, on the northern shore of Hong Kong Island, and Kowloon provided an ideal situation for the growth of one of the world's leading entrepôt ports.

PHYSICAL FEATURES

Hong Kong Island is approximately 17 km long and between 3 km and 8 km wide. An irregular range of hills rises abruptly from the sea; several peaks are over 300 m in height, and Victoria Peak reaches 554 m. Granites, basalt and other volcanic rocks account for the main geological formations. These rocks are most common, too, on Lantau and Lamma islands and in the Kowloon peninsula and New Territories, which are mostly hilly, rising to 957 m in Tai Mo Shan, and have rugged, deeply indented coastlines. The territory is poor in minerals and, apart from hillside areas of dense scrub, was largely stripped of natural vegetation by indiscriminate tree-felling during the Japanese occupation of 1941–45. The resultant erosion has been extensively repaired under a vigorous programme of reafforestation. Flat land and agricultural land are scarce everywhere. Reclamation of land from the sea for building purposes is very important, and since 1945 much additional land has been made available for housing and commercial development, as well as for projects like the international airport at Chek Lap Kok, off Lantau Island, which was opened in 1998. In 1996 major reclamation work at West Kowloon, which included the extension of Stonecutters Island, was substantially completed. Reclamation also continued to progress on Hong Kong Island and in the New Territories.

CLIMATE

The climate of Hong Kong is subtropical and governed by monsoons. Winter lasts from October to April, when the winds are from the north or north-east, while during the summer months from May to September south or south-westerly winds predominate. Average daily temperatures are highest in July with 29°C and lowest in January with 16°C. The wet summer is very humid. Annual rainfall averages 2,214 mm, some 80% of which falls between May and September. Devastating typhoons occasionally strike in summer.

Despite the high rainfall, it has proved increasingly difficult to supply sufficient domestic and industrial water, and most supplies are piped from the neighbouring Guangdong Province of China. The Plover Cove reservoir, inaugurated in 1969, trebled Hong Kong's reservoir capacity, and further reservoirs subsequently came into operation, including the world's first seabed reservoir. Nevertheless, in 1997 Hong Kong was dependent upon China for 70% of its water supply, compared with 45% in 1984. By the year 2000 the annual supply from China was scheduled to increase to 840m. cu m, from 690m. cu m in 1995, and by the year 2010 to 1,100m. cu m. Additional purchases may be made in years of low rainfall.

POPULATION

The population of Hong Kong in mid-2001 was officially estimated at 6,724,900, giving an average density of 6,124.5 persons per sq km. However, average density in the New Territories in mid-2000 was 3,520 per sq km, whereas for Hong Kong Island and Kowloon it was 17,200 and 44,210 respectively. In the Mong Kok district of Kowloon in the 1980s density was over 200,000. These figures represent some of the highest population densities in the world. In 1979 the population was greatly swelled by the entry of many thousands of illegal immigrants from China and 'boat people' from Viet Nam. The influx continued throughout the 1980s.

Hong Kong has experienced an extraordinary growth in population. Between 1841, when only about 5,000 people lived on the island, and 1941, the colony received successive waves of migrants; then the population was estimated at about 1.5m. There was a drastic reduction during the Japanese occupation (1941–45), but by 1949 the population had increased to 1,857,000. After the establishment of the People's Republic of China in 1949, large numbers of refugees arrived in Hong Kong, where the rate of natural increase was already high. Hong Kong's crude birth rate in 2001 was estimated at 7.2 per 1,000 (compared with 18.3 in 1975). At an estimated 3.1 per 1,000 registered live births in 2001, the infant mortality rate was among the lowest in Asia. The crude death rate in 2001 was estimated at 4.8 per 1,000 (compared with 4.9 in 1975). The proportion of the population under 15 years of age declined from 23% in 1986 to 17.2% in 2000, while those aged 65 years and over rose from 8% to 11.2%.

About 95% of the territory's population are of predominantly Chinese descent. The Cantonese form the largest community. About 60% of the population in 1991 were born in Hong Kong. The prospect of the territory's transfer to Chinese sovereignty in mid-1997 led to an exodus of skilled personnel, the total number of emigrants reaching a record 66,000 in 1992. It was estimated, however, that at least 12% of those who had emigrated in the 10 years to 1994 had subsequently returned to Hong Kong, many having secured residency rights in countries such as Australia and Canada.

History

N. J. MINERS

Revised by JAMES TANG

INTRODUCTION

On 1 July 1997 Hong Kong became a Special Administrative Region (SAR) of the People's Republic of China, thus ending more than 150 years of British colonial rule. The agreement for the reversion of Hong Kong's sovereignty to China was reached in the Sino-British Joint Declaration of 1984. The arrangement, known as 'one country, two systems', promised capitalist Hong Kong 'a high degree of autonomy', with the exception of foreign relations and defence, while the territory's political and economic systems, as well as its existing way of life, were to remain unchanged for at least 50 years, until 2047. The territory of the Hong Kong SAR (see below) is almost exactly the same as that acquired by the British in the 19th century.

EARLY DEVELOPMENT TO 1945

The colonial territory of Hong Kong was acquired by the United Kingdom (UK) in three stages. The First Opium War of 1840–42 began after the Chinese commissioner in Guangzhou (Canton) had seized and destroyed large stocks of opium held by the British traders there, who then left the city. The British Government demanded compensation and a commercial treaty, and an expedition was dispatched to enforce these demands. During the hostilities a naval force occupied the island of Hong Kong, which was ceded to the UK 'in perpetuity' by the Treaty of Nanjing (Nanking) of 1842. As soon as this was ratified, a colony was formally proclaimed in June 1843. Continuing disputes between the UK and China over trade and shipping led to renewed warfare in 1856. This was ended by the Convention of Beijing (Peking) of 1860, by which the peninsula of Kowloon on the mainland opposite the island was annexed.

Following China's defeat in the Sino-Japanese War of 1895, the Western powers seized the opportunity to extract further concessions. The UK demanded, and obtained in 1898, a 99-year lease on the mainland north of Kowloon, together with the adjoining islands. These New Territories increased the area of the colony from about 110 sq km to more than 1,000 sq km. The terms of the 1898 Convention of Beijing allowed the existing Chinese magistrates to remain in the old walled city of Kowloon, but in 1899 they were unilaterally expelled on the pretext that they had encouraged resistance to the British occupation. The Chinese Government protested at the time and reasserted a claim to jurisdiction over this small area in 1933, 1948 and 1962, although this was rejected by the Hong Kong courts. In 1994, with the agreement of the People's Republic of China, the area was cleared, levelled and converted into a public park.

The main reason for the British occupation of Hong Kong in 1841 was its magnificent harbour. Attracted by its free port status, the entrepôt trade between the West and China grew steadily for the next 100 years. The great trading companies set up their headquarters under the British flag; banks, insurance companies and other commercial enterprises were established to serve the China traders as well as shipbuilding, ship-repairing and other industries dependent on the port. At the same time the population grew from about 5,000 in 1841 to more than 500,000 in 1916 and over 1m. by 1939, of which fewer than 20,000 were non-Chinese. Chinese were allowed free access and the flow of migrants increased whenever China was disturbed by wars or rebellions, the process being reversed when peaceful conditions had been restored on the mainland. Apart from the settled farming population of the New Territories, relatively few Chinese regarded Hong Kong as their permanent home until after the Second World War. Most came to trade or seek employment and then returned to their home towns. Europeans were similarly transient, whether they were government officials or in private employment.

The colony's administration followed the usual crown colony pattern, with power concentrated in the hands of a Governor advised by nominated executive and legislative councils, on which government officials had an overall majority over the unofficial members. The first unofficial members were appointed to the Legislative Council in 1850, and the first Chinese in 1880; the first 'unofficials' in the Executive Council were appointed in 1896, and the first Chinese in 1926. In 1894, 1916 and 1922 the British residents pressed for an unofficial majority in the Legislative Council and the election of some or all of the 'unofficials' on a franchise confined to British subjects, citing the constitutional progress made in other colonies; but on all occasions the British Government was unwilling to allow the Chinese majority to be politically subjected to a small European minority. A sanitary board was set up in 1883 and this was made partly elective in 1887. In 1936 it was renamed the Urban Council, although its powers were not significantly increased.

Little of note happened in Hong Kong throughout this period, apart from commercial expansion, land reclamation and the building of reservoirs. There were a number of large-scale strikes in the early 1920s, but otherwise anti-foreigner agitation in China had little effect on Hong Kong's prosperity.

The growing threat of war in the late 1930s led to an increase in defence expenditure, which forced the imposition of income and profits taxes for the first time; this wartime expedient was made permanent in 1947. Japanese forces occupied most of the Chinese Province of Guangdong, north of the colony, in 1938, and in December 1941 overran Hong Kong. In August 1945 the Japanese authorities handed power back to the surviving colonial officials who had been interned with the rest of the British community throughout the occupation. A British naval force arrived in late August to install an interim military administration, thus forestalling pressures from the US Government for Hong Kong to be returned to China.

POST-WAR ISSUES

After the Japanese capture of Hong Kong in December 1941, a planning unit was formed in London to prepare for the post-war rehabilitation of the colony. Its members later staffed the interim military administration, which restored public services on a minimum basis. Civil government, on the traditional colonial pattern, was re-established in May 1946. Meanwhile, China was disrupted by civil war between the nationalist and communist armies, which ended with the communist victory in 1949. The UK recognized the new communist Government of China in 1950, having heavily reinforced the garrison in Hong Kong in 1949 to deter any possible Chinese attack. The only serious violation of the frontier occurred in 1967. The strength of the garrison was reduced at successive defence reviews. In 1992 special units of the Hong Kong Police Force assumed responsibility for the security of the border. All Gurkha troops left the territory in November 1996; one British battalion provided security until mid-1997, when it was replaced by soldiers of the Chinese People's Liberation Army.

During the Second World War the colony's population had declined to about 600,000, as a result of privation and mass deportations by the Japanese. The population quickly regained pre-war levels and rose to about 2m. in 1950, owing to a massive influx of refugees from the civil war in China. The pressures resulting from this inflow forced the colony to abandon its policy of free access, and the frontier was closed in 1950. Movement over the border was subsequently tightly controlled by the Chinese authorities, with the exception of a period during May 1962, when the frontier was unexpectedly opened and 120,000 refugees were allowed to leave. Individual escapees also attempted to enter clandestinely. From 1974 to 1980 any illegal immigrants who were apprehended in the frontier region were transferred to the Chinese authorities, but those who succeeded in reaching the urban areas were allowed to remain. This concession continued to encourage escape attempts. After a massive surge in illegal immigration in 1979–80 (when it was estimated that more than 200,000 people succeeded in settling in the colony in spite of the fact that 170,000 were captured and repatriated), it was announced in October 1980 that, in future, all illegal immigrants who were discovered anywhere in the colony would be repatriated. This announcement caused a sharp decline in illegal attempts to enter, but such immigration continued, and in 1997 an average of some 49 illegal immigrants were arrested daily and forcibly repatriated to China. The Chinese authorities permitted 150 people a day to cross the border, and more were entitled to settle in Hong Kong after China's resumption of sovereignty. From 1990 a total of 25,000 workers were allowed to enter Hong Kong each year on fixed-term contracts to relieve the labour shortage.

The problem of feeding the refugees and providing employment was made worse by the outbreak of the Korean War in 1950, which led to the imposition of an embargo on the export of strategic goods to China and gravely damaged Hong Kong's entrepôt trade. However, the refugees provided a pool of compliant, hard-working labour. Local businessmen and industrialists who had fled from Shanghai took advantage of this and, by making use of the colony's existing financial infrastructure and world-wide trading connections, they reorientated the economy towards manufacturing for export.

The refugees put an immense strain on all public services, and the newcomers were left to build themselves shanty towns which spread over the hillsides. A devastating fire at one of these shanty towns in 1953 prompted the Government to initiate a resettlement programme; huge estates were built, with rooms allocated on the scale of 2.3 sq m for each adult. The early designs provided few amenities, as the main consideration was speed of construction. The housing programme continued steadily, with additional expansion from 1972, when a 10-year programme to house a further 1.5m. people, mainly in new towns in the New Territories, was announced. At the same time, various government housing agencies were amalgamated into a new housing authority to assume responsibility for the planning, construction and management of all public housing in Hong Kong. By 1991 more than 50% of the population were living in government-provided housing.

From 1976 many refugees from Viet Nam attempted to reach Hong Kong by sea. Initially, most were accepted for resettlement in the USA, Canada, Australia and Europe. However, in 1982, after the resettlement countries had reduced their immigration quotas, Hong Kong adopted a policy of confining all newly-arrived Vietnamese in closed camps, in order to deter others from landing in the territory. Nevertheless, the numbers continued to increase. A particularly large influx in 1988 led the Hong Kong Government to abandon its policy of automatically granting refugee status to newly-arrived Vietnamese. All arrivals were subjected to a test, and those considered to be 'economic migrants' were classified as illegal immigrants and confined in detention centres, to await eventual repatriation to Viet Nam. This new policy, however, failed to act as a deterrent. Vietnamese continued to arrive in increasing numbers, in the hope that they could pass the screening procedure and secure passages to the USA, since the Government of Viet Nam refused to accept the forced repatriation of those who had been classified as economic migrants. At the end of 1991 Viet Nam finally agreed to accept a limited programme of mandatory repatriation. This significantly reduced the number of Vietnamese arriving in Hong Kong. About 12,000 of those facing mandatory repatriation volunteered to return to Viet Nam, and China demanded that all Vietnamese should be removed before July 1997. Many of those remaining in Hong Kong were determined to resist forcible repatriation by any available means, and there were intermittent riots and demonstrations in the camps. From early 1998 it was announced that Hong Kong would no longer conduct a 'port of first asylum' policy, whereby refugees were permitted to apply for asylum upon arriving in the territory. Some 1,200 refugees, 659 migrants and 743 illegal immigrants from Viet Nam remained in Hong Kong in March and negotiations were under way between the Hong Kong and British Governments to determine responsibility for their repatriation. Hong Kong's last remaining camp for Vietnamese refugees was closed on 31 May 2000. Inmates were granted residency in the SAR. Several of the refugees, however, tried to remain inside the camp on the grounds that they could not afford the price of housing in the territory and were without jobs.

From 1945 until 1982 the people of Hong Kong showed a noticeable apathy towards any form of political activity or agitation for democratic self-government. This political calm was disturbed only three times: in 1956 there were faction fights between communist and nationalist supporters; in 1966 there were three nights of rioting, provoked by an increase in fares on the cross-harbour ferry; and for several months in 1967 there were disturbances and bomb attacks, led by communist sympathizers who were inspired by the example of the 'Cultural Revolution' in China. These had ended by late 1967, with the restoration of order in China itself.

The next 15 years were a period of political calm and rapidly-growing economic prosperity, until 1982, when the start of the negotiations on Hong Kong's future caused an upsurge of political activity. Anxiety at the prospect of rule by China after 1997 led to an increase in emigration and investment overseas by those residents able to do so. The collapse of the property market and the consequent depressed sales of leases of crown land resulted in budget deficits in 1983, 1984 and 1985, which were financed by increases in taxation and government borrowing. Confidence in Hong Kong's future recovered, and the property market revived following the signing of the Sino-British agreement of 1984 (see below). The economy continued to expand, in spite of periodic crises in the relationship with China. There were no budget deficits between 1985 and 1995, and taxes were steadily reduced.

In 1986 plans by China to construct a nuclear power plant at Daya Bay, about 50 km from the centre of Hong Kong, aroused great public anxiety. A petition against the project attracted more than 1m. signatures. Despite this, the Chinese authorities concluded the major contracts in September 1986, thereby demonstrating their lack of concern for Hong Kong opinion. The plant began operations in 1994. Construction of a second nuclear plant at Daya Bay began in 1995.

The massacre of students in Tiananmen Square, in Beijing, in June 1989 and the forcible suppression of the pro-democracy movement throughout China had a devastating impact on local confidence in the future. Demonstrations involving up to 1m. people were held to protest against the slaughter. The property market and the stock exchange suffered very sharp falls. The number of emigrants, mostly to Canada, Australia and the USA, reached a record 66,200 in 1992. The outflow fluctuated thereafter, and the number of departures declined to 30,900 in 1997. Many sought to obtain passports of foreign countries to enable them to leave Hong Kong before China's resumption of sovereignty in mid-1997. In an attempt to restore confidence, the British Government agreed in 1990 to grant full British passports with the right of abode in the UK to 50,000 business executives, administrators and professional people, together with their immediate family members, making a total of 225,000 individuals. It was hoped that this would encourage key personnel to remain in Hong Kong, since they would have the assurance that they could leave for the UK at any time. However, China denounced this move as a plot to entrench British influence in Hong Kong, and insisted that it would not recognize these passports after 1997.

In other moves to boost confidence, in October 1989 the Governor announced plans to build a new international airport at Chek Lap Kok, near Lantau Island, a railway to link the airport to the city, and large new port facilities and container terminals in the west of the harbour. China objected strongly to the proposals, and without Beijing's agreement it would not have been possible to raise the private finance required. In July 1991 the UK and China signed a memorandum of understanding on the arrangements for building the new airport, but China continued to raise objections to the costs of the project, and tried to use its power to withhold consent in order to extract concessions on political issues. In particular, China opposed the proposals made by the new Governor, Chris Patten, to extend the franchise for the 1995 Legislative Council elections. In 1995 China finally agreed to the financial arrangements and to the composition of the Airport Authority. The opening of the new airport, built at a cost of some US $20,000m., was initially scheduled for April 1998, but was postponed until July, owing to delays in the construction of the express rail link. The inauguration of the airport was overshadowed by problems in the cargo handling systems, which resulted in the loss of thousands of consignments of food and other goods. The authorities were forced to divert cargo to the old airport or to facilities on the mainland.

In June 1991 the Hong Kong Government enacted a Bill of Rights to give effect in local law to the relevant provisions of the UN International Covenant on Civil and Political Rights. These provisions remained in force following the territory's transfer to Chinese sovereignty in mid-1997.

POLITICAL AND ADMINISTRATIVE DEVELOPMENT

Following the restoration of civil government in May 1946, the returning Governor promised a greater measure of self-government and, after inviting suggestions from the public, proposed that an elected Municipal Council, with wide powers over local affairs in the urban area, should be established. These plans for major constitutional reform were deferred after the communist victory in China in 1949, and were finally abandoned in 1952. From then until 1985, there were no further moves towards democratic government, largely in deference to China's dislike of any such changes. Instead, the number of appointed unofficial members on the Legislative Council was successively increased from eight in 1951 to 30 in 1984.

Under the terms of the 1984 Joint Declaration (see below), the legislature of the Hong Kong SAR would be constituted by election. Therefore, in 1985 the composition of the Legislative Council was substantially changed, to include 24 indirectly-elected members, 12 chosen by the district boards, Urban Council and Regional Council, and 12 by 'functional constituencies', composed of the representatives of the commercial and industrial sectors, trade unions and various professional bodies. These 24 elected members were outnumbered by the 22 appointed members and the 10 officials. In deference to China's wishes, only minor constitutional changes were made in 1988. In 1990 the British Foreign Secretary agreed with China that the 1991 Legislative Council would consist of 21 functional constituency members, 18 directly elected by universal franchise, 18 members appointed by the Governor, and three civil servants. Elections were held in September 1991. Of the 18 seats open to election by universal suffrage, 15 were won by the United Democrats (a liberal grouping led by Martin Lee—who subsequently became the Chairman of the Democratic Party of Hong Kong) and their allies. The new Legislative Council, inaugurated in October, had a majority of elected members for the first time in the territory's history, although most of the 21 members representing functional constituencies had been chosen by only a few hundred voters. Contrary to the normal constitutional practice in British colonies, none of the leaders of the United Democrats was invited to join the Executive Council.

In 1992 Sir David Wilson was replaced as Governor by Chris Patten, a Conservative politician who had lost his seat in the British general election. Three months after his arrival he announced detailed proposals for the conduct of the 1995 elections, without first consulting China. He proposed that the Legislative Council should conform to the model laid down in the Basic Law (see below), with 30 members elected by functional constituencies, 20 directly elected by geographical constituencies and 10 by an electoral college, but that the electorate for the nine new functional constituencies should be enlarged to 2.7m. voters and that the electorate for the 10 electoral college seats should consist of all the elected members of the District Boards. China denounced this plan as an attempt to increase the number of directly-elected seats beyond that laid down in the Basic Law. Negotiations were held with China during 1993, but no compromise could be found. Patten's original proposals were enacted into law by the Legislative Council in June 1994.

At the elections to the Legislative Council held in September 1995, for the first time all 60 seats were determined by election. A total of 920,567 people (36% of registered electors) voted for the 20 seats open to direct election on the basis of geographical constituencies. The Democratic Party of Hong Kong won 19 seats (12 by direct election, five by functional constituencies and two chosen by electoral college). About one-half of the members of the Council usually supported the Democratic Party of Hong Kong, but the Government was able to avoid any significant defeats in the legislature by energetic lobbying for the support of smaller parties and independent members.

From 1896 to 1992 members of the Legislative Council who were not officials were appointed by the Governor to sit on the Executive Council. After 1946 the unofficial members outnumbered the officials. In 1992 Patten ended this practice, making the membership of the Executive Council entirely separate from the Legislative Council. The Governor was empowered to reject the advice given to him by the majority of the Council (of which he also was a member) but, in practice, this never occurred.

In 1996 the Urban Council remained responsible for public health and sanitation, recreation, amenities and cultural services in the urban area. From 1995 the Council consisted entirely of elected members, with nine indirectly chosen by District Boards and 32 elected by all those over 18 years of age who had been resident in Hong Kong for at least seven years. A similar Regional Council served the New Territories. The Chinese Government objected strongly to the abolition of the seats for appointed members, and threatened to reconstitute both councils after 1997. Elections were held for the two councils in March 1995, at which 26% of the registered voters cast their ballots. The Democratic Party of Hong Kong and its allies won 31 of the 59 directly-elective seats.

Hong Kong is divided into 18 districts. In each of these there is a management committee of officials from various government departments working in the area, presided over by a senior administrative officer. This committee is assisted by an advisory district board. Between 1994 and mid-1997 all members of District Boards were elected by universal suffrage. However, from July 1997 the District Boards were replaced by Provisional District Boards, comprising members appointed by the Chief Executive of Hong Kong. The interests of the rural indigenous inhabitants of the New Territories are served by an elected advisory body, the Heung Yee Kuk. There are also advisory committees attached to most government departments.

SOVEREIGNTY NEGOTIATIONS

After the communist victory in the Chinese civil war in 1949, the People's Republic asserted that all the unequal treaties, forced upon China, were no longer recognized as binding; but the treaties of 1842, 1860 and 1898 were not formally abrogated. The Chinese Government was unwilling to clarify its intentions after 1997, when the lease on the New Territories expired, apart from giving intermittent assurances that the interests of investors would be protected.

In 1982 the UK decided to press China for a decision. Following the visit of the British Prime Minister, Margaret Thatcher, to China in September, negotiations commenced through diplomatic channels and continued for two years. In August 1984 agreement was reached on a Joint Declaration, which was subsequently approved by the British Parliament and ratified in May 1985. Under this agreement, the UK undertook to restore sovereignty over the whole of Hong Kong to China on 1 July 1997, upon the expiry of the lease on the New Territories. Until that date, the British Government was to continue to be responsible for the administration of the territory, but a Joint Liaison Group (JLG—see below), consisting of British and Chinese diplomatic representatives, was formed to consult on the implementation of the agreement, and to ensure a smooth transfer of sovereignty in 1997.

China, for its part, undertook that, after 1997, Hong Kong would be constituted as a Special Administrative Region (SAR, designated 'Hong Kong, China'), governed by its own inhabitants in accordance with its own legal code, except in matters of foreign affairs and defence, for a period of 50 years. It was to retain its status as a free port and separate customs territory, and the Hong Kong dollar was to remain a freely convertible currency. The region's social and economic systems were to remain unchanged, and freedom of speech, of the press, of association, of travel and of religion was to be guaranteed by law. Existing leases of land were to be recognized, and were to be extended to the year 2047.

From mid-1997 all existing Chinese residents of Hong Kong became citizens of the People's Republic of China. As such, they were forbidden by Chinese law to hold dual British nationality. Following approval of the Hong Kong agreement, the British Government announced a new form of nationality, to be effective from 1997, designated 'British National (Overseas)', which would entitle the holders to British consular protection when travelling outside China. This status conferred no right of abode in the UK and was not transferable to descendants. Non-Chinese residents of Hong Kong were not to be granted Chinese nationality after 1997. They were to be entitled to hold only the new British National (Overseas) passport, and there were fears that they might become, in effect, stateless. In September 1995 the Governor aroused much controversy when he urged the UK to give the right of abode to more than 3m. Hong Kong citizens.

A 59-member Basic Law Drafting Committee (BLDC) was formed in Beijing in June 1985, with the aim of drawing up a new Basic Law (Constitution) for Hong Kong, in accordance with Article 31 of the Chinese Constitution, which provides for special administrative regions within the People's Republic. The BLDC included 25 representatives from Hong Kong itself. In April 1988 the first draft of the Basic Law for Hong Kong was published, and public comments were invited. In the light of these criticisms, the draft was further revised and a second version was published in February 1989.

The final draft was adopted by the National People's Congress of China in April 1990. The Basic Law gives China the right to declare a state of emergency in the territory and the right to station Chinese troops there. The SAR is also required to enact laws prohibiting any acts of subversion against the Government of China and forbidding any political groups in the SAR from establishing ties with any foreign organizations. Because of these provisions, the Legislative Council passed, by a large majority, a motion in April 1990 expressing its disapproval of the Basic Law.

A Joint Liaison Group (JLG), consisting of five representatives each from China and the UK, was established to hold consultations on the implementation of the Joint Declaration and to oversee arrangements for a smooth transition to Chinese sovereignty. Agreement was reached on a number of issues between 1985 and 1989, including the clearance of the Kowloon Walled City. Following the Tiananmen massacre, and particularly after the arrival of Chris Patten, progress was much slower. China asserted its right to veto any policy decisions that encompassed 1997 and withheld its approval of proposals to adapt legislation and revise international agreements to take account of China's resumption of sovereignty. In 1994, after seven years of negotiation, China and the UK finally reached agreement on the disposal of the land occupied by the British garrison. More than one-half of the barracks sites were to be handed over to the Hong Kong Government for redevelopment. The remainder was to be used by the Chinese army and navy. In 1995 agreement was reached on the procedure for the establishment of a Court of Final Appeal, which was to replace the Privy Council after 1997.

In September 1996 China and the UK agreed on the arrangements for the ceremony marking the transfer of sovereignty, which was to take place at midnight on 30 June 1997. In January 1997 the two Governments reached agreement on defining the borders of the territory of Hong Kong and formally signed a memorandum on the boundary in June.

PREPARATIONS FOR THE RESUMPTION OF CHINESE SOVEREIGNTY

Following the breakdown of the 1993 talks over Chris Patten's reform proposals, the Chinese Government declared that it would establish a 'second stove' in order to ensure a smooth political transition. This unilateral action to create new political institutions for the SAR, from the Chinese perspective, was to be consistent with the Joint Declaration, the Basic Law and the understanding reached in 1990 between the Chinese Minister of Foreign Affairs and the British Foreign Secretary. In July 1993 the Chinese Government established a Preliminary Working Committee (PWC) to advise on and formulate proposals for the transition. The PWC, chaired by the Vice-Premier and Minister of Foreign Affairs, Qian Qichen, comprised key Chinese officials in charge of Hong Kong affairs, as well as prominent pro-Beijing government figures. There were five sub-groups with responsibilities for economic, political, legal, cultural, and social and security matters. Since the Chinese Government refused to accept the Legislative Council elected in 1995, the PWC proposed the establishment of a provisional council in order to avoid a power vacuum in the territory.

In January 1996 a 150-member Preparatory Committee (PC) for the Hong Kong SAR was formally established, to succeed the PWC. The PC, also headed by Qian Qichen, included 94 members from Hong Kong and 56 members from the mainland. Most Hong Kong members were known to be sympathetic to the Beijing Government's position on Hong Kong. While a number of legislative councillors were appointed to the PC, the Democratic Party of Hong Kong, the largest political party in the Legislative Council, was excluded. In March the PC decided that a 60-member Provisional Legislative Council (PLC) was to be established, which would commence operation after the election of the first Chief Executive of the SAR. It also decided that the PLC should cease operation upon the formation of the first Legislative Council of the SAR, while the term of the PLC was not to extend beyond 30 June 1998. All PLC members had to be permanent residents of Hong Kong, with up to 12 members holding non-Chinese nationality or the right of abode in foreign countries. Members of the PLC were to be chosen by a 400-member Selection Committee, which would also elect the SAR's first Chief Executive. The responsibilities of the PLC included: to enact, amend or appeal laws to ensure the proper functioning of the Hong Kong SAR; to examine and approve budgets proposed by the administration; to approve taxation and public expenditure; to receive and debate the policy address of the Chief Executive of the SAR; to endorse the appointment of the judges of the Court of Final Appeal and the Chief Judge of the High Court; to deal with other necessary legislative matters before the formation of the first SAR Legislative Council. The President of the PLC also had to participate in the nomination of the six Hong Kong members of the Committee for the Basic Law of the Standing Committee of the National People's Congress in Beijing.

In November 1996 the PC elected the 400-member Selection Committee from among 5,789 candidates. On 11 December Tung Chee-hwa, having defeated two other candidates (the former Chief Justice, (Sir) Yang Ti-liang, and businessman Peter Woo) in the final round of the selection process, was elected the first Chief Executive of the SAR Government by the Selection Committee. On 21 December the PLC's 60 members were elected from among 134 candidates. Thirty-three served concurrently in the existing Legislative Council, but the Democratic Party of Hong Kong boycotted the election. On 14 March 1997 the National People's Congress approved a PC report on the establishment of the PLC. Soon after its establishment, the PLC began operation in parallel to the Legislative Council, in the neighbouring town of Shenzhen, scrutinizing and passing bills. In June the PLC introduced legislation to restore colonial restrictions and to impose new conditions on public demonstrations and the establishment of political organizations in the SAR. Under the legislation, public demonstrations and political organizations could be banned in the interests of national security, defined as 'the safeguarding of the territorial integrity and the independence of the People's Republic of China'. Political organizations were, moreover, not permitted to have connections with foreign political organizations or with Taiwan.

THE SAR GOVERNMENT

On 1 July 1997, following the handover ceremony at midnight, the SAR Government was inaugurated at 1.30 a.m. The ceremonies were attended by 4,000 dignitaries, including ministers of foreign affairs from more than 40 countries and senior representatives of more than 40 international organizations. The newly-elected British Prime Minister and his Foreign Secretary, as well as the US Secretary of State, however, did not attend the inauguration, in an expression of their disapproval of the swearing-in of PLC members during the ceremony. Legislators from the Democratic Party of Hong Kong and a number of independent Legislative Councillors protested against the abolition of the Legislative Council on the balcony of the Council building, shortly after midnight, vowing to return by means of elections in 1998.

More than 4,000 People's Liberation Army troops were deployed to the Hong Kong garrison. With the consent of the British, a small number of unarmed military personnel entered the territory in April and May 1997, and an advance party of some 500 troops crossed the border a few hours before the handover ceremony. Twenty-two of the 23 principal officials were retained by the SAR administration. The only new appointment was that of the Secretary for Justice, who replaced a retired expatriate. The incoming Executive Council had 14 members, with a former senior Executive Council member as convener, three ex-officio members, the Chief Secretary, the Financial Secretary and the Secretary for Justice, and 10 unofficial members. In addition to the Chief Secretary and the Financial Secretary, two outgoing members of the previous Executive Council were reappointed. The Chief Executive also appointed a special adviser with close connections to the Beijing Government. In March 1999 Anson Chan, regarded by the international media as representing Hong Kong's conscience, agreed to continue serving as Chief Secretary for Administration for two years beyond her normal retirement age, until 2002, when the term of office of the Chief Executive was to end. In June 1999 the Government appointed Dr E. K. Yeoh, hitherto Chief Executive of the Hospital Authority, as Secretary for Health and Welfare. After the Secretary for Justice, Dr Yeoh was the second non-civil servant to be appointed to a senior civil service position by the SAR Government. The convener of the Executive Council, Dr Chung Sze-yuen, retired in late June. He was replaced by a fellow member of the Executive Council, Leung Chun-ying. In May 2000 Elsie Leung was reappointed as Secretary of Justice, for a further two years. In January 2001 Anson Chan unexpectedly announced that for personal reasons she would step down at the end of April, well before the expiry of Tung's first term. She was replaced by the hitherto Financial Secretary, Donald Tsang. Antony Leung, a former banker and member of the Executive Council, was appointed Financial Secretary. In 1999, meanwhile, the Government announced a civil service reform programme, including the introduction of performance-based pay, new entry and exit procedures and a lower starting salary. The initiative encountered resistance. In July 2002 thousands of civil servants took to the streets to demonstrate against the pay decreases, introduced by the Government in an effort to reduce civil service costs (as a measure to counter the SAR's budget deficit). While the public appeared to be supportive of the pay decreases, there were concerns that the administration had not handled the issue well and that as a result morale in the civil service had suffered.

The SAR Government replaced the existing local administration with the Provisional Urban Council, a Provisional Regional Council and 18 Provisional District Boards. While their responsibilities remained the same and all existing councillors and board members continued to serve, membership of these elected bodies was expanded with appointed members, many of whom had been unsuccessful in earlier elections. In April 1999 the SAR administration decided to restructure local government by abolishing the municipal and regional councils. The Government intended to assume responsibility for the public services offered by the councils. Existing district boards were to be replaced by district councils. While the public was dissatisfied with the performance of the two municipal councils, critics of the Government maintained that the restructuring was a retrograde step in terms of local democracy. In November the Democratic Party of Hong Kong threatened legal action if the plan were not abandoned, as it contravened the Basic Law. The Hong Kong SAR's first district elections took place on 28 November. The Democratic Party of Hong Kong won the largest number of elected seats (86), but the pro-Beijing Democratic Alliance for the Betterment of Hong Kong (DAB) substantially increased its representation, from 37 seats to 83.

One of the first acts of the SAR administration was the introduction of legislation to prevent an influx of mainland-born children of Hong Kong residents. These children were granted the right of abode in the territory by the Basic Law, but the Government insisted that they could be admitted only upon verification of their identities and in an orderly fashion, according to a quota system controlled by the mainland authorities.

Elections for the first Legislative Council of the SAR were held on 24 May 1998 and were conducted under new electoral arrangements. Of the 60 seats, 30 were elected by narrowly-defined functional constituencies, 20 were elected by proportional representation in geographically-based constituencies and 10 were chosen by an 800-member Election Committee. Pro-democracy parties criticized the reduction of the franchise under these new arrangements. Despite heavy rain, the people of Hong Kong turned out to vote in large numbers. With almost 1.5m. registered voters casting their ballots, the participation rate of 53.3% was the highest since the introduction of direct elections in Hong Kong. Most former Legislative Councillors who had boycotted the Provisional Legislative Council were elected to the new legislature.

The Democratic Party of Hong Kong, led by Martin Lee, returned to the Legislative Council with 13 seats, of which nine were obtained in the geographical constituencies. Although the Democratic Party of Hong Kong and other pro-democracy parties received solid support from the electorate and won most seats in the geographical constituencies (14 of the 20 seats) their overall political strength in the legislature was reduced. Together with the Frontier and the Citizens' Party, and liberal independents, the pro-democracy camp secured a total of 19 seats. Another pro-democracy group,the Association for Democracy and People's Livelihood, which had participated in the PLC, lost all its seats on the Council.

Pro-Beijing supporters dominated the functional constituencies and the electoral committee ballot and also achieved some seats in the geographical constituencies. The DAB, which won 10 seats, with five from geographical constituencies, benefited most from the new electoral system. The leader of the pro-business Liberal Party, Allen Lee, failed to win a seat in the geographical elections, but his party obtained 10 seats through the functional and election committee constituencies, while the Hong Kong Progressive Alliance managed to obtain five seats.

The powers of the new legislature were curbed by the Basic Law. Henceforth Legislative Councillors were not permitted to introduce bills related to public expenditure, the political structure or the operation of the government. The passage of private members' bills or motions also required the majority of votes of both groups of councillors—those elected through geographical constituencies, and those returned through functional constituencies and the election committee.

Although political forces in the first legislature were fragmented, the Legislative Council was more assertive than the PLC. Even before the new legislature convened, the seven major political parties, together with a number of like-minded independents, formed a temporary alliance in June 1998, demanding that the administration adopt new measures to address the economic downturn in Hong Kong. Tung Chee-hwa responded by announcing a series of government initiatives to improve the economic situation, including the abolition of savings tax for commercial corporations, the postponement of the sale of land by auction and tender until 31 March 1999, an increase in loans to home-buyers, and allocation of additional government funding to assist small and medium enterprises. The coalition was not maintained over constitutional and political issues. Senior civil servants were often required to respond to questions presented by the Legislative Council. In June 2000 the legislature overwhelmingly approved a vote of 'no confidence' in two senior officials, following a series of public housing scandals. One of the officials involved, the Secretary for Housing, Rosanna Wong, resigned shortly before the vote took place. The term of the Legislative Council ended on 30 June 2000. All the major political parties presented candidates for the elections to the second post-1997 legislature, which were held on 10 September 2000. The number of directly-elective seats was increased from 20 to 24, while the number of Council members selected by the Election Committee was reduced from 10 to six. (The ballot for Election Committee members, who were responsible for choosing those who were to occupy the Election Committee seats, had taken place in July.) Of the 60 seats on the Legislative Council the Democratic Party of Hong Kong secured a total of 12 (including nine by direct election), the DAB won 11 seats (including eight by direct election), and the Liberal Party won eight seats. The level of voter participation was 43.6% of the electorate. Following the resignation from the incoming Legislative Council on 19 September of a newly-elected member, Gary Cheng, the DAB's Vice-Chairman (owing to his admission of a conflict of interest between his role as a legislator and previously-undeclared business assets), a by-election took place on 10 December. The seat was won by Audrey Eu, an independent candidate and former chairperson of the Hong Kong Bar Association.

In March 2001 the Hong Kong Government introduced the Chief Executive Election Bill, interpreting the powers of the central Government in Beijing to remove the Chief Executive and providing detailed arrangements for the next election for the latter. Although the Government amended the Bill's provisions relating to the removal of the Chief Executive (after it was criticized by some legislators for giving unnecessary powers to the Chinese Government), following which the Bill was duly passed by the Legislative Council by 36 votes to 18 in July 2001, the approval of the new legislation was widely regarded as a set-back for Hong Kong's democratic progress.

An economic recession followed the financial turmoil that affected the Asian region from mid-1997, leading to the collapse of the Hong Kong property market, rising unemployment and negative economic growth. In August 1998 the Government launched a massive intervention in the financial markets, spending more than US $15,000m. in an attempt to maintain the stability of the currency and stock markets, in the face of manipulation by foreign speculators. Although the intervention was supported by the local business community, it undermined Hong Kong's reputation as a free economy, and at the time was criticized by the international media. However, many observers later accepted as necessary the authorities' involvement in the financial markets, owing to the exceptional situation. While the economic situation stabilized, the Government warned that economic difficulties were structural in nature. At the beginning of 2002 the Government forecast a modest real growth of 1% for the year, and in June the unemployment rate reached a record 7.4% (see Economy).

The issue of the right of abode raised questions as to the foundation of the rule of law and Hong Kong's autonomous status. On 29 January 1999 the Court of Final Appeal (CFA) ruled against the SAR Government's position that, according to Article 24 of the Basic Law, mainland children born of a Hong Kong permanent resident should be granted the right of abode in the territory only if at the time of their birth their parents had already become permanent residents. In delivering their verdict, the judges also maintained that the CFA had the authority to interpret the Basic Law. The ruling was questioned by mainland legal experts who had been involved with the drafting of the Basic Law and by other senior Chinese officials. In February, in response to a motion filed by the Department of Justice, the CFA declared that its ruling did not question the authority of the Standing Committee of the NPC. Human-rights groups argued that the Government's action, in seeking clarification from the Court, undermined the rule of law and judicial independence in Hong Kong. Claiming that the decision would lead to the influx of more than 1.6m. people from the mainland, the SAR authorities suggested that the CFA had misinterpreted the Basic Law. Supported by opinion polls, in May the SAR Government requested the State Council (Cabinet) of China to ask the Ninth NPC to interpret the relevant articles of the Basic Law. Pro-democracy legislators walked out of the Legislative Council Chamber in protest at the Government's decision. In late June the Standing Committee of the Ninth NPC ruled that the CFA's interpretation of the Basic Law was wrong and provided a new interpretation, which reduced the number of mainland children with the right of abode in Hong Kong to about 200,000.

In April 2000 a deputy director of the Liaison Office of the Central People's Government (CPG), formerly part of the Hong Kong branch of the Xinhua News Agency, suggested that the Hong Kong media should not disseminate the views of those who advocated the independence of Taiwan. In June another official from the Liaison Office warned the local business community not to deal with Taiwanese companies that support independence for Taiwan. Following both incidents, the Hong Kong Government reaffirmed that the local media remained free to report and comment on public issues, and that businesses in the SAR were at liberty to choose their business partners.

In January 2001 a CPG official stated that no organization or individual should be allowed to turn Hong Kong into the centre of activities for Falun Gong, a controversial religious group banned in the mainland since 1999. In June 2001 the Chief Executive declared the group to be an 'evil cult'. Nevertheless, the Government announced that it did not intend to introduce anti-cult legislation.

In July 2001 Li Shaomin, a US national who had been convicted in China of spying for Taiwan and who had spent five months in a mainland prison, was permitted by the Hong Kong Government to return to the SAR, where he worked as an academic. His case was widely seen as a test of the 'one country, two systems' arrangement with China. Li's employer, the City University of Hong Kong, decided to permit him to resume his teaching and research duties. He later returned to the USA when his leave application was unsucessful.

In December 2001 Tung Chee-hwa announced that he would stand for a second five-year term as Chief Executive, the election having been scheduled for 24 March 2002. The central Government in Beijing endorsed his candidacy. On the closing date for nominations at the end of February 2002, however, Tung was the only candidate with overwhelming support, having received 714 nominations from the 794-strong Selection Committee. On 4 March, therefore, the central Government formally appointed Tung for a second term, beginning on 1 July 2002.

The most important political change that Tung introduced was a new scheme for the appointment of senior officials. Under this scheme, all principal officials, defined as the Chief Secretary for Administration, the Financial Secretary, the Secretary for Justice, along with the 11 secretaries in charge of policy bureaux, were to become political appointees, with their terms of office not exceeding that of the Chief Executive who had appointed them. These senior officials, widely regarded as 'ministers', were also to be members of the Executive Council, thus turning it into a cabinet-style body. The principal officials would report directly to the Chief Executive and would have to accept total responsibility for their respective portfolios. The civil service remained a permanent service based on meritocracy. Amid criticisms that the 'ministers' were accountable only to the Chief Executive and not to the Legislative Council or to the public, in addition to concerns that the arrangements might not be consistent with the Basic Law, the new scheme was approved by the Legislative Council on 29 May 2002, less than six weeks after its first formal introduction there. In mid-June the Council approved the funding, and a Government resolution transferring statutory powers to the principal officials was passed by a vote of 36 to 21.

The 14 principal officials appointed by Tung included eight who had served under Tung in his first term. The three most senior officials, Donald Tsang (Chief Secretary), Antony Leung (Financial Secretary) and Elsie Leung (Secretary for Justice) remained unchanged. Tung appointed five new 'ministers' from business and the professions: the Secretary for Commerce, Industry and Technology, Henry Tang Ying-yen; the Secretary for Education and Manpower, Arthur Li Kwok-cheung; the Secretary for Home Affairs, Patrick Ho Chi-ping; the Secretary for the Environment, Transport and Works, Sarah Liao Sau-tung; and the Secretary for Financial Services and the Treasury, Frederick Ma Si-hang. In addition to the 14 principal officials, Tung appointed five non-official members to the Executive Council, including the leaders of two political parties—James Tien from the Liberal Party and Jasper Tsang Yok-sing from the DAB.

The Government tried to allay concerns about the political neutrality of the civil service under the new scheme by announcing that the Secretary for the Civil Service would be selected from within the civil service and would not lose civil servant status if he or she decided to return to the service upon the expiry of his or her term. The new scheme represented a significant political change. While pro-democracy groups opposed the scheme and denounced it as undemocratic, an accurate assessment of its political consequences for the SAR's governance would be possible only in the longer term.

While the international community remained generally impressed by the success of the 'one country, two systems' arrangement for Hong Kong, and while foreign governments continued to express satisfaction with Hong Kong's autonomy five years after the resumption of Chinese sovereignty, in 2002 there were concerns over the handling of demonstrators in Hong Kong and the use of immigration powers by the SAR authorities. In its six-monthly report on Hong Kong to Parliament, the British Government highlighted the arrests of some Falun Gong demonstrators and the handcuffing of two journalists covering a police operation to clear protesters demonstrating against the repatriation to the mainland of failed right-of-abode seekers. The SAR Government denied entry to the Chinese-US human rights activist, Harry Wu Hongda, who had been invited to speak at the Foreign Correspondents' Club in June. Falun Gong representatives in Hong Kong also claimed that almost 100 practitioners from abroad had been refused entry prior to the celebrations for the 5th anniversary of Hong Kong's transfer of sovereignty on 1 July 2002, an event attended by President Jiang Zemin.

Hong Kong took an active part in the worldwide efforts against terrorism during 2002 in its capacity as the President of the Financial Action Task Force on Money Laundering, based in Paris. Hong Kong police and customs authorities also established a special unit to address suspicious financial transactions. The Government introduced the UN (Anti-Terrorism Measures) Bill in April 2002, and it was approved in June with the amendment that the administration's power to list terrorist organizations that were not already designated as terrorist groups by the UN Security Council should be subject to judicial review.

Economy

FRANÇOIS GIPOULOUX

ECONOMIC DEVELOPMENT

From 1997 Hong Kong's economic performance was mitigated. After recovering quickly from the financial crisis that affected Asia from mid-1997, the problems facing the Special Administrative Region (SAR) in mid-2002 were more closely related to the downturn in the world economy and to the increasing integration of China's economy into the world trade system than to the territory's reversion to Chinese sovereignty in 1997. The average annual growth rate of the territory's gross domestic product (GDP) between 1996 and 2001 was 2.5%, half the rate achieved between1990 and1996. Taking the price deflation from 1999 into account, the value of Hong Kong's GDP at the end of 2001 was below the level of 1997. Hong Kong remains, however, a major international commercial centre, being one of the largest trading entities in goods and among the most significant financial centres in the world. Hong Kong continued to be classified as the world's freest market in 2002 by the US Heritage Foundation 2002 Index of Economic Freedom, and an advanced economy by the IMF from 1997. Compared with the previous year, GDP was forecast to increase by 1.0% in 2002, following a 0.1% increase in 2001. Per caput GDP was forecast to decrease by around 2.0% in 2002, after a 1.2% decline in 2001. Per caput GDP was forecast at HK $184,800 (or US $23,700) in 2002. Hong Kong is thus placed among the highest group of world economic rankings. Although the general standard of living of the Hong Kong population has significantly improved, however, the increase in wealth per caput has been very inequitably distributed. As a result, the lowest 10% of income earners receive less than one-half of that of the median, and less than one-sixth of the earnings of the top 10% of the working population.

Despite political interference in the functioning of its independent judiciary and perceived threats to the independence of the press, in economic terms Hong Kong's return to Chinese sovereignty appears to have proceeded relatively smoothly. Under the 'one country, two systems' concept, Hong Kong has charted its own course, with the exception of foreign affairs and defence. The SAR's mini-constitution—the Basic Law—guarantees that the capitalist system and way of life in Hong Kong will remain unchanged for 50 years. Hong Kong has been promised, and is exercising, a high degree of autonomy and continues, among other responsibilities, to manage its own economic policies and finances. It issues its own currency, enjoys a low and simple tax regime, maintains its own laws and common-law legal system, employs its own civil servants and remains a separate customs territory.

The Asian financial crisis (of 1997/98) provoked a downturn in real estate prices. Office and residential rental prices declined by 65% and 55% respectively from the peak reached in the third quarter of 1997. The regional financial turmoil brought about a fall in the Hong Kong stock and property markets, and a sharp rise in unemployment. The depressed economic conditions in most countries of the region in the late 1990s affected intra-regional trade. The subdued sentiment, risk sensitivity and financial stringency, which hampered consumption, investment and normal business operations, compounded the uncertainties.

However, despite the relatively severe upheaval that occurred, the basis of the economy remains strong. Banks' finances are generally sound and well supported—the Government holds substantial fiscal and foreign-exchange reserves and is not burdened by any substantial public debt. The corporate sector is reducing and rationalizing its operations for greater efficiency and competitiveness, and the labour force is adapting promptly to more stringent employment conditions. Inflation, which in 1997 stood at an average annual rate of 5.8% and was threatening to become a major problem, was replaced by deflation in 1998–99, thus causing some concern. The consumer price index fell by 3.7% in 2000, by 1.6% in 2001 and was forecast to decline by 2.2% in 2002. The downward trend in prices resulted from three factors: the poor performance of some Asian economies, which took advantage of the exchange rate situation to boost their economies; the competition emanating from China, where costs and prices are lower; and the decline in the real estate sector in Hong Kong. However, the economy as a whole displayed the profound flexibility that was required for it to withstand the ensuing difficulties. In addition, the enormous growth potential of the mainland should instil confidence in the longer-term outlook for the Hong Kong economy.

From the early 1980s the Hong Kong economy underwent considerable structural change. The contribution of the local manufacturing sector has declined significantly as a percentage of GDP, from almost 24% in 1980 to 19% in 1989 and 5.9% in 2000. There has been a corresponding growth in the services sector, from 68% in 1980 to 73% in 1989 and to 85.7% in 2000. Within the latter sector are the categories of finance, insurance, real estate and business services, which are indicative of the sophistication of a metropolitan economy. The contribution to GDP of this cluster of services more than doubled in value between 1985 and 1997, while the number of jobs provided by the services sector tripled. Hong Kong's predominance as a service-based economy is reflected in its communications network, one of the densest in the world. In turn, this shift to services requires measures to maintain and increase Hong Kong's international competitiveness in the sector, including training, language competence and the availability of reasonably-priced commercial office space. However, these figures can be misleading, and do not mean that Hong Kong does not depend significantly on manufacturing activities. For example, thousands of companies have switched some or all of their production to the mainland, and have been officially reclassified as trading rather than manufacturing entities, even though they may be local producers and their major activity remains the organization of production.

There is a broad consensus regarding the factors underlying Hong Kong's economic performance. For more than 40 years the colonial Government maintained reasonable stability of political institutions and supported a market regime that allowed for great flexibility of resource use and provided strong incentives to wealth acquisition, in the form of low income taxes and no taxes on capital gains. In addition, the world economy provided a favourable environment for growth through trade. The manufacturing base in Hong Kong was developed following the communists' assumption of power in China in 1949. Having been expelled from the mainland, the capitalists of Shanghai transferred their expertise in labour-intensive manufacturing, their commercial networks and some of their capital resources to Hong Kong. Their skills, combined with the availability of cheap labour, the entrepreneurial character of these refugees and the laissez-faire environment of the territory, produced impressive industrial results, propelling Hong Kong to a leading position in the labour-intensive manufacture of products such as textiles, and subsequently plastic flowers, rattan furniture, watches and clocks, electronics and precision machinery. By the early 1980s the manufacturing labour force that supported Hong Kong's production and export performance totalled almost 1m. workers.

During the post-War era from 1945, the Hong Kong Government adopted a policy of minimal interference, allowing market forces to prevail. The tax system is simple, and rates of taxation are low. The business profit tax is 16%, and the highest rate of personal income tax is 15% of salary. Owing to a system of generous allowances, 61% of the work-force pay no tax at all on their salaries. Furthermore, there are no taxes on capital gains, dividends or interest. The Government's policy of low taxation and prudent fiscal management enabled it, generally, to achieve surpluses on its consolidated account during the 1990s. Nevertheless, the Government plays a significant role in infrastructural development, healthcare services, public housing and land sales. Policy intervention was prompted mainly by strong popular pressure. For example, the post-War population inflow, and the huge shanty towns that it created, ultimately led to the establishment of a public housing programme. By 1982 40% of the population had been housed under the programme. Similarly, riots in 1966 led to an expansion of social services, such as a public assistance scheme covering the elderly, and the passage of employment legislation restricting child labour and mandating four rest days per month. From the 1990s the Government also became more pro-active in its support of high-technology development. It encourages applied research and development, and has plans to establish a science park.

Hong Kong is now a major regional centre for business in Asia; as of 1 June 2001 there were a total of 3,237 regional operations, representing a 7.9% increase over 2000. The total number of regional headquarters in 2001 rose from 855 in 2000 to 944, an increase of 10.4%. The previous record was 903 regional headquarters in 1997. The number of regional offices rose by 6.8%, from a total of 2,146 in 2000 to 2,293 in 2001. The USA headed the list of countries with the largest number of regional headquarters in Hong Kong, with a total of 221 companies. This was followed by Japan with 160 companies, and the United Kingdom with 90 companies.

POPULATION AND WORK-FORCE

The quality of Hong Kong's human resources has been an important factor in economic growth. In mid-2001 the population of the SAR totalled 6,724,900, representing an increase of 0.3m. compared with mid-1996. The population growth between mid-2000 and mid-2001 was moderate, at 1.1%. In the most recent projections, Hong Kong's population was expected to increase at an even lower average annual rate, of 0.9%, to reach 8.72m. in mid-2031. According to the Census and Statistics Department, migration would be the main source of growth in population, accounting for 93% during the 2002–31 period. Natural increase of the population would account for 7% during the same period. With a land area of less than 1,100 sq km, Hong Kong is one of the most densely-populated places in the world, the population density reaching 6,124.5 people per sq km in mid-2001. The highest density is found in Kowloon (43,201 inhabitants per sq km), while Hong Kong Island's density reached 16,635 persons per sq km and that of the New Territories and outlying islands 3,443. The proportion of Hong Kong's population living in Kowloon decreased from 32% in 1996 to 30.2 % in 2001, while the proportion living in the New Territories increased from 46.8% to almost 50%, a reflection of the Government's policy of developing new towns in the New Territories. The proportion of the population living on Hong Kong Island decreased from 21.1% to 19.9% during the same period. The annual population growth decreased from 3.3% in the 1960s, to 2.2% in the 1970s and 2.0% in the 1980s. The fall in population growth is attributed to a decline in the birth rate and to net migration. During the period 1990–2000 annual population growth averaged 1.8%. In 1986 the crude birth rate was 13.0 per 1,000 people; the rate declined to an estimated 7.2 per 1,000 in 2001. The population will continue to follow a continuous ageing trend. In 2001 16% of the population was aged under 15. This rate was expected to decrease to 12% by 2031. The proportion of those aged 65 and over was projected to rise significantly, from 11% in 2001 to 24% in 2031.

The population of Hong Kong is one of the most well-educated in the region. Moreover, the general educational level of the population improved markedly during 1990–2000. While 59.5% of the population aged 15 and over had attained secondary education and above in 1990, the percentage increased to 70.2% in 2000. Analysed by sex, the proportion of males having attained secondary education or above in 2000 was 74.0%, and 66.6% for females. The increase in education opportunities (school places provided by kindergartens, primary and secondary schools, technical institutes, and colleges as well as tertiary institutions) contributed to these major improvements in educational achievements.

In 2000 the total labour force was 3.38m. As the sectoral composition of the economy and the skill level of the population have changed, so has the occupational distribution of employment. The decline of the manufacturing sector has been dramatic: in 1990 it accounted for 28% of total employment, but by 2000 a mere 10.5% of the labour force were employed in the sector. The expansion of the services sector, meanwhile, has been impressive. There is no legal minimum wage in Hong Kong. In September 2001 the average wage rate for supervisory technical, clerical and miscellaneous non-production workers in the wholesale, retail and import-export trades, and restaurant and hotel sector was HK $12,067 per month (about US $1,547). In June 2001 a production manager in the manufacturing sector was earning an average of HK $32,900 (about US $4,220). Other staff in the manufacturing sector, such as a human resources manager, earned about HK $45,500 per month (about US $5,830). Other workers in the manufacturing sector earned HK $10,096 (US $1,294) per month. On the service side of the economy, accounting professionals in the financial sector earned HK $32,100 monthly (US $4,120) in June 2001, while a retail store manager earned HK $22,200 (US $2,850) monthly. In the same sector a marketing, sales, or product manager earned HK $36,700 (US $4,710). Hong Kong has always had one of the most fluid labour markets in the world. This is particularly true of the highly-skilled work-force, which has formed a large proportion of the immigrants to and emigrants from Hong Kong. The right to emigrate is guaranteed in the basic law. From 1992 (when there were 66,200 emigrants) to 2001 (10,600 emigrants), there has been a downward trend in emigration.

By international standards, Hong Kong's unemployment rate has been low, but the situation deteriorated in the late 1990s and again from 2001. As unemployment was unable to match the growth in labour supply amidst more widespread corporate downsizing and lay-offs, the unemployment rate surged to 6.1% during the fourth quarter of 2001, and reached a new record of 7.4% in June 2002. The median duration of unemployment in 2001 lengthened from 78 to 82 days, while the proportion of persons unemployed for three months or longer went up from 42% to 45%. The underemployment rate also rose appreciably from 2.6% in the fourth quarter of 2000 to 3.0% in the fourth quarter of 2001. Seasonally-adjusted unemployment rates rose to 7.1% in February–April 2002, reflecting a further deterioration of many major economic sectors including decoration and maintenance, manufacturing, restaurants, financing, sanitary services, education services and recreational services. Unemployment and underemployment are found mainly among the semi-skilled, such as production-related workers. On the other hand, Hong Kong labour mobility is high. During the final quarter of 2001, some 392,000 persons (or 12% of the work force) changed jobs. Extrapolating this high mobility rate for a period of one year, almost one-half of the work force would have changed jobs. Interestingly, some 48% of employed persons left their jobs essentially owing to dissatisfaction with their working conditions. This high mobility rate emphasizes the efficiency of the labour market since almost one-half of the 'job-hoppers' experienced less than one month of unemployment before being hired again. This high labour mobility is both a strong point (flexibility during crises) and a constraint during periods of rapid recovery. In those periods Hong Kong 'job-hoppers' have been heavily criticized by employers. Finally, despite the recent economic downturn, employment in the private sector increased by 14.4% between 1996 and 2001—a net creation of 174,000 jobs. The proportion of services in private employment increased from 79% in 1996 to 84% in 2001. Conversely, the manufacturing sector's contribution to employment in the private sector declined from 10.9% to 6.5%. Also noteworthy was the relative decline of Hong Kong's entrepôt function and its growing importance as a major financial and business services hub. The import-export trade lost 14,000 jobs from 1996 to 2001, while the financial and business services sectors created almost 124,000 jobs. Finally, the household service sector has been the main job provider for private employment: 146,000 jobs were created over five years, mainly in education, health and social services.

INDUSTRY

Hong Kong has long had a reputation for being a producer and exporter of manufactured goods. Most output is of light manufacturing, but Hong Kong also has construction, shipbuilding and aircraft engineering industries. About 80% of its manufactures are exported, with its main markets being China, the USA, Germany and Japan. Although declining, manufacturing continues to be an important sector of Hong Kong's economy. Mechanization, automation, and the relocation of labour-intensive and lower value-added manufacturing processes to mainland China have contributed to the decline in manufacturing employment. This has facilitated Hong Kong's development of more knowledge-based and higher value-added manufacturing. Thus, manufacturing productivity (gross output per employee) significantly increased (by more than 400%) between 1983 and 1999, with a further 2% increase in 2000.

There were around 19,000 manufacturing establishments in Hong Kong in 2000, employing 214,000 people. Many smaller enterprises are linked with larger factories through an efficient and flexible subcontracting network. This arrangement has enabled the manufacturing sector to respond swiftly to changes in external demand. The opening of mainland China, combined with low labour and land costs there, significantly altered the industrial landscape in Hong Kong. Local manufacturers relocated most of their productive capacities across the border through subcontract processing arrangements in mainland China. Therefore, the number of establishments and persons engaged in the local manufacturing sector decreased significantly between 1990 and 2000, while the average number of employees per establishment also declined. This decline has been offset, however, by a strong rise in labour productivity. Over the period 1990–1999 the annual average growth of the labour productivity index for the whole manufacturing sector was 7.1%. Among selected industry groups like electrical and electronic products, this ratio reached 16%. It is worth noting, moreover, that most of the firms that relocated their manufacturing processes to mainland China have continued to conduct export operations in Hong Kong as import-export firms. In doing so, they facilitate the import of goods produced by their associate manufacturing firms in the mainland for subsequent re-export to overseas markets. While those firms are now registered in the services sector, they often provide manufacturing-related technical support services (e.g. product design, sample and mould working, production planning, quality control) to the production activities in the mainland. The frontiers between manufacturing and non-manufacturing activities are thus becoming less distinct. It may be appropriate to take into account the contribution of trading firms with manufacturing-related activities in assessing the share of manufacturing in the economy. The proportion of import-export firms engaged in China out of the total number of firms (including all manufacturing-related activities) increased both in terms of the number of establishments (47.4% to 52.3%) and the number of employed persons (from 28.7% to 37.4%) between 1995 and 1999.

The clothing industry, which has played a pivotal role in Hong Kong's development, faces challenges from continued global economic restructuring and the accession of China to the World Trade Organization (WTO) in December 2001. With all quotas being abolished by 2004, China's removal of quota restrictions will allow Hong Kong manufacturers to market their mainland-origin products freely. Therefore, the relocation of Hong Kong manufacturers to the mainland to take advantage of its lower cost base will continue. In 2000 the clothing sector accounted for 42.8% of Hong Kong's domestic exports, with its total value having risen from HK $74,251m. in 1999 to HK $77,415m. in 2000. Re-exports of clothing were worth HK $99,308m. in 1999, increasing to HK $111,268m. in 2000. Nearly one-third of Hong Kong's total clothing exports in 1999 went to the US market, while EU countries accounted for one-fifth of the total.

The electronic industry exhibits a particular strength in the manufacture of consumer electronics (especially audio and video equipment). Hong Kong's advantage comes from efficient low-cost manufacturing, consumer product trend identification and aesthetic design capabilities. As electronic companies are moving into more technology-intensive products, the shift from low-profit-margin, mass-produced, labour-intensive products to more capital items and equipment products has sharpened the competition with other Asian suppliers. Owing to the rapid expansion in internet applications and sustained demand for telecommunication services, the market for related equipment is expected to be strong, and more intense competition from mainland suppliers will affect Hong Kong's exports to this market.

Being a major world exporter of toys, the SAR produces a wide range of these products, with a particular strength in plastic toys. Hong Kong is also a major exporter of other plastic products. Additionally, there are numerous local end-users, including plastic factories producing toys, packaging materials, shoes, housewares and casings of electrical and electronic consumer goods. Hong Kong is one of the world's principal manufacturers of watches and clocks.

TRADE AND INVESTMENT

In 2001 Hong Kong was the world's 10th largest trading entity. While China's opening up and implementation of economic reforms might have been expected to lead to a multiplication of channels for import and export all over the mainland, at least in coastal areas, and to a subsequent decrease of the relative position of Hong Kong in China's trade, in fact the reverse occurred. The proportion of China's trade sent to or through Hong Kong increased from 11% in 1978 to 40% in 2000. The reasons for this paradox are linked to Hong Kong's remarkable efficiency in providing a range of highly-sophisticated services and to the economy of scale and of scope inherent in an urban centre. In other words, China depends on Hong Kong for numerous services in the value added-chain, such as order-processing, financing, sourcing, production management, product design, quality control, marketing and shipping.

Hong Kong's total exports of goods (comprising re-exports and domestic exports) decreased by 3.0% in 2001, in contrast to a highly strong performance in 2000 when an increase of 17.1% was recorded. Among total exports of goods, re-exports fell by 4.6% in 2001, after a robust growth rate of 18.5% in 2000. Domestic exports decreased sharply, by 15.2% in 2001. This poor performance, the worse since 1962, contrasted with an increase of 7.5% in 2000. The decline is, however, less marked than in Asian economies specializing in electronics such as Singapore, Malaysia, the Republic of Korea, the Philippines and Taiwan, where exports contracted by between 9% and 17% during 2001. The influence of China has undoubtedly been a mitigating factor, absorbing 37.4% of Hong Kong's re-exports in 2001. The decrease in merchandise exports in 2001 was particularly distinct in the markets of the USA (where a contraction of 9% was recorded) and of the European Union (EU, which declined by 8%), while the East Asian market proved more resilient. Exports of goods to East Asia nevertheless recorded growth of 2% in 2000, although sharply down from the 20% growth attained in 2000. Using the competitive manufacturing base of the Chinese mainland, Hong Kong has continued to be the world's leading exporter of toys, clocks, calculators, radios, hairdressing equipment, telephone sets, travel goods and handbags, imitation jewellery and artificial flowers. Exports are of key importance for Hong Kong's domestic industrial performance, with many industries exporting 90% or more of their output. The element of advanced technology in exports remains low, so that Hong Kong has to rely heavily on competitive prices, prompt delivery and other basic factors to maintain its markets. In 2001 the Asia-Pacific region accounted for 67% of Hong Kong's trade and for 11 of the SAR's leading 20 trading partners. China is Hong Kong's largest trading partner (with exchanges totalling US $157,500m. in 2001), followed by the USA

(US $55,700m.), and the EU (US $46,800m.). Total exports to Japan also decreased by 13% compared with 2000. The strong performance of the external sector has also been underpinned by the improved competitiveness of Hong Kong's exports, owing to the cost/price adjustment ratio and productivity upgrading in the local economy. Domestic exports increased by 6.1% in 2000, while re-exports rose by 18.1% and accounted for about 85% of Hong Kong's total exports. The SAR's re-export growth was partly fuelled by the outward processing activities in Guangdong Province in southern China. Raw materials and semi-manufactures are exported to the mainland for processing, and the final products are subsequently returned to Hong Kong before being exported to overseas markets. In 2001 48% of Hong Kong's total exports to the mainland were for outward processing. On the other hand, 78% of Hong Kong imports from the mainland were related to outward processing.

The substantial contribution of re-exports reflects Hong Kong's role as an entrepôt. Re-exports used to be important in the pre-War and 1950s economy, but in the 1960s and 1970s their significance faded quite markedly. Revival began as links with China grew, and by the late 1980s re-exports drew level again with domestic exports. In the late 1990s, while domestic exports were stagnant or decreasing (disregarding the decline in 1998 owing to the Asian financial crisis), re-exports were still increasing dynamically, providing the momentum of growth for the Hong Kong economy. The mainland remained the largest market for Hong Kong's re-exports, accounting for 37.4% of re-exports in 2001. Other major markets included the USA (21.3%), Japan (6.3%), the United Kingdom (3.5%), Germany (3.4%), Taiwan (2.3%) and Singapore (2.0%). Exports of services attained a robust growth rate in 2000, at 14% in value terms to reach HK $334,000m., up significantly from the 8% increase registered in 1999. Offshore trade has also gained from the rapid expansion of regional trade. The deceleration in the economy of the USA in 2001, however, had an adverse impact on Hong Kong's export trade.

Foreign Investment

In 2000 flows of foreign direct investment (FDI) into Asia exceeded US $143,000m. (a 44% increase over 1999), of which 45% was invested in Hong Kong. FDI inflows to Hong Kong in 2000 increased sharply to reach US $64,000m., thus overtaking China to become the largest FDI recipient in Asia. It also represented four times the total inflows to the countries of the Association of South East Asian Nations (ASEAN). This upsurge in inflows can be attributed to three factors, according to the United Nations Conference on Trade and Development (UNCTAD): first, a general improvement in the local business environment; second, the imminence of China's accession to the WTO, which induced investors to deposit funds in Hong Kong in the form of long-term loans to their affiliates in anticipation of business opportunities on the mainland; and third, a prominent cross-border deal in the telecommunications sector, which was partly financed by capital raised through new shares issued to a parent company in the British Virgin Islands. This operation was recorded as capital inflow in Hong Kong. In the first nine months of 2001 foreign direct investment inflows remained strong, totalling US $20,800m.

China seemed to be the main investor in Hong Kong. At the end of 2000 the stock of FDI from the mainland amounted to US $143,000m. (31% of the total). There were in 2001–02 about 2,000 mainland-related enterprises operating in Hong Kong. Mainland-related enterprises are prominent in a wide range of activities, including property, car and life insurance, transport, finance and construction. In terms of manufacturing, mainland investment was mainly concentrated in two main industries—transport equipment and food and beverages.

Several major mainland-related companies have taken up equity stakes in some key infrastructure ventures in Hong Kong, including the Western Harbour Crossing, the Tate's Cairn Tunnel, Kwai Chung Container Terminals 4, 6, 7, and 8, the Northwest New Territories Landfill Project and the Tuen Mun River Trade Terminal.

Hong Kong continues to play a predominant role as a funding hub for business in the Asia-Pacific region. Hong Kong is also a major external investor. In 2000 Hong Kong was the source of US $59,400m. of outward investment. In terms of the cumulative amount on approval basis, Hong Kong is the largest investor in the Chinese mainland, and is among the leading investors in Indonesia, Taiwan, Thailand, Viet Nam and the Philippines. Among the 364,345 foreign-funded projects on the mainland by the end of 2000, 53% were associated with Hong Kong investors. Contracted and utilized capital inflows from Hong Kong were US $328,000m. and US $170,300m. respectively, accounting for 48% and 49% of the national total. According to government estimates, there were some 157,300 Hong Kong citizens working on the mainland, in connection with manufacturing, commerce, restaurants and hotels and other business services.

TOURISM

Tourism is a major source of foreign-exchange earnings and employment in Hong Kong. Hong Kong is an important transit destination in Asia. One factor in the long-term growth of the tourism industry is that the territory has been increasingly successful in attracting international conventions. The number of visitor arrivals in Hong Kong increased at an annual average rate of 7.1% between 1990 and 2000. With 13.7m. arrivals in 2001, the SAR registered a significant growth (5%) in the number of visitors compared with 2000. However, 65% of the visitors spent only one night in Hong Kong. Indeed, a great number of those arrivals are Taiwanese en route to mainland China. China remained the main source of visitors to Hong Kong, followed by Taiwan and Japan. The decline in tourism from the late 1990s could be attributed to the downturn in the economies in the region, which reduced the amount of disposable income for people to spend on tourism. In addition, owing to the pegging of the Hong Kong dollar to the US dollar, the SAR became a very expensive destination for visitors from other Asian countries and from Australia and New Zealand. Other Asian countries, most of which witnessed a significant depreciation in their currencies from 1997, became much cheaper destinations for tourists. In 2000, however, the number of tourists arrivals increased by 15.3% compared with the previous year to reach 13.06m. After declining in 1999, tourism earnings also improved noticeably in 2000 and 2001, reaching HK $58,392m. and HK $64,282m. respectively. In 2001 the decline in the number of tourists from Western Europe and from the USA, in particular, was offset by a surge in the number of visitors from mainland China (rising by 17.5%, to reach 4.4m.) owing to the relaxation of visa procedures and the increase in the number of tour operators.

INFRASTRUCTURE AND TRANSPORT

A modern and efficient infrastructure has supported Hong Kong's role as a trading entrepôt and regional financial and services centre. The SAR has the best natural deep-water port on the Chinese coast. For much of the 1990s Hong Kong was the busiest container port in the world, maintaining a narrow lead over Singapore in most years. In 2001 Hong Kong's eight privately-operated container terminals and mid-stream operators handled 17.8 m. 20-foot equivalent units (TEUs) of cargo. The Port Development Board expects container throughput to reach 32.8m. TEUs by the year 2016. This will require additional container terminals. The current eight terminals have 19 berths. The ninth container terminal (CT9), under construction on Tsing Yi Island, was scheduled for completion in late 2004.

The container traffic at Hong Kong consists of three distinct types. The largest category is direct shipment of containers carrying imports and exports to and from China (mainly Guangdong Province). A second category is transhipment of containers for other countries, and the final category is river transport, which is, strictly speaking, inland transport, in the same category as road and rail transport. The growth of direct traffic averaged 4.0% annually in the period 1995–99. The importance of transhipment declined over that period, contracting by an annual average of 0.4%, while river trade experienced a strong growth, averaging 25% during the same period.

Hong Kong faces increasing competition from neighbouring ports, with growing volumes of traffic hitherto transhipped to Hong Kong being rerouted to Shenzhen and other ports on the East China coast. Moreover, the eventual implementation of direct transport links between mainland China and Taiwan will lead to a decrease in Hong Kong's share of this trade (1m. TEUs or 6% of Hong Kong's total container throughput). In terms of basic monetary cost comparisons, Hong Kong is adversely affected by higher terminal handling charges than the Shenzhen ports and by the relatively high haulage costs to and from mainland China. However, Hong Kong enjoys several advantages in terms of non-monetary cost competitiveness. It benefits from a high port productivity, and has a higher frequency of calling (more than 80 international shipping lines with 400 container line services per week to over 500 destinations, and over 310 daily feeder services linking the Pearl River Delta area). Furthermore, Hong Kong enjoys well-developed and efficient logistics services allied to straightforward and transparent customs.

This is combined with world-class banking and financial institutions and experience in international trade practices, securing timely payments and document processing. Despite start-up problems during the first few weeks of operations, particularly for cargo movements, Hong Kong's new international airport at Chek Lap Kok, which was financed by the private sector and opened in July 1998, subsequently settled into a routine of efficiency. By 2001 Chek Lap Kok was the busiest international air cargo terminal in the world (2.08m. metric tons). About 65 international airlines operate some 3,800 flights weekly to some 130 destinations. The marine cargo terminal in the airport came into operation in March 2001. With 24-hour operations, two all-weather runways, an ability to handle all types of commercial aircraft, high-speed transport links from the terminal to the city, and the largest cargo-handling facility in the world, the new airport appeared to be well positioned to fulfil Hong Kong's aviation needs in the early part of the 21st century.

The two principal air carriers of the SAR registered mitigated results for 2001. Cathay Pacific recorded a 5% decrease in its passenger activity and an 8.5% decline in cargo handling. Dragonair, however, achieved a 12% increase in passenger traffic and 30% in air cargo.

The underground Mass Transit Railway (MTR), the privatization of which was approved in February 2000, extends to 77 km with five lines and 44 stations. Complementing the MTR are the modernized Kowloon–Canton (Guangzhou) Railway, which in 1999 handled more than 738,000 passenger journeys daily, and the Light Rail Transit system, which operates in the north-western New Territories and carried about 385,000 passengers each day. An ambitious transport infrastructure programme involves a total investment of more than HK $300,000m. (US $36,000m.). This includes an investment of about HK $200m. (US $25,600m.) on 12 railway projects and HK $100,000m. (US $12,800m.) on road projects. These rail projects will add more than 60 km to the existing 143 km of railway lines in Hong Kong and open up the north-west and north-east New Territories for further development. Additional rail projects totalling HK $100,000m. (US $12,800m.) proposed in the Railway Development Strategy 2000 will further expand the railway network from 200 km to 250 km by 2016. The road projects will add about 50 km of new roads (including two bridges and six tunnels) to Hong Kong's transport network. These will help to alleviate congestion in urban areas and provide vital new links to the New Territories.

Hong Kong is the largest teleport in Asia, and the territory has ambitions to become a leading regional telecommunication centre and internet and broadcasting hub. Satellite-based communications and television broadcasting services are provided via 36 satellite earth antennas. Hong Kong provides dedicated relay services for multinational companies, international press agencies and television channels to downlink or uplink their satellite signals over the Asia-Pacific region. Hong Kong is connected to nine submarine cable systems. Three overland systems have also been put into operation to service the growing traffic between Hong Kong and the mainland.

BANKING AND FINANCE

The Hong Kong Monetary Authority (HKMA) was established in 1993 by the merger of the Office of the Commissioner of Banking and the Office of the Exchange Fund. Hong Kong has a three-tier system of licensed banks, restricted licence banks and deposit-taking companies, collectively known as Authorized Institutions. Along with the increase in merger and acquisitions activities, the number of licensed banks has decreased slightly in recent years. At the end of 2001 there were 147 licensed banks, 49 restricted licensed banks, and 54 deposit-taking companies in Hong Kong, with 111 local representatives from over 40 countries. Total assets of all the authorized institutions in Hong Kong declined by 1.9% during 2000 to HK $6,659,000m. at year-end. The high number of branches (1,580) demonstrates the need for even the largest banks with world-wide operations to seek funds at the primary level; otherwise Hong Kong would surely be considered 'over-banked' at the retail level. This growth after 1978 reflected in part the Government's lifting of its 10-year moratorium on new banks in Hong Kong (there was one exception). In recent years the mainland has continued to increase its presence in Hong Kong's financial sector. Upon completion in 2001 of the merger of the Bank of China, (which started issuing Hong Kong dollar bank notes in May 1994) and 11 associate banks, the new entity was named the Bank of China (Hong Kong) and became the second largest banking group in the SAR after the Hongkong and Shanghai Banking Corporation. China's other three specialized banks, namely the People's Construction Bank of China, the Agricultural Bank of China, and the Industrial and Commercial Bank of China, obtained banking licences in 1995 and subsequently opened their first branch operations in Hong Kong. In June 1996 Shenzhen Development Bank, the only listed bank in the mainland, opened a representative office in Hong Kong. In 2001 there were 18 mainland–related authorized institutions operating in Hong Kong, of which 12 were licensed banks. The Bank of China was, in 2002, the second-largest bank in Hong Kong after the Hong Kong Bank Group. It was established on 1 October 2001 by restructuring the 10 members of the former Bank of China Group.

As part of the overall plan to reform and enhance the development of the banking sector, the Hong Kong Monetary Authority undertook further to deregulate the interest rate rules (IRRs). The first phase of deregulation took effect in July 2000. It removed the IRRs on time deposits with a maturity of less than seven days and the prohibition on benefits for deposits (other than Hong Kong dollar demand and saving deposits). The final phase of interest rate deregulation took effect in July 2001. It removed interest 'ceilings' on all types of deposits. Banks in Hong Kong have responded to deregulations in different ways with regard to their charging policy for account services, minimum balance requirements and tiering of interest rates.

In the early 21st century more than one-half of the assets and liabilities of the Hong Kong banks were foreign. This 'internationalization' of Hong Kong banking is an essential part of the strategy to underpin Hong Kong's political independence as an SAR with international economic ties. Hong Kong joined the Bank for International Settlements (BIS) in 1996. In early 1997 Hong Kong announced its support for the IMF's New Arrangements to Borrow (NAB) scheme. Hong Kong's involvement in this emergency fund was regarded as an important move towards consolidating its position as an international financial centre. In mid-1997 the SAR retained its membership of the Asian Development Bank (ADB) and of Asia-Pacific Economic Co-operation (APEC). In July 1999 the Government announced a series of initiatives based on a commissioned consultancy to suggest a reform programme to improve competitiveness and enhance the security and soundness of Hong Kong's banking sector. Among the major initiatives are simplification of the three-tier system, relaxation of the one branch (to three) policy for foreign banks, deregulation of remaining interest rate rules, measures to enhance depositor protection and the adoption of more formalized risk-based supervision.

The Stock Market and The Exchange Rate

After the 1973 share market speculative upsurge, more attention was paid to controlling the potential excesses of the financial sector. In August 1980 the Stock Exchange Unification Ordinance was enacted, which provided for the establishment of one exchange in place of the previous four. Under the ordinance, a unified Stock Exchange of Hong Kong began operations in April 1986, with the exclusive right to operate a market. All members of the existing exchanges were invited to apply for shares in the new exchange. This unification aimed to achieve a broader market, to increase the attractiveness of Hong Kong securities to overseas investors and to assist the better management of the market and more effective regulation of the stockbrokers.

The overall supervisory body is the Securities and Futures Commission, which began work in 1989. During the regional stock-market turmoil of late 1997 the Government was obliged to intervene (see below) after the securities and futures markets in Hong Kong experienced the most severe volatility ever recorded. A 1,438-point fall (13.7%) in the Hang Seng Index was registered on 28 October and a 1,705-point rebound (18.8%) on the following day. In 2000 the Stock Exchange of Hong Kong, the Hong Kong Futures Exchange and the Hong Kong Securities Clearing Company merged to form Hong Kong Exchanges and Clearing Ltd. Hong Kong has also developed a thriving capital market. The Hong Kong stock market, (the third-largest in terms of capitalization, in Asia behind Japan and China) as measured by the Hang Seng Index, underwent wide fluctuations during 2001, reflecting the movements in the US stock market. At the end of 2001 the Hang Seng Index closed at 11,397 points, still almost 25% below the level of 15,096 recorded at the end of 2000. The average daily turnover of US $8,200m. in 2001 was distinctly below that of the $12,700m. transacted in 2000. In common with other international stock markets, a sharp decline in the value of shares followed the terrorist attacks on the USA on 11 September. At the end of March 2002 Hong Kong's stock market capitalization was HK $3,924,000m. In August the Hang Seng Index fell below 10,000 points.

Linked to the pound sterling, then to the US dollar, the Hong Kong dollar floated freely between 1974 and 1983. During that period the Hong Kong dollar lost half of its value. In that context, therefore, the Hong Kong monetary authorities returned to the policy of a fixed exchange rate (pegging) to the US dollar. Since then, the parity has remained unchanged at HK $7.8 to US $1. The Hong Kong dollar is pegged to the US dollar through the linked exchange rate (LER) system. This pegging of the exchange rate came under severe attack during the financial turbulence of 1997, when the Hong Kong dollar was subjected to speculative pressure on several occasions. The overnight interbank interest rate surged briefly to 280% on 23 October 1997, under the automatic adjustment mechanism of the currency board system. The combination of the interest-rate rise and the asset price adjustments in both the securities and property sectors caused serious concern within the local community. In September 1999 the territory reaffirmed its commitment to the linked exchange rate mechanism, while other measures aimed to increase liquidity in the interbank money market. The currency board's system relies on three pillars: a fixed exchange rate; a monetary base covered at 100% at least by the currency reserves; and a money creation strictly subordinated to the variation of exchange reserves. Although the 'peg' has been denounced as a factor of rigidity by the Financial Secretary, and a *de facto* obstacle to economic recovery, the resistance of the 'peg' to speculative attacks during the Asian crisis gave the fixed exchange rate a strong credibility and a pivotal element in Hong Kong's autonomy within the framework of 'one country, two systems'.

Housing and the Property Market

About 735,000 residential flats were completed to meet the housing needs of the population between 1990 and 2000. From 1999 the completion of new flats per annum averaged a total of 80,000. The proportion of owner-occupiers increased sharply, from 42.6% in 1990 to 51.1% in 2000, while the proportion of tenants decreased from 51.9% to 45%. Among the 2m. domestic households in 2000, 32.1% resided in public rental housing and 50.7% in private permanent housing. The proportion of domestic households in subsidized sale flats increased from 6.5% in 1990 to 15.5% in 2000, while the proportion of domestic households in temporary housing declined from 5.4% to 1.2%. Prices of residential flats followed a downward trend in 2001. For 2001 as a whole, flat prices on average decreased by 134%. Having remained broadly stable in the first three quarters of 2001, the rental market for private residential flats weakened in the fourth quarter, giving a cumulative decline of 7% for the whole year. The sales market for office space, meanwhile, was weak for most of 2001, and the rental market also slackened considerably in that year. In a major change of policy, announced in September 2001, the Government declared a moratorium on the sale of subsidized public housing, in an attempt to revive the property market. Sales were to be suspended until June 2002, while drastic reductions in the supply of such homes were to remain in place until 2005/06.

RECENT POLICY

In the budget for 2002/03, delivered in March 2002, the Financial Secretary proposed no major amendments to Hong Kong's tax structure, leaving unchanged the rates of profits tax and salaries tax. The policy of strengthening Hong Kong as an international financial and high-value-added services centre remained in place. In addition, noting that the future of Hong Kong depended on the kind and value of services the SAR could deliver, the Financial Secretary reiterated the Government's commitment to upgrading the quality of human resources, by improving education and attracting outside talent. The Government was also to take initiatives to enhance flows of people, goods, capital, information and services to and from the Chinese mainland. A fiscal deficit of HK $65,600m. (equivalent to 5.2% of GDP) was likely to be recorded in the government account for 2001/02. With the Government continuing on a counter-cyclical fiscal policy, a deficit of HK $45,200m. was envisaged for 2002/03. A programme of 'one-off' relief measures was announced to assist the community, while civil service pay reductions were to become effective from October 2002. Fiscal deficits were likely to continue for some time before being restored to balance by 2006/07. To redress the fiscal imbalances, the growth of government spending was to be controlled at 2% in 2002/03 and at 1.5% thereafter, in order to reduce government spending to 20% of GDP by 2006/07.

In his fifth Policy Address, delivered in October 2001, the Chief Executive of Hong Kong announced a number of government initiatives to develop the territory for a prosperous future. Education headed the agenda, with an objective to accelerate the transition to the knowledge-based economy. Investment in education was set to increase every year for the subsequent five to 10 years, while the education system was to undergo changes, and a lifelong 'learning ladder' was to be developed. The Government also planned to press ahead with large-scale infrastructure projects, including linkages with the Pearl River Delta. Other initiatives included increasing 'greening' efforts to improve the living environment of Hong Kong. The Policy Speech 2001 also revealed some government measures to improve the business environment of Hong Kong. Financial assistance worth US $1,900m. was extended to small- and medium-sized enterprises through four new funds being established as a result of recommendations in the Small and Medium Enterprises Committee report released in June. The Policy Speech 2001 also addressed the prevailing economic hardship in several ways, including the creation of 30,000 job opportunities and the reduction in payments of local taxes. The Government also pledged to proceed with a number of major infrastructure projects to help Hong Kong maintain its status as a regional transport and business hub. Over the next 10 years investment totalling HK $600,000m. was to be spent, including HK $200,000m. from the two railway corporations. The main focus was to be on transport, land formation, port, housing, tourism-related developments, education, hospitals and improvements to the environment.

Statistical Survey

Source (unless otherwise stated): Census and Statistics Department, 19/F Wanchai Tower, 12 Harbour Rd, Hong Kong; tel. 25825073; fax 28271708; e-mail genenq@censtatd.gcn.gov.hk; internet www.info.gov.hk/censtatd/eng/hkstat/index2.html/.

Area and Population

AREA, POPULATION AND DENSITY

Land area (sq km)	1,098*
Population (census results)†	
15 March 1996	6,412,937
15 March 2001	
Males	3,285,344
Females	3,423,045
Total	6,708,389
Population (official estimates at mid-year)‡	
1999	6,605,500
2000	6,665,000
2001	6,724,900
Density (per sq km) at mid-2001	6,124.5

* 424 sq miles.

† All residents (including mobile residents) on the census date, including those who were temporarily absent from Hong Kong.

‡ Revised figures, referring to resident population, including mobile residents.

DISTRICTS (2001 census)

	Area (sq km)	Population*	Density (per sq km)
Hong Kong Island	80.28	1,335,469	16,635
Kowloon	46.85	2,023,979	43,201
New Territories	970.91	3,343,046	3,443
Total	1,098.04	6,702,494	6,104

* Excluding marine population (5,895).

PRINCIPAL TOWNS (population at 1996 census)

Kowloon*	1,988,515	Tai Po	271,661
Victoria (capital)	1,011,433	Tseun Wan	268,659
Tuen Mun	445,771	Sheung Shui	192,321
Sha Tin	445,383	Tsing Yu	185,495
Kwai Chung	285,231	Aberdeen	164,439

* Including New Kowloon.

BIRTHS, MARRIAGES AND DEATHS*

	Known live births		Registered marriages		Known deaths	
	Number	Rate (per '000)	Number	Rate (per '000)	Number	Rate (per '000)
1994	71,646	11.9	38,264	6.3	29,905	5.0
1995	68,836	11.2	38,786	6.3	31,183	5.1
1996	64,559†	10.2	37,045	5.9	32,049†	5.1
1997‡	60,379†	9.3	37,593	5.8	32,079†	4.9
1998‡	53,356†	7.9	31,673	4.7	32,680†	4.8
1999‡	50,513	7.5	31,287	4.6	33,387	4.8
2000‡	53,720	8.1	30,879	4.6	33,993	5.1
2001‡	49,144	7.3	32,825	4.9	33,305	5.0

* Excluding Vietnamese migrants.

† Figure calculated by year of registration.

‡ Provisional. Figures prior to 2000 have not been revised to take account of the results of the 2001 population census.

Expectation of life (years at birth, 2001, provisional): Males 77.0; Females 82.2.

ECONOMICALLY ACTIVE POPULATION
('000 persons aged 15 years and over, excl. armed forces)

	1998	1999	2000
Agriculture and fishing	9.4	9.4	9.3
Mining and quarrying	0.2	0.3	0.4
Manufacturing	385.6	359.4	338.1
Electricity, gas and water	17.9	17.1	16.6
Construction	309.5	289.2	303.2
Wholesale, retail and import/export trades, restaurants and hotels	961.6	941.3	985.2
Transport, storage and communications	353.0	342.7	358.7
Financing, insurance, real estate and business services	411.6	437.6	448.7
Community, social and personal services	701.3	736.3	754.2
Total employed	3,150.1	3,133.0	3,214.4
Unemployed	155.4	209.4	168.3
Total labour force	3,305.5	3,342.5	3,382.7
Males	1,971.4	1,963.7	1,959.8
Females	1,334.1	1,378.8	1,422.9

2001 (census results): Total employed 3,252,706 (incl. 23,599 unpaid family workers); Unemployed 185,286; Total labour force 3,437,992.

Source: mainly ILO, *Yearbook of Labour Statistics*.

Health and Welfare

KEY INDICATORS

Fertility (births per woman, 1995–2000)	1.2
Under-5 mortality rate (per 1,000 live births, provisional, 2001)	2.7
HIV/AIDS (% of persons aged 15–49, 1999)	0.06
Physicians (per 1,000 head, provisional, 2001)	1.5
Hospital beds (per 1,000 head, provisional, 2001)	5.2
Human Development Index (1999): ranking	24
value	0.880

For sources and definitions, see explanatory note on p. vi.

Agriculture

PRINCIPAL CROPS ('000 metric tons)

	1998	1999	2000
Lettuce*	5	5	5
Spinach*	12	12	12
Onions and shallots (green)*	4	4	4
Other vegetables*	44	34	34
Fruit	4	4*	4*

* FAO estimate(s).

Source: FAO.

LIVESTOCK (FAO estimates, '000 head, year ending September)

	1998	1999	2000
Cattle	40	32	32
Pigs	110	110	110
Chickens	3,000	3,000	3,000
Ducks	250	250	250

Source: FAO.

LIVESTOCK PRODUCTS ('000 metric tons)

	1998	1999	2000
Beef and veal*	19	18	18
Pig meat*	161	161	154
Poultry meat	55	65	67
Game meat†	6	6	6
Cattle hides (fresh)	3	3	3†

* Unofficial figures.
† FAO estimate(s).
Source: FAO.

Fishing

('000 metric tons, live weight)

	1997	1998	1999
Capture	186.0	180.0	127.8
Lizardfishes	8.1	6.6	5.0
Threadfin breams	20.0	19.4	14.0
Other marine fishes (incl. unspecified)	134.9	138.0	96.5
Shrimps and prawns	6.2	5.3	4.0
Squids	13.6	8.3	6.5
Aquaculture	8.3	6.4	6.0
Total catch	194.3	186.4	133.8

Source: FAO, *Yearbook of Fishery Statistics*.

Industry

SELECTED PRODUCTS
('000 metric tons, unless otherwise indicated)

	1997	1998	1999
Crude groundnut oil	50	n.a.	18
Uncooked macaroni and noodle products	93	99	127
Cigarettes (million)	20,929	13,470	n.a.
Cotton yarn (pure and mixed)	163.3	101.1	n.a.
Cotton woven fabrics (million sq m)	506	n.a.	n.a.
Knitted sweaters ('000)	176,766	146,438	117,738
Men's and boys' jackets ('000)	7,419	10,117	6,414
Men's and boys' trousers ('000)	44,086	41,953	32,937
Women's and girls' blouses ('000)	94,453	74,571	63,596
Women's and girls' dresses ('000)	6,457	6,612	5,668
Women's and girls' skirts, slacks and shorts ('000)	61,336	70,136	77,344
Men's and boys' shirts ('000)	85,198	49,139	41,040
Telephones ('000)	91	n.a.	n.a.
Watches ('000)	81,452	75,402	31,926
Electric energy (million kWh)	28,943	31,414	n.a.

Source: UN, *Industrial Commodity Statistics Yearbook*.

Finance

CURRENCY AND EXCHANGE RATES

Monetary Units
100 cents = 1 Hong Kong dollar (HK $).

Sterling, US Dollar and Euro Equivalents (31 May 2002)
£1 sterling = HK $11.439;
US $1 = HK $7.799;
€1 = HK $7.321;
HK $1,000 = £87.42 = US $128.22 = €136.59.

Average Exchange Rate (HK $ per US $)
1999 7.7575
2000 7.7912
2001 7.7988

BUDGET (HK $ million, year ending 31 March)

Revenue	1999/2000	2000/01	2001/02*
Direct taxes:			
Earnings and profits tax	66,914	73,870	77,900
Estate duty	1,272	1,503	1,400
Indirect taxes:			
Duties on petroleum products, beverages, tobacco and cosmetics	7,377	7,293	6,781
General rates (property tax)	7,132	14,428	12,470
Motor vehicle taxes	2,613	3,025	2,744
Royalties and concessions	1,577	1,767	1,903
Others	24,832	24,301	21,088
Fines, forfeitures and penalties	1,093	1,061	966
Receipts from properties and investments	6,986	7,579	8,269
Reimbursements and contributions	5,672	4,210	4,143
Operating revenue from utilities:			
Water	2,434	2,412	2,505
Others	892	885	913
Fees and charges	10,896	10,973	10,981
Interest receipts (operating revenue)	15,390	6,835	180
Land Fund (investment income)	21,388	12,681	—
Capital Works Reserve Fund (land sales and interest)	39,111	32,183	10,078
Capital Investment Fund	2,665	2,949	2,819
Loan funds	11,515	3,612	5,466
Other capital revenue	3,236	13,493	3,441
Total government revenue	232,995	225,060	174,047

Expenditure†	1999/2000	2000/01	2001/02*
Economic affairs and services	12,272	12,486	14,102
Internal security	20,171	20,937	21,941
Immigration	2,143	2,108	2,347
Other security services	3,568	3,698	3,775
Social welfare	27,616	28,165	30,731
Health services	31,894	32,753	34,016
Education	50,307	51,408	52,597
Environmental services	12,496	11,337	11,329
Recreation, culture and amenities	7,409	6,443	6,522
Other community and external affairs	1,721	1,819	1,953
Transport	6,559	6,395	6,333
Land and buildings	8,099	8,513	10,843
Water supply	8,275	7,912	7,765
Support	31,082	30,927	35,710
Housing	45,872	42,606	33,187
Total	269,484	267,507	273,151
Recurrent	195,272	198,619	213,220
Capital	74,212	68,888	59,931

* Revised estimates.
† Figures refer to consolidated expenditure by the public sector. Of the total, government expenditure, after deducting grants, debt repayments and equity injections, was (in HK $ million): 214,533 in 1999/2000; 224,791 in 2000/01; 239,345 (estimate) in 2001/02. Expenditure by other public-sector bodies (in HK $ million) was: 54,951 in 1999/2000; 42,716 in 2000/01; 33,806 (estimate) in 2001/02.

INTERNATIONAL RESERVES (US $ million at 31 December)

	1999	2000	2001
Gold*	19	18	19
Reserve position in the IMF	—	—	—
Foreign exchange†	96,236	107,542	111,155
Total	96,255	107,560	111,174

* National valuation.
† Including the foreign exchange reserves of the Hong Kong Special Administrative Region Government's Land Fund.
Source: IMF, *International Financial Statistics*.

MONEY SUPPLY (HK $ million at 31 December)

	1999	2000	2001
Currency outside banks	99,267	91,509	101,375
Demand deposits at banking institutions	85,348	93,052	109,509
Total money	184,615	184,561	210,884

Source: IMF, *International Financial Statistics.*

COST OF LIVING
(Consumer price index; base: October 1999–September 2000 = 100)

	1999	2000	2001
Foodstuffs	101.9	99.7	98.9
Housing	107.3	98.5	95.5
Fuel and light	97.3	100.7	98.7
Alcoholic drinks and tobacco	101.1	100.1	103.4
Clothing and footwear	109.2	97.9	93.4
Durable goods	103.7	98.7	91.7
Miscellaneous goods	99.6	100.5	101.8
Transport	99.4	100.3	100.7
Miscellaneous services	100.2	99.9	100.4
All items	103.2	99.4	97.8

NATIONAL ACCOUNTS
(HK $ million at current market prices)
Expenditure on the Gross Domestic Product

	1999	2000	2001*
Government final consumption expenditure	121,540	121,834	130,659
Private final consumption expenditure	732,821	735,072	739,037
Change in stocks	–10,612	16,194	–207
Gross domestic fixed capital formation	316,960	333,003	326,040
Total domestic expenditure	1,160,709	1,206,103	1,195,529
Exports of goods and services	1,637,609	1,901,314	1,816,744
Less Imports of goods and services	1,571,335	1,840,764	1,749,688
GDP in purchasers' values	1,226,983	1,266,653	1,262,585
GDP at constant 1990 prices	808,656	893,263	894,587

* Figures are provisional.

Gross Domestic Product by Economic Activity

	1998	1999	2000*
Agriculture and fishing	1,530	1,171	920
Mining and quarrying	301	307	241
Manufacturing	70,849	65,767	69,753
Electricity, gas and water	33,546	34,358	35,852
Construction	69,937	66,111	63,164
Wholesale, retail and import/ export trades, restaurants and hotels	288,081	282,194	308,410
Transport, storage and communications	107,958	108,957	121,104
Financing, insurance, real estate and business services	282,686	267,017	273,897
Community, social and personal services	232,963	245,722	250,555
Ownership of premises	170,660	162,488	152,737
Sub-total	1,258,510	1,234,091	1,276,633
Less Imputed bank service charges	89,446	94,580	95,945
GDP at factor cost	1,169,064	1,139,511	1,180,688
Indirect taxes, *less* subsidies	62,538	55,846	60,510
GDP in purchasers' values	1,231,602	1,195,357	1,241,198

* Figures are provisional.

BALANCE OF PAYMENTS (US $ million)

	1999	2000	2001
Exports of goods f.o.b.	174,719	202,698	190,926
Imports of goods f.o.b.	–177,878	–210,891	–199,257
Trade balance	–3,159	–8,193	–8,331
Exports of services	36,564	41,458	42,426
Imports of services	–24,869	–25,564	–25,079
Balance on goods and services	8,536	7,790	9,015
Other income received	47,031	53,494	48,010
Other income paid	–42,548	–50,699	–43,377
Balance on goods, services and income	13,019	10,586	13,649
Current transfers received	570	538	813
Current transfers paid	–2,109	–2,208	–2,495
Current balance	11,479	8,915	11,968
Capital account (net)	–1,780	–1,546	–1,162
Direct investment abroad	–19,349	–59,338	–8,981
Direct investment from abroad	24,587	61,883	22,834
Portfolio investment assets	–25,440	–22,022	–39,131
Portfolio investment liabilities	58,525	46,508	–531
Financial derivatives assets	21,297	8,414	17,508
Financial derivatives liabilities	–11,113	–8,182	–12,490
Other investment assets	42,963	18,279	58,243
Other investment liabilities	–90,410	–41,375	–42,599
Net errors and omissions	–732	–1,491	–977
Overall balance	10,028	10,044	4,684

Source: IMF, *International Financial Statistics.*

External Trade

PRINCIPAL COMMODITIES (HK $ million, excl. gold)

Imports	1998	1999	2000
Food and live animals	57,483	55,746	57,438
Chemicals and related products	91,219	89,941	104,559
Basic manufactures	264,148	249,758	282,506
Textile yarn, fabrics, made-up articles, etc.	104,439	97,455	106,875
Machinery and transport equipment	562,814	540,679	707,766
Office machines and automatic data-processing equipment	103,145	108,295	142,920
Telecommunications and sound recording and reproducing apparatus and equipment	130,886	119,257	161,627
Electrical machinery, apparatus and appliances n.e.s., and electrical parts thereof	195,561	212,589	288,955
Miscellaneous manufactured articles	378,286	388,999	432,398
Clothing (excl. footwear)	110,744	114,485	124,735
Footwear	44,982	41,304	44,149
Photographic apparatus, equipment and supplies, optical goods, watches and clocks	54,627	54,145	59,871
Total (incl. others)	1,429,092	1,392,718	1,657,962

Domestic exports	1998	1999	2000
Chemicals and related products	6,753	5,655	6,300
Basic manufactures	18,164	15,623	15,877
Textile yarn, fabrics, made-up articles, etc.	10,767	9,488	9,164
Machinery and transport equipment	46,471	39,731	44,846
Office machines and automatic data-processing equipment	8,922	8,254	7,303
Telecommunications and sound recording and reproducing apparatus and equipment	6,304	3,796	4,206
Electrical machinery, apparatus and appliances n.e.s., and electrical parts thereof	26,688	23,790	28,533
Miscellaneous manufactured articles	108,770	103,114	107,773
Clothing (excl. footwear)	74,874	74,251	77,415
Photographic apparatus, equipment and supplies, optical goods, watches and clocks	12,535	8,353	5,715
Total (incl. others)	188,454	170,600	180,967

Re-exports	1998	1999	2000
Chemicals and related products	66,565	66,951	74,983
Basic manufactures	197,442	189,740	216,264
Textile yarn, fabrics, made-up articles, etc.	90,234	85,710	95,573
Machinery and transport equipment	407,400	431,673	560,832
Office machines and automatic data-processing equipment	92,902	98,136	120,509
Telecommunications and sound recording and reproducing apparatus and equipment	114,348	114,325	148,663
Electrical machinery, apparatus and appliances n.e.s., and electrical parts thereof	132,040	156,479	220,611
Miscellaneous manufactured articles	426,262	440,260	492,212
Clothing (excl. footwear)	96,799	99,308	111,268
Footwear	51,913	47,840	50,534
Photographic apparatus, equipment and supplies, optical goods, watches and clocks	58,379	59,790	69,583
Total (incl. others)	1,159,195	1,178,400	1,391,722

2001 (HK $ million): Total imports 1,568,194; Domestic exports 153,520; Re-exports 1,327,467.

PRINCIPAL TRADING PARTNERS (HK $ million, excl. gold)

Imports	1999	2000	2001
China, People's Repub.	607,546	714,987	681,980
Germany	28,114	32,215	33,309
Japan	162,652	198,976	176,599
Korea, Repub.	65,432	80,600	70,791
Malaysia	30,010	37,906	39,200
Singapore	60,017	74,998	72,898
Taiwan	100,426	124,172	107,929
Thailand	22,798	28,001	27,370
United Kingdom	26,961	30,797	28,877
USA	98,572	112,801	104,941
Total (incl. others)	1,392,718	1,657,962	1,568,194

Domestic exports	1999	2000	2001
Canada	3,151	3,210	3,093
China, People's Repub.	50,414	54,158	49,547
France	3,081	2,730	n.a.
Germany	8,543	9,294	5,818
Japan	5,459	5,084	4,060
Netherlands	4,119	3,910	4,619
Singapore	3,682	4,716	2,650
Taiwan	5,101	6,104	5,346
United Kingdom	10,392	10,681	8,578
USA	51,358	54,438	47,589
Total (incl. others)	170,600	180,967	153,520

Re-exports	1999	2000	2001
China, People's Repub.	399,188	488,823	496,574
France	22,837	25,205	21,516
Germany	44,122	50,599	45,774
Japan	67,506	82,050	83,551
Korea, Repub.	19,793	26,978	24,640
Netherlands	19,422	20,373	20,693
Singapore	28,716	32,028	26,929
Taiwan	27,859	33,696	30,021
United Kingdom	45,541	52,356	46,764
USA	269,444	311,047	282,189
Total (incl. others)	1,178,400	1,391,722	1,327,467

Transport

RAILWAYS (traffic)

	1999	2000	2001
Passenger trains:			
Arrivals	2,595	2,925	3,001
Departures	2,596	2,925	3,001
Freight (in metric tons):			
Loaded	173,415	132,911	97,139
Unloaded	293,061	318,323	273,051

ROAD TRAFFIC (registered motor vehicles at 31 December)

	1999	2000	2001
Private cars	365,533	374,013	381,757
Private buses	447	451	485
Public buses	12,173	12,498	12,812
Private light buses	2,228	2,158	2,098
Public light buses	4,350	4,350	4,350
Taxis	18,138	18,138	18,138
Goods vehicles	130,374	128,656	126,233
Motorcycles	33,079	34,085	36,191
Government vehicles (excl. military vehicles)	7,368	7,242	7,127
Total (incl. others)	574,193	582,141	589,808

Note: Figures do not include tramcars.

SHIPPING

Merchant Fleet (registered at 31 December)

	1999	2000	2001
Number of vessels	479	560	646
Total displacement ('000 grt)	7,972.6	10,242.2	13,709.7

Source: Lloyd's Register-Fairplay, *World Fleet Statistics*.

Traffic (2001)

	Ocean-going vessels	River vessels
Vessels entered (number)	37,350	177,390
Passengers landed ('000)	9,779*	—
Passengers embarked ('000)	10,238*	—
Cargo landed ('000 metric tons)†	87,900	21,600
Cargo loaded ('000 metric tons)†	42,400	27,400

* Includes helicopter passengers to/from Macao.
† Provisional.

CIVIL AVIATION

	1999	2000	2001
Passengers:			
Arrivals	10,699,000	11,566,000	11,533,000
Departures	10,623,000	11,458,000	11,488,000
Freight (in metric tons):			
Landed	841,161	952,514	895,000*
Loaded	1,133,130	1,288,071	1,181,000*

* Provisional.

Tourism

VISITOR ARRIVALS BY COUNTRY OF RESIDENCE

	1999	2000	2001
Australia	304,407	352,409	324,156
Canada	226,185	253,095	249,707
China, People's Repub.	3,206,452	3,785,845	4,448,583
Germany	189,292	193,837	173,359
Indonesia	196,221	236,275	212,260
Japan	1,174,071	1,382,417	1,336,538
Korea, Repub.	291,015	372,639	425,732
Macao	416,839	449,947	532,391
Malaysia	277,355	314,857	286,338
Philippines	274,587	278,460	293,105
Singapore	370,156	450,569	421,513
Taiwan	2,063,027	2,385,739	2,418,827
Thailand	195,587	228,774	241,480
United Kingdom	333,973	367,938	360,581
USA and Guam	858,925	966,008	935,717
Total (incl. others)	11,328,272	13,059,477	13,725,332

Receipts from tourism: HK $52,986m. in 1999; HK $58,392m. in 2000; HK $64,282m. in 2001.

Source: Hong Kong Tourist Association, Hong Kong.

Communications Media

	1999	2000	2001
Television receivers ('000 in use)	2,884	3,105	n.a.
Telephones ('000 in use)	3,868.8	3,925.8	3,925.8
Facsimile machines (number in use)	384,000	404,000	411,000
Mobile cellular telephones ('000 subscribers)	4,275.0	5,447.3	5,701.7
Personal computers ('000 in use)	2,000	2,360	2,600
Internet users ('000)	1,734	2,283	3,100

1997 ('000 in use): Radio receivers 4,450.
1998: Daily newspapers 45; Periodicals 684.

Sources: partly UNESCO, *Statistical Yearbook*; UN, *Statistical Yearbook*; International Telecommunication Union.

Education

(2001/02*)

	Institutions	Full-time teachers§	Students
Kindergartens	784	9,159	156,202
Primary schools	815	22,845	493,075
Secondary schools	537	25,093	465,503
Special schools	74	1,671	9,511
Institute of Vocational Education†	1	1,033	54,825
Approved post-secondary college	2	117	4,180
Other post-secondary colleges	10	—	3,263
UGC-funded institutions‡	8	5,620	83,657
Open University Institute	1	105	26,923
Adult education institutions	1,415	—	184,288

* Provisional figure(s).
† Formed by merger of two technical colleges and seven technical institutes in 1999.
‡ Funded by the University Grants Committee.
§ As of 2000–01.

Adult literacy rate (UNESCO estimates): 93.5% (males 96.5%; females 90.2%) in 2000 (Source: UN Development Programme, *Human Development Report*).

Directory

The Constitution

Under the terms of the Basic Law of the Hong Kong Special Administrative Region, the Government comprises the Chief Executive, the Executive Council and the Legislative Council. The Chief Executive must be a Chinese citizen of at least 40 years of age; he is appointed for a five-year term, with a limit of two consecutive terms; in 2002 he was to be chosen by an 800-member Election Committee; he is accountable to the State Council of the People's Republic of China, and has no military authority; he appoints the Executive Council, judges and the principal government officials; he makes laws with the advice and consent of the legislature; he has a veto over legislation, but can be overruled by a two-thirds' majority; he may dissolve the legislature once in a term, but must resign if the legislative impasse continues with the new body. The Legislative Council has 60 members; 24 seats are directly elected under a system of proportional representation, 30 seats are elected by 'functional constituencies' (comprising professional and special interest groups) and six by an 800-member electoral college. The Legislative Council is responsible for enacting, revising and abrogating laws, for approving the budget, taxation and public expenditure, for debating the policy address of the Chief Executive and for approving the appointment of the judges of the Court of Final Appeal and of the Chief Justice of the High Court.

The Government

Chief Executive: TUNG CHEE-HWA (assumed office 1 July 1997).

EXECUTIVE COUNCIL
(September 2002)

Chairman: The Chief Executive.

Ex-Officio Members:

Chief Secretary for Administration: DONALD TSANG YAM-KUEN.

Financial Secretary: ANTONY LEUNG KAM-CHUNG.

Secretary for Justice: ELSIE LEUNG OI-SIE.

Secretary for Commerce, Industry and Technology: HENRY TANG YING-YEN.

Secretary for Housing, Planning and Lands: MICHAEL SUEN MING-YEUNG.

Secretary for Education and Manpower: ARTHUR LI KWOK-CHEUNG.

Secretary for Health, Welfare and Food: YEOH ENG-KIONG.

Secretary for the Civil Service: JOSEPH WONG WING-PING.

Secretary for Home Affairs: PATRICK HO CHI-PING.

Secretary for Security: REGINA IP LAU SUK-YEE.

Secretary for Economic Development and Labour: STEPHEN IP SHU-KWAN.

Secretary for the Environment, Transport and Works: SARAH LIAO SAU-TUNG.

Secretary for Financial Services and the Treasury: FREDERICK MA SI-HANG.

Secretary for Constitutional Affairs: STEPHEN LAM SUI-LUNG.

Non-Official Members: LEUNG CHUN-YING, JAMES TIEN PEI-CHUN, JASPER TSANG YOK-SING, CHENG YIU-TONG, ANDREW LIAO CHEUNG-SING.

LEGISLATIVE COUNCIL

The second Legislative Council to follow Hong Kong's transfer to Chinese sovereignty was elected on 10 September 2000. The Legislative Council comprises 60 members—30 chosen by functional constituencies, 24 (increased from 20 in the previous legislature) by direct election in five geographical constituencies and six (reduced from 10) by an 800-member Election Committee. The term of office of the Legislative Council commenced on 1 October 2000 and was to last for four years.

President: RITA FAN HSU LAI-TAI.

Election, 10 September 2000

Party	Directly-elective seats	Functional Constituency seats	Election Committee seats	Total seats
Democratic Party of Hong Kong	9	3	—	12
Democratic Alliance for the Betterment of Hong Kong	8	3	—	11
Liberal Party	—	8	—	8
Hong Kong Progressive Alliance	—	1	3	4
The Frontier	3	—	—	3
Association for Democracy and People's Livelihood	1	—	—	1
New Century Forum	—	1	1	2
Independents and others	3	14	2	19
Total	24	30	6	60

GOVERNMENT OFFICES

Executive Council: Central Government Offices, Lower Albert Rd, Central; tel. 28102545; fax 28450176.

Office of the Chief Executive: 5/F Main Wing, Central Government Offices, Lower Albert Rd, Central; tel. 28783300; fax 25090577.

Government Secretariat: Central Government Offices, Lower Albert Rd, Central; tel. 28102900; fax 28457895.

Government Information Services: Murray Bldg, Garden Rd, Central; tel. 28428777; fax 28459078; internet www.info.gov.hk.

Political Organizations

Association for Democracy and People's Livelihood (ADPL): Sun Beam Commercial Bldg, Room 1104, 469–471 Nathan Rd, Kowloon; tel. 27822699; fax 27823137; e-mail adpl@netvigator.com; internet www.adpl.org.hk; advocates democracy; Chair. FREDERICK FUNG KIN-KEE; Gen. Sec. TAM KWOK-KIU.

Citizens' Party: 1203 Dominion Centre, 43 Queen's Rd East, Wanchai; tel. 28930029; fax 21475796; e-mail enquiry@citizensparty.org; internet www.citizensparty.org; f. 1997; urges mass participation in politics; Leader CHRISTINE LOH.

Democratic Alliance for the Betterment of Hong Kong (DAB): SUP Tower, 12/F, 83 King's Rd, North Point; tel. 25280136; fax 25284339; e-mail info@dab.org.hk; internet www.dab.org.hk; f. 1992; pro-Beijing; supported return of Hong Kong to the motherland and implementation of the Basic Law; Chair. TSANG YOK-SING; Sec.-Gen. MA LIK.

Democratic Party of Hong Kong: Central Government Offices, Rooms 401–410, West Wing, 11 Ice House St, Central; tel. 25371469; fax 25374874; f. 1994 by merger of United Democrats of Hong Kong (UDHK—declared a formal political party in 1990) and Meeting Point; liberal grouping; advocates democracy; Chair. MARTIN LEE; Sec.-Gen. LAW CHI-KWONG.

The Frontier: Hong Kong House, Room 301, 11–19 Wellington St, Central; tel. 25372482; fax 28456203; f. 1996; pro-democracy movement, comprising teachers, students and trade unionists; Spokesperson EMILY LAU.

Hong Kong Democratic Foundation: Hong Kong House, Room 301, 17–19 Wellington St, Central; GPOB 12287; tel. 28696443; fax 28696318; advocates democracy; Chair. ALAN LUNG.

Hong Kong Progressive Alliance: c/o The Legislative Council, Hong Kong; tel. 25262316; fax 28450127; f. 1994; advocates close relationship with mainland China; 52-mem. organizing cttee drawn from business and professional community; Spokesman AMBROSE LAU.

Hong Kong Voice of Democracy: 7/F, 57 Peking Rd, Tsimshatsui; tel. 92676489; fax 27915801; internet www.democracy.org.hk; pro-democracy movement; Dir LAU SAN-CHING.

Liberal Democratic Foundation (LDF): Hong Kong; pro-Beijing.

Liberal Party: Shun Ho Tower, 2/F, 24–30 Ice House St, Central; tel. 28696833; fax 28453671; f. 1993 by mems of Co-operative Resources Centre (CRC); business-orientated; pro-Beijing; Leader ALLEN LEE PENG-FEI; Chair. JAMES TIEN.

New Hong Kong Alliance: 4/F, 14–15 Wo On Lane, Central; fax 28691110; pro-China.

The **Chinese Communist Party** (based in the People's Republic) and the **Kuomintang** (Nationalist Party of China, based in Taiwan) also maintain organizations.

Judicial System

The Court of Final Appeal was established on 1 July 1997 upon the commencement of the Hong Kong Court of Final Appeal Ordinance. It replaced the Privy Council in London as the highest appellate court in Hong Kong to safeguard the rule of law. The Court comprises five judges—the Chief Justice, three permanent judges and one non-permanent Hong Kong judge or one judge from another common-law jurisdiction.

The High Court consists of a Court of Appeal and a Court of First Instance. The Court of First Instance has unlimited jurisdiction in civil and criminal cases, while the District Court has limited jurisdiction. Appeals from these courts lie to the Court of Appeal, presided over by the Chief Judge or a Vice-President of the Court of Appeal with one or two Justices of Appeal. Appeals from Magistrates' Courts are heard by a Court of First Instance judge.

HIGH COURT

38 Queensway; tel. 28690869; fax 28690640: internet www.info.gov.hk/jud.

Chief Justice of the Court of Final Appeal: ANDREW K. N. LI.

Permanent Judges of the Court of Final Appeal: R. A. V. RIBEIRO, PATRICK S. O. CHAN, K. BOKHARY.

Chief Judge of the High Court: ARTHUR S. C. LEONG.

Justices of Appeal: K. H. WOO, M. STUART-MOORE, F. STOCK, Mrs D. LE PICHON, S. H. MAYO, A. G. ROGERS, M. K. C. WONG, B. R. KEITH, P. C. Y. CHEUNG.

Judges of the Court of First Instance: C. G. JACKSON, G. J. LUGAR-MAWSON, A. O. T. CHUNG, T. M. GALL, D. Y. K. YAM, W. S. Y. WAUNG, C. SEAGROATT, M. P. BURRELL, Ms C. CHU, Mrs V. S. BOKHARY, K. K. PANG, W. D. STONE, Ms C. M. BEESON, P. V. T. NGUYEN, M. J. HARTMANN, A. R. SUFFIAD, A. H. SAKHRANI, L. P. S. TONG, Miss S. S. H. KWAN, Mr Justice YEUNG, Mr Justice MA, Ms Justice YUEN.

OTHER COURTS

District Courts: There are 34 District Judges.

Magistrates' Courts: There are 59 Magistrates and 11 Special Magistrates, sitting in 9 magistracies.

Religion

The Chinese population is predominantly Buddhist. In 1994 the number of active Buddhists was estimated at between 650,000 and 700,000. Confucianism and Daoism are widely practised. The three religions are frequently found in the same temple. In 1999 there were some 527,000 Christians, approximately 80,000 Muslims, 12,000 Hindus, 1,000 Jews and 1,200 Sikhs. The Bahá'í faith and Zoroastrianism are also represented.

BUDDHISM

Hong Kong Buddhist Association: 1/F, 338 Lockhart Rd; tel. 25749371; fax 28340789; internet www.hkbuddhist.org; Pres. Ven. KOK KWONG.

CHRISTIANITY

Hong Kong Christian Council: 9/F, 33 Granville Rd, Kowloon; tel. 23687123; fax 27242131; e-mail hkcc@hkcc.org.hk; internet www.hkcc.org.hk; f. 1954; 21 mem. orgs; Chair. Rev. Li Ping-kwong; Gen. Sec. Rev. Eric So Shing-yit.

The Anglican Communion

Primate of Hong Kong Sheng Kung Hui and Bishop of Hong Kong Island and Macao: Most Rev. Peter K. K. Kwong, Bishop's House, 1 Lower Albert Rd, Central; tel. 25265355; fax 25212199; e-mail office1@hkskh.org.

Bishop of Eastern Kowloon: Rt Rev. Louis Tsui, Holy Trinity Bradbury Centre, 4/F, 139 Ma Tau Chung Rd, Kowloon; tel. 27139983; fax 27111609; e-mail ekoffice@ekhkskh.org.hk.

Bishop of Western Kowloon: Rt Rev. Thomas Soo, Ultra Grace Commercial Bldg, 15/F, 5 Jordan Rd, Kowloon; tel. 27830811; fax 27830799; e-mail hkskhdwk@netvigator.com.

The Lutheran Church

Evangelical Lutheran Church of Hong Kong: 50A Waterloo Rd, Kowloon; tel. 23885847; fax 23887539; e-mail info@elchk.org.hk; internet www.elchk.org.hk; 13,000 mems; Pres. Rev. Tso Shui-wan.

The Roman Catholic Church

For ecclesiastical purposes, Hong Kong forms a single diocese, nominally suffragan to the archdiocese of Canton (Guangzhou), China. According to Vatican sources, in 2000 there were an estimated 371,327 adherents in the territory, representing more than 5% of the total population.

Bishop of Hong Kong: Cardinal Joseph Zen Ze-kiun, Catholic Diocese Centre, 12/F, 16 Caine Rd; tel. 25241633; fax 25218737; e-mail bishophk@hk.super.net.

The Press

Hong Kong has a thriving press. At the end of 2000, according to government figures, there were 59 daily newspapers, including 32 Chinese-language and seven English-language dailies, and 717 periodicals.

PRINCIPAL DAILY NEWSPAPERS

English Language

Asian Wall Street Journal: GPOB 9825; tel. 25737121; fax 28345291; f. 1976; business; Editor Reginald Chua; circ. 65,378.

China Daily: Hong Kong edition of China's official English-language newspaper; launched 1997; Editor Liu Dizhong; circ. 11,000.

Hong Kong iMail: Sing Tao Bldg, 4/F, 1 Wang Kwong Rd, Kowloon Bay, Kowloon; tel. 27982798; fax 27953009; e-mail imail@hk-imail.com; internet www.hk-imail.com; f. 1949; Editor Andrew Lynch; circ. 45,000.

International Herald Tribune: 1201 K Wah Centre, 191 Java Rd, North Point; tel. 29221188; fax 29221190; internet www.iht.com; Correspondent Kevin Murphy.

South China Morning Post: Morning Post Centre, Dai Fat St, Tai Po Industrial Centre, Tai Po, New Territories; tel. 26808888; fax 26616984; internet www.scmp.com; f. 1903; CEO Owen Jonathan; Editor Robert Keatley; circ. 118,000.

Target Intelligent Report: Suite 2901, Bank of America Tower, 12 Harcourt Rd, Central; tel. 25730379; fax 28381597; e-mail info@targetnewspapers.com; internet www.targetnewspapers.com; f. 1972; financial news, commentary, politics, property, litigations, etc.

Chinese Language

Ching Pao: 3/F, 141 Queen's Rd East; tel. 25273836; f. 1956; Editor Mok Kong; circ. 120,000.

Hong Kong Commercial Daily: 1/F, 499 King's Rd, North Point; tel. 25905322; fax 25658947.

Hong Kong Daily News: All Flats, Hong Kong Industrial Bldg, 17/F, 444–452 Des Voeux Rd West; tel. 28555111; fax 28198717; internet www.hkdailynews.net; f. 1958; morning; CEO Peter Y. K. Kuo; Chief Editor K. K. Yeung; circ. 120,000.

Hong Kong Economic Journal: North Point Industrial Bldg, 22/F, 499 King's Rd; tel. 28567567; fax 28111070; e-mail info@hkej.com; Editor-in-Chief H. C. Chiu; circ. 70,000.

Hong Kong Economic Times: Kodak House, Block 2, Room 808, 321 Java Rd, North Point; tel. 28802888; fax 28111926; f. 1988; Publr Perry Mak; Chief Editor Eric Chan; circ. 64,565.

Hong Kong Sheung Po (Hong Kong Commercial Daily): 499 King's Rd, North Point; tel. 25640788; f. 1952; morning; Editor-in-Chief H. Cheung; circ. 110,000.

Hsin Wan Pao (New Evening Post): 342 Hennessy Rd, Wanchai; tel. 28911604; fax 28382307; f. 1950; Editor-in-Chief Chao Tse-lung; circ. 90,000.

Ming Pao Daily News: Block A, Ming Pao Industrial Centre, 15/F, 18 Ka Yip St, Chai Wan; tel. 25953111; fax 28982534; e-mail mingpao@mingpao.com; internet www.mingpao.com; f. 1959; morning; Chief Editor Paul Cheung; circ. 84,217.

Oriental Daily News: Oriental Press Centre, Wang Tai Rd, Kowloon Bay, Kowloon; tel. 27951111; fax 27955599; Chair. C. F. Ma; Editor-in-Chief Ma Kai Lun; circ. 650,000.

Ping Kuo Jih Pao (Apple Daily): Hong Kong; tel. 29908685; fax 23708908; f. 1995; Propr Jimmy Lai; Publr Loh Chan; circ. 400,000.

Seng Weng Evening News: f. 1957; Editor Wong Long-chau; circ. 60,000.

Sing Pao Daily News: Sing Pao Bldg, 101 King's Rd, North Point; tel. 25702201; fax 28870348; f. 1939; morning; Chief Editor Hon Chung-suen; circ. 229,250.

Sing Tao Daily: Sing Tao Bldg, 3/F, 1 Wang Kwong Rd, Kowloon Bay, Kowloon; tel. 27982575; fax 27953022; f. 1938; morning; Editor-in-Chief Luk Kam Wing; circ. 60,000.

Ta Kung Pao: 342 Hennessy Rd, Wanchai; tel. 25757181; fax 28345104; e-mail tkp@takungpao.com; internet www.takungpao.com; f. 1902; morning; supports People's Republic of China; Editor T. S. Tsang; circ. 150,000.

Tin Tin Yat Pao: Culturecom Centre, 10/F, 47 Hung To Rd, Kwun Tong, Kowloon; tel. 29507300; fax 23452285; f. 1960; Chief Editor Ip Kai-wing; circ. 199,258.

Wen Wei Po: Hing Wai Centre, 2–4/F, 7 Tin Wan Praya Rd, Aberdeen; tel. 28738288; fax 28730657; internet www.wenweipo.com; f. 1948; morning; communist; Dir Zhang Guo-liang; First Editor-in-Chief Cheung Ching-wan; circ. 200,000.

SELECTED PERIODICALS

English Language

Asian Business: c/o TPL Corporation (HK) Ltd, Block C, 10/F, Seaview Estate, 2–8 Watson Rd, North Point; tel. 25668381; fax 25080197; e-mail absales@asianbusiness.com.hk; internet www.asianbusinessnet.com; monthly; Publr and Executive Editor James Leung; circ. 75,000.

Asian Medical News: Pacific Plaza, 8/F, 410 Des Voeux Rd West; tel. 25595888; fax 25596910; e-mail amn@medimedia.com.hk; internet www.amn.com; f. 1979; monthly; Man. Editor Ross Garbett; circ. 28,300.

Asian Profile: Asian Research Service, GPOB 2232; tel. 25707227; fax 25128050; f. 1973; 6 a year; multi-disciplinary study of Asian affairs.

Business Traveller Asia/Pacific: Unit 404, Printing Hse, 6 Duddell St, Central; tel. 25119317; fax 25196846; e-mail enquiry@businesstravellerasia.com; f. 1982; consumer business travel; 12 a year; Publr Peggy Teo; Editor Jonathan Wall; circ. 23,320.

Far Eastern Economic Review: Central Plaza, 25/F, 18 Harbour Rd, Wanchai, GPOB 160; tel. 25084338; fax 25031549; e-mail review@feer.com; internet www.feer.com; f. 1946; weekly; Editor Michael Vatikiotis; circ. 95,570.

Hong Kong Electronics: Office Tower, Convention Plaza, 38/F, 1 Harbour Rd; tel. 25844333; fax 28240249; e-mail hktdc@tdc.org.ht; internet www.tdctrade.com; f. 1985; monthly; publ. by the Hong Kong Trade Development Council; Editor John Cairns; circ. 90,000.

Hong Kong Enterprise: Office Tower, Convention Plaza, 38/F, 1 Harbour Rd; tel. 25844333; fax 28240249; e-mail hktdc@tdc.org.hk; internet www.tdctrade.com; f. 1967; monthly; publ. by the Hong Kong Trade Development Council; Editor Tess Lugos; circ. 150,000.

Hong Kong Government Gazette: Govt Printing Dept, Cornwall House, Taikoo Trading Estate, 28 Tong Chong St, Quarry Bay; tel. 25649500; weekly.

Hong Kong Household: Office Tower, Convention Plaza, 38/F, 1 Harbour Rd, Wanchai; tel. 25844333; fax 28240249; e-mail hktdc@tdc.org.hk; internet www.tdctrade.com; f. 1983; publ. by the Hong Kong Trade Development Council; household and hardware products; 2 a year; Editor Tess Lugos; circ. 90,000.

Hong Kong Industrialist: Federation of Hong Kong Industries, Hankow Centre, 4/F, 5–15 Hankow Rd, Tsimshatsui, Kowloon; tel. 27323188; fax 27213494; e-mail fhki@fhki.org.hk; monthly; publ. by the Federation of Hong Kong Industries; Editor James Manning; circ. 6,000.

Hong Kong Trader: Office Tower, Convention Plaza, 38/F, 1 Harbour Rd, Wanchai; tel. 25844333; fax 28243485; e-mail trader@tdc.org.hk; internet www.tdc.org.hk/hktrader; f. 1983; publ. by the Hong Kong Trade Development Council; trade, economics, financial and general business news; monthly; Man. Editor SOPHY FISHER; circ. 70,000.

Official Hong Kong Guide: Wilson House, 3/F, 19–27 Wyndham St, Central; tel. 25215392; fax 25218638; f. 1982; monthly; information on sightseeing, shopping, dining, etc. for overseas visitors; Editor-in-Chief DEREK DAVIES; circ. 9,300.

Orientations: 17/F, 200 Lockhart Rd; tel. 25111368; fax 25074620; e-mail omag@netvigator.com; internet www.orientations.com.hk; f. 1970; 10 a year; arts of East Asia, the Indian subcontinent and South-East Asia; Publr and Editorial Dir ELIZABETH KNIGHT.

Reader's Digest (Asia Edn): 3 Ah Kung Ngam Village Rd, Shaukiwan; tel. 96906381; fax 96906389; e-mail friends@rdasia.com.hk; f. 1963; general topics; monthly; Editor PETER DOCKRILL; circ. 332,000.

Sunday Examiner: Catholic Diocese Centre, 11/F, 16 Caine Rd; tel. 25220487; fax 25369939; e-mail sundayex@catholic.org.hk; f. 1946; religious; weekly; Editor Fr JOHN J. CASEY; circ. 2,300.

Textile Asia: c/o Business Press Ltd, California Tower, 11/F, 30–32 D'Aguilar St, GPOB 185, Central; tel. 25233744; fax 28106966; e-mail texasia@netvigator.com; f. 1970; monthly; textile and clothing industry; Publr and Editor-in-Chief KAYSER W. SUNG; circ. 17,000.

Tradefinance Asia: Hong Kong monthly; Editor RICHARD TOURRET.

Travel Business Analyst: GPO Box 12761; tel. 25072310; e-mail TBAoffice@aol.com; internet www.travelbusinessanalyst.com; f. 1982; travel trade; monthly; Editor MURRAY BAILEY.

Chinese Language

Affairs Weekly: Hong Kong; tel. 28950801; fax 25767842; f. 1980; general interest; Editor WONG WAI MAN; circ. 130,000.

Cheng Ming Monthly: Hennessy Rd, POB 20370; tel. 25740664; Chief Editor WAN FAI.

City Magazine: Hang Seng Bldg, 7/F, 200 Hennessy Rd, Wanchai; tel. 28931393; fax 28388761; f. 1976; monthly; fashion, wine, cars, society, etc.; Publr JOHN K. C. CHAN; Chief Editor PETER WONG; circ. 30,000.

Contemporary Monthly: Unit 705, Westlands Centre, 20 Westlands Rd, Quarry Bay; tel. 25638122; fax 25632984; f. 1989; monthly; current affairs; 'China-watch'; Editor-in-Chief CHING CHEONG; circ. 50,000.

Disc Jockey: Fuk Keung Ind. Bldg, B2, 14/F, 66–68 Tong Mei Rd, Taikoktsui, Kowloon; tel. 23905461; fax 27893869; e-mail vinpres@netvigator.com; f. 1990; monthly; music; Publr VINCENT LEUNG; Editor ALGE CHEUNG; circ. 32,000.

Eastweek: Oriental Press Centre, Wang Tai Rd, Kowloon Bay, Kowloon; tel. 27951111; fax 27955599; f. 1992; weekly; general interest; Chair. C. F. MA; circ. 238,000.

Elegance HK: Aik San Bldg, 14/F, 14 Westlands Rd, Quarry Bay; tel. 2963011; fax 25658217; f. 1977; monthly; for thinking women; Chief Editor WINNIE YUEN; circ. 75,000.

Kung Kao Po (Catholic Chinese Weekly): 16 Caine Rd; tel. 25220487; fax 25213095; e-mail kkp@catholic.org.hk; internet kkp.catholic.org.hk; f. 1928; religious; weekly; Editor-in-Chief Fr LOUIS HA.

Lisa's Kitchen Bi-Weekly: Fuk Keung Ind. Bldg, B2, 14/F, 66–68 Tong Mei Rd, Taikoktsui, Kowloon; tel. 23910668; fax 27893869; f. 1984; recipes; Publr VINCENT LEUNG; circ. 50,000.

Metropolitan Weekly: f. 1983; weekly; entertainment, social news; Chief Editor CHARLES YOU; circ. 130,000.

Ming Pao Monthly: Ming Pao Industrial Centre, 15/F, Block A, 18 Ka Yip St, Chai Wan; tel. 25155107; fax 28982566; Chief Editor KOO SIU-SUN.

Motor Magazine: Prospect Mansion, Flat D, 1/F, 66–72 Paterson St, Causeway Bay; tel. 28822230; fax 28823949; f. 1990; Publr and Editor-in-Chief KENNETH LI; circ. 32,000. (Publication suspended, 2001.)

Next Magazine: 8 Chun Ying St, T. K. O. Industrial Estate West, Tseung Kwan O, Hong Kong; tel. 27442733; fax 29907210; internet www.nextmedia.com; f. 1989; weekly; news, business, lifestyle, entertainment; Editor-in-Chief CHEUNG KIM HUNG; circ. 172,708.

Open Magazine: Causeway Bay, POB 31429; tel. 28939197; fax 28915591; e-mail open@open.com.hk; internet www.open.com.hk; f. 1990; monthly; Chief Editor JIN CHONG; circ. 15,000.

Oriental Sunday: Oriental Press Centre, Wang Tai Rd, Kowloon Bay, Kowloon; tel. 27951111; fax 27952299; f. 1991; weekly; leisure magazine; Chair. C. F. MA; circ. 120,000.

Reader's Digest (Chinese Edn): Reader's Digest Association Far East Ltd, 3 Ah Kung Ngam Village Rd, Shaukiwan; tel. 28845590; fax 25671479; e-mail chrd@netvigator.com; f. 1965; monthly; Editor-in-Chief VICTOR FUNG KEUNG; circ. 295,000.

Today's Living: Prospect Mansion, Flat D, 1/F, 66–72 Paterson St, Causeway Bay; tel. 28822230; fax 28823949; e-mail magazine@todayliving.com; f. 1987; monthly; interior design; Publr and Editor-in-Chief KENNETH LI; circ. 35,000.

TV Week: 1 Leighton Rd, Causeway Bay; tel. 28366147; fax 28346717; f. 1967; weekly; Publr PETER CHOW; circ. 59,082.

Yazhou Zhoukan: Block A, Ming Pao Industrial Centre, 15/F, 18 Ka Yip St, Chai Wan; tel. 25155358; fax 25059662; e-mail loppoon@mingpao.com; internet www.yzzk.com; f. 1987; international Chinese news weekly; Chief Editor YAU LOP-POON; circ. 110,000.

Young Girl Magazine: Fuk Keung Ind. Bldg, B2, 14/F, 66–68 Tong Mei Rd, Taikoktsui, Kowloon; tel. 23910668; fax 27893869; f. 1987; biweekly; Publr VINCENT LEUNG; circ. 65,000.

Yuk Long TV Weekly: Hong Kong; tel. 25657883; fax 25659958; f. 1977; entertainment, fashion, etc.; Publr TONY WONG; circ. 82,508.

NEWS AGENCIES

International News Service: 2E Cheong Shing Mansion, 33–39 Wing Hing St, Causeway Bay; tel. 25665668; Rep. AU KIT MING.

Xinhua (New China) News Agency, Hong Kong SAR Bureau: 387 Queen's Rd East, Wanchai; tel. 28314126; f. 2000 from fmr news dept of branch office of Xinhua (responsibility for other activities being assumed by Liaison Office of the Central People's Government in the Hong Kong SAR); Dir ZHANG GUOLIANG.

Foreign Bureaux

Agence France-Presse (AFP): Telecom House, Room 1840, 18/F, 3 Gloucester Rd, Wanchai, GPOB 5613; tel. 28020224; fax 28027292; Regional Dir YVAN CHEMLA.

Agencia EFE (Spain): 10A Benny View House, 63–65 Wong Nai Chung Rd, Happy Valley; tel. 28080199; fax 28823101; Correspondent MIREN GUTIÉRREZ.

Associated Press (AP) (USA): 1282 New Mercury House, Waterfront Rd; tel. 25274324; Bureau Chief ROBERT LIU.

Central News Agency (CNA) Inc (Taiwan): Hong Kong Bureau Chief CONRAD LU.

Jiji Tsushin-Sha (Japan): 3503 Far East Finance Centre, 16 Harcourt Rd; tel. 25237112; fax 28459013; Bureau Man. KATSUHIKO KABASAWA.

Kyodo News Service (Japan): Unit 1303, 13/F, 9 Queen's Rd, Central; tel. 25249750; fax 28105591; e-mail tyoko@po.iijnet.or.jp; Correspondent TSUKASA YOKOYAMA.

Reuters Asia Ltd (United Kingdom): Hong Kong; tel. 258436363; Bureau Man. GEOFF WEETMAN.

United Press International (UPI) (USA): 1287 Telecom House, 3 Gloucester Rd, POB 5692; tel. 28020221; fax 28024972; Vice-Pres. (Asia) ARNOLD ZEITLIN; Editor (Asia) PAUL H. ANDERSON.

PRESS ASSOCIATIONS

Chinese Language Press Institute: Tower A, Sing Tao Bldg, 1 Wang Kwong Rd, Kowloon Bay, Kowloon; tel. 27982501; fax 27953017; Pres. AW SIAN.

Hong Kong Chinese Press Association: Rm 2208, 22/F, 33 Queen's Rd Central; tel. 28613622; fax 28661933; 13 mems; Chair. HUE PUE-YING.

Hong Kong Journalists Association: GPOB 11726; tel. 25910692; fax 25727329; e-mail hkja@hk.super.net; internet www.hkja.org.hk; f. 1968; 549 mems; Chair. MAK YIN-TING.

Newspaper Society of Hong Kong: Rm 904, 75–83 King's Rd, North Point; tel. 25713102; fax 25712627; f. 1954; Chair. LEE CHO JAT.

Publishers

Art House of Collectors HK Ltd: 37 Lyndhurst Terrace, Ground Floor, Central; tel. 28818026; fax 28904304; Dir. LI LAP FONG.

Asia 2000 Ltd: 15B The Parkside, 263 Hollywood Rd, Sheung Wan; tel. 25301409; fax 25261107; e-mail info@asia2000.com.hk; internet www.asia2000.com.hk; Asian studies, politics, photography, fiction; Man. Dir MICHAEL MORROW.

Asian Research Service: GPOB 2232; tel. 25707227; fax 25128050; f. 1972; maps, atlases, monographs on Asian studies and journals; Dir NELSON LEUNG.

Chinese University Press: Chinese University of Hong Kong, Sha Tin, New Territories; tel. 26096508; fax 26036692; e-mail cup@cuhk.edu.hk; internet www.cuhk.edu.hk/cupress; f. 1977; studies on China and Hong Kong and other academic works; Dir Dr STEVEN K. LUK.

Commercial Press (Hong Kong) Ltd: Eastern Central Plaza, 8/F, 3 Yiu Hing Rd, Shau Kei Wan; tel. 25651371; fax 25645277; e-mail webmaster@commercialpress.com.hk; internet www.commercial press.com.hk; f. 1897; trade books, dictionaries, textbooks, Chinese classics, art, etc.; Man. Dir and Chief Editor CHAN MAN HUNG.

Excerpta Medica Asia Ltd: 8/F, 67 Wyndham St; tel. 25243118; fax 28100687; f. 1980; sponsored medical publications, abstracts, journals etc.

Hoi Fung Publisher Co: 125 Lockhart Rd, 2/F, Wanchai; tel. 25286246; fax 25286249; Dir. K. K. TSE.

Hong Kong University Press: Hing Wai Centre, 14/F, 7 Tin Wan Praya Rd, Aberdeen; tel. 25502703; fax 28750734; e-mail hkupress@hkucc.hku.hk; internet www.hkupress.org; f. 1956; Publr COLIN DAY.

International Publishing Co: Rm 213–215, HK Industrial Technology Centre, 72 Tat Chee Ave, Kowloon Tong, Kowloon; tel. 23148882; fax 23192208; Admin. Man. KAREN CHOW.

Ismay Publications Ltd: C. C. Wu Building; tel. 25752270; Man. Dir MINNIE YEUNG.

Ling Kee Publishing Co Ltd: Zung Fu Industrial Bldg, 1067 King's Rd, Quarry Bay; tel. 25616151; fax 28111980; f. 1956; educational and reference; Chair. B. L. AU; Man. Dir K. W. AU.

Oxford University Press (China) Ltd: Warwick House, 18/F, 979 King's Rd, Taikoo Place, Quarry Bay; tel. 25163222; fax 25658491; e-mail oupchina@oupchina.com.hk; internet www.oupchina.com.hk; f. 1961; school textbooks, reference, academic and general works relating to Hong Kong, Taiwan and China; Regional Dir SIMON LI.

Taosheng Publishing House: Lutheran Bldg, 3/F, 50A Waterloo Rd, Yau Ma Tei, Kowloon; tel. 23887061; fax 27810413; e-mail taosheng@elchk.org.hk; Dir CHAN PUI TAK.

Textile Asia/Business Press Ltd: California Tower, 11/F, 30–32 D'Aguilar St, GPOB 185, Central; tel. 25233744; fax 28106966; e-mail texasia@netvigator.com; internet www.textileasia-business press.com; f. 1970; textile magazine; Man. Dir KAYSER W. SUNG.

The Woods Publishing Co: Li Yuen Building, 2/F, 7 Li Yuen St West, Central; tel. 25233002; fax 28453296; e-mail tybook@netvig ator.com; Production Man. TONG SZE HONG.

Times Publishing (Hong Kong) Ltd: Seaview Estate, Block C, 10/F, 2–8 Watson Rd, North Point; tel. 25668381; fax 25080255; e-mail abeditor@asianbusiness.com.hk; internet www.asianbusiness net.com; trade magazines and directories; CEO COLIN YAM; Executive Editor JAMES LEUNG.

Government Publishing House

Government Information Services: see Government Offices.

PUBLISHERS' ASSOCIATIONS

Hong Kong Publishers' and Distributors' Association: National Bldg, 4/F, 240–246 Nathan Rd, Kowloon; tel. 23674412; 45 mems; Chair. HO KAM-LING; Sec. HO NAI-CHI.

Society of Publishers in Asia: c/o Worldcom Hong Kong, 502–503 Admiralty Centre, Tower I, 18 Harcourt Rd, Admiralty; tel. 28654007; fax 28652559; e-mail worldcom@hkstar.com.

Broadcasting and Communications

TELECOMMUNICATIONS

Asia Satellite Telecommunications Co Ltd (AsiaSat): East Exchange Tower, 23–24/F, 38–40 Leighton Rd; tel. 28056666; fax 25043875; e-mail wpang@asiasat.com; internet www.asiasat .com; CEO PETER JACKSON.

Cable and Wireless HKT Ltd: Hongkong Telecom Tower, 39/F, Taikoo Place, 979 King's Rd, Quarry Bay; tel. 28882888; fax 28778877; e-mail info@cwhkt.com; internet www.cwhkt.com; fmrly Hong Kong Telecommunications; in 1998 acquired Pacific Link Communications to become largest mobile telephone operator in Hong Kong; monopoly on provision of international lines expired March 1998; full competition began Jan. 1999; CEO LINUS CHEUNG.

Regulatory Authority

Telecommunications Authority: statutory regulator, responsible for implementation of the Govt's pro-competition and pro-consumer policies; Dir.Gen. ANTHONY S. K. WONG.

Hutchison Telecom, New T and T Hong Kong Ltd, and New World Telecom also operate local services. In 2000 six companies were licensed to provide mobile telecommunications services, serving over 5.2m. customers.

BROADCASTING

Regulatory Authority

Broadcasting Authority: regulatory body; administers and issues broadcasting licences.

Radio

Hong Kong Commercial Broadcasting Co Ltd: 3 Broadcast Drive, KCPOB 73000; tel. 23365111; fax 23380021; e-mail comradio@crhk.com.hk; internet www.crhk.com.hk; f. 1959; broadcasts in English and Chinese on three radio frequencies; Chair. G. J. HO; Dir and CEO WINNIE YU.

Metro Broadcast Corpn Ltd (Metro Broadcast): Hong Kong; tel. 23649333; fax 23646577; e-mail tech@metroradio.com.hk; internet www.metroradio.com.hk; f. 1991; broadcasts on three channels in English, Cantonese and Mandarin; Gen. Man. CRAIG B. QUICK.

Radio Television Hong Kong: Broadcasting House, 30 Broadcast Drive, POB 70200, Kowloon Central PO; tel. 23396300; fax 23380279; e-mail rthk@hk.super.net; internet www.rthk.org.hk; f. 1928; govt-funded; 24-hour service in English and Chinese on seven radio channels; service in Putonghua inaugurated in 1997; Dir CHU PUI-HING.

Star Radio: Hutchison House, 12/F, 10 Harcourt Rd, Central; f. 1995; satellite broadcasts in Mandarin and English; Gen. Man. MIKE MACKAY.

Television

Asia Television Ltd (ATV): Television House, 81 Broadcast Drive, Kowloon; tel. 29928888; fax 23380438; e-mail atv@hkatv.com; internet www.hkatv.com; f. 1973; operates two commercial television services (English and Chinese) and produces television programmes; Dir and CEO FENG XIAO PING.

STAR Group Ltd: One Harbourfront, 8/F, 18 Tak Fung St, Hunghom, Kowloon; tel. 26218888; fax 26213050; internet www.startv.com; f. 1990; subsidiary of the News Corpn Ltd; broadcasts programming services via satellite to 300m. viewers in 53 countries across Asia, the Indian subcontinent and the Middle East; music, news, sport and entertainment broadcasts in English, Mandarin, Hindi, Japanese, Tagalog, Arabic, and Thai; subscription and free-to-air services on several channels; also owns radio stations in India; Chair. and CEO Exec. JAMES MURDOCH.

Radio Television Hong Kong: (see Radio); produces drama, documentary and public affairs programmes; also operates an educational service for transmission by two local commercial stations; Dir CHU PUI-HING (acting).

Television Broadcasts Ltd (TVB): TV City, Clearwater Bay Rd, Kowloon; tel. 23352288; fax 23581300; e-mail external .affairs@tvb.com.hk; internet www.tvb.com; f. 1967; operates Chinese and English language services; two colour networks; Exec. Chair. Sir RUN RUN SHAW; Man. Dir LOUIS PAGE.

Wharf Cable Ltd: Wharf Cable Tower, 4/F, 9 Hoi Shing Rd, Tsuen Wan; tel. 26115533; fax 24171511; f. 1993; 24-hour subscription service of news, sport and entertainment on 35 channels; carries BBC World Service Television; Chair. PETER WOO; Man. Dir STEPHEN NG.

Finance

(cap. = capital; res = reserves; dep. = deposits; m. = million; brs = branches; amounts in Hong Kong dollars unless otherwise stated)

BANKING

In April 2002 there were 141 licensed banks, of which 27 were locally incorporated, operating in Hong Kong. There were also 48 restricted licence banks (formerly known as licensed deposit-taking companies), 48 deposit-taking companies, and 105 foreign banks' representative offices.

Hong Kong Monetary Authority (HKMA): 30/F, 3 Garden Rd, Central; tel. 28788196; fax 28788197; e-mail hkma@hkma.gov.hk; internet www.hkma.gov.hk; f. 1993 by merger of Office of the Commissioner of Banking and Office of the Exchange Fund; carries out central banking functions; maintains Hong Kong dollar stability within the framework of the linked exchange rate system; supervises licensed banks, restricted licence banks and deposit-taking cos, their overseas brs and representative offices; manages foreign currency reserves; Chief Exec. JOSEPH YAM; Deputy Chief Execs DAVID CARSE, TONY LATTER, NORMAN CHAN.

Banks of Issue

Bank of China (Hong Kong) Ltd (People's Repub. of China): Bank of China Tower, 1 Garden Rd, Central; tel. 28266888; fax

28105963; internet www.bochk.com; f. 1917; became third bank of issue in May 1994; merged in Oct. 2001 with the local branches of 11 mainland banks (incl. Kwangtung Provincial Bank, Sin Hua Bank Ltd, China and the South Sea Bank Ltd, Kincheng Banking Corpn, China State Bank, National Commercial Bank Ltd, Yien Yieh Commercial Bank Ltd, Hua Chiao Commercial Bank Ltd and Po Sang Bank Ltd, to form the Bank of China (Hong Kong); Chair. LIU MINGKANG; Vice-Chair. and CEO LIU JINBAO; 369 brs.

The Hongkong and Shanghai Banking Corporation Ltd: 1 Queen's Rd, Central; tel. 28221111; fax 28101112; internet www.asiapacific.hsbc.com; f. 1865; personal and commercial banking; cap. 44,937m., res 38,192m., dep. 1,493,180m. (Dec. 2001); Chair. DAVID ELDON; more than 600 offices world-wide.

Standard Chartered Bank: Standard Chartered Bank Bldg, 4–4A Des Voeux Rd, Central; tel. 28203333; fax 28569129; internet www.standardchartered.com.hk; f. 1859; Group Exec. Dir (vacant).

Other Commercial Banks

Asia Commercial Bank Ltd: Asia Financial Centre, 120–122 Des Voeux Rd, Central; tel. 25419222; fax 25410009; internet www.asia-commercial.com; f. 1934; fmrly Commercial Bank of Hong Kong; cap. 810.0m., res 432.8m., dep. 12,466.6m. (Dec. 2000); Chair. and CEO ROBIN Y. H. CHAN; Gen. Man. and Exec. Dir STEPHEN TAN; 13 domestic, 1 overseas br.

Bank of East Asia Ltd: GPOB 31, 10 Des Voeux Rd, Central; tel. 28423200; fax 28459333; internet www.hkbea.com; inc in Hong Kong in 1918, absorbed United Chinese Bank Ltd in Aug. 2001; cap. 3,583.7m., res 13,211.6m., dep. etc. 154,887.5m. (Dec. 2001); Chair. and Chief Exec. DAVID K. P. LI; 90 brs in Hong Kong and 14 overseas brs.

Chekiang First Bank Ltd: Chekiang First Bank Centre, 1 Duddell St, Central; tel. 29221222; fax 28100531; e-mail contact@cfb.com.hk; internet www.cfb.com.hk; f. 1950; cap. 2,500m., res 1,105m., dep. 21,575.8m. (Dec. 2001); Chair. JAMES Z. M. KUNG; 18 brs.

Chiyu Banking Corpn Ltd: 78 Des Voeux Rd, Central; tel. 28430111; fax 25267420; f. 1947; cap. 300m., res 4,069.8m., dep. 23,189.9m. (Dec. 2000); Chair. TAN KONG PIAT; 15 brs.

CITIC Ka Wah Bank Ltd: 232 Des Voeux Rd, Central; tel. 25457131; fax 25417029; e-mail info@citickawahbank.com; internet: www.citickawahbank.com; f. 1922; cap. 2,595.5m., res 3,658.2m., dep. 49,715.5m. (Dec. 2001); Chair. KONG DAN; Pres. and CEO CAI ZHONGZHI; 26 domestic brs, 2 overseas brs.

Dah Sing Bank Ltd: Dah Sing Financial Centre, 36/F, 108 Gloucester Rd, Central; tel. 25078866; fax 25985052; e-mail ops@dahsing.com.hk; internet www.dahsing.com; f. 1947; cap. 800.0m., res 3,718.5m., dep. 38,506.4m. (Dec. 2001); Chair. DAVID S. Y. WONG; Man. Dir DEREK H. H. WONG; 37 domestic brs, 1 overseas br.

Dao Heng Bank Ltd: The Centre, 11/F, 99 Queen's Rd, Central; tel. 22188822; fax 22853822; e-mail webmaster@daoheng.com; internet www.daoheng.com; f. 1921; cap. 5,200m., res 8,221.3m., dep. 100,818.6m. (Dec. 2001); CEO RANDOLPH GORDON SULLIVAN; 44 domestic brs, 4 overseas brs.

DBS Kwong On Bank Ltd: 139 Queen's Rd, Central; tel. 28153636; fax 21678222; e-mail hkcs@dbs.com; internet www.dbs.com.hk; f. 1938, inc 1954 as Kwong On Bank, name changed 2000; subsidiary of the Development Bank of Singapore; cap. 750.0m., res 3,616m., dep. 27,206m. (Dec. 2000); Chair. RONALD LEUNG DING-BONG; Sr Man. Dir KENNETH T. M. LEUNG; 32 brs.

First Pacific Bank Ltd: First Pacific Bank Centre, 22/F, 56 Gloucester Rd, Wanchai; tel. 28239239; fax 28655151; e-mail info@firstpacbank.com; internet www.firstpacbank.com; f. 1922; fmrly The Hong Nin Savings Bank Ltd; merged with Far East Bank in 1989; cap. 1,248m., res 1,634.2m., dep. 20,096.5m. (Dec. 1999); Chair. DAVID LI KWOK-PO; Man. Dir DANIEL WAN YIM-KEUNG; 24 brs.

Hang Seng Bank Ltd: 83 Des Voeux Rd, Central; tel. 21981111; fax 28684047; e-mail ccd@hangseng.com; internet www.hangseng.com; f. 1933; cap. 9,559m., res 30,711m., dep. 408,295m. (Jun. 2002); Chair. DAVID ELDON; Vice-Chair. and CEO VINCENT CHENG; 155 domestic brs, 5 overseas brs.

Hongkong Chinese Bank Ltd: Lippo Centre, Floor Mezz. 1, 89 Queensway, Central; tel. 28676833; fax 28459221; internet www.hkcb.com.hk; f. 1954; cap. 2,393.3m., res 953.4m., dep. 20,332.3m. (Dec. 2000); Chair. MOCHTAR RIADY; Man. Dir and Chief Exec. RAYMOND LEE WING-HUNG; 21 domestic, 2 overseas brs.

Industrial and Commercial Bank of China (Asia): ICBC Tower, 122–126 Queen's Rd, Central; tel. 25343333; fax 28051166; internet www.icbcasia.com; f. 1964; fmrly Union Bank of Hong Kong; cap. 901.7m., res 1,420.7m., dep. 17,809.1m. (Dec. 2000); Chair. JIANG JIANQING; 21 brs.

International Bank of Asia Ltd: International Bank of Asia Bldg, 38 Des Voeux Rd, Central; tel. 28426222; fax 28101483; e-mail iba-info@iba.com.hk; internet www.iba.com.hk; f. 1982 as Sun Hung Kai Bank Ltd, name changed 1986; subsidiary of Arab Banking Corpn; cap. 1,172.2m., res 1,103.6m., dep. 24,027.9m. (Dec. 2001); Man. Dir and CEO MIKE M. MURAD; 26 brs.

Jian Sing Bank Ltd: 99–105 Des Voeux Rd, Central; tel. 25410088; fax 25447145; e-mail admin@jsb.com.hk; f. 1964 as Hongkong Industrial and Commercial Bank Ltd, acquired by Dah Sing Bank Ltd in 1987, 40% interest acquired by China Construction Bank in 1994, resulting in name change; cap. 300.0m., res 51.9m., dep. 2,415.1m. (Dec. 2000); Chair. ZHEFU LUO; CEO and Gen. Man. PATRICK P. T. HO.

Liu Chong Hing Bank Ltd: POB 2535, 24 Des Voeux Rd, Central; tel. 28417417; fax 28459134; e-mail intlcorrbankhk@lchbhk.com; internet www.lchbank.com; f. 1948; cap. 217.5m., res 5,578.5m., dep. 33,229.9m. (Dec. 2001); Chair. and Man. Dir LIU LIT-MAN; 36 domestic brs, 3 overseas brs.

Nanyang Commercial Bank Ltd: Nanyang Commercial Bank Bldg, 151 Des Voeux Rd, Central; tel. 25421111; fax 28153333; e-mail webmaster_nyc@bocgroup.com; internet www.nanyang-bank.com; f. 1949; cap. p.u. 600m., res 10,016.3m., dep. 72,204.4m. (Dec. 2000); Chair. ZHANG HONG-YI; 41 brs, 6 mainland brs, 1 overseas br.

Overseas Trust Bank Ltd: The Centre, 11/F, 99 Queen's Rd, Central; tel. 22188822; fax 22853822; e-mail corpcomm@daoheng.com; internet www.daoheng.com; f. 1955; under govt control 1985–93; cap. 2,000m., res 2,459.5m., dep. 25,835.6m. (Dec. 2000); Chair. PHILIPPE PAILLART; Man. Dir R. G. SULLIVAN; 28 domestic brs, 4 overseas brs.

Shanghai Commercial Bank Ltd: 12 Queen's Rd, Central; tel. 28415415; fax 28104623; e-mail contact@shacombank.com.hk; internet www.shacombank.com.hk; f. 1950; cap. 2,000m., res 6,845.6m., dep. 61,008.1m. (Dec. 2001); CEO, Man. Dir and Gen. Man. JOHN KAM-PAK YAN; 40 domestic brs, 4 overseas brs.

Standard Bank Asia Ltd (Standard Jardine Fleming Bank): 36/F, Two Pacific Place, 88 Queensway; tel. 28227888; fax 28227999; e-mail ashbanking@standardbank.com.hk; internet www.standardbank.com; f. 1970 as Jardine Fleming & Company Ltd, renamed Jardine Fleming Bank Ltd in 1993, absorbed by Standard Bank Investment Corpn Ltd and name changed as present in July 2001; cap. 66m., res 52.3m., dep. 1,571.4m. (Dec. 2001); Chair. PIETER PRINSLOO.

Tai Yau Bank Ltd: 130–32Des Voeux Rd, Central; tel. 25229002; fax 28685334; f. 1947; cap. 150.0m., res 176.5m., dep 1,469.9m. (Dec. 2000); Chair. KO FOOK KAU.

Wayfoong Finance Ltd: 10/F, Tower 1, HSBC Centre, 1 Sham Mong Rd, Kowloon; tel. 22888777; fax 22888722; f. 1960; owned by HSBC Holdings plc; cap. 300.0m., res 882.2m., dep. 1,747.9m. (Dec. 1999).

Wing Hang Bank Ltd: POB 514, 161 Queen's Rd, Central; tel. 28525111; fax 25410036; e-mail whbpsd@whbhk.com; internet www.whbhk.com; f. 1937; cap. 293.4m., res 5,123.0m., dep. 48,236.3m. (Dec. 2000); Chair. and Chief Exec. PATRICK Y. B. FUNG; 27 domestic brs, 14 overseas brs.

Wing Lung Bank Ltd: 45 Des Voeux Rd, Central; tel. 28268333; fax 28100592; e-mail wlb@winglungbank.com.hk; internet www.winglungbank.com; f. 1933; cap. 1,161.0m., res 6,250.0m., dep. 51,970.0m. (Dec. 2001); Chair. MICHAEL PO-KO WU; Exec. Dir and Gen. Man. CHE-SHUM CHUNG; 35 domestic brs, 2 overseas brs.

Principal Mainland Chinese and Foreign Banks

ABN AMRO Bank NV (Netherlands): Edinburgh Tower, 3–4/F, Landmark, 15 Queen's Rd, Central; tel. 28429211; fax 28459049; CEO (China) SERGIO RIAL; 3 brs.

American Express Bank Ltd (USA): One Pacific Place, 36/F, 88 Queensway, Central; tel. 28440688; fax 28453637; Senior Country Exec. DOUGLAS H. SHORT III; 3 brs.

Australia and New Zealand Banking Group Ltd: 27/F, One Exchange Square, 8 Connaught Place, Central; tel. 28437111; fax 28680089; Gen. Man. PETER RICHARDSON.

BA Asia Ltd: GPOB 799, 2/F, Bank of America Tower, 12 Harcourt Rd; tel. 28476666; fax 28100821; Chair. COLM MCCARTHY; Man. Dir. and CEO FREDERICK CHIN.

Bangkok Bank Public Co Ltd (Thailand): Bangkok Bank Bldg, 28 Des Voeux Rd, Central; tel. 28016688; fax 28451805; Gen. Man. CHEN MAN YING; 2 brs.

Bank of America (Asia) Ltd (USA): Devon House, 17/F, 979 King's Rd, Quarry Bay; tel. 25973333; fax 25972500; internet www.bankofamerica.com.hk; Pres. and CEO SAMUEL TSIEN; 13 brs.

Bank of Communications, Hong Kong Branch: 20 Pedder St, Central; tel. 28419611; fax 28106993; f. 1934; Gen. Man. FANG LIANKUI; 41 brs.

Bank of India: Ruttonjee House, 2/F, 11 Duddell St, Central; tel. 25240186; fax 28106149; e-mail boihk@netvigator.com; Chief Exec. O. P. GUPTA.

Bank of Scotland: Jardine House, 11/F, 1 Connaught Place, Central; tel. 25212155; fax 28459007; Sr Man. I. A. McKinney; 1 br.

Barclays Capital Asia Ltd: Citibank Tower, 42/F, 3 Garden Rd, Central; tel. 29032000; fax 29032999; internet www.barclayscapital.com; f. 1972; Chair. and CEO Robert A. Morrice.

BNP Paribas (France): Central Tower, 4–14/F, 28 Queen's Rd, Central; tel. 29098888; fax 25302707; e-mail didier.balme@bnpgroup.com; internet www.bnpparibas.com.hk; f. 1958; Man. Didier Balme; 2 brs.

Citibank, NA (USA): Citibank Tower, 39–40/F and 44–50/F, Citibank Plaza, 3 Garden Rd, Central; tel. 28688888; fax 23068111; 20 brs.

Commerzbank AG (Germany): Hong Kong Club Bldg, 21/F, 3A Chater Rd, Central; tel. 28429666; fax 28681414; 1 br.

Crédit Agricole Indosuez (France): One Exchange Square, 42–45/F, 8 Connaught Rd, Central; tel. 28489000; fax 28681406; Sr Country Officer Charles Reybet-Degat; 1 br.

Deutsche Bank AG (Germany): 51–56/F, Cheung Kong Center, 2 Queen's Rd, Central; tel. 22038888; fax 28459056; Gen. Mans Dr Michael Thomas, Reiner Rusch; 1 br.

Equitable PCI Bank (Philippines): 7/F, No. 1, Silver Fortune Plaza, Wellington St; tel. 28680323; fax 28100050; Vice-Pres. Paul Lang; 1 br.

Fortis Bank (Belgium): Fortis Bank Tower, 27/F, 77–79 Gloucester Rd, Wanchai; tel. 28230456; fax 25276851; e-mail info@fortisbank.com.hk; internet www.fortisbank.com.hk; Gen. Man. David Yu; 28 brs.

Indian Overseas Bank: POB 182, Ruttonjee House, 3/F, 11 Duddell St, Central; tel. 25227249; fax 28450159; 2 brs.

JP Morgan Chase Bank (USA): 39/F, One Exchange Square, Connaught Place, Central; tel. 28431234; fax 28414396.

Malayan Banking Berhad (Malaysia): Entertainment Bldg, 18–19/F, 30 Queen's Rd, Central; tel. 25227141; fax 28106013; trades in Hong Kong as Maybank; Man. Hwan Woon Han; 2 brs.

Mevas Bank: 36/F, Dah Sing Financial Centre, 108 Gloucester Rd; tel. 31013286; fax 31013298; e-mail contactus@mevas.com; internet www.mevas.com; Chair. David S. Y. Wong.

Mizuho Bank Ltd (Japan): 17/F, 2 Pacific Place, 88 Queensway, Admiralty; tel. 21033000; fax 28681421; Gen. Man. Takeshi Tanimura; 1 br.

National Bank of Pakistan: 18/F, ING Tower, 308–320 Des Voeux Rd, Central; tel. 25217321; fax 28451703; Gen. Man. Usman Aziz; 2 brs.

Oversea-Chinese Banking Corpn Ltd (Singapore): 9/F, 9 Queen's Rd, Central; tel. 28682086; fax 28453439; Gen. Man. Benjamin Yeung; 3 brs.

Philippine National Bank: 2/F, Wing's Bldg, 110–116 Queen's Rd, Central; tel. 25253638; fax 25253107; e-mail itdept@pnbhk.com; Sr Vice-Pres. and Gen. Man. Articer O. Quebal; 1 br.

N. M. Rothschild and Sons (Hong Kong) Ltd: 16/F, Alexandra House, 16–20 Chater Rd, Central; tel. 25255333; fax 28681773; Chair. Philip Brass.

Société Générale Asia Ltd (France): 40/F, Edinburgh Tower, The Landmark, 15 Queen's Rd; tel. 25838600; fax 28400738; CEO Jackson Cheung.

Sumitomo Mitsui Banking Corpn (SMBC) (Japan): 7–8F/, One International Finance Centre, 1 Harbour View St, Central; tel. 22062000; fax 22062888; Gen. Man. Toshio Morikawa; 1 br.

Tokyo-Mitsubishi International (HK) Ltd (Japan): 16/F, Tower 1, Admiralty Centre, 18 Harcourt Rd; tel. 25202460; fax 25291550; Man. Dir. and CEO Yoshiaki Watanabe.

UFJ International Finance Asia Ltd (Japan): 6/F, Hong Kong Club Bldg, 3A Chater Rd, Central; tel. 25334300; fax 28453518; CEO and Man. Dir Akihiko Kobayashi.

United Overseas Bank Ltd (Singapore): United Overseas Bank Bldg, 54–58 Des Voeux Rd, Central; tel. 28425666; fax 28105773; Sr Vice-Pres. and CEO Robert Chan Tze Leung; 5 brs.

Banking Associations

The Chinese Banks' Association Ltd: South China Bldg, 5/F, 1–3 Wyndham St, Central; tel. 25224789; fax 28775102; 1,666 mems; Chair. Bank of East Asia (represented by David K. P. Li).

The DTC Association (The Hong Kong Association of Restricted Licence Banks and Deposit-Taking Companies): Suite 3738, 37/F, Sun Hung Kai Centre, 30 Harbour Rd; tel. 25264079; fax 25230180.

The Hong Kong Association of Banks: GPOB 11391; tel. 25211169; fax 28685035; e-mail hkab@pacific.net.hk; internet www.hkab.org.hk; f. 1981 to succeed The Exchange Banks' Asscn of Hong Kong; all licensed banks in Hong Kong are required by law to be mems of this statutory body, whose function is to represent and further the interests of the banking sector; 134 mems; Chair. Hongkong and Shanghai Banking Corp. Ltd. (represented by Raymond Or); Sec. Rona Morgan.

STOCK EXCHANGE

Honk Kong Exchanges and Clearing Ltd: 1 International Finance Centre, 12/F, 1 Harbour View St, Central; tel. 25221122; fax 22953106; e-mail info@hkex.com.hk; internet www.hkex.com.hk; f. 2000 by unification of the Stock Exchange of Hong Kong, the Hong Kong Futures Exchange and the Hong Kong Securities Clearing Co; 572 mems; Chair. Lee Yeh Kwong; CEO Kwong Ki Chi.

In 1998 **Exchange Fund Investment Ltd** was established by the Government to manage its stock portfolio acquired during the intervention of August (Chair. Yang Ti-liang).

SUPERVISORY BODY

Securities and Futures Commission (SFC): Edinburgh Tower, 12/F, The Landmark, 15 Queen's Rd, Central; tel. 28409222; fax 28459553; e-mail enquiry@hksfc.org.hk; internet www.hksfc.org.hk; f. 1989 to supervise the stock and futures markets; Chair. Andrew Sheng; Dep. Chair. Laura Cha.

INSURANCE

In December 2001 there were 204 authorized insurance companies, including 105 overseas companies. The following are among the principal companies:

Asia Insurance Co Ltd: World-Wide House, 16/F, 19 Des Voeux Rd, Central; tel. 28677988; fax 28100218; e-mail kclau@asiainsurance.com.hk; internet www.asiainsurance.com.hk; Chair. Sebastian Ki Chit Lau.

CGU International Insurance plc: Cityplaza One, 9/F, Taikoo Shing; tel. 28940555; fax 28905741; e-mail cguasia.com; Gen. Man. Andrew Lo.

Hong Kong Export Credit Insurance Corpn: South Seas Centre, Tower I, 2/F, 75 Mody Rd, Tsim Sha Tsui East, Kowloon; fax 27226277; Commr D. K. Dowding.

Mercantile and General Reinsurance Co PLC: 13C On Hing Bldg, 1 On Hing Terrace, Central; tel. 28106160; fax 25217353; Man. T. W. Ho.

Ming An Insurance Co (HK) Ltd: Ming An Plaza, 19/F, 8 Sunning Rd, Causeway Bay; tel. 28151551; fax 25416567; e-mail mai@mingan.com.hk; internet www.mingan.com; Dir and Gen. Man. K. P. Cheng.

National Mutual Insurance Co (Bermuda) Ltd: 151 Gloucester Rd, Wanchai; tel. 25191111; fax 25987204; life and general insurance; Chair. Sir David Akers-Jones; CEO Terry Smith.

Prudential Assurance Co Ltd: Cityplaza 4, 10/F, 12 Taikoo Wan Rd, Taikoo Shing; tel. 29773888; fax 28776994; life and general; CEO James C. K. Wong.

Royal and Sun Alliance (Hong Kong) Ltd: Dorset House, 32/F, Taikoo Place, 979 King's Road, Quarry Bay; tel. 29683000; fax 29685111; Man. Dir Keith Land.

Summit Insurance (Asia) Ltd: Sunshine Plaza, 25/F, 253 Lockhart Rd, Wanchai; tel. 21059000; fax 25166992; e-mail psi@hcg.com.hk; internet www.hsinchong.com/summit; CEO Iu Po Sing.

Willis China (Hong Kong) Ltd: 17/F, AIA Plaza, 18 Hysan Ave, Causeway Bay; tel. 28270111; fax 28270966; www.willis.com; Man. Dir Kirk Austin.

Winterthur Swiss Insurance (Asia) Ltd: Dah Sing Financial Centre, 19/F, 108 Gloucester Rd, Wanchai; tel. 25986282; fax 25985838; Man. Dir Allan Yu.

Insurance Associations

Hong Kong Federation of Insurers (HKFI): First Pacific Bank Centre, Room 902, 9/F, 56 Gloucester Rd, Wanchai; tel. 25201868; fax 25201967; e-mail hkfi@hkfi.org.hk; internet www.hkfi.org.hk; f. 1988; 117 general insurance and 42 life insurance mems; Chair. Choy Chung Foo; Exec. Dir Louisa Fong.

Insurance Institute of Hong Kong: GPO Box 6747; tel. 25825601; fax 28276033; internet www.iihk.org.hk; f. 1967; Pres. Stephen Law.

Trade and Industry

Hong Kong Trade Development Council: Office Tower, 38/F, Convention Plaza, 1 Harbour Rd, Wanchai; tel. 1830668; fax 28240249; e-mail hktdc@tdc.org.hk; internet www.tdctrade.com; f. 1966; Chair. Peter Woo Kwong-ching; Exec. Dir Michael Sze.

Trade and Industry Department: Trade and Industry Department Tower, 700 Nathan Rd, Kowloon; tel. 23985333; fax 27892491; e-mail enqtid@tid.gcn.gov.hk; internet www.info.gov.hk/tid; Dir-Gen. JOSHUA LAW.

DEVELOPMENT ORGANIZATIONS

Hong Kong Housing Authority: 33 Fat Kwong St, Homantin, Kowloon; tel. 27615002; fax 27621110; f. 1973; plans, builds and manages public housing; Chair. DOMINIC WONG; Dir of Housing J. A. MILLER.

Hong Kong Productivity Council: HKPC Bldg, 78 Tat Chee Ave, Yau Yat Chuen, Kowloon Tong, Kowloon; tel. 27885678; fax 27885900; e-mail bettylee@hkpc.org; internet www.hkpc.org; f. 1967 to promote increased productivity of industry and to encourage optimum utilization of resources; council of 23 mems appointed by the Government, representing management, labour, academic and professional interests, and govt depts associated with productivity matters; Chair. KENNETH FANG; Exec. Dir THOMAS TANG.

Kadoorie Agricultural Aid Loan Fund: c/o Director of Agriculture, Fisheries and Conservation, Cheung Sha Wan Govt Offices, 5/F, 303 Cheung Sha Wan Rd, Kowloon; tel. 21506666; fax 23113731; e-mail afcdenq@afcd.gcn.gov.hk; f. 1954; provides low-interest loans to farmers; HK $9,035,000 was loaned in 2001/02.

J. E. Joseph Trust Fund: c/o Director of Agriculture, Fisheries and Conservation, Cheung Sha Wan Govt Offices, 5/F, 303 Cheung Sha Wan Rd, Kowloon; tel. 21506666; fax 23113731; e-mail afcdenq@afcd.gcn.gov.hk; f. 1954; grants low-interest credit facilities to farmers and farmers' co-operative socs; HK $5,050,000 was loaned in 2001/02.

CHAMBERS OF COMMERCE

Chinese Chamber of Commerce, Kowloon: 2/F, 8–10 Nga Tsin Long Rd, Kowloon; tel. 23822309; f. 1936; 234 mems; Chair. and Exec. Dir YEUNG CHOR-HANG.

The Chinese General Chamber of Commerce: 4/F, 24–25 Connaught Rd, Central; tel. 25256385; fax 28452610; e-mail cgcc@cgcc.org.hk; internet www.cgcc.org.hk; f. 1900; 6,000 mems; Chair. Dr CHAN YAU-HING.

Hong Kong General Chamber of Commerce: United Centre, 22/F, 95 Queensway, POB 852; tel. 25299229; fax 25279843; e-mail chamber@chamber.org.hk; internet www.chamber.org.hk; f. 1861; 4,000 mems; Chair. CHRISTOPHER CHENG; Dir EDEN WOON.

Kowloon Chamber of Commerce: KCC Bldg, 3/F, 2 Liberty Ave, Homantin, Kowloon; tel. 27600393; fax 27610166; e-mail kcc02@hkkcc.biz.com.hk; internet www.hkkcc.org.hk; f. 1938; 1,640 mems; Chair. TONG KWOK-WAH; Exec. Dir CHENG PO-WO.

FOREIGN TRADE ORGANIZATIONS

Hong Kong Chinese Importers' and Exporters' Association: Champion Bldg, 7–8/F, 287–291 Des Voeux Rd, Central; tel. 25448474; fax 25444677; e-mail info@hkciea.org.hk; internet www.hkciea.org.hk; f. 1954; 3,000 mems; Pres. HUI CHEUNG-CHING.

Hong Kong Exporters' Association: Room 824–825, Star House, 3 Salisbury Rd, Tsimshatsui, Kowloon; tel. 27309851; fax 27301869; e-mail exporter@exporters.org.hk; internet www.exporters.org.hk; f. 1955; 630 mems comprising leading merchants and manufacturing exporters; Pres. CLIFF K. SUN; Exec. Dir SHIRLEY SO.

INDUSTRIAL AND TRADE ASSOCIATIONS

Chinese Manufacturers' Association of Hong Kong: CMA Bldg, 64 Connaught Rd, Central; tel. 25456166; fax 25414541; e-mail info@cma.org.hk; internet www.cma.org.hk; f. 1934 to promote and protect industrial and trading interests; operates testing and certification laboratories; 3,700 mems; Pres. CHAN WING KEE; Exec. Dir FRANCIS T. M. LAU.

Federation of Hong Kong Garment Manufacturers: Cheung Lee Commercial Bldg, Room 401–3, 25 Kimberley Rd, Tsimshatsui, Kowloon; tel. 27211383; fax 23111062; e-mail fhkgmfrs@hkstar.com; f. 1964; 200 mems; Pres. CHOI HIN-TO; Sec.-Gen. ANTHONY K. K. TANG.

Federation of Hong Kong Industries (FKHI): Hankow Centre, 4/F, 5–15 Hankow Rd, Tsimshatsui, Kowloon; tel. 27323188; fax 27213494; e-mail fhki@fhki.org.hk; internet www.fhki.org.hk; f. 1960; 3,000 mems; Chair. HENRY Y. Y. TANG.

Federation of Hong Kong Watch Trades and Industries Ltd: Peter Bldg, Room 604, 58–62 Queen's Rd, Central; tel. 25233232; fax 28684485; e-mail hkwatch@netvigator.com; internet www.hkwatch.org; f. 1947; 700 mems; Chair. FRANK CHAU.

Hong Kong Association for the Advancement of Science and Technology Ltd: 2A, Tak Lee Commercial Bldg, 113–17 Wanchai Rd, Wanchai; tel. 28913388; fax 28381823; e-mail info@hkaast.org.hk; internet www.hkaast.org.hk; Pres. KO JAN MING.

Hong Kong Biotechnology Association Ltd: Rm 789, HITEC, 1 Trademart Drive, Kowloon Bay, Kowloon; tel. 26209955; fax 26201238; e-mail etang@hkbta.org.hk; internet www.hkbta.org.hk; Chair. LO YUK LAM.

Hong Kong Chinese Enterprises Association: Harbour Center, Room 2104–6, Harbour Centre, 25 Harbour Rd, Wanchai; tel. 28272831; fax 28272606; e-mail info@hkcea.com; internet www.hkcea.com; f. 1991; 1,000 mems; Chair. LIU JINBAO; Exec. Dir ZHOU JIE.

Hong Kong Chinese Textile Mills Association: 11/F, 38–40 Tai Po Rd, Sham Shiu Po, Kowloon; tel. 27778236; fax 27881836; f. 1931; 150 mems; Pres. LEE CHUNG-CHIU.

Hong Kong Construction Association Ltd: 3/F, 180–182 Hennessy Rd, Wanchai; tel. 25724414; fax 25727104; e-mail admin@hkca.com.hk; internet www.hkca.com.hk; f. 1920; 372 mems; Pres. JIMMY TSE; Sec.-Gen. PATRICK CHAN.

Hong Kong Electronic Industries Association Ltd: Rm 1201, 12/F, Harbour Crystal Centre, 100 Granville Rd, Tsimshatsui, Kowloon; tel. 27788328; fax 27882200; e-mail hkeia@hkeia.org.; internet www.hkeia.org; 370 mems; Chair. SAMSON TAM.

Hong Kong Garment Manufacturers Association: 401-3, Cheung Lee Commercial Bldg, 25 Kimberley Rd, Tsimshatsui, Kowloon; tel. 23052893; fax 23052493; e-mail mleung@textilecouncil.com; f. 1987; 40 mems; Chair. PETER WANG.

Hong Kong Information Technology Federation Ltd: Unit 3701, Windsor House, Causeway Bay; tel. 29238021; fax 25760181; e-mail info@hkitf.com; internet www.hkitf.org.hk; 250 mems; f. 1980; Pres. CHARLES MOK.

Hong Kong Jewellery and Jade Manufacturers Association: Flat A, 12/F, Kaiser Estate Phase 1, 41 Man Yue St, Hunghom, Kowloon; tel. 25430543; fax 28150164; e-mail hkjja@hkstar.com; internet www.jewellery-hk.org; f. 1965; 227 mems; Chair. CHARLES CHAN; Gen. Man. CATHERINE CHAN.

Hong Kong Jewelry Manufacturers' Association: Unit G, 2/F, Kaiser Estate Phase 2, 51 Man Yue St, Hunghom, Kowloon; tel. 27663002; fax 23623647; e-mail hkjma@jewelry.org.hk; internet www.jewelry.org.hk; f. 1988; 260 mems; Chair. DENNIS NG.

Hong Kong Knitwear Exporters and Manufacturers Association: Clothing Industry Training Authority, 3/F, Kowloon Bay Training Centre, 63 Tai Yip St, Kowloon; tel. 27552621; fax 27565672; f. 1966; 108 mems; Chair. WILLY LIN; Exec. Sec. SHIRLEY LIU.

Hong Kong and Kowloon Footwear Manufacturers' Association: Kam Fung Bldg, 3/F, Flat D, 8 Cleverly St, Sheung Wan; tel. and fax 25414499; 88 mems; Pres. LOK WAI-TO; Sec. LEE SUM-HUNG.

Hong Kong Optical Manufacturers' Association Ltd: 2/F, 11 Fa Yuen St, Mongkok, Kowloon; tel. 23326505; fax 27705786; e-mail hkoma@netvigator.com; internet www.hkoptical.org.hk; f. 1982; 114 mems; Pres. HUI LEUNG-WAH.

Hong Kong Plastics Manufacturers Association Ltd: Fu Yuen Bldg, 1/F, Flat B, 39–49 Wanchai Rd; tel. 25742230; fax 25742843; f. 1957; 200 mems; Chair. JEFFREY LAM; Pres. DENNIS H. S. TING.

Hong Kong Printers Association: 1/F, 48–50 Johnston Rd, Wanchai; tel. 25275050; fax 28610463; e-mail printers@hkprinters.org; internet www.hkprinters. org; f. 1939; 437 mems; Chair. HO KA-HUN; Exec. Dir LEE SHUN-HAY.

Hong Kong Rubber and Footwear Manufacturers' Association: Kar Tseuk Bldg, Block A, 2/F, 185 Prince Edward Rd, Kowloon; tel. 23812297; fax 23976927; f. 1948; 180 mems; Chair. CHEUNG KAM; Gen. Sec. LAI YUEN-MAN.

Hong Kong Sze Yap Commercial and Industrial Association: Cosco Tower, Unit 1205–6, 183 Queen's Rd, Central; tel. 25438095; fax 25449495; f. 1909; 1,082 mems; Chair. LOUIE CHICK-NAN; Sec. WONG KA CHUN.

Hong Kong Toys Council: Hankow Centre, 4/F, 5–15 Hankow Rd, Tsimshatsui, Kowloon; tel. 27323188; fax 27213494; e-mail fhki@fhki.org.hk; internet www.toyshk.org; f. 1986; 200 mems; Chair. SAMSON CHAN.

Hong Kong Watch Manufacturers' Association: Yu Wing Bldg, 3/F and 11/F, Unit A, 64–66 Wellington St, Central; tel. 25225238; fax 28106614; e-mail hkwma@netvigator.com; internet www.hkwma.org; 682 mems; Pres. STANLEY C. H. LAU; Sec.-Gen. TONY K. L. WONG.

Information and Software Industry Association Ltd: Suite 2, 8/F, Tower 6, China Hong Kong City, 33 Canton Rd, Tsimshatsui; tel. 26222867; fax 26222731; e-mail info@isia.org.hk; internet www.isia.org.hk; Chair. C. S. NG.

Internet and Telecom Association of Hong Kong: GPOB 13461; tel. 25042732; fax 25042752; e-mail info@itahk.org.hk; internet www.itahk.org.hk; 130 mems; Chair. TONY HAU.

New Territories Commercial and Industrial General Association Ltd: Cheong Hay Bldg, 2/F, 107 Hoi Pa St, Tsuen Wan; tel. 24145316; fax 24934130; f. 1973; 4,000 mems; Chair. H. L. WAN; Sec.-Gen. K. C. NGAN.

Real Estate Developers Association of Hong Kong: Worldwide House, Room 1403, 19 Des Voeux Rd, Central; tel. 28260111; fax 28452521; f. 1965; 750 mems; Pres. Dr STANLEY HO; Exec. Vice-Pres. THOMAS KWOK.

Textile Council of Hong Kong Ltd: 401-3, Cheung Lee Commercial Bldg, 25 Kimberley Rd, Tsimshatsui , Kowloon; tel. 23052893; fax 23052493; e-mail mleung@textilecouncil.com; f. 1989; 10 mems; Chair. ANDREW LEUNG; Exec. Dir MICHAEL LEUNG.

Toys Manufacturers' Association of Hong Kong Ltd: Room 1302, Metroplaza, Tower 2, 223 Hing Fong Rd, Kwai Chung, New Territories; tel 24221209; fax 24221639; e-mail tmhk@harbourring .com.hk; internet www.tmhk.net; 250 mems; Pres. ARTHUR CHAN; Sec. BECKY TO.

EMPLOYERS' ORGANIZATIONS

Employers' Federation of Hong Kong: Suite 2004, Sino Plaza, 255–257 Gloucester Rd, Causeway Bay; tel. 25280536; fax 28655285; e-mail efhk@efhk.org.hk; internet www.efhk.org.hk; f. 1947; 446 mems; Chair. JAMES C. NG; Exec. Dir JACKIE MA.

Hong Kong Factory Owners' Association Ltd: Wing Wong Bldg, 11/F, 557–559 Nathan Rd, Kowloon; tel. 23882372; fax 23857129; f. 1982;1,179 mems; Pres. HWANG JEN; Sec. TSANG CHUN WAH.

UTILITIES

Electricity

CLP Power Ltd: 147 Argyle St, Kowloon; tel. 26788111; fax 27604448; internet www.clpgroup.com; f. 1918; fmrly China Light and Power Co Ltd; generation and supply of electricity to Kowloon and the New Territories; Chair. MICHAEL D. KADOORIE; Man. Dir ROSS SAYERS.

Hongkong Electric Co Ltd: Electric Centre, 28 City Garden Rd, North Point; tel. 28433111; fax 28100506; e-mail mail@hec.com.hk; internet www.hec.com.hk; generation and supply of electricity to Hong Kong Island, and the islands of Ap Lei Chau and Lamma; Chair. GEORGE C. MAGNUS; Man. Dir K. S. TSO.

Gas

Gas Authority: all gas supply cos, gas installers and contractors are required to be registered with the Gas Authority. At the end of 2000 there were seven registered gas supply cos.

Hong Kong and China Gas Co Ltd: 23/F, 363 Java Rd, North Point; tel. 29633388; fax 25632233; internet www.towngas.com; production, distribution and marketing of town gas and gas appliances; operates two plants; Chair. LEE SHAU-KEE; Man. Dir ALFRED W. K. CHAN.

Water

Drainage Services Department: responsible for planning, designing, constructing, operating and maintaining the sewerage, sewage treatment and stormwater drainage infrastructures.

Water Supplies Department: tel. 28294709; fax 25881594; e-mail wsdinfo@wsd.gov.hk; internet www.info.gov.hk/wsd/; responsible for water supplies; approx. 2.4m. customers (2001).

MAJOR COMPANIES

The following are among Hong Kong's leading companies. Capital, reserves and sales are given in HK dollars unless otherwise stated.

Akai Holdings Ltd: Two Exchange Sq., 30/F, 8 Connaught Place, Central; tel. 25241043; fax 28453558; cap. and res US $405m., sales US $833m. (1998/99); fmrly Semi-Tech (Global) Co Ltd; investment holding co, its subsidiaries' activities incl. manufacturing, retailing and distribution of sewing machines, consumer durables, electronics and audio and video products; Chair. JAMES H. TING.

Amoy Properties Ltd: Standard Chartered Bank Bldg, 28/F, 4 Des Voeux Rd, Central; tel. 28790111; fax 28686086; e-mail amoy@ hanglung.com; internet www.hanglung.com/amoy/home.html; f. 1949; cap. and res 27,477m. (1999/2000), sales 257m. (1997/98); property investment and management, investment holding and carpark management; Chair. RONNIE CHICHUNG CHAN; Man. Dir NELSON WAI LEUNG YUEN; 807 employees.

Benzer Electronics Manufacturing Ltd: Kimley Comm. Bldg, 142–146 Queen's Rd, Central; tel. 25419118; fax 28519402; sales 7,750m. (1994); manufacture and sales of electrical goods; Gen. Man. RAJU BHALIA.

Brilliance China Automotive Holdings: Suites 2303–06, 23/F, Great Eagle Centre, 23 Harbour Rd, Wanchai; tel. 25237227; fax 25268472; internet www.brillianceauto.com; f. 1992; manufacture and distribution of minibuses; jt ventures with several mainland vehicle manufactures and Toyota (Japan); Chair. WU XIAOAN.

Cheung Kong (Holdings) Ltd: Cheung Kong Center, 7/F, 2 Queen's Rd, Central; tel. 21288888; fax 28452940; internet www.ckh.com.hk; cap. and res 141,743m., sales 8,193m. (1999); investment holding, project management, property development; Chair. Dr LI KA-SHING; Man. Dir VICTOR LI; 4,380 employees.

China Resources Enterprise Ltd: Rm 3908, China Resources Bldg, 26 Harbour Road, Wanchai; tel. 28271028; fax 25988453; e-mail creltd@cre.com.hk; internet www.cre.com.hk; f. 1992; revenue US $2,153.6m. (2000); food and beverages, distribution and trading, retailing; Chair. NING GAONING; Man. Dir SONG LIN.

Chow Sang Sang Holdings International Ltd: Chow Sang Sang Bldg, 4/F, 229 Nathan Rd, Kowloon; tel. 27300111; fax 27309683; cap. 110m., sales 4,317.0m. (1999); manufacturing, retailing and trading of jewellery, gold and other precious metals; Chair. CHOW KWEN-LIM; 1,370.

CITIC Pacific Ltd: CITIC Tower, 32/F, 1 Tim Mei Ave, Central; tel. 28202111; fax 28772771; e-mail contact@citicpacific.com; internet www.citicpacific.com; cap. and res 38,178m., sales 26,424m. (1999); investment holding, power generation, construction of roads, bridges and tunnels; Chair. LARRY YUNG CHI KIN; Man. Dir HENRY FAN HUNG LING; 10,490 employees.

Crocodile Garments Ltd: Lai Sun Commercial Centre, 10/F, 680 Cheung Sha Wan Rd, Kowloon; tel. 27853898; fax 27860190; e-mail raymond@crocodile.com.hk; internet www.crocodile.com.hk; cap. and res 470.7m., sales 652.5m. (1998/9); manufacture and sale of garments; Chair. LIM POR YEN; 1,700 employees.

Dah Chong Hong Holdings Ltd: Hang Seng Bldg, 12/F, 77 Des Voeux Rd, Central; tel. 28468111; fax 28459092; f. 1964; sales 8,900m. (1995, est.); manufacture and retail of foods; Chief Exec. JOSEPH PANG CHO HUNG.

Daido Concrete (H.K.) Ltd: Tai Po Industrial Estate, 3 Dai Shing St, New Territories; tel. 28867788; fax 25130110; internet www.daidohk.com; cap. and res 118.8m., sales 161.0m. (1999); manufacture and sale of concrete piles; trading in construction materials; Chair. PANG TAK CHUNG; 700 employees.

Dickson Concepts (International) Ltd: East Ocean Centre, 4/F, 98 Granville Rd, Tsimshatsui East, Kowloon; tel. 23113888; fax 23113323; internet www.irasia.com/listco/hk/dickson/index.htm; cap. and res. 1,054.1m., sales 3,050m. (1999/2000); investment holding; trading of luxury goods; Chair. DICKSON POON.

General Motors Overseas Corpn: Rm 1804, 2 Exchange Sq., 8 Connaught Place, Central; tel. 28464500; fax 28401193; sales 14,000m. (1995, est.); sales and servicing of motor vehicles.

Gold Peak Industries (Holdings) Ltd: Gold Peak Bldg, 8/F, 30 Kwai Wing Rd, Kwai Chung, New Territories; tel. 24271133; fax 24891879; e-mail gp@goldpeak.com; internet www.goldpeak.com; cap. and res 926.4m., sales 2,234.5m. (1997/98); manufacture and sale of batteries, car audio equipment, other electrical and electronic products; Chair. VICTOR C. W. LO; 13,100 employees.

Guangdong Investment Ltd: Guangdong Investment Tower, 29–30/F, 148 Connaught Rd, Central; tel. 28604368; fax 25284386; internet www.gdi.com.hk; cap. and res 4,414.8m., sales 5,359m. (1999); holding company, activities incl. travel, hotels, property, industrial investment and energy; Chair. WU JIESI; Man. Dir KANG DIAN.

Henderson Investment Ltd: World-Wide House, 6/F, 19 Des Voeux Rd, Central; tel. 29088888; fax 29088838; e-mail henderson@ hld.com; internet www.hld.com; cap. and res 18,459.1m., sales 817.2m. (1999/2000); property development and investment, investment holding; Chair. and Man. Dir Dr LEE SHAU KEE.

Hong Kong Land Holdings Ltd: 8/F, 1 Exchange Sq., 8 Connaught Place, Central; tel. 28428428; fax 28459226; internet www.hkland.com; sales US $387m. (2000); property investment and development; Chair. PERCY WEATHERALL; Man. Dir NICHOLAS SALLNOW-SMITH.

Hopewell Holdings Ltd: Hopewell Centre, 64/F, 183 Queen's Rd East; tel. 25284975; fax 28656276; cap. and res 13,642.6m., sales 1,509.6m. (1999/2000); property investment and management, road infrastructure and power station projects; Chair. Sir GORDON WU YING SHEUNG.

Hutchison Whampoa Ltd: Hutchison House, 22/F, 10 Harcourt Rd; tel. 21281188; fax 21281705; internet www.hutchison-whampoa .com; cap. and res 243.902m., sales 55,442m. (1999); investment holding and management company; Chair. LI KA-SHING; Man. Dir CANNING FOK; 42,510 employees.

Hysan Development Co Ltd: Manulife Plaza, 49/F, The Lee Gardens, 33 Hysan Ave; tel. 28955777; fax 25775219; internet www.hysan.com.hk; cap. and res 21,266m. (2001), sales 355m. (2001); property investment; Chair. and Man. Dir PETER T. C. LEE.

Inchcape Pacific Ltd: Standard Chartered Bank Bldg, 17/F, 4 Des Voeux Rd, Central; tel. 28424666; fax 28100031; motors, consumer and industrial, shipping services, buying services, business machines, inspection and testing, insurance services; Chair. Dr RAYMOND CH'IEN.

Jardine Matheson Ltd: Jardine House, 48/F, GPOB 70; tel. 28438288; fax 28459005; e-mail jml@jardines.com; internet www.jardines.com; f. 1832; group sales US $9,413m. (2001); property, hotels, consumer marketing, engineering and construction, insurance broking, supermarkets and motor trading, transportation; Man. Dir PERCY WEATHERALL; 130,000 employees.

Dairy Farm International Holdings Ltd: Devon House, 7/F, Taikoo Place, 979 King's Rd, Quarry Bay; tel. 28376483; fax 25769734; internet www.dairyfarmgroup.com; sales US $6,800m. (1999); international food and drugstore retailing; Chair. SIMON KESWICK; CEO RONALD FLOTO.

Jardine International Motor Holdings Ltd: Hong Kong; tel. 28957288; fax 28907017; internet www.jardine-matheson.com/motors.html; cap. and res US $396m., sales US $2,807m. (1999); sales and servicing of motor vehicles; Chair. A. J. L. NIGHTINGALE; 4,400 employees.

Jardine Pacific: Devon House, 25/F, Taikoo Place, 979 King's Rd; tel. 25792888; fax 8569868; internet www.jardines.com; f. 1989; sales US $1,588m. (1998); marketing and distribution, engineering and construction, aviation and shipping, property and financial services; Chair. ANTHONY NIGHTINGALE; 3,000 employees.

Johnson Electric Holdings Ltd: Johnson Bldg, 6–22 Dai Shun St, Tai Po Industrial Estate, Tai Po; internet www.johnsonelectric.com; New Territories; cap. and res. 385.2m., sales 677.1m. (1999/2000); design, manufacture and marketing of micromotors, investment and property holding; Chair. and Chief Exec. PATRICK WANG SHUI CHUNG.

Kader Holdings Co Ltd: 22 Kai Cheung Rd, Kowloon; tel. 27981688; fax 27961126; e-mail kader@kader.com.hk; internet www.kader.com.hk; f. 1989; cap. 66.5m., sales 430m. (2001); manufacture and sale of plastic and stuffed toys, electronic toys and model trains, property investment, investment holding and trading; Chair. and Non-Exec. Dir DENNIS H. S. TING; Man. Dir KENNETH W. S. TING.

Lai Sun Garment (International) Ltd: Lai Sun Commercial Centre, 11/F, 680 Cheung Sha Wan Rd, Kowloon; tel. 27410391; fax 27852775; e-mail advpr@laisun.com.hk; internet www.laisun.com.hk; cap. and res 3,132.2m., sales 2,966.9m. (1999/2000); manufacture and sales of garments; Chair. and Man. Dir LIM POR YEN; 2000 employees.

Lam Soon (Hong Kong) Ltd: 21 Dai Fu St, Tai Po Industrial Estate, New Territories; tel. 27432011; fax 27861480; sales 2,345.1m. (1998); investment holding co, its subsidiaries' activities incl. the processing and trading of edible oils, flour products, fruit juices, food products, detergents, electronic products and packaging; Chair. WHANG TAR CHOUNG; 1,700 employees.

Li & Fung Ltd: LiFung Tower, Cheung Sha Wan Rd, Kowloon; tel. 23002300; fax 23002000; internet www.lifung.com; f. 1906; manufacture and trade of consumer products; Chair. VICTOR K. FUNG; Man. Dir WILLIAM K. FUNG.

Luks Industrial Co Ltd: Cheong Wah Factory Bldg, 5/F, 39–41 Sheung Heung Rd, Kowloon; tel. 23620297; fax 27643067; cap. and res 1,276.6m., sales 1,116.7m. (1995); manufacture and sales of printed circuit boards, colour TVs; Chair. and Man. Dir LUK KING TIN.

New World Development Co Ltd: New World Tower, 30/F, 18 Queen's Rd, Central; tel 25231056; fax 28104673; e-mail newworld@nwd.com.hk; internet www.nwd.com.hk; cap. and res 58,208m., sales 20,535m. (1999/2000); property investment, construction and hotels; Exec. Chair. Dato' Dr CHENG YU-TUNG; Man. Dir CHENG KAR-SHUN; 16,512 employees.

Sanyo Electric (Hong Kong) Ltd: Chuan Kei Fty Bldg, 14/F, 15–23 Kin Hong St, Kwai Chung, New Territories; tel. 24269321; fax 24805901; sales 7,154m. (1994); mfr and retailer of consumer electronics; Dir TOSHIO KUSUMI; 3,000 employees.

Shanghai Industrial Holdings Ltd: Harcourt House, 26/F, 39 Gloucester Rd, Wanchai; internet www.sihl.com.hk; cap. and res 11,415.7m., sales 3,300.6m. (1999); manufacture, distribution and sale of cigarettes, packaging materials and printed products; Chair. CAI LAI XING; Man. Dir ZHUO FU MIN.

Shell Electric Mfg (Holding) Co Ltd: Shell Industrial Bldg, 12 Lee Chung St, Chai Wan Industrial District; tel. 25580181; fax 28972095; sales 1,295m. (1999); manufacturing and marketing of electric fans and other household appliances; Chair. Dr YUNG YAU; Man. Dir BILLY YUNG KWOK KEE; 5,200 employees.

Shougang Concord International Enterprises Co Ltd: First Pacific Bank Centre, 7/F, 51–57 Gloucester Tower, Wanchai; tel. 28612832; fax 28613972; sales 7,676m. (1995, est.); distribution of metal and ceramics, container services, mfr of kitchen equipment; Chair. ZHANG YAN-LIN; Man. Dir LIU SHIYING; 12,750 employees.

Shui On Holdings Ltd: Shui On Centre, 34/F, 6–8 Harbour Rd; tel. 28791888; fax 28024396; internet shuion.com; f. 1965; leading construction co, specializes in public-sector projects; Chair. VINCENT H. S. LO; Man. Dir FRANKIE Y. L. WONG.

Sime Darby Hong Kong Ltd: East Wing, Hennessy Centre, 28/F, 500 Hennessy Rd, Causeway Bay; tel. 28950777; fax 28905896; e-mail simedarbyHK@simenet.com; internet www.simenet.com; cap. and res 1,352m., sales 5,673m. (1999/2000); distribution of motor vehicles and heavy construction equipment, industrial, electrical and mechanical contracting, etc.; Chair. Tan Sri Dato' Seri AHMAD SARJI BIN ABDUL HAMID; Man. Dir JOHN HICKMAN BELL.

Sino Land Co Ltd: Tsim Sha Tsui Centre, 12/F, Salisbury Rd, Kowloon; tel. 27218388; fax 27235901; e-mail info@sino-land.com; internet www.sino-land.com; cap. and res 27,201.0m. (1999/2000), sales 904.5m. (1997/98); investment holding, share investment, property development and investment; Chair. ROBERT NG CHEE-SIONG.

Sterling Products: Kwai Chung; f. 1957; manufactures children's clothing; Man. Dir KENNETH WANG; Gen. Man. C. W. LEUNG.

Sun Hung Kai Properties Ltd: Sun Hung Kai Centre, 45/F, 30 Harbour Rd, Wanchai; tel. 28278111; fax 28272862; e-mail shkp@shkp.com.hk; internet www.shkp.com.hk; cap. and res 120,904m., sales 25,826m. (1999/2000); investment holding, property development and management; Chair. and Chief Exec. WALTER KWOK; Man. Dir PETER FUNG.

Swire Group: John Swire and Sons (HK) Ltd: Swire House, 4/F, 9 Connaught Road, Central; tel. 28408888; fax 25269365; shipping managers and agents, airline operators, aviation services, marine and aviation engineering, trading, China trade development, property development, operators of offshore oil drilling support equipment, and mfrs of soft drinks and paints, packagers and distributors of sugar; waste management; Chair. PETER D. A. SUTCH.

Swire Pacific Ltd: Two Pacific Place, 35/F, 88 Queensway; tel. 28408098; fax 25269365; internet www.swirepacific.com; cap. and res 68,093m., sales 16,862m. (1999); real estate; Chair. J. W. J. HUGHES-HALLETT.

Tem Fat Hing Fung Holdings: Cheung Fat Bldg, 16/F, 7–9 Hill Rd, Western District; tel. 28032888; fax 28581799; sales 7,785m. (1998); production and sale of gold bullion, gold ornaments and jewellery; Chair. RAYMOND CHAN FAT CHU; Man. Dir. ALEXANDER CHAN FAT LEUNG.

Tse Sui Luen Jewellery (International) Ltd: Summit Bldg, Ground Floor, Block B, 30 Man Yue St, Hunghom, Kowloon; tel. 23334221; fax 27640753; cap. and res 269.9m., sales 1,271.9m. (1999/2000); investment holding co, its subsidiaries' activities incl. manufacuring and marketing of jewellery products and property investment; Chair. TSE SUI LUEN; 1,048.

Tsim Sha Tsui Properties Ltd: Tsim Sha Tsui Centre, 12/F, Salisbury Rd, Kowloon; tel. 27218388; fax 27235901; e-mail info@sino-land.com; internet www.sino-land.com; cap. and res 10,532.4m., sales 2,039.7m. (1999/2000); investment holding, property development; Chair. ROBERT NG CHEE SIONG.

Unibros FE Ltd: Jardine House, Rm 2106, 1 Connaught Place, Central; tel. 25252072; fax 28453446; sales 15,100m. (1995, est.); sale of steel products.

Vitasoy International Holdings Ltd: 1 Kin Wong St, Tuen Mun, New Territories; tel. 24660333; fax 24563441; sales 1,691.5m. (1997/98); manufacture and distribution of food and beverages; Chair. and Man. Dir WINSTON L. Y. LAI; 2,020 employees.

A S Watson and Co Ltd: Watson House, 1–5 Wo Lin Hang Rd, Fo Tan, Shatin, New Territories; tel. 26068833; fax 26958833; sales 10,800m. (1995, est.); mfr of mineral water, fruit juices and ice cream; CEO SIMON MURRAY; 16,500 employees.

Wharf (Holdings) Ltd (The): Ocean Centre, 16/F, Harbour City, Canton Rd, Kowloon; tel. 21188118; fax 21188018; internet www.wharfholdings.com; f. 1886; cap. and res 54,645m. (2001), sales 11,725m. (2001); property investment and development, hotels, transport, telecommunications and multimedia; Chair. and Chief Exec. PETER K. C. WOO.

Wheelock & Co Ltd: Wheelock House, 23/F, 20 Pedder St; tel. 21182118; fax 21182018; e-mail teresatsang@wharfholdings.com; internet www.wheelockcompany.com; f. 1857; cap. and res 26,485m., sales 7,165m. (2001/02); merchant house and property investment; Chair. PETER K. C. WOO

Winsor Industrial Corpn Ltd: East Ocean Centre, 2/F, 98 Granville Rd, Tsimshatsui East, Kowloon; tel. 27311888; fax 28101199; cap. 129.8m., sales 1,115.8m. (1997/98); investment holding co, its subsidiaries' activities incl. manufacture of textiles, knitwear and other garments; Chair. and Man. Dir W. H. CHOU; 4,500 employees.

TRADE UNIONS

In December 2000 there were 638 trade unions in Hong Kong, comprising 594 employees' unions, 25 employers' associations and 19 mixed organizations.

Hong Kong and Kowloon Trades Union Council (TUC): Labour Bldg, 11 Chang Sha St, Kowloon; tel. 23845150; f. 1949; 66 affiliated unions, mostly covering the catering and building trades; 28,200 mems; supports Taiwan; affiliated to ICFTU; Officer-in-Charge WONG YIU KAM.

Hong Kong Confederation of Trade Unions: Wing Wong Commercial Bldg, 19/F, 557–559 Nathan Rd, Kowloon; tel. 27708668; fax 27707388; e-mail hkctu@hkctu.org.hk; internet www.hkctu.org.hk; registered Feb. 1990; 61 affiliated independent unions and federations; 156,000 mems; Chair. LAU CHIN-SHEK.

Hong Kong Federation of Trade Unions (FTU): 7/F, 50 Ma Tau Chung Rd, Tokwawan, Kowloon; tel. 27120231; fax 27608477; f. 1948; 171 member unions, mostly concentrated in shipyards, public transport, textile mills, construction, department stores, printing and public utilities; supports the People's Republic of China; 310,000 mems; Pres. CHENG YIU-TONG; Gen. Sec. CHAN JIK-KWEI.

Also active are the **Federation of Hong Kong and Kowloon Labour Unions** (31 affiliated unions with 21,700 mems) and the **Federation of Civil Service Unions** (29 affiliated unions with 12,000 mems).

Transport

Transport Department: Immigration Tower, 41/F, 7 Gloucester Rd, Wanchai; tel. 28042600; fax 28240433; internet www.info .gov.hk/td.

RAILWAYS

Kowloon–Canton Railway Corpn: KCRC House, 9 Lok King St, Fo Tan, Sha Tin, New Territories; tel. 26881333; fax 26880983; internet www.kcrc.com; operated by the Kowloon–Canton Railway Corpn, a public statutory body f. 1983; operates both heavy and light rail systems; the 34-km East Rail runs from the terminus at Hung Hom to the frontier at Lo Wu; through passenger services to Guangzhou (Canton), suspended in 1949, were resumed in 1979; the electrification and double-tracking of the entire length and redevelopment of all stations has been completed, and full electric train service came into operation in 1983; in 1988 a light railway network serving Tuen Mun, Yuen Long and Tin Shui Wai in the north-western New Territories was opened; passenger service extended to Foshan in 1993, Dongguan in 1994, Zhaoqing in 1995 and Shanghai in 1997; direct Kowloon–Beijing service commenced in May 1997; also freight services to several destinations in China; West Rail, a domestic passenger line linking Tuen Mun and Yuen Long with Kowloon, was scheduled to begin services in late 2003; three East Rail extensions due for completion in 2004; Chair. and CEO YUENG KAI-YIN.

MTR Corporation: MTR Tower, Telford Plaza, Kowloon Bay; tel. 29932111; fax 27988822; internet www.mtr.com.hk; f. 1975; privatized in 2000, shares commenced trading on Hong Kong Stock Exchange in Oct. 2000; network of 77 km of railway lines and 44 stations; the first section of the underground mass transit railway (MTR) system opened in 1979; a 15.6-km line from Kwun Tong to Central opened in 1980; a 10.5-km Tsuen Wan extension opened in 1982; the 12.5-km Island Line opened in 1985–86; in 1989 a second harbour crossing between Cha Kwo Ling and Quarry Bay, known as the Eastern Harbour Crossing, commenced operation, adding 4.6 km to the railway system; 34-km link to new airport at Chek Lap Kok and to Tung Chung New Town opened in mid-1998; an additional line, the Tseung Kwan O Extension, was under construction and was scheduled for completion by August 2002; additional lines were also planned for 2006; Chair. and Chief Exec. JACK C. K. SO.

TRAMWAYS

Hong Kong Tramways Ltd: Whitty Street Tram Depot, Connaught Rd West, Western District; tel. 21186338; fax 21186038; f. 1904; operates six routes and 161 double-deck trams between Kennedy Town and Shaukeiwan; Dir and Gen. Man. MICKY LEUNG.

ROADS

At the end of 2000 there were 1,904 km of roads and 1,023 highway structures. Almost all of them are concrete or asphalt surfaced. Owing to the hilly terrain, and the density of building development, the scope for substantial increase in the road network is limited. A new 29-km steel bridge linking Hong Kong's Lantau Island with Macao and Zhuhai City, in the Chinese province of Guangdong, was being planned in 2001, with studies being carried out to determine the project's financial and technological feasibility.

Highways Department: Ho Man Tin Government Offices, 5/F, 88 Chung Hau St, Ho Man Tin, Kowloon; tel. 27623333; fax 27145216; f. 1986; planning, design, construction and maintenance of the public road system; co-ordination of major highway projects; Dir. K. S. LEUNG.

FERRIES

Conventional ferries, hoverferries and catamarans operate between Hong Kong, China and Macao. There is also an extensive network of ferry services to outlying districts.

Hongkong and Yaumati Ferry Co Ltd: 98 Tam Kon Shan Rd, Ngau Kok Wan, North Tsing Yi, New Territories; tel. 23944294; fax 27869001; e-mail hkferry@hkf.com; internet www.hkf.com; licensed routes on ferry services, incl. cross-harbour, to outlying islands, excursion, vehicular and dangerous goods; fleet of 50 vessels (passenger ferries, vehicular ferries, hoverferries, catamarans, oil barges and floating pontoons); also operates hoverferry services between Hong Kong and Shekou and catamaran service to Macao; Gen. Man. DAVID C. S. HO.

Hongkong Macao Hydrofoil Co Ltd: Turbojet Ferry Services (Guangzhou) Ltd, 83 Hing Wah St West, Lai Chi Kok, Kowloon; operates services to Macao, Fu Yong (Shenzhen airport) and East River Guangzhou.

'Star' Ferry Co Ltd: Kowloon Point Pier, Tsimshatsui, Kowloon; tel. 21186223; fax 21186028; e-mail sf@starferry.com.hk; f. 1898; operates 13 passenger ferries between the Kowloon Peninsula and Central, the main business district of Hong Kong; between Central and Hung Hom; between Tsimshatsui and Wanchai; between Tsimshatsui and Central; and between Wanchai and Hung Hom; Man. JOHNNY LEUNG.

SHIPPING

Hong Kong is one of the world's largest shipping centres and is a major container port. Hong Kong was a British port of registry until the inauguration of a new and independent shipping register in December 1990. Following Hong Kong's reunification with the People's Republic of China, Hong Kong maintains full autonomy in its maritime policy. At the end of 2001 the register comprised a fleet of 646 vessels, totalling 13.7m. grt. The eight container terminals at Kwai Chung, which are privately-owned and operated, comprised 18 berths in 1998. The construction of a ninth terminal (CT9) commenced in 1998 and was expected to be operational by 2001. Lantau Island has been designated as the site for any future expansion.

Marine Department, Hong Kong Special Administrative Region Government: Harbour Bldg, 22/F, 38 Pier Rd, Central, GPOB 4155; tel. 28523001; fax 25449241; e-mail webmaster@ mardep.gcn.gov.hk; internet www.info.gov.hk/mardep; Dir of Marine S. Y. TSUI.

Shipping Companies

Anglo-Eastern Ship Management Ltd: Universal Trade Centre, 14/F, 3 Arbuthnot Rd, Central, POB 11400; tel. 28636111; fax 28612419; e-mail allhx470@gncomtext.com; internet www.webhk .com/angloeastern/; Chair. PETER CREMERS; Man. Dir MARCEL LIEDTS.

Chung Gai Ship Management Co Ltd: Admiralty Centre Tower 1, 31/F, 18 Harcourt Rd; tel. 25295541; fax 28656206; Chair. S. KODA; Man. Dir K. ICHIHARA.

Fairmont Shipping (HK) Ltd: Fairmont House, 21/F, 8 Cotton Tree Drive; tel. 25218338; fax 28104560; Man. CHARLES LEUNG.

Far East Enterprising Co (HK) Ltd: China Resources Bldg, 18–19/F, 26 Harbour Rd, Wanchai; tel. 28283668; fax 28275584; f. 1949; shipping, chartering, brokering; Gen. Man. WEI KUAN.

Gulfeast Shipmanagement Ltd: Great Eagle Centre, 9/F, 23 Harbour Rd, Wanchai; tel. 28313344; Finance Dir A. T. MIRMOHAMMADI.

Hong Kong Borneo Shipping Co Ltd: 815 International Bldg, 141 Des Voeux Rd, Central; tel. 25413797; fax 28153473; Pres. Datuk LAI FOOK KIM.

Hong Kong Ming Wah Shipping Co: Unit 3701, China Merchants Tower, 37/F, Shun Tak Centre, 168–200 Connaught Rd, Central; tel. 25172128; fax 25473482; e-mail mwins@cmhk.com; Chair. CHEUNG KING WA; Man. Dir and Vice-Chair. Capt. MAO SHI JIAN.

Island Navigation Corpn International Ltd: Harbour Centre, 28–29/F, 25 Harbour Rd, Wanchai; tel. 28333222; fax 28270001; Man. Dir F. S. SHIH.

Jardine Ship Management Ltd: Jardine Engineering House, 11/ F, 260 King's Rd, North Point; tel. 28074101; fax 28073351; e-mail jsmhk@ibm.net; Man. Dir Capt. PAUL UNDERHILL.

Oak Maritime (HK) Inc Ltd: 2301 China Resources Bldg, 26 Harbour Rd, Wanchai; tel. 25063866; fax 25063563; Chair. STEVE G. K. HSU; Pres. FRED C. P. TSAI.

Ocean Tramping Co Ltd: Hong Kong; tel. 25892645; fax 25461041; Chair. Z. M. GAO.

Orient Overseas Container Line Ltd: Harbour Centre, 31/F, 25 Harbour Rd, Wanchai; tel. 28333888; fax 25318122; internet www.oocl.com; member of the Grand Alliance of shipping cos (five partners); Chair. C. C. Tung.

Teh-Hu Cargocean Management Co Ltd: Unit B, Fortis Bank Tower, 15/F, 77–79 Gloucester Rd, Wanchai; tel. 25988688; fax 28249339; e-mail tehhuhk@on-nets.com; f. 1974; Man. Dir Kenneth K. W. Lo.

Wah Kwong Shipping Agency Co Ltd: Shanghai Industrial Investment Bldg, 26/F, 48–62 Hennessy Rd, POB 283; tel. 25279227; fax 28656544; e-mail wk@wahkwong.com.hk; Chair. George S. K. Chao.

Wah Tung Shipping Agency Co Ltd: China Resources Bldg, Rooms 2101–5, 21/F, 26 Harbour Rd, Wanchai; tel. 28272818; fax 28275361; e-mail mgr@watunship.com.hk; f. 1981; Dir and Gen. Man. B. L. Liu.

Wallem Shipmanagement Ltd: Hopewell Centre, 46/F, 183 Queen's Rd East; tel. 28768200; fax 28761234; e-mail rgb@wallem.com; Man. Dir R. G. Buchanan.

Worldwide Shipping Agency Ltd: Wheelock House, 6–7/F, 20 Pedder St; tel. 28423888; fax 28100617; Man. J. Wong.

Associations

Hong Kong Cargo-Vessel Traders' Association: 21–23 Man Wai Bldg, 2/F, Ferry Point, Kowloon; tel. 23847102; fax 27820342; 978 mems; Chair. Chow Yat-tak; Sec. Chan Bak.

Hong Kong Shipowners' Association: Queen's Centre, 12/F, 58–64 Queen's Rd East, Wanchai; tel. 25200206; fax 25298246; e-mail hksoa@hksoa.org.hk; internet www.hksoa.org.hk; 220 mems; Chair. K.H. Koo; Dir Arthur Bowring.

Hong Kong Shippers' Council: Rm 2407, Hopewell Centre, 183 Queen's Rd East; tel. 28340010; fax 28919787; e-mail shippers@hkshippers.org.hk; internet www.hkshippers.org.hk; 63 mems; Chair. Willy Lin; Exec. Dir Sunny Ho.

CIVIL AVIATION

By the end of 2000 Hong Kong was served by 64 foreign airlines. A new international airport, on the island of Chek Lap Kok, near Lantau Island, to replace that at Kai Tak, opened in July 1998, following delays in the construction of a connecting high-speed rail-link. The airport has two runways, with the capacity to handle 35m. passengers and 3m. metric tons of cargo per year. The second runway commenced operations in May 1999. A helicopter link with Macao was established in 1990.

Airport Authority of Hong Kong: Cheong Yip Rd, Hong Kong International Airport, Lantau; tel. 21887111; fax 28240717; f. 1995; Chair. Dr Victor Fung Kwok-king; CEO Dr David J. Pang.

Civil Aviation Department: Queensway Government Offices, 46/F, 66 Queensway; tel. 28674332; fax 28690093; e-mail enquiry@cad.gov.hk; internet www.info.gov.hk/cad/; Dir-Gen. Albert K. Y. Lam.

AHK Air Hong Kong Ltd: Units 3601–8, 36/F, Tower 1, Millennium City, 388 Kwun Tong Rd, Kowloon; tel. 27618588; fax 27618586; e-mail ahk.hq@airhongkong.com.hk; f. 1986; international cargo carrier; Chief Operating Officer Hunter Crawford.

Cathay Pacific Airways Ltd: South Tower, 5/F, Cathay Pacific City, 8 Scenic Rd, Hong Kong International Airport, Lantau; tel. 27475000; fax 28106563; internet www.cathaypacific.com/hk; f. 1946; services to more than 40 major cities in the Far East, Middle East, North America, Europe, South Africa, Australia and New Zealand; Chair. and CEO David Turnbull.

Hong Kong Dragon Airlines Ltd (Dragonair): Dragonair House, 11 Tung Fai Rd, Hong Kong International Airport, Lantau; tel. 31933193; fax 31933194; internet www.dragonair.com; f. 1985; scheduled and charter flights to 25 destinations in Asia, 16 of which are in mainland China; scheduled regional services include Phuket (Thailand), Hiroshima and Sendai (Japan), Kaohsiung (Taiwan), Phnom-Penh (Cambodia), Dhaka (Bangladesh), Bandar Seri Begawan (Brunei), and Kota Kinabalu (Malaysia); Dir and CEO Stanley Hui.

Tourism

Tourism is a major source of foreign exchange, tourist receipts reaching HK $64,282m. (including receipts from visitors from mainland China) in 2001. Some 13.7m. people visited Hong Kong in 2001. In December 2001 there were some 90 hotels, and the number of rooms available totalled 35,853. In November 1999 it was agreed that a new Disneyland theme park would be constructed in Hong Kong, to be opened in 2005. The Government expected the park to create a huge influx of tourists to the territory.

Hong Kong Tourist Association: Citicorp Centre, 9–11/F, 18 Whitfield Rd, North Point; tel. 28076543; fax 28076595; e-mail dm@hktourismboard.com; internet www.DiscoverHongKong.com; f. 1957; reconstituted as Hong Kong Tourism Board 1 April 2001; co-ordinates and promotes the tourist industry; has govt support and financial assistance; up to 20 mems of the Board represent the Govt, the private sector and the tourism industry; Chair. Selina Chow; Exec. Dir Clara Chong.

Defence

In July 1997 a garrison of 4,800 PLA troops was established in Hong Kong. The garrison can intervene in local matters only at the request of the Hong Kong Government, which remains responsible for internal security.

Defence Expenditure: Projected expenditure on internal security in 2001/02 totalled HK $21,941m.

Commander of the PLA Garrison in Hong Kong: Lt-Gen. Xiong Ziren.

Education

Full-time education is compulsory in Hong Kong between the ages of six and 15. Schools fall into three main categories: those wholly maintained by the Government; those administered by non-government organizations with government financial aid; and those administered independently by private organizations. There are also government-aided schools for children with special educational needs; in September 2001/02 they provided education for 9,511 children. The adult literacy rate in 2000 was estimated at 93.5% (males 96.5%; females 90.2%). Budgetary expenditure on education was estimated at HK $52,297m. for 2001/02.

PRE-PRIMARY AND PRIMARY SCHOOLS

Kindergartens are administered by private bodies without direct government assistance for children between the ages of three and five. The Government provides indirect assistance through rent and rate rebates to non-profit-making kindergartens, fee assistance for needy parents, etc. In 2001/02 there were 784 such schools, with a combined enrolment of 156,202. The age of entry into primary school is six, and the schools provide a six-year course of basic primary education. Primary school pupils totalled 493,075 in 2001/02. Compulsory primary education was first introduced in 1971 when fees were abolished in most of the primary schools in the public sector. There are nine government-subsidized primary schools and a number of private international schools catering for the education of English-speaking children. At the end of six years, every primary school-leaver is allocated a free place in a secondary school for three years. The method of allocation is based on parental choice and schools' internal assessments, monitored by an Academic Aptitude Test under the Secondary School Places Allocation scheme.

SECONDARY SCHOOLS

Junior secondary education (Secondary 1–3), which became compulsory in September 1979, has been free since September 1978. A centralized system of selection and allocation of subsidized school places for senior secondary education (Secondary 4–5), known as the Junior Secondary Education Assessment System, was first introduced in 1981, and was enhanced in 1988 by the adoption of the Mean Eligibility Allocation Method, which relieved all students from taking any public scaling test. Both the performance of students in the school internal assessments and parental choice form the basis for selection and allocation of Secondary 3 students to subsidized Secondary 4 places. Students may also choose to continue their studies in post-Secondary 3 craft courses offered by technical institutes and industrial training centres.

In 2001/02 there were 465,5603 secondary school pupils. There are three main types of secondary school in Hong Kong: grammar, technical and prevocational schools. The Hong Kong Certificate of Education Examination may be taken after a five-year course; a further course of two years leads to the Hong Kong Advanced Level Examination. The prevocational schools provide a five-year secondary course. Sixth-form classes were introduced in September 1992. Following the resumption of Chinese sovereignty in mid-1997, Cantonese was gradually to replace English as the official medium of instruction. Some 100 schools were to be allowed to retain English as the medium of instruction, provided that they fulfil certain criteria (eg. language capability of the students).

HIGHER EDUCATION

In late 1999 there were 10 institutions of higher education: City University of Hong Kong (CUHK), Hong Kong Baptist University (HKBU), Hong Kong Polytechnic University (HKPU), Lingnan University (LU), the Chinese University of Hong Kong (CUHK), the

Hong Kong University of Science and Technology (HKUST); the University of Hong Kong (HKU), the Open University of Hong Kong, the Hong Kong Academy for the Performing Arts and the Hong Kong Institute of Education. In September 1997 an estimated total of 109,019 full-time and part-time students were enrolled at the 10 institutions.

Technological training is also provided by the Vocational Training Council (VTC), which operates the Hong Kong Institute of Vocational Education (IVE) and 24 training centres. The IVE was founded in 1999 and incorporated two technical colleges and seven institutes. A total of 54,825 students were enrolled in 2001/02.

The four government-run colleges of education and the Institute of Languages in Education of merged to form the Hong Kong Institute of Education in 1994. The Institute provides training for teachers of kindergartens, primary and secondary schools, and offers full- and part-time courses of two and three years' duration. There were some 9,000 teacher-training students during 1998/99. The Government provides loans and grants for needy students.

Bibliography

GENERAL

Balke, G. *Hong Kong Voices*. Hong Kong, Longman, 1989.

Blyth, Sally, and Wotherspoon, Ian. *Hong Kong Remembers*. Oxford, Oxford University Press, 1997.

Bristow, Roger. *Hong Kong's New Towns: A Selective Review*. Hong Kong and New York, Oxford University Press, 1990.

Chan, Anthony. *Li Ka-shing*. Hong Kong, Oxford University Press, 1997.

Cheek-Milby, K., and Mushkat, Miron. *Hong Kong, The Challenge of Transformation*. Centre of Asian Studies, University of Hong Kong, 1989.

Cheng, Joseph Y. S., and Lo, Sonny S. H. (Eds). *From Colony to SAR: Hong Kong's Challenges Ahead*. Hong Kong, Chinese University Press, 1996.

Cheung, Fanny M. (Ed). *Engendering Hong Kong Society: A Gender Perspective of Women's Status*. Hong Kong, Chinese University Press, 1997.

Cheung, Stephen Y. L., and Sze, Stephen M. H. (Eds). *The Other Hong Kong Report 1996*. Hong Kong, Chinese University Press, 1996.

Cottrell, Robert. *The End of Hong Kong*. London, John Murray, 1993.

Cradock, Percy. *Experiences of China*. London, John Murray, 1994.

Evans, Gareth, and Tam, Maria. *Hong Kong: The Anthropology of a Chinese Metropolis*. Honolulu, HI, University of Hawaii Press, 1997.

Government Information Services Department. *Hong Kong 1998*. Hong Kong, Government Publications Centre, 1999.

Hughes, R. *Hong Kong: Borrowed Place, Borrowed Time*. London, André Deutsch, 1976.

Jao, Y. C., Leung Chi-keung, Wesley-Smith, P., and Wong Siu-lun (Eds). *Hong Kong and 1997: Strategies for the Future*. University of Hong Kong, 1985.

Jones, Catherine. *Promoting Prosperity: The Hong Kong Way of Social Policy*. Hong Kong, Chinese University Press, 1991.

Lau Siu-kai and Kuan Hsin-chi. *The Ethos of the Hong Kong Chinese*. Hong Kong, Chinese University Press, 1988.

Le Corre, Philippe. *Après Hong Kong*. Editions Autrement, 1997.

Lee, James. *Housing, Home Ownership and Social Change in Hong Kong*. Burlington, VT, Ashgate Publishing Co, 1999.

Lee, Rance P. L. (Ed.). *Corruption and Its Control in Hong Kong*. Hong Kong, Chinese University Press, 1981.

Leung, Benjamin K. P. (Ed.). *Social Issues in Hong Kong*. Oxford University Press, 1990.

Ma, Eric Kit-wai. *Culture, Politics and Television in Hong Kong*. London, Routledge, 1999.

Mok, Joshua K. H., and Chan, David K. K. (Eds). *Globalization and Education: The Quest for Quality Education in Hong Kong*. Hong Kong University Press, 2002.

Osgood, Cornelius. *The Chinese: A Study of a Hong Kong Community*. 3 vols. Tucson, University of Arizona Press, 1975.

Segal, Gerald. *The Fate of Hong Kong*. London, Simon and Schuster, 1993.

Wacks, Raymond (Ed.). *Civil Liberties in Hong Kong*. Oxford University Press, 1988.

The New Legal Order in Hong Kong. Hong Kong, Hong Kong University Press, 2000.

Wesley-Smith, Peter. *An Introduction to the Hong Kong Legal System*. Hong Kong, Oxford University Press, 3rd Edn, 1999.

Wilson, Dick. *Hong Kong! Hong Kong!* London, Unwin Hyman, 1990.

HISTORY AND POLITICS

Ash, Robert. F., Ferdinand, Peter, Hook, Brian, and Porter, Robin (Eds). *Hong Kong in Transition: One Country, Two Systems*. Richmond, Surrey, Curzon Press, 2002.

Bonavia, David. *Hong Kong 1997—The Final Settlement*. Bromley, Columbus Books, 1985.

Brown, J. M., and Foot, R. *Hong Kong's Transitions, 1842–1997*. London, Macmillan, 1997.

Buckley, Roger. *Hong Kong: The Road to 1997*. Cambridge, Cambridge University Press, 1997.

Butenhoff, Linda. *Social Movements and Political Reform in Hong Kong*. New York, Praeger, 1999.

Byrnes, Andrew, and Chan, Johannes (Eds). *Public Law and Human Rights: A Hong Kong Sourcebook*. Singapore, Butterworth, 1994.

Callick, Rowan. *Comrades and Capitalists, Hong Kong Since the Handover*. Sydney, University of New South Wales Press, 1998.

Cameron, Nigel. *The Illustrated History of Hong Kong*. Hong Kong, Oxford University Press, 1991.

Chan Lau Kit-ching. *China, Britain and Hong Kong: 1895–1945*. Hong Kong, Chinese University Press, 1991.

Chan, Ming K., Postiglione, Gerard A., and Vogel, Ezra F. (Eds). *The Hong Kong Reader: Passage to Chinese Sovereignty*. Armonk, NY, M. E. Sharpe, 1996.

Chan, Ming K., and Young, John D. (Eds). *Precarious Balance: Hong Kong Between China and Britain, 1842–1992*. Armonk, NY, M. E. Sharpe, 1994.

Chang, David. W., and Chuang, Richard. Y. *The Politics of Hong Kong's Reversion to China*. Basingstoke, Macmillan, 1997.

Cheek-Milby, Kathleen. *A Legislature Comes of Age: Hong Kong's Search for Influence and Identity*. Hong Kong, Oxford University Press, 1995.

Chi Kuen Lau. *Hong Kong's Colonial Legacy*. Hong Kong, Chinese University Press, 1998.

Crowell, Todd. *Farewell, My Colony: Last Days in the Life of British Hong Kong*. Hong Kong, Asia 2000, 1998.

Dimbleby, Jonathan. *The Last Governor—Chris Patten and the Handover of Hong Kong*. London, Little, Brown and Co, 1997.

Endacott, G. B. A. *A History of Hong Kong*. London, Oxford University Press, 1958.

Government and People in Hong Kong, 1841–1962: A Constitutional History. Hong Kong University Press, 1964.

Endacott, G. B., and Birch, A. H. *Hong Kong Eclipse*. Oxford University Press, 1978.

Fenby, Jonathan. *Dealing With the Dragon—A Year in the New Hong Kong*. London, Little, Brown and Co, 2000.

Flowerdew, John. *The Final Years of British Hong Kong—The Discourse of Colonial Withdrawal*. London, Macmillan, 1997.

Fok, K. C. *Lectures on Hong Kong History*. The Commercial Press (Hong Kong), 1990.

Ghai, Y. *Hong Kong's New Constitutional Order*. Hong Kong, Hong Kong University Press, 1997.

Hamilton, Gary G. (Ed.). *Cosmopolitan Capitalists*. Seattle, WA, University of Washington Press, 2000.

Harris, Peter. *Hong Kong: A Study in Bureaucratic Politics*. Heinemann Asia, 1978.

Hayes, James W. *The Hong Kong Region 1850–1911, Institutions and Leadership in Town and Countryside*. New Haven, CT, and London, William Dawson, 1977.

Horlemann, Ralf. *Hong Kong's Transition to Chinese Rule: The Limits of Autonomy*. Richmond, Surrey, Curzon Press, 2002.

Hsiung, James C. *Hong Kong the Super Paradox: Life After Return to China*. New York, St Martin's Press, 2000.

Keay, John. *Last Post: The End of the Empire in the Far East*. London, John Murray, 1997.

Kuan Hsin-chi, Lau Siu-kai, Louie Kin-shuen and Wong Ka-ying. *The 1995 Legislative Council Elections in Hong Kong*. Hong Kong, Chinese University Press, 1997.

Power Transfer and Electoral Politics: The First Legislative Election in the Hong Kong Special Administrative Region. Hong Kong, Chinese University Press, 1999.

Kwok, Reginald Yin-Wang, and So, Alvin Y. (Eds). *The Hong Kong-Guangdong Link: Partnership in Flux.* Armonk, NY, M. E. Sharpe, 1995.

Kwok, Rowena Y. F., Leung, Joan Y. H., and Scott, Ian (Eds). *Votes without Power: The Hong Kong Legislative Council Elections 1991.* Hong Kong University Press, 1992.

Lam, Jermain T. M. *The Political Dynamics of Hong Kong Under the Chinese Sovereignty.* Huntington, NY, Nova Science Publishers, 2000.

Lau Siu-kai and Louie Kin-shuen. *Hong Kong Tried Democracy: The 1991 Elections in Hong Kong.* Hong Kong, Chinese University Press, 1997.

The First Tung Chee-hwa Administration: The First Five Years of the Hong Kong Special Administrative Region. Hong Kong, Chinese University Press, 2002.

Lee Pui Tak. *Hong Kong Reintegrating with China: Political, Cultural and Social Dimensions.* Hong Kong University Press, 2001.

Lo Shiu-hing. *The Politics of Democratization in Hong Kong.* London, Macmillan, 1997.

Luard, E. *Britain and China.* London, Chatto and Windus, 1962.

McGurn, William. *Perfidious Albion: The Abandonment of Hong Kong 1997.* Washington, Ethics and Public Policy Center, 1992.

McMillen, Donald H., and DeGolyer, Michael E. (Eds). *One Culture, Many Systems: Politics in the Reunification of China.* Hong Kong, Chinese University Press, 1993.

Meyer, David R. *Hong Kong as a Global Metropolis.* Cambridge, Cambridge University Press, 2000.

Mills, A. *British Rule in Eastern Asia.* London, Oxford University Press, 1942.

Miners, N. J. *Hong Kong under Imperial Rule 1912–1941.* Oxford University Press, 1987.

The Government and Politics of Hong Kong (with post-handover update by James T. H. Tang). 5th Edn, Oxford University Press, 1998.

Morris, J. *Hong Kong: Epilogue to an Empire.* London, Penguin Books Ltd, 1988, revised 1997.

Ngo Tak-Wing. *Hong Kong's History: State and Society Under Colonial Rule.* London, Routledge, 1999.

Patten, Christopher. *East and West—The Last Governor of Hong Kong.* London, Macmillan, 1998.

Postiglione, G. A., and Tang, J. T. H. *Hong Kong's Reunion with China: The Global Dimensions.* Armonk, NY, M. E. Sharpe, 1997.

Pottinger, George. *Sir Henry Pottinger—First Governor of Hong Kong.* Far Thrupp, Sutton, 1997.

Rafferty, Kevin. *City on the Rocks: Hong Kong's Uncertain Future.* London and New York, Penguin-Viking, 1989.

Roberti, Mark. *The Fall of Hong Kong: China's Triumph and Britain's Betrayal.* Chichester, John Wiley, 1994, revised 1997.

Sayer, G. R. *Hong Kong: Birth, Adolescence and Coming of Age.* London, Oxford University Press, 1937.

Hong Kong, 1862–1919. Hong Kong University Press, 1975.

Scott, Ian. *Political Change and The Crisis of Legitimacy in Hong Kong.* Oxford University Press, 1989.

Scott, Ian (Ed.). *Institutional Change and the Political Transition in Hong Kong.* London, Palgrave, 1997.

So, Alvin Y. *Hong Kong's Embattled Democracy.* Baltimore, MD, The Johns Hopkins University Press. 1999.

Thomas, Nicholas. *Democracy Denied: Identity, Civil Society and Illiberal Democracy in Hong Kong.* Burlington, VT, Ashgate Publishing Co, 1999.

Tsai Jung-Fang. *Hong Kong in Chinese History: Community and Social Unrest in the British Colony, 1842–1913.* New York, Columbia University Press, 1995.

Tsang, Steve Y. S. *Democracy Shelved: Great Britain, China and Attempts at Constitutional Reform in Hong Kong 1945–1952.* Oxford University Press, 1988.

An Appointment with China. London, Tauris, 1997.

A Modern History of Hong Kong: 1841–1998. London, Tauris, 2002.

Vines, Stephen. *Hong Kong: China's New Colony.* London, Aurum Press, 1998.

Wang Enbao. *Hong Kong 1997: The Politics of Transition.* Boulder, CO, Lynne Rienner, 1995.

Wang Gungwu and Wong Siu-lun (Eds). *Hong Kong's Transition—A Decade after the Deal.* London, Oxford University Press, 1997.

Welsh, Frank. *A History of Hong Kong.* London, HarperCollins, 1993, revised 1997.

Wesley-Smith, P. *Unequal Treaty 1898–1997.* Oxford University Press, 1980.

Wesley-Smith, P., and Chen, Albert (Eds). *The Basic Law and Hong Kong's Future.* London, Butterworth, 1988.

Yahuda, Michael. *Hong Kong: China's Challenge.* London, Routledge, 1996.

ECONOMY

Cohen, Warren I., and Li, Zhao (Eds). *Hong Kong under Chinese Rule: The Economic and Political Implications of Reversion.* Cambridge University Press, 1998.

England, J., and Rear, J. *Industrial Relations and Law in Hong Kong.* Oxford University Press, 1981.

Enright, Michael, Scott, Edith, and Dodwell, David. *The Hong Kong Advantage.* Hong Kong, Oxford University Press, 1997.

Federation of Hong Kong Industries. *Hong Kong's Industrial Investment in the Pearl River Delta.* Hong Kong, 1992.

Fosh, Patricia, Chan, Andy W., and Chow, Wilson W. S. (Eds). *Hong Kong Management and Labour: Change and Continuity.* London, Routledge, 2000.

Freris, Andrew. *The Financial Markets of Hong Kong.* London, Routledge, 1991.

Hong Kong Government. *The Economic Background.* 1992.

Estimates of Gross Domestic Product 1961–1995. Census and Statistics Department, 1996.

Hong Kong in Figures. Census and Statistics Department, annual.

Hsia, Ronald, and Chau, L. *Industrialisation, Employment and Income Distribution.* London, Croom Helm, 1978.

Jao, Y. C. *Banking and Currency in Hong Kong, a Study of Post-War Financial Development.* London, Macmillan, 1974.

The Asian Financial Crisis and the Ordeal of Hong Kong. Westport, CT, Quorum Books, 2001.

Lam, Pun-Lee, and Chan, Sylvia. *Competition in Hong Kong's Gas Industry.* Hong Kong, Chinese University Press, 2000.

Lethbridge, David (Ed.). *The Business Environment in Hong Kong.* Oxford University Press, 4th Edn, 2000.

Mann, Richard I. (Ed.). *Business in Hongkong: Signposts for the 90s; A Positive View.* Toronto, Gateway Books, 1992.

McGuinness, Paul. *A Guide to the Equity Markets of Hong Kong.* New York, Oxford University Press, 2000.

Peebles, Gavin. *The Economy of Hong Kong.* New York, Oxford University Press, 1988.

Rowley, Chris, and Fitzgerald, Robert (Eds). *Managed in Hong Kong.* Ilford, Frank Cass, 2000.

Schenk, Catherine R. *Hong Kong as an International Financial Centre: Emergence and Development, 1945–65.* London, Routledge, 2001.

Yu, Tony Fu-Lai. *Entrepreneurship and Economic Development in Hong Kong.* London, Routledge, 1997.

MACAO

Physical and Social Geography

The Special Administrative Region (SAR) of Macao (or Macau as it was also known prior to its reversion from Portuguese to Chinese sovereignty in December 1999), is situated on the south-eastern coast of the People's Republic of China, at latitude 22°14′ N and longitude 113°35′ E. The territory comprises the narrow, hilly Macao peninsula of the Chinese district of Foshan, on which is situated the Cidade do Santo Nome de Deus de Macau, together with two small islands to the south, Taipa and Coloane. The highest peak, of 170.6m, is situated on the island of Coloane. The SAR covered an area of 25.40 sq km (9.81 sq miles) in 2000 (compared with 17.32 sq km in 1989). The peninsular area occupied 7.8 sq km of the total, the island of Taipa 6.2 sq km, Coloane 7.6 sq km and the reclaimed land between Taipa and Coloane 2.2 sq km. A major land-reclamation programme continued to progress in 2001. Macao lies some 64 km west of Hong Kong (across the Zhujiang (Pearl River) estuary), and 145 km south of the city of Guangzhou (Canton), the capital of Guangdong Province. In early 1998 it was announced that Macao and the Pearl River Water Resources Committee (PRWRC) of China were to conduct a joint study on the realignment of local waters, the land-reclamation projects having had a negative impact on water flow. In late 1998 Macao and the Land Department of Guangdong conducted a joint aerial land survey. The Macao peninsula is linked by two bridges (the first spanning 2.6 km and the second 4.4 km) to the island of Taipa, which in turn is connected to Coloane by a 2.2-km causeway. A second link with the mainland, the 1.5-km Lotus Bridge connecting Macao to Zhuhai (Guangdong Province), opened in December 1999. Plans for a 29-km bridge linking Macao with Hong Kong's Lantau Island and Zhuhai were under consideration in 2001, and plans for a third bridge between Macao and Taipa Island were approved in 2002. The climate is subtropical, with temperatures averaging 15°C in January and 29°C in July. The average annual rainfall is between 100 cm and about 200 cm. The highest levels of humidity and precipitation occur between April and September.

The census of August 2001 enumerated the population at 435,235, of whom 414,200, or 95.2%, held Chinese nationality, while 8,793 (2.0%) were of Portuguese nationality. (About 60% of the population were between 15 and 50 years of age at the census of 1996.) By December 2001 the population was estimated to have increased to 436,686. In 1990 more than 90% of the population resided on the Macao peninsula. At 16,926 persons per sq km in December 2001, the territory's population density was one of the highest in the world. In 2001 the birth rate stood at 7.5 per 1,000, and a death rate of 3.1 per 1,000 was recorded. The official languages are Chinese (Cantonese being the principal dialect) and Portuguese. English is also widely spoken, speakers of English outnumbering Portuguese-speakers. The predominant religions are Chinese Buddhism, Daoism, Confucianism and Roman Catholicism. The capital, the city of Macao, is situated on the peninsula.

History

FRANK H. H. KING

Revised since 1980 by the editorial staff

The territory was established as one of several trading posts by the Portuguese as early as 1537, the first Portuguese sailors having anchored in the Zhujiang (Pearl River) in 1513. A permanent settlement was established in 1557. Motivated by trade and missionary zeal, the Portuguese developed Macao as a base for their operations both in China and Japan, and penetration during Japan's 'Christian century' from 1543 involved close relations with Macao. The first Portuguese Governor was appointed in 1680. However, sovereignty remained vested in China; the Chinese residents were subject to a Chinese official, and Macao's Portuguese administration, virtually autonomous for the first 200 years, concerned itself with the governance of the Portuguese and, until the establishment of Hong Kong, with the growing presence of other European trading nations. The Portuguese paid an annual rent to China.

Macao was an uncertain base from which to expand trade with China. The Roman Catholic administration was unfriendly to Protestants, the Chinese authority was too close and restrictive, and the opium question and growing restlessness of the 'private' merchants undermined a system that had developed during the years of controlled and relatively limited 'company' trade.

The ceding of Hong Kong to Britain in 1842 revealed China's weakness, and in 1845 Portugal declared Macao a free port. In the consequent disputes Portugal drove out the Chinese officials, and the settlement was proclaimed Portuguese territory. This unilateral declaration was recognized by China in 1887 in return for provisions intended to facilitate the enforcement of its customs laws, particularly in regard to opium, by the Imperial Maritime Customs.

However, Macao's establishment as a colony did not restore prosperity. With the silting of its harbour, the diversion of its trade to Hong Kong, and the opening of the treaty ports as bases of trade and missionary work, Macao was left to handle the local distributive trade, while developing a reputation as a base for smuggling, gambling and other unsavoury activities. With the closing of the Hong Kong–China border in 1938, Macao's trade boomed, but this prosperity declined after 1942, when the colony became isolated as the only European settlement on the China coast not occupied by the Japanese during the Second World War.

In 1951 Macao was declared an overseas province of Portugal and elected a representative to the Portuguese legislature in Lisbon. Macao's economy depended largely on the gold trade, at that time illegal in Hong Kong, on gambling and tourism, and on an entrepôt business with China.

Macao's tranquillity was disrupted by communist riots in 1966–67, inspired by the 'Cultural Revolution' in mainland China. These were contained only after the Macao Government signed an agreement with Macao's Chinese Chamber of Commerce outlawing the activities of Chinese loyal to the Taiwan regime, paying compensation to the families of Chinese killed in the rioting, and refusing entry to refugees from China. However, China wished the Portuguese administration to continue, and on admission to the UN the Beijing Government affirmed that it regarded the future of Macao as an internal matter.

RECENT POLITICAL DEVELOPMENTS

After the military coup in Portugal in April 1974, the only Governor of an overseas territory to be retained in office was that of Macao. China refused to discuss the future of Macao with Portugal, and the revolutionary leaders became convinced that there was no demand for an independence which China would not, in any case, have tolerated. Nevertheless, the revolution caused considerable political activity in Macao. The Centro Democrático de Macau (CDM) was established to press for radical political reform and the removal of those connected with the former regime in Portugal. The conservative Associação para a Defesa dos Interesses de Macau (ADIM) was established, and in April 1975 defeated the CDM's candidate for Macao's representative to the Lisbon assembly. The Macao electorate reaffirmed its conservative bias when over 65% voted for right-wing parties in the Lisbon constituency.

Col Garcia Leandro, who succeeded Nobre de Carvalho at the end of his much-extended term as Governor in late 1974, correctly assessed China's position while being sufficiently flexible to recognize that Macao needed capitalism and was not ready for socialism. He initiated policies which, in effect, insulated Macao from the direct influence of a series of Portuguese governments which contained elements sympathetic to the USSR and which might have disrupted the delicate balance necessary for the continuation of Macao's existence. Thus, Leandro, who had at first dealt with the CDM, expelled many of its supporters, effectively assuring the success of the ADIM in elections to the Legislative Assembly in July 1976. Leandro also supported the enactment of legislation in Portugal (the Organic Law) which, in February 1976, appeared to give Macao virtual political autonomy.

Macao had thus become a special territory of Portugal with a Governor of ministerial rank appointed by the President of the Portuguese Republic, to whom he was responsible. The Governor was the executive authority and could issue decrees, a subject of continued controversy, and he remained independent of the Legislative Assembly with the right to veto legislation not passed by a two-thirds' majority. The composition of the Assembly reflected Macao's social and political structure, which was still divided into 'Chinese' and 'Portuguese', the latter self-determined on the basis of culture, language and religion—not on place of origin. Of the 17 members at that time, six were elected on a proportional basis, six were elected indirectly by designated organizations, and five were appointed by the Governor.

The 1976 elections confirmed Macao's conservative preference, with the ADIM receiving 55% of the 2,700 votes cast and winning four of the six seats. A group of young independents stood as the Grupo de Estudos para o Desenvolvimento Communitário de Macau (GEDEC), winning 17% of the vote, while the radical and once dominant CDM was less successful, but also elected a member. The Governor's appointees and those indirectly elected created an Assembly which was still recognizably Portuguese, confirming the Portuguese nature of the Government and avoiding the anomalous position of a Chinese population voting for non-communist parties on China's very borders.

Macao's international relations continued to be subject to the *de jure* approval of the President of Portugal and the *de facto* tolerance of China. In April 1978 the Chinese authorities acted on a long-standing request of Governor Leandro and invited him to visit several Chinese cities (excluding Beijing). It was the first visit by a Governor of Macao since the communist revolution but, while interpreted as confirmation of China's acceptance of Macao's status at that time, the visit was seen in the context of China's overall policy rather than as an endorsement of Leandro himself. Meanwhile, leaders of the Chinese community in Macao continued to participate in political events in China, including regular attendance at sessions of the National People's Congress in Beijing. Portugal and China established diplomatic relations in February 1979.

Governor Leandro, who correctly appraised Macao's needs in 1974, was frustrated in his desire to obtain greater local Chinese political participation, and his efforts to have the Macao population involved in the nomination of his successor were ineffective. His four-year administration was, however, marked by a more realistic planning orientation, marred in execution by administrative problems. Nevertheless, he changed patterns of thinking, set in motion basic economic reforms, and secured the passage of legislation that resulted in a more efficient taxation system and improvements to the local civil service.

The next Governor, Gen. Nuno de Melo Egídio, arrived in February 1979. Elections for the Legislative Assembly were due in late 1979, but in June the Assembly extended the term of the seven elected representatives for another year. This temporarily averted the constitutional crisis confronting the Governor in 1980, when the four-year-old Organic Law was due for review. A delegation of the representatives had visited Lisbon to discuss proposals to revise the 1976 Organic Law with politicians in the Portuguese legislature. Their proposals, which were to give the local population a greater influence in decisions concerning the administration of Macao, included plans to enlarge the Legislative Assembly from 17 to 21 members. All of these would, they proposed, be elected, thus reducing the Governor to a merely titular status. In March 1980, when Gen. Melo Egídio visited Beijing on the first 'official' visit by a Governor of Macao since its establishment as a Portuguese colony in 1557, the Chinese leader Deng Xiaoping, while expressing his approval of the stability of Macao, also made it clear that the Chinese Government opposed any change in the Organic Law. His views were echoed by sections of the local population in Macao; 97% of the population did not speak Portuguese, they took very little part in political life and were largely unaffected by the Portuguese administration.

The appointment in 1981 of Cdre (later Rear-Adm.) Vasco Almeida e Costa as Governor was evidence of an unspoken agreement between Beijing and Lisbon not to alter the legal status of Macao. Governor Almeida e Costa was determined to extend voting rights in Macao, to produce a more representative Assembly. Following a constitutional dispute in March 1984, after he had used his controversial authority to issue two administrative decrees without the approval of the Legislative Assembly (and had successfully introduced electoral reforms despite vigorous opposition), he requested President Eanes of Portugal to dissolve the Assembly. In August 1984 elections for a new Assembly were held, in which the Chinese majority were allowed to vote for the first time, regardless of their length of residence in the territory. Two of the six directly-elected seats were won by Chinese candidates, while the six indirectly-elected members, all Chinese, were returned unopposed. The Governor appointed four government officials and a Chinese businessman to complete the Assembly, which was thus, for the first time, dominated by ethnic Chinese deputies.

Governor Almeida e Costa resigned in January 1986. He was replaced as Governor by Joaquim Pinto Machado, who had hitherto been a professor of medicine and was little-known as a political figure. His appointment marked a break in the tradition of military governors for Macao, but his political inexperience placed him at a disadvantage. Within weeks of Pinto Machado's arrival, the likelihood of his departure was widely rumoured, and in May 1987, one year after his appointment, he resigned for reasons of 'institutional dignity'. He was replaced in August by Carlos Melancia, a former socialist deputy in the Assembly of the Republic, who had held ministerial posts in several Portuguese Governments led by Dr Mário Lopes Soares, subsequently the President of Portugal.

In May 1985, meanwhile, President Eanes visited Beijing and Macao, and it was announced that the Portuguese and Chinese Governments had agreed to hold formal talks about the territory's future. The first session of negotiations took place in June 1986, in Beijing, and further talks were held in September and October, when it was reported that 'broad agreement' had been reached. Portugal's acceptance of Chinese sovereignty greatly simplified subsequent negotiations, and on 13 April 1987, following the conclusion of the fourth round of talks, a joint declaration was formally signed in Beijing by the Portuguese and Chinese Governments, during an official visit to China by the Prime Minister of Portugal. According to the agreement, which was formally ratified in January 1988, Macao was to become a 'Special Administrative Region' (SAR) of the People's Republic, to be known as Macao, China, on 20 December 1999. Macao was thus to have the same status as that agreed (with effect from mid-1997) for Hong Kong, and was to enjoy autonomy in most matters except defence and foreign policy. A Sino-Portuguese Joint Liaison Group (JLG), established to oversee the transfer of power, held its inaugural meeting in Lisbon in April 1988.

Under the detailed arrangements for the transfer, a chief executive for Macao was to be appointed in 1999 by the Chinese Government, following 'elections or consultations to be held in Macao', and the territory's legislature was to contain 'a majority of elected members'. The inhabitants of Macao were to become Chinese citizens; the Chinese Government refused to allow the possibility of dual Sino-Portuguese citizenship, although Macao residents in possession of Portuguese passports were apparently to be permitted to retain them for travel purposes. The agreement provided for a 50-year period during which Macao would be permitted to retain its free-enterprise capitalist economy, and to be financially independent of China.

In August 1988 the establishment of a Macao Basic Law Drafting Committee was announced by the Chinese Government. Comprising 30 Chinese members and 19 representatives from Macao, the Committee was to draft a law determining the territory's future constitutional status within the People's Republic of China.

Triennial elections to the six directly elective seats in Macao's 17-seat Legislative Assembly were held in October 1988. In a low turn-out (representing fewer than 30% of the 67,492 registered voters), an informally constituted 'liberal' grouping increased its representation from one seat in the previous Assembly to three seats. These gains were achieved at the expense of the long-dominant 'grand alliance' of pro-Beijing and Macanese business interests. The new members hoped to influence the administration's policies on housing, education and workers' welfare.

In January 1989 it was announced that Portuguese passports were to be issued to about 100,000 ethnic Chinese inhabitants, born in Macao before October 1981, and it was anticipated that as many as a further 100,000 would be granted before 1999. Unlike their counterparts in the neighbouring British dependent territory of Hong Kong, therefore, these Macao residents (but not all) were to be granted the full rights of a citizen of the European Community (EC, now European Union—EU). In February 1989 President Mário Soares of Portugal visited Macao, in order to discuss the transfer of the territory's administration to China.

Following the violent suppression of the pro-democracy movement in China in June 1989, as many as 100,000 residents of Macao participated in demonstrations in the enclave to protest against the Chinese Government's action. The events in the People's Republic gave rise to much concern in Macao, and it was feared that many residents would wish to leave the territory prior to 1999. In August 1989, however, China assured Portugal that it would honour the agreement to maintain the capitalist system of the territory after 1999.

In March 1990 the implementation of a programme to grant permanent registration to parents of 4,200 Chinese residents, the latter having already secured the right of abode in Macao, developed into chaos when other illegal immigrants demanded a similar concession. The authorities decided to declare a general amnesty, but were unprepared for the numbers of illegal residents who rushed to take advantage of the scheme, thereby revealing the true extent of previous immigration from China. In the ensuing stampede by 50,000 illegal immigrants, desperate to obtain residency rights, about 200 persons were injured and 1,500 arrested, as the police attempted to control the situation. Border security was increased, in an effort to prevent any further illegal immigration from China.

In late March 1990 the Legislative Assembly approved the final draft of the territory's revised Organic Law. The Law was approved by the Portuguese Assembly of the Republic in mid-April, and granted Macao greater administrative, economic, financial and legislative autonomy, in advance of 1999. The powers of the Governor and of the Legislative Assembly, where six additional seats were to be created, were therefore increased. The post of military commander of the security forces was abolished, responsibility for security being assumed by a civilian Under-Secretary.

In June 1990 the Under-Secretary for Justice, Dr Manuel Magalhães e Silva, resigned, owing to differences of opinion on the issues of Macao's political structure and Sino-Portuguese relations. In the same month, while on a visit to Lisbon for consultations with the President and Prime Minister, Carlos Melancia rebuked the Chinese authorities for attempting to interfere in the internal affairs of Macao. This unprecedented reproach followed criticism of the Governor's compromising attitude towards the People's Republic of China.

Meanwhile, in February 1990, Carlos Melancia had been implicated in a financial scandal. It was alleged that the Governor had accepted 50m. escudos from a Federal German company which hoped to be awarded a consultancy contract for the construction of the new airport in Macao. In September Melancia was served with a summons in connection with the alleged bribery. Although he denied any involvement in the affair, the Governor resigned, and was replaced on an acting basis by the Under-Secretary for Economic Affairs, Dr Francisco Murteira Nabo. In September 1991 it was announced that Melancia and five others were to stand trial on charges of corruption. The trial opened in Lisbon in April 1993. At its conclusion in August the former Governor was acquitted on the grounds of insufficient evidence. In February 1994, however, it was announced that Melancia was to be retried, owing to irregularities in his defence case.

The ability of Portugal to maintain a stable administration in the territory had once again been called into question. Many observers believed that the enclave was being adversely affected by the political situation in Lisbon, as differences between the socialist President and centre-right Prime Minister were being reflected in rivalries between officials in Macao. In an attempt to restore confidence, therefore, President Soares visited the territory in November 1990. In January 1991, upon his re-election as Head of State, the President appointed Gen. Vasco Rocha Vieira (who had served as the territory's Chief of Staff in 1973/74 and as Under-Secretary for Public Works and Transport in 1974/75) to be the new Governor of Macao. In March 1991 the Legislative Assembly was expanded from 17 to 23 members. All seven Under-Secretaries were replaced in May.

Following his arrival in Macao, Gen. Rocha Vieira announced that China would be consulted on all future developments in the territory. The 10th meeting of the Sino-Portuguese JLG took place in Beijing in April 1991. Topics under regular discussion included the participation of Macao in international organizations, progress towards an increase in the number of local officials employed in the civil service (hitherto dominated by Portuguese and Macanese personnel) and the status of the Chinese language. The progress of the working group on the translation of local laws from Portuguese into Chinese was also examined, a particular problem being the lack of suitably-qualified bilingual legal personnel. (The training of civil servants was duly improved: the University of Macao opened new courses in administration, law and translation; and hundreds of civil servants were dispatched to Beijing or Lisbon for training.) It was agreed that Portuguese was to remain an official language after 1999. The two sides also reached agreement on the exchange of identity cards for those Macao residents who would require them in 1999. Regular meetings of the JLG continued.

In July 1991 the Macao Draft Basic Law was published by the authorities of the People's Republic of China. Confidence in the territory's future was enhanced by China's apparent flexibility on a number of issues. Unlike the Hong Kong Basic Law, that of Macao did not impose restrictions on holders of foreign passports assuming senior posts in the territory's administration after 1999, the only exception being the future Chief Executive. Furthermore, the draft contained no provision for the stationing of troops from China in Macao after the territory's return to Chinese administration.

In November 1991 the Governor of Macao visited the People's Republic of China, where it was confirmed that the 'one country, two systems' policy would operate in Macao from 1999. Following a visit to Portugal by the Chinese Premier in February 1992, the Governor of Macao stated that the territory was to retain 'great autonomy' after 1999. In March 1993 the final draft of the Basic Law of the Macao SAR was ratified by the National People's Congress in Beijing, which also approved the design of the future SAR's flag. The adoption of the legislation was welcomed by the Governor of Macao, who reiterated his desire for a smooth transfer of power in 1999. The Chief Executive of the SAR was to be selected by local representatives. The SAR's first Legislative Council was to comprise 23 members, of whom eight would be directly elected. Its term of office would expire in October 2001, when it would be expanded to 27 members, of whom 10 would be directly elected.

Meanwhile, elections to the Legislative Assembly were held in September 1992. The level of participation was higher than on previous occasions, with 59% of the registered electorate (albeit only 13.5% of the population) attending the polls. Fifty candidates contested the eight directly-elective seats, four of which were won by members of the main pro-Beijing parties, the União Promotora para o Progresso and the União para o Desenvolvimento.

Relations between Portugal and China remained cordial. In June 1993 the two countries reached agreement on all outstanding issues regarding the construction of the territory's airport and the future use of Chinese air space. Furthermore, Macao was to be permitted to negotiate air traffic agreements with other countries. In October, upon the conclusion of a three-day visit to Macao, President Soares expressed optimism regarding the territory's smooth transition to Chinese administration. In November President Jiang Zemin of China was warmly received in Lisbon, where he had discussions with both the Portuguese President and Prime Minister. In February 1994 the Chinese Minister of Communications visited Macao to discuss with the Governor the progress of the airport project.

In April 1994, during a visit to China, the Portuguese Prime Minister received an assurance that Chinese nationality would not be imposed on Macanese people of Portuguese descent, who would be able to retain their Portuguese passports. Speaking in Macao itself, the Prime Minister expressed confidence in the territory's future. Regarding the issue as increasingly one of foreign policy, he stated his desire to transfer jurisdiction over Macao from the Presidency of the Republic to the Government, despite the necessity for a constitutional amendment.

In July 1994 a group of local journalists dispatched a letter, alleging intimidation and persecution in Macao, to President Soares, urging him to intervene to defend the territory's press freedom. The journalists' appeal followed an incident involving the director of the daily *Gazeta Macaense*, who had been obliged to pay 300,000 escudos for reproducing an article from *Semanário*, a Lisbon weekly newspaper, and now faced trial. The territory's press had been critical of the Macao Supreme Court's decision to extradite ethnic Chinese to the mainland (despite the absence of any extradition treaty) to face criminal charges and the possibility of a death sentence.

Gen. Rocha Vieira embarked upon a second visit to China in August 1994. The Governor of Macao had discussions with the Chinese Minister of Foreign Affairs, who declared Sino-Portuguese relations to be sound but, as a result of a gaffe relating to the delegation's distribution to the press of a biography of Premier Li Peng containing uncomplimentary remarks, stressed the need for vigilance.

The draft of the new penal code for Macao did not incorporate the death penalty. In January 1995, during a visit to Portugal, Vice-Premier Zhu Rongji of China confirmed that the People's Republic would not impose the death penalty in Macao after 1999, regarding the question as a matter for the authorities of the future SAR. The new penal code, prohibiting capital punishment, took effect in January 1996.

On another visit to the territory in April 1995, President Soares emphasized the need for Macao to assert its identity, and stressed the importance of three issues: the modification of the territory's legislation; the rights of the individual; and the preservation of the Portuguese language. Travelling on to Beijing, accompanied by Gen. Rocha Vieira, the Portuguese President had successful discussions with his Chinese counterpart on various matters relating to the transition.

In May 1995, during a four-day visit to the territory, Lu Ping, the director of the mainland Hong Kong and Macao Affairs Office, proposed the swift establishment of a preparatory working committee (PWC) to facilitate the transfer of sovereignty. He urged that faster progress be made on the issues of the localization of civil servants and of the law, and on the use of Chinese as the official language. Lu Ping also expressed his desire that the reorganized legislative and municipal bodies to be elected in 1996–97 conform with the Basic Law.

In November 1995, following the change of government in Lisbon, the incoming Portuguese Minister of Foreign Affairs, Jaime Gama, urged that the rights and aspirations of the people of Macao be protected. In December, while attending the celebrations to mark the inauguration of the territory's new airport, President Soares had discussions with the Chinese Vice-President, Rong Yiren. During a four-day visit to Beijing in February 1996, Jaime Gama met President Jiang Zemin and other senior officials, describing the discussions as positive. While acknowledging the sound progress of recent years, Gama and the Chinese Minister of Foreign Affairs agreed on an acceleration in the pace of work of the Sino-Portuguese JLG. In March 1996 Gen. Rocha Vieira was reappointed Governor of Macao by the newly-elected President of Portugal, Jorge Sampaio. António Guterres, the new Portuguese Prime Minister, confirmed his desire for constitutional consensus regarding the transition of Macao. The JLG's 26th meeting took place in June 1996 in Macao.

At elections to the Legislative Assembly in September 1996, a total of 62 candidates from 12 electoral groupings contested the eight directly-elective seats. The pro-Beijing União Promotora para o Progresso received 15.2% of the votes and won two seats, while the União para o Desenvolvimento won 14.5% and retained one of its two seats. The business-orientated groups were more successful: the Associação Promotora para a Economia de Macau took 16.6% of the votes and secured two seats; the Convergência para o Desenvolvimento and the União Geral para o Desenvolvimento de Macau each won one seat. The pro-democracy Associação de Novo Macau Democrático also won one seat. The level of voter participation was 64%. The 23-member legislature was to remain in place beyond the transfer of sovereignty in 1999.

In October 1996 Portugal and China announced the establishment of a mechanism for regular consultation on matters pertaining to international relations. In the same month citizens of Macao joined a flotilla of small boats carrying activists from Taiwan and Hong Kong to protest against a right-wing Japanese group's construction of a lighthouse on the disputed Daioyu (or Senkaku) Islands, situated in the East China Sea (see Taiwan, p. 366). Having successfully evaded Japanese patrol vessels, the protesters raised the flags of China and Taiwan on the disputed islands. In November activists from around the world attended a three-day conference in Macao, in order to discuss their strategy for the protection of the islands.

During 1996 the rising level of violent criminal activity became a cause of increasing concern. Between January and December there were 14 bomb attacks, in addition to numerous brutal assaults. In November a Portuguese gambling inspector narrowly survived an attempt on his life by an unidentified gunman and, as attacks on local casino staff continued, three people were killed and three wounded in six separate incidents. Criminal violence continued to gather momentum in 1997, giving rise to fears for the future of the territory's vital tourism industry. Many attributed the alarming increase in organized crime to the opening of the airport in Macao, which was believed to have facilitated the entry of rival gangsters from mainland China, Taiwan and Hong Kong. In May, following the murder of three men believed to have associations with one such group of gangsters, the Chinese Government expressed its concern at the deterioration of public order in Macao and urged Portugal to observe its responsibility, as undertaken in the Sino-Portuguese joint declaration of 1987, to maintain the enclave's social stability during the transitional period, whilst pledging the enhanced co-operation of the Chinese security forces in the effort to curb organized crime in Macao.

The freedom of Macao's press was jeopardized in June 1997, when several Chinese-language newspapers, along with a television station, received threats instructing them to cease reporting on the activities of the notorious 14K triad, a 10,000-member secret society to which much of the violence had been attributed. In July, during a night of arson and shooting, an explosive device was detonated in the grounds of the Governor's palace, although it caused no serious damage. In the following month China deployed 500 armed police officers to reinforce the border with Macao in order to intensify its efforts to combat illegal immigration, contraband and the smuggling of arms into the enclave. Despite the approval in July of a law further to restrict activities such as extortion and 'protection rackets', organized crime continued unabated. In early October the police forces of Macao and China initiated a joint campaign against illegal immigration. In late October Leong Kwok-hon, an alleged leader of the 14K triad, was shot dead.

Meanwhile, the slow progress of the 'three localizations' (civil service, laws and the implementation of Chinese as an official language) continued to concern the Government of China. In mid-1996 almost 50% of senior government posts were still held by Portuguese expatriates. In January 1997 the Governor pledged to accelerate the process with regard to local legislation, the priority being the training of the requisite personnel. In the same month, during a visit to Portugal, the Chinese Minister of Foreign Affairs reiterated his confidence in the future of Macao. In February President Sampaio travelled to both Macao and China, where he urged respect for Macao's identity and for the Luso-Chinese declaration regarding the transfer of sovereignty. In December 1997 details of the establishment in Macao of the office of the Chinese Ministry of Foreign Affairs, which was to commence operations in December 1999, were announced. In January 1998 the Macao Government declared that 76.5% of 'leading and directing' posts in the civil service were now held by local officials.

In March 1998 the murder of a Portuguese gambling official, followed by the killing of a marine police-officer, prompted the Chinese authorities to reiterate their concern at the deteriorating situation in Macao. In the following month the driver of the territory's Under-Secretary for Public Security was shot dead. In April, by which month none of the 34 triad-related murders committed since January 1997 had been solved, the Portuguese and Chinese Governments agreed to co-operate in the exchange of information about organized criminal activities. Also in April 1998 the trial, on charges of breaching the gaming laws, of the head of the 14K triad, Wan Kuok-koi ('Broken Tooth'), was adjourned for two months, owing to the apparent reluctance of witnesses to appear in court. Following an attempted car-bomb attack on Macao's chief of police, António Marques Baptista, in early May Wan Kuok-koi was rearrested. The charge of the attempted murder of Marques Baptista, however, was dismissed by a judge three days later on the grounds of insufficient evidence. Wan Kuok-koi remained in prison, charged with other serious offences. (In April 1999 he was acquitted of charges of the coercion of croupiers, but was to stand trial again on charges of triad membership, illegal gambling activities and 'money laundering'.) The renewed detention in May 1998 of Wan Kuok-koi led to a spate of arson attacks. The Portuguese Government was reported to have dispatched intelligence officers to the enclave to reinforce the local security forces. In June Marques Baptista travelled to Beijing and Guangzhou for discussions on the problems of cross-border criminal activity and drug-trafficking.

In April 1998 the Portuguese Prime Minister, accompanied by his Minister of Foreign Affairs and a business delegation, paid an official visit to Macao, where he expressed confidence that after 1999 China would respect the civil rights and liberties of the territory. The delegation travelled on to China, where the Prime Minister had cordial discussions with both President Jiang Zemin and Premier Zhu Rongji.

The Preparatory Committee for the Establishment of the Macao SAR, which was to oversee the territory's transfer to Chinese sovereignty and was to comprise representatives from both the People's Republic and Macao, was inaugurated in Beijing in May 1998. Four subordinate working groups (supervising administrative, legal, economic, and social and cultural affairs) were subsequently established. The second plenary session of the Preparatory Committee was convened in July 1998, discussions encompassing issues such as the 'localization' of civil servants, public security and the drafting of the territory's fiscal budget for the year 2000. In July 1998, during a meeting with the Chinese Premier, the Governor of Macao requested an increase in the mainland's investment in the territory prior to the 1999 transfer of sovereignty.

In July 1998, as abductions continued and as it was revealed, furthermore, that the victims of kidnapping and ransom had included two serving members of the Legislative Assembly, President Jiang Zemin of China urged the triads of Macao to cease their campaign of intimidation. The police forces of Macao, Hong Kong and Guangdong Province launched 'S Plan', an operation aiming to curb the activities of rival criminal gangs. In August, in an apparent attempt to intimidate the judiciary, the territory's Attorney-General and his pregnant wife were shot and slightly wounded. In the following month five police officers and 10 journalists, who were investigating a bomb attack, were injured when a second bomb exploded.

In August 1998 representatives of the JLG agreed to intensify Luso-Chinese consultations on matters relating to the transitional period. In September, in response to the increasing security problems, China unexpectedly announced that, upon the transfer of sovereignty, it was to station troops in the territory. This abandonment of a previous assurance to the contrary caused much disquiet in Portugal, where the proposed deployment was deemed unnecessary. Although the Basic Law made no specific provision for the stationing of a mainland garrison, China asserted that it was to be ultimately responsible for the enclave's defence. By October, furthermore, about 4,000 soldiers of the People's Liberation Army (PLA) were on duty at various Chinese border posts adjacent to Macao. During a one-week visit to Beijing, the territory's Under-Secretary for Public Security had discussions with senior officials, including the Chinese Minister of Public Security. In mid-October the detention without bail of four alleged members of the 14K triad in connection with the May car-bombing and other incidents led, later in the day, to an outburst of automatic gunfire outside the courthouse.

In November 1998 procedures for the election of the 200 members of the Selection Committee were established by the Preparatory Committee. Responsible for the appointment of the members of Macao's post-1999 Government, the delegates of the Selection Committee were required to be permanent residents of the territory: 60 members were to be drawn from the business and financial communities, 50 from cultural, educational and professional spheres, 50 from labour, social service and religious circles and the remaining 40 were to be former political personages.

About 70 people were arrested in November 1998, when the authorities conducted raids on casinos believed to be engaged in illegal activities. In December an off-duty Portuguese prison warder was shot dead and a colleague wounded by a gunman, the pair having formed part of a contingent recently dispatched from Lisbon to improve security at the prison where Wan Kuok-koi was being held. At the end of December it was confirmed that Macao residents of wholly Chinese origin would be entitled to full mainland citizenship, while those of mixed Chinese and Portuguese descent would be obliged to decide between the two nationalities. In January 1999 protesters clashed with police during demonstrations to draw attention to the plight of numerous immigrant children, who had been brought illegally from China to Macao to join their legitimately-resident parents. Several arrests were made. The problem had first emerged in 1996 when, owing to inadequate conditions, the authorities had closed down an unofficial school attended by 200 children, who because of their irregular status were not entitled to the territory's education, health and social services.

In January 1999 a grenade attack killed one person, and the proprietor of a casino and suspected member of 14K was shot dead. In that month details of the composition of the future PLA garrison were disclosed. The troops were to comprise solely ground forces, totalling fewer than 1,000 soldiers and directly responsible to the Commander of the Guangzhou Military Unit. They would be permitted to intervene to maintain social order in the enclave only if the local police were unable to control major triad-related violence or if street demonstrations posed a threat of serious unrest. In March, during a trip to Macao (where he had discussions with the visiting Portuguese President), Qian Qichen, a Chinese Vice-Premier, indicated that an advance contingent of PLA soldiers would be deployed in Macao prior to the transfer of sovereignty. Other sources of contention between China and Portugal remained the unresolved question of the post-1999 status of those Macao residents who had been granted Portuguese nationality and also the issue of the court of final appeal.

In April 1999 an alleged member of the 14 Carats triad was shot dead by a gunman on a motor cycle. Also in April, at the first plenary meeting of the Selection Committee, candidates for the post of the SAR's Chief Executive were elected. Edmund Ho received 125 of the 200 votes, while Stanley Au garnered 65 votes. Three other candidates failed to secure the requisite minimum of 20 votes. Edmund Ho and Stanley Au, both bankers and regarded as moderate pro-business candidates, thus proceeded to the second round of voting by secret ballot, held in May. The successful contender, Edmund Ho, received 163 of the 199 votes cast, and confirmed his intention to address the problems of law and order, security and the economy. The Chief Executive-designate also fully endorsed China's decision to deploy troops in Macao.

During 1999, in co-operation with the Macao authorities, the police forces of Guangdong Province, and of Zhuhai in particular, initiated a new offensive against the criminal activities of the triads. China's desire to deploy an advance contingent of troops prior to December 1999, however, reportedly continued to be obstructed by Portugal. Furthermore, the announcement that, subject to certain conditions, the future garrison was to be granted law-enforcement powers raised various constitutional issues. Some observers feared the imposition of martial law, if organized crime were to continue unabated. Many Macao residents, however, appeared to welcome the mainland's decision to station troops in the enclave. In a further effort to address the deteriorating security situation, from December 1999 Macao's 5,800-member police force was to be restructured.

In July 1999 the penultimate meeting of the JLG took place in Lisbon. In August, in accordance with the nominations of the Chief Executive-designate, the composition of the Government of the future SAR was announced by the State Council in Beijing. Appointments included that of Florinda da Rosa Silva Chan as Secretary for Administration and Justice. Also in August an outspoken pro-Chinese member of the Legislative Assembly was attacked and injured by a group of unidentified assailants. This apparently random assault on a serving politician again focused attention on the decline in law and order in the enclave. In September the Governor urged improved co-operation with the authorities of Guangdong Province in order to combat organized crime, revealing that more than one-half of the inmates of Macao's prisons were not residents of the territory. In the same month it was reported that 90 former Gurkhas of the British army were being drafted in as prison warders, following the intimidation of local officers. In September the Chief Executive-designate announced the appointment of seven new members of the Legislative Council, which was to succeed the Legislative Assembly in December 1999. While the seven nominees of the Governor in the existing Legislative Assembly were thus to be replaced, 15 of the 16 elected members (one having resigned) were to remain in office as members of the successor Legislative Council. The composition of the 10-member Executive Council was also announced.

In October 1999 President Jiang Zemin paid a two-day visit to Portugal, following which it was declared that the outstanding question of the deployment of an advance contingent of Chinese troops in Macao had been resolved. The advance party was to be restricted to a technical mission, which entered the territory in early December. In November the 37th and last session of the JLG took place in Beijing, where in the same month the Governor of Macao held final discussions with President Jiang Zemin.

Meanwhile, in April 1999 Wan Kuok-koi had been acquitted of charges of coercing croupiers. In November the trial of Wan Kuok-koi on other serious charges concluded: he was found guilty of criminal association and other illegal gambling-related activities and sentenced to 15 years' imprisonment. Eight co-defendants, including Wan Kuok-koi's brother, received lesser sentences. In a separate trial Artur Chiang Calderon, a former police officer alleged to be Wan Kuok-koi's military adviser, received a prison sentence of 10 years and six months for involvement in organized crime. While two other defendants were also imprisoned, 19 were released on the grounds of insufficient evidence. As the transfer of the territory's sovereignty approached, by mid-December almost 40 people had been murdered in triad-related violence on the streets of Macao since January 1999.

In late November 1999 representatives of the JLG reached agreement on details regarding the deployment of Chinese troops in Macao and on the retention of Portuguese as an official language. At midnight on 19 December 1999, therefore, in a ceremony attended by the Presidents and heads of government of Portugal and China, the sovereignty of Macao was duly transferred; 12 hours later (only after the departure from the newly-inaugurated SAR of the Portuguese delegation), 500 soldiers of the 1,000-strong force of the PLA, in a convoy of armoured vehicles, crossed the border into Macao, where they were installed in a makeshift barracks in a vacant apartment building. Prior to the ceremony, however, it was reported that the authorities of Guangdong Province had detained almost 3,000 persons, including 15 residents of Macao, suspected of association with criminal gangs. The celebrations in Macao were also marred by the authorities' handling of demonstrations by members of Falun Gong, a religious movement recently outlawed in China. The expulsion from Macao of several members of the sect in the days preceding the territory's transfer and the arrest of 30 adherents on the final day of Portuguese sovereignty prompted strong criticism from President Jorge Sampaio of Portugal. Nevertheless, in an effort to consolidate relations with the EU, in May 2000 the first official overseas visit of the SAR's Chief Executive was to Europe, his itinerary including Portugal.

Meanwhile, a spate of arson of attacks on vehicles in February 2000 was followed by the fatal shooting, in a residential district of Macao, of a Hong Kong citizen believed to have triad connections. In March, in an important change to the immigration rules, it was announced that children of Chinese nationality whose parents were permanent residents of Macao would shortly be allowed to apply for residency permits. A monthly quota of 420 successful applicants was established, while the youngest children were to receive priority.

In May 2000 hundreds of demonstrators took part in a march to protest against Macao's high level of unemployment. This shortage of jobs was attributed to the territory's use of immigrant workers, mainly from mainland China and South-East Asia, who were estimated to total 28,000. During the ensuing clashes several police officers and one demonstrator were reportedly injured. Trade unions continued to organize protests, and in July (for the first time since the unrest arising from the Chinese Cultural Revolution of 1966) tear gas and water cannon were used to disperse about 200 demonstrators who were demanding that the immigration of foreign workers be halted by the Government. In the same month it was announced that, in early 2001, an office of the Macao SAR was to be established in Beijing, in order to promote links between the two Governments. In Guangzhou in August 2000, as cross-border crime continued to increase, senior officials of Macao's criminal investigation unit met their counterparts from China and Hong Kong for discussions on methods of improving co-operation. It was agreed that further meetings were henceforth to be held twice a year, alternately in Beijing and Macao.

Celebrations to mark the first anniversary in December 2000 of Macao's reversion to Chinese sovereignty were attended by President Jiang Zemin, who made a speech praising the local administration, but warning strongly against those seeking to use either of the SARs as a base for subversion. A number of Falun Gong adherents from Hong Kong who had attempted to enter Macao for the celebrations were expelled. The same fate befell two Hong Kong human rights activists who had hoped to petition Jiang Zemin during his stay in Macao about the human rights situation in the People's Republic. A group of Falun Gong members in Macao held a protest the day before the Chinese President's arrival. They were detained in custody and subsequently alleged that they had suffered police brutality.

In January 2001 China urged the USA to cease interfering in its internal affairs, following the signature by President Bill Clinton of the US Macao Policy Act, which related to the control of Macao's exports and the monitoring of its autonomy. In the same month voter registration began in Macao, in preparation for the expiry of the first Legislative Council's term of office in October and the election of a new assembly. In his Chinese Lunar New Year address on 23 January, Edmund Ho called for new efforts to revitalize the economy and achieve social progress.

The Governor of Guangdong Province, Lu Ruihua, made an official visit to Macao in early February to improve links between the two regions. At the same time, the Legislative Council announced plans to strengthen ties with legislative bodies in the mainland, and the Chairwoman of the Legislative Council, Susana Chou, visited Beijing and held talks with Vice-Premier

Qian Qichen. Also in February, a Macao resident was charged with publishing on-line articles about the Falun Gong.

Edmund Ho visited Beijing in early March 2001 to attend the fourth session of the Ninth National People's Congress, and held talks with President Jiang Zemin, who praised the former's achievements since the reversion of Macao to Chinese rule. On returning to Macao, Ho received the President of Estonia, Lennart Meri, who was touring the mainland and who thus became the first head of state to visit the SAR since its return to China. The two leaders discussed co-operation in the fields of tourism, trade, information technology (IT), and telecommunications, with Ho apparently seeking to learn from Estonia's experience in opening the telecommunications market. The EU announced in mid-March that SAR passport holders would, from May 2001, no longer require visas to enter EU countries. In the same month Jorge Neto Valente, a prominent lawyer and reputedly the wealthiest Portuguese person in Macao, was kidnapped by a gang, but freed in a dramatic police operation. The incident was the highest-profile kidnapping case in Macao since the return to Chinese rule.

The Macao, Hong Kong, and mainland police forces established a working group in mid-March 2001 to combat cross-border crime, with a special emphasis on narcotics, and in late March the Macao, Hong Kong, and Guangdong police forces conducted a joint anti-drug operation, 'Spring Thunder', resulting in the arrest of 1,243 suspected traffickers and producers, and the seizure of large quantities of heroin, ecstasy, and marijuana. As part of the growing campaign against crime, a Shanghai court sentenced to death a Macao-based gangster, Zeng Jijun, on charges of running a debt-recovering group, members of which had committed murder. Three of Zeng's associates were given long prison sentences.

In May 2001 Macao and Portugal signed an agreement to strengthen co-operation in the fields of economy, culture, public security, and justice during the visit of the Portuguese Minister of Foreign Affairs, Jaime Gama, the highest-ranking Portuguese official to visit Macao since its reversion to Chinese rule.

In early June 2001 Macao's Secretary for Security, Cheong Kuoc Va, visited Beijing and signed new crime-fighting accords aimed at reducing the trafficking of drugs, guns, and people. In mid-June Chief Executive Edmund Ho made his first official visit to the headquarters of the EU in Brussels, where he sought to promote contacts and exchanges between the SAR and the EU.

At the beginning of July 2001 China's most senior representative in Macao, Wang Qiren, died of cancer. Later in the month, another major campaign against illegal activities related to the triads was conducted by the Macao, Hong Kong, and Guangdong police forces, and was part of ongoing attempts to eradicate organized crime. At the end of the month, the Secretary for Security, Cheong Kuoc Va, reported that cases of violent crime had declined by 37.3% year-on-year in the first half of 2001, and murders, robberies, arson, drug-trafficking, and kidnapping had all decreased significantly over the same period. In a further sign of co-operation between Macao and the mainland against crime, the two sides signed an agreement on mutual judicial co-operation and assistance in late August, the first of its kind.

In September 2001 José Proença Branco and Choi Lai Hang were appointed police commander and customs chief respectively. Following the terrorist attacks in New York and Washington, DC, on 11 September, several Pakistanis were detained in Macao; however, it was quickly announced that the detentions were not connected to the world-wide terrorist searches that had been initiated. In the mean time, the Macao, Hong Kong, and Guangdong police departments began examining measures and directing activities aimed at fighting terrorism.

Elections to the Legislative Assembly (Council) were held on 24 September 2001, the first since Macao's reversion to Chinese rule. The number of seats was increased from 23 to 27: seven members were appointed by the Chief Executive, 10 elected directly and 10 indirectly. Of the 10 directly-elective seats, two seats each were won by the business-orientated CODEM, the pro-Beijing factions UPP and UPD and the pro-democracy ANMD. Two other factions won one seat each. Of the 10 indirectly-elective seats, four were won by the OMKC (a group representing business interests), and two seats each were one by the DCAR (a group representing welfare, cultural, educational, and sports interests), the CCCAE (a group representing labour), and the OMCY (a group representing professionals).

In mid-October 2001 China appointed Bai Zhijian as director of its liaison office in Macao, and later in the month Cui Shiping was selected as Macao's representative in the NPC, replacing the late Wang Qiren. At the same time, Edmund Ho attended the summit meeting of Asia-Pacific Economic Co-operation (APEC) in Shanghai, and the EU-Macao Joint Committee held a meeting in the SAR, aimed at improving trade, tourism and legal co-operation between the two entities. During late 2001, meanwhile, Macao increased co-operation with Hong Kong and the mainland in fighting crime and combating terrorism, amid reports that Russian mafias were becoming increasingly active in the SARs, and in mid-November the three police departments held an anti-drugs forum in Hong Kong. Later in the month, Edmund Ho announced that personal income tax would be waived and industrial and commercial taxes reduced for 2002, in order to alleviate the impact of the economic downturn. Ho also pledged to create 6,000 new jobs and invest more in infrastructure, and urged employers to avoid staff reductions.

In December 2001 the Government moved finally to break the 40-year monopoly on casinos and gambling held by Stanley Ho and his long-established company, the Sociedade de Turismo e Diversões de Macau (STDM). Under the new arrangements, some 21 companies, none of which was Chinese-owned, were to be permitted to bid for three new operating licences for casinos in the SAR. The intention was to improve the image of the gambling industry, ridding the territory of its reputation for vice and making it more business- and family-orientated. Meanwhile, Stanley Ho's daughter Pansy was playing an increasingly prominent role in managing the family businesses (which included the shipping, property and hotel conglomerate, Shun Tak holdings); in December the group opened a new convention and entertainment centre.

Also in December 2001 Edmund Ho paid a visit to Beijing, where he and President Jiang Zemin discussed the situation in Macao. In early January 2002 Ho visited the mainland city of Chongqing, seeking to reinforce economic ties between the two places, and stating that Macao would play a more active role in developing the region. Also in January, the Government granted permission to the Taipei Trade and Cultural Office (TTCO) to issue visas for Taiwan-bound visitors from Macao and the mainland. In February Li Peng, Chairman of the Standing Committee of the NPC, paid an official visit to Macao, where he held discussions with the Chief Executive of the SAR. During Li's visit, a leading Macao political activist, along with several activists from the Hong Kong-based 'April 5th Action Group', were arrested for planning to stage protests against Li for his role in the Tiananmen Square suppression of 1989 and in favour of the release of mainland political dissidents. The Hong Kong activists were immediately deported. At the same time the Hong Kong media reported that a Hong Kong-based cameraman had been beaten and had his camera destroyed by a Macao policeman when he attempted to film the interception of the activists. Other journalists also claimed to have been treated aggressively, their allegations being disputed by the Macao police.

In early March 2002 a new representative office of the Macao SAR was established in Beijing, with the aim of enhancing ties between the SAR and the central Government and mainland. Wu Beiming was named as its director. At its inaugural ceremony, Edmund Ho and Chinese Vice-Premier Qian Qichen praised the 'one country, two systems' model, and the director of the central government liaison office in Macao, Bai Zhijian, suggested that Macao might become a model for Taiwan's eventual reunification with the mainland.

On 1 April 2002 Stanley Ho's STDM formally relinquished its 40-year monopoly on casinos. However, Ho retained influence in the gambling sector after his Macao Gaming Holding Company (SJM) won an 18-year licence to operate casinos (see Economy, below). Also in early April, Edmund Ho attended the first annual conference of the Bo'ao Forum for Asia (BFA—a non-profit NGO), held on Hainan Island, China, where he met Hong Kong Chief Executive Tung Chee-hwa and Chinese Premier Zhu Rongji, as well as business leaders from both places.

The US Government in early April 2002 issued its second annual 'United States-Macao Policy Act Report' which stated that the SAR continued to develop in a positive direction, citing its support for the USA's anti-terrorism campaign, the opening of the economy, the reorganization of its customs services, efforts to counter organized crime, and the preservation of its own identity, including maintaining basic civil and human rights. As a result, Macao would continue to be accorded a special status distinct from mainland China under US law and policy. In the middle of the month the United Kingdom announced that it was granting visa-free access to holders of Macao SAR passports, and in late May the visiting Portuguese Minister of Foreign Affairs, António Martins da Cruz, also expressed confidence in Macao's future. In early June Macao hosted the Euro-China Business meeting, aimed at promoting small- and medium-sized enterprises in China to European investors. Also at this time, the Taiwanese Government eased restrictions on residents of Hong Kong and Macao applying for landing visas, essentially allowing those persons to obtain such visas on their first visit to Taiwan. However, in late July a Macao official criticized Taiwanese President Chen Shui-bian and accused him of seeking independence from the mainland.

In mid-June 2002 the Procurator-General, Ho Chio Meng, visited Portugal to promote judicial co-operation between the two territories, the first such visit by a Macao delegation since its return to Chinese rule. Later in the month José Chu was appointed director of the Public Administration and Civil Services Bureau of the SAR.

Meanwhile, the Macao police force continued to maintain co-operation with Hong Kong and the mainland. In late June it was announced that almost 1,000 people had been arrested in Hong Kong during a one-month operation with the Macao police aimed at reducing cross-border and organized crime. At the end of July the Secretary for Security, Cheong Kuoc Va, stated that although overall crime had increased by 1.8% during the first half of the year, serious crimes had registered significant decreases.

In early July 2002 Beijing appointed Wan Yongxiang as the special commissioner of the Office of Special Commissioner of the Chinese Ministry of Foreign Affairs in the Macao SAR, succeeding Yuan Tao, who had held that post since 1999, when the office was established. At the end of July the Government announced the introduction of new identity cards, to be introduced in December 2002. The cards were expected to function additionally as driving licences, border and medical access passes, and electronic payment methods.

The Russian Minister of Foreign Affairs, Igor Ivanov, visited Macao in late July 2002, mainly seeking to strengthen bilateral economic and trading ties, and encouraging Macao businesses to invest in Russia. In early August 2002 Edmund Ho visited the Chinese Autonomous Region of Nei Mongol (Inner Mongolia) in order to examine the possibility of developing ties with the Sino-Russian border region, and later in the month he visited Guangzhou, in southern China, to discuss further economic co-operation and the joint development of Hengqin island, which is under the jurisdiction of Zhuhai City but located very close to Macao.

Economy

Revised by the editorial staff

Macao's economy is based on tourism and textile manufacturing. Various development projects have been initiated in an attempt at diversification. Industries such as plastics, toy-making and electronics have been introduced, while efforts have been made to develop the service sector, especially finance, again with limited success. Export-orientated manufacturing has performed well, the value of merchandise exports increasing sharply in the 1980s and 1990s. However, exports decreased in 2001, reflecting a weakening demand in global markets.

In 1990, according to official estimates, Macao's gross domestic product (GDP), measured at current prices, rose to 27,895.5m. patacas. By 1995 GDP had increased to 55,333m. patacas, but it declined to 55,294m. in 1996. In 1997 GDP reached 55,894m. patacas. In 1998, however, GDP decreased to 51,902m. patacas. GDP declined further in 1999, to stand at an estimated 49,210m. patacas (about US $6,159m.), equivalent to 113,387 patacas (US $14,191) per head, but increased in 2000 to an estimated 49,742m. patacas, and to an estimated 49,802m. patacas in 2001. During 1990–95 the territory's GDP increased, in real terms, at an average annual rate of 6.0%. In 1996, however, real GDP contracted by 0.5% compared with the previous year. In 1997 and in 1998, in real terms, negative growth rates, of 0.3% and of 4.6% respectively, were again recorded. A negative growth rate of 2.9% was registered in 1999. The lower growth rates, which followed the particularly strong expansion of 13.3% recorded in 1992, and subsequent contraction of GDP were attributed to weak domestic demand, the lack of capital and of new technology, the shortage of skilled labour and the higher cost of salaries. GDP increased by a modest 4.6% in 2000, but expanded by less than 1.0% in 2001, reflecting the global economic slowdown. Between 1990 and 1999 the population increased at an average annual rate of 1.8%. According to the census of August 2001, the population totalled 435,235, rising to an estimated 436,686 in December 2001. The average annual rate of inflation (excluding rents) between 1990 and 1997 was 6.7%, declining to 3.5% in 1997 and to only 0.2% in 1998. Deflation rates of 3.2% in 1999, 1.6% in 2000, and 3.3% in 2001 were recorded. In 1998 the rate of unemployment rose to 4.6% of the labour force, many job losses being in the trade, tourism and construction sectors. In July 1998 the Government allocated 50m. patacas to various training initiatives, in an attempt to lessen the effects of unemployment. The unemployment rate was officially estimated at 6.4% in 1999, 6.8% in 2000, and 6.4% in 2001. Some sources, however, suggested that the level was much higher.

Macao continues its attempts to present attractive prospects for foreign investors. Tax and banking reform measures have been passed, and the gambling industry is on a sound base. The Macao Government Economic Committee was founded in February 1994. Its functions included the formulation of policies on industrial and commercial development, as well as on investment promotion. A law enacted in April 1995 aimed to attract overseas investment by offering the right of abode in Macao to entrepreneurs with substantial funds (at least US $250,000) at their disposal. The World Trade Center was established in 1995, and opened for business (on a site of newly-reclaimed land) in early 1996. In addition to providing information services, the Center offers exhibition and conference facilities.

As in the neighbouring Special Administrative Region (SAR) of Hong Kong, many skilled personnel were expected to leave the territory prior to its return to Chinese administration. In August 1994 the Macao Government announced the availability of stipends to public servants expressing their willingness to serve in Macao beyond 1999. Owing to a shortfall in government revenue, civil servants' wages were 'frozen' in 1998.

TOURISM

Despite attempts to diversify, the economy of Macao remains heavily dependent on tourism and the related gambling industry, with clientele coming mainly from Hong Kong at weekends. The Government's receipts from direct taxes on gambling increased from 2,048m. patacas in 1990, when they accounted for 41.2% of total budgetary revenue, to 5,269m. patacas in 1995, thus accounting for 60.8% of government revenue in that year. In 1996 the Government's receipts from gambling decreased to 4,954m. patacas, before rising to 6,013m. in 1997. In 1998, however, direct taxes from gambling yielded only 5,100m. patacas, contributing nevertheless more than 50% to the Government's revenue. In 2000 taxes on gambling accounted for an estimated 60% of the Government's total recurrent revenue. In the same year the contribution of tourism and gambling to GDP was estimated at 38%, while the 10 licensed casinos employed 6% of the labour force.

Visitor arrivals decreased from 8.15m. in 1996, to 7.0m. in 1997 and to 6.9m. in 1998, as a result of the Asian currency crisis and the upsurge of casino-related crime in the territory. The sharpest declines, of 43.6% in 1997 and of 74.0% in 1998, were in the numbers of Japanese visitors, the Government of Japan having been among those to warn citizens not to visit Macao. In 1999 total visitor arrivals rose to 7.4m., almost 57% of whom were residents of Hong Kong, and in 2000 total visitor arrivals had risen to 9,162,212, of whom 54% were residents of Hong Kong. In 2001 total visitor arrivals increased to a record 10,278,973, of whom 51% were residents of Hong Kong. Although a helicopter link between Macao and Hong Kong was established in 1990, most visitors from Hong Kong continue to travel by sea (51% in 2001). From 1993 the number of visitors from the People's Republic of China increased rapidly, tourists from the mainland reaching a total of 816,816 in 1998 (excluding visitors using a double-entry visa between January and July of that year), more than doubling to 1,645,193 in 1999, and rising to 2,274,713 in 2000 and 3,005,722 in 2001. Average per caput spending (excluding mainland Chinese visitors) declined to US $171.63 in 1999, a decrease of 1.38% compared with 1998. The average visitor from the People's Republic of China spent US $332.63 in 1999, a decline of 5.07% compared with the previous year. Following the territory's transfer of sovereignty in December 1999, passports remained necessary for mainland Chinese visitors to Macao, along with special passes issued by the Ministry of Public Security of the People's Republic.

Efforts are being made to broaden the base of the tourist industry, to encourage longer stays (the average length of sojourn being only 1.35 nights in 2001) and to attract overseas visitors to the territory's unique heritage. Programmes to restore and develop Macao's historic and religious monuments offer visitors opportunities for cultural insights perhaps lost in Hong Kong. The first preservation statutes were passed in 1976. Numerous sites have since been similarly protected. During the 1990s several new hotels were built, in which major US chains have interests. By December 2000 the number of hotels rated two-stars and above had risen to 38, of which 16 were four- and five-star establishments, while the number of hotel rooms totalled 8,886. In 2000 and 2001, however, the hotel occupancy rate reached only 57.6% and 60.1% respectively, compared with 79% in 1991.

By the mid-1990s a tourist activity centre was in operation, incorporating the Macao Grand Prix Museum, the Wine Museum, restaurants, conference halls, exhibition areas and other facilities. Other projects included a 360m.-patacas shopping centre (a joint venture with a major Japanese retailing company). In collaboration with a Taiwan-based enterprise, a 2,000m.-patacas complex, incorporating the territory's largest casino and office building, was constructed by the Sociedade de Turismo e Diversões de Macao (STDM). A new sports stadium, covering an area of 44,000 sq m on the island of Taipa, was inaugurated in early 1997. In 1998 plans for the redevelopment of the greyhound racecourse (which had a turnover of US $44m. in 1997) were announced. The construction of a 16,000-sq-m cultural centre, on a huge site of reclaimed land around the Outer Harbour, was completed in 1999. The complex comprises a museum block, housing the historical, archaeological and architectural collections of Macao, and a theatre block. A new 17-ha marine park, including a dolphin tank and aquarium, was planned for reclaimed land on Taipa Island. In July 2000 the SAR Government established a new body to prepare Macao for the Fourth East Asian Games in 2005, which had been awarded to Macao in 1996. In September 2001 construction began on a new 900m. patacas (US $112m.) Fisherman's Wharf amusement park, to be completed in 2003. The 140,000-sq m park will incorporate a seafood section (Dynasty Wharf), and the main amusements and rides area will be on 40,000 sq m of reclaimed land; the third section will comprise a marina, restaurants, bars and a nightclub (Legend Wharf). The centrepiece will be an 'artificial volcano'. The tourist project, Macao's largest since its return to Chinese rule, was being implemented by David Chow Kam Fai, a wealthy entertainment magnate who was also a member of the Legislative Assembly. Chow was widely believed to be a rival of STDM president Stanley Ho, even though Ho owned a stake in the project. Meanwhile, in December 2001 STDM opened the 338m-high Macao Tower Convention and Entertainment Centre, as part of plans to make the SAR more family-orientated and to shed its unsavoury image.

The tourism sector is dominated by STDM, a syndicate to which the territory's gambling monopoly was transferred in 1962 (see below). The company also has interests in the jetfoil service between Hong Kong and Macao, the local airport and Air Macao, various infrastructural operations and property projects, the electricity company, a television network and a supermarket chain. In 1996 the company's assets were estimated at HK $21,500m. STDM's contribution to Macao's budget is substantial, taxes levied on the company accounting for a large percentage of total government revenues (see above). In June 1997 the Sino-Portuguese Joint Liaison Group (JLG) reached agreement on the revision of Macao's gambling franchise. Under the revision, STDM was to pay tax of 31.8% on its revenues from casinos (increased from 30% and backdated to January 1996). In addition to an initial contribution of US $22.7m., STDM was also to contribute 1.6% of its annual gross takings to a new government-controlled Macao development foundation—see below (responsible for the operation of the cultural centre). In 1998 this annual contribution reached US $116m. Furthermore, the contract obliged STDM to guarantee marine transport operations and maintenance, to meet the cost of various public works and to match any government spending on tourism promotion. In 1997, however, STDM's net profits declined by 19.9% compared with the previous year. Profits continued to decline sharply in 1998, by an estimated 50%, but were estimated to have increased from US $98m. in 1999 to $184m. in 2000. STDM's gross takings, meanwhile, rose by 21% in 2000 compared with the previous year, to reach US $2m.

Meanwhile, the sharp increase in casino-related crime led to speculation that STDM might lose its long-standing monopoly in 2001 upon the expiry of its gambling franchise. In July 2000 it was announced that a special committee, chaired by the Chief Executive of the SAR, was to be established to study the future development and management of the gambling industry. STDM's gambling franchise had been renewed once in 1996. However, in December 2001 the Government decided against renewing STDM's monopoly, and the agreement finally expired in April 2002. Under the new arrangements, the Government announced in February 2002 that three companies had successfully bid for casino licences—the Las Vegas-backed Wynn Resorts (Macao) Ltd, the Galaxy Casino Co Ltd (a Hong Kong-Macao joint venture), and the Macao Gaming Holding Co (SJM—Sociedade de Jogos de Macau, a subsidiary of STDM), managed by Stanley Ho. The Gaming Industrial Regime, approved by the Legislative Assembly in August 2001, stipulated that casinos should contribute to the development of tourism, and that the SJM was to pay 35% of its total income to the SAR Government annually—up from 31.8% previously. Despite the loss of his monopoly, Stanley Ho was expected to retain a strong influence in the gambling sector, as his competitors needed time to develop a presence in the SAR. (STDM employed more than 10,000 people in its 11 casinos in 2001, and contributed approximately 30% of the SAR's GDP.) In late June 2002 the Government formally awarded Wynn Resorts (Macao) Ltd a 20-year contract to operate casinos. As a first step, Wynn would invest 4,000m. patacas in Macao over seven years, and open its first casino and hotel complex in 2006.

In June 1997 the JLG reached agreement on the establishment of a foundation, to be funded in part by a tax on gambling revenue (see above). The Macao Development and Co-operation Foundation, which replaced the Orient Foundation, became responsible for the promotion of academic research, science and technology, the arts, education and welfare, with particular emphasis on the preservation and development on the territory's cultural heritage. In August 2002 the Macao Foundation announced the construction of a new Macao Science Center, which would mainly serve educational purposes, but would also function as a convention centre and a tourist attraction. The Center, designed by renowned architect I. M. Pei, was to accommodate physics laboratories, an exhibition hall, a multi-media studio, a science ground for youngsters, an astronomical hall and a multi-purpose conference room.

In co-operation with the territory's large hotels, a tourism-training institute was established in the territory in 1995. Macao is a member of the Pacific Asia Travel Association (PATA) and of the World Tourism Organization. Following the territory's transfer of sovereignty in December 1999, further development of the hotel and tourism sector was envisaged.

INDUSTRY AND POWER

The manufacturing sector employed 21.7% of the economically-active population in 2001. The production of clothing and of knitwear remain by far the most important manufacturing industries. Clothing output decreased from more than 191.8m. units in 1998 to 182.0m. units in 1999, but increased to 222.4m. units in 2000. Output of knitwear rose from 27.7m. units in 1998 to 30.6m. units in 1999 and to 37.9m. units in 2000. From 1998, however, many garment manufacturers reported a substantial decrease in export orders for Japan (Macao's leading non-quota market), owing to that country's economic recession. Other products include footwear (13.3m. pairs being manufactured in 2000, compared with 8.9m. pairs in 1999, and 5.4m. in 1998), toys, fireworks, plastics and electronics. The number of manufacturing establishments decreased from 1,381 in 1998 to an estimated 1,227 in 1999 and to 1,212 in 2000.

The Concordia Industrial Park was established in the early 1990s on reclaimed land near the new airport, with the aim of stimulating investment and enhancing industrial diversification, with an emphasis on small and medium enterprises, and new technology ventures being particularly encouraged. Investors benefited from numerous property, industrial, and corporate tax exemptions, as well as low land prices. By 2000 total investment had risen to 643m. patacas, and the various companies' sales were projected at 867m. patacas in 2000, and at 1,058m. patacas in 2001. The industrial estate is promoted and managed by the Sociedade do Parque Industrial da Concordia—SPIC (established in 1993), of which 60% is owned by the Macao Government. The SPIC has in recent years established ties with the Chinese Academy of Sciences and the China Association of Science and Technology. Future plans envision an expansion of the Park to meet future demands for such space, and using the Park to promote foreign direct investment in the mainland, which would extend into Macao.

Regulations governing the entry of foreign workers were relaxed in 1988. In 2001 the total number of foreign workers was estimated at 26,000, mainly from the People's Republic of China and the Philippines, compared with 35,000 in 1995.

Macao possesses few natural resources. The People's Republic of China provides part of the SAR's water supply. In mid-1996 Guangdong Province announced the implementation of new measures to improve the quality of its water supplies to Macao. Four reservoirs in the Chinese city of Zhuhai supplied 150,000 cu m of water daily in 1999. In June 1984 Macao's electricity supply was linked to a China-based source. The People's Republic was initially to supply 10% of Macao's power requirement. In 1999 87% of the territory's electricity was domestically produced. Macao's two power stations have a total capacity of more than 400 MW, with additional facilities scheduled to enter into service during 2000–01. Total gross output of electricity rose from 1,477.7 kWh in 2000 to 1,510.4 kWh in 2001. Imports of fuels and lubricants accounted for 7.9% of total import costs in 2001, compared with 7.6% in 2000.

FOREIGN TRADE AND INVESTMENT

Macao's foreign trade expanded strongly in the 1980s, the trade surplus reaching a peak of 2,217m. patacas in 1987. The value of merchandise exports rose from 2,742m. patacas in 1980 to 13,638.2m. in 1990, 17,580.0m. in 1999 and to 20,380.4m. in 2000. In 2001, however, total exports decreased to 18,473.0m., owing to weaker demand in the USA and the European Union (EU). The trade surplus stood at 1,279.8m. patacas in 1999, when the cost of imports increased to 16,300.2m. patacas, and the surplus increased to 2,282.8m. patacas in 2000, the cost of imports in that year having risen to 18,097.6m. patacas. However, in 2001, when imports reached 19,170.4m. patacas, a trade deficit of 697.4m. patacas was recorded.

As a result of the policy of diversifying exports away from their heavy reliance on the textile sector, non-textile products accounted for almost 30% of overall shipments in 1989, compared with only 13% in 1980. During the 1990s, however, many non-textile operations were relocated to China and to South-East Asia, where labour costs were lower. From mid-1997 Macao's position was further weakened by the relative appreciation of the pataca against the currencies of its South-East Asian competitors. Exports of clothing decreased from 14,623.0m. patacas in 2000 to 13,202.0m. patacas (71.5% of the total). Exports of textile fabrics, however, increased from 1,245.1m. patacas in 2000 to 1,266.5m. patacas in 2001. The toy-making sector showed strong growth in the late 1980s, providing almost 10.2% of all exports in 1989. In the 1990s, however, exports of toys declined sharply, reaching only 35.0m. patacas (less than 0.2% of total exports) in 1999. Sales of electronic goods showed strong expansion in the early 1990s, the value of exports of radio and television sets rising from 321.5m. patacas in 1991 to 565.6m. in 1994. However, exports of electronics subsequently decreased, earning only 15.0m. patacas in 1998. Exports of machinery and apparatus declined from 388.0m. patacas in 1998 to 337.0m. in 1999, but rose to 418.3m. in 2000 and to 555.6m. in 2001.

The textile and garment sector therefore remains dominant, most exports having been regulated by the General Agreement on Tariffs and Trade (GATT, superseded by the World Trade Organization—WTO), an agency of which Macao became a member in January 1991. The quota limits established by the Multi-Fibre Arrangement (MFA) were due for renewal in 1991, but the existing agreement was extended until the end of 1992, pending a successful conclusion to the 'Uruguay Round' of GATT negotiations. Shortly before this conclusion in December 1993, the MFA was extended for a further year. It was envisaged that the provisions of the MFA would be phased out over a 10-year period. Meanwhile, an extension agreement between Macao and the USA (a major importer of the territory's textiles and garments) was signed in mid-1991. A two-year bilateral textile agreement was signed in January 1994. In September 1998, following the USA's expression of doubt that not all of Macao's textile exports were in fact manufactured in the enclave (in possible violation of country-of-origin regulations), the territory was warned that the situation was to be closely monitored. Macao became an associate member of the Economic and Social Commission for Asia and the Pacific (ESCAP) in 1991. In June 1992 Macao and the European Community (EC, now European Union—EU) signed a five-year trade and economic co-operation agreement, granting mutual preferential treatment on tariffs and other commercial matters. The agreement was extended in December 1997. Macao remained a 'privileged partner' of the EU after December 1999. Wishing to enhance links with the EU, in May 2000 the new Chief Executive of the SAR, Edmund Ho, paid an official visit to Portugal, which in January had assumed the EU's rotating presidency for a six-month period. Ho made his first official visit to the EU's headquarters in Brussels in mid-June 2001, seeking to promote contacts and exchanges between the two entities. Macao also retained its membership of the WTO after December 1999.

In 1997 the People's Republic of China became Macao's principal supplier, providing 28.6% of Macao's imports, surpassing Hong Kong (25.2%), and with Japan ranked third (8.5%). In 1998 China supplied almost 32.2% of Macao's imports, while Hong Kong provided 23.7% and Japan 7.7%. In 1999 more than 35.6% of Macao's imports were purchased from China, with Hong Kong accounting for 18.1% and Japan for 6.7%. In 2000 some 41.1% of Macao's imports originated from China, with 15.2% coming from Hong Kong, while Taiwan ranked third (9.5%). In 2001 China supplied 42.6% of Macao's imports, followed by Hong Kong (13.9%) and Taiwan (6.7%). Exports to the USA increased rapidly from the late 1970s, reaching 537m. patacas in 1980. By 1989 this figure had risen to 4,946m. patacas, representing more than one-third of Macao's total export trade. After fluctuating in subsequent years, the territory's exports to the USA rose to 8,140.7m. patacas (47.7% of the total) in 1998, 8,249.1m. patacas (46.9% of the total) in 1999, and a record 9,836.7m. patacas (48.3% of the total) in 2000. In 2001, however, Macao's exports to the USA decreased to 8,907.1m. patacas (48.2% of the total). China purchased 2,155.0m. patacas (11.7% of the total) of Macao's exports in 2001, compared with 2,079.8m. (10.2%) in 2000. Other important trading partners were Germany and the United Kingdom.

Macao actively seeks new markets through the promotion of official trade delegations.

Upon its return to Chinese sovereignty in December 1999, Macao was allowed to retain its system of free enterprise for a period of 50 years. The territory's status as a free port was also retained. Macao remained a separate customs territory, and its trade with China continued to be classified as foreign trade.

Between the late 1970s and 1995 it was estimated that mainland Chinese companies had invested a total of US $5,800m. in Macao. Economic co-operation between Macao and the neighbouring Chinese Special Economic Zone (SEZ) of Zhuhai, largely in the form of joint ventures, has increased. In early 1996 a bilateral seminar resulted in proposals for co-operation in areas such as aviation, industrial production, tourism and the joint promotion of an island development zone. Macao's involvement in China has also risen. By mid-1994 it was estimated that more than 3,900 joint ventures had been established on the mainland, entailing a total investment of US $1,200m. In 1997 alone Macao companies invested a total of US $10,000m. in 6,333 projects in China. During the first half of 2002 Macao experienced a sharp increase in foreign investment, inflows totalling 1,000m. patacas.

FINANCE AND BANKING

In the early 1990s overall economic buoyancy was reflected in the increased levels of expenditure in successive budgets, total spending rising from 5,489.9m. patacas in 1990 to 11,251.3m. in 1994, when a budgetary surplus of 1,559.9m. was recorded. In 1995, however, expenditure was reduced to 10,314.9m. patacas, while revenue declined to 11,033.8m. (from 12,811.2m. in 1994) to give a surplus of 718.9m. By 1997 expenditure had been reduced to 14,134.1m. patacas, while revenue had also declined, to 14,134.1m. (compared with 14,681.3m. and 14,711.3m. respectively in 1996). In 1998 the budget was projected to balance at 14,831.1m. patacas. Revenue was lower than anticipated, however, owing to a shortfall in receipts from gambling and from land leases (95% of land in Macao being owned by the Government). A budgetary deficit, equivalent to an estimated 1.5% of GDP, thus resulted. In 1999 expenditure was projected at only 9,805.4m. patacas, while revenue was expected to total 10,111.8m. patacas. The provisional budget for 2000 envisaged a reduction in expenditure to 8,501.7m. patacas, although it aimed to increase spending on anti-corruption measures; expenditure on health and education was to remain at a level similar to that of the previous year. Revenue was provisionally estimated at 8,815.9m. patacas in 2000. The provisional budget for 2001 envisaged expenditure of 15,220.8m. patacas and revenue of 15,641.6m. patacas.

In April 1977 the local currency's link with the Portuguese escudo was ended and a new parity of 1.075 (subsequently 1.030) patacas = HK $1 was established, an appreciation of about 38%. Exporters of merchandise were required to surrender 50% (subsequently 40%) of their foreign-exchange earnings to the official Exchange Fund. The banking system therefore had sufficient resources to maintain the value of the pataca, which continues to float with the Hong Kong dollar. The latter currency also circulates widely in Macao. Upon the territory's transfer of sovereignty, the pataca was retained and remained freely convertible.

A state-owned institution responsible for currency issue, the Instituto Emissor de Macau (IEM), was founded in 1980, nominally taking over this function from the Banco Nacional Ultramarino, which remained the Government's banker for the territory. In 1989 the IEM was replaced by the Autoridade Monetária e Cambial de Macau (AMCM, Monetary and Foreign Exchange Authority of Macao), now the Autoridade Monetária de Macau. Banknotes will continue to be issued by the Banco Nacional Ultramarino, acting as the Government's agent until at least 2010. Since October 1995 notes have also been issued by the Bank of China's branch in Macao.

Plans to revitalize the banking sector began in July 1982, when a new banking ordinance was passed, allowing for the establishment of development banks. The financial sector was declared open to competition, and six international and three Portuguese banks were granted full commercial licences. The aim was to establish an enlarged financial sector, providing a widening of financial services to support the growth of various business sectors. In 1987 legislation to permit offshore banking was introduced, allowing foreign companies to operate tax-free, apart from the payment of an annual fee. The level of offshore activity, however, has been disappointing. Also in 1987 Macao's largest bank, the Nan Tung Bank, was acquired by the Bank of China, the official foreign exchange bank of the People's Republic.

In 2001 a total of 21 registered banks were operating in Macao. In addition, a postal savings bank, established in 1935, is operated by the Government. The total assets of the commercial banking sector reached the equivalent of 295% of GDP in September 1998, compared with 207% in 1995.

Macao has no foreign-exchange controls or restrictions on capital flows. As a result, balance-of-payments data are not comprehensive. During 1990–98, however, the current account showed a consistent surplus. This reached US $2,700m. (equivalent to 37.4% of GDP) in 1996, before declining to US 2,400m. (38.8% of GDP) in 1998.

The Financial System Act, which aimed to improve the reputation of the territory's banks, took effect in September 1993. The legislation required banks to record the identity of those making unusually large transactions, in an attempt to curb the unauthorized acceptance of deposits. In June 1996, in an effort to combat organized crime, the first guidelines on the prevention of 'money-laundering' operations were issued. These underwent revision in 1999.

From December 1999 Macao began administering its own finances, and was to be exempt from taxes imposed by central government. Consumption taxes are levied on only a limited number of items, such as cigarettes and alcohol. The rates of income tax are lower than in the neighbouring SAR of Hong Kong.

DEVELOPMENT AND INFRASTRUCTURE

In 1998 the Government allocated 1,900m. patacas (of a total budget of 10,700m.) to infrastructural projects, an increase of 300m. patacas compared with the previous year. Until the 1990s, however, Macao's development was hindered by the territory's lack of infrastructure, the limitations of the electricity and water supplies, the shortage of skilled labour and the dearth of suitable building land.

In August 1979 the administration announced that it had prepared a land-use plan. The master plan was based on a massive land-reclamation scheme which required soil from China. However, none of the feasibility studies was made in consultation with the Chinese authorities, thus undermining the plan's validity. Nevertheless, between 1989 and 2000 alone Macao's land area was increased from 17.32 sq km to 25.40 sq km.

The shortage of land for development purposes has presented a serious problem. In February 1983 plans were announced for a joint-venture scheme, between Macao and the Zhuhai SEZ, to reclaim 110 ha of Macao's outer harbour area for urban development. A second reclamation project of similar size was planned for the Areia Preta area. These two projects are part of a major reclamation programme which would double Macao's land area. In 2000 work was under way on a reclamation scheme on both sides of an existing causeway joining Taipa and Coloane Islands. A new town called Cotai is to be built on this site, which would include a railway terminal serving a new planned passenger and freight route to Zhuhai and thence all the way to Guangzhou. The completion, in four stages, of the Nam Van Lakes project scheduled for the early 21st century, would enlarge the peninsular area by 20%. Details of this land-reclamation project, which originally was to cost US $1,400m., were announced in July 1993 by a prominent entrepreneur, following the scheme's approval by the People's Republic of China. The development was to incorporate hotels, offices, apartments and commercial malls, with residential and business accommodation for 60,000 people along a six-lane waterfront highway.

As a result of the establishment of diplomatic relations between Portugal and China in February 1979 and the subsequent growth of confidence in the future of the territory, there was a considerable rise in property prices in Macao. Land sold by the Portuguese administration a few years previously to encourage residential development had more than quadrupled in value by 1981.

The Government's receipts from land leases rose sharply in the early 1990s, reaching almost 40% of its total revenue (equivalent to 8.25% of GDP) in 1992. Having accounted for 25% of government revenue in 1993–94, receipts from land leases declined substantially during 1995–97 to make an average annual contribution to revenue of only 6% (or 1% of GDP). This decline in the property market, following a period of very strong growth in the construction sector, was also demonstrated by the sharp decrease in the number of buildings completed in 1997—only 1,150,000 sq m (of which 632,000 sq m represented residential property), compared with 1,908,000 sq m in 1996 (1,619,000 sq m being for residential purposes). This decline continued, with new gross floor area completed falling to 969,192 sq m in 1998, and to 668,778 sq m in 1999, reaching a new low of 370,315 sq m in 2000, but increasing to 404,325 sq m of new floor area in 2001.

Mainland Chinese speculation in both residential and commercial property resulted in a surplus of buildings. By 1996 there were an estimated 30,000–50,000 vacant apartments, mainly on the island of Taipa. In August 1996, in order to address the problem of the property surplus, the Government began to offer financial incentives, in the form of mortgage subsidies, to first-time buyers. Between January and June 1998 the number of real-estate transactions totalled 6,683, an increase of 1.6% compared with the corresponding period of 1997. The value of these transactions, however, declined by 56.9%, to stand at 4,300m. patacas. During the 1990s real interest rates increased markedly, reaching a level of 12.3% in September 1998. It was hoped that a series of reductions in interest rates in 1998/99 would stimulate the housing market.

In March 2000 the transfer to the SAR's Government of the assets of the Sino-Portuguese Land Group, established in 1988 to handle land concession matters, was completed. Comprising income from land leases and attendant earnings from banking deposits and investments, the Land Fund totalled 10,185m. patacas.

In March 1980, meanwhile, Chinese approval was secured for Macao's most ambitious project, an international airport. Following a feasibility study for its construction on reclaimed land and on piles off the island of Taipa, it was confirmed in 1987 that the project would proceed. By 1989 construction work at the new airport site had commenced. The cost of the airport scheme was originally estimated at some 3,500m. patacas, of which one-third was to be provided by the Government of the People's Republic of China. It was envisaged that the airport would not only enhance Macao's role as a point of entry to the People's Republic of China and afford the enclave access to international transport networks, but also improve investment conditions and provide new opportunities for the development of industries such as tourism. In 1990, however, it was reported that the consortium of Chinese companies involved in the project had been forced to reduce its proposed equity from 500m. patacas to just 130m., owing to the shortage of foreign exchange in China. Furthermore, ballast required for the reclamation work had not been delivered on schedule by the consortium. Nevertheless, the future of the project was assured, when three Macao businessmen agreed to finance the shortfall. In June 1993 Portugal and China reached agreement on all outstanding issues regarding the building of the airport. A regional airline, Air Macau, was formally established in 1994, with investment from the Civil Aviation Administration of China (CAAC) and with Portuguese and Macao interests. The airport was officially inaugurated in December 1995, at a final cost of 8,900m. patacas. The terminal has an annual capacity of 6m. passengers. By 2000 Air Macau was operating flights to several cities in China, Taiwan, Thailand, Japan, the Republic of Korea and the Philippines. Of particular significance was the opening by Air Macau of a direct route between Taiwan and mainland China, passengers no longer being required to change aircraft. Flights to and from the Democratic People's Republic of Korea (North Korea) by Koryo Air resumed in April 2002, and a new Air Macau route to Singapore was inaugurated in August 2002. In 2001 a total of 11 airlines operated more than 500 scheduled flights weekly to more than 30 destinations. The airport handled some 3.8 m. passengers in 2001, compared with 3.2m. in 2000 and 2.6m. in 1999. In 1998 the airport processed 65,167 tons of cargo. The volume of cargo handled declined to 53,118 tons in 1999, but recovered in 2000 to 68,084 tons, and 76,076 tons in 2001. In 2001 the airport's franchise was extended to 2039.

The regular catamaran, jetfoil and high-speed ferry services between Macao and Hong Kong are complemented by a helicopter service, which commenced in 1990. In conjunction with the construction of the airport, a new 4.4-km four-lane bridge providing an additional link between the island of Taipa and the peninsula of Macao opened in April 1994, having been completed at a cost of more than 600m. patacas. Other completed development plans include the construction of a deep-water harbour. The new port of Kao-ho, on the island of Coloane, began operations in 1990, handling both container and oil tanker traffic.

In mid-1997 a preliminary agreement was reached by the Sino-Portuguese Infrastructure Co-ordination Commission, which was established in April of that year, concerning the construction of a six-lane road bridge linking Macao with Zhuhai. The bridge, which was to cost US $12.29m. (financed equally by Macao and Zhuhai), was to extend from an area of reclaimed land between Taipa and Coloane to the island of Hengqin, situated off the coast of Zhuhai, and would provide a link with the planned Beijing–Zhuhai highway. Construction work began in June 1998, and the 1.5-km Lotus Bridge duly opened to traffic in December 1999. The Chinese Government was to develop the island of Hengqin as an international free trade zone. Following Macao's transfer of sovereignty in December 1999, the Chinese authorities planned greater integration of the SAR within the Zhujiang (Pearl River) Delta, particularly with regard to infrastructural development. Suggestions for the construction of a 37.9-km bridge between Macao and Hong Kong were made by the private sector in 1997. These plans developed into a proposal to build a new 29-km steel bridge linking Macao with Hong Kong's Lantau Island and Zhuhai, Guangdong Province. Feasibility studies to determine the project's financial and technical viability were being conducted in 2001. In August 2002 the Chon Tit (Macao) Investment and Development Co was chosen for the construction of a third bridge connecting downtown Macao with Taipa Island. The new 1,720-m, six-lane bridge would have two levels and cost 560.2m. patacas to build, over a 28-month period. The project would create 1,000 jobs and relieve congestion on the existing bridges.

Macao's telecommunications network has been extensively modernized. In May 1984 a new satellite ground station was inaugurated, establishing direct communications with Portugal, Japan and the UK, and in 1986 plans were announced to install a 15-km fibre optic cable between Macao and the Zhuhai SEZ, thus improving telecommunications links between the two territories. A fully digital telephone network was established in 1991. In 1995 the Companhia de Telecomunicações de Macau (CTM) began to provide internet services. By early 1996 CTM had signed agreements for the provision of mobile telephone services with three of China's inland localities: Beijing, Guangdong Province and Shanghai. In 1994, meanwhile, CTM announced a four-year plan, costing HK$1,700m., to develop new facilities, many of which formed part of the telecommunications infrastructure of the territory's new airport. Following Macao's transfer of sovereignty in December 1999, Portugal Telecom retained its 28% share in CTM. The former's management concession was renewed until 2001, thus granting CTM exclusive rights to provide fixed-line telephone services, data communications and leased lines. In June 2000 a new body, the Office for the Development of Telecommunications and Information Technology (GDTTI), was established, with a view to building a legal framework for the telecommunications sector, ensuring that services met the needs of the market, developing the communications infrastructure, issuing licenses, and maintaining quality control, price regulation and standardization of the network.

Statistical Survey

Source (unless otherwise indicated): Direcção dos Serviços de Estatística e Censos, Alameda Dr Carlos d'Assumpção 411–417, Dynasty Plaza, 17° andar, Macau; tel. 728188; fax 561884; e-mail info@dsec.gov.mo; internet www.dsec.gov.mo.

AREA AND POPULATION

Area (2001): 25.80 sq km (9.96 sq miles).

Population: 435,235 (males 208,865, females 226,370) at census of 23 August 2001 (414,200 inhabitants were of Chinese nationality and 8,793 inhabitants were of Portuguese nationality); 436,686 (official estimate) at 31 December 2001.

Density (31 December 2001): 16,926 per sq km.

Births, Marriages and Deaths (2001): Registered live births 3,241 (birth rate 7.5 per 1,000); Registered marriages 1,222 (marriage rate 2.8 per 1,000); Registered deaths 1,327 (death rate 3.1 per 1,000).

Expectation of Life (years at birth, 1996–99): 77.7 (males 76.2; females 80.2).

Economically Active Population (2001): Manufacturing 44,055; Production and distribution of electricity, gas and water 1,020; Construction 16,897; Wholesale and retail trade; repair of motor vehicles, motorcycles and personal and household goods 30,196; Hotels, restaurants and similar activities 22,437; Transport, storage and communications 14,524; Financial activities 6,078; Real estate, renting and services to companies 10,733; Public administration, defence and compulsory social security 15,971; Education 8,117; Health and social work 5,069; Other community, social and personal service activities 22,143; Private households with employed persons 4,839; Others 728; Total employed 202,807.

HEALTH AND WELFARE
Key Indicators

Under-5 Mortality Rate (per 1,000 live births, 2001): 5.25.

HIV/AIDS (% persons aged 15–49, 2001): 0.004.

Physicians (per 1,000 head, 2001): 2.04.

Hospital Beds (per 1,000 head, 2001): 2.24.

Human Development Index (1999): value 0.867.

For definitions, see explanatory note on p. vi.

AGRICULTURE, ETC.

Livestock ('000 head, year ending September 2000): Poultry 500 (FAO estimate). Source: FAO.

Livestock Products ('000 metric tons, 2000): Beef and veal 1.1; Pig meat 8.6*; Poultry meat 4.6; Hen eggs 0.8* (*FAO estimate). Source: FAO.

Fishing (FAO estimates, metric tons, live weight, 1999): Marine fishes 1,020; Shrimps and prawns 230; Other marine crustaceans 210; Total catch (incl. others) 1,500. Source: FAO, *Yearbook of Fishery Statistics*.

INDUSTRY

Production (2000): Wine 414,492 litres; Knitwear 37.92m. units; Footwear 13.26m. pairs; Clothing 222.35m. units; Furniture 48,457 units; Electric energy (2001) 1,510.4 million kWh.

FINANCE

Currency and Exchange Rates: 100 avos = 1 pataca. *Sterling, Dollar and Euro Equivalents* (31 May 2002): £1 sterling = 11.783 patacas; US $1 = 8.034 patacas; €1 = 7.541 patacas; 1,000 patacas = £84.87 = $124.47 = €132.60. *Average Exchange Rate* (patacas per US dollar): 7.992 in 1999; 8.026 in 2000; 8.034 in 2001. Note: The pataca has a fixed link with the value of the Hong Kong dollar (HK $1 = 1.030 patacas).

Budget (million patacas, 2001, provisional): *Total revenue:* 15,641.6 (direct taxes 7,547.4; indirect taxes 840.8; others 7,253.4). *Total expenditure:* 15,220.8.

International Reserves (US $ million at 31 December 2001): Foreign exchange 3,508.4; Total 3,508.4. Source: IMF, *International Financial Statistics*.

Money Supply (million patacas at 31 December 2001): Currency outside banks 1,977.4; Demand deposits at commercial banks 4,020.8; Total money 5,998.2. Source: IMF, *International Financial Statistics*.

Cost of Living (Consumer Price Index; base: Oct. 1999–Sept. 2000 = 100): All items 101.12 in 1999; 99.49 in 2000; 97.52 in 2001.

Gross Domestic Product (million patacas at current prices): 49,071 in 1999; 49,742 in 2000; 49,802 in 2001.

Expenditure on the Gross Domestic Product (million patacas at current prices, 2001): Government final consumption expenditure 6,062.7; Private final consumption expenditure 20,625.4; Increase in stocks 71.9; Gross fixed capital formation 5,194.6; *Total domestic expenditure* 31,954.6; Exports of goods and services 48,678.5; *Less* Imports of goods and services 30,831.0; *GDP in purchasers' values* 49,802.1.

Gross Domestic Product by Economic Activity (provisional, million patacas at current prices, 2000): Mining and quarrying 3.3; Manufacturing 4,137.9; Electricity, gas and water supply 1,216.6; Construction 1,056.2; Trade, restaurants and hotels 4,581.5; Transport, storage and communications 3,240.2; Financial intermediation, real estate, renting and business activities 10,345.4; Public administration, other community, social and personal services (incl. gambling) 20,582.8; *Sub-total* 45,164.0; *Less* Financial intermediation services indirectly measured 2,427.4; *GDP at basic prices* 42,736.6; Taxes on products (net) 6,603.1; *GDP in purchasers' values* 49,339.6.

EXTERNAL TRADE

Principal Commodities (million patacas, 2001): *Imports c.i.f.:* (distribution by SITC): Food and live animals 1,098.7; Beverages and tobacco 1,448.9 (Beverages 1,055.9); Mineral fuels, lubricants, etc. 1,516.0 (Petroleum, petroleum products, etc. 1,204.4); Chemicals and related products 682.4; Basic manufactures 7,465.0 (Textile yarn, fabrics, etc. 6,750.4); Machinery and transport equipment 3,446.3 (Electrical machinery, apparatus, etc. 1,720.8, Transport equipment and parts 813.8); Miscellaneous manufactured articles 3,259.0 (Clothing and accessories 1,955.1); Total (incl.others) 19,170.4. *Exports f.o.b.:* Textile yarn and thread 856.7; Textile fabrics 1,266.5; Machinery and mechanical appliances 555.6; Clothing 13,202.0; Footwear 645.9; Total (incl. others) 18,473.0.

Principal Trading Partners (million patacas, 2001): *Imports c.i.f.:* Australia 226.9; China, People's Republic 8,164.7; France 805.7; Germany 457.4; Hong Kong 2,660.2; Italy 200.7; Japan 1,041.2; Korea, Republic 1,139.1; Singapore 510.3; Taiwan 1,278.2; United Kingdom 512.6; USA 796.8; Total (incl. others) 19,170.4. *Exports f.o.b.:* Canada 349.9; China, People's Republic 2,155.0; France 786.3; Germany 1,418.1; Hong Kong 1,177.6; Netherlands 596.5; United Kingdom 1,180.2; USA 8,907.1; Total (incl. others) 18,473.0.

TRANSPORT

Road Traffic (motor vehicles in use, Dec. 2001): Light vehicles 52,379; Heavy vehicles 4,136; Motorcycles 58,250.

Shipping (international sea-borne freight traffic*, '000 metric tons, 2001): Goods loaded 146.2; Goods unloaded 72.8.

* Containerized cargo only.

TOURISM

Visitor Arrivals by Country of Residence (2001): China, People's Republic 3,005,722; Hong Kong 5,196,136; Taiwan 1,451,826; Total (incl. others) 10,278,973.

COMMUNICATIONS MEDIA

Radio Receivers (1997): 160,000 in use.

Television Receivers (2000): 125,115 in use.

Daily Newspapers (2001): 11.

Telephones (Dec. 2001): 176,450 main lines in use.

Facsimile Machines (1999): 6,290 in use.

Mobile Cellular Telephones (2001): 194,475 subscribers.

Personal Computers (2001): 60,390 households.

Internet Users (2001): 34,403.

Sources: partly International Telecommunication Union and UNESCO, *Statistical Yearbook*.

EDUCATION
(2000/01)

Kindergarten: 60 schools; 551 teachers; 14,978 pupils.

Primary: 81 schools; 1,747 teachers; 45,474 pupils.

Secondary (incl. technical colleges): 48 schools; 1,753 teachers; 35,850 pupils.

Higher: 11 institutes; 923 teachers; 8,358 students.

Notes: Figures for schools and teachers refer to all those for which the category is applicable. Some schools and teachers provide education at more than one level. Institutions of higher education refer to those recognized by the Government of Macao Special Administrative Region.

Adult Literacy Rate: 93.7% in 1996.

Directory

The Constitution

Under the terms of the Basic Law of the Macao Special Administrative Region (SAR), which took effect on 20 December 1999, the Macao SAR is an inalienable part of the People's Republic of China. The Macao SAR, which comprises the Macao peninsula and the islands of Taipa and Coloane, exercises a high degree of autonomy and enjoys executive, legislative and independent judicial power, including that of final adjudication. The executive authorities and legislature are composed of permanent residents of Macao. The socialist system and policies shall not be practised in the Macao SAR, and the existing capitalist system and way of life shall not be changed for 50 years. In addition to the Chinese language, the Portuguese language may also be used by the executive, legislative and judicial organs.

The central people's Government is responsible for foreign affairs and for defence. The Government of Macao is responsible for maintaining social order in the SAR. The central people's Government appoints and dismisses the Chief Executive, principal executive officials and Procurator-General.

The Chief Executive of the Macao SAR is accountable to the central people's Government. The Chief Executive shall be a Chinese national of no less than 40 years of age, who is a permanent resident of the region and who has resided in Macao for a continuous period of 20 years. He or she is elected locally by a broadly-representative Selection Committee and appointed by the central people's Government.

The Basic Law provides for a 300-member Election Committee, which serves a five-year term. The Election Committee shall be composed of 300 members from the following sectors; 100 members from industrial, commercial and financial sectors; 80 from cultural, educational, and professional sectors; 80 from labour, social welfare and religious sectors; and 40 from the Legislative Council, municipal organs, Macao deputies to the National People's Congress (NPC), and representatives of Macao members of the National Committee of the Chinese People's Political Consultative Conference (NCCPPCC). The Selection Committee responsible for the choice of the Chief Executive in 1999 comprised 200 members; 60 representatives of business and financial circles; 50 from cultural, educational and professional circles; 50 from labour, social welfare and religious circles; and 40 former politicians and Macao deputies to the NPC and representatives of Macao members of the NCCPPCC. The term of office of the Chief Executive of the Macao SAR is five years; he or she may serve two consecutive terms. The Chief Executive's functions include the appointment of a portion of the legislative councillors and the appointment or removal of members of the Executive Council.

With the exception of the first term (which was to expire on 15 October 2001), the term of office of members of the Legislative Council (commonly known as the Legislative Assembly) shall be four years. The second Legislative Council shall be composed of 27 members, of whom 10 shall be returned by direct election, 10 by indirect election and seven by appointment. The third and subsequent Legislative Councils shall comprise 29 members, of whom 12 shall be returned by direct election, 10 by indirect election and seven by appointment.

The Macao SAR shall maintain independent finances. The central people's Government shall not levy taxes in the SAR, which shall practise an independent taxation system. The Macao pataca will remain the legal currency. The Macao SAR shall retain its status as a free port and as a separate customs territory.

The Government

(September 2002)

Chief Executive: EDMUND H. W. HO.

Secretary for Administration and Justice: FLORINDA DA ROSA SILVA CHAN.

Secretary for Economy and Finance: FRANCIS TAM PAK YUEN.

Secretary for Security: CHEONG KUOC VA.

Secretary for Social and Cultural Affairs: FERNANDO CHUI SAI ON.

Secretary for Transport and Public Works: AO MAN LONG.

GOVERNMENT OFFICES

Office of the Chief Executive: Headquarters of the Government of the Macao Special Administrative Region, Av. da Praia Grande; tel. 726886; fax 726128; internet www.macau.gov.mo.

Office of the Secretary for Administration and Justice: Rua de S. Lourenço 28, Edif. dos Secretários; tel. 9895178; fax 726880; internet www.macau.gov.mo.

Office of the Secretary for Economy and Finance: Rua de S. Lourenço 28, Edif. dos Secretários; tel. 7978160; fax 726665.

Office of the Secretary for Security: Calçada dos Quarteis, Quartel de S. Francisco; tel. 7997510; fax 580702.

Office of the Secretary for Social and Cultural Affairs: Rua de S. Lourenço 28, Edif. dos Secretários; tel. 7978197; fax 725778.

Office of the Secretary for Transport and Public Works: Rua de S. Lourenço 28, Edif. dos Secretários, 1° andar; tel. 9895108; fax 727566.

Macao Government Information Bureau: Gabinete de Comunicação Social do Governo de Macau, Rua de S. Domingos 1, POB 706; tel. 332886; fax 336372; e-mail info@macau.gov.mo; internet www.macau.gov.mo; Dir VICTOR CHAN CHI PING.

Economic Services: Direcção dos Serviços de Economia, Rua Dr Pedro José Lobo 1–3, Edif. Luso Internacional, 25/F; tel. 386937; fax 590310; e-mail info@economia.gov.mo; internet www.economia.gov.mo.

EXECUTIVE COUNCIL

FLORINDA DA ROSA SILVA CHAN, FRANCIS TAM PAK YUEN, CHEONG KUOC VA, FERNANDO CHUI SAI ON, AO MAN LONG, TONG CHI KIN (Spokesman), LEONG HENG TENG, VICTOR NG, LIU CHAK WAN, MA IAO LAI.

Legislature

LEGISLATIVE COUNCIL (LEGISLATIVE ASSEMBLY)

Edif. da Assembléia Legislativa, Praça da Assembléia Legislativa, Aterros da Baía da Praia Grande; tel. 728377; fax 727857.

Following the election of 23 September 2001, the Legislative Assembly comprised 27 members: seven appointed by the Chief Executive, 10 elected directly and 10 indirectly. Members serve for four years. The Assembly chooses its President from among its members, by secret vote. At the election of September 2001, the business-orientated Convergência para o Desenvolvimento and União Geral para o Desenvolvimento de Macau (CODEM) each won two of the 10 directly-elective seats. The pro-Beijing candidates of the União Promotora para o Progresso (UPP) and of the União para o Desenvolvimento (UPD) won two seats each. The pro-democracy Associação de Novo Macau Democrático (ANMD) also took two seats. Four of the 10 directly-elective seats were taken by the OMKC, a group representing business interests. Groups representing various other interests occupied the remaining six seats. The Legislative Assembly was superseded, under the terms of the Basic Law, by the Legislative Council. In practice, however, the legislature continues to be referred to as the Legislative Assembly.

President: SUSANA CHOU.

Political Organizations

There are no formal political parties, but a number of registered civic associations exist and may participate in elections for the Legislative Assembly by presenting a list of candidates. These include the União Promotora para o Progresso (UNIPRO), Associação Promotora para a Economia de Macau (APPEM), União para o Desenvolvimento (UPD), Associação de Novo Macau Democrático (ANMD), Convergência para o Desenvolvimento (CODEM), União Geral para o Desenvolvimento de Macau (UDM), Associação de Amizade (AMI), Aliança para o Desenvolvimento da Economia (ADE), Associação dos Empregados e Assalariados (AEA) and Associação pela Democracia e Bem-Estar Social de Macau (ADBSM). Civic associations that are considerably active in civic, educational, and charity activities and services are: Associação Geral dos Operários de Macau (General Workers' Association of Macao), União Geral das Associações dos Moradores de Macau (Union of Neighbourhood Associations), Instituto do Novo Macau (New Macao Institute), Santa Casa Misericórdia (Charity Organization), Tong Sin Tong (Charity Organization), and Associação dos Trabalhadores da Função Pública de Macau (Macao Civil Servants Association).

Judicial System

Formal autonomy was granted to the territory's judiciary in 1993. A new penal code took effect in January 1996. Macao operates its own five major codes, namely the Penal Code, the Code of Criminal Procedure, the Civil Code, the Code of Civil Procedure and the Commercial Code. In March 1999 the authority of final appeal was granted to the supreme court of Macao, effective from June. The judicial system operates independently of the mainland Chinese system.

Court of Final Appeal: Praçeta 25 de Abril, Edif. dos Tribunais de Segunda Instância e Ultima Instância; tel. 3984107; fax 326744; Pres. SAM HOU FAI.

Procurator-General: HO CHIO MENG.

Religion

The majority of the Chinese residents profess Buddhism, and there are numerous Chinese places of worship, Daoism and Confucianism also being widely practised. The Protestant community numbers about 2,500. There are small Muslim and Hindu communities.

CHRISTIANITY

The Roman Catholic Church

Macao forms a single diocese, directly responsible to the Holy See. At 31 December 2000 there were 29,850 adherents in the territory.

Bishop of Macao: Rt Rev. DOMINGOS LAM KA TSEUNG, Paço Episcopal, Largo da Sé s/n, POB 324; tel. 309954; fax 309861; e-mail mdiocese@macau.ctm.net.

The Anglican Communion

Macao forms part of the Anglican diocese of Hong Kong (q.v.).

The Press

A new Press Law, prescribing journalists' rights and obligations, was enacted in August 1990.

PORTUGUESE LANGUAGE

Boletim Oficial: Rua da Imprensa Nacional, POB 33; tel. 573822; fax 596802; e-mail info@imprensa.macau.gov.mo; internet www.imprensa.macau.gov.mo; f. 1838; weekly govt gazette; Dir Dr ANTÓNIO GOMES MARTINS.

O Clarim: Rua Central 26-A; tel. 573860; fax 307867; e-mail clarim@macau.ctm.net; f. 1948; weekly; Editor ALBINO BENTO PAIS; circ. 1,500.

Hoje Macau: Rua Francisco H. Fernandes 23, Edif. Walorly 13/AF; tel. 752401; fax 752405; e-mail hoje@macau.ctm.net; internet www.macauhoje.ctm.net/; daily; Dir CARLOS MORAIS JOSÉ; circ. 1,000.

Jornal Tribuna de Macau: Av. Almeida Ribeiro 99, Edif. Comercial Nam Wah, 6 andar, Salas 603–05; tel. 378057; fax 337305; internet www.jtm.com.mo; f. 1998 through merger of Jornal de Macau (f. 1982) and Tribuna de Macau (f. 1982); daily; Dir JOSÉ FIRMINO DA ROCHA DINIS; circ. 1,000.

MacaU: Livros do Oriente, Av. Amizade 876, Edif. Marina Gardens, 15E; tel. 700320; fax 700423; e-mail rclilau@macau.ctm.net; internet www.booksmacau.com; f. 1992; monthly magazine.

Ponto Final: Rua de Roma Kin Heng Long, Edif. Heng Hoi Kok, 10/F; tel. 339566; fax 339563; e-mail pontofin@macau.ctm.net; internet www.pontofinal.com.mo; Dir RICARDO PINTO; circ. 1,500.

CHINESE LANGUAGE

Boletim Oficial: see above; Chinese edn.

Cheng Pou: Rua da Praia Grande 57–63, Edif. Hang Cheong, E–F; tel. 965972; fax 965741; daily; Dir KUNG SU KAN; Editor-in-Chief LEONG CHI CHUN; circ. 5,000.

Jornal Informação: Rua de Fran António 22, 1° C, Edif. Mei Fun; tel. 561557; fax 566575; weekly; Dir CHAO CHONG PENG; circ. 8,000.

Jornal San Wa Ou: Av. Venseslau de Morais 221, Edif. Ind. Nam Fong, 2a Fase, 15°, Bloco E; tel. 717569; fax 717572; e-mail correiro@macau.ctm.net; daily; Dir LAM CHONG; circ. 1,500.

Jornal 'Si-Si': Rua de Brás da Rosa 58, 2/F; tel. 974354; weekly; Dir and Editor-in-Chief CHEANG VENG PENG; circ. 3,000.

Jornal Va Kio: Rua da Alfândega 7–9; tel. 345888; fax 580638; f. 1937; daily; Dir CHIANG SAO MENG; Editor-in-Chief TANG CHOU KEI; circ. 21,000.

O Pulso de Macau: Rua Oito do Bairro Iao Hon S/N; Edif. Hong Tai, Apt F0588 R/C; fax 400284; weekly; Dir HO SI VO.

Ou Mun Iat Pou (Macao Daily News): Rua Pedro Nolasco da Silva 37; tel. 371688; fax 331998; f. 1958; daily; Dir LEI SENG CHUN; Editor-in-Chief LEI PANG CHU; circ. 100,000.

Semanário Desportivo de Macau: Estrada D. Maria II, Edif. Kin Chit Garden, 2 G–H; tel. 718259; fax 718285; weekly; sport; Dir FONG SIO LON; Editor-in-Chief FONG NIM LAM; circ. 2,000.

Semenário Recreativo de Macau: Av. Sidónio Pais 31 D, 3/F A; tel. 553216; fax 516792; weekly; Dir. IEONG CHEOK KONG; Editor-in-Chief TONG IOK WA.

Seng Pou (Star): Travessa da Caldeira 9; tel. 938387; fax 388192; f. 1963; daily; Dir KUOK KAM SENG; Deputy Editor-in-Chief TOU MAN KUM; circ. 6,000.

Sin Man Pou (Jornal do Cidadão): Rua dos Pescadores, Edif. Ind. Oceano, Bl. 11, 2/F–B; tel. 722111; fax 722133; f. 1944; daily; Dir and Editor-in-Chief KUNG MAN; circ. 8,000.

Tai Chung Pou: Rua Dr Lourenço; P. Marques 7A, 2/F; tel. 939888; fax 934114; f. 1933; daily; Dir VONG U. KONG; Editor-in-Chief SOU KIM KEONG; circ. 8,000.

Today Macau Journal: Pátio da Barca 20, R/C; tel. 215050; fax 210478; daily; Dir LAM VO I; Editor-in-Chief IU VENG ION; circ. 6,000.

NEWS AGENCIES

Associated Press (AP) (USA): POB 221; tel. 361204; fax 343220; Correspondent ADAM LEE.

China News Service: Av. Gov. Jaime Silveiro Marques, Edif. Zhu Kuan, 14/F, Y/Z; tel. 594585; fax 594585.

LUSA—Agência de Noticias de Portugal: Av. Conselheiro Ferreira de Almeida 95-A; tel. 967601; fax 967605; e-mail lusa2@macau.ctm.net; internet www.lusamacau.com; Dir JOÃO ROQUE.

Reuters (United Kingdom): Rua da Alfândega 69; tel. 345888; fax 930076; Correspondent HARALD BRUNING.

Xinhua (New China) News Agency Macao SAR Bureau: Av. Gov. Jaime Silvério Marques, Edif. Zhu Kuan, 13 andar-V; tel. 727710; fax 700548; Dir CHEN BOLIANG.

PRESS ASSOCIATIONS

Associação dos Jornalistas de Macau (Macao Journalists' Association): Rua Tomás Vieira, 70A R/C; tel. 921395; fax 921315; e-mail macauja@macau.ctm.net; internet home.macau.ctm.net/~macauja; f. 1999; Pres. CHEANG UT MENG.

Associação dos Trabalhadores da Imprensa de Macau: Travessa do Auto Novo 301–303, Edif. Cheng Peng; tel. 375245; Pres. TANG CHOU KEI.

Clube de Jornalistas de Macau: Travessa dos Alfaiates 8–10; tel. 921395; fax 921315; e-mail cjm@macau.ctm.net; Pres. DAVID CHAN CHI WA.

Macao Chinese Media Workers Association: Travessa do Matadouro, Edif. 3, 3B; tel. 939486; Pres. LEE PANG CHU.

Publishers

Associação Beneficência Leitores Jornal Ou Mun: Nova-Guia 339; tel. 711631; fax 711630.

Fundação Macau: Av. República 6; tel. 966777; fax 968658; internet www.fmac.org.mo.

Instituto Cultural de Macau: see under Tourism; publishes literature, social sciences and history.

Livros do Oriente: Av. Amizade 876, Edif. Marina Gardens, 15 E; tel. 700320; fax 700423; e-mail rclilau@macau.ctm.net; internet www.loriente.com; f. 1990; publishes in Portuguese, English and Chinese on regional history, culture, etc.; Gen. Man. ROGÉRIO BELTRÃO COELHO; Exec. Man. CECÍLIA JORGE.

Universidade de Macau—Centro de Publicações: POB 3001; tel. 3974506; fax 831694; e-mail PUB_GRP@umac.mo; internet www.umac.mo.pc; f. 1993; art, economics, education, political science, history, literature, management, social sciences, etc.; Head Dr ZHENG DEHUA.

GOVERNMENT PUBLISHER

Imprensa Oficial: Rua da Imprensa Nacional s/n; tel. 573822; fax 596802; e-mail helpdesk@imprensa.macau.gov.mo.

Broadcasting and Communications

TELECOMMUNICATIONS

Companhia de Telecomunicações de Macau, SARL (CTM): Rua de Lagos, Edif. Telecentro, Taipa; tel. 833833; fax 8913031; e-mail mktg@macau.ctm.net; internet www.ctm.com.mo; holds local telecommunications monopoly; shareholders include Cable and Wireless (51%) and Portugal Telecom (28%); Chair. LINUS CHEUNG; CEO DAVID KAY; 1,000 employees.

Regulatory Authority

Office for the Development of Telecommunications and Information Technology (GDTTI): Av. da Praia Grande 789, 3/F; tel. 3969161; fax 356328; e-mail ifx@gdtti.gov.mo; internet www.gdtti.gov.mo.

BROADCASTING

Radio

Rádio Vila Verde: Macao Jockey Club, Taipa; tel. 822163; private radio station; programmes in Chinese; Man. KOK HOI.

Television

Teledifusão de Macau, SARL (TDM): Rua Francisco Xavier Pereira 157-A, POB 446; tel. 335888 (Radio), 519188 (TV); fax 520208; privately-owned; two radio channels: **Rádio Macau** (Av. Dr Rodrigo Rodrigues, Edif. Nam Kwong, 7/F; fax 343220) in Portuguese, broadcasting 24 hours per day in Portuguese on **TDM Canal 1** (incl. broadcasts from RTP International in Portugal) and 17 hours per day in Chinese on **TDM Channel 2**; Chair. STANLEY HO; Exec. Vice-Chair. Dr MANUEL GONÇALVES.

Macao Satellite Television: Rua de Madrid S/N, Edif. Zhu Kuan, R/C, 'P'; tel. 786540; fax 752134; commenced transmissions in 2000; domestic and international broadcasts in Chinese aimed at Chinese-speaking audiences worldwide.

Macao is within transmission range of the Hong Kong television stations.

Cosmos Televisão por Satélite, SARL: Av. Infante D. Henrique 29, Edif. Va Iong, 4/F A; tel. 785731; fax 788234; commenced trial satellite transmissions in 1999, initially for three hours per day; by the year 2003 the company planned to provide up to six channels; Chair. NG FOK.

Finance

(cap. = capital; res = reserves; dep. = deposits; m. = million; brs = branches; amounts in patacas unless otherwise indicated)

BANKING

Macao has no foreign-exchange controls, its external payments system being fully liberalized on current and capital transactions. The Financial System Act, aiming to improve the reputation of the territory's banks and to comply with international standards, took effect in September 1993.

Issuing Authority

Autoridade Monetária de Macau—AMCM (Monetary Authority of Macao): Calçada do Gaio 24–26, POB 3017; tel. 568288; fax 325432; e-mail amcm@macau.ctm.net; internet www.amcm.macau.gov.mo; f. 1989 as Autoridade Monetária e Cambial de Macau (AMCM), to replace the Instituto Emissor de Macau; govt-owned; Pres. ANSELMO L. S. TENG.

Banks of Issue

Banco Nacional Ultramarino (BNU), SA: Av. Almeida Ribeiro 22, POB 465; tel. 355111; fax 355653; e-mail markt@bnu.com.mo; internet www.bnu.com.mo; f. 1864, est. in Macao 1902; Head Office in Lisbon; agent of Macao Government; Gen. Man. Dr HERCULANO J. SOUSA; 10 brs.

Bank of China: Bank of China Bldg, Av. Dr Mário Soares; tel. 781828; fax 781833; e-mail bocmacau@macau.ctm.net; f. 1950 as Nan Tung Bank, name changed 1987; authorized to issue banknotes from Oct. 1995; Gen. Man. ZHANG HONGYI; 24 brs.

Other Commercial Banks

Banco da América (Macau), SARL: Av. Almeida Ribeiro 70–76, POB 165; tel. 568821; fax 570386; f. 1937; fmrly Security Pacific Asian Bank (Banco de Cantão); cap. 100m., res 44.4m., dep. 1,123.0m. (Dec. 2000); Chair. SAMUEL NG TSIEN; Man. Dir KIN HONG CHEONG.

Banco Comercial de Macau, SA: Av. da Praia Grande 572, POB 545; tel. 7910000; fax 595817; e-mail bcmbank@bcm.com.mo; f. 1995; cap. 225m., res 316m., dep. 6,082m. (Dec. 2001); Chair. JORGE JARDIM GONÇALVES; CEO Dr MANUEL MARECOS DUARTE; 17 brs.

Banco Delta Asia, SARL: Av. Conselheiro Ferreira de Almeida 79; tel. 559898; fax 570068; e-mail contact@bdam.com; internet www.delta-asia.com; f. 1935; fmrly Banco Hang Sang; cap. 190.0m., res 50.6m., dep. 3,012.3m. (Dec. 2001); Chair. STANLEY AU; Exec. Dir PHILIP NG; 10 brs.

Banco Seng Heng, SARL: Seng Heng Bank Tower, Macao Landmark, Av. da Amizade; tel. 555222; fax 570758; e-mail sengheng@macau.ctm.net; internet www.senghengbank.com; f. 1972; cap. 150.0m., res 631.5m., dep. 10,726m. (Dec. 2000); Gen. Man. ALEX LI; 7 brs.

Banco Tai Fung, SARL: Tai Fung Bank Bldg, Av. Alameda Dr Carlos d'Assumpção 418; tel. 322323; fax 570737; e-mail tfbsecr@taifungbank.com; internet www.taifungbank.com; f. 1971; cap. 1,000m., dep. 18,950m. (Dec. 2001); Chair. FUNG KA YORK; Gen. Man. LONG RONGSHEN; 20 brs.

Banco Weng Hang, SA: Av. Almeida Ribeiro 241; tel. 335678; fax 576527; e-mail wenghang@macau.ctm.net; internet www.whbmac.com; f. 1973; subsidiary of Wing Hang Bank Ltd, Hong Kong; cap. 120m., res 490m., dep. 7,325m. (Dec. 2000); Chair. PATRICK FUNG YUK-BUN; Gen. Man. and Dir LEE TAK LIM; 10 brs.

Guangdong Development Bank: Av. da Praia Grande 269; tel. 323628; fax 323668; Gen. Man. GUO ZHI-HANG.

Luso International Banking Ltd: Av. Dr Mário Soares 47; tel. 378977; fax 578517; e-mail lusobank@lusobank.com.mo; internet www.lusobank.com.mo; f. 1974; cap. 151.5m., res 184m., dep. 6,245.8m. (Dec. 2000); Chair. WONG XI CHAO; Gen. Man. IP KAI MING; 10 brs.

Foreign Banks

Banco Comercial Português (Portugal): Av. da Praia Grande 594, BCM Bldg, 12/F; tel. 786769; fax 786772; Gen. Man. MANUEL D'ALMEIDA MARECO DUARTE.

Banco Espírito Santo do Oriente (Portugal): Av. Dr Mário Soares 323, Bank of China Bldg, 28/F, E–F; tel. 785222; fax 785228; e-mail besor@macau.ctm.net; f. 1996; subsidiary of Banco Espírito Santo, SA (Portugal); Exec. Dir JOÃO MANUEL AMBRÓSIO; Man. Dir Dr LUÍS MORAIS SARMENTO.

Bank of East Asia Ltd (Hong Kong): Av. da Praia Grande 697, Edif. Tai Wah R/C; tel. 335511; fax 337557; Gen. Man. LAI TZE HIM.

BNP Paribas (France): Av. Central Plaza, 10/F, Almeida Ribeiro 61; tel. 562777; fax 560626; f. 1979; Man. SANCO SZE.

Citibank NA (USA): Rua da Praia Grande 251–53; tel. 378188; fax 578451; Pres. DANIEL CHOW SHIU LUN.

Finibanco (Macau) SA (Portugal): Av. Sa Praia Grande 811; tel. 322678; fax 322680.

The Hongkong and Shanghai Banking Corporation Ltd (Hong Kong): Av. da Praia Grande 613–19; tel. 553669; fax 315421; e-mail hsbc@macau.ctm.net; f. 1972; CEO THOMAS YAM.

International Bank of Taipei (Taiwan): Av. Infante D. Henrique 52–58; tel. 715175; fax 715035; e-mail tppmonx@macau.ctm.net; f. 1996; fmrly Taipei Business Bank; Gen. Man. KEVIN CHIOU.

Liu Chong Hing Bank Ltd (Hong Kong): Av. da Praia Grande 693, Edif. Tai Wah, R/C; tel. 339982; fax 339990; Gen. Man. LAM MAN KING.

Overseas Trust Bank Limited (Hong Kong): Rua de Santa Clara 5–7E, Edif. Ribeiro, Loja C e D; tel. 329338; fax 323711; e-mail otbmacau@macau.ctm.net; Senior Man. LAU CHI KEUNG.

Standard Chartered Bank (UK): 8/F Office Tower, Macao Landmark, Av. de Amizade tel. 786111; fax 786222; f. 1982; Man. ABRAHAM WONG.

Banking Association

Associação de Bancos de Macau—ABM (The Macao Association of Banks): Av. da Praia Grande 575, Edif. 'Finanças', 15/F; tel. 511921; fax 346049; Chair. ZHANG HONGYI.

INSURANCE

ACE Seguradora, SA: Rua Dr. Pedro José Lobo 1–3, Luso Bank Bldg, 17/F, Apt 1701–02; tel. 557191; 570188; Rep. ANDY AU.

AIA Co (Bermuda) Ltd: Central Plaza, 13/F, Av. Almeida Ribeiro 61; tel. 9881888; fax 315900; Rep. ALEXANDRA FOO.

American Home Assurance Co: Av. Almeida Ribeiro 61, Central Plaza, 15/F, 'G'.

American International Assurance Co: Av. Almeida Ribeiro 61, Central Plaza, 13/F; tel. 9881888; fax 315900; life insurance; Rep. ALEXANDRA FOO CHEUK LING.

Asia Insurance Co Ltd: Rua do Dr Pedro José Lobo 1–3, Luso International Bank Bldg, 11/F, Units 1103–04; tel. 570439; fax 570438; non-life insurance; Rep. S. T. CHAN.

AXA China Region Insurance Company: Rua de Xangai 175, Edif. da Associação Comercial de Macau, 17/F; tel. 781188; fax 780022; life insurance; Rep. KANE CHOW.

CGU International Insurance plc: Av. da Praia Grande 693, Edif. Tai Wah A & B, 13/F; non-life insurance; tel. 923329; fax 923349; Man. VICTOR WU.

China Insurance Co Ltd: Av. Dr. Rodrigo Rodgrigues, Edif. Seguros da China, 19/F; non-life insurance.

China Life Insurance Co Ltd: Av. Dr Rodrigo Rodrigues Quarteirão 11, Lote A, Zape, China Insurance Bldg, 15/F; tel. 558918; fax 787287; e-mail cic@macau.ctm.net; Rep. CHENG MINGJIN.

Companhia de Seguros Fidelidade: Av. Almeida Ribeiro 22–38 (BNU); tel. 374072; fax 511085; life and non-life insurance; Man. LEONEL ALBERTO RANGE RODRIGUES.

Companhia de Seguros de Macau, SARL: Av. da Praia Grande 57, Centro Comercial Praia Grande, 18/F; tel. 555078; fax 551074; Gen. Man. IVAN CHEUNG.

Companhia de Seguros Delta SA: Av. da Praia Grande 369–71, Edif. Keng Ou, 13/F, D; tel. 337036; fax 337037; Rep. JOHNNY CHENG.

Crown Life Insurance Co: Av. da Praia Grande 287, Nam Yuet Commercial Centre, Bl. B, 8/F; tel. 570828; fax 570844; Rep. STEVEN SIU.

HSBC Insurance (Asia) Ltd: Av. Horta e Costa 122–124, 4/F, Rm A; tel. 212323; fax 217162; non-life insurance; Rep. JOHNNY HO MOON FAI.

Ing Life Insurance Co (Macao) Ltd: Av. Almeida Ribeiro 61, 11/F, Unit C and D; tel. 9886060; fax 9886100; Man. STEVEN CHIK YIU KAI.

Insurance Co of North America: Av. Almeida Ribeiro 32, Tai Fung Bank Bldg, Rm 806–7; tel. 557191; fax 570188; Rep. JOSEPH LO.

Luen Fung Hang Insurance Co Ltd: Rua de Pequim 202A–246, Macao Finance Centre, 6/F–A; tel. 700033; fax 700088; e-mail lfhins@macau.ctm.net; internet www.lfhins.com; non-life insurance; Rep. SI CHI HOK.

Macao Insurance Co: Av. da Praia Grande 429, Centro Comercial da Praia Grande, 18/F; non-life insurance.

Macao Life Insurance Co: Av. da Praia Grande 429, Centro Comercial da Praia Grande, 18/F; tel. 555078; fax 551074; Rep. MANUEL BALCÃO REIS.

Manulife (International) Ltd: Av. da Praia Grande 517, Edif. Comercial Nam Tung, 8/F, Unit B & C; tel. 3980388; fax 323312; internet www.manulife.com.hk; Rep. DANIEL TANG.

MassMutual Asia Ltd: Av. da Praia Grande 517, Edif. Nam Tung 16, 6/F; life insurance.

Min Xin Insurance Co Ltd: Rua do Dr Pedro José Lobo 1–3, Luso International Bank Bldg, 27/F, Rm 2704; non-life insurance; tel. 305684; fax 305600; Rep. PETER CHAN.

Mitsui Sumitomo Insurance Co Ltd: Rua Dr Pedro José Lobo 1–3, Edif. Banco Luso, 12/F, Apartment 1202; tel. 385917; fax 596667; non-life insurance; Rep. CARMEN PANG.

QBE Insurance (International) Ltd: Av. da Praia Grande 369–71, Edif. Keng On 'B', 9/F; tel. 323909; fax 323911; non-life insurance; Rep. SALLY SIU.

The Wing On Fire & Marine Insurance Co Ltd: Av. Almeida Ribeiro 61, Central Plaza, 7/F, Block E; tel. 356688; fax 333710; non-life insurance; Rep. CHIANG AO LAI LAI.

Winterthur Swiss Insurance (Macao) Ltd: Av. da Praia Grande 599, Edif. Comercial Rodrigues, 10/F, C; tel. 356618; fax 356800; non-life insurance; Man. ALLAN YU KIN NAM.

Insurers' Association

Federation of Macao Professional Insurance Intermediaries: Rua de Pequim 244–46, Macao Finance Centre, 6/F, G; tel. 703268; fax 703266; Rep. DAVID KONG.

Macao Insurance Agents and Brokers Association: Av. da Praia Grande 309, Nam Yuet Commercial Centre, 8/F, D; tel. 378901; fax 570848; Rep. JACK LI KWOK TAI.

Macao Insurers' Association: Av. da Praia Grande 575, Edif. 'Finanças', 15/F; tel. 511923; fax 337531; e-mail minsa@macau.ctm.net; Pres. VICTOR WU.

Trade and Industry

CHAMBER OF COMMERCE

Associação Comercial de Macau: Rua de Xangai 175, Edif. ACM, 5/F; tel. 576833; fax 594513; Pres. MA MAN KEI.

INDUSTRIAL AND TRADE ASSOCIATIONS

Associação dos Construtores Civis (Association of Building Development Cos): Rua do Campo 9–11; tel. 323854; fax 345710; Pres. CHUI TAK KEI.

Associação dos Exportadores e Importadores de Macau: Av. Infante D. Henrique 60–62, Centro Comercial 'Central', 3/F; tel. 375859; fax 512174; e-mail aeim@macau.ctm.net; exporters' and importers' asscn; Pres. VÍTOR NG.

Associação dos Industriais de Tecelagem e Fiação de Lã de Macau (Macao Weaving and Spinning of Wool Manufacturers' Asscn): Av. da Amizade 271, Edif. Kam Wa Kok, 6/F–A; tel. 553378; fax 511105; Pres. WONG SHOO KEE.

Associação Industrial de Macau: Rua Dr Pedro José Lobo 34–36, Edif. AIM, 17/F, POB 70; tel. 574125; fax 578305; e-mail aim@macau.ctm.net; internet www.madeinmacau.net; f. 1959; Pres. PETER PAN.

Centro de Produtividade e Transferência de Tecnologia de Macau (Macao Productivity and Technology Transfer Centre): Rua de Xangai 175, Edif. ACM, 6/F; tel. 781313; fax 788233; e-mail cpttm@cpttm.org.mo; internet www.cpttm.org.mo; vocational or professional training; Dir Dr ERIC YEUNG.

Euro-Info Centre Macao: Av. Sidónio Pais 1-A, Edif. Tung Hei Kok, R/C; tel. 713338; fax 713339; e-mail eic@macau.ctm.net; internet www.ieem.org.mo/eic/eicmacau.html; promotes trade with EU; Man. SAM LEI.

Instituto de Promoção do Comércio e do Investimento de Macau—IPIM (Macao Trade and Investment Promotion Institute): Av. da Amizade 918, World Trade Center Bldg, 3/F–4/F; tel. 710300; fax 590309; e-mail ipim@ipim.gov.mo; internet www.ipim.gov.mo; Pres. LEE PENG HONG.

SPIC—Concordia Industrial Park Ltd: Av. da Amizade 918, World Trade Center Bldg, 13/F A & B; tel. 786636; fax 785374; e-mail spic@macau.ctm.net; internet www.concordia-park.com; f. 1993; industrial park, promotion of investment and industrial diversification; Pres. of the Bd PAULINA Y. ALVES DOS SANTOS.

World Trade Center Macao, SARL: Av. da Amizade 918, Edif. World Trade Center, 16/F–19/F; tel. 727666; fax 727633; e-mail wtcmc@macau.ctm.net; internet www.wtc-macau.com; f. 1995; trade information and business services, office rentals, exhibition and conference facilities; Man. Dir Dr ANTÓNIO LEÇA DA VEIGA PAZ.

UTILITIES

Electricity

Companhia de Electricidade de Macau, SARL—CEM: Estrada D. Maria II 32–36, Edif. CEM; tel. 339933; fax 719760; f. 1972; sole distributor; Pres. Eng. CUSTÓDIO MIGUENS.

Water

Sociedade de Abastecimento de Aguas de Macau, SARL—SAAM: Av. do Conselheiro Borja 718; tel. 233332; fax 234660; e-mail info@saam.com.mo; internet www.saam.com.mo; f. 1984 as jt venture with Suez Lyonnaise des Eaux; Dir-Gen. JIM CONLON.

TRADE UNIONS

Macao Federation of Trade Unions: Rua Ribeira do Patane 2; tel. 576231; fax 553110; Pres. TONG SENG CHUN.

Transport

RAILWAYS

There are no railways in Macao. A plan to connect Macao with Zhuhai and Guangzhou (People's Republic of China) is under consideration. Construction of the Zhuhai–Guangzhou section was under way in 2001.

ROADS

In 2000 the public road network extended to 324.2 km. The peninsula of Macao is linked to the islands of Taipa and Coloane by two bridges and by a 2.2-km causeway respectively. The first bridge (2.6 km) opened in 1974. In conjunction with the construction of an airport on Taipa (see below), a new 4.4-km four-lane bridge to the mainland was opened in April 1994. A second connection to the mainland, the 1.5-km six-lane road bridge (the Lotus Bridge) linking Macao with Hengqin Island (in Zhuhai, Guangdong Province), opened to traffic in December 1999. A new 29-km steel bridge linking Macao with Hong Kong's Lantau Island and Zhuhai City, Guangdong Province, was being planned in 2001, with studies being carried out to determine the project's financial and technological feasibility.

SHIPPING

There are representatives of shipping agencies for international lines in Macao. There are passenger and cargo services to the People's Republic of China. Regular services between Macao and Hong Kong are run by the Hong Kong-based **New World First Ferry** and **Shun Tak-China Travel Ship Management Ltd** companies. The principal services carried 7.4m. passengers in 1997. A new terminal opened in late 1993. The new port of Kao-ho (on the island of Coloane), which handles cargo and operates container services, entered into service in 1991.

CTS Parkview Holdings Ltd: Av. Amizade, Porto Exterior, Terminal Marítimo de Macau, Sala 2006B; tel. 726789; fax 727112; purchased by STDM in 1998.

STDM Shipping Dept: Av. da Amizade Terminal Marítimo do Porto Exterior; tel. 726111; fax 726234; affiliated to Sociedade de Turismo e Diversões de Macau; Gen. Man. ALAN HO; Exec. Man. Capt. AUGUSTO LIZARDO.

Association

Associação de Agências de Navegação e Congêneres de Macau: Av. Horta e Costa 7D–E, POB 6133; tel. 528207; fax 302667; Pres. VONG KOK SENG.

Port Authority

Capitania dos Portos de Macau: Rampa da Barra, Quartel dos Mouros, POB 47; tel. 559922; fax 511986; e-mail webmaster@marine.gov.mo; internet www.marine.gov.mo.

CIVIL AVIATION

In August 1987 plans were approved for the construction of an international airport, on reclaimed land near the island of Taipa, and work began in 1989. The final cost of the project was 8,900m. patacas. Macao International Airport was officially opened in December 1995. In 2001 the airport handled a total of 3,805,306 passengers. The terminal has the capacity to handle 6m. passengers a year. Between January and December 2001 76,076 tons of cargo were processed. By 2001 a total of 11 airlines operated 507 scheduled flights weekly to 22 destinations, mostly in China, but also to the Democratic People's Republic of Korea, the Philippines, Singapore, Taiwan, and Thailand. A helicopter service between Hong Kong and Macao commenced in 1990: East Asia Airlines transported a total of 72,579 helicopter passengers in 1999.

AACM—Civil Aviation Authority Macao: Rua Dr Pedro José Lobo 1–3, Luso International Bldg, 26/F; tel. 511213; fax 338089; e-mail aacm@macau.ctm.net; internet www.macau-airport.gov.mo; f. 1991; Pres. RUI ALFREDO BALACÓ MOREIRA.

Administração de Aeroportos, Lda—ADA: Av. de João IV, Centro Comercial Iat Teng Hou, 5/F; tel. 711808; fax 711803; e-mail adamkt@macau.ctm.net; internet www.ada.com.mo; airport administration; Chair. DUNG JUN; Dir CARLOS SERUCA SALGADO.

CAM—Sociedade do Aeroporto Internacional de Macau, SARL: Av. Dr Mário Soares, Bank of China Bldg, 29/F; tel. 785448; fax 785465; e-mail cam@macau.ctm.net; internet www.macau-airport.gov.mo; f. 1989; airport owner, responsible for design, construction, development and international marketing of Macao International Airport; Chair. Eng. JOÃO MANUEL DE SOUZA MOREIRA.

Air Macau: Av. da Praia Grande 693, Edif. Tai Wah, 9/F–12/F, POB 1910; tel. 3966888; fax 3966866; e-mail airmacau@airmacau.com.mo; internet www.airmacau.com.mo; f. 1994; controlled by China National Aviation Corporation (Group) Macao Co Ltd; services to several cities in the People's Republic of China, the Republic of Korea, the Philippines, Taiwan and Thailand; other destinations planned; Chair. GU TIEFEI; Pres. SUN BO.

Tourism

Tourism is now a major industry, a substantial portion of the Government's revenue being derived from the territory's casinos. The other attractions are the cultural heritage and museums, dog-racing, horse-racing, and annual events such as Chinese New Year (January/February), the Macao Arts Festival (February/March), Dragon Boat Festival (May/June), the Macao International Fireworks Festival (September/October), the International Music Festival, (October) the Macao Grand Prix for racing cars and motorcycles (November) and the Macao International Marathon (December). At the end of 2001 there were 25 hotels of two-stars and above. A total of 9,030 hotel rooms were available in 2001. Average per caput visitor spending in that year was 1,389 patacas. Total visitor arrivals rose from 9.2m. in 2000 to 10.3m. in 2001. Of the latter figure, almost 5.2m. were arrivals from Hong Kong and 3.0m. from the People's Republic of China.

Macao Government Tourist Office (MGTO): Direcção dos Serviços de Turismo, Largo do Senado 9, Edif. Ritz, POB 3006; tel. 315566; fax 510104; e-mail mgto@macautourism.gov.mo; internet www.macautourism.gov.mo; Dir Eng. JOÃO MANUEL COSTA ANTUNES.

Instituto Cultural de Macau: Praçeta de Miramar 87U, Edif. San On; tel. 700391; fax 700405; e-mail postoffice@icm.gov.mo; internet www.icm.gov.mo; f. 1982; organizes performances, concerts, exhibitions, festivals, etc.; library facilities; Pres. HEIDI HO.

Macao Hotels Association: Rua Luís Gonzaga Gomes s/n, Bl. IV, r/c, Centro de Actividades Turísticas, Cabinet A; tel. 703416; fax 703415.

Sociedade de Turismo e Diversões de Macau (STDM), SARL: Hotel Lisboa, 9F, Old Wing, POB 3036; tel. 566065; fax 371981; e-mail stdmmdof@macau.ctm.net; operates 10 casinos, five hotels, tour companies, helicopter and jetfoil services from Hong Kong, etc.; Man. Dir Dr STANLEY HO.

Defence

The 1998 budget allocated 1,200m. patacas to Macao's security. Upon the territory's reversion to Chinese sovereignty in December 1999, troops of the People's Liberation Army (PLA) were stationed in Macao. The force comprises around 1,000 troops: a maximum of 500 soldiers are stationed in Macao, the remainder being positioned in Zhuhai, China, on the border with the SAR. The unit is directly responsible to the Commander of the Guangzhou Military Region and to the Central Military Commission. The Macao garrison is composed mainly of ground troops. Naval and air defence tasks are performed by the naval vessel unit of the PLA garrison in Hong Kong and by the air force unit in Huizhou. Subject to the request of the Macao SAR, the garrison may participate in law-enforcement and rescue operations in the SAR.

Commander of the PLA Garrison in Macao: Senior Colonel LIU LIANHUA.

Education

The rate of literacy among the population aged 15 and over in Macao was 91.3% in 2001, illiteracy being confined mainly to elderly women. The education system in Macao is structured as follows: pre-school education (lasting two years); primary preparatory year (one year); primary education (six years); secondary education (five–six years, divided into junior secondary of three years and senior secondary of two–three years). Schooling normally lasts from the ages of three to 17. In 2001/02 schools enrolled a total of 99,990 pupils: kindergarten 13,620; primary 43,886; secondary 41,840 (including technical and vocational students); and special education 2,461. From 1995/96 free education was extended from government schools to private schools. Private schools provide education for more than 90% of children. Of these schools 77% have joined the free education system, and together with the government schools they form the public school system, in which all pupils from primary preparatory year up to the junior secondary level (10 years) receive free tuition. Based on the four years of free education, compulsory education was implemented from 1999/2000. In 2001/02 the enrolment rate was as follows: pre-school education and primary preparatory year 86.9% (some families leave their children in China); primary education 104.2%; secondary education (including vocational and technical) 82.0%; and higher education 24.0%. Government expenditure on education and training in 2001 was 565m. patacas.

In higher learning, there are 12 public and private universities, polytechnic institutes and research centres, namely: the University of Macao, Macao Polytechnic Institute, Institute for Tourism Studies, Macao Security Forces Academy, Inter-University Institute of Macao, Asia International Open University (Macao), Institute of European Studies of Macao, Kiang Wu Nursing College of Macao, United Nations University/International Institute for Software Technology, Macao University of Science and Technology, Macao Institute of Management, and Macao Millennium College. Some 12,749 students attended courses offered by those institutions in the academic year 2000/01, ranging from the bacharelato (three-year courses) to doctorate programmes.

Bibliography

Berlie, J. A. (Ed.). *Macao 2000.* Oxford, Oxford University Press, 2000.

Boxer, C. R. *The Portuguese Seaborne Empire.* London, Hutchinson and Co, 1969.

Braga, J. M. *O primeiro acordo Luso-Chinês.* Macau, 1939.

The Western Pioneers and their Discovery of Macau. Macau, 1949.

Brookshaw, D. *Visions of China: Stories from Macau.* Hong Kong, Hong Kong University Press, 2002.

Do Carmo, Maria Helena. *Os Interesses dos Portugueses em Macau, na Primeira Metade do Século XVIII.* Macau, University of Macau Publications Centre, 1999.

Chan, S. S. *The Macau Economy.* Macau, University of Macau Publications Centre, 2000.

Cheng, Christina Miu Bing. *Macau: A Cultural Janus.* Hong Kong, Hong Kong University Press, 1999.

Coates, Austin. *A Macao Narrative.* Hong Kong, Oxford University Press, 1998.

Macao and the British, 1637–1842: Prelude to Hong Kong. Hong Kong, Oxford University Press, 1989.

Gomes, L. G. *Bibliografia Macaense.* Macau, Imprensa Nacional, 1973.

Guillén Núñez, César, and Leong Kai Tai. *Macao Streets.* Hong Kong, Oxford University Press, 1999.

Gunn, Geoffrey C. *Encountering Macau: A Portuguese City-state on the Periphery of China, 1557–1999.* Boulder, CO, Westview Press, 1996.

Ieong Wan Chong and Ricardo Chi Sen Siu. *Macau: A Model of Mini-Economy.* Macau, University of Macau Publications Centre, 1997.

Jesus, C. A. Montalto de. *Historic Macau.* Macau, Salesean Printing Press, 1926.

Leong Ka Tai, and Davies, S. *Macau.* Singapore, Times Editions, 1986.

Ljungstedt, A. *An Historical Sketch of the Portuguese Settlements in China.* Boston, 1936.

Lui Kwok Man. *Macau in Transition.* Macau, University of Macau Publications Centre, 2000.

Macau Research Group. *A Strategic Assessment of Macau, 2000 Edition.* Icon Group International, 2000.

McGivering, Jill. *Macao Remembers.* Hong Kong, Oxford University Press, 1999.

Mo, Timothy. *An Insular Possession.* London, Chatto and Windus, 1998.

Pons, Philippe. *Macao.* Paris, Le Promeneur, 2000.

Porter, Jonathan. *Macau: The Imaginary City.* Boulder, CO, Westview Press, 2000.

Ramos, Rufino et al. (Eds). *Population and Development in Macau.* Macau, University of Macau Publications Centre, 1994.

Macau and its Neighbors in Transition. Macau, University of Macau Publications Centre, 1997.

Macau and its Neighbors Towards the 21st Century. Macau, University of Macau Publications Centre, 1998.

Shipp, Steve. *Macau, China: A Political History of the Portuguese Colony's Transition to Chinese Rule.* Jefferson, NC, McFarland & Co, 1997.

Da Silva Diaz de Seabra, Isabel Leonor. *Relações Entre Macau e O Sião (Séculos XVIII–XIX).* Macau, University of Macau Publications Centre, 1999.

Sit, Victor F. S., et al. *Entrepreneurs and Enterprises in Macao: A Study in Industrial Development.* Hong Kong, Hong Kong University Press, 1991.

USA International Business Publications. *Macau Country Study Guide.* International Business Publications, 2000.

Macao Government and Policy Guide. International Business Publications, 2000.

Wesley-Smith, P. 'Macao' in Albert P. Blaustein (Ed.), *Constitutions of Dependencies and Special Sovereignties, Vol. III.* New York, Oceana Press, 1977.

Wong Hon Keung. *Economic Interaction Between Guangxi and Macau.* Macau, University of Macau Publications Centre, 1998.

Yee, Herbert S. *Macau in Transition: From Colony to Autonomous Region.* New York, St. Martin's Press, 2001.

CHINA (TAIWAN)

Physical and Social Geography

The Republic of China has, since 1949, been confined mainly to the province of Taiwan (comprising one large island and several much smaller ones), which lies off the south-east coast of the Chinese mainland. The territory under the Republic's effective jurisdiction consists of the island of Taiwan (also known as Formosa) and nearby islands, including the P'enghu (Pescadores) group, together with a few other islands which lie just off the mainland and form part of the province of Fujian (Fukien), west of Taiwan. The largest of these is Kinmen (Jinmen), also known as Quemoy, which (with three smaller islands) is about 10 km from the port of Xiamen (Amoy), while five other islands under Taiwan's control, mainly Matsu (Mazu), lie further north, near Fuzhou. The island of Taiwan itself is separated from the mainland by the Taiwan Strait, which is about 220 km wide at its broadest point and 130 km at the narrowest point. Taiwan is 36,006 sq km in area, measuring 394 km from north to south and, at its widest point, 144 km from east to west. The island straddles the Tropic of Cancer. The Central Range of mountains occupies almost 50% of the island, extending 270 km from north to south. At 3,952 m, Mount Jade is the island's highest point. Owing to the mountainous character of the relief, in 1998 less than 24% of the land area was cultivated, while forests covered more than 58%. The climate is subtropical in the north and tropical in the south, being strongly modified by oceanic and relief factors. Apart from the mountainous core, winter temperatures average 15°C and summer temperatures about 26°C. Monsoon rains visit the north-east in winter (October to March) but come to the south in summer, and are abundant, the mean annual average rainfall being 2,580 mm. Typhoons are often serious, particularly between July and September, when windward mountain slopes may receive as much as 300 mm of rain within 24 hours.

The population was 22,405,568 at 31 December 2001, giving Taiwan a population density of 619.1 per sq km, one of the highest in the world. In 1964 the rate of natural increase fell below 3.0% for the first time, declining steadily thereafter to stand at 0.59% in 2001. The crude birth rate in 2001 was 11.7 per 1,000 (compared with 44.8 per 1,000 in 1956), and the crude death rate in 2001 was 5.7 per 1,000 (compared with 8.0 per 1,000 in 1956). The death rate is one of the lowest in Asia, as is the infant mortality rate (deaths under one year of age per 1,000 live births), which was estimated at 5.9 in 2000. In 2001, 20.8% of Taiwan's population were estimated to be under 15 years of age; 70.4% were aged between 15 and 64; and 8.8% of the population were 65 and over (compared with 2.5% in 1962). With the expansion of industry, Taiwan's population has become increasingly urbanized. Between 1966 and 2000 the proportion living in towns of 100,000 or more inhabitants increased from 31.0% to 60.0%.

History

HISTORICAL BACKGROUND

The geographic location of the island of Taiwan has determined its history. Situated between the Malay archipelago, China and Japan, the island has had an eventful past. The original inhabitants were tribes of Malayan origin. China's relations with the island date from AD 607, but the first small Chinese settlements were not established there until the 14th century. During the 17th century Portuguese, Spanish and Dutch traders visited the island from time to time. In 1624 the Dutch settled the southern part. Two years later came the Spanish, who occupied the northern part. In 1642 the Dutch expelled the Spanish, and in 1661 the Dutch were, in turn, driven out by the Chinese Ming loyalist Zheng Zheng Gong (Coxinga) who ruled, with his sons, for 22 years. In 1663 the Qing emperor, Kang Xi, invaded and conquered the island, which became a part of his empire until it was ceded to the Japanese at the end of the Sino-Japanese war of 1895. During the period of independence and Qing rule, massive immigration from the mainland established the ethnic Chinese character of the island.

Following Japan's defeat in the Second World War, Taiwan became one of the provinces of the Republic of China, ruled by the Kuomintang (KMT, Nationalist Party). The leader of the KMT was Gen. Chiang Kai-shek, President of the Republic since 1928. Virtually all of Taiwan's exportable surpluses went to the Chinese mainland. In 1947 misgovernment by mainland officials led to a large-scale, but peaceful, political uprising, which was repressed with great brutality. In early 1949 the KMT regime, driven from the mainland by the Communists, moved to Taiwan's capital, Taipei, along with approximately 2m. soldiers, officials and their dependants. Thus, the island's population increased from 6.8m. to 7.5m. in 1950, excluding military personnel numbering 600,000. The KMT regime continued to assert that it was the rightful Chinese Government, in opposition to the People's Republic of China (proclaimed by the victorious Communists in 1949), and declared its intention to recover control of the mainland from the Communists. (For further details of events prior to 1949, see the chapter on the People's Republic of China.)

THE ESTABLISHMENT OF CHINESE NATIONALIST RULE AND SUBSEQUENT FOREIGN RELATIONS

Although its effective control was limited to Taiwan, the KMT regime continued to be dominated by politicians who had formerly been in power on the mainland. In support of the regime's claim to be the legitimate government of all China, Taiwan's legislative bodies were filled mainly by surviving mainland members, and the representatives of the island's native Taiwanese majority occupied only a minority of seats. Unable to replenish their mainland representation, the National Assembly (last elected fully in 1947) and other organs extended their terms of office indefinitely, although fewer than one-half of the original members were alive on Taiwan by the 1980s. While it promised eventually to reconquer the mainland, the KMT regime was largely preoccupied with ensuring its own survival, and promoting economic development, on Taiwan. Under the KMT Government, Taiwan achieved a remarkable record of economic growth, although the island's regeneration in the period after 1949 was assisted by massive US aid. The years 1951 and 1952 were notable for government reorganization. There followed a four-year (1953–56) period of adjustment and planning. In 1957 and 1958 the cumulative effect of domestic reform and US aid brought a great improvement in economic and other fields. The prominent developments of this period include the land reform programme, the rapid development of industry and the establishment of a system of nine-year free public education. The political domination of the island by immigrants from the mainland caused resentment among Taiwanese, and led to demands for increased democratization and for the recognition of Taiwan as a state independent of China. The KMT, however, consistently rejected demands for independence, constantly restating the party's long-standing policy of seeking political reunification, under KMT terms, with the mainland.

The KMT Government continued to represent China at the UN (and as a permanent member of the UN Security Council) until October 1971, when the People's Republic of China was admitted in place of Taiwan. Nationalist China was subsequently expelled from several other international organizations. In November 1991, however, as 'Chinese Taipei', Taiwan joined the Asia-Pacific Economic Co-operation forum (APEC). In September 1992, under the name of the 'Separate Customs Territory of Taiwan, P'enghu, Kinmen and Matsu', Taiwan was granted observer status at the General Agreement on Tariffs and Trade (GATT), and in 2000 discussions on its application for full membership of the successor World Trade Organization (WTO) continued. Taiwan was finally approved for membership of the body in late September 2001, after 11 years of bidding. In June 1995 Taiwan offered to make a donation of US $1,000m., to be used for the establishment of an international development fund, if the island were permitted to rejoin the UN. In September 2002, for the 10th consecutive year, the General Committee of the UN General Assembly rejected a proposal urging Taiwan's participation in the UN. However, Taiwan's leaders pledged to continue the island's campaign to gain re-entry. In April 1997 the Minister of Foreign Affairs announced that Taiwan had applied to be an observer of the World Health Organization (WHO) and would be seeking similar status in other UN agencies. Its application was unsuccessful, however, as was a second attempt to gain observer status in May 1998 and subsequent annual attempts, most recently in May 2002.

After 1971 a number of countries broke off diplomatic relations with Taiwan and recognized the People's Republic. The British Government established full diplomatic relations with Beijing in March 1972. When Tokyo sought a *rapprochement* with Beijing in September 1972, Taiwan broke off diplomatic relations with Japan. In August 1992 the Republic of Korea accorded recognition to the People's Republic of China, but unofficial links were to be maintained. In late 2002 the Government of Taiwan maintained formal diplomatic relations with some 27 countries. Taiwan's commercial relations with numerous countries continued to flourish.

In 1954 the USA, which refused to recognize the People's Republic of China, signed a mutual security treaty with the KMT Government, pledging to protect Taiwan and the Pescadores. In 1955 the islands of Kinmen (Quemoy) and Matsu, lying just off shore from the mainland, were included in the protected area. However, US documents declassified in 2002 revealed that in 1971 the USA had secretly pledged to China that it would not support Taiwan's independence, in exchange for Chinese assistance in ending the Viet Nam War. This had marked the beginning of a US shift away from Taiwan in favour of the People's Republic. In February 1973 the US Government announced that it would continue to maintain diplomatic relations with Taiwan but, at the same time, would set up an 'American mission' in Beijing and allow a 'Chinese liaison office' to open in Washington, DC. In December 1978, however, prior to a visit to Washington by Deng Xiaoping, the leader of the People's Republic, there was a dramatic change in US policy towards Taiwan. Diplomatic recognition was withdrawn from Taiwan as constituting the Republic of China, and the US embassy was closed. However, Taiwan, as an unrecognized but existing state, remained assured of continuing US protection and trade until some form of reconciliation between China and Taiwan could be brought about. China abandoned its denunciations of the Taiwan leadership, and, instead, offered suggestions for forms of autonomy for Taiwan within the People's Republic. These approaches were rejected by Taiwan, where public indignation was manifested against US policy. The USA also terminated the mutual security treaty with Taiwan. Commercial links were to be maintained. Taiwan's purchase of armaments from the USA remained a controversial issue. In August 1982 a joint Sino-US communiqué was published, in which the USA pledged to reduce gradually its sale of armaments to Taiwan. In April 1984 the US President, Ronald Reagan, gave an assurance that he would continue to support Taiwan, despite the improved relations between the USA and the People's Republic. In mid-1989 US relations with the People's Republic deteriorated sharply, following the Tiananmen Square massacre in Beijing. In September 1992 President Bush announced the sale of up to 150 F-16 fighter aircraft to Taiwan. The announcement was condemned by the People's Republic. In December Carla Hills, the US trade representative, became the first senior US government official to visit the island since the severance of diplomatic relations in early 1979.

In September 1994 the USA announced a modification of its policy towards Taiwan, henceforth permitting senior-level bilateral meetings to be held in US government offices. In December the US Secretary of Transportation visited the Ministry of Foreign Affairs in Taipei, the first US official of cabinet rank to visit Taiwan for more than 15 years. In June 1995 President Lee Teng-hui was permitted to make a four-day unofficial visit to the USA, where he gave a speech at Cornell University, his alma mater, and met members of the US Congress. This highly-significant visit by the Taiwanese Head of State provoked outrage in Beijing, and the Chinese ambassador to Washington was recalled. In January 1996 the Taiwanese Vice-President was granted a transit visa permitting him to disembark in the USA en route to Guatemala. In the following month he was accorded a similar privilege while travelling to Haiti and from El Salvador. In August the new Vice-President received a transit visa enabling him to spend two days in the USA, en route to the Dominican Republic, again arousing disapproval in Beijing. He was granted a similar concession in January 1997, on a journey to Nicaragua, and again in May 1998, en route to visit Taiwan's Central American allies.

In March 1996, as the mainland began a series of missile tests off the Taiwanese coast (see below), the USA stationed two naval convoys in waters east of the island representing the largest US deployment in Asia since 1975. US President Clinton agreed to the sale of Stinger anti-aircraft missiles and other defensive weapons. In September 1996 President Lee and the US Deputy Treasury Secretary, Lawrence Summers, met in Taipei for discussions, the most senior-level contact between the two sides since 1994. In November 1996 Taiwan welcomed the US State Department's pledge to continue to sell defensive weapons to the island. Some controversy arose in late 1996, however, when irregularities in the financing of President Clinton's re-election campaign, involving Taiwanese donors, were reported. Furthermore, it was alleged that a senior KMT official had offered an illicit contribution of US $15m. to the Democratic Party in Washington. In early 1997 the first of the Patriot anti-missile air defence systems, purchased from the USA under an arrangement made in 1993, were reported to have been deployed on Taiwan. The first of the F-16s were delivered to the island in April 1997. The Taiwanese Government expressed satisfaction at the USA's continued commitment to Taiwan's security, confirmed following the visit to the USA of the President of the People's Republic, Jiang Zemin, in October, and again in June 1998, during President Clinton's visit to the People's Republic. However, a statement by Clinton affirming that the USA would not support Taiwan's membership of the UN was sharply criticized in Taiwan. In late October 1998 the Taiwanese Chief of Staff, Gen. Tang Fei, made a secret two-week visit to the USA. This was regarded as an extremely sensitive matter, in view of the fact that Koo Chen-fu (see below) had recently met with Jiang Zemin. In the following month the People's Republic complained to the USA following the US Energy Secretary's visit to Taiwan. In January 1999 the People's Republic was angered by Taiwan's proposed inclusion in the US-led Theater Missile Defence (TMD) anti-missile system. Tensions continued throughout the year, and in August the USA reaffirmed its commitment to defend Taiwan against Chinese military action. In the following month, however, the USA again refused to support Taiwan's application for UN membership. In October of that year the island welcomed the adoption, albeit in modified form, of the Taiwan Security Enhancement Act (TSEA), establishing direct military links, by the International Relations Committee of the US House of Representatives, despite opposition from the Clinton administration. Reaction from the People's Republic was unfavourable, and its displeasure increased in early February 2000 when the House of Representatives overwhelmingly approved the Act. In April of that year the US Senate postponed consideration of the Act at the behest of the Taiwanese President-elect, Chen Shui-bian, in order not to antagonize Beijing during the sensitive period preceding his inauguration. In the same month the US Government announced that it had decided to defer the sale of four naval destroyers to Taiwan, although it was prepared to supply long-range radar and medium-range air-to-air missiles. In September the USA granted a transit visa to Taiwanese Vice-President Annette Lu to stay in New York *en route* to Central America. Lu subsequently declared that the stopover had marked a breakthrough in talks between the USA and Taiwan. In October China was angered by a resolution passed by the US Congress supporting Taiwan's participation in the UN and other international organizations.

The election of George W. Bush to the US Presidency in late 2000 was widely expected to boost US-Taiwan relations at the expense of US relations with the mainland, since Bush had used uncompromising rhetoric against the latter in his election campaign. This became more apparent after the crisis over the detention of a US spy plane and its crew following its collision with a Chinese fighter plane on 1 April 2001 (see the chapter on the People's Republic of China). Following that incident, in late April the USA agreed to sell Taiwan US $4,000m. worth of arms consisting of Kidd-class navy destroyers, Orion anti-submarine aircraft, diesel submarines, amphibious assault vehicles, and surface-to-air missiles and torpedoes, all of which would bolster the island's defences. However, the USA stopped short of selling Taiwan the advanced Aegis combat-radar system, for fear of provoking Beijing. At the same time President Bush said that the US would do whatever was necessary to defend Taiwan, in the event of an invasion by the mainland. Beijing was further angered by the visit of President Chen Shui-bian to the USA in late May 2001, when he met business leaders and members of the US Congress. Chen's visit was followed by that of his predecessor, Lee Teng-hui, in late June, as well as by a group of Taiwanese military and intelligence officials on an exchange programme, the first such exchange since 1979. Also in June, Taiwan successfully tested its US-made 'Patriot' air defence missiles for the first time.

In late August 2001 two US Navy aircraft carrier battle groups staged a one-day exercise in the South China Sea coinciding with Chinese military exercises in the Taiwan Straits, a further reminder that the USA was committed to protecting Taiwan. In October the Minister of National Defence, Wu Shih-wen, began finalizing the purchase of the naval destroyers offered earlier in the year, and the USA also offered Taiwan anti-tank missiles. In December the US House of Representatives approved the 2002 Defense Authorization Act, which included weapons sales to Taiwan and the promise of US help in acquiring submarines.

In January 2002 the Bush Administration rejected demands by a former US State Department official, Richard Holbrooke, that a fourth communiqué on US-Taiwan relations was needed, stating that the existing 1982 communiqué was satisfactory. At the same time, a delegation from a US 'think tank', consisting of retired generals and officials, visited the mainland, and subsequently Taiwan, where they met President Chen and other senior officials and discussed the island's security. Also in January, Vice-President Annette Lu made a brief stopover in New York, en route to South America, and former President Lee Teng-hui announced that he planned to visit the USA in May to raise Taiwan's profile. During his visit to Beijing in late February 2002, President Bush pledged to adhere to the 1979 Taiwan Relations Act—the first time a US President had stated this in China itself.

There were indications that the USA's long-standing 'strategic ambiguity' regarding Taiwan was gradually coming to an end in early 2002. In mid-March the Minister of National Defense, Gen. (retd) Tang Yao-ming visited the USA to attend a private three-day defence and security conference in Florida, where he met the US Deputy Secretary of Defense, Paul Wolfowitz, and Assistant Secretary of State James Kelly. During the conference, Wolfowitz reportedly stated that the USA would assist in training Taiwan's military in areas of command and doctrine. Several days later the Asia-Pacific Center for Security Studies, a 'think-tank' operating under the US Navy's Pacific Command, issued invitations for Taiwanese military personnel to attend a 12-week course on security issues—another indication of the greater access being given to the Taiwanese military by the USA. Tang was the first incumbent to make a non-transit visit to the USA since 1979, and the event emphasized the increasingly important security links between the two sides. China condemned Tang's visit as interference in its affairs and responded by denying permission for a US warship to visit Hong Kong in April. Meanwhile, the scandal in late March concerning former President Lee Teng-hui's co-operation with the island's intelligence services in secretly establishing an unauthorized fund (see below) embarrassed Taiwan and several US lobbying groups, which had received sums of this money. Lee subsequently postponed his planned visit to the USA. In mid-April, however, the US Under-Secretary of Commerce for International Trade, Grant Aldonas, became the highest-ranking official of George W. Bush's Administration to visit Taiwan, where he met Chen Shui-bian. The latter proposed establishing a free-trade pact with the USA and Japan.

In June 2002 it became known that a US defence contractor would probably build eight new diesel-electric submarines for Taiwan's navy, having purchased a share of a German company that produced the relevant designs; a high-level US delegation visited Taiwan in late July to discuss these arrangements. Also in July, the USA considered accelerating the transfer of advanced air-to-air missiles purchased by Taiwan but undelivered, and a US Department of Defense report warned that preparations for a conflict with Taiwan was the main factor behind Beijing's military build-up. However, the USA refrained from commenting on Chen's mention in early August of a possible referendum to determine the island's future. Premier Yu Shyi-kun and the Chairwoman of the Mainland Affairs Council, Tsai Ing-wen, made a brief stopover in New York, USA, at the same time, their visits being denounced by Beijing.

In early September 2002 a Vice-Minister of National Defense, Kang Ning-hsiang, and the Vice-Commander of the Navy both visited Washington, DC, to discuss the planned acquisition of four new Kidd-class destroyers. However, the high costs of the vessels jeopardized their purchase, at a time when Taiwan's defence budget was being reduced. Later in the month Wu Shu-chen, the wife of President Chen, began a private 10-day visit to the USA, seeking to raise the island's profile.

Meanwhile, reflecting the occasional political aspects of commercial relations with the USA, the Taiwanese Government in September 2002 urged the state-owned China Airlines to place a US $2,000m. order for US-manufactured Boeing aircraft for its fleet, rather than the rival European-manufactured Airbus. The outcome was expected to be decided by the end of 2002.

In January 1993, meanwhile, the official confirmation of Taiwan's purchase of 60 Mirage fighter aircraft from France again provoked strong protest from Beijing. In January 1994 Taiwan suffered a reverse when (following pressure from the People's Republic) France recognized Taiwan as an integral part of Chinese territory and agreed not to sell weapons to the island. In March 1995, however, it was reported that Taiwan was to purchase shoulder-fired anti-aircraft missiles from a French company. Despite speculation to the contrary, in 1996 the sale of these missiles, as well as the delivery of the Mirage aircraft and six Lafayette-class frigates, was confirmed. The first of the Mirages were delivered in May 1997. Delivery of the frigates was completed in March 1998. Plans by the USA to sell diesel submarines to Taiwan were blocked by Germany and the Netherlands in May 2001, however. The two countries, being the main owners of the design technology, were unwilling to raise tensions with Beijing by approving such a sale. In September an Australian firm emerged as the most likely supplier of the submarines when it was rumoured that a US defence company would take a 40% stake in the former. The impasse appeared to be resolved in mid-2002 when a US defence contractor took a stake in a German submarine manufacturer (see above).

Mainland displeasure was compounded in February 1993 when, for the first time in two decades, the Taiwanese Minister of Foreign Affairs paid a visit to Japan. In September 1994 pressure from Beijing resulted in the withdrawal of President Lee's invitation to attend the forthcoming Asian Games in Hiroshima. Instead, however, the Taiwanese Vice-Premier was permitted to visit Japan. Similarly, in July 1995 Japan announced that the Taiwanese Vice-Premier would not be permitted to attend a meeting of APEC members to be held in Osaka in November. Instead, President Lee was represented by Koo Chen-fu, Chairman of the Straits Exchange Foundation. (The latter also attended the APEC meeting in the Philippines in November 1996.) At the APEC summit meeting in Kuala Lumpur in November 1998, President Lee was represented by a Minister without Portfolio, Chiang Ping-kun, who had also attended the 1999 APEC conference, held in September in Auckland, New Zealand. Perng Fai-nan, the Governor of the Central Bank, represented President Chen Shui-bian at the APEC meeting in Brunei in November 2000.

In 1996 Taiwan's relations with Japan continued to be strained by the issue of adequate compensation for the thousands of Asian (mostly Korean) women used by Japanese troops for sexual purposes during the Second World War. In October Taiwan rejected a Japanese offer of nominal compensation for Taiwanese women. Relations deteriorated further in 1996 on account of a dispute relating to a group of uninhabited islets in the East China Sea: known as the Tiaoyutai (Diaoyu Dao) in Chinese, or Senkaku in Japanese, and situated about 200 km north-east of Taiwan and 300 km west of the Japanese island of Okinawa, the islands were claimed by Taiwan, China and Japan. In July, following the construction of a lighthouse on one of the islands by a Japanese right-wing group, the Taiwanese Ministry of Foreign Affairs lodged a strong protest over Japan's decision to incorporate the islands within its 200-mile (370-km) exclusive economic zone. Taiwan continued to urge that the dispute be settled by peaceful means. In early October further discussions with Japan on the question of Taiwanese fishing rights within the disputed waters ended without agreement. In the same month a flotilla of small boats, operated by activists from Taiwan, Hong Kong and Macao, succeeded in evading Japanese patrol vessels. Having reached the disputed islands, protesters raised the flags of Taiwan and of China. In May 1997 the Taiwanese Minister of Foreign Affairs expressed grave concern, following the landing and planting of their national flag on one of the disputed islands by a Japanese politician and three aides. A flotilla of 20 ships carrying about 200 protesters and journalists from Taiwan and Hong Kong set sail from the port of Shenao, ostensibly to participate in an international fishing contest. The boats were intercepted by Japanese coast-guard vessels and failed to gain access to the islands. In September 1997 an attempted parachute landing by Taiwanese activists also ended in failure. Reports in October that Japanese patrol boats were forcibly intercepting Taiwanese fishing vessels were a further cause for concern for the Taiwanese authorities. There was a significant development in relations between the two countries in November 1999, when the Governor of Tokyo paid an official visit to Taiwan. He was the most senior Japanese official to visit the island since the severing of diplomatic relations. The People's Republic condemned the visit, claiming that it undermined Sino-Japanese relations. Former President of Taiwan Lee Teng-hui made a private visit to Japan in late April 2001, ostensibly for medical treatment. In order to minimize tensions with Beijing, the Japanese authorities forbade Lee from making political statements while in Japan. In March 2002 it was revealed that Japanese politicians, including former Prime Minister Ryutaro Hashimoto, had received money from an unauthorized fund established by Lee in order to procure influence in Japan. However, the incident failed to damage bilateral relations, and in late 2001–early 2002 officials from both sides were investigating the possibility of establishing a free-trade agreement.

In March 1989, meanwhile, President Lee paid a state visit to Singapore, the first official visit overseas by a President of Taiwan for 12 years. In a further attempt to end diplomatic isolation, Lee said that he would visit any foreign country, even if it maintained diplomatic relations with Beijing. In February 1994 President Lee embarked upon an eight-day tour of South-East Asia. His itinerary incorporated the Philippines, Indonesia and Thailand, all three of which maintained diplomatic relations with the People's Republic of China. Although the tour was described as informal, President Lee had meetings with the three heads of state, leading to protests from Beijing. In May the Taiwanese President visited Nicaragua, Costa Rica, South Africa (the island's only remaining major diplomatic ally) and Swaziland. In April 1995 President Lee travelled to the United Arab Emirates and to Jordan. Although accompanied by senior members of the Executive Yuan, the visits were described as private (Taiwan having no diplomatic relations with these countries). In June the Taiwanese Premier visited Austria, Hungary and the Czech Republic, where he had private meetings with his Czech counterpart and with President Václav Havel. Again, the visits provoked strong protest from China. In August 1996, as Beijing continued to urge Pretoria to sever its diplomatic links with Taipei, Vice-Premier Hsu Li-teh led a delegation of government and business representatives to South Africa. In September, however, the Taiwanese Minister of Foreign Affairs was obliged to curtail an ostensibly private visit to Jakarta (where he was reported to have had discussions with his Indonesian counterpart), following protests from the People's Republic of China. In January 1997 the Vice-President was received by the Pope during a visit to the Holy See, the only European state that continued to recognize Taiwan. In the same month the Minister of Foreign Affairs embarked upon a tour of seven African nations, in order to consolidate relations. His itinerary included South Africa, despite that country's recent announcement of its intention to sever diplomatic relations with Taiwan (a major set-back to the island's campaign to gain wider international recognition). In March 1997 a six-day visit to Taiwan by the Dalai Lama was strongly condemned by the People's Republic of China, which denounced a meeting between President Lee and the exiled spiritual leader of Tibet as a 'collusion of splittists'. A second visit by the Dalai Lama, scheduled for July 1998, was postponed, following mainland China's criticism of the opening of a representative office of the Dalai Lama's religious foundation in Taiwan. However, the Dalai Lama visited Taiwan in March–April 2001 and held talks with President Chen, much to the anger of Beijing.

In July 1997, following the Bahamas' withdrawal of recognition from Taiwan and establishment of diplomatic relations with the People's Republic of China, the Taiwanese Minister of Foreign Affairs undertook an extensive tour of the countries of Central America and the Caribbean, in an effort to maintain their support. In September, during a tour of Central America (the six nations of the region having become the core of Taiwan's remaining diplomatic allies), President Lee attended an international conference on the development of the Panama Canal. The USA granted a transit visa to the Taiwanese President, enabling him to stop over in Hawaii en route to and from Central America. A visit to Europe in October by Vice-President Lien Chan was curtailed when pressure from Beijing forced the Spanish Government to withdraw an invitation. The Malaysian and Singaporean Prime Ministers met their Taiwanese counterpart in Taiwan in November, on their return from the APEC forum in Canada. The People's Republic expressed concern at the meetings.

In January 1998 the Taiwanese Premier, Vincent Siew, met senior officials during a visit to the Philippines and Singapore. It was believed that discussions had focused on the possibility of Taiwan extending economic assistance to those countries. Moreover, the Taiwanese Government expressed its intention to pursue the creation of a multilateral Asian fund, under the auspices of APEC, to support the ailing Asian economies. Relations with Taiwan's Asian neighbours were further strengthened in February, when a leading member of the KMT visited the Republic of Korea, again, it was understood, to discuss financial assistance in the wake of the Asian economic crisis. Negotiations between the Malaysian Deputy Prime Minister and Finance Minister and the Taiwanese Premier, held in Taiwan in February, also concentrated on economic and financial issues. Vincent Siew made a return visit to Malaysia in April. China was highly critical of these visits, accusing Taiwan of seeking to gain political advantage from the regional economic crisis. At the APEC meeting held in Kuala Lumpur, Malaysia, in November 1998 President Lee was represented by the Minister without Portfolio, Chiang Ping-kun, who also attended the 1999 APEC conference, held in September in Auckland, New Zealand.

In August 1999 the Taiwanese Government threatened to refuse entry to the island to Philippine labourers in retaliation for Manila's unilateral termination of its aviation agreement with Taipei. In October the Philippine authorities decided to close the country to Taiwanese aircraft. Access was, however, temporarily granted in November during talks on the renewal of the agreement. Negotiations faltered in December, but reached a successful conclusion in early 2000, thus permitting flights to the Philippines to resume. In March, however, the agreement collapsed, and flights were suspended again. In June the Taiwanese Government imposed a three-month ban on new work permits for Philippine nationals, citing interference by the Philippines' representative office in Taiwan concerning labour disputes. Any connection with the aviation dispute was denied. In September a new aviation agreement, enabling flights between Taipei and Manila to restart, was signed.

Following the withdrawal of diplomatic recognition by South Africa, in 1998 Taiwan made extensive efforts to maintain relations with the island's other allies. The Minister of Foreign Affairs visited eight African countries in February, and in April it was announced that Taiwan's overseas aid budget was to be substantially increased in an attempt to retain diplomatic support. In May the Vice-President, Lien Chan, visited Taiwan's Central American and Caribbean allies. China expressed serious concern in November at New Zealand's decision to grant Taiwanese officials in Wellington privileges accorded to accredited diplomats. Taiwan's strong economic position was a deciding factor in its diplomatic fortunes in late 1998 and in 1999. Following the loss of four allies during 1998, relations were established with the Marshall Islands in November of that year, and with the former Yugoslav republic of Macedonia in January 1999. The latter rapidly benefited from its contacts with Taiwan, receiving extensive aid following the Kosovo conflict. The Prime Minister of Papua New Guinea initiated diplomatic relations with Taiwan in early July 1999. Following his resignation later that month, recognition was withdrawn from Taiwan, allegedly because of a failure to adhere to correct procedures for the establishment of relations. Full diplomatic relations were established with Palau in December of that year, and Taiwan opened an embassy on the island in March 2000. In August 2000 the new Taiwanese President, Chen Shui-bian, embarked upon a tour of diplomatic allies in Central America and West Africa. In October Taiwan was concerned that it might lose a diplomatic ally when the Minister of Foreign Affairs of Solomon Islands unexpectedly cancelled a visit to Taipei and travelled instead to Beijing. The Premier of Solomon Islands did not attend a regional forum, instead visiting Taipei to make amends and to reiterate his commitment to maintaining relations. There was speculation that this commitment arose from a need for substantial financial assistance from Taiwan.

In November 2000, after eight years' suspension, the 25th Joint Conference of Korea-Taiwan Business Councils took place in Seoul. It was agreed that henceforth conferences would be held annually alternately in Taipei and Seoul, and Taiwan ultimately hoped for a resumption of ministerial-level discussions on the establishment of bilateral air links. In the same month the European Parliament passed a resolution on strengthening relations with Taiwan, and in December Taiwan and Egypt agreed to exchange representative offices. Also in December, France refused to grant a visa to the Taiwanese Minister of Justice.

Throughout 2001 Taiwan continued to seek a higher diplomatic profile. President Chen in late May began a tour of five Latin American nations—El Salvador, Guatemala, Panama, Paraguay, and Honduras—as part of Taiwan's 'dollar diplomacy'—a practice of giving aid and bringing investment in return for diplomatic recognition. While in El Salvador, Chen met eight regional leaders, who pledged support for Taiwan. Both Taiwan and the People's Republic of China were increasingly bidding for support in this region to boost their overall global standing. Taiwan was also in competition with China for support from Pacific island nations, five of which (Marshall Islands, Nauru, Palau, Solomon Islands, and Tuvalu) recognized Taiwan. Two of these nations, Solomon Islands and the Marshall Islands, were thought to be wavering in their support of Taiwan. In June the former Yugoslav republic of Macedonia announced that it would recognize the People's Republic of China, thus leading to a break in relations with Taiwan. In November Wu Shu-chen, wife of President Chen, travelled to Strasbourg, France, to accept the 'Prize for Freedom' awarded to her husband by Liberal International, a world grouping of liberal parties. Chen himself had been refused a visa by the European Union (EU).

On 1 January 2002 Taiwan formally became a member of the WTO. At the same time, it was reported that Taiwan had secretly been developing military and intelligence links with India, through mutual co-operation including bilateral visits of military personnel and the exchange of intelligence data. Also in January, Vice-President Lu visited Nicaragua and Paraguay, having visited The Gambia in December 2001. Vice-President Lu also visited Indonesia in mid-August 2002 and met several ministers, but not President Megawati Sukarnoputri, owing to pressure on the latter by Beijing. While in Indonesia, Lu discussed possible liquefied natural gas projects, investment and migrant labour. Taiwanese companies had in previous years invested US $17,000m. in Indonesia, the home of some 100,000 of Taiwan's migrant workers. President Chen completed a four-nation tour of Africa in early July 2002, having visited Senegal, São Tomé and Príncipe, Malawi and Swaziland. While en route to Swaziland, he was refused permission to land in South Africa, Pretoria being concerned not to offend Beijing.

In late July 2002 Taiwan broke off diplomatic relations with Nauru after the latter established relations with the People's Republic of China. In September Taiwan announced the opening of a trade and economic affairs representative office in Mongolia.

The question of the sovereignty of the Spratly Islands, situated in the South China Sea and believed to possess petroleum and natural gas resources, to which Taiwan and five other countries laid claim, remained unresolved in 2002. A contingent of Taiwanese marines is maintained on Taiping Island, the largest of the disputed islands, located some 1,574 km south-west of Taiwan. A satellite telecommunications link between Taiping and Kaohsiung was inaugurated in October 1995. In August 1993 Taiwan announced its intention to construct an airbase on Taiping Island, but in January 1996 the scheme was postponed. In late December 1998 the Legislative Yuan approved the first legal definition of Taiwan's sea borders. The Spratly Islands were claimed, as were the disputed Tiaoyutai Islands, within the 12- and 24-nautical mile zones.

RELATIONS WITH THE PEOPLE'S REPUBLIC AND REUNIFICATION INITIATIVES

In October 1981 Taiwan rejected the latest in a series of proposals from the People's Republic of China for reunification, whereby Taiwan would become a 'special administrative region' of China and would enjoy a high degree of autonomy, including the retention of its own armed forces. In 1982 the Taiwan Government implied that eventual reunification could be made possible by narrowing the economic gap between the two sides over time, and on the basis of Sun Yat-sen's 'Three Principles of the People'. In 1983 Deng Xiaoping indicated the possibility that, following reunification, Taiwan would retain the right to purchase military equipment from abroad, would be free to export where necessary to sustain its economic growth, would make its own legal decisions, fly its own flag, and issue passports and visas, while the mainland authorities would not send civilian or military personnel to Taiwan. Limitations on this autonomy would be that the People's Republic would speak for China in international affairs, while Taiwan would be designated Chinese Taipei, as agreed for the summer Olympic Games in 1984 and 1988, or China-Taiwan.

In October 1984, following the agreement between the People's Republic of China and the United Kingdom that the former would regain sovereignty over Hong Kong after 1997, Chinese leaders urged Taiwan to accept similar proposals for reunification on the basis of 'one country, two systems'. The KMT Government, however, insisted that Taiwan would never negotiate with Beijing until the mainland regime renounced communism, thus reasserting the rigid and fundamental 'three no's' policy (of 'no compromise, no contact and no negotiation with the mainland') on which its relationship with the People's Republic was based. In May 1986 Taiwan was induced to adopt a more flexible policy after a Taiwanese cargo aircraft was diverted to the mainland by a pilot who wished to defect; representatives from the airlines of the two countries held negotiations in Hong Kong, leading to the return of the aircraft (and two other crew members) to Taiwan. These discussions represented the first-ever direct contact between the two countries (although Taipei insisted that the talks were for humanitarian reasons only and did not indicate a change of policy). In March 1987, however, in accordance with the 'three no's' policy, Taiwan declared the agreement that had been concluded between the People's Republic of China and Portugal, regarding the return of Macao to Chinese sovereignty, to be null and void.

Questions of Taiwan's political evolution and of its future relations with the People's Republic of China were the principal determinants of the pace at which the KMT proceeded with the programme of political reform. While the opposition parties and liberal elements within the KMT generally recognized that Taiwan should adopt a more pragmatic foreign policy if it were to end its diplomatic isolation, the KMT was, until its 13th National Congress in July 1988, dominated by 'conservative' members who had fled the mainland with Chiang Kai-shek in 1947, and who feared that reform would undermine the *raisons d'être* of the KMT: that it constituted 'the legitimate Government of all China and that Taiwan formed a province of this polity', not an independent state. They thus opposed the increasing dominance of the KMT by native Taiwanese.

In October 1987 the Government announced the repeal of the 38-year ban on visits to the mainland by Taiwanese citizens, with the exception of civil servants and military personnel. (The latter regulations were relaxed in November 1998.) In so doing, the Government tacitly recognized that Taiwanese had, for some years, been making illegal visits to the mainland via Hong Kong. Between November 1987 and October 1990, according to the mainland authorities, almost 1.8m. Taiwanese visited (mainly via Hong Kong) the People's Republic. In late 1988 permission was extended to include visits by mainland Chinese to Taiwan for humanitarian purposes. In August 1991 it was announced that restrictions on immigration by ethnic Chinese persons from Hong Kong and Macao were to be relaxed. In 1991 a total of 948,800 Taiwan residents visited the mainland, followed by 1.5m. in 1992. In 1995 almost 1.3m. Taiwanese citizens travelled to the mainland, while visitors from the People's Republic to Taiwan numbered 42,634, the latter figure representing an increase of more than 80% compared with the previous year. A total of 42,491 mainland residents were permitted to visit Taiwan in 1997.

In November 1987 the opposition Democratic Progressive Party (DPP) approved a resolution declaring that Taiwanese had the freedom to demand independence for Taiwan. It was disclaimed, however, that this constituted a pro-independence policy on the part of the DPP. In January 1988 two opposition activists were imprisoned, on charges of sedition, for advocating Taiwanese independence. While there was evidence of a more flexible policy towards the People's Republic at the 13th National Congress of the KMT in July (when the ruling party authorized an increase in indirect imports from the mainland and in indirect Taiwanese investment in mainland projects), President Lee's restatement of the party's long-standing policy of seeking reunification under the KMT underlined the continuing necessity to satisfy 'conservative' sentiment within the party.

In April 1989 the Government announced that it was considering a 'one China, two governments' formula for its future relationship with the mainland, whereby China would be a single country under two administrations, one in Beijing and one in Taipei. In May a delegation led by the Minister of Finance attended a meeting of the Asian Development Bank (ADB) in Beijing, under the name of Taipei, China. Although the Government stressed that the delegation would not be allowed to hold talks with Chinese government officials, the visit, together with one made by a party of Taiwanese gymnasts a month earlier, represented a considerable relaxation in Taiwan's stance. Reconciliation initiatives were abruptly halted, however, by the violent suppression of the pro-democracy movement in Beijing in June 1989. The actions of the Chinese Government were strongly condemned by Taiwan. Nevertheless, in May 1990 President Lee suggested the opening of direct dialogue on a government-to-government basis with the People's Republic. The proposal, however, was rejected by Beijing, which continued to maintain that it would negotiate only on a party-to-party basis with the KMT.

In October 1990 the National Unification Council, chaired by President Lee, was formed. In the same month the Mainland Affairs Council, comprising heads of government departments and led by the Vice-Premier of the Executive Yuan, was founded. The DPP urged the Government to renounce its claim to sovereignty over mainland China and Mongolia. In November the Straits Exchange Foundation (SEF) was established for the purpose of handling civilian contacts with the People's Republic. In December President Lee announced that Taiwan would formally end the state of war with the mainland; the declaration of emergency was to be rescinded by May 1991, thus opening the way to improved relations with Beijing.

In February 1991 the National Unification Council put forward radical new proposals whereby Taiwan and the People's Republic of China might recognize each other as separate political entities. In March a national unification programme, which incorporated the demand that Taiwan be acknowledged as an independent and equal entity, was approved by the Central Standing Committee of the KMT. The programme also included a proposal for direct postal, commercial and shipping links between Taiwan and the mainland, this suggestion being well received in the People's Republic.

In April 1991 a delegation from the SEF travelled to Beijing for discussions, the first such delegation ever to visit the People's Republic. The talks were reported to have promoted understanding and consensus. In early May it was announced that the large financial rewards hitherto offered to members of the armed forces of the People's Republic who defected to Taiwan would no longer be available. In the following month the Premier of Taiwan reaffirmed that unification with the mainland would be pursued by peaceful and democratic means. Upon the second anniversary of the Tiananmen Square massacre, in June 1991 the Taiwanese authorities urged the Government of the People's Republic to cease its alleged persecution of pro-democracy activists.

In August 1991 a Beijing magazine published an informal 10-point plan for the eventual reunification of China, whereby Taiwan would become a special administrative region and retain its own legislative, administrative and judicial authority. Thus, for the first time, the 'one country, two systems' policy of the People's Republic was clearly stated. In the same month Deng Xiaoping and other senior leaders reportedly offered to travel from the mainland to Taiwan for the purpose of reunification talks.

Two senior envoys of the mainland Chinese Red Cross were allowed to enter Taiwan in August 1991 on a humanitarian mission, the first ever visit by official representatives of the People's Republic of China. As the Beijing Government continued to warn against independence for Taiwan, in September the island's President asserted that conditions were not appropriate for reunification wth the mainland and that Taiwan was a *de facto* sovereign and autonomous country. The President of the People's Republic indicated that force might be used to prevent the separation of Taiwan. In December the non-governmental Association for Relations across the Taiwan Straits (ARATS) was established in Beijing. In January 1992 the SEF protested to the People's Republic over the detention of a former pilot of the mainland air force who had defected to Taiwan in 1965 and, upon returning to his homeland for a family reunion in December 1991, had been arrested. He subsequently received a 15-year prison sentence. In May 1992 the National Unification Council's proposal for a non-aggression pact between Taiwan and the People's Republic was rejected.

In July 1992 the Taiwanese Government reiterated that it would not consider party-to-party talks with Beijing. In the same month President Lee urged the establishment of 'one country, one good system'. In mid-July statutes to permit the further expansion of economic and political links with the People's Republic were adopted by the Legislative Yuan. In August the vice-president of the mainland Red Cross travelled to the island, thus becoming the most senior representative of the People's Republic to visit Taiwan since 1949. Delegates from the SEF and ARATS met in Hong Kong in October 1992 for discussions. The Chairman of the Mainland Affairs Council, however, insisted upon the People's Republic's renunciation of the use of military force prior to any dialogue on the reunification question. At the end of the month the Government of Taiwan announced a further relaxation of restrictions on visits to the mainland by state employees. Upon taking office in February 1993, the new Premier of Taiwan confirmed the continuation of the 'One China' policy.

Historic talks between the Chairmen of the SEF and of the ARATS were held in Singapore in April 1993. Engaging in the highest level of contact since 1949, Taiwan and the People's Republic agreed on the establishment of a formal structure for future negotiations on economic and social issues. Agreements on the verification of official documents and on the registration of mail were also signed. One issue that remained unresolved, however, was that of adequate legal protection for Taiwanese investments in the People's Republic, the rapid increase in capital outflow to the mainland being of growing concern to the island's authorities.

In 1993 divisions between Taiwan's business sector and political groupings (the former advocating much closer links with the People's Republic, the latter urging greater caution) became evident. In January, and again later in the year, the Secretary-General of the SEF resigned, following disagreement with the Mainland Affairs Council.

In August 1993 the People's Republic issued a document entitled *The Taiwan Question and the Reunification of China*, reiterating its claim to sovereignty over the island. Relations were further strained by a series of aircraft hijackings to Taiwan from the mainland. A SEF-ARATS meeting, held in Taiwan in December 1993, attempted to address the issue of the repatriation of hijackers. Incidents of air piracy continued in 1994, prison sentences of up to 13 years being imposed on the hijackers by the Taiwanese authorities.

Further meetings between delegates of the SEF and ARATS were held in early 1994. Relations between Taiwan and the mainland deteriorated sharply in April, however, upon the disclosure of a tragedy in Zhejiang Province in the People's Republic: 24 Taiwanese tourists were among those robbed and killed on board a pleasure boat plying Qiandao Lake. Taiwanese outrage was compounded by the mainland's insensitive handling of the incident. Taiwan suspended all commercial and cultural exchanges with the People's Republic. In June three men were convicted of the murders and promptly executed. In February 1995 compensation totalling 1.2m. yuan was awarded to the victims' families by the People's Republic.

In July 1994 the Taiwanese Government released a White Paper on mainland affairs, urging that the division be acknowledged and the island accepted as a separate political entity. In August the SEF-ARATS talks were resumed when Tang Shubei, Vice-Chairman and Secretary-General of the ARATS, flew to Taipei for four days of discussions with his Taiwanese counterpart, Chiao Jen-ho. Tang thus became the most senior Communist Chinese official ever to visit the island. Although the visit was marred by opposition protesters, the two sides reached tentative agreement on several issues, including the repatriation of hijackers and illegal immigrants from Taiwan to the mainland. Procedures for the settlement of cross-Straits fishing disputes were also established. In mid-November relations were strained once again when, in an apparent accident during a training exercise, Taiwanese anti-aircraft shells landed on a mainland village, injuring several people. Nevertheless, in late November a further round of SEF-ARATS talks took place in Nanjing, at which agreement in principle on the procedure for the repatriation of hijackers and illegal immigrants was confirmed. Further progress was made at meetings in Beijing in January 1995, although no accord was signed.

It was announced in March 1995 that the functions of the SEF were to be enhanced. To improve co-ordination, the SEF board of directors would henceforth include government officials, while meetings of the Mainland Affairs Council would be attended by officials of the SEF. In the same month the Mainland Affairs Council approved a resolution providing for the relaxation of restrictions on visits by mainland officials and civilians.

President Jiang Zemin's Lunar New Year address, incorporating the mainland's 'eight-point' policy on Taiwan, was regarded as more conciliatory than hitherto. In April 1995, in response, President Lee proposed a 'six-point' programme for cross-Straits relations: unification according to the reality of separate rules; increased exchanges on the basis of Chinese culture; increased economic and trade relations; admission to international organizations on an equal footing; the renunciation of the use of force against each other; and joint participation in Hong Kong and Macao affairs. In late April, however, the eighth round of working-level SEF-ARATS discussions was postponed, owing to disagreement over the agenda.

In May 1995 the SEF Chairman, Koo Chen-fu, and his mainland counterpart, Wang Daohan, formally agreed to meet in Beijing in July. In June, however, this proposed second session of senior-level negotiations was postponed by the ARATS, in protest at President Lee's recent visit to the USA. Tension between the two sides increased in July, when the People's Republic unexpectedly announced that it was about to conduct an eight-day programme of guided missile and artillery-firing tests off the northern coast of Taiwan. A second series of exercises took place in August, again arousing much anxiety on the island. In mid-August President Jiang Zemin confirmed that the People's Republic would not renounce the use of force against Taiwan. Nevertheless, at the end of that month President Lee reaffirmed the KMT's commitment to reunification. In October President Jiang Zemin's offer to visit Taiwan in person was cautiously received on the island. President Lee confirmed his Government's anti-independence stance in November.

In January 1996 the Taiwanese Premier again urged the early resumption of cross-Straits dialogue. In February unconfirmed reports indicated that as many as 400,000 mainland troops had been mobilized around Fujian Province. In the same month, upon his appointment as Chairman of the Mainland Affairs Council, Chang King-yuh pledged to attempt to improve relations with the mainland. In early March, as Taiwan's first direct presidential election approached, the People's Republic began a new series of missile tests, including the firing of surface-to-surface missiles into an area off Taiwan's south-western coast, adjacent to the port of Kaohsiung, and into a zone off the north-eastern coast, near the port of Keelung. Live artillery exercises continued in the Taiwan Strait until after the election, arousing international concern. The USA deployed two naval task forces in the area (see above). In early April, as tension eased, the Mainland Affairs Council removed the ban on visits to Taiwan by officials of the People's Republic. At the end of April the SEF, which had lodged a strong protest with the ARATS during the missile tests of March, urged the resumption of bilateral discussions.

Upon his inauguration in May 1996, Taiwan's re-elected Head of State declared his readiness to visit the People's Republic for negotiations. In July President Lee reaffirmed his commitment to peaceful reunification, and urged the mainland to renounce the use of violence and to resume dialogue. In the same month visits to Taiwan by executives of the mainland's port authorities and of Air China (the flag carrier of the People's Republic) led to speculation that direct travel links between the two sides might be established. Other business delegations followed. The national oil corporations of Taiwan and of the People's Republic signed a joint exploration agreement. At the end of July, as bilateral relations continued to improve, the Mainland Affairs Council announced that Taiwanese governors and mayors were to be permitted to attend cultural activities and international functions in the People's Republic.

In October 1996 the Taiwanese Vice-Minister of Education, the most senior official to date, visited the People's Republic for discussions with his mainland counterparts. In November the Mainland Affairs Council announced that the permanent stationing of mainland media representatives in Taiwan was to be permitted. President Lee's renewed offer to travel to the People's Republic was rejected and, despite repeated SEF requests, Tang Shubei of the ARATS continued to assert that cross-Straits discussions could not resume owing to Taiwan's pursuit of its 'two Chinas' policy (a reference to President Lee's attempts to raise the diplomatic profile of the island). In January 1997, however, as the reversion of the entrepôt of Hong Kong to Chinese sovereignty approached, shipping representatives of Taiwan and of the People's Republic reached a preliminary consensus on the establishment of direct sea links. Under the terms of the agreement, which permitted mainland cargoes to be transhipped at Kaohsiung for onward passage to a third country but did not allow goods to enter the island's customs, five Taiwanese and six mainland shipping companies were granted permission to conduct cross-Straits cargo services. In April 1997, following the arrival in Kaohsiung of the first ship in 48 years to sail directly from the Chinese mainland to the island, the first Taiwanese-owned (but Panamanian-registered) vessel set sail for the port of Xiamen on a similarly historic voyage across the Taiwan Strait.

In March 1997 an unemployed journalist hijacked a Taiwanese airliner on an internal flight and, citing political repression on the island, forced the aircraft to fly to the mainland, where he requested asylum. The mainland authorities were commended for their handling of the incident, the aircraft returning to Taiwan later the same day. In May the SEF agreed to accept the Taiwanese hijacker, who was to face criminal charges upon his return to the island.

In July 1997, upon the reversion to Chinese sovereignty of the British colony of Hong Kong, President Lee firmly rejected the concept of 'one country, two systems' and any parallel with Taiwan, and strenuously refuted a suggestion by President Jiang Zemin that Taiwan would eventually follow the example of Hong Kong. In August Liu Gangchi, Deputy Secretary-General of the ARATS, arrived in Taipei, at the head of a 32-member delegation, to attend a seminar on the subject of China's modernization. In September the Taiwanese Minister of Finance and the Governor of the central bank were obliged to cancel a visit to Hong Kong, where they had planned to have informal discussions with delegates to the forthcoming IMF/World Bank meeting, owing to Hong Kong's failure to issue them with visas. The affair compounded fears that Taiwan's business dealings with Hong Kong might be jeopardized.

A call for the opening of political negotiations, made by the Minister of Foreign Affairs of the People's Republic in September 1997, was welcomed by the Mainland Affairs Council. However, the Taiwanese authorities continued to insist that Beijing remove all preconditions before the opening of dialogue. In November the Secretary-General of the SEF was invited by the ARATS to attend a seminar on the mainland in the following month. The SEF proposed instead that its Chairman head a delegation to the People's Republic. An interview given by President Lee to a Western newspaper, in which he referred to Taiwan's independence, caused anger on the part of the Beijing authorities.

The declaration by an ARATS official, in January 1998, that Taiwan did not need to recognize the Government of the People's Republic as the central Government as a precondition for dialogue was regarded as a significant concession on the part of the mainland authorities. However, Taiwan continued to insist that China abandon its demand that talks be conducted under its 'One China' principle. In February the ARATS sent a letter to the SEF requesting the resumption of political and economic dialogue between the two sides, and inviting a senior SEF official to visit the mainland. The SEF responded positively to the invitation in March, and proposed that a delegation be sent to the People's Republic to discuss procedural details, prior to a visit to the mainland by the SEF Chairman.

In April 1998 a delegation chaired by the newly-appointed Deputy Secretary-General of the SEF, Jan Jyh-horng, visited the People's Republic. Following negotiations with the ARATS, it was announced that the Chairman of the SEF would visit the People's Republic later in 1998 formally to resume the dialogue, which had been suspended since 1995. The visit was regarded as an important step towards restoring stability to Taiwan-China relations. The arrest on the mainland in May 1998 of four Taiwanese business executives on charges of espionage, and the visit to Malaysia by the Taiwanese Premier, in April, threatened to reverse the improvement in relations. However, in July the Chinese Minister of Science and Technology visited Taiwan, the first such visit by a mainland Minister since the civil war. This was followed later in the month by a formal visit to Taiwan by the Deputy Secretary-General of the ARATS. The kidnap and murder in August in the People's Republic of a Taiwanese local government official caused serious concern for the Taiwanese authorities. Furthermore, later in that month a Beijing court convicted the four Taiwanese businessmen on charges of espionage. In October Koo Chen-fu, the SEF Chairman, duly travelled to the People's Republic, where he met with President Jiang Zemin (the highest level of bilateral contact since 1949) and had discussions with his mainland counterpart and other senior officials. A four-point agreement was reached, allowing for increased communications between the two sides, but little was achieved in terms of a substantive breakthrough. However, the talks were considered to mark an important improvement in cross-Straits relations, and Wang Daohan accepted an invitation to visit Taiwan in March 1999. In January 1999 the ARATS invited the SEF Deputy Secretary-General to visit the People's Republic for talks in order to prepare for Wang Daohan's visit. The SEF made a counter-proposal that ARATS officials visit Taiwan to discuss preparations. In the following month, during a flight to the island of Kinmen, an SEF official was attacked by four Chinese convicted aircraft hijackers, who were part of a group being transferred to the nearby island prior to their repatriation to the mainland. During the following months Taiwan repatriated several hundred Chinese illegal immigrants. In March an ARATS delegation led by Deputy Secretary-General Lin Yafei visited Taiwan. It was agreed that Wang Daohan's visit would take place later in the year, but no date was set. In April President Lee reaffirmed that Beijing should recognize Taiwan as being of equal status. An SEF group went to Beijing in March, and preliminary agreement was reached that Wang Daohan would visit Taiwan in either mid-September or mid-October. In August, however, the ARATS suspended contacts with the SEF, following President Lee's insistence on the 'two-state theory' (see below), and it was confirmed in October that Wang Daohan would not visit Taiwan as long as it adhered to the theory.

Meanwhile, China was becoming increasingly demonstrative in its opposition to Taiwan's inclusion in the TMD system (see above). Ballistic missiles were deployed in mainland coastal regions facing Taiwan, and fears were heightened within the international community in July 1999, when the People's Republic announced that it had developed a neutron bomb, after declaring itself ready for war should Taiwan attempt to gain independence. This declaration was prompted by an interview given by President Lee to a German radio station, during which he asserted that relations with the People's Republic were 'state-to-state'. Chinese military exercises took place in the Taiwan Strait later that month, allegedly to intimidate Taiwan. Faced with this aggression and a lack of US support, Taiwan promised that it would not amend its Constitution to enshrine its claim to statehood in law. In August the USA reaffirmed its readiness to defend Taiwan against Chinese military action. Shortly afterwards the Taiwanese Government refused a request by Beijing that it retract the 'state-to-state' theory with regard to cross-Straits relations, and tension increased in late August when the KMT incorporated the 'two-state theory' into the party resolution, claiming that this would henceforth become the administrative guideline and priority of the Taiwanese authorities. Later that month the Mainland Affairs Council announced that former Taiwan government officials involved in affairs related to national intelligence or secrets were not to be permitted to travel to China within three years of leaving their posts. In September, however, following a severe earthquake in Taiwan that killed or injured several thousand people, China was among the many countries to offer emergency assistance to the island. Taiwan, however, accused the People's Republic of contravening humanitarian principles by trying to force other countries to seek its approval before offering help.

In February 2000 the People's Republic threatened to attack Taiwan if it indefinitely postponed reunification talks. The approval in the Legislative Yuan in March of a law providing for the first direct transport links between Taiwan's outlying islands and mainland China for 50 years did not substantially improve matters, and in April the Vice-President-elect, Annette Lu, was denounced by the Chinese media after she made 'separatist' remarks, televised in Hong Kong, declaring that Taiwan was only a 'remote relative and close neighbour' of China. A Taiwanese opposition group subsequently endorsed a motion to dismiss Lu for putting the island at risk by provoking China. In an attempt to improve relations with the People's Republic, President Chen offered to compromise and to reopen negotiations on the basis that each side was free to interpret the 'one China' formula as it saw fit. Chinese Premier Zhu Rongji rejected the suggestion, and questioned Taiwan's motives, effectively dispelling all hopes of restarting negotiations in the near future. In July 2000 the Chinese authorities responded angrily when the United Kingdom issued a visa to former President Lee Teng-hui, who continued to be perceived as a dissident by the People's Republic. Despite the fact that Lee's visa was for the purposes of a private visit by an individual, and specified as a condition that no public statements would be made during the trip, China cancelled ministerial-level contacts and official meetings with the United Kingdom, and threatened to take action against British trade interests.

In October 2000 Beijing published a policy document on its national defence, which confirmed that the People's Republic would use force to prevent Taiwanese secession, to stop occupation of the island, and also in the event of Taiwan indefinitely postponing reunification with the mainland. In November, however, there were signs of an improvement in relations when Wu Po-hsiung, the Vice-Chairman of the KMT, travelled to Beijing and met unofficially with Chinese Vice-Premier Qian Qichen. Wu was the most senior KMT official to visit mainland China for more than 50 years, and it was thought that Beijing was attempting to isolate Chen Shui-bian by consorting with his political rivals. During the meeting both sides agreed to hold important academic forums to discuss cross-Straits relations and to attempt to devise common positions. Qian stressed, however, the importance of Taiwan's recognition of the 'One China' principle before official negotiations could resume.

In November 2000 Taiwan announced that journalists from the People's Republic were to be granted permission to stay in Taiwan for periods of up to one month, during which time they would be invited to attend any press conferences called by the President's office and the Executive Yuan, in order to enhance cross-Straits exchanges and understanding. In the following month plans were announced for 'mini three links' with China, providing for direct trade, transport and postal links between Kinmen and Matsu islands and the mainland. The Taiwanese Government stressed, however, that any future direct links with Taiwan itself would be subject to rigorous security checks. In early January 2001 groups sailed from Kinmen and Matsu to Xiamen and Fuzhou, respectively, in the People's Republic. Beijing's response toward the initiative was guarded.

In March 2001 the press spokesman for the Fourth Session of the Ninth National People's Congress reiterated that China did not favour the confederal system of reunification, but rather the 'one country, two systems' model. Also in that month, exiled pro-democracy activist Wei Jingsheng visited Taiwan and had talks with Vice-President Lu. Cross-Straits relations had become strained by April following the visit of the Dalai Lama to Taiwan, and the forthcoming sale of weapons by the USA to Taiwan (see above).

In May 2001 President Chen announced that he aspired to become the first Taiwanese leader to visit the mainland since 1949 by attending the APEC forum to be held there in October; however, Beijing rejected Chen's offer. Although official cross-Straits relations were often hostile, ties continued to develop between Taiwan and the mainland, particularly in the business sphere. Many Taiwanese companies continued to invest in the mainland, and it was hoped that the growing economic interdependence between the two entities would reduce the risk of war. President Chen in late August endorsed a plan by a special advisory committee to expand economic and commercial links with the mainland, a reversal of the previous government's 'no haste, be patient' policy of limiting trade with the mainland for fear of becoming over-dependent on its main political enemy. The new policy of 'aggressive opening' included the removal of a US $50m. limit on individual investments in the mainland. Beijing responded coolly to Chen's initiative, stating that direct full transport links between the mainland and Taiwan would have to wait until Chen respected the 'One China' reunification formula, but a senior Chinese trade official stated that China would not block further Taiwanese investment. At the same time, state-owned oil companies from Taiwan and China announced plans to resume co-operative exploration of the Taiwan Straits. Beijing's reluctance to accept Chen's proposals reflected the fact that it had for years called for greater links with Taiwan which the latter had rejected, and was thus unwilling to embrace Taiwan too quickly. Chen's critics warned that his new policy would make Taiwan too economically dependent on the mainland. In September 2001 the Taiwanese Government approved a proposal allowing Chinese investment in Taiwan's land and property market, as part of the new opening to the mainland. The limit on individual investments in the mainland was formally removed on 7 November; restrictions on direct remits to and from the mainland via Taiwanese banks were also abolished.

In late October 2001, meanwhile, Taiwan boycotted the APEC summit meeting in Shanghai, following Beijing's refusal to allow Taiwan's chosen delegate, former Vice-President Li Yuan-tsu, to attend, on the grounds that he was not an 'economic' official. Despite this, the DPP deleted from its charter a vow to achieve the island's formal independence, since it was already a *de facto* separate entity. The change indicated a growing acceptance of the status quo by the DPP. It was hoped that the acceptance of China and Taiwan into the WTO in mid-November would improve cross-Straits relations, by enhancing communications in the field of trade.

The heavy defeat of the pro-mainland KMT by the pro-independence DPP at the legislative elections of December 2001 (see below) was initially seen as a reverse to cross-Straits relations; however, Beijing reacted with moderation to the event, in contrast to past bellicosity during elections, but insisted that Taiwan accept the 'One China' principle as a precondition for bilateral dialogue. Meanwhile, the Control Yuan reported that some 200 recently retired Taiwanese military and intelligence officials had visited Hong Kong and the mainland in violation of laws stipulating that they wait three years before doing so. There were fears that a number of these officials had divulged military secrets to mainland military officials, thereby jeopardizing the island's security.

In January 2002 the Government announced a new passport design incorporating the words 'issued in Taiwan' on the cover, ostensibly to differentiate clearly Taiwanese passports from mainland ones. The initiative was regarded disapprovingly by Beijing, as a sign of symbolic statehood. In mid-January the Government announced a list of more than 2,000 items that would thenceforth be legally importable from the mainland, mostly consumer but also agricultural goods, and at the same time facilitated direct transport links with the mainland. Later in the month, Chinese Vice-Premier Qian Qichen invited members of the DPP to visit the mainland, stating that most DPP members were not independence activists. President Chen welcomed Qian's remarks, and Premier Yu stated that he was planning to send a delegation to the mainland, but ruled out negotiations on the so-called '1992 consensus'. In February an unnamed senior Chinese official reportedly suggested, privately, that China was prepared to abandon its insistence that Taipei accept the 'One China' principle before commercial links could be realized.

In a sign of improving financial links, in early March 2002 Beijing announced that, for the first time, two Taiwanese banks would be allowed to open offices on the mainland. Taiwan would also allow mainland banks to establish offices on the island. At the end of the month, Taiwan eased restrictions on the island's companies investing in computer-chip manufacturing on the mainland; however, restrictions would remain on the number of plants established and type of chips produced. Underlying these restrictions was a fear that Taiwan's valuable electronics industry might become dependent on the mainland, and that the mainland might gain access to advanced semiconductor technology used to guide missiles. It was thought that Taiwan's efforts to open up to the mainland were being hampered by former President Lee Teng-hui's new political party, upon which the DPP depended to maintain a majority in the legislature and which generally favoured a slower approach to improving bilateral commercial relations.

At the beginning of May 2002 an official Chinese newspaper published Beijing's strongest criticism to date of President Chen, describing him as a 'troublemaker' who sought to damage bilateral relations, and criticizing his efforts to promote a separate 'Taiwanese' identity. The comments were thought to be a response to the strengthening of relations between Taiwan and the USA (see above). None the less, Taiwan at the same time reluctantly allowed China to ship more than 2,300 tons of water to its outlying islands in order to help relieve the worst drought in many years, an arrangement that would have been unthinkable a few years previously. Meanwhile, Chen in early May announced that he planned to send a DPP delegation to the mainland later in the year, in response to Qian Qichen's conciliatory speech in January. At the end of May the Mainland Affairs Council planned to introduce changes that would allow non-governmental organizations a greater role in promoting cross-Straits dialogue. Two state-owned oil companies from both sides at this time agreed upon a joint venture to explore petroleum and gas deposits in the straits. Taiwan's arrest in mid-June of one of its own military officers for passing military secrets to

China failed to damage these improving commercial links, but offered a reminder that the intelligence 'war' between the two sides was far from over. Earlier, in mid-April, Taiwan had dispatched several navy vessels to monitor a Chinese research vessel operating just outside Taiwanese waters, and had tested an indigenously developed air-defence missile in May. Despite mutual suspicions, several Taiwanese legislators and retired generals secretly travelled to Beijing in June and discussed defence issues with their mainland counterparts.

In late June 2002 Beijing urged business groups to play the major role in establishing direct transport links between the two territories. However, in early July the mainland's Bank of China demanded that Taiwanese banks sign an acknowledgement of the 'One China' principle before cross-Straits banking services could begin. Taipei immediately rejected such demands, accusing Beijing of seeking to introduce a political element into the financial links between them, and questioning the sincerity of China's goodwill.

Bilateral relations again deteriorated in late July 2002, however, when the Pacific island nation of Nauru transferred its recognition from Taiwan to the People's Republic of China, thereby undermining Taipei diplomatically and prompting Chen to warn that Taiwan might have to chart its own future path. At the same time Taiwan's Ministry of Defense warned in a biannual report that China's military spending was accelerating rapidly and that it would possess 600 short-range missiles targeting the island by 2005. Chen further incensed Beijing in early August by supporting demands for a referendum to determine the island's future, and referring to China and Taiwan as two countries. Although China warned against any such moves, Chen's rhetoric was believed to have reflected his frustration at the lack of a political breakthrough in cross-Straits relations, and was probably aimed at raising the DPP's popularity ahead of forthcoming mayoral elections. However, DPP officials stated that there had been no change in policy, and Chen subsequently softened his rhetoric. Taiwan then cancelled planned military exercises as a gesture of good faith, but Chen's comments delayed the introduction of direct transport links. At the end of July the Government announced that Chinese products could be advertised on the island and that Chinese employees of Taiwanese or foreign companies would be allowed to work in Taiwan. A Taiwanese semiconductor manufacturer, the world's largest, also announced plans to build a new factory on the Chinese mainland, in Shanghai.

The political atmosphere between China and Taiwan was likely to remain volatile, however, and in early September 2002 Chen described the mainland's threats against the island as a form of 'terrorism'.

INTERNAL POLITICAL DEVELOPMENTS

President Chiang Kai-shek remained in office until his death in April 1975. He was succeeded by the former Vice-President, Dr Yen Chia-kan, as Head of State, and by his son, Gen. Chiang Ching-kuo (who had been Premier since May 1972), as Chairman of the KMT. Chiang Ching-kuo succeeded Dr Yen as President in May 1978, when Sun Yun-suan became Premier.

Meanwhile, legislative elections were held in December 1972, for the first time in 24 years, to fill 53 seats in the National Assembly. The new members, elected for a fixed term of six years, joined 1,376 surviving 'life-term' members of the Assembly. In the December 1983 elections for 71 local seats in the Legislative Yuan, whose original republican membership had been reduced by attrition from 760 to 274 (with an average age of 77), the ruling KMT won 62 seats. In addition, 27 supplementary vacancies for overseas Chinese were filled by presidential appointment. Younger, well-qualified Taiwan-orientated members thus entered the Legislative Yuan. In March 1984 President Chiang Ching-kuo was re-elected for a second six-year term by the National Assembly. Lee Teng-hui, hitherto Governor of Taiwan Province, was elected Vice-President. Yu Kuo-hwa, a former Governor of the Central Bank, was appointed Premier in May, in place of Sun Yun-suan, and a major reshuffle of the Executive Yuan (cabinet) brought several younger politicians into the Government. At local elections in November 1985 the KMT won 80% of the seats.

The Ending of Martial Law and Progress towards Democracy

In 1986 the KMT announced its readiness to discuss four controversial issues: the possible establishment of new political parties, the status of the martial law (in force since 1949), the structure of provincial government in Taiwan, and the problem of the ageing political leadership. In September 135 leading opposition politicians formed the Democratic Progressive Party (DPP), in defiance of the KMT, and in preparation for the legislative elections that were due to be held in December. In October the KMT announced its intention to suspend martial law. The formation of rival political groups was also permitted. During 1987 three such organizations emerged: the Chinese Freedom Party (CFP), favouring improved relations with mainland China; the Democratic Liberal Party (DLP); and the Kungtang, or Labour Party. The Chinese Republican Party (CRP) was formed in 1988.

Elections for 84 seats in the National Assembly and 73 seats in the Legislative Yuan were held in December 1986. The KMT won 68 seats in the National Assembly and 59 in the Legislative Yuan, but the DPP received about one-quarter of the total votes cast, winning 11 seats in the Assembly and 12 in the Legislative Yuan, thus more than doubling the non-KMT representation. Following the opening of a new session of the Legislative Yuan in February 1987, the KMT began to implement its programme of reform. The most significant change was the termination of martial law, and its replacement in July by a new national security law, whereby political parties other than the KMT were permitted, civilians were removed from the jurisdiction of military courts, and military personnel no longer had the right to determine the acceptability of persons entering and leaving Taiwan. Despite the fact that the removal of martial law had been the principal aim of the DPP, the party remained opposed to the conditions with which opposition groups had to comply in order to gain legal recognition. The new law stated that opposition parties should honour the Constitution, support the Government's anti-communist policy and oppose separatism, but many DPP leaders argued that acceptance of these conditions would effectively recognize the right of the ruling KMT to regulate its own opposition. The question of the DPP's legal status thus remained unresolved.

The KMT also attempted to rejuvenate Taiwan's ageing leadership. Within the party, younger members advocating reform were promoted to positions of influence, and in April 1987 secured seven major posts in a reshuffle of the Executive Yuan. Among the younger members of the KMT, a strong movement in favour of the increased democratization of Taiwan's parliamentary system developed. In February 1988 a plan to restructure the legislative bodies, which had been initiated by President Chiang Ching-kuo in 1986, was approved by the Central Standing Committee of the KMT. Under its provisions, 'life-term' members of the Legislative Yuan and the National Assembly would be progressively reduced in number through death and voluntary retirement. Seats in the National Assembly and the Legislative Yuan would no longer be reserved for representatives of mainland constituencies, and there would be a corresponding increase in members representing Taiwanese constituencies.

Chiang Ching-kuo died in January 1988, and was succeeded by the Vice-President, Lee Teng-hui, who was designated to serve the remaining two years of President Chiang's term of office. Before his death, President Chiang had stated that Taiwan's future leadership should be provided by constitutional means, thus signalling the end of the Chiang 'dynasty'. President Lee was the first native Taiwanese to serve as President and was thus, potentially, at variance with the 'old guard' of mainland-orientated members of the KMT and the Legislative Yuan. The new President sought to strengthen the KMT's commitment to the programme of political reform and to the rejuvenation and 'Taiwanization' of the country's leadership. However, the slow pace at which the Government proceeded attracted criticism, not only from the DPP, but also from liberal elements within the KMT. In January 1988 the DPP sought to obstruct the adoption of two draft laws regarding the freedom of assembly and demonstration, and the formation of new political parties, claiming that their provisions would regulate too strictly the activities of the opposition. In April liberal representatives of the KMT in the Legislative Yuan began to intensify the campaign for a restructuring of the party, demanding that all 150 members of its Central Committee, and at least some of the 31 members of its Central Standing Committee, be elected to office. In May an initially peaceful demonstration by farmers in Taipei resulted in the most serious riots in Taiwan's recent history.

At the 13th National Congress of the KMT, held in July 1988, Lee promised to accelerate reform and to fortify 'the substance and function of democracy'. The party congress confirmed him in the chairmanship of the party and went on to elect most of his 180 nominees for membership of an expanded Central Committee. Two-thirds of the members of the new Central Committee were chosen, for the first time in the history of the KMT, by free elections and had not previously been members. The proportion of members who were native Taiwanese also increased sharply, from one-fifth to almost two-thirds. President Lee's appointments to the Central Standing Committee followed the same trend, in that 12 of its 31 members were replaced by representatives of the younger, liberal faction of the KMT. For the first time, also, the number of members of the Central Standing Committee who were native Taiwanese was greater than that of those born on the mainland. A reshuffle of the Executive Yuan in late July reflected the changes that had been accomplished at the National Congress of the KMT: new ministerial appointments resulted in a government comprising younger members. At the same time, President Lee promoted three urgent legislative measures: a draft revision of regulations concerning the registration of civic organizations and political parties; a retirement plan (with generous pensions) for those members of the Legislative Yuan, the Control Yuan and the National Assembly who had been elected by mainland constituencies in 1947; and a new law aiming to give greater autonomy to the Taiwan Provincial Government and its assembly.

The three measures became law in January 1989. In the following month the KMT became the first political party to register under the new legislation. However, the new laws were severely criticized by the DPP, which protested at the size of the retirement pensions being offered and at the terms of the Civic Organizations Law, which required that, in order to register, political parties undertook to reject communism and any notion of official political independence for Taiwan. Despite these objections, the DPP applied for official registration in April 1989. In May Yu Kuo-hwa resigned as Premier of the Executive Yuan and was replaced by Lee Huan, the Secretary-General of the KMT.

Partial elections to the Legislative Yuan and the Taiwan Provincial Assembly were held on 2 December 1989. A total of 101 seats in the Legislative Yuan were contested by the KMT, the DPP and several independent candidates. The KMT obtained 72 seats and the DPP won 21. By virtue of achieving more than 20 seats, the DPP secured the prerogative to propose legislation in the Legislative Yuan.

In February 1990 the opening of the National Assembly's 35-day plenary session, convened every six years to elect the country's President, was disrupted by DPP members' violent action in a protest against the continuing domination of the Assembly by elderly KMT politicians, who had been elected on the Chinese mainland prior to 1949 and who had never been obliged to seek re-election. At the Legislative Yuan, demonstrators attempted to prevent senior KMT members from entering the building, and the election of a KMT veteran as President of the legislature had to be postponed, when opposition members deliberately delayed the procedure. More than 80 people were injured during the ensuing street clashes between riot police and demonstrators.

In March 1990 DPP members were barred from the National Assembly for refusing to swear allegiance to 'The Republic of China', attempting instead to substitute 'Taiwan' upon taking the oath. A number of amendments to the Temporary Provisions, which for more than 40 years had permitted the effective suspension of the Constitution, were approved by the National Assembly in mid-March. Revisions included measures to strengthen the position of the mainland-elected KMT members, who were granted new powers to initiate and veto legislation, and also an amendment to permit the National Assembly to meet annually. The revisions were opposed not only by the DPP but also by more moderate members of the KMT, and led to a large protest rally in Taipei, which attracted an estimated 10,000 demonstrators, who continued to demand the abolition of the National Assembly and the holding of direct presidential elections. Nevertheless, President Lee was duly re-elected, unopposed, by the National Assembly for a six-year term, two rival KMT candidates having withdrawn from the contest. In April President Lee and the Chairman of the DPP met for discussions.

There was renewed unrest in May 1990, however, following President Lee's unexpected appointment as Premier of Gen. (retd) Hau Pei-tsun, the former Chief of the General Staff and, since December 1989, the Minister of National Defense. Outraged opposition members prevented Hau from addressing the National Assembly, which was unable to approve his nomination until the session was reconvened a few days later, police being summoned to the Assembly to restore order. Angry demonstrators, fearing a reversal of the process of democratic reform, again clashed with riot police on the streets of Taipei. A new Executive Yuan was appointed at the end of the month, and included a civilian as Minister of National Defense. New Ministers of Foreign Affairs and of Finance were appointed, but the majority of ministers retained their previous portfolios.

The National Affairs Conference (NAC), convened in late June 1990, was attended by 150 delegates from various sections of society. At the historic meeting, proposals for reform were presented for discussion. A Constitutional Reform Planning Group was subsequently established. The NAC also reached consensus on the issue of direct presidential elections, which would permit the citizens of Taiwan, rather than the ageing members of the National Assembly, to select the Head of State. Conservative members of the KMT were strongly opposed to this proposal.

Meanwhile, the Council of Grand Justices had ruled that elderly members of the National Assembly and of the Legislative Yuan should step down by the end of 1991. Constitutional reform was to be implemented in several stages: in April 1991 the Temporary Provisions, adopted in 1948, were to be abolished; in late 1991 a new National Assembly was to be elected by popular vote, the number of members being reduced and all elderly mainland-elected delegates being obliged to relinquish their seats; elections to the new Legislative Yuan were to take place in 1992. Meanwhile, in early December 1990 Huang Hwa, the leader of a faction of the DPP and independence activist, had received a 10-year prison sentence upon being found guilty of 'preparing to commit sedition'.

In April 1991 the National Assembly was convened, the session again being marred by violent clashes between KMT and DPP members. The DPP subsequently boycotted the session, arguing that a completely new constitution should be introduced and that elderly KMT delegates, who did not represent Taiwan constituencies, should not have the right to make amendments to the existing Constitution. As many as 20,000 demonstrators attended a protest march organized by the DPP. Nevertheless, the National Assembly duly approved the constitutional amendments, and at midnight on 30 April the 'period of mobilization for the suppression of the Communist rebellion' and the Temporary Provisions were formally terminated. The existence, but not the legitimacy, of the Government of the People's Republic was officially acknowledged by President Lee. Furthermore, Taiwan remained committed to its 'One China' policy. Martial law remained in force until November 1992 on the islands of Kinmen (Quemoy) and Matsu where, owing to their proximity to the mainland, it had not been lifted in mid-1987 as elsewhere in Taiwan. In May 1991 widespread protests, following the arrest of four advocates of independence, led to the abolition of the Statute of Punishment for Sedition. The law had been adopted in 1949 and had been frequently employed by the KMT to suppress political dissent.

A senior UN official arrived on the island in August 1991, the first such visit since Taiwan's withdrawal from the organization in 1971. Large-scale rallies calling for a referendum to be held on the issue of Taiwan's readmission to the UN, resulting in clashes between demonstrators and the security forces, took place in September and October.

In August 1991 the opposition DPP officially announced its alternative draft constitution for 'Taiwan', rather than for 'the Republic of China', thus acknowledging the *de facto* position regarding sovereignty. In late September, only one day after being reinstated in the Legislative Yuan, Huang Hsin-chieh, the Chairman of the DPP, relinquished his seat in the legislature and urged other senior deputies to do likewise. Huang Hsin-chieh had been deprived of his seat and imprisoned in 1980, following his conviction on charges of sedition. At the party congress in October 1991, Huang Hsin-chieh was replaced as DPP Chairman by Hsu Hsin-liang. Risking prosecution by the authorities, the DPP congress adopted a resolution henceforth to advocate the establishment of 'the Republic of Taiwan', and urged the Government to declare the island's independence.

Elections to the new 405-member National Assembly, which was to be responsible for amending the Constitution, were held on 21 December 1991. The 225 seats open to direct election were contested by a total of 667 candidates, presented by 17 parties. The campaign was dominated by the issue of whether Taiwan should become independent or seek reunification with the mainland. The opposition's independence proposal was overwhelmingly rejected by the electorate, the DPP suffering a humiliating defeat. The KMT secured a total of 318 seats (179 of which were won by direct election), while the DPP won 75 seats (41 by direct election).

In late 1991, in a new campaign to curb illegal dissident activity, the authorities arrested 14 independence activists, including members of the banned, US-based World United Formosans for Independence (WUFI). Several detainees were indicted on charges of sedition. Furthermore, the four dissidents, whose arrest in May had provoked widespread unrest, were brought to trial and found guilty of sedition, receiving short prison sentences. In January 1992 four WUFI members were found guilty of plotting to overthrow the Government. In February 20,000 demonstrators took part in a march in Taichung. The protesters' demands included the abolition of the sedition laws and the holding of a referendum on the issue of independence for the island. In the same month the Government released a report on the 1947 massacre of 18,000–28,000 civilians. For the first time the KMT leadership admitted responsibility for the violent suppression of the alleged communist rebels.

In March 1992, at a plenary session of the KMT Central Committee, agreement was reached on several issues, including a reduction in the President's term of office from six to four years. The principal question of arrangements for future presidential elections, however, remained unresolved. Liberal members continued to advocate direct election, while conservatives favoured a complex proxy system. In April street demonstrations were organized by the DPP to support demands for direct presidential elections. In May the National Assembly adopted eight amendments to the Constitution, one of which empowered the President to appoint members of the Control Yuan.

Meanwhile, the radical dissident, (Stella) Chen Wan-chen, who had established the pro-independence Organization for Taiwan Nation-Building upon her return from the USA in 1991, was sentenced to 46 months' imprisonment in March 1992, having been found guilty of 'preparing to commit sedition'. In May, however, Taiwan's severe sedition law was amended, non-violent acts ceasing to be a criminal offence. As a result, several independence activists, including Chen Wan-chen and Huang Hwa, were released from prison. Other dissidents were able to return from overseas exile. Nevertheless, in June (George) Chang Tsang-hung, the chairman of WUFI, who had returned from exile in the USA in December 1991, received a prison sentence of five (commuted from 10) years upon conviction on charges of sedition and attempted murder, involving the dispatch of letter-bombs to government officials in 1976. Chang was released for medical treatment in October 1992, and in March 1993 he was acquitted of the sedition charges, on the grounds of insufficient evidence.

The First Full Elections and KMT Disunity

Taiwan's first full elections since the establishment of Nationalist rule in 1949 were held in December 1992. The KMT retained 102 of the 161 seats in the Legislative Yuan. The DPP, however, garnered 31% of the votes and more than doubled its representation in the legislature, winning 50 seats. Following this set-back, the Premier and the KMT Secretary-General resigned. In February 1993 President Lee nominated the Governor of Taiwan Province, Lien Chan, for the premiership. The Legislative Yuan duly approved the appointment of Lien Chan, who thus became the island's first Premier of Taiwanese descent. The incoming Executive Yuan incorporated numerous new ministers.

There were violent scenes in the National Assembly in April 1993, when deputies of the DPP (which in recent months had modified its aggressive pro-independence stance, placing greater emphasis on the issues of corruption and social welfare) accused members of the KMT of malpractice in relation to the election of the Assembly's officers.

In May 1993 the growing rift between conservative and liberal members of the ruling party was illustrated by the resignation from the KMT of about 30 conservative rebels, and their formation of the New Alliance Nationalist Party. Furthermore, in June the Government was defeated in the Legislative Yuan, when a group of KMT deputies voted with the opposition to approve legislation on financial disclosure requirements for elected and appointed public officials. The unity of the KMT was further undermined in August, when six dissident legislators belonging to the New Kuomintang Alliance, which had registered as a political group in March, announced their decision to leave the ruling party in order to establish the New Party. The rebels included Wang Chien-shien, the former Minister of Finance. Nevertheless, in the same month, at the 14th KMT Congress, Lee Teng-hui was re-elected Chairman of the party. A new 31-member Central Standing Committee and 210-member Central Committee, comprising mainly Lee's supporters, were selected. In a conciliatory gesture by the KMT Chairman, four vice-chairmanships were created, the new positions being filled by representatives of different factions of the party.

In September 1993, following a series of bribery scandals, the Executive Yuan approved measures to combat corruption. The administrative reform plan included stricter supervision of public officials and harsher penalties for those found guilty of misconduct. In the same month a KMT member of the Legislative Yuan was sentenced to 14 years' imprisonment for bribery of voters during the 1992 election campaign; similar convictions followed. At local government elections held in November 1993, although its share of the votes declined to 47.5%, the KMT fared better than anticipated, securing 15 of the 23 posts at stake. The DPP, which accused the KMT of malpractice, received 41.5% of the votes cast, but won only six posts; it retained control of Taipei County. The DPP Chairman, Hsu Hsin-liang, resigned, and was replaced by Shih Ming-teh. Following allegations of extensive bribery at further local polls in early 1994 (at which the DPP and independent candidates made strong gains), the Ministry of Justice intensified its campaign against corruption. Proposals for constitutional amendments to permit the direct election in 1996 of the Taiwanese President by popular vote (rather than by electoral college) and to limit the powers of the Premier were approved by the National Assembly in July 1994.

At gubernatorial and mayoral elections in December 1994 the DPP took control of the Taipei mayoralty, in the first such direct polls for 30 years, while the KMT succeeded in retaining the provincial governorship of Taiwan, in the first ever popular election for the post, and the mayoralty of Kaohsiung. The New Party established itself as a major political force, its candidate for the mayoralty of Taipei receiving more votes than the KMT incumbent. Almost 77% of those eligible voted in the elections. A government reorganization followed.

In March 1995, in response to continuing allegations of corruption (the number of indictments now having exceeded 2,000), President Lee announced the appointment of a committee to investigate the financial activities of the KMT. In the same month, following the President's formal apology at a ceremony of commemoration in February, the Legislative Yuan approved a law granting compensation to the relatives of the victims of a massacre by Nationalist troops in 1947 (the 'February 28 Incident'), in which an estimated 18,000 native Taiwanese had been killed. (In June 1997 the Executive Yuan approved draft legislation to grant an amnesty to those involved in the incident.)

Fewer than 68% of those eligible voted at the elections to the Legislative Yuan held on 2 December 1995. A major campaign issue was that of corruption. The KMT received only 46% of the votes cast, and its strength declined to 85 of the 164 seats. The ruling party fared particularly badly in Taipei. Although it performed less well than anticipated, the DPP increased its representation to 54 seats. The New Party, which favoured reconciliation with the mainland, secured 21 seats. At the Legislative Yuan's first session in February 1996, Liu Sung-pan of the KMT only narrowly defeated a strong challenge from Shih Ming-teh of the DPP to secure re-election as the chamber's President.

The Presidential Election of 1996 and Beyond

The first direct presidential election was scheduled for March 1996, to coincide with the National Assembly polls. President Lee had declared his intention to stand for re-election in August 1995. In January 1996 Lien Chan offered to resign as Premier in order to support President Lee and to concentrate on his own vice-presidential campaign. He remained in office in an interim capacity. Other contenders for the presidency included the independent candidate and former President of the Judicial Yuan, Lin Yang-kang, supported by former Premier Hau Pei-tsun (both conservative former KMT Vice-Chairmen having campaigned on behalf of New Party candidates at the December elections and therefore having had their KMT membership revoked); Peng Ming-min of the DPP; and Chen Li-an, former President of the Control Yuan and previously Minister of National Defense, an independent Buddhist candidate. Wang Chien-shien of the New Party withdrew his candidacy in favour of the Lin-Hau alliance. The campaign was dominated by the issue of reunification with the mainland. In mid-March a DPP demonstration on the streets of Taipei, in support of demands for Taiwan's independence, was attended by 50,000 protesters.

At the presidential election, held on 23 March 1996, the incumbent President Lee received 54.0% of the votes cast, thus securing his re-election. His nearest rival, Peng Ming-min of the DPP, took 21.1% of the votes. The independent candidates, Lin Yang-kang and Chen Li-an, received 14.9% and 10.0% of the votes respectively. At the concurrent elections for the National Assembly, the KMT garnered 55% of the votes and took 183 of the 334 seats. The DPP won 99 seats and the New Party 46 seats. The Chairman of the DPP, Shih Ming-teh, resigned and Hsu Hsin-liang subsequently returned to the post.

On 20 May 1996 President Lee was sworn in for a four-year term. In June, however, the President's announcement of the composition of the new Executive Yuan aroused much controversy. Although several members retained their previous portfolios, the President (apparently under pressure from within the KMT and disregarding public concern at the rising levels of corruption and organized crime) demoted the popular Ministers of Justice (Ma Ying-jeou) and of Transportation and Communications, who had exposed malpractice and initiated campaigns against corruption. Other changes included the replacement of the Minister of Foreign Affairs, Fredrick Chien (who became Speaker of the National Assembly), by John Chang, the grandson of Chiang Kai-shek. The most controversial nomination, however, was the reappointment as Premier of Lien Chan, despite his recent election as the island's Vice-President. As fears of a constitutional crisis grew, opposition members of the Legislative Yuan, along with a number of KMT delegates, demanded that the President submit the membership of the Executive Yuan to the legislature for approval, and threatened to boycott the chamber's business. In October the Constitutional Court opened its hearing regarding the question of the island's Vice-President serving concurrently as Premier.

In October 1996 the Taiwan Independence Party was established by dissident members of the DPP. In the same month the Legislative Yuan approved the restoration of funding for a controversial fourth nuclear power plant, construction of which had been suspended in 1986. Thousands of anti-nuclear protesters demonstrated at the legislature, clashing with police and preventing Lien Chan from entering the building.

In December 1996 the multi-party National Development Conference (NDC), established to review the island's political system, held its inaugural meeting. The convention approved KMT proposals to abolish the Legislative Yuan's right to confirm the President's choice of Premier, to permit the legislature to introduce motions of 'no confidence' in the Premier and to empower the President to dismiss the legislature. The Provincial Governor, (James) Soong Chu-yu, subsequently tendered his resignation in protest at the NDC's recommendations that elections for the provincial governorship and assembly be abolished, as the first stage of the dissolution of the provincial apparatus. An historical legacy duplicating many of the functions of central and local government, the Provincial Government was responsible for the entire island, with the exception of the cities of Taipei and Kaohsiung. In January 1997 President Lee refused to accept the Governor's resignation, but the affair drew attention to the uneasy relationship between the island's President and its Governor, and brought to the fore the question of reunification with the mainland. The Provincial Government was abolished in December 1998.

In May 1997 more than 50,000 demonstrators, protesting against the Government's apparent inability to address the problem of increasing crime, demanded the resignation of President Lee. Three members of the Executive Yuan resigned, including the popular Minister without Portfolio and former Minister of Justice, Ma Ying-jeou, who expressed his deep shame at recent events. The appointment of Yeh Chin-feng as Minister of the Interior (the first woman to oversee Taiwan's police force) did little to appease the public, which remained highly suspicious of the alleged connections between senior politicians and the perpetrators of organized crime. In mid-May thousands of protesters, despairing of the rapid deterioration in social order, again took to the streets of Taipei, renewing their challenge to President Lee's leadership and demanding the immediate resignation of Premier Lien Chan. In late June, prior to the return to Chinese sovereignty of Hong Kong, a 'Say No to China' rally attracted as many as 70,000 supporters.

In July 1997 the National Assembly approved various constitutional reforms, including the 'freezing' of the Provincial Government. Other revisions that received approval were to empower the President of Taiwan to appoint the Premier without the Legislative Yuan's confirmation; the legislature was to be permitted to hold a binding vote of 'no confidence' in the Executive Yuan, while the President gained the right to dissolve the Legislative Yuan. In August the Premier and his entire Government resigned in order to permit a reallocation of portfolios. Vincent Siew, former Chairman of the Council for Economic Planning and Development and also of the Mainland Affairs Council, replaced Lien Chan as Premier. (Lien Chan retained the post of Vice-President.) John Chang was appointed Vice-Premier, and the new Minister of Foreign Affairs was Jason Hu. Following the installation of the new Executive Yuan, the Premier pledged to improve social order, further develop the economy, raise the island's standard of living and improve links with the People's Republic of China. In the same month President Lee Teng-hui was re-elected unopposed as Chairman of the ruling KMT.

The KMT experienced a serious set-back in elections at mayoral and magistrate levels, held on 29 November 1997. The opposition DPP, which had campaigned on a platform of more open government, secured 43% of the total votes, winning 12 of the 23 constituency posts contested, while the KMT achieved only 42% (eight posts). Voter turn-out was 65.9%. The outcome of the elections meant that more than 70% of Taiwan's population would come under DPP administration. Following the KMT's poor performance in the ballot, the Secretary-General of the party resigned, and was replaced by John Chang. A major reorganization of the party followed. Liu Chao-shiuan was appointed Vice-Premier in place of Chang.

At local elections, held in January 1998, the KMT won an overwhelming majority of the seats contested, while the DPP, in a reversal of fortune, performed badly. A minor cabinet reshuffle was carried out in early February.

In late March the Minister of Transportation and Communications resigned, assuming responsibility for two aeroplane crashes in Taiwan in early 1998, in which more than 200 people had died. In the following month the Minister of Justice tendered, and then subsequently withdrew, his resignation, citing pressure from lawmakers with connections to organized crime. However, in July he was forced to resign, following his mishandling of an alleged scandal concerning the acting head of the Investigation Bureau.

In June 1998 the first-ever direct election for the leadership of the DPP was held. Lin Yi-hsiung won a convincing victory, assuming the chairmanship of the party in August. Meanwhile, in local elections, in June, the KMT suffered a set-back, winning fewer than 50% of the seats contested. Independent candidates performed well. In August 17 new members were elected to the KMT Central Standing Committee, the 16 others being appointed by President Lee.

The Legislative Elections of December 1998 and Constitutional Issues

Elections to the newly-expanded 225-member Legislative Yuan took place on 5 December 1998; 68.1% of the electorate participated in the poll. The KMT won 46.4% of the votes cast, securing 125 seats, the DPP received 29.6% of the votes and won 72 seats, while the pro-unification New Party secured only 7.1% of the votes and 11 seats. The New Nation Alliance, a breakaway group from the DPP (formed in September), won only one seat (with 1.6% of the votes cast). The KMT's victory was widely attributed to its management of the economy, in view of the Asian financial crisis, the developments in cross-Straits dialogue and a decline in factionalism within the party in 1998. In the election (held simultaneously) to select the mayor of Taipei, the KMT candidate, Ma Ying-jeou (a former Minister of Justice), defeated the DPP incumbent, Chen Shui-bian. However, the DPP candidate for the office of mayor of Kaohsiung, Frank Hsieh, narrowly defeated the KMT incumbent. The KMT retained control of both city councils.

Owing to the DPP's poor performance at the elections, Lin Yu-hsiung offered his resignation as Chairman of the DPP, but withdrew it following overwhelming party support for his leadership. However, Chiou I-jen resigned as Secretary-General in December 1998 and was replaced by Yu Shyi-kun. Later that month Chao Shu-po, a Minister without Portfolio, was appointed Governor of Taiwan Province, replacing the elected incumbent, James Soong, as part of the plans to dismantle the Provincial Government, agreed in 1997. A minor reorganization of the Executive Yuan took place in late January 1999.

In March 1999 an unprecedented vote of 'no confidence' in the leadership of Premier Vincent Siew was defeated in the Legislative Yuan. The motion was presented by the opposition following Siew's reversal of his earlier position and his decision to reduce the tax on share transactions, apparently as a result of pressure from President Lee. The National Assembly passed a controversial constitutional amendment on 4 September, which, *inter alia*, extended the terms of the deputies from May 2000 to June 2002. Election to the assembly was henceforth to be on the basis of party proportional representation. Several politicians and critical citizens condemned the move as being 'against the public will'. Shortly afterwards, the KMT leadership expelled the Speaker of the National Assembly, Su Nan-cheng, from the party on the grounds that he had violated its policy on the tenure extension, thereby also removing him from his parliamentary seat and the post of speaker. There was widespread dissatisfaction regarding the National Assembly's action, and in March 2000 the Council of Grand Justices of the Judicial Yuan ruled it to be unconstitutional. Later that month the DPP and the KMT reached an agreement on the abolition of the body and the cancellation of elections scheduled for early May. In April the National Assembly convened, and approved a series of constitutional amendments, which effectively deprived the body of most of its powers, and reduced it to an ad hoc institution. The capacity to initiate constitutional amendments, to impeach the President or Vice-President, and to approve the appointment of senior officials, was transferred to the Legislative Yuan. The National Assembly was to retain the functions of ratifying constitutional amendments and impeachment proceedings, in which case 300 delegates, appointed by political parties according to a system of proportional representation, would convene for a session of a maximum duration of one month.

The Presidential Election of 2000 and Beyond

In November 1999 it was announced that a presidential election was to be held in March 2000. Five candidates registered: Lien Chan (with Vincent Siew as candidate for Vice-President) was the KMT nominee, while Chen Shui-bian, a former mayor of Taipei, was to stand for the DPP (with the feminist Annette Lu as vice-presidential candidate), and Li Ao was to represent the New Party; the former DPP Chairman, Hsu Hsin-liang, qualified as an independent candidate, as did James Soong, who was consequently expelled from the KMT, along with a number of his supporters. Jason Hu resigned as Minister of Foreign Affairs in November 1999 in order to direct the KMT's election campaign. He was replaced by Chang Che-shen, hitherto Director-General of the Government Information Office. It became evident in the following month, when Soong was publicly accused of embezzlement, that the election would be bitterly contested. Although Soong denied the charges, his popularity was affected. In January 2000 Lien Chan, in an attempt to regain the support of disillusioned voters, proposed that the KMT's extensive business holdings be placed in trust and that the party terminate its direct role in the management of the numerous companies in which it owned shares. The KMT adopted the proposal shortly afterwards. In a reflection of the tense political situation between Taiwan and China, Chen Shui-bian of the DPP modified the party's stance and pledged not to declare formal independence for the island unless Beijing attacked.

The presidential election, held on 18 March 2000, was won by Chen Shui-bian, who obtained 39.3% of the votes cast. James Soong, his closest rival, received 36.8% of the votes. (On the day after the election he founded the People First Party, in an attempt to take advantage of his popularity.) Lien Chan of the KMT secured only 23.1% of the votes. The remaining candidates obtained less than 1%. The poll attracted a high level of participation, 82.7% of the electorate taking part. (Upon his inauguration in May, Chen would thus become Taiwan's first non-KMT President since 1945.) Violence erupted as disappointed KMT supporters besieged the party's headquarters, attributing the KMT's defeat to the leadership's expulsion of James Soong and the resultant division of the party. Lee Teng-hui subsequently accepted responsibility for the defeat and resigned from the chairmanship of the party. Lien Chan assumed the leadership. As the KMT continued to dominate the Legislative Yuan, however, the party did not entirely relinquish its influence, and in early April gave permission for Tang Fei, a KMT member and hitherto Minister of National Defense, to serve as Premier (although he was to be suspended from party activities while in the post). Following protracted negotiations, the membership of the new Executive Yuan, which incorporated 11 DPP members and 13 KMT members, was approved in early May. The incoming Government largely lacked ministerial experience. Furthermore, the DPP's lack of a legislative majority impeded the passage of favourable legislation. The size of the budget deficit also made it difficult for the DPP to fulfil specific electoral pledges on health, housing and education. In July Frank Hsieh replaced Lin Yi-hsiung as Chairman of the DPP.

In July 2000 the Government was heavily criticized after a river accident in which four workers, stranded by a flash flood, drowned as a result of the authorities' failure to provide a rescue helicopter. While the various government departments deliberated over the allocation of responsiblity, the victims' final hours were broadcast live on national television. The Vice-Premier and Chairman of the Consumer Protection Commission Yu Shyi-kun subsequently resigned, as did senior officials of the emergency services. The Premier's offer of resignation was refused by President Chen Shui-bian. In October 2000, however, Tang Fei resigned as Premier, ostensibly owing to ill health. It was suggested that his departure from the post was due to the Government's failure to agree upon the fate of Taiwan's fourth nuclear power plant, the DPP being opposed to the project. (Later that month the Executive Yuan announced that construction of the plant was to be halted.) Vice-Premier Chang Chun-hsing was appointed Premier, and a minor government reorganization was effected. Changes included the appointment of Yen Ching-chang as Minister of Finance, his predecessor having resigned following a sharp decline in the stock market.

Political disputes over the construction of Taiwan's fourth nuclear power plant intensified later in October 2000. The Minister of Economic Affairs, Lin Hsin-yi, was expelled from the KMT for 'seriously opposing KMT policies and impairing the people's interests' after he had demonstrated his support for the cancellation of the project. At the end of the month Chang Chun-hsiung announced that the Executive Yuan had decided to halt construction of the plant for financial and economic reasons. Although environmentalists were pleased, citing Taiwan's inability to process nuclear waste and to cope with accidents, the KMT reacted furiously, rejecting the Government's right to cancel a project approved by the legislature, and, together with the New Party and the People First Party, immediately began collecting legislators' signatures for the recall (dismissal) of Chen Shui-bian. The opposition was not mollified by a subsequent apology from Chen, and shortly afterwards the Legislative Yuan passed revised legislation on the process for presidential impeachment. Owing to the controversy, KMT member Vincent Siew refused to act as the President's representative to the annual APEC forum in Brunei in November and was replaced by Perng Fai-nan, the Governor of the Central Bank. The dispute became so serious that the business community issued an unprecedented public statement that economic recovery should take priority over political differences, but in December some 10,000 protesters in Taipei demanded that Chen resign. In November the Government requested a constitutional interpretation on the issue from the Council of Grand Justices, which it agreed to be bound by. The Council ruled in mid-January 2001 that the Government should have sought the legislature's approval before halting construction of the plant, and in mid-February 2001 the Government decided immediately to resume construction of the plant. In March 2001 a minor government reorganization was effected. The most notable change was the appointment of Hu Ching-piao, hitherto a Minister without Portfolio, as Chairman of the Atomic Energy Council, replacing Hsia Der-yu. It was rumoured that Hsia had disagreed with Chang Chun-hsiung over the future of the nuclear plant.

Meanwhile, in September 2000 four retired naval officers and one still serving were arrested in connection with the suspected murder in 1993 of a naval captain, Yin Ching-feng, to prevent him from revealing a scandal surrounding Taiwan's 1991 purchase of French-built frigates. It was alleged that bribery had influenced the award of the contract, which had been abruptly withdrawn from a South Korean firm. In October the Control Yuan impeached three former naval admirals, including the former Commander-in-Chief of the Navy Adm. (retd) Yeh Chang-tung, for their involvement in the affair. In December the Taiwanese authorities appealed to the French Government for information to assist their investigations. The report of a two-year investigation by the Control Yuan, released in March 2002, strongly criticized the Ministry of National Defense and the navy command for failing to investigate fully Capt. Yin's murder, and recommended the court-martial of Adm. (retd) Yeh and former Prime Minister and Minister of National Defense, Hau Pei-tsun. The report also revealed that France had divulged to China confidential information regarding the deal. Several retired admirals went on trial for corruption in late April 2002.

By March 2001 President Chen had lost popularity within his DPP for softening his stance on two of its key policies—independence for Taiwan, and commitment to a nuclear power-free island. Fears emerged that the DPP could lose seats in legislative elections due in December, though polls showed that some 60% of the public supported construction of the nuclear plant. However, polls also showed Chen's popularity to be in decline, with much of the optimism that had greeted his inauguration being replaced with concerns about his inexperience and lack of power, his handling of the economy, and the political gridlock in domestic affairs, as well as the impasse in cross-Straits relations.

Concerns about the economy were heightened in May 2001 when 20,000 demonstrators from 18 trade unions marched in Taipei to protest against the Government's inability to reduce the unemployment rate, which at nearly 4% was at a 16-year high; furthermore, economic growth had declined to its lowest rate in 26 years. Later in the month Chen announced that he was planning to form the island's first coalition government after the December elections, in order to end the political infighting. In late June Chen received a major political boost when former President Lee Teng-hui offered his public support and suggested that he would back Chen in the December elections. Lee had disagreed with KMT leader Lien Chan, and his possible defection to Chen's support base threatened significantly to weaken the KMT. The emerging alliance between the two pro-independence leaders signalled a potential realignment in Taiwanese politics into pro-mainland and pro-independence forces, and seemed to end Beijing's goals of developing a strong pro-mainland political bloc on the island. There were also concerns that the realignment could further polarize society in this regard.

Moves toward such a political environment gained momentum in early July 2001, when the KMT issued a policy paper arguing that Taiwan's best option in terms of its relations with China was to form a 'confederation' with the mainland—the furthest that any political party had moved in calling for a union with China. The architect of the new KMT policy, Su Chi, described this as being 'somewhere in the middle ground between independence and unification', though the party had adopted a noticeably more pro-reunification stance under Lien Chan. However, the KMT's Central Standing Committee in late July refrained from adopting the proposal, reflecting the party's uncertainty over mainland policy. On 12 August 2001 a new political party, the Taiwan Solidarity Union (TSU), was formally launched with the support of former President Lee, and consisting of breakaway members of the KMT and DPP, led by former Interior Minister Huang Chu-wen. The party was formed in order to help President Chen win a majority in December's elections, an important goal given that the KMT had used its majority to block many of Chen's reforms during the previous one-year period. However, there were fears that the new party would drain support from Chen's DPP.

In July 2001 President Chen called for major governmental reforms, including reorganization, streamlining measures, anti-corruption action, and improved inter-departmental co-operation. At the end of August Chen also accepted proposals by a special advisory committee on closer economic relations with the mainland (see above).

The Legislative Elections of December 2001 and Subsequent Events

The last months of 2001 were dominated by campaigning for legislative elections. As support for the KMT waned, politics increasingly became an ethnic issue, with the KMT and People First Party (PFP) drawing their support from those who had fled the mainland in 1949 and their descendants (approximately 15% of the population), while native Taiwanese (who comprised 65% of the population) supported the DPP and the TSU. Despite the economic recession, Chen's popularity rose in the period prior to the elections, amid rumours that the DPP would form a coalition to secure a majority. The DPP hoped that a coalition would enable reforms to the legislature, notably the abolition of the multi-member constituencies in favour of a single-seat, 'first-past-the-post' system, thereby ending the need for candidates from the same party to compete against each other.

At the elections held on 1 December 2001 the DPP emerged as the biggest single party in the new legislature, having won 36.6% of the votes cast and 87 seats, but failed to win a majority. The KMT won 31.3% of votes and 68 seats, thereby losing its dominance of the Legislative Yuan for the first time in its history. The PFP came third, winning 20.3% of the votes and 46 seats, while the newly formed TSU came fourth, with 8.5% of the votes and 13 seats. The New Party won only 2.9% of the votes and one seat, while independents took nine seats. The level of voter participation was registered as 66.2%.

In the immediate aftermath of the elections, political manoeuvring to establish a coalition began, as the DPP and KMT sought to have their candidate elected as Vice-President of the Legislative Yuan. On 21 January 2002 President Chen reorganized the Executive Yuan, appointing his hitherto Secretary-General, Yu Shyi-kun, as Premier. The move was seen as a consolidation of the President's power, aimed at improving his prospects for re-election in 2004; the new Premier was also thought to be a more efficient administrator than his predecessor. Other notable appointments included Chen Shih-meng, hitherto deputy governor of the Central Bank, as the Secretary-General to the President, replacing Yu. Lin Hsin-i, hitherto Minister of Economic Affairs, was appointed Vice-Premier and Chairman of the Council for Economic Planning and Development, Eugene Chien, hitherto Deputy Secretary-General to the President, as Minister of Foreign Affairs, and Gen. Tang Yao-ming, hitherto Chief of the General Staff, as the new Minister of National Defense. Tang was the first native-born Taiwanese to hold the newly-augmented defence post in a mainlander-dominated military, and he was to oversee military reforms in early 2002. Lee Yung-san, Chairman of the International Commercial Bank of China, was appointed Minister of Finance, while Lee Ying-yuan, hitherto deputy representative in Washington, DC, was appointed Secretary-General to the Executive Yuan; however, the ministers in charge of mainland and overseas Chinese affairs were retained, suggesting a desire for continuity in relations with China.

In late January 2002 elections were held for provincial city and township councillors. Although the KMT won the largest number of seats in these elections, it failed to expand its popularity on a national level, with the results reflecting the KMT's competent organizational mobilization methods. At the beginning of February an alliance of the KMT and PFP ('pan-blue camp') successfully blocked the DPP-TSU ('pan-green camp') candidate for the post of Vice-President of the Legislative Yuan, electing Chiang Ping-kun of the KMT to that position. At the same time, the incumbent President of the legislature, Wang Jin-pyng of the KMT, was re-elected to his post. Following their success, officials from the KMT and PFP stated that they would consider presenting joint candidates for the mayoralties of Taipei and Kaohsiung in late 2002, and possibly the presidency itself in 2004, with Wang as their candidate for the latter post.

In February 2002 the KMT-PFP alliance immediately challenged the new Government by attempting to force it to accept revisions to legislation concerning local budget allocations, which had been approved by the outgoing Legislative Yuan in December 2001. However, in the decisive vote in the new Legislative Yuan, the KMT and PFP failed to secure the majority necessary to accomplish this, thereby giving the Government a minor victory. The narrowness of this victory, however, indicated that the KMT continued to pose a formidable obstacle to the new Government. An early set-back for the Government came in late March when the Minister of Economic Affairs, Christine Tsung, resigned, citing a hostile political environment, particularly in the Legislative Yuan. She was replaced by her deputy, Lin Yi-fu.

A major political scandal erupted in late March 2002 when one daily and one weekly newspaper reported that the Government of former President Lee Teng-hui had, in co-operation with the island's intelligence service (National Security Bureau—NSB), clandestinely established an unauthorized fund worth US $100m. to finance covert operations on the mainland and to further Taiwanese interests among influential lobby groups abroad, including the USA. Prosecutors immediately raided the offices of the two newspapers and seized the offending copies, accusing the editors of leaking state secrets, amid fears that freedom of the press would come under threat. The scandal threatened to damage Lee's position, as well as jeopardize espionage missions on the mainland and Taiwan's reputation for maintaining secret intelligence—it was widely believed that the source of the 'leaks' was a former NSB colonel who had embezzled US $5.5m. and then fled the island. Following the revelations, President Chen reiterated his commitment to press freedom and proposed new oversights for the NSB.

In early April 2002 the Executive Yuan approved plans to abolish the posts of Speaker and Deputy Speaker of the National Assembly, and replace them with that of a chairman of the session. In early May the Government revealed plans to reform the electoral system, which would reduce the number of seats in the Legislative Yuan from 225 to 150 and extend the term of legislators from three to four years. Some 90 seats would be filled from single-seat constituencies (thereby eliminating the need for candidates from the same party to compete against each other, as in the existing multi-seat constituencies), with the remaining seats divided proportionally among parties that gained more than 5% of the total vote. It was hoped that such reforms would make government more efficient and less dependent upon the availability of finance. A disadvantage of the system of multi-seat constituencies was that it required the participation of larger numbers of candidates and thus greater funding, thereby encouraging corruption.

Also in early May 2002, KMT Chairman Lien Chan announced that his party would form an official alliance with the PFP in order to strengthen opposition to the ruling DPP. However, plans for a joint candidacy in the 2004 presidential elections were hampered by regulations stipulating that the presidential and vice-presidential candidates must come from the same party. Meanwhile, in mid-May thousands of people demonstrated in favour of changing Taiwan's official name from the 'Republic of China' to 'Taiwan'—an initiative that was supported by 70% of respondents in an opinion poll conducted by the Ministry of Foreign Affairs in 2001, but strongly opposed by China.

In mid-June 2002 Premier Yu Shyi-kun appointed Liu Shyh-fang as the first female Secretary-General of the Executive Yuan, replacing Lee Ying-yuan, who was standing as the DPP's candidate in elections for the mayoralty of Taipei, in December. In late July President Chen Shui-bian formally assumed the chairmanship of the DPP, in a move designed to bring party policy into line with the Government. However, critics suggested that the dual leadership style was reminiscent of the excessively-strong executive characterized by the decades of KMT rule.

In mid-September 2002 the Executive Yuan approved drafts of the new Political Party Law, which would ban political parties from operating or investing in profit-making enterprises, and allow the Government to investigate and confiscate assets unlawfully obtained by political parties. Although ostensibly aimed at creating greater political fairness and financial openness, the draft legislation was viewed as being aimed at the KMT which, during the decades of its rule, had amassed a vast commercial fortune worth an estimated NT $53,750m. (US $1,600m.) in 2001. As a result, the KMT might be forced to sell many of its assets. Meanwhile, Taiwan's political forces were increasingly focused on elections for the mayoralties of Taipei and Kaohsiung, scheduled for December 2002, and widely regarded as a preparation for the 2004 presidential elections.

Economy

ROBERT F. ASH

Based on earlier contributions by PHILIP E. T. LEWIS and ATHAR HUSSAIN

ECONOMIC DEVELOPMENT

Since 1949 the economic development of Taiwan has been shaped by historical, geo-strategic and geo-economic factors. The main historical influences have been twofold. First, Taiwan's early post–1949 development capacity was enhanced by the legacy of important agricultural, industrial and infrastructural initiatives, undertaken by Japan during its colonization of Taiwan between 1895 and 1945. Second, the defeat during the Chinese Civil War of the forces of the Chinese Nationalist Party (Kuomintang—KMT) by those of the Chinese Communist Party (CCP), and the subsequent transfer, in 1949, of the Government of the Republic of China to Taiwan were cathartic events that prompted fundamental shifts in economic policy. These shifts, reinforced and underwritten by the USA, made possible a swift economic recovery and thereafter helped promote a pattern of rapid, sustained and equitable growth that contrasted markedly with the KMT Government's disappointing growth record during the 'Nanking Decade' in China (1928–37). Meanwhile, until the 1970s, China's alienation from most western countries (especially the USA) further served Taiwan's economic interests. Although almost universal recognition of the People's Republic as the sole legitimate government of China subsequently left Taiwan's international diplomatic and political status dangerously exposed, its buoyant economic growth (including its role as one of the world's most important trading nations) continued unaffected. Since the late 1980s, however, the accelerated expansion of cross-Strait trade and investment has increasingly become a key determinant of Taiwan's development trajectory.

Natural and geographical factors played an important part in shaping Taiwan's economic development. Its geographical location gave Taiwan a central, strategically important position in the Asia-Pacific trading region—especially along trade routes between Japan, Korea, China and South-East Asia. Also significant was the small size of Taiwan's economy ('smallness' being defined to embrace natural and human resources, as well as mere surface area). In contrast to the economic self-sufficiency to which mainland China has often aspired (and the fulfilment of which its continental scope has facilitated), inherent natural and market constraints forced Taiwan to look outwards in order to maintain its economic development momentum. Its external orientation has been one of the most critical and characteristic features of Taiwan's post–1949 economic development.

Taiwan generally lacks mineral and energy resources—indeed, no important mineral is found in significant quantities on the island. Thus, its energy requirements, as well as most raw materials for domestic industry, have had to be imported. The domestic coal industry is small, while onshore and offshore sources of petroleum and natural gas are of minor significance—Taiwan imports approximately 95% of its energy requirements.

ECONOMIC STRATEGY, GROWTH AND STRUCTURAL CHANGE

Following the recovery from wartime economic destruction and from the dislocation associated with the arrival in Taiwan of the exiled KMT Government, economic policy in the 1950s was dominated by efficiency-enhancing institutional and economic initiatives in agriculture (not least, the implementation of land reform) and import-substituting industrialization (ISI). One result of ISI was a significant rise in industry's share in GDP, from 20% in 1952 to 27% in 1960. By the end of the decade, however, import substitution was exhausted, and the Government of Chiang Kai-shek embarked upon a new strategy of export-led growth. This outward orientation—one that was to drive Taiwan's subsequent techno-industrial transformation—was perhaps the single most important watershed in Taiwan's post–1949 economic development. It has lasted to the present day and has been accompanied by one of the fastest-growing performances of any economy in the world.

Between the early 1950s and the first half of the 1960s, Taiwan succeeded in laying the foundations of self-sustaining growth. Economic growth rates were among the highest in the world (GDP growth averaged 8.3% per annum during 1952–65), while inflationary pressures remained modest. Yet a large part of the increase in output was absorbed by a rapid rise in population. Whether viewed through estimates of per caput income or more aggregate measures of national product, investment, exports, and growth data for the late 1960s and throughout the 1970s indicated an even more buoyant economic performance. Between 1966 and 1980 GDP grew at an average annual rate of 9.8%, while per caput income growth accelerated even more sharply.

Economic structural change after the 1960s reflected the impact of two new policy impulses: first, in the 1970s, the process of industrial deepening; second, in the 1980s, that of industrial upgrading and diversification. The effect of these initiatives was most noticeable in terms of adjustments to markets, ownership and industrial composition. In particular, as US aid and policy guidance receded, so Taiwan's own economic technocrats identified net market opportunities, which they sought to realize by fostering indigenous industrial entrepreneurship.

Even allowing for a declining trend in Taiwan's economic growth from 1980, GDP expansion during the 1980–2000 remained buoyant (averaging 7.9% annually during 1981–90; and 6.4% during 1991–2000). Unlike almost all its East and South East Asian neighbours, Taiwan emerged relatively unscathed from the Asian financial crisis of the late 1990s, having registered real GDP growth of 6.4% and 4.6% in 1997 and 1998 respectively. In 2000, however, average growth of 6.7% in the first three quarters of the year gave way to a lacklustre 3.8% expansion between October and November. This decline signified the onset of a deep recession—Taiwan's first in a generation—and in 2001 GDP growth actually decreased by 2.2%. This contraction was unprecedented in Taiwan's post–1949 experience, the previous low point having been reached in 1974 when, under the impact of the global oil crisis, GDP growth was just 1.2%. However, positive growth resumed in 2002, and one official forecast suggested that annual growth might exceed 3% by the end of the year.

Both internal and external factors contributed to this poor economic performance. Taiwan's strong external economic orientation made it particularly vulnerable to developments overseas, so that the global economic downturn associated with the bursting of the 'high-tech bubble' in the USA—still, along with mainland China, one of Taiwan's two most important export markets—took a severe toll on the economy during 2000–01. Domestic factors contributed too, as private-sector investment contracted, unemployment increased, private consumption growth slowed and deflationary pressures began to emerge. Political uncertainties associated with the election of President Chen Shui-bian—the first incumbent from a party other than the KMT since the establishment of the Republic of China in 1912—and the associated decline in the influence of the KMT itself also impinged on Taiwan's economic performance.

These difficulties notwithstanding, Taiwan's post-war record of economic growth was almost unparalleled globally. From a base of massive poverty, it became one of the most important trading nations—with a trade-GDP ratio of 46% in 2000—possessing one of the most competitive economies in the world. Taiwan also transformed itself into one of the major alternative centres of high-technology capability outside the USA, Western Europe and Japan—a position which the Chen Shui-bian Government is committed to strengthening through its plan to develop a knowledge-based economy. In 2001 Taiwan ranked third in the world (second on a per caput basis) in terms of the number of US patents awarded to it. Meanwhile, average per caput income in Taiwan increased from US $2,344 to US $8,111 between 1980 and 1990. It reached a peak in 2000 (US $14,188), before recessionary conditions reduced it to US $12,941 in 2001.

Underlying Taiwan's rapid, long-term growth has been a consistently high rate of domestic capital formation. Between the mid-1950s and the 1970s, domestic savings were insufficient to finance domestic investment, and Taiwan was forced to borrow from abroad. Between 1951 and 1965 US aid—cumulatively worth US $1,440m.—was also an important source of investment and defence spending. Since 1975, however, Taiwan has been a net overseas lender, and domestic savings have more than paid for domestic investment. In general, the high interest rate available to savers has reflected official policies, designed to yield a real return on their deposits.

Rapid economic growth from the 1950s was accompanied by major changes in the sectoral composition of the Taiwanese economy. Agriculture's share of total output decreased from almost 30% in 1960 to 1.9% in 2001. The contribution of industry, having peaked at 47.1% in 1986, decreased to 30.9%, as the service sector overtook it as the largest sector—accounting for more than two-thirds of GDP in 2001. The emerging pre-eminence of the service sector owed most to the buoyant growth performance of Taiwan's financial, insurance and commercial sectors.

Growth-driven structural changes were also accompanied by inter-industry shifts. For example, between the 1960s and 1980s food and food-processing, textiles, and wood and paper manufacturing all declined at the expense of increases in the output of machinery and electrical goods. Yet the most noteworthy development has been the more recent and spectacular enhancement of Taiwan's status as a manufacturer of electronic and information technology (IT) equipment of all kinds. By 1995, for example, it had become the third largest producer of such goods in the world, after Japan and the USA. Alongside declining production of televisions, radios, telephones and calculators in the 1990s, integrated circuit production recorded impressive expansion. Despite a sharp reduction in demand during and after the Asian financial crisis, output has averaged close to 15% growth annually since the early 1990s.

ECONOMIC POLICIES

In the years immediately after 1949, the Taiwanese economy depended heavily on the production and processing of food and agricultural products, using labour-intensive, low-technology manufacturing processes. The surplus output of such goods was exported mainly to the USA. Meanwhile, Japan and the USA provided more than two-thirds of much-needed foreign investment. The importance of these two countries, especially as a source of imports, has continued to the present day, although since the late 1980s their significance as a destination for Taiwanese exports has declined as the role of China (including Hong Kong) became increasingly important. In its initial stage, Taiwan's manufacturing growth, particularly in the production of electronic and electrical goods, was also mainly financed by US and Japanese capital.

After its removal to Taiwan, the KMT initially maintained tight controls over the economy. Subsequently, the need to restructure itself following the débâcle of the Civil War—an aspiration emphasized in advice from the USA—led it to promote a more market-orientated, free-enterprise system. This shift in emphasis at a time when its Chinese Communist rivals were putting in place a Soviet-style central planning system did not, however, eschew a continuing and significant degree of interventionism by the Government, characterized by the maintenance of state ownership and the implementation of trade restrictions to protect the nascent manufacturing sector against imports. Macroeconomic management was also highly interventionist by modern standards. Meanwhile, in the countryside, land reforms redistributed property rights, enabling former landowners to invest in urban businesses and encouraging farmers to increase productivity and output.

Beginning around the end of the 1950s, many earlier ISI policies were dismantled, as the Taiwanese economy was opened up and reorientated towards international markets. The immediate goal was to expand industrial exports in order to create employment and absorb surplus labour that was emerging in the agricultural sector; in the longer run, it was hoped that foreign-exchange earnings would become a major source of capital for financing further sustained growth. In the event, a combination of short-term export financing, tax incentives, import duty rebates, and foreign direct investment (FDI) were the policy means whereby export industries were further expanded. In particular, the 1961 Statute for the Encouragement of Investment offered tax benefits to export firms, including those in government-sponsored 'pioneer' sectors, such as electronics. At the same time, in export-processing zones, firms enjoyed a duty-free environment that favoured both production and export activities, and encouraged further FDI inflows. Significant too was the Government's establishment of 'industrial estates' throughout Taiwan, designed to make use of the abundant labour force.

Numerous firms benefited from these initiatives, which facilitated the establishment of new firms and laid the foundation for what became one of the hallmarks of Taiwan's industrialization—namely, the dominance of small and medium-scale enterprises (SMEs), rather than the concentration of large firms, such as the South Korean *chaebol*. Over time, the SMEs became the mainstay of Taiwan's industrial economy. By the mid-1980s their share of manufacturing output had reached almost half, their share of non-farm employment was more than 60% and they contributed a similar proportion of export earnings.

As a result of the Government's export promotion strategy, labour-intensive, export-orientated industries became the main engine of Taiwan's economic growth. In the 1970s, however, concern about the perceived 'shallowness' of the economy, as well as the threat posed by the declining supply of surplus labour (and consequent upward pressure on wages) and evidence of growing protectionism in some major markets (most notably, that of the USA), was reflected in proposals to embark on a programme of heavy and chemical industrialization (HCI). In the event, the impact of this initiative was much less marked than that of much more extensive HCI in the Republic of Korea (South Korea). There were two important consequences. First, Taiwan avoided massive foreign borrowing and reliance on big business in order to implement HCI, and thereby escaped the problems of high inflation, massive foreign debt and deteriorating income distribution that were later to confront South Korea. Second, Taiwan's mild HCI prevented the emergence of dominant, large-scale conglomerates and, instead of basic and petrochemical industries becoming the mainstay of the economy, Taiwan's industrial and export base continued to be dominated by labour-intensive items, such as textiles, garment and consumer electronics.

Against the background of calls for industrial upgrading, in the early 1980s the Government identified two 'strategic areas'—machinery and information industries—to play a key role in Taiwan's future industrial development. These were considered activities with good market potential, favourable linkage effects, high value-added, high-technology input, low energy use and a low pollution impact. Later, other high-technology sectors were added to the list. This was a watershed, as was the Government's decision for the first time to reward spending on research and development (R&D).

The most notable success of the new strategy was reflected in the rapid expansion of the information industry (especially, semiconductors and computers). Here, industrial policy embraced a comprehensive range of measures, including tax incentives, concessionary loans, R&D sponsorship, technology transfer, and infrastructural initiatives (for example, the establishment of Hsinchu Industrial Park). The rise of the semiconductor sector was attributable to a variety of factors, including the existence of buoyant global demand for components for the computer industry, access to a 'reverse brain drain' of Taiwanese-born, but US-trained experts (many of whom had experience of having worked in California's Silicon Valley), and the benefits of SMEs' flexibility and adaptability to the industry's short product cycle. The Government's continuing role in facilitating technology transfer and technology diffusion also did much to help generate rapid growth.

After 1987 previous restrictions on trade with, and subsequently investment in, mainland China were removed, precipitating a rapid increase in cross-Strait economic relations. As a result, the intervening years witnessed Taiwan's evolving relationship with the People's Republic of China become a major economic, as well as political issue. China's insistence that Taipei must accept Beijing's interpretation of the 'one China' principle has long been a major obstacle to political rapprochement across the Taiwan Straits. From 2000, reports that President Chen Shui-bian might hold a referendum on Taiwanese independence added to the political difficulties. Such profound problems have not, however, halted the momentum of cross-Straits trade and investment. To what extent Taiwan's growing trade dependence on the mainland will facilitate Beijing's ability to control its economy—and thereby accelerate national reunification—remains in the realms of speculation. Suffice to say that the Government in Taipei is inherently caught in the dilemma of whether to strengthen investment and trade links with China, at the risk of excessive dependence on its political adversary; or whether to seek to limit Taiwanese companies' access to the world's fastest growing economy, thereby sacrificing higher rates of growth at home. The island's accession (in January 2002) to the World Trade Organization (WTO) has become an additional key issue impinging on Taiwan's economic security. On the one hand, membership promises to help diversify its concentrated market dependencies (including vis-à-vis the People's Republic) and provide a firmer legal basis for the implementation of market access agreements. On the other hand, it will almost certainly force Taiwan to accept direct trade links with the mainland, which may further increase its dependence. Meanwhile, cross-Straits economic interactions have had major implications for domestic development through their impact on manufacturing industry and employment, manifested in widespread concern that Taiwan's economy is 'hollowing out'.

POPULATION AND WORK-FORCE

Taiwan is one of the most heavily-populated countries in the world, the density of its population exceeding that of any province in mainland China. Its total population in December 2001 was almost 22.41m. Since 1949 demographic pressures have derived largely from the influx of more than 1.5m. mainlanders during 1948–49 and a subsequent, albeit quite short-term, rise in the birth rate (in the early 1950s Taiwan's birth rate was among the highest in the world). In and after the 1960s deliberate fertility control measures facilitated a sharp fall in population growth, enabling Taiwan rapidly to complete its demographic transition. Underlying these demographic changes, there has been a major contraction in the share of population under the age of 15 (from 69% to 30% of total population between 1970 and 2000). At the same time, however, as life expectancy has increased, so the share of the over-65s has risen (from 5% to over 12%). Because more men than women fled the mainland after the KMT defeat in the Chinese Civil War, there is still an imbalance of males over females in Taiwan.

As the process of economic modernization gathered pace, Taiwan's population became increasingly urbanized. In 1920 the urban share of total population was a mere 4%—a figure that changed little in succeeding decades. Not until the 1960s, under the impact of rising farm productivity and expanding industrialization, did rural–urban migration get under way. Such, however, was the impact of structural change within the economy that by the early 1970s Taiwan's population had already become about two-thirds urban. By 1980 78% of Taiwanese lived in cities with a population of 50,000 or more—a higher proportion than in both Japan and the USA.

Having steadily risen since 1970, the labour participation rate (labour force as a proportion of the population aged 15 and over) has fallen slightly—from 59.2% to 57.2% between 1990 and 2001. Between 1952 and 1975 the total labour force increased from 3.06m. to 5.66m.—an average annual growth of 2.7%; since 1975 the rate of expansion has slowed to 2.1%, generating a work force of 9.83m. in 2001. From 1965 until 2000 the unemployment rate never exceeded 3%. In the wake of recessionary conditions during 2001, however, it rose sharply to 4.6%. This figure was unlikely to decrease significantly in 2002, the rate of unemployment during January–July having reached 5.11%.

Meanwhile, the Government has long placed a high premium on maintaining a productive and highly-skilled work-force. Recent legislative priorities have focused on the rights of workers, including workers' welfare, labour-management relations, health and safety issues, and fixing appropriate quotas for the hiring of foreign workers.

The share of agriculture in total employment, which was over 50% in the 1950s, has since declined to a mere 7.5%. The momentum of construction activity means that the absolute level of industrial employment has not yet peaked, although its share of employment has been in decline since 1987 (falling from 42.8% to 36% in 2001). Manufacturing employment has reflected these alterations, its share in total employment having declined from a peak of 35.2% in 1987 to 27.6% in 2001. The changes highlighted both the removal of more and more manufacturing off shore and improvements in productivity. The most important locus of employment growth has therefore been the service sector, which in 2001 had a work force of 5.2m., or 56.5% of the total.

In 1990 Taiwan liberalized its foreign labour policy in an attempt to remedy a serious labour shortage. At the end of 2000 310,000 foreign workers were employed on the island, 59% of whom were engaged in manufacturing and 13% in the construction industry. Most overseas workers came from Thailand, although the Philippines was also an important source of domestic helpers. Foreign workers also play an important role in the nursing, health care and catering sectors. Their positive economic contribution notwithstanding, foreign workers have at times been viewed as a threat to local employment, and at the end of 1998, the Government in Taipei signalled its intention to reduce the foreign labour quota for manufacturing industries by 10% in order to combat the rising level of unemployment.

Education has made a critical contribution to Taiwan's modern economic growth. Since 1968 education has been compulsory for all children for nine years, and an increasingly wide range of educational opportunities has been made available for those who have left school. In the 2000/01 academic year there were 7,998 registered schools at all levels; average class size was 35.5 pupils, with each teacher responsible, on average, for about 17 pupils.

Enrolment rates for children of primary school (aged 6–11) and secondary school (12–17) ages are close to 100%. With more than 60% of the 18–21 age group in education, university and college enrolment rates are also extremely high. In 2001 almost 24% of Taiwan's total population was in attendance at some kind of educational institution. Despite criticisms of the higher education sector for its supposed inflexibility and failure to address Taiwan's economic and social needs, it is noteworthy that in 2001 the most popular discipline in higher education was engineering, followed (in decreasing order) by commerce and business administration, medical science, and mathematics and computer science. Together, these four branches accounted for two-thirds of all students undergoing higher education. Almost 40,000 Taiwanese students were also enrolled in overseas universities, the most popular destination being the USA.

MANUFACTURING

At the beginning of the 1950s the manufacturing sector 'proper' accounted for a mere 13% of GDP, compared with 32% for agriculture, and for the remainder of the decade farm-processing remained the main industrial activity in Taiwan. However, following the switch from ISI to an export-led strategy, the 1960s and 1970s witnessed a rapid increase in the growth of manufacturing, as a result of which its share in GDP almost doubled, rising from 19.1% in 1960) to 36% in 1980. A further marginal expansion in manufacturing output growth continued into the 1980s, although since 1986 a consistent trend decline has been observable.

The changing pattern of industrial growth in Taiwan followed a familiar trajectory. Initially, export-driven growth was centred on the production of labour-intensive goods, such as textiles, plastics, plywood and electronic products. Subsequently, the shift to higher value-added activities was reflected in the accelerated development of capital-intensive, heavy industrial goods, including synthetic fibres, steel, machinery, cars and ships—a process given further impetus by the later HCI programme (see above). The most recent and, in terms of its economic impact, most significant change was towards knowledge- and skill-intensive production, the leading branches being semiconductors and associated products. The impact of this final shift was well illustrated by the finding that, in the 1990s, the share of industrial exports characterized by low technology intensity decreased from 49% to 17%, while that of high intensity increased from 18% to 42%. With labour costs rising and capital costs declining, the underlying pattern of industrial growth accorded with the principle of comparative advantage.

SMEs have made a vital contribution to industrial development in Taiwan. Not only have they made a greater contribution to foreign trade growth than their larger-scale counterparts, but—unlike big firms—they have done so without having been major recipients of government protection and incentives. About 97% of manufacturing enterprises are SMEs, they employ almost 80% of the manufacturing labour force and generate around 30% of the sector's sales (and about one-quarter of the value of associated exports). SMEs' strong outward orientation is highlighted in the finding that up to two-thirds of their output is exported, compared with about 35% for large-scale enterprises.

The promotion of SMEs may have reflected the KMT Government's wish to avoid the emergence of 'predatory capitalism' by encouraging competition among many firms and minimizing the discretionary element in industrial policy. The SMEs also maximized flexibility in production, enabling them to adjust quickly to changes in market conditions. At the same time, they have sometimes encountered serious financial difficulties, especially in their ability to engage in R&D. In their frequent role as sub-contractors for foreign firms, they have also struggled to create brand names in international markets.

Textiles

By the end of its period of colonization, Taiwan had become up to 30% self-sufficient in textiles, and after 1949 indigenous textile mills were further supplemented by the removal to Taiwan of equipment from the mainland. Between 1950 and 1980 textiles—both cotton and wool production—were a dominant sector, employing the largest share of industrial employment and generating more exports than any other single manufacturing activity. Initially, textiles benefited from abundant supplies of cheap labour, although rising wages subsequently shifted production towards synthetic and other 'speciality' products (at one time Taiwan ranked second to the

USA in terms of its production of synthetic fibres—estimated at 3.1m. tons in 2001). Textiles were also important because of the industry's linkages with the machinery and petrochemical sectors. At the beginning of the 1980s textile products (including finished garments) still accounted for about one-fifth of the total value of Taiwan's exports. Thereafter, however, the sector's export contribution declined steadily, reaching 15% in 1990 and barely 10% in 2000. Even so, garments and textile products still rank third in terms of the absolute value of associated exports (US $15,200m. in 2000). From the 1990s many of Taiwan's factories producing cheaper, lower-quality goods were relocated in China and South-East Asia.

Machine Tools

Machine tools are one of the most important heavy industries in a developing economy. In Taiwan's case, not only have they generated important forward linkages with the rest of the economy, but they have also contributed much to its defence infrastructure. Machine tool production grew rapidly in the 1970s, and by the following decade had gained a significant share in the world market—even to the extent of invoking a US request that it introduce export restrictions. Although widely regarded as a large-scale, heavily capital-intensive industry, machine tool firms in Taiwan are predominantly small-scale, their success being premised on their flexibility and ability to deliver high-quality products punctually. Between 1981 and 2000 machine tool exports increased, on average, by 12.3% annually; in 2001 the value of exports of machinery (including electrical machinery) was almost US $13,000m.

Petrochemicals

As with machine tools, the 1970s marked the 'take-off' period for petrochemical production in Taiwan, investment projects being sponsored by both government and the private sector. In the wake of rapid growth, by the end of the 1990s the industry's annual production value was in excess of US $12,000m. By the late 1990s Taiwan ranked in the leading 20 international producers of petrochemicals and was first in terms of polyvinyl chloride (PVC). In general, however, although output has been directed overwhelmingly towards meeting local requirements, large-scale petrochemical imports are still necessary in order to address what remains a large domestic demand deficit. Newly-completed projects—not least those of the dominant Formosa Plastics Group—promise significantly to relieve such difficulties in the near future.

Motor Vehicles

The performance of the motor vehicle industry (mainly cars, but also some buses and trucks) has, by Taiwan's standards, been disappointing. Production began in the 1960s and subsequently expanded rapidly, peaking at over 436,000 vehicles in 1992 (an average annual rate of expansion of almost 20% over the previous 27 years, albeit from a minimal initial base). Since 1992, in response to the vagaries of changing domestic demand, output growth has been more erratic; in particular, since 1998 production has decreased sharply, from 402,000 to 269,000 in 2001. Although rising incomes have made car ownership more popular (registered passenger cars numbered more than 4.8m. in 2001—almost all of them for private use), Taiwan's motorcycle industry remains buoyant, output (which peaked at 1.63m. in 1994) still exceeding 1.1m. in 2000.

For many years domestic automobile production benefited from protectionist policies, including the imposition of high imports tariffs and quantitative import bans and restrictions. The less favourable consequence of protection has, however, been low efficiency and poor competitiveness. Given that Japan has already succeeded in significantly penetrating the island's car market, Taiwan's accession to the WTO and the consequent need to reduce import tariffs raised serious questions about the industry's ability to survive in a more openly competitive environment.

Information Technology

The development of high-technology industries can be dated from two initiatives that started in 1980: first, the construction of a manufacturing plant by United Microelectronics Corporation; second, the beginning of operations at Taiwan's first science-based industrial park at Hsinchu. By the end of the 1980s more than 70 research-based companies had established plants at Hsinchu, and 10 years later the corresponding figure was in excess of 200 (with sales worth US $11,600m.). Meanwhile, the 1990s witnessed the establishment of a second government-sponsored science park in Tainan, while private-sector sites, such as that opened near Taipei by the Formosa Plastics Corporation, were also contributing to the development of high-technology manufacturing. Such facilities, assisted by the Ministry of Economic Affairs' Industrial Technology Research Institute (ITRI), are the principal means whereby technologies have been developed and transferred to domestic private enterprises.

By the end of the 1990s Taiwan had become the world's third largest manufacturer of IT products, behind the USA and Japan. With a total production value of US $39,900m. (domestic and overseas revenue combined), the IT industry had also become the single most important source of foreign exchange. Taiwan's 900 computer hardware manufacturers meanwhile provided jobs for some 100,000 employees. Laptop computers, monitors, desktop personal computers (PCs), and motherboards have come to account for about 80% of the production value of the IT industry. The administration of President Chen Shui-bian was explicit in its determination to further develop Taiwan as a knowledge-based economy.

The spectacular foreign-exchange contribution of IT and related products was illustrated by the fact that associated exports increased almost 20-fold between 1986 and 2000, registering an average annual growth rate of 21.4%. Up to 1997 the performance was even more outstanding, subsequent growth being affected by adverse international economic conditions. Most serious of all was the bursting of the US technological 'bubble', which was reflected in a 20% decline in IT exports in 2001. Even so, with earnings of US $15,600m. in 2001, the IT sector still accounted for almost 12.7% of the value of all Taiwan's exports.

The structure of Taiwan's IT industry resembles a pyramid. At the top, a small number of companies pursue costly and time-consuming product-innovating R&D activities, the results of which are translated into production by SMEs located at the bottom of the pyramid (SMEs account for about 85% of total IT output). As in other areas of manufacturing, inherent size constraints have prevented SMEs from themselves undertaking major R&D and marketing investment. In addition, heavy reliance on imports of key components and advanced technology from overseas has tied Taiwan's IT industry closely to the industries of the USA and Japan.

Since the late 1990s the benefits of cheap, but adequately skilled, labour and low rents have attracted Taiwanese entrepreneurs to relocate IT production facilities to China. One-half or more of Taiwanese high-technology goods are now assembled on the mainland, including most digital cameras, visual display units (VDUs) and an increasing share of other computer hardware. By the first half of 2000 42% of all Taiwanese PCs were manufactured in mainland China, as a result of which China displaced Taiwan as the world's third largest producer of such equipment (similarly, Taiwanese firms accounted for around three-quarters of the output value of computers and related goods produced on the mainland). Four of the five principal Taiwanese 'notebook PC' makers have production plants in China. Most recently and controversially, Taiwanese semiconductor manufacturers have also started to invest in China, chip-makers no doubt seeing burgeoning demand on the mainland (already worth US $15,000m. a year, and projected to reach US $40,000m. by 2025) as a way of offsetting possible future falls in demand elsewhere in the world.

INFRASTRUCTURE

Taiwan benefited from important infrastructural initiatives undertaken by the Japanese during their colonization of the island. Between the mid-1950s and the end of the 1970s the Government directed large-scale investment funds towards extending Taiwan's physical economic infrastructure. Most important of all were the 'Ten Major Construction Projects' implemented between 1973 and 1980, which facilitated major improvements in roads, and air and sea transport. In the 1980s infrastructural initiatives were accorded much lower priority, as a result of which quite serious problems of congestion began to emerge. Thus, from 1986 economic plans once more placed a high emphasis on infrastructural construction (now extended to include environmental improvements). At the start of the 21st century, such initiatives have continued to be regarded as a vital factor in generating continuing economic growth. In particular, the Chen Shui-bian Administration made clear its commitment to improving Taiwan's basic infrastructure through the expansion of airport passenger and cargo transport capacities, the extension of link roads between airports and harbours and the construction of broadband networks.

Since 1995 successive Taiwanese Governments have sought to promote the development of Taiwan into an Asia-Pacific Regional Operations Centre (APROC). This long-term proposal was intended to transform Taiwan into a business and investment hub in the region, embracing services and high technology, and providing multinational corporations (MNCs) with the manufacturing, air and sea transport, financial, telecommunications and media facilities essential for their efficient operation. The successful implementation of this project would greatly enhance Taiwan's regional economic status, with implications for its strategic security and ability to compete with other service and high-technology hubs, such as Hong Kong and Shanghai.

Transport and Communications

Since 1975 the total length of roads in Taiwan has doubled, reaching approximately 36,000 km. (including 20,635 km. of highways) in 2001. Even so, the pressure on major trunk routes is severe, making their further extension a high priority. Major highways, such as the Sun Yat-sen Freeway (the country's principal north–south route, connecting Taipei and Keelung), are often congested, and improvements are regarded as a major priority. Taiwan's rail network has advanced much less than that of its roads. Total track length is some 1,097.2 km—only 12% longer than in 1970. As a result, whereas average road length per head of total population had increased by more than 50% since 1970, the corresponding figure for railways showed a decline of almost 16%. These figures were reflected in figures for cargo and passenger transport. In 2000, for example, road and rail passengers totalled 1.3m., of whom almost 85% were carried by roads; roads carried 96% of combined rail and road traffic in the same year.

Taiwan's five international ports (Keelung, Kaohsiung, Taichung, Hualien and Suao) are capable of handling marine traffic, and service ocean vessels, of all sizes. In 2001 the total volume of cargo handled (loaded and unloaded) by these ports exceeded 550m. tons—just 14m. tons below the record level of 2000. The single most important of these ports is Kaohsiung which, in 2001, accounted for two-thirds of all cargo handled by the five ports. Since the 1960s there has been a rapid expansion of Taiwan-registered ships, their gross registered tonnage having risen from a mere 1.13m. tons in 1970 to 5.37m. tons in 2000. Cargo tonnage carried by such vessels has increased from 8.6 to 110.3m. tons.

There are two international airports in Taiwan: one is Chiang Kai-shek International Airport in Taoyuan, which serves Taipei and northern regions of the country; the other is Kaohsiung International Airport, which serves the south. Over 50 airlines fly to and within Taiwan. Between 1990 and 2000 the number of international flights rose from 60,691 to 138,379 (an average annual rate of expansion of 8.6%); in the same period domestic flights increased from 191,132 to 448,181 (8.9% growth per annum). In 2000 airports handled 46.4m. passengers—43% of them on international flights; freight traffic meanwhile totalled 1.62m. tons, of which 95% was internal cargo.

Energy

Taiwan has very limited natural resources, forcing it to import most of its raw materials and energy. Coal reserves, which are found in northern Taiwan, are negligible; petroleum and natural gas reserves are also scarce, being concentrated mainly in two northern counties of the island (Hsinchu and Miaoli). Total hydroelectric potential has been estimated at 5,047 MW, of which 1,912 MW have been developed, primarily along the major rivers.

In 1955 domestic sources provided almost three-quarters of Taiwan's total commercial energy supplies, 60% of which were derived from domestically-produced coal. By 1970 well over one-half of energy needs were being met from imports, and the overseas share subsequently continued to rise steadily. At the same time, dependence on coal gave way to dependence on oil. In 2000 energy imports—103,200m. litres in terms of oil equivalent—accounted for an astonishing 97% of total energy supplies. These imports included 54,600m. litres of crude petroleum and petroleum products (oil equivalent), worth US $8,100m., and 32,600m. litres (oil equivalent) of coal. The fact that energy consumption growth has been marginally less than GDP growth since the mid-1970s points to improved conservation and/or efficiency in the use of energy during this period.

From the late 1970s until the mid-1980s, there was a sharp increase in the share of nuclear energy in total power generation—from a mere 0.3% in 1977) to 52.4% in 1985. From the 1980s, however, plans to extend Taiwan's nuclear energy capacity became increasingly controversial and eventually, in late 2000, the Executive Yuan announced that a long-standing proposal to construct a fourth nuclear power plant would not, after all, be implemented. By 2000 the nuclear sector's share of power generation had fallen back to 23.6%—slightly less than in 1981.

In 2001 the industrial sector accounted for 57.1% of Taiwan's total energy consumption, compared with 24.1% for residential and commercial purposes, 15.7% for transport and 1.6% for agriculture (non-energy uses making up the balance).

TRADE

The outward orientation of Taiwan's development strategy and, in particular, the role of foreign trade (especially export promotion) have been important factors in the island's economic growth. Indeed, along with other leading Asian newly-industrializing countries (NICs), Taiwan's experience highlighted many traditional hallmarks of trade dependence. Foreign investment also played an important role in Taiwan's economic transformation. Since the late 1980s cross-Straits interactions have provided a new and crucial dimension to Taiwan's external economic relations—one that both complements and challenges its economic ties with other parts of the world.

The exhaustion of ISI by the late 1950s and the increasingly severe constraints imposed by limited domestic markets left export markets as the obvious alternative target for manufactured goods. Accordingly, at the end of the 1950s, the Government embarked on a more aggressive external-orientated strategy, as tariffs for domestic producers were lowered, protective measures for exporters introduced, and other accommodating measures (such as the establishment of export-processing zones) implemented. Education and labour training were also accorded priority in order to enhance the growth of manufacturing production for export.

Between 1960 and 1970 the value of Taiwan's merchandise trade rose six-and-a-half-fold, with annual growth averaging 20.6% (25% per annum for exports, and almost 18% for imports). For the time being, the balance of merchandise trade remained in deficit, although the trend was a declining one. Moreover, by 1970, industrial goods had already come to dominate exports, constituting almost 79% of total export value. Raw materials accounted for 63% of imports, compared with 32% for capital goods and 5% for consumption. While Japan generated 43% of Taiwan's imports, but absorbed only 9% of its exports, the corresponding figures for the USA were 24% and 38% respectively.

From the 1970s onwards, efforts were directed towards improving the quality and sophistication of exports, the most crucial feature of this process being the emergence of Taiwan as a major producer of electrical and electronics goods and, subsequently, of high-technology IT products. The dual processes of industrialization and technological upgrading facilitated the accelerated growth of exports. By 1984 the total value of Taiwan's foreign trade had reached US $52,400m., making it the 10th largest exporting country and 15th largest trading nation in the world.

Foreign trade expansion was a necessary condition of Taiwan's sustained economic growth, and from the 1960s the island's economy became increasingly trade dependent. By the 1980s Taiwan traded even more than Japan relative to the size of its economy: the combined value of imports and exports constituting 95% of GNP in 1980), compared with about 30% for Japan. Taiwan's export share alone was around 48%.

Until the late 1980s, the direction of such trade was overwhelmingly towards capitalist industrial countries and, above all, the USA and Japan. Fears that Taiwan might fall prey to the pessimistic predictions of dependency theory proved unfounded. Indeed, a major problem for Taiwan was its growing trade surplus vis-à-vis the USA, which peaked at US $16,000m. in 1987, compared with a mere US $1,200m. in 1976. The size of this bilateral surplus elicited protests from Washington, which were translated into Taiwan's subsequent removal from preferential tariff treatment by the USA. Yet although the deficit was later reduced, it is instructive that as recently as 2001, the surplus totalled US $9,425m.

By contrast, Taiwan's balance of trade with Japan has consistently deteriorated since the 1950s. By the mid-1980s its bilateral deficit averaged about US $3,000m.; by the end of that decade, it was more than US $6,000m.; and in 2001, US $13,089m. (though admittedly significantly below the record US $21,959m. of the previous year). Underlying these figures is the finding that successful efforts to increase Taiwanese exports to Japan were offset by soaring imports.

Besides Japan and the USA—and with China not a protagonist of significance until the end of the decade——trade with other Asian countries accounted for around 15% of Taiwan's foreign trade in the 1980s. The remaining balance was roughly shared between Western Europe and the Middle East. During and after the 1980s, however, two new developments occurred: one (of minor importance) was Taiwan's willingness to enter into trade relations with Russia, and Eastern Europe; the other—which rapidly became a key variable factor—was the initiation for the first time since 1949 of indirect trade links with the Chinese mainland (see below).

In global terms, Taiwan has enjoyed a trade surplus in every year since 1976, although it is noteworthy that were it not for the opening of trade links with China, a return to a global trade deficit would have taken place. The peak level of this surplus was reached in 1987, when it was US $18,700 (and when foreign exchange reserves totalled US $77,000m.—a remarkable rise on the US $9,000m. of just five years earlier). The previous year had seen Taiwan's export-to-GDP ratio also at its highest level (56.7%), and its import-to-GDP ratio at its lowest level (–37.4%). This burgeoning surplus put great pressure on the NT dollar and, following the devaluation of the US dollar in September 1985, there was a sharp appreciation of the Taiwanese currency—by 42% against the US dollar by the end of 1987 (the biggest such appreciation among all Asia's major currencies). The fact that 1987 marked the beginning of a contraction in Taiwan's merchandise trade surplus is, of course, no coincidence.

In general, until the onset of the Asian financial crisis in the late 1990s, Taiwan's foreign trade growth continued to be buoyant. During 1990–97, for example, the rate of expansion of Taiwan's global merchandise trade was almost 10% annually (8.9% for exports, and 11.1% for imports). In 1998, however, trade decreased by 9%, and exports, by 9.4%. The following two years witnessed recovery and further growth, which took the value of trade to a record US $288,300m. (exports reaching US $148,300m. and imports US $140,000m.). Yet such was the subsequent deterioration of external conditions that in 2001, foreign trade fell to US $230,104m.—a decline of more than 20%. The decline in exports in 2001 was some US $25,454m. A further measure of the relatively disappointing recent trade performance was reflected in the finding that in 2000, the export-to-GNP ratio was 47%, and the corresponding import-to-GNP ratio, 44.5%—both well below the 51–52% target set by the Council for Economic Planning and Development (CEPD) in the 1980s.

Exports

For many years, Taiwan has relied heavily on industrial products for its exports. In 1965 agricultural goods (including processed farm products) accounted for 54% of all exports. Thereafter, however, the share of industrial goods rose rapidly to reach 90% by the end of the 1970s—and over 98% in 2001. The USA, Hong Kong, Japan and (more recently) mainland China have been the major purchasers of Taiwanese goods. Other important export destinations include Singapore, the Netherlands, Germany and the United Kingdom.

In 1990 Hong Kong replaced Japan as the second largest export destination for Taiwanese products—a position that it has maintained through 2001 and the first half of 2002. Two main factors underlie Hong Kong's increased importance to Taiwan. The first reflects the successful implementation of the Government's efforts to diversify its export markets. The second stems from Taiwan's growing trade with China, which the Government insists must be carried out indirectly through a third party (usually Hong Kong). Although trade with Hong Kong has continued to expand, the rate of growth in recent years has declined, primarily because of the growing number of Taiwan-based industries that have invested in the mainland since the legalization of private exchanges in 1987.

For the second consecutive year, exports to Japan in 1998 were reduced, owing to the overall deceleration in Taiwan's foreign trade after years of steady growth, which recovered somewhat in 1999 and 2000. In 2001, however, there was another sharp decline, of 23%. Following 14 years of consistent growth, from 1996 export growth to Japan followed an erratic path, veering between expansion and contraction. In 1997 and 1998, for example, shipments to Japan fell back by 32%, before recovering to reach a record level of US $16,600m. in 2000; an improvement that attributed to increasing exports of Taiwanese IT products to Japan, as well as a rise in the output (mainly of electrical items and electronics) of Taiwanese-Japanese joint ventures based in Taiwan. These items were estimated to have accounted for almost half of all Taiwanese exports to Japan during these years.

European markets have also been targeted as part of Taiwan's diversification policy. The Netherlands, Germany and the United Kingdom were the leading European destinations for Taiwanese goods in 2001, their purchases (worth US $12,039m.) accounting for 54% of the value of exports to all European Union (EU) member states in 2001. In order to overcome the trade restrictions created by the EU single market, several of Taiwan's largest companies have gained footholds in the EU by establishing their own factories or by merging with existing local companies. Such investment has mostly been directed to the production of electric appliances, electronics and IT products.

Countries in South-East Asia have also emerged as strong trading partners, and become an important destination for Taiwanese foreign investment. Abundant cheap labour, raw materials and lower land prices are the familiar factors, which have attracted Taiwanese entrepreneurs Between 1986 and 1996 the share of Taiwanese exports purchased by member countries of the Association of South East Asian Nations (ASEAN) rose from 5% to just over 12%. This figure has not since been reattained, and in 2001 the ASEAN share declined to 10.5%.

Imports

Most of Taiwan's imports comprise raw materials and semi-finished goods required for production, although there has recently been a small increase in imports of consumer goods. Capital goods imports have steadily risen, their share accounting for over one-quarter of all imports. In 2000 the value of Taiwan's imports rose sharply to US $140,000m. (an annual rise of over 26% and 22% higher than the previous peak level of 1997). However, in 2001 total imports declined to US $107,238m., a 24.4% decrease on the previous year. In 2001 Asian countries accounted for more than one-half of Taiwan's imports, followed by members of the North American Free Trade Agreement (NAFTA—18.3%, with 17% from the USA alone), ASEAN (14.5%) and the EU (14%).

Cross-Straits Economic Ties

Trade relations with the mainland were historically extremely close, and in the early 1930s such exchanges probably accounted for about one-half of Taiwan's total trade, excluding Japan. Such relations were interrupted by the establishment in 1949 of the People's Republic of China and were only resumed in the 1980s, following an official announcement (July 1985) that while neither direct trade nor entrepreneurial contact would be permitted across the Taiwan Straits, entrepôt trade would no longer be prohibited. Since the end of the 1980s, Taiwan has become increasingly trade-dependent on the mainland economy, and by 2000 its total trade dependency ratio vis-à-vis China had risen to 11.2%—a figure that concealed a low import dependence, but a much higher (17.6%) reliance on the mainland as an export market. Taiwan's degree of export dependence on China is uniquely high in Taiwan's case. By contrast, China's trade dependence on Taiwan is both lower and more stable, although it is instructive that by 2001 Taiwan had become the second largest source of China's imports, accounting for 11.2% of the total.

Government statistics from Taipei show cross-Straits trade having risen from US $8,100m. to US $32,400m. between 1991 and 2000, implying an average annual growth rate of 16.7%. The unbalanced nature of such trade was reflected in the fact that in 2000 the value of Taiwanese exports to the mainland was estimated at US $26,200m., compared with reverse shipments that were worth only US $6,200m. The further implication was that Taiwan enjoyed a trade surplus of almost US $20,000m., compared with only US $5,800m. in 1991. Although such estimates no doubt accord with reality, their precision is subject to a significant margin of error.

Huge amounts of FDI have also flowed to China from Taiwan, although quantifying these capital flows is extremely difficult. Mainland official sources indicate that cumulative Taiwanese investment utilized in China totalled US $22,000m. by the end of 2000. Taiwan's Central Bank unofficially regarded this as a gross underestimate and suggested that a true figure was closer to US $100,000m., with 40,000–50,000 investment projects already in place. The likelihood is that with around 40% of all Taiwanese FDI now being directed to the mainland, China has already become an important link in the production chain of many Taiwanese firms. Guangdong, Zhejiang, Shanghai and Jiangsu are and will remain the principal investment destinations within China, although the geographical extent of Taiwanese FDI penetration in China is highlighted in the finding that Taiwan is also a major source of capital in Sichuan—the province at the heart of China's western regional development initiative. In 2002 there were also reports of plans to construct two Taiwan-invested industrial parks in Shanghai.

The extent of Taiwan's involvement in the mainland is also highlighted by the sheer number of Taiwanese business executives who live and work there. Several hundred thousand Taiwanese are permanently based in Shanghai, while there are said to be 30,000 resident Taiwanese managers, running 5,000 electronics factories that employ 2m. workers in Dongguan City in Guangdong's Pearl River Delta. Throughout China, Taiwan in 2000–02 employed at least 5m. Chinese workers.

The linked accession of China and Taiwan in December 2001 and January 2002 respectively to the WTO seems certain to accelerate the process of cross-Straits trade and investment. From Taiwan's perspective, a major implication of WTO membership will be the necessity, in accordance with WTO rules, to eliminate non-tariff barriers on Chinese goods. This process was already under way in January 2002. The Taiwanese Bureau of Foreign Trade issued a list of 2,126 items (including 901 agricultural products), which it stated would be added to the list of legal imports from China to Taiwan. The final list was expected to embrace almost 5,700 products, or 44% of all those included in Taiwan's tariff schedule. A further implication of the removal of such barriers will be to encourage more imports from China, which, in turn, is likely to reduce Taiwan's trade surplus vis-à-vis China.

Meanwhile, President Chen Shui-bian continued to face increasing pressure to relax investment restrictions. In October the Democratic Progressive Party (DPP) announced its decision to replace the supposedly outmoded 'no haste, be patient' policy on investment in China with a strategy of 'active opening and effective management'. Associated with this were the abandonment of previous restrictions on single investments of over US $50m. and a reduction in restricted investment categories, including PCs and chips.

WTO membership is also likely to end Taiwan's long-standing bans on direct shipping and air travel across the Straits. Although such links are not embraced by the 'Uruguay Round' of the negotiations of the predecessor General Agreement on Tariffs and Trade (GATT), their prevention would seem incompatible with the principle of most-favoured-nation treatment that lies at the heart of WTO rules. With direct links in place, transport costs will decrease, and trade can be expected to rise.

FINANCE

Taiwan's financial sector remained under notably tight central control until the end of the 1970s. By the following decade, however, changing circumstances—not least the oil crisis—dictated the first steps towards financial liberalization. Accordingly, price deregulation, including the abolition of interest rate controls, began to take place; and restrictions on capital movements were relaxed. Foreign exchange reforms were also introduced. Such changes served to facilitate more competitive financial behaviour and more efficient management. It was against this background that in 1989, Taiwan's Banking Law was revised, the principal effect being to remove controls on deposit and lending interest rates.

Loosening control by the Central Bank of China (CBC, Taiwan's central bank) over the money supply was, however, confined to the mid-1980s (the rate of expansion of M1B —currency and deposit money—in 1986–88 averaged 37.8%, compared with 13.3% for the previous three years). By the end of the 1980s, quite tight control had been reimposed, and since then money supply (M1B) expansion has not exceeded 16.9%.

A matter of growing concern in the 1990s was the deterioration in the financial position of Taiwan's banking sector. By the end of 1998 overdue bank loans had reached 4.5% of total lending, and while the major banks remained in profit, they felt compelled to set aside large reserves to meet lending losses. By the end of 2000 non-performing loans (NPLs) were estimated to be NT $773,500m., equivalent to 5.34% of all domestic bank loans, and a year later the figure was estimated to be at an all-time high of 8%. In 2000 some 10 Taiwanese banks were reported to have made losses, totalling NT $16,600m.

Since the beginning of 2001 the slow growth of money supply has been a source of anxiety, encouraging the CBC to ease its monetary policy (for example, the benchmark rediscount rate was lowered five times in 2001 to reach a record low). In the recessionary conditions of 2001, firms' demand for investment credit slackened, while the level of NPLs did little to encourage a proactive lending stance by banks. Nevertheless, having declined by 0.34% in 2000, in 2001, money supply (M1B) growth recovered, rising by 11.9%—a movement that continued in the first four months of 2002, when it increased further by more than 16%.

Membership of the WTO imposed new financial burdens on Taiwan, and from the late 1990s the Government introduced more financial deregulatory initiatives in anticipation of its accession. It has also shown itself to be in favour of the 'privatization' of banks—especially the three main commercial banks—most of which have traditionally been under state ownership or control (until 1991, 21 out of 24 Taiwanese banks were government-owned). Despite opposition from some quarters, several legislative and institutional initiatives have helped accelerate this process.

Meanwhile, in October 2000 an amendment to the Banking Law relaxed restrictions on the investment activities of Taiwanese banks, while increasing the ownership limit in other banks or financial companies from 15% to 25%. In December of the same year, in an attempt to encourage mergers involving foreign as well as domestic institutions, the 'Merger Act of Financial Institutions' was approved. In mid-2001 new financial reform laws were proposed, involving further liberalization and an acceleration of the consolidation of domestic banks. The 'Financial Holding Company Law' seeks to permit the establishment of integrated financial groups capable of offering a wide range of services, including banking, insurance and brokering. Insurance companies will also gain more freedom to formulate investment policies and develop new products. No less significant, in September 2001, control of 35 local financial institutions was transferred to 10 commercial banks.

In the 1990s financial liberalization was accompanied by a parallel process in Taiwan's stock exchange, which was opened to direct investment by foreign institutions (in 1991) and to foreign individuals (in 1996). Many domestic households now own stocks, although only a quite small proportion of business firms in Taiwan seek to issue shares for public trading. Despite the earlier initiatives, in October 1997 little more than 3% of Taiwan's stocks were owned by foreigners. In the event, this no doubt protected Taiwan from damaging capital flight of the kind that was so injurious to other economies during the Asian crisis. Conditions have, however, since changed —not least, under the impact of further legislative initiatives designed to facilitate share ownership by foreigners—and by mid-2000 foreign investors accounted for the ownership of 12.5% of Taiwanese stocks.

The year 1997 was very eventful for the domestic stock market. Following a 50% rise over three months to take the index to a record high of 10,256 points, it then suffered as a result of panic selling associated with the onset of the Asian financial crisis. By the end of 1997 the index had fallen back to 8,228, and by the end of 1998 to 6,418 points. Government efforts to halt the decline through the establishment of a US $9,000m. stabilization fund were less than successful, and by February 1999 the index had declined further to 5,475 points.

The index subsequently recovered, rising to over 8,600 points by June 1999. Yet the huge scale of capital outflows since 1997, alongside with ongoing securities liberalization, led some members of Taiwan's business community to question the logic of greater exposure to international markets. As it turned out, under the impact of economic and political factors (such as, in the latter case, uncertainties associated with the emergence of the DPP as a major new political force), stock market volatility continued. In 2000 the market lost more than 40% of its value; in 2001, it declined further, reaching less than 3,500 points in October. The hope in 2001–02 was that growing political stability in Taiwan, as well as the positive effect of improved economic conditions at home and abroad (especially in the USA), would generate greater stability in the stock market.

Statistical Survey

Source (unless otherwise stated): Bureau of Statistics, Directorate-General of Budget, Accounting and Statistics (DGBAS), Executive Yuan, 2 Kwang Chow St, Taipei 10729; tel. (2) 23710208; fax (2) 23319925; e-mail sicbs@emc.dgbas.gov.tw; internet www.dgbasey.gov.tw.

Area and Population

AREA, POPULATION AND DENSITY

Area (sq km)	36,006*
Population (census results)	
16 December 1990	20,393,628
16 December 2000	
Males	11,348,803
Females	10,818,356
Total	22,167,159
Population (official figures at 31 December)	
1999	22,034,096
2000	22,216,107
2001	22,405,568
Density (per sq km) at 31 December 2001	619.1

* 13,902 sq miles.

PRINCIPAL TOWNS
(population at 31 December 2001)

Taipei (capital)	2,633,802	Hsinchu	373,296
Kaohsiung	1,494,457	Taoyuan	338,361
Taichung	983,694	Chungli	329,913
Tainan	740,846	Fengshan	322,678
Panchiao	532,694	Hsintien	272,500
Chungho	401,619	Chiayi	267,993
Keelung	390,966	Changhwa	231,129
Shanchung	384,051	Yungho	229,383
Hsinchuang	376,584	Pingtung	215,245

BIRTHS, MARRIAGES AND DEATHS (registered)

	Live births		Marriages		Deaths	
	Number	Rate (per 1,000)	Number	Rate (per 1,000)	Number	Rate (per 1,000)
1994	322,938	15.31	170,864	8.10	113,866	5.40
1995	329,581	15.50	160,249	7.53	119,112	5.60
1996	325,545	15.18	169,424	7.90	122,489	5.71
1997	326,002	15.07	166,216	7.68	121,000	5.59
1998	271,450	12.43	145,976	6.69	123,180	5.64
1999	283,661	12.89	173,209	7.87	126,113	5.73
2000	305,312	13.76	181,642	8.19	125,958	5.68
2001	260,354	11.65	170,515	7.63	127,647	5.71

Expectation of life (years at birth, 2001): Males 72.8; Females 78.5.

ECONOMICALLY ACTIVE POPULATION
(annual averages, '000 persons aged 15 years and over*)

	1999	2000	2001
Agriculture, forestry and fishing	776	740	708
Mining and quarrying	11	11	10
Manufacturing	2,603	2,655	2,587
Construction	843	832	746
Electricity, gas and water	35	36	35
Commerce	2,130	2,163	2,165
Transport, storage and communications	476	481	486
Finance, insurance and real estate	406	412	410
Business services	284	313	339
Social, personal and related community services	1,502	1,534	1,570
Public administration	318	315	327
Total employed	9,385	9,491	9,383
Unemployed	283	293	450
Total labour force	9,668	9,784	9,832
Males	5,812	5,867	5,855
Females	3,856	3,917	3,977

* Excluding members of the armed forces and persons in institutional households.

Health and Welfare

KEY INDICATORS

Fertility (births per woman, 2001)	1.40
Under-5 mortality rate (per 1,000 live births, 2001)	1.43
HIV/AIDS (% of persons aged 15–49, 2001)	0.02
Physicians (per 1,000 head, 2001)	1.54
Hospital beds (per 1,000 head, 2001)	5.70
Health expenditure (2000): US $ per head (PPP)	758
% of GDP	5.4
public (% of total)	64.6
Human Development Index (1999): value	0.886

For definitions, see explanatory note on p. vi.

Agriculture

PRINCIPAL CROPS ('000 metric tons)

	1999	2000	2001
Potatoes	36.1	43.2	32.1
Rice*	1,558.6	1,540.1	1,396.3
Sweet potatoes	218.6	197.8	188.7
Sorghum	33.6	26.5	21.7
Maize	201.2	178.3	166.0
Tea	21.1	20.3	19.8
Tobacco	9.3	11.5	9.2
Groundnuts	67.2	79.1	56.1
Sugar cane	3,255.8	2,893.8	2,180.3
Bananas	212.5	198.5	204.7
Pineapples	348.5	357.5	388.7
Citrus fruit	486.5	440.4	463.5
Vegetables	3,513.8	3,262.2	3,046.2

* Figures are in terms of brown rice. The equivalent in paddy rice (in '000 metric tons) was: 1,916.3 in 1999; 1,906.1 in 2000; 1,723.9 in 2001.

LIVESTOCK ('000 head at 31 December)

	1999	2000	2001
Cattle	156.1	153.9	146.0
Buffaloes	9.2	7.8	6.5
Pigs	7,243.2	7,495.0	7,164.6
Sheep and goats	237.3	202.5	184.7
Chickens	121,512	117,885	117,310
Ducks	11,649	10,624	10,104
Geese	3,006	2,821	2,613
Turkeys	262	251	235

LIVESTOCK PRODUCTS

	1999	2000	2001
Beef (metric tons)	5,168	4,901	5,057
Pig meat (metric tons)	996,780	1,115,883	1,165,998
Goat meat (metric tons)	8,916	8,213	7,219
Chickens ('000 head)*	385,563	389,770	376,196
Ducks ('000 head)*	35,208	34,099	32,142
Geese ('000 head)*	7,464	6,503	6,330
Turkeys ('000 head)*	488	500	458
Milk (metric tons)	338,005	358,049	346,079
Duck eggs ('000)	485,629	478,452	481,789
Hen eggs ('000)	7,274,451	7,270,033	7,325,125

* Figures refer to numbers slaughtered.

Forestry

ROUNDWOOD REMOVALS ('000 cubic metres)

	1999	2000	2001
Industrial wood	23.3	21.1	26.4
Fuel wood	4.3	4.8	6.0
Total	27.6	25.9	32.4

Fishing*

('000 metric tons, live weight, incl. aquaculture)

	1999	2000	2001
Tilapias	57.3	49.3	82.9
Other freshwater fishes	23.4	22.5	19.2
Japanese eel	16.5	30.5	34.2
Milkfish	50.8	39.7	59.4
Pacific saury	12.5	27.9	39.8
Skipjack tuna	163.9	198.9	186.7
Albacore	64.3	66.1	64.1
Yellowfin tuna	95.0	94.3	109.6
Bigeye tuna	76.8	73.1	81.2
Chub mackerel	45.3	28.6	24.3
Sharks, rays, skates, etc.	42.7	48.1	44.2
Other fishes (incl. unspecified)	292.9	282.5	286.5
Total fish	941.4	961.5	1,032.1
Marine shrimps and prawns	35.9	35.4	29.2
Other crustaceans	6.7	9.2	9.8
Pacific cupped oyster	18.6	20.0	16.6
Common squids	15.9	13.1	13.7
Argentine shortfin squid	277.0	254.7	147.6
Flying squids	5.0	3.9	4.5
Other molluscs	0.5	0.3	0.3
Other aquatic animals	47.3	46.6	47.4
Total catch	1,348.8	1,344.7	1,301.2

* Figures exclude aquatic plants, totalling (in '000 metric tons) 15.5 in 1999; 12.7 in 2000; 15.7 in 2001.

Mining

(metric tons, unless otherwise indicated)

	1999	2000	2001
Coal	91,673	83,380	—
Crude petroleum ('000 litres)	47,105	37,172	44,380
Natural gas ('000 cu m)	855,623	746,824	849,158
Salt	76,916	69,523	66,150
Sulphur	194,811	205,588	223,659
Marble (raw material)	17,771,530	17,831,591	20,475,479
Dolomite	200,595	119,257	70,698

Industry

SELECTED PRODUCTS
('000 metric tons, unless otherwise indicated)

	1999	2000	2001
Wheat flour	738.2	785.5	784.3
Granulated sugar	286.0	230.2	201.8
Carbonated beverages ('000 litres)	461,032	436,897	442,241
Alcoholic beverages—excl. beer ('000 hectolitres)	2,482.0	2,507.4	2,482.4
Cigarettes (million)	22,735	21,064	22,226
Cotton yarn	353.6	337.6	313.6
Man-made fibres	3,227.9	n.a.	n.a.
Paper	1,246.2	1,259.9	1,114.6
Paperboard	3,073.5	3,233.9	2,590.5
Sulphuric acid	848.2	1,020.9	955.8
Spun yarn	485.9	439.6	360.3
Cement	18,283.2	17,572.3	18,127.6
Steel ingots	16,026.7	17,302.4	17,336.2
Sewing machines ('000 units)	2,778.2	2,947.2	2,630.0
Electric fans ('000 units)	23,800.3	22,278.5	21,602.4
Personal computers ('000 units)	12,959.1	16,431.7	16,650.6
Monitors ('000 units)	10,941.8	8,193.8	7,896.4
Radio cassette recorders ('000 units)	4,620.6	4,600.9	4,901.4
Radio receivers ('000 units)	2,156.6	2,038.1	1,985.8
Television receivers ('000 units)	1,021.5	1,154.6	927.6
Picture tubes ('000 units)	23,344.0	20,538.0	9,739
Integrated circuits (million units)	3,985.2	5,068.6	4,799.3
Electronic condensers (million units)	80,670.6	111,071.2	118,127.0
Telephone sets ('000 units)	6,629.5	4,722.4	1,911.0
Passenger motor cars (units)	341,133	367,725	266,237
Trucks and buses (units)	4,227	3,358	2,326
Bicycles ('000 units)	7,228.3	7,193.2	4,746.5
Ships ('000 dwt)*	665.5	868.0	1,014.3
Electric energy (million kWh)	160,570	175,165	178,358
Liquefied petroleum gas	746.3	943.2	975.2

* Excluding motor yachts.

Finance

CURRENCY AND EXCHANGE RATES

Monetary Units

100 cents = 1 New Taiwan dollar (NT $).

Sterling, US Dollar and Euro Equivalents (31 May 2002)

£1 sterling = NT $50.08;
US $1 = NT $34.15;
€1 = NT $32.05;
NT $1,000 = £19.97 = US $29.29 = €31.20.

Average Exchange Rate (NT $ per US $)

1999 32.270
2000 31.235
2001 33.813

BUDGET (NT $ million, year ending 31 December)

Revenue	1999/2000	2001	2002*
Taxes	1,280,657	841,480	878,447
Monopoly profits	77,316	58,718	—
Non-tax revenue from other sources	672,872	517,491	381,715
Total	2,030,845	1,417,689	1,260,162

* Estimates.

Expenditure	1999/2000	2001	2002*
General administration	234,929	167,013	167,571
National defence	343,282	237,752	227,581
Education, science and culture	367,635	257,442	275,196
Economic development	356,418	277,094	267,952
Social welfare	411,023	293,421	266,413
Community development and environmental protection	39,627	22,341	23,845
Pensions and survivors' benefits	195,395	121,967	131,872
Obligations	249,584	151,242	103,258
Subsidies to provincial and municipal governments	25,980	27,672	39,955
Other expenditure	6,273	4,234	15,082
Total	2,230,145	1,560,178	1,518,725

* Estimates.

Note: Figures refer to central government accounts, including Taiwan Province from 1999/2000. Owing to the modification of Budget Law, the financial year 1999/2000 was extended by six months to December 2000. Beginning in 2001, the financial year corresponds to the calendar year.

INTERNATIONAL RESERVES (US $ million at 31 December)

	1999	2000	2001
Gold*	4,861	4,628	4,361
Foreign exchange	106,200	106,742	122,211
Total	111,061	111,370	126,572

* National valuation.

MONEY SUPPLY (NT $ million at 31 December)

	1999	2000	2001
Currency outside banks	611,167	527,748	525,659
Demand deposits at deposit money banks	3,896,013	3,964,324	4,500,201
Total money	4,507,180	4,492,072	5,025,860

COST OF LIVING
(Consumer Price Index; base: 1996 = 100)

	1999	2000	2001
Food	102.97	103.13	102.12
Clothing	94.28	94.58	93.00
Housing	102.54	103.08	102.73
Transport and communications	99.33	102.70	103.87
Medicines and medical care	106.91	110.93	112.41
Education and entertainment	108.60	111.71	113.96
All items (incl. others)	102.78	104.07	104.06

NATIONAL ACCOUNTS (NT $ million in current prices)

National Income and Product

	1999	2000	2001
Compensation of employees	4,687,235	4,939,685	n.a.
Operating surplus	3,106,004	3,163,763	n.a.
Domestic factor incomes	7,793,239	8,103,448	8,064,676
Consumption of fixed capital	804,144	878,482	845,489
Gross domestic product (GDP) at factor cost	8,597,383	8,981,930	8,909,665
Indirect taxes	726,810	727,193	685,375
Less Subsidies	34,264	45,735	52,739
GDP in purchasers' values	9,289,929	9,663,388	9,542,301
Factor income from abroad	224,468	286,688	327,448
Less Factor income paid abroad	138,556	146,728	130,061
Gross national product (GNP)	9,375,841	9,803,348	9,739,688
Less Consumption of fixed capital	804,144	878,482	845,489
National income in market prices	8,571,697	8,924,866	8,894,199
Other current transfers from abroad	100,750	99,990	89,406
Less Other current transfers paid abroad	171,150	181,477	187,476
National disposable income	8,501,297	8,843,379	8,796,129

Expenditure on the Gross Domestic Product

	1999	2000	2001
Government final consumption expenditure	1,221,717	1,246,983	1,235,989
Private final consumption expenditure	5,641,313	5,981,274	6,065,088
Increase in stocks	46,628	-54,978	-97,106
Gross fixed capital formation	2,124,744	2,267,328	1,831,694
Total domestic expenditure	9,034,402	9,440,607	9,035,665
Exports of goods and services	4,486,094	5,260,994	4,822,800
Less Imports of goods and services	4,230,567	5,038,213	4,316,164
GDP in purchasers' values	9,289,929	9,663,388	9,542,301
GDP at constant 1996 prices	9,029,704	9,558,698	9,376,203

Gross Domestic Product by Economic Activity

	1999	2000	2001
Agriculture, hunting, forestry and fishing	237,531	201,810	182,524
Mining and quarrying	46,391	40,427	37,315
Manufacturing	2,470,012	2,550,380	2,415,497
Construction	358,300	329,567	284,875
Electricity, gas and water	207,749	208,325	209,651
Transport, storage and communications	625,637	648,571	664,161
Trade, restaurants and hotels	1,717,692	1,865,320	1,849,033
Finance, insurance and real estate*	1,890,388	1,937,655	1,946,952
Business services	237,144	261,783	267,792
Community, social and personal services	835,631	907,084	964,628
Government services	946,549	984,982	1,027,182
Other services	96,514	107,436	115,039
Sub-total	9,669,538	10,043,340	9,964,649
Value-added tax	173,642	178,160	164,026
Import duties	139,348	146,443	119,099
Less Imputed bank service charge	692,599	704,555	705,473
GDP in purchasers' values	9,289,929	9,663,388	9,542,301

* Including imputed rents of owner-occupied dwellings.

BALANCE OF PAYMENTS (US $ million)

	1999	2000	2001
Exports of goods f.o.b.	121,119	147,548	122,079
Imports of goods f.o.b.	-106,077	-133,529	-101,898
Trade balance	15,042	14,019	20,181
Exports of services	17,259	19,952	20,435
Imports of services	-24,405	-26,930	-24,700
Balance on goods and services	7,896	7,041	15,916
Other income received	6,965	9,166	9,327
Other income paid	-4,160	-4,698	-3,648
Balance on goods, services and income	10,701	11,509	21,595
Current transfers received	3,126	3,202	2,607
Current transfers paid	-5,443	-5,806	-5,341
Current balance	8,384	8,905	18,861
Capital account (net)	-173	-287	-163
Direct investment abroad	-4,420	-6,701	-5,480
Direct investment from abroad	2,926	4,928	4,109
Portfolio investment assets	-4,835	-10,087	-12,427
Portfolio investment liabilities	13,914	9,559	11,136
Other investment assets	2,334	-8,368	-1,837
Other investment liabilities	-699	2,650	3,776
Net errors and omissions	1,162	1,878	-622
Overall balance	18,593	2,477	17,353

External Trade

PRINCIPAL COMMODITIES (US $ million)

Imports c.i.f.	1999	2000	2001
Mineral products	9,145.6	14,094.0	12,763.6
Products of chemical or allied industries	10,596.4	13,085.1	10,231.9
Textiles and textile articles	2,873.8	2,896.9	2,358.6
Base metals and articles thereof	9,511.2	11,044.3	7,783.6
Machinery and mechanical appliances; electrical equipment; sound and television apparatus	50,598.4	66,033.5	47,549.3
Vehicles, aircraft, vessels and associated transport equipment	4,022.0	4,704.8	4,237.9
Optical, photographic, cinematographic, measuring, precision and medical apparatus; clocks and watches; musical instruments	6,186.2	9,116.3	6,213.5
Total (incl. others)	110,689.9	140,010.6	107,237.4

Exports f.o.b.	1999	2000	2001
Plastics, rubber and articles thereof	7,524.3	9,055.8	7,992.8
Textiles and textile articles	14,172.7	15,217.1	12,630.1
Base metals and articles thereof	11,606.9	13,518.6	11,330.9
Machinery and mechanical appliances; electrical equipment; sound and television apparatus	64,161.9	82,561.6	66,851.5
Vehicles, aircraft, vessels and associated transport equipment	5,151.9	5,752.8	4,441.6
Total (incl. others)	121,591.0	148,320.6	122,866.4

PRINCIPAL TRADING PARTNERS (US $ million)

Imports c.i.f.	1999	2000	2001
Australia	2,957.1	3,501.5	3,084.9
Canada	1,124.6	1,276.3	996.1
China, People's Republic	4,526.3	6,223.3	5,901.9
France	1,887.3	1,830.1	2,130.5
Germany	5,312.6	5,542.2	4,246.0
Hong Kong	2,092.9	2,186.6	1,848.9
Indonesia	2,291.4	3,015.1	2,523.4
Italy	1,308.5	1,391.5	1,084.1
Japan	30,591.0	38,557.9	25,848.4
Korea, Republic	7,192.8	8,988.1	6,705.1
Malaysia	3,882.0	5,325.4	4,213.7
Netherlands	1,705.7	2,087.4	1,524.2
Philippines	2,172.5	3,593.9	3,250.5
Russia	1,183.2	1,379.6	603.5
Saudi Arabia	1,383.6	2,690.5	2,745.4
Singapore	3,312.2	5,013.8	3,367.2
Switzerland	1,105.5	1,058.6	865.8
Thailand	2,383.4	2,768.0	2,181.0
United Kingdom	1,720.5	1,937.4	1,442.8
USA	19,693.1	25,126.2	18,229.2
Total (incl. others)	110,689.9	140,010.6	107,237.4

Exports f.o.b.	1999	2000	2001
Australia	1,847.4	1,828.0	1,362.7
Canada	1,750.5	1,882.2	1,564.3
China, People's Republic	2,536.9	4,217.5	4,745.4
France	1,584.1	1,637.6	1,166.0
Germany	4,076.6	4,891.4	4,480.4
Hong Kong*	26,012.1	31,336.3	26,961.4
Indonesia	1,298.6	1,733.7	1,474.6
Italy	1,326.5	1,484.5	1,254.5
Japan	11,900.3	16,599.4	12,759.0
Korea, Republic	2,604.9	3,907.8	3,275.6
Malaysia	2,848.1	3,611.7	3,061.4
Netherlands	4,214.3	4,933.8	4,229.2
Philippines	2,611.4	3,035.7	2,148.7
Singapore	3,818.3	5,455.8	4,051.5
Thailand	2,104.5	2,562.3	2,125.7
United Kingdom	3,830.3	4,508.5	3,329.3
USA	30,901.5	34,814.7	27,654.5
Viet Nam	1,341.6	1,663.5	1,726.9
Total (incl. others)	121,590.9	148,320.6	122,866.4

* The majority of Taiwan's exports to Hong Kong are re-exported.

Transport

RAILWAYS (traffic)

	1999	2000	2001
Passengers ('000)	309,815	460,311	476,214
Passenger-km ('000)	11,020,369	12,623,814	12,268,691
Freight ('000 metric tons)	25,993	22,261	19,287
Freight ton-km ('000)	1,314,912	1,179,056	1,009,863

ROAD TRAFFIC (motor vehicles in use at 31 December)

	1999	2000	2001
Passenger cars	4,509,430	4,716,217	4,825,581
Buses and coaches	23,798	23,923	24,053
Goods vehicles	779,912	808,586	830,673
Motorcycles and scooters	10,958,469	11,423,172	11,733,202

SHIPPING

Merchant Fleet (at 31 December)

	1999	2000	2001
Number of vessels	684	680	656
Total displacement ('000 grt)	5,371.4	5,086.2	4,617.9

Source: Lloyd's Register-Fairplay, *World Fleet Statistics*.

Sea-borne freight traffic ('000 metric tons)

	1999	2000	2001
Goods loaded	209,518	223,728	221,154
Goods unloaded	324,567	343,222	331,719

CIVIL AVIATION (traffic on scheduled services)

	1999	2000	2001
Passengers carried ('000)	50,342.2	46,430.5	44,114.7
Passenger-km (million)	41,698.8	45,755.8	n.a.
Freight carried ('000 metric tons)	1,447.5	1,620.0	1,310.2
Freight ton-km (million)	5,449.9	6,226.3	n.a.

Tourism

TOURIST ARRIVALS BY COUNTRY OF ORIGIN

	1999	2000	2001
Hong Kong	63,323	73,708	80,752
Indonesia	76,424	106,787	89,027
Japan	826,222	916,301	971,190
Korea, Republic	76,142	83,729	82,684
Malaysia	52,678	58,017	56,834
Philippines	123,000	84,088	69,118
Singapore	85,844	94,897	96,777
Thailand	137,972	133,185	116,420
USA	317,801	359,533	339,390
Overseas Chinese*	295,595	313,367	325,266
Total (incl. others)	2,411,248	2,624,037	2,617,137

* i.e. those bearing Taiwan passports.

Tourism receipts (US $ million): 3,571 in 1999; 3,738 in 2000; 3,990 in 2001.

Communications Media

	1999	2000	2001
Book production (titles)	30,871	34,533	36,546
Newspapers	384	445	454
Magazines	6,463	6,641	7,236
Television receivers ('000 in use)*	9,200	9,660	n.a.
Telephone subscribers ('000)	12,044	12,642	12,847
Mobile telephones ('000 in use)	11,541	17,874	21,633
Personal computers ('000 in use)*	4,353	4,964	5,000
Internet users ('000)*	4,540	6,260	7,550

Radio receivers (1994): more than 16 million in use.

* Source: International Telecommunication Union.

Education

(2001/02)

	Schools	Full-time teachers	Pupils/ Students
Pre-school	3,234	19,799	246,303
Primary	2,611	103,501	1,925,491
Secondary (incl. vocational)	1,181	98,609	1,684,449
Higher	154	44,769	1,187,225
Special	24	1,639	5,860
Supplementary	954	3,293	304,763
Total (incl. others)	8,158	271,610	5,354,091

Directory

The Constitution

On 1 January 1947 a new Constitution was promulgated for the Republic of China (confined to Taiwan since 1949). The form of government that was incorporated in the Constitution is based on a five-power system and has the major features of both cabinet and presidential government. A process of constitutional reform, initiated in 1991, continued in 2000. The following is a summary of the Constitution, as subsequently amended:

PRESIDENT

The President shall be directly elected by popular vote for a term of four years. Both the President and Vice-President are eligible for re-election to a second term. The President represents the country at all state functions, including foreign relations; commands land, sea and air forces, promulgates laws, issues mandates, concludes treaties, declares war, makes peace, declares martial law, grants amnesties, appoints and removes civil and military officers, and confers honours and decorations. The President convenes the National Assembly and, subject to certain limitations, may issue emergency orders to deal with national calamities and ensure national security; may dissolve the Legislative Yuan; also nominates the Premier (who may be appointed without the Legislative Yuan's confirmation), and the officials of the Judicial Yuan, the Examination Yuan and the Control Yuan.

NATIONAL ASSEMBLY

Three hundred delegates shall be elected by proportional representation to the National Assembly within three months of the expiration of a six-month period following the public announcement of a proposal by the Legislative Yuan to amend the Constitution or alter the national territory, or within three months of a petition initiated by the Legislative Yuan for the impeachment of the President or the Vice-President. Delegates to the National Assembly shall convene of their own accord within 10 days after the election results have been confirmed and shall remain in session for no more than one month. The term of office of the delegates to the National Assembly shall terminate on the last day of the convention. The powers of the National Assembly are: to vote on the Legislative Yuan's proposals to amend the Contitution or alter the National territory; to deliberate a petition for the impeachment of the President or the Vice-President initiated by the Legislative Yuan.

EXECUTIVE YUAN

The Executive Yuan is the highest administrative organ of the nation and is responsible to the Legislative Yuan; has three categories of subordinate organization:

Executive Yuan Council (policy-making organization)

Ministries and Commissions (executive organization)

Subordinate organization (19 bodies, including the Secretariat, Government Information Office, Directorate-General of Budget, Accounting and Statistics, Council for Economic Planning and Development, and Environmental Protection Administration).

LEGISLATIVE YUAN

The Legislative Yuan is the highest legislative organ of the State, empowered to hear administrative reports of the Executive Yuan, and to change government policy. It may hold a binding vote of 'no confidence' in the Executive Yuan. It comprises 225 members, 168 chosen by direct election from two special municipalities and other cities and counties, eight members are elected from and by aborigines, and eight from and by overseas Chinese. The remaining 41 members are elected from a nationwide constituency on the basis of proportional representation. Members serve for three years and are eligible for re-election.

JUDICIAL YUAN

The Judicial Yuan is the highest judicial organ of state and has charge of civil, criminal and administrative cases, and of cases concerning disciplinary measures against public functionaries (see Judicial System).

EXAMINATION YUAN

The Examination Yuan supervises examinations for entry into public offices, and deals with personnel questions of the civil service.

CONTROL YUAN

The Control Yuan is the highest control organ of the State, exercising powers of impeachment, censure and audit. Comprising 29 members serving a six-year term, nominated and (with the consent of the National Assembly) appointed by the President, the Control Yuan may impeach or censure a public functionary at central or local level, who is deemed guilty of violation of law or dereliction of duty, and shall refer the matter to the law courts for action in cases involving a criminal offence; may propose corrective measures to the Executive Yuan or to its subordinate organs.

The Government

HEAD OF STATE

President: CHEN SHUI-BIAN (inaugurated 20 May 2000).

Vice-President: HSU-LIEN ANNETTE LU.

Secretary-General: CHEN SHIH-MENG.

THE EXECUTIVE YUAN
(September 2002)

Premier: YU SHYI-KUN.

Vice-Premier and Chairman of the Council for Economic Planning and Development: LIN HSIN-I.

Secretary-General: LIU SHYH-FANG.

Ministers without Portfolio: TSAY CHING-YEN, HU SHENG-CHENG, CHEN CHI-NAN, HUANG HWEI-CHEN, LIN SHENG-FENG, KUO YAO-CHI (Chairwoman of the Public Construction Commission), YEH JIUNN-RONG.

Minister of the Interior: YU CHENG-HSIEN.

Minister of Foreign Affairs: EUGENE Y. H. CHIEN.

Minister of National Defense: Gen. (retd) TANG YAO-MING.

Minister of Finance: LEE YUNG-SAN.

Minister of Education: HUANG JONG-TSUN.

Minister of Justice: CHEN DING-NAN.

Minister of Economic Affairs: LIN YI-FU.

Minister of Transportation and Communications: LIN LING-SAN.

Minister of the Mongolian and Tibetan Affairs Commission: HSU CHIH-HSIUNG.

Minister of the Overseas Chinese Affairs Commission: CHANG FU-MEI.

Governor of the Central Bank of China: PERNG FAI-NAN.

Director-General of Directorate-General of Budget, Accounting and Statistics: LIN CHUAN.

Director-General of Central Personnel Administration: LEE YI-YIANG.

Director-General of the Government Information Office: ARTHUR IAP.

Minister of Health: LEE MING-LIANG.

Administrator of the Environmental Protection Administration: HAU LUNG-BIN.

Director-General of the Coast Guard Administration: WANG CHUN.

Director of the National Palace Museum: TU CHENG-SHENG

Chairwoman of the Mainland Affairs Council: TSAI ING-WEN.

Chairman of Veterans' Affairs Commission: YANG TE-CHIH.

Chairwoman of the National Youth Commission: LIN FANG-MEI.

Chairman of the Atomic Energy Council: OUYANG MIN-SHEN.

Chairman of the National Science Council: WEI CHE-HO.

Chairman of the Research, Development and Evaluation Commission: LIN CHIA-CHENG.

Chairman of the Council of Agriculture: FAN CHEN-TZUNG.

Chairwoman of the Council for Cultural Affairs: TCHEN YU-CHIOU.

Chairwoman of the Council of Labor Affairs: CHEN CHU.

Chairman of the Fair Trade Commission: HWANG TZONG-LEH.

Chairman of the Council of Aboriginal Affairs: CHEN CHIEN-NIEN.

Chairman of the National Council on Physical Fitness and Sports: LIN TE-FU.

Chairwoman of the Council for Hakka Affairs: YEH CHU-LAN.

MINISTRIES, COMMISSIONS, ETC.

Office of the President: Chiehshou Hall, 122 Chungking South Rd, Sec. 1, Taipei 100; tel. (2) 23718889; fax (2) 23611604; e-mail public@mail.oop.gov.tw; internet www.oop.gov.tw.

Ministry of Economic Affairs: 15 Foo Chou St, Taipei; tel. (2) 23212200; fax (2) 23919398; e-mail service@moea.gov.tw; internet www.moea.gov.tw.

Ministry of Education: 5 Chung Shan South Rd, Taipei 10040; tel. (2) 23566051; fax (2) 23976978; internet www.moe.gov.tw.

Ministry of Finance: 2 Ai Kuo West Rd, Taipei; tel. (2) 23228000; fax (2) 23965829; e-mail root@www.mof.gov.tw; internet www.mof.gov.tw.

Ministry of Foreign Affairs: 2 Chiehshou Rd, Taipei 10016; tel. (2) 23119292; fax (2) 23144972; internet www.mofa.gov.tw.

Ministry of the Interior: 5–9/F, 5 Hsu Chou Rd, Taipei; tel. (2) 23565005; fax (2) 23566201; e-mail gethics@mail.moi.gov.tw; internet www.moi.gov.tw.

Ministry of Justice: 130 Chungking South Rd, Sec. 1, Taipei 100 10036; tel. (2) 23146871; fax (2) 23896759; internet www.moj.gov.tw.

Ministry of National Defense: 2/F, 164 Po Ai Rd, Taipei; tel. (2) 23116117; fax (2) 23144221; internet www.ndmc.edu.tw.

Ministry of Transportation and Communications: 2 Chang Sha St, Sec. 1, Taipei; tel. (2) 23492900; fax (2) 23118587; e-mail motceyes@motc.gov.tw; internet www.motc.gov.tw.

Mongolian and Tibetan Affairs Commission: 4/F, 5 Hsu Chou Rd, Sec. 1, Taipei; tel. (2) 23566166; fax (2) 23566432; internet gopher://serv.hinet.net/11/government/department/EY/mtac.

Overseas Chinese Affairs Commission: 4/F, 5 Hsu Chou Rd, Taipei; tel. (2) 23566166; fax (2) 23566323; e-mail ocacinfo@mail.ocac.gov.tw; internet www.ocac.gov.tw.

Directorate-General of Budget, Accounting and Statistics: 2 Kwang Chow St, Taipei 100; tel. (2) 23710208; fax (2) 23319925; e-mail sicbs@emc.dgbasey.gov.tw; internet www.dgbas.gov.tw.

Government Information Office: 2 Tientsin St, Taipei; tel. (2) 33568888; fax (2) 23568733; e-mail service@mail.gio.gov.tw; internet www.gio.gov.tw.

Council of Aboriginal Affairs: 16–17/F, 4 Chung Hsiao West Rd, Sec. 1, Taipei; tel. (2) 23882122; fax (2) 23891967.

Council of Agriculture: see under Trade and Industry—Government Agencies.

Atomic Energy Council (AEC): 67 Lane 144, Kee Lung Rd, Sec. 4, Taipei; tel. (2) 23634027; fax (2) 23625617; internet www.aec.gov.tw.

Central Personnel Administration: 109 Huai Ning St, Taipei; tel. (2) 23111720; fax (2) 23715252; internet www.cpa.gov.tw.

Consumer Protection Commission: 1 Chung Hsiao East Rd, Sec. 1, Taipei; tel. (2) 23566600; fax (2) 23214538; e-mail tcpc@ms1.hinet.net; internet www.cpc.gov.tw.

Council for Cultural Affairs: 102 Ai Kuo East Rd, Taipei; tel. (2) 25225300; fax (2) 25519011; e-mail wwwadm@ccpdunx.ccpd.gov.tw; internet expo96.org.tw/cca/welcome_c.html.

Council for Economic Planning and Development: 9/F, 87 Nanking East Rd, Sec. 2, Taipei; tel. (2) 25225300; fax (2) 25519011; internet www.cepd.gov.tw.

Environmental Protection Administration: 41 Chung Hua Rd, Sec. 1, Taipei; tel. (2) 23117722; fax (2) 23116071; e-mail www@sun.epa.gov.tw; internet www.epa.gov.tw.

Fair Trade Commission: 12–14/F, 2-2 Chi Nan Rd, Sec. 2, Taipei; tel. (2) 23517588; fax (2) 23974997; e-mail ftcse@ftc.gov.tw; internet www.ftc.gov.tw.

Department of Health: 100 Ai Kuo East Rd, Taipei; tel. (2) 23210151; fax (2) 23122907; internet www.doh.gov.tw.

Council of Labor Affairs: 5–15/F, 132 Min Sheng East Rd, Sec. 3, Taipei; tel. (2) 27182512; fax (2) 25149240; internet gopher://192.192.46.131.

Mainland Affairs Council: 5–13/F, 2-2 Chi Nan Rd, Sec. 1, Taipei; tel. (2) 23975589; fax (2) 23975700; e-mail macst@mac.gov.tw; internet www.mac.gov.tw.

National Science Council: 17–22/F, 106 Ho Ping East Rd, Sec. 2, Taipei; tel. (2) 27377501; fax (2) 27377668; e-mail nsc@nsc.gov.tw; internet www.nsc.gov.tw.

National Youth Commission: 14/F, 5 Hsu Chou Rd, Taipei; tel. (2) 23566271; fax (2) 23566290; internet www.nyc.gov.tw.

Research, Development and Evaluation Commission: 7/F, 2-2 Chi Nan Rd, Sec. 1, Taipei; tel. (2) 23419066; fax (2) 23928133; e-mail service@rdec.gov.tw; internet rdec.gov.tw.

Veterans' Affairs Commission: 222 Chung Hsiao East Rd, Sec. 5, Taipei; tel. (2) 27255700; fax (2) 27253578; e-mail hsc@www.vac.gov.tw; internet vac.gov.tw.

President and Legislature

PRESIDENT

Election, 18 March 2000

Candidate	Votes	% of votes
Chen Shui-bian (Democratic Progressive Party—DPP)	4,977,737	39.3
James C. Y. Soong (Independent)	4,664,932	36.8
Lien Chan (Kuomintang—KMT)	2,925,513	23.1
Hsu Hsin-lian (Independent)	79,429	0.6
Li Ao (New Party—NP)	16,782	0.1
Total	12,664,393*	100.0

* Not including invalid or spoiled ballot papers, which numbered 122,278.

LI-FA YUAN
(Legislative Yuan)

The Legislative Yuan is the highest legislative organ of the State. It comprises 225 seats. The 168 directly-elected members come from two special municipalities and other cities and counties. Eight members are elected from and by aborigines, and eight from and by overseas Chinese. The remaining 41 members are elected from a nationwide constituency on the basis of proportional representation. Members serve for three years and are eligible for re-election.

President: WANG JIN-PYNG.

General Election, 1 December 2001

Party	% of votes	Seats
Democratic Progressive Party (DPP)	36.6	87
Kuomintang (KMT)	31.3	68
People First Party	20.3	46
Taiwan Solidarity Union (TSU)	8.5	13
New Party (NP)	2.9	1
Other	0.5	1
Independents	—	9
Total	100.0	225

Political Organizations

Legislation adopted in 1989 permitted political parties other than the KMT to function. By mid-2002 a total of 99 parties had registered with the Ministry of the Interior.

China Democratic Socialist Party (CDSP): 6/F, 7, Ho Ping East Rd, Sec. 3, Taipei; tel. (2) 27072883; f. 1932 by merger of National Socialists and Democratic Constitutionalists; aims to promote democracy, to protect fundamental freedoms, and to improve public welfare and social security; Chair. I BUH-LUEN; Sec.-Gen. KAO SHAO-CHUNG.

China Young Party: 12/F, 2 Shin Sheng South Rd, Sec. 3, Taipei; tel. (2) 23626715; f. 1923; aims to recover sovereignty over mainland China, to safeguard the Constitution and democracy, and to foster understanding between Taiwan and the non-communist world.

Chinese Republican Party (CRP): 3/F, 26 Lane 90, Jong Shuenn St, Sec. 2, Taipei; tel. (2) 29366572; f. 1988; advocates peaceful struggle for the salvation of China and the promotion of world peace; Chair. WANG YING-CHYUN.

Democratic Liberal Party (DLP): 4/F, 20 Lane 5, Ching Tyan, Taipei; tel. (2) 23121595; f. 1989; aims to promote political democracy and economic liberty for the people of Taiwan; Chair. HER WEI-KANG.

Democratic Progressive Party (DPP): 10/F, 30 Pei Ping East Rd, Taipei; tel. and fax (2) 23929989; e-mail foreign@dpp.org.tw; internet www.dpp.org.tw; f. 1986; advocates 'self-determination' for the people of Taiwan and UN membership; supports establishment of independent Taiwan following plebiscite; 140,000 mems; Chair. CHEN SHUI-BIAN; Sec.-Gen. CHANG CHUN-HSIUNG.

Democratic Union of Taiwan (DUT): 16/F, 15-1 Harng Joe South Rd, Sec. 1, Taipei; tel. (2) 23211531; f. 1998; Chair. HSU CHERNG-KUEN.

Green Party: 11/F-1, 273 Roosevelt Rd, Sec. 3, Taipei; tel. (2) 23621362; f. 1996 by breakaway faction of the DPP; Chair. CHEN GUANG-YEU.

Jiann Gwo Party (Taiwan Independence Party—TAIP): 2/F, 406 Guang Hwa 2 Rd, Kaohsiung; tel. (7) 7218127; internet www.taip .org.tw; f. 1996 by dissident mems of DPP; Chair. HER WEN-CHII; Sec.-Gen. LI SHENG-HSIUNG.

Kungtang (KT) (Labour Party): 2/F, 22 Kai Feng St, Sec. 2, Taipei; tel. (2) 23121472; fax (2) 23719687; e-mail no1hsieh@eagle .seed.net.tw; f. 1987; aims to become the main political movement of Taiwan's industrial work-force; 10,000 mems; Chair. JENG JAU-MING; Sec.-Gen. HSIEH CHENG-YI.

Kuomintang (KMT) (Nationalist Party of China): 11 Chung Shan South Rd, Taipei 100; tel. (2) 23121472; fax (2) 23434524; internet www.kmt.org.tw; f. 1894; fmr ruling party; aims to supplant communist rule in mainland China; supports democratic, constitutional government, and advocates the unification of China under the 'Three Principles of the People'; aims to promote market economy and equitable distribution of wealth; 2,523,984 mems; Chair. LIEN CHAN; Sec.-Gen. LIN FONG-CHENG.

Nationwide Democratic Non-Partisan Union (NDNU): c/o The Legislative Yuan, Taipei.

New Nation Alliance: 14/F, 9 Song Jiang Rd, Taipei; tel. (2) 23585643; f. 1998; promotes independence for Taiwan and the establishment of a 'new nation, new society and new culture'; Chair. PERNG BAE-SHEAN.

New Party (NP): 4/F, 65 Guang Fuh South Rd, Taipei; tel. (2) 27562222; fax (2) 27565750; e-mail npncs@ms2.hinet.net; internet www.np.org.tw; f. 1993 by dissident KMT legislators (hitherto mems of New Kuomintang Alliance faction); merged with China Social Democratic Party in late 1993; advocates co-operation with the KMT and DPP in negotiations with the People's Republic, the maintenance of security in the Taiwan Straits, the modernization of the island's defence systems, measures to combat government corruption, the support of small and medium businesses and the establishment of a universal social security system; 80,000 mems; Chair. HAO LONG-BIN; Sec.-Gen. LI BING-NAN.

People First Party (PFP): Taipei; f. 2000; internet www.pfp.org.tw; Chair. JAMES C. Y. SOONG; Sec.-Gen. DAVID J. C. CHUNG.

Taiwan Solidarity Union (TSU): 5/F, 180 Hoping East Rd, Taipei; tel. (2) 23678990; fax (2) 23678408; f. 2001, by a breakaway faction of the Kuomintang (KMT); Chair. HUANG CHU-WEN; Sec.-Gen. SHU CHIN-CHIANG.

Workers' Party: 2/F, 181 Fu-hsing South Rd, Taipei; tel. (2) 27555868; f. 1989 by breakaway faction of the Kungtang; radical; Leader LOU MEIWEN.

Various pro-independence groups (some based overseas and, until 1992, banned in Taiwan) are in operation. These include the **World United Formosans for Independence** (WUFI—4,000 mems world-wide; Chair. GEORGE CHANG) and the **Organization for Taiwan Nation-Building**.

Diplomatic Representation

EMBASSIES IN THE REPUBLIC OF CHINA

Belize: 11/F, 9 Lane 62, Tien Mou West Rd, Taipei 111; tel. (2) 28760894; fax (2) 28760896; e-mail embelroc@ms41.hinet.net; internet www.embassyofbelize.org.tw; Ambassador: WILLIAM QUINTO.

Burkina Faso: 6/F, 9-1, Lane 62, Tien Mou West Rd, Taipei 111; tel. (2) 28733096; fax (2) 28733071; e-mail abftap94@ms17.hinet.net; Ambassador: JACQUES Y. SAWADOGO.

Chad: 8/F, 9 Lane 62, Tien Mou West Rd, Taipei; tel. (2) 28742943; fax (2) 28742971; e-mail amchadtp@ms23.hinet.net; Ambassador: HISSEIN BRAHIM TAHA.

Costa Rica: 5/F, 9-1, Lane 62, Tien Mou West Rd, Taipei 111; tel. (2) 28752964; fax (2) 28753151; e-mail oscaralv@ficnet.net; Ambassador: OSCAR ALVAREZ.

Dominican Republic: 6/F, 9 Lane 62, Tien Mou West Rd, Taipei 111; tel. (2) 28751357; fax (2) 28752661; Ambassador: MIGUEL HERNÁNDEZ.

El Salvador: 2/F, 9 Lane 62, Tien Mou West Rd, Shih Lin, Taipei 111; tel. (2) 28763509; fax (2) 28763514; e-mail embasal.taipei@ msa.hinet.net; Ambassador: FRANCISCO RICARDO SANTANA BERRÍOS.

The Gambia: 9/F, 9-1 Lane 62, Tien Mou West Rd, Taipei 111; tel. (2) 28753911; fax (2) 28752775; Ambassador: JOHN-PAUL BOJANG.

Guatemala: 3/F, 9-1 Lane 62, Tien Mou West Rd, Taipei 111; tel. (2) 28756952; fax (2) 28740699; e-mail embchina@minex.gob.gt; Ambassador: MANUEL ERNESTO GALVEZ CORONADO.

Haiti: 8/F, 9-1 Lane 62, Tien Mou West Rd, Taipei 111; tel. (2) 28766718; fax (2) 28766719; Ambassador: LAFONTAINE SAINT-LOUIS.

Holy See: 87 Ai Kuo East Rd, Taipei 106 (Apostolic Nunciature); tel. (2) 23216847; fax (2) 23911926; e-mail aposnunc@tptsl.seed.net.tw; Chargé d'affaires: Mgr JAMES PATRICK GREEN.

Honduras: 9/F, 9 Lane 62, Tien Mou West Rd, Taipei 111; tel. (2) 28755507; fax (2) 28755726; e-mail honduras@ms9.hinet.net; internet www.hondurasinfo.hn; Ambassador: MARLENE VILLELA DE TALBOTT.

Liberia: 11/F, 9-1 Lane 62, Tien Mou West Rd, Taipei 111; tel. (2) 28751212; fax (2) 28751313; e-mail libemb@tpts5.seed.net.tw; Ambassador: JOHN CUMMINGS

Malawi: 2/F, 9 Lane 62, Tien Mou West Rd, Taipei 111; tel. (2) 28762284; fax (2) 28763545; Ambassador: EUNICE KAZEMBE.

Marshall Islands: 4/F, 9-1 Lane 62, Tien Mou West Rd, Taipei 111; tel. (2) 28734884; fax (2) 28734904; internet www.rmiembassy .org.tw; Ambassador: ALEX CARTER BING.

Nicaragua: 3/F, 9 Lane 62, Tien Mou West Rd, Taipei 111; tel. (2) 28749034; fax (2) 28749080; e-mail embni629@ms39.hinet.net; Ambassador: LUIS A WONG.

Palau: 8/F, 128 Min Sheng East Rd, Sec. 3, Taipei; tel. (2) 27197761; fax (2) 27197774; Ambassador: JOHNSON TORIBIONG.

Panama: 6/F, 111 Sung Kiang Rd, Taipei 104; tel. (2) 25099189; fax (2) 25099801; Ambassador: JOSÉ ANTONIO DOMÍNGUEZ.

Paraguay: 7/F, 9-1 Lane 62, Tien Mou West Rd, Taipei 111; tel. (2) 28736310; fax (2) 28736312; e-mail eptaipei@seed.net.tw; Ambassador: (vacant).

São Tomé and Príncipe: 3/F, 18 Chi-lin Rd, Taipei 104; tel. (2) 25114111; fax (2) 25116255; e-mail stproc@ms42.hinet.net; Ambassador: OVIDIO M. PEQUENO.

Senegal: 10/F, 9-1 Lane 62, Tien Mou West Rd, Taipei 111, tel. (2) 28766519; fax (2) 28734909; e-mail sngol@ms2.seeder.net; Ambassador: ADAMA SARR.

Solomon Islands: 7/F, 9-1 Lane 62, Tien Mou West Rd, Taipei 111; tel. (2) 28731168; fax (2) 28766442; Ambassador: SETH GUKUNA.

Swaziland: 10/F, 9 Lane 62, Tien Mou West Rd, Taipei 111; tel. (2) 28725934; fax (2) 28726511; Ambassador: MOSES MATHENDELE DLAMINI.

Judicial System

The power of judicial review is exercised by the Judicial Yuan's 16 Grand Justices nominated and appointed for nine years by the President of Taiwan with the consent of the National Assembly. The Grand Justices hold meetings to interpret the Constitution and unify the interpretation of laws and orders. From 2003 the Judicial Yuan shall have 15 Grand Justices, one of whom shall serve as its President and another as Vice-President, nominated and appointed by the President of Taiwan with the consent of the Legislative Yuan. The President of the Judicial Yuan is also the *ex-officio* chairman for the Plenary Session of the Grand Justices. The Ministry of Justice is under the jurisdiction of the Executive Yuan.

Judicial Yuan: 124 Chungking South Rd, Sec. 1, Taipei; tel. (2) 23141936; fax (2) 23898923; e-mail judicial@mail.judicial.gov.tw; internet www.judicial.gov.tw; Pres. WENG YUEH-SHENG; Vice-Pres. CHENG CHUNG-MO; Sec.-Gen. YANG JEN-SHOU; the highest judicial organ, and the interpreter of the constitution and national laws and ordinances; supervises the following:

Supreme Court: 6 Chang Sha St, Sec. 1, Taipei; tel. (2) 23141160; fax (2) 23114246; Court of third and final instance for civil and criminal cases; Pres. WU CHII-PIN.

High Courts: Courts of second instance for appeals of civil and criminal cases.

District Courts: Courts of first instance in civil, criminal and non-contentious cases.

Supreme Administrative Court: 1 Lane 126, Chungking South Rd, Sec. 1, Taipei; tel. (2) 23113691; fax (2) 23111791; e-mail jessie@judicial.gov.tw; Court of final resort in cases brought against govt agencies; Pres. JONG YAW-TANG.

High Administrative Courts: Courts of first instance in cases brought against government agencies.

Commission on Disciplinary Sanctions Against Functionaries: 124 Chungking South Rd, 3/F, Sec. 1, Taipei 10036; tel. (2) 23619375; fax (2) 23311934; decides on disciplinary measures against public functionaries impeached by the Control Yuan; Chief Commissioner LIN KUO-HSIEN.

Religion

According to the Ministry of the Interior, in 1999 34% of the population were adherents of Buddhism, 42% of Daoism (Taoism), 7.8% of I-Kuan Tao and 3.6% of Christianity.

BUDDHISM

Buddhist Association of Taiwan: Mahayana and Theravada schools; 1,613 group mems and more than 9.61m. adherents; Leader Ven. CHIN-HSIN.

CHRISTIANITY

The Roman Catholic Church

Taiwan comprises one archdiocese, six dioceses and one apostolic administrative area. In December 2000 there were 310,218 adherents.

Bishops' Conference: Chinese Regional Bishops' Conference, 34, Lane 32, Kuangfu South Rd, Taipei 10552; tel. (2) 25782355; fax (2) 25773874; e-mail bishconf@ms1.hinet.net; internet www.catholic .org.tw; f. 1967; Pres. Cardinal PAUL SHAN KUO-HSI, Bishop of Kaohsiung.

Archbishop of Taipei: Most Rev. JOSEPH TI-KANG, Archbishop's House, 94 Loli Rd, Taipei 10668; tel. (2) 27371311; fax (2) 27373710.

The Anglican Communion

Anglicans in Taiwan are adherents of the Protestant Episcopal Church. In 1999 the Church had 2,000 members.

Bishop of Taiwan: Rt Rev. DAVID JUNG-HSIN LAI, 7 Lane 105, Hangchow South Rd, Sec. 1, Taipei 100; tel. (2) 23411265; fax (2) 23962014; e-mail skhtpe@ms12.hinet.net; internet www.dfms.org/ taiwan.

Presbyterian Church

Tai-oan Ki-tok Tiu-Lo Kau-Hoe (Presbyterian Church in Taiwan): No. 3, Lane 269, Roosevelt Rd, Sec. 3, Taipei 106; tel. (2) 23625282; fax (2) 23628096; f. 1865; Gen. Sec. Rev. L. K. LO; 224,679 mems (2000).

DAOISM (TAOISM)

In 1999 there were about 4.54m. adherents. Temples numbered 8,604, and clergy totalled 33,850.

I-KUAN TAO

Introduced to Taiwan in the 1950s, this 'Religion of One Unity' is a modern, syncretic religion, drawn mainly from Confucian, Buddhist and Daoist principles and incorporating ancestor worship. In 1998 there were 93 temples and 18,000 family shrines. Adherents totalled 845,000.

ISLAM

Leader MOHAMMED MA CHA-JENG; 53,000 adherents in 1999.

The Press

In 1999 the number of registered newspapers stood at 367. The majority of newspapers are privately owned.

PRINCIPAL DAILIES

Taipei

Central Daily News: 260 Pa Teh Rd, Sec. 2, Taipei; tel. (2) 27765368; fax (2) 27775835; internet www.cdn.com.tw; f. 1928; morning; Chinese; official Kuomintang organ; Publr and CEO SHAW YU-MING; circ. 600,000.

The China Post: 8 Fu Shun St, Taipei 104; tel. (2) 25969971; fax (2) 25957962; e-mail cpost@msl.hinet.net; internet www .chinapost.com.tw; f. 1952; morning; English; Publr and Editor JACK HUANG; readership 250,000.

China Times: 132 Da Li St, Taipei; tel. (2) 23087111; fax (2) 23063312; f. 1950; morning; Chinese; Chair. YU CHI-CHUNG; Publr YU ALBERT CHIEN-HSIN; circ. 1.2m.

China Times Express: 132 Da Li St, Taipei; tel. (2) 23087111; fax (2) 23082221; e-mail chinaexpress@mail.chinatimes.com.tw; f. 1988; evening; Chinese; Publr S. F. LIN; Editor C. L. HUANG; circ. 400,000.

Commercial Times: 132 Da Li St, Taipei; tel. (2) 23087111; fax (2) 23069456; e-mail commercialtimes@mail.chinatimes.com.tw; f. 1978; morning; Chinese; Publr PENG CHWEI-MING; Editor-in-Chief PHILLIP CHEN; circ. 300,000.

Economic Daily News: 555 Chung Hsiao East Rd, Sec. 4, Taipei; tel. (2) 27681234; fax (2) 27600129; f. 1967; morning; Chinese; Publr WANG PI-CHEN.

The Great News: 216 Chen Teh Rd, Sec. 3, Taipei; tel. (2) 25973111; f. 1988; morning; also *The Great News Daily-Entertainment* (circ. 460,000).

Liberty Times: 11/F, 137 Nanking East Rd, Sec. 2, Taipei; tel. (2) 25042828; fax (2) 25042212; f. 1988; Publr WU A-MING; Editor-in-Chief ROGER CHEN.

Mandarin Daily News: 2 Foo Chou St, Taipei; tel. (2) 23921133; fax (2) 23410203; f. 1948; morning; Publr LIN LIANG.

Min Sheng Daily: 555 Chung Hsiao East Rd, Sec. 4, Taipei; tel. (2) 27681234; fax (2) 27560955; f. 1978; sport and leisure; Publr WANG SHAW-LAN.

Taiwan Hsin Sheng Pao: 260 Pa Teh Rd, Sec. 2, Taipei; tel. (2) 87723058; fax (2) 87723026; f. 1945; morning; Chinese; Publr LIU CHZ-SHIEN.

Taiwan News: 7/F, 88 Hsin Yi Rd, Sec. 2, Taipei 110; tel. (2) 23527666; fax (2) 23517666; e-mail editor@etaiwannews.com; internet www.etaiwannews.com; f. 1949; morning; English; Chair. and Publr LUIS KO.

United Daily News: 555 Chung Hsiao East Rd, Sec. 4, Taipei; tel. (2) 27681234; fax (2) 27632303; e-mail secretariat@udngroup .com.tw; f. 1951; morning; Publr WANG SHAW-LAN; Editor-in-Chief HUANG SHU-CHUAN; circ. 1.2m.

Provincial

China Daily News (Southern Edn): 57 Hsi Hwa St, Tainan; tel. (6) 2202691; fax (6) 2201804; f. 1946; morning; Publr LIU CHZ-SHIEN; circ. 670,000.

Keng Sheng Daily News: 36 Wuchuan St, Hualien; tel. (38) 340131; fax (38) 329664; f. 1947; morning; Publr HSIEH YING-YIN; circ. 50,000.

The Commons Daily: 180 Min Chuan 2 Rd, Kaohsiung; tel. (7) 3363131; fax (7) 3363604; f. 1950; frmrly Min Chung Daily News; morning; Executive-in-Chief WANG CHIN-HSIUNG; circ. 148,000.

Taiwan Daily News: 361 Wen Shin Rd, Sec. 3, Taichung; tel. (4) 22958511; fax (4) 2958950; f. 1964; morning; Publr ANTONIO CHIANG; Editor-in-Chief LIU CHIH TSUNG; circ. 250,000.

Taiwan Hsin Wen Daily News: 3 Woo Fu I Rd, Kaohsiung; tel. (7) 2226666; f. 1949; morning; Publr CHANG REI-TE.

Taiwan Times: 32 Kaonan Rd, Jen Wu Shan, Kaohsiung; tel. (7) 3428666; fax (7) 3102828; f. 1978; Publr WANG YUH-FA.

SELECTED PERIODICALS

Artist Magazine: 6/F, 147 Chung Ching South Rd, Sec. 1, Taipei; tel. (2) 23886715; fax (2) 23317096; e-mail artvenue@seed .net.tw; f. 1975; monthly; Publr HO CHENG KUANG; circ. 28,000.

Better Life Monthly: 11 Lane 199, Hsin-yih Rd, Sec. 4, Taipei; tel. (2) 27549588; fax (2) 27016068; e-mail bettlife@ms14.hinet.net; f. 1987; Publr JACK S. LIN.

Brain: 9/F, 47 Nanking East Rd, Sec. 4, Taipei; tel. (2) 27132644; fax (2) 27137318; f. 1977; monthly; Publr JOHNSON WU.

Business Weekly: 21/F, 62 Tun Hua South Rd, Sec. 2, Taipei; tel. (2) 27736611; fax (2) 27364620; f. 1987; Publr JIN WEI-TSUN.

Car Magazine: 1/F, 3 Lane 3, Tung-Shan St, Taipei; tel. (2) 23218128; fax (2) 23935614; e-mail carguide@ms13.hinet.net; f. 1982; monthly; Publr H. K. LIN; Editor-in-Chief TA-WEI LIN; circ. 85,000.

Central Monthly: 7/F, 11 Chung Shan South Rd, Taipei; tel. (2) 23433140; fax (2) 23435417; f. 1950; Publr HUANG HUI-TSEN.

China Times Weekly: 5/F, 25 Min Chuan East Rd, Sec. 6, Taipei; tel. (2) 27936000; fax (2) 27912238; f. 1978; weekly; Chinese; Editor CHANG KUO-LI; Publr CHUANG SHU-MING; circ. 180,000.

Commonwealth Monthly: 4/F, 87 Sung Chiang Rd, Taipei; tel. (2) 25078627; fax (2) 25079011; f. 1981; monthly; business; Pres. CHARLES H. C. KAO; Publr and Editor DIANE YING; circ. 83,000.

Cosmopolitan: 5/F, 8 Lane 181, Jiou-Tzung Rd, Nei Hu Area, Taipei; tel. (2) 287978900; fax (2) 287978990; e-mail hwaker@ ms13.hinet.net; f. 1992; monthly; Publr MINCHUN CHANG.

Country Road: 14 Wenchow St, Taipei; tel. (2) 23628148; fax (2) 23636724; e-mail h3628148@ms15.hinet.net; internet www.coa .gov.tw/magazine/fst/road.htm; f. 1975; monthly; Editor CHRISTINE S. L. YU; Publr KAO YU-HSIN.

Crown Magazine: 50, Alley 120, Tun Hua North Rd, Sec. 4, Taipei; tel. (2) 27168888; fax (2) 25148285; f. 1954; monthly; literature and arts; Publr PING HSIN TAO; Editor CHEN LIH-HWA; circ. 76,000.

Defense Technology Monthly: 6/F, 6 Nanking East Rd, Sec. 5, Taipei; tel. (2) 27669628; fax (2) 27666092; f. 1894; Publr J. D. Bih.

Earth Geographic Monthly: 4/F, 16 Lane 130 Min Chuan Rd, Hsin-Tien, Taipei; tel. (2) 22182218; fax (2) 22185418; f. 1988; Publr Hsu Chung-jung.

Elle-Taipei: 9/F, 5 Lane 30, Sec. 3, Min Sheng East Rd, Taipei; tel. (2) 87706168; fax (2) 87706178; e-mail jdewitt@hft.com.tw; f. 1991; monthly; women's magazine; Publr Jean de Witt; Editor-in-Chief Lena Yang; circ. 50,000.

Evergreen Monthly: 11/F, 2 Pa Teh Rd, Sec. 3, Taipei; tel. (2) 25782321; fax (2) 25786838; f. 1983; health care knowledge; Publr Liang Guang-ming; circ. 50,000.

Excellence Magazine: 3/F, 15 Lane 2, Sec. 2, Chien Kuo North Rd, Taipei; tel. (2) 25093578; fax (2) 25173607; f. 1984; monthly; business; Man. Lin Hsin-jyh; Editor-in-Chief Liu Jen; circ. 70,000.

Families Monthly: 11/F, 2 Pa Teh Rd, Sec. 3, Taipei; tel. (2) 25785078; fax (2) 25786838; f. 1976; family life; Editor-in-Chief Thelma Ku; circ. 155,000.

Foresight Investment Weekly: 7/F, 52 Nanking East Rd, Sec. 1, Taipei; tel. (2) 25512561; fax (2) 25119596; f. 1980; weekly; Dir and Publr Sun Wun Hsiung; Editor-in-Chief Wu Wen Shin; circ. 55,000.

Global Views Monthly: 2/F, 1 Lane 93, Taipei; tel. (2) 25173688; fax (2) 25078644; f. 1986; Pres. Charles H. C. Kao; Publr and Editor-in-Chief Wang Li-hsing.

Gourmet World: 4/F, 52 Hang Chou South Rd, Sec. 2, Taipei; tel. (2) 23972215; fax (2) 23412184; f. 1990; Publr Hsu Tang-jen.

Harvest Farm Magazine: 14 Wenchow St, Taipei; tel. (2) 23628148; fax (2) 23636724; e-mail h3628148@ms15.hinet.net; f. 1951; every 2 weeks; Publr Kao Yu-hsin; Editor Kao Ming-tang.

Information and Computer: 10/F, 116 Nang King East Rd, Taipei; tel. (2) 25422540; fax (2) 25310760; f. 1980; monthly; Chinese; Publr Lin Ferng-chin; Editor Jennifer Chiu; circ. 28,000.

Issues and Studies: Institute of International Relations, 64 Wan Shou Rd, Wenshan, Taipei 116; tel. (2) 29394921; fax (2) 29397352; e-mail scchang@nccu.edu.tw; internet www.iir.nccu.edu.tw; f. 1965; quarterly; English; Chinese studies and international affairs; Publr and Editor Ho Szu-yin.

Jade Biweekly Magazine: 7/F, 222 Sung Chiang Rd, Taipei; tel. (2) 25811665; fax (2) 25210586; f. 1982; economics, social affairs, leisure; Publr Hsu Chia-chung; circ. 98,000.

The Journalist: 16/F, 218 Tun Hua South Rd, Sec. 2, Taipei; tel. (2) 23779977; fax (2) 23775850; f. 1987; weekly; Publr Wang Shin-ching.

Ladies Magazine: 11/F, 3, 187 Shin Yi Rd, Sec. 4, Taipei; tel. (2) 27026908; fax (2) 27014090; f. 1978; monthly; Publr Cheng Chin-shan; Editor-in-Chief Theresa Lee; circ. 60,000.

Living: 6/F, 100 Ai Kuo East Rd, Hsin Tien, Taipei; tel. (2) 23222266; fax (2) 33225050; f. 1997; monthly; Publr Lisa Wu.

Madame Figaro: 5/F, 25 Min Chuan East Rd, Sec. 6, Taipei; tel. (2) 27929868; fax (2) 27928838; e-mail tina@mail.chinatimes.com.tw; f. 1993; fmrly *Marie Claire*; Publr Chang Shu-ming.

Management Magazine: 5/F, 220 Ta Tung Rd, Sec. 3, Hsichih, Taipei; tel. (2) 86471828; fax (2) 86471466; e-mail frankhung@mail.chinamgt.com; internet www.harment.com; f. 1973; monthly; Chinese; Publr and Editor Frank L. Hung; Pres. Kathy T. Kuo; circ. 65,000.

Money Monthly: 10/F, 289 Chung Hsiao East Rd, Taipei; tel. (2) 25149822; fax (2) 27154657; f. 1986; monthly; personal financial management; Publr Patrick Sun; Man. Editor Jennie Shue; circ. 55,000.

Music and Audiophile: 2/F, 2 Kingshan South Rd, Sec. 1, Taipei; tel. (2) 25684607; fax (2) 23958654; f. 1973; Publr Chang Kuo-ching; Editor-in-Chief Charles Huang.

National Palace Museum Bulletin: 211 Chih-shan Rd, Wai Shuang Hsi, Sec. 2, Taipei 11102; tel. (2) 28812021; fax (2) 28821440; e-mail service01@npm.gov.tw; internet www.npm.gov.tw; f. 1965; every 3 months; Chinese art history research in English; Publr and Dir Tu Cheng-sheng; Editor-in-Chief Wang Yao-ting; circ. 1,000.

National Palace Museum Monthly of Chinese Art: Wai Shuang Hsi, Shih Lin, Taipei 11102; tel. (2) 28821230; fax (2) 28821440; f. 1983; monthly in Chinese; Publr Tu Cheng-sheng; circ. 10,000.

Nong Nong Magazine: 7/F, 531-1 Chung Cheng Rd, Hsin Tien, Taipei; tel. (2) 22181828; fax (2) 22181081; e-mail group@nongnong.com.tw; f. 1984; monthly; women's interest; Publr Anthony Tsai; Editor Vivian Lin; circ. 70,000.

PC Home: 4/F, 100 Ai Kuo East Rd, Sec. 2, Taipei; tel. (2) 23965698; fax (2) 23926069; f. 1996; monthly; Publr Hung-tze Jang.

PC Office: 11/F, 8 Tun Hua North Rd, Taipei; tel. (2) 27815390; fax (2) 27780899; f. 1997; monthly; Publr Hung-tze Jang.

Reader's Digest (Chinese Edn): 3/F, 2 Ming Sheng East Rd, Sec. 5, Taipei; tel. (2) 27607262; fax (2) 27461588; monthly; Editor-in-Chief Annie Cheng.

Sinorama: 5/F, 54, Chunghsiao East Rd, Sec. 1, Taipei 100; tel. (2) 23922256; fax (2) 23970655; f. 1976; monthly; cultural; bilingual magazine with edns in Chinese with Japanese, Spanish and English; Publr Su Tza-ping; Editor-in-Chief Anna Y. Wang; circ. 110,000.

Studio Classroom: 10 Lane 62, Ta-Chih St, Taipei; tel. (2) 25338082; fax (2) 25331009; internet www.studioclassroom.com; f. 1962; monthly; Publr Doris Brougham.

Taipei Journal: 2 Tientsin St, Taipei 10041; tel. (2) 23970180; fax (2) 23568233; e-mail tj@mail.gio.gov.tw; internet taipeijournal.nat.gov.tw; f. 1964 (fmrly Free China Journal); weekly; English; news review; Publr Arthur Iap; Exec. Editor-in-Chief Michael Chen; circ. 30,000.

Taipei Review: 2 Tientsin St, Taipei 100; tel. (2) 23516419; e-mail tr@gio.gov.tw; f. 1951; monthly; English; illustrated; Publr Arthur Iap; Editor-in-Chief Andrew T. H. Cheng.

Taipei Times: 5/F, 137 Nanking East Rd, Sec. 2, Taipei; tel. (2) 25182728; fax (2) 25189154; internet www.taipeitimes.com; f. 1999; Publr Antonio Chiang.

Time Express: 7/F, 2, 76 Tun Hua South Rd, Sec. 2, Taipei; tel. (2) 27084410; fax (2) 27084420; f. 1973; monthly; Publr Richard C. C. Huang.

Unitas: 10/F, 180 Keelung Rd, Sec. 1, Taipei; tel. (2) 27666759; fax (2) 27567914; e-mail unitas@udngroup.com.tw; monthly; Chinese; literary journal; Publr Chang Pao-ching; Editor-in-Chief Hsu Hui-chih.

Vi Vi Magazine: 7/F, 550 Chung Hsiao East Rd, Sec. 5, Taipei; tel. (2) 27275336; fax (2) 27592031; f. 1984; monthly; women's interest; Pres. Tseng Ching-tang; circ. 60,000.

Vogue: 5/F, 232 Tun Hua North Rd, Taipei; tel. (2) 27172000; fax (2) 27172004; f. 1996; monthly; Publr Bentham Liu.

Wealth Magazine: 7/F, 52 Nanking East Rd, Sec. 1, Taipei; tel. (2) 25816196; fax (2) 25119596; f. 1974; monthly; finance; Pres. Tshai Yen-kuen; Editor Andy Lian; circ. 75,000.

Win Win Weekly: 7/F, 52 Nanking East Rd, Taipei; tel. (2) 25816196; fax (2) 25119596; f. 1996; Publr Gin-ho Hshie.

Youth Juvenile Monthly: 3/F, 66-1 Chung Cheng South Rd, Sec. 1, Taipei; tel. (2) 23112832; fax (2) 23612239; f. 1954; Publr Lee Chung-guai.

NEWS AGENCIES

Central News Agency (CNA): 209 Sung Chiang Rd, Taipei; tel. (2) 25051180; fax (2) 25078839; e-mail cnamark@ms9.hinet.net; internet www.cna.com.tw; f. 1924; news service in Chinese, English and Spanish; feature and photographic services; 12 domestic and 30 overseas bureaux; Pres. Hui Yuan-hui.

Foreign Bureaux

Agence France-Presse (AFP): Room 617, 6/F, 209 Sung Chiang Rd, Taipei; tel. (2) 25016395; fax (2) 25011881; e-mail AFPTPE@ms11.hitnet.tw; Bureau Chief Yang Hsin-hsin.

Associated Press (AP) (USA): Room 630, 6/F, 209 Sung Chiang Rd, Taipei; tel. (2) 25036651; fax (2) 25007133; Bureau Chief William Foreman.

Reuters (UK): 8/F, 196 Chien Kuo North Rd, Sec. 2, Taipei; tel. (2) 25080815; fax (2) 25080204; Bureau Chief Benjamin Kang Lim.

Publishers

There are 7,810 publishing houses. In 2001 a total of 40,235 titles were published.

Art Book Co: 1/F, 18 Lane 283, Roosevelt Rd, Sec. 3, Taipei; tel. (2) 23620578; fax (2) 23623594; Publr Ho Kung Shang.

Cheng Wen Publishing Co: 3/F, 277 Roosevelt Rd, Sec. 3, Taipei; tel. (2) 23628032; fax (2) 23660806; e-mail ccicncwp@ms17.hinet.net; Publr Larry C. Huang.

China Economic News Service (CENS): 555 Chung Hsiao East Rd, Sec. 4, Taipei 110; tel. (2) 27681234; fax (2) 27629143; e-mail webmaster@www.cens.com; internet www.cens.com; f. 1974; trade magazines.

China Times Publishing Co: 5/F, 240 Hoping West Rd, Sec. 3, Taipei; tel. (2) 23087111; fax (2) 23027844; e-mail ctpc@mse.hinet.net; internet www.publish.chinatimes.com.tw; f. 1975; Pres. Mo Chao-ping.

Chinese Culture University Press: 55 Hua Kang Rd, Yangmingshan, Taipei; tel. (2) 28611861; fax (2) 28617164; e-mail ccup@ccuo16.pccu.edu.tw; Publr Lee Fu-chen.

The Commercial Press Ltd: 37 Chungking South Rd, Sec. 1, Taipei; tel. (2) 23614739; fax (2) 23710274; e-mail cptw@ms12 .hinet.net; Man.-Editor TANG HAO-CHUAN.

Crown Publishing Co: 50 Lane 120, Tun Hua North Rd, Taipei; tel. (2) 27168888; fax (2) 27161793; e-mail magazine@crown.com.tw; internet www.crown.com.tw; Publr PHILIP PING.

The Eastern Publishing Co Ltd: 121 Chungking South Rd, Sec. 1, Taipei; tel. (2) 23114514; fax (2) 23814132; Publr CHENG LI-TSU.

Elite Publishing Co: 1/F, 33-1 Lane 113, Hsiamen St, Taipei 100; tel. (2) 23671021; fax (2) 23657047; e-mail elite113@ms12 .hinet.net; f. 1975; Publr KO CHING-HWA.

Far East Book Co: 10/F, 66-1 Chungking South Rd, Sec. 1, Taipei; tel. (2) 23118740; fax (2) 23114184; e-mail service@mail .fareast.com.tw; internet www.fareast.com.tw; art, education, history, physics, mathematics, law, literature, dictionaries, textbooks, language tapes, Chinese-English dictionary; Publr GEORGE C. L. PU.

International Cultural Enterprises: Rm 612, 6/F, 25 Po Ai Rd, Taipei 100; tel. (2) 23318080; fax (2) 23318090; e-mail itsits@ms69 .hinet.net; internet www.itsitsh.com.tw; Publr LAKE HU.

Kwang Fu Book Enterprises Co Ltd: 6/F, 38 Fushing North Rd, Taipei; tel. (2) 27410415; fax (2) 2718230; e-mail loatiao@kf.net.tw; internet www.kf.net; Publr C. H. LIN.

Kwang Hwa Publishing Co: 5/F, 54 Chung Hsiao East Rd, Sec. 1, Taipei; tel. (2) 23516419; fax (2) 23510821; e-mail service@sinorama .com.tw; internet www.sinorama.com.tw; Publr ARTHUR IAP.

Li-Ming Cultural Enterprise Co: 3/F, 49 Chungking South Rd, Sec. 1, Taipei 100; tel. (2) 23821233; fax (2) 23821244; e-mail liming2f@ms15.hinet.net; internet www.limingco.com.tw; Pres. SHEN FANG-SHIN.

Linking Publishing Co Ltd: 561 Chung Hsiao East Rd, Sec. 4, Taipei; tel. (2) 27683708; fax (2) 27634590; e-mail linking@udn group.com.tw; internet www.udngroup.com.tw/linkingp; Publr LIU KUO-JUEI.

San Min Book Co Ltd: 386 Fushing North Rd, Taipei; tel. (2) 25006600; fax (2) 25064000; e-mail sanmin@ms2.hinet.net; internet www.sanmin.com.tw; f. 1953; literature, history, philosophy, social sciences, dictionaries, art, politics, law; Publr LIU CHEN-CHIANG.

Senseio Business Group: 259 Tun Hua South Rd, Sec. 1, Taipei; tel. (2) 27037777; fax (2) 27049948; f. 1966; Publr LIAW SUSHI-IGU.

Sitak Publishing Group: 10/F, 15 Lane 174, Hsin Ming Rd, Neihu Dist, Taipei; tel. (2) 27911197; fax (2) 27955824; e-mail rights@sitak.com.tw; Publr CHU PAO-LOUNG; Dir KELLY CHU.

Taiwan Kaiming Book Co: 77 Chung Shan North Rd, Sec. 1, Taipei; tel. (2) 25510820; fax (2) 25212894; Publr LUCY CHOH LIU.

Tung Hua Book Co Ltd: 105 Ermei St, Taipei; tel. (2) 23114027; fax (2) 23116615; Publr CHARLES CHOH.

The World Book Co: 6/F, 99 Chungking South Rd, Sec. 1, Taipei; tel. (2) 23311616; fax (2) 23317963; e-mail wbc@ms2.hinet.net; internet www.worldbook.com.tw; f. 1921; literature, textbooks; Chair. YEN FENG-CHANG; Publr YEN ANGELA CHU.

Youth Cultural Enterprise Co Ltd: 3/F, 66-1 Chungking South Rd, Sec. 1, Taipei; tel. (2) 23112837; fax (2) 23113309; e-mail youth@ms2.hinet.net; internet www.youth.com.tw; Publr LEE CHUNG-KUEI.

Yuan Liou Publishing Co Ltd: 7F/5, 184 Ding Chou Rd, Sec. 3, Taipei 100; tel. (2) 23651212; fax (2) 23657979; e-mail ylib@ .ylib.com; internet www.ylib.com.; f. 1975; fiction, non-fiction, children's; Publr WANG JUNG-WEN.

Broadcasting and Communications

TELECOMMUNICATIONS

Directorate-General of Telecommunications: Ministry of Transportation and Communications, 16 Chinan Rd, Section 2, Taipei; tel. (2) 23433969; internet www.dgt.gov.tw; regulatory authority.

Chunghwa Telecommunications Co Ltd: 21 Hsinyi Rd, Sec. 1, Taipei; tel. (2) 23445385; fax (2) 23919166; internet www.cht.com.tw; f. 1996; state-controlled company, privatization commenced 2000; Chair. MAO CHI-KUO.

Far EasTone Telecom: 334 Sze Chuan Rd, Sec. 1, Taipei; tel. (2) 29505478; internet www.fareastone.com.tw; mobile telephone services.

KG Telecom: 43 Kuan Chien Rd, Taipei; tel. (2) 23888800; e-mail kgtweb@kgt.com.tw; internet www.kgt.com.tw; mobile telephone services.

Taiwan Cellular Corpn: internet www.twngsm.com.tw; f. 1998 as Pacific Cellular Corpn; mobile telephone and internet services; Pres. JOSEPH FAN.

BROADCASTING

Broadcasting stations are mostly commercial. The Ministry of Transportation and Communications determines power and frequencies, and the Government Information Office supervises the operation of all stations, whether private or governmental.

Radio

In July 2002 there were 143 radio broadcasting corporations in operation, and permission for the establishment of a further 30 radio stations was to be given by the end of 2002.

Broadcasting Corpn of China (BCC): 375 Sung Chiang Rd, Taipei 104; tel. (2) 25005555; fax (2) 25018793; e-mail ls@mail.bcc.com.tw; internet www.bcc.com.tw; f. 1928; domestic (6 networks and 1 channel) services; 9 local stations, 131 transmitters; Pres. LEE CHING-PING; Chair. CHAO SHOU-PO.

Central Broadcasting System (CBS): 55 Pei An Rd, Tachih, Taipei 104; tel. (2) 28856168; fax (2) 28852315; e-mail rtm@cbs.org.tw; internet www.cbs.org.tw; domestic and international service; Dir. CHOU TEN-RAY.

Cheng Sheng Broadcasting Corpn Ltd: 7/F, 66-1 Chungking South Rd, Sec. 1, Taipei; tel. (2) 23617231; fax (2) 23715665; internet www.csbc.com.tw; f. 1950; 6 stations, 3 relay stations; Chair. WENG YEN-CHING; Pres. PANG WEI-NANG.

International Community Radio Taipei (ICRT): 2/F, 373 Sung Chiang Rd, Taipei; tel. (2) 25184899; fax (2) 25183666; internet www.icrt.com.tw; predominantly English-language broadcaster; Gen. Man. DOC CASEY.

Kiss Radio: 34/F, 6 Min Chuan 2 Rd, Kaohsiung; tel. (7) 3365888; fax (7) 3364931; Pres. HELENA YUAN.

M-radio Broadcasting Corpn: 8/F, 1-18 Taichung Kang Rd, Sec. 2, Taichung City; tel. (4) 23235656; fax (4) 23231199; e-mail jason@mradio.com.tw; internet www.mradio.com.tw; Pres. SHEN CHIN-HWEI; Gen. Man. JASON C. LIN.

UFO Broadcasting Co Ltd: 25/F, 102 Roosevelt Rd, Sec. 2, Taipei; tel. (2) 23636600; fax (2) 23673083; Pres. JAW SHAU-KONG.

Voice of Taipei Broadcasting Co Ltd: 10/F, B Rm, 15-1 Han Chou South Rd, Sec. 1, Taipei; tel. (2) 23957255; fax (2) 23941855; Pres. NITA ING.

Television

Legislation to place cable broadcasting on a legal basis was adopted in mid-1993, and by June 2002 63 cable television companies were in operation. A non-commercial station, Public Television (PTV), went on air in July 1998. Legislation to place satellite broadcasting on a legal basis was adopted in February 1999, and by June 2002 122 satellite broadcasting channels (provided by 59 domestic and 16 international companies) and 3 domestic and 3 international Digital Broadcasting System (DBS) channels were in operation.

China Television Co (CTV): 120 Chung Yang Rd, Nan Kang District, Taipei; tel. (2) 27838308; fax (2) 27826007; e-mail pubr@mail.chinatv.com.tw; internet www.chinatv.com.tw; f. 1969; Pres. JIANG FENG-CHYI; Chair. SUMING CHENG.

Chinese Television System (CTS): 100 Kuang Fu South Rd, Taipei 10658; tel. (2) 27510321; fax (2) 27775414; e-mail public@ mail.cts.com.tw; internet www.cts.com.tw; f. 1971; cultural and educational; Chair. JOU RUNG-SHENG; Pres. SHI LU.

Formosa Television Co (FTV): 14/F, 30 Pa Teh Rd, Sec. 3, Taipei; tel. (2) 25702570; fax (2) 25773170; internet www.ftv.com.tw; f. 1997; Chair. TSAI TUNG-RONG: Pres. CHEN KANG-HSING.

Public Television Service Foundation (PTS): 90, Lane 95, Sec. 9, Kang Ning Rd, Neihu, Taipei; tel. (2) 26329533; fax (2) 26338124; e-mail pts@mail.pts.org.tw; internet www.pts.org.tw; Chair. FRANK WU; Pres. YUNG-PE LEE.

Taiwan Television Enterprise (TTV): 10 Pa Teh Rd, Sec. 3, Taipei 10560; tel. (2) 25781515; fax (2) 25799626; internet www.ttv.com.tw; f. 1962; Chair. LAI KUO-CHOU; Pres. JENG IOU.

Finance

(cap. = capital; dep. = deposits; m. = million; brs = branches; amounts in New Taiwan dollars unless otherwise stated)

BANKING

In June 1991 the Ministry of Finance granted 15 new banking licences to private banks. A 16th bank was authorized in May 1992; further authorizations followed. Restrictions on the establishment of offshore banking units were relaxed in 1994.

Central Bank

Central Bank of China: 2 Roosevelt Rd, Sec. 1, Taipei 100; tel. (2) 23936161; fax (2) 23571974; e-mail adminrol@mail.cbc.gov.tw; internet www.cbc.gov.tw; f. 1928; bank of issue; cap. 80,000m., dep. 4,829,374m. (Jul. 2002); Gov. PERNG FAI-NAN.

Domestic Banks

Bank of Taiwan: 120 Chungking South Rd, Sec. 1, Taipei 10036; tel. (2) 23493456; fax (2) 23315840; e-mail bot076@mail.bot.com.tw; internet www.bot.com.tw; f. 1899; cap. 32,000m., dep. 1,916,188m. (Dec. 2001); Chair. M. T. CHEN; Pres. SHENG-YANN LII; 129 brs, incl. 6 overseas; plans to merge with Central Trust of China and Land Bank of Taiwan in 2002 suspended.

Chiao Tung Bank: 91 Heng Yang Rd, Taipei 100; tel. (2) 23613000; fax (2) 23310398; e-mail dp092@ctnbank.com.tw; internet www.ctnbank.com.tw; f. 1907; fmrly Bank of Communications; cap. 24,400m., dep. 360,787m. (Dec. 2000); Chair. SHEN-CHIH CHENG; Pres. KUO HSIUNG-CHUANG; 34 brs, incl. 2 overseas.

Export-Import Bank of the Republic of China (Eximbank): 8/F, 3 Nan Hai Rd, Taipei 100; tel. (2) 23210511; fax (2) 23940630; e-mail eximbank@eximbank.com.tw; internet www.eximbank.com.tw; f. 1979; cap. 10,000m., dep. 14,075m. (Dec. 2000); Chair. PAULINE FU; Pres. HERBERT S. S. CHUNG; 3 brs.

Farmers Bank of China: 85 Nanking East Rd, Sec. 2, Taipei 104; tel. (2) 21003456; fax (2) 25515425; internet www.farmerbank.com.tw; f. 1933; cap. 12,474m., dep. 448,723m. (Dec. 2000); Chair. CHIEH-CHIEN CHAO; Pres. C. C. HUANG; 76 brs.

International Commercial Bank of China (ICBC): 100 Chi Lin Rd, Taipei 10424; tel. (2) 25633156; fax (2) 25611216; e-mail service@icbc.com.tw; internet www.icbc.com.tw/; f. 1912; cap. 33,157m., dep. 756,910m. (Dec. 2000); Chair. TZONG-YEONG LIN; Pres. Y. T. (MCKINNEY) TSAI; 82 brs, incl. 18 overseas.

Land Bank of Taiwan: 46 Kuan Chien Rd, Taipei 10038; tel. (2) 23483456; fax (2) 23757023; e-mail lbot@imail.landbank.com.tw; internet www.landbank.com.tw; f. 1946; dep. 1,291,720m. (Dec. 2000); Chair. CHI-LIN WEA; 110 brs; plans to merge with bank of Taiwan and Central Trust of China in 2002 suspended.

Taiwan Co-operative Bank: POB 33, 77 Kuan Chien Rd, Taipei 10038; tel. (2) 23118811; fax (2) 23890704; e-mail tacbid01@14.hinet.net; internet www.tcb-bank.com.tw; f. 1946; acts as central bank for co-operatives, and as major agricultural credit institution; cap. 20,034m., dep. 1,414,949m. (June 2000); Chair. W. H. LEE; Pres. MCKINNEY Y. T. TSAI; 144 brs.

Commercial Banks

Asia Pacific Bank: 66 Minchuan Rd, Taichung; tel. (4) 22271799; fax (4) 22265110; e-mail service@apacbank.com.tw; internet www.apacbank.com.tw; f. 1992; cap. 12,115m., dep. 148,837m. (Dec. 2000); Chair. CHIOU JIA-SHYONG; Pres. WU WEN KE; 35 brs.

Bank of Kaohsiung: 168 Po Ai 2nd Rd, Kaohsiung; tel. (7) 5570535; fax (7) 5580529; e-mail service@mail.bok.com.tw; internet www.bok.com.tw; f. 1982; cap. 4,487m., dep. 172,442m. (Dec. 2000); Chair. FLANDY SU; Pres. S. H. CHUANG; 31 brs.

Bank of Overseas Chinese: 8 Hsiang Yang Rd, Taipei 10014; tel. (2) 23715181; fax (2) 23814056; e-mail plan@mail.booc.com.tw; internet www.booc.com.tw; f. 1961; cap. 16,752m., dep. 238,008m. (Jun. 2001); Chair. CHUEN CHANG; Pres. WEN-LONG LIN; 56 brs.

Bank of Panhsin: 18 Cheng Tu St, Pan Chiao City, Taipei; tel. (2) 29629170; fax (2) 29572011; f. 1997; cap. 6,000m., dep. 77,602m. (Dec. 1999); Chair. L. P. HUI; Pres. JAMES J. C. CHEN; 28 brs.

Bank SinoPac: 9-1, Chien Kuo North Rd, Sec. 2, Taipei; tel. (2) 25082288; fax (2) 25083456; internet www.banksinopac.com.tw; f. 1992; cap. 17,577m., dep. 204,688m. (Dec. 2000); Chair. L. S. LIN; Pres. PAUL C. Y. LO; 35 brs.

Central Trust of China: 49 Wu Chang St, Sec. 1, Taipei 10006; tel. (2) 23111511; fax (2) 23611544; e-mail ctc17001@ctc.com.tw; internet www.ctoc.com.tw; f. 1935; cap. 10,000m., dep. 204,808m. (Dec. 2000); Chair. WANG RONG-JOU; Pres. JACK. H. HUANG; 19 brs; plans to merge with Bank of Taiwan and Land Bank of Taiwan in 2002 suspended.

Chang Hwa Commercial Bank Ltd: 38 Tsuyu Rd, Sec. 2, Taichung 40010; tel. (4) 2222001; fax (4) 2231170; e-mail customem@ms1.chb.com.tw; internet www.chb.com.tw; f. 1905; cap. 35,356m., dep. 1,072,837m. (Dec. 2001); Chair. PO-SHIN CHANG; Pres. MIKE S. E. CHANG; 153 brs, 7 overseas.

Chinatrust Commercial Bank: 3 Sung Shou Rd, Taipei; tel. (2) 27222002; fax (2) 27239775; internet www.chinatrust.com.tw; f. 1966; cap. 73,925m., dep. 610,252m. (Dec. 2001); Chair. JEFFREY L. S. KOO; 57 brs, 11 overseas.

The Chinese Bank: 6 Chung Hsiao West Rd, Sec. 1, Taipei; tel. (2) 23880506; fax (2) 23880334; internet www.chinesebank.com.tw; f. 1992; cap. 15,171m., dep. 190,400m. (Dec. 2000); Chair. WANG YOU-THENG; Pres. CHEN FEN; 30 brs.

Chinfon Commercial Bank: 1 Nanyang St, Taipei 100; tel. (2) 23114881; fax (2) 23141068; e-mail ibd@chinfonbank.com.tw; internet www.chinfonbank.com.tw; f. 1971; cap 11,128m., dep. 150,201m. (Dec. 2000); Chair. HUANG SHI-HUI; Pres GREGORY C. P. CHANG; 34 brs, 2 overseas.

Chung Shing Bank: 228–230 Sung Chiang Rd, Taipei; tel. (2) 25616601; fax (2) 25114389; internet www.csbank.com.tw; f. 1992; cap. 15,076m., dep. 186,529m. (Dec. 1999); Chair. PAN LUNG-CHEN; Pres. WAN-SAN S. CHIEN; 25 brs.

Cosmos Bank: 39 Tun Hua South Rd, Sec. 2, Taipei; tel. (2) 27011777; fax (2) 27541742; e-mail ibd@cosmosbank.com.tw; internet www.cosmosbank.com.tw; f. 1992; cap. 14,009m., dep. 174,374m. (Mar. 2002); Chair. HSUI SHENG-FA; Pres. C. C. HU; 35 brs.

COTA Commercial Bank: 32-1 Kung Yuan Rd, Taichung; tel. (4) 22245161; fax (4) 22275237; f. 1995; cap. 3,184m., dep. 53,906m. (Dec. 2001); Chair. LIAO CHUN-TSE; Pres CHANG YING-CHE; 18 brs.

E. Sun Commercial Bank: 77 Wuchang St, Sec. 1, Taipei; tel. (2) 23891313; fax (2) 23891115; e-mail esbintl@email.esunbank.com.tw; internet www.esunbank.com.tw; f. 1992; cap. 16,933m., dep. 215,066m. (Dec. 2000); Chair. HUANG YUNG-JEN; Pres. HOU YUNG-HSUNG; 36 brs.

EnTie Commercial Bank: 3/F, 158 Ming Sheng East Rd, Sec. 3, Taipei; tel. (2) 27189999; fax (2) 27187843; internet www.entiebank.com.tw; f. 1993; cap. 14,093m., dep. 177,418m. (Dec. 2000); Chair. YU-LING LIN; Pres. CHENG-DER LIU; 39 brs.

Far Eastern International Bank: 27/F, 207 Tun Hua South Rd, Sec. 2, Taipei; tel. (2) 23786868; fax (2) 23779000; e-mail 800@mail.feib.com.tw; internet www.feib.com.tw; f. 1992; cap. 15,248m., dep. 156,861m. (Jun. 2001); Chair. DOUGLAS T. HSU; Pres. ELI HONG; 30 brs.

First Commercial Bank: POB 395, 30 Chungking South Rd, Sec. 1, Taipei; tel. (2) 23481111; fax (2) 23610036; e-mail fcb@mail.firstbank.com.tw; internet www.firstbank.com.tw; f. 1899; cap. 38,216m., dep. 1,179,017m. (Dec. 2001); Chair. JEROME J. CHEN; Pres. TSENG CHIEN-CHUNG; 159 brs, 11 overseas.

Fubon Commercial Bank: 2/F, 169 Jen Ai Rd, Sec. 4, Taipei; tel. (2) 27716699; fax (2) 87716939; e-mail fubon@fubonbank.com.tw; internet www.fubonbank.com.tw; f. 1992; cap. 21,857m., dep. 227,481m. (Dec. 2001); Chair. CHEN S. YU; Pres. WANG CHUAN-HSI; 38 brs.

Grand Commercial Bank: 17 Chengteh Rd, Sec. 1, Taipei; tel. (2) 25562088; fax (2) 25561579; e-mail service@grandbank.com.tw; internet www.grandbank.com.tw; f. 1991; cap. 16,043m. (Dec. 2000), dep. 171,090m. (Dec. 2001); Chair. KAO CHIH-YEN; Pres. ALEXANDER T. Y. DEAN; 43 brs.

Hsinchu International Bank: 106 Chung Yang Rd, Hsinchu 300; tel. (3) 5245131; fax (3) 5250977; f. 1948; cap. 12,665m., dep. 245,378m. (Dec. 1999); Chair. S. Y. CHAN; Pres C. W. WU; 73 brs.

Hua Nan Commercial Bank Ltd: POB 989, 38 Chungking South Rd, Sec. 1, Taipei; tel. (2) 23713111; fax (2) 23821060; e-mail service@ms.hncb.com.tw; internet www.hncb.com.tw; f. 1919; cap. 35,198m., dep. 1,085,254m. (Dec. 2000); Chair. LIN MING-CHEN; Pres. HSU TEH-NAN; 138 brs, 5 overseas.

Hwa Tai Commercial Bank: 246 Chang An E. Rd, Sec. 2, Taipei; tel. (2) 27525252; fax (2) 27711495; f. 1999; cap. 3,300m., dep. 50,111m. (Dec. 1999); Chair. M. H. LIN; Pres. S. Y. WU: 18 brs.

International Bank of Taipei: 36 Nanking East Rd, Sec. 3, Taipei; tel. (2) 25063333; fax (2) 25062462; e-mail b630@ibtpe.com.tw; internet www.ibtpe.com.tw; f. 1948; cap. 18,038m., dep. 285,131m. (Dec. 2001); Chair. S. C. HO; Pres. K. C. YU; 88 brs.

Jih Sun International Bank: 6/F, 68 Sungchiang Rd, Taipei; tel. (2) 25615888; fax (2) 25218878; internet www.jihsunbank.com.tw; f. 1992, as Baodao Commercial Bank, assumed present name in December 2001; cap. 10,815m., dep. 148,405m. (May 2000); Chair. CHUN-KUAN CHEN; Pres. TA HAO CHUNG; 24 brs.

Kao Shin Commercial Bank: 75 Lih Wen Rd, Kaohsiung; tel. (7) 3460711; fax (7) 3502980; f. 1997; cap. 2,300m., dep. 48,244m. (Dec. 1999); Chair. C. N. HUANG; Pres. F. T. CHAO; 27 brs.

Lucky Bank: 35 Chung Hua Rd, Sec. 1, Taichung 403; tel. (4) 2259111; fax (4) 22258624; f. 1997; cap. 3,146m., dep. 74,753m. (Dec. 1999); Chair. C. C. CHANG; Pres. T. Y. SU; 27 brs.

Macoto Bank: 134 Hsi Chang St, Taipei; tel. (2) 23812160; fax (2) 23752538; e-mail master@makoto.com.tw; internet www.makotobank.com.tw; f. 1997; cap. 7,090m., dep. 157,472m. (Dec. 2001); Chair. C. I. LIN; Pres. SHERMAN CHUANG; 49 brs.

Pan Asia Bank: 3–4/F, 60-8 Chungkang Rd, Taichung; tel. (02) 23279998; fax (02) 23271565; e-mail pabkdbu@ms4.hinet.net; internet www.pab.com.tw; f. 1992; cap. 14,700m., dep. 153,431m. (Dec. 2000); Chair. KOH FEI-LO; Pres. YIN YI-NA; 35 brs.

Shanghai Commercial and Savings Bank Ltd: 2 Min Chuan East Rd, Sec. 1, Taipei 104; tel. (2) 25817111; fax (2) 25638539; internet www.scsb.com.tw; f. 1915; cap. 13,260m., dep. 282,726m. (Dec. 2000); Chair. H. C. YUNG; Pres. Y. P. CHEN; 58 brs.

Sunny Bank: 88 Shih Pai Rd, Sec. 1, Taipei 112; tel. (2) 28208166; fax (2) 28233414; f. 1997; cap. 3,800m., dep. 82,129m. (Dec. 1999); Chair. S. H. CHEN; Pres. C. W. CHEN; 22 brs.

Ta Chong Bank: 58 Chungcheng 2nd Rd, Kaohsiung; tel. (7) 2242220; fax (7) 2245251; e-mail service@tcbank.com.tw; internet www.tcbank.com.tw; f. 1992; cap. 13,563m., dep. 144,953m. (Dec. 1999); Chair. and Pres. CHEN TIEN-MAO; 38 brs.

Taichung Commercial Bank: 87 Min Chuan Rd, Taichung 403; tel. (4) 22236021; fax (4) 22240748; e-mail webmaster@ ms1.tcbbank.com.tw; internet www.tcbbank.com.tw; f. 1953; cap. 15,380m., dep. 181,772m. (Dec. 2000); Chair. Y. F. TSAI; Pres. Y. C. TSAI; 80 brs.

Taipeibank: 50 Chung Shan North Rd, Sec. 2, Taipei 10419; tel. (2) 25425656; fax (2) 25428870; e-mail br180@ms1.taipeibank.com.tw; internet www.taipeibank.com.tw; f. 1969; fmrly City Bank of Taipei; cap. 20,020m., dep. 527,800m. (Dec. 2000); Chair. CHI YUAN LIN; Pres. JESSE Y. DING; 73 brs, 2 overseas.

Taishin International Bank: 44 Chung Shan North Rd, Sec. 2, Taipei; tel. (2) 25683988; fax (2) 25234551; e-mail pr@taishinbank .com.tw; internet www.taishinbank.com.tw; f. 1992; absorbed Dah An Commercial Bank in February 2002; cap. 23,874m., dep. 247,254m. (Dec. 2000); Chair. THOMAS T. L. WU; Pres. JULIUS H. C. CHEN; 39 brs.

Taitung Business Bank: 354 Chung Hwa Rd, Sec. 1, Taitung 950; tel. (89) 331191; fax. (89) 331194; e-mail secretpb@ttbb.com.tw; internet www.ttbb.com.tw; f. 1955; Chair. KUWAN-MIN CHANG; Pres. H. I. YIN.

Taiwan Business Bank: 30 Tacheng St, Taipei; tel. (2) 25597171; fax (2) 25509245; e-mail tbb3688@hotmail.com; internet www.tbb.com.tw; f. 1915, reassumed present name 1994; cap. 35,878m., dep. 811,675m. (Dec. 2000); Chair. HSIAO CHIEH-JEN; Pres. LU HO-YI.

Union Bank of Taiwan: 109 Ming Sheng East Rd, Sec. 3, Taipei; tel. (2) 27180001; fax (2) 27137515; e-mail 014_0199@email.ubot .com.tw; internet www.ubot.com.tw; f. 1992; cap. US $444m., dep. US $4,615m. (Jun. 2002); Chair. C. C. HUANG; Pres. S. C. LEE; 40 brs.

United World Chinese Commercial Bank: 65 Kuan Chien Rd, POB 1670, Taipei 10038; tel. (2) 23125555; fax (2) 23311093; e-mail yinglin@uwccb.com.tw; internet www.uwccb.com.tw; f. 1975; cap. 34,176m., dep. 594,331m. (Dec. 2000); Chair. GREGORY K. H. WANG; Pres. C. C. TUNG; 74 brs, incl. 6 overseas.

There are also a number of Medium Business Banks throughout the country.

Community Financial System

The community financial institutions include both credit co-operatives and credit departments of farmers' and fishermen's associations. These local financial institutions focus upon providing savings and loan services for the community. At the end of 1999 there were 50 credit co-operatives, 287 credit departments of farmers' associations and 27 credit departments of fishermen's associations, with a combined total deposit balance of NT $2,339,000m., while outstanding loans amounted to NT $1,340,200m.

Foreign Banks

In December 2001 a total of 36 foreign banks were in operation in Taiwan.

STOCK EXCHANGE

In January 1991 the stock exchange was opened to direct investment by foreign institutions, and in March 1996 it was also opened to direct investment by foreign individuals. By the end of June 2000 463 foreign institutional investors had been approved to invest in the local securities market. Various liberalization measures have been introduced since 1994. In March 1999 the limits on both single and aggregate foreign investment in domestic shares were raised to 50% of the outstanding shares of a listed company. In November of that year the 'ceiling' of investment amount for each qualified foreign institutional investor in domestic securities markets was increased from US $600m. to US $1,200m.

Taiwan Stock Exchange Corpn: 13/F, 17 Po Ai Rd, Taipei 100; tel. (2) 23485678; fax (2) 23485324; f. 1962; Chair. C. Y. LEE.

Supervisory Body

Securities and Futures Commission: 85 Hsin Sheng South Rd, Sec. 1, Taipei; tel. (2) 87734202; fax (2) 8734134; Chair. CHU JAW-CHYUAN; Sec.-Gen. CHEN WEI-LUNG.

INSURANCE

In 1993 the Ministry of Finance issued eight new insurance licences, the first for more than 30 years. Two more were issued in 1994.

Allianz President General Insurance Co Ltd: 11/F, 69 Ming Sheng East Rd, Sec. 3, Taipei; tel. (2) 25157177; fax (2) 25077506; e-mail azpl@ms2.seeder.net; internet www.allianz.com.tw; f. 1995; Chair. NAN-TEN CHUNG; Gen. Man. NICHOLAS CHANG.

Cathay Life Insurance Co Ltd: 296 Jen Ai Rd, Sec. 4, Taipei 10650; tel. (2) 27551399; fax (2) 27551322; e-mail master@cathlife .com.tw; internet www.cathlife.com.tw; f. 1962; Chair. TSAI HONG-TU; Gen. Man. LIU CHIU-TE.

Central Insurance Co Ltd: 6 Chung Hsiao West Rd, Sec. 1, Taipei; tel. (2) 23819910; fax (2) 23116901; internet www.cins.com.tw; f. 1962; Chair. H. K. SHE; Gen. Man. C. C. HUANG.

Central Reinsurance Corpn: 53 Nanking East Rd, Sec. 2, Taipei; tel. (2) 25115211; fax (2) 25235350; e-mail chlin@crc.com.tw; internet www.crc.com.tw; f. 1968; Chair. CHING-HSIEN LIN; Pres. C. T. YANG.

Central Trust of China, Life Insurance Dept: 3–8/F, 69 Tun Hua South Rd, Sec. 2, Taipei; tel. (2) 27849151; fax (2) 27052214; e-mail sectrl@ctclife.com.tw; internet www.ctclife.com.tw; f. 1941; life insurance; Pres. EDWARD LO; Gen. Man. MAN-HSIUNG TSAI.

China Life Insurance Co Ltd: 122 Tun Hua North Rd, Taipei; tel. (2) 27196678; fax (2) 27125966; e-mail services@mail.chinalife .com.tw; internet www.chinalife.com.tw; f. 1963; Chair. C. F. KOO; Gen. Man. CHESTER C. Y. KOO.

China Mariners' Assurance Corpn Ltd: 11/F, 2 Kuan Chien Rd, Taipei; tel. (2) 23757676; fax (2) 23756363; internet www.cmac .com.tw; f. 1948; Chair. VINCENT M. S. FAN; Pres. W. H. HUNG.

Chung Kuo Insurance Co Ltd: 10–12/F, ICBC Bldg, 100 Chilin Rd, Taipei 10424; tel. (2) 25513345; fax (2) 25414046; f. 1931; fmrly China Insurance Co Ltd; Chair. S. Y. LIU; Pres. C. Y. LIU.

Chung Shing Life Insurance Co Ltd: 18/F, 200 Keelung Rd, Sec. 1, Taipei 110; tel. (2) 27583099; fax (2) 23451635; f. 1993; Chair. T. S. CHAO; Gen. Man. DAH-WEI CHEN.

The First Insurance Co Ltd: 54 Chung Hsiao East Rd, Sec. 1, Taipei; tel. (2) 23913271; fax (2) 23930685; f. 1962; Chair. C. H. LEE; Gen. Man. M. C. CHEN.

Fubon Insurance Co Ltd: 237 Chien Kuo South Rd, Sec. 1, Taipei; tel. (2) 27067890; fax (2) 27042915; internet www.fubon-ins.com.tw; f. 1961; Chair. TSAI MING-CHUNG; Gen. Man. T. M. SHIH.

Fubon Life Insurance Co Ltd: 14/F, 108 Tun Hua South Rd, Sec. 1, Taipei; tel. (2) 87716699; fax (2) 87715919; f. 1993; Chair. RICHARD M. TSAI; Gen. Man. CHIAO PEN TIAN.

Global Life Insurance Co Ltd: 18 Chung Yang South Rd, Sec. 2, Peitou, Taipei 11235; tel. (2) 28967899; fax (2) 28958312; f. 1993; Chair. JOHN TSENG; Gen. Man. ROBERT KUO.

Hontai Life Insurance Co Ltd: 7/F, 70 Cheng Teh Rd, Sec. 1, Taipei; tel. (2) 25595151; fax (2) 25562840; internet www.hontai .com.tw; f. 1994; frmrly Hung Fu Life Insurance Co; Chair. TONY SHE; Gen. Man. YU-CHIEH YANG.

Kuo Hua Insurance Co Ltd: 166 Chang An East Rd, Sec. 2, Taipei; tel. (2) 27514225; fax (2) 27819388; e-mail kh11601@kuohua.com.tw; internet www.kuohua.com.tw; f. 1962; Chair. and Gen. Man. J. B. WANG.

Kuo Hua Life Insurance Co Ltd: 42 Chung Shan North Rd, Sec. 2, Taipei; tel. (2) 25621101; fax (2) 25423832; internet www.khl.com.tw; f. 1963; Chair. JASON CHANG; Pres. WEN-PO WANG.

Mercuries Life Insurance Co Ltd: 6/F, 2 Lane 150, Hsin-Yi North Rd, Sec. 5, Taipei; tel. (2) 23455511; fax (2) 23456616; internet www.mli.com.tw; f. 1993; Chair. HARVEY TANG; Gen. Man. CHUNG-SHIN LU.

Mingtai Fire and Marine Insurance Co Ltd: 1 Jen Ai Rd, Sec. 4, Taipei; tel. (2) 27725678; fax (2) 27729932; internet www .mingtai.com.tw; f. 1961; Chair. LARRY P. C. LIN; Gen. Man. H. T. CHEN.

Nan Shan Life Insurance Co Ltd: 144 Min Chuan East Rd, Sec. 2, Taipei 104; tel. (2) 25013333; fax (2) 25012555; internet www.nanshanlife.com.tw; f. 1963; Chair. EDMUND TSE; Pres. SUNNY LIN.

Prudential Life Assurance Co Ltd: 12/F, 550 Chung Hsiao East Rd, Sec. 4, Taipei; tel. (2) 27582727; fax (2) 27086758; internet www.prudential-uk.com.tw; f. 1999; Chair. DOMINIC LEUNG KA KUI; CEO DAN L. TING.

Shin Fu Life Insurance Co Ltd: 8/F, 6 Chung Hsiao West Rd, Sec. 1, Taipei; tel. (2) 23817172; fax (2) 23817162; f. 1993; Chair. and Gen. Man. SONG CHI CHIENG.

Shin Kong Insurance Co Ltd: 15 Chien Kuo North Rd, Sec. 2, Taipei; tel. (2) 25075335; fax (2) 25074580; internet www.shinkong .com.tw; f. 1963; Chair. ANTHONY T. S. WU; Pres. YIH HSIUNG LEE.

Shin Kong Life Insurance Co Ltd: 66 Chung Hsiao West Rd, Sec. 1, Taipei; tel. (2) 23895858; fax (2) 23758688; internet www.skl.com.tw; f. 1963; Chair. EUGENE T. C. WU; Gen. Man. HONG-CHI CHENG.

Sinon Life Insurance Co Ltd: 11-2F, 155 Tsu Chih St, Taichung; tel. (4) 3721653; fax (4) 3722008; e-mail sinonlife@mail.sinonlife.com.tw; internet www.sinonlife.com.tw; f. 1993; Chair. PO-YEN HORNG; Gen. Man. P. T. LAI.

South China Insurance Co Ltd: 5/F, 560 Chung Hsiao East Rd, Sec. 4, Taipei; tel. and fax (2) 27298022; internet www.south-china.com.tw; f. 1963; Chair. C. F. LIAO; Pres. ALLAN I. R. HUANG.

Tai Ping Insurance Co Ltd: 3–5/F, 550 Chung Hsiao East Rd, Sec. 4, Taipei; tel. (2) 27582700; fax (2) 27295681; f. 1929; Chair. C. C. HUANG; Gen. Man. JAMES SUN.

Taian Insurance Co Ltd: 59 Kwantsien Rd, Taipei; tel. (2) 23819678; fax (2) 23315332; e-mail taian@mail.taian.com.tw; f. 1961; Chair. C. H. CHEN; Gen. Man. PATRICK S. LEE.

Taiwan Fire and Marine Insurance Co Ltd: 8–9/F, 49 Kuan Chien Rd, Jungjeng Chiu, Taipei; tel. (2) 23821666; fax (2) 23882555; e-mail tfmi@mail.tfmi.com.tw; internet www.tfmi.com.tw; f. 1948; Chair. W. Y. LEE; Gen. Man. JOSEPH N. S. CHANG.

Taiwan Life Insurance Co Ltd: 16–19/F, 17 Hsu Chang St, Taipei; tel. (2) 23116411; fax (2) 23759714; e-mail service1@twlife.com.tw; internet www.twlife.com.tw; f. 1947; Chair. PING-YU CHU; Pres. CHENG-TAO LIN.

Union Insurance Co Ltd: 12/F, 219 Chung Hsiao East Rd, Sec. 4, Taipei; tel. (2) 27765567; fax (2) 27737199; internet www.unionins.com.tw; f. 1963; Chair. S. H. CHIN; Gen. Man. FRANK S. WANG.

Zurich Insurance Taiwan Ltd: 56 Tun Hua North Rd, Taipei; tel. (2) 27752888; fax (2) 27416004; internet www.zurich.com.tw; f. 1961; Chair. DEAN T. CHIANG; Gen. Man. YUNG H. CHEN.

Trade and Industry

GOVERNMENT AGENCIES

Board of Foreign Trade (Ministry of Economic Affairs): 1 Houkow St, Taipei; tel. (2) 23510271; fax (2) 23513603; internet www.trade.gov.tw; Dir-Gen. WU WEN-YEA.

Council of Agriculture (COA): 37 Nan Hai Rd, Taipei 100; tel. (2) 23812991; fax (2) 23310341; e-mail webmaster@www.coa.gov.tw; f. 1984; govt agency directly under the Executive Yuan, with ministerial status; a policy-making body in charge of national agriculture, forestry, fisheries, the animal industry and food administration; promotes technology and provides external assistance; Chair. Dr CHEN HSI-HUANG; Sec.-Gen. Dr HUANG CHIN-RONG.

Industrial Development Bureau (Ministry of Economic Affairs): 41-3 Hsin Yi Rd, Sec. 3, Taipei; tel. (2) 27541255; fax (2) 27030160; internet www.moeaidb.gov.tw; Dir-Gen. CHEN CHAO-YIN.

Industrial Development and Investment Center (Ministry of Economic Affairs): 8/F, 71 Kuan Chien Rd, Taipei; tel. (2) 23892111; fax (2) 23820497; e-mail njlin@mail.idic.gov.tw; internet www.idic.gov.tw; f. 1959 to assist investment and planning; Dir-Gen. ANGELA T. CHU (acting).

CHAMBER OF COMMERCE

General Chamber of Commerce of the Republic of China: 6/F, 390 Fu Hsing South Rd, Sec. 1, Taipei; tel. (2) 27012671; fax (2) 27542107; f. 1946; 65 mems, incl. 40 nat. feds of trade asscns, 22 district export asscns and 3 district chambers of commerce; Chair. Dr GARY WANG; Sec.-Gen. CHIU JAW-SHIN.

INDUSTRIAL AND TRADE ASSOCIATIONS

China External Trade Development Council: 4/F, CETRA Tower, 333 Keelung Rd, Sec. 1, Taipei 110; tel. (2) 27255200; fax (2) 27576653; internet www.cetra.org.tw; trade promotion body; Sec.-Gen. HUANG CHIH-PENG.

China Productivity Center: 2/F, 79 Hsin Tai 5 Rd, Sec. 1, Hsichih, Taipei County; tel. (2) 26982989; fax (2) 26982976; f. 1956; management, technology, training, etc.; Pres. CHEN MING-CHANG.

Chinese National Association of Industry and Commerce: 13/F, 390 Fu Hsing South Rd, Sec. 1, Taipei; tel. (2) 27070111; fax (2) 27017601; Chair. JEFFREY L. S. KOO.

Chinese National Federation of Industries (CNFI): 12/F, 390 Fu Hsing South Rd, Sec. 1, Taipei; tel. (2) 27033500; fax (2) 27033982; e-mail cnfi@mail.industry.net.tw; internet www.cnfi.org.tw; f. 1948; 142 mem. asscns; Chair. LIN KUNG-CHUNG; Sec.-Gen. Y. H. KUO.

Taiwan Handicraft Promotion Centre: 1 Hsu Chou Rd, Taipei; tel. (2) 23933655; fax (2) 23937330; f. 1956; Pres. Y. C. WANG.

Trading Department of Central Trust of China: 49 Wuchang St, Sec. 1, Taipei 10006; tel. (2) 23111511; fax (2) 23821047; f. 1935; export and import agent for private and govt-owned enterprises.

UTILITIES

Electricity

Taiwan Power Co (Taipower): 242 Roosevelt Rd, Sec. 3, Taipei 100; tel. (2) 23651234; fax (2) 23678593; e-mail service@taipower.com.tw; internet www.taipower.com.tw; f. 1946; electricity generation; privatizating from 2001; Chair. LI NENG-BAI; Pres. LIN CHING-CHI.

Gas

The Great Taipei Gas Corpn: 5/F, 35 Kwang Fu North Rd, Taipei; tel. (2) 27684999; fax (2) 27630480; supply of gas and gas equipment.

Water

Taipei Water Dept: 131 Changxing St, Taipei; tel. (2) 7352141; fax (2) 7353185; f. 1907; responsible for water supply in Taipei and suburban areas; Commr LIN WEN-YUAN.

CO-OPERATIVES

In December 1999 there were 5,375 co-operatives, with a total membership of 5,679,976 and total capital of NT $46,000m. Of the specialized co-operatives the most important was the consumers' co-operative (4,440 co-ops).

The Co-operative League (f. 1940) is a national organization responsible for co-ordination, education and training and the movement's national and international interests (Chair. K. L. CHEN).

MAJOR COMPANIES

(cap. = capital; res = reserves; m. = million; amounts in New Taiwan dollars unless otherwise stated)

State Enterprises

A programme of partial privatization began in March 1989 (with the sale of shares in the China Steel Corporation), but has been subject to various delays. The following are the major state enterprises operating in 2002 under the Ministry of Economic Affairs:

China Shipbuilding Corpn: 3 Chung Kang Rd, Hsiao-kang, Kaohsiung; tel. (7) 8010111; fax (7) 8020805; internet www.csbcnet.com.tw; f. 1973; shipbuilding and repairing up to 1m. dwt; machinery mfrs; sales 19,467m. (1996/97); Chair. CHIANG HSU; Pres. FAN KUANG-NAN; 5,632 employees.

Chinese Petroleum Corpn: 83 Chung Hua Rd, Sec. 1, Taipei 10031; tel. (2) 23610221; fax (2) 23319645; internet www.cpc.com.tw; f. 1946; natural gas, petroleum products, petrochemical feedstocks; refineries at Kaohsiung and Taoyuan; sales 427,749m. (2001); Chair. C. T. KUO; Pres. WENENT W. P. PAN; 17,923 employees.

Taiwan Fertilizer Co Ltd: 90 Nan King East Rd, Sec. 2, Chung Shan District, Taipei 10408; tel. (2) 25422231; fax (2) 25634597; mfrs of compound fertilizers, urea, ammonium sulphate, calcium super-phosphate, melamine, sulphamic acid, etc.; sales 7,637m. (1997); Chair. WIU MAU-YING; Pres. YAU KUO; 1,708 employees.

Taiwan Machinery Manufacturing Corpn: 3 Tai Chi Rd, Hsiao-kang 29-87, Kaohsiung 81235; tel. (7) 8020111; fax (7) 8022129; f. 1946; machine mfg, shipbuilding and repairing, pre-fabricated steel frameworks, steel and iron casting, various steel products, and marine diesel engines; sales 2,541m. (1996/97); Chair. LIN I-HSIUNG; Pres. C. W. YUAN; 597 employees.

Taiwan Salt Industrial Corpn: 297 Chien Kan Rd, Sec. 1, Tainan 70203; tel. (6) 2610551; fax (6) 2649710; internet www.towns.com.tw; sales 2,204m. (1996/97); Chair. CHENG PAO-CHING; Pres. CHI HANG-WANG; 583 employees.

Taiwan Sugar Corpn: 266 Chien Kwo South Rd, Sec. 1, Taipei 106; tel. (2) 23261300; fax (2) 27067038; f. 1964; sugar, edible oils, pork, beverages, snacks, yeast, etc.; sales 32,586m. (2001); Chair. WU NAI-JEN; Pres. DAWN RAY-BEAN; 8,180 employees.

Selected Private Companies

Cement

Taiwan Cement Corpn: 16-5 Teh Wei St, Taipei; tel. (2) 25865101; fax (2) 25862337; f. 1950; cement mfrs and exporters; cap. and res 33,128m. (1997), sales 17,128m. (1998); Chair. C. F. KOO; Pres. C. Y. KOO; 1,773 employees.

Chemicals

Chi Mei Corpn: 59–1 San Chia Tsun, Jenteh Hsiang, Tainan; tel. (6) 2663000; fax (6) 2665588; f. 1960; mfr of resins and other chemical products; sales 39,173m. (1995); Chair. W. L. CHI; 1,500 employees.

China Petrochemical Development Corporation: 8–11/F, 12 Dong Hsing Rd, Taipei; tel. (2) 23969600; fax (2) 23517224; mfr of petroleum-related chemicals and their derivatives; cap. and res 20,049m., sales 10,778m. (1998); Pres. C. Y. Huang.

Formosa Chemicals and Fibre Corpn: 359 Chong Shan Rd, Sec. 3, Zhang Hwa; tel. (4) 7236101; f. 1965; mfrs of chemicals, pulp, rayon staple, yarns, cloth and nylon filament; cap. and res 57,273m., sales 40,615m. (1998); Pres. Wen-yuen Wang; 7,739 employees.

Kaohsiung Ammonium-Sulphate Corpn Ltd: 100–2 Chung Shan 3rd Rd, POB 52, Kaohsiung 80614; tel. (7) 3819369; fax (7) 3352346; mfrs of ammonium sulphate, nitric acid, oleum and sulphuric acid; Chair. Richard M. Chen; Gen. Man. Chen Hsien-hsiung; 890 employees.

Electrical and Electronics

Acer Inc: 21/F, 88 Hsintaiwuh Rd, Sec. 1, Hsih Chih Cheng, Taipei; tel. (2) 26961234; fax (2) 25455308; f. 1976; personal computers, multi-user systems, computer applications, laser printers, etc.; cap. and res 44,374m., sales 169,660m. (1998); Chair. Stan Shih; Pres. Simon Lin; 4,000 employees.

Advanced Semiconductor Engineering Inc: Rm 1901, 19/F, 333 Keelung Rd, Sec. 1, Taipei; tel. (2) 87805489; fax (2) 27576121; e-mail investor_relations@asek.asetwn.com.tw; f. 1984; integrated circuit packaging and testing; cap. and res 83,441m. (2000), sales 32,609m. (1999).

Advanced Technology (Taiwan) Corpn: 1 Industry E, 6th Rd, SBIP, Hsinchu; tel. (35) 777300; fax (35) 776464; mfr of semiconductors, etc.

Chung Hwa Picture Tubes Ltd: 1127 Ho Ping Rd, Ta Nan Tsun, Pateh Hsiang, Taoyuan; tel. (3) 3675151; fax (3) 3667612; f. 1971; mfr of electronic components; sales 23,180m. (1995); Pres. C. Y. Lin; 5,931 employees.

CMC Magnetics Corpn: 104 Min Chuan West Rd, Taipei; tel. (2) 25536247; fax (2) 25535311; f. 1978; mfr of blank CDs for audio, video and CD-ROM uses; cap. and res 4,152m., sales 2,704m. (1996); Chair. Bob M. H. Wong; 800 employees.

Compal Electronics Inc: 7/F, 319 Ba De Rd, Sec. 4, Taipei; tel. (2) 27468446; fax (2) 27607903; computers and accessories; cap. and res 18,368m. (1997), sales 36,978m. (1998); Chair. Rock Sheng-hsiung Hsu; 1,330 employees.

Compeq Manufacturing Co Ltd: POB 9-22, 91 Lane 814, Ta Hsin Rd, Shin-chuang Vil., Lu Chu Hsiang, Taoyuan; tel. (3) 3231111; fax (3) 3235577; f. 1973; mfr of computers and computer peripherals; cap. and res 7,808m. (1997), sales 10,301m. (1998); Chair. H. W. Chen; 1,676 employees.

Delta Electronics Inc: 31-1 Sing Pang Rd, Kui Shan Siang, Shan Ting Chun, Tao Yuen; f. 1971; electronic parts, colour monitors, etc.; cap. and res 13,245m., sales 26,136m. (1998); Pres. Mo Hsiung Chen; 3,400 employees.

First International Computer Inc: 6/F, 201–04 Tun Hua North Rd, Sungshan District, Taipei; tel. (2) 27174500; fax (2) 27120231; f. 1980; mfr of consumer electronics; cap. and res 13,711m. sales 30,269m. (1998); Pres. H. L. Wang; 1,600 employees.

Fortronics International Co Ltd: 14/F, 110 Fu Hsing Rd, Taoyuan; tel. (3) 3353925; fax (3) 3328117; f. 1984; semiconductors, resistors, integrated circuits, etc.; Dir Oliver Yu.

Goldentech Discrete Semiconductor Inc (TM): 4/F, 82 Pao Kao Rd, Hsintien, Taipei; tel. (2) 29178496; fax (2) 29149235; f. 1986; diodes, transistors, semiconductors, etc.; Dir John Lin.

GVC Corpn: 14/F, 76 Tun Hua South Rd, Sec. 2, Ta-an District, Taipei; tel. (2) 27552888; fax (2) 27552413; f. 1980; personal computers, computer peripherals; cap. and res 9,239m., sales 31,823m. (1997); Chair. Michael Chiang; 1000 employees.

Inventec Corpn: 66 Hou Kang St, Shih Lin District, Taipei; tel. (2) 28810721; fax (2) 28823605; computers and electronic products; cap. and res 14,709m., sales 46,164m. (1998); 2,739 employees.

Macronix International Co Ltd: 3 Creation 3rd Rd, Science-Based Industrial Park, Hsinchu; tel. (3) 5788888; fax (3) 5788887; internet www.macronix.com; f. 1989; mfr of semiconductors; cap. 18,000m., sales 12,000m. (1998); Pres. Ming Choi Wu; 1,800 employees.

Matsushita Electric Co Ltd: 579 Yuan Shan Rd, Chung Ho City, Taipei; tel. (2) 22235121; fax (2) 22271197; f. 1962; audio equipment, cooking, heating and laundry appliances, air conditioners and refrigerators; sales 30,636m. (1995); Chair. Yu Mein Hong; 4,000 employees.

Mitac International Corpn: 40, Wen Hua 2nd Rd, Kwei Shan Hsiang, Taoyuan; tel. (3) 3289000; fax (3) 3280928; design and manufacture of computers; cap. and res 6,614m., sales 61,546m. (1997); Chair. Matthew Miau.

Philips Electronic Building Elements Industries (Taiwan): 23–30/F, 66 Chung Hsiao West Rd, Section 1, Taipei; f. 1967; mfr of integrated circuits; sales 37,996m. (1995); Chair. Y. C. Lo; 2,806 employees.

Philips Electronic Industries (Taiwan) Ltd: Shih Kong Mitsukoshi Bldg, 22–24/F and 27–29/F, Chung Hsiao West Rd, Sec. 1, Taipei; tel. (2) 23887666; fax (2) 25155388; internet www .philips.com.tw; f. 1970; mfr of electronic components; sales 44,836m. (1995); Pres. Yi Chiang Lo; 5,267 employees.

Ritek Corpn: 42 Kuang Fu North Rd, Hsinchu Industrial Park, Hsinchu 30316; tel. (3) 5985696; fax (3) 5978684; e-mail rockkuan @ms4.hinet.net; f. 1989; mfr of blank CDs for audio, video and CD-ROM uses; cap. and res. 1,246m. (1996), sales 2,891m. (1997); Chair. Chin Tai Yeh; 200 employees.

Taiwan Semiconductor Manufacturing Co Ltd (TSMC): 121 Research Rd 3, Hsinchu Science Industrial Park, Hsinchu; tel. (3) 5780221; fax (3) 5781546; internet www.tsmc.com.tw; f. 1987; mfr of integrated circuits; cap. and res 83,297, sales 50,233m. (1998); Chair. and CEO Morris Chang; 3,412 employees.

Tatung Co Ltd: 22 Chung Shan North Rd, Sec. 3, Taipei 104; tel. (2) 25925252; fax (2) 25915185; f. 1918; household electric appliances, audio equipment, computers, telecommunications, wires and cables, heavy electrical apparatus, steel and machinery, material industry, construction and transport equipment; cap. and res 36,431m., sales 94,110m. (1998); Chair. T. S. Lin; Pres. W. S. Lin; 3,970 employees.

TECO Electric & Machinery Co Ltd: 156-2 Sung Chiang Rd, Taipei; tel. (2) 25621111; fax (2) 25312796; f. 1956; household appliances, commercial air conditioners, industrial motors and applications; cap. and res 24,113m., sales 20,415m. (1997); Chair. Theodore M. H. Huang; Pres. T. S. Hsieh; 3,400 employees.

United Microelectronics Corpn Ltd (UMC): 13 Chuang Hsin Rd 1, Science-Based Industrial Park, Hsinchu; tel. (35) 782258; fax (35) 774767; f. 1980; semiconductors, microcomputers, communications, etc.; cap. and res 76,262m., sales 18,431m. (1998); Chair. Robert Tsao; Pres. Hsuan Ming-chin; 2,285 employees.

Winbond Electronics Corpn: 4 Creation 3rd Rd, Science-Based Industrial Park, Hsinchu; tel. (3) 5770066; fax (3) 5789467; internet www.winbound.com.tw; design and production of very large-scale integrated circuits; cap. and res 42,316m., sales 15,658m. (1998); Pres. Din-Yuan Yang; 3,000 employees.

Yageo Corpn: 3/F, 223-1 Pao Chiao Rd, Hsin Tien, Taipei; tel. (2) 29177555; fax (2) 29174285; resistors; cap. and res 25,627m., sales 3,222m. (1998); Pres. Chen Tie-min; 973 employees.

Engineering

Aerospace Industrial Development Corpn: 111 Fu-Hsing North Rd, Lane 68, Taichung 407; tel. (4) 2590001; fax (4) 2562265; f. 1969; aircraft, aircraft engines design and manufacturing; sales 23,506m. (1996/97); Chair. Chuen Huei-tsai: Pres. Chin Hu; 4,243 employees.

China Motor Corpn: 11/F, 2 Tung Hua South Rd, Sec. 2, Ta-an District, Taipei; tel. (2) 23250000; fax (2) 27082913; f. 1969; mfr of motor vehicles; cap. and res 24,630m., sales 52,882m. (1998); Pres. H. Y. Lin; 2,471 employees.

Ford Lio Ho Motor Co: 705 Chung Hua Rd, Sec. 1, Chung Li City, Taoyuan; tel. (3) 4553131; fax (3) 4551474; f. 1972; motor vehicles; sales 47,100m. (1995); Pres. M. McKelvie; 2,700 employees.

Fortune Motors Co Ltd: 5/F, 270 Nanking East Rd, Sec. 3, Taipei; tel. (2) 27731111; fax (2) 27319436; f. 1975; wholesaler of motor vehicles; sales 34,889m. (1995); Pres. Hsi Jui Lin; 3,000 employees.

Ho Tai Motor Co Ltd: 8–14/F, 121 Sung Chiang Rd, Chung Shan District, Taipei; tel. (2) 25062121; fax (2) 25041749; internet www.hotaimotor.com.tw; f. 1947; mfr of motor vehicles; cap. and res 9,181m. (1997), sales 52,937m. (1999); Pres. S. D. Cheng; 1,200 employees.

Kuozui Motors Ltd: 11/F 121 Sung Chiang Rd, Taipei; tel. (3) 24529172; fax (3) 24519180; f. 1984; cars and trucks; sales 37,444m. (1995); Chair. Yen Huei Su; 2,000 employees.

Kwang Yang Motor Co Ltd: 35 Wan Hsing St, Sanmin District, Kaohsiung; tel. (7) 3822526; fax (7) 3852583; f. 1963; mfr of motor cycles; sales 24,175m. (1995); Pres. S. C. Wang; 2,819 employees.

Nan Yang Industries Co Ltd: 46 Fu Hsing North Rd, Taipei; tel. (2) 27526571; fax (2) 27724465; f. 1965; motor vehicle components and motor cycles; sales 24,125m. (1995); Pres. Chi Yung Hsu; 2,710 employees.

Ret-Ser Engineering Agency: 207 Sung Chiang Rd, Taipei; tel. (2) 25032233; fax (2) 25031113; f. 1956; construction and design; sales 29,700m. (1995); Pres. Yuan Yi Tseng; 9,451 employees.

Sanyang Industry: 3 Chung Hua Rd, Hukou, Hsinchu; tel. (2) 27912161; fax (2) 27912160; mfr of cars, motorcycles, etc.; cap. and res 12,010m., sales 31,271m. (1998); 3,550 employees.

Taiwan Aerospace Corpn (TAC): 17/F, 169 Jen-Ai Rd, Sec. 4, Taipei; tel. (2) 27716681; fax (2) 27716727; f. 1991; jet aircraft; Chair. JACK SUN; Pres. GEORGE K. LIU.

Yulong Motor Co Ltd: 39–1 Tsuen Po Kong Keng, West Lake Sanyi Village, Miaoli County; tel. (3) 7871801; f. 1953; cars and pick-up trucks; cap. and res 24,836m., sales 52,845m. (1997); Chair. VIVIAN W. SHUN-WEN; Pres. CHEN HWA LEE; 3,549 employees.

Food and Drink

President Enterprises Corpn: 301 Chung Chen Rd, Yan Harng, Yeong Kang Shiang, Tainan Hsien; tel. (6) 2532121; fax (6) 2532661; f. 1967; noodles, processed foods, soft drinks, etc.; cap. and res 39,202m., sales 29,204m. (1998); Pres. JASON C. S. LIN; CEO KAO CHIN-YEN; 30,923 employees.

Ve Dan Enterprises Corpn: POB 9, 65 Hsin An Rd, Shalu, Taichung; tel. (4) 6622111; fax (4) 6627351; monosodium glutamate, instant noodles and canned foods; sales 5,880m. (1998); Pres. JENG YANG; 2,000 employees.

Ve Wong Corpn: F5, 79 Chung Shan North Rd, Sec. 2, Taipei; tel. (2) 25717271; fax (2) 25629689; e-mail tradep@vewong.com.tw; internet www.vewong.com; processed food and drinks; sales 3,300m. (2000); Contact JOHN CHEN; 1,500 employees.

Weichuan Foods Corpn: 125 Sung Chiang Rd, Taipei; tel. (2) 25078221; fax (2) 25070623; f. 1953; milk products, monosodium glutamate, canned foods and soy sauce; cap. and res 6,802m., sales 12,156m. (1995); Pres. THOMAS NANTU HUANG; 3,314 employees.

Metals

China Steel Corpn: Lin Hai Industrial District, POB 47-29, 1 Chung Kang Rd, Hsiao Kang, Kaohsiung 81233; tel. (7) 8021111; fax (7) 8022511; e-mail f1000@mail.csc.com.tw; internet www.csc.com.tw; f. 1971; steel; state holding reduced to 40.6% in 1999; 16 subsidiaries; cap. and res 132,902m., sales 98,459m. (1998); Chair. C. Y. WANG; Pres. J. Y. CHEN; 8,895 employees.

China Wire & Cable Co Ltd: 4/F, 54-6 Chung Shan North Rd, Sec. 3, Taipei; tel. (2) 25917111; fax (2) 25922765; aluminium doors and windows; sales 2,686m., cap. and res 4,134m. (1997); Chair. CHEN CHIN-CHUN; 862 employees.

First Copper and Iron Industry Co: 11/F, 210 Nanking East Rd, Sec. 3, Taipei; tel. (2) 27717611; fax (2) 27213467; manufacture and sale of metals and alloys for industrial purposes; cap. and res 3,584m., sales 2,024m. (1998); Pres. WANG YUH-JEN.

Great China Metal Industry Co Ltd: Room 805, 293 Sung Chiang Rd, Taipei; tel. (2) 25030340; fax (2) 25081196; e-mail gcm1@ms17.hinet.net; aluminium cans; cap. and res 4,430m., sales 2,258m. (1997); Chair. CHIANG CHING-YI; 347 employees.

Tang Eng Iron Works Co Ltd: 458 Hsin Hsing Rd, Hu Kou Hsiang, Hsinchu Hsien; tel. (3) 5981721; fax (3) 5981646; f. 1940; stainless steel sheets and coils, steel bars, shapes etc., railway rolling stock, buses, general machinery, construction, bridge projects land development and transport business; sales 15,306m. (1997); Chair. YIN SHIU-HAU; Pres. YEN WEN-E; 2,259 employees.

Plastics and Glass

Formosa Plastics Corpn: 39 Chong Shang Rd, Kaohsiung; tel. (7) 3331101; e-mail pjlau@fpc.com.tw; internet www.fpc.com.tw; f. 1958; PVC products, footwear, polyester fibre, etc.; several affiliates; cap. and res 60,890m., sales 43,376m. (1998); Pres. WANG CHIN-SHU.

Nan Ya Plastics Corpn: f. 1958; largest affiliate, mfr of plastic products; cap. and res 68,706m., sales 125,188m. (1998); Chair. WANGYUNG-CHING; 16,370 employees.

Taiwan Glass Industrial Corpn: 11F, Taiwan Glass Bldg, 261 Nanking East Rd, Sec. 3, Sungshan District, Taipei 105; tel. (2) 27130333; fax (2) 27150333; f. 1964; cap. and res 21,964m., sales 12,237m. (1998); Chair. LIN YU-CHIA; Pres. LIN PO-FENG; 3,128 employees.

Textiles and Garments

Chung Shing Textile Co Ltd: 10/F, 123 Chung Hsiao East Rd, Sec. 2, Chengchung District, Taipei; tel. (2) 23971188; fax (2) 23963346; f. 1956; textiles and garments; sales 9,888m., cap. and res 8,817m. (1997); Chair. CHOU IN-SHIR; Pres. W. SHANG; 4,000 employees.

Far Eastern Textile Ltd: 38/F, Taipei Metro Tower, 207 Tun Hua Rd, Sec. 2, Taipei 106; tel. (2) 27338000; fax (2) 27369621; f. 1951; polyester staple, polyester filament, texturized yarn, cotton yarn, blended yarn, cotton clothing, shirts, underwear, pyjamas, pants/suits, bedsheets, etc; cap. and res 43,692m., sales 29,361m. (1997); Chair. DOUGLAS T. HSU; Pres. HSI CHIA-YI; 8,024 employees.

Hualon Corpn: 9/F, 351 Chung Shan Rd, Sec. 2, Taipei; tel. (2) 22266811; fax (2) 22266851; internet www.hualon.com.tw; f. 1967; mfr of fabrics and yarns; sales 28,741m. (1998); Pres. LIANG CHING-HSIUNG; 5,242 employees.

Pou Chen Corpn: 2 Fukong Rd, Fu Hsing Industrial Zone, Chang Hwa Hsien; tel. (4) 7695147; fax (4) 7695150; mfr of footwear; cap. and res 6,618m., sales 13,340m. (1997); Chair. CHI CHIEH TSAI; 2,800 employees.

Shin Kong Synthetic Fibres Corpn: 8/F, 123 Nan King East Rd, Sec. 2, Chung Shan, Taipei; tel. (2) 25071251; fax (2) 25072264; f. 1967; mfr of fabrics, yarns and silk; cap. and res 14,093m., sales 12,976m. (1998); Pres. TUNGLIANG WU; 2,475 employees.

Tai Yuen Textile Co Ltd: 8/F, 2 Tun Hua South Rd, Sec. 2, Taipei 106; tel. (2) 27552222; fax (2) 27061277; e-mail tyt070@email.taiyuen.com; internet www.taiyuen.com; f. 1951; yarn, cloth, denim, knitting fabrics, garments and sewing thread; Chair. VIVIAN WU YEN; Vice-Chair. C. J. WU; 3,000 employees.

Tainan Spinning Co Ltd: 511 Yu Nung Rd, Tung District, Tainan 701; tel. (2) 27589888; fax (2) 27582804; f. 1955; cotton, blended and synthetic yarns, etc; cap. and res 18,641m., sales 11,629m. (1998); Chair. WU HSIU-HUEI; Pres. CHUANG SHANG-HSIUNG; 2,824 employees.

Miscellaneous

Kunnan Enterprises Ltd: 33 Hsiang Ho Rd, Lee Lin Village, Tan Tzu Hsiang, Taichung; tel. (4) 5360183; fax (4) 9256491; sports equipment; sales 4,800m. (1991); Chair. LO KUN-NAN; 2,235 employees.

Yuen Foong Yu Paper Manufacturing Co Ltd: 14 Jeou Tang Rd, Da Xu Village, Kaohsiung Province; tel. (07) 6512611; f. 1950; mfr of paper products; cap. and res 13,867m., sales 17,431m. (1997); Chair. S. S. HO; Pres. S. C. HO; 4,200 employees.

TRADE UNIONS

Chinese Federation of Labour: 11/F, Back Bldg, 201–18 Tun Hua North Rd, Taipei; tel. (2) 27135111; fax (2) 27135116; e-mail cfllabor@ms10.hinet.net; f. 1954; mems: 48 federations of unions representing 2,985,955 workers; Pres. LIN HUI-KUAN.

National Federations

Chinese Federation of Postal Workers: 9/F, 45 Chungking South Rd, Sec. 2, Taipei 100; tel. (2) 23921380; fax (2) 23414510; e-mail cfpw@ms16.hinet.net; f. 1930; 27,957 mems; Pres. CHEN SHIAN-JUH.

National Chinese Seamen's Union: 8/F, 25 Nanking East Rd, Sec. 3, Taipei; tel. (2) 25150265; fax (2) 25078211; f. 1913; 21,705 mems; Pres. FANG FU-LIANG.

Taiwan Railway Labor Union: Rm 6044, 6/F, 3 Peiping West Rd, Taipei; tel. (2) 23896615; fax (2) 23896134; f. 1947; 15,579 mems; Pres. CHANG WEN-CHENG.

Regional Federations

Taiwan Federation of Textile and Dyeing Industry Workers' Unions (TFTDWU): 2 Lane 64, Chung Hsiao East Rd, Sec. 2, Taipei; tel. (2) 23415627; f. 1958; 11,906 mems; Chair. CHANG MING-KEN.

Taiwan Provincial Federation of Labour: 11/F, 44 Roosevelt Rd, Sec. 2, Taipei; tel. and fax (2) 23938080; f. 1948; 81 mem. unions and 1,571,826 mems; Pres. SHIH YUAN-LIN; Sec.-Gen. HUANG YAO-TUNG.

Transport

RAILWAYS

Taiwan Railway Administration (TRA): 3 Peiping West Rd, Taipei 10026; tel. (2) 23815226; fax (2) 23831367; f. 1891; a public utility under the Ministry of Communications and Transportation; operates both the west line and east line systems, with a route length of 1,097.2 km, of which 592.2 km are electrified; the west line is the main trunk line from Keelung, in the north, to Fangliao, in the south, with several branches; electrification of the main trunk line was completed in 1979; the east line runs along the east coast, linking Hualien with Taitung; the north link line, with a length of 79.2 km from Suao Sing to Hualien, was opened in 1980; the south link line, with a length of 98.2 km from Taitung Shin to Fangliao, opened in late 1991, completing the round-the-island system; construction of a high-speed link between Taipei and Kaohsiung (345 km) was scheduled for completion in 2005; Man. Dir T. P. CHEN.

There are also 1,440 km of private narrow-gauge track, operated by the Taiwan Sugar Corpn in conjunction with the Taiwan Forestry Bureau and other organizations. These railroads are mostly used for freight.

Construction of a five-line (including one elevated light rail line), 86.8-km, mass rapid-transit system (MRTS) in Taipei, incorporating links to the airport, began in 1987. The first 10.9-km section of the Mucha (light rail) line opened in March 1996 and the Tamshui line

(22.8 km) opened in December 1997. The Chungho and Hsintien lines, and part of the Nankang line, were in operation by 1999. The remainder of the network was scheduled for completion after 2006. A 42.7-km system is planned for Kaohsiung, scheduled for completion in the year 2007. MRT systems are also projected for Taoyuan, Hsinchu, Taichung and Tainan.

Taipei Rapid Transit Corporation: 7, Lane 48, Chung Shan North Rd, Sec. 2, Taipei; tel. (2) 0800033068; fax (2) 25115003; internet www.trtc.com.tw; f. 1994; 66.7 km (incl. 10.5 km light rail) open, with further lines under construction; Chair. LEE PO-WEN; Pres. RICHARD C. L. CHEN.

ROADS

There were 20,635 km of highways in 2001, most of them asphalt-paved. The Sun Yat-sen (North–South) Freeway was completed in 1978. Construction of a 505-km Second Freeway, which is to extend to Pingtung, in southern Taiwan, began in July 1987 and was scheduled to be completed by the end of 2003. Work on the Taipei–Ilan freeway began in 1991.

Taiwan Area National Expressway Bureau: 1 Lane 1, Hoping East Rd, Sec. 3, Taipei; tel. (2) 27078808; fax (2) 27017818; e-mail neebeyes@taneeb.gov.tw; internet www.taneeb.gov.tw; f. 1946; responsible for planning, design, construction and maintenance of provincial and county highways; Dir-Gen. CHENG WEN-LON.

Taiwan Area National Freeway Bureau: POB 75, Hsinchuang, Taipei 242; tel. (2) 29096141; fax (2) 29093218; internet www.freeway.gov.tw; f. 1970; Dir-Gen. HO NUAN-HSUAN.

Taiwan Motor Transport Co Ltd: 5/F, 17 Hsu Chang St, Taipei; tel. (2) 23715364; fax (2) 23820634; f. 1980; operates national bus service; Gen. Man. CHEN WU-SHIUNG.

SHIPPING

Taiwan has five international ports: Kaohsiung, Keelung, Taichung, Hualien and Suao. In 2001 the merchant fleet comprised 656 vessels, with a total displacement of 4,617,900 grt.

Evergreen Marine Corpn: 166 Ming Sheng East Rd, Sec. 2, Taipei 104; tel. (2) 25057766; fax (2) 25055256; f. 1968; world-wide container liner services; Indian subcontinent feeder service; two-way round-the-world services; Chair. KUO SHIUAN-YU; Pres. CHAN MING BO.

Taiwan Navigation Co Ltd: 29, Chi Nan Rd, Sec. 2, Taipei 104; tel. (2) 23941769; Chair. FRANK LU; Pres. I. Y. CHANG.

U-Ming Marine Transport Corpn: 29/F, Taipei Metro Tower, 207 Tun Hua South Rd, Sec. 2, Taipei; tel. (2) 27338000; fax (2) 27359900; world-wide tramp services; Chair. DOUGLAS HSU; Pres. C. K. ONG.

Uniglory Marine Corpn: 6/F, 172 Ming Sheng East Rd, Sec. 2, Taipei; tel. (2) 25019001; fax (2) 25086024; Chair. LOH YAO-FON; Pres. LEE MUN-CHI.

Wan Hai Lines Ltd: 10/F, 136 Sung Chiang Rd, Taipei; tel. (2) 25677961; fax (2) 25216000; f. 1965; regional container liner services; Chair. CHEN CHAO HON; Pres. CHEN PO TING.

Yang Ming Marine Transport Corpn (Yang Ming Line): 271 Ming de 1st Rd, Chidu, Keelung 206; tel. (2) 24559988; fax (2) 24559958; e-mail winsor@imail.yml.com.tw; internet www.yml.com.tw; f. 1972; world-wide container liner services, bulk carrier and supertanker services; Chair. T. H. CHEN; Pres. HUANG WANG-HSIU.

CIVIL AVIATION

There are two international airports, Chiang Kai-shek at Taoyuan, near Taipei, which opened in 1979 (a second passenger terminal and expansion of freight facilities being completed in 2000), and Hsiaokang, in Kaohsiung (where an international terminal building was inaugurated in 1997). There are also 14 domestic airports.

Civil Aeronautics Administration: 340 Tun Hua North Rd, Taipei; tel. (2) 23496000; fax (2) 23496277; e-mail gencaa@mail.caa.gov.tw; internet www.caa.gov.tw; Dir-Gen. BILLY K. C. CHANG.

China Air Lines Ltd (CAL): 131 Nanking East Rd, Sec. 3, Taipei; tel. (2) 25062345; fax (2) 25145786; internet www.china-airlines.com; f. 1959; international services to destinations in the Far East, Europe, the Middle East and the USA; Chair. Capt. Y. L. LEE; Pres. WEI HSING-HSIUNG.

EVA Airways: Eva Air Bldg, 376 Hsin-nan Rd, Sec. 1, Luchu, Taoyuan Hsien; tel. (3) 3515151; fax (3) 3510005; internet www.evaair.com.tw; f. 1989; subsidiary of Evergreen Group; commenced flights in 1991; services to destinations in Asia (incl. Hong Kong and Macao), the Middle East, Europe, North America, Australia and New Zealand; Chair. CHANG KUO-CHENG; Pres. KITTY YEN.

Far Eastern Air Transport Corpn (FAT): 5, Alley 123, Lane 405, Tun Hua North Rd, Taipei 10592; tel. (2) 7121555; fax (2) 7122428; internet www.fat.com.tw; f. 1957; domestic services and regional international services; Chair. and Pres. M. W. CHENG.

Mandarin Airlines (AE): 13/F, 134 Ming Sheng East Rd, Sec. 3, Taipei; tel. (2) 7171188; fax (2) 7170716; e-mail mandarin@mandarin-airlines.com; internet www.mandarin-airlines.com; f. 1991; subsidiary of CAL; merged with Formosa Airlines 1999; domestic and regional international services; Chair. Y. L. LEE; Pres. MICHAEL LO.

TransAsia Airways: 9/F, 139 Chengchou Rd, Taipei; tel. (2) 25575767; fax (2) 25570643; internet www.tna.com.tw; f. 1951; fmrly Foshing Airlines; domestic flights and international services; Chair. FAN CHIEH-CHIANG; Pres. SUN HUANG-HSIANG.

UNI Airways Corpn: 9/F, 260 Pah-Teh Rd, Sec. 2, Taipei; tel. (2) 27768576; fax (2) 87722029; internet www.uniair.com.tw; f. 1989; fmrly Makung Airlines; merged with Great China Airlines and Taiwan Airlines 1998; domestic flights and international services (to Kota Kinabalu, Malaysia; Bali, Indonesia; Phuket, Thailand); Chair and Pres. JENG KUNG-YEUN.

Tourism

The principal tourist attractions are the cuisine, the cultural artefacts and the island scenery. In 2001 there were 2,617,137 visitor arrivals (including 325,266 overseas Chinese) in Taiwan. Receipts from tourism in 2001 totalled US $3,991m.

Tourism Bureau, Ministry of Transportation and Communications: 9/F, 290 Chung Hsiao East Rd, Sec. 4, Taipei 106; tel. (2) 23491635; fax (2) 27735487; e-mail tbroc@tbroc.gov.tw; internet www.tbroc.gov.tw; f. 1972; Dir-Gen. CHANG SHUO-LAO.

Taiwan Visitors Association: 5/F, 9 Min Chuan East Rd, Sec. 2, Taipei; tel. (2) 25943261; fax (2) 25943265; internet www.tva.org.tw; f. 1956; promotes domestic and international tourism; Chair. STANLEY C. YEN.

Defence

In August 2001, according to Western sources, the armed forces totalled an estimated 370,000: army 240,000 (with deployments of 15,000–20,000 and 8,000–10,000, respectively, on the islands of Kinmen—Quemoy—and Matsu), navy 62,000 (including 30,000 marines), and air force 68,000. Paramilitary forces totalled 26,650. Reserves numbered 1,657,500. Military service is for 22 months.

Defence Expenditure: Budgeted at NT $244,248m. for 2001.

Chief of the General Staff: Adm. LI CHIEH.

Commander-in-Chief of the Army: Gen. HO SHOU-YEH.

Commander-in-Chief of the Navy: Adm. MIAO YUNG-CHING.

Commander-in-Chief of the Air Force: Gen. LI TIEN-YU.

Education

Taiwan's educational policy stresses national morality, the Chinese cultural tradition, scientific knowledge and the ability to work and to contribute to the community. Hence government policies have been mainly directed towards improving the quality and availability of education, accelerating the in-service training of teaching staff and co-ordinating education to the economic and social needs of the country. The central budget for 2002 allocated NT $275,196m. to education, science and culture.

ELEMENTARY AND SECONDARY EDUCATION

Pre-school kindergarten education is optional, although in 2000/01 243,090 children attended kindergartens. In 1968 an educational development programme was begun; this extended compulsory education for children of school-age to nine years. Children above school-age and adults who have had no education whatsoever receive education in the form of supplementary courses of six months' to one year's and 18 months' to two years' duration, which are held in national elementary schools. In 2001/02 there were 2,611 primary schools, with a total of 103,501 teachers and 1,925,491 pupils. With the extension of compulsory education to junior high school, the junior high school entrance examinations have been abolished.

Secondary, including vocational, education has shown substantial growth in past years, with 1,181 schools, 98,609 teachers and 1,684,449 pupils in 2001/02. There are three types of school: junior high, senior high and vocational. Senior high schools admit junior high school graduates and prepare them for higher education. They offer a three-year programme. Vocational schools also offer a three-year programme and provide training in agriculture, fisheries, commerce and industry, etc.

HIGHER AND ADULT EDUCATION

In 2000/01 there were 150 universities, junior colleges and independent colleges. Most of them offer postgraduate facilities. The great majority of courses are of four years' duration. Junior colleges provide two-, three- and five-year courses. Enrolment in higher education in 2001/02 was 1,187,225 students, with 44,769 teachers.

As part of the government policy to promote advanced education and academic standards, it has been encouraging existing universities to establish graduate schools with special budgets made available for the purpose. The Government also encourages the establishment of overseas Chinese institutes of higher learning for the study of Chinese as a means of promoting international understanding. During the 1980s rules were considerably relaxed to allow more students to go abroad for further education, mostly to the USA, Japan and Europe. Government lectureships and research professorships have been established to encourage Chinese scholars abroad to return to Taiwan.

In 1987 the nine teachers' junior colleges were upgraded to teachers' colleges. These admit senior secondary graduates for a four-year course. High school teachers are trained at normal universities.

In adult education, the main aim has been to raise the literacy rate and standard of general knowledge. In 2001/02 there were 954 supplementary schools, with an enrolment of 304,763. Chinese language, general knowledge, arithmetic, music and vocational skills are taught. Radio and television are an important component in the expansion of education. The Chinese Television Service and the Educational Broadcasting Station are both supervised by the Ministry of Education to broadcast cultural and educational programmes.

Bibliography

See also pp. 325–328.

GENERAL

Alagappa, Muthiah (Ed.). *Taiwan's Presidential Politics: Democratization and Cross-Strait Relations in the 21st Century*. Armonk, NY, M. E. Sharpe, 2001.

Aspalter, Christian. *Democratization and Welfare State Development in Taiwan*. Aldershot, Ashgate, 2002.

Aspalter, Christian, and Kepler, Johannes. *Understanding Modern Taiwan: Essays in Economics, Politics, and Social Policy*. Aldershot, Ashgate, 2001.

Republic of China Yearbook. Annual. Taipei, Kwang Hwa Publishing Co.

Bullard, Monte. *The Soldier and the Citizen—The Role of the Military in Taiwan's Development*. Armonk, NY, M. E. Sharpe, 1997.

Chao, Linda, and Myers, Ramon H. (Eds). *The First Chinese Democracy: Political Life in the Republic of China on Taiwan*. Baltimore, MD, Johns Hopkins University Press, 1999.

Cheng Tun-jen, and Haggard, Stephen (Eds). *Political Change in Taiwan*. Boulder, CO, Lynne Rienner Publishers, 1993.

Ching Cheong. *Will Taiwan Break Away: The Rise of Taiwanese Nationalism*. Singapore, World Scientific Publishing, 2001.

Ching, Leo T. S. *Becoming 'Japanese': Colonial Taiwan and the Politics of Identity Formation*. Berkeley, University of California Press, 2001.

Clough, Ralph N. *Island China*. Cambridge, MA, Harvard University Press, 1978.

Cohen, Marc J. *Taiwan at the Crossroads: Human Rights, Political Development and Social Change on the Beautiful Island*. Washington, DC, Asia Resource Centre, 1989.

Copper, John F. *China Diplomacy: The Washington-Taipei-Beijing Triangle*. Boulder, CO, Westview Press, 1993.

Words Across The Taiwan Straits. Lanham, MD, University Press of America, 1995.

Taiwan: Nation-State or Province? Boulder, CO, Westview Press, 1999.

As Taiwan Approaches the New Millennium. Lanham, MD, University Press of America, 2002.

Corcuff, Stephane (Ed.). *Memories of the Future: National Identity Issues and the Search for a New Taiwan*. Armonk, NY, M. E. Sharpe, 2002.

Crozier, Brian. *The Man Who Lost China: The First Full Biography of Chiang Kai-Shek*. London, Angus and Robertson, 1977.

Dell' Orto, Alessandro. *Place and Spirit in Taiwan*. Richmond, Surrey, Curzon Press, 2002.

Edmonds, Martin, and Tsai, Michael (Eds). *Defending Taiwan: The Future Vision of Taiwan's Defence Policy and Military Strategy*. London, RoutledgeCurzon, 2002.

Taiwan's Maritime Security. London, RoutledgeCurzon, 2002.

Edmonds, Richard L., and Goldstein, Steven M. (Eds). *Taiwan in the Twentieth Century: A Retrospective*. New York, Cambridge University Press, 2001.

Feldman, Harvey J. (Ed.). *Constitutional Reform and the Future of the Republic of China*. Armonk, NY, M. E. Sharpe, 1993.

Garver, John W. *The Sino-American Alliance—Nationalist China and American Cold War Strategy in Asia*. Armonk, NY, M. E. Sharpe, 1997.

Goddard, W. G. *Formosa: A Study in Chinese History*. London, Macmillan, 1966.

Herschensohn, Bruce. (Ed.). *Across the Taiwan Strait: Democracy: The Bridge Between Mainland China and Taiwan*. Lanham, MD, Lexington, 2002.

Hickey, Dennis Van Vranken. *Taiwan's Security in the Changing International System*. Boulder, CO, Lynne Rienner Publishers, 1997.

Hsiau A-Chin. *Contemporary Taiwanese Cultural Nationalism*. London, Routledge, 2000.

Hsu Long-Hsuen, and Chang Ming-Kai. *History of the Sino-Japanese War*. Chung Wu Publishing Co, 1971.

Kaplan, David E. *Fires of the Dragon: Politics, Murder and the Kuomintang*. New York, Atheneum, 1993.

Kiang, Clyde Y. *The Hakka Search for a Homeland*. Elgin, PA, Allegheny Press, 1991.

Klintworth, Gary. *New Taiwan, New China: Taiwan's Changing Role in the Asia-Pacific Region*. Melbourne, Longman, 1996.

Klintworth, Gary (Ed.). *Taiwan in the Asia-Pacific in the 1990s*. St Leonards, NSW, Allen and Unwin, 1994.

Lai Tse-han, Myers, Ramon H., and Wei Wou. *A Tragic Beginning: The Taiwan Uprising of February 28, 1947*. CA, Stanford University Press, 1992.

Lasater, Martin L. *The Changing of the Guard: President Clinton and the Security of Taiwan*. Boulder, CO, Westview Press, 1996.

The Taiwan Conundrum. Boulder, CO, Westview Press, 1999.

Lasater, Martin L., Yu, Peter Kien-Hong, Hsu, Kuang-Min, and Lym, Robyn (Eds). *Taiwan's Security in the Post-Deng Xiaoping Era*. London, Frank Cass, 2001.

Lee, David Tawei. *The Making of the Taiwan Relations Act: Twenty Years in Retrospect*. Oxford, Oxford University Press, 2000.

Leng Shao-chuan (Ed.). *Chiang Ching-Kuo's Leadership in the Development of the Republic of China on Taiwan*. Lanham, MD, University Press of America, 1994.

Long, Simon. *Taiwan: China's Last Frontier*. London, Macmillan, 1991.

Marsh, Robert M. *The Great Transformation—Social Change in Taipei, Taiwan Since the 1960s*. Armonk, NY, M. E. Sharpe, 1996.

Nadeau, Jules. *Twenty Million People—Made in Taiwan*. Montreal, Montreal Press, 1990.

Rawnsley, Gary D. *Taiwan's Informal Diplomacy and Propaganda*. New York, St Martin's Press, 2000.

Rigger, Shelley. *Politics in Taiwan*. London, Routledge, 1999.

From Opposition to Power: Taiwan's Democratic Progressive Party. Boulder, CO, Lynne Rienner Publishers, 2001.

Rubinstein, Murray A. (Ed.). *Taiwan: A New History*. Armonk, NY, M. E. Sharpe, 1999.

Shambaugh, David (Ed.). *Contemporary Taiwan*. Oxford, Clarendon Press, 1998.

Sheng, Lijun. *China's Dilemma: The Taiwan Issue*. London, I.B. Tauris, 2001.

Cross-Strait Relations Under Chen Shui-bian. Singapore, Institute of Southeast Asian Studies, 2002.

Skoggard, Ian A. *The Indigenous Dynamic in Taiwan's Postwar Development*. Armonk, NY, M. E. Sharpe, 1996.

Sutter, Robert G., and Johnson, William R. (Eds). *Taiwan in World Affairs*. Boulder, CO, Westview Press, 1996.

Swaine, Michael. *Taiwan: Foreign and Defense Policymaking 2001*. Santa Monica, CA, Rand, 2001.

Tan, Alexander C., Chan, Steven, and Jillson, Calvin (Eds). *Taiwan's National Security: Dilemmas and Opportunities*. Aldershot, Ashgate, 2001.

Taylor, Jay. *The Generalissimo's Son: Chiang Ching-Kuo and the Revolutions in China and Taiwan*. Cambridge, MA, Harvard University Press, 2000.

Tien Hung-mao. *The Great Transition: Political and Social Change in the Republic of China*. Stanford, CA, Hoover Institution Press, 1990.

Tien Hung-mao (Ed.). *Taiwan's Electoral Politics and Democratic Transition: Riding the Third Wave*. Armonk, NY, M. E. Sharpe, 1995.

Tien Hung-mao and Steve Tsang (Eds). *Democratization in Taiwan: Implications for China*. New York, St Martin's Press, 1999.

Tsang, Steve (Ed.). *Political Developments in Taiwan since 1949*. Honolulu, HI, University of Hawaii Press, 1993.

Wachman, Alan M. *Taiwan: National Identity and Democratization*. Armonk, NY, M. E. Sharpe, 1994.

Wu, Jaushieh Joseph. *Taiwan's Democratization: Forces Behind the New Momentum*. Hong Kong, Oxford University Press, 1995.

Yang, Maysing H. *Taiwan's Expanding Role in the International Arena*. Armonk, NY, M. E. Sharpe, 1997.

Yu, Peter Kien-Hong. *The Crab and Frog Motion Paradigm Shift: Decoding and Deciphering Taipei and Beijing's Dialectical Politics*. Lanham, MD, University Press of America, 2002.

Zhan Jun. *Ending the Chinese Civil War*. New York, St Martin's Press, 1994.

Zhao Suisheng (Ed.). *Across the Taiwan Strait: Mainland China, Taiwan, and the 1995–96 Crisis*. London, Routledge, 1999.

ECONOMY

Aberbach, Joel D., Dollar, David, and Sokoloff, Kenneth L. (Eds). *The Role of the State in Taiwan's Development*. Armonk, NY, M. E. Sharpe, 1995.

Center for Quality of Life Studies, Ming Teh Foundation. *Economic Development in Taiwan: A Selected Bibliography*. Taipei, 1984.

Champion, Steven R. *The Great Taiwan Bubble: The Rise and Fall of an Emerging Stock Market*. Berkeley, CA, Pacific View Press, 1998.

Chang Chun-yen, Yu Po-lung, Zhang Junyan, and Yu P.L. (Eds). *Made By Taiwan: Booming in the Information Technology Era*. River Edge, NJ, World Scientific Publishing, 2001.

Chang Han-yu, and Myers, R. H. *Japanese Colonial Development Policy in Taiwan 1895–1906: A Case of Bureaucratic Entrepreneurship*. The Journal of Asian Studies, Vol. XXII, No. 4, 1963.

Chen Fen-Ling. *Working Women and State Policies in Taiwan: A Study in Political Economy*. Basingstoke, Palgrave, 2000.

Chow, Peter Y. C., and Bates, Gill (Eds). *Weathering the Storm: Taiwan, Its Neighbours, and the Asian Financial Crisis*. Washington, DC, Brookings Institute Press, 2000.

Chow, Peter Y. C., and Liao, Kuang-sheng (Eds). *Taiwan in the Global Economy: From an Agrarian Economy to an Exporter of High-Tech Products*. New York, Praeger, 2002.

Directorate-General of Budget, Accounting and Statistics, Executive Yuan. *Statistical Yearbook of the Republic of China*. Taipei.

Galenson, Walter. *Economic Growth and Structural Change in Taiwan*. Ithaca, NY, Cornell University Press, 1979.

Gold, Thomas. *State and Society in the Taiwan Miracle*. Armonk, NY, M. E. Sharpe, 1986.

Ho, Samuel P. S. *Economic Development of Taiwan, 1860–1970*. New Haven, CT, Yale University Press, 1978.

Ho Yhi-Min. *Agricultural Development of Taiwan: 1903–1960*. Nashville, TN, Vanderbilt University Press, 1966.

Hsueh Li-Min, Hsu Chen-kuo, and Perkins, Dwight H. (Eds). *Industrialization and the State: The Changing Role of Government in Taiwan's Economy, 1945–1998*. Cambridge, MA, Harvard University Press, 2000.

International Business Publications. *Taiwan Business and Investment Opportunities Yearbook*. International Business Publications, 2002.

Jacoby, N. H. *An Evaluation of US Economic Aid to Free China 1951–1965*. New York, Praeger, 1967.

Kuo, Shirley W. Y. *The Taiwan Economy in Transition*. Boulder, CO, Westview Press, 1983.

Lee Teng-hui. *Intersectoral Capital Flows in the Economic Development of Taiwan 1895–1960*. Ithaca, NY, Cornell University Press, 1971.

Lin Ching-yuan. *Industrialization in Taiwan 1946–72*. New York, Praeger, 1973.

Mai, Chao-cheng, and Shih, Chien-sheng (Eds). *Taiwan's Economic Success Since 1980*. Cheltenham, Edward Elgar Publishing, 2001.

McBeath, Gerald. A. *Wealth and Freedom: Taiwan's New Political Economy*. Brookfield, VT, Ashgate, 1998.

Ranis, Gustav, Chu Yun-peng and Hu Sheng-cheng (Eds). *The Political Economy of Taiwan's Development Into the 21st Century*. Cheltenham, Edward Elgar Publishing, 1999.

Rubinstein, Murray A. (Ed.). *The Other Taiwan: 1945 to the Present*. Armonk, NY, M. E. Sharpe, 1995.

Shen Tsung-Han. *Agricultural Development on Taiwan since World War II*. Taipei, Mei Ya Publications Inc, 1971.

Wade, Robert. *Governing the Market: Economic Theory and the Role of Government in East Asian Industrialization*. Princeton, NJ, Princeton University Press, 1990.

EAST TIMOR

Physical and Social Geography

East Timor, which is styled Timor Loro Sa'e (Timor of the rising sun) in the principal indigenous language, Tetum, occupies the eastern half of the island of Timor, which lies off the north coast of Western Australia and extends between 8° 15′ and 10° 30′ S and 123° 20′ and 127° 10′ E. The western half of the island is Indonesian territory. In addition to the eastern half of Timor island, the territory also includes an enclave around Oecusse (Oekussi) Ambeno on the north-west coast of the island, and the islands of Ataúro (Pulo Cambing) and Jaco (Pulo Jako). East Timor occupies an area of 14,609 sq km (5,641 sq miles).

Timor's climate is dominated by intense monsoon rain, succeeded by a pronounced dry season. The north coast of the island has a brief rainy season from December to February; the south coast a double rainy season from December to June, with a respite in March. The mountainous spine of the island experiences heavy rains that feed torrential floods. Once every three to four years, however, the climatic phenomenon known as El Niño is likely to subject the island to serious drought.

Very irregular, rugged hills and mountains form the core of the island, which is split by a longitudinal series of depressions and by small, discontinuous plateaux. There are many extinct volcanoes. Some good soils have been formed from the older volcanic rock, but the dominant soil consists of soft clay, which does not support heavy vegetation.

The indigenous peoples are of mixed origin. The aboriginal population is composed mainly of Melanesians, who probably resulted from the fusion of a basic Papuan stock with immigrant Asian elements. Evidence exists, also, of an Australoid strain. These peoples were displaced from the more favoured areas by subsequent arrivals from Indonesia, while communities of Chinese and other Asians gained control of much of the commerce conducted on the island. In a UN registration process completed in June 2001, the population of East Timor totalled 737,811, about 90% of whom lived in rural areas. More than 250,000 people were displaced by the conflict of 1999. In mid-2001 more than 113,000 remained in refugee camps in neighbouring West Timor. In mid-2002 many had yet to return to East Timor.

History

ROBERT CRIBB

Only fragments are known of the early history of Timor. The island's name means 'east' and for at least a millennium Timor appears to have remained on the eastern fringe of the Indonesian commercial world, a source of sandalwood for trade to India and China and of slaves for markets in the archipelago. Indian and Islamic cultural influences on Timor were meagre, however, and there is no evidence of literacy or of large-scale state formation before 1600. Rather, it would appear that the island was divided among a fluctuating number of small polities headed by powerful chiefs, later known as *liurai*. Early European accounts report that these polities were grouped into two federations, generally referred to as the Wehale (Belu) and the Sonbai. While the nature of these federations is not clear, they certainly did not constitute co-ordinated political units. Timor's sandalwood attracted Portuguese interest in the mid-16th century, but the Portuguese preferred to establish their bases in the relative security of neighbouring Solor and Larantuka, rather than on the Timor coast itself. During the next century, however, Dominican missionaries converted many *liurai* to Catholicism, and the coastal regions of the island came increasingly under the domination of the so-called Topasses, or 'Black Portuguese'. The Topasses were descendants of Portuguese and other Western and Asian soldiers who married local women; they were rough adventurers who soon established a sphere of influence in western Timor. In the 1640s the Portuguese authorities attempted to assert control over the island by constructing a fort at Kupang at the western end of the island. This fort was no sooner constructed than it was seized in 1653 by the Dutch East Indies Company, which named it Castle Concordia. As Topass power grew under the rival de Hornay and da Costa families, however, the Dutch were unable to expand their power beyond the environs of Kupang. Portuguese influence in the region increased with the arrival of Catholic refugees from Makassar in Sulawesi, which the Dutch had conquered in 1660, but Timor itself remained firmly under the control of the Topasses. Successive Topass leaders received formal appointment as governors of the island from the Governor-General in Goa, and occasionally paid tax or tribute to the Portuguese crown from proceeds of trade in sandalwood, slaves, beeswax, gold and horses. In 1702 the Portuguese shifted their headquarters from Larantuka to Lifau, on the northern coast of west Timor, and appointed outsiders as governors. These governors led a miserable existence, besieged by the Topasses and harassed by the Dominicans, until 1769 when Governor António de Menezes moved his office to what was then the small settlement of Dili, further east along the coast. The Dutch, meanwhile, defeated a Topass attack on Kupang in 1749 and began slowly to expand their hegemony over the western part of the island, although they were never able to subdue the Topass strongholds around Lifau and in the inland region of Noimuti.

For about a century, neither colonial power did any more than continue to exploit the traditional trade of the island. However, from the mid-19th century, the development of modern colonialism and the fear of losing their colonies to newer, more dynamic colonial powers led both the Portuguese and the Dutch to begin to develop the island. The Portuguese began a programme of road-building, which enabled them to exercise closer control both of the *liurai* and of the general population. Coffee plantations were established, and a poll tax was imposed on all Timorese to encourage the growing of cash crops. Eventually the authority of the *liurai* was formally abolished, although they remained powerful local figures. In 1859 the Portuguese and the Dutch agreed to consolidate their territorial holdings, the Portuguese giving up Larantuka and outposts on other islands in exchange for the establishment of demarcated borders on Timor itself. Under a further treaty, in 1902 the two powers exchanged several small territories in the interior for the sake of a neater border, although the area around Lifau remained as a Portuguese enclave on the north coast, with the name Oecusse (Oekussi). Portugal's interference with the powers of the *liurai* led to a revolt in 1910–12 under Dom Boaventura, but the Timorese were defeated with the assistance of troops sent from Mozambique.

Portugal's cultural influence on East Timor was relatively limited. Although there was an official policy of encouragement of the adoption of Portuguese culture and Catholicism, the colonial authorities were often suspicious of the Catholic Church, and missionaries were banned from the colony for 40 years from 1834. As for general education, the colonial budget was minimal, and few funds were available for schooling. In consequence, even in 1950 adult literacy in East Timor was estimated at less than 5%, while less than 0.5% of the indigenous population of East Timor was classified as *civilizado*, that is, speaking Portuguese and having an income sufficient to maintain a 'civilized' life style. The remainder of the colonial élite was European, Chinese and mestizo. Portugal declared its neutrality at the start of the Second World War, and apprehension quickly grew in Australia and the Netherlands Indies that the Portuguese authorities in East Timor might accept a Japanese presence in the territory, much as the Vichy French authorities had allowed the Japanese access to French Indo-China. To forestall this possibility, Australia landed troops in Dili in mid-December 1941, despite Portuguese objections. These troops were not numerous enough to resist Japanese landings in mid-February 1942, but they retreated into the interior and undertook highly effective guerrilla warfare until they were evacuated in January 1943. The Japanese occupation appears to have been a very difficult time for the Timorese themselves, partly because of the guerrilla war and Allied and Japanese bombing, and partly because the impoverished territory was cut off from supplies of cloth and other consumer goods.

PRESSURES FOR DECOLONIZATION

By the end of the Second World War in 1945, Portugal's continued tenure of East Timor was by no means assured. Indonesian nationalists considered, and then rejected, the possibility of claiming the territory as a part of the new Indonesian Republic. More seriously, Australia proposed taking over the territory, perhaps with a United Nations (UN) mandate, to ensure that the island could serve as a base for a more effective forward line of defence in the event of another attack from the north. It appears that Portugal was able to stave off the Australian threat only by negotiating its intention to return to East Timor against NATO's interest in having access to the Azores, a Portuguese possession strategically located in the North Atlantic. During the 1950s, however, Portugal came under more general pressure to decolonize East Timor, pressure that even caused the delay of the country's entry into the UN in 1956. In 1951 Portugal declared East Timor, along with its other colonies, to be an overseas province, the subjects of which had the same (limited) political rights as metropolitan Portuguese. The UN, however, continued to consider the former colonies as non-self-governing territories. Whereas Portugal's African territories seemed destined for eventual independence, its three small Asian colonies, including East Timor, all appeared likely to be absorbed by their larger neighbours. India occupied Goa in 1961, and in 1968 China forced Portugal to acknowledge Macao as Chinese territory under Portuguese administration. Indonesian leaders appear to have assumed that East Timor would eventually be absorbed into Indonesia, but until 1968 Indonesia took no action to claim the territory, the Indonesian Government being occupied with the pursuit and consolidation of the archipelago's claim to formerly Dutch West New Guinea. However, Indonesian intelligence forces may have sponsored a brief rebellion in the territory in 1959 and a Government-in-exile shortly afterwards.

In April 1974, however, the future of East Timor was abruptly placed on the international political agenda following a coup by the armed forces in Lisbon. The new Portuguese Government lifted political restrictions and foreshadowed major political changes, which appeared to include the possibility of independence, with regard to the country's colonies. Within a month, two new Timorese political parties had emerged: the União Democrática Timorense (UDT, Timorese Democratic Union), which was led by plantation owners and senior officials from the Portuguese administration, advocated democratization and eventual independence from Portugal, while the Associação Social Democrática Timorense (ASDT, Timorese Social Democratic Association), which drew its membership from amongst younger professionals and intellectuals, argued for a more rapid transition to independence and for more extensive social reforms. A third party, the Associação Popular Democrática Timorense (Apodeti, Timorese Popular Democratic Association), which appears to have been sponsored from the outset by Indonesian intelligence organizations, proposed integration with Indonesia. The UDT was initially the most popular of the parties, but during 1974 it gradually lost support to the ASDT, which adopted an increasingly radical profile. In September 1974 the ASDT renamed itself Frente Revolucionária do Timor Leste Independente (Fretilin, Revolutionary Front for an Independent East Timor) and claimed to be the sole representative of the East Timorese people.

The assumption that East Timor's natural destiny was absorption by Indonesia remained dominant throughout the international community, however: Portugal was preoccupied with internal political difficulties and with the decolonization of its African colonies, and other international powers had no natural interest in the territory, while in Australia the Labor Government of Gough Whitlam believed that East Timor was too small and too poor for independence. In June 1974 the Indonesian Minister of Foreign Affairs, Adam Malik, formally stated that Indonesia respected East Timor's right to independence and had no intention of taking over the territory. The growing popularity and leftward political shift of Fretilin, however, added political weight to the arguments of Indonesian military and intelligence groups already in favour of annexation. Furthermore, less than a decade earlier, the Indonesian military had violently suppressed the Indonesian Communist Party, and in 1974 communist forces in Indo-China were clearly gaining influence. Under these circumstances, the Indonesian military feared that Fretilin would seek to establish a communist regime in East Timor and that such a regime would provide a base for 'subversion' in Indonesia itself. It appears that in about July 1974, therefore, sections of the Indonesian military intelligence initiated what became known as 'Operation Komodo', a broad-based strategy intended to secure the integration of East Timor into Indonesia. This strategy included the provision of funding and logistical assistance for supporters of integration, the promotion of the perception that East Timor was incapable of managing its own independence and the initiation of thinly concealed preparations for armed intervention in the territory.

In January 1975 local Portuguese officials, concerned by Indonesia's shift away from the acceptance of East Timorese independence, persuaded Fretilin and the UDT to form a coalition as the basis for a national transitional government to oversee the territory's passage to independence. From March local elections were held in several areas, most of which were won by Fretilin supporters; the colonial authorities tentatively scheduled the territory's accession to independence for the end of 1976. These arrangements had not been ratified by the Portuguese metropolitan government, however, which called a conference in Macau in May 1975 to discuss the decolonization of East Timor. Fretilin declined to attend the conference, apparently because its leaders regarded decolonization as a process that should be led from within East Timor itself, rather than by Lisbon, and because the movement objected to the inclusion of Apodeti in the negotiations. At about this time, Indonesian intelligence apparently warned UDT leaders that Indonesia would invade East Timor in order to prevent 'Communist' Fretilin from coming to power. The UDT responded first by pulling out of the coalition with Fretilin in May and then by staging a coup in Dili on 11 August with the assistance of the police force. The Portuguese Governor, Col Mário Lemos Pires, was under official instructions not to intervene and subsequently withdrew to the offshore island of Ataúro. Fretilin sympathizers in the local army units, however, launched a counter-attack, retaking Dili by 27 August and driving the remaining UDT forces across the border into Indonesian-controlled West Timor by the last week of September. From among the somewhat ramshackle collection of East Timorese parties and individuals displaced by Fretilin, Indonesian intelligence then assembled a coalition to demand integration. Meanwhile, Indonesian special forces, disguised as anti-Fretilin guerrillas, began to move into the territory, capturing the border town of Batugade on 8 October. However, difficult terrain and determined resistance by Fretilin forces, who had seized some NATO weaponry from the Portuguese, meant that Indonesian progress was slow. Only in late November, after the fall of the town of Atabae, did Fretilin conclude that Indonesian conquest was likely. On 28 November, in an attempt to galvanize domestic and international support, Fretilin declared East Timor's independence as the Democratic Republic of East Timor, with Francisco Xavier do Amaral as President. Indonesia responded with a naval and airborne attack on Dili on 7 December. The attack took place one day after the departure from Jakarta of the US President, Gerald Ford, who had been on an official visit to Indonesia. The US President and the Secretary of State, Henry Kissinger, were subsequently acknowledged to have given approval to the Indonesian invasion. The operation was officially claimed to have been the work of East Timorese opposed to Fretilin, assisted by Indonesian 'volunteers'; however, the invasion was in fact carried out by regular marines and troops from Indonesia's élite strategic reserve (KOSTRAD). In the period during and after the capture of Dili, Indonesian troops killed several hundred East Timorese civilians suspected of offering resistance or supporting Fretilin, and this pattern was repeated on a smaller scale as the Indonesian troops fanned out across the territory to take other centres. On 17 December Indonesia sponsored a 'provisional Government' of East Timor led by Apodeti and a number of UDT leaders, with Arnaldo dos Reis Araújo as acting Governor. In May 1976 a 'People's Assembly' of 37 specially-selected delegates formally petitioned Indonesia for integration, and on 17 July President Suharto of Indonesia formally declared the territory as the country's 27th province.

INDONESIAN RULE AND EAST TIMORESE RESISTANCE

Many observers expected that Indonesia would quickly achieve full control of East Timor and that the East Timorese would soon adjust to the new administration. In the event, however, Fretilin offered effective military resistance to the Indonesian armed forces in the countryside and retained a broad base of support amongst the East Timorese. Fretilin's military success was due to its access to modern weapons from the former Portuguese forces, to the fact that some of its troops had gained previous battle experience in Portugal's African colonies, and to the suitability of the East Timorese terrain for guerrilla warfare. Fretilin's popular support was based principally on the extensive political work carried out by the movement in rural areas since September 1974. In a society deprived of education, Fretilin activists had carried out extensive rural literacy programmes. They had also promoted the development of agricultural and trading co-operatives, which challenged the unpopular economic power of Chinese shopkeepers and wholesalers. At the same time, the activists refrained from suggesting major changes in traditional society, and so were able to win the support of many influential *liurai*. Reports on the three months of Fretilin administration in East Timor prior to the Indonesian attack on Dili suggest that Fretilin officials were generally efficient and humane. The contrasting brutality of Indonesian troops during the invasion, moreover, further alienated many East Timorese from the Indonesian cause. However, continuing warfare in the territory, together with Indonesia's resettling of villagers into strategic hamlets between 1977 and 1979, led to a famine in which perhaps 100,000 people died (of an original population of about 650,000). By the end of the resettlement campaign, Indonesia had succeeded in destroying the founding leadership of Fretilin and believed that the territory was under control.

Although the USA and Australia had made it clear that they would not intervene against Indonesia's occupation of East Timor, the UN Security Council passed a resolution on 23 December 1975 urging Indonesia's withdrawal from the territory and East Timorese self-determination. Indonesia refused to co-operate with a visit by the UN Secretary-General's special representative, Winspeare Guicciardi, and the Security Council passed a further resolution in April 1976 demanding that Indonesia withdraw from East Timor. There was, however, no significant international interest in pursuing the issue to the extent of the imposition of sanctions or other hostile measures. From 1976 to 1982 the UN General Assembly passed annual resolutions affirming the right of the East Timorese to self-determination and independence. Australia, however, gave *de jure* recognition to Indonesia's annexation of the territory in 1979.

Indonesia's policy in the territory was to suppress the independence movement while hoping that the slow acculturation of young East Timorese to Indonesian rule would gradually erode the resistance base. Substantial development aid was also allocated to the province, producing a dramatic improvement in communications, infrastructure and education. Bahasa Indonesia came to be widely spoken, and by 1993 more than 1,000 East Timorese were studying at Indonesian universities. Many East Timorese sought employment elsewhere in Indonesia, particularly in Bali. In December 1988 Indonesia opened East Timor to foreign tourists, and in April 1990 it disbanded the special military command in the territory. In April 1991 the Indonesian Government announced that only 200 Fretilin guerrillas remained and that the Indonesian security forces would not pursue them because they represented no danger. Throughout this period, however, Indonesian oppression of the East Timorese population continued: both the European Community (EC, now European Union—EU) and the international human rights organization, Amnesty International, found compelling evidence of widespread killing and systematic torture. Such Indonesian brutality created deep resentment among the East Timorese people, including those of the younger generation who remembered nothing but Indonesian rule. External interests, moreover, came to dominate the province's economy. A military-controlled company obtained an effective monopoly on the coffee crop—the province's main export commodity—while other Indonesian interests dominated the construction and service industries. An indefinite number of Indonesians migrated to the province, and these migrants tended to dominate the administration and to control the lower reaches of the East Timorese economy, so that only a relatively small proportion of the benefits of the province's economic growth reached indigenous East Timorese.

In the mid-1980s resistance re-emerged, led by the Fretilin commander, José Alexandre 'Xanana' Gusmão. This resistance both encouraged, and was encouraged by, renewed international support for the East Timorese cause. Portugal in particular reasserted its claim—which was supported by the UN—that it was legally the administering power in East Timor, and increasingly used its position in the EU to press the East Timorese case. The former Portuguese colonies in Africa were also sympathetic to East Timor's cause, and the issue remained a persistent source of tension in Indonesia's international relations. In 1990 the Indonesian Minister of Foreign Affairs, Ali Alatas, began discussions with Portugal, through the office of the UN Secretary-General, in the hope of reaching a solution that would allow Indonesia to gain international recognition as the legitimate governing power in East Timor, possibly by finding some special constitutional status for the territory within Indonesia. These negotiations, however, were overtaken by political events within East Timor and also within Indonesia itself.

On 12 November 1991 Indonesian security forces fired on a demonstration at the funeral in Dili of a Fretilin sympathizer, killing between 100 and 180 people. A further 100 witnesses were said to have been summarily executed shortly afterwards. However, foreign news crews had been present, and film of the massacre was smuggled out of the country and widely broadcast. Although the Indonesian armed forces initially claimed that only 19 had died and that the troops involved had been 'provoked' by Fretilin supporters, intense international pressure led President Suharto to establish a separate inquiry, which found that 50 had died and 90 had 'disappeared' in the incident. This rare public criticism of the army led to the court martial and conviction of 10 military personnel and the dismissal of two senior army officers. Widespread criticism followed, however, concerning the disparity between the sentences given to protesters and to members of the armed forces.

In November 1992 the resistance suffered a major set-back when Xanana Gusmão was captured near Dili. In May 1993 he was found guilty of rebellion, conspiracy, attempting to establish a separate state and illegal possession of arms, and was condemned to life imprisonment. Following a plea for clemency, however, the sentence was commuted to 20 years by Suharto in August. In June 1997 the senior guerrilla leader, David Alex, was apprehended by Indonesian forces and died in a military hospital soon after his capture. The circumstances of his death were highly controversial, with the resistance claiming that Alex had been tortured or poisoned. In March 1998 Konis Santana, the military commander and acting leader of Fretilin, died as the result of an accident; he was subsequently replaced as acting leader by Taur Matan Ruak.

Despite military successes, a senior officer of the Indonesian armed forces acknowledged in early 1994 that Indonesia had failed to win the support of the East Timorese, and suggested that it would take another two generations until Indonesian rule could be accepted. Even this gloomy prognosis was made to seem optimistic by the growing religious dimension of the conflict. The predominantly Catholic East Timorese were deeply offended by incidents such as the mistreatment of nuns, the desecration of a church, and general anti-Catholic remarks by Muslim Indonesian officials, while Indonesians, reluctant to see genuine nationalism behind the Timorese resistance, became increasingly inclined to blame the territory's recalcitrance on Catholic separatism. These issues were complicated by the growing numbers of Muslim Indonesian residents of the province, who sometimes felt targeted by East Timorese demonstrators.

The UN sent a special investigator, Bacre Waly Ndiaye, to report on conditions in East Timor in July 1994; his conclusion that a climate of fear and suspicion dominated the territory subsequently encouraged the UN Secretary-General, Boutros Boutros-Ghali, to organize contacts and then talks between Timorese groups for and against integration with Indonesia, in the hope that these discussions might lead to a consensus on the best future for the territory. In mid-December 1998 the UN special envoy, Jamsheed Marker, visited East Timor and held talks with Xanana Gusmão and the acting Bishop of Dili, Carlos Ximenes Belo.

Within the EU, Portugal was the most vociferous in condemning Indonesia and lobbying for a UN-supervised referendum in East Timor; in July 1992 Portugal blocked an economic co-operation treaty between the Association of South East Asian Nations (ASEAN) and the EC on these grounds. Portugal also began proceedings against Australia in the International Court of Justice, seeking a ruling against the so-called Timor Gap Treaty, concluded between Australia and Indonesia in 1991. The Treaty provided a legal framework for petroleum and gas exploration in the maritime zone between Australia and East Timor, which had not been covered by earlier Indonesian-Australian treaties. Portugal claimed that the agreement infringed both Portuguese sovereignty and the East Timorese right to self-determination. (Only Australia was named because Indonesia does not come under the court's jurisdiction.) In a judgment brought in June 1995, however, the Court ruled that it could not exercise jurisdiction because the central issue was the legality of actions by Indonesia, which had refused to present a case. Formal contacts between the Indonesian and Portuguese Governments, especially over the status of Portuguese culture in East Timor, took place in 1995 and 1996 but were for the most part inconclusive. In January 1996 Portugal began direct satellite television broadcasts to East Timor.

In June 1995, March 1996 and October 1997, All-Inclusive Intra-East Timorese Dialogues (AIETD) were held in Austria under UN auspices. Participants pressed for better protection of human rights in the territory, and in October 1997 adopted the name Loro Sai (Sa'e) for East Timor. On repeated occasions after late 1995, groups of young East Timorese entered foreign embassies in Jakarta to request political asylum; most were allowed to leave Indonesia. International awareness of East Timor was heightened in October 1996 when Bishop Carlos Ximenes Belo and resistance leader José Ramos Horta were jointly awarded the Nobel Peace Prize. The award especially enhanced Ramos Horta's campaign to seek international support for East Timorese self-determination, but there was little diplomatic movement until July 1997 when, with the apparent approval of President Suharto, President Nelson Mandela of South Africa met the imprisoned Xanana Gusmão for informal discussions. Despite high international hopes and an apparently amicable meeting between Mandela and Suharto on the issue, however, the Mandela initiative ended without result.

The accession of Bucharuddin Jusuf (B.J.) Habibie to the presidency of Indonesia following the downfall of President Suharto in May 1998 immediately raised expectations that East Timor would be dealt with as part of a more general plan to address problems left by the outgoing regime. Demonstrations against Indonesian rule continued, and the new President publicly suggested both that the territory might be given a new 'special' status within Indonesia and that troops might be withdrawn. Xanana Gusmão, however, was not among the numerous political prisoners released by the new regime immediately after the fall of Suharto, and there was initially no indication that Indonesia was prepared to contemplate independence for East Timor. In July speculation that the territory's status might be altered in the near future led thousands of non-East Timorese to flee to neighbouring East Nusa Tenggara province. At the end of the same month, the withdrawal from East Timor of hundreds of Indonesian troops began. In early August it was announced that Indonesia and Portugal had agreed to hold discussions on the possibility of 'wide-ranging' autonomy for the province.

On 27 January 1999, however, Indonesia surprised observers by announcing that, if East Timor rejected the autonomy programme that was being negotiated, it would consider allowing the province to become independent. Although the Indonesian Government was initially determined that the decision on the future of East Timor should not be reached on the basis of a referendum, it soon agreed to a UN-supervised poll in which all East Timorese would vote on whether to accept the autonomy proposals offered or to opt for independence, and signed an agreement with Portugal to this effect on 5 May, with the poll scheduled to be held on 8 August. Few observers had previously imagined that such a concession would be made, particularly since the Indonesian military was believed to view the relinquishing of East Timor as having dangerous implications for overall national security and as an insult to army prestige. However, the Indonesian Armed Forces commander, Gen. Wiranto, was reportedly receptive to arguments that the continued garrisoning of East Timor would weaken the army's capacity to maintain order elsewhere in the archipelago; some Muslim leaders were also reported to favour the removal of East Timor's predominantly Catholic population from the Indonesian body politic. Although all Indonesians resident in East Timor were to be permitted to vote in the poll, non-Timorese citizens constituted only a small minority of the population of 830,000 and since Timorese living in exile were also to be allowed to participate, a victory for the supporters of independence appeared likely. However, a virulent campaign of violence and intimidation waged by a number of anti-independence militia groups based within the territory threatened proceedings and appeared to cast some doubt on the certainty of a vote in favour of independence. The militia were accused of carrying out summary killings, kidnappings, looting, harassment and the forced recruitment of young East Timorese in order to sabotage the poll. Furthermore, it emerged that the Indonesian military itself was supporting, encouraging and training a number of the militias.

The violence continued to escalate throughout April and May 1999. In April anti-independence militia members shot and hacked to death 57 people in a churchyard in the town of Liquiça; further massacres were reported to have occurred in other areas of the territory, including Dili. Also in April Xanana Gusmão (who in February had been moved from Cipinang prison in Jakarta to serve out the remainder of his 20-year sentence under effective house arrest in the capital) abruptly reversed his previous position on the conflict in response to increasing violence by anti-independence militias and urged guerrilla fighters in Falintil (the military wing of Fretilin) to resume their struggle. The escalating violence in the territory, together with logistical difficulties, led the UN to postpone the referendum to 21 August and then to 30 August. On 18 June the rival pro-independence and integrationist factions signed a peace accord urging a cease-fire and disarmament in advance of the scheduled referendum.

Despite the continuing intimidation and violence, the referendum proceeded on 30 August 1999. About 98.5% of the electorate participated in the poll, which resulted in an overwhelming rejection, by 78.5% of voters, of autonomy proposals and an endorsement of independence for East Timor. The announcement of the result, however, precipitated a rapid descent into anarchy. As pro-Jakarta militias embarked upon a campaign of murder and destruction, which many observers believed to be premeditated, hundreds of civilians were killed, thousands were forced to flee their homes, and many buildings were destroyed in arson attacks. Anti-independence activists stormed the residence of the Nobel laureate, Bishop Carlos

Ximenes Belo, evicting at gunpoint some 6,000 refugees who had sought shelter in the compound, and then burned down the home of the bishop. Bishop Ximenes Belo was evacuated to Australia, while Xanana Gusmão took refuge in the British embassy in Jakarta, following his release from house arrest. Thousands of terrified civilians besieged the UN compound in Dili, the premises of other international agencies, churches and police stations in a desperate search for protection from the indiscriminate attacks of the militias.

On 7 September 1999 martial law was declared in the territory, and a curfew was imposed. The violence continued unabated, however, and in mid-September, with international concern rising, the Indonesian Government yielded to pressure and agreed to permit the deployment of a multinational peace-keeping force. Following a visit to Jakarta by the UN High Commissioner for Human Rights, Mary Robinson, the Indonesian President also agreed to the holding of an international inquiry into whether the country's army was responsible for the perpetration of the atrocities. As the massacre of innocent civilians continued, thousands of refugees were airlifted to safety in northern Australia, along with remaining employees of the UN (many local staff members of the UN Mission in East Timor (UNAMET) having been among the victims of the violence). Meanwhile, aid agencies warned that as many as 300,000 East Timorese people faced starvation if humanitarian assistance were not urgently provided: in East Timor itself the number of displaced persons was estimated at 200,000, many of whom were in hiding in the mountains, while a further 100,000 were believed to have been driven into neighbouring West Timor, where their fate was unknown.

The first contingent of several thousand peace-keeping troops, forming the International Force for East Timor (Interfet), landed in the territory on 20 September 1999. Led by Australia, which committed 4,500 troops, the force gradually restored order. Other substantial contributions to the operation were made by the Philippines and Thailand, each of which provided 1,000 soldiers. A week later the Indonesian armed forces formally relinquished responsibility for security to the multinational force. At the end of October, after 24 years as an occupying force, the last Indonesian soldiers left East Timor. Amid scenes of jubilation in Dili, Xanana Gusmão, who had recently returned to his homeland, was able personally to witness the Indonesian commanders' final departure.

UNTAET ADMINISTRATION

On 19 October 1999 the result of the referendum was ratified by the Indonesian legislature, thus permitting East Timor's accession to independence to proceed. Shortly thereafter, on 25 October, the UN Security Council established the United Nations Transitional Administration in East Timor (UNTAET) as an integrated peace-keeping operation fully responsible for the administration of East Timor during its transition to independence. UNTAET, with an initial mandate extending until 31 January 2001, was to exercise all judicial and executive authority in East Timor, to undertake the establishment and training of a new police force, and to assume responsibility for the co-ordination and provision of humanitarian assistance and emergency rehabilitation; Interfet was scheduled to be replaced as soon as possible by UNTAET's military component. Meanwhile, the UN also began a large-scale emergency humanitarian relief effort. The UN administration in East Timor faced two major areas of difficulty in the months following the referendum, however. First, in an already poverty-stricken territory, the restoration of basic services after the major destruction of infrastructure during the violence of September 1999 proved to be extremely difficult. Because of the large-scale destruction of houses, many people displaced in the violence were unable to return to their homes. The Indonesian professionals who had provided medical, agricultural, educational and technical services had all fled by the time the UN took control of East Timor, and foreign aid workers were not numerous enough adequately to replace them. In addition, although development aid worth US $523m. had been promised to East Timor by various sources in December 1999, by March 2000 only US $22m. had actually been provided. While construction work supplied some employment opportunities, there was little activity in other areas of the economy, and some sources estimated the unemployment rate in the territory to be as high as 80%. Because the Indonesian rupiah (which was itself extremely unstable in the late 1990s) remained the legal currency in the territory, East Timor's economy continued to be adversely affected by fluctuations in the Indonesian economy. Crime rates also increased, but could not be dealt with effectively because of the lack of any proper judicial system and prisons. In May 2000 only 700 of a total 1,610 international police officers promised for the civilian police force (CivPol) established by the UN had been deployed in the territory.

The second major area of difficulty faced by the UN administration concerned the various conflicts that emerged in East Timorese society following the referendum, as a consequence of the previous 25 years of Indonesian occupation and the violence of 1999. In particular, there were conflicts over the ownership of land that had changed hands as a result of political pressures, and tensions surrounding the issue of whether skilled East Timorese who had co-operated with the Indonesian authorities should be placed in positions of political responsibility in the newly-independent East Timor. Although Xanana Gusmão urged the national reconciliation of all East Timorese, tensions were often acute at local level, especially when alleged East Timorese members of pro-Indonesia militia groups returned home. There was considerable discussion over whether the reconciliation of the East Timorese people would be best served by placing militia leaders on trial, by announcing a general amnesty for those involved in the violence, or by installing some form of 'truth and reconciliation commission' as in South Africa.

Following his popularly acclaimed return to Dili in October, Xanana Gusmão met the UNTAET Transitional Administrator, Sérgio Vieira de Mello, in November, and reportedly communicated the concerns of local East Timorese organizations that they were being marginalized by UNTAET officials. In late November he visited Jakarta in order to establish relations with the Indonesian Government, and in early December he visited Australia, where he met with representatives of the Australian Government to discuss the Timor Gap Treaty. A memorandum outlining an agreement temporarily to preserve the provisions of the original Timor Gap Treaty was signed in February 2000 by the Australian Government and East Timor's UN administrators to enable the exploitation of resources in the area to continue; Indonesia had ceased to be party to the original Treaty when it relinquished control of East Timor in October 1999. In May 2000 Australia announced that it was willing to consider the further renegotiation of the treaty, possibly with a view to conceding rights to a larger share of the area's resources to East Timor.

On 1 December 1999 José Ramos Horta returned to East Timor after 24 years of exile. Ramos Horta, who commanded much popular support, urged the East Timorese people to show forgiveness towards their former oppressors and called for reconciliation between Indonesia and East Timor. On 2 December UNTAET established a 15-member National Consultative Council (NCC), comprising representatives of UNTAET itself, the National Council of Timorese Resistance (CNRT, the nationalist 'umbrella' organization including Fretilin), the Catholic church and groups that had formerly supported integration with Indonesia. The NCC's mandate was both to monitor the UNTAET administration and to advise on preparations for full independence. The NCC decided that Portuguese, rather than English, Bahasa Indonesia or the indigenous lingua franca, Tetum, would become the national language. However, other key issues such as how the East Timorese armed forces should be constructed, and the nature of the future electoral system, remained undecided. On 23 February 2000 the transfer of command of military operations in East Timor from Interfet to the UNTAET peace-keeping force was completed. The UNTAET force included contingents supplied by Australia, Bangladesh, Brazil, Canada, Fiji, Ireland, Jordan, Kenya, the Republic of Korea, Malaysia, New Zealand, Pakistan, the Philippines and Portugal.

In late January 2000 a panel appointed by the Indonesian Government to investigate human rights abuses in East Timor delivered its report to the Indonesian Attorney-General. The panel reportedly named 24 individuals whom it recommended should be prosecuted for their alleged involvement in violations of human rights in the territory. One of those named was the former Minister of Defence and Security and Commander-in-Chief of the Indonesian armed forces, Gen. Wiranto, who had since been appointed Co-ordinating Minister for Politics and Security in the Indonesian Government; also named were a number of senior military officers, as well as leaders of the pro-Jakarta militias responsible for the extreme violence perpetrated during the period following the referendum. However, pro-independence leaders in East Timor strongly criticized the report as inadequate. Also in late January the International Commission of Inquiry in East Timor recommended that the UN establish an independent international body to investigate allegations of human rights violations in East Timor, and an international tribunal to deal with the cases of those accused by the investigators. In February the recently-appointed President of Indonesia, Abdurrahman Wahid, visited East Timor and publicly apologized for the atrocities committed by the Indonesian armed forces during the Republic's occupation of the territory; during his visit Wahid laid wreaths at Dili's Santa Cruz cemetery—the site of the 1991 Dili massacre—and at a cemetery containing the graves of members of the Indonesian armed forces. Also in February 2000 Wahid reaffirmed the commitment of the Indonesian Government to the prosecution of any individuals implicated in the violation of human rights in East Timor. In the same month Wahid suspended Gen. Wiranto from the Indonesian Government. The UN Secretary-General, Kofi Annan, made an official visit to East Timor in mid-February, during which he pledged that investigations into violations of human rights in the territory would be carried out. The President of Portugal, Dr Jorge Sampaio, also made a three-day official visit to East Timor in that month, during which he expressed the solidarity of the people of Portugal with the East Timorese.

A number of mass graves containing the bodies of suspected victims of the violence perpetrated by the anti-independence militias both before and after the holding of the referendum in August 1999 were discovered in East Timor (including two in the Oecusse enclave) in late 1999 and early 2000. In early December 1999 Sonia Picado Sotela, the Chair of the International Commission of Inquiry in East Timor, confirmed that the team of UN investigators had discovered evidence of 'systematic killing'. The UN announced in March 2000 that at least 627 East Timorese had been killed in the violence that followed the referendum, although this estimate was likely to increase as investigations continued. By May 2000 approximately 161,000 East Timorese refugees had returned to the territory under official auspices, leaving about 150,000 in 185 camps in Indonesian-controlled West Timor. Although there were fears that these camps were dominated by pro-Indonesia militias who might use them as a base for attacks on East Timor, UNTAET was reluctant to press for the refugees' immediate return because of a lack of facilities to house and feed them. In September 2000 the office of the United Nations High Commissioner for Refugees (UNHCR) temporarily suspended its relief operations in West Timor following the brutal murder of three of the organization's representatives in the region by pro-Indonesia militia members. During early 2001 the repatriation of refugees resumed, in order to enable people to register to vote in the Constituent Assembly elections scheduled for August. In July the Indonesian authorities formally asked all remaining refugee families to choose between repatriation and resettlement elsewhere in Indonesia. Only 1.1%, representing 1,250 people, chose to return to East Timor. Some observers attributed this figure to intimidation in the camps and to reports of the harassment of returnees in East Timor, but others pointed out that most of those who wished to return had probably already done so.

On 5 April 2000 UNTAET signed an agreement with the Indonesian Government relating to Indonesia's co-operation in efforts to resolve judicial and human rights issues. The agreement allowed for the extradition of Indonesians to East Timor for trial on charges relating to the violence of 1999. Relations between East Timor and Indonesia remained tense, however. In July a 17-member team from the Indonesian Attorney-General's Office visited East Timor to investigate a limited number of cases of human rights violations relating to the violence that occurred in East Timor in 1999. In August 2000, however, an amendment to Indonesia's Constitution, introduced in the closing stages of the annual session of the country's principal legislative body, the Majelis Permusyawaratan Rakyat, appeared to contradict the assurances previously made to the international community by President Wahid concerning Indonesia's ability to conduct its own independent investigation into atrocities committed in East Timor by members of the country's armed forces. The amendment excluded military personnel from retroactive prosecution and (despite the suggestion of senior Indonesian legislators that the amendment would probably not apply to crimes such as genocide, war crimes and terrorism) was perceived by many international observers as a serious threat to the possibility of the prosecution of members of the Indonesian military believed responsible for recent human rights violations in East Timor. After the murder of the three UNHCR aid workers in West Timor, Indonesia agreed in October 2000 to disarm militias still active in its territory, but only a few hundred antiquated weapons were turned in. In the same month, moreover, Indonesia formally refused to extradite the militia leader, Eurico Guterres, accused of playing a leading role in the Liquiça massacre, promising that he would be tried under Indonesian law. After a three-month trial in early 2001 Guterres was finally convicted of weapons offences and sentenced to six months' imprisonment. In view of the time already spent in custody, however, he was released after serving only 23 days.

In June 2000 an agreement was reached between UNTAET and East Timorese leaders on the formation of a new transitional coalition Government, in which the two sides were to share political responsibility. The Cabinet of the new transitional Government, which was formally appointed on 15 July and met for the first time on 17 July, initially included four East Timorese cabinet ministers: João Carrascalão, President of the UDT and a Vice-President of the CNRT, was allocated responsibility for infrastructure; Mari Alkatiri, Secretary-General of Fretilin, was appointed Minister for Economic Affairs; Father Filomeno Jacob was appointed to oversee social affairs; and Ana Pessôa was placed in charge of internal administration. The new Cabinet also included four international representatives: Jean-Christian Cady, the UNTAET Deputy Special Representative of the Secretary General for Governance and Public Administration, was allocated responsibility for the police and emergency services, while the three remaining non-East Timorese cabinet members were to be responsible for the judicial affairs, finance and political affairs portfolios. Mariano Lopes da Cruz, an East Timorese national, was appointed as Inspector-General. It was reported that Xanana Gusmão, whilst having no formal position in the new Government, was to be consulted informally by Sérgio Vieira de Mello—who was to retain ultimate control over the approval of any draft legislation proposed to the Cabinet—with respect to all political decisions. On 14 July UNTAET approved the establishment of a 'National Council'—which consisted of 33 East Timorese representatives from the political, religious and private sectors—to advise the new Cabinet. The current NCC was to be dissolved at the first session of the new Council. On 20 October, however, the composition of an expanded, 36-member National Council was announced; the new East Timor National Council was to replace the 15-member NCC, which held its last meeting on that day. On 23 October Xanana Gusmão was elected leader of the new National Council. Earlier the same month, José Ramos Horta was appointed to the Cabinet of the transitional Government as Minister of Foreign Affairs, increasing the number of ministers in the Cabinet to nine.

Both Ramos Horta and Xanana Gusmão stressed their commitment to good relations with Indonesia, downplaying the need to prosecute Indonesian military commanders for their role in the violence and refusing to support the independence movements in the Indonesian provinces of Aceh and Irian Jaya (now Papua). In March 2000 Indonesia agreed to allow a land corridor to link the enclave of Oecusse to the rest of East Timor. In April 2001 East Timor and Indonesia reached an agreement on maintaining border security, and in April 2002 the two sides began a formal border demarcation survey. As interim Minister for Economic Affairs, Mari Alkatiri renegotiated the Timor Gap Treaty with Australia. In July 2001 the two sides reached the Timor Sea Arrangement, under which production from the so-called Joint Petroleum Development Area in the Timor Sea (formal ownership of which was still undecided) was to be divided 90:10 between East Timor and Australia. Although this arrangement appeared to favour East Timor, and was presented as a future economic mainstay for the new country, some observers argued that most of the indirect benefits of the Arrangement would flow to Australia.

On 20 August 2000, meanwhile, Xanana Gusmão retired as the Military Commander of Falintil to concentrate on his political role in the process of guiding East Timor towards full independence in advance of the general election, subsequently scheduled for August 2001. Xanana Gusmão relinquished control of the guerrilla army to his deputy, Taur Matan Ruak. Falintil was formally disbanded on 1 February 2001. Some 650 of its members were recruited into the newly-formed East Timor Defence Force (ETDF) and given immediate training as regular troops. The first of these trainees graduated in June, and Taur Matan Ruak was sworn in as Brigadier-General and commander of the ETDF. The remainder of Falintil was demobilized.

Although there was a widespread feeling that only Xanana Gusmão had public support for the future post of President of East Timor, he himself repeatedly said that he would not be a candidate, and on 28 March 2001 he resigned as chair of the National Council. In the vote for Gusmão's successor on 9 April, José Ramos Horta (reportedly supported by UNTAET) was defeated by Manuel Carrascalão, who criticized UNTAET for what he described as 'colonialist' practices. In August, after all the newly-registered political parties declared Xanana Gusmão to be their preferred candidate and also in response to the encouragement of the international community, he announced that he would in fact stand at the presidential election, scheduled for 2002.

On 4 July 2001 the 16 parties that had registered for the elections agreed on a National Unity Pact, which included a promise of mutual respect during the campaign and to honour the election results. Approximately 380,000 East Timorese were eligible to vote for the 88 members of a Constituent Assembly (13 of them chosen as district representatives, the rest by proportional representation). A transition period began on 15 July: the National Council was dissolved, members of the Transitional Cabinet who intended to play a political role resigned from their posts, and formal campaigning began. The Constituent Assembly was to draft a constitution for East Timor and was expected to complete its work before the expiry of the UN mandate on 31 January 2002. Sérgio Vieira de Mello promised that there would a gradual rather than an abrupt withdrawal of UN support.

At the election for the Constituent Assembly, conducted on 30 August 2001, Fretilin garnered 57% of the votes cast and secured a total of 55 seats (including 12 of the 13 district seats). Of the remaining 33 seats, the Partido Democrático (PD) won seven, the Partido Social Democrata (PSD) six and the Associação Social-Democrata Timorense (ASDT) also six. The composition of the new Cabinet, headed by Mari Alkatiri, was announced in September. Alkatiri, a member of East Timor's small Muslim community, who had lived in exile from 1975 to 1999, retained the portfolio of economic affairs, while José Ramos Horta continued as Minister of Foreign Affairs. Fretilin was allocated a total of nine cabinet posts. Two positions were occupied by PD members, with the remaining nine posts being assigned to various independents and experts.

The Constituent Assembly was initially expected to prepare East Timor's Constitution within 90 days, but the final document was not approved until 22 March 2002. The Constitution provided for parliamentary government with a five-year term and with a largely symbolic, but popularly-elected, President. A Standing Committee of Parliament was designated to act on behalf of the legislature when it was not in session. The assembly revived the name Democratic Republic of East Timor, used by the short-lived independent Fretilin Government in late 1975, and declared 28 November 1975 as the date of independence. Although the Constitution provided for an elected parliament of 52–65 members, the 88-member Constituent Assembly declared itself the first National Parliament of the new republic. The Constitution designated Portuguese and Tetum as official languages and permitted East Timorese to hold dual citizenship. It also provided for the separation of church and state but specifically refrained from outlawing discrimination on the basis of sexual orientation, although many other forms of discrimination were banned.

In January 2002 a Reception, Truth and Reconciliation Commission was established with a two-year mandate to address the difficult problem of reconciling those responsible for violence in the period from April 1974 to October 1999 with their victims and their victims' families. The aims of the commission were both to describe, acknowledge and record past human rights abuses along the lines of the post-apartheid South African Truth and Reconciliation Commission, and to devise procedures that would facilitate reconciliation at village level. The commission was not empowered to provide amnesties, and serious cases were to be dealt with in the courts. In Jakarta, meanwhile, in March 2002 the former governor of East Timor, Abílio Soares, was placed on trial, charged with knowingly permitting the mass violence of August–September 1999. Altogether, 18 high-ranking Indonesian officials were indicted, including three generals. The trial of Maj.-Gen. Tono Suratman, military commander of the province at the time of the violence, began in July 2002. When convicted in mid-August, Abílio Soares received a prison sentence of only three years, provoking international condemnation. Furthermore, the acquittal of the former police chief of East Timor, Timbo Salaen, along with several other officers, prompted human rights groups to demand the UN's intervention in the process.

Xanana Gusmão's overwhelming popularity was confirmed on 14 April 2002, when he was elected President of East Timor with nearly 83% of the votes cast.The only other candidate was Francisco Xavier do Amaral, who had served as President briefly in 1975 and who had declared his candidacy only for the sake of providing an alternative.

East Timor finally achieved independence on 20 May 2002 in a ceremony attended by the UN Secretary-General, Kofi Annan, and the Indonesian President, Megawati Sukarnoputri. The celebrations were marred, however, by the unauthorized arrival of six Indonesian warships in Dili harbour just before the ceremony, ostensibly to guard Megawati. The incident was widely seen as an attempt by sections of the Indonesian military to create an incident that would force Megawati to abandon her visit. In the event, however, the warships withdrew peacefully. President Gusmão swore in a new 24-member cabinet headed by Prime Minister Mari Alkatiri, and the UNTAET administration formally came to an end.

INDEPENDENCE

Independent East Timor faced several political problems. The ownership of property emerged as a major issue, as confiscation and forced sales in the Indonesian period had often led to several people having rival but legitimate claims to the same property. The issue of law and order was a problem, both because high unemployment encouraged robbery and because demobilized freedom fighters who were not included in the defence force formed a significant social group that readily accused the Government of betraying the ideals of the independence struggle. Tension continued also over the issue of reconciliation, with President Gusmão favouring a general amnesty, while some in Fretilin sought a more punitive approach. Furthermore, many observers noted a sharp personal tension between President Gusmão and Prime Minister Alkatiri. Gusmão fulfilled his election promise to act as a 'watchdog' by accusing parliamentarians of 'irresponsibility' after two sessions of the legislature failed to achieve a quorum and by criticizing the Government for failing to uphold the editorial independence of the state-run radio and television stations.

The UN presence remained in independent East Timor on a reduced scale in the form of the United Nations Mission of Support in East Timor (UNMISET), headed by a former Indian diplomat, Kamalesh Sharma. UNMISET's mandate, due to last two years only, was to maintain continuity in policing, to pay particular attention to gender and HIV policies and to supervise a continuing military presence of about 5,000 international troops. East Timor became a member of the UN itself in September 2002.

In international affairs, the new Government's priority was to ensure good relations with Indonesia so that issues of trade, border demarcation, militia remnants in West Timor and access to the Oecusse enclave could be resolved easily. Accordingly,

East Timor repeatedly assured Indonesia that it did not support the separatist movements in Aceh, Papua and elsewhere. President Gusmão visited Jakarta in early July 2002, when he and President Megawati announced a plan to promote economic co-operation between the two countries. The two sides also agreed to establish a joint commission to consider Indonesian claims for compensation for assets lost in East Timor when the territory became independent, although East Timor foreshadowed that it might refer to Indonesian exploitation and destruction of property in resisting those claims. Indonesia's claims referred both to infrastructure, such as roads, which it constructed during its rule of the territory, and to the private property of Indonesian citizens abandoned in 1999. At the same time, therefore, the East Timor Government was keen to anchor the country more firmly in the broader region. It signalled that it would seek membership of ASEAN, although Singapore was reportedly opposed to the entry of another economically weak country to the association. East Timor sought good relations with the People's Republic of China, which had previously recognized it in 1975 and which was the first country to establish formal diplomatic relations in 2002.

Relations with Australia were made difficult by disagreement over the maritime boundaries in the Timor Sea. Although the new Government signed a treaty with Australia on independence day to ratify the arrangement for exploiting petroleum and gas in the Timor Gap, Prime Minister Mari Alkatiri announced at the same time that this treaty did not establish a maritime border and that East Timor would pursue its claim to a much larger proportion of the disputed area, including the whole of the lucrative Greater Sunrise oilfield. East Timor's claim was based partly on changes in the law of the sea that give the median line on the sea's surface (which favours East Timor) priority over submarine features (which favour Australia), and partly on the moral grounds that substantial oil revenues might be necessary if East Timor were to achieve sustained development. Australia rejected the East Timorese claim, influenced by fears that concessions to East Timor might call into question its long-standing maritime border with Indonesia. In March 2002 Australia had withdrawn from International Court of Justice jurisdiction over maritime borders.

Meanwhile, the future of an estimated 50,000 East Timorese still in refugee camps in West Timor remained unresolved. President Gusmão urged them to return to their homeland and Indonesia announced plans to close the remaining camps in August 2002, but many refugees were reluctant to move, in some cases fearing retribution for their alleged roles in the 1999 violence.

Economy

BROAD ECONOMIC TRENDS

The Portuguese Colonial Era

Until the early 1970s East Timor was a remote outpost of the Portuguese colonial empire. During the 400 years or so of Portuguese colonial rule, which began in the latter half of the 16th century, the territory was largely neglected, with little progress being recorded in terms of economic or social development. Even after a change in its official status to that of an 'overseas province' of Portugal after the Second World War, the territory fared little better, reflecting in part the relative economic backwardness and resource constraints of Portugal itself. The situation was exacerbated by the political upheavals of the early 1970s, both in East Timor itself and in the metropolitan centre, which led eventually to Indonesian military intervention in 1975 and the formal integration of East Timor by Indonesia as the country's 27th province in 1976.

Indonesian Administration

The period of Indonesian rule, which ended amid chaos, brutal violence and widespread destruction in September 1999, was one of undeniable economic progress in East Timor, albeit in the context of severe political and social repression. The resentments engendered among the East Timorese population as a result of the oppressive Indonesian rule were reinforced by a number of economic grievances. These included the large-scale immigration into the province from other parts of the Indonesian archipelago of traders and professionals who were perceived to have gained a disproportionate advantage from the improvement in East Timor's economic circumstances and to have deprived the local population of its fair share of the benefits of this development. This perception was heightened by the tight control that the Indonesian military and business interests close to former President Suharto of Indonesia soon established over the territory's principal resource, namely, its production of high-quality arabica coffee.

Indonesian rule over East Timor became increasingly untenable in the 1990s in the face of growing pressure, from both within East Timor and abroad, for Indonesia to permit the territory to exercise its right to self-determination. This pressure increased as Indonesia descended into political, social and economic instability in the aftermath of the financial crisis that afflicted much of South-East Asia during 1997–98. Bucharuddin Jusuf (B. J.) Habibie, appointed President of Indonesia in May 1998, was eventually forced to permit a referendum among the East Timorese population as to whether they would prefer their territory to become independent or to remain a province of Indonesia. This decision had profound implications for the economy of East Timor. Soon after the announcement of the forthcoming referendum, the Indonesian military and other conservative factions within the Indonesian political élite mobilized armed militia gangs in East Timor to promote the pro-Indonesia cause. When, despite the mounting coercion and intimidation exercised by these groups, more than 78% of the population of East Timor voted in a referendum held on 30 August 1999 to sever the territory's ties with Indonesia, the response of these groups was uncompromising. In the killing and destruction that followed the announcement of the result of the referendum, they razed much of East Timor to the ground, completely decimating the territory's already weak economic infrastructure. At the same time, many of the non-indigenous professionals, tradesmen and administrators fled the territory, further undermining its capacity for recovery.

UN Transitional Administration

The havoc wreaked by the 'scorched earth' policy pursued by the pro-Indonesia militias in East Timor and their patrons outside the territory following the referendum of 1999 prompted a forceful international reaction. The UN Security Council subsequently agreed to the urgent dispatch of an Australian-led international peace-keeping force, Interfet, which entered East Timor in September 1999. By the time this intervention force entered East Timor and began to restore law and order, the territory's economy, which was already one of the poorest in Asia in both economic and social terms, had been almost completely devastated. According to the UN, at least 627 people were killed in the violence that followed the referendum, and many of the territory's fixed assets, including buildings, installations and equipment, had been destroyed, mostly by arson. The territory's infrastructural facilities were also targeted with particular vehemence.

Inevitably, this rampage prompted a sharp decline in all of East Timor's principal economic and social indicators, as exemplified by a World Bank estimate that GDP per caput had decreased by almost 50% in the weeks following the referendum. A subsequent report prepared by the UN and the World Bank pointed out that with a gross domestic product (GDP) per caput of US $424 in 1998, poverty rates had already been more than twice the average of those prevailing in Indonesia. East Timor thus had no effective economic reserves with which to counter the destruction of assets and livelihoods that followed the announcement of the referendum results in 1999.

Once Interfet had succeeded in restoring a degree of peace and law and order in East Timor, the responsibility for preparing the territory for independence fell to the United Nations Transitional Administration in East Timor (UNTAET), which was established in October 1999 by the UN Security Council. This task included rehabilitating the economic and institutional infrastructure, and laying the groundwork for the territory's sustainable development in the future.

The work of UNTAET was facilitated greatly by the compassion generated within the international donor community and by the extensive exposure given by the international media to the events surrounding the referendum on independence. Within two months of the landing of Interfet troops in Dili, the capital, a high-level meeting was called between the East Timorese national leadership and donor representatives in Tokyo in mid-December 1999, at which donors pledged a total of US $523m. for an ambitious relief and reconstruction programme for East Timor. This sum comprised US $157m. in support of an initial humanitarian relief programme and US $366m. in support of a longer-term programme to promote governance, administrative capacity-building and economic and social reconstruction.

The implementation of the humanitarian component of the programme had been largely completed by mid-2000, with the most pressing humanitarian needs having been met through relief operations undertaken by a variety of UN agencies and non-governmental organizations (NGOs). By the end of April 2000 these measures had resulted in the distribution of more than 35,000 tons of rice, 9,700 shelter kits and 50,000 sheets of roofing material for use as emergency shelter. The World Health Organization and the United Nations Population Fund had by this time also issued sufficient medical supplies and reproductive health kits to cover the needs of the local population.

With regard to the longer-term reconstruction component of the programme, the initial focus of operations following the Tokyo meeting was the establishment of a transitional administration capable of supporting the implementation of the programme. UNTAET was granted wide-ranging legislative and executive powers in support of its mandate to develop basic national institutions and to recruit, train and empower a corps of East Timorese civil servants to manage these institutions. To this end, UNTAET co-operated closely with the East Timorese leadership through the National Council of Timorese Resistance (more commonly known by its Portuguese acronym, CNRT) and the National Consultative Council (NCC). In its attempts to develop a suitable civil service infrastructure, however, UNTAET was faced with a disappointingly small pool of qualified personnel from which to draw its recruits. This was due partly to the fact that much of the territory's provincial civil service during the era of Indonesian rule had been staffed by non-East Timorese, and partly to the fact that many of the East Timorese who had worked for the Indonesian civil service had either fled the territory following the violence in 1999 or were distrusted by the new administration. To overcome this difficulty and provide a facility for the development of East Timor's future administrators, UNTAET opened a Civil Service Academy in May 2000.

The mandate of UNTAET ended with East Timor's transition to independence on 20 May 2002. Notwithstanding the many challenges it faced, the UN administration was widely acknowledged to have achieved its objectives with a relatively high degree of success. Apart from its efforts in the restoration of governance structures, UNTAET had succeeded in rehabilitating much of the territory's devastated physical and social infrastructure by the end of its mandate, and set the scene for a broader economic recovery. This success was underlined by an IMF report issued in June 2002, which noted that economic conditions in East Timor had improved steadily since mid-2000, with real GDP growth rates of 15% and 18% having been recorded in 2000 and 2001, respectively, as against a contraction of 34% in 1999. As a result, overall output had been restored to near pre-crisis levels by mid-2002.

Post-independence Development Strategy

By the latter half of 2001 the progress in post-conflict rehabilitation and the approaching deadline for the transfer of authority to an independent government prompted UNTAET and the newly installed Second Transitional Government to turn their attention to issues of longer-term economic development. A Planning Commission was therefore established to oversee the preparation of the National Development Plan shortly after the swearing-in of the new Council of Ministers on 20 September 2001. The plan was drafted on the basis of an exhaustive countrywide consultative process in order to engage the people of East Timor as fully as possible. To heighten the sense of public ownership of this plan, a popular version entitled *East Timor to 2020: Our Nation, Our Future* was issued on 11 May 2002 and distributed to every household in East Timor with a view to promoting a common national understanding of the respective roles and responsibilities of the Government and the community in achieving economic growth and development. The plan came into operation following East Timor's independence on 20 May 2002, and is intended to be implemented on a rolling basis consistent with the country's annual budgets.

The principal objectives of the National Development Plan are to reduce poverty and promote economic growth. It urges a combination of capacity-building measures (especially in the early implementation phases); co-ordinated efforts by various developmental participants (government, civil society, community organizations and NGOs) to reduce poverty; and a number of sector-specific strategies to overcome the impediments to poverty reduction and economic development. To achieve these goals, the plan proposes a phased approach: In the short term, priority will continue to be given to the building of an appropriate legislative framework and institutional capacities, as well as the further development of infrastructure, education and health; over the longer term, the foundations laid by these efforts will be built upon to achieve sustainable development funded by the anticipated increase in oil and gas revenues.

NATURAL AND HUMAN RESOURCES

East Timor has a total area of 14,609 sq km, including the coastal enclave of Oecusse (Oekussi) in the western half of the island of Timor, which is surrounded on all its land frontiers by Indonesian territory. The country has a rugged, mountainous terrain, relatively poor soils and a comparatively dry climate, which restricts its agricultural potential. It also has very limited onshore mineral deposits, although there are indications of significant crude petroleum reserves in the waters off its southern coasts.

The population of East Timor is relatively small, albeit not precisely quantifiable. Estimates prepared during the Portuguese era, which were based on numbers submitted to the colonial authorities by *liurai* (village headmen), but which are acknowledged to be unreliable, indicated a total population of 624,564 in 1973. The subsequent civil war and Indonesian military intervention took a heavy toll on the territory's population, both directly, through acts of war, and indirectly, through the hunger and disease that ensued. The first formal population census under Indonesian rule, conducted in 1980, thus showed a total population of 555,350. By the time of the next census in 1990 this number had risen to 747,750, and an inter-censal survey carried out in 1995 suggested a further increase in the population to 843,100. This latter overall figure included a substantial, but unknown, number of non-indigenous people, however, many of whom left East Timor in the unrest preceding and following the referendum on independence held in August 1999, together with some 213,000 East Timorese who had fled the violence to Indonesian-governed West Timor. The most widely-accepted estimates suggested that in mid-2002 the country had an overall population of some 750,000, with some 50,000 East Timorese still living as refugees in West Timor. The number of these refugees returning to East Timor accelerated particularly rapidly from the beginning of 2002 onwards, as the political and economic situation in East Timor stabilized and the Indonesian Government ceased food distributions to the refugee camps. In an attempt to resolve the situation, the Government of East Timor agreed to offer repatriation assistance to the remaining refugees until the end of August 2002.

AGRICULTURE

Agriculture forms the mainstay of the East Timorese economy, and accounts for the employment of more than 70% of the territory's labour force. The territory has historically produced a variety of food and commercial crops, and also has a history of animal husbandry and fisheries. Like the rest of the economy, however, the agricultural sector suffered serious dislocations as a result of the upheavals that followed the territory's vote for independence from Indonesia in 1999. A major reconstruction effort was therefore introduced by UNTAET, with financial support from the World Bank, for the agricultural sector. This effort comprised both a rapid-delivery component to facilitate the recovery of agricultural production levels, and a number of longer-term measures to ensure the sustained growth of the sector. To enable the achievement of its more immediate goal, the programme provided for the restoration of productive assets to farmers; the community-based repair of rural feeder roads and small irrigation systems; the provision of agricultural credits; the establishment of local radio services to provide information to farmers; and the development of five pilot agricultural service centres managed by private entrepreneurs or NGOs to provide support services to farmers. With regard to the longer-term objectives of the programme, major irrigation rehabilitation works and a substantial initiative to support coffee production and marketing were initiated. In addition, measures were also implemented to initiate watershed management and reafforestation measures, and to help local fishermen to restore their fishing capacity. While these measures had resulted in the recovery of both agricultural and fisheries production to pre-1999 levels by mid-2002, all the available evidence suggested that the post-independence Government would continue to place a high degree of emphasis on the development of the agricultural sector. This was highlighted in the National Development Plan, which stated that 'in the medium-term the agricultural sector, more than most, provides opportunities for economic growth, exports, employment and improvements in social welfare throughout East Timor'.

Food Crops

The principal food crops grown in the territory comprise maize (which is the chief staple of the local population) and rice, although small quantities of such other staples as cassava, sweet potatoes and soybeans are also produced in the territory. Data published by the Indonesian Central Statistical Agency suggested that the territory produced 36,848 tons of rice in 1998. This marked a significant increase over the corresponding figure of 8,005 tons in 1976, by which time the political unrest of the preceding years had resulted in food crop production falling to approximately one quarter of the level achieved in 1970 (which itself represented the peak level achieved in food crop production during the colonial period). The increase in production between 1976 and 1998 was attributable mainly to the extensive rehabilitation and expansion of irrigation systems. Meanwhile, production data for non-rice staples in 1998 indicated an output of 58,857 tons of maize, 32,092 tons of cassava, 11,549 tons of sweet potatoes, and 672 tons of soybeans.

The production of food crops was severely disrupted by the political upheavals and unrest of 1999, as a result of which UNTAET estimated that output of both rice and maize had declined to some 70% of pre-conflict levels in 2000. This decrease was attributed to a combination of factors, including a reduction in the planted area and dislocation of rural labour owing to the violence linked to the independence ballot, the destruction of irrigation schemes, and the loss of services from government and private-sector suppliers. To overcome these difficulties UNTAET accorded high priority to supporting a recovery in food crop production and introduced a number of programmes to bring more land under cultivation and to increase yields. These included restitution of farming household assets, rehabilitation of rural feeder roads and irrigation systems, and fertilizer demonstrations. By early 2002 these programmmes had enabled UNTAET to meet its ambitious target of increasing food production to 80%–120% of 1997 levels.

Cash Crops

The main commercial crop grown in East Timor is coffee, although small plantations of coconut, cloves and cocoa have also been established. In addition to the low-value robusta coffees grown in most of Indonesia, East Timor also produces substantial quantities of the high value arabica variety in the territory's higher elevations. East Timor's coffee plantations were originally established during the Portuguese colonial era, and during this period accounted for some 90% of the territory's export earnings. Production declined sharply in the transitional period of the mid-1970s as a result of the departure of Portuguese agricultural experts and the virtual abandonment of the coffee plantations. This led to a major replanting effort being initiated by the Indonesian authorities, with more than 1m. arabica and robusta seedlings being planted in the first four years of Indonesian rule. By 1994 coffee production had reached almost 8,800 tons, although it declined to less than 5,000 tons in 1997–98 as a result of the economic crisis affecting Indonesia and the effects of the drought caused by the weather phenomenon known as El Niño. In 1999 coffee production increased to around 10,000 tons, and much of the crop survived the destruction that followed the referendum.

One important feature of the East Timorese coffee industry during the era of Indonesian rule was the controversial marketing system employed by the Indonesian authorities: soon after the territory was integrated into Indonesia, a monopoly was established over the coffee market by PT Denok, a company associated with the Indonesian military, through the seizure of Portuguese-era coffee plantations and the forced sale of coffee by smallholders to PT Denok at artificially low prices. As a result of pressure from the US Government, this monopoly began to disintegrate in the mid-1990s, at which time a new system was put in place linking the Indonesian system of rural co-operatives to the US National Co-operative Business Association (NCBA) and providing local smallholders with significantly higher prices for their output. As a result of this arrangement, which remained in place even after the extensive political changes of 1999, the NCBA accounted for some 25% of the sale of East Timorese coffee. Another major purchaser of East Timorese coffee was the US-based Starbucks Corporation, cited in the media as one of East Timor's best clients.

One serious difficulty faced by East Timorese coffee producers as a result of the violence of 1999 was that all of the 'wet processing' facilities used for the processing of high-grade arabica coffee were badly damaged and inoperable, meaning that farmers were forced to 'dry-process' their coffee, which then fetched a much lower price. Although the coffee sector consequently did not escape entirely the widespread destruction of 1999, it remains in relatively good condition and is seen by both UNTAET and the national leadership of East Timor as one of the prime sources of potential future export earnings and fiscal revenues. The industry has also benefited from the fact that local trees have never been treated with pesticides or chemicals, thus allowing the coffee to gain organic certification and increasing its value on the environmentally-conscious Western markets. By the end of 2000 all of East Timor's 19 coffee-producing sub-districts had been declared organic zones. Some estimates suggested that the value of the country's coffee exports could rise to US $50m. per year in the near future, thus equivalent to almost one-half of its estimated GDP (of US $119m.) in 1999.

Apart from coffee, other important cash crops produced in East Timor include cloves, coconuts and cocoa. These were developed largely during the era of Indonesian rule in an effort to diversify East Timor's economic base away from its heavy dependence on coffee, which suffered sharp price fluctuations in the 1980s and early 1990s. Another cash crop developed under Indonesian rule was sugar cane, which is currently cultivated mainly by smallholders over an area of some 10,000 ha. In addition, small quantities of candlenut, coconut, Manila hemp and vanilla are also grown in East Timor. The National Development Plan provided for additional emphasis to be given to the cultivation of such cash crops as a source of employment and income creation in rural areas and of export earnings for the whole nation.

Animal Husbandry and Fisheries

Animal husbandry has traditionally played a significant role in the agricultural economy of East Timor, but was particularly badly affected by the political unrest of the mid-1970s. Concerted efforts made during the period of Indonesian rule to rebuild herds had a considerable impact, however, with the official statistics indicating that the total number of cattle in the territory more than doubled in the four years between 1978 and 1982. By the late 1980s the number of cattle in East Timor was officially estimated at approximately 63,600, with the number rising further to some 72,200 by the mid-1990s. The animal husbandry sector also suffered serious dislocations as a result of the violence that followed the independence ballot. UNTAET began to rehabilitate the sector through the restitution of livestock to poor farmers and the introduction of a wide-ranging livestock vaccination campaign in 2000.

The waters around East Timor have rich fisheries resources, which were largely neglected during Portuguese rule. Efforts to develop a viable commercial fishing industry during the period of Indonesian administration had a significant impact, however, and by the mid-1990s the territory produced more than 2m. tons of saltwater fish and 400 tons of freshwater fish per year. In 2000 the further development of the fisheries industry was widely perceived to represent one of the most promising sources of potential additional revenue. Draft strategic guidelines for the rehabilitation and development of the aquaculture and seafood industries were thus formulated in that year under the UNTAET administration, and subsistence fishing had recovered by 2002 with the assistance of a number of programmes administered by NGOs and the UN. The prospects for a commercialization of East Timor's fisheries were also being examined through a definition of the country's maritime boundaries with Indonesia and Australia, increased research into its offshore fish resources, training of industry personnel and the development of appropriate marketing networks. As a result of these measures, the National Development Plan proposed a 50% overall increase in production and a 25% increase in industry employment within five years.

Forestry

Although East Timor was officially reported to have a forested area of 170,484 ha in 1994, the forestry sector suffered from unsustainable land management and the clearing of land for agricultural use and fuel wood in the 1980s and 1990s, which has resulted in serious deforestation and associated soil degradation and erosion. Its principal products are such local timbers as cendana, eucalyptus, redwood and lontar palm. Sandalwood, which once covered many of the territory's mountains and hills, is viewed as another potentially important forestry crop, but is in need of extensive replanting. By 2000 this replanting had already been initiated, and an effort is being made to undertake a comprehensive inventory of East Timor's forestry resources and an analysis of their potential for development. In order to ensure the sustainable exploitation of these resources, the National Development Plan proposed the formulation of a Forestry Master Management Plan, and a number of specific action plans based on that master plan.

MINING

Onshore Resources

East Timor's main onshore mineral resource is high-grade, high-quality marble. Exploitation of this resource had already begun in the 1980s and 1990s, when marble was employed in the construction of many hotels, office buildings and shopping malls in the Indonesian capital, Jakarta. In addition, the country is also believed to have some reserves of silver and manganese.

Offshore Oil and Gas

The most notable mineral resources of East Timor are petroleum and natural gas, which are located mainly in the Timor Sea to the south of the country in the so-called 'Timor Gap' area between East Timor and Australia. In order to be able to proceed with the development of these resources, and despite the uncertainty surrounding the international status of these waters, the Governments of Australia and Indonesia signed a controversial petroleum production revenue-sharing agreement known as the Timor Gap Treaty in 1989. Under Australian pressure, this agreement implicitly demarcated the maritime border between the then Indonesian province of East Timor and Australia not along the median line between the two countries' coastlines, as provided for by the UN Convention on the Law of the Sea, but at the southern edge of the Timor Trough, an undersea trench lying considerably closer to Timor than to Australia, thereby giving Australia control over the larger share of the offshore petroleum and gas resources in that area. Operationally, the agreement provided for the establishment of a 'zone of co-operation' in the waters between East Timor and Australia, which was divided into three areas, and decreed that each country had the right to 90% of the petroleum revenues derived from the areas nearest to its own shores, with the other country having the right to the remaining 10%; in addition, both countries were to share equally the revenues derived from the central area known as 'zone of co-operation A' (ZOCA).

The signing of this agreement resulted in exploration and production concessions being awarded to a number of oil companies. Several of the fields covered by these concessions—the Elang, Kakatua and Kakatua North fields in the south-western corner of ZOCA—have already entered into production, with the first petroleum being extracted in July 1998. However, the royalties generated by these fields for the contracting states are still relatively small, at some US $2m.– $3m. Two much larger fields, Bayu-Undan lying 18 km to the south of the existing fields and Greater Sunrise lying partially within the north-eastern corner of ZOCA, remain to be developed. Bayu-Undan has estimated reserves of about 400m. barrels of natural gas condensate and other liquid hydrocarbons, and has the potential to generate tens of millions of US dollars in revenue, while Greater Sunrise has proved and probable recoverable reserves of some 8,400,000m. cu ft of natural gas and 320m. barrels of condensate.

Following the withdrawal of Indonesia from East Timor, the Indonesian Government acknowledged in October 1999 that it no longer retained any jurisdiction over the Timor Gap area. Negotiations were subsequently initiated involving UNTAET, Australia and the East Timorese national leadership on the amendment of the Timor Gap Treaty. Following extensive negotiations, provisional arrangements for the sharing of the hydrocarbon resources in the maritime border area between Australia and East Timor were concluded in July 2001, when a new Timor Sea Treaty was initialled by the Australian Government, UNTAET and a representative of the interim Government of East Timor. This agreement covers an area of 75,000 sq km between East Timor and Australia, which is now known as the Joint Petroleum Development Area (JPDA). Although the agreement ostensibly assigns 90% of the revenue from the area to East Timor and only 10% to Australia, it is widely acknowledged to be far less favourable to East Timor than these figures suggest because of a number of complex issues relating to the measurement of petroleum production, the definition of by-products, the taxation of the petroleum production and shipping activities, and the proposed siting of the Timor Sea natural gas processing industry in Darwin rather than in East Timor.

As this new agreement was negotiated by UNTAET on behalf of East Timor, it needed to be ratified by the new post-independence Government of East Timor. After tough negotiations with the Australian Government in the run-up to independence, the Second Transitional Government of East Timor established after the elections of August 2001 agreed to accept the Timor Sea Treaty, which was duly ratified shortly after the country gained sovereign independence in May 2002. In ratifying the treaty, however, the Government made it clear that it had done so without prejudice to its maritime claims, and in July 2002 both the National Parliament and the President of the newly independent country stressed their determination to seek a delineation of the maritime boundary between East Timor and Australia midway between the shorelines of the two countries. This would place the known Elang, Kakatua, Kakatua North, Bayu-Undan and Greater Sunrise petroleum and natural gas fields firmly within the territorial waters of East Timor, as they are located much closer to its shores than to those of Australia.

INFRASTRUCTURE

Transport and Communications

The transport and communications network established during the period of Portuguese rule was very limited, and was intended mainly to enable the colonial administration to achieve its tax-collection objectives and to facilitate the transport of the territory's coffee crop to external markets. The upgrading and expansion of these facilities became a major focus of government policy during the subsequent period of Indonesian administration, and considerable progress was achieved in this regard. Particularly significant results were recorded in the development of land transport services. Whereas only one paved road, 20 km in length and located in the capital, Dili, was built in East Timor during the era of Portuguese rule, by the mid-1990s the Indonesian Government had built more than 3,800 km of roads, including 428 km of paved highways, as well as 18 bridges. This achievement was accompanied by a sharp increase in the number of motor vehicles registered, as well as by the establishment of a number of bus routes linking East Timor's towns and villages. Progress was also made by the Indonesian Government in the development of East Timor's air transport infrastructure. In 1981 the construction of the Komoro airport in Dili was completed to complement the airport built at Baucau in the east of the territory. During Indonesian rule, these airports were served regularly by the two state-owned Indonesian airlines, PT Garuda Indonesia and PT Merpati Nusantara Airlines. East Timor was also connected to the rest of the Indonesian archipelago by regular scheduled passenger and cargo ship services.

East Timor's telecommunications system was also improved substantially under the Indonesian administration. Following the launching of the Palapa series of Indonesian telecommunications satellites from the mid-1970s, East Timor became linked through telephone and television circuits to all other Indonesian provinces and to the world beyond. To increase the efficiency of the telecommunications system, a new automatic telephone switching system was installed in Dili.

The transport and communications infrastructure was very badly damaged by the events of 1999. The road system fell into particularly serious disrepair, as the result of a combination of the impact of the post-referendum violence, the deceleration in repair and maintenance activities caused by the Indonesian economic crisis of 1997–98 and the subsequent wear imposed on the network by the heavy military vehicles of Interfet and the UNTAET peace-keeping force. Similarly, East Timor's ports and airports also suffered serious damage as a result of inadequate maintenance, the destruction of equipment and excessively heavy use in 1999/2000. High priority was therefore given to the restoration of the transport and communications infrastructure.

UNTAET launched a wide-ranging emergency rehabilitation programme soon after it assumed administrative control, and subsequently initiated a longer-term programme for the sustainable development of the sector. By the end of 2000 both the airport and the seaport of Dili had become operational, and significant progress had been made in road repairs and maintenance, especially with regard to the major arterial roads needed to ensure access to all of East Timor's important population centres. With these objectives achieved, UNTAET established comprehensive business plans for the aviation, ports and roads sectors by mid-2001, and also began the reconstruction of public buildings. Increasingly, moreover, it moved its rehabilitation efforts beyond the capital, Dili. Despite the progress made by UNTAET, it was widely acknowledged that much remained to be done, and the National Development Plan drafted by the new Government placed high priority on the restoration and/or establishment of required physical capabilities and public services.

SOCIAL DEVELOPMENT

Health

The healthcare situation in East Timor prior to the violence that followed the referendum in 1999 was poor, with key indicators of the population's overall state of health, such as life expectancy and infant mortality rates, showing that the territory lagged far behind Indonesia. At the time there were eight small district hospitals in the territory and one central referral hospital in Dili. The sector was managed by the Provincial Health Department, and the total health sector work-force numbered around 5,000 (including staff employed by the East Timor Provincial Health Department, staff directly employed by the Ministry of Health in Jakarta, and non-technical and administrative staff). In addition to the government-administered system, a loose network of 31 healthcare centres also existed, managed by various religious groups; these clinics provided basic curative care and some preventative services. There were also several private clinics and some Indonesian military health facilities.

Extensive destruction of health infrastructure by pro-Indonesia militias in 1999 caused the total breakdown of the healthcare system. The situation was exacerbated by the complete loss of all healthcare equipment and medication and by the departure of senior health staff from the central, district and sub-district levels of the healthcare system as a result of the violence, with a reported 130 of the territory's 160 doctors having left East Timor. Following Indonesia's withdrawal from East Timor in September 1999, immediate humanitarian assistance for health was provided by the International Committee of the Red Cross and various NGOs, supported by several UN agencies and, initially, some Interfet medical staff. Significant efforts were subsequently made to repair the damage inflicted during the period of post-referendum violence, with NGOs playing a particularly important role in this process. By June 2000 some 80 new health facilities had been established, supplemented by a number of mobile clinics. In addition, an operating Interim Health Authority was established in March 2000, while a training programme was initiated for district health officers and health laboratory services were also developed.

To speed up the recovery of the health services, a wide-ranging Health Sector Rehabilitation and Development Programme was launched in June 2000 by UNTAET, with financial support from the World Bank and a number of bilateral donors. This programme was expected to cost some US $38m. over a three-year period. It aimed to restore access to basic health services in the transitional period between the provision of humanitarian relief and the development of the health system, to begin the development of an effective health policy and health system, and to build local administrative capacities to implement and manage the health programme. By mid-2002 almost 90 community health centres had been established to provide basic services throughout the country, and a proposal had been submitted to the Cabinet for the rehabilitation/reconstruction of Dili National Hospital and five regional hospitals. Meanwhile, in February 2002 a new medical warehouse was established to supply medicines and other medical consumables to all districts of East Timor. The National Development Plan continued to give high priority to the health sector, with a special focus on primary health care, preventive medicine and the prevention of health hazards, and on reproductive health. Given the acute shortage of qualified East Timorese doctors, however, the health system appeared certain to remain dependent upon external assistance for some time to come.

Education

East Timor's education system had been developed to a certain extent under the Indonesian administration. Prior to the violence of 1999, there were 788 primary schools (including 140 private schools, most of which were administered by the Roman Catholic Church), 114 junior secondary schools, 37 senior secondary schools, and 17 vocational and technical schools. At the tertiary level, more than 1,500 East Timorese students were reported to have obtained university scholarships, mainly to the Indonesian universities of Malang, Jakarta and Denpasar. The University of East Timor was established in 1986. The rate of illiteracy in East Timor remained high during the period of Indonesian rule, however, at more than 50% in 1999, and the education provided by the system was often of poor quality, with technical education being particularly weak. Many teachers (the majority of whom, with the exception of teachers in the primary education sector, were non-East Timorese) were inadequately trained and poorly paid, and basic teaching equipment was also in short supply.

The education system was devastated by the extensive post-referendum violence. Approximately 95% of schools and other educational institutions were destroyed, and a large percentage (perhaps 70%–80%) of senior administrative staff and secondary school teachers was lost from the education system. The rehabilitation of the education system (to include the repair of classrooms, the supply of basic teaching and learning resources, and the establishment of a programme of teacher training) was therefore a priority concern of UNTAET. Soon after assuming control, the transitional administration developed a comprehensive three-stage School System Revitalization Programme (SSRP) with World Bank support to build upon the voluntarist measures already taken by local communities to revive the school system. The first stage of this programme, comprising a US $13.9m. Emergency School Readiness Project (ESRP), was launched in June 2000. It provided for the rehabilitation of 2,100 classrooms with the necessary furniture, books and other instructional materials, the building of new schools to replace those too badly damaged to be repaired, and measures to improve the quality of instruction. Subsequent stages of the SSRP would provide for further improvements to the school system in order to enhance the quality of education and attract the increased participation of parents, teachers and the broader community in the school improvement process.

At the tertiary level, the university was reopened in January 2001, with provisions being made for the enrolment of 4,500 students in degree programmes and 3,000 students in bridging courses. In addition, scholarships were provided to some 500 students in 2000 to attend courses at foreign universities. These activities were supplemented by various training programmes for civil servants, administrators, teachers and other professionals. With Portuguese having been restored, along with the local Tetum, as one of the country's two official languages, these programmes also included substantial Portuguese-language training components, funded primarily by Portugal.

FINANCE

Foreign Aid

The devastation caused by the post-referendum violence left East Timor heavily dependent on external financial assistance for its economic and social reconstruction. The international community responded vigorously to these needs; a first high-level meeting between the East Timorese national leadership and donor representatives was held in mid-December 1999 in Tokyo. This meeting was followed by six others in Lisbon in June 2000, Brussels in December 2000, Dili in March 2001, Canberra in June 2001, Oslo in December 2001 and Dili in May 2002. While underlining the donors' commitment to a co-ordinated effort to support the recovery and sustainable development of East Timor, these meetings were intended to monitor the performance of the technical co-operation activities financed by the foreign assistance, and to make appropriate adjustments where necessary.

At the first meeting in December 1999, the donors pledged US $523.2m. for a major three-year relief and reconstruction programme for East Timor (see above). These pledges were subsequently supplemented by a variety of other bilateral and multilateral commitments. Although the disbursement of these funds was initially somewhat slow as a result of the inevitable delays in formulating specific projects for their expenditure, the rate of disbursement began to accelerate significantly during the latter part of UNTAET's administration, when the availability of these foreign funds played a pre-eminent role in driving East Timor's economic recovery. The degree of the country's resulting dependence on external financial support was highlighted by the fact that of the estimated GDP per caput, US $431 in 2002, some US $400 had been contributed by foreign donors. Most of these foreign funds were made available in the form of grants rather than loans, moreover, so as not to burden the newly independent country, one of the poorest in the world, with an overhang of foreign debt.

To maximize the developmental impact of the externally-provided resources, the donor community agreed to co-ordinate their disbursement largely through two trust funds, the Consolidated Fund for East Timor (CFET), administered by UNTAET, and the Trust Fund for East Timor (TFET), administered by the World Bank in partnership with the Asian Development Bank (ADB). The former was intended principally to fund the administrative costs of government and to strengthen the capacity of the Timorese administration-in-waiting, while the latter was intended to finance economic reconstruction and development. Both were scheduled to be phased out by 2003 or 2004, upon completion of the post-crisis rehabilitation and recovery tasks for which they were established. Given East Timor's limited capacity for generating domestic revenues in the short term, however, the country was expected to remain dependent on external financial support for at least a few more years.

Fiscal Policy

As a relatively poor agricultural economy, dependent on coffee as its only significant export commodity, East Timor has historically been unable to cover its financial requirements. During the period of Indonesian rule it was dependent on external transfers for approximately 85% of its recurrent and capital expenditure. This dependence on external funding was greatly increased following the Indonesian withdrawal as a result of the collapse in domestic revenue-generating capacity and the sharp rise in capital spending required to rebuild the devastated infrastructure. UNTAET therefore placed considerable emphasis on establishing a framework for sustainable public finances and developing the associated financial management systems and human resources. By mid-2000 a Central Fiscal Authority had already been established as the precursor to a Ministry of Finance, which was given the responsibility of developing local capacities in the area of tax administration.

The first consolidated budget for East Timor, covering the 2000/01 fiscal year (from 1 July 2000), was presented at the second donors' meeting in Lisbon in June 2000. As subsequently revised in November 2000, this budget proposed a total expenditure of US $60.8m. and domestic revenues of US $25.1m. The resulting cash deficit of US $35.7m. was expected to be fully covered by grants pledged by external donors. The introduction of this budget was accompanied by the adoption of a series of measures relating to tax and user charges intended to generate the required domestic revenues, the achievement of which was also supported by a significant increase in oil revenues from the Timor Gap area. At the same time, an institutional framework was created for the responsible fiscal management of the economy. The task of the execution of the budget, including expenditure control and monitoring, was assigned to a new Treasury agency within the Central Fiscal Authority, which was established to develop the foundations for sound and transparent fiscal management and subsequently evolved into a full Ministry of Finance. In addition, the 2000/01 budget also provided for the establishment of an Economic Development Agency, to be responsible for business registration and the creation of an appropriate regulatory framework.

The budgets for 2001/02 and 2002/03, endorsed by the donors at the meetings held in Canberra in June 2001 and in Dili in May 2002 respectively, followed a broadly similar pattern to that of 2000/01 in that they projected significant deficits expected to be financed in large part from external sources. The medium-term fiscal framework developed for 2003/04 to 2005/06 suggests a gradual reversal of this pattern, however, with the large fiscal deficits being steadily reduced and then giving way to surpluses, once significant oil revenues begin to accrue from the development of the Bayu-Undan and, later, the Greater Sunrise natural gas and condensate fields. Preliminary estimates suggest that, even on the basis of the current revenue-sharing agreements with Australia, the Timor Sea reserves may yield up to US $3,000m. in petroleum revenue for East Timor within 20 years. The prospect of such a hydrocarbon 'bonanza' in the foreseeable future has given rise to fears that it might destabilize the economy of East Timor. Responding to these fears, the Government has indicated that it plans to save a significant proportion of its petroleum revenues, and to establish an 'oil fund' for this purpose, which will provide an insurance against unforeseen problems in the short term and a sustainable flow of income once the country's hydrocarbon resources have been depleted in the longer term.

Money and Banking

The devastation wreaked in the aftermath of the independence referendum also took its toll on the financial services sector in East Timor, which had suffered an almost total collapse as a result of the withdrawal of the Indonesian banks after September 1999. Although some progress had been made in reviving the banking system, it remained weak in mid-2002, when there were only two financial institutions—an Australian bank and Banco Nacional Ultramarino of Portugal—in operation in Dili. Both institutions were established in 2000 and provide mainly foreign-exchange services, although one began to provide loans to the private sector in mid-2000 under a small enterprise development project funded by the World Bank. The available data suggested that although current-account deposits had already risen by the end of 2000 to a level approximately equivalent to those held in September 1999 by the Indonesian banks then operating in East Timor, very little commercial bank credit had been extended, with the exception of loans issued under the TFET-funded small enterprise development project, owing to lack of adequate collateral. The prospects for a rapid expansion of the banking sector remained uncertain, although some large foreign banks, including an Indonesian bank, expressed an interest in opening branches in East Timor, and there was some local interest in the establishment of micro-financing institutions.

The lack of a single universally-accepted currency also posed a problem for an extended period of time. Although UNTAET chose the US dollar as East Timor's interim currency in January 2000, three other currencies—the Indonesian rupiah, the Portuguese escudo and the Australian dollar—remained in common use for at least a further 18 months. The Indonesian rupiah retained its influence as the currency used by the population at large, although its use was affected by the demonetization of several high-value banknotes by the Indonesian central bank in August 2000, which resulted in the emergence of a steeply-discounted secondary market for such notes in East Timor. The Australian dollar, meanwhile, continued to circulate mainly in Dili, where a relatively large expatriate Australian community had established itself. Despite its status as the official currency, the use of the US dollar by the local population was initially hampered by the slow execution of budgetary expenditures, the scarcity of low-denomination notes and coins, and the unfamiliarity of the currency. After mid-2001, however, the increased disbursement of TFET funds in particular resulted in an accelerated adoption of the currency, and by mid-2002 it was reported that the US dollar had begun to circulate widely throughout the country.

In early 2001 UNTAET established a Central Payments Office (CPO), subsequently renamed the Banking and Payments Authority (BPA), as a precursor to a central bank charged with the responsibilities of currency management, the making of payments and receipts on behalf of the East Timorese administration, and bank licensing and supervision.

ECONOMIC PROSPECTS

East Timor's relatively strong economic performance in 2000 and 2001, supported by both the externally funded economic rehabilitation measures and the presence of a large and relatively wealthy expatriate community, was unlikely to be sustained in the short term as the international donor community phased out its activities following the country's accession to independence in 2002. Most observers consequently anticipated a deceleration in the rate of economic growth for at least the next three to four years until oil revenues from the Timor Sea became available. In the mean time, the country was expected to remain heavily dependent on international support to finance its still substantial developmental needs in almost all social and economic fields. The weakening of the resource constraints resulting from the availability of substantial petroleum revenues by around 2006 will permit some acceleration of the development process, although this will continue to be restrained by insufficient technical and institutional capacities. Over time, however, these revenues will enable East Timor to overcome many of its current weaknesses and emerge as a prosperous hydrocarbon-based economy.

Statistical Survey

Sources (unless otherwise stated): Indonesian Central Bureau of Statistics, Jalan Dr Sutomo 8, Jakarta 10710, Indonesia; tel. (21) 363360; fax (21) 3857046; internet www.bps.go.id; IMF, *East Timor: Establishing the Foundations of Sound Macroeconomic Management*.

AREA AND POPULATION

Area: 14,609 sq km (5,641 sq miles).

Population: 555,350 at census of 31 October 1980; 747,750 (males 386,939, females 360,811) at census of 31 October 1990; 1998: 884,000; 2001 (UN registration): 737,811.

Density (2001): 50.5 per sq km.

Births and Deaths (UN estimates, annual averages): Birth rate per 1,000: 1985–90: 43.3; 1990–95: 36.8; 1995–2000: 29.4; Death rate per 1,000: 1985–90: 20.4; 1990–95: 17.5. 1995–2000: 14.8. Source: UN, *World Population Prospects: The 2000 Revision*.

Expectation of Life (UN estimates, years at birth, 1995–2000): 47.5 (males 46.7; females 48.4). Source: UN, *World Population Prospects: The 2000 Revision*.

Economically Active Population (survey, persons aged 10 years and over, August 1993): Total employed 336,490; Unemployed 5,397; Total labour force 341,887.

AGRICULTURE, ETC.

Principal Crops ('000 metric tons, 1996): Rice (paddy) 46; Maize 101; Cassava (Manioc) 66; Sweet potatoes 16; Soybeans 1; Potatoes 6; Cabbages 3; Mustard greens 2; Avocados 1; Mangoes 5; Oranges 1; Papayas 1; Pineapples 2; Bananas 4.

Livestock ('000 head, 1996): Cattle 137; Sheep 32; Goats 187; Pigs 378; Horses 32; Buffaloes 69; Chickens 1,021; Ducks 28.

Fishing (metric tons): Total catch 2,459 in 1994; 2,462 in 1995.

FINANCE

Currency and Exchange Rate: United States currency is used: 100 cents = 1 US dollar ($). *Sterling and Euro Equivalents* (31 May 2002): £1 sterling = US $1.4667; €1 = 93.87 US cents; US $100 = £68.18 = €106.53.

Budget (million rupiah, year ending 31 March 1999): *Revenue:* Federal tax revenue 106,225 (Income tax 47,964, Value-added tax and sales tax 23,485, Revenue-sharing 34,108); Provincial tax revenue 7,637 (Vehicle taxes 5,105, Vehicle ownership fees 2,399); Other receipts 3,012; Total 116,874.

Expenditure: Current expenditure 207,132 (Salaries and wages 146,529, Goods 36,474); Capital expenditure 319,956; Total 527,088.

Money Supply (estimate, '000 million rupiah, 31 December 1998): Currency in circulation 58.

Cost of Living (Consumer Price Index for Dili; base: year ending March 1989 = 100): 146.4 in 1994; 158.6 in 1995; 169.3 in 1996.

Gross Domestic Product (million rupiah at current prices): 996,000 in 1997; 1,272,000 in 1998; 1,878,000* in 1999. * Preliminary figure.

Balance of Payments: (estimates, US $ million, 1999): Exports of goods 46; Imports of goods –82; *Trade balance* –36; Services and other income (net) –12; *Balance on goods, services and income* –48; Current transfers 49; *Current balance* 1; Capital transfers 3; Other capital flows (net) –3; Net errors and omissions –1; *Overall balance* 0.

EXTERNAL TRADE

Principal Commodities (US $ million, 1998): *Imports:* Rice 13; Other foodstuffs 22; Petroleum products 14; Construction materials 20; Total (incl. others) 135. *Exports:* Products of agriculture, forestry and fishing 51 (Food crops 8, Other crops 28, Livestock 12); Products of manufacturing 3; Total (incl. others) 55.

Principal Trading Partner (US $ million, 1998): *Imports:* Indonesia 135. *Exports:* Indonesia 53.

TOURISM

Tourist Arrivals ('000 foreign visitors, excl. Indonesians, at hotels): 0.8 in 1996; 1.0 in 1997; 0.3 in 1998. Figures exclude arrivals at non-classified hotels: 204 in 1996; 245 in 1997; 41 in 1998.

Directory

The Constitution

The Constitution of the Democratic Republic of East Timor was promulgated by the Constituent Assembly on 22 March 2002 and became effective on 20 May 2002, when the nation formalized its independence. The main provisions of the Constitution are summarized below:

FUNDAMENTAL PRINCIPLES

The Democratic Republic of East Timor is a democratic, sovereign, independent and unitary state. Its territory comprises the historically defined eastern part of Timor island, the enclave of Oecussi, the island of Ataúro and the islet of Jaco. Oecussi Ambeno and Ataúro shall receive special administrative and economic treatment.

The fundamental objectives of the State include the following: to safeguard national sovereignty; to guarantee fundamental rights and freedoms; to defend political democracy; to promote the building of a society based on social justice; and to guarantee the effective equality of opportunities between women and men.

Sovereignty is vested in the people. The people shall exercise the political power through universal, free, equal, direct, secret and periodic suffrage and through other forms stated in the Constitution.

In matters of international relations, the Democratic Republic of East Timor shall establish relations of friendship and co-operation with all other peoples. It shall maintain privileged ties with countries whose official language is Portuguese.

The State shall recognize and respect the different religious denominations, which are free in their organization. Tetum and Portuguese shall be the official languages.

FUNDAMENTAL RIGHTS, DUTIES, LIBERTIES AND GUARANTEES

All citizens are equal before the law and no one shall be discriminated against on grounds of colour, race, marital status, gender, ethnic origin, language, social or economic status, political or ideological convictions, religion, education and physical or mental condition. Women and men shall have the same rights and duties in family, political, economic, social and cultural life. Rights, freedoms and safeguards are upheld by the State and include the following: the right to life; to personal freedom, security and integrity; to *habeas corpus*; to the inviolability of the home and of correspondence; to freedom of expression and conscience; to freedom of movement, assembly and association; and to participate in political life. Freedom of the press is guaranteed.

Rights and duties of citizens include the following: the right and the duty to work; the right to vote (at over 17 years of age); the right to petition; the right and duty to contribute towards the defence of sovereignty; the freedom to form trade unions and the right to strike; consumer rights; the right to private property; the duty to pay taxes; the right to health and medical care; the right to education and culture.

ORGANIZATION OF THE POLITICAL POWER

Political power lies with the people. The organs of sovereignty shall be the President of the Republic, the National Parliament, the Government and the Courts. They shall observe the principle of separation and interdependence of powers. There shall be free, direct, secret, personal and regular universal suffrage. No one shall hold political office for life.

PRESIDENT OF THE REPUBLIC

The President of the Republic is the Head of State and the Supreme Commander of the Defence Force. The President symbolizes and guarantees national independence and unity and the effective functioning of democratic institutions. The President of the Republic shall be elected by universal, free, direct, secret and personal suffrage. The candidate who receives more than half of the valid votes shall be elected President. Candidates shall be original citizens of the Democratic Republic of East Timor, at least 35 years of age, in possession of his/her full faculties and have been proposed by a minimum of 5,000 voters. The President shall hold office for five years. The President may not be re-elected for a third consecutive term of office.

The duties of the President include the following: to preside over the Supreme Council of Defence and Security and the Council of State; to set dates for elections; to convene extraordinary sessions of the National Parliament; to dissolve the National Parliament; to promulgate laws; to exercise the functions of the Supreme Commander of the Defence Force; to veto laws; to appoint and dismiss the Prime Minister and other Government members; to apply to the Supreme Court of Justice; to submit relevant issues of national interest to a referendum; to declare a State of Emergency following the authorization of the National Parliament; to appoint and dismiss diplomatic representatives; to accredit foreign diplomatic representatives; to declare war and make peace with the prior approval of the National Parliament.

COUNCIL OF STATE

The Council of State is the political advisory body of the President of the Republic. It is presided over by the President of the Republic and comprises former Presidents of the Republic who were not removed from office, the Speaker of the National Parliament, the Prime Minister, five citizens elected by the National Parliament and five citizens nominated by the President of the Republic.

NATIONAL PARLIAMENT

The National Parliament represents all Timorese citizens, and shall have a minimum of 52 and a maximum of 65 members, elected by universal, free, direct, equal, secret and personal suffrage for a term of five years. The duties of the National Parliament include the following: to enact legislation; to confer legislative authority on the Government; to approve plans and the Budget and monitor their execution; to ratify international treaties and conventions; to approve revisions of the Constitution; to propose to the President of the Republic that issues of national interest be submitted to a referendum. The legislative term shall comprise five legislative sessions, and each legislative session shall have the duration of one year.

GOVERNMENT

The Government is the supreme organ of public administration and is responsible for the formulation and execution of general policy. It shall comprise the Prime Minister, the Ministers and the Secretaries of State, and may include one or more Deputy Prime Ministers and Deputy Ministers. The Council of Ministers shall comprise the Prime Minister, the Deputy Prime Ministers, if any, and the Ministers. It shall be convened and presided over by the Prime Minister. The Prime Minister shall be appointed by the President of the Republic. Other members of the Government shall be appointed by the President at the proposal of the Prime Minister. The Government shall be responsible to the President and the National Parliament. The Government's programme shall be submitted to the National Parliament for consideration within 30 days of the appointment of the Government.

JUDICIARY

The Courts are independent organs of sovereignty with competence to administer justice. There shall be the Supreme Court of Justice and other courts of law, the High Administrative, Tax and Audit Court, other administrative courts of first instance and military courts. There may also be maritime courts and courts of arbitration.

It is the duty of the Public Prosecutors to represent the State. The Office of the Prosecutor-General shall be the highest authority in public prosecution and shall be presided over by the Prosecutor-General, who is appointed and dismissed by the President of the Republic. The Prosecutor-General shall serve for a term of six years.

ECONOMIC AND FINANCIAL ORGANIZATION

The economic organization of East Timor shall be based on the co-existence of the public, private, co-operative and social sectors of ownership, and on the combination of community forms with free initiative and business management. The State shall promote national investment. The State Budget shall be prepared by the Government and approved by the National Parliament. Its execution shall be monitored by the High Administrative, Tax and Audit Court and by the National Parliament.

NATIONAL DEFENCE AND SECURITY

The East Timor defence force—FALINTIL-ETDF—is composed exclusively of national citizens and shall be responsible for the provision of military defence to the Democratic Republic of East Timor. There shall be a single system of organization for the whole national territory. FALINTIL-ETDF shall act as a guarantor of national independence, territorial integrity and the freedom and security of the population against any external threat or aggression. The police shall guarantee the internal security of the citizens.

The Superior Council for Defence and Security is the consultative organ of the President of the Republic on matters relating to defence and security. It shall be presided over by the President of the Republic and shall include a higher number of civilian than military entities.

GUARANTEE AND REVISION OF THE CONSTITUTION

Declaration of unconstitutionality may be requested by: the President of the Republic; the Speaker of the National Parliament; the Prosecutor-General; the Prime Minister; one-fifth of the Members of the National Parliament; the Ombudsman.

Changes to the Constitution shall be approved by a majority of two-thirds of Members of Parliament and the President shall not refuse to promulgate a revision statute.

FINAL AND TRANSITIONAL PROVISIONS

Confirmation, accession and ratification of bilateral and multilateral conventions, treaties, agreements or alliances that took place before the Constitution entered into force shall be decided by the respective bodies concerned; the Democratic Republic of East Timor shall not be bound by any treaty, agreement or alliance not thus ratified. Any acts or contracts concerning natural resources entered into prior to the entry into force of the Constitution and not subsequently confirmed by the competent bodies shall not be recognized.

Indonesian and English shall be working languages, together with the official languages, for as long as is deemed necessary.

Acts committed between 25 April 1974 and 31 December 1999 that can be considered to be crimes of humanity, of genocide or of war shall be liable to criminal proceedings within the national or international courts.

The Government

Until 20 May 2002 all legislative and executive authority in East Timor was exercised by the United Nations Transitional Administration in East Timor (UNTAET). Under its guidance the Constituent Assembly promulgated a new Constitution on 22 March 2002 and the people of East Timor elected their first President on 14 April. Having satisfied both these preconditions East Timor was formally granted independence on 20 May, at which time the Constituent Assembly transformed itself into East Timor's first Parliament and the Government was formally inaugurated by the President. The Government was largely composed of the same Cabinet members who had constituted the pre-independence Council of Ministers.

Upon independence UNTAET was succeeded by the United Nations Mission of Support in East Timor (UNMISET—see Regional Organizations), which was to remain in the country for an initial period of one year. UNMISET's mandate comprised the following elements: to provide support to core administrative structures critical to the political stability and viability of the new country; to assist in interim law enforcement and public security; to aid in the development of a new law enforcement agency—the East Timor Police Force (ETPF); and to contribute to the maintenance of internal and external security. Downsizing of the mission was to take place as rapidly as possible and it was intended that, over a period of two years, all operational responsibilities would be fully devolved to the East Timorese authorities.

HEAD OF STATE

President: José Alexandre (Xanana) Gusmão (took office 20 May 2002).

CABINET
(September 2002)

Prime Minister and Minister for Economy and Development: Mari bin Amude Alkatiri.

Senior Minister for Foreign Affairs and Co-operation: José Ramos Horta.

Minister for Justice: Ana Maria Pessôa Pereira da Silva Pinto.

Minister for Finance: Madalena Brites Boavida.

Minister for Internal Administration: Rogério Tiago Lobato.

Minister for Health: Rui Maria de Araújo.

Minister for Transport, Communications and Public Works: Ovídio de Jesus Amaral.

Minister for Education, Culture, Youth and Sport: Armindo Maia.

Minister for Agriculture, Fisheries and Forestry: Estanislau Aleixo da Silva.

Secretary of State for Defence: Felix de Jesús Rodrigues.

Secretary of State for Labour and Solidarity: Arsênio Paixão Bano.

Secretary of State for Commerce and Industry: Arlindo Rangel.

Secretary of State for Tourism, Environment and Investment: José Texeira.

Secretary of State for the Council of Ministers: Gregorio José da Conceição Ferreira de Sousa.

Secretary of State for Parliamentary Affairs: Antoninho Bianco.

Secretary of State for Electricity and Water: Egídio de Jesus.

There are, in addition, seven Vice-Ministers.

MINISTRIES

Office of the President: Dili; e-mail op@gov.east-timor.org.

Office of the Prime Minister: Dili; e-mail opm@gov.east-timor.org.

Ministry of Agriculture, Forestry and Fisheries: Dili; e-mail agriculture@gov.east-timor.org.

Ministry of Economic Affairs and Planning: Dili; e-mail economic.affairs@gov.east-timor.org.

Ministry of Education, Culture, Youth and Sport: Dili; e-mail education@gov.east-timor.org.

Ministry of Finance: Dili; e-mail finance@gov.east-timor.org.

Ministry of Foreign Affairs: Dili; e-mail foreign.affairs@gov.east-timor.org.

Ministry of Health: Dili; e-mail health@gov.east-timor.org.

Ministry of Internal Administration: Dili; e-mail internal.admin@gov.east-timor.org.

Ministry of Justice: Dili; e-mail justice@gov.east-timor.org.

Ministry of Transport, Communications and Public Works: Dili; e-mail transport@gov.east-timor.org.

President and Legislature

PRESIDENT

Presidential Election, 14 April 2002

Candidate	Votes	%
José Alexandre Gusmão	301,634	82.69
Francisco Xavier do Amaral	63,146	17.31
Total	364,780	100.0

NATIONAL PARLIAMENT

A single-chamber Constituent Assembly was elected by popular vote on 30 August 2001. Its 88 members included 75 deputies elected under a national system of proportional representation and one representative from each of East Timor's 13 districts, elected under a 'first-past-the-post' system. Upon independence on 20 May 2002 the Constituent Assembly became the National Parliament; it held its inaugural session upon the same day.

Speaker: Francisco Guterres.

General Election, 30 August 2001

	Seats
Frente Revolucionária do Timor Leste Independente (Fretilin)	55
Partido Democrático (PD)	7
Associação Social-Democrata Timorense (ASDT)	6
Partido Social Democrata (PSD)	6
Klibur Oan Timor Asuwain (KOTA)	2
Partido Democrata Cristão (PDC)	2
Partido Nacionalista Timorense (PNT)	2
Partido do Povo de Timor (PPT)	2
União Democrática Timorense (UDT)	2
Partido Democrata Cristão de Timor (UDC/PDC)	1
Partido Liberal (PL)	1
Partido Socialista de Timor (PST)	1
Independent	1
Total	88

Political Organizations

Associação Popular Democrática de Timor Pro Referendo (Apodeti Pro Referendo) (Pro Referendum Popular Democratic

Association of Timor): c/o Frederico Almeida Santos Costa, CNRT Office, Balide, Dili; tel. (390) 324994; f. 1974 as Apodeti; adopted present name in August 2000; fmrly supported autonomous integration with Indonesia; Pres. and CNRT Permanent Council Rep. Frederico Almeida Santos Costa.

Associação Social-Democrata Timorense (ASDT) (Timor Social Democratic Association): Av. Direitos Humanos Lecidere, Dili; tel. (0408) 983331; f. 2001; Pres. Francisco Xavier do Amaral.

Barisan Rakyat Timor Timur (BRTT) (East Timor People's Front): fmrly supported autonomous integration with Indonesia; Pres. Francisco Lopes da Cruz.

Conselho Nacional da Resistência Timorense (CNRT) (National Council of Timorese Resistance): CNRT National Secretariat, Rua Caicoli, Balide, Dili: tel. (390) 311352; fax (390) 311345; e-mail xanana@minihub.org; f. 1998; alliance of fmr East Timorese resistance movements (Fretilin, the UDT and the defunct National Council of Maubere Resistance); Pres. José Alexandre (Xanana) Gusmão; Vice-Pres José Ramos Horta, Mário Viegas Carrascalão.

Conselho Popular pela Defesa da República Democrática de Timor Leste (CPD-RDTL) (Popular Council for the Defence of the Democratic Republic of East Timor): Opposite the Church, Balide, Dili; tel. (0409) 481462; f. 1999; promotes adoption of 1975 Constitution of Democratic Republic of East Timor; Spokesperson Cristiano da Costa.

Frente Revolucionária do Timor Leste Independente (Fretilin) (Revolutionary Front for an Independent East Timor): Rua dos Martires da Patria, Dili; tel. (390) 321409; internet www.geocities.com/SoHo/Study/4141/; f. 1974 to seek full independence for East Timor; entered into alliance with the UDT in 1986; Pres. Francisco Guterres; Sec. for International Relations José Ramos Horta.

Klibur Oan Timor Asuwain (KOTA) (Association of Timorese Heroes): Rua dos Martires da Patria, Fatuhada, Dili; tel. (390) 324661; e-mail clementinoamaral@hotmail.com; f. 1974 as pro-integration party; currently supports independence with Timorese traditions; Pres. Clementino dos Reis Amaral (acting).

Movement for the Reconciliation and Unity of the People of East Timor (MRUPT): f. 1997; Chair. Manuel Viegas Carrascalão.

Partai Liberal (PL) (Liberal Party): Talbessi Sentral, Dili; tel. (0408) 786448; Pres. Armando José Dourado da Silva.

Partido Democrata Cristão (PDC) (Christian Democrat Party): Former Escola Cartilha, Rua Quintal Kiik, Bairo Economico, Dili; tel. (390) 324683; e-mail arlindom@octa4.net.au; f. 2000; Pres. António Ximenes.

Partido Democrático (PD) (Democratic Party): 1 Rua Democracia, Pantai Kelapa, Dili; tel. (0419) 608421; e-mail flazama@hotmail.com; Pres. Fernando de Araújo.

Partido Democratik Maubere (PDM) (Maubere Democratic Party): Blok B II, 16 Surikmas Lama Kraik, Fatumeta, Dili; tel. (0407) 184508; e-mail pdm_party@hotmail.com; f. 2000; Pres. Paolo Pinto.

Partido Nacionalista Timorense (PNT) (Nationalist Party of Timor): Dili; tel. (390) 323518; Pres. Dr Abílio Araújo (acting).

Partido do Povo de Timor (PPT) (Timorese People's Party): Dili; tel. (0409) 568325; f. 2000; pro-integration; supported candidacy of Xanana Gusmão for presidency of East Timor; Pres. Dr Jacob Xavier.

Partido Republika National Timor Leste (PARENTIL) (National Republic Party of East Timor): Perumnar Bairopite Bob Madey Ran, Fahan Jalam, Ailobu Laran RTK; tel. (0419) 361393; Pres. Flaviano Pereira Lopez.

Partido Social Democrata Timor Lorosae (PSD) (Social Democrat Party of East Timor): Apartado 312, Correios de Dili, Dili; tel. (0418) 357027; e-mail psdtimor@hotmail.com; f. 2000; Pres. Mário Viegas Carrascalão.

Partido Socialista de Timor (PST) (Socialist Party of Timor): Rua Colegio das Madras, Balide, Dili; tel. (0407) 560246; e-mail kaynaga@hotmail.com; Marxist-Leninist Fretilin splinter group; Pres. Avelino da Silva.

Partido Trabalhista Timorense (PTT) (Timor Labour Party): 2B Rua Travessa de Befonte, 2 Bairro Formosa, Dili; tel. (390) 322807; f. 1974; Pres. Paulo Freitas da Silva.

União Democrática Timorense (UDT) (Timorese Democratic Union): Palapagoa Rua da India, Dili; tel. (409) 881453; e-mail uchimov2001@yahoo.com; internet www.unitel.net/udttimor; f. 1974; allied itself with Fretilin in 1986; Pres. João Carrascalão; Sec.-Gen. Domingos Oliveira.

União Democrata-Cristão de Timor (UDC/PDC) (Christian Democratic Union of Timor): 62 Rua Americo Thomaz, Mandarin, Dili; tel. (390) 325042; f. 1998; Pres. Vincente da Silva Guterres.

Diplomatic Representation

EMBASSIES IN EAST TIMOR

Australia: Av. dos Mártires da Pátria, Dili; tel. (390) 322111; fax (390) 323615; Ambassador: Paul Foley.

China, People's Republic: POB 131, Dili; tel. (438) 881918; fax (390) 325166; Ambassador: Guanfu Shao.

Indonesia: Kompleks Pertamina, Pantai Kelapa, Correios Timor Leste, Dili; tel. (390) 312333; fax (390) 312332; Ambassador: (vacant).

Japan: Pertamina 6, Dili; tel. (390) 323131; fax (390) 323130.

Korea, Democratic People's Republic: Dili.

Korea, Republic: Dili; e-mail koreadili@hotmail.com; internet www.mofat.go.kr/mission/emb/embassy_en.mof; Ambassador: Lim Byong-hyo.

Malaysia: Av. Almirante Americo Thomas, rue de Thomas, Mandarin, Dili; tel. (390) 311141; fax (390) 321805; e-mail mwdili@bigpond.com; Chargé d'affaires a.i.: Mohamed Rameez Yahaya.

Portugal: rue Dr António Carvalho, Dili; tel. (390) 312155; fax (390) 312526; Ambassador: Rui Quartim Santos.

Thailand: Central Maritime Hotel, Dili.

United Kingdom: Pantai Kelapa, Av. do Portugal, Dili; tel. (408) 010991; e-mail dili.fco@gtnet.gov.uk; Ambassador: Hamish St Clair Daniel.

USA: Av. do Portugal, Dili; tel. (390) 313205; fax (390) 313206; Chargé d'affaires a.i.: Shari Villarosa.

Judicial System

Until independence was granted on 20 May 2002 all legislative and executive authority with respect to the administration of the judiciary in East Timor was vested in UNTAET. During the transitional period of administration a two-tier court structure was established, consisting of District Courts and a Court of Appeal. The Constitution, promulgated in March 2002, specified that East Timor should have three categories of courts: the Supreme Court of Justice and other law courts; the High Administrative, Tax and Audit Court and other administrative courts of first instance; and military courts. The judiciary would be regulated by the Superior Council of the Judiciary, the function of which would be to oversee the judicial sector and, in particular, to control the appointment, promotion, discipline and dismissal of judges. The effectiveness of the newly-established judicial system was severely impaired by East Timor's lack of human and material resources. In July 2002 there were only 22 judges in East Timor, none of whom possessed more than two years of legal experience.

Office of the Prosecutor-General: Dili; Prosecutor-General Longuinhos Monteiro; Deputy Prosecutor-General Amandio Benevides.

Religion

In 1998 it was estimated that about 86.3% of the total population were Roman Catholic.

CHRISTIANITY

The Roman Catholic Church

East Timor comprises the dioceses of Dili and Baucau, directly responsible to the Holy See. In December 2000 the country had an estimated 750,047 Roman Catholics.

Bishop of Baucau: Rt Rev. Basílio do Nascimento Martins; Largo da Catedral, Baucau 88810; tel. (399) 21209; fax (399) 21380.

Bishop of Dili: Rt Rev. Carlos Filipe Ximenes Belo; Av. Direitos Humanos, Bidau Lecidere, CP 4, Dili 88010; tel. (390) 321177.

Protestant Church

Igreja Protestante iha Timor Lorosa'e: Jl. Raya Comoro, POB 1186, Dili 88110; tel. and fax (390) 323128; f. 1988 as Gereja Kristen Timor Timur (GKTT); adopted present name 2000; Moderator Rev. Francisco de Vasconcelos; 30,000 mems.

The Press

The office and printing plant of the largest newspaper in East Timor under Indonesian rule, *Suara Timor Timur* (Voice of East Timor, circulation of 8,000), were destroyed prior to the referendum on independence in August 1999. The Constitution promulgated in March 2002 guarantees freedom of the press in East Timor.

Lalenok (Mirror): Rua Gov. Celestino da Silva, Farol, Dili; tel. (390) 321607; e-mail lalenok@hotmail.com; f. 2000; publ. by Kamelin Media Group; Tetum; 3 a week; Dir Gen. and Chief Editor VIRGÍLIO DA SILVA GUTERRES; Editor JOSÉ MARIA POMPELA; circ. 300.

Lian Maubere: Dili; f. 1999; weekly.

Suara Timor Lorosae: Dili; daily.

The Official Gazette of East Timor: Dili; f. 1999 by UNTAET; forum for publication of all government regulations and directives, acts of organs or institutions of East Timor and other acts of public interest requiring general notification; published in English, Portuguese and Tetum, with translations in Bahasa Indonesia available on request.

Tais Timor: Dili; f. 2000; fmrly published by the Office of Communication and Public Information (OCPI) of the United Nations; Tetum, English, Portuguese and Bahasa Indonesia; every fortnight; distributed free of charge; circ. 75,000.

Talit@kum: Dili; f. 2000; news magazine; publ. by Kdadlak Media Group; Bahasa Indonesia; monthly; Chief Editor HUGO FERNANDEZ.

Timor Post: Rua D. Aleixo Corte Real No. 6, Dili; f. 2000; managed by editors and staff of the former *Suara Timor Timur*; Bahasa Indonesia, Tetum, Portuguese and English; daily; Chief Editor ADERITO HUGO DA COSTA

PRESS ASSOCIATION

Timor Lorosae Journalists Association (TLJA): Dili; f. 1999; Co-ordinator OTELIO OTE; Pres. VIRGÍLIO GUTERRES.

Broadcasting and Communications

TELECOMMUNICATIONS

Prior to the civil conflict in 1999, East Timor's telephone lines totalled about 12,000. Telecommunications transmission towers were reported to have suffered significant damage in the civil conflict. Indonesia withdrew its telecommunication services in September. A cellular telephone network service was subsequently provided by an Australian company. In July 2002 the Government granted a consortium led by Portugal Telecom a 15-year concession permitting it to establish and operate East Timor's telecommunications systems. Under the terms of the concession the consortium agreed to provide every district in East Timor with telecommunications services at the most inexpensive tariffs viable within 15 months. At the expiry of the concession in 2017 the telecommunications system was to be transferred to government control.

BROADCASTING

Following independence UNMISET transferred control of public television and radio in East Timor to the new Government. Legislation was passed in mid-2002 requesting the establishment of a Public Broadcasting Service controlled by an independent board of directors. In the interim MARIANO LOPES was appointed to serve as head of television and radio.

Radio

In May 2002 Radio UNTAET, launched by the UN, became Radio Timor-Leste, which broadcasts in four languages to an estimated 90% of East Timor's population. The Roman Catholic Church also operates a radio station, Radio Kamanak, while a third populist station, Voz Esperança, broadcasts in Dili. A fourth radio station, Radio Falintil FM, also operates in Dili. In 2000 the US radio station, Voice of America, began broadcasting to East Timor seven days a week in English, Portuguese and Bahasa Indonesia.

Television

TV Timor-Leste (TVTL): Dili; f. 2000 as Televisaun Timor Lorosa'e by UNTAET; adopted present name in May 2002; broadcasts in Tetum and Portuguese.

Finance

In January 2000 a Central Fiscal Authority was established by the UNTAET Transitional Administrator. This later became the country's Ministry of Finance. On 24 January the National Consultative Council formally adopted the US dollar as East Timor's transitional currency; however, the Indonesian rupiah continues to be widely used as a means of payment throughout the country.

BANKING

East Timor's banking system collapsed as a result of the violent unrest that afflicted the territory in 1999. In late 1999 Portugal's main overseas bank, Banco Nacional Ultramarino, opened a branch in Dili. In January 2001 the Australia and New Zealand Banking Group also opened a branch in the capital. In February the East Timor Central Payments Office was officially opened. This was succeeded in November 2001 by the Banking and Payments Authority, which was intended to function as a precursor to a central bank.

Banking and Payments Authority (BPA): Av. Bispo Medieros, POB 59, Dili; tel. (390) 313716; inaugurated Nov. 2001; regulates and supervises East Timor's financial system, formulates and implements payments system policies, provides banking services to East Timor's administration and foreign official institutions, manages fiscal reserves; fmrly Central Payments Office; Gen. Man. LUÍS QUINTANEIRO.

Foreign Banks

Australia and New Zealand Banking Group Ltd (ANZ) (Australia): POB 264, Unit 2, 17–19 Rua José Maria Marques, Dili; tel. (390) 324800; fax (390) 324822; e-mail etimor@anz.com; internet www.anz.com; retail and commercial banking services; Gen. Man. CHRIS DURMAN; Chief Operating Officer RICHARD HARE.

Banco Nacional Ultramarino (Portugal): Edif. BNU, Rua José Maria Marques, Dili; tel. (390) 323385; fax (390) 323994; e-mail timor@bnu.com.mo; internet www.bnu.pt; Dir-Gen. Dr TUBAL GONÇALVES.

Trade and Industry

UTILITIES

East Timor's total generating capacity amounted to some 40 MW. As a result of the civil conflict in 1999, some 13–23 power stations were reported to require repairs ranging from moderate maintenance to almost complete rehabilitation. The rehabilitation of the power sector was ongoing in 2002, with funding largely provided by foreign donors.

Transport

ROADS

The road network in East Timor is poorly designed and has suffered from long-term neglect. In December 1999 the World Bank reported that some 57% of East Timor's 1,414 km of paved roads were in poor or damaged condition. Many gravel roads are rough and potholed and are inaccessible to most vehicles. Some repair and maintenance work on the road network was being carried out in 2002, using funding supplied by external donors.

SHIPPING

East Timor's maritime infrastructure includes ports at Dili, Carabela and Com, smaller wharves at Oecusse (Oekussi) and Liquiça (Likisia), and slip-landing structures in Oecusse, Batugade and Suai. In November 2001, following its reconstruction, the management of the port at Dili was transferred to the Government. The port was expected to be a significant source of revenue.

CIVIL AVIATION

East Timor has two international airports and eight grass runways. At mid-2000 operators of international flights to East Timor included Qantas Airways and Air North of Australia. In June 2001, Dili Express Pte was the first Timor-based company to begin international flights, with a service to Singapore.

Defence

In October 1999, following the intervention of an international peace-keeping force, Interfet, the last of the occupying Indonesian armed forces departed from East Timor. Interfet was subsequently replaced by the armed forces of the United Nations Transitional Administration for East Timor (UNTAET). At independence on 20 May 2002 UNTAET was succeeded by the United Nations Mission of Support in East Timor (UNMISET). At 30 June 2002 the UNMISET peace-keeping force comprised: 4,789 military personnel; 119 military observers; and 939 civilian police. It was supported by 631 international and 660 local civilians. The maximum authorized strength was 5,000 troops, including 120 military observers and 1,250 civilian police. Provision was also made for 455 international civilian staff, 100 experts for a Civilian Support Group, 977 locally recruited staff and 241 UN Volunteers. The peace-keeping force was gradually to be replaced, through a two-year process of phased withdrawal, by an East Timor Defence Force (FALINTIL-ETDF), comprising a light infantry force of 1,500 regulars and 1,500 reservists. The first battalion of 600 members was recruited in February

2001 from the ranks of the former guerrilla army, FALINTIL, and the first ETDF troops were deployed into the peace-keeping structure in early August. A second deployment followed in September 2001. On 23 July 2002 the first battalion of FALINTIL-ETDF assumed responsibility from UNMISET's peace-keeping force for the district of Lautem—the first such transfer since the UN's arrival in the country in 1999.

Commander-in-Chief: Brig.-Gen. TAUR MATAN RUAK.

Force Commander: Maj.-Gen. TAN HUCK GIM (Singapore).

Chief Military Observer: (vacant).

Chief of Civilian Police: Chief Superintendent PETER MILLER (Canada).

Education

Prior to the civil conflict in 1999 there were 167,181 primary students at the 788 schools, 32,197 junior secondary students at 114 schools and 14,626 senior secondary students at 37 schools. Primary school enrolment included 70% of those in the relevant age-group and secondary enrolment about 39%. The 17 vocational and technical schools had 4,347 students. Some 4,000 students were engaged in further education at the university and the polytechnic in Dili, while an additional several thousand East Timorese were following courses at Indonesian universities. It was estimated that, as a result of the civil conflict in 1999, 75%–80% of primary and secondary schools were either partially or completely destroyed. Illiteracy rates were reported to be above 50% in 1999, with higher rates recorded for females than for males. In 2001 an estimated 236,000 students attended 900 schools in the country, with some 5,000 students engaged in further education at the National University of East Timor. The university was reopened in November 2000. By July 2001 UNTAET estimated that the number of usable classrooms within East Timor (following a massive rehabilitation programme that restored 2,000 classrooms to a basic, operational level) was only 14% below the 1999 pre-violence level. A total of 373 schools had been rehabilitated to a basic operational level.

Bibliography

See also Indonesia.

Aarons, Mark, and Domm, Robert. *East Timor: A Western Made Tragedy*. Sydney, Left Book Club, 1992.

Aditjondro, George J. *In the Shadow of Mount Ramelau: The Impact of the Occupation of East Timor*. Indonesian Documentation and Information Centre, 1994.

Alkatiri, Mari. *Statement on the National Development Plan for East Timor*. Donors' Meeting on East Timor, Dili, 14–15 May 2002.

Andersen, Tim. *Aidwatch Background Paper: Main Features of the Timor Sea Agreements*. Aidwatch, Sydney, May 2002.

Allied Geographical Section. *Area Study of Portuguese Timor*. London, 1943.

Auburn, F. M., Ong, David, and Forbes, Vivian L. *Dispute Resolution and the Timor Gap Treaty*. Nedlands, WA, Indian Ocean Centre for Peace Studies, University of Western Australia, 1994.

Audley-Charles, Michael Geoffrey. *The Geology of Portuguese Timor*. London, Geological Society of London, 1968.

Ball, Desmond, and McDonald, Hamish. *Death in Balibo, Lies in Canberra*. St Leonards, NSW, Allen & Unwin, 2000.

Bijlmer, Hendricus Johannes Tobias. *Outlines of the Anthropology of the Timor-Archipelago*. Weltevreden, Kolff, 1929.

Boxer, C. R. *The Topasses of Timor*. Amsterdam, Indisch Instituut, 1947.

Breen, Bob. *Mission Accomplished: East Timor*. St Leonards, NSW, Allen & Unwin, 2001.

Bruce, Robert H. *US Response to the East Timor Massacre: Historical Grounds for Scepticism about a Suggested Remedy*. Nedlands, WA, Indian Ocean Centre for Peace Studies, University of Western Australia, 1992.

Budiardjo, Carmel, and Liem Soei Liong. *The War against East Timor*. London, Zed Press, and Leichhardt, NSW, Pluto Press, 1984.

Callinan, Bernard. *Independent Company: the 2/2 and 2/4 Australian Independent Companies in Portuguese Timor, 1941–1943*. London, Heinemann, 1953.

Campaign for Independent East Timor. *East Timor on the Road to Independence: A Background Report*. Sydney, 1974.

Cardoso, Luís. *The Crossing: A Story of East Timor*. London, Granta Books, 2000.

Carey, Peter, and Bentley, G. Carter (Eds). *East Timor at the Crossroads: The Forging of a Nation*. Honolulu, HI, University of Hawaii Press, 1995.

Catholic Commission for Justice, Development and Peace. *The Church and East Timor: A Collection of Documents by National and International Catholic Church Agencies*. Melbourne, 1993.

Catholic Institute for International Relations. *International Law and the Question of East Timor*. London, 1995.

Cristalis, Irena. *Bitter Dawn: East Timor—A People's Story*. London, Zed Press, 2002.

Cultural Survival. *East Timor, Five Years after the Indonesia Invasion: Testimony Presented at the Decolonization Committee of the United Nations' General Assembly, October 1980*. Cambridge, MA, 1981.

Da Costa, Helder, and Soesastro, Hadi. 'Building East Timor's Economy' in *Comparing Experiences with State Building in Asia and Europe: The Cases of East Timor, Bosnia and Kosovo*. Council for Asia Europe Co-operation (CAEC), internet www.caec-asiaeurope.org/conference/publications/costasoesastro.pdf.

Departemen Luar Negeri, Indonesia. *Decolonization in East Timor*. Jakarta, Department of Information, 1977.

Departemen Penerangan, Indonesia. *Government Statements on the East-Timor Question*. Jakarta, 1975.

Department of Foreign Affairs and Trade, Australia. *Briefing Papers: International Court of Justice, Portugal v. Australia (concerning East Timor)*. Canberra, 1995.

Department of Information, Indonesia. *The Province of East Timor: Development in Progress*. Jakarta.

Downie, Sue, and Kingsbury, Damien (Eds). *The Independence Ballot in East Timor: Report of the Australian Volunteer Observer Group*. Clayton, Vic, Monash Asia Institute, 2001.

Dunn, James. *East Timor: The Balibo Incident in Perspective*. Broadway, NSW, The Australian Centre for Independent Journalism, 1995.

Timor: A People Betrayed. Sydney, ABC Books, 1996.

Fitzpatrick, Daniel. *Land Claims in East Timor*. Canberra, Asia Pacific Press, 2002.

Fox, James J., and Babo Soares, Dionísio (Eds). *East Timor: Out of the Ashes, the Destruction and Reconstruction of an Emerging State*. Bathurst, NSW, Crawford House, 1999.

Glover, Ian. *Archaeology in Eastern Timor, 1966–67*. Canberra, Department of Prehistory, Research School of Pacific Studies, Australian National University, 1986.

Greenlees, Don, and Garran, Robert. *Deliverance: the Inside Story of East Timor's Fight for Freedom*. Crow's Nest, NSW, Allen & Unwin, 2002.

Gunn, Geoffrey C. *Wartime Portuguese Timor: the Azores Connection*. Clayton, Vic, Monash University, Centre of Southeast Asian Studies, 1988.

Timor Loro Sae: 500 Years. Macao, Livros do Oriente, 1999.

A Critical View of Western Journalism and Scholarship on East Timor. Sydney, Journal of Contemporary Asia Publishers, 1994.

East Timor and the United Nations: The Case for Intervention. Lawrenceville, NJ, Red Sea Press, 1997.

Gusmão, Xanana. *To Resist Is To Win: The Autobiography of Xanana Gusmão*. Richmond, Vic, Aurora Books, 2000.

Head, Mike. 'New Timor Gap Treaty Secures Australian Control of Oil and Gas Projects', World Socialist Web Site, 11 July 2001, www.wsws.org/articles/2001/jul2001/timo-j11.shtml.

Hill, Hal, and Saldanha, João (Eds). *East Timor and Economic Development*. Singapore, Institute of Southeast Asian Studies, 2001.

East Timor: Development Challenges for the World's Newest Nation. Singapore, Institute of Southeast Asian Studies; and Canberra, Asia Pacific Press, Australian National University, 2001.

Hill, Helen. *Stirrings of Nationalism in East Timor: Fretilin 1974–1978: the Origins, Ideologies and Strategies of a Nationalist Movement*. (Otford, NSW, Otford Press, 2002.

Hoadley, J. Stephen. *The Future of Portuguese Timor: Dilemmas and Opportunities*. Singapore, Institute of Southeast Asian Studies, 1975.

Inbaraj, Sonny. *East Timor: Blood and Tears in Asean*. Chiang Mai, Silkworm Books, 1995.

International Commission of Jurists. *Tragedy in East Timor: Report on the Trials in Dili and Jakarta*. Geneva, 1992.

Report of the Trial of Xanana Gusmão in Dili, East Timor. Geneva, 1993.

International Monetary Fund. *Staff Statement*. Donors' Meeting on East Timor, Dili, 14–15 May 2002.

Jardine, Matthew. *East Timor: Genocide in Paradise*. Tucson, AZ, Odonian Press, 1995.

Joint Assessment Mission. *East Timor—Building a Nation: A Framework for Reconstruction and Development*. November 1999.

Agriculture Background Paper.

Health and Education Background Paper.

Macro-Economics Background Paper.

Jolliffe, Jill. *East Timor: Nationalism and Colonialism*. St Lucia, Qld, University of Queensland Press, 1978.

Cover-up: the Inside Story of the Balibo Five. Carlton North, Vic, Scribe, 2001.

Kim, Insu, and Schwarz, Stephen. *Birth of a Nation: East Timor Gains Independence, Faces Challenges of Economic Management, Poverty Alleviation*. IMF Survey, Volume 31, No. 11, 10 June 2002.

Kingsbury, Damien (Ed.). *Guns and Ballot Boxes: East Timor's Vote for Independence*. Melbourne, Vic, Monash Asia Institute, 2000.

Kohen, Arnold, and Taylor, John. *An Act of Genocide: Indonesia's Invasion of East Timor*. London, Tapol, 1979.

Kohen, Arnold S. *From the Place of the Dead: The Epic Struggles of Bishop Belo of East Timor*. New York, St Martin's Press, 1999.

Krieger, Heike (Ed.). *East Timor and the International Community: Basic Documents*. Cambridge, Cambridge University Press, 1997.

Lennox, Rowena. *Fighting Spirit of East Timor: The Life of Martinho da Costa Lopes*. Sydney, Pluto Press, 2000.

Martin, Ian. *Self-determination in East Timor: the United Nations, the Ballot, and International Intervention*. Boulder, CO, Lynne Rienner Publishers, 2001.

Martinkus, John. *A Dirty Little War*. Milsons Point, NSW, Random House, 2001.

McDonald, Hamish, et al. *Masters of Terror: Indonesia's Military and Violence in East Timor in 1999*. Canberra, Australian National University, Strategic and Defence Studies Centre, 2002.

Metzner, Joachim K. *Man and Environment in Eastern Timor: A Geoecological Analysis of the Baucau-Viqueque Area as a Possible Basis for Regional Planning*. Canberra, Development Studies Centre, Australian National University, 1997.

Middelkoop, Pieter. *Head Hunting in Timor and its Historical Implications*. Sydney, University of Sydney, 1963.

Ministério do Ultramar, Portugal. *Estatuto Político-administrativo da Província de Timor*. Lisbon, Agência-Geral do Ultramar, 1963.

Mubyarto, et al. *East Timor: The Impact of Integration: An Indonesian Socio-anthropological Study*. Northcote, Vic, Indonesia Resources and Information Program (IRIP), 1991.

Nicol, Bill. *Timor: The Stillborn Nation*. Melbourne, Vic, Widescope International, 1978.

Orentlicher, Diane. *Human Rights in Indonesia and East Timor*. New York, Human Rights Watch, 1988.

Ormeling, Ferdinand Jan. *The Timor Problem: A Geographical Interpretation of an Underdeveloped Island*. Groningen, Wolters, 1955.

Pinto, Constâncio, and Jardine, Matthew. *East Timor's Unfinished Struggle: Inside the Timorese Resistance*. Boston, MA, South End Press, 1997.

Ramos Horta, Arsénio. *The Eyewitness: Bitter Moments in East Timor Jungles*. Singapore, Usaha Quality Printers.

Ramos Horta, José. *Funu: Unfinished Saga of East Timor*. Trenton, NJ, Red Sea Press, 1987.

Retbøll, Torben (Ed.). *East Timor, Indonesia, and the Western Democracies: A Collection of Documents*. Copenhagen, International Work Group for Indigenous Affairs (IWGIA), 1980.

Roff, Sue Rabbitt. *East Timor: A Bibliography, 1970–1993*. Canberra, Peace Research Centre, 1994.

Timor's Anschluss: Indonesian and Australian Policy in East Timor, 1974–76. Leviston, NY, Edwin Mellen Press, 1992.

Rohland, Klaus. *Opening Remarks*. Donors' Meeting on East Timor, Dili, 14–15 May 2002.

Rothwell, Donald R., and Tsamenyi, Martin (Eds). *The Maritime Dimensions of Independent East Timor*. NSW, Centre for Maritime Policy, University of Wollongong, 2000.

Rowland, Ian. *Timor: including the Islands of Roti and Ndao*. Oxford and Santa Barbara, CA, Clio Press, 1992.

Schlicher, Monika. *Portugal in Ost-Timor: Eine Kritische Untersuchung zur Portugiesischen Kolonialgeschichte in Ost-Timor*. Hamburg, Abera, 1996.

Schulte Nordholt, H. G. *The Political System of the Atoni of Timor*. The Hague, M. Nijhoff, 1971.

Sherlock, Kevin P. *A Bibliography of Timor: Including East (formerly Portuguese) Timor, West (formerly Dutch) Timor, and the Island of Roti*. Canberra, Australian National University, 1980.

East Timor: Liurais and Chefes de Suco; Indigenous Authorities in 1952. Darwin, NT, 1983.

Sherman, Tom. *Second Report on the Deaths of Australian-based Journalists in East Timor in 1975*. Canberra, Department of Foreign Affairs and Trade, 1999.

Singh, Bilveer. *East Timor, Indonesia, and the World: Myths and Realities*. Kuala Lumpur, ADPR Consult (M), 1996.

Sousa Saldanha, João Mariano de. *The Political Economy of East Timor Development*. Jakarta, Pustaka Sinar Harapan, 1994.

Sousa Saldanha, João Mariano de (Ed.). *An Anthology: Essays on the Political Economy of East Timor*. Casuarina, NT, Centre for Southeast Asian Studies, Northern Territory University, 1995.

Stepan, Sasha. *Credibility Gap: Australia and the Timor Gap Treaty*. Canberra, Australian Council for Overseas Aid, 1990.

Subroto, Hendro. *Eyewitness to Integration of East Timor*. Jakarta, Pustaka Sinar Harapan, 1997.

Suter, Keith. *East Timor and West Irian*. London, Minority Rights Group, 1982.

Sword, Kirsty, and Walsh, Pat (Eds). *'Opening up': Travellers' Impressions of East Timor 1989–1991*. Fitzroy, Vic, Australia East Timor Association, 1991.

Tanter, Richard, Selden, Mark, and Shalom, Stephen R. (Eds). *Bitter Flowers, Sweet Flowers: East Timor, Indonesia, and the World Community*. Lanham, MD, Rowman & Littlefield Publishers, 2001.

Tapol, The Indonesian Human Rights Campaign. *East Timor: United Nations Resolutions, 1975–1982*. Thornton Heath, Surrey, Tapol, 1991.

Taylor, John G. *East Timor: the Price of Freedom*. New York, Zed Books, 1999.

Teklkamp, Gerard J. *De Ekonomische Struktuur van Portugees-Timor in de Twintigste Eeuw: Een Voorlopige Schets*. Amsterdam, Centrale Bibliotheek, Koninklijk Instituut voor de Tropen, 1975.

Traube, Elizabeth G. *Cosmology and Social Life: Ritual Exchange among the Mambai of East Timor*. Chicago, IL, University of Chicago Press, 1986.

Turner, Michele. *Telling East Timor: Personal Testimonies 1942–1992*. Kensington, NSW, New South Wales University Press, 1992.

United Nations Security Council. *Report of the Secretary-General on the United Nations Transitional Administration in East Timor*. United Nations, New York, 17 April 2002.

United Nations Transitional Administration in East Timor (UNTAET), World Bank and International Monetary Fund. *Background Paper for Donors' Meeting on East Timor, Lisbon, Portugal, June 22–23, 2000*. Washington, DC, World Bank, 2000.

Valdivieso, Luís M., et al. *East Timor: Establishing the Foundations of Sound Macroeconomic Management*. Washington, DC, IMF, August 2000.

Valdivieso, Luís M., and Lopez-Mejia, Alejandro. *East Timor: Macroeconomic Management on the Road to Independence*. Finance and Development, Volume 38, No. 1, March 2001.

Valdivieso, Luís M. *Staff Statement*. Donors' Meeting for East Timor, Canberra, 14–15 June 2001.

Vieira de Mello, Sérgio. *Statement*. Donors' Meeting on East Timor, Dili, 14–15 May 2002.

Way, Wendy (Ed). *Australia and the Indonesian Incorporation of Portuguese Timor. 1974–1976*. Carlton, Vic, Melbourne University Press, 2000.

Wiarda, Siqueira. *The Portuguese in Southeast Asia: Malacca, Moluccas, East Timor*. Hamburg, Abera Verlag, 1997.

Winters, Rebecca. *Buibere: Voice of East Timorese Women*. Nightcliff, Darwin, NT, East Timor International Support Centre, 1999.

Winters, Rebecca, and Kelly, Brian. *Children of the Resistance: the Current Situation in East Timor as seen through the Eyes of two Australian Tourists*. Darwin, NT, Australians for a Free East Timor, 1996.

World Bank, *Background Paper for Donors' Meeting on East Timor*. Donors' Meeting on East Timor, Dili, 14–15 May 2002.

INDIA

Physical and Social Geography

B. H. FARMER

The Republic of India is one of the largest countries in the world, with an area of 3,287,263 sq km (1,269,219 sq miles), including the Indian portion of Jammu and Kashmir, which is disputed between India and Pakistan. India stretches from 8° to 33° 15′ N, and from 68° 5′ to 97° 25′ E. Its northern frontiers are with Tibet (the Xizang Autonomous Region of the People's Republic of China), and with Nepal and Bhutan. On the north-west it bounds Pakistan; on the north-east it borders on Myanmar (formerly Burma); and in the east, Bangladesh. India's great southern peninsula stretches far down into the tropical waters of the Indian Ocean, where its territorial boundaries extend to the Andaman and Nicobar Islands, in the Bay of Bengal, and the Lakshadweep archipelago, in the Arabian Sea.

PHYSICAL FEATURES

India has three well-marked and, indeed, obvious relief regions: the Himalayan system in the north, the plateaux of the peninsula and, in between, the great plains of the Indus and Ganga (Ganges) basins.

The Himalayan system, between the Tibet plateau and the Indo-Gangetic plains, is made up of complex ranges arranged more or less in parallel, but in places combining and then dividing again, in others taking on the apparent form of a series of peaks divided by deep gorges rather than that of a range. The Great Himalaya is, in general, just such an array of giant peaks, mostly over 6,100 m in height, covered by perpetual snows, and nurturing great glaciers, which in turn feed the rivers flowing to the Indus, Ganga and Brahmaputra. The southernmost range of the system, the Siwaliks, presents a wall-like margin to the plains; while in the extreme north-east the whole system bends very sharply on crossing the Brahmaputra and forms the wild, forest-clad country of the Naga and other hills on the marches of Myanmar.

Peninsular India, the Deccan or South Country, begins at another but more broken wall that fringes the plains to the south, and stretches away to Kanyakumari, the southernmost extremity of India. The whole peninsula is built, fundamentally, of ancient and largely crystalline rocks which have been worn down through long geological ages and now form a series of plateaux, mostly sloping eastward and drained by great rivers, like the Mahanadi, Krishna and Godavari, flowing to the Bay of Bengal. Where plateaux end abruptly their edges present, from the lower plains or plateaux below, the appearance of mountain ranges. This feature is most evident in the Western Ghats, the great scarp overlooking the narrow western coastal plain. Two rivers, the Narmada and Tapti, flow east. Between them, and on east into the jungle country of Chota Nagpur, lies wild hilly territory that has done much to isolate the southern Deccan from the plains through long periods of Indian history. The Garo and Khasi Hills of Meghalaya form a detached piece of plateau country. In places there are variants on the ancient crystalline-rock plateau theme. Thus, in the north-eastern Deccan narrow, down-faulted basins preserve the most important of India's coal measures; while inland of Mumbai (formerly Bombay), and covering most of the state of Maharashtra, great basalt flows have given rise to distinctive countryside with broad open valleys floored by fertile, though difficult, *regur* (black cotton soils) separated by flat-topped hills. The west coast is fringed by a narrow alluvial plain. That on the east coast is generally wide, especially where it broadens out into the highly productive deltas of the great east-flowing rivers.

The Indo-Gangetic plain, between the Siwaliks and the northernmost plateau-edges of the Deccan, is one of the really great plains of the world. Consisting entirely of alluvium, it presents an appearance of monotonous flatness from the air or, indeed, to the uninitiated traveller on land. In fact, however, its general flatness conceals a great deal of variety. The fine muds and clays of the Ganga-Brahmaputra delta contrast, for instance, with the sands of the Rajasthan desert at the western extremity of the Indian portion of the plains. Almost everywhere, too, there is a contrast of floodplains (along the rivers) and naturally dry belts, often of older alluvium, well above the reach of even the highest floods.

CLIMATE

In northern India there are three seasons. A 'cool season' lasts from December to February, and brings average temperatures of 10°–15°C to Delhi and the Punjab, but with a high diurnal range (from as high as 26°C by day to freezing point or below at night) and, although this is the season of the 'dry' north-east monsoon, depressions from the north-west may bring rain to the Punjab and, indeed, further down the plains to the east. In the 'hot season' of the north temperatures rise until, in May, the average is 32°–35°C (as high as 48°C by day), and rain is very rare. With the 'burst' of the monsoon in June and July, temperatures fall and the rains begin, to last until September or October.

In the Ganga delta, to take another regional example, the 'cool season' is less cool than in Delhi (19°C average for January in Kolkata—formerly Calcutta), the hot season less hot (30°C May average), and the rains much heavier—there is hardly a year in which Kolkata's streets do not suffer serious flooding at least once. The 'hot season' is, moreover, punctuated by 'mango showers', which are even more significant in Assam.

In the peninsula, the coolness of the 'cool season' tends to be diminished as one goes south, as does the striking heat of the 'hot season', partly because in places such as Mumbai temperatures are never as high as in, say, Delhi, and partly because in the far south it is always hot, except where temperatures are mitigated by altitude. In Tamil Nadu, for example, average monthly temperatures vary only from 24°C in January to 32°C in May and June. In the peninsula, too, the south-west monsoon brings particularly heavy rains to the westward-facing scarps of the Western Ghats, which receive 200–250 cm in four months. The dry season also decreases southward till in Kerala, in the far south-west, it lasts for only a month or two. In Tamil Nadu, there is an almost complete reversal of the normal monsoonal rainfall regime: the heaviest rains fall in October to January (inclusive) and the south-west monsoon period is relatively dry.

The theme of contrast in Indian climate is best expressed by drawing attention to the tremendous difference between, on the one hand, the deserts of Rajasthan and the rather less dry sands of Ramanathapuram, in south-eastern Tamil Nadu, and, on the other, the verdant landscapes of the north-eastern Deccan and of Kerala.

SOILS AND VEGETATION

The soils of the Himalayan mountains and plateaux are generally thin, skeletal and infertile, except in intermontane basins or in areas of artificial terracing, and therefore artificial depth and fertility. The soils of the peninsula are also generally poor, though for a different reason—that in general they have been derived from long years of weathering from unpromising crystalline rocks. There are, however, noteworthy exceptions—particularly the rich alluvia, with a generally high potential for improvement by means of fertilizers, to be found in the east coast deltas of the Mahanadi, Godavari, Krishna and Kaveri, and the *regur* of the basalt areas of Maharashtra. The latter are naturally of quite high fertility and retain moisture (an important property in a monsoon climate, especially in the axis of semi-aridity that runs east of the Ghats through Pune) but are sticky, erodible and hard to cultivate when wet, and also difficult to irrigate satisfactorily. The soils of the plains are, by nature, generally much more fertile than those of the Himalayas or of the Deccan, though this does not apply to the sandier soils that are to be found (for example) in the Rajasthan desert, or to the leached soils of old alluvial terraces like those on the western margins of the Bengal delta. Yet infertility has tended to creep in as a result of human occupancy. This is partly, and very widely, a matter of long continued cultivation without adequate manuring, partly a matter of salinity and alkalinity induced by a causal chain that stretches from canal irrigation through rising water-tables to the capillary ascent of salts to the surface. The problem of salinity particularly afflicts the fields of Uttar Pradesh.

The tremendous variations in rainfall, not to say temperature and relief, to be met in India mean that there must have been, far back in time, very wide variations in natural vegetation. These probably ranged from near-desert or even complete desert (in Rajasthan); through thorn scrub (in semi-arid regions like the western Maharashtran Deccan) and tropical dry deciduous forest (in slightly wetter areas lying along a broad crescentic belt from the middle Ganga plains to Hyderabad and Chennai—formerly Madras) and moist tropical deciduous forest (in the north-east Deccan); to tropical wet evergreen forest, approaching rain forest (along the Western Ghats and in Kerala). There must also have been a complete altitudinal gradation from plains vegetation through deciduous and coniferous forests to montane vegetation in the Himalayas. Little natural vegetation of any sort survives in the plains or in the east and west coast deltas and coastal strips, except in rare groves; or, for that matter, over much of Tamil Nadu or the plateau areas of Maharashtra (apart from the still-forested eastern districts of the latter state). In all these regions, and many more, the landscape is dominated not by natural vegetation but by arable cultivation. Even in apparently uncultivated areas the natural vegetation has been modified out of all recognition. It may well be that part of the Rajasthan desert is man-made or, at any rate, degraded by man. The savannah-like jungles of parts of central India have developed from denser forest formations, by the action of man and his animals. Even the surviving forests of the north-east Deccan, dominated by *sal* (*Shorea robusta*, a useful timber tree), are often, if not generally, derived from more heterogeneous forests by the action of fire. Not surprisingly, India's forest resources, although not by any means inconsiderable, do not match its needs.

MINERALS

India possesses some of the largest and richest reserves of iron ore in the world. These occur particularly in the north-east Deccan, in the states of Bihar, Orissa and in the western part of West Bengal. Other deposits occur farther afield—for example, around Salem, in Tamil Nadu; in Karnataka; and in Goa. Altogether it has been estimated that India has reserves of no less than 22,000m. metric tons of iron ore. This is ample to supply the country's present industrial needs and to allow for exports. There are perhaps resources of 80,000m. tons of poor and medium coals, but only 2,500m. tons of coking coals. Some 95% of Indian production, and nearly all of the coking coal, comes from seams in the down-faulted basins in the north-east Deccan. It will be appreciated that the bulk of the iron ore reserves are in the same region. Elsewhere, there is a little coal in Assam and lignite in Rajasthan and Tamil Nadu.

India is rich in the non-ferrous minerals used in alloys, notably in manganese (of which India in most years is the second or third largest producer in the world; ores are found widely distributed in the Deccan). About 75% of the world's mica comes from India, notably from Bihar, Tamil Nadu and Rajasthan. The known reserves of various minerals in December 1976 were: haematite 9,000m. metric tons; magnetite 2,800m. tons; lignite 2,000m. tons; limestone 50,000m. tons; dolomite 1,800m. tons; china clay 365m. tons; fireclay 300m. tons; copper 333m. tons; kyanite 143m. tons; lead 120m. tons; zinc 101m. tons; manganese 98m. tons; nickel 78m. tons; and phosphorite 78m. tons. Onshore deposits of petroleum have been found in Assam, Gujarat and Nagaland, and offshore oilfields have been discovered in the western continental shelf off the Maharashtra coast, notably in the Mumbai High. Estimates of recoverable reserves vary but are officially put at about 1,500m. tons. There is no shortage of building-stone or of the raw materials for the cement industry.

POPULATION AND ETHNIC GROUPS

With a provisional population at the March 2001 census of 1,027,015,247 (including Sikkim and the Indian-held part of Jammu and Kashmir), India is the world's second most populous country. The population officially reached 1,000m. on 11 May 2000. The annual exponential rate of growth of population was about 2.2% in 1971–81, declining to 2.1% in 1981–91. The annual rate of growth declined again in 1991–2001, to 1.93%. At March 2001 the population density was 324 persons per sq km. By any standards, large areas of India are now over-populated; economic development is a constant race against population increase, and the control of future growth has become a major issue.

There are great variations in population density in the Indian countryside. There are very high densities of rural population in the rice-growing areas of the lower Ganga plain and in the Bengal delta; in parts of Assam; in parts of the eastern peninsular deltas and around Chennai; in Kerala; and in the coastal plains stretching from south of Mumbai north into Gujarat. Less spectacular, but still high densities are to be found in the upper Ganga plains and in the Punjab, in Assam, and in Tamil Nadu generally. At the other extreme, low densities occur in the Himalayas and Rajasthan desert (not surprisingly), in the jungle-covered hills and plateaux of the north-eastern Deccan (though these have been invaded by mining, by the iron and steel industry, and by agricultural colonists, refugees from Bangladesh); in inland Gujarat and Saurashtra; and in the marchland-hills that stretch from west to east in the region of the Narmada and Tapti. India also has its great and growing urban concentrations, especially in and around Mumbai, Kolkata and Chennai.

The peoples of India are extremely varied in composition. It is not particularly profitable to attempt to divide them into 'racial' groups distinguished by physical characteristics (though it may be of interest that representatives of what are often held to be primitive stocks may be met, especially among jungle tribes). It is more useful to consider the linguistic divisions of the Indian people, particularly since these in large measure form the basis for the current division of the federal union into states. The languages of north India are of the Indo-Aryan family, the most important member of which is Hindi, the language particularly of Uttar Pradesh and Haryana (now separated by an inter-state boundary from the Punjabi-speaking area to the west). Other members of the family (whose corresponding linguistic states will be readily identified) are Rajasthani, Bihari, Bengali, Oriya and Marathi. In south India the languages are of a quite different family, the Dravidian; and include Tamil (in Tamil Nadu), Malayalam (in Kerala), Telugu (in Andhra Pradesh), and Kannada (in Karnataka). There are also many tribal languages in the jungle areas and Tibetan languages in the Himalayas.

As is well known, Indian society is also divided into castes, each of which is endogamous and into one of which a man or woman enters irrevocably at birth. Status and, to some extent, occupation are still largely determined by caste, and caste considerations enter significantly into politics; although the scene is a complex and rapidly shifting one in many regions.

Religion is in India both a divisive and a cohesive force. Communal friction and disharmony are often largely a matter of religion, especially as between Hindus and Muslims in north India. Most of India's peoples, however, are, apart from certain tribal groups, united to a greater or lesser extent by cultural traits and the consciousness of a common heritage, and these derive in very large measure from age-old Hinduism.

History

DAVID TAYLOR

Based on an earlier article by PETER ROBB

India represents arguably the world's oldest continuous civilization, incorporating, as it does, certain features that seem traceable to the Indus valley culture of the middle of the third millennium BC. The continuity is attributable partly to an ability to digest internal and external challenges. Historically-documented reformers start with Mahavira, the founder of Jainism, and Gautama, the Buddha, in the sixth and fifth centuries BC, but include also Shankara (eighth to ninth centuries AD), greatest of the medieval Hindu philosophers, Guru Nanak (early 16th century), the first of the Sikh Gurus, and such 19th and 20th century reformers, revivalists and thinkers as Dayananda, Vivekananda and Gandhi. Invading conquerors, the harbingers of foreign influence, go back to the pastoralist Aryan migrants of pre-history; they include Alexander in the fourth century BC, White Huns in the fifth century AD, Afghans from the 12th century, Moguls from the 16th and Europeans from the 18th. India tended to absorb these changes or to superimpose them on existing practice: the price of this eclecticism was thus the almost endless diversity of India.

Social and religious forms have played the major part in providing unity, notably from the Aryan hymns of the *Rig Veda*, dating from perhaps 1500 BC and representing the beginnings of ritual and philosophy associated with Brahmanism, and from the commentaries and speculations known as the *Brahmanas* and *Upanishads* (800–500 BC), with their ideas of sacrifice and oneness. By contrast, political structures in India have ebbed and flowed over the millennia, though empires have played an important part in providing common experiences and promoting aspects of the tradition. Archaeological evidence now shows that the Indus valley civilization extended from the north of what is now Pakistan to Gujarat and western Uttar Pradesh, while between them the Magadha kingdom and its successor, the Mauryan empire, held sway over much of north India over a period of more than 300 years, reaching a climax under the great Emperor, Ashoka (273–232 BC). The Guptas too, with their efficient bureaucracy, flourished over an even larger area for almost 200 years from the fourth century AD, sponsoring great achievements in art, sciences, philosophy and law. In the south, too, Hindu powers arose, their influence sometimes stretching far beyond the subcontinent—the Palavas (AD 300–800), the Cholas (ninth to 13th century) and Vijayanagara (14th to 16th centuries). In the north, medieval Islamic empires were established: the Delhi sultanates (1211–1526) and then the great Moguls, particularly Akbar (1556–1605), whose authority and administrative system spread almost throughout the region. The British also played a unifying role as they came to rule more and more of the subcontinent after 1750, for they centralized and refined the bureaucracy, finances and military power of the State in India, they increased trade and improved communications, and they introduced a common language for some of the Indian élites and an assertive ethic and culture.

THE BRITISH IN INDIA

The British came to India as traders, and the East India Co was the original instrument of empire, lasting, in name, until 1858. Throughout their period in power the British preferred to rule with as light an influence as possible and often used Indian intermediaries and allies, but they inevitably strengthened the institutions for which they found a use. They introduced Western laws in regard to property, and a succession of Western concepts of the role and character of government. They allowed, if they did not positively encourage, the spread of ideas of equality, social justice, nationalism and representative democracy. Their revenue settlements, the building of telegraph lines, railways and canals, and the development of commercial agriculture subtly distorted the shape of rural society. In the towns, new classes appeared from among those whom the British had educated in English (mainly to serve in the administration, in minor roles) or those who had benefited from the British system and the functions that it called upon Indians to perform: there were merchants, landlords, officials, lawyers, doctors and teachers who had common interests which, to some extent, superseded caste, communal and regional differences. Some people of this kind came together after 1885 in an annual conference called the Indian National Congress.

In the 19th century the Government listened most to those whom they believed to head traditional social and political networks, but they also responded to English-educated Indians who were needed to run the administration and whose spokesmen carried weight in some quarters in Britain. These Indians stood out because of their class and education, and the constitutional concessions that the British made to them encouraged them to seek wider support. Controversies arose about how best to persuade the British to relinquish their power; those who advocated more active agitation and more permanent, popular organizations inevitably came into contact with religious movements. The rise of Mahatma Gandhi after 1920 represented a fusion of these forces, a rethinking of the approach of the Indian National Congress (widely referred to as simply Congress) and the incorporation of a wider range of people into the nationalist movement—changes, in fact, encouraged by the British reforms that Gandhi wished to boycott.

In the 1880s the British introduced a degree of local self-government (with powers to raise local revenue); in 1892, indirectly, and again in 1909, they conceded the elective principle in choosing who were to advise, though not control, the executive through the legislative councils. Finally between 1915 and 1919, an even more important breakthrough, they admitted publicly that they would eventually have to introduce responsible government, and in 1919 an Act of Parliament began this process by introducing shared control at the provincial level (diarchy). In 1935 this was extended to full control of provincial affairs under normal circumstances. Congress insisted, however, that without sovereignty political power would be meaningless, and persisted with its campaigns until independence was finally achieved in 1947. The timing of the transfer of power depended on the interaction of many factors, but the leading one was the mobilization of much of the population by Gandhi and Congress. This was a continuous process after 1919, but was marked by peaks of activity in 1919–22 (the Non-Co-operation Movement), 1930–32 (the Civil Disobedience Movement), and 1942–43 (the Quit India Movement).

As Congress came to occupy the pre-eminent position in Indian politics, so it had to address the question of India's cultural and social diversity. Most urgently, this meant the question of Hindu-Muslim relations, where the earlier ambiguity had been replaced by an improved categorization, influenced by British policies of classification and enumeration, for example through the introduction of decennial censuses. Although Congress leaders insisted that Congress was a movement for every Indian, Muslims were alarmed by what they perceived as the priority given to Hindu symbols and were themselves often caught up by the pan-Islamic movement of the time. Muslim élites, who had been favoured by the introduction of separate electorates in 1909, became increasingly concerned about their future as majority rule came closer. This anxiety was transmitted from the political classes, who hoped to inherit British power, through the *ulama* (the religious leadership) to the population at large. It was not helped by Congress insistence that it was an alternative government to the British, and thus superior in status to other political associations; the fact that the dangers were real, at least at the street level, was demonstrated in many savage communal riots, which though due to faults on both sides were obviously more alarming for the community in a minority. In the 1940s Muslim demands hardened, after the resignation of Congress ministries and the movement's subsequent outlawing because of Gandhi's 'Quit India' campaign. The British began to treat the Muslim League, which had at last consolidated its all-India status, as an equal with Congress. After the Second World War the British believed they could hold India only by force, and they had lost the will for this. Thus, after 1945, the British wanted to go, and when the Muslim League under Muhammad Ali Jinnah stood in their way, the British Prime Minister, Clement Attlee, and the last Viceroy, Lord Mountbatten of Burma, cut the knot and partitioned the country. The majority Muslim areas, never wholeheartedly behind the League (which had been led by men from the Muslim minority areas), found themselves yoked, for a time, as a new country: Pakistan.

INDEPENDENT INDIA AND THE RULE OF NEHRU

India became an independent dominion on 15 August 1947. The new Prime Minister, Jawaharlal Nehru, promised that it now would 'awake to life and freedom'. His administration, however, was marked by continuity as well as change. The immediate task was to restore the authority of the Government following a rising tide of panic and massacre as refugees fled from one part to the other of divided Punjab. Millions were uprooted and hundreds of thousands killed as the boundary force set up by Mountbatten proved wholly inadequate. Both the migration and the enormous death toll left permanent marks on India and Pakistan, but in the short term order was restored quite quickly. Its accomplishment, however, claimed the life of Gandhi, who had rushed to Delhi to try to stop the communal violence, and was assassinated in January 1948 by a Hindu extremist who seems to have considered him too conciliatory to the Muslims. Nehru told the nation 'the light has gone out'; but the shock of Gandhi's death restored it, at least for a time, by discrediting communalists.

It was necessary also to address the problem of the princely states, which numbered about 560, comprised two-fifths of the area of the subcontinent, and which varied enormously in size and population. Although in theory a state could opt for independence or for union with either India or Pakistan, in practice the withdrawal of British suzerainty made the first option difficult (if not impossible), while the second was a real choice only for those states adjacent to the borders between the two new countries. By independence day all but four had acceded to one or the other; and during 1948 the Home Minister, Vallabhbhai Patel, coerced and cajoled those that had joined India into being absorbed into the new Indian federation.

Two of the princely states that held aloof from the Indian Union were Junagadh (on the coast of Gujarat) and Hyderabad, the largest of them all. Both states had Muslim rulers (that of Hyderabad being known as the Nizam), but predominantly Hindu populations. Junagadh was occupied by Indian troops, after its prince opted for union with Pakistan, while Hyderabad was also occupied following the assumption of power by a local extremist group. Both states were subsequently taken into the Indian Union. (At the same time Kalat, situated in a remote desert area of Balochistan, was absorbed by Pakistan.) The remaining French colonial outposts on the subcontinent were later incorporated into India; Chandernagore in 1951, followed by Pondicherry, Karikal, Mahé and Yanam in 1954.

The state of Jammu and Kashmir, with its predominantly Muslim population and Hindu ruler, had also remained undecided, until October 1947 when Pathan tribesmen from Pakistan invaded in support of an internal rising. The Maharaja was promptly persuaded to opt for India, whose troops retained for him Jammu (with its Hindu-Sikh majority), Ladakh and the Vale of Kashmir. A 'popular' government was installed under Sheikh Abdullah, with a promise, embodied in a UN resolution, of a plebiscite to follow.

Unity was maintained within India firstly through the Constitution, which established the Indian Union as a secular parliamentary democracy on the Western model, with a federal structure but a strong centre. On 26 January 1950 India became a republic with a President as its constitutional head, but recognizing the British sovereign as head of the Commonwealth.

Indian unity was potentially threatened by the divisive element of language. Two issues were at stake. One was whether the state (previously provincial) boundaries should follow linguistic divisions. Some 14 language areas could be so demarcated, although inevitably there were inconsistencies and ambiguities. Although Gandhi had been an advocate of linguistic provinces, Nehru's initial stance after 1947 was to reject the redrawing of boundaries on the grounds that it would encourage local at the expense of national loyalties. However, it became clear that demands for linguistic states enjoyed widespread support, and in 1956 an extensive state reorganization, using language as the most important criterion, was carried out, which also allowed the distinction between former British and former princely areas to be abolished. In 1960 the erstwhile Bombay presidency was divided into Gujarat and Maharashtra, and in 1966 Haryana was created out of the Hindi-speaking but also predominantly Hindu areas of the Punjab, ostensibly on linguistic grounds, but, in fact, to form a Sikh-majority state in the new Punjab. On the north-east borders of the country, where predominantly tribal groups had been isolated during the colonial period, a number of local insurgencies, notably among the Naga and Mizo tribes, challenged the Government's authority. In 1962 the state of Nagaland was created out of the state of Assam, in the hope of placating some sections of the rebels.

The other linguistic issue was that of the national language. While the British had used English as the language of administration at the all-India level, Congress had become increasingly committed to the use of Hindi (sometimes referred to, for example by Gandhi, as Hindustani to avoid any Hindu overtone), the language spoken widely in northern India but not elsewhere. At independence it was decided to allow English to be used alongside Hindi as the country's official language for a limited period until 1965. As this date approached, however, it became clear that many non-Hindi speakers, especially in Tamil Nadu, wanted the use of English as an official language to continue, so as to counterbalance a possible dominance at the national level by Hindi speakers. Nehru had already taken a conciliatory line on the issue and his successors have continued to postpone the phasing out of English.

The supremacy of Congress in India's political life was ensured by the resolution of internal struggles in favour of Nehru, and from 1951 until the Chinese invasion in 1962 his influence was paramount. The assassination of Gandhi provided the occasion for an outright attack on communalist parties (as well as communalists within Congress) who had been encouraged by the war with Pakistan and the influx of Hindu refugees. The issue was further defused by the Nehru-Liaquat pact in 1950, temporarily settling the relations between India and Pakistan. At the first general election in 1951–52 communalist parties fared badly, and Congress scored an overwhelming victory.

The very success of Nehru's Congress posed a problem, however. In so far as Congress became the inevitable party of government after independence, it was bound to attract the ambitious and thus to find it difficult to evolve a consistent ideology: a compendium of more or less diverse interests could not also be a unified force for, say, socialism. For there did not evolve after independence, any more than before, a credible alternative party or parties of government. This lack resulted partly from deliberate Congress policy, partly from the wide slice of the political sphere encompassed by Congress as a result of its history as the central nationalist movement, and partly from the divisions among opposition groups. Potential or long-standing opposition leaders were ready to take office at times under Congress while permanent opposition groupings of any size proved elusive. The various opposition leaders, R. M. Lohia, Jayaprakash Narayan, Asok Mehta, J. B. Kripalani and so on, tended to be individualists rather than organization-men. Thus, under Nehru, the pre-eminence of Congress during the independence struggle was modified and preserved.

The initial Congress victory in the 1951–52 elections was followed by further victories in 1957 and 1962. Although Congress never quite succeeded in gaining an absolute majority of the popular vote, it far surpassed any other party, and, under India's 'first past the post' electoral system, easily won a majority of seats both at the national level and in almost all of the states, although the southern state of Kerala witnessed the world's first ever election of a Communist government in 1957.

There was broad continuity too, under Nehru, in the personnel of government. In spite of a certain shift in legislative and party membership towards agricultural classes and peasant castes, the beneficiaries tended to be those already dominant socially or economically; individuals whose ability and resources brought them to the top proved mostly to be members of dominant landholding castes. The monopoly of politics by an English-speaking professional élite, whose talents fitted them to negotiate with the British, may have continued slowly to be weakened as it began to be with the advent of popular agitation in the 1920s; but independence and democracy have also further emphasized the resilience of customary power structures, particularly the caste system, which had operated all along beside the British-inspired politicians.

Neither did change spread to the bureaucracy. Nehru opted for continuity among the administrators, partly through necessity, for the Congress cadres could not replace the bureaucracy the British had built. At the highest levels, it is true, political leaders displaced the administrator-rulers, often not receiving the advice of civil servants except on the bare question of legality, and combined bureaucratic and political functions. At lower levels, however, the executive functions of the higher civil servant remained, as for example in the district officer as the fount of authority in the locality. At the local level, government officials and police officers continued to be widely regarded as corrupt and inefficient.

Independence did change the priorities of government, even when policies continued existing trends. Thus, Nehru continued the social reforming tendencies which resulted from Western influence in British days, but with a determination impossible for alien rulers. He insisted on the secular nature of India's Government, on equality before the law (untouchability, as a status, was formally abolished under the Constitution), and on the passage of legislation providing, among other things, for divorce, monogamy, and equal rights of inheritance for Hindu women (although the Constitution called for a common civil code, the question of the status of Muslim family law was left unresolved). Under Nehru too, education was greatly expanded, but (repeating the mistake of the British) most notably at university and higher technical levels, and in towns; in the countryside the literacy rate has remained low, although gradually improving.

During the 1950s Nehru conducted foreign affairs with little interference. He began by supporting nationalist forces in Indonesia, mainland South-East Asia and elsewhere. Acutely aware of East–West tension, and of the dangers of a nuclear war in the post-1945 years, he declared the policy of non-involvement, and strove to build up a third force of uncommitted or non-aligned nations. This led him to welcome the communist rise to power in China in 1949 and brought him to the Bandung conference of Afro-Asian states in 1955.

This was the zenith of Nehru's international influence and from this moment his star seemed to decline. He was forthright in condemning the United Kingdom and France over Suez in 1956, but offended Indian right-wing opinion by being less clear on the issue of Soviet intervention in Hungary. In 1959 the Chinese decision to rule, instead of control, Tibet (Xizang), followed by the Dalai Lama's flight to India, put him under further pressure from right-wing opinion and embroiled him with China itself. It gradually became clear that China did not regard its border with India as settled, and, partly under pressure from public opinion and the army, Nehru agreed to a policy of asserting Indian presence up to the border it claimed. The dispute became serious with the discovery of a Chinese road across the desolate Aksai Chin plateau, to the north of Ladakh. Nehru made some bellicose speeches, and the Indians engaged in minor skirmishes. Suddenly, in 1962, the Chinese advanced in full force against apparently unprepared Indian positions, overran them, continued rapidly on into India, and then withdrew to their earlier positions. Thus, Nehru's plan for an unaligned bloc, to be led by India in close friendship with China, was finally destroyed, and the way was open for even closer ties with the USSR. In December 1961 India's remaining credit as a peacemaker was undermined with the occupation of the Portuguese enclaves of Goa, Daman and Diu, when Nehru finally abandoned, under heavy internal pressure, the unpromising negotiations with Portugal to have these territories accede to India without force.

INDIRA GANDHI'S RULE

The First Period, 1966–77

Although in the last 18 months of his life Nehru was much criticized, there were serious concerns about what would happen after his death. In the event, in May 1964, the transition was smooth and the succession passed to Lal Bahadur Shastri, not the most able nor the closest to Nehru among the members of the outgoing Government, but something of a consensus figure. Shastri soon found himself faced with three national crises; first, over the proclamation of Hindi as the sole official language in January 1965, followed by the Rann of Kutch incident with Pakistan in April and finally the three-weeks' war with Pakistan in September. His stature grew with this last event, in which India resisted Pakistan's efforts to seize Kashmir by force. He died, however, in January 1966, after going to Tashkent to meet the Pakistani President, Ayub Khan, and the Soviet Premier, Aleksei Kosygin. His successor was Nehru's daughter, Indira Gandhi, with the kingmaker, K. Kamaraj, in the background and the existing Congress team except for Morarji Desai, who left because he would be Prime Minister or nothing.

In 1967 the general election ended the nearly general domination of Congress in the states, and returned it to power at Delhi with a much reduced majority. Indira Gandhi continued as Prime Minister, but was now strengthened by a deal with Morarji Desai who became Deputy Premier and Finance Minister. In Madras (subsequently renamed Tamil Nadu) the strongly regionalist Dravida Munnetra Kazhagam (DMK) took power, and in Kerala communist rule was restored. Anti-Congress ministries were set up in several other states, but proved so unstable that mid-term elections were held from Haryana to West Bengal. The chief beneficiaries of the Congress losses were the left-wing pro-communist groups and the Hindu nationalist party, the Jana Sangh.

The Congress managers had supported Indira Gandhi as another consensus figure, and had no intention of reducing their influence in her favour, or condoning any substantial change in the Congress programme. The election results of 1967, however, had shaken their credibility, and shown to many, including Indira Gandhi, that Congress needed a new image and revitalized organization if it was to remain in power. It was not in Indira Gandhi's personal style, either, to leave the initiative in the hands of others. The crisis was precipitated by the death of the respected President Zakir Husain in May 1969. The presidency possesses considerable reserve powers which would have placed it in a key position in the event, as then seemed quite possible, of the next general election failing to give Congress an overall majority. The right wing adopted N. S. Reddy as the Congress candidate. Indira Gandhi retorted by implementing the long-standing Congress promise to nationalize the banks, by dismissing Desai from the finance ministry and by supporting the Vice-President, V. V. Giri, a left-wing Congress politician, for the presidency. His subsequent success in winning the post greatly strengthened her hand.

In November 1969 Congress openly split. Although in the legislature Indira Gandhi retained the support of a majority of the party's members, reflecting the support she commanded in the country as a whole, she was obliged to depend, in the first instance, on left-wing groups outside Congress to maintain a majority in the Lok Sabha (House of the People, the lower parliamentary house). In 1970 Congress success with communist allies in the Kerala elections encouraged the Prime Minister to dissolve the Lok Sabha. The elections of February–March 1971 proved a notable success, both for Indira Gandhi herself and her wing of Congress, which was initially known as Congress (R). Once again an effective opposition had failed to emerge, largely because Congress (R) occupied the middle ground ideologically and, by being in power, attracted recruits as the party of government. The rival Congress (O) was left with little positive policy; and the degree to which Indira Gandhi had commandeered the territory of the socialists was marked by their evident confusion about how to react to her.

Hard on the election results came a fresh crisis with Pakistan: its army's intervention in East Pakistan (now Bangladesh). India was faced with an immense refugee problem: about 7m. by August 1971, nearly all in West Bengal. First, India publicized the problem and asked for help. Next, it concluded in

August a treaty with the Soviet Union: 'non-alignment' was safeguarded, but the two countries promised mutual support, short of actual military involvement, in the event of either being attacked by a third. Finally, thus assured of non-interference, India first sheltered, then trained and armed, and finally gave support to Bangladeshi guerrilla forces along and across the border. These actions eventually resulted in open warfare between India and Pakistan. In December, after 11 days of fighting, India won a comprehensive victory in East Bengal, while maintaining its position in the west. In July 1972 Indira Gandhi and the President of Pakistan, Zulfikar Ali Bhutto, signed the Simla (later renamed Shimla) Agreement, in which both countries renounced the use of force and agreed to respect the cease-fire line in Kashmir and international borders elsewhere. They also agreed to discuss outstanding issues on a bilateral basis rather than taking them to international fora such as the UN.

However, the explosion of India's first nuclear device in May 1974 set back the improvement in relations with Pakistan, and resulted in much criticism throughout the world. India, apparently supreme in the subcontinent in 1971, once again found its position challenged. The fall of Mujib in Bangladesh in August 1975 brought into the open several disputes and fears of Indian dominance. The inclusion of Sikkim in the Indian Union (April 1975) led to strained relations with Nepal. Indian foreign policy later became more pragmatic. In mid-1976 agreement was reached with Pakistan on exchange of ambassadors and restoration of air links, and relations improved with China to the point of an exchange of ambassadors.

Indira Gandhi's personal position had been further strengthened by state elections in 1972. With Congress ministries in almost all states, she was able to secure Chief Ministers who would carry out her policies. Nevertheless, discontent grew as India was severely affected by drought in 1973 and 1974, while the world-wide petroleum crisis pushed up inflation and lowered the standard of living throughout Indian society. Unrest developed in a number of states, while in Gujarat and Bihar the veteran socialist, Jayaprakash Narayan, headed a popular campaign against the local Congress governments, alleging corruption. During 1974 he sought allies more widely and began to attack the central Government. His coalition lacked ideological coherence, including, as it did, parties both to the right and left of Congress, but in June 1975, as the Janata Front, it won control of the state government in Gujarat.

In June 1975 the Allahabad High Court found Indira Gandhi guilty of electoral malpractices in her own constituency in the 1971 election (although most observers considered them to have been rather trivial). Indira Gandhi then proclaimed a state of emergency and arrested large numbers of her opponents. The Houses of Parliament were recalled and, in the absence of non-Government members (other than the Communist Party of India), rapidly approved constitutional amendments to strengthen the executive and legislature, and to protect the Prime Minister through retrospective legislation.

The emergency saw some gains in administrative efficiency, an apparently successful attack on the 'black market' and some reduction in the predicted rate of inflation. Opponents were silenced where they were not imprisoned, news censorship was imposed and non-Congress state governments in Tamil Nadu and Gujarat were removed. In January 1977, however, Indira Gandhi unexpectedly announced that the general election, hitherto postponed, would be held in March, when the state of emergency would also be terminated. A number of its restrictions were immediately lifted. Three explanations for this manoeuvre seem more likely than others: that Indira Gandhi was misinformed about her popularity or, being informed, saw this as her last chance to gain a popular mandate; that she wished to allow the political advance of her second son, Sanjay, and members of his Youth Congress; and that, once again, she needed to outflank opponents within her own party, an idea supported by the resignation of Jagjivan Ram (who, it was suggested, had earlier advocated the Prime Minister's resignation) after the elections were announced.

The Janata Interlude, 1977–80

Congress faced a large number of straight contests, as the opposition groups had either come together formally in the Janata Party or had entered into electoral agreements, as was the case with Jagjivan Ram's new Congress for Democracy. The results must rank among the most extraordinary in recent times. Indira Gandhi lost her own seat in the Lok Sabha and Congress was defeated throughout north India, winning no seats at all in areas where they had always seemed invincible. Indira Gandhi had alienated local political machines through her assertions of central power and her encouragement of Sanjay, the middle classes through the attacks on the courts, the press and freedom of expression, the farmers through the development tax, the workers through the freezing of wages and the ban on strike action, and the poor through real or imagined excesses in slum clearance and sterilization. However, in the south, Congress and its allies improved their position: there, emergency measures were less effective and fewer leaders were imprisoned, Jagjivan Ram was less well-known and the Janata Party unimportant, the government-controlled radio was still the main source of outside information, and the major opposition party, Tamil Nadu's DMK, had been discredited by charges of corruption.

The first tasks for the Janata Government, under the leadership of Morarji Desai, were to dismantle the machinery of the state of emergency and to repair the Constitution. It had its successes. It transformed an electoral alliance into a ruling party, helped by the reluctant agreement of Jagjivan Ram and his supporters to merge with the majority. It secured its candidate, N. S. Reddy, as President in July 1977.

However, serious rifts soon appeared: they widened or narrowed in tandem with Indira Gandhi's fortunes. Politically unsuccessful in 1978, strongly criticized by the Shah Commission on the state of emergency and even subject to criminal charges, Indira Gandhi none the less won a Lok Sabha by-election in Karnataka in November 1978; by then her supporters had overall majorities in state assemblies in Karnataka and Andhra Pradesh, had formed a brief coalition in Maharashtra, and had become the major parliamentary opposition at the centre. Over the same period, the Janata Government threatened to disintegrate. The party rallied a little in 1979, however, while Indira Gandhi's supporters were themselves broken into factions by her quarrels with Devaraj Urs. At this point the Congress faction led by Indira Gandhi became known as Congress (I).

Gradually, however, Morarji Desai's huge majority disappeared, and the withdrawal of communist and socialist support forced his resignation in July 1979. President Reddy, in an unprecedented situation, first called on Y. B. Chavan, leader of the then official opposition, and later asked Charan Singh, former Minister of Finance and of Home Affairs in the Janata Government and now head of the Lok Dal, to form a government. Singh was dependent on the tacit support of Indira Gandhi, which was withdrawn as soon as he took office. Finally, ignoring the claims of Jagjivan Ram, who eventually succeeded Desai as Janata leader, the President dissolved Parliament in August. Elections to the Lok Sabha were held in January 1980.

The Final Phase, 1980–84

Indira Gandhi won an overwhelming victory, though with only 42% of the total vote. Sanjay Gandhi entered the Lok Sabha for the first time. Sanjay had come to have the support of men and women of his own generation and, because of his influence on the selection of candidates, many were elected with him. He was, of course, himself influential by virtue of being the heir apparent, and, when he met his death in an air crash in June 1980, this need continued to be felt. By 1981 some people spoke of the inevitable succession of his elder brother, Rajiv, and in June 1981 Rajiv won, by a large majority, Sanjay's former seat. In February 1983 he became General Secretary of the All-India Congress Committee.

Indira Gandhi's second term in office was overshadowed by the violent regional or religious separatism that was expressed in some communities, including those that had enjoyed economic advantages. In Assam and north-eastern India, feelings against Bengali residents, especially those who had migrated recently from Bangladesh, were expressed in murders, bomb outrages, strikes and a campaign of non-co-operation; in 1982 and 1983 many hundreds of lives were lost in this region. The most serious outbreaks of violence occurred, however, in the Punjab, where a militant Sikh secessionist movement had been smouldering for some years, and had, it is widely believed, been encouraged by Congress (I) in order to outflank the moderate wing of its local opponents, the Akali Dal, a Sikh-based political party which had held power between 1977 and 1980.

Certainly, Indira Gandhi succeeded in ousting the Akali Dal from office in the Punjab, but with tragic consequences. At first her Government faced demands from a small minority for a separate Sikh state ('Khalistan') and, more generally, for a settlement of grievances about land and water rights, communal recognition and the shared state capital at Chandigarh. By 1984, however, there was a growing polarization of Hindus and Sikhs, advanced chiefly by the killing of hundreds of people by terrorists. Reluctant to act, the Government came under severe pressure from Hindus. With considerable financial resources and discipline, Sikh followers of the extremist leader, Jarnail Singh Bhindranwale, transformed the Golden Temple at Amritsar into a terrorist stronghold. Communal polarization was completed by the storming of the Temple complex by the Indian army, the death of Bhindranwale and hundreds of his supporters, damage to sacred buildings, and an army blockade and curfew in the Punjab. Serious negotiations seemed for a time to be impossible, and foreign as well as communal relations worsened, with officially supported claims of Pakistani involvement and criticism of British failure to silence Sikhs in exile. The climax came, without breaking the impasse: Indira Gandhi was assassinated in October 1984 by Sikh members of her personal guard. Her death was followed by riots, especially in Delhi, in which many hundreds of Sikhs were massacred.

FROM INDIRA GANDHI TO NARASIMHA RAO

Rajiv Gandhi's Succession

In contrast to her father, Indira Gandhi had centralized and personalized power, weakening the judiciary, the Parliament and the party. Her attempts to control state as well as central politics had strained the Union and brought often no more than pyrrhic victories to her cause. The succession of her son, Rajiv, to lead the party and the Government—when he had so recently been regarded as unready for such responsibilities—was a comment not only on Indira Gandhi's dynastic ambitions but on her political legacy. The assassination, none the less, brought genuine feelings of outrage, especially among Hindus in north India, and a readiness to accept Rajiv as a true leader. His early command of events won respect, too, though also criticism of his failure to prevent the violence against Sikhs in the immediate aftermath of his mother's murder, and to eschew appeals to Hindu chauvinism during the campaigning for the Lok Sabha elections in December 1984. The results of the elections were an unprecedented triumph for Congress (I) in seats, and a solid gesture of support in terms of votes. National opposition was reduced to 44 seats among five parties out of the 508 seats contested. State elections in many areas in 1985 confirmed the strength of Rajiv Gandhi's position in most of the country.

The new Prime Minister's initial moves were conciliatory and progressive. He consulted with opposition leaders, promised to avoid interfering with the judiciary and embarked upon reforms to increase efficiency and reduce corruption. He soon became seen as representative of a new breed of technocrats, with an appeal to the younger generation. In particular, the 1985 budget, drawn up by the Minister of Finance, Vishwanath Pratap (V.P.) Singh, initiated a process of liberalization and restructuring which continues to the present and which, in some respects, marked the end of the Nehruvian approach to economic planning. Rajiv Gandhi also, in the face of opposition from some of his advisers, attempted to revitalize Congress (I) by promising internal party elections for the first time since the split of 1969.

In the short term, however, Rajiv Gandhi's most significant achievement was to reverse his mother's fiercely power-orientated centralizing approach and to talk seriously to the leaders of various regional movements. In August 1985 he signed an agreement in Assam limiting the voting rights of immigrants (mainly Bangladeshis), a move which led to the holding of state elections in December of the same year. These were won by the Asom Gana Parishad (AGP), which represented the militant Assamese groups.

Rajiv Gandhi's new conciliatory approach achieved what appeared to be its greatest success in July 1985, when he came to an agreement with the principal leader of the Akali Dal, Harchand Singh Longowal, under which fresh elections were to be held in the Punjab and some concessions were to be made to Sikh demands. The agreement seemed to have the potential to defuse separatist demands and bypass the militants. Although Longowal himself was assassinated by terrorists, the promised elections, which were held in September 1985, gave victory to the Akali Dal, and its leader, S. S. Barnala, became Chief Minister.

In June 1986 Laldenga, the leader of the Mizo National Front (MNF), signed a peace agreement with Rajiv Gandhi, thus ending 25 years of rebellion. The accord granted Mizoram limited autonomy in the drafting of local laws, independent trade with neighbouring foreign countries and a general amnesty for all Mizo rebels. Laldenga led an interim coalition government, formed by the MNF and Congress (I), until February 1987, when the MNF won an absolute majority at elections to the state assembly. In the same month, Mizoram and Arunachal Pradesh were officially admitted as the 23rd and 24th states of India, respectively, and in May the Union Territory of Goa became India's 25th state.

From the beginning of 1986, however, it became apparent that the 'honeymoon period' was over, and gradually problems began to accumulate which eventually overwhelmed the still-inexperienced Prime Minister. It was, in fact, in the Punjab where the situation first began to show signs of deterioration. The agreement with Longowal had left a number of issues unresolved. Protracted negotiations led to an increase in Sikh extremism and encouraged a temporary recapture of the Golden Temple by Sikh militants in early 1986. Measures to combat violence by the police and paramilitary forces, who were often accused of brutality and arbitrary executions of suspects, jeopardized the standing of the popular state government, and the ruling Akali Dal began to be plagued by internal dissent. On the other hand, the proposed concessions to the Sikhs, which were regarded as inadequate in the Punjab, gave rise to a strong reaction elsewhere, especially in the neighbouring state of Haryana. State elections were due to be held in Haryana in mid-1987 and, in an attempt to improve Congress (I)'s chances, Rajiv Gandhi dismissed the Barnala government in the Punjab in May of that year and introduced President's rule. However, not only did this move fail to prevent the defeat of Congress (I) in Haryana, it also ended any prospect of co-operation with moderate Sikhs in the Punjab. In addition, as Barnala had predicted, it also worsened the security situation, and in the late 1980s and into the early 1990s, thousands of people on all sides of the conflict died in the ensuing disturbances.

Other regional demands came to the fore in the late 1980s and created difficulties not only for Rajiv Gandhi's Government but also for state government leaders. In West Bengal in 1987, for example, a regional movement, led by the Gorkha National Liberation Front under Subhas Ghising, emerged in Darjeeling to demand a separate state for the Nepali speakers of the area. It was claimed by the communist state government of West Bengal that the regionalist agitation had been supported by Congress (I) in an attempt to destabilize it. At all events, an agreement was drawn up by the Minister of Home Affairs in July 1988, which attempted to reach a compromise. Under the agreement, a semi-autonomous Hill Development Council was established, which remained, however, within the framework of West Bengal. In Assam and other north-eastern states, there continued to be localized tribal insurgencies. In Tripura the Tripura National Volunteers were responsible for the deaths of several hundred people in the 1980s, but in August 1988 they were persuaded by the central Government to come to an agreement by which they ceased hostilities and abandoned their demands for a separate state in return for a number of specific concessions. In Assam the Bodo tribal group increased its pressure for a separate state in early 1989, but, again, a potentially explosive situation was defused by the opening up of peaceful negotiations between the separatists and government officials.

While the Punjab remained the most serious problem facing Rajiv Gandhi, he lost political momentum and credibility in other areas as well. Tension between rival castes and communities (particularly between Hindus and Muslims) grew, and there were several major outbreaks of violence. Within his own party,

Rajiv Gandhi's leadership came increasingly into question, as he failed to reconcile the various factions. In 1987, following a number of major electoral set-backs for Congress (I) (e.g. in Kerala and Haryana), several ministers resigned, notably V. P. Singh, who had been moved from the Ministry of Finance to the Ministry of Defence, allegedly because of pressure from businessmen who resented his efforts to eradicate malpractice and tax evasion. In July Singh and some other senior figures were expelled from Congress (I) for 'anti-party activities' and in October established their own Jan Morcha (People's Front), advocating more radical social change. It was against this background that allegations of financial corruption in the upper echelons of Congress (I) began to be made, especially regarding the 'Bofors affair', in which large payments appear to have been made to Indian agents by a Swedish company in connection with its sales of artillery to the Indian Government. Rajiv Gandhi's response to the mounting pressure was to fall back on the style of politics that had been identified with his mother. Several of her advisers, who had been moved aside, were brought back into favour and there was, again, a marked centralization of party authority. A more confrontational style appeared to be adopted by the central administration towards non-Congress (I) state governments. After the death in December 1987 of the popular Chief Minister of Tamil Nadu, M. G. Ramachandran, Congress (I) attempted to take advantage of a rift within his party, the All-India Anna Dravida Munnetra Kazhagam (AIADMK) to re-establish itself as a political force in the state. Presidential rule was imposed in January 1988 and AIADMK activists were arrested.

The opposition parties responded by seeking a common position from which to resist Congress (I). A new anti-Government alliance was formed at the end of 1987 and was strengthened in mid-1988 with the creation of the National Front (Rashtriya Morcha): a coalition of the four major centrist parties (the Indian National Congress (S), the Jan Morcha, the Janata Party and the Lok Dal (A)) and three major regional parties (the Asom Gana Parishad, the DMK and the Telugu Desam). In October the Jan Morcha, Janata Party and Lok Dal merged to form the Janata Dal (People's Party), which was to work in collaboration with the National Front. V. P. Singh, who in July had achieved a major parliamentary by-election victory in the Gandhi home territory of Allahabad, was elected President of the Janata Dal. Further opposition to Rajiv Gandhi's Government was incited by serious drought and social conflict that occurred in a number of different areas of the country.

In January 1989 Congress (I) was decisively defeated by the DMK in the elections to the state assembly in Tamil Nadu, following the period of presidential rule, but gained outright majorities over the regional parties in elections in the less significant states of Nagaland and Mizoram where local factors operated. During the remainder of 1989 both Congress (I) and the opposition fronts clearly began to prepare for the general election that was due to be held by the end of the year. While the opposition continued its campaign against alleged government corruption and inefficiency, it had difficulty in overcoming its own very marked internal quarrels. Apart from doing its utmost to exploit the internecine differences within the opposition, Congress (I) took steps to increase its popularity and political control. For example, in mid-1989 the Government proposed to consolidate the Panchayat Raj scheme (see Directory—The Constitution) so as to standardize and democratize local government on the basis of more regular elections and to strengthen its link with district-level planning.

As 1989 progressed, however, the political calculations of all the parties were affected by the increase in Hindu militancy, orchestrated by the so-called Sangh Parivar, a grouping of organizations headed by the Rashtriya Swayamsevak Sangh (RSS—National Volunteer Organization). The RSS originated prior to 1947, when it articulated communal Hindu unease with Congress policies. It was, indeed, banned in the early years of independence. Operating through organizations such as the fundamentalist Vishwa Hindu Parishad (VHP—World Hindu Council), and closely associated first with the Jana Sangh and then with the Bharatiya Janata Party (BJP—Indian People's Party), it had begun to make an impact in the early 1980s by exploiting citizens' uncertainties about their place in a rapidly-changing environment, both in India and worldwide. An episode in 1986, when for short-term political reasons Rajiv Gandhi's Government had introduced special legislation restricting the rights of divorced Muslim women, gave the RSS and its allies new opportunities. In 1984 a campaign was launched over the status of a disputed religious site in the town of Ayodhya in northern India. It was claimed that a disused 16th-century mosque (the Babri Masjid) stood on the site of the birthplace of the god Ram (Ram Janambhoomi) and that an ancient Hindu temple had been demolished to allow its construction. During 1989 those who advocated the building of a new temple on the site, including the BJP, organized a high-profile foundation ceremony at Ayodhya. Congress (I) was faced with the dilemma as to which attitude to adopt. In the end, it chose to appear accommodating towards the temple protagonists, thus, in effect, losing Muslim support while failing to curtail the BJP's strength. The Janata Dal, although it had an electoral understanding with the BJP, maintained a broadly secular posture.

The 1989 Elections and Coalition Government

Finally, Rajiv Gandhi called the general election a few weeks ahead of schedule and polling took place on 22–26 November 1989 for 525 of the 545 seats in the Lok Sabha, as well as for assemblies in a number of states. Assam did not take part in the elections, owing to tribal unrest and to the incomplete state of the electoral rolls. Congress (I) had clearly been damaged by the corruption charges and by the public perception that it had reverted to the patterns of the Indira Gandhi period, and won only 193 seats, which constituted a massive decline compared with its result in the general election of 1984. The party also lost control of the large northern states of Uttar Pradesh and Bihar in the concurrent state assembly elections. The Janata Dal won 141 seats in the Lok Sabha, and its allies in the National Front a further three. The BJP had been the main beneficiary of the recent surge in Hindu communal feeling and was able to secure 88 seats, mainly in the Hindi-speaking areas of northern and central India. The Communist Party of India—Marxist (which is well-established in West Bengal but enjoys only limited support elsewhere), together with the Communist Party of India, won 51 seats. Once all the votes had been counted, the balance of forces was such that almost any combination of parties was theoretically possible, but, in the end, the National Front was able to form a minority Government (the first minority Government in Indian history) with support from both the BJP and the communist parties. V. P. Singh was elected leader of the Janata Dal Parliamentary Party and thus became Prime Minister in early December, but only after performing complex and calculating manoeuvres to outflank his rival, Chandra Shekhar. To maintain a political balance, V. P. Singh appointed Devi Lal, the populist Chief Minister of Haryana, as Deputy Prime Minister.

Domestic events in India during V. P. Singh's period in office were dominated by a series of interrelated crises, which eventually overwhelmed the National Front Government. The first of these was the factional rivalry within the Government, which focused, in particular, on the ambitions of Devi Lal, the Deputy Prime Minister. In mid-July 1990 this culminated in a political confrontation, which led eventually to Devi Lal's dismissal. Partly to counter Devi Lal's retaliatory political challenge, and partly in an attempt to increase and strengthen his longer-term support, V. P. Singh then made the dramatic announcement that his Government planned to implement the recommendations of the Mandal Commission. This had been established by the Morarji Desai Government in the late 1970s to consider how best to improve the welfare of the more deprived sections of society. It was, in particular, concerned with the so-called 'other backward classes' (OBCs), who had not been eligible at the national level for the range of benefits in education and employment that had been given after independence to the former untouchables (Harijans) or 'scheduled castes'. The OBCs had become increasingly powerful in political terms, as they utilized their electoral strength. The Commission had proposed, in the absence of any better criterion, that jobs and other benefits within the central government sector should be allocated on the basis of caste. This recommendation, in fact, only reflected what was already being practised at state government level in much of the country, but was regarded, nevertheless, as a symbolic attack on the position of the urban middle class, which is drawn disproportionately from the upper castes. V. P. Singh's announcement provoked widespread unrest in northern Indian cities, and by early October 1990 about 40 students had, as a form of protest, committed suicide by self-immolation. Thereafter, however, attention shifted to the renewed BJP campaign over the disputed religious site at Ayodhya. Here, too, a strong element of political calculation was at work. The BJP leadership, through its high-profile campaign which was carried out with the avid support of the VHP, risked losing some of its core support in the cities. At the same time, however, the Ayodhya campaign was an opportunity to give the widest publicity to its ideological claim, through its slogan of *Hindutva* (Hinduness), that it represented the interests of India's majority. The means employed to convey this message was a *rath yatra* (procession) across India to Ayodhya led by L. K. Advani, the BJP President. The procession itself was halted by government action before it reached Ayodhya, but there was a major confrontation between security forces and demonstrators at the disputed shrine on 30 October, and a number of people were killed. Many arrests were made elsewhere, in an attempt to contain the disturbances. As a consequence of the confrontation, there were riots in many northern Indian cities, in which Muslims were the principal victims.

It was against this highly charged background that the BJP withdrew its support for the National Front Government. Following a series of complicated political manoeuvres behind the scenes and the defeat of V. P. Singh in a vote of 'no confidence', a new Government was formed in November 1990 by Chandra Shekhar, the erstwhile President of the Janata Dal who had defected from the party with a small group of supporters to form the Janata Dal (S) (which merged with the Janata Party in April 1991 to become the Samajwadi Party). The new Government was totally dependent, however, on the support of Congress (I). This was withdrawn in March 1991, and consequently there was no alternative other than to hold fresh elections, which were scheduled to take place over three days in late May. Unlike the situation in 1989, there was no co-operation on a nation-wide scale between the various political parties, except between the Janata Dal and the communist parties. Congress (I), the BJP and the Janata Dal each sought to exploit its particular appeal, on the basis of stability and experience, *Hindutva*, and caste-based social justice, respectively, while other parties, particularly the Samajwadi Party, tried to strenghen their position in particular states.

As the elections approached, it seemed likely that no party would win an outright majority, and that the political stalemate would continue. On 21 May 1991, however, after the first day's polling had taken place, Rajiv Gandhi was assassinated while campaigning in the southern state of Tamil Nadu. It seems almost certain that the assassination was carried out by members of the Liberation Tigers of Tamil Eelam (LTTE), who had suffered most as a result of India's intervention in Sri Lanka in 1987–90 (see below). The remaining elections were postponed while the funeral of the former Prime Minister took place, and were held in mid-June. The final results gave Congress (I) 227 of the 511 seats contested (its ally, the AIADMK, also regained control of Tamil Nadu with a convincing majority). This was a significant increase on the predicted figure and undoubtedly represented the effect of a 'sympathy wave'. More remarkable, however, was the success of the BJP, which increased its number of seats in the Lok Sabha from 88 to 119 and almost doubled its share of the vote.

The death of Rajiv Gandhi had left his party without any immediately obvious successor. In the end, P. V. Narasimha Rao, a long-standing Gandhi family loyalist who, at the same time, enjoyed wide respect within Congress (which had gradually shed its (I) suffix), was chosen as interim party President and assumed the premiership. Narasimha Rao's Council of Ministers represented a careful balance between existing factions and groups within Congress. In the early weeks of Narasimha Rao's Government, which lacked a majority in the Lok Sabha, it became clear that the other parties did not want yet another political upheaval and were prepared to allow the new Government, initially at least, an easy passage. With the exception of the BJP, the main parties abstained on a vote of confidence in July 1991, and the choice of Speaker was reached by consensus. At around the same time, the Congress candidate, Dr Shankar Dayal Sharma, was elected, without any serious opposition, to the country's presidency.

INDIA IN TRANSITION

The Narasimha Rao Government

While it was clear from the beginning of his premiership that Narasimha Rao would need to utilize all his political skills to face the multifarious challenges of Hindu nationalism, lower caste unrest and regional autonomist movements, he used the initial 'honeymoon' period of office to inaugurate a new and much more far-reaching phase of economic restructuring than any previously undertaken. The economy in 1991 was in a parlous state, and simultaneous foreign-exchange and fiscal crises meant that the country was on the verge of bankruptcy. In a bold move, Narasimha Rao appointed an economist and former Governor of the Reserve Bank of India, Dr Manmohan Singh, to the post of Minister of Finance. Dr Singh immediately carried out a number of emergency measures, including a substantial devaluation of the rupee and stringent curbs on imports. At the same time, help was sought from the IMF, and gradually the economic situation stabilized. It was widely felt that, in the longer term, a new departure in economic policy was necessary, and this was implemented in the July 1991 and February 1992 budgets. During this period, almost the whole of the apparatus of economic regulation was dismantled, the rupee was made partially convertible, the banking system overhauled and foreign investment encouraged. Some of these measures were unpopular with the opposition and with certain sections of Congress, and progress in some areas was impeded; for example, the removal of subsidies on fertilizer directly affected many farmers and therefore had to be modified. The rapid removal of controls also created the climate for a massive bank fraud in May 1992 linked to stock-exchange speculation. The most prominent figure in these events, Harshad Mehta, was arrested, but the ramifications were much wider and led, among other things, to the resignation of the Minister of Commerce. Nerver-theless, the rapidly expanding Indian middle class responded favourably to the new policies, and among the left-wing section of the population it was accepted that some of the new economic initiatives were long overdue.

The generally positive news on the economic front, however, was overshadowed by the return, with redoubled strength, of the Ayodhya question. The BJP had been buoyed by its success in the 1991 elections, and had also to satisfy the expectations of its many supporters who thought that the mosque would now be demolished and a temple constructed. In January 1992 an attempt on the part of the BJP to exploit the Kashmir issue (see below) went awry, but by the middle of the year it had begun to set deadlines for work to begin on the temple, and was able to use its control of the state government in Uttar Pradesh to good effect. Narasimha Rao's response was cautious and aimed at exhausting the BJP through discussion and legal manoeuvre. In November, however, the BJP launched yet another mass campaign. This culminated on 6 December with the demolition of the mosque at Ayodhya and the creation of a makeshift temple on the site. Claims and counterclaims were immediately made about who was responsible for these events. It was clear that neither the central Government nor the state government had been able to take the necessary swift action that might have averted the demolition, but whether this reflected incompetence or deliberate intent is unclear. Whatever the position adopted by the party leaders, the demolition of the mosque was clearly regarded as a great victory by many of the BJP's supporters. One consequence was an outbreak of rioting in many cities in which hundreds of lives (the majority Muslim) were lost. The worst-affected city was Mumbai, and in January 1993 renewed violence broke out there, resulting in more than 500 deaths, again mainly Muslim. On 12 March there were a number of bomb explosions in Mumbai, which caused about 250 casualties. The Government claimed that these latter incidents were linked to Pakistan intelligence agencies.

The Government's immediate response to the demolition of the mosque was to arrest the senior leadership of the BJP (although they were later released), ban the RSS, and dismiss the BJP state governments in Uttar Pradesh and in three other states. It was also announced that the mosque would be rebuilt.

This did not in fact happen and much of the rest of 1993 appeared to be characterized by political drift. In July a vote of 'no confidence' was moved in the Lok Sabha by virtually all the opposition parties; Narasimha Rao survived by a narrow margin of 14 votes, composed, for the most part, of defectors from another party who had been attracted by promises of reward. However, in the polls that were held in November in the states where the BJP governments had been dismissed, the BJP advance was very clearly halted. In Uttar Pradesh the BJP lost control, not to Congress, whose credibility had been unable to recover from the events at Ayodhya, but to a coalition of parties representing the interests of the OBCs, 'scheduled castes' and Muslims. In the remaining three states the BJP held one and lost two to Congress; it also gained control of the newly established legislative assembly in the capital, Delhi. With hindsight, it appeared to many observers that the Prime Minister had followed a successful strategy of defusing confrontation, although some critics argued that his actions had given the BJP added respectability.

The following year, 1994, was again a period of consolidation. The economic reforms were allowed to stand, and continued to show results, but there were few fresh initiatives and the Government went out of its way to emphasize its commitment to social welfare. Rao's administration was, however, vulnerable to opposition charges that it was too willing to accept external interference in economic management. This issue came to a head in the early part of the year with the launch by the opposition of a campaign against India signing the new General Agreement of Tariffs and Trade (GATT) accord, the so-called Dunkel draft. Other areas where the Congress Government was challenged included the question of corruption. In July and August there was a three-week boycott of Parliament by the opposition over what it regarded as lack of effective action following a parliamentary inquiry into the 1992 bank scandal (see above) in order to downplay the involvement of Congress ministers.

A series of state elections were held in two rounds in late 1994 and early 1995. These seemed to indicate that the political manoeuvring that had maintained the Prime Minister in power and had avoided renewed confrontation with the forces of Hindu nationalism had not succeeded in recruiting new support for Congress. Ten states went to the polls, six of which were among the largest in the country. Of these six, Congress succeeded only in winning in Orissa, where it defeated a fading Janata Dal government. In Bihar, however, the incumbent Janata Dal government, under the leadership of the caste-based politician, Laloo Prasad Yadav, easily deflected a Congress challenge. In the remaining four states Congress governments were defeated. In the south, Karnataka went to the Janata Dal, while in neighbouring Andhra Pradesh (the Prime Minister's home state), the former film star, N. T. Rama Rao, whose regionalist Telugu Desam party had held office earlier, returned to power despite a reputation for erratic policy making and implementation. In the west of the country, the two coastal states of Maharashtra (the capital of which is Mumbai) and Gujarat, which jointly formed the spearhead of India's economic development, were both lost to right-wing Hindu forces. In Gujarat the BJP had established a strong position, and its victory came as no surprise. In Maharashtra, however, there had been a realistic possibility of Congress retaining power, and its defeat at the hands of a coalition between the BJP and a local party, the Shiv Sena, whose views on communal questions were considerably more extreme, constituted a serious set-back.

A direct consequence of the defeats suffered in the first set of state elections was the emergence of a personal challenge to the Prime Minister from within the ruling party. When Narasimha Rao had been selected to lead Congress in 1991, there had been at least three other plausible contenders—Arjun Singh, N. D. Tewari and Sharad Pawar—each from a different region of the country and each with a somewhat different appeal. Now, in late 1994, however, the challenge came from Arjun Singh alone. Identifying with the left-wing element of the party, Singh claimed that the strategies of economic liberalization were harming the poor, and that Narasimha Rao had been too accommodating to the *Hindutva* forces. Following the initial electoral defeats, Arjun Singh resigned from the Council of Ministers in late December and subsequently from Congress. In conjunction with N. D. Tewari, he eventually forced a formal split in the party in May 1995. The newly-established All India Indira Congress (Tewari) was able to recruit dissident members of Congress in many states, but Singh himself was not an uncontroversial figure and consequently his appeal was limited.

As the 1996 elections approached, each party began to establish its agenda. Each had to balance an appeal to the electorate in terms of social justice and greater welfare for all with an awareness of the requirements of the new economic policies. Congress was able to accentuate the significant results that the new economic programmes were beginning to deliver, while claiming to remain a party that cared for the poor. Low inflation rates and good harvests seemed to favour its cause. The BJP emphasized that economic development could be achieved without allowing indiscriminate entry to foreign capital. It was able to dramatize this belief through its involvement in the struggle over the Dabhol power project, which constituted the first major foreign investment in India's electricity sector. When the BJP came to power in Maharashtra in 1995, almost its first action had been to cancel the project (although it was later renegotiated). This controversial move bolstered the party's image at the local level but may have lost it credibility in some quarters. The BJP continued to project itself as a strongly nationalist party, although with less stress on the Hindu component of national identity. The parties on the left and centre offered variations on the themes of social and economic justice, although the force of the job reservation issue diminished as the other main parties adopted versions of the same policy. On the other hand, regional issues and demands for increased powers for state governments began to assume greater significance. Wherever a party was in power, either at the national or at the state level, it introduced welfare programmes, for example the provision of subsidized meals, which were designed to benefit as many of the electorate as possible. In several states opposition parties made the introduction of prohibition a major electoral issue.

Despite the efforts of the parties to establish distinct identities in terms of policy, the more important questions revolved around image and personality. In January 1996 Prime Minister Rao attempted a bold gamble to outflank his rivals inside Congress and to discredit the opposition. He did this by allowing the disclosure of the names (often identified only by initials) in a diary kept by a Delhi-based industrialist and political intermediary, Surendra K. Jain. These names appeared to be connected to payments of large amounts of money for political favours. While a number of Congress ministers were listed, so too were opposition leaders, including L. K. Advani of the BJP and prominent Janata Dal figures. The Prime Minister's own name was subsequently implicated in the so-called Hawala (illegal money transfer) scandal, but he was also faced with more serious and potentially more damaging difficulties concerning the prosecution, on charges of cheating and criminal conspiracy, of a flamboyant faith healer and 'godman', Chandraswami, who had been consulted by generations of political leaders, including Rao himself.

The 1996 Elections and the United Front Government

As the 1996 elections approached, political alliances emerged and solidified. The BJP campaigned alongside the Shiv Sena, and arrived at understandings with the Akali Dal in Punjab and two smaller local parties. Congress was faced with the choice of which of the two major regional parties to ally itself with in Tamil Nadu; its decision to support the AIADMK, the ruling party, whose leader, the former film actress Jayalalitha Jayaram, had alienated many groups in the state, proved to be a serious error of judgement both in terms of popular support and because it impelled a number of important local members of Congress to leave and establish a rival party, the Tamil Maanila Congress. The Janata Dal and its allies continued to work together as the National Front, and had an electoral understanding with the Left Front, which represented the two major communist parties.

The general election itself, which was held over three days at the end of April and early May 1996, was relatively muted, largely owing to the Election Commission's stringent enforcement of limits on expenditure, although the turn-out was no lower than in the past. The results, as had been widely predicted, gave no party or group an overall majority. The largest party in terms of seats was the BJP, which won 160 seats, and with the support of the Shiv Sena and other smaller allies could count on an overall legislative strength of 194 seats. Congress gained 136 seats. Neither the BJP nor Congress, however, performed as well or as badly, respectively, as certain observers had predicted. The National Front and the Left Front together obtained 179 seats, with the remainder won by minor parties and independents. State elections held concurrently in a number of states generally confirmed the national trend. Congress lost power in the states of Assam, Haryana and Kerala, while the AIADMK was defeated in Tamil Nadu. In West Bengal the Left Front, which had ruled the state since 1977, was again returned to power, but with a reduced majority. On 15 May 1996, as soon as the electoral position was clear, the President asked the BJP under its new parliamentary leader, Atal Bihari Vajpayee, to form the new Government and to prove its majority within two weeks. Given the antagonism felt towards the BJP by the majority of other political parties, this proved impossible, and Vajpayee resigned on 28 May in anticipation of his Government's inevitable defeat in a parliamentary vote of confidence. In the mean time, the National and Left Fronts had merged to form an informal coalition known as the United Front (UF), which comprised a total of 13 parties, with the Janata Dal, the Samajwadi Party, the two communist parties and the regional DMK and Telugu Desam as its major components. With Congress prepared to lend external support, the UF was able to form a Government at the end of May. With no overwhelmingly powerful individual leader within the UF, several names had been put forward to head the coalition and therefore to assume the premiership. Eventually H. D. Deve Gowda was selected to lead the UF and the new Government. Although with only limited experience at national level, Deve Gowda had formerly held the position of Chief Minister of the state of Karnataka and was widely identified as a pragmatic political figure with an interest in further economic change and development. To hold the key finance portfolio the new Prime Minister chose Palaniappan Chidambaram, who had been Minister of State for Commerce under Narasimha Rao and a committed liberalizer. The other major portfolios were distributed on political grounds. The home affairs ministry was assigned to Indrajit Gupta, a member of the Communist Party of India, while a veteran politician, Inder Kumar Gujral, who was affiliated with the Janata Dal, was appointed Minister of External Affairs.

On assuming power, the UF drew up a 'common minimum programme', which committed it to a combination of pragmatic economic reform and anti-poverty policies. An early effort by P. Chidambaram to raise the prices of petroleum products achieved only partial success in the face of opposition not only from the BJP but also from the Minister's own supporters and allies. Other early signals of potential problems were the expulsion from the Janata Dal of another Karnataka politician and erstwhile aspirant for the prime ministership, Ramakrishna Hegde, the ongoing conflict between the two UF-ruled states of Karnataka and Tamil Nadu over the allocation of water resources, and a major corruption inquiry in Bihar, a bastion of UF support.

In September 1996 Narasimha Rao resigned from the leadership of Congress after he was ordered to stand trial for his alleged involvement in the Chandraswami case; the party presidency was assumed, on an acting basis, by the veteran politician, Sitaram Kesri. Later that month separate charges of forgery and criminal conspiracy (dating back to the former Prime Minister's tenure of the external affairs ministry in the 1980s) were made against the beleaguered Rao. Kesri moved quickly to establish his position. He succeeded in bringing back many former dissidents, such as Arjun Singh and Congress (Tewari), into the ranks of Congress and he also benefited, at least in the short term, from the decision by Sonia Gandhi, Rajiv's widow, to join the party in March 1997. In June Kesri, who in January had also become the party's parliamentary leader, was confirmed as party President, in Congress's first contested leadership poll since 1977, fending off a challenge from two significant rivals. While Narasimha Rao had established an understanding with Deve Gowda, this was not shared by Kesri, and strains soon began to develop between the opposition and the ruling power. In March 1997 Kesri finally launched his attack by threatening to withdraw Congress's support for the Government unless Deve Gowda resigned as Prime Minister. Although in some respects this threat might have been a bluff, since Congress would not necessarily have won any subsequent election, it nevertheless achieved its goal by forcing Deve Gowda's resignation in mid-April (following his defeat in a parliamentary vote of confidence). After considerable uncertainty, Inder Kumar Gujral, who had enjoyed a number of successes as Minister of External Affairs, was selected to be the new Prime Minister. While Gujral had a considerable reputation as an intellectual, his major problem was lack of any substantial political base outside Delhi; this meant that he would always be required to balance carefully the divergent elements in his coalition. The price of Congress support for the UF administration was regular consultation by the latter with Kesri and the playing down of inquiries that had been launched into Congress finances. More generally, the political climate made it very difficult for the Government to advance its economic programme, and important but potentially problematic decisions over matters such as domestic petroleum prices and the future of the insurance sector were postponed or evaded.

While the UF Government had managed to survive the resignation of Deve Gowda, it was confronted with other major problems which dominated the political scene for the rest of 1997, as every political party and individual leader manoeuvred for power and influence. Chief among these was the forced resignation in July followed by the arrest of Laloo Prasad Yadav, the Chief Minister of Bihar and President of the Janata Dal. The reason for these events was an allegation that Yadav had been involved in a major corruption scandal based on the supply of fodder for non-existent animals. Despite his resignation, Yadav continued to dominate the politics of his home state by contriving that his wife be appointed as Chief Minister in his place, and by forming a breakaway faction of his party, known as the Rashtriya Janata Dal (RJD). The RJD proceeded to play a key role in the national coalition, despite reservations being expressed by some other members, especially among the left-wing parties. The issue that finally led to the downfall of the UF Government was the protracted investigation into the assassination of Rajiv Gandhi. A commission of inquiry, the Jain commission, had been established to investigate alleged security lapses, and in November 1997 its draft report was 'leaked' to an Indian news magazine. Among its findings were criticisms of the DMK, the party that had been in power in Tamil Nadu in May 1991, at the time of the assassination, and was again in power at that time. Congress, encouraged by Sonia Gandhi who was anxious to ensure justice for her late husband, insisted that the DMK state administration be dismissed by the national Government on the grounds of the former's alleged links with Tamil terrorists. Prime Minister Gujral rejected Congress's demand, and was consequently forced to resign on 28 November when Congress withdrew its support for the Government, as earlier threatened. This constituted the third government collapse in less than two years. In early December the President dissolved the Lok Sabha following the inability of both Congress and the BJP to form an alternative coalition government. It was announced that Gujral would retain the premiership in an acting capacity pending the holding of a fresh general election in February/March 1998.

One consequence of the series of high-level corruption cases was the increased sensitivity of positions such as the Director of the Central Bureau of Investigation. Joginder Singh, who had overseen some of the most important cases and had gained a reputation as an independent if controversial figure, was moved from this post in June 1997, allegedly as a result of political pressure exerted on the Prime Minister from various quarters, including Congress. A lively debate also developed over the question of whether the appointment of senior judges should be made by the Government or by the Chief Justice. The President, however, continued to be regarded as above the political fray, and, as so often in the past, was widely seen as a key figure in maintaining Indian political stability. In July 1997 the widely respected Kocheril Raman Narayan was elected President almost unanimously by members of both Houses of Parliament and the state assemblies. Narayanan was notable both for his distinguished diplomatic career and for being the first President of India to come from a 'scheduled caste' (or 'untouchable') background.

The 1998 and 1999 Elections and the BJP in Power

Three main groupings contested the 1998 elections: the UF, Congress, and the BJP in alliance with a number of small local parties (most significantly the AIADMK in Tamil Nadu). The campaign, as in 1996, was relatively low-key, with all parties aiming to minimize areas of conflict and emphasize their commitment both to further economic liberalization and to programmes of social investment. There occurred, however, a series of fatal bomb explosions in Tamil Nadu, allegedly perpetrated by Islamist militants. The results gave each of the groupings some strength, but none of them achieved an overall majority. Congress won 142 seats in the Lok Sabha, which represented a mediocre but not disastrous performance. While the party's role in bringing down the UF Government was held against it, Congress's fortunes were helped considerably by Sonia Gandhi's decision to campaign actively for the first time (shortly after the elections she replaced Sitaram Kesri as the party's President). The various components of the UF enjoyed mixed results, depending on the strength of their respective regional bases and on the appeal of their leaders. While the Janata Dal performed badly, other elements of the grouping, for example the Telugu Desam in Andhra Pradesh and the CPI—M in West Bengal retained all or most of their strength. The biggest gainer overall, however, was the BJP, which increased its tally of legislative seats from 160 to 182. With the support of its pre-election allies, especially the AIADMK, which won 18 of the seats in Tamil Nadu, the BJP could count on approximately 250 seats, the largest bloc in the legislature but considerably fewer than the 273 seats needed to form a government. Although the constitutional position was not entirely clear, the President decided to ask Vajpayee of the BJP to form a government, and the latter assumed the premiership on 19 March. As in 1996, Vajpayee was given two weeks to garner sufficient support to win a parliamentary vote of confidence. This he did (by 274 votes to 261) on 28 March on the basis of the support of the Telugu Desam, which eventually left the UF, and the support of several small groupings. Nevertheless, it was clear from the very outset that Vajpayee's Government had only the most tenuous hold on power, and that the Prime Minister would need to exercise both tact and skill to retain his position. Within his own party he would have to face pressure for demonstrative action to fulfil the Hindu nationalist agenda of the more extremist members, while many of the Prime Minister's allies had very specific demands which they insisted be met. The AIADMK under Jayalalitha demanded that the DMK state government in Tamil Nadu be dismissed, while the Samata Party in Bihar and the All India Trinamool Congress in West Bengal made similar, if less strident, demands concerning their own state administrations. To do so, however, would have created serious political and constitutional problems for the central Government. As well as narrowly political demands, others were made regarding the division of water and other resources between states. Although the partners in the coalition Government produced a national Agenda for Governance to guide their actions, it was clear that government matters would not always proceed smoothly.

After a seemingly lacklustre few weeks in power, the new Government startled India and the rest of the world by exploding a series of underground nuclear test devices on 11 and 13 May 1998 (see below). This provocative action was initially greeted with huge popular enthusiasm, but Pakistan's tests in response, and an awareness of the negative international consequences (particularly the imposition of economic sanctions by the USA) soon led to a more measured domestic assessment. The budget, which was introduced in June by the Minister of Finance, Yashwant Sinha (an experienced former bureaucrat as well as BJP politician), was widely considered to be uninspired, and the almost immediate decision to rescind some of the measures, notably an increase in petrol prices, further eroded the Government's image. In early July, in the face of strong opposition from various groups, the Government was forced to defer a parliamentary bill proposing the reservation of one-third of seats in the Lok Sabha and in state legislatures for women (male deputies again prevented the introduction of the Women's Reservation Bill in December). In early August the Government approved draft bills providing for the creation of three new states (Uttaranchal, Vananchal and Chhattisgarh), but deferred another proposed piece of legislation to confer full statehood on Delhi.

Shortly after its accession to power, the demands of the smaller parties in the governing coalition created problems for the BJP. The most difficult partner was the AIADMK, whose leader, Jayalalitha, faced ongoing investigations into corruption allegations relating to her earlier period as Chief Minister of Tamil Nadu. In late June 1998 she appeared to be about to precipitate an internal political crisis, but the issue was eventually resolved. In the mean time, however, Congress, which was by now firmly under the control of Sonia Gandhi and her immediate colleagues, began to explore ways of destabilizing the Government by exploiting its internal divisions. In late November Congress performed well in state elections in Rajasthan, Delhi and Madhya Pradesh, defeating incumbent BJP governments in the first two. The dilemma facing Congress, however, was how to engineer the downfall of the BJP coalition in such a way as to enhance rather than damage its own position with the electorate. In April 1999 Sonia Gandhi thought that an opportune moment had arrived, and, with the help of the AIADMK, which withdrew from the ruling coalition (allegedly in protest at the earlier dismissal of the Chief of Staff of the Navy), was able to create a political stalemate, which the President resolved by forcing the Prime Minister to seek a vote of confidence. This was held on 17 April and resulted in the Government's defeat, although by the margin of only a single vote. The President then gave Sonia Gandhi the opportunity to assemble a new coalition. Her political skills were unequal to the task, however; putting together a coalition for the purpose of ousting a common enemy was very different from sharing the fruits of office among many different partners, as the BJP had earlier found to its cost. On 17 April, therefore, the Lok Sabha was dissolved, and fresh elections were called. Vajpayee and his Government remained in power in an acting capacity pending the holding of the polls.

Immediately after the elections were called, it was difficult to see exactly who or which party was likely to be the main beneficiary. Indeed, all political groups suffered to some extent from popular annoyance at the failure of the Vajpayee administration to survive. Sonia Gandhi had staked her reputation on being able to form a new government and her failure to do so damaged her standing both within the ranks of Congress as well as on a national level. Her foreign origins were used against her, and in May 1999 Sharad Pawar, the leader of Congress in the Lok Sabha until its dissolution and the most powerful of the old-guard party heads, was expelled from Congress for voicing public criticism on this point. The following month Pawar announced the establishment of a new party, the Nationalist Congress Party. Among the non-Congress parties apart from the BJP, new alliances emerged but without the capacity to dominate national politics. Back in June 1998 two major parties representing lower-caste interests in northern India—the Samajwadi Party and the Rashtriya Janata Dal—had formed a new grouping, known as the Rashtriya Loktantrik Morcha (National Democratic Front). All the opposition parties tried to capitalize on the anti-incumbency factor and on economic issues such as the soaring prices of basic commodities (notably onions, India's most basic staple after rice).

While the BJP seemed less well placed immediately after the dissolution of the Lok Sabha in April 1999, the subsequent hostilities with Pakistan (see below) had a very positive effect on the nationalist party's standing and in particular on that of the Prime Minister. The widely held perception that Vajpayee had responded with dignity and firmness to Pakistani provocation, and that India had, in effect, won the war had a major impact on public opinion.

In the general election, which was staggered over five weekends during September and early October 1999, the 24-member BJP-led alliance, known as the National Democratic Alliance (NDA) and comprising numerous minor regional parties with little shared ideology, won an outright majority in the Lok Sabha, with 299 of the 545 seats, while Congress and its allies obtained 134 seats. Although Sonia Gandhi won both of the seats that she contested herself in Karnataka and Uttar Pradesh, her lack of political experience, her weak grasp of Hindi and her foreign birth all contributed to Congress's worst electoral defeat since independence. Vajpayee was sworn in as Prime Minister for a third term, at the head of a large coalition Government, on 13 October.

State elections, both those that coincided with the general elections and those held in February 2000, demonstrated that, while the BJP was still the most successful political party in the country, it was far from unchallenged. In Maharashtra, which includes Mumbai, the BJP-Shiv Sena coalition was replaced in October 1999 by a Congress-led partnership with the Nationalist Congress Party. In February 2000 the BJP was successfully challenged in Bihar, where Laloo Prasad Yadav's RJD suffered defeat in the general elections, but performed unexpectedly well at the expense of the BJP in the February state elections, and after a few weeks formed a coalition with the support of Congress. By contrast, in Haryana the BJP and its allies retained power, and in Orissa they ousted the Congress Government. In addition to these electoral problems, the Prime Minister faced difficulties in managing the NDA coalition partners. In July 2000 events surrounding attempts to arrest and prosecute the founder of the Shiv Sena, Bal Thackeray, in connection with the riots of 1992–93 led to the resignation of Ram Jethmalani, the Minister of Law, Justice and Company Affairs. Even within the BJP there were critics who felt that Vajpayee was moving away from his party's core values. Claims that he was neglecting the demands of the RSS for greater stress on Hindu nationalism were reinforced in March 2000 when he conceded to pressure from Congress and some BJP allies to force the government of Gujarat to rescind its decision to remove the ban on civil servants becoming members of the RSS.

It was against this political background that Vajpayee and his colleagues had to struggle to implement their policies. Continued moves to restructure the economy provoked resistance from those who would be disadvantaged by the changes and, as in the past, measures announced in the budget had to be withdrawn. The large-scale project to build the Sardar Sarovar dam on the Narmada River in Gujarat, for example, encountered resistance from environmentalist activists representing the tens of thousands of people whom the dam would displace; at the same time the project found wide support among the intended beneficiaries. Pledges made during election campaigns to create new states for various ethnic groups were not easy to implement. In May 2000, however, the Government introduced three items of legislation to establish the states of Chhattisgarh, Jharkhand and Uttaranchal, and amended versions were finally passed by the Lok Sabha and Rajya Sabha in August. Meanwhile, natural disasters severely tested all levels of government. In October 1999, for example, shortly after the elections, a major cyclone ravaged the Congress-held state of Orissa and killed at least 10,000 people. The drought in Andhra Pradesh, Gujarat and Rajasthan in 2000 was another large-scale tragedy emphasizing the magnitude of the task facing all authorities. Worst of all, in January 2001 a devastating earthquake occurred in Gujarat, the epicentre being near the coastal town of Bhuj. It severely affected the surrounding remote town of Kutch and caused serious damage as far away as Ahmedabad. More than 30,000 were killed and over 1m. were made homeless. In October 2000 the Central Bureau of Investigation filed charges against three businessmen, the Hinduja brothers, for allegedly accepting bribes in the 'Bofors' affair (see above). In the same month the former Prime Minister, P. V. Narasimha Rao, was convicted of corruption. He was sentenced to three years' imprisonment and was fined Rs 100,000. He was acquitted of the charges in March 2002.

In 2001 the problems facing the NDA coalition further increased. A scandal involving senior government officials over bribe-taking for a defence contract, exposed by an internet news service, tehelka.com, in March, demonstrated the extent of corruption in the senior ranks of the Government. The President of the BJP, Bangaru Laxman, resigned. The Minister of Defence, George Fernandes, also resigned (but was reinstated in October); he was implicated by association after evidence showed the President of the Samata Party, Jaya Jaitley, accepting bribes at his official residence. Jaitley also resigned as leader of her party. The leader of the All India Trinamool Congress and Minister of Railways, Mamata Banerjee, used this opportunity to resign from the coalition and to gain some political capital. During 2001 a major state-owned financial institution, the Unit Trust of India, encountered serious difficulties. The Chairman, P. Subramanyam, resigned in early July and was later arrested on charges of conspiracy, abuse of public office and corruption. In March the President of the Bombay Stock Exchange, Anand Rathi, resigned amid allegations of manipulation of share prices; the Chairman of the Global Trust Bank also resigned. Vajpayee, himself, faced health problems and appeared tired and listless. The results of the state elections in May demonstrated the extent of the disquiet. The BJP performed badly in all four states. In Tamil Nadu the AIADMK returned to power, despite the conviction in October 2000 of Jayalalitha on corruption charges, for which she was sentenced to three years' imprisonment. She was sworn in as Chief Minister (an office she had previously held in 1991–96) but in order to remain in office she was instructed to win appeals against her convictions within six months. In June 2001 she ordered the arrest of her predecessor, M. Karunanidhi, in circumstances that were widely considered as retaliation for her own earlier arrest. The incident provoked extensive condemnation, prompting the central Government to force the Governor of Tamil Nadu, Fathima Beevi, to resign. In September the Supreme Court overturned Jayalalitha's appointment as Chief Minister. Congress fared well in the May state elections in Assam and Kerala. In West Bengal neither Congress nor the All India Trinamool Congress was able to displace the Left Front, which won its sixth successive victory and its first under Buddhadev Bhattacharya, the CPI (M) leader who had replaced Jyoti Basu on the latter's retirement. Congress attempted to exploit the situation, although Sonia Gandhi, who had been re-elected party leader in September 2000, had to deal with the continuing allegations surrounding the Bofors case (see above). Vajpayee also faced some unrest within his own party, especially after the failure of the summit meeting with Pakistan (see below). The Minister of Home Affairs, L. K. Advani, was considered by some to be a closer adherent to the BJP's core traditions and, therefore, a potential successor. In August 2001 Vajpayee tendered his resignation to his party, amid continuing disputes within the NDA and within the BJP. He was, however, persuaded to withdraw his offer. At the end of the month the All India Trinamool Congress and Pattali Makkal Katchi (which left in February) rejoined the NDA.

Meanwhile, at the end of 2000, communal tension between Hindus and Muslims increased, following Vajpayee's statement that the construction of the Ram Janmabhoomi, the Hindu temple, in Ayodhya was an expression of 'national sentiment that has yet to be realized' and part of the Government's agenda. Although the Prime Minister later attempted to diminish his remarks, declaring that he did not support the destruction of the Muslim Babri Masjid, the opposition demanded an immediate apology and forced the abrupt adjournment of the Lok Sabha and Rajya Sabha. Opposition members also demanded the resignation of three ministers, including L. K. Advani, who were charge-sheeted by the Central Bureau of Investigation in a case relating to the demolition of the Babri Masjid. Vajpayee rejected the demand; however, he confirmed that the Government would abide by the judgment of the Supreme Court. In January 2001 plans for a negotiated settlement over the religious site in Ayodhya suffered a set-back when the All India Babri Masjid Action Committee ruled out negotiations with the VHP. VHP leaders convened a religious parliament, the Dharma Sansad, at the Maha Kumbh Mela (the largest ever Hindu gathering, centring on Allahabad, Uttar Pradesh) in January–February. The Dharma Sansad stated that all obstacles impeding the construction of the temple should be removed by the relevant organizations by mid-March 2002. In February 2001 an Indian high court ruled that nearly 40 people could be brought to trial in connection with the destruction of the mosque in Ayodhya, and that, on technical grounds, senior BJP leaders would not be among the defendants. In view of this verdict, in May a special Central Bureau of Investigation court hearing also discontinued criminal proceedings against the ministers. However, a separate criminal case was registered against the BJP and VHP leaders. In the mean time, a commission of inquiry into the events in Ayodhya took place.

The year 2002 witnessed a continuation of previous trends but with heightened tensions and difficulties, both domestically and regionally. Despite the Prime Minister's renewed attempts to resolve the dispute over the religious site in Ayodhya, the All India Babri Masjid Action Committee refused to enter negotiations with the uncompromising VHP. In the mean time, the VHP continued its plans to construct a temple at the site. In early February the BJP declared in its manifesto for state elections in Uttar Pradesh that it would abide by a court decision or a negotiated settlement between the Hindu and Muslim groups over the disputed site. As the deadline set by the Dharma Sansad, to begin building the temple in mid-March approached, hundreds of Hindu activists assembled in Ayodhya to take part in the illegal construction. In late February a major outbreak of communal violence occurred in the BJP-held state of Gujarat after a train carrying Hindu activists returning from a rally at Ayodhya was attacked by a suspected group of Muslims. Some 60 Hindu activists were killed in the attack. In the days and weeks that followed, up to 2,000 people, mainly Muslims, were killed in horrific circumstances in towns and cities across the state, including the commercial capital Ahmedabad. The Chief Minister of Gujarat, Narendra Modi, was heavily criticized for his inaction during the riots, and it was widely reported that the local police did little to protect those under attack. Eventually, after considerable criticism from opposition parties, Modi resigned in July. Meanwhile, in February state elections took place in four states, including the country's largest—Uttar Pradesh. The results demonstrated clearly the decline in the BJP's fortunes. In Uttar Pradesh the party lost almost one-half of its seats. No evident winner emerged from the election, although the Samajwadi Party, a representative of various less-privileged sections of the population, secured the largest number of seats. Eventually, Ms Mayawati, the General Secretary of the Bahujan Samaj Party—also representing the poorer sections of society—formed a coalition government with the BJP for the third time, and was appointed the state's Chief Minister. Congress enjoyed victory and formed governments in Punjab, Uttaranchal and Manipur, giving a welcome boost to the party. In the same month Jayalalitha, who had succeeded in having her convictions overturned in December 2001, returned to the Tamil Nadu state assembly and immediately took over as Chief Minister.

The BJP appeared to flounder somewhat after its poor performance at the state elections. Its tough stance towards Pakistan (see below) was generally popular but did not deliver a great deal of additional political support. In July 2002 a government reorganization took place in which Jaswant Singh and Yashwant Sinha, the Ministers of Foreign Affairs and Finance, respectively, exchanged portfolios. In May a member of the Shiv Sena, Manohar Joshi, was chosen as the new Speaker of the Lok Sabha, in a perceived attempt to strengthen the right-wing element within the Government. However, the Government's candidate for the presidential election, held in July, was Aavul Pakkiri Jainulabidin Abdul Kalam, a Muslim from South India who was closely associated over many years with the development of the country's missile and nuclear programmes. He won an overwhelming majority in the election. In the following month a more orthodox figure, Bhairon Singh Shekhawat (a former BJP Chief Minister of Rajasthan), was elected Vice-President.

REGIONAL PROBLEMS

Even before independence the unity of India was a major concern of the country's political leaders. The partition of 1947, in which large areas in the north-west and north-east (West Pakistan and East Pakistan) were detached in the name of religion, heightened anxiety over other apparently divisive political movements claiming autonomy or separation. The linguistic reorganization of the states of the Indian Union (see above) provided a framework in which the conflicts over language were reduced to a minimum. However, states have frequently clashed with each other and with the Centre over the allocation of financial and other resources. Some of the most intractable problems in South India have arisen over the sharing of water resources. Although these disputes have often created severe political pressure, they have never taken the form of direct challenges to the integrity of India. However, mainly in the more peripheral parts of the country, a series of separatist and autonomist movements have placed great strain on the Indian Government, both in the past and at present. In the Punjab, the crisis that had begun in the late 1970s (see above) continued until the early 1990s, when a combination of severe police repression (leading to widespread allegations of human rights abuses) and political overtures led to a tacit settlement between the Government and the mainstream Sikh political parties. Although there was a brief resurgence of violence in 1995, when the Congress Chief Minister, Beant Singh, was killed by a car-bomb, it proved to be an isolated incident. Since the 1996 national elections, the Akali Dal has been the dominant political force in the state. In state elections in February 1997 and again in the 1998 and 1999 parliamentary elections, the Akali Dal established an electoral alliance with the BJP, thus demonstrating the Indian political system's capacity to bring together parties with divergent views. The Akali Dal was also represented in the Vajpayee Government, which was formed in March 1998. The 2002 state elections (see above) returned Congress to power in Punjab under Amarinder Singh, whose ancestors had been the rulers of the state of Patiala, a major Sikh centre.

Separatist or autonomist movements continue to operate throughout north-eastern India, notably in Tripura, Nagaland and Assam. Most of them are based around particular tribal groupings, who use violence against those perceived as outsiders as well as against the security forces. Substantial numbers of people have been killed in ambushes and other acts of violence. The national Government aims to achieve political settlements with the separatist groups where possible, as in the 1993 agreement with the Bodo tribal group in Assam, which provided for the establishment of a local council, and in agreements with two separate Naga groups in 1997 and 2000. When this is not possible, however, the Government tends to resort to the use of military force in an attempt to repress the movements. One of the most prominent of the separatist groups is the United Liberation Front of Assam (ULFA), a militant Maoist group which emerged in the 1980s and seeks the outright secession of the state from India. ULFA was outlawed by the central Government in 1990, but continued its armed activity against the state. In late 2000 there was a sharp upsurge in the ULFA's terrorist activities. Bodo insurgency was also renewed in the late 1990s, but a cease-fire was negotiated in March 2000, and extended in September by one year. In mid-June 2001 the Government agreed to a cease-fire with separatist groups in Manipur. In the same month the Government extended the scope of its existing cease-fire with Nagaland to include the National Socialist Council of Nagaland (Khaplang)—NSCN (K), along with all underground organizations in north-east India, and offered to involve the NSCN (K) and the NSCN (Isak Muivah—IM) in peace negotiations. The decision to extend the cease-fire to Naga groups in the neighbouring states of Assam, Manipur and Arunachal Pradesh, as well as Nagaland, gave rise to fears of the creation of a 'greater Nagaland' as part of an eventual settlement. Strikes and violent protests took place in Manipur. In an effort to curb the violence, the Prime Minister consulted the leaders of the seven north-eastern states of India in July and subsequently announced the Government's decision to limit the cease-fire to the state of Nagaland.

In mid-2000 ethnic tensions in the southern states of Karnataka and Tamil Nadu were aggravated following the kidnapping of the renowned South Indian actor, Rajkumar, by the notorious Tamil criminal, Veerappan, at the end of July. In return for Rajkumar's release, Veerappan demanded financial compensation for the Tamil people affected by the ethnic riots that had occurred in 1991, recognition of Tamil as one of the languages used in government business in Karnataka and the release of prisoners in the state, charged under an anti-terrorist law. The abduction caused outbursts of violence by supporters of Rajkumar in Karnataka. The state governments of Karnataka and Tamil Nadu responded to the kidnapping by sending a mediator to negotiate with Veerappan and eventually agreed to meet the conditions set by the abductor. This stance was criticized by the general public and by the Supreme Court, which in November overruled the decision on the early release from prison of 51 of Veerappan's allies. A week later Rajkumar was unexpectedly released. Officials denied that they had paid a ransom, and Veerappan remained at large. A former Karnataka state minister and advocate of firmer action against Veerappan, H. Nagappa, was kidnapped by the Tamil criminal in August 2002. Veerappan reportedly demanded the release of a number of prisoners in return for Nagappa's release.

Although the situations in Punjab and north-eastern India remained major security issues throughout the 1980s, the most protracted and, in many ways, most serious of the regional problems confronting India was the Kashmir crisis. Following the initial conflict in 1947–48, the cease-fire line (the Line of Control—LoC—as it was renamed in 1972) effectively defined the division of the state between Indian- and Pakistani-controlled sections and the wars with Pakistan in 1965 and 1971 made little change to this. India eventually renounced its commitment to a plebiscite under UN auspices, arguing that Pakistan had never acted in good faith.

Sheikh Abdullah, who had initially supported accession to India and had emerged as the dominant political figure in Kashmir after 1947, but who then began to talk of independence, was imprisoned, without trial, for many years, while Kashmir was dominated by politicians who toed the official line and relied on Indian support. In 1954 the Kashmir assembly proclaimed that it had joined the Indian Union. Sheikh Abdullah eventually accepted Kashmir's position in India and returned to the state as Chief Minister from 1975 until his death in 1982. He was succeeded by his son, Dr Farooq Abdullah. Although Farooq and his party, the Jammu and Kashmir National Conference (JKNC), in alliance with Congress (I)—which later became known simply as Congress—succeeded in winning state elections in 1987 (which many observers believed were rigged), he failed to establish a rapport with the people of Kashmir. It was against this background that political forces in the state that wanted either accession to Pakistan or, increasingly, independence became more prominent and more militant, particularly the outlawed Jammu and Kashmir Liberation Front (JKLF). They were able to enforce an effective boycott of the national elections in November 1989 and, thenceforth, the violence escalated, with fierce clashes between militants and security forces. The entire Srinagar area was placed under an indefinite curfew, and many more troops were sent in. Dr Farooq Abdullah's Government resigned in January 1990, and the state was placed under direct rule from Delhi, with power in Srinagar shared between bureaucrats and military leaders. In May the principal Muslim religious leader in Kashmir, Mirwaiz Maulvi Muhammad Farooq, was murdered (by whom is not clear) and his funeral was the occasion for another major clash in which many people died.

Over the next few years the level of violence escalated, with both sides accusing the other of atrocities. In October 1993 there was a major incident in the town of Bijbehara, in which nearly 40 protesters were killed by the security forces. In the same month militants seized the revered Hazrat Bal mosque in Srinagar, in an effort to provoke the Government into action that would further alienate the population. In the face of a deliberate policy of restraint on the part of the Government, however, the militants were eventually forced into a negotiated surrender. In May 1995, however, a similar episode in the town of Charar-e-Sharief ended less agreeably, with the total destruction of a 15th-century shrine and with each side blaming the other. Another negative development in this year was the taking by a previously unknown Islamist separatist group called Al-Faran of foreign tourists as hostages (a Norwegian hostage was executed by his captors in August 1995; others are missing and believed to be dead).

In addition to attempting to gain the ascendancy militarily, from 1994 the Government tried to initiate a political dialogue with the Kashmiri separatists. Selected militant leaders were released, the JKLF declared a cease-fire and in 1996 elections were held to Jammu and Kashmir's Lok Sabha seats, although it was widely believed that the security forces had coerced many people into voting in the face of a boycott declared by the main pro-militant political grouping. State elections were then held in September, and attracted a substantially higher turn-out, despite continuing calls for a boycott. Dr Farooq Abdullah and the JKNC returned to power on the basis of a pledge to find a negotiated solution within the framework of the Indian Union. Although Dr Abdullah began by promising to talk to the militant leaders and also established a committee to consider the vexed question of regional divisions within the state (notably between the Muslim-majority areas and the Hindu and Buddhist regions in the north and south), the political impetus inspired by the elections soon began to wane. Although at a lesser level than in the early 1990s, militant activity continued to be a major problem, increasingly perpetrated by Islamist non-Kashmiri groups from outside of Kashmir, for example Pakistan and Afghanistan, and on occasion, as in June 1998 and March 2000, members of the Hindu and Sikh minorities were massacred for purely sectarian reasons. The accession to power of the BJP Government in March 1998 led to no immediate change in policy with regard to the situation in Jammu and Kashmir. Although he had earlier been associated with the UF, Dr Abdullah made a point of keeping on good terms with the new central administration, in which his son became a Minister. He failed to extend his own political base, however, and often appeared vulnerable to charges of ineffectiveness.

At the beginning of 2000 the situation in Kashmir deteriorated, but in early April there were indications that India was willing to re-establish dialogue. Leaders of the All-Party Hurriyat Conference (APHC), who had been arrested during the 1999 general election campaign, were released in April and May. The APHC represented a wide range of anti-India political opinion. In July one of the main militant groups, the Hizbul Mujahideen, declared a three-month cease-fire. The gesture obtained a quick and positive response from the Indian Government: the Indian Army suspended all offensive operations against the Kashmiri militants for the first time in 11 years. Other militant groups, however, denounced the cessation of hostilities as a betrayal and continued their violent campaign, in an attempt to disrupt the peace effort. At the beginning of August the Hizbul Mujahideen ended the cease-fire, despite the fact that the Vajpayee Government had allowed the group to raise demands that extended beyond the scope of the Indian Constitution, although the Government was committed to a solution within it. The leader of the group attributed the failure of negotiations to India's opposition to a tripartite discussion including representatives of Pakistan. Vajpayee accused Pakistan of orchestrating the events and of encouraging divisions amongst militant leaders, while the APHC was criticized for impeding the peace process. Dr Abdullah had attempted to seize the initiative at the end of June by successfully urging the state assembly to adopt a resolution demanding that the state revert to the degree of autonomy it had enjoyed before 1954; the resolution, however, was rejected by both the Vajpayee Government and militant groups.

In November 2000 the Indian Government declared the suspension of combat operations against Kashmiri militant groups during the holy Muslim month of Ramadan. This unilateral cease-fire began at the end of November and was renewed periodically, despite an increased casualty rate among Indian soldiers and a high-profile attack on the historic Red Fort in Delhi in December. The majority of national parties and foreign governments supported the cessation of hostilities. The APHC welcomed the development and offered to enter negotiations with the Pakistani authorities in order to prepare for tripartite discussions. The Hizbul Mujahideen and other militant groups, however, rejected the offer and continued their campaign of violence. In December Pakistan extended an invitation to the APHC to participate in joint preparations for the establishment of negotiations, and proposed that tripartite dialogue begin after Ramadan, pending which the APHC should participate in bilateral dialogue with the Indian Government and Pakistani authorities, respectively. India reiterated that it was prepared to enter dialogue with Pakistan once the violence ended. However, India's proposed negotiations with Kashmiri separatist leaders failed to take place, partly because of a reluctance to allow the APHC to establish its own dialogue with Pakistan. Although Abdul Ghani Lone, a leading APHC figure, was permitted to make a private visit to Islamabad in November, passport applications for a delegation of leaders were subsequently refused. The cease-fire ended in May 2001, and during Indo-Pakistani negotiations in July violence in the region escalated. From December 2001 the situation within Kashmir precipitated a major crisis between India and Pakistan (see below). In May 2002 Lone was assassinated; the perpetrators, however, remained unknown. As a result of the crisis and the associated militant activity within Kashmir, the Indian authorities adopted a less conciliatory approach towards politicians associated with the APHC. In early August it was announced that state elections in Jammu and Kashmir were to take place in four phases, from mid-September to early October. The APHC announced that it would boycott the election. Islamist militant groups declared their intention to disrupt the campaign and the voting. In mid-September, during the election campaign, the State Minister of Law and Parliamentary Affairs, Mushtaq Ahmed Lone, was killed by suspected separatist groups.

From the very beginning of the present Kashmir crisis, Pakistan took a keen interest in developments and argued vigorously for the rights of the Muslim Kashmiris and its own unheeded demand for a UN-authorized plebiscite. India, on the other hand, was more concerned with the way that the crisis had been orchestrated, in its opinion, from the Pakistan side of the border. The Indian Government claimed that arms were being provided to the Kashmiri militants by official Pakistan sources and that guerrilla training camps existed in Pakistan-held Kashmir (known as Azad Kashmir). Pakistan strenuously denied that it was officially involved in the uprising and stressed that Muslim Kashmiris were fighting for self-determination. Both India and Pakistan put their armed forces in a state of increased readiness, but neither side showed any desire to precipitate a war. The talks that were instigated by India and Pakistan in early 1997 and again in 2001 regarding the Kashmir crisis opened up new possibilities, although many of the political groups in the state itself expressed grave anxiety that their interests had to be taken into account in any permanent settlement. For many this meant that Jammu and Kashmir should be given substantial autonomy with respect to both India and Pakistan.

FOREIGN RELATIONS

India's relations with its neighbours have been fraught with difficulties. While India considered itself as the natural leader of the region, this attitude was often resented by the smaller countries, especially when, under the leadership of Indira Gandhi, India began to assert its superior power more directly. India was also concerned that domestic problems on its borders might have negative consequences for itself.

In the case of Sri Lanka, India initially maintained stable and friendly relations, but in the 1980s found itself drawn into the civil war between the Sinhalese-dominated Government and the Tamil minority, led by the Liberation Tigers of Tamil Eelam (LTTE), who enjoyed considerable support among India's own Tamil people. India was also concerned that external powers, the USA in particular, might begin to play a part. As the Sri Lankan army appeared, in 1987, to be gaining the advantage, but at a high cost in terms of civilian casualties in the Tamil areas of Sri Lanka, the Indian Government put considerable pressure on Sri Lanka to accept an India-mediated agreement with the LTTE and to invite an Indian Peace-Keeping Force (IPKF) to oversee the agreement. An accord was signed between Rajiv Gandhi and the Sri Lankan President, J. R. Jayewardene, in July 1987 and Indian troops were immediately dispatched to Tamil areas in Sri Lanka. Although, initially, the Indo-Sri Lankan accord brought Rajiv Gandhi considerable domestic dividends, the situation rapidly turned against him as the Indian troops, which, by February 1988, numbered about 50,000, struggled to persuade the Tamil guerrillas to surrender their arms and to abide by the terms of the agreement. The IPKF encountered considerable resistance from the Tamil militants, especially during the siege of the Tamil stronghold in Jaffna in October 1987. Following the gradual implementation of the peace accord, however, several thousand IPKF troops were withdrawn from Sri Lanka in the latter half of 1988 and early 1989. In August 1989 an agreement between India and Sri Lanka was signed in Colombo, in which India stated that it would immediately cease hostilities against the Tamil guerrillas and that it would make 'all efforts' to withdraw its 43,000 troops from Sri Lanka by 31 December, while, for its part, the Sri Lankan Government agreed to strengthen the civil administration as early as possible to ensure peace and normality in the Tamil-dominated northern and eastern provinces, and to establish a peace committee to coincide with the start of the cease-fire. The completed withdrawal of Indian troops from Sri Lanka was, in fact, accomplished by the end of March 1990, although violent conflict in the island flared up again very shortly afterwards. The flow of Sri Lankan refugees into Tamil Nadu increased considerably. By late 1991 the number of Sri Lankans in refugee camps in Tamil Nadu was estimated at more than 200,000. The assassination of the former Indian Prime Minister, Rajiv Gandhi, almost certainly by members of the LTTE, completed India's disenchantment with the latter organization. Measures were subsequently taken by the state government in Tamil Nadu to suppress LTTE activity within the state, and also to begin the process of repatriating refugees. The repatriation programme proved a slow and difficult process. In May 1992 the LTTE was officially banned in India. India was subsequently supportive of the Sri Lankan Government's efforts to defeat the LTTE and achieve a negotiated settlement within a Sri Lankan framework. Where necessary, it also took action against local South Indian politicians who had links with the LTTE.

India inherited the colonial view of Nepal as an important buffer state (between itself and China) and played a significant role in the country's internal politics. Relations between the two deteriorated in early 1989, when India decided not to renew the two treaties determining trade and transit, insisting that a common treaty covering both issues be negotiated. Nepal refused, stressing the importance of keeping the treaties separate on the grounds that Indo-Nepalese trade issues are negotiable, whereas the right of transit is a recognized right of land-locked countries. India responded by closing most of the transit points through which most of Nepal's trade is conducted. It was widely believed that another matter aggravating the dispute was Nepal's recent acquisition of Chinese-made military equipment, which, according to India, violated the Treaty of Peace and Friendship of 1950. Following several rounds of high-level talks, a joint agreement was signed by the two countries in June 1990, restoring trade relations and reopening the transit points. Chandra Shekhar visited Kathmandu in February 1991 (the first official visit to Nepal by an Indian Prime Minister since 1977), shortly after it was announced that the first free elections there were to be held in May. Following these elections a generally pro-Congress Government took office in Nepal, and Indo-Nepalese relations were more or less restored to their earlier state. The Nepalese Prime Minister, G. P. Koirala, visited India in December 1991. Although Koirala was defeated in elections in 1994, his left-wing successor (who himself lost his post after only a few months) was reluctant to alienate India, although his election campaign had included a great deal of anti-India rhetoric. In June 1997 the new Indian Prime Minister, Inder Kumar Gujral, made a visit to Nepal and announced the opening of a transit route through north-east India between Nepal and Bangladesh. Gujral and the Nepalese Prime Minister, Lokendra Bahadur Chand, also agreed that there should be a review of the 1950 treaty between the two countries. However, an outbreak of anti-Indian violence in December 2000 over a minor incident demonstrated the extent of popular suspicion.

Relations with Bangladesh obviously started on a high note, given India's role in the 1971 conflict, but, particularly after the assassination of the Bangladesh Prime Minister, Sheikh Mujibur Rahman, in August 1975 (see chapter on Bangladesh), successive Bangladesh leaders have been wary of what they view as India's 'big-brother' approach. The most important bilateral issue for a long period of time was the distribution of the Ganges waters following the controversial construction of a barrage on the Indian side of the border. Fruitless negotiations regarding this question extended over many years, but finally in December 1996 Gujral concluded an agreement with Bangladesh which seemed to be fair and acceptable to both countries. Unresolved issues remain, including the dispute over territorial rights to pockets of land or enclaves along the irregular border, despite intermittent efforts to resolve these problems. Local border disputes therefore have occurred over the years, leading to occasional clashes. In April 2001 the worst fighting since 1976 took place, on the border between the Indian state of Meghalaya and Bangladesh. Some 16 Indian border troops and three members of the Bangladesh Rifles were killed. Indians were outraged by the alleged maltreatment of Indian soldiers before their deaths. The situation was brought under control, and both sides agreed to take part in negotiations. Subsequently, two joint working groups were established to review the undemarcated section of the border and the exchange of enclaves, although a further clash occurred in March 2002.

Relations with the People's Republic of China remained very restricted for many years after the 1962 war, not least because of China's links with Pakistan. India's long-standing friendship with Viet Nam was also an obstacle to an improvement in Indo-Chinese relations, especially around 1980. Regular official-level meetings were held during the 1980s but little progress was made. A visit to China by Rajiv Gandhi in December 1988, however, proved a turning point. Trade links were gradually improved and talks were held on the border question. In 1993 Narasimha Rao visited Beijing (returning a visit by the Chinese Premier, Li Peng, in 1991) and signed an agreement allowing for a reduction in military confrontation along the disputed border. This process was taken further when the Chinese President, Jiang Zemin, visited New Delhi in November 1996. Yet despite the gradual improvement in relations, India signalled on many occasions that it was unhappy with the nuclear asymmetry between the two countries and with what it perceived as China's willingness to transfer missiles and missile technology to Pakistan. India's relations with China suffered badly following the 1998 nuclear tests, in part because of China's belief that India was using a fabricated threat from China to justify its actions. However, in June of the following year the Indian Minister of External Affairs visited Beijing to reinstigate dialogue. During border negotiations in November 2000, India and China exchanged detailed maps of the middle sector of the Line of Actual Control: a significant step towards resolving differences. In January 2001 Li Peng, Chairman of the National People's Congress, visited India. The focus of his successor's visit one year later was economic issues.

Relations between India and Pakistan have been tense since 1947 and have been marked by three wars and numerous lesser clashes. The fate of Jammu and Kashmir (see above) has been the most important issue, serving also as a symbol for the broader conflicts and rivalries between the two countries. In addition, in recent years India has become anxious that Pakistan is attempting to tilt the balance of power by acquiring nuclear weapons. In 1987 army manoeuvres close to the Pakistan border seemed to presage new conflict, but in December 1988 Rajiv Gandhi visited Islamabad for discussions with Pakistan's new Prime Minister, Benazir Bhutto. At this meeting, which constituted the first official visit of an Indian Prime Minister to Pakistan for nearly 25 years, the two leaders signed three agreements, including a formal pledge not to attack each other's nuclear installations. In June 1989 India and Pakistan moved one step closer to defusing the tension created by the confrontation over the Siachen Glacier in the sensitive Kashmir border area, when high-level talks were held in Islamabad, at which the two countries agreed to attempt to find a formula to bring about the eventual complete withdrawal of their troops from the area. Since the end of 1989, however, the renewed crisis in Kashmir has meant that relations have been very largely frozen, although the agreement not to attack each other's nuclear installations came into effect in January 1991. India gained a notable diplomatic victory in February 1994 when it was able to force the withdrawal, at the UN Commission on Human Rights, of a hostile resolution put forward by Pakistan condemning alleged human rights abuses by Indian security forces in Kashmir. In June 1994 the Indian army had begun to deploy a new missile, named the Prithvi, which has the capacity to reach most of Pakistan. While the 'arms race' between the two countries continued, with claims on both sides concerning the other's missile programmes, talks (which had been suspended since 1994) were resumed in March 1997, both at official and at ministerial level. Of most significance were the negotiations between India and Pakistan's Foreign Secretaries, which took place in Islamabad in late June. These talks resulted in an agreement to establish a series of working parties to consider groups of issues, which were to be considered separately from each other. One such group of issues specifically related to Jammu and Kashmir. Although the two sides' perception of what the agenda for such talks would be differed drastically, the very fact that they were to take place opened up the possibility of long-term convergence. From September 1997, however, the talks process lapsed.

The nuclear tests of May 1998 (see below) marked a low point in Indo-Pakistani relations, but talks resumed towards the end of that year and in February 1999, in an unprecedented gesture, Prime Minister Vajpayee crossed the land border between the two countries (inaugurating the first passenger bus service between India and Pakistan) and visited Lahore, the capital of the Pakistani province of Punjab and the home city of the Pakistani Prime Minister, Nawaz Sharif. Vajpayee and Sharif signed the Lahore Declaration on 21 February, which, with its pledges regarding peace and nuclear security, was patently designed to allay world-wide fears of a nuclear 'flashpoint' in South Asia, and committed two sides to working towards better relations and to implementing a range of confidence-building measures. In March the two foreign ministers agreed a timetable for further talks.

At the very time that the Lahore Declaration was signed, however, preparations had been under way in Pakistan for an audacious move along the LoC in Kashmir. In early May 1999 it became clear to the Indian army that guerrilla groups, probably reinforced by regular Pakistani troops, had occupied positions on the Indian side of the cease-fire line, near the town of Kargil, thus posing a threat to a vital communication line to the Ladakh region. Air-strikes launched by the Indian air force at the end of the month failed to dislodge the infiltrators, and the army was forced into a lengthy and costly campaign in which at least 400 Indian soldiers died and two Indian military aircraft were shot down. By mid-July, however, the Indian forces had gained the upper hand in the conflict, and the Indian military dominance combined with diplomatic pressure applied by the USA eventually led to a Pakistani withdrawal. Despite some demands from various sectors of the population, the Indian Government refused to allow its troops to cross the LoC into Pakistani-held territory, and thereby strengthened its position internationally. World opinion was generally very supportive of India, and the presumed Pakistani attempt to force the 'internationalization' of the Kashmir issue was thwarted. On 10 August there was renewed tension when India shot down a Pakistani naval patrol aircraft near Pakistan's border with Gujarat, killing all 16 people on board; Pakistan retaliated the following day by firing at Indian military helicopters in the same area. Skirmishing continued along the LoC, and in December 1999 tension was further heightened following the hijack of an Indian Airlines plane by militants with strong Pakistani connections. India was forced to release several prominent Islamist militants from Indian prisons in exchange for the safe return of the captive passengers and crew. Following unsuccessful attempts to enter negotiations with local Kashmiri groups (see above), in May 2001 Vajpayee issued an unexpected invitation to Gen. Musharraf to visit India for discussions. The Pakistani leader, who had recently named himself President, duly attended the momentous negotiations in Agra in mid-July. Despite hopes of a dramatic breakthrough, the discussions broke down after both leaders failed to agree on a concluding joint communiqué. Pakistan remained insistent that the two sides agree that Kashmir was the principal issue, while India was resolute that Kashmir be discussed only in the context of cross-border terrorism. Nevertheless, the Indian Prime Minister accepted President Musharraf's invitation to visit Pakistan. Meanwhile, both sides continued to develop their missile programmes. In April 1999 and January 2001 India tested its Agni II missile, which was capable of carrying nuclear warheads; this was matched by Pakistan's comparable test of its Ghauri II missile.

The conflict reached a new stage at the end of 2001 when on 13 December militants gained access to the grounds of the union parliament in New Delhi and attempted to launch an apparent suicide attack on a parliament building. Although no political leaders died, nine people (including a number of policemen, some security officials and a groundsman) were killed and some 25 were injured in the assault; the five assailants were also killed. The attack was seen as an assault on democracy, and was blamed by India on Pakistani intelligence agencies; no proof was produced, however, to support this allegation. By the end of the month positions on both sides of the LoC were reinforced; eventually, up to 1m. troops were mobilized on both sides of the border on a high state of alert, exchanging gunfire daily. President Musharraf's speech in mid-January 2002, in which he promised to combat Pakistan-based militant groups, and subsequent arrests of some of the most prominent militant leaders, combined with international pressure to defuse the tension between the neighbouring countries had a positive effect in the short term. However, following a further militant attack on an Indian army camp in Jammu in mid-May, in which a number of civilians, including women and children, were killed, the two countries appeared to be on the brink of war again, with the attendant risk of a nuclear exchange. Many politicians and publicists, supporting the argument that India would be doing no more in dealing with terrorism than the USA after the September 2001 attacks on New York and Washington, DC, demanded decisive action against militant bases in Pakistan, while Pakistan made it clear that, under certain circumstances, it would not rule out first use of nuclear weapons. Intense diplomatic efforts, most notably by the US Government, which sent the Deputy Secretary of State to visit both countries in early June and the Secretary of Defense Donald Rumsfeld later in the month, appeared to have played a major role in defusing the immediate crisis, although troops on both sides remained in position. Visits in July by the British Foreign Secretary Jack Straw and by the US Secretary of State Gen. Colin Powell in late July were attempts to encourage further dialogue but produced no immediate result.

Indo-US relations had begun to improve during the late 1980s, despite the feeling in India that the USA was always more favourably disposed to Pakistan and China and unwilling to afford India its rightful standing in world affairs. India's recently introduced programme of economic reform was widely welcomed by the USA, and Indian policy-makers recognized the importance of US goodwill to its future investment and trade opportunities. Nevertheless, US efforts to persuade India to reverse its nuclear and rocket programmes through discussions and negotiations with Pakistan, together with concerns in some quarters about the long-term consequences for India's freedom of action if what was seen as a US-inspired economic reform programme were fully implemented, meant that the path has not been an easy one. In 1992 an agreement between India and Russia regarding the supply of rocket engines from the latter provoked a threat of sanctions from the USA and the suspension of the arrangement. During a visit to India by the US Secretary of Defense in January 1995 a 'landmark' agreement on defence and security co-operation was signed by the two countries. India's nuclear tests in May 1998 were a set-back to its relations with the USA; although sanctions were imposed, they were generally regarded as primarily symbolic. In March 2000 President Clinton made a six-day visit to India, which was widely regarded as initiating a new era in bilateral relations. Abandoning any effort to give India and Pakistan equal weight, the US President seemed to endorse India's position that the Kashmir question was a local matter and of no direct concern to the international community. India reciprocated by indicating that it would maintain a de facto halt to further nuclear tests. In September 2000 the Indian Prime Minister visited the USA and was accorded the honour of addressing a joint session of Congress. In response to the terrorist attacks on US mainland targets on 11 September 2001, India offered full support to the USA and its counter-terrorism initiatives. In late September US President George W. Bush announced an end to the military and economic sanctions imposed against India and Pakistan in 1998. India was disappointed, however, with US Secretary of State Gen. Colin Powell's apparent leaning towards the Pakistan-held view that the Kashmir question was a matter of international concern, during his visit to the region in October. During the crisis between India and Pakistan in 2002 (see above) the USA appeared to be sympathetic to Indian concerns over cross-border infiltration and terrorism.

Although the context of the Indo-Russian relationship has changed drastically since the end of the Cold War, it remains important to both sides. A visit by the Indian Prime Minister to the USA in May 1994 was closely followed at the end of June by a trip to Moscow. The following month it was announced that the controversial Russian rocket engines would be supplied to India, albeit without any transfer of technology. In October 1996 India and Russia signed a defence co-operation agreement (later extended to 2010), and in December India signed a US $1,800m. contract to purchase 40 fighter aircraft from Russia. In June 1998 Russia defied a G-8 ban on exporting nuclear technology to India by agreeing to supply the latter with two nuclear reactors, and in December the Russian Prime Minister visited Delhi, in part to demonstrate diplomatic support for India in the face of Western criticism of the nuclear tests earlier in the year. During Russian President Vladimir Putin's visit to India in October 2000, the two countries signed a declaration of 'strategic partnership', which involved co-operation on defence, economic matters and international terrorism issues. India signed a contract to purchase 50 Sukhoi-30 fighter aircraft from Russia, with a licence to manufacture 150 more. The deal, reportedly worth more than US $3,000m., was finalized in December. In February 2001 India agreed to buy 310 Russian T-90 tanks, at an estimated cost of US $700m. In June the two countries successfully conducted a joint test of a new supersonic cruise missile. At the Conference on Interaction and Confidence-Building Measures in Asia in June 2002 at Almaty, Kazakhstan, Putin attempted to act as a mediator between India and Pakistan, without success.

India's nuclear ambitions, as indicated above, have always been an issue in its international relations, both with Pakistan and China, and with the West. Although the 1974 test had not led to any immediate development, it was clear that India was steadily acquiring the technological capacity to move ahead, if it so wished. Its long-standing refusal to sign the Nuclear Non-Proliferation Treaty (NPT) was repeated at the 1995 conference at which the treaty was renewed. In mid-1996, in a move that provoked widespread international condemnation, India decided not to be party to the Comprehensive Test Ban Treaty (CTBT), which it had earlier supported, so long as the existing nuclear powers were unwilling to commit themselves to a strict timetable for full nuclear disarmament. In early April 1998 Pakistan provoked stern condemnation from the new right-wing Government in India following its successful test-firing of a new intermediate-range missile (capable of reaching deep into Indian territory). In the following month the arms race escalated dramatically and to potentially dangerous proportions when India took a momentous decision to explode five nuclear test devices and to claim thereby that it was now a nuclear-weapons state. This action should also be considered in the light of India's progress in developing missiles capable of carrying nuclear warheads. At least three reasons can be proffered as to why the new BJP Government carried out the nuclear tests. First, according to an official announcement, the Government was concerned at the growing power of China, and felt it necessary to take long-term measures to maintain a measure of equality between the two most prominent countries in Asia. Second, there was concern over Pakistan's nuclear programme, and the possibility that, with help from China, it might have moved ahead of India in certain respects. Third, India's future position as a major world power, entitled, for example, to a permanent seat on the UN Security Council, was believed to depend on its ability to match the existing nuclear powers. India's controversial decision led to two immediate consequences—Pakistan responded with its own series of nuclear tests, and the USA, with limited support from other countries, subsequently imposed economic sanctions on both India and Pakistan until such time as they had signed the NPT and the CTBT and taken steps to reverse their nuclear programmes. Having made its point in no uncertain terms, Indian policy seemed to be to attempt to negotiate a deal with the USA. Immediately after the tests a self-imposed moratorium on further testing was announced, followed by intense diplomatic activity. By mid-2001, however, no further substantive progress had been made. With regard to Pakistan, India stated that it was prepared to hold bilateral talks aimed at a 'no-first-use' agreement. However, both countries seemed more concerned about gaining the diplomatic initiative than holding serious discussions. The Indo-Pakistani hostilities of 1999 and the crisis of 2002 raised the possibility of an actual nuclear conflict between the two sides.

Economy

SANJAYA BARU

In 2000 India became a nation of more than 1,000m. people. The size and diversity are the two most distinctive features of the Indian economy. India is a vast country, in terms both of its area and of its population. It has a total area of about 3.3m. sq km, making it the third largest among the developing countries, exceeded only by the People's Republic of China and Brazil. In terms of population, however, India is second only to China, the one other nation in the world with a population exceeding 1,000m. India's diversity is both regional and structural, and, consequently, any average statistic for India conceals both this diversity and the disparity in levels of development. Regionally, India extends from the subtropical deltaic regions of the east and the south, to the semi-arid plains and plateaux of central India; from the areas of heavy, seasonal monsoon rains to the desert lands of Rajasthan. There are, on the one hand, relatively prosperous states, such as Gujarat, Maharashtra, Haryana and Punjab, where the levels of income per caput are much higher than the national average, and are growing rapidly. There are, on the other hand, backward, poverty-ridden states, such as Bihar, Madhya Pradesh and parts of eastern and north-eastern India, where there is little apparent development of economic activity. To sum up, wide inter-regional inequalities in almost all indicators of development are an important defining feature of the Indian subcontinent.

In terms of its overall economic structure, India remains a primarily rural and agricultural country, but there are also well-developed areas of industrial production. Indian agriculture is diverse, including small-scale peasant farmers, who cultivate subsistence holdings under traditional practices, as well as relatively large-scale farmers, who have learned to use modern inputs, such as chemical fertilizers or pump irrigation, to practise high-productivity, commercial agriculture. Similarly, at one extreme, India's manufacturing sector produces basic industrial inputs such as steel, cement and chemicals, as well as fairly sophisticated heavy machinery, while, at the other, there is a very large and dynamic 'informal' sector, producing a wide range of products by means of 'back-yard' technologies.

Almost two centuries of British colonial rule ended on 15 August 1947, when India became independent. Colonial policy during the inter-war period (1918–39) sought to foster some industrial and agricultural development by investing in the required infrastructure, but at independence the Indian economy had not fully recovered from the ravages wreaked by the 19th century processes of enforced commercialization in agriculture and de-industrialization, coupled with the drain of economic surpluses through the levy of 'home charges'. The first half of the 20th century witnessed a decline in levels of industrial productivity and in the rates of growth of agricultural output in some parts of India, thus accentuating inter-regional inequalities and constricting the home market in manufactured goods. The more reliable estimates of economic activity during this period indicate that the output of major food crops expanded at a rate lower than the rate of increase of population, thus depressing the standard of living. In turn, this acted as a constraint on the growth of industrial activity. This resulted from the adverse ratio of population to agricultural land, the effects of which on agricultural productivity were not offset by any significant changes in technology or investment in infrastructure. The output of commercial non-food crops expanded at a faster rate than that of food crops, partly in response to the export demand, for example in jute, and partly in response to growing domestic demand for sugar and oilseeds. Indian industry, the growth of which can be directly attributed to the policy of 'discriminating protection' which was pursued after the mid-1920s, was restricted largely to consumer goods, such as cotton textiles, sugar, paper and a few chemicals and engineering goods, and was mostly confined to a small number of urban centres. Up until the 1950s, Indian industry was dependent on imports for all its requirements of capital goods and machinery. While the United Kingdom was the major source of all such imports, the proportion has declined over the years, as both domestic production and imports from other advanced industrial economies have increased.

India had a stable and efficient administration, both fiscal and legal, and fairly well-developed means of communication, especially railway transport and shipping. There was an uneven educational system, which neglected primary education and literacy for the masses, but produced an adequate supply of people with higher education for recruitment into the lower levels of administration and the professions. A very small industrial labour force, and an even smaller number of industrialists, provided a base that could be built upon for the future.

ECONOMIC RESOURCES

India has a rich base of natural resources, many of which remain inadequately exploited. This potential, together with a large number of underemployed people and underutilized assets, make it possible for India to aim for a much higher rate of economic growth, if productivity and efficiency are improved. India's major problem, however, is the size and rate of growth of its population.

The most recent decennial census was conducted in February 2001, and provisional national and state population totals were released in the following month. India's population was estimated at 1,027,015,247. By 2016 India's population is expected to exceed 1,250m. According to the census, of the total population of 1,027m., about 742m. live in rural areas and 285m. in urban areas. Since 1991 the net increase in population in rural areas between 1991 and 2001 was 113m. while in urban areas it was 68m. The percentage decadal growth of population in rural and urban areas during the same period was estimated to be 17.9% and 31.2% respectively. The percentage of urban population in relation to total population had increased by 2.1% compared with 1991, to reach 27.8% in 2001. The annual rate of growth of total population in 1991–2001 was 2.76%, compared with 2.88% in 1981–91. Based on the 2001 census, the annual exponential rate of growth of population was estimated at 1.93%, which compares favourably with the annual rate recorded in 1981–91 (2.14%).

The country-wide average population growth rate was a sum of wide regional variations. Southern India recorded much lower rates of growth of population, with the lowest rate, of 0.90%, being recorded by the southern state of Kerala. The highest rate of growth of population of 4.97% was recorded by the north-eastern state of Nagaland. The density of the population increased from 142 per sq km in 1961 to 324 in 2001, with the highest density of 880 per sq km being recorded in Bihar and the lowest, 13, recorded by Arunachal Pradesh in the north-east. Among urban centres, Kolkata (formerly Calcutta) has the highest density, with 23,783 per sq km recorded in 1999. In 1999 India's crude birth rate (per 1,000) was estimated to be 26.1, compared with 45 in 1965, and the crude death rate (per 1,000) was calculated at 8.7, in comparison with 20 in 1965. The total fertility rate, which was 6.2 births per woman in 1965, had declined to 3.1 by 2000. In 1990–98 about 43% of the population in the relevant age-group was estimated to be using contraceptives. Despite these trends, an improvement in life expectancy from around 44–46 years in the mid-1960s to 61 by 2000, has made population growth a major problem for India, diminishing the significance of post-independence economic growth in per caput terms. The infant mortality rate, which is a useful guide to the level of social welfare, declined from 150 per 1,000 live births in 1965 to 69 per 1,000 in 2000. Although lower than the average (of 80 per 1,000) for low-income countries, this compares poorly with China's rate of 32. Whereas 37% of the population in 1990 were estimated to be in the age-group of 0–14 years, it was projected that by 2025 the proportion would fall to 24%. Similarly, the percentage of the population in the 15–64 age-group was projected to rise from 58.6% to 68.4%.

The population is largely rural, with about 72% of the total residing in approximately 600,000 villages. While the overall urban proportion of the population is small, total numbers are large: in 1981 there were about 160m. inhabitants in urban areas, of whom about 60% or more resided in the larger cities, i.e. those with a population of 100,000 or more. According to the 2001 census, the urban population was an estimated 285m. The four largest urban agglomerations, Mumbai (formerly Bombay), Kolkata, Delhi and Chennai (formerly Madras), had a combined population of about 49m. Since the late 1970s, cities such as Bangalore, Ahmedabad and Hyderabad have also expanded rapidly as new industrial centres. Tamil Nadu is the most urbanized state, with 43.9% of its population living in urban areas, followed by Maharashtra (42.4%) and Gujarat (37.4%). Bihar is the least urbanized, with just 10.5% of its population living in urban areas.

Of India's total area of around 3.3m. sq km, about 55% is available for cultivation. The remainder consists of forests, deserts, land in urban use, meadows and pasture, or fallow land. Of the cultivable land, only about 33% is under assured irrigation, despite a substantial expansion of irrigation facilities since the 1960s. The remainder is dependent upon rain-fed agriculture. The pattern of rainfall, under the south-eastern and the south-western monsoons, is highly seasonal and highly variable. Except in the extreme south, most of the rain falls in the summer months of June to September, and is essential for prosperity and survival. A small but essential amount of rain falls in the winter, allowing some areas to grow winter food crops in addition to summer crops. The monsoon rains are highly unreliable from year to year, in terms both of their timing and of the amount of rain that they bring. An additional problem is that the amount of rainfall varies widely across the country, diminishing rapidly from east to west; areas where average rainfall is low also suffer from the high variability.

Because the economy is dependent upon agriculture for food and incomes, and because agriculture is critically dependent on the monsoon, the fear that inadequate rainfall in every third or fifth year is likely to produce unfavourable conditions affects the populace and government planners. Much of India's farmland is of poor natural fertility, being subject to erosion, salinity or leaching: the result of years of population pressure on a poor agricultural economy. In addition, the land that is available for cultivation is distributed very unequally among the farming population. The land itself is being subjected to environmental pressures, the long-term effects of which may be catastrophic but are incalculable. The growing demand for fuelwood, for energy needs, is leading to large-scale deforestation and soil erosion which, if not halted or reversed, may have serious effects on agricultural productivity and the social environment.

NATIONAL INCOME AND STRUCTURE OF PRODUCTION

Estimates of India's gross national product (GNP), and consequently of national income per head, may be derived from two main sources, which offer differing estimates. These are either official Indian sources, which provide estimates in terms of Indian rupees, or estimates in US dollars, provided by international institutions such as the World Bank. There are a number of reasons for such discrepancies, and, in any case, US dollar values provide only an approximation to levels of real income in India. This is chiefly because relative price ratios differ between countries, and a typical Indian 'basket' of commodities would cost less to buy in India than in the USA. However, while the actual rupee and US dollar values of levels of GNP or incomes may not correspond to their values in terms of foreign currencies at official rates of exchange, the general trend in rates of growth indicates similar conclusions.

In 2001 India's gross domestic product (GDP) was estimated to be US $456,990m. GDP per caput was approximately US $456. India experienced a steady acceleration of its national income growth in the 20th century. Following near zero growth between 1900 and 1950, India's GDP grew at an average annual rate of about 3.5% between 1950 and 1980, and at an average annual rate of approximately 5.6% in the period 1980–2000. The early 1990s witnessed an acceleration of GDP growth to 6.7% per annum in 1992/93 to 1996/97, driven by a 7.6% growth in industrial production and 7.6% rise in service-sector income. However, a deceleration in industrial growth to less than 4.0% and in agricultural growth to about 1.5% adversely affected overall GDP growth in 1997/98 to 2001/02, with annual GDP growth rates declining to 5.5%. In 2002/03 economic growth was expected to be between 5.5% and 6.0%.

On a purchasing-power parity (PPP) basis—as estimated by the World Bank—India's GDP per caput was reckoned to be US $2,358 in 2000. On a PPP basis, India stood as the fifth largest economy in the world in 2000, with an estimated GDP of US $1,689,000m., compared with the USA's GDP of US $8,511,000m. and China's GDP of US $4,420,000m. Using the argument that market exchange rates do not reflect their PPP equivalents, owing to differences in the relative value of traded versus non-traded output, the IMF has adopted the view that PPP estimates of per caput income represent more accurately the distribution of real income across the world. While in PPP terms India was the fifth largest economy, after the USA, China, Japan and Germany, in US dollar terms and at market rates of exchange the Indian economy was estimated to be the world's 13th largest economy in 2000. The acceleration of economic growth in the 1990s was accompanied by structural shifts in the composition of Indian GDP. The share of the agricultural sector declined, while that of industry and services increased, with the services sector emerging as the largest component of GDP, accounting for as much as 45% of national income in 1999.

Despite its low-income status, in recent years India has recorded an impressive improvement, even by international standards, in real GDP growth. Compared with the near zero growth in output in British India during 1900–50 and the long-term annual average growth rate of 3.5% during 1950–80, real GDP increased by an annual average of about 5.0% in 1980–90 and an estimated 6.1% in 1992–2001. An important characteristic of income growth in India is the year-to-year fluctuation, induced largely by uncertain rainfall conditions which still play a crucial role in influencing output growth in agriculture, and thereby income levels in both the rural and urban sectors of the economy. Between 1980 and 1990 the annual rate of growth of the economy fluctuated widely around the average, ranging from 3.5% to around 11.0%. With the country's population increasing by more than 2% annually, a 5% growth in real GDP meant that average GDP per head rose, in real terms, by only about 3.0% per year between 1980 and 1990. This was, however, an improvement on the performance recorded during the two preceding decades and was largely due to an expansion in the services sector (see below). Taking 1950/51 as the base year, India's GDP per head had increased about threefold, in real terms, by 1982/83. At current prices, however, the increase was nearer 15 times, the difference being explained by rising inflation. As with the rate of growth of output, the rate of inflation over the past few decades has also been uneven.

Estimates of per caput incomes, low as they are by international standards, give a misleading picture of the standard of living that most Indians enjoy for two major reasons. First, valuations in terms of the market exchange rate do not accurately portray the real purchasing power of income for reasons discussed above. Second, the averages conceal wide disparities in income across both social groups and regions. For example, some parts of western and southern India are as prosperous as the majority of South-East Asian economies, just as the top 5% of the Indian population enjoys a standard of living comparable to most upper-middle to upper income economies. However, at least one-third of the population lives below the officially defined 'poverty line'. There are varying estimates of the incidence of poverty in India. Alternative sources of data, as well as varying definitions of poverty, have contributed to a continued controversy among academic economists and policy-makers on the actual incidence of poverty in India as well as on trend of change. What is largely undisputed is that as a percentage of the population, the percentage of people living below the poverty line has declined from more than 50% in the 1960s to around 30% in the late 1990s. In absolute numbers, however, this represents an increase. Some estimates suggest an even steeper decline to around 20%, while others claim more modest progress, with those in poverty accounting for at least 40% of the population. There has also been discussion on the impact of the recent acceleration of growth in the 1990s, and the policies of trade liberalization, on poverty. Critics of the Government's policies claim that higher growth has not 'trickled down' to the poor and, consequently, there has been no improvement in their status. Economists in the Planning Commission claim that the statistics are not comprehensive and do not capture structural changes under way in the economy. The question of the impact of higher growth on poverty and inequality in India remains largely unanswered, awaiting further research. It is clear, however, that some regions of the country have succeeded in lowering the incidence of poverty better than others. On the whole, peninsular India has made greater progress than the plains of north India.

The pattern of extremely distorted distribution of assets and incomes has shaped almost all other trends in the Indian economy, ranging from agricultural production to the over-expansion of the services sector. The rapid growth of the services sector in India is partly explained by the expansion of a sophisticated business economy in urban areas, but is largely explained by an excessive increase in government expenditure on a wide range of subsidies, employment-generating programmes, etc. In recent years subsidies of fertilizer sales, food supplies and of urban transport, defence expenditure and export promotion measures have also contributed to the rise in non-productive expenditure.

Not surprisingly, the structure of production has changed during the process of economic growth in India. In 1950/51 agriculture and allied activities contributed 58% of total national income, while manufacturing, construction and mining (industrial sector), together accounted for 17%, and the services sector (including defence and public administration) contributed the remaining 25%. By 2001 the three sectors contributed 24.9%, 26.9% and 48.2%, respectively. The phenomenal increase in the size of the services sector is in part a reflection of the deceleration of industrial production in the latter half of the 1990s and in part represents the growth of the financial, government, tourism and trade sectors. Although the economy has been undergoing a process of structural change, this change has not been of a kind associated with the growth of modern, large-scale industry, and the non-factory sector continues to account for a very large share of total manufacturing output. The expansion in the services sector has mainly been due to the growth of bureaucracy (including civil, police and defence services) and of banking, insurance and trading activity. These are activities in which employment expansion has been more rapid than productivity levels, partly on account of the fact that the Government, which accounts for a large share of income in these sectors, has been forced to provide jobs even when economic activity has not increased, thus creating a large pool of unproductive labour. In general, however, in terms of the structure of employment, the economy has undergone little change. Agriculture still accounts for an overwhelmingly large percentage of the total labour force, employing slightly more than 60% of the total, with industry coming a poor third, after services (with around 19%), and accounting for only about 11%. These figures indicate the limited ability of the modern industrial sector to absorb the growing labour force, partly compounded by its relatively low weight in total output and partly by the dominance of a capital-intensive technology, which creates few job opportunities per unit of capital invested. As a rough estimate, the capital cost of each job being created is perhaps 20 times as much in organized industry as in agriculture. While much of the recent expansion in industrial activity has been in the private sector, it is the public sector that has, throughout the past few decades, provided greater employment, with its share in total industrial employment estimated at nearly 70% in 1996. Recent reductions in public-sector investment and the process of rationalization in the private corporate sector make the prospects for industrial employment even bleaker.

Although employment in the organized large-scale manufacturing sector has not increased in recent years, there is evidence to suggest that overall employment growth in the economy kept pace with population growth until the mid-1990s and decelerated thereafter. Employment increased in the rural non-farm and urban informal sectors. However, while the growth rate of employment in 1987/88 to 1993/94 was estimated to be 2.43%, compared with a lower rate in the preceding two decades, between 1993/94 and 1999/2000 overall employment was estimated to have grown by only 1.0%. Analysts believe that the deceleration in employment growth was mainly due to the decline in employment generation in the public sector and a slower growth in agricultural employment. The positive growth in employment in the service sector and in non-farm businesses has not compensated for the loss in on-farm and organized industrial sector employment.

These figures provide a mixed illustration of the process of economic growth in India, but, on the positive side, there has been a very encouraging increase in the rate of domestic savings in the economy. As a proportion of GDP, gross domestic savings more than doubled from around 12% in the early 1960s to 26% in 1996/97. However, a disturbing trend emerged in the late 1990s, with the savings rate declining to around 23.0% in the late 1990s (23.4% in 2000/01). This is almost entirely due to a decrease in public-sector savings, which declined from a peak of 5.0% in the mid-1970s to a negative figure of –1.7% in 2000/01, thus implying dissaving. The contribution of household savings doubled, from less than 10% of GDP in the 1950s and 1960s to as much as 20.9% in 2000/01. The share of the private corporate-sector savings increased from around 1% of GDP in the 1950s and 1960s to 4.2% in 2000/01.

With the rate of net investment at around 19% in the early 1980s, the overall contribution of foreign capital (official aid flows plus private lending) was quantitatively small, being about 2% or less of net output. However, with economic liberalization and the opening up of many sectors to foreign direct and portfolio investment, there has been a marked increase in foreign capital inflows. India altered its strategy of resource mobilization in the 1990s, moving in favour of increased foreign direct investment (FDI) and reducing its dependence on external debt. Consequently, the external debt-to-GDP ratio decreased from 41% in 1991/92 to 21.5% in 2000/01. The debt-service ratio (debt-servicing as a share of earnings from exports of goods and services) declined from a peak of 35.3% in 1990/91 to 17.1% in 2000/01. At the end of March 2001 total debt stock, long- and short-term, (amounting to US $100,356m.) as a ratio of GDP (approximately US $456,990m.) was estimated at 21.9%. The ratio of short-term debt to total external debt also decreased from a peak of 10.2% in March 1991 to 3.4% at the end of March 2001.

While aiming to achieve a lower debt-to-GDP ratio, India pursued increased capital flows through FDI and portfolio investment. Investment by foreign institutional investors (FIIs) in the Indian capital market increased from virtually nil in 1990/91 to almost US $4,000m. in the mid-1990s. The annual flow of portfolio investment declined after the Asian financial crisis and in 2000/01 reached an estimated US $2,760m. FDI flows increased from an annual inflow of around US $300m. in 1992/93 to a high of US $3,557m. in 1997/98, before declining to about US $2,300m. in the late 1990s. In 2000/01 the annual inflow of FDI reached an estimated US $2,339m.; in 2001/02 the total was expected to have exceeded US $3,000m. In the early 21st century India continued to attract less FDI than East and South-East Asia; however, the Government remained committed to a more open external economic policy, welcoming both portfolio investment as well as FDI.

By developing-country standards, India's inflation rate is not very high. The long-term average annual rate of inflation (measured by the wholesale price index) for 1960–90 reached about 8%. The 1990s began with a much higher rate of inflation, with an annual average of more than 10% in 1990–95, and ended with low levels of inflation, with an annual average of between 4% and 5.0% in 1999/2000. The decline in inflation was largely due to increased commercial competition resulting from reduced tariffs and a more liberal trade regime. Despite an increase in food and energy prices, depressed industrial prices—as a result of stagnant demand—curbed the rate of inflation in 2000/01 to less than 2.0%. The annual rate of inflation, measured on the basis of point-to-point variations in the wholesale price index, decreased from more than 5.0% in August 2001 to an historically low level of 1.1% in February 2002. The rate of inflation remained around this level in the first half of 2002.

AGRICULTURE

India is a major producer of a number of agricultural commodities, including rice, groundnuts, sugar cane (of which it is the world's leading producer) and tea, although its share of world trade in these commodities is generally low. Domestic production is dominated by food grains (cereals and pulses), which constitute roughly two-thirds of total agricultural output. The bulk of India's production of food grains consists of cereals, principally rice, wheat, sorghum (*jowar*), maize and various forms of millet, mainly cat-tail millet (*bajra*). Less than 8% of the production of food grains is provided by pulses, which are a useful source of vegetable protein for consumers. A series of good monsoons in the 1990s was followed by two years of less than normal rainfall. In 2002 the monsoon began on a weak note, raising fears of inadequate ground water availability, as well as crop failure. Uneven and scarce rainfall presages reduced crop production, led to higher vegetable prices and reduced hydroelectric power (HEP) generation. However, India's high foodgrain stocks, totalling more than 50m. metric tons, and abundant foreign-exchange reserves mean that a failed monsoon need not result in food shortages or high food prices. Foodgrain production reached an estimated 211.2m. tons in 2001/02. Meanwhile, India has become a net exporter of both wheat and rice. The expected production of major crops in 2001/02 was as follows (in tons): milled rice 90.8m.; wheat 73.5m.; coarse grain 33.1m.; pulses 13.8m.; oilseeds 21.2m.; sugar cane 289.4m. India's increased openness to trade in agriculture has enabled it to overcome yearly fluctuations in output.

Between 1960 and the early 1980s India's total agricultural production expanded at an average annual rate of just under 2%. Between 1967/68 and 1995/96 the average annual rate of output of food grains increased by 2.7% (rice by 2.9%, wheat by 4.7% and pulses by 0.9%). In the 1990s there was a rise in the rate of growth of production of pulses, but a decline in the growth of production of rice and wheat. The volume of output is, however, highly sensitive to the nature of the monsoon, and can fluctuate widely and unpredictably from year to year. One of the important features of the Indian economy in recent years has been the 'drought-proofing' of the industrial sector, with the result that the impact of poor agricultural harvests is not felt with the same intensity, as in the past, in the urban and industrial sectors. However, two consecutive years of weak monsoons have renewed concerns about the probable negative impact of reduced rainfall on rural incomes and industrial-sector growth.

There are two important growing seasons in India: the *kharif*, or the summer season, especially important for rice; and the *rabi*, or the winter season, during which most of the wheat is grown. The *kharif* crop is particularly dependent on the monsoon rains, although failure of the winter rains can damage the *rabi* crops also. However, the latter is becoming increasingly reliant on irrigation and, to that extent, a little more protected from the vagaries of the climate. Compared with an irrigation potential of 22.6m. ha at the time of India's independence, recent estimates of the country's 'Ultimate Irrigation Potential' amount to 139.9m. ha. By 2002 the total land area under irrigation had risen to 94.7m. ha; by 2003 this was expected to increase to 100m. ha, of which about 37% would be cultivated by major and medium irrigation projects and 63% through minor irrigation projects. During the 1950s and the early 1960s, the bulk of the increase in India's output of food grains resulted from an expansion of the area sown. However, the supply of cultivable land has practically reached its limit, with increasing competition for land between food grains and non-food crops. Recent increases in output have resulted chiefly from improvements in yields, especially for wheat, but also for rice and *bajra*, particularly on irrigated land planted with new high-yielding varieties (HYV). By international standards, however, yields are still very low, and practices such as multiple cropping affect only a small proportion of the total cultivable area.

There is naturally some doubt as to whether India can succeed in producing enough food for its growing population. Here the evidence is rather contradictory, and future prospects are not easy to determine. On the one hand, the rate of increase in the country's total production of food grains has barely kept pace with the rate of population growth. On the other hand, net imports of food have declined significantly in recent years, especially as a proportion of total availability. Net imports of food have been less than 2% of total supply in the 1990s so far, compared with an estimated 8%–10% in the 1960s and 5%–8% in the 1970s. The view that India is achieving self-sufficiency in food has to be qualified, without denying the very substantial progress that the country has made towards this objective. The effective economic demand for food depends not on population growth, but on increases in purchasing power. The persistence of large-scale poverty in India reflects the limited growth in purchasing power of potential consumers of food grains.

Non-food crops have expanded less rapidly in terms of output and yield, particularly those that are not plantation crops, as are tea and coffee. Owing to an increase in the profitability of producing food crops, there has been little increase in the area under non-food crops, and there has been no comparable development of high-yielding varieties for these crops. An exception, to some extent, is sugar cane, production of which reached 301m. metric tons in 2000/01. In 1989/90 India emerged as the world's largest producer of sugar, despite which there is a shortage of the commodity in the domestic market, where rapid urbanization, combined with changes in food intake patterns, increased the consumption of sugar in India (which is still, however, much lower than average global consumption). India is also a major producer of tea, and production reached 848,000 tons in 2000/01. Government policy favours the satisfaction of domestic demand for tea (India is the world's leading consumer), as with many other consumer goods, and treats export supplies, to some extent, as a residual item, partly to ward off inflationary pressures.

An important feature of Indian agriculture in recent years has been the widening of inter-regional disparities in agricultural production, productivity and standards of living. While regions serviced by assured irrigation (particularly north-western India and the deltaic regions of peninsular India) have prospered, dry land and semi-arid regions have not done so well. The inability to transfer the success of the 'green revolution' to dry-land farming has widened the divide, in terms of standards of living, between dry and wet regions. Consequently, food consumption levels are also uneven and the incidence of poverty and malnourishment varies widely across the country.

Despite major technological advances, the national average rate of growth of agricultural production has not accelerated beyond the 2.8% long-term trend rate (1950–90). While growth was largely concentrated in a few crops—mainly rice, wheat and sugar cane—in a few regions (mainly north-western India and the delta regions of peninsular India), more recently eastern India, especially Bengal, has also experienced high agricultural growth. As a result of good monsoons and increased public expenditure in the agricultural sector in the 1990s (equivalent to 8% of GDP), there has been some improvement in overall agricultural output in recent years.

Policy-makers believe that to sustain overall economic growth of more than 7.0%, Indian agriculture will have to expand by at least 4.0% per annum, a target that was met in the early 1990s, but not since ensured. Higher agricultural growth is contingent upon increased public investment in irrigation, rural roads, agricultural research and extension services and soil conservation. New public investment will, however, require the reduction of input subsidies, especially subsidies for fertilizer use, irrigation water and power. Equally, it also requires the removal of restrictions on trade, particularly the movement of agricultural produce within the country. After a hesitant attempt to reduce fertilizer subsidies in the early 1990s, and a policy reversal in the mid-1990s, the Government subsequently resumed its strategy of subsidy reduction. A decline in capital formation in the agricultural sector has emerged as a major concern for policy-makers and agricultural planners. Although some state governments have been investing funds in rural infrastructure, particularly in irrigation and road-building, widespread neglect in productivity improvement and inadequate investment in new technology continue. India will have to increase land productivity and rural incomes in order to accelerate the rate of economic growth.

INDUSTRY AND INFRASTRUCTURE

At independence in 1947, India was producing a limited range of industrial products. These consisted of cotton textiles, jute, some iron and steel, a few consumer goods, but very little machinery. Most of the demand for manufactured goods was met through imports. Thus, in the 1950s, more than one-third of total steel supplies were imported, as was 70% of textile machinery, almost 100% of sugar-mill machinery and about 90% of metal-working machinery. By the late 1960s, imports of these industrial products had declined significantly: to less than 15% of the total iron and steel supply, a little over one-half of metal-working and textile machinery, and hardly any sugar-milling equipment. These circumstances coincided with a period during which the absolute level of demand for almost all of these commodities had increased substantially. Other figures provide further evidence of the rapid growth and diversification of industrial production in India, to such an extent that India in the 1980s could reasonably be included as one of the so-called Newly Industrialized Countries (NICs). While this rapidly diminishing dependence on imports was achieved, Indian industry has been characterized by a relatively low level of productivity and a lack of competitiveness in international markets, which has hampered India's export efforts.

In recent years the structure of industrial production has undergone significant change, with chemical-based industries increasing their share of industrial production at the expense of agro-based industries. Three characteristics of the pattern of industrial growth may be noted. First, statistics are most readily available for the organized sector of industry, which is defined in terms of units consisting of 10 or more workers using power or of 20 or more without power. Much of the industrial activity is carried out by smaller units. There are no reliable statistics relating to the behaviour of this so-called 'unorganized' or informal sector, but it is believed to be growing rapidly. Second, within the organized sector, the distribution of employment and output is extremely unbalanced. In the early 1980s only 6.3% of factories had capital of more than Rs 2m. However, these provided 60.6% of total employment in the organized sector, and produced 80% of the value added. By contrast, 38.2% of the factories had capital of less than Rs 100,000; they provided 11.5% of employment and only 4.1% of value added. Third, the growth of industrial production has been uneven, with fluctuations between different years and between regions. In terms of variations over time, industrial growth was most rapid in the period up to the mid-1960s. The rate of growth of industrial production slowed thereafter, but recovered in the early 1980s. Compared with an average annual rate of growth of industrial production of 4.1% for the period 1965–80, output increased at the rate of 7.3% during 1981–91.

The 1990s witnessed an acceleration in industrial production in the first half of the decade, with the index of industrial production (IIP) recording a peak growth rate of 12.8% in 1995/96, and a subsequent deceleration of growth from 1997. According to the index, which was revised in 1998, industrial production grew at more than 10.0% in the mid-1990s, but decelerated to an average of around 6.0% in the second half of the 1990s. In April–December 2001 it was estimated to be no more than 2.3%, the lowest rate of growth in more than a decade. The decline in industrial growth was largely attributed to a sharp deceleration in the growth of the manufacturing sector. The official explanation was that the decline was the product of both normal business and investment cycles and the adjustment delays expected during corporate restructuring. Prolonged high real interest rates, infrastructure constraints in the power and transport sectors, and delays in establishing credible institutional and regulatory framework for private participation in some principal sectors have all been identified as factors contributing to the deceleration. Economists also believe that the surge in consumer demand, owing to the liberalization of trade policy in the early 1990s and the substantial increase in government salaries in the late 1990s, might have become exhausted; unless a new phase of investment to stimulate demand is introduced, it will be difficult to accelerate industrial production.

In the 1950s the annual average per caput consumption of electricity was about 4.5 kWh. In 1999/2000 this was estimated to be 69.2 kWh. India is a major coal-mining country, with total coal production (excluding lignite) of an estimated 309.6m. metric tons in 2000/01, compared with a mere 32m. tons in 1950/51. Power is generated by hydro-, thermal-, nuclear- and gas-based installations. In 1950/51 total energy generated was 6,600m. kWh, of which 2,500m. kWh was generated by HEP and 2,600m. kWh by thermal power. In 1999/2000 total energy generated was 532,200m. kWh, of which HEP accounted for 80,600m. kWh, thermal power accounted for 386,800m. kWh and nuclear power accounted for 13,300m. kWh. The policy of permitting private investment in power generation contributed to an increase in the share of non-utilities in energy generation. In 1999/2000 non-utilities generated 51,500m kWh compared with 25,100m. kWh in 1990/91.

A major constraint on India's economic growth is inadequate and poor-quality electric power. Thermal plants account for 74% of total power generation (India has the fourth-largest coal reserves in the world) and HEP plants (often dependent on monsoons) for 24%; the remaining 2% is contributed by nuclear power. Low productivity of underground mines, high ash content and low calorific value are some of the shortcomings of India's coal industry. In recent years the Government has liberalized coal-mining policies, permitting private investment in mining, and deregulating coal prices and retail trade.

Indian crude petroleum production did not keep pace with increased demand in the 1990s, and India's dependence on imported energy is projected to increase further. Between 1990 and 2020 oil demand is expected to quadruple, while oil imports are expected to increase eight-fold. In 1990 indigenous oil accounted for 60% of total consumption, while imported oil accounted for 40%. However, by 2000 this ratio was reversed with imported oil accounting for more than 60% of consumption. By 2010 oil imports are expected to be almost 75% of total consumption. Refinery throughput of crude oil was estimated to be 103.4m. metric tons in 2000/01, with domestic production estimated at 32.4m. tons and net imports accounting for 74.1m. tons. Although India remains self-sufficient in coal, and coal will continue to be the most important source of energy, imported oil and natural gas are expected to become significant sources of energy. Hence, ensuring reliable supplies of imported oil and gas will be a major security concern for India.

Infrastructure has become a key area of reform and privatization under the Government's new economic policies. While public investment was traditionally the main source of funding for new projects in the infrastructure sector, including power, roads, ports, communication, transportation, etc., the Government now permits private investors, both domestic and foreign, to invest in these areas. The inability of the Government to fulfil the 1992–97 Five-Year Plan power target of 30,000 MW, has also encouraged it to look for innovative ways of financing new investment. Against a target of 3,299 MW of additional generation capacity, 4,242 MW of capacity was actually added in 1998/99. Of this, 1,575 MW was created in the private sector (against a target of 1,830 MW) by independent power producers, 991.6 MW was created in the public-sector utilities owned by the central Government and 1,675 MW in utilities owned by state governments. Several state governments have already restructured the state electricity boards (SEB), dividing them into separate generation and distribution companies. Improvement in plant efficiency, reduction of transmission and distribution losses, and punishment of power theft are essential to ensure better efficiency of SEBs.

The generation and distribution of electricity remains an area of major policy reform. After failing to attract adequate private investment into generation, and encountering problems with power purchase, best exemplified by the travails of the Dabhol Power Company (mainly owned by the US company, Enron) in the state of Maharashtra, the central and state Governments have now shifted focus to SEB reform and the privatization of distribution. Power utilities in Delhi and various other cities have already been privatized. In 2002 the union Government proposed an electricity bill, which would create the legal framework for the privatization of distribution and the regulation of utilities.

As mentioned above, India's dependence on imported fuels has risen. Petroleum imports constitute more than 30% of the cost of total imports. The decrease in global petroleum prices has until recently masked the increase in imports. However, the recent rise in prices was expected to exert renewed pressure on India's import bill. India imports most of its petroleum requirements from the Middle East, but is exploring the possibility of tapping the petroleum and natural gas resources of Bangladesh, Iran, Oman and the Central Asian Republics.

The major consumers of energy in India are the industrial and the transport sectors, which together account for about 70% of consumption. Industry remains a heavy consumer of coal-based energy and of electricity, while in transport there has been a substantial change-over from coal to petroleum, owing partly to the expansion of road transport, and partly to the increasing use of diesel-powered, rather than coal-based, locomotives on India's railways.

For a very large and very poor country, India has a well-developed and relatively efficient transport system. An elaborate railway network, first created in the mid-19th century, continues to function. Most of the locomotives are powered by diesel fuel, and, increasingly, the track is being electrified. Railways and highways have been the focus of infrastructure modernization in the early 21st century. The National Highways Authority of India is engaged in a major construction exercise to build four-lane highways throughout India, linking the six major cities and the medium-sized cities located between them. Road construction is also under way. Major investment by the World Bank and private donors has facilitated the project. Away from these, quality and all-weather availability declines, and rural roads are poorly-developed and inadequately maintained, thus adding considerably to the problems of marketing agricultural products. However, even these matters vary from one state to another. In the more developed states like Andhra Pradesh, Maharashtra and Tamil Nadu, even rural roads are being renewed.

India's shipping sector is the second largest in Asia, and there are substantial shipbuilding facilities. At the end of 2001 the total registered merchant fleet comprised 1,018 vessels, with a total displacement of almost 6.7m. grt. India has several well-established seaports, notably Mumbai and Kolkata, and has invested in the establishment and development of a number of new ones, such as Visakhapatnam, Mormugao and Paradip (Paradeep). The modernization of shipping and port-handling has been another area of increased activity in the early 21st century.

From the 1950s, enterprises in the public sector were designed to play a strategic role in India's industrial development. A large part of total industrial output originates in the public sector. In the early 1980s public-sector industries, which consisted mainly of modern large-scale enterprises, provided about 26% of total factory employment and 70% of fixed industrial capital. Joint-sector enterprises provided an additional 5%–6% of both output and employment. Enterprises in the public sector may be divided into two categories: manufacturing enterprises and service enterprises. Among the former is the Steel Authority of India, which is the largest industrial public-sector body in terms of investment (Rs 46,000m. in the early 1980s). Other important operations include the Fertilizer Corporation of India Ltd, Bharat Heavy Electricals Ltd and Hindustan Machine Tools (HMT) Ltd. Among the service enterprises are a number of major trading companies, such as the Food Corporation of India and the Minerals and Metals Trading Corporation.

India has developed a substantial volume of industrial production, which is able to satisfy the bulk of domestic demand for manufactured commodities. Indian industry produces a wide variety of products, ranging from consumer goods to fairly advanced forms of capital equipment. The country has developed a substantial domestic defence potential, and is now moving into the assembly, production and, more recently, the export of fairly advanced military equipment, under collaboration agreements. India is one of the very few developing countries that has an indigenously created potential for using nuclear power, avowedly directed towards peaceful uses. India has been involved in establishing fertilizer factories and other production facilities under 'turn-key' arrangements in other developing countries. Indian multinational corporations now operate in a number of East African, Middle Eastern and South-East Asian countries. The productivity of Indian industries, however, is often well below international levels, which has made it difficult for India to maintain or advance its share in world trade in a number of traditional and new commodities. This lack of competitiveness is often revealed in other ways, e.g. in long delivery dates, unreliability of supply, or in poor or variable quality of some exports. Indian industry is also regarded as being slow to adopt new technologies or improved designs, and as being technologically backward.

While the public sector remains an important feature of Indian industry, since 1991 successive governments have initiated policies to reduce public ownership, end public monopolies, expose public enterprises to market competition at home and abroad and, eventually, to privatize the public sector. The governing National Democratic Alliance (NDA), which took office in October 1999, placed privatization of the public sector at the centre of its policy agenda. It created a Ministry of Disinvestment which handles the process of disinvestment and privatization. As a result, private investment, including FDI, is now permitted in all infrastructure industries including power, telecommunications, coal, civil aviation, and in the financial sector, including insurance. Independent regulatory authorities have been established in the spheres of power, telecommunications and insurance, to ensure equal treatment for public- and private-sector companies. Only the railways remain entirely in the public sector. However, in this area too, the Government is permitting private companies to offer services ranging from manufacture of wagons to catering. In 2001/02 the Government successfully privatized several major public enterprises across a range of industries, including a bread-making firm, an aluminium company, a telecommunications firm, an oil company and several hotels. Overcoming political controversy and initial allegations of corruption, the highly regarded Minister of Disinvestment and of Development of the North-Eastern Region, Arun Shourie, has been able to push through a wide-ranging programme of privatization. Considering the pace at which the process advanced in early 2002, it appeared likely that the Government would reach its annual target of Rs 100,000m. from the privatization programme.

The Governing NDA has continued the previous government's policy of opening India up to FDI. Despite the nervousness in global markets and the uncertainty caused by the terrorist attacks on the USA in September 2001, India succeeded in attracting increased amounts of foreign investment. Whereas in the 1980s India witnessed a minimal inflow of FDI and no foreign portfolio investment in the capital market, in 1996/97 foreign investment reached a peak of almost US $6,000m. Foreign capital flows reduced thereafter, particularly after the Asian financial crisis in 1997/98. However, in 2001/02 India managed to attract nearly US $3,000m. of FDI. Foreign investment flows increased further in 2002.

A decline in production and in capital formation in the manufacturing sector began to cause major concern from 1999. The growth rate in production recorded by the IIP declined from an already low 6.6% in 1999/2000 to 2.8% in 2001/02. In April–June 2002 the index showed a marginal growth, signalling a revival of demand. It was expected that industrial growth would be higher in 2002/03, compared with the poor performance in 2001/02. A weak monsoon in 2002 could still adversely affect industrial recovery; however, companies remained confident about the prospects of higher demand for manufactured goods and the revival of investment in the industrial sector. Public investment in the infrastructure sector in 2001/02, especially in road construction, and increased private investment in housing, have helped to stimulate demand for several basic industries, such as iron and steel, cement and plastics. A sharp increase in automobile and two-wheeled vehicle sales has stimulated growth in the automobile industry. Early forecasts suggest that in 2002/03 industrial growth may reach around 5.0%; the services sector is expected to grow by 7.0%. The UN Industrial Development Organization's *Industrial Development Report 2002/03* placed India 50th in a list of 87 industrializing countries in terms of its international competitiveness. The report underscores the critical importance of investing in skills, research and development and infrastructure to enhance the global competitiveness of Indian industry.

TRADE AND BALANCE OF PAYMENTS

There has been a fundamental reorientation in India's external economic policies over the last decade. After independence in 1947 India pursued a strategy of import-substituting industrialization. While India's share in world trade in 1950 was 1.8%, it declined over the ensuing 40 years of inward-orientated industrial development to a low of 0.4% in the mid-1980s. By the early 2000s India's share had increased to 0.7%. The Government set a medium-term target of increasing this to 1.0% by 2007. In the mean time, the share of exports in GDP rose from 5.8% in 1991/92 to 10.1% in 2000/01. Furthermore, India's share of trade in GDP grew from 13.3% in 1991/92 to 19.2% in 2000/01, indicating the country's increased trade openness.

Although India has pursued a more outward-orientated economic policy since the early 1980s, the decisive shift in policy occurred in 1991 when the Government responded to a balance-of-payments crisis by radically altering its industrial and trade policies. Since the introduction of reforms in 1991, India's import-weighted average tariff rate for all products has been reduced from 87% to 30% in 1998/99. The maximum tariff rate was gradually reduced from over 200% in 1990/91 to 45% by 1998/99. In mid-2000 the lowest average tariff rate of 16% was on agricultural products and the highest (39%) on consumer goods; capital goods and intermediate goods attracted a customs duty rate of around 30%. India had phased out all quantitative restrictions (QRs) on imports by April 2001, following a settlement with the USA and the European Union (EU), which had earlier complained to the World Trade Organization (WTO) about India's continued use of QRs. Fears that the removal of QRs might encourage uncontrolled growth of imports hitherto have not materialized. India's non-oil trade deficit declined in 2001/02, mainly owing to subdued non-oil import growth.

While India has moved away from being a commodity-exporting economy (its exports in the 1950s and 1960s were mainly tea, tobacco, plantation crops, and suchlike), in the 1990s gems and jewellery, garments and textiles, engineering goods, chemicals and leather were the principal exports. In March 2002 the Ministry of Commerce published a medium-term export strategy for 2002–07, which aimed to increase India's share of world exports from the current 0.6% to 1.0% by 2007. The strategy document identified Argentina, Australia, Brazil, Canada, Hong Kong, Indonesia, Israel, Japan, the Republic of Korea, Mexico, Norway, Poland, Russia, Saudi Arabia, Singapore, South Africa, Switzerland, Taiwan, Thailand, Turkey, the United Arab Emirates, the USA and the EU as India's 'focus markets'. The potential sectors identified for export promotion were engineering goods, textiles, gems and jewellery, chemicals, agricultural commodities (including marine and plantation crops), leather and leather products and electronics. While India has a low share of world merchandise trade, its share of trade in computer software services has grown rapidly. Indian trade statistics do not account for the software services trade. According to available data, software service exports grew at an average annual rate of 52.5% in 1995–2000. In 2000/01 the growth rate had increased to an estimated 57%, with the total software service export trade amounting to US $6,300m. India aimed to increase annual software exports to US $10,000m. by 2005.

India's exports (in US dollar terms) increased at an average annual rate of 10% between 1992/93 and 1999/2000, compared with 7.6% between 1980/81 and 1991/92. Import growth, which averaged 8.5% per year (in US dollar terms) between 1980/81 and 1991/92, increased to an annual average rate of 13.4% in 1992/93–1999/2000. However, from April 2001 to February 2002 India's merchandise exports increased by only 0.1%, compared with a 20.6% growth over the same period one year previously. Some improvement has since been recorded and by the end of March 2003 exports are expected to have increased by 10%. The USA and the EU account for nearly one-half of India's external trade. The USA remains India's single largest trading partner, accounting for 21% of India's exports in 2000/01. The most striking development in the trade sector in recent years has been the emergence of 'Greater China' (China and Hong Kong) as India's second-largest trading partner (when the EU is not viewed as a single unit), accounting for 7.8% of India's exports in 2000/01. In recent years India has increasingly emphasized economic co-operation with its Asian neighbours; consequently, India's trade with Asia, particularly South and South-East Asia, has increased.

An improvement in India's external trade profile was also accompanied by an accumulation of foreign-exchange reserves. At the time of the balance-of-payments crisis in early 1991, India's foreign-exchange reserves declined to less than US $1,000m. The policy of external trade and investment liberalization and of opening up the Indian stock market to investment by foreign institutional investors, yielded rich dividends in terms of a rapid accumulation of foreign-exchange reserves. From less than US $1,000m. in 1991, India's reserves reached a record figure of more than US $56,000m. in mid-June 2002, representing the value of more than eight months of imports of goods and services. From 1997 India was adversely affected by the Asian financial crisis, which caused a deceleration in external capital flows, mainly on account of diminishing portfolio investment. The buoyancy in capital flows, the continued high inflow of remittances from Indians abroad (mainly in the Persian (Arabian) Gulf region) and a positive outlook for India among emerging markets helped keep India's current-account deficit at low and manageable levels. Compared with a current-account deficit to GDP ratio of more than 3.0% in the crisis year of 1991, in the period 1995–2000 the ratio was between 1.0% and 1.5%. India's external debt profile has remained stable. The debt stock to GDP ratio has decreased from 41% in 1991/92 to 21.5% in 2000/01, the debt-service ratio also declined from 30% in 1991/92 to 17% in 2000/01 and short-term debt accounts for less than 5.0% of total debt in 2000, compared with 8.3% in 1991/92. A low current-account deficit, stable reserves and a modest rate of inflation (a low 2.0% in mid-2002 compared with the long-term average of more than 8.0%) created the conditions identified by an expert group as the minimum macroeconomic requirements for India to permit full capital-account convertibility. It is likely that India would have announced this had the Asian financial crisis and the more recent uncertainties in the global economy not intervened.

Steadily rising foreign-exchange reserves, a stable exchange rate (maintained by the Reserve Bank of India's policy of 'managed float') and a low current-account deficit (narrowing to near balance in August 2002) constitute the three major strengths of India's external economic profile. The shortcomings, however, are that merchandise export growth remains low and the trade deficit, created in 2001/02 by rising oil prices, is increasingly bridged by earnings on the 'invisibles' account, mainly from an inflow of remittances from Indians abroad and software earnings. India has managed to stabilize its external debt and to insulate the domestic economy from the inflationary consequences of rising foreign-exchange reserves.

ECONOMIC POLICY AND RECENT PERFORMANCE

For the first three decades following independence, India consciously sought to build a mixed economy. One of the main objectives of general economic policy was to redress the weaknesses inherent in a developing economy with a poor capital and infrastructural base. State intervention and investment were justified on the grounds of 'private investment failure'. The Second Five-Year Plan (1955–60) witnessed heavy public investment in the core industrial sector as well as in transport and communications. While this was politically advertised as being the basis for the building of a 'socialistic pattern of society', in reality, public investment, both in industry and agriculture, was supplemented by private investment, which laid the foundations for the growth of indigenous business enterprise.

India's protected industrial sector thrived during the 1960s. However, a series of poor monsoons, two wars with Pakistan (in 1965 and 1971) and rising social and political discontent curbed productive investment, leading to a deceleration in the rate of growth of industrial production throughout the 1970s. In order to adjust to this low-growth phase and in response to pressures from new business groups (both domestic and non-resident Indians), a series of policy changes were carried out, liberalizing the highly-regulated economy and making production for exports, rather than for the internal market, relatively profitable. The first phase of this new liberal economic policy was introduced in 1978–80. The rise in the cost of petroleum on the world market in 1979, however, forced the Government to revert to a more regulated economy.

The second phase of economic liberalization was implemented during the early months of Rajiv Gandhi's premiership. The 1985/86 budget heralded the arrival of a more liberal tax and investment regime that was expected to stimulate production and demand through supply-side policies.

Compared with the low economic growth rate of the 1970s (with an average annual GDP growth rate of 3.5%), the 1980s witnessed moderate to high growth with an average annual GDP growth rate of about 5.0%. This increase was largely due to a steep increase in public expenditure and investment. The liberalization of imports facilitated access to new technologies, which, in turn, encouraged expansion in the consumer durables, electronics and petrochemicals industries. The Government had not, however, protected itself against an excessive level of borrowing, both domestically and internationally. India's excellent sovereign credit rating allowed it easy access to global financial markets in the late 1980s, and both long- and short-term debts were rapidly accumulated.

Given the high accumulation of debt and the concomitant burden of debt servicing, and in the absence of an adequate growth in exports, India found itself unable to withstand the adverse effects of the Gulf crisis in mid-1990. Partly on account of this and partly on account of the poor political assessments of credit-rating agencies, which believed that a minority Government would be unable to pursue policies that would stabilize the Indian economy, India's credit rating began to slip in the latter half of 1990. By early 1991 its rating had reached a nadir, having fallen from the highest ranking to below investment grade, and foreign-exchange reserves had decreased to less than US $1,000m. Faced with the risk of default, the Government imposed draconian import control measures, borrowed extensively from the IMF and, in July 1991, devalued the rupee by 20%.

The balance-of-payments crisis of mid-1991 coincided with the arrival in office of a new Congress Party Government led by Prime Minister P. V. Narasimha Rao, with the highly-regarded economist and former Governor of the Reserve Bank of India, Dr Manmohan Singh, as Minister of Finance. The Rao-Singh team utilized the opportunity opened by the payments crisis to make the Indian economy accessible to foreign trade and investment flows. Implementing a traditional structural adjustment programme designed with the assistance of the World Bank and the IMF, India liberalized its trade and investment policies, announced a programme of fiscal stabilization aimed at reducing the fiscal deficit from more than 8.5% of GDP to 5.0%, instigated a policy for phasing out short-term external debt exposure and reduced the current-account deficit from more than 3.0% of GDP to less than 2.0% within a year. Along with this medium-term adjustment and stabilization programme, the Government gradually introduced extensive changes in industrial and tax policies.

The policies to transform the Indian economy from an 'inward-orientated', import-substituting model of industrial development to an 'outward-orientated' model were further developed by successive governments throughout the 1990s. As a result, the policies not only prevented external default, but also helped to increase India's foreign-exchange assets several-fold within a short period of time, from less than US $1,000m. in 1991 to more than US $25,000m. in 1994. There was a sharp decrease in both fiscal and current-account deficits and an improvement in the external debt profile. India's recovery from a balance-of-payments crisis is regarded as one of the fastest achieved under an IMF-World Bank adjustment and stabilization programme. In part, the success of the Indian strategy lay in the ability of the authorities to ensure relative freedom from the IMF-World Bank orthodoxy, in order to pursue an unorthodox and unconventional approach to fiscal and balance-of-payments correction. As well as stabilizing the economy, these policies also helped to accelerate the rate of growth of the Indian economy. Compared with the long-term rate of growth of around 4.0% during 1950–90, the Indian economy was able to register a rate of growth of over 6.0% in the period 1992–99. This acceleration of growth was accompanied by a decline in the rate of inflation. According to the UN Development Programme's *Human Development Report 2000*, India's human development indicators also showed an improvement in the 1990s. India, once considered a country with *low* human development, has advanced to the category of *medium* human development. According to the *Human Development Report 2002*, India's rank in a list of 173 countries had improved to 124. However, evidence on the distributional impact of higher growth is still inconclusive. As in many other parts of the world, including many richer economies, higher growth is likely to have been accompanied by increased inequalities. There is a continuous debate among statisticians and economists in India as to whether higher growth has worsened poverty or, at best, left it unaltered. Few believe that there has been direct beneficial impact of this growth on poverty. Most, however, seem to concede that inequality may have increased.

The improved performance of the economy in the 1990s appears impressive when compared with the record of India's experience in the first eight decades of the 20th century. However, by comparison with its East and South-East Asian neighbours, India is still rather backward. Clearly, the challenge facing India today is to grow faster, increase its share of world trade and improve its human development indicators if it wishes to catch up with China by 2010. India remains committed to a more liberal trade and investment policy; in mid-2000 new areas of the economy, including the electronic media and telecommunications were fully opened up to foreign investors. Although India was a reluctant participant in earlier rounds of trade negotiations in the General Agreement on Tariffs and Trade (GATT) and subsequently the World Trade Organization (WTO), in recent years the country has been an active advocate of liberal trade rules within a multilateral framework. India has actively opposed all forms of protectionism, including neo-protectionist initiatives, which seek to link trade policy to labour and environmental standards.

Despite the contentious political and intellectual debates regarding economic policy issues in India, successive governments representing a wide range of political parties have gradually pushed through economic reforms. However, two major challenges remain: accelerating the rate of growth of agricultural production and productivity as well as of employment in rural areas, both on farm and in non-farm activity; and reforming public enterprises and securing returns to wide-ranging public investment in all sectors. Governments remain politically constrained from making consumers pay for water, including irrigation water, and power. They have been unsuccessful in reducing the workforce in overstaffed public enterprises and government offices. The biggest policy challenge is improving the productivity of existing investment.

Nevertheless, the liberal trade and investment regime has encouraged private enterprise to grow in areas where markets are readily available for products and services. The most promising area of growth has been the services sector, which by the end of the 1990s accounted for about 40% of GDP. In this sector, software services have emerged as an important area of growth, income, employment and exports. India's sustained investment in good-quality higher education, particularly in engineering, has helped transform India into a 'software superpower'. Other sectors experiencing growth include pharmaceuticals, chemicals and petrochemicals, automobiles, consumer durables and plastics. Most of these industries are, however, emerging in the western and southern states of India and around New Delhi, leaving north and north-eastern India relatively deprived and static. Increasing regional inequalities in growth remain an area of concern for India, with peninsular India growing at a much faster pace than the land-locked regions of northern and north-eastern India.

While India's various governments comprising political parties that span the ideological spectrum have continued the radical economic policy, the most consistent critics of the policies of economic liberalization have been the small group of socialist and communist parties that control provincial governments in the states of West Bengal and Kerala. Even these parties have been pragmatic in office, whilst criticizing the policies of the central Government, a body in which they have never shared power. The major areas of policy difference between them and the ruling political parties relate to foreign portfolio investment and privatization of public enterprises. Another political group that has remained critical of India's increased openness to foreign trade and investment is the right-wing protectionst organization called the Swadeshi Jagran Manch (Self-Reliance Awareness Platform), which draws inspiration from the ruling political party, the Bharatiya Janata Party (BJP), but remains critical of the latter's economic policies. The BJP and influential regional political parties, such as the Telugu Desam (in Andhra Pradesh) and the Dravida Munnetra Kazhakam (in Tamil

Nadu), which are members of the ruling NDA, have demonstrated that they support continuation of the policies of economic reform, liberalization and privatization initiated by Congress when in office in 1991–96. It is important to note that while Congress is itself in the midst of a debate on its economic policy orientation, as the principle opposition party, it, nevertheless, continues with the policies of fiscal reform and privatization in the 14 states in which it has gained power. Frustratingly for reformers, most political parties when in opposition dispute the very policies they sponsor when in government. Notwithstanding this ideological flux and the intense debate on policy within the country, India appears set on the course of greater trade and investment liberalization and privatization of the public sector.

Apart from dealing with the impact of a weak monsoon, the immediate challenge for policy-makers in 2002/03 is to foster a recovery of industrial production and investment in the economy. The estimated rate of growth for the Ninth Five-Year Plan (1997–2002) was about 5.5%, lower than the targeted 6.5%. The Government attributed this shortfall to the impact of the Asian financial crisis, the sanctions imposed on India after the nuclear tests in 1998, the escalation of the Kashmir crisis to a 'near-war' situation with Pakistan in the Kargil area in 1999 and the global economic slowdown in 2001/02. Against this background, the Government set a target of 8.0% growth for the Tenth Five-Year Plan (2002–07). If India is to boost the rate of economic growth from around 6.0% to 8.0% in 2002–07, a huge increase in investment and a significant improvement in productivity of capital and labour will be required. Equally, the Government will have to reduce the domestic debt and the unsustainably high level of fiscal deficit, which in mid-2002 had reached more than 10% of GDP. Fiscal reform and privatization are vital in achieving these goals. Government, on a central and state level, will also have to pursue vigorously economic reform, particularly in the infrastructure sector, and sustain higher levels of income and spending in the rural areas.

The Indian economy is capable of registering a rate of growth rate of 6.0%–7.0% in the medium term. If India succeeds in sustaining even 6.5% growth in 2002–12, it will still manage to reduce poverty and encourage industrial growth. According to the Tenth Five-Year Plan document, in order to achieve these targets, an increase in both new investment and the productivity of existing investment is required. Growth in investment will have to be generated primarily by the private sector, which accounts for about two-thirds of all investment in the economy. Increased flow of FDI was one source of private investment quoted by the document. Furthermore, reforms of labour legislation are necessary to promote investment in employment-generating ventures. The document also stated that the completion of reforms already started, as well as new reform initiatives, which encompass fundamental fiscal changes, and reform of relatively untouched sectors and institutional and legal areas was required to create 'an environment in which productive investment flourishes'. Since the Chinese economy has been registering lower growth rates in recent years, India has the potential to emerge as the world's fastest growing economy, as long as the Government remains focused on economic and governance reforms.

Statistical Survey

Source (unless otherwise stated): Central Statistical Organization, Ministry of Statistics and Programme Implementation, Sardar Patel Bhavan, Patel Chowk, New Delhi 110 001; tel. (11) 3732150; fax (11) 3342384; e-mail moscc@bol.net.in; internet mospi.nic.in.

Area and Population

AREA, POPULATION AND DENSITY*

Area (sq km)	3,166,414†
Population (census results)	
1 March 1991‡§	846,302,688
1 March 2001‖ ¶	
Males	531,277,078
Females	495,738,169
Total	1,027,015,247
Population (official estimates at mid-year)**	
1999	986,611,000
2000	1,002,142,000
2001	1,017,544,000
Density (per sq km) at March 2001	324

* Including Sikkim (incorporated into India on 26 April 1975) and the Indian-held part of Jammu and Kashmir.

† 1,222,559 sq miles.

‡ Excluding adjustment for underenumeration, estimated at 1.5%.

§ Including estimate for the Indian-held part of Jammu and Kashmir.

‖ Provisional results.

¶ Including estimates for certain areas in the states of Gujarat and Himachal Pradesh where the census could not be conducted, owing to recent natural disasters.

** Not adjusted to take account of the 2001 census results.

Source: Registrar General of India.

STATES AND TERRITORIES (population at 2001 census)

	Capital	Area (sq km)	Population (provisional)	Density (per sq km)
States				
Andhra Pradesh	Hyderabad	275,069	75,727,541	275
Arunachal Pradesh[1]	Itanagar	83,743	1,091,117	13
Assam	Dispur	78,438	26,638,407	340
Bihar*	Patna	94,163	82,878,796	880
Chhattisgarh	Raipur	135,191	20,795,956	154
Goa[5]	Panaji	3,702	1,343,998	363
Gujarat	Gandhinagar	196,022	50,596,992	258
Haryana	Chandigarh[2]	44,212	21,082,989	477
Himachal Pradesh	Shimla	55,673	6,077,248	109
Jammu and Kashmir[3]	Srinagar	101,387	10,069,917	99
Jharkhand†	Ranchi	79,714	26,909,428	338
Karnataka	Bangalore	191,791	52,733,958	275
Kerala	Thiruvananthapuram (Trivandrum)	38,863	31,838,619	819
Madhya Pradesh*	Bhopal	308,245	60,385,118	196
Maharashtra	Mumbai (Bombay)	307,713	96,752,247	314
Manipur	Imphal	22,327	2,388,634	107
Meghalaya	Shillong	22,429	2,306,069	103
Mizoram[4]	Aizawl	21,081	891,058	42

— *continued*	Capital	Area (sq km)	Population (provisional)	Density (per sq km)
Nagaland	Kohima	16,579	1,988,636	120
Orissa	Bhubaneswar	155,707	36,706,920	236
Punjab	Chandigarh[2]	50,362	24,289,296	482
Rajasthan	Jaipur	342,239	56,473,122	165
Sikkim	Gangtok	7,096	540,493	76
Tamil Nadu	Chennai (Madras)	130,058	62,110,839	478
Tripura	Agartala	10,486	3,191,168	304
Uttaranchal*	Dehradun	53,483	8,479,562	159
Uttar Pradesh*	Lucknow	240,928	166,052,859	689
West Bengal	Kolkata (Calcutta)	88,752	80,221,171	904
Territories				
Andaman and Nicobar Islands	Port Blair	8,249	356,265	43
Chandigarh[2]	Chandigarh	114	900,914	7,902
Dadra and Nagar Haveli	Silvassa	491	220,451	449
Daman and Diu[5]	Daman	112	158,059	1,411
Delhi	Delhi	1,483	13,782,976	9,294
Lakshadweep	Kavaratti	32	60,595	1,894
Pondicherry	Pondicherry	480	973,829	2,029

* Chhattisgarh, Jharkhand and Uttaranchal (formerly parts of Madhya Pradesh, Bihar and Uttar Pradesh respectively) were granted statehood in November 2000; figures for area and population have been adjusted accordingly.

[1] Arunachal Pradesh was granted statehood in February 1987.

[2] Chandigarh forms a separate Union Territory, not within Haryana or Punjab. As part of a scheme for a transfer of territory between the two states, Chandigarh was due to be incorporated into Punjab on 26 January 1986, but the transfer was postponed.

[3] Figures refer only to the Indian-held part of the territory.

[4] Mizoram was granted statehood in February 1987.

[5] Goa was granted statehood in May 1987. Daman and Diu remain a Union Territory.

Source: *Census of India*, 2001.

PRINCIPAL TOWNS (provisional population at 2001 census*)

Town	Population	Town	Population
Greater Mumbai (Bombay)	11,914,398	Ranchi	846,454
Delhi	9,817,439	Jodhpur	846,408
Kolkata (Calcutta)	4,580,544	Gwalior	826,919
Bangalore	4,292,223	Vijayawada (Vijayavada)	825,436
Chennai (Madras)	4,216,268	Chandigarh	808,796
Ahmedabad	3,515,361	Guwahati	808,021
Hyderabad	3,449,878	Hubli-Dharwar	786,018
Pune (Poona)	2,540,069	Tiruchirapalli	746,062
Kanpur (Cawnpore)	2,532,138	Thiruvananthapuram (Trivandrum)	744,739
Surat	2,433,787	Mysore	742,261
Jaipur (Jeypore)	2,324,319	Jalandhar	701,223
Lucknow	2,207,340	Bareilly	699,839
Nagpur	2,051,320	Kota	695,899
Indore	1,597,441	Salem	693,236
Bhopal	1,433,875	Aligarh	667,732
Ludhiana	1,395,053	Bhubaneswar	647,302
Patna	1,376,950	Moradabad	641,240
Vadodara (Baroda)	1,306,035	Gorakhpur	624,570
Thane (Thana)	1,261,517	Raipur	605,131
Agra	1,259,979	Kochi (Cochin)	596,473
Kalyan	1,193,266	Jamshedpur	570,349
Varanasi (Banaras)	1,100,748	Bhilai Nagar	553,837
Nashik	1,076,967	Amravati	549,370
Meerut	1,074,229	Cuttack	535,139
Faridabad Complex	1,054,981	Bikaner	529,007
Haora (Howrah)	1,008,704	Warangal	528,570
Pimpri-Chinchwad	1,006,417	Guntur	514,707
Allahabad	990,298	Bhavnagar	510,958
Amritsar	975,695	Durgapur	492,996
Visakhapatnam (Vizag)	969,608	Ajmer	485,197
Ghaziabad	968,521	Kolhapur	485,183
Rajkot	966,642	Ulhasnagar	472,943
Jabalpur (Jubbulpore)	951,469	Saharanpur	452,925
Coimbatore	923,085	Jamnagar	447,734
Madurai	922,913	Bhatpara	441,957
Srinagar	894,940	Kozhikode (Calicut)	436,527
Solapur	873,037	Ujjain	429,933
Aurangabad	872,667	Bokaro Steel City	394,173
		Jhansi	383,248
		Rajahmundry	313,347

* Figures refer to the city proper in each case.

Capital: New Delhi, provisional population 294,783 at 2001 census.

Provisional population of principal urban agglomerations at 2001 census: Greater Mumbai (Bombay) 16,368,084; Kolkata (Calcutta) 13,216,546; Delhi 12,791,458; Chennai (Madras) 6,424,624; Banglaore 5,686,844; Hyderabad 5,533,640; Ahmedabad 4,519,278; Pune (Poona) 3,755,525; Surat 2,811,466; Kanpur 2,690,486; Jaipur (Jeypore) 2,324,319; Lucknow 2,266,933; Nagpur 2,122,965; Patna 1,707,429; Indore 1,639,044; Vadodara (Baroda) 1,492,398; Bhopal 1,454,830; Coimbatore 1,446,034; Ludhiana 1,395,053; Kochi (Cochin) 1,355,406; Visakhapatnam (Vizag) 1,329,472; Agra 1,321,410; Varanasi (Banaras) 1,211,749; Madurai 1,194,665; Meerut 1,167,399; Nashik 1,152,048; Jabalpur (Jubbulpore) 1,117,200; Jamshedpur 1,101,804; Asansol 1,090,171; Dhanbad 1,064,357; Faridabad 1,054,981; Allahabad 1,049,579; Amritsar 1,011,327; Vijayawada (Vijayavada) 1,011,152; Rajkot 1,002,160.

BIRTHS AND DEATHS

(estimates, based on Sample Registration Scheme)

	1997	1998	1999*
Birth rate (per 1,000)	27.2	26.4	26.1
Death rate (per 1,000)	8.9	9.0	8.7

* Provisional figures.

Expectation of life (WHO estimates, years at birth, 2000): Males 59.8; Females 62.7 (Source: WHO, *World Health Report*).

ECONOMICALLY ACTIVE POPULATION
(persons aged five years and over, 1991 census, excluding Jammu and Kashmir)

	Males	Females	Total
Agriculture, hunting, forestry and fishing	139,361,719	51,979,110	191,340,829
Mining and quarrying	1,536,919	214,356	1,751,275
Manufacturing	23,969,433	4,702,046	28,671,479
Construction	5,122,468	420,737	5,543,205
Trade and commerce	19,862,725	1,433,612	21,296,337
Transport, storage and communications	7,810,126	207,620	8,017,746
Other services	23,995,194	5,316,428	29,311,622
Total employed	221,658,584	64,273,909	285,932,493
Marginal workers	2,705,223	25,493,654	28,198,877
Total labour force	224,363,807	89,767,563	314,131,370

Unemployment (work applicants at 31 December, '000 persons aged 14 years and over): 40,090 (males 30,563; females 9,526) in 1998; 40,371 (males 30,438; females 9,933) in 1999; 41,344 (males 30,887; females 10,457) in 2000 (Source: ILO).

2001 census (provisional): Main workers 313,173,394 (males 240,520,672, females 72,652,722); Marginal workers 89,338,796 (males 34,943,064, females 54,395,732); Total 402,512,190 (males 275,463,736, females 127,048,454).

Health and Welfare

KEY INDICATORS

Fertility (births per woman, 2000)	3.1
Under-5 mortality rate (per 1,000 live births, 2000)	96
HIV/AIDS (% of persons aged 15–49, 2001)	0.79
Physicians (per 1,000 head, 1999)	0.52
Hospital beds (per 1,000 head, 1999)	0.92
Health expenditure (1998): US $ per head (PPP)	110
% of GDP	5.1
public (% of total)	18.0
Access to water (% of persons, 2000)	88
Access to sanitation (% of persons, 2000)	31
Human Development Index (2000): ranking	124
value	0.577

For sources and definitions, see explanatory note on p. vi.

Agriculture

PRINCIPAL CROPS ('000 metric tons, year ending 30 June)

	1998/99	1999/2000	2000/01
Rice (milled)	86,080	89,680	84,870
Sorghum (Jowar)	8,410	8,690	7,720
Cat-tail millet (Bajra)	6,950	5,780	7,060
Maize	11,150	11,510	12,070
Finger millet (Ragi)	2,610	2,290	2,740
Small millets	670	620	600
Wheat	71,290	76,370	68,760
Barley	1,540	1,450	1,430
Total cereals	188,700	196,390	185,250
Chick-peas (Gram)	6,800	5,120	3,520
Pigeon-peas (Tur)	2,710	2,690	2,260
Dry beans, dry peas, lentils and other pulses	5,700	5,600	4,890
Total food grains	203,910	209,800	195,920
Groundnuts (in shell)	8,980	5,250	6,220
Sesame seed	530	480	590
Rapeseed and mustard	5,660	5,790	4,210
Linseed	270	240	190
Castor beans	840	770	870
Total edible oil seeds (incl. others)	24,750	20,710	18,400

— continued	1998/99	1999/2000	2000/01
Cotton lint*	12,290	11,530	9,650
Jute†	8,840	9,420	9,250
Kenaf (Mesta)†	970	1,130	1,230
Tea (made)	850	816	827
Sugar cane:			
production gur	28,870	29,930	29,920
production cane	288,720	299,320	299,210
Tobacco (leaves)	700	609	600
Potatoes	22,490	24,700	22,100

* Production in '000 bales of 170 kg each.
† Production in '000 bales of 180 kg each.

Source: Directorate of Economics and Statistics, Ministry of Agriculture and Ministry of Commerce (for tea).

LIVESTOCK ('000 head, year ending September)

	1998	1999	2000
Cattle*	212,121	214,877	218,800
Sheep*	57,100	57,600	57,900
Goats*	121,362	122,530	123,000
Pigs	16,005*	16,500†	16,500†
Horses†	990	990	990
Asses†	1,000	1,000	1,000
Mules†	200	200	200
Buffaloes*	90,909	92,090	93,772
Camels†	1,030	1,030	1,030
Chickens†	375,000	382,500	402,000

* Unofficial figure(s). † FAO estimate(s).

Source: FAO.

LIVESTOCK PRODUCTS ('000 metric tons)

	1998	1999	2000
Beef and veal	1,401	1,421	1,442
Buffalo meat	1,380	1,410	1,421
Mutton and lamb	226	228	229
Goat meat	462	466	467
Pig meat	543	560	560
Poultry meat	540	559	575
Cows' milk	35,500*	36,000*	30,900†
Buffaloes' milk	35,850*	38,000*	39,000†
Goats' milk	3,150*	3,180*	3,200†
Butter	160*	175*	175†
Ghee	1,440*	1,575*	1,575†
Hen eggs*	1,658	1,733	1,782
Wool:			
greasy†	44	44	44
clean	31*	31†	31†
Cattle and buffalo hides (fresh)	942	954	971
Sheepskins (fresh)	51	52	52
Goatskins (fresh)	127	128	128

* Unofficial figure(s). † FAO estimate(s).

Source: FAO.

Forestry

ROUNDWOOD REMOVALS ('000 cubic metres, excl. bark)

	1998	1999	2000
Sawlogs, veneer logs and logs for sleepers	18,350	17,350	16,500
Other industrial wood*	5,598	5,688	5,688
Fuel wood*	293,215	295,248	297,310
Total	317,163	318,286	319,498

* FAO estimates.

Source: FAO.

SAWNWOOD PRODUCTION
('000 cubic metres, incl. railway sleepers)

	1998	1999	2000
Coniferous sawnwood	1,200	1,200	1,100
Broadleaved sawnwood	7,200	7,200	6,800
Total	8,400	8,400	7,900

Source: FAO.

Fishing

('000 metric tons, live weight)

	1997	1998	1999
Capture	3,517.1	3,214.8	3,316.8
Bombay-duck (Bummalo)	213.1	179.8	190.1
Croakers and drums	313.2	272.2	314.8
Indian oil-sardine (sardinella)	212.1	209.1	148.7
Indian mackerel	190.4	171.0	187.7
Aquaculture	1,862.3	2,029.6	2,035.5
Roho labeo	519.3	570.1	556.7
Mrigal carp	480.0	520.0	517.0
Catla	510.0	550.0	541.0
Total catch	5,379.4	5,244.4	5,352.3

Source: FAO, *Yearbook of Fishery Statistics.*

Mining

('000 metric tons, unless otherwise indicated)

	1998/99	1999/2000	2000/01*
Coal	292,270	304,000	310,000
Lignite	23,419	21,847	24,000
Iron ore†	72,230	74,946	79,210
Manganese ore†	1,538	1,586	1,556
Bauxite	6,610	7,050	7,893
Chalk (Fireclay)	470	400	348
Kaolin (China clay)	741	806	791
Dolomite	2,922	2,815	2,964
Gypsum	2,267	3,247	2,707
Limestone	113,000	129,000	126,000
Crude petroleum	33,000	32,000	32,000
Sea salt	11,964	15,585	13,584
Chromium ore†	1,418	1,738	1,952
Phosphorite	1,262	1,192	1,253
Kyanite	6	6	4
Magnesite	350	326	317
Steatite	482	557	553
Copper ore†	4,200	3,100	n.a.
Lead concentrates†	63	63	54
Zinc concentrates†	350	360	365
Mica—crude (metric tons)	1,484	1,807	1,111
Gold (kilograms)	2,683	2,586	7,554
Diamonds (carats)	34,580	40,956	57,406
Natural gas (million cu m)‡	25,706	26,884	27,860

* Provisional figures.

† Figures refer to gross weight. The estimated metal content is: Iron 63%; Manganese 40%; Chromium 30%; Copper 1.2%; Lead 70%; Zinc 60%.

‡ Figures refer to gas utilized.

Source: Indian Bureau of Mines.

Industry

SELECTED PRODUCTS ('000 metric tons, unless otherwise indicated)

	1998/99	1999/2000	2000/01
Refined sugar*	15,539	17,470	19,250
Cotton cloth (million sq metres)	17,948	18,989	19,718
Jute manufactures	1,587	1,591	1,625
Paper and paper board	3,117	3,459	3,090
Soda ash	1,377	1,515	1,631
Fertilizers	13,897	14,286	14,770
Petroleum products	64,500	79,900	96,600
Cement	88,000	100,400	99,500
Pig-iron (saleable)	2,998	3,184	3,063
Finished steel	23,800	27,200	29,300
Aluminium (metric tons)	536,800	497,900	620,400
Diesel engines—stationery (number)	432,300	348,300	306,000
Sewing machines (number)	64,800	59,800	48,800
Television receivers (number)	2,460,000	2,561,600	n.a.
Electric fans (number)	5,700,000	5,800,000	5,200,000
Passenger cars and multipurpose vehicles	503,795	699,200	632,200
Commercial vehicles (number)	135,823	173,469	152,000
Motor cycles, mopeds and scooters (number)	3,374,498	3,722,000	3,755,000
Bicycles (number)	10,373,000	13,733,000	14,974,000

* Figures relate to crop year (beginning November) and are in respect of cane sugar only.

Finance

CURRENCY AND EXCHANGE RATES

Monetary Units

100 paise (singular: paisa) = 1 Indian rupee.

Sterling, Dollar and Euro Equivalents (31 May 2002)

£1 sterling = 71.92 rupees;
US $1 = 49.03 rupees;
€1 = 46.02 rupees;
1,000 Indian rupees = £13.91 = $20.40 = €21.73.

Average Exchange Rate (rupees per US $)

1999	43.055
2000	44.942
2001	47.186

UNION BUDGET (million rupees, year ending 31 March)

Revenue	2000/01*	2001/02†	2002/03‡
Tax revenue (net)	1,366,580.7	1,423,488.2	1,729,647.5
Customs receipts	475,422.0	431,700.0	451,930.0
Union excise duties	685,261.3	745,200.0	914,330.0
Corporation Tax	356,962.7	390,590.0	486,160.0
Other taxes on income	317,639.8	344,380.0	425,240.0
Other taxes and duties	50,744.0	55,064.4	80,340.0
Less States' share of tax revenue	516,875.2	528,446.2	612,352.5
Less Surcharge transferred to National Calamity Contingency Fund	2,573.9	15,000.0	16,000.0
Other current revenue	559,655.4	702,242.0	721,401.5
Interest receipts (net)	327,961.7	378,000.0	416,600.1
Dividends and profits	135,746.8	182,916.1	188,050.0
Receipts of Union Territories	4,468.4	4,840.9	5,080.0
External grants	8,134.7	8,260.0	8,590.9
Other receipts (net)	84,960.3	128,225.0	103,080.5
Less Write-off of loans	1,616.5	—	—
Recoveries of loans (net)	120,463.3	151,430.0	176,800.0
Disinvestment of equity in public-sector enterprises	21,254.0	50,000.0	120,000.0
Total	2,067,953.4	2,327,160.2	2,747,849.0

Expenditure	2000/01*	2001/02†	2002/03‡
Central Ministries/Departments	2,888,348.1	3,238,824.0	3,619,263.5
Agriculture and Co-operation	60,900.1	22,533.6	23,670.0
Fertilizers	99,497.1	128,967.5	117,652.5
Defence	602,676.5	678,101.7	766,111.6
Economic Affairs	1,169,130.8	1,250,715.2	1,381,721.5
Food and Public Distribution	124,336.1	178,818.9	214,585.5
Home Affairs	103,586.4	107,404.4	120,945.7
Education and Literacy	79,160.3	80,703.3	97,917.1
Rural Development	60,599.6	106,256.2	102,894.1
Road Transport and Highways	70,294.9	75,797.4	77,100.6
State Plans	340,141.0	375,933.8	453,610.8
Union Territories	27,617.2	29,606.2	30,220.4
Total	3,256,106.3	3,644,364.0	4,103,094.7
Current§	2,778,574.7	3,043,052.6	3,404,827.9
Capital	477,531.6	601,311.4	698,266.8

* Provisional.

† Revised estimates.

‡ Forecasts.

§ Including interest payments (million rupees): 993,142.1 in 2000/01; 1,072,572.7 in 2001/02; 1,173,901.8 in 2002/03.

Source: Government of India, Annual Budget Papers, 2002/03.

INTERNATIONAL RESERVES (US $ million at 31 December)

	1999	2000	2001
Gold*	2,403	2,252	2,329
IMF special drawing rights	4	2	5
Reserve position in IMF	671	637	614
Foreign exchange	31,992	37,264	45,251
Total	35,070	40,154	48,199

* National valuation (9,085 rupees per troy ounce in 1999; 9,153 rupees per ounce in 2000; 9,756 rupees per ounce in 2001).

Source: IMF, *International Financial Statistics*.

MONEY SUPPLY
(million rupees, last Friday of year ending 31 March)

	1999/2000	2000/01	2001/02
Currency with the public	1,890,820	2,095,500	2,414,000
Demand deposits with banks	1,496,810	1,662,700	1,782,840
Other deposits with Reserve Bank	30,330	36,290	28,500
Total money	3,417,960	3,794,490	4,225,340

Source: Reserve Bank of India.

COST OF LIVING
(Consumer Price Index for Industrial Workers; base: 1990 = 100)

	1997	1998	1999
Food (incl. beverages)	199.0	228.8	232.5
Fuel and light	177.8	193.3	205.6
Clothing (incl. footwear)	184.9	192.8	199.3
Rent	161.0	201.1	236.3
All items (incl. others)	192.5	217.7	228.0

2000: Food (incl. beverages) 236.6; All items 237.1 (Source: ILO, *Yearbook of Labour Statistics*).

2001: Food (incl. beverages) 241.9; All items 246.2 (Source: UN, *Monthly Bulletin of Statistics*).

NATIONAL ACCOUNTS
('000 million rupees at current prices, year ending 31 March)

National Income and Product

	1998/99	1999/2000	2000/01
Domestic factor incomes*	14,494.2	15,732.1	16,974.0
Consumption of fixed capital	1,666.1	1,824.3	1,984.4
Gross domestic product at factor cost	16,160.3	17,556.4	18,958.4
Indirect taxes *Less* Subsidies	1,422.4	1,740.0	1,921.5
GDP in purchasers' values	17,582.8	19,296.4	20,879.9
Factor income from abroad *Less* Factor income paid abroad	−149.7	−154.3	−174.1
Gross national product	17,433.1	19,142.1	20,705.7
Less Consumption of fixed capital	1,666.1	1,824.3	1,984.4
National income in market prices	15,767.0	17,317.8	18,721.3
Other current transfers from abroad	434.9	532.8	587.6
Less Other current transfers paid abroad	2.5	1.5	3.4
National disposable income	16,199.4	17,849.2	19,305.4

* Compensation of employees and the operating surplus of enterprises.

Expenditure on the Gross Domestic Product

	1998/99	1999/2000	2000/01*
Government final consumption expenditure	2,117.7	2,481.3	2,759.0
Private final consumption expenditure	11,359.3	12,614.5	13,395.9
Increase in stocks	−11.9	322.2	212.2
Gross fixed capital formation	3,732.1	4,169.4	4,569.8
Total domestic expenditure	17,197.2	19,587.4	20,936.9
Exports of goods and services	1,952.8	2,277.0	2,901.8
Less Imports of goods and services	2,247.4	2,657.0	3,060.9
Statistical discrepancy	680.2	89.1	102.1
GDP in purchasers' values	17,582.8	19,296.4	20,879.9

* Estimates.

Gross Domestic Product by Economic Activity
(at current factor cost)

	1998/99	1999/2000	2000/01*
Agriculture	1,232.4	4,214.0	4,300.9
Forestry and logging	185.7	189.6	195.4
Fishing	180.8	201.9	223.5
Mining and quarrying	351.1	405.2	446.5
Manufacturing	2,517.9	2,668.9	2,997.5
Electricity, gas and water supply	424.8	438.9	495.3
Construction	919.2	1,054.4	1,164.3
Trade, hotels and restaurants	2,247.3	2,415.4	2,612.9
Transport, storage and communications	1,113.1	1,241.9	1,383.3
Banking and insurance	958.1	1,190.8	1,165.5
Real estate and business services	857.6	1,014.9	1,201.0
Public administration and defence	992.9	1,153.0	1,246.2
Other services	1,179.3	1,367.6	1,526.1
Total	16,160.3	17,556.4	18,958.4

* Provisional estimates.

BALANCE OF PAYMENTS (US $ million)

	1998	1999	2000
Exports of goods f.o.b.	34,076	36,877	43,132
Imports of goods f.o.b.	-44,828	-45,556	-55,325
Trade balance	-10,752	-8,679	-12,193
Exports of services	11,691	14,509	18,331
Imports of services	-14,540	-17,271	-19,913
Balance on goods and services	-13,601	-11,441	-13,775
Other income received	1,806	1,919	2,280
Other income paid	-5,443	-5,629	-6,156
Balance on goods, services and income	-17,238	-15,151	-17,651
Current transfers received	10,402	11,958	13,504
Current transfers paid	-67	-35	-51
Current balance	-6,903	-3,228	-4,198
Direct investment abroad	-48	-79	-335
Direct investment from abroad	2,635	2,169	2,315
Portfolio investment liabilities	-601	2,317	1,619
Other investment assets	-3,239	-450	-1,136
Other investment liabilities	9,837	5,623	7,152
Net errors and omissions	1,390	313	670
Overall balance	3,071	6,664	6,087

Source: IMF, *International Financial Statistics.*

OFFICIAL DEVELOPMENT ASSISTANCE (US $ million)

	1996	1997	1998
Bilateral donors	1,013.6	910.4	894.4
Multilateral donors	883.6	730.6	700.2
Total	1,897.2	1,641.0	1,594.6
Grants	997.9	876.3	787.6
Loans	899.3	764.7	807.0
Per caput assistance (US $)	2.0	1.7	1.6

Source: UN, *Statistical Yearbook for Asia and the Pacific.*

External Trade

PRINCIPAL COMMODITIES
(million rupees, year ending 31 March)

Imports c.i.f.	1998/99	1999/2000	2000/01
Mineral fuels, lubricants, etc.	269,190	546,490	714,970
Fixed vegetable oils (edible)	75,890	80,460	60,930
Organic chemicals	59,120	66,640	63,640
Inorganic chemicals	53,780	57,550	49,250
Pearls, precious and semi-precious stones	158,200	235,560	221,010
Non-electrical machinery	255,760	118,950	124,270
Electronic goods	100,360	129,720	170,860
Total (incl. others)	1,783,310	2,152,360	2,308,730

Exports f.o.b.	1998/99	1999/2000	2000/01
Marine products	43,690	51,250	63,670
Rice	62,810	31,260	29,430
Cotton fabrics, yarn, etc.	116,610	133,880	160,300
Ready-made garments	183,640	206,490	254,780
Leather and leather manufactures	68,470	68,900	89,140
Gems and jewellery	249,450	327,160	337,340
Engineering products	163,640	190,820	266,580
Chemicals and related products	122,270	203,950	272,470
Total (incl. others)	1,397,530	1,595,610	2,035,710

Source: Ministry of Commerce.

PRINCIPAL TRADING PARTNERS
(million rupees, year ending 31 March)

Imports c.i.f.	1998/99	1999/2000	2000/01
Australia	60,790	46,860	48,550
Bahrain	19,780	16,280	9,250
Belgium	121,020	159,510	131,110
France	30,270	31,120	29,270
Germany	90,050	79,790	80,380
Hong Kong	18,900	35,440	38,930
Indonesia	34,880	41,550	41,580
Iran	19,220	54,200	9,640
Italy	45,780	31,830	33,050
Japan	103,730	109,880	84,150
Korea, Republic	58,660	52,250	40,830
Kuwait	63,150	82,850	5,140
Malaysia	67,760	87,700	53,760
Netherlands	19,520	20,400	19,980
Nigeria	49,540	126,890	2,910
Russia	30,210	35,220	31,390
Saudi Arabia	77,050	130,750	28,370
Singapore	58,230	66,490	66,870
Switzerland	123,780	112,660	144,360
United Arab Emirates	72,410	101,140	30,110
United Kingdom	110,280	117,630	144,720
USA	153,140	154,440	137,730
Total (incl. others)	1,783,310	2,152,360	2,308,730*

* Including imports from unspecified countries (million rupees): 675,910.

Exports f.o.b.	1998/99	1999/2000	2000/01
Australia	16,300	17,470	18,540
Bangladesh	41,890	27,570	42,720
Belgium	54,180	59,260	67,180
Canada	19,900	25,050	29,990
China, People's Republic	17,970	23,340	37,980
France	34,910	38,880	46,600
Germany	77,910	75,320	87,150
Hong Kong	79,120	108,810	120,650
Israel	14,940	21,650	21,580
Italy	44,380	48,520	59,790
Japan	69,500	73,030	81,980
Korea, Republic	12,950	20,650	20,590
Malaysia	13,530	19,370	27,780
Netherlands	32,120	38,380	40,210
Russia	29,850	41,070	40,610
Saudi Arabia	32,570	32,170	37,600
Singapore	21,770	29,150	40,070
Spain	21,010	23,740	30,440
Sri Lanka	18,390	21,630	29,240
Thailand	13,500	19,480	24,220
United Arab Emirates	78,570	90,250	118,670
United Kingdom	78,060	88,170	105,020
USA	302,890	363,800	425,100
Total (incl. others)	1,397,530	1,595,610	2,035,710

Source: Ministry of Commerce.

Transport

RAILWAYS (million, year ending 31 March)

	1998/99	1999/2000	2000/01
Passengers	4,411	4,585	4,833
Passenger-km	403,900	430,666	457,022
Freight (metric tons)	420.9	478.2	504.2
Freight (metric ton-km)	281,500	308,039	315,516

Source: Railway Board, Ministry of Railways.

ROAD TRAFFIC ('000 motor vehicles in use at 31 March)

	1998	1999*	2000*
Private cars, jeeps and taxis	5,056	5,528	5,937
Buses and coaches	535	470	487
Goods vehicles	2,529	2,544	2,656
Motor cycles and scooters	28,342	31,212	33,540
Others	4,477	4,999	5,294
Total	40,939	44,753	47,914

* Provisional figures.

Source: Transport Research Division, Ministry of Surface Transport.

SHIPPING

Merchant Fleet (registered at 31 December)

	1999	2000	2001
Vessels	971	987	1,018
Displacement ('000 grt)	6,914.8	6,662.1	6,688.2

Source: Lloyd's Register-Fairplay, *World Fleet Statistics*.

International Sea-borne Traffic (year ending 31 March)

	1998/99	1999/2000	2000/01
Vessels* ('000 nrt):			
Entered	48,512	60,850	55,466
Cleared	39,031	41,187	38,043
Freight† ('000 metric tons):			
Loaded	101,247	110,301	135,331
Unloaded	186,797	225,049	233,007

* Excluding minor and intermediate ports.

† Including bunkers.

Sources: Transport Research Division, Ministry of Surface Transport; Directorate General of Commercial Intelligence and Statistics.

CIVIL AVIATION (traffic)

	1998/99	1999/2000	2000/01
Kilometres flown ('000)	187,046	193,417	202,955
Passenger-km ('000)	23,909,446	24,623,528	26,215,657
Freight ton-km ('000)	517,102	532,611	548,994
Mail ton-km ('000)	28,707	33,838	33,241

Source: Directorate General of Civil Aviation.

Tourism

FOREIGN VISITORS BY COUNTRY OF ORIGIN*

	1999	2000	2001
Australia	73,041	53,995	52,691
Canada	82,892	84,013	88,600
CIS	34,620	35,988	24,831
France	85,891	100,022	102,434
Germany	85,033	83,881	80,011
Italy	50,677	50,419	41,351
Japan	79,373	98,159	80,634
Malaysia	52,613	60,513	57,869
Netherlands	48,826	46,370	42,368
Singapore	53,310	46,612	42,824
Sri Lanka	120,072	129,193	112,813
United Kingdom	345,085	432,624	405,472
USA	251,925	348,292	329,147
Total (incl. others)	2,024,131	2,180,039	2,053,208

* Figures exclude nationals of Bangladesh and Pakistan. Including these, the total was 2,481,928 in 1999, 2,649,378 in 2000 and 2,537,282 in 2001.

Source: Ministry of Tourism.

Receipts from tourism (million rupees): 129,510 in 1999; 142,380 in 2000; 143,440 in 2001.

Communications Media

	1998	1999	2000
Television receivers ('000 in use)	70,000	75,000	79,000
Telephones ('000 main lines in use)	21,593.7	26,511.3	32,436.1
Mobile cellular telephones ('000 in use)	1,195.4	1,195.4	3,577.1
Personal computers ('000 in use)	2,700	3,300	4,600
Internet users ('000)	1,400	2,800	5,000
Daily newspapers	4,890	5,157	5,364
Non-daily newspapers and other periodicals	n.a.	41,161	43,781

1997: Radio receivers ('000 in use) 116,000; Facsimile machines ('000 in use) 100*.

2001: Telephones ('000 main lines in use) 34,732.1; Mobile cellular telephones ('000 in use) 5,725.2; Internet users ('000) 7,000.

* Year ending 31 March.

Sources: International Telecommunication Union; UN, *Statistical Yearbook*; Register of Newspapers for India; Ministry of Information and Broadcasting.

Education

(1999/2000*)

	Institutions	Teachers	Students
Primary	641,695	1,919,340	113,612,541
Middle	198,004	1,297,805	42,065,198
Secondary (High school); Higher secondary (New pattern); Intermediate/pre-degree/junior college	116,820	1,720,430	28,214,457

* Provisional figures.

Source: Ministry of Human Resource Development, *Annual Report 2000/01*.

Adult literacy rate (UNESCO estimates): 57.2% (males 68.4%; females 45.4%) in 2000 (Source: UN Human Development Programme, *Human Development Report*).

Directory

The Constitution

The Constitution of India, adopted by the Constituent Assembly on 26 November 1949, was inaugurated on 26 January 1950. The Preamble declares that the People of India solemnly resolve to constitute a Sovereign Democratic Republic and to secure to all its citizens justice, liberty, equality and fraternity. There are 397 articles and nine schedules, which form a comprehensive document.

UNION OF STATES

The Union of India comprises 28 states, six Union Territories and one National Capital Territory. There are provisions for the formation and admission of new states.

The Constitution confers citizenship on a threefold basis of birth, descent, and residence. Provisions are made for refugees who have migrated from Pakistan and for persons of Indian origin residing abroad.

FUNDAMENTAL RIGHTS AND DIRECTIVE PRINCIPLES

The rights of the citizen contained in Part III of the Constitution are declared fundamental and enforceable in law. 'Untouchability' is abolished and its practice in any form is a punishable offence. The Directive Principles of State Policy provide a code intended to ensure promotion of the economic, social and educational welfare of the State in future legislation.

THE PRESIDENT

The President is the head of the Union, exercising all executive powers on the advice of the Council of Ministers responsible to Parliament. He is elected by an electoral college consisting of elected members of both Houses of Parliament and the Legislatures of the States. The President holds office for a term of five years and is eligible for re-election. He may be impeached for violation of the Constitution. The Vice-President is the ex officio Chairman of the Rajya Sabha and is elected by a joint sitting of both Houses of Parliament.

THE PARLIAMENT

The Parliament of the Union consists of the President and two Houses: the Rajya Sabha (Council of States) and the Lok Sabha (House of the People). The Rajya Sabha consists of 245 members, of whom a number are nominated by the President. One-third of its members retire every two years. Elections are indirect, each state's legislative quota being elected by the members of the state's legislative assembly. The Lok Sahba has 543 members elected by adult franchise; not more than 13 represent the Union Territories and National Capital Territory. Two members are nominated by the President to represent the Anglo-Indian community.

GOVERNMENT OF THE STATES

The governmental machinery of states closely resembles that of the Union. Each of these states has a governor at its head appointed by the President for a term of five years to exercise executive power on the advice of a council of ministers. The states' legislatures consist of the Governor and either one house (legislative assembly) or two houses (legislative assembly and legislative council). The term of the assembly is five years, but the council is not subject to dissolution.

LANGUAGE

The Constitution provides that the official language of the Union shall be Hindi. (The English language will continue to be an associate language for many official purposes.)

LEGISLATION—FEDERAL SYSTEM

The Constitution provides that bills, other than money bills, can be introduced in either House. To become law, they must be passed by both Houses and receive the assent of the President. In financial affairs, the authority of the Lower House is final. The various subjects of legislation are enumerated on three lists in the seventh schedule of the Constitution: the Union List, containing nearly 100 entries, including external affairs, defence, communications and atomic energy; the State List, containing 65 entries, including local government, police, public health, education; and the Concurrent List, with over 40 entries, including criminal law, marriage and divorce, labour welfare. The Constitution vests residuary authority in the Centre. All matters not enumerated in the Concurrent or State Lists will be deemed to be included in the Union List, and in the event of conflict between Union and State Law on any subject enumerated in the Concurrent List the Union Law will prevail. In time of emergency Parliament may even exercise powers otherwise exclusively vested in the states. Under Article 356, 'If the President on receipt of a report from the government of a state or otherwise is satisfied that a situation has arisen in which the Government of the state cannot be carried on in accordance with the provisions of this Constitution, the President may by Proclamation: (a) assume to himself all or any of the functions of the government of the state and all or any of the powers of the governor or any body or authority in the state other than the Legislature of the state; (b) declare that the powers of the Legislature of the state shall be exercisable by or under the authority of Parliament; (c) make such incidental provisions as appear to the President to be necessary': provided that none of the powers of a High Court be assumed by the President or suspended in any way. Unless such a Proclamation is approved by both Houses of Parliament, it ceases to operate after two months. A Proclamation so approved ceases to operate after six months, unless renewed by Parliament. Its renewal cannot be extended beyond a total period of three years. An independent judiciary exists to define and interpret the Constitution and to resolve constitutional disputes arising between states, or between a state and the Government of India.

OTHER PROVISIONS

Other Provisions of the Constitution deal with the administration of tribal areas, relations between the Union and states, inter-state trade and finance.

AMENDMENTS

The Constitution is flexible in character, and a simple process of amendment has been adopted. For amendment of provisions concerning the Supreme Courts and the High Courts, the distribution of legislative powers between the Union and the states, the representation of the states in Parliament, etc., the amendment must be passed by both Houses of Parliament and must further be ratified by the legislatures of not less than half the states. In other cases no reference to the state legislatures is necessary.

Numerous amendments were adopted in August 1975, following the declaration of a state of emergency in June. The Constitution (39th Amendment) Bill laid down that the President's reasons for proclaiming an emergency may not be challenged in any court. Under the Constitution (40th Amendment) Bill, 38 existing laws may not be challenged before any court on the ground of violation of fundamental rights. Thus detainees under the Maintenance of Internal Security Act could not be told the grounds of their detention and were forbidden bail and any claim to liberty through natural or common law. The Constitution (41st Amendment) Bill provided that the President, Prime Minister and state Governors should be immune from criminal prosecution for life and from civil prosecution during their term of office.

In November 1976 a 59-clause Constitution (42nd Amendment) Bill was approved by Parliament and came into force in January 1977. Some of the provisions of the Bill are that the Indian Democratic Republic shall be named a 'Democratic Secular and Socialist Republic'; that the President 'shall act in accordance with' the advice given to him by the Prime Minister and the Council of Ministers, and, acting at the Prime Minister's direction, shall be empowered for two years to amend the Constitution by executive order, in any way beneficial to the enforcement of the whole; that the term of the Lok Sabha and of the State Assemblies shall be extended from five to six years; that there shall be no limitation on the constituent power of Parliament to amend the Constitution, and that India's Supreme Court shall be barred from hearing petitions challenging constitutional amendments; that strikes shall be forbidden in the public services and the Union Government have the power to deploy police or other forces under its own superintendence and control in any state. Directive Principles are given precedence over Fundamental Rights: 10 basic duties of citizens are listed, including the duty to 'defend the country and render national service when called upon to do so'.

The Janata Party Government, which came into power in March 1977, promised to amend the Constitution during the year, so as to 'restore the balance between the people and Parliament, Parliament and the judiciary, the judiciary and the executive, the states and the centre, and the citizen and the Government that the founding fathers of the Constitution had worked out'. The Constitution (43rd Amendment) Bill, passed by Parliament in December 1977, the Constitution (44th Amendment) Bill, passed by Parliament in December 1977 and later redesignated the 43rd Amendment, and the Constitution (45th Amendment) Bill, passed by Parliament in December 1978 and later redesignated the 44th Amendment, reversed most of the changes enacted by the Constitution (42nd Amendment) Bill. The 44th Amendment is particularly detailed on emergency provisions: An emergency may not be proclaimed unless 'the security of India or any part of its territory was threatened by war or external aggression or by armed rebellion.' Its introduction must be approved by a two-thirds majority of Parliament within a month, and after six months the emergency may be continued only with the approval of Parliament. Among the provisions left unchanged after these Bills were a section subordinating Fundamental Rights to Directive Principles and a clause empowering the central Government to deploy armed forces under its control in any state without the state government's consent. In May 1980 the Indian Supreme Court repealed sections 4 and 55 of the 42nd Amendment Act, thus curtailing Parliament's power to enforce directive principles and to amend the Constitution. The death penalty was declared constitutionally valid.

The 53rd Amendment to the Constitution, approved by Parliament in August 1986, granted statehood to the Union Territory of Mizoram; the 55th Amendment, approved in December 1986, granted statehood to the Union Territory of Arunachal Pradesh; and the 57th Amendment, approved in May 1987, granted statehood to the Union Territory of Goa (Daman and Diu remain, however, as a Union Territory). The 59th Amendment, approved in March 1988, empowered the Government to impose a state of emergency in Punjab, on the grounds of internal disturbances. In December 1988 the minimum voting age was lowered from 21 to 18 years. The 71st Amendment, approved in August 1992, gave official language status to Nepali, Konkani and Manipuri. In August 2000 legislation to permit the establishment of three new states, Chhattisgarh, Jharkhand and Uttaranchal, was approved by Parliament. The 93rd amendment, approved in May 2002, ensured free and compulsory education for children from the age of six to 14.

THE PANCHAYAT RAJ SCHEME

This scheme is designed to decentralize the powers of the Union and State Governments. It is based on the Panchayat (Village Council) and the Gram Sabha (Village Parliament) and envisages the gradual transference of local government from state to local authority. Revenue and internal security will remain state responsibilities at present. By 1978 the scheme had been introduced in all the states except Meghalaya, Nagaland and 23 out of 31 districts in Bihar. The Panchayat operated in all the Union Territories except Lakshadweep, Mizoram (which became India's 23rd state in February 1987) and Pondicherry. The 72nd Amendment, approved in late 1992, provided for direct elections to the Panchayats, members of which were to have a tenure of five years.

The Government

President: Aavul Pakkiri Jainulabidin Abdul Kalam (sworn in 25 July 2002).

Vice-President: Bhairon Singh Shekhawat (sworn in 19 August 2002).

COUNCIL OF MINISTERS
(August 2002)

A coalition of the Bharatiya Janata Party (BJP), the Biju Janata Dal (BJD), the Dravida Munnetra Kazhagam (DMK), the Shiv Sena (SS), the Shiromani Akali Dal (SAD), Jammu and Kashmir National Conference, the Marumalarchi Dravida Munnetra Kazhagam (MDMK), the Janata Dal (United) (JD—U), the Samata Party (SP), the Rashtriya Lok Dal (RLD), the All India Trinamool Congress, the Pattali Makkal Katchi and Independents (Ind.).

Prime Minister*: Atal Bihari Vajpayee (BJP).

Deputy Prime Minister and Minister of Home Affairs: Lal Krishna Advani (BJP).

Minister of External Affairs: Yashwant Sinha (BJP).

Minister of Finance and Company Affairs: Jaswant Singh (BJP).

Minister of Defence: George Fernandes (SP).

Minister of Health and Family Welfare: Shatrughan Sinha (BJP).

Minister of Tourism and Culture: Jagmohan (BJP).

Minister of Agriculture: Ajit Singh (RLD).

Minister of Environment and Forests: T. R. Baalu (DMK).

Minister of Urban Development and Poverty Alleviation: Ananth Kumar (BJP).

Minister of Labour: Sahib Singh Verma (BJP).

Minister of Human Resource Development, of Ocean Development and of Science and Technology: Dr Murli Manohar Joshi (BJP).

Minister of Disinvestment and of Development of the North-Eastern Region: Arun Shourie (BJP).

Minister of Law and Justice: K. Jana Krishnamurthy (BJP).

Minister of Power: Anant Gangaram Geete (SS).

Minister of Communications and Information Technology and of Parliamentary Affairs: Pramod Mahajan (BJP).

Minister of Commerce and Industry: Murasoli Maran (DMK).

Minister of Petroleum and Natural Gas: Ram Naik (BJP).

Minister of Tribal Affairs: Juel Oram (BJP).

Minister of Social Justice and Empowerment: Dr Satya Narayan Jatiya (BJP).

Minister of Information and Broadcasting: Sushma Swaraj (BJP).

Minister of Rural Development: Shanta Kumar (BJP).

Minister of Chemicals and Fertilizers: Sukhdev Singh Dhindsa (SAD).

Minister of Textiles: Kashiram Rana (BJP).

Minister of Consumer Affairs, and Food and Public Distribution: Sharad Yadav (JD—U).

Minister of Civil Aviation: Syed Shahnawaz Hussain (BJP).

Minister of Water Resources: Arjun Charan Sethi (BJP).

Minister of Youth Affairs and Sports: Vikram Verma (BJP).

Minister of Railways: Nitish Kumar (SP).

Minister of Coal and Mines: Uma Bharati (BJP).

Minister of Agro and Rural Industries: Kariya Munda (BJP).

Minister of Shipping: Ved Prakash Goyal (BJP).

Minister of Heavy Industries and Public Enterprises: Balasaheb Vikhe Patil (SS).

Ministers of State with Independent Charge

Minister of State for Road Transport and Highways: Maj.-Gen. B. C. Khanduri (BJP).

Minister of State for Non-Conventional Energy Sources: M. Kannapan (MDMK).

Minister of State for Steel: B. K. Tripathy (BJD).

Minister of State for Small-scale Industries, of Personnel, Public Grievances and Pensions, and of Atomic Energy and Space: Vasundara Raje (BJP).

Minister of State for Food-Processing Industries: N. T. Shanmugham (PMK).

There are, in addition, 40 Ministers of State without independent charge.

* The Prime Minister is also in charge of ministries and departments not allotted to others.

MINISTRIES

President's Office: Rashtrapati Bhavan, New Delhi 110 004; tel. (11) 3015321; fax (11) 3017290; internet www.goidirectory.nic.in.

Vice-President's Office: 6 Maulana Azad Rd, New Delhi 110 011; tel. (11) 3016344; fax (11) 3018124.

Prime Minister's Office: South Block, New Delhi 110 011; tel. (11) 3013040; fax (11) 3016857; internet www.pmindia.nic.in.

Ministry of Agriculture: Krishi Bhavan, Dr Rajendra Prasad Rd, New Delhi 110 001; tel. (11) 3382651; fax (11) 3386004.

Ministry of Atomic Energy: South Block, New Delhi 110 011; tel. (11) 3011773; fax (11) 3013843.

Ministry of Chemicals and Fertilizers: Shastri Bhavan, New Delhi 110 001; tel. (11) 3383695; fax (11) 3386222.

Ministry of Civil Aviation: Rajiv Gandhi Bhavan, Safdarjung Airport, New Delhi 110 023; tel. (11) 4610358; fax (11) 4610354; e-mail web@civilav.delhi.nic.in; internet www.civilaviation.nic.in.

Ministry of Coal and Mines: Shram Shakti Bhavan, Rafi Marg, New Delhi 110 001; tel. (11) 3384884; fax (11) 3387738; e-mail secy.moc@sb.nic.in; internet www.coal.nic.in.

Ministry of Commerce and Industry: Udyog Bhavan, New Delhi 110 011; tel. (11) 3012107; fax (11) 3014335; internet www.commin.nic.in.

Ministry of Communications: Sanchar Bhavan, 20 Asoka Rd, New Delhi 110 001; tel. (11) 3719898; fax (11) 3782344.

Ministry of Consumer Affairs, Food and Public Distribution: Krishi Bhavan, New Delhi 110 001; tel. (11) 3384882; fax (11) 3388302; internet www.fcamin.nic.in.

Ministry of Defence: South Block, New Delhi 110 011; tel. (11) 3012380; internet www.mod.nic.in.

Ministry of Disinvestment: 132 Yojana Bhavan, Sansad Marg, New Delhi 110 001; tel. (11) 3711094; fax (11) 3710492.

Ministry of Electronics: Electronics Niketan, 6 CGO Complex, New Delhi 110 003; tel. (11) 4364041; fax (11) 4363134.

Ministry of Environment and Forests: Paryavaran Bhavan, CGO Complex Phase II, Lodi Rd, New Delhi 110 003; tel. (11) 4360721; fax (11) 4360678; e-mail secy@menf.delhi.nic.in; internet www.envfor.nic.in.

Ministry of External Affairs: South Block, New Delhi 110 011; tel. (11) 3012318; fax (11) 3010700; internet www.meadev.nic.in.

Ministry of Finance and Company Affairs: North Block, New Delhi 110 001; tel. (11) 3012611; fax (11) 3012477; e-mail jsdea@finance.delhi.nic.in; internet www.finmin.nic.in.

Ministry of Food-Processing Industries: Panchsheel Bhavan, Khelgaon Marg, New Delhi 110 049; tel. (11) 6493225; fax (11) 6493228.

Ministry of Health and Family Welfare: Nirman Bhavan, New Delhi 110 011; tel. (11) 3018863; fax (11) 3014252; e-mail secyhlth@mohfw.delhi.nic.in; internet www.mohfw.nic.in.

Ministry of Heavy Industries and Public Enterprises: Udyog Bhavan, New Delhi 110 011; tel. (11) 3012433; fax (11) 3011770.

Ministry of Home Affairs: North Block, New Delhi 110 001; tel. (11) 3011989; fax (11) 3015750; e-mail mhaweb@mhant.delhi.nic.in; internet www.mha.nic.in.

Ministry of Human Resource Development: Shastri Bhavan, New Delhi 110 001; tel. (11) 3386995; fax (11) 3384093.

Ministry of Information and Broadcasting: Shastri Bhavan, New Delhi 110 001; tel. (11) 3382639; fax (11) 3383513; internet www.mib.nic.in.

Ministry of Information Technology: Electronics Niketan, 6, CGO Complex, Lodi Rd, New Delhi 110 003; tel. (11) 4364041; internet www.mit.gov.in.

Ministry of Labour: Shram Shakti Bhavan, Rafi Marg, New Delhi 110 001; tel. (11) 3710265; fax (11) 3711708; e-mail labour@lisd.delhi.nic.in; internet www.labour.nic.in.

Ministry of Law and Justice: Shastri Bhavan, Dr Rajendra Prasad Rd, New Delhi 110 001; tel. (11) 3384777; fax (11) 3387259; e-mail lawmin@caselaw.delhi.nic.in; internet www.nic.in/lawmin/.

Ministry of Non-Conventional Energy Sources: Block 14, CGO Complex, New Delhi 110 003; tel. (11) 4361481; fax (11) 4361298; e-mail secymnes@ren02.nic.in; internet www.mnes.nic.in.

Ministry of Ocean Development: Block 12, CGO Complex, Lodi Rd, New Delhi 110 003; tel. (11) 4360874; fax (11) 4360779.

Ministry of Parliamentary Affairs: Parliament House, New Delhi 110 001; tel. (11) 3017663; fax (11) 3017726; e-mail parlmin@sansad.nic.in; internet www.mpa.nic.in.

Ministry of Personnel, Public Grievances and Pensions: North Block, New Delhi 110 001; tel. (11) 3014848; fax (11) 3012432; e-mail pgweb@arpg.delhi.nic.in; internet www.persmin.nic.in.

Ministry of Petroleum and Natural Gas: Shastri Bhavan, New Delhi 110 001; tel. (11) 3383501; fax (11) 3384787; e-mail dspdi.png@sb.nic.in; internet www.petroleum.nic.in.

Ministry of Power: Shram Shakti Bhavan, New Delhi 110 001; tel. (11) 3710271; fax (11) 3717519; internet www.powermin.nic.in.

Ministry of Railways: Rail Bhavan, Raisina Rd, New Delhi 110 001; tel. (11) 3384010; fax (11) 3384481; e-mail crb@del2.vsnl.net.in; internet www.indianrailway.com.

Ministry of Road Transport and Highways: Parivahan Bhavan, 1 Sansad Marg, New Delhi 110 001; tel. (11) 3714938; fax (11) 3714324; internet www.nic.in/most.

Ministry of Rural Development: Krishi Bhavan, New Delhi 110 001; tel. (11) 3384467; fax (11) 3782502; e-mail arunbhat@rural.delhi.nic.in; internet www.rural.nic.in.

Ministry of Science and Technology: Technology Bhavan, New Mehrauli Rd, New Delhi 110 016; tel. (11) 6511439; fax (11) 6863847; internet www.mst.nic.in.

Ministry of Small-scale Industries and Agro and Rural Industries: Udyog Bhavan, New Delhi, 110 011; tel. (11) 3013045; internet www.ssi.nic.in.

Ministry of Social Justice and Empowerment: Shastri Bhavan, Dr Rajendra Prasad Rd, New Delhi 110 001; tel. (11) 3382683; fax (11) 3384918; e-mail secywel@sb.nic.in; internet www.socialjustice.nic.in.

Ministry of Statistics and Programme Implementation: Sardar Patel Bhavan, Patel Chowk, New Delhi 110 001; tel. (11) 3732150; fax (11) 3732067; e-mail moscc@bol.net.in; internet mospi.nic.in.

Ministry of Steel: Udyog Bhavan, New Delhi 110 011; tel. (11) 3015489; fax (11) 3013236; e-mail dvs@ub.nic.in; internet www.nic.in/steel.

Ministry of Textiles: Udyog Bhavan, New Delhi 110 011; tel. (11) 3011769; fax (11) 3013711; e-mail textiles@ub.delhi.nic.in; internet www.texmin.nic.in.

Ministry of Tourism and Culture: Transport Bhavan, Parliament St, New Delhi 110 001; tel. (11) 3711792; fax (11) 3710518.

Ministry of Tribal Affairs: Rm 212.D, Shastri Bhavan, New Delhi; tel. (11) 3381652; e-mail dirtdb.wel@sb.nic.in; internet www.tribal.nic.in.

Ministry of Urban Development and Poverty Alleviation: Nirman Bhavan, New Delhi 110 011; tel. (11) 3018495; fax (11) 3014459; e-mail secyurban@alpha.nic.in; internet www.urbanindia.nic.in.

Ministry of Water Resources: Shram Shakti Bhavan, Rafi Marg, New Delhi 110 001; tel. (11) 3710305; fax (11) 3710253; internet www.wrmin.nic.in.

Ministry of Youth Affairs and Sports: Shastri Bhavan, Dr Rajendra Prasad Rd, New Delhi 110 001; tel. (11) 3382897; fax (11) 3387418; internet www.yas.nic.in.

Legislature

PARLIAMENT

Rajya Sabha
(Council of States)

Most of the members of the Rajya Sabha are indirectly elected by the State Assemblies for six years, with one-third retiring every two years. The remaining members are nominated by the President.

Chairman: BHAIRON SINGH SHEKHAWAT.

Deputy Chairman: NAJMA HEPPTULLAH.

Distribution of Seats, August 2002

Party	Seats
Congress*	60
Janata Dal	2
Communist Party of India—Marxist	13
Telugu Desam	13
Bharatiya Janata Party	50
Samajwadi Party	8
Rashtriya Janata Dal	8
Dravida Munnetra Kazhagam	8
Shiromani Akali Dal	4
Biju Janata Dal	4
Tamil Maanila Congress	2
Nationalist Congress Party	3
Samata Party	2
Muslim League	2
All-India Anna Dravida Munnetra Kazhagam	9
Communist Party of India	5
Jammu and Kashmir National Conference (F)	3
Shiv Sena	5
Bahujan Samaj Party	4
Revolutionary Socialist Party	3
Indian National Lok Dal	4
Independents and others	22
Nominated	11
Total	245

* Formerly known as the Congress (Indira) Party, or Congress (I); name gradually changed to the Congress Party in the early to mid-1990s.

Lok Sabha
(House of the People)

Speaker: MANOHAR JOSHI.

General Election, 5, 11, 18 and 25 September and 3 October 1999

Party	Seats
National Democratic Alliance	299
Bharatiya Janata Party	182
Dravida Munnetra Kazhagam	12
Marumalarchi Dravida Munnetra Kazhagam	4
Pattali Makkal Katchi	5
Janata Dal (United)	20
Shiv Sena	15
Shiromani Akali Dal	2
Indian National League	4
Himachal Vikash Congress	1
Telugu Desam	29
Biju Janata Dal	10
All India Trinamool Congress	8
Sikkim Democratic Front	1
Manipur State Congress Party	1
Jammu and Kashmir National Conference	4
M.G.R. Anna D.M. Kazhagam	1
Congress and allies	134
Congress	112
Rashtriya Janata Dal	7
All-India Anna Dravida Munnetra Kazhagam	10
Muslim League Kerala State Committee	2
Rashtriya Lok Dal	2
Kerala Congress (M)	1
Bahujan Samaj Party	14
Communist Party of India	4
Communist Party of India—Marxist	32
Samajwadi Party	26
Nationalist Congress Party	7
Revolutionary Socialist Party	3
Asom Gana Parishad	1
Peasants' and Workers' Party of India	1
Janata Dal (Secular)	1
Independents and others	20
Nominated	2*
Vacant	1
Total	545

* Nominated by the President to represent the Anglo-Indian community.

State Governments

(August 2002)

ANDHRA PRADESH

(Capital—Hyderabad)

Governor: Dr CHAKRAVARTY RANGARAJAN.

Chief Minister: N. CHANDRABABU NAIDU (Telugu Desam).

Legislative Assembly: 294 seats (Telugu Desam 180, Congress 90, Communist—CPI—M 2, Bharatiya Janata Party 12, independents and others 9, vacant 1).

ARUNACHAL PRADESH

(Capital—Itanagar)

Governor: ARVIND DAVE.

Chief Minister: MUKUT MITHI (Congress).

Legislative Assembly: 60 seats (Congress 53, Nationalist Congress Party 4, Arunachal Congress 1, independents 2).

ASSAM

(Capital—Dispur)

Governor: Lt-Gen. (retd) S. K. SINHA.

Chief Minister: TARUN GOGOI (Congress).

Legislative Assembly: 126 seats (Congress 70, Asom Gana Parishad 20, Bharatiya Janata Party 8, Nationalist Congress Party 3, All-India Trinamool Congress 1, independents and others 23, vacant 1).

BIHAR

(Capital—Patna)

Governor: VINOD CHANDRA PANDE.

Chief Minister: RABRI DEVI (Rashtriya Janata Dal).

Legislative Assembly: 243 seats (Rashtriya Janata Dal 114, Bharatiya Janata Party 35, Congress 12, Samata Party 29, Janata Dal (United) 18, Bahujan Samaj Party 5, Communist—CPI 6, Communist—CPI—M 2, Communist—Marxist-Leninist (Liberation) 6, independents and others 16).

Legislative Council: 96 seats.

CHHATTISGARH

(Capital—Raipur)

Governor: DINESH NANDAN SAHAYA.

Chief Minister: AJIT JOGI (Congress).

Legislative Assembly: 90 seats (Congress 62, Bharatiya Janata Party 23, Bahujan Samaj Party 3, others 2).

GOA

(Capital—Panaji)

Governor: KIDAR NATH SAHANI.

Chief Minister: MANOHAR PARRIKAR (Bharatiya Janata Party).

Legislative Assembly: 40 seats (Bharatiya Janata Party 17, Congress 16, United Goans Democratic Party 3, Maharashtrawadi Gomantak Party 2, others 2).

GUJARAT

(Capital—Gandhinagar)

Governor: SUNDAR SINGH BHANDARI.

Chief Minister: NARENDRA MODI (acting).

The Assembly was dissolved in mid-July 2002.

HARYANA

(Capital—Chandigarh)

Governor: BABU PARMANAND.

Chief Minister: OM PRAKASH CHAUTALA (Indian National Lok Dal).

Legislative Assembly: 90 seats (Congress 21, Indian National Lok Dal 46, Haryana Vikas Party 2, Bharatiya Janata Party 6, National Congress Party 1, Republican Party of India 1, Bahujan Samaj Party 1, independents and others 12).

HIMACHAL PRADESH

(Capital—Shimla)

Governor: SURAJ BHAN.

Chief Minister: PREM KUMAR DHUMAL (Bharatiya Janata Party).

Legislative Assembly: 68 seats (Congress 31, Bharatiya Janata Party 28, Himachal Vikas Congress 4, independents 1, vacant 4).

JAMMU AND KASHMIR

(Capitals—(Summer) Srinagar, (Winter) Jammu)

Governor: GIRISH CHANDRA SAXENA.

Chief Minister: (vacant).

Legislative Assembly: 87 seats (Jammu and Kashmir National Conference 28, Congress 20, People's Democratic Party 16, independents and others 23).

Legislative Council: 36 seats.

The State was placed under Governor's rule in mid-October 2002 after political parties failed to establish a coalition government following state elections.

JHARKHAND

(Capital—Ranchi)

Governor: M. RAMA JOIS.

Chief Minister: BABULAL MARANDI (Bharatiya Janata Party).

Legislative Assembly: 81 seats (Bharatiya Janata Party 32, Congress 11, Jharkhand Mukti Morcha 12, Rashtriya Janata Dal 9, Samata Party 4, Janata Dal—U 4, others 9).

KARNATAKA

(Capital—Bangalore)

Governor: T. N. CHATURVEDI.

Chief Minister: SOMANAHALLI MALLIAM KRISHNA (Congress).

Legislative Assembly: 224 seats (Congress 132, Bharatiya Janata Party 44, Janata Dal (Secular) 19, Janata Dal (United) 9, independents and others 20).

Legislative Council: 75 seats.

KERALA

(Capital—Thiruvananthapuram)

Governor: SIKANDER BAKHT.

Chief Minister: A. K. ANTHONY (Congress).

Legislative Assembly: 140 seats (Congress 63, Communist—CPI—M 23, Muslim League 16, Kerala Congress (M) 9, Communist—CPI 7, Janata Dal (S) 3, Nationalist Congress Party 2, Kerala Congress 2, Kerala Congress (Joseph) 2, Revolutionary Socialist Party 2, independents and others 11).

MADHYA PRADESH

(Capital—Bhopal)

Governor: Dr Bhai Mahavir.

Chief Minister: Digvijay Singh (Congress).

Legislative Assembly: 230 seats (Congress 126, Bharatiya Janata Party 80, Bahujan Samaj Party 9, Samajwadi Party 4, independents and others 11).

MAHARASHTRA

(Capital—Mumbai)

Governor: Mohammad Fazal.

Chief Minister: Vilasrao Desmukh (Congress).

Legislative Assembly: 288 seats (Congress 75, Shiv Sena 69, Nationalist Congress Party 58, Bharatiya Janata Party 56, Janata Dal (Secular) 2, Peasants' and Workers' Party 5, Bharatiya Bahujan Mahasangh 3, Communist—CPI—M 2, Samajwadi Party 2, independents and others 16).

Legislative Council: 78 seats.

MANIPUR

(Capital—Imphal)

Governor: Ved Prakash Marwah.

Chief Minister: Okram Ibobi Singh (Congress).

Legislative Assembly: 60 seats (Congress 20, Federal Party of Manipur 13, Manipur State Congress Party 7, Communist—CPI 5, Bharatiya Janata Party 4, Nationalist Congress Party 3, Samata Party 3, Manipur People's Party 2, others 3).

MEGHALAYA

(Capital—Shillong)

Governor: M. M. Jacob.

Chief Minister: Flinder Anderson Khonglam (Nationalist Congress Party).

Legislative Assembly: 60 seats (Congress 16, Nationalist Congress Party 9, United Democratic Party 20, Bharatiya Janata Party 3, People's Democratic Movement 3, Hills State People's Democratic Party 3, independents and others 6).

MIZORAM

(Capital—Aizawl)

Governor: Amolak Rattan Kohli.

Chief Minister: Zoramthanga (Mizo National Front).

Legislative Assembly: 40 seats (Mizo National Front 21, Congress 6, Mizo People's Conference 12, others 1).

NAGALAND

(Capital—Kohima)

Governor: Shyamal Dutta.

Chief Minister: S. C. Jamir (Congress).

Legislative Assembly: 60 seats (Congress 53, independents and others 10).

ORISSA

(Capital—Bhubaneswar)

Governor: M. M. Rajendran.

Chief Minister: Naveen Patnaik (Biju Janata Dal).

Legislative Assembly: 147 seats (Biju Janata Dal 68, Bharatiya Janata Party 38, Congress 26, Jharkhand Mukti Morcha 3, Communist—CPI 1, Communist—CPI—M 1, Janata Dal (Secular) 1, All India Trinamool Congress 1, independents 8).

PUNJAB

(Capital—Chandigarh)

Governor: Lt-Gen. (retd) J. F. R. Jacob.

Chief Minister: Amarinder Singh (Congress).

Legislative Assembly: 117 seats (Congress 63, Shiromani Akali Dal 41, Bharatiya Janata Party 3, independents and others 10).

RAJASTHAN

(Capital—Jaipur)

Governor: Anshuman Singh.

Chief Minister: Ashok Gehlot (Congress).

Legislative Assembly: 200 seats (Congress 150, Bharatiya Janata Party 33, Janata Dal 3, Communist—CPI—M 1, Bahujan Samaj Party 2, independents and others 8, vacant 3).

SIKKIM

(Capital—Gangtok)

Governor: V. Rama Rao.

Chief Minister: Pawan Kumar Chamling (Sikkim Democratic Front).

Legislative Assembly: 32 seats (Sikkim Democratic Front 25, Sikkim Sangram Parishad 7).

TAMIL NADU

(Capital—Chennai)

Governor: P. S. Ramamohan Rao.

Chief Minister: Jayaram Jayalalitha (All-India Anna Dravida Munnetra Kazhagam).

Legislative Assembly: 234 seats (All-India Anna Dravida Munnetra Kazhagam 132, Dravida Munnetra Kazhagam 27, Tamil Maanila Congress 23, Pattali Makkal Katchi 20, Congress 7, Communist—CPI—M 6, Communist—CPI 5, Bharatiya Janata Party 4, All India Forward Bloc 1, independents and others 9).

TRIPURA

(Capital—Agartala)

Governor: Lt-Gen. (retd) K. M. Seth.

Chief Minister: Manik Sarkar (Communist—CPI—M).

Legislative Assembly: 60 seats (Communist—CPI—M 38, Congress 13, Tripura Upajati Juba Samity 4, independents and others 5).

UTTARANCHAL

(Capital—Dehradun)

Governor: Surjit Singh Barnala.

Chief Minister: Narain Dutt Tiwari (Congress).

Legislative Assembly: 70 seats (Congress 36, Bharatiya Janata Party 19, Bahujan Samaj Party 7, independents and others 8).

UTTAR PRADESH

(Capital—Lucknow)

Governor: Vishnu Kant Shastri.

Chief Minister: Ms Mayawati (Bahujan Samaj Party).

Legislative Assembly: 403 seats (Samajwadi Party 143, Bahujan Samaj Party 99, Bharatiya Janata Party 88, Congress 25, Rashtriya Lok Dal 14, Rashtriya Kranti Party 4, Communist—CPI—M 2, Janata Dal—United 2, independents and others 26).

Legislative Council: 108 seats.

WEST BENGAL

(Capital—Kolkata)

Governor: Viren J. Shah.

Chief Minister: Buddhadev Bhattacharya (Communist—CPI—M).

Legislative Assembly: 294 seats (Communist—CPI—M 143, All India Trinamool Congress 60, Congress 26, All India Forward Bloc 25, Revolutionary Socialist Party 17, Communist—CPI 7, independents and others 16).

UNION TERRITORIES

Andaman and Nicobar Islands (Headquarters—Port Blair):

Lt-Gov.: Nagendra Nath Jha.

Chandigarh (Headquarters—Chandigarh):

Administrator: Lt. Gen (retd) J. F. R. Jacob.

Chandigarh was to be incorporated into Punjab state on 26 January 1986, but the transfer was postponed indefinitely.

Dadra and Nagar Haveli (Headquarters—Silvassa):

Administrator: O. P. Kelkar.

Daman and Diu (Headquarters—Daman):

Administrator: O. P. Kelkar.

Lakshadweep (Headquarters—Kavaratti):

Administrator: K. S. Mehra.

Pondicherry (Capital—Pondicherry):

Lt-Gov.: K. R. Malkani.

Chief Minister: N. Rangasamy (Congress).

Assembly: 30 seats (Congress 13, DMK 12, AIADMK 3, Tamil Maanila Congress 2).

NATIONAL CAPITAL TERRITORY

Delhi (Headquarters—Delhi):

Lt-Gov.: Vijay Kumar Kapoor.

Chief Minister: Sheila Dixit (Congress).

Assembly: 70 seats (Congress 52, Bharatiya Janata Party 15, Janata Dal 1, independents 2).

Political Organizations

MAJOR NATIONAL POLITICAL ORGANIZATIONS

All India Congress Committee (I): 24 Akbar Rd, New Delhi 110 011; tel. (11) 3019080; fax (11) 3017047; internet www.indiancongress.org; f. 1978, as Indian National Congress (I), as a breakaway group under Indira Gandhi; name of party gradually changed to Indian National Congress or Congress Party in the early to mid-1990s; merged with Tamil Maanila Congress in 2002; Pres. Sonia Gandhi; Gen. Secs Ambika Soni, Kamal Nath, Mahavir Prasad, Motilal Vora, Oscar Fernandes, Vylar Ravi; 35m. mems (1998).

Bahujan Samaj Party (Majority Society Party): c/o Lok Sabha, New Delhi; promotes the rights of the *Harijans* ('Untouchables') of India; Leader Kanshi Ram; Gen. Sec. Ms Mayawati.

Bharatiya Janata Party (BJP) (Indian People's Party): 11 Ashok Rd, New Delhi 110 001; tel. (11) 3382234; fax (11) 3782163; e-mail bjpco@del3.vsnl.net.in; internet www.bjp.org; f. 1980 as a breakaway group from Janata Party; radical right-wing Hindu party; Pres. K. M. Venkaiah Naidu; Gen. Secs Rajnath Singh, Arun Jaitley, Mukhtar Abbas Naqvi, Sanjay Joshi, Anita Arya; 10.5m. mems.

Communist Party of India (CPI): Ajoy Bhavan, Kotla Marg, New Delhi 110 002; tel. (11) 3235546; fax (11) 3235543; e-mail cpi@vsnl.com; internet www.cpofindia.org; f. 1925; advocates the establishment of a socialist society led by the working class, and ultimately of a communist society; nine-mem. central secretariat; Gen. Sec. Ardhendu Bhushan Bardhan; 555,010 mems (2000).

Communist Party of India—Marxist (CPI—M): A. K. Gopalan Bhavan, 27–29 Bhai Vir Singh Marg, New Delhi 110 001; tel. (11) 3747435; fax (11) 3747483; e-mail cpim@vsnl.com; internet www.del.vsnl.net.in/cpim; f. 1964 as pro-Beijing breakaway group from the CPI; declared its independence of Beijing in 1968 and is managed by a central committee of 73 mems and a politburo of 17 mems; Leaders Buddhadev Bhattacharya, Jyoti Basu, Prakash Karat, Sitaram Yechury, Somnath Chatterjee; Gen. Sec. Harkishan Singh Surjeet; 717,645 mems (1998).

Janata Dal (People's Party): 7 Jantar Mantar Rd, New Delhi 110 001; tel. (11) 3368833; fax (11) 3368138; f. 1988 as a merger of parties within the Rashtriya Morcha; advocates non-alignment, the eradication of poverty, unemployment and wide disparities in wealth, and the protection of minorities; 136-mem. National Executive; Pres. Sharad Yadav; Sec.-Gen. Dr Bapu Kaldate; split into two factions in July 1999—Janata Dal (United), headed by Sharad Yadav, and Janata Dal (Secular), headed by H. D. Deve Gowda.

Nationalist Congress Party (NCP): 10 Dr Bishambhar Das Marg, New Delhi 110001; tel. (11) 3359218; fax (11) 3352112; f. 1999 as breakaway faction of Congress; Pres. Sharad Pawar; Gen. Secs Tariq Anwar, P. A. Sangma, T. B. Peethambaran, Dr Jagannath Mishra.

MAJOR REGIONAL POLITICAL ORGANIZATIONS

Akhil Bharat Hindu Mahasabha: Hindu Mahasabha Bhavan, Mandir Marg, New Delhi 110 001; tel. (11) 3342087; fax (11) 3363105; f. 1915; seeks the establishment of a democratic Hindu state; Pres. Dinesh Chandra Tyagi; Gen. Sec. Dr Madanlal Goyal; 525,000 mems.

All-India Anna Dravida Munnetra Kazhagam (AIADMK) (All-India Anna Dravidian Progressive Assen): Lloyd's Rd, Chennai 600 004; f. 1972; breakaway group from the DMK; Chair. (vacant); Gen. Sec. C. Jayaram Jayalalitha.

All India Forward Bloc: 28 Gurudwara Rakabganj Rd, New Delhi 110 001; tel. and fax (11) 3714131; e-mail dbiswas@sansad.nic.in; f. 1940 by Netaji Subhash Chandra Bose; socialist aims, including nationalization of major industries, land reform and redistribution, and the establishment of a union of socialist republics through revolution; Chair. D. D. Shastri; Gen. Sec. Debabrata Biswas; 900,000 mems (1999).

All India Trinamool Congress: 125-D, Parliament House, New Delhi 110 001; tel. (11) 3034355; internet www.trinamool.org; Leader Mamata Banerjee.

Asom Gana Parishad (AGP) (Assam People's Council): Golaghat, Assam; f. 1985; draws support from the All-Assam Gana Sangram Parishad and the All-Assam Students' Union (Pres. Keshab Mahanta; Gen. Sec. Atul Bora); advocates the unity of India in diversity and a united Assam; Pres. Brindaban Goswami; a breakaway faction formed a new central exec. committee under Pulakesh Barua in April 1991.

Dravida Munnetra Kazhagam (DMK): Anna Arivalayam, Teynampet, Chennai 600 018; f. 1949; aims at full autonomy for states (primarily Tamil Nadu) within the Union, to establish regional languages as state languages and English as the official language pending the recognition of regional languages as official languages of the Union; Pres. Muthuvel Karunanidhi; Gen. Sec. K. Anbazhagan; more than 4m. mems.

Indian National Lok Dal: c/o Rajya Sabha, New Delhi.

Jammu and Kashmir National Conference (JKNC): Mujahid Manzil, Srinagar 190 002; tel. 71500; fmrly All Jammu and Kashmir National Conference, f. 1931, renamed 1939, reactivated 1975; state-based party campaigning for internal autonomy and responsible self-govt; Pres. Omar Abdullah; Gen. Sec. Sheikh Nazir Ahmad; 1m. mems.

Jharkhand Mukti Morcha: c/o Rajya Sabha, New Delhi.

Pattali Makkal Katchi: Chennai; Leader Dr Ramadas.

Peasants' and Workers' Party of India: Mahatma Phule Rd, Naigaum, Mumbai 400 014; f. 1949; Marxist; seeks to nationalize all basic industries, to promote industrialization, and to establish a unitary state with provincial boundaries drawn on a linguistic basis; Gen. Sec. Dajiba Desai; c. 10,000 mems.

Rashtriya Loktantrik Morcha (National Democratic Front): New Delhi; f. 1998; Convenor Mulayam Singh Yadav; includes:

Rashtriya Janata Dal (RJD) (National People's Party): New Delhi; f. 1997 as a breakaway group from Janata Dal; Leader Laloo Prasad Yadav.

Samajwadi Party (Socialist Party): New Delhi; f. 1991 by the merger of the Janata Dal (S) and the Janata Party; Pres. Mulayam Singh Yadav; Gen. Sec. Amar Singh.

Republican Party of India (RPI): Ensa Hutments, I Block, Azad Maidan, Fort, Mumbai 400 001; tel. (22) 2621888; main aim is to realize the aims and objects set out in the preamble to the 1950 Constitution; Pres. Prakash Rao Ambedkar; Gen. Sec. Ramdas Athavale; 100,000 mems.

Revolutionary Socialist Party: c/o Lok Sabha, New Delhi.

Samata Party: 220 VP House, Rafi Marg, New Delhi 110 001; tel. (11) 3352280; fax (11) 3350349; f. 1994; Pres. George Fernandes.

Shiromani Akali Dal: Baradan Shri Darbar Sahib, Amritsar; f. 1920; merged with Congress Party 1958–62; Sikh party composed of several factions both moderate and militant; seeks the establishment of an autonomous Sikh state of 'Khalistan'; Pres. (Shiromani Akali Dal—Badal) Prakash Singh Badal; Sec.-Gen. (Shiromani Akali Dal—Badal) Gurdev Singh Dhindsa.

Shiv Sena: Shiv Sena Bhavan, Ram Ganesh Gadkari Chowk, Dadar, Mumbai 400 028; tel. (22) 4309128; e-mail senabhavan@shivsena.org; internet www.shivsena.org; f. 1966; militant Hindu group; Pres. Balashaheb 'Bal' Thackeray.

Telugu Desam (Telugu Nation): 3-5-910, Himayatnagar, Hyderabad 500 029; tel. (842) 237290; f. 1982; state-based party (Andhra Pradesh); campaigns against rural poverty and social prejudice; Pres. N. Chandrababu Naidu.

Diplomatic Representation

EMBASSIES AND HIGH COMMISSIONS IN INDIA

Afghanistan: 5/50F Shanti Path, Chanakyapuri, New Delhi 110 021; tel. (11) 6886625; fax (11) 6875439; Ambassador: Masood Khalili.

Algeria: E-6/5 Vasant Vihar, New Delhi 110 057; tel. (11) 6146706; fax (11) 6147033; e-mail embalg@nda.vsnl.net.in; Ambassador: Abdelkrim Belarbi.

Argentina: B-8/9 Vasant Vihar, Paschmi Marg, New Delhi 110 057; tel. (11) 6148411; fax (11) 6146506; e-mail eindi@mantraonline.com; Ambassador: Gerardo Biritos.

Australia: 1/50-G Shanti Path, Chanakyapuri, New Delhi 110 021; tel. (11) 6888223; fax (11) 6885199; internet www.ausgovindia.com; High Commissioner: Penny Wensley.

Austria: EP/13 Chandragupta Marg, Chanakyapuri, New Delhi 110 021; tel. (11) 6889037; fax (11) 6886929; e-mail aedelhi@del2.vsnl.net.in; Ambassador: Dr Herbert Traxl.

Bangladesh: 56 Ring Rd, Lajpat Nagar-III, New Delhi 110 024; tel. (11) 6834065; fax (11) 6839237; High Commissioner: Tufail Karim Haider.

Belarus: 163 Jor Bagh, New Delhi 110 003; tel. (11) 4694518; fax (11) 4697029; e-mail embelind@del6.vsnl.net.in; Ambassador: Uladzimir A. Sakalovsky.

Belgium: 50N, Shanti Path, Chanakyapuri, New Delhi 110 021; tel. (11) 6889851; fax (11) 6885821; e-mail ambabel@del2.vsnl.net.in; Ambassador: Guy Trouveroy.

Bhutan: Chandragupta Marg, Chanakyapuri, New Delhi 110 021; tel. (11) 6889807; fax (11) 6876710; Ambassador: Lyonpo Dago Tshering.

Bosnia and Herzegovina: 57 Poorvi Marg, Vasant Vihar, New Delhi 110 057; tel. (11) 6147415; fax (11) 6143042; Ambassador: Novak Todorović.

Brazil: 8 Aurangzeb Rd, New Delhi 110 011; tel. (11) 3017301; fax (11) 3793684; e-mail brasindi@vsnl.com; Ambassador: Vera Barrouin Machado.

Brunei: A-42 Vasant Marg, Vasant Vihar, New Delhi 110 057; tel. (11) 6148340; fax (11) 6142101; High Commissioner: Dato' Paduka Haji Abdul Mokti Haji Mohammad Daud.

Bulgaria: 16/17 Chandragupta Marg, Chanakyapuri, New Delhi 110 021; tel. (11) 6115550; fax (11) 6876190; e-mail bulemb@mantraonline.com; Ambassador: Edvin Sugarev.

Burkina Faso: C-12, Anand Niketan, New Delhi 110 016; tel. (11) 4671678; fax (11) 4671745; e-mail emburnd@bol.net.in; Ambassador Albert E. Kiemde.

Cambodia: N-14 Panchsheel Park, New Delhi 110 017; tel. (11) 6495092; fax (11) 6495093; Ambassador: Sim Suong.

Canada: Shanti Path, Chanakyapuri, New Delhi 110 021; tel. (11) 6876500; fax (11) 6876579; e-mail domcan.delhi@delhi01.x400.gc.ca; High Commissioner: Peter S. Sutherland.

Chile: 146 Jorbagh, New Delhi 110 003; tel. (11) 4617123; fax (11) 4617102; e-mail embassyofchile@hotmail.com; Ambassador: Manuel Cárdenas.

China, People's Republic: 50D Shanti Path, Chanakyapuri, New Delhi 110 021; tel. (11) 6881249; fax (11) 6882024; internet www.chinaembassy-india.com; Ambassador: Hua Jun-duo.

Colombia: 82D Malcha Marg, Chanakyapuri, New Delhi 110 021; tel. (11) 6110773; fax (11) 6112486; Ambassador: María Clara Betancur.

Congo, Democratic Republic: B-39 Soami Nagar, New Delhi 110 017; tel. (11) 6222796; fax (11) 6227226; Ambassador: Kitenge Nkumbi Kasongo.

Croatia: 70 Ring Rd, Lajpat Nagar-III, New Delhi 110 024; tel. (11) 6924761; fax (11) 6924763; e-mail croemnd@del1.vsnl.net.in; Ambassador: Dr Zoran Andrić.

Cuba: E-1/9 Vasant Vihar, New Delhi 110 057; tel. (11) 6143849; fax (11) 6143806; e-mail embcuind@ndf; Ambassador: Olga Chamero Trias.

Cyprus: 106 Jor Bagh, New Delhi 110 003; tel. (11) 4697503; fax (11) 4628828; e-mail cyprus@del3.vsnl.net.in; High Commissioner: Rea Yiordamlis.

Czech Republic: 50M Niti Marg, Chanakyapuri, New Delhi 110 021; tel. (11) 6110205; fax (11) 6886221; e-mail newdelhi@embassy.mzv.cz; Ambassador: Jaromír Novotný.

Denmark: 11 Aurangzeb Rd, New Delhi 110 011; tel. (11) 3010900; fax (11) 3010961; e-mail denmark@vsnl.com; internet www.denmarkindia.com; Ambassador: Michael Sternberg.

Egypt: 1/50M Niti Marg, Chanakyapuri, New Delhi 110 021; tel. (11) 6114096; fax (11) 6885355; e-mail egypt@del2.vsnl.net.in; Ambassador: Gehad Madi.

Ethiopia: 7/50G Satya Marg, Chanakyapuri, New Delhi 110 021; tel. (11) 6119513; fax (11) 6875731; e-mail delethem@bol.net.in; Ambassador: Desta Erifo.

Finland: E–3 Nyaya Marg, Chanakyapuri, New Delhi 110 021; tel. (11) 6115258; fax (11) 6886713; e-mail sanomat.NDE@formin.fi; internet www.finembindia.com; Ambassador: Glen Lindholm.

France: 2/50E Shanti Path, Chanakyapuri, New Delhi 110 021; tel. (11) 6118790; fax (11) 6872305; Ambassador: Bernard de Montferrand.

Germany: 6 Block 50G, Shanti Path, Chanakyapuri, New Delhi 110 021; tel. (11) 6871831; fax (11) 6873117; e-mail germany@vsnl.com; internet www.germanembassy-india.org; Ambassador: Heimo Richter.

Ghana: 50-N Satya Marg, Chanakyapuri, New Delhi 110 021; tel. (11) 6883298; fax (11) 6883202; High Commissioner: (vacant).

Greece: 32 Dr S. Radhakrishnan Marg, Chanakyapuri, New Delhi 110 021; tel. (11) 6880700; fax (11) 6888010; e-mail hellemb@id.eth.net; Ambassador: Yannis-Alexis Zepos.

Holy See: 50C Niti Marg, Chanakyapuri, New Delhi 110 021 (Apostolic Nunciature); tel. (11) 6889184; fax (11) 6874286; e-mail nuntius@bol.net.in; Pro-Nuncio: Most Rev. Lorenzo Baldisseri, Titular Archbishop of Diocletiana.

Hungary: Plot 2, 50M Niti Marg, Chanakyapuri, New Delhi 110 021; tel. (11) 6114737; fax (11) 6886742; e-mail huembdel@giasdl01.vsnl.net.in; Ambassador: László Fodor.

Indonesia: 50A Chanakyapuri, New Delhi 110 021; tel. (11) 6114100; fax (11) 6885460; e-mail iembassy@giasdl01.vsnl.net.in; Ambassador: Zakaria Soemin Taatmadja.

Iran: 5 Barakhamba Road, New Delhi 110 001; tel. (11) 3329600; fax (11) 3325493; Ambassador: Mir Mahmoud-Moussavi Khameneh.

Iraq: 169–171 Jor Bagh, New Delhi 110 003; tel. (11) 4618011; fax (11) 4631547; Ambassador: Salah al-Mukhtar.

Ireland: 13 Jor Bagh, New Delhi 110 003; tel. (11) 4626733; fax (11) 4697053; Ambassador: Philip McDonogh.

Israel: 3 Aurangzeb Rd, New Delhi 110 011; tel. (11) 3013238; fax (11) 3014298; e-mail israelem@vsnl.com; Ambassador: David Aphek.

Italy: 50E Chandragupta Marg, Chanakyapuri, New Delhi 110 021; tel. (11) 6114355; fax (11) 6873889; e-mail italemb@del3.vsnl.net.in; internet www.italembdelhi.com; Ambassador: Benedetto Amari.

Japan: Plots 4–5, 50G Shanti Path, Chanakyapuri, New Delhi 110 021; tel. (11) 6876581; fax (11) 6885587; Ambassador: Hiroshi Hirabayashi.

Jordan: 1/21 Shanti Niketan, New Delhi 110 021; tel. (11) 6889857; fax (11) 6883763; e-mail jordemb@ndf.vsnl.net.in; Ambassador: Nabil Talhouni.

Kazakhstan: 4 Olof Palme Marg, Vasant Vihar, New Delhi 110 057; tel. (11) 6144779; fax (11) 6144778; e-mail embaskaz@giasdl01.vsnl.net.in; Ambassador: Askar O. Shakirov.

Kenya: E-66 Vasant Marg, Vasant Vihar, New Delhi 110 057; tel. (11) 6146537; fax (11) 6146550; High Commissioner: L. O. Amayo.

Korea, Democratic People's Republic: D-14 Maharani Bagh, New Delhi 110 065; tel. (11) 6829644; fax (11) 6829645; Ambassador: Jang Kwang Son.

Korea, Republic: 9 Chandragupta Marg, Chanakyapuri, POB 5416, New Delhi 110 021; tel. (11) 6885412; fax (11) 6884840; Ambassador: Kwon Soon-Tae.

Kuwait: 5A Shanti Path, Chanakyapuri, New Delhi 110 021; tel. (11) 4100791; fax (11) 6881115; Ambassador: Abdullah Ahmed al-Murad.

Kyrgyzstan: Sufdaryagung A 1/6, New Delhi; tel. (11) 4108008; fax (11) 4108009; e-mail kyrghyz@netscape.net; Ambassador: Osmonakun Ibraimov.

Laos: New Delhi; Ambassador: Kideng Thammavong.

Lebanon: 10 Sardar Patel Marg, Chanakyapuri, New Delhi 110 021; tel. (11) 3013174; fax (11) 3015555; e-mail lebanemb@giasdl01.vsnl.net.in; Ambassador: Dr Jean Daniel.

Libya: 22 Golf Links, New Delhi 110 003; tel. (11) 4697717; fax (11) 4633005; Secretary of People's Bureau: Nuri el-Fituri al-Madani.

Malaysia: 50M Satya Marg, Chanakyapuri, New Delhi 110 021; tel. (11) 6111291; fax (11) 6881538; e-mail hcom@del2.vsnl.net.in; High Commissioner: Dato' S. K. Choo.

Mauritius: 41 Jesus and Mary Marg, Chanakyapuri, New Delhi 110 021; tel. (11) 4102161; fax (11) 412194; e-mail mhcnd@bol.net.in; High Commissioner: D. Seewoo.

Mexico: B-33 Friends Colony (West), New Delhi 110 065; tel. (11) 6932860; fax (11) 6932864; Ambassador: Julio Faesler Carlisle.

Mongolia: 34 Archbishop Makarios Marg, New Delhi 110 003; tel. (11) 4631728; fax (11) 4633240; e-mail embassy.mongolia@gems.vsnl.net.in; Ambassador: Oidovyn Nyamdavaa.

Morocco: 33 Archbishop Makarios Marg, New Delhi 110 003; tel. (11) 4636920; fax (11) 4636925; e-mail sifamand@giasdl01.vsnl.net.in; internet www.moroccoembindia.com; Ambassador: Mohamed Louafa.

Myanmar: 3/50F Nyaya Marg, Chanakyapuri, New Delhi 110 021; tel. (11) 6889007; fax (11) 6877942; e-mail myandeli@nda.vsnl.net.in; Ambassador: U Kyaw Tau.

Namibia: A-2/6 Vasant Vihar, New Delhi 110 057; tel. (11) 6144772; fax (11) 6146120; e-mail nhcdelhi@del2.vsnl.net.in; High Commissioner: Joel Kaapanda.

Nepal: Barakhamba Rd, New Delhi 110 001; tel. (11) 3329218; fax (11) 3326857; e-mail rned.ramjnki@axcess.net.in; Ambassador: Dr Bhekh B. Thapa.

Netherlands: 6/50F Shanti Path, Chanakyapuri, New Delhi 110 021; tel. (11) 6884951; fax (11) 6884956; e-mail nlembas@giasdl01.vsnl.net.in; Ambassador: P. F. C. Koch.

New Zealand: 50N Nyaya Marg, Chanakyapuri, New Delhi 110 021; tel. (11) 6883170; fax (11) 6883165; e-mail nzhc@ndf.vsnl.net.in; High Commissioner: Caroline McDonald.

Nigeria: 21 Olof Palme Marg, Vasant Vihar, New Delhi 110 057; tel. (11) 6146221; fax (11) 6146617; e-mail nhcnd@nde.vsnl.in; High Commissioner: KABIRU AHMED.

Norway: 50C Shanti Path, Chanakyapuri, New Delhi 110 021; tel. (11) 6873532; fax (11) 6873814; e-mail noramb@vsnl.com; Ambassador: TRULS HANEVOLD.

Oman: 16 Olof Palme Marg, New Delhi 110 057; tel. (11) 6144798; fax (11) 6146478; Ambassador: KHALIFA BIN ALI BIN ESSA AL-HARTHY.

Pakistan: 2/50G Shanti Path, Chanakyapuri, New Delhi 110 021; tel. (11) 4676004; fax (11) 6872339; High Commissioner: ASHRAF JEHANGIR QAZI.

Peru: G-15 Maharani Bagh, New Delhi 110 065; tel. (11) 6312610; fax (11) 6312557; e-mail info@embaperuindia.com; internet www.embaperuindia.com; Ambassador: LUIS HERNÁNDEZ.

Philippines: 50N Nyaya Marg, Chanakyapuri, New Delhi 110 021; tel. (11) 6889091; fax (11) 6876401; e-mail phndelhi@del2.vsnl.net.in; Ambassador: JOSÉ P. DEL ROSARIO, Jr.

Poland: 50M Shanti Path, Chanakyapuri, New Delhi 110 021; tel. (11) 6889211; fax (11) 6871914; e-mail gorski@del2.vsnl.net.in; Ambassador: Dr KRZYSZTOF MAJKA.

Portugal: 13 Sundar Nagar, New Delhi 110 003; tel. (11) 4601262; fax (11) 4601252; e-mail embportin@ndf.vsnl.net.in; internet www.embportindia.com; Ambassador: MANUEL MARCELO CURTO.

Qatar: G-5 Anand Niketan, New Delhi 110 021; tel. (11) 6117988; fax (11) 6886080; Ambassador: YOUSEF H. AL-SAI.

Romania: A-52 Vasant Marg, Vasant Vihar, New Delhi 110 057; tel. (11) 6140447; fax (11) 6140611; e-mail emrond@hotmail.com; Ambassador: PETRU PETRA.

Russia: Shanti Path, Chanakyapuri, New Delhi 110 021; tel. (11) 6873799; fax (11) 6876823; Ambassador: ALEKSANDR KADAKIN.

Saudi Arabia: D-12, New Delhi South Extension Part II, New Delhi 110 049; tel. (11) 6252470; fax (11) 6259333; Ambassador: A. REHMAN N. ALOHALY.

Senegal: 30 Paschimi Marg, Vasant Vihar, New Delhi 110 057; tel. (11) 6143720; fax (11) 6145809; Ambassador: AHMED EL MANSOUR DIOP.

Singapore: E-6 Chandragupta Marg, Chanakyapuri, New Delhi 110 021; tel. (11) 6885659; fax (11) 6886798; e-mail singhnd@giasdl01.vsnl.net.in; High Commissioner: CHAK MUM SEE.

Slovakia: 50M Niti Marg, Chanakyapuri, New Delhi 110 021; tel. (11) 6889071; fax (11) 6877941; e-mail skdelhi@giasdl01.vsnl.net.in; Ambassador: LADISLAV VOLKO.

Somalia: A-17, Defence Colony, New Delhi 110 024; tel. (11) 4619559; Ambassador: MOHAMED OSMAN OMAR.

South Africa: B-18 Vasant Marg, Vasant Vihar, New Delhi 110 057; tel. (11) 6149411; fax (11) 6143105; e-mail highcommissioner@sahc-india.com; High Commissioner: M. E. NKOANA MASHABANE.

Spain: 12 Prithviraj Rd, New Delhi 110 011; tel. (11) 3792085; fax (11) 3793375; Ambassador: DON ALBERTO ESCUDERO.

Sri Lanka: 27 Kautilya Marg, Chanakyapuri, New Delhi 110 021; tel. (11) 3010201; fax (11) 3793604; e-mail lankacom@del2.vsnl.net.in; High Commissioner: SENAKA BANDARANAYAKE.

Sudan: Plot No. 3, Shanti Path, Chanakyapuri, New Delhi 110 021; tel. (11) 6873785; fax (11) 6883758; Ambassador: AWED EL KARIM FADLALLA.

Sweden: Nyaya Marg, Chanakyapuri, New Delhi 110 021; tel. (11) 6875760; fax (11) 6885401; e-mail embassy.new.delhi@sida.se; Ambassador: (vacant).

Switzerland: Nyaya Marg, Chanakyapuri, New Delhi 110 021; tel. (11) 6878372; fax (11) 6873093; e-mail swienidel@vsnl.com; Ambassador: Dr WALTER B. GYGER.

Syria: D-5/8, Vasant Vihar, New Delhi 110 057; tel. (11) 6140285; fax (11) 6143107; Ambassador: MOHSEN AL-KHAYER.

Tanzania: 10/1 Sarv Priya Vihar, New Delhi 110 016; tel. (11) 6853046; fax (11) 6968408; High Commissioner: AHMED K. M. KIWIANUKA.

Thailand: 56N Nyaya Marg, Chanakyapuri, New Delhi 110 021; tel. (11) 6118103; fax (11) 6872029; e-mail thaiemb@nda.vsnl.net.in; Ambassador: BANDHIT SOTIPALALIT.

Trinidad and Tobago: 131 Jor Bagh, New Delhi 110 003; tel. (11) 4618186; fax (11) 4624581; e-mail hcreptt@giasdl01.vsnl.net.in; High Commissioner: TEDWIN HERBERT (acting).

Tunisia: 23 Paschimi Marg, Vasant Vihar, New Delhi 110 057; tel. (11) 6145346; fax (11) 6145301; e-mail embtun@nde.vsnl.net.in; Ambassador: ELYES KASRI.

Turkey: 50N Nyaya Marg, Chanakyapuri, New Delhi 110 021; tel. (11) 6889054; fax (11) 6881409; e-mail tembdelhi@mantraonline.com; Ambassador: HASAN GOGUS.

Turkmenistan: 1/13 Shanti Niketan, New Delhi 110 021; tel. (11) 6118409; fax (11) 6118332; e-mail turkmind@del3.vsnl.net.in; Ambassador: ASHIR ATAEV.

Uganda: B-3/26 Vasant Vihar, New Delhi 110 057; tel. (11) 6144413; fax (11) 6144405; e-mail ughcom@ndb.vsnl.net.in; High Commissioner: JULIET BETTY K. KAJUMBA (acting).

Ukraine: 46 Paschimi Marg, Vasant Vihar, New Delhi 110 057; tel. (11) 6146041; fax (11) 6146043; e-mail embassy@bol.net.in; Ambassador: OLEH Y. SEMENETS.

United Arab Emirates: EP–12 Chandragupt Marg, New Delhi 110 021; tel. (11) 6872937; fax (11) 6873272; Ambassador: AHMED ABDULLAH AL-MUSALLY.

United Kingdom: Shanti Path, Chanakyapuri, New Delhi 110 021; tel. (11) 6872161; fax (11) 6872882; e-mail bhcndpa@del2.vsnl.net.in; internet www.ukinindia.org; High Commissioner: Sir ROBERTSON YOUNG.

USA: Shanti Path, Chanakyapuri, New Delhi 110 021; tel. (11) 4198000; fax (11) 4190060; Ambassador: ROBERT D. BLACKWILL.

Uruguay: A 16/2 Vasant Vihar, New Delhi 110 057; tel. (11) 6151991; fax (11) 6144306; e-mail uruind@del3.vsnl.net.in; Ambassador: ENRIQUE ANCHORDOQUI.

Uzbekistan: EP-40 Dr S. Radhakrishnan Marg, Chanakyapuri, New Delhi 110 021; tel. (11) 4670774; fax (11) 4670773; Ambassador: Dr IBRAHIM MAVLANOV.

Venezuela: N-114 Panchshila Park, New Delhi 110 017; tel. (11) 6496913; fax (11) 6491686; e-mail embavene@del2.vsnl.net.in; Ambassador: WALTER MÁRQUEZ.

Viet Nam: 17 Kautilya Marg, Chanakyapuri, New Delhi 110 021; tel. (11) 3012123; fax (11) 3017714; e-mail sqdelhi@del3.vsnl.net.in; Ambassador: PHAM SY TAM.

Yemen: J-16, Hauz Khas, New Delhi 110 016; tel. (11) 6602481; fax (11) 6602483; Ambassador: Dr MOHAMED SAAD ALI.

Yugoslavia: 3/50G Niti Marg, Chanakyapuri, New Delhi 110 021; tel. (11) 6873661; fax (11) 6885535; e-mail zvezda@del2.vsnl.net.in; Ambassador: Dr CEDOMIR STRABAC.

Zambia: C-79 Anand Niketan, New Delhi 110 021; tel. (11) 4101289; fax (11) 4101520; e-mail zambiand@nde.vsnl.net.in; High Commissioner: Prof. MOSES MUSONDA.

Zimbabwe: F-63 Poorvi Marg, Vasant Vihar, New Delhi 110 057; tel. (11) 6140430; fax (11) 6154316; e-mail zimdelhi@vsnl.net; High Commissioner: LUCIA MUVINGI.

Judicial System

THE SUPREME COURT

The Supreme Court, consisting of a Chief Justice and not more than 25 judges appointed by the President, exercises exclusive jurisdiction in any dispute between the Union and the states (although there are certain restrictions where an acceding state is involved). It has appellate jurisdiction over any judgment, decree or order of the High Court where that Court certifies that either a substantial question of law or the interpretation of the Constitution is involved. The Supreme Court can enforce fundamental rights and issue writs covering habeas corpus, mandamus, prohibition, quo warranto and certiorari. The Supreme Court is a court of record and has the power to punish for its contempt.

Provision is made for the appointment by the Chief Justice of India of judges of High Courts as ad hoc judges at sittings of the Supreme Court for specified periods, and for the attendance of retired judges at sittings of the Supreme Court. The Supreme Court has advisory jurisdiction in respect of questions which may be referred to it by the President for opinion. The Supreme Court is also empowered to hear appeals against a sentence of death passed by a State High Court in reversal of an order of acquittal by a lower court, and in a case in which a High Court has granted a certificate of fitness.

The Supreme Court also hears appeals which are certified by High Courts to be fit for appeal, subject to rules made by the Court. Parliament may, by law, confer on the Supreme Court any further powers of appeal.

The judges hold office until the age of 65 years.

Supreme Court: New Delhi; tel. (11) 3388942; fax (11) 3383792; internet www.caselaw.delhi.nic.in@bssc-cl.

Chief Justice of India: BHUPINDER NATH KIRPAL.

Judges of the Supreme Court: BRIJESH KUMAR, S. RAJENDRA BABU, ASHOK BHAN, P. VENKATARAMA REDDY, SYED SHAH MOHAMMED QUADRI, DORAISWAMY RAJU, Y. K. SABHARWAL, HOTOI KHETOHO SEMA, BISHWANATH AGARWAL, VISHESHWAR NATH KHARE, RUMA PAL, S. N. VARIAVA, SHIVRAJ V. PATIL, K. G. BALAKRISHNAN, G. B. PATTANAIK, MANHARLAL BHIKHALAL SHAH, B. N. SRIKRISHNA, UMESH CHANDRA BANERJEE, RAMESH CHANDRA

LAHOTI, SANTOSH HEGDE, S. B. SINHA, S. N. PHUKAN, ARIJIT PASSAYAT, BISHESHWAR PRASAD SINGH, ARUN KUMAR.

Attorney-General: SOLI J. SORABJEE.

HIGH COURTS

The High Courts are the Courts of Appeal from the lower courts, and their decisions are final except in cases where appeal lies to the Supreme Court.

LOWER COURTS

Provision is made in the Code of Criminal Procedure for the constitution of lower criminal courts called Courts of Session and Courts of Magistrates. The Courts of Session are competent to try all persons duly committed for trial, and inflict any punishment authorized by the law. The President and the local government concerned exercise the prerogative of mercy.

The constitution of inferior civil courts is determined by regulations within each state.

Religion

BUDDHISM

The Buddhists in Ladakh (Jammu and Kashmir) are followers of the Dalai Lama. Head Lama of Ladakh: KAUSHAK SAKULA, Dalgate, Srinagar, Kashmir. In 1991 there were 6.3m. Buddhists in India, representing 0.80% of the population.

Mahabodhi Society of India: 4-A, Bankim Chatterjee St, Kolkata 700 073; tel. and fax (33) 2415214; 11 centres in India, five centres world-wide; Pres. KALASURI M. WIPULASARA MAHA THERO; Gen. Sec. Dr D. REWATHA THERO.

HINDUISM

In 1991 there were 672.6m. Hindus in India, representing 82.4% of the population.

International Society for Krishna Consciousness: Sri Mayapur Chandrodaya Mandir, Sri Mayapur Dham, District Nadia; tel. (3472) 45233; f. 1966; 300 centres world-wide.

Rashtriya Swayamsevak Sangh (RSS) (National Volunteer Organization): Dr Hedgewar Bhawan, Mahal, Nagpur 440 002; tel. (712) 720150; fax (712) 721589; e-mail vishwa@rss.org; internet www.rss.org; f. 1925; 30,000 *shakhas* (spiritual centres), 50,000 working centres; Pres. K. S. SUDARSHAN; Gen. Sec. MOHAN BHAGWAT.

Sarvadeshik Arya Pratinidhi Sabha: Asaf Ali Rd, Near Ram Lila Maidan, New Delhi 110 002; tel. (11) 3274771; e-mail vedicgod@nda.vsnl.net.in; internet www.whereisgod.com; f. 1875 by Maharshi Dayanand Saraswati; Pres. DEV RATNA ARYA; Sec. VED BRAT SHARMA.

Vishwa Hindu Parishad (VHP) (World Hindu Council): Sankat Mochan Ashram, Ramakrishna Puram VI, New Delhi 110 022; tel. (11) 6178992; fax (11) 6195527; e-mail asmita@ndc.vsnl.net.in; internet www.vhp.org; f. 1964; Pres. VISHNU HARI DALMIA; Gen. Sec. Dr PRAVEEN TOGADIA.

ISLAM

Muslims are divided into two main sects, Shi'as and Sunnis. Most of the Indian Muslims are Sunnis. At the 1991 census Islam had 95.2m. adherents (11.2% of the population).

Jamiat Ulama-i-Hind (The Assembly of Muslim Religious Leaders of India): 1 Bahadur Shah Zafar Marg, New Delhi 110 002; tel. (11) 3311455; fax (11) 3316173; e-mail info@jamiatulamahind.org; internet www.jamiatulamahind.org; f. 1919; Pres. ASAD MADANI; Gen. Sec. Maulana MAHMOOD MADANI.

SIKHISM

In 1991 there were 16.3m. Sikhs (comprising 2.0% of the population), the majority living in the Punjab.

Sikh Gurdwara Prabandhak Committee: Darbar Sahab, Amritsar 143 001; tel. (183) 553956; fax (183) 553919; internet www.sgpc.net; f. 1925; highest authority in Sikhism; Pres. Prof. KIRPAL SINGH BADUNGAR; Jathedar Shri Akal Takht Saheb JOGINDER SINGH VEDANTI.

OTHER INDIAN FAITHS

Jainism: 3.4m. adherents (1991 census), 0.4% of the population.

Zoroastrians: More than 120,000 Parsis practise the Zoroastrian religion.

CHRISTIANITY

According to the 1991 census, Christians represented 2.3% of the population in India.

National Council of Churches in India: Christian Council Lodge, Civil Lines, POB 205, Nagpur 440 001, Maharashtra; tel. (712) 531312; fax (712) 520554; e-mail nccindia@nagpur.dot.net.in; internet www.nccindia.org; f. 1914; mems: 26 reformed and three orthodox churches, 18 regional Christian councils, 14 All-India ecumenical orgs and seven related agencies; represents c. 10m. mems; Pres. Most Rev. GEEVARGHESE MAR COORILOS; Gen. Sec. Rev. Dr IPE JOSEPH.

Orthodox Churches

Malankara Orthodox Syrian Church: Devalokam, Kottayam 686 038, Kerala; tel. (481) 578500; fax (481) 570569; c. 2.5m. mems (1995); 22 bishops, 21 dioceses, 1,340 parishes; Catholicos of the East and Malankara Metropolitan: HH BASELIUS MARTHOMA MATHEWS II; Asscn Sec. A. K. THOMAS.

Mar Thoma Syrian Church of Malabar: Mar Thoma Sabha Office, Poolatheen, Tiruvalla 689 101, Kerala; tel. (473) 630313; fax (473) 630327; e-mail marthoma@vsnl.com; c. 1m. mems (2001); Metropolitan: Most Rev. Dr PHILIPOSE MAR CHRYSOSTOM MAR THOMA; Sec. Rev. Dr P. G. PHILIP.

The Malankara Jacobite Syrian Orthodox Church is also represented.

Protestant Churches

Church of North India (CNI): CNI Bhavan, 16 Pandit Pant Marg, New Delhi 110 001; tel. (11) 3716513; fax (11) 3716901; e-mail gscni@ndb.vsnl.net.in; internet www.cnisynod.org; f. 1970 by merger of the Church of India (fmrly known as the Church of India, Pakistan, Burma and Ceylon), the Council of the Baptist Churches in Northern India, the Methodist Church (British and Australasian Conferences), the United Church of Northern India (a union of Presbyterians and Congregationalists, f. 1924), the Church of the Brethren in India, and the Disciples of Christ; comprises 26 dioceses; c. 1.2m. mems (1999); Moderator Most Rev. Z. JAMES TEROM, Bishop of Chota Nagpur; Gen. Sec. Dr VIDYA SAGAR LALL.

Church of South India (CSI): CSI Centre, 5 Whites Rd, Chennai 600 014; tel. (44) 8521566; fax (44) 8524121; e-mail csi@vsnl.com; internet www.csisynod.org; f. 1947 by merger of the Weslyan Methodist Church in South India, the South India United Church (itself a union of churches in the Congregational and Presbyterian/Reformed traditions) and the four southern dioceses of the (Anglican) Church of India; comprises 21 dioceses (incl. one in Sri Lanka); c. 2.8m. mems (2000); Moderator Most Rev. K. J. SAMUEL, Bishop of East Kerala; Gen. Sec. Rev. G. DYVASIRVADAM.

Methodist Church in India: Methodist Centre, 21 YMCA Rd, Mumbai 400 008; tel. and fax (22) 3074137; e-mail gensecmci@vsnl.com; f. 1856 as the Methodist Church in Southern Asia; 600,000 mems (1998); Gen. Sec. Rev. TARANATH S. SAGAR.

Samavesam of Telugu Baptist Churches: C. A. M. Compound, Nellore 524 003, Andhra Pradesh; tel. (861) 24177; f. 1962; comprises 856 independent Baptist churches; 578,295 mems (1995); Gen. Sec. Rev. T. NATHANIEL.

United Evangelical Lutheran Churches in India: 94 Purasawalkam High Rd, Kilpauk, Chennai 600 010; tel. (44) 5325659; fax (44) 6421870; e-mail gurukul@giasmdo1.vsnl.net.in; internet www.gltc.edu; f. 1975; 10 constituent denominations: Andhra Evangelical Lutheran Church, Arcot Lutheran Church, Evangelical Lutheran Church in Madhya Pradesh, Gossner Evangelical Lutheran Church in Chotanagpur and Assam, India Evangelical Lutheran Church, Jeypore Evangelical Lutheran Church, Northern Evangelical Lutheran Church, South Andhra Lutheran Church, Good Samaritan Evangelical Lutheran Church and Tamil Evangelical Lutheran Church; c. 1.3m. mems; Pres. Bishop JOHN FRANKLIN; Exec. Sec. Dr K. RAJARATNAM.

Other denominations active in the country include the Assembly of the Presbyterian Church in North East India, the Bengal-Orissa-Bihar Baptist Convention (6,000 mems), the Chaldean Syrian Church of the East, the Convention of the Baptist Churches of Northern Circars, the Council of Baptist Churches of North East India, the Council of Baptist Churches of Northern India, the Hindustani Convent Church and the Mennonite Church in India.

The Roman Catholic Church

India comprises 25 archdioceses and 120 dioceses. These include four archdioceses and 20 dioceses of the the Syro-Malabar rite, and one archdiocese and three dioceses of the Syro-Malankara rite. The archdiocese of Goa and Daman is also the seat of the Patriarch of the East Indies. The remaining archdioceses are metropolitan sees. In December 2000 there were an estimated 16.7m. adherents of the Roman Catholic faith in the country.

Catholic Bishops' Conference of India (CBCI): CBCI Centre, 1 Ashok Place, Goledakkhana, New Delhi 110 001; tel. (11) 3344470; fax (11) 3364615; e-mail cbci@vsnl.com; internet www.cbcisite.com;

f. 1944; Pres. Most Rev. CYRIL MAR BASELIOS MALANCHARUVIL, Archbishop of Thiruvananthapuram; Sec.-Gen. Most Rev. PERCIVAL JOSEPH FERNANDEZ, Auxiliary Bishop of Bombay (Mumbai).

Latin Rite

Conference of Catholic Bishops of India (CCBI): CCBI Secretariat, Divya Deepti Sadan, 2nd Floor, 9–10 Bhai Vir Singh Marg, POB 680, New Delhi 110 001; tel. (11) 3364222; fax (11) 3364343; e-mail cbci@vsnl.com; internet www.cbcisite.com; f. 1994; Pres. Most Rev. TELESPHORO P. TOPPO, Archbishop of Ranchi.

Patriarch of the East Indies: Most Rev. RAUL NICOLAU GONSALVES (Archbishop of Goa and Daman), Paço Patriarcal, POB 216, Altinho, Panaji, Goa 403 001; tel. (832) 223353; fax (832) 224139; e-mail archbp@goatelecom.com.

Archbishop of Agra: Most Rev. Dr OSWALD GRACIAS, Cathedral House, Wazirpura Rd, Agra 282 003; tel. (562) 351318; fax (562) 353939; e-mail abpossie@sancharnet.in.

Archbishop of Bangalore: Most Rev. IGNATIUS PAUL PINTO, Archbishop's House, 75 Miller's Rd, Bangalore 560 046; tel. (80) 3330438; fax (80) 3330838; e-mail bgarchdi@bgl.vsnl.net.in.

Archbishop of Bhopal: Most Rev. PASCHAL TOPNO, Archbishop's House, 33 Ahmedabad Palace Rd, Bhopal 462 001; tel. (755) 540829; fax (755) 544737; e-mail adbhopal@vsnl.com; internet cbci.org/bhopal.htm.

Archbishop of Bombay (Mumbai): Cardinal IVAN DIAS, Archbishop's House, 21 Nathalal Parekh Marg, Fort, Mumbai 400 001; tel. (22) 2021093; fax (22) 2853872; e-mail bombaydiocese@vsnl.com; internet www.archbom.org.

Archbishop of Calcutta (Kolkata): Most Rev. LUCAS SIRKAR, Archbishop's House, 32 Park St, Kolkata 700 016; tel. and fax (33) 2807015; e-mail bls@cal2.vsnl.net.in.

Archbishop of Cuttack-Bhubaneswar: Most Rev. RAPHAEL CHEENATH, Archbishop's House, Satya Nagar, Bhubaneswar 751 007; tel. (674) 502234; fax (674) 501817; e-mail crcdc@mail.com.

Archbishop of Delhi: Most Rev. VINCENT M. CONCESSAO, Archbishop's House, 1 Ashok Place, Goledakkhana, New Delhi 110 001; tel. (11) 3343457; fax (11) 3746575; e-mail archbish@vsnl.com.

Archbishop of Guwahati: Most Rev. THOMAS MENAMPARAMPIL, Archbishop's House, POB 100, Guwahati 781 001; tel. (361) 547664; fax (361) 520588; e-mail bishop@gw1.dot.net.in; internet www.peacetoall.com.

Archbishop of Hyderabad: Most Rev. MARAMPUDI JOJI, Archbishop's House, Sardar Patel Rd, Secunderabad 500 003; tel. (40) 7805545; fax (40) 7718089; e-mail abphydmjoji@rediffmail.com.

Archbishop of Imphal: Most Rev. JOSEPH MITTATHANY, Archbishop's House, POB 35, Imphal 795 001; tel. (385) 421292; fax (385) 421293; e-mail jmittathany@hotmail.com.

Archbishop of Madras (Chennai) and Mylapore: Most Rev. JAMES MASILAMONY ARUL DAS, Archbishop's House, 21 San Thome High Rd, Chennai 600 004; tel. (44) 4941102; fax (44) 4941999; e-mail archmsml@vsnl.com.

Archbishop of Madurai: Most Rev. MARIANUS AROKIASAMY, Archbishop's House, K. Pudur, Madurai 625 007; tel. (452) 566198; fax (452) 566630; e-mail anupro@eth.net; internet www.maduraiarchdiocese.org.

Archbishop of Nagpur: Most Rev. ABRAHAM VIRUTHAKULANGARA, Archbishop's House, 25 Kamptee Rd, Mohan Nagar, Nagpur 440 001; tel. (712) 533239; fax (712) 527906; e-mail abpabrah@nagpur.dot.net.in.

Archbishop of Patna: Most Rev. BENEDICT JOHN OSTA, Archbishop's House, Bankipore, Patna 800 004; tel. (612) 673811; fax (612) 664816; e-mail archbishop@satyam.net.in.

Archbishop of Pondicherry and Cuddalore: Most Rev. Dr S. MICHAEL AUGUSTINE, Archbishop's House, Cathedral St, POB 193, Pondicherry 605 001; tel. (413) 334748; fax (413) 339911; e-mail abppondi@satyam.net.in; internet www.pondyarchdiocese.org.in.

Archbishop of Ranchi: Most Rev. TELESPHORE P. TOPPO, Archbishop's House, Purulia Rd, POB 5, Ranchi 834 001; tel. (651) 204728; fax (651) 304844; e-mail rca@vitalmail.com.

Archbishop of Shillong: Most Rev. DOMINIC JALA, Archbishop's House, Shillong 793 003; tel. (364) 223355; fax (364) 211306; e-mail jala@dte.vsnl.net.in.

Archbishop of Verapoly: Most Rev. DANIEL ACHARUPARAMBIL, Latin Archbishop's House, POB 2581, Kochi 682 031; tel. (484) 372892; fax (484) 360911; e-mail vpoly@vsnl.com; internet www.verapolyarchdiocese.org.

Archbishop of Visakhapatnam: Most Rev. MARIADAS KAGITHAPU, Archbishop's House, Maharanipeta, Visakhapatnam 530 002; tel. (891) 706428; fax (891) 704404; e-mail kmariadas@satyam.net.in.

Syro-Malabar Rite

Major Archbishop of Ernakulam-Angamaly: Cardinal MAR VARKEY VITHAYATHIL, Major Archbishop's House, Ernakulam, POB 10, Kochi 682 031; tel. (484) 352629; fax (484) 366028; e-mail abperang@md3.vsnl.net.in; internet www.ernakulamarchdiocese.org.

Archbishop of Changanacherry: Most Rev. JOSEPH MAR POWATHIL, Archbishop's House, POB 20, Changanacherry 686 101; tel. (481) 420040; fax (481) 422540; e-mail abpchry@md2.vsnl.net.in; internet www.archdiocesechanganacherry.org.

Archbishop of Tellicherry: Most Rev. GEORGE VALIAMATTAM, Archbishop's House, POB 70, Tellicherry 670 101; tel. and fax (490) 341058; e-mail diocese@eth.net.

Archbishop of Trichur: Most Rev. JACOB THOOMKUZHY, Archbishop's House, Trichur 680 005; tel. (487) 333325; fax (487) 338204; e-mail carbit@md4.vsnl.net.in; internet archdioceseoftrichur.org.

Syro-Malankara Rite

Archbishop of Thiruvananthapuram: Most Rev. CYRIL MAR BASELIOS MALANCHARUVIL, Archbishop's House, Pattom, Thiruvananthapuram 695 004; tel. (471) 541643; fax (471) 541635; e-mail archbp03@md3.vsnl.net.in; internet www.malankara.net.

BAHÁ'Í FAITH

National Spiritual Assembly: Bahá'í House, 6 Canning Rd, POB 19, New Delhi 110 001; tel. (11) 3386458; fax (11) 3782178; e-mail nsaindia@bahaindia.org; internet www.bahaindia.org; c. 2m. mems; Sec.-Gen. Prof. M. D. TELI.

The Press

Freedom of the Press was guaranteed under the 1950 Constitution. In 1979 a Press Council was established (its predecessor was abolished in 1975), the function of which was to uphold the freedom of the press and maintain and improve journalistic standards.

The growth of a thriving press has been inhibited by cultural barriers caused by religious, social and linguistic differences. Consequently the English-language press, with its appeal to the educated middle-class urban readership throughout the states, has retained its dominance. The English-language metropolitan dailies are some of the widest circulating and most influential newspapers. The main Indian language dailies, by paying attention to rural affairs, cater for the increasingly literate non-anglophone provincial population. Most Indian-language papers have a relatively small circulation.

The majority of publications in India are under individual ownership (77% in 1999), and they claim a large part of the total circulation (60% in 1999). The most powerful groups, owned by joint stock companies, publish most of the large English dailies and frequently have considerable private commercial and industrial holdings. Four of the major groups are as follows:

Times of India Group (controlled by family of the late ASHOK JAIN): dailies: *The Times of India* (published in 11 regional centres), *Economic Times*, the Hindi *Navbharat Times* and *Sandhya Times*, the Marathi *Maharashtra Times* (Mumbai); periodicals: the English fortnightlies *Femina* and *Filmfare*.

Indian Express Group (controlled by the family of the late RAMNATH GOENKA): publishes nine dailies including the *Indian Express*, the Marathi *Lokasatta*, the Tamil *Dinamani*, the Telugu *Andhra Prabha*, the Kannada *Kannada Prabha* and the English *Financial Express*; six periodicals including the English weeklies the *Indian Express* (Sunday edition), *Screen*, the Telugu *Andhra Prabha Illustrated Weekly* and the Tamil *Dinamani Kadir* (weekly).

Hindustan Times Group (controlled by the K. K. BIRLA family): dailies: the *Hindustan Times* (published from 10 regional centres), *Pradeep* (Patna) and the Hindi *Hindustan* (Delhi, Lucknow, Patna and Ranchi); periodicals: the weekly *Overseas Hindustan Times* and the Hindi monthly *Nandan* and *Kadambini* (New Delhi).

Ananda Bazar Patrika Group (controlled by AVEEK SARKAR and family): dailies: the *Ananda Bazar Patrika* (Kolkata) and the English *The Telegraph* (Guwahati, Kolkata and Siliguri); periodicals include: *Business World*, Bengali weekly *Anandamela*, Bengali fortnightly *Desh*, Bengali monthly *Anandalok* and the Bengali monthly *Sananda*.

PRINCIPAL DAILIES

Delhi (incl. New Delhi)

The Asian Age: L-11, South Extension Part II, New Delhi 110 049; tel. (11) 6250573; fax (11) 6251179; internet www.asianage.com; f. 1994; morning; English; also publ. from Bangalore, Bhubaneswar, Mumbai, Kolkata and London; Editor-in-Chief M. J. AKBAR.

Business Standard: Pratap Bhavan, 5 Bahadur Shah Zafar Marg, New Delhi 110 002; tel. (11) 3720202; fax (11) 3720201; e-mail editor@business-standard.com; internet www.business-standard.com; morning; English; also publ. from Kolkata, Ahmedabad, Bangalore, Chennai, Hyderabad and Mumbai; Editor T. N. Ninan; combined circ. 63,800.

Daily Milap: 8a Bahadur Shah Zafar Marg, New Delhi 110 002; tel. (11) 3317651; fax (11) 3319166; e-mail info@milap.com; internet www.milap.com; f. 1923; Urdu; nationalist; Man. Editor Punam Suri; Chief Editor Navin Suri; circ. 31,250.

Daily Pratap: Pratap Bhawan, 5 Bahadur Shah Zafar Marg, New Delhi 110 002; tel. (11) 3318572; fax (11) 3318276; f. 1919; Urdu; Editor K. Narendra; circ. 26,700.

Delhi Mid Day: World Trade Tower, Barakhamba Lane, New Delhi 110 001; tel. (11) 3414224; fax (11) 3412491; e-mail delhimidday@hotmail.com; f. 1989; Editor Sanjay Kapoor.

The Economic Times: 7 Bahadur Shah Zafar Marg, New Delhi 110 002; tel. (11) 3302000; fax (11) 3323346; internet www.economictimes.com; f. 1961; English; also publ. from Kolkata, Ahmedabad, Bangalore, Hyderabad, Chennai and Mumbai; Editor (Delhi) Arindam Sengupta; combined circ. 432,300, circ. (Delhi) 124,700.

Financial Express: Bahadur Shah Zafar Marg, New Delhi 110 002; tel. (11) 3702100; fax (11) 3702164; e-mail editor@financialexpress.com; internet www.financialexpress.com; f. 1961; morning; English; also publ. from Ahmedabad (in Gujarati), Mumbai, Bangalore, Kolkata and Chennai; Editor Sanjaya Baru; combined circ. 30,800.

The Hindu: INS Bldg, Rafi Marg, New Delhi 110 001; tel. (11) 3715426; fax (11) 3718158; f. 1878; morning; English; also publ. from eight other regional centres; Editor N. Ravi; combined circ. 904,700.

Hindustan: 18/20 Kasturba Gandhi Marg, New Delhi 110 001; tel. (11) 3361234; fax (11) 3704645; f. 1936; morning; Hindi; also publ. from Lucknow, Muzaffarpur, Ranchi, Bhagalpur, Varanasi and Patna; Editor Chandra Prakash Gupta; combined circ. 659,100.

The Hindustan Times: 18/20 Kasturba Gandhi Marg, New Delhi 110 001; tel. (11) 3704612; fax (11) 3704589; internet www.hindustantimes.com; f. 1923; morning; English; also publ. from nine regional centres; Editor Vir Sanghvi; circ. (Delhi) 777,750, combined circ. 878,300.

Indian Express: Bahadur Shah Zafar Marg, New Delhi 110 002; tel. (11) 6511015; fax (11) 6511615; internet www.indianexpress.com; f. 1953; English; also publ. from seven other towns; Man. Editor Vivek Goenka; Editor-in-Chief Shekhar Gupta; combined circ. 688,878, circ. (New Delhi, Jammu and Chandigarh) 138,100.

Janasatta: 9/10 Bahadur Shah Zafar Marg, New Delhi 110 002; f. 1983; Hindi; tel. (11) 3702100; fax (11) 3702141; also publ. from Kolkata; Editor-in-Chief Prabhash Joshi; Exec. Editor Om Thanvi.

National Herald: Herald House 5a, Bahadur Shah Zafar Marg, New Delhi 110 002; tel. (11) 3315950; fax (11) 3313458; f. 1938; English; nationalist; Editor T. V. Venkitachalam; circ. 33,000.

Navbharat Times: 7 Bahadur Shah Zafar Marg, New Delhi 110 002; tel. (11) 3492041; fax (11) 3492168; f. 1947; Hindi; also publ. from Mumbai; Editor Ramesh Chandra; combined circ. 501,500, circ. (Delhi) 328,100.

The Pioneer: Link House, 3 Bahadur Shah Zafar Marg, New Delhi 110 002; tel. (11) 3755271; fax (11) 3755275; e-mail pioneer@del2.vsnl.net.in; internet www.dailypioneer.com; f. 1865; also publ. from Lucknow; Editor Chandan Mitra combined circ. 154,000, circ. (Delhi) 78,000.

Punjab Kesari: Romesh Bhavan, 2 Printing Press Complex, nr Wazirpur DTC Depot, Ring Rd, Delhi 110 035; tel. (11) 7194459; fax (11) 7194470; e-mail ashwanik@nda.vsnl.net.in; Hindi; also publ. from Jalandhar and Ambala; Editor Ashwini Kumar; circ. 363,300 (Delhi), combined circ. 869,200.

Rashtriya Sahara: Amba Deep, Kasturba Gandhi Marg, New Delhi 110 001; tel. (11) 3755316; fax (11) 3755317; morning; Hindi; also publ. from Lucknow and Gorakhpur; Resident Editor Nishit Joshi; circ. 121,000 (New Delhi), 104,300 (Lucknow).

Sandhya Times: 7 Bahadur Shah Zafar Marg, New Delhi 110 002; tel (11) 3492162; fax (11) 3492047; f. 1979; Hindi; evening; Editor Sat Soni; circ. 64,200.

The Statesman: Statesman House, 148 Barakhamba Rd, New Delhi 110 001; tel. (11) 3315911; fax (11) 3315295; e-mail thestatesman@vsnl.com; internet www.thestatesman.net; f. 1875; English; also publ. from Kolkata and Siliguri; Editor-in-Chief C. R. Irani; combined circ. 174,000.

The Times of India: 7 Bahadur Shah Zafar Marg, New Delhi 110 002; tel. (11) 3492049; fax (11) 3351606; internet www.timesofindia.com; f. 1838; English; also publ. from 10 other towns; Exec. Man. Editor Dileep Padgaonkar; combined circ. 1,939,000.

Andhra Pradesh

Hyderabad

Deccan Chronicle: 36 Sarojini Devi Rd, Hyderabad 500 003; tel. (40) 7803930; fax (40) 7805256; f. 1938; English; Editor-in-Chief M. J. Akbar; Editor A. T. Jayanti; circ. 238,900.

Eenadu: Somajiguda, Hyderabad 500 082; tel. (40) 3318181; fax (40) 3318555; e-mail eenadu@hd2.vsnl.net.in; internet www.eenadu.net; f. 1974; Telugu; also publ. from 14 other towns; Chief Editor Ramoji Rao; combined circ. 841,900.

Newstime: 6-3-570 Somajiguda, Hyderabad 500 482; tel. (40) 318181; fax (40) 318555; f. 1984; also publ. from Vijaywada and Visakhapatnam; Editor Ramoji Rao; circ. 60,000.

Rahnuma-e-Deccan: 12-2-837/A/3, Asif Nagar, Hyderabad 500 028; tel. (40) 3534943; fax (40) 3534945; e-mail rahnumadeccan@email.com; f. 1949; morning; Urdu; independent; Chief Editor Syed Vicaruddin; circ. 25,000.

Siasat Daily: Jawaharlal Nehru Rd, Hyderabad 500 001; tel. (40) 4603666; fax (40) 4603188; e-mail siasat@hd1.vsnl.net.in; internet www.siasat.com; f. 1949; morning; Urdu; Editor Zahid Ali Khan; circ. 45,844.

Vijayawada

Andhra Jyoti: Andhra Jyoti Bldg, POB 712, Vijayawada 520 010; tel. (866) 474532; f. 1960; Telugu; also publ. from Hyderabad, Visakhapatnam and Tirupati; Editor Nanduri Ramamohan Rao; combined circ. 78,600.

Andhra Prabha: 16-1-28, Kolandareddy Rd, Poornanandampet, Vijayawada 520 003; tel. (866) 571351; internet www.andhraprabha.com; f. 1935; Telugu; also publ. from Bangalore, Hyderabad, Chennai and Visakhapatnam; Editor V. V. Deekshitulu; combined circ. 24,500.

New Indian Express: 16-1-28, Kolandareddy Rd, Poornanandampet, Vijayawada 520 003; tel. (866) 571351; English; also publ. from Bangalore, Belgaum, Kochi, Kozhikode, Thiruvananthapuram, Madurai, Chennai, Hyderabad, Visakhapatnam, Coimbatore and Bhubaneswar; Man. Editor Manoj Kumar Sonthalia; Editor (Andhra Pradesh) P. S. Sundaram; combined circ. 251,900.

Assam

Guwahati

Asomiya Pratidin: Maniram Dewan Rd, Guwahati 781 003; tel. (361) 540420; fax (361) 524634; e-mail protidin@gw1.vsnl.net.in; morning; Assamese; also published from Dibrugarh; circ. 103,400.

Assam Tribune: Tribune Bldgs, Maniram Dewan Rd, Chandmari, Guwahati 781 003; tel. (361) 661357; fax (361) 666398; e-mail webmaster@assamtribune.com; internet www.assamtribune.com; f. 1939; English; Man. Dir and Editor P. G. Baruah; circ. 53,500.

Dainik Agradoot: Agradoot Bhavan, Dispur, Guwahati 781 006; tel. (361) 261923; fax (361) 260655; e-mail agradoot@sify.com; internet www.dainikagradoot.com; f. 1995; Assamese; Editor K. S. Deka; circ. 74,500.

Dainik Assam: Tribune Bldgs, Maniram Dewan Rd, Chandmari, Guwahati 781 003; tel. (361) 541360; fax (361) 516356; e-mail webmaster@assamtribune.com; internet www.assamtribune.com; f. 1965; Assamese; Editor Anil Baruah; circ. 16,700.

The North East Daily: Maniram Dewan Rd, Chandmari, Guwahati 781 003; tel. (361) 524594; fax (361) 524634; e-mail protidin@gw1.vsnl.net.in; Assamese; circ. 34,891.

Jorhat

Dainik Janambhumi: Nehru Park Rd, Jorhat 785 001; tel. (376) 3320033; fax (376) 3321713; e-mail clarionl@sancharnet.in; f. 1972; Assamese; also published from Guwahati; Editor Deva Kr. Borah; circ. 26,500.

Bihar

Patna

Aryavarta: Mazharul Haque Path, Patna 800 001; tel. (612) 230716; fax (612) 222350; e-mail aryavart@dte.vsnl.net.in; morning; Hindi; Editor Bhaktishwar Jha.

Hindustan Times: Buddha Marg, Patna 800 001; tel. (612) 223434; fax (612) 226120; f. 1918; morning; English; also publ. from nine regional centres; Editor Vir Sanghvi; combined circ. 878,300.

Indian Nation: Mazharul Haque Path, Patna 800 001; tel. (612) 237780; fax (612) 222350; e-mail aryavart@dte.vsnl.net.in; morning; English; Editor Bhaktishwar Jha.

The Times of India: Times House, Fraser Rd, Patna 800 001; tel. (612) 226301; fax (612) 233525; also publ. from New Delhi, Mumbai, Ahmedabad, Bangalore and Lucknow; Man. Editor Ramesh Chandra; circ. 20,900.

Chhattisgarh
Raipur

Dainik Bhaskar: Press Complex, Rajbandha Mandan, G. E. Rd, Raipur 492 001; tel. (771) 535277; fax (771) 535255; Hindi; morning; Editor R. C. Agrawal; circ. 81,500.

Deshbandhu: Deshbandhu Complex, Ramsagarpara Layout, Raipur 492 001; tel. (771) 534911; fax (771) 534955; Hindi; also publ. from Jabalpur, Satna, Bilaspur and Bhopal; Chief Editor Lalit Surjan; circ. 53,600 (Raipur), 19,300 (Satna), 24,240 (Bhopal), 19,637 (Jabalpur), 27,300 (Bilaspur).

Goa
Panaji

Gomantak: Gomantak Bhavan, St Inez, Panaji, Goa 403 001; tel. (832) 422700; fax (832) 422701; f. 1962; morning; Marathi and English edns; Editor Laxman T. Joshi; circ. 16,700 (Marathi), 5,200 (English).

Navhind Times: Navhind Bhavan, Rua Ismail Gracias, POB 161, Panaji, Goa 403 001; tel. (832) 225685; fax (832) 224258; e-mail navhind@goa1.dot.net.in; internet www.navhindtimes.com; f. 1963; morning; English; Editor Arun Sinha; circ. 32,700.

Gujarat
Ahmedabad

Gujarat Samachar: Gujarat Samachar Bhavan, Khanpur, Ahmedabad 380 001; tel. (79) 5504010; fax (79) 5502000; f. 1930; morning; Gujarati; also publ. from Surat, Rajkot, Vadodara, Mumbai, London and New York; Editor Shantibhai Shah; combined circ. 1,010,000.

Indian Express: 5th Floor, Sanidhya Bldg, Ashram Rd, Ahmedabad 380 009; tel. (79) 6583023; fax (79) 6575826; e-mail praman@express2.indexp.co.in; f. 1968; English; also publ. in 10 other towns; Man. Editor Vivek Goenka; Chief Editor Shekhar Gupta; circ. (Ahmedabad and Vadodara) 28,200.

Lokasatta—Janasatta: Mirzapur Rd, POB 188, Ahmedabad 380 001; tel. (79) 5507307; fax (79) 5507708; f. 1953; morning; Gujarati; also publ. from Rajkot and Vadodara; Man. Editor Vivek Goenka; combined circ. 23,700.

Sandesh: Sandesh Bhavan, Lad Society Rd, Ahmedabad 380 054; tel. (79) 6765480; fax (79) 6754796; e-mail advt@sandesh.com; internet www.sandesh.com; f. 1923; Gujarati; also publ. from Bhavnagar, Vadodara, Rajkot and Surat; Editor Falgunbhai C. Patel; combined circ. 756,696.

The Times of India: 139 Ashram Rd, POB 4046, Ahmedabad 380 009; tel. (79) 6582151; fax (79) 6583758; f. 1968; English; also publ. from Mumbai, Delhi, Bangalore, Patna and Lucknow; Resident Editor Kingshuk Nag; circ. (Ahmedabad) 122,700.

Western Times: 'Western House', Marutnandan Complex, Madalpur, Ahmedabad 380 006; tel. (79) 6576037; fax (79) 6577421; e-mail western@icenet.net.in; f. 1967; English and Gujarati edns; also publ. (in Gujarati) from eight other towns; Man. Editor Nikunj Patel; Editor Ramu Patel; circ. (Ahmedabad) 25,364 (English), 39,359 (Gujarati).

Bhuj

Kutchmitra: Kutchmitra Bhavan, nr Indirabai Park, Bhuj 370 001; tel. (2832) 52090; fax (2832) 50271; e-mail kutchmitra@rediffmail.com; f. 1947; Propr Saurashtra Trust; Editor Kirti Khatri; circ. 39,389.

Rajkot

Jai Hind: Jai Hind Press Bldg, Babubhai Shah Marg, POB 59, Rajkot 360 001; tel. (281) 440511; fax (281) 448677; e-mail jaihind@satyam.net.in; f. 1948; morning and evening (in Rajkot as *Sanj Samachar*); Gujarati; also publ. from Ahmedabad; Editor Y. N. Shah; combined circ. 101,400.

Phulchhab: Phulchhab Bhavan, Phulchhab Chowk, Rajkot 360 001; tel. (281) 444611; fax (281) 448751; f. 1950; morning; Gujarati; Propr Saurashtra Trust; Editor Dinesh Raja; circ. 84,500.

Surat

Gujaratmitra and Gujaratdarpan: Gujaratmitra Bhavan, nr Old Civil Hospital, Sonifalia, Surat 395 003; tel. (261) 3478703; fax (261) 3478700; e-mail gujaratmitra@satyam.net.in; f. 1863; morning; Gujarati; Editor B. P. Reshamwala; circ. 90,023.

Jammu and Kashmir
Jammu

Himalayan Mail: Srinagar; f. 1996; English.

Kashmir Times: Residency Rd, Jammu 180 001; tel. (191) 543676; fax (191) 542028; e-mail kashmirtimes@hotmail.com; internet www.kashmirtimes.com; f. 1955; morning; English and Hindi; Editor Prabodh Jamwal.

Srinagar

Srinagar Times: Badshah Bridge, Srinagar; f. 1969; Urdu; Editor S. F. Mohammed; circ. 14,000.

Jharkhand
Ranchi

Aj: Main Rd, Ranchi 834 001; tel. (651) 311416; fax (651) 306224; Hindi; morning; also publ. from eight other cities; Editor Shardul V. Gupta; circ. 59,000.

Hindustan: Circular Court, Circular Rd, Ranchi 834 001; tel. (651) 205811; Hindi; morning; also publ. from Patna, Delhi, Bhagalpur, Lucknow and Muzaffarpur; Editor Chandra Prakash; combined circ. 659,100.

Ranchi Express: 55 Baralal St, Ranchi 834 001; tel. (651) 206320; fax (651) 203466; f. 1963; Hindi; morning; Editor Ajay Maroo; circ. 75,200.

Karnataka
Bangalore

Deccan Herald: 75 Mahatma Gandhi Rd, Bangalore 560 001; tel. (80) 5588999; fax (80) 5586443; e-mail ads@deccanherald.co.in; internet www.deccanherald.com; f. 1948; morning; English; also publ. from Hubli-Dharwar and Gulbarga; Editor-in-Chief K. N. Shanth Kumar; combined circ. 159,500.

Kannada Prabha: Express Bldgs, 1 Queen's Rd, Bangalore 560 001; tel. (80) 2866893; fax (80) 2866617; e-mail bexpress@bgl.vsnl.net.in; internet www.kannadaprabha.com; f. 1967; morning; Kannada; also publ. from Belgaum and Hyderabad; Editor Y. N. Krishnamurthy; circ. 70,200.

New Indian Express: 1 Queen's Rd, Bangalore 560 001; tel. (80) 2256893; fax (80) 2256617; f. 1965; English; also publ. from Kochi, Hyderabad, Chennai, Madurai, Vijayawada and Vizianagaram; Man. Editor Manoj Kumar Sonthalia; combined circ. 251,900.

Prajavani: 75 Mahatma Gandhi Rd, Bangalore 560 001; tel. (80) 5588999; fax (80) 5586443; e-mail ads@deccanherald.co.in; internet www.prajavani.net; f. 1948; morning; Kannada; also publ. from Hubli-Dharwar and Gulbarga; Editor-in-Chief K. N. Shanth Kumar; combined circ. 286,000.

Hubli-Dharwar

Samyukta Karnataka: Koppikar Rd, Hubli 580 020; tel. (836) 364303; fax (836) 362760; e-mail info@samyuktakarnataka.com; internet www.samyuktakarnataka.com; f. 1933; Kannada; also publ. from Bangalore and Gulburga; Man. Editor K. Shama Rao; combined circ. 121,100.

Manipal

Udayavani: Udayavani Bldg, Press Corner, Manipal 576 119; tel. (8252) 70845; fax (8252) 70563; f. 1970; Kannada; Editor T. Satish U. Pai; circ. 153,000.

Kerala
Kottayam

Deepika: POB 7, Kottayam 686 001; tel. (481) 566706; fax (481) 567947; e-mail deepika@md2.vsnl.net.in; internet www.deepika.com; f. 1887; Malayalam; independent; also publ. from Kannur, Kochi, Thiruvananthapuram and Thrissur; Man. Dir Jose T. Pattara; combined circ. 180,000.

Malayala Manorama: K. K. Rd, POB 26, Kottayam 686 001; tel. (481) 563646; fax (481) 562479; e-mail editor@malayalamanorama.com; internet www.malayalamanorama.com; f. 1890; also publ. from Kozhikode, Thiruvananthapuram, Palakkad, Kannur, Kollam, Thrissur and Kochi; morning; Malayalam; Man. Dir and Editor Mammen Mathew; Chief Editor K. M. Mathew; combined circ. 1,243,400.

Kozhikode

Deshabhimani: 11/127 Convent Rd, Kozhikode 673 032; tel. (495) 77286; f. 1946; morning; Malayalam; publ. by the CPI—M; also publ. from Kochi and Thiruvananthapuram; Chief Editor S. Ramachandran Pillai; combined circ. 171,000.

Mathrubhumi: Mathrubhumi Bldgs, K. P. Kesava Menon Rd, POB 46, Kozhikode 673 001; tel. (495) 366655; fax (495) 366656; e-mail mathrelt@md2.vsnl.net.in; f. 1923; Malayalam; Editor R. Gopalakrishnan; also publ. from Thiruvananthapuram, Kannur, Thrissur, Kollam, Malappuram, Kottayam and Kochi; combined circ. 891,000.

Thiruvananthapuram

Kerala Kaumudi: POB 77, Pettah, Thiruvananthapuram 695 024; tel. (471) 461050; fax (471) 461985; e-mail sreeni@giasmd01.vsnl .net.in; internet www.keralakaumudi.com; f. 1911; Malayalam; also publ. from Kollam, Alappuzha, Kochi, Kannur and Kozhikode; Editor-in-Chief M. S. MANI; combined circ. 140,100.

Thrissur

Express: POB 15, Trichur 680 001; tel. 25800; f. 1944; Malayalam; Editor K. BALAKRISHNAN; circ. 68,200.

Madhya Pradesh

Bhopal

Dainik Bhaskar: 6 Dwarka Sadan, Habibganj Rd, Bhopal 462 011; tel. (755) 551601; f. 1958; morning; Hindi; also publ. from Indore, Raipur, Jhansi, Bhopal, Bilaspur and Gwalior; Chief Editor R. C. AGARWAL; circ. 139,200 (Bhopal), 55,800 (Gwalior), 26,300 (Bilaspur), 174,500 (Indore), 81,500 (Raipur).

Indore

Naidunia: 60/1 Babu Labhchand Chhajlani Marg, Indore 452 009; tel. (731) 763111; fax (731) 763120; e-mail naidunia@edi.com; internet www.naidunia.com; f. 1947; morning; Hindi; Chief Editor ABHAY CHHAJLANI; circ. 133,600.

Maharashtra

Kolhapur

Pudhari: 2318, 'C' Ward, Kolhapur 416 002; tel. (231) 22251; fax (231) 22256; f. 1974; Marathi; Editor P. G. JADHAV; circ. 192,500.

Mumbai

Afternoon Despatch and Courier: 6 Nanabhai Lane, Fort, Mumbai 400 001; tel. (22) 2871616; fax (22) 2870371; e-mail aftnet@ bom2.vsnl.net.in; internet www.afternoondc.com; evening; English; Editor BEHRAM CONTRACTOR; circ. 65,800.

The Daily: Asia Publishing House, Mody Bay Estate, Calicut St, Mumbai 400 038; tel. (22) 2653104; fax (22) 2619773; f. 1981; Editor RAJIV BAJAJ; circ. 38,700.

The Economic Times: Times of India Bldg, Dr Dadabhai Naoroji Rd, Mumbai 400 001; tel. (22) 2620271; fax (22) 2620144; e-mail etbom@timesgroup.com; internet www.economictimes.com; f. 1961; also publ. from New Delhi, Kolkata, Ahmedabad, Hyderabad, Chennai and Bangalore; English; Exec. Editor JAIDEEP BOSE; combined circ. 432,300, circ. (Mumbai) 146,100.

Financial Express: Express Towers, Nariman Point, Mumbai 400 021; tel. (22) 2022627; fax (22) 2886402; e-mail iemumbai@express .indexp.co.in; internet www.financialexpress.com; f. 1961; morning; English; also publ. from New Delhi, Bangalore, Kolkata, Coimbatore, Kochi, Ahmedabad (Gujarati) and Chennai; Man. Editor VIVEK GOENKA; Editor SANJAYA BARU; combined circ. (English) 30,800.

The Free Press Journal: Free Press House, 215 Free Press Journal Rd, Nariman Point, Mumbai 400 021; tel. (22) 2874566; fax (22) 2874688; e-mail freepress@bom2.vsnl.net.in; f. 1930; English; also publ. from Indore; Man. Editor G. L. LAKHOTIA; combined circ. 87,000.

Indian Express: Express Towers, Nariman Point, Mumbai 400 021; tel. (22) 2022627; fax (22) 2022139; f. 1940; English; also publ. from Pune and Nagpur; Man. Editor VIVEK GOENKA; Chief Editor SHEKHAR GUPTA; combined circ. 191,900.

Inquilab: 156 D. J. Dadajee Rd, Tardeo, Mumbai 400 034; tel. (22) 4942586; fax (22) 4936571; e-mail azizk@mid-day.mailserve.net; internet www.inquilab.com; f. 1938; morning; Urdu; Editor FUZAIL JAFFEREY; circ. 40,100.

Janmabhoomi: Janmabhoomi Bhavan, Janmabhoomi Marg, Fort, POB 62, Mumbai 400 001; tel. (22) 2870831; fax (22) 2874097; e-mail bhoomi@bom3.vsnl.net.in; f. 1934; evening; Gujarati; Propr Saurashtra Trust; Editor KUNDAN VYAS; circ. 60,700.

Lokasatta: Express Towers, Nariman Point, Mumbai 400 021; tel. (22) 2022627; fax (22) 2022139; internet www.loksatta.com; f. 1948; morning (incl. Sunday); Marathi; also publ. from Pune, Nagpur and Ahmednagar; Editor Dr AROON TIKEKAR; combined circ. 369,400.

Maharashtra Times: Dr Dadabhai Naoroji Rd, POB 213, Mumbai 400 001; tel. (22) 2620271; fax (22) 2620144; f. 1962; Marathi; Editor KUMAR KETKAR; circ. 189,300.

Mid-Day: 64 Sitaram Mills Compound, N. M. Joshi Marg, Lower Parel, Mumbai 400 011; tel. (22) 3054545; fax (22) 3054861; e-mail mid-day@giasbm01.vsnl.net.in; internet www.mid-day.com; f. 1979; daily and Sunday; English; Editor AYAZ MEMON; circ. 128,600.

Mumbai Samachar: Red House, Syed Abdulla Brelvi Rd, Fort, Mumbai 400 001; tel. (22) 2045531; fax (22) 2046642; f. 1822; morning and Sunday; Gujarati; political, social and commercial; Editor PINKY DALAL; circ. 114,700.

Navakal: 13 Shenviwadi, Khadilkar Rd, Girgaun, Mumbai 400 004; tel. (22) 353585; f. 1923; Marathi; Editor N. Y. KHADILKAR; circ. 213,500.

Navbharat Times: Dr Dadabhai Naoroji Rd, Mumbai 400 001; tel. (22) 2620382; f. 1950; Hindi; also publ. from New Delhi, Jaipur, Patna and Lucknow; circ. (Mumbai) 173,400.

Navshakti: Free Press House, 215 Nariman Point, Mumbai 400 021; tel. (22) 2874566; f. 1932; Marathi; Editor D. B. JOSHI; circ. 65,000.

Sakal: Sakal Bhavan, Plot No. 42-B, Sector No. 11, CBD Belapur, Navi Mumbai 400 614; tel. (22) 7574327; fax (22) 7574280; e-mail sakal@vsnl.in; f. 1970; daily; Marathi; also publ. from Pune, Aurangabad, Nasik, Kolhapur and Solapur; Editor ANIL MOHAN TAKALKAR; combined circ. 604,103.

The Times of India: The Times of India Bldg, Dr Dadabhai Naoroji Rd, Mumbai 400 001; tel. (22) 2620271; fax (22) 2620144; e-mail toieditorial@timesgroup.com; internet www.timesofindia.com; f. 1838; morning; English; also publ. from 10 regional centres; Exec. Man. Editor DILEEP PADGAONKAR; circ. (Mumbai and Pune) 648,800, combined circ. 1,939,000.

Nagpur

Hitavada: Wardha Rd, Nagpur 440 012; tel. (712) 523155; fax (712) 535093; e-mail hitavada@nagpur.dot.net.in; f. 1911; morning; English; also publ. from Raipur and Jabalpur; Man. Editor BANWARILAL PUROHIT; Editor V. PHANSHIKAR; circ. 55,700.

Lokmat: Lokmat Bhavan, Wardha Rd, Nagpur 440 012; tel. (712) 523527; fax (712) 526923; also publ. from Jalgaon, Akola, Pune, Nasik and Aurangabad; Marathi; **Lokmat Samachar** (Hindi) publ. from Nagpur, Akola and Aurangabad; **Lokmat Times** (English) publ. from Nagpur and Aurangabad; Editor VIJAY DARDA; combined circ. (Marathi) 454,900, (Hindi) 61,500.

Nava Bharat: Nava Bharat Bhavan, Cotton Market, Nagpur 440 018; tel. (712) 726677; f. 1938; morning; Hindi; also publ. from 10 other cities; Editor-in-Chief R. G. MAHESWARI; combined circ. 631,100.

Tarun Bharat: 28 Farmland, Ramdaspeth, Nagpur 440 010; tel. (712) 525052; e-mail ibharat@nagpur.dot.net.in; f. 1941; Marathi; independent; also publ. from Belgaum; Gen. Man. RAMDAS MULEY; Editor SUDHIR PATHAK; circ. (Nagpur) 57,100, combined circ. 164,000.

Pune

Kesari: 568 Narayan Peth, Pune 411 030; tel. (20) 4459250; fax (20) 4451677; f. 1881; Marathi; also publ. from Solapur, Kolhapur, Chiplun, Ahmednagar and Sangli; Editor ARVIND VYANKATESH GOKHALE; circ. (Pune) 47,500.

Sakal: 595 Budhwar Peth, Pune 411 002; tel. (20) 4455500; fax (20) 4450583; e-mail sakal@giaspn01.vsnl.net.in; www.esakal.com; f. 1932; daily; Marathi; also publ. from Mumbai, Nashik, Aurangabad and Kolhapur; Editor ANANT DIXIT; Man. Dir and Man. Editor PRATAP PAWAR; combined circ. 650,000.

Orissa

Bhubaneswar

Dharitri: B-26, Industrial Estate, Bhubaneswar 751 010; tel. (674) 580101; fax (674) 580795; e-mail dharitri@mail.com; internet www.dharitri.com; evening and morning; Oriya; Editor TATHAGATA SATPATHY; circ. 160,500.

Pragativadi: 178-B, Mancheswar Industrial Estate, Bhubaneswar 751 010; tel. (674) 580298; fax (674) 582636; e-mail pragativadi@ yahoo.com; Exec. Editor SAMAHIT BAL; circ. 119,000.

Cuttack

Prajatantra: Prajatantra Bldgs, Behari Baug, Cuttack 753 002; tel. (671) 603071; fax (671) 603063; f. 1947; Oriya; Editor BHARTRUHARI MAHTAB; circ. 119,300.

Samaj: Cuttack; tel. (671) 20994; fax (671) 601044; f. 1919; Oriya; also publ. from Sambalpur; circ. 149,400.

Punjab

Chandigarh

The Tribune: Sector 29C, Chandigarh 160 020; tel. (172) 655065; fax (172) 655054; e-mail tribunet@ch1.dot.net.in; internet www .tribuneindia.com; f. 1881 (English edn), f. 1978 (Hindi and Punjabi edns); Editor (all edns) HARI JAISINGH; Editor (Hindi edn) VIJAY SAIGHAL; Editor (Punjabi edn) G. S. BHULLAR; circ. 231,700 (English), 52,600 (Hindi), 74,000 (Punjabi).

Jalandhar

Ajit: Ajit Bhavan, Nehru Garden Rd, Jalandhar 144 001; tel. 55960; f. 1955; Punjabi; Man. Editor S. BARJINDER SINGH; circ. 227,600.

Hind Samachar: Civil Lines, Jalandhar 144 001; tel. (181) 280104; fax (181) 280113; f. 1948; morning; Urdu; also publ. from Ambala Cantt; Editor-in-Chief Vijay Kumar Chopra; Jt Editor Avinash Chopra; combined circ. 44,144.

Jag Bani: Civil Lines, Jalandhar 144 001; tel. (181) 280104; fax (181) 280113; f. 1978; morning; Punjabi; Editor-in-Chief Vijay Kumar Chopra; Jt Editor Avinash Chopra; circ. 199,021.

Punjab Kesari: Civil Lines, Jalandhar 144 001; tel. (181) 280104; fax (181) 280113; f. 1965; morning; Hindi; also publ. from Delhi and Ambala; Editor-in-Chief Vijay Kumar Chopra; Jt Editor Avinash Chopra; combined circ. 869,220.

Rajasthan

Jaipur

Rajasthan Patrika: Kesargarh, Jawahar Lal Nehru Marg, Jaipur 302 004; tel. (141) 561582; fax (141) 566011; e-mail info@rajasthan_patrika.com; internet www.rajasthan_patrika.com; f. 1956; Hindi edn also publ. from eight other towns; Editor Moti Chand Kochar; combined circ. (Hindi) 597,100.

Rashtradoot: M.I. Rd, POB 30, Jaipur 302 001; tel. (141) 372634; fax (141) 373513; f. 1951; Hindi; also publ. from Kota, Udaipur, Ajmer and Bikaner; CEO Somesh Sharma; Chief Editor Rajesh Sharma; circ. 368,482 (Jaipur), 76,763 (Kota), 45,250 (Bikaner), 38,023 (Udaipur), 27,514 (Ajmer).

Tamil Nadu

Chennai (Madras)

Daily Thanthi: 46 E.V.K. Sampath Rd, POB 467, Chennai 600 007; tel. (44) 5387731; fax (44) 5380069; f. 1949; Tamil; also publ. from Bangalore, Coimbatore, Cuddalore, Erode, Madurai, Nagercoil, Salem, Tiruchi, Tirunelveli, Pondicherry and Vellore; Gen. Man. D. Rajiah; Editor R. Thiruvadi; combined circ. 601,500.

Dinakaran: 106/107 Kutchery Rd, Mylapore, POB 358, Chennai 600 004; tel. (44) 4941006; fax (44) 4951008; e-mail dinakaran@dinakaran.com; internet www.dinakaran.com; f. 1977; Tamil; also publ. from Madurai, Tiruchirapalli, Vellore, Tirunelveli, Salem and Coimbatore; Man. Dir K. Kumaran; Editor D. Paulraj; combined circ. 351,872.

Dinamalar: 21, Casa Major Rd, Egmore, Chennai 600 008; tel. (44) 8267106; e-mail malar@md3.vsnl.net.in; internet www.dinamalar.com; f. 1951; Tamil; also publ. from nine other towns; Editor R. Krishnamoorthy; combined circ. 491,100.

Dinamani: Express Estates, Mount Rd, Chennai 600 002; tel. (44) 8520751; fax (44) 8524500; e-mail express@giasmd01.vsnl.net.in; internet www.dinamani.com; f. 1934; morning; Tamil; also publ. from Madurai, Coimbatore and Bangalore; Editor T. Sambandam; combined circ. 158,300.

Financial Express: Vasanthi Medical Center, 30/20 Pycrofts Garden Rd, Chennai 600 006; tel. (44) 8231112; fax (44) 8231489; internet www.financialexpress.com; f. 1961; morning; English; also publ. from Mumbai, Ahmedabad (in Gujarati), Bangalore, Kochi, Kolkata and New Delhi; Man. Editor Vivek Goenka; combined circ. 32,594.

The Hindu: Kasturi Bldgs, 859/860 Anna Salai, Chennai 600 002; tel. (44) 8413344; fax (44) 8415325; e-mail wsvcs@thehindu.co.in; internet www.hinduonnet.com; f. 1878; morning; English; independent; also publ. from 10 other regional centres; Publr S. Rangarajan; Editor N. Ravi; combined circ. 904,700.

The Hindu Business Line: Kasturi Bldgs, 859/860 Anna Salai, Chennai 600 002; tel. (44) 8589060; fax (44) 8545703; internet www.hindubusinessline.com; f. 1994; morning; English; also publ. from 10 other regional centres; Publr S. Rangarajan; Editor N. Ram; combined circ. 39,700.

Murasoli: 93 Kodambakkam High Rd, Chennai 600 034; tel. (44) 470044; f. 1960; organ of the DMK; Tamil; Editor S. Selvam; circ. 54,000.

New Indian Express: Express Estates, Anna Salai, Chennai 600 002; tel. (44) 8461818; fax (44) 8461830; e-mail newexpress@vsnl.com; internet www.newindpress.com; f. 1932 as Indian Express; morning; English; also publ. from 11 other cities; Man. Editor Manoj Kumar Sonthalia; combined circ. 251,900.

Tripura

Agartala

Dainik Sambad: 11 Jagannath Bari Rd, POB 2, Agartala 799 001; tel. (381) 226676; fax (381) 224845; f. 1966; Bengali; morning; Editor Bhupendra Chandra Datta Bhaumik; circ. 42,400.

Uttaranchal

Dehradun

Amar Ujala: Shed 2, Patel Nagar Industrial Estate, Dehradun 248 003; tel. (135) 723870; fax (135) 721776; Hindi; morning; also publ. from 10 other cities; Editor Ajay K. Agrawal; combined circ. 637,500.

Uttar Pradesh

Agra

Amar Ujala: Sikandra Rd, Agra 282 007; tel. (562) 321600; fax (562) 322181; e-mail amarujal@nde.vsnl.net.in; internet www.amarujala.org; f. 1948; Hindi; also publ. from Bareilly, Allahabad, Jhansi, Kanpur, Moradabad, Chandigarh and Meerut; Editor Ajay K. Agarwal; circ. 148,800 (Agra), 56,400 (Bareilly), 48,100 (Moradabad), 107,300 (Meerut), 95,700 (Kanpur), 66,600 (Allahabad and Varanasi), 12,600 (Jhansi).

Allahabad

Amrita Prabhat: 10 Edmonstone Rd, Allahabad 211 001; tel. (532) 600654; f. 1977; Hindi; Editor Tamal Kanti Ghosh; circ. 44,000.

Northern India Patrika: 10 Edmonstone Rd, Allahabad 211 001; tel. (532) 600654; fax (532) 605394; f. 1959; English; Editor V. S. Datta; circ. 46,000.

Kanpur

Dainik Jagran: Jagran Bldg, 2 Sarvodaya Nagar, Kanpur 208 005; tel. (512) 216161; fax (512) 216972; e-mail jpl@jagran.com; internet www.jagran.com; f. 1942; Hindi; also publ. from 15 other cities; Editor Narendra Mohan; combined circ. 1,378,386.

Vyapar Sandesh: 26/104 Birhana Rd, Kanpur 208 001; tel. (512) 352066; f. 1958; Hindi; commercial news and economic trends; Editor Hari Shankar Sharma; circ. 17,000.

Lucknow

National Herald: Lucknow; f. 1938 Lucknow, 1968 Delhi; English; Editor-in-Chief D. V. Venkitachalam.

The Pioneer: 20 Vidhan Sabha Marg, Lucknow 226 001; tel. (522) 2812820; fax (522) 2812814; f. 1865; English; also publ. from New Delhi; Editor Chandan Mitra; combined circ. 136,000.

Swatantra Bharat: 1st Floor, Suraj Deep Complex, 1 Jopling Rd, Lucknow 226 001; tel. (522) 209301; fax (522) 209308; e-mail sbharat@lw1.vsnl.net.in; f. 1947; Hindi; also publ. from Kanpur; Editor K. K. Srivastava; circ. 66,058 (Lucknow), 48,511 (Kanpur).

Varanasi

Aj: Aj Bhavan, Sant Kabir Rd, Kabirchaura, Varanasi 221 001; tel. (542) 393981; fax (542) 393989; f. 1920; Hindi; also publ. from Gorakhpur, Patna, Allahabad, Ranchi, Agra, Bareilly, Lucknow, Jamshedpur, Dhanbad and Kanpur; Editor Shardul Vikram Gupta; circ. 64,000 (Agra), 57,800 (Allahabad), 54,300 (Gorakhpur), 230,000 (Kanpur), 29,300 (Jamshedpur), 78,900 (Lucknow), 190,900 (Patna), 58,900 (Ranchi), 230,000 (Varanasi).

West Bengal

Kolkata (Calcutta)

Aajkaal: 96 Raja Rammohan Sarani, Kolkata 700 009; tel. (33) 3509803; fax (33) 3500877; e-mail aajkaal@cal.vsnl.net.in; f. 1981; morning; Bengali; Chief Editor Pratap K. Roy; circ. 154,600.

Ananda Bazar Patrika: 6 Prafulla Sarkar St, Kolkata 700 001; tel. (33) 2374880; fax (33) 2253241; internet www.anandabazar.com; f. 1922; morning; Bengali; also publ. from Siliguri; Editor Aveek Sarkar; circ. 888,900.

Bartaman: 76A Acharya J.C. Bose Rd, Kolkata 700 014; tel. (33) 2443907; fax (33) 2441215; f. 1984; also publ. from Siliguri; Editor Barun Sengupta; circ. 473,200.

Business Standard: Church Lane, Kolkata 700 001; tel. (33) 278000; fax (33) 2253241; f. 1975; morning; also publ. from New Delhi, Ahmedabad, Hyderabad, Bangalore, Chennai and Mumbai; English; Editor T. N. Ninan; combined circ. 63,800.

The Economic Times: 105/7A, S. N. Banerjee Rd, Kolkata 700 014; tel. (33) 294232; fax (33) 292400; English; also publ. from Ahmedabad, Delhi, Bangalore, Chennai, Hyderabad and Mumbai; circ. (Kolkata) 51,700.

Financial Express: 83 B. K. Pal Ave, Kolkata 700 005; morning; English; also publ. from Mumbai, Ahmedabad, Bangalore, Coimbatore, Kochi, Chennai and New Delhi; Man. Editor Vivek Goenka; combined circ. 30,800.

Ganashakti: 74A A. J. C. Bose Rd, Kolkata 700 016; tel. (33) 2458950; fax (33) 2448090; e-mail mail@ganashakti.co.in; internet www.ganashakti.com; f. 1967; morning; Bengali; also publ. from Siliguri; Editor Dipen Ghosh; circ. 114,300.

Himalchuli: 7 Old Court House St, Kolkata 700 001; tel. (33) 207618; fax (33) 206663; f. 1982; Nepali; Editor S. C. Talukdar; circ. 42,494.

Sambad Pratidin: 20 Prafulla Sarkar St, Kolkata 700 072; tel. (33) 2253707; fax (33) 2252536; e-mail pratidin@cal2.vsnl.net.in;

internet www.sangbadpratidin.com; morning; Bengali; Editor SWAPAN SADHAN BASU; circ. 273,700.

Sandhya Aajkaal: 96 Raja Rammohan Sarani, Kolkata 700 009; tel. (33) 3509803; fax (33) 3500877; evening; Bengali; Chief Editor PRATAP K. ROY; circ. 25,300.

Sanmarg: 160C Chittaranjan Ave, Kolkata 700 007; tel. (33) 2414800; fax (33) 2415087; e-mail sanmarg@vsnl.com; f. 1948; Hindi; Editor RAMAWATAR GUPTA; circ. 106,100.

The Statesman: Statesman House, 4 Chowringhee Sq., Kolkata 700 001; tel. (33) 2257070; fax (33) 2250118; f. 1875; morning; English; independent; also publ. from New Delhi and Siliguri; Editor-in-Chief C. R. IRANI; combined circ. 174,000.

The Telegraph: 6 Prafulla Sarkar St, Kolkata 700 001; tel. (33) 2374880; fax (33) 2253240; e-mail thetelegraphindia@newscom.com; f. 1982; English; also publ. from Guwahati; Editor AVEEK SARKAR; circ. 288,400.

Uttar Banga Sambad: 7 Old Court House St, Kolkata 700 001; tel. (33) 2207618; fax (33) 2206663; f. 1980; Bengali; Editor S. C. TALUKDAR; circ. 107,000.

Vishwamitra: 74 Lenin Sarani, Kolkata 700 013; tel. (33) 2441139; fax (33) 2446393; e-mail vismtra@cal2.vsnl.net.in; f. 1915; morning; Hindi; commercial; Editor PRAKASH CHANDRA AGRAWALLA; combined circ. 91,006.

SELECTED PERIODICALS

Delhi and New Delhi

Alive: Delhi Press Bldg, E-3, Jhandewala Estate, Rani Jhansi Rd, New Delhi 110 055; tel. (11) 3529557; fax (11) 3625020; e-mail advertising@delhipressgroup.com; f. 1940; monthly; English; political and cultural; Editor VISHWA NATH; circ. 4,781.

Bal Bharati: Patiala House, Publications Division, Ministry of Information and Broadcasting, Delhi; tel. (11) 387038; f. 1948; monthly; Hindi; for children; Editor SHIV KUMAR; circ. 30,000.

Biswin Sadi: B-1, Nizamuddin West, New Delhi 110 013; tel. (11) 4626556; f. 1937; monthly; Urdu; Editor Z. REHMAN NAYYAR; circ. 32,000.

Business Today: F-26 Connaught Place, New Delhi 110 001; tel. (11) 3315801; fax (11) 3318385; e-mail btoday@giasdl01.vsnl.net.in; internet www.business-today.com; fortnightly; English; Editor SANJAY NARAYAN; circ. 110,100.

Careers Digest: 21 Shankar Market, Delhi 110 001; tel. (11) 44726; f. 1963; monthly; English; Editor O. P. VARMA; circ. 35,000.

Catholic India: CBCI Centre, 1 Ashok Place, Goldakkhana, New Delhi 110 001; tel. (11) 3344470; fax (11) 3364615; e-mail cbci@vsnl.com; internet www.cbcisite.com; quarterly.

Champak: Delhi Press Bldg, E-3, Jhandewala Estate, Rani Jhansi Rd, New Delhi 110 055; tel. (11) 3529557; fax (11) 3625020; f. 1969; fortnightly (Hindi, English, Gujarati and Marathi edns); monthly (Kannada edn); children; Editor VISHWA NATH; combined circ. 166,338.

Children's World: Nehru House, 4 Bahadur Shah Zafar Marg, New Delhi 110 002; tel. (11) 3316970; fax (11) 3721090; e-mail cbtnd@vsnl.com; internet www.childrensbooktrust.com; f. 1968; monthly; English; Editor NAVIN MENON; circ. 25,000.

Competition Refresher: 2767, Bright House, Daryaganj, New Delhi 110 002; tel. (11) 3282226; fax (11) 3269227; e-mail psbright@ndf.vsnl.net.in; internet www.brightcareers.com; f. 1984; monthly; English; Chief Editor, Publr and Man. Dir PRITAM SINGH BRIGHT; circ. 175,000.

Competition Success Review: 604 Prabhat Kiran Bldg, Rajendra Place, Delhi 110 008; tel. (11) 5712898; fax (11) 5754647; monthly; English; f. 1964; Editor S. K. SACHDEVA; circ. 262,000.

Computers Today: Marina Arcade, G-59 Connaught Circus, New Delhi 110 001; tel. (11) 3736233; fax (11) 3725506; e-mail ctoday@india-today.com; f. 1984; Editor J. SRIHARI RAJU; circ. 46,300.

Cricket Samrat: L–1, Kanchan House, Najafgarh Rd, Commercial Complex, nr Milan Cinema, New Delhi 110 015; tel. (11) 5191175; fax (11) 5469581; f. 1978; monthly; Hindi; Editor ANAND DEWAN; circ. 64,500.

Employment News: Government of India, East Block IV, Level 5, R. K. Puram, New Delhi 110 066; tel. (11) 6193316; fax (11) 6193012; e-mail empnews@bol.net.in; f. 1976; weekly; Hindi, Urdu and English edns; Gen. Man. and Chief Editor SUBHASH SETIA; Editor RANJANA DEV SARMAH; combined circ. 550,000.

Filmi Duniya: 16 Darya Ganj, New Delhi 110 002; tel. (11) 3278087; fax (11) 3279341; f. 1958; monthly; Hindi; Chief Editor NARENDRA KUMAR; circ. 132,100.

Filmi Kaliyan: 4675-B/21 Ansari Rd, New Delhi 110 002; tel. (11) 3272080; f. 1969; monthly; Hindi; cinema; Editor-in-Chief V. S. DEWAN; circ. 82,400.

Global Travel Express: 26F Rajiv Gandhi Chowk (Connaught Place), New Delhi 110 001; tel. (11) 3312329; fax (11) 462136; e-mail nri@ndf.vsnl.net.in; f. 1993; monthly; English; travel and tourism; Chief Editor HARBHAJAN SINGH; Editor GURINDER SINGH; circ. 28,499.

Grih Shobha: Delhi Press Bldg, E-3 Jhandewala Estate, Rani Jhansi Rd, New Delhi 110 055; tel. (11) 3529557; fax (11) 3625020; e-mail grihshobha@delhipressgroup.com; f. 1979; monthly; Tamil, Kannada, Marathi, Hindi and Gujarati edns; women's interests; Editor VISHWA NATH; circ. 90,960 (Kannada), 62,244 (Gujarati), 135,651 (Marathi), 328,224 (Hindi).

India Perspectives: Room 149B 'A' Wing, Shastri Bhavan, New Delhi 110 001; tel. (11) 3389471; f. 1988; Editor BHARAT BHUSHAN.

India Today: F 14/15, Connaught Place, New Delhi 110 001; tel. (11) 3315801; fax (11) 3316180; e-mail letters.editor@intoday.com; internet www.india-today.com; f. 1975; English, Tamil, Telugu, Malayalam and Hindi; weekly; Editor PRABHU CHAWLA; Editor-in-Chief AROON PURIE; circ. 432,100 (English), 336,900 (Hindi), 52,000 (Tamil), 48,200 (Malayalam), 58,300 (Telugu).

Indian Observer: 26F Rajiv Gandhi Chowk (Connaught Place), New Delhi 110 001; tel. (11) 3312329; fax (11) 4621636; e-mail nri@ndf.vsnl.net.in; f. 1964; fortnightly; English; Editor HARBHAJAN SINGH; circ. 31,684.

Indian Railways: 411 Rail Bhavan, Raisina Rd, New Delhi 110 001; tel. (11) 3383540; fax (11) 3384481; f. 1956; monthly; English; publ. by the Ministry of Railways (Railway Board); Editor S. K. SINGH; circ. 12,000.

Journal of Industry and Trade: Ministry of Commerce, Delhi 110 011; tel. (11) 3016664; f. 1952; monthly; English; Man. Dir A. C. BANERJEE; circ. 2,000.

Junior Science Refresher: 2769, Bright House, Daryaganj, New Delhi 110 002; tel. (11) 3282226; fax (11) 3269227; e-mail psbright@ndf.vsnl.net.in; internet www.brightcareers.com; f. 1987; monthly; English; Chief Editor, Publr and Man. Dir PRITAM SINGH BRIGHT; circ. 118,000.

Kadambini: Hindustan Times House, Kasturba Gandhi Marg, New Delhi 110 001; tel. (11) 3704581; fax (11) 3704600; e-mail rajendrawasthy@hindustantimes.com; f. 1960; monthly; Hindi; Editor RAJENDRA AWASTHY; circ. 90,000.

Krishak Samachar: Bharat Krishak Samaj, Dr Panjabrao Deshmukh Krishak Bhavan, A-1 Nizamuddin West, New Delhi 110 013; tel. (11) 4619508; e-mail ffi@mantraonline.com; f. 1957; monthly; English and Hindi edns; agriculture; Editor Dr. KRISHAN BIR CHAUDHARY; circ. (English) 6,000, (Hindi) 17,000.

Kurukshetra: Ministry of Rural Development, Room No. 655/661, 'A' Wing, Nirman Bhavan, New Delhi 110 011; tel. (11) 3015014; fax (11) 3386879; monthly; English; rural development; Editor P. V. RAO; circ. 14,000.

Mainstream: 145/1D Shahpur Jat, 1st Floor, nr Asiad Village, New Delhi 110 049; tel. (11) 6497188; fax (11) 6569352; English; weekly; politics and current affairs; Editor SUMIT CHAKRAVARTTY.

Mayapuri: A-5, Mayapuri Phase 1, New Delhi 110 064; tel. (11) 5138596; fax (11) 5133120; e-mail mayapuri@hotmail.com; f. 1974; weekly; Hindi; cinema; Editor A. P. BAJAJ; circ. 146,144.

Mukta: Delhi Press Bldg, E-3 Jhandewala Estate, Rani Jhansi Rd, New Delhi 110 055; tel. (11) 3529557; fax (11) 3625020; e-mail advertising@delhipressgroup.com; f. 1979; monthly; Hindi, Gujarati and Marathi edns; youth; Editor VISHWA NATH; circ. 14,910.

Nandan: Hindustan Times House, Kasturba Gandhi Marg, New Delhi 110 001; tel. (11) 3704562; fax (11) 3704600; e-mail jbharti@hindustantimes.com; f. 1963 monthly; Hindi; Editor JAI PRAKASH BHARTI; circ. 87,700.

New Age: 15 Kotla Rd, Delhi 110 055; tel. (11) 3230762; fax (11) 3235543; e-mail cpindia@del2.vsnl.net.in; f. 1953; main organ of the Communist Party of India; weekly; English; Editor SHAMEEM FAIZEE; circ. 215,000.

Organiser: Sanskriti Bhavan, D. B. Gupta Rd, Jhandewalan, New Delhi 110 055; tel. (11) 3626977; fax (11) 3516635; e-mail chari_s@vsnl.com; internet www.organiser.org; f. 1947; weekly; English; Editor SESHADRI CHARI; circ. 44,100.

Outlook: AB-10 Safdarjung Enclave, New Delhi 110 029; tel. (11) 6191421; fax (11) 6191420; e-mail outlook@outlookindia.com; internet www.outlookindia.com; f. 1995; weekly; Editor-in-Chief VINOD MEHTA; circ. 247,110.

Panchjanya: Sanskriti Bhavan, Deshbandhu Gupta Marg, Jhandewala, New Delhi 110 055; tel. (11) 3514244; fax (11) 3558613; e-mail panch@nde.vsnl.net.in; f. 1947; weekly; Hindi; general interest; nationalist; Chair. S. N. BANSAL; Editor TARUN VIJAY; circ. 59,300.

Proven Trade Contacts: Narang Tower, 46 Community Centre, Naraina Phase I, New Delhi 110 028; tel. (11) 5892020; fax (11) 5892026; e-mail tc@narang.com; internet www.webptc.com; f. 1992;

monthly; medical/surgical/scientific/pharmaceutical trade promotion; circ. 12,000 in 125 countries; Contact VIVEK NARANG.

Punjabi Digest: 209 Hemkunt House, 6 Rajendra Place, POB 2549, New Delhi 110 008; tel. (11) 5715225; fax (11) 5761023; f. 1971; literary monthly; Gurmukhi; Chief Editor Sardar S. B. SINGH; circ. 84,200.

Rangbhumi: 5A/15 Ansari Rd, Darya Ganj, Delhi 110 002; tel. (11) 3274667; f. 1941; Hindi; films; Editor S. K. GUPTA; circ. 30,000.

Sainik Samachar: Block L-1, Church Rd, New Delhi 110 001; tel. (11) 3019668; f. 1909; pictorial fortnightly for India's armed forces; English, Hindi, Urdu, Tamil, Punjabi, Telugu, Marathi, Kannada, Gorkhali, Malayalam, Bengali, Assamese and Oriya edns; Editor P. K. PATTAYANAK; circ. 20,000.

Saras Salil: Delhi Press Bldg, E-3, Jhandewala Estate, Rani Jhansi Rd, New Delhi 110 055; tel. (11) 3529557; fax (11) 3625020; f. 1993; fortnightly; Hindi; Editor VISHWA NATH; circ. 1,111,900.

Sarita: Delhi Press Bldg, E-3, Jhandewala Estate, Rani Jhansi Rd, New Delhi 110 055; tel. (11) 3529557; fax (11) 3525020; e-mail advertising@delhipressgroup.com; f. 1945; fortnightly; Hindi; family magazine; Editor VISHWA NATH; circ. 127,170.

Shama: 13/14 Asaf Ali Rd, New Delhi 110 002; tel. (11) 3232674; fax (11) 3235167; f. 1939; monthly; Urdu; art and literature; Editors M. YUNUS DEHLVI, IDREES DEHLVI, ILYAS DEHLVI; circ. 58,000.

Suman Saurabh: Delhi Press Bldg, E-3 Jhandewala Estate, Rani Jhansi Rd, New Delhi 110 055; tel. (11) 3529557; fax (11) 3625020; f. 1983; monthly; Hindi; youth; Editor VISHWA NATH; circ. 45,900.

Sushama: 13/14 Asaf Ali Rd, New Delhi 110 002; tel. (11) 3232674; fax (11) 3235167; f. 1959; monthly; Hindi; art and literature; Editors IDREES DEHLVI, ILYAS DEHLVI, YUNUS DEHLVI; circ. 30,000.

Trade Union Record: 24 Canning Lane, New Delhi 110 001; tel. (11) 3387320; fax (11) 3386427; f. 1930; fortnightly; English and Hindi edns; Editor SANTOSH KUMAR.

Vigyan Pragati: PID Bldg, Dr K. S. Krishnan Marg, New Delhi 110 012; tel. (11) 5785647; fax (11) 5731353; f. 1952; monthly; Hindi; popular science; Editor DEEKSHA BIST; circ. 100,000.

Woman's Era: Delhi Press Bldg, E-3, Jhandewala Estate, Rani Jhansi Rd, New Delhi 110 055; tel. (11) 3529557; fax (11) 3625020; f. 1973; fortnightly; English; women's interests; Editor VISHWA NATH; circ. 87,000.

Yojana: Yojana Bhavan, Sansad Marg, New Delhi 110 001; tel. (11) 3710473; e-mail yojana@techpilgrim.com; f. 1957; monthly; English, Tamil, Bengali, Marathi, Gujarati, Assamese, Malayalam, Telugu, Kannada, Punjabi, Urdu, Oriya and Hindi edns; Chief Editor SUBHASH SETIA; circ. 72,000.

Andhra Pradesh

Hyderabad

Andhra Prabha Illustrated Weekly: 591 Lower Tank Bund Rd, Express Centre, Domalaguda, Hyderabad 500 029; tel. (40) 233586; f. 1952; weekly; Telugu; Editor POTTURI VENKATESWARA RAO; circ. 21,800.

Secunderabad

Andhra Bhoomi Sachitra Vara Patrika: 36 Sarojini Devi Rd, Secunderabad 500 003; tel. (842) 7802346; fax (842) 7805256; f. 1977; weekly; Telugu; Editor T. VENKATRAM REDDY; circ. 46,900.

Vijayawada

Andhra Jyoti Sachitra Vara Patrika: Vijayawada 520 010; tel. (866) 474532; f. 1967; weekly; Telugu; Editor PURANAM SUBRAMANYA SARMA; circ. 59,000.

Bala Jyoti: Labbipet, Vijayawada 520 010; tel. (866) 474532; f. 1980; monthly; Telugu; Assoc. Editor A. SASIKANT SATAKARNI; circ. 12,500.

Jyoti Chitra: Andhra Jyoti Bldgs, Vijayawada 520 010; tel. (866) 474532; f. 1977; weekly; Telugu; Editor T. KUTUMBA RAO; circ. 20,100.

Swati Saparivara Patrika: Anil Bldgs, Suryaraopet, POB 339, Vijayawada 520 002; tel. (866) 431862; fax (866) 430433; e-mail vjwswati@sancharnet.in; f. 1984; weekly; Telugu; Editor VEMURI BALARAM; circ. 263,374.

Vanita Jyoti: Labbipet, POB 712, Vijayawada 520 010; tel. (866) 474532; f. 1978; monthly; Telugu; Asst Editor J. SATYANARAYANA; circ. 13,100.

Assam

Guwahati

Agradoot: Agradoot Bhavan, Dispur, Guwahati 781 006; tel. (361) 261923; fax (361) 260655; e-mail agradoot@sify.com; f. 1971; bi-weekly; Assamese; Editor K. S. DEKA; circ. 45,000.

Asam Bani: Tribune Bldg, Guwahati 781 003; tel. (361) 661356; fax (361) 660594; e-mail dileepchandan@yahoo.com; internet www.assamtribune.com; f. 1955; weekly; Assamese; Editor DILEEP CHANDAN; circ. 14,000.

Sadin: Maniram Dewan Rd, Chandmari, Guwahati 781 003; tel. (361) 524594; fax (361) 524634; e-mail protidin@gw1.vsnl.net.in; weekly; Assamese; circ. 44,700.

Bihar

Patna

Anand Digest: Govind Mitra Rd, Patna 800 004; tel. (612) 656557; fax (612) 225192; f. 1981; monthly; Hindi; family magazine; Editor Dr S. S. SINGH; circ. 44,500.

Balak: Govind Mitra Rd, POB 5, Patna 800 004; tel. (612) 650341; f. 1926; monthly; Hindi; children's; Editor S. R. SARAN; circ. 32,000.

Gujarat

Ahmedabad

Akhand Anand: Anand Bhavan, Relief Rd, POB 123, Ahmedabad 380 001; tel. (79) 357482; f. 1947; monthly; Gujarati; Pres. ANAND AMIN; Editor PRAKASH N. SHAH; circ. 10,000.

Chitralok: Gujarat Samachar Bhavan, Khanpur, POB 254, Ahmedabad 380 001; tel. (79) 5504010; fax (79) 5502000; f. 1952; weekly; Gujarati; films; Man. Editor SHREYANS S. SHAH; circ. 20,000.

Sakhi: Sakhi Publications, Jai Hind Press Bldg, nr Gujarat Chamber, Ashram Rd, Navrangpura, Ahmedabad 380 009; tel. (79) 6581734; fax (79) 6587681; f. 1984; fortnightly; Gujarati; women's; Man. Editor NITA Y. SHAH; Editor Y. N. SHAH; circ. 10,000.

Shree: Gujarat Samachar Bhavan, Khanpur, Ahmedabad 380 001; tel. (79) 5504010; fax (79) 5502000; f. 1964; weekly; Gujarati; women's; Editor SMRUTIBEN SHAH; circ. 20,000.

Stree: Sandesh Bhavan, Lad Society Rd, Ahmedabad 380 054; tel. (79) 6765480; fax (79) 6753587; e-mail stree@sandesh.com; internet www.sandesh.com; 1962; weekly; Gujarati; Jt Editors RITABEN PATEL, LILABEN PATEL; circ. 42,170.

Zagmag: Gujarat Samachar Bhavan, Khanpur, Ahmedabad 380 001; tel. (79) 22821; f. 1952; weekly; Gujarati; for children; Editor BAHUBALI S. SHAH; circ. 38,000.

Rajkot

Amruta: Jai Hind Publications, Jai Hind Press Bldg, Babubhai Shah Marg, Rajkot 360 001; tel. (281) 440513; fax (281) 448677; f. 1967; weekly; Gujarati; films; Editor Y. N. SHAH; circ. 27,000.

Niranjan: Jai Hind Publications, Jai Hind Press Bldg, Babubhai Shah Marg, Rajkot 360 001; tel. (281) 440517; fax (281) 448677; f. 1972; fortnightly; Gujarati; children's; Editor N. R. SHAH; circ. 15,000.

Parmarth: Jai Hind Publications, Jai Hind Press Bldg, Babubhai Shah Marg, Rajkot 360 001; tel. (281) 440511; fax (281) 448677; monthly; Gujarati; philosophy and religion; Editor Y. N. SHAH; circ. 30,000.

Phulwadi: Jai Hind Publications, Jai Hind Press Bldg, Babubhai Shah Marg, Rajkot 360 001; tel. (281) 440513; fax (281) 448677; f. 1967; weekly; Gujarati; for children; Editor Y. N. SHAH; circ. 27,000.

Karnataka

Bangalore

Mayura: 75 Mahatma Gandhi Rd, Bangalore 560 001; tel. (80) 5588999; fax (80) 5587179; e-mail ads@deccanherald.co.in; f. 1968; monthly; Kannada; Editor-in-Chief K. N. SHANTH KUMAR; circ. 39,200.

New Leader: 93 North Rd, St Mary's Town, Bangalore 560 005; f. 1887; weekly; English; Editor Rt Rev. HERMAN D'SOUZA; circ. 10,000.

Prajamata: North Anjaneya Temple Rd, Basavangudi, Bangalore 560 004; tel. (80) 602481; f. 1931; weekly; Kannada; news and current affairs; Chief Editor G. V. ANJI; circ. 28,377.

Sudha: 75 Mahatma Gandhi Rd, Bangalore 560 001; tel. (80) 5588999; fax (80) 5587179; e-mail ads@deccanherald.co.in; f. 1965; weekly; Kannada; Editor-in-Chief K. N. HARI KUMAR; circ. 85,500.

Manipal

Taranga: Udayavani Bldg, Press Corner, Manipal 576 119; tel. (8252) 70845; fax (8252) 70563; e-mail taranga@manipalpress.com; internet www.udayavani.com; f. 1983; weekly; Kannada; Editor-in-Chief SANDHYA S. PAI; circ. 105,000.

Kerala

Kochi

The Week: Malayala Manorama Buildings, POB 4278, Kochi 682 036; tel. (484) 316285; fax (484) 315745; e-mail editor@

theweek.com; internet www.the_week.com; f. 1982; weekly; English; current affairs; Chief Editor MAMMEN MATHEW; Editor PHILIP MATHEW; circ. 177,531.

Kottayam

Balarama: MM Publications Ltd, POB 226, Erayilkadavu, Kottayam 686 001; tel. (481) 563721; fax (481) 564393; e-mail vanbal@satyam.net.in; f. 1972; children's weekly; Malayalam; Chief Editor BINA MATHEW; Senior Man. V. SAJEEV GEORGE; circ. 245,080.

Malayala Manorama: K. K. Rd, POB 26, Kottayam 686 001; tel. (481) 563646; fax (481) 562479; e-mail editor@malayalamanorama.com; internet www.malayalamanorama.com; f. 1937; weekly; Malayalam; also publ. from Kozhikode; Man. Dir and Editor MAMMEN MATHEW; Chief Editor MAMMEN VARGHESE; combined circ. 896,793.

Manorajyam: Manorajyam Bldg, M. C. Rd, Kottayam 686 039; tel. (481) 61203; f. 1967; weekly; Malayalam; Publr R. KALYANARAMAN; circ. 50,900.

Vanitha: MM Publications Ltd, POB 226, Erayilkadavu, Kottayam 686 001; tel. (481) 563721; fax (481) 564393; e-mail vanbal@satyam.net.in; f. 1975; women's fortnightly; Malayalam; Chief Editor Mrs K. M. MATHEW; Senior Man. V. SAJEEV GEORGE; circ. 435,105.

Kozhikode

Arogya Masika: Mathrubhumi Bldgs, K. P. Kesava Menon Rd, Kozhikode 673 001; tel. (495) 765381; fax (495) 760138; e-mail arogyamasika@mat1.mathrubhumi.co.in; monthly; Malayalam; health; Man. Editor P. V. CHANDRAN; circ. 135,000.

Chitrabhumi: Mathrubhumi Bldgs, K. P. Kesava Menon Rd, Kozhikode 673 001; tel. (495) 366655; fax (495) 366656; weekly; Malayalam; films; Editor M. T. VASUDEVAN NAIR; circ. 34,500.

Grihalakshmi: Mathrubhumi Bldgs, K. P. Kesava Menon Rd, POB 46, Kozhikode 673 001; tel. (495) 366655; fax (495) 366656; e-mail mathrclt@md2.vsnl.net.in; internet www.mathrubhumi.com; f. 1979; monthly; Malayalam; women's; Editor K. K. SREEDHARAN NAIR; circ. 108,000.

Mathrubhumi Illustrated Weekly: Mathrubhumi Bldgs, K. P. Kesava Menon Rd, POB 46, Kozhikode 673 001; tel. (495) 366655; fax (495) 56656; f. 1923; weekly; Malayalam; Editor M. T. VASUDEVAN NAIR; circ. 64,000.

Sports Masika: Mathrubhumi Bldgs, K. P. Kesava Menon Rd, Kozhikode 673 001; tel. (495) 366655; fax (495) 366656; monthly; Malayalam; sport; Exec. Editor V. RAJAGOPAL; circ. 77,400.

Quilon

Karala Sabdam: Thevally, Quilon 691 009; tel. (474) 72403; fax (474) 740710; f. 1962; weekly; Malayalam; Man. Editor B. A. RAJAKRISHNAN; circ. 66,600.

Nana: Therally, Quilon 691 009; tel. 2403; weekly; Malayalam; Man. Editor B. A. RAJAKRISHNAN; circ. 50,500.

Thiruvananthapuram

Kalakaumudi: Kaumudi Bldgs, Pettah, Thiruvananthapuram 695 024; tel. (471) 443531; fax (471) 442895; e-mail kalakaumudi@vsnl.com; f. 1975; weekly; Malayalam; Chief Editor M. S. MANI; Gen. Man. ABRAHAM EAPEN; circ. 73,000.

Vellinakshatram: Kaumudi Bldgs, Pettah, Thiruvananthapuram 695 024; tel. (471) 443531; fax (471) 442895; e-mail kalakaumudi@vsnl.com; internet www.vellinakshatram.com; f. 1987; film weekly; Malayalam; Editor PRASAD LAKSHMANAN; Man. Editor SUKUMARAN MANI; circ. 55,000.

Madhya Pradesh
Bhopal

Krishak Jagat: 14 Indira Press Complex, M. P. Nagar, POB 37, Bhopal 462 011; tel. (755) 768452; fax (755) 760449; e-mail krishjag@sanchar.net.in; internet www.krishakjagatindia.com; f. 1946; weekly; Hindi; agriculture; Chief Editor VIJAY KUMAR BONDRIYA; Editor SUNIL GANGRADE; circ. 100,000.

Maharashtra
Mumbai

Abhiyaan: Abhiyaan Press and Publications Ltd, 4A/B, Government Industrial Estate, Charkop, Kandivli (W), Mumbai 400 067; tel. (22) 8687515; fax (22) 8680991; f. 1986; weekly; Gujarati; Dir DILIP PATEL; Editor VINOD PANDYA; circ. 140,900.

Arogya Sanjeevani: C-14 Royal Industrial Estate, 5-B Naigaum Cross Rd, Wadala, Mumbai 400 031; tel. (22) 4138723; fax (22) 4133610; e-mail woman@bol.net.in; f. 1990; quarterly; Hindi; Editor SAROJ SHUKLA; circ. 62,907.

Auto India: Nirmal, Nariman Point, Mumbai 400 021; tel. (22) 2883946; fax (22) 2883940; e-mail editor@auto-india.com; f. 1994; monthly; Editor RAJ WARRIOR; circ. 63,900.

Bhavan's Journal: Bharatiya Vidya Bhavan, Mumbai 400 007; tel. (22) 3634462; fax (22) 3630058; f. 1954; fortnightly; English; literary; Man. Editor J. H. DAVE; Editor S. RAMAKRISHNAN; circ. 25,000.

Blitz News Magazine: Saiman House, off Sayani Rd, Prabhadevi, Mumbai 400 025; tel. (22) 4372474; fax (22) 4229048; f. 1941; weekly; English; Editor-in-Chief M. J. AKBAR; combined circ. 419,000.

Bombay Samachar: Red House, Sayed Brelvi Rd, Mumbai 400 001; tel. (22) 2045531; fax (22) 2046642; f. 1822; weekly; Gujarati; Editor JEHANBUX D. DARUWALA; circ. 124,500.

Business India: Nirmal, 14th Floor, Nariman Point, Mumbai 400 021; tel. (22) 2883943; fax (22) 2883940; f. 1978; fortnightly; English; Publr ASHOK ADVANI; circ. 88,100.

Business World: 25–28 Atlanta, 2nd Floor, Nariman Point, Mumbai 400 021; tel. (22) 2851352; fax (22) 2870310; f. 1980; weekly; English; Editor AVEEK SARKAR; circ. 89,500.

Chitralekha: 62 Vaju Kotak Marg, Fort, Mumbai 400 001; tel. (22) 2614730; fax (22) 2615895; e-mail advertise@chitralekha.com; f. 1950 (Gujarati), f. 1989 (Marathi); weekly; Gujarati and Marathi; Editors BHARAT SHELANI, GYANESH MAHARAO; circ. 251,059 (Gujarati), 112,239 (Marathi).

Cine Blitz Film Monthly: 17/17H Cawasji Patel St, Fort, Mumbai 400 001; tel. (22) 2044143; fax (22) 2047984; f. 1974; English; Editor RITA K. MEHTA; circ. 184,100.

Debonair: Maurya Publications (Pvt) Ltd, 20/21, Juhu Centaur Hotel, Juhu Tara Rd, POB 18292, Mumbai 400 049; tel. (22) 6116632; fax (22) 6152677; e-mail maurya@debonairindia.com; f. 1972; monthly; English; Publr CHAITANYA PRABHU; CEO JOSEPH MASCARENHAS; circ. 110,000.

Economic and Political Weekly: Hitkari House, 284 Shahid Bhagatsingh Rd, Mumbai 400 001; tel. (22) 2696073; fax (22) 2696072; e-mail epw@vsnl.com; internet www.epw.org.in; f. 1966; English; Editor KRISHNA RAJ; circ. 132,800.

Femina: Times of India Bldg, Dr Dadabhai Naoroji Rd, Mumbai 400 001; tel. and fax (22) 2731385; e-mail femina@timesgroup.com; internet www.feminaindia.com; f. 1959; fortnightly; English; Editor SATHYA SARAN; circ. 116,000.

Filmfare: Times of India Bldg, Dr Dadabhai Naoroji Rd, Mumbai 400 001; tel. (22) 2731187; fax (22) 2731401; internet www.filmfare.com; f. 1952; fortnightly; English; Exec. Editor SHASHI BALIGA; circ. 156,400.

Financing Agriculture: 1st Floor, Dhanraj Mahal, Chhatrapati Shivaji Maharaj Marg, Mumbai 400 001; tel. (22) 2028924; fax (22) 2028966; e-mail afcl@vsnl.com; internet www.afcindia.com; quarterly.

G: 62 Vaju Kotak Marg, Fort, Mumbai 400 001; tel. (22) 2614730; fax (22) 2615395; e-mail advertise@chitralekha.com; f. 1989; monthly; English; Editor BHAWNA SOMAYA; circ. 61,437.

Gentleman: Mumbai; e-mail gent@bom3.vsnl.net.in; f. 1980; monthly; English; Editor PREMNATH NAIR (acting).

Indian PEN: Theosophy Hall, 40 New Marine Lines, Mumbai 400 020; tel. (22) 2032175; e-mail ambika.sirkar@gems.vsnl.net.in; f. 1934; quarterly; organ of Indian Centre of the International PEN; Editor RANJIT HOSKOTE.

Janmabhoomi-Pravasi: Janmabhoomi Bhavan, Janmabhoomi Marg, Fort, POB 62, Mumbai 400 001; tel. (22) 2870831; fax (22) 2874097; e-mail bhoomi@bom3.vsnl.net.in; f. 1939; weekly; Gujarati; Propr Saurashtra Trust; Editor KUNDAN VYAS; circ. 104,700.

JEE: 62 Vaju Kotak Marg, Fort, Mumbai 400 001; tel. (22) 2614730; fax (22) 2615895; e-mail advertise@chitralekha.com; fortnightly; Gujarati and Marathi; Editor MADHURI KOTAK; circ. 92,160 (Gujarati), 30,150 (Marathi).

Meri Saheli: C-14 Royal Industrial Estate, 5-B Naigaum Cross Rd, Wadala, Mumbai 400 031; tel. (22) 4182797; fax (22) 4133610; e-mail woman@bol.net.in; f. 1987; monthly; Hindi; Editor HEMA MALINI; circ. 292,200.

Movie: Mahalaxmi Chambers, 5th Floor, 22 Bhulabhai Desai Rd, Mumbai 400 026; tel. (22) 4935636; fax (22) 4938406; f. 1981; monthly; English; Editor DINESH RAHEJA; circ. 70,700.

New Woman: C-14 Royal Industrial Estate, 5-B Naigaum Cross Rd, Wadala, Mumbai 400 031; tel. (22) 4138723; fax (22) 4133610; e-mail woman@bol.net.in; f. 1996; monthly; English; Editor HEMA MALINI; circ. 79,962.

Onlooker: Free Press House, 215 Free Press Journal Marg, Nariman Point, Mumbai 400 021; tel. (22) 2874566; f. 1939; fortnightly; English; news magazine; Exec. Editor K. SRINIVASAN; circ. 61,000.

Reader's Digest: Orient House, Adi Marzban Path, Ballard Estate, Mumbai 400 001; tel. (22) 2617291; fax (22) 2613347; f. 1954; monthly; English; Publr and Editor ASHOK MAHADEVAN; circ. 389,378.

Savvy: Magna Publishing Co Ltd, Magna House, 100/E Old Prabhadevi Rd, Prabhadevi, Mumbai 400 025; tel. (22) 4362270; fax (22) 4306523; e-mail savvy@magnamags.com; internet www.magnamags.com; f. 1984; monthly; English; Editor SAIRA MENEZES; circ. 99,500.

Screen: Mumbai; f. 1951; film weekly; English; Editor UDAYA TARA NAYAR; circ. 90,000.

Society: Magna Publishing Co Ltd, Magna House, 100/E Old Prabhadevi Rd, Prabhadevi, Mumbai 400 025; tel. (22) 4362270; fax (22) 4306523; f. 1979; monthly; English; Editor LALITHA GOPALAN; circ. 67,200.

Star and Style: Maurya Publications (Pvt) Ltd, 20/21, Juhu Centaur Hotel, Juhu Tara Rd, POB 18292, Mumbai 400 049; tel. (22) 6116632; fax (22) 6152677; e-mail maurya@bom3.vsnl.net.in; f. 1965; bimonthly; English; film; Publr/Editor NISHI PREM; circ. 60,000.

Stardust: Magna Publishing Co Ltd, Magna House, 100/E Old Prabhadevi Rd, Prabhadevi, Mumbai 400 025; tel. (22) 4362270; fax (22) 4306523; e-mail stardust@bom1.vsnl.net.in; internet www.stardustindia.com; f. 1985; monthly; English; Editor ASHWIN VARDE; circ. 308,000.

Vyapar: Janmabhoomi Bhavan, Janmabhoomi Marg, POB 62, Fort, Mumbai 400 001; tel. (22) 2870831; fax (22) 2874097; e-mail rajeshbhayani@hotmail.com; f. 1949 (Gujarati), 1987 (Hindi); Gujarati (2 a week) and Hindi (weekly); commerce; Propr Saurashtra Trust; Editor RAJESH M. BHAYANI; circ. 30,900 (Gujarati), 16,600 (Hindi).

Yuvdarhsan: c/o Warsha Publications Pvt Ltd, Warsha House, 6 Zakaria Bunder Rd, Sewri, Mumbai 400 015; tel. (22) 441843; f. 1975; weekly; Gujarati; Editor and Man. Dir R. M. BHUTTA; circ. 18,600.

Nagpur

All India Reporter: AIR Ltd, Congress Nagar, POB 209, Nagpur 440 012; tel. (712) 534321; fax (712) 526283; e-mail air@allindiareporter.com; internet www.allindiareporter.com; f. 1914; weekly and monthly; English; law journals; Chief Editor V. R. MANOHAR; circ. 55,500.

Rajasthan

Jaipur

Balhans: Kesargarh, Jawahar Lal Nehru Marg, Jaipur 302 004; tel. (141) 561582; fax (141) 566011; e-mail ads@rajasthanpatrika.com; internet www.rajasthanpatrika.com; fortnightly; Hindi; circ. 31,800.

Itwari Patrika: Kesargarh, Jawahar Lal Nehru Marg, Jaipur 302 004; tel. (141) 561582; fax (141) 566011; weekly; Hindi; circ. 12,000.

Rashtradoot Saptahik: HO, M.I. Rd, POB 30, Jaipur 302 001; tel. (141) 372634; fax (141) 373513; f. 1983; Hindi; also publ. from Kota and Bikaner; Chief Editor and Man. Editor RAJESH SHARMA; CEO SOMESH SHARMA; combined circ. 167,500.

Tamil Nadu

Chennai (Madras)

Aishwarya: 325 N. S. K. Salai, Chennai 600 024; tel. (44) 422064; f. 1990; weekly; Tamil; general; Editor K. NATARAJAN; circ. 20,000.

Ambulimama: 82 Defence Officers Colony, Ekkatuthangal, Chennai 600 097; e-mail chandamama@vsnl.com; f. 1947; children's monthly; Tamil; Editor B. VISWANATHA REDDI; circ. 65,000.

Ambuli Ammavan: 82 Defence Officers Colony, Ekkatuthangal, Chennai 600 097; e-mail chandamama@vsnl.com; f. 1970; children's monthly; Malayalam; Editor B. VISWANATHA REDDI; circ. 12,000.

Ananda Vikatan: 757 Anna Salai, Chennai 600 002; tel. (44) 8524054; fax (44) 8523819; e-mail editor@vikatan.com; internet www.vikatan.com; f. 1924; weekly; Tamil; Editor and Man. Dir S. BALASUBRAMANIAN; circ. 316,700.

Aval Vikatan: 757 Anna Salai, Chennai 600 002; tel. (44) 8524054; fax (44) 8523819; e-mail editor@vikatan.com; internet www.vikatan.com; f 1998; fortnightly; Tamil; Editor B. SRINIVASAN; circ. 165,718.

Chandamama: 82 Defence Officers Colony, Ekkatuthangal, Chennai 600 097; e-mail chandamama@vsnl.com; f. 1947; children's monthly; Hindi, Gujarati, Telugu, Kannada, English, Sanskrit, Bengali, Assamese; Editor B. VISWANATHA REDDI; combined circ. 420,000.

Chandoba: 82 Defence Officers Colony, Ekkatuthangal, Chennai 600 097; e-mail chandamama@vsnl.com; f. 1952; children's monthly; Marathi; Editor B. VISWANATHA REDDI; circ. 93,000.

Chutti Vikatan: 757 Anna Salai, Chennai 600 002; tel. (44) 8524054; fax (44) 8523819; e-mail editor@vikatan.com; internet www.vikatan.com; f. 1999; monthly; Tamil; Editor B. SRINIVASAN; Man. Dir S. BALASUBRAMANIAN; circ. 75,000.

Devi: 727 Anna Salai, Chennai 600 006; tel. (44) 8521428; f. 1979; weekly; Tamil; Editor B. RAMACHANDRA ADITYAN; circ. 84,600.

Dinamani Kadir: Express Estate, Mount Rd, Chennai 600 002; tel. (44) 8520751; fax (44) 8524500; weekly; Editor G. KASTURI RANGAN (acting); circ. 55,000.

Frontline: Kasturi Bldgs, 859/860 Anna Salai, Chennai 600 002; tel. (44) 8589060; fax (44) 8545703; f. 1984; fortnightly; English; Publr S. RANGARAJAN; Editor N. RAM; circ. 67,225.

Hindu International Edition: 859/860 Anna Salai, Chennai 600 002; tel. (44) 8413344; fax (44) 8415325; f. 1975; weekly; English; Editor N. RAVI; circ. 3,000.

Jahnamamu (Oriya): 82 Defence Officers Colony, Ekkatuthangal, Chennai 600 097; e-mail chandamama@vsnl.com; f. 1972; children's monthly; Editor B. VISWANATHA REDDI; circ. 111,000.

Junior Vikatan: 757 Anna Salai, Chennai 600 002; tel. (44) 8524054; fax (44) 8523819; e-mail editor@vikatan.com; internet www.vikatan.com; f. 1983; 2 times a week; Tamil; Editor and Man. Dir S. BALASUBRAMANIAN; circ. 189,100.

Kalai Magal: POB 604, Chennai 600 004; tel. (44) 843099; f. 1932; monthly; Tamil; literary and cultural; Editor R. NARAYANASWAMY; circ. 10,200.

Kalkandu: 306 Purasaivakkam High Rd, Chennai 600 010; f. 1948; weekly; Tamil; Editor P. V. PARTHASARTHY; circ. 55,000.

Kalki: 47 Jawaharlal Nehru Rd, Ekkatuthangal, Chennai 600 097; tel. (44) 2345621; e-mail kalkiweekly@vsnl.com; internet www.kalkiweekly.com; f. 1941; weekly; Tamil; literary and cultural; Editor SEETHA RAVI; circ. 55,000.

Kumudam: 151 Purasawalkam High Rd, Chennai 600 010; tel. (44) 6422146; fax (44) 6425041; e-mail kumudam@giasmd01.vsnl.net.in; f. 1947; weekly; Tamil; Editor Dr S. A. P. JAWAHAR PALANIAPPAN; circ. 371,700.

Kungumam: 93A Kodambakkam High Rd, Chennai 600 034; tel. (44) 8268177; f. 1978; weekly; Tamil; Editor PARASAKTHI; circ. 82,100.

Malaimathi: Chennai; f. 1958; weekly; Tamil; Editor P. S. ELANGO; circ. 48,100.

Muththaram: 93A Kogambakkam High Rd, Chennai 600 034; tel. (44) 476306; f. 1980; weekly; Tamil; Editor Sri PARASAKTHI; circ. 19,100.

Pesum Padam: Chennai; tel. (44) 422064; f. 1942; monthly; Tamil; films; Man. Editor K. NATARAJAN; circ. 34,700.

Picturpost: Chennai; tel. (44) 422064; f. 1943; monthly; English; films; Man. Editor K. NATARAJAN; circ. 11,000.

Rajam: Chennai; tel. (44) 422064; f. 1986; monthly; Tamil; women's interests; Man. Dir and Editor K. NATARAJAN; circ. 32,677.

Rani Muthu: 1091 Periyar E.V.R. High Rd, Chennai 600 007; tel. (44) 5324771; e-mail raniweekly@vsnl.net; f. 1969; fortnightly; Tamil; Editor A. MA. SAMY; circ. 64,951.

Rani Weekly: 1091 Periyar E.V.R. High Rd, Chennai 600 007; tel. (44) 5324771; e-mail raniweekly@vsnl.net; f. 1962; Tamil; Editor A. MA. SAMY; circ. 170,424.

Sportstar: Kasturi Bldgs, 859/860 Anna Salai, Chennai 600 002; tel. (44) 8413344; fax (44) 8415325; f. 1978; weekly; English; Publr S. RANGARAJAN; Editor N. RAM; circ. 52,900.

Thuglak: 46 Greenways Rd, Chennai 600 028; tel. (44) 4936913; fax (44) 4936915; f. 1970; weekly; Tamil; Editor CHO S. RAMASWAMY; circ. 149,100.

Vellore

Madha Jothidam: 3 Arasamaram St, Vellore 632 004; f. 1949; monthly; Tamil; astrology; Editor and Publr A. K. THULASIRAMAN; circ. 8,000.

Uttar Pradesh

Allahabad

Nutan Kahaniyan: 15 Sheo Charan Lal Rd, Allahabad 211 003; tel. (532) 400612; f. 1975; Hindi; monthly; Chief Editor K. K. BHARGAVA; circ. 167,500.

West Bengal

Kolkata (Calcutta)

All India Appointment Gazette: 7 Old Court House St, Kolkata 700 001; tel. (33) 2206663; fax (33) 2296548; f. 1973; 2 a week; English; Editor S. C. TALUKDAR; circ. 158,900.

Anandalok: 6 Prafulla Sarkar St, Kolkata 700 001; tel. (33) 2374880; fax (33) 2253240; f. 1975; fortnightly; Bengali; film; Editor DULENDRA BHOWMIK; circ. 55,200.

Anandamela: 6 Prafulla Sarkar St, Kolkata 700 001; tel. (33) 2216600; fax (33) 2253240; f. 1975; weekly; Bengali; juvenile; Editor DEBASHIS BANDOPADHYAY; circ. 41,400.

Contemporary Tea Time: 1/2 Old Court House Corner, POB 14, Kolkata 700 001; tel. (33) 2200099; fax (33) 2435753; e-mail calcutta@ctl.co.in; internet www.ctl.co.in; f. 1988; quarterly; English; tea industry; Exec. Editor GITA NARAYANI; circ. 5,000.

Desh: 6 Prafulla Sarkar St, Kolkata 700 001; tel. (33) 2374880; fax (33) 2253240; f. 1933; fortnightly; Bengali; literary; Editor AVEEK SARKAR; circ. 67,300.

Investment Preview: 7 Old Court House St, Kolkata 700 001; tel. (33) 2206663; fax (33) 296548; f. 1992; weekly; English; Editor S. C. TALUKDAR; circ. 53,845.

Khela: 96 Raja Rammohan Sarani, Kolkata 700 009; tel. (33) 3509803; f. 1981; weekly; Bengali; sports; Editor ASOKE DASGUPTA; circ. 10,500.

Naba Kallol: 11 Jhamapookur Lane, Kolkata 700 009; tel. (33) 354294; f. 1960; monthly; Bengali; Editor P. K. MAZUMDAR; circ. 26,600.

Neetee: 4 Sukhlal Johari Lane, Kolkata; f. 1955; weekly; English; Editor M. P. PODDAR.

Prabuddha Bharata (Awakened India): 5 Dehi Entally Rd, Kolkata 700 014; tel. (33) 2440898; fax (33) 2450050; e-mail advaita@vsnl.com; internet www.advaitaonline.com; f. 1896; monthly; art, culture, religion and philosophy; Publr SWAMI BODHASARANANDA; circ. 7,500.

Sananda: 6 Prafulla Sarkar St, Kolkata 700 001; tel. (33) 2374880; fax (33) 2253241; f. 1986; monthly; Bengali; Editor APARNA SEN; circ. 126,200.

Saptahik Bartaman: 76A J. C. Bose Rd, Kolkata 700 014; tel. (33) 2448208; fax (33) 2441215; f. 1988; weekly; Bengali; Editor BARUN SENGUPTA; circ. 112,900.

Screen: P-5, Kalakar St, Kolkata 700 070; f. 1960; weekly; Hindi; Editor M. P. PODDAR; circ. 58,000.

Statesman: Statesman House, 4 Chowringhee Sq., Kolkata 700 001; tel. (33) 2257070; fax (33) 2250118; f. 1875; overseas weekly; English; Editor-in-Chief C. R. IRANI.

Suktara: 11 Jhamapooker Lane, Kolkata 700 009; tel. (33) 355294; f. 1948; monthly; Bengali; juvenile; Editor M. MAJUMDAR; circ. 36,700.

NEWS AGENCIES

Press Trust of India Ltd: 4 Parliament St, New Delhi 110 001; tel. (11) 3717642; fax (11) 3718714; f. 1947, re-established 1978; Chair. VIJAY KUMAR CHOPRA; Gen. Man. M. K. RAZDAN.

United News of India (UNI): 9 Rafi Marg, New Delhi 110 001; tel. (11) 3711700; fax (11) 3716211; e-mail uninet@del2.vsnl.net.in; f. 1961; Indian language news in Hindi and Urdu; English wire service; World TV News Service (UNISCAN); photograph service; graphics service; special services covering banking and business; brs in 90 centres in India; Chair. ARUN ARORA; Gen. Man. and Chief Editor VIRENDER MOHAN.

Foreign Bureaux

Agence France-Presse (AFP): 56 Janpath, 3rd Floor, New Delhi 110 001; tel. (11) 3738700; fax (11) 3311105; e-mail afpdelhi@afp.com; Bureau Chief RÉNÉ SLAMA.

Agencia EFE (Spain): 72 Jor Bagh, New Delhi 110 003; tel. (11) 4618092; fax (11) 4615013; Correspondent ISABEL CALLEJA SOLERA.

Agenzia Nazionale Stampa Associata (ANSA) (Italy): C-179 Defence Colony, New Delhi 110 024; tel. (11) 4615004; fax (11) 4640190; e-mail natale@giasdl01.vsnl.net.in; Bureau Chief BENIAMINO NATALE.

Associated Press (AP) (USA): 6B Jor Bagh Lane, New Delhi 110 003; tel. (11) 4698682; fax (11) 4616870; e-mail bbrown@ap.org; Bureau Chief BETH DUFF BROWN.

Deutsche Presse-Agentur (dpa) (Germany): 39 Golf Links, New Delhi 110 003; tel. (11) 4617792; fax (11) 4635772; e-mail dpadelhi@vsnl.com; Chief Rep. JÜRGEN HEIN.

Informatsionnoye Telegrafnoye Agentstvo Rossii—Telegrafnoye Agentstvo Suverennykh Stran (ITAR—TASS) (Russia): 3 Vasant Vihar, New Delhi 110 057; tel. (11) 6142351; fax (11) 6146292; Bureau Chief STANISLAV BYCHKOV.

Inter Press Service (IPS) (Italy): 49 (F.F.) Defence Colony Market, New Delhi 110 024; tel. (11) 4634154; fax (11) 4624725; Correspondent ANN NINAN.

Islamic Republic News Agency (IRNA) (Iran): SF-204, Jor Bagh, New Delhi 110 003; tel. (11) 4632009; fax (11) 4643369; e-mail irna@del2.vsnl.net.in; Bureau Chief RAMEZANALI YOUSEFI.

Kyodo News Service (Japan): 308 World Trade Centre, Babar Rd, New Delhi 110 001; tel. (11) 3411954; fax (11) 3414756; Bureau Chief KAZUMASA KOIKE.

Reuters (UK): 1 Kautilya Marg, Chanakyapuri, New Delhi 110 021; tel. (11) 3012024; fax (11) 3014043; e-mail delhi.newsroom@reuters.com; Bureau Chief MYRA MACDONALD.

United Press International (UPI) (USA): 706, Sector 7B, Chandigarh 160 019; tel. (172) 794017; fax (172) 790591; e-mail hsnanda@glide.net.in; Bureau Chief HARBAKSH SINGH NANDA.

Xinhua (New China) News Agency (People's Republic of China): B-3/60, Safdarjung Enclave, New Delhi 110 029; tel. (11) 610886; fax (11) 6190657; Chief ZHOU XIAOZHENG.

The following agencies are also represented: Associated Press of Pakistan, A. P. Dow Jones, Bloomberg Business News, Depthnews, Knight-Ridder Financial News, Middle East News Agency and Viet Nam News Agency.

CO-ORDINATING BODIES

Press Information Bureau: Shastri Bhavan, Dr Rajendra Prasad Rd, New Delhi 110 001; tel. (11) 3383643; fax (11) 3383169; internet www.pib.nic.in; f. 1946 to co-ordinate press affairs for the govt; represents newspaper managements, journalists, news agencies, parliament; has power to examine journalists under oath and may censor objectionable material; Prin. Information Officer N. J. KRISHNA.

Registrar of Newspapers for India: Ministry of Information and Broadcasting, West Block 8, Wing 2, Ramakrishna Puram, New Delhi 110 066; tel. (11) 6018788; f. 1956 as a statutory body to collect press statistics; maintains a register of all Indian newspapers; Registrar G. D. BELIYA.

PRESS ASSOCIATIONS

All-India Newspaper Editors' Conference: 36–37 Northend Complex, Rama Krishna Ashram Marg, New Delhi 110 001; tel. (11) 3364519; fax (11) 3317499; f. 1940; c. 400 mems; Pres. VISHWA BANDHU GUPTA; Sec.-Gen. RAMU PATEL.

All India Small and Medium Newspapers' Federation: 26-F Rajiv Gandhi Chowk (Connaught Place), New Delhi 110 001; tel. (11) 3326000; e-mail nri@ndf.vsnl.net.in; c. 9,000 mems; Pres. HARBHAJAN SINGH; Gen. Secs B. C. GUPTA, B. M. SHARMA.

The Foreign Correspondents' Club of South Asia: AB-19 Mathura Rd, New Delhi 110 001; tel. (11) 3388535; fax (11) 3385517; e-mail fcc@fccsouthasia.org; internet www.fccsouthasia.org; 327 mems; Pres. S. VENKATANARAYAN; Man. KIRAN KAPUR.

Indian Federation of Working Journalists: A-4/199 Basant Lane, Nr Railway Central Hospital, New Delhi 110 001; tel. (11) 3348894; fax (11) 3348871; f. 1950; 27,000 mems; Pres. K. VIKRAM RAO; Sec.-Gen. PARMANAND PANDEY.

Indian Journalists' Association: New Delhi; Pres. VIJAY DUTT; Gen. Sec. A. K. DHAR.

Indian Languages Newspapers' Asscn: Janmabhoomi Bhavan, Janmabhoomi Marg, POB 10029, Fort, Mumbai 400 001; tel. (22) 2870537; f. 1941; 320 mems; Pres. VIJAY KUMAR BONDRIYA; Hon. Gen. Secs PRADEEP G. DESHPANDE, KRISHNA SHEWDIKAR, LALIT SHRIMAL.

Indian Newspaper Society: INS Bldg, Rafi Marg, New Delhi 110 001; tel. (11) 3715401; fax (11) 3723800; e-mail indnews@nde.vsnl.net.in; f. 1939; 676 mems; Pres. PRATAP PAWAR; Sec.-Gen. P. K. LAHIRI.

National Union of Journalists (India): 7 Jantar Mantar Rd, 2nd Floor, New Delhi 110 001; tel. (11) 3368610; fax (11) 3369664; e-mail nujindia@ndf.vsnl.in; internet www.education.vsnl.com/nujindia; f. 1972; 12,000 mems; Pres. SHYAM KHOSLA; Sec.-Gen. P. K. ROY.

Press Club of India: 1 Raisina Rd, New Delhi 110 001; tel. 3719844; f. 1948; 4,500 mems; Pres. PRAKASH PATRA; Sec.-Gen. SANJEEV ACHARYA.

Press Council of India: Faridkot House, Ground Floor, Copernicus Marg, New Delhi 110 001; tel. (11) 3381681; established under an Act of Parliament to preserve the freedom of the press and maintain and improve the standards of newspapers and news agencies in India; 28 mems; Chair. Justice JAICHANDRA REDDY; Sec. REVA KHETRAPAL.

Press Institute of India: Sapru House Annexe, Barakhamba Rd, New Delhi 110 001; tel. (11) 3318066; fax (11) 3311975; e-mail presinst@reno2.nic.in; f. 1963; 29 mem. newspapers and other orgs; Chair. NARESH MOHAN; Dir AJIT BHATTACHARJEA.

Publishers

Delhi and New Delhi

Affiliated East-West Press (Pvt) Ltd: G-1/16 Ansari Rd, Daryaganj, New Delhi 110 002; tel. (11) 3264180; fax (11) 3260538; e-mail affiliat@vsnl.com; internet www.aewpress.com; textbooks and reference books; also represents scientific societies; Dirs SUNNY MALIK, KAMAL MALIK.

Allied Publishers (Pvt) Ltd: 13/14 Asaf Ali Rd, New Delhi 110 002; tel. (11) 3233002; fax (11) 3235967; e-mail aplnd@del2.vsnl.net.in; academic and general; Man. Dir S. M. SACHDEV.

Amerind Publishing Co (Pvt) Ltd: Oxford Bldg, N-56 Connaught Circus, New Delhi 110 001; tel. (11) 3314957; fax (11) 3322639; f. 1970; offices at Kolkata, Mumbai and New York; scientific and technical; Dirs MOHAN PRIMLANI, GULAB PRIMLANI.

Arnold Heinman Publishers (India) Pvt Ltd: New Delhi; f. 1969 as Arnold Publishers (India) Pvt Ltd; literature and general; Man. Dir G. A. VAZIRANI.

Atma Ram and Sons: 1376 Kashmere Gate, POB 1429, Delhi 110 006; tel. (11) 3973082; f. 1909; scientific, technical, humanities, medical; Man. Dir S. PURI; Dir Y. PURI.

B.I. Publications Pvt Ltd: 13 Daryaganj, New Delhi 110 002; tel. (11) 3274443; fax (11) 3261290; e-mail bidel@ndb.vsnl.net.in; f. 1959; academic, general and professional; Man. Dir K. S. MANI.

S. Chand and Co Ltd: 7361 Ram Nagar, Qutab Rd, near New Delhi Railway Station, New Delhi 110 055; tel. (11) 3672080; fax (11) 3677446; e-mail schand@vsnl.com; internet www.schandgroup.com; f. 1917; educational and general in English and Hindi; also book exports and imports; Man. Dir RAVINDRA KUMAR GUPTA.

Children's Book House: A-4 Ring Rd, South Extension Part I, POB 3854, New Delhi 110 049; tel. (11) 4636030; fax (11) 4636011; e-mail neeta@giasdl01.vsnl.net.in; internet www.neetaprakashan.com; f. 1952; educational and general; Dir R. S. GUPTA.

Children's Book Trust: Nehru House, 4 Bahadur Shah Zafar Marg, New Delhi 110 002; tel. (11) 3316970; fax (11) 3721090; e-mail cbtnd@vsnl.com; internet www.childrensbooktrust.com; f. 1957; children's books in English and other Indian languages; Editor C. G. R. KURUP; Gen. Man. RAVI SHANKAR.

Concept Publishing Co: A/15-16, Commercial Block, Mohan Garden, New Delhi 110 059; tel. (11) 5351460; fax (11) 5357103; e-mail publishing@conceptpub.com; f. 1975; geography, rural and urban development, education, sociology, economics, anthropology, agriculture, religion, history, law, philosophy, information sciences, ecology; Man. Dir ASHOK KUMAR MITTAL; Man. Editor D. N. GULATI.

Frank Bros and Co (Publishers) Ltd: 4675A Ansari Rd, 21 Darya Ganj, New Delhi 110 002; tel. (11) 3263393; fax (11) 3269032; e-mail fbros@ndb.vsnl.net.in; f. 1930; children's and educational books; Chair. R. C. GOVIL.

Global Business Press: GT Rd, 18–19 Dilshad Garden, Delhi 110 095; tel. (11) 2297792; fax (11) 2282332; business, management and computers; Dir SHEKHAR MALHOTRA.

Heritage Publishers: 32 Prakash Apartments, 5 Ansari Rd, Darya Ganj, New Delhi 110 002; tel. (11) 3266258; fax (11) 3263050; e-mail heritage@nda.vsnl.net.in; f. 1973; social sciences, art and architecture, technical, medical, scientific; Propr and Dir B. R. CHAWLA.

Hind Pocket Books (Pvt) Ltd: 18–19 Dilshad Garden, Delhi 110 095; tel. (11) 2297792; fax (11) 2282332; e-mail gbp@del2.vsnl.net.in; f. 1958; fiction and non-fiction paperbacks in English, Hindi, Punjabi, Malayalam and Urdu; Chair DINANATH MALHOTRA; Exec. Dir SHEKHAR MALHOTRA.

Hindustan Publishing Corpn (India): 4805/24 Bharat Ram Rd, Daryaganj, New Delhi 110 002; tel. (11) 3254401; fax (11) 6193511; e-mail hpc@hpc.cc; internet www.hpc.cc; archaeology, pure and applied sciences, geology, sociology, anthropology, economics; Man. Partner P. C. KUMAR.

Kali for Women: B1/8 Hauz Khas, New Delhi 110 016; tel. (11) 6964497; fax (11) 6864497; e-mail kaliw@del2.vsnl.net.in; women's studies, social sciences, humanities, general non-fiction, fiction, etc.; Heads of Organization URVASHI BUTALIA, RITU MENON.

Lalit Kala Akademi: Rabindra Bhavan, New Delhi 110 001; tel. (11) 3387241; fax (11) 3782485; e-mail lka@lalitkala.org.in; internet www.lalitkala.org.in; books on Indian art; Exec. Editor SHARDA GUPTA.

Lancers Books: POB 4236, New Delhi 110 048; tel. (11) 6241617; fax (11) 6992063; e-mail lanbooks@aol.com; f. 1977; politics (with special emphasis on north-east India), defence; Propr S. KUMAR.

Madhuban Educational Books: 576 Masjid Rd, Jangpura, New Delhi 110 014; tel. (11) 4314605; fax (11) 4310879; e-mail helpline@vikaspublishing.com; internet www.gobookshopping.com; f. 1969; school books, children's books; Chair. and Man. Dir CHANDER M. CHAWLA.

Motilal Banarsidass Publishers (Pvt) Ltd: 41 U.A. Bungalow Rd, Jawahar Nagar, Delhi 110 007; tel. (11) 3911985; fax (11) 3930689; e-mail mlbd@vsnl.com; internet www.mlbd.com; f. 1903; religion, philosophy, astrology, yoga, linguistic, in English and Sanskrit; Man. Dir J. P. JAIN; 7 brs.

Munshiram Manoharlal Publishers Pvt Ltd: 54 Rani Jhansi Rd, POB 5715, New Delhi 110 055; tel. (11) 3671668; fax (11) 3612745; e-mail mrml@mantraonline.com; f. 1952; Indian art, architecture, archaeology, religion, music, law, medicine, dance, dictionaries, travel, history, politics, numismatics, Buddhism, philosophy, sociology, etc.; Publishing Dir DEVENDRA JAIN; Dir ASHOK JAIN.

National Book Trust: A-5 Green Park, New Delhi 110 016; tel. (11) 6569962; fax (11) 6851795; e-mail nbtindia@ndb.vsnl.net.in; f. 1957; autonomous organization established by the Ministry of Human Resources Development to produce and encourage the production of good literary works; Chair. Dr SITAKANT MAHAPATRA; Dir NIRMAL KANTHI BHATACHARJEE.

National Council of Educational Research and Training (NCERT): Sri Aurobindo Marg, New Delhi 110 016; tel. (11) 6562708; fax (11) 6851070; e-mail dirc@glasdlo1.vsnl.net.in; f. 1961; school textbooks, teachers' guides, research monographs, journals, etc.; CEO PURAN DHAND.

Neeta Prakashan: A-4 Ring Rd, South Extension Part I, POB 3853, New Delhi 110 049; tel. (11) 4636010; fax (11) 4636011; e-mail neeta@giasdl01.vsnl.net.in; internet www.neetaprakashan.com; f. 1960; educational, children's, general; Dir RAKESH GUPTA.

New Age International Pvt Ltd: 4835/24 Ansari Rd, Daryaganj, New Delhi 110 002; tel. (11) 3278348; fax (11) 3267437; e-mail del.nail@axcess.net.in; f. 1966; science, engineering, technology, management, humanities, social science; Dir K. K. GUPTA.

Oxford and IBH Publishing Co (Pvt) Ltd: 66 Janpath, New Delhi 110 001; tel. (11) 3324578; fax (11) 3710090; e-mail oxford@vsnl.com; f. 1964; science, technology and reference in English; Dir VIJAY PRIMLANI; Man. Dir MOHAN PRIMLANI.

Oxford University Press: YMCA Library Bldg, 1st Floor, Jai Singh Rd, POB 43, New Delhi 110 001; tel. (11) 3747124; fax (11) 3360897; e-mail mk@oupin.com; f. 1912; educational, scientific, medical, general and reference; Man. Dir MANZAR KHAN.

Penguin Books India (Pvt) Ltd: 11 Community Centre, Panchsheel Park, New Delhi 110 017; tel. (11) 6494401; fax (11) 6494403; e-mail penguin@del2.vsnl.net.in; f. 1987; Indian literature and general non-fiction in English; Chair. PETER FIELD; CEO and Publr DAVID DAVIDAR.

People's Publishing House (Pvt) Ltd: 5E Rani Jhansi Rd, New Delhi 110 055; tel. (11) 7524701; f. 1947; Marxism, Leninism, peasant movt; Dir SHAMEEM FAIZEE.

Pitambar Publishing Co Pvt Ltd: 888 East Park Rd, Karol Bagh, New Delhi 110 005; tel. (11) 3670067; fax (11) 3676058; e-mail pitambar@bol.net.in; internet www.pitambar.com; academic, children's books, textbooks and general; Man. Dir ANAND BHUSHAN; 5 brs.

Prentice-Hall of India (Pvt) Ltd: M-97 Connaught Circus, New Delhi 110 001; tel. (11) 2143344; fax (11) 3717179; e-mail phi@phindia.com; internet www.phindia.com; f. 1963; university-level text and reference books; Man. Dir A. K. GHOSH.

Pustak Mahal: 10B Netaji Subhas Marg, Daryaganj, New Delhi 110 002; tel. (11) 3272783; fax (11) 3260518; e-mail pustakmahal@vsnl.com; children's, general, computers, religious, encyclopaedia; Man. Dir RAM AVTAR GUPTA.

Rajkamal Prakashan (Pvt) Ltd: 1B Netaji Subhas Marg, New Delhi 110 002; tel. (11) 3274463; fax (11) 3278144; e-mail rajkamalprakashan@email.com; f. 1946; Hindi; literary; also literary journal and monthly trade journal; Man. Dir ASHOK MAHESHWARI.

Rajpal and Sons: 1590 Madrasa Rd, Kashmere Gate, Delhi 110 006; tel. (11) 3865483; fax (11) 3867791; e-mail orienpbk@ndb.vsnl.net.in; f. 1891; humanities, social sciences, art, juvenile; Hindi; Chair VISHWANATH MALHOTRA.

RIS (Research and Information System) for the Non-Aligned and Other Developing Countries: Zone IV-B, Fourth Floor, India Habitat Centre, Lodhi Rd, New Delhi 110 003; tel. (11) 4682176; fax (11) 4682173; e-mail risnodec@del2.vsnl.net.in; internet www.ris.org.in; f. 1983; current and economic affairs involving non-aligned and developing countries; Dir-Gen. Dr V. R. PANCHAMUKHI.

Rupa & Co: 7/16 Ansari Rd, Daryaganj, POB 7017, New Delhi 110 002; tel. (11) 3278586; fax (11) 3277294; e-mail del.rupaco@axcess.net.in; internet www.rupaandco.com; f. 1936; Chief Exec. R. K. MEHRA.

Sage Publications India Pvt Ltd: 32 M-Block Market, Greater Kailash-1, POB 4215, New Delhi 110 048; tel. (11) 6491293; fax (11) 6491295; e-mail sageind@nda.vsnl.net.in; internet www.indiasage

.com; f. 1981; social science, development studies, business and management studies; Man. Dir TEJESHWAR SINGH.

Sahitya Akademi: Rabindra Bhavan, 35 Ferozeshah Rd, New Delhi 110 001; tel. (11) 3364207; fax (11) 3382428; e-mail secy@ndb.vsnl.net.in; internet www.sahitya-akademi.org; f. 1956; bibliographies, translations, monographs, encyclopaedias, literary classics, etc.; Pres. RAMAKANTA RATH; Sec. Dr K. SATCHIDANANDAN.

Scholar Publishing House (P) Ltd: 85 Model Basti, New Delhi 110 005; tel. (11) 3541299; fax (11) 3676565; e-mail scholar@vsnl.com; internet www.scholargroup.com; f. 1968; educational; Man. Dir RAJESH RANADE.

Shiksha Bharati: 1590 Madrasa Rd, Kashmere Gate, Delhi 110 006; tel. (11) 3869812; fax (11) 3867791; e-mail orientpbk@vsnl.com; f. 1955; textbooks, creative literature, popular science and juvenile in Hindi and English; Editor MEERA JOHRI.

Sterling Publishers (Pvt) Ltd: A-59 Okhla Industrial Area, Phase II, New Delhi 110 020; tel. (11) 6387070; fax (11) 6383788; e-mail ghai@nde.vsnl.net.in; internet www.sterlingpublishers.com; f. 1965; academic books on the humanities and social sciences, children's books, computer books, management books, paperbacks; Chair. and Man. Dir S. K. GHAI; Gen. Man. A. J. SEHGAL.

Tata McGraw-Hill Publishing Co Ltd: 7 West Patel Nagar, New Delhi 110 008; tel. (11) 5819304; fax (11) 5819302; e-mail info_india@mcgraw-hill.com; internet www.tatamcgrawhill.com; f. 1970; engineering, computers, sciences, medicine, management, humanities, social sciences; Chair. Dr F. A. MEHTA; Man. Dir Dr N. SUBRAHMANYAM.

Vikas Publishing House (Pvt) Ltd: 576 Masjid Rd, Jangpura, New Delhi 110 014; tel. (11) 4314605; fax (11) 4310879; e-mail helpline@vikaspublishing.com; internet www.gobookshopping.com; f. 1969; computers, management, commerce, sciences, engineering, textbooks; Chair. and Man. Dir CHANDER M. CHAWLA.

A. H. Wheeler & Co Ltd: 411 Surya Kiran Bldg, 19 K. G. Marg, New Delhi 110 001; tel. (11) 3312629; fax (11) 3357798; e-mail wheelerpub@mantraonline.com; f. 1958; textbooks, reference books, computer science and information technology, electronics, management, telecommunications, social sciences, etc.; Exec. Pres. ALOK BANERJEE.

Chennai (Madras)

Higginbothams Ltd: 814 Anna Salai, POB 311, Chennai 600 002; tel. (44) 8520640; fax (44) 8528101; e-mail higginbothams@vsnl.com; f. 1844; general; Dir S. CHANDRASEKHAR.

B. G. Paul and Co: 4 Francis Joseph St, Chennai; f. 1923; general, educational and oriental; Man. K. NILAKANTAN.

T. R. Publications Pvt Ltd: PMG Complex, 2nd Floor, 57 South Usman Rd, T. Nagar, Chennai 600 017; tel. (44) 4340765; fax (44) 4348837; e-mail trgeetha@giasmd01.vsnl.net.in; internet www.trpubs.com; Chief Exec. S. GEETHA.

Kolkata (Calcutta)

Academic Publishers: 12/1A Bankim Chatterjee St, POB 12341, Kolkata 700 073; tel. (33) 2414857; fax (33) 2413702; e-mail acabooks@cal.vsnl.net.in; f. 1958; textbooks, management, medical, technical; Man. Partner B. K. DHUR.

Advaita Ashrama: 5 Dehi Entally Rd, Kolkata 700 014; tel. (33) 2164000; fax (33) 2450050; e-mail advaita@vsnl.com; internet www.advaitaonline.com; f. 1899; religion, philosophy, spiritualism, Vedanta; publication centre of Ramakrishna Math and Ramakrishna Mission; Publication Man. Swami MUMUKSHANANDA.

Allied Book Agency: 18A Shyama Charan De St, Kolkata 700 073; tel. (33) 312594; general and academic; Dir B. SARKAR.

Ananda Publishers (Pvt) Ltd: 45 Beniatola Lane, Kolkata 700 009; tel. (33) 2414352; fax (33) 2253240; e-mail ananda@cal3.vsnl.net.in; literature, general; Dir A. SARKAR; Man. Dir S. MITRA.

Assam Review Publishing Co: 27A Waterloo St, 1st Floor, Kolkata 700 069; tel. (33) 2482251; fax (33) 2482251; e-mail teknokom@satyam.net.in; f. 1926; publrs of *The Assam Review and Tea News* (monthly) and *The Assam Directory and Tea Areas Handbook* (annually); Chief Exec. GOBINDALAL BANERJEE.

Book Land (Pvt) Ltd: Kolkata; tel. (33) 2414158; economics, politics, history and general; Dir SUBHANKAR BASU.

Chuckervertty, Chatterjee and Co Ltd: 15 College Sq., Kolkata 700 073; tel. (33) 2416425; Man. Dir MALA MAZUMDAR.

Eastern Law House (Pvt) Ltd: 54 Ganesh Chunder Ave, Kolkata 700 013; tel. (33) 2374989; fax (33) 2150491; e-mail elh@cal.vsnl.net.in; f. 1918; legal, commercial and accountancy; Dir ASOK DE; br. in New Delhi.

Firma KLM Private Ltd: 257B B. B. Ganguly St, Kolkata 700 012; tel. (33) 2374391; fax (33) 2217294; e-mail fklm@satyam.net.in; f. 1950; Indology, scholarly in English, Bengali, Sanskrit and Hindi, alternative medicine; Man. Dir R. N. MUKHERJI.

Intertrade Publications (India) (Pvt) Ltd: 55 Gariahat Rd, POB 10210, Kolkata 700 019; tel. (33) 474872; f. 1954; economics, medicine, law, history and trade directories; Man. Dir Dr K. K. ROY.

A. Mukherjee and Co (Pvt) Ltd: 2 Bankim Chatterjee St, Kolkata 700 073; tel. (33) 311406; fax (33) 7448172; f. 1940; educational and general in Bengali and English; Man. Dir RAJEEV NEOGI.

Naya Prokash: 206 Bidhan Sarani, POB 11468, Kolkata 700 006; tel. (33) 2414709; fax (33) 5382897; e-mail npsales@cal2.vsnl.net.in; f. 1960; agriculture, horticulture, Indology, history, political science; Man. Dir P. S. BASU.

New Era Publishing Co: 31 Gauri Bari Lane, Kolkata 700 004; f. 1944; Propr Dr P. N. MITRA; Man. S. K. MITRA.

W. Newman and Co Ltd: 3 Old Court House St, Kolkata 700 069; tel. (33) 2489436; f. 1854; general; Man. K. M. BANTIA.

Punthi Pustak: 136/4B Bidhan Sarani, Kolkata 700 004; tel. (33) 558473; religion, history, philosophy; Propr S. K. BHATTACHARYA.

Renaissance Publishers (Pvt) Ltd: 15 Bankim Chatterjee St, Kolkata 700 012; f. 1949; politics, philosophy, history; Man. Dir J. C. GOSWAMI.

Saraswati Library: 206 Bidhan Sarani, Kolkata 700 006; tel. (33) 345492; f. 1914; history, philosophy, religion, literature; Man. Partner B. BHATTACHARJEE.

M. C. Sarkar and Sons (Pvt) Ltd: 14 Bankim Chatterjee St, Kolkata 700 073; tel. (33) 312490; f. 1910; reference; Dirs SUPRIYA SARKAR, SAMIT SARKAR.

Visva-Bharati: 6 Acharya Jagadish Bose Rd, Kolkata 700 017; tel. (33) 2479868; f. 1923; literature; Dir ASHOKE MUKHOPADHYAY.

Mumbai

Bharatiya Vidya Bhavan: Munshi Sadan, Kulapati K. M. Munshi Marg, Mumbai 400 007; tel. (22) 4950916; fax (22) 3630058; e-mail brbhavan@bom7.vsnl.net.in; f. 1938; art, literature, culture, education, philosophy, religion, history of India; various periodicals in English, Hindi, Sanskrit and other Indian languages; Pres. R. VENKATARAMAN; Sec.-Gen. S. RAMAKRISHNAN.

Blackie and Son (Pvt) Ltd: Blackie House, 103–105 Walchand Hirachand Marg, POB 381, Mumbai 400 001; tel. (22) 261410; f. 1901; educational, scientific and technical, general and juvenile; Man. Dir D. R. BHAGI.

Himalaya Publishing House: 'Ramdoot', Dr Bhalerao Marg (Kelewadi), Girgaon, Mumbai 400 004; tel. (22) 3860170; fax (22) 3877178; e-mail himpub@vsnl.net.in; f. 1976; textbooks and research work; Dir MEENA PANDEY; CEO D. P. PANDEY.

India Book House (Pvt) Ltd: 412 Tulsiani Chambers, Nariman Point, Mumbai 400 021; tel. (22) 2840165; fax (22) 2835099; e-mail info@ibhworld.com; Man. Dir DEEPAK MIRCHANDANI.

International Book House (Pvt) Ltd: Indian Mercantile Mansions (Extension), Madame Cama Rd, Mumbai 400 039; tel. (22) 2021634; fax (22) 2851109; e-mail ibh@vsnl.com; internet www.intbh.com; f. 1941; general, educational, scientific, technical, engineering, social sciences, humanities and law; Man. Dir S. K. GUPTA; Exec. Dir SANJEEV GUPTA.

Jaico Publishing House: 127 Mahatma Gandhi Rd, opposite Mumbai University, Mumbai 400 023; tel. (22) 2676702; fax (22) 2656412; e-mail jaicopub@vsnl.com; f. 1947; general paperbacks, management, computer and engineering books, etc.; imports scientific, medical, technical and educational books; Man. Dir ASHWIN J. SHAH.

Popular Prakashan (Pvt) Ltd: 35c Pandit Madan Mohan Malaviya Marg, Tardeo, Popular Press Bldg, opp. Roche, Mumbai 400 034; tel. (22) 4941656; fax (22) 4945294; e-mail popularprakashan@vsnl.com; f. 1968; sociology, biographies, religion, philosophy, fiction, arts, music, current affairs, medicine, history, politics and administration in English and Marathi; Man. Dir R. G. BHATKAL.

Somaiya Publications (Pvt) Ltd: 172 Mumbai Marathi Granthasangrahalaya Marg, Dadar, Mumbai 400 014; tel. (22) 4130230; fax (22) 2047297; e-mail somaiyabooks@rediffmail.com; internet www.somaiya.com; f. 1967; economics, sociology, history, politics, mathematics, sciences, language, literature, education, psychology, religion, philosophy, logic; Chair. Dr S. K. SOMAIYA.

Taraporevala, Sons and Co (Pvt) Ltd D.B.: 210 Dr Dadabhai Naoroji Rd, Fort, Mumbai 400 001; tel. (22) 2071433; f. 1864; Indian art, culture, history, sociology, scientific, technical and general in English; Chief Exec. R. J. TARAPOREVALA.

N. M. Tripathi (Pvt) Ltd: 164 Shamaldas Gandhi Marg, Mumbai 400 002; tel. (22) 2013651; f. 1888; general in English and Gujarati; Chair. A. S. PANDYA; Man. Dir KARTIK R. TRIPATHI.

Other Towns

Bharat Bharati Prakashan & Co: Western Kutchery Rd, Meerut 250 001; tel. 663698; f. 1952; textbooks; Man. Dir Surendra Agarwal.

Bharati Bhawan: Thakurbari Rd, Kadamkuan, Patna 800 003; tel. (612) 671356; fax (612) 670010; e-mail bbpdpat@giascl01.vsnl.com; f. 1942; educational and juvenile; Man. Partner Tarit Kumar Bose.

Bishen Singh Mahendra Pal Singh: 23A New Connaught Place, POB 137, Dehradun 248 001; tel. (135) 655748; fax (135) 650107; e-mail bsmps@del2.vsnl.net.in; internet www.bishensinghbooks.com; f. 1957; botany, forestry, agriculture; Dirs Gajendra Singh Gahlot, Abhimanyu Gahlot.

Catholic Press: Ranchi 834 001, Bihar; f. 1928; books and periodicals; Dir William Tigga.

Chugh Publications: 2 Strachey Rd, POB 101, Allahabad; tel. (532) 623063; sociology, economics, history, general; Propr Ramesh Kumar Chugh.

Geetha Book House: K. R. Circle, Mysore 570 001; tel. (821) 33589; f. 1959; general; Dirs M. Gopala Krishna, M. Gururaja Rao.

Kalyani Publishers: 1/1 Rajinder Nagar, Civil Lines, Ludhiana, Punjab 141 008; tel. (161) 745756; fax (161) 745872; textbooks; Dir Usha Raj Kumar.

Kitabistan: 30 Chak, Allahabad 211 003; tel. (532) 653219; f. 1932; general, agriculture, govt publs in English, Hindi, Urdu, Farsi and Arabic; Partners A. U. Khan, Sultan Zaman.

Krishna Prakashan Media (P) Ltd: (Unit) Goel Publishing House, 11 Shivaji Rd, Meerut 250 001; tel. (121) 642946; fax (121) 645855; textbooks; Man. Dir Satyendra Kumar Rastogi; Dir Anita Rastogi.

The Law Book Co (Pvt) Ltd: 18B Sardar Patel Marg, Civil Lines, POB 1004, Allahabad 211 001; tel. (532) 624905; fax (532) 420852; e-mail baggal@nae.vsnl.net.in; f. 1929; legal texts in English; Dir Anil Bagga; Man. Dir L. R. Bagga.

Macmillan India Ltd: 315/316 Raheja Chambers, 12 Museum Rd, Bangalore 560 001; tel. (80) 5594120; fax (80) 5588713; e-mail chandra291@vsnl.com; school and university books in English; general; Pres. and Man. Dir Rajiv Beri; Dir (Technical) Debashish Banerjee.

Navajivan Publishing House: PO Navajivan, Ahmedabad 380 014; tel. (79) 7540635; f. 1919; Gandhiana and related social science; in English, Hindi and Gujarati; Man. Trustee Jitendra Desai; Sales Man. Kapil Rawal.

Nem Chand and Bros: Civil Lines, Roorkee 247 667; tel. (1332) 72258; fax (1332) 73258; f. 1951; engineering textbooks and journals.

Pilgrims Publishing: Pilgrims Book House, B27/98-A-8 Nawabganj Rd, Durga Kund, Varanasi 221 001; tel. (542) 312456; fax (542) 314059; e-mail pilgrims@satyam.net.in; internet www.pilgrimsbooks.com; f. 1986; first edition and reprint books on Nepal, Tibet, India and the Himalayas; Man. Editor Chaitanya Nagar.

Orient Longman Ltd: 3-6-272 Himayat Nagar, Hyderabad 500 029; tel. (40) 3224305; fax (40) 3222900; e-mail orlongco@hd2.dot.net.in; f. 1948; educational, technical, general and children's in English and almost all Indian languages; Chair. Shanta Rameshwar Rao; Dirs Dr Nandini Rao, J. Krishnadev Rao.

Publication Bureau: Panjab University, Chandigarh 160 014; tel. (172) 541782; f. 1948; textbooks, academic and general; Man. H. R. Grover.

Publication Bureau: Punjabi University, Patiala 147 002; tel. (175) 2826650; university-level text and reference books; Head of Bureau S. Sukhdial Singh.

Ram Prasad and Sons: Hospital Rd, Agra 282 003; tel. (562) 367904; fax (562) 360906; e-mail ea_08@yahoo.com; f. 1905; agricultural, arts, history, commerce, education, general, pure and applied science, economics, sociology; Dirs R. N., B. N., Y. N. and Ravi Agarwal; Man. S. N. Agarwal; br. in Bhopal.

Government Publishing House

Publications Division: Ministry of Information and Broadcasting, Govt of India, Patiala House, New Delhi 110 001; tel. (11) 3386879; fax (11) 3386879; e-mail pubdiv1@bol.net.in; internet www.nic.in/indiapublications; f. 1941; culture, art, literature, planning and development, general; also 21 periodicals in English and several Indian languages; Dir P. S. Bhatnagar.

PUBLISHERS' ASSOCIATIONS

Bombay Booksellers' and Publishers' Association: No. 25, 6th Floor, Bldg No. 3, Navjivan Commercial Premises Co-op Society Ltd, Dr Bhadkamkar Marg, Mumbai 400 008; tel. (22) 3088691; f. 1961; 400 mems; Pres. K. M. Varghese; Gen. Sec. B. S. Fernandes.

Delhi State Booksellers' and Publishers' Association: 3026/7H Shiv Chowk, (South Patel Nagar) Ranjit Nagar, New Delhi 110 008; tel. (11) 5772748; fax (11) 5786769; e-mail rpnbooks@indiatimes.com; f. 1943; 400 mems; Pres. Dr S. K. Bhatia; Sec. Ranbir Singh.

Federation of Educational Publishers in India: 19 Rani Jhansi Rd, New Delhi 110 055; tel. (11) 3522697; fax (11) 3636103; f. 1987; 14 affiliated asscns; 168 mems; 24 associated mems; Pres. R. K. Gupta; Sec.-Gen. Kamal Arora.

Federation of Indian Publishers: Federation House, 18/1-C Institutional Area, nr JNU, New Delhi 110 067; tel. (11) 6964847; fax (11) 6864054; e-mail fipl@satyam.net.in; internet www.federationofindianpublishers.com; 18 affiliated asscns; 159 mems; Pres. Debajyoti Datta; Hon. Gen. Sec. Narendra Kumar.

Akhil Bharatiya Hindi Prakashak Sangh: A-2/1, Krishan Nagar, Delhi 110 051; tel. (11) 2219398; f. 1954; 400 mems; Pres. Inder Sengar; Gen. Sec. Arun Kumar Sharma.

All Assam Publishers' and Booksellers' Association: College Hostel Rd, Panbazar, Guwahati 780 001; tel. (361) 634790; fax (361) 513886; Pres. Nabin Baruah; Sec. J. N. Dutta Baruah.

All India Urdu Publications' and Booksellers' Association: 3243 Kuchatarachand, Daryaganj, New Delhi 110 002; tel. (11) 3257189; fax (11) 3265480; e-mail aakif@del3.vsnl.net.in; internet www.aakif.com; f. 1988; 150 mems; Pres. Dr Khaliq Anjum; Gen. Sec. S. M. Zafar Ali.

Booksellers' and Publishers' Association of South India: 8, II Floor, Sun Plaza, G. N. Chetty Rd, Chennai 600 006; 158 mems; Pres. S. Chandrasekar; Sec. Ravi Chopra.

Gujarati Sahitya Prakashak Vikreta Mandal: Navajivan Trust, P.O. Navajivan, Ahmedabad 380 014; tel. (79) 7540635; 125 mems; Pres. Jitendra Desai; Sec. K. N. Madrasi.

Karnataka Publishers' Association: 88 Mysore Rd, Bangalore 560 018; tel. (80) 601638; Pres. Prof. H. R. Dasegowda; Sec. S. V. Srinivasa Rao.

Kerala Publishers' and Booksellers' Association: Piaco Bldg, Jew St, Kochi 682 011; 30 mems; Pres. D. C. Kizhakemuri; Sec. E. K. Sekhar.

Marathi Prakashak Parishad: Amber Chambers, Appa Balwant Chowk, Pune 411 002; tel. (212) 4451219; fax (212) 4454086; 100 mems; Pres. A. G. Kulkarni.

Orissa Publishers' and Booksellers' Association: Binodbihari, Cuttack 753 002; tel. (671) 612855; f. 1973–74; 280 mems; Pres. Subhendu Sekhar Ratha; Sec. Bhikari Charan Mohapatra.

Paschimbanga Prakasak Sabha: 206 Bidhan Sarani, Kolkata 700 006; tel. (33) 3504534; fax (33) 2413852; Pres. Amitabha Sen; Gen. Sec. T. Saha.

Publishers' Association of West Bengal: 6-B, Ramanath Mazumder St, Kolkata 700 009; tel. (33) 325580; 164 mems; Pres. Mohit Kumar Basu; Gen. Sec. Shankari Bhusan Nayak.

Publishers' and Booksellers' Association of Bengal: 93 Mahatma Gandhi Rd, Kolkata 700 007; tel. (33) 2411993; f. 1912; 4,500 mems; Pres. Dulal Bhattashali; Gen. Sec. Chitta Singha Roy.

Punjabi Publishers' Association: Satnam Singh, Singh Brothers, Bazar Mai Sewan, Amritsar 143 006; tel. (183) 45787; Sec. Satnam Singh.

Vijayawada Publishers' Association: 27-1-68, Karl Marx Rd, Vijayawada 520 002; tel. (866) 433353; fax (866) 426348; 41 mems; Pres. Dupati Vijay Kumar; Sec. U. N. Yogi.

Federation of Publishers' and Booksellers' Associations in India: 2nd Floor, 84 Darya Ganj, New Delhi 110 002; tel. (11) 3272845; fax (11) 3281227; 16 affiliated asscns; 550 mems; Pres. S. C. Sethi; Sec. K. P. R. Nair.

Publishers' and Booksellers' Guild: Guild House, 2B Jhamapukur Lane, Kolkata 700 009; tel. (33) 3544417; fax (33) 3604566; e-mail guild@cal2.vsnl.net.in; internet www.kolkatabookfair2002.com; f. 1975; 37 mems; organizes annual Kolkata Book Fair; Pres. Jayant Manaktala; Sec. Kalyan Shah.

UP Publishers' and Booksellers' Association: 111-A/243 Ashok Nagar, Kanpur 208 012; asscn for Uttar Pradesh state.

Broadcasting and Communications

TELECOMMUNICATIONS

Telecom Regulatory Authority of India (TRAI): 16th Floor, Jawahar Vyapar Bhavan 1, Tolstoy Marg, New Delhi 110 001; tel. (11) 3357815; fax (11) 3738708; e-mail trai@del2.vsnl.net.in; internet www.trai.gov.in; f. 1998; Chair. S. S. Sodhi; Vice-Chair. Bal Krishan Zutshi.

Bharti Telenet Ltd: Indore; f. 1998; India's first privately-owned telephone network; Exec. Dir Bhagwan Khurana.

Ericsson: POB 10912, New Delhi 110 066.

ITI (Indian Telephone Industries) Ltd: 45/1 Magrath Rd, Bangalore 560 025; tel. (80) 5366116; fax (80) 5593188; internet www.itiltdindia.com; f. 1948; mfrs of all types of telecommunication equipment, incl. telephones, automatic exchanges and long-distance transmission equipment; also produces optical fibre equipment and microwave equipment; will manufacture all ground communication equipment for the 22 earth stations of the Indian National Satellite; in conjunction with the Post and Telegraph Department, a newly designed 2,000-line exchange has been completed; Chair. and Man. Dir Lakshmi G. Menon.

Mahanagar Telephone Nigam Ltd (MTNL): Jeevan Bharati Tower, 124 Connaught Circus, New Delhi 110 001; tel. (11) 3742212; fax (11) 3314243; e-mail cmd@bol.net.in; internet www.mtnl.net.in; f. 1986; 66% state-owned; owns and operates telephone networks in Mumbai and Delhi; Chair. and Man. Dir Narinder Sharma.

Videsh Sanchar Nigam Ltd (VSNL): Lok Manya Videsh Sanchar Bhawan, Kasinath Dhuru Marg, Prabhadevi, Mumbai 400 028; tel. (22) 4322959; fax (22) 4365689; e-mail helpdesk@giaspn01.vsnl.net.in; internet www.vsnl.com; f. 1986; 26% state-owned; 25% owned by the Tata Group; Chair. Ratan N. Tata; Man. Dir S. K. Gupta.

BROADCASTING

Prasar Bharati (Broadcasting Corpn of India): New Delhi; autonomous body; oversees operations of state-owned radio and television services; f. 1997; Chief Exec. K. S. Sarma.

Radio

All India Radio (AIR): Akashvani Bhavan, Parliament St, New Delhi 110 001; tel. (11) 3715411; fax (11) 3714061; broadcasting is controlled by the Ministry of Information and Broadcasting and is primarily govt-financed; operates a network of 208 stations and 332 transmitters (grouped into four zones— north, south, east and west), covering 98.8% of the population and over 90% of the total area of the country; Dir-Gen. T. R. Malakar.

The News Services Division of AIR, centralized in New Delhi, is one of the largest news organizations in the world. It has 45 regional news units, which broadcast 316 bulletins daily in 24 languages and 38 dialects. Eighty four bulletins in 19 languages are broadcast in the Home Services, 139 regional bulletins in 64 languages and dialects, and 64 bulletins in 25 languages in the External Services.

Television

Doordarshan India (Television India): Mandi House, Doordarshan Bhavan, Copernicus Marg, New Delhi 110 001; tel. (11) 3385958; fax (11) 3386507; f. 1976; broadcasting is controlled by the Ministry of Information and Broadcasting and is govt-financed; programmes: 280 hours weekly; 5 All-India channels, 11 regional language satellite channels, 5 state networks and 1 international channel; Dir-Gen. Dr S. Y. Qureshi.

In January 2002 74.8% of the country's area and 87.9% of the population were covered by the TV network. There were 1,231 transmitters in operation in that month. By 2000 51 programme production centres and nine relay centres had been established.

Finance

(cap. = capital; p.u. = paid up; res = reserves; dep. = deposits; m. = million; brs = branches; amounts in rupees)

BANKING

State Banks

Reserve Bank of India: Central Office Bldg, Shahid Bhagat Singh Rd, POB 10007, Mumbai 400 001; tel. (22) 2661602; fax (22) 2658269; e-mail rbiprd@giasbm01.vsnl.net.in; internet www.rbi.org.in; f. 1934; nationalized 1949; sole bank of issue; cap. 50m., res 65,000m., dep. 806,463.9m. (Dec. 2000); Gov. Dr Bimal Jalan; Dep. Govs Dr Rakesh Mohan, S. P. Talwar, Jagdish Capoor; 4 offices and 14 brs.

State Bank of India: Corporate Centre, Madame Cama Rd, POB 10121, Mumbai 400 021; tel. (22) 2022426; fax (22) 2851391; e-mail sbiid@boms.vsnl.net.in; internet www.sbi.co.in; f. 1955; cap. p.u. 5,263m., res and surplus 146,980.8m., dep. 2,705,601.4m. (March 2002); 7 associates, 7 domestic subsidiaries/affiliates, 3 foreign subsidiaries, 4 jt ventures abroad; Chair. Janaki Ballabh; Man. Dirs A. K. Batra, P. N. Venkatachalam; 9,085 brs (incl. 51 overseas brs and rep. offices in 31 countries).

State-owned Commercial Banks

Fourteen of India's major commercial banks were nationalized in 1969 and a further six in 1980. They are managed by 15-mem. boards of directors (two directors to be appointed by the central Government, one employee director, one representing employees who are not workmen, one representing depositors, three representing farmers, workers, artisans, etc., five representing persons with special knowledge or experience, one Reserve Bank of India official and one Government of India official). The Department of Banking of the Ministry of Finance controls all banking operations.

There were 65,931 branches of public-sector and other commercial banks in June 2001.

Aggregate deposits of all scheduled commercial banks amounted to Rs 10,677,070m. in December 2001.

Allahabad Bank: 2 Netaji Subhas Rd, Kolkata 700 001; tel. (33) 2208668; fax (33) 2488323; e-mail albfd@giascl01.vsnl.net.in; internet www.allahabadbank.com/; f. 1865; nationalized 1969; cap. p.u. 2,467m., res 7,338m., dep. 226,660m. (March 2002); Chair. and Man. Dir B. Samal; 1,915 brs.

Andhra Bank: Andhra Bank Bldgs, Saifabad, 5-9-11 Secretariat Rd, Hyderabad 500 004; tel. (40) 3230001; fax (40) 3211050; e-mail andhrabank.fedho@gnhyd; internet www.andhrabankindia.com; f. 1923; nationalized 1980; cap. p.u. 4,500m., res 4,339m., dep. 184,908m. (March 2002); Chair. and Man. Dir B. Vasanthan; 980 brs and 87 extension counters.

Bank of Baroda: 1st Floor, Mackinnon Mackenzie Bldg, 4 Shoorji Vallabhdas Marg, Ballard Pier, 10046, Mumbai 400 001; tel. (22) 2615065; fax (22) 2620408; e-mail bobio@calva.com; internet www.bankofbaroda.com; f. 1908; nationalized 1969; merged with Benares State Bank in 2002; cap. 2,943.3m., res 35,334.2m., dep. 618,045m. (March 2002); Chair. and Man. Dir P. S. Shenoy; 2,641 brs in India, 38 brs overseas.

Bank of India: Express Towers, Nariman Point, POB 234, Mumbai 400 021; tel. (22) 2023167; fax (22) 2022831; e-mail cmdboi@bom5.vsnl.net.in; internet www.bankofindia.com; f. 1906; nationalized 1969; cap. 4,880.8m., res and surplus 21,637.2m., dep. 608,330m. (March 2002); Chair. and Man. Dir K. V. Krishnamurthy; 2,528 brs in India, 19 brs overseas.

Bank of Maharashtra: 'Lokmangal', 1501 Shivajinagar, Pune 411 005; tel. (212) 5532731; fax (212) 5533246; e-mail bomcocmd@vsnl.com; internet www.bank-of-maharashtra.com; f. 1935; nationalized 1969; cap. 3,305.1m., res 3,672m., dep. 191,306.3m. (March 2002); Chair. and Man. Dir S. C. Basu; 1,179 brs.

Canara Bank: 112 Jayachamarajendra Rd, POB 6648, Bangalore 560 002; tel. (812) 2221581; fax (812) 2222704; e-mail canbank@blr.vsnl.net.in; internet www.canbankindia.com; f. 1906; nationalized 1969; cap. 5,778.7m., res 28,936.3m., dep. 640,300.1m. (March 2002); Chair. and Man. Dir R. V. Shastri; 2,348 brs in India, 1 br. overseas.

Central Bank of India: Chandermukhi, Nariman Point, Mumbai 400 021; tel. (22) 2026428; fax (22) 2044336; e-mail cbicpp@b01.net.in; internet www.centralbankofindia.com; f. 1911; nationalized 1969; cap. 11,241.4m., res and surplus 8,726m., dep. 471,373.8m. (March 2002); Chair. and Man. Dir Dr Dalbir Singh; 3,115 brs.

Corporation Bank: Mangaladevi Temple Rd, POB 88, Mangalore 575 001; tel. (824) 426416; fax (824) 444617; e-mail rmd@corpbank.co.in; internet www.corpbank.com; f. 1906; nationalized 1980; cap. 1,434.4m., res 19,603.8m., dep. 189,240m. (March 2002); Chair. and Man. Dir K. Cherian Varghese; Exec. Dir P. K. Gupta; 652 brs.

Dena Bank: Maker Towers 'E', 7th–10th Floor, Cuffe Parade, Colaba, POB 6058, Mumbai 400 005; tel. (22) 2189151; fax (22) 2189046; e-mail dena@giasbom01.vsnl.net.in; internet www.denabank.com; f. 1938 as Devkaran Nanjee Banking Co Ltd; nationalized 1969; cap. 2,068.2m., res and surplus 6,213.7m., dep. 153,546.9m. (March 2002); Chair. and Man. Dir A. G. Joshi; 1,134 brs.

Indian Bank: 31 Rajaji Salai, POB 1866, Chennai 600 001; tel. (44) 5233231; fax (44) 5231278; e-mail indbank@giasmd01.vsnl.net.in; internet www.indian-bank.com; f. 1907; nationalized 1969; cap. 38,039.6m., res 3,812.5m., dep. 240,388m. (March 2002); Chair. and Man. Dir Ranjana Kumar; Exec. Dir M. B. N. Rao; 1,424 brs.

Indian Overseas Bank: 762 Anna Salai, POB 3765, Chennai 600 002; tel. (44) 8524171; fax (44) 8523595; e-mail iobfx@vsnl.com; internet www.iob.com; f. 1937; nationalized 1969; cap. 4,448m., res 3,172.2m., dep. 309,460m. (March 2002); Chair. and Man. Dir S. C. Gupta; Exec. Dir R. Natarajan; 1,438 brs.

Oriental Bank of Commerce: Harsha Bhavan, E Block, Connaught Place, POB 329, New Delhi 110 001; tel. (11) 3323444; fax (11) 3321514; e-mail obc@obcindia.com; internet www.obcindia.com; f. 1943; nationalized 1980; cap. 1,925.4m., res 14,271.9m., dep. 284,884m. (March 2002); Chair. and Man. Dir B. D. Narang; 533 brs.

Punjab and Sind Bank: 21 Bank House, Rajendra Place, New Delhi 110 008; tel. (11) 5768831; fax (11) 5751765; internet www.punjabandsindbank.com; f. 1908; nationalized 1980; cap. 2,430.6m., res 1,307.4m., dep. 94,966m. (March 1999); Chair. and Man. Dir N. S. GUJRAL; Exec. Dir M. S. KAPUR; 811 brs.

Punjab National Bank: 7 Bhikaiji Cama Place, Africa Ave, New Delhi 110 066; tel. (11) 6102303; fax (11) 6196456; e-mail pnbibd@ndf.vsnl.net.in; internet www.pnbindia.com; f. 1895; nationalized 1969; merged with New Bank of India in 1993; cap. 2,122.4m., res 26,658m., dep. 641,234.8m. (March 2002); Chair. and Man. Dir S. S. KOHLI; Exec. Dir K. R. CHABRIA; 4,268 brs.

Syndicate Bank: POB 1, Manipal 576 119; tel. (8252) 71181; fax (8252) 70266; e-mail idcb@syndicatebank.com; internet www.syndicatebank.com; f. 1925 as Canara Industrial and Banking Syndicate Ltd; name changed as above 1964; nationalized 1969; cap. 4,719.4m., res 7,467.0m., dep. 285,480m. (March 2002); Chair. and Man. Dir MICHAEL BASTIAN; 1,948 brs.

UCO Bank: 10 Biplabi Trailokya Maharaj Sarani (Brabourne Rd), POB 2455, Kolkata 700 001; tel. (33) 2254120; fax (33) 2253986; e-mail hoidiv.calcutta@ucobank.wiprobt.ems.vsnl.net.in; internet www.ucobank.com; f. 1943 as United Commercial Bank Ltd; nationalized 1969; name changed as above 1985; cap. 22,645.2m., res 4,969.5m., dep. 268,487.7m. (March 2002); Chair. and Man. Dir V. P. SHETTY; Exec. Dir M. M. VAISH; 1,797 brs.

Union Bank of India: Union Bank Bhavan, 239 Vidhan Bhavan Marg, Nariman Point, Mumbai 400 021; tel. (22) 2023060; fax (22) 2025238; e-mail union@bom3.vsnl.net.in; internet www.unionbankofindia.com; f. 1919; nationalized 1969; cap. 3,380m., res 17,690m., dep. 397,939m. (March 2002); Chair. and Man. Dir V. LEELADHAR; 2,023 brs.

United Bank of India: 16 Old Court House St, Kolkata 700 001; tel. (33) 2487471; fax (33) 2485852; e-mail utbihoc@giascl01.vsnl.net.in; internet www.unitedbankofindia.com; f. 1950; nationalized 1969; cap. 18,108.7m., res 1,583.2m., dep. 196,106.6m. (March 2002); Chair. and Man. Dir MADHUKAR; Exec. Dir G. R. SUNDARAVADIVEL; 1,316 brs.

Vijaya Bank: 41/2 Mahatma Gandhi Rd, Bangalore 560 001; tel. (80) 5584066; fax (80) 5588853; e-mail vijbank@bgl.vsnl.net.in; internet www.vijayabank.com; f. 1931; nationalized 1980; cap. 3,335.2m., res 3,295.1m., dep. 146,810m. (March 2002); Chair. and Man. Dir M. S. KAPUR; 842 brs.

Principal Private Banks

The Bank of Rajasthan Ltd: C-3 Sardar Patel Marg, Jaipur 302 001; tel. (141) 381222; fax (141) 381123; e-mail borit@jp1.dot.net.in; internet www.bankofrajasthan.com; f. 1943; cap. p.u. 1,003.7m., res 1,104.8m., dep. 39,599.8m. (March 2002); Chair. PRAVIN KUMAR TAYAL; Man. Dir K. M. BHATTACHARYA; 307 brs.

Bharat Overseas Bank Ltd: Habeeb Towers, 196 Anna Salai, Chennai 600 002; tel. (44) 8525686; fax (44) 8524700; e-mail bobl@md3.vsnl.net.in; internet www.boblonline.com; f. 1973; cap. 157.5m., res 1,072.8m., dep. 18,232.6m. (March 2002); Chair. G. KRISHNAMURTHY; Gen. Man. G. CHANDRAN; 77 brs.

Bombay Mercantile Co-operative Bank Ltd: 78 Mohammed Ali Rd, Mumbai 400 003; tel. (22) 3425961; fax (22) 3433385; e-mail bmcb@bom5.vsnl.net.in; f. 1939; cap. 126m., res 1,696.6m., dep. 27,756.3m. (March 2000); Chair. A. R. KIDWAI; Man. Dir A. Q. SIDDIQUI; 53 brs.

The Catholic Syrian Bank Ltd: St Mary's College Rd, POB 502, Trichur 680 020; tel. (487) 333020; fax (487) 333435; e-mail csbho@md2.vsnl.net.in; internet www.casybank.com; f. 1920; cap. 99.9m., res 401.8m., dep. 31,910m. (March 2002); Chair. and CEO N. R. ACHAN; Gen. Man. JOHN J. ALAPATT; 284 brs.

Centurion Bank Ltd: 1201 Raheja Centre, Free Press Journal Marg, Nariman Point, Mumbai 400 021; tel. (22) 2047234; fax (22) 2845860; e-mail cblho@bom3.vsnl.net.in; internet www.centurionbank.com; f. 1995; cap. 1,524.7m., res 215.9m., dep. 47,048.3m. (March 2000); Chair. and Man. Dir V. JANAKIRAMAN.

City Union Bank Ltd: 149 TSR (Big) St, Kumbakonam 612 001; tel. (435) 432322; fax (435) 431746; e-mail cub@vsnl.com; internet www.cityunion.com; f. 1904; cap. 240.0m., res 797.4m., dep. 19,737m. (March 2002); Chair. V. NARYANAN; Chief Gen. Man. K. VENKATARAMAN; 114 brs.

The Federal Bank Ltd: Federal Towers, POB 103, Alwaye 683 101; tel. (484) 623620; fax (484) 621687; e-mail nrihelp@federalbank.co.in; internet www.federal-bank.com; f. 1931; cap. 217.2m., res and surplus 4,186.6m., dep. 88,650m. (March 2002); Chair. K. P. PADMAKUMAR; 410 brs.

Global Trust Bank Ltd: 303-48-3 Sardar Patel Rd, Secunderabad 500 003; tel. (40) 7819333; fax (40) 7815879; e-mail ask@globaltrustbank.com; internet www.globaltrustbank.com; f. 1994; cap. p.u. 1,214m., res 2,729.6m., dep. 77,342.3m. (March 2001); Man. Dir SUDHAKAR GANDE; Exec. Dir SRIDHAR SUBASRI; 96 brs.

ICICI Bank: ICICI Towers, 4th Floor, South Tower, Bandra–Kurla Complex, Bandra (East), Mumbai 400 051; tel. (22) 6531414; fax (22) 6531167; e-mail sinorhn@icicibank.com; internet www.icicibank.com; f. 1994; cap. 2,203.6m., res and surplus 10,922.6m., dep. 163,782m. (March 2001); Man. Dir and CEO H. N. SINOR; 389 brs.

IndusInd Bank Ltd: IndusInd House, 425 Dadasaheb Bhadkamkar Marg, Lamington Rd, nr Opera House, Mumbai 400 004; tel. (22) 3859901; fax (22) 3859913; e-mail glob@indusind.com; internet www.indusind.com; f. 1994; cap. 1,590.2m., res 3,854.1m., dep. 71,871.3m. (March 2001); Chair. R. J. SHAHANEY; Man. Dir BHASKAR GHOSE; 77 brs.

Jammu and Kashmir Bank Ltd: Corporate Headquarters, M. A. Rd, Srinagar 190 001; tel. (194) 481930; fax (194) 481923; e-mail jkbcosgr@jkbmail.com; internet www.jkbank.org; f. 1938; cap. p.u. 481.1m., res 8,889.2m., dep 129,111.1m. (March 2002); Chair. and CEO M. Y. KHAN; 440 brs.

The Karnataka Bank Ltd: POB 716, Kodialbail, Mangalore 575 003; tel. (824) 440751; fax (824) 441212; e-mail info@ktkbank.com; internet www.thekarnatakabankltd.com; f. 1924; cap. 135m., dep. 70,015m. (March 2002); Chair. and CEO Mr ANANTHAKRISHNA; 357 brs.

The Karur Vysya Bank Ltd: Erode Rd, POB 21, Karur 639 002; tel. (4324) 32520; fax (4324) 30202; e-mail kvbid@giasmd01.vsnl.net.in; f. 1916; cap. 60.0m., res 3,227.8m., dep. 41,800.6m. (March 2002); Chair. P. T. KUPPUSWAMY; Sr Gen. Man. V. DEVARAJAN; 213 brs.

Lakshmi Vilas Bank Ltd: Kathaparai, Salem Rd, POB 2, Karur 639 006; tel. (4324) 320057; fax (4324) 320068; e-mail lvbho.cppd@gecsl.com; internet www.lakshmivilasbankltd.com; f. 1926; cap. 115.1m., res 1,529.1m., dep. 22,776.4m. (March 2001); Chair. A. KRISHNAMOORTHY; 211 brs.

The Sangli Bank Ltd: Rajwada Chowk, POB 158, Sangli 416 416; tel. (233) 73611; fax (233) 77156; f. 1916; cap. p.u. 60.2m., dep. 7,303.6m. (March 1995); Chair. and CEO SURESH D. JOSHI; Gen. Man. Dr V. PRASANNA BHAT; 178 brs.

The South Indian Bank Ltd: SIB House, Mission Quarters, Thrissur 680 001, Kerala; tel. (487) 420020; fax (487) 442021; e-mail head@southindianbank.com; internet www.southindianbank.com; f. 1929; cap. 357.4m., res 2,388.6m., dep. 59,197m. (March 2002); Chair. and CEO A. SETHUMADHAVAN; 380 brs.

Tamilnad Mercantile Bank Ltd: 57 Victoria Extension Rd, Tuticorin 628 002; tel. (461) 321932; fax (461) 322994; f. 1921 as Nadar Bank, name changed as above 1962; cap. 2.8m., res 2,764.3m., dep. 31,980.7m. (March 2001); Chair. S. KRISHNAMURTHY; 160 brs.

The United Western Bank Ltd: 172/4 Raviwar Peth, Shivaji Circle, POB 2, Satara 415 001; tel. (2162) 20517; fax (2162) 23374; internet www.uwbankindia.com; f. 1936; cap. 298.9m., res and surplus 1,967.7m., dep. 43,488.4m. (March 2000); Chair. and Chief Exec. P. N. JOSHI; Gen. Man. V. G. PALKAR; 227 brs.

The Vysya Bank Ltd: 72 St Marks Rd, Bangalore 560 001; tel. (80) 2272021; fax (80) 2272220; e-mail ibdbby.vbl@gnbom.global.net.in; internet www.vysbank.com; f. 1930; cap. 226.2m., res 6,301.2m., dep. 80,680m. (March 2002); Chair. K. R. RAMAMOORTHY; Dir K. BALASUBRAMANIAN; 484 brs.

Foreign Banks

ABN AMRO Bank NV (Netherlands): 14 Veer Nariman Rd, POB 97, Mumbai 400 023; tel. (22) 2042331; CEO ROMESH SOBTI; 11 brs.

Abu Dhabi Commercial Bank (UAE): Rehmat Manzil, 75-B Veer Nariman Rd, Mumbai 400 020; tel. (22) 2830235; fax (22) 2870686; Chief Exec. KHALIFA MOHAMMAD HUSSEIN; 1 br.

American Express Bank Ltd (USA): 7th Floor, Maker Chambers IV, 211 Nariman Point, Mumbai 400 021; tel. (22) 2833293; fax (22) 2872968; Country Head STEVE MARTIN; 4 brs.

Banca Nazionale del Lavoro Spa (Italy): 61 Maker Chambers VI, Nariman Point, Mumbai 400 021; tel. (22) 2047763; fax (22) 2023482; Rep. L. S. AGARWAL.

Bank Muscat SAOG (Oman): 29 Infantry Rd, Bangalore 560 001; tel. (80) 2867755; fax (80) 2862214; e-mail bmiimgt@bgl.vsnl.net.in; CEO SAMIT GHOSH; 1 br.

Bank of America NA (USA): Express Towers, POB 10080, Nariman Point, Mumbai 400 021; tel. (22) 2852882; fax (22) 2029016; Country Man. VISHWAVIR AHUJA; 3 brs.

Bank of Bahrain and Kuwait BSC: Jolly Maker Chambers II, Ground Floor, POB 11692, 225 Nariman Point, Mumbai 400 021; tel. (22) 2823698; fax (22) 2044458; Gen. Man. and CEO K. S. KRISHNAKUMAR; 2 brs.

Bank of Ceylon: 1090 Poonamallee High Rd, Chennai 600 084; tel. (44) 6420972; fax (44) 5325590; e-mail ceybank@md3.vsnl.net.in; internet www.bocindia.com; Asst Vice-Pres. B. KARTHIK; Country Man. N. V. MOORTHY.

Bank of Nova Scotia (Canada): Mittal Tower B, Nariman Point, Mumbai 400 021; tel. (22) 2832822; fax (22) 2873125; Sr Vice-Pres. and CEO (India) DOUGLAS H. STEWART; Vice-Pres. and Man. BHASKAR DESAI; 4 brs.

Bank of Tokyo-Mitsubishi Ltd (Japan): Jeevan Prakash, Sir P. Mehta Rd, Mumbai 400 001; tel. (22) 2660564; fax (22) 2661787; Regional Rep. for India and Gen. Man. KUNIHIKO NISHIHARA; 4 brs.

Barclays Bank PLC (UK): 21–23 Maker Chambers VI, 2nd Floor, Nariman Point, Mumbai 400 021; tel. (22) 2044353; fax (22) 2043238; CEO AJAY SONDHI; 2 brs.

BNP Paribas (France): French Bank Bldg, 62 Homji St, Fort, Mumbai 400 001; tel. (22) 2660822; fax (22) 2679709; e-mail mumbai-1.admin@asia.bnpparibas.com; internet www.bnpparibas.co.in; cap. Rs 352m., res Rs 1,700m., dep. Rs 16,300m. (2002); Chief Exec. and Country Man. JONATHAN LYON; 8 brs.

Chinatrust Commercial Bank (Taiwan): 21-A Janpath, New Delhi 110 001; tel. (11) 3356001; fax (11) 3731815; e-mail ctcbindd@ndf.vsnl.net.in; internet www.chinatrustindia.com; Gen. Man. and CEO ROBERT C. F. WANG; 1 br.

Citibank, NA (USA): Sakhar Bhavan, 230 Backbay Reclamation, Nariman Point, Mumbai 400 021; tel. (22) 2025499; internet www.citibank.com/india; CEO SANJAY NAYAR; 16 brs.

Commerzbank AG (Germany): Free Press House, 215 Free Press Journal Rd, Nariman Point, Mumbai 400 021; tel. (22) 2885510; fax (22) 2885524; Gen. Mans G. SHEKHAR, PETER KENYON-MUIR; 2 brs.

Crédit Agricole Indosuez (France): Ramon House, 169 Backbay Reclamation, Mumbai 400 020; tel. (22) 2045104; fax (22) 2049108; Sr Country Officer ALAIN BUTZBACH; Gen. Man. NIRENDU MAZUMDAR.

Crédit Lyonnais (France): Apeejay House, 3rd Floor, 3 Dinshaw Vachha Rd, Mumbai 400 020; tel. (22) 2330300; fax (22) 2351888; Chief Exec. and Country Man. JEAN-YVES LE PAULMIER; 4 brs.

Deutsche Bank AG (Germany): DB House, Hazarimal Somani Marg, Fort, POB 1142, Mumbai 400 001; tel. (22) 2074720; fax (22) 2075047; Chief Country Officer DOUGLAS NEILSON; 5 brs.

Development Bank of Singapore Ltd: Free Press House, 14th Floor, Nariman Point, Mumbai 400 021; tel. (22) 2388888; fax (22) 2388899; internet www.dbs.com; 1 br.

Dresdner Bank (Germany): Hoechst House, Nariman Point, Mumbai 400 021; tel. (22) 2850009; 2 brs.

Fuji Bank Ltd (Japan): Maker Chambers III, 1st Floor, Jamnalal Bajaj Rd, Nariman Point, Mumbai 400 021; tel. (22) 2886638; fax (22) 2886640; CEO (India) and Gen. Man. TATSUJI TAMAKA; 1 br.

Hongkong and Shanghai Banking Corpn Ltd (Hong Kong): 52–60 Mahatma Gandhi Rd, POB 128, Mumbai 400 001; tel. (22) 2674921; fax (22) 2658309; internet www.hongkongbank.com; CEO and Country Head NIALL S. K. BOOKER; 30 brs.

ING Bank (Netherlands): Hoechst House, 7th Floor, 193 Backbay Reclamation, Nariman Point, Mumbai 400 005; tel. (22) 2029876; fax (22) 2046134; e-mail atul.sahasrabuddhe@asia.ing.com; Country Head ATUL SAHASRABUDDHE; 2 brs.

JP Morgan Chase Manhattan Bank: Mafatlal Centre, 9/F, Nariman Point, Mumbai 400 021; tel. (22) 2855666; fax (22) 2027772; Man. Dir and Sr Country Officer (India and South Asia) DOMINIC PRICE; 1 br.

Mashreq Bank PSC (United Arab Emirates): Air-India Bldg, Nariman Point, Mumbai 400 021; tel. (22) 2026096; fax (22) 2831278; CEO SUNEIL KUCCHAL.

Oman International Bank SAOG (Oman): 201 Raheja Centre, Free Press Journal Marg, Nariman Point, Mumbai 400 021; tel. (22) 2324848; fax (22) 2875626; e-mail oibind@bom3.vsnl.net.in; Country Man. G. PATTIBIRAMAN; 2 brs.

Société Générale (France): Maker Chambers IV, Bajaj Marg, Nariman Point, POB 11635, Mumbai 400 021; tel. (22) 2870909; fax (22) 2045459; e-mail sg.mumbai@sgib.com; CEO PAUL H. RUSCH; 4 brs.

Sonali Bank (Bangladesh): 'Apeejay House', 15 Park St, Kolkata 700 016; tel. (33) 247998; Dep. Gen. Man. SIRAJUDDIN AHMED; 1 br.

Standard Chartered Grindlays Bank (UK): New Excelsior Bldg, 4th Floor, A. K. Naik Marg, POB 1806, Mumbai 400 001; tel. (22) 2075409; fax (22) 2072550; e-mail vkrishn@scbindia.mhs.compuserve.com; Chief Exec. JASPAL S. BINDRA; 61 brs.

State Bank of Mauritius Ltd: 101, Raheja Centre, 1st Floor, Free Press Journal Marg, Nariman Point, Mumbai 400 021; tel. (22) 2842965; fax (22) 2842966; Gen. Man. and CEO P. THONDRAYEN; 2 brs.

Sumitomo Bank (Japan): 15/F Jolly Maker Chamber No. 2, 225 Nariman Point, Mumbai 400 021; tel. (22) 2880025; fax (22) 2880026; CEO and Gen. Man. KOZO OTSUBO.

UFJ Bank Ltd (Japan): Mercantile House, Upper Ground Floor, 15 Kasturba Gandhi Marg, New Delhi 110 001; tel. (11) 3318008; fax (11) 3315162; f. 1933 as Sanwa Bank, name changed to above following merger with Tokai Bank in Jan. 2002; Gen. Man. NOBUO OJI.

Banking Organizations

Indian Banks' Association: Stadium House, 6th Floor, Block 3, Veer Nariman Rd, Churchgate, Mumbai 400 020; tel. (22) 2844999; fax (22) 2835638; e-mail ibastadium@vsnl.net; internet www.iba.org.in; 156 mems; Chair. Dr DALBIR SINGH; Sec. K. C. CHOWDHARY.

Indian Institute of Bankers: 'The Arcade', World Trade Centre, 2nd Floor, East Wing, Cuffe Parade, Mumbai 400 005; tel. (22) 2187003; fax (22) 2185147; e-mail iibgen@bom5.vsnl.net.in; internet www.iib.org.in; f. 1928; 343,202 mems; Pres. V. LEELADHAR; Chief Sec. R. H. SARMA.

National Institute of Bank Management: NIBM Post Office, Kondhwe Khurd, Pune 411 048; tel. (20) 6833080; fax (20) 6834478; e-mail director@nibm.ernet.in; internet www.nibmindia.com; f. 1969; Dir Dr ASISH SAHA.

DEVELOPMENT FINANCE ORGANIZATIONS

Agricultural Finance Corporation Ltd: Dhanraj Mahal, 1st Floor, Chhatrapati Shivaji Maharaj Marg, Mumbai 400 001; tel. (22) 2028924; fax (22) 2028966; e-mail afcl@vsnl.com; internet www.afcindia.com; f. 1968 by a consortium of 45 public- and private-sector commercial banks including development finance institutions to help increase the flow of investment and credit into agriculture and rural development projects; provides project consultancy services to commercial banks, Union and State govts, public-sector corpns, the World Bank, the ADB, FAO, the International Fund for Agricultural Development and other institutions and to individuals; undertakes techno-economic and investment surveys in agriculture and agro-industries etc.; publishes quarterly journal Financing Agriculture; 3 regional offices and 9 br. offices; cap. p.u. 150m., res and surplus 20.5m. (March 2001); Chair. Dr. JAGDISH KAPOOR; Man. Dir A. M. ALAM.

Export-Import Bank of India: Centre 1, Floor 21, World Trade Centre, Cuffe Parade, Mumbai 400 005; tel. (22) 2185272; fax (22) 2182572; e-mail eximind@vsnl.com; internet www.eximbankindia.com; f. 1982; cap. 6,499.9m., res 12,026.4m., dep. 2,797.2m. (March 2002); offices in Bangalore, Chennai, Kolkata, New Delhi, Pune, Ahmedabad, Johannesburg, Budapest, Rome, Singapore and Washington, DC; Man. Dir T. C. VENKAT SUBRAMANIAN; Exec. Dir R. M. V. RAMAN.

Housing Development Finance Corpn Ltd (HDFC): Ramon House, 169 Backbay Reclamation, Mumbai 400 020; tel. (22) 2820282; fax (22) 2046758; e-mail library@hdfcindia.com; internet www.hdfcindia.com; provides loans to individuals and corporate bodies; Chair. DEEPAK S. PAREKH; Man. Dir KEKI M. MISTRY; 109 brs.

ICICI Ltd: ICICI Towers, Bandra-Kurla Complex, Mumbai 400 051; tel. (11) 6531414; fax (11) 6531122; internet www.icici.com; f. 1955 as Industrial Credit and Investment Corpn of India Ltd to assist industrial enterprises by providing finance in both rupee and foreign currencies in the form of long- or medium-term loans or equity participation, guaranteeing loans from other private investment sources, furnishing managerial, technological and administration advice to industry; also offers suppliers' and buyers' credit, export development capital, asset credit, technology finance, instalment sale and equipment leasing facilities, and infrastructure finance; zonal offices at Mumbai, Kolkata, Chennai, New Delhi, Vadodara, Pune, Bangalore, Hyderabad and Coimbatore; development office at Guwahati (Assam); equity share cap. 4,781.4m., res 41,921.8m. (March 1998); Chair. N. VAGHUL; Man. Dir K. V. KAMATH.

Industrial Development Bank of India (IDBI): IDBI Tower, WTC Complex, Cuffe Parade, Colaba, Mumbai 400 005; tel. (22) 2189117; fax (22) 2180930; internet www.idbi.com; f. 1964, reorg. 1976; 72.1% govt-owned; India's premier financial institution for providing direct finance, refinance of industrial loans and bills, finance to large- and medium-sized industries, and for extending financial services, such as merchant banking and forex services, to the corporate sector; 5 zonal offices and 38 br. offices; cap. 6,528m., res 84,738m., dep. 410,828.9m. (March 2001); Chair. and Man. Dir P. P. VORA.

Small Industries Development Bank of India: 10/10 Madan Mohan Malviya Marg, Lucknow 226 001; tel. (522) 209517; fax (522) 209514; e-mail snairan@sidbi.com; internet www.sidbi.com; f. 1990; wholly-owned subsidiary of Industrial Development Bank of India; promotes, finances and develops small-scale industries; cap. p.u. 4,500m., res 24,240m. (March 2000); Chair. P. B. NIMBALKAR; 39 offices.

Industrial Finance Corpn of India Ltd: IFCI Tower, 61 Nehru Place, New Delhi 110 019; tel. (11) 6487444; fax (11) 6488471; e-mail ifci@giasd01.vsnl.net.in; internet www.ifciltd.com; f. 1948 to provide medium- and long-term finance to cos and co-operative socs in India, engaged in manufacture, preservation or processing of goods, shipping, mining, hotels and power generation and distribution; promotes industrialization of less developed areas, and sponsors training in management techniques and development banking; cap. p.u. 10,679.5m., res 4,976.7m. (March 2002); Chair. and Man. Dir V. P. SINGH; 13 regional offices and 4 other offices.

Industrial Investment Bank of India: 19 Netaji Subhas Rd, Kolkata 700 001; tel. (33) 2209941; fax (33) 2207182; e-mail iibiho@vsnl.com; internet www.iibiltd.com; Chair. and Man. Dir Dr B. SAMAL (acting).

National Bank for Agriculture and Rural Development: Plot no. C-24, G Block, Bandra-Kurla Complex, Bangra (E), Mumbai 400 051; tel. (22) 6539060; e-mail nabpro@bom7.vsnl.net.in; internet www.nabard.org; f. 1982 to provide credit for agricultural and rural development through commercial, co-operative and regional rural banks; cap. p.u. 20,000m., res 29,479m. (March 2000); held 50% each by the cen. Govt and the Reserve Bank; Chair. Y. C. NANDA; Man. Dir M. V. S. CHALAPATI RAO; 17 regional offices, 10 sub-offices and 5 training establishments.

STOCK EXCHANGES

There are 24 stock exchanges (with a total of more than 9,985 listed companies) in India, including:

National Stock Exchange of India Ltd: Exchange Plaza, Bandra Kurla Complex, Bandra (East), Mumbai 400 051; tel. (22) 6598100; fax (22) 6598120; e-mail cc_nse@nse.co.in; internet www.nseindia.com; f. 1994; Chair. P. P. VORA; Man. Dir RAVI NARAIN.

Ahmedabad Share and Stock Brokers' Association: Kamdhenu Complex, opposite Sahajanand College, Panjarapole, Ambawadi, Ahmedabad 380 015; tel. (79) 6307971; fax (79) 6308877; e-mail ase@satyam.net.in; f. 1894; 299 mems; Pres. ATUL M. CHOKSHI; Exec. Dir RAJIV DESAI.

Bangalore Stock Exchange Ltd: 51 Stock Exchange Towers, 1st Corss, J. C. Rd, Bangalore 560 027; tel. (812) 2995234; fax (80) 2995242; e-mail edbgse@blr.vsnl.net.in; 234 mems; Pres. JAGDISH V. AHUJA; Exec. Dir K. KAMALA.

Bombay Stock Exchange: Phiroze Jeejeebhoy Towers, 25th Floor, Dalal St, Fort, Mumbai 400 001; tel. (22) 2655861; fax (22) 2655720; e-mail webmaster@bseindia.com; internet www.bseindia.com; f. 1875; 638 mems; Pres. DEENA MEHTA; Exec. Dir. A. N. JOSHI; Sec. A. A. TIRODKAR.

Calcutta Stock Exchange Association Ltd: 7 Lyons Range, Kolkata 700 001; tel. (33) 2206928; fax (33) 2104486; e-mail secretary@cse.india.com; internet www.cse-india.com; f. 1908; 917 mems; Pres. SUPRIYA GUPTA; Sec. P. K. RAY.

Delhi Stock Exchange Association Ltd: DSE House, 3/1 Asaf Ali Rd, New Delhi 110 002; tel. (11) 3292170; fax (11) 3292174; e-mail dse@vsnl.com; f. 1947; 356 mems; Pres. VIJAY BHUSAN; Exec. Dir P. K. SINGHAL.

Ludhiana Stock Exchange Association Ltd: Feroze Gandhi Market, Ludhiana 141 001; tel. (161) 412316; fax (161) 404748; e-mail lse@satyam.net.in; f. 1981; 301 mems; Pres. R. C. SINGAL; Gen. Man. H. S. SIDHU.

Madras Stock Exchange Ltd: Exchange Bldg, 11 Second Line Beach, POB 183, Chennai 600 001; tel. (44) 5221085; fax (44) 5244897; e-mail mseed@md3.vsnl.net.in; f. 1760; 171 mems; Pres. D. N. DAS; Exec. Dir P. J. MATHEW.

Mangalore Stock Exchange: Rama Bhavan Complex, 4th Floor, Kodialbail, Mangalore 575 003; tel. (824) 440581; fax (824) 440736; 146 mems; Pres. RAMESH RAI; Exec. Dir UMESH P. MASKERI.

Thiruvananthapuram Stock Exchange: Thiruvananthapuram; Dir JOSE JOHN.

Uttar Pradesh Stock Exchange Association Ltd: 14/113 Civil Lines, Kanpur 208 001; tel. (512) 293174; fax (512) 293175; e-mail upse@lw1.vsnl.net.in; 520 mems; Pres. R. K. AGARWAL; Exec. Dir Dr J. N. GUPTA.

The other recognized stock exchanges are: Hyderabad, Madhya Pradesh (Indore), Kochi, Pune, Guwahati, Jaipur, Bhubaneswar (Orissa), Coimbatore, Saurashtra, Meerut, Vadodara and Magadh (Patna).

INSURANCE

In January 1973 all Indian and foreign insurance companies were nationalized. The general insurance business in India is now transacted by only four companies, subsidiaries of the General Insurance Corpn of India, formed under the 1972 General Insurance Business Nationalisation Act. The Insurance Regulatory Development Authority Bill, approved by the legislature in December 1999, established a regulatory authority for the insurance sector and henceforth permitted up to 26% investment by foreign companies in new domestic, private-sector insurance companies.

General Insurance Corpn of India (GIC): 'Suraksha', 170 J. Tata Rd, Churchgate, Mumbai 400 020; tel. (22) 2833046; fax (22) 2855423; e-mail sengupt@gic.nic.in; internet www.gic.nic.in; f. 1973 by the reorg. of 107 private non-life insurance cos (incl. brs of foreign cos operating in the country) as the four subsidiaries listed below; Chair. P. C. GHOSH; Man. Dir P. B. RAMANUJAN.

National Insurance Co Ltd: 3 Middleton St, Kolkata 700 071; tel. (33) 2472130; fax (33) 2402369; e-mail poddar-an@national.nic.in; internet www.national.nic.in; Chair. and Man. Dir M. S. WADHWA; 19 regional offices, 254 divisional offices and 690 branch offices.

New India Assurance Co Ltd: New India Assurance Bldg, 87 Mahatma Gandhi Rd, Fort, Mumbai 400 001; tel. (22) 2674617; fax (22) 2652811; e-mail knb@niacl.com; internet www.niacl.com; f. 1919; Chair. and Man. Dir K. N. BHANDARI; 26 regional offices, 393 divisional offices, 703 branch offices and 37 overseas offices; Chair. and Man. Dir R. BERI.

The Oriental Insurance Co Ltd: Oriental House, A-25/27 Asaf Ali Rd, New Delhi 110 002; tel. (11) 3279221; fax (11) 3263175; e-mail bdbanerjee@oriental.nic.in; internet www.orientalinsurance.nic.in; Chair. and Man. Dir S. L. MOHAN.

United India Insurance Co Ltd: 24 Whites Rd, Chennai 600 014; tel. (44) 8520161; fax (44) 8525280; e-mail knb@united.nic.in; internet www.united.nic.in; Chair. and Man. Dir V. JAGANNATHAN.

Life Insurance Corpn of India (LIC): 'Yogakshema', Jeevan Bima Marg, Mumbai 400 021; tel. (22) 2021383; fax (22) 2020274; e-mail liccreos@bom3.vsnl.net.in; internet www.licindia.com; f. 1956; controls all life insurance business; Chair. S. B. MATHUR; Man. Dirs A. RAMAMURTHY and N. C. SHARMA; 100 divisional offices, 2,048 brs and three overseas offices.

Trade and Industry

GOVERNMENT AGENCIES AND DEVELOPMENT ORGANIZATIONS

Coal India Ltd: 10 Netaji Subhas Rd, Kolkata 700 001; tel. (33) 2488099; fax (33) 2483373; internet www.coalindia.nic.in; cen. govt holding co with eight subsidiaries; responsible for almost total (more than 90%) exploration for, planning and production of coal mines; owns 498 coal mines throughout India; marketing of coal and its products; cap. p.u. Rs 72,205.4m., res and surplus Rs 15,985m., sales Rs 7,832m. (March 2001); Chair. and Man. Dir N. K. SHARMA; 660,000 employees (1995).

Cotton Corpn of India Ltd: Plot No. 3A, Sector No. 10, CBD Belapur, Navi Mumbai 400 614; tel. (22) 7579217; fax (22) 7576030; e-mail ccimum@bom7.vsnl.net.in; internet www.cotcorp.com; f. 1970 as an agency in the public sector for the purchase, sale and distribution of home-produced cotton and imported cotton staple fibre; exports long staple cotton; cap. p.u. Rs 250m., res and surplus Rs 2,046.8m., sales Rs 6,810m. (March 2001); Chair. and Man. Dir VISHWA NATH.

Export Credit Guarantee Corpn of India Ltd: Express Towers, 10th Floor, Nariman Point, Mumbai 400 021; tel. (22) 2044519; fax (22) 2829968; e-mail ecgcedp@bom2.vsnl.net.in; internet www.ecgcindia.com; f. 1957 to insure for risks involved in exports on credit terms and to supplement credit facilities by issuing guarantees, etc.; cap. Rs 3,400m., res Rs 3,629m. (March 2000); Chair. and Man. Dir P. M. A. HAKEEM; 23 brs.

Fertilizer Corpn of India Ltd: 'Madhuban', 55 Nehru Place, New Delhi 110 019; tel. (11) 6444971; fax (11) 6416694; e-mail fci@fci.hub.nic.in; internet www.fert-india.com; f. 1961; fertilizer factories at Sindri (Jharkand), Gorakhpur (Uttar Pradesh), Talcher (Orissa) and Ramagundam (Andhra Pradesh), producing nitrogenous and some industrial products; cap. Rs 7,467.4m., sales Rs 7,832m. (March 2001); Chair. and Man. Dir Dr SUDHIR KRISHNA.

Food Corpn of India: 16–20 Barakhamba Lane, New Delhi 110 001; tel. (11) 3413871; fax (11) 3413231; f. 1965 to undertake trading in food grains on a commercial scale but within the framework of an overall govt policy; to provide farmers an assured price for their produce; to supply food grains to the consumer at reasonable prices; also purchases, stores, distributes and sells food grains and other foodstuffs and arranges imports and handling of food grains and fertilizers at the ports; distributes sugar in a number of states and has set up rice mills; cap. p.u. Rs 22,945m., sales Rs 214,210m. (March 2001); Chair. BHURE LAL; Man. Dir R. N. DAS; 65,131 employees.

Handicrafts and Handlooms Exports Corpn of India Ltd: 5th Floor, Jawahar Vyapar Bhavan Annexe, 1 Tolstoy Marg, New Delhi 110 001; tel. (11) 3701086; fax (11) 3701051; e-mail hhecnd@ndc.vsnl.net.in; internet www.hhecworld.com; f. 1958; govt undertaking dealing in export of handicrafts, handloom goods, ready-to-wear clothes, carpets, jute, leather and precious jewellery, and import of bullion and raw silk; promotes exports and trade development; cap. p.u. Rs 118.2m., res and surplus Rs 89.5m. (March 2001); Chair. and Man. Dir K. K. SINHA.

Housing and Urban Development Corpn Ltd: HUDCO Bhavan, India Habitat Centre, Lodhi Rd, New Delhi 110 003; tel. (11) 4648160; fax (11) 4625308; internet www.hudcoindia.com; f. 1970; to finance and undertake housing and urban development programmes including the establishment of new or satellite towns and building material industries; cap. p.u. Rs 11,780m., res and surplus Rs 7,626.5m., sales 18,764m. (March 2001); 21 brs; Chair. and Man. Dir PANKAJ JAIN; Sec. GOPAL KRISHAN.

India Trade Promotion Organisation (ITPO): Pragati Bhavan, Pragati Maidan, Lal Bahadur Shastri Marg, New Delhi 110 001; tel. (11) 3371540; fax (11) 3318142; e-mail itpo@giasdl10.vsnl.net.in; internet www.indiatrade promotion.org; f. 1992 following merger; promotes selective development of exports of high quality products; arranges investment in export-orientated ventures undertaken by India with foreign collaboration; organizes trade fairs; operates Trade Information Centre; cap. p.u. Rs 2.5m., res and surplus Rs 2,102.1m. (March 2001); regional offices in Bangalore, Mumbai, Kolkata and Chennai, and international offices in Frankfurt, New York, Moscow, São Paulo and Tokyo; Chair. and Man. Dir J. VASUDEVAN; Exec. Dir K. T. CHACKO.

Jute Corpn of India Ltd: 15-N, Nellie Sengupta Sarani, 7th Floor, Kolkata 700 087; tel. (33) 2166770; fax (33) 2166771; e-mail jutecorp@vsnl.net.in; f. 1971; objects: (i) to undertake price support operations in respect of raw jute; (ii) to ensure remunerative prices to producers through efficient marketing; (iii) to operate a buffer stock to stabilize raw jute prices; (iv) to handle the import and export of raw jute; (v) to promote the export of jute goods; cap. p.u. Rs 50m., sales Rs 786.3m. (March 2001); Chair. and Man. Dir A. K. KHASTAGIR.

Minerals and Metals Trading Corpn of India Ltd (MMTC): Scope Complex, Core-1, 7 Institutional Areas, Lodi Rd, New Delhi 110 003; tel. (11) 4362200; fax (11) 4360724; e-mail cpmr@mmtclimited.com; internet www.mmtclimited.com; f. 1963; export of iron and manganese ore, ferro-manganese, finished stainless steel products, engineering, agricultural and marine products, textiles, leather items, chemicals and pharmaceuticals, mica, coal and other minor minerals; import of steel, non-ferrous metals, rough diamonds, fertilizers, etc. for supply to industrial units in the country; cap. p.u. Rs 500m., res Rs 5,361.8m., sales Rs 53,383.7m. (March 2001); 9 regional offices and 16 sub-regional offices in India; foreign offices in Japan, the Republic of Korea, Jordan and Romania; Chair. and Man. Dir SHIV DAYAL KAPOOR; 3,246 employees.

National Co-operative Development Corpn: 4 Siri Institutional Area, Hauz Khas, New Delhi 110 016; tel. (11) 6567475; fax (11) 6962370; e-mail cdadmin@ncdc.delhi.nic.in; internet www.ncdc.nic.in; f. 1963 to plan, promote and finance country-wide programmes through co-operative societies for the production, processing, marketing, storage, export and import of agricultural produce, foodstuffs and notified commodities; also programmes for the development of poultry, dairy, fish products, coir, handlooms, distribution of consumer articles in rural areas and minor forest produce in the co-operative sector; 15 regional and state directorates; Pres. AJIT SINGH; Man. Dir P. K. MISHRA.

National Industrial Development Corpn Ltd: Chanakya Bhavan, Africa Ave, New Delhi 110 021; tel. (11) 4670153; fax (11) 6876166; e-mail nidc123@del2.vsnl.net.in; internet www.exploreindia.com/nidc; f. 1954; consultative engineering, management and infrastructure services to cen. and state govts, public and private sector enterprises, the UN and overseas investors; cap. p.u. Rs 187m. (March 2001); Chair. and Man. Dir PRANAB GHOSH.

National Mineral Development Corpn Ltd: Khanij Bhavan, 10-3-311/A Castle Hills, Masab Tank, POB 1352, Hyderabad 500 028; tel. (40) 3538713; fax (40) 3538711; e-mail nmdchyd@hdl.vsnl.net.in; internet www.nmdc-india.com; f. 1958; cen. govt undertaking; to exploit minerals (excluding coal, atomic minerals, lignite, petroleum and natural gas) in public sector; may buy, take on lease or otherwise acquire mines for prospecting, development and exploitation; iron ore mines at Bailadila-11C, Bailadila-14 and Bailadila-5 in Madhya Pradesh, and at Donimalai in Karnataka State; new 5m. metric ton iron ore mine under construction at Bailadila-10/11A; diamond mines at Panna in Madhya Pradesh; research and development laboratories and consultancy services covering all aspects of mineral exploitation at Hyderabad; investigates mineral projects; cap. p.u. Rs 1,321.6m., res and surplus Rs 8,188.6m. (March 2000); Chair. and Man. Dir P. R. TRIPATHI.

National Productivity Council: Utpadakta Bhavan, Lodi Rd, New Delhi 110 003; tel. (11) 4643778; fax (11) 4615002; e-mail npc@ren02.nic.in; internet www.npcindia.org; f. 1958 to increase productivity and to improve quality by improved techniques which aim at efficient and proper utilization of available resources; autonomous body representing national orgs of employers and labour, govt ministries, professional orgs, local productivity councils, small-scale industries and other interests; 12 regional directorates, 2 regional offices; 75 mems; Chair. V. GOVINDARAJAN; Dir-Gen. A. K. GOSWAMI.

National Research Development Corpn: 20–22 Zamroodpur Community Centre, Kailash Colony Extension, New Delhi 110 048; tel. (11) 6417821; fax (11) 6460506; e-mail nrdc@giasd101.vsnl.net.in; internet www.nrdcindia.com; f. 1953 to stimulate development and commercial exploitation of new inventions with financial and technical aid; finances development projects to set up demonstration units in collaboration with industry; exports technology; cap. p.u. Rs 44.2m., res and surplus Rs 45.3m. (March 2001); Man. Dir N. K. SHARMA.

National Seeds Corpn Ltd: Beej Bhavan, Pusa, New Delhi 110 012; tel. (11) 5852379; fax (11) 5766462; e-mail nsc@vsnl.com; f. 1963 to improve and develop the seed industry; cap. p.u. Rs 206.2m., res and surplus Rs 207.4m., sales Rs 642.3m. (March 2001); Chair. and Man. Dir KUMAR BHATIA.

The National Small Industries Corpn Ltd: NSIC Bhavan, Okhla Industrial Estate, New Delhi 110 020; tel. (11) 6926275; fax (11) 6926820; e-mail cmd@nsicindia.com; internet www.nsicindia.com; f. 1955 to aid, advise, finance, protect and promote the interests of small industries; establishes and supplies machinery for small industries in other developing countries on turn-key basis; cap. p.u. Rs 1,679.9m. (March 2001); all shares held by the Govt; Chair. and Man. Dir RAJIV BHATNAGAR.

PEC Ltd: 'Hansalaya', 15 Barakhamba Rd, New Delhi 110 001; tel. (11) 3313619; fax (11) 3314797; e-mail pec@pecltd.org; internet www.pecltd.org; f. 1971; export of engineering, industrial and railway equipment; undertakes turn-key and other projects and management consultancy abroad; countertrade, trading in agrocommodities, construction materials (steel, cement, clinkers, etc.) and fertilizers; cap. p.u. Rs 15m., res and surplus Rs 209.7m. (March 2001); Chair. and Man. Dir A. K. SRIVASTAVA.

Rehabilitation Industries Corpn Ltd: 25 Mirza Ghalib St, Kolkata 700 016; tel. (33) 2441185; fax (33) 2451055; f. 1959 to create employment opportunities through multi-product industries, ranging from consumer goods to engineering products and services, for refugees from Bangladesh and migrants from Pakistan, repatriates from Myanmar and Sri Lanka, and other immigrants of Indian extraction; cap. p.u. Rs 47.6m. (March 2000); Chair. and Man. Dir ASHOK BASU.

State Farms Corpn of India Ltd: Farm Bhavan, 14–15 Nehru Place, New Delhi 110 019; tel. (11) 6446903; fax (11) 6226898; e-mail sfci@vsnl.net; f. 1969 to administer the central state farms; activities include the production of quality seeds of high-yielding varieties of wheat, paddy, maize, bajra and jowar; advises on soil conservation, reclamation and development of waste and forest land; consultancy services on farm mechanization; auth. cap. Rs 241.9m., res and surplus Rs 385.6m. (March 2001); Chair. BHASKAR BARUA; Man. Dir JOGINDER SINGH.

State Trading Corpn of India Ltd: Jawahar Vyapar Bhavan, Tolstoy Marg, New Delhi 110 001; tel. (11) 3701100; fax (11) 3701123; e-mail stcindia@vsnl.net; internet www.stcindia.com; f. 1956; govt undertaking dealing in exports and imports; cap. p.u. Rs 300m., res and surplus Rs 3,219.6m. (March 2002); 10 regional brs, 5 sub-brs and 1 office overseas; Chair. and Man. Dir S. M. DEWAN; 1,069 employees (2002).

Steel Authority of India Ltd (SAIL): Ispat Bhavan, Lodi Rd, POB 3049, New Delhi 110 003; tel. (11) 4367481; fax (11) 4367015; e-mail sail.co@vsnl.co; internet www.sail.co.in; f. 1973 to provide co-ordinated development of the steel industry in the public sector; integrated steel plants at Bhilai, Bokaro, Durgapur, Rourkela; alloys steel plants at Durgapur and Salem; subsidiaries: Visvesvaraya Iron and Steel Ltd (Karnataka), Indian Iron and Steel Co (West Bengal) and Maharashtra Elektrosmelt Ltd; combined crude steel capacity is 12.5m. metric tons annually; equity cap. Rs 41,304m., res and surplus Rs 11,599.7m., sales Rs 160,471.4m. (March 2002); Chair. and Man. Dir ARVIND PANDE; Dir (Finance) V. S. JAIN; 160,000 employees (2000).

Tea Board of India: 14 B. T. M. Sarani (Brabourne Rd), POB 2172, Kolkata 700 001; tel. (33) 251411; fax (33) 2251417; provides financial assistance to tea research stations; sponsors and finances independent research projects in universities and tech. institutions to supplement the work of tea research establishments; also promotes tea production and export; Chair. NABA KRISHNA DAS.

CHAMBERS OF COMMERCE

Associated Chambers of Commerce and Industry of India (ASSOCHAM): 11 Community Centre, Zamrudpur, New Delhi 110 048; tel. (11) 6292310; fax (11) 6451981; e-mail assocham@sansad.nic.in; internet www.assocham.org; f. 1920; a central org. of 350 chambers of commerce and industry and industrial asscns representing more than 100,000 cos throughout India; 6 promoter chambers, 125 ordinary mems, 40 patron mems and 500 corporate associates; Pres. K. K. Nohria; Sec.-Gen. Jayant Bhuyan.

Federation of Indian Chambers of Commerce and Industry (FICCI): Federation House, Tansen Marg, New Delhi 110 001; tel. (11) 3738760; fax (11) 3320714; e-mail ficci.bisnet@gems.vsnl.net.in; internet www.bisnetindia.com; f. 1927; 430 ordinary mems, 50 corporate mems, 1,150 assoc. mems, 190 cttee mems; Pres. Rajendra S. Lodha; Sec.-Gen. Dr Amit Mitra.

ICC India: Federation House, Tansen Marg, New Delhi 110 001; tel. (11) 3738760; fax (11) 3320714; e-mail iccindia@del2.vsnl .net.in; internet www.iccindiaonline.org; f. 1929; 53 org. mems, 481 assoc. mems, 8 patron mems, 118 cttee mems; Pres. Arunachalam Vellayan; Exec. Dir M. K. Sanghi.

Associated Chambers of Commerce and Industry of Uttar Pradesh: 2/122 Vijaya Khand, Gomti Nagar, Lucknow 226 016; tel. (522) 301956; fax (522) 301958; e-mail asochmup@lw1.vsnl.net.in; 495 mems; Pres. U. K. Modi; Sec.-Gen. R. K. Jain.

Bengal Chamber of Commerce and Industry: 6 Netaji Subhas Rd, Kolkata 700 001; tel. (33) 2203733; fax (33) 2201289; e-mail bencham@cal3.vsnl.net.in; f. 1853; 210 mems; Pres. S. K. Dhall; Sec. Pradip Das Gupta.

Bengal National Chamber of Commerce and Industry: 23 R. N. Mukherjee Rd, Kolkata 700 001; tel. (33) 2482951; fax (33) 2487058; e-mail bncci@bncci.com; internet www.bncci.com; f. 1887; 500 mems, 35 affiliated industrial and trading asscns; Pres. N. Saha; Sec. D. P. Nag.

Bharat Chamber of Commerce: 9 Park Mansions, 2nd Floor, 57-A Park Street, Kolkata, 700 016; tel. (33) 2299591; fax (33) 2294947; f. 1900; c. 500 mems; Pres. B. M. Bangur; Sec. K. Sarma.

Bihar Chamber of Commerce: Khem Chand Chaudhary Marg, POB 71, Patna 800 001; tel. (612) 670535; fax (612) 689505; e-mail secgen@dte.vsnl.net.in; f. 1926; 600 ordinary mems, 125 org. mems, 10 life mems; Pres. P. L. Khaitan; Sec.-Gen. Giridhari Lal Saraf.

Bombay Chamber of Commerce and Industry: Mackinnon Mackenzie Bldg, 4 Shoorji Vallabhdas Rd, Ballard Estate, POB 473, Mumbai 400 001; tel. (22) 2614681; fax (22) 2621213; e-mail bcci@bombaychamber.com; internet www.bombaychamber.com; f. 1836; 824 ordinary mems, 526 assoc. mems, 75 hon. mems; Pres. K. Ramachandran; Exec. Dir L. A. D'Souza.

Calcutta Chamber of Commerce: 18h Park St, Stephen Court, Kolkata 700 071; tel. (33) 2290758; fax (33) 2298961; e-mail calchamb@cal3.vsnl.net.in; 450 mems; Pres. P. D. Tulsan; Sec.-Gen. Amit Dey.

Chamber of Commerce and Industry (Regd): O.B 31, Rail Head Complex, Jammu 180 012; tel. (191) 472266; fax (191) 472255; 1,069 mems; Pres. Ram Sahai; Sec.-Gen. Rajendra Motial.

Cochin Chamber of Commerce and Industry: Bristow Rd, Willingdon Island, POB 503, Kochi 682 003; tel. (484) 668349; fax (484) 668651; e-mail chamber@md2.vsnl.net.in; internet www .cochinchamber.com; f. 1857; 176 mems; Pres. V. R. Nair; Sec. Eapen Kalapurakal.

Federation of Andhra Pradesh Chambers of Commerce and Industry: 11-6-841, Red Hills, POB 14, Hyderabad 500 004; tel. (40) 3393658; fax (40) 3395083; e-mail info@fapcci.org; internet www.fapcci.org; f. 1917; 2,300 mems; Pres. S. Thirumalai; Sec. G. Hemlata.

Federation of Karnataka Chambers of Commerce and Industry: Kempegowda Rd, Bangalore 560 009; tel. (80) 2262355; fax (80) 2251826; e-mail fkcci@mantraonline.com; internet www.fkcci.net; f. 1916; 2,150 mems; Pres. M. Satyanarayana Swamy; Sec. C. Manohar.

Federation of Madhya Pradesh Chambers of Commerce and Industry: Udyog Bhavan, 129a Malviya Nagar, Bhopal 462 003; tel. (755) 573612; fax (755) 551451; e-mail fmcci@bom6.vsnl.net.in; f. 1975; 500 ordinary mems, 58 asscn mems; Pres. Ranjit Vithaldas; Sec.-Gen. Prafulla Maheshwari.

Goa Chamber of Commerce and Industry: Goa Chamber Bldg, Rua de Ormuz, POB 59, Panaji 403 001; tel. (832) 224223; fax (832) 429010; e-mail gcci@goatelecom.com; internet www.goachamber .org; f. 1908; 450 mems; Pres. Nitin Kunkolienkar; Sec. Air Cmmdre (retd) P. K. Pinto.

Gujarat Chamber of Commerce and Industry: Shri Ambica Mills, Gujarat Chamber Bldg, Ashram Rd, POB 4045, Ahmedabad 380 009; tel. (79) 6582301; fax (79) 6587992; e-mail bis@gujaratchamber.org; internet www.gujaratchamber.org; f. 1949; 7,713 mems; Pres. Kalyan J. Shah; Sec.-Gen. S. C. Shah.

Indian Chamber of Commerce: India Exchange, 4 India Exchange Place, Kolkata 700 001; tel. (33) 2203243; fax (33) 2213377; e-mail ceo@indianchamber.org; internet www .indianchamber.org; f. 1925; 300 ordinary mems, 42 assoc. mems, 20 corporate group mems, 17 affiliated asscns; Pres. A. V. Lodha; Sec.-Gen. Nazeeb Arif.

Indian Chamber of Commerce and Industry: Four Square House, 49 Community Centre, New Friends Colony, New Delhi 110 065; tel. (11) 6836468; fax (11) 6840775; e-mail iccind@yahoo.com.in; Pres. L. K. Modi; Hon. Sec. R. P. Swami.

Indian Merchants' Chamber: IMC Bldg, IMC Marg, Churchgate, Mumbai 400 020; tel. (22) 2046633; fax (22) 2048508; e-mail imc@imcnet.org; internet www.imcnet.org; f. 1907; 185 asscn mems, 2,700 mem. firms; Pres. Suresh Kotak; Sec. P. N. Mogre.

Karnataka Chamber of Commerce and Industry: Karnataka Chamber Bldg, J. C. Nagar, Hubli 580 020; tel. (836) 365223; fax (836) 360933; e-mail kccihble@blr.vsnl.net.in; internet www .kccihubli.com; f. 1928; 2,500 mems; Pres. Madan B. Desai; Hon. Sec. Mohan Tenginkai.

Madhya Pradesh Chamber of Commerce and Industry: Chamber Bhavan, Sanatan Dharam Mandir Marg, Gwalior 474 009; tel. (751) 332916; fax (751) 323844; f. 1906; 1,705 mems; Pres. Govindas Agarwal; Sec. Deepak Agarwal.

Madras Chamber of Commerce and Industry: Karumuttu Centre, 634 Anna Salai, Chennai 600 035; tel. (44) 4349452; fax (44) 4349164; e-mail mascham@md3.vsnl.net.in; internet www .mascham.com; f. 1836; 287 mem. firms, 48 assoc., 16 affiliated, 11 honorary, 3 others; Pres. K. V. Shetty; Sec. R. Subramanian.

Maharashtra Chamber of Commerce and Industry: Oricon House, 6th Floor, 12 K. Dubhash Marg, Fort, Mumbai 400 001; tel. (22) 2855859; fax (22) 2855861; e-mail maharashtrachamber@vsnl.com; f. 1927; 1,954 mems; Pres. A. R. Anandpara; Sec.-Gen. Dilip Salvekar.

Mahratta Chamber of Commerce, Industries and Agriculture: Tilak Rd, POB 525, Pune 411 002; tel. (20) 4440371; fax (20) 4447902; e-mail mccipune@vsnl.com; internet www.mcciapune.com; f. 1934; 1,381 mems; Pres. Arun Firodia; Dir.-Gen. D. K. Abhyankar.

Merchants' Chamber of Commerce: 15b Hemanta Basu Sarani, Kolkata 700 001; tel. (33) 2483123; fax (33) 2488657; e-mail mercham@cal.vsnl.net.in; internet www.mercham.org; f. 1901; 600 mems; Pres. Sushil Dhandhania; Dir-Gen. R. K. Sen.

Merchants' Chamber of Uttar Pradesh: 14/76 Civil Lines, Kanpur 208 001; tel. (512) 531306; fax (512) 547292; e-mail mercham@vsnl.net.in; internet merchantschamber-up.com; f. 1932; 180 mems; Pres. S. N. Gupta; Sec. P. N. Dixit.

North India Chamber of Commerce and Industry: 9 Gandhi Rd, Dehra Dun, Uttar Pradesh; tel. (935) 23479; f. 1967; 105 ordinary mems, 29 asscn mems, 7 mem. firms, 91 assoc. mems; Pres. Dev Pandhi; Hon. Sec. Ashok K. Narang.

Oriental Chamber of Commerce: 6a Dr Rajendra Prasad Sarani (Clive Row), Kolkata 700 001; tel. (33) 2202120; fax (33) 2203609; e-mail orientchamb@vsnl.net; f. 1932; 245 ordinary mems, 3 assoc. mems; Pres. Samar Mohan Saha; Sec. Kazi Abu Zober.

PHD Chamber of Commerce and Industry: PHD House, Thapar Floor, 4/2 Siri Institutional Area, opp. Asian Games Village, POB 130, New Delhi 110 016; tel. (11) 6863801; fax (11) 6863135; e-mail phdcci@del2.vsnl.net.in; internet www.phdcci.org; f. 1905; 1,600 mems, 110 asscn mems; Pres. Arun Kapur; Sec.-Gen. Dr B. P. Dhaka.

Rajasthan Chamber of Commerce and Industry: Rajasthan Chamber Bhavan, M.I. Rd, Jaipur 302 003; tel. (141) 565163; fax (141) 561419; e-mail rajcham@jpl.vsnl.net.in; internet www .rajchamber.com; 1,000 mems; Pres. S. K. Mansinghka; Hon. Sec.-Gen. Dr K. L. Jain.

Southern India Chamber of Commerce and Industry: Indian Chamber Bldgs, 6 Esplanade, POB 1208, Chennai 600 108; tel. (44) 5342228; fax (44) 5341876; e-mail sicci@md3.vsnl.net.in; f. 1909; 1,000 mems; Pres. R. Muthu; Sec. J. Prasad Davids.

Upper India Chamber of Commerce: 14/113 Civil Lines, POB 63, Kanpur 208 001; tel. (512) 543905; fax (512) 210684; f. 1888; 127 mems; Pres. Dilip Bhargava; Sec. S. P. Srivastava.

Utkal Chamber of Commerce and Industry Ltd: Barabati Stadium, Cuttack 753 005; tel. (671) 301211; fax (671) 302059; f. 1964; 225 mems; Pres. Dr S. K. Tamotia; Sec. Shashi Sekhar Samal.

Uttar Pradesh Chamber of Commerce: 15/197 Civil Lines, Kanpur 208 001; tel. 211696; f. 1914; 200 mems; Pres. Dr B. K. Modi; Sec. Aftab Sami.

INDUSTRIAL AND TRADE ASSOCIATIONS

Ahmedabad Textile Mills' Association: Ashram Rd, Navrangpura, POB 4056, Ahmedabad 380 009; tel. (79) 6582273; fax (79) 6588574; f. 1891; 21 mems; Pres. Arvind Kumar Somany; Sec.-Gen. Abhinava Shukla.

All India Federation of Master Printers: A-370, 2nd Floor, Defence Colony, New Delhi 110 024; tel. (11) 4601570; fax (11) 4624808; f. 1953; e-mail aifmp@vsnl.com; 49 affiliates, 800 mems; Pres. C. R. Janardhana; Hon. Gen. Sec. P. Chander.

All India Manufacturers' Organization (AIMO): Jeevan Sahakar, 4th Floor, Sir P.M. Rd, Fort, Mumbai 400 001; tel. (22) 2661016; fax (22) 2660838; f. 1941; 800 mems; Pres. KAMALKUMAR R. DUJODWALA; Hon. Gen. Sec. SURESH DEORA.

All India Plastics Manufacturers' Association: AIPMA House, A-52, St No. 1, MIDC, Andheri (East), Mumbai 400 093; tel. (22) 8217324; fax (22) 8216390; e-mail aipma@bom2.vsnl.net.in; internet www.aipma.org; f. 1947; 220 mems; Chair. MOHAN K. JAIN; Hon. Sec. AJAY DESAI.

All India Shippers' Council: Federation House, Tansen Marg, New Delhi 110 001; tel. (11) 3738760; fax (11) 3320714; f. 1967; 200 mems; Chair. RAMU S. DEORA; Sec. M. Y. REDDY.

Association of Man-made Fibre Industry of India: Resham Bhavan, 78 Veer Nariman Rd, Mumbai 400 020; tel. (22) 2040009; fax (22) 2049172; f. 1954; 7 mems; Pres. P. S. SHARMA; Sec. S. K. MARATHE.

Automotive Component Manufacturers' Association of India: 6th Floor, The Capital Court, Olof Parme Marg, Munirka, New Delhi 110 067; tel. (11) 6160315; fax (11) 6160317; e-mail acma@vsnl.com; internet www.acmainfo.com; 413 mems; Pres. DEEP KAPURIA; Exec. Dir VISHNU MATHUR.

Automotive Tyre Manufacturers' Association: PHD House, opp. Asian Games Village, Siri Fort Institutional Area, New Delhi 110 016; tel. (11) 6851187; fax (11) 6864799; e-mail atma@nda.vsnl.net.in; internet www.atmaindia.net.in; 11 mems; Chair. RAGHUPATI SINGHANIA; Dir-Gen. D. RAVINDRAN.

Bharat Krishak Samaj (Farmers' Forum, India): Dr Panjabrao Deshmukh Krishak Bhavan, A-1 Nizamuddin West, New Delhi 110 013; tel. (11) 4619508; fax (11) 4619509; e-mail ffi@mantraonline.com; f. 1954; national farmers' org.; 5m. ordinary mems, 70,000 life mems; Chair. Dr BAL RAM JAKHAR; Exec. Chair./Gen. Sec. Dr KRISHAN BIR CHAUDHARY.

Bombay Metal Exchange Ltd: 88/90, Gulalwadi, Kika St, 1st Floor, Mumbai 400 004; tel. (22) 2421964; fax (22) 2422640; e-mail bme@bom8.vsnl.net.in; promotes trade and industry in non-ferrous metals; 460 mems; Pres. ASHOK G. BAFNA; Sec. T. S. B. IYER.

Bombay Shroffs Association: 233 Shaikh Memon St, Mumbai 400 002; tel. (22) 3425588; f. 1910; 350 mems; Pres. KISHORE J. SHAH; Hon. Secs RAJNIKANT O. DHARIA, PRANLAL R. SHETH.

Calcutta Flour Mills Association: 25/B Shakespeare Sarani, Kolkata 700 017; tel. (33) 2476723; fax (33) 2475944; e-mail swaika@vsnl.com; f. 1932; 28 mems; Chair. NAVNEET SWAIKA; Hon. Sec. RAVI BHAGAT.

Calcutta Tea Traders' Association: 6 Netaji Subhas Rd, Kolkata 700 001; tel. (33) 2201574; fax (33) 2201289; f. 1886; 1,490 mems; Chair. ARUN GROVER; Sec. J. KALYANA SUNDARAM.

Cement Manufacturers' Association: Vishnu Kiran Chambers, 2142-47 Gurudwara Rd, Karol Bagh, New Delhi 110 005; tel. (11) 5763206; fax (11) 5738476; e-mail cmand@vsnl.com; internet cmaindia.org; 54 mems; 125 major cement plants; Pres. T. M. M. NAMBIAR; Sec.-Gen. A. V. SRINIVASAN.

Confederation of Indian Industry (CII): 23 Institutional Area, Lodi Rd, New Delhi 110 003; tel. (11) 4629994; fax (11) 4626149; e-mail cii@ciionline.org; internet www.ciionline.org; f. 1974; 3,800 mem. cos; Pres. ASHOK SOOTA; Dir-Gen. TARUN DAS.

Consumer Electronics and Television Manufacturers' Association (CETMA): J-13, Jangpura Extension, New Delhi 110 014; tel. (11) 4327777; fax (11) 4321616; e-mail cetmadel@ndb.vsnl.net.in; Pres. RAJEEV KARWAL; Sec.-Gen. SURESH KHANNA.

East India Cotton Association: Cotton Exchange Bldg, 9th Floor, 175 Kalbadevi Rd, Marwari Bazar, Mumbai 400 002; tel. (22) 2014876; fax (22) 2015578; e-mail eica@bom8.vsnl.net.in; f. 1921; 417 mems; Pres. SURESH A. KOTAK; Gen. Sec. HEMANT MULKY.

Electronic Component Industries Association (ELCINA): ELCINA House, 422 Okhla Industrial Estate, New Delhi 110 020; tel. (11) 6928053; fax (11) 6923440; e-mail elcina@del2.vsnl.net.in; internet www.elcina.com; f. 1967; 300 mems; Pres. B. S. SETHIA; Sec.-Gen. SOMNATH CHATTERJEE.

Federation of Automobile Dealers Associations: 805 Surya Kiran, 19 Kasturba Gandhi Marg, New Delhi 110 001; tel. (11) 3320046; fax (11) 3320093; e-mail fadadelhi@vsnl.net; internet www.fadaweb.com; f. 1964; Pres. KAILASH GUPTA; Sec.-Gen. GULSHAN AHUJA; 1,100 mems.

Federation of Gujarat Industries: Sidcup Tower, 4th Floor, Near Marble Arch, Race Course, Vadodara 390 007; tel. (265) 311101; fax (265) 339054; e-mail info@federationofgujarat.org; internet www.federationofgujarat.org; f. 1918; 350 mems; Pres. SHIVINDER SINGH CHAWLA; Sec.-Gen. Dr PARESH RAVAL.

Federation of Hotel and Restaurant Associations of India: B-82 Himalaya House, 23 K. G. Marg, New Delhi 110 001; tel. (11) 3323770; fax (11) 3322645; e-mail fhrai@vsnl.com; internet www.fhrai.com; Sec.-Gen. SHYAM SURI.

Federation of Indian Export Organisations: PHD House, 3rd Floor, Siri Institutional Area, Hauz Khas, New Delhi 110 016; tel. (11) 6851310; fax (11) 6863087; e-mail fieo@nda.vsnl.net.in; internet www.fieo.com; f. 1965; 5,900 mems; Pres. P. D. PATODIA; Dir-Gen. RANJIT LALL.

The Fertiliser Association of India: 10 Shaheed Jit Singh Marg, New Delhi 110 067; tel. (11) 6517305; fax (11) 6960052; e-mail fai@vsnl.com; internet www.fertindia.com; f. 1955; 1,695 mems; Chair. AJAY SHRIRAM; Dir-Gen. (vacant).

Grain, Rice and Oilseeds Merchants' Association: 14-C, Groma House, 2nd Floor, Sector 19, Vashi, Navi Mumbai 400 703; tel. (22) 7897454; fax (22) 7897458; e-mail groma@vsnl.com; internet www.groma.org; f. 1899; 1,200 mems; Pres. KALYAN J. SHAH; Sec. S. C. SHAH.

Indian Drug Manufacturers' Association: 102B Poonam Chambers, Dr A. B. Rd, Worli, Mumbai 400 018; tel. (22) 4944624; fax (22) 4950723; e-mail idma@giasbm01.vsnl.net.in; 600 mems; Pres. N. H. ISRANI; Sec.-Gen. I. A. ALVA.

Indian Electrical and Electronics Manufacturers' Association (IEEMA): 501 Kakad Chambers, 132 Dr Annie Besant Rd, Worli, Mumbai 400 018; tel. (22) 4936528; fax (22) 4932705; e-mail mumbai@ieema.org; internet www.ieema.org; f. 1948; 400 mems; Pres. R. N. MUKHIJA; Sec.-Gen. SUNIL P. MORE.

Indian Jute Mills Association: Royal Exchange, 6 Netaji Subhas Rd, Kolkata 700 001; tel. (33) 2209918; fax (33) 2205643; e-mail ijma@cal2.vsnl.net.in; sponsors and operates export promotion, research and product development; regulates labour relations; 33 mems; Pres. R. K. PODDAR; Sec. SARIT RAY.

Indian Leather Products Association: Suite 6, Chatterjee International Centre, 14th Floor, 33-A, J. L. Nehru Rd, Kolkata 700 071; tel. (33) 2267102; fax (33) 2468339; e-mail ilpa@cal2.vsnl.net.in; 120 mems; Pres. PARESH RAJDA; Exec. Dir P. K. DEY.

Indian Machine Tool Manufacturers' Association: 17 Nangal Raya Commercial Complex, New Delhi 110 046; tel. (11) 5592814; fax (11) 5599882; e-mail imtma@del2.vsnl.net.in; internet www.imtma.org; 400 mems; Pres. V. S. GOINDI; Sec. A. MUKHERJEE.

Indian Mining Association: 6 Netaji Subhas Rd, Kolkata 700 001; tel. (33) 263861; f. 1892; 50 mems; Sec. K. MUKERJEE.

Indian Mining Federation: 135 Biplabi Rash Behari Basu Rd, 2nd Floor, Kolkata 700 001; tel. (33) 2428975; f. 1913; 40 mems; Chair. V. K. ARORA; Sec. S. K. GHOSE.

Indian Motion Picture Producers' Association: IMPPA House, Dr Ambedkar Rd, Bandra (West), Mumbai 400 050; tel. (22) 6486344; fax (22) 6480757; f. 1938; 1,700 mems; SHAKTI SAMANTA; Sec. SHASHANK JARE.

Indian National Shipowners' Association: 22 Maker Tower, F, Cuffe Parade, Mumbai 400 005; tel. (22) 2182103; fax (22) 2182104; e-mail insamum@vsnl.com; internet www.indianshipowners.com; f. 1929; 31 mems; Pres. P. K. SRIVASTARA; Sec.-Gen. S. S. KULKARNI.

Indian Oilseeds & Produce Exporters' Association (IOPEA): 78/79 Bajaj Bhavan, Nariman Point, Mumbai 400 021; tel. (22) 2023225; fax (22) 2029236; e-mail iopea@bom3.vsnl.net.in; internet www.iopea.org; f. 1956; 350 mems; Chair. KISHOR BHEDA; Sec. A. N. SUBRAMANIAN.

Indian Paper Mills Association: India Exchange, 8th Floor, India Exchange Place, Kolkata 700 001; tel. (33) 2203242; fax (33) 2204495; f. 1939; 37 mems; Pres. K. K. KHEMKA; Sec. B. GHOSH.

Indian Refractory Makers' Association: 5 Lala Lajpat Rai Sarani, 4th Floor, Kolkata 700 020; tel. (33) 2810868; fax (33) 2814357; e-mail irma@giascl01.vsnl.net.in; internet www.irmaindia.org; 85 mems; Chair. Dr M. MUKHOPADHYAY; Exec. Dir P. DAS GUPTA.

Indian Soap and Toiletries Makers' Association: 614 Raheja Centre, Free Press Journal Marg, Mumbai 400 021; tel. (22) 2824115; fax (22) 2853649; e-mail istma@bom3.vsnl.net.in; 38 mems; Pres. B. V. PATEL; Sec.-Gen. R. HARIHARAN.

Indian Sugar Mills Association: 'Sugar House', 39 Nehru Place, New Delhi 110 019; tel. (11) 6472554; fax (11) 6472409; e-mail sugarmil@nda.vsnl.net.in; f. 1932; 215 mems; Pres. RAM V. TYAGARAJAN; Dir-Gen. S. L. JAIN.

Indian Tea Association: Royal Exchange, 6 Netaji Subhas Rd, Kolkata 700 001; tel. (33) 2102474; fax (33) 2434301; e-mail ita@cal2.vsnl.net.in; internet www.indiatea.org; f. 1881; 63 mem. cos; 483 tea estates; Chair. BHARAT BAJORIA; Sec.-Gen. D. CHAKRABARTI.

Indian Woollen Mills' Federation: Churchgate Chambers, 7th Floor, 5 New Marine Lines, Mumbai 400 020; tel. (22) 2624372; fax (22) 2624675; e-mail iwmf@bom3.vsnl.net.in; f. 1963; 50 mems; Chair. V. K. BHARTIA; Sec.-Gen. A. C. CHAUDHURY.

Industries and Commerce Association: ICO Association Rd, POB 70, Dhanbad 826 001; tel. (326) 303147; fax (326) 303787; f. 1933; 70 mems; Pres. B. N. SINGH; Sec. K. R. CHAKRAVARTY.

Jute Balers' Association: 12 India Exchange Place, Kolkata 700 001; tel. (33) 2201491; f. 1909; 300 mems; Chair. NIRMAL KUMAR BHUTORIA; Sec. SUJIT CHOUDHURY.

Maharashtra Motor Parts Dealers' Association: 13 Kala Bhavan, 3 Mathew Rd, Mumbai 400 004; tel. (22) 3614468; 375 mems; Pres. J. C. UNADKAT; Sec. J. R. CHANDAWALLA.

Millowners' Association, Mumbai: Elphinstone Bldg, 10 Veer Nariman Rd, Fort, POB 95, Mumbai 400 001; tel. (22) 2040411; fax (22) 2832611; f. 1875; 23 mem. cos; Chair. NANDAN S. DAMANI; Sec.-Gen. V. Y. TAMHANE.

Mumbai Motor Merchants' Association Ltd: 304 Sukh Sagar, N. S. Patkar Marg, Mumbai 400 007; tel. (22) 8112769; 409 mems; Pres. S. TARLOCHAN SINGH ANAND; Gen. Sec. S. BHUPINDER SINGH SETHI.

Mumbai Textile Merchants' Mahajan: 250 Sheikh Memon St, Mumbai 400 002; tel. (22) 2065750; fax (22) 2000311; f. 1881; 1,900 mems; Pres. SURENDRA TULSIDAS SAVAI; Hon. Secs DHIRAJ S. KOTHARI, RAJESH B. PATEL.

National Association of Software and Service Companies (NASSCOM): International Youth Centre, Uma Shankar Dixit Marg, Chanakyapuri, New Delhi 110 021; tel. (11) 3010199; fax (11) 3015452; e-mail nasscom@nasscom.org; internet www.nasscom.org; more than 650 mems; Pres. KIRAN KARNIK.

Organisation of Pharmaceutical Producers of India (OPPI): Thomas Cook Bldg, 1st Floor, 324 Dr Dadabhoy Naoroji Rd, Fort, Mumbai 400 001; tel. (22) 2045509; fax (22) 2044705; e-mail india oppi@vsnl.com; internet www.indiaoppi.com; 66 ordinary mems, 7 associate mems; Pres. RANJIT SHAHANI; Sec.-Gen. R. D. JOSHI.

Society of Indian Automobile Manufacturers: Core 4B, 5th Floor, India Habitat Centre, Lodhi Rd, New Delhi 110 003; tel. (11) 4647810; fax (11) 4648222; e-mail siamsoc@bol.net.in; f. 1960; 35 mems; Pres. R. SESHASAYEE; Exec. Dir RAJAT NANDI.

Southern India Mills' Association: 44 Racecourse, Coimbatore 641 018, Tamil Nadu; tel. (422) 211391; fax (422) 217160; e-mail simacbe@vsnl.com; f. 1933; 358 mems; Chair. MANIKAM RAMASWAMI; Sec. P. R. SUBRAMANIAN.

Surgical Manufacturers and Traders' Association: 60 Darya Ganj, New Delhi 110 002; tel. (11) 3271027; fax (11) 3258576; e-mail raviawasthi@hotmail.com; Pres. RAMESH BHASIN; Sec. RAVI AWASTHI.

Synthetic and Art Silk Mills' Association Ltd: 3rd Floor, Sasmira Bldg, Sasmira Marg, Worli, Mumbai 400 025; tel. (22) 4945372; fax (22) 4938350; e-mail sasma_100@pacific.net.in; f. 1939; 150 mems; Chair. V. S. CHALKE; Gen. Sec. K. A. SAMUEL.

Telecom Equipment Manufacturers' Association of India (TEMA): PHD House, 4th Floor, R. K. Dalmia Wing, opp Asian Games Village, New Delhi 110 016; tel. (11) 6859621; fax (11) 6859620; e-mail tema@vsnl.com; internet www.tematelecom.org; Pres. N. K. GOYAL; Exec. Dir. S. K. KHANNA.

Travel Agents' Association of India: 2D Lawrence and Mayo House, 276 Dr D. N. Rd, Mumbai 400 001; tel. (22) 2074022; fax (22) 2074559; e-mail travels@bom2.vsnl.net.in; 1,700 mems; Pres. JEHANGIR KATGARA; Hon. Sec.-Gen. SHUBHADA JOSHI.

United Planters' Association of Southern India (UPASI): Glenview, POB 11, Coonoor 643 101; tel. (423) 30270; fax (423) 32030; e-mail upasi@vsnl.com; f. 1893; 920 mems; Pres. P. S. WALLIA; Sec.-Gen. ULLAS MENON.

EMPLOYERS' ORGANIZATIONS

Council of Indian Employers: Federation House, Tansen Marg, New Delhi 110 001; tel. (11) 3738760; fax (11) 3320714; f. 1956; comprises:

All India Organisation of Employers (AIOE): Federation House, Tansen Marg, New Delhi 110 001; tel. (11) 3738760; fax (11) 3320714; f. 1932; 210 mems (incl. 158 associate mems); Pres. N. SRINIVASAN; Sec.-Gen. Dr AMIT MITRA.

Employers' Federation of India (EFI): Army and Navy Bldg, 148 Mahatma Gandhi Rd, Mumbai 400 001; tel. (22) 2844232; fax (22) 2843028; e-mail efisolar@vsnl.com; f. 1933; 28 asscn mems, 182 ordinary mems, 18 hon. mems; Pres. Dr RAM S. TARNEJA; Sec.-Gen. SHARAD S. PATIL.

Standing Conference of Public Enterprises (SCOPE): SCOPE Complex, 1st Floor, Core No. 8, 7 Lodi Rd, New Delhi 110 003; tel. (11) 4360101; fax (11) 4361371; e-mail scope@niesco .delhi.nic.in; internet www.niesco.delhi.nic.in; f. 1973; representative body of all central public enterprises in India; advises the Govt and public enterprises on matters of major policy and co-ordination; trade enquiries, regarding imports and exports of commodities, carried out on behalf of mems; 198 mems; Chair. D. K. VARMA; Sec.-Gen. (vacant).

Employers' Association of Northern India: 14/113 Civil Lines, POB 344, Kanpur 208 001; tel. (512) 210513; f. 1937; 190 mems; Chair. RAJIV KEHR; Sec.-Gen. P. DUBEY.

Employers' Federation of Southern India: Karumuttu Centre, 1st Floor, 634 Anna Salai, Chennai 600 035; tel. (44) 4349452; fax (44) 4349164; e-mail efsi@vsnl.net; f. 1920; 493 mems; Pres. R. VISWANATHAN; Sec. T. M. JAWAHARLAL.

UTILITIES

Electricity

Central Electricity Authority (CEA): Sewa Bhavan, R. K. Puram, New Delhi 110 066; tel. (11) 6108476; fax (11) 6105619; e-mail cea-edp@hub.nic.in; internet www.cea.nic.in; responsible for technical co-ordination and supervision of electricity programmes; advises Ministry of Power on all technical, financial and economic issues; Chair. H. L. BAJAJ.

Bombay Suburban Electric Supply Ltd: 6th Floor, Nagin Mahal, 82 Veer Nariman Rd, Mumbai 400 020; tel. (22) 2043287; fax (22) 2041280; internet www.bses.com; f. 1929; has monopoly in supply of electricity to Mumbai; Chair. and Man. Dir S. S. DUA (acting).

Calcutta Electricity Supply Corpn Ltd (CESC): CESC House, Chouringhee Sq., Kolkata 700 001; tel. (33) 2256040; fax (33) 2256334; f. 1978; generation and supply of electricity; Chair. R. P. GOENKA; Man. Dir SUMANTRA BANERJEE.

Damodar Valley Corpn: DVC Towers, VIP Rd, Kolkata 700 054; tel. (33) 3551935; fax (33) 3551937; e-mail dvchq@wb.nic.in; f. 1948 to administer the first multipurpose river valley project in India, the Damodar Valley Project, which aims at unified development of irrigation, flood control and power generation in West Bengal and Jharkhand; operates nine power stations, incl. thermal, hydel and gas turbine; power generating capacity 2,761.5 MW (1999); Chair. J. C. JETLI.

Dabhol Power Co: Dabhol; 65% owned by Enron (USA), 15% owned by the Maharashtra State Electricity Board (MSEB), 10% owned by Bechtel Enterprises Inc. (USA) and 10% owned by General Electric Co (USA); administered a two-phase project to establish plants with a power-generating capacity of 2,184 MW; first phase completed in 1999, second phase near completion in 2001; supplied electricity to the MSEB on a build-own-operate basis; production suspended in May 2001, following financial disagreements between Enron and the MSEB; sale of company under way in mid-2002; Man. Dir MOHAN GURUNATH.

Essar Power Ltd: Essar House, Mahalaxmi, Mumbai 400 034; tel. (22) 4950606; fax (22) 4954787; Chair. S. N. RUIA.

National Hydroelectric Power Corporation: Sector 33, Faridabad 121 003; fax (91) 5278020; e-mail yprasad@nhpc.nic.in; internet www.nhpcindia.com; f. 1975; Chair and Man. Dir YOGENDRA PRASAD.

National Thermal Power Corporation Ltd: Core-7, SCOPE Complex, Lodi Rd, New Delhi 110 003; tel. (11) 4360100; fax (11) 4361018; e-mail pr@ntpcn.ernet.in; internet www.ntpc.net; f. 1975; operates 11 coal-fired and five gas-fired power stations throughout India; Chair. and Man. Dir C. P. JAIN; 24,000 employees.

Noida Power Co Ltd: Commercial Complex, H Block, Alpha Sector II, Greater Noida, Uttar Pradesh 201 308; tel. (120) 4326559; fax (120) 4326448; f. 1922; distribution of electricity; Chair. and Man. Dir USHA CHATRATH; CEO P. NEOGI.

Nuclear Power Corporation of India Ltd: Commerce Center-1, World Trade Centre, Cuffe Parade, Mumbai 400 005; tel. (22) 2182171; fax (22) 2180109; internet www.npcil.org; Chair. and Man. Dir V. K. CHATURVEDI.

Power Grid Corporation of India Ltd: B-9, Qutab Institutional Area, Katwaria Sarai, New Delhi 110 016; tel. (11) 6560121; fax (11) 6560039; internet www.powergridindia.com; f. 1989; responsible for formation of national power grid; Chair. and Man. Dir R. P. SINGH.

Tata Power Co Ltd: Bombay House, 24 Homi Mody St, Mumbai 400 001; tel. (22) 2048331; fax (22) 2040505; generation, transmission and distribution of electrical energy; Chair. RATAN N. TATA; Man. Dir FIRDOSE VANDREWALA.

Thana Electric Supply Co Ltd: Asian Bldg, 1st Floor, 17 Ramji Kamani Marg, Ballard Estate, Mumbai 400 001; tel. (22) 2615444; fax (22) 2611069; e-mail thanaele@bom2.vsnl.net.in; f. 1927; Man. Dir SURESH S. MEMMADY.

Gas

Gas Authority of India Ltd: 16 Bhikaji Cama Place, R. K. Puram, Delhi 110 066; tel. (11) 6172580; fax (11) 6185941; e-mail pbanerjee @gail.com.in; internet www.nic.in/gail; f. 1984; 80% state-owned; transports, processes and markets natural gas; constructing gas-based petrochemical complex; Chair. and Man. Dir PROSHANTO BANERJEE; 1,513 employees.

Water

Brihanmumbai Municipal Corporation (Hydraulic Engineers' Department): Municipal Corporation Offices, Ground Floor,

Annex Bldg, Mahapalika Marg, Mumbai 400 001; tel. (22) 2620025; fax (22) 2700532; Head Eng. S. N. TURKAR.

Calcutta Municipal Corporation (Water Supply Department): 5 S. N. Banerjee Rd, Kolkata 700 013; tel. (33) 2444518; fax (33) 2442578; f. 1870; Chief Municipal Eng. DIBYENDU ROY CHOWDHURY.

Chennai Metropolitan Water Supply and Sewerage Board: No. 1 Pumping Station Rd, Chintadripet, Chennai 600 002; tel. (44) 8525717; fax (44) 831243; f. 1978; Chair. and Man. Dir SANTHA SHEELA NAIR.

Delhi Jal Board: Varunalaya Phase II, Karol Bagh, New Delhi 110 005; tel. and fax (11) 3516261; e-mail prodjb@bol.net.in; internet www.delhijalboard.com; f. as Delhi Water Supply and Sewage Disposal Undertaking, reconstituted as above in 1998; part of the Delhi Municipal Corporation (f. 1957); production and distribution of potable water and treatment and disposal of waste water in Delhi; Chair. SHEILA DIXIT.

MAJOR COMPANIES

Government Industrial Undertakings

The following are some of the more important industrial and commercial undertakings in which the Government holds a controlling interest.

Bharat Coking Coal Ltd: Koyla Bhawan, Koyla Nagar, Dhanbad 826 005; tel. (326) 263030; fax (326) 262227; f. 1972; cap. p.u. Rs 2,188.8m., sales Rs 20,714m. (March 2001); a subsidiary of Coal India Ltd; manages coking coal mines nationalized in 1972; Chair. and Man. Dir B. N. PAN.

Bharat Electronics Ltd: Regd and Corporate Office, 116/2 Race Course Rd, Bangalore 560 001; tel. (80) 2267322; fax (80) 2258410; e-mail imd@bel-india.com; internet www.bel-india.com; f. 1954; cap. p.u. Rs 800m., res and surplus Rs 5,647.8m., sales Rs 17,153.3m. (March 2001); mfrs of communications and radar equipment and electronic components; 9 manufacturing units; Chair. and Man. Dir Dr V. K. KOSHY; 15,700 employees.

Bharat Heavy Electricals Ltd: BHEL House, Siri Fort, New Delhi 110 049; tel. (11) 6001010; fax (11) 6493021; internet www.bhel.com; f. 1964; cap. p.u. Rs 2,447.6m., res and surplus Rs 42,306.1m., sales Rs 63,478m. (March 2001); integrated global service in power generation, transmission and utilization equipment; plants at Bhopal, Jhansi, Haridwar, Hyderabad, Bangalore and Tiruchirappalli; overseas offices in Dubai, United Arab Emirates, and South-East Asia; Chair. and Man. Dir K. G. RAMACHANDRAN; 53,800 employees.

Bharat Petroleum Corpn Ltd: Bharat Bhavan, 4 and 6 Currimbhoy Rd, Ballard Estate, POB 688, Mumbai 400 001; tel. (22) 2713000; fax (22) 2632951; e-mail infor@bharatpetroleum.com; internet www.bharatpetroleum.com; f. 1928 as Burmah-Shell Oil Storage and Distributing Co of India Ltd, nationalized 1976; cap. p.u. Rs 3,000m., res and surplus Rs 36,974m., sales Rs 459,312m. (March 2002); refinery at Trombay with crude processing capacity of 6.6m. metric tons a year; mfrs of MS, superior kerosene, aviation turbine fuel, high speed diesel oil, light diesel oil, bitumen, liquefied petroleum gas (LPG), solvents, naphtha, mineral turpentine and low sulphur heavy stock; owns eight port installations, six inland installations, two bunkering installations, one lubricating oil blending plant, 11 pipeline TOPS, 67 company-operated depots, 64 commission operated/special agreement depots, 26 dispatch units, 33 LPG-bottling plants, 16 aviation service stations, 1,345 LPG distributorships and 4,489 retail outlets throughout India; Chair. and Man. Dir SARTHAK BEHURIA; 12,638 employees (2000).

Bongaigaon Refinery and Petrochemicals Ltd: Dhaligaon, Bongaigaon District, Assam 783 385; tel. (3664) 41230; fax (3664) 41203; internet www.brplindia.com; oil refinery and petrochemical plant producing transportation and industrial fuels, DMT and PSF; cap. p.u. Rs 1,998m., res and surplus Rs 3,686m., sales Rs 12,553m. (March 2001); Chair. and Man. Dir B. K. GOGOI.

Cement Corpn of India Ltd: Core-5, SCOPE Complex, 7 Lodhi Rd, POB 3061, New Delhi 110 003; tel. (11) 4360158; fax (11) 4360464; e-mail ccisystem@vsnl.com; internet www.business.vsnl.com/cci; f. 1965; cap. Rs 4,187m., sales Rs 749m. (March 2001); establishes cement factories and sells cement in various parts of the country; surveys and prospects for limestone deposits; 10 operating factories in six states and in the Union Territory of Delhi; also offers consultancy services from concept to commissioning; Chair. and Man. Dir K. TEKCHANDANI.

Central Coalfields Ltd: Darbhanga House, Ranchi 834 001; tel. (651) 301606; fax (651) 301624; e-mail cclcmd@dte.vsnl.net.in; internet www.ccl.nic.in; f. 1975; cap. p.u. Rs 9,400m., sales Rs 24,887m. (March 2001); wholly-owned subsidiary of Coal India Ltd; Chair. and Man. Dir S. K. VERMA; Sec. M. M. GANGOPADHYAY.

Chennai Petroleum Corporation Ltd: 536 Anna Salai, Chennai 600 018; tel. (44) 454633; fax (44) 451783; oil refinery in Tamil Nadu; cap pu. Rs 1,490m.; res and surplus Rs 8,829m., sales Rs 71,326m. (March 2002); Chair. and Man. Dir S. RAMMOHAN.

Eastern Coalfields Ltd: Sanctoria, PO Dishergarh 713 333, Burdwin; tel. (341) 520053; fax (341) 520459; f. 1975; cap. p.u. Rs 22,184.5m., sales Rs 24,887m. (March 2001); subsidiary of Coal India Ltd; Chair. and Man. Dir ASHOK MEHTA.

Engineers India Ltd: El House, 1 Bhikaiji Cama Place, New Delhi 110 066; tel. (11) 6102121; fax (11) 6178210; e-mail eil.mktg@eil.co.in; internet www.engineersindia.com; provides engineering consultancy in India and abroad with specialization in the fields of petroleum refineries, pipelines, oil and gas processing, petrochemicals, offshore platforms, ports and terminals, metallurgy, fertilizers, power, chemicals; cap. p.u. Rs 561.6m., res and surplus Rs 6,562.5m., sales Rs 5,369.9m. (March 2002); Chair. and Man. Dir M. K. DALAL.

The Fertilizers and Chemicals Travancore Ltd (FACT): POB 14, Udyogamandal 683 501, Kochi; tel. (484) 541101; fax (484) 532475; f. 1943; cap. p.u. Rs 3,547.7m., res and surplus Rs 634.6m., sales Rs 17,622m. (March 2002); major shareholdings were acquired by Govt in 1963; mfrs of fertilizers, chemicals and petrochemicals (caprolactam); Chair. and Man. Dir T. T. THOMAS.

Gujarat State Fertilizers Co Ltd: PO Fertilizernager, Vadodara 391 750; tel. (265) 372451; fax (265) 372746; internet www.gsfclimited.com; cap. p.u. Rs 797.3m., res and surplus Rs 13,783.5m. (March 1999); Man. Dir BALWANT SINGH.

Heavy Engineering Corpn Ltd: Plant Plaza Rd, Ranchi 834 004; tel. (651) 408192; fax (651) 408571; e-mail hec@bitsmart.com; internet www.hecltd.com; f. 1958; cap. p.u. Rs 4,481m., res and surplus Rs 104m., sales Rs 1,591m. (March 2001); operates a heavy machine building plant, a foundry forge plant and a heavy machine tools plant; project and consultancy division; Chair. and Man. Dir G. P. PANDEY.

Hindustan Aeronautics Ltd: Corporate Office, 15/1 Cubbon Rd, POB 5150, Bangalore 560 001; tel. (80) 2866637; fax (80) 2868758; e-mail chairman@hal-india.com; internet www.hal-india.com; f. 1964; cap. p.u. Rs 1,205m., res and surplus Rs 13,791m., sales Rs 24,466m. (March 2001); mfrs of aircraft, helicopters, aero-engines, airborne electronic equipment and accessories; undertakes overhaul of aircraft, etc.; main customer is the Indian air force; 14 factories and nine design bureaux; Chair. N. R. MOHANTY; 34,448 employees.

Hindustan Cables Ltd: 9 Lajpat Rai Sarani, Kolkata 700 020; tel. (33) 2471808; fax (33) 2471657; cable factories at Rupnarainpur in West Bengal, Hyderabad, and Naini in Allahabad; cap. p.u. Rs 994m., res and surplus Rs 804m. (March 1995); Chair. and Man. Dir N. K. AGRAWAL.

Hindustan Copper Ltd: Tamra Bhavan, 1 Ashutosh Chowdhury Ave, Kolkata 700 019; tel. (33) 2400423; fax (33) 2408478; f. 1967; cap. Rs 5,436m., sales Rs 6,559m. (March 2001); responsible for the development of Indian Copper Complex, Ghatsila, in Bihar, Khetri Copper Complex, in Rajasthan, Taloja Copper Project in Maharashtra, and Malanjkhand Copper Project in Madhya Pradesh; annual capacity: 50,000 metric tons of finished copper (1994); Chair. and Man. Dir BALARAM K. MENON; c. 20,000 employees.

Hindustan Fertilizer Corpn Ltd: Madhuban, 55 Nehru Place, New Delhi 110 019; tel. (11) 6489520; fax (11) 6488652; e-mail hfcl1@vsnl.com; cap. p.u. Rs 8,846m., sales Rs 785m. (March 2001); operates Namrup fertilizer plant; Chair. and Man. Dir N. K. BORAH.

Hindustan Newsprint Ltd: Newsprint Nagar, Kerala 686 616; tel. (482) 656211; fax (482) 656777; e-mail hnl@vsnl.com; internet www.hnlonline.com; f. 1982; newsprint factory in Kerala; cap. p.u. Rs 825.4m., res and surplus Rs 1,116.6m., sales Rs 103,923m. (2000); Man. Dir N. P. PRABHU; 1,205 employees.

Hindustan Paper Corporation Ltd: Ruby Bldg, 75-C, Park St, Kolkata 700 016; tel. (33) 2296901; fax (33) 2494996; internet www.hindpaper.com; operates several paper mills; cap. p.u. Rs 6,914m., res and surplus Rs 66.6m., sales Rs 5,315m. (March 2001); Chair. and Man. Dir RAJI PHILIP.

Hindustan Petroleum Corpn Ltd: Petroleum House, 17 Jamshedji Tata Rd, Churchgate, Mumbai 400 020; tel. (22) 2026151; fax (22) 2872992; f. 1952 as Esso Standard Refining Co of India Ltd; fully nationalized 1976; cap. Rs 3,388.1m., res and surplus Rs 55,589m., sales Rs 471,799.3m. (March 2001); petroleum refining, manufacture of lubricating oil base stocks and marketing of petroleum products; refinery at Mahul (capacity 5.5m. metric tons a year), producing petrol, kerosene, diesel oils, fuel oils, solvents, LPG, asphalts, etc., and at Visakhapatnam (AP) (capacity 7.5m. metric tons a year), producing liquid petroleum gas, naphtha, motor gasoline, aviation turbine fuel, mineral turpentine, kerosene, etc.; lube refinery at Mahul uses crude from fuel refinery; designed capacity of 335,000 metric tons a year; has about 19.5% share in the Indian oil market; Chair. and Man. Dir M. B. LAL; Dir (Finance) S. D. GUPTA; 11,598 employees.

HMT (Hindustan Machine Tools) Ltd: 59 Bellary Rd, Bangalore 560 032; tel. (80) 3330333; fax (80) 3338547; f. 1953; cap. p.u. Rs 4,682m., sales Rs 3,452m. (March 2001); India's largest machine tools and watch mfr with units at Aurangabad, Bangalore, Pinjore

(Haryana), Kalamassery (Kerala), Hyderabad, Ajmer, Tumkur and Srinagar; 3 subsidiaries; Chair. and Man. Dir M. S. Zahed; 29,211 employees.

IBP Co Ltd: IBP House, 34A Nirmal Chandra St, Kolkata 700 013; tel. (33) 2365818; fax (33) 2155557; internet www.ibpoil.com; cap. p.u. Rs 221.5m., res and surplus Rs 3,469.3m., sales Rs 83,884m. (March 2001); a subsidiary of Indian Oil Corpn Ltd; manufacture and marketing of petroleum products; Chair. and Man. Dir Arun Jyoti.

Indian Iron and Steel Co Ltd: 50 Chowringhee Rd, Kolkata 700 071; tel. (33) 2828372; fax (33) 2826621; e-mail iisco@wbnic.in; internet www.iiscosteel.com; f. 1918; cap. p.u. Rs 3,876.7m., res and surplus Rs 35.0m., sales Rs 9,413.7m. (March 2001); a subsidiary of Steel Authority of India Ltd (SAIL); major establishments include iron and steel works at Burnpur, collieries at Chasnalla and iron ore mines and foundry at Kulti and the township of Burnpur and Kulti, West Bengal; Exec. Dir A. K. Jaiswal.

Indian Oil Corpn Ltd: SCOPE Complex, Core-2, 7 Institutional Area, Lodi Rd, New Delhi 110 003; tel. (11) 4360101; fax (11) 4362607; f. 1964; cap. p.u. Rs 7,786.7m., res and surplus Rs 145,324m., sales Rs 1,149m. (March 2002); the Refineries and Pipelines Division in New Delhi manages six refineries; the division lays pipelines and manages the Gauhati–Siliguri, Haldia–Barauni–Kanpur, Haldia–Maurigram–Rajbandh, Salaya–Koyali–Mathura, Kandla–Bhatindaand Koyali–Ahmedabad oil pipelines; the Marketing Division in Mumbai distributes petroleum products and has about 55% share in the Indian oil market; lube blending plant at Chennai; Research and Development Centre at Faridabad; Indian Oil Blending Ltd, a wholly-owned subsidiary, has blending plants at Kolkata and Mumbai; Assam Oil Division manages Digboi Refinery (Assam) and markets petroleum products in the north-east; Chair. M. S. Ramachandran; 33,287 employees.

Instrumentation Ltd: Kota 324 005; tel. (744) 424591; fax (744) 424322; e-mail ilkotain@jpl.dot.net.in; internet www.ilpgt.com; f. 1964; cap. p.u. Rs 240.5m., res and surplus Rs 10.1m., sales Rs 1,067.4m. (March 2001); the largest mfrs of industrial process control instruments in India; designs, builds, erects and commissions instrumentation systems; manufactures control valves and allied items with the technical collaboration of Japan, gas analysers used in pollution control with Germany and modernized process control instruments with the UK; plants at Kota, Jaipur and Palghat; Chair. and Man. Dir Niranjan Sinha; Man. (Admin.) D. C. Gupta.

Kochi Refineries Ltd: Ambalamugal, Ernakulam 682 302; tel. (484) 780261; fax (484) 720855; oil refinery at Kochi; cap. p.u. Rs 1,384.7m., res and surplus Rs 9,994.3m., sales Rs 66,540.8m. (March 2002); Chair. S. Behuria; Man. Dir B. K. Menon.

National Aluminium Company Ltd: Nalco Bhawan, P/1 Nayapalli, Bhubaneswar 751 013; tel. (674) 301988; fax (674) 301290; internet nalcoindia.com; aluminium plant in Orissa; cap. p.u. Rs 6,443m., res and surplus Rs 25,809.3m., sales Rs 24,086.0m. (March 2002); Chair. and Man. Dir C. Venkataramana.

National Fertilizers Ltd: Core-3, SCOPE Complex, Lodi Rd, New Delhi 110 003; tel. (11) 4360821; fax (11) 4361553; cap. p.u. Rs 4,906m., res and surplus Rs 9,165m., sales Rs 28,887.4m. (March 2001); Man. Dir P. S. Grewal.

National Textile Corporation Ltd: Scope Complex, Core No. IV, 7 Lodhi Rd, New Delhi 110 003; tel. (11) 4362417; fax (11) 4361112; internet www.ntc-entyee.com; operates a large number of textile mills throughout the country; cap. p.u. Rs 5,121m., res Rs 952m., sales Rs 799m. (March 2001); Chair. and Man. Dir K. M. Chadha.

Neyveli Lignite Corpn Ltd: Neyveli, Cuddalore District, Tamil Nadu 607 801; tel. (4142) 52280; fax (4142) 52646; f. 1956; cap. p.u. Rs 16,777.1m., res and surplus Rs 32,903.1m., sales Rs 21,890.2m. (March 2001); activities include lignite mining, power generation, production of urea and carbonized briquettes; Chair. and Man. Dir S. Jayamaran.

Northern Coalfields Ltd: Singrauli Colliery, Sidhi 486 889; tel. (7805) 66635; fax (7805) 66640; internet www.ncl.nic.in; cap. p.u. Rs 5,776.7m., res and surplus Rs 20,677.3m., sales Rs 27,397m. (March 2001); Chair. and Man. Dir Mithilesh Kumar Sinha; Dir (Finance) D. K. Mitra; 17,006 employees.

Oil India Ltd: Allahabad Bank Bldg, 17 Parliament St, POB 203, New Delhi 110 001; tel. (11) 3360841; fax (11) 3340962; e-mail oilindia@oil.delhi.nic.in; internet www.oilindia.nic.in; f. 1959; cap. p.u. Rs 2,140m., res and surplus Rs 28,629.5m., sales Rs 19,757m. (March 2001); formed as a result of an agreement between the Govt of India, the Burmah Oil Co Ltd and the Assam Oil Co Ltd, for the development of new oilfields in Assam; the company has mining leases for the exploration and production of crude petroleum and natural gas in Naharkatiya, Hugrijan, Moran, Doom Doma (Assam) and Ningru (Arunachal Pradesh), and petroleum exploration licences in Assam, Orissa, Rajasthan, Arunachal Pradesh, Uttar Pradesh and offshore areas of Saurashtra; it supplies crude petroleum to the refineries at Barauni, Guwahati, Bongaigaon, Digboi and Numaligarh; it supplies natural gas to the Rajasthan Electricity Board; it is also engaged in the transport of oil and the sale of gas; for this purpose the company has constructed and is operating a network of pipelines; the company also produces liquefied petroleum gas; Chair. and Man. Dir Ranjit Kumar Dutta.

Oil and Natural Gas Corporation Ltd (ONGC): Jeevan Bharati, Tower II, 8th Floor, 124 Indira Chowk, New Delhi 110 001; tel. (11) 3310156; fax (11) 3316413; internet www.ongcindia.com; f. 1956 as the Oil and Natural Gas Commission, name changed as above in 1994; cap. Rs 14,259m., res and surplus Rs 278,359.1m., sales Rs 236,473.1m. (March 2002); petroleum exploration and exploitation in India and abroad; crude petroleum production 28.9m. metric tons (1996/97); Chair. and Man. Dir Subir Raha; 43,700 employees.

Projects and Development India Ltd: A-14, Sector 1, Noida 201 301; tel. (91) 4529851; fax (91) 4529801; e-mail pdilnoida@vsnl.com; cap. p.u. Rs 535.2m., sales Rs 277m. (March 2002); a design engineering and technical consultancy organization in the field of fertilizers, industrial chemicals, petroleum, gas and pollution monitoring; Chair. and Man. Dir A. C. Saini; brs in Vadodara, Kolkata, Mumbai and Chennai.

Rashtriya Chemicals and Fertilizers Ltd: 'Priyadarshini', Eastern Express Highway, Mumbai 400 022; tel. (22) 4045001; fax (22) 4045111; e-mail cmdsec@vsnl.com; f. 1978; cap. p.u. Rs 5,517m., res and surplus Rs 8,150.8m., sales Rs 21,083.1m. (March 2001); operates Trombay and Thal Fertilizers and Industrial Chemicals plant; expansion projects and proposed new projects and jt ventures abroad; Chair. and Man. Dir D. K. Varma; Dir (Finance) S. Balan.

South Eastern Coalfields Ltd: Seepat Rd, Bilaspur, Madhya Pradesh 495 006; tel. (7752) 40170; fax (7752) 40306; cap. p.u. Rs 6,597m., res and surplus Rs 12,835m., sales Rs 35,559m. (March 2001); Chair. and Man. Dir Mukti Nath Jha.

Tea Trading Corpn of India Ltd: 7 Wood St, 2nd Floor, Kolkata 700 016; tel. (33) 3701192; fax (33) 3701092; f. 1973; cap. p.u. Rs 111.4m., sales Rs 34.3m. (March 2001); promotes the export and local sale of tea; owns and manages tea estates; processes and manufactures tea in blended and packaged form; is expanding into export of seafoods and processed fruit and food products; Man. Dir P. K. Gupta.

Western Coalfields Ltd: Coal Estate, Civil Lines, Nagpur 440 001; tel. (712) 511381; fax (712) 525302; e-mail wclcmd@nagpur.dot.net.in; f. 1975; cap. p.u. Rs 2,971m., res and surplus Rs 9,069m., sales Rs 26,854m. (March 2001); wholly-owned subsidiary of Coal India Ltd; Chair. and Man. Dir S. V. Chaoji.

Private Companies

The following are among India's major industrial enterprises in the private sector, listed by industry.

Automobile Industry

Ashok Leyland Ltd: 19 Rajaji Salai, POB 1305, Chennai 600 001; tel. (44) 5342141; fax (44) 5342493; e-mail al@webindia.com; internet www.ashokleyland.com; f. 1948; cap. Rs 1,189.3m., res (excl. revaluation res) Rs 8,915m. (March 2002), sales Rs 22,610m. (2000/01); mfrs of light, medium and heavy duty commercial vehicles, industrial and marine diesel engines and spare parts; six factories; Chair. R. J. Shahaney; Man. Dir R. Seshasayee; 14,345 employees (March 1999).

Bajaj Auto Ltd: Mumbai-Pune Rd, Akurdi, Pune 411 035; tel. (20) 7402851; fax (20) 7407397; e-mail exp4@bajajauto.globalnet.ems.vsnl.net.in; internet www.bajajauto.com; f. 1945; cap. Rs 1,011.8m., res Rs 27,645.9m., sales Rs 37,170m. (March 2002); sold more than 1.33m. units in 1997/98; manufactures and sells scooters, motorcycles, mopeds, three-wheelers, etc.; two subsidiaries: Bajaj Auto Holdings Ltd and Bajaj Auto Finance Ltd; Chair. and Man. Dir Rahul Bajaj; more than 21,000 employees.

Bajaj Tempo Ltd: Mumbai-Pune Rd, Akurdi, Pune 411 035; tel. (20) 7476381; fax (20) 7470889; e-mail tempoindia@vsnl.com; internet www.tempoindia.com; cap. p.u. Rs 132m., sales Rs 5,200m. (March 2002); mfrs of light commercial vehicles, three-wheelers, tractors and engines; Chair. and Man. Dir Abhay N. Firodia.

Daewoo Motors India Ltd: A-1 Surajpur Industrial Area, Surajpur 203 207; tel. (11) 914569243; fax (11) 914569818; cap. p.u. Rs 5,112m., sales Rs 9,140.5m. (March 2001); mfrs of commercial vehicles and passenger cars; Man. Dir and CEO D. W. Kim.

Daimler Chrysler India Pvt Ltd: Sector 15A, Chikhali Village, Pimpri, Pune 411 018; tel. (20) 772781; fax (20) 773597; Man. Dir and CEO Hans-Michael Huber.

Eicher Motors Ltd: Eicher House, 12 Commercial Complex, Greater Kailash-II (Masjid Moth), New Delhi 110 048; tel. (11) 6445521; fax (11) 6431929; e-mail ssandilya@eicher.co.in; internet www.eicherworld.com; mfrs of commercial vehicles; cap. p.u.

Rs 200m., res and surplus Rs 513.2m. (March 2002); Chair. S. Sandilya; Man. Dir Rakesh Kalra.

Escorts Ltd: A-36, Mohan Co-op Industrial Estate, Mathura Rd, New Delhi 110 044; tel. (11) 3310145; fax (11) 3310271; f. 1942; manufactures and sells motor cycles, tractors, pistons, self-propelled mobile cranes, road construction equipment, röntgen equipment, hydraulic shock absorbers, etc.; five subsidiaries; cap. p.u. Rs 722.3m., res and surplus Rs 7,073.2m., sales Rs 11,080m. (March 2002); Chair. and Man. Dir Rajan Nanda.

Fiat India Automobiles Ltd: LBS Marg, Kurla, Mumbai 400 070; tel. (22) 5142186; fax (22) 5147107; mfrs of passenger cars; Man. Dir Maurizio Paolo Bianchi.

Ford India Ltd: Via S. P. Koil Post, Chengalpattu 603 204; tel. (4114) 54375; fax (4114) 54278; internet www.india.ford.com; mfrs of passenger cars; Chair. Terry de Jockheere; Pres. and Man. Dir David Friedman.

General Motors India Ltd: GF VIPPS Centre, 2 LSC Masjid Moth, Greater Kailash II, New Delhi 110 048; tel. (11) 6443301; fax (11) 6485934; e-mail p.balendran@gm.co.in; internet opelindia.com; f. 1995; mfrs of passenger cars; Pres. and Man. Dir Aditya Vij.

Hero Honda Motors Ltd: 34 Basant Lok, Vasant Vihar, New Delhi 110 057; tel. (11) 6872451; fax (11) 6873321; internet www.herohonda.com; f. 1984; cap. p.u. Rs 399.4m., res and surplus Rs 6,458.2m., sales Rs 44,650m. (March 2002); mfrs of motor cycles; Chair. and Man. Dir Brijmohan Lall Munjal.

Hindustan Motors Ltd: Birla Bldg, 9/1 R. N. Mukherjee Rd, Kolkata 700 001; tel. (33) 2201680; fax (33) 2480055; f. 1942; cap. p.u. Rs 1,613m., res Rs 176.7m., sales Rs 10,010m. (March 2002); mfrs of cars, truck chassis, cranes, presses, excavators, steel structurals, steel castings and forgings at factory at Hindmotor (West Bengal); dumpers, crawler/wheeled tractors, motorized scrappers and front-end loaders at factory in Trivellore (Tamil Nadu); power shift transmissions and torque converters at Hosur (Tamil Nadu), engines and transmissions for cars at Pithampur (Madhya Pradesh) and buses and trucks at Vadodara (Gujarat); two subsidiaries: Hindustan Motor Finance Corpn Ltd and Hindustan Export Ltd; Chair. Chandra Kant Birla; Man. Dir A. Sankaranarayan; 15,000 employees (1995).

Honda Siel Cars India Ltd: Plot No. A-1, Sector 40/41, Surajpur-Kasna Rd, Greater Noida Industrial Development Area, Uttar Pradesh 203 207; tel. (11) 914561268; fax (11) 914561261; Pres. and CEO H. Yamada.

Hyundai Motor India Ltd: Plot No. H-1, Sipcot Industrial Park, Irrungattukottai, Sriperumbudur Taluk, Kancheepuram 602 105; tel. (4111) 56111; fax (4111) 56280; mfrs of passenger cars; Man. Dir J. I. Kim.

Kinetic Motor Company Ltd: Neeta Towers, Mumbai-Pune Rd, Dapodi, Pune 411 012; tel. (20) 7124903; fax (20) 7124906; cap. p.u. Rs 150.4m., res Rs 509m., sales Rs 3,290m. (March 2002); mfrs of two-wheel vehicles; Man. Dir Hideo Tanaka.

LML Ltd: C-3, Panki Industrial Estate, Kanpur 208 022; tel. (512) 691181; fax (512) 691191; e-mail lmlknp@lml-india.com; cap. p.u. Rs 437m.; res. Rs 7,223.5m., sales Rs 5,180m. (March 2001); mfrs of scooters; Chair. M. R. B. Punja; Man. Dir D. K. Singhania.

Maharashtra Scooters Ltd: Mumbai-Pune Rd, Akurdi, Pune 411 035; tel. (20) 772851; fax (20) 773398; cap. p.u. Rs 114m., sales Rs 1,040m. (March 2002); Chair. Rahul Bajaj; Man. Dir Ranjit Gupta.

Mahindra and Mahindra Ltd: Gateway Bldg, Apollo Bunder, Mumbai 400 001; tel. (22) 4931441; fax (22) 4975193; internet www.mahindraworld.com; f. 1945; cap. p.u. Rs 1,105m., res Rs 13,800.8m., sales Rs 32,730m. (March 2002); mfrs of 'Mahindra' range of vehicles, tractors and agricultural implements, industrial engines, industrial process and control instruments; trades in steel and machine tools, exports and imports chemicals, engineering goods, diesel engines, oilfield services, telecommunications, construction and road building, etc.; 13 subsidiaries; Chair. Keshub Mahindra; Man. Dir Anand G. Mahindra; 19,000 employees (1998).

Majestic Auto Ltd: 601 International Trade Tower, Nehru Place, New Delhi 110 019; tel. (11) 6216666; fax (11) 6475194; cap. p.u. Rs 65.5m., res Rs 399m. (March 1996); mfrs of motor cycles and mopeds; Chair. O. P. Munjal; Man. Dir Pankaj Munjal.

Maruti Udyog Ltd: 11th Floor, Jeevan Prakash Bldg, 25 Kasturba Gandhi Marg, New Delhi 110 001; tel. (11) 3316831; fax (11) 3318754; cap. p.u. Rs 1,323m., res and surplus Rs 24,515m., sales Rs 92,533m. (March 2001); largest mfrs of passenger cars and light utility commercial vehicles in collaboration with Suzuki Motor Co of Japan; Chair. Shinzo Nakanishi; Man. Dir Jagdish Khattar; 4,968 employees.

Motor Industries Co Ltd: Hosur Rd, Adugodi, POB 3000, Bangalore 560 030; tel. (80) 2220088; fax (80 2212728; f. 1951; owned by Bosch of Germany; manufactures automotive components; cap. p.u. Rs 341m., res and surplus Rs 3,725m., sales Rs 14,550m. (Dec. 2001); Man. Dir Andreas Nobis.

Swaraj Mazda Ltd: SCO 204–205, Sector 34-A, Chandigarh 160 022; tel. (172) 647700; fax (172) 615111; mfrs of light commercial vehicles; cap. p.u. Rs 105m., res Rs 69.4m., sales Rs 2,950m. (March 2002); Vice Chair. and Man. Dir Yash Mahajan.

Tata Engineering and Locomotive Co Ltd (TELCO): Bombay House, 24 Homi Mody St, Hutatma Chowk, Mumbai 400 001; tel. (22) 2049131; fax (22) 2045474; internet www.telcoindia.com; f. 1945; cap. p.u. Rs 2,559m., res Rs 29,978.8m., sales Rs 89,180.6m. (March 2002); manufactures and sells Tata Diesel truck and bus chassis, light commercial vehicles, passenger cars; factories at Jamshedpur, Lucknow, Dharwar and Pune; Chair. Ratan Tata; 22,414 employees (2002).

Toyota Kirloskar Motor Ltd: Plot No. 1, Bidadi Industrial Area, Ramnagar Taluk, Bangalore (Rural) District 562 109; tel. (8113) 87001; fax (8113) 87078; mfrs of utility vehicles and passenger cars; Man. Dir. S. Yamazaki.

TVS Motor Company Ltd: Jayalakshmi Estates, 5th Floor, 8 Haddows Rd, Chennai 600 006; tel. (44) 8272233; fax (44) 8257121; cap. p.u. Rs 231m., res Rs 3,003m., sales Rs 19,300m. (March 2002); mfrs of mopeds, motor cycles and scooters; Man. Dir Venu Srinivasan.

Volvo India Pvt Ltd: 201 Embassy Sq., 148 Infantry Rd, Bangalore 560 003; tel. (80) 2282910; fax (80) 2284448; Man. Dir Ulf Nordqvist.

Yamaha Motor India Ltd: 19/6 Mathura Rd, Faribad 12 006; tel. (129) 284931; fax (129) 284841; mfrs of motorcycles; Man. Dir Masahiko Shibuya.

Biotechnology

Biocon India Group: 20 K. M. Hosur Rd, Electronic City, Bangalore 561 229; tel. (80) 8523434; fax (80) 8523423; e-mail contact.us@bioconindia.com; internet www.biocon.com; f. 1978; comprises Biocon India Ltd—involved in the research, development and manufacture of healthcare pharmaceutical products and industrial enzymes—and the contract research organization Syngene International Ltd; subsidiary of Syngene: Clinigene International; Chair. Kiran Mazumdar-Shaw.

Cipla Ltd: Mumbai Central, 289 J. B. B. Marg, Mumbai 400 008; tel. (22) 3095521; fax (22) 3070013; internet www.cipla.com; f. 1935; sales Rs 6,170m. (1999); research and development; manufacture and sale of drugs; Chair. and Man. Dir Dr Yusuf K. Hamied; 2,227 employees.

Dr Reddy's Laboratories Ltd: 7-1-27 Ameerpet, Hyderabad 500 016; tel. (40) 3731946; fax (40) 3731855; e-mail corpcom@drreddys.com; internet www.drreddys.com; f. 1984; research, development, manufacture and marketing of pharmaceutical products; research in molecular biology and infectious diseases; cap. and res Rs 3,794.7m., sales Rs 4,930.2m. (March 2002); Chair. Dr K. A. Reddy.

Greenearth Biotechnologies Ltd: 14A Jigani Industrial Area, Bangalore 562106; tel. (80) 8398793; fax (80) 8394936; e-mail sjn@greenearthbiotech.com; internet www.greenearthbiotech.com.

Maharashtra Hybrid Seeds Co Ltd: Resham Bhavan, 4th Floor, 78 Veer Nariman Point, Mumbai 400 020; tel. (22) 2049497; fax (22) 2047871; e-mail rbarwale@mahyco.com; research, production and processing of cereals, oilseeds, pulses and vegetables; production of agro-based food products; research in biotechnology, biochemistry and plant-breeding; Man. Dir R. B. Barwale.

Ranbaxy Laboratories Ltd: 19 New Place, New Delhi 110 019; tel. (11) 6452666; fax (11) 6002088; internet www.ranbaxy.com; f. 1961; manufactures therapeutic and pharmaceutical products; cap. and res Rs 14,553m., sales 17,459m. (2000); Man. Dir and CEO D. S. Brar; 8,000 employees (2002).

Shantha Biotechnics (Pvt) Ltd: Serene Chambers, 3rd Floor, Rd 7, Banjara Hills, Hyderabad 500 034; tel. (40) 3543010; fax (40) 3548476; e-mail shantha@hd1.vsnl.net.in; internet www.shanthabiotech.com; research, development and production of drugs and vaccines; Chair. K. V. Reddy.

Cement Industry

Associated Cement Companies Ltd: Cement House, 121 Maharashi Karve Rd, POB 11025, Mumbai 400 020; tel. (22) 2039122; fax (22) 2080076; f. 1936; cap. Rs 1,709m., res Rs 8,581m., sales Rs 28,110m. (March 2002); manufacture and sale of cement (11 cement works in eight states), refractories (Katni). Subsidiaries: The Cement Marketing Co of India Ltd, ACC-Nihon Castings Ltd, Webel Electro Ceramics Ltd and Associated Tyre Machinery Co Ltd; Chair. Tarun Das; Man. Dir T. M. M. Nambiar; 15,283 employees.

India Cements Ltd: 4th Floor, Dhun Bldg, 827 Anna Salai, Chennai 600 002; tel. (44) 8521526; fax (44) 8520702; f. 1946; cap. Rs 1,384.8m., res and surplus Rs 6,025.1m., sales Rs 11,440m. (March 2002); mfrs of cement, cement clinker, grinding media, malleable cast iron material, etc.; factories at Sankarnagar (Tirunelveli District), Sankaridrug (Salem District); Chair. and Man. Dir N. SRINIVASAN; 6,000 employees.

Mysore Cements Ltd: Industry House, 45 Race Course Rd, Bangalore 560 001; tel. (812) 264907; fax (812) 262165; f. 1958; cap. p.u. Rs 687m., sales Rs 2,980m. (March 2002); Chair. S. K. BIRLA; Man. Dir N. L. HAMIRWASIA.

OCL India: B-47 Connaught Place, New Delhi 110 001; tel. (11) 3321212; fax (11) 3731333; e-mail ocl@nda.vsnl.net.in; f. 1949; fmrly Orissa Cement Ltd; manufactures cement and refractories; factory at Rajgangpur in Orissa; four subsidiaries; cap. Rs 71.8m., res Rs 1,337.3m. (March 2000), sales Rs 2,800m. (2000/01); Jt Pres. R. H. DALMIA (refractories), A. H. DALMIA (cement).

Shree Cement Ltd: Bangur Nagar, POB 33, Beawar 305 901; tel. (1462) 20010; fax (1462) 21868; f. 1979; cap. p.u. Rs 348.4m., res Rs 1,770.5m., sales Rs 3,970m. (March 2002); capacity of 2m. metric tons per year; Chair. and Man. Dir B. G. BANGUR.

Chemicals and Fertilizers

See also under Cotton Textiles.

Atul Ltd: Atul 396 020, Valsad District, Gujarat; tel. (2632) 33261; fax (2632) 33619; e-mail ho@atul.co.in; internet www.atul.co.in; f. 1947; cap. p.u. Rs 296.7m., sales Rs 5,580m. (March 2002); mfrs of dyes, dye intermediates, chemicals, pesticides and pharmaceutical intermediates; six subsidiaries; Man. Dir SUNIL SIDDHARTH LALBHAI.

Coromandel Fertilisers Ltd: Coromandel House, 1-2-10 Sardar Patel Rd, Secunderabad 500 003; tel. (842) 842034; fax (842) 844117; f. 1961; manufactures and markets chemical fertilizers; cap. p.u. Rs 194.6m., res and surplus Rs 2,170.8m., sales Rs 6,150m. (March 2002); Chair. Dr BHARAT RAM; Pres. and Man. Dir R. S. NANDA.

Gujarat Heavy Chemicals Ltd: Bhikubhai Chambers, Swastik Society, Naurangpura, Ahmedabad 380 009; cap. p.u. Rs 932.5m., res Rs 1,699m., sales Rs 3,620m. (March 2002); Chair. K. V. HARIHAN DAS; Man. Dir S. K. MUKHERJEE.

ICI India Ltd: 34 Chowringhee, POB 9093, Kolkata 700 071; tel. (33) 298688; fax (33) 296330; f. 1954; cap. Rs 408.7m., res Rs 3,626.2m., sales Rs 6,430m. (March 2002); mfrs of commercial blasting explosives, nitrocellulose, paints, rubber chemicals, polythene, pharmaceuticals etc.; factories in West Bengal, Bihar, Andhra Pradesh, Maharashtra and Tamil Nadu; Chair. Dr ASHOK GANGULY; Man. Dir ADITYA NARAYAN; 4,100 employees (1994).

Indian Organic Chemicals Ltd: Chemtex House, Main St, Sector 12, Hiranandani Gdns, Powai, Mumbai 400 076; tel. (22) 5780625; fax (22) 5793924; f. 1960; cap. p.u. Rs 334.7m., res Rs 860m. (March 1996); manufactures and sells polyester staple fibre, organic chemicals, etc.; Chair. and Man. Dir S. B. GHIA.

Indian Petrochemicals Corpn Ltd: PO Petrochemicals Township, Gujarat 391 345; tel. (265) 375876; fax (265) 375063; e-mail cmd@ipclmail.com; f. 1969; cap. Rs 2,490.5m., res and surplus Rs 29,461.3m. (March 2001); Chair. MUKESH AMBANI; 13,013 employees.

National Organic Chemical Industries Ltd: Mafatlal Chambers, 'B' Wing, N. M. Joshi Marg, Lower Parel (East), Mumbai 400 013; tel. (22) 3016566; fax (22) 3016570; f. 1961; merged with Polyolefins Industries Ltd in 1994; manufactures and sells petrochemicals, polymers, rubber chemicals and plastics; cap. p.u. Rs 1,226.1m., res Rs 2,903.2m., sales Rs 6,420m. (March 2002); Chair. ARVIND N. MAFATLAL; Vice-Chair. and Man. Dir Dr N. M. DHULDHOYA; 2,190 employees (2001).

Southern Petrochemical Industries Corporation Ltd (SPIC): 97 Mount Rd, Chennai 600 032; tel. (44) 2350245; fax (44) 2352163; e-mail spiccorp@spic.co.in; internet www.spic-india.com; f. 1969; manufactures and sells fertilizers, caustic soda, etc.; cap. p.u. Rs 880.5m., res and surplus Rs 5,015.9m., sales Rs 21,950m. (March 2001); manufacturing plants at Tuticorin, Cuddalore and Manali; Chair. M. A. CHIDAMBARAM; Man. Dir BABU K. VERGHESE.

Tata Chemicals Ltd: Bombay House, 24 Homi Mody St, Mumbai 400 001; tel. (22) 2049131; fax (22) 2851132; f. 1939; owns and operates the largest inorganic chemical complex in India and a gas-based fertilizer project; cap. p.u. Rs 1,807m., res and surplus Rs 13,706.6m., sales Rs 13,871.0m. (March 2002); Chair. RATAN TATA; Man. Dir PRASAD R. MENON.

Computer Services

Infosys Technologies Ltd: Plot 44, 3rd Cross, Electronic City, Hosur Rd, Bangalore 561 229; tel. (80) 8520261; fax (80) 8520352; e-mail infosys@inf.com; internet www.inf.com; f. 1981; cap. Rs 331m., sales Rs 26,040m. (March 2002); developer, producer and exporter of software products; Chair. and CEO NARAYANA N. R. MURTHY.

Satyam Computer Services Ltd: 1st Floor, Mayfair Centre, 1-83303/36 Sardar Patel Rd, Secunderabad 500 003; fax (40) 840058; e-mail corporatecommunications@satyam.com; internet www.satyam.com; f. 1987; cap. p.u. Rs 629m., sales Rs 17,320m. (March 2002); develops software products; Chair. B. RAMALINGA RAJU; Man. Dir B. R. RAJU.

Tata Consultancy Services: 11th Floor, Air India Bldg, Nariman Point, Mumbai 400 021; tel. (22) 2024827; fax (22) 2040711; e-mail tcs.corpffice@mumbai.tcs.co.in; internet www.tcs.com; f. 1968; provides computer consultancy services; more than 100 offices worldwide; CEO S. RAMADORAI.

Wipro Corporation: Du Parc Trinity, 17 M. G. Rd, Bangalore 560 001; tel. (80) 5092598; fax (80) 5596751; e-mail kannnv@wiprosys.soft.net; internet www.wipro.com; f. 1945; cap. p.u. Rs 465m., sales Rs 34,680m. (March 2002); develops software systems, as well as manufacturing household goods and hospital equipment; Chair. AZIM HASHIM PREMJI.

Construction

The Hindustan Construction Co Ltd: Hincon House, L.B.S. Marg, Vikhroli (West), Mumbai 400 038; tel. (22) 5775959; fax (22) 5777568; e-mail hccnet@bom3.vsnl.net.in; internet www.hccindia.com; f. 1926; cap. p.u. Rs 200.3m., res and surplus Rs 549.9m., sales Rs 3,950m. (March 2002); constructs concrete dams, railways and hydro tunnels, power houses, docks, jetties, barrages, industrial structures, environmental engineering projects, bridges, highways, etc.; major projects: Maneri Bhali, Salal, Idamalayar and Kadamparai hydroelectric works, Teesta, Mahananda barrages, tunnelling by shield method for Kolkata Metro, Narora atomic power project, Barauni, Titagarh, Farakka and Ramagundam thermal power projects, Cochin tanker terminal and fertilizer berths at Cochin port, construction at Upper Kolab dam, Tezpur bridge over the River Brahmaputra in Assam, SSSF project for Tarapur atomic power station, Expressway Mumbai Pune, etc.; brs in New Delhi, Kolkata and Chennai; civil works in Iraq, Malawi and Tanzania; subsidiary: Ganga Construction Ltd; Chair. and Man. Dir AJIT GULABCHAND.

Cotton Textiles, Jute, Man-Made Fibres

Arvind Mills Ltd: Railwaypura Post, Naroda Rd, POB 10010, Ahmedabad 380 025; tel. (79) 2148282; fax (79) 2121396; f. 1931; cap. Rs 1,396.4m., res and surplus Rs 2,409.2m., sales Rs 18,730m. (March 2002); manufactures and sells cotton textiles and blended fabrics; also deals in telecommunications products and electronics; two subsidiaries; Chair. and Man. Dir ARVIND N. LALBHAI.

Birla Corpn Ltd: Birla Bldg, 9/1 R. N. Mukherjee Rd, Kolkata 700 001; tel. (33) 2201680; fax (33) 2487988; f. 1919; cap. Rs 770m., res Rs 1,330m. (March 2000), sales Rs 8,680m. (2000/01); manufacture and sale of jute goods, automobile trimmings, steel foundry items, PVC floor covering and wallpapers, calcium carbide, oxy-acetylene gases, staple and synthetic fibre yarn, cement, jute carpets and webbing; one subsidiary; Chair. PRIYAMBADA BIRLA; Man. Dir K. C. MITTAL.

Birla VXL Ltd: 9/1, R. N. Mukherjee Rd, Kolkata 700 001; tel. (33) 280135; fax (33) 289110; f. 1948; fmrly VXL India Ltd; manufactures and sells wool tops, yarns, worsted and blended fabrics, carpets, electricity meters, relays, control panels and special high precision items, vegetable oils etc.; factories at Amritsar, Faridabad, Harda, Jamnagar and Joka; cap. Rs 651m., res Rs 1,686.6m. (June 1998), sales Rs 3,351m. (2000/01); five subsidiaries; Chair. SUDARSHAN K. BIRLA; Pres. C. L. RATHI.

The Bombay Dyeing and Manufacturing Co Ltd: Neville House, J. N. Heredia Marg, Ballard Estate, Mumbai 400 038; tel. (22) 268071; fax (22) 265622; f. 1879; cap. p.u. Rs 392m., res Rs 6,289.4m. (March 2000), sales Rs 7,940m. (March 2002); mfrs and exporters of cotton yarn and textiles, and blends of cotton and synthetic fibres; two mills and a processing plant in Mumbai, one mill at Jamnagar, a processing plant at Roha (Maharashtra) and a dimethyl terephthatate plant at Patalganga (Maharashtra); three subsidiaries; Chair. NUSLI N. WADIA; Man. Dir NINU KHANNA; 10,650 employees.

Century Enka Ltd: 7th Floor Bakhtawar, Nariman Point, Mumbai 400 021; tel. (22) 2027375; f. 1965; cap. p.u. Rs 286m., res and surplus Rs 7,090m. (March 2002), sales Rs 7,540m. (2000/01); Chair. B. K. BIRLA.

Century Textiles and Industries Ltd: Century Bhavan, Dr Annie Besant Rd, Worli, Mumbai 400 025; tel. (22) 4300351; fax (22) 4309491; f. 1897; cap. p.u. Rs 930m., res Rs 10,349.7m. (March 2001), sales Rs 21,970m. (March 2002); mfrs of cotton textiles and yarn; cotton yarn mill at Worli (Mumbai), plants at Satrati (Madhya Pradesh) producing viscose rayon yarn, tyre yarn and caustic soda, plants at Kalyan (Maharashtra), portland cement plants at Baikunth, Sarlanagar (Madhya Pradesh) and Gadchandur (Maharashtra), minerals and chemicals plant at Jamnagar (Gujarat), and pulp and paper plants at Lalkua (Uttar Pradesh); co is also engaged in tramp shipping, the building and development of land and property, and floriculture activities; Chair. B. K. BIRLA.

Grasim Industries Ltd: Century Bhavan, Dr Annie Besant Rd, Mumbai 400 025; tel. (22) 4308491; fax (22) 4227586; f. 1947; cap.

Rs 916.9m., res Rs 26,849.5m. (March 2000), sales Rs 43,870m. (March 2002); fmrly the Gwalior Rayon Silk Manufacturing (Weaving) Co Ltd; mfrs of viscose staple fibre; dissolving pulp and paper; man-made fabrics; cotton textiles; also mfrs of rayon and allied chemical plant and machinery; Chair. KUMAR MANGALAM BIRLA; Pres. INDU H. PAREKH; 15,000 employees.

JCT Ltd: Thapar House, 124 Janpath, New Delhi 110 001; tel. (11) 3329608; fax (11) 3327707; f. 1946; manufactures polyester blended and cotton fabrics and nylon/polyester filament and cotton yarn; textile mills at Phagwara and Srinagar and ginning factories at Abohar, Khanna and Jagraon; four subsidiaries; cap. Rs 859.2m., res Rs 1,034.7m., sales Rs 4,900m. (March 2002); Chair. M. M. THAPAR.

Kesoram Industries Ltd: A. J. C. Bose Rd, Kolkata 700 017; tel. (33) 2209454; fax (33) 2209455; e-mail kesoram.cal@gncal.global net.ems.vsnl.net.in; f. 1919; cap. p.u. Rs 482m., res Rs 2,871.3m., sales Rs 11,270m. (March 2002); mfrs of cotton textiles and piece goods, rayon yarn, transparent paper, cellulose film, sulphuric acid, carbon disulphide, cast iron spun pipes and fittings, cement, refractories, etc.; two subsidiaries: Bharat General and Textile Industries Ltd and KICM Investment Ltd; factories in West Bengal, Andhra Pradesh and Karnataka; Chair. B. K. BIRLA.

Mafatlal Industries Ltd: Mafatlal House, Backbay Reclamation, Mumbai 400 020; tel. (22) 2026944; fax (22) 2027750; f. 1913; cap. p.u. Rs 499.9m., res Rs 2,359m. (March 2001), sales Rs 2,860m. (March 2002); manufactures and sells textile goods and yarn, ready-made garments, plastic processing machines, electronic professional grade connectors, flurione chemicals, and dyes and intermediates of chemicals; two subsidiaries; Chair. and Sr Pres. ARVIND N. MAFATLAL; Exec. Dir PRAFUL R. AMIN.

Raymond Ltd: New Hind House, Narottam Morarjee Marg, Ballard Estate, Mumbai 400 038; tel. (22) 4151415; f. 1925; manufactures and sells wool/blended suiting fabrics, furnishing fabrics, rugs, blankets, knitting yarn, steel files and rasps, twist drills, garments; plants in Maharashtra and Madhya Pradesh; cap. Rs 613.8m., res Rs 8,338.8m., sales Rs 8,680m. (March 2002); Chair. and Man. Dir GAUTAM SINGHANIA.

Reliance Industries Ltd: Maker Chambers IV, 222 Nariman Point, Mumbai 400 021; tel. (22) 2831633; fax (22) 2042268; internet www.ril.com; f. 1973; cap. Rs 10,534.5m., res Rs 109,411m., sales Rs 242,860m. (March 2002); mfrs and sellers of blended and synthetic yarn polyester staple fibre and of synthetic and worsted fabrics; petrochemicals; Chair. MUKESH D. AMBANI; Man. Dir ANIL AMBANI; 14,255 employees.

Electrical Goods

Blue Star Ltd: Kasturi Bldgs, Mohan T. Advani Chowk, Jamshedji Tata Rd, Mumbai 400 020; tel. (22) 2020868; fax (22) 2824043; e-mail ccm@bluestarindia.com; internet www.bluestarindia.com; cap. p.u. Rs 193m., res and surplus Rs 921.1m., sales Rs 4,914m. (2001/02); air-conditioning, electronics, industrial and commercial equipment; Chair and CEO ASHOK M. ADVANI.

BPL Ltd: Dynamic House, 64 Church St, POB 5194, Bangalore 560 001; tel. (80) 5588388; fax (80) 5586971; f. 1963; manufacturers consumer and domestic electrical goods; cap. p.u. Rs 277m. (March 2001) sales Rs 11,940m. (March 2002); Chair. T. P. G. NAMBIAR; Vice-Chair. and Man. Dir AJIT G. NAMBIAR.

Crompton Greaves Ltd: CG International, 'Jagruti', 2nd Floor, Kanjurmarg (E), Mumbai 400 042; tel. (22) 5782451; fax (22) 5774066; e-mail cgi@cgl.co.in; internet www.cgl.co.in/international/; f. 1937; manufactures, distributes and exports electrical and electronics equipment systems, power and industrial transformers, industrial and commercial motors; cap. p.u. Rs 524m., res and surplus Rs 5,058m. (March 1997); sales Rs 14,730m. (March 2002); sales offices and manufacturing units throughout India; Chair. K. K. NOHRIA; Man. Dir S. M. TOCHAN.

Eveready Industries India Ltd: 1 Middleton St, Kolkata 700 071; tel. (33) 2400748; fax (33) 2402059; f. 1934; fmrly Union Carbide India Ltd; cap. p.u. Rs 557.8m., res Rs 1,855.3m., sales Rs 8,050m. (March 2002); mfrs of all types of dry cells and batteries for radio and telecommunication purposes, zinc alloys, etc.; one subsidiary: Nepal Battery Co Ltd; Chair. B. M. KHAITAN.

Philips India Ltd: Shivsagar Estate, Block 'A', Dr Annie Besant Rd, Mumbai 400 018; tel. (22) 4964590; fax (22) 4938722; e-mail p.virmani@pin.philips.com; f. 1930; cap. p.u. Rs 453.3m., res Rs 1,017.6m., sales Rs 15,066m. (Dec. 2001); mfrs of consumer electronics, lighting products, domestic appliances, industrial electronics and electronic components; factories at Kolkata, Kalwa-Thane and Pune; three subsidiaries; Chair. D. N. GHOSH; Man. Dir K. RAMACHANDRAN; 5,594 employees.

Siemans Ltd: 130 Pandurang Budhkar Marg, Worli, Mumbai 400 018; tel. (22) 4931350; fax (22) 4940552; f. 1957; cap. p.u. Rs 336.3m., res and surplus Rs 2,873.7m., sales Rs 11,570m. (Sept. 2001); railway signalling, electrical and electronic equipment, telecommunications, etc.; Man. Dir J. SCHUBERT.

Videocon International Ltd: 1601 Maker Chamber V, Nariman Point, Mumbai 400 021; tel. (22) 2871632; fax (22) 2873258; manufactures consumer electronics; cap. p.u. Rs 213m. (March 2001), sales Rs 32,510m. (2000/01); Man. Dir V. N. DHOOT.

Voltas Ltd: Volkart Bldg, 19 J. N. Heredia Marg, Ballard Estate, POB 900, Mumbai 400 001; tel. (22) 2618131; fax (22) 2618504; f. 1954; cap. Rs 331m., res Rs 1,172.9m. (March 2001), sales Rs 8,660m. (March 2002); an integrated marketing, engineering and manufacturing company with country-wide selling and service organization; mfrs of air-conditioning and refrigeration equipment, pumps, beverages, agrochemicals, capillary tubes, thermostats, CNC machines, water coolers, mining and drilling machinery, fork-lift trucks, power capacitators and air and water pollution control equipment; Chair. ISHAAT HUSSAIN; Man. Dir NAWSHIR KHURODY; 5,807 employees (2000).

Industrial and Building Supplies

BOC India Ltd: Oxygen House, P-43 Taratala Rd, Kolkata 700 088; tel. (33) 4014708; fax (33) 4014974; f. 1935; cap. p.u. Rs 491m., sales Rs 2,700m. (March 2002), res Rs 1,549m. (March 2000); mfrs and suppliers of industrial and medical gases, including special gases and gas mixtures of ultra high purity; medical and surgical equipment; oxygen (liquid and gaseous), acetylene and nitrous oxide plants; high-pressure industrial and medical pipelines; factories and depots all over India; mem. of The BOC Group, UK; Chair. J. N. SAPRU; Man. Dir SANJEEV LAMBA; 660 employees.

Larsen and Toubro Ltd: L & T House, Narottam Morarji Marg, Ballard Estate, POB 278, Mumbai 400 001; tel. (22) 2618181; fax (22) 2620223; e-mail mn-adv@lth.ltindia.com; internet www .larsentoubro.com; f. 1938; cap. p.u. Rs 2,485.5m., res Rs 37,127.2m., sales Rs 83,590m. (March 2002); construction-related equipment; plants and machinery for chemical, fertilizer, cement, food-processing, steel, paper and power industries; material handling and processing plants; civil, mechanical and electrical construction; cement; industrial electronics; computer accessories; computer software; switchgear; industrial valves; packaging; shipping; plastic and rubber-processing machinery; three subsidiaries and seven associate cos; Chair. Emeritus H. HOLCK-LARSEN; Man. Dir and CEO A. M. NAIK; 25,000 employees.

Texmaco Ltd: Birla Bldg, 9/1 R. N. Mukherjee Rd, Kolkata 700 001; tel. (33) 2489101; fax (33) 2205833; e-mail texmaco@cal.vsnl .net.in; f. 1939; cap. p.u. Rs 51.6m., res Rs 628.4m. (March 2000), sales Rs 1,410m. (1999/2000); mfrs of textile machinery, textiles, rolling stock, boilers of all types, sugar mill machinery, steel and cast iron castings, machine tools, heavy, medium and light structurals and other engineering goods; a cement plant is under construction and the corpn has diversified into shipping; Chair. K. K. BIRLA; Pres. RAMESH MAHESWARI.

Metals

Bharat Aluminium Co Ltd: Core VI, Scope Complex, 7 Lodi Rd, New Delhi 110 003; tel. (11) 4360091; fax (11) 4360035; f. 1965; cap. p.u. Rs 4,888.5m., res and surplus Rs 1,351.4m. (March 1995); partially privatized in 2001, 49% state-owned, 51% owned by Sterlite Industries; operates an integrated aluminium project at Korba (Madhya Pradesh); plans to set up alumina plants in Andhra Pradesh; Chair. and Man. Dir S. K. GHOSH.

Essar Steel Ltd: Essar House, 11 K. K. Marg, Mahalaxmi, Mumbai 400 034; tel. (22) 4950606; fax (22) 4954283; cap. p.u. Rs 3,309m., res and surplus Rs 15,861.2m., sales Rs 20,140m. (March 2002); mfrs of hot briquetted iron and hot rolled steel coils; Chair. S. N. RUIA; Man. Dir J. MEHRA.

GKW (Guest Keen Williams) Ltd: 3A Shakespeare Sarani, Kolkata 700 071; tel. (33) 674761; f. 1931; cap. p.u. Rs 296m., res and surplus Rs 941.6m. (March 1997); mfrs of metal pressings, alloys and special steels, industrial fasteners, automative forgings, electrical stamping and laminations, strip wound cores, railway track fasteners and accessories; factories in West Bengal, Karnataka and Maharashtra; Man. Dir J. D. CURRAVALA; Vice-Chair. K. K. BANGUR.

Hindalco Industries Ltd: Century Bhavan, 3rd Floor, Dr Annie Besant Rd, Worli, Mumbai 400 025; tel. (22) 4626666; fax (22) 4227586; ajjhala@worli.hindalco.com; internet www.hindalco.com; f. 1958 as Hindustan Aluminium Corpn Ltd; cap. p.u. Rs 744.6m., res and surplus Rs 56,429.1m., sales Rs 23,310m. (March 2002); produces aluminium, rolled products, extruded products, conductor and commercial rods; subsidiaries: Minerals and Minerals Ltd, Renuka Investments and Finance Ltd, Renukeshwar Investments and Finance Ltd, Indian Aluminium Co Ltd and Annapurna Foils Ltd; Chair. KUMAR MANGALAM BIRLA.

Hindustan Zinc Ltd: Yashad Bhavan, Yashadgarh, Udaipur 313 004; tel. (294) 529182; fax (294) 526443; e-mail hzludr@ ndp.vsnl.net.in; internet www.hzlindia.com; f. 1966; cap. p.u. Rs 4,225.3m., res and surplus Rs 7,377.3m., sales Rs 16,130.5m.

(March 2001); partially privatized in 2002; 26% owned by Sterlite Industries Ltd; develops mining and smelting capacities for metal, particularly zinc and lead; units: zinc smelter, Debari, Rajasthan and Vishakhapatnam, Andhra Pradesh, lead smelter, Tundoo, Bihar and zinc lead smelter, Putholi, Rajasthan; produces zinc ingots, cadmium, refined lead, refined silver, sulphuric acid, etc.; Chair. and Man. Dir K. K. KAURA.

Indian Aluminium Co Ltd: 1 Middleton St, POB 361, Kolkata 700 071; tel. (33) 2402210; fax (33) 2403964; f. 1938; cap. p.u. Rs 711m., res Rs 7,009m. (March 2000); owns and operates bauxite mines (Lohardaga in Bihar, and Chandgad and Durgmanwadi in Maharashtra); alumina plants (Muri in Bihar: 80,000 tons per annum) (Belgaum in Karnataka: 260,000 tons); smelters (Alupuram in Kerala: 21,000 tons) (Hirakud in Orissa: 30,000 tons) (Belgaum: 66,000 tons); sheet mills (Belur in West Bengal: 50,000 tons) (Taloja in Maharashtra: 40,000 tons); extrusion plant (Alupuram in Kerala: 8,000 tons); foil plant (Kalwa in Maharashtra: 6,000 tons); Chair. KUMARMANGALAM BIRLA; CEO S. K. TAMOTIA; 7,699 employees.

Ispat Industries Ltd: 71 Park St, Kolkata 700 016; tel. (33) 2495102; fax (33) 2493050; internet www.ispatgroup.com; cap. p.u. Rs 6,858m., res Rs 9,027.6m. (March 2000), sales Rs 18,380m. (March 2002); Chair. M. L. MITTAL; Man. Dir P. K. MITTAL.

Lloyds Steel Industries Ltd: Lloyds House, 954 Appasaheb Marathe Marg, Prabhadevi, Mumbai 400 025; tel. (22) 4225287; fax (22) 4201236; cap. p.u. Rs 424.3m., res Rs 1,645.2m. (March 1994); Chair. and Man. Dir R. N. GUPTA.

Mukand Ltd: Bajaj Bhavan, Jamnalal Bajaj Marg, Mumbai 400 021; tel. (22) 2822222; fax (22) 2021174; internet www.mukand.com; manufactures high carbon steel, alloy steel, stainless steel, billets, bars, rods, EOT cranes etc.; cap. Rs 1,239m., res Rs 3,732m. (March 2000); Chair. RAHUL BAJAJ; Pres. and Dir SUKETU V. SHAH.

Sterlite Industries Ltd: B-10/4 Waluj MIDC Industrial Area, Waluj, Aurangabad 431 133; (240) 554583; fax (240) 554590; e-mail silho@bom3.vsnl.net.in; internet www.sterlite.com; f. 1975; mfrs copper products; sales Rs 20,346m. (June 1999); Chair. and Man. Dir ANIL AGRAWAL.

Sunflag Iron and Steel Co Ltd: 33 Mount Rd, Sadar, Nagpur 440 001; manufactures iron and mild and alloy steel rolled products; cap. p.u. Rs 1,622.0m., res and surplus Rs 157.6m., sales Rs 4,064.8m. (March 2002); Chair. P. B. BHARDWAJ; Jt Man. Dir PRANAB BHARDWAJ.

The Tata Iron and Steel Co Ltd: Bombay House, 24 Homi Mody St, Fort, Mumbai 400 023; tel. (22) 2049131; fax (22) 2049522; e-mail tatasteelho@tata.com; internet tatasteel.com; f. 1907; took over Indian Tube Co Ltd in 1986; cap. Rs 3,679.7m., res and surplus Rs 30,779.9m., sales Rs 67,080m. (March 2002); integrated iron and steel plant at Jamshedpur (Bihar) with licensed annual saleable steel capacity of 2.1m. metric tons; main steel products comprise sheets, narrow strips, plates, structurals, bars, billets, high silicon sheets, rolled rings, rails, wheels, axles and agricultural implements such as hoes, picks, beaters; by-products such as benzol, ammonium sulphate; subsidiaries: Tata Refractories Ltd, The Tata Pigments Ltd, Special Sheets Ltd, and Kalamati Investment Co Ltd; Chair. RATAN N. TATA; Man. Dir B. MUTHURAMAN; 46,234 employees.

Paper

Andhra Pradesh Paper Mills Ltd: 501–509 Swapnalok Complex, 92/93 Sarojini Devi Rd, Secunderabad 500 003; tel. (40) 813715; fax (40) 813717; e-mail venkathv@rediffmail.com; f. 1964; cap. p.u. Rs 118.3m., res and surplus Rs 1,551m., sales Rs 4,237.6m. (March 2002); manufactures pulp and paper; Chair. L. N. BANGUR; Exec. Dir R. C. MALL.

Ballarpur Industries Ltd: Thapar House, 124 Janpath, New Delhi 110 001; tel. (11) 3368332; fax (11) 3368729; f. 1945; manufactures and sells writing, printing, industrial and speciality papers, building materials and chemicals; mills in Maharashtra, Haryana, Karnataka, Andhra Pradesh and Orissa; five subsidiaries; cap. Rs 715.5m., res Rs 7,663.3m., sales Rs 15,676.1m. (June 2001); Chair. L. M. THAPAR; Pres. and Man. Dir GAUTAM THAPAR.

J. K. Corpn Ltd: Nehru House, 4 Bahadur Shah Zafar Marg, POB 7057, New Delhi 110 002; tel. (11) 3311112; fax (11) 3712680; f. 1938; cap. p.u. Rs 496.3m., res Rs 1,768.4m., sales Rs 11,928m. (Sept. 2001); mfrs of writing, printing, coated and speciality papers, strawboard, greyboard and cement; factories in Orissa, Madhya Pradesh, Rajasthan; Chair. and Man. Dir HARI SHANKAR SINGHANIA.

Orient Paper and Industries Ltd: 9/1 R. N. Mukherjee Rd, Kolkata 700 001; tel. (33) 2204370; fax (33) 2430490; f. 1936; equity cap. Rs 148m., res Rs 283.7m. (March 2000), sales Rs 5,610m. (2000/01); there are paper mills at Brajrajnagar (Orissa), with a capacity of 76,000 metric tons per year, and at Amlai (Madhya Pradesh), with a capacity of 95,000 tons per year; in addition, there is a cement plant with an annual capacity of 1.18m. tons at Devapur (Andhra Pradesh); also manufactures electric fans at plants in West Bengal and Haryana (1.7m. produced annually); Chair. C. K. BIRLA.

Rubber

Apollo Tyres Ltd: 7 Institutional Area, Sector-22, Gurgaon 122 001; tel. (124) 6383002; fax (124) 6383021; e-mail info@apollotyres.com; f. 1972; cap. p.u. Rs 363.2m., res and surplus Rs 2,824m., sales Rs 17,101.4m. (March 2002); manufactures, markets and exports of automobile tyres, tubes and flaps; Chair. RAUNAQ SINGH; Vice-Chair. and Man. Dir ONKAR SINGH KANWAR; 6,000 employees.

CEAT Ltd: 254 E Dr Annie Besant Rd, Worli, Mumbai 400 018; tel. (22) 4930621; fax (22) 4928342; f. 1958; manufactures automobile tyres and rubber products; cap. Rs 352m., res Rs 3,105m. (March 2000), sales Rs 11,140m. (March 2002); Chair. R. P. GOENKA; Man. Dir (vacant).

Dunlop India Ltd: 57B Mirza Ghalib St, Kolkata 700 016; tel. (33) 2494502; fax (33) 2499622; f. 1926; cap. p.u. Rs 189.9m., res Rs 231.6m. (Dec. 1998); mfrs of tyres and tubes for bicycles, automobiles, aircraft, earth-moving equipment, tractors, conveyor and transmission belting, hoses, bicycle rims and Metalastik products; factories at Sahaganj and Ambattur; one subsidiary: India Tyre and Rubber Co (India) Ltd; Chair. M. R. CHHABRIA; Man. Dir (vacant); 10,394 employees.

Goodyear India Ltd: Godrej Bhavan, 3rd Floor, Mathura Rd, New Delhi 110 065; tel. (11) 6836567; fax (11) 6836170; f. 1960; mfr of automobile tyres, tubes, fan belts, etc.; cap. p.u. Rs 230.7m., res and surplus Rs 632.3m., sales Rs 4,990m. (Dec. 2001); Chair. and Man. Dir LUIS C. CENEVIZ; 1,700 employees (1995).

J. K. Industries Ltd: Link House, 3 Bahadur Shah Zafar Marg, New Delhi 110 001; manufactures and sells automotive tyres and tubes; cap. Rs 345.4m., res Rs 3,778.6m. (March 2001), sales Rs 13,410m. (March 2002); Chair. HARI SHANKAR SINGHANIA; Man. Dir RAGHUPATI SINGHANIA.

MRF Ltd: 124 Greames Rd, Chennai 600 006; tel. (44) 8252777; fax (44) 832523; f. 1960; cap. p.u. Rs 42.4m., res and surplus Rs 5,265.1m., sales Rs 17,140m. (Sept. 2001); manufactures and markets automobile and bicycle tyres and tubes, tread rubber and other rubber products; two subsidiaries: Funskool (India) Ltd and Crystal Investments and Finance Co Ltd; Chair. and Man. Dir K. M. MAMMEN MAPPILLAI.

Synthetics and Chemicals Ltd: 7 Jamshedji Tata Rd, Churchgate Reclamation, Mumbai 400 020; tel. (22) 220161; fax (22) 2870299; f. 1960; cap. p.u. Rs 264.5m., res and surplus Rs 829.7m. (March 1999), sales Rs 710m. (1998/99); mfrs of synthetic rubbers, including styrene-butadiene rubbers (SBR), acrylonitrile-butadiene rubbers (NBR) and synthetic latices; Chair. and Man. Dir SURESH T. KILACHAND; 2,000 employees.

Miscellaneous

Duncans Industries Ltd: Duncan House, 31 Netaji Subhas Rd, Kolkata 700 001; tel. (33) 2200962; fax (33) 2486021; cap. p.u. Rs 532.2m., res and surplus Rs 2,667.8m. (March 2000); manufacture and sale of tea and fertilizers, trading of tobacco, etc.; 16 subsidiaries; Chair. G. P. GOENKA; Man. Dir V. P. KAUSHIK.

Exide Industries Ltd: Exide House, 59E Chowringhee Rd, Kolkata 700 020; tel. (33) 2478326; fax (33) 2479819; f. 1947; fmrly Chloride Industries Ltd; cap. p.u. Rs 357.3m., res and surplus Rs 2,309.7m. (March 2002); manufactures batteries; factories in West Bengal and Maharashtra; one subsidiary; Chair. and Man. Dir S. B. GANGULY.

Gujarat Co-op Milk Marketing Federation Ltd: 10 Amul Dairy Rd, Anand, Gujarat 388 001; tel. (2692) 58506; fax (2692) 40208; e-mail gcmmf@amul.com; internet www.amul.com; f. 1973; manufacturer of milk and milk products; sales Rs 22,185.2m. (2000); Chair. Dr V. KURIEN; Man. Dir B. M. VYAS; 700 employees.

Hindustan Lever Ltd (HLL): Hindustan Lever House, 165/166 Backbay Reclamation, POB 409, Mumbai 400 020; tel. (22) 2870622; fax (22) 2850552; f. 1933; cap. p.u. Rs 2,201.2m., res and surplus Rs 28,229m., sales Rs 109,719m. (Dec. 2001); manufacture and sale of washing products, toilet preparations, di-ammonium phosphate, seeds, plant growth nutrient, food, beverages, marine products, leather goods, fine chemicals and exports; 16 subsidiaries; Chair. M. S. BANGA; 36,000 employees (2000).

ITC Ltd: Virginia House, 37 Chowringhee, POB 89, Kolkata 700 071; tel. (33) 2499371; fax (33) 2452251; f. 1910; fmrly India Tobacco Co.; cap. Rs 2,475.1m., res and surplus Rs 41,039.7m., sales Rs 50,590m. (March 2002); manufacture and sale of cigarettes and smoking tobaccos; printed and packaging material; development of tobacco and tobacco cultivation; tobacco exports; manufacture of speciality papers; financial services; hoteliering; travel and tourism; 11 major subsidiaries and group cos; Chair. YOGESH DEVESHWAR; 20,000 employees (1995).

Shaw Wallace & Co: 4 Bankshall St, Kolkata 700 001; tel. (33) 2485601; fax (33) 2486908; f. 1946; manufacturers and traders in agrochemicals, fertilizers, synthetic detergents, leather footwear, beer and liqueurs, tea etc.; cap. Rs 480.1m., res Rs 219.0m. (June

2000), sales Rs 2,400m. (March 2002); Chair. VIDYA MANOHAR CHHABRIA; Exec. Dir KOMAL C. WAZIR.

Tata Tea Ltd: 1 Bishop Lefroy Rd, Kolkata 700 020; tel. (33) 2470747; fax (33) 2471891; e-mail tatatea@tata.com; internet www.tata.com; f. 1962; cap. p.u. Rs 562.2m., res and surplus Rs 9,117.6m., sales Rs 7,613.3m. (March 2002); cultivates, manufactures and sells tea, coffee and allied products; owns 55 tea estates and one coffee estate; four subsidiaries; acquired the Tetley tea business in March 2000; Chair. RATAN N. TATA; Man. Dir HOMI R. KHUSROKHAN; 57,736 employees (2002).

UB Group: UB House, 1 Vital Mallya Rd, Bangalore 560 001; tel. (80) 2272806; fax (80) 2274890; India's only indigenous multinational, operating in 24 countries with a diversified range of interests, including brewing, spirits, life sciences, engineering, petrochemicals, fertilizers, financial services, information technology and aviation; sales in India Rs 24,588m. (1994), world-wide sales Rs 42,000m.(1995); Chair. VIJAY MALLYA.

Williamson Magor and Co Ltd: 4 Mangoe Lane, Surendra Mohan Ghosh Sarani, Kolkata 700 001; tel. (33) 2483655; fax (33) 2486659; f. 1868; cultivation, manufacture, sale and export of tea; sales Rs 12,668m. (1995); Chair. B. M. KHAITAN; Man. Dir DEEPAK KHAITAN; 100,000 employees (1995).

TRADE UNIONS

Indian National Trade Union Congress (INTUC): 4 Bhai Veer Singh Marg, New Delhi 110 001; tel. (11) 3747768; fax (11) 3364244; e-mail intuchq@del3.vsnl.net.in; f. 1947; 4,411 affiliated unions with a total membership of 6,839,440; affiliated to ICFTU; 27 state brs and 29 nat. feds; Pres. G. SANJEEVA REDDY; Gen. Sec. RAJENDRA PRASAD SINGH.

Indian National Cement Workers' Federation: Mazdoor Karyalaya, Congress House, Mumbai 400 004; tel. (22) 3871809; fax (22) 3870981; 49,000 mems; 38 affiliated unions; Pres. H. N. TRIVEDI; Gen. Sec. N. NANJAPPAN.

Indian National Chemical Workers' Federation: Tel Rasayan Bhavan, Tilak Rd, Dadar, Mumbai 400 014; tel. (22) 4121742; fax (22) 4130950; 35,000 mems; Pres. RAJA KULKARNI; Gen. Sec. R. D. BHARADWAJ.

Indian National Electricity Workers' Federation: 392 Sector 21-B, Faridabad 121 001; tel. (129) 215089; fax (129) 215868; e-mail inef@ndf.vsnl.net.in; f. 1950; 187,641 mems; 146 affiliated unions; Pres. D. P. PATHAK; Gen. Sec. S. L. PASSEY.

Indian National Metal Workers' Federation: 35 K Rd, Jamshedpur 831 001; tel. (657) 431475; Pres. N. K. BHATT; Gen. Sec. S. GOPESHWAR.

Indian National Mineworkers' Federation: Imperial House, CJ-66 Salt Lake, Kolkata 700 091; tel. (33) 3345586; fax (33) 3372158; e-mail imme@vsnl.com; f. 1949; 351,454 mems in 139 affiliated unions; Pres. RAJENDRA P. SINGH; Gen. Sec. S. Q. ZAMA.

Indian National Paper Mill Workers' Federation: 6/B, LIGH, Barkatpura, Hyderabad 500 027; tel. (40) 7564706; Pres. G. SANJEEVA REDDY; Gen. Sec. R. CHANDRASEKHARAN.

Indian National Port and Dock Workers' Federation: 15 Coal Dock Rd, Kolkata 700 043; tel. (33) 455929; f. 1954; 18 affiliated unions; 81,000 mems; Pres. JANAKI MUKHERJEE; Gen. Sec. G. KALAN.

Indian National Sugar Mills Workers' Federation: A-176, Darulsafa Marg, Lucknow 226 001; tel. (522) 247638; 100 affiliated unions; 40,000 mems; Pres. ASHOK KUMAR SINGH; Gen. Sec. P. K. SHARMA.

Indian National Textile Workers' Federation: 27 Burjorji Bharucha Marg, Mumbai 400 023; tel. (22) 2671577; f. 1948; 400 affiliated unions; 363,790 mems; Pres. P. L. SUBHAIAH; Gen. Sec. HARIBHAU NAIK.

Indian National Transport Workers' Federation: Bus Mazdoor Karyalaya, L/1, Hathital Colony, Jabalpur 482 001; tel. (761) 429210; 263 affiliated unions; 327,961 mems; Pres. G. SANJEEVA REDDY; Gen. Sec. K. S. VERMA.

National Federation of Petroleum Workers: Tel Rasayan Bhavan, Tilak Rd, Dadar, Mumbai 400 014; tel. (22) 4181742; fax (22) 4130950; f. 1959; 22,340 mems; Pres. RAJA KULKARNI; Gen. Sec. S. N. SURVE.

Bharatiya Mazdoor Sangh: Ram Naresh Bhavan, Tilak Gali, Pahar Ganj, New Delhi 110 055; tel. (11) 7524212; fax (11) 7520654; f. 1955; 3,507 affiliated unions with a total membership of 3,117,324 mems; 24 state brs; 28 nat. feds; Pres. RAMAN GIRDHAR SHAH; Gen. Sec. HASMUKH DAVE.

Centre of Indian Trade Unions: BTR Bhavan, 13-A Rouse Ave, New Delhi 110 002; tel. (11) 3221306; fax (11) 3221284; e-mail citu@vsnl.com; f. 1970; 3,250,000 mems; 24 state and union territory brs; 3,900 affiliated unions, 10 nat. federations; Pres. E. BALANANDAN; Gen. Sec. M. K. PANDHE.

Assam Chah Karmachari Sangha: POB 13, Dibrugarh 786 001; tel. 20870; 13,553 mems; 20 brs; Pres. G. C. SARMAH; Gen. Sec. A. K. BHATTACHARYA.

All-India Trade Union Congress (AITUC): 24 Canning Lane, New Delhi 110 001; tel. (11) 3387320; fax (11) 3386427; e-mail aitucong@bol.net.in; f. 1920; affiliated to WFTU; 3m. mems, 3,000 affiliated unions; 26 state brs, 10 national federations; Pres. J. CHITHARANJAN; Gen. Sec. GURUDAS DASGUPTA.

Major affiliated unions:

Annamalai Plantation Workers' Union: Valparai, Via Pollachi, Tamil Nadu; over 21,000 mems.

Zilla Cha Bagan Workers' Union: Mal, Jalpaiguri, West Bengal; 15,000 mems; Pres. NEHAR MUKHERJEE; Gen. Sec. BIMAL DAS GUPTA.

United Trades Union Congress (UTUC): 249 Bepin Behari Ganguly St, Kolkata 700 012; tel. (33) 275609; f. 1949; 584,523 mems from 413 affiliated unions; 10 state brs and 6 nat. feds; Pres. P. C. JOHN; Gen. Sec. S. R. SEN GUPTA.

Major affiliated unions:

All India Farm Labour Union: Patna; c. 35,000 mems; Pres. MAHENDRA SINGH TIKAIT.

Bengal Provincial Chatkal Mazdoor Union: Kolkata; textile workers; 28,330 mems.

Hind Mazdoor Sabha (HMS): 'Shrama-Sadhana', 57 D. V. Pradhan Rd, Hindu Colony, Dadar (East), Mumbai 400 014; tel. (22) 4144336; fax (22) 4102759; e-mail mki@vsnl.com; f. 1948; affiliated to ICFTU; 4.8m. mems from 2,700 affiliated unions; 20 state councils; 18 nat. industrial feds; Pres. PRABHU NARAYAN SINGH; Gen. Sec. UMRAOMAL PUROHIT.

Major affiliated unions:

Colliery Mazdoor Congress (Coalminers' Union): Pres. MADHU DANDAVATE; Gen. Sec. JAYANTA PODDER.

Mumbai Port Trust Dock and General Employees' Union: Pres. Dr SHANTI PATEL; Gen. Sec. S. K. SHETYE.

South Central Railway Mazdoor Union: 7C Railway Bldg, Accounts Office Compound, Secunderabad 500 371; tel. (40) 7821351; e-mail scrmu@hotmail.com; internet www.scrmu.org; f. 1966; 89,150 mems; Pres. K. S. N. MURTHY; Gen. Sec. N. SUNDARESAN; 135 brs.

Transport and Dock Workers' Union: Gen. Sec. MANOHAR KOTWAL.

West Bengal Cha Mazdoor Sabha: Cha Shramik Bhavan, Jalpaiguri 735 101, West Bengal; tel. (3561) 31140; fax (3561) 30349; f. 1947; 55,000 mems; Pres. Prof. SUSHIL ROY; Gen. Sec. SAMIR ROY.

Western Railway Employees' Union: Pres. JAGDISH AJMERA; Gen. Sec. UMRAOMAL PUROHIT.

Confederation of Central Government Employees and Workers: 4B/6 Ganga Ram Hospital Marg, New Delhi 110 060; tel. (11) 587804; 1.2m. mems; Pres. S. MADHUSUDAN; Sec.-Gen. S. K. VYAS.

Affiliated union:

National Federation of Post, Telephone and Telegraph Employees (NFPTTE): C-1/2 Baird Rd, New Delhi 110 001; tel. (11) 322545; f. 1954; 221,880 mems (est.); Pres. R. G. SHARMA; Gen. Sec. O. P. GUPTA.

All India Bank Employees' Association (AIBEA): 3B Lall Bazar St, 1st Floor, Kolkata 700 001; tel. (33) 2489371; fax (33) 2486072; e-mail aibea@cal2.vsnl.net.in; 27 state units, 710 affiliated unions, 525,000 mems; Pres. SURESH D. DHOPESWARKAR; Gen. Sec. TARAKESWAR CHAKRABORTI.

All India Defence Employees' Federation (AIDEF): Survey No. 81, Elphinstone Rd, Khadki, Pune 411 003; tel. (212) 318761; 350 affiliated unions; 400,000 mems; Pres. SAMUEL AUGUSTINE; Gen. Sec. D. LOBO.

All India Port and Dock Workers' Federation: 9 Second Line Beach, Chennai 600 001; tel. (44) 5224222; fax (44) 5225983; f. 1948; 100,000 mems in 34 affiliated unions; Pres. S. R. KULKARNI; Gen. Sec. S. C. C. ANTHONY PILLAI.

All India Railwaymen's Federation (AIRF): 4 State Entry Rd, New Delhi 110 055; tel. (11) 3343493; fax (11) 3363167; e-mail airf@ndb.vsnl.net.in; f. 1924; 1,024,310 mems (2000); 17 affiliated unions; Pres. UMRAOMAL PUROHIT; Gen. Sec. J. P. CHAUBEY.

National Federation of Indian Railwaymen (NFIR): 3 Chelmsford Rd, New Delhi 110 055; tel. (11) 3343305; fax (11) 3744013; e-mail nfir@satyam.net.in; f. 1952; 19 affiliated unions; 916,629 mems (2000); Pres. MAHENDRA PRATAP; Gen. Sec. M. RAGHAVAIAH.

Transport

RAILWAYS

India's railway system is the largest in Asia and the fourth largest in the world. In 2000 the total length of Indian railways exceeded 63,028 route-km. The network carried 12m. passengers and more than 1m. metric tons of freight traffic per day. The Government exercises direct or indirect control over all railways through the Railway Board. India's largest railway construction project of the 20th century, the 760-km Konkan railway line (which took seven years and almost US $1,000m. to build), was officially opened in January 1998.

A 16.45-km underground railway, which carries more than 1m. people daily, was completed in Kolkata in 1995.

Ministry of Railways (Railway Board): Rail Bhavan, Raisina Rd, New Delhi 110 001; tel. (11) 3384010; fax (11) 3384481; e-mail crb@del2.vsnl.net.in; internet www.indianrailways.com; Chair. I. I. M. S. Rana.

Zonal Railways

The railways are grouped into 15 zones:

Central: Chhatrapati Shivaji Terminus (Victoria Terminus), Mumbai 400 001; tel. (22) 2621230; fax (22) 2624555; e-mail gmcr@bom2.vsnl.net.in; internet www.cr-mumbai.com; Gen. Man. S. P. S. Jain.

East Central: Hajipur; tel. (6224) 74728; fax (6224) 74738; f. 1996; Officer on Special Duty K. K. Agarwal.

East Coast: Bhubaneswar 751 023; tel. (674) 300773; fax (674) 440753; e-mail bishtbms@hotmail.com; internet webind.com/eastcoastrailway; f. 1996; Officer on Special Duty Surender Jain.

Eastern: 17 Netaji Subhas Rd, Kolkata 700 001; tel. (33) 2207596; fax (33) 2480370; Gen. Man. S. C. Sengupta.

North Central: Allahabad; tel. (532) 624530; fax (532) 624841; e-mail secyncr@hotmail.com; f. 1996; Officer on Special Duty G. C. Sandle.

North Eastern: Gorakhpur 273 012; tel. (551) 201041; fax (551) 201842; e-mail gmner@nda.vsnl.net.in; Gen. Man. Om Prakash.

North Western: Jaipur; tel. (141) 222695; fax (141) 222936; Officer on Special Duty S. P. Chaudhury.

Northeast Frontier: Maligaon, Guwahati 781 011; tel. (361) 570422; fax (361) 571124; f. 1958; Gen. Man. Vipin Nanda.

Northern: Baroda House, Kasturba Gandhi Marg, New Delhi 110 001; tel. (11) 3387227; fax (11) 3384503; e-mail nragm@vsnl.com; Gen. Man. R. K. Singh.

South Central: Rm 312, 3rd Floor, Rail Nilayam, Secunderabad 500 071; tel. (40) 7822874; fax (40) 825316; internet www.scrailway.gov.in; Gen. Man. S. M. Singla.

South Eastern: 11 Garden Reach Rd Kolkata 700 043; tel. (33) 4397876; fax (33) 4397826; e-mail gm@ser.railnet.gov.in; internet www.serailway.com; Gen. Man. V. N. Garg.

South Western: Bangalore; tel. (80) 2205773; fax (80) 2282787; f. 1996; Officer on Special Duty V. Vijayalakshmi.

Southern: Park Town, Chennai 600 003; tel. (44) 5353157; fax (44) 5351439; internet www.srailway.com; Gen. Man. V. Anand.

West Central: Jabalpur; tel. (761) 627444; fax (761) 328133; e-mail osdwcr@yahoo.com; f. 1996; Officer on Special Duty V. K. Bhargav.

Western: Churchgate, Mumbai 400 020; tel. (22) 2005670; fax (22) 2017631; internet www.westernrailwayindia.com; Gen. Man. V. D. Gupta.

ROADS

In December 2001 there were an estimated 3.15m. km of roads in India, 58,112 km of which were national highways. About 50% of the total road network was paved. In January 1999 the Government launched the ambitious 500,000m. rupee National Highways Development project, which included plans to build an east–west corridor linking Silchar with Porbandar and a north–south corridor linking Kashmir with Kanyakumari, as well as a circuit of roads linking the four main cities of Mumbai, Chennai, Kolkata and New Delhi.

Ministry of Road Transport (and Highways): Transport Bhavan, 1 Parliament St, New Delhi 110 001; tel. (11) 3715159; responsible for the construction and maintenance of India's system of national highways, with a total length of 58,112 km in 2001, connecting the state capitals and major ports and linking with the highway systems of neighbouring countries. This system includes 172 national highways which constitute the main trunk roads of the country.

Border Roads Development Board: f. 1960 to accelerate the economic development of the north and north-eastern border areas; it has constructed 29,229 km and improved 34,306 km of roads, and maintains about 16,872 km in the border areas.

National Highways Authority of India: G-5&6, Sector 10, Dwarka, New Delhi 110 045; tel. (11) 5080390; fax (11) 5080360; e-mail nhai@vsnl.com; internet www.nhai.org; f. 1995; planning, designing, construction and maintenance of national highways; under Ministry of Road Transport; Chair. Deepak Dasgupta.

INLAND WATERWAYS

About 14,500 km of rivers are navigable by power-driven craft, and 3,700 km by large country boats. Services are mainly on the Ganga and Brahmaputra and their tributaries, the Godavari, the Mahanadi, the Narmada, the Tapti and the Krishna.

Central Inland Water Transport Corpn Ltd: 4 Fairlie Place, Kolkata 700 001; tel. (33) 2202321; fax (33) 2436164; e-mail ciwtc@cal3.vsnl.net.in; internet www.ciwtc.com; f. 1967; inland water transport services in Bangladesh and the east and north-east Indian states; also shipbuilding and repairing, general engineering, lightering of ships and barge services; Chair. and Man. Dir S. C. Dua.

SHIPPING

In March 2002 India was 14th on the list of principal merchant fleets of the world. In mid-2001 the fleet had 515 ships, with a total displacement of 7.07m. grt. There were some 102 shipping companies operating in India in January 2000. The major ports are Chennai, Haldia, Jawaharlal Nehru (at Nhava Sheva near Mumbai), Kandla, Kochi, Kolkata, Mormugao, Mumbai, New Mangalore, Paradip (Paradeep), Tuticorin and Visakha (Visakhapatnam).

Chennai (Madras)

South India Shipping Corpn Ltd: Chennai; Chair. J. H. Tarapore; Man. Dir F. G. Dastur.

Kolkata (Calcutta)

India Steamship Co Ltd: India Steamship House, 21 Hemanta Basu Sarani, POB 2090, Kolkata 700 001; tel. (33) 2481171; fax (33) 2488133; e-mail india.steamship@gems.vsnl.net.in; f. 1928; cargo services; Chair. K. K. Birla; Man. Dir Ashok Kak; br in Delhi.

Surrendra Overseas Ltd: Apeejay House, 15 Park St, Kolkata 700 016; tel. (33) 2172372; fax (33) 2179596; e-mail solcal@apeejaygroup.com; internet www.apeejaygroup.com; shipowners; Chair. Jit Paul.

Mumbai (Bombay)

Century Shipping Ltd: Mumbai; tel. (22) 2022734; fax (22) 2027274; Chair. B. K. Birla; Pres. N. M. Jain.

Chowgule & Co (Pvt) Ltd: Bakhtawar, 3rd Floor, Nariman Point, POB 11596, Mumbai 400 021; tel. (22) 2026822; fax (22) 2024845; f. 1963; Chair. Vishwasrao Dattaji Chowgule; Man. Dir Shivajirao Dattaji Chowgule.

Essar Shipping Ltd: Essar House, 11 Keshavrao Khadye Marg, Mahalaxmi, Mumbai 400 034; tel. (22) 4950606; fax (22) 4950607; f. 1975; Chair. S. N. Ruia; Man. Dir Sanjay Mehta.

The Great Eastern Shipping Co Ltd: Ocean House, 134/A Dr Annie Besant Rd, Worli, Mumbai 400 018; tel. (22) 4922100; fax (22) 4925900; internet www.greatship.com; f. 1948; cargo services; Exec. Chair. K. M. Sheth; Man. Dir Bharat Sheth; br. in New Delhi.

Shipping Corpn of India Ltd: Shipping House, 245 Madame Cama Rd, Mumbai 400 021; tel. (22) 2026666; fax (22) 2026905; e-mail mail@sci.co.in; internet www.shipindia.com; f. 1961 as a govt undertaking; Chair. and Man. Dir P. K. Srivastava; brs in Kolkata, New Delhi, Chennai and London.

Tolani Shipping Co Ltd: 10A Bakhtawar, Nariman Point, Mumbai 400 021; tel. (22) 2026878; fax (22) 2870697; e-mail ops@tolanigroup.com; Chair. and Man. Dir Dr N. P. Tolani.

Varun Shipping Co Ltd: 3rd Floor, Laxmi Bldg, 6 Shoorji Vallabhdas Marg, Ballard Estate, Mumbai 400 001; tel. (22) 2658114; fax (22) 2621723; f. 1971; Chair. and Man. Dir Arun Mehta.

CIVIL AVIATION

There are five main international airports and 90 domestic airports and 27 civil enclaves. By mid-1998 nine airports (in Mumbai, Delhi, Chennai, Kolkata, Hyderabad, Ahmedabad, Goa, Bangalore and Thiruvananthapuram) had been identified for expansion/upgrading. The process of long-term leasing of Mumbai, Delhi, Chennai, Kolkata airports was under way in 2002 and was scheduled for completion in 2003.

Airports Authority of India: Rajiv Gandhi Bhavan, Safdarjung Airport, New Delhi 110 003; tel. (11) 4632950; fax (11) 4632990; e-mail aaichmn@vsnl.net.in; manages the international and domestic airports; Chair. S. K. Narula.

Air-India: Air-India Bldg, 218 Backbay Reclamation, Nariman Point, Mumbai 400 021; tel. (22) 2024142; fax (22) 2023686; e-mail hqpsai@bom3.vsnl.net.in; internet www.airindia.com; f. 1932 as Tata Airlines; renamed Air-India in 1946; in 1953 became a state corpn responsible for international flights; services to 46 online stations (incl. 2 cargo stations) and 84 offline offices throughout the world; Chair. K. Roy Paul; Man. Dir J. N. Gogoi.

Alliance Air-Airline Allied Services: 1st Floor, Domestic Arrival Terminal, Indira Gandhi International Airport, Palam, New Delhi 110 037; tel. (11) 5662458; fax (11) 5662006; e-mail aaslmd@del2.net.in; internet www.allianceair-india.com/; f. 1996; 100% owned by Indian Airlines; scheduled passenger services to regional destinations; Man. Dir Manek Paes.

Archana Airways: 41A Friends Colony (East), Mathura Rd, New Delhi 110 065; tel. (11) 6842001; fax (11) 6847762; f. 1991; commenced operations 1993; scheduled and charter passenger services to domestic destinations; Dir/Chair. A. K. Bhartiya; Man. Dir N. K. Bhartiya.

Blue Dart Express: 88–89 Old International Terminal, Meenambakkam Airport, Chennai 600027; tel. (44) 2334995; fax (44) 2349067; e-mail bdal@md2.vsnl.net.in; internet www.bluedart.com; f. 1983 as Blue Dart Courier Services; name changed as above in 1990; air express transport co; Chair. Tushar K. Jani; Chief Exec. Niteen Gupte.

Continental Aviation: E-4/130 Arera Colony, Bhopal 462 016; tel. (755) 566625; fax (755) 563447; domestic passenger services; Gen. Man. Sam Verma.

Elbee Airlines: SM House, 11 Sahakar House, Vile Parla East, Mumbai 400 057; tel. (22) 8237006; fax (22) 8227201; e-mail elbeebom@bom4.vsnl.net.in; internet www.elbeenet.com/elbeeair.htm; f. 1994; scheduled and charter cargo services to domestic destinations; Chief Exec. Ashis Nain.

Gujarat Airways Ltd: 1st Floor, Sapana Shopping Centre, 20 Vishwas Colony, Alkapuri, Vadodara 390 005; tel. (265) 330864; fax (265) 339628; e-mail info@gujaratairways.com; internet www.gujaratairways.com; f. 1994; commenced operations 1995; scheduled services to domestic destinations; Chair. G. N. Patel; Man. Dir R. C. Sharma.

Indian Airlines: Airlines House, 113 Gurudwara Rakabganj Rd, New Delhi 110 001; tel. (11) 3716236; fax (11) 3719440; e-mail cmdial@vsnl.com; internet www.nic.in/indian-airlines; f. 1953; state corpn responsible for regional and domestic flights; services to 63 cities throughout India and to 16 destinations in the Middle East and the Far East; Chair. and Man. Dir Sunil Arora.

Jagson Airlines: 12E Vandana Bldg, 11 Tolstoy Marg, New Delhi 110 001; tel. (11) 3721594; fax (11) 3324693; e-mail jagson@id.eth.net; f. 1991; scheduled and charter passenger services to domestic destinations; Chair. Jagdish Gupta; Man. Dir Pradeep Gupta.

Jet Airways (India) Ltd: S. M. Centre, 1st Floor, Andheri-Kurla Rd, Andheri (East), Mumbai 400 059; tel. (22) 8505080; fax (22) 8505631; internet www.jetairways.com; f. 1992; commenced operations 1993; private co; scheduled passenger services to domestic and regional destinations; Chair. and Man. Dir Naresh Goyal; Exec. Dir Saroj K. Datta.

NEPC Airlines: 36 Wallajah Rd, Chennai 600 002; tel. (44) 848075; fax (44) 447353; f. 1994; private co; passenger services to domestic destinations; Chair. and Man. Dir Ravi Prakash Khemka.

Sahara Airlines: Dr Gopaldas Bhawan, 3rd Floor, 28 Barakhamba Rd, New Delhi 110 001; tel. (11) 3326851; fax (11) 375510; e-mail ukbose@saharaairline.com; internet www.saharaairline.com; f. 1991, as Sahara India Airlines; commenced operations 1993; private co; scheduled passenger and cargo services to domestic destinations; Chair. Subrata R. Sahara; CEO U. K. Bose.

TransBharat Aviation Ltd: 201 Laxmi Bhavan, 72 Nehru Place, Delhi 110 019; tel. (11) 6419600; fax (11) 3313353; f. 1990; commenced operations 1991; charter services throughout India.

UP Airways Ltd: Roopali House, A-2 Defence Colony, New Delhi 110 024; tel. (11) 4646290; fax (11) 4646292; e-mail sgsimpex@del3.vsnl.net.in; private co; charter services to domestic destinations; Chair. and Man. Dir Subhash Gulati; Chief Exec. Capt. H. S. Bedi.

Tourism

The tourist attractions of India include its scenery, its historic forts, palaces and temples, and its rich variety of wild life. Tourist infrastructure has recently been expanded by the provision of more luxury hotels and improved means of transport. In 2000 there were about 2.64m. foreign visitors to India, and revenue from tourism totalled an estimated 144,754m. rupees.

Ministry of Tourism: Transport Bhavan, Parliament St, New Delhi 110 001; tel. (11) 3711792; fax (11) 3710518; formulates and administers govt policy for promotion of tourism; plans the organization and development of tourist facilities; operates tourist information offices in India and overseas; Dir-Gen. V. K. Duggal.

India Tourism Development Corpn Ltd: SCOPE Complex, Core 8, 6th Floor, 7 Lodi Rd, New Delhi 110 003; tel. (11) 4360303; fax (11) 4360233; e-mail itdcscope@usa.net; internet www.theashokgroup.com; f. 1966; operates Ashok Group of hotels (largest hotel chain owner), resort accommodation, tourist transport services, duty-free shops and a travel agency and provides consultancy and management services; Chair. and Man. Dir Ashwani Lohani.

Defence

At 1 August 2001 India's total armed forces numbered 1,263,000: army 1,100,000, navy 53,000 (incl. naval air force), air force 110,000. Active paramilitary forces totalled 1,089,700 men, including the 174,000-strong Border Security Force (based mainly in the troubled state of Jammu and Kashmir). Military service is voluntary, although the Constitution states that every citizen has a fundamental duty to perform national service when called upon to do so.

Defence Budget (2002/03): Estimated at Rs 650,000m.

Chair. of Joint Chiefs of Staff Committee: Gen. Sundarajan Padmanabhan.

Chief of Staff of the Army: Gen. Sundararajan Padmanabhan.

Chief of Staff of the Navy: Adm. Madhabendra Singh.

Chief of Staff of the Air Force: Air Chief Marshal S. Krishnaswamy.

Education

Under the Constitution, education in India is primarily the responsibility of the individual state governments, although the central Government has several direct responsibilities, some specified in the Constitution, as for example, responsibility for the Central Universities, all higher institutions, promotion and propagation of Hindi, co-ordination and maintenance of higher education standards, scientific and technological research and welfare of Indian students abroad.

Education in India is administered centrally by the Ministry of Human Resources Development (Department of Education). At state level, there is an Education Minister. There are facilities for free primary education (lower and upper stages) in all the states. Priority has been given to an expansion in elementary and community education as well as in education for girls. An amendment to the Constitution, approved in May 2002, ensures free and compulsory education for children from the age of six to 14.

ELEMENTARY EDUCATION

The notable characteristic of elementary education in India is the use of what is known as basic education. There is an activity-centred curriculum which educates through socially useful, productive activities such as spinning, weaving, gardening, leather work, book craft, domestic crafts, pottery, elementary engineering, etc. The emphasis is on introducing important features of basic education in non-basic schools. Basic education is the national pattern of all elementary education and all elementary schools will ultimately be brought over to the basic system. Twenty per cent already have, and the rest are gradually being converted under an 'orientation' system for teachers.

In lower primary classes, for children between 6 and 11 years of age, the total number of pupils increased from 50m. in 1965 to 110.9m. in 1998/99. Enrolment in higher primary or middle schools (age-group 11–14 years) in that year was 40.4m. Similarly, the number of primary (lower and higher) schools increased from 466,862 in 1965/66 to 839,699 in 1999/2000.

SECONDARY EDUCATION

Education at this level is provided for those between the ages of 14 and 17. Many state governments have taken steps to reorganize secondary schools, resulting in great expansion since 1965. In 1999/2000 there were 116,820 secondary and higher secondary schools with about 28.2m. pupils and 1.72m. teachers.

Most schools follow what is known as the 'three language formula' which comprises teaching of: the regional dialect, Hindi and English. Much emphasis is now also being laid on physical training, which has become a compulsory subject.

HIGHER AND ADULT EDUCATION

The universities are for the most part autonomous as regards administration. The University Grants Commission is responsible for the promotion and co-ordination of university education and has the authority to make appropriate grants and to implement development schemes.

India had a total of 245 universities and institutions with university status in 2000/01, and some 12,342 university and affiliated colleges. University enrolment was 8.0m. in 2001/02.

A National Council for Higher Education in Rural Areas was established in 1953 to advise the Government on all matters relating to the development of rural higher education. In 1977 there were 10 rural institutes functioning in seven states, most of them affiliated to the state university.

Educational work is being undertaken for the eradication of illiteracy, education in citizenship, cultural and recreational activities and organization of youth and women's groups for community development. A National Board for Adult Education has been set up, but the state governments are largely responsible for adult education programmes. The main emphasis is on improving literacy rates, especially in rural areas; there are also Urban Adult Education Programmes and in 1976 a major programme of non-formal education was launched for the 15–25 age group. The rate of literacy rose from 43.6% of the adult population in 1981 to 65.4% in 2001, which is still, however, far lower than the literacy rate of most developing countries at comparable levels of economic development.

Bibliography

GENERAL

Allchin, F. R., and Allchin, B. *The Rise of Civilisation in India and Pakistan.* Cambridge University Press, 1983.

Basham, A. L. *The Wonder that was India.* New York, NY, Hawthorn, 1963.

A Cultural History of India. Oxford, Clarendon Press.

Butalia, Urvashi (Ed.). *Speaking Peace: Women's Voices From Kashmir.* New Delhi, Kali for Women, 2002.

Chaudhuri, Nirad. *The Autobiography of an Unknown Indian.* London, Macmillan, 1951.

Crawley, W., and Page, David. *Satellites over South Asia: Broadcasting Culture and the Public Interest.* London, Sage Publications, 2001.

Crossette, Barbara. *India: Facing the Twenty-First Century.* Bloomington, IN, Indiana University Press, 1993.

De Bary, W. Theodore. (Ed.). *Sources of Indian Tradition. 2 vols.* New York, NY, and London, Columbia University Press, 1958.

Hiro, Dilip. *Inside India Today.* London, Routledge and Kegan Paul, 1976.

Johnson, B. L. C. *India: Resources and Development.* London, Heinemann, 1978.

Khilnani, Sunil. *The Idea of India.* London, Hamish Hamilton, 1997.

Lal, Deepak. *The Hindu Equilibrium, Vol. I: Cultural Stability and Economic Stagnation in India (1500 BC–AD 1980); Vol. II: Aspects of Indian Labour.* Oxford University Press, 1989.

Lewis, Norman. *A Goddess in the Stones: Travels in India.* London, Jonathan Cape, 1991.

Mehta, Ved. *A New India.* London, Penguin, 1978.

Naipaul, V. S. *India: A Wounded Civilization.* London, André Deutsch, 1977.

India: A Million Mutinies Now. London, Heinemann, 1990.

Pandey, Gyanendra (Ed.). *Hindus and Others: The Question of Identity in India Today.* New Delhi, Viking Penguin, 1993.

Robinson, Francis (Ed.). *Cambridge Encyclopedia of India.* Cambridge University Press, 1989.

Rushdie, S. *Midnight's Children.* London, Cape, 1981.

Sen, Mala. *Death by Fire: Sati, Dowry Death and Female Infanticide in Modern India.* London, Weidenfeld and Nicolson, 2001.

Sinha, Arun. *Against the Few: Struggles of India's Rural Poor.* London, Zed Books, 1992.

Singh, R. L. (Ed.). *India: Regional Studies.* Kolkata, for 21st International Geog. Congress by Indian Nat. Cttee for Geography, 1968.

Spate, O. H. K. and Learmonth, A. T. A. *India and Pakistan.* 3rd edn, London, Methuen, 1967.

Tully, Mark. *No Full Stops in India.* London, Viking, 1991.

Varma, Pavan K. *Mansions at Dusk: The Havelis of Old Delhi.* New Delhi, Spantech, 1991.

Westwood, J. N. *Railways of India.* 1974.

Wolpert, Stanley. *India.* Berkeley, CA, University of California Press, 1993.

HISTORY AND POLITICS

Ahmad, Aziz. *Islamic Modernization in India and Pakistan 1857–1964.* London and New York, Oxford University Press, 1966.

Akbar, M. J. *Nehru: The Making of India.* London, Viking, 1989.

India: The Siege Within. London, Penguin, 1985.

Riot after Riot: Reports on Caste and Communal Violence in India. New Delhi, Penguin Books India Ltd, 1988.

Alavi, H., and Harriss, J. (Eds). *South Asia, Sociology of 'Developing Societies'.* London, Macmillan, 1989.

Andersen, Walter, and Damle, S. *The Brotherhood in Saffron.* Boulder, CO, Westview Press, 1987.

Appadorai, A. (Ed.) *Documents on Political Thought in Modern India.* Oxford University Press, 1977.

Ayoob, Mohammed. *India, Pakistan and Bangladesh: Search for a New Relationship.* New Delhi, Indian Council of World Affairs, 1975.

Azad, Abul Kalam. *India Wins Freedom.* Hyderabad, Orient Longman Ltd, 1989.

Baker, C. J., and Washbrook, D. A. *South India, Political Institutions and Political Change 1880–1920.* Delhi, Macmillan, 1975.

Bayly, C. A. *The Local Roots of Indian Politics, Allahabad 1880–1920.* Oxford, Clarendon Press, 1975.

Indian Society and the Making of the British Empire. Cambridge University Press, 1988.

Bayly, Susan. *Caste, Society and Politics in India from the 18th Century to the Modern Day.* Cambridge University Press, 1999.

Bhargava, Rajeev (Ed.). *Secularism and its Critics.* Delhi, Oxford University Press, 1998.

Bhattacharjea, Ajit. *Jayaprakash Narayan: A Political Biography.* New Delhi.

Blackburn, R. *Explosion in the Sub-Continent.* London, Penguin, 1974.

Bose, Sugata, and Jalal, Ayesha (Eds). *Nationalism, Democracy and Development: State and Politics in India.* Delhi, Oxford University Press, 1997.

Bradnock, R. W. *India's Foreign Policy since 1971.* London, Pinter, 1990.

Brass, Paul R. *Language, Religion and Politics in North India.* London, Cambridge University Press, 1975.

The Politics of India since Independence. Cambridge University Press, 1990.

Brown, Judith M. *Gandhi and Civil Disobedience: The Mahatma in Indian Politics, 1928–1934.* Cambridge University Press, 1977.

Gandhi: Prisoner of Hope. New Haven, CT, Yale University Press, 1989.

Modern India: The Origins of an Asian Democracy. New Delhi, Oxford University Press, 2nd edn, 1994.

Chandra, Bipan, et al. *India's Struggle for Independence.* Harmondsworth, Penguin, 1989.

Chatterjee, Partha (Ed.). *State and Politics in India.* Delhi, Oxford University Press, 1997.

Chellaney, Brahma. *Nuclear Proliferation: the US-Indian Conflict.* London, Sangam Books, 1993.

Cohen, Stephen Philip. *India: Emerging Power.* Washington, DC, The Brookings Institution, 2001.

Collins, L., and Lapierre, D. *Freedom at Midnight.* London, Collins, 1975.

Copland, Ian. *The Princes of India in the Endgame of Empire, 1917–1947.* Cambridge University Press, 1997.

Dasgupta, C. *War and Diplomacy in Kashmir 1947–48.* London, Sage Publications, 2002.

Derrett, J. Duncan M. *Religion, Law and the State in India.* London, Faber and Faber.

Dewey, Clive, and Hopkins, A. G. (Eds). *The Imperial Impact.* London, Athlone Press, 1977.

Donaldson, R. H. *Soviet Policy towards India: Ideology and Strategy.* 1974.

Edwardes, Michael. *British India 1772–1947*. London, Sidgwick and Jackson, 1967.

The Myth of the Mahatma. London, Constable, 1987.

Epstein, T. S. *South India: Yesterday, Today and Tomorrow*. 1973.

Fairservis, Walter A., Jr. *The Roots of Ancient India*. Chicago, IL, and London, 2nd edn, University of Chicago, 1975.

Farwell, Byron. *Armies of the Raj*. London, Viking, 1990.

Fay, Peter Ward. *The Forgotten Army: India's Armed Struggle for Independence, 1942–45*. University of Michigan, 1994.

Findly, Ellison Banks. *Nur Jahan: Empress of Mughal India*. New York, NY, and Oxford, Oxford University Press, 1993.

Frank, Katherine. *The Life of Indira Nehru Gandhi*. London, HarperCollins, 2002, 2nd edn.

Frankel, Francine R. *India's Green Revolution: Political Costs of Economic Growth*. 1971.

India's Political Economy, 1947–77: The Gradual Revolution. Princeton, NJ, Princeton University Press, 1979.

Frankel, Francine R., and Rao, M. S. A. (Eds). *Dominance and State Power in Modern India. 2 vols*. Delhi, Oxford University Press, 1989 and 1990.

Franklin, Michael (Ed.). *Representing India—Indian Culture and Imperial Control in Eighteenth Century British Orientalist Discourse*. London, Routledge, 2000.

French, Patrick. *Liberty or Death: India's Journey to Independence and Division*. London, HarperCollins, 1998.

Fuchs, Stephen. *The Aboriginal Tribes of India*. Macmillan, 1973.

Galanter, Marc. *Competing Equalities*. Berkeley, CA, University of California Press, 1984.

Gandhi, Sonia (Ed.). *Freedom's Daughter: Letters between Indira and Jawaharlal Nehru 1922–39*. London, Hodder and Stoughton Ltd, 1989.

Rajiv. New Delhi, Viking, 1992.

(Ed.) *Two Alone, Two Together: Letters between Indira Gandhi and Jawaharlal Nehru, 1940–64*. London, Hodder and Stoughton Ltd, 1992.

Ganguly, Sumit. *Conflict Unending*. Oxford, Oxford University Press, 2002.

Gopal, Sarvepalli. *Jawaharlal Nehru. 3 vols*. London, Cape, 1975–84.

Gordon, Leonard A. *Brothers Against the Raj: A Biography of Indian Nationalists Sarat and Subhas Chandra Bose*. New York, NY, Columbia University Press, 1992.

Gould, Harold A., and Ganguly, Sumit. (Eds). *The Hope and the Reality: US-Indian Relations from Roosevelt to Reagan*. Boulder, CO, Westview Press, 1993.

Griffith, Kenneth. *The Discovery of Nehru: An Experience of India*. London, Michael Joseph, 1990.

Guha, Ramachandra. *Savaging the Civilized: Verrier Elwin, His Tribals, and India*. University of Chicago Press, 1999.

Habibullah, A. B. M. *The Foundation of Muslim Rule in India*. 2nd edn, Allahabad, 1961.

Hansen, Thomas, and Jaffrelot, Christophe (Eds). *The BJP and the Compulsions of Politics in India*. Delhi, Oxford University Press, 1998.

Hardgrave, Robert, and Kochanek, Stanley. *India: Government and Politics in a Developing Nation*. 4th edn, New York, NY, Harcourt, Brace, Jovanovich, 1986.

Hardy, Peter. *The Muslims of British India*. Cambridge University Press, 1972.

Harrison, Selig S., and Kemp, Geoffrey. *India and America after the Cold War*. Washington, 1993.

Hasan, Mushirul. *Nationalism and Communal Politics in India, 1885–1930*. New Delhi, Manohar, 1991.

(Ed.). *India's Partition: Process, Strategy and Mobilization*. Oxford University Press, 1993.

Legacy of a Divided Nation: India's Muslims since Independence. London, C. Hurst & Co (Publishers) Ltd, 1997.

Hazarika, Sanjoy. *Strangers of the Mist: Tales of War and Peace from India's Northeast*. New Delhi, Viking Press, 1995.

Healy, Kathleen. *Rajiv Gandhi: The Years of Power*. New Delhi, Vikas Publishing House, 1989.

Hurtig, Christiane. *Les Maharajas et la Politique dans l'Inde Contemporaine*. Paris, Presses de la Fondation Nationale des Sciences Politiques, 1988.

Israel, Milton. *Propaganda and the Press in the Indian Nationalist Struggle, 1920–1947*. Cambridge University Press, South Asian Studies 56, 1994.

Jain, J. P. *Nuclear India*. New Delhi, Radiant Publishers, 1974.

Jalal, Ayesha. *Democracy and Authoritarianism in South Asia*. Cambridge University Press, 1995.

James, Lawrence. *Raj: The Making and Unmaking of British India*. London, Little, Brown & Co, 1997.

Jeffrey, Robin (Ed.). *People, Princes and Paramount Power: Society and Politics in the Indian Princely States*. Oxford University Press, 1979.

What's Happening to India? London, Macmillan, 1988.

Jha, Prem Shankar. *In the Eye of the Cyclone: The Crisis in Indian Democracy*. New Delhi, Viking Penguin, 1993.

Kashmir 1947: Rival Versions of History. New Delhi, Oxford University Press, 1995.

Johnson, G. *Provincial Politics and Indian Nationalism. Bombay and the Indian National Congress 1880–1915*. Cambridge University Press, 1974.

Joshi, G. N. *Constitution of India*. 6th edn, 1975.

Kapur, Ashok. *India's Nuclear Option: Atomic Diplomacy and Decision Making*. New York, NY, Praeger, 1976.

Kapur, Rajiv A. *Sikh Separatism: The Politics of Faith*. London, Allen and Unwin, 1986.

Keay, John. *The Honourable Company: A History of the English East India Company*. London, HarperCollins, 1992.

India: A History. London, HarperCollins, 2000.

Khurshid, Salman. *Beyond Terrorism—New Hope for Kashmir*. New Delhi, UBSPD Publishers, 1994.

King, Robert D. *Nehru and the Language Politics of India*. New Delhi, Oxford University Press, 1997.

Kohli, Atul. *Democracy and Disorder*. Cambridge University Press, 1990.

Kohli, Atul (Ed.). *The Success of India's Democracy*. Cambridge University Press, 2001.

Kopf, D. A. *British Orientalism and the Bengal Renaissance*. Berkeley and Los Angeles, CA, University of California, 1969.

Kothari, Rajani. *State against Democracy: In Search of Humane Governance*. New Delhi, Ajanta, 1988.

(Ed.). *Caste in Indian Politics*. New Delhi, Orient Longmans, 1970.

Kulke, Hermann, and Rothermund, Dietmar. *A History of India*. 3rd Edn, London, Routledge, 1997.

Lamb, Alastair. *Crisis in Kashmir, 1947–1966*. London, Routledge and Kegan Paul, 1966.

Lipton, M., and Firn, J. *The Erosion of a Relationship: India and Britain since 1960*. Oxford University Press for the Institute of International Affairs, 1975.

Longer, V. *The Defence and Foreign Policies of India*. New Delhi, Sterling Publishers Pvt Ltd, 1988.

Lumby, E. W. R. *The Transfer of Power in India*. London, Allen and Unwin, 1954.

Malhotra, Inder. *Indira Gandhi: A Personal and Political Biography*. London, Hodder and Stoughton, 1990.

Manor, James (Ed.). *Nehru to the Nineties: The Changing Office of the Prime Minister of India*. New Delhi, Viking Press, 1994.

Mansergh, Nicholas, Lumby, E. W., and Moon, Penderel (Eds). *India: The Transfer of Power, 1942–47, 12 vols*. London, HMSO, 1970–83.

Mansingh, Surjit. *India's Search for Power: Mrs Gandhi's Foreign Policy 1966–82*. London, Sage Publications, 1984.

Marshall, P. J. (Ed.). *Problems of Empire, Britain and India 1757–1813*. London, Allen and Unwin, 1968.

Bengal: The British Bridgehead. Cambridge University Press, 1988.

Masani, Zareer. *Indira Gandhi: A Biography*. London, 1974.

Indian Tales of the Raj. London, BBC Books, 1988.

Masselos, J. (Ed.). *Struggling and Ruling*. New Delhi, Sterling Publishers Ltd, 1987.

Mehrotra, S. R. *India and the Commonwealth 1885–1929*. London, Allen and Unwin, 1965.

Mehta, Ved. *Mahatma Gandhi and his Apostles*. London, André Deutsch, 1977.

Rajiv Gandhi and Rama's Kingdom. Yale University Press, 1995.

Menon, V. P. *The Integration of the Indian States*. Mumbai, Orient Longmans, 1956.

The Transfer of Power in India. Mumbai, Orient Longmans, 1957.

Mernissi, Fatima. *The Forgotten Queens of Islam*. London, Polity Press, 1993.

Mitra, Ashok. *Calcutta Diary*. 1977.

Hoodlum Years. Mumbai, Orient Longmans, 1978.

Moon, Sir Penderel. *The British Conquest and Dominion of India.* London, Gerald Duckworth and Co Ltd, 1989.

Strangers in India. London, Faber and Faber, 1944.

Moore, R. J. *Liberalism and Indian Politics 1872–1922.* London, Edward Arnold, 1966.

The Crisis of Indian Unity. Oxford, Clarendon Press, 1975.

Nanda, B. R. (Ed.). *Indian Foreign Policy: The Nehru Years.* Delhi and Mumbai, Vikas Publishing House, 1976.

Socialism in India. Delhi, 1972.

Nossiter, T. J. *Communism in Kerala: a Study in Political Adaptation.* London, Hurst, for Royal Institute of International Affairs, London, 1980.

Marxist State Governments in India. London, Pinter, 1988.

Nugent, Nicholas. *Rajiv Gandhi—Son of a Dynasty.* London, BBC Books, 1990.

Padgaonkar, Dileep. *When Bombay Burned.* Delhi, UBSPD, 1994.

Pandey, Gyanendra. *The Construction of Communalism in Colonial North India.* New Delhi, Oxford University Press, 1993.

Pearson, M. N. *The Portuguese in India.* Cambridge University Press, 1988.

Perkovich, George. *India's Nuclear Bomb: The Impact on Global Proliferation.* Berkeley, CA, University of California Press, 2000.

Philips, C. H., and Wainwright, Mary (Eds). *Indian Society and the Beginnings of Modernization.* London, SOAS, 1976.

Prasad, Bimla. *The Origins of Indian Foreign Policy.* Kolkata, Bookland, 1960.

Ramunny, Murkot. *The World of Nagas.* New Delhi, Northern Book Centre, 1988.

Read, Anthony, and Fisher, David. *The Proudest Day: India's Long Road to Independence.* London, Jonathan Cape, 1998.

Robb, P. G. *The Government of India and Reform.* Oxford University Press, 1976.

Robinson, F. C. R. *Separatism among Indian Muslims. The Politics of the United Provinces' Muslims 1860–1923.* Cambridge University Press, 1974.

Rudolph, L. I., and S. H. *The Modernity of Tradition.* Chicago, 1967.

In Pursuit of Lakshmi: The Political Economy of the Indian State. University of Chicago Press, 1987.

Sahgal, Nayantara. *Indira Gandhi: Emergence and Style.* Vikas Publications, 1978.

Sarkar, Sumit. *Modern India 1885–1947.* New Delhi, Macmillan, 1983.

Sathyamurthy, T. V. (Ed.). *Class Formation and Political Transformation in Post-Colonial India.* Delhi, Oxford University Press, 1998.

(Ed.). *Region, Religion, Caste, Gender and Culture in Contemporary India.* Delhi, Oxford University Press, 1998.

Schwartzberg, J. E. (Ed.). *An Historical Atlas of South Asia.* London and Chicago, IL, University of Chicago Press, 1978.

Scott, Paul. *The Raj Quartet.* London, Heinemann, 1976.

Seal, Anil. *The Emergence of Indian Nationalism.* Cambridge University Press, 1967.

Sen, Amartya, and Dreze, Jean. *India: Development and Participation.* Oxford, Oxford University Press, 2002.

Sen, Mala. *India's Bandit Queen: The True Story of Phoolan Devi.* London, HarperCollins, 1992.

Sen Gupta, B. *Soviet-Asian Relations in the 1970s and Beyond: Interpretational Study.* 1976.

Shukla, Satyendra R. *Sikkim. The Story of Integration.* New Delhi, S. Chand and Co (Pvt) Ltd, 1976.

Singh, Amarinder. *A Ridge Too Far: War in the Kargil Heights 1999.* Bharat Rakshak, 2001

Singh, B.P., and Varma, K. Pavan (Eds). *The Millennium Book on New Delhi.* New York, NY, Oxford University Press, 2001.

Singh, Khushwant. *A History of the Sikhs. 2 vols.* 1964–66.

Singh, Prakash. *Kohima to Kashmir: On the Terrorist Trail.* New Delhi, Rupa & Co, 2001.

Singh, Tavleen. *Kashmir: A Tragedy of Errors.* New Delhi, Viking Press, 1995.

Singh, V. B., and Bose, Shankar. *Data Handbook on Lok Sabha Elections 1952–80.* London, Sage Publications, 1985.

Sisson, Richard, and Rose, Leo E. *War and Secession: Pakistan, India and the Creation of Bangladesh.* Berkeley, CA, University of California Press, 1990.

Sisson, Richard, and Wolpert, Stanley (Eds). *Congress and Indian Nationalism.* Berkeley and Los Angeles, CA, University of California Press, 1988.

Smith, D. E. *India as a Secular State.* Princeton, NJ, Princeton University Press, 1963.

Spear, Percival. *A History of India, Vol II.* Harmondsworth, Penguin Books, 1965.

Srivastava, C. P. *Lal Bahadur Shastri, Prime Minister of India 1964–66: A Life of Truth in Politics.* Oxford University Press, 1994.

Stern, Robert W. *Changing India.* Cambridge University Press, 1993.

Stokes, Eric. *The Peasant and the Raj.* Cambridge University Press, 1978.

Suntharalingam, R. *Indian Nationalism. An Historical Analysis.* New Delhi, Vikas, 1983.

Tandon, Prakash. *Punjabi Century 1857–1957.* University of California, 1968.

Tellis, Ashley. *India's Emerging Nuclear Posture.* Oxford, Oxford University Press, 2001.

Thakur, Ramesh. *The Government and Politics of India.* London, Macmillan, 1995.

Thapar, R. A. *History of India, Vol. I.* Harmondsworth, Penguin Books, 1966.

Asoka and the Decline of the Mauryas.

Tinker, Hugh. *Experiment with Freedom: India and Pakistan, 1947.* London, Oxford University Press, 1967.

India and Pakistan: A Political Analysis. London, 2nd edn, Pall Mall Press, 1967.

South Asia: A Short History. London, Pall Mall Press, 1966.

Tomlinson, B. R. *The Indian National Congress and the Raj 1929–1942.* London, Macmillan, 1976.

Tully, Mark, and Jacob, Satish. *Amritsar: Mrs Gandhi's Last Battle.* London, Cape, 1985.

Tully, Mark, and Masani, Zareer. *From Raj to Rajiv.* London, BBC Books, 1988.

Vanaik, Achin. *The Painful Transition: Bourgeois Democracy in India.* London, Verso, 1990.

The Furies of Indian Communalism: Religion, Modernity and Secularisation. London, Verso, 1997.

Wavell, Lord (Ed. Moon, P.). *The Viceroy's Journal.* 1973.

Weiner, Myron (Ed.). *State Politics in India.* London, Oxford University Press.

Party Politics in India: The Development of a Multi-Party System. Princeton, NJ, Princeton University Press, 1957.

The Child and the State in India: Child Labour and Education Policy in Perspective. Princeton University Press, 1991.

Weiner, Myron, and Katzenstein, Mary. *India's Preferential Policies.* University of Chicago Press, 1981.

Wolpert, Stanley. *A New History of India.* New York, Oxford University Press, 1976.

Gandhi's Passion: The Life and Legacy of Mahatma Gandhi. New York, NY, Oxford University Press, 2001.

ECONOMY

Ahluwalia, Isher, and Little, I. M. D. *India's Economic Reforms and Development: Essays for Manmohan Singh.* New Delhi, Oxford University Press, 1997.

Bagchi, A. K. *Private Investment in India, 1900-1939.* Cambridge University Press, 1972.

Change and Choice in Indian Industry. Kolkata, K. P. Bagchi and Co, 1980.

Balasubramanyam, V. N. *The Economy of India.* London, Weidenfeld and Nicolson, 1986.

Bardhan, Pranab. *The Political Economy of Development in India.* Oxford University Press, 1984.

Bardhan, Pranab, Dhatta-Chaudhuri, M., and Krishnan, T. N. (Eds). *Development and Change: Essays in Honour of Professor K. N. Raj.* Delhi, Oxford University Press, 1993.

Baru, Rama V. *Private Health Care in India.* New Delhi, Sage Publications Ltd, 1999.

Baru, Sanjaya. *The Political Economy of Indian Sugar: State Intervention and Structural Change.* Delhi, Oxford University Press, 1989.

Baru, Sanjaya, and Chaudhuri, Saumitra. *Mid-Year Review of the Indian Economy, 1997–98.* New Delhi, Konark Publishers, 1998.

Basu, S. K. *Studies in Economic Problems.* Mumbai, Asia Publishing House, 1965.

Bauer, P. T. *Indian Economic Policy and Development.* London, Allen and Unwin; New York, Praeger, 1961.

Bhaduri, A., and Nayyar, D. *An Intelligent Person's Guide to Economic Liberalisation in India*. Delhi, Penguin Books India (Pvt) Ltd,1996.

Bhagwati, Jagdish. *India in Transition. Freeing the Economy.* Oxford, Clarendon Press, 1993.

Bhagwati, J., and Desai, P. *India: Planning for Industrialisation.* Oxford University Press, 1974.

Bhalla, G. S. (Ed.). *Economic Liberalisation and Indian Agriculture.* Delhi, Institute for Studies in Industrial Development, 1994.

Bhatt, V. V. *Aspects of Economic Change and Policy in India, 1800–1960.* Mumbai, Allied Publishers, 1962.

A Decade of Performance of Industrial Development Bank of India. World Bank Paper.

Blyn, G. *Agricultural Trends in India, 1891–1941: Output, Availability and Productivity.* Philadelphia, 1966.

Brahmananda, P. R., and Panchamukhi, V. R. *Development Process of the Indian Economy.* Mumbai, Himalaya Publishing House, 1987.

Byres, Terence J. *State and Development Planning in India.* New Delhi, Oxford University Press, 1994.

The Indian Economy: Major Debates Since Independence. New Delhi, Oxford University Press, 1998.

Cassen, R. H. *India: Population, Economy and Society.* London, Macmillan, 1977.

Chakravarti, Sukhamoy. *Development Planning: The Indian Experience.* Oxford, Clarendon Press, 1987.

Selected Economic Writings. Delhi, Oxford University Press, 1993.

Chandavarkar, Rajnarayan. *The Origins of Industrial Capitalism in India.* Cambridge, Cambridge University Press, 1995.

Chandok, H. L., and the Policy Group. *India Database: The Economy.* 2 vols. Delhi, Living Media India Ltd, 1990.

Chaudhuri, P. *The Indian Economy: Poverty and Development.* London, Crosby Lockwood Staples, 1978.

Chelliah, Raja J. *Essays in Fiscal and Financial Sector Reforms in India.* New Delhi, Oxford University Press, 1999.

Choudhury, R. A., Gamkhar, S., and Ghose, A. *The Indian Economy and its Performance since Independence.* New Delhi, Oxford University Press, 1990.

Das, Gurcharan. *India Unbound.* Knopf, 2nd edn, 2001.

Dasgupta, B. *The Oil Industry in India; Some Economic Aspects.* 1971.

Agrarian Changes and the New Technology in India. Geneva, UNRISD, 1977.

Datta, Amlan. *An Introduction to India's Economic Development since the Nineteenth Century.* Mumbai, Popular Prakashan (Pvt) Ltd, 1989.

Desai, Meghnad, et al. *Agrarian Power and Agrarian Productivity in South Asia.* Berkeley, CA, University of California Press, 1984.

Drèze, Jean, and Sen, Amartya. *India: Economic Development and Social Opportunity.* New Delhi, Oxford University Press, 1995.

Indian Development: Selected Regional Perspectives. New Delhi, Oxford University Press, 1999.

Dutt, R. C. *Economic History of India.* Delhi, Publications Division, 1960.

Economist Intelligence Unit: *India to 1990: How Far Will Reform Go?* London, The Economist Publications, 1986.

Epstein, T. A. *Economic Development and Social Change in South India.* Mumbai, Oxford University Press, 1962.

Etienne, Gilbert (translation by Mothersole, Megan). *Studies in Indian Agriculture: the Art of the Possible.* Berkeley, CA, University of California Press, 1968.

Farmer, B. H. *Agricultural Colonization in India since Independence.* Oxford University Press, 1974.

(Ed.). *Green Revolution? Technology and Changes in Rice Growing Areas of Tamil Nadu and Sri Lanka.* London, Macmillan, 1977.

Federation of Indian Chambers of Commerce and Industry (FICCI). *Footprints of Enterprise: Indian Business Through the Ages.* New Delhi, Oxford University Press, 1998.

Fonseca, A. J. *Wage Issues in a Developing Economy: The Indian Experience.* Bombay, 1975; Delhi, Kolkata, Chennai, 1976; Oxford University Press.

Frankel, Francine R., Hasan, Zoya, Bhargava, Rajeev and Arora, Balveer. *Transforming India: Social and Political Dynamics of Democracy.* Oxford University Press, 2000.

Goldsmith, R. W. *The Financial Development of India, 1860–1977.* Yale University Press, 1984.

Guha, Ashok (Ed.). *Economic Liberalisation, Industrial Structure and Growth in India.* Oxford University Press, 1989.

Gupta, Dipankar. *Mistaken Modernity: India Between Worlds.* HarperCollins, 2001.

Gupta, S. P. *Mid Year Review of the Indian Economy, 1995–96.* Delhi, Konark Publishers, 1996.

Gurumurthi, S. *Fiscal Federalism in India.* New Delhi, Vikas Publishing House, 1994.

Gyan, Chand. The Socialist Transformation of the Indian Economy. London, Allen and Unwin, 1965.

Hanson, A. H. *The Process of Planning: A Study of India's Five-Year Plans 1950–1964.* London, Oxford University Press, 1966.

Harriss-White, Barbara, and Subramaniam, S. *Illfare in India, Essays on India's Social Sector.* New Delhi, Sage Publications Ltd, 1999.

Henderson, P. D. *India: The Energy Sector.* Delhi, 1975; London, 1976. Published for the World Bank by Oxford University Press.

Herring, Ronald. *Land to the Tiller.* New Haven, CT, Yale University Press, 1983.

Jalan, Bimal. *India's Economic Crisis: The Way Ahead.* Delhi, Oxford University Press, 1991.

(Ed.) *Indian Economy: Problems and Prospects.* New Delhi, Viking, 1992.

Jenkins, Rob. *Democratic Politics and Economic Reform In India.* Cambridge, Cambridge University Press, 1999.

Jha, Prem Shankar. *The Economy of India.* Delhi, Oxford University Press, 1979.

Joshi, Vijay and Little, I. M. D. *India: Macroeconomics and Political Economy, 1964–1991.* Delhi, Oxford University Press, 1994.

India's Economic Reforms, 1991–2001. Delhi, Oxford University Press, 1996.

Karlekar, Hiranmay (Ed.). *Independent India: The First Fifty Years.* Oxford University Press, 1999.

Kelkar, Vijay, and Rao, V. V. Bhanoji. *India: Development Policy Imperatives.* Delhi, Tata McGraw-Hill Publishing Co Ltd, 1996.

Khusro, A. M. *Unfinished Agenda, India and the World Economy.* New Delhi, Wiley Eastern Ltd, 1994.

Lal, Deepak. *Unfinished Business: India in the World Economy.* Oxford University Press, 1999.

Lala, R. M. *Beyond the Last Blue Mountain: A Life of J. R. D. Tata.* New Delhi, Penguin Books, 1992.

Lucas, R. E. B., and Papanek, G. F. *The Indian Economy, Recent Developments and Future Prospects.* Boulder, CO, Westview Press, 1988.

Maddison, A. *Class Structure and Economic Growth: India and Pakistan since the Moguls.* 1971.

Malyarov, O. V. *The Role of the State in the Socio-Economic Structure of India.* New Delhi, Vikas Publishing House, 1983.

Mehta, B. *India and the World Oil Crisis.* 1974.

Mellor, John W. *The New Economics of Growth: A Strategy for India and the Developing World.* Ithaca and London, Cornell University Press, 1976.

Mongia, J. N. (Ed.). *Readings in Indian Labour and Social Welfare.* Delhi, Atma Ram, 1976.

Mookherjee, Dilip (Ed.). *Indian Industry, Policies and Performance.* Delhi, Oxford University Press, 1994.

Mukherjee, Sadhan. *India's Economic Relations with the USA and the USSR.* New Delhi, Sterling Publishers Pvt. Ltd, 1978.

Nair, K. *Three Bowls of Rice: India & Japan, A Century of Effort.* East Lansing, MI, Michigan State University Press, 1973.

Nayar, B. R. *India's Mixed Economy.* Mumbai, Popular Prakashan Ltd, 1989.

Nayyar, Deepak (Ed.). *Industrial Growth and Stagnation.* New Delhi, Oxford University Press, 1994.

Nayyar, Deepak, and Badhuri, Amit. *An Intelligent Person's Guide to Economic Liberalisation in India.* New Delhi, Penguin, 1991.

Papola, T. S., and Rodgers, G. (Eds). *Labour Institutions and Economic Development in India.* London, International Labour Office, 1993.

Parikh, Kirit (Ed.). *Mid Year Review of the Indian Economy, 1994–95.* Delhi, Konark Publishers, 1995.

(Ed.) India Development Report, 1997.

Delhi, Oxford University Press, 1997.

Patel, I. G. *Glimpses of Indian Economic Policy.* Oxford University Press, 2002.

Raj, K. N. *Organisational Issues in Indian Agriculture.* Oxford University Press, 1990.

Rajghatta, Chidanand. *The Horse that Flew: How India's Silicon Gurus Spread their Wings.* New Delhi, HarperCollins, 2002.

Rangarajan, C. *Indian Economy: Essays on Money and Finance.* New Delhi, UBS Publishers and Distributors, 1998.

Rao, V. K. R. V., and Narain, Dharm. *Foreign Aid and India's Economic Development*. London, Asia Publishing House, 1964.

India's National Income 1950–1980. London, Sage Publications, 1983.

Reddy, Y. Venugopal. *Monetary and Financial Sector Reforms in India.* New Delhi, UBS Publishers and Distributors, 2000.

Rosen, G. *Democracy and Economic Change in India*. Cambridge University Press for University of California Press, 2nd edn, 1967.

Sachs, Jeffrey D., Varshney, Ashutosh, and Bajpai, Nirupam. *India in the Era of Economic Reforms.* Oxford University Press, 1999.

Sainath, P. *Everbody Loves a Good Drought: Life in India's Poorest Districts*. Delhi, Penguin Books India (Pvt) Ltd, 1997.

Sandesara, J. C. *Industrial Policy and Planning—1947 to 1991: Tendencies, Interpretations and Issues.* Delhi, Sage Publications, 1992.

Satyamurthy, T. V. (Ed.). *Industry and Agriculture in India since Independence*. Delhi, Oxford University Press, 1995.

Sharma, Shalendra D. *Development and Democracy in India.* Boulder, CO, Lynne Rienner, 1999.

Singh, Charan. *India's Economic Policy: The Gandhian Blueprint.* New Delhi, Vikas Publishing House, 1978.

Srinivasan, T. N. *India's Economic Reforms.* Oxford, Oxford University Press, 2000.

Streeten, P., and Lipton, M. (Eds). *The Crisis of Indian Planning.* London, Oxford University Press, 1968.

Swamy, S. *Economic Growth in China and India 1952–1970*. 1973.

Tripathi, D. (Ed.). *Business and Politics in India: A Historical Perspective.* Delhi, Manohar Publications, 1991.

Turner, R. (Ed.). *India's Urban Future*. Berkeley and Los Angeles, CA, University of California Press; London, Cambridge University Press, 1962.

Varshney, A. *Democracy, Development and the Countryside*. Cambridge, Cambridge University Press, 1995.

Vedavalli, R. *Private Foreign Investment and Economic Development: A Case Study of Petroleum in India*. London, Cambridge University Press, 1976.

Wadhva, C. D. *Some Problems of India's Economic Policy*. 1973.

Zinkin, Maurice, and Ward, Barbara. *Why Help India?* London, Pergamon Press, 1963.

INDONESIA

Physical and Social Geography

HARVEY DEMAINE

With revisions by ROBERT CRIBB

The Republic of Indonesia, which today comprises the same area as the former Netherlands East Indies, lies along the Equator between the south-eastern tip of the Asian mainland and Australia. Its western and southern coasts abut on the Indian Ocean; to the north it faces the Straits of Melaka (Malacca) and the South China Sea; and the remote northern shore of Papua (formerly Irian Jaya) province has frontage on to the Pacific Ocean. Indonesia's only land frontiers are with Papua New Guinea, to the east of (West) Papua, with East Timor (which acceded to independence in May 2002), and with the Malaysian states of Sarawak and Sabah, which occupy northern Borneo; almost all of the remainder of Bórneo comprises the Indonesian territory of Kalimantan.

Indonesia extends more than 4,800 km from east to west and 2,000 km from north to south. However, nearly four-fifths of the area between these outer extremities consists of sea, and the total land surface of Indonesia covers 1,922,570 sq km (742,308 sq miles).

PHYSICAL FEATURES

The country consists of about 17,500 islands of extremely varied size and character, of which some 6,000 are inhabited. The largest exclusively Indonesian island is Sumatra (Sumatera), covering 482,393 sq km, though this is exceeded by the Indonesian segment, comprising 547,891 sq km or about two-thirds, of Borneo. These islands are followed in size by the 421,981 sq km of Papua, then by Sulawesi (Celebes), with 191,800 sq km, and by Java (Jawa), which, with the neighbouring island of Madura, totals 127,499 sq km. The remaining areas are much smaller islands, comprising Bali, the Nusa Tenggara group and the small scattered islands of the Maluku (Moluccas) group, which lie between Sulawesi and Papua.

Differences in size also reflect fundamental differences in geological structure. All the large islands except Sulawesi stand on one of two great continental shelves: the Sunda Shelf, representing a prolongation of the Asian mainland, covered by the shallow waters of the Straits of Melaka, the Java Sea and the southernmost part of the South China Sea; and the Sahul Shelf, which is covered by the shallow Arafura Sea and links New Guinea with Australia. In Sumatra, Java and north-eastern Borneo and West Papua there are pronounced mountain ranges facing the deep seas along the outer edges of the shelves, and extensive lowland tracts, facing the shallow inner seas whose coastlines reveal evidence of recent submergence. In contrast to the larger islands of western and eastern Indonesia, most of those lying between the two shelves, including Sulawesi as well as those of the Nusa Tenggara and Maluku groups, rise steeply from deep seas on all sides, with only extremely narrow coastal plains.

The recent mountain building in most parts of the archipelago is related to widespread vulcanicity, much of which is still in the active stage. Except in Borneo and West Papua, the culminating relief normally consists of volcanic cones, many of which exceed 3,000 m in altitude, though the loftiest peaks of all are the non-volcanic Punjak Jaya (5,000 m) and Idenburg-top (4,800 m) in the Snow mountains of West Papua. The archipelago is also subject to earthquakes and associated tsunami ('tidal' waves). In December 1992 approximately 2,500 people died in Flores as a consequence of tremors and inundation, and in 1993 and 1994 more than 400 died after earthquakes off the south-west coast of Sumatra and the south coast of Java.

Although the most extensive lowlands occur along the eastern coast of Sumatra and the southern coasts of Borneo and Papua, the larger part of all three lowland areas consists of tidal swamp which, until very recently, has been virtually ignored for cultivation purposes, and still constitutes a major obstacle to the opening up of the better-drained areas further inland. Reclamation is under way in some of these lands, as part of the transmigration programme, but it still cannot match that of the narrower coastal lowlands of the smaller central island of Java.

NATURAL RESOURCES

The much greater fertility of the soils of the eastern two-thirds of Java and nearby Bali, by comparison with nearly all the rest of Indonesia, except a small part of interior and coastal north-eastern Sumatra, arises from the neutral-basic character (as opposed to the prevailingly acidic composition elsewhere) of the volcanic ejecta from which they are derived. In the remaining nine-tenths or more of Indonesia, the soils—whether volcanically derived or not—are altogether poorer in quality than they are popularly assumed to be; indeed, they are not noticeably better than in most other parts of the humid tropics.

There is much controversy about the scale of Indonesia's mineral wealth. Exploration is still continuing in many parts of the archipelago, and substantial deposits certainly exist, particularly of hydrocarbons. Despite the country's wealth of hydrocarbon deposits, growing domestic consumption of petroleum products is leading Indonesia to diversify its energy sources. Exploration and extraction of coal are being expanded, and sources of geothermal energy are being exploited on a small scale. Although overshadowed by the hydrocarbon sector, which makes a major contribution to the economy, there are significant reserves of tin, bauxite, copper, nickel, gold and silver.

CLIMATE AND VEGETATION

Climatically the greater part of Indonesia may be described as maritime equatorial, with consistently high temperatures (except at higher altitudes) and heavy rainfall in all seasons, though in many parts of western Indonesia there are distinct peak periods of exceptionally heavy rain when either the north-east or the south-west monsoon winds are blowing on shore. However, the eastern half of Java, Bali, southern Sulawesi and Nusa Tenggara, which lie further to the south and nearer to the Australian desert, experience a clearly marked dry season during the period of the south-east monsoon between June/July and September/October. The south-east monsoon subsequently changes direction, to become the south-west monsoon over western Indonesia. In Pontianak, situated almost exactly on the Equator on the west coast of Borneo, the monthly mean temperature varies only from 25.6°C in December to 26.7°C in July, and average monthly rainfall varies from 160 mm in July to 400 mm in December. The total annual rainfall is 3,200 mm. Surabaya, in eastern Java, shows even less variation in mean monthly temperature, which ranges between 26.1°C and 26.7°C throughout the year. It has four months (December–March) with over 240 mm of rain, and four others (July–October) with less than 50 mm, out of an annual total of 1,735 mm.

Nearly all of Indonesia, in its natural state, supports very dense vegetation, with significant variations, including tidal swamps, normal lowlands, lower slopes, and higher altitudes. Natural forests (which covered 109.8m. ha in 1995, or approximately 57% of Indonesia's land area) become progressively thinner as one goes eastwards from central Java to Timor, and over much of Nusa Tenggara the vegetation is better described as scrub.

POPULATION AND CULTURE

With a population of 206,264,595 according to the results of the June 2000 census, Indonesia ranks as the fourth most populous country in the world, after the People's Republic of China, India and the USA. Despite a programme of family planning, Indonesia's population increased at an average rate of 1.49% per year over the period 1990–2000. So large a population, spread over so vast and fragmented a territory, presents wide variations, notably in ethnic type, religion and language. Java, Madura and Bali, which comprise about one-thirteenth of the total area of Indonesia, contain almost two-thirds of its population. This situation has persisted, despite extensive efforts to shift population out of Java and Bali from as early as 1905 under colonization schemes, latterly known as 'transmigration'.

Archaeological evidence suggests that the archipelago was sparsely populated from at least 50,000 years ago by people of Austromelanesian (Papuan) stock. The Austromelanesians achieved higher population densities only in New Guinea, where there is evidence of intensive cultivation of taro and other crops from about 7000 BC. In the western two-thirds of the archipelago, the Austromelanesians were later largely displaced by Austronesians, seafaring people from the island of Taiwan, who began to move southwards from about 4000 BC and who went on, in a series of great migrations, to colonize Polynesia and Madagascar. The considerable physical differences between ethnic groups in Indonesia is now thought to be related to different levels of mixing between the two peoples, with the older Austromelanesian elements progressively stronger in the eastern part of the archipelago.

Nearly 90% of the Indonesian population was Muslim in 1993. The character of Indonesian Islam, however, varies widely from region to region. The peoples of the coastal regions of Western Indonesia are predominantly Muslim, although their religious practice varies considerably according to the influence of local custom or *adat*. The strongly Muslim Minangkabau of West Sumatra, for instance, maintain a matrilineal system of inheritance directly at variance with normal Islamic practice, and local customs are important even in Aceh (far northern Sumatra), which is traditionally regarded as the staunchest Muslim region. In the interior of Java, earlier Hindu and animist influences are strong, producing a belief system known as *Kejawen* which is only broadly recognizable as Muslim. In the interior of the other larger islands, some of the formerly animist ethnic groups have been converted to Islam (such as the Gayo and Alas in northern Sumatra) or Christianity (such as the neighbouring Bataks and the Minahasans of North Sulawesi). Christian missionary influence is strongest in eastern Indonesia. Hinduism remains the religion of the island of Bali and of a few small enclaves in Java, but the traditional religion of the Dayaks of Borneo has also been given official recognition as a form of Hinduism, although it bears only a passing resemblance to the religion practised in Bali. Christianity, Buddhism and Confucianism are strong amongst the Chinese minority. Small animist communities remain in many regions, but official policy requires all Indonesians in time to accept one of the larger religions.

Over 270 Austronesian languages and 180 Papuan languages have been recognized in Indonesia, but only 13 of these have more than 1m. speakers. The national language is a development of Malay, the language of Srivijaya and of other early states on the Melaka Strait. In the pre-colonial era Malay had spread widely as a trading lingua franca, and as the language of Islam in the archipelago. The Dutch strengthened its position by using it as a major language of administration, law and education. The Indonesian nationalist movement formally adopted Malay as the national language in 1929, and called it 'Indonesian' (Bahasa Indonesia). Since independence the vocabulary of Indonesian has expanded enormously. Indonesian is now used exclusively at all but the initial levels of the education system and is the only language of public affairs.

Besides its indigenous population, Indonesia has one of the largest Chinese communities in South-East Asia. This community may have totalled nearly 3m. Although a substantial proportion of the Chinese were born and brought up in Indonesia, accepted citizenship and became 'Indonesianized', up to one-half remained without citizenship and a source of friction in the society, as demonstrated during the riots of 1998 (see History). The Chinese and smaller non-indigenous groups, such as Arabs and Eurasians, are largely concentrated in the urban areas. The cities have grown rapidly in recent years, with Jakarta's population rising from 4.6m. in 1971 to an estimated 11.4m. in 2001.

History

ROBERT CRIBB

HISTORICAL BACKGROUND

From about AD 100 the rise of Asia's great maritime trade route, linking India and China through South-East Asia, drew the small hunting, fishing and agricultural communities of the Indonesian archipelago into a broader world of civilization and commerce. Newly-rich local rulers, trading in spices, resins and fragrant woods, justified their acquired wealth by adopting Indian political ideology, turning themselves into Hindu god-kings and providing a conduit through which Hindu ideas spread unevenly to the mass of the people. Srivijaya on the Sumatra coast (c. 700–1200) and Majapahit in the interior of Java (c. 1300–1450) emerged as the greatest early states, their influence covering much of the western archipelago. Islam arrived on the trade routes from India in about 1100, and during subsequent centuries largely displaced Hinduism and Buddhism as the formal religion of the courts and of society, although in practice it fused with Indian and local religions into distinctive Indonesian forms.

Colonial Rule

European traders and raiders were present in the archipelago from the early 16th century, but only gradually did the Dutch East Indies Company turn its scattered forts and trading posts into a colonial empire. The company focused initially on trade and soon became involved in plantations, but it was finally unable to cope with the complexities of colonial administration and the metropolitan Dutch Government took over the colony in 1799. After a brief period of British occupation under Sir Stamford Raffles (1811–16), the Dutch authorities launched an era of intensive colonial exploitation on Java known as the Cultivation System. Many authorities have argued that this exploitation brought about the long-term impoverishment of the island, though empirical evidence is equivocal. From the 1870s Western private enterprise was allowed to operate in the colony, leading to a spectacular expansion of plantation agriculture outside Java (Jawa), especially in East Sumatra (Sumatera). Petroleum extraction in Sumatra and Borneo (Kalimantan) also became important. During the four decades to 1910, the Dutch largely completed their military conquest of the archipelago. The Dutch preserved many of the traditional rulers of the archipelago as agents of colonial rule, and established a complicated legal system under which the traditional native law (*adat*) in each region was codified and applied to indigenous people. The result was a form of racial classification in which the population was divided into Europeans, Natives and 'Foreign Orientals' (principally Chinese), with differing rights and duties. Only Natives were permitted to own land, but they had fewer political and legal rights. The Chinese community, which included both recent immigrants and locally-born families with a long history in the archipelago, came to occupy a middle position in society, dominating small- and medium-scale commerce to the exclusion of indigenous Indonesians.

The disruption of indigenous society by Western economic penetration and the emergence of a small educated élite, trained especially to serve the increasingly complex government and private bureaucracies, led to the rise of a nationalist movement in the early 20th century. Islamic and communist influences were initially strong in this movement, but by the late 1920s the movement was dominated by 'secular' nationalists, notably Sukarno, Hatta and Sjahrir. The movement extracted few concessions from the colonial authorities and remained politically weak until the Japanese occupation (1942–45), which removed the Dutch and raised hopes of rapid independence.

INDEPENDENCE

In the confusion following the Japanese surrender, Sukarno and Hatta declared independence on 17 August 1945, becoming President and Vice-President respectively of the new Republic of Indonesia. More than four years of fighting and negotiation with the Dutch ensued, however, before the formal transfer of sovereignty on 27 December 1949. By January 1949 the Dutch had reconquered most of the archipelago, but they were defeated by a combination of guerrilla resistance and foreign pressure; the USA, in particular, became convinced of the moderate credentials of the Indonesian nationalists, and wished to avoid a prolonged struggle which might encourage the growth of communism. The transfer of sovereignty left Indonesia with a federal system, devised by the Dutch to isolate radical forces on Java and Sumatra; the Republic of Indonesia declared in 1945 was thus a constituent state of the 14-member Republic of the United States of Indonesia. The other states were quickly dissolved, and in August 1950 Indonesia returned to a unitary structure. Against Indonesian wishes, however, the Dutch retained the territory of West New Guinea (later West Irian, renamed Irian Jaya and subsequently Papua) on the grounds that it was ethnically distinct from the rest of Indonesia.

Parliamentary Democracy, 1950–57

Under the 1950 Constitution, political power was vested in a legislature, with Prime Ministers and their cabinets responsible for executive government. Although the legislature was unelected (most members were present by virtue of their roles in one or other of the many deliberative bodies created by both sides during the war of independence), it was diverse and appears to have represented the main social forces and currents of political thought in the country. Because of this diversity, governments were invariably coalitions and were vulnerable to defections; few lasted longer than a year in office. Indonesia lacked the human and infrastructural resources to deal rapidly and effectively with the social and economic problems left by colonialism, and the performance of these governments was thus generally disappointing. Expectations had been raised by the independence struggle and could not easily be met. The political parties themselves undermined their own standing and performance by discord, corruption and partisan appointments to the civil service. The country also faced rebellions: in South Maluku (the Moluccas) a conservative, largely Christian movement attempted to secede, while in parts of Java, Sumatra and Celebes (Sulawesi) the Darul Islam movement attempted to impose an Islamic state. Many people also resented the failure of successive governments to dislodge the Dutch from West New Guinea, though Indonesia's international status was improved when it hosted the Afro-Asian Conference in Bandung in 1955.

At the first national elections in 1955 Java-based parties and those towards the left gained the greatest support, although no party came close to a majority. The continuing impasse in Jakarta, together with growing alarm in the islands outside Java, led in 1956 to local mutinies in Sumatra, an island that generated much of Indonesia's export revenue. The mutinies developed into full rebellions in 1957, although their aim was to recover central power, not to secede. In response to the crisis, President Sukarno declared martial law in 1957, and during the next two years gradually replaced the parliamentary system with authoritarian rule based on the original 1945 Constitution adopted at the beginning of the war for independence.

Guided Democracy, 1959–65

Sukarno called his authoritarian system 'Guided Democracy', but for the most part it was a retreat from democracy. The elected legislature was replaced by an appointed one; cabinets were chosen by and responsible to the President. Political activity was restricted, and two parties were banned. The army, which had by then defeated the regional rebellions, became deeply involved in the administration under martial law, and also assumed a major role in the economy as managers of Dutch enterprises that had been nationalized in 1957. Although conservative in structure and social policy, 'Guided Democracy' was radical in rhetoric and ideology. Sukarno proclaimed a continuing revolution in the name of the poor and oppressed, and he increasingly incorporated Marxist elements into state ideology. Although he enjoyed unrivalled oratorical power over the Indonesian masses, he also made extensive use of the Partai Komunis Indonesia (PKI—Indonesian Communist Party) in mobilizing popular support. The communists had created by far the most effective party structure in the country and had won 16.4% of the vote in the 1955 elections, but probably enjoyed the support of between one-third and one-half of the population by 1965. 'Guided Democracy' delivered few tangible benefits to Indonesians. Sukarno showed little interest in day-to-day administration, and the fabric of the country gradually deteriorated; by 1965 Indonesia was one of the poorest countries in the world. The little radical legislation that he did sponsor (notably in the area of land reform) failed to be implemented, owing to bureaucratic inertia and the resistance of local powers. Sukarno's recovery of West New Guinea in 1963 by a mixture of bluff and shrewd international diplomacy won him enormous credit with Indonesians, but his confrontation with Malaysia (1963–66), which he regarded as an undemocratic and neocolonial 'puppet' of the British, brought no such success.

Although the PKI held virtually none of the levers of power, there was widespread speculation that its broader ideological influence would deliver it control of Indonesia on the death of Sukarno, who by 1965 was visibly ageing and appeared to be losing political control. Such a prospect, however, provoked concern within the Muslim community and in the army, which remained the most powerful institution in the country. Deepening social and ideological conflict, exacerbated by declining economic conditions, led to a sense of impending crisis. On 30 September 1965 a group of left-wing junior army officers staged a limited coup against the more conservative High Command in order to forestall a rumoured army coup a few days later. Both Sukarno and the PKI probably had some knowledge of the plot, although there is no reliable evidence that either took part in planning it. Poor execution of the coup (most but not all of the targeted generals were killed), however, apparently led the plotters to expand it into a full-scale seizure of power, for which they were utterly unprepared. Their movement, therefore, was easily suppressed by the senior surviving general, Suharto.

Sukarno remained formally in office, but between October 1965 and March 1966 Suharto steadily eroded his power, preventing his exercise of authority in the Government and countering his still formidable oratorical skills by establishing what became known as the 'New Order' coalition of Muslims, students, economic managers and the armed forces, which demanded a radical change of policy direction towards economic recovery. During the same period the PKI was proscribed. Probably about 500,000 party members and sympathizers (from a claimed membership of 3m.) were killed, some by the armed forces, some by anti-communist vigilantes, and more than 1.5m. were detained for various periods. Suharto became acting President in March 1967 and full President a year later. Sukarno was held under house arrest until his death in 1970.

SUHARTO AND THE NEW ORDER

Suharto's new regime presented itself as a managerial government with the task of restoring stability to politics and growth to the economy. Suharto left much of the management of the Indonesian economy to a team of US-trained economists, who worked closely with the Inter-Governmental Group for Indonesia (IGGI), an international consortium of aid donors to Indonesia. Although they maintained the large state sector of the economy inherited from the period of 'Guided Democracy', they opened the Indonesian economy to foreign investment, first in mining and forestry, and later in industrial manufacture. Indonesia benefited especially from the rapid increase in petroleum prices, and was able to underwrite a massive programme of infrastructural investment as a base for growth (see Economy). The new Government also began programmes aimed at addressing the problems of rapid population growth. A major and effective family-planning campaign was launched. The long-standing policy of encouraging people from densely-populated Java and Bali to move to less-populated regions in the other islands was expanded, with World Bank finance, to a massive population transfer that encompassed 1.5m. people between 1969 and 1982. New techniques for cultivating rice were also introduced, leading to a spectacular expansion of production, with self-sufficiency being achieved in 1982.

Suharto swiftly abandoned the left-wing rhetoric of 'Guided Democracy', but refrained from installing any ideology in its place. Instead, he elevated as a national symbol the *Pancasila*, five principles expounded by Sukarno just before the declaration of independence. These principles were: belief in God, national unity, humanitarianism, social justice and democracy. Sukarno had expressed them in deliberately general terms (belief in God, for instance, referred to belief in any supreme deity, not just belief in Allah or the Christian God) in order to transcend emerging ideological differences within the nationalist movement on the eve of independence. Suharto now used the *Pancasila* to deny the central symbolic space in Indonesian politics to any ideology, and he often portrayed his regime as representing a desirable middle course between the left (communism) and the right (fundamentalist Islam).

The armed forces played a crucial role in the new Government. They provided the main security and intelligence apparatus in the form of the Operational Command for the Restoration of Security and Order (Kopkamtib). Those who had been involved in the abortive 1965 coup were rigorously pursued, and involvement was interpreted so broadly that most leftist dissent was encompassed. The armed forces also increased their role in administration through the doctrine of *dwifungsi* or dual function, which held that the concern of the armed forces was not simply national defence but also the actual conduct of government in the interests of good administration. A powerful myth began to develop that the armed forces had played the principal role in securing independence in the 1940s, that it had done so in the face of obstruction and betrayal by the civilian authorities and that it therefore retained a special right and duty to supervise and take charge of the conduct of government. Under *dwifungsi*, serving and retired army officers took a wide variety of posts, from the level of cabinet minister down to village head.

In order to meet domestic and international expectations of a restoration of democracy, elections took place in July 1971, but under conditions designed to ensure a government victory. During the preceding months and years, the authorities comprehensively undermined the surviving parties, often intervening directly in their internal affairs to ensure that they were controlled by groups sympathetic to the armed forces. More important, the Government introduced the doctrine of 'monoloyalty', under which government officials were permitted to support only the Government at election time; other political parties thus lost the influential backing they had previously received from various sections of the bureaucracy, especially in the countryside. At the same time, the Government decreed the so-called 'floating mass policy', under which the mass of Indonesians were not to be exposed to political campaigning except during the brief, defined campaign period before elections; this was ostensibly to avoid distracting people from the tasks of national development. For the election campaign itself, contestants were screened by security officials before being permitted to stand, and public questioning of government policy was not permitted (although the implementation of policy might be challenged). In addition, inter-ethnic, inter-religious or inter-'group' (i.e. class) issues were not permitted to be discussed publicly at any time. In 1973, after the elections, the Government further weakened the parties by forcing them to merge into two fractious federations: the Partai Persatuan Pembangunan (PPP—United Development Party), comprising the four Muslim parties, and the Partai Demokrasi Indonesia (PDI—Indonesian Democratic Party), composed of the remaining parties.

Government candidates contested the 1971 elections as the Sekretariat Bersama Golongan Karya (Joint Secretariat of Functional Groups, also known as Sekber Golkar, or simply Golkar), an organization that had played a minor role under 'Guided Democracy' as an army-dominated co-ordinating body for anti-communist trade unions and other associations. Golkar, however, was not a political party; it had no individual membership and virtually no identity except during the election period, and was thus exempt from many of the restrictions on the parties, as well as enjoying the support of the bureaucracy and the armed forces. Golkar received 63% of the vote in the 1971 elections, and its share of the vote remained largely unchanged in the elections until the end of Suharto's 'New Order'. Serious discontent began to arise in Indonesia during the mid-1970s, however. Student groups, in particular, protested against the perceived lack of true democracy, the hardships being caused to ordinary Indonesians by the rapid modernization programme and the corruption of the ruling group. The President's wife, Siti Hartinah (Tien), was among those accused of appropriating funds from the Government and of abusing her position to obtain favours and to attract exorbitant commissions. Concern that the exceptionally high revenue derived from petroleum exports was being squandered was later vindicated when the state oil company, Pertamina, came close to bankruptcy in 1975–76. There was much resentment too of the business relations between 'New Order' figures and Chinese Indonesian business-owners (*cukong*). This dissent culminated in the Malari riots of 1974.

Towards a 'Pancasila State', 1975–88

Disturbed by this dissent, Suharto launched an ambitious programme to turn the *Pancasila* from a symbol into a national ideology. In a major programme of ideological construction, the *Pancasila's* set of vague unifying principles became a comprehensive ideology, with the Government exclusively responsible for formulation and interpretation. The *Pancasila* was held to prescribe a society modelled on the traditional family, in which parental authority was respected and in which individual interest was subordinate to the well-being of the community. *Pancasila* labour relations, for instance, implied that there could be no conflict of interests between workers and management and that strikes were inherently anti-social. In emphasizing authority, the *Pancasila* also reinforced Suharto's presidential authority, and some observers began to liken his style to that of a traditional Javanese king.

Opposition to the new interpretation of the *Pancasila* came first from a group of older politicians associated with the parliamentary period and the early 'New Order'. In 1980 they signed the Petition of 50, objecting to Suharto's new doctrines and urging the legislature to review (i.e. reject) them. The strongest reaction to the new *Pancasila*, however, came from religious groups, when the Government insisted in the early 1980s that all social organizations adopt the *Pancasila* as their sole basic principle (*azas tunggal*), placing it even above religious principles. Deep disquiet over this requirement prompted violent protests, including a demonstration in Tanjung Priok, the port area of Jakarta, in which at least 18 people (perhaps 100 or more) were shot by security forces. One of the largest factions of the Muslim PPP withdrew from the party in consequence of the new requirement.

The years 1975–88 were also a time of continued political repression. Muslim militants especially were often arrested and tried, but the Government maintained that the banned PKI remained a threat and periodically dismissed officials on the grounds of tenuous left-wing connections. In late 1982, in response to an escalation of crime in Indonesia's major cities, the authorities launched the *petrus*, or 'mysterious killings' campaign, in which known and suspected small-scale criminals were sought out and killed in vigilante-style operations.

None the less, these were also years in which the Suharto Government deftly refined economic and social policy. Pertamina was rehabilitated, and the regime reacted promptly and efficiently to the collapse of petroleum prices. As the impossibility of significantly diminishing Java's population by means of transmigration became apparent, the goals of the programme were shifted to economic development in the other islands, the resettlement of people displaced by development projects and natural disasters, and the establishment of politically reliable Javanese settler communities in potentially secessionist regions. Economic development proceeded and, by the late 1980s, the country was in a position to emulate the achievements of the East Asian newly-industrializing countries.

Suharto's Final Decade, 1988–98

From the late 1980s, the question of the succession increasingly overshadowed the political agenda in President Suharto's

Indonesia. Born in 1921, Suharto had long passed normal retirement age; however, he gave no indication of selecting a successor. During the approach to each of the successive five-yearly MPR sessions, at which the President was elected, Suharto hinted that he expected his next term to be his last; but once he was elected, these hints gradually gave way to expressions of willingness to stand for a further term, if that were the will of the MPR. Few observers inside or outside the country could foresee any circumstances that would force Suharto from office, and most believed that only death or serious illness would end his rule. The political order was commonly described as being in 'a state of waiting', and it was widely felt that policy-making was being seriously hampered by the efforts of major political figures to position themselves in preparation for Suharto's demise.

Within élite circles, much attention focused on the Vice-Presidency. This position is one of little power in itself, but is of significance as the Vice-President automatically succeeds to the presidency if the President dies or steps down. Suharto's early Vice-Presidents had all been men with weak power bases of their own, who were therefore unlikely to challenge his power. By the late 1980s, however, the military had become increasingly concerned that Suharto's sudden death might leave them with an unacceptable President. In 1993, therefore, the army engineered a series of public endorsements of its Commander, Gen. Try Sutrisno, in order to secure his election to the Vice-Presidency. As a former presidential adjutant without conspicuous presidential talents, Try was by no means unacceptable to Suharto, and his presence in office did little to allay the general feeling that the future of Indonesia after Suharto was still very uncertain.

Outside élite circles, there was a growing perception that Indonesia might be destined for a more liberal political order. During the 1990s the Government's emphasis on the *Pancasila* as the central principle for all social activity perceptibly diminished. Although the *azas tunggal* requirement remained in place, the Government seemed not to be attempting to impose ideological conformity with any great vigour. Instead, it appeared to accept that decision-making in a complex and diverse society must be the outcome of negotiation among various ideological, religious and social groups. In his independence day speech in August 1990 the President stated that there was no need to fear differences of opinion within society. His remarks were followed by measures both to relax the censorship of the press and to limit the sanctions against publications deemed to have offended political proprieties. In May 1996 the People's Consultative Assembly began to discuss legislation to end the Government's monopoly of news services. Although there was no more than a modest easing of political repression, these statements and actions were in sharp contrast to the official position in the late 1970s when the *Pancasila* state was being constructed.

These policy alterations reflected broader changes in Indonesian society under the 'New Order'. Growing prosperity and an increasingly complex economy and society had led to better education, improved living standards and greater international awareness for a substantial new middle class of bureaucrats, professionals and entrepreneurs. These groups were keen to obtain greater political influence and to see a more regularized economic and administrative order; without necessarily wanting a democracy that enfranchised the poor, they desired a political system in which power and influence were no longer reserved for a small civilian and military élite. These aspirations were generally described as a wish for 'openness' (*keterbukaan*, itself a direct translation of *glasnost*).

More or less independent political organizations became increasingly prominent. A new Muslim organization, the Ikatan Cendekiawan Muslim Indonesia (ICMI, Association of Muslim Intellectuals), which was founded in December 1990 and led by Suharto's protégé, the Minister of State for Research and Technology, Prof. Dr Ir Bucharuddin Jusuf (B. J.) Habibie, became a frequent contributor to public debate. In 1991 the Chairman of the Nahdlatul Ulama (NU—Council of Scholars, Indonesia's largest Muslim organization), Abdurrahman Wahid, founded the Democracy Forum, comprising 45 prominent Indonesian intellectuals, including a number of Christians. In 1993, moreover, the formerly ineffective PDI elected to its chair Megawati Sukarnoputri (a daughter of the late President Sukarno), whose dynamic leadership appeared to be winning greater public support for the party. There even appeared to be limited space for more radical organizations, with the Government failing to suppress the student-worker coalition, Infight, or the illegal Partai Rakyat Demokrasi (PRD—People's Democratic Party), while several nominally social organizations were founded with names close to or even identical with those of parties from the 1950s. In May 1996 Sri Bintang Pamungkas, a former PPP parliamentarian who had been expelled from the legislature in 1995 for allegedly challenging the *Pancasila*, founded the Partai Uni Demokrasi Indonesia (United Democratic Party of Indonesia). In 1995 it was announced that parliamentary seats reserved for the armed forces would be reduced from 100 to 75 at the next election. In early 1996 there was increasing public discussion of the electoral system, and suggestions for a number of reforms that would remove some of Golkar's advantages were made. It was suggested, for instance, that polling day should be a public holiday, so that voters would not have to vote at their place of work, where they were more easily subject to pressure. In March a group of political activists established an independent election monitoring committee.

In the early phase of this apparent political relaxation, Suharto appeared to be moving closer to Islam than earlier in his presidency. He adopted the given name Mohamed after his pilgrimage to Mecca in 1991; in the March 1993 government reorganization those primarily responsible for the country's economic policy since 1988, Prof. Dr Johannes B. Sumarlin, Adrianus Mooy and Radius Prawiro (all Western-educated Christians), were replaced, leaving only three Christians in the Cabinet; and in November 1993 he halted a controversial state lottery, which had been strongly criticized by Muslims on religious and social grounds. Habibie, moreover, was often mentioned as Suharto's likely choice for Vice-President in 1998. Habibie, however, came under pressure from mid-1995. Senior military figures publicly reaffirmed the armed forces' commitment to Golkar, raising the possibility that they might try to displace the civilian Chairman, Harmoko, considered an ally of Habibie, at the next congress. Harmoko himself attracted public opprobrium in July when he misquoted a common Muslim prayer. Several incidents, moreover, illustrated the Government's determination not to allow greater openness to move very far towards political liberalization. In June 1994 Harmoko, who was also the Minister of Information, revoked the publishing licences of three widely-read weekly newspapers, including the well-established and respected journal, *Tempo*. The ban was believed to stem from *Tempo*'s coverage of a controversial decision to purchase for the armed forces 39 warships from the former East German navy, in which Habibie had played a major role. Harmoko's ban was overruled by a Jakarta court in May 1995, but in June 1996 the Supreme Court upheld a government appeal against this decision. Later in 1995 three members of the Alliance of Independent Journalists, which had been formed in August 1994 in the wake of the *Tempo* ban, were arrested and charged with displaying 'public hatred' for the Government. In May 1996 the founder of the Partai Uni Demokrasi Indonesia, Sri Bintang Pamungkas, was sentenced to nearly three years' imprisonment on dubious charges of insulting the President. Leading military figures also continued to draw public attention to an allegedly dangerous clandestine opposition linked to the banned communist party. Accusations of membership of what were called *organisasi tanpa bentuk* or 'formless organizations' were used in an attempt to discredit critics of the Government, such as the academic, George Aditjondro, the trade unionist, Muchtar Pakpahan, and the novelist, Pramoedya Ananta Toer. Government figures also publicly threatened several non-governmental organizations active in human rights and environmental issues, especially the Legal Aid Institute (LBH) and the environmental forum (WALHI). In August 1996 an investigative journalist writing on land affairs, Fuad Muhammad Syafruddin, died after an attack on his home by an unidentified intruder. The security forces also targeted radical Islamic groups for arrests and interrogations. On several occasions in the 1990s members of the security forces were punished for their roles in killing demonstrators, but for the most part the penalties imposed were slight in comparison with those imposed on the demonstrators themselves. Cynicism about the legal process was also exacerbated by the escape from Cipinang prison of Eddy Tansil, a businessman serving a 20-year sentence for defrauding a state bank of US $430m. A subsequent investigation revealed that Tansil had enjoyed substantial privileges during his imprisonment.

With the *Pancasila's* plausibility on the wane, and in the context of increased popular expectations of government propriety, these events provoked an increasing dissatisfaction with the 'New Order', despite its clear economic achievements. This dissatisfaction was compounded by a growing awareness of the extent to which Suharto's family members had profited from their position. Three of Suharto's six children, in particular, had built up substantial and diverse business interests based apparently on privileged access to government contracts, licences and subsidies: the President's youngest son, Hutomo ('Tommy') Mandala Putra, for example, had obtained exclusive rights for the purchase of cloves from farmers, which he then exploited in order to make substantial profits from resale to industrial users. Friends of the President, whose business interests were intertwined with those of his children, profited from monopolies over flour, tin-plate, plywood and many other important commodities. Even in the late 1980s, there was a consensus that curbing the privileges of Suharto's children would be the single most popular measure that any new President could take; it was also widely felt that Suharto was holding on to power to give his children time to consolidate their positions as legitimate business-owners, so that they would continue to prosper once he was no longer President.

During the 1990s, however, there were increasing indications that Suharto was not simply aiming to consolidate his family's economic position, but was planning in due course to transfer power to a small coterie of his family and friends. In October 1993 leadership positions in Golkar were assumed by two of Suharto's own children and seven children of former government figures close to Suharto. At the same time, the President also removed or transferred a number of senior military figures linked to the campaign that had installed Gen. Try Sutrisno as Vice-President, and he appeared to be promoting his son-in-law, Gen. Prabowo Subianto, the head of the army's special forces, as a military guarantor for his family's fortunes under the next President.

As the 1997 parliamentary elections approached, the new leader of the PDI, Megawati Sukarnoputri, appeared to be the main beneficiary of this discontent. Taking advantage of somewhat romanticized memories of her father as a President who cared for the underprivileged, she appeared likely to lead the PDI to a record vote, and there was even speculation that her party would nominate her as a presidential candidate in 1998. To avoid this possibility, government figures began to organize a series of manoeuvres to destroy Megawati's power. First, officials in East Java allowed internal party opponents of Megawati to establish a rival regional board, and prohibited her from visiting the province to seek a resolution. Not only was East Java Indonesia's most populous province, and one of its richest, but the President's daughter, Siti Hardiyanti Rukmana (Tutut), was Golkar's campaign director there for the 1997 elections, and the Government appeared determined to ensure that the relatively disappointing Golkar result in East Java in 1992 was not repeated. In June 1996 government supporters within the PDI engineered a special party congress of dubious legality, which removed Megawati as leader and installed her predecessor, Soerjadi. A sharp attack on Megawati by the Commander-in-Chief of the Armed Forces, Gen. Feisal Tanjung, an invited speaker at the congress, indicated the end of a period in which army figures saw her as a useful balance to Habibie and the dominant civilian group in Golkar. As the congress met, however, Megawati mobilized her supporters in rallies in Jakarta and other cities, prepared court cases to reclaim the party leadership and asserted publicly that the PDI would win 80%–85% of the vote if free and fair elections were held. She also announced that her opponents had been expelled from the party, and refused to surrender the party headquarters to them. The NU leader, Abdurrahman Wahid, meanwhile signed a remarkable public petition warning that the Government's authoritarian nature, and its tolerance of social injustice, threatened to create a culture of violence in Indonesia.

On 27 July 1996 armed vigilantes from the Soerjadi faction stormed the PDI headquarters in Jakarta, with military support, evicting Megawati's supporters and provoking two days of rioting in the capital. Disturbances on a smaller scale continued in other cities during the following weeks. To defuse the growing conflict with the Megawati faction, the Government moved quickly to blame the disturbances on the underground PRD, which was portrayed as a successor to the Communist Party. The PRD leader, Budiman Sudjatmiko, and other prominent activists were arrested; in April 1997 they were convicted of subversion and given sentences ranging from three to 15 years. By contrast, most PDI members arrested at the same time were acquitted or given token sentences. Megawati herself was careful not to encourage violence, and tried to have her exclusion from the party overruled in the courts. None the less, in October 1996 the courts refused to hear Megawati's case; she was not permitted to recover any of her former influence in the party, and she and her supporters were excluded from the PDI candidate lists for the forthcoming general election. The authorities also prevented her supporters from opening a rival party headquarters.

The misfortunes of the PDI reinvigorated the PPP, which had suffered from internal division and lack of funds and which had been humiliated in previous months by the public defection to Golkar of several former leading supporters. The dour personality of the party Chairman, Ismael Hassan Metareum, once a liability, now enhanced the party's image as a serious contestant, but the PPP benefited most of all from growing signs that it was winning the support of discontented PDI supporters. As the election approached, a widespread, illicit and parallel campaign developed under the slogan 'Mega-Bintang', literally 'superstar', but in this context an encouragement to Megawati supporters to vote for the PPP, whose electoral symbol is a star. PPP rallies were massively attended, and it appeared that the PPP might possibly oust Golkar from first place in the Jakarta capital district, which it had not done since 1982.

Soerjadi's standing was further weakened in October 1996, when the National Commission on Human Rights published a report on the events of July which concluded that the raid on the PDI headquarters had not been carried out by Soerjadi supporters but by specially-recruited thugs with military backing. This analysis was confirmed shortly before the 1997 election, when persons involved in the action complained publicly that they had still not been paid for their services. The report blamed the subsequent riots directly on government provocation, rather than on allegedly subversive groups such as the PRD, and concluded with a recommendation that those involved in the seizure should be prosecuted.

The months leading up to the election witnessed several outbreaks of religious and ethnic tension. In Situbondo (East Java) in October 1996, Tasikmalaya (West Java) in December, and Rengasdengklok (West Java) in January 1997, Muslim mobs burned churches, temples and shops associated with local Chinese Indonesians. There was further violence in the PPP stronghold of Pekalongan (Central Java) in March and May. Yet more serious was a prolonged clash between indigenous Dayaks and Madurese immigrants in the province of West Kalimantan, which lasted from December 1996 until March 1997. Several hundred people were killed, several thousand fled their homes and there were rumours of cannibalism and the ritual mutilation of victims' corpses.

The Government formally permitted an election campaign period of 25 days before the poll on 29 May 1997, but Golkar (and, to a much lesser extent, the PPP) began campaigning earlier by holding supposedly closed 'meetings with cadres'. In Central Java, moreover, the provincial Government launched a major programme to paint public objects yellow, the Golkar colour. During the official campaign period itself the Government imposed a strict roster so that no two parties were campaigning in the same region on the same day, thus effectively allowing each party only eight or nine days campaigning in each province. As in previous elections, the authorities maintained a visibly heavy security presence, both to prevent disturbances and to create an atmosphere of threat, but there was extensive localized violence in Jakarta and some other centres. The campaign was notable for the extent to which both Golkar and the PPP campaigned with promises of specific actions, such as improving education or public transport (in past elections, the contestants were generally barred from making specific policy proposals and had instead resorted to more general appeals); Golkar figures also issued barely-veiled threats that areas failing to support Golkar would receive fewer development funds. The PDI campaign, by contrast, was lacklustre, and was further undermined by Megawati's announcement shortly before polling that she would abstain from voting.

In the event, the election delivered an unprecedented victory to Golkar, which won every province and received 74.51% of the votes nationally. The PPP also improved its performance, winning 22.43% (up from 15.97% in 1992), while the PDI vote plummeted to 3.07% from its previous figure of 14.9%. Soerjadi himself failed to win a seat. The result greatly disappointed PPP supporters, who had expected to win about 35% of the vote and who at once accused the Government of fraud and manipulation. According to official figures, 93.38% of the electorate took part in the election. However, it was widely rumoured that many government officials had voted twice—at home and at the office—and that counting procedures had been fraudulent. Party supporters in Madura rioted and destroyed ballot boxes, forcing a repoll in some districts.

The election victory appeared to leave President Suharto firmly in control of the political order; immediately after the election, he further confirmed his authority by transferring the victorious Golkar Chairman, Harmoko, from his post as Minister of Information to the ill-defined position of Minister of State for Special Affairs. (Subsequently, in October 1997, Harmoko was appointed Speaker of the Legislature.) The dissident PRD was formally banned in September and the formal process leading to Suharto's nomination for a seventh term as President began in October. However, the social tensions that had preceded the election failed to dissipate; three days of anti-Chinese violence rocked Ujung Pandang and there was widespread anticipation of further unrest. The sense of foreboding was exacerbated by serious forest fires in Sumatra, Kalimantan, Irian Jaya and elsewhere, which covered large areas of the archipelago with a thick blanket of smoke, often for periods of several weeks. The unrestrained clearing of forest (much of it previously logged) and of swamp areas for agricultural projects was acknowledged as the principal cause of the fires: a large-scale plan to grow rice on what were once the peat swamps of Central Kalimantan appeared to have been the origin of much of the devastation, although the rapid expansion of rubber and oil palm plantations was also blamed. The smoke from the fires seriously hampered communications, forcing the cancellation of hundreds of commercial airline flights and paralysing tourism in many areas of the country. The cost in terms of damage to the health of 60m.–80m. people cannot be calculated. Although fires affected some areas in Java, the capital, Jakarta, was largely unaffected, and the authorities showed little intention of taking any action to address the problem, relying instead on the anticipated onset of the annual rains in December.

During the same period, Indonesia was being drawn steadily into the economic crisis that had begun in Thailand in mid-1997. Although the decline in the value of the rupiah was partly a consequence of 'contagion' from the rest of the region, it was also exacerbated by international concerns over the high levels of indebtedness amongst large Indonesian companies, many of which were associated with President Suharto's circle. The decline in the rupiah worsened the debt crisis, forcing Indonesia to request assistance from the IMF in October. The resulting IMF rescue programme, however, went much further than the Government had expected, demanding a substantial limitation of the privileges enjoyed by Suharto's family and friends and also a reduction in government expenditure in areas that were an important source of patronage, both within and outside élite circles.

The crisis had immediate and far-reaching implications for the economy. External credit for Indonesian companies dried up, and even those firms that were not seriously indebted were unable to obtain finance for routine operations. Factories and construction projects were closed down, forcing millions of workers out of employment. The price of imported goods (including staples such as wheat flour) rose dramatically, compounding the hardship. Unrest spread rapidly, precipitating riots in dozens of cities and towns across the archipelago. Shops and other businesses owned by members of the Chinese community, who were blamed for increasing prices and accused of sending money out of the country, were especially targeted. The crisis worsened as it became clear that the Suharto Government did not intend to implement the IMF programme rapidly or sincerely, and as international money markets forced the value of the rupiah still lower. By mid-January 1998 an extensive range of public figures had begun to urge Suharto to step down at the MPR session scheduled for March 1998. In the last week of January the markets drove the rupiah down to an unprecedented 15,000 to the US dollar, after Suharto indicated that he would choose as his Vice-President the Minister of State for Research and Technology, B. J. Habibie, whose reputation as a proponent of economic nationalism and expensive technological projects ran directly counter to the IMF's insistence on economic austerity and openness.

Both inside and outside Indonesia, at this point, there was hope that the President would respond to the obvious discontent with imaginative and responsible measures, but also fear of cataclysmic disorder if he were to step down. Two of the main opposition leaders, the ousted PDI leader, Megawati Sukarnoputri, and the leader of the Muhammadiyah, Amien Rais, began to collaborate and both gave support to a common opposition movement called Siaga. A third influential leader, Abdurrahman Wahid of the Nahdlatul Ulama, was more hesitant, however, and his political career received a temporary set-back when he suffered a severe stroke in January 1998. As the election approached, the growing sentiment in favour of a new President also fuelled a short-lived movement to secure the selection of Emil Salim, a respected economist and former Minister of the Environment who had spoken out publicly in favour of reform, as Vice-President; with Suharto firmly in control of the MPR, however, this movement made no progress. On 10 March Suharto was duly re-elected as President. Habibie was installed as Vice-President. As a concession to the President's increasing frailty, it was announced that Habibie would take charge of multilateral international relations; however, there was no indication that he would take any significant role in administration. In February, prior to the election, Suharto had consolidated his position by appointing his son-in-law, Gen. Prabowo, as head of the army's strategic reserve, KOSTRAD. Following his election victory, Suharto further strengthened his position by appointing a Cabinet that concentrated power in his immediate circle of friends and family but which left Habibie's followers rather poorly represented: Suharto's business associate, Mohamad 'Bob' Hasan, became Minister of Trade and Industry; his daughter, Tutut, became Minister of Social Affairs; and Tutut's close friend, Gen. (retd) Hartono, assumed the influential home affairs portfolio.

The composition of the new Cabinet, together with the fact that the main points of continuing dispute between the IMF and the Suharto Government concerned the economic privileges that continued to be enjoyed by Suharto's family members and associates, largely exhausted any hopes that Suharto himself might permit significant political and economic reforms in Indonesia. The IMF appeared to acknowledge this by conceding much ground in a new agreement with the Indonesian Government reached in April 1998. Within the country, however, a ground swell of discontent was emerging, expressed first in a growing number of student demonstrations in the cities and subsequently in riots in centres across the archipelago. Meanwhile, the political opposition to Suharto grew more confident, with Amien Rais taking a particularly prominent role and abandoning his former Islamist stridency. In a process reminiscent of the events of 1965, disparate opposition groups played down their differences and adopted a single slogan, *reformasi* (reform), as a code for the simple goal of removing Suharto from office. As the popular movement against Suharto gathered momentum, signs of disunity began to appear within the military: elements of the armed forces launched a campaign of kidnapping, torture and intimidation of student activists, but on 1 May 1998 the armed forces chief of staff, Gen. Wiranto, disavowed the kidnappings and announced an inquiry into them. The Government appeared also to be giving ground: in late April the Minister of Justice, Muladi, promised unspecified reforms; his promises were echoed by Hartono. The timetable for and the extent of such reforms was kept vague, however.

On 5 May 1998, when the Government announced a 70% increase in fuel prices as part of its agreement with the IMF to cut state subsidies, the violence escalated abruptly. As in January, the main targets of the violence were members of Indonesia's ethnic Chinese minority. In April and early May tens of thousands of Chinese Indonesians fled to neighbouring Singapore and Malaysia in search of refuge from the violence. Within days of the riots of 5 May, members of the legislature, senior figures from within the regime, and even Vice-President Habibie's ICMI, began to demand immediate reform. Some military units were even seen enthusiastically greeting student protesters and protecting them from riot police. Suharto's departure from the country on 9 May for a meeting of the G-15 group (of leaders of developing countries) in Cairo, Egypt, aroused speculation that he might choose to stay in exile. As the violence continued, however, alternative speculation emerged that pro-Suharto elements in the military were deliberately exacerbating the unrest to provide the pretext for a military crack-down, out of which Gen. Prabowo would emerge to wield greater power. Street violence in Jakarta reached a peak on 14 May, when armed gangs took control of large parts of the city. An estimated 500 people died; 3,000 buildings were burnt and many thousands of vehicles were also destroyed. A further 700 people were reported to have been killed in other centres.

On 18 May 1998, three days after Suharto's return from Cairo, his former supporter, Harmoko, astounded observers by demanding the President's resignation and by then publicly threatening Suharto with impeachment if he failed to step down. Suharto endeavoured to recover the initiative by offering immediate political reforms, including the appointment of a new Cabinet, and the holding of an election in early 1999, followed by an MPR session to elect a new President; he also reversed the fuel price increase, the original announcement of which had precipitated the worst disturbances. Although these pledges won the apparent support of Gen. Wiranto and of NU leader, Abdurrahman Wahid, both of whom feared that instability would ensue if Suharto were to resign abruptly, they failed to appease the protest movement. Finally, following the resignation on the evening of 20 May of the 14 economic ministers in Suharto's Cabinet, Gen. Wiranto visited the President late at night to inform him that the military could no longer guarantee security in Jakarta if he remained in office. The following morning Suharto announced his resignation, stating 'I find it difficult to carry out my duty as the country's ruler'. Vice-President Habibie was sworn in immediately as his successor, and Gen. Wiranto promised to defend Suharto and his family.

PRESIDENT B. J. HABIBIE, 1998–99

Suharto's resignation certainly saved Indonesia from even greater turmoil; however, it also raised new uncertainties. President Habibie's relations with the armed forces were considered poor following the naval acquisitions issue of 1994, his capacity to manage the economy was widely doubted in view of his reputation for promoting prestigious but costly projects, and he was also widely perceived as a protégé of his predecessor and as possibly no more than a tool, subject to continuing manipulation by Suharto. In the event, Habibie managed his first months in office rather astutely, balancing the continuing demand for reform against the power of entrenched interests. He at once dubbed his Government the 'Reform Order', and supported Gen. Wiranto in his dismissal of Suharto's son-in-law, Gen. Prabowo, from his command position in KOSTRAD (Prabowo was dismissed from the armed forces in August 1998 and subsequently went into exile in Jordan). Habibie also released prominent political prisoners, including Muchtar Pakpahan and Sri Bintang Pamungkas, encouraged government departments to sever their business ties with enterprises owned by the Suharto family, and foreshadowed the implementation of electoral reform, with the announcement that new elections would take place in 1999. The President also visited homes and businesses in Jakarta's Chinatown, which had been attacked in the riots of May 1998, and publicly expressed his sympathy for the plight of ethnic Chinese victims of the violence. In June the Government announced a liberalization of the censorship laws and an investigation into the wealth of state officials, and it was widely rumoured that the Suharto family interests were also to be subject to investigation. However, both the extent and the timetable of most of these reforms fell short of the demands that students and others had made of the Suharto regime, and there was widespread impatience with the pace of change under Habibie.

In the early days of his presidency, Habibie announced that he would not serve out the remainder of Suharto's term (1998–2003), and called a special session of the MPR on 10–13 November 1998 to authorize the holding of new parliamentary elections. The MPR limited the President and Vice-President to a maximum of two five-year terms of office each, decreed that the number of seats in the DPR held by nominated representatives of the military should be reduced, and provided for the establishment of a Commission on General Elections (Komisi Pemilihan Umum, KPU), within which all contesting parties would be represented, to oversee the poll. Greatest attention focused, however, on the revised election laws, which were drafted by a committee of academic experts known as the Team of Seven and approved with some significant amendments by the DPR on 28 January 1999. The new law relating to political parties provided that only parties with branches in at least nine of the country's 27 provinces would be permitted to contest the election and that they should have branches in at least half the districts in those provinces; this measure was intended to ensure that only parties with a national orientation would contest the election. In addition, the law provided that a party must win at least 2% of the seats in the MPR to be permitted to compete in the elections scheduled for 2004. Although candidates were required to be 'loyal to the *Pancasila*' and the Communist Party remained banned, the former requirement that all political organizations accept the *Pancasila* as their sole basic principle gave way to the milder provision that the parties should certify that their principles and programmes did not contradict the *Pancasila*. In contrast with previous elections, at which government employees had been impelled to support Golkar, the new laws prohibited Indonesia's 4.1m. civil servants on active duty from campaigning. In addition, the armed forces announced that they would maintain neutrality in the election.

Although the Team of Seven proposed that a predominantly district-based system of election should replace the proportional system of the Suharto era (in which each province effectively constituted a single electorate), the DPR retained the proportional system, with the complex proviso that each party should link each candidate to a district and that the successful candidates would be drawn from the districts where the party had performed best. The DPR also preserved a long-standing arrangement which gave extra weighting to provinces in the more sparsely-populated outer islands over those in densely-populated Java. Following intense debate and vehement student protests, the DPR agreed to reduce the number of seats in the legislature allocated to the military from 75 to 38; in addition, the military presence in provincial and district assemblies was reduced from 20% to 10%. It was also announced that the membership of the MPR was to be reduced from 1,000 to 700 (500 of whom would comprise the members of the DPR while, of the remainder, 135 were to be elected by the provincial assemblies and 65 appointed by the KPU to represent social organizations).

Soon after May 1998, in anticipation of the new laws, political parties began to form on a wide variety of ideological, ethnic and religious bases. By early 1999 more than 200 new parties had been created; however, only 48 met the criteria for competing in the forthcoming election. Most observers agreed that Megawati's wing of the PDI, reconstituted as the PDI—Perjuangan (PDI—P—Struggle PDI) would perform well, and that the Partai Kebangkitan Bangsa (PKB, National Awakening Party) of Abdurrahman Wahid had a secure base amongst the traditionalist rural Muslims of East Java; the potential of the other parties, including Golkar, however, remained extremely uncertain. Particularly unclear was whether Golkar's prestige as the party of government would help it to survive the loss of military and civil service support and the defection of former supporters to new parties. This uncertainty bedevilled attempts by the parties to foreshadow the kind of partners they might seek to work with after the election, in the likely event that no party won a majority. A semi-formal alliance between party leaders Megawati, Amien Rais and Abdurrahman Wahid showed signs of serious strains as soon as it was announced. A further source of tension and uncertainty was the position of former President Suharto. Although Gen. Wiranto had promised to defend Suharto and his family following the transfer of the presidency to Habibie, the latter's Government faced enormous public pressure to investigate the Suharto family's accumulation of wealth during the era of the New Order. Suharto himself denied any wrong-doing, but the slow progress of investigations by the Attorney General and the lack of any clear results gave rise to strong suspicions that the Habibie Government was not being as thorough in its investigation as perhaps it might, possibly out of fear that too close an examination might compromise other leading government figures. Although the former President and several members of his family were questioned, at mid-1999 only Suharto's youngest son, Hutomo ('Tommy') Mandala Putra, faced prosecution (see below). There was also suspicion that Suharto retained considerable informal influence over the military and in some civilian circles and that he was using this influence not only to protect himself but to maintain a sway over political developments.

Meanwhile, serious violence broke out in several parts of the country. In Jakarta in mid-November 1998, in the worst violence since the riots of May, at least 16 people were killed and more than 400 injured when students and civilians clashed with soldiers outside the building where a four-day special session of the MPR was being held. Further riots occurred in Jakarta in late November, in which at least another 14 people died during confrontations between Muslims and Christians. In East Java in late 1998 at least 182 Muslim clerics and alleged black magicians were killed over a period of several months in a spate of savage and apparently organized murders blamed on unidentified 'ninja' and verified by an official investigation in December 1998 (the investigation failed, however, to draw any conclusion as to the identity of the perpetrators). In Maluku violent clashes between Muslims and Christians broke out in early 1999, with several hundred deaths reported; a number of those who died were killed by the military, who were drafted into the region in an attempt to restore order. Meanwhile, in West Kalimantan, indigenous Dayaks resumed their hunting of Madurese settlers, this time with support from the majority Malay population; by late March, more than 165 Madurese were reported to have been killed, with numerous reports of the mutilation and cannibalization of the bodies of many of the victims. Many thousands of Madurese fled the province.

In the countryside, moreover, dozens of land disputes erupted, a legacy of the high-handed expropriation of landowners during the Suharto era and a disturbing reminder of the bitter land conflicts of the early 1960s. In some regions there were violent protests against corrupt or oppressive local officials, or against destructive or polluting factories. Gen. Wiranto's proposal to counter such violence by establishing a 40,000-strong civilian auxiliary militia was met with some incredulity. Also in early 1999 it emerged that the military's prestige and self-confidence had been damaged by its association with political repression during the Suharto years to a greater extent than anticipated, and the armed forces remained uncertain of how best to fulfil their role. Particularly significant in provoking a questioning of the role and conduct of the armed forces was the publication in November 1998 of a report containing the findings of a panel appointed by the Government to investigate the riots in May: while the report gave no single figure for the number of people killed or injured, the panel found that elements of the military had acted as provocateurs during the riots (with particular suspicion falling on a unit led by Gen. Prabowo) and concluded that the riots had been 'created as part of a political struggle at the level of the élite'. (The panel recommended that further investigation be carried out into the causes of the violent unrest and also found, contrary to earlier official statements, that a number of rapes had taken place during the riots.) Military leaders announced that they would 'redefine, reposition and reactualize' their place in Indonesian society, implying that their role in politics and administration would be diminished, but the precise nature of any intended changes was far from clear. In an attempt to reduce the military's association with petty repression, the police force (part of the military since 1962) was formally separated from the armed forces on 1 April 1999; however, the police force remained under the control of the Ministry of Defence. The armed forces also resumed their revolutionary-era name, Tentara Nasional Indonesia (TNI—the Indonesian National Defence Forces), in place of the Suharto-era name, ABRI (the Armed Forces of the Republic of Indonesia).

Although the election campaign dominated politics during the first half of 1999, the Habibie Government continued an extensive programme of reform. In April the DPR passed a new law providing for the election of district heads (*bupati*) by the district assemblies, rather than through appointment by Jakarta, and transferring a wide range of administrative functions to the provinces and districts (*kabupaten* and *kotamadya*); another law provided that provinces would receive a greater share of revenue from natural resources such as oil, gas, fisheries and timber. In a presidential decree announced in May, Habibie removed a ban on the use and teaching of the Mandarin Chinese language and also outlawed discrimination on the grounds of ethnic origin. Given the level of tension prevalent throughout the archipelago, the election campaign itself proceeded with surprising calm. Although some violent clashes occurred, the various parties were aware that widespread violence might well result in the cancellation of the elections and consequently kept outdoor rallies to a minimum. The PDI—P's campaign emphasized the party's commitment to extensive reform and the righting of the injustices of the Suharto era, while the Golkar campaign focused on a promise of moderate reform, stability and the administrative experience of the party. To varying degrees, the Muslim parties stressed the need to strengthen the Islamic character of the State, and accused the PDI—P of being dominated by Christians, Hindus and non-committed Muslims. These accusations in turn reinforced the PDI—P's standing as the party most likely to defend religious and ethnic minorities, although initially it remained vehemently opposed to any fragmentation of the country.

The day on which the polls were held, 7 June 1999, was declared a public holiday in order to eliminate any potential intimidation of voters by their employers. Approximately 118m. people voted (a turn-out of 91%). The final results of the poll were not announced until mid-July. Although foreign observers had pronounced the election itself fair, the subsequent delay in the announcement of the outcome gave rise to suspicions that results were being tampered with. None the less, most observers concluded that the slowness was a consequence of lack of infrastructure (the military communications facilities used in previous counts were not available) and of inexperience. The slow accumulation of voting tallies allowed the public to adjust to some unexpected results: although Megawati's PDI—P led the poll as expected, with 34% of the votes, its nearest rival proved to be Golkar, whose sluggish performance in much of Java, especially in the cities, was balanced by the achievement of impressive results in the outer islands, especially in eastern Indonesia. Although Golkar received 20% of the national vote, the weighting given to outer islands meant that the party won 120 seats (26% of the total) as compared with the PDI—P's 154. As expected, Abdurrahman Wahid's PKB did well in East Java, but the Partai Amanat Nasional (PAN, National Mandate Party) of Amien Rais performed relatively poorly, receiving only 7% of the vote. Formerly closely associated with the modernist Muslim Muhammadiyah movement and with arguments for making Indonesia more clearly Muslim, Rais had campaigned energetically and had sought to broaden his appeal to Christians, Chinese and more secular Muslims; however, this strategy appeared to cause the alienation of his own base while failing to allay the suspicions of those other constituencies. In third place in the poll was the PPP, the principal Muslim party of the Suharto era, with 11% of the vote and 59 seats. The party had campaigned on general Islamic principles without defining a clear ideology, but it appeared to have benefited from its reputation for defying Suharto during the New Order era and its consistent reformist position in the MPR following Habibie's accession to the Presidency, as well as from its well-developed national organization. In addition to these five parties, some 14 smaller parties won seats in the MPR (although their combined share of the vote was only about 7%). A number of small parties, some of which had failed to win a seat, withheld formal ratification of the election results, but they were subsequently overruled by President Habibie, who finally endorsed the results on 3 August.

During the election campaign, each of the parties nominated a preferred candidate for the presidency, which was originally scheduled to be decided by the MPR in November 1999. The Indonesian Constitution provided no clear guidance on whether the successful candidate would require a majority of votes in the MPR or merely a plurality; however, in mid-1999 there existed a general consensus that the next President would need a base of support broader than any single party and that extensive negotiations would be necessary to construct any potential coalition. With the PDI—P and Golkar leading the polls, Megawati and Habibie initially emerged as the main candidates for the presidency. Habibie's prospects, however, were seriously damaged by factionalism within Golkar and by allegations that he had helped to channel funds originally intended for the recapitalization of the struggling Bank Bali into his wing of Golkar. He was also widely perceived to have mishandled the East Timor issue: many Indonesians felt that the country had been humiliated by the overwhelming vote in favour of independence by the East Timorese in August 1999 and by the subsequent introduction of foreign peace-keeping troops into the territory. Megawati's prospects, meanwhile, were impaired by her apparent remoteness: she made few public speeches during the election campaign and showed no interest in lobbying other parties for support. Concealed threats from PDI—P members that there would be violence if she were not elected, and indications of 'money politics' in the PDI—P also raised doubts about Megawati's capacity to improve the standards of government if she were to come to power. Megawati's position was further weakened by the public statements of some Muslim leaders, including Abdurrahman Wahid, to the effect that a woman should not become President in a predominantly Muslim country.

Meanwhile, Amien Rais recovered from his electoral set-back by assembling a coalition of Muslim parties called Poros Tengah (Central Axis), which aimed to give its member parties a powerful collective voice in the proceedings, as a means of exerting pressure with a view to increasing future influence in government. As the date of the MPR vote approached, both Habibie and Megawati appeared increasingly unlikely to succeed; however, no clear alternatives had emerged. On 20 October 1999, only hours before the rescheduled vote was due to take place, Habibie withdrew his candidacy, following the rejection of his presidential record by the MPR in a secret ballot. Poros Tengah and much of Golkar then transferred their support to Abdurrahman Wahid (also known as Gus Dur), even though Wahid's party, the PKB, was not part of the Poros Tengah coalition. Wahid was subsequently elected President by the MPR, securing a total of 373 votes; Megawati received 313 votes. The announcement of Wahid's victory provoked outrage among Megawati's supporters, leading to violence in Jakarta and elsewhere. On 21 October, however, the MPR voted to appoint Megawati as Vice-President.

PRESIDENT ABDURRAHMAN WAHID, 1999–2001

President Wahid's new Cabinet, announced on 26 October 1999, was large (consisting of 36 members) and was drawn from many parties, reflecting both Wahid's desire to include in the new political order all the major forces in Indonesian society and to discharge the political debts he had incurred in winning the presidency. Poros Tengah, however, with more than one-third of the seats in the DPR, secured half the posts in the Cabinet, whereas Golkar, which held one-quarter of the elected seats in the DPR, was allocated only four positions in the Cabinet. Many observers questioned whether such a diverse and unwieldy Cabinet, led by a President who was blind and in ill health, would be capable of effectively addressing the country's pressing economic problems. However, President Wahid's tolerant, inclusive style of leadership initially appeared ideal for easing the political tensions that had developed during and after the Suharto era. Wahid's credentials as an opposition leader during the Suharto era were strong, but he made it clear that he had no interest in avenging the wrongs of the New Order; as a pious Muslim he was acceptable to Islamic modernists, but he also had a strong record of respect and tolerance for other religious traditions. Wahid continued President Habibie's policy of seeking to reintegrate the Chinese community into Indonesian political and cultural life, lifting restrictions on the public celebration of Chinese festivals and including a Chinese Indonesian, Kwik Kian Gie, in his Cabinet, in the senior post of Co-ordinating Minister for the Economy, Finance and Industry. He also invited Indonesians exiled by Suharto to return home. The President abolished the Ministries of Information and Social Affairs (both of which had been closely associated with the Suharto-era apparatus for the political control of society), and he regularly appeared before the legislature to answer questions on his administration. While the new President attempted a radical reform of the notoriously corrupt judiciary, he also appeared to have achieved some success in reducing the political power of the military. Although Gen. Wiranto became Co-ordinating Minister for Political Affairs and Security, and although six members of the new Cabinet had a military background, a civilian, Yuwono Sudarsono, held the post of Minister of Defence, and for the first time in recent history a naval officer, Adm. Widodo Adi Sutjipto, was appointed Commander-in-Chief of the Armed Forces. The number of military officers included in the presidential staff was also sharply reduced.

The President's commitment to regularizing the political order was undermined, however, by his own opaque political style. His public statements were often impulsive, contradictory and made without consulting his advisers or Cabinet. In November 1999, only a month after installing the Cabinet, Wahid dismissed the Co-ordinating Minister for People's Welfare and Poverty Alleviation, and PPP leader, Hamzah Haz, on unspecified charges of corruption, which were never pursued. The President appeared to veer between detachment from the process of government and undue intervention in administrative detail. Wahid was also rumoured to be manipulated by 'whisperers' who took advantage of his blindness to further their own political advantage, and doubts over his state of health were raised repeatedly. Meanwhile, hopes that Vice-President Megawati would take a more active role than her predecessors were disappointed, as she continued her inactive approach to politics. On the other hand, with a divided Cabinet, a passive Vice-President, and a vast civilian and military bureaucracy whose capacity and loyalty was in doubt, the President had little choice but to embark upon a complex series of manoeuvres, amid shifting alliances, to ensure that at least some of his policy goals were achieved.

In early 2000 Wahid removed Gen. Wiranto from his powerful cabinet position after Indonesia's National Human Rights Commission on 31 January found the General responsible for the violence that followed East Timor's referendum on independence in August 1999. Travelling in Europe and Asia at the time, the President announced that he had asked Wiranto to resign. Wiranto resisted, however, and over a period of nearly a fortnight the two men exchanged public comments through the media. Amid rumours of the possibility of a military coup, Wahid agreed on 13 February 2000 to allow Wiranto to retain his post until the Attorney-General had investigated the issue, but on the following day the Cabinet Secretary announced that Wiranto had been suspended from his position. He was replaced by the Minister of Home Affairs, Gen. (retd) Suryadi Sudirja. Wiranto subsequently resigned in mid-May.

Rivalry between ministers and lack of co-ordination between government departments became a serious problem, to the extent that the Minister of State for Regional Autonomy, Ryaas Rasyid, threatened to resign over the issue. Even before the end of 1999, moreover, allegations had begun to emerge of corruption and the abuse of power within the new Government. Many cabinet ministers appeared to be turning their departments into party fiefdoms, as had happened in the 1950s. In April 2000 President Wahid dismissed the Minister of State for Investment and Development of State Enterprises, Laksamana Sukardi of the PDI—P, and the Minister of Trade and Industry, Yusuf Kalla of the so-called 'black' (pro-Habibie) wing of Golkar, later suggesting that both Ministers were guilty of corruption. Such accusations had often been heard previously against Kalla. Sukardi, however, was a respected and capable Minister; his dismissal appeared to reflect the fact that he had pressed too hard for rapid reform and had thus lost support within his own party. Wahid shocked the legislature in July when he uncharacteristically refused to explain his reasons for dismissing the Ministers. Misgivings also grew over the increasing business activities of Wahid's own organization, the Nahdlatul Ulama, and of the President's brother, Hasyim Wahid, who, despite a lack of economic experience, had been secretly appointed adviser to the Indonesian Bank Restructuring Agency (IBRA). Still more disturbing was an affair in early 2000 in which the President's masseur, Suwondo, was alleged to have solicited US $4.1m. from the deputy chief of the state logistical agency, BULOG. According to official accounts, the funds were a 'private' bribe paid to Suwondo by the deputy chief of the agency, Sapuan, who was subsequently formally dismissed from his post. The Sultan of Brunei was also reported to have illegally given US $2m. to Wahid for unspecified purposes. Wahid's appointment of the NU chairperson, Rozy Munir, as Minister for State Industries also encouraged rumours that he intended to exploit those industries—traditionally a major source of graft—for the NU's use in future election campaigns. In addition, the President appeared to be seeking ways to protect some of the most heavily-indebted Suharto-era business conglomerates from the full effects of economic restructuring. Observers suspected that he anticipated substantial donations to the PKB in return.

By mid-2000 President Wahid's political 'honeymoon' was clearly over, and there was growing speculation over whether the forces unhappy with his policies and style of leadership might combine to remove him from office. Wahid was summoned to give an account of his actions at the annual MPR session on 7–18 August, but escaped formal censure, as party leaders feared that action against him might precipitate mass unrest, and because they obtained what they believed was a promise from Wahid to relinquish major policy-making powers to Megawati. With the MPR session safely over, however, he claimed that only 'administrative' duties, and not decision-making powers, were to be transferred to the Vice-President, and on 23 August 2000 he announced the formation of a new 26-member Cabinet. The incoming Cabinet included considerably fewer representatives of Megawati's PDI—P, reportedly resulting in serious tensions between the President and the Vice-President. Two of the most influential cabinet posts were allocated to Wahid loyalists: Susilo Bambang Yudhoyono was appointed Co-ordinating Minister for Political Affairs, Security and Social Welfare, while Rizal Ramli was designated Co-ordinating Minister for the Economy, Finance and Industry, replacing Kwik Kian Gie, who had previously resigned from the post. The lack of a clear alternative candidate for the presidency, however, remained one of Wahid's strengths.

The investigation of alleged wrongdoing by former President Suharto, which had stalled under President Habibie, resumed under President Wahid. Suharto suffered a stroke in 1999, which reportedly impaired his speech, and he twice failed to appear for questioning by the Attorney-General's Office, his lawyers arguing that he was too ill. In April 2000 the former President was banned from leaving Jakarta. The Attorney-General announced in July that Suharto would go on trial in August. President Wahid had previously stated, however, that the formal establishment of Suharto's guilt was more important than any punishment and had declared that he would pardon the former President if he were found guilty.

The most serious problem facing the Wahid Government, however, was the rise of communal violence in Maluku, where Christians and Muslims were in approximately equal numbers. Hostility between the two communities was based partly on traditional rivalries, exacerbated by a rise of religious orthodoxy on both sides. Migration into the province by Muslim traders during recent decades and the growing administrative dominance of Muslim officials had also served to accentuate the Christians' increasing sense of being beleaguered. However, the violence was precipitated principally by rivalry between Christian and Muslim gangs in Jakarta and in the provincial capital, Ambon, and then exacerbated by rumours of the massacre, rape and torture of members of each religious community and the desecration of places of worship. Sporadic violence following the fall of Suharto developed into a local civil war, with Christian and Muslim militias launching attacks on each other's villages and places of worship. By the end of 2001 more than 6,000 people were reported to have been killed, some 500,000 had been displaced, downtown Ambon had been destroyed, and the province was becoming increasingly partitioned into separate Christian and Muslim cantons. The formal separation of the predominantly Muslim northern districts of the region as the new province of North Maluku in late 1999 did nothing to resolve the tensions. Given the army's record of aggravating tensions in Aceh and Irian Jaya, the President was reluctant to yield to military calls for the introduction of martial law in Maluku. In July 2000, however, Wahid also rejected suggestions that UN troops be sent to the province to quell the violence. Wahid placed Vice-President Megawati in charge of seeking a solution to the violence, but her limited activities had no apparent effect on the tensions, and her demonstrated lack of commitment to the project was widely criticized. In May 2000 local Muslims were joined by a so-called Laskar Jihad (Holy War Militia) from Java, which eventually numbered an estimated 3,000 fighters. There was much speculation that the violence in the province was being encouraged by external forces, perhaps with a view to destabilizing the Wahid Government, or perhaps simply for local commercial reasons. By mid-2000 clear evidence had emerged that local army units were supporting the Muslims whilst the local police backed the Christians.

Meanwhile, levels of violence throughout the archipelago increased considerably. Bombs exploded in Jakarta on several occasions. In January 2000 Muslim demonstrators launched arson attacks on churches and Christian businesses in Lombok, and there were many reports of new militia groups training in Java. Members of the Cabinet also regularly received death threats. In May the offices of the Surabaya-based newspaper, the *Jawa Pos*, which had published accusations of corruption against President Wahid and his relatives, were attacked by a paramilitary force associated with Wahid's supporters. A series of apparently co-ordinated bomb blasts at Jakarta churches on Christmas Eve 2000 claimed 16 lives. Communal violence reportedly resulted in the deaths of 200 people in Sulawesi in June. Furthermore, clashes between indigenous Dayaks and immigrant Madurese in West Kalimantan claimed an estimated 500 lives in February 2001, and about 50,000 Madurese were displaced. Many of the bombings showed a degree of technical sophistication that aroused suspicions that sections of the military might have been involved. The violence and general insecurity across the archipelago was estimated to have displaced perhaps 1m. people in 18 provinces.

During his first year in office, Wahid attempted to establish greater control over the military by supporting the promotion of reforming officers, but these attempts generated a hostile reaction in military circles. The August 2000 session of the MPR was also perceived to have made a number of concessions to the military, including the introduction of a constitutional amendment that excluded military personnel from prosecution for crimes committed prior to the enactment of the legislation used to prosecute them; this particular amendment was feared by many international observers seriously to threaten the possibility of the prosecution of members of the Indonesian military believed responsible for recent human rights violations in the former province of East Timor. Doubts concerning the commitment of the Indonesian Government to the trial of military personnel suspected of involvement in gross human rights violations in East Timor were further consolidated in early September when Gen. Wiranto's name was not included in a list announced by the Attorney-General's office of 19 suspects named in connection with such violations. Legislation was also passed to extend military representation in the MPR until 2009, four years after the date at which the military had been scheduled to lose its remaining 38 seats in the House.

Potentially even more important than reforms to the military, however, was the process of administrative decentralization implemented under Wahid's presidency. Planning for a greater delegation of authority to district and municipality governments (the administrative level below the provinces) had begun under Suharto, and enabling legislation was passed during Habibie's term. A specifically appointed State Minister for Regional Autonomy, Ryaas Rasyid, oversaw early preparations for decentralization. In one of Wahid's arbitrary changes of direction, however, Rasyid was shifted to an unrelated portfolio in August 2000. The decision to devolve authority to Indonesia's approximately 350 districts and municipalities, rather than to provinces, was taken to diminish the risk that the provinces might develop a desire for self-rule and attempt to secede, but it raised serious questions over the administrative capacity of such small units and over the likely social consequences for resource-poor districts. Popular aspirations, moreover, continued to focus on the provincial level, with public pressure leading to the establishment of three new provinces (Gorontalo, Banten and Bangka-Belitung) in late 2000, with strong campaigns under way for the creation of several more.

On 31 August 2000 the trial of former President Suharto was adjourned for a fortnight after the defendant, who in early August had been formally charged with corruption arising from his 30 years in power, failed to appear in court to hear the charges against him. Following claims by Suharto's lawyers that their client was seriously ill and not fit to stand trial, the judge allowed the defence team two weeks in which to prepare the testimony of the former President's 23 doctors, detailing the defendant's condition. In late September all corruption charges against Suharto were dismissed after an independent team of doctors declared that the former President was mentally and physically unfit to stand trial. In early November, however, the Jakarta High Court ruled that the trial was to resume. In mid-September, meanwhile, President Wahid announced that he had ordered the arrest of Suharto's youngest son, Tommy. Supporters of the former President and his family were suspected of involvement in a series of bomb threats and explosions in Jakarta in August and September. In one attack in mid-September at least 15 people were killed when a bomb exploded in the basement of the Jakarta Stock Exchange. The police declined to arrest Tommy without evidence, whereupon President Wahid sought to dismiss the police chief. Tommy was later sentenced to 18 months' imprisonment on separate corruption charges, but disappeared before he could be detained. In July 2001 Syafiuddin Kartasasmita, the judge who had sentenced Tommy, was assassinated by apparently professional gunmen in Jakarta; the gunmen later admitted in custody that they had been paid by Tommy.

In February 2001 the DPR formally censured Wahid over the BULOG and Brunei corruption allegations, thus taking the first step towards formal impeachment. The President's reputation as a democrat was further damaged by his failure to rebuke NU loyalists in Central and East Java who responded to the DPR decision by ransacking the Golkar and PAN offices and threatening to march on Jakarta to defend the President. The impeachment process, meanwhile, was accompanied by demonstrations by both opponents and supporters of Wahid. In March thousands of students took to the streets of Jakarta demanding the President's resignation. In May the DPR issued a second formal memorandum claiming unsatisfactory performance on the part of Wahid (just two days previously he had been cleared of corruption charges in the Brunei and BULOG scandals by the Attorney General, Marzuki Darusman), and on this basis requested the MPR to call a special session to impeach the President. Since the MPR was in practice a somewhat augmented DPR, the working body of the assembly agreed, calling the session for 1 August. Wahid responded by describing the DPR's action as unconstitutional and threatening that his supporters would resort to violence. He reshuffled his Cabinet on 3 June and again on 12 June; the first reshuffle was a major reorganization that removed Susilo Bambang Yudhoyono and the second led to the replacement of his Minister for Finance, Prijadi Praptosuharjo. The President also attempted to dismiss the head of the national police, Gen. Surojo Bimantoro, although Wahid made no attempt to obtain the requisite approval of the DPR. Bimantoro subsequently refused to accept his dismissal, and reshuffled 100 police officers in June, in a demonstration of defiance.

The President announced on 9 July 2001 that he would declare a state of emergency on 20 July if a compromise were not reached. The declaration was not made on the latter date, however, and Wahid merely delayed the deadline for reconciliation to 31 July, the day before the impeachment hearing of the MPR. A special session convened on 21 July, but was boycotted by Wahid's PKB and the small Christian party, Partai Demokrasi Kasih Bangsa (PDKB). The assembly speaker, Amien Rais, requested the President to deliver an account of his actions, to which Wahid replied that the session was illegal and that he would not attend. He separately met military MPR representatives and threatened them with dismissal if they continued to support the session. In the early hours of 23 July Wahid declared a state of civil emergency, suspended the MPR, the DPR, and Golkar, and announced that new elections would be held within a year. Later that morning, however, the Supreme Court issued an advisory opinion that the President's declaration was illegal, while the chief of the Jakarta police force announced that he would accept orders only from the Vice-President and would protect the security of the MPR session. The MPR itself then declared that the President had no constitutional authority to attempt to suspend it and that he had violated his oath of office in trying to do so; Amien Rais demanded an immediate impeachment hearing. That afternoon the assembly formally voted unanimously to dismiss Abdurrahman Wahid and to elevate Megawati Sukarnoputri to the country's presidency. Three days later the PPP leader, Hamzah Haz, defeated four other candidates, including the Golkar leader, Akbar Tandjung, and the former Co-ordinating Minister for Political Affairs, Security and Social Welfare, Susilo Bambang Yudhoyono, for election as Vice-President. Although Hamzah Haz had been among those rejecting a female president on Islamic principles in 1999, he appeared to be Megawati's preferred candidate and received strong PDI—P support in the ballot.

PRESIDENT MEGAWATI SUKARNOPUTRI, 2001–

Delays in the announcement of the composition of the new Cabinet led to widespread fears that Megawati was already weakened by the bargaining among the various power groups. However, her Cabinet, announced on 9 August 2001, offered an impressive blend of technocratic skill and political connections. Susilo Bambang Yudhoyono returned as Co-ordinating Minister for Political Affairs, Security and Social Welfare, with Dorodjatun Kuntjoro-Jakti as Co-ordinating Minister for the Economy, Finance and Industry and Yusuf Kalla as Co-ordinating Minister for People's Welfare. Many observers were disappointed, however, with her selection as Attorney General of M. A. Rahman, generally described as unremarkable. Vigorous reform of Indonesia's notoriously corrupt legal system was widely considered essential for the restoration of domestic and international confidence in the country. International risk surveys consistently identified Indonesia as having one of the highest perceived levels of corruption in Asia and the world, and addressing this problem through the courts was considered a high priority.

None the less, Megawati's election brought with it a powerful sense of relief and hope for stability and reconciliation. Her placid personality appeared to satisfy a widespread desire that the President should play a calming and moderating role, rather than spearheading changes to the Constitution, the legal system, the administrative structure or Indonesian political culture in general. Her first major speech as President, delivered on 16 August 2001, seemed to have been written by bureaucrats who intended to implement the policies she announced. However, the Government remained seriously constrained by a lack of revenue, which meant that the implementation of many desirable measures simply remained beyond the capacity of the Government. The far-reaching decentralization of 1 January 2001 had also succeeded in placing many important areas of policy beyond the reach of the central Government. In November 2001 the MPR agreed to amend the Constitution to provide for the direct election of the President and Vice-President following the first round of voting, for a constitutional court to review legislation and for a bicameral legislature, with a new upper house representing the regions. In August 2002 the MPR finally approved more detailed plans providing for the direct election of the President—provision was made for the establishment of an electoral process by which, if no candidate polled more than 50% of the votes, a second round of voting would be held. It was also decided that the 38 seats reserved for the military within the legislature would be abolished by 2004, five years ahead of the previously established schedule. However, requests for the introduction of Islamic law were rejected.

In August 2001 Megawati's decision to revoke Wahid's dismissal of the corrupt Bimantoro as Chief of Police raised fears that efforts to combat official corruption would end. In January 2002 the Government announced that the payment period granted to major shareholders of failed banks—all of them associates of Suharto—would be extended to 10 years, meaning that these debts were unlikely ever to be repaid (this decision was reversed in March). The Ministry of Information, which had sought to manage public access to news under Suharto and which had been abolished by Habibie, was to some extent re-established in the form of the State Ministry of Communications and Information (an office under the control of the Co-ordinating Minister for Political Affairs, Security and Social Welfare) in August 2001, and in March 2002 an Australian journalist was barred from the country because of his work on human rights issues. Shortly after Megawati came to power, moreover, the authorities arrested a number of activists under laws against 'sowing hatred' from the colonial era, which had not been used since the fall of Suharto. None the less, Megawati surprised observers in July 2001 by establishing *ad hoc* human rights tribunals to try TNI members for excesses in Tanjung Priok in 1984 and in East Timor between April and August 1999.

On 14 March 2002 the trial began of 18 military officers, civilian officials and militia members accused of complicity in an attack on a church in Suai, East Timor, in which 26 people were killed. The defendants, none of whom were in custody during the trial, included: Abílio Soares, the last Indonesian Governor of East Timor; Maj.-Gen. Damiri, the regional military commander; and Eurico Guterres, the most prominent militia leader. The defence advanced a wide range of claims, including: the assertion that the violence was a product of local tensions; that the court had no jurisdiction over events in East Timor; and that the court was a tool of hostile foreign powers. In August 2002 the Indonesian judiciary was subjected to widespread international condemnation when the special tribunal returned its first verdicts relating to the violence in East Timor. While Abílio Soares was convicted and given a three-year prison term for gross human rights violations, a sentence criticized for its leniency, the former Chief of Police in East Timor, Timbul Salaen, and five other officers were acquitted of all the charges against them. The verdicts prompted demands from human rights organizations for UN intervention in the process.

Indonesia's dysfunctional legal system remained a major problem. Tommy Suharto remained at large for 12 months following his conviction on corruption charges. While a fugitive, he was declared to be the main suspect in the murder of Justice Syafiuddin Kartasasmita, one of the Supreme Court judges who had found him guilty. The police officially intensified their search for him, but with no success. When former President Abdurrahman Wahid accused the police of protecting Tommy, Bimantoro brought a charge of slander against him. Alternative rumours surfaced that Wahid himself had connived in Tommy's disappearance in exchange for payment. In October 2001, however, the Supreme Court overruled Tommy's conviction. On 28 November Tommy was finally arrested, in a seizure portrayed as a triumph of police investigation. In March 2002 he stood trial, charged with possession of weapons and with ordering the murder of Kartasasmita. During the trial, which was broadcast on both television and radio, Tommy boasted that the police had helped him to visit his family regularly during his flight. One of Tommy's lawyers was herself charged with trying to bribe prosecution witnesses, and the Jakarta police officer who had arrested him was investigated for smuggling luxury cars into Indonesia. Tommy was found guilty on 26 July and sentenced to 15 years in prison; it emerged later that during his trial he had been living in considerable comfort in a well-appointed cell in Jakarta's Cipinang prison, protected by his own bodyguard, visited freely by friends and family, and permitted to take regular leave. In early August Tommy announced that he did not intend to appeal against his conviction.

In March 2002 Akbar Tandjung, Speaker of the DPR and Chairman of Golkar, was arrested and put on trial on charges of sequestering funds for his party's election campaign from the state logistical agency, BULOG. During the course of the trial, it emerged that most of the parties had received a share of these illegal BULOG funds, said to amount to US $350m. In September 2002 Tandjung was found guilty of misusing state funds and sentenced to three years in prison. He remained at liberty pending an appeal. Meanwhile, the Governor of the Central Bank, Syahril Sabirin, was sentenced to a three-year prison term in March for his role in the Bank Bali scandal, and Ginanjar Kartasasmita, a senior economic minister in the Suharto era, was questioned over decisions he made in the 1990s. Many of these trials and investigations, however, were criticized: in some cases, the defendants seemed to have been selected for political reasons; in others the charges appeared to have been chosen in order to increase the possibility of an acquittal or to minimize the severity of the eventual sentence. The criticism was to some extent borne out in August 2002 when the Court of Appeal overruled Sabirin's conviction for corruption. Sabirin had retained his position as Governor throughout the appeals process.

Excluding such high profile cases, the legal system seemed incapable of addressing the high levels of violent crime in society, political violence or the deep-seated corruption of the judiciary. Suspected petty criminals were routinely beaten to death by crowds in many centres. Piracy was a serious problem in the Strait of Melaka (Malacca). The police also failed to prevent an attack on the offices of the human rights organization Kontras in March 2002. Despite the widespread perception that justice was 'for sale' in the courts, no judges were charged successfully with any offence. In December 2001 the DPR approved legislation placing the police under the direct command of the country's President, but this measure seemed unlikely to improve the probity or effectiveness of police operations. The new legislation gave the police exclusive responsibility for internal security, but the military authorities made it clear that they considered this area to remain within their remit. The incapacity of the Government was also exposed by its inadequate response to serious floods in Java in early 2002.

Serious factional splits within all the major parties, moreover, obstructed the DPR's legislative role; it ended its third session in April 2002 having completed deliberations on only four of 24 items of legislation before it, and one of those bills was passed with votes from only 49 of the 489 members.

Decentralization also seriously undermined the unity of the armed forces and police by opening new opportunities for local and regional commanders to develop lucrative commercial arrangements with regional authorities. The Government planned a review of the decentralization process with the aim of restoring key powers to the centre, but that review was unlikely to be completed before the general election scheduled to be held in 2004.

Progress was, however, made in resolving two of Indonesia's worst communal conflicts. In central Sulawesi, where violence had broken out in late 1999 and had cost an estimated 2,000 lives over a two-year period, representatives from the two sides agreed to meet in the southern town of Malino, where they reached a peace settlement. The success of this agreement encouraged the Government to schedule a similar meeting in Malino in February 2002, bringing together the warring parties in Maluku. This meeting led to an agreement, known as 'Malino II', which included a provision that the Laskar Jihad forces should leave Maluku. The Laskar Jihad itself rejected this provision and promised to stay in the region to undertake 'humanitarian' work. On 28 April an unidentified gang attacked the Christian village of Soya, killing 12 people and setting fire to a 450-year old church. Vice-President Hamzah Haz supported the Laskar Jihad decision to remain in Maluku, commenting that the province was not yet safe for Muslims, but he visited Soya and made a donation to the cost of rebuilding the church.

The efforts of politicians to position themselves for the forthcoming elections became increasingly apparent during 2002. In May Hamzah Haz visited Laskar Jihad commander Ja'far Umar Thalib, who had recently been arrested for agitation and for slandering the President; he had made a speech in which he allegedly stated that he would kill all the relatives of former President Sukarno, including President Megawati. Haz described the visit as 'private'. Later in the month the Vice-President also visited an Islamic boarding school run by Abu Bakar Ba'asyir, accused by the Government of Singapore of having links with the international terrorist organization al-Qa'ida. On 12 October 2002 a devastating car bomb exploded outside a night-club on the island of Bali, killing an estimated 200 people, including many Australian tourists. Islamist terrorists were believed to be responsible. In response to international pressure, an emergency anti-terrorism decree was passed. Abu Bakar Ba'asyir was formally detained on suspicion of involvement in several bombings that had occurred in December 2000.

SEPARATIST MOVEMENTS

Despite the archipelago's ethnic diversity, Indonesia experienced surprisingly few separatist movements during the first 50 years of independence. Regional movements generally sought only greater autonomy or aimed primarily to change the nature of the central Government rather than to achieve independence. During the 1970s, however, important separatist movements emerged in the provinces of Aceh and Irian Jaya, and from 1975 Indonesia faced persistent nationalist resistance in the occupied territory of East Timor. After the fall of President Suharto in 1998, all these movements gathered momentum, and in 1999 a referendum on independence was held in East Timor leading to Indonesia's withdrawal from the territory in October of that year (see the chapter on East Timor). Demands for independence were voiced for the first time in other provinces, notably in the resource-rich provinces of Riau and East Kalimantan, but also in Bali and South Sulawesi. It seemed likely, however, that these new calls were intended principally to stake a claim for greater autonomy within Indonesia, rather than being envisaged as a serious contribution to the disintegration of the Republic.

Aceh

Aceh, the northernmost region of Sumatra, was an independent sultanate until the late 19th century, when it was conquered by the Dutch in a ferocious campaign. With a reputation as Indonesia's most staunchly Muslim region, Aceh was never fully subdued by the colonial power, and was one of the first areas where Indonesians took effective control from the Japanese after the declaration of independence in 1945. The Dutch never attempted to reoccupy the region, and Aceh ended the war of independence as a full province of the Indonesian Republic. After 1950 the Acehnese quickly became disillusioned with the Republic's leadership, which was generally perceived as corrupt, neglectful and 'un-Islamic'. The removal of Aceh's provincial status was also resented. A rebellion erupted in September 1953 under Daud Beureu'eh, and the Aceh revolt formally joined the broader Darul Islam movement for an Islamic Indonesia. Conciliatory policies by the central Government and a willingness to compromise on the part of the Acehnese, however, ended the revolt in the late 1950s. In 1959 Aceh became a special territory (Daerah Istimewa), with considerable autonomy in religious and educational affairs.

Dissent re-emerged in the mid-1970s, provoked by the exploitation by the central Government of natural gas and coal fields in Aceh; many Acehnese felt that Aceh was receiving none of the benefits of these operations. Migration and transmigration of other Indonesians into the province together with the growing power of the central Government led to a feeling that the region's autonomy was being eroded. Hasan di Tiro formed the Gerakan Aceh Merdeka (GAM—Free Aceh Movement) in 1976 and declared independence in 1977. This small rebellion was quickly suppressed by the army, although Tiro later established a government-in-exile in Sweden.

Opposition to the central Government arose again in 1989, led by the National Liberation Front Acheh Sumatra. In 1990 Aceh was made a 'military operations zone', thus allowing the armed forces far greater freedom to counter the rebellion. The armed forces were accused of using excessive and indiscriminate force in their subsequent operations, and it was estimated that by mid-1991, when the rebellion had been largely suppressed, about 1,000 Acehnese had been killed. This figure continued to rise over subsequent years, and there were persistent reports of torture, kidnapping and sexual assault by the security forces. In July 1993 the human rights group Amnesty International produced a report accusing the Government of protecting those members of the armed forces responsible for atrocities in Aceh, thus enabling them to act with impunity. Following the downfall of Suharto in May 1998, Aceh's status as a military operations zone was revoked in June, and in August 1,000 troops were withdrawn from the province. Gen. Wiranto also made a public apology for past military excesses. Following rioting in September, however, the withdrawal of troops was suspended. Although President Habibie's decentralization measures were intended to defuse some of the resentment underlying the Aceh revolt by giving the province a greater share of oil and gas revenues, public opinion in Aceh became increasingly sympathetic towards the notion of independence. Violence continued to escalate in the province over the months following the accession of President Habibie. In January 1999 27 soldiers were court-martialled over the deaths in custody of four Acehnese earlier the same month, but military violence in the countryside continued. Tension remained high in the province, and was exacerbated by the discovery of several mass graves of people killed by the army during security operations. Voter turn-out in the legislative elections of 7 June was low in many districts, and violence continued to escalate following the poll as GAM guerrillas intensified their campaign for independence for the province. On 23 July 57 Acehnese students and their teacher were killed by the military in an attack on the village of Beutong Ateuh in western Aceh, and by late August 200 Acehnese were reported to have been killed by the Indonesian armed forces since the instigation in June of a renewed military campaign in an attempt by the central Government to suppress the uprising.

On coming to power in October 1999, President Wahid foreshadowed a referendum on independence in the territory. In response, Acehnese nationalists belonging to the Aceh Referendum Information Centre (SIRA) organized a pro-referendum rally in the provincial capital, Banda Aceh, on 7–8 November, reportedly attended by 1m. people. The prospect of a referendum, however, was rejected by the army. Whereas East Timor was, in some respects, accepted as having been a special case, independence for Aceh seemed likely to precipitate the disintegration of Indonesia. Sections of the armed forces were also widely believed to have interests in Aceh's lucrative but illegal marijuana industry. Furthermore, the Acehnese independence movement was seriously divided and lacked the international support that had helped the East Timorese movement to achieve its aim. Although there were signs of some material support from Acehnese living in Malaysia, Malaysia itself emphatically declined to support independence for the province. By early 2000 President Wahid appeared to have withdrawn from the idea of a referendum on independence for Aceh, suggesting instead greater autonomy for the province, together with a larger share of revenue from natural resources and the limited introduction of Islamic law. This offer failed to satisfy the nationalists, however, and violence continued in Aceh. By mid-2000 more than 300,000 people out of the province's total population of 4m. were reported to have been displaced by the violence, and GAM was said to control about half the villages in the province. In May 2000, in Geneva, Switzerland, the Indonesian Government and Acehnese rebel representatives agreed upon a three-month cease-fire ('humanitarian pause'), which took effect on 2 June. Also in May 24 junior soldiers and one civilian were sentenced to various terms of imprisonment for the murder in July 1999 of the 58 Acehnese in Beutong Ateuh; the trial was criticized by both Acehnese community groups, who had demanded the death penalty for the accused, and human rights lawyers, who called for a wider trial of crimes against humanity in the province. The cease-fire was later extended to January 2001, but appeared to have little influence on the level of violence. Pressure on the Government was increased by continued attacks on the major LNG plant in Aceh (see Economy). In April 2001 President Wahid signed an instruction for the police to assist the military in Aceh, effectively signalling a return to repressive strategies. An estimated 1,500 people were killed in 2001, mostly by the military, but some by GAM, which increasingly targeted Javanese settlers.

Aside from maintaining military pressure on GAM, the Government's main strategy for combating the insurgency was to prepare an enhanced autonomy plan for Aceh, giving the provincial Government a greater share of gas revenue and imposing Islamic law within the province. The necessary legislation was drafted under Wahid's presidency but was signed into law by Megawati as one of her first acts in office. Although apparently generous in the autonomy it gives to Aceh, the legislation was widely criticized by Acehnese for failing to deal with the military presence. Many Acehnese, moreover, regarded the implementation of Islamic law as a cynical attempt to alienate modern-minded Acehnese from the traditional religious leaders whose power was thereby enhanced. Although there was a common perception in Jakarta that the main orientation of the Acehnese movement was Islamic, GAM had never proposed an Islamic state, and its relations with radical Muslim groups in Java were poor. GAM, in fact, condemned the terrorist attacks on the USA of 11 September 2001 (see below) more strongly than the Indonesian Government. The autonomy measures came into force on 1 January 2002, when the province was renamed Nanggroë Aceh Darussalam (NAD—Islamic State of Aceh). The new regional Government was permitted to retain 70% of provincial revenues and began in March to implement its version of Islamic law by imposing a dress code. There was no movement, however, on the issue of human rights. Although President Megawati apologized to the Acehnese for past oppression on 16 August 2001, she insisted that the province would not be permitted to leave Indonesia and that armed separatist movements would not be tolerated. She also eventually obtained the release of five GAM negotiators who had been arrested by police in July 2001 during negotiations with the Government, but the time taken to achieve this release indicated the depth of resistance within the armed forces to any compromise with the rebels. From early 2002 military leaders adopted an increasingly stringent public policy towards separatism, and the military presence in Aceh rose to about 17,000. On 22 January 2002 army units trapped and killed the GAM military leader, Abdullah Syafei, and in the same month the Iskandar Muda military command (Kodam) covering Aceh was restored. None the less, discussions between government and GAM representatives on the issue of restoring security took place in Geneva in May 2002.

Papua

The western half of the island of New Guinea had been a part of the Netherlands Indies before the Second World War, but it was scarcely integrated with the remainder of the colony and was inhabited by Melanesians who were ethnically different from the Malay peoples who dominated the rest of Indonesia. Partly on these grounds and partly to assuage the humiliation of defeat in the Indonesian war of independence, the Netherlands decided in 1949 to retain control of the region, envisaging its eventual self-determination. This decision, bitterly resented by Indonesians, led to more than a decade of diplomatic activity, which culminated in the transfer of the colony to Indonesia under UN auspices in 1962–63. Indonesia named the region Irian Barat (West Irian), but in 1972 changed it to Irian Jaya (Victorious Irian).

Under the UN agreement, the opinion of the indigenous population was to be heard in an 'Act of Free Choice' five years after integration, but this act was not internationally guaranteed or supervised and Indonesia carried it out in 1968 in a way that made acceptance of Indonesian rule mandatory. Resentment against Indonesian rule soon emerged. Indonesian authorities had little respect for traditional Papuan dress and custom, and attempted to impose Indonesian culture. The region became a major destination for internal migration and transmigration, and the less-educated local people often found themselves unable to compete with new inhabitants for bureaucratic, professional and other skilled jobs. Logging and copper-mining in the region, moreover, became major sources of export revenue for the Indonesian Government, while few funds seemed to reach the province.

A rebellion erupted in 1965, led by the Organisasi Papua Merdeka (OPM—Free Papua Movement) and unrest has continued in the province ever since. Seth Rumkorem declared a Republic of West Papua in 1971 and a major uprising took place in 1977. Despite grandiose claims, the movement controlled no significant territory by the early 1990s, although its forces were able to range widely in the difficult terrain and take sanctuary across the border in Papua New Guinea. In 1984 about 10,000 refugees crossed the border into Papua New Guinea (see also Foreign Relations, below).

Human rights organizations continue to report allegations of torture, killing, intimidation and cultural suppression in the province. Most recently attention has focused on the huge Freeport mine near the province's southern coast, which is Indonesia's largest source of gold and copper. Since mid-1994 the mine authorities have been accused of complicity with Indonesian military forces in the deaths of more than 60 local people who protested at environmental degradation and what they saw as the privileged position of outsiders in the mining industry. In January 1996 the OPM launched a bid for greater international attention by kidnapping 26 people, including seven foreigners, in the south-east of the province. The OPM later released 15 of them, but the remainder were freed in an operation by Indonesian special forces in May, during which the OPM killed two Indonesian hostages. In August 1996 Indonesian forces freed several Indonesian forestry workers taken hostage by another OPM group. Five people were reported to have been killed by soldiers in Jayapura, the provincial capital, in July 1998, during a demonstration pressing for the secession of the province from Indonesia.

In the months immediately after the fall of President Suharto, Irian Jaya was relatively quiet. In early October 1998 the Indonesian Government revoked the status of Irian Jaya as a 'military operations zone' following the conclusion of a ceasefire agreement with the OPM in late September; however, this action was not followed by any withdrawal of Indonesian troops from the province. The movement towards independence for East Timor (see below), however, encouraged the Irianese to begin pressing the case for independence for the region. In late February 1999 100 tribal leaders raised the issue of independence at a meeting with President Habibie, and pro-independence banners began to appear in the larger centres. However, Irian Jaya's immediate prospects for independence were weaker than those of East Timor, because 40% of the province's 2m. people are of non-Irianese descent, because its copper and gold mines are important to the national economy, and because it was formerly a part of the Netherlands Indies.

In September 1999 President Habibie announced that the province of Irian Jaya would be divided into three. Although ostensibly intended to bring administration closer to the people, the move was widely perceived as a device to split the region's independence movement. On coming to power in October, President Wahid revoked the partition, and in December announced that the province's name would be changed from Irian Jaya to Papua. (The central authorities, however, subsequently declined to ratify the change; nationalists, meanwhile, preferred the name of West Papua, Papua alone being widely used within the province itself but also being the traditional name for the southern part of Papua New Guinea.) The President, nevertheless, resisted any suggestion of independence for the territory, and the police and army continued to arrest Papuans for raising the nationalist flag; the flag was formally banned again on 1 December 2000. On 23–25 February 2000 an unofficial congress of the Papuan People met in Jayapura, formally repudiated the 1968 'Act of Free Choice' and began planning strategies for achieving independence for the province. Although, according to various reports, Indonesian military and intelligence operations had largely defeated or compromised the OPM as a resistance force, the example of East Timor had demonstrated to independence movements in other parts of the archipelago the critical importance of an international campaign and of a visible protest movement in the cities. The congress held in Jayapura in February 2000 was therefore dominated by urban non-governmental organizations rather than guerrillas. In response to the activities of the independence movement, the Indonesian military authorities apparently began to develop and support local pro-Indonesia militia groups similar to those used in East Timor. In 2001 these militia began receiving help from the Java-based radical Muslim Laskar Jihad. On 4 June a political congress held in the province, attended by about 3,000 Papuans, declared that the territory had never been legally integrated into Indonesia. The claim was immediately rebuffed by the Indonesian Government. In July, however, members of the Presidium Dewan Papua (PDP—Papua Presidium Council) held talks with President Wahid in Jakarta and renewed their demand for independence for the territory.

In October 2000 the Minister of Defence announced that a tougher line on separatism would be taken in the province. In November Theys Eluay, a moderate leader of the PDP, and four others were charged with sedition; shortly afterwards, on 11 November, Eluay was assassinated after attending a dinner with the local army commander. An official investigation later concluded that members of the military were responsible for the murder. Legislation was also drafted, however, for special autonomy for the province, along lines broadly similar to those in Aceh, though without the implementation of Islamic law in the mainly Christian province. The progress of this law through the legislature was delayed by the long struggle in Jakarta to unseat President Wahid, and by disagreement over the percentage of resource income that was to be retained by the provincial government. When the special autonomy bill was finally approved on 22 October 2001, it provided that 80% of revenue from forestry and fishery and 70% from oil and gas would be retained by Papua. The bill confirmed the province's name as Papua and legalized the use of the Papuan flag. The legislation took effect on 1 January 2002.

In late August 2002 two US citizens and one Indonesian were killed following an attack on a vehicle convoy at the Freeport mine. While the Government suspected the involvement of the OPM, there was speculation that the Indonesian military might have staged the incident in order to attract support for its ongoing campaign against rebel militias in the area. To date, the attack was the worst incident involving foreign nationals to have taken place in the province.

FOREIGN RELATIONS

Since independence Indonesia has prided itself on maintaining an 'active and independent' foreign policy. During the 1950s Indonesia was a founder-member of the Non-aligned Movement (NAM), and assumed the chairmanship of the organization in September 1992. However, Indonesia's dependent position in the international economy has never permitted it the freedom of action that it professes. During 'Guided Democracy', Sukarno turned to the USSR and the People's Republic of China for support, and from 1965–66 'New Order' Indonesia solicited funds from Western donors.

The centre-piece of Indonesian foreign policy is its membership of the Association of South East Asian Nations (ASEAN), which it founded with Malaysia, the Philippines, Singapore and Thailand in 1967. Indonesia also played a major role in establishing the Asia-Pacific Economic Co-operation forum (APEC), and hosted the November 1994 APEC summit meeting in Bogor. ASEAN's original aims emphasized regional economic co-operation as a means of diminishing threats to internal security, but it has worked most effectively in defusing conflicts between its members and in creating a united diplomatic front on broader international issues. ASEAN support, for instance, helped to limit the damage to Indonesia's international reputation caused by its invasion and protracted pacification of East Timor and by its repeated disregard for UN resolutions on the colony.

Indonesian suspicion of China has been a major feature of foreign policy since 1965–66, when the military accused China of supporting the PKI and the attempted coup. Indonesia severed diplomatic relations with China in 1967. Poor relations were compounded by long-term doubts about the loyalty of Indonesia's ethnic Chinese minority and a belief that China might seek to take advantage of their support. To prevent such intervention, Indonesia banned the import of material written in Chinese characters. In May 1985, however, the two countries began to discuss the resumption of direct trade links, and in April 1988 Indonesia announced that it was willing to establish full diplomatic relations, provided China gave an assurance that it would not seek to interfere in Indonesia's internal affairs. Diplomatic relations were finally restored in August 1990, after Indonesia undertook to repay debts to China incurred during the period of 'Guided Democracy'. President Suharto visited China in November 1990. Relations between Indonesia and China suffered a set-back in 1998 when, some six weeks after the perpetration of terrible violence against ethnic Chinese Indonesians around the time of the fall of Suharto in May, China issued a sharp diplomatic protest against the violence and gave prominent coverage in the state-controlled media to reports of the gruesome rapes, arson and murders. China's response was perhaps prompted by the indignation and anger at the violence expressed by overseas Chinese in general; however, for those who wished to emphasize the primary loyalty of ethnic Chinese Indonesians to Indonesia, rather than to China, this display of Chinese interest was less than welcome. Following his accession to the presidency, President Habibie publicly expressed his sympathy for the plight of the ethnic Chinese victims of violence. Subsequently, in May 1999 as part of an ongoing programme of general reform, Habibie lifted a ban that had existed on the use and teaching of the Mandarin Chinese language within Indonesia.

Indonesia aspires to be recognized as the major power in South-East Asia, and welcomed the withdrawal of the former USSR from its base in Cam Ranh Bay in Viet Nam and of the USA from Subic Bay in the Philippines. Indonesia has also been involved in diplomatic efforts to resolve long-standing regional conflicts. From June 1991 it hosted several informal meetings attended by representatives of Brunei, China, Malaysia, the Philippines, Taiwan and Viet Nam to discuss these countries' conflicting claims to all or parts of the Spratly Islands in the South China Sea, which are strategically important and show considerable potential for petroleum exploitation. The meetings resulted in a joint statement agreeing to resolve the dispute peacefully. Paradoxically, Indonesia's bilateral relations with Malaysia became strained in 1993 by a dispute over two islands, Sipadan and Ligitan, off the coast of Sabah. (The dispute was submitted to the International Court of Justice (ICJ) in the Hague, the Netherlands, in June 2002.) In April 1995 the Indonesian armed forces increased patrols in the South China Sea after China re-emphasized its claim to seas near the Natuna archipelago, which Indonesia has traditionally claimed. Indonesia also assumed an active diplomatic role in the long-running conflicts in Indo-China. From July 1988 Indonesia hosted a series of informal meetings between the contending Cambodian factions and, with France, Indonesia jointly chaired the Paris International Conference on Cambodia from August 1989. Indonesia contributed troops to the UN Transitional Authority in Cambodia prior to the elections of 1993. In July 1996 Indonesia hosted a series of meetings between ASEAN ministers of foreign affairs and inter-nation 'dialogue partners' (Australia, Canada, China, the EU, India, Japan, New Zealand, Russia, the Republic of Korea and the USA) to discuss regional security and international trade. Smoke from forest fires in Indonesia seriously disrupted commerce and communications and also damaged public health in Singapore and Malaysia during the second half of 1997. Although both countries played down suggestions of tension with Indonesia, they were clearly irritated by Indonesia's failure to address the problem more promptly. President Suharto twice apologized publicly to the neighbouring countries for the haze. Indonesia's relations with Malaysia were also strained by the forced repatriation in early 1998 of thousands of Indonesian workers from Malaysia as a result of the impact of the regional economic crisis; many of those repatriated reported brutal treatment in detention centres prior to their removal.

Indonesia's relations with the West have been periodically disrupted by disagreements over human rights and over East Timor, whose annexation by Indonesia remained widely unrecognized internationally in the late 1990s, prior to the referendum held in August 1999. In March 1992, after the Dutch Government linked the continuation of aid to an improvement in Indonesia's human rights performance, Indonesia angrily rejected all Dutch aid and dissolved IGGI, which had been chaired by the Netherlands. A new international aid consortium, the Consultative Group on Indonesia (CGI—chaired by the World Bank and including 18 countries and 13 multilateral aid agencies, but excluding the Netherlands), met in Paris, France, in July 1992 to assume the functions of IGGI. In early 1994 the USA threatened to remove Indonesia's trade privileges unless it took steps to conform to ILO standards for labour conditions. US pressure also played a major role in the early release from detention of Muchtar Pakpahan, the head of an independent (and thus technically illegal) trade union, who had been sentenced to nearly three years' imprisonment for his labour activities in November 1994. The events surrounding Megawati's expulsion from the PDI leadership led the USA to postpone the sale to Indonesia of nine F-16 fighter aircraft in September 1996; the US position was weak, however, as it was known to have had difficulty in finding a buyer for the aircraft. In June 1997 Indonesia itself cancelled the sale, on the grounds of unacceptable US criticism over the alleged abuse of human rights in the country. The British Government pledged to review the sale of 16 *Hawk* fighter aircraft to Indonesia, but allowed the sale to proceed after the Indonesian Government made it clear that it would simply buy from elsewhere. The continuing resistance in East Timor strengthened the international campaign to maintain pressure on Indonesia over its occupation of the territory.

Within the EU, Portugal was perhaps the most vociferous in condemning Indonesia and lobbying for a UN-supervised referendum in East Timor; in July 1992 Portugal blocked an economic co-operation treaty between ASEAN and the EC on these grounds. Portugal also began proceedings against Australia in the ICJ, seeking a ruling against the so-called Timor Gap Treaty, concluded between Australia and Indonesia in 1991. The Treaty provided a legal framework for petroleum and gas exploration in the maritime zone between Australia and East Timor, which had not been covered by earlier Indonesian-Australian treaties. Portugal claimed that the agreement infringed both Portuguese sovereignty and the East Timorese right to self-determination. (Only Australia was named because Indonesia does not come under the court's jurisdiction.) In a judgment brought in June 1995, however, the Court ruled that it could not exercise jurisdiction because the central issue was the legality of actions by Indonesia, which had refused to present a case. Formal contacts between the Indonesian and Portuguese Governments, especially over the status of Portuguese culture in East Timor, took place in 1995 and 1996 but were for the most part inconclusive. In January 1996 Portugal began direct satellite television broadcasts to East Timor. Indonesia's relations with Australia, which had been increasingly close in the early 1990s, soured when widespread public protests in Australia forced Indonesia to withdraw the nomination of Lt-Gen. Herman Mantiri as ambassador to Canberra. Mantiri was targeted because of remarks he made in 1991, apparently defending the Dili massacre. The rift with Australia appeared to have been healed when the two countries signed a security agreement in December 1995. Although not amounting to a formal alliance, the agreement binds the two sides to consult on security matters and to consider possible joint measures. None the less, in June 1996 Indonesia remained sensitive enough to the Mantiri affair to reject as Australia's ambassador-designate to Jakarta a diplomat known to have written critically of the Suharto family's business activities in internal government reports. Indonesia accepted a new envoy in September. In March 1997 the two countries signed a treaty concerning seabed and 'economic zone' boundaries. Following the downfall of President Suharto in May 1998, relations between Indonesia and Australia were significantly affected by the issue of East Timor; in January 1999 the Indonesian Government expressed its 'deep regret' at Australia's announcement earlier the same month that it was to change its policy on the territory and actively promote 'self-determination' in East Timor. Following the announcement in March 1999 that the Indonesian Government was to allow the East Timorese people to vote on the issue of independence, Australia continued to attempt to establish a role for itself in the process of the definition of the future of the province. In early May Indonesia and Portugal signed a UN-sponsored accord on East Timor which allowed for total independence for the territory if the East Timorese people voted to reject autonomy proposals offered by Indonesia in the referendum scheduled to be held in August. On 28 December, following Indonesia's withdrawal from East Timor in October after the territory's population voted in favour of independence, diplomatic relations between Indonesia and Portugal (which had been severed in 1975) were restored. Meanwhile, however, Indonesia's relations with Australia deteriorated, following the latter's involvement in peace-keeping operations in East Timor after the referendum. Furthermore, many members of the Indonesian élite deeply resented Australia's wider role in the detachment of East Timor from Indonesia, as well as the public claim made by the Australian Prime Minister, John Howard, that he had 'stood up' to Indonesia over the issue. There was also widespread suspicion in Indonesia that official Australian support for the territorial integrity of Indonesia might not endure in response to increasing public pressure in favour of independence for the Indonesian province of Irian Jaya (now Papua—see above). Relations improved in June 2001, when Wahid finally made an official visit to Australia, the first by an Indonesian President for 26 years.

On 31 January 2000 the UN Commission on Human Rights recommended that an international tribunal be established to try Indonesian military personnel and other individuals suspected of involvement in the violence in East Timor in August and September 1999. In late February 2000, however, UN Secretary-General Kofi Annan stated that the Indonesian legal process should be allowed to run its course before the establishment of any such tribunal. In January the EU lifted an embargo on military assistance to Indonesia, which it had imposed in an attempt to force Indonesia to repatriate displaced East Timorese from West Timor and to bring to justice those responsible for the violence in the territory. A similar embargo imposed by the USA remained in place, however. During a visit to Indonesia in April, the US commander in the Pacific, Adm. Dennis Blair, publicly criticized the human rights record of the Indonesian military and predicted that military co-operation between the USA and Indonesia would not be resumed in the foreseeable future.

Indonesia's relations with Papua New Guinea were strained by the disputed common border issue and by the question of the OPM. The Papua New Guinea Government scrupulously refrained from assisting the separatists: in May 1990 the OPM leader, Melkianus Salossa, was arrested in Papua New Guinea and deported to Indonesia, where he received a life sentence, and since October 1990 a new border agreement has enabled the exchange of military intelligence and the conduct of joint border patrols. However, the insecure border and widespread sympathy for the OPM in Papua New Guinea meant that the rebels periodically obtained support and sanctuary across the border. Papua New Guinea was angered by regular incursions of Indonesian troops and aircraft into its territory and by Indonesia's crude and corrupt attempts to buy influence in Port Moresby.

In September 1996 the last Vietnamese refugees held on the island of Galang, south of Singapore, were repatriated. Suharto's term as Chairman of the NAM, which began in 1992, came to an end in 1995, but the President continued to seek a high international profile in the meetings of ASEAN and APEC until his downfall in 1998. In June 1997 Indonesia joined a new Islamic grouping, the Developing Eight (D-8), which also included Bangladesh, Egypt, Iran, Malaysia, Nigeria, Pakistan and Turkey; the grouping aims to promote mutual economic co-operation, as well as global peace, justice and equality.

The economic crisis of 1997 and the fall of President Suharto in 1998 turned Indonesian attention inward and distracted attention and energy from international politics. ASEAN, in particular, was notably less effective during this period without the driving force of Indonesia behind it. Although Western countries generally welcomed President Habibie's reform programme, they expressed some doubts about the depth of Indonesia's commitment to fundamental change. The early months of President Wahid's leadership, in late 1999 and early 2000, were characterized by a hectic programme of foreign travel intended to strengthen his Government's credentials, to win international support for Wahid's own political position from within Indonesia itself, and to restore business confidence in the country's future. Wahid spent the major part of his first month in office outside Indonesia, and by March 2000 the President had visited 34 foreign countries. In February 2000 President Wahid visited East Timor for the first time since the Timorese people's vote for independence, in an attempt to begin the process of Indonesia's reconciliation with the territory. Relations with Singapore were strained by occasional dismissive remarks from the Indonesian President, while relations with the USA deteriorated over repeated outspoken criticism of Indonesian policy made by the US ambassador to Jakarta, Robert Gelbard. President Wahid shared former President Suharto's long-term aim of establishing Indonesia's credentials as a leader in both East Asia and the Islamic world, and he publicly commented on the need of both groupings to establish a higher profile and a greater degree of independence from external powers, especially the USA.

Relations between the new Megawati Government and Australia were strained almost immediately after the President's accession in mid-2001 by the issue of refugees, asylum-seekers and illegal immigrants, mainly from South Asia and the Middle East, who passed through Indonesia while attempting to reach Australia. The issue was one of great controversy in Australia but was of little direct importance to Indonesia, which objected to Australian claims that it should be doing more to prevent unauthorized migrants from passing through its territory.

On 19 September 2001 a scheduled visit to Washington, DC, by President Megawati proceeded despite the terrorist attacks on New York and Washington only eight days previously. In her discussions with President George W. Bush, Megawati offered support for the USA's campaign against terrorism, receiving in exchange promises of financial aid and improved access to defence equipment. The US response to the attacks, however, added greatly to Megawati's difficulties. The US attack on Afghanistan was widely condemned in Muslim circles. There were protests against the US bombing in several Indonesian cities and demands for a boycott of US goods and firms. Radical Muslim groups began 'sweeping' tourist areas in Jakarta, Central Java and Makassar to tell US citizens to leave the country. The authorities later estimated that 1.3m. tourists had cancelled visits to Indonesia as a result. Some Islamic groups began to recruit volunteers to join the Taliban forces in Afghanistan, and cabinet ministers made conflicting statements about whether such actions were legal. None the less, with a widespread perception in Indonesia that the USA had over-reacted to the attacks, the Government was reluctant to be seen to be acting against Islam at the behest of the USA. Whereas individuals with al-Qa'ida connections, including at least three Indonesians, were arrested in neighbouring South-East Asian countries, Megawati's Government sought to downplay the issue, arguing that there was no proven Indonesian involvement with Islamic terrorism. In October Megawati stated publicly that she did not wish to see any country use violence against another, even in retaliation. Several moderate Muslim leaders argued that a harsh reaction would strengthen Islamic radicalism, rather than controlling it, but some reports indicated that the authorities were quietly keeping Muslim radicals under tighter control. In early 2002 the USA and Indonesia agreed that the former would provide US $10m. to train Indonesian police in counter-terrorism techniques and to train bank officials in the tracing of terrorist financial transactions. On 18 July the US Senate Appropriations Committee voted to abandon conditions on providing US military training to the Indonesian armed forces, thus enabling the Indonesian military to participate in the US Department of Defense's International Military Education and Training programme (IMET). The Pentagon had argued that it needed Indonesia's co-operation in the global war on terrorism and that this war should take precedence over human rights considerations.

Economy

SARWAR O. H. HOBOHM

Revised for this edition by the editorial staff

Indonesia is the fourth most populous country in the world: a child born on the island of Lombok on 4 February 1997 was officially designated as the country's 200 millionth inhabitant. According to the results of the census of June 2000, the total population had risen to almost 206.3m. With substantial deposits of petroleum, natural gas and other minerals, as well as the capacity to produce a wide range of agricultural commodities, Indonesia is also one of the world's most richly-endowed countries in terms of natural resources. Yet the country remains relatively poor, and achieved the status of a 'middle-income' country, by World Bank criteria, only in 1981, when its national income per caput first exceeded the threshold of US $500. After some brief set-backs in the mid-1980s the Indonesian economy recorded almost a decade of rapid economic growth, and by 1996 the country's gross domestic product (GDP) had risen to US $1,155 per head. However, the Asian financial crisis, which began in the latter half of 1997 and intensified during 1998, prompted a sharp regression in this figure, both because of a decline in the volume of output and a fall in its value in terms of US dollars, owing to a severe devaluation of the national currency, the rupiah. Official national accounts data showed that GDP per caput decreased to US $1,080 in 1997, and declined sharply to some US $470 in 1998, before increasing to US $680 in 1999 and US $715 in 2000, as a result of both a recovery in the value of the rupiah and a real growth in output. This pattern of recovery suffered a set-back in 2001, when a slowdown in economic growth and a sharp depreciation of the rupiah resulted in a decline in GDP per caput to US $690.

The Indonesian economy is also characterized by a variety of distributional imbalances. The results of the 2000 population census showed that 60.4% of Indonesia's population lived on the three islands of Java (Jawa), Madura and Bali, which together comprised only 7.2% of the country's total land area. These islands also represent the most fertile regions of Indonesia, and are the most heavily urbanized and most developed areas, both industrially and infrastructurally. These advantages are, to a considerable extent, offset by the three islands' high population density, and they also contain areas of extreme poverty. This variation in income levels is emphasized by periodic surveys of consumption expenditure conducted by the Central Bureau of Statistics: these indicated that in 1999, for example, the poorest 40% of the population accounted for only 21.7% of total consumption expenditure, while the wealthiest 20% of the population accounted for 40.6% of the total.

ECONOMIC DECLINE AND RECOVERY, 1949–69

At independence Indonesia inherited an economy that had already been seriously disrupted by three years of Japanese wartime occupation and a four-year armed struggle for independence. The following two decades were characterized by dislocation and decline, as weak international commodity markets combined with domestic political upheavals and economic mismanagement to prevent the effective rehabilitation of the economy. This culminated in the virtual collapse of the economy by the mid-1960s.

Following the political crisis of 1965–66, President Suharto assumed office and adopted economic stability and development as the principal objectives of his 'New Order' Government. A comprehensive programme for the restoration of economic stability and growth was prepared with the assistance of the IMF, and significant measures were adopted to restore the economy's external balance. The rupiah was devalued, a relatively liberal Foreign Investment Law was introduced in 1967, and a debt-rescheduling agreement was reached in the same year with Indonesia's foreign creditors. The Western creditors, who had combined to form the Inter-Governmental Group for Indonesia (IGGI) also agreed to resume aid payments to Indonesia, which facilitated the rapid stabilization of the economy in the late 1960s. By 1969 it had become possible for Indonesia's economic policy-makers to move towards the more ambitious goal of generating economic growth and development.

ECONOMIC PLANNING AND GROWTH, 1969-97

This goal was pursued through a series of five-year Development Plans, known by the acronym Repelita, the first of which was initiated on 1 April 1969 at the beginning of the 1969/70 fiscal year. These Plans did not constitute comprehensive proposals for thoroughgoing state-controlled change with fixed sectoral targets; rather, they represented guidelines for public-sector investment projects, and also sought to encourage and guide private investment. Public expenditure targets under these Plans were generally quite ambitious, and their implementation required considerable quantities of external financial resources, although this dependence on foreign aid declined gradually. Five such plans had been implemented in full by the end of the 1993/94 fiscal year on 31 March 1994. The sixth plan was disrupted by the onset of the Asian financial crisis of 1997–98, and the ensuing economic and political upheavals, which resulted in a breakdown of the planning system.

Repelita I

The formulation of Repelita I (1969/70–73/74) by the National Planning Development Board (Bappenas) established the pattern for all subsequent development planning in Indonesia. The Plan involved expenditure of US $2,000m. and aimed to achieve an average real annual GDP growth rate of 4.7%. Its main emphasis was on agricultural and infrastructural development. With only a few exceptions, such as rice production, most of the Plan targets were achieved or surpassed, with a real annual GDP growth rate of 8.6% being recorded.

Repelita II

Repelita II (1974/75–78/79) granted a high priority to the generation of employment and the even distribution of economic development, *inter alia*, by facilitating the process of state-assisted resettlement ('transmigration') from the main islands to the 'outer' islands. Some 28% of the Government's domestically-funded capital expenditure was thus committed to regional and social development. Agriculture, and especially the production of rice and other food crops, continued to receive priority, as did infrastructural development. Supported by earnings from petroleum and liquefied natural gas (LNG), which was produced and exported on a large scale from 1978 onwards, an impressive average annual real GDP growth rate of 7.7% was achieved during this period.

Repelita III

Repelita III (1979/80–83/84) retained many of the goals of the two previous five-year Plans, including the achievement of rice self-sufficiency, a more equal distribution of the fruits of development, and increased private-sector participation in industrial development. The Plan also envisaged an increase in the production of non-oil and non-gas traded goods, such as agricultural commodities, forestry products, non-petroleum minerals and, above all, labour-intensive manufactures. The implementation of the Plan was disrupted by persistent volatility in world petroleum prices, which prompted the Government to devalue the rupiah on two occasions—once by almost 34% in November 1978, shortly before the Plan came into effect; and once by a further 28% in March 1983. The latter devaluation was accompanied by a decision to rephase 47 large capital- and import-intensive development projects, involving a projected investment of US $21,000m., and to initiate a programme of structural adjustment. Despite these difficulties, real GDP growth over the Plan period averaged 5.7% per year.

Repelita IV

Repelita IV (1984/85–88/89) had three major objectives: the absorption of 9.3m. new workers; the growth of high-technology industries; and the promotion of non-oil and non-gas exports, to help to achieve a real annual average GDP growth rate of 5%. In order to facilitate an increased private-sector contribution to the achievement of the Plan targets, an extensive liberalization of the economy was effected, which included reforms of Indonesia's taxation system, financial institutions, customs and port-handling formalities, and licensing procedures for private investments. As a result of these measures, the value of non-oil and non-gas exports exceeded the combined value of oil and natural gas exports for the first time in more than a decade in 1987, and continued to expand further in 1988 and 1989. In overall terms, the economy achieved a real average annual growth rate of 5.2% over the Plan period.

Repelita V

Repelita V (1989/90–93/94) established a target for annual GDP growth of 5% in real terms, in order to generate adequate employment opportunities for the anticipated increase of 3% per year in the labour force from 74.5m. to 86.4m. between 1988 and 1993. A particularly high target of 10% average annual growth was set for the non-oil and non-gas manufacturing sector, which was expected to account for much of the projected growth in labour absorption and export earnings during the Plan period. About 55% of the total investment of Rp. 239,000,000m. projected by the Plan was to be provided by the private sector, with public funding being aimed primarily at the development of Indonesia's infrastructure and human resources. Many of the Plan's targets were achieved or exceeded and the economy recorded a real average growth rate of about 8.3% per year. The manufacturing sector grew by an average 10.2% per year, with its non-hydrocarbon component expanding by 11.6% per year. As a result of these developments, manufacturing superseded agriculture for the first time in 1991, becoming the most important sector in the Indonesian economy.

Repelita VI

Repelita VI came into effect on 1 April 1994. It represented the first phase of the 25-year Second Long-Term Development Period, known by its Indonesian acronym as PJPT II, which also commenced on that date and was intended to lead to the beginning of Indonesia's development as a modern industrialized economy. To achieve this goal, PJPT II projected a real annual average GDP growth rate of more than 7%, with the manufacturing industry providing the main impetus for this growth. This was projected to result in a fourfold increase in real per caput incomes and an increase in the share of manufacturing industry in GDP to more than 32.5% by the end of PJPT II.

The targets for Repelita VI itself were more modest, and provided for an annual average GDP growth rate of 6.2% in real terms. The most rapid growth, of 9.4% per year, was expected to be recorded by the manufacturing sector, with its non-oil and non-gas component projected to expand by 10.3% per year. The achievement of these targets was expected to require a total investment of Rp. 660,000,000m., of which the private sector was expected to account for 73.4%. The vast bulk of this investment was to be generated within Indonesia itself, with foreign funding amounting to less than 6% in net terms (i.e. after adjustments for debt-service payments and the repatriation of profits and dividends). As in Repelita V, investment in the productive sectors was to be left mainly to private entrepreneurs, allowing the Government to concentrate its development expenditure in such fields as infrastructure and human resources.

Official statistics indicated that Indonesia's economic performance had significantly exceeded the Government's targets during the first three years of Repelita VI. GDP was officially estimated to have grown in real terms by 7.5% in 1994, 8.2% in 1995 and 7.8% in 1996, with manufacturing industry expanding by 12.4%, 10.9% and 11.6% in these three years respectively; the utilities, construction and financial services industries also recorded double-digit growth in these three years. With the population estimated to be increasing at less than 2% per year, these economic growth rates implied a substantial annual increase in per caput income levels. A reversal of this favourable trend began in mid-1997, however, as Indonesia succumbed to the Asian economic crisis, with a steady deceleration in quarterly rates of GDP growth from 8.5% in the first quarter to a mere 1.3% in the fourth quarter, causing the annual rate to average only 4.7% in 1997. This deterioration in Indonesia's economic performance continued into 1998, with estimates released by the Central Bureau of Statistics indicating a contraction in GDP by 13.0% in that year.

INDONESIA AND THE ASIAN FINANCIAL CRISIS, 1997–98

Indonesia was affected particularly seriously by the Asian financial crisis, which began in mid-1997 with speculative assaults on the currencies of Thailand, the Philippines and Malaysia. Indonesia initially appeared less vulnerable to these attacks, both because its currency was not pegged as firmly to the US dollar as those of its neighbours, and because its macroeconomic basis appeared more solid, with high rates of GDP growth, low inflation and a much lower ratio between the deficit on the current account of its balance of payments and its GDP. The initial attacks on the rupiah consequently came several weeks after those on the other South-East Asian currencies, and appeared less concentrated. On 14 August, however, the Indonesian authorities were forced to float the rupiah, causing it to depreciate from the previously-established trading range of Rp. 2,378–2,682 per US dollar to Rp. 2,830 by the end of the day. This effective devaluation had a serious impact on Indonesia's corporate and banking sector, which carried substantial volumes of unsecured short-term offshore loans that became much more difficult to service from their largely rupiah-based earnings.

During the weeks following the flotation of the currency the Government announced a number of measures to restore stability, including the imposition of selective foreign-exchange controls and the introduction of a wide-ranging set of policy measures to boost market confidence, comprising, *inter alia*, the removal of all remaining restrictions on foreign investment and the postponement of several large-scale infrastructure projects. However, while these measures helped to forestall further attacks on the rupiah for a time, the threat to the international solvency of Indonesia's banks and businesses caused by the depreciation of the rupiah continued to undermine market sentiment. In October, following a renewed assault on the rupiah in late September by both the international markets and domestic companies seeking dollars to pay or secure their foreign debts, the Government turned to the IMF for assistance. A US $23,000m. rescue programme was subsequently announced by the IMF, the World Bank and the Asian Development Bank (ADB), which included a US $5,000m. commitment of Indonesia's own external assets and was supported by a second tier of bilateral aid commitments of US $15,000m. from Japan, Singapore, the USA, Australia and Malaysia. The programme was conditional on the Indonesian Government's implementation of a wide range of reforms in the areas of fiscal and monetary policy, the restructuring of the financial sector, and the deregulation of the economy.

The enforcement of these conditions proved extremely difficult, however, as they frequently conflicted with the interests of the politically influential conglomerates owned by President Suharto's relatives and associates, which dominated the Indonesian business sector. Increasingly frequent cases of the Government reneging on its reform commitments provoked a further loss of confidence in international financial markets, which were already under pressure as the continued weakness of the rupiah threatened to push many of Indonesia's corporations to the brink of insolvency. As the financial crisis began to jeopardize the real economy, causing inflation and unemployment to increase, political and social tensions also began to rise, most often manifesting themselves in riots and attacks on the economically-powerful ethnic Chinese business community, which served further to erode public confidence.

In an effort to revive the economy, in February 1998 the Government proposed pegging the rupiah to the US dollar at an exchange rate of approximately Rp. 5,000 per dollar by means of a currency board mechanism. This proposal was opposed by Indonesia's major donors, however, and the bitter wrangling that ensued between the Indonesian Government and the donors over the following weeks, culminating in the announcement on 5 March of the suspension of the IMF support programme, led to a further weakening of international confidence in the Indonesian economy. The situation was exacerbated a few days later by the election of the long-standing Minister of State for Research and Technology, B. J. Habibie, to the vice-presidency. Widely known for his free-spending tendencies and enthusiasm for high-technology projects, Habibie's election provoked concern on the financial markets, which was heightened by Suharto's appointment of his daughter Siti Hardiyanti Rukmana, a controversial businesswoman, and several other close business associates to the Cabinet following his re-election as President.

The period immediately after President Suharto's re-election witnessed a resumption of discussions between the Indonesian Government and the IMF, as well as the renewal of efforts to resolve the growing crisis within the Indonesian banking system and of negotiations with the country's external creditors to reschedule private-sector debts of almost US $80,000m. The conclusion in April 1998 of a new, third, agreement with the IMF, and modest progress on the banking reform and debt-rescheduling issues, appeared to offer some hope of an end to the crisis. The markets remained wary, however, and reports soon began to emerge of renewed government regression in the reform process. In May, partly to assuage these concerns, the Government announced a sharp cut in subsidies on fuel, energy and public transport, which resulted in a dramatic increase in the prices of these goods and services, shortly before the governing body of the IMF was scheduled to decide on the disbursement of the next tranche of its financial support programme. These price increases precipitated widespread rioting and an intensification of public protest by the country's students, which eventually led to the abdication of President Suharto on 21 May, after 32 years in power, and his succession by the Vice-President, B. J. Habibie.

By this time, the Indonesian economy had been severely damaged, with international trade having stalled owing to lack of access to finance, GDP having contracted by an officially-estimated rate of 6.2% in the first quarter of 1998, inflation having surged to levels not seen since the mid-1960s, and unemployment having risen to almost 15% of the total workforce of an estimated 90m. Moreover, the change in leadership prompted a renewed moratorium on official aid payments, as the IMF and other multilateral and bilateral donors sought to assess the implications of Habibie's accession to the presidency. Although a further revision of the IMF rescue programme was agreed in June 1998, the damage caused to the economy since mid-1997 had been serious. The principal economic indicators for 1998 as a whole, although more encouraging than the predictions of most analysts, showed a decline in GDP by 13.1% and an inflation rate of 57.7%. A shift in the balance of the current account from a traditional deficit of some US $4,900m. in 1997 to a surplus of US $4,100m. was only due to a decline in the value of imports, from US $46,200m. to US $31,900m.

In view of this severe economic downturn and the attendant social and humanitarian threats, both the IMF and the World Bank reversed their earlier hard-line stance in the latter half of 1998 and began to encourage the Indonesian Government to pursue more expansionary fiscal and economic policies. This culminated in the signing, on 20 October, of a new letter of intent between the IMF and the Indonesian Government, which provided, *inter alia*, for a strengthening of the latter's employment-creation and food-distribution programmes. These developments, combined with intensified efforts to restructure the domestic banking sector and to resolve the corporate offshore debt problem, helped to arrest the economic downturn in the third quarter of 1998.

FALTERING RECOVERY, 1999–

The incipient recovery of the latter half of 1998 continued to strengthen during 1999. It was supported by the comparatively peaceful nature of the legislative election held in June (with the benchmark Jakarta stock index rising by 12% to a 23-month high on the day after the election) and the election of Abdurrahman Wahid to the presidency in October, both of which events generated hopes of a comprehensive break with the past and a greater commitment to economic reform. Official data thus indicated a modest expansion of GDP by 0.8% in real terms in 1999, with inflation easing dramatically to 20.5%, interest rates declining to about 20%–25%, and both the rupiah and the stock market gaining ground.

However, the sustainability of this recovery remained fraught with a number of problems. The banking sector continued to be burdened with high levels of bad debt, estimated in some cases to account for as much as 75%–85% of total loans, and was further undermined in mid-1999 by revelations that one of the country's major banks, Bank Bali, had made illicit payments to a company associated with a leading figure of the ruling Golkar party. Meanwhile, the corporate sector continued to be constrained by its high level of offshore debt, officially estimated at US $65,600m. in mid-1999. Unemployment remained high, and at mid-1999 some 25% of the population were reported to be living in absolute poverty. Furthermore, although the current account of the balance of payments remained in surplus for much of the post-crisis period, this principally reflected a high degree of import compression, which itself threatened to restrain the short-term growth prospects of the economy. In addition, shifts in the relative production costs and prices of a wide range of products caused by the regional economic crisis have significantly altered the competitiveness structures of various

Indonesian industries, and have given rise to the need for extensive inter- and intra-sectoral restructuring.

Despite these problems, the economy recorded a relatively promising performance in 2000, with GDP expanding by 5.2% in real terms, on the basis of a strong growth in exports and a recovery in domestic demand. The rate of inflation also slowed to a mere 3.7%, allowing the monetary authorities to ease interest rates to an average of some 13.5% in an effort to support a continued acceleration of GDP growth. However, these favourable trends were increasingly undermined by a steady deterioration in the political situation, which manifested itself in numerous scandals within the Government, infighting within the political élite in Jakarta, increasing separatist and sectarian violence in several of Indonesia's outlying provinces, and rising crime levels throughout the country. These political difficulties also hampered the Government's ability to meet the deadlines set by the IMF for its economic reform programme, which resulted in a renewed moratorium on the disbursement of IMF funds in December 2000.

During the first half of 2001 the Indonesian economy's capacity to sustain its improved performance of the previous year had become increasingly weak, as political stability was damaged by parliamentary efforts to impeach President Abdurrahman Wahid for alleged corruption and incompetence, while Indonesia's access to foreign financial support continued to be blocked by the IMF's refusal to release payments. The resulting erosion of business confidence led to a sharp downturn in the capital and currency markets, with the exchange rate of the rupiah falling from an average of some Rp. 8,400 to the US dollar in 2000 to more than Rp. 11,000 from April 2001 onwards. By mid-2001 this dramatic deterioration in Indonesia's financial markets had begun to jeopardize the country's prospects for continued economic recovery, as the depreciation of the rupiah significantly raised the costs to both the Government and the corporate sector of servicing their substantial external debts.

Following the inauguration of Megawati Sukarnoputri as the country's President in August 2001, however, the IMF and the Government signed a letter of intent, thus enabling the release of previously unavailable loans and leading to hopes of a revival of the faltering economic recovery. Although Megawati's accession to the presidency also resulted in the restoration of a degree of political stability, the rehabilitation of the economy was interrupted as a result of the global economic uncertainty precipitated by the terrorist attacks on the USA on 11 September 2001. Preliminary data, therefore, suggested that in 2001 the real rate of GDP growth declined to some 3.3%, with inflation rising to 11.5% and causing a renewed, if modest, increase in Bank Indonesia's discount rate to 14.5% by the end of the year. The year-end exchange rate subsequently stood at Rp. 10,400 to the US dollar.

The first half of 2002 witnessed an improvement in Indonesia's economic performance, largely in response to the increased political stability and the resulting growth in market confidence as the Government continued to implement its agreement with the IMF approximately on schedule. The rupiah had strengthened to a rate of below 9,000 to the US dollar by the end of July 2002, and the composite index of the Jakarta Stock Exchange rose from 392 at the end of December 2001 to a peak of 551 on 16 April 2002 (making it one of the best performing markets in the world), before declining again, to some 460, by the end of July. Inflationary pressures started to ease, with only minimal movements being recorded in the consumer price index between March and July 2002. Economic growth began to accelerate, with quarterly data indicating a 2.47% growth in GDP between the last quarter of 2001 and the first quarter of 2002, compared with a decline of 1.47% between the preceding two quarters.

AGRICULTURE

Until it was superseded by manufacturing in 1991, agriculture was the predominant sector of the Indonesian economy in terms of output, although it still accounted for almost 20% of GDP in that year. It remains the most important sector in terms of employment, however, with a national labour force survey showing that it engaged 43.8% of the working population in 2001. The agricultural sector is divided into five subsectors—food crops, cash crops, animal husbandry, fishing, and forestry—of which the food-crop subdivision is the most important in terms of income and employment generation. The other subdivisions play a significant role as earners of non-oil and non-gas export revenues, and were estimated to account for approximately 20% of such earnings in 2001 in both unprocessed and processed forms.

Food Crops

The predominant food crops are rice and other 'secondary' (*palawija*) food staples such as maize, cassava, sweet potatoes and soybeans. Food crops form the most important component of the agricultural sector, and during the five years to 2000 they accounted for approximately 52.0% of agricultural GDP. These crops are usually cultivated on relatively small land-holdings (seldom exceeding 1 ha in size) and under highly complex traditional tenurial relationships, which have historically ensured an adequate level of subsistence for all members of the rural community.

Rice is by far the most important food crop, and is also the preferred staple of the vast majority of Indonesians. Successive governments in the first four decades after independence therefore viewed the achievement and maintenance of rice self-sufficiency as a principal policy objective, and launched several programmes aimed at encouraging farmers to apply productivity-enhancing cultivation techniques and the increased use of purchased inputs such as higher-yielding seeds, chemical fertilizers and pesticides. The impact of these programmes was dramatic, and was enhanced by substantial investment in irrigation infrastructure during the 1970s, which permitted an expansion of cultivated area and multiple cropping. Between 1969 and 1984 gross annual production of milled rice increased at an average annual rate of 5.1%, from 12.3m. tons to 25.9m. tons, while the harvested area increased by almost 22%, from 8m. ha to approximately 9.8m. ha. As a result of these developments, the long-cherished goal of self-sufficiency in rice was reached by 1984/85.

After 1985 the growth of rice production became much more erratic, with sharp increases of output in 1992 and 1995 being interspersed with periods of stagnation or contraction. This was due in part to unfavourable weather conditions and pest infestations, and in part to shifts in government policy, which aimed to match output growth with the growth in demand. Official production data suggest that the steady recovery in production of milled rice, from 26.3m. tons in 1994 to 28.8m. tons in 1996, was reversed in 1997, when production fell to 27.7m. tons, owing to the protracted droughts caused by the intense climatic phenomenon known as El Niño. A further small decline was recorded in 1998, largely as a result of continued adverse weather conditions and the inability of farmers to pay the sharply-increased prices of imported fertilizers and other production inputs. Improved climatic and economic conditions permitted a recovery in rice production to 28.4m. tons in 1999 and 29.0m. tons in 2000, however, temporarily allaying fears about Indonesia's food security, which had been heightened in the aftermath of the economic crisis of 1997–98 as a consequence of serious concerns regarding the country's ability to cover the gap in domestic production through imports. Subsequently, however, these fears re-emerged, following a 4.5% decline in production to 27.7m. tons in 2001; official projections indicated a further decline, of 1.9%, to 27.2m. tons in 2002.

In contrast to the emphasis placed on the intensification of rice production, relatively little effort was made to expand production of the secondary food staples. Consequently, output of these crops remained virtually stagnant during the 1970s, and the production increases that did occur were due to an expansion in planted area rather than to improved yields, which remained low by international standards. Considerable production increases were, however, achieved in the 1980s and early 1990s, with output of maize rising from 3.6m. tons in 1980 to 8.0m. tons in 1992, while annual output of cassava increased from 13.8m. tons to 16.5m. tons, and that of soybeans from 680,000 tons to 1.9m. tons, during the same period. Meanwhile, production of groundnuts increased from 424,000 tons to 739,000 tons. The output of most of these products, except cassava, declined sharply in 1993, owing to adverse weather conditions, but recovered, albeit erratically, in 1994–96. Official data for 1996 showed that the output of maize had risen to the unprecedented level of 9.3m. tons, while that of cassava had reached a record high of 17.0m. tons. The output of sweet potatoes, groundnuts and soybeans remained close to the average of the previous five years, however, at 2.0m. tons, 738,000 tons and 1.5m. tons, respectively. The output of all of these crops declined significantly in 1997, however, as a result of the droughts induced by El Niño, with only a modest and partial recovery being recorded in 1998–2000, followed by further declines in 2001 as climatic and economic conditions deteriorated again.

Cash Crops

Indonesia is an important producer of a wide range of cash crops, including rubber, palm oil, copra, coffee, tea, cocoa, sugar and tobacco. Most of these commodities are grown on commercial plantations as well as smallholdings, and are destined primarily for export. Although the increasing importance of petroleum export earnings in the 1970s caused a decline in the contribution of agricultural exports, whose share of total export value fell from 70% in 1969 to less than 9% in 1983, increasing anxiety about an impending decline in world petroleum prices at the end of the 1970s prompted a reversal of the neglect suffered by the cash crops sector during the early 1970s. Considerable efforts were therefore made during the 1980s and 1990s to promote the growth of cash-crop production.

To increase the productivity of existing plantings, 'intensification' programmes were introduced for annual crops grown principally by smallholders, such as sugar and tobacco. These programmes, involving the provision of extension services and subsidized credit and inputs, were accompanied by similar programmes covering smallholder producers of major perennial cash crops, who were encouraged to replant their stands with higher-yielding varieties, and to employ yield-increasing cultivation techniques. The development of new acreage was also encouraged, *inter alia* through a 'nucleus estate and smallholder' programme providing for the establishment of smallholdings supported by commercial plantations.

Production of most major agricultural commodities expanded considerably during the 1980s and 1990s. National income statistics show that the combined real value (in constant prices) of 'farm non-food crops' and 'estate crops' more than doubled between the late 1970s and the mid-1990s, and continued to rise in the latter half of the decade. There has been considerable variation between crops, however, largely in response to market conditions and to the degree of government support granted to particular commodities. These factors have significantly affected the performance of the principal agricultural export commodities.

Owing to previous neglect of the industry, rubber production increased only sporadically during the 1970s, while efforts were made to rehabilitate the industry. These efforts resulted in rapid increases in production from the late 1970s onwards. This growth trend was cut short, however, by a sharp decline in international rubber prices in 1982, which reduced tappers' incentives; output declined to only 900,000 tons in 1982, compared with 1.05m. tons in the previous year. By 1985 production had recovered to approximately 1981 levels (despite continuing weak prices), as more of the area planted and replanted during the late 1970s became productive. Production subsequently increased steadily to an officially-estimated figure of 1.57m. tons in 1996, before declining marginally to around 1.55m. tons in 1997 as a result of the regional economic crisis and adverse weather conditions. Since then, Indonesia's production of rubber has risen steadily to an estimated 1.75m. tons in 2000. This output level was exceeded only by that of Thailand.

The production of palm oil received considerable encouragement from the Government from 1970, and annual output increased from 216,500 tons in that year to an estimated 6.3m. tons in 2000. Similarly, efforts were also made to promote the growth of coconut oil production, particularly since the mid-1980s. Although palm oil was intended primarily for export, shipments have occasionally been restricted in times of poor harvest in order to ensure adequate supplies of vegetable oil in the domestic market. The most recent attempt of this kind to restrain the rising domestic price of cooking oil was made in January 1998, when the Government introduced an indefinite ban on exports of palm oil. This measure contradicted the open-markets policies pursued by the IMF, however, and an agreement subsequently reached in April of that year specifically provided for the ban to be replaced by a 40% export tax later in the same month, which would itself be gradually phased out as circumstances permitted. As a result of these measures, exports of palm oil declined to less than 1.5m. tons in 1998 from almost 2.9m. tons in 1997, before increasing steadily to an estimated 4.5m. tons in 2001.

Indonesia is one of the world's largest producers of coffee, and output of its mainly *robusta* varieties increased steadily, from 186,300 tons in 1970 to more than 459,000 tons in 1996. Although output declined to 428,000 tons in 1997 as a result of poor weather conditions and the deteriorating economic environment, the subsequent years to 2000 witnessed a recovery to some 510,000–515,000m. tons. Until 1989 Indonesia's exports were subject to stringent quotas imposed by the International Coffee Organization (ICO), which often amounted to less than one-half of total output. The suspension of the ICO's export quotas in July 1989 permitted Indonesia to increase the volume of its coffee exports by almost 18%, from 352,300 tons in 1989 to 414,900 tons in 1990, which enabled it to recover some of the losses incurred as a result of the ensuing fall in prices. However, the volume of exports declined to 249,800 tons in 1992, owing to an excess of coffee on the world markets. Declining supplies and the introduction of a retention scheme by major producers to limit exports resulted in a recovery in the world coffee market in 1993, however, and in an increase in Indonesia's exports to 329,500 tons. Although the following two years witnessed a renewed decline to 226,200 tons by 1995, exports recovered to 362,800 tons in 1996, before falling again to 307,900 tons in 1997. In 1998 exports recovered to 355,700 tons, before declining in the subsequent three years to an estimated 230,000 tons by 2001.

The production of cocoa, which was first planted on a large scale in the mid-1970s, has gained dramatically in importance in Indonesia, which has now become one of the world's largest producers. Output was estimated at 207,150 tons in 1992 and increased steadily to 374,000 tons in 1996, before declining to some 330,000 tons in 1997 as a result of the phenomenon known as El Niño and the economic crisis. Output growth was resumed in 1998, however, and was estimated to have reached 471,000 tons by 2000, before decreasing modestly in 2001, owing to the persistent weaknesses in Indonesia's overall social and economic environment, as well as to adverse weather conditions. The crop has also become an increasingly important export commodity, with the volume of cocoa-bean exports having risen from a mere 6,800 tons in 1981 to 336,700 tons in 2000, before declining to an estimated 316,400 tons in 2001.

Animal Husbandry and Fishing

All the main products of animal husbandry recorded impressive growth between the early 1970s and mid-1990s, with annual meat production increasing from 314,000 tons to 1.63m. tons, egg production from 59,000 tons to 780,000 tons, and milk from 29m. litres to 441m. litres during the period 1970–96. The output of all of these products declined sharply in 1997–98 as a result of the economic crisis, however, and the recovery in subsequent years was relatively slow. Official estimates thus suggested that meat production amounted to a mere 1.45m. tons in 2001, while the production of eggs and milk amounted to 794,000 tons and 505m. litres respectively. Despite efforts to promote the growth of this sector in recent decades, *inter alia* through the import of large numbers of breeding animals, including pigs, dairy and beef cattle, and poultry, in the late 1980s and early 1990s, animal husbandry remains relatively underdeveloped in Indonesia, contributing only about 2.1% of GDP in 2001. The sector was also seriously affected by the economic crisis in 1997–98, and in particular by the depreciation in the value of the rupiah, which raised the cost of imported animal feed and affected the profitability of the commercial animal husbandry enterprises. This resulted in the culling of substantial numbers of dairy animals and poultry during the crisis and the immediate post-crisis period.

In 1982 international recognition of the concept of the archipelagic state permitted Indonesia to declare the waters separating its many islands as an exclusive economic zone (EEZ), giving the country undisputed control over the vast marine fisheries resources of this sea area. These resources began to be developed in 1987, both through the issuing of licences to foreign fishing fleets, and the encouragement of private (including foreign) investment in the fishing industry; particular emphasis was given to shrimp and tuna fisheries. The Government is also seeking to enhance the potential of Indonesia's freshwater fisheries, which provide the bulk of animal protein consumed in Indonesia, through the promotion of freshwater shrimp hatcheries and a nucleus fishpond scheme, similar to the expansion programme for cash crops. Indonesia's shrimp hatcheries, which operated predominantly on a commercial basis, also suffered as a result of the economic crisis.

Forestry

With an estimated 110m. ha, or approximately 57% of its land area covered by forest in 1995, Indonesia has some of the most extensive concentrations of tropical hardwoods in the world. These were exploited at a rapid rate in the late 1960s and, after heavy foreign investment was attracted into the industry during the 1970s, Indonesia's annual output of industrial logs increased from only 4m. cu m in 1963 to an average of 22.2m. cu m between 1974 and 1980, remaining at about this level for much of the following two decades. As the bulk of this production was destined for export, timber became the third most important export commodity, after petroleum and natural gas, during this period.

Following a government decision in 1980 to increase the content of domestic value added in its forestry exports, the export of raw logs was gradually reduced, and in 1985 it was prohibited altogether until June 1992, when the ban was replaced by a high export tax. The promotion of local processing resulted in a rapid increase in plywood production, which rose from about 1m. cu m in 1980 to a peak of 9.9m. cu m in the year to March 1994. After remaining in excess of 9m. cu m during the following two years, however, output declined sharply as the economic crisis drove many producers out of business, and by 1999 production had fallen to approximately 4.6m. cu m. The production of sawn timber also expanded rapidly, reaching 10.9m. cu m in 1989/90, and thereafter fluctuated within the 10m.–12m. cu m range annually until 1997–98, before declining to less than 2.1m. cu m in 1999. The remainder of the domestic wood-processing industry is devoted to the manufacture of veneers, and smaller quantities of furniture and wooden handicrafts.

Despite the continued exploitation of Indonesia's forestry resources, the Government reacted with concern to the environmental implications of indiscriminate logging practices, which characterized the industry during its early years of growth. From the early 1980s the Government increasingly required logging companies to introduce selective cutting policies, and in 1985 the practice of total tree felling was banned. Emphasis was also placed on reafforestation, and logging companies were given the choice of either providing reafforestation deposits, or of carrying out compulsory reafforestation themselves. In September 2000 the Government reimposed a total ban on the export of raw logs. These efforts to protect the country's forestry resources have been only partially successful, however, as witnessed by widespread forest fires in Sumatra and Kalimantan that have become an almost regular feature since the mid-1990s; these frequently generate huge clouds of smoke, which are carried over much of South-East Asia. Many of these fires are set deliberately, both by subsistence farmers practising traditional 'slash-and-burn' methods of cultivation and by large-scale plantation owners seeking to clear the forest for new cash-crop estates.

In addition to tropical rain forests, Indonesia also has sizeable teak plantations. Other significant forestry products are rattan, resins and copal. In order to promote the domestic rattan-processing industry, the Government banned all exports of raw rattan (with effect from January 1987) and of semi-processed rattan products (from July 1988). As with logs, however, this ban was replaced by an export tax in June 1992.

MINING

Petroleum and Natural Gas

The petroleum and natural gas industries have played a crucial role in providing Indonesia with resources to fund its developmental programmes. Owing to the heavy dependence of the economy on such industries for both its foreign exchange and fiscal revenues, the country's prosperity has been closely linked to fluctuations in international petroleum markets. Even after several years of efforts to promote alternative sectors of the economy and the collapse in petroleum and gas revenues, following the international decline in petroleum prices in 1986, the petroleum and natural gas industries have continued to make a disproportionately large contribution to government resources.

According to Indonesian law, sovereign ownership of the country's mineral resources is vested collectively in the Indonesian people, on whose behalf the State (currently through the Department of Mines and Energy) administers all aspects of their exploitation. In the case of petroleum and natural gas, this function has traditionally been delegated to state-owned oil companies, of which the latest, Pertamina, was formed in 1968 by the merger of two existing companies. This statutory provision resulted in a revocation, in 1960, of the concessions that had earlier been granted to foreign oil companies, but, as a result of the technical and financial constraints facing state-owned corporations, foreign oil companies were permitted to continue operating in Indonesia, as contractors of state companies, under several forms of agreement, the most common of which being the profit-sharing contract.

Foreign investment in the Indonesian petroleum industry has been actively encouraged since 1966, and some 285 production-sharing and other contracts had been signed by mid-2001, of which about 130 have subsequently lapsed. Heavy investment, encouraged by the oil price rises of the 1970s, resulted in a rapid increase in output, from 189m. barrels in 1967 to a record 615m. barrels in 1977. Thereafter, fluctuating international supply and demand caused production levels gradually to be reduced to an average of 585m. barrels per year during the period 1978–81. The Organization of the Petroleum Exporting Countries (OPEC) subsequently attempted to maintain prices through the imposition of output restraints, which led to a further decline in Indonesia's production, with annual output levels fluctuating between 484m. barrels and 588m. barrels between 1982 and 2001.

In addition to the proven and probable reserves of some 10,400m. barrels of petroleum, Indonesia had known reserves of natural gas amounting to 114,200,000m. cu ft (equivalent to approximately 20,000m. barrels of petroleum) at the end of 1998. More than one-half of these reserves are located off shore, especially near the Natuna Islands in the South China Sea and near the Bird's Head area of Papua (formerly Irian Jaya—see History). The commercial exploitation of these reserves began in 1977/78, when two major natural gas fields at Arun, in the province of Aceh in northern Sumatra, and Badak, in East Kalimantan, were brought into production, and facilities were established to permit the production of LNG.

The initial development of the LNG industry was linked with the signing of several long-term export contracts to Japan in 1973 and 1981. These contracts were extended until 2011 in mid-1995, and have been supplemented by a number of other sales agreements with Japanese, South Korean and Taiwanese utilities during the past two decades. This growing international demand for LNG, reinforced by the increasing domestic use of natural gas to generate power and to fuel large manufacturing plants, has resulted in a steady expansion of the natural gas production and liquefaction industries. By 1997 Indonesia's production of natural gas and LNG had risen to 3,166,750m. cu ft (corresponding to about 542m. barrels) and 1,402,621,000m. British thermal units (20.6m. tons), respectively, although output of both natural gas and LNG declined modestly in 1998, as a result of the economic crisis. After a recovery in 1999–2000, the production of both natural gas and LNG came under severe threat in 2001 after mounting political unrest in Aceh caused the operator of the Arun field to shut down production in March of that year. Although this stoppage was only temporary, with a phased resumption of production beginning in July, widespread concerns over security issues remained.

With the Arun and Badak fields being gradually depleted, the need to develop new fields had become increasingly urgent in the early 1990s if Indonesia was to be able to meet these commitments. Negotiations on the development of the Natuna field were begun in 1991 between the Indonesian authorities and the US corporation, Exxon, which led to the signing of a formal agreement between the two parties in January 1995. The development of the Natuna field, involving an expected investment of US $35,000m.–$40,000m. over a period of 30 years, proceeded rapidly, and commercial production began on 8 August 2002 with the inauguration of a 96-km pipeline to Malaysia. The volume of sales under the 20-year contract with Malaysia was expected to rise from 100m. cu ft per day in 2002 to 250m. cu ft per day by 2004. However, the heavy costs of developing the Natuna field are expected to prevent the early development of two other large offshore fields, the Wiriager Deep and Muturi fields, discovered near the western coast of Papua in 1996 and 1997 respectively.

Indonesia is also seeking to increase production and exports of liquefied petroleum gas (LPG), which until 1987 was produced almost entirely as a by-product of the refining of crude petroleum. A 1986 agreement to supply 2m. tons of LPG per year to Japan, from 1988 onwards, has led to the construction of specifically-designed LPG facilities at the Arun and Badak natural gas processing plants. In response to an earlier contract signed with Japan in 1983, for the delivery of some 450,000 tons of butane and propane per year, a fractionation plant was also established in 1986 on Bintan island, near Singapore. Between 1981 and 1995 the production of LPG increased from 560,000 tons to 3.9m. tons, before decreasing gradually to less than 2.1m. tons in 2000 in response to declining demand and increased external competition in export markets.

Other Minerals

In addition to petroleum and natural gas, Indonesia has significant (but, in many cases, unquantified) reserves of a variety of other minerals, including coal, tin, bauxite, copper, nickel, iron sands, gold and silver. Most of these are localized, and are frequently situated in remote areas, so that their exploitation often involves high costs.

Indonesia has substantial reserves of coal, estimated at 36,300m. tons at the end of 1995. In order to restrict the growth of domestic petroleum consumption (especially in the production of electricity), a major effort has been made to expand the use of coal as a source of fuel, thereby increasing coal production from 304,000 tons in 1980 to 76.8m. tons in 2000. This effort has involved the expansion of the main existing coalfields at Bukit Asam, in South Sumatra, and Ombilin, in West Sumatra, the promotion of increased exploration, and the development of new fields. It has been accompanied by a sharp increase in coal exports from 2.5m. tons in 1989 to almost 57.2m. tons in 2000, making Indonesia the world's third largest exporter of coal after Australia and South Africa.

Indonesia is one of the world's leading producers of tin. This is mined primarily by a state-owned company, PT Tambang Timah, which was partially privatized in October 1995, on the islands of Bangka and Belitung, off the eastern coast of Sumatra. The devaluation of the rupiah by 30.7% in relation to the US dollar in September 1986, combined with stringent cost-cutting, enabled PT Tambang Timah to remain competitive in the latter half of the 1980s, despite the collapse in world prices following the 1985–86 tin trading crisis; Indonesian tin production rose steadily to a peak of 31,300 tons in 1989. Output fluctuated between 28,200 tons and 30,700 tons in the following years to 1994, largely in response to the imposition of supply controls by the Association of Tin Producing Countries (ATPC) from 1 March 1987. Having been restored to profitability, a proportion of the company's shares were floated in London and Jakarta in October 1995. A firm market recovery in the second half of 1995 and a decision by the ATPC countries to abandon their export restraints with effect from 1 July 1996 resulted in a significant improvement in the industry's outlook. This was underlined by a steady increase in production from 30,610 tons in 1994 to almost 55,200 tons in 1997. Output declined to less than 54,000 tons in 1998, however, largely as a result of the impact of the regional economic crisis, and continued to contract, to 47,753 tons, in 1999, before recovering to 50,166 tons in 2000.

West Borneo and the Riau archipelago are the main sources of Indonesia's bauxite, which is mined on the islands of Tembeling, Kelong, Dendang and Bintan by another state-owned company, PT Aneka Tambang. Other major hard minerals include nickel, which is mined at several locations in Celebes (Sulawesi), principally by the Canadian-owned Inco at Soroako and PT Aneka Tambang at Pomalaa, and copper, which is mined solely by a US company, PT Freeport Indonesia Inc, in a controversial large-scale mining operation in the province of Papua. Copper deposits have also been found in Sumatra, Borneo, Java and Celebes. A recovery in international prices for most of these metals after mid-1987 prompted significant increases in mining output and mineral exports. By 1992 production of nickel ore had increased to 2.50m. tons (gross weight) and, although it declined to 1.98m. tons in 1993, it had risen again to almost 3.43m. tons by 1996 before falling back to approximately 2.83m. tons in 1997. Subsequently it increased again, to 3.35m. tons in 2000. Production of copper concentrate increased from approximately 190,000 tons (gross weight) in 1984 to 3.19m. tons in 2000.

In the mid-1980s Indonesia initiated a major programme to expand its output of precious metals, and of gold in particular. Accordingly, more than 100 contracts were awarded to private companies to explore for gold during 1985–87. It was hoped that as many as 600 further contracts would be signed in the following years, and that the programme would increase Indonesia's production of gold to 150 tons per year by the late 1990s, from 3.3 tons in 1986. Although the implementation of this programme was hindered by a number of infrastructural constraints and the growing problem of illegal mining on concessions offered to private mining companies, output increased substantially to a peak of 129.0 tons in 1999 before declining to 117.6 tons in 2000. Approximately one-half of this total amount was produced by PT Freeport Indonesia at its copper mine in Papua.

MANUFACTURING

During the first two decades after independence, few efforts were made to develop Indonesia's embryonic manufacturing sector. Indeed, many of the relatively unsophisticated industries that did exist fell into decline, as a result not only of the general economic difficulties but also of specific measures such as the expropriation of many foreign-owned enterprises and the replacement of expatriate managements with poorly-trained and ineffectual bureaucracies. By the mid-1960s, therefore, Indonesia's manufacturing sector, which consisted almost entirely of handicrafts and a small textile industry, accounted for less than 10% of GDP.

Following the accession to power of the 'New Order' Government of President Suharto in 1966, however, high priority began to be given to industrial development. While the Government played an active part in this process, through the establishment of numerous state-owned enterprises and through equity participation in large numbers of private enterprises, it also sought to encourage private investors, both domestic and foreign, to contribute to Indonesia's industrialization. This resulted in the rapid expansion of manufacturing industry, so that by the mid-1990s Indonesia had the capacity to produce a wide variety of goods ranging from handicrafts to high-technology aerospace products. In 1991 the manufacturing sector superseded agriculture as the largest contributor to GDP, and by 1997 it had acquired a share of almost 27% of GDP.

The industrialization strategy initially adopted by the Indonesian Government was characterized by the establishment of import-substitution enterprises at all levels of manufacturing, including several in which the country has only a questionable comparative advantage. These enterprises therefore required considerable protection, through tariff and non-tariff barriers, which tended to perpetuate inefficiency. As industrialization became increasingly 'upstream', these inefficiencies were compounded by the obligation of 'downstream' producers to procure inputs from domestic producers of capital and intermediate goods, or from officially-licensed importers, who had little cause to reduce their selling prices much below those charged by domestic suppliers. This gave rise to the much-debated 'high-cost economy' and the lack of international competitiveness suffered by much of Indonesia's manufacturing industry, and also stimulated a series of liberalizing reforms aimed at improving the export potential of Indonesia's manufactured products in response to the 1986 depression in world petroleum prices.

These measures proved very successful and a strong growth in manufactured exports took place after 1987. Particularly encouraging was the fact that the increase in traditional exports of semi-processed raw materials was accompanied by a corresponding rise in exports of manufactured end-use products, such as cement, iron and steel products, and motor vehicles.

Of Indonesia's main products, most consumer goods, such as processed foods and beverages, tobacco products, textiles and garments, motor vehicle components and assemblies, and electrical appliances, are produced by the private manufacturing sector, often in joint ventures with foreign companies. In many of the capital and intermediate goods industries, such as chemicals, cement, glass, fertilizers, ceramics, machinery and basic metal products, the Government plays an important role, with the private sector excluded from some industries, such as those producing fertilizers. In addition to more 'formal' industries, the Government has also promoted the establishment of small-scale enterprises, often involving the production of handicrafts and organized on a co-operative basis, as a means of generating employment in rural areas.

One of the major objectives of Indonesia's industrialization policy has been to add value to domestically-produced raw materials. Consequently, a variety of processing industries has been set up, ranging from relatively small-scale units for the processing of agricultural commodities and forestry products (including food-processing enterprises, crumb rubber factories, processing plants for crude palm oil, plywood mills and sawmills and establishments for the manufacture of rattan products) to several large-scale petrochemical plants located in various parts of Indonesia, as well as processing units for Indonesia's hard minerals, of which the aluminium smelter on the Asahan river in North Sumatra is the most significant.

Another important goal has been the installation of a domestic manufacturing capacity for industries defined as having strategic importance, which has resulted in the establishment of a number of (usually state-owned) high-technology industries in such fields as telecommunications and shipbuilding, as well as an aerospace industry, based in Bandung. A particularly controversial example of this policy to develop a domestic manufacturing base for certain industries was a decision announced in February 1996 to provide special tax and tariff incentives to a private company owned by one of President Suharto's sons to produce a national car with an eventual local content of more than 60%. However, under the terms of the financing agreements reached with the IMF in 1997–98, this approach to industrialization was being reconsidered, with the national car project having been suspended as a consequence of the economic crisis and subsequently revived as a regular joint venture with a South Korean company.

The manufacturing sector was particularly badly affected by the regional financial crisis from 1997. Having drawn heavily on offshore loans in earlier years, the sector was largely insolvent by mid-1998, and many jobs had been lost. Declining demand in the domestic market and the inability to raise trade credits to finance imports of components or exports of finished products exacerbated the situation. Consequently, manufacturing value added decreased by 11.4% in 1998, with its share in GDP declining from almost 27% in 1997 to approximately 25% in 1998. With the sector recording a growth of 3.8% in 1999, 5.5% in 2000, and 4.3% in 2001, its share of GDP had recovered to about 26% by 2000. In the aftermath of the financial crisis, moreover, the Government began to reconsider the conglomerate-based industrialization strategy adopted in the past, and planned to focus more on the promotion of small and medium-sized enterprises in the future.

INFRASTRUCTURE

Transport

At the time of the 'New Order' Government's accession to power, Indonesia's transport infrastructure was limited, and in an extremely poor state of repair. In the following three decades, however, great emphasis was placed on the rehabilitation and expansion of transport facilities, with public investment in the transportation and tourism sectors averaging 18% of total government capital spending during Repelitas I and II, almost 13% during Repelita III, 15% during Repelita IV and 20% during Repelita V. Priority continued to be given to infrastructure development in Repelita VI (1994/95–1998/99), under which the transport sector was scheduled to receive 21.5% of total projected capital expenditure. This target was exceeded in the first four years of the plan period, when the share of public spending on transport and communications averaged almost 22% in each year. Despite significant improvements brought about by these investments, many transport facilities remain inadequate and continue to inhibit economic development. Their effectiveness has suffered further in the aftermath of the 1997/98 crisis, as the resulting financial constraints have reduced repair and maintenance activities and contributed to a deterioration of the existing infrastructure.

In 1999 Indonesia had a total road length of 355,951 km, almost 60% of which was located in Sumatra, Java and Bali. On these islands most cities are now connected by highways or secondary roads, and several major motorway projects have been completed. Indonesia's railway services are limited to the islands of Java (including Madura), where most major cities are connected, and Sumatra, where three separate networks, with a total track length of some 6,500 km, operate in the northern, western and southern parts of the island. A major programme to rehabilitate the country's rail services, initiated in 1981, had resulted, by mid-1999, in the renovation or replacement of about 3,000 passenger carriages and some 27,000 freight wagons. Proposals to establish a 150-km network to facilitate commuter travel between Jakarta and its suburbs, as well as an underground mass rapid transit system in central Jakarta, have also been developed. However, the implementation of such projects has been delayed by the effects of the economic crisis. River transport plays an important role in several regions, notably Kalimantan and eastern Sumatra; in the 1999/2000 fiscal year 70.2m. passengers and 27.8m. tons of freight were transported by this means.

Considerable efforts have been made to expand and upgrade ports and shipping since the mid-1980s. An ambitious six-year port modernization programme, financed in part by the World Bank and the ADB, was initiated in 1985. In 1984, in an attempt to modernize the country's ageing merchant fleet, the authorities introduced a policy whereby all cargo vessels of more than 25 years of age were to be replaced with locally-designed and -built freighters. This policy had to be suspended in 1988, owing to the inability of the local shipbuilding industry to provide adequate numbers of replacement vessels. Inter-island passenger shipping was also being improved, through the introduction of new liners, funded partially with aid from the Federal Republic of Germany.

Air transport in Indonesia is relatively well developed, with 61 recognized main airports in mid-2002, most of which were capable of handling aircraft of at least Fokker F-28 size. The largest airline is the state-owned Garuda Indonesia, which operated an all-jet fleet of 49 aircraft in mid-2002. A number of other airlines, mostly privately-owned, operate domestic and regional services. The country's civil aviation sector was negatively affected by the regional economic crisis and political unrest in late 1997 and early 1998, with a number of the smaller, privately-owned carriers suffering particularly as a result of rising costs and declining revenues. In mid-1999 Sempati Air became the first serious casualty of the crisis when it was declared bankrupt.

Electric Power

Indonesia's power-generating capacity expanded rapidly between 1966 and 1998, from approximately 650 MW to some 21,000 MW, most of which was operated by the state-owned power generating company, Perusahaan Listrik Negara (PLN, now Perusahaan Umum Listrik—PUL). As late as 1980, some 95% of Indonesia's electricity was generated by oil- or gas-fuelled plants, but by 2000, as a result of a deliberate diversification policy, oil- and gas-fuelled plants (including combined-cycle plants) accounted for less than 50% of Indonesia's power-generating capacity, with the remainder being generated by coal-fired steam, hydropower and geothermal power plants. Indonesia's power-generating capacity was officially projected to reach 22,000 MW by the year 2000. Approximately one-half of this additional capacity was to be installed by PUL, with the remainder being established by private companies under 'build-operate-transfer' contracts with the state-owned company. However, the onset of the regional economic crisis in 1997 resulted in the indefinite suspension of these projects, and in a modest decline in power production in 1999 and 2000 to slightly more than 20,000 MW.

TRADE

For more than a decade from the mid-1970s, Indonesia's export trade was dominated by crude petroleum and natural gas, which, between 1980 and 1985, accounted for an average of 76% of total export revenue. Consequently, Indonesia's export earnings became heavily dependent on the vagaries of the international energy markets during this period. After 1986, however, the Indonesian Government adopted a wide range of measures aimed at promoting the expansion of non-hydrocarbon exports, which resulted in a significant shift in the composition of Indonesia's exports. In 1987 the value of non-oil and non-gas exports exceeded the value of petroleum and gas exports for the first time in almost 15 years. This trend was reinforced in the following years, and the share of petroleum and gas exports declined steadily; with only a brief interruption in 1990 caused by the sharp increase in international energy prices as a result of the Iraqi invasion of Kuwait; the share had fallen to approximately 24% by 1996. Another temporary increase in this share, to 29%, occurred in 1997, owing to the high energy prices prevailing in the early part of that year, following which the sector's share declined to a mere 16% of total export revenue in 1998. In 1999–2001, however, this share increased markedly, to approximately 23%, owing initially to the severe contraction of non-oil and non-gas exports caused by continuing effects of the economic crisis, and subsequently to the sharp increase in world oil prices in 2000 and their continued stability in 2001.

Indonesia's merchandise trade has consistently recorded a surplus. Even in the early 1980s, when weakening international oil prices caused a decline in export earnings, the trade surplus was sustained by appropriate government policy measures and the general deceleration of economic activity, the combination of which reduced import demand. The renewed growth in export earnings in the late 1980s caused a steady increase in the trade surplus, from US $2,458m. in 1986 to US $6,664m. in 1989, although this trend was reversed in the following years as increased imports, associated with a rapid acceleration in the growth of domestic consumption and investment, prompted a progressive reduction of the surplus to US $4,801m. in 1991. After recovering to US $8,231m. in 1993, the trade surplus began to contract again, narrowing progressively to US $5,129m. in 1996. A sharp reversal in this trend occurred in 1997 as a result of the Asian financial crisis, which prompted an increase in the surplus to US $25,042m. by 2000, largely as a result of the strong compression of imports prompted by the devaluation of the rupiah and the general economic downturn during this period. Preliminary data for 2001 suggested a renewed reduction in the surplus on the merchandise account to US $21,647m., reflecting a significant decline in exports owing to the deceleration of economic growth in that year.

The surplus on the merchandise account has usually been more than offset by a consistent deficit on invisible items, resulting from interest payments on Indonesia's external debt and the repatriation of profits by foreign investors, and also from Indonesia's heavy dependence on foreign transport services. Indonesia's current account was therefore in deficit for most of the 1980s and 1990s. This deficit increased particularly sharply from US $2,790m. in 1994 to US $7,663m. in 1996, before narrowing to US $4,889m. in 1997 as the regional economic crisis prompted a reduction in trade and a slowdown in debt repayments and profit repatriation. These developments resulted in the recording of a highly unusual surplus of US $4,096m. on Indonesia's current account in 1998, which increased steadily to US $7,985m. by 2000, before easing to an estimated US $4,977m. in 2001.

Apart from petroleum and gas, which, despite their diminished importance, remain the country's principal export products, the bulk of Indonesia's exports consist of primary and semi-processed agricultural and mineral commodities. The most important of these have traditionally been rubber, coffee, tin, shrimps and palm oil. Exports of logs, which accounted for 7.6% of total exports in 1980, declined into virtual insignificance in the following years and were replaced by exports of processed wood, which in 1994 contributed almost 13% of total export value. This share declined gradually to approximately 9% in 1997 and 1998, and further to some 7% in 2000 and 2001, owing to marketing problems and increased foreign competition in Indonesia's main export markets. Another group of manufactured exports that expanded rapidly during the 1980s but suffered a similar contraction in the mid-1990s was textiles and garments. Its share of total exports increased from 0.4% in 1980 to 17.8% in 1992, but subsequently declined to 9.7% by 1997 before recovering sharply to 14.8% in 1998 and 17.8% in 1999 as exports of other products contracted more rapidly. This trend was reversed in 2000, however, when the increase in petroleum prices raised the value of the oil and gas component of Indonesia's external trade. Following efforts to promote non-oil and -gas exports, a wide range of other manufactured goods also began to assume an increasingly important share of the country's exports in the early and mid-1990s, although this trend was arrested by the impact on the manufacturing sector of the regional economic crisis which began in 1997. Indonesia's imports, meanwhile, consisted largely of capital and intermediate goods between the mid-1980s and 2001, as the domestic expansion of rice production and import-substituting manufacturing caused imports of consumer goods to be sharply reduced.

Indonesia's trade was traditionally biased towards Japan, the USA and Singapore, which together accounted for approximately 77% of exports and 52% of imports during the 1980s. This pattern changed only modestly in the following decade. Japan remained the most important trading partner in 2001, purchasing approximately 23% of Indonesia's exports and supplying 15% of imports, while the USA accounted for 14% of Indonesia's exports and 10% of its imports in the same year. Singapore remained the third most important destination for Indonesia's exports and supplier of its imports in 2001, accounting for some 10% of Indonesia's total exports and imports, but in the early 1990s was occasionally surpassed as an import supplier by Germany and the Republic of Korea.

TOURISM

The tourism industry in Indonesia developed rapidly from the 1980s, as the country emerged as an increasingly important long-haul destination for tourists from Europe, the Americas and the Asia-Pacific region. This development was actively encouraged by the Government, which took a conscious decision in the mid-1980s to promote the industry as a means of creating employment, generating foreign exchange and stimulating the economic and social development of some of the country's more remote, but touristically attractive, regions. This resulted in an easing of the previously highly restrictive visa requirements for foreign visitors in 1983, and the introduction of several promotional campaigns by the national airline, Garuda Indonesia. In subsequent years, a number of additional measures were taken to support the growth of the industry, including the further liberalization of entry regulations, the encouragement of private-sector investment in tourism-related facilities, the establishment of an increasing number of 'gateway' airports and seaports and the development of the associated infrastructure, and the progressive opening of regional airports to foreign carriers. Considerable efforts also continued to be made to publicize Indonesia's tourism potential in the major overseas markets, which culminated in the launching of a 'Visit Indonesia Year' campaign in 1991 and its subsequent extension, under a 'Visit Indonesia Decade' banner, to the year 2000.

These measures had a dramatic impact. Over the following years the increasingly intensive promotion of the industry prompted a sharp acceleration of its expansion, with the number of tourist arrivals exceeding 1m. in 1987, 2m. in 1990, 3m. in 1992, 4m. in 1994, and 5m. in 1996 and 1997 (in which years the value of receipts from tourism was recorded as US $6,308m. and US $5,321m., respectively). This growth in tourist arrivals and spending was accompanied by a corresponding increase in tourist facilities, as exemplified by a rise in the number of star-rated hotel rooms from 34,300 in 1980 to almost 70,000 in 1996, and an increase in the number of travel agencies operating in Indonesia from 330 to 2,225 during the same period. However, the tourism industry suffered a serious set-back as a result of the political unrest and economic crisis of 1997/98, which led to a sharp decline in the number of tourist arrivals to approximately 4.6m. in 1998, in which year the value of receipts from tourism was recorded as US $3,459m. In 1999 the number of tourist arrivals rose marginally, to 4.7m., but continued social and political instability depressed the number to below 4.2m. in both 2000 and 2001.

FOREIGN AID AND INVESTMENT

The ambitious development programmes that Indonesia has introduced since the late 1960s have necessitated enormous investments of capital. Since these capital needs have been considerably in excess of Indonesia's own resources, even in the 1970s (when there was a dramatic increase in petroleum revenues), a significant proportion of investment requirements have been met from abroad, in the form of commercial and concessional loans, as well as direct foreign investments.

Aid

Indonesia has substantial foreign borrowings, estimated at some US $131,200m. at the end of 2001, the major part of which have historically been incurred by the Government and state-owned enterprises. According to data published by the central bank, the total disbursed volume of such loans amounted to approximately US $71,400m. at the end of 2001. The remaining debt of US $60,300m. was held by the private sector. The overall figure included US $25,200m. in short-term debt (with an original maturity of up to one year), the vast bulk of which was held by the private sector. The majority of Indonesia's public-sector debt derives from loans that were disbursed through the IGGI consortium, which co-ordinated the official financial assistance that Western donors provided to Indonesia until 1991. IGGI's annual commitments were running at approximately US $2,400m. during the early 1980s, although they increased steadily in subsequent years to US $4,750m. in 1991.

In March 1992, angered by the human rights conditions attached to its aid by the Dutch Government (which traditionally held the chairmanship of IGGI), the Indonesian Government rejected all further Dutch aid and requested the dissolution of IGGI. IGGI was replaced by the Consultative Group for Indonesia (CGI), chaired by the World Bank, which held its first meeting in Paris, France, in July 1992, when it pledged an annual total of US $4,940m. This was progressively increased to US $5,360m. by the CGI's fourth meeting in July 1995, and was reduced only marginally to US $5,260m. at its fifth meeting in June 1996. This level was left broadly unchanged at the Group's sixth meeting in July 1997, and was increased to approximately US $5,900m. at the seventh meeting held in July 1999. At its next pledging session in October 2000 the CGI approved budget support loans of US $4,800m. for the Government, as well as US $530m. in loans for technical co-operation projects implemented through non-governmental organizations. Much of the budgetary support loan remained undisbursed as late as mid-2001, however, owing to the lenders' concerns over the slow implementation of the IMF-sponsored reform programme and the unstable political situation in Indonesia. The situation began to improve following the accession of Megawati Sukarnoputri to the presidency in August 2001, and at the next CGI meeting held in October of that year the CGI pledged a further US $3,140m. for 2002.

The liberalization of regulations governing foreign borrowing by Indonesian banks and firms also prompted a rapid rise in the private sector's foreign indebtedness. The volume of this debt was estimated to have increased by almost US $6,000m. in 1990 alone. This caused considerable concern in the Government, which sought to exercise increasingly forceful forms of moral suasion to limit overseas borrowing by private enterprises, and in September 1991 formed a special inter-ministerial team to examine the commercial borrowing plans of all investment projects involving official participation. However, these measures failed to restrain the growth of corporate offshore debt incurred by the Indonesian banking sector and many of the country's business conglomerates, and this debt played a significant role in precipitating and exacerbating the financial and economic crisis of 1997–98.

Forecasts prepared by the World Bank suggested that Indonesia's debt repayment schedule would have peaked in the first half of 2002. In order to ease the resulting pressures, the Government sought to negotiate debt-rescheduling agreements with both its official and private creditors. The first such agreement was concluded in April 2002 with the 'Paris Club' of official creditors, which provided for a rescheduling of US $5,400m. from the total debt-service obligations of US $7,500m. falling due between 1 April 2002 and 31 December 2003. This was followed by an announcement in June 2002 that the 'London Club' of commercial creditors had similarly agreed, in principle, to extend the servicing of a number of loans taken out by the Indonesian Government in 1995–97. The outlook for the repayment of Indonesia's large volume of private sector debt was more difficult. In early 2002 it was announced that three Indonesian firms had defaulted on debts totalling some US $1,500m., and further defaults appeared likely, even though most Indonesian firms preferred to reach some agreement with their creditors involving a combination of debt restructuring, debt forgiveness and deferred payments.

Investment

During the early years of the 'New Order' Government, high priority was given to attracting foreign investment, and the enactment of the Foreign Investment Law of 1967 granted investors a high degree of protection and a wide range of privileges. As Indonesia's resource position improved during the 1970s, the number of restrictions placed on foreign investors began to increase, but after mid-1984 many of these restrictions were relaxed.

Between 1967 and the end of 2001 foreign investment projects worth about US $250,000m. had been approved by a national investment co-ordinating board, the Badan Koordinasi Penanaman Modal (BKPM), although this total excluded investments in the petroleum, natural gas and financial sectors, which were beyond the BKPM's jurisdiction. Considerable concern was aroused by a significant decrease in the number of investment applications during the early 1980s, reflecting the dissatisfaction of potential investors with the restrictions placed on their activities by the Government. This prompted the Government to initiate a process of deregulation to attract foreign investment which began to take effect in 1987. The value of projects approved by the BKPM increased steadily in subsequent years, and peaked at US $10,292m. in 1992, before declining to approximately US $8,100m. in 1993. The upward trend resumed after the introduction of a particularly wide-ranging set of deregulatory reforms in mid-1994, with the total value of foreign investment projects approved in that year by the BKPM amounting to US $23,700m. This upward trend persisted in 1995, when the BKPM approved projects worth almost US $40,000m., but suffered a set-back in 1996, when the value of approved projects declined to approximately US $30,000m. A modest recovery was recorded in 1997, when the value of approved projects rose to US $33,833m. However, the deepening financial and economic crisis resulted in a sharp reduction in the value of approved projects to US $13,563m. in 1998 and US $10,891m. in 1999, although a recovery to US $15,283m. was recorded in 2000. This recovery proved temporary, however, and the volume of approved investment fell again, to less than US $9,000m., in 2001. Furthermore, the available data suggest that only a relatively small proportion (estimated at about 33%) of approved investment projects had actually been implemented by the end of 2001.

The sectoral distribution of these investments has been heavily biased towards manufacturing, which had received about 70% of approved domestic and 65% of approved foreign capital investment by the end of 2001. Apart from the manufacturing sector, such investment has been channelled mainly into agriculture, tourism, infrastructure and financial services. Interest in infrastructural investment, including power generation and transport services, rose particularly rapidly after mid-1994, when new deregulation measures opened these sectors to foreign participation.

FINANCE

The economic turmoil of the early 1960s left Indonesia with a thoroughly disrupted financial system. Rampant inflation, caused by persistently large budgetary deficits, an absence of monetary restraint, and the isolation of the state-run banking system from market forces, had caused major disruptions to the country's financial structure. Between 1966 and the mid-1990s considerable efforts were made to stabilize the financial sector, but these efforts were undermined by the liberalization policies introduced after the mid-1980s and their abuse by an increasingly corrupt and politically well-connected business élite. The financial sector was consequently ill-prepared to withstand the financial crisis of 1997/98, and its poor handling by the Government and multinational agencies such as the IMF.

Fiscal Policy

In response to the economic crisis of the mid-1960s, President Suharto's 'New Order' Government committed itself to the principle of a balanced budget—implying the absence of budget deficits financed from domestic sources—shortly after assuming office in 1966. The somewhat unorthodox definition of a balanced budget employed by the Suharto Government permitted receipts of foreign aid to be classified as revenues, rather than as means through which to finance a deficit, however, and the Government retained the option of using surplus revenues to increase its deposits at the central bank. These deposits could then be drawn upon for extrabudgetary funding of government spending in times of reduced revenues. Consequently, the nominal budgetary balance often concealed quite substantial deficits. This pattern persisted until 1997, when an agreement was reached with the IMF introducing more standard budgeting practices; it allowed a (domestically funded) budget deficit equivalent to 3.5% of GDP in the 1998/99 fiscal year to counteract the contraction caused by the ongoing economic crisis. Such deficits, albeit with a gradually declining magnitude, have been permitted in subsequent years, with the deficit for 2002 being fixed at 2.5% of GDP.

A number of other major fiscal policy reforms have also been introduced in the post-Suharto era. After a transitional nine-month budget period from 1 April to 31 December 2000, the fiscal year was adjusted to coincide with the calendar year from 2001. At the same time a wide-ranging decentralization of the budgetary process was introduced, with the generation of public revenues and expenditure being devolved to the provincial and district level to a large extent. This resulted in a dramatic reduction in the central Government's revenues, and threatened to increase the prosperity gap between the densely-populated and resource-poor provinces of Java and the less heavily-populated, resource-rich provinces in the outer islands. The devolution of many fiscal powers to the district level caused particularly serious problems, as it created considerable differences in local taxation levels and generated widespread uncertainty among personal and corporate taxpayers. More recently the Government has been attempting to remove some of these excesses by shifting many of the powers held at district level to the provincial level. A comprehensive restructuring of Indonesia's archaic and arcane tax system was undertaken during the 1980s, with further wide-ranging reforms being introduced in late 1994. These measures involved the introduction of a simplified income tax code, value-added tax, and revised property tax and stamp duty regulations. Forceful measures were also taken to enforce these taxes. This resulted in substantial increases in the Government's non-oil and non-gas domestic revenues (excluding foreign aid flows), in nominal terms, from Rp. 4,913,000m. in the fiscal year 1983/84 to Rp. 197,600,000m. in 2001.

Government spending is divided into the usual categories of recurrent and capital expenditure, and has historically been an important element in the generation of employment and national income. The State employs some 17% of the labour force, and public contracts have been a major source of income for a number of private sector suppliers. Changes in Indonesia's economic fortunes in the mid-1980s necessitated a deceleration in the rate of growth of public expenditure and caused greater emphasis to be shifted from capital expenditure to the less capital- and import-intensive recurrent expenditure, in an effort to maintain domestic demand and the economic growth rate. Even within the capital budget, increasing emphasis was given to agricultural and infrastructural development, which provided the greatest domestic benefits. In the late 1980s the growth of capital expenditure began to accelerate again, as structural adjustments and rising inflows of foreign funds made more resources available, and as mounting population pressure emphasized the urgent need for an acceleration of economic growth rates. The volume of capital expenditure in 1999/2000 was thus more than five times as high in nominal rupiah terms as the recorded capital expenditure in 1989/90. In 2001 the central Government's development expenditures amounted to some 15% of total government expenditures.

Money and Banking

Indonesia's financial sector is headed by Bank Indonesia, the central bank. For almost two decades, until the late 1980s, commercial banking was dominated by five large state-owned banks. In addition there were 11 foreign branch banks (whose activities were, however, confined to the Jakarta area) and some 70 private banks, of which 10 were licensed to deal in foreign exchange. The banking industry also comprised a state-owned national development bank, as well as provincial development banks in each of Indonesia's 27 provinces, and a state-owned savings bank. Fourteen 'non-bank financial institutions', performing a variety of merchant-banking functions, had also been established. By the end of 1988 there were also more than 80 leasing companies, 90 insurance companies, and a stock exchange, which had traded since 1977.

The restoration of fiscal balance in the late 1960s was accompanied by a reimposition of monetary control and wide-ranging reforms of financial sector institutions. While the controls enabled a non-inflationary development of priority sectors to take place, there were considerable inefficiencies in the mobilization and allocation of resources. Following the 1983 reductions in the price of petroleum, therefore, a significant reform of the banking sector took place, and there was a return to indirect forms of monetary control. Most of the previously-imposed credit and interest-rate restrictions had been abolished by 1987, and had been replaced by a variety of indirect means of regulating liquidity, including money-market securities and discount window facilities to generate liquidity and assist banks facing temporary shortages, as well as special forms of discount instruments, known as Bank Indonesia Certificates, to reduce surplus liquidity.

The reform process continued into the late 1980s and early 1990s, and culminated in the introduction of new banking legislation in 1992. The reforms were aimed at simplifying the structure of the banking system and facilitating an enhanced mobilization of investable resources, while simultaneously ensuring the efficient use of these resources in productive investments. The categories of recognized banking institutions were reduced to two—commercial banks and small-scale credit banks—and many of the remaining restraints on banking were withdrawn: foreign branch banks operating in Jakarta were given permission to open sub-branches in six regional capitals; domestic banks were allowed to form joint-venture banks with international institutions which maintained representative offices in Jakarta; the upper limit on offshore borrowing by Indonesian commercial banks was removed; privately-owned banks were granted permission to compete with state-owned banks in attracting deposits from the parastatal enterprises; and licensing requirements for dealing in foreign exchange were relaxed.

Efforts were also made to invigorate the Indonesian Stock Exchange by partially opening it to foreign institutional investors. This policy was reinforced by the provision of a wide range of incentives to encourage the flotation on the Jakarta Stock Exchange of domestically-incorporated firms and equalizing the taxes applicable to interest earned from time and savings deposits and dividends received on equity holdings. A special 'over-the-counter' stock exchange was established in Jakarta, and private entrepreneurs were given permission to create privately-owned regional stock markets in several provincial capitals, with one stock exchange being established in Surabaya. Measures were also taken to encourage the entry of new firms, including foreign joint ventures, into the leasing, factoring, venture capital, securities trading, credit-card and consumer finance industries.

The new reforms stimulated a dramatic expansion of the Indonesian financial sector. By the end of 1989 no fewer than 14 new joint-venture banks, 26 locally-owned private commercial banks and 250 secondary banks had been licensed by Bank Indonesia, while existing banks had opened more than 700 new branches. This growth continued in the following years, and by the end of 1996 the number of commercial banks totalled 239, while the number of secondary banks had risen to 9,276. In the capital markets the number of companies listed on the Jakarta Stock Exchange, which began computerized trading in mid-1995, increased from 24 in 1988 to almost 290 by the end of 1996. Its growth was accompanied by the emergence of a strong overseas interest in the Indonesian capital markets, with a number of major international brokerages establishing a presence in Indonesia.

This unrestrained growth of the financial sector inevitably gave rise to fears about its viability, which were reinforced by a number of bank failures and several well-publicized scandals involving banks and securities firms. In addition, the precipitous increase in the money supply that was associated with this expansion of financial institutions placed considerable strains on Indonesia's economic stability and threatened to fuel a significant acceleration of inflation. To counteract these developments, the Indonesian authorities began to intensify their supervision of the country's financial intermediaries from mid-1990 onwards, while at the same time taking measures to limit the growth of domestic liquidity. These policies, which resulted in temporary surges in interest rates to 30% per annum, were sustained in 1991 and the first half of 1992, and had considerable success in restraining the excessive expansion of the economy and in curbing inflation, albeit at the cost of precipitating a mild recession. These developments also had serious implications for the financial sector, as the banks experienced increased repayment arrears, owing to the inability of their over-extended customers to meet their debt-service obligations, and the stock markets stagnated because of the reduced liquidity in the economy.

Having succeeded in curbing the inflationary pressures of the previous two years, and concerned to prevent a further deepening of the recession, the Government began to relax its stringent monetary policies from mid-1992. By June 1993 interest rates had declined to their lowest levels in seven years, which stimulated a strong economic recovery in the following years. The Government subsequently began to tighten monetary policy, and there was a modest rise in interest rates as the renewed surge in economic activity provoked a resurgence of inflationary pressures. Efforts were also being made to address the issue of bad debt, which in April 1995 was estimated at Rp. 9,780,000m., representing 4.2% of the assets of the banking system.

These measures enabled Indonesia to maintain a comparatively high degree of monetary stability until mid-1997, but proved unable to withstand the turmoil precipitated by the Thai financial crisis which then erupted. This caused the Indonesian currency and capital markets to come under severe speculative pressure in the second half of the year, and a corresponding collapse of the rupiah's exchange rate and the prices of shares in companies listed on the Indonesian stock markets.

The rationalization of the financial sector, involving in particular a restructuring of the banking system, is a major priority of the reform measures the Indonesian Government agreed to undertake as part of the rescue programme negotiated with the IMF in 1997–98. The first step in this direction was taken in November 1997, when the Government announced plans to close 16 banks known to be burdened by a high level of bad debt. This was followed in January 1998 by the establishment of the Indonesian Bank Restructuring Agency (IBRA), which was assigned the task of rehabilitating the highly-indebted financial and corporate sectors, and acquired control of almost US $70,000m. in the form of both equity and debt from the banks that had failed during the financial crisis. IBRA was intended to strengthen the industry by consolidating the large number of existing, and often troubled, banks into a few solid entities through a combination of closures, mergers, recapitalization and privatizations by 2004. This rescue plan, which also provided for the surviving banks to raise their capital adequacy ratios (CARs) to 8% by 2001, was to be funded through the issue of government bonds worth a total of Rp. 157,600,000m.

The results of the financial sector rehabilitation programme have been inconsistent. While four of the state-owned commercial banks were successfully merged into a single new institution, PT Bank Mandiri, in July 1999, the sale of IBRA assets proved particularly difficult for various reasons. These included: low offer prices; machinations by politically influential former owners seeking to buy back their assets; nationalistic reservations concerning the sale of national assets to foreigners; and, following the introduction of the decentralization measures of 2001, political difficulties at the local level.

Although the process of restoring the banking system to some degree of health has largely been achieved in the interim, the sale of the remaining banks in IBRA's portfolio has continued to give rise to numerous legal and political complications. It was not until April 2002, after some two years of uncertainty, that IBRA finally sold a 51% stake in Bank Central Asia, once the flagship of the highly influential Salim conglomerate, and the largest domestically owned private bank in Indonesia, to a US company, Farallon Capital Management. The sale of several other banks was scheduled for 2002, but after IBRA's failure to divest itself of a similar share in the medium-sized Bank Niaga in mid-June, this effort was postponed indefinitely.

ECONOMIC PROSPECTS

The Asian financial crisis of the late 1990s took a heavy toll in Indonesia. Although by 2000 the economy had stabilized to some degree—with inflation having been reduced almost to a single-digit figure, interest rates having been lowered, and a surplus having been achieved on the current account of the balance of payments—the situation deteriorated again in 2001, largely owing to the ongoing political uncertainty prevailing in the country. This continued to erode both domestic and international confidence in Indonesia's future, and played a major role in precipitating a serious weakening of the capital and currency markets. By mid-2001 this deterioration in the financial markets had begun to place in jeopardy Indonesia's prospects for continued economic recovery.

Megawati Sukarnoputri's appointment as President in August 2001 helped to restore a degree of investor confidence, and preliminary indicators suggested that the economy's performance would improve markedly in 2002 in comparison with 2001. Provided that the country's overall stability was maintained, economic expansion was expected to continue in the second half of 2002 and into 2003. Concerns had been raised about the prospect of the legislative and presidential elections scheduled to take place in 2004; it was feared that these might provoke renewed political instability from mid-2003, once the campaign period had begun. This would, inevitably, also have an impact upon Indonesia's economic performance, deterring private investors and undermining the willingness of foreign donors to continue to provide Indonesia with the large volume of foreign support still needed if the economy were to be revitalized to pre-crisis levels.

Statistical Survey

Source (unless otherwise stated): Badan Pusat Statistik (Central Bureau of Statistics/Statistics Indonesia), Jalan Dr Sutomo 6–8, Jakarta 10710; tel. (21) 3507057; fax (21) 3857046; e-mail bpshq@bps.go.id; internet www.bps.go.id.

Note: Unless otherwise stated, figures for East Timor (occupied by Indonesia between July 1976 and October 1999) are not included in the tables.

Area and Population

AREA, POPULATION AND DENSITY

Area (sq km)	1,922,570*
Population (census results)	
31 October 1990	178,631,196
30 June 2000	
Males	103,417,180
Females	102,847,415
Total	206,264,595
Density (per sq km) at 30 June 2000	107.3

* 742,308 sq miles.

ISLANDS (population at 2000 census)*

	Area (sq km)	Population	Density (per sq km)
Jawa (Java) and Madura	127,499	121,352,608	951.8
Sumatera (Sumatra)	482,393	43,309,707	89.8
Sulawesi (Celebes)	191,800	14,946,488	77.9
Kalimantan	547,891	11,331,558	20.7
Nusa Tenggara†	67,502	7,961,540	117.9
Bali	5,633	3,151,162	559.4
Maluku (Moluccas)	77,871	1,990,598	25.6
Papua‡	421,981	2,220,934	5.3
Total	1,922,570	206,264,595	107.3

* Figures refer to provincial divisions, each based on a large island or group of islands but also including adjacent small islands.
† Comprising most of the Lesser Sunda Islands, principally Flores, Lombok, Sumba, Sumbawa and part of Timor.
‡ Formerly Irian Jaya (West Papua).

PRINCIPAL TOWNS (estimated population at 31 December 1996)

Jakarta (capital)	9,341,400
Surabaya	2,743,400
Bandung	2,429,000
Medan	1,942,000
Palembang	1,394,300
Semarang	1,366,500
Ujung Pandang (Makassar)	1,121,300
Malang	775,900
Padang	739,500
Banjarmasin	544,700
Surakarta	518,600
Pontianak	459,100
Yogyakarta (Jogjakarta)	421,000

Mid-2000 (UN estimates, '000 persons, incl. suburbs): Jakarta 11,018; Bandung 3,409; Surabaya 2,461; Medan 1,879; Palembang 1,422; Ujung Pandang 1,051 (Source: UN, *World Urbanization Prospects: The 2001 Revision*).

Mid-2001 (UN estimate, '000 persons, incl. suburbs): Jakarta 11,429 (Source: UN, *World Urbanization Prospects: The 2001 Revision*).

BIRTHS AND DEATHS (UN estimates, annual averages)

	1985–90	1990–95	1995–00
Birth rate (per 1,000)	28.0	24.9	22.5
Death rate (per 1,000)	9.3	8.3	7.5

Source: UN, *World Population Prospects: The 2000 Revision*.

Expectation of life (WHO estimates, years at birth, 2000): Males 63.4; Females 67.4 (Source: WHO, *World Health Report*).

Birth rate (per 1,000): 22.9 in 1997; 22.8 in 1998; 22.4 in 1999. Source: UN, *Statistical Yearbook for Asia and the Pacific*.

Death rate (per 1,000): 7.5 in 1997; 7.7 in 1998; 7.5 in 1999. Source: UN, *Statistical Yearbook for Asia and the Pacific*.

ECONOMICALLY ACTIVE POPULATION (persons aged 15 years and over)

	1999	2000*	2001
Agriculture, hunting, forestry and fishing	38,378,133	40,676,713	39,743,908
Mining and quarrying	725,739	n.a.	n.a.
Manufacturing	11,515,955	11,641,756	12,086,122
Electricity, gas and water	188,321	n.a.	n.a.
Construction	3,415,147	3,497,232	3,837,554
Trade, restaurants and hotels	17,529,099	18,489,005	17,469,129
Transport, storage and communications	4,206,067	4,553,855	4,448,279
Financing, insurance, real estate and business services	633,744	882,600	1,127,823
Public services	12,224,654	9,574,009	11,003,482
Activities not adequately defined	—	522,560†	1,091,120†
Total employed	88,816,859	89,837,730	90,807,417
Unemployed	6,030,319	5,813,231	8,005,031
Total labour force	94,847,178	95,650,961	98,812,448

* Excluding Maluku province.
† Includes Mining and quarrying and electricity, gas and water.

Health and Welfare

KEY INDICATORS

Fertility (births per woman, 2000)	2.4
Under-5 mortality rate (per 1,000 live births, 2000)	48
HIV/AIDS (% of persons aged 15–49, 2001)	0.10
Physicians (per 1,000 head, 1994)	0.16
Hospital beds (per 1,000 head, 1994)	0.66
Health expenditure (1998): US $ per head (PPP)	54
% of GDP	2.7
public (% of total)	25.5
Access to water (% of persons, 2000)	76
Access to sanitation (% of persons, 2000)	66
Human Development Index (2000): ranking	110
value	0.684

For sources and definitions, see explanatory note on p. vi.

Agriculture

PRINCIPAL CROPS ('000 metric tons, incl. East Timor)

	1998	1999	2000
Rice (paddy)	49,200	50,866	51,000
Maize	10,169	9,204	9,169
Potatoes	998	924	924*
Sweet potatoes	1,935	1,627	1,627*
Cassava (Manioc)	14,696	16,347	16,347*
Other roots and tubers*	350	350	350
Sugar cane†	27,180	23,500	21,400
Dry beans*	900	900	900
Soybeans	1,306	1,383	1,198
Groundnuts (in shell)	1,217	1,161	1,000†
Coconuts†	14,341	15,529	16,235
Palm kernels	1,303	1,490†	1,600†
Cabbages	1,660	1,750*	1,750*
Tomatoes	334	324	324*
Pumpkins, squash and gourds*	150	150	150
Cucumbers and gherkins	566	580*	580*
Aubergines (Eggplants)	320	340*	340*
Chillies and green peppers	374	497	497*
Dry onions	559	805	805*
Garlic	84	63	63*
Green beans	186	172	172*
Carrots	333	286	286*
Other vegetables*	1,385	1,429	1,429
Oranges	614	645	645*
Avocados	131	122	122*
Mangoes	600	827	827*
Pineapples	327	317	317*
Bananas	3,177	3,377	3,377*
Papayas	490	450	450
Other fruits and berries*	1,682	1,740	1,740
Cashew nuts	69	75*	75*
Coffee (green)	455	417†	430†
Cocoa beans	334	344	362†
Tea (made)	166	168	168*
Tobacco (leaves)	138	141	141*
Natural rubber	1,564	1,488	1,488*

* FAO estimate(s). † Unofficial figure(s).

Source: FAO.

LIVESTOCK ('000 head, incl. East Timor; year ending September)

	1998	1999	2000*
Cattle	11,634	12,102	12,102
Sheep	7,144	7,502	7,502
Goats	13,560	14,121	14,121
Pigs	7,798	9,353	9,353
Horses	567	579	579
Buffaloes	2,829	2,859	2,859
Chickens	645,998	726,907	800,000
Ducks	25,950	26,284	26,284

* FAO estimates.

Source: FAO.

LIVESTOCK PRODUCTS ('000 metric tons, incl. East Timor)

	1998	1999	2000
Beef and veal	343	309	351
Buffalo meat	46	48	51
Mutton and lamb	34	32	36
Goat meat	48	45	48
Pig meat	622	748	748
Poultry meat	621	620	732
Cows' milk	375	436	498
Sheep's milk	86	90	90
Goats' milk	232	232	232
Hen eggs	393	525	576
Other poultry eggs	137	116	120
Wool: greasy	24	24	24
Cattle and buffalo hides	56	57	57*
Sheepskins	8	8	8
Goatskins	11	11	11

Note: Figures for meat refer to inspected production only, i.e. from animals slaughtered under government supervision.

* FAO estimate.

Source: FAO.

Forestry

ROUNDWOOD REMOVALS ('000 cubic metres, excluding bark)

	1997	1998	1999
Sawlogs, veneer logs and logs for sleepers:			
Coniferous	333	n.a.	n.a.
Non-coniferous	32,250	21,815	24,861
Pulpwood	11,547*	6,197	3,248
Other industrial wood	3,158	3,204	3,249
Fuel wood	154,772	157,023	159,243
Total	202,060	188,239	190,601

* FAO estimate.

2000: Production as in 1999 (FAO estimates).

Source: FAO, *Yearbook of Forest Products*.

SAWNWOOD PRODUCTION
('000 cubic metres, including railway sleepers)

	1997	1998	1999
Coniferous (softwood)	138	n.a.	n.a.
Broadleaved (hardwood)	7,100	2,523	2,427
Total	7,238	2,523	2,427

2000: Production as in 1999 (FAO estimates).

Source: FAO, *Yearbook of Forest Products*.

Fishing

('000 metric tons, live weight)

	1997	1998	1999
Capture	3,790.8	3,964.9	4,149.4
Scads	276.9	277.6	291.1
Goldstripe sardinella	156.9	174.7	183.2
Bali sardinella	138.6	154.0	161.5
'Stolephorus' anchovies	183.6	166.8	175.0
Skipjack tuna	187.2	227.1	238.1
Yellowfin tuna	116.2	168.1	176.3
Indian mackerels	201.4	204.8	214.7
Aquaculture	662.5	629.8	647.6
Common carp	146.7	109.9	115.6
Milkfish	142.7	158.7	160.0
Total catch	4,453.3	4,594.7	4,797.0

Note: Figures exclude aquatic plants ('000 metric tons): 126.0 (capture 11.0, aquaculture 115.0) in 1997; 47.5 (capture 7.5, aquaculture 40.0) in 1998; 49.8 (capture 7.8, aquaculture 42.0) in 1999. Also excluded are crocodiles, recorded by number rather than by weight. The number of crocodiles caught was: 250 in 1997; 11,647 in 1998; 7,661 in 1999.

Source: FAO, *Yearbook of Fishery Statistics*.

Mining

('000 metric tons, unless otherwise indicated)

	1998	1999	2000
Crude petroleum (million barrels)‡	568.2	547.6	516.1
Natural gas (million cubic metres)	84,333	86,863	82,334
Bauxite	1,055	1,116	1,551
Coal	61,146	72,618	76,800§
Nickel*	74.1	89.1	98.2
Copper*	780.8	766.0	1,012.1
Tin ore (metric tons)*	53,959	47,754	51,629
Gold (kg)†	124,018	127,184	124,596
Silver (kg)†	348,987	288,200	255,578

* Figures refer to the metal content of ores and concentrates.
† Including gold and silver in copper concentrate.
‡ Including condensate.
§ Estimate.

Source: US Geological Survey.

Industry

SELECTED PRODUCTS ('000 metric tons, unless otherwise indicated)

	1996	1997	1998
Refined sugar	2,564	n.a.	1,793
Cigarettes (million)	n.a.	220,157	271,177
Veneer sheets ('000 cubic metres)	50	50	1,110
Plywood ('000 cubic metres)	9,575	9,600	7,015
Newsprint	267	390	478
Other printing and writing paper	1,236	1,510	1,855
Other paper and paperboard*†	2,618	2,922	3,154
Nitrogenous fertilizers*†‡	2,986	2,993	2,899
Jet fuel	1,167	990	1,150†
Motor spirit (petrol)	7,155	7,950	7,302†
Naphthas	1,673	929	522†
Kerosene	6,894	6,159	6,956†
Gas-diesel oil	14,400†	12,275†	13,423†
Residual fuel oils	10,200†	12,000†	11,560†
Lubricating oils	240†	220†	211†
Liquefied petroleum gas	3,179	2,945	2,344†
Rubber tyres ('000)§	n.a.	23,388	25,701
Cement	24,648	20,702	22,344†
Aluminium (unwrought)‖¶	223.2	219.4	133.4
Tin (unwrought, metric tons)†‖¶	48,960	52,577	54,000
Radio receivers ('000)	n.a.	4,177	n.a.
Passenger motor cars ('000)**	n.a.	42	6
Electric energy (million kWh)†	78,117	84,096	90,027
Gas from gasworks (terajoules)	29,528	20,134	26,715†

1999: Veneer sheets ('000 cubic metres) 927; Plywood ('000 cubic metres) 4,437; Newsprint ('000 metric tons) 532; Other printing and writing paper ('000 metric tons) 2,733; Cement ('000 metric tons) 24,024†.

* Data from FAO.
† Provisional or estimated production.
‡ Production in terms of nitrogen.
§ For road motor vehicles, excluding bicycles and motorcycles.
‖ Primary metal production only.
¶ Data from *World Metal Statistics*.
** Vehicles assembled from imported parts.

Source: mainly UN, *Industrial Commodity Statistics Yearbook*.

Palm oil ('000 metric tons): 4,899 in 1996; 5,385 in 1997; 5,902 in 1998; 6,250 (unofficial figure) in 1999; 6,950 (unofficial figure) in 2000; 7,135 (estimate) in 2001. Source: FAO.

Raw sugar (centrifugal, '000 metric tons): 2,160 in 1996; 2,187 in 1997; 1,846 in 1998; 1,690 (unofficial figure) in 1999; 1,600 (unofficial figure) in 2000; 1,700 (unofficial figure) in 2001. Source: FAO.

Finance

CURRENCY AND EXCHANGE RATES

Monetary Units

100 sen = 1 rupiah (Rp.).

Sterling, Dollar and Euro Equivalents (31 May 2002)

£1 sterling = 12,885.0 rupiah;
US $1 = 8,785.0 rupiah;
€1 = 8,246.5 rupiah;
100,000 rupiah = £7.761 = $11.383 = €12.126.

Average Exchange Rate (rupiah per US $)

1999 7,855.2
2000 8,421.8
2001 10,260.9

BUDGET ('000 million rupiah, year ending 31 March)

Revenue	1997/98	1998/99	1999/2000*
Tax revenue	101,493.2	143,701.8	171,296.8
Taxes on income, profits, etc.	64,947.3	97,297.4	118,164.4
General sales, turnover or VAT	25,198.8	27,728.7	33,087.1
Excises	5,101.2	7,730.3	10,381.2
Taxes on international trade	3,127.2	6,956.6	5,025.3
Import duties	2,998.7	2,316.4	4,177.0
Export duties	128.5	4,640.2	848.3
Other current revenue	10,782.3	12,200.0	17,131.7
Profit receipts	2,340.7	3,428.3	5,430.4
Other	8,441.6†	8,771.7	11,701.3
Total	112,275.5	155,901.8	188,428.5

Expenditure	1997/98	1998/99	1999/2000*
Current expenditure	73,921.1	125,900.0	155,880.3
Personnel (central govt.)	17,269.0	22,656.2	32,105.5
Pensions	4,225.0	5,310.0	9,205.0
Material	8,999.3	9,838.6	9,971.3
Armed forces	1,825.4	2,671.9	2,117.8
Transfers to regions	11,060.5	13,074.2	17,341.2
Interest on external debt	11,262.9	24,650.0	20,615.0
Gross interest costs of bank restructuring	0.0	8,384.8	22,230.4
Subsidies	21,120.9	41,799.3	47,024.6
Petroleum	9,814.3	28,606.6	35,839.1
Food	10,598.7	6,426.7	5,415.4
Other	11,306.6	13,192.7	11,185.5
Other	2,383.1	2,825.0	4,474.5
Development expenditure (including net lending)	44,651.0	55,252.0	49,020.0
General public services	1,011.2	1,083.4	924.5
Education	5,145.0	7,072.9	7,742.7
Health, family planning and welfare	2,051.3	4,150.0	4,488.2
Housing and water supply	1,333.4	2,435.9‡	2,121.9‡
Other community and social services	1,581.6	2,261.4	2,568.3
Manpower and transmigration	1,368.3	1,933.8	2,058.1
Economic services	17,564.0	23,506.0	16,038.1
Agriculture and irrigation§	3,268.5	7,126.0‖	3,604.6‖
Electricity	4,448.9	5,829.3	3,799.4
Transport and tourism	7,711.7	8,756.4	6,361.4
Trade and co-operatives¶	998.8	895.3**	1,642.6**
Regional, business and environment	7,045.9	11,456.7	15,607.3
Regional development	6,019.0	10,558.3	11,648.7
Investment through banking system	381.4	256.7	3,171.1
Total	118,572.1	181,152.0	204,900.3

* Figures are provisional.
† Including privatization proceeds.
‡ Excluding credit for low-cost housing.
§ Excluding fertilizer subsidies.
‖ Excluding farming loans and credit for plantation.
¶ Excluding bank restructuring costs.
** Excluding co-operatives credit and loans for primary-level co-operatives' members.

Source: IMF, *Indonesia: Statistical Appendix* (October 2000).

INTERNATIONAL RESERVES (US $ million at 31 December)

	1999	2000	2001
Gold*	812	766	772
IMF special drawing rights	—	32	16
Reserve position in IMF	200	190	183
Foreign exchange	26,245	28,280	27,048
Total	27,257	29,268	28,019

* Valued at market-related prices.

Source: IMF, *International Financial Statistics.*

MONEY SUPPLY ('000 million rupiah at 31 December)

	1999	2000	2001
Currency outside banks	58,353	72,371	76,342
Demand deposits at deposit money banks	55,327	78,102	93,146
Total money (incl. others)	114,562	156,785	170,509

Source: IMF, *International Financial Statistics.*

COST OF LIVING (Consumer Price Index; base: 1996 = 100)*

	1999	2000	2001
Food (incl. beverages)	242.5	249.0	267.1
Non-food	177.3	190.2	213.4
All items	202.7	210.3	234.5

* Excluding East Timor since November 1999.

Source: Asian Development Bank, *Key Indicators of Developing Asian and Pacific Countries.*

NATIONAL ACCOUNTS ('000 million rupiah at current prices)

National Income and Product

	1991	1992	1993
Domestic factor incomes*	201,118	229,946	262,575
Consumption of fixed capital	11,380	13,045	14,907
Gross domestic product (GDP) at factor cost	212,498	242,991	247,668
Indirect taxes, *less* subsidies	15,004	17,795	20,544
GDP in purchasers' values	227,502	260,786	268,212
Net factor income from abroad	-10,913	-12,542	-12,553
Gross national product (GNP)	216,960	248,233	255,659
Less Consumption of fixed capital	11,380	13,045	-14,907
National income in market prices	205,580	235,188	240,752

* Compensation of employees and the operating surplus of enterprises. The amount is obtained as a residual.

Source: UN, *National Accounts Statistics.*

Expenditure on the Gross Domestic Product

	1999	2000	2001
Government final consumption expenditure	72,631	90,780	110,837
Private final consumption expenditure	813,183	867,997	999,266
Increase in stocks*	-96,461	-81,385	-56,820
Gross fixed capital formation	221,472	268,669	310,909
Total domestic expenditure	1,010,825	1,146,061	1,364,192
Exports of goods and services	390,560	542,992	612,482
Less Imports of goods and services	301,654	407,036	485,700
GDP in purchasers' values	1,099,732	1,282,018	1,490,974
GDP at constant 1993 prices	379,352	397,934	411,132

* Figures obtained as a residual.

Source: Asian Development Bank, *Key Indicators of Developing Asian and Pacific Countries.*

Gross Domestic Product by Economic Activity

	1999	2000	2001
Agriculture, forestry and fishing	215,687	218,301	244,381
Mining and quarrying	109,925	176,640	202,680
Manufacturing	285,874	335,339	389,321
Electricity, gas and water	13,429	15,072	17,286
Construction	67,616	76,091	84,045
Trade, hotels and restaurants	175,835	194,910	239,959
Transport, storage and communications	55,190	64,550	79,825
Finance, insurance, real estate and business services	71,220	79,477	92,459
Public administration	56,745	69,460	81,851
Other services	48,210	52,177	59,167
Total	1,099,732	1,282,018	1,490,974

Source: Asian Development Bank, *Key Indicators of Developing Asian and Pacific Countries.*

BALANCE OF PAYMENTS (US $ million)

	1998	1999	2000
Exports of goods f.o.b.	50,371	51,242	65,406
Imports of goods f.o.b.	-31,942	-30,598	-40,366
Trade balance	18,429	20,644	25,040
Exports of services	4,479	4,579	5,213
Imports of services	-11,961	-11,553	-15,011
Balance on goods and services	10,947	13,670	15,242
Other income received	1,910	1,891	2,456
Other income paid	-10,099	-11,690	-11,529
Balance on goods, services and income	2,758	3,871	6,169
Current transfers received	1,338	1,914	1,816
Current balance	4,096	5,785	7,985
Direct investment abroad	-44	-72	-150
Direct investment from abroad	-356	-2,745	-4,550
Portfolio investment liabilities	-1,878	-1,792	-1,909
Other investment liabilities	-7,360	-1,332	-1,287
Net errors and omissions	1,849	2,128	3,637
Overall balance	-3,693	1,972	3,726

Source: IMF, *International Financial Statistics.*

External Trade

PRINCIPAL COMMODITIES (distribution by SITC, US $ million)

Imports c.i.f.	1996	1997	1998
Food and live animals	3,926.6	2,979.8	2,611.7
Cereals and cereal preparations	2,002.5	1,106.1	1,567.9
Rice	766.4	109.0	861.2
Crude materials (inedible) except fuels	3,441.3	2,958.8	2,349.1
Textile fibres and waste	1,261.3	1,034.0	976.0
Mineral fuels, lubricants, etc.	3,775.0	4,142.0	2,752.4
Crude petroleum oils, etc.	1,519.0	1,467.1	1,058.3
Refined petroleum products	2,086.2	2,451.7	1,611.7
Gas oils	963.6	1,173.1	893.2
Chemicals and related products	5,876.9	5,768.9	4,030.0
Organic chemicals	2,226.8	2,222.9	1,491.5
Basic manufactures	6,844.7	6,715.4	4,671.0
Textile yarn, fabrics, etc.	1,288.4	1,172.9	1,036.6
Iron and steel	2,370.8	2,286.4	1,478.6
Machinery and transport equipment	17,458.6	17,499.8	9,902.9
Power-generating machinery and equipment	1,968.6	1,877.0	1,154.5

Imports c.i.f. — *continued*	1996	1997	1998
Machinery specialized for particular industries	4,118.4	3,959.4	2,702.2
General industrial machinery, equipment and parts	3,629.2	3,682.3	2,394.3
Telecommunications and sound equipment	1,766.3	1,778.8	504.8
Other electrical machinery, apparatus, etc.	1,868.4	2,110.7	1,228.4
Road vehicles and parts*	2,673.5	2,593.0	940.0
Parts and accessories for cars, buses, lorries, etc.*	1,359.5	1,297.2	388.0
Total (incl. others)	42,928.5	41,679.8	27,336.9

* Excluding tyres, engines and electrical parts.

Source: UN, *International Trade Statistics Yearbook.*

Exports f.o.b.	1997	1998	1999
Food and live animals	3,531.4	3,717.4	3,643.8
Fish, crustaceans and molluscs	1,619.4	1,614.4	1,526.3
Coffee, tea, cocoa and spices	1,285.1	1,516.3	1,288.5
Crude materials (inedible) except fuels	4,357.8	3,719.2	3,396.6
Ores and concentrates of non-ferrous base metals	1,718.2	1,453.3	1,451.6
Mineral fuels, lubricants, etc.	13,153.9	9,429.4	11,191.3
Petroleum, petroleum products, etc.	6,822.4	4,264.3	5,528.6
Crude petroleum oils, etc.	5,480.0	3,348.6	4,517.3
Petroleum gases, etc., in the liquefied state	4,840.1	3,815.5	4,357.0
Animal and vegetable oils, fats and waxes	2,282.1	1,520.7	1,825.9
Fixed vegetable oils, fluid or solid, crude, refined or purified	2,174.9	1,152.1	1,674.4
Chemicals and related products	1,869.4	2,086.6	2,354.9
Basic manufactures	9,778.8	8,832.6	11,125.4
Wood and cork manufactures (excl. furniture)	4,445.3	2,714.4	3,306.6
Veneers, plywood, etc.	3,729.1	2,207.2	2,515.8
Plywood of wood sheets	3,410.6	2,077.9	2,256.3
Paper, paperboard, etc.	939.6	1,439.9	1,975.3
Textile yarn, fabrics, etc.	2,268.9	2,358.0	3,028.6
Machinery and transport equipment	4,620.0	4,654.6	5,271.6
Telecommunications and sound equipment	1,752.8	1,360.5	1,468.1
Miscellaneous manufactured articles	6,876.0	6,603.6	8,171.7
Clothing and accessories (excl. footwear)	2,952.8	2,681.2	3,914.9
Footwear	1,477.2	1,156.7	1,541.1
Jewellery, goldsmiths' and silversmiths' wares, etc.	703.4	1,661.7	174.2
Total (incl. others)	53,443.6	48,847.5	48,665.5

Source: UN, *International Trade Statistics Yearbook.*

PRINCIPAL TRADING PARTNERS (US $ million)*

Imports c.i.f.	1999	2000	2001
Australia	1,460.4	1,693.8	1,814.2
Canada	421.2	638.3	356.6
China, People's Republic	1,242.2	2,022.0	1,842.6
France	371.6	400.0	396.9
Germany	1,398.5	1,244.7	1,300.5
Hong Kong	227.5	342.4	257.4
Italy	276.9	345.1	407.5
Japan	2,913.3	5,397.3	4,689.4
Korea, Republic	1,330.1	2,082,6	2,209.4
Malaysia	605.6	1,128.8	n.a.
Netherlands	346.7	434,4	343.9
Singapore	2,525.9	3,788.6	3,147.0
Taiwan	784.1	1,269.7	1,071.1
Thailand	933.4	1,109.1	n.a.
United Kingdom	511.2	557.3	643.0
USA	2,839.0	3,390.3	3,207.6
Total (incl. others)	24,003.3	33,514.8	30,962.1

Exports f.o.b.	1999	2000	2001
Australia	1,484.8	1,519.4	1,844.8
Belgium/Luxembourg	696.5	840.6	n.a.
China, People's Republic	2,008.9	2,767.7	2,200.6
France	503.2	718.3	662.6
Germany	1,233.9	1,443.1	1,296.9
Hong Kong	1,330.0	1,554.1	1,290.3
Italy	655.5	757.8	621.9
Japan	10,397.2	14,415.2	13,010.1
Korea, Republic	3,319.8	4,317.9	3,772.4
Malaysia	1,335.9	1,971.8	n.a.
Netherlands	1,543.6	1,837.4	1,498.2
Philippines	694.7	819.5	n.a.
Singapore	4,930.5	6,562.4	5,363.8
Spain	741.6	932.2	n.a.
Taiwan	1,757.5	2,378.3	2,188.0
Thailand	812.7	1,026.5	n.a.
United Kingdom	1,176.1	1,507.9	1,383.1
USA	6,896.5	8,475.4	7,748.7
Total (incl. others)	48,665.4	62,124.0	56,320.9

* Imports by country of production; exports by country of consumption. Figures include trade in gold.

Transport

RAILWAYS (traffic)

	1998	1999	2000
Passengers embarked (million)	170	187	192
Passenger-km (million)	16,340*	n.a.	n.a.
Freight loaded ('000 tons)	18,129	19,302	19,545
Freight ton-km (million)	5,368*	n.a.	n.a.

* Estimate.

Source: Indonesian State Railways.

ROAD TRAFFIC (motor vehicles registered at 31 December)

	1998*	1999	2000†
Passenger cars	2,769,375	2,897,803	3,038,913
Lorries and trucks	1,586,721	1,628,531	1,707,134
Buses and coaches	626,680	644,667	666,280
Motor cycles	12,628,991	13,053,148	13,563,017

* Including East Timor.

† Preliminary figures.

Source: State Police of Indonesia.

SHIPPING

Merchant Fleet (registered at 31 December)

	1999	2000	2001
Number of vessels	2,369	2,480	2,528
Displacement ('000 grt)	3,241.5	3,384.2	3,613.1

Source: Lloyd's Register-Fairplay, *World Fleet Statistics.*

Sea-borne Freight Traffic ('000 metric tons)

	1998	1999	2000*
International:			
Goods loaded	133,700	139,340	145,217
Goods unloaded	47,138	43,477	40,100
Domestic:			
Goods loaded	113,487	113,633	154,728
Goods unloaded	119,795	122,368	124,996

* Preliminary figures.

CIVIL AVIATION (traffic on scheduled services)

	1996	1997	1998
Kilometres flown (million)	256	199	155
Passengers carried ('000)	17,139	12,937	9,603
Passenger-km (million)	25,081	23,718	15,974
Total ton-km (million)	2,986	2,797	1,826

Source: UN, *Statistical Yearbook*.

Tourism

FOREIGN TOURIST ARRIVALS

Country of Residence	1998	1999	2000
Australia	394,543	531,211	459,994
France	70,396	78,613	93,477
Germany	141,314	169,083	151,897
Japan	469,409	606,102	643,794
Korea, Republic	177,852	220,440	213,762
Malaysia	491,597	440,212	475,845
Netherlands	81,507	86,022	105,109
Philippines	104,192	46,177	79,682
Singapore	1,446,660	1,332,877	1,427,886
Taiwan	281,959	349,247	356,436
United Kingdom	137,600	138,296	161,662
USA	150,042	151,763	176,379
Total (incl. others)	4,606,416	4,727,520	5,064,217

Receipts from tourism (US $ million): 4,331 in 1998; 4,710 in 1999; 5,749 in 2000 (Source: World Tourism Organization).

Communications Media

	1999	2000	2001
Television receivers ('000 in use)	30,000	31,700	n.a.
Telephones ('000 main lines in use)	6,080.2	6,662.6	7,949.3
Mobile cellular telephones ('000 subscribers)	2,221.0	3,669.3	5,303.0
Personal computers ('000 in use)	1,900	2,100	2,300
Internet users ('000)	900	2,000	4,000

Facsimile machines (number in use, 1997): 185,000*.
Radio receivers ('000 in use, 1997): 31,500†.
Daily newspapers (1996): Number: 69; Average circulation: 4,665,000†.
Non-daily newspapers (1996): Number: 94; Average circulation: 4,696,000†.

* Estimate(s).

† Source: UNESCO, *Statistical Yearbook*.

Source (unless otherwise indicated): International Telecommunication Union.

Education

(1999/2000)

	Institutions	Teachers	Pupils and Students
Primary schools	150,197	1,141,168	25,614,836
General junior secondary schools	20,866	441,174	7,600,093
General senior secondary schools	7,900	n.a.	2,896,864
Vocational senior secondary schools	4,169	n.a.	1,882,061
Universities	1,634	194,828	3,126,307

Source: Ministry of Education and Culture.

Adult literacy rate (UNESCO estimates): 86.9% (males 91.8%; females 82.0%) in 2000 (Source: UN Development Programme, *Human Development Report*).

Directory

The Constitution

Indonesia had three provisional Constitutions: in August 1945, February 1950 and August 1950. In July 1959 the Constitution of 1945 was re-enacted by presidential decree. The General Elections Law of 1969 supplemented the 1945 Constitution, which has been adopted permanently by the Majelis Permusyawaratan Rakyat (MPR—People's Consultative Assembly). Amendments made to the Constitution in 2001 and 2002 were to take effect in 2004, when Indonesia was scheduled to hold its next general election. The following is a summary of the Constitution's main provisions, with subsequent amendments:

GENERAL PRINCIPLES

The 1945 Constitution consists of 37 articles, four transitional clauses and two additional provisions, and is preceded by a preamble. The preamble contains an indictment of all forms of colonialism, an account of Indonesia's struggle for independence, the declaration of that independence and a statement of fundamental aims and principles. Indonesia's National Independence, according to the text of the preamble, has the state form of a Republic, with sovereignty residing in the People, and is based upon five fundamental principles, the *pancasila*:

1. Belief in the One Supreme God.
2. Just and Civilized Humanity.
3. The Unity of Indonesia.
4. Democracy led by the wisdom of deliberations (*musyawarah*) and consensus among representatives.
5. Social Justice for all the people of Indonesia.

STATE ORGANS

Majelis Permusyawaratan Rakyat—MPR (People's Consultative Assembly)

Sovereignty is in the hands of the People and is exercised in full by the MPR as the embodiment of the whole Indonesian People. The MPR is the highest authority of the State, and is to be distinguished from the legislative body proper (Dewan Perwakilan Rakyat, see below), which is incorporated within the MPR. The bicameral MPR, with a total of 700 members (reduced from 1,000 in 1999), is composed of the members of the DPR and the DPD (see below). Elections to the MPR are held every five years. The MPR sits at least once every five years, and its primary competence is to determine the Constitution and the broad lines of the policy of the State and the Government. It also inaugurates the President and Vice-President, who are responsible for implementing that policy. All decisions are taken unanimously in keeping with the traditions of *musyawarah*.

The President

The highest executive of the Government, the President, holds office for a term of five years and may be re-elected once. As Mandatory of the MPR he must execute the policy of the State according to the Decrees determined by the MPR during its Fourth General and Special Sessions. In conducting the administration of the State, authority and responsibility are concentrated in the President. The Ministers of the State are his assistants and are responsible only to him. The President and Vice-President are to be directly elected on a single ticket (until November 2001 the MPR had exercised the power to elect them). If no candidate succeeds in obtaining more than one-half of the votes cast in a general election, a second round of voting shall be held. The President and Vice-President may be dismissed by the MPR on the proposal of the Dewan Perwakilan Rakyat if it is proven that he/she has either violated the law or no longer meets the requirements of his/her office. The President may not freeze or dissolve the Dewan.

Dewan Perwakilan Rakyat (House of Representatives)

The legislative branch of the State, the Dewan Perwakilan Rakyat, sits at least once a year. Its members are all directly elected. Every statute requires the approval of the Dewan. Members of the Dewan have the right to submit draft bills which require ratification by the President, who has the right of veto. In times of emergency the President may enact ordinances which have the force of law, but such Ordinances must be ratified by the Dewan during the following session or be revoked.

Dewan Perwakilan Daerah—DPD (House of Representatives of the Regions)

The Dewan Perwakilan Daerah is the second chamber of the MPR. Its members are directly elected from every province. Each province has an equal number of members and total membership of the DPD is no more than one-third of the total membership of the DPR. The DPD sits at least once a year. It may propose to the DPR Bills relating to regional autonomy, the relationship between central and local government, the formation, expansion and merger of regions, the management of natural and other economic resources, and the financial balance between the centre and the localities. It may also participate in the discussion of such Bills and oversee the implementation of regional laws, as well as the State Budget, taxation, education and religion.

Dewan Pertimbangan Agung—DPA (Supreme Advisory Council)

The DPA is an advisory body assisting the President who chooses its members from political parties, functional groups and groups of prominent persons.

Mahkamah Agung (Supreme Court)

The judicial branch of the State, the Supreme Court and the other courts of law (public courts, religious courts, military tribunals, administrative courts and a Constitutional Court) are independent of the Executive in exercising their judicial powers. There is an independent Judicial Commission which is authorized to propose candidates for appointment as justices of the Supreme Court and to ensure the good behaviour of judges. Its members are appointed and dismissed by the President with the approval of the DPR.

Badan Pemeriksa Keuangan (Supreme Audit Board)

Controls the accountability of public finance, enjoys investigatory powers and is independent of the Executive. Its findings are presented to the Dewan.

The Government

HEAD OF STATE

President: MEGAWATI SUKARNOPUTRI (inaugurated 23 July 2001).

Vice-President: HAMZAH HAZ.

CABINET
(September 2002)

Co-ordinating Minister for Political Affairs, Security and Social Welfare: Gen. (retd) SUSILO BAMBANG YUDHOYONO.

Co-ordinating Minister for the Economy, Finance and Industry: DORODJATUN KUNTJORO-JAKTI.

Co-ordinating Minister for People's Welfare: JUSUF KALLA.

Minister of Home Affairs and Regional Autonomy: Lt-Gen. (retd) HARI SABARNO.

Minister of Foreign Affairs: HASSAN WIRAYUDA.

Minister of Defence: MATORI ABDUL DJALIL.

Minister of Maritime Affairs and Fisheries: ROCHIMIN DAHURI.

Minister for Justice and Human Rights Affairs: YUSRIL IHZA.

Minister of Finance and State Enterprises Development: BOEDIONO.

Minister of Industry and Trade: RINI SUWANDI.

Minister of Agriculture: Prof. Dr Ir BUNGARAN SARAGIH.

Minister of Forestry: M. PRAKOSA.

Minister of Energy and Mineral Resources: Dr Ir PURNOMO YUSGIANTORO.

Minister of Transportation and Telecommunication: Lt-Gen. (retd) AGUM GUMELAR.

Minister of Manpower and Transmigration: JACOB NUWA WEA.

Minister of National Education: ABDUL MALIK FAJAR.

Minister of Health: Dr AHMAD SUYUDI.

Minister of Social Affairs: BACHTIAR CHAMSYAH.

Minister of Religious Affairs: SAID AQIEL MUNAWAR.

Minister of Resettlement and Regional Infrastructure Development: SOENARNO.

Minister of State for Culture and Tourism: Drs I. GDE ARDIKA.

Minister of State for Research and Technology: HATTA RAJASA.

Minister of State for Co-operatives and Small- and Medium-Sized Businesses: ALIMARWAN HANAN.

Minister of State for the Environment: NABIEL MAKARIM.

Minister of State for Women's Empowerment: Sri REDJEKI SOEMARYOTO.

Minister of State for Administrative Reform: FEISAL TAMIN.

Minister of State for State Enterprises: LAKSAMANA SUKARDI.

Minister of State for Communications and Information: SYAMSUL MU'ARIF.

Minister of State for Eastern Indonesian Development: MANUEL KAISIEPO.

Minister of State for National Development Planning: KWIK KIAN GIE.

Officials with the rank of Minister of State:

Attorney-General: MUHAMMAD ABDUL RACHMAN.

State Secretary: BAMBANG KESOWO.

MINISTRIES

Office of the President: Istana Merdeka, Jakarta; tel. (21) 3840946.

Office of the Vice-President: Jalan Merdeka Selatan 6, Jakarta; tel. (21) 363539.

Office of the Attorney-General: Jalan Sultan Hasanuddin 1, Kebayoran Baru, Jakarta; tel. (21) 7221377; fax (21) 7392576; e-mail kejagung@kejaksaan.go.id; internet www.kejaksaan.go.id.

Office of the Cabinet Secretary: Jalan Veteran 18, Jakarta Pusat; tel. (21) 3810973.

Office of the Co-ordinating Minister for Political Affairs, Security and Social Welfare: Jalan Medan Merdeka Barat 15, Jakarta 10110; tel. (21) 3849453; fax (21) 3450918.

Office of the Co-ordinating Minister for the Economy, Finance and Industry: Jalan Taman Suropati 2, Jakarta 10310; tel. (21) 3849063; fax (21) 334779.

Office of the State Secretary: Jalan Veteran 17, Jakarta 10110; tel. (21) 3849043; fax (21) 3452685; internet www.ri.go.id.

Ministry of Agriculture and Forestry: Jalan Harsono R.M. 3, Gedung D-Lantai 4, Ragunan, Pasar Minggu, Jakarta Selatan 12550; tel. (21) 7822638; fax (21) 7816385; e-mail eko@deptan.go.id; internet www.deptan.go.id.

Ministry of Defence: Jalan Medan Merdeka Barat 13–14, Jakarta Pusat; tel. (21) 3456184; fax (21) 3440023; e-mail postmaster@dephan.go.id; internet www.dephan.go.id.

Ministry of Finance and State Enterprises Development: Jalan Lapangan Banteng Timur 2-4, Jakarta 10710; tel. (21) 3814324; fax (21) 353710; internet www.depkeu.go.id.

Ministry of Foreign Affairs: Jalan Taman Pejambon 6, Jakarta 10410; tel. (21) 3441508; fax (21) 3805511; e-mail guestbook@dfa-deplu.go.id; internet www.deplu.go.id.

Ministry of Health and Social Welfare: Jalan H. R. Rasuna Said, Block X5, Kav. 4-9, Jakarta 12950; tel. (21) 5201587; fax (21) 5203874; e-mail webadmin@depkes.go.id; internet www.depkes.go.id.

Ministry of Home Affairs and Regional Autonomy: Jalan Merdeka Utara 7–8, Gedung Utama Lt. 4, Jakarta Pusat 10110; tel. (21) 3842222; fax (21) 372812; e-mail dpod@indosat.net.id; internet www.depdagri.go.id.

Ministry of Industry and Trade: Jalan Jenderal Gatot Subroto, Kav. 52–53, 2nd Floor, Jakarta Selatan; tel. (21) 5256458; fax (21) 5229592; e-mail men-indag@dprin.go.id; internet www.deprin.go.id.

Ministry of Justice and Human Rights Affairs: Jalan H. R. Rasuna Said, Kav. 4–5, Kuningan, Jakarta Pusat; tel. (21) 5253004; fax (21) 5253095; internet www.depkehham.go.id.

Ministry of Manpower and Transmigration: Jalan Jenderal Gatot Subroto, Kav. 51, Jakarta Selatan 12950; tel. (21) 5255683; fax (21) 515669; internet www.nakertrans.go.id.

Ministry of Mines and Mineral Resources: Jalan Merdeka Selatan 18, Jakarta 10110; tel. (21) 3804242; fax (21) 3847461; e-mail pulahta@setjen.dpe.go.id; internet www.dpe.go.id.

Ministry of National Education: Jalan Jenderal Sudirman, Senayan, Jakarta Pusat; tel. (21) 5731618; fax (21) 5736870; internet www.depdiknas.go.id.

Ministry of Religious Affairs: Jalan Lapangan Banteng Barat 3–4, Jakarta Pusat; tel. (21) 3811436; fax (21) 380836; internet www.depag.go.id.

Ministry of Transportation and Telecommunication: Jalan Merdeka Barat 8, Jakarta 10110; tel. (21) 3811308; fax (21) 3451657; e-mail pusdatin@rad.net.id; internet www.dephub.go.id.

Office of the Minister of State for Co-operatives and Small- and Medium-Sized Businesses: Jalan H. R. Rasuna Said, Kav. 3–5, POB 177, Jakarta Selatan 12940; tel. (21) 5204366; fax (21) 5204383; internet www.depkop.go.id.

Office of the Minister of State for the Environment: Jalan D. I. Panjaitan, Kebon Nanas Lt. II, Jakarta 134110; tel. (21) 8580103; fax (21) 8580101; internet www.bapedal.go.id.

Office of the Minister of State for Research and Technology: BPP Teknologi II Bldg, Jalan M. H. Thamrin 8, Jakarta Pusat 10340; tel. (21) 3169166; fax (21) 3101952; e-mail webmstr@ristek.go.id; internet www.ristek.go.id.

Office of the Minister of State for Women's Affairs: Jalan Medan Merdeka Barat 15, Jakarta 10110; tel. (21) 3805563; fax (21) 3805562; e-mail birum@menperta.go.id.

OTHER GOVERNMENT BODIES

Dewan Pertimbangan Agung—DPA (Supreme Advisory Council): Jalan Merdeka Utara 15, Jakarta; tel. (21) 362369; internet www.dpa.go.id; Chair. Gen. (retd) ACHMAD TIRTOSUDIRO; Sec.-Gen. SUTOYO.

Badan Pemeriksa Keuangan—BPK (Supreme Audit Board): Jalan Gatot Subroto 31, Jakarta; tel. (21) 584081; internet www.bpk.go.id; Chair. Prof. Dr SATRIO BUDIHARDJO JUDONO; Vice-Chair. Drs BAMBANG TRIADJI.

Legislature

MAJELIS PERMUSYAWARATAN RAKYAT—MPR
(People's Consultative Assembly)

Jalan Jendral Gatot Subroto 6, Jakarta 10270; tel. (21) 5715268: fax (21) 5715611; e-mail kotaksurat@mpr.go.id; internet www.mpr.go.id.

The Majelis Permusyawaratan Rakyat (MPR—People's Consultative Assembly) consists of the 500 members of the Dewan Perwakilan Rakyat (House of Representatives) and 200 other appointees (reduced from 500 in 1999), including regional delegates and representatives of various professions. In late 2002 the Constitution was amended to provide for the direct election of all members of the MPR at the next general election, scheduled to be held in 2004. The MPR was to be a bicameral institution comprising the Dewan Perwakilan Rakyat and the Dewan Perwakilan Daerah (House of Representatives of the Regions).

Speaker: Dr AMIEN RAIS.

	Seats
Members of the Dewan Perwakilan Rakyat	500
Regional representatives	135
Professional representatives	65
Total	700

Dewan Perwakilan Rakyat
(House of Representatives)

Jalan Gatot Subroto 16, Jakarta; tel. (21) 586833; e-mail humas-dpr@dpr.go.id; internet www.dpr.go.id.

Following the election of June 1999 the Dewan Perwakilan Rakyat (House of Representatives) comprised 500 members; of these, 462 were directly elected (increased from 425) and 38 were nominated by the President from the armed forces (reduced from 75). In 2002 the Constitution was amended to provide for the direct election of all members of the Dewan at the next general election, scheduled to be held in 2004. The role of the armed forces in the Dewan was thus to be abolished.

Speaker: Ir AKBAR TANDJUNG.

General Election, 7 June 1999

	Seats
Partai Demokrasi Indonesia Perjuangan (PDI—P)	154
Partai Golongan Karya (Golkar)	120
Partai Persatuan Pembangunan (PPP)	59
Partai Kebangkitan Bangsa (PKB)	51
Partai Amanat Nasional (PAN)	35
Partai Bulan Bintang (PBB)	13
Partai Keadilan (PK)	6
Partai Keadilan dan Persatuan (PKP)	6
Partai Demokrasi Kasih Bangsa (PDKB)	3
Partai Nahdlatul Umat (PNU)	3
Partai Bhinneka Tunggal Ika	3
Partai Demokrasi Indonesia (PDI)	2
Others	7
Appointed members*	38
Total	500

* Members of the political wing of the Indonesian National Defence Forces (TNI).

Political Organizations

Prior to 1998, electoral legislation permitted only three organizations (Golkar, the PDI and PPP) to contest elections. Following the replacement of President Suharto in May 1998, political restrictions were relaxed and new parties were allowed to form (with the only condition being that all parties must adhere to the *pancasila* and reject communism); by early 1999, more than 200 new political parties were reported to have been established.

Barisan Nasional (National Front): Jakarta; f. 1998; committed to ensuring that Indonesia remains a secular state; Sec.-Gen. RACHMAT WITOELAR.

Chinese Indonesian Reform Party: Jakarta; e-mail lieus@parti.or.id; f. 1998.

Indonesian National Unity: Jakarta; f. 1995 by fmr mems of Sukarno's National Party; seeks full implementation of 1945 Constitution; Chair. SUPENI.

Indonesian Reform Party (PPI): Jakarta; f. 1998; Gen. Chair. CHANDRA KUWATLI; Sec.-Gen. Dr H. ACE MULYADI.

Islamic Indonesian Party (PII): Jakarta; f. 1998; Pres. SUUD BAJEBER; Sec.-Gen. SYAIFUL MUNIR.

National Brotherhood Foundation: Jakarta; f. 1995; Chair. KHARIS SUHUD.

New Indonesian National Party: Jakarta; f. 1998.

Partai Amanat Nasional (PAN) (National Mandate Party): c/o Dewan Perwakilan Rakyat, Jalan Gatot Subroto 16, Jakarta; f. 1998; aims to achieve democracy, progress and social justice, to limit the length of the presidential term of office and to increase autonomy in the provinces; Gen. Chair. Dr AMIEN RAIS; Sec.-Gen. FAISAL BASRI.

Partai Bhinneka Tunggal Ika (PBI): c/o Dewan Perwakilan Rakyat, Jalan Gatot Subroto 16, Jakarta.

Partai Bulan Bintang (PBB) (Cresent Moon and Star Party): c/o Dewan Perwakilan Rakyat, Jalan Gatot Subroto 16, Jakarta; f. 1998; Leader YUSRIL IHZA MAHENDRA.

Partai Demokrasi Indonesia (PDI) (Indonesian Democratic Party): Jalan Diponegoro 58, Jakarta 10310; tel. (21) 336331; fax (21) 5201630; f. 1973 by the merger of five nationalist and Christian parties; Chair. SOERJADI (installed to replace Megawati Sukarnoputri as leader of the party in a government-orchestrated coup in 1996).

Partai Demokrasi Indonesia Perjuangan (PDI—P) (Indonesian Democratic Struggle Party): c/o Dewan Perwakilan Rakyat, Jalan Gatot Subroto 16, Jakarta; established by Megawati Sukarnoputri, fmr leader of the Partai Demokrasi Indonesia (PDI—see above), following her removal from the leadership of the PDI by the Government in 1996; Chair. MEGAWATI SUKARNOPUTRI.

Partai Demokrasi Kasih Bangsa (PDKB) (The Nation Compassion Democratic Party): Sekretariat, Kompleks Widuri Indah Blok A-4, Jalan Palmerah Barat 353, Jakarta Selatan 12210; tel. (21) 53673648; fax (21) 5330973; e-mail pdkb@pdkb.or.id; internet www.pdkb.or.id.

Partai Golongan Karya (Golkar) (Functional Group): Jalan Anggrek Nellimurni, Jakarta 11480; tel. (21) 5302222; fax (21) 5303380; f. 1964; reorg. 1971; 23m. mems (1999); Co-ordinator of Advisors Haji HARMOKO; Pres. and Chair. Ir AKBAR TANDJUNG; Sec.-Gen. BUDI HARSONO.

Partai Keadilan (PK) (Justice Party): c/o Dewan Perwakilan Rakyat, Jalan Gatot Subroto 16, Jakarta; e-mail partai@keadilan.or.id; internet www.keadilan.or.id; f. 1998; Islamic; Pres. Dr NUR MAHMUDI ISMA'IL; Sec.-Gen. LUTHFI HASAN ISHAAQ.

Partai Keadilan dan Persatuan (PKP) (Justice and Unity Party): c/o Dewan Perwakilan Rakyat, Jalan Gatot Subroto 16, Jakarta; internet www.pkp.or.id; f. 1999; Gen. Chair. EDI SUDRADJAT.

Partai Kebangkitan Bangsa (PKB) (National Awakening Party): Jakarta; e-mail fahmi201@yahoo.com; internet www.pkb.org; Islamic; f. 1998; Chair. of Exec. Council KIAI Haji MA'RUF AMIN; Chair. of Advisory Council Haji MATORI ABDUL JALIL.

Partai Kebangkitan Umat (PKU) (Islamic Awakening Party): c/o Dewan Perwakilan Rakyat, Jalan Gatot Subroto 16, Jakarta; f. 1998 by clerics and members of the Nahdlatul Ulama, with the aim of promoting the adoption of Islamic law in Indonesia.

Partai Nahdlatul Umat (PNU): c/o Dewan Perwakilan Rakyat, Jalan Gatot Subroto 16, Jakarta; Islamic party.

Partai Pembauran (Assimilation Party): Jakarta; f. 1998; Chinese.

Partai Persatuan Pembangunan (PPP) (United Development Party): Jalan Diponegoro 60, Jakarta 10310; tel. (21) 336338; fax (21) 3908070; e-mail dpp@ppp.or.id; internet www.ppp.or.id; f. 1973 by the merger of four Islamic parties; Leader HAMZAH HAZ; Sec.-Gen. ALI MARWAN HANAN.

Partai Rakyat Demokrasi (PRD) (People's Democratic Party): Jakarta; Chair. BUDIMAN SUJATMIKO.

Partai Tionghoa Indonesia (The Indonesian-Chinese Party): Jakarta; f. 1998; Chinese.

Partai Uni Demokrasi Indonesia (PUDI) (Democratic Union Party of Indonesia): Jakarta; e-mail sribintangpamungkas@e-mail.com; internet www.pudi.or.id; f. 1996; Chair. Sri BINTANG PAMUNGKAS.

Other groups with political influence include:

Ikatan Cendekiawan Muslim Indonesia (ICMI) (Association of Indonesian Muslim Intellectuals): Gedung BPPT, Jalan M. H. Thamrin 8, Jakarta; tel. (21) 3410382; e-mail nama_anda@icmi.or.id; internet www.icmi.or.id; f. 1990 with government support; Chair. ACHMAD TIRTOSUDIRO; Sec.-Gen. ADI SASONO.

Masyumi Baru: Jalan Pangkalan Asem 12, Cempaka Putih Ba, Jakarta Pusat; tel. (21) 4225774; fax (21) 7353077; Sec.-Gen. RIDWAN SAIDI.

Muhammadiyah: Jalan Menteng Raya 62, Jakarta Pusat; tel. (21) 3903024; fax (21) 3141582; internet www.muhammadiyah.or.id; second largest Muslim organization; f. 1912; 28m. mems; Chair. SYAFII MA'AIRF.

Nahdlatul Ulama (NU) (Council of Scholars): Jalan H. Agus Salim 112, Jakarta Pusat; tel. (21) 336250; largest Muslim organization; 30m. mems; Chair. AHMAD HASYIM.

Syarikat Islam: Jalan Taman Amir Hamzah Nomor 2, Jakarta; tel. (21) 31906037.

The following groups remain in conflict with the Government:

Gerakan Aceh Merdeka (GAM) (Free Aceh Movement): based in Aceh; f. 1976; seeks independence from Indonesia; Leader HASAN DI TIRO; Military Commdr MUZZAKIR MANAF.

National Liberation Front Acheh Sumatra: based in Aceh; f. 1989; seeks independence from Indonesia.

Organisasi Papua Merdeka (OPM) (Free Papua Movement): based in Papua; f. 1963; seeks unification with Papua New Guinea; Chair. MOZES WEROR; Leader KELLY KWALIK.

Presidium Dewan Papua (PDP) (Papua Presidium Council): based in Papua; seeks independence from Indonesia; internet www.westpapua.net; Chair. (vacant); Vice-Chair. TOM BEANAL.

Diplomatic Representation

EMBASSIES IN INDONESIA

Afghanistan: Jalan Dr Kusuma Atmaja 15, Jakarta; tel. (21) 333169; fax (21) 335390; Chargé d'affaires: ABDUL GHAFUR BAHER.

Algeria: Jalan H. R. Rasuna Said, Kav. 10-1, Kuningan, Jakarta 12950; tel. (21) 5254719; fax (21) 5254654; e-mail ambalyak@rad.net.id; Ambassador: SOUFIANE MIMOUNI.

Argentina: Menara Mulia, Suite 1901, Jalan Jenderal Gatot Subroto Kav. 9–11, Jakarta 12930; tel. (21) 5265661; fax (21) 5265664; e-mail embargen@cbn.net.id; Ambassador: JOSÉ LUIS MIGNINI.

Australia: Jalan H. R. Rasuna Said, Kav. C15-16, Kuningan, Jakarta 12940; tel. (21) 25505555; fax (21) 5227101; e-mail public.affairsjakt@dfat.gov.au; internet www.austembjak.or.id; Ambassador: RICHARD SMITH.

Austria: Jalan Diponegoro 44, Jakarta 10310; tel. (21) 338101; fax (21) 3904927; e-mail jakarta-ob@bmaa.gv.at; internet www.austrian.embassy.or.id; Ambassador: Dr BERNHARD ZIMBURG.

Bangladesh: Jalan Denpasar Raya 3, Block A-13, Kav. 10, Kuningan, Jakarta 12950; tel. (21) 5221574; fax (21) 5261807; e-mail bdootjak@dnet.net.id; internet www.bangladeshembassyjakarta.or.id; Ambassador: Maj.-Gen. Dr M. AFSARUL QADER.

Belgium: Deutsche Bank Bldg, 16th Floor, Jalan Imam Bonjol 80, Jakarta 10310; tel. (21) 3162030; fax (21) 3162035; e-mail jakarta@diplobel.org; Ambassador: LUK DARRAS.

Bosnia and Herzegovina: Menara Imperium, 11th Floor, Suite D-2, Metropolitan Kuningan Super Blok, Kav. 1, Jalan H. R. Rasuna Said, Jakarta 12980; tel. (21) 83703022; fax (21) 83703029; Ambassador: ZDRAVKO RAJIĆ.

Brazil: Menara Mulia, Suite 1602, Jalan Jenderal Gatot Subroto, Kav. 9, Jakarta 12930; tel. (21) 5265656; fax (21) 5265659; e-mail brasemb@rad.net.id; Ambassador: JADIEL FERREIRA DE OLIVEIRA.

Brunei: Wisma GKBI, Suite 1901, Jalan Jenderal Sudirman 28, Jakarta Selatan 10210; tel. (21) 5741437; fax (21) 5741463; Ambassador: Dato' Haji MOHAMMAD AMIN BIN Haji ABDUL RAHIM.

Bulgaria: Jalan Imam Bonjol 34–36, Jakarta 10310; tel. (21) 39040489; fax (21) 3904049; e-mail bgemb.jkt@centrin.net.id; Ambassador: GATYU GATEV.

Cambodia: Panin Bank Plaza JL, 4th Floor, 52 Palmera Utara, Jakarta 11480; tel. (21) 5483643; fax (21) 5483684; e-mail recjkt@cabi.net.id.

Canada: World Trade Centre, 6th Floor, Jalan Jenderal Sudirman, Kav. 29–31, POB 8324/JKS, Jakarta 12920; tel. (21) 5250709; fax (21) 5712251; e-mail canadianembassy.jkrta@dfait-maeci.gc.ca; internet www.dfait-maeci.gc.ca/jakarta/; Ambassador: FERRY DE KERCKHOVE.

Chile: Bina Mulia Bldg, 7th Floor, Jalan H. R. Rasuna Said, Kav. 10, Kuningan, Jakarta 12950; tel. (21) 5201131; fax (21) 5201955; e-mail emchijak@indosat.net.id; Ambassador: SINCLAIR MANLEY JAMES.

China, People's Republic: Jalan Mega Kuningan 2, Karet Kuningan, Jakarta 12950; tel. (21) 5761038; fax (21) 5761034; e-mail enbsychn@cbn.net.id; internet www.chinaembassy-indonesia.or.id; Ambassador: LU SHUMIN.

Colombia: Central Plaza Bldg, 16th Floor, Jalan Jenderal Sudirman, Kav. 48, Jakarta; tel. (21) 516446; fax (21) 5207717; e-mail emcolin@rad.net.id; Ambassador: LUIS FERNANDO ANGEL.

Croatia: Menara Mulia Bldg, Suite 2101, Jalan Gatot Subroto, Kav. 9–11, Jakarta 12930; tel. (21) 5257822; fax (21) 5204073; e-mail croemb@rad.net.id; internet www.croatemb.or.id; Ambassador: BORIS MITOVIĆ.

Cuba: Taman Puri, Jalan Opal, Blok K-1, Permata Hijau, Jakarta 12210; tel (21) 5304293; fax (21) 53676906; e-mail cubaindo@cbn.net.id; Ambassador: MIGUEL ANGEL RAMÍREZ RAMOS.

Czech Republic: Jalan Gereja Theresia 20, POB 1319, Jakarta Pusat 10350; tel. (21) 3904075; fax (21) 336282; e-mail jakarta@embassy.mzv.cz; internet www.czech-embassy.or.id; Ambassador: MILAN SARAPATKA.

Denmark: Menara Rajawali, 25th Floor, Jalan Mega Kuningan, Lot 5.1, Jakarta 12950; tel. (21) 5761478; fax (21) 5761535; e-mail jktamb@um.dk; internet www.emb-denmark.or.id; Ambassador: MICHAEL STERNBERG.

Egypt: Jalan Teuku Umar 68, Jakarta 10350; tel. (21) 331141; fax (21) 3105073; e-mail egypt@indosat.net.id; Ambassador: AHMAD NABIL ELSALAWY.

Finland: Menara Rajawali, 9th Floor, Jalan Mega Kuningan, Kawasan Mega Kuningan, Jakarta 12950; tel. (21) 5761650; fax (21) 5761631; e-mail sanomat.jak@formin.fi; internet www.finembjak.com; Ambassador: MATTI PULLINEN.

France: Jalan M. H. Thamrin 20, Jakarta 10350; tel. (21) 3142807; fax (21) 3143338; e-mail ambassade@ambafrance-id.org; internet www.ambafrance-indonesie.org; Ambassador: HERVÉ LADSOUS.

Germany: Jalan M. H. Thamrin 1, Jakarta 10310; tel. (21) 3901750; fax (21) 3901757; e-mail germany@rad.net.id; internet www.deutschebotschaft-jakarta.or.id; Ambassador: Dr GERHARD FULDA.

Greece: Plaza 89, 12th Floor, Suite 1203, Jalan H. R. Rasuna Said, Kav. X-7 No. 6, Kuningan, Jakarta 12540; tel. (21) 5207776; fax (21) 5207753; e-mail grembas@cbn.net.id; internet www.greekembassy.or.id; Ambassador: CONSTANTIN DRAKATIS.

Holy See: Jalan Merdeka Timur 18, POB 4227, Jakarta Pusat (Apostolic Nunciature); tel. (21) 3841142; fax (21) 3841143; e-mail vatjak@cbn.net.id; Apostolic Nuncio: Most Rev. RENZO FRATINI, Titular Archbishop of Botriana.

Hungary: 36 Jalan H. R. Rasuna Said, Kav. X/3, Kuningan, Jakarta 12950; tel. (21) 5203459; fax (21) 5203461; e-mail huembjkt@rad.net.id; internet www.huembjkt.or.id; Ambassador: GYÖRGY BUSZTIN.

India: Jalan H. R. Rasuna Said, Kav. S/1, Kuningan, Jakarta 12950; tel. (21) 5204150; fax (21) 5204160; e-mail eoiisi@indo.net.id; internet www.eoijakarta.or.id; Ambassador: SHYAM SARAN.

Iran: Jalan Hos Cokroaminoto 110, Menteng, Jakarta Pusat 10310; tel. (21) 331391; fax (21) 3107860; e-mail irembjkt@indo.net.id; internet www.iranembassy.or.id; Ambassador: SEYED MOHSEN NABAVI.

Iraq: Jalan Teuku Umar 38, Jakarta 10350; tel. (21) 4214067; fax (21) 4214066; e-mail iraqembi@rad.net.id; Chargé d'affaires: MUSTAFA MUHAMMAD TAWFIQ.

Italy: Jalan Diponegoro 45, Jakarta 10310; tel. (21) 337445; fax (21) 337422; e-mail italemba@italambjkt.or.id; internet www.italambjkt.or.id; Ambassador: FRANCESCO MARIA GRECO.

Japan: Menara Thamrin, 7th–10th Floors, Jalan M. H. Thamrin Kav. 3, Jakarta 10350; tel. (21) 324308; fax (21) 325460; internet www.id.emb-japan.go.jp; Ambassador: TAIZO WATANABE.

Jordan: Jalan Denpasar Raya, Blok A XIII, Kav. 1–2, Jakarta 12950; tel. (21) 5204400; fax (21) 5202447; e-mail jordanem@cbn.net.id; internet www.jordanembassy.or.id; Ambassador: MOHAMED ALI DAHER.

Korea, Democratic People's Republic: Jalan H. R. Rasuna Said, Kav. X.5, Jakarta; tel. (21) 5210181; fax (21) 5210183; Ambassador: JANG CHANG-CHON.

Korea, Republic: Jalan Jenderal Gatot Subroto 57, Jakarta Selatan; tel. (21) 5201915; fax (21) 5254159; Ambassador: KIM JAE-SUP.

Kuwait: Jalan Denpasar Raya, Blok A XII, Kuningan, Jakarta 12950; tel. (21) 5202477; fax (21) 5204359; e-mail ami@Kuwait-toplist.com; Ambassador: JASEM M. J. AL-MUBARAKI.

Laos: Jalan Patra Kuningan XIV 1-A, Kuningan, Jakarta 12950; tel. (21) 5229602; fax (21) 5229601; e-mail laoemjkt@cabi.net.id; Ambassador: SOMPHET KHOUSAKOUN.

Lebanon: Jalan YBR V 82, Kuningan, Jakarta 12950; tel. (21) 5253074; fax (21) 5207121; Ambassador: NAZIH ACHOUR.

Libya: Jalan Pekalongan 24, Jakarta; tel. (21) 335308; fax (21) 335726; Chargé d'affaires a.i.: TAJEDDIN A. JERBI.

Malaysia: Jalan H. R. Rasuna Said, Kav. X/6, Kuningan, Jakarta 12950; tel. (21) 5224947; fax (21) 5224974; e-mail mwjakarta@indosat.net.id; Ambassador: Datuk RASTAM MOHAMMAD ISA.

Mali: Jalan Mendawai III 18, Kebayoran Baru, Jakarta 12130; tel. (21) 7208472; fax (21) 7229589; e-mail ambamali@indosat.net.id; Ambassador: AMADOU N'DIAYE.

Marshall Islands: Jalan Brawijaya Raya 17, Jakarta 12160; tel. (21) 7248565; fax (21) 7248566; e-mail marshall@idola.net.id.

Mexico: Menara Mulia Bldg, Suite 2306, Jalan Gatot Subroto, Kav. 9–11, Jakarta 12930; tel. (21) 5203980; fax (21) 5203978; e-mail embmexic@rad.net.id; Ambassador: SERGIO LEY-LÓPEZ.

Morocco: Suite 512, 5th Floor, South Tower, Kuningan Plaza, Jalan H. R. Rasuna Said C-11-14, Jakarta 12940; tel. (21) 5200773; fax (21) 5200586; e-mail sifamajakar@cbn.net.id; Ambassador: M. ABDERAHMAN DRISSI ALAMI.

Mozambique: Wisma GKBI, 37th Floor, Suite 3709, Jalan Jenderal Sudirman 28, Jakarta 10210; tel. (21) 5740901; fax (21) 5740907; e-mail embamoc@cbn.net.id.

Myanmar: Jalan Haji Agus Salim 109, Jakarta Selatan; tel. (21) 320440; fax (21) 327204; e-mail myanmar@cbn.net.id; Ambassador: U NYO WIN.

Netherlands: Jalan H. R. Rasuna Said, Kav. S/3, Kuningan, Jakarta 12950; tel. (21) 5251515; fax (21) 5700734; e-mail jak-ea@minbuza.nl; internet www.netherlandsembassy.or.id; Ambassador: Baron S. VAN HEEMSTRA.

New Zealand: BRI II Bldg, 23rd Floor, Jalan Jenderal Sudirman, Kav. 44–46, Jakarta; tel. (21) 5709460; fax (21) 5709457; e-mail nzembjak@cbn.net.id; Ambassador: CHRIS ELDER.

Nigeria: Jalan Tamam Patra xiv/11–11A, Kuningan Timur, POB 3649, Jakarta Selatan 12950; tel. (21) 5260922; fax (21) 5260924; e-mail embnig@centrin.net.id; Ambassador: SAIDU MOHAMMED.

Norway: Menara Rajawali Bldg, 25th Floor, Kawasan Mega Kuningan, Jakarta 12950; tel. (21) 5761523; fax (21) 5761537; e-mail emb.jakarta@mfa.no; internet www.norwayemb-indonesia.org; Ambassador: SJUR TORGERSEN.

Pakistan: Jalan Teuku Umar 50, Jakarta 10350; tel. (21) 3144008; fax (21) 3103945; e-mail parepjkt@rad.net.id; Ambassador: MATAHAR HUSEIN.

Panama: World Trade Centre, 8th Floor, Jalan Jenderal Sudirman, Kav. 29–31, Jakarta 12920; tel. (21) 5711867; fax (21) 5711933; e-mail panacon@pacific.net.id; Ambassador: VIRGINIA WEDEN DE ACOSTA.

Papua New Guinea: Panin Bank Centre, 6th Floor, Jalan Jenderal Sudirman 1, Jakarta 10270; tel. (21) 7251218; fax (21) 7201012; e-mail kdujkt@cbn.net.id; Ambassador: TARCY ERI.

Peru: Menara Rajawali Bldg, 12th Floor, Jalan Mega Kuningan, Lot 5.1, Kawasan Mega Kuningan, Jakarta 12950; tel. (21) 5761820; fax (21) 5761825; e-mail embaperu@cbn.net.id; Ambassador: NILO FIGUEROA CORTAVARRIA.

Philippines: Jalan Imam Bonjol 6–8, Jakarta 10310; tel. (21) 3155118; fax (21) 3151167; e-mail phjkt@indo.net.id; Ambassador: RAFAEL E. SEGUIS.

Poland: Jalan H. R. Rasuna Said, Kav. X Blok IV/3, Jakarta Selatan 12950; tel. (21) 2525948; fax (21) 2525958; e-mail plembjkt@net.id; Ambassador: KRZYSZTOF SZUMSKI.

Portugal: Bina Mulia Bldg I, 7th Floor, Jalan H. R. Rasuna Said Kav. X, Kuningan, Jakarta 12950; tel. (21) 5265103; fax (21) 5271981; e-mail porembjak@cbn.net.id; Ambassador: ANA MARIA ROSA MARTINS GOMES.

Qatar: Jalan Taman Ubud I, No. 5, Kuningan Timur, Jakarta 12920; tel. (21) 5277751; fax (21) 5277754; e-mail jakarta@mofa.gov.qa; Ambassador: ABDULLA MOHAMMED TALEB AL-MARI.

Romania: Jalan Teuku Cik Ditiro 42A, Menteng, Jakarta Pusat; tel. (21) 3106240; fax (21) 3907759; e-mail romind@cbn.net.id; Ambassador: GHEORGHE SAVUICA.

Russia: Jalan H. R. Rasuna Said, Kav. X-6, Jakarta; tel. (21) 5222912; e-mail rusembjkt@dnet.net.id; Ambassador: VLADIMIR Y. PLOTNIKOV.

Saudi Arabia: Jalan M. T. Haryono Kav. 27, Cawang Atas, Jakarta Timur; tel. (21) 8011533; fax (21) 3905864; e-mail idemb@mofa.gov.sa; Ambassador: ABDULLAH A. ALIM.

Singapore: Jalan H. R. Rasuna Said, Blok X/4, Kav. 2, Kuningan, Jakarta 12950; tel. (21) 5201489; fax (21) 5201486; e-mail denpasar@pacific.net.id; internet www.mfa.gov.sg/jkt; Ambassador: EDWARD LEE.

Slovakia: Jalan Prof. Mohammed Yamin 29, POB 1368, Jakarta Pusat; tel. (21) 3101068; fax (21) 3101180; e-mail slovemby@indo.net.id; Ambassador: MILAN LAJČIAK.

South Africa: Suite 705, Wisma GKBI, Jalan Jenderal Sudirman 28, Jakarta 10210; tel. (21) 5740660; fax (21) 5740661; e-mail saembhom@mweb.co.id; internet www.saembassy-jakarta.or.id; Ambassador: NORMAN M. MASHABANE.

Spain: Jalan H. Agus Salim 61, Jakarta 10350; tel. (21) 335937; fax (21) 325996; e-mail embespid@mail.mae.es; Ambassador: ANTONIO SÁNCHEZ JARA.

Sri Lanka: Jalan Diponegoro 70, Jakarta 10320; tel. (21) 3161886; fax (21) 3107962; e-mail lankaemb@rad.net.id; Ambassador: H. J. K. R. BANDARA.

Sudan: Wisma Bank Dharmala, 7th Floor, Suite 01, Jalan Jenderal Sudirman, Kav. 28, Jakarta 12920; tel. (21) 5212099; fax (21) 5212077; e-mail leen@cbn.net.id; Ambassador: SIDIQ YOUSIF ABU-AGLA.

Sweden: Menara Rajawali Bldg, 9th Floor, Jalan Mega Kuningan, Lot 5.1, Kawasan Mega Kuningan, Jakarta 12950; POB 2824, Jakarta 10001; tel. (21) 5762690; fax (21) 5762691; e-mail sweden@cbn.net.id; internet www.swedemb-jakarta.com; Ambassador: HARALD SANDBERG.

Switzerland: Jalan H. R. Rasuna Said X-3/2, Kuningan, Jakarta Selatan 12950; tel. (21) 5256061; fax (21) 5202289; e-mail vertretung@jak.rep.admin.ch; internet www.swissembassy.or.id; Ambassador: GEORGES MARTIN.

Syria: Jalan Karang Asem I/8, Jakarta 12950; tel. (21) 515991; fax (21) 5202511; Ambassador: NADIM DOUAY.

Thailand: Jalan Imam Bonjol 74, Jakarta 10310; tel. (21) 3904052; fax (21) 3107469; e-mail thaijkt@indo.net.id; Ambassador: CHAIYONG SATJIPANON.

Tunisia: Wisma Dharmala Sakti, 11th Floor, Jalan Jenderal Sudirman 32, Jakarta 10220; tel. (21) 5703432; fax (21) 5700016; e-mail embtun@uninet.net.id; Ambassador: MAHMOUD BESSROUR.

Turkey: Jalan H. R. Rasuna Said, Kav. 1, Kuningan, Jakarta 12950; tel. (21) 5256250; fax (21) 5226056; e-mail cakabe@cbn.net.id; Ambassador: FERYAL ÇOTUR.

Ukraine: WTC Bldg, 8th Floor, Jalan Jenderal Sudirman, Kav. 29–31, Jakarta 12084; tel. (21) 5211700; fax (21) 5211710; e-mail uaembas@rad.net.id; Chargé d'affaires a.i.: SERGIY NIKSHICH.

United Arab Emirates: Jalan Prof. Dr Satrio, Kav. 16-17, Jakarta 12950; tel. (21) 5206518; fax (21) 5206526; e-mail uaeemb@rad.net.id; Ambassador: MOHAMMED SULTAN AL-SOWAIDI.

United Kingdom: Jalan M. H. Thamrin 75, Jakarta 10310; tel. (21) 3156264; fax (21) 3926263; e-mail britem2@ibm.net.id; internet www.britain-in-indonesia.or.id; Ambassador: RICHARD GOZNEY.

USA: Jalan Merdeka Selatan 4-5, Jakarta 10110; tel. (21) 34359000; fax (21) 3857189; e-mail jakconsul@state.gov; internet www.usembassyjakarta.org; Ambassador: RALPH (SKIP) BOYCE.

Uzbekistan: Menara Mulia Bldg, Suite 2401, 24th Floor, Jalan Jenderal Gatot Subroto, Kav. 9–11, Jakarta 12930; tel. (21) 5222581; fax (21) 5222582; e-mail registan@indo.net.id.

Venezuela: Menara Mulia Bldg, 20th Floor, Suite 2005, Jalan Jenderal Gatot Subroto, Kav. 9–11, Jakarta Selatan 12930; tel. (21) 5227547; fax (21) 5227549; e-mail evenjakt@indo.net.id; Ambassador: LUIS EDUARDO SOTO.

Viet Nam: Jalan Teuku Umar 25, Jakarta; tel. (21) 3100358; fax (21) 3100359; e-mail embvnam@uninet.net.id; Ambassador: NGUYEN DANG QUANG.

Yemen: Jalan Yusuf Adiwinata 29, Jakarta; tel. (21) 3904074; fax (21) 4214946; Ambassador: ABDUL WAHAD FARAH.

Yugoslavia: Jalan Hos Cokroaminoto 109, Jakarta 10310; tel. (21) 3143560; fax (21) 3143613; e-mail ambajaka@rad.net.id; Ambassador: VELJKO ČAGOROVIĆ.

Judicial System

There is one codified criminal law for the whole of Indonesia. In December 1989 the Islamic Judicature Bill, giving wider powers to Shariah courts, was approved by the Dewan Perwakilan Rakyat (House of Representatives). The new law gave Muslim courts authority over civil matters, such as marriage. Muslims may still choose to appear before a secular court. Europeans are subject to the Code of Civil Law published in the State Gazette in 1847. Alien orientals (i.e. Arabs, Indians, etc.) and Chinese are subject to certain parts of the Code of Civil Law and the Code of Commerce. The work of codifying this law has started, but, in view of the great complexity and diversity of customary law, it may be expected to take a considerable time to achieve.

Supreme Court (Mahkamah Agung): Jalan Merdeka Utara 9–13, Jakarta 10110; tel. (21) 3843348; fax (21) 3811057; e-mail pansekjen@mari.go.id; internet www.mari.go.id; the final court of appeal.

Chief Justice: Prof. BAGIR MANAN.

Deputy Chief Justice: H. TAUFIK.

High Courts in Jakarta, Surabaya, Medan, Makassar, Banda Aceh, Padang, Palembang, Bandung, Semarang, Banjarmasin, Menado, Denpasar, Ambon and Jayapura deal with appeals from the District Courts.

District Courts deal with marriage, divorce and reconciliation.

Religion

All citizens are required to state their religion. According to a survey in 1985, 86.9% of the population were Muslims, while 9.6% were Christians, 1.9% were Hindus, 1.0% were Buddhists and 0.6% professed adherence to tribal religions.

Five national religious councils—representing the Islamic, Catholic, Protestant, Hindu and Buddhist religious traditions—were established to serve as liaison bodies between religious adherents and the Government and to advise the Government on the application of religious principles to various elements of national life.

ISLAM

In 1993 nearly 90% of Indonesians were Muslims. Indonesia has the world's largest Muslim population.

Majelis Ulama Indonesia (MUI) (Indonesian Ulama Council): Komp. Masjid Istiqlal, Jalan Taman Wijaya Kesuma, Jakarta 10710; tel. (21) 3455471; fax (21) 3855412; internet www.mui.or.id; central Muslim organization; Chair. SAHAL MAHFUDZ; Sec.-Gen. DIEN SYAMSUDDIN.

CHRISTIANITY

Persekutuan Gereja-Gereja di Indonesia (Communion of Churches in Indonesia): Jalan Salemba Raya 10, Jakarta 10430; tel. (21) 3908119; fax (21) 3150457; e-mail pgi@bit.net.id; internet www.pgi.or.id; f. 1950; 70 mem. churches; Chair. Rev. Dr SULARSO SOPATER; Gen. Sec. Rev. Dr JOSEPH M. PATTIASINA.

The Roman Catholic Church

Indonesia comprises eight archdioceses and 26 dioceses. At 31 December 2000 there were an estimated 6,289,326 adherents in Indonesia (excluding the territory of East Timor), representing 3.3% of the population.

Bishops' Conference: Konferensi Waligereja Indonesia (KWI), Jalan Cut Meutia 10, POB 3044, Jakarta 10002; tel. (21) 336422; fax (21) 3918527; e-mail kwi@parokinet.org; f. 1973; Pres. Cardinal JULIUS RIYADI DARMAATMADJA, Archbishop of Jakarta.

Archbishop of Ende: Most Rev. ABDON LONGINUS DA CUNHA, Keuskupan Agung, POB 210, Jalan Katedral 5, Ndona-Ende 86312, Flores; tel. (381) 21176; fax (381) 21606; e-mail uskup@ende.parokinet.org

Archbishop of Jakarta: Cardinal JULIUS RIYADI DARMAATMADJA, Keuskupan Agung, Jalan Katedral 7, Jakarta 10710; tel. (21) 3813345; fax (21) 3855681.

Archbishop of Kupang: Most Rev. PETER TURANG, Keuskupan Agung Kupang, Jalan Thamrin, Oepoi, Kupang 85111, Timor NTT; tel. (380) 826199; fax (380) 833331.

Archbishop of Makassar: Most Rev. JOHANNES LIKU ADA', Keuskupan Agung, Jalan Thamrin 5–7, Makassar 90111, Sulawesi Selatan; tel. (411) 315744; fax (411) 326674; e-mail pseupg@indosat.net.id.

Archbishop of Medan: Most Rev. ALFRED GONTI PIUS DATUBARA, Jalan Imam Bonjol 39, POB 1191, Medan 20152, Sumatra Utara; tel. (61) 4519768; fax (61) 4145745; e-mail mar39@indosat.net.id.

Archbishop of Merauke: Most Rev. JACOBUS DUIVENVOORDE, Keuskupan Agung, Jalan Mandala 30, Merauke 99602, Irian Jaya (Papua); tel. (971) 321011; fax (971) 321311.

Archbishop of Pontianak: Most Rev. HIERONYMUS HERCULANUS BUMBUN, Keuskupan Agung, Jalan A. R. Hakin 92A, POB 1119, Pontianak 78011, Kalimantan Barat; tel. (561) 732382; fax (561) 738785; e-mail kap@pontianak.wasantara.net.id.

Archbishop of Semarang: Most Rev. IGNATIUS SUHARYO HARDJOATMODJO, Keuskupan Agung, Jalan Pandanaran 13, Semarang 50231; tel. (24) 312276; fax (24) 414741; e-mail uskup@semarang.parokinet.org.

Other Christian Churches

Protestant Church in Indonesia (Gereja Protestan di Indonesia): Jalan Medan Merdeka Timur 10, Jakarta 10110; tel. (21) 3519003; fax (21) 34830224; consists of 10 churches of Calvinistic tradition; 2,789,155 mems, 3,841 congregations, 1,965 pastors (1998); Chair. Rev. Dr D. J. LUMENTA.

Numerous other Protestant communities exist throughout Indonesia, mainly organized on a local basis. The largest of these (1985 memberships) are: the Batak Protestant Christian Church (1,875,143); the Christian Church in Central Sulawesi (100,000); the Christian Evangelical Church in Minahasa (730,000); the Christian Protestant Church in Indonesia (210,924); the East Java Christian Church (123,850); the Evangelical Christian Church in Irian Jaya (Papua—360,000); the Evangelical Christian Church of Sangir-Talaud (190,000); the Indonesian Christian Church/Huria Kristen Indonesia (316,525); the Javanese Christian Churches (121,500); the Kalimantan Evangelical Church (182,217); the Karo Batak Protestant Church (164,288); the Nias Protestant Christian Church (250,000); the Protestant Church in the Moluccas (575,000); the Simalungun Protestant Christian Church (155,000); and the Toraja Church (250,000).

BUDDHISM

All-Indonesia Buddhist Association: Jakarta.

Indonesian Buddhist Council: Jakarta.

HINDUISM

Hindu Dharma Council: Jakarta.

The Press

In August 1990 the Government announced that censorship of both the local and foreign press was to be relaxed and that the authorities would refrain from revoking the licences of newspapers that violated legislation governing the press. In practice, however, there was little change in the Government's policy towards the press. In June 1994 the Government revoked the publishing licences of three principal news magazines, *Tempo, Editor* and *DeTik*. Following the resignation of President Suharto in May 1998, the new Government undertook to allow freedom of expression. *DeTik* magazine subsequently resumed publication under the new name, *DeTak,* in July; *Tempo* magazine resumed publication in October.

PRINCIPAL DAILIES

Bali

Harian Pagi Umum (Bali Post): Jalan Kepudang 67A, Denpasar 80232; internet www.balipost.co.id; f. 1948; daily (Indonesian edn), weekly (English edn); Editor K. NADHA; circ. 25,000.

Java

Angkatan Bersenjata: Jalan Kramat Raya 94, Jakarta Pusat; tel. (21) 46071; fax (21) 366870.

Bandung Post: Jalan Lodaya 38A, Bandung 40264; tel. (22) 305124; fax (22) 302882; internet www.bandung-post.com; f. 1979; Chief Editor AHMAD SAELAN; Dir AHMAD JUSACC.

Berita Buana: Jalan Tahah Abang Dua 33–35, Jakarta 10110; tel. (21) 5487175; fax (21) 5491555; f. 1970; internet www.beritabuana.net; relaunched 1990; Indonesian; circ. 150,000.

Berita Yudha: Jalan Letjenderal Haryono MT22, Jakarta; tel. (21) 8298331; f. 1971; Indonesian; Editor SUNARDI; circ. 50,000.

Bisnis Indonesia: Wisma Bisnis Indonesia, Jalan Letjenderal S. Parman, Kav. 12, Slipi, Jakarta 11480; tel. (21) 5305869; fax (21) 5305868; e-mail iklana@bisnis.co.id; internet www.bisnis.com; f. 1985; available online; Indonesian; Editor SUKAMDANI S. GITOSARDJONO; circ. 60,000.

Harian Berita Sore: Jakarta; e-mail edy@beritasore.com; internet www.beritasore.com; Indonesian.

Harian Indonesia (Indonesia Rze Pao): Jalan Toko Tiga Seberang 21, POB 4755, Jakarta 11120; tel. (21) 6295948; fax (21) 6297830; e-mail info@harian-indonesia.com; internet www.harian-indonesia.com; f. 1966; Chinese; Editor W. D. SUKISMAN; Dir HADI WIBOWO; circ. 42,000.

Harian Terbit: Jalan Pulogadung 15, Kawasan Industri Pulogadung, Jakarta 13920; tel. (21) 4602953; fax (21) 4602950; f. 1972; Indonesian; Editor H. R. S. HADIKAMAJAYA; circ. 125,000.

Harian Umum AB: CTC Bldg, 2nd Floor, Kramat Raya 94, Jakarta Pusat; f. 1965; official armed forces journal; Dir GOENARSO; Editor-in-Chief N. SOEPANGAT; circ. 80,000.

The Indonesia Times: Jalan Pulo Lentut 12, Jakarta Timur; tel. (21) 4611280; fax (21) 375012; e-mail info@webpacific.com; internet www.indonesiatimes.com; f. 1974; English; Editor TRIBUANA SAID; circ. 35,000.

Indonesian Observer: Wisma Indovision, 11th Floor, Jalan Raya Panjang Blok Z/III, Green Garden, Jakarta 11520; tel. (21) 5818855; fax (21) 58302414; internet www.indonesian-observer.com; f. 1955; English; independent; Editor TAUFIK DARUSMAN; circ. 25,000.

Jakarta Post: Jalan Palmerah Selatan 15, Jakarta 10270; tel. (21) 5300476; fax (21) 5492685; e-mail editorial@thejakartapost.com; internet www.thejakartapost.com; f. 1983; English; Chief Editor RAYMOND TORUAN; circ. 50,000.

Jawa Pos: Graha Pena Bldg, 4th and 5th Floors, Achmad Yani 88, Surabaya 60234; tel. (31) 8283333; fax (31) 8285555; internet www.jawapos.co.id; f. 1949; Indonesian; CEO DAHLAN ISKAN; circ. 120,000.

Jepara Pos: Jepara; internet www.jeparapos.com; Indonesian.

Kedaulatan Rakyat: Jalan P. Mangkubumi 40–42, Yogyakarta; tel. (274) 65685; fax (274) 63125; internet www.kr.co.id; f. 1945; Indonesian; independent; Editor IMAN SUTRISNO; circ. 50,000.

Kompas: Jalan Palmerah Selatan 26–28, Jakarta; tel. (21) 5483008; fax (21) 5305868; internet www.kompas.com; f. 1965; Indonesian; Editor Drs JAKOB OETAMA; circ. 523,453.

Media Indonesia Daily: Jalan Pilar Mas Raya, Kav. A-D, Kedoya Selatan, Kebon Jeruk, Jakarta 11520; tel. (21) 5812088; fax (21) 5812105; e-mail redaksi@mediaindonesia.co.id; internet www.mediaindo.co.id; f. 1989; fmrly Prioritas; Indonesian; Publr SURYA PALOH; Editor DJAFAR H. ASSEGAFF; circ. 2,000.

Merdeka: Jalan Raya Kebayoran Lama 17, Jakarta Selatan 12210; tel. (21) 5556059; fax (21) 5556063; f. 1945; Indonesian; independent; Dir and Chief Editor B. M. DIAH; circ. 130,000.

Neraca: Jalan Jambrut 2–4, Jakarta; tel. (21) 323969; fax (21) 3101873.

Pelita (Torch): Jalan Jenderal Sudirman 65, Jakarta; f. 1974; Indonesian; Muslim; Editor AKBAR TANJUNG; circ. 80,000.

Pewarta Surabaya: Jalan Karet 23, POB 85, Surabaya; f. 1905; Indonesian; Editor RADEN DJAROT SOEBIANTORO; circ. 10,000.

Pikiran Rakyat: Jalan Asia-Afrika 77, Bandung 40111; tel. (22) 51216; internet www.pikiran-rakyat.com; f. 1950; Indonesian; independent; Editor BRAM M. DARMAPRAWIRA; circ. 150,000.

Pos Kota: Yayasan Antar Kota, Jalan Gajah Mada 100, Jakarta 10130; tel. (21) 6290874; e-mail iklankilat@poskota.net; internet www.poskota.co.id; f. 1970; Indonesian; Editor H. SOFYAN LUBIS; circ. 500,000.

Republika: Jalan Warung Buncit Raya 37, Jakarta 12510; tel. (21) 7803747; fax (21) 7800420; internet www.republika.co.id; f. 1993; organ of ICMI; Chief Editor PARNI HADI.

Sinar Pagi: Jalan Letjenderal Haryono MT22, Jakarta Selatan.

Suara Karya: Jalan Bangka II/2, Kebayoran Baru, Jakarta Selatan 12720; tel. (21) 7192656; fax (21) 71790784; internet www.suarakarya-online.com; f. 1971; Indonesian; Editor SYAMSUL BASRI; circ. 100,000.

Suara Merdeka: Jalan Pandanaran 30, Semarang 50241; tel. (24) 412660; fax (24) 411116; internet www.suaramerdeka.com; f. 1950; Indonesian; Publr Ir BUDI SANTOSO; Editor SUWARNO; circ. 200,000.

Suara Pembaruan: Jalan Dewi Sartika 136/D, Cawang, Jakarta 13630; tel. (21) 8013208; fax (21) 8007262; e-mail koransp@suarapembaruan.com; internet www.suarapembaruan.com; f. 1987; licence revoked in 1986 as Sinar Harapan (Ray of Hope); Publr Dr ALBERT HASIBUAN.

Surabaya Post: Jalan Taman Ade Irma Nasution 1, Surayaba; tel. (31) 45394; fax (31) 519585; internet www.surabayapost.co.id; f. 1953; independent; Publr Mrs TUTY AZIS; Editor IMAM PUJONO; circ. 115,000.

Wawasan: Bapak Mahmud, Jalan Letjen Suprapto, Brigjen Katamso 1, Medan 20151; tel. (24) 4150858; fax (24) 4510025; e-mail waspada@waspada.co.id; internet www.waspada.co.id; f. 1986; Indonesian; Chief Editor H. PRABUDI SAID; circ. 65,000.

Kalimantan

Banjarmasin Post: Jalan Haryono MT 54–143, Banjarmasin; tel. (511) 54370; fax (511) 66123; e-mail bpost@Indomedia.com; internet www.indomedia.com/bpost/; f. 1971; Indonesian; Chief Editor H. BASUKI SUBIANTO; circ. 50,000.

Gawi Manuntung: Jalan Pangeran Samudra 97B, Banjarmasin; f. 1972; Indonesian; Editor M. ALI SRI INDRADJAYA; circ. 5,000.

Harian Umum Akcaya: Jalan Veteran 1, Pontianak.

Lampung Post: Jalan Pangkal Pinang, Lampung.

Manuntung: Jalan Jenderal Sudirman RT XVI 82, Balikpapan 76144; tel. (542) 35359; internet www.manuntung.co.id; largest newspaper in East Borneo.

Maluku

Pos Maluku: Jalan Raya Pattimura 19, Ambon; tel. (911) 44614.

Suara Maluku: Komplex Perdagangan Mardikas, Block D3/11A, Ternate; tel. (911) 44590.

Papua

Berita Karya: Jayapura.

Cendrawasih Post: Jayapura; Editor RUSTAM MADUBUN.

Teropong: Jalan Halmahera, Jayapura.

Riau

Riau Pos: Pekanbaru, Riau; internet www.riaupos.com; circ. 40,000.

Sulawesi

Bulletin Sulut: Jalan Korengkeng 38, Lt II Manado, 95114, Sulawesi Utara.

Cahaya Siang: Jalan Kembang II 2, Manado, 95114, Sulawesi Utara; tel. (431) 61054; fax (431) 63393.

Fajar (Dawn): Makassar; circ. 35,000.

Manado Post: Manado Post Centre, Jalan Babe Palar 54, Manado; tel. (431) 855558; fax (431) 860398; internet www.mdopost.net.

Pedoman Rakyat: Jalan H. A. Mappanyukki 28, Makassar; f. 1947; independent; Editor M. BASIR; circ. 30,000.

Suluh Merdeka: Jalan R. W. Mongsidi 4/96, POB 1105, Manado, 95110; tel. and fax (431) 866150.

Tegas: Jalan Mappanyukki 28, Makassar; tel. (411) 3960.

Wenang Post: Jalan R. W. Mongsidi 4/96, POB 1105, Manado 95115; tel. and fax (431) 866150; weekly.

Sumatra

Harian Analisa: Jalan Jenderal A. Yani 37–43, Medan; tel. (61) 326655; fax (61) 514031; internet www.analisadaily.com; f. 1972; Indonesian; Editor SOFFYAN; circ. 75,000.

Harian Haluan: Jalan Damar 59 C/F, Padang; f. 1948; Editor-in-Chief RIVAI MARLAUT; circ. 40,000.

Harian Umum Nasional Waspada: Jalan Brigjenderal 1 Katamso, Medan 20151; tel. (61) 4150858; fax (61) 4510025; e-mail waspada@indosat.net.id; internet www.waspada.co.id; f. 1947; Indonesian; Editor-in-Chief H. PRABUDI SAID.

Mimbar Umum: Merah, Medan; tel. (61) 517807; f. 1947; Indonesian; independent; Editor MOHD LUD LUBIS; circ. 55,000.

Serambi Indonesia: Jalan T. Nyak Arief 159, Lampriek, Banda Aceh; e-mail serambi@indomedia.com; internet www.indomedia.com/serambi/.

Sinar Indonesia Baru: Jalan Brigjenderal Katamso 66, Medan 20151; tel. (61) 4512530; fax (61) 438150; e-mail redaksi@hariansib.com; internet www.hariansib.com; f. 1970; Indonesian; Chief Editor G. M. PANGGABEAN; circ. 150,000.

Suara Rakyat Semesta: Jalan K. H. Ashari 52, Palembang; Indonesian; Editor DJADIL ABDULLAH; circ. 10,000.

Waspada: Jalan Jenderal Sudirman, cnr Jalan Brigjenderal Katamso 1, Medan 20151; tel. (61) 550858; fax (61) 510025; f. 1947; Indonesian; Chief Editor ANI IDRUS; circ. 60,000 (daily), 55,000 (Sunday).

PRINCIPAL PERIODICALS

Amanah: Jalan Garuda 69, Kemayoran, Jakarta; tel. (21) 410254; fortnightly; Muslim current affairs; Indonesian; Man. Dir MASKUN ISKANDAR; circ. 180,000.

Berita Negara: Jalan Pertjetakan Negara 21, Kotakpos 2111, Jakarta; tel. (21) 4207251; fax (21) 4207251; f. 1951; 2 a week; official gazette.

Bobo: PT Gramedia, Jalan Kebahagiaan 4-14, Jakarta 11140; tel. (21) 6297809; fax (21) 6390080; f. 1973; weekly; children's magazine; Editor TINEKE LATUMETEN; circ. 240,000.

Bola: Yayasan Tunas Raga, Jalan Palmerah Selatan 17, Jakarta 10270; tel. and fax (21) 5483008; internet www.bolanews.com; 2 a week; Tue. and Fri.; sports magazine; Indonesian; Chief Editor IAN SITUMORANG; circ. 715,000.

Buana Minggu: Jalan Tanah Abang Dua 33, Jakarta Pusat 10110; tel. (21) 364190; weekly; Sunday; Indonesian; Editor WINOTO PARARTHO; circ. 193,450.

Business News: Jalan H. Abdul Muis 70, Jakarta 10160; tel. (21) 3848207; fax (21) 3454280; f. 1956; 3 a week (Indonesian edn), 2 a week (English edn); Chief Editor SANJOTO SASTROMIHARDJO; circ. 15,000.

Citra: Gramedia Bldg, Unit 11, 5th Floor, Jalan Palmerah Selatan 24-26, Jakarta 10270; tel. (21) 5483008; fax (21) 5494035; e-mail citra@gramedia-majalah.com; internet www.tabloid-citra.com; f. 1990; weekly; TV and film programmes, music trends and celebrity news; Chief Editor H. MAMAN SUHERMAN; circ. 239,000

Depthnews Indonesia: Jalan Jatinegara Barat III/6, Jakarta 13310; tel. (21) 8194994; fax (21) 8195501; f. 1972; weekly; publ. by Press Foundation of Indonesia; Editor SUMONO MUSTOFFA.

Dunia Wanita: Jalan Brigjenderal, Katamso 1, Medan; tel. (61) 4150858; fax (61) 4510025; e-mail waspada@indosat.net.id; f. 1949; fortnightly; Indonesian; women's tabloid; Chief Editor Dr RAYATI SYAFRIN; circ. 10,000.

Economic Review: c/o Bank BNI, Strategic Planning Division, Jalan Jenderal Sudirman, Kav. 1, POB 2955, Jakarta 10220; tel. (21) 5728606; fax (21) 5728456; internet www.economicreview.net; f. 1966; 4 a year; English.

Ekonomi Indonesia: Jalan Merdeka, Timur 11–12, Jakarta; tel. (21) 494458; monthly; English; economic journal; Editor Z. ACHMAD; circ. 20,000.

Eksekutif: Jalan R. S. Fatmawati 20, Jakarta 12430; tel. (21) 7659218; fax (21) 7504018; e-mail eksek@pacific.net.id; internet www.pacific.net.id/eksekutif/.

Femina: Jalan H. R. Rasuna Said, Blok B, Kav. 32–33, Jakarta Selatan; tel. (21) 5209370; fax (21) 5209366; e-mail info@femina-online.com; internet www.femina-online.com; f. 1972; weekly; women's magazine; Publr SOFJAN ALISJAHBANA; Editor WIDARTI GUNAWAN; circ. 130,000.

Forum: Kebayoran Centre, 12A–14, Jalan Kebayoran Baru, Welbak, Jakarta 12240; tel. (21) 7255625; fax (21) 7255645.

Gadis Magazine: Jalan H. R. Rasuna Said, Blok B, Kav. 32–33, Jakarta 12910; tel. (21) 5253816; fax (21) 5262131; e-mail gadis@indosat.net.id; internet www.gadis-online.com; f. 1973; every 10 days; Indonesian; teen lifestyle magazine; Editor-in-Chief PETTY S. F.; circ. 100,000.

Gamma: Jakarta; internet www.gamma.co.id; f. 1999; by fmr employees of *Tempo* and *Gatra*.

Gatra: Gedung Gatra, Jalan Kalibata Timur IV/15, Jakarta 12740; tel. (21) 7973535; fax (21) 79196923; e-mail gatra@gatra.com; internet www.gatra.com; f. 1994 by fmr employees of *Tempo* (banned 1994–1998); Gen. Man. and Editor-in-Chief WIDI YARMANTO.

Gugat (Accuse): Surabaya; politics, law and crime; weekly; circ. 250,000.

Hai: Gramedia, Jalan Palmerah Selatan 22, Jakarta 10270; tel. (21) 5483008; fax (21) 6390080; f. 1973; weekly; youth magazine; Editor ARSWENDO ATMOWILOTO; circ. 70,000.

Indonesia Business News: Wisma Bisnis Indonesia, Jalan Letjenderal S. Parman, Kav. 12, Slipi, Jakarta 11410; tel. (21) 5304016; fax (21) 5305868; English.

Indonesia Business Weekly: Jalan Letjenderal S. Parman, Kav. 12, Slipi, Jakarta 11410; tel. (21) 5304016; fax (21) 5305868; English; Editor TAUFIK DARUSMAN.

Indonesia Magazine: 20 Jalan Merdeka Barat, Jakarta; tel. (21) 352015; f. 1969; monthly; English; Chair. G. DWIPAYANA; Editor-in-Chief HADELY HASIBUAN; circ. 15,000.

Intisari (Digest): Jalan Palmerah Selatan 24–26, Gedung Unit II, 5th Floor, Jakarta 10270; tel. (21) 5483008; fax (21) 53696525; e-mail intisari@gramedia-majalah.com; internet www.intisari-online.com; f. 1963; monthly; Indonesian; popular science, health, technology, crime and general interest; Editors AL. HERU KUSTARA, IRAWATI; circ. 141,000.

Jakarta Jakarta: Gramedia Bldg, Unit II, 5th Floor, Jalan Palmerah Selatan No. 24–26, Jakarta 10270; tel. (21) 5483008; fax (21) 5494035; f. 1985; weekly; food, fun, fashion and celebrity news; circ. 70,000.

Keluarga: Jalan Sangaji 11, Jakarta; fortnightly; women's and family magazine; Editor S. DAHONO.

Majalah Ekonomis: POB 4195, Jakarta; monthly; English; business; Chief Editor S. ARIFIN HUTABARAT; circ. 20,000.

Majalah Kedokteran Indonesia (Journal of the Indonesian Medical Assen): Jalan Kesehatan 111/29, Jakarta 11/16; f. 1951; monthly; Indonesian, English.

Manglé: Jalan Lodaya 19–21, 40262 Bandung; tel. (22) 411438; f. 1957; weekly; Sundanese; Chief Editor Drs OEJANG DARAJATOEN; circ. 74,000.

Matra: Grafity Pers, Kompleks Buncit Raya Permai, Kav. 1, Jalan Warung, POB 3476, Jakarta; tel. (21) 515952; f. 1986; monthly; men's magazine; general interest and current affairs; Editor-in-Chief (vacant); circ. 100,000.

Mimbar Kabinet Pembangunan: Jalan Merdeka-Barat 7, Jakarta; f. 1966; monthly; Indonesian; publ. by Dept of Information.

Mutiara: Jalan Dewi Sartika 136D, Cawang, Jakarta Timur; general interest; Publr H. G. RORIMPANDEY.

Nova: PT Gramedia, Gedung Unit II, Lantai V, Jalan Palmerah Selatan No. 24–26, Jakarta 10270; tel. (21) 5483008; fax (21) 5483146; weekly; Wed.; women's interest; Indonesian; Editor KOES SABANDIYAH; circ. 618,267.

Oposisi: Jakarta; weekly; politics; circ. 400,000.

Otomotif: Gramedia Bldg, Unit II, 5th Floor, Jalan Palmerah Selatan 24–26, Jakarta 10270; tel. (21) 5490666; fax (21) 5494035; e-mail iklanmjl@ub.net.id; f. 1990; weekly; automotive specialist tabloid; circ. 215,763.

Peraba: Bintaran Kidul 5, Yogyakarta; weekly; Indonesian and Javanese; Roman Catholic; Editor W. KARTOSOEHARSONO.

Pertani PT: Jalan Pasar Minggu, Kalibata, POB 247/KBY, Jakarta Selatan; tel. (21) 793108; f. 1974; monthly; Indonesian; agricultural; Pres. Dir Ir RUSLI YAHYA.

Petisi: Surabaya; weekly; Editor CHOIRUL ANAM.

Rajawali: Jakarta; monthly; Indonesian; civil aviation and tourism; Dir R. A. J. LUMENTA; Man. Editor KARYONO ADHY.

Selecta: Kebon Kacang 29/4, Jakarta; fortnightly; illustrated; Editor SAMSUDIN LUBIS; circ. 80,000.

Simponi: Jakarta; f. 1994 by former employees of *DeTik* (banned 1994–98).

Sinar Jaya: Jakarta Selatan; fortnightly; agriculture; Chief Editor Ir SURYONO PROJOPRANOTO.

Swasembada: Gedung Chandra Lt 2, Jalan M. H. Thamrin 20, Jakarta 10310; tel. (21) 3103316.

Tempo: Gedung Tempo, 8th Floor, Jalan H. R. Rasuna Said, Kav. C-17, Kuningan, Jakarta 12940; tel. (21) 5201022; fax (21) 5200092; internet www.tempo.co.id; f. 1971; weekly; Editor-in-Chief BAMBANG HARYMURTI.

Tiara: Gramedia Bldg, Unit 11, 5th Floor, Jalan Palmerah Selatan 24–26, Jakarta 10270; tel (21) 5483008; fax (21) 5494035; f. 1990; fortnightly; lifestyles, features and celebrity news; circ. 47,000.

Ummat: Jakarta; Islamic; sponsored by ICMI.

NEWS AGENCIES

Antara (Indonesian National News Agency): Wisma Antara, 3rd, 19th and 20th Floors, 17 Jalan Merdeka Selatan, POB 1257, Jakarta 10110; tel. (21) 3802383; fax (21) 3840970; e-mail antara@antara.co.id; internet www.antara.co.id; f. 1937; 20 radio, seven television, 96 newspaper, eight foreign newspaper, seven tabloid, seven magazine, two news agency, nine embassy and seven dotcom subscribers in 2001; 26 brs in Indonesia, six overseas brs/correspondents; four bulletins in Indonesian and one in English; monitoring service of stock exchanges world-wide; photo service; Exec. Editor HERU PURWANTO; Man. Dir MOHAMAD SOBARY.

Kantorberita Nasional Indonesia (KNI News Service): Jalan Jatinegara Barat III/6, Jakarta Timur 13310; tel. (21) 811003; fax (21) 8195501; f. 1966; independent national news agency; foreign and domestic news in Indonesian; Dir and Editor-in-Chief Drs SUMONO MUSTOFFA; Exec. Editor HARIM NURROCHADI.

Foreign Bureaux

Agence France-Presse (AFP): Jalan Indramayu 18, Jakarta Pusat 10310; tel. (21) 3336082; fax (21) 3809186; Chief Correspondent PASCAL MALLET.

Agenzia Nazionale Stampa Associata (ANSA) (Italy): Jalan Petogogan 1 Go-2 No, 13 Kompleks RRI, Kebayoran Baru, Jakarta Selatan; tel. (21) 7391996; fax (21) 7392247; Correspondent HERYTNO PUJOWIDAGDO.

Associated Press (AP) (USA): Deutsche Bank Bldg, 14th Floor, No. 1403–1404, Jalan Imam Bonjol 80, Jakarta 10310; tel. (21) 39831269; fax (21) 39831270; e-mail gspencer@ap.org; Chief of Bureau GEOFF SPENCER.

Central News Agency Inc (CNA) (Taiwan): Jalan Gelong Baru Timur 1-13, Jakarta Barat; tel. and fax (21) 5600266; Bureau Chief WU PIN-CHIANG.

Informatsionnoye Telegrafnoye Agentstvo Rossii—Telegrafnoye Agentstvo Suverennykh Stran (ITAR—TASS) (Russia): Jalan Surabaya 7 Menteng, Jakarta Pusat 10310; tel. and fax (21) 3155283; e-mail ab1952@indosat.net.id; Correspondent ANDREY ALEKSANDROVICH BYTCHKOV.

Inter Press Service (IPS) (Italy): Gedung Dewan Pers, 4th Floor, Jalan Kebon Sirih 34, Jakarta 10110; tel. (21) 3453131; fax (21) 3453175; Chief Correspondent ABDUL RAZAK.

Jiji Tsushin (Japan): Jalan Raya Bogor 109B, Jakarta; tel. (21) 8090509; Correspondent MARGA RAHARJA.

Kyodo Tsushin (Japan): Skyline Bldg, 11th Floor, Jalan M. H. Thamrin 9, Jakarta 10310; tel. (21) 345012; Correspondent MASAYUKI KITAMURA.

Reuters (United Kingdom): Wisma Antara, 6th Floor, Jalan Medan Merdeka Selatan 17, Jakarta 10110; tel. (21) 3846364; fax (21) 3448404; Bureau Chief JONATHAN THATCHER.

United Press International (UPI) (USA): Wisma Antara, 14th Floor, Jalan Medan Merdeka Selatan 17, Jakarta; tel. (21) 341056; Bureau Chief JOHN HAIL.

Xinhua (New China) News Agency (People's Republic of China): Jakarta.

PRESS ASSOCIATIONS

Aliansi Jurnalis Indpenden (AJI) (Alliance of Independent Journalists): Jakarta; internet www.aji.or.id; f. 1994; unofficial; aims to promote freedom of the press; Sec.-Gen. AHMAD TAUFIK.

Persatuan Wartawan Indonesia (Indonesian Journalists' Asscn): Gedung Dewan Pers, 4th Floor, Jalan Kebon Sirih 34, Jakarta 10110; tel. (21) 353131; fax (21) 353175; f. 1946; government-controlled; 5,041 mems (April 1991); Chair. TARMAN AGAM; Gen. Sec. H. SOFJAN LUBIS.

Serikat Penerbit Suratkabar (SPS) (Indonesian Newspaper Publishers' Asscn): Gedung Dewan Pers, 6th Floor, Jalan Kebon Sirih 34, Jakarta 10110; tel. (21) 3459671; fax (21) 3862373; e-mail sps-pst@dnet.net.id; internet www.dnet.net.id/sps; f. 1946; Exec. Chair. Drs S. L. BATUBARA; Sec.-Gen. Drs AMIR E. SIREGAR.

Yayasan Pembina Pers Indonesia (Press Foundation of Indonesia): Jalan Jatinegara Barat III/6, Jakarta 13310; tel. (21) 8194994; f. 1967; Chair. SUGIARSO SUROYO, MOCHTAR LUBIS.

Publishers

JAKARTA

Aries Lima/New Aqua Press PT: Jalan Rawagelan II/4, Jakarta Timur; tel. (21) 4897566; general and children's; Pres. TUTI SUNDARI AZMI.

Aya Media Pustaka PT: Wijaya Grand Centre C/2, Jalan Dharmawangsa III, Jakarta 12160; tel. (21) 7206903; fax (21) 7201401; children's; Dir Drs ARIANTO TUGIYO.

PT Balai Pustaka: Jalan Gunung Sahari Raya 4, POB 1029, Jakarta 10710; tel. and fax (21) 3855733; e-mail bp1917@hotmail.com; internet www.balaiperaga.com; f. 1917; children's, school textbooks, literary, scientific publs and periodicals; Dir R. SISWADI.

Bhratara Niaga Media PT: Jalan Oto Iskandardinata III/29F, Jakarta 13340; tel. (21) 8502050; fax (21) 8191858; f. 1986; fmrly Bhratara Karya Aksara; university and educational textbooks; Man. Dir AHMAD JAYUSMAN.

Bina Rena Pariwara PT: Jalan Pejaten Raya 5-E, Pasar Minggu, Jakarta 12510; tel. (21) 7901931; fax (21) 7901939; e-mail hasanbas@softhome.net; f. 1988; financial, social science, economic, Islamic, children's; Dir Drs HASAN BASRI.

Bulan Bintang PT: Jalan Kramat Kwitang 1/8, Jakarta 10420; tel. (21) 3901651; fax (21) 3107027; f. 1954; Islamic, social science, natural and applied sciences, art; Pres. AMRAN ZAMZAMI; Man. Dir FAUZI AMELZ.

Bumi Aksara PT: Jalan Sawo Raya 18, Rawamanguu, Jakarta 13220; tel. (21) 4717049; fax (21) 4700989; f. 1990; university textbooks; Dir H. AMIR HAMZAH.

Cakrawala Cinta PT: Jalan Minyak I/12B, Duren Tiga, Jakarta 12760; tel. (21) 7990725; fax (21) 7974076; f. 1984; science; Dir Drs M. TORSINA.

Centre for Strategic and International Studies (CSIS): Jalan Tanah Abang III/23–27, Jakarta 10160; tel. (21) 3865532; fax (21) 3847517; e-mail csis@pacific.net.id; internet www.csis.or.id; f. 1971; political and social sciences; Dir Dr DAOED JOESOEF.

Cipta Adi Pustaka: Graha Compaka Mas Blok C 22, Jalan Cempaka Putih Raya, Jakarta Pusat; tel. (21) 4213821; fax (21) 4269315; f. 1986; encyclopedias; Dir BUDI SANTOSO.

Dian Rakyat PT: Jalan Rawagelas I/4, Kaw. Industri Pulo Gadung, Jakarta; tel. (21) 4604444; fax (21) 4609115; f. 1966; general; Dir H. MOHAMMED AIS.

Djambatan PT: Jalan Wijaya I/39, Jakarta 12170; tel. (21) 7203199; fax (21) 7227989; f. 1954; children's, textbooks, social sciences, fiction; Dir SJARIFUDIN SJAMSUDIN.

Dunia Pustaka Jaya: Jalan Rawa Bambu Rt. 003/07 38, Komp. BATAN, Pasar Minggu, Jakarta Selatan 12520; tel. (21) 7891875; fax (21) 3909320; f. 1971; fiction, religion, essays, poetry, drama, criticism, art, philosophy and children's; Man. A. RIVAI.

EGC Medical Publications: Jalan Agung Jaya III/2, Sunter Agung Podomoro, Jakarta 14350; tel. (21) 686351; fax (21) 686352; e-mail egc_arcan@hotmail.com; f. 1978; medical and public health, nursing, dentistry; Dir IMELDA DHARMA.

Elex Media Komputindo: Jalan Palmerah Selatan 22, Kompas–Gramedia Bldg, 6th Floor, Jakarta 10270; tel. (21) 53699059; fax (21) 5326219; e-mail elex@elexmedia.co.id; internet www.elexmedia.co.id; f. 1985; publishing (management, computing, software and merchandising); Dir AL. ADHI MARDHIYONO.

Erlangga PT: Kami Melayani II, Pengetahuan, Jalan H. Baping 100, Ciracas, Jakarta 13740; tel. (21) 8717006; fax (21) 8717011; e-mail erlprom@rad.net.id; internet www.erlangga.com; f. 1952; secondary school and university textbooks; Man. Dir GUNAWAN HUTAURUK.

Gaya Favorit Press: Jalan H. R. Rasuna Said, Blok B, Kav. 32–33, Jakarta 12910; tel. (21) 5209370; fax (21) 5209366; f. 1971; fiction, popular science and children's; Vice-Pres. MIRTA KARTOHADIPRODJO; Man. Dir WIDARTI GUNAWAN.

Gema Insani Press: Jalan Kalibata Utara II/84, Jakarta 12740; tel. (21) 7984391; fax (21) 7984388; e-mail gipnet@indosat.net.id; internet www.gemainsani.co.id; f. 1986; Islamic; Dir UMAR BASYARAHIL.

Ghalia Indonesia: Jalan Pramuka Raya 4, Jakarta 13140; tel. (21) 8584330; fax (21) 8502334; f. 1972; children's and general science, textbooks; Man. Dir LUKMAN SAAD.

Gramedia Widyasarana Indonesia: Jalan Palmerah Selatan 22, Lantai IV, POB 615, Jakarta 10270; tel. (21) 5483008; fax (21) 5300545; f. 1973; university textbooks, general non-fiction, children's and magazines; Gen. Man. ALFONS TARYADI.

Gunung Mulia PT: Jalan Kwitang 22–23, Jakarta 10420; tel. (21) 3901208; fax (21) 3901633; e-mail corp.off@bpkgm.com; internet www.bpkgm.com; f. 1951; general, children's, Christian; Pres. Dir ICHSAN GUNAWAN, Dir V. N. LEIMENA.

Hidakarya Agung PT: Jalan Kebon Kosong F/74, Kemayoran, Jakarta Pusat; tel. (21) 4241074; Dir MAHDIARTI MACHMUD.

Ichtiar: Jalan Majapahit 6, Jakarta Pusat; tel. (21) 3841226; f. 1957; textbooks, law, social sciences, economics; Dir JOHN SEMERU.

Indira PT: Jalan Borobudur 20, Jakarta 10320; tel. (21) 882754; f. 1953; general science and children's; Man. Dir BAMBANG P. WAHYUDI.

Kinta CV: Jalan Kemanggisan Ilir V/110, Pal Merah, Jakarta Barat; tel. (21) 5494751; f. 1950; textbooks, social science, general; Man. Drs MOHAMAD SALEH.

LP 3 ES: Jalan Letjen. S. Parman 81, Jakarta 11420; tel. (21) 5674211; fax (21) 5683785; e-mail lp3es@indo.net.id; f. 1971; general; Dir IMAM AHMAD.

Masagung Group: Gedung Idayu, Jalan Kwitang 13, POB 2260, Jakarta 10420; tel. (21) 3154890; fax (21) 3154889; f. 1986; general, religious, textbooks, science; Pres. H. ABDURRAHMAN MASAGUNG.

Midas Surya Grafindo PT: Jalan Kesehatan 54, Cijantung, Jakarta 13760; tel. (21) 8400414; fax (21) 8400270; f. 1984; children's; Dir Drs FRANS HENDRAWAN.

Mutiara Sumber Widya PT: Jalan Kramat II 55, Jakarta; tel. (21) 3926043; fax (21) 3160313; f. 1951; textbooks, Islamic, social sciences, general and children's; Pres. FADJRAA OEMAR.

Penebar Swadya PT: Jalan Gunung Sahari III/7, Jakarta Pusat; tel. (21) 4204402; fax (21) 4214821; agriculture, animal husbandry, fisheries; Dir Drs ANTHONIUS RIYANTO.

Penerbit Universitas Indonesia: Jalan Salemba Raya 4, Jakarta; tel. (21) 335373; f. 1969; science; Man. S. E. LEGOWO.

Pradnya Paramita PT: Jalan Bunga 8–8A, Matraman, Jakarta 13140; tel. (21) 8504944; e-mail pradnya@centrin.net.id; f. 1973; children's, general, educational, technical and social science; Pres. Dir WILLY LALUYAN.

Pustaka Antara PT: Jalan Taman Kebon Sirih III/13, Jakarta Pusat 10250; tel. (21) 3156994; fax (21) 322745; e-mail nacelod@indonet.id; f. 1952; textbooks, political, Islamic, children's and general; Man. Dir AIDA JOESOEF AHMAD.

Pustaka Binaman Pressindo: Bina Manajemen Bldg, Jalan Menteng Raya 9–15, Jakarta 10340; tel. (21) 2300313; fax (21) 2302047; e-mail pustaka@bit.net.id; f. 1981; management; Dir Ir MAKFUDIN WIRYA ATMAJA.

Pustaka Sinar Harapan PT: Jalan Dewi Sartika 136D, Jakarta 13630; tel. (21) 8093208; fax (21) 8091652; f. 1981; general science, fiction, comics, children's; Dir W. M. NAIDEN.

Pustaka Utma Grafiti PT: Jalan Utan Kayu 68EFG, Utan Kayu Utara, Jakarta 13120; tel. (21) 8567502; fax (21) 8573387; f. 1981; social sciences, humanities and children's books; Dir ZULKIFLY LUBIS.

Rajagrafindo Persada PT: Jalan Pelepah Hijau IV TN-1 14–15, Kelapa Gading Permai, Jakarta 14240; tel. (21) 4529409; fax (21) 4520951; f. 1980; general science and religion; Dir Drs ZUBAIDI.

Rineka Cipta PT: Blok B/5, Jalan Jenderal Sudirman, Kav. 36A, Bendungan Hilir, Jakarta 10210; tel. (21) 5737646; fax (21) 5711985; f. 1990 by merger of Aksara Baru (f. 1972) and Bina Aksara; general science and university texts; Dir Dr H. SUARDI.

Rosda Jayaputra PT: Jalan Kembang 4, Jakarta 10420; tel. (21) 3904984; fax (21) 3901703; f. 1981; general science; Dir H. ROZALI USMAN.

Sastra Hudaya: Jalan Kalasan 1, Jakarta Pusat; tel. (21) 882321; f. 1967; religious, textbooks, children's and general; Man. ADAM SALEH.

Tintamas Indonesia: Jalan Kramat Raya 60, Jakarta 10420; tel. and fax (21) 3911459; f. 1947; history, modern science and culture, especially Islamic; Man. Miss MARHAMAH DJAMBEK.

Tira Pustaka: Jalan Cemara Raya 1, Kav. 10D, Jaka Permai, Jaka Sampurna, Bekasi 17145; tel. (21) 8841277; fax (21) 8842736; e-mail Tirapus@cbn.net.id; f. 1977; translations, children's; Dir ROBERT B. WIDJAJA.

Widjaya: Jalan Pecenongan 48C, Jakarta Pusat; tel. (21) 3813446; f. 1950; textbooks, children's, religious and general; Man. DIDI LUTHAN.

Yasaguna: Jalan Minangkabau 44, POB 422, Jakarta Selatan; tel. (21) 8290422; f. 1964; agricultural, children's, handicrafts; Dir HILMAN MADEWA.

Bandung

Alma'arif: Jalan Tamblong 48–50, Bandung; tel. (22) 4264454; fax (22) 4239194; f. 1949; textbooks, religious and general; Man. H. M. BAHARTHAH.

Alumni PT: Jalan Bukit Pakar Timur II/109, Bandung 40197; tel. (22) 2501251; fax (22) 2503044; f. 1968; university and school textbooks; Dir EDDY DAMIAN.

Angkasa: Jalan Merdeka 6, POB 1353 BD, Bandung 40111; tel. (22) 4204795; fax (22) 439183; Dir H. FACHRI SAID.

Armico: Jalan Madurasa Utara 10, Cigereleng, Bandung 40253; tel. (22) 5202234; fax (22) 5201972; f. 1980; school textbooks; Dir Ir ARSIL TANJUNG.

Citra Aditya Bakti PT: Jalan Geusanulun 17, Bandung 40115; tel. (22) 438251; fax (22) 438635; f. 1985; general science; Dir Ir IWAN TANUATMADJA.

Diponegoro Publishing House: Jalan Mohammad Toha 44–46, Bandung 40252; tel. and fax (22) 5201215; e-mail dpnegoro@indosat.net.id; f. 1963; Islamic, textbooks, fiction, non-fiction, general; Man. H. A. DAHLAN.

Epsilon Group: Jalan Marga Asri 3, Margacinta, Bandung 40287; tel. (22) 7567826; f. 1985; school textbooks; Dir Drs BAHRUDIN.

Eresco PT: Jalan Megger Girang 98, Bandung 40254; tel. (22) 5205985; fax (22) 5205984; f. 1957; scientific and general; Man. Drs ARFAN ROZALI.

Ganeca Exact Bandung: Jalan Kiaracondong 167, Pagauban, Bandung 40283; tel. (22) 701519; fax (22) 775329; f. 1982; school textbooks; Dir Ir KETUT SUARDHARA LINGGIH.

Mizan Pustaka PT: Jalan Yodkali 16, Bandung 40124; tel. (22) 7200931; fax (22) 7207038; e-mail info@mizan.com; internet www.mizan.com; f. 1983; Islamic and general books; Pres. Dir HAIDAR BAGIR; Man. Dir PUTUT WIDJANARKO.

Penerbit ITB: Jalan Ganesa 10, Bandung 40132; tel. and fax (22) 2504257; e-mail itbpress@bdg.centrin.net.id; f. 1971; academic books; Dir EMMY SUPARKA; Chief Editor SOFIA MANSOOR-NIKSOLIHIN.

Putra A. Bardin: Jalan Ganesya 4, Bandung; tel. (22) 2504319; f. 1998; textbooks, scientific and general; Dir NAI A. BARDIN.

Remaja Rosdakarya PT: Jalan Ciateul 34–36, POB 284, Bandung 40252; tel. (22) 5200287; fax (22) 5202529; textbooks and children's fiction; Pres. ROZALI USMAN.

Sarana Panca Karyam PT: Jalan Kopo 633 KM 13/4, Bandung 40014; f. 1986; general; Dir WIMPY S. IBRAHIM.

Tarsito PT: Jalan Guntur 20, Bandung 40262; tel. (22) 304915; fax (22) 314630; academic; Dir T. SITORUS.

Flores

Nusa Indah: Jalan El Tari, Ende 86318, Flores; tel. (0381) 21502; fax (0381) 22373; f. 1970; religious and general; Dir LUKAS BATMOMOLIN.

Kudus

Menara Kudus: Jalan Menara 4, Kudus 59315; tel. (291) 371143; fax (291) 36474; f. 1958; Islamic; Man. CHILMAN NAJIB.

Medan

Hasmar: Jalan Letjenderal Haryono M. T. 1, POB 446, Medan 20231; tel. (61) 24181; f. 1962; primary school textbooks; Dir HASBULLAH LUBIS; Man. AMRAN SAID RANGKUTI.

Impola: Jalan H. M. Joni 46, Medan 20217; tel. (61) 711415; f. 1984; school textbooks; Dir PAMILANG M. SITUMORANG.

Madju: Jalan Amaliun 37, Medan 20215; tel. (61) 711990; fax (61) 717753; f. 1950; textbooks, children's and general; Pres. H. MOHAMED ARBIE; Man. Dir Drs ALFIAN ARBIE.

Masco: Jalan Sisingamangaraja 191, Medan 20218; tel. (61) 713375; f. 1992; school textbooks; Dir P. M. SITUMORANG.

Monora: Jalan Letjenderal Jamin Ginting 583, Medan 20156; tel. (61) 812667; fax (61) 812669; f. 1968; school textbooks; Dir CHAIRIL ANWAR.

Semarang

Aneka Ilmu: Jalan Raya Semarang Demak Km 8.5, Sayung, Demak; tel. (24) 580335; fax (24) 582903; f. 1983; general and school textbooks; Dir H. SUWANTO.

Effhar COY PT: Jalan Dorang 7, Semarang 50173; tel. (24) 3511172; fax (24) 3551540; e-mail effhar_dahara@yahoo.com; f. 1976; general books; Dir H. DARADJAT HARAHAP.

Intan Pariwara: Jalan Beringin, Klaten Utara, Kotak Pos III, Kotif Klaten, Jawa-Tengah; tel. (272) 22441; fax (272) 22021; school textbooks; Pres. SOETIKNO.

Mandira PT: Jalan Letjenderal M. T. Haryono 501, Semarang 50241; tel. (24) 316150; fax (24) 415092; f. 1962; Dir Ir A. HARIYANTO.

Mandira Jaya Abadi PT: Jalan Letjenderal M. T. Haryono 501, Semarang 50241; tel. (24) 519547; fax (24) 542189; e-mail mjabadi@indosat.net.id; f. 1981; Dir Ir A. HARIYANTO.

Solo

Pabelan PT: Jalan Raya Pajang, Kertasura KM 8, Solo 57162; tel. (271) 743975; fax (271) 714775; f. 1983; school textbooks; Dir AGUNG SASONGKO.

Tiga Serangkai PT: Jalan Dr Supomo 23, Solo; tel. (271) 714344; fax (271) 713607; f. 1977; school textbooks; Dir ABDULLAH.

Surabaya

Airlangga University Press: Kampus C, Jalan Mulyorejo, Surabaya; tel. (31) 5992246; fax (31) 5992248; e-mail aupsby@rad.net.id; academic; Dir Dr ARIFAAN RAZAK.

Bina Ilmu PT: Jalan Tunjungan 53E, Surabaya 60275; tel. (31) 5323214; fax (31) 5315421; f. 1973; school textbooks, Islamic; Pres. ARIEFIN NOOR.

Bintang: Jalan Potroagung III/41C, Surabaya; tel. (31) 3770687; fax (31) 3715941; school textbooks; Dir AGUS WINARNO.

Grip PT: Jalan Rungkut Permai II/C–11, Surabaya; tel. (31) 22564; f. 1958; textbooks and general; Man. Mrs SURIPTO.

Jaya Baya: Jalan Embong Malang 69H, POB 250, Surabaya 60001; tel. (31) 41169; f. 1945; religion, philosophy and ethics; Man. TADJIB ERMADI.

Sinar Wijaya: Jalan Raya Sawo VII/58, Bringin-Lakarsantri, Surabaya; tel. (31) 706615; general; Dir DULRADJAK.

Yogyakarta

Andi Publishers: Jalan Beo 38–40, Yogyakarta 55281; tel. (274) 561881; fax (274) 588282; e-mail andi_pub@indo.net.id; f. 1980; Christian, computing, business, management and technical; Dir J. H. GONDOWIJOYO.

BPFE PT: Jalan Gambiran 37, Yogyakarta 55161; tel. (274) 373760; fax (274) 380819; f. 1984; university textbooks; Dir Drs INDRIYO GITOSUDARMO.

Centhini Yayasan: Gg. Bekisar UH V/716 E–1, Yogyakarta 55161; tel. (274) 383148; f. 1984; Javanese Culture; Chair. H. KARKONO KAMAJAYA.

Gadjah Mada University Press: Jalan Grafika 1, Campus UGM, Bulaksumur, Yogyakarta 55231; tel. (274) 902727; fax (274) 561037; f. 1971; university textbooks; Dir Drs H. SUKAMTO.

Indonesia UP: Gg. Bekisar UH V/716 E–1, Yogyakarta 55161; tel. (274) 383148; f. 1950; general science; Dir H. KARKONO KAMAJAYA.

Kanisius Publr: Jalan Cempaka 9, Deresan, POB 1125, Yogyakarta 55281; tel. (274) 588783; fax (274) 563349; e-mail office@

kanisius.co.id; internet www.kanisius.co.id; f. 1922; children's, textbooks, Christian and general; Man. E. SURONO.

Kedaulatan Rakyat PT: Jalan P. Mangkubumi 40–42, Yogyakarta; tel. (274) 2163; Dir DRONO HARDJUSUWONGSO.

Penerbit Tiara Wacana Yogya: Jalan Kaliurang KM 7, 8 Kopen 16, Banteng, Yogyakarta 55581; tel. and fax (274) 880683; f. 1986; university textbooks and general science; Dir SITORESMI PRABUNINGRAT.

Government Publishing House

Balai Pustaka PT (Persero) (State Publishing and Printing House): Jalan Gunung Sahari Raya 4, Gedung Balai Pustaka, 7th Floor, Jakarta Pusat 10710; tel. (21) 3447003; fax (21) 3446555; e-mail mail@balaiperaga.com; internet www.balaiperaga.com; history, anthropology, politics, philosophy, medical, arts and literature; Pres. Dir H. R. SISWADI IDRIS.

PUBLISHERS' ASSOCIATION

Ikatan Penerbit Indonesia (IKAPI) (Asscn of Indonesian Book Publishers): Jalan Kalipasir 32, Jakarta 10330; tel. (21) 3141907; fax (21) 3146050; e-mail sekretariat@ikapi.or.id; internet www.ikapi.or.id; f. 1950; 631 mems (Jan. 2000); Pres. ARSELAN HARAHAP; Sec.-Gen. SAHAR L. HASSAN.

Broadcasting and Communications

TELECOMMUNICATIONS

Directorate-General of Posts and Telecommunications (Postel): Gedung Sapta Pesona, Jalan Medan Merdeka Barat 17, Jakarta 10110; tel. (21) 3835912; fax (21) 3860754; e-mail admin@postel.go.id; internet www.postel.go.id; Dir Gen. SASMITO DIRDJO; Dep. Dir-Gen. R. SAKSONO SOEDARSO.

PT Indosat (Persero) Tbk: Jalan Medan Merdeka Barat 21, POB 2905, Jakarta 10110; tel. (21) 3802614; fax (21) 3458155; e-mail sant@indosat.com; internet www.indosat.com; telecommunications; partially privatized in 1994; Pres. WIDYA PURNAMA.

PT Satelit Palapa Indonesia (SATELINDO): Jalan Daan Mogot Km 11, Jakarta 11710; tel. (21) 5451745; fax (21) 5451748; e-mail webmaster@satelindo.co.id; internet www.satelindo.co.id; Pres. Dir JOHNY SWANDI SJAM.

PT Telekomunikasi Indonesia Tbk (TELKOM): Corporate Office, Jalan Japati No. 1, Bandung 40133; tel. (22) 4521510; fax (22) 440313; internet www.telkom.co.id; domestic telecommunications; 24.2% of share capital was transferred to the private sector in 1995; CEO ASMAN AKHIR NASUTION.

BROADCASTING

Regulatory Authority

Directorate-General of Radio, Television and Film: Jalan Merdeka Barat 9, Jakarta 10110; Dep. Dir M. ARSYAD SUBIK.

Radio

Radio Republik Indonesia (RRI): Jalan Medan Merdeka Barat 4–5, Jakarta 10110; tel. (21) 3846817; fax (21) 3457134; e-mail rri@rrionline.com; internet www.rrionline.com; f. 1945; 49 stations; Dir SURYANTA SALEH; Dep. Dirs FACHRUDDIN SOEKARNO (Overseas Service), ABDUL ROCHIM (Programming), SUKRI (Programme Development), SAZLI RAIS (Administration), CHAERUL ZEN (News).

Voice of Indonesia: Jalan Medan Merdeka Barat 4–5, POB 1157, Jakarta; tel. (21) 3456811; international service provided by Radio Republik Indonesia; daily broadcasts in Arabic, English, French, German, Bahasa Indonesia, Japanese, Bahasa Malaysia, Mandarin, Spanish and Thai.

Television

In March 1989 Indonesia's first private commercial television station began broadcasting to the Jakarta area. In 1996 there were five privately-owned television stations in operation.

PT Cakrawala Andalas Televisi (ANTEVE): Gedung Sentra Mulia, 18th Floor, Jalan H. R. Rasuna Said, Kav. X-6 No. 8, Jakarta 12940; tel. (21) 5222086; fax (21) 5222087; e-mail ancorcom@uninet.net.id; internet www.anteve.uninet.net.id; f. 1993; private channel; broadcasting to 10 cities; Pres. Dir H. R. AGUNG LAKSONO; Gen. Man. CEO NENNY SOEMAWINATA.

PT Rajawali Citra Televisi Indonesia (RCTI): Jalan Raya Pejuangan 3, Kebon Jeruk, Jakarta 11000; tel. (21) 5303540; fax (21) 5493852; e-mail webmaster@rcti.co.id; internet www.rcti.co.id; f. 1989; first private channel; 20-year licence; Pres. Dir M. S. RALIE SIREGAR; Vice-Pres. ALEX KUMARA.

PT Surya Citra Televisi (SCTV): GRHA SCTV, 2nd Floor, Jalan Gatot Subroto, Kav. 21, Jakarta 12930; tel. (21) 5225555; fax (21) 5224777; e-mail pr@sctv.co.id; internet www.sctv.co.id; f. 1990; private channel broadcasting nationally; Pres. Dir Dr Ir AGUS MULYANTO.

PT CIPTA TPI: Jalan Pintu II—Taman Mini Indonesia Indah, Pondok Gede, Jakarta Timur 13810; tel. (21) 8412473; fax (21) 8412470; e-mail info@tpi.co.id; internet www.tpi.co.id; f. 1991; private channel funded by commercial advertising; Pres. Dir SITI HARDIJANTI RUKMANA.

Televisi Republik Indonesia (TVRI): TVRI Senayan, Jalan Gerbang Pemuda, Senayan, Jakarta; tel. (21) 5733135; fax (21) 5732408; e-mail info@tvrisby.com; internet www.tvrisby.com; f. 1962; state-controlled; Man. Dir AZIS HUSEIN.

Finance

(cap. = capital; auth. = authorized; p.u. = paid up; res = reserves; dep. = deposits; m. = million; brs = branches; amounts in rupiah)

BANKING

In December 1996 there were 9,276 banks, with 14,956 branches, in operation in Indonesia, including seven state commercial banks, 27 regional government banks, 164 private national banks and 41 foreign and joint-venture banks. At the end of March 1995 total bank deposits stood at 167,123,000m. rupiah. A programme of extensive reform of the banking sector was ongoing in 2002, under the auspices of the Indonesian Bank Restructuring Agency (IBRA, see Government Agencies, below).

Central Bank

Bank Indonesia: Jalan M. H. Thamrin 2, Pusat, Jakarta 10002; tel. (21) 2310408; fax (21) 2311058; e-mail humasbi@bi.go.id; internet www.bi.go.id; f. 1828; nationalized as central bank in 1953; cap. 2,606,000m., res 116,570,000m., dep. 322,904,000m. (Dec. 2000); Gov. Dr SYAHRIL SABIRIN; 42 brs.

State Banks

In late December 1997 the Government announced that four of the state-owned banks—Bank Bumi Daya, Bank Dagang Negara, Bank Ekspor Impor Indonesia and Bank Pembangunan Indonesia—were to merge; the four banks subsequently merged into a single new institution, PT Bank Mandiri, which was established in July 1999.

PT Bank Ekspor Indonesia (Persero): Gedung Brs Efek, Menara II Lt. 8, Jalan Sudirman, Kav. 52–53, Jakarta; tel. (21) 5154638; fax (21) 5154639; internet www.bexi.co.id.

PT Bank Mandiri (Persero): Plaza Mandiri, Jalan Jenderal Gatot Subroto, Kav. 36-38, Jakarta 12190; tel. (21) 5265045; fax (21) 5268246; internet www.bankmandiri.co.id; f. 1999 as a result of the merger of four state-owned banks—PT Bank Bumi Daya, PT Bank Dagang Negara, PT Bank Ekspor Impor Indonesia and PT Bank Pembangunan Indonesia; cap. 4,251m., res 175,219m., dep. 163,923m. (Dec. 2000); Pres. Commissioner BINHADI; Pres. Dir E. C. W. NELOE.

PT Bank Negara Indonesia (Persero) Tbk: Jalan Jenderal Sudirman, Kav. 1, BP 2955, Jakarta 10220; tel. (21) 2511946; fax (21) 2511221; e-mail hin@bni.co.id; internet www.bni.co.id; f. 1946; commercial bank; specializes in credits to the industrial sector; cap. 7,091,336m., res 57,505,154m., dep. 86,273,706m. (Dec. 2000); Pres. Dir SAIFUDDIEN HASAN; 585 local brs, 6 overseas brs.

PT Bank Rakyat Indonesia (Persero): Jalan Jenderal Sudirman, Kav. 44–46, BP 94, Jakarta 10210; tel. (21) 2510244; fax (21) 2500077; internet www.bri.co.id; f. 1895, present name since 1946; commercial and foreign exchange bank; specializing in agricultural smallholdings and rural development; state-owned; cap. 1,728,000m., res 29,341,025m., dep. 50,522,731m. (Dec. 2000); Pres. Dir DJOKOSANTOSO MOELJONO; 323 brs.

PT Bank Tabungan Negara (Persero): 10th Floor, Bank BTN Tower Bldg, Jalan Gajah Mada 1, Jakarta 10130; tel. (21) 6336789; fax (21) 6336704; e-mail webadmin@btn.co.id; internet www.btn.co.id; f. 1964; commercial bank; state-owned; cap. 15,093,540m., dep. 16,712,526m. (Dec. 2000); Chair. DARMIN NASUTION; 37 brs.

Commercial Banks

PT ANZ Panin Bank: Panin Bank Centre, Jalan Jenderal Sudirman (Senayan), Jakarta 10270; tel. (21) 5750300; fax (21) 5727447; internet www.anz.com/indonesia; f. 1990 as Westpac Panin Bank; 85%-owned by the Australia and New Zealand Banking Group Ltd; cap. 50,000m., dep. 972,000m. (Dec. 2000); Pres. Dir SCOTT ARMSTRONG.

Bank Artha Graha: Bank Artha Graha Tower, 5th Floor, Jalan Jenderal Sudirman, Kav. 52–53, Jakarta 12920; tel. (21) 5152168; fax (21) 5152162; e-mail agraha@rad.net.id; f. 1967; merged with PT Bank Arta Pratama in 1999; cap. 75,000m., dep. 340,344m. (Dec. 1993); Pres. Dir ANTON B. S. HUDYANA; Chair. LETJEN; 64 brs.

PT Bank Bali: Gedung Bank Bali, 19th Floor, Jalan Jenderal Sudirman, Kav. 27, Jakarta 12920; tel. (21) 5237899; fax (21) 2500811; internet www.bankbali.co.id; f. 1954; scheduled to merge with PT Bank Universal, PT Bank Prima Express, PT Bank Arthamedia and PT Bank Patriot by Dec. 2002; cap. 5,691,698m., res 201,598m., dep. 9,860,617m. (Dec. 2000); Pres. Commissioner I. NYOMAN SOEWANDA; 270 brs.

PT Bank Central Asia (BCA): Wisma BCA, 5th Floor, Jalan Jenderal Sudirman, Kav. 22–23, Jakarta 12920; tel. (21) 5711250; fax (21) 5701865; internet www.klikbca.com; f. 1957; placed under the supervision of the Indonesian Bank Restructuring Agency in May 1998; 51% share sold to Farallon Capital Management (USA) in March 2002; cap. 1,471,993m., res 4,814,280m., dep. 86,072,502m. (Dec. 2000); Chair. MUHAMMAD DJOEANA KOESOEMAHARDJA; 796 brs.

PT Bank Dagang Bali: Jalan Gajah Mada 2, Denpasar, Bali; tel. (361) 263736; fax (361) 231226; e-mail bdbBank@yahoo.com; f. 1970; cap. 51,000m., res 3,774m., dep. 1,112,303m. (Dec. 2000); Pres. Dir I. GUSTI MADE OKA; Chair. GUSTI AYU NYOMEN SAYANG.

PT Bank Danamon Indonesia Tbk: Wisma Bank Danamon, Jalan Jenderal Sudirman, Kav. 45, Jakarta 12930; tel. (21) 5770551; fax (21) 5770704; internet www.danamon.co.id; f. 1956; placed under the supervision of the Indonesian Bank Restructuring Agency in April 1998, merged with PT Bank Tiara Asia in July 2000, with PT Tamara Bank in August 2000, and with PT Bank Duta and PT Bank Nusa Nasional in September 2000; cap. 3,562,261m., res 32,994,432m., dep. 30,643,895m. (Dec. 2000); Chair. PETER B. STOCK; Pres. Dir ARWIN RASYID; 737 brs.

Bank Internasional Indonesia (BII): Plaza BII, Jalan M. H. Thamrin 51, Kav. 22, Jakarta 10350; tel. (21) 2300888; fax (21) 2301494; e-mail bii-info@idola.net.id; internet www.bii.co.id; cap. 13,054,731m., res 1,442,194m., dep. 28,784,389m. (Dec. 2000); Chair. RUSLI PRAKARSA; Pres. Dir HIROSHI TADANO; 249 brs.

PT Bank Mayapada Internasional: Arthaloka Bldg, Ground & 1st Floor, Jalan Jenderal Sudirman, Kav. 2, Jakarta 10220; tel. (21) 2511588; fax (21) 2511539; e-mail mayapada@bankmayapada.com; internet www.bankmayapada.com; f. 1989; cap. 164,145m., dep. 925,394m. (Dec. 2000); Chair. TAHIR; Pres. Dir HARYONO TJAHJARIJADI; 5 brs, 7 sub-brs.

PT Bank Mizuho Indonesia: Plaza B11, 24th Floor, Menara 2, Jalan M. H. Thamrin 51, Jakarta 10350; tel. (21) 3925222; fax (21) 3926354; frmly PT Bank Fuji International Indonesia; f. 1989; cap. 144,375m., res 25,908m., dep. 1,431,883m. (Dec. 1998); Pres. Dir TAKAO ENDO.

PT Bank Muamalat Indonesia (BMI): Arthaloka Bldg, Jalan Jenderal Sudirman 2, Jakarta 10220; tel. (21) 2511414; fax (21) 2511453; internet www.muamalatbank.com; Indonesia's first Islamic bank; cap. 165,593m. (July 2000); Pres. Dir A. RIAWAN AMIN; Chair. ABBAS ADHAR.

PT Bank Niaga: Graha Niaga, Jalan Jenderal Sudirman, Kav. 58, Jakarta 12190; tel. (21) 2505252; fax (21) 2505205; e-mail caniaga@attglobal.net; internet www.bankniaga.com; f. 1955; cap. 359,270m., res 557,805m., dep. 12,614,890m. (Dec. 1999); Pres. Commissioner SUKANTO REKSOHADIPRODJO; Pres. Dir PETER B. STOK; 96 brs.

PT Bank NISP Tbk: Jalan Taman Cibeunying Selatan 31, Jakarta 40114; tel. (22) 7234123; fax (22) 7100466; e-mail nisp@bank nisp.com; internet www.banknisp.com; f. 1941; cap. 274,611m., dep. 2,740,549m. (Dec. 1999); Pres. Dir PRAMUKTI SURJAUDAJA; Chair. KARMAKA SURJANDAJA; 59 brs.

PT Bank Prima Express: Jalan Roa Malaka Selatan 67, Jakarta 11230; tel. (21) 6906377; fax (21) 6908606; e-mail primex@rad.net.id; f. 1956 as Bank Tani Nasional PT; scheduled to merge into PT Bank Bali by Dec. 2002; cap. 167,000m., res 484,071m., dep. 1,522,444m. (Dec. 2000); Chair. BUDI PURWANTO; Pres. MICHAEL HUTABARAT; 16 brs.

PT Bank Rabobank International Indonesia: Plaza 89, 9th Floor, Jalan H. R. Rasuna Said, Kav. X-7, Jakarta 12940; tel. (21) 2520876; fax (21) 2520875; internet www.rabobank.com; cap. 350,000m., res 2,741m., dep. 1,010,012m. (Dec. 1999); Pres. and Dir HANS WINKELMOLEN.

PT Bank Sumitomo Mitsui Indonesia: Summitmas II, 10th Floor, Jalan Jenderal Sudirman, Kav. 61–62, Jakarta 12069; tel. (21) 5227011; fax (21) 5227022; f. 1989; fmrly PT Bank Sumitomo Indonesia, merged with PT Bank Sakura Swadharma in April 2001; cap. 753,191m., dep. 2,050,876m. (Dec. 1999); Pres. Dir YOSHIRO MORIMOTO; 1 br.

PT Bank UFJ Indonesia: Bank Bali Tower, 4th–5th Floors, Jalan Jenderal Sudirman, Kav. 27, Jakarta 12920; tel. (21) 2500401; fax (21) 2500410; f. 1989 as PT Sanwa Indonesia Bank; fmrly PT Bank Sanwa Indonesia; name changed as above Oct. 2001 following merger with PT Tokai Lippo Bank; cap. 600,000m., dep. 1,748,023m. (Dec. 2000); Pres. Dir MAKOTO KANEKO; Chair. RYOSUKE TAMAKOSHI.

PT Bank Universal: Plaza Setiabudi, Atrium Bldg, 2nd Floor, Jalan H. R. Rasuna Said, Kav. 62, Jakarta 12920; tel. (21) 5210550; fax (21) 5210588; e-mail info@bankuniversal.co.id; internet www.bankuniversal.co.id; f. 1990; to merge into PT Bank Bali by Dec. 2002; cap. 849,196m., res 4,734,630m., dep. 9,099,995m. (Dec. 1999); Pres. Dir STEPHEN Z. SATYAHADI; Chair. THEODORE PERMADI RACHMAT; 65 brs.

PT Hagabank: Jalan Abdul Muis 28, Jakarta 10160; tel. (21) 2312888; fax (21) 2312250; e-mail info@hagabank.com; internet www.hagabank.com; f. 1989; cap. 65,000m., res -939m., dep. 1,484,928m. (Dec. 2000); Pres. DANNY HARTONO; Chair. TIMOTY E. MARNANDUS.

PT Korea Exchange Bank Danamon: Suite 1201, 12th Floor, Wisma GKBI, Jalan Jenderal Sudirman, Kav. 28, Selatan, Jakarta; tel. (21) 5741030; fax (21) 5741032; e-mail kebd@idola.net.id; cap. 150,000m., dep. 542,739m. (Dec. 2000); Pres. NAM HAENG WAN; Chair. HONG YOUNG CHEUL.

PT Lippo Bank: Gedung Menara Asia, Jalan Raya Diponegoro 101, Lippo Karawaci, Tangerang 15810; tel. (21) 5460555; fax (21) 5460816; e-mail info_crc@lippobank.co.id; internet www.lippobank .co.id; f. 1948; cap. 811,494m., res 10,416,818m., dep. 18,938,719m. (Dec. 2000); Chair. MOCHTAR T. RIADY; Pres. Dir and CEO EDDY SINDORO; 310 brs.

PT Pan Indonesia Tbk (Panin Bank): Panin Bank Centre, 11th Floor, Jalan Jenderal Sudirman, Senayan, Jakarta 10270; tel. (21) 2700545; fax (21) 2700340; e-mail jasman@panin.co.id; internet www.panin.co.id; f. 1971; cap. 1,488,888m., res 1,082,472m., dep. 11,019,510m. (Dec. 2000); Chair. FUADY MOURAD; Pres. H. ROSTIAN SJAMSUDIN; 116 brs, 2 overseas brs.

PT Pesona Kriyadana: Jalan Pecenongan 84, POB 1471, Jakarta 10120; tel. (21) 3458103; fax (21) 3451617; f. 1974; fmrly Overseas Express Bank, Bank Utama; cap. 85,000m., res 16,039m., dep. 1,944,241m. (Dec. 1995); Chair. A. SUBOWO; Pres. Dir JANPIE SIAHAAN; 8 brs.

Foreign Banks

ABN AMRO Bank NV (Netherlands): Jalan Ir H. Juanda 23–24, POB 2950, Jakarta 10029; tel. (21) 2312777; fax (21) 2313222; internet www.abnamro.co.id; Man. C. J. DE KONING; 15 brs.

Bangkok Bank Public Company Ltd (Thailand): Jalan M. H. Thamrin 3, Jakarta 10110; POB 4165, Jakarta 11041; tel. (21) 2311008; fax (21) 3853881; f. 1968; Gen. Man. PRASARN TUNTASOOD.

Bank of America NA (USA): Jakarta Stock Exchange Bldg Tower 1, 22nd Floor, Jalan Jenderal Sudirman, Kav. 52–53, Jakarta 12190; POB 4931 JKTM, Jakarta 12049; tel. (21) 5158000; fax (21) 5158088; e-mail rahul.goswamy@bankofamerica.com; f. 1968; Man. Dir and Country Man. RAHUL GOSWAMY.

Bank of Tokyo-Mitsubishi Ltd (Japan): Midplaza Bldg, 1st–3rd Floors, Jalan Jenderal Sudirman, Kav. 10–11, POB 2711, Jakarta 10227; tel. (21) 5706185; fax (21) 5731927; e-mail pip@botm.co.id; internet www.btmjkt.com; Gen. Man. HIDEYUKI ABE.

Citibank NA (USA): Citibank Tower, Jalan Jenderal Sudirman, Kav. 54-55, Jakarta 12910; tel. (21) 52962277; fax (21) 52969303; internet www.citibank.co.id; f. 1912; Vice-Pres JAMES F. HUNT, EDWIN GERUNGAN, ROBERT THORNTON.

Deutsche Bank, AG (Germany): Deutsche Bank Bldg, Jalan Iman Bonjol 80, Jakarta 10310; POB 1135, Jakarta 10011; tel. (21) 3904792; fax (21) 335252; Gen. Man. HEINZ POEHLSEN.

Hongkong and Shanghai Banking Corpn Ltd (Hong Kong): 1st–5th Floors, World Trade Centre, Jalan Jenderal Sudirman, Kav. 29–31, Jakarta 12920; POB 2307, Jakarta 10023; tel. (21) 5246222; fax (21) 5211103; internet www.hsbc.co.id; CEO P. C. L. HOLBERTON; 6 brs.

The JP Morgan Chase Bank, NA (USA): Chase Plaza, 5th Floor, Jalan Jenderal Sudirman, Kav. 21, POB 311/JKT, Jakarta 12920; tel. (21) 5712213; fax (21) 5703690; Vice-Pres. and Sr Officer PETER NICE.

Standard Chartered Bank (United Kingdom): Wisma Standard Chartered Bank, Jalan Jenderal Sudirman, Kav. 33-A, Jakarta 10220; POB 57 JKWK, Jakarta 10350; tel. (21) 2513333; fax (21) 5721234; internet www.standardchartered.com/id/index.html; Chief Exec. DAVID HAWKINS; 5 brs.

Banking Association

The Association of Indonesian National Private Commercial Banks (Perhimpunan Bank-Bank Umum Nasional Swasta—PERBANAS): Jalan Perbanas, Karet Kuningan, Setiabudi, Jakarta

12940; tel. (21) 5223038; fax (21) 5223037; e-mail secretariat@perbanas.web.id; internet www.perbanas.web.id; f. 1952; 94 mems; Chair. GUNARNI SOEWORO; Sec.-Gen. WIBOWO NGASERIN.

STOCK EXCHANGES

At the end of January 2000 278 companies were listed on the Jakarta Stock Exchange, and market capitalization was 410,520,769m. rupiah. At the end of August 2002 there were 287 companies listed on the Jakarta Stock Exchange.

Bursa Paralel: PT Bursa Paralel Indonesia, Gedung Bursa, Jalan Medan Merdeka Selatan 14, Jakarta; tel. (21) 3810963; fax (21) 3810989; f. 1987.

Jakarta Stock Exchange (JSX): PT Bursa Efek Jakarta, Jakarta Stock Exchange Bldg, 4th Floor, Jalan Jenderal Sudirman, Kav. 52–53, Jakarta 12190; tel. (21) 5150515; fax (21) 5150330; e-mail webmaster@jsx.co.id; internet www.jsx.co.id; PT Bursa Efek Jakarta, the managing firm of the JSX was transferred to the private sector in April 1992; 197 securities houses constitute the members and the shareholders of the exchange, each company owning one share; Pres. Dir ERRY FIRMANSYAH.

Surabaya Stock Exchange: 5th Floor, Gedung Medan Pemuda, Jalan Pemuda 27–31, Surabaya 60271; tel. (31) 5340888; fax (31) 5342888; e-mail helpdesk@bes.co.id; internet www.bes.co.id; f. 1989; Chair. NATAKOESOEMAH.

Regulatory Authority

Badan Pengawas Pasar Modal (BAPEPAM) (Capital Market Supervisory Agency): Jalan Medan Merdeka Selatan 14, Jakarta 10110; POB 1439; tel. (21) 365509; fax (21) 361460; Chair. BACELIUS RURU; Exec. Sec. M. IRSAN NASARUDIN.

INSURANCE

In August 1996 there were 163 insurance companies, comprising 98 non-life companies, 56 life companies, four reinsurance companies and five social insurance companies.

Insurance Supervisory Authority of Indonesia: Directorate of Financial Institutions, Ministry of Finance, Jalan Dr Wahidin, Jakarta 10710; tel. (21) 3451210; fax (21) 3849504; Dir SOPHAR L. TORUAN.

Selected Life Insurance Companies

PT Asuransi AIA Indonesia: Bank Panin Senayan, 7th and 8th Floors, Jalan Jenderal Sudirman, Senayan, Jakarta 10270; tel. (21) 5721388; fax (21) 5721389; f. 1975; Pres. Dir HARRY HARMAIN DIAH.

PT Asuransi Allianz Aken Life: Summitmas II, 20th Floor, Jalan Jenderal Sudirman, Kav. 61–62, Jakarta 12190; tel. (21) 2522470; fax (21) 2523246; e-mail general@allianz.co.id; internet www.allianz.co.id; Pres. Dir Dr PETER ENARES.

Asuransi Jiwa Bersama Bumiputera 1912: Wisma Bumiputera, Lt. 17–21, Jalan Jenderal Sudirman, Kav. 75, Jakarta 12910; tel. (21) 5703812; fax (21) 5712837; Pres. Drs H. SUGUARTO; Dir H. SURATNO HADISUWITO.

PT Asuransi Jiwa Buana Putra: Jalan Salemba Tengah 23, Jakarta Pusat; tel. (21) 3908835; fax (21) 3908810; f. 1974; Pres. SUBAGYO SUTJITRO; Dir H. M. FATHONI SUSILO.

PT Asuransi Jiwa Bumiputera John Hancock: Plaza Mashill, 7th Floor, Jalan Jenderal Sudirman, Kav. 25, Jakarta 12920; tel. (21) 5228857; fax (21) 5228819; e-mail iby@pacific.net.id; internet www.jhancock.co.id; life insurance and pension schemes; CEO DAVID W. COTTRELL.

PT Asuransi Jiwa Central Asia Raya: Wisma Asia, 10th–11th Floors, Jalan S. Parman, Kav. 79, Slipi, Jakarta 11420; tel. (21) 5637901; fax (21) 5637902; e-mail service@car.co.id; internet www.car.co.id; Man. Dir DJONNY WIGUNA.

PT Asuransi Jiwasraya (Persero): Jalan H. Juanda 34, Jakarta 10120; tel. (21) 3845031; fax (21) 3862344; e-mail asuransi@jiwasraya.co.id; internet www.jiwasraya.co.id; f. 1959; Pres. and CEO HERRIS B. SIMANDJUNTAK.

PT Asuransi Jiwa 'Panin Putra': Jalan Pintu Besar Selatan 52A, Jakarta 11110; tel. (21) 672586; fax (21) 676354; f. 1974; Pres. Dir SUJONO SOEPENO; Chair. NUGROHO TJOKROWIRONO.

PT Asuransi Jiwa Pura Nusantara: Wisma Bank Dharnala, Lt. 20–21, Jalan Jenderal Sudirman, Jakarta 12920; tel. (21) 5211990; fax (21) 5212001; Dir MURNIATY KARTONO.

PT Asuransi Lippo Life: Menara Matahari Lippo Life Bldg, Lt. 7, Jalan Bulevar Palem Raya 7, Lippo Karawaci, Tangerang 15811; tel. (21) 5475433; fax (21) 5475401; f. 1983; life insurance, pensions, healthcare.

PT Asuransi Panin Life: Panin Bank Plaza, 5th Floor, Jalan Palmerah Utara 52, Jakarta 11480; tel. (21) 5484870; fax (21) 5484570; Pres. NUGROHO TJOKROWIRONO; Dir SUJONO SUPENO.

Bumi Asih Jaya Life Insurance Co Ltd: Jalan Matraman Raya 165–167, Jakarta 13140; tel. (21) 2800700 fax (21) 8509669; e-mail baj@bajlife.com; f. 1967; Chair. P. SITOMPUL; Pres. VIRGO HUTAGALUNG.

Bumiputera 1912 Mutual Life Insurance Co: Wisma Bumiputera, 18th–21st Floors, Jalan Jenderal Sudirman, Kav. 75, Jakarta 12910; tel. (21) 2512154; fax (21) 2512172; e-mail spw@bumiputera.com; f. 1912; Pres. SUPARWANTO.

Koperasi Asuransi Indonesia: Jalan Iskandarsyah I/26, Jakarta; tel. (21) 7207879; fax (21) 7207451; Dir H. J. V. SUGIMAN.

Selected Non-Life Insurance Companies

PT Asuransi Bina Arta Tbk: Wisma Dharmala Sakti, 8th Floor, Jalan Jenderal Sudirman, Kav. 32, Jakarta 10220; tel. (21) 5708157; fax (21) 5708166; e-mail dharins@uninet.net.id; Pres. SUHANDA WIRAATMADJA; Vice-Pres. M. MULYATNO.

PT Asuransi Bintang Tbk: Jalan R. S. Fatmawati 32, Jakarta 12430; tel. (21) 7504872; fax (21) 7506197; e-mail bintang@asuransibintang.com; internet www.asuransibintang.com; f. 1955; general insurance; Pres. Dir ARIYANTI SULIYANTO.

PT Asuransi Buana Independen: Jalan Pintu Besar Selatan 78, Jakarta 11110; tel. (21) 6904331; fax (21) 6263005; Exec. Vice-Pres. SUSANTY PURNAMA.

PT Asuransi Central Asia: Wisma Asia, 12th–15th Floors, Jalan Letjen S. Parman, Kav. 79, Slipi, Jakarta 11420; tel. (21) 5637933; fax (21) 5638029; e-mail cust-aca@aca.co.id; internet www.aca.co.id; Pres. ANTHONY SALIM; Dir TEDDY HAILAMSAH.

PT Asuransi Danamon: Gedung Danamon Asuransi, Jalan H. R. Rasuna Said, Kav. C10, Jakarta 12920; tel. (21) 516512; fax (21) 516832; Chair. USMAN ADMADJAJA; Pres. Dir OTIS WUISAN.

PT Asuransi Dayin Mitra: Jalan Raden Saleh Raya, Kav. 1B–1D, Jakarta 10430; tel. (21) 3153577; fax (21) 39129; e-mail nuning@dayinmitra.co.id; internet www.dayinmitra.co.id; f. 1982; general insurance; Man. Dir LARSOEN HAKER.

PT Asuransi Indrapura: Jakarta; tel. (21) 5703729; fax (21) 5705000; f. 1954; Presiding Dir ROBERT TEGUH.

PT Asuransi Jasa Indonesia: Jalan Letjenderal M. T. Haryono, Kav. 61, Jakarta 12780; tel. (21) 7994508; e-mail jasindo@jasindo.co.id; internet www.jasindo.co.id; Pres. Dr Ir BAMBANG SUBIANTO; Dir AMIR IMAM POERO.

PT Asuransi Parolamas: Komplek Golden Plaza, Blok G 39–42, Jalan R. S. Farmawati 15, Jakarta 12420; tel. (21) 7508983; fax (21) 7506339; internet www.parolamas.co.id; Pres. TJUT RUKMA; Dir Drs SYARIFUDDIN HARAHAP.

PT Asuransi Ramayana: Jalan Kebon Sirih 49, Jakarta 10343; tel. (21) 337148; fax (21) 334825; f. 1956; Chair. R. G. DOERIAT; Pres. Dir F. WIDYASANTO.

PT Asuransi Tri Pakarta: Jalan Paletehan I/18, Jakarta 12160; tel. (21) 711850; fax (21) 7394748; Pres. Drs M. MAINGGOLAN; Dir HUSNI RUSTAM.

PT Asuransi Wahana Tata: Jalan H. R. Rasuna Said, Kav. 12, Jakarta 12920; tel. (21) 5203145; fax (21) 5203146; internet www.aswata.co.id; Chair. S. SUGIARSO; Pres. RUDY WANANDI.

PT Lloyd Indonesia: Jalan Tiang Bendera 34-1, Jakarta 11230; tel. (21) 677195; Dir JOHNY BASUKI.

Berdikari Insurance Company: Jalan Merdeka Barat 1, Jakarta 10002; tel. (21) 3841339; fax (21) 3440586; e-mail ho@berdikari-insurance.com; internet www.berdikari-insurance.com; Pres. HOTBONAR SINAGA.

PT Maskapai Asuransi Indonesia (MAI): Jalan Sultan Hasanuddin 53–54, Kebayoran Baru, Jakarta Selatan 12160; tel. (21) 7204250; fax (21) 7256980; e-mail ptmai@cbn.net.id; Pres. Dir J. TRI WAHONO.

PT Maskapai Asuransi Jasa Tania: Gedung Agro Bank, Lt. 4, Jalan Teuku Cik Ditiro 14, Jakarta 10350; tel. (21) 3101912; fax (21) 323089; Pres. H. R. SUTEDJIO; Dir Drs H. ABELLAH.

PT Maskapai Asuransi Timur Jauh: Jalan Medan Merdeka Barat 1, Jakarta Pusat; tel. (21) 370266; f. 1954; Pres. Dir BUSTANIL ARIFIN; Dirs V. H. KOLONDAM, SOEBAKTI HARSONO.

PT Pan Union Insurance: Panin Bank Plaza, Lt. 6, Jalan Palmerah Utara 52, Jakarta 11480; tel. (21) 5480669; fax (21) 5484047; e-mail paninins@cbn.net.id; Chair. CHANDRA R. GUNAWAN; Pres. NIZARWAN HARAHAP.

PT Perusahaan Maskapai Asuransi Murni: Jalan Roa Malaka Selatan 21–23, Jakarta Barat; tel. (21) 679968; f. 1953; Dirs HASAN DAY, HOED IBRAHIM, R. SOEGIATNA PROBOPINILIH.

PT Pool Asuransi Indonesia: Blok A–IV Utara, Jalan Muara Karang Raya 293, Jakarta 14450; tel. (21) 6621946; fax (21) 6678021; f. 1958; Pres. BAMBANG GUNAWAN TANUJAYA; Dir TANDJUNG SUSANTO.

PT Tugu Pratama Indonesia: Wisma Tugu I, Jalan H. R. Rasuna Said, Kav. C8-9, Jakarta 12940; tel. (21) 52961777; fax (21) 52961555; e-mail tpi@tugu.com; internet www.tugu.com; f. 1981; general insurance; Chair. AINUN NA'IM; Pres. BAHDER MUNIR SJAMSOEDDIN.

Joint Ventures

PT Asuransi AIU Indonesia: Panin Bank Bldg, 3rd Floor, Jalan Jenderal Sudirman, Senayan, Jakarta 10270; tel. (21) 5720888; fax (21) 5703759; Pres. Dir PETER MEYER; Dirs SWANDI KENDY, GUNAWAN TJIU.

PT Asuransi Jayasraya: Jalan M. H. Thamrin 9, Jakarta; tel. (21) 324207; Dirs SUPARTONO, SADAO SUZUKI.

PT Asuransi Jiwa EKA Life: Wisma EKA Jiwa, 9th Floor, Jalan Mangga Dua Raya, Jakarta 10730; tel. (21) 6257808; fax (21) 6257837; e-mail cs@ekalife.co.id; internet www.ekalife.co.id; Pres. Dir HENRY C. SURYANAGA.

PT Asuransi Mitsui Marine Indonesia: Menara Thamrin, 14th Floor, Jalan M. H. Thamrin, Kav. 3, Jakarta 10340; tel. (21) 2303432; fax (21) 2302930; internet www.mitsuimarine.co.id; Pres. Dir S. AOSHIMA; Vice-Pres. PUTU WIDNYANA.

PT Asuransi Royal Indrapura: Jakarta Stock Exchange Bldg, 29th Floor, Jalan Jenderal Sudirman, Kav. 52–53, Jakarta 12190; tel. (21) 5151222; fax (21) 5151771; Pres. Dir Ir MINTARTO HALIM; Man. Dir MORAY B. MARTIN.

Insurance Association

Dewan Asuransi Indonesia (Insurance Council of Indonesia): Jalan Majapahit 34, Blok V/29, Jakarta 10160; tel. (21) 363264; fax (21) 354307; f. 1957; Chair. MUNIR SIAMSOEDDIN; Gen. Sec. SOEDJIWO.

Trade and Industry

GOVERNMENT AGENCIES

Agency for Strategic Industries (BPIS): Jakarta; f. 1989; co-ordinates for production of capital goods.

Badan Pengkajian dan Penerapan Teknologi—BPPT (Agency for the Assessment and Application of Technology): Jalan M. H. Thamrin 8, Jakarta 10340; tel. (21) 3162222; e-mail webmaster@bppt.go.id; internet www.bppt.go.id.

Badan Penyehatan Perbankan Nasional—BPPN (Indonesian Bank Restructuring Agency—IBRA): Wisma Danamon Aetna Life, Lantai 15, Jalan Jenderal Sudirman, Kav. 45–46, Jakarta 12930; tel. (21) 5770952; fax (21) 5772301; e-mail bppncare@bppn.go.id; internet www.bppn.go.id; f. 1998 to restructure the banking sector; Chair. SYAFRUDDIN TUMENGGUNG; Sr Dep. Chair. ARWIN RASYID.

Badan Tenaga Nuklir Nasional—BATAN (National Nuclear Energy Agency): Jalan Kuningan Barat, Mampang Prapatan, Jakarta 12710; tel. (21) 5251109; fax (21) 5251110; e-mail humas@batan.go.id; internet www.batan.go.id.

Badan Urusan Logistik—BULOG (National Logistics Agency): Jalan Jenderal Gatot Subroto 49, POB 2345, Jakarta 12950; tel. and fax (21) 5256482; e-mail rotu03@bulog.go.id; internet www.bulog.go.id; Chair. WIDJANARKO PUSPOYO.

National Agency for Export Development (NAFED): Jalan Gajah Mada 8, Jakarta 10310; tel. (21) 3841082; fax (21) 6338360; e-mail nafed@nafed.go.id; internet www.nafed.go.id.

National Economic Council: Jakarta; f. 1999; 13-member council formed to advise the President on economic policy; Chair. EMIL SALIM; Sec.-Gen. Sri MULYANI INDRAWATI.

DEVELOPMENT ORGANIZATIONS

Badan Koordinasi Penanaman Modal (BKPM) (Investment Co-ordinating Board): Jalan Jenderal Gatot Subroto 44, POB 3186, Jakarta 12190; tel. (21) 5252008; fax (21) 5254945; e-mail sysadm@bkpm.go.id; internet www.bkpm.go.id; f. 1976; Chair. THEO F. TOEMION.

Badan Perencanaan Pembangunan Nasional—Bappenas (National Planning Development Board): Jalan Taman Suropati 2, Jakarta 10310; tel. (21) 336207; fax (21) 3145374; e-mail admin@bappenas.go.id; internet www.bappenas.go.id; formulates Indonesia's national economic development plans; Chair. KWIK KIAN GIE.

Commercial Advisory Foundation in Indonesia (CAFI): Jalan Probolinggo 5, Jakarta 10350; tel. (21) 3156013; fax (21) 3156014; f. 1958; information, economic regulations bulletin, consultancy and translation services; Chair. JOYCE SOSROHADIKOESOEMO; Man. Dir LEILA RIDWAN SOSROHADIKOESOEMO.

CHAMBER OF COMMERCE

Kamar Dagang dan Industri Indonesia (KADIN) (Indonesian Chamber of Commerce and Industry): Chandra Bldg, 3rd–5th Floors, Jalan M. H. Thamrin 20, Jakarta 10350; tel. (21) 324000; fax (21) 3150241; f. 1969; 27 regional offices throughout Indonesia; Chair. Ir ABURIZAL BAKRIE; Sec.-Gen. Ir IMAN SUCIPTO UMAR.

INDUSTRIAL AND TRADE ASSOCIATIONS

Association of Indonesian Automotive Industries (GAIKINDO): Jalan H. O. S. Cokroaminoto 6, Jakarta 10350; tel. (21) 3102754; fax (21) 332100.

Association of Indonesian Beverage Industries (ASRIM): Jalan M. Ikhwan Mais 8, Jakarta Pusat; tel. (21) 3841222; fax (21) 3842294.

Association of Indonesian Coal Industries (ABBI): Perum Batu Bara Bldg, Jalan Supomo 10, Jakarta Selatan; tel. (21) 8295608.

Association of Indonesian Coffee Exporters (AICE): Jalan R. P. Soeroso 20, Jakarta 10330; tel. (21) 3106765; fax (21) 3144115; Chair. OESMAN SOEDARGO.

Association of Indonesian Heavy Equipment Industries (HINABI): c/o PT Traktor Nusantara, Jalan Pulogadung 32, Jakarta 13930; tel. (21) 4703932; fax (21) 4713940.

Association of Indonesian Tea Producers (ATI): Jalan Sindangsirna 4, Bandung 40153; tel. (22) 2038966; fax (22) 2031455; e-mail ptpnviii@pop.rad.net.id.

Association of State-Owned Companies: CTC Bldg, Jalan Kramat Raya 94–96, Jakarta; tel. (21) 346071; co-ordinates the activities of state-owned enterprises; Pres. ODANG.

Electric and Electronic Appliance Manufacturers' Association: Jalan Pangeran, Blok 20/A-1D, Jakarta; tel. (21) 6480059.

GINSI (Importers' Assen of Indonesia): Oil Center Bldg, 1st Floor, Jalan M. H. Thamrin 55, Jakarta 10350; tel. (21) 39837395; fax (21) 39837394; f. 1956; 2,921 mems (1996); Chair. AMIRUDIN SAUD; Sec.-Gen. MUSTAFA KEMAL.

Indonesian Cocoa Association (AKI): Jalan Brawijaya VII/5, Kebayoran Baru, Jakarta 12160; tel. (21) 771721; fax (21) 7203487.

Indonesian Cement Association: Graha Purnayudha, Jalan Jenderal Sudirman, Jakarta; tel. (21) 5207603; fax (21) 5207188.

Indonesian Exporters' Federation: Menara Sudirman, 8th Floor, Jalan Jenderal Sudirman, Kav. 60, Jakarta 12190; tel. (21) 5226522; fax (21) 5203303; Chair. HAMID IBRAHIM GANIE.

Indonesian Footwear Association (APRISINDO): Gedung Langlang Asia Ruang A, Jalan Daan Mogot 151, Jakarta Barat 11510; tel. (21) 5664157; fax (21) 5604671; e-mail aprisindo@vision.net.id; Chair. ANTON J. SUPIT.

Indonesian Furniture Industry and Handicraft Association (ASMINDO): Jalan Pegambiran 5A, 3rd Floor, Rawamangun Jakarta 13220; tel. (21) 47864028; fax (21) 47864031; e-mail asmindo@indo.net.id; internet www.furniture-indonesia.com/asmindo; Chair. DJALAL KAMAL.

Indonesian Nutmeg Exporters' Association: Jalan Hayam Wuruk 103, Jakarta; tel. (21) 6297432.

Indonesian Palm Oil Producers' Association: Jalan Pulo Mas IIID/1, Jakarta; tel. (21) 4892635; Chair. NUKMAN NASUTION.

Indonesian Precious Metals Association: Jalan Wahid Hasyim 45, Jakarta; tel. (21) 3841771.

Indonesian Pulp and Paper Association: Jalan Cimandiri 6, Jakarta 10330; tel. (21) 326084; fax (21) 3140168.

Indonesian Textile Association (API): Panin Bank Centre, 3rd Floor, Jalan Jenderal Sudirman 1, Jakarta Pusat 10270; tel. (21) 7396094; fax (21) 7396341; f. 1974; Sec.-Gen. DANANG D. JOEDONAGORO.

Indonesian Tobacco Association: Jalan H. Agus Salim 85, Jakarta 10350; tel. (21) 3140627; fax (21) 325181; Pres. H. A. ISMAIL.

Masyarakat Perhutanan Indonesia (MPI) (Indonesian Forestry Community): Gedung Manggala Wanabakti, 9th Floor, Wing B/Blok IV, Jalan Jenderal Gatot Subroto, Jakarta Pusat 10270; tel. (21) 5733010; fax (21) 5732564; f. 1974; nine mems; Pres. M. HASAN.

National Board of Arbitration (BANI): Menara Kadin Indonesia, 29th Floor, Jalan H. R. Rasuna Said, Kav. 2–3, Jakarta 12950; tel. and fax (21) 5274716; e-mail bani-arb@indo.net.id; f. 1977; resolves company disputes; Chair. Prof. H. PRIYATNA ABDURRASYID.

Rubber Association of Indonesia (Gapkindo): Jalan Cideng Barat 62A, Jakarta; tel. (21) 3846813; fax (21) 3846811; e-mail karetind@indosat.net.id; Exec. Dir SUHARTO HONGGOKUSUMO.

Shippers' Council of Indonesia: Jalan Kramat Raya 4–6, Jakarta; Pres. R. S. PARTOKUSUMO.

UTILITIES

Electricity

PT Perusahaan Umum Listrick Negara (PLN): Jalan Trunojoyo, Blok M1/135, Kebayaran Baru, Jakarta Selatan 12160; tel. (21)

7261875; fax (21) 7204929; e-mail webmaster@pln.co.id; internet www.pln.co.id; state-owned electricity co; Pres. EDDIE WIDYONO.

Gas

PT Perusahaan Pertambangan Minyak dan Gas Bumi Negara (PERTAMINA): Jalan Medan Merdeka Timur IA, Jakarta 10110; tel. (21) 3815111; fax (21) 363585; internet www.pertamina.com; f. 1957; state-owned petroleum and natural gas mining enterprise; Pres., Dir and CEO BAIHAKI HAKIM.

Perusahaan Gas Negara (PGN) (Public Gas Corporation): Jakarta; e-mail webmaster@pgn.co.id; internet www.pgn.co.id; monopoly of domestic gas distribution; Pres. Dir W. M. P. SIMANDJUNTAK.

Water

PDAM DKI Jakarta (PAM JAYA): Jalan Penjernihan 11, Pejompongan, Jakarta 10210; tel. (21) 5704250; fax (21) 5711796; f. 1977; responsible for the water supply systems of Jakarta; Pres. Dir Ir H. MUZAHIEM MOKHTAR.

PDAM Kodya Dati II Bandung: Jalan Badaksinga 10, Bandung 40132; tel. (22) 2509030; fax (22) 2508063; e-mail pdambdg@elga.net.id; f. 1974; responsible for the water supply and sewerage systems of Bandung; Pres. Dir Ir SOENITIYOSO HADI PRATIKTO.

PDAM Tirtanadi Medan: Jalan Sisingamangaraja 1, Medan 20212; tel. (61) 571666; fax (61) 572771; f. 1979; manages the water supply of Medan and nearby towns and cities; Man. Dir Ir KUMALA SIREGAR.

CO-OPERATIVES

In 1996 there were 48,391 primary and secondary co-operatives in Indonesia; membership of primary co-operatives was 27,006,000 in the same year.

Indonesian Co-operative Council (DEKOPIN): Jakarta; Pres. Sri EDY SWASONO.

MAJOR COMPANIES

(cap. = capital; res = reserves; m. = million)

State Enterprises

PT ASEAN Aceh Fertilizer: POB 09, Lhok Seumawe, North Aceh; tel. (645) 56933; fax (645) 56660; f. 1979; company owned by ASEAN governments (Indonesia 60%, Malaysia 13%, Thailand 13%, Philippines 13%, Singapore 1%); produces ammonia and urea; sales Rp. 341,500m. (1996); Pres. ZAENAL SOEDJAIS; 850 employees.

PT Barata Indonesia: Jalan Ngagel 109, Surabaya 60240; tel. (31) 5673942; fax (31) 5673642; f. 1971; manufacture of heavy construction and industrial equipment; Pres. Dir IMAM KARTONO; 3,500 employees.

PT Boma Bisma Indra (BBI): Jalan Ngagel 155–157, Surabaya 60246; tel. (31) 5670295; fax (31) 5671022; e-mail bbimark@rad.net.id; f. 1971; engineering services and the manufacture of industrial plant equipment; sales Rp. 210,000m. (1998); Pres. Dir Ir SOETRISNO SOETOMO; 2,100 employees.

PT Cipta Niaga: Jalan Malaka 7–9, POB 4314/JAK, Jakarta 11230; tel. (21) 6912823; fax (21) 6912471; e-mail h_office@cn-kp.co.id; internet www.cn-kp.co.id; f. 1964; import and distribution of basic goods, bulk articles, sundries, provisions and drinks, and export of Indonesian produce; Pres. Dir EDDIE M. GUNADI.

PT Dahana: Jalan Letjenderal Basir Surya, POB 117, Cibeurem, Tasikmalaya; tel. (265) 331853; fax (265) 334819; manufacture of dynamite and other industrial explosives and accessories.

PT Dharma Niaga Ltd: Jalan Kalibesar Barat 11, Jakarta 11230; tel. (21) 6903430; fax (21) 6906533; f. 1970; import, export, distribution, installation, after sales service; sales Rp. 450,000m. (1996); Pres. Drs BENARTO; 1,200 employees.

PT Industri Pesawat Terbang Nusantara (IPTN): Jalan Pajajaran 154, Bandung 40174; tel. (22) 631846; fax (22) 631696; f. 1976; aircraft manufacture; Chair. ASHADI TJAHJADI; 16,000 employees.

INKA: Jalan Yos Sudarso 71, Madiun; tel. (351) 452271; fax (351) 452275; f. 1981; manufacture of railway rolling stock; Exec. Dir Ir ISTANTORO.

INTI: Jalan Moch Toha 77, Bandung 40253; tel. (22) 502784; f. 1974; manufacture of telecommunications equipment.

PT Krakatau Steel: Wisma Baja 4th–8th Floors, 54 Jalan Gatot Subroto, Jakarta Selatan 12960; tel. (21) 510266; fax (21) 5204208; f. 1971; mfr of metals and metal products; sales Rp. 2,600,000m. (1996); Chair. T. ARIWIBOWO; Pres. Ir SOETORO MANGOENSOEWARGO; 7,000 employees.

LEN Industri: Sukarno Hatta 442, Bandung 40254; tel. (22) 5202682; fax (22) 5202695; e-mail marketing@len.co.id; f. 1965 as the National Electrotechnics Research Institute, became a state-owned company in 1991; manufactures electronic products and components; Pres. Dir E. FEBRUANUS.

PT Mega Eltra: Jalan Menteng Raya 27, Jakarta 13250; tel. (21) 3909018; fax (21) 3102937; f. 1960; building co and trader in cement, pharmaceuticals, chemicals and machinery; sales Rp. 280,000m. (1996); Chair. R. LENG KONG; Pres. Dir AMIR SAJAP; 600 employees.

PT Nurtanio: BPP Teknologi Bldg, Jalan M. H. Thamrin 8, Jakarta; tel. (2) 322395; aerospace.

PT PAL Indonesia (Persero): POB 1134, Ujung, Surabaya 60155; tel. (31) 3292275; fax (31) 3292493; e-mail pal-mbd@surabaya.wasantara.net.id; f. 1980; shipbuilding and general engineering; Pres. Dir ADWIN H. SURYOHADIPROJO; 3,369 employees.

Perum Perhutani (State Forest Corporation): Gedung Manggala Wanabakti, Blok IV/Lantai 4, Jalan Gatot Subroto, Senayan, Jakarta Pusat; tel. (21) 587090; fax (21) 583616; f. 1973; Pres. Dir Ir WARDONO SALEH.

PT Petrokimina Gresik: Jalan Jenderal Akhmad Yani, Gresik 61119, East Java; tel. (31) 3981811; fax (31) 3981722; e-mail pkg@indo.net.id; internet www.petrogres.co.id; f. 1975; produces fertilizers, ammonia and other related products; sales Rp. 754,000m. (1996); Pres. Dir ARIFIN TASRIF; 3,871 employees.

PT Pindad (Persero): Jalan Jenderal Gatot Subroto 517, Bandung 40284; tel. (22) 7312073; fax (22) 7304095; e-mail info@pindad.com; manufacture of products for commercial and military markets; Pres. Dir BUDI SANTOSO.

PT Pos Indonesia (Persero): Jalan Banda 30, Bandung 40115; tel. (21) 4213640; fax (22) 4205717; e-mail dirut@pos.wasantara.net.id; f. 1927; provides communication, logistic and financial services; sales Rp. 559,000m. (1996); Chair. DJAKARIA PURAWIJAYA.

PT Pupuk Iskandar Muda: Jalan Medan-Banda Aceh, Lhok Seumawe, North Aceh; tel. (645) 22049; fax (645) 22699; f. 1982; produces ammonia and urea; sales Rp. 185,000m. (1996); Pres. Dir Ir OMAY K. WIRAATMADJA; 1,200 employees.

PT Pupuk Sriwwijaya (PT Pusri): Jalan Taman Anggrek, Kemanggisan Jaya, Jakarta 11480; tel. (21) 5481208; fax (21) 5480607; e-mail sutadji@cabi.net.id; internet www.pusri.co.id; f. 1959; produces ammonia and urea; sales Rp. 2,495,000m. (1996); Pres. Dir Ir SUHADI; 6,000 employees.

PT Semen Gresik (Persero) Tbk: Gedung Graham Irama, 11th Floor, Jalan H. R. Rasuna Said, Kuningan, Jakarta 12950; tel. (31) 3981732; fax (31) 3983209; e-mail ptsg@sg.sggrp.com; internet www.sggrp.com; f. 1969; cement plant; cap. and res Rp. 2,981,248m., sales Rp. 3,596,410m. (2000); Pres. Dir URIP TIMURYONO.

PT Tambang Batubara Bukit Asam (PTBA): Jalan Prof. Dr Supomo SH10, Jakarta 12870; tel. (21) 8295608; fax (21) 8297642; merged with Perum Tambang Batubara in 1990; coal-mining.

PT Timah Tbk: Jalan Teuku Cik Ditiro 56A, Jakarta 10310; tel. (21) 3101185; fax (21) 3101187; e-mail timah@pt.timah.co.id; internet www.pttimah.com; tin-mining; partially privatized in 1995; Chair. WIMPY S. TJATJEP; Pres. THOBRANI ALWI.

Management Board

General Management Board of the State Trading Corporations (BPU-PNN): Jakarta; f. 1961; Pres. Col SUHARDIMAN.

Private Companies

Agribusiness

PT Central Proteinaprima: SHS Bldg, Jalan Ancol Barat, Blok A/5E 10 Ancol, Jakarta Utara; tel. (21) 6909958; fax (21) 6909956; e-mail cpprima@indoexchange.com; f. 1988; mfr of animal feeds; cap. and res Rp. 442,671m., sales Rp. 2,885,305m. (1998); Pres. Dir FRANCISCUS AFFANDY; 4,100 employees.

PT Charoen Pokphand: Jalan Ancol VIII/I, Ancol Barat, Jakarta 14430; tel. (21) 5152858; fax (21) 6905640; e-mail charoen@indoexchange.com; f. 1972; mfr of livestock feeds, poultry farming; cap. and res Rp. 282,967m. (1998), sales Rp. 2,378,746m. (1999); Pres. Dir SUMET JIARAVANON.

PT Dharmala Agrifood: Wisma Dharmala Sakti, 20th Floor, Jalan Jenderal Sudirman, Kav. 32, Jakarta; tel. (21) 5704434; fax (21) 5708166; e-mail dharagri@indoexchange.com; f. 1970; mfr of animal feeds, poultry farming, trading of rice and maize; cap. and res Rp. 177,573m., sales Rp. 270,603m. (1996); Pres. Dir THOMAS CHANDRA; 1,000 employees.

PT Japfa Comfeed Indonesia: Japfa II Bldg, Jalan Daan Mogot 9, Km 12, Jakarta 11730; tel. (21) 5448710; fax (21) 5448709; e-mail info@japfacomfeed.co.id; internet www.japfacomfeed.co.id; f. 1971; mfr of animal feeds, poultry and aquaculture farming; sales Rp. 2,402,590.6m. (1999); Pres. Dir HANDOJO SANTOSA; 10,500 employees.

Salim Group: Wisma BCA, 11th Floor, Jalan Jenderal Sudirman, Kav. 23, Jakarta; tel. (21) 5711002; fax (21) 5711581.

PT Sinar Mas Multiartha: BII Plaza, Tower III, 7th Floor, Room 702, Jalan M. H. Thamrin 51, Jakarta 10350; tel. (21) 3925660; fax (21) 3925788; cap. and res Rp. 9,233,307m., sales Rp. 8,404,602 (1998); Chair. EDWARD H. HADIDJAJA.

Food Processing

PT Canning Indonesia Products: 101 Jalan Diponegoro, Denpasar 80113, Bali; tel. (361) 228816; fax (361) 222555; e-mail pronas brand@lycos.com; f. 1948; mfr of food and beverages; sales Rp. 25,000m. (1996); Pres. Dir AUDI H. NATAWIRJA; 327 employees.

PT Indofood Sukses Makmur Tbk: Gedung Ariobimo Central, 12th Floor, Jalan H. R. Rasuna Said, X-2 Kav. 5, Kuningan, Jakarta 12950; tel. (21) 5228822; fax (21) 5226014; e-mail indofood@indo exchange.com; f. 1990; mfr of food, incl. noodles; cap. and res Rp. 625,978m. (1998), sales Rp. 11,548,598m. (1999); Pres. Dir EVA RIYANTI HUTAPEA; 23,000 employees.

PT Mayora Indah: Gedung Mayora, Jalan Tomang Raya 21–23, Jakarta 11440; tel. (21) 5655311; fax (21) 5655323; e-mail mayora@indoexchange.com; mfr of processed food products; cap. and res Rp. 556,277m. (1997), sales Rp. 544,110m. (1999); Chair. JOGI HENDRA ATMADJA; 7,000 employees.

PT Multi Bintang Indonesia: Jalan Daan Mogot Km 19, POB 3264, Jakarta 10032; tel. (21) 6190108; fax (21) 6190190; e-mail multiindo@indoexchange.com; producer and distributor of alcoholic and non-alcoholic beverages; cap. and res Rp. 215,109m., sales Rp. 508,249m. (2000); Pres. Dir HERMAN P. P. M. HOFHUIS; 850 employees.

PT SMART Corporation (Sinar Mas Agro Resources and Technology): BII Bldg, Tower II, 28th Floor, Jalan M. H. Thamrin, 51 Kav. 22, Jakarta 10350; tel. (21) 3925777; fax (21) 3184501; e-mail investor@smart-corp.com; internet www.smart-corp.com; f. 1962; food and soft drinks mfr and plantation owner (tea, banana, coconut, rubber); cap. and res Rp. 249,816m., sales Rp. 1,007,356m. (1997); Pres. MUKTAR WIDJAJA; 10,000 employees.

Heavy Equipment

PT Bakrie and Brothers Tbk: Wisma Bakrie, Lot 6, Jalan H.R. Rasuna Said, Kav. B-1, Jakarta 12920; tel. (21) 5250212; fax (21) 5207141; bakri@indoexchange.com; f. 1990; steel and pipe mfr, automotives construction, telecommunications, infrastructure support, etc.; cap. and res Rp. 1,373,156m. (1997), sales Rp. 3,521,917m. (1998); Pres. TANRI ABENG; 15,000 employees.

PT Komatsu Indonesia: Jalan Raya Cakung, Cilincing Km 4, Jakarta 14140; tel. (21) 4400611; fax (21) 4400615; e-mail komatsu@ indoexchange.com; internet www.komi.co.id; f. 1982; mfr of construction equipment; total assets Rp. 375,695m. (1997), sales Rp. 549,606m. (1999); Pres. Dir HIROSHI OKADO; 840 employees.

PT United Tractors: Jalan Raya Bekasi Km 22, Cakung, Jakarta 13910; tel. (21) 4605949; fax (21) 4600657; e-mail ir@unitedtractors .com; internet www.unitedtractors.com; f. 1972; distributor of heavy equipment; cap. Rp. 656,880m., sales Rp. 5,193,532m. (2000); Pres. HAGIANTO KUMALA; 7,200 employees.

Mining

PT Aneka Tambang Tbk: POB 4150, Jakarta 12041; Gedung Aneka Tambang, Jalan Letjen. T.B. Simatupang/Lingkar Solatan, Tanjung Barat, Jakarta 12530; tel. (21) 7891234; fax (21) 7891224; e-mail tambang@indoexchange.com; internet www.antam.co.id; f. 1968; exploration, mining, processing and marketing of nickel ore, ferro-nickel, bauxite, iron, sand, gold and silver; cap. and res Rp. 1,302,145m.; sales Rp. 1,021,911 (1998); Pres. ADITYA SUMANAGARA.

PT International Nickel Indonesia Tbk: Bapindo Plaza II, 22nd Floor, Jalan Jenderal Sudirman, Kav. 54–55, Jakarta; tel. (21) 5249000; fax (21) 5249020; e-mail inco@indoexchange.com; f. 1968; nickel mining and processing; cap. and res Rp. 728,466m., sales Rp. 401,607m. (2000); Pres. and CEO RUMENGAN MUSU; 2,360 employees.

Motor Vehicle Assembly

PT Astra International Tbk: Wisma 46, Kota BNI, Lantai 8, Jalan Jenderal Sudirman, Kav. 1, Jakarta 10220; tel. (21) 5711555; fax (21) 5714232; internet www.astra.co.id; f. 1957; car mfr, heavy industry, financial and non-financial services; cap. and res Rp. 2,568,324m. (1997), sales Rp. 28,403,770m. (2000); Pres. Dir THEODORE PERMADI RACHMAT; 91,000 employees.

PT Federal Motor: 1 Jalan Yos Sudarso Sunter, Jakarta 14350; tel. (21) 6518080; fax (21) 6521889; e-mail yozardi@federal.co.id; internet www.federal.co.id; f. 1971; mfr of motor cycles, parts and accessories; sales US $250m. (1997); Pres. Dir BUDI SETIADHARMA; 1,650 employees.

Paper

PT Indah Kiat Pulp and Paper Corpn Tbk: Bll Plaza, Menara II Lantai 7, Jalan M. H Thamrin 52, Jakarta 10350; tel. (21) 5380001; fax (21) 5380200; e-mail indahkiat@indoexchange.com; f. 1976; cap. and res Rp. 7,847,512m. (1997), sales Rp. 10,048,366m. (1999); Pres. Dir TEGUH GANDA WIDJAYA; 16,000 employees.

PT Pabrik Kertas Tjiwi Kimia: Jalan Raya Surabaya, Mojokerto Km 44, Sidoardjo, Jawa Timur; tel. (321) 21574; fax (321) 21615; internet www.tjiwi.co.id; f. 1972; mfr of writing and printing paper, stationery products and general office products; sales Rp. 6,678,877m. (1999); Chair. YUDI SETIAWAN LIN; 10,500 employees.

PT Surabaya Agung Industri Pulp and Kertas: Jalan Kedungdoro 60, 8th–10th Floors, Surabaya 60251; tel. (31) 5482003; fax (31) 5482039; e-mail ird@suryakertas.com; internet www .suryakertas.com; f. 1973; producer of paper and packaging materials; cap. and res Rp. 357,042m., sales Rp. 655,700m. (1998); Pres. Dir TIRTOMULYADI SULISTYO; 1,800 employees.

Petrochemicals

PT Continental Carbon Indonesia: Jalan Kebon Sirih 63, Jakarta; tel. (21) 3907939; fax (21) 3907929; production of carbon black; Pres. Dir LILI SOEMANTRI.

PT Eastern Polymer: Jalan Cilincing Raya, Tanjung Priok, North Jakarta; tel. (21) 4301167; fax (21) 496083; jt venture with Mitsubishi Corpn (50%) and PT Anugrah Daya Laksana (50%); production of PVC resin; Pres. Dir MOTONOBU TOKUDA.

PT Indochlor Prakarsa: Wisma Bimoli, 3rd Floor, Jalan Jembatab Tiga Block F & G, Jakarta 14440; tel. (21) 6603601; fax (21) 6603610; produces caustic soda, hydrochloric acid and liquid chlorine; Pres. Dir GAUTAMA SETIAWAN.

PT Petrokimia Nusantara Interindo: Plaza 89, Suite 705, Jalan H. R. Rasuna Said, Kav. X-7 No 6, Jakarta 12490; tel. (21) 5222722; fax (21) 5209360; production of polyethylene; Pres. Dir Dr JAMES WHITE.

PT Standard Toyo Polymer: Permata Plaza Bldg, 9th Floor, Jalan M. H. Thamrin 57, Jakarta 10310; tel. (21) 3903132; jt venture between Tosoh Corpn and Mitsui Corpn (50%) and local companies (50%); production of PVC resin; Pres. Dir NORIO MARSUYAMA.

PT Tri Polyta Indonesia Tbk: Menara Kebon Sirih, 12th Floor, Jalan Kebon Sirih 17–19, Jakarta 10340; tel. (21) 3929828; fax (21) 3929818; internet www.tripolyta.com; production of polypropylene, acrylic acid and acrylic ester; sales Rp. 1,134,115m. (1999); Pres. Dir IMAM SUCIPTO UMAR.

PT Unggul Indah Cahaya Tbk: Wisma UIC, 2nd Floor, Jalan Jenderal Gatot Subroto, Kav. 6–7, Jakarta 12930; tel. (21) 57905100; fax (21) 57905111; e-mail corp_sect@uic.co.id; f. 1983; chemicals mfr and processor; cap. and res Rp. 495,646m., sales Rp. 1,257,997m. (1999); Pres. HARTONO GUNAWAN; 320 employees.

Pharmaceuticals

PT Darya-Varia Laboratoria Tbk: Graha Darya-Varia, 2nd–3rd Floors, Jalan Melawai Raya 93, Kebayoran Baru, Jakarta Selatan 12130; tel. (21) 7258010; fax (21) 7258011; e-mail info@darya -varia.com; internet www.darya-varia.com; f. 1976; mfr of pharmaceuticals and consumer healthcare products; cap. and res Rp. 280,000m. (1999), sales Rp. 430,701m. (2000); Chair. PHILIP A. TOWNSEND; 1,793 employees.

PT Enseval Putera Megatrading Tbk (EPM): 10 Jalan Pulo Lentut, Kawasan Industri Pulo Gadung, Jakarta 13920; tel. (21) 4682242; fax (21) 4682241; e-mail enseval@indoexchange.com; internet www.enseval.com; f. 1988; distribution of pharmaceuticals, cosmetics, medical products, consumer products and raw materials; cap. and res Rp. 118,430m. (1997), sales Rp. 1,264,937m. (1999); Pres. Dir BUDI DHARMA WREKSOATMODJO; 2,000 employees.

PT Kalbe Farma: Jalan Jend A Yani, Pulo Mas, Jakarta 13210; tel. (21) 8997333; fax (21) 8972874; e-mail kalbeibd@pacific.net.id; internet www.kalbefarma.com; f. 1966; mfr of healthcare products, pharmaceuticals and veterinary products; cap. and res. Rp. U161,763m. (1998), sales Rp. 1,119,238m. (1999); Pres. Dir. JOHANNES SETIJONO; 1,550 employees.

PT Merck Indonesia: Jalan T. B. Simatupang 8, Pasar Rebo, Jakarta 13760; tel. (21) 8400081; fax (21) 8400492; e-mail merck@ indoexchange.com; f. 1970; mfr of pharmaceuticals and medicines; res Rp. 123,280m., sales Rp. 136,255m. (2001); Pres. Dir R. G. STOCK; Vice-Pres. Dir S. KOESDIANTO.

PT Nellco Indopharma: Jalan Kebon Jeruk 18/6, Jakarta 11160; tel. (21) 6297562; fax (21) 6297753; f. 1963; production of pharmaceutical goods; Pres. Dir RUDY CHANDRA.

PT Surya Hidup Satwa: Jalan Angol Barat Blok A-5E/10, Jakarta 14430; tel. (21) 6909958; fax (21) 6909957; e-mail suryahidup@ indoexchange.com; f. 1976; mfr and distribution of veterinary products and animal husbandry equipment; cap. and res Rp. 454,667m., sales Rp. 3,840,857m. (1998); Pres. Dir FREDDIE HADIWIBOWO; 150 employees.

PT Tempo Scan Pacific Tbk: Gedung Bina Mulia II, Jalan H. R. Rasuna Said, Kav. 11, Jakarta 12950; tel. (21) 5201858; fax (21) 5201857; e-mail tempo@indoexchange.com; f. 1970; mfr of pharmaceutical, personal care and cosmetic products; sales Rp. 1,331,509m. (1999); Chair. DIAN PARAMITA TAMZIL; Pres. Dir HANDOJO SELAMET; 3,200 employees.

PT Unilever Indonesia: Graha Unilever, Jalan Gatot Subroto, Kav. 15, Jakarta 12930; tel. (21) 5262112; fax (21) 5262044; e-mail unilever@indoexchange.com; f. 1933; mfr of personal care and home care products; cap. and res Rp. 900,000m., sales Rp. 4,100,000m. (1999); Chair. SRI HARTINA URIP SIMEON.

Plastics

PT Industri Dinar Makmur: Jalan Palmerah Utara 69–71, Jakarta 10270; tel. (21) 5481205; fax (21) 5483412; specializes in styrofoam and air bubble film; Dir ICHWAN HARTONO.

PT Pioneer Plastic Ltd: Jalan Bandengan Utara 43, Jakarta Utara 14440; tel. (21) 6690908; fax (21) 6694431; f. 1954; mfr of plastic hardware products; Pres. PANDJI WISAKSANA; 200 employees.

PT Sinar Panah Industry Co: Jalan Padamulya IV, Gg. Karung 39, Jakarta 11330; tel. (21) 6317947; fax (21) 6318168; f. 1963; Man. HENDRA WIDJAJA.

Rubber

PT Bakrie Sumatera Plantations Tbk: Kisaran 21202, Kabupaten Asahan, North Sumatera; tel. (623) 41508; fax (623) 41066; e-mail bakriesum@indoexchange.com; f. 1911; owner and operator of rubber plantations; cap. and res Rp. 225,108m., sales Rp. 825,027m. (1997); Pres. Dir HARI WITONO; 5,150 employees.

PT Gajah Tunggal: Wisma Hayam Wuruk, 10th Floor, Jalan Hayam Wuruk, Kav. 8, Jakarta 10120; tel. (21) 3805916; fax (21) 3804908; e-mail gajah@indoexchange.com; internet www.gt-tires.com; f. 1951; produces automotive tyres; cap. and res Rp. 1,395,387m. (1997), sales Rp. 3,969,842m. (1999); Pres. Dir R. KASENDA; 13,600 employees.

PT Goodyear Indonesia: POB 5, Jalan Pemuda 27, Bogor 16161; tel. (251) 326593; fax (251) 328088; e-mail goodyear@indoexchange.com; internet www.goodyear-indonesia.com; f. 1935; mfr of tyres, inner tubes and other related rubber products; cap. and res Rp. 125,615m. (1997), sales Rp. 535,114m. (1999); Pres. Dir GOTTFRIED HESS; 850 employees.

PT Hevea Latex and Rubber Works: Jalan Dr Setiabudhi 276A, Bandung 40143; tel. (22) 211149; fax (22) 212840; f. 1949; mfrs and exporters of sports and other shoes, rubber articles; Dir Ir SUGIRI.

PT Sepatu Bata: Jalan Taman Pahlawan Kalibata, Jakarta 12750; tel. (21) 7992008; fax (21) 7995679; e-mail jakarta@bataindonesia.com; internet www.bata.com; mfr of shoes and other footwear products; cap. and res Rp. 38,637m., sales Rp. 128,320m. (1997); Chair. G. L. ZANACCO.

Textiles

PT Argo Pantes Tbk: Wisma Argo Manunggal, 16th Floor, Jalan Gatot Subroto 95, Kav. 22, Jakarta 12930; tel. (21) 2520065; fax (21) 2520028; e-mail argo@indoexchange.com; internet www.argo.co.id; f. 1977; textiles mfr; sales Rp. 1,084,571m. (1999); Pres. Dir A. MOEIS; 6,500 employees.

PT Panasia Indosyntec: Jalan Garuda 153/74, Bandung 40184; tel. (22) 6034123; fax (22) 6036434; e-mail panafil@panasiagroup.co.id; internet www.panasiagroup.co.id; f. 1973; producer of integrated textiles and selected clothing; sales Rp. 444,000m. (1995); Pres. Dir AWONG HIDJALA; 8,000 employees.

PT Indorama Synthetics: Graha Irama, 17th Floor, Jalan H. R. Rasuna Said, Blok X-1, Kav. 1–2, Jakarta 12950; tel. (21) 5261555; fax (21) 5261501; e-mail corporate@indorama.com; internet www.indorama.com; f. 1974; mfr of polyester products and spun yarns; cap. and res US $223m., sales US $319m. (2001); Man. Dir S. P. LOHIA.

PT Polysindo Eka Perkasa Tbk: Kiara Payung Village, Klari District, Karawang, West Java; tel. (267) 431971; fax (267) 431975; e-mail polysindo@indoexchange.com; mfr of raw materials for the textile industry; cap. and res Rp. 209,534m., sales Rp. 2,175,670m. (1997); Pres. MARIMUTU SINIVASAN.

PT Textile Manufacturing Co Jaya Tbk: Kiara Payung Village, Klari District, West Java; tel. (267) 432400; fax (267) 432307; mfr of textiles; cap. and res Rp. 96,796m. (1997), sales Rp. 2,352,933m. (1999); Pres. Dir MARIMUTU SINIVASAN; 2,650 employees.

Timber

PT Barito Pacific Timber: Wisma Barito Pacific, Tower B, 9th Floor, Jalan Jenderal S. Parman, Kav. 62–63, Jakarta 11410; tel. (21) 5306711; fax (21) 5306680; e-mail barito@indoexchange.com; internet www.barito.co.id; f. 1979; producer and processor of timber and wood; cap. and res Rp. 1,989,881m. (1997), sales Rp. 1,929,206m. (1998); Pres. Dir YOHANNES HARDIAN WIDJANARKO; 28,500 employees.

PT Inti Indorayon Utama: 20th Floor, BNI Bldg, Jalan Jenderal Sudirman, Kav. 1, Jakarta 10220; tel. (21) 5706047; fax (21) 5702606; e-mail indorayon@indoexchange.com; f. 1983; mfr of processed wood products; cap. and res Rp. 207,699m. (1997), sales Rp. 768,292m. (1999); Pres. Dir H. DARLIN; 5,500 employees.

PT Surya Dumai Industri Tbk: Wisma 77, 7th Floor, Jalan S. Parman, Kav. 77 Slipi, Jakarta 11410; tel. (21) 53670888; fax (21) 53671888; e-mail kulimco@idola.net.id; producer of wood-based products and operator of forest and timber estate concessions; cap. and res Rp. 365,463m., sales Rp. 677,535m. (1998); Chair. CITRA GUNAWAN.

Tobacco

PT Gudang Garam (Perusahaan Rokok Tjap): Jalan Semampir II/1, Kediri 64121, East Java; tel. (354) 682091; fax (354) 681555; e-mail gg@indoexchange.com; f. 1973; producer of clove cigarettes; cap. and res Rp. 6,111,108m., sales Rp. 14,964,674m. (2000); Pres. Dir DJAJUSMAN SUROWIJONO; 43,000 employees.

PT Hanjaya Mandala Sampoerna: Jalan Rungkut Industri Raya 14–18, Surabaya 60293; tel. (31) 8431699; fax (31) 8430986; e-mail sampoerna@indoexchange.com; internet www.indoexchange.com/sampoerna; f. 1963; producer of clove cigarettes; cap. and res Rp. 1,634,523m. (1998), sales Rp. 7,412,032m. (1999); Chair. AGA SAMPOERNA; Pres. PUTERA SAMPOERNA; 19,000 employees.

PT Perusahaan Rokok Tjap Bentoel: Jalan Raya Karanglo, Banjar Arum, Singosari, Malang 65153, East Java; tel. (341) 49000; fax (341) 54710; f. 1930; mfr of clove cigarettes; sales Rp. 610,000m. (1994); Pres. BUDHIWIDJAYA KUSUMANEGARA; 8,000 employees.

Miscellaneous

PT Aneka Kimia Raya: Wisma AKR, 8th Floor, Jalan Panjang 5, Kabon Geruk, Jakarta 11530; tel. (21) 5311110; fax (21) 5311388; e-mail akr@indoexchange.com; f. 1977; mfr of industrial chemicals; cap. and res Rp. 138,955m. (1997), sales Rp. 1,058,868m. (1999); Pres. Dir H. ADIKOSOEMO; 546 employees.

PT Asahimas Flat Glass Co Ltd: Jalan Ancol IX/5, Ancol Barat, Jakarta 14430; tel. (21) 6904041; fax (21) 6904705; e-mail corporate-secretary@amfg.co.id; internet www.amfg.co.id; f. 1971; mfr of plate glass and other glass products; cap. and res Rp. 443,156m., sales Rp. 786,477m. (1999); Pres. Dir MITSURU JIBIKI; 2,617 employees.

PT Bayu Buana: Jalan Ir. H. Juanda III 12A, Jakarta 10120; tel. (21) 3801705; fax (21) 3861955; e-mail bayu@indoexchange.com; internet www.bayu.buana.co.id; f. 1972; operator of travel agency, fast food services, retail and leisure services; cap. and res Rp. 56,767m. (1997), sales Rp. 472,315m. (1999); Pres. Dir TYRONE KASKAM AWAN; 400 employees.

PT Bimantara Citra Tbk: Menara Kebon Sirih, Jalan Kebon Sirih 17–19, Jakarta 10340; tel. (21) 3909211; fax (21) 3909207; e-mail alex@bimantara.co.id; internet www.bimantara.co.id; f. 1981; holding company with primary interests in advertising and mass media; cap. and res Rp. 860,884m., sales Rp. 1,442,889m. (1998); Pres. Dir JOSEPH DHARMABRATA; 9,750 employees.

PT Ciputra Development Tbk: Jalan Prof. Dr Satrio, Kav. 6, Karet Kuningan, Jakarta 12940; tel. (21) 5225858; fax (21) 5205262; e-mail investor@ciputra.com; internet www.ciputra.com; f. 1981; real estate and property development; cap. and res Rp. 862,500m., sales Rp. 268,102m. (2000); Pres. Dir Ir CIPUTRA; 3,865 employees.

PT Dharmala Sakti Sejahtera Tbk: Wisma Dharmala Sakti, 20th Floor, Jalan Jenderal Sudirman 32, Jakarta 10220; tel. (21) 5704456; fax (21) 5703438; e-mail dharsakti@indoexchange.com; f. 1981; large conglomerate with primary interests in banking and finance; cap. and res Rp. 237,173m., sales Rp. 792,703m. (1997); Pres. Dir TJAN SOEN ENG; 1,900 employees.

PT Duta Pertiwi Tbk: ITC Bldg, 7th–8th Floors, Jalan Mangga Dua Raya, Jakarta 14430; tel. (21) 6019788; fax (21) 6017039; e-mail duti@simasred.com; internet www.simasred.com; f. 1982; property and real estate development and investment; cap. and res Rp. 1,221,916m., sales Rp. 604,992m. (2000); Pres. Dir MUKTAR WIDJAJA; 2,088 employees.

PT Indocement Tunggal Prakarsa Tbk: Wisma Indosement, 8th Floor, Jalan Jenderal Sudirman, Kav. 70–71, Jakarta 12910; tel. (21) 2512121; fax (21) 2510066; e-mail corpsec@ibm.net; internet www.indocement.co.id; f. 1973; cement producer; cap. and res Rp. 1,843,817m. (1996), sales Rp. 1,758,966m. (1999); Pres. Dir SUDWIKATMONO; 7,000 employees.

PT Matahari Putra Prima Tbk: Menara Matahari–Lippo Life, 20th Floor, 7 Blvd Palem Raya, Lippo Karawari 12000, Tangerang 15811; tel. (21) 5469333; fax (21) 5475444; e-mail dannykjg@

matahari.co.id; internet www.matahari.co.id; f. 1986; owner and operator of Indonesia's largest department store chain (81 stores); cap. and res Rp. 1,127,162m. (1998), sales Rp. 4,265,183m. (2001); Chair. Dr CHENG CHENG WEN; Pres. Dir BENYAMIN J. MAILOOL.

PT Modern Photo Film Tbk: Jalan Matraman Raya 12, Jakarta 13150; tel. (21) 2801000; fax (21) 8581620; e-mail modernpho@indoexchange.com; f. 1971; mfr of photography products; cap. and res Rp. 229,531m. (1997), sales Rp. 1,520,682m. (1999); Pres. SUNGKONO HONORIS; 3,400 employees.

PT Mulialand Tbk: Plaza Kuningan, Menara Utara, 10th Floor, Jalan H. R. Rasuna Said, Kav. C11–14, Jakarta 12940; tel. (21) 5207729; fax (21) 5200795; e-mail mulialand@indoexchange.com; f. 1987; property development and real estate investment, leasing of office blocks and residential apartments; cap. and res Rp. 509,651m., sales Rp. 698,190m. (1998); Chair. JOKO SOERGIARTO TJANDRA; 140 employees.

PT Ramayana Lestari Sentosa Tbk: Jalan K. H. Wahid Hasyim 220A-B, Jakarta 10250; tel. (21) 3920480; fax (21) 3920484; e-mail ramayana@indoexchange.com; f. 1983; operator of department stores and supermarkets; cap. and res Rp. 564,424m. (1997), sales Rp. 1,654,293m. (1999); Chair. AGUS MAKMUR; 16,500 employees.

PT Supreme Cable Manufacturing Corporation Tbk: Jalan Kabon Sirih 71, Jakarta 10340; tel. (21) 3100525; fax (21) 331119; e-mail sucaco@indoexchange.com; f. 1970; mfr of cable, metal goods and alloys and plastic products and materials; cap. and res Rp. –30,922m. (1997), sales Rp. 312,833m. (1999); Pres. Dir ELLY SOEPONO; 800 employees.

PT Tigaraksa Satria Tbk: Tira Bldg, Jalan H. R. Rasuna Said, Kav. B3, Jakarta 12920; tel. (21) 5254208; fax (21) 5222413; e-mail tigaraksa@indoexchange.com; f. 1986; distributor of food products, personal care products, household products and garments; cap. and res Rp. 237,233m., sales Rp. 730,285m. (1998); Pres. Dir GIN SUGIANTO; 700 employees.

PT Warna Agung: Kompleks Delta Bldg, Blok C 3–6, Jalan Suryopranoto, Kav. 1–9, Jakarta 10160; tel. (21) 3808711; fax (21) 3809721; f. 1969; mfr of paints, emulsions and other related products; sales Rp. 24,000m. (1994); Chair. L. MOELJONO; Dir F. SUTADJI; 400 employees.

PT Wicaksana Overseas International: Jalan Ancol Barat VII, Blok A5D 2, Jakarta 14430; tel. (21) 6927293; fax (21) 6909436; e-mail wicaksana@indoexchange.com; internet www.wicaksanaweb.com; f. 1973; distributor of consumer goods; sales Rp. 2,572,638m. (1999); Pres. BACHTIAR YUSUF; 2,800 employees.

TRADE UNIONS

Serikat Buruh Sejahtera Indonesia (SBSI) (Indonesian Prosperity Trade Union Central Board): Jakarta; f. 1998; application for official registration rejected in May 1998; 1,228,875 mems in 168 branches in 27 provinces throughout Indonesia; Gen. Chair. MUCHTAR PAKPAHAN; Gen. Sec. SUNARTY.

Federasi Serikat Pekerja Seluruh Indonesia (FSPSI) (Federation of All Indonesian Trades Unions): Jalan Raya Pasar Minggu Km 17 No. 9, Jakarta 12740; tel. (21) 7974359; fax (21) 7974361; f. 1973, renamed 1995; sole officially recognized National Trade Union Centre; comprises 18 national industrial unions; 5.1m. mems in February 1999; Gen. Chair. JACOB NUWA WEA; Gen. Sec. SJUKUR SARTO.

Transport

Directorate General of Land Transport and Inland Waterways: Ministry of Transportation and Telecommunication, Jalan Medan Merdeka Barat 8, Jakarta 10110; tel. (21) 3456332; fax (21) 3451657; Dir-Gen. SOEJONO.

RAILWAYS

There are railways on Java, Madura and Sumatra, totalling 6,458 km in 1996, of which 125 km were electrified.

In 1995 a memorandum of understanding was signed by a consortium of European, Japanese and Indonesian companies for the construction of a subway system in Jakarta. However, in 2002 construction had not yet begun owing to the Government's inability to fund the project, which was expected to cost US $1,500m. to implement.

Perusahan Umum Kereta Api (PERUMKA): Jalan Perintis Kermedekaan 1, Bandung 40117, Java; tel. (22) 430031; fax (22) 430062; six regional offices; transferred to the private sector in 1991; Chief Dir Drs ANWAR SUPRIADI.

ROADS

There is an adequate road network on Java, Sumatra, Sulawesi, Kalimantan, Bali and Madura, but on most of the other islands traffic is by jungle track or river boat. In 1997 the road network in Indonesia totalled 342,700 km; 27,357 km were main roads and 40,490 km were secondary roads. About 158,670 km of the network were paved.

Directorate General of Highways: Ministry of Public Works, Jalan Pattimura 20, Kebayoran Baru, Jakarta Selatan 12110; tel. (21) 7262805; fax (21) 7260769; Dir-Gen. Ir SURYATIN SASTROMIJOYO.

SHIPPING

The Ministry of Communications controls 349 ports and harbours, of which the four main ports of Tanjung Priok (near Jakarta), Tanjung Perak (near Surabaya), Belawan (near Medan) and Makassar (formerly Ujung Pandang, in South Sulawesi) have been designated gateway ports for nearly all international shipping to deal with Indonesia's exports and are supported by 15 collector ports. Of the ports and harbours, 127 are classified as capable of handling ocean-going shipping.

Directorate General of Sea Communications: Ministry of Communications, Jalan Medan Merdeka Barat 8, Jakarta 10110; tel. (21) 3456332; Dir-Gen. SOENTORO.

Indonesian National Ship Owners' Association (INSA): Jalan Gunung Sahari 79, Jakarta Pusat; tel. (21) 414908; fax (21) 416388; Pres. H. HARTOTO HADIKUSUMO.

Shipping Companies

Indonesian Oriental Lines, PT Perusahaan Pelayaran Nusantara: Jalan Raya Pelabuhan Nusantara, POB 2062, Jakarta 10001; tel. (21) 494344; Pres. Dir A. J. SINGH.

PT Jakarta Lloyd: Jalan Agus Salim 28, Jakarta Pusat 10340; tel. (21) 331301; fax (21) 333514; f. 1950; services to USA, Europe, Japan, Australia and the Middle East; Pres. Dir Drs M. MUNTAQA.

PT Karana Line: Jalan Kali Besar Timur 30, POB 1081, Jakarta 11110; tel. (21) 6907381; fax (21) 6908365; Pres. Dir BAMBANG EDIYANTO.

PT Pelayaran Bahtera Adhiguna (Persero): Jalan Kalibesar Timur 10–12, POB 4313, Jakarta 11043; tel. (21) 6912613; fax (21) 6901450; f. 1971; Pres. H. DJAJASUDHARMA.

PT Pelayaran Nasional Indonesia (PELNI): Jalan Angkasa 18, Jakarta; tel. (21) 4211921; fax (21) 491623; internet www.pelni.com; state-owned; national shipping co; Pres. Dir ISNOOR HARYANTO.

PT Pelayaran Samudera Admiral Lines: Jalan Gunung Sahari 79–80, Jakarta 10610; POB 1476, Jakarta 10014; tel. (21) 4247908; fax (21) 4206267; e-mail admiral@uninet.net.id; Pres. Dir DJOKO SOETOPO.

PT (Persero) Pann Multi Finance: Pann Bldg, Jalan Cikini IV/11, POB 3377, Jakarta 10330; tel. (21) 322003; fax (21) 322980; state-controlled; Pres. Dir W. NAYOAN; Dir HAMID HADIJAYA.

PT Perusahaan Pelayaran Gesuri Lloyd: Gesuri Lloyd Bldg, Jalan Tiang Bendera IV 45, Jakarta 11230; tel. (21) 6904000; fax (21) 6904190; e-mail gesuri@indosat.net.id; internet www.gesuri.co.id; f. 1963; Pres. FRANKIE NURIMBA.

PT Perusahaan Pelayaran 'Nusa Tenggara': Kantor Pusat, Jalan Raya Pelabuhan Benoa, POB 3069, Denpasar 80222, Bali; tel. (361) 723608; fax (361) 722059; e-mail ntship@indo.net.id; Man. Dir KETUT DERESTHA.

PT Perusahaan Pelayaran Samudera 'Samudera Indonesia': Jalan Kali Besar Barat 43, POB 1244, Jakarta; tel. (21) 671093; fax (21) 674242; Chair. and Dir SOEDARPO SASTROSATOMO; Exec. Dir RANDY EFFENDI.

PT Perusahaan Pelayaran Samudera Trikora Lloyd: Bank Bumi Daya Bldg, 2nd and 3rd Floors, Jalan Malaka 1, Jakarta 11230; POB 4076, Jakarta 11001; tel. (21) 6907751; fax (21) 6907757; f. 1964; Pres. Dir GANESHA SOEGIHARTO; Man. Dir P. R. S. VAN HEEREN.

PT Perusahaan Pertambangan Minyak dan Gas Bumi Negara (PERTAMINA): Directorate for Shipping, Harbour and Communication, Jalan Yos Sudarso 32–34, POB 327, Tanjung Priok, Jakarta; tel. (21) 4301086; fax (21) 4301492; state-owned; tanker services; Pres. and Chair. Dr IBNU SUTOWO.

CIVIL AVIATION

The first stage of a new international airport, the Sukarno-Hatta Airport, at Cengkareng, near Jakarta, was opened in 1985, to complement Halim Perdanakusuma Airport, which was to handle charter and general flights only. A new terminal was opened at Sukarno-Hatta in 1991, vastly enlarging airport capacity. Construction of an international passenger terminal at the Frans Kaisepo Airport, in Papua (then Irian Jaya), was completed in 1988. Other international airports include Ngurah Rai Airport at Denpasar (Bali), Polonia Airport in Medan (North Sumatra), Juanda Airport, near Surabaya (East Java), Sam Ratulangi Airport in Manado (North Sulawesi) and Hasanuddin Airport, near Makassar (formerly

Ujung Pandang, South Sulawesi). There are a total of 72 airports, six of which are capable of accommodating wide-bodied aircraft. Domestic air services link the major cities, and international services are provided by the state airline, PT Garuda Indonesia, by its subsidiary, PT Merpati Nusantara Airlines, and by numerous foreign airlines. In December 1990 it was announced that private airlines equipped with jet-engined aircraft would be allowed to serve international routes.

In 2000 the Government announced a policy of liberalization for the airline industry. This led to a dramatic increase in the number of airlines operating in Indonesia; in July 2002 Indonesia had 25 domestic airlines, compared to five in 2000. Of these, only 16 new companies had begun operations by July 2002.

Directorate-General of Air Communications: Jalan Arief Rahman Hakim 3, Jakarta 10340; tel. (21) 3914235; fax (21) 3914239; Dir-Gen. ZAINUDDIN SIKADO.

Awair International: Graha Aktiva Bldg, Jalan H. R. Rasuna Said, Jakarta; tel. and fax (21) 5203598; internet www.awairlines .com; f. 2000; scheduled domestic passenger services from Jakarta; Pres. YASSIR ISMAIL.

Bayu Indonesia Air (BYU): Jalan Bikatamsu 29E, Jakarta; f. 1975; tel. (21) 4515588; fax (21) 4515777; international services; Man. Dir PERMADI WIRATANUNINGRAT.

PT Bouraq Indonesia Airlines (BOU): Jalan Angkasa 1–3, POB 2965, Kemayoran, Jakarta 10720; tel. (21) 6288815; fax (21) 6008729; internet www.bouraq.com; f. 1970; private company; scheduled regional and domestic passenger and cargo services linking Jakarta with points in Java, Borneo, Sulawesi, Bali, Timor and Tawau (Malaysia); Pres. Dir DANNY SUMENDAP.

Carstensz Papua Airlines (CPA): Papua; f. 2002; domestic services.

Citilink: Jakarta; internet www.ga-citilink.com; f. 2001; subsidiary of PT Garuda Indonesia; provides shuttle services between domestic destinations.

Deraya Air Taxi (DRY): Terminal Bldg, 1st Floor, Rm 150/HT, Halim Perdanakusuma Airport, Jakarta 13610; tel. (21) 8093627; fax (21) 8095770; internet www.boedihardjogroup.com; scheduled and charter passenger and cargo services to domestic and regional destinations; Pres. Dir SITI RAHAYU SUMADI.

Dirgantara Air Service (DAS): POB 6154, Terminal Bldg, Halim Perdanakusuma Airport, Rm 231, Jakarta 13610; tel. (21) 8093372; fax (21) 8094348; charter services from Jakarta, Barjarmas and Pontianak to destinations in West Kalimantan; Pres. MAKKI PERDANAKUSUMA.

PT Garuda Indonesia: Garuda Indonesia Bldg, Jalan Merdeka Selatan 13, Jakarta 10110; tel. (21) 2311801; fax (21) 2311962; internet www.garuda.co.id; f. 1949; state airline; operates scheduled domestic, regional and international services to destinations in Europe, the USA, the Middle East, Australasia and the Far East; Pres. and CEO INDRA SETIAWAN.

Indonesia Air Transport—IAT (IDA): Pondok Cabe Aerodrome, POB 2485, Jakarta; tel. (21) 7490213; fax (21) 7491287; charter passenger and cargo services to domestic, regional and international destinations; f. 1968; Man. Dir AZMAR MUALIM.

Indonesian Airlines: Jakarta; f. 1999; domestic services; Pres. RUDY SETYOPURNOMO.

Lion Mentari Airlines: Gedung Jaya, 7th Floor, Jalan M. H. Thamrin 12, Jakarta 10340; tel. (21) 331838; fax (21) 327808; internet www.lionairlines.com; f. 1999; domestic and international services; Pres. Dir RUSDI KILANA.

PT Mandala Airlines: Jalan Tomang Raya, Kav. 35–37, Jakarta 11440; tel. (21) 4206646; fax (21) 4249491; internet www.mandala .co.id; f. 1969; privately-owned; scheduled regional and domestic passenger and cargo services; Pres. and Dir GUNADI SUGOTO.

PT Merpati Nusantara Airlines: Jalan Angkasa, Blok 15, Kav. 2–3, Jakarta 10720; tel. (21) 6546789; fax (21) 6540620; e-mail lt13@indosat.net.id; internet www.merpati.co.id; f. 1962; subsidiary of PT Garuda Indonesia; domestic and regional services to Australia and Malaysia; Chair. MUCHTARUDIN SIREGAR; Pres. WAHYU HIDAYAT.

Pelita Air Service: Jalan Abdul Muls 52–56A, Jakarta 10160; tel. (21) 2312030; fax (21) 2312216; internet www.pelita-air.co.id; f. 1970; domestic services; Pres. Dir SOERATMAN.

Star Air: Jalan Gunung Sahari Raya 57 A-B, POB 4724, Jakarta 10610; f. 2000; scheduled international and domestic passenger services from Jakarta to Balikpapan, Medan and Surabaya; CEO ALE SUGIARTO.

Sumut Airlines: North Sumatra; f. 2002; domestic services.

Tourism

Indonesia's tourist industry is based mainly on the islands of Java, famous for its volcanic scenery and religious temples, and Bali, renowned for its scenery and Hindu-Buddhist temples and religious festivals. Lombok, Sumatra and Sulawesi are also increasingly popular. Domestic tourism within Indonesia has also increased significantly. In 2000 5.1m. foreign tourists visited Indonesia, compared with 4.7m. in 1999 and 4.6m. in 1998. Foreign-exchange earnings from tourism declined from US $5,321m. in 1997 to US $3,459m. in 1998.

Department of Culture and Tourism: Jalan Medan Merdeka Barat 16–19, Jakarta Pusat; tel. (21) 3838805; fax (21) 3848245; internet www.indonesiatourisminfo.com; f. 1957; Chair. I. GEDE ARDIKA.

Indonesia Tourism Promotion Board: Wisma Nugra Santana, 9th Floor, Jalan Jenderal Sudirman 7–8, Jakarta 10220; tel. (21) 5704879; fax (21) 5704855; e-mail itpb@cbn.net.id; internet www .goindo.com; private body; promotes national and international tourism; Chair. PONTJO SUTOWO; CEO GATOT SOEMARTONO.

Defence

In August 2001 the total strength of the armed forces was an estimated 297,000: army 230,000, navy 40,000, and air force 27,000; paramilitary forces comprised some 195,000 police, including a mobile brigade of 14,000 and 12,000 marines. Military service, which is selective, lasts for two years.

Defence Expenditure: Budgeted at an estimated 14,300,000m. rupiah in 2001.

Commander-in-Chief of the Armed Forces: Gen. ENDRIARTONO SUTARTO.

Chief of Staff of the Army: Lt-Gen. RYAMIZARD RYACUDU.

Chief of Staff of the Navy: Adm. BERNARD KENT SONDAKH.

Chief of Staff of the Air Force: Air Chief Marshal CHAPPY HAKIM.

Education

Education is controlled mainly by the Ministry of Education and Culture, but the Ministry of Religious Affairs also operates Islamic religious schools (*madrasahs*) at the primary level.

Primary education, beginning at seven years of age and lasting for six years, was made compulsory in 1987. In 1993 it was announced that compulsory education was to be expanded to nine years. Secondary education begins at 13 years of age and lasts for a further six years, comprising three years of junior secondary education and a further three years of senior secondary education. A further three years of academic level or five years of higher education may follow.

As a proportion of children in the relevant age-group, enrolment at primary level in 1996 was equivalent to 113% (males 115%; females 110%); enrolment at secondary level in the same year was equivalent to 56% of children in the relevant age-group.

Technical and vocational education is the least developed aspect of the educational system, but vocational subjects have been introduced in the secondary schools. In 1997/98, according to preliminary data, there were 1,862,060 pupils at 4,006 vocational senior secondary schools.

In 1997/98, according to preliminary data, there were 1,391 universities, with a total enrolment of 2.1m. In 1996 enrolment at tertiary level was equivalent to 11% of the relevant population.

In 1999/2000 the Government spent an estimated 7,742,700m. rupiah, representing approximately 3.8% of total estimated budgetary expenditure, on education.

Bibliography

GENERAL

Cribb, Robert. *Historical Dictionary of Indonesia.* Metuchen, NJ, Scarecrow Press, 1992.

Historical Atlas of Indonesia. Richmond, Surrey, Curzon Press, 2000.

Hardjono, Joan (Ed.). *Indonesia: Resources, Environment, Ecology.* Kuala Lumpur, Oxford University Press, 1991.

Wilhelm, Donald. *Emerging Indonesia.* London, Quiller Press, 1985.

HISTORY AND POLITICS

Abaza, Mona. *Changing Images of Three Generations of Azharites in Indonesia.* Singapore, Institute of Southeast Asian Studies, 1993.

Alatas, Ali. *A Voice for a Just Peace.* Singapore, Institute of Southeast Asian Studies, 2001.

Ananta, Aris. *Human Development During the Indonesian Crisis.* Singapore, Institute of Southeast Asian Studies, 2002.

Andaya, Leonard Y. *The World of Maluku: Eastern Indonesia in the Early Modern Period.* Honolulu, University of Hawaii Press, 1993.

Anderson, Benedict. *Language and Power: Exploring Political Cultures in Indonesia.* Ithaca, NY, and London, Cornell University Press, 1991.

Antlöv, Hans, and Cederroth, Sven. *Elections in Indonesia: The New Order and Beyond.* Richmond, Surrey, Curzon Press, 2001.

Antons, Christoph. *Intellectual Property Law in Indonesia.* Boston, MA, Kluwer Law International, 2000.

Anwar, Dewi Fortuna. *Indonesia in ASEAN: Foreign Policy and Regionalism.* Singapore, Institute of Southeast Asian Studies, 1994.

Aragon, Lorraine V. *Fields of the Lord: Animism, Christian Minorities, and State Development in Indonesia.* Richmond, Surrey, Curzon Press, 2000.

Aspinall, Edward, Feith, Herb, and van Klinken, Gerry (Eds). *The Last Days of President Suharto.* Clayton, Vic, Monash Asia Institute, 1999.

Baker, R. W., Soesastro, M. H., Kristiadi, J., and Ramage, D. E. (Eds). *Indonesia—The Challenge of Change.* Singapore, Institute of Southeast Asian Studies, 1999.

Barber, Charles Victor, and Schweithelm, James. *Trial by fire: forest fires and forestry policy in Indonesia's era of crisis and reform.* Washington, DC, World Resources Institute, 2000.

Barton, Greg. *Abdurrahman Wahid: Muslim Democrat, Indonesian President.* Sydney, University of New South Wales Press, 2002.

Bellwood, Peter. *Prehistory of the Indo-Malaysian Archipelago.* Sydney, Academic Press, 1985.

Boland, B. J. *The Struggle of Islam in Modern Indonesia.* Leiden, Koninklijk Instituut voor Taal-, Land- en Volkenkunde, 1971.

Bourchier, David, and Legge, John (Eds). *Democracy in Indonesia: 1950s and 1990s.* Clayton, Vic, Monash University Centre of Southeast Asian Studies, 1994.

Bourchier, David, and Hadiz, Vedi (Eds). *Indonesian Politics and Society.* London, Routledge, 2001.

Bresnan, John. *Managing Indonesia: the Modern Political Economy.* New York, Columbia University Press, 1993.

Buchholt, Helmut, and Mai, Ulrich (Eds). *Continuity, Change and Aspirations: Social and Cultural Life in Minahasa, Indonesia.* Singapore, Institute of Southeast Asian Studies, 1994.

Challis, Roland. *Shadow of a Revolution: Indonesia and the Generals.* Stroud, Gloucs., Sutton Publishing, 2001.

Cleary, Mark, and Eaton, Peter. *Borneo: change and development.* Kuala Lumpur, Oxford University Press, 1995.

Coppel, Charles A. *Indonesian Chinese in Crisis.* Kuala Lumpur, Oxford University Press, 1983.

Coppel, Charles (Ed.). *Violent Conflicts in Indonesia: Analysis, Representation, Resolution.* Richmond, Surrey, Curzon Press, 2001.

Cribb, Robert (Ed.). *The Indonesian Killings of 1965–1966: Studies from Java and Bali.* Clayton, Vic, Monash University, 1991.

Cribb, Robert, and Brown, Colin. *Modern Indonesia: a History since 1945.* London, Longman, 1995.

Crouch, Harold. *The Army and Politics in Indonesia.* Ithaca, NY, Cornell University Press, 1978.

Dahm, Bernhard. *History of Indonesia in the Twentieth Century.* London, Praeger, 1971.

Effendy, Bahtiar. *Islam & the State: The Transformation of Islamic Political Ideas and Practices in Indonesia.* Singapore, Institute of Southeast Asian Studies, 2001.

Eklöf, Stefan. *Indonesian Politics in Crisis: the Long Fall of Suharto 1996–98.* Copenhagen, Nordic Institute of Asian Studies, 1999.

Elson, R. E. *Suharto: a Political Biography.* Cambridge, Cambridge University Press, 2001.

Emmerson, Donald K. (Ed.). *Indonesia beyond Suharto: Polity, Economy, Society, Transition.* New York, M. E. Sharpe, 1999.

Feith, Herbert. *The Decline of Constitutional Democracy in Indonesia.* Ithaca, NY, Cornell University Press, 1970.

Forrester, Geoff (Ed.). *Post-Soeharto Indonesia: Renewal or Chaos?* Singapore, Institute of Southeast Asian Studies, 1999.

Frederick, William H. *Visions and Heat: The Making of the Indonesian Revolution.* Athens, OH, Ohio University Press, 1988.

Friend, Theodore. *The Blue-eyed Enemy: Japan against the West in Java and Luzon, 1942–1945.* Princeton, NJ, Princeton University Press, 1988.

Furnivall, J. S. *Netherlands India: A Study of Plural Economy.* Cambridge, Cambridge University Press, 1939.

Gardner, Paul F. *Shared Hopes, Separate Fears: Fifty Years of US-Indonesian Relations.* Boulder, CO, Westview Press, 1997.

Geertz, Clifford. *The Religion of Java.* University of Chicago Press, 1976.

Gooszen, Hans. *A Demographic History of the Indonesian Archipelago, 1880–1942.* Singapore, Institute of Southeast Asian Studies, 2000.

Hadiwinata, Bob S. *The Politics of NGOs in Indonesia: Developing Democracy and Managing a Movement.* London, RoutledgeCurzon, 2002.

Hadiz, Vedi. *Workers and the State in New Order Indonesia.* London, Routledge, 1997.

Hall, Kenneth R. *Maritime Trade and State Development in early Southeast Asia.* Honolulu, University of Hawaii Press, 1985.

Halldorsson, Jon O. *Authoritarian Imperatives: The Political Economy of State and Democratization in Indonesia.* Richmond, Surrey, Curzon Press, 2001.

Hefner, Robert W. *Civil Islam: Muslims and Democratization in Indonesia.* Princeton, NJ, Princeton University Press, 2000.

Hill, Hal (Ed.). *Indonesia's New Order: the Dynamics of Socio-economic Transformation.* St Leonards, NSW, Allen and Unwin, 1994.

Honna, Jun. *Military and Democracy in Indonesia.* London, RoutledgeCurzon, 2002.

Hughes, John. *Indonesian Upheaval.* New York, Fawcett, 1967.

Jackson, Karl D., and Pye, Lucian W. (Eds). *Political Power and Communication in Indonesia.* Berkeley, University of California Press, 1978.

Jenkins, David. *Suharto and his Generals: Indonesian Military Politics 1975–1983.* Ithaca, NY, Cornell Modern Indonesia Project, 1984.

Jones, Gavin W., and Hull, Terence H. *Indonesia Assessment—Population and Human Resources.* Singapore, Institute of Southeast Asian Studies, 1997.

Kahin, Audrey R. (Ed.). *Regional Dynamics of the Indonesian Revolution: Unity from Diversity.* Honolulu, University of Hawaii Press, 1985.

Kahin, Audrey R., and Kahin, George McTurnan. *Subversion as Foreign Policy: The Secret Eisenhower and Dulles Debacle in Indonesia.* New York, New Press, 1995.

Kahin, George McTurnan. *Nationalism and Revolution in Indonesia.* Ithaca, NY, Cornell University Press, 1952.

Kell, Tim. *The Roots of the Acehnese Rebellion 1989–1992.* Ithaca, NY, Cornell University Southeast Asia Program, 1995.

Kingsbury, Damien (Ed.). *The Presidency of Abdurrahman Wahid: An Assessment After the First Year.* Clayton, Vic, Monash Asia Institute, 2001.

Kingsbury, Damien, and Aveling, Harry (Eds). *Autonomy and Disintegration in Indonesia.* London, RoutledgeCurzon, 2002.

Koentjaraningrat. *Javanese Culture.* Singapore, Oxford University Press, 1985.

Kumar, Ann, and McGlynn, John H. (Eds). *Illuminations: The Writing Traditions of Indonesia.* Weatherhill, 1996.

Legge, J. D. *Sukarno: A Political Biography.* Harmondsworth, Penguin, 1973.

Leifer, Michael. *Indonesia's Foreign Policy.* London, Allen and Unwin, 1983.

Leithe, Denise. *The Politics of Power: Freeport in Suharto's Indonesia.* Honolulu, University of Hawaii Press, 2002.

Lloyd, Grayson J., and Smith, Shannon L. (Eds). *Indonesia Today: Challenges of History.* Singapore, Institute of Southeast Asian Studies, 2001.

Lowry, Bob. *Indonesian Defence Policy and the Indonesian Armed Forces.* Canberra, Australian National University, 1993.

Lubis, Todung Mulya. *In Search of Human Rights: Legal-Political Dilemmas of Indonesia's New Order, 1966-1990.* Jakarta, Gramedia Pustaka Utama, 1994.

MacFarling, Ian. *The Dual Function of the Indonesian Armed Forces: Military Politics in Indonesia.* Canberra, Australian Defence Studies Centre, 1996.

Mackie, J. A. C. *Konfrontasi: The Indonesia-Malaysia Dispute, 1963–1966.* Kuala Lumpur, Oxford University Press, 1974.

Manning, Chris, and Peter Van Diermen, (Eds). *Indonesia in Transition: Social Aspects of Reformasi and Crisis.* Singapore, Institute of Southeast Asian Studies, 2000.

May, Brian. *The Indonesian Tragedy.* London, Routledge and Kegan Paul, 1978.

McDonald, Hamish. *Suharto's Indonesia.* Melbourne, Fontana, 1980.

McVey, Ruth T. *The Rise of Indonesian Communism.* Ithaca, NY, Cornell University Press, 1965.

Moertono, Soemarsaid. *State and Statecraft in Old Java: a Study of the Later Mataram Period, 16th to 19th Century.* Ithaca, NY, Cornell Modern Indonesia Project, 1974.

Mortimer, Rex (Ed.). *Showcase State: The Illusion of Indonesia's 'Accelerated Modernisation'.* Sydney, Angus and Robertson, 1973.

Mortimer, Rex. *Indonesian Communism under Sukarno: Ideology and Politics, 1959–1965.* Ithaca, NY, Cornell University Press, 1974.

Nasution, Adnan Buyung. *The Aspiration for Constitutional Government in Indonesia: A Socio-legal Study of the Indonesian Konstituante 1956–1959.* Jakarta, Pustaka Sinar Harapan, 1993.

Nishihara, Masashi. *Golkar and the Indonesian Elections of 1971.* Ithaca, NY, Cornell Modern Indonesia Project, 1972.

Oey-Gardiner, Mayling, and Bianpoen, Carla (Eds). *Indonesian Women: The Journey Continues.* Canberra, Australian National University, Research School of Pacific and Asian Studies, 2000.

O'Rourke, Kevin. *Reformasi: the Struggle for Power in post-Soeharto Indonesia.* Crow's Nest, NSW, Allen and Unwin, 2002.

Osborne, Robin. *Indonesia's Secret War: The Guerrilla Struggle in Irian Jaya.* Sydney, Allen and Unwin, 1985.

Otten, Mariël. *Transmigrasi, Myths and Realities: Indonesian Resettlement Policy, 1965–1985.* Copenhagen, International Workshop for Indigenous Affairs, 1986.

Pangaribuan, Robinson. *The Indonesian State Secretariat 1945–1993.* Perth, Murdoch University, 1995.

Pemberton, John. *On the Subject of 'Java'.* Ithaca, NY, Cornell University Press, 1994.

Penders, C. L. M. *Indonesia 1945–1962: Dutch Decolonisation and the West New Guinea Debacle.* Richmond, Surrey, Curzon Press, 2001.

Philpott, Simon. *Rethinking Indonesia: Postcolonial Theory, Authoritarianism and Identity.* New York, St Martin's Press, 2000.

Porter, Donald. *Managing Politics and Islam in Indonesia.* Richmond, Surrey, Curzon Press, 2002.

Ramage, Douglas. *Politics in Indonesia: Democracy, Islam and the Ideology of Tolerance.* London, Routledge, 1995.

Ramstedt, Martin (Ed.). *'Hinduism' in Modern Indonesia: Hindu Dharma Indonesia between Local, National and Global Interest.* Richmond, Surrey, Curzon Press, 2001.

Reeve, David. *Golkar of Indonesia: An Alternative to the Party System.* Singapore, Oxford University Press, 1985.

Reid, Anthony J. S. *The Indonesian National Revolution 1945–1950.* Hawthorn, Vic, Longmans, 1974.

Southeast Asia and the Age of Commerce, 1450–1680, Volume one: The Land Below the Winds. New Haven, CT, Yale University Press, 1988.

Southeast Asia and the Age of Commerce, 1450–1680, Volume two: Expansion and Crisis. New Haven, CT, Yale University Press, 1993.

Reuter, Thomas (Ed.). *Inequality, Crisis and Social Change in Indonesia: the Muted Worlds of Bali.* London, RoutledgeCurzon, 2002.

Ricklefs, M. C. *A History of Modern Indonesia since c. 1200.* Basingstoke, Hampshire, Palgrave Macmillan, 2001.

Robinson, Geoffrey. *The Dark Side of Paradise: Political Violence in Bali.* Ithaca, NY, Cornell University Press, 1995.

Robinson, Kathryn, and Bessell, Sharon (Eds). *Women in Indonesia: Gender, Equity and Development.* Singapore, Institute of Southeast Asian Studies, 2002.

Roeder, O. G. *The Smiling General: President Soeharto of Indonesia.* Jakarta, Gunung Agung, 1969.

Romano, Angela. *Politics and the Press in Indonesia: Understanding an Evolving Political Culture.* Richmond, Surrey, Curzon Press, 2002.

Rosser, Andrew. *The Politics of Liberalization in Indonesia: State, Market and Power.* Richmond, Surrey, Curzon Press, 2001.

Sajoo, Amyn B. *Pluralism in 'Old Societies and New States': Emerging ASEAN Contexts.* Singapore, Institute of Southeast Asian Studies, 1994.

Salim, Arskal, and Azra, Azyumardi (Eds). *Shari'a and Politics in Modern Indonesia.* Singapore, Institute of Southeast Asian Studies, 2002.

Saltford, John. *The United Nations and the Indonesian Takeover of West Papua, 1962–1969: the Anatomy of a Betrayal.* Richmond, Surrey, Curzon Press, 2002.

Schwarz, Adam. *A Nation in Waiting: Indonesia in the 1990s.* St Leonards, NSW, Allen and Unwin, 1994.

Sen, Krishna, and Hill, David T. *Media,Culture and Politics in Indonesia.* Melbourne, Oxford University Press, 2000.

Singh, Bilveer. *ABRI and the Security of Southeast Asia: The Role and Thinking of General L. Benny Murdani.* Singapore Institute of International Affairs, 1994.

Sjamsuddin, Nazaruddin. *The Republican Revolt: a Study of the Acehnese Rebellion.* Singapore, Institute of Southeast Asian Studies, 1985.

Smith, Anthony L. *Strategic Centrality: Indonesia's Changing Role in ASEAN.* Singapore, Institute of Southeast Asian Studies, 2000.

Soesastro, Hadi, Smith, Anthony L., and Ling, Han Mui (Eds). *Governance in Indonesia: Challenges Facing the Megawati Presidency.* Singapore, Institute of Southeast Asian Studies, 2002.

Southwood, Julie, and Flanagan, Patrick. *Indonesia: Law, Propaganda and Terror.* London, Zed Books, 1983.

Sukma, Rizal. *Islam in Indonesian Foreign Policy: Domestic Weakness and Dilemma of Dual Identity.* London, Routledge, 2001.

Indonesia and China: The Politics of a Troubled Relationship. London, Routledge, 1999.

Sundhaussen, Ulf. *The Road to Power: Indonesian Military Politics 1945–1967.* Kuala Lumpur, Oxford University Press, 1982.

Suryadinata, Leo. *Political Parties and the 1982 General Election in Indonesia.* Singapore, Institute of Southeast Asian Studies, 1982.

Elections and Politics in Indonesia. Singapore, Institute of Southeast Asian Studies, 2001.

Sutherland, Heather. *The Making of a Bureaucratic Elite: the Colonial Transformation of the Javanese Priyayi.* Singapore, Heinemann, 1979.

Tan, T. K. (Ed.). *Sukarno's Guided Indonesia.* Brisbane, Jacaranda Press, 1967.

Taylor, Jean Gelman. *The Social World of Batavia: European and Eurasian in Dutch Asia.* Madison, WI, University of Wisconsin Press, 1983.

Thoolen, Hans (Ed.). *Indonesia and the Rule of Law: Twenty Years of 'New Order' Government.* London, Pinter, 1987.

Toer, Pramoedya Ananta. *This Earth of Mankind.* Ringwood, Vic, Penguin, 1982.

Child of All Nations. Ringwood, Vic, Penguin, 1984.

The Mute's Soliloquy: A Memoir by Pramoedya Ananta Toer. New York, NY, Hyperion, 1999.

Uhlin, Anders. *Indonesia and the 'Third Wave of Democratization': The Indonesian Pro-Democracy Movement in a Changing World.* Richmond, Curzon Press, 1998.

van Dijk, C. *Rebellion under the Banner of Islam: the Darul Islam in Indonesia.* The Hague, Martinus Nijhoff, 1981.

A Country in Despair: Indonesia between 1997 and 2000. Leiden, KITLV Press, 2001.

Vatikiotis, Michael R. J. *Indonesian Politics Under Suharto: Order, Development and Pressure for Change.* London and New York, Routledge, 1993.

Vickers, Adrian. *Bali: a Paradise Created.* Ringwood, Vic, Penguin, 1989.

Vlekke, Bernard H. M. *Nusantara, a History of the East Indian Archipelago.* Cambridge, MA, Harvard University Press, 1945.

Way, Wendy (Ed.). *Australia and the Indonesian Incorporation of Portuguese Timor, 1974-1976.* Carlton, Vic, Melbourne University Press, 2000.

Weatherbee, Donald E. *Ideology in Indonesia: Sukarno's Indonesian Revolution.* New Haven, CT, Yale University Southeast Asian Studies, 1966.

Weinstein, Franklin B. *Indonesian Foreign Policy and the Dilemma of Dependence: from Sukarno to Suharto.* Ithaca, NY, Cornell University Press, 1974.

Wertheim, W. F. *Indonesian Society in Transition.* The Hague, van Hoeve, 2nd Edn, 1959.

Wessel, Ingrid, and Wimhöfer, Georgia (Eds). *Violence in Indonesia.* Hamburg, Abera, 2001.

Wiener, Margaret J. *Visible and Invisible Realms: Power, Magic and the Colonial Conquest of Bali.* Chicago, University of Chicago Press, 1995.

ECONOMY

Alexander, P., Boomgaard, P., and White, B. *In the Shadow of Agriculture: Non-farm Activities in the Javanese Economy, Past and Present.* Amsterdam, Royal Tropical Institute, 1991.

Anmar, M. A., and Omura, K. (Eds). *Local Development in Indonesia.* Tokyo, Institute of Developing Economies, 1994.

Arndt, H. W. *The Indonesian Economy: Collected Papers.* Singapore, Chopmen Publishers, 1983.

Arndt, H. W., and Hill, Hal. *Southeast Asia's Economic Crisis—Origins, Lessons and the Way Forward.* Singapore, Institute of Southeast Asian Studies, 1999.

Australian National University. *Bulletin of Indonesian Economic Studies.* Canberra, 3 a year.

Bank Indonesia. *Report for the Financial Year.* Jakarta, annually.

Barlow, Colin, and Hardjono, Joan (Eds). *Indonesia Assessment 1995: Development in Eastern Indonesia.* Singapore, Institute of Southeast Asian Studies, 1996.

Binhadi. *Financial Sector Deregulation, Banking Development and Monetary Policy: The Indonesian Experience (1983–1993).* Jakarta, Indonesian Bankers' Institute, 1995.

Booth, A. *Agricultural Development in Indonesia.* Sydney, Wellington and London, Allen and Unwin, 1988.

Booth, A. (Ed.). *The Oil Boom and After: Indonesian Economic Policy and Performance in the Soeharto Era.* Singapore, Oxford University Press, 1992.

Booth, A., and McCawley, P. (Eds). *The Indonesian Economy during the Soeharto Era.* Kuala Lumpur, Oxford University Press, 1981.

Booth, A., O'Malley, W. J., and Weidemann, A. (Eds). *Indonesian Economic History of the Dutch Colonial Era.* New Haven, CT, Yale University Press, 1988.

Bresnan, John. *Managing Indonesia—The Modern Political Economy.* New York, Columbia University Press, 1993.

Chalmers, Ian, and Hadiz, Vedi (Eds). *The Politics of Economic Development in Indonesia: Contending Perspectives.* London, Routledge, 1997.

Cole, David C., and Slade, Betty F. *Building a Modern Financial System—The Indonesian Experience.* Cambridge, Cambridge University Press, 1996.

Cribb, Robert (Ed.). *The Late Colonial State in Indonesia: Political and Economic Foundations of the Netherlands Indies, 1880–1942.* Leiden, KITLV Press, 1994.

Dick, H. *The Indonesian Interisland Shipping Industry: An Analysis of Competition and Regulation.* Singapore, Institute of Southeast Asian Studies, 1987.

Dick, H., Fox, J. J., and Mackie, J. A. C. *Balanced Development: East Java in the New Order.* Singapore, Oxford University Press, 1993.

Dickie, R. B., and Layman, T. A. *Foreign Investment and Government Policy in the Third World: Forging Common Interests in Indonesia and Beyond.* London, Macmillan, 1988.

Dirkse, J. P., et al. (Eds). *Development and Social Welfare: Indonesia's Experiences Under the New Order.* Leiden, KITLV Press, 1993.

Drake, C. *National Integration in Indonesia: Patterns and Policies.* Honolulu, University of Hawaii Press, 1989.

Economist Intelligence Unit. *Country Forecast: Indonesia.* London, quarterly.

Country Profile: Indonesia. London, annually.

Country Report: Indonesia. London, quarterly.

Quarterly Economic Review: Indonesia. London, quarterly.

Faulkner, George. *Business Indonesia: A Practical Insight into Doing Business in Indonesia.* Sydney, Business & Professional Publishing, 1995.

Fenton, Robert. *The Indonesian Plywood Industry: A Study of the Statistical Base, the Value-added Effects and the Forest Impact.* Singapore, Institute of Southeast Asian Studies, 1996.

Financial Times Business Information Ltd. *Banking in the Far East 1993: Structures and Sources of Finance.* London, 1993.

Gérard, Françoise, and Ruf, François (Eds). *Agriculture in Crisis: People, Commodities and Natural Resources in Indonesia 1996–2001.* Richmond, Surrey, Curzon Press, 2001.

Glover, David, and Jessup, Timothy (Eds). *Indonesia's Fires and Haze—The Cost of Catastrophe.* Singapore, Institute of Southeast Asian Studies, 1999.

Goeltom, Miranda S. *Indonesia's Financial Liberalization: An Analysis of 1981–88 Panel Data.* Singapore, Institute of Southeast Asian Studies, 1995.

Hardjono, J. M. *Transmigration in Indonesia.* Kuala Lumpur, Oxford University Press, 1977.

Hardjono, J. M. (Ed.). *Indonesia: Resources, Ecology and Environment.* Singapore, Oxford University Press, 1991.

Hayami, Yujiro, and Kawagoe, Toshihito. *The Agrarian Origins of Commerce and Industry: A Study of Peasant Marketing in Indonesia.* New York, St Martins Press, 1993.

Heij, Gitte. *Tax Administration and Compliance in Indonesia.* Murdoch University, Western Australia, Asia Research Centre on Social, Political and Economic Change, 1994.

Hicks, G. L., and McNicoll, G. *The Indonesian Economy, 1950–67: A Bibliography.* New Haven, CT, Yale University Press, 1968.

Hill, Hal. *Foreign Investment and Industrialization in Indonesia.* Singapore, Oxford University Press, 1988.

'Indonesia's Textile and Garment Industries: Developments in an Asian Perspective'. *Occasional Paper No. 87.* Singapore, Institute of Southeast Asian Studies, 1992.

The Indonesian Economy since 1966: Southeast Asia's Emerging Giant. Melbourne, Cambridge University Press, 1996.

Indonesia's Industrial Transformation. Singapore, Institute of Southeast Asian Studies, 1997.

The Indonesian Economy in Crisis—Causes, Consequences and Lessons. Singapore, Institute of Southeast Asian Studies, 1999.

The Indonesian Economy. Cambridge, Cambridge University Press, 2000.

Hill, Hal (Ed.). *Unity and Diversity: Regional Economic Development in Indonesia since 1970.* Singapore, Oxford University Press, 1989.

Hill, Hal, and Thee Kian Wie. *Indonesia Assessment—Indonesia's Technological Challenge.* Singapore, Institute of Southeast Asian Studies, 1998.

Hoadley, Mason C. *Towards a Feudal Mode of Production in West Java, 1680–1800.* Singapore, Institute of Southeast Asian Studies, 1994.

Hobohm, S. O. H. *Indonesia to 1991: Can Momentum be Regained?* London, Economist Intelligence Unit, 1987.

Indonesia to 1993: Breakthrough in the Balance. London, Economist Intelligence Unit, 1989.

Khatkhate, Deena. 'The Regulatory Impediments to the Private Industrial Sector Development in Asia—A Comparative Study'. *World Bank Discussion Paper 177.* Washington, DC, World Bank, 1993.

Li, Tania (Ed.). *Transforming the Indonesian Uplands: Marginality, Power and Production.* Singapore, Institute of Southeast Asian Studies, 1999.

Lindblad, J. Th. *Historical Foundations of a National Economy in Indonesia, 1890s–1990s.* Amsterdam, North Holland and the Royal Netherlands Academy of Arts and Sciences, 1996.

MacIntyre, Andrew. *Business and Politics in Indonesia.* Sydney, Allen and Unwin, in association with the Asian Studies Association of Australia, 1991.

Mackie, J. A. C. *The Indonesian Economy: 1950–1963.* In *Studien zur Entwicklung in Süd- und Ostasien, Neue Folge, Teil 3, Indonesien.* Frankfurt am Main, Berlin, Alfred Metzner Verlag, 1964.

Maddison, A., and Prince, G. (Eds). *Economic Growth in Indonesia 1820–1940.* Dordrecht, Foris Publications, 1989.

Mann, Richard. *Economic Crisis in Indonesia—The Full Story.* Jakarta, Gateway Books, 1998.

Plots & Schemes that brought down Soeharto. Jakarta, Gateway Books, 1998.

Business in Indonesia—Changes, Challenges, Opportunities. Jakarta, Gateway Books, 1999.

Manning, Chris. *Indonesian Labour in Transition: An East Asian Success Story?* Cambridge, Cambridge University Press, 1998.

Manning, C., and Hardjono, J. (Eds). *Indonesia Assessment 1993—Labour: Sharing in the Benefits of Growth?* Canberra, Australian National University, 1993.

Manning, Chris, and Van Diermen (Eds). *Indonesia in Transition: Social Aspects of Reformasi and Crisis.* Singapore, Institute of Southeast Asian Studies, 2000.

Martokoesoemo, S.B. *Beyond the Frontiers of Indonesian Banking and Finance: Financial Intermediation to Mobilize the Potential of Small Entrepreneurs.* Rotterdam, Labyrint Publication, 1993.

McLeod, Ross H. *Indonesia's Crisis and Future Prospects.* In Karl D. Jackson (Ed.). *Asian Contagion—The Causes and Consequences of a Financial Crisis.* Singapore, Institute of Southeast Asian Studies, 1999.

Indonesia. In Ross H. McLeod and Ross Garnaut (Eds). *East Asia in Crisis—From Being a Miracle to Needing One.* London, Routledge, 1998.

McLeod, Ross H. (Ed.). *Indonesia Assessment 1994: Finance as a Key Sector in Indonesia's Development.* Canberra, Australian National University, and Singapore, Institute of Southeast Asian Studies, 1994.

Mears, L. A. *Rice Marketing in the Republic of Indonesia.* Jakarta, PT Pembangunan, 1961.

The New Rice Economy of Indonesia. Yogyakarta, Gadjah Mada University Press, 1981.

Montes, Manuel F., and Abdusalamov, Muhammad Ali. *Indonesia: Reaping the Market.* In K. S. Jomo (Ed.). Tigers in Trouble—Financial Governance, Liberalisation and Crises in East Asia. London, Zed Books, 1998.

Montes, Manuel. *The Currency Crisis in Southeast Asia.* Singapore, Institute of Southeast Asian Studies, 1999.

Mortimer, R. (Ed.). *Showcase State: The Illusion of Indonesia's 'Accelerated Modernization'.* Sydney, Angus and Robertson, 1973.

Palmer, Ingrid. *The Indonesian Economy since 1965: A Case Study of Political Economy.* London, Frank Cass, 1977.

Pangestu, Mari, and Sato, Yuri. *Waves of Change in Indonesia's Manufacturing Industry.* Tokyo, Institute of Developing Economies, 1997.

Patten, R. H., and Rosengard, J. K. *Progress with Profits: The Development of Rural Banking in Indonesia.* San Francisco, International Centre for Economic Growth and Harvard Institute for International Development, 1991.

Pearson, Scott, et al. *Rice Policy in Indonesia.* Ithaca, NY, and London, Cornell University Press, 1991.

Penny, D. H., and Singarimbun. *Population and Poverty in Rural Java: Some Economic Arithmetic from Sriharjo.* Ithaca, NY, Cornell University, 1973.

Pierce, Carol J., and Resosudarmo, Ida Pradnja (Eds). *Which Way Forward? Forests, Policy and People in Indonesia.* Singapore, Institute of Southeast Asian Studies, 2002.

Piggott, R. R., et al. *Food Price Policy in Indonesia.* Canberra, Australian Centre for International Agricultural Research, 1993.

Poot, H., Kuyvenhoven, A., and Jansen, J. *Industrialization and Trade in Indonesia.* Yogyakarta, Gadjah Mada University Press, 1990.

Prawiro, Radius. *Indonesia's Struggle for Economic Development—Pragmatism in Action.* Kuala Lumpur, Oxford University Press, 1998.

Robison, R. *Indonesia: The Rise of Capital.* Sydney, Allen and Unwin, 1986.

Power and Economy in Suharto's Indonesia. Manila and Wollongong, Journal of Contemporary Asia Publishers, 1990.

Singh, Bilveer. *The Indonesian Military Business Complex: Origins, Course and Future.* Canberra, Strategic and Defence Studies Centre, Australian National University, 2001.

Smith, Anthony L. (Ed.). *Gus Dur and the Indonesian Economy.* Singapore, Institute of Southeast Asian Studies, 2001.

Smith, Shannon L. D. *Indonesian Political Economy: Developing Batam.* Singapore, Institute of Southeast Asian Studies, 2001.

Soemardjan, S. *Indonesia: A Socio-Economic Profile.* New Delhi, Sterling Publishers, 1988.

Sousa Saldanha, João Mariano de. *The Political Economy of East Timor Development.* Translated by Theresia Slamet and P. G. Kattopo. Jakarta, Pustaka Sinar Harapan, 1994.

Thee Kian Wie and Yoshihara, K. 'Foreign and Domestic Capital in Indonesian Industrialization' in *Southeast Asian Studies* Vol 24, No. 4, March 1987.

Thorbecke, Erik, et al. *Adjustment and Equity in Indonesia.* Paris, OECD Development Centre Studies, 1992.

Turner, Sarah. *Indonesia's Small Entrepreneurs: Trading on the Margins.* London, RoutledgeCurzon, 2002.

United Nations Industrial Development Organization (UNIDO). *Indonesia: Industrial Development Review.* London, Economist Intelligence Unit, 1993.

Van Dierman, Peter. *Small Business in Indonesia.* Aldershot, Ashgate, 1997.

Winters, Jeffrey A. *Power in Motion: Capital Mobility and the Indonesian State.* Ithaca, NY, Cornell University Press, 1996.

Woo, W. T., Glassburner, B., and Nasution, A. *Macroeconomic Policies, Crises, and Long-Term Growth in Indonesia, 1965–90.* Washington, DC, World Bank, 1994.

JAPAN

Physical and Social Geography

JOHN SARGENT

The archipelago comprising Japan, or Nihon Koku (Land of the Rising Sun), lies to the east of the Asian mainland in an arc stretching from latitude 45° N to latitude 24° N, covering a land area of 377,855 sq km (145,891 sq miles). The Tsushima Strait, which separates Japan from Korea, is about 190 km wide, while 800 km of open sea lie between Japan and the nearest point on the coast of the Chinese mainland. Four large and closely grouped islands—Hokkaido, Honshu, Shikoku, and Kyushu—constitute 98% of the territory of Japan, the remainder being made up by numerous smaller islands.

PHYSICAL FEATURES

The Japanese islands belong to a belt of recent mountain-building which extends around the rim of the Pacific Ocean, and which is characterized by frequent volcanic activity and crustal movement. Around the fringes of the western Pacific, this belt takes the form of a complex series of island arcs, stretching southwards from the Aleutians and including Japan. In the Japanese islands, the Kurile, Kamchatka, Bonin, Ryukyu and Korean arcs converge. Where two or more of these major arcs meet, as in Hokkaido and in central Honshu, conspicuous knots of highland occur. In the latter area, the Japan Alps, which rise to more than 3,000 m above sea-level, form the highest terrain in the country, although the highest single peak, Mt Fuji (3,776 m), is an extinct volcano unrelated to the fold mountains of the Alps.

Three major zones of active volcanoes and hot springs occur: in Hokkaido, in northern and central Honshu, and in southern Kyushu. Further evidence of crustal instability is provided by the occurrence, each year, of over a thousand earth tremors. Earthquakes strong enough to cause damage to buildings are, however, less frequent, and occur, on average, once every five years.

While the major arcs determine the basic alignment of the main mountain ranges, complex folding and faulting has resulted in an intricate mosaic of landform types, in which rugged, forested mountains alternate with small pockets of intensively cultivated lowland.

In the mountains, short, fast-flowing torrents, fed by melt-water in the spring and by heavy rains in the summer, have carved a landscape which is characterized by steep and sharply angled slopes. Narrow, severely eroded ridges predominate and rounded surfaces are rare. Although the mountain torrents provide many opportunities for the generation of hydroelectric power, marked seasonal changes in precipitation cause wide fluctuations in the rate of flow, and consequently hinder the efficient operation of hydroelectric plant throughout the year.

The extreme scarcity of level land is one of the salient features of the geography of Japan. In a country where the population was the eighth largest in the world in mid-1998, only 15% of the total land area is cultivable. Thus, the small areas of lowland, which contain not only most of the cultivated land but also all the major concentrations of population and industry, are of vital importance.

Most Japanese lowlands consist of small coastal plains which have been formed through the regular deposition of river-borne alluvium. On encountering the low-lying land of the coastal plain, the typical torrent becomes a sluggish river which meanders across the gently sloping surface of the plain, to terminate in a shallow estuary. The river bed is usually raised above the surface of the surrounding plain, and the braided channel is contained by levees, both man-made and natural. Most alluvial plains are bounded inland by rugged upland, and many are flanked by discontinuous benches of old and poorly consolidated alluvial material. None of the alluvial plains of Japan is extensive: the Kanto, which is the largest, has an area of only 12,800 sq km. Many plains are merely small pockets of nearly level land, closely hemmed in by the sea and the steeply sloping mountains.

The coastline of Japan is long and intricate. On the Pacific coast, where major faults cut across the prevailing grain of the land, large bays, flanked by relatively extensive alluvial plains, are conspicuous features. Three of these bay-head plains—the Kanto, the Nobi and the Kansai—contain more than one-third of the population of the country, and more than one-half of its industrial output. Further west along the Pacific coast, two narrow channels lead into the sheltered waters of the Inland Sea, which occupies a zone of subsidence between Shikoku and western Honshu. By contrast with the Pacific coasts, the Japan Sea coastline is fairly smooth. The overall insularity of Japan may be indicated by reference to the fact that very few parts of the country are more than 100 km from the sea.

CLIMATE

While relief conditions in Japan often impose severe limits upon economic activity, climatic conditions are, on the whole, more favourable. Japanese summers are of sufficient warmth and humidity to allow the widespread cultivation of paddy rice; yet cold, dry winters clearly differentiate Japan from those countries of subtropical and tropical Asia, where constant heat prohibits prolonged human effort.

The climate of Japan, like the climates of the rest of Monsoon Asia, is characterized by a marked seasonal alternation in the direction of the prevailing winds. In winter, in association with the establishment of a centre of high atmospheric pressure over Siberia, cold, dry air masses flow outwards from the continent. During their passage over the Japan Sea, these air masses are warmed in their lower layers, and pick up moisture, which, when the air masses rise on contact with the Japanese coast, is precipitated in the form of snow. Thus, winter weather along the Japan Sea coastlands is dull, cloudy and characterized by heavy falls of snow. By contrast, the Pacific side of the country experiences cold, dry weather, with low amounts of cloud. Near the Pacific coast, winter temperatures are ameliorated by the influence of the warm Kuro Shio sea current.

Besides this contrast between the two sides of the country, a latitudinal variation in temperature, similar to that of the Atlantic seaboard of the USA, is also apparent. Thus, north of latitude 38° N, average January temperatures fall below 0°C, and reach −10°C in Hokkaido. In this northern zone, winter weather conditions prohibit the double cropping that is elsewhere characteristic of Japanese agriculture. South of latitude 38° N, January temperatures gradually rise, reaching 4°C at Tokyo, and 6°C at Kagoshima in southern Kyushu.

After mid-March, the winter pattern of atmospheric circulation begins to change, with high pressure developing over the Aleutians, and low pressure over Siberia. In association with these unstable conditions, the first of the two annual rainfall maxima occurs, with the onset of the Bai-u rains in June. By July, however, the high pressure centre to the east of Japan has fully developed, and, with low pressure prevailing over the continent, a south-easterly flow of warm, moist air covers the entire country. On the Pacific coast, August temperatures rise to over 26°C, and the weather becomes unpleasantly hot and humid. To the north, however, August temperatures are lower, reaching only 18°C in Hokkaido.

In late August and early September the Pacific high pressure centre begins to weaken, and the second rainfall maximum occurs, with the arrival of typhoons, or tropical cyclones, which travel northwards to Japan from the equatorial regions of the Pacific Ocean. These severe storms, which frequently coincide with the rice harvest, cause widespread damage. By October, high pressure has again developed over Siberia, and the north-westerly winter monsoon is consequently re-established.

Annual precipitation in Japan varies from 850 mm in eastern Hokkaido to more than 3,000 mm in the mountains of central Honshu, and in those parts of the Pacific coast which are fully exposed to the force of the late summer typhoons.

RESOURCES

Although about 67% of the total area of Japan is forested, not all of the forest cover is commercially valuable, and large areas of woodland must be preserved to prevent soil erosion. Because many houses are still built of wood, the demand for timber is high, and the domestic output is supplemented by imports.

In terms of value, and also of volume, the Japanese fish catch is one of the world's largest. Seafood provides a large proportion of the protein content of the average Japanese diet, and demand is therefore high. Rich fishing grounds occur in both the Japan Sea and the Pacific Ocean to the east of Japan.

Japan has few mineral resources, and industry is heavily dependent upon imported raw materials and fuels. Japan's coal is of poor to medium quality, and seams are thin and badly faulted. The two main coalfields are located towards the extremities of the country, in Hokkaido and in northern Kyushu. Japanese coal deposits are particularly weak in coking coal, much of which is imported, mainly from the USA and Australia. The small Japanese oilfields, which are located in north-east Honshu, supply a minimal percentage of domestic fuel demand. Japan is heavily dependent on foreign iron ores, imported mainly from Australia, Brazil and India. Many other minerals are mined, but none exists in large quantities. Japan is self-sufficient only in limestone and sulphur.

POPULATION

In 1867, on the eve of modernization, the population of Japan was already approximately 30m., a level at which it had remained, with little fluctuation, for the preceding 150 years. With industrialization, the population increased rapidly and by 1930 had reached 65m. After the Second World War, the population policy initiated by the Japanese Government succeeded in drastically lowering the rate of population increase, and during the second half of the 20th century the growth rate closely corresponded to the rates prevailing in Western Europe. In the early 21st century, however, Japan's fertility rate continued to decline steadily, prompting the authorities to express concern.

The population of Japan, according to census results, was 126,925,843 on 1 October 2000. By mid-2002 the population had risen to an estimated 127,450,000, representing an average density of 337.3 persons per sq km. Only 15% of Japan's land area is cultivable lowland, and the population density in these areas is among the highest in the world. Three conspicuous urban-industrial concentrations are centred upon Tokyo, Osaka and Nagoya. Japan is by far the most urbanized country in Asia. Tokyo, the capital of Japan and one of the largest cities in the world, had an estimated population of 8,135,000 on 1 October 2000.

Apart from the very small number of Ainu (a people who exhibit certain Caucasian characteristics), the Japanese population has been, since early times, ethnically and linguistically uniform. The racial origins of the Japanese remain conjectural, but both Mongol and southern Pacific strains are apparent in the present-day population.

History up to 1952

RICHARD STORRY

ANTIQUITY AND THE MIDDLE AGES

It is generally agreed that the ancestors of the Japanese must have been immigrants from the mainland of Asia. It is also claimed that there was probably some migration to Japan from the islands of South-East Asia, but the whole subject is still one of pure conjecture. What does seem undeniable is that the forebears of the small and dwindling Ainu communities of Hokkaido once occupied the whole country and were in fact the original inhabitants. Be that as it may, an elaborate mythology surrounds the origins of Japan and the Japanese. This declares, for example, that the country itself was created by the gods, and that the first Emperor, Jimmu (c. 660 BC), was a direct descendant, in the fifth generation, of the sun goddess.

Yamato Period

At all events, it seems probable that the invading immigrants from Asia, who no doubt crossed over from Korea, gradually forced their way eastward from Kyushu along the shores of the Inland Sea, until, around the beginning of the Christian era, they found themselves in the fertile Kansai plain (the modern Kyoto-Osaka region). Here, in the Yamato district, they established an ordered society under chieftains who became priest-kings, dedicated to the cult of the Sun.

This early Japanese society was profoundly influenced by the civilizations of Korea and China. The Chinese ideographic script is only one important and very striking example of many cultural importations from or through Korea. Of even greater significance was the introduction of Buddhism in the sixth century AD. It was at this stage that the existing body of religious practices, associated with sun worship and animism, became known as Shinto, or 'The Way of the Gods'. Neither the theology of Buddhism, nor the ethics of Confucianism (another import from the continent) made Shinto superfluous. Old beliefs existed side by side with the new; and in course of time, as one would expect, Chinese ideas of religion, of morality, of artistic excellence, of good government, of sound agriculture, were adapted to Japanese conditions and thus underwent a degree of change in the process.

Nara and Heian Periods

At the beginning of the eighth century Nara became the capital, being built on the contemporary Chinese model. This was the heyday of the early Buddhist sects in Japan; and the splendid temples surviving at Nara have a particular interest today, since they are the best remaining examples anywhere of Chinese architecture of the Tang period. Nara was intended to be a permanent capital. This was, in fact, Heian-kyo, later to be known as Kyoto, founded in 794 and constructed, like Nara, on the model of the Chinese capital. It was to be the home of the Japanese imperial family until 1868. The establishment of this city marks the opening of the Heian age (794–1185), a period remarkable for the artistic sophistication of the court and metropolitan aristocracy.

By the middle of the 12th century effective power in Kyoto was in the hands of a warrior household, the Taira. Their great rivals were another family, the Minamoto. At first the Taira carried all before them; and Kiyomori, the head of the family, ruled Japan in the Emperor's name for a generation. After his death in 1181, however, the tables were turned; and in a final battle, in 1185, the Minamoto annihilated their enemies. Thereafter the leader of the Minamoto, Yoritomo, set up a new system of government, known as the *Bakufu* (literally 'camp office'), at Kamakura in the east of the country, far from the imperial capital. The Emperor gave Yoritomo the title *Sei-i Tai Shogun*, or 'Barbarian-subduing Generalissimo'—usually abbreviated, in Western use, as 'Shogun'.

Kamakura Period

The original purpose of Yoritomo's *Bakufu* was the control and administration of the Japanese warrior class, which was now a distinct entity, and one that was rapidly becoming all-powerful in society. The Japanese fighting man was already a member of an élite class by the 12th century. The true rulers of the country from that time forward, until the late 19th century, would tend nearly always to belong to the warrior class. Not for a moment did this class seek to overthrow the imperial dynasty. The idea was indeed unthinkable, since the

Emperor's line was descended from the sun goddess. So ceremonious respect was always paid to the Kyoto court; but it was exceptional, and usually a sign of uncharacteristic weakness, for any warrior administration to allow the reality of power to slip back into the hands of the imperial household. Every Shogun governed in the Emperor's name and received his appointment from the Emperor.

The Kamakura *Bakufu* lasted until well into the 14th century. Yoritomo was a man of exceptional energy, organizing ability, and ruthlessness, who did not hesitate to pursue a vendetta against his own younger half-brother Yoshitsune, who as a military commander had been chiefly responsible for the ultimate defeat of the Taira. Yoritomo died in 1199. His successors in the office of Shogun were leaders of inferior calibre, and the *Bakufu* was run by the house of Hojo, related to the Minamoto by marriage. It was the Hojo who rallied the country in resistance to the Mongol invasions of 1274 and 1281. Japanese martial courage was a vital element in the discomfiture of the invaders; but the decisive factor, both in 1274 and 1281, seems to have been the storms which wrecked the Mongol ships lying off the coast. With some justice the Japanese described the great typhoon of 1281 as a *kami-kaze*, or 'divine wind'.

Some 50 years later both the Hojo family and the Kamakura *Bakufu* were overthrown in the course of a civil war. The climax occurred in 1331 when, with their enemies overrunning Kamakura, the Hojo and their supporters—more than 800 in all—committed *seppuku*, the formal term for the act of *hara-kiri*, the warrior's suicide by self-disembowelling.

Muromachi Period

Over the succeeding 250 years and more there was great disorder, including much bitter fighting in and near Kyoto. A new *Bakufu* was established, this time in the Muromachi district of the capital, with members of the Ashikaga house (of the Minamoto line) holding office as Shogun. From the fall of Kamakura to the latter half of the 16th century political events, so often shaped by domestic warfare, were extremely complicated. This period was marked not only by civil war but also by economic growth and artistic achievement. The breakdown of central government gave at least some provincial lords the freedom and incentive to embark on foreign trade on their own account, especially with China. One consequence of this commerce was a substantial importation in the 15th century of copper cash from China, which promoted the growth of money instead of rice as a medium for exchange. At the same time painting, classical drama, architecture, landscape gardening, ceramics, the tea ceremony, flower arrangement—a great deal of what is recognized today as Japan's magnificent cultural heritage—blossomed in these stormy years. Here Zen Buddhism, in all its manifestations, played a central part. Japan presented a paradoxical scene of savagery and civilization, of barbarism and beauty, intertwined.

TOKUGAWA RULE

Effective central government and internal peace were not finally secured until the early years of the 17th century, after Ieyasu founded the Tokugawa *Bakufu* in Yedo (the modern Tokyo), giving the whole country a domestic order that would endure until the coming of US and European men-of-war in the 1850s. Tokugawa Ieyasu built on the work already performed by two notable captains, Oda Nobunaga (1534–82) and Toyotomi Hideyoshi (1536–98). The former contrived, before his death, to unify about one-half of the provinces of Japan. Hideyoshi, the son of a foot-soldier, was one of Nobunaga's commanders. Within 10 years of Nobunaga's death he made himself master of the whole country, with the help of a wise and cautious ally, Tokugawa Ieyasu.

The 'Closed Country'

After Hideyoshi's death Ieyasu lost little time in making his own position supreme. He defeated his most formidable rivals in battle in 1600, and three years later he was appointed Shogun by the Emperor. The history of Japan in Ashikaga days taught him, no doubt, the lesson that the Shogun's government was best conducted, like Yoritomo's regime, well away from Kyoto. At any rate, he made Yedo Castle the headquarters of his administration.

Ieyasu and his immediate descendants adopted a number of important measures to buttress the dominant position of the Tokugawa house (a branch of the seemingly indestructible Minamoto line). Careful watch at all times was kept on those lords considered to be unreliable. Yet a more effective way of controlling all feudatories was the rule, strictly enforced, that they spend part of every year in the Shogun's capital at Yedo. It was also decreed that when a lord returned to his own province he must leave his wife and family behind him, in Yedo.

Moreover, the Tokugawa *Bakufu* adopted a policy of severe national isolation. From 1628 only the Chinese and Dutch were allowed in, as traders, and their commerce was confined to the port of Nagasaki, where the handful of Dutch merchants was restricted to the tiny island of Deshima. No other foreigners were granted access. No Japanese was permitted to go abroad. Vessels above a certain tonnage could not be built. The modest foreign trade at Nagasaki was a Tokugawa monopoly, controlled by officials appointed by Yedo.

This situation, known as *sakoku* or the 'closed country', was not broken until 1853 and 1854, when Cdre Matthew Perry's squadron of US warships visited Yedo (now Tokyo) Bay. On his second visit Perry secured *Bakufu* consent to the opening of two ports and the acceptance, at a future date, of a resident US consul. The door having been forced ajar, it was soon widened. Other powers lost no time in following the example of the USA, and a decade after Perry's expedition a community of foreign diplomats and traders had settled on Japanese soil.

While none of Japan's leaders really welcomed this intrusion by the West, some were implacable in their hostility, insisting that the 'barbarians' be expelled. Others perceived the weakness of their country and argued that it must come to terms with the situation, learning the techniques of modern Western civilization. Only then would Japan attain the necessary power to hold its own. At the cost of much humiliation—a great deal of pride had to be swallowed—the second, more realistic, course was adopted as the national policy.

THE RISE OF IMPERIAL JAPAN

Modernization followed the domestic transformation known as the Meiji Restoration. The Tokugawa Shogunate had lost face from the moment the first concessions were made to Perry and other intruders. Eventually, in 1868, the much weakened *Bakufu* was overthrown by provincial lords from the south-west, acting in concert and impelled by a coalition of their own most vigorous, far-sighted, warrior retainers. The Emperor, still in his teens, was persuaded to leave Kyoto for Yedo, which was renamed Tokyo and became the new capital. Nominally, full governing powers were 'restored' to the ancient monarchy, but the young Emperor, Meiji, reigned rather than governed. Real power was exercised by an oligarchy composed almost entirely of the provincial warriors (all of them young or still in the prime of life) who had engineered the downfall of the Shogunate. These men, the Meiji modernizers, dominated Japanese politics, actively or from their retirement, for the best part of 50 years. The pace of modernization, with the abolition of so many cherished customs and privileges, inevitably gave acute offence to many conservatives. There was more than one unsuccessful armed rising against the Government in the decade following the Restoration of 1868.

The heritage of Confucian ethics, with their strong emphasis on loyalty to seniors and superiors, fortified the traditions of Shinto, with its veneration of the imperial house, in sustaining a spirit of harmony and hard work, deeply influencing the great majority of the people. Educational indoctrination played a significant part here. The Meiji Government founded an impressive structure of schools, colleges and universities. In 1890 the Emperor issued his famous *Rescript on Education*, an exhortation commending the nation's fundamental ethical code to all young people. The Rescript, stressing the patriotic virtues of obedience and self-sacrifice, was read aloud in all schools on days of national festival and commemoration.

A constitution promulgated in 1889, setting up a bicameral legislature, represented a concession by the oligarchy to the growing demand for some form of national legislative assembly. However, the powers of the Diet (as the new legislature was known) were modest. Nevertheless, the party leaders in the Diet soon became a serious irritant to the Government.

Wars with China and Russia

Domestic political squabbles, however, were put aside in the face of a crisis with China over Korea, in 1894, which led to a war in which Japan won spectacular victories on land and at sea. By the Treaty of Shimonoseki (1895) China surrendered to Japan the island of Taiwan (Formosa) and the Liaodong peninsula in South Manzhou (Manchuria), including Lushun (Port Arthur). Within a few days Japan was forced by Russia, Germany and France to waive its claim to Manzhou. A few years later Russia established itself in control of Lushun and its hinterland. Revenge came in the Russo-Japanese War of 1904–05, which was a much more costly affair for Japan in terms of men and material resources than the Sino-Japanese War had been, 10 years earlier. However, Japan's victories, including the destruction of the Tsar's Baltic fleet in the Tsushima Strait in May 1905, were dramatic, and Asia in particular was deeply moved by what happened.

THE TAISHO ERA

The death of Emperor Meiji in 1912 was decidedly a landmark, the end of a not inglorious chapter. For the Meiji era was Japan's Victorian age, when despite set-backs and disappointments everything seemed to move forward. The new Emperor proved to be mentally unstable, and in 1921 his eldest son, Crown Prince Hirohito, became regent, succeeding to the throne at the end of 1926.

The period 1912–26 is known as the Taisho era, after the title chosen for the reign of Meiji's successor. It is noteworthy for three important developments and one shocking disaster. In the first place, thanks to the World War of 1914–18, the nation's economic power began to swell in dynamic fashion, as Japanese shipyards, factories and foundries were overwhelmed with orders from the Allied countries. Secondly, as Britain's ally, Japan invaded and occupied Shandong (Shantung), Germany's leased territory in China, bringing Japan firmly into China's affairs. The temptation to dictate to China could not be resisted, with the result that Chinese dislike and distrust of Japan increased dramatically, setting the tone of relations between the two countries for years to come. Thirdly, Lenin's triumph in Russia gave some impetus to protest movements created by the contrast in the standards of living between those who had been enriched by the war and the poorer sections of the urban working class. Left-wing groups began to obtain a measure of representation in the Diet; democracy appeared to be coming into vogue. Then, in September 1923, more than one-half of the city of Tokyo and the whole of Yokohama were destroyed in a series of earth tremors and subsequent fires. In recorded history there have been few comparable natural disasters so calamitous in loss of life and destruction of property.

THE PRE-WAR SHOWA PERIOD

After Emperor Taisho's death in 1926 his successor chose as the title for the new reign two Chinese characters, Sho Wa, which can be translated as 'Bright Harmony'. The years that followed, however, belied the promise implicit in these words. A Prime Minister, Hamaguchi, was shot and wounded by a nationalist fanatic in 1930, and died some months later from his injuries. In 1932 another Prime Minister, Inukai, was assassinated; and in 1936 two former premiers, Saito Makoto and Takahashi Korekiyo, were shot down in their homes by parties of mutinous troops. These and other instances of civil bloodshed and violence were among the more lurid symptoms of a wave of irrational nationalist hysteria prompted partly by events on the continent of Asia and in part by the economic consequences for Japan of the world depression, which hit the country hard at the beginning of the 1930s. Unrest and dissatisfaction exploded in anger against Diet politicians, wealthy capitalists, and liberal-minded men at the palace and in other influential positions. Public opinion came to regard such figures as weak, corrupt and incompetent. The man in uniform, on the other hand, was back in favour, and in power. For in the early autumn of 1931 Japanese forces in South Manzhou carried out a coup against the Chinese in Shenyang (Mukden), and this soon developed into the forcible seizure of all Manzhou.

Military Expansion in Asia

Condemned by the League of Nations for aggression in Manzhou, Japan left that body in 1933. Manzhou became a vassal state (Manchukuo), an apanage of the Empire, dominated by the army and only in name more independent than Taiwan, or Korea, which had been annexed in 1910. Domination of Manzhou led to involvement in northern China, and out of this came undeclared war in mid-1937. By the end of that year Japan and China were locked in a combat that did not end until 1945. As the war continued, Japan's relations with other powers underwent a change. It drew closer to Nazi Germany and Fascist Italy, eventually joining them in full alliance in September 1940. Increasingly, both the United Kingdom and the USA, powers that supported the Chinese Government in Chongqing, were seen as potential enemies.

In July 1941 Vichy France agreed to the Japanese occupation of bases in the Saigon area—bases in northern French Indo-China had been occupied by Japan in the previous year. The move southward seemed a clear threat to both Malaya and the Netherlands East Indies. It indicated, too, that for the time being, at least, Japan was not going to join its ally Germany in the assault on the USSR. There was an immediate response by the British Commonwealth, the USA and the Netherlands, in the form of a virtual embargo on all trade with Japan. This was serious, for it meant that petroleum imports into that country had to cease. US-Japanese talks were inconclusive. Inexorably, Japan drifted towards armed confrontation with the Western powers.

The Sino-Japanese War of 1894–95 and the Russo-Japanese War of 1904–05 had started with surprise attacks by the Japanese navy. On 7 December 1941 Japan followed the same strategy, attacking the US fleet at Pearl Harbor in Hawaii. Later in the same month, Japanese forces invaded Hong Kong, Malaya, Singapore and the Netherlands East Indies.

THE PACIFIC WAR

For the first six months the Japanese advance was virtually unhindered. Hong Kong, Malaya, Singapore, Java and the Indies, the Philippines, Burma and the Andaman Islands, New Britain and the Solomons all fell to Japanese arms. There had, however, been a grave miscalculation of the spirit and resources of the nation's principal enemies. Allied submarines, US island-hopping strategy and superior fire-power led to a reversal of Japan's position. From mid-1944 the tide turned against Japan. By mid-1945 military collapse was imminent. US air raids had inflicted fearful punishment. The merchant fleet, like the battle fleet, had practically ceased to exist. Germany was out of the war. The USSR was an unknown but menacing factor, returning no answer to pleas that it should act as a mediator.

The Potsdam proclamation at the end of July 1945 seemed to leave the Government unmoved, although in reality the Premier, the aged Baron Suzuki, was seeking ways and means of ending the war short of abject capitulation. On 6 August the first atomic bomb laid waste Hiroshima. On 9 August the second descended on the suburbs of Nagasaki. Between those dates the Soviet army overran Manchukuo. In this supreme crisis the nation's leaders were divided between those who favoured surrender (with the proviso that the monarchy be maintained) and those who were ready to fight on in spite of everything. It was the Emperor, invited to give an unprecedented decision of his own, who tipped the balance by declaring that the Potsdam terms must be accepted.

THE OCCUPATION

US Gen. Douglas MacArthur represented all the Allies in Japan, but the occupation was nevertheless an almost exclusively US undertaking and to a very great extent MacArthur took his own decisions, without direct reference to Washington. He rejected the view that the Japanese would be better off without the age-old institution of the monarchy. He felt that the Emperor was a stabilizing factor in a society shaken to its roots by the capitulation. Popular regard for the Emperor, however, no longer rested on the belief that he partook of divinity because of his descent from the sun goddess. When, at the beginning of 1946, the Emperor formally renounced his 'divinity', it created little interest among most Japanese.

In his administration of Japan, MacArthur acted through the Japanese Government, a procedure that worked smoothly in nearly every instance. Between conquerors and conquered there was indeed a harmony that nobody could have foreseen during the years of warfare. The Japanese, however, can be intensely pragmatic. The events of 1945 seemed to demonstrate that their own way of conducting affairs was inefficient and harmful to themselves. So when the US occupying forces arrived, and once it was clear that their general behaviour was by no means vengeful and oppressive, the Japanese were ready to be their pupils in all manner of activities.

Political, Economic and Social Reforms

The guiding theme of the occupation, in the early days especially, was disarmament and democratization. A new Constitution, promulgated in 1946, reflected both these aims. One clause stated that the Japanese people renounced war; and it went on to say that 'land, sea, and air forces, as well as other war potential, will never be maintained'. A further clause laid down that the Prime Minister and his Cabinet colleagues must be civilians. The other articles of the Constitution reflected the authentic spirit of North American democracy, with full emphasis on the rights of the individual. Sovereignty of the people was declared. The Emperor was made 'the symbol of the State and of the unity of the people', and it was affirmed that he derived his position 'from the will of the people'.

Although undeniably US-inspired, the post-war Constitution captured the imagination of the Japanese. To this day its defenders are sufficiently numerous to make it unlikely that the Constitution will be so radically amended as to change its basic character. Amendment requires the assent of two-thirds of the members of both houses of the Diet, confirmed by a referendum of the people as a whole.

Another measure of profound social and political importance, instigated by MacArthur's headquarters, was the land reform programme. Thousands of tenant farmers were able to obtain ownership of the land they cultivated. Up to the war a depressed class, the farmers of Japan, thanks to the land reform, became firm, if not always satisfied, upholders of the political status quo. Left-wing parties found the farming vote difficult to entice. The average farmer, freed from the burden of rent and assured of sales for his crop at guaranteed prices, was not impressed by advocates of collectivization and other projects of agrarian socialism.

The educational system was comprehensively reformed. In terms of organization and syllabus it was reworked to a pattern resembling that of the USA. The famous *Rescript on Education*, needless to say, was discarded, and there was a thorough revision of school-books concerned with history, political science and ethics.

These manifold and generally liberating changes were not far short of revolutionary in character. Political freedom gave the parties of the Left an opportunity to exploit these changes, and to make them even more far-reaching. However, except for the period between May 1947 and March 1948, when a coalition Government under Tetsu Katayama of the Socialist Party was in office, electoral success always attended the conservative parties. Until the end of 1954 the political scene was dominated by Shigeru Yoshida; and, even after his retirement, the old man was influential, as adviser to successive Governments, until his death in 1967.

Consolidation of Relations with the West

As the international situation hardened into the Cold War, the attitude of MacArthur's headquarters underwent a subtle but definite change. The emphasis shifted from reform to rehabilitation. In particular, as the armies of Mao Zedong began to gain ground in China, and as it became clear that US influence on the Chinese mainland might soon be eliminated, the importance of Japan's future role in the non-communist world was perceived with growing clarity. After the Korean War broke out in June 1950 it seemed all the more desirable, and in fact urgent, to nourish the revival of Japan. In other words Japan was now regarded not as a recent enemy but rather as a new friend and junior ally. In these circumstances the disarmament clause of the Constitution appeared as an embarrassment. In practice, however, it was to be blandly ignored.

The US military occupation lasted until 1952. This was much longer than had been planned. Soon after his basic reforms had been introduced, MacArthur had decided that the situation called for a treaty of peace. When he was dismissed by President Truman in 1951 the Japanese feared that progress towards a peace treaty would be checked. However, on 8 September the treaty was concluded at San Francisco between Japan and 48 nations (but not the USSR). It was a magnanimous settlement, free from punitive clauses, although Japan's territorial losses were confirmed. On the same day a bilateral security pact was signed by Japan and the USA. In this, Japan asked the USA to retain its forces in and around the Japanese islands as a defence against outside attack. When all the signatories of the San Francisco Treaty had ratified the document, it came into force; on 28 April 1952 Japan became, once again, formally an independent state.

Recent History

AKIRA YAMAZAKI

Revised for this edition by LESLEY CONNORS

THE POST-WAR POLITICAL ORDER

The reforms introduced during the US military occupation created the institutional framework within which Japan was to conduct its social and political life. The conservative political forces, under the guidance of Shigeru Yoshida (Prime Minister in 1946–47 and 1948–54) and bolstered by the return to the Kokkai (Diet) of pre-war political leaders who had been purged, were divided between two main parties, the Liberals and the Democrats, but were united in their desire to change the institutional framework and to reverse many of the democratic reforms. The conservatives were confronted by a vigorous opposition, dominated by the Japan Socialist Party (JSP), which regarded any attempt to tamper with the reforms and, above all, with the Constitution (particularly Article 9, the 'peace clause', whereby Japan renounces the use of war) as a potential threat to return Japan to the militarism of the 1930s and 1940s.

The contest between these groups was resolved in 1955, at which time the foundations of the post-war political order were established. At a general election for the House of Representatives (the lower house of the Diet) in February 1955, the JSP received 29.2% of the total votes and won 156 of the 467 seats in the chamber. The JSP thus controlled the minimum number of seats (one-third of the total) necessary to obstruct any proposed revision of the post-war Constitution. However, the radical policies (and even more radical rhetoric) of the JSP alarmed business interests, who were organized in the Japan Federation of Economic Organizations (KEIDANREN). Business leaders urged the Liberals and the Democrats (who had together won 63.2% of the votes and 297 seats at the election) to merge into a single party, which they did in November 1955. The new party, the Liberal-Democratic Party (LDP), governed Japan from 1955 until 1993 (returning to office in 1994, initially as part of a coalition Government), leading the country during a period of remarkable economic expansion.

The advantages that the LDP enjoyed were overwhelming: as the incumbent governing party, it obtained the political benefits of the 'economic miracle', while Japan's electoral arrangements provided an additional asset for the LDP. At the national level, the opposition parties were unable to achieve as much support, even temporarily, as they had locally. A high degree of ideological fragmentation precluded any serious possibility that the opposition could replace the LDP in government. Some of the opposition parties, notably the Komeito ('Clean Government Party'), the Democratic Socialist Party (DSP) and the New Liberal Club (NLC), were more inclined to co-operate with the LDP than with the increasingly isolated Japanese Communist Party (JCP).

Furthermore, the opposition parties were hampered by the uneven distribution of parliamentary constituencies. For many years successive LDP Governments steadfastly refused to allow any revision of electoral boundaries, to take account of population movements, with the result that the rural areas, where support for the LDP was strong, were substantially over-represented in the Diet. In April 1976 the Supreme Court ruled that the allocation of seats in the House of Representatives was unconstitutional, owing to 'mal-apportionment', which denied equal rights to urban voters (as guaranteed by the Japanese Constitution). In 1990 the LDP leadership announced its commitment to the implementation of comprehensive changes to the procedure for the allocation of seats to the lower house (see below).

Finance was another factor behind the success of the LDP. Politics in Japan, and particularly elections, are spectacularly expensive: the officially reported income of the political parties in 1990 (not an unusually expensive year) was US $700m., which was probably little more than one-quarter of their actual income. To win elections, a political party must be able to raise enormous funds. The LDP traditionally enjoyed a close relationship with the business community, thus the party was well placed to obtain large-scale financial support. One estimate suggested that Japanese business interests transferred more than 45,000m. yen per year to the LDP.

LIBERAL-DEMOCRATIC GOVERNMENTS

Nobusuke Kishi became Prime Minister in February 1957, and held office until July 1960, when he was succeeded by Hayato Ikeda. In November 1964 Ikeda resigned, owing to ill health, and was replaced by Eisaku Sato. Japan enjoyed strong economic growth under Ikeda and Sato. The latter remained in office until July 1972, when he was succeeded by Kakuei Tanaka, hitherto the Minister of International Trade and Industry.

Meanwhile, many of Japan's outer islands, surrendered to the USA at the time of the 1945 armistice, were restored to Japanese sovereignty. The Tokara Archipelago and the Amami Islands (parts of the Ryukyu group) had been restored to Japan in December 1951 and December 1953, respectively. The Bonin Islands and the remainder of the Ryukyu Islands (including Okinawa) reverted to Japan in June 1968 and May 1972, respectively.

1972–82

Tanaka's period of tenure as Prime Minister was characterized primarily by scandals, illustrating the problem of widespread corporate involvement in Japanese politics, although initially more noteworthy was Japan's recognition of the People's Republic of China in September 1972. During his premiership, Tanaka allegedly accepted bribes totalling 500m. yen from the Marubeni Corporation, a representative in Japan of the Lockheed Aircraft Corporation (a leading US aerospace company). Following a severe reduction in the LDP's majority in the House of Councillors (upper house of the Diet) at elections held in July 1974, Tanaka's hold on the premiership became tenuous. In December he resigned in favour of Takeo Miki, a former Deputy Prime Minister. Tanaka was subsequently arrested, in July 1976, on charges of accepting bribes, and resigned from the LDP. Largely as a result of voters' disapproval of the LDP's alleged involvement in corruption, the party lost its majority in the House of Representatives in December. Miki was forced to resign, and was succeeded by Takeo Fukuda, who had resigned in November as Deputy Prime Minister.

At the elections held in July 1977 for the House of Councillors Fukuda was unable to reverse the LDP's decline. He was defeated in the LDP presidential election by Masayoshi Ohira, the party's Secretary-General, who became Prime Minister in December 1978. Although Ohira managed to retain his position as Prime Minister following the election of October 1979 to the House of Representatives (when the LDP once again failed to obtain a majority and there were significant gains by the JCP), the Government was defeated on a motion of 'no confidence' in the House of Representatives in May 1980. The lower house was thus dissolved, and at elections held in June the LDP received 47.9% of the total votes and won 284 of the 511 seats. A compromise candidate, Zenko Suzuki, was elected President of the LDP in July, and was subsequently appointed Prime Minister. Suzuki's Government was beset by serious economic problems and growing factionalism within the LDP. As the economic crisis worsened, Suzuki was forced to resign as Prime Minister and President of the LDP in October 1982.

The Nakasone Administration

Suzuki's successor was Yasuhiro Nakasone, who was supported by the Suzuki and Tanaka factions of the LDP. At elections in June 1983 the LDP increased its strength in the upper house from 134 to 137 members in the 252-seat chamber. This result was seen as an endorsement of Nakasone's policies of increased spending on defence, closer ties with the USA and greater Japanese involvement in international affairs.

In October 1983, after judicial proceedings lasting seven years, a Tokyo court found Tanaka, the former Prime Minister, guilty of accepting bribes. He immediately began appeal proceedings against the conviction and the sentence, and refused to relinquish his legislative seat, which led to a boycott of the Diet by the opposition. This forced Nakasone to dissolve the House of Representatives in preparation for a premature general election in December 1983. The election campaign was dominated by the issues of political ethics and Nakasone's forthright style of leadership. The LDP suffered its worst reverse to date, losing 36 seats (and its majority) in the lower house. Nakasone was placed second (behind Takeo Fukuda) in his district, whereas Tanaka was returned with an overwhelming majority. The Komeito, the DSP and the JSP gained seats, while the JCP and the NLC lost seats. A coalition was formed between the LDP, the NLC (which had split from the LDP over the Tanaka affair in 1976) and several independents, and Nakasone remained as President of the LDP, promising to reduce Tanaka's influence. Six members of Tanaka's faction, however, held posts in Nakasone's new Cabinet.

Nakasone's domestic policy was based on the 'three reforms': administrative reforms, particularly of government-controlled enterprises such as telecommunications and railways; fiscal reforms, to enable the Government to balance its budget after many years of persistent deficit; and educational reforms, to liberalize the rigid examination-dominated system.

In November 1984 Nakasone was re-elected as President of the LDP, guaranteeing him a further two years in office as Prime Minister, the first to serve a second term since Eisaku Sato (1964–72). Nakasone was committed to raising Japan's international status by fostering friendly relations with other world leaders. He made successful tours to the USA, Australia and South-East Asia in 1984, and to Europe in 1985. However, there was continued concern in the European Community (EC, now European Union—EU) over trade protectionism in Japan, and in the USA over the imbalance of bilateral trade.

In May 1986 an agreement was reached on a redistribution of seats in the House of Representatives between urban and rural constituencies, reducing the maximum ratio of discrepancy in constituency size to less than 3:1, the limit that the Supreme Court had stipulated as permissible. Following this agreement, the lower house was dissolved in June, enabling the holding of a general election to coincide with the triennial election for one-half of the seats in the House of Councillors. Polling for both houses of the Diet took place in July and produced decisive victories for the LDP. In the election for the House of Representatives, the LDP received 49.4% of the votes, its highest level of electoral support since 1963, and won a record 304 of the 512 seats. The LDP, therefore, was able to dispense with its coalition partner, the NLC (which disbanded in August and rejoined the LDP).

Nakasone's second term as President of the LDP (a position that had to be held in order to be Prime Minister) ended in October 1986, and party rules prohibited a third term. However, the leaders of the five main LDP factions agreed to change the party's rules to permit a one-year extension of a President's term, with the approval of two-thirds of the LDP members of the Diet. Nakasone was confirmed as party President in September.

In September 1983, meanwhile, Masashi Ishibashi became Chairman of the JSP and initiated a shift from the party's traditional left-wing policies towards a position closer to the centre of the political spectrum. The JSP's moderation resulted in a slight increase in support at the 1983 general election, and a policy of further moderation was implemented, which brought about the end of the domination of the Marxist-orientated Shakaishugi Kyokai (Socialist Association) within the party. At the 1986 election, however, the JSP's less extreme image failed to attract voters, and the party lost 26 of the 112 seats won in 1983. This disastrous result brought about Ishibashi's resignation and the appointment, in September 1986, of Takako Doi, the first woman to lead a major Japanese political party.

Following the 1986 elections, Nakasone's priorities were to oversee an untroubled transfer to private-sector control of the Japanese National Railways (JNR), to alleviate economic tensions with the USA, while maintaining a high level of Japanese exports in spite of the sharp rise in the value of Japan's currency, and to reform both the education and tax systems. The JNR was successfully reorganized in April 1987, but Nakasone failed to make significant progress in the three remaining areas. Educational reforms remained under discussion by a specially-established council, while proposed reforms to the tax system were withdrawn in April 1987, after the LDP suffered a serious defeat in the unified local elections. In spite of Nakasone's efforts, economic tensions with the USA continued, as the current-account surplus on Japan's balance of payments maintained its growth.

Meanwhile, Tanaka's illness led to the disintegration of his faction. In July 1987 Noboru Takeshita (who had been appointed Secretary-General of the LDP after the 1986 election) announced the formation of a major new grouping within the LDP, the Takeshita faction. He gained the support of 113 other members of the Tanaka faction, while around 20 Tanaka faction members remained with Susumu Nikaido, a former Vice-President of the LDP and the second most powerful man in the Tanaka faction. In October Nakasone nominated Takeshita as his successor.

The Takeshita Administration

On 6 November 1987 the Diet was convened and Takeshita was formally elected as Prime Minister. In the new Cabinet, Takeshita carefully maintained a balance among the five major factions of the LDP. He claimed that he would work to continue Nakasone's domestic and foreign policies (seeking the former Prime Minister's advice on foreign affairs), with particular emphasis on correcting the external trade imbalance, further liberalizing the financial market, reforming the tax system, land policy and the education system.

In contrast to its failure to stem the rapid rise in land prices, the Takeshita administration initially achieved steady progress in easing friction with overseas trading partners. The restrictions on imports in the agricultural sector were abolished, while US companies were permitted greater access to the Japanese domestic construction market. Trade tensions worsened, however, during Takeshita's tenure of office. The primary cause of concern was the continuing trade imbalance between Japan and the USA (the US trade deficit with Japan still accounted for about one-third of the USA's total world trade deficit). In May 1989 the situation deteriorated when the USA named Japan, together with India and Brazil, as unfair trading partners.

The implementation of a programme of tax reform, which Nakasone had failed to achieve, was one of the most important issues confronting Takeshita's Government. In June 1988 the LDP's tax deliberation council proposed the introduction of a new indirect tax (a general consumption tax or a form of value-added tax), which was to be levied at a 3% rate. This proposal encountered widespread disapproval, however, both from the general public and from the opposition parties.

Takeshita and the LDP suffered a serious political reversal in June 1988, when several leading figures in the party, including Nakasone, Shintaro Abe, Kiichi Miyazawa and Takeshita himself, were alleged to have been indirectly involved in share-trading irregularities with the Recruit Cosmos Company. Although these politicians strenuously denied any knowledge of, or involvement in, such transactions, the Prime Minister expressed his concern that these allegations would alienate public opinion from the proposals for tax reform and hinder their progress towards approval by the Diet. As the situation regarding the Recruit affair became increasingly serious, the opposition demanded the resignation of the alleged participants and the commissioning of a full parliamentary investigation into the alleged share transactions. In November, in exchange for the establishment of a committee to investigate the affair, the House of Representatives approved the tax reform measures (which constituted the most wide-ranging revision of the tax system for 40 years); they were approved by the House of Councillors in the following month.

In late 1988 and early 1989 three ministers, including the Deputy Prime Minister and Finance Minister, Kiichi Miyazawa, were forced to resign from their posts, owing to their alleged involvement in the Recruit affair. Hiromasa Ezoe, who founded the Recruit group, was said to have given large amounts of shares and money, totalling some 1,300m. yen, to many leading politicians and bureaucrats, in an attempt to buy influence and to help to expand his business empire.

In late April 1989 Takeshita suddenly resigned from his post. There were several factors leading to his decision: Takeshita, personally, was found to have received political contributions worth more than 150m. yen from the Recruit group in the form of pre-listed shares and money; the Takeshita Cabinet, whose position was severely damaged by the shares scandal and public outrage over the introduction of the 3% consumption tax in April, saw its public approval rating fall to less than 10%; and, finally, there was a growing consensus among LDP officials that Takeshita's continued leadership would adversely affect the party's prospects in the elections to the House of Councillors at the end of July. Hard-pressed to find a candidate who was not only willing to accept the position but also suitable (three of the leading contenders, Michio Watanabe, Kiichi Miyazawa and Shintaro Abe, were, temporarily at least, out of the question, since they had all received pre-listed Recruit shares), Takeshita finally nominated Sosuke Uno, the incumbent Minister of Foreign Affairs. Uno was elected Prime Minister at a Diet session on 2 June, becoming the first Japanese Prime Minister, since the LDP was founded in 1955, not to command his own political faction.

At the end of May 1989, following an eight-month investigation, public prosecutors indicted 13 people (eight on charges of offering bribes, and five for allegedly accepting them). Two of those indicted were politicians: Takao Fujinami, an LDP member belonging to the Nakasone faction, and Katsuya Ikeda, a former Deputy Secretary-General of the Komeito. At the same time, under heavy criticism from members of the opposition as well as from his own party, Nakasone resigned from his faction and from the LDP, assuming complete moral responsibility for the Recruit affair, since it had occurred during his administration. However, on the same day as his resignation, Nakasone announced that he would continue to undertake his political activities and that he would not resign from his seat in the Diet.

The Showa era came to an end when, after a long illness, Emperor Hirohito, who had reigned since 1926 (and who was, thus, the longest-reigning monarch in Japan's history), died in January 1989. He was succeeded by his son, Akihito, and the Government announced that the new era was to be known as the Heisei ('achievement of universal peace') era.

The Uno Administration

Within days of Uno's appointment in June 1989, the LDP was confronted with further scandal, when a Japanese magazine published allegations that Uno had paid a geisha girl for a five-month sexual affair in 1985/86. In response to these allegations (on which Uno refused to comment), there were demands for the immediate resignation of the new Prime Minister from outraged women's groups and from various members of the opposition. The LDP's fears of waning support appeared to be confirmed in July 1989, when the ruling party lost its majority in the House of Councillors for the first time in history. At elections for one-half of the seats in the upper house, the LDP obtained only 27% of the total votes, while the JSP received 35%. The leader of the JSP, Takako Doi, attracted widespread support during the election campaign. Women voters, expressing disgust at the corruption in male-dominated politics, were attracted by the image of an intellectual female political leader. Consequently, Uno offered to resign as soon as the LDP had decided on a suitable successor, assuming total responsibility for his party's defeat. On 8 August the LDP chose the relatively unknown Toshiki Kaifu, a former Minister of Education and a member of the small faction led by Toshio Komoto, to replace Uno as the party's President and as the new Prime Minister. Although the House of Councillors' ballot rejected Kaifu as the new Prime Minister in favour of Takako Doi, the decision of the lower house was adopted (in accordance with constitutional procedures). This was the first time in 41 years that the two houses of the Diet had disagreed over the choice of Prime Minister.

The Kaifu Administration

At the end of August 1989 the LDP suffered another reversal when the Chief Cabinet Secretary was forced to resign, owing to a sex scandal. Nevertheless, Kaifu swiftly gained the approval of the electorate, owing to his untainted political record and his promise to revise the consumption tax. In October Kaifu was re-elected unopposed as President of the LDP for a two-year term.

Meanwhile, in August 1989 the JSP, in an apparent move to broaden its base of support, unanimously approved a change of policy that would commit it to retaining the Japanese-US bilateral security treaty (see below) and a free-market economy in the event of the establishment of a coalition government.

At the election for the House of Representatives held in February 1990 the LDP was returned to power with a large measure of support. The LDP received 46.1% of the votes cast and secured 275 of the 512 seats in the lower house. The JSP made substantial gains, winning 136 seats. The election results were significant in demonstrating not only the willingness of the electorate to forgive past indiscretions (many major politicians who had been implicated in recent scandals were returned to the lower house, including former Prime Ministers Nakasone and Uno) but also the possibility of a future polarization of voters, with the role of the smaller parties becoming increasingly insignificant.

In May 1990 Prime Minister Kaifu announced his commitment to the implementation of the electoral reforms that had been proposed in April. The proposals, for the House of Representatives, included a plan to replace the present multi-seat constituencies with a combination of single seats and proportional representation. Although the proposals were presented as an attempt to counter electoral corruption, LDP members expressed fears that the changes would invest more power in party committees responsible for nominating candidates, and would therefore increase the scope for bribery.

Kaifu's domestic and international standing altered significantly following Iraq's invasion of Kuwait in August 1990, and the subsequent outbreak of hostilities in the Persian (Arabian) Gulf region. In September Japan announced a US $4,000m.-contribution to the international effort to force an unconditional Iraqi withdrawal from Kuwait. Controversial legislation, which provided for the dispatch to the Gulf area of some 2,000 non-combatant personnel, encountered severe opposition and provoked widespread discussion on the constitutional legitimacy of the deployment of Japanese personnel (in any capacity) in such a conflict. The proposals were withdrawn in November. Nevertheless, Kaifu was reported to be considering resignation until, later that month, the LDP won a by-election to the upper house. In January 1991, following repeated demands by the USA for a greater financial commitment (and a swifter disbursement of funds already pledged), the Kaifu Government announced plans to increase its contribution by US $9,000m. and to provide aircraft for the transport of refugees in the Gulf region. Opposition to the proposal within Japan was again vociferous.

Meanwhile, a developing power struggle within the LDP had also weakened Kaifu's political authority. Former Prime Minister Takeshita took advantage of diplomatic and political errors committed by Shin Kanemaru, the leader of the LDP faction that supported Kaifu, to ease his way back into a position of prominence in the LDP. In order to bolster his preparations for a return to the political forum, Takeshita also promoted Nakasone's return to the party, together with that of Kiichi Miyazawa. In June 1991 Kaifu broached the controversial issue of political reform by requesting that the LDP endorse a series of electoral reform bills. This initiative, following a year's deliberation of the issue within the party, was viewed as an attempt not only to regain public confidence but also to obstruct the efforts of tainted party leaders to return to office when Kaifu's LDP presidential term expired in October. Later that month, however, the Diet rejected Kaifu's proposals, leaving the way open for Kiichi Miyazawa.

Having successfully prevented the Government from dispatching Self-Defence Force (SDF) personnel overseas during the Gulf War, the JSP was unable to sustain popular support for its strict pacifist stance. Although the party, in a bid to attract wider support, had changed the English rendering of its name to the Social Democratic Party of Japan (SDPJ) in February 1991, it suffered defeat on an unprecedented scale in the unified local elections in April. The set-back forced the party to discard the abolition of the consumption tax, and to approve the LDP's proposal to revise the tax in the following month. In July the SDPJ leader, Takako Doi, resigned and the party selected a new leader, Makoto Tanabe, from its conservative wing.

The Miyazawa Administration

At the election for the presidency of the LDP in October 1991 Miyazawa (with the support of Shin Kanemaru, a former Deputy Prime Minister) defeated Michio Watanabe and Hiroshi Mitsuzuka. Miyazawa attempted to win control of the ruling party by strengthening his long-established links with Takeshita, Watanabe and Mitsuzuka on the one hand, and by establishing new ties with Kanemaru on the other. Watanabe was appointed to the posts of Deputy Prime Minister and Minister of Foreign Affairs. However, a bitter feud developed between Kanemaru and Takeshita over the allocation of posts within the party executive and the Cabinet. The new Cabinet comprised the same proportion of the LDP's four major factions as its predecessor, but with the Takeshita faction obtaining more of the senior portfolios than it had previously held.

The new Prime Minister attempted to enact controversial legislation to allow SDF troops to serve abroad on UN peace-keeping missions. Realizing the need to gain Kanemaru's full support, Miyazawa repeatedly requested that he assume the post of LDP Vice-President. In January 1992 Kanemaru at last accepted the offer, together with Miyazawa's pledge of loyalty. Subsequently, the peace-keeping legislation was approved, with the support of the Komeito and the DSP, on the condition that SDF personnel join only non-military operations. The legislation was enacted in June 1992, in spite of opposition from the SDPJ.

In July 1992 the LDP recovered from a period of apparent unpopularity to achieve unexpected gains in elections to the upper house of the Diet. Although the LDP failed to recapture the majority that it had lost in 1989, the results provided the Miyazawa Government with significant encouragement. The dominant Takeshita faction of the LDP, however, was beset by crisis when, following further investigations into the activities of the Sagawa Kyubin transport company, it emerged that the latter's former president, Hiroyasu Watanabe, had made an unreported 500m.-yen donation to Shin Kanemaru in February 1990. In late August 1992 Kanemaru was forced to resign as LDP Vice-President, offering also to resign as head of the Takeshita faction, since he faced the charge of violating the Political Funds Control Law. However, he avoided trial by issuing a written statement to the authorities, in which he admitted the charge. The Tokyo Summary Court responded with a fine of 200,000 yen, prompting a public outcry over the failure to prosecute this case more resolutely. Kanemaru returned to his duties as head of the Takeshita faction for two weeks, only to yield to mounting pressure and resign from the Diet in mid-October. Two days prior to the opening of an extraordinary Diet session in late October, Ichiro Ozawa, a protégé of Kanemaru, announced the split of his group of 36 lower house members from the Takeshita faction, following his failure to obtain the chairmanship. Further changes in the political map occurred with the formation in early November of the Sirius Group of 27 reform-minded Diet members belonging to the SDPJ, Social Democratic Federation and RENGO, the trade union organization. Other such party and cross-party groups increased in prominence and number, reflecting the growing demand for political and electoral reform. As the trials connected to the Sagawa Kyubin scandal continued, seven leading LDP politicians, including Kanemaru, were accused of dealings with an extreme rightist group and with an organized crime gang in 1987, during Takeshita's ascent to the leadership of the party.

In a bid to restore confidence in the embattled Government, Miyazawa reshuffled the Cabinet in December 1992. Changes included the appointment of Hajime Funada as Director-General of the Economic Planning Agency, at 39 the youngest-ever member of a post-war cabinet. Seiroku Kajiyama, Ozawa's rival, became the LDP's Secretary-General. Political and electoral reforms were postponed until after the completion of the budget in April 1993.

With the arrest of Kanemaru and his secretary, Masahisa Haibara, in March 1993, on suspicion of evading the payment of 1,040m. yen in tax, groups seeking political reform within the Diet gained fresh momentum. Each of the established parties, apart from the Communists, assembled proposals for changes to the electoral system. While the LDP's preference was for a single-member constituency system, the opposition parties produced a variety of suggestions, which incorporated elements of proportional representation. Within the ruling party itself, differences between younger Diet members and their seniors emerged, as the former, led by Ozawa and his ally, Tsutomu Hata, encouraged an agreement with the opposition parties. A cross-party consensus was needed for any legislation to pass through the upper house, where the LDP was in the minority.

In June 1993 the LDP confirmed that it would not compromise its proposal to meet the demands of the opposition, thus effectively abandoning the reforms. The lower house adopted a no-confidence motion against the Miyazawa Government by 255 to 220 votes; 39 LDP members, including 34 members of the Hata-Ozawa group, voted against their party, while 16 other LDP politicians did not vote. The Hata-Ozawa group, consisting of 44 members of the LDP, immediately formed a new party called the Japan Renewal Party (JRP, Shinseito), in order to contest the forthcoming general election, called for July. Another group of 10 LDP Diet members also broke away to form the New Party (Shinto/Sakigake).

The election for the House of Representatives, held on 18 July 1993, marked the end of uninterrupted LDP rule. Apart from the record low turn-out of 67%, voting patterns changed surprisingly little. The LDP won 223 of the 511 seats, slightly more than it had held immediately prior to the election, but still well short of an overall majority. The SDPJ fared particularly badly, its number of seats being almost halved to 70. Of the parties formed by ex-LDP members, the JRP and New Party Sakigake won 55 and 13 seats respectively, most of which had been occupied by LDP members. The performance of the other recently-established party, the Japan New Party (JNP) led by Morihiro Hosokawa, which fielded no incumbent candidates, was impressive, its 35 seats being secured mainly in urban constituencies and in the same marginal seats where new political parties had enjoyed success in the past. The remaining parties managed to maintain their strength in the lower house: the Komeito took 51 seats, the JCP 15, the DSP 15 and the Social Democratic Federation/United Social Democratic Party (USDP) four, while candidates with no party affiliations won 30 seats. Nevertheless, the LDP remained a potent electoral force.

THE END OF UNINTERRUPTED LDP RULE AND ESTABLISHMENT OF A COALITION GOVERNMENT

Following the election of July 1993, therefore, Prime Minister Miyazawa resigned, since there was no prospect of his party regaining its majority in the lower house. Amidst widespread expectations that the LDP would remain in power, either as a minority government, or as part of a coalition government, the other non-communist parties formed an alliance to oust the LDP. Thus, Morihiro Hosokawa, possessor of an illustrious aristocratic lineage and leader of the JNP, became Japan's first non-LDP Prime Minister for 38 years, defeating the new LDP President, Yohei Kono, by 262 votes to 224. Hosokawa formed a coalition Government, which included representatives of all the coalition partners. However, there was some dissatisfaction within the SDPJ concerning the distribution of key government posts. In spite of being the largest coalition partner, the SDPJ secured relatively few important positions, although its Chairman, Sadao Yamahana, was appointed Minister Responsible for Political Reform; the party was also allocated the Home Affairs, Construction and Transport portfolios. Tsutomu Hata, one of the JRP's leaders, became Deputy Prime Minister and Minister of Foreign Affairs, while his party also took responsibility for the crucial Ministries of Finance, and of International Trade and Industry. The sense of irritation within the SDPJ was exacerbated by its failure to obtain the position of Chief Cabinet Secretary, or even one of the two Deputy Chief Cabinet Secretary posts, leaving the party with no influence over the direction and co-ordination of policy. The former SDPJ Chairman, Takako Doi, who might have articulated such disaffection, was silenced by her reluctant acceptance of the post of Speaker of the lower house. Yamahana was replaced as Chairman of the SDPJ by Tomiichi Murayama in September 1993.

One of the Hosokawa Government's outstanding achievements was the approval of legislation on political reform, which was surrounded by much controversy until its final passage through the Diet in late January 1994. Under the new electoral system, Japan's 511 medium-sized, multi-member constituencies in the House of Representatives were to be replaced by 500 seats, 300 of which were to be filled from single-member constituencies in a 'first-past-the-post' contest, and the remaining 200 in 11 regional blocks by proportional representation. New funding rules allowed politicians to receive a maximum of 500,000 yen per year from each company wishing to donate, for the next five years, after which time payments to individual politicians from businesses would be illegal. Under the reforms, a 40% increase in state funding for political parties was also promised. The legislation was approved despite strong opposition from within the coalition, owing to a late agreement between Hosokawa and the LDP President. Their compromise thus met LDP demands for an increased number of single-member constituencies, for 11 regional rather than one national proportional representation list, and for no immediate termination of corporate donations to individual politicians.

Encouraged by record public approval ratings, Hosokawa promised further, wide-ranging reform. Economic strategy was revised by the Economic Reform Research Council, under the chairmanship of Gaishi Hiraiwa. The co-operation of Hiraiwa, who was Chairman of Japan's leading business association, KEIDANREN, reinforced the impression of change in the relationship between business and politics. This had already been suggested by KEIDANREN's decision in mid-1993 to abandon its role as a conduit for funds to the LDP, although its members remained free to contribute at their own discretion. These developments reflected trends in trade unions, which were disengaging themselves from exclusive relationships with their former political partners.

Although the Socialists were recognized as a potential source of instability within the coalition, the breakdown of the relationship between Hosokawa and his close ally, Masayoshi Takemura, leader of New Party Sakigake, was unexpected. The apparent cause of the rift was the sudden announcement by the Prime Minister in February 1994 of his intention to introduce a 6,000,000m.-yen reduction in income and residential taxes, while planning to establish a national welfare tax of 7% in 1997. This initiative was taken without wide consultation of the coalition partners. The rise in indirect taxation, from its current level of 3%, was strongly opposed not only by the SDPJ, which threatened to leave the coalition, but also by Chief Cabinet Secretary Takemura, who made public his view that the Prime Minister should reconsider this policy. Hosokawa, therefore, was forced to withdraw the proposed tax increases.

Perceptions of relationships within the coalition altered. After Hosokawa tried to reorganize the Cabinet in late February 1994, he appeared to be drawing closer to Ichiro Ozawa and the JRP-Komeito grouping within the coalition, and away from Takemura's New Party Sakigake group, with which Hosokawa had previously suggested he wanted the JNP to merge. Hosokawa was understood to be seeking to remove Takemura as Chief Cabinet Secretary. In early March, however, Hosokawa was forced to abandon his planned reshuffle amidst mounting opposition within the coalition.

The 1994/95 budget was agreed by the Cabinet in mid-February 1994. The opposition, however, prevented its being approved by directing political discussion to details of a 100m.-yen loan received by Hosokawa, during his time as Governor of Kumamoto, from the scandal-tainted Sagawa Kyubin distribution company. This, together with speculation surrounding the Prime Minister's former share dealings, fuelled intense discussion in the Diet. In June Hosokawa was forced to give sworn testimony in the Diet concerning his financial activities.

With the coalition becoming increasingly fragile, Hosokawa resigned on 8 April 1994 amid controversy over his financial dealings. During the subsequent negotiations between the coalition partners regarding the succession to the premiership, the differences between the SDPJ and the JRP over tax policy and the North Korean nuclear issue (see below) became apparent. Tsutomu Hata of the JRP and Michio Watanabe were both potential candidates for the premiership. Watanabe, however, eventually decided against leaving the LDP along with some of his supporters, and on 25 April Tsutomu Hata was chosen as Prime Minister. The SDPJ was offended by the creation in the lower house of a parliamentary organization, Kaishin (Reform), comprising the JRP, JNP, DSP and two smaller political groupings (subsequently joined by the Komeito), which had facilitated Hata's appointment. Hata was therefore obliged to form a minority Government, without the SDPJ and New Party Sakigake, which pledged support only until the passage of all budget legislation through the Diet in mid-June.

This political realignment encouraged Satsuki Eda in May 1994 to dissolve the USDP and merge the party with the JNP. Within weeks, however, the JNP itself faced an uncertain future. Keigo Ouchi was replaced as leader of the DSP by Takashi Yonezawa in early June. Largely paralysed by the Government's minority status, Hata resigned as Prime Minister on 25 June; a general election was not called. In a surprise development, the SDPJ united with the LDP and New Party Sakigake to secure the election of Tomiichi Murayama, the SDPJ Chairman, as Prime Minister on 29 June, the first Socialist Prime Minister for 47 years. In the House of Representatives' ballot Murayama defeated Toshiki Kaifu, the former LDP Prime Minister, who had left the LDP to join Ozawa, by 261 to 214 votes. Many LDP members opposed Murayama's election, and even within the SDPJ there was disapproval, especially following Murayama's statement that the unarmed neutrality policy of the SDPJ was outdated and that he no longer considered the SDF to be unconstitutional.

In August 1994 leaders of the major Japanese opposition parties, at the instigation of former Prime Ministers Hata, Hosokawa and Kaifu, agreed to establish a consultative body, as a first step towards founding a joint party to counter the LDP-New Party Sakigake-SDPJ coalition Government. In the same month Murayama appointed Sohei Miyashita, the former Director-General of the Defence Agency, as the Director-General of the Environment Agency in place of Shin Sakurai, who had angered China and the Republic of Korea by denying Japan's 'war of aggression' in the Pacific during the Second World War. Sakurai was the second Cabinet member to resign within three months over controversial remarks about Japan's war record; Shigeto Nagano, the Minister of Justice, had been forced to resign in May after describing the 1937 Nanjing massacre (in which more than 300,000 Chinese citizens were killed by Japanese soldiers) as a 'fabrication'.

The longer the SDPJ remained in government, the more difficult it became for it to appeal to traditional supporters. In late September 1994 Murayama announced an increase in the consumption tax, from 3% to 5%, to take effect in April 1997. Although, in mitigation, a two-tiered reduction in income and residential taxes of some 5,500,000m. yen was to be introduced, it seemed ironic that a Socialist Prime Minister should announce this increase in tax, the introduction of which his party had so long opposed. The SDPJ was widely considered the party most likely to threaten the coalition Government's stability, but rather than its pacifist wing, it was those on the right of the SDPJ who began to endanger the party. In October 1994 Murayama was forced to question another of his party's former policy commitments, when he suggested that the construction of further nuclear power plants might be unavoidable. The following day, to Murayama's apparent consternation, the Secretary-General of the SDPJ, Wataru Kubo, echoed those proposing the dissolution of the party and the formation of a new party of social democrats and liberals. Kubo planned to co-operate with Sadao Yamahana, who was poised to lead his own faction out of the SDPJ.

Meanwhile, among the opposition parties, although the Shinseito, the Komeito, DSP, JNP and LDP splinter groups had largely agreed by September 1994 that they should merge, misgivings remained among some of the smaller partners that the Shinseito and the Komeito would dominate a new opposition party. Difficulties were also experienced in negotiating the inclusion of the Komeito's party machinery in these plans, the party being the only one of the prospective partners to have a national organization. In late October significant differences on foreign policy emerged between the Komeito and the Shinseito. Ozawa urged Japan to become an 'ordinary country', whereas the Komeito reaffirmed its position that Japan should not become involved in peace-keeping operations or any collective security system that required the use of force.

Driven by electoral realities, however, the Komeito opted to divide into two groups. The first comprised all 52 Komeito lower-house members and a majority (24) of its upper-house members. This group was to participate in the anticipated merger of the opposition parties. The second group, which included those not standing for election to the House of Councillors in 1995 and all Komeito local politicians (approximately 3,000), retained the party's machinery, including its newspaper and its headquarters. This arrangement was approved at the party's extraordinary congress in early December 1994. A few days later the New Frontier Party (Shinshinto), comprising all the major opposition parties with the exception of the JCP, held its inaugural congress, during which the former LDP Prime Minister, Toshiki Kaifu, was elected leader, defeating Hata and Yonezawa. Ozawa was elected unopposed as the new party's Secretary-General.

In January 1995 Yamahana began negotiations in preparation for the creation of a new party, claiming the support of as many as 30 SDPJ Diet members. Unable to ignore the momentum that these developments were creating, the SDPJ leadership sought a delay and promised to introduce measures to form a new party at a party congress scheduled to be held in February. Yamahana, however, made it clear that a split in the party was imminent.

On 18 January 1995 the country suffered its worst disaster since the Second World War when a massive earthquake struck the Kobe region, killing more than 6,000 people. The scale of this calamity effectively postponed the dissolution of the SDPJ; politics was thrown into hiatus for several weeks, as public and media attention focused on the efforts to bring relief to the disaster area. In the aftermath of the earthquake, the Government was severely criticized (and subsequently acknowledged responsibility) for the poor co-ordination of the relief operation.

In mid-February 1995 it emerged that two credit unions had been involved in questionable financial dealings with two senior members of the New Frontier Party (Shinshinto) and a number of senior officials of the Ministry of Finance. At the same time, the coalition became involved in a dispute with the Ministry of Finance over attempts by the Cabinet to streamline special public corporations. At issue was a proposal, opposed by the Ministry of Finance, to merge the Japan Development Bank with the Export-Import Bank. In the following month the Minister of Finance, Masayoshi Takemura, was forced to retract the proposal, promising instead to merge the Export-Import Bank with the Overseas Co-operation Fund.

In March 1995 12 people died and more than 5,000 were injured, when a poisonous gas, sarin, was released into the Tokyo underground railway system. The religious sect, Aum Shinrikyo, which was believed to be responsible for a similar incident in Matsumoto in 1994, was widely suspected of launching the attack, although the sect's leader, Shoko Asahara, initially denied that Aum Shinrikyo had been involved. Following a further gas attack in Yokohama in April 1995, a number of sect members were detained by the authorities, and in June Asahara was indicted on a charge of murder. The sect was declared bankrupt in March 1996 and the trial of Asahara opened in the following month. In September Asahara and two other members of the sect were instructed to pay some US $7.3m. in compensation to victims of the Tokyo incident. Attempts by the Ministry of Justice to outlaw the sect, on the grounds that it had engaged in subversive activities, were unsuccessful; however, the sect was denied legal status as a religious organization.

The gas attack in Tokyo, and the sensation generated in the media by the sporadic acts of terrorism that followed, kept party politics at a low ebb. This was reflected in the unified local elections held in April 1995. Despite the election of independent candidates, Yukio Aoshima and Nokku Yokoyama (both former comedians), in the Tokyo and Osaka gubernatorial elections, it was hard to detect anything but apathy in the record low turn-out registered in the vote for members of Japan's local assemblies and local chief executives. In accordance with his campaign pledges, Aoshima took a controversial decision in May to halt the Tokyo Exposition, despite the 98,200m.-yen loss that was expected to ensue. In the same month the SDPJ established a working group to study policy in preparation for the creation of a new party. Yamahana had resigned from the SDPJ earlier in the month.

Following considerable disagreement in the Diet, during which New Party Sakigake threatened to withdraw from the coalition if an apology for Japanese actions in the war were not adopted, a resolution was passed in June 1995 to commemorate the 50th anniversary of the end of the Second World War. The New Frontier Party (Shinshinto) boycotted the vote, while the resolution was openly criticized by a group of 160 LDP Diet members, led by Seisuke Okuno, who objected to the labelling of Japan as an aggressor, preferring to characterize the war as one of liberation for the peoples of Asia. The resolution was also widely criticized as insufficiently explicit by nations whose citizens had been prisoners of the Japanese army during the Second World War.

In late June 1995 a total of some 29,900m. yen was allocated to political organizations in the country's first distribution of subsidies to political parties. In elections to the House of Councillors, held in July, the coalition parties suffered as the electorate registered a post-war record low turn-out of 44.5%. With one-half of the 252 seats being contested, the LDP won 49 seats, the SDPJ 16 and New Party Sakigake three. The New Frontier Party (Shinshinto), benefiting from the strong organizational support of the Soka Gakkai religious organization, was aided by the low turn-out and was able to win some 40 seats. The defeat prompted some LDP Diet members to question Kono's leadership. In August Murayama undertook a major reorganization of the Cabinet. Isamu Miyazaki, an independent civil servant, was appointed Director-General of the Economic Planning Agency. Yohei Kono announced that he would not seek re-election in September to the presidency of the LDP, and was succeeded by Ryutaro Hashimoto, the Minister of International Trade and Industry.

In October 1995 the Minister of Justice was obliged to resign, following allegations that he had accepted an unreported loan of 200m. yen from a Buddhist group. The Director-General of the Management and Co-ordination Agency resigned in November, owing to controversy arising from his suggestion that Japanese colonial rule over Korea had been of some benefit.

Murayama announced his resignation as Prime Minister on 5 January 1996. The three-party coalition continued to govern under the premiership of the LDP President, Ryutaro Hashimoto, whose experience as Minister of Finance and of International Trade and Industry was well respected by Japanese business leaders and US officials. Hashimoto's first task as Prime Minister was to gain Diet approval for the 1996 draft budget, which included expenditure of 685,000m. yen for the liquidation of seven insolvent housing loan companies (*jusen*). The use of public funds for the settlement of the *jusen* issue aroused considerable opposition. In March the New Frontier Party (Shinshinto) organized a parliamentary 'sit-in' to obstruct the Budget Committee meetings of the House of Representatives. Budget deliberations resumed when the Government agreed to the party's demand for an inquiry regarding the alleged acceptance by the LDP Secretary-General, Koichi Kato, of illegal political donations. No action was taken against Kato as a result of this inquiry, and the budget proposals were approved eventually in May with little revision; however, the liquidation of the *jusen* was postponed, pending the introduction of a tighter financial regulatory system.

In early 1996 the Hashimoto administration conducted an investigation into the Ministry of Health and Welfare's poor management of HIV-tainted blood products, which had infected about 1,800 haemophiliac patients with the virus in the 1980s. Led by the Minister of Health and Welfare, Naoto Kan (a Sakigake member), the investigation revealed the irresponsible conduct of the Ministry's officials and of the medical experts involved in delaying the decision to recall tainted products. In August charges of professional negligence were brought against the former head of a government advisory body on AIDS, and in the following month several senior officials from the pharmaceutical company involved in the sale of the contaminated blood products were also arrested. Their trial opened in March 1997.

The opposition New Frontier Party (Shinshinto) elected Ichiro Ozawa as President in December 1995. The contest for the party leadership, however, aggravated the internal division between the Ozawa group and the Hata-Hosokawa group, inviting speculation about a possible dissolution of the party. While this did not occur, individual members expressed opposition to Ozawa's policies. Other parties also experienced internal problems. Some local organizations opposed the transformation of the SDPJ, under Murayama's chairmanship, into a moderate liberal party, and an independent New Socialist Party was formed by left-wing members of the SDPJ. In September 1996, as the end of her term as Speaker of the House of Representatives approached, Takako Doi agreed to resume the leadership of the SDPJ, replacing Murayama. In August Masayoshi Takemura resigned as leader of the New Party Sakigake, the smallest coalition partner, and in the same month the Secretary-General of the party, Yukio Hatoyama, also resigned. With Naoto Kan and several members of the SDPJ, he formed a new party in September, the Democratic Party of Japan (DPJ). Hatoyama felt that New Party Sakigake's electoral prospects had been damaged by the poor performance of its leader, Takemura, during the latter's tenure as Minister of Finance. In late August Shoichi Ide and Hiroyuki Sonoda became leader and Secretary-General, respectively, of New Party Sakigake.

THE ELECTION OF OCTOBER 1996

Such developments indicated that the parties and individual politicians were preparing for a general election, which Hashimoto duly declared would take place on 20 October 1996. The election was to be the first for the lower house to be held under the new electoral system of 300 single-seat constituencies and 200 proportional-representation seats. In an effort to strengthen the electoral bases in new single-member districts, the parties promoted co-operation even with formerly rival organizations. The LDP, for example, approached labour unions, and the New Frontier Party (Shinshinto) received some support from local labour union organizations that refused to support the new SDPJ. At the election the LDP won 239 of the 500 seats in the House of Representatives. The New Frontier Party (Shinshinto) secured 156 seats, the recently-formed DPJ 52 seats, the JCP 26 seats and the SDPJ 15 seats. New Party Sakigake won only two seats. The low turn-out (59%) was regarded as an indication of widespread electoral disillusionment with all the political parties.

At an extraordinary session of the Diet, convened on 7 November 1996, Ryutaro Hashimoto was re-elected Prime Minister, winning a majority in the first ballot in both houses, with the support not only of his own LDP, but also members of the SDPJ and New Party Sakigake. Both the SDPJ, which attributed its loss of seats to its political relationship with the LDP, and New Party Sakigake entered into a policy agreement with the LDP, but decided to remain outside the Government. Thus, the new Cabinet, inaugurated later that day, consisted entirely of LDP members—the first single-party LDP administration since August 1993. The LDP also secured the co-operation of both the New Frontier Party (Shinshinto) and the DPJ, while maintaining the basic framework of the LDP-SDPJ-New Party Sakigake policy accord. Despite criticism from party members seeking yet closer co-operation with the New Frontier Party (Shinshinto), the LDP leadership emphasized the importance of maintaining the unofficial coalition agreement, which highlighted administrative reform as a priority.

The incoming Government was almost immediately beset by corruption scandals, when it was alleged that some 10 LDP members, among them the Ministers of Finance and of Health and Welfare, had received political donations from Junichi Izui, the owner of an oil company, who had been detained on charges of tax evasion. Although not illegal in themselves, the payments should have been disclosed, following the introduction of new legislation concerning political funds. In a further corruption scandal, a Deputy Minister of Health and Welfare was forced to resign after being accused of accepting bribes from the developer of a nursing home. He was subsequently arrested and, at the opening of his trial in March 1997, pleaded guilty to charges of bribery.

THE INTRODUCTION OF ADMINISTRATIVE AND ECONOMIC REFORM

A programme of comprehensive administrative and economic reforms was inaugurated by the new administration, with the establishment of special commissions, chaired by the Prime Minister, to examine a reorganization of ministries and to investigate ways of reducing government expenditure. These commissions proposed a reduction in the number of central ministries, an increase in the powers of the Prime Minister, the establishment of an effective crisis management system to be headed by the Prime Minister, and a review of the structure of public investment. In February 1997 the Government released details of a series of financial deregulation measures: among other reforms, government control over the financial sector was to be reduced and a new financial supervisory agency was to be established, to assume responsibility for some of the Ministry of Finance's regulatory duties. Social welfare reforms were also introduced, with revisions to the national health insurance system and the introduction of a nursing assistance insurance scheme. The Government's management of the nuclear programme was comprehensively reviewed, following two accidents, in December 1995 and March 1997, at plants managed by the Power Reactor and Nuclear Fuel Development Corporation, a public organization supervised by the Science and Technology Agency. Allegations that the corporation had failed to report a further 11 radiation leaks over the previous three years served to heighten public disquiet over Japan's nuclear research and development programme.

In elections to the Tokyo Metropolitan Assembly, held in June 1997, the LDP performed well; moreover, with the defection to the party of several New Frontier Party (Shinshinto) members, the LDP increased its number of seats in the House of Representatives to 247. Meanwhile, the New Frontier Party (Shinshinto) experienced serious internal difficulties as junior members began openly to criticize Ozawa, following the party's dismal performance in the 1996 general election. In January 1997, together with several supporters, Tsutomu Hata, a co-founder of the party, left the New Frontier Party (Shinshinto) to form a new party, the Sun Party (Taiyoto), and in June Hosokawa also relinquished his membership. The New Frontier Party (Shinshinto) sustained a defeat in the elections to the Tokyo Metropolitan Assembly, failing to win a single seat. In July, faced with the apparent decline in the party's influence, several New Frontier Party (Shinshinto) members formed a parliamentary faction with members of the DPJ and the Sun Party. The JCP continued to attract voters who were frustrated with the major parties, and became the second largest party in the Tokyo Metropolitan Assembly.

In September 1997 Hashimoto was re-elected unopposed to the presidency of the LDP. A wide-ranging cabinet reorganization was effected on 11 September, but the appointment of Koko Sato, who had been convicted on charges of bribery, as Director-General of the Management and Co-ordination Agency caused widespread anger, and he was forced to resign shortly afterwards. Meanwhile, the LDP regained its majority in the House of Representatives, following a series of defections by members of the New Frontier Party (Shinshinto). Following further defections from the party, the New Frontier Party (Shinshinto) was dissolved in December. Several new opposition parties were established by former members of the New Frontier Party (Shinshinto), including the Liberal Party (LP), led by Ichiro Ozawa. A subsequent realignment of six political parties, including the DPJ, in January 1998, resulted in the formation of an opposition grouping, Minyuren, that was to constitute the largest opposition force in the Diet. In March the members of Minyuren announced their integration into the DPJ, to form a single party, led by Naoto Kan. The new DPJ was formally established in late April, and became the second largest party in the House of Representatives; Naoto Kan and Tsutomu Hata were elected as President of the party and Secretary-General, respectively.

Meanwhile, in late 1997 a series of corruption scandals, involving substantial payments to corporate racketeers by leading financial institutions, had a severe impact on the Japanese economy. The crisis was exacerbated by an increase in the rate of the unpopular consumption tax, in April, from 3% to 5%, and a decrease in public expenditure (as part of the Government's fiscal reforms), which resulted in a significant weakening in consumer demand. The collapse of several prominent financial institutions in November, and the threat of further bankruptcies, deepened the economic crisis. The Government announced a series of measures designed to encourage economic growth, including a reduction in taxes and, in a major reversal of policy, proposed the use of public money to support the banking system. The credibility of the Ministry of Finance was, however, weakened in late January 1998, when two senior officials were arrested on suspicion of accepting bribes from banks. The Minister of Finance, Hiroshi Mitsuzuka, resigned, accepting full moral responsibility for the affair. He was replaced by Hikaru Matsunaga. The repercussions of the bribery scandal widened in early 1998, as other banks were implicated in the affair. The Bank of Japan, the central bank, subsequently began an internal investigation into its own practices, and in March the Governor resigned, as a result of further bribery allegations made against a senior bank official. He was replaced by Masaru Hayami. Trials of those implicated in the financial scandals continued in 1998–2000.

Attempts to stimulate the Japanese economy continued in early 1998. Several important financial deregulation measures, including those concerning the liberalization of the telecommunications market, retail outlets and foreign-exchange transactions, became effective on 1 April, designated as the Japanese equivalent of the 'Big Bang' liberalization process that had already been undertaken by the London and New York financial markets. Legislation for the reorganization of government ministries was approved by the Diet in June, whereby, from the year 2001, the number of central ministries and agencies was to be reduced from 22 to 13. Hashimoto, however, was not able to enforce effective measures to revive the Japanese economy. Restricted by his commitment to achieve a balanced budget, and confronted with the problem of non-performing loans, totalling some 77,000,000m. yen (subsequently revised upwards, to 87,500,000m. yen), that had been accumulated by Japanese financial institutions, Hashimoto was unable to introduce significant tax cuts, the measure that many analysts considered necessary for economic revival. The economy continued to stagnate during 1998, with declines recorded in consumer spending, the construction industry and manufacturing. Hashimoto was increasingly criticized for his lack of decisive action, and in June the SDPJ and New Party Sakigake left the governing coalition.

In preparation for the election for one-half of the seats in the House of Councillors, the Government issued proposals in late May 1998 for public spending totalling some 16,000,000m. yen. The plan, however, failed to revive Hashimoto's popularity and boost public confidence in his administration of the economy, and in the election to the upper house, held on 12 July, the LDP performed poorly, losing 17 of its 61 seats contested. The DPJ, by contrast, won 27 seats, bringing its total to 47, and the JCP more than doubled its representation, taking 15 seats. Electoral turn-out was low, at some 58%. Hashimoto resigned as President of the LDP, assuming responsibility for the party's failure at the election, and was replaced by Keizo Obuchi, formerly Minister of Foreign Affairs, and leader of the largest faction in the LDP. Despite the party's preference for a consensus candidate, the election for LDP President was unusually open, and two other candidates, Seiroku Kajiyama, whose economic policies were favoured by business leaders, and Junichiro Koizumi, who was popular with the electorate, also contested the ballot of party members in the Diet. All three candidates were unanimous, however, in emphasizing the need for permanent tax cuts and reform of the tax system. Obuchi was subsequently elected Prime Minister, on 30 July, at an extraordinary session of the Diet, despite the election by the House of Councillors of an opposition candidate, Naoto Kan, as their choice for Prime Minister. The decision of the lower house, nevertheless, prevailed.

Obuchi's Government, appointed on his election, and designated an 'economic reform' cabinet, comprised a large number of hereditary politicians. The appointment of Kiichi Miyazawa, a former Prime Minister, as Minister of Finance, was, however, welcomed by some observers, owing to his financial expertise. Doubts nevertheless remained about the new Government's commitment to economic reform, and Obuchi's administration failed to attract the support of the electorate, achieving extremely low approval ratings. In his inaugural policy address to the legislature Obuchi announced that attempts to achieve a balanced budget were to be postponed, and proposed additional tax cuts, to the value of 7,000,000m. yen. His reluctance to commit the Government to the closure of failing banks and to a fundamental restructuring of the banking sector, however, led to a further weakening of confidence in the Japanese economy. Following weeks of negotiations, in October 1998 the Diet approved banking legislation which included provisions for the nationalization of failing banks, as demanded by the opposition. In November the Government presented a 24,000,000m.-yen programme aimed at revitalizing the country's economy, but ruled out a reduction in the consumption tax.

In November 1998 Komei merged with Shinto Heiwa (New Peace Party, founded in 1997) to form New Komeito, which thus became the second-largest opposition party. In the same month Fukushiro Nukaga, the Director-General of the Defence Agency, resigned from the Government to assume responsibility for a procurement scandal involving his agency. In mid-November the LDP and the LP reached a basic accord on the formation of a coalition, which would still remain short of a majority in the upper house. In early January 1999, following intense discussions, agreement was reached on coalition policies. Ozawa appeared to have won concessions on a number of proposals that the LP wanted to be submitted for consideration by the Diet in forthcoming sessions, including a reduction in the number of seats determined by proportional representation in the House of Representatives from 200 to 150 and provision for an expansion of Japan's participation in UN peace-keeping operations. The Cabinet was reshuffled to include the LP, with the number of ministers reduced from 20 to 18 (excluding the Prime Minister). Takeshi Noda of the LP, the only new member of the Cabinet, was appointed as Minister of Home Affairs. At the end of January the Government adopted an administrative reform plan, which aimed to reduce further the number of cabinet ministers and public servants and to establish an economic and fiscal policy committee. Draft legislation on the implementation of the plan was introduced to the Diet in April. In March Shozaburo Nakamura resigned as Minister of Justice following allegations of repeated abuse of power.

Local elections in April 1999 were largely unremarkable; 11 of the 12 governorships contested were won by the incumbents, all standing as independents. The 19-candidate gubernatorial election for Tokyo created by far the most interest. The convincing victory of Shintaro Ishihara, a nationalist writer and a former Minister of Transport under the LDP (although now unaffiliated), was regarded as an embarrassment for the ruling party, which had supported Yasushi Akashi, a former senior UN official. Ishihara immediately provoked controversy, making a series of inflammatory comments about the 1937 Nanjing massacre and criticizing the Chinese Government, which responded angrily, prompting the Japanese Government to distance itself publicly from the new Governor's remarks.

In June 1999 the Government voted to grant official legal status to the *de facto* national flag (*Hinomaru*) and anthem (*Kimigayo*), despite considerable opposition owing to their association with Japan's militaristic past. The necessary legislation was subsequently approved by the Diet, however, and became effective in mid-August. Meanwhile, in July New Komeito agreed to join the ruling LDP-LP coalition, giving the Government a new majority in the upper house and expanding its control in the lower house to more than 70% of the seats. Negotiations on policy initiatives proved difficult, however, and were still continuing in September, owing to differences over a number of contentious issues such as constitutional revision and New Komeito's opposition to a reduction in the number of seats in the lower house, as favoured by the LP. Obuchi was re-elected to the presidency of the LDP in September, defeating Koichi Kato, a former Secretary-General of the party, and Taku Yamasaki, a former policy chief. Naoto Kan, however, failed to retain the presidency of the DPJ, and was replaced by Yukio Hatoyama.

A new Cabinet was appointed in October 1999. The Minister of Finance, Kiichi Miyazawa, and the Director-General of the Economic Planning Agency retained their portfolios, while Michio Ochi was appointed Chairman of the Financial Reconstruction Commission. The LP and New Komeito each received one cabinet post. A basic accord on coalition policy included an agreement to seek a reduction in the number of seats in the House of Representatives, initially by 20 and subsequently by a further 30.

At the end of September 1999 a serious accident at a uranium-processing plant at Tokaimura, which raised levels of radiation to 15,000 times the normal level, severely undermined public confidence in the safety of Japan's nuclear industry. Furthermore, in November it was revealed that in recent inspections by government officials, 15 of 17 nuclear facilities had failed to meet the required health and safety standards. In December legislation was enacted that aimed to prevent accidents and to improve procedures for the management of any future incidents at nuclear power facilities. In February 2000 the Government announced that a total of 439 people had been exposed to radiation in the Tokaimura accident (compared with initial estimates of 69), and by April two workers from the plant had died from radiation exposure.

Trials continued in 1997–99 of members of Aum Shrinrikyo, the cult believed to be responsible for the sarin gas attack on the Tokyo underground railway system in 1995. In September 1999 Masato Yokoyama, a leading member of the cult, became the first of those accused to receive the death sentence; at least five other cult members had been sentenced to death by mid-2000. In late 1999 the Diet enacted legislation aimed at curbing the activities of Aum Shrinrikyo and, in an attempt to prevent any such restriction, the cult's leaders announced a suspension of all external activities, and acknowledged culpability for a number of crimes, including the gas attack. In January 2000 the cult announced that its name was to change to Aleph Shrinrikyo, and that it no longer considered Shoko Asahara, on trial for his part in the gas attack, to be its leader. In February, following a police raid on Aum Shinrikyo premises, it was revealed that a number of major companies and government agencies had placed orders for computer software with a firm believed to be a major source of revenue for Aum Shinrikyo; the Defence Agency subsequently announced that it was to abandon software purchased from the company for use by the SDF.

At the end of 1999 media reflections on the past 12 months reported that the popular mood was still pessimistic, despite the Economic Planning Agency's October statement that the economy was 'continuing a moderate improvement'. In fact, the country was back in recession, following a second consecutive quarter of negative growth from October to December. Consumer spending remained weak, overcapacity was still a problem, and unemployment continued to rise. The very fabric of Japan seemed to be fragmenting, as juvenile involvement in serious crimes rose, various police scandals were uncovered, rocket launches by Japan's Space Agency failed, railway tunnels collapsed and nuclear-power workers ladled radioactive material with buckets. There was persistent scepticism regarding the fate of the administrative reforms that had been adopted in July and about the Government's commitment to fiscal discipline. The new coalition, which was regularly threatened with withdrawal by Ozawa and the LP, did not inspire confidence in rational decision-making, and the promise made to Ozawa that priority would be given during the forthcoming Diet session to the bill to reduce the number of seats in the House of Representatives indicated difficulties to come.

Unpopular as the three-party alliance was, its significance became apparent as Obuchi was forced, in the interests of keeping his coalition together, to honour his promise to Ozawa of electoral reform. The coalition between the LP and the LDP had been underpinned by Obuchi's agreement to reduce the number of seats determined by proportional representation by 50. The New Komeito, a party that was heavily dependent on these seats and passionately opposed to the proposed legislation, was, in turn, promised a lesser reduction in proportional-representation seats, of only 20, to be followed by a reduction of 30 single-member seats at a later date. The nature of the divisions between the alliance parties meant that no compromise was possible with the principal opposition party, the DPJ, which, as the potential second party in a two-party system, was strongly in favour of a reduction in the number of proportional-representation seats from 200 to 150. However, the size of the coalition rendered a compromise unnecessary. In February 2000, without committee debate, and despite a boycott of the Diet by opposition parties, legislation was passed to reduce the number of proportional-representation seats in the House of Representatives from 500 to 480. The action strongly recalled an earlier era of 'snap votes'. The reinforced majority of the expanded coalition, and the Government's success in enacting the controversial legislation on security, the flag and the anthem, aroused old fears, and the opposition parties responded by reverting to the old tactics of boycott. Between 20 January and 9 February the Government ruled unopposed.

Meanwhile, in January 2000 multi-party commissions had been established in both houses to review the Constitution over a five-year period. The commissions were discussion bodies only and were not permitted to submit legislation to the Diet. However, their range of discussion was broad and included both the structure of the bicameral legislature itself and Article 9. The inauguration of the commissions was a significant development, which marked a new openness and a wide agreement on the need for debate. A poll taken as the commissions began their work suggested that 50.6% of people supported constitutional amendment, compared with 44.9% in 1997, while only 24.1% opposed any amendment, compared with 31.0% three years earlier.

The first ordinary session of the Diet in 2000 was different, owing not only to the boycott and the 'alternative Diet' established by the opposition, but also to the implementation of changes to Diet procedure, which ended the system of responses being given by bureaucrats on behalf of ministers. The end of the 100-year-old practice was expected to enliven Diet debate, and was regarded as a means of educating a new style of politician and facilitating the shift to a more politician-led pattern of policy-making. To that end, the cabinet reshuffle in October 1999 had brought the appointment of parliamentary vice-ministers with particular expertise in the areas covered by their ministries. Vice-ministerial appointments thus included senior people who might previously have been appointed to a cabinet position. Among these was Nishimura Shingo, of the LP, who was forced to resign from the Defence Agency after arguing that the Diet should debate the possibility of Japan acquiring nuclear weapons. The goal of politician-led governance was also behind the inauguration of a Prime Minister's question time. However, the new Diet standing committee, which became the forum for the 40-minute weekly debate between the Prime Minister and the leaders of the opposition parties, failed to win critical acclaim.

In addition to the strong parliamentary opposition, the Government was also undermined by a number of scandals during 2000. In February the Chairman of the Financial Reconstruction Commission, Michio Ochi, was forced to resign after he remarked that he would endeavour to ensure that bank inspections were lenient, and in that month a personal aide to the Prime Minister was accused of misappropriating shares, which he later traded. In March a number of incidents of police misconduct at a senior level resulted in disciplinary action being taken against the chief of the National Police Agency.

In February 2000, meanwhile, Japan's first female governor took office in Osaka, having won a by-election necessitated by the resignation of the previous incumbent after his indictment in December 1999 for sexually harassing a female member of his staff during his election campaign earlier in that year. In April 2000 a second female governor was voted into office in southern Japan. Japan's governors, and local government, played an increasingly prominent role, drawing attention to their desire for greater autonomy. Growing opposition to a number of government projects became evident in 2000; a project to construct a nuclear-power plant in Mie Prefecture was stopped, and in a referendum held in Tokushima, on Shikoku island, in January 90% of the electorate voted against a proposed dam across the Yoshino River (although senior ministers announced that the project would proceed, as local referendums are not legally binding). In February Governor Ishihara of Tokyo proposed that a tax be levied on major banks based on the size of their business rather than their profits; he was criticized by the central Government, which had previously been the only body able to introduce taxes. Ishihara attracted criticism from the foreign residents of Tokyo, and from neighbouring countries, in April, when, in an address to members of the SDF, he blamed foreign residents for a number of serious crimes and referred to them as *sangokujin*, a derogatory wartime term for people from Taiwan and Korea. He also angered the People's Republic of China by visiting Taiwan in November 1999, following an earthquake, and again in May 2000 for the inauguration of the latter's new President, Chen Shui-bian, despite having refused an invitation to visit China as part of celebrations to mark the anniversary of the establishment of relations between Beijing and Tokyo.

Friction within the ruling coalition continued throughout the early months of 2000, as the LP pushed for the consideration of elements of its policy programme, such as the upgrading of the Defence Agency to a ministry and the revision of education legislation, policies that were opposed by New Komeito. As elections to the House of Representatives drew inexorably closer, tension mounted over which coalition candidates would be endorsed. Finally, on 1 April Ozawa told Obuchi that he intended to withdraw the LP from the coalition. On the following day Obuchi suffered a stroke and went into a coma from which he never regained consciousness.

The handling of Obuchi's collapse, and the manner of the subsequent appointment of Secretary-General Yoshiro Mori, head of the third-largest faction in the LDP, as Prime Minister, led many to believe that nothing had changed in the conception of the nature of leadership since the end of the 1955 system. There was criticism of the secrecy surrounding Obuchi's hospitalization, which was kept from the public for more than 20 hours. There was criticism too that Mori was selected to succeed Obuchi as leader of the LDP, and consequently as Prime Minister, by a few politicians in the traditional smoke-filled rooms. The events in the first days following Obuchi's stroke exposed the lack of adequate legislation to prevent a political vacuum in such circumstances. (The Government has since clarified the law, designating a ranking of five ministers to assume the premiership, starting with the Chief Cabinet Secretary.)

Mori immediately announced his commitment to the economic and political reform initiatives of his predecessor, and in early April formed a coalition with New Komeito and a new party, Hoshuto (New Conservative Party, formed by 26 members of the LP on 3 April 2000). All ministers from the Obuchi administration were reappointed to their posts.

Obuchi's death was just one element of a dramatic change in the cast of leading political characters. During April 2000 both Seiroku Kajiyama, a former Chief Cabinet Secretary, and former Prime Minister Noboru Takeshita, hospitalized since April 1999 but still involved in behind-the-scenes manoeuvring, announced their retirement from politics and from the LDP; both men died shortly afterwards. Former Prime Minister Ryutaro Hashimoto was appointed head of the Takeshita faction of the LDP, which had been led by Obuchi prior to his stroke. The physical decline of the old guard, combined with party realignments and a need for expertise that the older politicians lacked, at a time when the demand for greater political input into, and accountability for, policy-making was growing, resulted in greater prominence for the younger generation of politicians. The generational rifts became embarrassingly public in 1993. By 2000, however, the 'policy-making new generation', *seisaku shinjinrui*, was appearing in live television debates, drafting private members' bills, demanding structural change within the parties and rejecting factional discipline.

Following his appointment as Prime Minister, Mori made a number of controversial public statements, expressing imperialist views. He was heavily criticized by the opposition and the media and was forced to issue apologies, although he did not retract his remarks. Shortly prior to the elections, newspaper surveys showed that some 50% of the electorate remained undecided on how to cast their vote; Mori expressed the view that these voters should 'sleep in' on election day, later claiming that his intent was to urge unaligned voters to abstain rather than vote against the LDP, although some concern was expressed as Japan tried to combat voter apathy.

The election, which was held on 25 June 2000, was the first that the LDP had contested as part of a coalition and the first in which it did not present candidates for every seat. The LDP won the most seats (233), although its representation was reduced (from 239 at the 1996 election), and many of its key political figures, including current and former cabinet ministers, lost their seats, particularly in metropolitan areas. The DPJ increased its representation to 127 seats. New Komeito won 31 seats, the LP 22 seats, Hoshuto 20 seats and the SDPJ 19 seats. Only the JCP among the opposition parties suffered a loss of seats. Down six seats, from 26 to 20, the JCP was left without the minimum number of members required to propose legislation to the lower house. The party has since shown a greater inclination to co-operate with the other opposition parties. The LDP benefited from the electoral system, which gives rural areas (where the LDP has strong support) disproportionately high representation. Tradition and family connections remained important, with two candidates (the brother of Noboru Takeshita and the daughter of Keizo Obuchi) winning seats despite their lack of political credentials and experience. Only 62.5% of those eligible participated in the election.

Following the June 2000 election, questions were immediately raised about how long the new Mori administration could survive in the light of the difficulties it faced: further bribery scandals, a reduced mandate, Mori's own poor ratings, LDP factionalism and rivalries, and the need to balance the coalition both in the Cabinet and in terms of policy-making. One week after the appointment of his second Cabinet, in July, only 11% of the public wanted Mori to remain as Prime Minister, while 38.2% wanted him to go and 46.9% were unhappy but resigned (*shikata ga nai*). Meanwhile, within the LDP itself, there were growing demands for Mori's resignation from a cross-factional group of younger Diet members, who were fearful of the coalition losing its majority in the next elections to the House of Councillors.

A summit of G-8 industrialized nations was held in Japan in July 2000. Although riots had been predicted, and Obuchi had been widely condemned for selecting Okinawa as the host site, the summit was uneventful and produced little of substance. At the end of August the Atomic Energy Commission released its long-term programme for 'research, development and utilization of nuclear energy'. In a clear response to the accident at Tokaimura in the previous year, and the debate that it had provoked, numerical targets were removed from the draft plan, with important implications for the future of the nuclear energy programme.

The Diet reconvened in September 2000. In the new session electoral reform again became a source of conflict between the Government and opposition parties. In October an amendment to the existing electoral system for the upper house, whereby voters cast their ballots for parties, to one in which electors could choose to vote either for a party or for an individual candidate, was proposed by the governing coalition. The issue was again the subject of dispute within the coalition, and compromise between the Government and the opposition, which argued that the proposed changes would make campaigning in elections more costly, was elusive. In a repetition of the events of January, the opposition parties commenced a boycott of Diet proceedings in protest against the Government forcing the bill through the upper house. The boycott, which lasted 18 days, ended following an agreement between the governing coalition and the opposition to debate the bill in the House of Representatives. The legislation, which was enacted in late October, also reduced the number of seats in the upper house, from 252 to 247.

Throughout September and October 2000 there was considerable public demand for the suspension of outdated, meaningless public-works projects. In November the coalition parties approved the cancellation of 255 such projects, at an estimated saving of 2,500,000m. yen. Popular alienation from the major parties continued, and trust was undermined by ongoing revelations of misconduct. A leading LDP politician, the Chief Cabinet Secretary, Hidenao Nakagawa, resigned in October after it was alleged, *inter alia*, that he had links to a right-wing activist and had conducted an extramarital affair. Once again the scandal provoked demands for Mori's resignation and criticism of the Prime Minister by senior officials within his own party.

In early November 2000 the leaders of two LDP factions, Koichi Kato and Taku Yamasaki, joined the campaign to force Mori to resign and threatened to abstain if the opposition parties were to propose a vote of no confidence. With a total of 72 members in the House of Representatives, abstention by the Kato and Yamasaki factions was not sufficient to result in the approval of such an opposition motion. Opposition from Miyazawa (Kato's former faction leader and political mentor), a lack of public support for the move, together with splits within the factions over the wisdom of leaving the relative safety of the LDP prior to elections to the upper house, which were scheduled for July 2001, brought the rebellion to a muted end and left Kato seriously, if not permanently, damaged.

Mori survived the November no-confidence vote and two weeks later, in December 2000, reshuffled his Cabinet to include former Prime Minister Hashimoto in the post of Minister of State for the Development of Okinawa and the Settlement of the Northern Territories, areas of particular involvement for Hashimoto during his own premiership. The appointment was well received in the business community, but provoked suggestions that Hashimoto was positioning himself for a return to power.

The new Diet session opened at the end of January 2001, with apologies for the most recent scandal (the misuse of funds by officials of the Ministry of Foreign Affairs) and a plea for the speedy passage of the budget. The new Diet was declared by Mori to be a 'Reform Diet', which would bring about the rebirth of the country. Mori particularly emphasized the role of information technology and education reform in this process. He was also positive about the prospects for structural reforms and for Japan's economic recovery. When the Diet reconvened, the restructuring of central government ministries and agencies was largely complete. A new Cabinet Office had been created, under the control of the Prime Minister, which was ranked higher than other ministries and charged with inter-ministry policy co-ordination. Within the new Cabinet Office, a new Council on Economic and Fiscal Policy, led by the Prime Minister, had been established to address budgetary, financial and economic issues. The Cabinet Secretariat had been strengthened and expanded, and 22 other ministries had been consolidated down to 12. New political posts were established in each of the ministries and agencies to increase political input into the policy-making process. The administrative reforms had a number of objectives, including increased transparency and streamlining, but the major aim was to enable greater political leadership to be assumed by the Prime Minister and the Cabinet.

Despite the enhanced powers afforded to the Prime Minister by the administrative reforms (the ability to propose policy, majority voting in the Cabinet, greater control over appointments, etc.), Mori continued to be a 'lame-duck' Prime Minister throughout the early months of the year, suffering from one scandal after another. The coalition parties were made even less sanguine about their prospects in the election when the DPJ, the LP and the SDP agreed, at the end of March 2001, to put forward joint opposition candidates in 13 of 27 single-seat constituencies. In the mean time fear was mounting, both inside and outside Japan, that continuing economic problems could lead to a political and social crisis, and also that, without a transformation of the nature of political leadership, the economic problems could not be addressed.

At the beginning of April 2001 another reform came into effect, requiring the disclosure of administrative documents on request, although there were suggestions that many documents had been disposed of in the January restructuring. These institutional changes were important, but so too were the people who were to implement them. In April 2001 four candidates contested the presidency of the LDP, a first since the election of Yasuhiro Nakasone as President in 1982. The four were Ryutaro Hashimoto, Junichiro Koizumi, Taro Aso and Shizuka

Kamei. The favourite to win was former Prime Minister Hashimoto, the leader of the largest faction of the LDP, with more than 100 members. Koizumi, who had just resigned as Chairman of the Mori faction, had high public ratings, but had alienated significant sections of the LDP with his plans for the privatization of the postal services. At a time when other traditional sources of LDP support, such as the construction industry and agricultural unions, were losing their ability to gather votes, this was regarded as important and worried Koizumi's supporters, who included Koichi Kato and Taku Yamazaki. Kamei and Aso were outsiders. The system used by the LDP to elect its President has varied over time. On this occasion, the election took place in two stages: a prefectural membership vote, which accounted for 30% of the total, followed by a vote by LDP Diet members. The nature of the election process proved crucial. Although there was much political manoeuvring between the LDP factions, and within the factions between the generations, the overwhelming support of the local branches of the party for Koizumi, who ran on a platform of 'Change the LDP, Change Japan', was decisive, and the LDP Diet members also backed him. Overall, Koizumi won 298 of the 478 presidency votes, while Hashimoto won 155. With the support of the coalition, Koizumi was confirmed as Prime Minister by the Diet.

Koizumi, perceived as eccentric, a reformist and a nationalist, rapidly became a political phenomenon, with unparalleled popularity ratings. His appointment was widely regarded in Japan as signalling a 'seismic shift' within the LDP and, by extension, within the political world as a whole. Nevertheless, Koizumi's ostensibly non-factional appointments to leadership positions within the LDP and to the Cabinet demonstrated the need to keep the party and the coalition, as well as the nation, behind him. Although seven ministers were retained from the previous Mori administration, the new Cabinet contained an unprecedented five women, including Makiko Tanaka as Minister of Foreign Affairs. It also included three non-Diet members, most notably Heizo Takenaka, a pro-reformist economics professor at Keio University and adviser to two previous Cabinets, as Minister of State in charge of Economic and Fiscal Policy and Information Technology Policy, and Nobuteru Ishihara, the son of the controversial Governor of Tokyo, and one of the LDP 'Young Turks', as Minister of State in charge of Administrative Reform and Regulatory Reform. The perception that Koizumi's inaugural speech lacked policy detail, however, did nothing to undermine his cult status, although it may have contributed to his decision to create teams of personal advisers to draft reform proposals on a range of subjects.

Koizumi's depiction in the foreign press as a nationalist was further encouraged by his announcement that he would visit the Yasukuni Shrine on 15 August 2001, the 56th anniversary of the end of the Second World War, and by his vocal support for constitutional revision, beginning with the public election of the Prime Minister, but also embracing changes that would allow Japan to exercise the right of collective security. On this, as on many other issues, Koizumi's political philosophy and policies were close to those of former Prime Minister Nakasone, who strongly supported Koizumi, comparing the new Prime Minister's reforms with his own 'final settlement of post-war politics'. Early indications that Koizumi was prepared to exercise political leadership came in May 2001, with his agreement, against the advice of the Ministry of Justice and the Ministry of Health, Labour and Welfare, to the payment of compensation to leprosy sufferers detained in sanitation centres. More significantly, in June Koizumi moved to impose his own guide-lines for the 2002/03 budget.

In June 2001 an initiative drastically to reform the legal system, which had been overshadowed and delayed by the drama of the LDP presidential election and the appointment of the new Prime Minister, resulted in the Final Report of the Judicial Reform Council and government support for its recommendations. A bill to increase the number of lawyers (from 20,000 to 50,000 by 2018); to open postgraduate law schools in 2004; to increase the pass rate in law studies from 3% to 70%–80%; to introduce juries or lay judges in criminal trials; and to shorten trials and introduce trial deadlines was to be considered by the Diet later in the year. These legal reforms were likely to be of great social and economic significance as Japan endeavoured to become a law-based society, competitive internationally and able to attract investment. The Koizumi reform plan, drafted by the Council on Economic and Fiscal Policy, was also published in June. The overall short-term objectives of the plan were to eradicate bad loans and to implement reforms in seven areas, including privatization, deregulation, the encouragement of entrepreneurial activity and fiscal reform. The longer-term aim was for private-sector demand to become the driving force of the economy. The proposals reiterated the promise to reduce the issuance of new government bonds in the 2002/03 budget, to 30,000,000m. yen, and to that end, to decrease public works, reform special public corporations and reduce central government grants to local administrations.

Elections to the Tokyo Metropolitan Assembly in early July 2001, in which the LDP secured five additional seats, were regarded as an expression of 'Koizumi fever' and an indication of what the LDP might expect in the elections to the House of Councillors scheduled for later in the month. The new electoral system for the upper house, which allowed votes for individuals as well as parties, led, predictably, to a large number of celebrity candidates. The results of the elections, which were held on 29 July, were even better than anticipated for the LDP, which regained Tokyo and Osaka (lost in 1998), and took 25 of the 27 contested single-seat constituencies. Overall, the coalition won 79 of the 121 contested seats, giving the Government a useful majority of 140 seats in the 247-member chamber. Although Koizumi hailed the results as a mandate for reform, the stock market fell on the following day to a 16-year low, driven by two conflicting fears: firstly, that Koizumi would fail to carry out reform owing to LDP opposition, and secondly, that his reforms would lead rapidly to short-term bankruptcies and loss of corporate earnings. Two consecutive quarters of decline in industrial production since the beginning of the year also compounded these concerns. There were questions in some quarters about the prospects for the Prime Minister's structural reforms. However, Koizumi's public support, the absence of a viable challenger within the LDP and the lack of concerted opposition from outside placed him in a strong position.

At the beginning of September 2001 the Ministry of Finance, together with the Council on Economic and Fiscal Policy, under the Prime Minister, began to consider ministry budget requests for 2002/03. Early indications suggested that the initial requests, which had increased by 3.6% from the previous year, despite the Council's guide-lines urging a 10% reduction, demonstrated heavy involvement by the bureaucracy and LDP policy committees (*zoku*), and little response to Koizumi's request for a new balance to be achieved in budget allocations through targeted, rather than across-the-board, cuts. Koizumi's attempts to give budgetary priority to seven specific areas (environment, the ageing society, local revitalization, urban redevelopment, science, education and information technology (IT)) were undermined by equivocation between ministries and by a failure to persuade the new so-called 'super ministries' to make any changes to the budgetary share of their constituent ministries and agencies. This was particularly evident in the requests from the newly-created Ministry of Land, Infrastructure and Transport. In the first few days of September, the main stock market index declined to its lowest point since 1989, unemployment rose to the highest levels on record and gross domestic product (GDP) for the second quarter of 2001 showed 0.8% negative growth.

The crisis precipitated by the terrorist attacks on the USA on 11 September 2001 gave the Prime Minister the opportunity to exercise the sort of decisive leadership that the structural reforms of the last several years had been designed to enhance. However, the impact of the terrorist attacks on the Japanese stock market was instantaneous. On 12 September the Nikkei index plummeted again, this time to below 10,000 points (its lowest level in 17 years), thus threatening the already beleaguered banking sector and prompting an announcement from Koizumi that the attacks on the USA would not be allowed to slow down the pace of Japan's reforms, including the disposal of non-performing loans. The events of September prolonged Koizumi's political 'honeymoon' for a short while and suppressed growing opposition within the LDP to his political and economic reforms, but the pace of reform was slow. However, Koizumi's non-consensual and decisive leadership style and his reliance on private advisory bodies created a groundswell of opposition within the LDP policy committees and within the LDP leadership itself. His attacks on the faction system in general, and the *Keiseikai* in particular, left him isolated within the party and caused the pace of reform to decelerate.

Koizumi's weakness within the party was in some ways his strength. His relative lack of dependency on the factional leadership, his distance from the vested interests that maintain themselves through public works and his independent sources of policy expertise gave him public popularity that in turn protected him and his reform programme from attack by the LDP. For Koizumi, therefore, maintaining his popularity was vital. Polls conducted in November 2001 showed that his approval ratings had risen even higher for the first three months of the administration before suffering a downturn during mid-2001.

Although Koizumi retained his exceptionally high ratings throughout late 2001, the media began to focus on his failure to deliver reform. The restructuring of the public corporations, one of Koizumi's central aims and one of his more popular reforms, showed signs of failing under concerted opposition both from the ministries, which provide more than half the corporations' directors, and the *zoku,* to which the corporations provide funding in return for political favours. Koizumi's efforts to dissolve or privatize public corporations, the details for which were to be submitted to the Diet in January 2002 had, by September, produced plans for the dissolution of only five of the 163 corporations. The reforms suffered a further set-back with the report by the Government Secretariat for the Promotion of Administrative Reform in early October that recommended the abolition or privatization of only 34 public corporations. In mid-November, Koizumi attempted to take the initiative with an announcement firstly that the Housing Loan Corporation should be abolished, rather than privatized, and secondly that the four major road corporations should suspend construction of 2,383 km of highway and expect an end to government subsidies in the fiscal year 2003.

An outbreak of bovine spongiform encephalopathy (BSE, or so-called mad cow disease), the first outside Europe, was confirmed in September and brought another ministry into the glare of adverse publicity. The Ministry of Agriculture, Forestry and Fisheries (MAFF) stood accused of failing to heed WHO warnings on the use of meat and bone meal feed, and of failing to provide adequate crisis management. The failures were attributed to the lack of cohesion within the ministry, despite previous efforts to restructure it. The Ministry's structural problems were greatly exacerbated by the strength of LDP Diet member links with agricultural interests and their influence on civil servants. One-half of the annual MAFF budget of around 3,000,000m. yen was spent on public works, a sum equal to 20% of the total spending on public works.

The outbreak of BSE, along with the decline in IT production and the impact of the terrorist attacks in the USA, forced the Cabinet Office to lower its projected economic growth rate from 1.7% to −1% and led the Ministry of Finance to warn of the possibility of a contraction of GDP for the fiscal year 2001 and of a fourth consecutive year of negative economic growth; the longest experienced since the beginning of the Meiji era. The ongoing recession was blamed for a rise of nearly 18% in serious crimes between 2000 and 2001, mainly the result of a massive increase in armed robbery and arson. The unemployment rate for September rose to 5.3%, with the construction sector and IT industries continuing to suffer the most severe job losses. In addition to the redundancies, many larger companies began to implement wage reductions. The response of the Minister for Health, Labour and Welfare to the September figures was to declare that the employment situation had entered a state of emergency. The situation continued to worsen especially for males in the transport, communication, manufacturing and construction sectors. The response of RENGO (Japanese Trade Union Confederation) was to abandon the post-war *shunto* system of annual unified wage increase demands and to fight wage cuts and job insecurity. The shift towards a merit-based system is a function of restructuring and unemployment but it also reflects a growing desire for a more competition-orientated society and a decline in the number of people who want an egalitarian society with a minimal gap between the rich and the poor.

Demographic issues, in particular declining population growth and an ageing society, continued to attract attention. Official figures showed population growth at its slowest since the Second World War, the first ever decline in the 'productive age group' (aged between 15 and 64 years), and those in the 'old' category (aged over 65 years) exceeding the 'young' (children under 15 years) for the first time since records began in 1920. Related to this, the average age of marriage continued to rise, although unmarried cohabitation and the number of children born out of wedlock remained low. Figures released in February 2002 suggested that the situation was graver than previously predicted and that an ongoing decline in the fertility rate would result in Japan's population peaking in 2006, one year earlier than expected. By 2050 the population will have declined to 100.59m. people, 35% of whom will be over 65, double the figure at the beginning of the 21st century. Of the total population in 2050, it is anticipated that only 54% will be of working age.

The implications of a decreasing population for the social welfare system are stark. One immediate effect of the downward revision of predicted fertility rates to 1.39 from 1.61 is on the percentage of salary that will need to be paid in pension contributions, which will increase as the declining numbers of those in work have to support a growing population of retirees. The percentage cost of healthcare to GDP is expected to more than double, to 18%, by 2025; public expenditure will grow by 7.5% of GDP over the same period, in order to pay for the ageing population. Despite the urgent need for a sustainable social security system, plans for medical insurance reform and pension reform put forward by the Government met strong opposition from LDP *zoku*.

Since the mid 1970s Japan has also seen a net outflow of skilled workers through migration. One possible way of addressing the demographic stagnation that is such an obstacle to economic growth would be changes to the immigration laws to encourage inward migration. Minor amendments in the early 1990s brought slight increases in the numbers of certain types of immigrant. However, following the attacks on the USA in September 2001, the Government's seven-point plan strengthened international co-operation and information exchange on immigration controls, and further opening of national borders were not anticipated in the near future. Koizumi instructed the Ministry of Health, Labour and Welfare to produce plans by September 2002 to encourage higher birth rates. These are expected to go well beyond the provision of nursery care and to include financial incentives, paternity leave and low-interest loans for higher education.

The birth of Princess Toshi (Aiko), the first child of the Crown Prince and Princess, took place in December 2001. In accordance with the Imperial Household Law, the younger brother of the Crown Prince remained second in line to the throne, but the birth drew further debate on the need for revision of the law to allow female succession. The proposal attracted widespread support from the public and also among members of the Diet who, under the post-war Constitution, would be required to enact the changes.

Media evaluations of the workings of the new government structure, one year after its inception, reported rigidity in bureaucratic structures, and continued bureaucratic dominance. There appeared to be little transfer of actual power from the bureaucracy, despite increased formal powers for the Prime Minister's Office, the creation of the Financial Services Agency and the Council on Economic and Fiscal Policy (CEFP), and the introduction of senior vice-ministers and parliamentary secretaries. The media viewed the reshuffle of a number of these vice-ministers and parliamentary secretaries in January 2002 as a retreat by Koizumi on faction-based appointments and a victory for Hashimoto. In July 2002 a review of the functions of the CEFP was ordered amid fears that it was not fulfilling its original purpose of transferring responsibility for economic and fiscal policy from the bureaucracy to the Prime Minister and Cabinet. Reforms to the Diet, such as the introduction of Prime Minister's 'question time' and the abolition of the practice whereby bureaucrats answered on behalf of ministers, did not attract greater public attention to the Diet nor render its work any more meaningful.

Koizumi's dismissal of Tanaka Makiko on 29 January 2002 after weeks of pressure from the LDP, despite his pledge not to reshuffle his Cabinet during his term of office, appeared to precipitate a sharp decline in the Prime Minister's popularity. Predictions of a return to factional politics and an end to the prospects for reform caused falls in the stock market, in government bonds and in the value of the yen. Tanaka claimed that the Prime Minister had broken his pledges on reform and was allowing his Cabinet to be run by former Prime Minister Mori. The opposition DPJ began to behave like an opposition party and criticized Koizumi's handling of the economy, rising unemployment and the growing number of scandals involving senior members of the LDP. For the first time Koizumi was no longer able to use the promise of an approach to the DPJ as a credible threat to control the LDP.

In early March 2002 one of Koizumi's two closest allies, Kato Koichi, resigned following the arrest of the former head of his Tokyo office on charges of tax evasion and accepting bribes for facilitating the allocation of public works. Kato's resignation from the LDP followed that of the former Director-General of the Hokkaido and Okinawa Development Agency, Suzuki Muneo, on charges of malpractice. The scandals focused attention on the urgent need to address the issues of the relationship of LDP Diet members and the bureaucracy with regard to policy-making. Koizumi's rising unpopularity, along with a decline in support for the LDP, prompted coalition fears of adverse voter reaction at the forthcoming elections.

Almost simultaneously with the resignations, a draft report was produced by the LDP National Vision Project Headquarters under Koizumi, and submitted to the Prime Minister without prior consideration by the General Council. The report, which proposed a study of measures to create a cabinet-led system and deny influence to politicians with vested interests, drew an angry response from the LDP, both for its content and the manner of its introduction. The proposals included cabinet drafting of all bills and policies, restrictions on contact between backbench politicians and bureaucrats, and an end to approval of bills by party committees before submission to the Diet. The report, and its rejection by the LDP, was best viewed in the context of Koizumi's attempt to open up the postal delivery service to private competition, which, under the LDP operating methods, might be derailed by one dissenting LDP vote. In an attempt to re-establish his reformist credentials, the Prime Minister also proposed restricting political donations from public works contractors and reviewing the fund-raising role of local branches of political parties.

Restructuring of the postal services remained the basis of Koizumi's reform programme because of the implications for controlling vested interest politics. It was opposed by many in the LDP for the same reasons. In an unusual step, the four postal bills were submitted to the Diet without the support of the LDP, and the passage of the legislation secured only after some modification of the content and the promise of a cabinet reshuffle. The compromises resulted in requirements for entering the mail delivery sector being pitched at a level that would exclude most private companies. The extended Diet session ended on 31 July 2002.

Following the Prime Minister's North Korean initiative, his popularity improved. This initiative, and the strong expectation that Hatoyama would be re-elected as leader of the DPJ in the forthcoming elections for party president, gave rise to speculation that Koizumi would call a general election. In late September 2002 Koizumi effected a cabinet reorganization. Hakuo Yanagisawa, Minister of State responsible for the Financial Services Agency and regarded as an opponent of reform, was among those replaced.

JAPAN'S FOREIGN RELATIONS

In the 20 years following the Second World War, successive Japanese Governments sought to shelter the country behind its alliance with the USA, and to avoid independent commitments in foreign policy. When Japan signed the San Francisco Treaty in 1951, it also signed a bilateral security treaty with the USA, whereby the Japanese Government granted the use of military bases in Japan exclusively to the USA in return for a US commitment to provide military support to Japan in the event of external aggression. Japan has since then functioned as a main base for US forces in eastern Asia, its sole military obligation being to defend its own territory. Thus, Japan will not go to the defence of its ally if the USA is attacked elsewhere. The insistence of the USA that Japan rearm was a significant factor in the reawakening of Japanese foreign policy.

Prime Minister Hosokawa expended every effort to promote Japan's international status, embarking in September 1993 upon a visit to New York, where he met President Clinton and also addressed the General Assembly of the United Nations (UN). Although a long-standing US demand to liberalize the Japanese rice market was met in December, it was significant that the agricultural trade accord was drafted by the Secretariat of the General Agreement on Tariffs and Trade (GATT), and accepted by Japan in the context of the successful attempt to complete the Uruguay Round of negotiations. The agreement gave foreign rice-producers access to Japanese domestic markets, beginning with 4% of the market and rising to 8% over six years, after which rice would be subject to a tariff system.

In its relations with the USA, Japan was unable to demonstrate any shift in policy, resisting efforts by the Clinton administration to introduce numerical targets as 'objective criteria' in the trade negotiations at the Washington Summit in July 1994. The failure of these talks, with Hosokawa's rejection of US demands, was heralded in Japan as an indication of a new maturity in the bilateral relationship. Japan's policy towards the USA subsequently began to follow two different directions. On the one hand, in negotiations on the automobile trade, an uncompromising position was maintained, despite US demands for concessions. On the other hand, however, Japan was prepared to meet US expectations in areas such as Japanese involvement in UN activities, and security ties with the USA (for the latter see below).

After 10 months of trade negotiations at the sub-cabinet level, the USA expressed strong dissatisfaction with the proportion of Japanese government contracts awarded to non-Japanese firms. A 60-day consultation period was established, following the expiry of which the USA promised that retaliatory sanctions would be imposed against Japan. While agreement was reached by early October 1994 in three of the four main areas under discussion, the two sides had yet to resolve their dispute over the automobile trade. Following the failure of the trade negotiations in early May 1995, the USA threatened to impose severe sanctions on a number of luxury car models. Japan responded by lodging a complaint with the World Trade Organization (WTO), on the grounds that the USA's actions violated the WTO Agreement and other international accords. The USA retaliated by filing a complaint of its own. Prime Minister Murayama found some support for Japan's position on a visit to EU leaders in Paris in June, but the USA added the threat of further sanctions on Japanese air cargo after access to flights was not granted to a US carrier. In late June, immediately prior to the introduction of US sanctions, an agreement was reached, whereby Japan promised to allow an increase in the proportion of US-manufactured parts bought by Japanese car-makers in North America, and to guarantee that Japanese manufacturers would not contravene their 1994 purchase plans. An agreement on the air cargo dispute was also reached in July 1995, although discussions continued on perceived obstacles to foreign competition in the Japanese photographic film market.

Japanese-US trade negotiations in 1996 continued to focus on the opening of the Japanese market. Specific areas of contention included photographic film and insurance, and discussions began on the renegotiation of two previous agreements on semiconductors and airline routes, which were due to expire in that year. Agreement on the issue of semiconductors was reached in August, whereby two new bodies were to be established to regulate the market. However, in the wake of the events in Okinawa (see below), Prime Minister Hashimoto and President Clinton were more concerned with reinforcing the bilateral security relationship than trade disputes in late 1996 and early 1997. At a meeting in April 1997 they discussed co-operation in regional affairs, focusing on the issue of stability in the Korean peninsula. As Japan's trade surplus with the USA increased in early 1997, with notably, a growth in the export of automobiles, it was feared that the friction over trade issues might intensify. The USA continued to put pressure on Japan to open its market further and to transform its export-orientated economy to one based on the domestic market. In September the USA imposed large fines on three Japanese shipping companies, following complaints about restrictive harbour practices in Japan; however, an agreement to reform Japanese port operations was concluded shortly thereafter. Negotiations on increased access to airline routes for Japanese and US carriers were also successfully concluded in January 1998.

During 1998 the USA became increasingly concerned about the deceleration of the Japanese economy and its impact on other Asian economies, already severely depressed by the regional currency crisis. Discussion of Japan's economic and financial problems was the focus of the G-7 summit meeting in April. During a two-day visit to Japan in November, President Clinton urged the Government to implement measures rapidly to encourage domestic demand, reform the banking sector and liberalize the country's markets, reinforcing earlier warnings that it risked provoking protectionist measures. The USA was also critical of Japan's refusal to lower tariffs on rice and forestry and fisheries products, or to curb low-priced steel exports to the USA. Japan's trade surplus with the USA continued to increase, growing by some 33% in 1998, to reach its highest level since 1987. In May 1999, during a six-day visit by Prime Minister Obuchi to the USA (the first such official state visit in 12 years), Clinton praised Obuchi's efforts to stimulate economic recovery and welcomed Japanese plans for further deregulation in several sectors, including telecommunications, energy, housing and financial services. Meanwhile, the dispute over Japanese steel exports had escalated. A ruling, in April, by the US Department of Commerce that Japan had 'dumped' hot-rolled steel into the US market was endorsed, in June, by the US International Trade Commission, and punitive duties were subsequently imposed. In November Japan brought a complaint before the WTO against the US ruling.

Stability in the Asia-Pacific region is a vital consideration in Japanese foreign policy, since Japan depends on regional markets for a substantial proportion of its foreign trade, as well as for its imports of vital raw materials. In January 1993, on a tour of member countries of the Association of South East Asian Nations (ASEAN), Prime Minister Miyazawa outlined his policy for the area, which included regional co-operation, a commitment to economic openness in the Asia-Pacific area, and a fuller political and security dialogue among ASEAN countries. In August the incoming Prime Minister, Hosokawa, promised to initiate a new era in Japan's relations with its neighbours by making a full apology for Japan's war record in his first policy speech. However, political pressure forced him to moderate his language and to state that Japan would not pay compensation to victims of Japanese aggression. On a tour of the Philippines, Viet Nam, Malaysia and Singapore in late August 1994, Prime Minister Murayama emphasized Japan's responsibility and remorse for its actions in the Second World War, and its desire for reconciliation. Shortly afterwards, and on the same theme, Murayama announced the 'Peace, Friendship and Exchange Initiative', a 100,000m.-yen programme to promote historical studies and exchanges among Asian nations. Murayama chaired the Asia-Pacific Economic Co-operation (APEC) meeting in Osaka in November 1995, as part of Japan's commitment to regional co-operation. Although Japan's close security co-operation with the USA sometimes caused concern among its Asia-Pacific neighbours, Japan's relations with these countries remained stable in the late 1990s. Hashimoto visited ASEAN countries in January 1997, and the Japanese Minister of Foreign Affairs participated in the meeting of ASEAN and other foreign ministers in July. However, the Asian economic crisis that began in late 1997 threatened to disrupt Japan's trading relations with its neighbours. At the annual IMF-World Bank conference, held in late 1997 in Hong Kong, Japan proposed the establishment of an Asian Monetary Fund, a regional organization in which only Asian countries would participate. Strong objections were voiced by the USA and European countries, which advocated a more international response to the crisis. Japan responded by co-operating with the USA and international financial institutions in providing aid for, among other countries, Thailand and Indonesia. However, Asian Governments remained dissatisfied with Japan's response to the crisis, fearing that the weakness of the Japanese currency would prevent regional economic re covery by inhibiting a growth in exports. In response to increasing international pressure, in October 1998 the Japanese Government announced a US $30,000m.-aid 'package' for Asian countries, and in November the USA and Japan presented a joint initiative for growth and economic recovery in the region. In addition, at an ASEAN summit meeting, held in Hanoi, Viet Nam, in December, Japan pledged further assistance, in the form of loans worth some US $5,000m., to be disbursed over a three-year period.

In May 1990 Japan's relations with the Republic of Korea, which had been strained since the Second World War, were greatly improved following a visit by President Roh Tae-Woo, during which Prime Minister Kaifu offered an unequivocal apology for Japanese colonial aggressions on the Korean peninsula in the past, and promised to improve legislation protecting the basic rights of those Koreans and their descendants resident in Japan, by 1993. In February 1995 Prime Minister Murayama publicly acknowledged that Japan had been responsible, in part, for the post-war division of the Korean peninsula. He was forced to retract the statement, however, following bitter controversy in the Diet. In June the Diet issued a resolution expressing deep regret for the atrocities committed by Japanese troops during the Second World War. The resolution, which was timed to coincide with the 50th anniversary of the end of the war, was widely criticized, however, by former prisoners of war of the Japanese, as insufficiently explicit and for being a personal statement by the Prime Minister, rather than a representation of the views of the Government as a whole. In August Murayama formally reiterated the statement of remorse, expressing 'a heartfelt apology' and admitting that Japanese national policy during the Second World War had been 'mistaken'. He discounted, however, the possibility of individual compensation payments by the Government to Asian (mostly Korean) women, used by Japanese troops for sexual purposes during the war ('comfort women'), preferring to advocate the creation of a private fund to collect donations from the Japanese people.

In February 1996 a report issued by the UN criticized Japan's treatment of the 'comfort women' and urged it to accept full responsibility for its actions. The first payments from the private fund, created to provide compensation to the victims, were disbursed in August, together with a letter of apology from Hashimoto, to four Philippine women. Further payments were made in January 1997 to several South Korean victims, but the majority of groups representing the women refused to accept payment from the fund, demanding that compensation be forthcoming from official, rather than private, sources. In April 1998, however, in the first such ruling, a Japanese district court ordered the Government to compensate three former 'comfort women' from South Korea. Meanwhile, in June 1996 Hashimoto met the South Korean President, Kim Young-Sam, to discuss bilateral co-operation in economic and security affairs. Relations with the Republic of Korea were strained in late 1996 over a territorial dispute concerning a group of islands, to which both countries laid claim.

Relations with the Republic of Korea deteriorated in early 1998, when Japan unilaterally terminated a bilateral fisheries agreement, following the failure of negotiations concerning the renewal of the accord. Discussions were held at intervals during 1998 to attempt to renegotiate the terms of the agreement. The Japanese Government contributed financial aid to the Republic of Korea as part of the international effort to stimulate its economic recovery. Japan's relations with the Republic of Korea improved considerably in October, during a four-day visit to Tokyo by President Kim Dae-Jung. A joint declaration was signed by the South Korean President and Prime Minister Obuchi, in which Japan apologized for its conduct towards Korea during the period of Japanese colonial rule. Emperor Akihito also expressed deep sorrow for the suffering inflicted on the Korean people. In addition, the Republic of Korea agreed to revoke a ban on the import of various Japanese goods, while Japan promised US $3,000m. in aid to the Republic of Korea in support of its efforts to stimulate economic recovery. In November the two countries concluded negotiations on the renewal of their bilateral fisheries agreement, which came into effect in January 1999. An agreement to modify some of the terms of the accord was reached in March, following a series of differences over its implementation. Increased co-operation was emphasized during a visit by Obuchi to the Republic of Korea later that month, when both countries agreed to strengthen bilateral economic relations, and Japan pledged further aid to the

Republic of Korea. At the end of May 2000 Prime Minister Mori visited Seoul and held a meeting with President Kim Dae-Jung, in which he affirmed Japan's support for the forthcoming inter-Korean summit and advocated close co-operation between Japan and the Republic of Korea with a view to establishing peace and stability on the Korean peninsula.

Japan's attempts to establish full diplomatic relations with the Democratic People's Republic of Korea (North Korea) in early 1991 were hindered by the latter's insistence that Japan make financial reparations for losses sustained during and following Japan's colonial rule of Korea in 1910–45. The refusal of the Democratic People's Republic of Korea to allow inspection of its nuclear facilities featured prominently on Japan's national and international agenda. Japan stressed the need to find a diplomatic solution and any substantial support for military intervention was ruled out. In March 1995 a delegation comprising members of all three parties in the Japanese Government visited North Korea to prepare for negotiations on the establishment of normal relations between the two countries. Japan provided emergency aid to the Democratic People's Republic of Korea in 1995/96, when a serious food shortage appeared to threaten the stability of the Korean peninsula. The Japanese Government supported a US initiative of dialogue involving the Democratic People's Republic of Korea, the People's Republic of China and the USA, aimed at negotiating a formal peace treaty between the two Korean states. Concerns that the Democratic People's Republic of Korea had developed a missile capable of reaching Japanese territory resulted in the suspension of food aid in early 1997, but relations improved slightly later in that year, when agreement was reached concerning the issue of visits to relatives in Japan by Japanese nationals resident in the Democratic People's Republic of Korea. The first such visits took place in November. It was announced in August that the two countries were to conduct negotiations aimed at restoring full diplomatic relations. It was subsequently reported that the Japanese Government had pledged some US $27m. in food aid to the Democratic People's Republic of Korea. However, food aid and negotiations on the resumption of full diplomatic relations, which had commenced following the visit to the Democratic People's Republic of Korea by an LDP delegation, were suspended in mid-1998, following the testing by North Korea of a suspected missile in the sea near Japan. Tensions were exacerbated in March 1999, when two suspected North Korean spy ships, which had infiltrated Japanese waters, were pursued and fired on by Japanese naval forces, in the first such operation since the establishment of the Japanese SDF. In September the Japanese Government welcomed North Korea's agreement with the USA to suspend its reported plans to test a new long-range missile, but remained cautious regarding any easing of sanctions against Pyongyang. In October unofficial talks were held in Singapore between Japanese and North Korean government officials, and Japan subsequently lifted a ban on charter flights to North Korea. Following a visit to North Korea by a multi-party delegation of Diet members in December, the Japanese Government announced that it would resume the provision of food aid. Later that month intergovernmental preparatory talks on re-establishing diplomatic relations were held in China, following an agreement between Japanese and North Korean Red Cross officials on humanitarian issues, most notably the commitment by the Red Cross organization of North Korea to urge its Government to co-operate in an investigation into the fate of some 10 missing Japanese nationals, believed by Japan to have been abducted by North Korean agents in the 1970s and 1980s. Official talks on the normalization of diplomatic relations were held in April and August 2000. A number of issues were discussed, including compensation for the Japanese colonial rule of Korea, although no substantive progress was made; a third round of talks was held in October.

In 1978 a treaty of peace and friendship was signed with the People's Republic of China. During an official visit to China in August 1988, Prime Minister Takeshita announced that Japan would advance 810,000m. yen in loans to China between 1990 and 1995. These loans were withheld following the massacre by Chinese troops in Tiananmen Square, Beijing, in June 1989, but were released in mid-1990 following the Chinese Government's declaration, in January, that a state of martial law no longer existed. There was further dissatisfaction with the Chinese Government in early 1992, when Chinese sovereignty was declared over the Ryukyu island group, which was claimed by Japan. Nevertheless, good relations between the two countries were bolstered by visits to China by Emperor Akihito in October 1992 and by Prime Minister Hosokawa in March 1994. Having protested strongly against the resumption of French nuclear testing in the Pacific, in August Japan announced that it would suspend economic aid to China, following renewed nuclear testing by the Chinese Government. The provision of economic aid was resumed in early 1997, following a moratorium on Chinese nuclear testing.

In mid-1996 Japan's relations with both China and Taiwan were strained when a group of nationalists, the Japan Youth Federation, built a lighthouse and war memorial on the Senkaku Islands (or Diaoyu Islands in Chinese), a group of uninhabited islets situated in the East China Sea, to which all three countries laid claim. The situation was further aggravated in September by the drowning of a Hong Kong citizen during a protest against Japan's claim to the islands. In October a flotilla of small boats, operated by 300 activists from Taiwan, Hong Kong and Macao evaded Japanese patrol vessels and raised the flags of China and Taiwan on the disputed islands. However, Japan sought to defuse tensions with China and Taiwan by withholding official recognition of the lighthouse.

In September 1997 Prime Minister Hashimoto visited China to commemorate the 25th anniversary of the normalization of relations between the two countries. China expressed concern at the revised US-Japanese security arrangements, following a statement by a senior Japanese minister that the area around Taiwan might be covered under the new guide-lines. Procedures for the removal of chemical weapons, deployed in China by Japanese forces during the Second World War, were also discussed. Japan's economic policy was criticized by the Chinese Government in 1998, which feared that the weakening yen would force a devaluation of the Chinese currency. In November, during a six-day state visit by the Chinese head of state, Obuchi and President Jiang Zemin issued (but declined to sign) a joint declaration on friendship and co-operation, in which Japan expressed deep remorse for past aggression against China. China was reported to be displeased by the lack of a written apology, however, and remained concerned by the implications of US-Japanese defence arrangements regarding Taiwan. A subsequent US-Japanese agreement to initiate joint technical research on the development of a theatre missile defence system, followed by the Japanese Diet's approval, in May 1999, of legislation on the implementation of the revised US-Japanese defence guidelines provoked severe criticism from China, despite Japan's insistence that military co-operation with the USA was purely defensive. In July a meeting in Beijing between Obuchi and the Chinese Premier, Zhu Rongji, resulted in the formalization of a bilateral agreement on China's entry to the WTO, following several months of intense negotiations on the liberalization of trade in services.

Japan and the USSR were, historically and geopolitically, rivals for supremacy in north-eastern Asia, over which they disputed control in large- and small-scale wars. Mutual mistrust was maintained from the end of the Second World War until the mid-1980s. Japan's treaty of peace and friendship, signed with the People's Republic of China in 1978, signalled an end to Japan's policy of maintaining equal distance from both China and the USSR. Japan's relations with the USSR were further strained by the Soviet military intervention in Afghanistan, in December 1979, and by the concomitant reinforcement of Soviet territory to the north of Japan. There was, however, a noticeable improvement in relations between Japan and the USSR in 1986. In January the Soviet Minister of Foreign Affairs, Eduard Shevardnadze, visited Japan (the first such visit by a Soviet Minister of Foreign Affairs for 10 years). The two countries agreed to improve economic and trade relations and to resume regular ministerial consultations.

The major obstacle to any substantial improvement in Soviet-Japanese relations was the seemingly intractable dispute over the Northern Territories. Japan has a strong claim to two islands, Habomai and Shikotan, which were formerly administered as part of Hokkaido. In addition, Japan claims Etorofu (Iturup) and Kunashiri (Kunashir), which, together with the rest of the Chishima (Kurile) chain and the southern part of

Karafuto (Sakhalin), were captured by Soviet forces during the closing stages of the Second World War. Following a visit to Tokyo by the Soviet Minister of Foreign Affairs in December 1988, Japan and the USSR agreed to establish a high-level joint working group to negotiate the future of the disputed territory and the conclusion of a peace treaty. After the dissolution of the Soviet Union at the end of 1991, the President of the Russian Federation, Boris Yeltsin, reconfirmed the existence of this territorial dilemma.

The G-7 Summit of industrialized nations, held in Tokyo in July 1993, provided the opportunity for Yeltsin to visit Japan, two proposed trips having been cancelled in the previous 12 months. However, despite his presence, no solution was found to the dispute over the Northern Territories. The US $500m. in bilateral aid promised to Yeltsin at the Summit fell far short of the US $4,000m. that President Clinton had initially suggested as a privatization fund. Despite US pressure, Japan's continuing reservations towards the provision of aid for Russia reflected both its frustration that the resolution of its territorial claims was still distant, as well as the development of more assertive diplomacy. Yeltsin also visited Tokyo in October, when the Northern Territories were discussed, although to little effect.

Bilateral negotiations over the status of the disputed territory opened in March 1995. Relations between the two countries steadily improved, and a commitment was made to resume negotiations on the signing of a peace treaty to bring a formal conclusion to the Second World War. In November 1996 Japan indicated that it was prepared to resume the disbursement of a US $500m.-aid 'package', withheld since 1991, and in May 1997 the Japanese Government abandoned its opposition to Russia's proposed membership of the G-7 group. Russian plans for joint development of the mineral and fishing resources of the disputed territory were followed, in July, by an outline agreement on the jurisdiction of the islands. A meeting between Hashimoto and Yeltsin later in that month resulted in the forging of a new diplomatic policy, based on 'trust, mutual benefit and long-term prospects'. At an informal summit meeting, held between Yeltsin and Hashimoto in Krasnoyarsk, Russia, in November, the two parties agreed to work towards the conclusion of a formal peace treaty by the year 2000. A series of measures aimed at encouraging Japanese assistance in the revival of the Russian economy were also discussed. Bilateral negotiations resulted in the conclusion of a framework fisheries agreement in December 1997. Yeltsin visited Japan in April 1998, and the Japanese Government's commitment to an improvement in bilateral relations was confirmed by its offer of financial aid, in the form of loans, and an expansion in economic co-operation. No further progress was made in the status of the disputed islands. The Japanese Government indicated its support for Russia's application for membership of the WTO and APEC. Further discussions between Yeltsin and Obuchi, held during the G-8 summit meeting in Cologne, Germany, in June 1999, were to be followed by a visit to Tokyo by the Russian President later that year. At the beginning of September Japan agreed to resume lending to Russia, which had been suspended since the Russian Government had effectively devalued the rouble and defaulted on some of its debts in mid-1998. At the same time an accord was concluded on improved access to the disputed islands for former Japanese inhabitants.

Negotiations on the territorial dispute achieved little progress during 2000, a major obstacle being the issue of how many of the islands should be returned. Despite Russian President Vladimir Putin's repudiation of Japan's claim to any of the islands during his first official visit to Tokyo in September, Russia subsequently offered to abide by a 1956 declaration that it would relinquish two of the islands after the signature of a peace treaty, but Japan initially rejected this partial solution. Talks held in March 2001 on the interpretation of the 1956 declaration proved inconclusive, although Prime Minister Mori and President Putin reaffirmed that the declaration would ultimately form the basis for a peace treaty. Further discussions were to be held in October 2001, at which the Japanese Government was expected to insist on negotiating the return of all four disputed islands, rather than only two. Meanwhile, in November 2000 a former Japanese naval officer on trial in Tokyo admitted spying for Russia. There was outrage in Japan at the fact that the crime carried possible punishments that were perceived as being extremely lenient in relation to the severity of the offence.

The sharp increase in world petroleum prices in 1973–74 illustrated the vulnerability of the Japanese economy to developments in the international arena. Japan's increasingly pragmatic approach in foreign affairs was demonstrated by its support for the Arab countries in its pronouncements on Middle East issues, thus ensuring a continuing supply of petroleum. Moreover, its growing involvement in world affairs was signalled by the financial aid granted to the international effort to force the Iraqi withdrawal from Kuwait in 1991. In September 1995 Prime Minister Murayama visited the Middle East. During meetings with the Syrian President, Hafiz al-Assad, the Israeli Prime Minister, Itzhak Rabin, and the Palestinian leader, Yasser Arafat, Murayama pledged economic aid to the Middle East, the promotion of trade with the region and Japan's involvement in the UN Disengagement Observer Force (UNDOF) operation in the Golan Heights.

In September 1994 the possibility that Japan was soon to be given a permanent seat on the UN Security Council receded, following a UN report that called for further discussion on the issue. Earlier, Japan's Minister of Foreign Affairs had anticipated that it would take time for Japan to be accorded a permanent seat, and he emphasized that this could only be on condition that its contributions to UN activities did not involve the use of force. During the late 1990s the Japanese Government campaigned for a greater proportion of senior-level positions within the UN to be allocated to Japanese personnel, as a reflection of its contribution to the UN budget. From January 1997 until January 1999 Japan held a non-permanent seat on the UN Security Council, while continuing to seek permanent membership. Prime Minister Mori addressed the UN General Assembly on this issue in October 2000 and also advocated Japan's membership to a gathering of Asian and African nations. Japan had the strong backing of the United Kingdom and lukewarm support from Russia and the People's Republic of China, but controversy over the whole idea of permanent membership meant that no new developments were expected in the near future, despite the fact that Japan was the second-largest contributor to the UN in 2000, being responsible for more than 20% of the total budget.

Japan's foreign relations generally failed to flourish under the leadership of the Mori Cabinet, which seemed to lack a coherent national vision or strategy. Mori's propensity to make inappropriate remarks and his mishandling of various issues drew a constant barrage of criticism in the domestic media, which was taken up by the foreign press, thereby undermining respect for him abroad and any capacity for international leadership. The Okinawa summit of G-8 nations, which contributed little of value to Japan's international standing, saw Mori become the butt of Western jokes. Unable to overcome its economic problems, Japan suffered a loss of confidence domestically and also found its only diplomatic tool seriously blunted. Even Japan's official development assistance (ODA), which since the early 1990s had assumed an increasing significance in the country's efforts to define a more proactive international role for itself, has been under pressure since 1997 and was reduced in the 2002/03 budget by 10%. Revelations of scandals involving misuse of funds within the Ministry of Foreign Affairs and the subsequent dismissal of top officials, including the ambassadors to the USA and the United Kingdom, have left the ministry weakened. Disputes between senior officials and the new Minister of Foreign Affairs in the Koizumi Cabinet, Makiko Tanaka, have also made them less effective.

Economic issues were also a source of friction between Japan and its allies in 2001, with Japan subjected to conflicting demands for economic reform and deregulation and for disposal of its bad debts and adoption of import targets. Measures taken by Japan in April against the import of three agricultural products—leeks, shiitake mushrooms and *tatami* reeds—from the People's Republic of China led to broad tariff increases by the Chinese against a number of Japanese industrial products, including automobiles. Trade difficulties with China are symptomatic of attempts to deal with the shifting power balance in the region, as Japan formulates its strategy to position itself advantageously as China's economic and military strength grows. The Ministry of Economy, Trade and Industry's policy document on international trade, which was published in May, warned of heightening competition with China for economic leadership within the region, as China experienced outstanding levels of growth, and predicted that Japanese industry would relocate to China. The Japanese Government welcomed the new administration of President George W. Bush in the USA and its shift from a policy of 'strategic partnership' with China to one of 'engagement'. A number of regional conferences in 2001 took as their theme the need for a new regional framework and for efforts to balance the emergent strength of China. The Malaysian Prime Minister, Mahathir bin Mohamad, proposed an international currency for use in international trade. Sub-regional economic co-operation and bilateral free trade, as well as the creation of an East Asia free-trade area, were all under discussion. Diplomatic and security questions were identified as possible areas of difficulty for Prime Minister Koizumi. Disputes over the contents of Japanese textbooks continued to strain relations with both China and the Republic of Korea under the Koizumi Cabinet, which, in early June, refused to make any of a number of requested revisions to a textbook produced by the Japanese Society for History Textbook Reform, which seeks to teach historical pride in the nation. Tensions were exacerbated by the perception of Koizumi as a dangerous nationalist by those countries.

The repercussions of the terrorist attacks on the USA in September 2001, three days after the 50th anniversary of the signing of the San Francisco Peace Treaty and the US-Japan Security Treaty, dominated many of Japan's subsequent international relations. The US-Japan relationship improved to a level not seen since the days of the 'Ron-Yasu' relationship enjoyed by US President Reagan and Nakasone in the 1980s. Koizumi's own aggressive image meant that his normalization of Japan's foreign policy necessitated skilful diplomacy if it were not to be perceived as a threat to the stability of the region. As a consequence, at the same time as Japan was drawn into a more active global role, for example in its contributions to peace-keeping operations and in its initiatives for a UN-sponsored World Summit on the reconstruction of Afghanistan, it also become more closely involved in regional activity on both a bilateral and multilateral level. Koizumi's regional offensive encompassed a meeting with Jiang Zemin in October 2001, visits to five ASEAN nations in January 2002, the signing of a New-Age Economic Partnership with Singapore and participation in the first annual Boao Economic Forum for Asia in the Chinese province of Hainan in April when he argued in favour of an Asian free-trade zone. These initiatives were also driven by concern over China's rapid economic and military growth and by that country's proposals for a China-ASEAN free-trade agreement; demands were made in Japan for drastic reductions in ODA to China. In May 2002 tensions were exacerbated when the Chinese seized North Korean nationals seeking refuge in the Japanese consulate in Shenyang.

An unexpected official visit to the Yasukuni Shrine by Koizumi in April 2002 resulted in the cancellation of a visit to Japan by the South Korean Minister of National Defence and led 800 South Koreans to join a pending legal action against the Prime Minister for unconstitutional behaviour. The joint hosting of the 2002 football World Cup in June brought an increase in co-operation and cultural exchange between Japan and South Korea. This, along with the initiation of a joint history study group, contributed to a steady improvement in relations between the two countries. Economic relations were strengthened by an investment alliance and by progress in talks for a broader free-trade agreement. Although Japan did not agree with the Bush Administration's description of North Korea, Iraq and Iran as an 'axis of evil', North Korea continued to be a source of growing concern, with a worsening of the situation on the Korean Peninsula and incursions into Japanese waters by what were believed to be North Korean spy ships. The relationship took a dramatic turn in mid-September when Koizumi returned from an unprecedented visit to Pyongyang with an apology for the abduction of 12 Japanese nationals by North Korea during the 1970s and 1980s, and the news that eight of the abductees had died. Progress was made in other areas, with the North Korean Government promising to continue its moratorium on missile test launches, to respect international agreements on nuclear weapons inspections and to halt operations on spy ships in Japanese waters.

NATIONAL SECURITY, DEFENCE AND REARMAMENT

Serious consideration of rearmament, in order to make Japan both an economic and a military power, would have been welcomed by the USA in the 1970s, but there were many fundamental obstacles. Constitutional revision was one prerequisite, since Article 9 of Japan's post-war Constitution is usually interpreted to mean that Japan's armed forces are for defence only, must remain relatively small in number and cannot be equipped with inter-continental ballistic missiles. However, any attempt to revise the Constitution would cause a major domestic political crisis. Moreover, rearmament would be bitterly contested in South-East Asia, where anti-Japanese sentiment remains very strong. Attention, therefore, was turned to alternative solutions, which included, in 1979, Prime Minister Ohira's plan for 'comprehensive security'. Briefly, this proposal envisaged a commitment by Japan to promote the integrity of the geopolitical structures within which it conducts its economic relations. For example, Egypt was identified as the key to regional stability in the Middle East, and so became an important beneficiary of Japan's foreign aid, as did Indonesia, a major supplier of petroleum to Japan after 1973. Prime Minister Nakasone favoured the creation of a strong defence force and a broader role for Japan in regional affairs. In matters of defence, Nakasone sought to make concessions to the USA, so as to reduce friction in (or at least divert attention from) the less tractable problems of trade.

In Japan, as elsewhere, global economic recession led to fiscal austerity, which, in turn, compromised the defence programme for 1983–87. Despite an average increase of 6.5% per year in military expenditure, the programme's aims were not fully realized. At the same time, Nakasone's decision to permit the transfer to the USA of new technologies with military applications indicated a change of policy, which was welcomed in the USA. In January 1987 the Japanese Government announced that it was to abandon its self-imposed limit on defence expenditure of 1% of the gross national product (GNP), which had operated since 1976. Defence spending equivalent to 1.004% of the forecast GNP was proposed for 1987/88; it was also announced that defence expenditure would be maintained at about this level until 1991. This decision was welcomed by the USA but harshly criticized by the USSR and the People's Republic of China. Nakasone, however, stressed that the Government did not intend to re-establish Japan as a major military power.

In March 1991 the Government reduced defence expenditure from the budget proposals for the financial year ending 31 March 1992, partly to persuade the Komeito to approve Japan's pledged additional US $9,000m.-contribution to the Gulf War effort, but also to reflect domestic concern that previous levels of defence expenditure were no longer necessary. Compared with the previous year, proposed defence spending was to rise by less than 4% in 1992/93.

After failing to win the approval of the Diet for proposals to send SDF personnel overseas in November 1990, the LDP agreed with the Komeito and the DSP that the Government would establish a new body to participate in UN peace-keeping operations. Although the Komeito initially insisted that SDF personnel be excluded from the new body, the proposal was finally approved on the condition that SDF personnel be confined to non-combat duties. In July 1991 the three political parties dispatched a mission to Cambodia and other Asian countries to assess the possibility of Japanese involvement in a UN-sponsored peace plan for Cambodia. In September 1992 683 Japanese personnel, including some civilian police officers, were sent to Cambodia to participate in the UN Transitional Authority in Cambodia (UNTAC) mission. The death of two Japanese personnel in Cambodia, in early 1993, heightened domestic opposition to Japan's involvement in UN peace-keeping operations. In September 1995 it was announced that SDF personnel would participate in a UN observer force in Israel from February 1996. In November 1999 the ruling parties agreed to postpone the consideration of a proposal to expand Japan's participation in UN peace-keeping operations.

The report of the Advisory Group on Defence Issues, commissioned by Hosokawa's Government, was published in August 1994. The report urged a reduction in SDF personnel from some 274,000 to 240,000, recognizing the difficulty that the SDF ground forces had faced in achieving full recruitment. The proposals were largely adopted in early January 1995 in a draft document on new defence policy guidelines. The report also called for reductions in aircraft and ships, the modernization of Japan's defence capability, and improvements in command, communications and intelligence. A case was also made for co-operation with the USA on the development of weapons systems such as anti-ballistic missile defences.

In a bid to counter the difficulties being experienced in their economic relationship, Japan and the USA sought to strengthen their security relationship. In early 1995 Japan's Defence Agency undertook a review of the bilateral security treaty to expand the financial support accorded by Japan to US operations overseas.

In September 1995 a 12-year-old girl was raped by three US servicemen in Okinawa. The incident led to nation-wide demonstrations against the three men (who were found guilty and sentenced to prison terms in March 1996) and against the Government's policy on Japanese-US security arrangements. Public support for the 35-year-old mutual security treaty declined sharply. In view of such public discontent, Governor Masahide Ota of Okinawa refused to approve the continued use of land by US military forces when the Defence Agency requested an extension of the leases demanding a review of the Japanese-US security arrangements in general, and of the Status of Forces Agreement in particular. A referendum, held in Okinawa in September 1996, revealed that the majority of residents favoured a reduction in the number of US bases. Nevertheless, later in that month Ota reversed his decison and agreed to sign the documents renewing the leases. In December it was announced that the USA was to return some 20% of the land used for military bases and to build a floating offshore helicopter base; there was, however, to be no significant reduction in the number of troops stationed in Okinawa. In order to reduce the financial and other obligations borne by Okinawa, some US military exercises were relocated to other prefectures, and the Government also began to negotiate special measures to promote economic development in the region. In December 1997, in a non-binding referendum held in Nago, Okinawa, to assess public opinion concerning the construction of the offshore helicopter base, the majority of voters rejected the proposal. The Mayor of Nago, who advocated the construction of the base in return for measures to stimulate the region's economy, tendered his resignation. Governor Ota stated his opposition to the proposed base. The new Mayor, elected in February 1998, initially approved of the helicopter base, but subsequently announced that he would support Ota in opposing the construction. In November 1998 Keiichi Inamine defeated Ota in the Okinawa gubernatorial election. Inamine, who had been supported by the LDP, presented an alternative solution, in an attempt to gain government support for the local economy, proposing that a military-commercial airport be built in northern Okinawa and leased to the USA for a period of 15 years. In December a US military site was officially returned to the Japanese Government, the first of the 11 bases to be returned under the 1996 agreement. In December 1999 Inamine's proposal for the relocation of the US air base to northern Okinawa was approved by both the local authorities and the Japanese Government, with the Henoko district of Nago chosen as the site for the new airport; at the same time funding was allocated for a 10-year development plan for the area. Negotiations with the USA, which opposed any time limit on its use of the airport, subsequently took place; although it had been hoped that negotiations would be concluded by July 2000, when the summit of G-8 nations was held in Nago, no agreement was reached by that time. In March, during a visit by the US Secretary of Defense, William Cohen, some agreements were concluded, giving Japan control of the US Kadena air base and resolving an air pollution problem in Kanagawa prefecture, but the central issues of a time limit on US use of the new airport and of the level of Japan's payments to the USA as a host nation to its military forces remained unresolved.

Following the signing of a US-Japan Joint Declaration on Security in April 1996 by President Clinton and Prime Minister Hashimoto, the review of the Guidelines for Japan-US Defense Co-operation (compiled in November 1978) continued in 1997, and culminated in the issuing of a joint statement detailing the new Guidelines in mid-September. China expressed concern at the provisions of the new agreement, which envisaged enhanced co-operation between the USA and Japan, not only on Japanese territory, but also in situations in unspecified areas around Japan. Despite opposition from its coalition partners, in April 1998 the LDP Government approved legislation to define the operations of the SDF under the revised Guidelines. The legislation was enacted in May 1999, prompting criticism from China and Russia. Its approval was ensured by an agreement between the LDP, its new coalition partner, the LP, and New Komeito to exclude a clause that would have allowed the inspection of unidentified foreign ships by the SDF, with the aim of enforcing economic sanctions; separate legislation on this issue was expected to be proposed later in the year. In August 1999 the Japanese Government formally approved a memorandum of understanding with the USA stipulating details of joint technical research on the development of a theatre missile defence system, which aims to detect and shoot down incoming ballistic missiles within a 3,000-km radius. The Defence Agency has estimated that Japan will have to allocate up to 30,000m. yen to the controversial research project over a period of five years.

Instability on the Korean peninsula was a cause of concern for the Japanese Government in 1998, particularly following the testing of a suspected missile by the Democratic People's Republic of Korea (see above). Officials from the ministries of foreign affairs and defence of the Republic of Korea and Japan agreed to convene regular bilateral security meetings. The incursion into Japanese waters of two suspected North Korean spy ships in March 1999 prompted the first-ever invocation of legislation allowing naval forces to engage in maritime policing operations (see above). The incident also provided the first opportunity for the South Korean and Japanese armed forces to operate a new 'emergency liaison system', which had been established as a result of a recent bilateral security agreement. The Japanese Government criticized India and Pakistan for conducting nuclear tests in mid-1998, and suspended grants of non-humanitarian aid and loans to India in response to the tests. A series of missile tests carried out by India and Pakistan in April 1999 again provoked criticism from Japan. Relations had improved by the end of 1999; in late 1999 and early 2000 the Indian Ministers of External Affairs and of Defence paid official visits to Tokyo, and in February 2000 former Prime Minister Ryutaro Hashimoto visited India as a special envoy. During his visit he had urged India to sign the UN's Comprehensive Test Ban Treaty, although he also indicated that Japan had no desire for bilateral relations to be determined by India's response to the Treaty. In late August Yoshiro Mori visited India as part of a tour of South Asia, in his first overseas trip as Prime Minster.

As part of efforts to combat increasing piracy in South-East Asia, Japan advocated the creation of a regional patrol for these waters. Although constitutionally unable to provide members of its navy for this task, Japan proposed the involvement of its coastguard, a non-military organization, in a regional force. In May 2000 Japan hosted a conference of coastguard officials from 15 Asian nations, at which the problem of piracy, and possible solutions, were discussed.

A new five-year mid-term defence programme was adopted in December 2000, in response to the changing nature of security threats in the post-Cold War world and to demands for a greater international contribution to peace by Japan. The new defence programme was to develop readiness to deal with nuclear, biological and chemical threats and terrorist attacks and was intended to bring Japan's defence capability to the levels prescribed in the national defence programme outline.

Under the Mori Cabinet, the old issues that bedevilled the US-Japanese relationship continued. Military bases in Okinawa contributed to anti-American feeling in the wake of rising crime in the area. US demands for a greater contribution to the maintenance of regional security from Japan grew under the new Bush administration, and the question of what role Japan should play under the new Guidelines remained unresolved.

The sinking of the fisheries training ship, the *Ehime-Maru*, by a US nuclear submarine in February 2001 exacerbated this growing anti-US nationalism.

In 2001 Japan maintained its official position of 'understanding' the missile defence initiative and its support for joint US-Japanese technical studies, while steadfastly avoiding any decision on whether it would enter into joint development of the Theater Missile Defense system. However, criticisms of the initiative by Minister of Foreign Affairs Makiko Tanaka and a hardline stance on the part of the Bush administration, which refused to distinguish between support for short-range theatre missile defence and long-range national missile defence, suggested that the issue would prove difficult to resolve.

Unusually, security and defence issues were the main focus of Junichiro Koizumi's first press conference after his appointment as Prime Minister in April 2001. Koizumi emphasized the need to avoid the sort of international isolation that had led to the last war, the importance of the US-Japan Security Alliance, and the value of changing the Constitution over time to recognize the right to existence of the SDF and to take part in collective self-defence.

The terrorist attacks on the USA in September 2001 and President Bush's insistence on co-operation from the rest of the world in the so-called 'war on terrorism' revived unpleasant memories in Japan of the tensions created by the character and timing of Japan's contributions to the Gulf War in the early 1990s. Such memories clearly contributed to the speed and strength of the Government's response. Despite the USA's later omission of Japan from the list of countries contributing to the war on terrorism, the Prime Minister's response was rapid and positive, going further than ever before towards normalizing Japan's international role, although without leading to any change in the Government's interpretation of its ability to exercise the right to collective defence. The Government's seven-point response plan, which included legislation to allow deployment of the SDF as theatre support, the dispatch of information-gathering warships as far as the Indian Ocean and the resumption of aid to India and Pakistan, received a mixed response domestically. Overall, however, the terrorist attacks contributed to the continuing erosion of domestic hostility towards a broader international role for Japan.

Anti-terrorism legislation was implemented on 2 November 2001, effective for two years but with the possibility of subsequent renewal. The legislation allowed for the dispatch of the SDF to non-combat zones in areas of conflict, subject to consent by the host government and to approval by the Diet within 20 days of troops being dispatched, or at the start of a new session. Such troops were given expanded powers to use weapons to protect refugees and injured foreign servicemen. In mid-November two destroyers and a supply ship sailed for the Indian Ocean in the first of several SDF contributions.

With various restraints being eroded by the events of September 2001 and the subsequent 'war on terrorism', the other major legislation introduced in the 2002 ordinary Diet session consisted of three defence bills, one setting out the response to a direct foreign military attack or expected attack, and the others revising the Self Defence Forces Law and the Law on the Establishment of the Security Council. Efforts to create a new framework to deal with national emergencies began in the mid-1970s, one reason perhaps why the prevailing legislation did not include responses to terrorism or incursions into Japan's territorial waters, despite the urgings of Koizumi. The new legislation would provide for an emergency headquarters in the Cabinet Office headed by the Prime Minister and establishes that government would make plans to deal with military emergencies on the basis of UN Security Council recommendations. The legislation would also grant the Prime Minister extended powers to direct the operations of local government and reduce restrictions on the domestic activities of the SDF. Debate on the bills was postponed until the next session of the Diet, which was scheduled to begin in mid-October 2002. Japan's effort to improve crisis management was also to include the launch of four surveillance satellites in February 2003.

Economy

BRUCE HENRY LAMBERT

INTRODUCTION AND OVERVIEW

At the start of the 21st century, Japan finds itself in the position of having to adjust to demands for deregulation and for a scaling-down of government, while conversely responding to calls for visionary leadership and the effective priming of a weakened economy. Since the 1990s the Japanese populace has had to contend with economic stagnation, the gradual exposure of corporate financial mismanagement, and continuing revelations of deficiencies in regulation. Associated problems have included rising unemployment, political instability, a steady dismantling of familiar institutional arrangements and a seeming loss of confidence in ethical values. It is increasingly difficult for people to remember, let alone to reconcile, the exhilarating days of the late 1980s, when the economy was booming and Japanese corporate expansion was seen as a major threat to other businesses around the world. Nevertheless, Japan remains a wealthy nation. In 2001 Japan accounted for 70% of total East Asian gross domestic product (GDP) and for 59% of total combined GDP for East, South-East and South Asia. Japan's per caput GDP for 2001 was equivalent to US $32,600, a figure fifth among the world's 30 wealthiest nations belonging to the Organisation for Economic Co-operation and Development (OECD). When considered in terms of purchasing-power parity (PPP—comparing costs for a common basket of goods and services), the adjusted per caput GDP of Japan (at $26,500) equalled that of Germany, tied 14th of the 30 OECD nations. Even this figure was still 5% higher than the average for the 15 members of the European Union (EU), although only 73% of the figure of $36,500 enjoyed in the USA; (Luxembourg has the OECD's highest PPP-adjusted GDP at $49,800). The Cabinet Office figure for Japan's real GDP in 2001 was 531,055,600m. yen (at 1995 prices), a contraction of 0.6% from the previous year. However, Japan officially emerged from recession in the first quarter of 2002; GDP increased by 1.4% from the previous quarter, aided by growth in exports and consumer spending.

Japan has comparatively low crime rates, and the people for the most part receive good health care. The Japanese have the longest life expectancy of any nation in the world. Tax and interest rates are low, and income is quite equitably distributed; the people are well-educated, city streets are clean, and government is small and contracting. The national infrastructure is up-to-date and well-developed (though exposed to potential disasters such as earthquakes). Therefore, Japan is in a rather good position. The people have high standards, and history has given them reason to expect to persevere through various challenges. Prime Minister Junichiro Koizumi came to power in April 2001 promising major changes and 'structural reform with nothing off-limits'. During his early months in office, while doing little of substance, his popularity rating exceeded 80%; but by early 2002, his approval rating in polls had plummeted to 40%, with a 44% disapproval rating. The causes for such decline included the dismissal of the popular Minister of Foreign Affairs, Makiko Tanaka, a perceived inability to implement substantive reforms, and a series of government scandals that increased the public's distrust of both civil servants and politicians. The Japanese people want to believe that there are better days ahead, but a key problem at present is that Japan is now near the technological frontier. It is more difficult to find proven and unambiguous models to emulate, and the path ahead is unclear.

This essay provides an overview of the contemporary Japanese economy along with explanation of many of the more novel features that affect the economy, including national policy, Japanese management systems, and relationships with government and the wider outside world. A key point might be borne in mind from the 1989 work of one analyst, Tessa Morris-Suzuki, *A History of Japanese Economic Thought*: the term 'economics' in Japan (*keizai*) has its roots in *keikoku saimin / keisei saimin*: 'administering the nation and relieving the suffering of the people'. Economics in Japan thus involves not simply an objective and detached allocation analysis of scarce resources, but the Confucian ideal of holding together the social fabric of the nation.

HISTORICAL BACKGROUND

Planning and public administration in Japan have a long history, and at times systemic controls have been very comprehensive. At the start of the Edo period in the 17th century, public administration systems put a number of stringent demands on society. One policy imposed was national seclusion (where leaving or entering Japan became punishable by death). Another policy required detailed reporting of all vital statistics for each area and family (and many of these records survive today). The system of *sankin kotai* that existed between 1635 and 1862 imposed limits on ambitious regional lords, who were required to spend alternate years in Edo (now Tokyo) and to leave their families behind as hostages when they returned to their domains. Other controls limited regional financial power: local lords were responsible for collecting and paying taxes imposed by the central Government, and their personal funds were deliberately kept in check through the expenditures involved in visiting the capital, maintaining two households, offering periodic bountiful gifts to the Shogunate, and maintaining roads and infrastructure to specifications and standards set by the central Government.

In the mid-19th century, Japan was forced by foreign powers to end more than 200 years of seclusion. This led to the disintegration of many of the above systems and relaxed a wide variety of rules. Feudal institutions drastically broke down: common people were allowed to take surnames and to travel freely, samurai were released from service and had to find new work, and boisterous anti-order dances swept the country (where, for example, people entered the homes of those more prosperous and helped themselves to food and drink, chanting 'eejanaika'— or 'what's the problem?'). The change from a feudal system to a more market-orientated economy brought a large measure of confusion and even chaos to the world of commerce. Numerous severe market shocks developed from the large-scale resumption of foreign trade and from the introduction of new foreign products. A revolutionary change to Western-style garments brought sharp alterations in demand for many items, with concurrent effects on employment. Social and technological rigidities made it difficult to adapt quickly. Many industries were suddenly and directly undercut by the import of competing items, while other industries (such as sword-making) suffered massive decreases in demand, based on new regulations and changing tastes and style. Such huge social displacement and change brought with it not only distribution channel breakdown and widespread malpractice that continued for many years, but also more serious problems: selective assassination and violent civil uprising (for the first 20 years after Japan's reopening, foreigners and those who supported them were often under threat). Market order was reimposed by co-ordinated self-regulation among businesses, supported by state authority; and these early corporatist restraining mechanisms were a precursor to some that can be found today.

Early Manufacturing and Trade

From 1854, when the so-called 'Black Ships' of the US navy threatened to bombard Tokyo and forced the Japanese to trade with the outside world, until well into the 1880s, most of Japan's actual import and export transactions were being conducted by foreign traders. This system was slow to change, as these foreign traders were not keen to share their knowledge and expertise with Japanese who might supplant them. The Meiji Government also found it difficult to give potential domestic traders substantial assistance, owing to Japan's international treaties of commerce. The Government itself was at first quite active in promoting industrialization through its programme to 'increase production and promote industry'. Modern technology was introduced from overseas, and several thousand foreign experts from numerous fields were hired by the government to teach, consult, and assist Japan in modernizing. The central Government had inherited various operations such as shipyards and mines from the Tokugawa Shogunate, and to these were added railways and a number of model factories, the most notable in the textile industry, including silk-reeling, cotton-spinning, and woollen mills.

During the 1870s the authorities rushed to modernize Japan by way of an increasingly wide range of government projects. In the early 1880s, however, it became clear that state resources were seriously overextended. The Government decided to divest itself of direct administration of many factories and production facilities, and offered them to private investors. At first, only loss-making factories were scheduled to be sold, but by 1884 the Government had begun to sell off profitable facilities such as mines, often at nominal prices. Strategic munitions and communications facilities remained under government control, however, later to be joined by the huge Yawata Iron and Steel Works. Most companies were not sold on the open market. The key to procuring government-owned operations was often an existing special relationship between business insiders and government (a *seisho* relationship). Such divestiture to protégés would now not be tolerated, and even then it was a problem: insider dealings precipitated substantial public outrage in the Hokkaido Colonization Office Scandal of 1881. The Government did not develop a more equitable system or maximize immediate government income; certain buyers were favoured because the Meiji leaders wanted the businesses to succeed. To that purpose they minimized uncertainty and used a shortlist of preferred contractors: businesses and individuals with proven entrepreneurial and managerial skills, whose efforts were then supported. It must be remembered that in Japan at that time few people had substantive relevant experience of managing these new large-scale industries. The country had been closed off and fragmented in many ways up to the time of the Meiji Restoration in 1868; the clan-related strife of the Ansei Purge of 1858 and the Boshin War of the late 1860s had a negative effect on many organizations, and others were damaged by the loss of feudal patronage with the fall of the Shogunate. Two of the three major merchant houses (Ono and Shimada) collapsed under these changes, and Mitsui barely survived the transition; smaller merchant houses greatly suffered or became insolvent. The Meiji Government of the 1880s chose a risk-avoiding strategy favouring preferred firms, and such privileges were based upon an expectation of future service to the state.

The Government followed up its divestiture sales with another important move: becoming the key customer to many of these newly-privatized firms. This may have been particularly important with novel products with which people were unfamiliar, such as new electrical, glass or chemical products. Government purchases in these areas allowed such industries to generate important economies-of-scale with production and made many businesses viable. At the same time that the Government was selling various business operations to the private sector, it was becoming more active in both supporting and regulating private enterprise. Government adjusted its oversight of private sector institutions in the direction of more interference. Businesses learned to exist under trying circumstances, or they perished. The main complaints by Japanese businessmen in the latter half of the 19th century were with what the business world saw as onerous taxation by government and their need to compete with imports. Yet because tariff rates were fixed by treaty, the Government was hampered in both flexibility and revenue-raising ability. The first tariff treaties were the so-called Ansei Commercial Treaties signed in 1858, which had been pressed on Japan by five nations: the United Kingdom, France, the Netherlands, Russia, and the USA. These had set tariffs on a sliding scale, ranging from 5% to 35% of sale price depending on the commodity. A revised tariff convention signed in June 1866 between the Shogunate and the Five Powers reduced tariffs to a flat 5% of declared value, and this remained in force throughout the period of Japan's modernization. Full tariff autonomy was not achieved until the conclusion of a new set of treaties in 1911. After waiting so long to regain control of such sovereign protectionist measures, it is not surprising that subsequent Japanese governments were loathe to lay them aside.

Relationships Between Business and Government

Business in Japan, wary of charges of profiteering and selfishness, has needed carefully to state its case that investment risk and hard work justify a reasonable return. Mobilizing resources for production and serving the nation is far more attractive than the pursuit of profit. The motives of businessmen were harshly questioned, while politicians and bureaucrats were honoured for their service to others. Certainly in feudal times merchants were deliberately and explicitly ranked below warriors, farmers and artisans on the social scale (*shi-no-ko-sho*). Japanese society in the modern period has not been widely recognized as inhospitable to mercantile pursuits. Yet from the Meiji Restoration in 1868 through to the end of the Second World War, Japanese business needed at times to struggle creatively in order to maintain a system of private enterprise. Private capital and independent direction and management of enterprise were severely and repeatedly threatened by the State. Such efforts at government hegemony into management were carefully resisted, a process that gave rise to protective mechanisms among businesses.

In the early 20th century Japanese business owners developed increasingly astute ways of dealing with government and with their own employees. Industrial disturbances and the organization of labour occurred to a minor extent, but an ideal workplace format was expected to operate as a family, under paternalistic ownership with similarities to feudal times. The Government repeatedly sought to guide and even control business strategy, but was typically hesitant to interfere logistically in such matters as friction with labour. To some degree, a mutually-beneficial collaboration between major Japanese business interests and government was strengthened by the divestiture programme of the 1880s. Congenial relationships between the highest ranks of business and of government subsequently proved difficult to modify, and some businesses came to expect treatment with largesse. Many relationships were further consolidated through intermarriage and adult adoption. The resulting family networks often remain vigorous and powerful today. Small and medium-sized firms, on the other hand, tend to receive little assistance.

In the aftermath of the First World War, Japan's economy was in particular need of adjustment. Exports to Europe had quickly declined with the advent there of peace and reconstruction. This foreign market contraction raised pressures in Japan for adjustment in manufacturing and marketing techniques and pricing, for co-ordination between firms, and for government to take a more active role in encouraging trade. A major early dispute (in what was to be a long struggle) between business and the national government bureaucracy came in 1918, when the Government proposed the Munitions Industries Mobilization Law. The law sought to impose government administration of wartime factory production in the event of future hostilities. The business world, supported by the newly-formed Industry Club of Japan, strongly resisted what it saw as a bureaucratic venture into its domain, but the Government prevailed. In 1929 (in the midst of peace-time), the Resources Investigation Law was passed. This legislation set up a system requiring firms to report on their resource and production potential, and the Ministry of Commerce and Industry was authorized to conduct inspections to verify reported figures. Later, as warfare on the Asian continent intensified, in September 1937 the Diet passed the Law for Temporary Measures for Imports and Exports which allowed the Commerce Ministry to regulate trade without consultation. Change pervaded Japanese society at all levels after 1939. The war in Manchuria had been going on since 1931, and over the course of the decade the people of Japan had become accustomed to not only escalating commodity deprivations but also the concepts of domestic propaganda and 'spiritual mobilization'. Exhortations to behave as Japanese and not mimic the West went so far as to include a 1939 ban on permanent waves for the hair and a condemnation of tennis. The war footing required popular co-operation and self-censorship, and external overt controls continued to expand.

Control Associations

The Important Industries Association Ordinance of 30 August 1941 established a format of control associations (*toseikai*) for all vital industries. At first each control association was under the leadership of the chief executive of the industry's top firm (which in effect transferred control to the major *zaibatsu* groups such as Mitsui, Mitsubishi, Yasuda and Sumitomo). This was not the leadership format desired by government economic planners but a compromise forged with business leaders with the aim of eliciting their support and participation. This format soon changed however: each control association was required to have a full-time president, and each such president became a quasi-government official whose directives had force of law.

So-called reform bureaucrats repeatedly tried to extend their command over business, hoping to take control from the 'selfish' interests of the capitalist owners. Direct administration was partly stymied by the political influence of big business, and partly by the military, who demanded their own direct influence over munitions-related industries. More radical change was successfully resisted owing to the unacceptability of expected costs: direct bureaucratic administration would involve great uncertainty and a huge short-term set-back as administrators would have to learn production system basics.

While industry was shaken by these various developments, not all pressures were generated from outside the business world. The *zaibatsu* and the largest firms were each actively seeking to increase their group domains, often at the expense of the small and medium-sized producers. Many huge newer companies (called *shin-zaibatsu*) had grown quickly in the 1930s with the expansion of opportunities in Japan's colonial markets. Yet as war escalated and continued, large shares of many businesses were lost to the old established *zaibatsu*. The control association system also furthered the decline of the newer ventures because the associations were generally under the direction of the largest firms, usually from the largest *zaibatsu* groups. The control system actively encouraged the consolidation or voluntary domination of small firms. Control association rules changed quickly, were often vague, and were difficult to resist without special assistance.

One question that has yet to be adequately charted in Japanese economic history is the extent to which the wartime control organization left a legacy to the post-war world. It has been common in Japan to belittle links with repudiated wartime institutions, yet institutional innovations of that period influence trade associations and economic federations even to the present. During wartime those who had a stake in private enterprise were forced to combine their energies and work together both for the good of the nation and for their own self-preservation. The struggles of internal factionalism were fought privately; publicity could threaten the survival of the overall system of private administration of capital and property. The control associations served as high-level forums (throughout and past the end of the war) where the large industrial capitalist cliques thrashed out differences. Control association leadership demanded excellent managerial skills such as resourcefulness, agility and creativity, the ability to keep informed, and an advanced aptitude for mediation. Such talents are always of use, and it is thus not surprising that many of these leaders continued to direct Japan's business world in the post-war years.

The Post-War Years

The post-war occupation authorities ordered the purging of certain remaining wartime Japanese political and economic leaders. Further changes in the business world stemmed from the *zaibatsu* dissolution and economic deconcentration programmes, and new anti-trust legislation. At the end of the war, wealth and power were also targeted. The peerage was dissolved. Living expenses were limited by statute, and 56 key people from 10 *zaibatsu* families were required to submit full monthly details of their household accounts. The occupation authorities chose to use the Japanese central government bureaucracy to administer the country and implement their directives, and the balance of power in Japanese society shifted in a number of ways. The bureaucracy quickly became stronger than ever through the restriction or elimination of competing administrative elements: politicians were purged, *zaibatsu* were dissolved, and the military was disbanded. Upper-level wartime bureaucrats were purged to some extent, but the economic ministries were barely affected. The bureaucracy was instead suddenly in a very favourable position to receive timely intelligence. It had a measure of power in being able selectively to screen information it collected for the occupation authorities, and it could choose the level of vigour with which it implemented directives.

The *zaibatsu* dissolution programme of the post-war period yielded mixed results. One of the major changes was an influx of new talent into the senior managerial ranks of the major corporations, and a concurrent decline in the influence of the founding families. The widespread advent of professional managers took away some of the onus of corporations being vehicles merely for the private profit of big capital, and increasingly open public ownership gave corporations a more social character. Undesired bureaucratic manipulation continued, but companies now could claim more convincingly to be caretakers of the savings of many from throughout society. Of course, the post-war *keiretsu* business groups rose from the remains of the *zaibatsu*, and to this day exert substantial influence on the economy.

The early post-war years were extremely difficult owing to lack of capital, raw materials, and markets. The occupation forces themselves generated an increasing amount of business, and this improved considerably with the advent of special procurement orders for the Korean War of the early 1950s and for reconstruction afterwards. Overall, Japan's business world rather quickly recovered influence, and was heavily involved with determining details of post-war development, including framing much of the detail of what became the San Francisco Peace Treaty of September 1951. The Korean War provided an economic boost for Japan, and the steadily-increasing involvement of the USA in Viet-Nam and Indo-China propelled the Japanese economy even further. This era of high-speed growth was marked by protected domestic markets, export promotion and subsidies, high levels of investment and low corporate interest rates. Japan's hard-working populace was rewarded for its diligence by recognizable improvements in living standards; incomes doubled and doubled again. From the foundation of the Liberal Democratic Party (LDP) in 1955, a pact had been struck between business, politicians and the bureaucracy, each supporting the other. The People's Political Association (*Kokumin Seiji Kyokai*) was the funding conduit from business to the political world, closely linked with political fund-raising by the Keidanren business federation. The People's Political Association went through a few organizational changes after its beginning as the Economic Reconstruction Council in January 1955. It played an important role in the so-called '1955 system' by which the LDP came to be formed and through which it held uninterrupted power for 38 years. The Keidanren political funding programme was substantial: in 1991 the system transferred 13,000m. yen (US $125.0m.) into politics and in 1989 reportedly contributed 30,000m. yen ($241.5m.).

Business helped the bureaucracy in offering lucrative *amakudari* (or 'descent from heaven') appointments to retired bureaucrats. The politicians, each with only a small personal staff, are beholden to the bureaucrats (and to some extent the party and faction leadership) for research and background support in their efforts to draft laws and effectively implement policy. Throughout all of this, the US Government was a background ally, with tens of thousands of troops in Japan and a vested interest in Japan remaining a bastion of market-driven capitalism and a staging area for US anti-Communist activities in the Asian region. Although relations between Japan and the USA were quite solid, the so-called 'Nixon shocks' of going off the gold standard and of ending the Bretton Woods agreement, and *rapprochement* with the People's Republic of China, caught many in Japan unawares. These factors combined with the effects of the oil shocks and an economic slowdown to force many in Japan to recognize that the strategic interests of Japan and the USA could diverge considerably.

The focus of economic progress in the post-war years has shifted from heavy industry to lighter manufacturing to value-added high technology and services. There is hope to move even more to knowledge-intensive industries such as software development or cutting-edge biotechnology. One of the weak dimensions of the Japanese infrastructure, however, is that it has not been very accepting of diversity, or supportive of exploration. The rule of orthodoxy and consensus has taken strong root in Japan, to the detriment of that which is different, creative and unorthodox. Opportunity for the inward migration of non-Japanese talent is also limited, and the local environment is not well prepared for approaches in other than the Japanese language. Singapore or the San Francisco Bay area, for example, seem more fertile ground than Japan for future-orientated global knowledge-intensive industries.

AGRICULTURE AND FOOD SUPPLY

Since the early 1990s agriculture has contracted in relative importance in all the OECD nations when compared with industry and services. In terms of its contribution to the overall economy, in 2000 the Japanese agricultural sector contributed 1.4% of gross value added (compared with 2.6% in 1989); industry contributed 32.8% and services 66.8%. Agriculture in the USA had only slightly more relative weight than in Japan, of 1.6% in 2000 (down from 2.0% in 1989). Yet the costs involved with agriculture in these two nations differ enormously. The OECD's *Agricultural Policies in OECD Countries* (2001) estimated total agricultural producer supports in Japan at US $54,900m., or 59% of the value of production (US producer supports were 21% of production value; the figure for the 15 EU members was 35%).

Although Japanese agriculture is declining in relative significance, that which remains is highly cherished and considered by many to be vital to national well-being and security. Japan is now a modern society, and a large proportion of the citizenry have a complex diet and cosmopolitan tastes. An enduring key indicator, sure to make news and generate comment in Japan, is the annual announcement of per caput consumption of rice. The figure is steadily decreasing. In 1960 annual consumption per head was 114.9 kg. By 1980 this figure had declined to 78.9 kg, and in 2000 annual consumption averaged only 64.6 kg, equivalent to a decrease of 44% since 1960.

Rice is often called the staple food of the Japanese people, but judging from consumption patterns it appears that rice is now merely one of many important foods. The importance of rice-derived calories and rice-derived protein has dwindled. Japanese rice prices are four to seven times higher than world prices owing to import controls. Wheat-based products, potential substitute foods, remain under partial control and are also as yet highly priced in Japan. Rice has without doubt been quite important in the past, both in terms of diet and also in terms of supplying a livelihood for a large number of rural people who were often otherwise untrained. Yet rice (along with tea-leaves and silkworms) is no longer a cornerstone for the tax system and the overall economy, as it was in the past.

On a calorific basis, domestic food production supplies only 40% of total consumption. Notwithstanding government pledges to raise the figure, it continues to decline, owing to a widespread demand for low consumer prices. Japan is officially resistant to accepting its dependence on external, non-Japanese suppliers (there is similar sentiment in the labour market with respect to its casual use of foreign specialists and labourers). The issue of food security involves questions of the nutritive value of different crops, and the efficient use of land area. Various forms of fish-farming, soybean production, multiple cropping, etc., are alternative farming-type uses of land that might be more efficient and better suit Japan. It is important to consider the scarcity of land in Japan and the cost of occupation of such land by any form of marginally-productive farming.

A large proportion of Japanese people now live in coastal urban areas. National average population density was 335.8 people per sq km in 2000, but more than three-quarters of the population live in urban areas or those defined as densely-inhabited districts (DIDs) where population density exceeds 4,000 per sq km.

INDUSTRY

Japan's total manufacturing output for the year 2000 was 5.2% higher than in 1995. This moderate improvement did not compare well with the average for the EU countries (up 16.6%), the OECD overall (up 23.0%) or such growth in the USA (up 30.9%). Conditions further deteriorated for Japanese manufacturing in 2001, with third-quarter seasonally adjusted manufacturing production equivalent to only 94.4% of 1995 levels. Because of

Japan's relatively poor economic environment, many firms have reduced their capital investment in recent years, and much corporate capital stock is now obsolete.

Japan is a nation with few natural resources, but the country has been remarkably slow to embrace the global trading regime. Protectionist import barriers have been erected and dismantled repeatedly over Japan's history, but at present the number of such barriers is low and declining, and there is new enthusiasm for trade. Some raw materials are still regulated, but markets for finished goods are open and at least officially in conformity with World Trade Organization (WTO) rules. Japan's government and its exporting manufacturers seem to have belatedly realized that high-priced raw materials lead to high-priced finished products that limit the domestic market. If domestically-produced products are expensive to manufacture, there is little possibility of developing export markets. In areas with market controls, Japanese firms have found themselves underpriced and losing market share to imports by foreign-based firms using raw materials purchased at standard world prices. In other cases (especially with foods), Japanese firms import semi-finished goods rather than basic raw materials because of a gap between domestic and world prices. Import controls speed up the 'hollowing-out' of industry as factories move abroad in an attempt to remain competitive.

In Western Europe and also in the USA, waning or non-competitive industries have had their eclipse prolonged through domestic policies involving subsidies or protectionist tariffs. Political pressures are an unavoidable but not insurmountable part of the policy process, involving considerations of employment, regional development, and economic parity problems, along with the concerns of vested interests. In many cases it is only possible to delay, not completely to avoid, the temporary problem of displacement and loss of jobs. Governments often act to ease such a period of industrial reorganization through information, education, or capital-transfer endowments. Efforts to ignore underlying structural weakness, however, do nothing to stimulate improvement. Instead, the structural weakness becomes a continuous and often increasing drain on the nation's economic vitality.

For manufacturers, Japan's high relative costs of intermediate inputs and labour do not compare well with those available in nearby China or the countries of the Association of South East Asian Nations (ASEAN). A major development of the 1980s was the improved economic and investment climate in these neighbouring countries, leading to a major movement of manufacturers and their suppliers to the lower-cost venues. Some in Japan have resented such moves, as foreign overseas workers undercut Japanese labour, and the firms may use the threat of relocation as a way to exact concessions over wages and benefits. For many firms, however, there has been little choice but to move abroad; there was no other way to produce the quality, low-cost manufactured goods required to compete in the increasingly global markets at home and abroad. A surprising aspect of this 'hollowing-out', and a cause for complaint by some overseas nations, has been that most of the more highly-skilled jobs have remained in Japan, as have many of the key research and development functions.

Japan's future industrial competitiveness will be affected by the consequences of an ageing population: in coming decades a diminishing proportion of working-age people will be supporting a larger proportion of citizens who have retired. On the positive side, Japan has been largely successful with its general education system and preparing the next generation of productive adults; OECD figures give Japan an upper secondary graduation rate of 94.9%, the highest of any member state (the rate in the USA is 78.2%).

TRADE AND BALANCE OF PAYMENTS

Japan has a very high reliance on trade, and a strong vested interest in the continuation of the international trading system. Modern Japan is highly dependent on imported foodstuffs, and would not easily or stoically support itself on rice and roots if its borders were closed. The problems of ploughing, cultivation and harvesting become quite complicated without imported tractor fuel and fertilizers. It therefore seems an inescapable fact that Japan must trade. Productive capacity is geared to trade (domestic and international), and the population has various raw material requirements that can only be satisfied by it. Like it or not, Japan's prosperity seems to be contingent on the continuity of peaceful international trade, and this would seem to deserve an expenditure of resources toward maintaining the trading system.

Japan continues to be in a good position in terms of foreign-exchange reserves, with official reserve assets valued at roughly US $446,000m. at the end of July 2002. The balance of payments remains strongly positive, but figures for 2001 showed a contraction in yen terms in both current account and trade balance from the previous year's figures. Japan's current-account surplus at the end of fiscal 2001 was 10,627,500m. yen, or 17.4% less than the previous year (which in turn was 31.6% less than in the fiscal year 1998). The positive balance in 2001 from trade in goods was 8,527,000m. yen (down 32.1% from the previous year). Exports decreased in 2001 by 5.2%, totalling 48,979,200m. yen in value, and imports rose by 3.6% to 42,415,500m. yen. Since 1980 Japan's import of manufactured goods has risen from 6% of GDP to almost 9%. The USA's imports in 1980 were also equivalent to 6% of GDP, and have now increased to 16%. Japan is also, of course, an important market for many Asian producers; 40% of Japan's imports come from Asia, and an improvement in Japan's vitality would help nearby nations more fully to recover from the regional economic crisis of 1997–98. In July 2001 *The Oriental Economist Report* claimed that 75% of the increase in Japan's imports emanated from 'captive imports' from overseas affiliates of Japanese firms (a further claim was that 80% of export growth was a result of shipments to overseas affiliates). As for services, Japan is a net importer; the 2001 negative balance of 5,315,000m. yen was a 3.5% decline from the previous year. The positive balance from trade in goods was thus 160% of Japan's net negative balance for services.

Japan's international investment position also remains strongly positive, with net assets at the end of 2001 of 179,257,000m. yen. Private-sector funds represented 69.5% of this total, of which banks accounted for 21.2%, or 14.7% of the overall total; these overseas net assets of Japanese banks grew by 20.6% compared with the year 2000. Investments overseas by the Japanese Government and Japanese banks thus comprised 45.2% of Japan's international position.

Bilateral and International Negotiations

Trade specialists from both Japan's public and private sectors are regularly involved in bilateral trade discussions. Probably the most important are those between Japan and the USA (where a 'Framework for a New Economic Partnership'—agreed in 1993 and renewed in 1995—promises an 'Enhanced Initiative on Deregulation'), and between Japan and the EU (which holds annual summit meetings and a joint Regulatory Reform Dialogue, and established a 10-year 'Action Plan' from the year 2000). There are differing tones to these discussions, with the USA typically being much more confrontational and the EU seeking mutual understanding. None the less, in both cases the Governments typically exchange suggestions with hundreds of proposals for reforms.

A major achievement was the signing of Japan's first Mutual Recognition Agreement (MRA) on 4 April 2001 with the EU. The MRA streamlines export procedures for telecommunications equipment, electrical products, chemicals and pharmaceuticals by allowing approved overseas facilities to assess a product's conformity to legal standards and technical regulations. Re-examination is no longer required for customs entry, and the European Commission expects savings to be substantial: up to €400m. on €21,000m. of such annual trade. Japan has participated energetically in ASEAN + 3, bringing together the 10 ASEAN member states with Japan, China and South Korea. Their Chiang Mai Initiative, signed in May 2000, has led Japan to become partner to various regional bilateral swap arrangements, whereby ASEAN +3 Governments will support the financial markets of partner states in times of crisis. Japan is active in other major international organizations and multilateral forums such as the UN and the OECD, and is an active participant in the WTO. By the end of July 2002, Japan had been respondent (the country complained against) in 13 of 262 developed country disputes filed with the WTO, and had brought 11 cases as complainant. The most publicized case arose following the decision by the US Government in March 2002 to impose tariffs of up to 30% on imports of steel. However, Japan withdrew its complaint in August 2002 after the USA declared certain steel items exempt from tariffs.

FINANCE

The 'Bubble' Economy and its Aftermath

In the late 1980s rampant real estate speculation combined with loose lending policies to elevate both the Japanese stock market and the overall economy. Real estate steadily and spectacularly rose in value from 1985 to late 1990, in many cases tripling or quadrupling in value. Interest rates were low, and regulatory oversight was often remarkably lax during these 'bubble years'. In general expectation of continuing growth, it became possible to borrow 120%–150% of the value of land. Businesses found they could borrow easily for expansion or for speculation, although many companies shifted their sourcing for funds from bank loans to equity financing, issuing convertible or warrant bonds. The stock market was also booming. In 1987 capital gains from securities and real estate transactions exceeded nominal GDP by 40%, and it was estimated that total Japanese land valuation was four times the value of the entire USA. After the Plaza Accord of September 1985, as the value of the yen greatly increased (from 243 yen to 120 yen per US dollar by the end of 1987), imports became relatively less expensive and personal consumption of luxury goods grew rapidly. One negative aspect of the real estate boom was that those renting apartments or homes in formerly less-affluent urban areas were sometimes forced to move out by developers' intimidatory tactics. Working people seeking to buy a home or apartment did not find the situation much easier: many gave up, others took out novel multi-generation 75-year mortgages, with their adult children as co-signers. Seeking to curb speculation, the Bank of Japan on 31 May 1989 raised the official discount rate (ODR) to 3.25% from a then-historic low of 2.5%. Soon four further rate increases had raised the ODR to 6% by 30 August 1990. This compounded concerns among Japanese banks about implementation of the 1988 Basle Capital Accord, which required banks doing international business to show capital adequacy by maintaining a reserve (or 'BIS ratio') of 8% on risk-adjusted assets.

Introduction of a 3% national consumption tax in April 1989 (along with promised further rate increases) restrained consumer spending. Meanwhile, regulations were introduced in 1990 setting lending limits on real estate projects, and a new land tax was announced in December 1990 (to take effect in 1992). These all contributed to price reversals. On the stock market, the Nikkei 225 Average suffered a 20-month collapse, declining from 38,915.87 points to 14,309.41, between 29 December 1989 and 18 August 1992; and as the economy experienced massive asset deflation, non-payment of loans began to become a problem for banks. The full extent of the problem was largely concealed, which increased uncertainty and led to many Japanese becoming vastly more prudent with their money. Banks reportedly became much stricter with new borrowers, even while they steadily supported and cancelled existing non-performing loans. Efforts to revive consumer spending were largely unsuccessful, although the ODR was reduced repeatedly from 1 July 1991 to 4 February 1993 until it had returned to 2.5%, and then cut even further so that at August 2002 it was 0.10%. At that date the short-term interest rate stood at 0.05%, a level previously considered impossible.

The bursting of this 'bubble' left many banks exposed and in trouble, owing to bad debts. Yet as the 1990s continued there was a marked lack of economic hopefulness; and the relative stagnation has continued to date. From the early 1990s it was widely held that Japanese banks were vastly under-reporting their non-performing loans, and this was belatedly confirmed; the cumulative bad debts have now led eventually to several bank failures. A 'Japan Premium' surcharge (which rose to 100 basis points in late 1997) came to be imposed by international markets on Japanese borrowing because of uncertainty over bad debt accounting. The banking crisis came to a head in 1998 (and real economic growth in that year contracted by 2.5%). The Financial Function Early Strengthening Law, has allowed the use of public funds to recapitalize financial institutions seeking to dispose of bad loans. Institutions applying for a capital injection (25 had received such funds as of early 2001) are required to construct and submit a 'plan for restoring sound management', and the Prime Minister and Cabinet Office are charged with monitoring implementation. This substantial inflow of public funds has provided at least a temporary respite, and has finally led to changes in government oversight structure. In early 2001 a total of 40 Japanese financial institutions (including five banks) were in receivership under the Financial Reconstruction Law; and the year brought more than 20,000 corporate bankruptcies. Although by 2002 the Japanese people had witnessed gradual revelations of negative information for more than 10 years, ordinary bank depositors had not yet lost money. Japan has a comprehensive system of deposit insurance, but it has increasingly been the source of much friction. Such insurance has been unlimited, but from April 2002 government guarantees for time deposits were restricted to 10m. yen per account; this 'pay-off' limit was due to be similarly introduced for ordinary (demand) savings accounts in 2003, but there were fears that depositors might withdraw their funds from weakly-performing banks, causing them to collapse.

Japan's Financial Services Agency reported that non-performing loans at Japanese banks rose from 36,800,000m. yen in September 2001 to 43,200,000m. yen at the end of March 2002 (when combined net losses for Japanese banks stood at 4,900,000m. yen). In 2001 the International Monetary Fund (IMF) estimated Japan's bad debt at 95,000,000m. yen (US $766,000m.), of which a potential 60% would need to be completely cancelled. The total bad debt was estimated by others, however, at nearly 150,000,000m. yen ($1,250,000m., or about 30% of Japan's GDP), and 1m. job losses are predicted if strict foreclosure is applied. There is much argument over such figures because the true extent of the problem is unknown. Japanese banks now rate the likelihood of loan recovery (there are two different four-category systems), but only 30% of firms that went bankrupt in 2000 had been rated as 'at risk of failure' (according to *The Oriental Economist Report*, July 2001). Special inspections by the Financial Services Agency from late 2001 of 149 major debtors led to 71 of them (and 58% of the total loans) being reclassified downwards. Clearly, therefore, much remained doubtful. The Resolution and Collection Corporation has been criticized for failing to act decisively with foreclosures; criticism has arisen that overpaying for purchases of non-performing assets at 'market rates' will provide public subsidies to bad managers. The final accounting is still unclear, but the long delay in dealing with these problems effectively has allowed substantial transfers of both debts and assets between firms, the securitization of debt, and a diffusion of responsibility for the uncollectable debt. This is a highly remarkable point: since 1992 Japan's financial institutions have cancelled the staggering sum of 81,540,000m. yen in bad loans (as of March 2002), and the end is yet to come, but very little attention has been directed at personal accountability or mismanagement among lenders, and barely more among borrowers. In September 2002 the Government announced plans to purchase shares from banks in financial difficulties, in an attempt to save them from bankruptcy.

The 'Big Bang'

Japan's 'Big Bang' was a diverse range of measures for financial-sector deregulation that was announced in 1996 and gradually implemented from April 1998. One major change has been with foreign-exchange liberalization, another has given the central bank (the Bank of Japan) greater autonomy. On the level of commercial finance reform, a further change has been the introduction of mark-to-market accounting, where financial assets such as land and securities are measured at market price rather than as formerly by book (purchase) value. Furthermore, it used to be the case that banks, trust banks, life and casualty insurance companies, and securities brokers all had clearly defined domains. This is no longer true, and the previously compartmentalized financial services system has now been widely deregulated. The newly-competitive climate has struck at the core of the formerly tight relationships among such firms. All main financial firms are part of extended industry groups, *keiretsu*, and most have far-reaching cross-shareholding and business relationships with counterpart financial firms active in other domains, but such firms (or their subsidiaries) are now increasingly in direct competition. The lowering of barriers has created some anomalies. For example, banks have posted their employees to affiliated securities firms to learn about the business (in order to develop the ability to offer such functions themselves). The securities firms, partly owned by and beholden to the banks, were thus in the difficult position of having to train their future competition. An ongoing major realignment has also been taking place among banks, with numerous mergers creating what seems likely to be four major banking groups; a substantial change from the 23 major banks that were operating in 1990. Public confidence in these new 'mega-banks' has been undermined by the highly-publicized logistical problems of merging computer systems and transaction security arrangements.

Savings and Pensions

A special institution in the Japanese financial world is the Postal Savings System of small-volume personal savings. The Postal Savings System exists alongside private banks, and has long been a point of convenience in that any post office was an access point to savings. However, with national mutual access now widely available online between banks via automatic teller machines, the system is no longer as remarkable for access to funds. What remains remarkable is that Japan's Postal Savings and Insurance System is the world's largest financial organization, with deposits of more than 370,000,000m. yen (US $3,100,000m.). The postal system is in the process of being dismantled and partially privatized, as many claim that there is now no reason for government to be in the banking business. The Government has been criticized for utilizing such postal savings as a source for funds outside the regular budget, and as yet no schedule for privatization has been finalized. None the less, as the use of these funds by public corporations declines, it appears likely that such funds in the near future will increasingly be used to purchase securities, both domestic and overseas.

Japan's rate of gross saving as percentage of disposable income is high: in 1999 of the 29 OECD nations, only South Korean households, at 33.5%, saved more than those of Japan, with 29.9%. There is a perceived need to save in order to provide for an uncertain future. Many efforts have been made by government to boost consumer spending. Some believed that a new-denomination 2,000-yen banknote would help encourage spending (the notes proved unpopular, however); tax cuts and the widespread issuance of 20,000-yen shopping vouchers (to elderly people, and to families with children aged 15 and under) have also been tried, but to little effect.

The demographic trend of Japan's ageing society is one of the concerns of Japan's fourth Economic Structural Reform Plan (running until 2005). Many Japanese who look at Japan's banking and finance difficulties have come to worry about the possibility that their pensions may be under threat. Their fears are not misplaced. Returns on investment tend to be low. Mismanagement threatens both public and private pension funds. On the implementation level, there is further concern about the many who fail to contribute to the National Pension Programme. There is also uncertainty about pensions keeping pace with an unpredictable future cost of living.

Prices, Wages and Unemployment

From a 1995 base the consumer price index in Japan had risen by an average annual rate of only 0.1% over the six years to December 2001, having begun to decrease in 1999. Compared with 2000 when a decrease of 0.6% was recorded, consumer prices declined by 1.2% in 2001, thus leading to the third consecutive year of deflation. Consumer prices continued to decline in 2002. Compensation per employee contracted by 1% between 1997 and 1998, and decreased again by, 0.3%, in 1999. According to the IMF, the level of unemployment rose from only 2.1% of the labour force in 1990 to 3.2% in 1995, and continued to increase steadily during the late 1990s. The OECD standardized unemployment rate for Japan as of mid-2001 was 4.7%. While the Japanese considered this very high, the OECD average was 6.3% and the EU average rate was 7.7%. By December 2001, however, Japan's rate of unemployment had exceeded 5.0% and in March 2002, according to the IMF, reached 5.7%, before declining slightly in subsequent months. Re-employment of middle-aged workers remained a problem, with many large firms' rates of pay based on seniority, and promotion possible on an internal basis only. The inflexibility of the system operates against the recruitment of employees mid-way through their career who try to join a new company, and helps explain the fervour with which many workers cling to their jobs.

Government Funding

Fortunately for the public, the Japanese Government takes a relatively small percentage of income in tax: total government tax receipts as a proportion of GDP placed Japan 28th of the 30 OECD nations in 1999 (above Mexico and South Korea). In September 2002 the Government announced plans to reduce taxation by around 1,500,000m. yen (US $12,000m.) in an effort to stimulate the stagnant economy. In 1999, among the OECD nations, Japan had the lowest percentage of GDP expended on general government (final government consumption 10.2%; this compared with 15.2% in the USA and the 15 EU countries' average of 20.1%). Japan's proportion of government employment to total employment is about 6%, which compares favourably to figures for the USA, Germany and the United Kingdom (all at 15%), France (25%) and Sweden (32%). Furthermore, the Japanese figure has not varied by a full percentage point since 1970.

One problem, however, is that Japan also maintains 77 state-supported public corporations and 86 semi-governmental agencies. They draw substantial off-budget funds from the Fiscal Investment and Loan Program (FILP); funds come largely from the Postal Savings System, with distributions handled by the Trust Fund Bureau of the Ministry of Finance. Originally, these special public corporations were mostly for post-war infrastructural development projects, when private capital was unavailable, but now there are alternative funding sources and often competition from the private sector for such business. The organizations have also been criticized for providing lucrative posts for retired bureaucrats. Their subsidies for the fiscal year ending March 2002 totalled 5,300,000m. yen (of the total 24,000,000m. yen allocated from the FILP). Many of these organizations reportedly have huge sums in unreconciled bad debts as well, and have been able to evade inquiry into their long-term strategic viability through political and bureaucratic machinations. The Government decided in December 2001 to abolish 17 of the organizations and privatize 45; another 38 are scheduled to be reorganized into independent administrative agencies. Negotiations are under way about the future of the other organizations. The process has provoked great discussion about the extent government subsidies and public services should operate in a market economy. Few will support mismanagement or profligacy, but a key question is whether privatization is the proper course. The entities under review include organizations for domestic and overseas development, labour and social welfare, scientific promotion, scholarships, consumer affairs, road development and public broadcasting, where market allocation of resources is often suboptimal. Nation-wide universal service by the postal system, for example, is highly desirable but often inefficient; there are fears that privatization will lead to the closing of rural services and accelerate migration away from the countryside. Attention has largely been focused, however, on the intransigence of vested interests within these organizations, on their ties to the ruling Liberal Democratic Party (LDP), and on links to each associated ministry, where retiring bureaucrats still expect offers of employment. There is also debate on reform focusing on the format and role of state-run universities, which are also becoming subject to criticism.

Foreign Aid

Japan was the world's principal aid donor in terms of total flow of funds from 1992 until 2000, but budget reductions and a depreciation of the yen in 2001 led to the USA regaining the primary position. Japan's net official development assistance (ODA) declined by 18.1% to US $9,678m. in that year (the USA gave $10,884m. and combined EU national donations were $26,004m.). Both the USA and Japan are often criticized for not giving more. In 2001 Japan ranked 19th of the 22 member nations within the OECD's Development Assistance Committee (DAC) in the proportion of gross national income (GNI) allocated to ODA (0.23%), while the USA was last among DAC nations, with 0.11%; Denmark gave the highest proportion of GNI at

1.01%. Controversy continues to dog Japan for its use of soft loans, and for blunt statements such as that in 2001 by an official of the Fisheries Agency that Japan uses ODA to reward poorer, smaller nations that support its policy goals in international forums such as the International Whaling Commission. China, an increasingly serious economic rival, saw its total aid reduced by 25% in 2002/03.

Defence Spending

Expenditures on Japan's national defence are substantial in gross terms, but a relatively low 0.96% of GDP (a 1976 cabinet decision seeks to keep the figure below 1%). Such spending levels are made possible by the alliance with the USA under the Japan-US Defense Guidelines. According to Japan's Defence Agency, defence expenditure in 2001 accounted for 6.0% of Japan's national finance expenses.

The Quest for Fiscal Responsibility

One continuing cause for concern has been Japan's rising public debt, which at the end of 2002 was scheduled to reach about 140% of GDP (693,000,000m. yen), according to the Ministry of Finance. This amount is markedly higher than for other major nations (US government debt is about 58% of GDP), and foreign credit-rating agencies have cited the figure as a reason for downgrading Japan's credit rating. The Bank of Japan highlights the fact that discounts and interest on Japanese government bonds consumed 22.8% of the national budget, in contrast to 13.5% in the USA, 16.5% in Germany, and 6.3% in France. Japan's fiscal deficit for the year ending March 2001 was 36.9% (deficit as percentage of expenditures). There has been some fiscal tightening, but regardless of government rhetoric, the figure shows every sign of continuing to grow, partly because it is still uncertain to what extent the Government will guarantee the growing amount of *zaito* bonds being issued by semi-public organizations.

Public works projects are the traditional outlet for special large-scale government expenditures, and these continue, although there is increasing public awareness of overspending and occasional repercussions against environmental impact. Prime Minister Koizumi promised a number of far-reaching reforms, but one that was uncommonly specific was a budgetary pledge to keep government bond issues below 30,000,000m. yen for the fiscal year 2003. In terms of economic 'pump-priming', this limit may generate new interest in resource allocation and investment efficiency, as economic impact and demand multipliers can vary greatly among projects. A further consideration is to develop an expanded use of private finance initiatives (PFI), where private capital is allowed to develop, to construct and/or to manage major projects of the type now administered by government. The United Kingdom reportedly uses the PFI method for 40% of national projects, and many such public/private systems have been successfully developed in other parts of Asia. Within Japan, a municipal government facility now being constructed via PFI in the city of Chiba will cost an estimated 50% less than if managed by the public sector. It will be good for the economy if the national Government can realize better efficiencies through such methods, but as with open public bidding being undercut by collusion, oversight will remain a problem.

The private sector is also actively proposing novel ways to boost the economy. A bid to raise standard household electricity voltage from 100 to 230 volts has been promoted since late 2000 by the Federation of Electric Power Companies and the Japan Electrical Manufacturers' Association. The upgrading and change-over would require 15 years, improving power transmission efficiency and saving 7,000m. kWh of electricity annually, or 0.8% of total electrical output. The cost for new infrastructure would be substantial, however, requiring around 80,000m. yen annually for new heavy electrical equipment, and similar expenditures for household appliances (which would almost all need to be replaced). While producers are keen on this demand-boosting measure, having proposed that tax concessions would offset expected consumer resistance, the Ministry of Economy, Trade and Industry (METI) has thus far taken a slow and cautious position.

The Stock Market

Although there is general pessimism about the economy and the market, some industries and shares have performed well. Booms and reversals often occur in parallel in world-wide markets, and following the US market there was a general withdrawal from high-technology and information technology shares in mid-2001. Although some analysts predicted a firming market for 2001, the benchmark Nikkei 225 Stock Average declined markedly during 2001 and into 2002. There were numerous fluctuations, and a fall to 9,420.85 points, the lowest closing index since 7 January 1985, was recorded on 6 February 2002. In early October 2002, furthermore, the index fell below 9,000 points for the first time since 1983—a very long way from the historic high set on 29 December 1989 of 38,915.87. The Topix index (all First Section firms on the Tokyo Stock Exchange) fell by 17% in the fiscal year ending March 2002, and had declined by another 10% by early August 2002.

Exchange Rate

Japan is the world's second largest national economy, and much attention and influence emanate from its relationship to the largest: the USA. The yen–dollar exchange rate has varied substantially over the past years. Annual daily average per US dollar for 1998 was 130.9 yen; this was up 15% to 113.9 yen in 1999; up 6% to 107.8 in 2000; and down 11% to 121.5 in 2001; the yen-dollar rate stood at 117.6 in mid-August 2002. The Japanese Government might be tempted to intervene and drive the yen lower (in order to stimulate exports and restrict imports), but this will also lower the capital adequacy (BIS-ratios) of Japanese banks with dollar-denominated loans on their books, and possibly force foreclosure on loans to shore up capital.

Inward Foreign Direct Investment

Japan's officially reported inward foreign direct investment (FDI) flow for 2000 was 0.61% of GDP (Japan was the lowest of the 28 OECD nations reporting; the US figure was 2.87%; the combined figure for Belgium-Luxembourg was highest at 35.83% of GDP). Japan's outward flow of FDI was 1.04% of GDP (only five of 27 OECD nations reported a lower figure). One explanation for Japan's distance from the norm is that Japanese language and society are barriers to outsiders, who fail to recognize opportunity; if they do so, it is difficult to set up and do business in Japan. Until recently there were onerous restrictions on foreign businesses in Japan, but the worst of such legal barriers have now been removed. The improved business climate is due in part to pressures being put on the Japanese Government by foreign governments, at the urging of Japan-based foreign businesses. The American Chamber of Commerce in Japan is a good example of an activist, pro-active organization systematically working for improvement; it collects anecdotes and data, and has steadily built up a network of local and home contacts to promote identified problems it seeks to change. Yet there was still both tacit and more organized resistance to foreign capital in 2002. Shinsei Bank (purchased in 2000 by the Ripplewood investment fund of the USA) has had problems with regulators and resorted to complaining publicly about being left out of repayment schedules by borrower Daiei, while Japanese creditors were being repaid. When Nestlé was being considered as a possible rescuer for Snow Brand Milk Products Co (after the Japanese firm and its subsidiary experienced food poisoning and mislabelling scandals), a Ministry of Agriculture, Forestry and Fisheries official was quoted as saying that partnership with a foreign firm would be unwise. Japan's Minister of State responsible for the Financial Services Agency, Hakuo Yanagisawa, voiced similar sentiments in opposing the sale of a large interest in Aozora Bank by Softbank to US investment fund Cerberus, saying in parliamentary committee that the sale would call into question Softbank's sense of responsibility. It might best be asked why in a market economy this is an issue for the government bureaucracy.

DEREGULATION AND REORGANIZATION

The business world is increasingly pluralistic, yet Japan remains highly adept at exchange of information, co-ordination of efforts, and co-operation. Much of this success is due to the astute use of trade associations and the major business federation, the Keidanren. Business forums, such as the Keizai Doyukai and the Japan Chamber of Commerce and Industry, and various government advisory committees, are also important to bring together and brief key leaders from various parts of the economy.

For many hundreds of years Japan has had a highly-regulated society, with government exercising active control through laws and licensing, as well as through the offering of extra-judicial 'guidance'. Deregulation has now occurred in many realms, but such facts take time to be fully recognized by those who might grasp new opportunities. Vagueness and diffused responsibility are well-known attributes of the Japanese political economy. Many believe that a measure of ambiguity allows for smoother, more harmonious relations. The inter-relationships of the Japanese ministries, and between ministries and those they regulate, can still often be vague and ill-defined. One example is in the practice of'administrative guidance', where a regulatory office within the government bureaucracy strongly suggests that a firm operate in a certain way. Such guidance does not have the rule of law. In some cases it will indicate forthcoming legislation, in other cases it is simply a warning for self-restraint so as not to cause 'excessive competition' or 'market instability'. Most firms seem to find it in their better interest to keep the regulators happy through compliance. The professional bureaucracy of the Japanese Government has been damaged and in decline since the early 1990s. Staff numbers have been reduced, and the highly-popular process of deregulation has shifted the initiative away from bureaucratic officialdom. The vast majority of Japanese government officials are hired directly after graduating from non-technical undergraduate university programmes, and then trained at work; mid-career appointments from outside government are rare. These are people who have been considered the best and the brightest in Japan, with a high sense of professionalism and *esprit de corps*. During the 1990s, however, scandal affected many ministries. Deregulation has also disrupted the post-retirement system of *amakudari*, where early-retiring officials are systematically placed into high-level private sector posts. Many individual officials have thus been led to feel that their financial future may be in question. These career problems have the potential to give rise to even more misconduct, scandal, and a further downward spiral for Japanese officialdom.

In early 2001 the Japanese Government substantially reorganized itself, separating off some services as independent offices and decreasing the number of ministries and agencies from 23 to 13. The full impact of these changes has yet to become apparent: there will be gradual rationalization and realization of efficiencies and an eventual 10% reduction in government staff totals. The immediate effect has been a reshuffling of supervisory responsibilities. The newly-formed Cabinet Office combines the functions of the former Prime Minister's Office, the Economic Planning Agency, the Okinawa Development Agency and the Financial Services Agency (FSA). The Cabinet Office also includes the Council on Economic and Fiscal Policy, which is charged with drafting the national budget (a responsibility formerly in the realm of the Ministry of Finance—MOF), and the newly-created Financial Crisis Management Meeting, responsible for policies to forestall any threatened systemic financial crisis. The MOF is considered a substantial loser in the reshuffle, but it could have been worse, as in the planning stages of government realignment, MOF bureaucrats managed to circumvent an even more radical dismantling of functions. Another major new conglomeration is the Ministry of Land, Infrastructure and Transport (MLIT), formed from the National Land Agency, the Ministry of Construction, the Ministry of Transport and the Hokkaido Development Agency. MLIT handles approximately 80% of Japan's public works budgets, which are coming under increasing focus for being profligate (and in some cases unnecessary and unwanted). A further forthcoming organizational change will be with postal operations: mail, postal savings and postal insurance, now part of the Postal Services Agency, an external organ of the Ministry of Public Management, Home Affairs, Posts and Telecommunications, are expected to be relaunched in future as a public corporation with privatized components. In July 2002 legislation allowing private firms to enter the state-run delivery market was approved. Various other key organizational changes have occurred; but other than eventual cost savings, their main substantive impact has been to shake up the work-life complacency and institutional loyalties of the affected government employees.

Various vested interests and political considerations continued to impede Prime Minister Koizumi's efforts with deregulation. One evolving area of promise is the planned creation of Special Regulatory Reform Zones; these should allow experimental deregulation on a limited scale, and results can be compared to mainstream conditions. If areas outside the Zones suddenly become less competitive, they can be expected to press for regulatory changes, broadening the deregulatory coalition.

The Telecommunications Sector

Japanese telecommunication services are said to be among the most expensive in the world, costing several times more than similar services in, for example, the USA and the United Kingdom. Although competition has been permitted since 1985, and fees have declined sharply, many still complain about the high interconnection fees charged by Nippon Telegraph and Telephone (NTT), the former national carrier. The NTT group is gradually facing competition from local networks and markets. NTT's rates must be approved by the Japanese Government (which by law must hold at least one-third of NTT shares, and in 2001 owned 53%). After pressure from the US Government, which claimed that the high rates stifled competition and cross-subsidized other services, NTT interconnection charges were scheduled for further reductions, but complaints continue. It has been argued that high access costs limit some households' access to internet services and thus hold back the development of a computer-literate population, and that as a result Japan's international competitiveness with information technology suffers directly. The NTT firms must provide universal service (as designated 'qualified telecommunications carriers') for which they can receive subsidies.

One of Japan's most-watched companies recently has been NTT DoCoMo, now the nation's largest firm in terms of market capitalization. Newspapers and magazines regularly featured details of its products and prospects, and its launch, in late 2001, of next-stage 3-G mobile services to the fashionable i-mode system, which added convenient internet and e-mail functions to new telephone handsets. In mid-2002 there were more than 28m. i-mode subscribers (of over 70m. wireless subscribers in all Japan) and NTT DoCoMo had a 60.5% market share of all mobile and car phone revenues. The technology at the consumer end is appealing; its development has benefited from synergies with Japan's electronic manufacturers and highly advanced production engineering, as well as a technically-literate populace. However the industry is linked to government in that NTT DoCoMo owes much to its specially-favoured position, being 67% owned by NTT, which in turn is 53% owned by the Government. Such a condition is far from a paragon of market virtue. The gradual development of the e-Japan strategy is, similarly, bringing government (politicians and civil servants) and large corporations together, while seeming neglectful of smaller scale businesses and any promotion of entrepreneurism.

MANAGEMENT SYSTEMS AND SHAREHOLDER RELATIONS

The great majority (more than 90%) of Japan's major corporate shareholders' meetings are staged on the same day at the same time, which logistically limits the role of individual shareholders. The typical explanation for this is that professional racketeers, *sokaiya*, sometimes disrupt shareholder meetings; their attendance is limited by holding thousands of shareholder meetings all at once. Yet the opinions of legitimate shareholders are also stifled. This serves the interests of corporate managers rather than those of shareholders, who miss the chance to question and guide management strategy. A related artifice is that these firms release their financial results on a common day one month before the meeting; owing to the sudden volume of information, poor results often escape careful media scrutiny. This approach to shareholder relations is very different from elsewhere in the world, with important ramifications, including a firm's ability to retain earnings and thus to lower its cost of capital, which has an impact on international competitiveness. Such corporate governance results in unique costs and benefits across Japan's mixed group of corporate stakeholders; most directly it is a problem for information flow in that the annual shareholders' meetings may be deliberately orchestrated so as not to operate as a check on management. The high reliance of Japanese corporate finance on retained earnings, derived from the relative freedom of managers from shareholder governance, also allows firms to avoid the discipline that might be imposed by other sources of external finance.

Shareholders are beginning to complain, and there is a growing trend toward activism. This includes pressure from foreign shareholders. The California Public Employees' Retirement System (CalPERS), with many thousands of millions of US dollars of investments in Japan, has published a list of guide-lines for better Japanese corporate governance. They have led unsuccessful proxy efforts to keep certain managers who have admitted corruption from being readmitted to corporate boards. Institutional Shareholder Services have made similar efforts, thus far without success. The Japanese domestic group Shareholders Ombudsman has also been working for change, and domestic pension fund managers have been driven to increased activism by legal requirements that they vote to maximize the value of their portfolio components.

In early December 1997 Japan's Ministry of Justice requested that corporations avoid the practice of holding annual shareholders' meetings on the same day, and also noted problems with efforts at keeping meetings as short as possible. Japan's National Police Agency, the Business Sector Advisory Group on Corporate Governance of the OECD, and the Tokyo Stock Exchange have also raised the call for reform, focusing on the use of *sokaiya* but also including criticism of meeting timing, the independence of auditors, the low returns on equity and low corporate dividend rate in Japan, etc. The system is increasingly difficult to justify. Yet change would alter many fundamental Japanese business formulas and relationships. It is interesting that the Japanese government bureaucracy and the Cabinet have only recently begun to take an active role in condemning the practice of holding simultaneous annual shareholders' meetings. A cynical argument is that the belated interest in part might be retaliation for the fact that business has been critical of bureaucratic corruption; business has also been agitating for limits on public official staffing numbers under the banner of deregulation.

Most large Japanese firms have a core group of institutional shareholders (major banks, insurance companies, institutional customers and suppliers) who hold stable blocks of stock and participate in cross-shareholding relationships. These shareholders are most interested in managing their own firms—they are not 'activist' shareholders. Their investment interest has often been to develop an existing business relationship rather than to seek dividends or capital gains. With cross-shareholding, teams of managers from different firms do not publicly criticize the others because to do so could result in the same thing happening to them. They instead provide their proxy votes in support of management. Cross-shareholding between firms thus contributes to a mutually-forgiving approach to excesses. Such an approach is convenient for a management team, but shortsighted when a firm loses the benefit of checks by expert shareholders that might improve its operations. In most cases, however, the senior management teams logistically are unable to attend each other's shareholder meetings because they are conducting their own at the same time.

Some reform will eventually come about, but because modifying the system threatens the stability of existing management, hitherto there has been little support for change among business leaders. Reform of the basic structure of shareholder relationships in Japan strikes at the heart of corporate stability. There have been efforts in the past few years among a few dozen firms to stagger their meetings away from the common day, but quiet efforts have yet to solve the problem; it has not disappeared, and a growing stridency for change by shareholders will probably lead to stronger legal measures towards instituting reform and an improvement in accurate information flow.

There are a number of other noteworthy Japanese management practices, which have a substantial impact on corporate performance. These include leadership personnel policies, extensive use of ancillary or affiliate organizations by government ministries and agencies, and the already-mentioned practice of adopting retired government officials into private firms as *amakudari* corporate executives. Notable also are a growing number of recent shareholder lawsuits in Japan, where corporate managers and directors have been ordered to pay thousands of millions of yen in compensation for losses due to mismanagement or breach of trust. The Keidanren business federation is seeking legal reform to restrict potential individual liability, but in view of recent corporate scandals in the USA, most notably involving Enron and WorldCom, its efforts might be better directed at encouraging more diligent corporate oversight.

EMERGING ISSUES

Research and Development Spending

Japan continues to invest heavily in research and development (R&D), with total R&D spending in 2000 at 2.98% of GDP, third in the OECD behind Sweden (3.78%) and Finland (3.37%). The Council for Science and Technology, a government advisory committee, designed the basis of the current five-year R&D plan with specific focus on four strategic areas: nanotechnology, life sciences, telecommunications, and the environment. There is to be a major increase in the award of competitively-based research grants. Overall, government was expected to contribute an average of 4,800,000m. yen per year, compared with 3,500,000m. yen in 1999. In Japan's private sector, many dozens of firms are among the best in the world, investing heavily in both technical research and human capital. Japan's private sector financed 72.42% of R&D spending in 2000 (government financed 19.58%): the highest proportion of private R&D spending in the OECD. Although the total outlays are large, it is insufficient if others are spending greater sums in more effective ways.

Neighbourhood Retailers

Japan has many small-scale elderly retailers whose post-retirement businesses have been termed a 'tolerated inefficiency', and whose work is supported by government as a means both to maintain employment and to nurture social welfare. Neighbourhood shops are often the most convenient for elderly people who go shopping on foot, and the shopkeepers contribute to maintaining a sense of local community. Yet uncompetitive businesses are increasingly criticized as contributing to congestion. They take up important space; their supplier deliveries slow down traffic. Until the recent past they were able to obstruct the introduction of larger-scale retailers into their neighbourhoods (although this is now more difficult). The fact that there is both friction and discussion over acceptable means of doing business would seem to be a good sign for Japan's economy, although resolution seems unlikely without a great amount of distress.

Increased Transparency

Increased transparency and improved administrative responsiveness can significantly reduce corporate overheads and stimulate competition, thus leading to lower costs for consumers. Japanese governmental efforts at regulatory reform and transparency have recently led to the development of a new and important responsiveness. The Economic Structural Reform Plan, adopted on 1 December 2000 and scheduled for implementation by 2005, specifies some 260 reforms. One of the more far-reaching is that the Japanese Government will adopt a 'no-action letter' system in which firms can request clarification of regulations, and ministries and agencies will be required within a fixed period to respond in writing. The FSA has already begun such a service, and the Ministry of Economy, Trade and Industry (METI) is considering the possibility of posting its responses on the internet. This type of transparency will further undermine *amakudari*, as there will be less need to employ retired bureaucrats to help navigate through opaque regulations.

Since April 2001 banks have been required to revise their accounting systems and adopt mark-to-market rules (allowing for adjustment of contract prices to market prices). At issue is compliance with the need to maintain minimum capital adequacy reserves (BIS ratios of capital/risk assets) of 8%, as required to conduct international business.

In today's Japan, most sectors and industries have become accustomed to the fact that favoured insider relationships are increasingly difficult to develop, and expensive to maintain. Structural changes that require strategic adjustment are occurring more and more regularly. Unlike in the past, areas of imperfect competition are more quickly identified and seized upon by either domestic or international firms—in many cases as a matter of survival. In recent years substantial deregulation in retailing, telecommunications, and the air transport industries (among others) has taken place; competition has markedly increased, more choices are available and prices are lower.

In summary, one point is clear: Japan does not have a history of seeking market-based solutions. Governments of the past have been prone to intervention, and the people are accustomed to such a role for government. Vested interests in Japan are strong and astute and will continue to resist any threats to their advantageous position. Great effort has already been expended on redesigning economic systems to be more robustly competitive. For future prosperity, the Japanese people may yet wish to employ increased resources on attending to transparency and give greater heed to compliance and accountability.

Statistical Survey

Source (unless otherwise stated): Statistics Bureau and Statistics Center, Ministry of Public Management, Home Affairs, Posts and Telecommunications, 19-1, Wakamatsu-cho, Shinjuku-ku, Tokyo 162-8668; tel. (3) 3202-1111; fax (3) 5273-1181; e-mail webmaster@stat.go.jp; internet www.stat.go.jp.

Area and Population

AREA, POPULATION AND DENSITY

Area (sq km)	377,864*
Population (census results)†	
1 October 1995	125,570,246
1 October 2000	
Males	62,110,764
Females	64,815,079
Total	126,925,843
Population (official estimates at mid-year)	
2000	126,870,000
2001	127,130,000
2002	127,450,000
Density (per sq km) at mid-2002	337.3

* 145,894 sq miles.

† Excluding foreign military and diplomatic personnel and their dependants.

PRINCIPAL CITIES (population at census of 1 October 1995)*

Tokyo (capital)†	7,967,614	Fukuyama	374,517
Yokohama	3,307,136	Fujisawa	368,651
Osaka	2,602,421	Takatsuki	362,270
Nagoya	2,152,184	Iwaki	360,598
Sapporo	1,757,025	Asahikawa	360,568
Kyoto	1,463,822	Machida	360,525
Kobe	1,423,792	Nara	359,218
Fukuoka	1,284,795	Nagano	358,516
Kawasaki	1,202,820	Toyohashi	352,982
Hiroshima	1,108,888	Suita	342,760
Kitakyushu	1,019,598	Toyota	341,079
Sendai	971,297	Takamatsu	331,004
Chiba	856,878	Koriyama	326,833
Sakai	802,993	Toyama	325,375
Kumamoto	650,341	Kawagoe	323,353
Okayama	615,757	Okazaki	322,621
Sagamihara	570,597	Kochi	321,999
Hamamatsu	561,606	Tokorozawa	320,406
Kagoshima	546,282	Kashiwa	317,750
Funabashi	540,817	Akita	311,948
Higashiosaka	517,232	Naha	301,890
Hachioji	503,363	Miyazaki	300,068
Niigata	494,769	Hakodate	298,881
Amagasaki	488,586	Koshigaya	298,253
Shizuoka	474,092	Aomori	294,167
Himeji	470,986	Akashi	287,606
Matsudo	461,503	Morioka	286,478
Matsuyama	460,968	Yokkaichi	285,779
Kanazawa	453,975	Fukushima	285,754
Urawa	453,300	Maebashi	284,788
Kawaguchi	448,854	Kasugai	277,589
Ichikawa	440,555	Ichihara	277,061
Nagasaki	438,635	Yao	276,664

PRINCIPAL CITIES — *continued* (population at census of 1 October 1995)*

Utsunomiya	435,357	Otsu	276,332
Omiya	433,755	Tokushima	268,706
Yokosuka	432,193	Ichinomiya	267,362
Oita	426,979	Kakogawa	260,567
Kurashiki	422,836	Shimonoseki	259,795
Gifu	407,134	Neyagawa	258,443
Hirakata	400,144	Ibaraki	258,233
Toyonaka	398,908	Fukui	255,604
Wakayama	393,885	Yamagata	254,488
Nishinomiya	390,389	Hiratsuka	253,822

* Except for Tokyo, the data for each city refer to an urban county (*shi*), an administrative division which may include some scattered or rural population as well as an urban centre.

† The figure refers to the 23 wards (*ku*) of the old city. The population of Tokyo-to (Tokyo Prefecture) was 11,773,605 (12,064,000 in 2000).

2000 census (provisional population, '000): Tokyo 8,135; Yokohama 3,427; Osaka 2,599; Nagoya 2,172; Sapporo 1,822; Kobe 1,493; Kyoto 1,468; Fukuoka 1,341; Kawasaki 1,250; Hiroshima 1,126; Kitakyushu 1,011; Sendai 1,008.

BIRTHS, MARRIAGES AND DEATHS*

	Registered live births		Registered marriages†		Registered deaths	
	Number	Rate (per 1,000)	Number	Rate (per 1,000)	Number	Rate (per 1,000)
1993	1,188,282	9.6	792,658	6.4	878,532	7.1
1994	1,238,328	10.0	782,738	6.3	875,933	7.1
1995	1,187,064	9.6	791,888	6.4	922,139	7.4
1996	1,206,555	9.7	795,080	6.4	896,211	7.2
1997	1,191,665	9.5	775,651	6.2	913,402	7.3
1998	1,203,147	9.6	784,595	6.3	936,484	7.5
1999	1,177,669	9.4	762,011	6.1	982,031	7.8
2000	1,190,547	9.5	798,138	6.4	961,653	7.7
2001	1,170,662	9.3	799,999	6.4	970,331	7.7

* Figures relate only to Japanese nationals in Japan.

† Data are tabulated by year of registration rather than by year of occurrence.

Expectation of life (WHO estimates, years at birth, 2000): Males 77.5; Females 84.7 (Source: WHO, *World Health Report*).

ECONOMICALLY ACTIVE POPULATION*
(annual averages, '000 persons aged 15 years and over)

	1999	2000	2001
Agriculture and forestry	3,070	2,970	2,860
Fishing and aquatic culture	280	290	270
Mining and quarrying	60	50	50
Manufacturing	13,450	13,210	12,840
Electricity, gas and water	380	340	340
Construction	6,570	6,530	6,320
Wholesale and retail trade and restaurants	14,830	14,740	14,730
Transport, storage and communications	4,060	4,140	4,070
Financing, insurance, real estate and business services	5,990	6,160	22,190
Community, social and personal services (incl. hotels)	15,520	15,640	
Activities not adequately defined	410	390	450
Total employed	64,620	64,460	64,120
Unemployed	3,170	3,200	3,400
Total labour force	67,790	67,660	67,520
Males	40,240	40,140	39,920
Females	27,550	27,530	27,600

* Figures are rounded to the nearest 10,000 persons.

Health and Welfare

KEY INDICATORS

Fertility (births per woman, 2000)	1.4
Under-5 mortality rate (per 1,000 live births, 2000)	4
HIV/AIDS (% of persons aged 15–49, 2000)	<0.10
Physicians (per 1,000 head, 1996)	1.93
Hospital beds (per 1,000 head, 1998)	16.5
Health expenditure (1998): US $ per head (PPP)	1,763
% of GDP	7.5
public (% of total)	78.1
Human Development Index (2000): ranking	9
value	0.933

For sources and definitions, see explanatory note on p. vi.

Agriculture

PRINCIPAL CROPS ('000 metric tons)

	1998	1999	2000
Wheat	569.5	583.1	688.7
Rice (paddy)	11,200.0	11,468.8	11,863.0
Barley	143.6	205.3	214.3
Potatoes	3,073.0	2,963.0	2,900.0*
Sweet potatoes	1,139.0	1,008.0	1,073.4
Taro (Coco yam)	258.4	247.7	247.7*
Yams	178.9	200.0*	200.0*
Other roots and tubers	72.0	70.0*	70.0*
Sugar cane	1,664.0	1,570.0	1,512.0
Sugar beets	4,164.0	3,787.0	3,800.0
Dry beans	102.4	102.0	103.5
Soybeans (Soya beans)	158.0	187.2	235.0
Cabbages	2,397.0	2,550.0	2,600.0*
Lettuce	506.3	540.5	540.0*
Spinach	322.3	329.0	330.0*
Tomatoes	763.6	768.7	804.4
Cauliflowers	102.0	115.9	115.9
Pumpkins, squash and gourds	257.8	265.6	253.6
Cucumbers and gherkins	746.3	765.9	766.7
Aubergines (Eggplants)	458.8	473.2	476.9
Chillies and green peppers	160.0	165.1	170.9
Green onions and shallots	508.5	532.3	532.3*
Dry onions	1,355.0	1,205.0	1,049.0
Green beans	66.3	62.0	63.9
Carrots	648.1	676.7	676.7*
Green corn	286.0	300.0*	300.0*
Mushrooms	74.2	70.5	67.5
Other vegetables	3,031.2*	3,077.8†	3,086.0*
Watermelons	603.2	595.3	580.6
Cantaloupes and other melons	299.0	300.0*	300.0*
Grapes	232.9	242.0	237.5
Apples	879.1	927.7	799.6
Pears	409.7	415.7	423.8
Peaches and nectarines	169.7	158.1	174.6
Plums	95.6	119.1	119.1
Oranges	124.0	111.0†	102.0†
Tangerines, mandarins, clementines and satsumas	1,194.0	1,447.0	1,143.0
Other citrus fruit	280.0	300.0*	300.0
Persimmons	260.1	286.0	278.8
Strawberries	181.1	203.1	205.3
Other fruits and berries	78.8†	75.6*	75.9*
Tea (made)	82.6	88.5	88.5
Tobacco (leaves)	64.0	64.7	60.8

* FAO estimate(s). † Unofficial figure.

Source: FAO.

LIVESTOCK ('000 head at 30 September)

	1998	1999	2000
Horses*	28	22	22
Cattle	4,708	4,658	4,588
Pigs	9,904	9,879	9,880
Sheep*	13	12	11
Goats*	29	31	31
Poultry	303,022	286,250	297,000*

* FAO estimate(s). † Unofficial figure.

Source: FAO.

LIVESTOCK PRODUCTS ('000 metric tons)

	1998	1999	2000
Beef and veal	529.3	540.4	530.0*
Pig meat	1,285.9	1,277.1	1,269.0
Poultry meat	1,211.7	1,211.3	1,195.4
Cows' milk	8,572.4	8,459.7	8,497.0
Butter	88.9	85.3	87.6
Cheese	123.8	123.7	126.2
Poultry eggs	2,531.0	2,534.6	2,527.3
Cattle hides (fresh)	33.0*	33.0†	32.0†

* Unofficial figure. † FAO estimate.

Source: FAO.

Forestry

ROUNDWOOD REMOVALS ('000 cubic metres, excl. bark)

	1998	1999	2000
Sawlogs, veneer logs and logs for sleepers	13,556	13,402	12,936
Pulpwood	5,421	5,024	4,717
Other industrial wood	339	341	334
Fuel wood	264	308	134
Total	19,580	19,075	18,121

Source: FAO.

SAWNWOOD PRODUCTION
('000 cubic metres, incl. railway sleepers)

	1998	1999	2000
Coniferous (softwood)	17,788	17,270	16,479
Broadleaved (hardwood)	837	682	615
Total	18,625	17,952	17,094

Source: FAO.

Fishing

('000 metric tons, live weight)

	1997	1998	1999
Capture	5,926.1	5,263.4	5,176.5
Chum salmon (Keta or Dog salmon)	269.2	206.6	182.9
Alaska (Walleye) pollock	338.8	316.0	382.4
Atka mackerel	206.8	241.0	169.5
Pacific saury (Skipper)	290.8	145.0	141.0
Japanese jack mackerel	323.1	311.3	211.1
Japanese pilchard (sardine)	284.1	167.1	351.2
Japanese anchovy	233.1	470.6	484.2
Skipjack tuna (Oceanic skipjack)	311.5	385.4	287.3
Chub mackerel	849.0	511.2	381.9
Yesso scallop	261.2	287.8	299.6
Japanese flying squid	366.0	180.7	237.3
Aquaculture	806.5	766.8	759.3
Pacific cupped oyster	218.1	199.5	205.3
Yesso scallop	254.1	226.1	216.0
Total catch	6,732.6	6,030.2	5,935.7

Note: Figures exclude aquatic plants ('000 metric tons): 683.2 (capture 149.9, aquaculture 533.3) in 1997; 640.6 (capture 116.9, aquaculture 523.7) in 1998; 676.9 (capture 120.9, aquaculture 556.0) in 1999. Also excluded are aquatic mammals (generally recorded by number rather than by weight), pearls, corals and sponges. The number of whales and dolphins caught was: 20,710 in 1997; 13,884 in 1998; 17,730 in 1999 (figures include whales caught during the Antarctic summer season beginning in the year prior to the year stated). The catch of other aquatic mammals (in '000 metric tons) was: 1.9 in 1997; 1.2 in 1998; 1.7 in 1999. For the remaining categories, catches (in metric tons) were: Pearls 48.5 in 1997, 29.1 in 1998, 24.8 in 1999; Corals (including FAO estimates) 5.1 in 1997, 6.9 in 1998, 5.2 in 1999; Sponges (FAO estimates) 5.0 in 1997, 4.0 in 1998, 4.0 in 1999.

Source: FAO, *Yearbook of Fishery Statistics.*

Mining

('000 metric tons, unless otherwise indicated)

	1998	1999	2000
Hard coal	3,663	3,906	3,149
Zinc ore*	68	64	64
Iron ore†	2	2	2
Silica stone	16,236	15,548	15,578
Limestone	183,955	180,193	185,569
Copper ore (metric tons)*	1,070	1,038	1,211
Lead ore (metric tons)*	6,198	6,074	8,835
Gold ore (kg)*	8,601	9,405	8,400
Crude petroleum ('000 barrels)	4,982	4,592	4,654
Natural gas (million cu m)	2,301	2,280	2,453

* Figures refer to the metal content of ores.

† Figures refer to gross weight. The estimated iron content is 54%.

Source: US Geological Survey.

Industry

SELECTED PRODUCTS
('000 metric tons, unless otherwise indicated)

	1997	1998	1999
Refined sugar	2,311	n.a.	n.a.
Cotton yarn—pure (metric tons)	169,141	160,381	157,941
Cotton yarn—mixed (metric tons)	14,378	13,046	13,059
Woven cotton fabrics—pure and mixed (million sq m)	917	842	774
Flax, ramie and hemp yarn (metric tons)	1,411	682	998
Linen fabrics ('000 sq m)	4,039	3,070	3,577
Woven silk fabrics—pure and mixed ('000 sq m)	55,381	40,440	34,564
Wool yarn—pure and mixed (metric tons)	62,439	46,637	41,997
Woven woollen fabrics—pure and mixed ('000 sq m)[1]	246,966	212,862	199,058
Rayon continuous filaments (metric tons)	43,374	40,127	33,980
Acetate continuous filaments (metric tons)	29,900	27,762	24,204
Rayon discontinuous fibres (metric tons)	110,796	96,611	77,294
Acetate discontinuous fibres (metric tons)[2]	76,036	71,989	80,536
Woven rayon fabrics—pure and mixed (million sq m)[1]	416.3	361	325
Woven acetate fabrics—pure and mixed (million sq m)[1]	39.4	28	27
Non-cellulosic continuous filaments (metric tons)	736,476	683,458	664,280
Non-cellulosic discontinuous fibres (metric tons)	825,847	803,558	754,033
Woven synthetic fabrics (million sq m)[1,3]	2,040.6	1,743	1,581
Leather footwear ('000 pairs)[4]	47,573	42,573	37,546
Mechanical wood pulp	1,674	1,598	1,474
Chemical wood pulp[5]	9,812	9,390	9,497
Newsprint	3,192.3	3,265	3,295
Other printing and writing paper	11,092.4	10,887	11,330
Other paper	3,983	3,704	3,769
Paperboard	12,746.8	12,031	12,338
Synthetic rubber	1,591.9	1,520	1,577
Motor vehicle tyres ('000)	170,800	166,956	171,083
Rubber footwear ('000 pairs)	19,052	13,954	12,775
Ethylene—Ethene	7,416.1	7,076	7,687
Propylene—Propene	5,408.6	5,101	5,520
Benzene—Benzol	4,502.0	4,203	4,459
Toluene—Toluol	1,418.7	1,349	1,488
Xylenes—Xylol	4,634.0	4,340	4,641
Ethyl alcohol—95% (kilolitres)	283,319	265,027	263,633
Sulphuric acid—100%	6,828	6,739	6,493
Caustic soda—Sodium hydroxide	4,391	4,252	4,345
Soda ash—Sodium carbonate	801.2	722	722
Ammonium sulphate	1,779.8	1,618	1,716
Nitrogenous fertilizers (a)[6]	854	762	751
Phosphate fertilizers (b)[6]	472	422	399
Liquefied petroleum gas	5,904	4,777	4,871
Naphtha (million litres)	19,234	18,003	17,978

— continued	1997	1998	1999
Motor spirit—Gasoline (million litres)[7]	53,534	55,316	56,316
Kerosene (million litres)	27,620	27,685	26,669
Jet fuel (million litres)	9,224	10,526	10,451
Gas oil (million litres)	48,153	46,071	44,536
Heavy fuel oil (million litres)	74,297	71,782	69,305
Lubricating oil (million litres)	2,833	2,630	2,693
Petroleum bitumen—Asphalt	5,886	5,492	5,596
Coke-oven coke	41,224	39,568	36,473
Cement	91,938	81,328	80,120
Pig-iron	78,519	74,981	74,520
Ferro-alloys[8]	1,004.4	903	847
Crude steel	104,545	93,548	94,192
Aluminium—unwrought: primary	363	309	311
Electrolytic copper	1,278.7	1,277	342
Refined lead—unwrought (metric tons)	227,953	227,571	227,122
Electrolytic, distilled and rectified zinc—unwrought (metric tons)	603,112	607,899	633,383
Calculating machines ('000)	3,238	2,705	2,402
Video disk players ('000)	1,214.5	171	43
Television receivers ('000)[9]	6,672	5,569	3,444
Merchant vessels launched ('000 grt)	9,963	10,563	n.a.
Passenger motor cars ('000)	8,491.4	8,056	8,100
Lorries and trucks ('000)	2,421.4	1,937	1,746
Motorcycles, scooters and mopeds ('000)	2,675.7	2,636	2,252
Cameras ('000)	12,275	11,977	10,326
Watches and clocks ('000)[10]	541,070	594,963	552,269
Construction: new dwellings started ('000)	1,387.0	n.a.	1,223.5
Electric energy (million kWh)[11]	1,037,938	1,046,288	n.a.

[1] Including finished fabrics.
[2] Including cigarette filtration tow.
[3] Including blankets made of synthetic fibres.
[4] Sales.
[5] Including pulp prepared by semi-chemical processes.
[6] Figures refer to the 12 months ending 30 June of the year stated and are in terms of (a) nitrogen, 100%, and (b) phosphoric acid, 100%.
[7] Including aviation gasoline.
[8] Including silico-chromium.
[9] Figures refer to colour television receivers only.
[10] Including watch and clock movements.
[11] Twelve months beginning 1 April of the year stated.

Source: partly UN, *Industrial Commodity Statistics Yearbook.*

Finance

CURRENCY AND EXCHANGE RATES

Monetary Units

100 sen = 1 yen.

Sterling, Dollar and Euro Equivalents (31 May 2002)

£1 sterling = 182.46 yen;
US $1 = 124.40 yen;
€1 = 116.77 yen;
1,000 yen = £5.481 = $8.039 = €8.564.

Average Exchange Rate (yen per US $)

1999 113.91
2000 107.77
2001 121.53

BUDGET ('000 million yen, year ending 31 March)*

Revenue	1999/2000†	2000/01‡	2001/02‡
Tax revenue	44,094	47,148	49,222
Individual income tax	15,067	18,680	18,572
Corporate income tax	9,799	9,947	11,839
Consumption tax	10,376	9,856	10,129
Liquor tax	1,867	1,860	n.a.
Gasoline tax	2,045	2,078	n.a.
Tobacco tax	896	900	n.a.
Stamp duties	1,584	1,511	1,505
Other receipts	3,766	3,718	3,607
Total	49,444	52,377	54,334

Expenditure	1999/2000†	2000/01‡	2001/02‡
Defence	4,915	4,936	4,955
Social security	19,112	16,767	17,555
Public works	12,235	9,431	9,435
Servicing of national debt§	20,272	21,965	17,171
Interest payments	10,907	10,743	n.a.
Transfer of local allocation tax to local governments	12,444	14,016	15,921
Total (incl. others)	89,019	84,987	82,652

* Figures refer only to the operations of the General Account budget. Data exclude transactions of other accounts controlled by the central Government: two mutual aid associations and four special accounts (including other social security funds).
† Revised forecasts.
‡ Initial forecasts.
§ Including the repayment of debt principal and administrative costs.

Source: Ministry of Finance, Tokyo.

INTERNATIONAL RESERVES (US $ million at 31 December)

	1999	2000	2001
Gold*	1,164	1,119	1,082
IMF special drawing rights	2,656	2,437	2,377
Reserve position in IMF	6,552	5,253	5,051
Foreign exchange	277,708	347,212	387,727
Total	288,080	356,021	396,237

* Valued at SDR 35 per troy ounce.

Source: IMF, *International Financial Statistics.*

MONEY SUPPLY ('000 million yen at 31 December)

	1999	2000	2001
Currency outside banks	59,404	61,947	66,676
Demand deposits at deposit money banks	180,133	185,911	215,109
Total money	239,537	247,858	281,785

Source: IMF, *International Financial Statistics.*

COST OF LIVING

(Consumer Price Index; average of monthly figures; base: 2000 = 100)

	1998	1999	2001
Food (incl. beverages)	102.5	102.0	99.4
Housing	99.9	99.8	100.2
Rent	99.6	99.6	100.4
Fuel, light and water charges	100.0	98.4	100.6
Clothing and footwear	101.3	101.1	97.8
Miscellaneous	99.4	100.4	99.8
All items	101.0	100.7	99.3

NATIONAL ACCOUNTS ('000 million yen at current prices)

National Income and Product

	1998	1999	2000
Compensation of employees	281,781.6	277,152.8	279,617.1
Operating surplus	94,932.6	96,072.1	93,906.8
Domestic factor incomes	376,714.2	373,224.9	373,523.9
Consumption of fixed capital	95,805.1	95,739.5	97,951.1
Statistical discrepancy	3,896.5	4,073.6	3,666.1
Gross domestic product (GDP) at factor cost	476,415.8	473,038.0	475,141.1
Indirect taxes	42,958.1	43,002.4	43,142.0
Less Subsidies	3,539.1	4,203.3	4,749.0
GDP in purchasers' values	515,834.8	511,837.1	513,534.0
Factor income received from abroad	14,108.3	11,445.1	11,574.8
Less Factor income paid abroad	7,168.8	5,061.3	5,153.5
Gross national product (GNP)	522,774.3	518,220.9	519,955.3
Statistical discrepancy	–3,896.5	–4,073.6	–3,666.1
Less Consumption of fixed capital	95,805.1	95,739.5	97,951.1
National income in market prices	423,072.7	418,407.8	418,338.1
Other current transfers from abroad	1,733.0	1,360.0	1,423.7
Less Other current transfers paid abroad	2,588.6	2,584.2	2,284.9
National disposable income	422,217.1	417,183.6	417,476.9

Expenditure on the Gross Domestic Product

	1999	2000	2001†
Government final consumption expenditure	82,876.0	85,730.8	88,312.1
Private final consumption expenditure	288,763.5	287,230.7	283,651.5
Increase in stocks	–1,713.7	–1,794.9	–1,708.2
Gross fixed capital formation	134,018.9	135,051.8	128,165.8
Total domestic expenditure	503,944.7	506,218.4	500,129.3
Exports of goods and services	51,143.5	55,255.9	52,567.0
Less Imports of goods and services	43,251.1	47,940.4	49,392.8
GDP in purchasers' values*	511,837.1	513,534.0	503,303.5
GDP at constant 1995 prices	521,826.9	534,148.2	531,055.6

* Including adjustment.
† Provisional figures.

Gross Domestic Product by Economic Activity

	1998	1999	2000
Agriculture, hunting, forestry and fishing	8,250.7	7,583.2	6,995.6
Mining and quarrying	742.5	655.0	636.4
Manufacturing	113,472.2	110,988.8	110,926.9
Electricity, gas and water	18,912.3	19,031.3	19,118.5
Construction	39,739.9	38,495.5	37,635.8
Wholesale and retail trade	77,381.6	73,099.1	71,450.8
Transport, storage and communications	34,652.3	32,935.5	32,909.3
Finance and insurance	29,315.5	33,045.4	32,643.5
Real estate and business activities*	102,830.5	103,690.1	106,448.7
Public administration	26,604.0	27,060.2	27,601.9
Other government services	14,203.6	14,207.3	14,021.3
Other community, social and personal services	61,275.9	62,165.1	64,222.8
Private non-profit services to households	10,094.5	10,001.3	9,341.4
Sub-total	537,475.6	532,957.8	533,952.7
Import duties	2,928.9	2,940.9	3,165.0
Less Imputed bank service charge	24,854.8	24,806.6	23,738.2
Less Consumption taxes for gross capital formation	3,611.4	3,328.6	3,511.5
Statistical discrepancy	3,896.5	4,073.6	3,666.1
GDP in purchasers' values	515,834.8	511,837.1	513,534.0

* Including imputed rents of owner-occupied dwellings.

BALANCE OF PAYMENTS (US $ million)

	1999	2000	2001
Exports of goods f.o.b.	403,694	459,513	383,592
Imports of goods f.o.b.	–280,369	–342,797	–313,378
Trade balance	123,325	116,716	70,214
Exports of services	60,998	69,238	64,515
Imports of services	–115,158	–116,864	–108,249
Balance on goods and services	69,165	69,091	26,480
Other income received	188,272	206,935	190,823
Other income paid	–138,432	–149,313	–120,118
Balance on goods, services and income	119,004	126,713	97,185
Current transfers received	6,212	7,381	6,152
Current transfers paid	–18,350	–17,211	–14,056
Current balance	106,865	116,883	89,280
Capital account (net)	–16,467	–9,259	–2,869
Direct investment abroad	–22,267	–31,534	–38,497
Direct investment from abroad	12,308	8,227	6,191
Portfolio investment assets	–154,410	–83,362	–106,788
Portfolio investment liabilities	126,929	47,387	60,503
Financial derivatives assets	–12,426	–2,996	15,063
Financial derivatives liabilities	17,535	1,100	–15,158
Other investment assets	266,340	–4,148	46,588
Other investment liabilities	–265,117	–10,211	–17,550
Net errors and omissions	16,966	16,869	3,724
Overall balance	76,256	48,955	40,487

Source: IMF, *International Financial Statistics*.

JAPANESE DEVELOPMENT ASSISTANCE

(net disbursement basis, US $ million)*

	1998	1999	2000
Official:			
Bilateral assistance:			
Grants	4,949	5,539	5,813
Grant assistance	2,168	2,340	2,109
Technical assistance	2,782	3,199	3,705
Loans	3,657	4,959	3,827
Total	8,606	10,498	9,640
Contributions to multilateral institutions	2,126	4,888	3,779
Total	10,732	15,386	13,419
Other official flows:			
Export credits	1,620	–755	–1,552
Equities and other bilateral assets, etc.	8,560	7,242	–3,052
Transfers to multilateral institutions	2,076	1,231	–252
Total	12,257	7,718	–4,856
Total official	22,989	23,104	8,563
Private flows:			
Export credits	–3,905	–2,292	–358
Direct investment and others	11,613	7,882	6,191
Bilateral investment in securities, etc.	–3,037	–4,546	478
Transfers to multilateral institutions	–4,579	–4,114	–52
Grants from private voluntary agencies	203	261	231
Total private	295	–2,809	6,490
Grand total	23,282	20,295	15,053

* Excluding aid to Eastern Europe.

External Trade

PRINCIPAL COMMODITIES (million yen)

Imports c.i.f.	1999	2000	2001
Food and live animals	5,040,063	4,966,400	5,250,600
Fish and fish preparations*	1,647,257	1,650,088	1,626,474
Crude materials (inedible) except fuels	2,550,759	2,642,000	2,586,100
Mineral fuels, lubricants, etc.	5,646,300	8,316,600	8,523,700
Petroleum and petroleum products	3,696,152	5,772,043	5,621,462
Crude and partly refined petroleum	3,040,166	4,818,853	4,718,360
Gas (natural and manufactured)	1,314,922	1,934,747	2,125,873
Chemicals	2,636,936	2,855,000	3,101,100
Machinery and transport equipment	11,045,403	12,924,000	13,215,900
Non-electric machinery	3,753,000	n.a.	n.a.
Office machines	2,259,548	2,904,233	2,764,027
Thermionic valves, tubes, etc.	1,532,974	2,139,923	1,909,535
Miscellaneous manufactured articles	n.a.	n.a.	n.a.
Clothing (excl. footwear)	1,855,506	2,115,377	2,318,293
Total (incl. others)†	35,268,008	40,938,423	42,415,533

* Including crustacea and molluscs.
† Including re-imports not classified according to kind.

Exports f.o.b.	1999	2000	2001
Chemicals	3,503,000	3,804,700	3,738,800
Basic manufactures	n.a.	n.a.	n.a.
Iron and steel	1,533,471	1,600,262	1,649,543
Machinery and transport equipment	32,508,684	35,594,800	32,895,700
Non-electric machinery	10,151,195	11,096,400	10,229,500
Power-generating machinery	1,514,557	1,635,451	1,720,184
Office machines	3,057,154	3,094,226	2,820,710
Automatic data-processing machines	1,647,785	1,600,555	1,535,273
Electrical machinery, apparatus, etc.	11,564,384	13,670,200	11,533,300
Thermionic valves, tubes, etc.	3,726,048	4,575,803	3,647,382
Electronic integrated circuits	2,307,400	2,933,751	2,372,424
Transport equipment	10,793,105	10,828,200	11,132,900
Road motor vehicles and parts*	7,094,811	6,930,054	7,210,812
Passenger cars (excl. buses)	6,226,149	6,123,022	6,421,641
Parts for cars, buses, lorries, etc.*	1,636,732	1,864,212	1,880,380
Miscellaneous manufactured articles	n.a.	n.a.	n.a.
Scientific instruments, watches, etc.	2,403,965	2,772,590	2,629,101
Scientific instruments and photographic equipment	2,240,592	2,625,666	2,504,480
Total (incl. others)†	47,547,556	51,654,198	48,979,244

* Excluding tyres, engines and electrical parts.
† Including re-exports not classified according to kind.

Source: Ministry of Finance.

PRINCIPAL TRADING PARTNERS (million yen)*

Imports c.i.f.	1999	2000	2001
Australia	1,456,995	1,595,908	1,755,871
Canada	900,255	938,485	941,469
China, People's Republic	4,875,385	5,941,358	7,026,677
France	699,010	691,297	750,358
Germany	1,307,034	1,371,925	1,505,798
Indonesia	1,429,002	1,766,187	1,805,632
Iran	355,989	577,787	609,819
Ireland	335,491	399,108	441,373
Italy	572,892	572,761	654,978
Korea, Republic	1,824,286	2,204,703	2,088,356
Kuwait	342,975	538,281	538,096
Malaysia	1,241,390	1,562,726	1,561,324
Philippines	603,437	776,247	778,879
Qatar	392,382	632,000	731,801
Russia	428,543	493,791	468,419
Saudi Arabia	944,329	1,531,277	1,496,299
Singapore	618,188	693,625	653,684
Switzerland	382,292	354,262	399,228
Taiwan	1,455,915	1,930,161	1,722,643
Thailand	1,008,226	1,142,346	1,260,472
United Arab Emirates	1,001,012	1,599,649	1,559,855
United Kingdom	674,111	709,180	729,016
USA	7,639,510	7,778,861	7,671,481
Total (incl. others)	35,268,008	40,938,423	42,415,533

Exports f.o.b.	1999	2000	2001
Australia	961,664	923,830	933,178
Belgium	569,822	564,615	555,798
Canada	788,693	805,939	797,113
China, People's Republic	2,657,428	3,274,448	3,763,723
France	775,731	803,801	758,786
Germany	2,121,636	2,155,178	1,896,740
Hong Kong	2,507,213	2,929,696	2,826,044
Indonesia	551,041	817,745	777,704
Italy	578,147	624,309	584,615
Korea, Republic	2,606,234	3,308,751	3,071,871
Malaysia	1,264,899	1,496,627	1,337,217
Mexico	500,173	561,557	496,995
Netherlands	1,367,273	1,356,814	1,393,132
Panama	775,000	695,408	586,630
Philippines	996,864	1,105,654	995,303
Singapore	1,854,167	2,243,914	1,786,059
Taiwan	3,276,252	3,874,042	2,942,227
Thailand	1,284,801	1,469,397	1,442,488
United Kingdom	1,616,321	1,598,434	1,474,989
USA	14,605,315	15,355,867	14,711,055
Total (incl. others)	47,547,556	51,654,198	48,979,244

* Imports by country of production; exports by country of last consignment.

Transport

RAILWAYS (traffic)

	1999	2000
National railways:		
Passengers (million)	8,720	8,670
Freight ton-km (million)	22,270	21,860
Private railways:		
Passengers (million)	13,030	12,980
Freight ton-km (million)	270	280

ROAD TRAFFIC ('000 motor vehicles owned, year ending 31 March)

	1998/99	1999/2000	2000/01
Passenger cars	41,783	42,056	42,365
Buses and coaches	237	236	236
Trucks, incl. trailers	8,476	8,266	8,106
Special use vehicles	1,306	1,386	1,431
Heavy use vehicles	319	321	323
Light two-wheeled vehicles	1,269	1,288	1,308
Light motor vehicles	20,298	21,030	21,755
Total	73,688	74,583	75,525

SHIPPING

Merchant Fleet (registered at 31 December)

	1999	2000	2001
Number of vessels	8,462	8,012	7,924
Total displacement ('000 grt)	17,063	15,257	16,653

Source: Lloyd's Register-Fairplay, *World Fleet Statistics*.

International Sea-borne Traffic

	1998	1999	2000
Vessels entered:			
Number	63,950	65,593	n.a.
Total displacement ('000 net tons)	425,193	446,482	n.a.
Goods ('000 metric tons):			
Loaded	100,905	101,995	101,727
Unloaded	730,217	748,855	787,987

CIVIL AVIATION (traffic on scheduled services)

	1996	1997	1998
Kilometres flown (million)	727	777	828
Passengers carried ('000)	95,914	94,998	101,701
Passenger-km (million)	141,812	151,048	154,402
Total ton-km (million)	19,142	20,627	20,806

Source: UN, *Statistical Yearbook*.

Tourism

FOREIGN TOURIST ARRIVALS
(excl. Japanese nationals resident abroad)

Country of Nationality	1998	1999	2000
Australia	123,681	135,303	147,393
Canada	106,884	106,734	119,168
China, People's Republic	267,180	294,937	351,788
Germany	86,194	87,132	88,309
Hong Kong	356,861	252,870	243,149
Korea, Republic	724,445	942,674	1,064,390
Philippines	82,346	93,346	112,182
Taiwan	843,088	931,411	912,814
United Kingdom	181,533	182,894	192,930
USA	666,700	697,630	725,954
Total (incl. others)	4,106,057	4,437,863	4,757,146

Receipts from tourism (US $ million): 3,742 in 1998; 3,428 in 1999; 3,374 in 2000.

Communications Media

	1999	2000	2001
Television receivers ('000 in use)	91,000	92,000	n.a.
Telephones ('000 main lines in use)	70,530.0	74,343.6	76,000.0
Mobile cellular telephones ('000 subscribers)	56,845.6	66,784.4	72,795.9
Personal computers ('000 in use)	36,300	40,000	44,400
Internet users ('000)	27,060	47,080	57,900
Book production:			
Titles	65,026	65,065	n.a.
Copies (million)	1,368	1,420	n.a.
Daily newspapers:			
Number	121	122	124
Circulation ('000 copies)	72,218	n.a.	n.a.

Radio receivers ('000 in use): 120,500 in 1997.
Facsimile machines ('000 in use): 16,000 in 1997.

Sources: Foreign Press Center, *Facts and Figures of Japan*; UNESCO, *Statistical Yearbook*; UN, *Statistical Yearbook*; International Telecommunication Union.

Education

(2000)

	Institutions	Teachers	Students
Elementary schools	24,106	408,000	7,366,000
Lower secondary schools	11,209	258,000	4,104,000
Upper secondary schools	5,478	269,000	4,166,000
Colleges of technology	62	4,000	57,000
Junior colleges	572	17,000	328,000
Graduate schools and universities	649	151,000	2,740,000

Directory

The Constitution

The Constitution of Japan was promulgated on 3 November 1946 and came into force on 3 May 1947. The following is a summary of its major provisions, with subsequent amendments:

THE EMPEROR

Articles 1–8. The Emperor derives his position from the will of the people. In the performance of any state act as defined in the Constitution, he must seek the advice and approval of the Cabinet, though he may delegate the exercise of his functions, which include: (i) the appointment of the Prime Minister and the Chief Justice of the Supreme Court; (ii) promulgation of laws, cabinet orders, treaties and constitutional amendments; (iii) the convocation of the Diet, dissolution of the House of Representatives and proclamation of elections to the Diet; (iv) the appointment and dismissal of Ministers of State, the granting of amnesties, reprieves and pardons, and the ratification of treaties, conventions or protocols; (v) the awarding of honours and performance of ceremonial functions.

RENUNCIATION OF WAR

Article 9. Japan renounces for ever the use of war as a means of settling international disputes.

Articles 10–40 refer to the legal and human rights of individuals guaranteed by the Constitution.

THE DIET

Articles 41–64. The Diet is convened once a year, is the highest organ of state power and has exclusive legislative authority. It comprises the House of Representatives (480 seats—300 single-seat constituencies and 180 determined by proportional representation) and the House of Councillors (247 seats). The members of the former are elected for four years whilst those of the latter are elected for six years and election for approximately one-half of the members takes place every three years. If the House of Representatives is dissolved, a general election must take place within 40 days and the Diet must be convoked within 30 days of the date of the election. Extraordinary sessions of the Diet may be convened by the Cabinet when one-quarter or more of the members of either House request it. Emergency sessions of the House of Councillors may also be held. A quorum of at least one-third of the Diet members is needed to carry out parliamentary business. Any decision arising therefrom must be passed by a majority vote of those present. A bill becomes law having passed both Houses, except as provided by the Constitution. If the House of Councillors either vetoes or fails to take action within 60 days upon a bill already passed by the House of Representatives, the bill becomes law when passed a second time by the House of Representatives, by at least a two-thirds majority of those members present.

The Budget must first be submitted to the House of Representatives. If, when it is approved by the House of Representatives, the House of Councillors votes against it or fails to take action on it within 30 days, or failing agreement being reached by a joint committee of both Houses, a decision of the House of Representatives shall be the decision of the Diet. The above procedure also applies in respect of the conclusion of treaties.

THE EXECUTIVE

Articles 65–75. Executive power is vested in the Cabinet, consisting of a Prime Minister and such other Ministers as may be appointed. The Cabinet is collectively responsible to the Diet. The Prime Minister is designated from among members of the Diet by a resolution thereof.

If the House of Representatives and the House of Councillors disagree on the designation of the Prime Minister, and if no agreement can be reached even through a joint committee of both Houses, provided for by law, or if the House of Councillors fails to make designation within 10 days, exclusive of the period of recess, after the House of Representatives has made designation, the decision of the House of Representatives shall be the decision of the Diet.

The Prime Minister appoints and may remove other Ministers, a majority of whom must be from the Diet. If the House of Representatives passes a no-confidence motion or rejects a confidence motion, the whole Cabinet resigns, unless the House of Representatives is dissolved within 10 days. When there is a vacancy in the post of Prime Minister, or upon the first convocation of the Diet after a general election of members of the House of Representatives, the whole Cabinet resigns.

The Prime Minister submits bills, reports on national affairs and foreign relations to the Diet. He exercises control and supervision over various administrative branches of the Government. The Cabinet's primary functions (in addition to administrative ones) are to: (a) administer the law faithfully; (b) conduct State affairs; (c) conclude treaties subject to prior (or subsequent) Diet approval; (d) administer the civil service in accordance with law; (e) prepare and present the budget to the Diet; (f) enact Cabinet orders in order to make effective legal and constitutional provisions; (g) decide on amnesties, reprieves or pardons. All laws and Cabinet orders are signed by the competent Minister of State and countersigned by the Prime Minister. The Ministers of State, during their tenure of office, are not subject to legal action without the consent of the Prime Minister. However, the right to take that action is not impaired.

Articles 76–95. Relate to the Judiciary, Finance and Local Government.

AMENDMENTS

Article 96. Amendments to the Constitution are initiated by the Diet, through a concurring vote of two-thirds or more of all the members of each House and are submitted to the people for ratification, which requires the affirmative vote of a majority of all votes cast at a special referendum or at such election as the Diet may specify.

Amendments when so ratified must immediately be promulgated by the Emperor in the name of the people, as an integral part of the Constitution.

Articles 97–99 outline the Supreme Law, while Articles 100–103 consist of Supplementary Provisions.

The Government

HEAD OF STATE

His Imperial Majesty AKIHITO, Emperor of Japan (succeeded to the throne 7 January 1989).

THE CABINET

(September 2002)

A coalition of the Liberal Democratic Party (LDP), Hoshuto and New Komeito. All ministers were members of the LDP, unless otherwise specified.

Prime Minister: JUNICHIRO KOIZUMI.

Minister of Public Management, Home Affairs, Posts and Telecommunications: TORANOSUKE KATAYAMA.

Minister of Justice: MAYUMI MORIYAMA.

Minister of Foreign Affairs: YORIKO KAWAGUCHI (non-politician).

Minister of Finance: MASAJURO SHIOKAWA.

Minister of Education, Culture, Sports, Science and Technology: ATSUKO TOYAMA (non-politician).

Minister of Health, Labour and Welfare: CHIKARA SAKAGUCHI (New Komeito).

Minister of Agriculture, Forestry and Fisheries: TADAMORI OSHIMA.

Minister of Economy, Trade and Industry: TAKEO HIRANUMA.

Minister of Land, Infrastructure and Transport: CHIKAGE OGI (Hoshuto).

Minister of the Environment: SHUNICHI SUZUKI.

Minister responsible for Disaster Prevention: YOSHIDA KONOIKE.

Minister of State and Chief Cabinet Secretary (Gender Equality): YASUO FUKUDA.

Minister of State and Chairman of the National Public Safety Commission: SADAKAZU TANIGAKI.

Minister of State and Director-General of the Defence Agency: SHIGERU ISHIBA.

Minister of State for Development of Okinawa and Northern Territories Affairs, Science and Technology Policy: HIROYUKI HOSODA.

Minister of State (Financial Services Agency and Economic and Fiscal Policy, Information Technology Policy): HEIZO TAKENAKA (non-politician).

Minister of State (Administrative Reform, Regulatory Reform): NOBUTERU ISHIHARA.

MINISTRIES

Imperial Household Agency: 1-1, Chiyoda, Chiyoda-ku, Tokyo 100-8111; tel. (3) 3213-1111; fax (3) 3282-1407; e-mail information@kunaicho.go.jp; internet www.kunaicho.go.jp.

Prime Minister's Office: 1-6-1, Nagata-cho, Chiyoda-ku, Tokyo 100-8968; tel. (3) 3581-2361; fax (3) 3581-1910; internet www.kantei.go.jp.

Cabinet Office: 1-6-1, Nagata-cho, Chiyoda-ku, Tokyo 100-8914; tel. (3) 5253-2111; internet www.cao.go.jp.

Ministry of Agriculture, Forestry and Fisheries: 1-2-1, Kasumigaseki, Chiyoda-ku, Tokyo 100-8950; tel. (3) 3502-8111; fax (3) 3592-7697; e-mail white56@sc.maff.go.jp; internet www.maff.go.jp.

Ministry of Disaster Prevention: Tokyo.

Ministry of Economy, Trade and Industry: 1-3-1, Kasumigaseki, Chiyoda-ku, Tokyo 100-8901; tel. (3) 3501-1511; fax (3) 3501-6942; e-mail webmail@meti.go.jp; internet www.meti.go.jp.

Ministry of Education, Culture, Sports, Science and Technology: 3-2-2, Kasumigaseki, Chiyoda-ku, Tokyo 100-8959; tel. (3) 5253-4111; fax (3) 3595-2017; internet www.mext.go.jp.

Ministry of the Environment: 1-2-2, Kasumigaseki, Chiyoda-ku, Tokyo 100-8975; tel. (3) 3581-3351; fax (3) 3502-0308; e-mail moe@eanet.go.jp; internet www.env.go.jp.

Ministry of Finance: 3-1-1, Kasumigaseki, Chiyoda-ku, Tokyo 100-8940; tel. (3) 3581-4111; fax (3) 5251-2667; e-mail info@mof.go.jp; internet www.mof.go.jp.

Ministry of Foreign Affairs: 2-11-1, Shiba-Koen, Minato-ku, Tokyo 105-8519; tel. (3) 3580-3311; fax (3) 3581-2667; e-mail webmaster@mofa.go.jp; internet www.mofa.go.jp.

Ministry of Health, Labour and Welfare: 1-2-2, Kasumigaseki, Chiyoda-ku, Tokyo 100-8916; tel. (3) 5253-1111; fax (3) 3501-2532; internet www.mhlw.go.jp.

Ministry of Justice: 1-1-1, Kasumigaseki, Chiyoda-ku, Tokyo 100-8977; tel. (3) 3580-4111; fax (3) 3592-7011; e-mail webmaster@moj.go.jp; internet www.moj.go.jp.

Ministry of Land, Infrastructure and Transport: 2-1-3, Kasumigaseki, Chiyoda-ku, Tokyo 100-8918; tel. (3) 5253-8111; fax (3) 3580-7982; e-mail webmaster@mlit.go.jp; internet www.mlit.go.jp.

Ministry of Public Management, Home Affairs, Posts and Telecommunications: 2-1-2, Kasumigaseki, Chiyoda-ku, Tokyo 100-8926; tel. (3) 5253-5111; fax (3) 3504-0265; internet www.soumu.go.jp.

Defence Agency: 5-1 Ichigaya, Honmura-cho, Shinkuju-ku, Tokyo 162-8801; tel. (3) 3268-3111; e-mail info@jda.go.jp; internet www.jda.go.jp.

Financial Services Agency: 3-1-1 Kasumigaseki, Chiyoda-ku, Tokyo 100-8967; tel. (3) 3506-6000; internet www.fsa.go.jp.

National Public Safety Commission: 2-1-2, Kasumigaseki, Chiyoda-ku, Tokyo 100-8974; tel. (3) 3581-0141; internet www.npsc.go.jp.

Legislature

KOKKAI
(Diet)

The Diet consists of two Chambers: the House of Councillors (upper house) and the House of Representatives (lower house). The members of the House of Representatives are elected for a period of four years (subject to dissolution). Following the enactment of reform legislation in December 1994, the number of members in the House of Representatives was reduced to 500 (from 511) at the general election of October 1996. Further legislation was enacted in February 2000, reducing the number of members in the House of Representatives to 480, comprising 300 single-seat constituencies and 180 seats determined by proportional representation. For the House of Councillors, which has 247 members (following legislation enacted in October 2000: previously the membership had been 252), the term of office is six years, with approximately one-half of the members elected every three years.

House of Councillors

Speaker: HIROYUKI KURATA.

Party	Seats after elections*	
	12 July 1998	29 July 2001
Liberal-Democratic Party	102	110
Democratic Party of Japan	47	60
Komei†	22	23
Japanese Communist Party	23	20
Social Democratic Party of Japan	13	8
Liberal Party	12	8
Hoshuto	—	5
New Party Sakigake‡	3	—
Kaikaku (Reform) Club	3	—
Dai-Niin Club	1	—
Independents	26	8
Other parties	—	5
Total	252	247

* Approximately one-half of the seats are renewable every three years. At the 2001 election 48 of the 121 seats were allocated on the basis of proportional representation.

† Renamed New Komeito in November 1998 following merger with Shinto Heiwa.

‡ Dissolved October 1998; new party (Party Sakigake) formed; absorbed by Democratic Party of Japan in March 2001.

House of Representatives

Speaker: TAMISUKE WATANUKI.

General Election, 25 June 2000

Party	Seats
Liberal-Democratic Party	233
Democratic Party of Japan	127
New Komeito	31
Liberal Party	22
Japanese Communist Party	20
Social Democratic Party of Japan	19
Hoshuto	7
Independents and others	21
Total	480

Political Organizations

The Political Funds Regulation Law provides that any organization wishing to support a candidate for an elective public office must be registered as a political party. There are more than 10,000 registered parties in the country, mostly of local or regional significance.

21st Century: 1-7-1, Nagato-cho, Chiyoda-ku, Tokyo; tel. (3) 3581-5111; f. 1996 by four independent mems of House of Representatives; Chair. HAJIME FUNADA.

Dai-Niin Club: Rm 531, Sangiin Kaikan, 2-1-1, Nagata-cho, Chiyoda-ku, Tokyo 100-0014; tel. (3) 3508-8531; e-mail info@niinkuraba.gr.jp; successor to the Green Wind Club (Ryukufukai), which originated in the House of Councillors in 1946–47.

Democratic Party of Japan—DPJ: 1-11-1, Nagata-cho, Chiyoda-ku, Tokyo 100-0014; tel. (3) 3595-9988; e-mail democrat@smn.co.jp; internet www.dpj.or.jp; f. 1998 by the integration into the original DPJ (f. 1996) of the Democratic Reform League, Minseito and Shinto Yuai; advocates a cabinet formed and controlled by the people; absorbed Party Sakigake in March 2001; Pres. YUKIO HATOYAMA: Sec.-Gen. KANSEI NAKANO.

Japanese Communist Party—JCP: 4-26-7, Sendagaya, Shibuya-ku, Tokyo 151-8586; tel. (3) 3403-6111; fax (3) 3746-0767; e-mail intl@jcp.jp; internet www.jcp.or.jp; f. 1922; 400,000 mems (2002); Chair. of Cen. Cttee TETSUZO FUWA; Chair. of Exec. Cttee KAZUO SHII.

Kaikaku (Reform) Club: Sabo Kaikan Bldg, 2-7-5, Hirakawa-cho, Chiyoda-ku, Tokyo 102-0093; tel. (3) 5211-3331; f. 1997; Pres. TATSUO OZAWA.

Liberal Party (LP): Kokusai Kogyo Bldg, 2-2-12, Akasaka, Minato-ku, Tokyo 107-0052; tel. (3) 5562-7111; fax (3) 5562-7122; internet www.jiyuto.or.jp; f. 1998; Pres. ICHIRO OZAWA; Sec.-Gen. HIROHISA FUJII.

Liberal-Democratic Party—LDP (Jiyu-Minshuto): 1-11-23, Nagata-cho, Chiyoda-ku, Tokyo 100-8910; tel. (3) 3581-6211; e-mail koho@ldp.jimin.or.jp; internet www.jimin.jp/; f. 1955; advocates the establishment of a welfare state, the promotion of industrial development, the improvement of educational and cultural facilities and constitutional reform as needed; 2,369,252 mems (2001); Pres. JUN-

ICHIRO KOIZUMI; Sec.-Gen. TAKU YAMASAKI; Chair. of Gen. Council MITSUO HORIUCHI; Chair of Policy Research Council TARO ASO.

New Conservative Party: 2-7-5, Hirakawa-cho, Chiyoda-ku, Tokyo 102-0093; tel. (3) 5212-5111; fax (3) 5212-4111; internet www.hoshutoh.com; f. 2000 by 26 fmr mems of the LP; Pres. TAKESHI NODA; Sec.-Gen. TOSHIHIRO NAKAI.

New Komeito: 17, Minami-Motomachi, Shinjuku-ku, Tokyo 160-0012; tel. (3) 3353-0111; e-mail info@komei.or.jp; internet www.komei.or.jp/; f. 1964 as Komeito, renamed as Komei 1994 following defection of a number of mems to the New Frontier Party (Shinshinto, dissolved Dec. 1997); absorbed Reimei Club Jan. 1998; renamed as above Nov. 1998 following merger of Komei and Shinto Heiwa; advocates political moderation, humanism and globalism, and policies respecting 'dignity of human life'; 350,000 mems (2001); Representative TAKENORI KANZAKI; Sec.-Gen. TETSUZO FUYUSHIBA.

New Socialist Party: Sanken Bldg, 6th Floor, 4-3-7, Hachobori, Chuo-ku, Tokyo 104-0032; tel. (3) 3551-3980; e-mail honbu@sinsyakai.or.jp; internet www.sinsyakai.or.jp; f. 1996 by left-wing defectors from SDPJ; opposed to US military bases on Okinawa and to introduction in 1996 of new electoral system; seeks to establish an ecological socio-economic system; Chair. TATSUKUNI KOMORI; Sec.-Gen. KEN-ICHI UENO.

Sangiin Club: Tokyo; f. 1998; Leader MOTOO SHIINA.

Social Democratic Party of Japan—SDPJ (Shakai Minshuto): 1-8-1, Nagata-cho, Chiyoda-ku, Tokyo 100-0014; tel. (3) 3580-1171; fax (3) 3580-0691; e-mail sdpjmail@omnics.co.jp; internet www.sdp.or.jp; f. 1945 as the Japan Socialist Party (JSP); adopted present name in 1996; seeks the establishment of collective non-aggression and a mutual security system, including Japan, the USA, the CIS and the People's Republic of China; 115,000 mems (1994); Chair. TAKAKO DOI; Sec.-Gen. SADAO FUCHIGAMI.

Diplomatic Representation

EMBASSIES IN JAPAN

Afghanistan: Olympia Annex Apt 503, 6-31-21, Jingumae, Shibuya-ku, Tokyo 150-0001; tel. (3) 3407-7900; fax (3) 3400-7912; Chargé d'affaires a.i.: RAHMATULLAH AMIR.

Algeria: 2-10-67, Mita, Meguro-ku, Tokyo 153-0062; tel. (3) 3711-2661; fax (3) 3710-6534; e-mail ambalgto@twics.com; Ambassador: BOUDJEMAA DELMI.

Angola: 2-10-24 Daizawa, Setagaya-ku, Tokyo 155-0032; tel. (3) 5430-7879; fax (3) 5712-7481; e-mail angolamd@s3.ocv.ne.jp.

Argentina: 2-14-14, Moto Azabu, Minato-ku, Tokyo 106-0046; tel. (3) 5420-7101; fax (3) 5420-7109; internet www.embargentina.or.jp; Ambassador: ALFREDO VICENTE CHIARADIA.

Australia: 2-1-14, Mita, Minato-ku, Tokyo 108-8361; tel. (3) 5232-4111; fax (3) 5232-4149; internet www.australia.or.jp; Ambassador: JOHN MCCARTHY.

Austria: 1-1-20, Moto Azabu, Minato-ku, Tokyo 106-0046; tel. (3) 3451-8281; fax (3) 3451-8283; e-mail austria@gol.com; internet www.austria.or.jp; Ambassador: HANS DIETMAR SCHWEISGUT.

Bangladesh: 4-15-15, Meguro, Meguro-ku, Tokyo 153-0063; tel. (3) 5704-0216; fax (3) 5704-1696; Ambassador: S. M. RASHED AHMED.

Belarus: 4-14-12, Shirogane K House, Shirogane, Minato-ku, Tokyo 108-0072; tel. (3) 3448-1623; fax (3) 3448-1624; e-mail belarus@japan.co.jp; Ambassador: PETR K. KRAVCHANKA.

Belgium: 5, Niban-cho, Chiyoda-ku, Tokyo 102-0084; tel. (3) 3262-0191; fax (3) 3262-0651; e-mail tokyo@diplobel.org; Ambassador: Baron PATRICK NOTHOMB.

Bolivia: Kowa Bldg, No. 38, Room 804, 4-12-24, Nishi Azabu, Minato-ku, Tokyo 106-0031; tel (3) 3499-5441; fax (3) 3499-5443; e-mail emboltk@interlink.or.jp; Ambassador: EUDORO GALINDO ANZE.

Bosnia and Herzegovina: 3-4 Rokuban-cho, Chiyoda-ku, Tokyo 102-0085; tel. (3) 3556-4151.

Brazil: 2-11-12, Kita Aoyama, Minato-ku, Tokyo 107-0061; tel. (3) 3404-5211; fax (3) 3405-5846; internet www.brasemb.or.jp; Ambassador: FERNANDO GUIMARÃES REIS.

Brunei: 6-5-2, Kita Shinagawa, Shinagawa-ku, Tokyo 141-0001; tel. (3) 3447-7997; fax (3) 3447-9260; Ambassador: P. S. N. YUSUF.

Bulgaria: 5-36-3, Yoyogi, Shibuya-ku, Tokyo 151-0053; tel. (3) 3465-1021; fax (3) 3465-1031; e-mail bulemb@gol.com; Ambassador: PETAR ANDONOV.

Burkina Faso: Apt 301, Hiroo Glisten Hills, 3-1-17, Hiroo, Shibuya-ku, Tokyo 150-0012; tel. (3) 3400-7919; fax (3) 3400-6945; Ambassador: W. RAYMOND EDOUARD OUÉDRAOGO.

Burundi: 6-5-3, Kita-Shinagawa, Shinagawa-ku, Tokyo 141; tel. (3) 3443-7321; fax (3) 3443-7720; Ambassador: GABRIEL NDIHOKUBWAYO.

Cambodia: 8-6-9, Akasaka, Minato-ku, Tokyo 107-0052; tel. (3) 5412-8521; fax (3) 5412-8526; e-mail aap33850@hkg.odn.ne.jp; Ambassador: ING KIETH.

Cameroon: 3-27-16, Nozawa, Setagaya-ku, Tokyo 154-0003; tel. (3) 5430-4381; fax (3) 5430-6489; e-mail ambacamtokyo@gol.com; Chargé d'affaires a.i.: MBELLA MBELLA LEJEUNE.

Canada: 7-3-38, Akasaka, Minato-ku, Tokyo 107-8503; tel. (3) 5412-6200; fax (3) 5412-6249; internet www.canadanet.or.jp; Ambassador: ROBERT G. WRIGHT.

Chile: Nihon Seimei Akabanebashi Bldg, 8th Floor, 3-1-14, Shiba, Minato-ku, Tokyo 105-0014; tel. (3) 3452-7561; fax (3) 3452-4457; e-mail embajada@chile.or.jp; internet www2.tky.3web.ne.jp/~oficomtc/main.htm; Ambassador: DEMETRIO INFANTE.

China, People's Republic: 3-4-33, Moto Azabu, Minato-ku, Tokyo 106-0046; tel. (3) 3403-3380; fax (3) 3403-3345; internet www.china-embassy.or.jp; Ambassador: WU DAWEI.

Colombia: 3-10-53, Kami Osaki, Shinagawa-ku, Tokyo 141-0021; tel. (3) 3440-6451; fax (3) 3440-6724; internet www.colombianembassy.org/html/homejp.htm; Ambassador: RICARDO GUTIÉRREZ.

Congo, Democratic Republic: Harajuku Green Heights, Room 701, 3-53-17, Sendagaya, Shibuya-ku, Tokyo 151-0051; tel. (3) 3423-3981; fax (3) 3423-3984; Chargé d'affaires: NGAMBANI ZI-MIZELE.

Costa Rica: Kowa Bldg, No. 38, Room 901, 4-12-24, Nishi Azabu, Minato-ku, Tokyo 106-0031; tel. (3) 3486-1812; fax (3) 3486-1813; Chargé d'affaires a.i.: ANA LUCÍA NASSAR SOTO.

Côte d'Ivoire: 2-19-12, Uehara, Shibuya-ku, Tokyo 151-0064; tel. (3) 5454-1401; fax (3) 5454-1405; e-mail ambacijp@gol.com; Chargé d'affaires a.i.: THOMAS A. YAPO.

Croatia: 3-3-100, Hiroo, Shibuya-ku, Tokyo 150-0012; tel. (3) 5469-3014; fax (3) 5469-3015; e-mail veltok@hpo.net; Ambassador: DRAGO BOVAČ.

Cuba: 1-28-4 Higashi-Azabu, Minato-ku, Tokyo 106-0044; tel. (3) 5570-3182; internet www.cyborg.ne.jp/~embcubaj; Ambassador: ERNESTO MELÉNDEZ BACHS.

Czech Republic: 2-16-14, Hiroo, Shibuya-ku, Tokyo 150-0012; tel. (3) 3400-8122; fax (3) 3400-8124; e-mail tokyo@embassy.mzv.cz; internet embassy.kcom.ne.jp/czech; internet www.mzv.cz; Ambassador: KAREL ZEBRAKOVSKY.

Denmark: 29-6, Sarugaku-cho, Shibuya-ku, Tokyo 150-0033; tel. (3) 3496-3001; fax (3) 3496-3440; e-mail embassy.tokyo@denmark.or.jp; internet www.denmark.or.jp; Ambassador: POUL HOINESS.

Djibouti: 5-18-10, Shimo Meguro, Meguro-ku, Tokyo 153-0064; tel. (3) 5704-0682; fax (3) 5725-8305; Ambassador: RACHAD AHMED SALEH FARAH.

Dominican Republic: Kowa Bldg, No. 38, Room 904, 4-12-24, Nishi Azabu, Minato-ku, Tokyo 106-0031; tel. (3) 3499-6020; fax (3) 3499-2627.

Ecuador: Kowa Bldg, No. 38, Room 806, 4-12-24, Nishi Azabu, Minato-ku, Tokyo 106-0031; tel. (3) 3499-2800; fax (3) 3499-4400; internet www.embassy-avenue.or.jp/ecuador/index-j.htm; Ambassador: MARCELO AVILA.

Egypt: 1-5-4, Aobadai, Meguro-ku, Tokyo 153-0042; tel. (3) 3770-8022; fax (3) 3770-8021; internet embassy.kcom.ne.jp/egypt/index.html; Ambassador: Dr MAHMOUD KAREM.

El Salvador: Kowa Bldg, No. 38, 8th Floor, 4-12-24, Nishi Azabu, Minato-ku, Tokyo 106-0031; tel. (3) 3499-4461; fax (3) 3486-7022; e-mail embesal@gol.com; Ambassador: RICARDO PAREDES-OSORIO.

Estonia: Akasaka Royal Office Bldg, 3rd Floor, 6-9-17, Akasaka, Minato-ku, Tokyo 107; tel. (3) 5545-7171; fax (3) 5545-7172; e-mail embassy.tokyo@mfa.ee; Ambassador: MARK SINISOO.

Ethiopia: 3-4-1, Takanawa, Minato-ku, Tokyo 108-0074; tel. (3) 5420-6860; fax (3) 5420-6866; ethioemb@gol.com; Ambassador: MAHDI AHMED.

Fiji: Noa Bldg, 14th Floor, 2-3-5, Azabudai, Minato-ku, Tokyo 106-0041; tel. (3) 3587-2038; fax (3) 3587-2563; e-mail fijiemb@hotmail.com; Ambassador: Ratu SEREMAIA CAVUILATI.

Finland: 3-5-39, Minami Azabu, Minato-ku, Tokyo 106-8561; tel. (3) 5447-6000; fax (3) 5447-6042; e-mail info@finland.or.jp; internet www.finland.or.jp; Ambassador: EERO KALEVI SALOVAARA.

France: 4-11-44, Minami Azabu, Minato-ku, Tokyo 106-8514; tel. (3) 5420-8800; fax (3) 5420-8917; e-mail ambafrance.tokyo@diplomatie.fr; internet www.ambafrance-jp.org; Ambassador: MAURICE GOURDAULT-MONTAGNE.

Gabon: 1-34-11, Higashigaoka, Meguro-ku, Tokyo 152-0021; tel. (3) 5430-9171; Ambassador: VINCENT BOULÉ.

Germany: 4-5-10, Minami Azabu, Minato-ku, Tokyo 106-0047; tel. (3) 5791-7700; fax (3) 3473-4243; e-mail germtoky@ma.rosenet.ne.jp; internet www.germanembassy-japan.org; Ambassador: HENRIK SCHMIEGLOW.

Ghana: 1-5-21, Nishi Azabu, Minato-ku, Tokyo 106-0031; tel. (3) 5410-8631; fax (3) 5410-8635; e-mail mission@ghanaembassy.or.jp; internet www.ghanaembassy.or.jp; Ambassador: Dr Barfuor Adje-Barwuah.

Greece: 3-16-30, Nishi Azabu, Minato-ku, Tokyo 106-0031; tel. (3) 3403-0871; fax (3) 3402-4642; e-mail greekemb@gol.com; Ambassador: Kyriakos Rodoussakis.

Guatemala: Kowa Bldg, No. 38, Room 905, 4-12-24, Nishi Azabu, Minato-ku, Tokyo 106-0031; tel. (3) 3400-1830; fax (3) 3400-1820; e-mail embguate@twics.com; Ambassador: Antonio Roberto Castellanos López.

Guinea: 12-9, Hachiyama-cho, Shibuya-ku, Tokyo 150-0035; tel. (3) 3770-4640; fax (3) 3770-4643; e-mail ambagui-tokyo@gol.com; Chargé d'affaires a.i.: Jean-Pierre Diawara.

Haiti: Kowa Bldg, No. 38, Room 906, 4-12-24, Nishi Azabu, Minato-ku, Tokyo 106; tel. (3) 3486-7096; fax (3) 3486-7070; Ambassador: Marcel Duret.

Holy See: Apostolic Nunciature, 9-2, Sanban-cho, Chiyoda-ku, Tokyo 102-0075; tel. (3) 3263-6851; fax (3) 3263-6060; Apostolic Nuncio: Most Rev. Ambrose B. de Paoli, Titular Archbishop of Lares.

Honduras: Kowa Bldg, No. 38, Room 802, 8th Floor, 4-12-24, Nishi Azabu, Minato-ku, Tokyo 106-0031; tel. (3) 3409-1150; fax (3) 3409-0305; e-mail honduras@interlink.or.jp; Ambassador: Edgardo Sevilla Idiáquez.

Hungary: 2-17-14, Mita, Minato-ku, Tokyo 108-0073; tel. (3) 3798-8801; fax (3) 3798-8812; e-mail huembtio@attmail.com; internet www2.gol.com/users/huembtio; Ambassador: Dr Zoltán Sűdy.

India: 2-2-11, Kudan Minami, Chiyoda-ku, Tokyo 102-0074; tel. (3) 3262-2391; fax (3) 3234-4866; internet embassy.kcom.ne.jp/embnet/india.html; Ambassador: Siddharth Singh.

Indonesia: 5-2-9, Higashi Gotanda, Shinagawa-ku, Tokyo 141-0022; tel. (3) 3441-4201; fax (3) 3447-1697; Ambassador: Soemadi D. M. Brotodiningrat.

Iran: 3-10-32, Minami Azabu, Minato-ku, Tokyo 106-0047; tel. (3) 3446-8011; fax (3) 3446-9002; internet www2.gol.com/users/sjei/indexjapanese.html; Ambassador: Ali Majedi.

Iraq: 8-4-7, Akasaka, Minato-ku, Tokyo 107-0052; tel. (3) 3423-1727; fax (3) 3402-8636; Chargé d'affaires a.i.: Muhsin M. Ali.

Ireland: Ireland House, 2-10-7, Kojimachi, Chiyoda-ku, Tokyo 102-0083; tel. (3) 3263-0695; fax (3) 3265-2275; internet www.embassy-avenue.jp/ireland/; Ambassador: Pádraig Murphy.

Israel: 3, Niban-cho, Chiyoda-ku, Tokyo 102-0084; tel. (3) 3264-0911; fax (3) 3264-0791; e-mail israel@gol.com; internet www.israelembassy-tokyo.com; Ambassador: Yitzhak Lior.

Italy: 2-5-4, Mita, Minato-ku, Tokyo 108-8302; tel. (3) 3453-5291; fax (3) 3456-2319; e-mail itembtky@gol.com; internet sunsite.sut.ac.jp/embitaly; Ambassador: Gabriele Menegatti.

Jamaica: Toranomon Yatsuka Bldg, 2nd Floor, 1-1-11, Atago, Minato-ku, Tokyo 105-0002; tel. (3) 3435-1861; fax (3) 3435-1864; e-mail secrat@jamaicaemb.or.jp; Ambassador: Dr Earl A. Carr.

Jordan: Chiyoda House, 4th Floor, 2-17-8, Nagata-cho, Chiyoda-ku, Tokyo 100-0014; tel. (3) 3580-5856; fax (3) 3593-9385; internet www2.giganet.net/private/users/emb-jord; Ambassador: Samir Naouri.

Kazakhstan: 5-9-8 Himonya, Meguro-ku, Tokyo 152-0023; tel. (3) 3791-5273.

Kenya: 3-24-3, Yakumo, Meguro-ku, Tokyo 152-0023; tel. (3) 3723-4006; fax (3) 3723-4488; e-mail kenrepj@ma.kcom.ne.jp; internet embassy.kcom.ne.jp/kenya; Ambassador: Mary Donde Odinga.

Korea, Republic: 1-2-5, Minami Azabu, Minato-ku, Tokyo 106-0047; tel. (3) 3452-7611; fax (3) 5232-6911; internet www.mofat.go.kr/embassy_htm/asia/japan/japanese/jp_japan; Ambassador: Cho Se-Hyung.

Kuwait: 4-13-12, Mita, Minato-ku, Tokyo 108-0073; tel. (3) 3455-0361; fax (3) 3456-6290; internet kuwait-embassy.or.jp; Ambassador: Sheikh Azzam Mubarak Sabah al-Sabah.

Laos: 3-3-22, Nishi Azabu, Minato-ku, Tokyo 106-0031; tel. (3) 5411-2291; fax (3) 5411-2293; Ambassador: Soukthavone Keola.

Lebanon: Chiyoda House, 5th Floor, 2-17-8, Nagata-cho, Chiyoda-ku, Tokyo 100-0014; tel. (3) 3580-1227; fax (3) 3580-2281; e-mail ambaliba@japan.co.jp; Ambassador: Jaafar Moawi.

Liberia: Sugi Terrace 201, 3-13-11, Okusawa, Setagaya-ku, Tokyo 158; tel. (3) 3726-5711; fax (3) 3726-5712; Chargé d'affaires a.i.: Harry Tah Freeman.

Libya: 10-14, Daikanyama-cho, Shibuya-ku, Tokyo 150-0034; tel. (3) 3477-0701; fax (3) 3464-0420; Secretary of the People's Bureau: Sulaiman Abu Baker Badi (acting).

Lithuania: Rm. 401, 7-11-12 Roppongi, Minato-ku, Tokyo 106-0032; tel. (3) 5414-3433; fax (3) 5414-3434; e-mail lithemb@gol.com; internet www2.gol.com/users/lithemb.

Luxembourg: Niban-cho TS Bldg, 4th Floor, 2-1, Niban-cho, Chiyoda-ku, Tokyo 102-0084; tel. (3) 3265-9621; fax (3) 3265-9624; internet www.luxembourg.or.jp; Ambassador: Pierre Gramegna.

Madagascar: 2-3-23, Moto Azabu, Minato-ku, Tokyo 106; tel. (3) 3446-7252; fax (3) 3446-7078; Ambassador: Cyrille Fida.

Malawi: Takanawa-Kaisei Bldg, 7th Floor, 3-4-1, Takanawa, Minato-ku, Tokyo 108-0074; tel. (3) 3449-3010; fax (3) 3449-3220; e-mail malawi@mx1.ttcn.ne.jp; internet embassy.kcom.ne.jp/malawi; Ambassador: Bright S. M. Mangulama.

Malaysia: 20-16, Nanpeidai-cho, Shibuya-ku, Tokyo 150-0036; tel. (3) 3476-3840; fax (3) 3476-4971; e-mail maltokyo@kln.gov.my; Ambassador: Dato' Marzuki Mohammad Noor.

Marshall Islands: Meiji Park Heights 101, 9-9, Minamimotomachi, Shinjuku-ku, Tokyo 106; tel. (3) 5379-1701; fax (3) 5379-1810; Ambassador: Mack T. Kaminaga.

Mauritania: 5-17-5, Kita Shinagawa, Shinagawa-ku, Tokyo 141-0001; tel. (3) 3449-3810; fax (3) 3449-3822; Ambassador: Ba Aliou Ibra.

Mexico: 2-15-1, Nagata-cho, Chiyoda-ku, Tokyo 100-0014; tel. (3) 3581-1131; fax (3) 3581-4058; e-mail embamex@twics.com; internet www.embassy-avenue.jp/mexico/index; Ambassador: Carlos de Icaza.

Micronesia: Reinanzaka Bldg, 2nd Floor, 1-14-2, Akasaka, Minato-ku, Tokyo 107-0052; tel. (3) 3585-5456; fax (3) 3585-5348; e-mail fsmemb@fsmemb.or.jp; Ambassador: Alik L. Alik.

Mongolia: Pine Crest Mansion, 21-4, Kamiyama-cho, Shibuya-ku, Tokyo 150-0047; tel. (3) 3469-2088; fax (3) 3469-2216; e-mail embmong@gol.com; internet www.embassy.avenue.jp/mongolia/index-j.htm; Ambassador: Jambyu Batjargal.

Morocco: Silva Kingdom Bldg, 5th–6th Floors, 3-16-3, Sendagaya, Shibuya-ku, Tokyo 151-0051; tel. (3) 3478-3271; fax (3) 3402-0898; Ambassador: Saad Eddin Taib.

Mozambique: 6th Floor, 3-12-17 Mita, Minato-ku, Tokyo 105-0014; tel. (3) 5419-0973; Chargé d'affaires a.i.: Artur Jossefa Jamo.

Myanmar: 4-8-26, Kita Shinagawa, Shinagawa-ku, Tokyo 140-0001; tel. (3) 3441-9291; fax (3) 3447-7394; Ambassador: U Soe Win.

Nepal: 7-14-9, Todoroki, Setagaya-ku, Tokyo 158-0082; tel. (3) 3705-5558; fax (3) 3705-8264; e-mail nepembjp@big.or.jp; internet www.nepal.co.jp/embassy.html; Ambassador: Kedar Bhakta Mathema.

Netherlands: 3-6-3, Shiba Koen, Minato-ku, Tokyo 105-0011; tel. (3) 5401-0411; fax (3) 5401-0420; e-mail nlgovtok@oranda.or.jp; internet www.oranda.or.jp; Ambassador: Egbert F. Jacobs.

New Zealand: 20-40, Kamiyama-cho, Shibuya-ku, Tokyo 150-0047; tel. (3) 3467-2271; fax (3) 3467-2278; e-mail nzemb.tky@mail.com; internet www.nzembassy.com./japan; Ambassador: Philip Gibson.

Nicaragua: Kowa Bldg, No. 38, Room 903, 9th Floor, 4-12-24, Nishi Azabu, Minato-ku, Tokyo 106; tel. (3) 3499-0400; fax (3) 3499-3800; Ambassador: Dr Harry Bodán-Shields.

Nigeria: 5-11-17, Shimo-Meguro, Meguro-ku, Tokyo 153-0064; tel. (3) 5721-5391; fax (3) 5721-5342; internet www.crisscross.com/users/nigeriaemb/home.htm; Ambassador: Emmanuel Oseimiegha Otiotio.

Norway: 5-12-2, Minami Azabu, Minato-ku, Tokyo 106-0047; tel. (3) 3440-2611; fax (3) 3440-2620; e-mail emb.tokyo@mfa.no; internet www.norway.or.jp; Ambassador: Odd Fosseidbråten.

Oman: 2-28-11, Sendagaya, Shibuya-ku, Tokyo 151-0051; tel. (3) 3402-0877; fax (3) 3404-1334; e-mail omanemb@gol.com; Ambassador: Mohammed Ali al-Khusaiby.

Pakistan: 2-14-9, Moto Azabu, Minato-ku, Tokyo 106-0046; tel. (3) 3454-4861; fax (3) 3457-0341; e-mail pakemb@gol.com; Ambassador: Touqir Hussain.

Palau: Rm 201, 1-1, Katamachi, Shinjuku-ku, Tokyo 160-0001; tel. (3) 3354-5500; Ambassador: Masao Salvador.

Panama: Kowa Bldg, No. 38, Room 902, 4-12-24, Nishi Azabu, Minato-ku, Tokyo 106-0031; tel. (3) 3499-3741; fax (3) 5485-3548; e-mail panaemb@gol.com; internet www.embassy-avenue.jp/panama/index-j.html; Ambassador: José A. Sosa.

Papua New Guinea: Mita Kokusai Bldg, Room 313, 3rd Floor, 1-4-28, Mita, Minato-ku, Tokyo 108; tel. (3) 3454-7801; fax (3) 3454-7275; Ambassador: Aiwa Olmi.

Paraguay: 3-12-9, Kami-Osaki, Shinagawa-ku, Tokyo 141-0021; tel. (3) 5485-3101; fax (3) 5485-3103; e-mail embapar@gol.com; internet www.embassy-avenue.jp/paraguay/index-j.htm; Ambassador: Dr Miguel A. Solano López.

Peru: 4-4-27, Higashi, Shibuya-ku, Tokyo 150-0011; tel. (3) 3406-4243; fax (3) 3409-7589; e-mail 1-tokio@ma.kcom.ne.jp; Ambassador: Juan Aurich Montero (acting).

Philippines: 5-15-5, Roppongi, Minato-ku, Tokyo 106-8537; tel. (3) 5562-1600; e-mail phpjp@gol.com; internet www.rptokyo.org; Ambassador: Romeo Abelardo Arguelles.

Poland: 4-5-14, Mita, Minato-ku, Tokyo 108-0074; tel. (3) 3280-2881; Ambassador: JERZY POMIANOWSKI.

Portugal: Kamiura-Kojimachi Bldg, 5th Floor, 3-10-3, Kojimachi, Chiyoda-ku, Tokyo 102-0083; tel. (3) 5212-7322; fax (3) 5226-0616; e-mail embportj@ma.kcom.ne.jp; internet www.pnsnet.co.jp/users/cltembpt; Ambassador: MANUEL GERVÁSIO DE ALMEIDA LEITE.

Qatar: 2-3-28, Moto-Azabu, Minato-ku, Tokyo 106-0046; tel. (3) 5475-0611; Ambassador: RIYADH ALI AL-ANSARI.

Romania: 3-16-19, Nishi Azabu, Minato-ku, Tokyo 106-0031; tel. (3) 3479-0311; fax (3) 3479-0312; e-mail romembjp@gol.com; internet www2.gol.com/users/romembjp/; Ambassador: ION PASCU.

Russia: 2-1-1, Azabu-dai, Minato-ku, Tokyo 106-0041; tel. (3) 3583-4224; fax (3) 3505-0593; internet www.embassy-avenue.jp/russia/index-j.html; Ambassador: ALEKSANDR N. PANOV.

Rwanda: Kowa Bldg, No. 38, 4-12-24, Nishi Azabu, Minato-ku, Tokyo 106; tel. (3) 3486-7801; fax (3) 3409-2434; Ambassador: MATANGUHA ZEPHYR.

Saudi Arabia: 1-8-4, Roppongi, Minato-ku, Tokyo 106-0032; tel. (3) 3589-5241; fax (3) 3589-5200; Ambassador: MOHAMED BASHIR KURDI.

Senegal: 1-3-4, Aobadai, Meguro-ku, Tokyo 153-0042; tel. (3) 3464-8451; fax (3) 3464-8452; e-mail senegal@senegal.jp; Ambassador: GABRIEL ALEXANDRE SAR.

Singapore: 5-12-3, Roppongi, Minato-ku, Tokyo 106-0032; tel. (3) 3586-9111; fax (3) 3582-1085; Ambassador: LIM CHIN BENG.

Slovakia: POB 35, 2-16-14, Hiroo, Shibuya-ku, Tokyo 150-8691; tel. (3) 3400-8122; fax (3) 3406-6215; e-mail zutokio@twics.com; internet www.embassy-avenue.jp/slovakia/index-j.html; Ambassador: JÚLIUS HAUSER.

Slovenia: 7-5-15, Akasaka, Minato-ku, Tokyo 107-0052; tel. (3) 5570-6275; fax (3) 5570-6075; Chargé d'affaires a.i.: BERNARD ŠRAJNET.

South Africa: 414 Zenkyoren Bldg, 4th Floor, 2-7-9, Hirakawa-cho, Chiyoda-ku, Tokyo 102-0093; tel. (3) 3265-3366; fax (3) 3265-1108; e-mail sajapan@rsatk.com; internet www.rsatk.com; Ambassador: KARAMCHUND MACKERDHUJ.

Spain: 1-3-29, Roppongi, Minato-ku, Tokyo 106-0032; tel. (3) 3583-8531; fax (3) 3582-8627; e-mail embspjp@mail.mae.es; Ambassador: JUAN LEÑA CASAS.

Sri Lanka: 2-1-54, Takanawa, Minato-ku, Tokyo 108-0074; tel. (3) 3440-6911; fax (3) 3440-6914; e-mail lankaemb@sphere.ne.jp; internet www.embassy-avenue.jp/srilanka/index.html; Ambassador: KARUNATILAKA AMUNUGAMA.

Sudan: 2-7-11, Shirogane, Minato-ku, Tokyo 108-0072; tel. (3) 3280-3161; Ambassador: Dr AWAD MURSI TAHA.

Sweden: 1-10-3-100, Roppongi, Minato-ku, Tokyo 106-0032; tel. (3) 5562-5050; fax (3) 5562-9095; e-mail ambassaden.tokyo@foreign.ministry.se; internet www.sweden.or.jp; Ambassador: KRISTER KUMLIN.

Switzerland: 5-9-12, Minami Azabu, Minato-ku, Tokyo 106-8589; tel. (3) 3473-0121; fax (3) 3473-6090; e-mail vertretung@tok.rep.admin.ch; internet www.eda.admin.ch/Tokyo; Ambassador: JACQUES REVERDIN.

Syria: Homat Jade, 6-19-45, Akasaka, Minato-ku, Tokyo 107-0052; tel. (3) 3586-8977; fax (3) 3586-8979; Chargé d'affaires a.i.: HAMZAH HAMZAH.

Tanzania: 4-21-9, Kami Yoga, Setagaya-ku, Tokyo 158-0098; tel. (3) 3425-4531; fax (3) 3425-7844; e-mail tzrepjp@gol.com; Ambassador: ELLY E. E. MTANGO.

Thailand: 3-14-6, Kami Osaki, Shinagawa-ku, Tokyo 141-0021; tel. (3) 3447-2247; fax (3) 3442-6750; e-mail thaitke@crisscross.com; Ambassador: CHAWAT ARTHAYUKTI.

Tunisia: 3-6-6, Kudan-Minami, Chiyoda-ku, Tokyo 102-0074; tel. (3) 3511-6622; fax (3) 3511-6600; Ambassador: SALAH HANNACHI.

Turkey: 2-33-6, Jingumae, Shibuya-ku, Tokyo 150-0001; tel. (3) 3470-5131; fax (3) 3470-5136; e-mail embassy@turkey.jp; internet www.turkey.jp; Ambassador: YAMAN BAŞKUT.

Uganda: 4-10-1, Himonya, Meguro-ku, Tokyo 152-0003; tel. (3) 3715-1097; e-mail ugabassy@crisscross.com.

Ukraine: 3-15-6, Nishi Azabu, Minato-ku, Tokyo 106-0046; tel. (3) 5474-9770; fax (3) 5474-9772; e-mail ukremb@rose.ocn.ne.jp; Ambassador: YURIY KOSTENKO.

United Arab Emirates: 9-10, Nanpeidai-cho, Shibuya-ku, Tokyo 150-0036; tel. (3) 5489-0804; fax (3) 5489-0813; e-mail uae-emb@onyx.dti.ne.jp; Ambassador: AHMED ALI HAMAD ALMUALLA.

United Kingdom: 1, Ichiban-cho, Chiyoda-ku, Tokyo 102-8381; tel. (3) 5211-1100; fax (3) 5275-3164; e-mail embassy@fco.gov.uk; internet www.uknow.or.jp; Ambassador: Sir STEPHEN GOMERSALL.

USA: 1-10-5, Akasaka, Minato-ku, Tokyo 107-8420; tel. (3) 3224-5000; e-mail ustkyecn@ppp.bekkoame.or.jp; internet usembassy.state.gov/tokyo/wwwhjmain.html; Ambassador: HOWARD H. BAKER.

Uruguay: Kowa Bldg, No. 38, Room 908, 4-12-24, Nishi Azabu, Minato-ku, Tokyo 106-0031; tel. (3) 3486-1888; fax (3) 3486-9872; Ambassador: ZULMA GUELMAN.

Uzbekistan: 5-11-8, Shimo-Meguro, Meguro-ku, Tokyo 153-0064; tel. (3) 3760-5625.

Venezuela: Kowa Bldg, No. 38, Room 703, 4-12-24, Nishi Azabu, Minato-ku, Tokyo 106-0031; tel. (3) 3409-1501; fax (3) 3409-1505; e-mail embavene@interlink.or.jp; internet sunsite.sut.ac.jp/embassy/venemb/embvenez.html; Ambassador: Dr CARLOS ENRIQUE NONES.

Viet Nam: 50-11, Moto Yoyogi-cho, Shibuya-ku, Tokyo 151-0062; tel. (3) 3466-3313; fax (3) 3466-3391; Ambassador: NGUYEN TAM CHIEN.

Yemen: Kowa Bldg, No. 38, Room 807, 4-12-24, Nishi Azabu, Minato-ku, Tokyo 106-0031; tel. (3) 3499-7151; fax (3) 3499-4577; Chargé d'affaires a.i.: ABDULRAHMAN M. AL-HOTHI.

Yugoslavia: 4-7-24, Kita-Shinagawa, Shinagawa-ku, Tokyo 140-0001; tel. (3) 3447-3571; fax (3) 3447-3573; e-mail embtokyo@twics.com; internet www.twics.com/~embtokyo/home.htm; Chargé d'affaires a.i.: NEMANJA JOVIĆ.

Zambia: 1-10-2, Ebara, Shinagawa-ku, Tokyo 142-0063; tel. (3) 3491-0121; fax (3) 3491-0123; e-mail shulamusakanya@hotmail.com; Chargé d'affaires a.i.: SHULA-PATRICK MUSAKANYA.

Zimbabwe: 5-9-10, Shiroganedai, Minato-ku, Tokyo 108; tel. (3) 3280-0331; fax (3) 3280-0466; e-mail zimtokyo@chive.ocn.ne.jp; Ambassador: Dr ANDREW H. MTETWA.

Judicial System

The basic principles of the legal system are set forth in the Constitution, which lays down that judicial power is vested in the Supreme Court and in such inferior courts as are established by law, and enunciates the principle that no organ or agency of the Executive shall be given final judicial power. Judges are to be independent in the exercise of their conscience, and may not be removed except by public impeachment, unless judicially declared mentally or physically incompetent to perform official duties. The justices of the Supreme Court are appointed by the Cabinet, the sole exception being the Chief Justice, who is appointed by the Emperor after designation by the Cabinet.

The Court Organization Law, which came into force on 3 May 1947, decreed the constitution of the Supreme Court and the establishment of four types of lower court—High, District, Family (established 1 January 1949) and Summary Courts. The constitution and functions of the courts are as follows:

SUPREME COURT

4-2, Hayabusa-cho, Chiyoda-ku, Tokyo 102-8651; tel. (3) 3264-8111; fax (3) 3221-8975; internet www.courts.go.jp.

This court is the highest legal authority in the land, and consists of a Chief Justice and 14 associate justices. It has jurisdiction over Jokoku (Jokoku appeals) and Kokoku (Kokoku appeals), prescribed in codes of procedure. It conducts its hearings and renders decisions through a Grand Bench or three Petty Benches. Both are collegiate bodies, the former consisting of all justices of the Court, and the latter of five justices. A Supreme Court Rule prescribes which cases are to be handled by the respective Benches. It is, however, laid down by law that the Petty Bench cannot make decisions as to the constitutionality of a statute, ordinance, regulation, or disposition, or as to cases in which an opinion concerning the interpretation and application of the Constitution, or of any laws or ordinances, is at variance with a previous decision of the Supreme Court.

Chief Justice: SHIGERU YAMAGUCHI.

Secretary-General: YUKIO HORIGOME.

LOWER COURTS

High Court

A High Court conducts its hearings and renders decisions through a collegiate body, consisting of three judges, though for cases of insurrection the number of judges must be five. The Court has jurisdiction over the following matters:

Koso appeals from judgments in the first instance rendered by District Courts, from judgments rendered by Family Courts, and from judgments concerning criminal cases rendered by Summary Courts.

Kokoku appeals against rulings and orders rendered by District Courts and Family Courts, and against rulings and orders concerning criminal cases rendered by Summary Courts, except those coming within the jurisdiction of the Supreme Court.

Jokoku appeals from judgments in the second instance rendered by District Courts and from judgments rendered by Summary Courts, except those concerning criminal cases.

Actions in the first instance relating to cases of insurrection.

Presidents: TOKUJI IZUMI (Tokyo), YOSHIO OKADA (Osaka), REISUKE SHIMADA (Nagoya), TOYOZO UEDA (Hiroshima), TOSHIMARO KOJO (Fukuoka), FUMIYA SATO (Sendai), KAZUO KATO (Sapporo), FUMIO ARAI (Takamatsu).

District Court

A District Court conducts hearings and renders decisions through a single judge or, for certain types of cases, through a collegiate body of three judges. It has jurisdiction over the following matters:

Actions in the first instance, except offences relating to insurrection, claims where the subject matter of the action does not exceed 900,000 yen, and offences liable to a fine or lesser penalty.

Koso appeals from judgments rendered by Summary Courts, except those concerning criminal cases.

Kokoku appeals against rulings and orders rendered by Summary Courts, except those coming within the jurisdiction of the Supreme Court and High Courts.

Family Court

A Family Court handles cases through a single judge in case of rendering judgments or decisions. However, in accordance with the provisions of other statutes, it conducts its hearings and renders decisions through a collegiate body of three judges. A conciliation is effected through a collegiate body consisting of a judge and two or more members of the conciliation committee selected from among citizens.

It has jurisdiction over the following matters:

Judgment and conciliation with regard to cases relating to family as provided for by the Law for Adjudgment of Domestic Relations.

Judgment with regard to the matters of protection of juveniles as provided for by the Juvenile Law.

Actions in the first instance relating to adult criminal cases of violation of the Labour Standard Law, the Law for Prohibiting Liquors to Minors, or other laws especially enacted for protection of juveniles.

Summary Court

A Summary Court handles cases through a single judge, and has jurisdiction in the first instance over the following matters:

Claims where the value of the subject matter does not exceed 900,000 yen (excluding claims for cancellation or change of administrative dispositions).

Actions which relate to offences liable to a fine or lesser penalty, offences liable to a fine as an optional penalty, and certain specified offences such as habitual gambling and larceny.

A Summary Court cannot impose imprisonment or a graver penalty. When it deems proper the imposition of a sentence of imprisonment or a graver penalty, it must transfer such cases to a District Court, but it can impose imprisonment with labour not exceeding three years for certain specified offences.

Religion

The traditional religions of Japan are Shintoism and Buddhism. Neither is exclusive, and many Japanese subscribe at least nominally to both. Since 1945 a number of new religions (Shinko Shukyo) have evolved, based on a fusion of Shinto, Buddhist, Daoist, Confucian and Christian beliefs. In 1995 there were some 184,000 religious organizations registered in Japan, according to the Ministry of Education.

SHINTOISM

Shintoism is an indigenous religious system embracing the worship of ancestors and of nature. It is divided into two cults: national Shintoism, which is represented by the shrines; and sectarian Shintoism, which developed during the second half of the 19th century. In 1868 Shinto was designated a national religion and all Shinto shrines acquired the privileged status of a national institution. Complete freedom of religion was introduced in 1947, and state support of Shinto was prohibited. In the mid-1990s there were 81,307 shrines, 90,309 priests and 106.6m. adherents.

BUDDHISM

World Buddhist Fellowship: Rev. FUJI NAKAYAMA, Hozenji Buddhist Temple, 3-24-2, Akabane-dai, Kita-ku, Tokyo.

CHRISTIANITY

In 1993 the Christian population was estimated at 1,050,938.

National Christian Council in Japan: Japan Christian Centre, 2-3-18-24, Nishi Waseda, Shinjuku-ku, Tokyo 169-0051; tel. (3) 3203-0372; fax (3) 3204-9495; e-mail ncc-j@jca.apc.org; internet www.jca.apc.org/ncc-j; f. 1923; 14 mems (churches and other bodies), 19 assoc. mems; Chair. REIKO SUZUKI; Gen. Sec. Rev. KENICHI OTSU.

The Anglican Communion

Anglican Church in Japan (Nippon Sei Ko Kai): 65, Yarai-cho, Shinjuku-ku, Tokyo 162-0805; tel. (3) 5228-3171; fax (3) 5228-3175; e-mail general-sec.po@nskk.org; internet www.nskk.org; f. 1887; 11 dioceses; Primate of Japan Most Rev. JAMES T. UNO, Bishop of Kita-Kanto; Gen. Sec. LAURENCE Y. MINABE; 57,878 mems (2001).

The Orthodox Church

Japanese Orthodox Church (Nippon Haristosu Seikyoukai): Holy Resurrection Cathedral (Nicolai-Do), 4-1-3, Kanda Surugadai, Chiyoda-ku, Tokyo 101; tel. (3) 3291-1885; fax (3) 3291-1886; e-mail ocj@gol.com; three dioceses; Archbishop of Tokyo, Primate and Metropolitan of All Japan Most Rev. DANIEL; 24,821 mems.

Protestant Church

United Church of Christ in Japan (Nihon Kirisuto Kyodan): Japan Christian Center, Room 31, 2-3-18, Nishi Waseda, Shinjuku-ku, Tokyo 169-0051; tel. (3) 3202-0541; fax (3) 3207-3918; e-mail ecumeni-c@uccj.org; f. 1941; union of 34 Congregational, Methodist, Presbyterian, Reformed and other Protestant denominations; Moderator Rev. SEISHI OJIMA; Gen. Sec. Rev. NOBORU TAKEMAE; 200,627 mems (2000).

The Roman Catholic Church

Japan comprises three archdioceses and 13 dioceses, and the Apostolic Prefecture of Karafuto. There were an estimated 511,063 adherents at 31 December 2000.

Catholic Bishops' Conference of Japan (Chuo Kyogikai): 2-10-10, Shiomi, Koto-ku, Tokyo 135-8585; tel. (3) 5632-4411; fax (3) 5632-4457; e-mail cbcj-has@ja2.so-net.ne.jp; internet www.cbcj.catholic.jp; Pres. Most Rev. AUGUSTINE JUN-ICHI NOMURA, Bishop of Nagoya.

Archbishop of Nagasaki: Most Rev. FRANCIS XAVIER KANAME SHIMAMOTO, Archbishop's House, 1-1, Hashiguchi-machi, Nagasaki-shi, Nagasaki-ken 852-8114; tel. (95) 843-4188; fax (95) 843-4322.

Archbishop of Osaka: Most Rev. LEO JUN IKENAGA, Archbishop's House, 2-24-22, Tamatsukuri, Chuo-ku, Osaka 540-0004; tel. (6) 6941-9700; fax (6) 6946-1345.

Archbishop of Tokyo: Most Rev. PETER TAKEO OKADA, Archbishop's House, 3-16-15, Sekiguchi, Bunkyo-ku, Tokyo 112-0014; tel. (3) 3943-2301; fax (3) 3944-8511; e-mail peter2000@nifty.com.

Other Christian Churches

Japan Baptist Convention: 1-2-4, Minami Urawa, Saitama-shi, Saitama 336-0017; tel. (48) 883-1091; fax (48) 883-1092; f. 1947; Pres. Rev. HIDETSUGU ANDO; Gen. Sec. Rev. SEIYA YAMASHITA; 33,139 mems (March 2001).

Japan Baptist Union: 2-3-18, Nishi Waseda, Shinjuku-ku, Tokyo 169-0051; tel. (3) 3202-0053; fax (3) 3202-0054; e-mail generalsecretary@jbu.or.jp; f. 1958; Moderator KUNIHIKO AMANO; Gen. Sec. KAZUO OYA; 4,615 mems.

Japan Evangelical Lutheran Church: 1-1, Sadohara-cho, Ichigaya-shi, Shinjuku-ku, Tokyo 162-0842; tel. (3) 3260-8631; fax (3) 3268-3589; e-mail s-matsuoka@jelc.or.jp; internet www.jelc.or.jp; f. 1893; Moderator Rev. MASATOSHI YAMANOUCHI; Gen. Sec. Rev. SHUN-ICHIRO MATSUOKA; 21,967 mems (2000).

Korean Christian Church in Japan: Room 52, Japan Christian Center, 2-3-18, Nishi Waseda, Shinjuku-ku, Tokyo 169-0051; tel. (3) 3202-5398; fax (3) 3202-4977; e-mail kccj@kb3.so-net.ne.jp; f. 1909; Moderator KIM DUK-HWA; Gen. Sec. KANG YOUNG-IL; 7,000 mems (2001).

Among other denominations active in Japan are the Christian Catholic Church, the German Evangelical Church and the Tokyo Union Church.

OTHER COMMUNITIES

Bahá'í Faith

The National Spiritual Assembly of the Bahá'ís of Japan: 7-2-13, Shinjuku, Shinjuku-ku, Tokyo 160-0022; tel. (3) 3209-7521; fax (3) 3204-0773; e-mail nsajpn@tka.att.ne.jp; internet www.bahaijp.org.

Judaism

Jewish Community of Japan: 3-8-8 Hiro, Shibuya-ku, Tokyo 150-0012; tel. (3) 3400-2559; e-mail jccjapan@gol.com; internet www.jccjapan.or.jp; Leader Rabbi ELLIOTT M. MARMON.

Islam

Islam has been active in Japan since the late 19th century. There is a small Muslim community, maintaining several mosques, including those at Kobe, Nagoya, Chiba and Isesaki, the Arabic Islamic Institute and the Islamic Center in Tokyo. The construction of Tokyo Central mosque was ongoing in 1999.

Islamic Center, Japan: 1-16-11, Ohara, Setagaya-ku, Tokyo 156-0041; tel. (3) 3460-6169; fax (3) 3460-6105; e-mail islamcpj@islamcenter.or.jp; internet www.islamcenter.or.jp; f. 1965; Chair. Dr SALIH SAMARRAI.

The New Religions

Many new cults have emerged in Japan since the end of the Second World War. Collectively these are known as the New Religions (Shinko Shukyo), among the most important of which are Tenrikyo, Omotokyo, Soka Gakkai, Rissho Kosei-kai, Kofuku-no-Kagaku, Agonshu and Aum Shinrikyo. (Following the indictment on charges of murder of several members of Aum Shinrikyo, including its leader, SHOKO ASAHARA, the cult lost its legal status as a religious organization in 1996. In January 2000 the cult announced its intention to change its name to Aleph. At that time it named a new leader, TATSUKO MURAOKA.)

Kofuku-no-Kagaku (Institute for Research in Human Happiness): Tokyo; f. 1986; believes its founder to be reincarnation of Buddha; 8.25m. mems; Leader RYUHO OKAWA.

Rissho Kosei-kai: 2-11-1, Wada Suginami-ku, Tokyo 166-8537; tel. (3) 3380-5185; fax (3) 3381-9792; internet www.kosei-kai.or.jp; f. 1938; Buddhist lay organization based on the teaching of the Lotus Sutra, active inter-faith co-operation towards peace; Pres. Rev. Dr NICHIKO NIWANO; 6.3m. mems with 245 brs world-wide (2000).

Soka Gakkai: 32, Shinano-machi, Shinjuku-ku, Tokyo 160-8583; tel. (3) 5360-9830; fax (3) 5360-9885; e-mail webmaster@en.sokagakkai.or.jp; internet www.sokagakkai.or.jp; f. 1930; society of lay practitioners of the Buddhism of Nichiren; membership of 8.21m. households (2000); group promotes activities in education, international cultural exchange and consensus-building towards peace, based on the humanist world view of Buddhism; Hon. Pres. DAISAKU IKEDA; Pres. EINOSUKE AKIYA.

The Press

In December 2000 there were 122 daily newspapers in Japan. Their average circulation was the highest in the world, and the circulation per head of population was also among the highest, at 573 copies per 1,000 inhabitants in 1999. The large number of weekly news journals is a notable feature of the Japanese press. At December 1998 a total of 2,763 periodicals were produced, 85 of which were weekly publications. Technically the Japanese press is highly advanced, and the major newspapers are issued in simultaneous editions in the main centres.

The two newspapers with the largest circulations are the *Yomiuri Shimbun* and *Asahi Shimbun*. Other influential papers include *Mainichi Shimbun, Nihon Keizai Shimbun, Chunichi Shimbun* and *Sankei Shimbun*.

NATIONAL DAILIES

Asahi Shimbun: 5-3-2, Tsukiji, Chuo-ku, Tokyo 104-8011; tel. (3) 3545-0131; fax (3) 3545-0358; internet www.asahi.com; f. 1879; also published by Osaka, Seibu and Nagoya head offices and Hokkaido branch office; Pres. SHINICHI HAKOSHIMA; Dir and Exec. Editor MASAO KIMIWADA; circ. morning 8.3m., evening 4.1m.

Mainichi Shimbun: 1-1-1, Hitotsubashi, Chiyoda-ku, Tokyo 100-8051; tel. (3) 3212-0321; fax (3) 3211-3598; internet www.mainichi.co.jp; f. 1882; also published by Osaka, Seibu and Chubu head offices, and Hokkaido branch office; Pres. AKIRA SAITO; Man. Dir and Editor-in-Chief MASATOU KITAMURA; circ. morning 4.0m., evening 1.7m.

Nihon Keizai Shimbun: 1-9-5, Otemachi, Chiyoda-ku, Tokyo 100-8066; tel. (3) 3270-0251; fax (3) 5255-2661; internet www.nikkei.co.jp; f. 1876; also published by Osaka head office and Sapporo, Nagoya and Seibu branch offices; Pres. TAKUHIKO TSURUTA; Dir and Man. Editor YASUO HIRATA; circ. morning 3.0m., evening 1.7m.

Sankei Shimbun: 1-7-2, Otemachi, Chiyoda-ku, Tokyo 100-8077; tel. (3) 3231-7111; internet www.sankei.co.jp; f. 1933; also published by Osaka head office; Man. Dir and Editor NAGAYOSHI SUMIDA; circ. morning 2.0m., evening 905,771.

Yomiuri Shimbun: 1-7-1, Otemachi, Chiyoda-ku, Tokyo 100-8055; tel. (3) 3242-1111; e-mail webmaster@yomiuri.co.jp; internet www.yomiuri.co.jp; f. 1874; also published by Osaka, Seibu and Chubu head offices, and Hokkaido and Hokuriku branch offices; Pres. and Editor-in-Chief TSUNEO WATANABE; circ. morning 10.2m., evening 4.3m.

PRINCIPAL LOCAL DAILIES

Tokyo

Daily Sports: 1-20-3, Osaki, Shinagawa-ku, Tokyo 141-8585; tel. (3) 5434-1752; f. 1948; morning; Man. Dir HIROHISA KARUO; circ. 400,254.

The Daily Yomiuri: 1-7-1, Otemachi, Chiyoda-ku, Tokyo 100-8055; tel. (3) 3242-1111; f. 1955; morning; Man. Editor TSUTOMU YAMAGUCHI; circ. 51,421.

Dempa Shimbun: 1-11-15, Higashi Gotanda, Shinagawa-ku, Tokyo 141-8790; tel. (3) 3445-6111; fax (3) 3444-7515; f. 1950; morning; Pres. TETSUO HIRAYAMA; Man. Editor TOSHIO KASUYA; circ. 298,000.

Hochi Shimbun: 4-6-49, Kohnan, Minato-ku, Tokyo 108-8485; tel. (3) 5479-1111; internet www.yomiuri.co.jp/hochi/home.htm; f. 1872; morning; Pres. MASARU FUSHIMI; Man. Editor TATSUE AOKI; circ. 755,670.

The Japan Times: 4-5-4, Shibaura, Minato-ku, Tokyo 108-8071; tel. (3) 3453-5312; internet www.japantimes.co.jp; f. 1897; morning; English; Chair. and Pres. TOSHIAKI OGASAWARA; Dir and Editor-in-Chief YUTAKA MATAEBARA; circ. 61,929.

The Mainichi Daily News: 1-1-1, Hitotsubashi, Chiyoda-ku, Tokyo 100-8051; tel. (3) 3212-0321; f. 1922; morning; English; also publ. from Osaka; Man. Editor TETSUO TOKIZAWA; combined circ. 49,200.

Naigai Times: 1-1-15, Ariake, Koto-ku, Tokyo 135-0063; tel. (3) 5564-7021; fax (3) 5564-1022; e-mail info@naigai-times.co.jp; f. 1949; evening; Pres. MITSUGU ONDA; Vice-Pres. and Editor-in-Chief KEN-ICHIRO KURIHARA; circ. 410,000.

Nihon Kaiji Shimbun (Japan Maritime Daily): 5-19-2, Shimbashi, Minato-ku, Tokyo 105-0004; tel. (3) 3436-3221; internet www.jmd.co.jp; f. 1942; morning; Man. Editor OSAMI ENDO; circ. 55,000.

Nihon Kogyo Shimbun: 1-7-2, Otemachi, Chiyoda-ku, Tokyo 100-8125; tel. (3) 3231-7111; internet www.jij.co.jp; f. 1933; morning; industrial, business and financial; Man. Editor YOSHIMI KURA; circ. 408,444.

Nihon Nogyo Shimbun (Agriculture): 2-3, Akihabara, Taito-ku, Tokyo 110-8722; tel. (3) 5295-7411; fax (3) 3253-0980; f. 1928; morning; Man. Editor YASUNORI INOUE; circ. 423,840.

Nihon Sen-i Shimbun (Textile and Fashion): 13-10, Nihonbashi-kobunacho, Chuo-ku, Tokyo 103-0024; tel. (3) 5649-8711; f. 1943; morning; Man. Editor KIYOSHIGE SEIRYU; circ. 116,000.

Nikkan Kogyo Shimbun (Industrial Daily News): 1-8-10, Kudan-kita, Chiyoda-ku, Tokyo 102-8181; tel. (3) 3222-7111; fax (3) 3262-6031; internet www.nikkan.co.jp; f. 1915; morning; Man. Editor HIDEO WATANABE; circ. 533,145.

Nikkan Sports News: 3-5-10, Tsukiji, Chuo-ku, Tokyo 104-8055; tel. (3) 5550-8888; fax (3) 5550-8901; internet www.nikkansports.com; f. 1946; morning; Man. Editor YUKIHIRO MORI; circ. 993,240.

Sankei Sports: 1-7-2, Otemachi, Chiyoda-ku, Tokyo 100-8077; tel. (3) 3231-7111; internet www.xusxus.com; f. 1963; morning; Man. Editor YUKIO INADA; circ. 809,245.

Shipping and Trade News: Tokyo News Service Ltd, Tsukiji Hamarikyu Bldg, 5-3-3, Tsukiji, Chuo-ku, Tokyo 104-8004; tel. (3) 3542-6511; fax (3) 3542-5086; internet www.tvguide.or.jp; f. 1949; English; Man. Editor TAKASHI INOUE; circ. 15,000.

Sports Nippon: 2-1-30, Ecchujima, Koto-ku, Tokyo 135-8735; tel. (3) 3820-0700; internet www.mainichi.co.jp/suponichi; f. 1949; morning; Man. Editor SUSUMU KOMURO; circ. 929,421.

Suisan Keizai Shimbun (Fisheries): 6-8-19, Roppongi, Minato-ku, Tokyo 106-0032; tel. (3) 3404-6531; fax (3) 3404-0863; f. 1948; morning; Man. Editor KOSHI TORINOUMI; circ. 61,000.

Tokyo Chunichi Sports: 2-3-13, Kohnan, Minato-ku, Tokyo 108-8010; tel. (3) 3471-2211; f. 1956; evening; Head Officer TETSUO TANAKA; circ. 330,431.

Tokyo Shimbun: 2-3-13, Kohnan, Minato-ku, Tokyo 108-8010; tel. (3) 3471-2211; fax (3) 3471-1851; internet www.tokyo-np.co.jp; f. 1942; Man. Editor KATSUHIKO SAKAI; circ. morning 655,970, evening 354,191.

Tokyo Sports: 2-1-30, Ecchujima, Koto-ku, Tokyo 135-8721; tel. (3) 3820-0801; f. 1959; evening; Man. Editor YASUO SAKURAI; circ. 1,321,250.

Yukan Fuji: 1-7-2, Otemachi, Chiyoda-ku, Tokyo 100-8077; tel. (3) 3231-7111; fax (3) 3246-0377; internet www.zakzak.co.jp; f. 1969; evening; Man. Editor MASAMI KATO; circ. 268,984.

Osaka District

Daily Sports: 1-18-11, Edobori, Nishi-ku, Osaka 550-0002; tel. (6) 6443-0421; f. 1948; morning; Man. Editor TOSHIAKI MITANI; circ. 562,715.

The Mainichi Daily News: 3-4-5, Umeda, Kita-ku, Osaka 530-8251; tel. (6) 6345-1551; f. 1922; morning; English; Man. Editor KATSUYA FUKUNAGA.

Nikkan Sports: 5-92-1, Hattori-kotobuki-cho, Toyonaka 561-8585; tel. (6) 6867-2811; internet www.nikkansports.com/osaka; f. 1950; morning; Man. Editor Katsuo Furukawa; circ. 513,498.

Osaka Shimbun: 2-4-9, Umeda, Kita-ku, Osaka 530-8279; tel. (6) 6343-1221; internet www.osakanews.com; f. 1922; evening; Man. Editor Kaoru Yura; circ. 88,887.

Osaka Sports: Osaka Ekimae Daiichi Bldg, 4th Floor, 1-3-1-400, Umeda, Kita-ku, Osaka 530-0001; tel. (6) 6345-7657; f. 1968; evening; Head Officer Kazuomi Tanaka; circ. 470,660.

Sankei Sports: 2-4-9, Umeda, Kita-ku, Osaka 530-8277; tel. (6) 6343-1221; f. 1955; morning; Man. Editor Masaki Yoshida; circ. 552,519.

Sports Nippon: 3-4-5, Umeda, Kita-ku, Osaka 530-8278; tel. (6) 6346-8500; f. 1949; morning; Man. Editor Hidetoshi Ishihara; circ. 477,300.

Kanto District

Chiba Nippo (Chiba Daily News): 4-14-10, Chuo, Chuo-ku, Chiba 260-0013; tel. (43) 222-9211; internet www.chibanippo.co.jp; f. 1957; morning; Man. Editor Noboru Hayashi; circ. 190,187.

Ibaraki Shimbun: 2-15, Kitami-cho, Mito 310-8686; tel. (292) 21-3121; internet www.ibaraki-np.co.jp; f. 1891; morning; Pres. and Editor-in-Chief Tadanori Tomosue; circ. 117,240.

Jomo Shimbun: 1-50-21, Furuichi-machi, Maebashi 371-8666; tel. (272) 54-9911; internet www.jomo-news.co.jp; f. 1887; morning; Man. Editor Mutsuo Odagiri; circ. 296,111.

Joyo Shimbun: 2-7-6, Manabe, Tsuchiura 300-0051; tel. (298) 21-1780; internet www.tsukuba.com; f. 1948; morning; Pres. Mineo Iwanami; Man. Editor Akira Saito; circ. 88,700.

Kanagawa Shimbun: 6-145, Hanasaki-cho, Nishi-ku, Yokohama 220-8588; tel. (45) 411-2222; internet www.kanagawa-np.co.jp; f. 1890; morning; Man. Editor Nobuyuki Chiba; circ. 238,203.

Saitama Shimbun: 6-12-11, Kishi-cho, Urawa 336-8686; tel. (48) 862-3371; internet www.saitama-np.co.jp; f. 1944; morning; Man. Editor Yotaro Numata; circ. 162,071.

Shimotsuke Shimbun: 1-8-11, Showa, Utsunomiya 320-8686; tel. (286) 25-1111; internet www.shimotsuke.co.jp; f. 1884; morning; Man. Dir and Editor-in-Chief Eisuke Toda; circ. 306,072.

Tohoku District
(North-east Honshu)

Akita Sakigake Shimpo: 1-1, San-no-rinkai-machi, Akita 010-8601; tel. (18) 888-1800; fax (188) 23-1780; internet www.sakigake.co.jp; f. 1874; Man. Editor Shigeaki Maekawa; circ. 263,246.

Daily Tohoku: 1-3-12, Shiroshita, Hachinohe 031-8601; tel. (178) 44-5111; f. 1945; morning; Man. Editor Tokoju Yoshida; circ. 104,935.

Fukushima Mimpo: 13-17, Ota-machi, Fukushima 960-8602; tel. (245) 31-4111; internet www.fukushima-minpo.co.jp; f. 1892; Pres. and Editor-in-Chief Tsutomu Hanada; circ. morning 308,353, evening 9,489.

Fukushima Minyu: 4-29, Yanagi-machi, Fukushima 960-8648; tel. (245) 23-1191; internet www.minyu; f. 1895; Man. Editor Kenji Kanno; circ. morning 201,414, evening 6,066.

Hokuu Shimpo: 3-2, Nishi-dori-machi, Noshiro 016-0891. (185) 54-3150; f. 1895; morning; Chair. Koichi Yamaki; circ. 31,490.

Ishinomaki Shimbun: 2-1-28, Sumiyoshi-machi, Ishinomaki 986; tel. (225) 22-3201; f. 1946; evening; Man. Editor Masatoshi Sato; circ. 13,050.

Iwate Nichi-nichi Shimbun: 60, Minamishin-machi, Ichinoseki 021-8686; tel. (191) 26-5114; internet www.isop.ne.jp/iwanichi; f. 1923; morning; Pres. Takeshi Yamagishi; Man. Editor Seiichi Watanabe; circ. 59,850.

Iwate Nippo: 3-7, Uchimaru, Morioka 020-8622; tel. (196) 53-4111; internet www.iwate-np.co.jp; f. 1876; Man. Editor Tokuo Miyazawa; circ. morning 230,073, evening 229,815.

Kahoku Shimpo: 1-2-28, Itsutsubashi, Aoba-ku, Sendai 980-8660; tel. (22) 211-1111; fax (22) 224-7947; internet www.kahoku.co.jp; f. 1897; Exec. Dir and Man. Editor Masahiko Ichiriki; circ. morning 503,318, evening 133,855.

Mutsu Shimpo: 2-1, Shimo-shirogane-cho, Hirosaki 036-8356; tel. (172) 34-3111; f. 1946; morning; Man. Editor Yuji Sato; circ. 53,500.

Shonai Nippo: 8-29, Baba-cho, Tsuruoka 997-8691; tel. (235) 22-1480; f. 1946; morning; Pres. Takao Sato; Man. Editor Masayuki Hashimoto; circ. 19,100.

To-o Nippo: 78, Kanbayashi, Yatsuyaku, Aomori 030-0180; tel. (177) 39-1111; internet www.toonippo.co.jp; f. 1888; Exec. Dir Yoshio Wajima and Man. Editor Takao Shiokoshi; circ. morning 262,532, evening 258,590.

Yamagata Shimbun: 2-5-12, Hatagomachi, Yamagata 990-8550; tel. (236) 22-5271; internet www.yamagata-np.co.jp; f. 1876; Man. Editor Toshinobu Shiono; circ. morning 213,057, evening 213,008.

Yonezawa Shimbun: 3-3-7, Monto-cho, Yonezawa 992-0039; tel. (238) 22-4411; f. 1879; morning; Man. Dir and Editor-in-Chief Makoto Sato; circ. 13,750.

Chubu District
(Central Honshu)

Chubu Keizai Shimbun: 4-4-12, Meieki, Nakamura-ku, Nagoya 450-8561; tel. (52) 561-5215; f. 1946; morning; Man. Editor Norimitsu Inagaki; circ. 97,000.

Chukyo Sports: Chunichi Kosoku Offset Insatsu Bldg, 4-3-9, Kinjo, Naka-ku, Nagoya 460-0847; tel. (52) 982-1911; f. 1968; evening; circ. 289,430; Head Officer Osamu Suetsugu.

Chunichi Shimbun: 1-6-1, San-no-maru, Naka-ku, Nagoya 460-8511; tel. (52) 201-8811; internet www.chunichi.ne.jp; f. 1942; Man. Editor Nobuaki Koide; circ. morning 2.7m., evening 748,635.

Chunichi Sports: 1-6-1, San-no-maru, Naka-ku, Nagoya 460-8511; tel. (52) 201-8811; f. 1954; evening; Head Officer Yasuhiko Aiba; circ. 631,429.

Gifu Shimbun: 10, Imakomachi, Gifu 500-8577; tel. (582) 64-1151; internet www.jic-gifu.or.jp/np; f. 1881; Exec. Dir and Man. Editor Tadashi Tanaka; circ. morning 170,176, evening 31,775.

Higashi-Aichi Shimbun: 62, Torinawate, Shinsakae-machi, Toyohashi 441-8666; tel. (532) 32-3111; f. 1957; morning; Man. Editor Yoshiyuki Suzuki; circ. 52,300.

Nagano Nippo: 3-1323-1, Takashima, Suwa 392-8611; tel. (266) 52-2000; f. 1901; morning; Man. Editor Etsuo Koizumi; circ. 73,000.

Nagoya Times: 1-3-10, Marunouchi, Naka-ku, Nagoya 460-8530; tel. (52) 231-1331; f. 1946; evening; Man. Editor Naoki Kito; circ. 146,137.

Shinano Mainichi Shimbun: 657, Minamiagata-machi, Nagano 380-8546; tel. (26) 236-3000; fax (26) 236-3197; internet www.shinmai.co.jp; f. 1873; Man. Editor Seiichi Inomata; circ. morning 469,801, evening 55,625.

Shizuoka Shimbun: 3-1-1, Toro, Shizuoka 422-8033; tel. (54) 284-8900; internet www.sbs-np.co.jp; f. 1941; Man. Editor Hisao Ishihara; circ. morning 730,746, evening 730,782.

Yamanashi Nichi-Nichi Shimbun: 2-6-10, Kitaguchi, Kofu 400-8515; tel. (552) 31-3000; internet www.sannichi.co.jp; f. 1872; morning; Man. Editor Katsuhito Nishikawa; circ. 205,758.

Hokuriku District
(North Coastal Honshu)

Fukui Shimbun: 1-1-14, Haruyama, Fukui 910-8552; tel. (776) 23-5111; internet www.fukuishimbun.co.jp; f. 1899; morning; Man. Editor Kazuo Uchida; circ. 202,280.

Hokkoku Shimbun: 2-5-1, Korinbo, Kanazawa 920-8588; tel. (762) 63-2111; internet www.hokkoku.co.jp; f. 1893; Man. Editor Wataru Inagaki; circ. morning 328,532, evening 97,051.

Hokuriku Chunichi Shimbun: 2-7-15, Kohrinbo, Kanazawa 920-8573; tel. (762) 61-3111; internet www.hokuriku.chunichi.co.jp; f. 1960; Man. Editor Kanji Komiya; circ. morning 116,719, evening 12,820.

Kitanippon Shimbun: 2-14, Azumi-cho, Toyama 930-8680; tel. (764) 45-3300; internet www.kitanippon.co.jp; f. 1884; Dir and Man. Editor Minoru Kawata; circ. morning 223,033, evening 29,959.

Niigata Nippo: 772-2, Zenku, Niigata 950-1189; tel. (25) 378-9111; internet www.niigata-nippo.co.jp; f. 1942; Dir and Man. Editor Michiei Takahashi; circ. morning 496,567, evening 66,836.

Toyama Shimbun: 5-1, Ote-machi, Toyama 930-8520; tel. (764) 91-8111; internet www.toyama.hokkoku.co.jp; f. 1923; morning; Man. Editor Sachio Miyamoto; circ. 42,988.

Kinki District
(West Central Honshu)

Daily Sports: 1-5-7, Higashikawasaki-cho, Chuo-ku, Kobe 650-0044; tel. (78) 362-7100; morning; Man. Editor Takashi Hirai.

Ise Shimbun: 34-6, Honmachi, Tsu 514-0831; tel. (592) 24-0003; internet www.isenp.co.jp; f. 1878; morning; Man. Editor Fujio Yamamoto; circ. 100,550.

Kii Minpo: 100, Akizucho, Tanabe 646-8660; tel. (739) 22-7171; internet www.agara.co.jp; f. 1911; evening; Man. Editor Kazusada Tanigami; circ. 38,165.

Kobe Shimbun: 1-5-7, Higashikawasaki-cho, Chuo-ku, Kobe 650-8571; tel. (78) 362-7100; internet www.kobe-np.co.jp; f. 1898; Man. Editor Masao Maekawa; circ. morning 545,854, evening 268,787.

Kyoto Shimbun: 239, Shoshoi-machi, Ebisugawa-agaru, Karasuma-dori, Nakagyo-ku, Kyoto 604-8577; tel. (75) 241-5430; internet www.kyoto-np.co.jp; f. 1879; Man. Editor OSAMU SAITO; circ. morning 505,723, evening 319,313.

Nara Shimbun: 606, Sanjo-machi, Nara 630-8686; tel. (742) 26-1331; internet www.nara-shimbun.com; f. 1946; morning; Dir and Man. Editor HISAMI SAKAMOTO; circ. 118,064.

Chugoku District
(Western Honshu)

Chugoku Shimbun: 7-1, Dobashi-cho, Naka-ku, Hiroshima 730-8677; tel. (82) 236-2111; fax (82) 236-2321; e-mail denshi@hiroshima-cdas.or.jp; internet www.chugoku-np.co.jp; f. 1892; Man. Editor NOBUYUKI AOKI; circ. morning 734,589, evening 85,089.

Nihonkai Shimbun: 2-137, Tomiyasu, Tottori 680-8678; tel. (857) 21-2888; internet www.nnn.co.jp; f. 1976; morning; Man. Editor KOTARO TAMURA; circ. 101,768.

Okayama Nichi-Nichi Shimbun: 6-30, Hon-cho, Okayama 700-8678; tel. (86) 231-4211; f. 1946; evening; Man. Dir and Man. Editor TAKASHI ANDO; circ. 45,000.

San-In Chuo Shimpo: 383, Tono-machi, Matsue 690-8668; tel. (852) 32-3440; f. 1882; morning; Man. Editor MASAMI MOCHIDA; circ. 172,605.

Sanyo Shimbun: 2-1-23, Yanagi-machi, Okayama 700-8634; tel. (86) 231-2210; internet www.sanyo.oni.co.jp; f. 1879; Man. Dir and Man. Editor TAKAMASA KOSHIMUNE; circ. morning 454,263, evening 71,200.

Ube Jiho: 3-6-1, Kotobuki-cho, Ube 755-8557; tel. (836) 31-1511; f. 1912; evening; Exec. Dir and Man. Editor KAZUYA WAKI; circ. 42,550.

Yamaguchi Shimbun: 1-1-7, Higashi-Yamato-cho, Shimonoseki 750-8506; tel. (832) 66-3211; internet www.minato-yamaguchi.co.jp; f. 1946; morning; Man. Editor SHOICHI SASAKI; circ. 84,000.

Shikoku Island

Ehime Shimbun: 1-12-1, Otemachi, Matsuyama 790-8511; tel. (899) 35-2111; internet www.ehime-np.co.jp; f. 1876; morning; Man. Editor RYOJI YANO; circ. 319,522.

Kochi Shimbun: 3-2-15, Honmachi, Kochi 780-8572; tel. (888) 22-2111; internet www.kochinews.co.jp; f. 1904; Dir and Man. Editor KENGO FUJITO; circ. morning 233,319, evening 146,276.

Shikoku Shimbun: 15-1, Nakano-cho, Takamatsu 760-8572; tel. (878) 33-1111; internet www.shikoku-np.co.jp; f. 1889; morning; Man. Editor JUNJI YAMASHITA; circ. 208,816.

Tokushima Shimbun: 2-5-2, Naka-Tokushima-cho, Tokushima 770-8572; tel. (886) 55-7373; fax (866) 54-0165; internet www.topics.or.jp; f. 1944; Dir and Man. Editor HIROSHI MATSUMURA; circ. morning 253,184, evening 52,203.

Hokkaido Island

Doshin Sports: 3-6, Odori-nishi, Chuo-ku, Sapporo 060-8711; tel. (11) 241-1230; internet douspo.aurora-net.or.jp; f. 1982; morning; Pres. KOSUKE SAKAI; circ. 139,178.

Hokkai Times: 10-6, Nishi, Minami-Ichijo, Chuo-ku, Sapporo 060; tel. (11) 231-0131; f. 1946; Man. Editor KOKI ITO; circ. morning 120,736.

Hokkaido Shimbun: 3-6, Odori-nishi, Chuo-ku, Sapporo 060-8711; tel. (11) 221-2111; internet www.aurora-net.or.jp; f. 1942; Man. Editor RYOZO ODAGIRI; circ. morning 1.2m., evening 740,264.

Kushiro Shimbun: 7-3, Kurogane-cho, Kushiro 085-8650; tel. (154) 22-1111; internet www.hokkai.or.jp/senshin/index.html; f. 1946; morning; Man. Editor YUTAKA ITO; circ. 55,686.

Muroran Mimpo: 1-3-16, Hon-cho, Muroran 051-8550; tel. (143) 22-5121; internet www.muromin.mnw.jp; f. 1945; Man. Editor TSUTOMO KUDO; circ. morning 60,300, evening 52,500.

Nikkan Sports: 3-1-30, Higashi, Kita-3 jo, Chuo-ku, Sapporo 060-0033; tel. (11) 242-3900; fax (11) 231-5470; internet www.kita-nikkan.co.jp; f. 1962; morning; Pres. SATOSHI KATO; circ. 160,355.

Tokachi Mainichi Shimbun: 8-2, Minami, Higashi-Ichijo, Obihiro 080-8688; tel. (155) 22-2121; fax (155) 25-2700; internet www.tokachi.co.jp; f. 1919; evening; Dir and Man. Editor TOSHIAKI NAKAHASHI; circ. 89,264.

Tomakomai Mimpo: 3-1-8, Wakakusa-cho, Tomakomai 053-8611; tel. (144) 32-5311; internet www.tomamin.co.jp; f. 1950; evening; Dir and Man. Editor RYUICHI KUDO; circ. 60,676.

Yomiuri Shimbun: 4-1, Nishi, Kita-4 jo, Chuo-ku, Sapporo 060-8656; tel. (11) 242-3111; f. 1959; Head Officer TSUTOMO IKEDA; circ. morning 261,747, evening 81,283.

Kyushu Island

Kagoshima Shimpo: 7-28, Jonan-cho, Kagoshima 892-8551; tel. (99) 226-2100; internet www.kagoshimashimpo.com; f. 1959; morning; Dir and Man. Editor JUNSUKE KINOSHITA; circ. 39,330.

Kumamoto Nichi-Nichi Shimbun: 172, Yoyasu-machi, Kumamoto 860-8506; tel. (96) 361-3111; internet www.kumanichi.co.jp; f. 1942; Man. Editor HIROSHI KAWARABATA; circ. morning 389,528, evening 101,795.

Kyushu Sports: Fukuoka Tenjin Center Bldg, 2-14-8, Tenjin-cho, Chuo-ku, Fukuoka 810-0001; tel. (92) 781-7401; f. 1966; morning; Head Officer HIROSHI MITOMI; circ. 449,850.

Minami Nippon Shimbun: 1-9-33, Yojirou, Kagoshima 890-8603; tel. (99) 813-5001; fax (99) 813-5016; e-mail tuusin@po.minc.ne.jp; internet www.minaminippon.co.jp; f. 1881; Man. Editor KEITEN NISHIMURA; circ. morning 401,938, evening 27,959.

Miyazaki Nichi-Nichi Shimbun: 1-1-33, Takachihodori, Miyazaki 880-8570; tel. (985) 26-9315; internet www.the-miyanichi.co.jp; f. 1940; morning; Man. Editor MASAAKI MINAMIMURA; circ. 236,083.

Nagasaki Shimbun: 3-1, Mori-machi, Nagasaki 852-8601; tel. (958) 44-2111; internet www.nagasaki-np.co.jp; f. 1889; Dir and Man. Editor SADAKATSU HONDA; circ. morning 200,128.

Nankai Nichi-Nichi Shimbun: 10-3, Nagahama-cho, Naze 894-8601; tel. (997) 53-2121; internet www.amami.or.jp/nankai; f. 1946; morning; Man. Editor TERUMI MATSUI; circ. 24,038.

Nishi Nippon Shimbun: 1-4-1, Tenjin, Chuo-ku, Fukuoka 810-8721; tel. (92) 711-5555; internet www.nishinippon.co.jp; f. 1877; Exec. Dir and Man. Editor TAKAMICHI TAMAGAWA; circ. morning 834,800, evening 188,444.

Nishi Nippon Sports: 1-4-1, Tenjin, Chuo-ku, Fukuoka 810; tel. (92) 711-5555; f. 1954; Man. Editor KENJI ISHIZAKI; circ. 184,119.

Oita Godo Shimbun: 3-9-15, Funai-machi, Oita 870-8605; tel. (975) 36-2121; internet www.oita-press.co.jp; f. 1886; Dir and Man. Editor MASAKATSU TANABE; circ. morning 245,257, evening 245,227.

Okinawa Times: 2-2-2, Kumoji, Naha 900-8678; tel. (98) 860-3000; internet www.okinawatimes.co.jp; f. 1948; Dir and Man. Editor MASAO KISHIMOTO; circ. morning 204,420, evening 204,420.

Ryukyu Shimpo: 1-10-3, Izumizaki, Naha 900-8525; tel. (98) 865-5111; internet www.ryukyushimpo.co.jp; f. 1893; Man. Editor TOMOKAZU TAKAMINE; circ. 200,936.

Saga Shimbun: 3-2-23, Tenjin, Saga 840-8585; tel. (952) 28-2111; fax (952) 29-4829; internet www.saga-s.co.jp; f. 1884; morning; Man. Editor TERUHIKO WASHIZAKI; circ. 138,079.

Yaeyama Mainichi Shimbun: 614, Tonoshiro, Ishigaki 907-0004; tel. (9808) 2-2121; internet www.cosmos.ne.jp/~mainichi; f. 1950; morning; Exec. Dir and Man. Editor YOSHIO UECHI; circ. 14,500.

WEEKLIES

An-An: Magazine House, 3-13-10, Ginza, Chuo-ku, Tokyo 104-03; tel. (3) 3545-7050; fax (3) 3546-0034; f. 1970; fashion; Editor MIYOKO YODOGAWA; circ. 650,000.

Asahi Graphic: Asahi Shimbun Publishing Dept, 5-3-2, Tsukiji, Chuo-ku, Tokyo 104-11; tel. (3) 3545-0131; f. 1923; pictorial review; Editor KIYOKAZU TANNO; circ. 120,000.

Diamond Weekly: Diamond Inc, 1-4-2, Kasumigaseki, Chiyoda-ku, Tokyo 100; tel. (3) 3504-6250; f. 1913; economics; Editor YUTAKA IWASA; circ. 78,000.

Focus: Shincho-Sha, 71, Yaraicho, Shinjuku-ku, Tokyo 162; tel. (3) 3266-5271; fax (3) 3266-5390; politics, economics, sport; Editor KAZUMASA TAJIMA; circ. 850,000.

Friday: Kodan-Sha Co Ltd, 2-12-21, Otowa, Bunkyo-ku, Tokyo 112; tel. (3) 5395-3440; fax (3) 3943-8582; current affairs; Editor-in-Chief TETSU SUZUKI; circ. 1m.

Hanako: Magazine House, 3-13-10, Ginza, Chuo-ku, Tokyo 104-03; tel. (3) 3545-7070; fax (3) 3546-0994; f. 1988; consumer guide; Editor KOJI TOMONO; circ. 350,000.

Nikkei Business: Nikkei Business Publications Inc, 2-7-6, Hirakawa-cho, Chiyoda-ku, Tokyo 102-8622; tel. (3) 5210-8101; fax (3) 5210-8520; internet www.nikkeibp.co.jp; f. 1969; Editor-in-Chief HIROTOMO NOMURA; circ. 350,000.

Shukan Asahi: Asahi Shimbun Publishing Dept, 5-3-2, Tsukiji, Chuo-ku, Tokyo 104-8011; tel. (3) 3545-0131; f. 1922; general interest; Editor-in-Chief AKIRA KATO; circ. 482,000.

Shukan Bunshun: Bungei-Shunju Ltd, 3-23, Kioicho, Chiyoda-ku, Tokyo 102; tel. (3) 3265-1211; f. 1959; general interest; Editor KIYONDO MATSUI; circ. 800,000.

Shukan Gendai: Kodan-Sha Co Ltd, 2-12-21, Otowa, Bunkyo-ku, Tokyo 112; tel. (3) 5395-3438; fax (3) 3943-7815; f. 1959; general; Editor-in-Chief TETSU SUZUKI; circ. 930,000.

Shukan Josei: Shufu-To-Seikatsu Sha Ltd, 3-5-7, Kyobashi, Chuo-ku, Tokyo 104; tel. (3) 3563-5130; fax (3) 3563-2073; f. 1957; women's interest; Editor Hideo Kikuchi; circ. 638,000.

Shukan Post: Shogakukan Publishing Co Ltd, 2-3-1, Hitotsubashi, Chiyoda-ku, Tokyo 101-01; tel. (3) 3230-5951; f. 1969; general; Editor Norimichi Okanari; circ. 696,000.

Shukan Shincho: Shincho-Sha, 71, Yarai-cho, Shinjuku-ku, Tokyo 162-8711; tel. (3) 3266-5311; fax (3) 3266-5622; f. 1956; general interest; Editor Hiroshi Matsuda; circ. 521,000.

Shukan SPA: Fuso-Sha Co, 1-15-1, Kaigan, Minato-ku, Tokyo 105; tel. (3) 5403-8875; f. 1952; general interest; Editor-in-Chief Toshihiko Sato; circ. 400,000.

Shukan ST: Japan Times Ltd, 4-5-4, Shibaura, Minato-ku, Tokyo 108-0023; tel. (3) 3452-4077; fax (3) 3452-3303; e-mail shukanst@japantimes.co.jp; f. 1951; English and Japanese; Editor Mitsuru Tanaka; circ. 150,000.

Shukan Yomiuri: Yomiuri Shimbun Publication Dept, 1-2-1, Kiyosumi, Koto-ku, Tokyo 135; tel. (3) 5245-7001; f. 1938; general interest; Editor Shini Kageyama; circ. 453,000.

Sunday Mainichi: Mainichi Newspapers Publishing Dept, 1-1-1, Hitotsubashi, Chiyoda-ku, Tokyo 100-51; tel. (3) 3212-0321; fax (3) 3212-0769; f. 1922; general interest; Editor Kenji Miki; circ. 237,000.

Tenji Mainichi: Mainichi Newspapers Publishing Dept, 3-4-5, Umeda, Osaka; tel. (6) 6346-8386; fax (6) 6346-8385; f. 1922; in Japanese braille; Editor Tadamitsu Morioka; circ. 12,000.

Weekly Economist: Mainichi Newspapers Publishing Dept, 1-1-1, Hitotsubashi, Chiyoda-ku, Tokyo 100-51; tel. (3) 3212-0321; f. 1923; Editorial Chief Nobuhiro Shudo; circ. 120,000.

Weekly Toyo Keizai: Toyo Keizai Inc, 1-2-1, Hongoku-cho, Nihonbashi, Chuo-ku, Tokyo 103-8345; tel. (3) 3246-5655; fax (3) 3270-0159; e-mail sub@toyokeizai.co.jp; internet www.toyokeizai.co.jp; f. 1895; business, economics, finance, and corporate information; Editor Toshiki Ota; circ. 62,000.

PERIODICALS

All Yomimono: Bungei-Shunju Ltd, 3-23, Kioicho, Chiyoda-ku, Tokyo 102; tel. (3) 3265-1211; fax (3) 3239-5481; f. 1930; monthly; popular fiction; Editor Koichi Sasamoto; circ. 95,796.

Any: 1-3-14, Hirakawa-cho, Chiyoda-ku, Tokyo 102; tel. (3) 5276-2200; fax (3) 5276-2209; f. 1989; every 2 weeks; women's interest; Editor Yukio Miwa; circ. 380,000.

Asahi Camera: Asahi Shimbun Publishing Dept, 5-3-2, Tsukiji, Chuo-ku, Tokyo 104-8011; tel. (3) 3545-0131; fax (3) 5565-3286; f. 1926; monthly; photography; Editor Hiroshi Hirose; circ. 90,000.

Balloon: Shufunotomo Co Ltd, 2-9, Kanda Surugadai, Chiyoda-ku, Tokyo 101; tel. (3) 3294-1132; fax (3) 3291-5093; f. 1986; monthly; expectant mothers; Dir Mariko Hosoda; circ. 250,000.

Brutus: Magazine House, 3-13-10, Ginza, Chuo-ku, Tokyo 104-03; tel. (3) 3545-7000; fax (3) 3546-0034; f. 1980; every 2 weeks; men's interest; Editor Koichi Tetsuka; circ. 250,000.

Bungei-Shunju: Bungei-Shunju Ltd, 3-23, Kioicho, Chiyoda-ku, Tokyo 102-8008; tel. (3) 3265-1211; fax (3) 3221-6623; internet bunshun.topica.ne.jp; f. 1923; monthly; general; Pres. Masaru Shiraishi; Editor Kiyondo Matsui; circ. 656,000.

Business Tokyo: Keizaikai Bldg, 2-13-18, Minami-Aoyama, Minato-ku, Tokyo 105; tel. (3) 3423-8500; fax (3) 3423-8505; f. 1987; monthly; Dir Takuo Ida; Editor Anthony Paul; circ. 125,000.

Chuokoron: Chuokoron-Sha Inc, 2-8-7, Kyobashi, Chuo-ku, Tokyo 104; tel. (3) 3563-1866; fax (3) 3561-5920; f. 1887; monthly; general interest; Chief Editor Kazuho Miya; circ. 100,000.

Clique: Magazine House, 3-13-10, Ginza, Chuo-ku, Tokyo 104-03; tel. (3) 3545-7080; fax (3) 3546-0034; f. 1989; every 2 weeks; women's interest; Editor Takako Noguchi; circ. 250,000.

Croissant: Magazine House, 3-13-10, Ginza, Chuo-ku, Tokyo 104-03; tel. (3) 3545-7111; fax (3) 3546-0034; f. 1977; every 2 weeks; home; Editor Masaaki Takeuchi; circ. 600,000.

Fujinkoron: Chuokoron-Sha Inc, 2-8-7, Kyobashi, Chuo-ku, Tokyo 104; tel. (3) 3563-1866; fax (3) 3561-5920; f. 1916; women's literary monthly; Editor Yukiko Yukawa; circ. 185,341.

Geijutsu Shincho: Shincho-Sha, 71, Yarai-cho, Shinjuku-ku, Tokyo 162-8711; tel. (3) 3266-5381; fax (3) 3266-5387; e-mail geishin@shinchosha.co.jp; f. 1950; monthly; fine arts, music, architecture, films, drama and design; Editor-in-Chief Kazuhiro Nagai; circ. 50,000.

Gendai: Kodan-Sha Ltd, 2-12-21, Otowa, Bunkyo-ku, Tokyo 112; tel. (3) 5395-3517; fax (3) 3945-9128; f. 1966; monthly; cultural and political; Editor Shunkichi Yabuki; circ. 250,000.

Gunzo: Kodan-Sha Ltd, 2-12-21, Otowa, Bunkyo-ku, Tokyo 112; tel. (3) 5395-3501; fax (3) 5395-5626; f. 1946; literary monthly; Editor Katsuo Watanabe; circ. 30,000.

Hot-Dog Press: Kodan-Sha Ltd, 2-12-21, Otowa, Bunkyo-ku, Tokyo 112-01; tel. (3) 5395-3473; fax (3) 3945-9128; every 2 weeks; men's interest; Editor Atsuhide Kokubo; circ. 650,000.

Ie-no-Hikari (Light of Home): Ie-no-Hikari Asscn, 11, Ichigaya Funagawaramachi, Shinjuku-ku, Tokyo 162-8448; tel. (3) 3266-9013; fax (3) 3266-9052; e-mail hikari@mxd.meshnet.or.jp; internet www.mediagalaxy.co.jp/ienohikarinet; f. 1925; monthly; rural and general interest; Pres. Shuzo Suzuki; Editor Kazuo Nakano; circ. 928,000.

Japan Company Handbook: Toyo Keizai Inc, 1-2-1, Nihonbashi Hongoku-cho, Chuo-ku, Tokyo 103-8345; tel. (3) 3246-5621; fax (3) 3246-5473; e-mail sub@toyokeizai.co.jp; internet www.toyokeizai.co.jp; f. 1974; quarterly; English; Editor Masaki Hara; total circ. 100,000.

Jitsugyo No Nihon: Jitsugyo No Nihon-Sha Ltd, 1-3-9, Ginza, Chuo-ku, Tokyo 104; tel. (3) 3562-1967; fax (3) 2564-2382; f. 1897; monthly; economics and business; Editor Toshio Kawajiri; circ. 60,000.

Junon: Shufu-To-Seikatsu Sha Ltd, 3-5-7, Kyobashi, Chuo-ku, Tokyo 104; tel. (3) 3563-5132; fax (3) 5250-7081; f. 1973; monthly; television and entertainment; circ. 560,000.

Kagaku (Science): Iwanami Shoten Publishers, 2-5-5, Hitotsubashi, Chiyoda-ku, Tokyo 102; tel. (3) 5210-4070; fax (3) 5210-4073; f. 1931; Editor Nobuaki Miyabe; circ. 29,000.

Kagaku Asahi: Asahi Shimbun Publishing Dept, 5-3-2, Tsukiji, Chuo-ku, Tokyo 104-8011; tel. (3) 5540-7810; fax (3) 3546-2404; f. 1941; monthly; scientific; Editor Toshihiro Sasaki; circ. 105,000.

Keizaijin: Kansai Economic Federation, Nakanoshima Center Bldg, 6-2-27, Nakanoshima, Kita-ku, Osaka 530-6691; tel. (6) 6441-0101; fax (6) 6443-5347; internet www.kankeiren.or.jp; f. 1947; monthly; economics; Editor M. Yasutake; circ. 2,600.

Lettuce Club: SS Communications, 11-2, Ban-cho, Chiyoda-ku, Tokyo 102; tel. (3) 5276-2151; fax (3) 5276-2229; f. 1987; every 2 weeks; cookery; Editor Mitsuru Nakaya; circ. 800,000.

Money Japan: SS Communications, 11-2, Ban-cho, Chiyoda-ku, Tokyo 102; tel. (3) 5276-2220; fax (3) 5276-2229; internet www.sscom.co.jp/money; f. 1985; monthly; finance; Editor Toshio Kobayashi; circ. 500,000.

Popeye: Magazine House, 3-13-10, Ginza, Chuo-ku, Tokyo 104-8003; tel. (3) 3545-7160; fax (3) 3545-9026; f. 1976; every 2 weeks; fashion, youth interest; Editor Katsumi Namaizawa; circ. 320,000.

President: President Inc, Bridgestone Hirakawacho Bldg, 2-13-12, Hirakawa-cho, Chiyoda-ku, Tokyo 102; tel. (3) 3237-3737; fax (3) 3237-3748; internet www.president.co.jp; f. 1963; monthly; business; Editor Kayoko Abe; circ. 263,308.

Ray: Shufunotomo Co Ltd, 2-9, Kanda Surugadai, Chiyoda-ku, Tokyo 101; tel. (3) 3294-1163; fax (3) 3291-5093; f. 1988; monthly; women's interest; Editor Tatsuro Nakanishi; circ. 450,000.

Ryoko Yomiuri: Ryoko Yomiuri Publications Inc, 2-2-15, Ginza, Chuo-ku, Tokyo 104; tel. (3) 3561-8911; fax (3) 3561-8950; f. 1966; monthly; travel; Editor Tetsuo Kinugawa; circ. 470,000.

Sekai: Iwanami Shoten Publishers, 2-5-5, Hitotsubashi, Chiyoda-ku, Tokyo 101; tel. (3) 5210-4141; fax (3) 5210-4144; internet www.iwanami.co.jp/sekai; f. 1946; monthly; review of world and domestic affairs; Editor Atsushi Okamoto; circ. 120,000.

Shinkenchiku: Shinkenchiku-Sha Co Ltd, 2-31-2, Yushima, Bunkyo-ku, Tokyo 113-8501; tel. (3) 3811-7101; fax (3) 3812-8229; e-mail ja-business@japan-architect.co.jp; internet www.japan-architect.co.jp; f. 1925; monthly; architecture; Editor Yasuhiro Teramatsu; circ. 87,000.

Shiso (Thought): Iwanami Shoten Publishers, 2-5-5, Hitotsubashi, Chiyoda-ku, Tokyo 101-8002; tel. (3) 5210-4055; fax (3) 5210-4037; e-mail shiso@iwanami.co.jp; internet www.iwanami.co.jp/shiso; f. 1921; monthly; philosophy, social sciences and humanities; Editor Kiyoshi Kojima; circ. 20,000.

Shosetsu Shincho: Shincho-Sha, 71, Yarai-cho, Shinjuku-ku, Tokyo 162-8711; tel. (3) 3266-5241; fax (3) 3266-5412; internet www.shincho.net/magazines/shosetsushincho; f. 1947; monthly; literature; Editor-in-Chief Tsuyoshi Menjo; circ. 80,000.

Shufunotomo: Shufunotomo Co Ltd, 2-9, Kanda Surugadai, Chiyoda-ku, Tokyo 101; tel. (3) 5280-7531; fax (3) 5280-7431; f. 1917; monthly; home and lifestyle; Editor Kyoko Furuto; circ. 450,000.

So-en: Bunka Publishing Bureau, 4-12-7, Hon-cho, Shibuya-ku, Tokyo 151; tel. (3) 3299-2531; fax (3) 3370-3712; f. 1936; fashion monthly; Editor Keiko Sasaki; circ. 270,000.

NEWS AGENCIES

Jiji Tsushin (Jiji Press Ltd): Shisei-Kaikan, 1-3, Hibiya Park, Chiyoda-ku, Tokyo 100-8568; tel. (3) 3591-1111; e-mail info@

jiji.co.jp; internet www.jiji.com; f. 1945; Pres. MASATOSHI MURAKAMI; Man. Dir and Man. Editor MASAKI SUGIURA.

Kyodo Tsushin (Kyodo News): 2-2-5, Toranomon, Minato-ku, Tokyo 105-8474; tel. (3) 5573-8081; fax (3) 5573-2268; e-mail kokusai@kyodonews.jp; internet http://home.kyodo.co.jp; f. 1945; Pres. ICHIRO SAITA; Man. Editor TOSHIEI KOKUBU.

Radiopress Inc: R-Bldg Shinjuku, 5F, 33-8, Wakamatsu-cho, Shinjuku-ku, Tokyo 162-0056; tel. (3) 5273-2171; fax (3) 5273-2180; e-mail rptokyo@oak.ocn.ne.jp; f. 1945; provides news from China, the former USSR, Democratic People's Repub. of Korea, Viet Nam and elsewhere to the press and govt offices; Pres. YOSHITOMO TANAKA.

Sun Telephoto: Palaceside Bldg, 1-1-1, Hitotsubashi, Chiyoda-ku, Tokyo 100-0003; tel. (3) 3213-6771; e-mail webmaster@suntele.co.jp; internet www.suntele.co.jp; f. 1952; Pres. KOZO TAKINO; Man. Editor KIYOSHI HIRAI.

Foreign Bureaux

Agence France-Presse (AFP): Asahi Shimbun Bldg, 11th Floor, 5-3-2, Tsukiji, Chuo-ku, Tokyo 104-0045; tel. (3) 3545-3061; fax (3) 3546-2594; Bureau Chief PHILIPPE RIES.

Agencia EFE (Spain): Kyodo Tsushin Bldg, 9th Floor, 2-2-5, Toranomon, Minato-ku, Tokyo 105-0001; tel. (3) 3585-8940; fax (3) 3585-8948; Bureau Chief CARLOS DOMÍNGUEZ.

Agenzia Nazionale Stampa Associata (ANSA) (Italy): Kyodo Tsushin Bldg, 9th Floor, 2-2-5, Toranomon, Minato-ku, Tokyo 105-0001; tel. (3) 3584-6667; fax (3) 3584-5114; Bureau Chief ALBERTO ZANCONATO.

Antara (Indonesia): Kyodo Tsushin Bldg, 9th Floor, 2-2-5, Toranomon, Minato-ku, Tokyo 105-0001; tel. (3) 3584-4234; fax (3) 3584-4591; Correspondent MARIA ANDRIANA.

Associated Press (AP) (USA): Asahi Shimbun Bldg, 11th Floor, 5-3-2, Tsukiji, Chuo-ku, Tokyo 104-0045; tel. (3) 3545-5902; fax (3) 3545-0895; internet www.ap.org; Bureau Chief MYRON L. BELKIND.

Central News Agency (Taiwan): 3-7-3-302, Shimo-meguro, Meguro-ku, Tokyo 153-0064; tel. (3) 3495-2046; fax (3) 3495-2066; Bureau Chief CHANG FANG MIN.

Deutsche Presse-Agentur (dpa) (Germany): Nippon Press Center, 3rd Floor, 2-2-1, Uchisaiwai-cho, Chiyoda-ku, Tokyo 100-0011; tel. (3) 3580-6629; fax (3) 3593-7888; Bureau Chief LARS NICOLAYSEN.

Informatsionnoye Telegrafnoye Agentstvo Rossii—Telegrafnoye Agentstvo Suverennykh Stran (ITAR—TASS) (Russia): 1-5-1, Hon-cho, Shibuya-ku, Tokyo 151-0071; tel. (3) 3377-0380; fax (3) 3378-0606; Bureau Chief VASILII GOLOVNIN.

Inter Press Service (IPS) (Italy): 1-15-19, Ishikawa-machi, Ota-ku, Tokyo 145-0061; tel. (3) 3726-7944; fax (3) 3726-7896; Correspondent SUVENDRINI KAKUCHI.

Magyar Távirati Iroda (MTI) (Hungary): 1-3-4-306, Okamoto, Setagaya-ku, Tokyo 157-0076; tel. (3) 3708-3093; fax (3) 3708-2703; Bureau Chief JÁNOS MARTON.

Reuters (UK): Shuwa Kamiya-cho Bldg, 5th Floor, 4-3-13, Toranomon, Minato-ku, Tokyo 105-0001; tel. (3) 3432-4141; fax (3) 3433-2921; Editor WILLIAM SPOSATO.

Rossiiskoye Informatsionnoye Agentstvo—Novosti (RIA—Novosti) (Russia): 3-9-13 Higashi-gotanda, Shinagawa-ku, Tokyo 141-0022; tel. (3) 3441-9241; fax (3) 3447-3538; e-mail riatokyo@ma.hcom.ne.jp; Bureau Chief VIATCHESLAV BANTINE.

United Press International (UPI) (USA): Ferrare Bldg, 4th Floor, 1-24-15, Ebisu, Shibuya-ku, Tokyo 150-0013; tel. (3) 5421-1333; fax (3) 5421-1339; Bureau Chief RUTH YOUNGBLOOD.

Xinhua (New China) News Agency (People's Republic of China): 3-35-23, Ebisu, Shibuya-ku, Tokyo 150-0013; tel. (3) 3441-3766; fax (3) 3446-3995; Bureau Chief WANG DAJUN.

Yonhap (United) News Agency (Republic of Korea): Kyodo Tsushin Bldg, 2-2-5, Toranomon, Minato-ku, Tokyo 105-0001; tel. (3) 3584-4681; fax (3) 3584-4021; f. 1945; Bureau Chief MOON YOUNG SHIK.

PRESS ASSOCIATIONS

Foreign Correspondents' Club of Japan: 20th Floor, 1-7-1, Yuraku-cho, Chiyoda-ku, Tokyo 100-0006; tel. (3) 3211-3161; fax (3) 3211-3168; e-mail yoda@fccj.or.jp; internet www.fccj.or.jp; f. 1945; 193 companies; Pres. HANS VAN DER LUGT; Man. SEISHI YODA.

Foreign Press Center: Nippon Press Center Bldg, 6th Floor, 2-2-1, Uchisaiwai-cho, Chiyoda-ku, Tokyo 100-0011; tel. (3) 3501-3401; fax (3) 3501-3622; internet www.nttls.co.jp/fpc; f. 1976; est. by the Japan Newspaper Publrs' and Editors' Asscn and the Japan Fed. of Economic Orgs; provides services to the foreign press; Pres. YOSHIO HATANO; Man. Dir MASAHIKO ISHIZUKA.

Nihon Shinbun Kyokai (The Japan Newspaper Publishers and Editors Asscn): Nippon Press Center Bldg, 2-2-1, Uchisaiwai-cho, Chiyoda-ku, Tokyo 100-8543; tel. (3) 3591-3462; fax (3) 3591-6149; e-mail s_intl@pressnet.or.jp; internet www.pressnet.or.jp; f. 1946; mems include 154 companies (112 daily newspapers, 4 news agencies and 38 radio and TV companies); Chair. TSUNEO WATANABE; Man. Dir and Sec.-Gen. SHIGEMI MURAKAMI.

Nihon Zasshi Kyokai (Japan Magazine Publishers Asscn): 1-7, Kanda Surugadai, Chiyoda-ku, Tokyo 101-0062; tel. (3) 3291-0775; fax (3) 3293-6239; f. 1956; 85 mems; Pres. HARUHIKO ISHIKAWA; Sec. GENYA INUI.

Publishers

Akane Shobo Co Ltd: 3-2-1, Nishikanda, Chiyoda-ku, Tokyo 101-0065; tel. (3) 3263-0641; fax (3) 3263-5440; f. 1949; juvenile; Pres. MASAHARU OKAMOTO.

Akita Publishing Co Ltd: 2-10-8, Iidabashi, Chiyoda-ku, Tokyo 102-8101; tel. (3) 3264-7011; fax (3) 3265-5906; f. 1948; social sciences, history, juvenile; Chair. SADAO AKITA; Pres. SADAMI AKITA.

ALC Press Inc: 2-54-12, Eifuku, Suginami-ku, Tokyo 168-0064; tel. (3) 3323-1101; fax (3) 3327-1022; e-mail menet@alc.co.jp; internet www.alc.co.jp; f. 1969; linguistics, educational materials, dictionary, juvenile; Pres. TERUMARO HIRAMOTO.

Asahi Shimbun Publications Division: 5-3-2, Tsukiji, Chuo-ku, Tokyo 104-8011; tel. (3) 3545-0131; fax (3) 5540-7682; f. 1879; general; Pres. MUNEYUKI MATSUSHITA; Dir of Publications HISAO KUWASHIMA.

Asakura Publishing Co Ltd: 6-29, Shin Ogawa-machi, Shinjuku-ku, Tokyo 162-8707; tel. (3) 3260-0141; fax (3) 3260-0180; e-mail edit@asakura.co.jp; internet www.asakura.co.jp; f. 1929; natural science, medicine, social sciences; Pres. KUNIZO ASAKURA.

Baifukan Co Ltd: 4-3-12, Kudan Minami, Chiyoda-ku, Tokyo 102-8260; tel. (3) 3262-5256; fax (3) 3262-5276; f. 1924; engineering, natural and social sciences, psychology; Pres. ITARU YAMAMOTO.

Baseball Magazine-Sha: 3-10-10, Misaki-cho, Chiyoda-ku, Tokyo 101-8381; tel. (3) 3238-0081; fax (3) 3238-0106; internet www.bbm-japan.com; f. 1946; sports, physical education, recreation, travel; Chair. TSUNEO IKEDA; Pres. TETSUO IKEDA.

Bijutsu Shuppan-Sha Ltd: Inaoka Kudan Bldg, 6th Floor, 2-36, Kanda Jimbo-cho, Chiyoda-ku, Tokyo 101-8417; tel. (3) 3234-2151; fax (3) 3234-9451; f. 1905; fine arts, graphic design; Pres. ATSUSHI OSHITA.

Bonjinsha Co Ltd: 1-3-13, Hirakawa-cho, Chiyoda-ku, Tokyo 102-0093; tel. (3) 3263-3959; fax (3) 3263-3116; f. 1973; Japanese language teaching materials; Pres. HISAMITSU TANAKA.

Bungeishunju Ltd: 3-23, Kioi-cho, Chiyoda-ku, Tokyo 102-8008; tel. (3) 3265-1211; fax (3) 3239-5482; internet www.bunshun.co.jp; f. 1923; fiction, general literature, recreation, economics, sociology; Dir MASARU SHIRAISHI.

Chikuma Shobo: Komuro Bldg, 2-5-3, Kuramae, Taito-ku, Tokyo 111-8755; tel. (3) 5687-2671; fax (3) 5687-1585; e-mail webinfo@chikumashobo.co.jp; internet www.chikumashobo.co.jp; f. 1940; general literature, fiction, history, juvenile, fine arts; Pres. AKIO KIKUCHI.

Child-Honsha Co Ltd: 5-24-21, Koishikawa, Bunkyo-ku, Tokyo 112-8512; tel. (3) 3813-3781; fax (3) 3813-3765; f. 1930; juvenile; Pres. YOSHIAKI SHIMAZAKI.

Chuokoron-Shinsha Inc: 2-8-7, Kyobashi, Chuo-ku, Tokyo 104-8320; tel. (3) 3563-1261; fax (3) 3561-5920; f. 1886; philosophy, history, sociology, general literature; Pres. JIN NAKAMURA.

Corona Publishing Co Ltd: 4-46-10, Sengoku, Bunkyo-ku, Tokyo 112-0011; tel. (3) 3941-3131; fax (3) 3941-3137; e-mail info@coronasha.co.jp; internet www.coronosha.co.jp; f. 1927; electronics business publs; Pres. TATSUMI GORAI.

Dempa Publications Inc: 1-11-15, Higashi Gotanda, Shinagawa-ku, Tokyo 141-0022; tel. (3) 3445-6111; fax (3) 3445-6101; f. 1950; electronics, personal computer software, juvenile, trade newspapers; Pres. TETSUO HIRAYAMA.

Diamond Inc: 6-12-17, Jingumae, Shibuya-ku, Tokyo 150-8409; tel. (3) 5778-7203; fax (3) 5778-6612; e-mail mitachi@diamond.co.jp; internet www.diamond.co.jp; f. 1913; business, management, economics, financial; Pres. YUTAKA IWASA.

Dohosha Ltd: TAS Bldg, 2-5-2, Nishikanda, Chiyoda-ku, Tokyo 101-0065; tel. (3) 5276-0831; fax (3) 5276-0840; e-mail intl@doho-sha.co.jp; internet www.doho-sha.co.jp; f. 1997; general works, architecture, art, Buddhism, business, children's education, cooking, flower arranging, gardening, medicine.

Froebel-Kan Co Ltd: 6-14-9, Honkomagome, Bunkyo-ku, Tokyo 113-8611; tel. (3) 5395-6614; fax (3) 5395-6639; e-mail info-e@

froebel-kan.co.jp; internet www.froebel-kan.co.jp; f. 1907; juvenile, educational; Pres. MAMORU KITABAYASHI; Dir MITSUHIRO TADA.

Fukuinkan Shoten Publishers Inc: 6-6-3, Honkomagome, Bunkyo-ku, Tokyo 113-8686; tel. (3) 3942-2151; fax (3) 3942-1401; f. 1952; juvenile; Pres. SHIRO TOKITA; Chair. KATSUMI SATO.

Gakken Co Ltd: 4-40-5, Kamiikedai, Ohta-ku, Tokyo 145-8502; tel. (3) 3726-8111; fax (3) 3493-3338; f. 1946; juvenile, educational, art, encyclopaedias, dictionaries; Pres. KAZUHIKO SAWADA.

Graphic-sha Publishing Co Ltd: 1-9-12, Kudan Kita, Chiyoda-ku, Tokyo 102-0073; tel. (3) 3263-4318; fax (3) 3263-5297; e-mail info@graphicsha.co.jp; internet www.graphicsha.co.jp; f. 1963; art, design, architecture, manga techniques, hobbies; Pres. SEIICHI SUGAYA.

Gyosei Corpn: 4-30-16, Ogikubo, Suginami-ku, Tokyo 167-8088; tel. (3) 5349-6666; fax (3) 5349-6677; e-mail business@gyosei.co.jp; internet www.gyosei.co.jp; f. 1893; law, education, science, politics, business, art, language, literature, juvenile; Pres. MOTOO FUJISAWA.

Hakusui-Sha Co Ltd: 3-24, Kanda Ogawa-machi, Chiyoda-ku, Tokyo 101-0052; tel. (3) 3291-7821; fax (3) 3291-7810; f. 1915; general literature, science and languages; Pres. KAZUAKI FUJIWARA.

Hayakawa Publishing Inc: 2-2, Kanda-Tacho, Chiyoda-ku, Tokyo 101-0046; tel. (3) 3252-3111; fax (3) 3254-1550; f. 1945; science fiction, mystery, autobiography, literature, fantasy; Pres. HIROSHI HAYAKAWA.

Heibonsha Ltd: 2-29-4 Hakusan, Bunkyo-ku, Tokyo 112-0001; tel. (3) 3818-0641; fax (3) 3818-0754; internet www.heibonsha.co.jp; f. 1914; encyclopaedias, art, history, geography, literature, science; Pres. NAOTO SHIMONAKA.

Hirokawa Publishing Co: 3-27-14, Hongo, Bunkyo-ku, Tokyo 113-0033; tel. (3) 3815-3651; fax (3) 5684-7030; f. 1925; natural sciences, medicine, pharmacy, nursing, chemistry; Pres. SETSUO HIROKAWA.

Hoikusha Publishing Co: 1-6-12, Kawamata, Higashi, Osaka 577-0063; tel. (6) 6788-4470; fax (6) 6788-4970; internet www.hoikusha.co.jp; f. 1947; natural science, juvenile, fine arts, geography; Pres. YUKI IMAI.

Hokuryukan Co Ltd: 3-8-14, Takanawa, Minato-ku, Tokyo 108-0074; tel. (3) 5449-4591; fax (3) 5449-4950; e-mail hk-ns@mk1.macnet.or.jp; internet www.macnet.or.jp/co/hk-ns; f. 1891; natural science, medical science, juvenile, dictionaries; Pres. HISAKO FUKUDA.

The Hokuseido Press: 3-32-4, Honkomagome, Bunkyo-ku, Tokyo 113-0021; tel. (3) 3827-0511; fax (3) 3827-0567; f. 1914; regional non-fiction, dictionaries, textbooks; Pres. MASAZO YAMAMOTO.

Ie-No-Hikari Association: 11, Funagawara-cho, Ichigaya, Shinjuku-ku, Tokyo 162-8448; tel. (3) 3266-9000; fax (3) 3266-9048; e-mail hikari@mxd.meshnet.or.jp; internet www.mediagalaxy.co.jp/ienohikarinet; f. 1925; social science, agriculture; Chair. SHUZO SUZUKI; Pres. KATSURO KAWAGUCHI.

Igaku-Shoin Ltd: 5-24-3, Hongo, Bunkyo-ku, Tokyo 113-8719; tel. (3) 3817-5610; fax (3) 3815-4114; e-mail info@igaku-shoin.co; internet www.igaku-shoin.co.jp; f. 1944; medicine, nursing; Pres. YU KANEHARA.

Institute for Financial Affairs Inc (KINZAI): 19, Minami-Motomachi, Shinjuku-ku, Tokyo 160-8519; tel. (3) 3358-1161; fax (3) 3359-7947; e-mail JDI04072@nifty.ne.jp; internet www.kinzai.or.jp; f. 1950; finance and economics, banking laws and regulations, accounting; Pres. MASATERU YOSHIDA.

Ishiyaku Publishers Inc: 1-7-10, Honkomagome, Bunkyo-ku, Tokyo 113-8612; tel. (3) 5395-7600; fax (3) 5395-7606; internet www.ishiyaku.co.jp; f. 1921; medicine, dentistry, rehabilitation, nursing, nutrition and pharmaceutics; Pres. KATSUJI FUJITA.

Iwanami Shoten, Publishers: 2-5-5, Hitotsubashi, Chiyoda-ku, Tokyo 101-8002; tel. (3) 5210-4000; fax (3) 5210-4039; e-mail rights@iwanami.co.jp; internet www.iwanami.co.jp; f. 1913; natural and social sciences, humanities, literature, fine arts, juvenile, dictionaries; Pres. NOBUKAZU OTSUKA.

Japan Broadcast Publishing Co Ltd: 41-1, Udagawa-cho, Shibuya-ku, Tokyo 150-8081; tel. (3) 3464-7311; fax (3) 3780-3353; e-mail webmaster@npb.nhk-grp.co.jp; internet www.nhk-grp.co.jp/npb; f. 1931; foreign language textbooks, gardening, home economics, sociology, education, art, juvenile; Pres. TATSUO ANDO.

Japan External Trade Organization (JETRO): 2-2-5, Toranomon, Minato-ku, Tokyo 105-8466; tel. (3) 3582-5511; fax (3) 3587-2485; internet www.jetro.go.jp; f. 1958; trade, economics, investment.

Japan Publications Trading Co Ltd: 1-2-1, Sarugaku-cho, Chiyoda-ku, Tokyo 101-0064; tel. (3) 3292-3751; fax (3) 3292-0410; e-mail jpt@po.iijnet.or.jp; internet www.jptco.co.jp; f. 1942; general works, art, health, sports; Pres. SATOMI NAKABAYASHI.

The Japan Times Ltd: 4-5-4, Shibaura, Minato-ku, Tokyo 108-0023; tel. (3) 3453-2013; fax (3) 3453-8023; e-mail jt-books@kt.rim.or.jp; internet bookclub.japantimes.co.jp; f. 1897; linguistics, culture, business; Pres. TOSHIAKI OGASAWARA.

Japan Travel Bureau Inc: Shibuya Nomura Bldg, 1-10-8, Dogenzaka, Shibuya-ku, Tokyo 150-8558; tel. (3) 3477-9521; fax (3) 3477-9538; internet www.jtb.co.jp; f. 1912; travel, geography, history, fine arts, languages; Vice-Pres. MITSUMASA IWATA.

Jimbun Shoin: 9, Nishiuchihata-cho, Takeda, Fushimi-ku, Kyoto 612-8447; tel. (75) 603-1344; fax (75) 603-1814; e-mail edjimbun@mbox.kyoto-inet.or.jp; internet www.jimbunshoin.co.jp; f. 1922; general literature, philosophy, fiction, social science, religion, fine arts; Pres. MUTSUHISA WATANABE.

Kadokawa Shoten Publishing Co Ltd: 2-13-3, Fujimi, Chiyoda-ku, Tokyo 102-0071; tel. (3) 3238-8611; fax (3) 3238-8612; f. 1945; literature, history, dictionaries, religion, fine arts, books on tape, compact discs, CD-ROM, comics, animation, video cassettes, computer games; Pres. TSUGUHIKO KADOKAWA.

Kaibundo Publishing Co Ltd: 2-5-4, Suido, Bunkyo-ku, Tokyo 112-0005; tel. (3) 5684-6289; fax (3) 3815-3953; e-mail LED04737@nifty.ne.jp; f. 1914; marine affairs, natural science, engineering, industry; Pres. YOSHIHIRO OKADA.

Kaiseisha Publishing Co Ltd: 3-5, Ichigaya Sadohara-cho, Shinjuku-ku, Tokyo 162-8450; tel. (3) 3260-3229; fax (3) 3260-3540; e-mail foreign@kaiseisha.co.jp; internet www.kaiseisha.co.jp; f. 1936; juvenile; Pres. MASAKI IMAMURA.

Kanehara & Co Ltd: 2-31-14, Yushima, Bunkyo-ku, Tokyo 113-8687; tel. (3) 3811-7185; fax (3) 3813-0288; f. 1875; medical, agricultural, engineering and scientific; Pres. SABURO KOMURO.

Kenkyusha Ltd: 2-11-3, Fujimi, Chiyoda-ku, Tokyo 102-8152; tel. (3) 3288-7711; fax (3) 3288-7821; e-mail kenkyusha-hanbai@in.aix.or.jp; internet www2.aix.or.jp/kenkyusha; f. 1907; bilingual dictionaries; Pres. KATSUYUKI IKEGAMI.

Kinokuniya Co Ltd: 5-38-1, Sakuragaoka, Setagaya-ku, Tokyo 156-8691; tel. (3) 3439-0172; fax (3) 3439-0173; e-mail publish@kinokuniya.co.jp; internet www.kinokuniya.co.jp; f. 1927; humanities, social science, natural science; Pres. OSAMU MATSUBARA.

Kodansha International Ltd: 1-17-14, Otowa, Bunkyo-ku, Tokyo 112-8652; tel. (3) 3944-6492; fax (3) 3944-6323; e-mail sales@kodansha-intl.co.jp; f. 1963; art, business, cookery, crafts, gardening, language, literature, martial arts; Pres. SAWAKO NOMA.

Kodansha Ltd: 2-12-21, Otowa, Bunkyo-ku, Tokyo 112-8001; tel. (3) 5395-3574; fax (3) 3944-9915; f. 1909; fine arts, fiction, literature, juvenile, comics, dictionaries; Pres. SAWAKO NOMA.

Kosei Publishing Co Ltd: 2-7-1, Wada, Suginami-ku, Tokyo 166-8535; tel. (3) 5385-2319; fax (3) 5385-2331; e-mail kspub@mail.kosei-shuppan.co.jp; internet www.kosei-shuppan.co.jp; f. 1966; general works, philosophy, religion, history, pedagogy, social science, art, juvenile; Pres. TEIZO KURIYAMA.

Kyoritsu Shuppan Co Ltd: 4-6-19, Kohinata, Bunkyo-ku, Tokyo 112-8700; tel. (3) 3947-2511; fax (3) 3947-2539; e-mail kyoritsu@po.iijnet.or.jp; internet www.kyoritsu-pub.co.jp; f. 1926; scientific and technical; Pres. MITSUAKI NANJO.

Maruzen Co Ltd: 3-9-2, Nihonbashi, Chuo-ku, Tokyo 103-8244; tel. (3) 3272-0521; fax (3) 3272-0693; internet www.maruzen.co.jp; f. 1869; general works; Pres. SEISHIRO MURATA.

Medical Friend Co Ltd: 3-2-4, Kudan Kita, Chiyoda-ku, Tokyo 102-0073; tel. (3) 3264-6611; fax (3) 3261-6602; f. 1947; medical and allied science, nursing; Pres. KAZUHARU OGURA.

Minerva Shobo: 1, Tsutsumi dani-cho, Hinooka, Yamashina-ku, Kyoto 607-8494; tel. (75) 581-5191; fax (75) 581-0589; e-mail info@minervashobo.co.jp; internet www.minervashobo.co.jp; f. 1948; general non-fiction and reference; Pres. KEIZO SUGITA.

Misuzu Shobo Ltd: 5-32-21, Hongo, Bunkyo-ku, Tokyo 113-0033; tel. (3) 3815-9181; fax (3) 3818-8497; f. 1947; general, philosophy, history, psychiatry, literature, science, art; Pres. KEIJI KATO.

Morikita Shuppan Co Ltd: 1-4-11, Fujimi, Chiyoda-ku, Tokyo 102-0071; tel. (3) 3265-8341; fax (3) 3264-8709; e-mail info@morikita.co.jp; internet www.morikita.co.jp; f. 1950; natural science, engineering; Pres. HAJIME MORIKITA.

Nakayama-Shoten Co Ltd: 1-25-14, Hakusan, Bunkyo-ku, Tokyo 113-8666; tel. (3) 3813-1101; fax (3) 3816-1015; e-mail eigyo@nakayamashoten.co.jp; internet www.nakayamashoten.co.jp; f. 1948; medicine, biology, zoology; Pres. TADASHI HIRATA.

Nanzando Co Ltd: 4-1-11, Yushima, Bunkyo-ku, Tokyo; tel. (3) 5689-7868; fax (3) 5689-7869; e-mail info@nanzando.com; internet www.nanzando.com; medical reference, paperbacks; Pres. HAJIME SUZUKI.

Nigensha Publishing Co Ltd: 2-2, Kanda Jimbo-cho, Chiyoda-ku, Tokyo 101-8419; tel. (3) 5210-4733; fax (3) 5210-4723; e-mail sales@nigensha.co.jp; internet www.nigensha.co.jp; f. 1953; calligraphy, fine arts, art reproductions, cars, watches; Pres. TAKAO WATANABE.

Nihon Keizai Shimbun Inc, Publications Bureau: 1-9-5, Otemachi, Chiyoda-ku, Tokyo 100-0004; tel. (3) 3270-0251; fax (3) 5255-2864; f. 1876; economics, business, politics, fine arts, video cassettes, CD-ROM; Pres. TOYOHIKO KOBAYASHI.

Nihon Vogue Co Ltd: 3-23, Ichigaya Honmura-cho, Shinjuku-ku, Tokyo 162-8705; tel. (3) 5261-5139; fax (3) 3269-8726; e-mail asai@tezukuritown.com; internet www.tezukuritown.com; f. 1954; quilt, needlecraft, handicraft, knitting, decorative painting, pressed flowers; Pres. NOBUAKI SETO.

Nippon Jitsugyo Publishing Co Ltd: 3-2-12, Hongo, Bunkyo-ku, Tokyo 113-0033; tel. (3) 3814-5651; fax (3) 3818-2723; e-mail int@njg.co.jp; internet www.njg.co.jp; f. 1950; business, management, finance and accounting, sales and marketing; Chair. and CEO YOICHIRO NAKAMURA.

Obunsha Co Ltd: 78, Yarai-cho, Shinjuku-ku, Tokyo 162-0805; tel. (3) 3266-6000; fax (3) 3266-6291; f. 1931; internet www.obunsha.co.jp; textbooks, reference, general science and fiction, magazines, encyclopaedias, dictionaries; software; audio-visual aids; CEO FUMIO AKAO.

Ohmsha Ltd: 3-1, Kanda Nishiki-cho, Chiyoda-ku, Tokyo 101-8460; tel. (3) 3233-0641; fax (3) 3233-2426; e-mail kaigaika@ohmsha.co.jp; internet http://www.ohmsha.co.jp/index_e.htm; f. 1914; engineering, technical and scientific; Pres. SEIJI SATO; Dir M. MORI.

Ondorisha Publishers Ltd: 11-11, Nishigoken-cho, Shinjuku-ku, Tokyo 162-8708; tel. (3) 3268-3101; fax (3) 3235-3530; f. 1945; knitting, embroidery, patchwork, handicraft books; Pres. HIDEAKI TAKEUCHI.

Ongaku No Tomo Sha Corpn (ONT): 6-30, Kagurazaka, Shinjuku-ku, Tokyo 162-0825; tel. (3) 3235-2111; fax (3) 3235-2119; internet www.ongakunotomo.co.jp; f. 1941; compact discs, videograms, music magazines, music books, music data, music textbooks; Pres. JUN MEGURO.

PHP Institute Inc: 11, Kitanouchi-cho, Nishikujo, Minami-ku, Kyoto 601-8411; tel. (75) 681-4431; fax (75) 681-9921; internet www.php.co.jp; f. 1946; social science; Pres. MASAHARU MATSUSHITA.

Poplar Publishing Co Ltd: 5, Suga-cho, Shinjuku-ku, Tokyo 160-8565; tel. (3) 3357-2216; fax (3) 3351-0736; e-mail henshu@poplar.co.jp; internet www.poplar.co.jp; f. 1947; children's; Pres. HARUO TANAKA.

Sanseido Co Ltd: 2-22-14, Misaki-cho, Chiyoda-ku, Tokyo 101-8371; tel. (3) 3230-9411; fax (3) 3230-9547; f. 1881; dictionaries, educational, languages, social and natural science; Chair. HISANORI UENO; Pres. TOSHIO GOMI.

Sanshusha Publishing Co Ltd: 1-5-34, Shitaya, Taito-ku, Tokyo 110-0004; tel. (3) 3842-1711; fax (3) 3845-3965; e-mail maeda_k@sanshusha.or.jp; internet www.sanshusha.co.jp; f. 1938; languages, dictionaries, philosophy, sociology, electronic publishing (CD-ROM); Pres. KANJI MAEDA.

Seibundo-Shinkosha Co Ltd: 3-3-1, Hongo, Bunkyo-ku, Tokyo 113-0033; tel. (3) 5800-5775; fax (3) 5800-5773; f. 1912; technical, scientific, design, general non-fiction; Pres. MINORU TAKITA.

Sekai Bunka Publishing Inc: 4-2-29, Kudan-Kita, Chiyoda-ku, Tokyo 102-8187; tel. (3) 3262-5111; fax (3) 3221-6843; internet www.sekaibunka.com; f. 1946; history, natural science, geography, education, art, literature, juvenile; Pres. TSUTOMU SUZUKI.

Shincho-Sha Co Ltd: 71, Yarai-cho, Shinjuku-ku, Tokyo 162-8711; tel. (3) 3266-5411; fax (3) 3266-5534; e-mail shinchosha@webshincho.com; internet www.webshincho.com; f. 1896; general literature, fiction, non-fiction, fine arts, philosophy; Pres. TAKANOBU SATO.

Shinkenchiku-Sha Co Ltd: 2-31-2, Yushima, Bunkyo-ku, Tokyo 113-8501; tel. (3) 3811-7101; fax (3) 3812-8229; e-mail ja-business@japan-architect.co.jp; internet www.japan-architect.co.jp; f. 1925; architecture; Pres. NOBUYUKI YOSHIDA.

Shogakukan Inc: 2-3-1, Hitotsubashi, Chiyoda-ku, Tokyo 101-8001; tel. (3) 3230-5526; fax (3) 3288-9653; internet www.shogakukan.co.jp; f. 1922; juvenile, education, geography, history, encyclopaedias, dictionaries; Pres. MASAHIRO OHGA.

Shokabo Publishing Co Ltd: 8-1, Yomban-cho, Chiyoda-ku, Tokyo 102-0081; tel. (3) 3262-9166; fax (3) 3262-7257; e-mail info@shokabo.co.jp; internet www.shokabo.co.jp; f. 1895; natural science, engineering; Pres. TATSUJI YOSHINO.

Shokokusha Publishing Co Ltd: 25, Saka-machi, Shinjuku-ku, Tokyo 160-0002; tel. (3) 3359-3231; fax (3) 3357-3961; e-mail eigyo@shokokusha.co.jp; f. 1932; architectural, technical and fine arts; Pres. TAKESHI GOTO.

Shueisha Inc: 2-5-10, Hitotsubashi, Chiyoda-ku, Tokyo 101-8050; tel. (3) 3230-6320; fax (3) 3262-1309; f. 1925; literature, fine arts, language, juvenile, comics; Pres. and CEO TAMIO KOJIMA.

Shufunotomo Co Ltd: 2-9, Kanda Surugadai, Chiyoda-ku, Tokyo 101-8911; tel. (3) 5280-7567; fax (3) 5280-7568; e-mail international@shufunotomo.co.jp; internet www.shufunotomo.co.jp; f. 1916; domestic science, fine arts, gardening, handicraft, cookery and magazines; Pres. KUNIHIKO MURAMATSU.

Shunju-Sha: 2-18-6, Soto-Kanda, Chiyoda-ku, Tokyo 101-0021; tel. (3) 3255-9614; fax (3) 3255-9370; f. 1918; philosophy, religion, literary, economics, music; Pres. AKIRA KANDA; Man. RYUTARO SUZUKI.

Taishukan Publishing Co Ltd: 3-24, Kanda-Nishiki-cho, Chiyoda-ku, Tokyo 101-8466; tel. (3) 3294-2221; fax (3) 3295-4107; internet www.taishukan.co.jp; f. 1918; reference, Japanese and foreign languages, sports, dictionaries, audio-visual aids; Pres. KAZUYUKI SUZUKI.

Tankosha Publishing Co Ltd: 19-1, Miyanishi-cho Murasakino, Kita-ku, Kyoto 603-8691; tel. (75) 432-5151; fax (75) 432-0273; e-mail tankosha@magical.egg.or.jp; internet tankosha.topica.ne.jp; f. 1949; tea ceremony, fine arts, history; Pres. YOSHITO NAYA.

Teikoku-Shoin Co Ltd: 3-29, Kanda Jimbo-cho, Chiyoda-ku, Tokyo 101-0051; tel. (3) 3262-0834; fax (3) 3262-7770; e-mail kenkyu@teikokushoin.co.jp; f. 1926; geography, atlases, maps, textbooks; Pres. MUTSUO SHIRAHAMA.

Tokai University Press: 2-28-4, Tomigaya, Shibuya-ku, Tokyo 151-8677; tel. (3) 5478-0891; fax (3) 5478-0870; f. 1962; social science, cultural science, natural science, engineering, art; Pres. TATSURO MATSUMAE.

Tokuma Shoten Publishing Co Ltd: 1-1-16, Higashi Shimbashi, Minato-ku, Tokyo 105-8055; tel. (3) 3573-0111; fax (3) 3573-8788; e-mail info@tokuma.com; internet www.tokuma.com; f. 1954; Japanese classics, history, fiction, juvenile; Pres. YASUYOSHI TOKUMA.

Tokyo News Service Ltd: Tsukiji Hamarikyu Bldg, 5-3-3, Tsukiji, Chuo-ku, Tokyo 104; tel. (3) 3542-6511; fax (3) 3545-3628; f. 1947; shipping, trade and television guides; Pres. T. OKUYAMA.

Tokyo Shoseki Co Ltd: 2-17-1, Horifune, Kita-ku, Tokyo 114-8524; tel. (3) 5390-7513; fax (3) 5390-7409; internet www.tokyoshoseki.co.jp; f. 1909; textbooks, reference books, cultural and educational books; Pres. YOSHIKATSU KAWAUCHI.

Tokyo Sogen-Sha Co Ltd: 1-5, Shin-Ogawa-machi, Shinjuku-ku, Tokyo 162-0814; tel. (3) 3268-8201; fax (3) 3268-8230; f. 1954; mystery and detective stories, science fiction, literature; Pres. YASUNOBU TOGAWA.

Tuttle Publishing Co Inc: Yaekari Bldg, 3rd Floor, 5-4-12 Osaki, Shinagawa-ku, Tokyo 141-0032; tel. (3) 5437-0171; fax (44) 5437-0755; e-mail tuttle@gol.com; internet www.tuttlepublishing.com; f. 1948; books on Japanese and Asian religion, history, social science, arts, languages, literature, juvenile, cookery; Pres. ERIC OEY.

United Nations University Press: 5-53-70, Jingumae, Shibuya-ku, Tokyo 150-8925; tel. (3) 3499-2811; fax (3) 3499-2828; e-mail sales@hq.unu.edu; internet www.unu.edu/unupress; f. 1975; social sciences, humanities, pure and applied natural sciences; Rector HANS J. H. VAN GINKEL.

University of Tokyo Press: 7-3-1, Hongo, Bunkyo-ku, Tokyo 113-8654; tel. (3) 3811-0964; fax (3) 3815-1426; e-mail info@utp.or.jp; f. 1951; natural and social sciences, humanities; Japanese and English; Chair. MASARU NISHIO; Man. Dir TADASHI YAMASHITA.

Weekly Toyo Keizai: 1-2-1, Nihonbashi, Hongoku-cho, Chuo-ku, Tokyo 103-8345; tel. (3) 3246-5655; fax (3) 3231-0906; e-mail sub@toyokeizai.co.jp; internet www.toyokeizai.co.jp; f. 1895; economics, business, finance and corporate, information; Pres. HIROSHI TAKAHASHI.

Yama-Kei Publishers Co Ltd: 1-1-33, Shiba-Daimon, Minato-ku, Tokyo 105-0012; tel. (3) 3436-4021; fax (3) 3438-1949; f. 1930; natural science, geography, mountaineering; Pres. YOSHIMITSU KAWASAKI.

Yohan: 3-14-9, Okubo, Shinjuku-ku, Tokyo 169-0072; tel. (3) 3208-0181; fax (3) 3209-0288; internet www.yohan.co.jp; f. 1963; social science, language, art, juvenile, dictionary; Pres. MASANORI WATANABE.

Yuhikaku Publishing Co Ltd: 2-17, Kanda Jimbo-cho, Chiyoda-ku, Tokyo 101-0051; tel. (3) 3264-1312; fax (3) 3264-5030; f. 1877; social sciences, law, economics; Pres. TADATAKA EGUSA.

Yuzankaku Shuppan: 2-6-9, Fujimi, Chiyoda-ku, Tokyo 102; tel. (3) 3262-3231; fax (3) 3262-6938; e-mail yuzan@cf.mbn.or.jp; internet www.nepto.co.jp/yuzankaku; f. 1916; history, fine arts, religion, archaeology; Pres. KEIKO NAGASAKA.

Zoshindo Juken Kenkyusha Co Ltd: 2-19-15, Shinmachi, Nishi-ku, Osaka 550-0013; tel. (6) 6532-1581; fax (6) 6532-1588; e-mail zoshindo@mbox.inet-osaka.or.jp; internet www.zoshindo.co.jp; f. 1890; educational, juvenile; Pres. AKITAKA OKAMATO.

Government Publishing House

Government Publications' Service Centre: 1-2-1, Kasumigaseki, Chiyoda-ku, Tokyo 100-0013; tel. (3) 3504-3885; fax (3) 3504-3889.

PUBLISHERS' ASSOCIATIONS

Japan Book Publishers Association: 6, Fukuro-machi, Shinjuku-ku, Tokyo 162-0828; tel. (3) 3268-1301; fax (3) 3268-1196; internet www.jbpa.or.jp; f. 1957; 499 mems; Pres. TAKAO WATANABE; Exec. Dir TOSHIKAZU GOMI.

Publishers' Association for Cultural Exchange, Japan: 1-2-1, Sarugaku-cho, Chiyoda-ku, Tokyo 101-0064; tel. (3) 3291-5685; fax (3) 3233-3645; e-mail office@pace.or.jp; internet www.pace.or.jp; f. 1953; 135 mems; Pres. Dr TATSURO MATSUMAE; Man. Dir YASUKO KORENAGA.

Broadcasting and Communications

TELECOMMUNICATIONS

International Digital Communications: 5-20-8, Asakusabashi, Taito-ku, Tokyo 111; tel. (3) 5820-5080; fax (3) 5820-5363; f. 1985; 53% owned by Cable and Wireless Communications (UK); Pres. SIMON CUNNINGHAM.

Japan Telecom Co Ltd: 4-7-1, Hatchobori, Chuo-ku, Tokyo 104-8508; tel. (3) 5540-8417; fax (3) 5540-8485; internet www.japan-telecom.co.jp; 30% owned by alliance of British Telecommunications PLC (UK) and American Telegraph and Telephone Corpn (USA); Chair. HARUO MURAKAMI; Pres. BILL MORROW.

KDDI Corpn: KDDI Bldg, 2-3-2, Nishi Shinjuku, Shinjuku-ku, Tokyo 163-03; tel. (3) 3347-7111; fax (3) 3347-6470; internet www.kddi.com; f. 2000 by merger of DDI Corpn, Kokusai Denshin Denwa Corpn (KDD) and Nippon Idou Tsushin Corpn (IDO); major international telecommunications carrier; Chair. JIRO USHIO; Pres. TADASHI ONODERA.

Nippon Telegraph and Telephone Corpn: 2-3-1, Otemachi, Chiyoda-ku, Tokyo 100-0004; tel. (3) 5359-2122; e-mail hyamada@yamato.ntt.jp; operates local, long-distance and international services; largest telecommunications co in Japan; Chair. SHIGEO SAWADA; Pres. JUN-ICHIRO MIYAZU.

NTT DoCoMo: 2-11-1 Nagatacho, Chiyoda-ku, Tokyo 100-6150; tel. (3) 5156-1111; fax (3) 5156-0271; internet www.nttdocomo.com; f. 1991; operates mobile phone network; Pres. KEIJI TACHIKAWA.

Tokyo Telecommunication Network Co Inc: 4-9-25, Shibaura, Minato-ku, Tokyo 108; tel. (3) 5476-0091; fax (3) 5476-7625.

KDDI, Digital Phone and Digital TU-KA also operate mobile telecommunication services in Japan.

BROADCASTING

NHK (Japan Broadcasting Corporation): 2-2-1, Jinnan, Shibuya, Tokyo 150-8001; tel. (3) 3465-1111; fax (3) 3469-8110; e-mail webmaster@www.nhk.or.jp; internet www.nhk.or.jp; f. 1925 (fmrly Nippon Hose Kyokai, NHK (Japan Broadcasting Corpn); Japan's sole public broadcaster; operates five TV channels (incl. two terrestrial services—general TV and educational TV, two digital satellite services—BS-1 and BS-2 and a digital Hi-Vision service—HDTV), three radio channels, Radio 1, Radio 2, and FM Radio, and three worldwide services, NHK World TV, NHK World Premium and NHK World Radio Japan; headquarters in Tokyo, regional headquarters in Osaka, Nagoya, Hiroshima, Fukuoka, Sendai, Sapporo and Matsuyama; Pres. KATSUJI EBISAWA.

National Association of Commercial Broadcasters in Japan (NAB-J): 3-23, Kioi-cho, Chiyoda-ku, Tokyo 102-8577; tel. (3) 5213-7727; fax (3) 5213-7730; internet www.nab.or.jp; f. 1951; asscn of 201 companies (133 TV cos, 110 radio cos). Among these companies, 42 operate both radio and TV, with 664 radio stations and 8,315 TV stations (incl. relay stations). Pres. SEIICHIRO UJIIE; Exec. Dir AKIRA SAKAI.

In June 2000 there were a total of 99 commercial radio broadcasting companies and 127 commercial television companies operating in Japan. Some of the most important companies are:

Asahi Hoso—Asahi Broadcasting Corpn: 2-2-48, Ohyodominami, Kita-ku, Osaka 531-8501; tel. (6) 6458-5321; fax (6) 6458-3672; internet www.asahi.co.jp; Pres. TOSHIHARU SHIBATA.

Asahi National Broadcasting Co Ltd—TV Asahi: 1-1-1, Roppongi, Minato-ku, Tokyo 106; tel. (3) 3587-5412; fax (3) 3586-6369; internet www.tv-asahi.co.jp; f. 1957; Pres. KUNIO ITO.

Bunka Hoso—Nippon Cultural Broadcasting, Inc: 1-5, Wakaba, Shinjuku-ku, Tokyo 160-8002; tel. (3) 3357-1111; fax (3) 3357-1140; internet www.joqr.co.jp; f. 1952; Pres. SHIGEKI SATO.

Chubu-Nippon Broadcasting Co Ltd: 1-2-8, Shinsakae, Naka-ku, Nagoya 460-8405; tel. (052) 241-8111; fax (052) 259-1303; internet www.cbc-nagoya.co.jp; Pres. KEN-ICHI YOKOYAMA.

Fuji Television Network, Inc: 2-4-8, Daiba, Minato-ku, Tokyo 137-8088; tel. (3) 5500-8888; fax (3) 5500-8027; internet www.fujitv.co.jp; f. 1959; Pres. HISASHI HIEDA.

Kansai TV Hoso (KTV)—Kansai : 2-1-7, Ogimachi, Kita-ku, Osaka 530-8408; tel. (6) 6314-8888; internet www.ktv.co.jp; Pres. NOBUO MAKIHATA.

Mainichi Hoso (MBS)—Mainichi Broadcasting System, Inc: 17-1, Chayamachi, Kita-ku, Osaka 530-8304; tel. (6) 6359-1123; fax (6) 6359-3503; internet mbs.co.jp; Pres. MASAHIRO YAMAMOTO.

Nippon Hoso—Nippon Broadcasting System, Inc: 2-4-8, Daiba, Minato-ku, Tokyo 137-8686; tel. (3) 5500-1234; internet www.1242.com; f. 1954; Pres. MICHIYASU KAWAUCHI.

Nippon TV Hoso-MO (NTV)—Nippon Television Network Corpn: 14, Niban-cho, Chiyoda-ku, Tokyo 102-8004; tel. (3) 5275-1111; fax (3) 5275-4501; internet www.ntv.co.jp; f. 1953; Pres. SEIICHIRO UJIIE.

Okinawa TV Hoso (OTV)—Okinawa Television Broadcasting Co Ltd: 1-2-20, Kumoji, Naha 900-8588; tel. (988) 63-2111; fax (988) 61-0193; internet www.otv.co.jp; f. 1959; Pres. BUNKI TOMA.

Radio Tampa—Nihon Short-Wave Broadcasting Co: 1-9-15, Akasaka, Minato-ku, Tokyo 107-8373; tel. (3) 3583-8151; fax (3) 3583-7441; internet www.tampa.co.jp; f. 1954; Pres. TAMIO IKEDA.

Ryukyu Hoso (RBC)—Ryukyu Broadcasting Co: 2-3-1, Kumoji, Naha 900-8711; tel. (98) 867-2151; fax (98) 864-5732; internet www.rbc-ryukyu.co.jp; f. 1954; Pres. YOSHIO ISHIGAKE.

TV Osaka (TVO)—Television Osaka, Inc: 1-2-18, Otemae, Chuo-ku, Osaka 540-8519; tel. (6) 6947-0019; fax (6) 6946-9796; internet www.tv-osaka.co.jp; f. 1982; Pres. MAKOTO FUKAGAWA.

TV Tokyo (TX)—Television Tokyo Channel 12 Ltd: 4-3-12, Toranomon, Minato-ku, Tokyo 105-8012; tel. (3) 3432-1212; fax (3) 5473-3447; internet www.tv-tokyo.co.jp; f. 1964; Pres. YUTAKA ICHIKI.

Tokyo -Hoso (TBS)—Tokyo Broadcasting System, Inc: 5-3-6, Akasaka, Minato-ku, Tokyo 107-8006; tel. (3) 3746-1111; fax (3) 3588-6378; internet www.tbs.co.jp/index.html; f. 1951; Chair. HIROSHI SHIHO; Pres. YUKIO SUNAHARA.

Yomiuri TV Hoso (YTV)—Yomiuri Telecasting Corporation: 2-2-33, Shiromi, Chuo-ku, Osaka 540-8510; tel. (6) 6947-2111; internet www.ytv.co.jp; f. 1958; 20 hrs colour broadcasting daily; Pres. TOMONARI DOI.

Satellite, Cable and Digital Television

In addition to the two broadcast satellite services that NHK introduced in 1989, a number of commercial satellite stations are in operation. Cable television is available in many urban areas, and in 1996/97 there were some 12.6m. subscribers to cable services in Japan. Satellite digital television services, which first became available in 1996, are provided by Japan Digital Broadcasting Services (f. 1998 by the merger of PerfecTV and JSkyB) and DirecTV. Terrestrial digital services were scheduled to be introduced by 2000.

Finance

(cap. = capital; p.u. = paid up; res = reserves; dep. = deposits; m. = million; brs = branches; amounts in yen)

BANKING

Japan's central bank and bank of issue is the Bank of Japan. More than one-half of the credit business of the country is handled by 136 private commercial banks, seven trust banks and three long-term credit banks, collectively designated 'All Banks'. At October 1998 the private commercial banks had total assets of 641,000,000m. yen, the trust banks had total assets of 62,000,000m. yen and the long-term credit banks had total assets of 72,000,000m. yen.

Of the former category, the most important are the city banks, of which there are 10, some of which have a long and distinguished history, originating in the time of the *zaibatsu*, the private entrepreneurial organizations on which Japan's capital wealth was built before the Second World War. Although the *zaibatsu* were abolished as integral industrial and commercial enterprises during the Allied Occupation, the several businesses and industries which bear the former *zaibatsu* names, such as Mitsubishi, Mitsui and Sumitomo, continue to flourish and to give each other mutual assistance through their respective banks and trust corporations.

Among the commercial banks, the Bank of Tokyo-Mitsubishi specializes in foreign-exchange business, while the Industrial Bank of Japan finances capital investment by industry. Shinsei Bank and Nippon Credit Bank also specialize in industrial finance; the work of these three privately-owned banks is supplemented by the government-controlled Development Bank of Japan.

The Government has established a number of other specialized institutions to provide services that are not offered by the private banks. Thus the Japan Bank for International Cooperation advances credit for the export of heavy industrial products and the import of raw materials in bulk. A Housing Loan Corporation assists firms in building housing for their employees, while the Agriculture, Forestry and Fisheries Finance Corporation provides loans to the named industries for equipment purchases. Similar services are provided for small enterprises by the Japanese Finance Corporation for Small Business.

An important financial role is played by co-operatives and by the many small enterprise institutions. Each prefecture has its own federation of co-operatives, with the Central Co-operative Bank of Agriculture and Forestry as the common central financial institution. This bank also acts as an agent for the government-controlled Agriculture, Forestry and Fisheries Finance Corporation.

There are also two types of private financial institutions for small business. There were 342 Credit Co-operatives, with total assets of 22,000,000m. yen, and 400 Shinkin Banks (credit associations), with total assets of 113,000,000m. yen at October 1998, which lend only to members. The latter also receive deposits.

The most common form of savings is through the government-operated Postal Savings System, which collects small savings from the public by means of the post office network. Total deposits amounted to 248,000,000m. yen in November 1998. The funds thus made available are used as loan funds by government financial institutions, through the Ministry of Finance's Trust Fund Bureau.

Clearing houses operate in each major city of Japan, and total 182 institutions. The largest are those of Tokyo and Osaka.

In June 1998 the Financial Supervisory Agency was established to regulate Japan's financial institutions.

Central Bank

Nippon Ginko (Bank of Japan): 2-1-1, Hongoku-cho, Nihonbashi, Chuo-ku, Tokyo 100-8630; tel. (3) 3279-1111; fax (3) 5200-2256; internet www.boj.or.jp; f. 1882; cap. and res 2,831,600m., dep. 41,823,400m. (March 2002); Gov. Masaru Hayami; Dep. Govs Sakuya Fujiwara, Yutaka Yamaguchi; 33 brs.

Principal Commercial Banks

Asahi Bank Ltd: 1-1-2, Otemachi, Chiyoda-ku, Tokyo 100-8106; tel. (3) 3287-2111; fax (3) 3212-3484; internet www.asahibank.co.jp; f. 1945 as Kyowa Bank Ltd; merged with Saitama Bank Ltd (f. 1943) in 1991; adopted present name in 1992; to merge with Daiwa Bank in 2002; cap. 403,380m., res 914,252m., dep. 26,357,595m. (March 2001); Chair. Tadashi Tanaka; Pres. Tatsuro Itoh; 424 brs.

Ashikaga Bank Ltd: 4-1-25, Sakura, Utsunomiya, Tochigi 320-8610; tel. (286) 22-0111; e-mail ashigin@ssctnet.or.jp; internet www.ashikagabank.co.jp; f. 1895; cap. 132,446m., res 98,934m., dep. 5,083,099m. (March 2000); Chair. Yoshio Yanagita; Pres. Shin Iizuka; 140 brs.

Bank of Fukuoka Ltd: 2-13-1, Tenjin, Chuo-ku, Fukuoka 810-8727; tel. (92) 723-2131; fax (92) 711-1746; f. 1945; cap. 58,657m., res 272,349m., dep. 5,805,102m. (March 2000); Chair. Kiyoshi Teramoto; Pres. Ryoji Tsukuda; 189 brs.

Bank of Tokyo-Mitsubishi Ltd: 2-7-1, Marunouchi, Chiyoda-ku, Tokyo 100-8388; tel. (3) 93240-1111; fax (3) 93240-4197; internet www.btm.co.jp; f. 1996 as a result of merger between Bank of Tokyo Ltd (f. 1946) and Mitsubishi Bank Ltd (f. 1880); specializes in international banking and financial business; cap. 785,970m., res 1,391,469m., dep. 62,606,410m. (March 2001); Chair. Satoru Kishi; Pres. Shigemitsu Miki; 805 brs.

Bank of Yokohama Ltd: 3-1-1, Minatomirai, Nishi-ku, Yokohama, Kanagawa 220-8611; tel. (45) 225-1111; fax (45) 225-1160; e-mail iroffice@hamagin.co.jp; internet www.boy.co.jp; f. 1920; cap. 184,800m., res 183,399m., dep. 9,192,156m. (March 2002); Pres. and CEO Sadaaki Hirasawa; 185 brs.

Chiba Bank Ltd: 1-2, Chiba-minato, Chuo-ku, Chiba 260-8720; tel. (43) 245-1111; e-mail 27528400@people.or.jp; internet www.chibabank.co.jp; f. 1943; cap. 106,888m., res 194,702m., dep. 6,870,950m. (March 2000); Chair. Takashi Tamaki; Pres. Tsuneo Hayakawa; 163 brs.

Dai-Ichi Kangyo Bank Ltd: 1-1-5, Uchisaiwai-cho, Chiyoda-ku, Tokyo 100-0011; tel. (3) 3596-1111; fax (3) 3596-2179; internet www.dkb.co.jp; f. 1971; jt holding co established with Fuji Bank Ltd and Nippon Kogyo Ginko in September 2000, prior to full merger by early 2002; cap. 858,784m., res 1,519,755m., dep. 40,012,121m. (March 2000); Pres. and CEO Katsuyuki Sugita; 353 brs.

Daiwa Bank Ltd: 2-2-1, Bingo-machi, Chuo-ku, Osaka 540-8610; tel. (6) 6271-1221; internet www.daiwabank.co.jp; f. 1918; to merge with Asahi Bank in 2002; cap. 465,158m., res 452,813m., dep 12,772,280m. (March 2001); Chair. Takashi Kaiho; Pres. Yasuhisa Katsuta; 182 brs.

Fuji Bank Ltd: 1-5-5, Otemachi, Chiyoda-ku, Tokyo 100-0004; tel. (3) 3216-2211; internet www.fujibank.co.jp; f. 1880; jt holding co with Dai-Ichi Kangyo Bank Ltd and Nippon Kogyo Ginko established Sept. 2000, prior to full merger by early 2002; cap. 1,039,543m., res 1,239,276m., dep. 38,961,618m. (March 2000); Chair. Toru Hashimoto; Pres. Yoshiro Yamamoto; 293 brs.

Hachijuni Bank: 178-8 Okada, Nagano-shi, Nagano 380-8682; tel. (26) 227-1182; fax (26) 226-5077; internet www.82bank.co.jp; f. 1931; cap. 52,243m., res 74,745m., dep. 5,137,760m. (March 2000); Pres. Minoru Chino.

Hokuriku Bank Ltd: 1-2-26, Tsutsumichodori, Toyama 930-8637; tel. (764) 237-111; fax (764) 915-908; e-mail kokusaibu@hokugin.co.jp; internet www.hokugin.co.jp; f. 1877; cap. 120,842m., res 145,857m., dep. 5,440,960m. (March 2000); Pres. Shinichiro Inushima; 191 brs.

Japan Net Bank: internet www.japannetbank.co.jp; f. 2000; Japan's first internet-only bank.

Joyo Bank Ltd: 2-5-5, Minamimachi, Mito-shi, Ibaraki 310-0021; tel. (29) 231-2151; fax (29) 255-6522; e-mail joyointl@po.net-ibaraki.ne.jp; internet www.joyobank.co.jp; f. 1935; cap. 85,113m., res 326,961m., dep. 6,340,849m. (March 2001); Chair. Toranosuke Nishino; Pres. Isao Shibuya; 186 brs.

North Pacific Bank: 3-11 Odori Nishi, Chuo-ku, Sapporo 060-8661; tel. (11) 261-1416; fax (11) 232-6921; f. 1917, as Hokuyo Sogo Bank Ltd; assumed present name in 1989; cap. 49,223m., res 71,088m., dep 5,153,501m. (March 2001); Chair. Masanao Takei; Pres. Iwao Takamuki.

Shizuoka Bank Ltd: 1-10, Gofuku-cho, Shizuoka 420-8761; tel. (54) 261-3131; fax (54) 344-0090; internet www.shizuokabank.co.jp; f. 1943; cap. 90,845m., res 246,227m., dep. 7,203,883m. (March 2001); Chair. Soichiro Kamiya; Pres. Yasuo Matsuura; 199 brs.

Sumitomo Mitsui Banking Corpn: 1-2 Yurakucho, Chiyoda-ku, Tokyo 100-0006; tel. (3) 2501-1111; internet www.smbc.co.jp; f. 1895; merged with Sakura Bank Ltd in April 2001 and assumed present name; cap. 752,848m., res 764,376m., dep. 52,651,617m. (March 2001); Chair. Akishige Okada; Pres. Yoshifumi Nishikawa; 351 brs.

UFJ Bank Ltd: 3-5-6, Fushimi-machi, Chuo-ku, Osaka-shi, Osaka; internet www.ufj.co.jp; f. April 2001, following merger of Sanwa Bank, Tokai Bank, and Toyo Trust and Banking (see above); cap. 1,000,000m. (Dec. 2001); dep. 51,107,000m. (Sept. 2001); Pres. Masashi Teranishi.

Principal Trust Banks

Chuo Mitsui Trust and Banking Co Ltd: 3-33-1, Shiba, Minato-ku, Chuo-ku, Tokyo 105-8574; tel. (3) 5232-3331; fax (3) 5232-8864; internet www.chuomitsui.co.jp; f. 1962 as Chuo Trust and Banking Co Ltd, name changed as above in 2000, following merger with Mitsui Trust and Banking Co Ltd; cap. 170,966m., res 166,803m., dep. 3,594,827m. (March 2000); Chair. Hisao Muramoto; Pres. Kiichiro Furusawa; 169 brs.

Mitsubishi Trust and Banking Corporation: 2-11-1 Nagatacho, Chiyoda-ku, Tokyo 100-8212; tel. (3) 3212-1211; fax (3) 3519-3367; internet www.mitsubishi-trust.co.jp; f. 1927; absorbed Nippon Trust Bank Ltd and Tokyo Trust Bank Ltd in Oct. 2001; cap. 292,794m., res 562,883m., dep. 11,359,018m. (March 2001); Chair. Toyoshi Nakano; Pres. Akio Utsumi; 54 brs.

Sumitomo Trust and Banking Co Ltd: 4-5-33, Kitahama, Chuo-ku, Osaka 540-8639; tel. (6) 6220-2121; fax (6) 6220-2043; e-mail ipda@sumitomotrust.co.jp; internet www.sumitomotrust.co.jp; f. 1925; cap. 283,985m., res 302,861m., dep. 9,782,090m. (March 2001); Chair. Hitoshi Hurakami; Pres. Atsushi Takahashi; 57 brs.

UFJ Trust Bank: 1-4-3, Marunouchi, Chiyoda-ku, Tokyo 100-0005; tel. (3) 3287-2211; fax (3) 3201-1448; f. 1959, as Toyo Trust and Banking; merged with Sanwa Bank Ltd and Tokai Bank Ltd in April 2001 to form UFJ Holdings Ltd (see above); cap. 280,471m., res 263,357m., dep. 3,952,347m. (March 2000); Pres. Yasukuni Doi; 56 brs.

Yasuda Trust and Banking Co Ltd: 1-2-1, Yaesu, Chuo-ku, Tokyo 103-8670; tel. (3) 3278-8111; fax (3) 3281-6947; internet www.ytb.co.jp; f. 1925; cap. 337,231m., res 13,905m., dep. 4,549,580m. (March 2001); Pres. and CEO Hiroaki Etoh; 50 brs.

Long-Term Credit Banks

Aozora: 1-13-10, Kudan-kita, Chiyoda-ku, Tokyo 102-8660; tel. (3) 3263-1111; fax (3) 3265-7024; e-mail sora@aozora.co.jp; internet www.aozora.co.jp; f. 1957; nationalized Dec. 1998, sold to consortium led by Softbank Corpn in Aug. 2000; fmrly The Nippon Credit Bank, name changed as above 2001; cap. 419,781m., res 33,333m., dep. 4,650,510m. (March 2001); Pres. and CEO Hiroshi Maruyama; Man. Exec. Dir Yuji Inagaki; 17 brs.

Nippon Kogyo Ginko (The Industrial Bank of Japan Ltd): 1-3-3, Marunouchi, Chiyoda-ku, Tokyo 100-8210; tel. (3) 3214-1111; fax (3) 3201-7643; internet www.ibjbank.co.jp; f. 1902; jt holding co with Dai-Ichi Kangyo Bank Ltd and Fuji Bank Ltd established in Sept. 2000, prior to full merger by early 2002; medium- and long-term financing; cap. 673,605m., res 650,501m., dep. 28,041,940m. (March 1999); Pres. and CEO MASAO NISHIMURA; 23 domestic brs, 20 overseas brs.

Shinsei Bank Ltd: 2-1-8, Uchisaiwai-cho, Chiyoda-ku, Tokyo 100-8501; tel. (3) 5511-5111; fax (3) 5511-5505; internet www.shinseibank.co.jp; f. 1952 as The Long-Term Credit Bank of Japan; nationalized Oct. 1998, sold to Ripplewood Holdings (USA), renamed as above June 2000; cap. 180,853m., res 305,343m., dep. 7,595,821m. (March 2001); Chair. MASAMOTO YASHIRO; 23 brs.

Co-operative Bank

Shinkin Central Bank: 3-8-1, Kyobashi, Chuo-ku, Tokyo 104-0031; tel. (3) 3563-4111; fax (3) 3563-7553; internet www.shinkin.co.jp; f. 1950; cap. 290,998m., res 494,202m., dep. 22,116,995m. (March 2001); Chair. YUKIHIKO NAGANO; Pres. YASUTAKA MIYAMOTO; 17 brs.

Principal Government Credit Institutions

Agriculture, Forestry and Fisheries Finance Corporation: Koko Bldg, 1-9-3, Otemachi, Chiyoda-ku, Tokyo 100-0004; tel. (3) 3270-2261; e-mail intl@afc.go.jp; internet www.afc.go.jp; f. 1953; finances mainly plant and equipment investment; Gov. TOSHIHIKO TSURUOKA; Dep. Gov. SHIGEO OHARA; 22 brs.

Development Bank of Japan: 1-9-1, Otemachi, Chiyoda-ku, Tokyo 100-0004; tel. (3) 3244-1770; fax (3) 3245-1938; e-mail safukas@dbj.go.jp; internet www.dbj.go.jp; f. 1951 as the Japan Development Bank; renamed Oct. 1999 following consolidation with the Hokkaido and Tohoku Development Finance Public Corpn; provides long-term loans; subscribes for corporate bonds; guarantees corporate obligations; invests in specific projects; borrows funds from Govt and abroad; issues external bonds and notes; provides market information and consulting services for prospective entrants to Japanese market; cap. 1,039,386m. (March 2001), res 455,768m. (March 1999), dep. 15,096,100m. (March 1998); Gov. TAKESHI KOMURA; Dep. Govs KUNITAKA KAJITA, TAKASHI MATSUKAWA; 10 domestic brs, 6 overseas brs.

Housing Loan Corporation: 1-4-10, Koraku, Bunkyo-ku, Tokyo 112-8570; tel. (3) 3812-1111; fax (3) 5800-8257; internet www.jyukou.go.jp; f. 1950 to provide long-term capital for the construction of housing at low interest rates; cap. 97,200m. (1994); Pres. SUSUMU TAKAHASHI; Vice-Pres. HIROYUKI ITOU; 12 brs.

Japan Bank for International Cooperation (JBIC): 1-4-1, Otemachi, Chiyoda-ku, Tokyo 100-8144; tel. (3) 5218-3101; fax (3) 5218-3955; internet www.jbic.go.jp; f. 1999 by merger of The Export-Import Bank of Japan (f. 1950) and The Overseas Economic Co-operation Fund (f. 1961); governmental financial institution, responsible for Japan's external economic policy and co-operation activities; cap. 6,679,944m. (March 2000); Gov. KYOSUKE SHINOZAWA.

Japan Finance Corporation for Small Business: Koko Bldg, 1-9-3, Otemachi, Chiyoda-ku, Tokyo 100-0004; tel. (3) 3270-1271; internet www.jfs.go.jp; f. 1953 to promote long-term growth and development of small businesses by providing the necessary funds and information on their use in accordance with national policy; cap. 433,715m. (Jan. 2002); wholly subscribed by Govt; Gov. TOMIO TSUTSUMI; Vice-Gov. SOHEI HIDAKA; 58 brs.

National Life Finance Corporation: Koko Bldg, 1-9-3, Otemachi, Chiyoda-ku, Tokyo 100-0004; tel. (3) 3270-1361; internet www.kokukin.go.jp; f. 1999 following consolidation of The People's Finance Corpn (f. 1949 to provide business funds, particularly to small enterprises unable to obtain loans from banks and other private financial institutions) and the Environmental Sanitation Business Finance Corpn (f. 1967 to improve sanitary facilities); cap. 290,771m. (March 2000); Gov. MAMORU OZAKI; Dep. Gov. MASAAKI TSUCHIDA; 152 brs.

Norinchukin Bank (Central Co-operative Bank for Agriculture, Forestry and Fisheries): 1-13-2, Yuraku-cho, Chiyoda-ku, Tokyo 100; tel. (3) 3279-0111; fax (3) 3218-5177; internet www.nochubank.or.jp; f. 1923; main banker to agricultural, forestry and fisheries co-operatives; receives deposits from individual co-operatives, federations and agricultural enterprises; extends loans to these and to local govt authorities and public corpns; adjusts excess and shortage of funds within co-operative system; issues debentures, invests funds and engages in other regular banking business; cap. 1,124,999m., res 723,455m., dep. 47,245,076m. (March 2001); Pres. HIROFUMI UENO; Dep. Pres. HIROHISA ISHIHARA; 39 brs.

Shoko Chukin Bank (Central Co-operative Bank for Commerce and Industry): 2-10-17, Yaesu, Chuo-ku, Tokyo 104-0028; tel. (3) 3272-6111; fax (3) 3272-6169; e-mail JDK06560@nifty.ne.jp; internet www.shokochukin.go.jp; f. 1936 to provide general banking services to facilitate finance for smaller enterprise co-operatives and other organizations formed mainly by small- and medium-sized enterprises; issues debentures; cap. 474,865m., res 24,410m., dep. 12,947,345m. (March 2000); Pres. YUKIHARU KODAMA; Dep. Pres. SHIGENORI SHIODA; 99 brs.

Other government financial institutions include the Japan Finance Corpn for Municipal Enterprises, the Small Business Credit Insurance Corpn and the Okinawa Development Finance Corpn.

Principal Foreign Banks

In March 1999 there were 88 foreign banks operating in Japan.

ABN AMRO Bank NV (Netherlands): Atago Green Hills MORI Tower, 32nd Floor, 2-5-1, Atago, Minato-ku, Tokyo 105-6231; tel. (3) 5405-6500; fax (3) 5405-6900; Br. Man. ATSUSHI WATANABE.

Bangkok Bank Public Co Ltd (Thailand): Bangkok Bank Bldg, 2-8-10, Nishi Shinbashi, Minato-ku, Tokyo 105-0003; tel. (3) 3503-3333; fax (3) 3502-6420; Senior Vice-Pres. and Gen. Man. (Japan) THAWEE PHUANGKETKEOW; br. in Osaka.

Bank of America NA: Sanno Park Tower, 15th Floor, 2-11-1, Nagatacho, Chiyoda-ku, Tokyo 100-6115; tel. (3) 3508-5800; fax (3) 3508-5811; Sr Vice-Pres. and Regional Man. Japan, Australia and Korea ARUN DUGGAL.

Bank of India: Mitsubishi Denki Bldg, 2-2-3, Marunouchi, Chiyoda-ku, Tokyo 100-0005; tel. (3) 3212-0911; fax (3) 3214-8667; e-mail boitok@gol.com; CEO (Japan) P. SIVARAMAN; br. in Osaka.

Bank Negara Indonesia (Persero): Rm 117-18, Kokusai Bldg, 3-1-1, Marunouchi, Chiyoda-ku, Tokyo 100-0005; tel. (3) 3214-5621; fax (3) 3201-2633; e-mail tky-br@ptbni.co.jp; Gen. Man. SURYO DANISWORO.

Bank One NA (USA): Hibiya Central Bldg, 7th Floor, 1-2-9, Nishi Shinbashi, Minato-ku, Tokyo 105; tel. (3) 3596-8700; fax (3) 3596-8744; Sr Vice-Pres. and Gen. Man. YOSHIO KITAZAWA.

Barclays Bank PLC (UK): Urbannet Otemachi Bldg, 15th Floor, 2-2-2, Otemachi, Chiyoda-ku, Tokyo 100-0004; tel. (3) 3276-5100; fax (3) 3276-5085; CEO ANDY SIMMONDS.

Bayerische Hypo- und Vereinsbank AG (Germany): Otemachi 1st Sq. East Tower, 17th Floor, 1-5-1, Otemachi, Chiyoda-ku, Tokyo 100-0004; tel. (3) 3284-1341; fax (3) 3284-1370; Exec. Dirs Prof. PETER BARON, KENJI AKAGI.

BNP Paribas (France): Tokyo Sankei Bldg, 22rd Floor, 1-7-2, Otemachi, Chiyoda-ku, Tokyo 100-0004; tel. (3) 5290-1000; fax (3) 5290-1111; internet www.bnpparibas.co.jp; CEO (Japan) ERIC MARTIN; Representative in Japan HIROAKI INOUE; br. in Osaka.

Citibank NA (USA): Pan Japan Bldg, 1st Floor, 3-8-17, Akasaka Minato-ku, Tokyo 107; tel. (3) 3584-6321; fax (3) 3584-2924; Country Corporate Officer MASAMOTO YASHIRO; 20 brs.

Commerzbank AG (Germany): Nippon Press Center Bldg, 2nd Floor, 2-2-1, Uchisaiwai-cho, Chiyoda-ku, Tokyo 100-0011; tel. (3) 3502-4371; fax (3) 3508-7545; Gen. Man. NORIO YATOMI.

Crédit Agricole Indosuez (France): Indosuez Bldg, 3-29-1, Kanda Jimbo-cho, Chiyoda-ku, Tokyo 101; tel. (3) 3261-3001; fax (3) 3261-0426; Sr Country Exec. FRANÇOIS BEYER.

Deutsche Bank AG (Germany): Sanno Park Tower, 2-11-1 Nagatacho, Chiyoda-ku, Tokyo 100-6170; tel. (3) 5156-4000; fax (3) 5156-6070; CEO and Chief Country Officer JOHN MACFARLANE; brs in Osaka and Nagoya.

The Hongkong and Shanghai Banking Corpn Ltd (Hong Kong): HSBC Bldg, 3-11-1, Nihonbashi, Chuo-ku, Tokyo 103-0027; tel. (3) 5203-3000; fax (3) 5203-3108; CEO NORMAN A. WILSON; br. in Osaka.

International Commercial Bank of China (Taiwan): Togin Bldg, 1-4-2, Marunouchi, Chiyoda-ku, Tokyo 100; tel. (3) 3211-2501; fax (3) 3216-5686; Sr Vice-Pres. and Gen. Man. SHIOW-SHYONG LAI; br. in Osaka.

JP Morgan Chase Bank (USA): Akasaka Park Bldg, 11th–13th Floors, 5-2-20, Akasaka, Minato-ku, Tokyo 107; tel. (3) 5570-7500; fax (3) 5570-7960; Man. Dir and Gen. Man. NORMAN J. T. SCOTT; br. in Osaka.

Korea Exchange Bank (Republic of Korea): Shin Kokusai Bldg, 3-4-1, Marunouchi, Chiyoda-ku, Tokyo 100; tel. (3) 3216-3561; fax (3) 3214-4491; f. 1967; Acting Gen. Man. CHO YOUNG-HYO; brs in Osaka and Fukuoka.

Lloyds TSB Bank PLC (UK): Akasaka Twin Tower New Bldg, 2-11-7, Akasaka, Minato-ku, Tokyo 107; tel. (3) 3589-7700; fax (3) 3589-7722; Principal Man. (Japan) G. M. HARRIS.

Morgan Guaranty Trust Co of New York (USA): Akasaka Park Bldg, 5-2-20, Akasaka, Minato-ku, Tokyo 107-6151; tel. (3) 5573-1100; Man. Dir TAKESHI FUJIMAKI.

National Bank of Pakistan: S. K. Bldg, 3rd Floor, 2-7-4, Nishi Shinbashi, Minato-ku, Tokyo 105; tel. (3) 3502-0331; fax (3) 3502-0359; f. 1949; Gen. Man. ZIAULLAH KHAN.

Oversea-Chinese Banking Corpn Ltd (Singapore): Akasaka Twin Tower, 15th Floor, 2-17-22, Akasaka, Minato-ku, Tokyo 107-0052; tel. (3) 5570-3421; fax (3) 5570-3426; Gen. Man. ONG SING YIK.

Société Générale (France): Ark Mori Bldg, 1-12-32, Akasaka, Minato-ku, Tokyo 107-6014; tel. (3) 5549-5800; fax (3) 5549-5809; Chief Operating Officer SHOZO NURISHI; br. in Osaka.

Standard Chartered Bank (UK): 21st Floor, Sanno Park Tower, 2-11-1, Nagata-cho, Chiyoda-ku, Tokyo 100-6155; tel. (3) 5511-1200; fax (3) 5511-9333; Chief Exec. (Japan) JULIAN WYNTER.

State Bank of India: 352 South Tower, Yuraku-cho Denki Bldg, 1-7-1, Yuraku-cho, Chiyoda-ku, Tokyo 100-0006; tel. (3) 3284-0085; fax (3) 3201-5750; e-mail sbitok@gol.com; internet www.sbijapan.com; CEO J. K. SINHA; br. in Osaka.

UBS AG: Urbannet Otemachi Bldg, 2-2-2, Otemachi, Chiyoda-ku, Tokyo 100-0004; tel. (3) 5201-8585; fax (3) 5201-8099; Man. MITSURU TSUNEMI.

Union de Banques Arabes et Françaises (UBAF) (France): Sumitomo Jimbocho Bldg, 8th Floor, 3-25, Kanda Jimbocho, Chiyoda-ku, Tokyo 101-0051; tel. (3) 3263-8821; fax (3) 3263-8820; e-mail antoine.homsy@ubaf.fr; Gen. Man. (Japan) ANTOINE R. HOMSY; br. in Osaka.

Westdeutsche Landesbank (Germany): Fukoku Seimei Bldg, 2-2-2, Uchisaiwaicho, Chiyoda-ku, Tokyo 100-0011; tel. (3) 5510-6200; fax (3) 5510-6299; Gen. Man. PETER CLERMONT.

Bankers' Associations

Japanese Bankers Association: 1-3-1, Marunouchi, Chiyoda-ku, Tokyo 100-8216; tel. (3) 3216-3761; fax (3) 3201-5608; internet www.zenginkyo.or.jp; f. 1945; fmrly Federation of Bankers Associations of Japan; 140 full mems, 46 associate mems, 72 special mems; Chair. MASASHI TERANISHI.

Tokyo Bankers Association, Inc: 1-3-1, Marunouchi, Chiyoda-ku, Tokyo 100-8216; tel. (3) 3216-3761; fax (3) 3201-5608; f. 1945; 116 mem. banks; conducts the above Association's administrative business; Chair. MASASHI TERANISHI; Vice-Chair. MASARI UGAI.

National Association of Labour Banks: 2-5-15, Kanda Surugadai, Chiyoda-ku, Tokyo 101-0062; tel. (3) 3295-6721; fax (3) 3295-6752; Pres. TETSUEI TOKUGAWA.

Regional Banks Association of Japan: 3-1-2, Uchikanda, Chiyoda-ku, Tokyo 101-0047; tel. (3) 3252-5171; fax (3) 3254-8664; f. 1936; 64 mem. banks; Chair. SADAAKI HIROSAWA.

Second Association of Regional Banks: 5, Sanban-cho, Chiyoda-ku, Tokyo 102-0075; tel. (3) 3262-2181; fax (3) 3262-2339; f. 1989 (fmrly National Asscn of Sogo Banks); 65 commercial banks; Chair. MASANAO TAKEI.

STOCK EXCHANGES

Fukuoka Securities Exchange: 2-14-2, Tenjin, Chuo-ku, Fukuoka 810-0001; tel. (92) 741-8231; internet www.fse.or.jp; Pres. FUBITO SHIMOMURA.

Hiroshima Stock Exchange: 14-18, Kanayama-cho, Naka-ku, Hiroshima 730-0022; tel. (82) 541-1121; f. 1949; 20 mems; Pres. MASARU NANKO.

Jasdaq Market: 1-14-8 Nihonbashi-Ningyocho, Chuo-ku, Tokyo 103-0013; tel. (3) 5641-1818; internet www.jasdaq.co.jp.

Kyoto Securities Exchange: 66, Tachiuri Nishimachi, Shijodori, Higashitoin Higashi-iru, Shimogyo-ku, Kyoto 600-8007; tel. (75) 221-1171; Pres. IICHI NAKAMURA.

Nagoya Stock Exchange: 3-3-17, Sakae, Naka-ku, Nagoya 460-0008; tel. (52) 262-3172; fax (52) 241-1527; e-mail kikaku@nse.or.jp; internet www.nse.or.jp; f. 1949; Pres. HIROSHI FUJITA; Sr Exec. Dir KAZUNORI ISHIMOTO.

Nasdaq Japan Market: 23rd Floor, Akasaka, Minato-ku, Tokyo 107-6023; tel. (3) 5563-8210; internet www.nasdaq-japan.com.

Niigata Securities Exchange: 1245, Hachibancho, Kami-Okawamaedori, Niigata 951-8068; tel. (252) 222-4181; Pres. KYUUZOU NAKATA.

Osaka Securities Exchange: 1-6-10, Kitahama, Chuo-ku, Osaka 541-0041; tel. (6) 4706-0875; fax (6) 6231-2639; internet www.ose.or.jp; f. 1949; 103 regular mems, 5 special participants; Chair. HIROTARO HIGUCHI; Pres. GORO TATSUMI.

Sapporo Securities Exchange: 5-14-1, Nishi, Minami Ichijo, Chuo-ku, Sapporo 060-0061; tel. (11) 241-6171; Pres. YOSHIRO ITOH.

Tokyo Stock Exchange Inc: 2-1, Nihonbashi, Kabuto-cho, Chuo-ku, Tokyo 103-8220; tel. (3) 3666-0141; fax (3) 3662-0547; internet www.tse.or.jp; f. 1949; 114 participants (incl. 22 foreign participants) (Dec. 2001); Pres. and CEO MASAAKI TSUCHIDA; Exec. Vice-Pres. and CFO YOSHIMASA YAMASHITA.

Supervisory Body

The Securities and Exchange Surveillance Commission: 3-1-1, Kasumigaseki, Chiyoda-ku, Tokyo 100; tel. (3) 3581-7868; fax (3) 5251-2136; f. 1992 for the surveillance of securities and financial futures transactions; Chair. TOSHIHIRO MIZUHARA.

INSURANCE

Principal Life Companies

Aetna Heiwa Life Insurance Co Ltd: 3-2-16, Ginza, Chuo-ku, Tokyo 104-8119; tel. (3) 3563-8111; fax (3) 3374-7114; f. 1907; Pres. BARRY S. HALPERN.

American Family Life Assurance Co of Columbus AFLAC Japan: Shinjuku Mitsui Bldg, 12th Floor, 2-1-1, Nishishinjuku, Shinjuku-ku, Tokyo 163-0456; tel. (3) 3344-2701; fax (3) 0424-41-3001; f. 1974; Chair. YOSHIKI OTAKE; Pres. HIDEFUMI MATSUI.

American Life Insurance Co (Japan): 1-1-3, Marunouchi, Chiyoda-ku, Tokyo 100-0005; tel. (3) 3284-4111; fax (3) 3284-3874; f. 1972; Chair. HIROSHI FUJINO; Pres. SEIKI TOKUNI.

Aoba Life Insurance Co Ltd: 3-6-30, Aobadai, Meguro-ku, Tokyo 153-8523; tel. (3) 3462-0007; fax (3) 3780-8169; Pres. TAKASHI KASAGAMI.

Asahi Mutual Life Insurance Co: 1-7-3, Nishishinjuku, Shinjuku-ku, Tokyo 163-8611; tel. (3) 3342-3111; fax (3) 3346-9397; internet www.asahi-life.co.jp; f. 1888; Pres. YUZURU FUJITA.

AXA Nichidan Life Insurance Co Ltd: 1-2-19 Higashi, Shibuya-ku, Tokyo 150-8020; tel. (3) 3407-6231; fax (3) 5466-7131; internet www.axa-nichidan.co.jp; Pres. MICHAEL W. SHORT.

Cardif Assurance Vie: 3-25-2, Toranomon, Minato-ku, Tokyo 105-0001; tel. (3) 5776-6230; fax (3) 5776-6236; f. 2000; Pres. ATSUSHI SAKAUCHI.

Chiyoda Mutual Life Insurance Co: 2-19-18, Kamimeguro, Meguro-ku, Tokyo 153-8611; tel. (3) 5704-5111; fax (3) 3719-6605; internet www.chiyoda-life.co.jp; f. 1904; declared bankrupt October 2000; Pres. REIJI YONEYAMA.

Chiyodakasai EBISU Life Insurance Co Ltd: Ebisu MF Bldg, 6th Floor, 4-6-1, Ebisu Shibuya-ku, Tokyo 150-0013; tel. (3) 5420-8282; fax (3) 5420-8273; f. 1996; Pres. SHIGEJI MINOSHIMA.

Daido Life Insurance Co: 1-2-1, Edobori Nishi-ku, Osaka City, Osaka 550-0002; tel. (6) 6447-6111; fax (6) 6447-6315; f. 1902; Pres. NAOTERU MIYATO.

Daihyaku Mutual Life Insurance Co: 3-1-4, Shibuya, Shibuya-ku, Tokyo 150-8670; tel. (3) 3498-2294; fax (3) 3400-9313; e-mail kikaku@daihyaku-life.co.jp; internet www.daihyaku-life.co.jp; f. 1914; declared bankrupt June 2000; Pres. MITSUMASA AKIYAMI.

Dai-ichi Mutual Life Insurance Co: 1-13-1, Yuraku-cho, Chiyoda-ku, Tokyo 100-8411; tel. (3) 3216-1211; fax (3) 5221-8139; f. 1902; Chair. TAKAHIDE SAKURAI; Pres. TOMIJIRO MORITA.

Dai-Tokyo Happy Life Insurance Co Ltd: Shijuku Square Tower, 17th Floor, 6-22-1, Nishishinjuku, Shinjuku-ku, Tokyo 163-1131; tel. (3) 5323-6411; fax (3) 5323-6419; f. 1996; Pres. HITOSHI HASUNUMA.

DIY Life Insurance Co Ltd: 5-68-2, Nakano, Nakano-ku, Tokyo 164-0001; tel. (3) 5345-7603; fax (3) 5345-7608; f. 1999; Pres. HITOSHI KASE.

Fuji Life Insurance Co Ltd: 1-18-17, Minamisenba, Chuo-ku, Osaka-shi 542-0081; tel. (6) 6261-0284; fax (6) 6261-0113; f. 1996; Pres. YOSHIAKI YONEMURA.

Fukoku Mutual Life Insurance Co: 2-2-2, Uchisaiwai-cho, Chiyoda-ku, Tokyo 100-0011; tel. (3) 3508-1101; fax (3) 3597-0383; f. 1923; Chair. TAKASHI KOBAYASHI; Pres. TOMOFUMI AKIYAMA.

GE Edison Life Insurance Co: Shibuya Markcity, 1-12-1, Dogenzaka, Shibuya-ku, Tokyo 150-8674; tel. (3) 5457-8100; fax (3) 5457-8017; Chair. MICHAEL D. FRAIZER; Pres. and CEO K. RONE BALDWIN.

Gibraltar Life Insurance Co Ltd: 4-4-1, Nihonbashi, Hongoku-cho, Chuo-ku, Tokyo 103-0021; tel. (3) 3270-8511; fax (3) 3231-8276; internet www.gib-life.co.jp; f. 1947; fmrly Kyoei Life Insurance Co Ltd, declared bankrupt Oct. 2000; Pres. KAZUO MAEDA.

ING Life Insurance Co Ltd: 26th Floor, New Otani Garden Court, 4-1, Kioi-cho, Chiyoda-ku, Tokyo 102-0094; tel. (3) 5210-0300; fax (3) 5210-0430; f. 1985; Pres. MAKOTO CHIBA.

Koa Life Insurance Co Ltd: 3-7-3, Kasumigaseki, Chiyoda-ku, Tokyo 100-0013; tel. (3) 3593-3111; fax (3) 5512-6651; intermet www.koa.co.jp; f. 1996; Pres. AKIO OKADA.

Kyoei Kasai Shinrai Life Insurance Co Ltd: J. City Bldg, 5-8-20, Takamatsu, Nerima-ku, Tokyo 179-0075; tel. (3) 5372-2100; fax (3) 5372-7701; f. 1996; Pres. YOSHIHIRO TOKUMITSU.

Manulife Life Insurance Co: 4-34-1, Kokuryo-cho, Chofu-shi, Tokyo 182-8621; tel. (3) 2442-7120; fax (3) 2442-7977; e-mail trevor_matthews@manulife.com; internet www.manulife.co.jp; f. 1999 (fmrly Manulife Century Life Insurance Co); Pres. and CEO TREVOR MATTHEWS.

Meiji Life Insurance Co: 2-1-1, Marunouchi, Chiyoda-ku, Tokyo 100-0005; tel. (3) 3283-8111; fax (3) 3215-5219; internet www.meiji-life.co.jp; f. 1881; to merge with Yasuda Mutual Life Insurance Co in April 2004; Chair. KENJIRO HATA; Pres. RYOTARO KANEKO.

Mitsui Mirai Life Insurance Co Ltd: Mitsui Kaijyo Nihonbashi Bldg, 1-3-16, Nihonbashi, Chuo-ku, Tokyo 103-0027; tel. (3) 5202-2811; fax (3) 5202-2997; f. 1996; Pres. KATSUYA WATANABE.

Mitsui Mutual Life Insurance Co: 1-2-3, Otemachi, Chiyoda-ku, Tokyo 100-8123; tel. (3) 3211-6111; fax (3) 5252-7265; internet www.mitsui-seimei.co.jp; f. 1927; Chair. KOSHIRO SAKATA; Pres. AKIRA MIYAKE.

Nichido Life Insurance Co Ltd: 4-2-3, Toranomon, Minato-ku, Tokyo 105-0001; tel. (3) 5403-1700; fax (3) 5403-1707; f. 1996; to merge with Tokio Marine Life Insurance Co in 2002; Pres. YOSHIAKI MIYAMOTO.

NICOS Life Insurance Co Ltd: Hongo MK Bldg, 1-28-34, Hongo, Bunkyo-ku, Tokyo 113-8414; tel. (3) 5803-3111; fax (3) 5803-3199; internet www.nicos-life.co.jp; f. 1986; Pres. RENE MULLER.

Nippon Fire Partner Life Insurance Co Ltd: 3-4-2, Tsukiji, Chuo-ku, Tokyo 104-8407; tel. (3) 5565-8080; fax (3) 5565-8365; f. 1996; Pres. HIRONOBU HARA.

Nippon Life Insurance Co (Nissay): 3-5-12, Imabashi, Chuo-ku, Osaka 541-8501; tel. (6) 6209-4500; f. 1889; Chair. JOSEI ITOH; Pres. IKUO UNO.

Orico Life Insurance Co Ltd: Sunshine 60, 26th Floor, 3-1-1, Higashi Ikebukuro, Toshima-ku, Tokyo 170-6026; tel. (3) 5391-3051; fax (3) 5391-3060; f. 1990; Chair. HIROSHI ARAI; Pres. TAKASHI SATO.

ORIX Life Insurance Corpn: Shinjuku Chuo Bldg, 5-17-5, Shinjuku, Shinjuku-ku, Tokyo 160-0022; tel. (3) 5272-2700; fax (3) 5272-2720; f. 1991; Chair. SHOGO KAJINISHI; Pres. SHINOBU SHIRAISHI.

Prudential Life Insurance Co Ltd: 1-7, Kojimachi, Chiyoda-ku, Tokyo 102-0083; tel. (3) 3221-0961; fax (3) 3221-2305; f. 1987; Chair. KIYOFUMI SAKAGUCHI; Pres. ICHIRO KONO.

Saison Life Insurance Co Ltd: Sunshine Sixty Bldg, 39th Floor, 3-1-1, Higashi Ikebukuro, Toshima-ku, Tokyo 170-6067; tel. (3) 3983-6666; fax (3) 2980-0598; internet www.saison-life.co.jp; f. 1975; Chair. and Pres. TOSHIO TAKEUCHI.

Skandia Life Insurance Co (Japan) Ltd: 5-6-6, Hiroo, Shibuya-ku, Tokyo 150-0012; tel. (3) 5488-1500; fax (3) 5488-1501; f. 1996; Pres. SUMIO SHIMOYAMA.

Sony Life Insurance Co Ltd: 1-1-1, Minami-Aoyama, Minato-ku, Tokyo 107-8585; tel. (3) 3475-8811; fax (3) 3475-8914; Chair. TSUNAO HASHIMOTO; Pres. KEN IWAKI.

Sumitomo Life Insurance Co: 7-18-24, Tsukiji, Chuo-ku, Tokyo 104-8430; tel. (3) 5550-1100; fax (3) 5550-1160; f. 1907; Chair. TOSHIOMI URAGAMI; Pres. KOICHI YOSHIDA.

Sumitomo Marine Yu-Yu Life Insurance Co Ltd: 2-27-1, Shinkawa, Chuo-ku, Tokyo 104-0033; tel. (3) 5541-3111; fax (3) 5541-3976; f. 1996; Pres. KATSUHIRO ISHII.

T & D Financial Life Insurance Co: 1-5-2, Uchisaiwai-cho, Chiyoda-ku, Tokyo 100-8555; tel. (3) 3504-2211; fax (3) 3593-0785; f. 1895; fmrly Tokyo Mutual Life Insurance Co; Pres. OSAMU MIZUYAMA.

Taisho Life Insurance Co Ltd: 1-9-1, Yurakucho, Chiyoda-ku, Tokyo 100-0006; tel. (3) 3281-7651; fax (3) 5223-2299; f. 1913; Pres. GEN SHIMURA.

Taiyo Mutual Life Insurance Co: 2-11-2, Nihonbashi, Chuo-ku, Tokyo 103-0027; tel. (3) 3272-6211; fax (3) 3272-1460; Pres. MASAHIRO YOSHIIKE.

Tokio Marine Life Insurance Co Ltd: Tokio Marine New Bldg, 1-2-1, Marunouchi, Chiyoda-ku, Tokyo 100-0005; tel. (3) 5223-2111; fax (3) 5223-2165; internet www.tokiomarine-life.co.jp; f. 1996; to merge with Nichido Life Insurance Co in 2002; Pres. SUKEAKI OHTA.

Yamato Mutual Life Insurance Co: 1-1-7, Uchisaiwai-cho, Chiyoda-ku, Tokyo 100-0011; tel. (3) 3508-3111; fax (3) 3508-3118; f. 1911; Pres. KEIJI NONOMIYA.

Yasuda Kasai Himawari Life Insurance Co Ltd: 2-1-1, Nishi-Shinjuku, Shinjuku-ku, Tokyo 163-0434; tel. (3) 3348-7011; fax (3) 3346-9415; f. 1981 (fmrly INA Himawari Life Insurance Co Ltd); Chair. (vacant); Pres. MAKOTO YOSHIDA.

Yasuda Mutual Life Insurance Co: 1-9-1, Nishi-Shinjuku, Shinjuku-ku, Tokyo 169-8701; tel. (3) 3342-7111; fax (3) 3349-8104; f. 1880; to merge with Meiji Life Insurance Co in April 2004; Chair. YUJI OSHIMA; Pres. MIKIHIKO MIYAMOTO.

Zurich Life Insurance Co Ltd: Shinanomachi Rengakan, 35, Shinanomachi, Shinjuku-ku, Tokyo 160-0016; tel. (3) 5361-2700; fax (3) 5361-2728; f. 1996; Pres. KENICHI NOGAMI.

Principal Non-Life Companies

ACE Insurance: Arco Tower, 1-8-1, Shimomeguro, Meguro-ku, Tokyo 153-0064; tel. (3) 5740-0600; fax (3) 5740-0608; internet www.ace-insurance.co.jp; f. 1999; Chair. FUMIO TOKUHIRA; Pres. TAKASHI OHKAWA.

Allianz Fire and Marine Insurance Japan Ltd: MITA N. N. Bldg, 4th Floor, 4-1-23, Shiba, Minato-ku, Tokyo 108-0014; tel. (3) 5442-6500; fax (3) 5442-6509; e-mail admin@allianz.co.jp; f. 1990; Chair. HEINZ DOLLBERG; Pres. ALEXANDER ANKEL.

The Asahi Fire and Marine Insurance Co Ltd: 2-6-2, Kaji-cho, Chiyoda-ku, Tokyo 101-8655; tel. (3) 3254-2211; fax (3) 3254-2296; e-mail asahifmi@blue.ocn.ne.jp; f. 1951; Pres. MORIYA NOGUCHI.

AXA Non-Life Insurance Co Ltd: Ariake Frontier Bldg, Tower A, 3-1-25, Ariake Koto-ku, Tokyo 135-0063; tel. (3) 3570-8900; fax (3) 3570-8911; f. 1998; Pres. GUY MARCILLAT.

The Chiyoda Fire and Marine Insurance Co Ltd: 1-28-1, Ebisu, Shibuya-ku, Tokyo 150-8488; tel. (3) 5424-9288; fax (3) 5424-9382; bought by Dai-Tokyo Fire and Marine Insurance Co in 2000, to combine in April 2001; f. 1897; Pres. KOJI FUKUDA.

The Daido Fire and Marine Insurance Co Ltd: 1-12-1, Kumoji, Naha-shi, Okinawa 900-8586; tel. (98) 867-1161; fax (98) 862-8362; f. 1971; Pres. MUNEMASA URA.

The Daiichi Mutual Fire and Marine Insurance Co: Ochanumizu-Kyoun-Building, 2-2 Kanda Surugadai, Chiyoda-ku, Tokyo 101-0062; tel. (3) 3518-6727; fax (3) 3518-6732; f. 1949; dissolved March 2001.

The Dai-ichi Property and Casualty Insurance Co Ltd: 1-2-10, Hirakawa-cho, Chiyoda-ku, Tokyo 102-0093; tel. (3) 5213-3124; fax (3) 5213-3306; f. 1996; Pres. TSUYOSHI SHINOHARA.

The Dai-Tokyo Fire and Marine Insurance Co Ltd: 3-25-3, Yoyogi, Shibuya-ku, Tokyo 151-8530; tel. (3) 5371-6122; fax (3) 5371-6248; internet www.daitokyo.index.or.jp; f. 1918; bought Chiyoda Fire and Marine Insurance Co in 2000; Chair. HAJIME OZAWA; Pres. AKIRA SESHIMO.

The Dowa Fire and Marine Insurance Co Ltd: St Luke's Tower, 8-1, Akashi-cho, Chuo-ku, Tokyo 104-8556; tel. (3) 5550-0254; fax (3) 5550-0318; internet www.dowafire.co.jp; f. 1944; Chair. MASAO OKAZAKI; Pres. SHUICHIRO SUDO.

The Fuji Fire and Marine Insurance Co Ltd: 1-18-11, Minamisenba, Chuo-ku, Osaka 542-8567; tel. (6) 6271-2741; fax (6) 6266-7115; internet www.fujikasai.co.jp; f. 1918; Pres. YASUO ODA.

The Japan Earthquake Reinsurance Co Ltd: Kobuna-cho, Fuji Plaza, 4th Floor, 8-1, Nihonbashi, Kobuna-cho, Chuo-ku, Tokyo 103-0024; tel. (3) 3664-6107; fax (3) 3664-6169; e-mail kanri@nihonjishin.co.jp; f. 1966; Pres. KAZUMOTO ADACHI.

JI Accident & Fire Insurance Co Ltd: A1 Bldg, 20-5, Ichibancho, Chiyoda-ku, Tokyo 102-0082; tel. (3) 3237-2045; fax (3) 3237-2250; internet www.jihoken.co.jp; f. 1989; Pres. TSUKASA IMURA.

The Kyoei Mutual Fire and Marine Insurance Co: 1-18-6, Shimbashi, Minato-ku, Tokyo 105-8604; tel. (3) 3504-2335; fax (3) 3508-7680; e-mail reins.intl@kyoeikasai.co.jp; internet www.kyoeikasai.co.jp; f. 1942; Chair. HIDEJI SUZUKI; Pres. WATARU OZAWA.

Meiji General Insurance Co Ltd: 2-11-1, Kanda-tsukasa-cho, Chiyoda-ku, Tokyo 101-0048; tel. (3) 3257-3141; fax (3) 3257-3295; e-mail nobuo.shimoda@meiji-life.co.jp; internet meiji-general.aaapc.co.jp; f. 1996; Pres. SEISUKE ADACHI.

Mitsui Marine and Fire Insurance Co Ltd: 3-9, Kanda Surugadai, Chiyoda-ku, Tokyo 101-8011; tel. (3) 3259-3111; fax (3) 3291-5467; internet www.mitsuimarine.co.jp; f. 1918; Pres. TAKEO INOKUCHI.

Mitsui Seimei General Insurance Co Ltd: 2-1-1, Toranomon, Minato-ku, Tokyo 105-0001; tel. (3) 3224-2830; fax (3) 3224-2677; f. 1996; Pres. KIYOSHI MATSUOKA.

The Nichido Fire and Marine Insurance Co Ltd: 5-3-16, Ginza, Chuo-ku, Tokyo 104-0061; tel. (3) 3289-1066; fax (3) 3574-0646; e-mail nichido@mu2.so-net.ne.jp; internet www.mediagalaxy.co.jp/nichido; f. 1914; Chair. IKUO EGASHIRA; Pres. TAKASHI AIHARA.

The Nipponkoa Insurance Co Ltd: 2-2-10, Nihonbashi, Chuo-ku, Tokyo 103-8255; tel. (3) 3272-8111; fax (3) 5229-3385; internet www.nihonkasai.co.jp; f. 1892 (fmrly The Nippon Fire and Marine Insurance Co Ltd before merging with The Koa Fire and Marine Insurance Co Ltd); Pres. and CEO KEN MATSUZAWA.

The Nissan Fire and Marine Insurance Co Ltd: 2-9-5, Kita-Aoyama, Minato-ku, Tokyo 107-8654; tel. (3) 3746-6516; fax (3) 3470-1308; e-mail webmas@nissan-ins.co.jp; internet www.nissan-ins.co.jp; f. 1911; Chair. FUMIYA KAWATE; Pres. RYUTARO SATO.

Nissay General Insurance Co Ltd: Shinjuku NS Bldg, 25th Floor, 2-4-1, Nishi-Shinjuku, Shinjuku-ku, Tokyo 163-0888; tel. (3) 5325-7932; fax (3) 5325-8149; f. 1996; Pres. TADAO NISHIOKA.

The Nisshin Fire and Marine Insurance Co Ltd: 2-3 Kanda Surugadai, Chiyoda-ku, Tokyo 100-8329; tel. (3) 5282-5534; fax (3) 5282-5582; e-mail nisshin@mb.infoweb.ne.jp; internet www.nisshinfire.co.jp; f. 1908; Pres. MICHIO NODA.

Saison Automobile and Fire Insurance Co Ltd: Sunshine 60 Bldg, 3-1-1, Higashi Ikebukuro, Toshima-ku, Tokyo 170-6068; tel. (3) 3988-2572; fax (3) 3980-7367; internet www.ins-saison.co.jp; f. 1982; Pres. Tomonori Kanai.

Secom General Insurance Co Ltd: 2-6-2, Hirakawa-cho, Chiyoda-ku, Tokyo 103-8645; tel. (3) 5216-6129; fax (3) 5216-6149; internet www.secom-sonpo.co.jp; Pres. Seiji Yamanaka.

Sony Assurance Inc.: Aromia Square 11F, 5-37-1, Kamata, Ota-ku, Tokyo 144-8721; tel. (3) 5744-0300; fax (3) 5744-0480; internet www.sonysonpo.co.jp; f. 1999; Pres. Shinieh Yamamoto.

The Sumi-Sei General Insurance Co Ltd: Sumitomo Life Yotsuya Bldg, 8-2, Honshio-cho, Shinjuku-ku, Tokyo 160-0003; tel. (3) 5360-6229; fax (3) 5360-6991; f. 1996; Chair. Hideo Nishimoto; Pres. Hideki Ishii.

The Sumitomo Marine and Fire Insurance Co Ltd: 2-27-2, Shinkawa, Chuo-ku, Tokyo 104-8252; tel. (3) 3297-6663; fax (3) 3297-6882; internet www.sumitomomarine.co.jp; f. 1944; Chair. Takashi Onoda; Pres. Hiroyuki Uemura.

The Taisei Fire and Marine Insurance Co Ltd: 4-2-1, Kudan-Kita, Chiyoda-ku, Tokyo 102-0073; tel. (3) 3222-3096; fax (3) 3234-4073; e-mail saiho@taiseikasai.co.jp; internet www.taiseikasai.co.jp; f. 1950; Pres. Ichiro Ozawa.

Taiyo Fire and Marine Insurance Co Ltd: 7-7, Niban-cho, Chiyoda-ku, Tokyo 102-0084; tel. (3) 5226-3117; fax (3) 5226-3133; f. 1951; Chair. Yuji Yamashita; Pres. Tsunaie Kanie.

The Toa Reinsurance Co Ltd: 3-6, Kanda Surugadai, Chiyoda-ku, Tokyo 101-8703; tel. (3) 3253-3177; fax (3) 3253-5298; f. 1940; Dir Takaya Imashimizu.

The Tokio Marine and Fire Insurance Co Ltd (Tokio Kaijo): 1-2-1, Marunouchi, Chiyoda-ku, Tokyo 100-8050; tel. (3) 3285-1900; fax (3) 5223-3040; internet www.tokiomarine.co.jp; f. 1879; Chair. Shunji Kono; Pres. Koukei Higuchi.

The Yasuda Fire and Marine Insurance Co Ltd: 1-26-1, Nishi-Shinjuku, Shinjuku-ku, Tokyo 160-8338; tel. (3) 3349-3111; fax (3) 5381-7406; internet www.yasuda.co.jp; f. 1887; Chair. Koichi Ariyoshi; Pres. Hiroshi Hirano.

The Yasuda General Insurance Co Ltd: Shinjuku MAYNDS Tower, 29th Floor, 2-1-1, Yoyogi, Shibuya-ku, Tokyo 151-0053; tel. (3) 5352-8129; fax (3) 5352-8213; e-mail uwdept@mx7.mesh.ne.jp; f. 1996; Chair. Shigeo Fujino; Pres. Ieji Yoshioka.

The Post Office also operates life insurance and annuity plans.

Insurance Associations

Japan Trade and Investment Insurance Organization (Boeki Hoken Kiko): 6th Floor, 2-8-6, Nishi-Shinjuku, Minato-ku, Tokyo 105-0003; tel. (3) 3580-0321; internet www.jtio.or.jp; Pres. Yukio Otsu.

The Life Insurance Association of Japan (Seimei Hoken Kyokai): New Kokusai Bldg, 3-4-1, Marunouchi, Chiyoda-ku, Tokyo 100-0005; tel. (3) 3286-2652; fax (3) 3286-2630; internet www.seiho.or.jp; f. 1908; 42 mem. cos; Chair. Shinichi Yokoyama; Senior Man. Dir Shigeru Suwa.

The Marine and Fire Insurance Association of Japan Inc (Nihon Songai Hoken Kyokai): Non-Life Insurance Bldg, 2-9, Kanda Awaji-cho, Chiyoda-ku, Tokyo 101-8335; tel. (3) 3255-1437; fax (3) 3255-1234; e-mail kokusai@sonpo.or.jp; internet www.sonpo.or.jp; f. 1946; 26 mems; Chair. Kunio Ishihara; Exec. Dir Eiji Ni.

Non-Life Insurance Rating Organization of Japan: Banzai Bldg, 2-31-19, Shiba, Minato-ku, Tokyo 105-0014; tel. (3) 3233-4755; fax (3) 5258-7658; e-mail choki@grp.nliro.or.jp; internet www.nliro.or.jp; f. 1964; 45 mems (July 2001); Chair. Akio Morishima; Senior Exec. Dir. Masahiro Ishii.

Trade and Industry

CHAMBERS OF COMMERCE AND INDUSTRY

The Japan Chamber of Commerce and Industry (Nippon Shoko Kaigi-sho): 3-2-2, Marunouchi, Chiyoda-ku, Tokyo 100-0005; tel. (3) 3283-7851; fax (3) 3216-6497; e-mail info@jcci.or.jp; internet www.jcci.or.jp/home-e; f. 1922; the cen. org. of all chambers of commerce and industry in Japan; mems 521 local chambers of commerce and industry; Chair. Kosaku Inaba; Pres. Shoichi Tanimura.

Principal chambers include:

Kobe Chamber of Commerce and Industry: 6-1, Minatojima-nakamachi, Chuo-ku, Kobe 650-8543; tel. (78) 303-5806; fax (78) 306-2348; e-mail info@kcci.hyogo-iic.ne.jp; f. 1878; 12,700 mems; Chair. Hiroshi Ohba; Pres. Hiroshi Miyamichi.

Kyoto Chamber of Commerce and Industry: 240, Shoshoi-cho, Ebisugawa-agaru, Karasumadori, Nakakyo-ku, Kyoto 604-0862; tel. (75) 212-6450; fax (75) 251-0743; e-mail kyoto@kyo.or.jp; f. 1882; 13,008 mems; Chair. Kazuo Inamori; Pres. Osamu Kobori.

Nagoya Chamber of Commerce and Industry: 2-10-19, Sakae, Naka-ku, Nagoya, Aichi 460-8422; tel. (52) 223-5722; fax (52) 232-5751; f. 1881; 20,622 mems; Chair. Seitaro Taniguchi; Pres. Yoshiki Kobayashi.

Naha Chamber of Commerce and Industry: 2-2-10, Kume Naha, Okinawa; tel. (98) 868-3758; fax (98) 866-9834; e-mail cci-naha@cosmos.ne.jp; f. 1927; 4,874 mems; Chair. Akira Sakima; Pres. Kosei Yonemura.

Osaka Chamber of Commerce and Industry: 2-8, Hommachi-bashi, Chuo-ku, Osaka 540-0029; tel. (6) 6944-6400; fax (6) 6944-6248; e-mail intl@osaka.cci.or.jp; internet www.osaka.cci.or.jp; f. 1878; 36,666 mems; Chair. Wa Tashiro; Pres. Takao Ohno.

Tokyo Chamber of Commerce and Industry: 3-2-2, Marunouchi, Chiyoda-ku, Tokyo 100-0005; tel. (3) 3283-7756; fax (3) 3216-6497; e-mail webmaster@tokyo-cci.or.jp; f. 1878; 118,642 mems; Chair. Kosaku Inaba; Pres. Shoichi Tanimura.

Yokohama Chamber of Commerce and Industry: Sangyo Boueki Center Bldg, 8th Floor, Yamashita-cho, Naka-ku, Yokohama 231-8524; tel. (45) 671-7400; fax (45) 671-7410; e-mail info@yokohama-cci.or.jp; f. 1880; 14,965 mems; Chair. Masayoshi Takanashi; Pres. Namio Oba.

INDUSTRIAL AND TRADE ASSOCATIONS

General

The Association for the Promotion of International Trade, Japan (JAPIT): 1-26-5, Toranomon, Minato-ku, Tokyo; tel. (3) 3506-8261; fax (3) 3506-8260; f. 1954 to promote trade with the People's Repub. of China; 700 mems; Chair. Yoshio Nakata; Pres. Yoshio Sakurauchi.

Industry Club of Japan: 1-4-6, Marunouchi, Chiyoda-ku, Tokyo; tel. (3) 3281-1711; f. 1917 to develop closer relations between industrialists at home and abroad and promote expansion of Japanese business activities; c. 1,600 mems; Pres. Gaishi Hiraiwa; Exec. Dir Kouichirou Shinno.

Japan Commercial Arbitration Association: Taishoseimei Hibiya Bldg, 1-9-1, Yurakucho, Chiyoda-ku, Tokyo 100-1006; tel. (3) 3287-3061; fax (3) 3287-3064; f. 1950; 1,012 mems; provides facilities for mediation, conciliation and arbitration in international trade disputes; Pres. Nobuo Yamaguchi.

Japan External Trade Organization (JETRO): 2-2-5, Toranomon, Minato-ku, Tokyo 105-8466; tel. (3) 3582-5511; fax (3) 3582-5662; e-mail seh@jetro.go.jp; internet www.jetro.go.jp; f. 1958; information for international trade, investment, import promotion, exhibitions of foreign products; Chair. and CEO Osamu Watanabe; Pres. Hiroshi Tsukamoto.

Japan Federation of Economic Organizations (KEIDANREN): 1-9-4, Otemachi, Chiyoda-ku, Tokyo 100-8188; tel. (3) 3279-1411; fax (3) 5255-6253; f. 1946; to merge with Japan Federation of Employers' Associations (Nikkeiren) by May 2001; private non-profit asscn researching domestic and international economic problems and providing policy recommendations; mems: 120 industrial orgs, 1,007 corpns (1999); Chair. Takashi Imai; Pres. Kozo Uchida.

Japan Federation of Smaller Enterprise Organizations (JFSEO) (Nippon Chusokigyo Dantai Renmei): 2-8-4, Nihonbashi, Kayaba-cho, Chuo-ku, Tokyo 103-0025; tel. (3) 3669-6862; f. 1948; 18 mems and c. 1,000 co-operative socs; Pres. Masataka Toyoda; Chair. of Int. Affairs Seiichi Ono.

Japan General Merchandise Exporters' Association: 2-4-1, Hamamatsu-cho, Minato-ku, Tokyo; tel. (3) 3435-3471; fax (3) 3434-6739; f. 1953; 40 mems; Pres. Tadayoshi Nakazawa.

Japan Productivity Center for Socio-Economic Development (JPC-SED) (Shakai Keizai Seisansei Honbu): 3-1-1, Shibuya, Shibuya-ku, Tokyo 150-8307; tel. (3) 3409-1112; fax (3) 3409-1986; f. 1994 following merger between Japan Productivity Center and Social Economic Congress of Japan; 10,000 mems; concerned with management problems and research into productivity; Chair. Masao Kamei; Pres. Ario Orita.

Keizai Doyukai (Japan Association of Corporate Executives): Palace Bldg, 8th Floor, 1-1-1, Marunouchi, Chiyoda-ku, Tokyo 100-0005; tel. (3) 3211-1271; fax (3) 3212-3774; e-mail contact@doyukai.or.jp; internet www.doyukai.or.jp; f. 1946; mems: c. 1,400; corporate executives concerned with national and international economic and social policies; Chair. Yotaro Kobayashi.

Nihon Boeki-Kai (Japan Foreign Trade Council, Inc): World Trade Center Bldg, 6th Floor, 2-4-1, Hamamatsu-cho, Minato-ku, Tokyo 105-6106; tel. (3) 3435-5952; fax (3) 3435-5969; e-mail mail@jftc.or.jp; internet www.jftc.or.jp; f. 1947; 192 mems; Chair. Kenji Miyahara; Exec. Man. Dir Keisuke Takanashi; Man. Dir Hisao Ikegami.

Chemicals

Federation of Pharmaceutical Manufacturers' Associations of Japan: Tokyo Yakugyo Bldg, 2-1-5, Nihonbashi Honcho, Chuo-ku, Tokyo 103-0023; tel. (3) 3270-0581; fax (3) 3241-2090; Pres. TADASHI SUZUKI.

Japan Chemical Industry Association: Tokyo Club Bldg, 3-2-6, Kasumigaseki, Chiyoda-ku, Tokyo 100-0013; tel. (3) 3580-0751; fax (3) 3580-0764; internet www.nikkakyo.org; f. 1948; 266 mems; Pres. AKIO KOSAI.

Japan Cosmetic Industry Association: Hatsumei Bldg, 2-9-14, Toranomon, Minato-ku, Tokyo 105-0001; tel. (3) 3502-0576; fax (3) 3502-0829; f. 1959; 687 mem. cos; Chair. REIJIRO KOBAYASHI.

Japan Gas Association: 1-15-12, Toranomon, Minato-ku, Tokyo 105-0001; tel. (3) 3502-0116; fax (3) 3502-3676; f. 1947; Chair. SHINICHIRO RYOKI; Vice-Chair. and Sr Man. Dir KOSHIRO GODA.

Japan Perfumery and Flavouring Association: Saeki No. 3 Bldg, 3rd Floor, 37 Kandakony-cho, Chiyoda-ku, Tokyo 101-0035; tel. and fax (3) 3526-7855; f. 1947; Chair. TOKAJIRO HASEGAWA.

Photo-Sensitized Materials Manufacturers' Association: JCII Bldg, 25, Ichiban-cho, Chiyoda-ku, Tokyo 102-0082; tel. (3) 5276-3561; fax (3) 5276-3563; f. 1948; Pres. MASAYUKI MUNEYUKI.

Fishing and Pearl Cultivation

Japan Fisheries Association (Dainippon Suisankai): Sankaido Bldg, 1-9-13, Akasaka, Minato-ku, Tokyo 107-0052; tel. (3) 3585-6683; fax (3) 3582-2337; internet www.suisankai.or.jp; Pres. HIROYA SANO.

Japan Pearl Export and Processing Co-operative Association: 3-7, Kyobashi, Chuo-ko, Tokyo; f. 1951; 130 mems.

Japan Pearl Exporters' Association: 122, Higashi-machi, Chuo-ku, Kobe; tel. (78) 331-4031; fax (78) 331-4345; e-mail jpeakobe@lime.ocn.ne.jp; internet www.japan-pearl.com; f. 1954; 56 mems; Pres. HIDEO KANAI.

Paper and Printing

Japan Federation of Printing Industries: 1-16-8, Shintomi, Chuo-ku, Tokyo 104; tel. (3) 3553-6051; fax (3) 3553-6079; Pres. HIROMICHI FUJITA.

Japan Paper Association: Kami Parupu Bldg, 3-9-11, Ginza, Chuo-ku, Tokyo 104-8139; tel. (3) 3248-4801; fax (3) 3248-4826; internet www.jpa.gr.jp; f. 1946; 54 mems; Chair. MASAO KOBAYASHI; Pres. KIYOSHI SAKAI.

Japan Paper Exporters' Association: Kami Parupu Bldg, 3-9-11, Ginza, Chuo-ku, Tokyo 104-8139; tel. (3) 3248-4831; fax (3) 3248-4834; e-mail japex@green.an.egg.or.jp; f. 1952; 37 mems; Chair. KENTARO NAGAOKA.

Japan Paper Importers' Association: Kami Parupu Bldg, 3-9-11, Ginza, Chuo-ku, Tokyo 104-8139; tel. (3) 3248-4832; fax (3) 3248-4834; e-mail japim@yacht.ocn.ne.jp; f. 1981; 27 mems; Chair. NOBUO KATSUMATA.

Japan Paper Products Manufacturers' Association: 4-2-6, Kotobuki, Taito-ku, Tokyo; tel. (3) 3543-2411; f. 1949; Exec. Dir KIYOSHI SATOH.

Mining and Petroleum

Asbestos Cement Products Association: Takahashi Bldg, 7-10-8, Ginza, Chuo-ku, Tokyo; tel. (3) 3571-1359; f. 1937; Chair. KOSHIRO SHIMIZU.

Japan Cement Association: Hattori Bldg, 1-10-3, Kyobashi, Chuo-ku, Tokyo 104-0031; tel. (3) 3561-8632; fax (3) 3567-8570; f. 1948; 20 mem. cos; Chair. KAZUTSUGU HIRAGA; Exec. Man. Dir HIROFUMI YAMASHITA.

Japan Coal Association: Hibiya Park Bldg, 1-8-1, Yuraku-cho, Chiyoda-ku, Tokyo 100; tel. (3) 3271-3481; fax (3) 3214-0585; Chair. TADASHI HARADA.

Japan Mining Industry Association: Shuwa Toranomon Bldg, No. 3, 1-21-8 Toranomon, Minato-ku, Tokyo 105-0001; tel. (3) 3502-7451; fax (3) 3591-9841; f. 1948; 60 mem. cos; Chair. AKIRA NISHIKAWA; Pres. A. SHINOZAKI; Dir-Gen. H. HIYAMA.

Japan Petrochemical Industry Association: 2nd Floor, 2-1-1, Uchisaiwai-cho, Chiyoda-ku, Tokyo 100-0011; tel. (3) 3501-2151; internet www.jpca.or.jp; Chair. MITSUO OHASHI.

Japan Petroleum Development Association: Keidanren Bldg, 1-9-4, Otemachi, Chiyoda-ku, Tokyo 100; tel. (3) 3279-5841; fax (3) 3279-5844; f. 1961; Chair. TAMOTSU SHOYA.

Metals

Japan Aluminium Association (JAA): Tsukamoto-Sozan Bldg, 4-2-15, Ginza, Chuo-ku, Tokyo 104-0061; tel. (3) 3538-0221; fax (3) 3538-0233; f. 1999 by merger of Japan Aluminium Federation and Japan Light Metal Association; Chair. SHIGESATO SATO.

Japan Brass Makers' Association: 1-12-22, Tsukiji, Chuo-ku, Tokyo 104-0045; tel. (3) 3542-6551; fax (3) 3542-6556; e-mail jbmajwcc@copper-brass.gr.jp; internet www.copper-brass.gr.jp; f. 1948; 62 mems; Pres. S. SATO; Man. Dir J. HATANO.

Japan Iron and Steel Exporters' Association: Tekko Kaikan Bldg, 3-2-10, Nihonbashi Kayaba-cho, Chuo-ku, Tokyo 103-0025; tel. (3) 3669-4818; fax (3) 3661-0798; f. 1953; mems 17 mfrs, 27 dealers; Chair. AKIRA CHIHAYA.

The Japan Iron and Steel Federation: Keidanren Bldg, 1-9-4, Otemachi, Chiyoda-ku, Tokyo 100-0004; tel. (3) 3279-3612; fax (3) 3245-0144; internet www.jisf.or.jp; f. 1948; Chair. AKIRA CHIHAYA.

Japan Stainless Steel Association: Tekko Bldg, 3-2-10, Nihonbashi Kayaba-cho, Chuo-ku, Tokyo 103; tel. (3) 3669-4431; fax (3) 3669-4431; e-mail yabe@jssa.gr.jp; internet www.jssa.gr.jp; Pres. MIKIO KATOH; Exec. Dir TAKEO YABE.

The Kozai Club: Tekko Bldg, 3-2-10, Nihonbashi Kayaba-cho, Chuo-ku, Tokyo 103-0025; tel. (3) 3669-4815; fax (3) 3667-0245; f. 1947; mems 39 mfrs, 69 dealers; Chair. AKIRA CHIHAYA.

Steel Castings and Forgings Association of Japan (JSCFA): Uchikanda DNK Bldg, 2-15-2, Uchikanda, Chiyoda-ku, Tokyo 101-0047; tel. (3) 3255-3961; fax (3) 3255-3965; e-mail jscfa@aqua.famille.ne.jp; f. 1972; mems 48 cos, 54 plants; Exec. Dir SADAO HARA.

Machinery and Precision Equipment

Electronic Industries Association of Japan: 3-2-2, Marunouchi, Chiyoda-ku, Tokyo 100-0005; tel. (3) 3213-5861; fax (3) 3213-5863; e-mail pao@eiaj.or.jp; internet www.eiaj.or.jp; f. 1948; 540 mems; Chair. FUMIO SATO.

Japan Camera Industry Association: JCII Bldg, 25, Ichibancho, Chiyoda-ku, Tokyo 102-0082; tel. (3) 5276-3891; fax (3) 5276-3893; internet www.photo-jcia.gr.jp; f. 1954; Pres. MASATOSHI KISHIMOTO.

Japan Clock and Watch Association: Kudan Sky Bldg, 1-12-11, Kudan-kita, Chiyoda-ku, Tokyo 102-0073; tel. (3) 5276-3411; fax (3) 5276-3414; internet www.jcwa.or.jp; Chair. HIROSHI HARUTA.

Japan Electric Association: 1-7-1, Yuraku-cho, Chiyoda-ku, Tokyo 100-0006; tel. (3) 3216-0551; fax (3) 3214-6005; f. 1921; 4,610 mems; Pres. TATSUO KAWAI.

Japan Electric Measuring Instruments Manufacturers' Association (JEMIMA): 1-9-10, Toranomon, Minato-ku, Tokyo 105-0001; tel. (3) 3502-0601; fax (3) 3502-0600; e-mail watanabe@jemima.or.jp; internet www.jemima.or.jp; 125 mems; Sec. Gen. KATSUHIKO WATANABE.

Japan Electrical Manufacturers' Association: 2-4-15, Nagata-cho, Chiyoda-ku, Tokyo 100-0014; tel. (3) 3581-4841; fax (3) 3593-3198; internet www.jema-net.or.jp; f. 1948; 245 mems; Chair. TAIZO NISHIMURO.

Japan Energy Association: Houwa Mita Tsunasaka Bldg, 2-7-7, Mita, Minato-ku, Tokyo 108-0073; tel. (3) 3451-1651; fax (3) 3451-1360; e-mail common@jea-wec.or.jp; internet www.jea-wec.or.jp; f. 1950; 142 mems; Chair. SHIGE-ETSU MIYAHARA; Exec. Dir HAJIME MURATA.

Japan Machine Tool Builders' Association: Kikai Shinko Bldg, 3-5-8, Shiba Koen, Minato-ku, Tokyo 105-0011; tel. (3) 3434-3961; fax (3) 3434-3763; f. 1951; 112 mems; Chair. TOYO KATO; Exec. Dir S. ABE.

Japan Machinery Center for Trade and Investment (JMC): Kikai Shinko Bldg, 3-5-8, Shiba Koen, Minato-ku, Tokyo 105-0011; tel. (3) 3431-9507; fax (3) 3436-6455; Pres. ISAO YONEKURA.

The Japan Machinery Federation: Kikai Shinko Bldg, 3-5-8, Shiba Koen, Minato-ku, Tokyo 105-0011; tel. (3) 3434-5381; fax (3) 3434-2666; f. 1952; Pres. SHOICHI SADA; Exec. Vice-Pres. SHINICHI NAKANISHI.

Japan Machinery Importers' Association: Koyo Bldg, 8th Floor, 1-2-11, Toranomon, Minato-ku, Tokyo 105-0001; tel. (3) 3503-9736; fax (3) 3503-9779; f. 1957; 94 mems; Pres. ISAO YONEKURA.

Japan Microscope Manufacturers' Association: c/o Olympus Optical Co Ltd, 2-43-2, Hatagaya, Shibuya-ku, Tokyo 151-0072; tel. (3) 3377-2139; fax (3) 3377-2139; e-mail jmma@olympus.co.jp; f. 1954; 31 mems; Chair. T. SHIMOYAMA.

Japan Motion Picture Equipment Industrial Association: Kikai Shinko Bldg, 3-5-8, Shiba Koen, Minato-ku, Tokyo 105; tel. (3) 3434-3911; fax (3) 3434-3912; Pres. MASAO SHIKATA; Gen. Sec. TERUHIRO KATO.

Japan Optical Industry Association: Kikai Shinko Bldg, 3-5-8, Shiba Koen, Minato-ku, Tokyo 105-0011; tel. (3) 3431-7073; f. 1946; 200 mems; Chair. SHIGEO ONO; Exec. Dir M. SUZUKI.

The Japan Society of Industrial Machinery Manufacturers: Kikai Shinko Bldg, 3-5-8, Shiba Koen, Minato-ku, Tokyo 105-0011;

tel. (3) 3434-6821; fax (3) 3434-4767; e-mail obd@jsim.or.jp; internet www.jsim.or.jp; f. 1948; 213 mems; Exec. Man. Dir KOJI FUJISAKI; Pres. KENTARO AIKAWA.

Japan Textile Machinery Association: Kikai Shinko Bldg, Room 310, 3-5-8, Shiba Koen, Minato-ku, Tokyo 105; tel. (3) 3434-3821; fax (3) 3434-3043; f. 1951; Pres. JUNICHI MURATA.

Textiles

Central Raw Silk Association of Japan: 1-9-4, Yuraku-cho, Chiyoda-ku, Tokyo; tel. (3) 3214-5777; fax (3) 3214-5778.

Japan Chemical Fibers Association: Seni Kaikan, 3-1-11, Nihonbashi-Honcho, Chuo-ku, Tokyo 103-0023; tel. (3) 3241-2311; fax (3) 3246-0823; internet www.fcc.co.jp/JCFA; f. 1948; 41 mems, 9 assoc. mems; Pres. KATSUHIKO HIRAI; Dir-Gen. KUNIO YAGI.

Japan Cotton and Staple Fibre Weavers' Association: 1-8-7, Nishi-Azabu, Minato-ku, Tokyo; tel. (3) 3403-9671.

Japan Silk Spinners' Association: f. 1948; 95 mem. firms; Chair. ICHIJI OHTANI.

Japan Spinners' Association: Mengyo Kaikan Bldg, 2-5-8, Bingomachi, Chuo-ku, Osaka 541-0051; tel. (6) 6231-8431; fax (6) 6229-1590; e-mail spinas@cotton.or.jp; internet www.jsa-jp.org/; f. 1948; Exec. Dir HARUTA MUTO.

Transport Machinery

Japan Association of Rolling Stock Industries: Awajicho Suny Bldg, 1-2, Kanda-Sudacho, Chiyoda-ku, Tokyo 101-0041; tel. (3) 3257-1901.

Japan Auto Parts Industries Association: 1-16-15, Takanawa, Minato-ku, Tokyo 108-0074; tel. (3) 3445-4211; fax (3) 3447-5372; e-mail japiaint@green.am.egg.or.jp; f. 1948; 530 mem. firms; Chair. TSUNEO ISHIMARU; Exec. Dir K. SHIBASAKI.

Japan Automobile Manufacturers Association, Inc (JAMA): Otemachi Bldg, 1-6-1, Otemachi, Chiyoda-ku, Tokyo 100-0004; tel. (3) 5219-6660; fax (3) 3287-2073; e-mail kaigai_tky@mta.jama.or.jp; internet www.jama.or.jp; f. 1967; 14 mem. firms; Chair. YOSHIHIDE MUNEKUNI; Pres. TAKAO SUZUKI.

Japan Bicycle Manufacturers' Association: 1-9-3, Akasaka, Minato-ku, Tokyo 107; tel. (3) 3583-3123; fax (3) 3589-3125; f. 1955.

Japan Ship Exporters' Association: Nippon-Zaidan Bldg, 1-15-16, Toranomon, Minato-ku, Tokyo 105-0001; tel. (3) 3502-2094; fax (3) 3508-2058; e-mail postmaster@jsea.or.jp; 38 mems; Exec. Man. Dir YUICHI WATANABE.

Japanese Marine Equipment Association: Kaiyo Senpaku Bldg, 15-16, Toranomon, Minato-ku, Tokyo 105-0001; tel. (3) 3502-2041; fax (3) 3591-2206; e-mail info@jsmea.or.jp; internet www.jsmea.or.jp; f. 1956; 240 mems; Pres. TADAO YAMAOKA.

Japanese Shipowners' Association: Kaiun Bldg, 2-6-4, Hirakawa-cho, Chiyoda-ku, Tokyo 102-0093; tel. (3) 3264-7171; fax (3) 3262-4760; Pres. KENTARO KAWAMURA.

Shipbuilders' Association of Japan: 1-15-16, Toranomon, Minato-ku, Tokyo 105-0001; tel. (3) 3502-2010; fax (3) 3502-2816; internet www.sajn.or.jp; f. 1947; 21 mems; Chair. TOSHIMICHI OKANO.

Society of Japanese Aerospace Companies Inc (SJAC): Toshin-Tameike Bldg, 2nd Floor, 1-1-14, Akasaka, Minato-ku, Tokyo 107-0052; tel. (3) 3585-0511; fax (3) 3585-0541; e-mail miwa-shuichi@sjac.or.jp; internet www.sjac.or.jp; f. 1952; reorg. 1974; 117 mems, 41 assoc. mems; Chair. TOSHIFUMI TAKEI; Pres. TAKATOSHI HOSOYA.

Miscellaneous

Communications Industry Association of Japan (CIA-J): Sankei Bldg, 1-7-2, Otemachi, Chiyoda-ku, Tokyo 100-0004; tel. (3) 3231-3005; fax (3) 3231-3110; e-mail admin@ciaj.or.jp; internet www.ciaj.or.jp; f. 1948; non-profit org. of telecommunications equipment mfrs; 236 mems; Chair. TADASHI SEKIZAWA; Pres. YUTAKA HAYASHI.

Japan Canners' Association: Yurakuchu Denki Bldg, 1-7-1, Yuraku-cho, Chiyoda-ku, Tokyo 100-0006; tel. (3) 3213-4751; fax (3) 3211-1430; Pres. KEINOSUKE HISAI.

Japan Hardwood Exporters' Association: Matsuda Bldg, 1-9-1, Ironai, Otaru, Hokkaido 047; tel. (134) 23-8411; fax (134) 22-7150; 7 mems.

Japan Lumber Importers' Association: Yushi Kogyo Bldg, 3-13-11, Nihonbashi, Chuo-ku, Tokyo 103; tel. (3) 3271-0926; fax (3) 3271-0928; f. 1950; 130 mems; Pres. SHOICHI TANAKA.

Japan Plastics Industry Federation: Kaseihin-Kaikan, 5-8-17, Roppongi, Minato-ku, Tokyo 106-0032; tel. (3) 3586-9761; fax (3) 3586-9760; internet www.jpif.gr.jp; Chair. AKIO SATO.

Japan Plywood Manufacturers' Association: Meisan Bldg, 1-18-17, Nishi-Shimbashi, Minato-ku, Tokyo 105; tel. (3) 3591-9246; fax (3) 3591-9240; f. 1965; 92 mems; Pres. HIROSHI INOUE.

Japan Pottery Manufacturers' Federation: Toto Bldg, 1-1-28, Toranomon, Minato-ku, Tokyo; tel. (3) 3503-6761.

The Japan Rubber Manufacturers Association: Tobu Bldg, 1-5-26, Moto Akasaka, Minato-ku, Tokyo 107-0051; tel. (3) 3408-7101; fax (3) 3408-7106; f. 1950; 124 mems; Pres. YASUO TOMINAGA.

Japan Spirits and Liquors Makers' Association: Koura Daiichi Bldg, 7th Floor, 1-1-6, Nihonbashi-Kayaba-cho, Chuo-ku, Tokyo 103; tel. (3) 3668-4621.

Japan Sugar Import and Export Council: Osima Bldg 1–3, Nihonbashi Koamicho, Chuo-ku, Tokyo; tel. (3) 3571-2362; fax (3) 3571-2363; 16 mems.

Japan Sugar Refiners' Association: 5-7, Sanban-cho, Chiyoda-ku, Tokyo 102; tel. (3) 3288-1151; fax (3) 3288-3399; f. 1949; 17 mems; Sr Man. Dir KATSUYUKI SUZUKI.

Japan Tea Exporters' Association: 17, Kitaban-cho, Shizuoka, Shizuoka Prefecture 420-0005; tel. (54) 271-3428; fax (54) 271-2177; e-mail japantea2000@ybb.ne.jp; 33 mems.

Japan Toy Association: 4-22-4, Higashi-Komagata, Sumida-ku, Tokyo 130; tel. (3) 3829-2513; fax (3) 3829-2549; Chair. MAKOTO YAMASHINA.

Motion Picture Producers' Association of Japan, Inc: Tokyu Ginza Bldg, 2-15-2, Ginza, Chuo-ku, Tokyo 104-0061; tel. (3) 3547-1800; fax (3) 3547-0909; e-mail eiren@mc.neweb.ne.jp; internet www2.neweb.ne.jp/wd/eiren; Pres. ISAO MATSUOKA.

EMPLOYERS' ORGANIZATION

Japan Business Federation (JBF) (Nihon Keieisha Dantai Renmei): Palace Bldg, 5th Floor, 1-1-1, Marunouchi, Chiyoda-ku, Tokyo 100-0005; tel. (3) 3213-4454; fax (3) 3213-4455; e-mail intldiv@nikkeiren.or.jp; internet www.nikkeiren.or.jp; f. 1948; 1540 mem. asscns; Chair. HIROSHI OKUDA; Dir-Gen. RYUKOH WADA.

UTILITIES

Electricity

Chubu Electric Power Co Inc: 1, Higashi-Shincho, Higashi-ku, Nagoya 461-8680; tel. (52) 951-8211; fax (52) 962-4624; internet www.chuden.co.jp; Chair. KOHEI ABE; Pres. HIROJI OTA.

Chugoku Electric Power Co Inc: 4-33, Komachi, Naka-ku, Hiroshima 730-8701; tel. (82) 241-0211; fax (82) 523-6185; e-mail angel@inet.energia.co.jp; internet www.energia.co.jp; f. 1951; Chair. SHITOMI TAKASU; Pres. SHIGEO SHIRAKURA.

Hokkaido Electric Power Co Inc: internet www.hepco.co.jp; Chair. KAZUO TODA; Pres. SEIJI IZUMI.

Hokuriku Electric Power Co Inc: internet www.rikuden.co.jp.

Kansai Electric Power Co Inc: 3-3-22, Nakanoshima, Kita-ku, Osaka 530-8270; tel. (6) 6441-8821; fax (6) 6441-8598; e-mail postmaster@kepco.co.jp; internet www.kepco.co.jp; Chair. YOSHIHISA AKIYAMA; Pres. H. ISHIKAWA.

Kyushu Electric Power Co Inc: 2-1-82, Watanabe-dori, Chuo-ku, Fukuoka 810-8726; tel. (92) 726-1649; fax (92) 731-8719; internet www.kyuden.co.jp;; Chair. MICHISADA KAMATA.

Shikoku Electric Power Co Inc: 2-5, Marunouchi, Takamatsu 760-8573; tel. (878) 21-5061; fax (878) 26-1250; e-mail postmaster@yonden.co.jp; internet www.yonden.co.jp; Chair. HIROSHI YAMAMOTO; Pres. KOZO KONDO.

Tohoku Electric Power Co Inc: 3-7-1, Ichiban-cho, Aoba-ku, Sendai 980; tel. (22) 225-2111; fax (22) 222-2881; e-mail webmaster@tohoku-epco.co.jp; internet www.tohoku-epco.co.jp; Chair. TERUYUKI AKEMA; Pres. TOSHIAKI YASHIMA.

Tokyo Electric Power Co Inc: 1-1-3, Uchisaiwai-cho, Chiyoda-ku, Tokyo 100; tel. (3) 3501-8111; fax (3) 3592-1795; internet www.tepco.co.jp; Chair. SHOH NASU; Pres. N. MINAMI.

Gas

Osaka Gas Co Ltd: e-mail intlstaff@osakagas.co.jp; internet www.osakagas.co.jp.

Toho Gas Co Ltd: 19-18, Sakurada-cho, Atsuta-ko, Nagoya 456; tel. (52) 871-3511; internet www.tohogas.co.jp; f. 1922; Chair. SUSUMU OGAWA; Pres. SADAHIKO SIMIZU.

Tokyo Gas Co Inc: 1-5-20, Kaigan, Minato-ku, Tokyo 105; tel. (3) 3433-2111; fax (3) 5472-5385; internet www.tokyo-gas.co.jp: f. 1885; Chair. HIROSHI WATANABE; Pres. H. UEHARA.

CO-OPERATIVE ORGANIZATION

Nikkenkyo (Council of Japan Construction Industry Employees' Unions): Moriyama Bldg, 1-31-16, Takadanobaba, Shinjuku-ku, Tokyo 169; tel. (3) 5285-3870; fax (3) 5285-3879; Pres. NOBORU SEKIGUCHI.

MAJOR COMPANIES

(cap. = capital; res = reserves; m. = million; amounts in yen, unless otherwise indicated)

Ajinomoto Co Inc: 1-15-1, Kyobashi, Chuo-ku, Tokyo 104-8315; tel. (3) 5250-8111; fax (3) 5250-8293; internet www.ajinomoto.co.jp/ajinomoto/company/other.htm; f. 1909; cap. and res US $2,917.5m., sales US $7,326.8m. (2000/01); mfrs and distributors of seasonings, edible oils, processed foods, beverages, dairy products, pharmaceuticals, amino acids, speciality chemicals; Pres. KUNIO EGASHIRA; 22,379 employees.

Asahi Glass Co Ltd: 1-12-1, Yurakucho, Chiyoda-ku, Tokyo 100-8405; tel. (3) 3218-5555; fax (3) 3201-5390; internet www.agc.co.jp; f. 1907; cap. and res 503,585m., sales 1,257,052m. (1999/2000); manufacture and sale of flat glass, TV bulbs, alkali and other chemicals, refractories and electronics; associated companies and subsidiaries in Belgium, India, Indonesia, Singapore, Thailand and the USA; Chair. HIROMICHI SEYA; Pres. S. ISHIZU; 7,453 employees.

Asahi Kasei Corpn: Hibiya-Mitsui Bldg, 1-1-2, Yuraku-cho, Chiyoda-ku, Tokyo 100-8440; tel. (3) 3507-2060; fax (3) 3507-2495; e-mail asahi@om.asahi-kasei.co.jp; internet www.asahi-kasei.co.jp; f. 1931; cap. and res 496,825m., sales 1,195,393m. (2002/03); manufacture and sale of chemicals and plastics, housing and construction materials, fibres and textiles, electronics, membranes and systems, biotechnology and medical products, engineering, and others; Chair. NOBUO YAMAGUCHI; Pres. KAZUMOTO YAMAMOTO; 26,227 employees.

Bridgestone Corpn: 1-10-1, Kyobashi, Chuo-ku, Tokyo 104-8340; tel. (3) 3567-0111; fax (3) 3535-2553; internet www.bridgestone.co.jp; f. 1931; cap. and res 769,640m., sales 2,006,902m. (2000); mfrs of rubber tyres and tubes, shock absorbers, conveyor belts, hoses, foam rubber, polyurethane foam, golf balls; Chair. and Pres. SHIGEO WATANABE; 101,489 employees.

Canon Inc: 3-30-2, Shimomaruko, Ohta-ku, Tokyo 146-8501; tel. (3) 3758-2111; fax (3) 5482-5135; internet www.canon.com; cap. and res 1,298,914m., sales 2,781,303m. (2000); mfrs of cameras, business machines etc.; Chair. FUJIO MITARAI; 81,009 employees.

Casio Computer Co Ltd: 1-6-2, Hon-machi, Shibuya-ku, Tokyo 151-8543; tel. (3) 5334-4111; fax (3) 5334-4669; e-mail webmaster@casio.co.jp; internet www.casio.co.jp; f. 1957; cap. and res 162,375m., sales 443,930m. (2000/01); manufacture and sale of electronic calculators, digital watches, electronic musical instruments, liquid crystal televisions, Japanese language word processors; Chair. TOSHIO KASHIO; Pres. KAZUO KASHIO; 19,325 employees.

Citizen Watch Co Ltd: 6-1-12, Tanashi-cho, Nishi-Tokyo City, Tokyo 188-8511; tel. (4) 2466-1231; fax (3) 2466-1280; e-mail info@citizen.co.jp; internet www.citizen.co.jp; f. 1930; cap. and res 219,564m., sales 378,338m. (2000/01); manufacture and sale of wristwatches and parts, machine tools and tools, jewellery and eyeglasses, information and electronic equipment, precision machine and precision measuring instruments; Chair. HIROSHI HARUTA; 17,530 employees.

Cosmo Oil Co Ltd: 1-1-1, Shibaura, Minato-ku, Tokyo 105-8528; tel. (3) 3798-3211; fax (3) 3798-3411; internet www.cosmo-oil.co.jp; f. 1986; cap. and res 151,886m., sales 1,845,841m. (2000/01); importing of petroleum, refining, sales and distribution of petroleum products and related activities; Chair. and CEO KEIICHIRO OKABE; 1,970 employees.

Dai Nippon Printing Co Ltd: 1-1-1, Ichigaya Kaga-cho, Shinjuku-ku, Tokyo 162-8001; tel. (3) 3266-2111; fax (3) 5225-8239; e-mail info@mail.dnp.co.jp; internet www.dnp.co.jp; f. 1876; cap. and res 905,752m., sales 1,286,703m. (1999/2000); printing, packaging, paper products, plastics, precision electronic products; Chair. and Pres. YOSHITOSHI KITAJIMA; 35,347 employees.

Daido Steel Co Ltd: 1-11-18, Nishiki, Naka-ku, Nagoya, 460-8581; tel. (52) 201-5112; fax (52) 221-9268; internet www.daido.co.jp; f. 1950; cap. and res 37,172m., sales 245,334m. (2000/01); metal refining, steel, etc.; Chair. KANJI TOMITA; Pres. TSUYOSHI TAKAYAMA; 4,662 employees.

Daihatsu Motor Co Ltd: 1-1, Daihatsu-cho, Ikeda, Osaka 563-8651; tel. (727) 51-8811; fax (727) 53-6880; internet www.daihatsu.co.jp; f. 1907; subsidiary of Toyota Motor Corpn; cap. and res 192,422m., sales 998,785m. (2000/01); Chair. IICHI SHINGU; Pres. TAKAYA YAMADA; 22,265 employees.

Dainippon Ink & Chemicals Inc: DIC Bldg, 3-7-20, Nihonbashi, Chuo-ku-ku, Tokyo 103-8233; tel. (3) 3272-4511; fax (3) 3278-8558; e-mail webmaster@dic.co.jp; internet www.dic.co.jp; f. 1937; cap. and res 178,658m., sales 939,216m. (1999/2000); manufacture and sale of printing inks, printing supplies, machinery, chemicals, imaging and reprographic products, synthetic resins, resin-related products, petrochemicals, packaging materials, plastic compounds, colourants, plastic moulded products, building materials, pressure-sensitive adhesive materials and biochemicals; Pres. KOZO OKUMURA; 30,972 employees.

Denso Corpn: 1-1, Showa-cho, Kariya-shi, Aichi 448-8661; tel. (566) 25-5511; fax (566) 25-4537; e-mail admin@web.denso.co.jp; internet www.denso.co.jp; f. 1949; cap. and res 1,304,400m., sales 1,883,407m. (1999/2000); car electrical equipment, air conditioners, automobile parts; Chair. AKIRA TAKAHASHI; Pres. and CEO HIROMU OKABE; 80,795 employees.

Fuji Electric Co Ltd: Gate City Ohsaki, East Tower, 1-11-2, Ohsaki, Shinagawa-ku, Tokyo 141-0032; tel. (3) 5435-7111; fax (3) 5435-7486; e-mail info@fujielectric.co.jp; internet www.fujielectric.co.jp; cap. and res 153,945m., sales 851,830m. (1999/2000); manufacture of electrical machinery; Pres. and CEO KUNIHIKO SAWA; 11,060 employees.

Fuji Heavy Industries Co Ltd: 1-7-2, Nishishinjuku, Shinjuku-ku, Tokyo 160-8316; tel. (3) 3347-2111; fax (3) 3347-2338; internet www.fhi.co.jp; cap. and res 357,455m., sales 1,311,887m. (2000/01); motor vehicles and industrial products; Pres. and CEO TAKESHI TANAKA; 13,600 employees.

Fuji Photo Film Co Ltd: 2-26-30, Nishi Azabu, Minato-ku, Tokyo 106-8620; tel. (3) 3406-2111; fax (3) 3406-2193; internet www.home.fujifilm.com; f. 1934; cap. and res 1,454,121m., sales 1,401,791m. (1999/2000); films and photographic materials, magnetic tapes, carbonless copying paper; Chair. and CEO MINORU OHNISHI; Pres. SHIGETAKA KOMORI; 37,151 employees.

Fujitsu Ltd: Marunouchi Center Bldg, 1-6-1, Marunouchi, Chiyoda-ku, Tokyo 100-8211; tel. (3) 3216-3211; fax (3) 3216-9365; e-mail pr_mailbox@hq.fujitsu.co.jp; internet www.fujitsu.co.jp; f. 1935; cap. and res 947,852m., sales 5,255,102m. (1999/2000); manufacture and sale of electronic computers and data processing equipment, telephone equipment, etc.; Chair. TADASHI SEKIZAWA; Pres. NAOYUKI AKIKUSA; 167,000 employees.

Furukawa Electric Co Ltd: 2-6-1, Marunouchi, Chiyoda-ku, Tokyo 100-8322; tel. (3) 3286-3001; fax (3) 3286-3694; e-mail pub@ho.furukawa.co.jp; internet www.furukawa.co.jp; f. 1896; cap. and res 217,286m., sales 696,569m. (1999/2000); manufacture and sale of electric, telephone and optic-fibre wires, cables and non-ferrous metal products; Chair. KENGO TOMOMATSU; Pres. JYUNNOSUKE FURUKAWA; 8,685 employees.

Hino Motors Ltd: 3-1-1, Hinodai, Hino-shi, Tokyo 191-8660; tel. (42) 586-5011; fax (3) 5419-9363; internet www.hino.co.jp; f. 1942; cap. 39,573m., sales 703,998m. (2000/01); diesel trucks and buses; Chair. IWAO OKIJIMA; Pres. TADAAKI JAGAWA; 9,070 employees.

Hitachi Ltd: 4-6, Kanda Suragadai, Chiyoda-ku, Tokyo 101-8010; tel. (3) 3258-1111; fax (3) 3258-5480; e-mail webmaster@hitachi.co.jp; internet www.hitachi.co.jp; f. 1910; cap. and res 2,876,212m., sales 8,001,203m. (1999/2000); manufacture and sale of power systems, information and communication systems, electronic devices, industrial machinery, metals, chemicals, wire, cable and other products; Chair. TSUTOMU KANAI; Pres. ETSUHIKO SHOYAMA; 337,911 employees.

Hitachi Zosen Corpn: 1-7-89, Nanko-kita, Suminoe-ku, Osaka 559-8559; tel. (6) 6569-0001; fax (6) 6569-0002; internet www.hitachizosen.co.jp; f. 1881; cap. and res 55,405m., sales 475,360m. (1999/2000); ship-building, ship repairing, conversion, manufacture of diesel engines, offshore equipment, marine auxiliary machinery and fittings; mfrs of industrial machinery and plant for chemicals, paper, petroleum, sugar, cement and iron, steel bridges and steel structures, environmental equipment; Chair. and CEO YOSHIHIRO FUJII; Pres. ISOH MINAMI; 10,867 employees.

Honda Motor Co Ltd: 2-1-1, Minami-Aoyama, Minato-ku, Tokyo 107-8556; tel. (3) 3423-1111; fax (3) 5412-1515; internet www.honda.co.jp/english; f. 1948; cap. and res 2,230,291m., sales 6,463,830m. (2000/01); mfrs of automobiles, motorcycles, power tillers, general purpose engines, outboard motors, lawn mowers and portable generators; 24 foreign subsidiaries; Chair. YOSHIHIDE MUNEKUNI; Pres. HIROYUKI YOSHINO; 101,100 employees.

Hoya Corpn: 2-7-5, Naka-Ochiai, Shinjuku-ku, Tokyo 161-8525; tel. (3) 3952-1151; fax (3) 3952-1314; internet www.hoya.co.jp; cap. and res 175,146m., sales 201,110m. (1999/2000); mfrs of medical and opthalmic equipment; Pres. and CEO HIROSHI SUZUKI; 2,381 employees.

Idemitsu Kosan Co Ltd: 3-1-1, Marunouchi, Chiyoda-ku, Tokyo 100; tel. (3) 3213-3115; internet www.idemitsu.co.jp; f. 1911; cap. and res 80,111m., sales 2,186,726m. (1999/2000); manufacture and sale of petroleum products and petrochemicals, and related enterprises; Pres. MASARU YAMATO; 4,592 employees.

Ishikawajima-Harima Heavy Industries Co Ltd: 2-2-1, Otemachi, Chiyoda-ku, Tokyo 100-8182; tel. (3) 3244-5111; fax (3) 3244-5131; internet www.ihi.co.jp; f. 1853; sales 1,082,402m. (Mar. 2002); rocket and satellite propulsion systems, jet engines, gas turbine power generation systems, storage systems, process plants, solid waste treatment systems, container cranes, unloaders, physical distribution systems, bridges, industrial machinery, compressors, semiconductor and LCD panel equipment, parking systems, ozone-based deodorizing and disinfecting equipment, shipbuilding and ship repair service, manufactures, aircraft gas turbines, nuclear power equipment, material handling equipment, iron and steel manufacturing plant, mining and civil engineering machinery, hydro- and thermal electric generating equipment, pneumatic and hydraulic machinery, chemical plant, steel structures, power plants, aero-engines, space utilities, turbochargers, construction machinery; Chair. (vacant); Pres. MOTOTSUGU ITO; 10,966 employees.

Isuzu Motors Ltd: 6-26-1, Minami-Oi, Shinagawa-ku, Tokyo 140-8722; tel. (3) 5471-1111; fax (3) 5471-1042; e-mail pr@notes .isuzu.co.jp; internet www.isuzu.co.jp; f. 1937; cap. 160,166m., sales 1,569,199m. (2000/01), total assets 1,843,053m. (1998/99); manufacture and sale of trucks, buses, sports utility vehicles, components and engines; Chair. TAKESHI INOH; Pres. YOSHINORI IDA; 30,232 employees.

Japan Energy Corpn: 2-10-1, Toranomon, Minato-ku, Tokyo 105-8407; tel. (3) 5573-6188; fax (3) 5573-6773; e-mail ask@j-energy.co.jp; internet www.j-energy.co.jp; f. 1905; present name 1993, fmrly Nikko Kyodo Co (following merger of Nippon Mining Co Ltd and Kyodo Oil Co Ltd in 1992); cap. and res 115,400m., sales 1,941,576m. (1999/2000); petroleum resource exploration and development; refining and marketing of petroleum products; pharmaceuticals and biotechnologies; manufacture and marketing of electronic materials, optoelectronics and electronics components; Chair., Pres. and CEO AKIHIKO NOMIYAMA; 3,795 employees.

Japan Tobacco Inc (JT): 2-2-1, Toranomon, Minato-ku, Tokyo 105-8422; tel. (3) 3582-3111; fax (3) 5572-1441; internet www.jti.co.jp; f. 1985; cap. and res 1,526,583m., sales 4,501,701m. (March 2001); tobacco, pharmaceuticals, food, agribusiness, real estate, engineering; Chair. TADASHI OGAWA; Pres. and CEO KATSUHIKO HONDA; 15,588 employees.

Kanebo Ltd: 3-20-20, Kaigan, Minato-ku, Tokyo 108-8080; tel. (3) 5446-3002; fax (3) 5446-3027; e-mail webmaster@kanebo.co.jp; internet www.kanebo.co.jp; f. 1887; cap. and res 31,340, sales 555,495m. (2000/01); manufacture, bleaching, dyeing, processing and sale of cotton yarns, cloth and thread, worsted and woollen yarns, woollen fabrics, nylon and polyester yarns and fabrics, carpets, spun silk yarns, silk thread spun from waste, silkworm eggs, silk fabrics, rayon staple, spun rayon yarns and fabrics, synthetic resins; cosmetics, pharmaceuticals and industrial materials; Pres. and Chair. TAKASHI HOASHI; 2,860 employees.

Kao Corpn: 1-14-10, Nihonbashi Kayabacho, Chuo-ku, Tokyo 103-8210; tel. (3) 3660-7111; fax (3) 3660-7103; internet www.kao.co.jp; cap. and res 428,369m., sales 846,922m. (1999/2000); health and household; Pres. TAKUYA GOTO; 6,086 employees.

Kawasaki Heavy Industries Ltd: Kobe Crystal Tower 1-1-3, Higashi-Kawasakicho, Chuo-ku, Kobe 650-8680; tel. (78) 371-9530; fax (3) 3432-4759; e-mail webadmin@khi.co.jp; internet www.khi.co.jp; f. 1896; cap. and res 167,670m., sales 1,149,698m. (1999/2000); manufacture and sale of ships, rolling stock, aircraft, machinery, engines and motorcycles, plant engineering; Chair. TOSHIO KAMEI; Pres. MASAMOTO TAZAKI; 29,772 employees.

Kawasaki Steel Corpn: Hibiya Kokusai Bldg, 2-2-3, Uchisaiwaicho, Chiyoda-ku, Tokyo 100-0011; tel. (3) 3597-3111; fax (3) 3597-4860; internet www.kawasaki-steel.co.jp; f. 1950; cap. and res 305,567m., sales 1,315,560m. (2000/01); manufacture and sale of steel, advanced materials, silicon wafers, gases, opto-electronic products, consumer durables and chemical products, sale of super-microcomputers, provision of construction, information, computer software, data communications and engineering services; Pres. KANJI EMOTO; 10,215 employees.

Kirin Brewery Co Ltd: 2-10-1, Shinkawa, Chuo-ku, Tokyo 104-8288; tel. (3) 5540-3411; fax (3) 5540-3547; internet www.kirin.co.jp; f. 1907; cap. and res 768,486m., sales 1,073,208m. (2000); production and sale of beer, soft drinks, dairy foods, pharmaceuticals, engineering and information systems; Pres. YASUHIRO SATO; 6,502 employees.

Kobe Steel Ltd: 5-9-12, Kita-Shinagawa, Shinagawa-ku, Tokyo 141-8688; tel. (3) 5739-6010; fax (3) 5739-5971; e-mail www-admin@kobelco.co.jp; internet www.kobelco.co.jp; f. 1905; sales 1,198,014m.; cap. 215,170,000m. (2001/02); manufacture and sale of iron and steel products, aluminium and copper products, industrial machinery, construction machinery; real estate; Chair. MASAHIRO KUMAMOTO; Pres. and CEO KOSHI MIZUKOSHI; 26,908 employees.

Komatsu Ltd: 2-3-6, Akasaka, Minato-ku, Tokyo 107-8414; tel. (3) 5561-2616; fax (3) 3505-9662; e-mail info@komatsu.co.jp; internet www.komatsu.com; f. 1921; cap. and res 474,257m., sales 1,096,369m. (2000/01); mfrs of construction equipment and industrial machinery including bulldozers, motor graders, wheel loaders, dump trucks, hydraulic excavators, presses, machine tools, arc welding robots and diesel engines; Chair. TETSUYA KATADA; Pres. SATORU ANZAKI; 28,522 employees.

Konica Corpn: Shinjuku Nomura Bldg, 1-26-2, Nishi-Shinjuku, Shinjuku-ku, Tokyo 163-0512; tel. (3) 3349-5251; fax (3) 3349-5290; internet www.konica.co.jp; cap. 160,259m., sales 560,900m. (2000/01); Chair. TOMIJI UEMATSU; Pres. and CEO FUMIO IWAI; 4,180 employees.

Kubota Corpn: 1-2-47, Shikitsuhigashi, Naniwa-ku, Osaka 556-8601; tel. (6) 6648-2111; fax (6) 6648-3862; internet www.kubota .co.jp; f. 1890; cap. and res 434,979m., sales 994,493m. (2000/01); manufacture and sale of ductile iron pipes, pumps, valves, spiral-welded steel pipes, polyvinyl chloride pipes, tractors, combines, engines, miniexcavators, general farming equipment, cement roofing materials, fire-resistant sidings, sale and installation of environmental control plant and other steel structures, building materials; Chair. OSAMU OKAMOTO; Pres. YOSHIKUNI DOBASHI; 14,594 employees.

Kyocera Corpn: 6, Takeda Tobadono-cho, Fushimi-ku, Kyoto 612-8501; tel. (75) 604-3500; fax (75) 604-3501; e-mail webmaster@ kyocera.co.jp; internet www.kyocera.co.jp; cap. 1,022,065m., sales 1,285,053m. (2000/ 01); manufacture of fine ceramic parts, semiconductor parts, electronic components and equipment, optical instruments and consumer-related products; Chair. KENSUKE ITOH; Pres. YASUO NISHIGUCHI; 53,000 employees.

Maruha Corpn (Maruha k.k.): 1-1-2, Otemachi, Chiyoda-ku, Tokyo 100-8608; tel. (3) 3216-0821; fax (3) 3216-2082; internet www.maruha.co.jp; f. 1880; name changed from Taiyo Fishery Co Ltd Sept. 1993; cap. and res 22,914m., sales 941,329m. (1999/2000); fishing, processing and sale of agricultural marine and meat products; canned and frozen salmon, crab, etc.; food processing, marine transport, export and import; refrigeration, ice production and cold storage; manufacture and sale of pharmaceuticals, organic fertilizers and sugar; culture and sale of pearls; breeding and sale of mink; Pres. KEIJIRO NAKABE; 1,314 employees.

Matsushita Electric Industrial Co Ltd: 1006 Oaza Kadoma, Kadoma-shi, Osaka 571-8501; tel. (6) 6908-1121; fax (6) 6908-2351; internet www.panasonic.co.jp/global; f. 1918; cap. and res 3,467,191m., sales 7,299,390,119m. (1999/2000); manufacture of electrical and electronic home appliances; 11 major subsidiaries in Japan; manufacturing and sales companies in 47 countries; Chair. YOICHI MORISHITA; Pres. KUNIO NAKAMURA; 290,448 employees.

Matsushita Electric Works Ltd: 1048 Kadoma, Kadoma-shi, Osaka 571-8686; tel. (6) 6908-1131; fax (6) 6909-6244; e-mail webmaster@mew.co.jp; internet www.mew.co.jp; f. 1918; cap. and res 529,852m., sales 1,181,091m. (1999/2000); lighting equipment, housing and building materials, electrical construction materials, electric appliances, plastic and electronic materials and automation components; Chair. KIYOSUKE IMAI; Pres. KAZUSHIGE NISHIDA; 41,234 employees.

Mazda Motor Corpn: 3-1, Shinchi, Fuchu-cho, Aki-gun, Hiroshima 730-8670; tel. (82) 282-1111; fax (82) 287-5190; internet www.mazda .co.jp; f. 1920; fmrly Toyo Kogyo Co Ltd; 33%-owned by Ford Motor Co (USA); cap. and res 234,467m., sales 2,161,572m. (1999/2000); manufacture and sale of 'Mazda' passenger cars and commercial vehicles; subsidiaries in Japan, Australia, Belgium, the USA, Canada, Colombia, Indonesia, New Zealand, Italy, Portugal, Spain and Germany; Chair. KAZUHIDE WATANABE; Pres. MARK FIELDS; 43,818 employees.

Mitsubishi Chemical Corpn: 2-5-2, Marunouchi, Chiyoda-ku, Tokyo 100-0005; tel. (3) 3283-6254; fax (3) 3283-6287; e-mail mccpr@cc.m-kagaku.co.jp; internet www.m-kagaku.co.jp; f. 1994 by merger; cap. and res 395,271m., sales 1,669,924m. (1999/2000); Japan's largest integrated chemical co; manufacture and sale of coke and coal-tar derivatives, dyestuffs and intermediates, caustic soda, organic solvents and chemicals, reagents, ammonia derivatives, inorganic chemicals, pesticides and herbicides, fertilizers, food additives and pharmaceutical intermediates; Chair. AKIRA MIURA; Pres. and CEO KANJI SHONO; 10,430 employees.

Mitsubishi Electric Corpn: Mitsubishi Denki Bldg, 2-2-3, Marunouchi, Chiyoda-ku, Tokyo 100; tel. (3) 3218-2111; fax (3) 3218-2431; e-mail prd.prdesk@hq.melco.co.jp; internet www.mitsubishi electric.com; f. 1921; cap. and res 596,450m., sales 4,129,493m. (2000/01); manufacture and sale of electrical machinery and equipment (for power plant, mining, ships, locomotives and other rolling stock, aircraft), electronic products and systems, domestic electric appliances, radio communication equipment, radio and television sets, meters and relaying equipment, fluorescent lamps, lighting, fixtures, refrigerators, lifts, electric tools, sewing machines; Pres. ICHIRO TANIGUCHI; 116,588 employees.

Mitsubishi Heavy Industries Ltd: 2-5-1, Marunouchi, Chiyoda-ku, Tokyo 100-8315; tel. (3) 3212-3111; fax (3) 3212-9860; internet www.mhi.co.jp; f. 1870; cap. and res 1,245,064m., sales 2,875,039m. (1999/2000); shipbuilding, ship repairing, power systems, chemical plant and machinery, industrial machinery, heavy machinery, rolling stock, precision machinery, steel structures, construction machinery, refrigerating and air-conditioning machinery, engines, aircraft, special purpose vehicles, space systems; major subsidiaries in Japan, Brazil and other countries; Chair. NOBUYUKI MASUDA; Pres. TAKASHI NISHIOKA; 39,304 employees.

Mitsubishi Materials Corpn: 1-5-1, Otemachi, Chiyoda-ku, Tokyo 100-8117; tel. (3) 5252-5201; fax (3) 5252-5272; e-mail www.adm@mmc.co.jp; internet www.mmc.co.jp; cap. and res 231,559m., sales 986,884m. (1999/2000); metal and metal forming; Chair. YUMI AKIMOTO; Pres. AKIRA NISHIKAWA; 6,556 employees.

Mitsubishi Motors Corpn: 5-33-8, Shiba, Minato-ku, Tokyo 108-8410; tel. (3) 3456-1111; fax (3) 5232-7747; internet www.mitsubishi-motors.co.jp; cap. and res 347,363m., sales 3,334,974m. (1999/2000); manufacture of motor vehicles; Chair. TAKEMUNE KIMURA; Pres. TAKASHI SONOBE; 25,846 employees.

Mitsui Chemicals, Inc.: Kasumigaseki Bldg, 3-2-5, Kasumigaseki, Chiyoda-ku, Tokyo 100-6070; tel. (3) 3592-4105; fax (3) 3592-4213; internet www.mitsui-chem.co.jp; f. 1997; by merger of Mitsui Petrochemical Industries Ltd and Mitsui Toatsu Chemicals; cap. and res 345,690m., sales 884,246m. (1999/2000); industrial chemicals, fertilizers, dyestuffs, fine chemicals, agricultural and pharmaceuticals, adhesives, electric materials and resins, etc.; Chair. SHIGENORI KODA; Pres. HIROYUKI NAKANISHI; 5,792 employees.

Mitsui Engineering & Shipbuilding Co Ltd: 5-6-4, Tsukiji, Chuo-ku, Tokyo 104-8439; tel. (3) 3544-3147; fax (3) 3544-3050; e-mail prdept@mes.co.jp; internet www.mes.co.jp; f. 1917; cap. and res 104,998m., sales 456,657m. (1999/2000); shipbuilding and industrial machinery; Pres. TOSHIMICHI OKANO; 3,931 employees.

NEC Corpn: 5-7-1, Shiba, Minato-ku, Tokyo 108-8001; tel. (3) 3454-1111; fax (3) 3798-1510; internet www.nec-global.com; f. 1899; cap. and res 976,953m., sales 4,991,447m. (1999/2000); integrating computers and communications, manufacture and sale of telephone switching systems, carrier transmission and terminals, digital radio and satellite communications, broadcasting electronic data processing and industrial electronic systems, electronic devices and consumer electronic products; Chair. HAJIME SASAKI; Pres. KOJI NISHIGAKI; 152,450 employees.

Nintendo Co Ltd: 60 Fukuine, Kamitoba Hokotate-cho, Minami-ku, Kyoto 601-8501; tel. (75) 662-9600; fax (75) 662-9615; internet www.nintendo.com; cap. and res 935,075m., sales 554,886m. (2001/02); manufacture of electronic video games systems; Pres. SATORU IWATA; 3,073 employees.

Nippon Meat Packers Inc: 3-6-14, Minami-honmachi, Chuo-ku, Osaka 541-0054; tel. (6) 6282-3031; fax (6) 6282-1056; internet www.nipponham.co.jp; sales 881,616m. (1999/2000), total assets US $4,446.6m. (1997/98); Chair. YOSHINORI OKOSO; Pres. HIROJI OHKOSO; 3,441 employees.

Nippon Mitsubishi Oil Corpn: 1-3-12, Nishi Shimbashi, Minato-ku, Tokyo 105-8412; tel. (3) 3502-1135; fax (3) 3502-9352; internet www.nmoc.co.jp; f. 1999 by merger of Mitsubishi Oil Co Ltd and Nippon Oil Co Ltd; cap. and res 840,971m., sales 3,594,911m. (1999/2000); refining and marketing of petroleum products; Chair. FUMIAKI WATARI; 10,539 employees.

Nippon Paper Industries Co Ltd: 1-12-1, Yuraku-cho, Chiyoda-ku, Tokyo 100-0006; tel. (3) 3218-8000; fax (3) 3214-5226; e-mail pub@npaper.co.jp; internet www.npaper.co.jp; f. 1993 by merger between Jujo Paper and Sanyo-Kokusaku Pulp Co Ltd; paper, pulp, chemical, wood products; cap. and res 342,367m., sales 906,041m. (1999/2000); Chair. TAKESHIRO MIYASHITA; Pres. MASAO KOBAYASHI; 6,009 employees.

Nippon Steel Corpn: Shin Nittetsu Bldg, 2-6-3, Otemachi, Chiyoda-ku, Tokyo 100-8071; tel. (3) 3242-4111; fax (3) 3275-5641; e-mail www-info@www.nsc.co.jp; internet www.nsc.co.jp; f. 1950; cap. and res 844,702m., sales 2,680,611,409m. (2000); Chair. TAKASHI IMAI; Pres. AKIRA CHIHAIYA; 19,816 employees.

Nippon Suisan Kaisha Ltd: 2-6-2, Otemachi, Chiyoda-ku, Tokyo 100-8686; tel. (3) 3244-7000; fax (3) 3244-7085; e-mail home@nissui.co.jp; internet www.nissui.co.jp; f. 1911; sales 472,300m. (1999/2000); marine fisheries and fish products; food processing; cargo and tanker services; Pres. YASUO KUNII; 1,790 employees.

Nissan Motor Co Ltd: 2, Takara-cho, Kanagawa-ku, Yokohama; tel. (5) 5565-2147; internet www.nissan.co.jp; f. 1933; cap. and res 884,252m., sales 5,977,075m. (1999/2000); manufacture and sale of automobiles, rockets, textile machinery, other machines and appliances and parts; Chair. and CEO YOSHIKAZU HANAWA; Pres. and Chief Operating Officer CARLOS GHOSN; 136,397 employees.

Nissan Shatai Co Ltd: 10-1, Amanuma, Hiratsuka-shi, Kanagawa-ken 254-8610; tel. (463) 21-8001; fax (463) 21-8155; f. 1949; sales 499,545m. (1999/2000); auto-bodies for passenger cars and small trucks; Pres. KAZUTAKA KOBATAKE; 4,836 employees.

Nisshin Steel Co Ltd: Shinkokusai Bldg, 3-4-1, Marunouchi, Chiyoda-ku, Tokyo 100-8366; tel. (3) 3216-5511; fax (3) 3214-1895; internet www.nisshin-steel.co.jp; f. 1928; cap. and res 244,998m., sales 430,955m. (1999/2000); mfrs of coated steel, stainless steel, special steel and various secondary products; Chair., Pres. and CEO M. TANAKA; 5,040 employees.

NKK Corpn: 1-1-2, Marunouchi, Chiyoda-ku, Tokyo 100-8202; tel. (3) 3212-7111; fax (3) 3214-8401; internet www.nkk.co.jp/en; f. 1912; cap. and res 256,771m., sales 1,685,391m. (1999/2000); manufacture and sale of pig iron, steel ingots, tubes, plates, sheets, bars, special steels and ferro-alloys, coal-derived chemicals, refractories and slag wool; engineering and construction of pipelines, steel plants, steel structures, water treatment plants, waste incineration plants, ships; urban development, electronics; Chair. SHUNKICHI MIYOSHI; Pres. and CEO YOICHI SHIMOGAICHI; 39,603 employees.

Oji Paper Co Ltd: 4-7-5, Ginza, Chuo-ku, Tokyo 104-0061; tel. (3) 3563-1111; fax (3) 3563-1135; e-mail info@ojipaper.co.jp; internet www.ojipaper.co.jp; f. 1873 (name changed 1996); cap. and res 433,715m., sales 1,205,474m. (1999/2000); newsprint, packing paper and printing paper; Chair. TAKAO OTSUBO; Pres. MASAHIKO OHKUNI; 14,044 employees.

Oki Electric Industry Co Ltd: 1-7-12, Toranomon, Minato-ku, Tokyo 105-8460; tel. (3) 3501-3111; fax (3) 3581-5522; e-mail www-admin@www.oki.co.jp; internet www.oki.co.jp; f. 1949; cap. and res 142,563m., sales 669,776m. (1999/2000); Chair. SHIKO SAWAMURA; Pres. and CEO KATSUMASA SHINOZUKA; 8,760 employees.

Omron Corpn: Karasuma Nanajo, Shimogyo-ku, Kyoto 600-8530; tel. (75) 344-7000; fax (75) 344-7001; internet www.omron.co.jp; cap. and res 336,062m., sales 555,358m. (1999/2000); mfr of advanced computer, communications and control technologies; Chair. NOBUO TATEISI; Pres. and CEO YOSHIO TATEISI; 23,742 employees.

Pioneer Corpn: 1-4-1, Meguro, Meguro-ku, Tokyo 153-8654; tel. (3) 3494-1111; fax (3) 3495-4431; e-mail pioneer_ir@post.pioneer.co.jp; internet www.pioneer.co.jp; f. 1938; cap. and res 308,697m., sales 615,871m. (1999/2000); electronics; Chair. KANYA MATSUMOTO; Pres. KANEO ITO; 27,414 employees.

Ricoh Co Ltd: 1-15-5, Minami-Aoyama, Minato-ku, Tokyo 107-8544; tel. (3) 3479-3111; fax (3) 3403-1578; internet www.ricoh.co.jp; cap. and res 541,506m., sales 1,447,157m. (1999/2000); electronics; Chair. HIROSHI HAMADA; Pres. MASAMITSU SAKURAI; 12,392 employees.

Sankyo Co Ltd: 3-5-1, Nihonbashi Honcho, Chuo-ku, Tokyo 103-8426; tel. (3) 5255-7111; fax (3) 5255-7035; internet www.sankyo.co.jp; f. 1899; cap. and res 604,505m., sales 589,732m. (1999/2000); health and household; Chair. YOSHIBUMI KAWAMURA; Pres. TETSUO TAKATO; 10,760 employees.

Sanyo Electric Co Ltd: 2-5-5, Keihan Hondori, Moriguchi City, Osaka 570-8677; tel. (6) 6991-1181; fax (6) 6991-5411; internet www.sanyo.co.jp; f. 1947; cap. and res 652,322m., sales 2,157,318m. (2000/01); manufacture and sale of electrical and electronic machinery and appliances—refrigerators, washing machines, electric fans, television and radio sets, bicycle dynamos, personal computers, commercial air conditioning systems etc.; Chair. SATOSHI IUE; Pres. SADAO KONDO; 76,176 employees.

Sekisui Chemical Co Ltd: 2-4-4, Nishi-Tenma, Kita-ku, Osaka 530-8565; tel. (6) 6365-4122; fax (6) 6365-4370; internet www.sekisui.co.jp; cap. and res 372,734m., sales 920,040m. (1999/2000); chemicals, building materials etc.; Chair. KAORU HIROTA; Pres. NAOTAKE OHKUBO; 5,176 employees.

Sharp Corpn: 22-22, Nagaike-cho, Abeno-ku, Osaka 545-8522; tel. (6) 6621-1221; fax (6) 6628-1653; internet www.sharp.co.jp; f. 1912; cap. and res 943,515m., sales 2,012,858m. (2000/01); manufacture and sale of consumer electronic products, information systems and electronic components; Pres. KATSUHIKO MACHIDA; 49,748 employees.

Shin-Etsu Chemical Co Ltd: 2-6-1, Otemachi, Chiyoda-ku, Tokyo 100-0004; tel. (3) 3246-5011; fax (3) 3246-5350; e-mail sec-pr@shinetsu.co.jp; internet www.shinetsu.co.jp; cap. and res 714,996m., sales 807,485m. (2000/01); Pres. CHIHIRO KANAGAWA; 19,398 employees.

Shiseido Co Ltd: 7-5-5, Ginza, Chuo-ku, Tokyo 104-8010; tel. (3) 3572-5111; fax (3) 3572-6973; internet www.shiseido.co.jp/e; f. 1872; cap. and res 397,065m., sales 596,643m. (1999/2000); manufacture and export of cosmetics and toiletries; Chair. YOSHIHARU FUKUHARA; Pres. and CEO AKIRA GEMMA; 23,688 employees.

Showa Denko KK: 1-13-9, Shiba Daimon, Minato-ku, Tokyo 105-8518; tel. (3) 5470-3111; fax (3) 3436-2625; e-mail pr_office@hq.sdk.co.jp; internet www.sdk.co.jp; f. 1939; cap. and res 111,965m., sales 746,999m. (2000); manufacture and sale of bulk and speciality chemicals, plastics, ferro-alloys, electronics materials, electrodes and abrasives; Chair. MAKOTO MURATA; Pres. MITSUO OHASHI; 12,475 employees.

Showa Shell Sekiyu KK: 2-3-2, Daiba, Minato-ku, Tokyo 135-8074; tel. (3) 5531-5601; fax (3) 5531-5609; f. 1942; cap. 34,197m. (2000), sales 1,639,475m. (1999); petroleum; Chair. HARUYUKI NIIMI; Pres. TAMOTSU YAMAZAKI; 1,130 employees.

Snow Brand Milk Products Co Ltd: 13, Honshio-cho, Shinjuku-ku, Tokyo 160-8575; tel. (3) 3226-2111; fax (3) 3226-2150; internet www.snowbrand.co.jp; f. 1950; cap. and res 27,809m., sales 1,140,763m. (2000/01); mfrs of liquid milk, condensed and powdered milk, butter, cheese, ice-cream, infant foods, instant foods, margarine, fruit juices, frozen foods; also imported wine distribution; Chair. KATSUYA SHONO; Pres. KOHEI NISHI; 15,380 employees.

Sony Corpn: 6-7-35, Kitashinagawa, Shinagawa-ku, Tokyo 141-0001; tel. (3) 5448-2111; fax (3) 5448-2244; internet www.world.sony.com; f. 1946; cap. and res 2,315,453m., sales 7,314,824m. (2000/01); manufacture and sale of electronic appliances, including professional and consumer audio and video equipment; production and distribution of music, motion pictures and television programmes; Chair. and CEO NORIO OHGA; Pres. and Chief Operating Officer NOBUYUKI IDEI; 181,800 employees.

Sumitomo Chemical Co Ltd: 2-27-1, Shinkawa, Chuo-ku, Tokyo 104-8260; tel. (3) 5543-5102; fax (3) 5543-5901; internet www.sumitomo-chem.co.jp; f. 1913; cap. and res 331,271m. (1999/2000), sales 1,040,950m. (2000/01); manufacture and sale of chemical fertilizers, dyestuffs, agricultural chemicals, intermediates, organic and inorganic industrial chemicals, synthetic resins, finishing resins, synthetic rubber and rubber chemicals; many subsidiaries; Chair. AKIO KOSAI; Pres. HIROMASA YONEKURA; 5,410 employees.

Sumitomo Electric Industries Ltd: 4-5-33, Kitahama, Chuo-ku, Osaka 541-0041; tel. (6) 6220-4141; fax (6) 6222-3380; e-mail www@prs.sei.co.jp; internet www.sei.co.jp; f. 1911; sales 1,478,740m. (2000/01); mfrs of electric wires and optical-fibre cables, high carbon steel wires; sintered alloy products; rubber and plastic products; disc brakes; radio-frequency products; Chair. and CEO NORITAKA KURAUCHI; Pres. NORIO OKAYAMA; 70,936 employees.

Sumitomo Heavy Industries Ltd: 5-9-11, Kitashinagawa, Shinagawa-ku, Tokyo 141-8686; tel. (3) 5488-8335; fax (3) 5488-8056; e-mail webadmin@shi.co.jp; internet www.shi.co.jp; f. 1934; cap. and res 64,829m. (1999/2000), sales 513,753m. (2000/01); industrial machinery and shipbuilding; Chair. MITOSHI OZAWA; Pres. and CEO YOSHIO HINO; 13,794 employees.

Sumitomo Metal Industries Ltd: 4-5-33, Kitahama, Chuo-ku, Osaka 541-0041; tel. (6) 6220-5111; fax (6) 6223-0305; internet www.sumikin.co.jp; f. 1897; cap. and res 502,249m. (1998/99), sales 1,497,641m. (2000/01); manufacture and sale of pig iron, steel ingots, steel bars, shapes, wire rods, tubes, pipes, castings, forgings, rolling stock parts, engineering; 100 subsidiaries in Japan; 8 offices abroad; Chair. REIJIRO MORI; Pres. HIROSHI SHIMOZUMA; 11,655 employees.

Sumitomo Metal Mining Co Ltd: 5-11-3, Shimbashi, Minato-ku, Tokyo 105-8716; tel. (3) 3436-7701; fax (3) 3434-2215; internet www.smm.co.jp; cap. and res 226,795m. (1998/99), sales 375,352m. (2000/01); Chair. AKIHIKO SHINOZAKI; Pres. KOICHI FUKUSHIMA; 2,670 employees.

Suzuki Motor Corpn: 300 Takatsuka, Hamamatsu, Shizuoka 432-8611; tel. (53) 440-2030; fax (53) 440-2776; internet www.suzuki.co.jp; f. 1920; cap. 119,736m., sales 1,668,251m. (2001/02); motor vehicles, outboard motors, power products, prefabricated houses; Pres. and COO MASAO TODA; Chair. and CEO OSAMU SUZUKI; 14,620 employees.

Taiheiyo Cement Corpn: 3-8-1, Nishi Kanda, Chiyoda-ku, Tokyo 101-8357; tel. (3) 5214-1520; fax (3) 5214-1707; e-mail webmaster@taiheiyo-cement.co.jp; internet www.taiheiyo-cement.co.jp/menu.html; fmrly Chichibu Onoda Cement Corpn; cap. and res 163,835m., sales 1,001,638m. (2000/01); building materials; Chair. and CEO KAZUSUKE IMAMURA; Pres. MICHIO KIMURA; 2,600 employees.

Taisei Corpn: 1-25-1, Nishi-Shinjuku, Shinjuku-ku, Tokyo 163-0606; tel. (3) 3348-1111; fax (3) 3345-1386; internet www.taisei.co.jp; f. 1873; cap. and res 175,545m. (1999/2000), sales 1,750,391m. (2000/01); engineering, construction; Chair. OSAMU HIRASHIMA; Pres. KANJI HAYAMA; 10,190 employees.

Takeda Chemical Industries Ltd: 4-1-1, Doshomachi, Chuo-ku, Osaka 540-8645; tel. (6) 6204-2111; fax (6) 6204-2880; internet www.takeda.co.jp; f. 1925; cap. and res 1,212,864m., sales 963,480m. (2000/01); mfrs and distributors of pharmaceuticals, industrial chemicals, OTC drugs, food additives; enriched foods and drinks, agricultural chemicals, fertilizers; Chair. M. FUJINO; Pres. and CEO KUNIO TAKEDA; 16,254 employees.

TDK Corpn: 1-13-1, Nihonbashi, Chuo-ku, Tokyo 103-8272; tel. (3) 3278-5111; fax (3) 5201-7110; internet www.tdk.co.jp; f. 1935; cap. and res 637,749m., sales 689,911m. (2000/01); mfrs of recording media and electronic materials and components; Chair. YUTAKA OTOSHI; Pres. and CEO HAJIME SAWABE; 29,747 employees.

Teijin Ltd: 1-6-7, Minami-Honmachi, Chuo-ku, Osaka 541-8587. (6) 6268-2132; fax (6) 6268-3205; internet www.teijin.co.jp; f. 1918; cap. and res 70,787m., sales 761,409m. (2000/01); mfrs of fibres, yarns and fabrics from polyester, fibres (Teijin Tetoron), nylon, polyvinyl chloride fibre (Teijin Teviron), acetate, acrylic fibre (Teijin Beslon), polycarbonate resin (Panlite), acetate resin (Tenex), petrochemicals, pharmaceuticals; 75 subsidiaries; Chair. HIROSHI ITAGAKI; Pres. SHOSAKU YASUI; 5,220 employees.

Tomen Corpn: 3-2-18, Nakanoshimai, Kita-ku, Osaka 530-8622; tel. (6) 6447-9333; fax (6) 5208-9062; internet www.tomen.co.jp; f. 1920; cap. and res 493m. (1999/2000), sales 2,516,523m. (2000/01); distributors of natural resources and manufactured goods; Pres. MORIHIKO TASHIRO; 1,300 employees.

Toppan Printing Co Ltd: 1, Kanda Izumi-cho, Chiyoda-ku, Tokyo 101-0024; tel. (3) 3835-5741; fax (3) 3835-0674; e-mail kouhou@toppan.co.jp; internet www.toppan.co.jp; f. 1900; cap. and res 707,489m., sales 1,296,195m. (2001/02); Chair. H. FUJITA; Pres. NAOKI ADACHI; 1,610 employees.

Toray Industries Inc: Toray Bldg, 2-2-1, Nihonbashi-Muromachi, Chuo-ku, Tokyo 103-8666; tel. (3) 3245-5111; fax (3) 3245-5459; internet www.toray.co.jp; f. 1926; cap. and res 418,115m., sales 1,075,371m. (2000/01); mfrs of nylon, Toray Tetoron (polyester fibre), Toraylon (acrylic fibre), Torayca (carbon fibre), pharmaceuticals and medical equipment, plastics and chemicals; Chair. KATSUNOSUKE MAEDA; Pres. and CEO KATSUHIKO HIRAI; 8,790 employees.

Toshiba Corpn: 1-1-1, Shibaura, Minato-ku, Tokyo 105-8001; tel. (3) 3457-2096; fax (3) 5444-9202; internet www.toshiba.co.jp; f. 1875; cap. and res 982,128m. (1999/2000), sales 5,951,357m. (2000/01); manufacture, sale and export of electric appliances, apparatus and instruments; heavy electric machinery; overseas offices in 24 countries; Chair. TAIZO NISHIMURO; Pres. and CEO TADASHI OKAMURA; 52,265 employees.

Tostem Inax Holiding Corpn: 2-1-1, Ojima, Koto-ku, Tokyo 136-8535; tel. (3) 3638-8115; fax (3) 3638-8343; internet www.tostem.co.jp; cap. and res 373,697m., sales 716,471m. (2000/01); housing and building sashes, housing materials, fabricated home products; Chair. and CEO KENJIRO USHIODA; Pres. and Chief Operating Officer EIICHI TOBITA; 13,536 employees.

Toyo Seikan Kaisha Ltd: 1-3-1, Uchisaiwai-cho, Chiyoda-ku, Tokyo 100-8522; tel. (3) 3508-2113; fax (3) 3592-9471; sales 719,021m. (2000/01); metal products; Chair. YOSHIRO TAKASAKI; Pres. HIROFUMI MIKI; 5,825 employees.

Toyobo Co Ltd: 2-2-8, Dojima Hama, Kita-ku, Osaka 530-8230; tel (6) 6348-3137; fax (6) 6348-3149; internet www.toyobo.co.jp; f. 1882; cap. and res 43,341m., sales 402,876m. (2000/01); manufacture; Chair. MINORU SHIBATA; Pres. JUNJI TSUMURA; 4,080 employees.

Toyota Auto Body Co Ltd: 100, Kanayama, Ichiriyama-cho, Kariya, Aichi 448-8666; tel. (566) 36-2121; fax (566) 36-9113; sales 556,531m. (2000/01); Chair. AKIRA IIJIMA; Pres. RISUKE KUBOCHI; 7,889 employees.

Toyota Industries Corpn: 2-1, Toyodacho Kariya-shi, Aichi 448-8671; tel. (566) 22-2511; fax (566) 27-5650; internet www.Toyota-industries.com/textile/; f. 1926 (fmrly Toyoda Automatic Loom Works Ltd); cap. and res 316,293m., sales 625,772m. (1999/2000); transport manufacture; Chair. CHISEI ISOGAI; Pres. TADASHI ISHIKAWA; 9,580 employees.

Toyota Motor Corpn: 1, Toyota-cho, Toyota, Aichi 471-8571; tel. (565) 28-2121; fax (565) 23-5800; internet www.global.toyota.com; f. 1937; cap. and res 7,114,567m., sales 13,424,423m. (2000/01); manufacture and sale of passenger cars, trucks, forklifts and parts; Chair. HIROSHI OKUDA; Pres. FUJIO CHO; 66,000 employees.

UBE Industries Ltd: 1978–96, Kogushi, Ube City, Yamaguchi, 775-8633; tel. (8) 3631-1111; fax (8) 5419-6230; internet www.ube.co.jp; f. 1897; cap. and res 94,345m., sales 535,007m. (2000/01); production, processing and sale of coal, limestone, chemical fertilizers, sulphuric acid, nitric acid, oxalic acid, ammonium nitrate, ammonia, pharmaceuticals, cement, caprolactam, high pressure polyethylene, industrial machinery and equipment, cast steel products, synthetic rubbers; Chair. MAOMI NAGAHIRO; Pres. KAZUMASA TSUNEMI; 3,630 employees.

Yamaha Corpn: 10-1, Nakazawa-cho, Hamamatsu, Shizuoka 430-0904; tel. (53) 460-2071; fax (53) 456-1109; e-mail seki-sab@post.yamaha.co.jp; internet www.yamaha.co.jp; cap. 285,330m., sales 519,104m. (2000/2001); musical instruments, electronic devices; Pres. SHUJI ITO; 22,277 employees.

Yamaha Motor Co Ltd: 2500, Shingai Iwata-shi, Shizuokaken 438-8501; tel. (538) 32-1117; fax (538) 32-1131; internet www.yamaha-motor.co.jp; f. 1955; cap. and res 148,955m., sales 884,054m. (2000/01); mfrs of motorcycles, outboard motors, boats, snowmobiles; Pres. TORU HASEGAWA; 26,464 employees.

TRADE UNIONS

A feature of Japan's trade union movement is that the unions are usually based on single enterprises, embracing workers of different occupations in that enterprise. In June 1994 there were 32,581 unions; union membership stood at 12.5m. workers in 1996. In November 1989 the two largest confederations, SOHYO and RENGO, merged to form the Japan Trade Union Confederation (JTUC—RENGO).

Japanese Trade Union Confederation (JTUC–RENGO): 3-2-11, Kanda Surugadai, Chiyoda-ku, Tokyo 101-0062; tel. (3) 5295-0550; fax (3) 5295-0548; e-mail jtuc-kokusai@sv.rengo-net.or.jp; internet www.jtuc-rengo.or.jp; f. 1989; 7.7m. mems; Pres. ETSUYA WASHIO.

Principal Affiliated Unions

Ceramics Rengo (All-Japan Federation of Ceramics Industry Workers): 3-11, Heigocho, Mizuho-ku, Nagoya-shi, Aichi 467; tel. (52) 882-4562; fax (52) 882-9960; 30,083 mems; Pres. TSUNEYOSHI HAYAKAWA.

Chain Rokyo (Chain-store Labour Unions' Council): 3rd Floor, 2-29-8, Higashi-ikebukuro, Toshima-ku, Tokyo 170; tel. (3) 5951-1031; fax (3) 5951-1051; 40,015 mems; Pres. TOSHIFUMI HIRANO.

CSG Rengo (Japanese Federation of Chemical, Service and General Workers' Unions): Yuai Bldg, 8th Floor, 2-20-12, Shiba, Minato-ku, Tokyo 105; tel. (3) 3453-3801; fax (3) 3454-2236; f. 1951; 228,137 mems; Pres. DAISAKU KOUCHIYAMA.

Denki Rengo (Japanese Electrical, Electronic & Information Union): Denkirengo Bldg, 1-10-3, Mita, Minato-ku, Tokyo 108-8326; tel. (3) 3455-6911; fax (3) 3452-5406; internet www.jeiu.or.jp; f. 1953; 756,000 mems; Pres. KATSUTOSHI SUZUKI.

Denryoku Soren (Federation of Electric Power Related Industry Workers' Unions of Japan): TDS Mita 7-13, 3rd Floor, Mita Z-Chome, Minato-ku, Tokyo 108-0073; tel. (3) 3454-0231; fax (3) 3798-1470; e-mail info@denryokusoren.or.jp; internet www.denryoku soren.or.jp; 255,278 mems; Pres. NORIO TSUMAKI.

Dokiro (Hokkaido Seasonal Workers' Union): Hokuro Bldg, Kita 4, Nishi 12, Chuo-ku, Sapporo, Hokkaido 060; tel. (11) 261-5775; fax (11) 272-2255; 19,063 mems; Pres. YOSHIZO ODAWARA.

Gomu Rengo (Japanese Rubber Workers' Union Confederation): 2-3-3, Mejiro, Toshima-ku, Tokyo 171; tel. (3) 3984-3343; fax (3) 3984-5862; 60,070 mems; Pres. YASUO FURUKAWA.

Hitetsu Rengo (Japanese Metal Mine Workers' Union): Gotanda Metalion Bldg, 5-21-15, Higashi-gotanda, Shinagawa-ku, Tokyo 141; tel. (3) 5420-1881; fax (3) 5420-1880; 23,500 mems; Pres. SHOUZOU HIMENO.

Insatsu Roren (Federation of Printing Information Media Workers' Unions): Yuai-kaikan, 7th Floor, 2-20-12, Shiba, Minato-ku, Tokyo 105-0014; tel. (3) 5442-0191; fax (3) 5442-0219; 22,303 mems; Pres. HIROFUMI NAKABAYASHI.

JA Rengo (All-Japan Agriculture Co-operative Staff Members' Union): 964-1, Toyotomicho-mikage, Himeji-shi, Hyogo 679-21; tel. and fax (792) 64-3618; 2,772 mems; Pres. YUTAKA OKADA.

Japan Federation of Service and Distributive Workers Unions: New State Manor Bldg, 3rd Floor, 2-23-1, Yoyogi, Shibuya-ku, Tokyo 151-0053; tel. (3) 3370-4121; fax (3) 3370-1640; internet www.jsd-union.org; 170,000 mems; Pres. MITSUO NAGUMO.

Jichi Roren (National Federation of Prefectural and Municipal Workers' Unions): 1-15-22, Oji-honcho, Kita-ku, Tokyo 114; tel. and fax (3) 3907-1584; 5,728 mems; Pres. NOBUO UENO.

Jichiro (All-Japan Prefectural and Municipal Workers' Union): Jichiro Bldg, 1, Rokubancho, Chiyoda-ku, Tokyo 102-0085; tel. (3) 3263-0263; fax (3) 5210-7422; internet www.jichiro.gr.jp; f. 1951; 1,004,000 mems; Pres. MORISHIGE GOTO.

Jidosha Soren (Confederation of Japan Automobile Workers' Unions): U-Life Center, 1-4-26, Kaigan, Minato-ku, Tokyo 105-8523; tel. (3) 3434-7641; fax (3) 3434-7428; internet www.jaw.or.jp; f. 1972; 728,000 mems; Pres. YUJI KATO.

Jiunro (Japan Automobile Drivers' Union): 2-3-12, Nakameguro, Meguro-ku, Tokyo 153; tel. (3) 3711-9387; fax (3) 3719-2624; 1,958 mems; Pres. SADAO KANEZUKA.

JR-Rengo (Japan Railway Trade Unions Confederation): TOKO Bldg, 9th Floor, 1-8-10, Nihonbashi-muromachi, Chuo-ku, Tokyo 103; tel. (3) 3270-4590; fax (3) 3270-4429; 78,418 mems; Pres. KAZUAKI KUZUNO.

JR Soren (Japan Confederation of Railway Workers' Unions): Meguro-satsuki Bldg, 3-2-13, Nishi-gotanda, Shinagawa-ku, Tokyo 141-0031; tel. (3) 3491-7191; fax (3) 3491-7192; internet www.jr -souren.com; 87,000 mems; Pres. YUJI ODA.

Jyoho Roren (Japan Federation of Telecommunications, Electronic Information and Allied Workers): Zendentsu-rodo Bldg, 3-6, Kanda Surugadai, Chiyoda-ku, Tokyo 101-0062; tel. (3) 3219-2231; fax (3) 3253-3268; 265,132 mems; Pres. KAZUO SASAMORI.

Kagaku League 21 (Japanese Federation of Chemistry Workers' Unions): Senbai Bldg, 5-26-30, Shiba, Minato-ku, Tokyo 108-8389; tel. (3) 3452-5591; fax (3) 3454-7464; internet www.jec-u.com; formed by merger of Goka Roren and Zenkoku Kagaku; 104,000 mems; Pres. KATUTOSHI KATO.

Kagaku Soren (Japanese Federation of Chemical Workers' Unions): Kyodo Bldg, 7th Floor, 2-4-10, Higashi-shinbashi, Minato-ku, Tokyo 105; tel. (3) 5401-2268; fax (3) 5401-2263; Pres. HIROKAZU IWASAKI.

Kaiin Kumiai (All-Japan Seamen's Union): 7-15-26, Roppongi, Minato-ku, Tokyo 106-0032; tel. (3) 5410-8330; fax (3) 5410-8336; internet www.jsu.or.jp; 35,000 mems; Pres. SAKAE IDEMOTO.

Kamipa Rengo (Japanese Federation of Pulp and Paper Workers' Unions): 2-12-4, Kita Aoyama, Minato-ku, Tokyo 107-0061; tel. (3) 3402-7656; fax (3) 3402-7659; 50,858 mems; Pres. TUNEO MUKAI.

Kensetsu Rengo (Japan Construction Trade Union Confederation): Yuai Bldg, 7th Floor, 2-20-12, Shiba, Minato-ku, Tokyo 105; tel. (3) 3454-0951; fax (3) 3453-0582; 13,199 mems; Pres. MASAYASU TERASAWA.

Kinzoku Kikai (National Metal and Machinery Workers' Unions of Japan): 6-2, Sakuraokacho, Shibuya-ku, Tokyo 150-0031; tel. (3) 3463-4231; fax (3) 3463-7391; f. 1989; 205,082 mems; Pres. MASAOKI KITAURA.

Kokko Soren (Japan General Federation of National Public Service Employees' Unions): 1-2-1, Kasumigaseki, Chiyoda-ku, Tokyo 100; tel. (3) 3508-4990; fax (3) 5512-7555; 40,370 mems; Pres. MARUYAMA KENZO.

Koku Domei (Japanese Confederation of Aviation Labour): Nikkokiso Bldg, 2nd Floor, 1-6-3, Haneda-kuko, Ota-ku, Tokyo 144; tel. (3) 3747-7642; fax (3) 3747-7647; 16,310 mems; Pres. KATSUMI UTAGAWA.

Kokuzei Roso (Japanese Confederation of National Tax Unions): R154, Okurasho Bldg, 3-1-1, Kasumigaseki, Chiyoda-ku, Tokyo 100; tel. (3) 3581-2573; fax (3) 3581-3843; 40,128 mems; Pres. TATSUO SASAKI.

Kotsu Roren (Japan Federation of Transport Workers' Unions): Yuai Bldg, 3rd Floor, 2-20-12, Shiba, Minato-ku 105-0014; tel. (3) 3451-7243; fax (3) 3454-7393; 97,239 mems; Pres. SHIGEO MAKI.

Koun-Domei (Japanese Confederation of Port and Transport Workers' Unions): 5-10-2, Kamata, Ota-ku, Tokyo 144-0052; tel. (3) 3733-5285; fax (3) 3733-5280; f. 1987; 1,638 mems; Pres. SAKAE IDEMOTO.

Leisure Service Rengo (Japan Federation of Leisure Service Industries Workers' Unions): Zosen Bldg, 4th Floor, 3-5-6, Misakicho, Chiyoda-ku, Tokyo 101-0061; tel. (3) 3230-1724; fax (3) 3239-1553; 47,601 mems; Pres. HIROSHI SAWADA.

NHK Roren (Federation of All-NHK Labour Unions): NHK, 2-2-1, Jinnan, Shibuya-ku, Tokyo 150; tel. (3) 3485-6007; fax (3) 3469-9271; 12,526 mems; Pres. YASUZO SUDO.

Nichirinro (National Forest Workers' Union of Japan): 1-2-1, Kasumigaseki, Chiyoda-ku, Tokyo 100; tel. (3) 3580-8891; fax (3) 3580-1596; Pres. KOH IKEGAMI.

Nikkyoso (Japan Teachers' Union): Japan Education Hall, 2-6-2, Hitotsubashi, Chiyoda-ku, Tokyo 101-0003; tel. (3) 3265-2171; fax (3) 3230-0172; internet www.jtu-net.or.jp; f. 1947; 400,000 mems; Pres. NAGAKAZU SAKAKIBARA.

Rosai Roren (National Federation of Zenrosai Workers' Unions): 2-12-10, Yoyogi, Shibuya-ku, Tokyo 151; tel. (3) 3299-0161; fax (3) 3299-0126; 2,091 mems; Pres. TADASHI TAKACHI.

Seiho Roren (National Federation of Life Insurance Workers' Unions): Tanaka Bldg, 3-19-5, Yushima, Bunkyo-ku, Tokyo 113-0034; tel. (3) 3837-2031; fax (3) 3837-2037; 414,021 mems; Pres. YOHTARU KOHNO.

Seiroren (Labour Federation of Government Related Organizations): Hasaka Bldg, 4th-6th Floors, 1-10-3, Kanda-ogawacho, Chiyoda-ku, Tokyo 101; tel. (3) 5295-6360; fax (3) 5295-6362; Chair. MITSURU WATANABE.

Sekiyu Roren (Japan Confederation of Petroleum Industry Workers' Union): NKK Bldg, 7th Floor, 2-18-2, Nishi-shinbashi, Minato-ku, Tokyo 105; tel. (3) 3578-1315; fax (3) 3578-3455; 28,807 mems; Pres. HIROSHI MOCHIMARU.

Sen'i Seikatsu Roren (Japan Federation of Textile Clothing Workers' Unions of Japan): Katakura Bldg, 3-1-2, Kyobashi, Chuo-ku, Tokyo 104; tel. (3) 3281-4806; fax (3) 3274-3165; 4,598 mems; Pres. KATSUYOSHI SAKAI.

Shigen Roren (Federation of Japanese Metal Resources Workers' Unions): Roppongi Azeria Bldg, 1-3-8, Nishi-azabu, Minato-ku, Tokyo 106; tel. (3) 3402-6666; fax (3) 3402-6667; Pres. MINORU TAKAHASHI.

Shin Unten (F10-Drivers' Craft Union): 4th Floor, 3-25-6, Negishi, Taito-ku, Tokyo 110; tel. (3) 5603-1015; fax (3) 5603-5351; 4,435 mems; Pres. SHOHEI SHINOZAKI.

Shinkagaku (National Organization of All Chemical Workers): MF Bldg, 2nd Floor, 2-3-3, Fujimi, Chiyoda-ku, Tokyo 102; tel. (3) 3239-2933; fax (3) 3239-2932; 8,400 mems; Pres. HISASHI YASUI.

Shinrin Roren (Japanese Federation of Forest and Wood Workers' Unions): 3-28-7, Otsuka, Bunkyo-ku, Tokyo 112; tel. (3) 3945-6385; fax (3) 3945-6477; 13,928 mems; Pres. ISAO SASAKI.

Shitetsu Soren (General Federation of Private Railway Workers' Unions): 4-3-5, Takanawa, Minato-ku, Tokyo 108-0074; tel. (3) 3473-0166; fax (3) 3447-3927; f. 1947; 160,000 mems; Pres. RYOICHI IKEMURA.

Shokuhin Rengo (Japan Federation of Foods and Tobacco Workers' Unions): Hiroo Office Bldg, 8th Floor, 1-3-18, Hiroo, Shibuya-ku, Tokyo 150; tel. (3) 3446-2082; fax (3) 3446-6779; f. 1991; 116,370 mems; Pres. SHIGERU MASUDA.

Shokuhin Rokyo (Food Industry Workers' Union Council (FIWUC)): ST Bldg, 6th Floor, 4-9-4, Hatchyoubori, Chuo-ku, Tokyo 104; tel. (3) 3555-7671; fax (3) 3555-7760; Pres. TAROU FUJIE.

Sonpo Roren (Federation of Non-Life Insurance Workers' Unions of Japan): Kanda MS Bldg, 4th Floor, 27, Kanda-higashimatsushitacho, Chiyoda-ku, Tokyo 101; tel. (3) 5295-0071; fax (3) 5295-0073; Pres. KUNIO MATSUMOTO.

Tanro (Japan Coal Miners' Union): Hokkaido Rodosha Bldg, 2nd Floor, Kita-11, Nishi-4, Kita-ku, Sapporo-shi, Hokkaido 001; tel. (11) 717-0291; fax (11) 717-0295; 1,353 mems; Pres. KAZUO SAKUMA.

Tanshokukyo (Association of Japan Coal Mining Staff Unions): 2-30, Nishiminatomachi, Omuta-shi, Fukuoka 836; tel. (944) 52-3883; fax (944) 52-3853; Pres. KEIZO UMEKI.

Tekko Roren (Japan Federation of Steel Workers' Unions): I&S Riverside Bldg, 4th Floor, 1-23-4, Shinkawa, Chuo-ku, Tokyo 104-0033; tel. (3) 3555-0401; fax (3) 3555-0407; internet www.tekkororen.or.jp; 135,000 mems; Pres. TAKESHI OGINO.

Tokei Roso (Statistics Labour Union Management and Co-ordination Agency): 19-1, Somucho, Wakamatsucho, Shinjuku-ku, Tokyo 162; tel. (3) 3202-1111; fax (3) 3205-3850; Pres. TOSHIAKI MAGARA.

Toshiko (The All-Japan Municipal Transport Workers' Union): 3-1-35, Shibaura, Minato-ku, Tokyo 108; tel. (3) 3451-5221; fax (3) 3452-2977; 43,612 mems; Pres. SHUNICHI SUZUKI.

Unyu Roren (All-Japan Federation of Transport Workers' Union): Zennittsu Kasumigaseki Bldg, 5th Floor, 3-3-3, Kasumigaseki, Chiyoda-ku, Tokyo 100-0013; tel. (3) 3503-2171; fax (3) 3503-2176; f. 1968; 143,084 mems; Pres. KAZUMARO SUZUKI.

Zeikan Roren (Federation of Japanese Customs Personnel Labour Unions): 3-1-1, Kasumigaseki, Chiyoda-ku, Tokyo 100; tel. and fax (3) 3593-1788; Pres. RIKIO SUDO.

Zen Insatsu (All-Printing Agency Workers' Union): 3-59-12, Nishigahara, Kita-ku, Tokyo 114; tel. (3) 3910-7131; fax (3) 3910-7155; 5,431 mems; Chair. TOSHIO KATAKURA.

Zen Yusei (All-Japan Postal Labour Union): 1-20-6, Sendagaya, Shibuya-ku, Tokyo 151; tel. (3) 3478-7101; fax (3) 5474-7085; 77,573 mems; Pres. NOBUAKI IZAWA.

Zenchuro (All-Japan Garrison Forces Labour Union): 3-41-8, Shiba, Minato-ku, Tokyo 105; tel. (3) 3455-5971; fax (3) 3455-5973; Pres. EIBUN MEDORUMA.

Zendensen (All- Japan Electric Wire Labour Union): 1-11-6, Hatanodai, Shinagawa-ku, Tokyo 142; tel. (3) 3785-2991; fax (3) 3785-2995; Pres. NAOKI TOKUNAGA.

Zen-eien (National Cinema and Theatre Workers' Union): Hibiya Park Bldg, 1-8-1, Yurakucho, Chiyoda-ku, Tokyo 100; tel. (3) 3201-4476; fax (3) 3214-0597; Pres. SADAHIRO MATSUURA.

Zengin Rengo (All-Japan Federative Council of Bank Labour Unions): R904, Kyodo Bldg, 16-8, Nihonbashi-Kodenmacho, Chuo-ku, Tokyo 103; tel. and fax (3) 3661-4886; 32,104 mems; Pres. KIKUO HATTORI.

Zenjiko Roren (National Federation of Automobile Transport Workers' Unions): 3-7-9, Sendagaya, Shibuya-ku, Tokyo 151; tel. (3) 3408-0875; fax (3) 3497-0107; Pres. OSAMU MIMASHI.

Zenkairen (All-Japan Shipping Labour Union): Shinbashi Ekimae Bldg, No. 1, 8th Floor, 2-20-15, Shinbashi, Minato-ku, Tokyo 105; tel. (3) 3573-2401; fax (3) 3573-2404; Chair. MASAHIKO SATO.

Zenkin Rengo (Japanese Federation of Metal Industry Unions): Yuai Bldg, 5th Floor, 2-20-12, Shiba, Minato-ku, Tokyo 105-0014; tel. (3) 3451-2141; fax (3) 3452-0239; f. 1989; 310,818 mems; Pres. MITSURO HATTORI.

Zenkoku Gas (Federation of Gas Workers' Unions of Japan): 5-11-1, Omori-nishi, Ota-ku, Tokyo 143; tel. (3) 5493-8381; fax (3) 5493-8216; 31,499 mems; Pres. AKIO HAMAUZU.

Zenkoku Keiba Rengo (National Federation of Horse-racing Workers): 2500, Mikoma, Miho-mura, Inashiki-gun, Ibaragi 300-04; tel. (298) 85-0402; fax (298) 85-0416; Pres. TOYOHIKO OKUMURA.

Zenkoku Nodanro (National Federation of Agricultural, Forestry and Fishery Corporations' Workers' Unions): 1-5-8, Hamamatsucho, Minato-ku, Tokyo 105; tel. (3) 3437-0931; fax (3) 3437-0681; 26,010 mems; Pres. SHIN-ICHIRO OKADA.

Zenkoku Semento (National Federation of Cement Workers' Unions of Japan): 5-29-2, Shinbashi, Minato-ku, Tokyo 105; tel. (3) 3436-3666; fax (3) 3436-3668; Pres. KIYONORI URAKAWA.

Zenkoku-Ippan (National Council of General Amalgamated Workers' Unions): Zosen Bldg, 5th Floor, 3-5-6, Misakicho, Chiyoda-ku, Tokyo 101-0061; tel. (3) 3230-4071; fax (3) 3230-4360; 54,708 mems; Pres. YASUHIKO MATSUI.

Zenkyoro (National Race Workers' Union): Nihon Kyoiku Kaikan, 7th Floor, 2-6-2, Hitotsubashi, Chiyoda-ku, Tokyo 101; tel. (3) 5210-5156; fax (3) 5210-5157; 24,720 mems; Pres. SHIMAKO YOSHIDA.

Zennitto (Japan Painting Workers' Union): Shin-osaka Communication Plaza, 1st Floor, 1-6-36, Nishi-miyahara, Yodogawa-ku, Osaka-shi, Osaka 532; tel. (6) 6393-8677; fax (6) 6393-8533; Pres. SEIICHI UOZA.

Zenrokin (Federation of Labour Bank Workers' Unions of Japan): Nakano Bldg, 3rd Floor, 1-11, Kanda-Awajicho, Chiyoda-ku, Tokyo 101; tel. (3) 3256-1015; fax (3) 3256-1045; Pres. EIICHI KAKU.

Zensen Domei (Japanese Federation of Textile, Garment, Chemical, Commercial, Food and Allied Industries Workers' Unions): 4-8-16, Kudanminami, Chiyoda-ku, Tokyo 102-0074; tel. (3) 3288-3549; fax (3) 3288-3728; e-mail kokusai@zensen.or.jp; internet www.zensen.or.jp; f. 1946; 1,246 affiliates; 613,810 mems; Pres. TSUYOSHI TAKAGI.

Zensuido (All-Japan Water Supply Workers' Union): 1-4-1, Hongo, Bunkyo-ku, Tokyo 113; tel. (3) 3816-4132; fax (3) 3818-1430; 33,522 mems; Pres. KAZUMASA KATO.

Zentanko (National Union of Coal Mine Workers): Yuai Bldg, 6th Floor, 2-20-12, Shiba, Minato-ku, Tokyo 105; tel. (3) 3453-4721; fax (3) 3453-6457; Pres. AKIRA YASUNAGA.

Zentei (Japan Postal Workers' Union): 1-2-7, Koraku, Bunkyo-ku, Tokyo 112-0004; tel. (3) 3812-4260; fax (3) 5684-7201; internet www.zentei.or.jp; 156,784 mems; Pres. SUSUMU TAKATO.

Zenzohei (All-Mint Labour Union): 1-1-79, Temma, Kita-ku, Osaka-shi, Osaka 530; tel. and fax (6) 6354-2389; Pres. CHIKASHI HIGUCHI.

Zenzosen-kikai (All-Japan Shipbuilding and Engineering Union): Zosen Bldg, 6th Floor, 3-5-6, Misakicho, Chiyoda-ku, Tokyo 101; tel. (3) 3265-1921; fax (3) 3265-1870; Pres. YOSHIMI FUNATSU.

Zosen Juki Roren (Japan Confederation of Shipbuilding and Engineering Workers' Unions): Yuai Kaikan Bldg, 4th Floor, 2-20-12, Shiba, Minato-ku, Tokyo 105-0014; tel. (3) 3451-6783; fax (3) 3451-6935; e-mail zosenjuki@mth.biglobe.ne.jp; 111,405 mems; Pres. MASAYUKI YOSHII.

Transport

RAILWAYS

Japan Railways (JR) Group: 1-6-5, Marunouchi, Chiyoda-ku, Tokyo 100-0005; tel. (3) 3215-9649; fax (3) 3213-5291; internet www.japanrail.com; fmrly the state-controlled Japanese National Railways (JNR); reorg. and transferred to private-sector control in 1987; the high-speed Shinkansen rail network consists of the Tokaido line (Tokyo to Shin-Osaka, 552.6 km), the Sanyo line (Shin-Osaka to Hakata, 623.3 km), the Tohoku line (Tokyo to Morioka, 535.3 km) and the Joetsu line (Omiya to Niigata, 303.6 km). The 4-km link between Ueno and Tokyo stations was opened in June 1991. The Yamagata Shinkansen (Fukushima to Yamagata, 87 km) was converted in 1992 from a conventional railway line. It is operated as a branch of the Tohoku Shinkansen with through trains from Tokyo, though not at full Shinkansen speeds. In 1997 the total railway route length was about 36,634 km.

Central Japan Railway Co: Yaesu Center Bldg, 1-6-6, Yaesu, Chuo-ku, Tokyo 103-8288; tel. (3) 3274-9727; fax (3) 5255-6780; internet www.jr-central.co.jp; f. 1987; also operates travel agency services, etc.; Chair. HIROSHI SUDA; Pres. YOSHIYUKI KASAI.

East Japan Railway Co: 2-2-2, Yoyogi, Shibuya-ku, Tokyo 151-8578; tel. (3) 5334-1151; fax (3) 5334-1110; internet www.jreast.co.jp; privatized in 1987; Pres. MUTSUTAKE OTSUKA.

Hokkaido Railway Co: West 15-chome, Kita 11-jo, Chuo-ku, Sapporo 060-8644; tel. (11) 700-5717; fax (11) 700-5719; e-mail keieki@jrhokkaido.co.jp; internet www.jrhokkaido.co.jp; Chair. YOSHIHIRO OHMORI; Pres. SHINICHI SAKAMOTO.

Japan Freight Railway Co: 2-3-19, Koraku, Bynkyo-ku, Tokyo 112-0004; tel (3) 3816-9722; internet www.jrfreight.co.jp; Chair. MASASHI HASHIMOTO; Pres. YASUSHI TANAHASHI.

Kyushu Railway Co: 3-25-21, Hakataekimae, Hakata-ku, Fukuoka 812-8566; tel. (92) 474-2501; fax (92) 474-9745; internet www.jrkyushu.co.jp; Chair. K. TANAKA; Pres. S. ISHIHARA.

Shikoku Railway Co: 8-33, Hamano-cho, Takamatsu, Kagawa 760-8580; tel. (87) 825-1622; fax (87) 825-1623; internet www.jr-shikoku.co.jp; Chair. HIROATSU ITO; Pres. TOSHIYUKI UMEHARA.

West Japan Railway Co: 2-4-24, Shibata, Kita-ku, Osaka 530-8341; tel. (6) 6375-8981; fax (6) 6375-8919; e-mail wjr01020@mxy.meshnet.or.jp; internet www.westjr.co.jp; scheduled for privatization in 2001; Chair. MASATAKA IDE; Pres. SHOJIRO NANYA.

Other Principal Private Companies

Hankyu Corpn: 1-16-1, Shibata, Kita-ku, Osaka 530-8389; tel. (6) 6373-5092; fax (6) 6373-5670; e-mail koho@hankyu.co.jp; internet www.hankyu.co.jp; f. 1907; links Osaka, Kyoto, Kobe and Takarazuka; Chair. KOHEI KOBAYASHI; Pres. T. OHASHI.

Hanshin Electric Railway Co Ltd: 1-1-24, Ebie, Fukushima-ku, Osaka 553; tel. (6) 6457-2123; f. 1899; Chair. S. KUMA; Pres. M. TEZUKA.

Keihan Electric Railway Co Ltd: 1-2-27, Shiromi, Chuo-ku, Osaka 540; tel. (6) 6944-2521; fax (6) 6944-2501; internet www.keihan.co.jp; f. 1906; Chair. MINORU MIYASHITA; Pres. A. KIMBA.

Keihin Express Electric Railway Co Ltd: 2-20-20, Takanawa, Minato-ku, Tokyo 108-8625; tel. (3) 3280-9120; fax (3) 3280-9199; internet www.keikyu.co.jp; f. 1899; Chair. ICHIRO HIRAMATSU; Pres. M. KOTANI.

Keio Electric Railway Co Ltd: 1-9-1, Sekido, Tama City, Tokyo 206-8052; tel. (42) 337-3106; fax (42) 374-9322; internet www.keio.co.jp; f. 1913; Chair. K. KUWAYAMA; Pres. H. NISHIYAMA.

Keisei Electric Railway Co Ltd: 1-10-3, Oshiage, Sumida-ku, Tokyo 131; tel. (3) 3621-2242; fax (3) 3621-2233; internet www.keisei.co.jp; f. 1909; Chair. (vacant); Pres. M. SATO.

Kinki Nippon Railway Co Ltd: 6-1-55, Uehommachi, Tennoji-ku, Osaka 543-8585; tel. (6) 6775-3444; fax (6) 6775-3468; internet www.kintetsu.co.jp; f. 1910; Chair. WA TASHIRO; Pres. AKIO TSUJII.

Nagoya Railroad Co Ltd: 1-2-4, Meieki, Nakamura-ku, Nagoya-shi 450; tel. (52) 571-2111; fax (52) 581-6060; e-mail info@meitetsu.co.jp; internet www.meitetsu.co.jp; Chair. S. TANIGUCHI; Pres. S. MINOURA.

Nankai Electric Railway Co Ltd: 5-1-60, Namba, Chuo-ku, Osaka 542; tel. (6) 6644-7121; internet www.nankai.co.jp; Pres. SHIGERU YOSHIMURA; Vice-Pres. K. OKAMOTO.

Nishi-Nippon Railroad Co Ltd: 1-11-17, Tenjin-cho, Chuo-ku, Fukuoka 810; tel. (92) 761-6631; fax (92) 722-1405; internet www.nnr.co.jp; serves northern Kyushu; Chair. H. YOSHIMOTO; Pres. G. KIMOTO.

Odakyu Electric Railway Co Ltd: 1-8-3, Nishi Shinjuku, Shinjuku-ku, Tokyo 160; tel. (3) 3349-2151; fax (3) 3346-1899; internet www.odakyu-group.co.jp; f. 1948; Chair. TATSUZO TOSHIMITSU; Pres. M. KITANAKA.

Sanyo Electric Railway Co Ltd: 3-1-1, Oyashiki-dori, Nagata-ku, Kobe 653; tel. (78) 611-2211; Pres. T. WATANABE.

Seibu Railway Co Ltd: 1-11-1, Kasunokidai, Tokorozawa-shi, Saitama 359; tel. (429) 26-2035; fax (429) 26-2237; internet www.seibu-group.co.jp/railways; f. 1894; Pres. YOSHIAKI TSUTSUMI.

Tobu Railway Co Ltd: 1-1-2, Oshiage, Sumida-ku, Tokyo 131-8522; tel. (3) 3621-5057; internet www.tobu.co.jp; f. 1897; Chair. KAICHIRO NEZU; Pres. TAKASHIGE UCHIDA.

Tokyo Express Electric Railway Co Ltd: 5-6, Nanpeidai-cho, Shibuya-ku, Tokyo 150; tel. (3) 3477-6111; fax (3) 3496-2965; e-mail public@tokyu.co.jp; internet www.tokyu.co.jp; f. 1922; Pres. S. SHIMUZU.

Principal Subways, Monorails and Tunnels

Subway services operate in Tokyo, Osaka, Kobe, Nagoya, Sapporo, Yokohama, Kyoto, Sendai and Fukuoka with a combined network of about 500 km. Most new subway lines are directly linked with existing private railway terminals which connect the cities with suburban areas.

The first commercial monorail system was introduced in 1964 with straddle-type cars between central Tokyo and Tokyo International Airport, a distance of 13 km. In 1988 the total length of monorail was 38.6 km.

In 1985 the 54-km Seikan Tunnel (the world's longest undersea tunnel), linking the islands of Honshu and Hokkaido, was completed. Electric rail services through the tunnel began operating in March 1988.

Fukuoka City Subway: Fukuoka Municipal Transportation Bureau, 2-5-31, Daimyo, Chuo-ku, Fukuoka 810-0041; tel. (92) 732-4107; fax (92) 721-0754; internet subway.city.fukuoka.jp; 2 lines of 17.8 km open; Dir KENNICHIROU NISHI.

Kobe Rapid Transit: 6-5-1, Kanocho, Chuo-ku, Kobe 650; tel. (78) 331-8181; 22.7 km open; Dir YASUO MAENO.

Kyoto Rapid Transit: 48, Bojocho Mibu, Nakakyo-ku, Kyoto 604; tel. (75) 822-9115; fax (75) 822-9240; 26.4 km open; Chair. T. TANABE.

Nagoya Subway: City of Nagoya Transportation Bureau, City Hall West Annex, 3-1-1, Sannomaru, Naka-ku, Nagoya 460-8508; tel. (52) 972-3824; fax (52) 972-3849; internet www.kotsu.city.nagoya.jp; 78.2 km open (2001); Dir-Gen. TAKAYASU TSUKAMOTO.

Osaka Monorail: 5-1-1, Higashi-machi, Shin-Senri, Toyonakashi, Osaka 565; tel. (6) 871-8280; fax (6) 871-8284; 113.5 km open; Gen. Man. S. OKA.

Osaka Underground Railway: Osaka Municipal Transportation Bureau, 1-11-53, Kujominami, Nishi-ku, Osaka 550; tel. (6) 6582-1101; fax (6) 6582-7997; f. 1933; 120 km open in 1998; the 6.6 km computer-controlled 'New Tram' service began between Suminoe-koen and Nakafuto in 1981; a seventh line between Kyobashi and Tsurumi-ryokuchi was opened in 1990; Gen. Man. HARUMI SAKAI.

Sapporo Transportation Bureau: Higashi, 2-4-1, Oyachi, Atsubetsu-ku, Sapporo 004; tel. (11) 896-2708; fax (11) 896-2790; f. 1971; 3 lines of 48 km open in 1993/94; Dir T. IKEGAMI.

Sendai City Subway: Sendai City Transportation Bureau, 1-4-15, Kimachidori, Aoba-ku, Sendai-shi, Miyagi-ken 980-0801; tel. (22) 224-5502; fax (22) 224-6839; internet www.comminet.or.jp/~kotsu-s; 15.4 km open; Dir T. IWAMA.

Tokyo Underground Railway: Teito Rapid Transit Authority, 3-19-6, Higashi Ueno, Taito-ku, Tokyo 110-0015; tel. (3) 3837-7046; fax (3) 3837-7048; internet www.tokyometro.go.jp; f. 1941; Pres. YASUTOSHI TSUCHISAKA; 177.2 km open.

Yokohama Rapid Transit: Municipal Transportation Bureau, 1-1, Minato-cho, Naka-ku, Yokohama 231-80; tel. (45) 671-3201; fax (45) 664-3266; 40.4 km open; Dir-Gen. MICHINORI KISHIDA.

ROADS

In December 1999 Japan's road network extended to an estimated 1,161,894 km, including 6,455 km of motorways and 53,685 km of highways. In May 1999 work was completed on a 29-year project to construct three routes, consisting of a total of 19 bridges, between the islands of Honshu and Shikoku across the Seto inland sea, at a cost of some US $25,000m.

There is a national omnibus service, 60 publicly-operated services and 298 privately-operated services.

Japan Highway Public Corpn: 3-3-2, Kasumigaseki, Chiyoda-ku, Tokyo 100-8979; tel. (3) 3506-0111; privatization plans announced in Dec. 2001.

SHIPPING

Shipping in Japan is subject to the supervision of the Ministry of Transport. At 31 December 2001 the Japanese merchant fleet (7,924 vessels) had a total displacement of 16,653,028 grt. The main ports are Tokyo, Yokohama, Nagoya and Osaka. The rebuilding of the port at Kobe, severely damaged by an earthquake in January 1995, was completed in 1997.

Principal Companies

Daiichi Chuo Kisen Kaisha: Dowa Bldg, 3-7-13, Toyoi, Koto-ku, Tokyo 103-8271; tel. (3) 5634-2276; fax (3) 5634-2262; f. 1960; liner and tramp services; Pres. MAHIKO SAOTOME.

Iino Kaiun Kaisha Ltd: Iino Bldg, 2-1-1, Uchisaiwai-cho, Chiyoda-ku, Tokyo 100; tel. (3) 3506-3037; fax (3) 3508-4121; f. 1918; cargo and tanker services; Chair. T. CHIBA; Pres. A. KARINO.

Kansai Kisen KK: Osaka Bldg, 3-6-32, Nakanoshima, Kita-ku, Osaka 552; tel. (6) 6574-9131; fax (6) 6574-9149; f. 1942; domestic passenger services; Pres. TOSHIKAZU EGUCHI.

Kawasaki Kisen Kaisha Ltd (K Line): 1-2-9, Nishi Shinbashi, Minato-ku, Tokyo 105-8421; tel. (3) 3595-5082; fax (3) 3595-5001; e-mail otaki@email.kline.co.jp; internet www.kline.co.jp; f. 1919; containers, cars, LNG, LPG and oil tankers, bulk carriers; Chair. of Bd I. SHINTANI; Exec. Vice-Pres. Z. WAKABAYASHI.

Nippon Yusen Kaisha (NYK) Line: 2-3-2, Marunouchi, Chiyoda-ku, Tokyo 100-0005; tel. (3) 3284-5151; fax (3) 3284-6361; e-mail prteam@jp.nykline.com; internet www.nykline.com; f. 1885; merged with Showa Line Ltd in 1998; world-wide container, cargo, pure car and truck carriers, tanker and bulk carrying services; Chair. JIRO NEMOTO; Pres. KENTARO KAWAMURA.

Nissho Shipping Co Ltd: 33, Mori Bldg, 7th Floor, 3-8-21, Toranomon, Minato-ku, Tokyo 105; tel. (3) 3438-3511; fax (3) 3438-3566; f. 1943; Pres. MINORU IKEDA.

OSK Mitsui Ltd: Shosen Mitsui Bldg, 2-1-1, Toranomon, Minato-ku, Tokyo 105-91; tel. (3) 3587-7092; fax (3) 3587-7734; f. 1942; merged with Navix Line Ltd in 1999; world-wide container, liner, tramp, and specialized carrier and tanker services; Chair. SUSUMU TEMPORIN; Pres. MASAHURU IKUTA.

Ryukyu Kaiun KK: 1-24-11, Nishi-machi, Naha, Okinawa 900; tel. (98) 868-8161; fax (98) 868-8561; cargo and passenger services on domestic routes; Pres. M. AZAMA.

Taiheiyo Kaiun Co Ltd: Mitakokusai Bldg, 23rd Floor, 1-4-28, Minato-ku, Tokyo 100; tel. (3) 5445-5805; fax (3) 5445-5806; f. 1951; cargo and tanker services; Pres. SANROKURO YAMAJI.

CIVIL AVIATION

There are international airports at Tokyo (Haneda and Narita), Osaka, Nagoya, and Fukuoka. In 1991 the Government approved a plan to build five new airports, and to expand 17 existing ones. This project was expected to take five years to complete and to cost

US $25,000m. There are proposals to build new airports at Shizuoka, Nagoya and Kobe. In September 1994 the world's first offshore international airport (Kansai International Airport) was opened in Osaka Bay, and a second runway was due for completion in 2007. In April 2002 a second runway was opened at Narita. In December 2001 plans were approved for a fourth runway at Haneda. At March 1999 a total of 85 airports were in operation.

Air Do: 6, Nishi, Kita 5, Chuo-ku, Sapporo; tel. (11) 252-5533; fax (11) 252-5580; e-mail postbear@airdo.co.jp; internet www.airdo.co.jp; f. 1996; domestic service between Tokyo and Sapporo; Pres. AKIRA NAKAMURA.

Air Nippon: 3-5-10, Haneda Airport, Ota-ku, Tokyo 144-0041; tel. (3) 5462-1911; fax (3) 5462-1941; internet www.ananet.or.jp/ank; f. 1974; formerly Nihon Kinkyori Airways; international and domestic passenger services; Pres. and CEO YUZURU MASUMOTO.

All Nippon Airways—ANA: 3-5-10 Haneda Airport, Ota-ku, Tokyo 144-0041; tel. (3) 5756-5675; fax (3) 5756-5679; internet www.ana.co.jp; f. 1952; operates domestic passenger and freight services; scheduled international services to the Far East, Australasia, the USA and Europe; charter services world-wide; Pres. and CEO KICHI-SABURO NOMURA.

Hokkaido Air System: Hokkadama-cho Airport, Sapporo-shi, Shigashi-ku, Sapporo 063; tel. (11) 781-1247; fax (11) 784-1716; internet www.hac-air.co.jp; f. 1997; domestic services on Hokkaido; Pres. TAKESHI KANDI.

JALways Co Ltd: JAL Bldg, 18th Floor, 2-4-11, Higashi-Shinagawa, Shinagawa-ku, Tokyo 140-8647; tel. (3) 5460-6830; fax (3) 5460-6839; e-mail jazgz@jaz.jalgroup.or.jp; internet www.jalways.co.jp; f. 1990; subsidiary of JAL; domestic and international scheduled and charter services; Chair. JIRO SAGARA; Pres. YUKIO OHTANI.

Japan Air Commuter: 8-2-2, Fumoto, Mizobe-cho, Aira-gun, Kagoshima 899-64; tel. (995) 582151; fax (995) 582673; e-mail info@jac.co.jp; internet www.jac.co.jp; f. 1983; subsidiary of Japan Air System; domestic services; Chair. YOSHITOMI ONO.

Japan Air System: JAS M1 Bldg, 3-5-1, Haneda Airport, Ota-ku, Tokyo 144-0041; tel. (3) 5756-4022; fax (3) 5473-4109; internet www.jas.co.jp; f. 1971; domestic and international services; plans to co-ordinate services with Northwest Airlines (USA) announced in 1995; to merge with JAL in late 2002; Chair. TAKESHI MASHIMA; Pres. HIROMI FUNABIKI.

Japan Airlines Co Ltd—JAL (Nihon Koku Kabushiki Kaisha): JAL Bldg, 2-4-11, Higashi-Shinagawa, Shinagawa-ku, Tokyo 140; tel. (3) 5460-3121; fax (3) 5460-3936; internet www.jal.co.jp; f. 1951; fully transferred to private-sector control in 1987; domestic and international services to Australasia, the Far East, North America, South America and Europe; to merge with Japan Air System in late 2002; Pres. ISAO KANEKO.

Japan Asia Airways Co: JAL Bldg, 19th Floor, 2-4-11. Higashi-shinagawa, Shinagawa-ku, Tokyo 140-0002; tel. (3) 5460-7285; fax (3) 5460-7286; e-mail jaabz@jaa.jalgroup.or.jp; internet www.japanasia.co.jp; f. 1975; subsidiary of JAL; international services from Tokyo, Osaka, Nagoya and Okinawa to Hong Kong and Taiwan; Chair. TEIICHI KURIBAYASHI; Pres. OSAMU IGARASHI.

Japan TransOcean Air: 3-24, Yamashita-cho, Naha-shi, Okinawa 900; tel. (988) 572112; fax (988) 582581; internet www.jal.co.jp/jta; f. 1967, present name since 1993; subsidiary of JAL; inter-island service in Okinawa; Chair. KEIICHI INAMINE; Pres. MICHIO OKUNO.

Nakanihon Airlines—NAL: Nagoya Airport, Toyoyama-cho, Nishikasugai-gun, Aichi 480-0202; tel. (568) 285405; fax (568) 285417; internet www.nals.co.jp; f. 1988; regional and domestic services; Pres. AKIRA HIRABAYASHI.

Skymark Airlines: World Trade Center, Bldg 3F, 2-4-1, Hamamatsucho, Minato-ku, Tokyo 105-6103; tel. (3) 5402-6767; fax (3) 5402-6770; e-mail info@skymark.co.jp; internet www.skymark.co.jp; f. 1997; domestic services; Chair. HIDEO SAWADA; Pres TAKASHI IDE.

Tourism

The ancient capital of Kyoto, pagodas and temples, forests and mountains, traditional festivals and the classical Kabuki theatre are some of the many tourist attractions of Japan. In 2000 there were 4,757,000 foreign visitors to Japan, and receipts from tourism totalled US $3,374m.

Department of Tourism: 2-1-3, Kasumigaseki, Chiyoda-ku, Tokyo 100; tel. (3) 3580-4488; fax (3) 3580-7901; f. 1946; a dept of the Ministry of Transport; Dir-Gen. KIMITAKA FUJINO.

Japan National Tourist Organization: Tokyo Kotsu Kaikan Bldg, 2-10-1, Yuraku-cho, Chiyoda-ku, Tokyo 100-0006; tel. (3) 3216-1901; fax (3) 3216-1846; internet www.jnto.go.jp; Pres. HIDEAKI MUKAIYMA.

Japan Travel Bureau Inc: 1-6-4, Marunouchi, Chiyoda-ku, Tokyo 100-0005; tel. (3) 3284-7028; f. 1912; 10,297 mems; Chair. I. MATSU-HASHI; Pres. R. FUNAYAMA.

Defence

At 1 August 2001 the armed forces totalled some 239,800 (148,700 Ground Self-Defence Force, 44,200 Maritime Self-Defence Force, 45,400 Air Self-Defence Force and 1,500 Joint Staff Council). The Ground Self-Defence Force is equipped with Japanese-made weapons including tanks and anti-aircraft guns, and has at its disposal surface-to-air missiles (SAM). The Maritime Self-Defence Force has 16 submarines, 42 destroyers and 12 frigates, as well as 30 mine-sweepers, three patrol combatant crafts, eight landing ships and various other vessels. The Air Self-Defence Force has 297 combat aircraft plus trainers and six SAM missile groups. Military service is voluntary. US forces in Japan at 1 August 2001 totalled 38,830.

Defence Expenditure: Budgeted for 2001/02: 4,955,000m. yen.

Chairman of the Joint Staff Council: Gen. SHOJI TAKEGOUCHI.

Chief of Staff for Ground Self-Defence Force: Gen. MASAHIRO NAKATANI.

Chief of Staff of Maritime Self-Defence Force: Adm. TORU ISHI-KAWA.

Chief of Staff of Air Self-Defence Force: Gen. IKUO TOTAKE.

Education

Immediately after the Second World War, with the introduction of democratic ideas into Japan, the educational system underwent extensive reform. General standards of education are very high, especially in mathematics and foreign languages. The standard of literacy among the Japanese has been almost 100% since before 1900. The Ministry of Education administers education at all levels and provides guidance, advice and financial assistance to local authorities. In each of the 47 prefectures and 3,255 municipalities, boards of education are responsible for upper secondary and special schools, while municipal boards maintain public elementary and lower secondary schools. Central government expenditure on education and science was expected to amount to 6,473,100m. yen for the 1999/2000 financial year. Each level of government provides for education with funds derived from its own revenue including taxes. The central Government may also grant subsidies where appropriate. The Government offers a scholarship system to able students with financial difficulties, who are expected to return the money within 20 years of graduation. Steadily increasing numbers of young people from Asian countries are coming to Japan for technical training at scientific and technological institutes and at factories.

PRE-SCHOOL EDUCATION

In 2000 there were 14,451 kindergartens (yochien) for children between three and five years of age, in which 1.8m. children were enrolled. Most kindergartens are privately-controlled.

ELEMENTARY AND LOWER SCHOOL EDUCATION

All children between six and 15 are required to attend six-year elementary schools (Shogakko) and three-year lower secondary schools (Chugakko). All children are provided with textbooks free of charge, while children of needy families are assisted in paying for school lunches and educational excursions by the Government and the local bodies concerned. Enrolment is almost 100%; there were 7.4m. pupils in 24,106 elementary schools and 4.1m. pupils in 11,209 lower secondary schools in 2000.

SECONDARY EDUCATION

There are three types of course available: full-time (which last for three years), part-time and correspondence (both of which last for four years). In 2000 there were 5,478 upper secondary schools (or high schools) in Japan, with an enrolment of 4.2m.

HIGHER EDUCATION

There were 649 universities and graduate schools, and 634 junior and technical colleges in 2000. The universities offer courses extending from three to four years and, in most cases, postgraduate courses for a master's degree in two years and a doctorate in three years. Junior colleges offer two- or three-year courses, credits for which can count towards a first degree. The technical colleges admit lower secondary school students for five years. The number of students in graduate schools and universities in 2000 was 2.7m., and in junior and technical colleges 385,000. Teacher training is offered in both universities and junior colleges.

Bibliography

GENERAL

Barrett, Brendan F. D., and Therivel, Riki. *Environmental Policy and Impact Assessment in Japan.* London and New York, Routledge, 1992.

Beasley, W. G. (Ed.). *Modern Japan: Aspects of History, Literature and Society.* London, Allen and Unwin, 1975.

Befu, Harumi, and Guichard-Anguis, Sylvie (Eds). *Globalizing Japan—Ethnography of the Japanese Presence in Asia, Europe and America.* London, Routledge, 2001.

Bestor, Theodore C. *Neighbourhood Tokyo.* Stanford, CA, Stanford University Press, 1989.

Bowring, Richard, and Kornicki, Peter (Eds). *The Cambridge Encyclopedia of Japan.* Cambridge, Cambridge University Press, 1993.

Buck, David N. *Responding to Chaos—Tradition, Technology, Society and Order in Japanese Design.* London, Routledge, 2000.

Buckley, Roger. *Japan Today.* Cambridge, Cambridge University Press, revised edn, 1999.

Buckley, Sandra. *Encyclopedia of Contemporary Japanese Culture.* London, Routledge, 2001.

Bunce, W. K. *Religions in Japan.* Rutland, VT, Charles E. Tuttle.

Clamoner, John. *Difference and Modernity: Social Theory and Contemporary Japanese Society.* Tokyo, Sophia University, 1996.

Craig, Timothy. J. *Inside the World of Japanese Popular Culture.* Armonk, NY, M. E. Sharpe, 2000.

Dore, Ronald. *Taking Japan Seriously: A Confucian Perspective on Leading Social Issues.* London, The Athlone Press, 1988.

Dore, R., and Sinha, R. (Eds). *Japan and the World Depression: Then and Now.* New York, St Martin's Press, 1987.

Downer, Lesley. *On the Narrow Road to the Deep North: Journey into a Lost Japan.* London, Jonathan Cape, 1989.

Fingleton, E. *Blindside: Why Japan is Still on Track to Overtake the U.S. by the Year 2000.* New York, Houghton Mifflin, 1995.

Hall, Ivan P. *Cartels of the Mind: Japan's Intellectual Closed Shop.* New York, W. W. Norton, 1998.

Hendry, Joy (Ed.). *Interpreting Japanese Society—Anthropological Approaches.* London, Routledge, 1998.

Hendry, Joy, and Raveri, Massimo (Eds). *Japan at Play.* London, Routledge, 2001.

Hood, Christopher, P. *Japanese Education Reform—Nakasone's Legacy.* London, Routledge, 2001.

Hosokawa, Morihiro. *The Time to Act is Now: Thoughts for a New Japan.* Tokyo, NTT Mediascope Inc, 1994.

Ishida, R. *Geography of Japan.* Tokyo, Kokusai Bunka Shinkokai, 1961.

Johnson, Sheila K. *The Japanese through American Eyes.* Stanford, CA, Stanford University Press, 1988.

Kaplan, David E., and Marshal, A. *The Cult at the End of the World.* London, Arrow Books, 1996.

Kato, Shuichi. *Japan: Spirit and Form.* Tokyo, Charles E. Tuttle, 1995.

Katzenstein, Peter J., and Shiraishi, Takashi. *Network Power: Japan and Asia.* Ithaca, NY, Cornell University Press, 1997.

Kerr, Alex. (trans. Fishman, B.). *Lost Japan.* Hawthorn, Vic, Lonely Planet, 1996.

Dogs and Demons: Tales From the Dark Side of Japan. New York, Hill and Wang, 2001.

Kodansha. *Japan: An Illustrated Encyclopedia.* London, Kodansha Europe, 1993.

Japan: Profile of a Nation. London, Kodansha Europe, 1995.

Lie, John. *Multi-Ethnic Japan.* Cambridge, MA, Harvard University Press, 2001.

Lockwood, William M. *The Economic Development of Japan.* Princeton, NJ, Princeton University Press, 1954.

Lockwood, William W. (Ed.). *The State and Economic Enterprise in Postwar Japan.* Princeton, NJ, Princeton University Press, 1965.

Maher, John C., and MacDonald, Gaynor (Eds). *Diversity in Japanese Culture and Language.* London, Kegan Paul International, 1996.

Maswood, Javed S. *Japan and East Asian Regionalism.* London, Routledge, 2000.

McGregor, Richard. *Japan Swings: Politics, Culture and Sex in the New Japan.* St Leonards, NSW, Allen and Unwin, 1996.

McVeigh, Brian J. *The Nature of the Japanese State—Rationality and Rituality.* London, Routledge, 1998.

Minichiello, Sharon A. (Ed.). *Japan's Competing Modernities—Issues in Culture and Democracy, 1900–1930.* Honolulu, HI, University of Hawaii Press, 1998.

Mulgan, Aurelia George. *The Politics of Agriculture in Japan.* London, Routledge, 2000.

Naff, C. *About Face: How I Stumbled onto Japan's Social Revolution.* New York, Kodansha International, 1995.

Nakane, C. *Japanese Society.* London, Weidenfeld and Nicolson, 1970.

Nakayama, Shigeru. *Science, Technology and Society in Postwar Japan.* London, Kegan Paul International, 1992.

Oe, Kenzaburo (trans. Yamanouchi, Hisaki). *Japan, the Ambiguous and Myself.* Tokyo, Kodansha International, 1996.

Ozawa, Ichiro. *Blueprint for a New Japan.* New York, Kodansha International, 1994.

Pezeu-Massabuau, J. (trans. Blum, P. C.). *The Japanese Islands: A Physical and Social Geography.* Rutland, VT, Charles E. Tuttle.

Pharr, Susan J., and Kraus, Ellis S. *Media and Politics in Japan.* Honolulu, HI, University of Hawaii Press, 1996.

Reischauer, Edwin O. *The Japanese.* Cambridge, MA, Harvard University Press, 1977.

Richie, Donald. *Different People: Pictures of some Japanese.* Tokyo, Kodansha, 1988.

Sale, Murray. *A Day in the Life of Japan.* London, William Collins and Sons Ltd, 1986.

Sargent, John. *Perspectives on Japan—Towards the Twenty-First Century.* Richmond, Surrey, Curzon Press, 1999.

Starr, Don. Japan: *A Historical and Cultural Dictionary.* Richmond, Surrey, Curzon Press, 2001.

Takeda, Kiyoko. *The Dual Image of the Japanese Emperor.* London, Macmillan Education, 1989.

Thomsen, H. *The New Religions of Japan.* Rutland, VT, Charles E. Tuttle, 1963.

Tipton, Elise. *Modern Japan–A Social and Political History..* London, Routledge, 2002.

Tsunoda de Bary, Keene. *Sources of the Japanese Tradition.* New York, Columbia University Press, 1958.

Upham, Frank K. *Law and Social Change in Postwar Japan.* Cambridge, MA, Harvard University Press, 1988.

Weiner, Michael. *Japan's Minorities—The Illusion of Homogeneity.* London, Routledge, 1996.

Wilson, W. *The Sun at Noon: An Anatomy of Modern Japan.* London, Hamish Hamilton, 1986.

Williams, Dominic. *A Dictionary of Japanese Financial Terms.* Richmond, Surrey, Curzon Press, 1995.

Wong, Anny. *The Roots of Japan's Environmental Policies.* London, Routledge, 2001.

HISTORY

Allen, Louis. *The End of the War in Asia.* London, Hart-Davis, MacGibbon, 1976.

Allinson, Gary D. *Japan's Postwar History.* Ithaca, NY, Cornell University Press, 1997.

Beasley, William G. *The Meiji Restoration.* London, Oxford University Press, 1973.

Behr, Edward. *Hirohito: Behind the Myth.* London, Hamish Hamilton, 1989.

Bix, Herbert P. *Peasant Protest in Japan 1590–1884.* New Haven, CT, Yale University Press, 1986.

Hirohito and the Making of Modern Japan. New York, NY, Harper Collins, 2000.

Blacker, Carmen. *The Japanese Enlightenment.* Cambridge, Cambridge University Press, 1964.

Dore, Ronald P. (Ed.). *Aspects of Social Change in Modern Japan.* Princeton, NJ, Princeton University Press, 1967.

Dower, John W. *Origins of the Modern Japanese State.* New York, Pantheon Books, 1975.

War Without Mercy: Race and Power in the Pacific War. New York, Pantheon Books, 1986.

Embracing Defeat: Japan in the Wake of World War II. New York, W. W. Norton, 1999.

Drifte, Reinhard. *Japan's Foreign Policy in the 1990s: From Economic Superpower to What Power?* Basingstoke, Macmillan, 1996.

Duus, Peter. *The Rise of Modern Japan.* Boston, MA, Houghton Mifflin, 1976.

Duus, Peter (Ed.). *The Cambridge History of Japan, Volume 6: The Twentieth Century.* New York, Cambridge University Press, 1989.

Duus, Peter, Myers, Ramon H., and Peattie, Mark R. (Eds). *The Japanese Wartime Empire 1931–1945.* Ewing, NJ, Princeton University Press, 1996.

Giffard, Sydney. *Japan among the Powers: 1890–1990.* New Haven, CT, Yale University Press, 1994.

Gordon, Andrew (Ed.). *Postwar Japan as History.* Berkeley, University of California Press, 1993.

Hall, John W. *Japan: From Prehistory to Modern Times.* London, Weidenfeld and Nicolson, 1970.

Harries, Meirion and Susie. *Soldiers of the Sun.* London, Heinemann, 1992.

Harvey, Robert. *The Undefeated: The Rise, Fall and Rise of Greater Japan.* London, Macmillan, 1995.

Havens, Thomas R. H. *Valley of Darkness: The Japanese People and World War Two.* New York, W. W. Norton, 1978.

Fire Across the Sea: the Vietnam War and Japan 1965–75. Princeton, NJ, Princeton University Press, 1988.

Hirschmeier, Johannes, and Yui, Tsunehiko. *The Development of Japanese Business, 1600–1973.* London, Allen and Unwin, 1975.

Hoyt, Edwin P. *Japan's War: The Great Pacific Conflict.* London, Hutchinson, 1986.

Inkster, Ian. *Japanese Industrialisation—Historical and Cultural Perspectives.* London, Routledge, 2001.

Jansen, Marius B. *The Making of Modern Japan.* Harvard, MA, Harvard University Press, 2001.

Junju Banno. *Democracy in Pre-War Japan—Concepts of Government, 1871–1937: Collected Essays.* London, Routledge, 2000.

Kamija, Morinosuke. *The Emergence of Japan as a World Power: 1895–1925.* Rutland, VT, Charles E. Tuttle, 1968.

Modern Japan's Foreign Policy. Rutland, VT, Charles E. Tuttle, 1969.

Korhonen, Pekka. *Japan and Asia-Pacific Integration: Pacific Romances 1968–1996.* London, Routledge, 1998.

Kornicki, Peter (Ed.). *Meiji Japan—Political, Economic and Social History 1868–1912.* London, Routledge, 1998.

LaFeber, Walter. *The Clash: A History of US-Japan Relations.* New York, W. W. Norton, 1997.

Large, Stephen S. (Ed.). *Showa Japan—Political, Economic and Social History 1926–1989.* London, Routledge, 1998.

Lehmann, Jean-Pierre. *The Image of Japan 1850–1905: From Feudal Isolation to World Power.* London, Allen and Unwin, 1978.

Livingston, Jon, Moore, Joe, and Oldfather, Felicia (Eds). *The Japan Reader 1: Imperial Japan: 1800–1945.* London, Penguin, 1976.

The Japan Reader 2: Postwar Japan 1945 to the Present. London, Penguin, 1976.

Lu, David J. *Japan—A Documentary History (Two Vols).* Armonk, NY, M. E. Sharpe, 1996.

Maddox, Robert J. *Weapons for Victory: The Hiroshima Decision Fifty Years Later.* Columbia, MO, University of Missouri Press, 1995.

Martin, Peter. *The Chrysanthemum Throne—A History of the Emperors of Japan.* Honolulu, HI, University of Hawaii Press, 1998.

Morley, James W. *Dilemmas of Growth in Prewar Japan.* Princeton, NJ, Princeton University Press, 1971.

Murakami, Haruki. *Underground: The Tokyo Gas Attack and the Japanese Psyche.* London, Harvill, 2001.

Murdoch, James. *A History of Japan (Three Vols).* London, Routledge, 1999.

Nakamura, James I. *Agricultural Production and the Economic Development of Japan 1873–1922.* Princeton, NJ, Princeton University Press, 1966.

Nish, Ian. *The Story of Japan.* London, Faber, 1968.

Japanese Foreign Policy, 1869–1942: Kasumigaseki to Miyakezaka. London, Routledge and Kegan Paul, 1977.

Packard, Jerrold M. *Sons of Heaven: A Portrait of the Japanese Monarchy.* London, MacDonald Queen Anne Press, 1988.

Rose, Cardine. *Interpreting History in Sino-Japanese Relations—A Case Study in Political Decision Making.* London, Routledge, 1998.

Ruoff, Kenneth J. *The People's Emperor: Democracy and the Japanese Monarchy, 1945–1995.* Harvard, MA, Harvard University Press, 2002.

Sansom, George B. *The Western World and Japan.* London, Cresset Press, 1950.

A History of Japan. London, Cresset Press, 1958–64.

Shibusawa, Masahide. *Japan and the Asian Pacific Region: Profile of Change.* London, Croom Helm, 1984.

Shillony, Ben-Ami. *Politics and Culture in Wartime Japan.* Oxford, Clarendon Press, 1988.

Smith, Dennis B. *Japan since 1945.* Basingstoke, Macmillan, 1995.

Storry, Richard. *A History of Modern Japan.* London, Penguin.

Japan and the Decline of the West in Asia 1894–1943. London, Macmillan Press, 1979.

Tsouras, Peter G. *Rising Sun Victorious.* London, Greenhill Books, 2001.

Weintraub, Stanley. *The Last Great Victory: The End of World War II July–August 1945.* New York, E.P. Dutton, 1995.

Wetzler, Peter. *Hirohito and War—Imperial Tradition and Military Decision Making in Pre-war Japan.* Honolulu, HI, University of Hawaii Press, 1998.

Wilson, Sandra. *The Manchurian Crisis and Japanese Society, 1931–33.* London, Routledge, 2001.

Yahara, Col Hiromichi. *The Battle for Okinawa.* New York, Wiley and Sons, 1995.

Yoshiaki Yoshimi. *Comfort Women: Sexual Slavery in the Japanese Military During World War II.* New York, NY, Columbia University Press, 2001.

POLITICS

Abe, Hitoshi, Shindo, Muneyuki, and Kawato, Sadafumi. *The Government and Politics of Japan.* Tokyo, Tokyo University Press, 1994.

Allinson, Gary D., and Sone, Yasuhiro (Eds). *Political Dynamics in Contemporary Japan.* Princeton, NJ, Princeton University Press, 1993.

Christensen, Ray. *Ending the LDP Hegemony: Party Cooperation in Japan.* Honolulu, University of Hawai'i Press, 2000.

Curtis, Gerald L. *The Logic of Japanese Politics: Leaders, Institutions, and the Limits of Change.* New York, Columbia University Press, 1999.

Curtis, Gerald L. (Ed.). *Japan's Foreign Policy After the Cold War: Coping With Change.* Armonk, NY, M. E. Sharpe, 1993.

Dore, Ronald. *Japan, Internationalism and the UN.* London, Routledge, 1997.

Funabashi, Yoichi (Ed.). *Japan's International Agenda.* New York, New York University Press, 1994.

Garby, Craig C., and Brown Bullock, Mary (Eds). *Japan: A New Kind of Superpower?* Washington, DC, The Woodrow Wilson Center Press, 1994.

Harries, M., and Harries, S. *Sheathing the Sword: The Demilitarization of Japan.* London, Hamish Hamilton, 1987.

Hayes, Louis D. *Introduction to Japanese Politics.* Armonk, NY, M. E. Sharpe, 2000.

Hook, Glenn D., et al. *Japan's International Relations—Politics, Economics and Security.* London, Routledge, 2000.

Hook, Glenn D., and McCormack, Gavan (Eds). *The Japanese Constitution—Documents and Analysis.* London, Routledge, 2000.

Hrebenar, Ronald J. *Japan's New Party System.* Boulder, CO, Westview Press, 2000.

Hughes, Christopher W. *Japan's Economic Power and Security—Japan and North Korea.* London, Routledge, 1999.

Hunsberger, Warren S. *Japan's Quest—The Search for International Role, Recognition and Respect.* Armonk, NY, M. E. Sharpe, 1996.

Inoguchi, Takashi, and Jain, Purnendra (Eds). *Japanese Foreign Policy Today.* New York, St Martin's Press, 2000.

Ishihara, Shintaro. *The Japan That Can Say No.* London, Simon and Schuster, 1991.

Jain, Purnendra, and Inoguchi, Takashi. *Japanese Politics Today.* Basingstoke, Macmillan, 1997.

Johnson, Chalmers. *Japan: Who Governs? The Rise of the Developmental State.* New York, W.W. Norton, 1995.

Johnsonn, Stephen. *Opposition Politics in Japan—Strategies under a One-Party Dominant Regime.* London, Routledge, 2000.

Kataoka, Tetsuya (Ed.). *Creating Single-Party Democracy: Japan's Postwar Political System.* Stanford, CA, Hoover Institution Press, 1993.

Kishima, Takako. *Political Life in Japan: Democracy in a Reversible World.* Princeton University Press, 1992.

Kohno, Masaru. *Japan's Postwar Party Politics.* Princeton, NJ, Princeton University Press, 1997.

Kyogoku, Jun-ichi. *The Political Dynamics of Modern Japan.* Tokyo, University of Tokyo Press, 1987.

Lee, Chong-Sik. *Japan and Korea: The Political Dimension.* Stanford, CA, Hoover Institution Press, 1986.

Masumi, Junnosuke. *Contemporary Politics in Japan.* Berkeley, University of California Press, 1995.

McCormack, Gavan, and Sugimoto, Yoshio (Eds). *Democracy in Contemporary Japan.* Armonk, NY, M. E. Sharpe, 1986.

Mendl, Wolf. *Japan's Asia Policy—Regional Security and Global Interests.* London, Routledge, 1997.

Millard, Mike. *Leaving Japan—Observations on the Dysfunctional U.S.-Japan Relationship.* Armonk, NY, M. E. Sharpe, 2000.

Mitchell, Richard H. *Political Bribery in Japan.* Honolulu, HI, University of Hawaii Press, 1996.

Nakano, Minoru. *The Policy-Making Process in Contemporary Japan.* Basingstoke, Macmillan, 1996.

Nakasone, Yasuhiro. *Japan—A State Strategy for the Twenty-First Century.* London, RoutledgeCurzon, 2002.

Pempel, T. J. (Ed.). *Policymaking in Contemporary Japan.* Ithaca, NY, Cornell University Press, 1977.

Reischauer, E. O. *The United States and Japan.* Cambridge, MA, Harvard University Press.

Richardson, Bradley M. *Japanese Democracy: Power, Coordination and Performance.* New Haven, CT, Yale University Press, 1997.

Schwartz, Frank J. *Advice and Consent—The Politics of Consultation in Japan.* Cambridge, Cambridge University Press, 1999.

Stegewerns, Dick. *Nationalism and Internationalism in Imperial Japan.* London, RoutledgeCurzon, 2002.

Stephan, John J. *The Kuril Islands: Russo-Japanese Frontier in the Pacific.* Oxford, Clarendon Press, 1975.

Stockwin, J. A. A. *Governing Japan: Divided Politics in a Major Economy.* Oxford, Blackwell, 1999.

Stockwin, J. A. A., et al. *Dynamic and Immobilist Politics in Japan.* Honolulu, University of Hawaii Press, 1988.

Upham, Frank K. *Law and Social Change in Postwar Japan.* Cambridge, MA, Harvard University Press, 1987.

Van Wolferen, Karel. *The Enigma of Japanese Power: People and Politics in a Stateless Nation.* London, Macmillan, 1989.

Yanaga, Chitoshi. *Japanese People and Politics.* New York, John Wiley, 1956.

Yoshida, Shigeru. *Japan's Decisive Century.* New York, Praeger, 1967.

ECONOMY

Abegglen, James C., and Stalk, George, Jr. *Kaisha—The Japanese Corporation—How Marketing, and Manpower Strategy, Not Management Style, Make the Japanese World Pace-setters.* New York, Basic Books, 1985.

Allen, George C. *An Economic History of Modern Japan.* London, Macmillan, 1981.

Japan's Economic Expansion. London, Oxford University Press, 1965.

Aoki, M. (Ed.). *The Economic Analysis of the Japanese Firm.* Amsterdam, Elsevier Science Publishers, 1984.

Aoki, Masahiko. *Information, Incentives, and Bargaining in the Japanese Economy.* New York, Cambridge University Press, 1988.

Argy, Victor. *The Japanese Economy.* Basingstoke, Macmillan, 1996.

Balassa, Bela, and Noland, Marcus. *Japan in the World Economy.* Washington, Institute for International Economics, 1990.

Basu, Dipak R., and Miroshnik, Victoria. *Japanese Foreign Investments, 1970–1998: Perspectives and Analyses.* Armonk, NY, M. E. Sharpe, 2000.

Beechler, Schon, and Stucker, Kristin (Eds). *Japanese Business.* London, Routledge, 1997.

Bergsten, Fred, and Cline, William R. *The United States–Japan Economic Problem.* Washington, Institute for International Economics, 1985.

Boltho, Andrea. Japan: *An Economic Survey 1953–1973.* Oxford University Press, 1976.

Boyer, Robert, and Yamanda, Toshio (Eds). *Japanese Capitalism in Crisis—A 'Regulationist' Interpretation.* London, Routledge, 2000.

Calder, Kent E. *Strategic Capitalism—Private Business and Public Purpose in Japanese Industrial Finance.* Princeton, NJ, Princeton University Press, 1993.

Carlile, Lonny E., and Tilton, Mark (Eds). *Is Japan Really Changing its Ways? Regulatory Reform and the Japanese Economy.* Washington, DC, Brookings Institution Press, 1998.

Choate, Pat. *Agents of Influence: How Japan's Lobbyists in the United States Manipulate America's Political and Economic System.* New York, Alfred A. Knopf, 1990.

Dattel, Eugene. *The Sun that Never Rose—The Inside Story of Japan's Failed Attempt at Global Financial Dominance.* Chicago, Probus, 1994.

Drysdale, Peter. *International Economic Pluralism: Economic Policy in Asia and the Pacific.* Sydney, Columbia University Press and Allen and Unwin, 1988.

Drysdale, Peter, and Gower, Luke (Eds). *The Japanese Economy.* London, Routledge, 1998.

Drysdale, Peter, Viviani, Nancy, Akio, Watanabe, and Ippei, Yamazawa. *The Australia-Japan Relationship: Towards the Year 2000.* Canberra, Australia-Japan Research Centre/Japan Centre for Economic Research, 1989.

Economic Planning Agency (Japanese Government). *Economic Survey of Japan.* Tokyo, Okurasho Insatsu Kyoku, annual.

Ezrati, Milton. *Kawari.* Reading, MA, Perseus Books, 1999.

Fallows, James. *Looking at the Sun—The Rise of the New East Asian Economic and Political System.* New York, Pantheon Books, 1994.

Flath, David. *The Japanese Economy.* Oxford, Oxford University Press, 2000.

Francks, Penelope. *Japanese Economic Development: Theory and Practice.* 2nd Edn, London, Routledge, 1999.

Freedman, Craig (Ed.). *Why Did Japan Stumble? Causes and Cures.* Cheltenham, Edward Elgar, 1999.

Economic Reform in Japan—Can the Japanese Change? Cheltenham, Edward Elgar Publishing, 2001.

Funabishi, Yoichi (Ed.). *Japan's International Agenda.* New York, New York University Press, 1994.

Gerlach, Michael. *Alliance Capitalism—The Social Organization of Japanese Business.* Berkeley, University of California Press, 1992.

Hartcher, Peter. *The Ministry.* Boston, MA, Harvard Business School Press, 1998.

Hasegawa, Harukiyo, and Hook, Glenn D. (Eds). *Japanese Business Management—Restructuring for Low Growth and Globalisation.* London, Routledge, 1997.

Hayes, Declan. *Japan's Big Bang: The Deregulation and Revitalisation of the Japanese Economy.* Rutland, VT, Charles E. Tuttle, 2000.

Hester, William R. *Japanese Industrial Targeting.* London, Macmillan, 1992.

Higashi, Chikara, and Lauter, Peter. *The Internationalisation of the Japanese Economy.* Boston, Kluwer Academic Publishers, 1990.

Holstein, William J. *The Japanese Power Game: What It Means For America.* Maxwell-Macmillan International, 1991.

Hook, Glenn, D. (Ed). *Political Economy of Japanese Globalization.* London, Routledge, 2001.

Horne, James. *Japan's Financial Markets—Conflict and Consensus in Policymaking.* Sydney, Allen and Unwin, 1985.

Hsu, Robert C. *The MIT Encyclopedia of the Japanese Economy.* Cambridge, MA, MIT Press, 1995.

Hughes, Christopher W. *Japan's Economic Power and Security.* London, Routledge, 1999.

Hunter, Janet (Ed.). *Japanese Economic History, 1930–1960.* London, Routledge, 2000.

Inoguchi, Takashi, and Okimoto, Daniel I. (Eds). *The Political Economy of Japan: The Changing International Context, Vol. 2.* Stanford, CA, Stanford University Press, 1988.

Ito, Takatoshi. *The Japanese Economy.* Cambridge, Massachusetts Institute of Technology, 1992.

Johnson, Chalmers. *MITI and the Japanese Miracle: The Growth of Industrial Policy, 1925–1975.* Stanford, CA, Stanford University Press, 1982.

Katz, Richard. Japan: *The System that Soured—The Rise and Fall of the Japanese Economic Miracle.* Armonk, NY, M. E. Sharpe, 1998.

Komiya, Ryutaro, Masahiro, Okuno, and Kotaro, Suzumura (Eds). *Industrial Policy in Japan.* Tokyo, Academic Press, 1988.

Koppel, Bruce M., and Orr, Jr, Robert M. (Eds). *Japan's Foreign Aid: Power and Policy in a New Era.* Boulder, CO, Westview Press, 1993.

Kosai, Yutaka, and Ogino, Yoshitaro. *The Contemporary Japanese Economy.* Armonk, NY, M. E. Sharpe, 1985.

Kumon, Shumpei, and Rosovsky, Henry (Eds). *The Political Economy of Japan: Cultural and Social Dynamics, Vol. 3.* Stanford, CA, Stanford University Press, 1992.

Lincoln, Edward J. *Japan Facing Economic Maturity*. Washington, DC, Brookings Institution, 1988.

McKenzie, C., and Stutchbury, M. (Eds). *The Yen and Japanese Financial Markets*. Sydney, Allen and Unwin, 1992.

Makiko, Yamada. *Japan's Top Management from the Inside (Studies in the Modern Japanese Economy)*. Hampshire, Palgrave, 1998.

Makoto, Itoh. *The Japanese Economy Reconsidered*. New York, NY, St Martins Press.

Masafumi, Matsuba. *The Contemporary Japanese Economy—Between Civil Society and Corporation-Centered Society*. Singapore, Institute of Southeast Asian Studies, 2001.

Masasuke, Ide. *Japanese Corporate Finance and International Competition: Japanese Capitalism Versus American Capitalism (Studies in The Modern Japanese Economy)*. Hampshire, Palgrave, 1998.

Matsumoto, Koji. *The Rise of the Japanese Corporate System*. Kegan Paul International, 1992.

Matsushita, Mitsuo. *International Trade and Competition Law in Japan*. Oxford, Oxford University Press, 1993.

Mendl, Wolf. *Japan and Southeast Asia: International Relations*. London, Routledge, 2001.

Mikanagi, Yumiko. *Japan's Trade Policy—Action or Reaction?* London, Routledge, 1996.

Minami, Ryoshin. *The Economic Development of Japan*. London, Macmillan, 1986.

Mirza, Hafiz. *Japan's Economic Empire—Foreign Investment by Japanese Companies Before the Pacific War*. Richmond, Surrey, Curzon Press, 2000.

Miyashita, Kenichi, and Russell, David. Keiretsu: *Inside the Hidden Japanese Conglomerates*. New York, McGraw-Hill, 1994.

Morris-Suzuki, Tessa. *The Technological Transformation of Japan*. Cambridge, Cambridge University Press, 1995.

Nakamura, Takafusa. *The Postwar Japanese Economy: Its Development and Structure*. Tokyo, University of Tokyo Press, 1982.

Nathan, John. Sony: *The Private Life*. Boston, MA, and New York, Houghton Mifflin, 1999.

Nihon Keizai Shimbunsha (Ed.). *Industrial Review of Japan*. Tokyo, Nihon Keizai Shimbunsha, annual.

Okabe, Mitsuaki. *Cross Shareholdings in Japan—A New Unified Perspective of the Economic System*. Cheltenham, Edward Elgar Publishing, 2002.

Ohkawa, Kazushi, and Rosovsky, Henry. *Japanese Economic Growth in Trend Acceleration in the Twentieth Century*. Stanford, CA, Stanford University Press, 1973.

Ohno, Kenichi, and Ohno, Izumi (Eds). *Japanese Views on Economic Development—Diverse Paths to the Market*. London, Routledge, 1998.

Okimoto, Daniel I. *Between MITI and the Market: Japanese Industrial Policy for High Technology*. Stanford, CA, Stanford University Press, 1990.

Orr, Robert M. *The Emergence of Japan's Foreign Aid Power*. New York, Columbia University Press, 1991.

Patrick, Hugh, and Meissner, Larry (Eds). *Japanese Industrialization and its Social Consequences*. Berkeley and London, University of California Press, for the Social Sciences Research Council, 1977.

Pempel, T. J. *Regime Shift: Comparative Dynamics of the Japanese Political Economy, Cornell Studies in Political Economy*. Ithaca, NY, Cornell University Press, 1998.

Prestowitz Jr, Clyde V. *Trading Places—How We are Giving our Future to Japan and How to Reclaim it*. New York, Basic Books, 1989.

Rafferty, Kevin. *Inside Japan's Power Houses: The Culture, Mystique and Future of Japan's Greatest Corporations*. London, Weidenfeld and Nicolson, 1995.

Reszat, Beate. *The Japanese Foreign Exchange Market*. London, Routledge, 1997.

Samuels, Richard J. *Rich Nation, Strong Army—National Security and the Technological Transformation of Japan*. Ithaca, NY, Cornell University Press, 1994.

Sato, Kazuo. *The Transformation of the Japanese Economy*. Armonk, NY, M. E. Sharpe, 1999.

The Japanese Economy—A Primer. Armonk, NY, M. E. Sharpe, 1999.

Sato, Ryuzo. *The Chrysanthemum and the Eagle: The Future of US-Japan Relations*. New York, New York University Press, 1994.

Schmieglow, Michele and Henrik. *Strategic Pragmatism: Japanese Lessons in the Use of Economic Theory*. New York, Praeger, 1990.

Schodt, Frederik L. *America and the Four Japans: Friend, Foe, Model, Mirror*. Berkeley, CA, Stone Bridge Press, 1994.

Sheard, Paul (Ed.). *International Adjustment and the Japanese Firm*. Sydney, Allen and Unwin, 1992.

Shibata, Tokue (Ed.). *Japan's Public Sector—How the Government is Financed*. Tokyo, University of Tokyo Press, 1993.

Suzuki, Yoshio. *Money and Banking in Contemporary Japan: The Theoretical Setting and its Applications*. New Haven, CT, Yale University Press, 1980.

Money, Finance and Macroeconomic Performance in Japan. New Haven, CT, Yale University Press, 1986.

Suzuki, Yoshio (Ed.). *The Japanese Financial System*, Tokyo, Bank of Japan, 1995.

Tachibanaki, Toshiaki. *Public Policies and the Japanese Economy: Savings, Investments, Unemployment, Inequality*. Basingstoke, Macmillan, 1996.

Taggart Murphy, R. *The Real Price of Japanese Money*. London, Weidenfeld & Nicolson, 1996.

Tasker, Peter. *Inside Japan: Wealth, Work and Power in the New Japanese Empire*. London, Sidgwick and Jackson, 1988.

The Weight of the Yen. New York, Norton, 1996.

Thurow, Lester. *Head to Head: The Coming Economic Battle Among Japan, Europe and America*. New York, William Morrow, 1992.

Tolliday, Steven. *The Economic Development of Modern Japan, 1868–1945—From the Meiji Restoration to the Second World War*. Cheltenham, Edward Elgar Publishing, 2001.

The Economic Development of Modern Japan, 1945–1995. Cheltenham, Edward Elgar Publishing, 2001.

Tsutsui, William M. (Ed.) *Banking in Japan*. London, Routledge, 1999.

van Wolferen, Karel. *The Enigma of Japanese Power—People and Politics in a Stateless Nation*. London, Macmillan, 1989.

Vestel, James. *Planning for Change: Industrial Policy and Japanese Economic Development 1945–1990*. Oxford, Oxford University Press, 1994.

Williams, David. *Japan: Beyond the End of History*. London, Routledge, 1994.

Wood, Christopher. *The Bubble Economy: The Japanese Economic Collapse*. London, Sidgwick and Jackson, 1992.

The End of Japan Inc.: How the New Japan Will Look. New York, Simon & Schuster, 1995.

Woronoff, Jon. *Japan's Commercial Empire*. Armonk, NY, M. E. Sharpe, 1985.

The Japanese Economic Crisis. Basingstoke, Macmillan, 1996.

Yamamura, Kozo (Ed.). *Policy and Trade Issues of the Japanese Economy—American and Japanese Perspectives*. Seattle, University of Washington Press, 1982.

Yamamura, Kozo, and Yasukichi, Yasuba (Eds). *The Political Economy of Japan: Vol. 1, The Domestic Transformation*. Stanford, CA, Stanford University Press, 1985.

Yamashita, Shoichi (Ed.). *Transfer of Japanese Technology and Management to Asean Countries*. Tokyo, University of Tokyo Press, 1991.

Yoshihara, Kunio. *Japanese Economic Development*. Tokyo, Oxford University Press, 1986.

KOREA

Physical and Social Geography

JOHN SARGENT

The total area of Korea is 223,337 sq km (86,231 sq miles), comprising the Democratic People's Republic of Korea (North Korea), the Republic of Korea (South Korea) and the demilitarized zone (DMZ) between them. North Korea has an area of 122,762 sq km (47,399 sq miles) and South Korea an area of 99,313 sq km (38,345 sq miles). The DMZ covers 1,262 sq km (487 sq miles). The Korean peninsula is bordered to the north by the People's Republic of China, and has a very short frontier with the Russian Federation in the north-east.

PHYSICAL FEATURES

Korea is predominantly an area of ancient folding, although in the south-east, where a relatively small zone of recent rocks occurs, a close geological similarity with Japan may be detected. Unlike Japan, the peninsula contains no active volcanoes and earthquakes are rare.

Although, outside the extreme north, few mountains rise to more than 1,650 m, rugged upland, typically blanketed in either pine forest or scrub, predominates throughout the peninsula. Cultivated lowland forms only 20% of the combined area of North and South Korea.

Two broad masses of highland determine the basic relief pattern of the peninsula. In the north the Changpai Shan and Tumen ranges form an extensive area of mountain terrain, aligned from south-west to north-east, and separating the peninsula proper from the uplands of eastern Manzhou (Manchuria) in the People's Republic of China. A second mountain chain runs for almost the entire length of the peninsula, close to, and parallel with, the eastern coast. Thus, in the peninsula proper, the main lowland areas, which are also the areas of maximum population density, are found in the west and south.

The rivers of Korea, which are short and fast-flowing, drain mainly westwards into the Huang Hai (Yellow Sea). Of the two countries, North Korea, with its many mountain torrents, is especially well endowed with opportunities for hydroelectric generation. Wide seasonal variations in the rate of flow, however, tend to hamper the efficient operation of hydroelectric plants.

In contrast with the east coast of the peninsula, which is smooth and precipitous, the intricate western and southern coasts are well endowed with good natural harbours, an asset which, however, is partly offset by an unusually wide tidal range.

CLIMATE

In its main elements, the climate of Korea is more continental than marine, and is thus characterized by a wide seasonal range in temperature. In winter, with the establishment of a high pressure centre over Siberia and Mongolia, winds are predominantly from the north and north-west. North Korea in winter is extremely cold, with January temperatures falling, in the mountains, to below -13°C. Owing to the warming influence of the surrounding seas, winter temperatures gradually rise towards the south of the peninsula, but only in the extreme southern coastlands do January temperatures rise above freezing point. Winter precipitation is light, and falls mainly in the form of snow, which, in the north, lies for long periods.

In the southern and western lowlands summers are hot and humid, with July temperatures rising to 26°C. In mid-summer violent cloudbursts occur, often causing severe soil erosion and landslides. In the extreme north-east summers are cooler, and July temperatures rarely rise above 17°C.

Annual precipitation, of which more than one-half falls in the summer months, varies from about 600 mm in the north-east to more than 1,500 mm in the south.

NATURAL RESOURCES

Although 70% of the total area of Korea is forested, high-quality timber is virtually limited to the mountains of North Korea, where extensive areas of larch, pine and fir provide a valuable resource. Elsewhere, excessive felling has caused the forest cover to degenerate into poor scrub.

Korea is fairly rich in mineral resources, but most deposits are concentrated in the north, where large-scale mining operations were begun by the Japanese before the Second World War. In North Korea the main iron-mining areas are located south of Pyongyang, and in the vicinity of Chongjin in the extreme north-east.

Throughout Korea many other minerals, including copper, sulphur, lead, zinc, tungsten, gold, silver and magnesite, are mined.

POPULATION

At mid-2001 the estimated population of North Korea was 22,428,000, while that of South Korea was 47,343,000, giving a combined total of some 70m. The population of the Korean peninsula has thus more than doubled since 1954, when the combined total was 30m. The population of South Korea was estimated at 47,640,000 at mid-2002.

Population density is higher in South Korea (479.5 per sq km in 2001) than in North Korea (an estimated 182.7 per sq km in 2001), but mean density figures conceal the crowding of population on the limited area of agricultural land, which is a salient characteristic of the geography of South Korea.

In 1970 about 40% of the population of South Korea was concentrated in cities with populations of 100,000 and over. According to the final results of the census of 1 November 2000, Seoul, the capital of South Korea, had a population of 9,853,972, while Busan, with 3,655,437 inhabitants, was the second largest city, followed by Daegu (2,473,990) and Incheon (2,466,338). In 1985 the urbanization rate was 65%, with 24% of the population concentrated in Seoul.

According to the 1993 census results, the population of Pyongyang, the capital of North Korea, was 2,741,260. The other two principal cities are Hamhung, with a population of 709,730, and Chongjin, the leading port of the north-east coast, with 582,480.

History up to the Korean War

ANDREW C. NAHM

HISTORICAL BACKGROUND

Political History

Tribal units of the Puyo people (later known as Koreans) emerged in c. 3000 BC, when the Tungusic people migrated into south Manzhou (Manchuria) and the Korean peninsula, bringing with them their Ural-Altaic tongue, shamanistic religion and a palaeolithic culture. A mythological figure named Tan'gun is said to have consolidated tribal units into a 'kingdom' named Choson in the northern part of Korea in 2333 BC. Ancient Choson of the Tan'gun, the Kija and the Wiman dynasties lasted some 2,225 years, but it was overthrown by the Chinese in 108 BC. The Chinese colonies in the north-western region of Korea lasted until the fourth century AD.

A new kingdom of Koguryo, which emerged in 37 BC in the southern region of Manzhou, along the Yalu River, and later extended into the Korean peninsula, ended Chinese domination in Korea and successfully defended its territory against Chinese aggression in the late sixth and early seventh centuries. Meanwhile, tribal federations which existed in the central and southern regions of the peninsula were consolidated into the kingdoms of Paekche and Silla in 18 BC and 57 BC respectively, ushering in the 'Three Kingdom' period in Korean history.

Silla destroyed Paekche in AD 663 and Koguryo in 668, in collaboration with China, so unifying Korea. However, the kingdom of Koryo, which rose in the central region in 918, brought about the demise of Silla in 935. Korea (Corea) is the Western version of Koryo. During the Koryo period the political system became similar to that of China, and in the 13th century Korea became a vassal to China, then ruled by the Yuan dynasty (established by the Mongol conquest).

In 1392 Gen. Yi Song-Gye overthrew the Koryo dynasty, which had suffered invasions by the Khitans in the 10th century and by the Mongols in the 13th century. He established the Yi dynasty and renamed the kingdom Choson, with Seoul as the new capital. The Yi dynasty brought the entire Korean peninsula and the island of Jeju (Cheju) under its rule, and it governed the kingdom with a Confucian bureaucracy manned by an élite class of scholar-officials. Korea became increasingly Confucianized as a vassal to China, then under the Ming dynasty.

While the power struggle among scholar-officials and between the monarchy and bureaucracy weakened the foundation of the nation, Korea suffered much from Japanese invasions in the late 16th century and Manzhou invasions in the early 17th century. Following the opening of Korea to the West in 1882, an international power struggle developed in Korea, initially between China and Japan, and then between Russia and Japan. The Japanese victories in the Sino-Japanese War of 1894–95 and the Russo-Japanese War of 1904–5 virtually sealed the fate of Korea, although nationalistic reformists made gallant efforts to save the sinking nation.

Despite the repeated invasions of foreign aggressors, Korea maintained its independence and preserved its national territory. However, in 1905 Korea became a Japanese protectorate, and in 1910 was annexed by Japan, ending the rule of the Yi dynasty as well as Korea's independence. The Japanese colonial rule in Korea was highly repressive and exploitative. Freedom of speech and press was non-existent, human rights were completely disregarded, farm lands were confiscated under various pretexts, economic and educational opportunities were extremely limited, and Korean workers and peasants alike were exploited under the repressive rule of the Japanese.

The Koreans retaliated in various ways. On 1 March 1919 some 2m. Koreans demonstrated peacefully, expressing their desire to be free from Japanese colonialism and to restore national independence under the principle of self-determination and the concept of 'one people, one nation.' A provisional government of Korea in exile (established in Shanghai in April 1919), and various non-violent as well as militant organizations of overseas Koreans, kept alive hopes for the eventual restoration of the Korean nation.

Economic and Social Development

An agricultural life developed during the bronze and iron ages (c. 2000 BC–AD 200), and a fully-fledged agricultural economy grew during the 'Three Kingdom' period, when land was monopolized by the aristocrats and cultivated by peasants who constituted the majority of the population. Domestic commerce did not develop until after the 10th century, but foreign trade with China and Japan had flourished during the 'Three Kingdom' and the unified periods.

The anti-commercialism of Confucianism did not encourage commercial economy to grow. However, as cities and towns expanded during the Yi period, government-approved commercial enterprises, as well as rural markets and fairs, increased in number, and cottage industries developed rapidly. Land continued to be owned by the gentry class (*yangban*), and cultivated by peasants and slaves.

Social evolution brought about the stratification of the people into the landed gentry and the toiling masses. The toiling masses were classified into 'good people' or 'common people,' who were engaged in agriculture, and 'the low-born', who were engaged in trade, manufacturing of goods and other lesser occupations. The *yangban* formed the educated and land-owning class of the Yi period, and provided all high-ranking government officials. The 'middle people' class provided the middle- and lower-ranking officials. Only those who passed the civil service examinations were qualified to be government officials during the Yi period.

Modern commerce and industry developed during the Japanese colonial period. Food production was accelerated to feed the ever-growing number of Japanese as an increasing amount of Korean rice was exported to Japan. Rapid industrial growth came after the Japanese invasions of Manzhou and China proper in the 1930s. With this, the number of industrial workers increased rapidly as the influence of the gentry class diminished.

Cultural History

During and after the period of Chinese domination of the north-western region of Korea, the sinification of Korean culture occurred. Buddhism, which migrated from China to Korea during the third century AD, reached its zenith following the unification of Korea by Silla. Many historic and renowned Buddhist temples, pagodas, statues of Buddha and Buddhist writings were produced by the Koreans during the 'Three Kingdom' and the unified Silla periods.

Buddhism became the state religion of Koryo. With the growing influence of Buddhism, book-printing techniques became advanced and sophisticated. *Tripitaka Koreana*, a Buddhist text of over 81,000 pages, and other Buddhist works were printed in Korea with movable type (wooden and metal blocks) in the 13th and 14th centuries.

Confucianism spread slowly but, after the establishment of the Tang dynasty in China in the early seventh century, Confucian influence grew strong in Korea. The increasing influence of Chinese culture had led to the development of native songs, called *hyangga*, as well as the creation of a system of writing Korean words in Chinese, called *idu*, during the unified Silla period. During the Koryo and Yi periods, scholarship grew rapidly as more books on early Korean history, geography and other subjects were published by Confucian scholars. All scholarly books were written in the Chinese language.

The adoption of neo-Confucianism as the state creed and rapid Confucianization of political and social patterns and institutions during the Yi period brought about a sudden decline of

Buddhism. At the same time, the growing number of public and private schools of Confucian and Chinese learning, and the introduction of the Chinese civil service examination system, resulted in the rise of an educated élite.

The adoption and promulgation of a new Korean script, commonly called *han'geul* ('Korean Letters'), by King Sejong in 1446 constituted an important milestone in the cultural history of Korea. With this, the Korean form of poetry, called *sijo*, flourished, as it enabled more Koreans to become literate.

The *Sirhak* ('Practical Learning') school of reformist Confucian scholars not only stimulated the development of a new interpretation of Confucianism, but also Korean studies, including historical and geographical studies, during and after the 17th century. Genre and folk painters, together with folk musicians, dancers and players, contributed greatly, not only to the preservation, but also to the growth, of a distinctive Korean folk culture during the Yi period, as novels and travelogues, written in *han'geul*, appeared.

The arrival and growth of Roman Catholicism and the 'Western Learning' after the 18th century, and the establishment of contacts with the West after 1882, led to the modernization of Korea. The creation of a modern educational system and the introduction of Western culture during the late Yi and Japanese colonial periods brought about a rapid increase of an educated population, and the growth of modern culture and the number of Christians.

The Japanese endeavoured to impose their culture on Korea by forcing Korean people to adopt Shintoism and to change their names to read like Japanese names. Efforts made by the Japanese to destroy the language and the racial and cultural identity of the Koreans were to no avail.

Liberation and Partition

On 15 August 1945 the Japanese surrendered to the Allies. The Cairo Declaration of December 1943, issued by the British and US leaders and Chiang Kai-shek of China, had stated that 'in due course Korea shall become free and independent'. The USSR accepted the Cairo agreement, but proposals made by the USA in 1945 led to the division of Korea into two military zones: the area south of the 38th parallel line under US occupation and the northern area under Soviet control.

The Japanese Governor-General in Korea had persuaded Yo Un-Hyong, a prominent left-wing nationalist (socialist), to form a political body to maintain law and order at the end of the Japanese colonial rule. The Committee for the Preparation of the National Construction of Korea was thus organized. After Japan's surrender, Korean political prisoners were freed and the committee began to function as a government. Provincial, district and local committees were organized to maintain law and order. On 6 September 1945, two days before the arrival of US occupation forces, the committee called a 'National Assembly' and established a 'People's Republic of Korea', claiming jurisdiction over the whole country. Meanwhile, Soviet troops, which had entered Korea in early August, quickly moved southward as they crushed Japanese resistance, and within a month the entire northern half of Korea had come under Soviet occupation.

The US occupation authority accepted the surrender of Korea from the Japanese Governor-General, but, unlike the Soviet authorities in the North, refused to recognize the legitimacy of either the 'People's Republic' or the provisional Government of Korea, based in China. The United States Army Military Government in Korea (USAMGIK) was established and operated until the proclamation of South Korea's independence in August 1948.

Exiled political leaders returned to Korea toward the end of 1945—Dr Syngman Rhee from the USA, Kim Ku and Dr Kim Kyu-Sik from China, and Kim Il Sung and other communists from the USSR and China. Pak Hon Yong, a communist who had been released from Japanese imprisonment, quickly formed the communist South Korean Workers' Party in the US-occupied zone. Freedom of political activity permitted by USAMGIK resulted in a proliferation of political parties and social organizations of all political orientations, each vying for prominence. USAMGIK attempted in vain to bring about a coalition of moderate nationalists and the non-communist left wing.

In December 1945 representatives of the UK, the USA and the USSR entered into the Moscow agreement, providing for a five-year trusteeship for Korea under a four-power regime (China was the fourth power), with a view to establishing an independent and united nation of Korea. Despite violent anti-trusteeship demonstrations, the Allied occupation authorities resolved to implement the Moscow plan. Then, abruptly, the communists throughout Korea changed their attitude in favour of the Moscow plan, splitting the Korean people into two opposing camps. In the US-occupied zone left-wing organizations created serious political and economic problems. Communist-directed labour strikes became widespread, and terrorism of both right- and left-wing organizations became rampant.

A joint US-Soviet commission was formed to establish a national government of Korea in consultation with Korean political and social organizations. The first session of the joint commission was held in Seoul, the capital of the South, in March–May 1946. The Soviet delegate insisted that only 'democratic' organizations should participate and that only organizations which supported the Moscow agreement were 'democratic'. It became clear that the USSR sought to establish a national government of Korea dominated by the communists. In May 1947 the second session of the joint commission, held in the northern capital Pyongyang, similarly failed to achieve any agreement and in June the commission's business was suspended indefinitely.

Realizing that the establishment of Korean unity and of a national government was a remote possibility, USAMGIK adopted new plans for South Korea. The Soviet occupation authority likewise proceeded to establish a client regime under Kim Il Sung. All anti-Soviet and anti-communist organizations were either dissolved or placed under communist leadership. A centralized, communist state began to emerge in the North, as Kim Il Sung formed his own party in defiance of Pak Hon Yong, head of the South Korean Workers' Party, whose headquarters were in Seoul.

The USA established a South Korean interim Legislative Assembly in late 1946, and in May 1947 an interim Government was created, both under moderate nationalists. These actions were bitterly criticized by right-wing leaders such as Dr Rhee and Kim Ku. The relationship between the USA and the right-wing nationalists worsened, while terrorist activities created an extremely uneasy situation. Several prominent politicians were assassinated. Neither the interim Legislative Assembly nor the interim Government was effective, for both were regarded by the conservative nationalists as US protégés attempting to prolong the US military occupation of Korea.

In September 1947 the US Government discarded the Moscow plan and placed the Korean question before the UN. The UN General Assembly formed the UN Temporary Commission on Korea in November and authorized it to conduct a national election in Korea to create a national government for the whole country.

The UN decision was welcomed by the USA and by most people in South Korea. The Soviet occupation authority and the Korean communists in the North, however, rejected the UN plan, and did not allow the UN Temporary Commission to visit North Korea. It soon became apparent that the UN plan would not work in the whole of Korea, and the Commission adopted an alternative plan to hold elections in those areas where it was possible, namely in South Korea only. It was assumed by the Commission that UN-sponsored and supervised elections would be held in the North in the near future, that a National Assembly created by the first democratic elections in Korea would represent the entire country, that the government to be established would be that of all Korea, and that the people in the North would elect their representatives to the National Assembly at a later date.

Whereas the right-wing nationalists welcomed such an alternative plan, the moderate and progressive nationalists, such as Kim Kyu-Sik, the head of the Democratic Independence Party, as well as Kim Ku, an extreme right-wing nationalist, vehemently opposed it, fearing that it would turn the temporary division of Korea into a permanent political partition. They visited North Korea and talked with Kim Il Sung and other communists, but failed to achieve their objective.

The Soviet authorities in the North had already begun to transfer power to the Supreme People's Assembly and the Central People's Committee, both established in early 1947. Dr Rhee's organization, the National Society for the Acceleration of Korean Independence, advocated the immediate independence of South Korea. The UN-sponsored elections held in the South in May 1948 created a National Assembly, heavily dominated by the right wing. About 7.5m. people, or 75% of the electorate, elected 198 of 210 representatives from the South, while 100 unfilled seats in the 310-member Assembly were reserved for North Korean representatives. The National Assembly drew up a democratic Constitution for the Republic of Korea. Dr Rhee was elected the first President of the Republic of Korea, whose legitimacy was immediately recognized by the UN. On 15 August 1948 the Republic of Korea was inaugurated, and the US occupation came to an end.

In August 1948 the communists in the North held an election and established the new 527-member Supreme People's Assembly of the Democratic People's Republic of Korea (DPRK), which was proclaimed on 9 September.

THE KOREAN WAR, 1950–53

(This section was contributed by the Editor)

US forces were withdrawn from South Korea in June 1949, leaving only a small military mission. South Korea's own forces were weaker than those of the North, which had been built up with Soviet help. Increased tension between the North and the South culminated in the Korean War, beginning on 25 June 1950, when a North Korean force of over 60,000 troops, supported by Soviet-built tanks, crossed the 38th parallel and invaded the South. Four days later the North Koreans captured Seoul; US forces, whose assistance was requested by the Seoul Government, arrived on 30 June.

In response to North Korea's attack, the UN mounted a collective defence action in support of South Korea. Armed forces from 16 UN member states, attached to a unified command under the USA, were sent to help repel the invasion. Meanwhile, the North Koreans continued their drive southwards, advancing so rapidly that they soon occupied most of South Korea, leaving UN troops confined to the south-east corner of the peninsula. Following sea-borne landings by UN forces at Incheon, near Seoul, in September 1950, the invaders were driven back and UN troops advanced into North Korea, capturing Pyongyang in October and reaching the Chinese frontier on the Yalu River in November.

In October 1950 the People's Republic of China sent troops to assist North Korea: 200,000 Chinese crossed the Yalu River into Korea, forcing the evacuation of South Korean and UN troops. The Chinese advanced into South Korea but were driven back by a UN counter-attack in April 1951.

Peace negotiations began in July 1951, but hostilities continued until an armistice agreement was concluded on 27 July 1953. The war caused more than 800,000 casualties in South Korea and enormous damage to property. The 1953 cease-fire line, roughly along the 38th parallel, remains the boundary between North and South Korea, with a narrow demilitarized zone (DMZ) separating the two frontiers.

THE DEMOCRATIC PEOPLE'S REPUBLIC OF KOREA

History

ANDREW C. NAHM

Updated by AIDAN FOSTER-CARTER

INTRODUCTION

Strong nationalist leadership, with potentially large popular support, was available in North Korea when the Second World War ended. It consisted chiefly of democratically-inclined, Western missionary-educated individuals, of whom the most outstanding leader was Cho Man Shik. In August 1945 the Japanese Governor in Pyongyang relinquished control to Cho and a newly-formed Provincial People's Committee. In the same month Soviet troops reached Pyongyang, accepted the legitimacy of the committee, and approved Cho as Chairman of the Five Provinces Administrative Bureau, formed to act as the indigenous government organ for North Korea.

In September 1945 Kim Il Sung, a young communist, who had led a guerrilla group of Korean communists in south-eastern Manzhou (Manchuria), returned to Korea with Soviet troops. Kim, however, had to cope with the 'domestic' communists who challenged his 'Kapsan' or 'partisan' faction. Two further groups of communists returned to North Korea following its liberation from the Japanese: one associated with the Soviet Army known as the 'Soviet faction', the other from Yanan, China, under the leadership of Kim Tu Bong of the Korean Independence League. In the early power struggle among the communists, Hyon Chun Hyok, the leader of the 'domestic' faction, was assassinated in September 1945. In the following month Kim Il Sung formed the North Korean Central Bureau of the Korean Communist Party (KCP) in order to consolidate his political position. In this he received covert support from the USSR.

Cho Man Shik organized the Korean Democratic Party (KDP), which received the support of the majority of the people, but his uncompromising stand against the Moscow plan for a five-year trusteeship of the Allied powers led to his downfall in January 1946. He was promptly placed under house arrest, and many members of the KDP fled to South Korea.

After the departure of the nationalists, a North Korean Provisional People's Committee was established in February 1946, with Kim Il Sung as Chairman and Kim Tu Bong as Vice-Chairman. The USSR accorded government status to the Committee. Kim Tu Bong formed the New People's Party (NPP) in March, to expand his power base, and managed to increase his party's membership. In July the North Korean Central Bureau of the KCP and the NPP merged to form the North Korean Workers' Party, with Kim Tu Bong as its Chairman and Kim Il Sung as Vice-Chairman. Real power, however, was in the hands of the latter.

In early 1947 the Supreme People's Assembly (SPA) was established as the highest legislative body in North Korea, and the Assembly, in turn, established a Central People's Committee to exercise executive authority. The Committee's first major act was to direct land reforms. No real attempts were made to establish collective farms, and the land which was distributed to landless peasants became the private property of the cultivators. It was not until the end of the Korean War, in 1953, that the agricultural 'co-operativization' programme was inaugurated. Land reform was followed by the nationalization of industry, transport, communications and financial institutions.

In early 1948 Pak Hon Yong, with other leaders of the communist South Korean Workers' Party, fled from the South when the party was outlawed by the US occupation authority. Pak, who enjoyed strong support from the 'domestic' faction, felt that he, instead of Kim Il Sung, should lead the movement in Korea. However, he was unable to achieve his objectives, and he grudgingly accepted a position subordinate to that of Kim.

THE ESTABLISHMENT OF THE DEMOCRATIC PEOPLE'S REPUBLIC

After refusing to allow the United Nations Temporary Commission on Korea to visit North Korea and to conduct elections there, Kim Il Sung established a separate, pro-USSR state. In August 1948 elections were held in the North for a new SPA. The newly-created Assembly drafted a Constitution, ratified it on 8 September and proclaimed the Democratic People's Republic of Korea (DPRK) on the following day. Kim Il Sung was named Premier, while Pak Hon Yong was made Vice-Premier and Minister for Foreign Affairs. In June 1949 the merger of the North Korean Workers' Party and the South Korean Workers' Party brought about a unified communist party, the Korean Workers' Party (KWP), with Kim as its Chairman and Pak as its Vice-Chairman. The establishment of the DPRK entrenched the temporary military division of Korea as a permanent political partition. The USSR announced the withdrawal of its troops from North Korea, completing the process in December 1949. However, a large number of Soviet advisers in various fields remained.

During 1950 North Korea substantially increased the size and strength of its armed forces with Soviet supplies. In June the North Korean invasion of the South precipitated the Korean War (see p. 652), inflicting great damage on both sides. During and after the unsuccessful attempt to conquer South Korea, Kim Il Sung purged many of his enemies, including Pak Hon Yong. Conflict among the surviving communist leaders, however, did not end, and Kim Tu Bong remained a formidable figure. Kim Il Sung's economic reconstruction programme, which emphasized the development of heavy industry, met strong opposition. The debate lasted until 1956, when Kim Tu Bong fell from power. Meanwhile, the 'Yanan' faction attacked the growing personality cult of Kim Il Sung; he counter-attacked, forcing some 'Yanan' communists to flee to China. The USSR and China effected a temporary reconciliation, but leaders of the 'Yanan' faction were systematically relegated to less important posts or eased entirely out of power. By 1958 it had ceased to pose any further threat, and Kim Il Sung continued to consolidate his position of unassailability during the following decade.

DEVELOPMENTS DURING THE 1970s

Following the announcement of the 1972 joint North-South agreement to open dialogue for the peaceful unification of the peninsula, the KWP proposed amendments to the Constitution. General elections to the fifth SPA were held in December. The newly-elected representatives adopted a socialist Constitution, and elected Kim Il Sung and Kim Il as President and Premier, respectively. For the first time, the North Korean Constitution stated the capital to be Pyongyang, not Seoul. It also elevated the Central People's Committee, headed by the President, to become the highest organ of state, while an Administration Council, headed by the Premier, was established as the DPRK's cabinet.

In 1973 North Korea gained observer status at the UN. This status nullified both the branding of North Korea as an aggressor in 1950 and the view that the Government of South Korea was the only lawful government in Korea. Both Koreas were invited to the UN General Assembly in November 1973 for a debate on the Korean question. North Korea was also given membership of the UN Conference on Trade and Development in May 1973.

In February 1974 the Central Committee of the KWP launched the 'Three Great Revolutions': ideological, technical and cultural. It emphasized the promotion of a self-orientated, self-reliant and independent ideology, or *juche* thought. The KWP also reorganized the structure of the Administration Council and reshuffled its membership twice in 1974. Kim Yong Ju, younger brother of Kim Il Sung, who had been regarded as heir apparent, was demoted in the party hierarchy, while Kim Il Sung's son, Kim Jong Il, rose in rank as a possible successor to his father. Significantly, a military leader, Gen. O Jin U, also rose in rank within the KWP.

One of North Korea's major objectives in the mid-1970s was the intensification of diplomatic activity to strengthen ties between non-aligned nations. The ministerial conference of the Non-aligned nations in Lima, Peru, in August 1975 voted to accept North Korea's application for participation.

Economic problems increasingly troubled the Pyongyang regime. Critical shortages of food and commodities were reported in the mid-1970s. In 1977 North Korea signed a new trade pact with the People's Republic of China, and an economic and technical co-operation agreement with the USSR. It was reported that the USSR had made large shipments of military goods to North Korea and had sent technical advisers in 1977.

During 1978 an important ideological-political campaign was undertaken to strengthen *juche* thought. A renewed drive to promote the 'Three Revolutions' was reportedly led by Kim Jong Il. In April a new socialist labour law was promulgated, which called for a change in the way of life for workers—eight hours of work, eight hours of rest, and eight hours of study of Kim Il Sung's *juche* thought.

The visits to Pyongyang by China's then Premier, Hua Guofeng, and his Vice-Premier, Deng Xiaoping, in 1978, and the trade agreement between Pyongyang and Beijing, seemed to have improved Sino-North Korean ties. China reportedly promised to supply more petroleum and greater economic assistance. Pyongyang dealt cautiously with the new Sino-US relationship and, while criticizing the Vietnamese invasion of Kampuchea (now Cambodia), eschewed any comments on China's punitive war against Viet Nam.

The new trade agreement between Moscow and Pyongyang, Vice-President Pak Song Chol's visit to Moscow in January 1979, and increasing contacts between Soviet and North Korean military leaders appeared to indicate a growing solidarity between the two countries. North Korea provided special privileges to the USSR in the port of Rajin on the north-eastern coast, making it a Soviet 'leased' territory and a Soviet naval base.

THE EMERGENCE OF KIM JONG IL

After conducting intense campaigns to select reliable and loyal supporters of Kim Il Sung's son, Kim Jong Il, as delegates, the Sixth Congress of the KWP met in early October 1980, the first such congress since 1970. Many significant structural and personnel changes in the party hierarchy were made. Although Kim Jong Il was not officially designated as successor to his father, as anticipated, he became a key member of several crucial committees in the party. A new five-member Standing Committee of the Political Committee (Politburo) of the Central Committee of the KWP was established, and Kim Il Sung became its Chairman, thus strengthening the concentration of power in the hands of a few. Many new members of the Central Committee and its subcommittees were supporters of Kim Jong Il, and it was reported that those who opposed his succession to power were removed from other key positions in the party, Government and military.

In April 1981 elections were held for members of provincial, city and county people's assemblies in the usual manner: one candidate named by the KWP for each position and a 100% turn-out of voters. In February 1982 elections were held to the SPA, and the Seventh Assembly emerged in early April. It approved the reappointment of the President, three Vice-Presidents, the Premier and 13 Vice-Premiers, but, contrary to expectations, it failed to name Kim Jong Il as a Vice-President.

Shortly before the convening of the SPA, the Central Committee of the KWP met, followed by a joint conference in mid-April 1982 of the Central Committee and the SPA. Both meetings failed to resolve the question of succession. Meanwhile, the power struggle intensified between the respective supporters of Kim Jong Il and his half-brother, Kim Pyong Il, son of Kim Il Sung's second wife. While the political turmoil surrounding the issue of succession increased instability in North Korea, several armed clashes between the military and workers occurred in Chongjin, in the north-east, in September 1981, followed in June 1982 by civil disturbances in Nampo, near Pyongyang, involving Koreans who had come to North Korea from Japan. Some 500 workers were reported to have been killed in the clashes in the north-eastern regions, while many fled into Soviet territory. For undisclosed reasons, an emergency meeting of the Central Committee of the KWP was convened in April 1982, and it was reported that some 12 generals and a large number of party leaders were purged in July. Furthermore, Choe Hyon, an experienced politician and a key member of the Central Committee of the ruling KWP, died in April, amid rumours that he had been murdered. However, Gen. O Jin U, a staunch supporter of Kim Jong Il, was retained as Minister of the People's Armed Forces.

It became known in April 1982 that there were several concentration camps for political dissidents and 'undesirables' in north-east Korea. More than 100,000 persons, including 23,000 Koreans who emigrated from Japan to North Korea, were reported to have been among the internees. (A report issued in January 1992 by the US Department of State estimated there to be a total of 12 concentration camps in North Korea, in which between 105,000 and 150,000 political prisoners were being detained.)

THE 1980s: SURVIVAL OF THE STALINIST REGIME

Elections were held in March 1983 to choose members for the local people's committees. The second session of the Seventh SPA met in April and elected Rim Chun Chu as Vice-President, succeeding Kang Ryang Uk. At the same time, it elected Yang Hyong Sop as Chairman of the SPA. Both were believed to be trusted supporters of Kim Jong Il.

The defection of a North Korean airman, in his fighter aircraft, to South Korea in February 1983, a labour uprising in Yanggang (North Hamgyong Province) and mass riots among workers in Wonsan (Kangwon Province) in April created serious domestic problems. It was reported that some 500 air force officers were purged on charges of disloyalty. As a result of the Rangoon (Yangon) bombing incident of October 1983 (see below), which was allegedly planned by North Korean agents, the intra-party struggle between moderates and radicals intensified.

In January 1984 Ri Jong Ok was dismissed from the premiership, a post he had held since 1977, and replaced by Kang Song San. Ri became a Vice-President. In early March 1984 Vice-President Kim Il, who had been critical of the junior Kim, died after a long illness. His death effectively marked the conclusion of the period of dominance by the 'old guard' of political leaders who had been associates of Kim Il Sung before he came to power.

The Government took a significant economic step in September 1984, announcing a new joint-venture law. It sought capital investment in North Korea on the part of foreign nations, particularly those of the West and Japan. This action was regarded as an admission of the failure of North Korea's 'self-reliant', closed economic policy. According to a Chinese source, the North Korean Government allowed some farmers to have private plots and fishermen to have private shops on a limited basis.

In August 1984 North Korea's official radio station confirmed, for the first time in a public broadcast, that Kim Jong Il would succeed his father as President, claiming that the transfer of power had been 'internationally acknowledged'. When the Central Committee met in early December, Kim Il Sung resumed direct control over economic and international affairs, including policy toward South Korea, which had been under the direction of Kim Jong Il. It was reported that there was conflict between the hard-line, pro-Soviet faction of the junior Kim, and the moderates who had been pro-China.

Frequent changes of personnel in the KWP Politburo and the Administration Council, effected during 1985 and 1986, were interpreted as an indication of North Korea's complex economic problems. In November 1986 unfounded reports that Kim Il

Sung had been assassinated focused international attention on Pyongyang, and led to speculation that there had been an attempted *coup d'état*. However, stability was apparently restored promptly, and, after elections to the Eighth SPA, held in the same month (when its 655 members were elected unopposed), Kim Il Sung was re-elected President, and a new Administration Council was formed. Ri Kun Mo, a member of the Central People's Committee, became Premier, replacing Kang Song San.

In February 1988 Gen. Choe Kwang replaced Gen. O Kuk Ryol as Chief of General Staff of the Korean People's Army (KPA). Gen. O was regarded as a close ally of Kim Jong Il. His replacement by Gen. Choe, a veteran associate of Kim Il Sung, led to speculation among foreign observers that the President had strengthened his position to the detriment of his son, owing possibly to a series of economic failures for which the latter was allegedly responsible.

In December 1988 Ri Kun Mo resigned as Premier, reportedly because of ill health, and was replaced by Yon Hyong Muk, a former Vice-Premier and a member of the KWP Politburo. In late 1988 suspicions increased that Kim Il Sung was reclaiming much of Kim Jong Il's power in favour of Kim Pyong Il. However, in April 1989, when the then General Secretary of the Chinese Communist Party, Zhao Ziyang, visited Pyongyang, Kim Jong Il played a conspicuous diplomatic role.

In July 1989 North Korea hosted the 13th World Festival of Youth and Students, both in an attempt to enhance the country's international image, and, it was surmised, as a rival event to the Olympic Games held in Seoul in 1988. More than 15,000 delegates from 165 countries (including one student from South Korea) participated in the festival, which was the largest international event ever staged in North Korea.

The announcement in February 1990 that elections to the SPA would be held on 22 April, six months ahead of schedule, led to renewed speculation that Kim Il Sung was preparing to transfer presidential power to Kim Jong Il. In the event, however, Kim Il Sung was re-elected President, although the junior Kim did acquire his first state (as distinct from party) post: in late May he was elected First Vice-Chairman of the National Defence Commission, a body responsible to the Central People's Committee.

Following the elections to the SPA, the number of seats in the Assembly was increased from 655 to 687. In a concession to statistical impossibility, the electoral turn-out was put at only 99.78%, rather than the usual 100%, excluding those abroad or at sea. All 100% of those who did vote, however, were claimed to have supported the single approved list of candidates.

CRACKS IN THE MONOLITH

Compared with the momentous developments in inter-Korean and foreign relations in the early 1990s (see below), North Korean domestic politics showed few overt signs of change during the same period. Recurrent speculation that Kim Jong Il would formally take over from Kim Il Sung reached a peak in early 1992, when father and son celebrated, respectively, their 80th and 50th birthdays, but once again proved premature. The younger Kim's role did, however, become more emphasized, and there was a noticeable intensification of 'loyalty campaigns' for the promotion of his personality cult. In December 1991 Kim Jong Il was appointed Supreme Commander of the KPA, a post hitherto constitutionally reserved for the President. One month later, a major policy statement issued in the junior Kim's name declared North Korea's unwavering allegiance to socialism (notwithstanding its demise elsewhere), including an explicit rebuttal of any market-orientated economic reforms.

Such public continuity and defiance, however, scarcely concealed the pressures for change in a country increasingly isolated and impoverished. Defectors (including the first diplomat ever to do so) revealed that even major enterprises were often inoperative owing to shortages of power and raw materials, and that senior officials were now openly critical of party economic policy. Rumours of unrest also continued. Japanese press reports that young Soviet-trained army officers had, in February 1991, attempted a coup against Kim Jong Il were predictably denied in Pyongyang. Better attested were demonstrations in the north-western border town of Shinuiju in August by some 7,000 people, protesting against food shortages and working conditions.

During 1992 several measures, seemingly designed to quell discontent, were adopted by the Government. In February, immediately before Kim Jong Il's customarily lavish birthday celebrations, it was announced that wages were to be increased by an average of 43.4%. Two months later, the SPA approved the budget for 1992, which included an increase of 11.6% in expenditure on social welfare (compared with an increase of only 3.5% in the 1991 budget). Efforts to placate the armed forces were also apparent. In April 1992 the celebrations of Armed Forces Day were given an unusually high profile, and included the first military parade in seven years and promotions for several hundred senior officers. In the same month Kim Il Sung was given the title of Grand Marshal, while his former rank of Marshal was conferred on Kim Jong Il and on O Jin U, Minister of the People's Armed Forces and hitherto Vice-Marshal.

There was a minor reshuffle of the Administration Council in December 1992, which included the replacement of Yon Hyong Muk as Premier by Kang Song San, an economist who had previously held the post in 1984–86. His appointment was interpreted by foreign observers as an attempt to provide fresh stimulus for economic reform. However, the fact that Kang was neither seen in public nor mentioned for several months subsequently led to speculation that his reputed reformist tendencies had fallen foul of close confidants of Kim Jong Il.

Two further promotions at the same time raised hopes of a liberalization in Pyongyang. Both Vice-Premier Kim Tal Hyon and Kim Yong Sun attained candidate (alternate) membership of the Politburo. Moreover, the former, who had impressed his hosts during a business-orientated visit to South Korea in July 1992, relinquished responsibility for external economic affairs to become Chairman of the State Planning Commission. In April 1993 Kim Yong Sun, who (as the KWP's international secretary) had also impressed foreign opinion, replaced Choe Tae Bok as the party's secretary for reunification. Initial hopes for a new openness proved unfounded, however, since from late 1992 North Korea reverted to more hardline positions.

Legislative changes showed a similar ambivalence. In October 1992 the SPA adopted three new laws on foreign investment and joint ventures. However, the overall commitment to centrally-planned socialism remained unchanged, and indeed was constantly reaffirmed. Meanwhile, certain constitutional amendments had been made in April 1992, although they were not published (except several months later in South Korea). Principal among the changes were the deletion of the last remaining references to Marxism-Leninism, and the upgrading of the National Defence Commission (now chaired by Kim Jong Il, and the highest military organ of state power) to become the most senior executive body below the President.

The first party youth congress in 12 years was held in February 1993, amid fulsome pledges of loyalty to both the 'Great Leader' (Kim Il Sung) and the 'Dear Leader' (Kim Jong Il). No full KWP congress had been convened since 1980, possibly because North Korea's crises were by then so deep that such a gathering could not be successfully staged. Furthermore, the country's growing economic hardships were reflected in the budget for 1993, which envisaged substantially-reduced increases in expenditure as compared with 1992. Both Kim Il Sung's birthday and that of his son were much less lavishly celebrated in 1993 than in the previous year.

Kim Jong Il was not seen in public between late April and late July 1993, when he re-emerged for the 40th anniversary of what North Korea proclaims as its 'victory' in the Korean War. There were reports that he had been treated for a heart condition (related to his alleged unhealthy lifestyle). An intriguing alternative version was that he had suffered a nervous breakdown after an upbraiding by his father on account of various policy errors, above all North Korea's threatened withdrawal from the Treaty on the Non-Proliferation of Nuclear Weapons (see below).

Important economic and political changes took place at the end of 1993. In what may have been the first admission ever of failure by Pyongyang, the KWP Central Committee announced, in early December, that the Seven-Year Plan (1987–93) had not been fulfilled. It was to be followed by a three-year 'adjustment period', giving priority to agriculture, light industry and foreign trade. As scapegoat for these economic failures, Kim Tal Hyon was removed from his post of Chairman of the State Planning

Commission and reportedly allocated the even more onerous task of directing the Sunchon Vinalon Works—a perennially underperforming favourite project of Kim Il Sung. His replacement was the previously unknown Hong Sok Hyong, who formerly managed the Kimchaek Iron and Steel Complex (the largest in the country).

What attracted most attention was the return to political life of Kim Il Sung's younger brother, Kim Yong Ju, after a 17-year absence, as both a full member of the Politburo and one of four state Vice-Presidents. Kim Yong Ju's reappearance now, however, was interpreted less as the emergence of a rival to Kim Jong Il than as evidence of a continuing need to bolster the 'Dear Leader' as successor with the overt backing of such a senior figure. Also appointed as Vice-President was Kim Pyong Shik, a returnee from Japan, who earlier in 1993 had assumed the chairmanship of the 'puppet' Korean Social Democratic Party.

The hardships of ordinary North Koreans, meanwhile, intensified, and in 1994 the trickle of defectors increased both in quantity and 'quality', the latter including two sons-in-law of government ministers. All painted a grim picture of deteriorating economic conditions and tight political control. The former was confirmed by the 1994 budget, which for the second successive year anticipated only modest increases in expenditure. It was revealed, however, that actual spending on social services in 1993 had needed to be greater than that originally budgeted for.

THE DEATH OF KIM IL SUNG AND BEYOND

Questions as to how long the world's last remaining Stalinist regime could endure unchanged acquired a sharp new focus in mid-1994. On 8 July, after almost 46 years in power, Kim Il Sung died, reportedly of a heart attack. Amid extraordinary scenes of mass mourning, Kim Jong Il was named as head of the funeral committee and, as in the past, he was generally referred to as the inheritor of his father's work. North Korea's first year without its founding 'Great Leader' presented a mixture of continuity and ambiguity. Continuity was evident in the style of the regime, where internally the cult of Kim Il Sung continued unabated, culminating in his embalmed body being placed on display in his former palace, now referred to as the 'holy land of *juche*'. There was continuity, too, in personnel, with few major new appointments among the ruling élite. The second most powerful figure in the regime, Marshal O Jin U, died in February 1995; his successor as Minister of the People's Armed Forces, Marshal Choe Kwang, was announced only in October. North Korea's stance toward the wider world also displayed elements of continuity, with characteristic militancy of rhetoric shown toward South Korea, Japan and the USA.

However, there was also growing ambiguity in North Korean political life. More than a year after the death of Kim Il Sung, his son and heir-presumptive, Kim Jong Il, had still not been officially appointed to any of the three top posts: General Secretary of the KWP, state President, and Chairman of the party's Central Military Commission. This was not the only failure of due process. General elections to the SPA (due to have been held by April 1995) did not take place, and the Assembly (still operational, albeit technically unconstitutional) failed to hold its annual meeting to consider the state budget. Amid increasingly unconvincing excuses of the need to observe a period of national mourning, the official media continued to treat Kim Jong Il as *de facto* leader, particularly in 1995, referring to him as the 'Great Leader'. Kim, however, remained as reclusive as ever, invisible to public view for long periods at a time. His appearances were confined mainly to army units and military occasions, which suggested that Kim's acceptance by the armed forces was not yet complete. The rise to prominence in early 1995 of several Vice-Marshals of the KPA, who were believed to be sympathetic to Kim, was interpreted as a further attempt by Kim to enhance his prestige among the military. Meanwhile, speculation continued that Kim Jong Il was in poor health. As in the past, there were rumours of coup attempts and popular unrest.

At the same time, however, there were signs of attempts to change. These included an international sports festival, held in Pyongyang in April 1995, which was attended by several thousand foreign visitors. More substantially, the nuclear agreement with the USA, signed in October 1994 (see below), gradually began to be implemented in the ensuing months, despite many difficulties. North Korea also expanded efforts to attract foreign (including South Korean) firms to invest in its only free economic and trade zone, at Rajin-Sonbong, in the north-east of the country. However, hopes for a more general turn toward economic reform, as in China and Viet Nam, remained unfulfilled. Rather, works by Kim Jong Il continued to inveigh against private ownership, pluralism and any effort to 'pollute' pure socialism.

The impression that North Korea was lacking in any form of effective leadership continued into 1996. Despite several occasions when Kim Jong Il might have been officially inaugurated, no ceremony took place. Kim Jong Il continued to be treated by the media as *de facto* leader, and to appear periodically, both at major state occasions and local 'guidance' visits. As before, these visits were confined mainly to army units.

Analysts' opinions were divided as to whether the 'Dear Leader' was quietly consolidating his grip on power, was the hesitant arbiter of an ongoing struggle between hardliners and reformers, or merely a figurehead for senior officers in the KPA. There were several indications that the military were in the ascendant. In October 1995 the 50th anniversary of the KWP was celebrated more as an army than a party affair. At official events, senior Vice-Marshals were given higher precedence than party and state representatives. One of these, Kim Kwang Jin, made two extremely bellicose speeches in March and July 1996, warning that it was only a matter of time before an inter-Korean war broke out, and threatening that North Korea would be the first to attack. In other respects, however, such as the nuclear issue (see below), North Korea was pragmatic and co-operative.

There was little overt sign of the problems attendant upon any political succession. Two senior figures, Vice-President Kim Yong Ju and Premier Kang Song San, hardly appeared in public in the first half of 1996; yet in July both were cited as still in office, with their membership of the Politburo intact. Kim Jong Il was said to favour some Vice-Ministers, such as the First Deputy Minister of Foreign Affairs, Kang Sok Ju, who seemed to be acting as Minister—for example, with regard to nuclear negotiations—while his nominal superior, Kim Yong Nam, appeared on ceremonial occasions.

The uncertainties over the situation in North Korea were not confined to the higher echelons of society. Ordinary citizens saw their already spartan living standards further eroded as the economy, still unreformed, contracted throughout the 1990s. Furthermore, the main farming areas in the west of the country were badly damaged in August 1995 by the worst floods of the century, forcing the 'hermit kingdom' to appeal for help from the international community. Foreign aid workers were given unprecedented access to the country, and were impressed by the degree of organization of the Government and the stoicism of the people, in the face of ever-worsening living conditions. Further flooding in mid-1996 threatened to exacerbate an already critical situation.

It was also clear, however, that, apart from the natural disaster, North Korea's major problems—both in agriculture, and on a more general level—were structural, and thus demanded bold new policies of reform. Without such steps, then even in this most controlled of societies there can be no guarantee that an ever more impoverished citizenry will remain quiescent indefinitely; the growing numbers of defectors, albeit still perhaps surprisingly few, are an indication of the worsening situation.

This curious combination of political uncertainty and economic decline persisted well into 1997. Despite earlier indications, the third anniversary of Kim Il Sung's death passed in July without the formal inauguration of Kim Jong Il. However, the mourning period was officially declared to be over, prompting renewed speculation that the junior Kim would soon succeed his father officially, although some analysts regarded it as too risky to essay the pomp and circumstance of a 'coronation' while the country was gripped by famine. Nevertheless, in April 1997 Kim Jong Il presided over a typical parade in Pyongyang, taking the salute (in front of Western television cameras, for the first time) from goose-stepping soldiers who did not appear to be noticeably underfed.

None the less, questions persisted as to who, if anyone, was really leading North Korea. A 'leaked' speech by Kim Jong Il, published in Seoul in April 1997, revealed him to be well aware of his country's plight (not least, the food shortages) and its vulnerability. Yet he disavowed any responsibility for the economy, declaring that his job was to guide the party and army. The latter aspect was clearly more in evidence: most of Kim's appearances were still on military occasions and the role of the KPA (both symbolic and real) continued to increase, including the drafting of soldiers to assist with farming.

The long-delayed reshuffle seemed to be under way in February 1997, when the defection of the senior leader, Hwang Jang Yop (see North-South Relations), appeared to precipitate a spate of morbidity. Both the Minister of the People's Armed Forces, Marshal Choe Kwang, and his deputy, Kim Kwang Jin, died within a week of one another. The latter was replaced by the head of the navy, Vice-Marshal Kim Il Chol, who by late 1998 had also assumed the responsibilities of Choe Kwang. The most powerful man in the military was evidently Vice-Marshal Jo Myong Rok, head of the KPA Political Bureau and Kim Jong Il's constant companion.

Meanwhile, North Korea's condolences on the death of the Chinese leader, Deng Xiaoping, in February 1997 were sent by Hong Song Nam as acting Premier, implying that Kang Song San had been dismissed. The impression of a purge was strengthened by Choe Kwang's funeral committee, from which several senior, pro-reform figures were absent. Besides Kang, these included the former Premier, Yon Hyong Muk, and the Minister of the Metal Industry, Choe Yong Rim. Perplexingly, however, all these absentees subsequently reappeared (if briefly) at major ceremonies in April and July. To mark the third anniversary of the passing of the 'Great Leader', North Korea introduced a new 'Juche' calendar, starting from 1912, his year of birth. If Pyongyang's aim was to keep the world guessing as to its true intentions, it certainly succeeded.

From late 1997 there were some signs of moves towards political normalization, at least by North Korea's own standards. The official rationale was that, following the end of the three years of official mourning for Kim Il Sung, normal life could now resume. Thus, on 8 October, Kim Jong Il at last assumed one of his late father's two vacant posts, becoming General Secretary of the KWP. The manner of his elevation was, however, unorthodox, being by acclamation at a series of provincial party conferences, rather than through election by the Central Committee, as laid down in the KWP's rules. There is still no sign that the Central Committee has actually met since Kim Il Sung's death, and there is no immediate prospect of a full party Congress, none having been convened since 1980. The legislature, however, has been revived. The elections for the SPA, which should have been held in 1995, finally took place on 26 July 1998. As ever, the electorate was presented with a single list of candidates, which it reportedly endorsed unanimously: some 99.85% of electors voted (that is, all North Koreans except those who were abroad or at sea), and fully 100% of voters supported the candidates.

The 10th SPA was duly convened in September 1998, the 50th anniversary of the foundation of the DPRK; the expected and long-awaited appointment of Kim Jong Il as President did not, however, occur. In a surprise move, the Constitution was amended to elevate Kim Il Sung posthumously to the rank of 'Eternal President' and thus perpetual Head of State. The chairmanship of the National Defence Commission (the highest military office, to which Kim Jong Il had been re-elected, having stood for election in a military constituency) was defined as the most senior position in the state hierarchy. Kim Jong Il consequently assumed the role of *de facto* Head of State, while remaining in the shadow of his father. The 10th SPA, like the Ninth, had 687 members. Usually the number increases at each election, so there was speculation that famine had taken its toll on population growth. Of the 687 members, as many as 443 (or 64%) were new, indicating that Kim Jong Il was at last able to promote his own generation and supporters. Military predominance was striking, with some 50 younger generals included among the new deputies. The composition of the assembly was also a guide to the ongoing power struggles in Pyongyang. Absentees included Kim Song Ae, Kim Il Sung's widow (and Kim Jong Il's stepmother); Kang Song San, at last officially replaced as Premier by Hong Song Nam (as part of the extensive government reorganization of September 1998); and several officials who in the past had handled relations with South Korea, including Kim Tal Hyon (who had been regarded as a possible candidate for the premiership). On the other hand, Vice-President Kim Yong Ju, Kim Jong Il's uncle and once his rival for the succession, retained an SPA seat despite being all but invisible since the death of his brother, Kim Il Sung.

Politics in North Korea also proceeded behind the scenes and by harsher means. Several reports claimed that So Kwan Hi, the long-serving Party Secretary for agriculture, was executed during late 1997, presumably as a scapegoat for the ongoing food crisis. The head of the youth league, Choe Ryong Hae (a friend of Kim Jong Il since childhood), was purged in January 1998 after reports that several youth league officials had been executed for spying for South Korea. It was reported in October that Kim Jong U, formerly the reformist Chairman of the DPRK Committee for the Promotion of External Economic Cooperation, had been executed.

In April 1999 the SPA resumed the annual sessions to consider the budget, which had lapsed since the death of Kim Il Sung in 1994. Unusually, some 50 of the newly-elected members were absent, prompting speculation of continuing purges. The budget itself gave only broad magnitudes, but these revealed that both revenue and expenditure had declined by one-half in the five years since figures were last published: a fact that passed almost without comment. The SPA approved a new economic planning law during the same session. Several other economic laws were also announced during 1999, covering specific areas such as agriculture, forestry, and even fish-breeding. Most of this legislation appeared to codify rather than alter existing arrangements, and gave the impression of a 'rearguard action' by the centre, to try to exert control over an economy which *de facto* had become increasingly anarchic, as the old planned economy had broken down. The revised Constitution of September 1998 gave slightly more scope to private enterprise and market forces, but the amendments failed to keep pace with the actual situation, even though in theory the DPRK remained bonded to communism and hostile to any explicit market reforms. In June 1999 a major policy statement proclaimed a 'military-first' policy, giving defence absolute priority.

Kim Jong Il himself remained elusive, although his 'on the spot guidance' broadened from visits to military bases to include more economic sites (many of them run by the military). He continued to delegate the head of state's task of meeting foreigners to Kim Yong Nam, the former Minister of Foreign Affairs, in his new capacity as President of the SPA Presidium. From mid-2000, however, Kim Jong Il adopted a less reclusive attitude and a startling change of image, if only for the purposes of external display. Within two months he met the heads of state of China, South Korea and Russia, while his polite but affable manner at the North-South summit, which took place in mid-June, impressed television viewers in South Korea. His behaviour was also revealing when entertaining South Korean media executives, whom he had invited to Pyongyang in August. Accounts of this lengthy luncheon, accompanied by much alcohol, showed the North Korean leader as effusive, yet still enigmatic and somewhat eccentric.

How, when, or even whether North Korea's apparent new openness to the outside world (see below) would be translated into domestic political and/or economic change remained ambiguous. Hitherto Kim Jong Il had explicitly and frequently inveighed against reform as a betrayal of socialism. He hinted to his Southern guests, however, that a long-overdue KWP Congress would be held in late 2000, at which the Party's statutes might be changed to excise the goal of communizing South Korea, despite the fact that this would necessitate the purging of officials loyal to his late father, Kim Il Sung. By late 2002 no Congress had yet been held or further mentioned. While the KWP formally remained the ruling party, its real power in relation to either the military or Kim Jong Il's circle was not evident. Nor was it clear who served on the Politburo, or even whether the Central Committee meets regularly. It was possible that the Party might gain a new lease of life if relaunched as a harbinger of 'Dengist' reforms, without which any South Korean or other foreign aid would have only limited revitalizing effects.

Whether the 'Dear Leader' was ready to commit himself irreversibly to a path of reform remained to be seen in late 2000.

The ambiguity continued in 2001, which began promisingly with a clearly business-orientated visit by Kim Jong Il to Shanghai, China (see below), and the publication by him of maxims emphasizing the need to adapt to new times. However, by late 2001 none of this had been translated into action. In fact, the year was largely devoid of overt domestic political activity of any kind. In April 2001 the SPA met for just one day, instead of the usual three. As well as passing a budget, the few figures of which suggested that the economy might have levelled out, the SPA ratified laws on copyright and the processing trade, although no details of these were given. This failure to change suggested fierce debate behind the scenes. Seoul press sources reported that Kim Yong Sun, the party secretary in charge of dialogue with South Korea, spent a week under arrest in March 2001, before Kim Jong Il ordered his release. The implication was that the initial hostility of the new US administration under President George W. Bush undermined North Korea's more reform-minded figures and strengthened the position of its hardliners: this interpretation was supported by the suspension of talks with South Korea (see below). Meanwhile, the world had its first glimpse of yet another Kim, the 'Dear Leader's' son and reputed heir, Kim Jong Nam, in an incident that did little to improve North Korea's reputation for bizarre behaviour. In May 2001 the young Kim and his family were detained on entering Japan at Narita airport, having been found to be travelling under false names and on fake Dominican Republic passports. They admitted their identity, stated that they hoped to visit the Disneyland theme park, and were swiftly deported to Beijing. This embarrassment seemed a set-back to possible plans to appoint Kim Jong Nam as his father's official successor.

In March 2002 the Kim Il Sung Socialist Youth League met for the first time in six years. Amid much mention of the need to inherit revolutionary traditions, no details were announced. In April it became known that Shin Il Nam, hitherto a Vice-Minister of Public Security, had been appointed Vice-Premier and Chairman of the Commission for Capital Construction. In August Japanese sources reported that a different son, Kim Hyon (also known as Kim Hyon Nam), had been appointed head of the KWP's propaganda and agitation department. If confirmed, this was the same route by which the young Kim Jong Il had begun his ascent to power, and might herald Kim Hyon's position as heir-apparent.

The year 2002 also witnessed two major anniversaries: Kim Jong Il's 60th birthday—in Korea a key event, called *hwan'gap*—in February, and the 90th anniversary of his late father's birth, in April. Both were celebrated with the usual lavish displays. This ceremonial mode continued with North Korea's largest-ever mass arts and gymnastics festival, called *Arirang*, held from May to August. Despite denials, this appeared as if it was intended to counter the football World Cup in South Korea; yet poor marketing meant that few foreign visitors attended. Substantive politics was harder to discern. As in 2001, the SPA convened for just a single day, in March. Besides approving the budget, it discussed an (unrevealed) 'organizational matter', and approved a law on land management, thought to be aimed at curbing illicit private use of land and resources, a practice that had spread since the famine of the late 1990s.

The latter part of 2002, however, brought radical changes in economic management, possibly auguring a long-awaited definitive turn to reform. No formal announcements had been made; officials, when pressed, spoke of 'perfecting socialism'. Thus, the full scope of the innovations was unclear. Their core consisted of drastic increases in prices, broadly to match those in the 'black market', and concomitant—but lesser, and uneven—wage increases. Some subsidies remained, but in general people and firms alike were thenceforth required to pay, and firms allowed to charge, the real cost of goods and services.

Sceptics suggested that the aim was to curb, not enhance, the free market: for instance to get household savings, often held at home in dollars or yuan, back into won and into banks. Yet other reports implied deeper change, including rumours of experimental private farm projects (the form in which market reform began in China). Remarkably, downsizing of unproductive labour was said to extend even to the Party, at least at the 'grass roots'; with drastic cuts in the hitherto ubiquitous and intrusive apparatus of political and guidance secretaries, agitprop teams, and the like in enterprises and even in the KPA. Such measures were highly likely to have political repercussions. If successful and well received, they may be extended, and in due time proclaimed as a new turn; perhaps at the long-awaited KWP Congress. If the measures were to prove unsuccessful, however, some analysts feared hyperinflation and that the result might destabilize the regime. If Kim Jong Il was prepared to take that risk, this suggested a belated realization that to take no action was not an option, and no less perilous.

NORTH-SOUTH RELATIONS

(AIDAN FOSTER-CARTER)

Relations (or the lack thereof) between North and South Korea must be understood against a very particular and, indeed, unique background. Both the Democratic People's Republic of Korea and the Republic of Korea still claim, as they have done ever since their founding in 1948, to be the sole legitimate government on the peninsula. Constitutionally and legally, each still defines the other as an enemy. Indeed, they remain technically at war, inasmuch as the Korean War (1950–53) concluded only with an armistice, not a peace treaty (and South Korea did not even sign the armistice).

Against that background, for most of the subsequent four decades both regimes not only eschewed all mutual contacts but also forced their citizens, on pain of draconian penalties, to do likewise. Quite unlike former East and West Germans, North and South Koreans have never been able to write to or telephone one another, let alone visit. Several million people have thus spent almost half a century utterly cut off from close relatives, not knowing if they are alive or dead. Each regime has also suppressed all but negative information about the other. As a result, over the years the two Koreas (unlike the two former Germanys) have become strangers as well as enemies, a fact that has added to the already huge incubus of mutual mistrust.

Only since the early 1990s have there been real signs of change, although as yet no substantial breakthrough has occurred. In earlier years there had been several attempts at dialogue, all abortive. The first began with secret visits in 1971, at which time both Korean states were alarmed by the recent US-Chinese *rapprochement*. This led to a joint statement on 4 July 1972, and the establishment of a South-North Co-ordinating Committee (SNCC). Red Cross talks also began, with the aim of arranging family reunions. Although SNCC meetings continued until 1975 and Red Cross talks until 1978, neither produced any result. The same was true of a further brief round of dialogue in 1979–80, during the democratic interlude in South Korea between the assassination of President Park Chung-Hee and Chun Doo-Hwan's coup.

Meanwhile, North Korea did nothing to enhance its trustworthiness, committing regular acts of aggression against the South. In August 1974 a North Korean resident of Japan shot at President Park, killing his wife. In the late 1970s South Korea discovered the existence of several tunnels, dug under the demilitarized zone (DMZ) separating the two countries, large enough for an invading force from the North. In October 1983, while on a visit to Rangoon, Burma (now Yangon, Myanmar), President Chun Doo-Hwan narrowly escaped an assassination attempt, which, however, killed 17 members of his entourage, including four cabinet ministers. The attack was believed to have been perpetrated by North Korean agents.

Perhaps because of the opprobrium incurred by the Rangoon bombing incident, North Korea subsequently adopted a different approach. What may have been intended only as a propagandist offer of 'aid' to South Korea, after severe floods occurred there in late 1984, was shrewdly accepted by Seoul. This led to a year of three-tiered dialogue in 1985, comprising economic, parliamentary and Red Cross talks. Only the last bore fruit, in the first reunion of separated families, which took place in September.

North Korea suspended all dialogue in early 1986 in protest against the annual 'Team Spirit' US-South Korean military exercises, and resumed its duplicitous policy: negotiating (unsuccessfully) with the International Olympic Committee to host part of the 1988 Seoul Olympic Games, only to bomb a South Korean civilian airliner in November 1987, causing the loss of 115 lives. None the less, South Korea's growing economic and diplomatic strength (symbolized by the full participation in the 1988 Olympics by China, Eastern Europe and the USSR, even though, at that point, none recognized Seoul) brought the North back into the negotiating process, albeit sporadically. Red Cross talks resumed in 1988, although planned family reunions in late 1989 failed to take place. There was, however, some progress in the sporting arena. The first ever inter-Korean football matches were held in Pyongyang and Seoul in late 1990, and in the following year joint Korean teams participated in two international sporting events. However, North and South Korea sent separate teams to the 1992 Barcelona Olympics.

Meanwhile, although there was no resumption of economic talks, in 1988 South Korea initiated indirect trade with the North. Direct inter-Korean trade, which began in late 1990, increased rapidly in 1991, and was equivalent to some US $210m. annually by 1992, when the South became the North's fourth largest trading partner (after China, Russia and Japan).

In the political arena, the first ever talks between the countries' heads of government finally took place in September 1990. The three such meetings in that year were largely symbolic, and the premiers did not meet again until October 1991. However, progress was made in mid-1991, when North Korea withdrew its long-standing objection to both Korean states joining the UN as separate entities (if only because it became clear that neither the USSR nor China would any longer veto South Korea's unilateral application). Both Koreas were thus admitted to the UN in September 1991. (They were already members of most of its specialized agencies, including the FAO, WHO and UNESCO.)

At the resumption of the prime-ministerial talks in October 1991, both parties agreed on the title, and envisaged provisions, of an accord governing future inter-Korean relations. Under the 'Agreement on Reconciliation, Non-aggression and Exchanges and Co-operation', which was signed in December and ratified in February 1992, North and South pledged, *inter alia*, to desist from mutual slander and sabotage, and to promote economic and other co-operation, as well as the reunion of separated family members. The accord was widely hailed as a milestone, and subsequent premiers' meetings, in May and September 1992, resulted in agreements to fulfil its provisions, as well as to establish several joint commissions.

Thereafter, however, relations worsened and the agreement remained largely unimplemented. In late 1992 South Korea was angered by the discovery on its territory of a large-scale northern espionage operation, while North Korea criticized the South's decision to resume in 1993 the 'Team Spirit' exercises (which had been suspended in 1992). The projected ninth meeting of premiers in December 1992 was cancelled, and such meetings were not subsequently resumed.

The main impediment to a real improvement in inter-Korean relations was the question of suspected nuclear ambitions (see below). Although the accord of December 1991 omitted any reference to nuclear issues, a separate agreement was signed later that month to create a bilateral Joint Nuclear Control Committee (JNCC). This made no progress, however, with North Korea opposing the South's demand for unannounced inspections, while Seoul resisted Pyongyang's demand to open all the US bases stationed on its territory to northern scrutiny.

The visit to South Korea of Kim Tal Hyon, the North Korean Vice-Premier in charge of trade and investment, who toured a range of factories and met prominent business leaders as well as the then President, Roh Tae-Woo, in July 1992, brought hopes of a breakthrough. While North Korea desperately needed southern aid and investment, it still seemed reluctant or unable to convince the South (and indeed the world) that it had unequivocally abandoned any nuclear ambitions; indeed, prior to October 2002, it had always denied ever having had a military-nuclear programme. Such suspicions were only enhanced by Pyongyang's announced intention, in March 1993, of withdrawing from the Treaty on the Non-Proliferation of Nuclear Weapons, which it had signed in 1985 (see below). The nuclear issue continued to blight inter-Korean relations throughout the remainder of 1993, not least because of Pyongyang's insistence on negotiating with Washington rather than Seoul. There were contacts in the 'peace village' of Panmunjom (in the DMZ) in October 1993 and March 1994, but both proved abortive; at the latter, the chief northern delegate threatened to reduce Seoul to 'a sea of fire'. This was on a par with other North Korean rhetoric, which included regular denunciations of the southern President, not to mention a call by the Chief of General Staff of the KPA, Vice-Marshal Choe Kwang, in a speech to soldiers in late 1993, for 'reunification with guns'.

Despite tense relations between the two Governments, however, their companies continued to do business. Inter-Korean trade in 1993 totalled some US $195m., slightly less than in 1992. With over 90% comprising southern purchases, this represented an important source of revenue for Pyongyang. Although Seoul still banned its companies from strengthening these ties by investing in the North, the fact that businessmen from both Koreas were now in regular contact (mainly in China) provided some hope—as with Taiwan and the People's Republic of China—of a slow improvement in their political relationship, too.

Just such an improvement became dramatically apparent in June 1994, when the former US President, Jimmy Carter, returned from Pyongyang (see below) with an offer from Kim Il Sung for a summit meeting with his South Korean counterpart. Kim Young-Sam accepted with alacrity, and two highly successful planning meetings were held at Panmunjom. Following the death of Kim Il Sung on 8 July, however, the summit (which had been arranged for 25–27 July) was postponed. Not only did the summit not take place in the ensuing months (technically North Korea remained without a Head of State), but North-South relations became markedly worse. Pyongyang professed outrage when Seoul failed to issue any condolence on the death of Kim Il Sung and acted harshly against the few southern radicals who did so. Northern denunciations of Kim Young-Sam, former dissident though he was, were, if anything, more virulent than they ever had been against the generals who preceded him.

The new bilateral relationship with Washington, engendered by the Geneva nuclear agreement of October 1994 (see below), had the advantage, from Pyongyang's viewpoint, of excluding Seoul—at least formally. Although this remained the North's official position, in practice by mid-1995 North Korea had accepted South Korean light-water reactors and engineers to build them. The North also continued business links with South Korean companies (if not with their Government), and in July 1995 13 technicians of the Daewoo conglomerate became the first southerners since 1953 to settle in the North with both Governments' approval. The technicians were to supervise Daewoo's new export factory at the port of Nampo, a pioneer venture which other southern firms were thought likely to emulate.

Yet the North's policy of ignoring or bypassing the South Korean Government was hardly sustainable as a long-term strategy, particularly in the light of the agreements signed in 1991–92 (albeit only partially implemented). In June 1995 North Korea appeared to have changed its tactics, accepting an offer of rice aid from the South, following a request for similar aid from Japan in the previous month (see below). However, the first ship was forced to fly the northern flag on its arrival in the port of Chongjin (for which Pyongyang later apologized), while in August another southern vessel was detained on spying charges. South Korea was aggrieved that its generosity did not elicit a similar spirit on the part of the North.

Such incidents embittered both the public and official moods in Seoul. When the floods of 1995 (see above) led to fresh appeals by the UN and the Red Cross for food aid to North Korea, South Korea was reluctant to oblige. The Government gave US $3m. in June 1996 and allowed small shipments from the Red Cross, but tried to prevent church groups and other private organizations from sending food aid to the North independently.

In so far as the rice aid of 1995 failed to herald the desired improvement in inter-Korean relations, both states must share the responsibility, albeit not equally. North Korea, which was willing to hold discussions and even sign agreements with the South in the early 1990s, had no convincing reason for its subsequent refusal of such dialogue. Its professed insistence on signing a peace treaty with the USA with the exclusion of South Korea, was patently unrealistic, while its continuous denigration of former President Kim Young-Sam was unacceptable practice by international standards. Yet the South Korean President was widely seen as having no clear or consistent strategy towards Pyongyang, oscillating between an uncompromising attitude and a more relaxed stance.

As ever, spies and refugees enlivened inter-Korean relations in the mid-1990s, while doing nothing to improve them. The report of Kim Dong Sik, a northern agent captured after a gun battle in October 1995, was worthy of any spy novel; he landed by midget submarine after a decade of training, which had included the use of full-scale models of areas of Seoul. In July 1996 another alleged spy was arrested after living for more than a decade in South Korea disguised as a Lebanese-Filipino history professor. Two dramatic incidents affected inter-Korean relations during 1996–97. In mid-September 1996 a North Korean submarine ran aground off South Korea's east coast. In the ensuing manhunt, all but two of its crew of 26 died (some by their own hands, apparently; one was captured alive and one escaped). Seoul's fury was only assuaged in December when, pressed by the USA, Pyongyang perfunctorily apologized for what, it still claimed, was an accident caused by engine trouble. Then in mid-February 1997 Hwang Jang Yop, one of North Korea's most senior leaders, sought asylum in the South Korean embassy in Beijing, China, while returning from a visit to Japan. Ranked 25th in the hierarchy, Hwang was the main theorist of North Korea's official ideology of *juche*, and was currently serving as party secretary and Chairman of the SPA foreign affairs committee. This defection was awkward for China, but the situation was eventually resolved by sending Hwang first to a third country, the Philippines, before allowing him to enter South Korea. Once in Seoul, Hwang warned that his former comrades were serious in threatening to attack the South. Even before Hwang's arrival, an earlier high-ranking defector had been assassinated near Seoul by unknown gunmen.

While both these events were set-backs for inter-Korean relations, there were also more positive signs. In particular, nuclear co-operation through KEDO reached the stage where ground-breaking for construction of the new light-water reactors (LWRs) began in mid-August 1997. Several dozen South Korean engineers were already on site at Shinpo, southern ships had delivered machinery and materials, and a telephone link with South Korea was in service. KEDO's office at Shinpo included the first South Korean diplomats ever to be based in North Korea.

In 1997 South Korea also appeared to be easing its restrictions on southern businesses wishing to invest in North Korea. In May five more companies received permission to explore joint ventures. Though the parlous state of the northern economy dampened optimism somewhat, in April North-South trade reached US $37.4m., its highest-ever monthly total. While infinitesimal to South Korea, annual trade of some US $200m.–$300m. in recent years suffices to make it North Korea's third-largest trading partner, after China and Japan. South Korea also announced its support for the North's bid to join the Asian Development Bank, which, however, was obstructed by Japanese opposition. Meanwhile, negotiations concerning the opening of North Korean airspace—if only maritime, so far—to flights to and from Seoul finally yielded results in April 1998, so that the tiny numbers of North and South Koreans in regular contact with one another now include air traffic controllers.

In general, North Korea continued its venomous diatribes against the South and, in particular, Kim Young-Sam during 1997, while South Korea, for its part, appeared ambivalent, not to say inconsistent, over how to approach the North. This was particularly evident over the issue of North Korea's food shortage. Although South Korea did give some relatively small amounts of aid, both in response to UN appeals and bilaterally through the Red Cross (the latter including actual visits by southern officials to the North, from China, to deliver 50,000 tons of grain), it often seemed more concerned either to play down the severity of the North's suffering, or to suggest that Pyongyang should help itself by spending less on the military and by privatizing the country's farms. This uncompromising approach placed Seoul somewhat at odds with the USA, where the Clinton administration remained committed to seeking engagement with Pyongyang and, in particular, to persuading it to enter four-way talks (see below).

The prospects for inter-Korean relations improved markedly with the election of Kim Dae-Jung as South Korea's President in December 1997. Kim Dae-Jung had long preached, and once in office immediately began to practise, a so-called 'sunshine' policy towards Pyongyang, involving consistent openness towards the North (while maintaining a strong security posture), in the belief that this would eventually elicit a positive response. The policy entails a distinction between governmental and private (including business) contacts, and a much more relaxed attitude towards the latter whatever the vicissitudes of the former. The acknowledged model here is relations between China and Taiwan. The first official North-South talks since the death of Kim Il Sung (there had been others which were quasi-governmental) took place in April 1998. Held in Beijing to discuss a northern request for fertilizer, the talks failed when South Korea linked this issue to its own demands for progress on family reunions. Yet, in a break from the past, Seoul made no effort to prevent the transfer of private southern aid to the North. The pace of civilian and business contacts thus increased in 1998, even though the South's economic crisis took its toll on inter-Korean trade, which declined in the first half of the year by almost 50%, to US $77m.

During mid-1998 inter-Korean relations were dominated by dramatic, if contradictory, developments. In mid-June, Chung Ju-Yung, the founder of the Hyundai group, South Korea's largest conglomerate, crossed the normally impenetrable DMZ at Panmunjom, bringing 500 cattle as a gift for his home town near Wonsan. During his week-long visit, Chung Ju-Yung also discussed a wide range of potential joint ventures between Hyundai and North Korean interests. The most dramatic involved a plan to run daily tour boats to Mount Kumgang, just north of the DMZ; this commenced in November 1998 and represented the first opportunity for South Korean tourists to set foot in the North. This breakthrough seemed jeopardized, however, when, during Chung Ju-Yung's visit to North Korea, a southern fishing boat caught a small northern spy submarine in its nets. When the submarine was eventually towed to port, its crew of nine were found to have killed themselves (or each other). Then in July, a dead North Korean frogman was found on a southern beach. In the past such provocations would certainly have led Seoul to forbid Hyundai to continue with its plans. It was indicative of Kim Dae-Jung's imagination and courage that on this occasion no such linkage was made, and, after a short delay, Hyundai was allowed to proceed.

During 1999 Hyundai's tourism project proved a major advancement for the 'sunshine' policy, with more than 80,000 southern tourists making the journey north in the first eight months alone. There was, however, criticism that Hyundai's payments to Pyongyang—which were to total almost US $1,000m. over six years—might be funding the North's military. The growing scepticism in Seoul reflected the failure of 'sunshine' to generate wider warmth. In June 1999 fresh talks in Beijing on fertilizer and family reunions broke down, even though South Korea softened its stance and sent fertilizer without preconditions. Meanwhile, on 15 June the two Koreas' navies fought a brief gun battle for the first time since the Korean War. North Korean boats were fishing for crab in the Yellow Sea south of the Northern Limit Line (NLL), which Pyongyang did not accept and, unusually, held their positions when challenged by southern patrol boats. After several days of confrontation the South resorted to ramming, and the North opened fire; however, one of its boats was sunk (with a reported 80 dead) and three others were badly damaged. Remarkably, both the Beijing talks and fertilizer deliveries—by sea, close to the combat area—continued throughout, and despite, this contretemps. The gun battle may have reassured Kim Dae-Jung's domestic critics that 'sunshine' did not mean appeasement, and the policy remained in place. In August a workers' team from the militant Korean Confederation of Trade Unions was allowed to travel north to play soccer with northern counterparts.

The 'sunshine' policy finally achieved results in 2000. In March Kim Dae-Jung's offer in his 'Berlin Declaration' of Southern aid to rebuild Northern infrastructure led to secret talks in China, and the announcement in April of the first ever North-South summit meeting. This momentous event duly occurred on 13–15 June, after a last-minute 24-hour delay. Kim Dae-Jung made the first ever official direct flight between Seoul and Pyongyang. Kim Jong Il met him at the airport with a full honour guard of the KPA's three services. South Korean television viewers—but not their Northern counterparts, who saw only the formalities—marvelled at the friendly persona of a man hitherto viewed as a completely evil figure. After two days of public affability and private tough negotiations, the two leaders signed a brief declaration pledging further progress. The document's only substantive stipulation was the reunion of separated families, duly held on 15–18 August when two sets of 100 elderly Koreans flew in each direction to meet relatives whom they had not seen for 50 years. Two further reunions took place in December 2000 and February 2001 (but a third, scheduled for October, was cancelled). In the following month the first (and by mid-2002 the only) exchange of personal mail—involving some 300 letters from each side—was permitted between North and South Korean families.

The bilateral summit meeting and family reunions ushered in a wider inter-Korean peace process. Ministerial meetings to follow the summit began in Seoul at the end of July 2000, with a second round held in Pyongyang at the end of August and two further sessions thereafter. The first session agreed to reconnect railway lines across the DMZ: a goal endorsed by Kim Jong Il soon afterwards, with work inaugurated by Kim Dae-Jung in September. In a related development, Hyundai won Kim Jong Il's approval to build a vast industrial estate in, and run tour buses to, Kaesong, the ancient Korean capital just north of the DMZ. If this project were to materialize, it would be comparable to the relationship between Shenzhen, in the People's Republic of China, and Hong Kong: serving both to link the two economies and as a basis for growth in the North. There were also positive security implications if the DMZ were to become a thoroughfare, instead of an all but impassable barrier. Economic talks were also held, during which a basic framework for business co-operation was agreed. North Korea's Minister of the People's Armed Forces, Vice-Marshal Kim Il Chol, visited Seoul in September, but would only discuss railways (the re-linking of which is being carried out by the army on both sides); no return visit was arranged.

These promising beginnings ground to a halt in 2001. In January economic talks broke down when the South refused a technically unfeasible northern demand for the immediate supply of electricity. In the following month North Korea agreed, but failed to ratify a protocol on joint railway building within the DMZ; construction work on its side had barely begun. In March the North pulled out of the fifth ministerial talks only hours before they were due to start. Thereafter it refused all official contact with South Korea for six months, seemingly as a corollary of its annoyance with the new US administration, except for sending a condolence delegation on the death of the Hyundai patriarch, Chung Ju-Yung. A further southern donation of fertilizer in May did not soften this stance. Indeed, June saw a reversion to provocation, when several northern merchant ships took short cuts through southern waters. The restrained response of the South Korean navy angered hard-liners in the South; as did a later incident, when a few members of a South Korean unification activists' delegation, allowed to visit Pyongyang for Liberation Day celebrations on 15 August, appeared to support DPRK positions. The controversy that this generated brought down South Korea's ruling coalition (see below).

All this gravely weakened the position of Kim Dae-Jung. By late 2001 most South Koreans endorsed the opposition's criticism of the 'sunshine' policy as appeasement. North Korea's erratic behaviour did not help matters. It accepted a fifth round of ministerial talks in September, only to cancel family reunions, at short notice in October, on the pretext of South Korea's heightened state of alert after the 11 September terrorist attacks on the USA. A sixth round of ministerial talks in November, held (at the North's insistence) at Mount Kumgang, ended with no agreement to meet further; the South's unification minister was dismissed soon after. Official relations thus remained suspended; although, in a major change from past policy, business and private contacts continued. So did links through KEDO: an unpublicized northern team inspected South Korean nuclear facilities in December, and other delegations followed in 2002. In December 2001 also, Hyundai sharply reduced its Mount Kumgang tours because of falling demand.

In February 2002 North Korea cancelled a joint celebration of the Lunar New Year for which the southern civic delegates had already arrived at Mount Kumgang. President Bush's designation in January of North Korea as part of an 'axis of evil' alarmed Kim Dae-Jung; in April he sent his adviser Lim Dong-Won, the sunshine policy's *eminence grise*, to try to persuade Kim Jong Il to agree to talks with the USA. This visit also revived North-South dialogue: April witnessed a fourth round of family reunions, now at Mount Kumgang (on the North's insistence, again) rather than in the two capitals. In May, however, North Korea withdrew from economic discussions at a day's notice. It also disregarded all entreaties to share in the football World Cup co-hosted by South Korea and Japan, but did broadcast highlights of some matches held in the South.

Yet private and semi-official contacts burgeoned. Official subsidies revived Mount Kumgang tourism. South Korean firms established several business and educational joint ventures in information technology (IT), including a college and Pyongyang's first internet café. In June 2002 South Korea's assistant Minister of Information and Communication led a delegation from major companies to Pyongyang; but North Korea later denied reports that agreement had been reached to install mobile telephone services in Pyongyang and Nampo, and no further detail emerged from this. Provincial links continued: Jeju sent oranges, and Gangwon (divided by the DMZ, and later to be badly hit by typhoon Rusa in late August) jointly sprayed against pine pests. In June 320 members of a South Korean Christian aid NGO, when denied a promised church service in Pyongyang, held their own impromptu worship in a hotel; however, they were not impeded. In May, in an encounter that would have startled their parents, Kim Jong Il hosted a dinner for Park Chung-Hee's daughter Park Geun-Hye, herself a possible presidential candidate. Kim also agreed to a friendly football match in September.

On 29 June 2002 relations sharply deteriorated when North Korean warships without warning fired on and sank a southern patrol boat in the Yellow Sea, killing five crew members. As in the 1999 incident, for which this may have been revenge, this occurred in disputed maritime border seas during the crab-fishing season. Yet it was wholly unexpected, prompting further criticism of the 'sunshine' policy and of the South Korean navy's lack of preparedness; the southern Minister of National Defence was dismissed a fortnight later. Within a month, however, North Korea expressed 'regret', and this sufficed for dialogue to resume. The seventh ministerial talks, held in Seoul in August, arranged a full roster of further meetings in specific areas. Economic discussions later that month set a timetable to open two cross-border road and rail links: not only the previously agreed route near Seoul, work on which had stalled, but a second corridor near the east coast. North Korea also agreed to take part in the Asian Games to be staged in Busan in October—the first time it had ever participated in an international event held in South Korea—in contrast to its eschewal of the football World Cup. Nearly 700 North Korean athletes took part in the event. There were even rumours that Kim Jong Il might attend the opening ceremony, to make a long-awaited return visit, regarding this as less risky—politically and otherwise—than a full second summit meeting in Seoul.

Caution was in order regarding how much or how soon any of this would be realized, given the intermittent pattern and disappointments of the past. Yet North Korea's economic changes and its wider diplomatic outreach suggested that this time Kim Jong Il might be serious: not least, to act before Kim Dae-Jung's departure from office in February 2003. Cross-border links were the touchstone. If these were to proceed, allowing the Kaesong project to go ahead, the security, economic and political climate on the peninsula would be definitively transformed. On a positive note, ceremonies were held on both sides of the DMZ on 18 September 2002 to mark the beginning of the reconstruction of rail links between the two Koreas—with the first reconnection possible as early as November. However, if the North were to retreat again, a probably less sympathetic new President in South Korea, combined with intensified US pressure, would presage a further deterioration in relations.

FOREIGN RELATIONS

(AIDAN FOSTER-CARTER)

Despite (or, perhaps, because of) North Korea's roots in Soviet military government, it has been the regime's consistent goal to emphasize and maximize what its own slogans call *chaju, chalip, chawi*: independence in politics, economics and defence. In practice, this has largely meant a refusal to be beholden to—let alone a satellite of—either of its giant neighbours and erstwhile sponsors, the USSR and China, while simultaneously exhibiting unremitting hostility towards the USA, Japan and, of course, South Korea. Although the Sino-Soviet dispute enabled Kim Il Sung for many years to play off Moscow against Beijing and receive aid from both, the end of the Cold War and the collapse of the USSR have exposed Pyongyang's vaunted self-reliance as ultimately self-defeating isolation and friendlessness.

North Korean foreign policy has undergone several phases over the years. During the 1950s Pyongyang emphasized its adherence to the communist bloc, receiving both military aid during the Korean War (1950–53) and assistance for reconstruction thereafter from the USSR, China and Eastern Europe. Yet already there were quarrels with Moscow over how best to use Soviet aid, with North Korea preferring to develop its own heavy industry rather than join the Council for Mutual Economic Assistance (CMEA). Meanwhile, although Japan had relations with neither Korean government at this stage, more than 75,000 pro-communist Koreans in Japan (mainly of southern origin) emigrated to the new socialist fatherland in the late 1950s.

In the wake of the public Sino-Soviet split in the early 1960s, Pyongyang demonstrated broad sympathy with Beijing's more revolutionary position, which led to the temporary suspension of Soviet aid. North Korea's own bellicosity peaked in 1968, with its seizure of the *USS Pueblo* and its dispatch of a commando unit to attack the presidential mansion in Seoul.

By contrast, the 1970s were an era of broadening contacts. Suspicious of China's amenability to US 'ping-pong diplomacy', North Korea not only repaired relations with Moscow but sought new allies, particularly in the Third World and the Non-aligned Movement (which it joined in 1975). Other initiatives were less successful. Pyongyang's breakthrough in establishing diplomatic relations with the four Nordic countries (its first such ties in the West) was marred shortly thereafter when, in 1976, all four of its ambassadors were expelled, their staff accused of systematic smuggling (a practice in which North Korean diplomats have allegedly been engaged ever since). Similarly, what seemed a useful development of economic ties with Japan and Western European countries came to an abrupt halt when it became clear that Pyongyang had no overt intention of paying for several hundred million dollars' worth of capital equipment imported in the early 1970s. These debts still remain unsettled.

By the early 1980s North Korea's relations with many of its communist allies showed signs of deterioration. Neither Moscow nor Beijing approved at first of the official designation of Kim Jong Il as his father's successor, although China at length relented and, in 1983, invited the 'Dear Leader' on his first known trip there.

This did not, however, prevent a distinct inclination towards the USSR in the mid-1980s, inspired perhaps by suspicion of Deng Xiaoping's reforms, yet continuing into the Gorbachev era. In 1984 Kim Il Sung visited Moscow for the first time in 23 years, and also spent several weeks touring Eastern Europe. He returned to meet Gorbachev in 1986, in which year joint Soviet-North Korean naval exercises were undertaken. In addition, the North Korean Government granted port facilities and overflying rights to the Soviet fleet and air force, reportedly in return for the supply of Soviet MiG-23 fighters and surface-to-air missiles. Soviet-North Korean trade grew rapidly, with North Korean imports more than quadrupling in the four years between 1984 and 1988.

However, within a period of less than five years, a series of set-backs comprehensively undermined North Korea's foreign policy orientations of the previous four decades. It was inevitable that the lure of South Korea's far greater economic prospects (coupled with the skilful diplomacy of Seoul's 'nordpolitik') would eventually lead pragmatists such as Deng and Gorbachev to qualify their inherited Cold War loyalties towards a Pyongyang which they increasingly considered a political and economic liability. Although China moved first to begin trading with Seoul, it was the USSR under Gorbachev's leadership that dealt both the diplomatic and financial *coup de grâce*: first by establishing full diplomatic relations with South Korea in September 1990, and then by stipulating that, from January 1991, its trade with North Korea would be conducted in convertible currencies at world market prices. This caused Pyongyang's total trade volume to decline by more than US $1,100m. (almost one-quarter) in 1991. Although the demise of the USSR itself afforded a certain grim satisfaction, Russia's President Yeltsin had no vestige of comradeship with the Pyongyang regime.

The cooling of relations with Moscow left China as North Korea's only major ally, although even this relationship was qualified by increasing impatience in Beijing, as much over Kim Il Sung's failure to embrace economic reform as for his suspected nuclear ambitions (see below). With reformers once again dominant in the Chinese leadership, economic ties with Seoul rapidly increased and, in August 1992, full diplomatic relations were established between China and South Korea, much to the consternation of Pyongyang. Since then Sino-North Korean relations have deteriorated significantly. Although China has opposed UN action against North Korea over the nuclear issue, its support has been tenuous at best.

In the light of these shifts of allegiance, North Korea has had no option but to try to repair relations with its traditional enemies. In late 1990 a breakthrough with Japan seemed likely, after a highly successful visit to Pyongyang by Shin Kanemaru, the senior mediator of the ruling Liberal-Democratic Party. Yet, eight rounds of talks, held in 1991–92, on the possible normalization of diplomatic relations between North Korea and Japan made no progress, due to intransigent demands from both sides. None the less, regular charter flights between the two countries led to an increase in unofficial contacts and visits, although not yet to the aid and investment which North Korea desperately needs. Relations with Japan were severely strained in May 1993, following North Korea's successful testing of the Rodong-1 medium-range missile in the Sea of Japan. According to US intelligence reports, the missile would be capable of reaching most of Japan's major cities (and possibly of carrying either a conventional or a nuclear warhead).

Contacts with the USA also increased considerably in the early 1990s, although diplomatic relations have yet to be established. North Korea on four occasions returned the remains of US soldiers who went missing in action during the Korean War, and several high-level US delegations, including retired senior political and military figures (and even the evangelist, Rev. Billy Graham), visited Pyongyang. In January 1992 the KWP's international secretary, Kim Yong Sun, visited New York for discussions with the US Under-Secretary of State (although one year later he was refused a visa to attend ceremonies marking the inauguration of President Clinton). US-North Korean discussions did, however, resume in mid-1993 over the nuclear issue.

For both Washington and Tokyo, a major obstacle to better relations with Pyongyang was and remained their suspicion that North Korea was seeking to develop nuclear weapons. In July 1991, after several years of prevarication, North Korea finally agreed a draft Nuclear Safeguards Agreement (NSA) with the International Atomic Energy Agency (IAEA), permitting the outside inspection of North Korean nuclear facilities. Following the announcement by President Bush of proposals to withdraw all US tactical nuclear weapons world-wide, and President Roh Tae-Woo's confirmation that none remained in South Korea, North Korea signed the NSA in January 1992. Moreover, Pyongyang subsequently submitted an unexpectedly detailed report on its nuclear facilities, almost one month ahead of schedule. The IAEA Director-General visited North Korea in May 1992 and formal IAEA inspections began later that month.

Yet, despite this unprecedented progress, suspicions were not allayed. Indeed, one large building at the Yongbyon installation, north of Pyongyang, was believed by some outside observers to be a nuclear-reprocessing plant. Likewise, North Korea's apparent attempts to obstruct the separate inter-Korean mutual nuclear inspections (see below) aroused widespread mistrust. Finally, though not part of the nuclear issue as such, the fact that North Korea sold improved *Scud* missiles to Iran and Syria in exchange for petroleum, did nothing to enhance relations with the West.

All these issues came to a head in 1993. In January North Korea refused to allow special inspections (as demanded by the IAEA) of two sites at Yongbyon, which were thought likely to reveal that more plutonium had been extracted than Pyongyang had admitted. Then, in an unprecedented move, on 12 March North Korea announced that it was to withdraw from the Treaty on the Non-Proliferation of Nuclear Weapons (the Non-Proliferation Treaty—NPT), which it had signed with the IAEA in 1985. This led to protracted diplomatic activity between Washington, Seoul and Tokyo, as well as muted criticism by the UN Security Council (in part because China would not support decisive action at this stage). However, the main channel for defusing the crisis was the holding of two rounds of direct talks between North Korea and the USA in mid-1993, which resulted in North Korea suspending implementation of its withdrawal from the NPT.

Despite this hopeful sign, the nuclear crisis continued for a further year. In May 1993 international concern about North Korea's weapons programme was heightened following the successful testing of an intermediate-range missile, the Rodong-1 (see above). Negotiations between North Korea and the USA, and separate inter-Korean talks, continued during the latter part of the year, but with no tangible results. Although some IAEA monitoring and intermittent inspection activities at Yongbyon were permitted, it remained uncertain whether North Korea had already succeeded in producing a nuclear weapon. Alarm was aroused again in May 1994, when North Korea began replacing spent fuel rods without effective supervision, prompting the IAEA to suggest the imposition of international sanctions. The situation deteriorated further on 13 June, when North Korea retaliated by announcing its complete withdrawal from the IAEA (and not merely the NPT), although in fact inspectors subsequently remained at Yongbyon. Meanwhile, the USA began to lobby the UN Security Council to impose sanctions on North Korea, despite objections by China and Russia and an unenthusiastic response from Japan.

The rising sense of crisis was defused in mid-June 1994, when the former US President Jimmy Carter visited Pyongyang. After 10 hours of talks with Kim Il Sung, he returned with two offers: a summit meeting with South Korea (see above), and a pledge to suspend North Korea's nuclear programme. While the latter was vague, it sufficed for Washington to resume high-level talks. When the third round commenced in Geneva on 8 July, however, Kim Il Sung was already dead—although the announcement of his death came only on the following day. The talks were duly postponed. None the less, following several subsequent rounds, a 'framework agreement' between North Korea and the USA was signed in Geneva in October. In essence, Pyongyang agreed to close down its nuclear site at Yongbyon in exchange for substantial compensation, principally in the form of new light-water reactors (LWRs) worth some US $4,500m., as well as up to 500,000 tons of heavy fuel oil annually during the estimated 10 years' construction period of the LWRs.

Although not written into the agreement, it was understood that South Korea would play a key part, both as supplier and main financier of the LWRs, and as a core member, with the USA and Japan, of KEDO, the consortium that was to supervise the entire project. North Korea initially protested bitterly against Seoul's involvement, and for several months it seemed as if the Geneva accord might collapse. By August 1995, however, Pyongyang tacitly abandoned its opposition to the South's *de facto* participation.

The Geneva nuclear accord perhaps set the pattern for a new development in North Korean foreign policy, which might be termed 'militant mendicancy'. Thus, in May 1995, a North Korean delegation visiting Japan made an unprecedented request for rice as aid. Not only was this granted, but South Korea insisted that the North should also, and first, accept free rice from fellow Koreans (see above). This has produced the remarkable spectacle of the North Korean regime being in effect sustained by its three oldest and bitterest foes—whom it continues to denounce—without any proviso requiring Pyongyang to reform or mend its ways. Such a contradictory mix can only be transitional. If aid is to continue, Kim Jong Il will soon have to prove more widely accommodating than his father was.

One test will be the quest for a peace treaty on the peninsula. North Korea has continued to undermine the existing armistice agreements. In March 1995 it expelled the Polish observers of the Neutral Nations Supervisory Commission at Panmunjom, following which it closed its side of the Joint Security Area to all comers from the South. The North's professed aim was a bilateral peace treaty with the USA, excluding the South. Pyongyang continued to pursue this quixotic quest in 1996, declaring on 4 April that it would no longer observe protocol in the DMZ, and raising tension with a few symbolic incursions into the southern half of the zone. This prompted the USA and South Korea to propose four-way talks with North Korea and China.

In any case, Pyongyang had *de facto* achieved the direct line of communication to Washington which it had long sought. While there were no formal ties, and talks on an exchange of liaison offices stalled, there were now regular contacts between the US State Department and the North Korean UN mission in New York. Discussions on missile control were held in Berlin, Germany, in April 1996, albeit without result. Progress was also made on 'missing in action' (MIA) issues: the USA paid US $2m. (in cash, at Panmunjom) for remains that had already been returned, and US investigators were, for the first time, allowed to search directly inside North Korea. In early 1996 there were also many visits to the USA, including separate delegations led by two leading reformists, Kim Jong U and Ri Jong Hyok.

However, all this was regarded as appeasement in some quarters, both in Seoul and in the Republican Party in the USA. In June 1996 Congress granted barely one-half of the modest US $25m. sought by the White House as the US contribution to KEDO's oil shipments. This was regrettable, since KEDO has achieved the remarkable feat of turning what had been the peninsula's worst risk into its best hope. Not only has North Korea abandoned its initial hostility to the South's leading role in the project, but for much of 1995–96 its delegates were in New York taking constructive part in negotiations over the text of the agreement. South Korean engineers now travel routinely to the LWR site at Shinpo, albeit via Beijing, and in August 1997 construction work began at the site.

Pyongyang also made overtures to Tokyo about resuming negotiations towards establishing diplomatic relations. Cautious as ever, Japan insisted that North Korea must first accept the four-way talks with South Korea and the USA. None the less, regular contacts continued. In July 1996 Kim Jong U toured several Japanese cities to try to encourage investment in the Rajin-Sonbong free zone, but had little success. (Kim Jong U subsequently fell from favour, and in 1998 was reported to have been executed; other reports denied this.)

With its old (and former) allies too, North Korea experienced mixed fortunes. China's avowed support for inter-Korean dialogue annoyed the North, but China, for its part, is equally irritated at Kim Jong Il's refusal of economic reform, not least because Beijing has been continually obliged to offer the country vital assistance. In July 1996 the 35th anniversary of the Sino-North Korean friendship treaty was marked by the exchange of middle-ranking delegations, as well as by a rare visit to Nampo by a Chinese naval flotilla.

Meanwhile, Moscow, which created North Korea and sustained it until the beginning of the collapse of the USSR in 1990, occupied a much less significant position in North Korea's foreign relations. In April 1996 a Deputy Chairman of the Russian Government, Vitalii Ignatenko, led the first major delegation from the new Russia to Pyongyang. There was talk of resuming economic co-operation: most major North Korean industrial installations were originally Soviet aid projects; but since both countries are in economic difficulties, not to mention Pyongyang's huge debts to Moscow, prospects for co-operation are not bright. They did not improve in 1997, when North Korea criticized Russia for supplying ultra-modern armaments (including tanks) to South Korea, in payment of debts.

North Korea's foreign relations neither changed nor advanced greatly during 1996–97. With no Head of State yet inaugurated, there were few high-ranking visitors either to or from Pyongyang, which appeared more isolated than ever. Only with China were there regular exchanges of delegations, and most of these were low-level. Still, as seen in the defection of Hwang Jang Yop (see above), Beijing remained concerned for North Korea's sensitivities, even as its economic and other links with South Korea continued to progress smoothly. China was also the biggest provider of food aid to North Korea. This was so, despite China's displeasure at the somewhat unlikely warming of relations between North Korea and Taiwan: worlds apart ideologically, yet perhaps united in their pariah status. In January 1997 an agreement was signed, whereby North Korea would dispose of low-grade nuclear waste from Taiwan, in a contract believed to be worth more than US $100m. South Korea protested vociferously, and this project seems to have been abandoned.

Elsewhere, in the first half of 1997 Japan began to adopt a more rigid policy towards North Korea than it had previously. The seizure in April of amphetamines worth US $90m. on a North Korean ship in a Japanese port did not improve relations. Unlike the USA, or even South Korea, Japan declined to respond to the UN's increasingly desperate appeals for food aid for North Korea. (It had supplied 500,000 tons of rice in 1995, and received scant gratitude.) Japan insisted that improved relations, including aid, would depend on Pyongyang making concessions, including the disclosure of details of the alleged kidnappings of Japanese citizens in the 1970s. In late August, however, agreement was reached between the two countries, whereby some now-elderly Japanese wives of Koreans who settled in North Korea in the 1950s and 1960s were to be allowed to visit their native land for the first time. Only with the USA, ironically, did North Korea enjoyed improving relations. Washington was swift to respond to UN appeals for food aid, and bilateral contacts continued in areas ranging from further joint digging for MIA remains, to talks about Pyongyang's missile development and sales. Several senior US politicians visited North Korea, usually by military aircraft, which would have been unthinkable in the past. Washington's main aim was to persuade North Korea to agree to attend the four-way talks first proposed in April 1996. After much prevarication by Pyongyang, preliminary discussions were held in New York, USA, on 5 August 1997. China, the fourth party (which was also initially hesitant), became much more positive about the proposal during 1997.

Full four-way talks finally commenced in Geneva, Switzerland, in December 1997, and were followed by more substantial discussions in March 1998. These were, however, unsuccessful, owing to wide differences over the agenda, with North Korea demanding that this should include the withdrawal of US troops from the peninsula. Further four-way talks took place in October; agreement was reached on the establishment of two subcommittees, with a view to instituting a permanent peace mechanism. Otherwise, North Korea's foreign relations remained fairly constant during 1998. Of the four major powers, Russia continued to count the least, in stark contrast to its predominance in the Soviet era. Efforts to revise the 1961 friendship treaty, not least in order to strike out its commitment to mutual military assistance, stalled for several years, until 1999 (see below). China, by contrast, continued to shore up Pyongyang with aid, even as its ties with Seoul become ever closer. Senior-level dialogue with the North went into abeyance for a decade, whereas Chinese and South Korean leaders exchanged regular bilateral visits as well as meeting in multilateral fora such as Asia-Pacific Economic Co-operation (APEC) and Asia-Europe Meeting (ASEM). Beijing's long-term aim is to displace the USA as the broker of choice between the two Koreas.

Relations with Japan continued to follow an uneven course. The first ever home visits of two groups of elderly Japanese-born wives of North Koreans were finally realized in late 1997 and early 1998. Thereafter, however, the kidnap issue—in particular, anger in Japan at what was seen as a perfunctory 'investigation' of the matter by Pyongyang—once again cast a shadow, preventing the resumption of talks towards restoring diplomatic ties. At the end of August 1998 relations deteriorated, when Japan accused Pyongyang of test-firing an unarmed Taepo Dong medium-range missile over its territory. In a strange twist, the North Korean regime subsequently claimed that the object launched had, in fact, been a satellite intended to broadcast patriotic music. That rocket launch, whatever its purpose, has had a lasting effect on North Korea's relations with its main foes. Japanese opinion and policy have hardened, both towards Pyongyang and on defence issues more generally; all the more so after a further provocation in March 1999, when the Japanese navy pursued and fired on two intruding boats, which were later traced to the North Korean port of Chongjin. Unlike South Korea and the USA, Japan still gave no food aid to the DPRK, and considered further sanctions such as banning remittances sent by pro-North Koreans living in Japan. The possibility, widely canvassed in mid-1999, that Pyongyang might test another missile carried a real risk that Japan would withdraw from KEDO; which in turn threatened to reopen the North Korean nuclear issue and reactivate the tensions of mid-1994.

The USA shared Japan's alarm at the DPRK's missile activities, albeit more with regard to proliferation: purchasers include Libya, Syria, Iran and Pakistan. In the past Pyongyang had hinted it might be 'bought off', as with its nuclear programme; but this seemed less likely after the NATO bombing of Yugoslavia in early 1999. Missiles were only one cause of US concern during 1998–99; the other being a large construction site at Kumchang-ri, near the disused nuclear site at Yongbyon, which was feared to be a covert continuation of nuclear activity. Kumchang-ri dominated US-North Korean relations for many months, until in May 1999 a US inspection team pronounced it 'clean'. While denying any link, Washington simultaneously announced a further 400,000 metric tons of grain in aid. The USA continued to be the mainstay of the UN World Food Programme's aid to North Korea, this operation being its largest ever, prior to Afghanistan in 2001–02. Meanwhile, under pressure from Republican critics in the US Congress, in November 1998 the Clinton Administration appointed William Perry, a former Secretary of Defense, to carry out a full review of US policy towards North Korea. Perry visited Pyongyang in May 1999, and his report was published in September of that year. It offered substantial incentives, in exchange for a definitive and verifiable end to the DPRK's nuclear and missile ambitions. During talks in Berlin, Germany, in mid-September the USA lifted sanctions on trade and travel in return for a promise by the DPRK that it would refrain from testing long-range missiles until 2003. As for allies (past or present), in March 1999 a new treaty with Russia was at last agreed, to replace that of 1961 with the former USSR. This was assumed to exclude the military support provided for in the old version. The treaty was signed during a visit to Pyongyang by the Russian Minister of Foreign Affairs, Igor Ivanov, in February 2000; it was ratified by North Korea in April of that year. With China effectively remaining North Korea's sole ally and source of finance, a high-level delegation visited Beijing in June 1999 for the first time in eight years. Led by Kim Yong Nam, the delegates included the Premier and the Ministers of Defence and Foreign Affairs—but no economic cadres, to China's reported annoyance. Multilaterally, the quadripartite talks involving the two Koreas, China and the USA continued to be held in Geneva, the sixth round taking place in August 1999, but with no obvious progress. As of late 2002, this particular forum had not reconvened.

From the latter part of 1999 onwards North Korea's diplomacy took a striking new turn, with conscious efforts made both to restore old relationships and foster new alliances. The first sign was a wide range of meetings held at the UN in September 1999 by the North Korean Minister of Foreign Affairs, Paek Nam Sun. In January 2000 Italy became the first G-7 country to establish full diplomatic relations with the DPRK. Later in the year Kuwait, the Philippines and Australia followed suit; the latter resuming ties first forged in 1975 but abruptly severed by Pyongyang soon after. In October 2000 the United Kingdom announced that it planned to normalize diplomatic relations with North Korea, and duly did so in December. Meanwhile, in July, Paek travelled to Bangkok, Thailand, for North Korea's admission as the 23rd member of the ASEAN Regional Forum (ARF), at which Canada and New Zealand also announced plans to establish relations. Paek also held unprecedented meetings with his South Korean, US and Japanese counterparts.

With the USA, progress continued. In October 2000 Vice-Marshal Jo Myong Rok, North Korea's most powerful military figure, visited Washington as a special envoy of Kim Jong Il. This led in the same month to a visit to Pyongyang by the US Secretary of State, Madeleine Albright. President Clinton was ready to follow to sign an agreement on missiles, but this foundered on verification difficulties. Agreement also eluded high-level bilateral talks with Japan, in abeyance since 1992, of which three rounds were held in 2000. Despite a show of cordiality, the two sides' agendas remained far apart. North Korea demanded compensation of up to US $10,000m. for Japanese colonial rule prior to 1945, whereas Japan continued to prioritize its missile and abduction concerns. There was no obvious way to overcome this impasse. However, in 2000 Japan gave 100,000 tons of food aid to the DPRK for the first time in several years, and was permitted to monitor its distribution. A third visit home by Japanese wives of North Koreans—the first since 1998—took place in September.

The most important development was a new effort to improve relations with the DPRK's original major allies. In May 2000 Kim Jong Il made an unofficial, and initially secret, visit to China, his first overseas trip since 1983. As well as meeting President Jiang Zemin and other leaders, he toured a computer factory and was quoted—for the first time—explicitly praising China's reform programme. This visit prepared Kim Jong Il for hosting Kim Dae-Jung a fortnight afterwards. One month later the 'Dear Leader' welcomed the President of the Russian Federation, Vladimir Putin, as the first ever Russian or Soviet leader to visit the DPRK. By this simple gesture, in a trip lasting less than 24 hours, Putin reversed a decade of hostility which had begun when the then President of the USSR, Mikhail Gorbachev, hastily forged ties with Seoul in 1990; and reconfirmed Moscow's importance with regard to the possible reunification of Korea, later presenting the G-8 with an offer by Kim Jong Il to abandon his missile programme in return for access to satellite-launching facilities. The 'Dear Leader's' later comment that this was said in jest left Moscow unamused, and was a reminder that rebuilding ties might not be straightforward. Furthermore, North Korea owed the Russian Federation some US $3,000m.

The year 2001 was also an active one for DPRK diplomacy, but with more mixed results. Ties with the USA suffered a setback when the new Republican administration under President George W. Bush expressed mistrust towards North Korea, prompting Pyongyang to suspend inter-Korean dialogue as well. By June the USA decided that it would, after all, talk to North Korea, but by late 2001 the latter had yet to respond. No further talks were held with Japan, which Pyongyang denounced (as did Seoul) for a new schools' history textbook that glossed over pre-1945 atrocities, and for Prime Minister Koizumi's visit to the Yasukuni shrine which commemorates (among others) convicted war criminals. With other Western countries, however, there was more progress. By June 2001 13 of the 15 member states of the European Union (EU), and the organization as such, had restored full diplomatic relations with the DPRK; the exceptions were France, which cites human rights concerns, and Ireland. In May a high-level EU delegation led by the Swedish Prime Minister, Göran Persson, had visited Pyongyang and met Kim Jong Il, in what was interpreted as a prompt to President Bush to resume dialogue. It was reported that the DPRK leader had pledged to maintain his country's moratorium on missile testing until 2003. Other states establishing relations with North Korea during 2001 included Brazil and Turkey.

As in 2000, however, the main trend was restoring good relations with old allies. In January 2001 Kim Jong Il paid his second visit to China in nine months. Again nominally secret, this was mainly to Shanghai and clearly business-related: the week-long itinerary took in several joint-venture factories and even the Stock Exchange, raising hopes (as yet unfulfilled) that North Korea may at last adopt market reforms. In September President Jiang Zemin reciprocated, with the first visit to Pyongyang by a senior Chinese leader in over a decade. Behind the formal warmth, Jiang would have pressed the case for reform (not least to save Beijing the cost of supporting the DPRK's economy, and coping with an outflow of hungry North Korean refugees); and openly called on his hosts to resume dialogue with South Korea, which they promptly did.

Relations with Russia also deepened. An expected visit by Kim Jong Il in April 2001 did not materialize, but his defence minister returned from Moscow with reported pledges of unspecified new military co-operation. The 'Dear Leader' finally made the journey to Russia in August: by special train, taking over three weeks and causing many complaints as stations along the route were cleared of normal traffic as he passed. A joint statement with President Putin referred to Russian 'understanding' of the DPRK's demand for US troops to leave South Korea. Reports also suggested that a deal had been concluded to repay the DPRK's Soviet-era debts, mainly by sending contract labour (whose working conditions the *Moscow Times* likened to serfdom). As this implies, not all Russians endorse their Government's efforts for renewed friendship with this relic of Stalinism.

The events of 11 September 2001 cast an especially long shadow for North Korea. The country remained on the US State Department's list of nations alleged to sponsor terrorism; if mainly for sheltering a number of Japanese hijackers since 1970, rather than any recent transgressions. No links to the Islamist militant group Al-Qa'ida were seriously alleged, and the DPRK swiftly condemned the terrorist attacks on the USA—but went on to criticize the US war in Afghanistan. For its part, Washington for the first time cited North Korea's suspected biological weapons programme as a major threat, in addition to its nuclear and missile concerns. Besides such weapons of mass destruction (WMD), the Bush Administration also gave notice that the DPRK's conventional force posture was unacceptably threatening. In January 2002 President Bush notoriously grouped North Korea with Iraq and Iran as an alleged 'axis of evil'. Pyongyang replied in kind, making any resumption of talks unlikely. None the less, MIA co-operation and US food aid continued. In December 2001 the pursuit and sinking by the Japanese navy of a suspected North Korean spy ship, later salvaged, did nothing for either Pyongyang's relations with Tokyo or its wider reputation.

The DPRK's image also suffered from a growing diplomatic problem in which it was, curiously, both cause and bystander. North Korean fugitives in China—numbering up to 300,000, none of whom Beijing acknowledged as refugees—became more militant in 2002; aided by foreign NGOs, several sought asylum in foreign embassies. Chinese police intrusions to seize them caused disputes with both South Korea and Japan; yet in the end all, including those arrested—numbering more than 80 as of September 2002—were allowed to travel to Seoul via third countries. The price of freedom for the few was a campaign of suppression in the border region, with many more migrants arrested and deported to an uncertain fate. It was doubtful if signs of reform in North Korea, or repression there and in China, could stem this tide from swelling over time, to destabilizing effect.

In early 2002 DPRK diplomacy temporarily turned away from the major powers, and seemed mainly to be motivated by economic needs. The Minister of Foreign Trade toured western Europe, while the titular Head of State, Kim Yong Nam went to Thailand and Malaysia, securing rice and palm oil on generous terms. At home Kim Jong Il hosted Indonesia's president, Megawati Sukarnoputri (their late fathers were close associates), who then travelled on to Seoul. The ever less reclusive 'Dear Leader' also visited the Russian embassy in Pyongyang three times in as many months. In July Russia's Minister of Foreign Affairs, after visiting both Koreas, declared Kim Jong Il ready for dialogue 'without preconditions'.

This duly ushered in a new bout of North Korean goodwill diplomacy. In Brunei in July, Paek Nam Sun returned to the ARF, having been absent in 2001. An informal meeting with the US Secretary of State, Colin Powell, was the first high-level contact with the Bush Administration. Paek professed eagerness for a visit by the US Assistant Secretary of State for East Asian and Pacific Affairs, James Kelly, on which Pyongyang had earlier stalled; but in October 2002 the visit finally took place, the discussions being described as useful. In August, however, a less senior envoy, Jack Pritchard, represented the USA at KEDO's LWR ground-breaking ceremony in Shinpo; he urged North Korea to submit to full IAEA inspections. The timing of these was contentious—the USA wanted them to proceed immediately, but the DPRK—like the former Clinton Administration—maintained that they were not mandatory until at least 2005.

With Tokyo there was faster movement. In Brunei Paek signed a joint statement with his Japanese counterpart, Yoriko Kawaguchi. Within a month, bilateral Red Cross and diplomatic talks were held in Pyongyang, cordially, but with no visible progress. However, Junichiro Koizumi made an historic visit to Pyongyang on 17 September 2002, becoming the first Japanese Prime Minister ever to do so. This seemed to represent a considerable risk, in view of the outstanding disputes between the two countries. The most significant outcome of Koizumi's summit meeting with Kim Jong Il was the latter's admission that North Korean agents had indeed kidnapped 11 or 12

Japanese nationals in the 1970s and 1980s, and of these, only five were still alive. Pyongyang's long silence on the issue had been an obstacle to the resumption of talks on the normalization of diplomatic relations, and the revelation shocked the Japanese public. Kim apologized for the kidnappings, blaming rogue military elements, and agreed to return the surviving Japanese; Koizumi apologized for Japan's colonization of the Korean peninsula. Kim also told Koizumi that he would allow international inspections of North Korea's nuclear facilities, and would maintain the moratorium on missile-testing beyond 2003. However, Tokyo's immediate response was unclear.

Koizumi's sudden enthusiasm for summit meetings might have been inspired by Vladimir Putin, who in Vladivostok in August met Kim Jong Il for the third time in as many years. The Russian President pressed for inter-Korean rail links, which could create an 'iron silk road'—a freight route from South Korea to Europe via Siberia, which Putin hoped would encourage economic development in Russia's depressed Far East. For his part, Kim Jong Il reportedly sought modern weapons, and visited factories in the region as well as a Russian Orthodox church. (Although not officially acknowledged, Kim was born in Khabarovsk in 1942, where his father was in exile.)

With inter-Korean links also improving, as of late 2002 prospects looked propitious once more for détente and dialogue. Past precedent, however, warned that the peninsula's political situation could quickly deteriorate again. Much had depended upon Koizumi's visit, any solid progress, threatening to leave the USA isolated in an aggressive stance. Yet if Kim Jong Il were to renege once again, the likely election in December 2002 of a more hard-line President in South Korea might leave North Korea facing sceptical or hostile leaders in all three of its main foes. With the USA displaying greater militancy, and a host of WMD and other issues awaiting discussion (much less settlement), there could be no guarantee in late 2002 that the DPRK's relations with the wider world would necessarily proceed more smoothly or normally in the future, particularly following the country's unexpected confirmation of the existence of its nuclear programme in October.

Economy

ROBERT F. ASH

Based on an earlier article by JOSEPH S. CHUNG

Following the introduction of a highly centralized planning system based on the former Soviet model, and radical economic initiatives introduced during both the interim post-war Soviet occupation of North Korea (1945–48) and the formal establishment of the Democratic People's Republic of Korea (DPRK) on 9 September 1948, the economy has been characterized by a strong orientation towards the socialization of production and productive relationships. By the end of 1958, the full socialist transformation of North Korea had been completed, laying the foundations of what was one of the world's most highly centralized and planned economic systems—and what has become, since the implementation of market-orientated reform in the former USSR, China and other previously socialist countries, the most monocratic and autarchic economic regime left in the world.

There is a consensus that, even allowing for the impressive rate of economic growth that was sometimes achieved, central planning systems have generated severe problems of waste and inefficiency. In the case of North Korea, there is no doubt that the Government's rigid adherence to central planning has inhibited economic growth and constrained its long-term economic performance. Until the early 1960s, it is true that economic expansion was rapid, but this performance owed more to recovery from a war-ravaged economy (following Japan's surrender and withdrawal in 1945, and, subsequently, the Korean War truce agreement in 1953), than to net growth. Even so, the rate of economic expansion in North Korea (averaging some 12% annually) exceeded that of the South until the late 1960s, and not until around the middle of the following decade did South Korea's aggregate GNP surpass that of North Korea. In per caput terms, the emerging pre-eminence of the South occurred even later.

Economic growth in all communist regimes has been driven by the physical accumulation of resources (especially capital), rather than by qualitative improvements. In this respect, North Korea is no exception, a capital accumulation rate—and its corollary, minimal consumption improvements—rather than productivity gains having facilitated economic expansion. Over time, infrastructural bottlenecks and associated difficulties have grown increasingly serious, highlighting the need to enhance efficiency through the better use of resources and the adoption of more advanced technology in order to maintain and increase the growth momentum.

Throughout its existence, North Korea's development strategy has been guided by the ideology of *juche*, or 'self-reliance' (a notion whose application has extended also to the realm of politics). *Juche* has quasi-mythical overtones, although the idea of '*juche* for economic development' was first articulated by President Kim Il Sung in December 1956. It dominated the formulation and implementation of economic development until well after Kim's death in 1994 and, under the pretext of making working people the masters of agricultural and industrial undertakings, facilitated a continuing emphasis on the need to generate an independent, self-reliant economy. Indeed, despite a willingness to embrace modest market-orientated policies in recent years, the notion of *juche* has remained a dominant economic organizational principle in North Korea.

Following the death of his father, Kim Il Sung, North Korea's new paramount leader, Kim Jong Il continued to defend socialist ownership and the consolidation and development of a socialist economic system embodying the *juche* ideal of self-reliance, while emphatically rejecting the introduction of capitalist methods. These principles were echoed in various official pronouncements, and underlined in the advocacy of reliance on exhortations, mass social mobilization and production campaigns designed to increase output.

The flexibility with which *juche* can be interpreted does not, however, necessarily make it incompatible with economic liberalization. From this perspective, it is salutary that a constitutional amendment, introduced in 1998, made reference to privatization, material incentives and profitability, while also apparently endorsing North Korea's pursuit of a planned, socialist and self-reliant economy. In the same year Pyongyang sought advice from the World Bank on the establishment of a market economy. It remained premature to speculate about the outcome of such initiatives: on the one hand, the North Korean Government has shown itself eager to expand foreign trade, encourage foreign investment and embrace modern technology; on the other hand, it has also continued to show considerable determination not to allow market-orientated reforms to jeopardize central control over key national assets.

At the beginning of the 21st century, North Korea faces severe economic problems. These are largely attributable to the inward-looking policies of the past, which, as in other former socialist countries, placed undue emphasis on heavy industry at the expense of welfare-enhancing consumer goods and services, as well as downgrading the role of foreign trade and inhibiting technology transfer. The outcome was to offer protection to domestic industries behind artificial barriers, and thereby prevent the emergence of internationally competitive industries driven by the principle of comparative advantage. This, in turn, led not only to a serious shortage of foreign exchange, but also exacerbated North Korea's growing foreign indebtedness. In the first half of the 1970s, for example, North Korea's outstanding foreign debt doubled to well over US $500m., resulting in it becoming the first communist country to default on its debt. More than three-quarters of this debt was owed to non-communist countries and an important consequence was that from 1975, North Korea was, for many years, cut off from access to advanced Western technology. Notwithstanding the critical need to maintain imports of foreign technology and capital in the interests of economic modernization, North Korea's isolation only served to underline the emphasis on self-reliance.

North Korea has also faced shortages in skilled labour, modern equipment and technology, which have persisted to the present day. Capacity under-utilization, reflecting congestion in the energy, transport and mining sectors, and inadequate infrastructural investment, have further impeded development. In addition, excessive bureaucracy, a shortage of fertile arable land and the absence of modern farming methods and equipment have resulted in a disappointing agricultural performance, giving rise to persistent food shortages, widespread malnutrition and starvation. After persistent reports of food supply problems and rationing for several years, North Korea officially acknowledged that, as a result of damage caused in 1995 and 1996 by the heaviest floods of the century, the country faced serious food shortages. To date, such shortages have not been eliminated (see below).

Many would argue that North Korea's economic salvation lies in the direction of gradual, if not radical economic reform, embracing Chinese-style market-orientated reforms and an opening of the economy to the outside world. As a long-term goal, this is a process that may be facilitated by Korean unification, although the potential short-term economic and social costs of integration are likely to be considerable. Yet to say this is not to ignore important initiatives to encourage foreign investment in North Korea. For example, as early as 1991, the Government in Pyongyang urged the creation of special economic zones and designated the 621-sq km Rajin-Sonbong Strip on the north-eastern coast as a 'Free Economic and Trade Zone', in imitation of the Chinese model. Whether, however, the North Korean Government will prove itself capable of using reform to turn around its economy, it remains impossible to say and the possibility of wholesale collapse still cannot be ruled out.

RESOURCE BASE, ECONOMIC GROWTH AND STRUCTURAL CHANGE

North Korea occupies about 55% of the total area of the Korean peninsula. Of its total surface area, only about 14% is arable. A generally harsh climate restricts the output of arable farming to one crop per year, although a high irrigation ratio helps offset the high summer concentration of rainfall, as well as providing relief in the face of frequent spring droughts. Natural soil fertility is less favourable than in South Korea and the average 'natural' farm size is small (probably less than 2 ha—and more likely 0.55 ha per member of the agricultural labour force). Yet the emergence of serious food shortages in recent years cannot simply be attributed to a lack of fertile land, nor, as the experiences of other Asian countries demonstrate, is small farm size necessarily inimical to the achievement of high yields and sustained agricultural growth.

Serious demographic losses (estimated at around 1.5m. persons) during the Korean War (1950–53) and migration to the South, as well as a relatively low population density exacerbated labour scarcities in North Korea. The average rate of natural increase of total population was close to 2% per annum in the 1990s, although there is also evidence of a declining trend rate. As of July 2001, the total population was estimated to be 21,968,228 and growing at 1.2% p.a. (birth rate, 19.1 per 1,000; death rate, 6.9 per 1,000). Recent data point to a remarkably low age dependency ratio, with 68% of the total population between the ages of 15 and 64. The share of the total population under 15 was 25.5% in 2001, compared with 6.9% aged 65 years -and above.

The maintenance of large armed forces (with more than 1m. members in 2002—the fifth largest army in the world) has increased the shortage of civilian labour in North Korea and encouraged the involvement of armed personnel in civilian projects. The labour force in 2000 was estimated at 9.6m. (of whom 36% were employed in agricultural work).

North Korea is well endowed with mineral resources, compared with the South, although its mineral industry remains under-developed and primitive because of the lack of modern equipment and technology. Telecommunications too have remained seriously under-developed. The shortage of modern equipment and vehicles appears to be the main problem facing both land and marine transport. In the absence of known deposits of petroleum, North Korea's electricity production (about 32,000m. kWh in 1998) derives from fossil fuel (34.4%) and hydropower sources (65.6%). The implied energy constraint—especially stagnating coal production—has inhibited industrial expansion. The development of the mining, power and metal industries, as well as rail transport, was given the highest economic priority by the Government in the late 1980s and early 1990s. However, in the mid-1990s emphasis was switched to agriculture, light industry and foreign trade: a somewhat surprising development and an implicit admission of past economic policy having failed.

The pursuit of an unbalanced development strategy, geared towards maximizing heavy industrial growth, has been reflected in significant structural change within the North Korean economy. At the time of partition, agriculture (including fishing and forestry) generated almost two-thirds of GDP, compared with an industrial contribution of under 20%. By 1999 the agricultural share had fallen to 30%—or even less—while that of industry had risen to 42%. (Services, meanwhile, accounted for an estimated 28% of GDP.) Such figures certainly attest to substantial industrial growth—above all, the expansion of heavy and military industries. From a comparative perspective, they also reveal the agricultural and, especially, industrial contributions to GDP to be higher in North Korea than in low-income countries taken as a whole, but point to a seriously lagging tertiary sector performance.

However, underlying this superficially impressive industrial growth performance, qualitative indicators suggest a much less buoyant picture. For example, industrial plants—most of them under strict state ownership and control—reportedly operated at an average 30% below capacity for years prior to Kim Il Sung's death, and, by the late 1990s, were believed to be functioning at about 20% of capacity. In any case, high industrial growth in North Korea was not translated into significant improvements in living standards, owing to the disproportionately high allocation of resources to heavy industry and military sectors of the economy.

Judged by its record of published economic data, North Korea is one of the most secretive countries in the world. The questionable reliability and ambiguities of limited official data pose additional problems in assessing the country's economic performance. Despite such problems and other difficulties associated with estimating the national output of a communist country on a US dollar basis, quantitative insights are available into North Korea's recent economic performance. The general picture that emerges is one of long-term positive growth (compared with average national income growth of some 9% per annum during 1960–90) followed by a serious contraction after 1991, when economic ties with the USSR and Eastern bloc countries collapsed. Negative growth during this period was exacerbated by problems of energy shortages, the poor maintenance of existing industrial facilities, technological backwardness and inadequate investment. (Some suggest that by the second half of the 1990s, investment had fallen below the replacement level, leading to a contracting capital stock.) Thus, the period 1991–98 saw a steady contraction in economic output (by 5.1% in 1991, 7.1% in 1992, 4.2% in 1993, 1.8% in 1994, 4.6% in 1995, 3.7% in 1996, 6.8% in 1997 and 1.1% in 1998)—a trend that was only reversed in 1999, thanks mainly to higher farm production and, more significantly, foreign aid (estimated at US $650m. in 1999). In 1999 and 2000, real GDP growth was estimated to be 6.2% and 1.3% respectively. On the basis of purchasing power parity (PPP), a recent figure puts North Korean GDP in 2000 to have been about US $19,000m—perhaps 1% above that of the previous year. Implied in this figure is an average per caput income, measured on a PPP basis, of around US $1,000 (contrasting with US $757, based on the World Bank Atlas approach).

With its goal of achieving self-sufficiency and its pursuit of an inward-looking developmental policy that has rejected integration into the international economic order, North Korea's strategy most closely resembles that of China under the leadership of Mao Zedong. North Korea is also one of the world's most highly defence-constrained economies. Official estimates suggest that the share of spending on defence has fallen steadily, from a peak of 32% in 1968 to under 15% today (a planned figure of 14.5% was given for 2000). However, defence expenditure is notoriously difficult to assess, and Western sources suggest that more than 25%—even up to 33%, according to some—of GDP (US $5,600m.) may be allocated to the military sector.

In 1984, in order to stimulate the economy, North Korea made an unprecedented change to its previously rigid insistence on self-sufficiency, by announcing its willingness to implement joint ventures with foreign companies (including those from capitalist countries). This development was a logical progression from the new foreign economic policy that had been contained in the January 1984 decision of the Supreme People's Assembly (SPA), in which reference was made to the need to expand economic co-operation and technical exchange, as well as trade, with Western countries. Some have viewed this readiness to accept foreign direct investment as the clearest indication of North Korea's slow but steady progression towards a modernization of its economy. It remains to be seen, however, to what extent recent diplomatic initiatives and co-operative commercial projects reflect Pyongyang's readiness to accept the limits to national self-sufficiency.

PLANNING

As early as the interim post-war Soviet occupation of North Korea (1945–48), the North Korean Interim People's Committee introduced a series of radical economic reforms (including land reform and the nationalization of major industries) which signalled a strong orientation towards the socialization of productive relationships and the introduction of a centralized planning system on the Soviet model. Following the formal establishment of the DPRK on 9 September 1948, the new Government launched its first Two-Year Plan (1949–50), by which it sought to consolidate the foundations of a self-reliant national economy. This process was, however, interrupted by the Korean War (1950–53).

From the end of the Korean War until 1984 North Korea's economic policy was conducted within the framework of five development plans. As a result of revisions, early fulfilment and delays, the dates of these plans are somewhat confusing and discontinuous: a Three-Year (Post-war Reconstruction) Plan (1954–56); a Five-Year Plan (actually 1957–60); the first Seven-Year Plan (actually 1961–70); a Six-Year Plan (1971–76); and, with the designation of 1977 as a year of readjustment, the second Seven-Year Plan (1978–84). Following a two-year adjustment period, the third Seven-Year Plan (1987–93), was announced by President Kim Il Sung in 1986. However, the process of orderly planning has been seriously undermined as a result of the severe economic problems of the 1990s and beyond.

The division of Korea after Japan's defeat in 1945 left North Korea in possession of about two-thirds of the peninsula's heavy industrial facilities and infrastructure. With post-war economic rehabilitation completed during the 1954–56 Plan, the country made substantial progress under the 1957–60 Plan towards establishing a firm foundation for industrialization, as envisaged in Plan targets. During this period the 'socialization' process was completed, and the *chollima* movement (which took its name from a legendary flying horse, symbolizing rapid progress) was introduced. Not until the first Seven-Year Plan, however, did the process of industrialization begin in earnest. This was the period in which economic and infrastructural bottlenecks first emerged, forcing the Government to extend the Plan and to adjust its policy in order to accommodate economic and military needs. As a result, some of the planned targets for 1961–70 remained unfulfilled. In the subsequent 1971–76 Plan, the basic objectives were unchanged, although greater emphasis was now placed on technological up-grading, the attainment of self-sufficiency in industrial raw materials, the development of energy industries, raising the quality of products and restoring sectional balances.

The Six-Year Plan (1971–76) was notable for its attempt to revise North Korea's policy of self-reliance in favour of seeking greater access to foreign capital and technology. The success of this strategy was reflected in the fulfilment of major economic targets ahead of plan. At the same time, however, increased capital and technology imports generated increasing foreign debts, which, in turn, led to problems of debt repayment. As a result, North Korea became the first communist country to default on its debt, preventing further purchases of advanced Western technology and forcing it to return to the previous strategy of self-reliance.

Thus, the major thrust of the 1978–84 Plan was the achievement of self-reliance—an associated aim being the lessening of dependence on Soviet economic aid—modernization, and 'scientization', as well as the promotion of the export of manufactured goods. Modernization meant increasing mechanization and automation, while 'scientization' was the North Korean term for introducing more modern production and management techniques. Available evidence suggests that the results of the 1978–84 Plan were disappointing—all the more so, given that major targets were set no higher than those of the previous Plan. The seriousness of continuing economic problems was reflected in the paucity of public official statements or proclamations on the 1978–84 Plan. Even North Korean officials recognized that the targeted growth of net material product (NMP) and several major commodities had not been fulfilled, and their suggestion that NMP growth had averaged 8.8% per annum has also been widely questioned. Nor is it likely that the total industrial output increased at an average rate of 12.2% per annum, as claimed, compared with a planned rate of 12.1%. The fact that three years elapsed before the formulation of the next economic plan is another indicator of the failure of the 1978–84 Plan and of the severity of the economic problems that already confronted North Korea in the mid-1980s.

The targets of the third Seven-Year Plan (1987–93), announced in April 1987, were generally less ambitious than those of previous Plans, reflecting persistent economic shortcomings and a more realistic approach by economic planners. Modernization and 'scientization' were again at the heart of the Plan, which called for average annual industrial growth of 10% (compared with 12% said to have been achieved in 1978–84). The country's NMP was targeted to increase by 70% during the Plan period, compared with the alleged 80% under the previous Plan. Annual production of crude steel was projected to reach 10m. metric tons—significantly lower than the previous target of 15m. tons per year, announced in 1980. By contrast, the projected annual production of non-ferrous metals and aquatic products, two of North Korea's most important export commodities, was increased to 1.7m. tons and 11m. tons, respectively, compared with earlier goals of 1.5m. tons and 5m. tons.

At the conclusion of the Plan, in December 1993, it was officially conceded that the Plan's targets had not been fulfilled, as a result of the difficulties associated with the demise of the USSR and the former socialist bloc. Gross industrial output was said to have expanded by only 50% over the Plan period (an average annual growth rate of 5.6%), although even this disappointing figure was questioned by Western sources. The only other production figures released by the North Korean authorities for 1987–93 were: power (an increase of 30%), coal (40%), non-ferrous metal ores (60%), steel (30%) and chemical fertilizers (50%). Significantly, all five were below the planned growth rates.

The enormity of North Korea's economic problems—the result of years of planning deficiencies, and now exacerbated by developments taking place elsewhere in the communist world—were reflected in the Government's inability to formulate a new long-term economic programme. After 1994 formal economic planning was replaced by greater emphasis of rhetoric, urging the workforce to 'rally under the Red Banner, continue on their arduous march and demonstrate their revolutionary zeal'. At the same time, the years 1994–97 were designated a 'period of adjustment in socialist economic construction'. Few quantitative targets were announced for this transitional period, other than planned increases in textile production (20%), fruit and meat output (both by 30%), chemical fibre and synthetic resin production (10%) and power output (30%). In recognition of North Korea's need to produce more and better consumer goods and to solve its increasingly severe food problem, greater emphasis was to be given to agriculture, light industry and foreign trade, while efforts would be made to maintain the development momentum of the coal and power industries, and to expand rail transport.

This transitional programme must be judged as another failure, for rather than consolidation taking place, the mid-1990s witnessed further economic decline. Potentially significant developments were the introduction of constitutional amendments (in September 1998), providing for greater private enterprise and market reform, and (in early 1999) the Government's adoption of a new economic planning law, which codified the principles and system of the centralized economy. As the experience of China shows, efforts to integrate reform into a socialist system pose huge difficulties. From this perspective, North Korea's simultaneous commitment to planning—much greater than that of the Chinese Government—and a degree of economic liberalization lie uneasily with one another. The seriousness of Pyongyang's reformist ambitions have yet to be demonstrated and in the meantime there is evidence that the Government may be using diplomacy (not least, the external desire to bring peace and stability to the Korean peninsula) in order to obtain secure foreign exchange and maximize additional resources under the pretext of humanitarian assistance. It is, for example, significant that North Korea has become the main recipient of US aid in Asia.

ECONOMIC PROSPECTS AND KOREAN REUNIFICATION

The economic implications for North Korea of reunification with the South have been the subject of much speculation. So opaque is the screen behind which North Korea operates that interpreting its motives vis-à-vis recent diplomatic initiatives—the most important of which include normalization of relations with various countries and the June 2000 Pyongyang Summit between the two Korean Presidents, Kim Dae-Jung and Kim Jong Il—is extremely difficult.

In the wake of the summit meeting in Seoul, discussions by working-level groups subsequently began to discuss matters such as the settlement of payments, mutual investment protection, the avoidance of double taxation and the arbitration of disputes. It would be premature to predict the outcome of such talks, and even two years after the Pyongyang Summit, there is no guarantee of deepening bilateral economic co-operation, through trade liberalization—let alone the establishment of a free-trade area or some other form of economic union. Perhaps the most promising development has been the agreement of the two Governments to resume contacts, following the visit to Pyongyang, in April 2002, by the South Korean presidential envoy, Lim Dong-Won.

In any case, Pyongyang's verbal commitment to economic reform—a clear prerequisite of inter-Korean economic integration—has been greeted by widespread scepticism. Some, for example, have argued that the true motive behind North Korean diplomatic activity in recent years has been to enhance its economic advantage by maximizing foreign exchange and foreign aid. The difficulties of interpreting developments in North Korea were exemplified by the different reactions to reports in July 2002 to the effect that tax measures abolished in 1974 were to be revived. Suffice to say that authoritative sources that regarded such moves as evidence of Pyongyang's determination to introduce market elements into its economy were matched by those that remained convinced that the North Korean Government's true intent was to reinforce state control over an expanding 'underground' economy.

Also effective from July 2002, prices and wages were simultaneously increased in an effort to enhance economic management and thereby improve living standards. Thus, alongside major rises in prices of basic goods, including staple foods (rice up from 0.08 to 44 won per kg.), transport (bus fares up from 0.1 to 2 won), accommodation and energy (electricity rates up from 0.035 to 1.8 won/kWh), workers' basic wages were also raised from 110 won to 2,000 won. The underlying rationale of the price increases was to eliminate the serious fiscal drain resulting from the use of state subsidies and to allow prices to reflect the true cost of production.

Even if market-orientated reforms were proven to be lasting, China's experience since the early 1980s is a warning of the high risks of such a strategy—not least, in terms of widening income differentials and the emergence of attendant economic and social strains. Furthermore, so serious were the shortages of essential raw materials and energy that it cannot simply be taken for granted that even a genuine reformist commitment by Kim Jong Il would be translated into the successful implementation of economic reform. China may appear to be, and probably is, the most obvious model for North Korea to follow (in January 2001 a delegation from Pyongyang, led by Kim Jong Il himself, visited Beijing and Shanghai in order to familiarize itself with the Chinese reformist development strategy). However, the political obstacles to market-orientated reform faced by North Korea—not least, the existence of a fundamental ideological challenge from Seoul—are much greater than those that have confronted Beijing. Nor are North Korea's base economic conditions as favourable as those enjoyed by China at the end of the 1980s. In short, it is not impossible that, far from facilitating sustained growth, insurmountable barriers could lead to economic collapse in North Korea.

To date, clear expressions of co-operation between North Korea and the outside world are few. However, two deserve recognition: first, the establishment, in 1991, of the Rajin-Sonbong Special Economic Zone (SEZ); and second, the 1998 agreement with Hyundai to develop the tourist potential of Mount Kumgang and—potentially far more important—to create a new industrial park in North Korea (probably at Kaesong). If the target of attracting 1.5m. visitors to Mount Kumgang by 2005 is fulfilled, associated revenue could reach US $450m. per year—sufficient, if not misappropriated for party purposes, to pay for vital food imports.

Attempts have been made to estimate the cost of rehabilitation programmes in the North, designed to facilitate economic integration between the two Koreas. Thus, rural energy rehabilitation has been costed at US $2,000–$3,000m. over five years, while the corresponding figure for a more comprehensive programme aimed at stimulating energy improvements throughout the economy has been estimated at US $20,000m.–$50,000m. over a 20-year period. A South Korean source has suggested that some US $6,000m. would be required in order to upgrade North Korea's economic infrastructure to South Korea's 1990 level. Elsewhere, it has been suggested that unification could require the expenditure of more than 8% of South Korea's national product in order to bring per caput income in the North to about the South's level.

What seems certain is that the nature of North Korea's state system (and for that matter, that of South Korea too) will make the process of economic integration as difficult, if not more so, than that of the reunification of Germany, and integration within the European Union (EU). The income disparities between North and South Korea are, for example, much greater than those between the former West and East Germany, and the costs of reunification are likely to be much higher. At the beginning of the 1990s, the Korea Development Institute (KDI) estimated that total reunification costs would be US $240,000m. In view of South Korea's subsequent growth and the North's economic stagnation, that figure doubtless should nowbe revised considerably upwards. The clear message contained in all these estimates is that the economic challenge facing Pyongyang and Seoul should not be underestimated.

AGRICULTURE, FORESTRY AND FISHING

About 80% of North Korea's total surface area consists of mountains and uplands, which extend close to the east coast. Plains are mainly concentrated in the west of the country and constitute the major agricultural base. The arable land ratio is about 14%.

In the far north, summer lasts only about two months, shortening the growing season considerably, but further south a typical growing season lasts a minimum of four months. North Korea's moist climate is conducive to forest growth, but high-quality timber is limited to the northern interior, where extensive forests of larch, spruce, fir and pine provide the basis of the timber industry. Domestic timber shortages are offset by substantial imports from the eastern territories of the CIS. Years of clearing forest lands for farming have reduced the total forest area from 9.9m. ha in the 1970s to 9.2m. ha in 2000. In an attempt to meet the increasing demand for timber, as well as to conserve forest resources, a new forestry law was enacted in December 1992 since when the Government has consistently implemented mass mobilization afforestation campaigns. Even so, it would be premature to claim any significant improvement yet in reforestation efforts.

The Land Reform Act of March 1946 sought to abolish tenancy and redistribute land to the farmers. The outcome was further to reduce the average size of the already small farms, while improving the distribution of land ownership. Private farming persisted until the end of the Korean War, but thereafter, as collectivization intensified, fell into decline until, by August 1958, it had completely disappeared. Since then, farming has been conducted within the framework of co-operative farms (collectives) or state farms. In the 1980s it was estimated that North Korea had about 3,800 co-operative and 180 state farms, the former managing more than 90% of the total cultivated land. One impact of collectivization was to increase average farm size. In the mid-1990s, however, the Government began to advocate the gradual transfer of collective farms to state ownership, which is considered to be more ideologically sound. Recent estimates by the Food and Agriculture Organization (FAO) suggest that North Korea's total arable area is about 1.9m. ha, of which 0.4m. ha comprise high-quality, permanently-irrigated land, 0.7m. ha. medium-quality, semi-irrigated land capable of supporting rice production, and 0.8m. ha low-quality land suitable for cultivating other cereal crops.

In 1976, in an effort to extend the arable area, North Korea launched a so-called 'nature remaking programme'. Its major objectives were to complete the irrigation of non-paddy lands, to reclaim 100,000 ha of new land, to build 150,000 ha–200,000 ha of terraced fields, to reclaim tidal land, and to conduct work on afforestation and water conservation projects. Subsequently, the third Seven Year Plan (1987–93) set out the goal of reclaiming some 300,000 ha of tidal land, most of it to be used for growing rice. In fact, subsequent reclamation work was slow and according to South Korean estimates, only 28,400 ha had been reclaimed by March 1995.

Central to North Korea's agricultural strategy has been the extension of irrigation. Following success in providing permanent irrigation for rice farmers, the focus of irrigation projects shifted to non-paddy fields, where, even allowing for a 40% rise in irrigated non-paddy fields, irrigation provision has remained less well-established. In early 1994 there were reportedly 40,000 km of irrigation waterways, which, together with 1,770 reservoirs and 26,000 pumping stations, supplied water to about 70% of the country's agricultural land. In 1989 a project was initiated to build a 400 km-long canal, by diverting the flow of the Taedong River along the west coast of North Korea. As part of the irrigation system, the canal was intended to provide water to rural areas and newly-reclaimed tideland in South Hwanghae and South Pyongan provinces. By late 1990 a total of 800 km of large and small irrigation waterways had been completed; in December 1995 the Kangryong Waterway (40 km) was the latest to be constructed.

If improved irrigation provision has been central to North Korea's farm strategy, the Government has also sought to raise farm yields through an expansion of mechanization (rice planting was already basically—95%—mechanized in the 1980s) and electrification, deep ploughing, close planting and the intensive use of fertilizers. In the face of recent declines in food production, there have also been attempts to introduce double cropping. The extent of technological backwardness in North Korean agriculture is reflected in the finding that in 1984, there were only seven tractors per 100 ha in the plains and six in the intermediate and mountainous areas—a situation which seems unlikely to have significantly changed in subsequent years. The average application of fertilizers was 1.3 tons and 1.2 tons per ha, respectively, for paddy and non-paddy fields in 1977, but although the 1984 target of 2.0 tons per ha is claimed to have been achieved, the plan to raise this figure to 2.5 tons by 1993 was not fulfilled. Such figures do not, however, indicate the distribution of fertilizer use, and in 1991 the UN warned that North Korea's intensive use of farm chemicals was causing substantial land degradation and water pollution.

North Korea claimed to have fulfilled the planned annual output of 10m. tons of grain (cereals and pulses) in 1984 (the last year for which such data were made public)—a figure that, according to Western estimates, rose to over 12m. tons by 1989. Some would argue, however, that such estimates considerably exaggerate the reality of North Korea's grain production during these years. In any case, the Government's stated goal was to raise annual grain output to 15m. tons by 1993. Nevertheless, such was the severity of agricultural decline in the wake of severe natural disasters (mainly flooding) and structural constraints associated with the central planning system that, according to Western estimates, average annual output fell to 4m. tons in 1993–94, and to a mere 3.7m. tons in 1996–98. The Government itself conceded that the destruction, by 1996, of 330,000 ha of arable land (18% of the total) had generated a loss of 1.9m. tons of grain (US $1,500m., in financial terms). By 1999 North Korean sources indicated that total grain output had recovered to around 4.3m. tons (8.6% more than in 1998)—still well below the 6.2m. tons needed to satisfy domestic requirements. Worse still, South Korean sources suggested a 15% decline in production in 2000, to 3.6m. tons, generating a food deficit of more than 2m. tons.

Paddy rice and maize are the two most important crops in North Korea, followed by wheat, barley, millet, sorghum, oats and rye. The output of potatoes is usually sizeable (estimated by FAO at 1.6m. tons in 1997, but subsequently revised downwards, probably conservatively, to 510,000 tons). Although an inferior 'grain', potatoes have high calorific yields and it is significant that recent years have seen an emphasis on the expansion of the sown potato area. It is estimated that total potato output registered a rise of 390,000 tons in 2000. Preferred cereals for consumption include rice and maize (and, to a lesser extent, wheat), while beans are an important source of energy. Rice was an important export item until the mid-1980s, although in recent years North Korea has begun to import rice (from Thailand, South Korea and other countries), as well as some wheat. FAO estimated that, between 1997 and 1998, rice imports rose from US $104m. to US $112m. (the value of wheat imports, meanwhile, having fallen sharply from US $80.5m. to US $48m. In 2000 domestic production of rice and maize was 1.42m. and 1.44m. tons (down, respectively, by 12.9% and 25% below the levels of 1999). The output of beans, wheat and barley also registered declines.

The consequence of deteriorating grain production in the 1990s has been increasingly serious food shortages that have persisted to the present day. The response of the North Korean Government was to urge its people to follow a 'two-meals-a-day' campaign and, unprecedentedly, to request assistance from various UN and other international organizations, as well as from developed countries. During the two-year period of 1992–93, grain imports are estimated to have already reached 1.9m. tons (almost a third of food requirements). Meanwhile, as the crisis deepened, policy-makers sought to accord a higher priority to agriculture, not least through more frequent 'on-the-spot guidance' sessions by senior officials. In early 1996 the authorities reportedly also began to allocate additional resources to affected farms, providing fertilizer, farm machinery and manpower (including members of the armed forces). However, despite some temporary amelioration, the underlying situation remained critical and, during 1997, resulted in further famine, which continued in 1998 and 1999. Between May and August 2000, insufficient rainfall and unseasonably hot weather caused the worst drought for 50 years; and in September strong tropical storms destroyed more crops. An official statement later confirmed that 1.4m. tons of grain had been lost from the annual harvest.

In 2001 FAO estimated that, in 2001/02, North Korea's total cereal demand would be 5.01m. tons. Given a predicted cereal harvest of 3.54m. tons—incidentally, the best harvest since 1995/96— FAO's projected deficit was 1.47m. tons. After deducting likely imports, food aid and concessional food imports were expected to total 1.37m. tons.

In short, since the mid-1990s, severe food shortages have persisted, resulting in malnutrition, starvation and famine-related diseases. According to Hwang Jang Yop, a senior diplomat who defected from North Korea in 1997, some 2.5m. people died as a result of famine in 1995–98, a figure that is in line with the more generally cited estimate of around 2m. deaths. Such figures suggested that over 10% of the population could have died from starvation or malnutrition-related disease. What was certain was that food aid notwithstanding, malnutrition rates were among the highest in the world. Food shortages also gave rise to large-scale emigration, so that by 1998 between 100,000 and 400,000 were estimated to have tried, mainly unsuccessfully, to flee across the Tumen River border into China.

Although climatic factors have played their part in generating food deficits in recent years, structural defects have been a more significant contributory factor. Until systemic changes have been introduced that can address such problems, food aid was likely to be needed for many years to come. Meanwhile, the continuing severity of food shortages was confirmed in a report by the UN World Food Programme (WFP), which indicated in 2001 that most North Koreans were seeking to survive on a daily rice ration of 150–200 grams. Indeed, shortages were reported even to have spread to Pyongyang itself.

In addition to increased grain imports, food aid has played a critical role in preventing even more dire consequences of famine. The importance of such aid was emphasized by a report in April 2002, which stated that North Korea would run out of food if further international food donations were not immediately made available. It was estimated that the international community extended US $1,080m. of relief aid to North Korea between mid-1995 and the end of 1998. In late 1999 UN officials announced plans to generate US $331.7m. in aid donations to North Korea (of which the majority was to be allocated to food aid, especially among children under six and agricultural restoration). In January 2001 agreement was reached whereby the International Fund for Agricultural Development (IFAD) would provide US $41.7m. ($24.4m. in the form of a loan, and $17.3m. as free aid) in order to help raise grain production. The following month, the WFP announced its intention to grant 810,000 tons of food and US $93m. for the purposes of humanitarian famine relief to an estimated 7.6m. North Koreans thought to be suffering from hunger. Bilateral assistance has also been important, the most important donors being the USA and Japan.

With a coastline of some 17,000 km, a mixture of warm and cold ocean currents, and many rivers and streams, North Korea has considerable potential for fishery development. The principal fishing grounds are in the coastal areas of the Sea of Japan to the east, and the Yellow Sea to the west. The catch from the Sea of Japan includes pollock, octopus, anchovy, sardine, flatfish, cod, sandfish, herring and mackerel. Species caught in the Yellow Sea include yellow corbina, hairtail stingray, sand eel and shrimp. Deep-sea fishing, which was first undertaken on a large scale in the 1970s, includes catches of herring, mackerel, pike and yellowtail. The main fishery ports are Shinpo, Kimchaek and the deep-sea fishery bases of Yanghwa and Hongwon. Besides the fishery stations, smaller fishery co-operatives are located along both coasts in traditional fishing centres. North Korea claimed to have achieved the 1978–84 Plan annual output target of 3.5m. tons of marine products. The 1987–93 Plan envisaged the modernization and expansion of the fishery industry. Instead, however, the total catch in 1995 was a mere 0.3m. tons, declining to 0.2m. tons in 1997. In early 1995 North Korea possessed an estimated 40,000 fishing vessels, including 3,750-ton vessels for deep-sea fishing and 450-ton vessels for offshore fishing. In the wake of emerging energy shortages (see below), sea-fishing and associated fish-processing activities declined, with repercussions for exports of marine products.

MINING

With 80%–90% of the important mineral deposits of the peninsula concentrated within its borders, North Korea is relatively well endowed in natural resources. Most important among the minerals are coal, iron ore, lead, magnesite, zinc, tungsten, mica, fluorite and precious metals. According to South Korean estimates, output in the mining sector decreased by 6.6% in 1998.

North Korean petroleum exploration began as long ago as 1965, but to date has yielded zero output, necessitating reliance on imports. Nevertheless, petroleum exploration continued, although it was severely constrained by high drilling costs. The most likely locations of petroleum deposits were the West Sea Bay and Anju Basin. However, Swedish, British, Japanese and Australian petroleum companies owned petroleum exploration concessions off the west and east coasts of North Korea. Joint explorations with South Korea's Korean National Oil Company (KNOC) might be expected to expand in the foreseeable future. North Korea's deposits of coal have been estimated at 12,000m. tons, of which about 80% are anthracite, bituminous coal requirements being imported, mainly from China. The country's coal mines, located largely in South Pyongan Province, produced 27m. tons of anthracite in 1995. Despite a steady increase in the 1980s, coal production has lagged behind the growing energy needs of the industrial sector, creating a persistent energy shortage. In the absence of petroleum and natural gas reserves, more than one-third of North Korea's electricity output is generated by coal-powered thermal plants (the remainder being derived from hydro power sources), so that the relatively weak performance of the coal industry has been a significant constraint on North Korean economic growth—a situation compounded by falling petroleum imports during the 1990s, caused by shortages of foreign exchange. Inadequate transport facilities have only aggravated the energy problem, while ageing mining equipment, inefficiencies associated with the need to mine deeper seams, the low level of mechanization and the lack of advanced equipment have also contributed to the comparative stagnation in the output of coal and other minerals. Efforts since the 1978–84 Plan have mainly centred on the reconstruction and expansion of the Anju District Coal Mining Complex, constructed in the 1970s with Soviet aid. In early 1991 a second mining facility, with a potential of 300,000 tons per year, was added to the complex, as part of a plan to increase the annual capacity to 650,000 tons. Despite these efforts, recent estimates indicate that the production of anthracite continued to decline in the second half of the 1990s (with falls of 11.4% in 1996 and 1.9% in 1997).

Iron ore, with known reserves of about 3,000m. metric tons, is very important to domestic industry and has also been a major source of foreign exchange. According to Western estimates, output increased from 8m. tons in 1985 to 10m. tons in 1988, but thereafter stagnated. Indeed, in the mid-1990s output declined significantly, from 4.6m. tons in 1994 to a mere 2.9m. tons in 1997. In the 1980s new mines at Tokson and Sohaeri were added to the earlier mines at Musan, Unryul, Tokson, Tokyon, Chaeyong and Hasong, all of which have benefited from large-scale state investment. The Chongpyong mine in South Hamgyong Province was commissioned in 1991.

North Korea is especially rich in magnesite, with reserves—mainly concentrated in the Tanchon District in the north-east—estimated at 6.5m tons. It remains the second-largest producer of magnesia products after China, having previously been the largest producer in the world. Mining of magnesite and production of its derivative, clinker, are important both for supporting the domestic refractory industry and for exports. The completion of expansion projects at the Tanchon magnesia plant, and the construction of the Unsong crushing and screening plant in the Tanchon District in 1987, raised the production capacity of clinker to 2m. tons per year. The 1994 agreement by North Korea and the USA to lift restrictions on bilateral trade offered an important new market for clinker, facilitating a large-scale expansion of North Korea's magnesite production capacity. In June 1995 the first North Korean trade mission to visit the USA concluded an agreement to export 100,000 tons of magnesite to a US company. In August 2000 a US mining company announced that it had formed a joint venture with the Korea Magnesia Clinker Industry group to mine, process and export magnesia products from North Korea. The first phase of the project envisaged the export of 200,000 metric tons of magnesia products to the USA and Asia.

Other minerals produced in large quantities by North Korea are lead, zinc, tungsten, graphite, mercury, phosphates, nickel, gold, silver, fluorspar and sulphur. Both zinc and lead ore are smelted domestically (at Tanchon, Nampo, Komdok, Haeju and Mungyong) and zinc and lead ingots are major exports. In 1994 North Korea produced an estimated 200,000 tons of high-grade electrolytic zinc and 80,000 tons of lead. A joint-venture project to redevelop the Unsan gold mine began operation in April 1987, and the first shipment of gold to Japan (totalling some 100 kg) was reported three months later. Unsan is potentially one of the world's major gold mines, with deposits estimated at more than 1,000 tons. The 1990 target was 2 tons, with an eventual annual production target of 10 tons.

MANUFACTURING

Under the impact of its Soviet-style planning system, North Korea has prioritized the development of heavy industry, in the ostensible belief that this would ultimately benefit light and domestic consumer industries. As a development strategy this approach has been a failure and even when rapid heavy industrial growth has taken place, quantitative expansion has often been at the expense of major qualitative deficiencies. In particular, excessive emphasis on machine-building (the basis for the munitions industry) generated a distorted industrial structure, and the orthodoxy that rapid heavy industrial development would enhance living standards through its ultimate promotion of agricultural and consumer goods industries has proven wholly unfounded. In general, the inwardly-orientated nature of North Korea's industrial strategy for many years contributed to inefficiency and low productivity. Hence, recent reform initiatives, whereby the Government has indicated a willingness to embrace a greater role for prices, markets and other 'orthodox' economic criteria, such as profitability, in order to enhance manufacturing production efficiency. At the beginning of the 21st century, heavy industry accounted for one-half of total production in North Korea.

Notwithstanding North Korean claims to have fulfilled the second Seven-Year Plan (1978–84) target of increasing industrial gross value output by 120%, it is unlikely that the implied average annual growth of 12.2% was really achieved, given that most major industrial commodities expanded by much less than this during the same period (for example, output increases of 78% for electric power, 50% for coal, 85% for steel, 78% for cement, 50% for tractors, 45% for textiles, and 80% for chemical fibres). In the third Seven-Year Plan (1987–93), official claims that industrial growth rose by 5.6% per annum were contested by Western sources, which suggested that industrial output had, in fact, declined. In any case, the years from 1994 to 1997 were designated a period of 'adjustment in socialist economic construction', with emphasis shifted from mining, power and metallurgical industries to agriculture, light industry and trade. The readjustment of economic priorities, which incidentally mirrors those undertaken by China in the wake of its own 'great famine' (1959–61), no doubt reflects the severity of North Korea's agricultural crisis and the urgent need to restore food supplies. That difficulties facing farmers had severe knock-on effects on industry can hardly be doubted: even official estimates indicate a fall in industrial output of almost two-thirds between 1992 and 1996. Construction is likely to have been similarly hit, some sources suggesting that investment had fallen below replacement level, thereby causing a contraction in the capital stock. In 1997 and 1998 manufacturing output fell, respectively, by 16.8% and 3.3%. Subsequently, however, heavy industrial development was re-emphasized, although Bank of Korea estimates that heavy and chemical industry expanded by 11.6% and construction by 24.3% in 1999 have been questioned by sceptical observers.

Machine-Building and Metallurgy

The machine-building industry is central to any strategy aimed at achieving industrial self-sufficiency, supplying machinery for domestic industry and agriculture (notably tractors and other farm machinery). In North Korea, it has also made available an extensive range of military equipment, including rifles, mortars, machine-guns, multiple rocket launchers, artillery, anti-aircraft weapons, tanks, personnel carriers, patrol craft and frigates, missile-equipped fast attack craft and amphibious vessels, submarines, medium-range *Scud*-type surface-to-surface missiles, and long-range *Taepo Dong* missiles. The industry accounted for only 5.1% of total industrial output in 1946, but its contribution had expanded to about one-third of the total by the early 1980s. In more recent years, however, production levels have declined.

The machine-building industry is capable of producing 5,000-metre boring machines, 300-hp bulldozers, 10,000-ton power presses, 50,000-kilovolt-ampere generators, 200,000-kilovolt-ampere transformers for power production, 3,000-hp locomotives, 20,000-ton ships, 7,000-hp electric locomotives, 100-ton freight cars and 10-cu m excavators for construction and mining. Such impressive quantitative measures are, however, belied by the poor quality of North Korean machinery, the technological level of which is well below international standards. From the mid-1970s North Korea began to import advanced machinery and equipment from developed Western countries. The 1987–93 Plan sought to modernize the machine-building industry by introducing high-speed, precision machines and equipment, and in early 1990 the Huichon machine-building complex was claimed to have initiated a flexible manufacturing process by adding robots to its numerically-controlled machine tools—an example expected to be followed by other plants. From the present perspective, accelerated economic reform and, in particular, the extension of joint ventures would appear to offer North Korea's best opportunity to pursue technological upgrading in its machine-building industry.

With an annual production capacity of 10m. tons of steel, the Kimchaek Iron Works replaced the Hwanghae Iron Works (in Songrim) as the largest North Korean centre for the production of iron and steel. Kimchaek is located in Chongjin, near the Musan iron ore mine, and has estimated deposits of 100m. tons. Other steel mills are found elsewhere in Chongjin, as well as at Taean. The disappointing performance of the metallurgical industry is highlighted in estimates for 1995, made by the US Bureau of Mines, which showed total output of pig iron, crude steel and rolled steel to have been, respectively, 6.6m., 8.1m. and 4m. tons—figures that can be compared with the unfulfilled targets for 1984 of 6.4m.–7m. tons (pig-iron and granulated iron), 7.4m.–9m. tons (crude steel) and 5.6m.–6m. tons (rolled steel). Outdated technology, shortages of coking coal and the low purity of domestic iron ore have posed serious constraints on the growth of the iron and steel industry. In the past, in addition to the construction of new and/or extension of existing facilities, mass mobilization campaigns to collect scrap iron have also been used in order to alleviate the steel shortage. At best, however, such efforts have been only partially successful, and in 2001 Kim Jong Il himself spoke of the need for technological modernization of the steel industry. It is significant too that in March 2001 Yonhap (the South Korean News Agency) quoted North Korean sources to the effect that South Korean steel firms should be encouraged to set up steel mills in the North. Meanwhile, in 2000 steel imports from China rose from 9,600 tons to 24,000 tons (a rise of 150%—but up 70% in value terms).

Chemicals

Because of its importance to agriculture, the chemical fertilizer industry has been the beneficiary of large-scale investment. Most fertilizers are produced by the giant Hungnam fertilizer plant, which has an annual capacity of 1m. tons, generating 770,000 tons in 1997. Official sources in Pyongyang suggest that chemical fertilizer output rose from 3m. to 4.7m. tons between 1976 and 1984 (an average annual increase of 5.9%), and increased further to 5.6m. tons by 1989 (3.6% per annum). Yet such figures are viewed sceptically in the West, where North Korea's annual production capacity was estimated to be only 3.5m. tons in 1995. It is clear too that industrial collapse in the 1990s had serious implications for fertilizer supplies: in particular, oil shortages have impacted seriously on the production of urea and ammonium sulphate (the main fertilizers used in North Korea). Imports have helped to a limited extent in offsetting domestic shortages and in 2000, in a gesture intended to demonstrate its support for economic rehabilitation in the North, South Korea sent 300,000 tons of fertilizer, valued at about US $90m. Other international donations of fertilizers, designed to enhance food production, have also assisted in increasing supplies of this vital input. The impact of fertilizer use on farm production depends on generating the right mix and quality, not just the increasing the physical volume of fertilizers. From this perspective, completion of the Sariwon complex, the construction of which began in 1998, will be a significant event, raising national potassium fertilizer production capacity to 510,000 tons.

Important integrated chemical plants include the Chongyun Works (located in the Anju District, north of Pyongyang), the construction of which began, with French assistance, during the Six-Year Plan (1971–76). It is the country's first petrochemical complex, designed to produce ethylene, polyethylene, acrylonitrite and urea, using crude petroleum supplied by the nearby refinery at Sonbong (formerly Unggi). In addition to building two large-scale vinalon plants, for more than a decade North Korea has also produced chemical fibres based on petrochemistry, at Chongnyun and other more recently-built plants. The annual production target for chemical fibres in the terminal year of the 1987–93 Plan was 225,000 tons, while that for synthetic resins and plastics was set at 500,000 tons. Annual production of chemical fibres in 1989–93 was estimated by foreign observers to be 177,000 tons.

Textiles

At the heart of North Korea's textile industry is the Pyongyang integrated textile mill, built with Soviet assistance in the late 1950s. Its production derives mainly from locally-produced synthetics, such as vinalon and petrochemically-based fibres, as well as cotton and silk. Although Pyongyang remains the centre of the national textile industry, plants in Shinuiju and Sariwon have become increasingly important in recent years. North Korea's output of textile fabrics increased by 78% during the 1978–84 Plan (an average annual growth rate of 8.6%), thereby supposedly fulfilling the 1984 target of 800m. m of cloth. Meanwhile, a combination of machine imports from Japan and upgrading of existing equipment facilitated an expansion of knitwear products, derived from domestically-produced orlon. The intention was to increase the annual output of textile fabrics to 1,500m. m by 1993. This target is, however, unlikely to have been fulfilled, and overseas estimates indicate that textile production at the beginning of the 1990s was no more than 680m. m. A much more salutary reminder of the severity of economic conditions in more recent years is the suggestion, made by South Korean sources, that North Korea's textile production had fallen to a mere 120m. m by the late 1990s. Nevertheless, textiles remain one of the most important sources of foreign exchange.

SERVICES

Until 1984 all outlets for the provision of services and the distribution of goods, including retail shops, were either state-owned or run as co-operatives. Following the introduction in 1984 of the so-called '3 August Consumer Goods Movement', local governments were permitted to establish, within their districts, direct sales outlets for the distribution of consumer goods produced locally with locally available resources. By the early 1990s, the total number of shops, service establishments and 'food-processing and storage bases' was estimated to be 130,000. However, outside the special economic zones, markets, in which farmers were allowed to sell surplus farm products, products raised on private plots, and a range of non-farm products at free-market prices reflecting scarcity values, have been the only exception to monopoly powers exercised by the State. The expectation is that such outlets will expand and increase in number, if and as economic reforms continue. Meanwhile, South Korean estimates indicate that at the end of the 1990s tertiary sector output was growing, on average, by about 1% a year.

INFRASTRUCTURE

Transport

By the 1970s transport bottlenecks were blamed for the failure to fulfil major targets under the Six-Year Plan (1971–76), when difficulties in delivering raw materials (especially coal) and semi-finished goods were already inhibiting expansion of the mining and manufacturing sectors, adversely affecting the energy situation and impeding foreign trade. The existence of such problems was reflected in renewed emphasis on modernizing and extending the freight capacity of railway, road and marine transport. The expansion and renovation of port facilities also benefited from large-scale investment funding in order to alleviate problems in the handling of cargo at North Korea's ports. Even so, transport problems persisted during the 1990s, the development of rail services being singled out for special attention.

With a total route length of 5,214 km at April 2000, the railway system has remained North Korea's principal means of transport, handling about 90% of the country's freight, and 70% of its passenger traffic. Most of the rail system comprises only single track and much of it would be widely regarded as obsolescent. Nevertheless, recent statistics indicate an electrification ratio of about 70% (but in excess of 85% for standard gauge railways, which account for some 80% of the total). This is important for a mountainous country like North Korea, since electrification enhances the traction capability of railways. Meanwhile, efforts continue to improve rail access to remote areas, and to areas near the Chinese border.

During 2000 and 2001 construction work continued in an effort to reconnect the 486-km inter-Korean Kyongui railway line, which, prior to the division of the Korean Peninsula, ran from Shinuiju in the North through Pyongyang to Seoul in the South. The two sides have also agreed to construct a highway to run parallel to the railway and such work is also under way. To these ends, the South Korean Government decided in February 2001 to allocate US $143m. to associated construction. Once opened, the railway was expected to facilitate not only inter-Korean travel, but also to enhance rail links with Russia, China and Japan. During a visit to Pyongyang in March 2001 the Russian President, Vladimir Putin, spoke of his Government's interest in assisting in a project that would reconnect the Trans-Korean and Trans-Siberian railways. Subsequently, the two countries signed an agreement on railway transport co-operation.

Fuel constraints and the near-absence of private automobiles have relegated road transport to a secondary role. Recent estimates suggest that the total road network is 31,200 km, although a mere 6.4% of this (just under 2,000 km) is paved. There also exists a network of some 682 km of multi-lane highways, the construction of which began in the 1970s. This includes an expressway, connecting Pyongyang and Kaesong (a distance of 170 km), which was completed in April 1992. Other expressways link Pyongyang and Nampo (53 km), Pyongyang and Wonsan on the east coast (172 km), Pyongyang and Sunan (15 km), and Wonsan and Mount Kumgang (114 km). A 135-km highway, known as the Tourist Expressway, connecting Pyongyang and Hyangsan, via Anju, was also completed in October 1995. Local transport between villages is provided by rural bus services, while bus and tram services operate in towns and cities. In 1973 an extravagantly-furbished, 32 km-long underground railway system was completed in Pyongyang.

Water transport plays a minor but growing role in freight and passenger traffic. The total length of inland waterways is 2,253 km, most of which is navigable only by small craft. In November 1995 the creation of a marine transport system in the port of Rajin-Sonbong Free Economic and Trade Zone was announced, as part of the Tumen Delta development project. This initiative, jointly implemented by North Korea and China's Yanbian Sea Transport Corporation, may be seen as part of North Korea's economic reform efforts, designed to connect Rajin with Yanji City (China) and Busan (South Korea) and thereby save shipping time and transport costs in the interests of enhancing inter-Korean trade. No less important as a sign of the modest opening of the North Korean economy—and perhaps a portent for the future—has been the opening of container operations between Incheon (South Korea) and Nampo in the north. As of 2001, North Korea's merchant fleet comprised 176 ships (1,000 grt or over), including more than 90 cargo vessels, four bulk carriers and one oil tanker.

North Korea possesses 87 airports, only 39 of which have paved runways, and its international air connections remain largely undeveloped. Regular flights (once or twice a week) connect Pyongyang to Moscow and Khabarovsk (Russia), Beijing, Macao and Shenyang (China), Nagoya (Japan), Bangkok (Thailand), Berlin (Germany) and Sofia (Bulgaria). In addition, there are irregular flights between Pyongyang and Eastern European, Middle Eastern and African destinations. Internal flights are very restricted, serving mainly to connect Pyongyang with the port cities of Hamhung and Chongjin. A significant development was the signing in Bangkok, in October 1997, of an agreement with South Korea, allowing foreign commercial flights through North Korean airspace. In March 2001 it was also revealed that DHL Korea was offering delivery services for parcels—not letters or cash—to selected destinations (including Pyongyang, Rajin-Sonbong, Hamhung and Nampo). Only corporations authorized to do business with North Korea are, however, able to take advantage of such facilities.

Energy

North Korea's importance as a producer of fuel and energy emerged in the pre-partition period, when the North, through the Japanese-built Sup'ung hydroelectric plant, supplied more than 90% of electricity in the peninsula. Following partition, several large hydroelectric plants, as well as smaller localized power plants (both thermal and hydroelectric) were constructed. From the 1970s, North Korea sought increasingly to use coal as an energy source (by 1999, coal accounted for 77% of primary energy consumption, the rest coming from hydropower). This major shift in energy policy was a response to the perceived disadvantages of hydroelectric plants, such as high initial costs, the long construction period and instability engendered by prolonged drought. However, against the advantage of being able to site coal-based power plants close to industrial and heavily populated areas are disadvantages associated with the poor quality and inaccessibility of coal deposits. In 1999 coal production was an estimated 85.5m. short tons, compared with consumption of 87.6m. short tons.

In the 1980s widespread construction of small and medium-scale hydroelectric plants got under way, especially in the mountainous provinces of Hamgyong, Jagang and Ryanggang. Some 1,300 of such plants were reported to be operational by the end of 1994. Such construction continues, a recent North Korean report (of December 2000) revealing that some 250 small and medium-scale power plants, with a generating capacity of 50,000 kWh, had been constructed in the previous few years, thereby facilitating the attainment of electricity self-sufficiency in Jagang Province.

In 1999 North Korea's electricity production was estimated to be 28,600m. kWh. Of this, 34.6% was derived from fossil fuel and 65.4% from hydroelectric sources. Electricity consumption was estimated at 26,598m. kWh. This surplus notwithstanding, electricity shortages persisted and power failures remained common.

Overall, an unfavourable domestic energy balance has necessitated petroleum imports in order to offset supply shortages. For the time being, oil accounts for a mere 10% of total primary energy consumption, supplies being wholly imported. For example, crude petroleum is imported from Russia to supply the Sobong (Unggi) refinery, near the Russian border, which provides fuel oil to the nearby 200-MW thermal power station—the country's only oil-fired electricity plant. North Korea's other petroleum refinery, built with Chinese aid at Bonghwa—receives crude petroleum from China and produces petrol (motor spirit) and industrial oils. In 1990 North Korea and the USSR concluded an agreement, at the latter's insistence, under which, from 1 January 1991, bilateral trade was to be conducted in convertible currencies and payments for Soviet petroleum were to be made at world market prices. As a result of the agreement and in the face of deteriorating relations between the two countries (at least, until the mid-1990s), between 1990 and 1992 North Korean imports of crude petroleum declined from 500,000 tons to 30,000 tons. The outcome was to make China the single most important source of petroleum imports, although when, in late 1992, Beijing imposed similar trading regulations, North Korea was forced to turn to the Middle East for crude petroleum supplies. Such temporizing manoeuvres were not, however, wholly successful and, in March 1996, worsening energy shortages prompted Kim Jong Il to instruct all factories and enterprises to reduce their use of coal and other energy sources, emphasizing that the deficit in raw materials and energy supply had become the most urgent problem facing the country.

A Soviet-designed nuclear research reactor, with a generating capacity of about 3 MW, was reportedly installed in Pyongyang as early as 1959. However, it is believed that a North Korean-Soviet agreement signed in 1985, whereby the USSR would construct a 1,760-MW nuclear power plant in North Korea, was never fulfilled (for more details of North Korea's nuclear installations, see History). In October 1994 North Korea and the USA signed a 'framework agreement' whereby Pyongyang agreed to suspend the development of nuclear weapons in exchange for the construction of two light-water reactors (LWRs) worth US $4,500m., in addition to receiving as much as 500,000 tons of petroleum annually for the duration of the construction period (forecast at 10 years). The project is managed by a consortium known as the Korean Peninsula Energy Development Organization (KEDO), whose three core members are Japan, the USA and South Korea. South Korea's state-run Korea Electric Power Corpn is the prime contractor for the project. Initial construction work commenced in August 1997, with some 5,000 South Korean engineers expected to work on the project. Progress towards its completion has, however, all too predictably been bedevilled by political disagreements. In May 2000, for example, North Korea demanded compensation in the form of food aid from the USA (which the latter refused to grant) for the delay in building the reactors, which, it argued, had exacerbated North Korea's already acute energy crisis. Because of such problems, the original completion date of 2003 of the first LWR was revised to 2008. An interesting question was whether the 1994 agreement could really meet North Korea's economic needs (rather than accommodate international concerns about its nuclear weapons programme). It was, for example, argued that a better approach might be to abandon the agreement in favour of upgrading the existing electrical grid and constructing new, efficient electricity-generating systems that ultimately might facilitate exports to the South. The 1994 agreement was placed in serious doubt following Pyongyang's admission in October 2002 that it had maintained a secret nuclear programme.

Such problems highlight the peculiar obstacles that make progress towards enhancing energy supplies in North Korea. As a result, even allowing for continuing domestic construction of small- and medium-scale facilities, increased investment in the power industry (for example, investment under the 2000 budget was intended to rise by 15.4%) and higher imports, improvements in the provision of energy will be slow. Large-scale infrastructural construction will also be necessary (North Korea possesses a mere 37 km and 180 km of pipelines to carry crude petroleum and its products). In short, it is safe to suppose that energy constraints will continue to impede North Korean economic growth into the foreseeable future.

Telecommunications

Telecommunications remain seriously under-developed in North Korea. In 1997, only 1.1m. main telephone lines were estimated to be in use and even today, the development of mobile phones has yet to begin. International connections are mainly made through Beijing and Moscow, although since the second half of the 1990s a direct telephone line has been established with South Korea. In March 2001 a Chinese source cited an official of the North Korean Central Science and Technology Information Agency to the effect that North Korea possessed a national e-mail network, known as 'Kuang Myong'. The report revealed, however, that the network only allows users to log on from within North Korea and that its content was limited to providing science and technology information.

Recent estimates suggest that there were about 3.36m. radios and 1.2m. television sets available to the North Korean population in 1997—an average of 15.5 and 5 per 100 persons, respectively.

In 2000 there was just one Internet Service Provider in North Korea. However, by 2001 North Korea had established six official websites, and in May of that year it joined Intelsat (the international commercial satellite telecommunications organization). In October 2001 North Korea launched its first e-mail service provider, known as 'Silibank'.

FINANCE

In the absence of a private sector, public (or government) finance in a planned economy plays the principal role in seeking to mobilize domestic savings for investment purposes and ensure financial equilibrium in the economy. There exist in North Korea a central government budget and local government budget—the two being consolidated into the national (state) budget. By the late 1980s central government revenue accounted for 85% of total revenue. The central government budget is largely financed from the central government's net income, transfers from local governments and other revenue sources. Revenue for the local government budget derives from local industrial and other sources, as well as from central government subsidies.

In 1995 government expenditure was estimated to constitute about 91% of GNP. The principal sources of revenue under the state budget were turnover (sales) taxes and state enterprise profits. The largest share of budget expenditure is allocated to economic development (officially put at 67.8% of total spending in 1994), followed by socio-cultural services (19%) and defence (11.6%). In reality, however, defence spending is much higher than these figures (for example, US and Australian government agencies have suggested such spending to have been as high as 25%–30% of the national budget), constituting a major fiscal drain. Peaceful reunification—or even simply political accommodation between North and South Korea—should permit a reduction in military expenditure and thereby allow a significant reallocation of resources to more productive economic ends. Apart from fiscal benefits, demobilization would also, by making more labour available, boost the expansion of labour-intensive light industrial manufactures, perhaps along the lines of China's township and village enterprises.

Like other formerly socialist countries, North Korea has traditionally pursued a conservative budgetary policy, through the maintenance of a balanced budget or generation of a budget surplus. In 1993, for example, official estimates pointed to a surplus of 328.2m. won. Notwithstanding a contraction in revenue of 3.2%, plans for 1994 looked to the attainment of a balanced budget. Because of the deepening economic crisis, the publication of budgetary data ceased in 1995, and only fragmentary information was subsequently made available. The combination of planned increases in revenue (by 3.1%) and spending (by 1.9%) together with a projected balanced budget (20,405m. won) implied that North Korea had suffered a budget deficit of 234m. won in the previous year. Data released in April 2001 suggest that a small surplus (of some 61m. won) was in fact achieved in 2000. Plans for 2001 looked for further increases in revenue (by 3.2%) and spending (by 2.9%)—figures which, if fulfilled, would generate another balanced budget of 21,571m. won. The same plans provided for a 16% rise in capital construction in 2001, as well as a 14.5% increase in military expenditure. It was not known to what extent these plans had been fulfilled.

Another way of improving North Korea's financial viability is to seek integration in international financial institutions. Thus, in 2000 North Korea submitted an application to join the Asian Development Bank (ADB). Hostility to such membership from the USA is one factor that has impeded efforts to improve North Korea's international financial profile.

FOREIGN TRADE AND FOREIGN INVESTMENT

A corollary of North Korea's self-reliant development policy has been, at least until recently, a downgrading of the role of foreign trade. As in other communist countries, the Government has pursued an essentially conservative and passive trade policy that emphasizes import-substitution in support of its programme of heavy industrialization. In other words, using its foreign relations merely to provide the goods trade has been primarily orientated towards importing the machinery, equipment and raw materials necessary to fulfil the output targets of successive economic plans, and to relieve unplanned shortages. Exports have been used mainly to pay for such imports, as well as to dispose of unplanned surpluses. This passive strategy has been reflected in a level of foreign trade that is much smaller than might have been expected of a country of North Korea's size and structure. The trade share, having peaked at 29.4% of GNP in 1975, thereafter fell sharply to 20% in 1985—and a mere 10% 10 years later. By way of comparison, at the end of the 1990s, the corresponding figure for South Korea was 50%–55%.

Even allowing for an expansion in trade with capitalist countries, these figures also reflected the declining role of foreign trade resulting from the onset of economic difficulties in the 1990s. Thus, having grown on average by 9.4% per annum during 1960–90 to reach US $4,800m. in 1990, the combined value of exports and imports subsequently declined sharply. By 1996, for example, exports had fallen to an estimated US $730m. (from US $1,700m. in 1990)—a downward trend which, despite being halted in 1997, was subsequently intensified (with exports of US $680m. and US $515.0m. in 1998 and 1999 respectively). Exports subsequently increased to US $565.8m. and US $650.2m. in 2000 and 2001 respectively. The decline in imports was less marked, but still significant (a fall from US $2,900m. in 1990 to US $964.6m. in 1999). However, imports increased to US $1,406.5m. and US $1,620.3m. in 2000 and 2001 respectively. In 1998 North Korea's trade turnover was estimated to be a mere US $1,400m. Implied in these figures was a foreign trade deficit of US $450m. in 1999. This deficit worsened, to US $840.7m. in 2000, and US $970.1m. in 2001. The estimates could usefully be compared with the corresponding figures for South Korea in 2000 (exports US $172,267.5m.; imports US $160,481.0m.) and 2001 (exports US $150,439.1m.; imports US $141,097.8m.).

In support of its economic modernization programme, in the early 1970s North Korea sought to use massive imports of advanced machinery and equipment from Western Europe and Japan. During the first half of the 1970s its trade balance steadily deteriorated and, unable to repay loans incurred as a result of such imports, in January 1976 it attracted world-wide notoriety when it became the first communist country to default on its foreign debt. Declining prices for North Korea's principal exports, rising import costs associated with the 1973 oil price rise, global recession and domestic transport difficulties—all contributed to the growing trade deficit and debt problem. In any case, the default resulted in a severe curtailment of Western credits to North Korea. Thereafter, its debt position continued to worsen, rising to US $5,200m. in 1988, and US $11,900m. in 1997. After the decision, in early 1999, by the Dutch investment bank, ING Barings, to cease operations in North Korea, the Government was forced to conduct international banking transactions through a limited number of banks in Japan and Macao.

Ideological and economic imperatives ensured that until the 1990s, North Korea's principal trading partners were other communist countries. Between 1955 and 1988, for example, trade with other communist countries rose, on average, by 11% per annum to reach US $3,290m. (compared with a trade turnover of US $600m. in 1995). Most important of all was the former Soviet Union, which in 1990 still accounted for 57% of North Korea's total foreign trade. The subsequent collapse of the USSR was a major watershed and in a single year, the former USSR's share had fallen to a mere 17.3% (in 1991). Nor has this decline been halted: by 1995 Russia was the source of 5% of North Korea's imports, and the destination for a mere 1% of its exports. An earlier watershed had, however, occurred in the 1970s, when North Korea began to purchase much-needed capital goods from capitalist countries (especially Japan). Between 1965 and 1975 bilateral trade vis-à-vis Japan rose by 23% per annum (North Korean imports increasing by 27% annually)—and during the next decade, by a further 6% per annum. Japan's leading role has been maintained to the present day, absorbing almost over one-third of North Korea's exports in 2000 and 2001, and about 15% of its imports during the same period.

For the 20 years after 1965 bilateral trade between North Korea and China rose by over 5% per annum, until it reached US $2,100m. (almost 15% of the DPRK's foreign trade). Thereafter, China's importance as a trading partner declined: by 1990 the value of bilateral trade had fallen to US $545m. (about 10%), and by 1999 to US $370m. Such, however, was the impact of the dramatic contraction in trade with the former USSR that China, meanwhile, emerged as North Korea's largest trading partner (in relative terms), accounting for about 30% of its total trade in 1999. In January 2001 a Chinese source reaffirmed China's role as North Korea's main trading partner, citing the shipment of exports worth US $438m. during January–November 2001 (in the same period, border trade with China's Liaoning Province was valued at US $75.6m.—54% more than during the same period of 1999). Overall, China was North Korea's principal trading partner in 2000 and 2001, accounting for 24.7% and 32.6% of North Korea's total trade in those years respectively. Other important trading partners, accounting for nearly 10% of total trade, were India and Thailand, the latter having only recently increased trade with North Korea.

In November 1988, for the first time since the Korean War, limited indirect trade with South Korea was resumed. Just two years later direct inter-Korean trade got under way, its value rising to US $210m. by 1992. By the end of the decade—and notwithstanding the temporary negative impact of the Asian financial crisis—inter-Korean trade had reached a record level of US $333.4m. (including some US $200m. in tour fees associated with the Mount Kumgang project), making South Korea the North's third largest trading partner. In 2000 bilateral trade increased further, to US $425m., pushing South Korea into second place after China. In the first seven months of 2002 inter-Korean trade rose by a reported 8.6%. Processing trade, especially of textile products, accounted for over half of such trade, although processed electronic imports from North Korea are expected to assume increasing importance in the coming years. Since 1991 North Korea has recorded an average annual surplus of about US $115m. in inter-Korean trade.

The fall of communist regimes in Eastern Europe and the dissolution of the USSR, as well as the insistence by both Russia and China on abandoning barter trading systems in favour of charging international prices for oil and other products, and the rapid expansion of inter-Korean trade, all suggest that a significant realignment of North Korea's economic relations is under way. At the same time, inefficiencies and infrastructural constraints (for example, low product quality and lack of variety, poor packaging, failure to meet delivery dates, and limited transport and harbour facilities) have continued to impede North Korean efforts to expand exports and increase much-needed foreign exchange earnings.

North Korea's principal exports include non-ferrous metals (mostly zinc, lead, barytes and gold), iron and steel, textile yarn and fabrics, military equipment, cement, vegetables and fishery products. The main imports are advanced machinery, transport equipment, high-grade iron and steel products, crude petroleum, coking coal, grain, chemicals and some consumer goods.

Throughout its existence, North Korea has almost consistently suffered an unfavourable trade balance. This remained the norm throughout the 1990s, although, despite falling farm exports, the deficit is estimated to have declined from US $700m. in 1991 to around US $300m. in 1998. This improvement was interrupted in 1999, when North Korea's global deficit rose to US $450m. (US $260m. in January–June alone). In recent years North Korea's current-account deficit and foreign debt difficulties have been alleviated by inflows of convertible currency from pro-Pyongyang Koreans living in Japan. Such contributions and remittances reportedly ranged from US $600m. to US $1,000m. per year—the latter figure approximating to total annual North Korean exports in the early 1990s.

The introduction, in 1984, of a joint-venture law (revised in 1994) signalled North Korea's willingness to use—by its own standards—radical means in order to acquire Western capital and technology. Initially, such efforts achieved only limited success. Indeed, the Ministry of Joint-Venture Industry, established in 1988, was closed down in 1990 and its responsibilities transferred to the General Bureau of Joint Venture, under the External Economic Affairs Commission. Of an estimated 140 joint ventures under way by 1994, about three-quarters involved companies owned by pro-Pyongyang Korean residents of Japan. Most of them were small, with an average capitalization of under US $1m.

Meanwhile, it was expected that government plans to establish special economic zones would stimulate further joint-venture activities, as well as encourage involvement by South Korean companies. Attempts to attract foreign capital into the Rajin-Sonbong Free Economic and Trade Zone, which was established in the Tumen River delta in 1991, were initially largely unsuccessful. By the end of 1997, for example, it was reported that although 111 contracts (worth some US $751m.) had been agreed, only 77 of them were under way, with associated utilized investment of US $57m. The Tumen River project was sponsored by the UNDP and the first specifically inter-Korean joint-venture agreement—with the South Korean Daewoo conglomerate—was concluded in January 1992, when the North Korean Government began to enact new laws designed to offer even more preferential treatment to foreign investors than that available under Chinese laws. In practice, foreign-exchange shortages, infrastructural deficiencies, uncooperative bureaucrats and low levels of skilled labour have prevented North Korea from realizing any significant benefits from the Rajin-Sonbong project, leading some to judge it to be a failure. Its future, according to some outside observers, may lie more in the direction of acting as a regional, trans-shipment base for North Korean exports to China.

The construction, in the late 1980s and early 1990s, of an international telecommunications centre, a new international airport and international hotels is a clear expression of North Korea's willingness to open the country to foreign tourism in order to improve its invisible trade balance. The most significant initiative in this context was the commencement, in November 1998, of a joint venture involving the South Korean conglomerate, Hyundai, to send daily tour boats to Mount Kumgang, representing the only ever opportunity for South Korean tourists to visit the North. By May 2000 North Korea had earned some US $180m. from the project, and in July of that year the Pyongyang authorities put forward the suggestion that Hyundai should develop a high-technology zone in the same area—a proposal unlikely to be realized in the near future. Indeed, in the face of major losses on the project, in January and February 2001, it was revealed that Hyundai was seeking to halve its monthly royalty payment on the Mount Kumgang project from US$12m. to US $6m.—this in spite of well over a quarter of a million tourist visits to the region.

Such difficulties notwithstanding, it was likely that North Korea would persist in its efforts to encourage greater foreign involvement in its economic development. In 2001 a South Korean source reported that China and North Korea had reached agreement on the creation of a 'second Shenzhen' through the establishment of an economic zone based on Shinuiju and Dandong, which would act as a distribution centre for light industrial goods. (In 1999 Shinuiju had already been proposed to Hyundai as a special economic zone and industrial complex.) In late September 2002 Yang Bin, a wealthy Chinese-born businessman with Dutch citizenship and Chairman of the Euro-Asia Group, was appointed Chief Executive of the Shinuiju Special Administrative Region, seemingly confirming Pyongyang's commitment to Chinese-style economic reforms. In addition, since 2000 Pyongyang has made extensive efforts to establish diplomatic relations with wealthier nations such as the United Kingdom, Italy, Australia, the Philippines and other countries—initiatives clearly not unconnected with its desire to accelerate economic growth and development. In July of the same year North Korea also became a member of the ASEAN Regional Forum (ARF).

Statistical Survey

Area and Population

AREA, POPULATION AND DENSITY*

Area (sq km)	122,762†
Population (census results)	
31 December 1993	
Males	10,329,699
Females	10,883,679
Total	21,213,378
Population (UN estimates at mid-year)‡	
1999	22,110,000
2000	22,268,000
2001	22,428,000
Density (per sq km) at mid-2001	182.7

* Excluding the demilitarized zone between North and South Korea, with an area of 1,262 sq km (487 sq miles).

† 47,399 sq miles.

‡ Source: UN, *World Population Prospects: The 2000 Revision*.

PRINCIPAL TOWNS (population at 1993 census)

Pyongyang (capital)	2,741,260	Wonsan	300,148
Nampo	731,448	Pyongsong	272,934
Hamhung	709,730	Sariwon	254,146
Chongjin	582,480	Haeju	229,172
Kaesong	334,433	Kanggye	223,410
Shinuiju	326,011	Hyesan	178,020

Source: UN, *Demographic Yearbook*.

BIRTHS AND DEATHS (UN estimates, annual averages)

	1985–90	1990–95	1995–2000
Birth rate (per 1,000)	20.6	20.8	18.6
Death rate (per 1,000)	5.8	7.0	10.4

Expectation of life (UN estimates, years at birth, 1995–2000): 63.1 (males 60.5; females 66.0).

Source: UN, *World Population Prospects: The 2000 Revision*.

ECONOMICALLY ACTIVE POPULATION
(ILO estimates, '000 persons at mid-1980)

	Males	Females	Total
Agriculture, etc.	1,484	1,870	3,355
Industry	1,654	719	2,373
Services	1,103	1,007	2,110
Total labour force	4,241	3,597	7,838

Source: ILO, *Economically Active Population Estimates and Projections, 1950–2025*.

Mid-2000 (estimates in '000): Agriculture, etc. 3,439; Total labour force 11,421 (Source: FAO).

Health and Welfare

KEY INDICATORS

Fertility (births per woman, 2000)	2.1
Under-5 mortality rate (per 1,000 live births, 2000)	30
HIV/AIDS (% of persons aged 15–49, 1994)	<0.01
Health expenditure (1998): US $ per head (PPP)	30
% of GDP	3.0
public (% of total)	83.5
Access to water (% of persons, 2000)	100
Access to sanitation (% of persons, 2000)	99

For sources and definitions, see explanatory note on p. vi.

Agriculture

PRINCIPAL CROPS
('000 metric tons)

	1998	1999	2000
Wheat*	165	97	50
Rice (paddy)	2,307	2,343	1,690
Barley	90	55*	29*
Maize	1,765	1,235	1,041
Rye†	70	75	75
Oats†	10	10	11
Millet†	10	20	45
Sorghum†	5	10	10
Potatoes	1,269	1,473	1,870
Sweet potatoes*	423	490	290
Pulses†	280	280	280
Soybeans (Soya beans)	340*	340*	350†
Cottonseed†	22	23	23
Cabbages†	625	625	630
Tomatoes†	61	62	62
Pumpkins, squash and gourds†	83	83	85
Cucumbers and gherkins†	64	64	64
Aubergines (Eggplants)†	42	42	42
Chillies and green peppers†	54	55	55
Green onions and shallots†	85	90	90
Dry onions†	80	82	82
Garlic†	73	75	80
Other vegetables†	2,205	2,206	2,406
Apples†	640	650	650
Pears†	125	125	130
Peaches and nectarines†	100	110	110
Watermelons†	103	103	104
Cantaloupes and other melons†	108	108	110
Other fruits and berries†	455	460	460
Tobacco (leaves)†	62	62	63
Hemp fibre†	12	12	13
Cotton (lint)†	11	11	11

* Unofficial figure(s). † FAO estimate(s).

Source: FAO.

LIVESTOCK ('000 head, year ending September)

	1998	1999	2000
Horses*	44	45	45
Cattle	565	577	579
Pigs	2,475	2,970	3,120
Sheep	165	185	185
Goats	1,508	1,900	2,276
Chickens	9,427	11,200	15,733
Ducks	1,372	1,624	2,078
Rabbits	2,795	5,202	11,475

* FAO estimates.

Source: FAO.

LIVESTOCK PRODUCTS ('000 metric tons)

	1998	1999	2000
Beef and veal	19.5	20.0	20.0
Goat meat	6.8	9.0	9.9
Pig meat	111.5	133.8	140.0
Poultry meat	20.4	23.4	26.8
Cows' milk*	85.0	86.0	90.0
Poultry eggs*	83.0	95.0	95.0
Cattle hides (fresh)	2.7	2.8	2.8

* FAO estimates.

Source: FAO.

Forestry

ROUNDWOOD REMOVALS
(FAO estimates, '000 cubic metres, excl. bark)

	1998	1999	2000
Sawlogs, veneer logs and logs for sleepers	1,000	1,000	1,000
Other industrial wood	500	500	500
Fuel wood	5,356	5,429	5,503
Total	6,856	6,929	7,003

Sawnwood production ('000 cubic metres, incl. railway sleepers): 280 (coniferous 185, broadleaved 95) per year in 1970–2000 (FAO estimates).

Source: FAO.

Fishing

('000 metric tons, live weight)

	1997	1998*	1999*
Capture	236.5	220.0	210.0
Freshwater fishes	20.0	20.0	20.0
Alaska pollock	66.6	60.0	55.0
Other marine fishes	120.3	114.9	109.9
Marine crustaceans	15.3	15.0	15.0
Squids	14.2	10.0	10.0
Aquaculture	70.2	68.5	68.5
Molluscs	66.6	65.0	65.0
Total catch	306.6	288.5	278.5

Note: Figures exclude aquatic plants ('000 metric tons, aquaculture only): 419.1 in 1997; 413.0* in 1998; 413.0* in 1999.

* FAO estimate(s).

Source: FAO, *Yearbook of Fishery Statistics.*

Mining

(estimates, '000 metric tons, unless otherwise indicated)

	1998	1999	2000
Hard coal	55,000	50,000	50,000
Brown coal and lignite	30,000	30,000	30,000
Iron ore: gross weight	700	700	700
metal content	300	300	300
Copper ore*	14	14	14
Lead ore*	70	70	70
Zinc ore*	200	190	190
Tungsten concentrates (metric tons)*	800	700	700
Silver (metric tons)*	45	40	40
Gold (kg)*	4,500	4,500	5,000
Magnesite (crude)	1,500	1,000	1,000
Phosphate rock†	450	350	350
Fluorspar‡	30	25	25
Barite (Barytes)	100	70	70
Salt (unrefined)	550	500	500
Graphite (natural)	35	33	30
Talc, soapstone and pyrophyllite	150	120	120

Note: No recent data are available for the production of molybdenum ore and asbestos.

* Figures refer to the metal content of ores and concentrates.

† Figures refer to gross weight. The phosphoric acid content (estimates, '000 metric tons) was: 142 in 1998; 105 in 1999; 105 in 2000.

‡ Metallurgical grade.

Source: US Geological Survey.

Industry

SELECTED PRODUCTS
('000 metric tons, unless otherwise indicated)

	1995	1996	1997
Nitrogenous fertilizers *	75	72	72
Motor spirit (petrol)†	960	950	930
Kerosene†	205	200	190
Gas-diesel (Distillate fuel) oils†	1,040	1,035	1,025
Residual fuel oils†	605	600	590
Coke-oven coke (excl. breeze)†	3,500	3,450	3,400
Cement†‡	17,000	17,000	17,000
Pig-iron†‡	500	500	450
Crude steel†‡	1,500	1,000	1,000
Refined copper (unwrought)†‡	27	28	28
Lead (primary metal)†‡	75	75	75
Zinc (primary metal)†‡	200	200	200
Electric energy (million kWh)†	36,000	35,000	33,990

* Output is measured in terms of nitrogen.

† Provisional or estimated figures.

‡ Data from the US Geological Survey.

Source: mainly UN, *Industrial Commodity Statistics Yearbook.*

1998 (estimates, '000 metric tons): Nitrogenous fertilizers 72; Cement 17,000; Pig-iron 250; Crude steel 1,000; Refined copper (unwrought) 28; Lead (primary metal) 75; Zinc (primary metal) 180.

1999 (estimates, '000 metric tons): Cement 16,000; Pig-iron 250; Crude steel 1,000; Refined copper (unwrought) 25; Lead (primary metal) 70; Zinc (primary metal) 180.

2000 (estimates, '000 metric tons): Cement 15,000; Pig-iron 250; Crude steel 1,000; Refined copper (unwrought) 25; Lead (primary metal) 70; Zinc (primary metal) 200.

Source: mainly US Geological Survey.

Finance

CURRENCY AND EXCHANGE RATES

Monetary Units

100 chon (jun) = 1 won.

Sterling, Dollar and Euro Equivalents (31 May 2002)

£1 sterling = 3.153 won;
US $1 = 2.150 won;
€1 = 2.018 won;
100 won = £31.71 = $46.51 = €49.55.

Note: In August 2002 it was reported that a currency reform had been introduced, whereby the exchange rate was adjusted from US $1 = 2.15 won to $1 = 150 won: a devaluation of 98.6%.

BUDGET (projected, million won)

	1992	1993	1994
Revenue	39,500.9	40,449.9	41,525.2
Expenditure	39,500.9	40,449.9	41,525.2
Economic development	26,675.1	27,423.8	28,164.0
Socio-cultural sector	7,730.6	7,751.5	8,218.3
Defence	4,582.1	4,692.2	4,816.9
Administration and management	513.1	582.4	326.0

1998 (estimates, million won): Total revenue 19,790.8; Total expenditure 20,015.2.

1999 (estimates, million won): Total revenue 19,801.0; Total expenditure 20,018.2.

2000 (estimates, million won): Total revenue 20,955.0; Total expenditure 20,903.0.

2001 (projected, million won): Total revenue 21,571.0; Total expenditure 21,571.0.

2002 (projected, million won): Total revenue 22,174.0; Total expenditure 22,174.0.

NATIONAL ACCOUNTS

Gross Domestic Product by Economic Activity (% of total)

	1997	1998	1999
Agriculture, forestry and fishing	28.9	29.6	31.4
Mining	6.7	6.6	7.3
Manufacturing	18.8	19.0	18.3
Electricity, gas and water	4.3	4.2	4.5
Construction	6.3	5.1	6.1
Government services	25.1	25.3	22.8
Other services	9.9	10.2	9.6
Total	100.0	100.0	100.0

Source: Bank of Korea (Republic of Korea).

External Trade

PRINCIPAL COMMODITIES (US $ million)*

Imports	1999	2000	2001
Live animals and animal products	101.3	20.3	73.9
Vegetable products		159.0	221.0
Animal or vegetable fats and oils; prepared edible fats; animal or vegetable waxes; Prepared foodstuffs; beverages, spirits and vinegar; tobacco and manufactured substitutes	58.2	89.1	89.9
Mineral products	141.0	171.2	231.1
Products of chemical or allied industries	96.4	108.4	123.4
Plastics, rubber and articles thereof	51.0	67.5	66.0
Textiles and textile articles	127.1	171.9	203.9
Base metals and articles thereof	59.0	85.2	100.4
Machinery and mechanical appliances; electrical equipment; sound and television apparatus	135.6	205.1	243.8
Vehicles, aircraft, vessels and associated transport equipment	102.2	146.2	88.4
Total (incl. others)	964.6	1,406.5	1,620.3

Exports	1999	2000	2001
Live animals and animal products	87.8	97.9	158.4
Vegetable products	22.5	30.3	42.0
Mineral products	22.6	43.2	50.5
Products of chemical or allied industries; Plastics, rubber and articles thereof	39.9	44.9	44.6
Wood, cork and articles thereof; wood charcoal; manufactures of straw, esparto, etc.	16.2	10.9	5.6
Textiles and textile articles	130.6	140.0	140.5
Natural or cultured pearls, precious or semi-precious stones, precious metals and articles thereof; imitation jewellery; coin	21.4	9.8	14.1
Base metals and articles thereof	46.5	43.9	60.2
Machinery and mechanical appliances; electrical equipment, sound and television apparatus	81.3	105.2	97.9
Total (incl. others)	515.0	565.8	650.2

* Excluding trade with the Republic of Korea (US $ million): Imports 211.8 in 1999, 272.8 in 2000, 226.8 in 2001; Exports 121.6 in 1999, 152.4 in 2000, 176.2 in 2001.

Source: Korea Trade-Investment Promotion Agency (KOTRA), Republic of Korea.

PRINCIPAL TRADING PARTNERS (US $ million)*

Imports	1999	2000	2001
China, People's Republic	328.7	450.8	573.1
Germany	32.6	53.6	82.1
Hong Kong	60.5	68.5	42.6
India	98.0	142.9	154.8
Japan	147.8	206.8	249.1
Russia	48.5	42.9	63.8
Singapore	48.1	46.2	112.3
Spain	n.a.	15.3	31.6
Taiwan	11.7	n.a.	n.a.
Thailand	34.7	188.3	109.6
United Kingdom	22.1	25.3	40.7
USA	11.3	n.a.	n.a.
Total (incl. others)	964.6	1,406.5	1,620.3

Exports	1999	2000	2001
Bangladesh	24.2	n.a.	n.a.
China, People's Republic	41.7	37.2	166.7
Germany	23.7	25.6	22.8
Hong Kong	63.3	46.4	38.0
India	44.3	25.5	3.1
Japan	202.6	256.9	225.6
Spain	n.a.	12.7	12.6
Thailand	3.2	19.5	24.9
Total (incl. others)	515.0	565.8	650.2

* Excluding trade with the Republic of Korea (US $ million): Imports 211.8 in 1999, 272.8 in 2000, 226.8 in 2001; Exports 121.6 in 1999, 152.4 in 2000, 176.2 in 2001.

Source: Korea Trade-Investment Promotion Agency (KOTRA), Republic of Korea.

Transport

SHIPPING

Merchant Fleet (registered at 31 December)

	1999	2000	2001
Number of vessels	171	176	176
Total displacement ('000 grt)	657.8	652.6	697.8

Source: Lloyd's Register-Fairplay, *World Fleet Statistics*.

International Sea-Borne Freight Traffic (estimates, '000 metric tons)

	1988	1989	1990
Goods loaded	630	640	635
Goods unloaded	5,386	5,500	5,520

Source: UN, *Monthly Bulletin of Statistics*.

CIVIL AVIATION (traffic on scheduled services)

	1995	1996	1997
Kilometres flown (million)	3	3	5
Passengers carried ('000)	254	254	280
Passenger-km (million)	207	207	286
Total ton-km (million)	22	22	30

Source: UN, *Statistical Yearbook*.

Tourism

	1996	1997	1998
Tourist arrivals ('000)	127	128	130

Source: World Tourism Organization, mainly *Yearbook of Tourism Statistics*.

Communications Media

	1994	1995	1996
Radio receivers ('000 in use)	2,950	3,000	3,300
Television receivers ('000 in use)	1,000	1,050	1,090
Telephones ('000 main lines in use)*	1,100	1,100	1,100
Telefax stations (number in use)	3,000*	n.a.	n.a.
Daily newspapers:			
Number	11	11*	3
Average circulation ('000 copies)*	5,000	5,000	4,500

* Estimate(s).

1997 ('000 in use): Radio receivers 3,360; Television receivers 1,200.

Sources: UNESCO, *Statistical Yearbook*; UN, *Statistical Yearbook*.

Education

(1987/88)

	Institutions	Teachers	Students
Pre-primary	16,964	35,000	728,000
Primary	4,810*	59,000	1,543,000
Secondary	4,840*	111,000	2,468,000
Universities and colleges	519†	23,000	325,000
Other tertiary	n.a.	4,000	65,000

* 1997 figure.

† Of which 46 were university-level institutions and 473 were colleges (1986).

Source: mainly UNESCO, *Statistical Yearbook*.

Directory

The Constitution

A new Constitution was adopted on 27 December 1972. According to South Korean sources, several amendments were made in April 1992, including the deletion of references to Marxism-Leninism, the extension of the term of the Supreme People's Assembly from four to five years, and the promotion of limited 'economic openness'. Extensive amendments to the Constitution were approved on 5 September 1998. The main provisions of the revised Constitution are summarized below:

The Democratic People's Republic of Korea is an independent socialist state; the revolutionary traditions of the State are stressed (its ideological basis being the *Juche* idea of the Korean Workers' Party), as is the desire to achieve national reunification by peaceful means on the basis of national independence. The Late President Kim Il Sung is the Eternal President of the Republic.

National sovereignty rests with the working people, who exercise power through the Supreme People's Assembly and Local People's Assemblies at lower levels, which are elected by universal, equal and direct suffrage by secret ballot.

The foundation of an independent national economy, based on socialist and *Juche* principles, is stressed. The means of production are owned solely by the State and socialist co-operative organizations.

Culture and education provide the working people with knowledge to advance a socialist way of life. Education is free, universal and compulsory for 11 years.

Defence is emphasized, as well as the rights of overseas nationals, the principles of friendly relations between nations based on equality, mutual respect and non-interference, proletarian internationalism, support for national liberation struggles and due observance of law.

The basic rights and duties of citizens are laid down and guaranteed. These include the right to vote and to be elected (for citizens who are more than 17 years of age), to work (the working day being eight hours), to free medical care and material assistance for the old, infirm or disabled, and to political asylum. National defence is the supreme duty of citizens.

THE STRUCTURE OF STATE

The Supreme People's Assembly

The Supreme People's Assembly is the highest organ of state power, exercises legislative power and is elected by direct, equal, universal and secret ballot for a term of five years. Its chief functions are: (i) to adopt, amend or supplement legal or constitutional enactments; (ii) to determine state policy; (iii) to elect the Chairman of the National Defence Commission; (iv) to elect the Vice-Chairmen and other members of the National Defence Commission (on the recommendation of the Chairman of the National Defence Commission); (v) to elect the President and other members of the Presidium of the Supreme People's Assembly, the Premier of the Cabinet, the President of the Central Court and other legal officials; (vi) to appoint the Vice-Premiers and other members of the Cabinet (on the recommendation of the Premier of the Cabinet); (vii) to approve the State Plan and Budget; (viii) to receive a report on the work of the Cabinet and adopt measures, if necessary; (ix) to decide on the ratification or abrogation of treaties. It holds regular and extraordinary sessions, the former being once or twice a year, the latter as necessary at the request of at least one-third of the deputies. Legislative enactments are adopted when approved by more than one-half of those deputies present. The Constitution is amended and supplemented when approved by more than two-thirds of the total number of deputies.

The National Defence Commission

The National Defence Commission, which consists of a Chairman, first Vice-Chairman, other Vice-Chairmen and members, is the highest military organ of state power, and is accountable to the Supreme People's Assembly. The National Defence Commission directs and commands the armed forces and guides defence affairs. The Chairman of the National Defence Commission serves a five-year term of office and has the most senior post in the state hierarchy.

The Presidium of the Supreme People's Assembly

The Presidium of the Supreme People's Assembly, which consists of a President, Vice-Presidents, secretaries and members, is the highest organ of power in the intervals between sessions of the Supreme People's Assembly, to which it is accountable. It exercises the following chief functions: (i) to convene sessions of the Supreme People's Assembly; (ii) to examine and approve new legislation, the State Plan and the State Budget, when the Supreme People's Assembly is in recess; (iii) to interpret the Constitution and legislative enactments; (iv) to supervise the observance of laws of State organs; (v) to organize elections to the Supreme People's Assembly and Local People's Assemblies; (vi) to form or abolish ministries or commissions of the Cabinet; (vii) to appoint or remove Vice-Premiers and other cabinet or ministry members, on the recommendation of the Premier, when the Supreme People's Assembly is not in session; (viii) to elect or transfer judges of the Central Court; (ix) to ratify or abrogate treaties concluded with other countries; (x) to appoint or recall diplomatic envoys; (xi) to confer decorations, medals, honorary titles and diplomatic ranks; (xii) to grant general amnesties or special pardon. The President of the Presidium represents the State and receives credentials and letters of recall of diplomatic representatives accredited by a foreign state.

The Cabinet

The Cabinet is the administrative and executive body of the Supreme People's Assembly and a general state management organ. It serves a five-year term and comprises the Premier, Vice-Premiers, Chairmen of Commissions and other necessary members. Its major functions are the following: (i) to adopt measures to execute state policy; (ii) to guide the work of ministries and other organs responsible to it; (iii) to establish and remove direct organs of the Cabinet and main administrative economic organizations; (iv) to draft the State Plan and adopt measures to make it effective; (v) to compile the State Budget and to implement its provisions; (vi) to organize and execute the work of all sectors of the economy, as well as education, science, culture, health and environmental protection; (vii) to adopt measures to strengthen the monetary and banking system; (viii) to adopt measures to maintain social order, protect State interests and guarantee citizens' rights; (ix) to conclude treaties; (x) to abolish decisions and directives of economic administrative organs which run counter to those of the Cabinet. The Cabinet is accountable to the Supreme People's Assembly.

Local People's Assemblies

The Local People's Assemblies and Committees of the province (or municipality directly under central authority), city (or district) and county are local organs of power. The Local People's Assemblies consist of deputies elected by direct, equal, universal and secret ballot. The Local People's Committees consist of a Chairman, Vice-Chairmen, secretaries and members. The Local People's Assemblies and Committees serve a four-year term and exercise local budgetary functions, elect local administrative and judicial personnel and carry out the decisions at local level of higher executive and administrative organs.

THE JUDICIARY

Justice is administered by the Central Court (the highest judicial organ of the State), local courts and the Special Court. Judges and other legal officials are elected by the Supreme People's Assembly. The Central Court protects state property, constitutional rights, guarantees that all state bodies and citizens observe state laws, and executes judgments. Justice is administered by the court comprising one judge and two people's assessors. The court is independent and judicially impartial. Judicial affairs are conducted by the Central Procurator's Office, which exposes and institutes criminal proceedings against accused persons. The Office of the Central Procurator is responsible to the Chairman of the National Defence Commission, the Supreme People's Assembly and the Central People's Committee.

The Government

HEAD OF STATE

President: (President Kim Il Sung died on 8 July 1994 and was declared 'Eternal President' in September 1998).

Chairman of the National Defence Commission: Marshal Kim Jong Il.

First Vice-Chairman: Vice-Marshal Jo Myong Rok.

Vice-Chairmen: Vice-Marshal Kim Il Chol, Vice-Marshal Ri Yong Mu.

Other members: Vice-Marshal Kim Yong Chun, Yon Hyong Muk, Marshal Ri Ul Sol, Vice-Marshal Paek Hak Rim, Jon Byong Ho, Kim Chol Man.

CABINET
(September 2002)

Premier: Hong Song Nam.

Vice-Premiers: Jo Chang Dok, Kwak Pom Gi.

Vice-Premier and Chairman of the Commission for Capital Construction: Col-Gen. Shin Il Nam.

Minister of Foreign Affairs: Paek Nam Sun.

Minister of Public Security: Vice-Marshal Paek Hak Rim.

Minister of the People's Armed Forces: Vice-Marshal Kim Il Chol.

Chairman of the State Planning Commission: Pak Nam Gi.

Minister of Power and Coal Industry: O Gwang Hong.

Minister of Extractive Industries: Son Jong Ho.

Minister of Metal and Machine-Building Industries: Jon Sung Hun.

Minister of Construction and Building Materials Industries: Jo Yun Hui.

Minister of the Electronics Industry: O Su Yong.

Minister of Railways: Kim Yong Sam.

Minister of Land and Marine Transport: Kim Yong Il.

Minister of Agriculture: Kim Chang Shik.

Minister of Chemical Industry: Pak Pong Ju.

Minister of Light Industry: Ri Ju O.

Minister of Foreign Trade: Ri Kwang Gun.

Minister of Forestry: Ri Sang Mu.

Minister of Fisheries: Ri Song Ung.

Minister of City Management: Choe Jong Gon.

Minister of Land and Environmental Protection: Jang Il Son.

Minister of State Construction Control: Pae Tal Jun.

Minister of Commerce: Ri Yong Son.

Minister of Procurement and Food Administration: Choe Nam Gyun.

Minister of Education: Pyon Yong Rip.

Minister of Post and Telecommunications: Ri Kum Bom.

Minister of Culture: Kang Nung Su.

Minister of Finance: Mun Il Bong.

Minister of Labour: Ri Won Il.

Minister of Public Health: Kim Su Hak.

Minister of State Inspection: Kim Ui Sun.

Chairman of the Physical Culture and Sports Guidance Committee: Pak Myong Chol.

President of the National Academy of Sciences: Ri Kwang Ho.

President of the Central Bank: Kim Wan Su.

Director of the Central Statistics Bureau: Kim Chang Su.

Chief Secretary of the Cabinet: Jong Mun San.

MINISTRIES

All Ministries and Commissions are in Pyongyang.

Legislature

CHOE KO IN MIN HOE UI
(Supreme People's Assembly)

The 687 members of the 10th Supreme People's Assembly (SPA) were elected unopposed for a five-year term on 26 July 1998. Its permanent body is the Presidium.

Chairman: Choe Tae Bok.

Vice-Chairmen: Chang Chol, Ryo Won Gu.

President of the Presidium: Kim Yong Nam.

Vice-Presidents of the Presidium: Yang Hyong Sop, Kim Yong Dae.

Political Organizations

Democratic Front for the Reunification of the Fatherland: Pyongyang; f. 1946; a vanguard organization comprising political parties and mass working people's organizations seeking the unification of North and South Korea; Mems of Presidium Pak Song Chol, Ryom Tae Jun, Yang Hyong Sop, Jong Tu Hwan, Ri Yong Su, Jong Shin Hyok, Kim Pong Ju, Pyon Chang Bok, Ryu Mi Yong, Ryo Won Gu, Yun Ki Bok, Kang Ryon Hak.

The component parties are:

Chondoist Chongu Party: Pyongyang; tel. (2) 334241; f. 1946; supports policies of Korean Workers' Party; follows the guiding principle of *Innaechon* (the realization of 'heaven on earth'); Chair. Ryu Mi Yong.

Korean Social Democratic Party (KSDP) (Joson Sahoeminjudang): Pyongyang; tel. (2) 5211981; fax (2) 3814410; f. 1945; advocates national independence and a democratic socialist society; supports policies of Korean Workers' Party; Chair. Kim Yong Dae; First Vice-Chair. Kang Pyong Hak.

Korean Workers' Party (KWP): Pyongyang; f. 1945; merged with the South Korean Workers' Party in 1949; the guiding principle is the *Juche* idea, based on the concept that man is the master and arbiter of all things; 3m. mems; Gen. Sec. Marshal Kim Jong Il.

Sixth Central Committee

General Secretary: Marshal Kim Jong Il.

Politburo

Presidium: Marshal Kim Jong Il.

Full Members:

Kim Yong Nam, Pak Song Chol, Kim Yong Ju, Kye Ung Tae, Jon Byong Ho, Han Song Ryong.

Alternate Members:

Hong Song Nam, Yon Hyong Muk, Yang Hyong Sop, Choe Tae Bok, Kim Chol Man, Choe Yong Rim, Ri Son Shil.

Secretariat:

Marshal Kim Jong Il, Kye Ung Tae, Jon Byong Ho, Han Song Ryong, Choe Tae Bok, Kim Ki Nam, Kim Kuk Tae, Kim Jung Rin, So Kwan Hi, Kim Yong Sun, Jong Ha Chol.

The component mass working people's organizations are:

General Federation of Trade Unions of Korea (GFTUK).

Kim Il Sung Socialist Youth League.

Korean Democratic Women's Union (KDWU).

Union of Agricultural Working People of Korea.

(See under Trade Unions.)

There is one opposition organization in exile, with branches in Tokyo (Japan), Moscow (Russia) and Beijing (People's Republic of China):

Salvation Front for the Democratic Unification of Chosun: f. early 1990s; seeks the overthrow of the Kim dynasty, the establishment of democracy in the DPRK and Korean reunification; Chair. PAK KAP DONG.

Diplomatic Representation

EMBASSIES IN THE DEMOCRATIC PEOPLE'S REPUBLIC OF KOREA

Algeria: Munsudong, Taedongkang District, Pyongyang; tel. (2) 90372; Ambassador: MOKHTAR REGUIEG.

Benin: Pyongyang; Ambassador: A. OGIST.

Bulgaria: Munsudong, Taedongkang District, Pyongyang; tel. (2) 3817341; Ambassador: YORDAN MUTAFCHIYEV.

China, People's Republic: Pyongyang; tel. (2) 3813116; fax (2) 3813425; Ambassador: WU DONGHE.

Cuba: POB 5, Pyongyang; tel. (2) 3817370; fax (2) 3817703; Ambassador: ESTEBAN LOBAINA ROMERO.

Egypt: Pyongyang; tel. (2) 3817406; fax (2) 3817611; Ambassador: MAHMUD MUHAMMAD FARAQ ZAYN.

Ethiopia: POB 55, Munsudong, Taedongkang District, Pyongyang; tel. (2) 3817750; fax (2) 3817618; Chargé d'affaires: FEKADE S.G. MESKEL.

India: Block 53, Munsudong, Taehak St, Taedongkang District, Pyongyang; tel. (2) 3817274; fax (2) 3817619; Ambassador: R. P. SINGH.

Indonesia: 5 Foreigners' Bldg, Munsudong, Taedongkang District, Pyongyang; tel. (2) 3817386; fax (2) 3817612; e-mail kbripyg@public.east.cn.net; Ambassador: BUCHARI EFFENDI.

Iran: Munhungdong, Monsu St, Taedongkang District, Pyongyang; tel. (2) 3817492; fax (2) 3817612; Ambassador: MOHAMMAD GANJIDOOST.

Laos: Pyongyang; Ambassador: KHAMKENG SAYAKEO.

Libya: Pyongyang; Secretary of People's Bureau: AHMED AMER AL-MUAKKAF.

Mali: Pyongyang; Ambassador: NAKOUNTE DIAKITÉ.

Mongolia: Pyongyang; tel. (2) 3817324; Ambassador: J. LOMBO.

Nigeria: POB 535, Pyongyang; tel. (2) 3817286; fax (2) 3817613; Ambassador: ADOGA ONAH.

Pakistan: Munsudong, Taedongkang District, Pyongyang; tel. (2) 3817479; fax 3817622; Ambassador: SULTAN HABIB.

Poland: Munsudong, Taedongkang District, Pyongyang; tel. (2) 3817327; fax (2) 3817634; Ambassador: WOJCIECH KALUZA.

Romania: Munhengdong, Pyongyang; tel. (2) 3817336; Ambassador: NICOLAE GIRBA.

Russia: Shinyangdong, Chung Kuyuck, Pyongyang; tel. (2) 3813101; fax (2) 3813427; Ambassador: ANDREI KARLOV.

Syria: Munsudong, Taedongkang District, Pyongyang; tel. (2) 349323; Ambassador: YASSER AL-FARRA.

Thailand: Pyongyang; Ambassador: NIKHOM TANTEMSAPYA.

United Kingdom: Munsudong, Pyongyang; tel. (2) 3817980; fax (2) 3817985; Ambassador: DAVID SLINN.

Viet Nam: Munsudong, Taedongkang District, Pyongyang; tel. (2) 3817353; fax (2) 3817632; Ambassador: LE XUAN VINH.

Yugoslavia: Pyongyang; Ambassador: LJUBOMIR DJUKIĆ.

Judicial System

The judicial organs include the Central Court, the Court of the Province (or city under central authority) and the People's Court. Each court is composed of judges and people's assessors.

Procurators supervise the ordinances and regulations of all ministries and the decisions and directives of local organs of state power to ensure that they conform to the Constitution, laws and decrees, as well as to the decisions and other measures of the Cabinet. Procurators bring suits against criminals in the name of the State, and participate in civil cases to protect the interests of the State and citizens.

Central Court: Pyongyang; the highest judicial organ; supervises the work of all courts.

President: KIM BYONG RYUL.

First Vice-President: YUN MYONG GUK.

Central Procurator's Office: supervises work of procurator's offices in provinces, cities and counties.

Procurator-General: CHOE YONG RIM.

Religion

The religions that are officially reported to be practised in the DPRK are Buddhism, Christianity and Chundo Kyo, a religion peculiar to Korea combining elements of Buddhism and Christianity. Religious co-ordinating bodies are believed to be under strict state control.

Korean Religious Believers Council: Pyongyang; f. 1989; brings together members of religious organizations in North Korea; Chair. JANG JAE ON.

BUDDHISM

In 1995, according to North Korean sources, there were some 60 Buddhist temples and an estimated 300 monks in the DPRK; the number of believers was about 10,000.

Korean Buddhists Federation: POB 77, Pyongyang; tel. (2) 43698; fax (2) 3812100; f. 1945; Chair. Cen. Cttee PAK TAE HWA; Sec. SHIM SANG RYON.

CHRISTIANITY

In 1995, according to North Korean sources, there were approximately 13,000 Christians (including 3,000 Roman Catholics) in the country, many of whom worshipped in house churches (of which there were about 500).

Korean Christians Federation: Pyongyang; f. 1946; Chair. Cen. Cttee KANG YONG SOP; Sec. O KYONG U.

The Roman Catholic Church

For ecclesiastical purposes, North and South Korea are nominally under a unified jurisdiction. North Korea contains two dioceses (Hamhung and Pyongyang), both suffragan to the archdiocese of Seoul (in South Korea), and the territorial abbacy of Tokwon (Tokugen), directly responsible to the Holy See.

Korean Roman Catholics Association: Changchung 1-dong, Songyo District, Pyongyang; tel. (2) 23492; f. 1988; Chair. Cen. Cttee JANG JAE ON; Vice-Chair. MUN CHANG HAK.

Diocese of Hamhung: Catholic Mission, Hamhung; Bishop (vacant); Apostolic Administrator of Hamhung and of the Abbacy of Tokwon: Fr PLACIDUS DONG-HO RI, 134-1 Waekwan-dong Kwan Eub, Chil kok kun, Gyeongbuk 718-800, Republic of Korea; tel. (545) 970-2000.

Diocese of Pyongyang: Catholic Mission, Pyongyang; Bishop Rt Rev. FRANCIS HONG YONG HO (absent); Apostolic Administrator Most Rev. NICHOLAS CHEONG JIN-SUK, Archbishop of Seoul.

CHUNDO KYO

Korean Chundoists Association: Pyongyang; tel. (2) 334241; f. 1946; Chair. of Central Guidance Cttee RYU MI YONG.

The Press

PRINCIPAL NEWSPAPERS

Choldo Sinmun: Pyongyang; f. 1947; every two days.

Joson Inmingun (Korean People's Army Daily): Pyongyang; f. 1948; daily; Editor-in-Chief RI TAE BONG.

Kyowon Sinmun: Pyongyang; f. 1948; publ. by the Education Commission; weekly.

Minju Choson (Democratic Korea): Pyongyang; f. 1946; govt organ; 6 a week; Editor-in-Chief KIM JONG SUK; circ. 200,000.

Nongup Kunroja: Pyongyang; publ. of Cen. Cttee of the Union of Agricultural Working People of Korea.

Pyongyang Sinmun: Pyongyang; f. 1957; general news; 6 a week; Editor-in-Chief SONG RAK GYUN.

Rodong Chongnyon (Working Youth): Pyongyang; f. 1946; organ of the Cen. Cttee of the Kim Il Sung Socialist Youth League; 6 a week; Editor-in-Chief RI JONG GI.

Rodong Sinmun (Labour Daily): Pyongyang; f. 1946; organ of the Cen. Cttee of the Korean Workers' Party; daily; Editor-in-Chief CHOE CHIL NAM; circ. 1.5m.

Rodongja Sinmun (Workers' Newspaper): Pyongyang; f. 1945; organ of the Gen. Fed. of Trade Unions of Korea; Editor-in-Chief Ri Song Ju.

Saenal (New Day): Pyongyang; f. 1971; publ. by the Kim Il Sung Socialist Youth League; 2 a week; Deputy Editor Choe Sang In.

Sonyon Sinmun: Pyongyang; f. 1946; publ. by the Kim Il Sung Socialist Youth League; 2 a week; circ. 120,000.

Tongil Sinbo: Kangan 1-dong, Youth Ave, Songyo District, Pyongyang; f. 1972; non-affiliated; weekly; Chief Editor Jo Hyon Yong; circ. 300,000.

PRINCIPAL PERIODICALS

Chollima: Pyongyang; popular magazine; monthly.

Choson (Korea): Pyongyang; social, economic, political and cultural; bi-monthly.

Choson Minju Juuiinmin Gonghwaguk Palmyonggongbo (Official Report of Inventions in the DPRK): Pyongyang; 6 a year.

Choson Munhak (Korean Literature): Pyongyang; organ of the Cen. Cttee of the Korean Writers' Union; monthly.

Choson Yesul (Korean Arts): Pyongyang; organ of the Cen. Cttee of the Gen. Fed. of Unions of Literature and Arts of Korea; monthly.

Economics: POB 73, Pyongyang; fax (2) 3814410; quarterly.

History: POB 73, Pyongyang; fax (2) 3814410; quarterly.

Hwahakgwa Hwahakgoneop: Pyongyang; organ of the Hamhung br. of the Korean Acad. of Sciences; chemistry and chemical engineering; 6 a year.

Jokook Tongil: Kangan 1-dong, Youth Ave, Songyo District, Pyongyang; organ of the Cttee for the Peaceful Unification of Korea; f. 1961; monthly; Chief Editor Li Myong Gyu; circ. 70,000.

Korean Medicine: POB 73, Pyongyang; fax (2) 3814410; quarterly.

Kunroja (Workers): 1 Munshindong, Tongdaewon, Pyongyang; f. 1946; organ of the Cen. Cttee of the Korean Workers' Party; monthly; Editor-in-Chief Ryang Kyong Bok; circ. 300,000.

Kwahakwon Tongbo (Bulletins of the Academy of Science): POB 73, Pyongyang; fax (2) 3814410; organ of the Standing Cttee of the Korean Acad. of Sciences; 6 a year.

Mulri (Physics): POB 73, Pyongyang; fax (2) 3814410; quarterly.

Munhwao Haksup (Study of Korean Language): POB 73, Pyongyang; fax (2) 3814410; publ. by the Publishing House of the Acad. of Social Sciences; quarterly.

Philosophy: PO Box 73, Pyongyang; fax (2) 3814410; quarterly.

Punsok Hwahak (Analysis): POB 73, Pyongyang; fax (2) 3814410; organ of the Cen. Analytical Inst. of the Korean Acad. of Sciences; quarterly.

Ryoksagwahak (Historical Science): Pyongyang; publ. by the Acad. of Social Sciences; quarterly.

Saengmulhak (Biology): POB, Pyongyang; fax (2) 3814410; publ. by the Korea Science and Encyclopedia Publishing House; quarterly.

Sahoekwahak (Social Science): Pyongyang; publ. by the Acad. of Social Sciences; 6 a year.

Suhakkwa Mulli: Pyongyang; organ of the Physics and Mathematics Cttee of the Korean Acad. of Sciences; quarterly.

FOREIGN LANGUAGE PUBLICATIONS

The Democratic People's Republic of Korea: Korea Pictorial, Pyongyang; f. 1956; illustrated news; Korean, Russian, Chinese, English, French, Arabic and Spanish edns; monthly; Editor-in-Chief Han Pom Chik.

Foreign Trade of the DPRK: Foreign Trade Publishing House, Potonggang District, Pyongyang; economic developments and export promotion; English, French, Japanese, Russian and Spanish edns; monthly.

Korea: Pyongyang; f. 1956; illustrated; Korean, Arabic, Chinese, English, French, Spanish and Russian edns; monthly.

Korea Today: Foreign Languages Publishing House, Pyongyang; current affairs; Chinese, English, French, Russian and Spanish edns; monthly; Vice-Dir and Editor-in-Chief Han Pong Chan.

Korean Women: Pyongyang; English and French edns; quarterly.

Korean Youth and Students: Pyongyang; English and French edns; monthly.

The Pyongyang Times: Sochondong, Sosong District, Pyongyang; tel. (2) 51951; English, Spanish and French edns; weekly.

NEWS AGENCIES

Korean Central News Agency (KCNA): Potonggangdong 1, Potonggang District, Pyongyang; internet www.kcna.co.jp; f. 1946; sole distributing agency for news in the DPRK; publs daily bulletins in English, Russian, French and Spanish; Dir-Gen. Kim Ki Ryong.

Foreign Bureaux

Informatsionnoye Telegrafnoye Agentstvo Rossii—Telegrafnoye Agentstvo Suverennykh Stran (ITAR—TASS) (Russia): Munsudong, Bldg 4, Flat 30, Taedongkang District, Pyongyang; tel. (2) 3817318; Correspondent Aleksandr Valiyev.

The Xinhua (New China) News Agency (People's Republic of China) is also represented in the DPRK.

Press Association

Korean Journalists Union: Pyongyang; tel. (2) 36897; f. 1946; assists in the ideological work of the Korean Workers' Party; Chair. Cen. Cttee Kim Song Guk.

Publishers

Academy of Sciences Publishing House: Nammundong, Central District, Pyongyang; tel. (2) 51956; f. 1953.

Academy of Social Sciences Publishing House: Pyongyang; Dir Choe Kwan Shik.

Agricultural Press: Pyongyang; labour, industrial relations; Pres. Ho Kyong Pil.

Central Science and Technology Information Agency: Pyongyang; f. 1963; Dir Ri Ja Bang.

Education Publishing House: Pyongyang; f. 1945; Pres. Kim Chang Son.

Foreign Language Press Group: Sochondong, Sosong District, Pyongyang; tel. (2) 841342; fax (2) 812100; f. 1949; Dir Choe Kyong Guk.

Foreign Language Publishing House: Oesong District, Pyongyang; Dir Song Ki Hyon.

Higher Educational Books Publishing House: Pyongyang; f. 1960; Pres. Ju Il Jung.

Industrial Publishing House: Pyongyang; f. 1948; technical and economic; Dir Kim Tong Su.

Kim Il Sung University Publishing House: Pyongyang; f. 1965.

Korea Science and Encyclopedia Publishing House: POB 73, Pyongyang; tel. (2) 18111; fax (2) 3814410; publishes numerous periodicals and monographs; f. 1952; Dir Gen. Kim Yong Il; Dir of International Co-operation Jean Bahng.

Korean People's Army Publishing House: Pyongyang; Pres. Yun Myong Do.

Korean Social Democratic Party Publishing House: Pyongyang; tel. (2) 3818038; fax (2) 3814410; f. 1946; publishes quarterly journal *Joson Sahoemingjudang* (in Korean) and *KSDP Says* (in English); Dir Choe Won Jun.

Korean Workers' Party Publishing House: Pyongyang; f. 1945; fiction, politics; Dir Ryang Kyong Bok.

Kumsong Youth Publishing House: Pyongyang; f. 1946; Dir Han Jong Sop.

Literature and Art Publishing House: Pyongyang; f. by merger of Mass Culture Publishing House and Publishing House of the Gen. Fed. of Literary and Art Unions; Dir Gen. Jo Kyong Hwan.

Transportation Publishing House: Namgyodong, Hyongjaesan District, Pyongyang; f. 1952; travel; Editor Paek Jong Han.

Working People's Organizations Publishing House: Pyongyang; f. 1946; fiction, government, political science; Dir Pak Se Hyok.

WRITERS' UNION

Korean Writers' Union: Pyongyang; Chair. Cen. Cttee Kim Pyong Hun.

Broadcasting and Communications

TELECOMMUNICATIONS

Korea Post and Telecommunications Co: Pyongyang; Dir Kim Hyon Jong.

BROADCASTING

Regulatory Authorities

DPRK Radio and Television Broadcasting Committee: see Radio, below.

Pyongyang Municipal Broadcasting Committee: Pyongyang; Chair. Kang Chun Shik.

Radio

DPRK Radio and Television Broadcasting Committee: Jonsungdong, Moranbong District, Pyongyang; tel. (2) 3816035; fax (2) 3812100; programmes relayed nationally with local programmes supplied by local radio cttees; loudspeakers are installed in factories and in open spaces in all towns; home broadcasting 22 hours daily; foreign broadcasts in Russian, Chinese, English, French, German, Japanese, Spanish and Arabic; Chair. CHA SUNG SU.

Television

General Bureau of Television: Gen. Dir CHA SUNG SU.

DPRK Radio and Television Broadcasting Committee: (see Radio).

Kaesong Television: Kaesong; broadcasts five hours on weekdays, 11 hours at weekends.

Korean Central Television Station: Ministry of Post and Telecommunications, Pyongyang; broadcasts five hours daily; satellite broadcasts commenced Oct. 1999.

Mansudae Television Station: Mansudae, Pyongyang; f. 1983; broadcasts nine hours of cultural programmes, music and dance, foreign films and news reports at weekends.

Finance

(cap. = capital; res = reserves; dep. = deposits; m. = million; brs = branches)

BANKING

During 1946–47 all banking institutions in North Korea, apart from the Central Bank and the Farmers Bank, were abolished. The Farmers Bank was merged with the Central Bank in 1959. The Foreign Trade Bank (f. 1959) conducts the international business of the Central Bank. Other banks, established in the late 1970s, are responsible for the foreign-exchange and external payment business of North Korean foreign trade enterprises.

The entry into force of the Joint-Venture Act in 1984 permitted the establishment of joint-venture banks, designed to attract investment into North Korea by Koreans resident overseas. The Foreign Investment Banking Act was approved in 1993.

Central Bank

Central Bank of the DPRK: Munsudong, Seungri St 58-1, Central District, Pyongyang; tel. (2) 3338196; fax (2) 3814624; f. 1946; bank of issue; supervisory and control bank; Pres. KIM WAN SU; 227 brs.

State Banks

Changgwang Credit Bank: Saemaeul 1-dong, Pyongchon District, Pyongyang; tel. (2) 18111; fax (2) 3814793; f. 1983; commercial, joint-stock and state bank; cap. 601.0m. won, res 1,194.2m. won, dep. 10,765.8m. won (Dec. 1997); Chair. KIM CHOL HWAN; Pres. KYE CHANG HO; 172 brs.

Credit Bank of Korea: Chongryu 1-dong, Munsu St, Otandong, Central District, Pyongyang; tel. (2) 3818285; fax (2) 3817806; f. 1986 as International Credit Bank, name changed 1989; Pres. LI SUN BOK; Vice-Pres. SON YONG SUN.

Foreign Trade Bank of the DPRK: FTB Bldg, Jungsongdong, Seungri St, Central District, Pyongyang; tel. (2) 3815270; fax (2) 3814467; f. 1959; deals in international settlements and all banking business; Pres. KIM JUN CHOL; 11 brs.

International Industrial Development Bank: Jongpyong-dong, Pyongchon District, Pyongyang; tel. (2) 3818610; fax (2) 3814427; f. 2001; Pres. SHIN DOK SONG.

Korea Daesong Bank: Segoridong, Gyongheung St, Potonggang District, Pyongyang; tel. (2) 3818221; fax (2) 3814576; f. 1978; Pres. RI HONG.

Koryo Bank: Ponghwadong, Potonggang District, Pyongyang; tel. (2) 3818168; fax (2) 3814033; f. 1989 as Koryo Finance Joint Venture Co, name changed 1994; co-operative, development, regional, savings and universal bank; Pres. LI CHANG HWAN; 10 brs.

Kumgang Bank: Jungsongdong, Central District, Pyongyang; tel. (2) 3818532; fax (2) 3814467; f. 1979; Chair. KIM JANG HO.

Joint-Venture Banks

Korea Commercial Bank: f. 1988; joint venture with Koreans resident in the USA.

Korea Joint Financial Co: f. 1988; joint venture with Koreans resident in the USA.

Korea Joint Bank: Ryugyongdong, Potonggang District, Pyongyang; tel. (2) 3818151; fax (2) 3814410; f. 1989 with co-operation of the Federation of Korean Traders and Industrialists in Japan; cap. US $1,932.5m. (1994); Chair PAK IL RAK; Vice-Pres. KIM SONG HWAN; 6 brs.

Korea Nagwon Joint Financial Co: f. 1987 by Nagwon Trade Co and a Japanese co.

Korea Rakwon Joint Banking Co: Pyongyang; Man. Dir HO POK DOK.

Korea United Development Bank: Central District, Pyongyang; tel. (2) 3814165; fax (2) 3814497; f. 1991; 51% owned by Zhongce Investment Corpn (Hong Kong), 49% owned by Osandok General Bureau; cap. US $60m.; Pres. KIM SE HO.

Koryo Joint Finance Co: Pyongyang; Dir KIM YONG GU.

Foreign-Investment Banks

Golden Triangle Bank: Rajin-Sonbong Free Economic and Trade Zone; f. 1995.

Daesong Credit Development Bank: Potonggang Hotel, 301 Ansan-dong, Pyongchon District, Pyongyang; tel. (2) 3814866; fax (2) 3814723; f. 1996 as Peregrine-Daesong Development Bank; jt venture between Oriental Commercial Holdings Ltd (Hong Kong) and Korea Daesong Bank; Man. NIGEL COWIE.

INSURANCE

State Insurance Bureau: Central District, Pyongyang; tel. (2) 38196; handles all life, fire, accident, marine, hull insurance and reinsurance.

Korea Foreign Insurance Co (Chosunbohom): Central District, Pyongyang; tel. (2) 3818024; fax (2) 3814464; f. 1974; conducts marine, motor, aviation and fire insurance, reinsurance of all classes, and all foreign insurance; brs in Chongjin, Hungnam and Nampo, and agencies in foreign ports; overseas representative offices in Chile, France, Germany, Pakistan, Singapore; Pres. RI JANG SU.

Korea International Insurance Co: Pyongyang; Dir (vacant).

Korea Mannyon Insurance Co: Pyongyang; Pres. PAK IL HYONG.

Trade and Industry

GOVERNMENT AGENCIES

DPRK Committee for the Promotion of External Economic Co-operation: Jungsongdong, Central District, Pyongyang; tel. (2) 333974; fax (2) 3814498; Chair. KIM YONG SUL.

DPRK Committee for the Promotion of International Trade: Central District, Pyongyang; Pres. RI SONG ROK; Chair. KIM JONG GI.

Economic Co-operation Management Bureau: Ministry of Foreign Trade, Pyongyang; f. 1998; Dir KIM YONG SUL.

Korea International Joint Venture Promotion Committee: Pyongyang; Chair. RI KWANG GUN.

Korean Association for the Promotion of Asian Trade: Pyongyang; Pres. RI SONG ROK.

Korean International General Joint Venture Co: Pyongyang; f. 1986; promotes joint economic ventures with foreign countries; Man. Dir KANG JONG MO.

Korean General Merchandise Export and Import Corpn: Pyongyang.

INDUSTRIAL AND TRADE ASSOCIATIONS

Korea Building Materials Trading Co: Central District, Pyongyang; chemical building materials, woods, timbers, cement, sheet glass, etc; Dir SHIN TONG BOM.

Korea Cement Export Corpn: Central District, Pyongyang; f. 1982; cement and building materials.

Korea Cereals Export and Import Corpn: Central District, Pyongyang; high-quality vegetable starches, etc.

Korea Chemicals Export and Import Corpn: Central District, Pyongyang; petroleum and petroleum products, raw materials for the chemical industry, rubber and rubber products, fertilizers, etc.

Korea Daesong Jeil Trading Corpn: Potonggang District, Pyongyang; machinery and equipment, chemical products, textiles, agricultural products, etc.

Korea Daesong Jesam Trading Corpn: Potonggang District, Pyongyang; remedies for diabetes, tonics, etc.

Korea Ferrous Metals Export and Import Corpn: Potonggang District, Pyongyang; steel products.

Korea Film Export and Import Corpn: Daedongmundong, Central District, POB 113, Pyongyang; tel. (2) 180008034; fax (2) 3814410; f. 1956; feature films, cartoons, scientific and documentary films; Dir-Gen. CHOE HYOK U.

Korea First Equipment Export and Import Co: Central District, Pyongyang; tel. (2) 334825; f. 1960; export and import of ferrous and non-ferrous metallurgical plants, geological exploration and mining equipment, communication equipment, machinebuilding plant, etc.; construction of public facilities such as airports, hotels, tourist facilities, etc.; joint-venture business in similar projects; Pres. CHAE WON CHOL.

Korea Foodstuffs Export and Import Corpn: Tongdaewon District, Pyongyang; cereals, wines, meat, canned foods, fruits, cigarettes, etc.

Korea Fruit and Vegetables Export Corpn: Central District, Pyongyang; tel. (2) 35117; vegetables, fruit and their products.

Korea General Co for Economic Co-operation: Central District, Pyongyang; overseas construction, equipment for hydroelectric power plants, equipment for rice-cleaning mills.

Korea General Export and Import Corpn: Central District, Pyongyang; plate glass, tiles, granite, locks, medicinal herbs, foodstuffs and light industrial products.

Korea General Machine Co: Pyongyang; Dir RA IN GYUN.

Korea Hyopdong Trading Corpn: Central District, Pyongyang; fabrics, glass products, ceramics, chemical goods, building materials, foodstuffs, machinery, etc.

Korea Industrial Technology Co: Pyongyang; Pres. KWON YONG SON.

Korea International Chemical Joint Venture Co: Pyongyang; Chair. RYO SONG GUN.

Korea International Joint Venture Co: Pyongyang; Man. Dir HONG SONG NAM.

Korea Jangsu Trading Co: Potonggang District, Pyongyang; medicinal products and clinical equipment.

Korea Jeil Equipment Export and Import Corpn: Jungsongdong, Central District, Pyongyang; tel. (2) 334825; f. 1960; ferrous and non-ferrous metallurgical plant, geological exploration and mining equipment, power plant, communications and broadcasting equipment, machine-building equipment, railway equipment, construction of public facilities; Pres. CHO JANG DOK.

Korea Jesam Equipment Export and Import Corpn: Central District, Pyongyang; chemical, textile, pharmaceutical and light industry plant.

Korea Koryo Trading Corpn: Pyongyang; Dir KIM HUI DUK.

Korea Kwangmyong Trading Corpn: Central District, Pyongyang; dried herbs, dried and pickled vegetables; Dir CHOE JONG HUNG.

Korea Light Industry Import-Export Co: Juchetab St, Tongdaewon District, Pyongyang; tel. (2) 37661; exports silk, cigarettes, canned goods, drinking glasses, ceramics, handbags, pens, plastic flowers, musical instruments, etc.; imports chemicals, dyestuffs, machinery, etc.; Dir CHOE PYONG HYON.

Korea Machine Tool Trading Corpn: Pyongyang; Dir KIM KWANG RYOP.

Korea Machinery and Equipment Export and Import Corpn: Potonggang District, Pyongyang; tel. (2) 333449; f. 1948; metallurgical machinery and equipment, electric machines, building machinery, farm machinery, diesel engines, etc.

Korea Maibong Trading Corpn: Central District, Pyongyang; non-ferrous metal ingots and allied products, non-metallic minerals, agricultural and marine products.

Korea Manpung Trading Corpn: Central District, Pyongyang; chemical and agricultural products, machinery and equipment.

Korea Mansu Trading Corpn: Chollima St, Central District, POB 250, Pyongyang; tel. (2) 43075; fax (2) 812100; f. 1974; antibiotics, pharmaceuticals, vitamin compounds, drugs, medicinal herbs; Dir KIM JANG HUN.

Korea Marine Products Export and Import Corpn: Central District, Pyongyang; canned, frozen, dried, salted and smoked fish, fishing equipment and supplies.

Korea Minerals Export and Import Corpn: Central District, Pyongyang; minerals, solid fuel, graphite, precious stones, etc.

Korea Namheung Trading Co: Tongdaewon District, Pyongyang; high-purity reagents, synthetic resins, vinyl films, essential oils, menthol and peppermint oil.

Korea Non-ferrous Metals Export and Import Corpn: Potonggang District, Pyongyang.

Korea Okyru Trading Corpn: Central District, Pyongyang; agricultural and marine products, household goods, clothing, chemical and light industrial products.

Korea Ponghwa Contractual Joint Venture Co: Pyongyang; Dir RIM TONG CHON.

Korea Ponghwa General Trading Corpn: Central District, Pyongyang; machinery, metal products, minerals and chemicals.

Korea Publications Export and Import Corpn: Yokjondong, Yonggwang St, Central District, Pyongyang; tel. (2) 3818536; fax (2) 3814404; f. 1948; export of books, periodicals, postcards, paintings, cassettes, videos, CDs, CD-ROMs, postage stamps and records; import of books; Pres. RI YONG.

Korea Pyongchon Trading Co: Central District, Pyongyang; axles, springs, spikes, bolts and bicycles.

Korea Pyongyang Trading Co Ltd: Central District, POB 550, Pyongyang; pig iron, steel, magnesia clinker, textiles, etc.

Korea Rungra Co: Pyongyang; Dir CHOE HENG UNG.

Korea Rungrado Trading Corpn: Potonggang District, Pyongyang; food and animal products; Gen. Dir PAK KYU HONG.

Korea Ryongaksan General Trading Corpn: Pyongyang; Gen. Dir HAN YU RO.

Korea Samcholli General Corpn: Pyongyang; Dir JONG UN OP.

Korea Senbong Trading Corpn: Central District, Pyongyang; ferrous and non-ferrous metals, rolled steels, mineral ores, chemicals, etc.

Korea Somyu Hyopdong Trading Corpn: Oesong District, Pyongyang; clothing and textiles.

Korea Songhwa Trading Corpn: Oesong District, Pyongyang; ceramics, glass, hardware, leaf tobaccos, fruit and wines.

Korea Technology Corpn: Central District, Pyongyang; scientific and technical co-operation.

Korea Unha Trading Corpn: Tongdaewon District, Pyongyang; clothing and fibres.

Kwangmyong Trading Group of Korea: Pyongyang; Pres. CHOE JONG HUN.

TRADE UNIONS

General Federation of Trade Unions of Korea (GFTUK): POB 333, Pyongyang; fax (2) 3814427; f. 1945; 1.6m. mems (1986); six affiliated unions; Chair. RYOM SUN GIL.

Metals, Engineering, Mining and Power Industries Workers' Union: Pyongyang; Chair. RI JU JIN.

Light and Chemical Industries and Commerce Union: Pyongyang; Chair. MUN SOK NAM.

Union of Public Employees: Pyongyang; Chair. PAK SEI HYOK.

Union of Construction and Forestry Workers: Pyongyang; Chair. SON YONG JUN.

Union of Educational and Cultural Workers: Pyongyang; Chair. PAK CHUN GEUN.

Union of Transport Workers and Fishermen: Pyongyang; Chair. CHOE RYONG SU.

General Federation of Agricultural and Forestry Technique of Korea: Chung Kuyuck Nammundong, Pyongyang; f. 1946; 523,000 mems.

General Federation of Unions of Literature and Arts of Korea: Pyongyang; f. 1946; seven br. unions; Chair. Cen. Cttee CHANG CHOL.

Kim Il Sung Socialist Youth League: Pyongyang; fmrly League of Socialist Working Youth of Korea; First Sec. KIM GYONG HO.

Korean Architects' Union: Pyongyang; f. 1954; 500 mems; Chair. Cen. Cttee PAE TAL JUN.

Korean Democratic Lawyers' Association: Ryonhwa 1, Central District, Pyongyang; fax (2) 3814644; f. 1954; Chair. HAM HAK SONG.

Korean Democratic Scientists' Association: Pyongyang; f. 1956.

Korean Democratic Women's Union: Jungsongdong, Central District, Pyongyang; fax (2) 3814416; f. 1945; Chief Officer PAK SUN HUI.

Korean General Federation of Science and Technology: Jungsongdong, Seungri St, Central District, Pyongyang; tel. (2) 3224389; fax (2) 3814410; f. 1946; 550,000 mems; Chair. Cen. Cttee CHOE HUI JONG.

Korean Medical Association: Pyongyang; f. 1970; Chair. CHOE CHANG SHIK.

Union of Agricultural Working People of Korea: Pyongyang; f. 1965 to replace fmr Korean Peasants' Union; 2.4m. mems; Chair. Cen. Cttee SUNG SANG SOP.

Transport

RAILWAYS

Railways were responsible for some 62% of passenger journeys in 1991 and for some 74% of the volume of freight transported in 1997.

At April 2000 the total length of track was 5,214 km, of which some 79% was electrified. There are international train services to Moscow (Russia) and Beijing (People's Republic of China). Construction work on the reconnection of the Kyongui (West coast, Shinuiju–Seoul) and East Coast Line (Wonsan–Seoul) began in September 2002; the former was expected to be completed by the end of that year, and the latter by September 2003. Eventually the two would be linked to the Trans-China and Trans-Siberian railways respectively, greatly enhancing the region's transportation links.

There is an underground railway system in Pyongyang, comprising two lines with a combined length of 22 km. Unspecified plans to expand the system were announced in February 2002.

ROADS

In 2000, according to South Korean estimates, the road network totalled 23,407 km (of which only about 8% was paved), including 682 km of multi-lane highways.

INLAND WATERWAYS

The Yalu (Amnok-gang) and Taedong, Tumen and Ryesong are the most important commercial rivers. Regular passenger and freight services: Nampo–Chosan–Supung; Chungsu–Shinuiju–Dasado; Nampo–Jeudo; Pyongyang–Nampo.

SHIPPING

The principal ports are Nampo, Wonsan, Chongjin, Rajin, Hungnam, Songnim and Haeju. In 1997 North Korean ports had a combined capacity for handling 35m. tons of cargo. At 31 December 2001 North Korea's merchant fleet comprised 176 vessels, with a combined displacement of 697,804 grt.

Korea Chartering Corpn: Central District, Pyongyang; arranges cargo transportation and chartering.

Korea Daehung Shipping Co: 1-1, Zungguyok, Pyongyang.

Korea East Sea Shipping Co: Pyongyang; Dir RI TUK HYON.

Korea Foreign Transportation Corpn: Central District, Pyongyang; arranges transportation of export and import cargoes (transit goods and charters).

Korean-Polish Shipping Co Ltd: Moranbong District, Pyongyang; tel. (2) 3814384; fax (2) 3814607; f. 1967; maritime trade mainly with Polish, Far East and DPRK ports.

Korea Tonghae Shipping Co: Changgwang St, Central District, POB 120, Pyongyang; tel. (2) 345805; fax (2) 3814583; arranges transportation by Korean vessels.

Ocean Maritime Management Co Ltd: Tonghungdong, Central District, Pyongyang.

Ocean Shipping Agency of the DPRK: Moranbong District, POB 21, Pyongyang; tel. (2) 3818100; fax (2) 3814531; Pres. O JONG HO.

CIVIL AVIATION

The international airport is at Sunan, 24 km from Pyongyang.

Chosonminhang/General Civil Aviation Bureau of the DPRK: Sunan Airport, Sunan District, Pyongyang; tel. (2) 37917; fax (2) 3814625; f. 1954; internal services and external flights by Air Koryo to Beijing and Shenyang (People's Republic of China), Bangkok (Thailand), Macao, Nagoya (Japan), Moscow, Khabarovsk and Vladivostok (Russia), Sofia (Bulgaria) and Berlin (Germany); charter services are operated to Asia, Africa and Europe; Pres. KIM YO UNG.

Tourism

The DPRK was formally admitted to the World Tourism Organization in 1987. Tourism is permitted only in officially accompanied parties. In 1999 there were more than 60 international hotels (including nine in Pyongyang) with 7,500 beds. Tourist arrivals totalled 128,000 in 1997. A feasibility study was undertaken in 1992 regarding the development of Mount Kumgang as a tourist attraction. The study proposed the construction of an international airport at Kumnan and of a number of hotels and leisure facilities in the Wonsan area. Local ports were also to be upgraded. It was hoped that the development, scheduled to cost some US $20,000m. and to be completed by 2004, would attract 3m. tourists to the area each year. In November 1998 some 800 South Korean tourists visited Mount Kumgang, as part of a joint venture mounted by the North Korean authorities and Hyundai, the South Korean conglomerate. By November 2000 only 350,000 South Korean tourists had visited the attraction. In 1996 it was reported that proposals had been made to create a tourist resort in the Rajin-Sonbong Free Economic and Trade Zone, in the north-east of the country. It was announced that hotels to accommodate some 5,000 people were to be constructed, as well as an airport to service the area. There were reports in 1998 that a heliport had been opened in the Zone, and in 1999 the resort was completed. Mount Chilbo, Mount Kuwol, Mount Jongbang and the Ryongmum Cave were transformed into new tourist destinations in that year. In August 2000 plans were announced for the development, jointly with China, of the western part of Mount Paektu, Korea's highest mountain, as a tourist resort.

Korea International Tourist Bureau: Pyongyang; Pres. HAN PYONG UN.

Korean International Youth Tourist Co: Mankyongdae District, Pyongyang; tel. (2) 73406; f. 1985; Dir HWANG CHUN YONG.

Kumgangsan International Tourist Co: Central District, Pyongyang; tel. (2) 31562; fax (2) 3812100; f. 1988.

National Tourism Administration of the DPRK: Central District, Pyongyang; tel. (2) 3818901; fax (2) 3817607; f. 1986; state-run tourism promotion organization; Dir RYO SUNG CHOL.

Ryohaengsa (Korea International Travel Company): Central District, Pyongyang; tel. (2) 3817201; fax (2) 3817607; f. 1953; has relations with more than 200 tourist companies throughout the world; Pres. CHO SONG HUN.

State General Bureau of Tourism: Pyongyang; Pres. RYO SUNG CHOL.

Defence

In August 2001 armed forces were estimated to total 1,082,000: army 950,000; navy 46,000; air force 86,000. There are also 189,000 security and border guards, and a workers' and peasants' militia ('Red Guards') numbering about 3.5m. Military service is selective: army for five to eight years, navy for five to 10 years and air force for three to four years.

Defence Expenditure: Budgeted at an estimated 2,960m. won for 2001.

Supreme Commander of the Korean People's Army and Chairman of the National Defence Commission: Marshal KIM JONG IL.

Chief of General Staff of the Korean People's Army: Vice-Marshal KIM YONG CHUN.

Commander of the Air Force: Col-Gen. O KUM CHOL.

Commander of the Navy: Gen. KIM YUN SHIM.

Education

Universal, compulsory primary and secondary education were introduced in 1956 and 1958, respectively, and are provided at state expense. Free and compulsory 11-year education in state schools was introduced in 1975. Children enter kindergarten at five years of age, and primary school at the age of six. After four years, they advance to senior middle school for six years. In 1987/88 there were 1.5m. primary school students and 2.5m. secondary school students. In that year some 325,000 students were enrolled in university-level institutions (of which there were 519 in 1986). In 1988 the Government announced the creation of new educational establishments, including one university, eight colleges, three factory colleges, two farmers' colleges and five special schools. English is compulsory as a second language from the age of 14. The adult literacy rate was estimated at 99% in 1984. In March 2001 the Ministry of Education announced plans for the establishment of a university of information science and technology in Pyongyang, in co-operation with a South Korean education foundation. The new university was due to offer a postgraduate degree course from September 2002 and undergraduate courses from 2003.

Bibliography

See pp. 731–734.

THE REPUBLIC OF KOREA

History

ANDREW C. NAHM

Updated by AIDAN FOSTER-CARTER

(For details of the Korean War and earlier history, see pp. 649–652)

THE FIRST REPUBLIC, 1948–60

The foundation of the Republic was hardly settled when a communist-inspired military rebellion broke out in October 1948. The rebellion was crushed, but it demoralized the nation and increased the repressive character of the Government. The democratic aspirations and trends of the pre-Korean War period diminished as the Government became more autocratic during and after the war. Political and social conditions became chaotic as economic hardships multiplied.

Faced by a series of crises, President Syngman Rhee and his Liberal Party (LP, established in 1952) acted high-handedly towards their opponents, and various constitutional amendments were forced through the National Assembly. In July 1952 the National Assembly adopted one such amendment to elect the President by popular vote, and the election, conducted under martial law, was won by Dr Rhee. In 1954 the National Assembly adopted another series of amendments, including the exemption of the incumbent President from the two-term constitutional limitation in office, and the abolition of the post of Prime Minister.

In the 1956 presidential election, a new opposition Democratic Party (DP), founded in 1955, nominated candidates for the offices of President and Vice-President. The sudden death of the presidential candidate of the opposition party assured victory for the 81-year-old Dr Rhee, but the DP candidate, Chang Myon, defeated the LP candidate for the vice-presidency.

As corruption among government officials and LP members, as well as repression by the police, increased, a widespread desire for change developed, particularly among urban voters. At elections to the National Assembly in 1958, the DP substantially increased its number of seats. Aware of the danger of losing absolute control, the LP-dominated National Assembly repealed local autonomy laws, and passed a new national security law.

The death of the DP candidate, Dr Cho Pyong-Ok, some weeks before the fourth presidential elections, contributed to the re-election of Dr Rhee in March 1960, following a campaign characterized by violence and intimidation of opposition candidates and supporters. Popular reaction against the corrupt and fraudulent practices of the administration increased, and fierce student riots erupted throughout the country. The student uprising of 19 April forced President Rhee and his Government to resign one week subsequently. A caretaker Government was established under Ho Chong, and in mid-June the National Assembly adopted a constitutional amendment instituting a strong parliamentary system, reducing the presidency to a figurehead office, and resurrecting the office of Prime Minister. In August the National Assembly elected Yun Po-Son as President and Chang Myon as Prime Minister; thus, the Second Republic emerged.

With the exception of the Land Reform Law of 1949, the First Republic achieved no positive success in the economic field. In the post-Korean War period a degree of economic recovery was achieved with aid from UN agencies and the USA, but South Korea remained economically backward, suffering shortages of power, fuel, food and consumer goods.

THE SECOND REPUBLIC, 1960–61

The Second Republic was hampered from the start: it had no mandate from the people, and both President Yun and Prime Minister Chang lacked fortitude and practical ability. The Chang administration was indecisive in dealing with former leaders of the Rhee regime and proved unable to deal effectively with ideological and social differences between political and sectional groups, while gaining no new support nor the loyalty of the people. Divisions emerged within the DP, and no solutions to economic and social problems appeared imminent. With the exception of the (totally ineffective) Five-Year Plan, the Chang administration failed to adopt measures for solving the country's serious economic problems. Meanwhile, there were renewed demonstrations, as communist influence spread among students. Agitation by students for direct negotiations with their North Korean counterparts, aimed at reunification of the country, compounded by shortages of food and jobs, increased the perceived threat to national security.

MILITARY RULE, 1961–63

On 16 May 1961 a military junta, led by a small group of young army officers headed by Maj.-Gen. Park Chung-Hee, overthrew the Chang administration. The junta dissolved the National Assembly, banned all political activity, and declared martial law, prohibiting student demonstrations and censoring the press. Lt-Gen. Chang Do-Yong, the army chief of staff, became Chairman of a Supreme Council for National Reconstruction. President Yun remained in office, but the Government was in the hands of the military. Pledges were issued by the Supreme Council, upholding anti-communism and adherence to the UN, envisaging a strengthening of links with the USA and the Western bloc, and promising a wide-ranging programme of economic and political reform, as well as the eventual restoration of civilian rule.

The Supreme Council acted as a legislative body, and a 'national reconstruction extraordinary measures law' replaced the Constitution. In July 1961, when Gen. Chang was arrested for alleged anti-revolutionary conspiracy, Gen. Park assumed the chairmanship of the Supreme Council. In August Gen. Park announced that political activity would be permitted in early 1963, as a prelude to the restoration of a civilian government. A constitutional amendment was passed by national referendum in December 1962, restoring a strong presidential system while limiting presidential office to two four-year terms. When President Yun resigned in March 1962, Gen. Park was appointed acting President.

In January 1963 the revolutionaries formed the Democratic Republican Party (DRP), which nominated Gen. Park as its presidential candidate. In mid-March a plot to overthrow the military Government was allegedly uncovered and the acting President announced that a plebiscite would be held on a four-year extension of military rule. The reaction was strongly negative, and in July civilian government was promised within a year. In August Gen. Park retired from the army and became an active presidential candidate of the DRP. Freedom of political activity was restored for those not charged with past political crimes. The opposition forces were afflicted by divisions; Yun Po-Son eventually emerged as the candidate of the Civil Rule Party. The election in October resulted in victory by a narrow margin for Gen. Park, and at National Assembly elections, held in November, the DRP won an overwhelming majority of the votes. Civilian constitutional rule was restored on 17 December 1963, with the inauguration of President Park and the convening of the Assembly.

THE THIRD REPUBLIC, 1963–72

Despite the establishment of a civilian government, all important positions in the administration were occupied by ex-military men, and the National Assembly was fully controlled by the DRP, headed by President Park. Although considerable economic development was achieved under the two Five-Year

Plans (1962–66 and 1967–71), the Third Republic faced many domestic difficulties. In March 1964 large-scale student demonstrations broke out in Seoul, in protest at negotiations being conducted with Japan to normalize relations between the two countries. Despite demonstrations in opposition, the Government dispatched troops to South Viet Nam in co-operation with the USA, declared martial law in June 1965 in the Seoul area, and concluded the treaty normalizing relations with Japan.

In order to promote a parliamentary democracy, if not to weaken the power of the ruling party, minor parties formed a coalition grouping, the New Democratic Party (NDP), in January 1967. However, in the May 1967 presidential election, the incumbent President defeated Yun Po-Son, nominee of the NDP, again by a large margin, and the ruling party won a substantial majority of seats in the National Assembly. Following the disclosure of electoral irregularities involving the ruling party, the NDP demanded the nullification of the results and called for a fresh election.

Prompted by the growing popularity of the NDP in urban areas, the increase in threats from North Korea, and the realization that President Park's aims of 'national regeneration' were not forthcoming, the ruling party proposed a constitutional amendment in order to allow the incumbent President to serve a third term of office. This was adopted in September 1969 at a session of the National Assembly (boycotted by the NDP). A national referendum, held in October, approved the amendment. In the seventh presidential election, held in April 1971, President Park defeated Kim Dae-Jung, nominee of the NDP, by a narrow margin.

On 4 July 1972 Seoul and Pyongyang simultaneously issued a statement which announced the opening of dialogue between North and South to achieve national unification by peaceful means without outside intervention. A North-South Co-ordinating Committee was duly established for the purpose.

THE FOURTH REPUBLIC, 1972–79

The two Five-Year Plans, spanning the period 1962–71, had established a sound foundation, and the economic future of the nation seemed brighter. The sudden changes in the international situation, due to the Sino-US *détente* and new developments in North-South relations since 1972, provided the ruling party with convenient pretexts to perpetuate President Park's rule. As a result, the Government proclaimed martial law in October 1972, dissolved the National Assembly, and suspended the 1962 Constitution in order to pave the way for Park's continued rule. A new Constitution was proposed by the Extraordinary State Council and approved in a referendum in November.

The new Constitution, known as the *Yusin* ('Revitalizing Reform') Constitution, gave the President greatly expanded powers, authorizing him to issue emergency decrees and establish the National Conference for Unification (NCU) as an electoral college. In December 1972 the NCU, with 2,359 members, was established, and it elected Park to serve a new six-year term. Thus, the Fourth Republic emerged.

At the elections of February 1973, the DRP won 71 of the 146 directly-elective seats of the National Assembly. Meanwhile, a new political movement, named *Yujonghoe* ('Political Fraternity for the Revitalizing Reform'), was established as a companion organization to the DRP, and 73 of its members were elected by the NCU, on the President's recommendation, to serve a three-year term in the National Assembly. Thus, President Park was assured an absolute majority.

South Korea witnessed tremendous economic growth during the period of the third Five-Year Plan (1972–76) and the fourth Five-Year Plan (which began in 1977), accompanied by rapid industrialization and an increase in per caput income. This, in turn, brought about remarkable educational and cultural development. However, the increasing autocracy and bureaucratism of the administration, coupled with corruption, caused the democratic movement to suffer, as freedom of speech and the press, and other civil rights were suppressed or violated, and the number of political dissidents increased.

The kidnapping in 1973 of Kim Dae-Jung (who had been campaigning against Park in the USA and Japan) from Tokyo to South Korea by agents of the Korean Central Intelligence Agency (KCIA) created serious problems for Seoul with the US and Japanese Governments. On the domestic scene, anti-Government agitation and demands for the abolition of the 1972 *Yusin* Constitution continued to cause political instability in 1974 and after. To address the unrest, the Government banned all anti-Government activities and agitation for constitutional reform, rendering the political situation more unstable. Against this background of tension, President Park's wife was killed in August in an assassination attempt against Park by a North Korean agent. In the following two months, the ban was lifted, but the opposition NDP and others relentlessly pressed for constitutional reform and the release of political prisoners.

The Presidential Emergency Measure for Safeguarding National Security, which was proclaimed in May 1975 (ostensibly to strengthen national security against a mounting threat of aggression from North Korea, following the fall of South Viet Nam), only antagonized the dissidents further. The new measure imposed further prohibition on opponents of the 1972 Constitution and banned student demonstrations (with limited success). In March 1978 the three most prominent dissident leaders issued a joint statement, demanding the abolition of the 1972 Constitution and the complete restoration of human rights. The re-election in May 1978 of President Park to serve a further six-year term exacerbated the situation, as student unrest, supported by the opposition party, caused greater political turmoil.

At elections to the National Assembly in December 1978, the DRP received only 31.7% of the votes cast, while the NDP won 32.9%; however, the election of 22 independent candidates was a clear display of the voters' displeasure with both parties. President Park carried out a major ministerial reshuffle in that month, and released 1,004 prisoners, including Kim Dae-Jung.

From June 1979 until the complete military take-over of the Government in May 1980, South Korea encountered daunting political, social and economic problems. In July 1979 the NDP elected Kim Young-Sam as its new President. However, Kim's anti-Government speeches and press interviews led to the suspension of his presidency, and then to his expulsion from the National Assembly. In October all the NDP legislators tendered their resignations in protest. A power struggle within the NDP ensued, although the resignation notices were returned. Some conciliatory measures taken by President Park, such as the release of more political and 'model' prisoners in mid-1979, did not satisfy the dissidents and students. The resulting protests led to a serious uprising in Busan and other southern cities in October 1979, and students in Seoul prepared for a large-scale uprising towards the end of that month. In the midst of the crisis, Kim Chae-Kyu, director of the KCIA, shot and killed President Park on 26 October. The Prime Minister, Choi Kyu-Ha, was named acting President, as martial law was proclaimed. Kim Jong-Pil assumed the presidency of the DRP. The cancellation of Emergency Decree No. 9 was announced in December, and the termination of the *Yusin* rule was effected. A further 1,640 prisoners were pardoned in December.

THE INTERIM PERIOD, 1979–81

The NCU elected Choi Kyu-Ha as the new President of the Republic on 6 December 1979, and a new State Council (cabinet), headed by Shin Hyun-Hwack, emerged. Park's assassin, Kim Chae-Kyu, and his accomplices were executed in May 1980. Meanwhile, a power struggle within the DRP, as well as within the military leadership, developed. In December 1979 Lt-Gen. Chun Doo-Hwan, Commander of the Defence Security Command, led a coup within the armed forces, removing the martial law commander and making himself a new 'strong man' in the country.

In April 1980 there was more violent anti-Government agitation by students and the NDP (the presidency of which had been resumed by Kim Young-Sam). The appointment of Gen. Chun Doo-Hwan as acting director of the KCIA in April only inflamed the situation further. More campus rallies followed in May, demanding the immediate end of martial law, the adoption of a new constitution without delay, and the resignation of Gen. Chun. Troops were mobilized, and in mid-May martial law was extended throughout the country. Some 30 political leaders, including Kim Jong-Pil and Kim Dae-Jung, were arrested for interrogation. Kim Young-Sam was placed under house arrest and the National Assembly was closed, as were colleges, while all political activities, assemblages and public demonstrations were banned. In spite of these restrictions, students and dissidents took over the city of Gwangju on 19 May, after several days of bloody clashes with paratroopers and police. This uprising, which became known as the 'Gwangju Incident', was violently suppressed by the army, with the loss of nearly 200 lives.

On 20 May 1980 all members of the State Council tendered their resignation, and a new State Council (headed by the acting Prime Minister, Park Choong-Hoon) emerged. Meanwhile, as riots spread to other cities, the martial law command brought charges against Kim Dae-Jung for alleged seditious activities, including a plot to overthrow the Government by force, and for instigating student uprisings and the Gwangju rebellion. A Special Committee for National Security Measures (SCNSM) was formed on 31 May. President Choi became its chairman but real power rested with Gen. Chun and 15 other army generals, appointed by him to the SCNSM. With the establishment of the SCNSM, Gen. Chun resigned as acting director of the KCIA; however, as Chairman of the Standing Committee of the SCNSM, he still exercised absolute power.

President Choi unexpectedly stepped down in August 1980. On 27 August the electoral college chose Chun to be the next President, and on 2 September he was inaugurated. On that date an all-civilian State Council, headed by Nam Duck-Woo, took office. President Chun made it known that he intended to offer himself as a candidate for the presidency under the new Constitution. Kim Dae-Jung was sentenced to death, although this sentence was subsequently suspended. The National Assembly, which had been in recess since May, dissolved itself in late September. In October a national referendum was held to approve a new Constitution. Meanwhile, the Legislative Council for National Security (LCNS) was created to replace the SCNSM. All members of the LCNS were appointed by President Chun. The Government carried out intensive investigations and purged some 835 politicians in November. Some key political leaders of both parties, such as Kim Jong-Pil and Kim Young-Sam, were not only deprived of rights to participate in the political process, but were imprisoned during the investigation period. Although later released, they were placed under house arrest.

THE FIFTH REPUBLIC, 1981–88

The partial lifting of martial law was announced in January 1981. With this, new political parties were organized and a new electoral college of 5,278 members was created by popular election in February. On 25 February the new electoral college elected the incumbent President as the 12th President of the Republic, to serve a single seven-year term of office under the new Constitution, which banned re-election. On 3 March President Chun was inaugurated, and the Fifth Republic emerged. A new State Council was formed, with Nam Duck-Woo remaining as Prime Minister. Later in the month elections were held to the new 276-member National Assembly. The Democratic Justice Party (DJP), headed by President Chun, won 151 seats and became the majority party, while the newly-formed Democratic Korea Party (DKP) secured 81 seats. With the establishment of the new National Assembly, the LCNS was dissolved. The KCIA was renamed the Agency for National Security Planning (ANSP) in April.

In January 1982 Yoo Chang-Soon, a former politician, replaced Nam Duck-Woo as Prime Minister and four other ministers were replaced. Some concessions to the wishes of the students and others were made by the Government, and Chun pledged that he would retire at the end of his term in 1988, thus becoming South Korea's first head of state to transfer power constitutionally. In January 1982 the midnight curfew, in force since September 1945, was lifted, except in the area near the demilitarized zone (DMZ) and along the coasts. In March 1982 some 2,860 prisoners were granted amnesty, which included the reduction of the life sentence for Kim Dae-Jung to a 20-year term.

A financial scandal, involving relatives of the wife of President Chun, precipitated another crisis in May 1982. As a result, there was a large-scale reorganization of the State Council, in which 11 ministers were replaced. Meanwhile, Kim Young-Sam, former leader of the now defunct NDP, was put under house arrest. In late June Chun appointed Kim Sang-Hyop, a respected educational leader, as the new Prime Minister. In December Kim Dae-Jung was released from prison and allowed to visit the USA for medical treatment.

South Korea's political climate was relatively calm for most of 1983, despite some campus disturbances in the latter part of the year. There was widespread shock and dismay in September at the shooting-down by the USSR of a Korean Air Lines passenger jet (which had apparently strayed into Soviet airspace), with the loss of 269 lives. In October President Chun embarked upon an overseas tour of several Asian and Australasian countries. However, his trip was cut short by an assassination attempt against him in Rangoon, Burma (now Yangon, Myanmar), allegedly perpetrated by North Korean agents. A bomb exploded at a mausoleum only minutes before the arrival of President Chun, killing 17 South Korean officials, among whom were the Deputy Prime Minister, three other ministers, three vice-ministers and two key members of the President's personal staff. Following the Rangoon incident, the surviving ministers tendered their resignations *en bloc*. Chin Iee-Chong, hitherto Chairman of the DJP, was appointed Prime Minister.

In February 1984 President Chun restored the political rights of 202 of the politicians who had been purged in 1981. However, 99 remained on the political blacklist, including Kim Jong-Pil, Kim Dae-Jung and Kim Young-Sam. In November Chun restored political rights to a further 84 persons. The drive launched by a group of former politicians who had regained their political rights brought about the formation of the New Korea Democratic Party (NKDP) in January 1985. Shortly after this, and just before the February general election, Kim Dae-Jung returned to Seoul from the USA, ending his self-imposed exile.

In the election to the National Assembly, held in mid-February 1985, the ruling DJP retained its majority, with 148 seats in the 276-member Assembly. Significantly, the NKDP (67 seats) won the majority of urban votes. President Chun reshuffled the State Council, appointing Lho Shin-Yong as Prime Minister and 12 other new ministers.

In April 1985 the Government restored political rights to the remaining 14 persons, including Kim Jong-Pil, Kim Dae-Jung and Kim Young-Sam, who had been on the political blacklist since 1980. Mass defections from the DKP and some defections from the Korea National Party increased the NKDP representation in the Assembly to 102 seats. Kim Young-Sam officially joined the NKDP in March 1986, and became adviser to the party President, Lee Min-Woo.

In March and April 1986 mass rallies were held, demanding constitutional reform and the resignation of President Chun. In June Chun finally agreed to the formation of a special parliamentary committee to discuss constitutional reform, which was to include members of the opposition parties; in the same month a special session of the National Assembly was convened to consider the findings of the committee, and negotiations continued for the remainder of the year. The NKDP proposed a new system of government, based on direct presidential elections. The DJP, however, favoured a system centred on a powerful Prime Minister, elected by the National Assembly, with greater responsibility to be accorded to the State Council, while the role of the President would be mainly ceremonial. The negotiations made little progress, despite a major concession by the NKDP when Kim Dae-Jung announced in November that he would not stand as a presidential candidate if the DJP accepted the NKDP's proposals.

In January 1987 the death of a university student, following torture in police custody, led to a new wave of anti-Government rallies and to the dismissal by President Chun of the Minister of Home Affairs and of the Chief of Police. Meanwhile, internal divisions were developing within the NKDP. In December 1986 the NKDP President, Lee Min-Woo, indicated his willingness to consider the Government's reform programme. While Lee's conditional endorsement of DJP proposals was supported by some members of the NKDP leadership, Kim Dae-Jung and Kim Young-Sam and 74 of the party's 90 National Assembly members left the NKDP and formed the Reunification Democratic Party (RDP).

In an unexpected move in April 1987, President Chun announced the suspension of the reform process until the conclusion of the Seoul Olympic Games in 1988. While he reaffirmed his commitment to relinquish the presidency in February 1988, he indicated that the election of his successor would take place within the framework of the existing electoral college system. This precipitated an angry popular reaction against the Government, resulting in further violent clashes with riot police.

At its inaugural meeting in May 1987, the RDP elected Kim Young-Sam to the chairmanship and issued a strong denunciation of Chun's suspension of the reform process. The DJP responded by refusing to recognize the RDP as the main opposition party; in mid-May it reallocated committee chairmanships in the National Assembly, electing new chairmen without the participation of RDP members. In late May, following new disclosures about the circumstances of the death in January of the student under detention by the Seoul police, new riots erupted. In an attempt to stem the continued unrest, a reorganization of the State Council was effected, which included the appointment of a new Prime Minister, Lee Han-Key. The nomination, in early June, of Roh Tae-Woo, the Chairman of the DJP, as the ruling party's presidential candidate exacerbated anti-Government sentiment still further.

The RDP organized mass rallies in support of its demands for immediate constitutional reform, and violent confrontations between demonstrators and riot police became a daily occurrence. The US Government sent a diplomatic mission to advise the South Korean Government against the introduction of martial law. In late June 1987, after having conferred with former presidents Yun and Choi, as well as with Cardinal Stephen Sou-Hwan Kim (the Roman Catholic Archbishop of Seoul) and other religious leaders, President Chun met Kim Young-Sam in an unsuccessful attempt to seek solutions to the country's political crisis. Chun refused, however, to offer any concessions with regard to the opposition's principal demands. The RDP responded by mobilizing mass support for a 'great peace march', with tens of thousands taking to the streets of Seoul. Kim Young-Sam and other opposition leaders were arrested, and Kim Dae-Jung was returned to house arrest. This restriction on Kim Dae-Jung's freedom had been imposed more than 50 times since his return from exile in 1985.

Such was the extent of the national crisis that, in late June 1987, Roh Tae-Woo informed President Chun that he would relinquish both the DJP chairmanship and his presidential candidature if the main demands of the RDP for electoral reform were not met. Under pressure from the DJP leadership, from international (and particularly US) opinion and from the continuing public disorder, Chun acceded, and negotiations for a new constitutional framework were announced.

In a conciliatory move, in July 1987, the Government granted amnesty and the restoration of their civil rights to some 2,335 political prisoners, including Kim Dae-Jung. President Chun relinquished the presidency of the DJP (to which Roh Tae-Woo was elected in early August), and reorganized the State Council, appointing Kim Chung-Yul (a former air force chief of staff and Minister of Defence) as Prime Minister, and reorganizing eight other portfolios. In late August the DJP and the RDP agreed on the basic outline of a new Constitution; it was announced that a public referendum on a draft Constitution would be held in October, and that a direct presidential election would be conducted in December.

Following these announcements, industrial unrest increased, while students continued to hold anti-Government demonstrations. More than 500 industrial disputes broke out, mainly in the motor vehicle, mining and shipbuilding industries. By mid-October 1987, however, nearly all the disputes had been settled, the Government having conceded a hurried revision of labour laws, guaranteeing workers' rights to form trade unions and to conduct collective bargaining.

Negotiations between Kim Dae-Jung and Kim Young-Sam failed to achieve agreement on a single RDP presidential candidate. In mid-October 1987 Kim Young-Sam declared his candidacy, and in early November Kim Dae-Jung, together with 27 of the RDP's National Assembly members, formed the Peace and Democracy Party (PDP), which selected Kim Dae-Jung as its presidential candidate. The formation of the PDP resulted in the virtual dissolution of the Korea National Party and the NKDP. Meanwhile, Kim Jong-Pil revived the DRP, renaming it the New Democratic Republican Party (NDRP), and was chosen as its presidential candidate.

In October 1987 the National Assembly approved a constitutional amendment providing for direct presidential elections, and the new Constitution (to take effect in February 1988) was submitted to a national referendum. Some 20m., or 78.2%, of the eligible voters cast their ballots, 93.3% of which were in favour of the new Constitution. The first direct presidential election for 16 years took place on 16 December 1987. Some 23m. voters, representing 89.2% of the eligible electorate, cast their ballots; Roh Tae-Woo was elected President for a non-renewable five-year term of office, receiving 36.6% of the total votes cast. Kim Dae-Jung and Kim Young-Sam each received about 27% of the votes cast. While they both alleged electoral fraud, and although many irregularities were reported, it appeared that the principal cause of Roh Tae-Woo's victory was the opposition's failure to unite in support of a single candidate.

THE SIXTH REPUBLIC, 1988–

On 25 February 1988 Roh Tae-Woo was inaugurated as President. In his inaugural address, he proclaimed that the era of 'ordinary people' had arrived, and that 'the day when freedom and human rights could be relegated in the name of economic growth and national security has ended.' Shortly before his inauguration, Roh had appointed a new State Council, with Lee Hyun-Jae (a former President of Seoul University) as Prime Minister.

At the general election, which took place in late April 1988 under the newly-adopted electoral law, four major parties (the DJP, the PDP, the RDP and the NDRP) competed for 299 seats. Of 26m. eligible voters, 75.8% turned out to elect 224 district representatives. The DJP secured the most seats but failed to win a majority in the National Assembly while the PDP, led by Kim Dae-Jung, became the main opposition party.

The Sixth Republic granted an increased measure of autonomy to national and private universities, and permitted the organization of student associations, thus expanding the initiatives taken during the period of the Fifth Republic. It also liberalized the press law, revoking the ban on the works of artists and writers who had defected to the North and allowing the circulation of certain North Korean publications. Restrictions on foreign travel were eased considerably. A campaign to bring to justice those who had been involved in political corruption resulted in the indictment of Chun Kyung-Hwan, a brother of former President Chun, and two of his brothers-in-law, who, as leading officials of the New Community Movement, were alleged to have embezzled US $9.7m. In April 1988, in response to this scandal, former President Chun resigned from all of the public offices that he held.

In late May and June 1988 thousands of students in Seoul and Gwangju took part in anti-Government and anti-US demonstrations, in commemoration of the uprising of May 1980. Demonstrations continued throughout June, July and August 1988. In many instances these led to violent confrontations between students and riot police, giving rise to fears that civil unrest would disrupt the Olympic Games in Seoul in September–October. In the event, the common perception of the Games as a matter affecting national prestige, shared by both the Government and the majority of the population, prevailed, and the Games were concluded successfully. A panel of the National Assembly began public hearings on alleged official corruption and violations of human rights during the Fifth Republic. As the opposition parties increased their pressure for the punishment of ex-President Chun and his aides, the anti-Government National Council of Student Representatives (Chondaehyop) intensified its activities, holding mass rallies and staging campus riots.

In November 1988 Chun apologized to the nation for the misdeeds of the Fifth Republic in a nation-wide televised address; he subsequently returned his property to the state and retreated with his wife to a Buddhist monastery in Gangwon Province. Meanwhile, the Government arrested 47 former advisers and officials of the Chun administration and put them on trial. However, the three opposition parties and the electorate were not satisfied with the measures taken. In order to alleviate tension, Roh reorganized the State Council in early December, replacing 21 of its 25 members and appointing Dr Kang Young-

Hoon (a former ambassador to the United Kingdom) as Prime Minister.

In January 1989 some 200 anti-Government groups formed the Pan-National Coalition of the Democratic Movement (Chonminyon) and, in conjunction with Chondaehyop, intensified protest and strike activities. As these events, together with the clandestine visit in March to North Korea by a Presbyterian minister (the Rev. Moon Ik-Hwan) and three others, created a new political crisis, the Minister of Government Administration, Kim Yong-Kap, resigned, warning against the growing threat of 'leftist tendencies'. Confronted by this new crisis, Roh announced, in March 1989, the indefinite postponement of a referendum to provide an interim appraisal of his first year in office, causing a new wave of protests. The citizens of Gwangju held a week-long rally, to commemorate the ninth anniversary of the events of 1980, without resorting to violence. However, further demonstrations resulted in injuries to a large number of students and policemen.

The political situation altered dramatically in January 1990, when it was announced that the RDP and the NDRP would merge with the ruling DJP to form a new party, the Democratic Liberal Party (DLP). While this move secured for the DLP control of more than two-thirds of the seats in the National Assembly (the DJP having lacked a majority), the broader aim of creating Japanese-style consensus politics was not attained in the months following the merger. Outside the new ruling bloc, the PDP, which was effectively isolated as the sole opposition party in the National Assembly, complained of a virtual coup, while the public responded by rejecting one DLP candidate and nearly ousting another at by-elections for the National Assembly in April, in what should have been safe DLP seats. A public opinion poll put the DLP's popularity as low as 14%, and a new opposition party, the Democratic Party (DP), was formed, largely comprising members of the RDP opposed to the merger.

In March 1990 President Roh announced a major reshuffle of the State Council, in which 15 of its 27 members, including all the economic ministers, were replaced. In late April industrial unrest flared up again, followed by student demonstrations. In late July some 200,000 people participated in a rally in Seoul to protest at the approval by the National Assembly of several items of controversial legislation, which included proposals to restructure the military leadership and to reorganize the broadcasting media. Shortly afterwards, all the opposition members of the National Assembly tendered their resignation in protest at the contentious legislation. They also demanded the dissolution of the National Assembly and the holding of a general election two years before that scheduled for 1992. However, the DLP claimed that the resignations were illegal and would not be accepted. The PDP deputies returned to the National Assembly only in mid-November, following an agreement with the DLP that local council elections would be held, as demanded by the PDP, in the first half of 1991, to be followed by gubernatorial and mayoral elections in 1992. The DLP also agreed to abandon plans for constitutional amendments, whereby executive power, currently vested in the President, would be transferred to the State Council. In late December there was an extensive government reshuffle, in which Kang Young-Hoon was replaced as Prime Minister by Ro Jai-Bong, hitherto chief presidential secretary.

The revelation of two new scandals dominated domestic political affairs in early 1991. The first incident involved the acceptance of bribes by high-ranking officials and prompted Roh to effect a minor government reshuffle in February. The second scandal was the beating to death by police of a student protester in an anti-Government rally in April, which precipitated weeks of widespread demonstrations, and also inspired the suicides of several students and others in protest. In response, Roh appointed a new Minister of Home Affairs in late April, and in the following month legislation was introduced to tighten control over the police and to relax the National Security Law. These concessions were, however, undermined by the hasty manner in which both measures were passed through the National Assembly, to the outrage of many opposition members who wished to debate more comprehensive reforms.

During May 1991 public unrest escalated to a level unprecedented during President Roh's tenure of office, as demonstrations by students and workers occurred throughout the country. The 11th anniversary of the 'Gwangju Incident' again occasioned widespread unrest, and in Gwangju itself more than 100,000 people were estimated to have participated in anti-Government activity. In late May the second government reshuffle of the year took place, and included the replacement of Ro Jai-Bong as Prime Minister by Chung Won-Shik, a former Minister of Education. Following the reorganization, an amnesty for more than 250 political detainees was announced.

Meanwhile, the Government drew some comfort from its results in the first local elections to be held in South Korea for 30 years. The DLP won 65% of the seats in the elections to provincial and large city councils in June, securing control of 11 out of 15 assemblies (in fact, all except the opposition's south-western strongholds of the two Jeolla provinces and the city of Gwangju, and Jeju island, where independents gained a narrow majority). However, opposition parties secured almost as many votes but were disadvantaged by the 'first past the post' electoral system. The smaller opposition DP suffered particularly: its 14% of the votes cast secured it only 2.4% of the seats. However, its seats were at least distributed across the country, whereas the 19% of the seats and 22% of the votes cast obtained by the newly-established New Democratic Party (NDP, created in April by a merger of the PDP with the smaller, dissident Party for New Democratic Alliance) remained overwhelmingly confined to the south-west, excluding some successes in Seoul. In September 1991 Kim Dae-Jung and Lee Ki-Taek agreed to a merger of their respective parties, the NDP and the DP, to form a stronger opposition front. The new party retained the latter's name: the Democratic Party (DP).

The main political development in the latter part of 1991 was a serious altercation between the Government and the Hyundai *chaebol* (conglomerate), in particular its founder and honorary chairman, Chung Ju-Yung. What was widely regarded as a politically-motivated investigation into Hyundai share dealings resulted in claims for 136,000m. won (almost US $170m.) in unpaid taxes being brought against Chung and members of his family. In January 1992 Chung severed formal ties with Hyundai and formed a new political party, the Unification National Party (UNP), which attracted a mixed membership, including former dissidents, malcontents and media personalities. The UNP performed well, as did the DP, in the elections to the 14th National Assembly, held in late March. The DLP suffered a humiliating set-back, securing only 38.5% of the votes cast, as opposed to the 73% which its then separate pre-merger component parties had totalled in the 1988 general elections. The DLP thus emerged with 149 seats, one short of an absolute majority in the 299-member Assembly (although enough independents had been won over by the time the Assembly opened in July to ensure a working majority). The opposition DP obtained 97 seats (having won 29.2% of the votes cast), including 25 of the 44 seats in Seoul, as well as an expected clear majority of the seats in Kim Dae-Jung's heartland in the south-west; however, it gained only a handful of seats elsewhere. By contrast, the UNP's 31 seats and 17.4% of the votes cast were more evenly distributed nation-wide.

The emergence of the UNP (which subsequently changed its name to the United People's Party, UPP) added a new dimension to the presidential elections, which were due to be held in December 1992. In May the DLP chose the former opposition leader, Kim Young-Sam, as its candidate, by a majority of two to one over his rival, Lee Jong-Chan. Initially there were fears that Lee, who had the support of Kim Young-Sam's many enemies among the ex-DJP old guard core of the DLP, might split the party by leading a 'walk-out' of anti-Kim elements. This prospect receded, however, owing to divisions among these elements, pressure from Roh Tae-Woo, and above all the realization that such a split might allow the opposition to win. In late August Kim replaced Roh as DLP President.

In other respects, the domestic political scene during 1992 appeared relatively stable. The Government succeeded in postponing a third round of elections (mayoral and gubernatorial), on the grounds that three elections in one year would be prohibitively expensive. Both student and labour activism were more muted than in previous years, except for a brief outbreak of pro-North Korean demonstrations in some universities in early 1992. In June and October President Roh effected the second and third partial government reshuffles of the year. The latter was presented as the formation of a politically neutral State Council to guarantee a fair presidential election, and included the odd spectacle of the entire Government, as well as the President, resigning from the ruling party.

The Presidency of Kim Young-Sam

The presidential election, on 18 December 1992, gave a convincing victory to Kim Young-Sam, who received some 42% of the votes cast. Kim thus became the first South Korean President since 1960 not to have a military background. Of the six other candidates, his nearest rivals were Kim Dae-Jung, with 34% of the votes cast, and Chung Ju-Yung, with 16%. Kim Dae-Jung, after his third presidential defeat, announced his retirement from politics. Chung Ju-Yung resigned as President of the UPP in early 1993, following allegations that he had embezzled Hyundai finances to fund his election campaign. Subsequent defections from the UPP caused the party to lose its status as a parliamentary negotiating group, and in 1994 the UPP merged with a smaller opposition party.

The opposition was further weakened by the new President's unexpected emergence as a radical reformer. In a campaign against corruption, which won him widespread approval, Kim publicly declared his own assets and forced the entire political élite to follow his example. This was an astute political move, since it exposed many of the ex-DJP old guard in the DLP as possessing wealth that they were hard put to explain, and thus weakened their position *vis-à-vis* the President's own faction. At first it seemed as if this campaign might go awry, when three newly-appointed ministers and several key presidential aides were also caught in the net and forced to resign on various charges of corruption. However, the main casualties were enemies of the President.

By mid-1993 the net appeared to be widening. The military were also targeted, and a number of senior officers were removed, charged either with corruption or association with the military coup of December 1979. The President's official redefinition of this event as a 'coup-like incident' raised the possibility that he might even bring to book his own two immediate predecessors as its instigators. However, Kim's real aim was more probably to impose his authority firmly on the ruling party without going so far as to risk splitting it. The popularity of this anti-corruption drive accounted for the DLP winning five out of six by-elections held in April and June 1993, including seats in Seoul that the opposition had been expected to take.

Other areas of political life in the first half of 1993 showed continuity, even conservatism. The usual May student riots were firmly quelled, as was unrest in July at the Hyundai motor works in Ulsan—itself an exception to a generally quiescent labour situation. Elsewhere, a number of dissident figures expressed support for President Kim, whose overall position appeared strong. The same mixture of radicalism and conservatism continued during the latter part of 1993. The President's reform drive reached its peak in August, when a ban was announced on bank accounts held under false names. This was an issue that previous administrations had not dared to address, and in the event the severity of the initial decree was mitigated by various concessions.

Another bold step was Kim's announcement in December 1993 that his Government would ratify the recently-concluded Uruguay Round of the General Agreement on Tariffs and Trade (GATT), even though this contravened his campaign pledge never to permit the opening of South Korea's rice market to foreign competition. The violent public demonstrations that followed this policy change prompted Kim to effect a major government reorganization in mid-December. The lack-lustre Hwang In-Sung was replaced as Prime Minister by Lee Hoi-Chang, who, as Chairman of the Board of Audit and Inspection, had played a major role in the President's crusade against corruption. The new Prime Minister's tenure lasted barely four months, however. He resigned on 22 April 1994, after a dispute over his exclusion from a new committee established to co-ordinate policy towards North Korea. Lee Yung-Duk succeeded him as Prime Minister, while the veteran Lee Hong-Koo resumed the unification portfolio (in which capacity he had earlier served under Roh Tae-Woo).

Lee Hoi-Chang's departure caused a degree of disappointment, as did two scandals that emerged in early 1994, which implicated Kim Young-Sam in financial malpractices. Although the President managed to evade prosecution, during 1994 his stance became more conservative. In June strikes staged by railway workers ended with mass arrests. One month subsequently radical students mourning the death of Kim Il Sung received the same treatment—prompting some opposition legislators to accuse the Government of 'McCarthyism' and over-reaction.

In late 1994 and the first half of 1995 the Government's popularity declined markedly. One reason for this was a series of man-made disasters, of which three were especially perturbing. In October 1994 the Songsu road bridge across the Han river in Seoul collapsed, killing 32 people. In April 1995 a gas explosion on a subway construction site in Daegu caused more than 100 deaths. However, these disasters were overshadowed by the collapse, in late June, of the luxury Sampoong department store in Seoul (which had been built as recently as 1989), with the loss of 458 lives. In the resultant public outcry, the Government was blamed for inadequate safety regulations to prevent disasters, and was accused of ill-co-ordinated responses when they occurred. Moreover, officials were alleged to have accepted bribes to overlook shoddy work and malpractice in the construction industry.

Accidents aside, there was also a sense of instability within the administration. A major restructuring of the State Council in December 1994, only one year after the last reshuffle, prompted criticism that when in opposition Kim Young-Sam had condemned such frequent turnovers. Lee Hong-Koo was promoted to the post of Prime Minister, while other appointments were regarded as conciliatory gestures to the increasingly restive ex-DJP old guard in the ruling party.

Further ministerial changes were effected in 1995, including the dismissal of Lee Hyung-Koo, the Minister of Labour, who was accused of corruption. His dismissal was unfortunately timed, occurring amidst harsh government action against worker protest. In early June, in an act unprecedented under past military regimes or even Japanese colonial rule, riot police stormed the Catholic Myeongdong Cathedral and a leading Buddhist temple in Seoul to seize 13 trade union leaders from the state telecommunications agency, Korea Telecom, who had sought sanctuary there.

In August 1995 one of the President's closest confidants, Seo Seok-Jai, the Minister of Government Administration, provoked an outcry by an unguarded comment to journalists that a former President was in possession of a huge political 'slush fund', which had allegedly been deposited under false and borrowed names in various accounts. Seo's prompt resignation and partial retraction, however, did not quell rumours. For a while there had been no great public support for opposition attempts to have Chun Doo-Hwan and Roh Tae-Woo prosecuted for their role in the 1979 coup and the Gwangju massacre of 1980. (In October 1994 a tribunal investigating the 1979 coup had found that Chun and Roh had participated in a 'premeditated military rebellion' but it had decided not to prosecute the former Presidents; likewise, in July 1995, during an official investigation into the Gwangju events, Chun and Roh were cleared of having committed 'homicide aimed at achieving insurrection'.) The scandal deepened in late October 1995, when Roh Tae-Woo, in an emotional televised address, admitted to having amassed 500,000m. won (some US $650m.) in illicit political funds during his term of office. In early November Roh appeared before the Chief Justice's office for cross-examination. After a second interrogation in mid-November, Roh was arrested on charges of corruption.

Even before this scandal, and only days before the Sampoong disaster, the electorate delivered a rebuke to the Government in South Korea's first full local elections for 34 years, held on 27 June 1995. The DLP won only five of the 15 major gubernatorial and mayoral posts, followed by the DP, which took four (including the mayorship of Seoul). Four posts were also won by the United Liberal Democratic Party (ULDP), which had been established in March by defectors from the DLP; the new party's President was Kim Jong-Pil, who had resigned (or had been forced out) as DLP Chairman in January.

The DP also performed well in major city and provincial council elections, winning 355 of the total 875 seats, followed by the DLP (286), independents (151) and the ULDP (83). However, the DP's satisfaction was short-lived: Kim Dae-Jung, the party's former leader and continuing *éminence grise*, announced in mid-July 1995 that he was returning to political life and would found his own party. This, the National Congress for New Politics (NCNP), was formally constituted in early September, severely undermining the DP, as 54 of its 96 deputies defected to the new party.

For the remainder of 1995 and into early 1996, however, party politics and local government were eclipsed by the public disgrace of those formerly in power. The charges against Roh Tae-Woo were widened to include the coup of December 1979 and the Gwangju massacre of May 1980; in December 1995 another ex-President, Chun Doo-Hwan, was also arrested on these charges and his trial began in February 1996. He was subsequently arraigned for accumulating illicit funds even greater than those of Roh. The prosecutors requested that Chun receive the death penalty and Roh life imprisonment, and in late August they were sentenced accordingly; however, these terms were subsequently commuted to life and 17 years, respectively.

This astonishing turn of events reflected a deliberate political decision by Kim Young-Sam, once the scandal of Roh's illicit funds had become public, to bring down, once and for all, those who had previously dominated the ruling party. Although a popular course of action to take—most of the nation was glad to see these former influential figures, in particular Chun, brought to justice—it was potentially risky, since it depended on the President being able to distance himself entirely from his predecessors' corrupt activities. Kim Dae-Jung, himself damaged by an admission that even he had taken US $2m. from Roh, made every attempt to draw Kim Young-Sam's name into the scandal. Yet despite the many uncertainties surrounding the source of funds for Kim Young-Sam's 1992 election campaign, and the arrest in March 1996 of his close aide, Chang Hak-Ro, on corruption charges, the reputation of the President, an adroit politician, remained untarnished.

In December 1995 Kim renamed the ruling party the New Korea Party (NKP) and Lee Soo-Sung, the president of Seoul National University, replaced Lee Hong-Koo as Prime Minister. Further government changes took place in an attempt to reassure the business community. In elections for the National Assembly, held on 11 April 1996, the NKP obtained 139 of the 299 seats, including most of the seats in Seoul (the first time that a ruling party had achieved this). The NCNP took 79, which was fewer than it had hoped, mostly in the south-west. Kim Dae-Jung failed to win a seat, having placed himself too far down the list of appointed candidates in a display of overconfidence. The ULD increased their tally of members from 32 to 50, while the DP, already poorly represented, was reduced to 15 seats.

Although the ruling party was thus 11 votes short of a working majority, it had acquired the necessary majority by the time the Assembly convened in June 1996, having persuaded 12 DP and independent members to join. This provoked protests from the NCNP and the ULD, who worked together to delay the Assembly's normal business until July. This unlikely co-operation—Kim Jong-Pil founded the fearsome KCIA, which had tried to assassinate Kim Dae-Jung in 1973—proved surprisingly durable.

August 1996 was notable not only for the sentencing of former Presidents Chun and Roh, but also for the severity with which the annual pro-unification rallies by radical students were suppressed. The students were besieged for several days in Yonsei University, Seoul, before an assault was launched by police, which destroyed the building. One riot policeman was killed and more than 5,000 students taken into custody, the largest number ever arrested. The latter half of 1996 also witnessed a remarkable rate of attrition among ministers, with many dismissals and resignations taking place in the months prior to Kim Young-Sam's customary cabinet reorganization in mid-December, when a further nine ministers were relieved of their posts. In late December 1996, having spent much of that year failing to persuade both sides of industry to agree on labour law reform, the Government approved legislation that gave employers enhanced powers of engagement and dismissal, but which failed to legalize the powerful Korean Confederation of Trade Unions (KCTU). To add insult to injury, the legislation was passed at a swift dawn session of the National Assembly, of which the opposition was not informed. A predictable reaction followed, with the KCTU attracting wide support for strikes, which cost more than US $3,000m. in lost production. However, legislation incorporating a compromise was approved in March, which recognized the KCTU, while postponing the introduction of greater flexibility for employers.

By then, however, the nation's attention was elsewhere. In mid-January 1997 the Hanbo group, South Korea's 14th largest *chaebol* (conglomerate), was declared bankrupt with debts of some US $6,000m., largely incurred through the failure of a steel mill project, rapidly revealed to be both ill-advised and corrupt. For a President whose clean image had already been tarnished by accusations that his election campaign might have drawn on the illicit funds of his predecessor, the procession of senior aides, ministers, bank chairmen and others who were implicated in 'Hanbogate', as the scandal soon became known, was a severe set-back. Yet more serious were separate charges of influence-peddling against his own son, Kim Hyun-Chul; in October 1997 Kim junior was found guilty of receiving bribes and of tax evasion.

These humiliations severely weakened the President's position as his term in office drew to a close. Attempts to lessen the implications of the scandals included yet more cabinet reorganizations. In early March Goh Kun, a known incorruptible, became Kim Young-Sam's sixth Prime Minister in four years. The entire economics team was replaced, and an experienced former Minister of Finance, Kang Kyung-Shik, was appointed Deputy Prime Minister in charge of the economy, while Lim Chang-Yul became Minister of Trade. Efforts by the new team to promote financial reform, the urgency of which had been illustrated by the near or total collapse of several further conglomerates after Hanbo, none the less faced obstacles, not only through the reluctance of politicians to address unpopular issues in an election year, but also from bureaucratic wrangling between the Bank of Korea and the Ministry of Finance and the Economy over spheres of influence and regulatory responsibilities.

Kim Young-Sam's weakness benefited the democratic process, however, by ensuring that his successor (the Constitution allows only a single, five-year term) could not be personally chosen. In mid-July 1997 an NKP convention approved Lee Hoi-Chang, the former Prime Minister, as its candidate for the presidential election. In September the increasingly unpopular Kim resigned as President of the NKP and was replaced by Lee. Allegations that Lee's sons had evaded military service, however, proved damaging. Factional disunity in the NKP was highlighted by the decision of Rhee In-Je (who had challenged Lee for the party's nomination) to resign from the party and announce his intention to stand in the election. In the event Rhee's act was decisive, as it split the ruling bloc.

The Presidency of Kim Dae-Jung

The outcome of the presidential election, held on 18 December 1997, was a triumph at last for Kim Dae-Jung, some 26 years after his first bid for the presidency, and represented a new milestone for South Korean democracy, with the first ever transfer of power to the opposition. On a turn-out of 80% of the electorate, Kim won 40.3% of the votes cast, only just ahead of Lee (38.7%), while Rhee trailed in third place (19.2%). The contest had narrowed to these three main candidates, with Kim Jong-Pil of the ULD withdrawing his candidacy in favour of Kim Dae-Jung (representing the NCNP) in exchange for promises of the premiership and of constitutional change, to be effected by 2000, with a view to giving the Prime Minister more power. Similarly, Lee had been boosted by the decision of Cho Soon, a former governor of the Bank of Korea (and one-time political protégé of Kim Dae-Jung) who was representing the ailing DP, to merge that party with the NKP, thus forming the Grand National Party (GNP) and presenting a more effective challenge to the new NCNP-ULD alliance. Regional loyalties were once again much in evidence. As ever, the Jeolla provinces in the south-west voted *en masse* for their favourite politician, Kim Dae-Jung, and Kim Jong-Pil's heartland, the usually conservative Chungcheong provinces in the centre-west, also duly delivered a majority to Kim Dae-Jung. Conversely, in the south-eastern Gyeongsang provinces, which had furnished all previous presidents since 1961, the votes were split between Lee and Rhee. The outcome was thus decided in the greater Seoul region, comprising the capital, the surrounding Gyeonggi province and the port of Incheon, where 40% of voters lived.

The unprecedented opposition victory also reflected popular anger at the Kim Young-Sam administration's handling of the economy. This had reached crisis point in November 1997, when South Korea was forced (having hitherto denied any such intention) to seek emergency rescue loans from the IMF. At a total of over US $57,000m., this was the largest-ever such rescue 'package' released by the IMF and was perceived as a national humiliation by many Koreans. The 'IMF era' at once transformed the context for politics and policy, and thus presented significant difficulties for the new President. Kim Dae-Jung initially announced that he would renegotiate with the IMF. Once elected, however, he rapidly took a leading role in calming markets, and emerged as a champion of deregulation and liberalization, rather than as the populist that his background might have suggested. Such intervention, while not strictly constitutional (Kim did not take office formally until 25 February 1998), averted disaster during what would otherwise have been a dangerous power vacuum at a crucial time. This pattern continued after his inauguration, with the introduction of a series of reforms that were radical by past standards. New legislation to allow labour flexibility, which had provoked such a backlash under Kim Young-Sam, was passed, and a tripartite commission of management, labour and government was set up. By August the unemployment rate had tripled to over 7% without provoking more than sporadic strikes. The exception was a confrontation at Hyundai Motor, the first large *chaebol* to declare compulsory redundancies. Even here there were, by late August, signs that the new regime's preference for consensus over confrontation—itself a novelty in Korean politics—might avert a forcible solution.

Yet Kim Dae-Jung also faced great obstacles. In the formal political arena, the GNP held a majority in the National Assembly. It refused to confirm Kim Jong-Pil as Prime Minister until August 1998; prior to that he was designated as 'acting' premier. As such he was not permitted to form a cabinet, although, fortunately, the outgoing Prime Minister, Goh Kun, agreed to do this, appointing a State Council in March (see below). Goh later joined the NCNP, for whom, in June, he was elected Mayor of Seoul in local elections which boosted support for the new ruling coalition. Parliamentary infighting rendered the National Assembly largely inactive from May to August, provoking widespread popular disgust. The NCNP-ULD strategy was to break the GNP's hold on the legislative body by encouraging defections to the ruling camp, and this looked likely eventually to produce a working majority for the Government. Even so, society at large remained apprehensive of, if not hostile to, the new paeans to market capitalism. Importantly, suspicion was not confined to workers and civil servants, who feared the potential effects of downsizing, smaller government, and privatization. Equally hostile were the *chaebol*, whose reckless overexpansion was, by common consent, to blame for the nation's financial plight, but which showed little inclination to follow government advice and rectify their affairs by means of the rationalization of activities, sale of assets, debt reduction and more transparent accounting. Given the size and power of, in particular, the largest conglomerates, it was not obvious how an administration avowedly committed to market forces could intervene to force the *chaebol* to change.

On an organizational level, the new Government instituted several changes in early 1998. The two posts of Deputy Prime Minister, which formerly accompanied the economy and unification portfolios, were abolished. Responsibility for foreign trade and foreign affairs was combined under the new Ministry of Foreign Affairs and Trade, while the Ministry of Commerce, Industry and Economy replaced the former Ministry of Trade, Industry and Economy. The Ministries of Home Affairs and Government were merged. Two new bodies were created: the Financial Supervisory Commission, which replaced three old regulatory bodies for banks, insurance and the stock market, and the Planning and Budget Commission, within the Office of the President; those institutions that lost powers were resentful, notably the Ministry of Finance and the Economy and the Bank of Korea, resulting in rivalry and arguments over policy. Compromise was evident in Kim Dae-Jung's first Cabinet, announced in March 1998, which allocated seven posts to the NCNP and five to the ULD. Non-party appointees included the Minister of Finance and the Economy, Lee Kyu-Song, who had held the same post a decade previously and was regarded as a scion of the old 'Korea Inc.' Fears that he would clash with the Presidential Secretary for Economics, Kim Tae-Dong, a professor famously critical of the *chaebol*, were eased when the latter was quickly transferred to another post. (In general, Kim Dae-Jung pledged not to continue the habit of frequent changes of personnel.) Other interesting appointments included that of the unification Minister, Kang In-Duk, whose hardline reputation and KCIA background did not prevent his implementation of Kim Dae-Jung's 'sunshine policy' (see North-South Relations, p. 658). Another ex-KCIA figure, Lee Jong-Chan, returned to head the Agency for National Security Planning (NSP); it was subsequently further retitled, as the National Intelligence Service, in a bid to distance itself from an insalubrious past, which included efforts at every election to tarnish Kim Dae-Jung as a pro-communist, culminating in 1997 in alleged co-operation with its equivalent in Pyongyang to forge the required documents.

More generally, Kim Dae-Jung's desire for reconciliation was seen in the release from prison, four days after his election victory, of ex-Presidents Chun Doo-Hwan and Roh Tae-Woo. In a break with the tradition of persecuting one's presidential predecessors, he resisted calls for Kim Young-Sam to be called to account for the 1997 financial crisis, although hearings on this were promised. He also offered amnesty to political prisoners who promised to obey the law, a softening of the previous insistence that they renounce their leftist beliefs. Many, however, refused this offer, leaving South Korea still holding some of the world's longest-serving prisoners of conscience. Most have subsequently been released in any case.

The Government's drive for restructuring continued undiminished in 1999, winning praise for South Korea as the leading force of economic reform in Asia. A much faster economic recovery than expected also helped to ease the difficulties of transition. Kim Dae-Jung's insistence that 'capital has no nationality' won growing acceptance, and foreign investment was increasingly welcomed rather than feared. This change of attitude was facilitated by widespread recognition that the culprits of the 1997 crisis were the *chaebol*, and their stubborn refusal to reform. This applied especially to the 'big five'—Hyundai, Samsung, Daewoo, LG and SK—which deemed themselves too big to fail. In 1999 Daewoo in effect went bankrupt, with debts eventually revealed to total some US $80,000m. The Government intervened to prevent a second financial crisis, dismantling the group and attempting to sell its viable parts. The proposed sale of Daewoo Motor to the Ford Motor Co collapsed in September 2000, however, following Ford's investigation of the company's finances. Amidst criticism that reform of the *chaebol* was not proceeding fast enough, during 2000 Hyundai's financial position became a serious cause for concern. The controlling Chung family fought for supremacy within the group but then pledged in June to withdraw from the *chaebol's* management.

Further reorganization of government was effected in 1999, mainly in connection with Kim Dae-Jung's first major reshuffle in late May. The Planning and Budget Commission became a fully-fledged ministry, with the reformer Jin Nyum retaining the portfolio. With another reform figure, Kang Bong-Kyun, appointed at its head, the normally conservative Ministry of Finance and the Economy was expected to vie with the new Financial Supervisory Commission for control of restructuring. Other cabinet changes affected a further 10 portfolios, including defence, unification, commerce and industry. Two months earlier the ministers responsible for science and maritime affairs had also been replaced. Overall, the changes were regarded as strengthening the positions of Kim Dae-Jung, the NCNP and those favouring reform. In mid-1999 a series of scandals ended Kim Dae-Jung's initial period of political harmony and lost the ruling coalition two by-elections in early June (although, at the end of March it had gained two seats from the GNP). The wife of the new Minister of Justice, Kim Tae-Joung, was accused of accepting fur coats from the wife of a tycoon being tried for corruption. Nothing was proved, but the Minister was later dismissed over another matter: during his tenure of the post of Prosecutor-General, a drunk underling had boasted of fomenting a strike at the national mint as a pretext to take action against trade-union militants. The new Minister of the Environment, Son Sook, an actress, resigned after only one month for accepting gifts of US $20,000 from businessmen during a performance in Moscow when already appointed to the post. All this, however, besides being rather bizarre, was of little significance compared with the large-scale corruption under previous regimes.

Parliamentary and party politics remained mostly unedifying in 1999, with the National Assembly idle for long periods owing to infighting between government and opposition. The ruling coalition too became strained, with the ULD frustrated at its leader Kim Jong-Pil's agreement not to press for constitutional changes which would have given him, as Prime Minister, more power. In January 2000 Kim Jong-Pil resigned as premier. He was replaced by another ULD figure, Park Tae-Joon, the founder of the Pohang Iron and Steel Co (POSCO), the world's largest steel-maker, still partly state-owned. A wider reorganization of the administration followed, with Lee Hun-Jai, the dynamic reformer heading the Financial Supervisory Commission, taking over as Minister of Finance and the Economy. The following portfolios were also reallocated: foreign affairs and trade; commerce, industry and energy; government administration and home affairs; education; construction and transportation; and maritime affairs and fisheries. Earlier, a new Minister of Unification and head of national intelligence had been appointed.

With legislative elections approaching, the ULD ended its coalition with Kim Dae-Jung's party, itself relaunched as the Millennium Democratic Party (MDP) in a bid to widen its appeal. The MDP had hoped to absorb the ULD, but Kim Jong-Pil objected to the MDP's support for the posting on the internet (use of which had spread rapidly in South Korea) by civic groups of blacklists of politicians deemed unfit for office, whether as corrupt, opportunists, idle, or involved with past military regimes. Kim Jong-Pil himself was so named, as were many other ULD representatives. Confusingly, Park Tae-Joon and other ULD ministers remained in government positions, while the ULD declared itself an opposition party and put up its own candidates against the MDP. The result was the ULD's decimation in elections for the 16th National Assembly on 13 April 2000, held under controversially revised rules that reduced the number of seats from 299 to 273: 227 were directly elective on a 'first-past-the-post' basis, and 46 were chosen from party lists based on the share of the overall vote. The ULD's representation declined from 50 to 17 seats, with the party losing ground even in its regional heartland of Chungchong, south of Seoul. Three days prior to the election it was announced that a summit meeting was to take place in June between Kim Dae-Jung and the North Korean leader, Kim Jong Il. (Kim Dae-Jung was awarded the Nobel Peace Prize in October in recognition of his progress towards reconciliation with North Korea.) Although the opposition condemned the timing of the announcement as electioneering, it did not appear to benefit the MDP significantly as the MDP's tally only rose from 98 to 115, well short of the majority it had hoped for. The GNP remained the largest party, gaining 11 seats to reach 133, four short of overall control. A small new party, the Democratic People's Party, took two seats, and there were six independents (most pro-MDP). Regional loyalties persisted in some areas; the GNP took 64 out of 65 seats in the Gyeongsang provinces in the south-east, while the MDP won 25 out of 29 in Jeolla in the south-west.

This result meant that political manoeuvring would continue. After briefly approaching the GNP, Kim Dae-Jung chose to rebuild his alliance with the rump of the ULD, which furnished a third Prime Minister, Lee Han-Dong, in May 2000 when Park Tae-Joon had to resign over a tax scandal. The fact that Lee had lately been a senior figure in the GNP did nothing to improve relations between the Government and the opposition, and the new Assembly, like its predecessor, remained largely paralysed by boycotts and infighting. A cabinet reshuffle followed in August 2000. The security team—comprising foreign affairs, defence, unification, and national intelligence—was retained, to stress continuity and to reward success in North Korean relations after June's breakthrough summit meeting (see Relations with North Korea, above). Economics ministers, however, were removed, owing to a perceived slackening and drift in the progress towards reform. After only seven months, Lee Hun-Jai was replaced at the Ministry of Finance and the Economy by Jin Nyum, hitherto Minister of Planning and Budget, who was succeeded by Jeon Yun-Churl, previously head of the Fair Trade Commission, the main anti-trust body. The Ministers of Education, Labour, Health and Welfare, Agriculture, and Commerce, Industry and Energy were also replaced as well as the heads of several cabinet-level agencies. With both the Ministry of Finance and the Economy and the Ministry of Commerce, Industry and Energy now allocated to their fourth minister in 30 months, Kim Dae-Jung's pledge to avoid the over-frequent cabinet changes of previous administrations looked somewhat meaningless. The turnover of personnel continued when the new Minister of Education resigned after just three weeks, on suspicion of involvement in a scandal; this was closely followed by the resignation of the Minister of Culture and Tourism, Park Jie-Won, a key figure in the secret talks which led to the North-South summit meeting.

Despite the summit's success, in domestic affairs the Government appeared to lose some control. An ill-conceived health-care reform brought doctors and pharmacists out on strike in mid-2000, angered the public, and cost some US $3,000m. The parties continued to disagree, delaying the next session of the National Assembly for a month. Even the awarding in October 2000 to Kim Dae-Jung of the Nobel Peace Prize, the first ever of any Nobel prize to a Korean, did not improve the national mood.

The year 2001 witnessed a further weakening of the President's administration. In January the MDP lent four parliamentary deputies to the ULD, to give the latter the numbers needed to become a recognized floor group. In the same month two posts of Deputy Prime Minister were reinstated: one, as was the case previously, was allocated to the Minister of Finance and the Economy; the other was a new post of Education and Human Resources Development—with yet another new education minister. At the same time, the Presidential Commission on Women's Affairs, which was created under Kim Dae-Jung, was upgraded to become the Ministry of Gender Equality.

In March 2001 there was yet another reshuffle, as the MDP formalized its coalition with the ULD and the tiny Democratic People's Party (DPP) to gain a narrow majority in the National Assembly. Nine ministers, three other officials of cabinet rank and two senior presidential secretaries were replaced, with a similar removal of vice-ministers soon after. The DPP's Han Seung-Soo, a former ambassador to the USA, became the Minister of Foreign Affairs and Trade, bespeaking a need for better relations with the new US administration under President George W. Bush (see below). Others replaced were the Ministers of Construction and Transportation, National Defence, Government Administration and Home Affairs, Health and Welfare, Information and Communication, Science and Technology, and Unification. The Government's economic team was retained, despite criticisms of falling growth and a retreat from reform, the latter including a series of subventions to ailing companies in the Hyundai group. Other commentators condemned the President for appointing nine professional politicians, including three ULD placemen, and six from his home region of Jeolla in the south-west of the country. The turnover continued: in May an incoming Minister of Justice set a new record, serving for just 43 hours after the 'leak' of a letter in which he pledged fealty to Kim Dae-Jung in feudal tones.

Politics outside the legislature also became more fractious, with a resurgence of violent strikes and demonstrations, including action at Daewoo Motor, where some workers (but not a majority) opposed its proposed sale to General Motors. A tax audit of leading newspapers, most critical of the Government, led to substantial fines totalling around US $390m. and accusations, including some from abroad, of an attack on press freedom. The *chaebol*, hitherto on the defensive, successfully demanded an easing of deadlines for restructuring. Dissension grew over the 'sunshine' policy, as Pyongyang broke off talks, provoked the South with naval incursions and manipulated a visiting southern delegation (see above). As a result, in September 2001 the conservative ULD joined the GNP to pass a vote dismissing the Minister of Unification, Lim Dong-Won.

Although this had no binding force, Lim resigned (he was promptly made a special adviser to the President), as did the entire State Council. ULD ministers were dismissed, while the ULD in turn expelled Lee Han-Dong for agreeing to stay on as Prime Minister. For separate reasons, the rapid turnover of ministers reached a new level of absurdity when South Korea had four different transport ministers in the space of six weeks during August and September 2001. In October the MDP lost three by-elections to the GNP. Soon after, Kim Dae-Jung symbolically resigned from the party presidency.

If 2001 was a difficult year for Kim Dae-Jung, the year 2002 proved to be even worse. In a curious repetition of Kim Young-Sam's final year and despite the key difference of a strong economy (for which he received scant credit) a President who had begun as a reformer appeared likely to leave office regarded as a liability, beset by scandals. Furthermore, like his predecessor, Kim Dae-Jung had to witness the imprisonment of two sons for alleged corruption and influence-peddling, as part of a series of scandals which, if small by past standards, showed the limits of the reform process; involving as it did close associates, as well as kin, of a leader who had claimed moral superiority. Institutions too, notably the tax and intelligence services and the prosecution office, were shown as being involved in past or present corrupt practices. This was likely to remain a challenge for the next President.

What South Korea surely did not need was endless cabinet reshuffles. Yet on 29 January 2002 there was yet another reallocation of portfolios, drawing general criticism except for the appointment of a woman, Park Sun-Sook, as presidential spokesperson. Lee Sang-Joo became the administration's seventh Minister of Education, while the Minister of Unification, Hong Soon-Young, was removed as a result of the failure of inter-Korean talks. The vaunted aim was to create a politically neutral cabinet, and four MDP-affiliated ministers lost their posts; however, two of the new ministers were also MDP members, with another a ULD supporter. An unfortunate loss was the experienced Minister of Foreign Affairs and Trade, Han Seung-Soo, again ostensibly on the grounds of removing party political figures (although the DPP, as such, was of no consequence), just as he was arranging a delicate visit by US President George W. Bush. The new ministers responsible for unification and foreign affairs, Jeong Se-Hyun and Choi Sung-Hong, were both formerly vice-ministers for their respective portfolios.

As the presidential election approached, the MDP won some plaudits for introducing Korea's first-ever primary elections, which in March 2002 produced an unexpected momentum (dubbed the 'Roh Wind') for an unlikely candidate: Roh Moo-Hyun, a populist lawyer and outsider. This worried Washington, DC, as Roh had never visited the USA and had once demanded the withdrawal of US troops. However, his popularity rose only briefly. By September, trailing in the opinion polls, he looked set to be withdrawn by leading power-brokers in the MDP as the usual pre-poll realignments to assemble a winning coalition gathered pace. An early bid by Park Geun-Hye, daughter of the late Park Chung-Hee, who in February left the GNP to form her own Korean Coalition for the Future, made little impact. Instead, the leading contender was Chung Mong-Joon, an independent legislator, scion of the Hyundai business conglomerate, and—above all—organizer of South Korea's co-hosting of the association football World Cup 2002. Taking advantage of the team's unexpected success (it reached the semi-finals) and the euphoria that this generated, Chung declared his candidacy in mid-September; although it remained unclear if he would seek to replace Roh as MDP candidate or would form a new party. Opinion polls suggested he would win in the former case, but that in a three-way contest the GNP's Lee Hoi-Chang would appear to be the best placed. Yet with the election scheduled for 19 December, and Lee losing support after the resurgence of allegations that his sons had evaded military service (which had contributed to his defeat in 1997), as of September 2002 the eventual outcome of the contest to become the next South Korean President remained uncertain.

Two tests of public opinion were the local elections held on 13 June and by-elections on 8 August 2002. The GNP achieved a decisive victory at both, the former by 3.9m. votes, the largest margin in Korean electoral history. Winning 11 of the 13 by-elections brought control of the National Assembly, which the party used to veto two successive presidential nominations for the post of Prime Minister after yet another reshuffle on 11 July. Kim Dae-Jung's initial choice was Chang Sang, the female President of Ewha Woman's University. The transgressions for which the legislature voted against first her and then the unrelated Chang Dae-Whan, a (male) newspaper proprietor, hardly seemed grave enough to warrant risking a power vacuum, should the President be incapacitated. Kim Dae-Jung, a weary 78, had twice been hospitalized in 2002, most recently with pneumonia. In early October Kim Suk-Soo, a career judge and former Head of the National Election Commission (formerly Central Election Management Committee), was appointed Prime Minister, his nomination having been confirmed by the National Assembly.

Kim's latest reshuffle brought no respite. The premiership apart, the outgoing Minister of Justice indicated that he had been removed for failing to protect the President's sons, while the dismissed Minister of Health and Welfare blamed foreign pharmaceutical companies. Also replaced were the Ministers of Information and Communication, and National Defence, the latter owing to the Yellow Sea naval battle (see relations with North Korea). Lee Jun, the new minister, was, as customary, a former general—and also a previous head of Korea Telecom, as was the new information minister, Lee Sang-Chul. Whatever the outcome of the elections in December 2002, South Korea's next president, whose term was to run from February 2003 until 2008, would do well to try to render the political arena in Seoul more stable, less corrupt and better tempered.

RELATIONS WITH NORTH KOREA

See p. 658.

FOREIGN RELATIONS

(AIDAN FOSTER-CARTER)

South Korean foreign policy, ever since the state's proclamation in 1948, has been shaped by the circumstances of the Cold War partition of Korea. As the successor to three years of US military government, the Republic of Korea has consistently cleaved to the USA to an extent unique in Asia, symbolized by the continued presence of 37,000 US forces (with nuclear arms until late 1991). Nor has this been a one-way relationship, since South Korea was the only other country to commit substantial troop levels to the US war effort in Viet Nam in the late 1960s. This relationship has been strengthened by regular senior-level visits over the years, including President Bush's trip to Seoul in January 1992 and a similarly positive visit by his successor, President Clinton, in July 1993. It has had its costs, notably North Korea's propaganda victory in the 1970s, when it achieved its aim of excluding Seoul from the Non-aligned Movement as an alleged 'lackey' of Washington. Such allegations, however, underestimate the considerable freedom of manoeuvre afforded to successive leaders in Seoul, owing to a shrewd perception and manipulation of their small country's large strategic importance to the USA. South Korea's growth as an economic power has led to some friction with the USA over trade issues since the late 1980s, when Seoul benefited from an enormous trade surplus; by the late 1990s a large deficit had replaced the surplus, which was also a source of tension. There was also anxiety in mid-1992, when the targeting of ethnic Korean businesses during rioting in Los Angeles led not only to understandable concern in Seoul but also to what some in the USA perceived as unwarranted interference by South Korean political figures.

Much more significant in the longer term are the effects of successful 'nordpolitik' (see below) and the ending of the Cold War, both of which reflect a reassertion of geopolitics over ideology and have led to better relations with South Korea's close neighbours, Russia and the People's Republic of China. Yet the linchpin still remains Seoul's tie to Washington, as testified by their close co-operation in the early 1990s in pursuing the issue of North Korea's suspected nuclear programme.

By contrast, South Korea's other major strategic relationship, that with Japan, has always been more problematic. Korean resentment against Japan's harsh colonial rule in the first half of the 20th century runs deep, and has been regularly reinforced by allegations, for example, of continued discrimination against the Korean minority in Japan or of attempts by the Japanese Government to 'whitewash' the imperialist period. One such issue concerned the so-called 'comfort women': as many as 200,000 mostly Korean young women and girls who were forcibly recruited in the late 1930s and early 1940s for the sexual use of Japanese troops. The problem lay in the Japanese Government's persistent efforts to deny the overwhelming evidence of official complicity, to rule out any question of compensation, and to avoid a full and frank apology. These issues plagued the visit by the Japanese Prime Minister, Kiichi Miyazawa, to Seoul in January 1992. However, in August 1993 the Japanese Government admitted for the first time that Korean and other Asian women had been forced to serve in Japanese military brothels, and offered full official apologies. None the less, such animosities did not prevent Japan from becoming South Korea's second largest trading partner and principal source of imports, especially of technology (although Seoul's large deficit on this trade had become yet another issue of contention). Despite the ties of geography, history, economics and culture that link South Korea and Japan, the political relationship would surely continue to be delicate.

A notable feature of South Korea's foreign policy in recent years has been its so-called 'nordpolitik', namely the replacement of unqualified anti-communism by a more subtle wooing of China and the former USSR. This has been highly successful in both its direct and indirect aims: to forge better ties with those powerful neighbours, and thereby to pressurize their ally, North Korea, into a more accommodating attitude. The key turning-point of 'nordpolitik' was the 1988 Seoul Olympiad. Of North Korea's communist allies, only Cuba, Ethiopia and Albania heeded its call for a boycott, while China, the USSR and the remaining Eastern European countries all participated. In the following year Hungary, Poland and Yugoslavia all established diplomatic relations with South Korea (prompting fierce denunciations by Pyongyang), a process which became more general with the collapse of communist rule in Eastern Europe.

The decisive step was the USSR's full recognition of South Korea in September 1990, accompanied by close personal ties between Presidents Gorbachev and Roh (who met three times within a 10-month period during 1990/91). With the subsequent demise of the USSR, these relations were continued not only with Russia but also with other republics of the CIS. President Yeltsin visited Seoul in November 1992, and gave assurances that Moscow no longer supported the North Korean regime. The Presidents of Kazakhstan and Uzbekistan (both of whose populations include Korean ethnic minorities, deported by Stalin to Central Asia from the Soviet Far East during the 1930s) had already visited South Korea.

With China, the *rapprochement* was more protracted. Trade began fitfully in the early 1980s, and a large Chinese team attended the Asian Games, held in Seoul in 1986. Since the late 1980s Sino-South Korean trade has increased rapidly, and trade offices were opened in Seoul and Beijing in 1991. In the following year there was a further strengthening of ties, culminating in the establishment of full diplomatic relations in August (and the consequent severance of ties by Taiwan). Still stronger links were subsequently forged between China and South Korea, including high-level visits in both directions and accelerating trade and investment.

Aside from these fundamental relationships with the above-mentioned four powers—inevitable given Korea's geopolitical position as (in the words of a Korean proverb) a 'shrimp among whales'—South Korean foreign policy has mainly been dictated by two factors: growing economic success (until the economic decline of the late 1990s) and rivalry with North Korea. Sometimes these have gone in harness, for instance in ensuring good relations with Western European nations (although there has been some friction on trade issues with the EU). Elsewhere, they have diverged, as in Africa, where the contest for influence led both Koreas to open embassies wherever they could, at considerable expense. While Pyongyang has now begun to draw back, Seoul is still extending its network, as former supporters of the North, such as Algeria, Angola and Tanzania, have finally extended recognition to South Korea as well.

Closer to home, in December 1992 South Korea restored relations with Viet Nam, severed since 1975. As with China, trade links preceded diplomatic ties; and Hanoi seemingly bore no grudge for the South Korean involvement on the Saigon side during the Viet Nam War. The other Indo-Chinese states appeared less susceptible to South Korean advances, especially Cambodia: Prince Sihanouk was an old friend of Kim Il Sung, who had a palace built for him in Pyongyang.

While President Kim Young-Sam's initial priorities were domestic—like those of Bill Clinton, who also took office in early 1993—he subsequently visited all four major powers involved in Korea. Starting with the USA in November 1993, he then travelled to both Japan and China in March 1994. He completed his tour of the quartet with a visit to Russia (and also Uzbekistan) in June.

In general, this 'quadrangular diplomacy' (as it was officially called) inevitably revolved around the North Korean nuclear issue in 1993–95. Seoul pursued close policy co-ordination with Washington and Tokyo on the matter, while with Moscow and Beijing it became a question of strengthening what were still very new ties. The relationship with China, in particular, expanded rapidly, underpinned by increasing trade, and amounted to a *de facto* shift away from South Korea's traditional dependence on the USA.

As regards Japan, President Kim Young-Sam set himself the task of overcoming the legacy of bitterness dating back to Japan's colonial rule in Korea, and there was an easing of restrictions on Japanese cultural items, such as films and music. Kim developed very cordial relations with Morihiro Hosokawa, whose resignation as Japan's Prime Minister, in April 1994, was regretted in Seoul. The visit to South Korea in July of the new Japanese Prime Minister, Tomiichi Murayama, was significant in that his Social Democratic Party had traditionally maintained friendly ties with Pyongyang, while not recognizing Seoul. In August 1995 South Korea acknowledged a statement made by Murayama on the occasion of the 50th anniversary of the end of the Second World War, in which the Japanese Prime Minister expressed 'deep reflection and sincere apologies' for Japanese colonial aggression.

There were no major foreign policy developments during 1994–95. The core relationship with Washington was consolidated—as it perhaps needed to be, given the strains caused by the new US relationship with North Korea (see above)—by two visits to the USA by Kim Young-Sam in 1995: first in July for the dedication of the (long overdue) Korean War memorial in Washington, and then in October for the UN's 50th anniversary celebrations. Kim also made his first official visit to Europe in March, travelling to six countries: the United Kingdom, France, Germany, Belgium, Denmark and the Czech Republic. The meetings of the Asia-Pacific Economic Co-operation (APEC) forum in November 1994 provided an occasion for Kim to visit Australia and the Philippines, as well as the host nation, Indonesia.

The most important official visits to South Korea during this period were from former foes. In November 1994 China's Premier, Li Peng, became the most senior Beijing leader yet to come to Seoul; a year later this new friendship was sealed with a state visit by President Jiang Zemin. Scarcely less significant was the arrival in May 1995 of Gen. Pavel Grachev, the Russian Minister of Defence, accompanied by many of Moscow's élite. Various agreements were concluded, including the exchange of military intelligence, which was sure to anger Pyongyang (and possibly displease Beijing).

Relations with Japan were tested in 1996. In addition to dissatisfaction at Japan's failure to be properly contrite for its past aggression, two more immediate issues dominated. A dispute arose over a group of islets, called Dokdo (in Korean) or Takeshima (in Japanese), long claimed by both countries but newly salient with their adoption of 200-nautical-mile exclusive economic zones; there was also rivalry over staging the football World Cup in 2002, which became so hostile that in June 1996 FIFA, the international football federation, took the unprecedented step of offering it to them both to co-host. Despite these problems, practical co-operation on North Korea and other issues was not affected.

To a lesser extent, ties with the USA were tested too. In May 1996 students demonstrated against the presence of US forces in the country, demanding that the USA accept some responsibility for the Gwangju massacre. These were followed by further demonstrations in August 1996 at Yonsei University,

Seoul, in which students were barricaded in the university, demanding reunification with North Korea and the withdrawal of US troops. Following a nine-day siege, riot police stormed the building and 5,715 students were detained. Seoul remained wary of the Clinton administration's overtures to Pyongyang. As far as the security of the country was concerned, South Korea chafed alike at US procrastination in revising the Status of Forces Agreement (SOFA) so as to give Korean courts more jurisdiction over errant GIs, and at restrictions on its own right to develop missiles to counter the threat from North Korea. There was resentment at pressure from Washington for easier access to the Korean market for US goods, the more so since South Korea had accumulated a large trade deficit with the USA. Yet underlying relations remained sound, and were strengthened by Clinton's visit to Seoul in April 1996.

Seoul also extended its foreign policy interests beyond the peninsula and the four major powers, a reflection of its position as the world's 11th largest economy. Kim Young-Sam attended the first Asia-Europe meeting (ASEM) in February 1996 in Bangkok, Thailand, and took the opportunity to visit India and Singapore, where, as in the whole Asian region, South Korea has substantial and expanding business interests. Such interests also extend to the Middle East; in January 1996 South Korea became a non-permanent member of the UN Security Council (for a two-year term), and sanctions or other measures against Iran, Iraq or Libya could be problematic for Seoul, since it has or has had strong commercial ties with all three. South Korea is a dutiful supplier of personnel and funds to UN peace-keeping operations around the world.

The year 1996 was long ago set as the target for South Korea to become a full member of the Organisation for Economic Co-operation and Development (OECD). In the course of negotiations, the realization that this symbol of Seoul's attainment of full developed country status also carries responsibilities (in the form of faster market-opening and deregulation than might have been wished) prompted occasional doubts. South Korea was formally invited to join the OECD in October 1996 and became the 29th member of that organization in December.

The once extensive, but now dwindling, list of countries refusing to recognize South Korea decreased further in 1996. The involvement of the North Korean embassy in a forged currency scandal gave the Cambodian Government its chance to overrule King Sihanouk's objections to the recognition of South Korea. Hun Sen, one of Cambodia's then Co-Prime Ministers, visited Seoul in July, and it was agreed to exchange missions. South Korea already had flourishing ties with Viet Nam, despite having fought for the former South Viet Nam, and with Laos.

In September 1996 South Korea's foreign policy moved in a new direction when Kim Young-Sam visited Central and South America. During his time in Guatemala he held meetings with leaders of the five other Central American countries, who requested increased South Korean investment in their economies, and he then visited Chile, Argentina, Brazil and Peru, with all of which South Korea maintains good political relations and rapidly-expanding commercial links. He omitted to visit Mexico, possibly because Roh Tae-Woo had been there in 1991, but paid a separate visit in June 1997. The Colombian President had, earlier, visited Seoul. Kim had also planned to visit several countries in Europe in March, but had to cancel his travels due to the internal political problems in South Korea.

For the most part, however, South Korea's foreign links centred on the quartet of major powers interested in maintaining stability on the peninsula. Relations with the USA remained broadly good, despite differences over how to deal with the North Korean leadership, and the occasional trade dispute. Several high-ranking US officials visited Seoul in early 1997: Vice-President Al Gore and the Speaker of the House of Representatives, Newt Gingrich, as well as the newly-appointed Secretaries of State and of Defense, Madeleine Albright and William Cohen. In June Kim Young-Sam briefly met President Clinton, while attending the UN summit on the environment in New York. Relations with Japan were also mostly positive, and included close co-operation over policy towards North Korea. In June and July 1997, however, there was anger in Seoul when Japan detained five South Korean boats for allegedly fishing in Japanese waters.

Among South Korea's newer allies, relations with China were undamaged after the defection of Hwang Jang Yop (see the chapter on North Korea). Sino-South Korean amity is now regularly reinforced when the Presidents meet at APEC sessions, or when their Ministers of Foreign Affairs conduct meetings at the Association of South East Asian Nations (ASEAN) Regional Forum, whereas North Korea no longer has such ready access to the Chinese leadership. As far as Russia is concerned, the Minister of Foreign Affairs, Yevgenii Primakov, was the most senior of several Russian visitors to South Korea in mid-1997. He announced that a direct line of communication was to be set up between the respective leaderships; needless to say, the post-communist Russia has no such channel to the North Korean administration. Russia's hopes of selling an anti-missile defence system and jet fighter planes to South Korea, however, appeared likely to be vetoed by the USA, which expected its ally to continue to buy US-made military equipment.

The election of President Kim Dae-Jung in December 1997 signalled no major changes in South Korean external policy, with the important exception of North Korea. The fact that Kim had lived as a political exile in the USA and Japan, and so was well connected in both Washington and Tokyo, was expected to promote warmer relations with these two major allies. Thus, in June 1998, he made a cordial trip to the USA, where he was fêted as a rare Asian leader wholly in favour of both democracy and free markets. Unlike his predecessor, Kim Dae-Jung also shared the Clinton administration's preference for engagement with North Korea. At another level, the US rescue of South Korea from the brink of default at the end of 1997 increased Seoul's debt to Washington, both literally and metaphorically, a situation which over time might need to be handled with care, given Korean pride and sensitivity to charges of 'flunkeyism'. Kim Dae-Jung inherited a slightly more complex relationship with Tokyo, owing to long-running animosity over such issues as 'comfort women', fishing rights, and the Dokdo/Takeshima islets. In addition, South Koreans shared the rest of Asia's concern at Japan's economic stagnation, with the added twist that the Asian financial crisis pitted South Korean exports against Japanese. On the other hand, Kim Dae-Jung's connections with Japan, as well as the fact that Prime Minister Kim Jong-Pil was the very man who, in 1965, negotiated the first post-war formal relations between the two countries, were positive factors. In any case, a visit by Kim Dae-Jung to Tokyo in early October 1998 proved a huge success, resulting in greatly improved relations between the two countries and mutual pledges to co-operate fully henceforth in strengthening bilateral economic, security and cultural ties. The Japanese Prime Minister, Keizo Obuchi, publicly apologized (Tokyo's first such official expression of regret ever) for Japan's conduct towards South Korea during its occupation of the peninsula between 1910 and 1945. In the economic arena South Korea agreed to remove a number of restrictions on Japanese imports, while Tokyo announced that it would commit US $3,000m. in addition to existing financial assistance to its neighbour. A year of vigorous and successful presidential diplomacy ended busily, with a visit to China in November, followed by two regional summits—APEC in Kuala Lumpur, Malaysia, and ASEAN in Hanoi, Viet Nam—and a visit to Seoul by US President Clinton. Kim Dae-Jung's stay in China was as cordial as that in Japan. The steady strengthening of ties with Beijing deepened further in August 1999, when for the first time a South Korean Minister of Defence visited China. Any military co-operation between these former Cold War adversaries will no doubt proceed carefully, for fear of upsetting Pyongyang, and perhaps also Washington.

In March 1999 Kim Dae-Jung welcomed the Japanese Prime Minister, Keizo Obuchi, to Seoul. His own first journey of the year was in May, to Russia and Mongolia. Relations with Moscow had been damaged in mid-1998 by the expulsion of a South Korean diplomat for spying, an affair which eventually led to the resignation of Seoul's Minister of Foreign Affairs. A longer-running issue was Russia's debt of US $1,700m. dating from loans extended by Roh Tae-Woo in 1990 as a reward for diplomatic relations. Seoul was reluctant to accept Moscow's offer to repay its debt in military equipment, preferably submarines. More widely, Russia resented being excluded from multilateral fora on the peninsula, be it the four-party talks or the Korean Peninsula Energy Development Organization (see the chapter on North Korea). The Russian Minister of Defence visited Seoul in September 1999. In July 1999 Kim Dae-Jung made a second visit as President to the USA (and a first to Canada). This was not quite the success of the year before; his hosts were disconcerted when Kim requested that South Korea be allowed to develop missiles with a range of 500 km, rather than the 300 km recently agreed in principle. None the less, relations remained good, and were reaffirmed in September by a three-way summit with Keizo Obuchi in Auckland, New Zealand, to show a common front against any new missile launch by North Korea. This took place just before the APEC meeting, which Kim Dae-Jung combined with bilateral visits to Australia and New Zealand. In November he visited Manila for the 'ASEAN + 3' meetings, where he met the Chinese and Japanese Prime Ministers: the first summit for that particular troika, and one of several signs of Kim's Asianist—but not anti-Western—proclivities. All this consolidated his reputation as South Korea's most internationally-minded leader to date.

During 2000 Kim extended his focus to Europe, with visits in March to France, Germany, Italy, and the Vatican (he is a devout Catholic). He had visited the United Kingdom in 1998 for the Asia-Europe (ASEM) meetings, which Seoul hosted in October 2000. In a speech in Berlin, he offered aid to rebuild North Korean infrastructure, an offer that led to inter-Korean summit talks being announced a month later. Relations with Japan continued to improve despite the death of Keizo Obuchi, whose funeral in June gave Kim Dae-Jung the chance to meet his successor, Yoshiro Mori, as well as Bill Clinton.

Relations with the USA faced new challenges in 2000. Allegations surfaced that US troops had massacred civilian refugees early in the Korean War at a village called Nogun-ri; both Governments set up official inquiries into this. It subsequently emerged that two US soldiers who had testified to being present at the massacre were in fact located elsewhere at the time of the killings. Anti-US sentiment was also heightened by an accident at a bombing range at Maehyang-ri, south-west of Seoul, which provoked a protest campaign; as well as by revelations of a toxic leak into the Han river from a US base in Seoul. The north-south summit implicitly raised the question of an eventual withdrawal of the 37,000 US troops stationed in South Korea; though Kim Dae-Jung insisted that Kim Jong Il had accepted his argument that they should stay to perform a regional peace-keeping role. This backdrop made it no easier to revise the Status of Forces Agreement (SOFA), which governs US troops in Korea. A fresh agreement was finally concluded in December, after five years of negotiation.

As for Seoul's newer links, relations with the People's Republic of China remained good, despite protests in January 2000 when Beijing repatriated seven young North Korean refugees (earlier expelled from Russia). There was criticism of the Government for being too meek towards China on the refugee issue and other matters, such as its refusal to grant a visa to the Dalai Lama (the spiritual leader of Tibet), or to congratulate the new President of Taiwan, Chen Shui-ban, whose triumph as a former opposition leader elected as President paralleled Kim Dae-Jung's own trajectory. Kim Dae-Jung publicly welcomed Vladimir Putin's election as Russian President, though the latter's prompt visit to Pyongyang discomforted some in Seoul. Multilaterally, the third Asia Europe Meeting (ASEM), which South Korea hosted in October, was the largest event ever held in South Korea's diplomatic history, with over 20 heads of state or government attending. The United Kingdom and Germany used the occasion to announce their intention to open ties with North Korea, as a boost for the 'sunshine' policy. In November Kim Dae-Jung took a prominent role as usual in two regional summits, the APEC in Brunei and the 'ASEAN + 3' in Singapore, with state visits there and to Indonesia. The President rounded off a remarkable year with visits to Sweden and Norway, where he received his Nobel Peace Prize.

The year 2001 proved to be much less successful, however. Fears that the new US administration would harm détente with North Korea proved correct in March, when Kim Dae-Jung became the first Asian leader to visit President George W. Bush, who publicly voiced mistrust of the DPRK. By contrast his Secretary of State, Colin Powell, expressed readiness to continue engagement, a view that subsequently prevailed, but not before damage had already been done. It did not help that before Kim's visit a joint statement with Russia's President Putin, who visited Seoul in February, strongly supported the 1972 Anti-Ballistic Missile Treaty (ABM), which Bush's missile defence proposals were set to breach. Relations improved as a result of the massive terrorist attacks perpetrated against US targets in September 2001, which brought strong sympathy from South Korea and a reaffirmation of security ties with the USA.

Meanwhile, Kim Dae-Jung's efforts to forge better ties with Japan met a set-back. A new history textbook to be used in Japanese schools, that concealed that country's pre-1945 aggression, caused strong repercussions in both Koreas and in China, and were compounded by Prime Minister Koizumi's visit to the Yasukuni shrine in August 2001. By contrast, relations with China remained good despite the latter's persecution of North Korean refugees, and a growing perception of China as an economic competitor. Senior visitors to Seoul included Li Peng. Later in 2001 Kim Dae-Jung made his customary forays to the APEC and 'ASEAN + 3' meetings. Ever at ease in Europe, Kim's politics being essentially 'Christian Democrat' in nature, in December 2001 he visited the United Kingdom, Norway and Hungary; he became the first Asian leader to address the European Parliament in Strasbourg. A planned visit to Latin America, which would have been his first, was postponed.

In 2002 foreign affairs provided no solace from domestic problems which, along with ill health, prevented the President from travelling as much as he had hoped. In January President Bush's 'axis of evil' speech was difficult to reconcile with the 'sunshine' policy. In the circumstances, Bush's visit to Seoul in February went off better than many had feared. Wider relations with the USA were strong enough to survive this and other challenges, including an accident in which a vehicle of the US forces killed two teenage girls, provoking the usual conflict over jurisdiction—yet (significantly) no serious demands for US troops to leave. There was dismay, however, at a decision to buy South Korea's next-generation combat aircraft from the USA. The choice of the latter's F-15K *Eagle* fighter was widely seen as a political decision, considering the technical superiority of France's Dassault *Rafale*. Other trade disputes were less fraught. A nationalist rebuff which prevented a US firm, Micron, from buying the chip-maker Hynix was balanced by General Motors' agreement to take over Daewoo Motor.

Relations with Japan were improved in 2002 by the two nations' co-hosting, albeit with largely separate organization, of the football World Cup. This afforded opportunities for mutual visits by Koizumi for the opening and Kim for the closing matches, as well as the first visit to post-war Korea by a member of the Japanese royal family (but not yet the Emperor or Crown Prince). Kim was also glad of Koizumi's unexpected decision to visit North Korea, as an indication of support for the 'sunshine' approach as against that of the 'axis of evil'. It was surprising, therefore, that Seoul persisted in a seemingly trivial campaign to have the sea between the two countries renamed from the Sea of Japan to the East Sea.

Ties with Russia were not especially close in 2002, despite agreement to settle a long-standing Moscow debt in part by South Korean weapons purchases. The Minister of Foreign Affairs, Igor Ivanov, visited both Koreas in July. Kim Dae-Jung endorsed President Putin's decision to prioritize the improvement of relations with Pyongyang. One shared interest was in an 'iron silk road', a rail freight route linking South Korea to Europe via Siberia. Yet this depended not only on Kim Jong Il's consent, but on investing US $3,000m. to upgrade North Korea's decrepit network. Moscow hoped that Seoul would finance this.

Also in 2002 some overdue realism entered South Korea's hitherto rather ingenuous view of China. Trade disputes enhanced the image of a tough economic competitor; while the sight of Chinese police beating South Korean diplomats in Beijing, who (for once) were protecting North Korean refugees, was salutary also. Even so, not only was the Dalai Lama again refused a visa, but Asiana Airlines declined even to carry him from India to Mongolia via Seoul. South Korea's priority with China remained a perceived need to maintain Beijing's engagement, especially in putting pressure on North Korea to make peace and introduce reforms. For their part, Chinese leaders in September pressed the visiting GNP leader, Lee Hoi-Chang, to continue engagement with Pyongyang, if he were elected President.

Besides 'nordpolitik', from 2003 the main challenges for South Korea's next President would be to keep the alliance with the USA in good form; to build a more mature relationship with Japan, based on future shared interests rather than previous disagreements; and to consider carefully how close Seoul should become to Beijing. If North-South relations were to improve definitively, a movement away from the USA towards China might become hard to resist, but not otherwise.

Economy

ROBERT F. ASH

Based on an earlier article by JOSEPH S. CHUNG

Until comparatively recently South Korea operated a mixed economic system. On the one hand, the country adhered to the basic tenets of private enterprise and a market economy; on the other hand, it followed a highly visible policy of government intervention. Through planning, direct or indirect ownership and control of enterprises and financial institutions, regulation of foreign exchange, and the implementation of appropriate monetary and fiscal policies, the Government played a crucial role in making market adjustments and maximizing incentives in pursuit of the fulfilment of its desired economic, social, political and cultural objectives. However, economic success, the increasing complexity of the economy, the emergence of a more democratic and pluralistic society (including greater participation in decision-making by different interest groups), and increasing international competitiveness were major factors in bringing about, from the late 1980s, a decline in the Government's role in the South Korean economy. Thus, the 1990s witnessed significant progress towards privatization and away from 'command capitalism'. The reformist thrust of government economic policy was underlined by renewed emphasis on the need for greater efficiency, improved labour productivity and enhanced competitiveness in order to meet the demands of globalization. The admission of South Korea, in December 1996, to membership of the Organisation for Economic Co-operation and Development (OECD) was another watershed, which heightened the importance of economic reform. So, from a negative aspect, was the impact of the Asian financial crisis, which highlighted long-standing structural weaknesses in the South Korean economy.

The process of measuring the effect of the Asian crisis was sensitive to the method of calculation. Bank of Korea estimates, given in 1995 constant prices, indicated that decelerating, but still positive, growth in 1997 was followed by negative growth in 1998, when GDP contracted by 6.7%. Thereafter, impressive recovery was shown to have taken place, GDP growth averaging 7.7% per year during 1999–2001 (with successive annual increases of 10.9%, 9.3% and 3%). By contrast, however, US dollar estimates based on the World Bank Atlas approach showed the post-1996 decrease in GDP continuing into 1998, before beginning to recover. In any case, what was not in doubt was that during 2000 and 2001, GDP growth was once more buoyant. Indeed, early in 2002, some observers expressed concern that the Korean economy might be 'overheating'. Such worries notwithstanding, economic growth remained impressive through the first half of the year, GDP accelerating from 5.7% to 6.3% during the first two quarters of 2002.

RESOURCE BASE, ECONOMIC GROWTH AND STRUCTURAL CHANGE

South Korea occupies only about 45% of the total area of the Korean peninsula, although its total population (estimated at 47.64m. in mid-2002) is more than double that of North Korea. Its total surface area is some 99,000 sq km, but little more than 20% of this is cultivable land (the remainder being shared between forest—65%–70% of total surface area—and land used to meet urban and transport needs). Such statistics emphasize the high density of population—479.7 persons per sq km.—which is only exceeded in Asia by Bangladesh, Hong Kong, Singapore and Taiwan.

As in the North, the main demographic impact of the Korean War was on mortality, which rose sharply between 1950 and 1953. Total military and civilian casualties attributable to the war were almost 2m. (of which deaths totalled some 600,000). Thereafter, however, a remarkable transformation occurred. Between 1955 and 1975 the death rate declined sharply (from 33 per 1,000 to 15 per 1,000), which, combined with a decelerating birth rate, resulted in the annual rate of natural increase falling below 2%. The deceleration in population growth continued until, by the end of the 1990s, it was a mere 1.1% per annum. Recent data point to a remarkably low age dependency ratio, with 71% of total population being between the ages of 15 and 64 (compared with 63% in 1980). Children below the age of 15 constituted 23% of total population in 2001. In the same year the economically active population numbered 22.18m., of whom 21.36m. (96.3%) were employed. Of these, 10.3% were engaged in agriculture, forestry and fishing; 27.1% in industry (with 19.7% in manufacturing); and 62.6% in the services sector.

Rapid urbanization has been a notable characteristic of demographic change in South Korea. In 1955 the urban share of total population was less than 25%. By 1975 the corresponding figure was already over 50%, and by the end of the 1980s it had reached 70%. The most important urban centres are Seoul and Busan, which, by 1990, already contained well over half of urban population—and 33% of total population.

South Korea contains quite rich concentrations of iron ore in the north-east of the country, although no more than 20% of these are thought to be high-grade. It also has significant reserves of limestone (the basis of the cement industry and so critically important for construction purposes), as well as minor deposits of gold, silver and copper. Its energy resources—mainly located in the north-east—are limited to anthracite coal, firewood and hydroelectric power. Total coal reserves have been estimated at about 1,500m. metric tons, of which perhaps 545m. tons are recoverable. In any case, dependence on coal as an energy source has fallen in favour of greater reliance on imported petroleum.

The social and economic legacy of the Korean War was devastating. In addition to casualties, some 1.5m. refugees from the North had to be accommodated. Physical damage to property has been calculated at the equivalent of South Korea's entire gross national product (GNP) for 1953, or at more than 10 times the then annual rate of fixed capital investment. Levels of production in all sectors were well below the previous peak levels of the early 1940s. Meanwhile, output in 1953 was heavily directed towards agriculture, with manufacturing production accounting for less than 9% of GNP. Such conditions dictated that economic rehabilitation, reconstruction and stabilization assumed the highest priority. In part thanks to large-scale US aid, these goals were fulfilled fairly quickly, and by 1957, war damage had been repaired and prices stabilized. Thereafter, however, until the military coup of 16 May 1961 brought Park Chung-Hee to power, the pace of South Korea's economic expansion slowed considerably.

The launch of the First Five-Year Plan (1962–66) was an important watershed in South Korea's post-war development, not only because it marked a break between different magnitudes of growth, but also because it embodied a distinctly new policy approach. The speed of transformation after the 1962 'take-off' was remarkable. By 1970 South Korea had already acquired the status of a 'newly-industrializing economy'; by 1986 it had reached the stage of self-sustaining growth, with domestic savings more than able to finance investment and with the balance of payments shifting from chronic deficit into surplus (thereby obviating the need for aid or overseas borrowing). The World Bank *World Development Report* (2000–2001) placed South Korea in the category of 'upper middle-income' countries and, in terms of per caput GNP, ranked it 59th among the 132 listed countries.

In the wake of the Korean War, massive inflows of aid facilitated quite rapid economic reconstruction, albeit accompanied by severe inflationary pressures. By the end of the 1950s, South Korea's productive facilities had been restored. Thereafter, between the First (1962–66) and Sixth (1987–91) Five-Year Plans—and driven by a rapid and sustained expansion of exports—South Korea's GNP grew, on average, by over 9% per annum. Although this average estimate conceals quite large year-to-year fluctuations, the rapid and mutually-reinforcing expansion of output, income and exports during these years was accompanied by increasing shares of savings, investment and foreign trade in national income. Much slower economic expansion in the 1990s (GNP increased by 5.7% per annum during 1990–99) reflected slowing growth in the early 1990s and, in 1997–98, the impact of the Asian financial crisis. In 2000 South Korea's aggregate GDP was US $461,700m.—a figure exceeded by only 10 other countries. In the same year its average per caput income was estimated to be US $9,770 (13.7% above the 1999 level)—but as much as 70% higher in purchasing-power parity terms. A further sign of economic recovery was that Korean GDP in 2001 was some 25% higher than on the eve of the crisis period.

The momentum of rapid growth from the 1960s until the end of the 1980s reflected the deliberate choice of a strategy designed to maximize growth through the pursuit of outward-orientated policies. Export-led growth was an imperative that dominated South Korea's development plans and replaced the earlier emphasis on import-substitution. Other complementary measures were adopted. Not least, the existence of an abundant supply of highly-skilled, highly-educated, disciplined and, at least initially, cheap labour, a readiness to use advanced foreign capital and technology, the growth of an indigenous managerial class and a growing research and development (R&D) capacity all contributed to the success of the export-led growth strategy. From a demand perspective, rising real wages that benefited a wide cross-section of the population, especially in the urban sector, also facilitated the emergence of a sizeable middle class that possessed considerable purchasing power.

Under the impact of rapid and sustained growth over several decades, the structure of the South Korean economy has undergone dramatic change. Predictably, the role of agriculture as a source of GDP has given way to that of industry (especially manufacturing industry) and, latterly, services. In the mid-1960s the farm sector still accounted for about 40% of GDP, compared with some 16% from industry, and 44% from services. In 2001 the corresponding figures were 5.2%, 44.9% (36% for manufacturing alone) and 49.9%.

A characteristic institutional feature of South Korea's economy has been the dominant role played by *chaebol*, or conglomerates—a Korean version of the Japanese *zaibatsu*. Such domination may well have disadvantaged the growth of small and medium-scale enterprises (SMEs) of the kind that have played such a vital role in Taiwan's post-war economic growth. Following almost 14,000 SME bankruptcies in 1995, the following year witnessed the establishment of a Small and Medium Business Administration, intended to promote more sustained SME growth. Its potential role was, however, overtaken by the onset of the financial crisis, and by the end of 1998 the failure of 22,828 SMEs had been recorded. Meanwhile, the collapse, in 1997, of one of the largest *chaebol*—the Hanbo Steel and Construction Corporation—compounded South Korea's political, as well as economic problems by implicating the Kim Young-Sam administration in its failure. This and other *chaebol* collapses had severe repercussions for the country's financial system, underlining the need for radical corporate and financial restructuring throughout the economy.

At the beginning of the 21st century, even allowing for significant recovery since 1999, South Korea still faced major challenges, which must be met if the country is to return to high and sustained growth. They include the implementation of further corporate and financial restructuring, as well as the formulation of effective measures to accommodate the growth of protective sentiments in the USA, Japan and EU member states—precisely the countries which, in the past, have absorbed a high share of Korean exports.

THE FINANCIAL CRISIS OF 1997 AND BEYOND

With the benefit of hindsight, it is clear that despite its record over several decades of high growth and rising living standards, as of the mid-1990s the South Korean economy faced deeply-rooted structural problems. Such problems were the major contributory factors, which precipitated the severe financial dislocation and economic collapse that affected South Korea, and other Asian countries, during 1997–98. Even before the onset of the Asian crisis, bankruptcy proceedings against a major *chaebol*—the Hanbo group—had served notice of the scale of difficulties facing the Government in Seoul. In July 1997 another *chaebol* (the Kia Group) defaulted on loans amounting to 2,770m. won. Efforts to rescue the situation were unsuccessful and the crisis deepened, leading to severe pressure on the national currency and stock market. The banking sector was particularly affected by the conglomerate bankruptcies, and the incidence of non-performing loans increased sharply in the second half of 1997. Against this background, fears began to grow that the Government might find itself with insufficient foreign currency reserves to service its foreign debt.

Central to understanding this rapid economic and financial deterioration are the close links that had evolved over many years between the Government, banks and *chaebol*. These links concealed underlying serious economic weaknesses, whilst creating an 'economic bubble', characterized by excessive investment in productive capacity and the over-valuation of the domestic currency. In the absence of adequate regulatory and supervisory controls, the financial system lacked transparency. With tacit acceptance by the Government, industrial projects were duplicated, generating excess capacity. Meanwhile, many *chaebol* had invested aggressively—and frequently in disregard of normal risk analysis—on the basis of profligate loans from domestic financial institutions, while also funding long-term investments by recourse to short-term foreign capital markets.

By the end of 1997 capital flight had become a serious problem, as foreign investors withdrew capital and many Koreans moved their savings overseas. Local firms sought to avoid hard-currency exposure and export revenue declined. Such developments brought further pressure to bear on stock prices and on land values, which both fell sharply. Despite intervention by the Bank of Korea, the won continued to slide, and by the end of the year it had lost more than half of its value *vis-à-vis* the US dollar.

After protracted negotiations, on 3 December 1997 IMF officials agreed a US $57,000m. loan agreement ($10,000m. to be made available as 'accelerated aid')—the largest rescue programme ever undertaken by the Fund. In return, the South Korean Government undertook to introduce more rigorous fiscal and monetary policies (including the maintenance of high interest rates), to strengthen regulatory control mechanisms, implement restructuring of banks and industrial corporations, firm up labour market reform, and enhance financial transparency in both public and private sectors.

Severe economic and associated social strains were in evidence throughout 1998. Annual GDP contracted by 5.8% and the unemployment rate rose from 3.1% to 7.9%; labour unrest and social demoralization were exacerbated by a rapid salary depreciation, mounting personal bankruptcies, and sharp increases in the prices of foreign consumer goods and energy imports. In July deepening recessionary conditions led the IMF to relax the fiscal and monetary conditions of its loan 'package'. Meanwhile, however, with the won successfully stabilized, in the second half of 1998, the Government—now headed by a new President, Kim Dae-Jung—introduced measures designed to stimulate domestic demand. Interest rates fell, expenditure was increased to provide support for the unemployed, and efforts to promote financial and corporate restructuring were intensified.

President Kim's efforts to strengthen discipline and control over South Korea's *chaebol* met with only partial success. Nor, given their preoccupation with self-survival, were the banks well placed to facilitate corporate restructuring. (The scale of banking sector problems was evidenced in estimates showing that the value of their non-performing loans was 160,000,000m.

won—far in excess of the 64,000,000m. won made available by the Government to buy back bad loans and recapitalize the banking system.) For example, when, in June 1998, 55 *chaebol* were declared 'non-viable' and refused further funding from banks, 20 of these that belonged to the five biggest conglomerates remained in business. Even after December 1998, when these five *chaebol* were instructed to limit their debts through mergers and asset disposal, strong resistance to reform continued. Yet, as the near-bankruptcy of the Daewoo Group (South Korea's second largest conglomerate) demonstrated in July 1999, the need for change remained imperative.

As indicated above, a major strand in *chaebol* restructuring plans was the reduction of their extremely high level of indebtedness, which was thought to be one of the principal reasons for the severity of South Korea's financial crisis. Although the largest *chaebol* failed to lower their debt-to-equity ratios below 200% (the level imposed by the Government in 1999), the average debt-to-equity ratio was more than halved, falling from more than 500% prior to the 1997 crisis to 225% in mid-2000. However, much of this decline was due to equity issuance rather than debt reduction.

Rationalization of the banking sector progressed more rapidly. Yet despite the closure of five large commercial banks and 16 smaller merchant banks, and notwithstanding the extension, as of early 2000, of 102,000,000m. won in government rescue packages, it remained clear that further reform and consolidation (including the disposal of government holdings in banking institutions) would have to be forthcoming.

South Korea's economic performance improved markedly in 1999, the contraction in GDP of the previous year (by 6.7%) being transformed into positive growth of 10.9%. An easing of fiscal and monetary policy kept interest rates low and helped stabilize the currency (the won reaching a two-year high). Meanwhile, private consumption spending and business investment rose sharply (by 10.1% and 46.8%, respectively). As annual manufacturing growth accelerated to 21%, the rate of unemployment began to decline (from 6.8% to 6.3%). Overseas demand for South Korean goods meanwhile strengthened, and by the end of the year the current-account surplus was US $24,500m., compared with a deficit of US $8,200 two years previously. Foreign-currency reserves continued their recovery from the low point of 1997, when they were just US $19,710m., to reach almost US $74,000m. Compared with foreign direct investment (FDI) inflows of US $5,400m. in 1998, by September 1999 FDI inflows had already reached an estimated US $15,000m. It was against this background that President Kim Dae-Jung claimed that his Government had 'completely overcome' the financial crisis—and this without full recourse to the IMF rescue 'package'.

Owing to a sharp slowdown in private consumption in the final quarter, GDP growth in 2000 was reduced to 9.3%—slightly lower than the 9.5% growth expected as of the end of 1999. Indeed, by the end of 2000, it was clear that rapid expansion during 1999 and in the first half of 2000 had not subsequently been maintained (growth in the second half of the year barely exceeding that of the second quarter alone). Stagnation in traditional manufacturing industries (for example, textiles and car production) was partly to blame, but the major contributory factor was falling domestic demand. A similar, but less pronounced pattern was apparent in the external sector, where export growth was 23.5% during January–September, but thereafter slowed to around 18%. By the end of the year the current-account surplus had been halved from US $24,500m. (at the end of 1999) to US $12,240m., and in 2001 it was further reduced to US $8,600m.

The domestic economic contraction notwithstanding, net flows of foreign direct investment (FDI) remained quite buoyant in 2000, reaching US $3,300m. in November (compared with a corresponding figure of US $3,900m. in 1999). Owing to a strong performance on its capital account, South Korea's foreign-exchange reserves reached a record level of US $95,900m., 30% above the level of the previous end-year. Following a reduction from 6.8% to 6.3% between 1998 and 1999, in 2000 the unemployment rate fell much more sharply (to 4.1%), and in 2001 the decline continued, to reach 3.7% (and 3.2% for the second half of the year).

South Korea's recovery from the economic crisis of 1997–98 was indeed striking and, despite a deceleration in 2001, economic growth in 2002 was buoyant. Doubts remained, however, about the long-term sustainability of such growth. The slowdown in GDP and export growth might be attributable to weakening external demand and its repercussions on domestic investment demand. From this perspective, improved economic conditions in the USA (which remained South Korea's most important export destination) promised the possibility of renewed and accelerated growth; likewise, for the time being, rapidly-rising consumer demand, encouraged by retail lending on a massive scale. (In mid-2002 loans to individuals and households were estimated to have absorbed about one-half of all lending by Korean banks and other financial institutions.) There was, however, a danger that the uncontrolled expansion of consumer credit might eventually necessitate the introduction of harsh measures to call in loans and/or reduce their level, thereby inhibiting further growth.

An even more fundamental point concerned the South Korean Government's ability to address the need for further corporate restructuring by enhancing competition in order to reduce the power of the *chaebol*. To this end, a major advance in 2002 was the purchase by General Motors (GM) of the bankrupt Daewoo Motor. The deal reportedly committed GM to paying US $251m. for a 42% stake—67% when other payments by GM's partners were taken into account—and taking over US $573m. of Daewoo's debts. Unfortunately, no sooner had the Daewoo deal been announced than it emerged that a proposal whereby Micron Technology would take over another fatally indebted Korean company—Hynix—had been rejected. The Hynix case merely underlined the continuing serious challenge of corporate restructuring in South Korea.

Overall, if South Korea is to improve its place in the global economy, it is incumbent on the Government to retreat even further from economic intervention by consolidating reforms (including banking reforms) and putting in place an effective legal and regulatory framework that will facilitate increased competitiveness by autonomous decision-making enterprises. At the same time, R & D and educational investment must be increased in order to make the South Korean economy a truly knowledge-based economy that can compete effectively in the global environment.

PLANNING

Since 1962 the South Korean Government has used formal economic planning as a means of exercising a major influence on the behaviour of the private sector and on the direction of economic development. Although the Government's 'indicative' plan has not directly compelled enterprises to adhere strictly to specific targets, it has brought indirect pressure to bear through the market mechanism. Thus, enterprises have been expected to conform to the basic objectives of the plan, while the Government has resorted to fiscal, monetary and other measures in order to fulfil planned targets. The existence of a private sector and the absence of compulsion highlights the peculiarly 'managerial approach' inherent in the Korean economy—a major contrast with the former Soviet planned system, which sought to integrate all major economic inputs and outputs in accordance with preconceived objectives and priorities through a vertical hierarchy in which orders are issued from higher to lower administrative levels. The Korean experience has been one of planning conducted in the context of a market-based economic system.

Except for the Fourth Five-Year Plan (1977–81), during which South Korea faced a serious recession, GDP growth has consistently over-fulfilled targeted rates. A common theme in all the plans has been a strong emphasis on the outward orientation of national economic development—in particular, the need for export expansion. In other particulars, policy thrusts of successive plans differed. For example, under the First Five-Year Plan (1962–66), a major priority was the expansion of infrastructural capital in electric power, railways, ports and communications, in order to obviate resource and other physical obstacles to development. In the Second Plan (1967–71), special attention was directed to the growth of electronic and petrochemical industries, as well as to raising farm incomes by maintaining high prices for rice (the staple crop). Priority development of heavy and chemical industries—especially steel, petrochemicals and ship-building—was strongly in evidence in the Third Plan (1972–76) and defined a major new policy thrust in South Korea's development strategy. In the Fourth Plan initiatives focused on industrial development based on the intensive use of technology and skilled labour. The same Plan, for the first time, also stressed the importance of social development, based on higher government welfare spending as a means of promoting a more equal distribution of income.

Under the Fifth (1982–86) and Sixth (1987–91) Plans, the strategy of export-led growth was strongly reaffirmed alongside unprecedented efforts to liberalize domestic markets, intended to dismantle regulations that had previously constrained the South Korean economy in its attempt to adjust to changing internal and external environments. In the simultaneous search for welfare and efficiency improvements, the Plans also articulated the need for more balanced sectoral and regional development.

In 1993 a revised Five-Year Plan was introduced. Within the framework of a targeted growth rate of 6.9%, the new Plan sought to elevate South Korea into the ranks of advanced economies and to lay the economic foundation for eventual reunification with the North. In line with the requirements of OECD membership, measures were introduced in an effort to combat official corruption and to initiate structural reforms within the economy. To these ends, three separate sub-plans were formulated, embracing deregulation, financial liberalization, and the management of foreign exchange and capital flows.

AGRICULTURE

South Korea is a mountainous country. Only 20% of the surface area (1.9m. ha) is arable, 65% being designated as forest land. The Taebaek range, which runs from north to south along the east coast, is the watershed of the Korean peninsula and the source of the country's principal rivers (the Han, Nakdong and Kum). South Korea's farming is concentrated mainly in these river basins and in the surrounding plains in the west and south. Owing to its more favourable climate and longer growing seasons (between 170 and 226 days), South Korea is more suited to farming than the North—especially in the cultivation of rice. This is the main crop, with paddy fields accounting for some three-fifths of the total cultivated area. Other food crops include barley, beans, potatoes and wheat, among which barley production has been promoted in order to conserve rice.

In the 1950s Korea remained a typical pre-industrial country, in which almost half of GDP derived from agriculture and an even larger proportion of its workforce was engaged in farming. Thereafter, however, the vigorous industrialization and export drive transformed this agrarian character: between 1960 and the early 1980s, the share of agriculture in GDP fell to about 15%, while the rural sector's share of total population declined from 58% to less than 25%. In 2001 agriculture accounted for just 5.2% of GDP and 10.3% of total employment. Although such figures highlight the relatively low productivity of the farming sector, viewed from an international perspective South Korea's record of agricultural growth since the early 1960s has exceeded the world average, as well as that of many Asian countries.

The Land Reform Acts of 1947 and 1948 abolished tenancy and defined the legal framework in which small owner-operated farms emerged. The rural population, which remained almost static at slightly more than 15m. until 1969, thereafter steadily declined. The contraction in the agricultural labour force (from 63.1% in 1963 to about 12% at the end of the 1990s) was not, however, matched by a parallel decline in average farm size, which actually rose, to 1.34 ha in 1997.

Despite the use of price subsidies, government farm purchases and import restrictions, the economic role of agriculture has gradually weakened. In particular, deficiencies associated with the small-scale nature and labour-intensive operation of farms, an ageing farm population and inefficiencies in the farm marketing system have meant that improvements in agricultural productivity have lagged substantially behind those in the industrial sector. One consequence—exacerbated by growing international pressure to open its domestic markets for rice and other agricultural products—was a rise in food imports to the extent that by the early 1990s the value of such sales was in excess of US $7,150m., making South Korea the sixth largest importer of farm products in the world.

In 2000 Korea's agricultural sector was adversely affected by the country's first outbreak of foot-and-mouth disease for 70 years. Emergency plans were drafted, providing for the destruction of 350,000 cattle and pigs in affected areas. Regional neighbours suspended imports of South Korean beef, pork and dairy products.

Food Production

Rice has dominated South Korea's agricultural production. In 2000 the annual rice harvest was 5.3m. metric tons, accounting for 72% of total crop output. Next in importance were radishes, which contributed a further 20% of total production. In order of importance, the balance of remaining food output was made up by barley, soyabeans, sweet and white potatoes, maize and wheat. For many years South Korea has been dependent on imports in order to satisfy domestic food demand, and in 2000 its trade account in food and live animals showed a deficit of US $4,100m.

Fisheries

South Korea has a long coastline, and fishing remains important for its contribution to national diet, livelihood and exports. Although accounting for only 0.5% of the labour force, South Korea's aquatic production is typically well in excess of 3m. metric tons, generating exports valued at US $1,640m. in 1996. Since the 1970s, structural changes have facilitated the emergence of South Korea's ocean-fishing industry as one of the most important in the world. Whether this position can be maintained in the face of the imposition of exclusive fishing zones by countries such as Russia and the USA, as well as the introduction of stricter fishery regulations for resource management, remains to be seen.

Forest Products

Although two-thirds of South Korea's surface area is forest land, and the country's moist climate is conducive to forest development, indiscriminate felling before 1945 depleted most of the original tree cover. Nation-wide afforestation and soil conservation campaigns have, however, successfully reversed the trend. Major tree species include red pine, Korean white pine, larch and oak. Lumbering, mainly of coniferous trees, is limited to the mountains of Gangwon and Gyeongsang Provinces, but contributes only a fraction of domestic timber needs. In 1997 88% of wood used domestically was imported.

MINING

In the absence of any known reserves of petroleum and possessing only 10%–20% of the Korean peninsula's mineral deposits, South Korea is poorly endowed with natural resources. Nevertheless, more than 50 different minerals have been found, of which the most important are graphite, anthracite coal, fluorite, salt, limestone, gold, silver, tungsten and some iron ore. As a result of ever-increasing domestic industrial requirements, the value of South Korea's exports of minerals (talc, agalmatolite, tungsten and graphite) has been far exceeded by the value of imports (especially iron, zinc, copper and aluminium ores). In an attempt to enhance the provision of minerals, South Korean enterprises have used joint ventures in order to participate in mineral extraction projects in resource-rich countries, such as Australia, Canada, Indonesia and the USA. Thus, in 1991 about 15% of South Korea's total overseas direct investment was in the mining sector.

In absolute terms, the value of mining production reached its peak level in 1997, although, since the early 1980s, the mining sector's share in GDP has never exceeded 1.5%.

Coal

Coal, mostly anthracite, is one of South Korea's leading mineral resources, with estimated deposits of 1,500m. metric tons. After reaching a peak of 24.3m. tons in 1987, anthracite production steadily declined to a mere 4.2m. tons in 2000. Rising domestic demand and declining production have necessitated imports of anthracite, mainly for domestic heating and cooking—this in addition to overseas purchases of coking coal for the iron and steel industry. The average annual cost of coal imports doubled between 1986 and 1990, to reach US $2,400m. at the time of the onset of the financial crisis in 1997.

Metallic Minerals

Notwithstanding estimated deposits of 120m. metric tons (mostly magnetite), the peak output level of iron ore (677,100 tons in 1989) has not subsequently been re-attained. In particular, production has fallen sharply in recent years from 631,500 tons in 1997 to 336,200 tons in 2000. Ore reserves (metal content) for lead, zinc, copper and tungsten are, respectively, 492m., 738m., 105m. and 100m. tons. Production of lead and especially zinc ore has declined markedly since the early 1980s (for example, between 1983 and 1997 total output of zinc ore fell from 113,900 tons to 16,800 tons). Other ores mined in South Korea include copper, gold, silver, molybdenum and tungsten—the tungsten mine at Sangdong being the second largest in the world.

Non-metallic Minerals

With estimated deposits of 30m. metric tons of amorphous graphite and 2.6m. tons of crystalline graphite, the country is one of the principal world sources of natural graphite. The production of amorphous graphite (at 75% purity) dramatically declined from its peak level of 107,767 tons in 1988 to a mere 1,820 tons in 1995. Meanwhile, total output of crystalline graphite was 1,552 tons in 1991. Production of fluorite (at 80% purity) declined rapidly in the 1980s, with output falling from 6,159 tons in 1981 to just 50 tons in 1993. Limestone is abundant in South Korea, with reserves estimated at 1,500m. tons, and output rose steadily from the early 1980s to reach 88m. tons (at 50% purity) by the mid-1990s. Limestone deposits have been the basis of the cement industry—and, in turn, of construction activities, which, in both the agricultural and industrial sectors, expanded rapidly in support of national economic growth momentum. In 1997, at the time of the onset of the financial crisis, cement production totalled 60.3m. tons, although it fell sharply to 46.8m. tons the following year. Cement exports have also been an important foreign exchange earner for South Korea. Kaolin production is also substantial, with output approaching 3m. tons in 1995. In addition, there are significant sources of uranium ore, with estimated reserves of 56m. tons (at 0.3%–0.4% uranium content).

MANUFACTURING

South Korea's labour-intensive consumer goods industry has succeeded quite well in meeting the demands of growing domestic and foreign markets. In the early 1970s, however, the early bias towards light manufacturing industry shifted towards more capital-intensive activities, such as machine-building, engineering, ship-building, whole plant construction, and the production of electronic goods, transport equipment and petrochemicals. Defence-related heavy industries have also been a high priority. From the 1980s, increasing emphasis was given to high-technology industries, including the production of automatic data-processing equipment. Implicit in this strategy was a recognition of South Korea's comparative advantage, based on a scarcity of natural resources, side by side with an abundance of skilled labour.

As a stimulus to rapid and sustained national economic growth, the expansion of exports has played a critically important role. The penetration of global markets has required South Korean manufacturing enterprises to become efficient and internationally competitive. This was achieved through the provision of incentives that facilitated a reduction in costs, the attainment of optimal scales of production and the introduction of productivity-enhancing innovations. In addition, the forces of international competition gave impetus to specialized production in those areas in which the country maximized its comparative advantage. By such means, South Korea has been able to create world-class industries in car manufacturing, the production of semiconductors, information processing, telecommunications, nuclear energy and shipbuilding.

Between 1965 and 1980 the average rate of growth of manufacturing output was a remarkable 16.4% per annum—a figure that fell to a still impressive 12% during 1980–90. The further halving of output growth to 6.2% per year between 1990 and 1999 was largely a reflection of the impact of the financial and economic crisis of 1997 and 1998. During 1990–96 manufacturing production grew, in real terms, by 8.3% per annum, but having decelerated to 6.8% in 1997, in 1998 output fell by 7.4%. The strength of subsequent recovery is suggested by the finding that in 1999 and 2000 annual real growth was 21% and 15.9%, respectively. Shipbuilding, semiconductors and car production played a notable role in this recovery. In 2001 the growth of manufacturing slowed, with total output up by only 1.7%.

Textiles

South Korea is one of the world's largest producers of textiles and its textile industry has made a major contribution to domestic employment, exports and economic growth. Growing protectionism in the wake of increasing competition from other low-wage economies has, in recent years, encouraged major textile enterprises to diversify into other fields, embodying high and biotechnology. In the late 1980s textiles were replaced by electronics as South Korea's largest single export item. In 1997 the value of textile exports was US $18,500m. and accounted for 13.6% of total export value (compared with 28.6% in 1980). Meanwhile, between 1980 and 1997 the textile sector's share of total manufacturing employment fell from 24.7% to 8.7%. Under the impact of the financial crisis, in 1998 the value of textile exports fell to US $16,700m., or 12.6% of total export value.

Petroleum Refining

Petroleum refining has become increasingly important to the South Korean economy, as the structure of energy supplies has shifted away from coal. From about 10% in 1965, the share of petroleum in total energy supplies increased to 63% in 1978. As a result of growing reliance on nuclear power, this figure subsequently declined (to 47% in 1988), although in line with rising national energy consumption, total petroleum consumption rose, on average, by 3.9% per annum in 1978–88. In 1997 petroleum accounted for 59.3% of total energy consumption. Owing to the decline in international petroleum prices, the value of crude petroleum imports fell from US $5,572m. in 1985 to an annual average of US $3,578m. during 1986–88 (physical imports having risen from 27m. metric tons to 31.4m. tons in the same period). As a result, petroleum accounted for only 7.1% of the value of the country's total imports in 1988, compared with 17.9% in 1985. This trend was, however, reversed in 1989 and 1990, when a sharp rise in petroleum prices, resulting from the Gulf War, raised the cost of imports to US $4,933m. and US $6,386m. By 1997 the corresponding figure had risen further to US $17,712m., accounting for 12.2% of the value of all imports, and in 1998 and 1999 crude petroleum imports averaged little more than US $13,000m. They rebounded in 2000 (to US $25,200m., but fell back slightly, to US $21,370m., in 2001, when Korea's net petroleum imports were estimated to be equivalent to about 3% of GDP.

Rising industrial demand for fuel oil is satisfied by domestic refineries, whose combined capacity at the end of 1997 was some 2.5m. b/d, or about 70 times greater than in 1964. Although exploration projects began in the early 1970s, no domestic petroleum sources have yet been discovered. As a result, all South Korea's crude petroleum has to be imported, mostly from Middle Eastern countries.

Chemicals

The construction, in 1959, of the Chungju Fertilizer Plant marked the beginning of South Korea's development of an indigenous chemical industry. Prior to this, all chemical fertilizer requirements were imported. In 1968, however, chemical fertilizer self-sufficiency had been secured, and in 1976 South Korea became a net exporter of fertilizers. The peak level of production (2.51m. metric tons) was reached in 1994—a figure which subsequently fell back to 1.94m. tons in 1999, before recovering to 2.18m. tons in 2000.

Diversification of the chemical industry has been under way since the 1960s. Major products include sulphuric acid, ammonia, compressed oxygen, dye, insecticides, polyethylene, polypropylene, polyvinyl chloride, polyester fibres and acrylic fibres. The chemical industry attracted 8.5% of foreign direct investment approvals in 1998, compared with 3.4% in 1997. In 2000 chemicals and chemical products earned US $13,800m. of foreign exchange and accounted for 8.0% of the total value of exports (compared with 3.9% in 1990). The corresponding figures for 2001 were US $10,800m. and 8.3%.

Metallurgy

The construction, in 1973, of the Pohang Iron and Steel Co (POSCO)—South Korea's first integrated steel plant—was an important watershed in the development of a national steel industry. POSCO subsequently became the second largest steel complex in the world, and by 1996, with an annual production capacity of some 40m. metric tons, South Korea had become the world's fifth-largest producer of steel. Meanwhile, production of pig-iron reached 24.8m. tons in 2000. In 1997, however, domestic demand for steel fell back sharply, and three of the country's largest producers were declared bankrupt. Despite a fall in the price of steel and a consequent quite sharp decline in the value of POSCO's steel exports, in the first half of 2000 South Korea was still the fourth-largest steel exporter to the USA.

Shipbuilding and Car Industries

Construction of new plants during the late 1960s laid the groundwork for a shift of emphasis in the 1970s, from production of light machinery products and simple metal-working machinery to the manufacture of transport and communications equipment, industrial machinery, precision machinery, textile machinery, and electric and electronic appliances.

When, in 1993, it received 38% of global shipbuilding orders, South Korea overtook Japan to become the world's largest shipbuilder. Helped by the rapidly rising value of the yen, South Korea received orders in that year for 186 vessels, with a displacement of 8.9m. grt and worth US $7,350m. (an increase of 291.3% over 1992). By 1995, in terms of tonnage, Daewoo Shipbuilding had become the largest shipbuilding company in the world in 1995, followed by Hyundai, Samsung and Hanjin. In 1993 these companies already accounted for some 85% of the country's total constructed tonnage, employees and turnover.

Although South Korea has not been able consistently to maintain its lead over Japan in terms of shipbuilding orders, the industry has generally succeeded in maintaining its momentum of buoyant growth. Following reductions in exports sales both in 1997 and 1999, the following years saw recovery to new peak levels, and in 2000 the value of shipping exports reached a record US $8,230m. (4.8% of total export value).

In the early 1980s the motor vehicle industry was adversely affected by the world recession, with total production declining from 203,100 to 121,000 vehicles in a single year (1979–80). By 1983 production had reattained and exceeded its former (1979) peak level, and thereafter the industry underwent rapid expansion until, by 1997, output had reached 2,828,730 vehicles (2,313,160 passenger cars, 282,127 lorries and 233,433 buses). The outcome was to make South Korea the fifth largest motor vehicle manufacturer in the world.

South Korea began to export motor vehicles to Canada in 1983, and had begun to penetrate the European market by 1985. The country's automobile producers passed another watershed when, in the mid-1980s, it entered the US market (in 1986 Hyundai's 'Excel' model was the most successful new foreign car ever to enter the US car market). The value of exported passenger cars rose from US $87.4m. in 1983 to a record US $3,336.1m. in 1988. There followed a short period of declining exports, but by 1993 recovery and renewed growth had taken exports to a new peak of US $3,892.3m. The momentum of export growth slowed only marginally in 1998, and in 2001 the value of passenger car exports was US $12,030m. This sustained growth in the motor industry reflected a successful exploration of both domestic as well as overseas markets. With increasing international competitiveness in the industry, tariffs on passenger cars have been reduced in recent years, although they still remain high. By the end of the 1990s, motor vehicle exports accounted for nearly 7% of South Korea's total export value, and in 2001 they had risen to an estimated 8%. In 2001 passenger cars were the third largest category of exports, after electrical and electronic products (US $47,359.7m., a figure more than US $14,600 below the record level of 2000), and machinery (US $11,640.4m.).

Electronics

The origins of the electronics industry lie in the assembly, in the early 1960s, of vacuum tube radios from imported parts. Subsequently, South Korea's electronics industry expanded rapidly, and in 1969 it received full-scale government support, when the Electronics Industry Promotion Law was promoted, designating electronics as a priority industry and recognizing its strategic export potential. The implementation of a comprehensive eight-year development programme was accompanied by major inflows of foreign capital and technology, which played a crucial role in generating 'foreign-led' electronics exports. In the early 1970s the manufacture of electronic components (such as transistors, diodes, integrated circuits, radio receivers and parts for monochrome television receivers) dominated. After 1974, colour television receivers were produced, fuelling a fast expansion in consumer electronics. By the end of the 1970s, South Korean-made products included electronic calculators and watches, and in 1979 the country had become one of the most important global producers of video-cassette recorders (VCRs).

The production and export of computers and peripheral equipment also expanded rapidly, as computer manufacturers began to pursue a policy of import substitution. With a total output and export value of US $23,531m. and US $15,200m., respectively, by 1988, the industry already accounted for 13.4% of GNP and 25.0% of total exports. In that year South Korea was the sixth largest exporter of electronic goods in the world and electronics had surpassed textiles as the country's principal export item. In 1992 South Korea became one of the five largest electronics-producing countries in the world, with overseas sales accounting for 25.9% of total exports—a figure that rose to 30.6% in the first half of 1999.

The growth of semiconductor production was considered essential if a country is to secure an internationally competitive position in high-technology areas, especially in the production of automatic data-processing equipment. Thus, as in Taiwan, semiconductors have played a major role in the development of South Korea's electronics industry. Indeed, by the mid-1990s, it had become one of the foremost international producers of semiconductors, South Korean companies having established global brand name recognition for their products. Helped by strong growth in the global market for semiconductor chips, Samsung Electronics garnered 10.8% of the world's memory chip market in 1993, thus becoming the seventh largest semiconductor chip producer in the world. In the same year South Korea's share in the global semiconductor market was 17.9%—and 23.6% in the dynamic random access memory (DRAM) chip market. Manufacturers have, however, remained dependent on Japan for the supply of many of the components that they use, although in 1993 a number of Japanese electronics and machinery manufacturers began themselves to purchase electronic parts and components from South Korean companies. The experience of the USA and other countries emphasized the critical need to allocate increasing investment to R&D in order to enhance international competitiveness, and it is instructive that in the early 1990s the three leading electronics manufacturers—Samsung, Daewoo and LG (formerly Lucky Goldstar)—substantially increased their R&D expenditure. Meanwhile, by the mid-1990s South Korea ranked second in the world in terms of production capacity of VCRs, microwave ovens, fax machines and videocassette tapes, and third for colour television receivers and telephones. In March 1996 Samsung initiated a DRAM plant in Texas—its first semiconductor facility to be located in the USA, attesting to the globalization of the country's electronic industry. Following a sharp decline in inflows during the previous year, in 1998 the electronics industry attracted 15.5% of all foreign direct investment approvals.

In 2001, of a total of US $47,360m. earned from exports of electrical and electronic goods, electrical home appliances accounted for 14.2%; semiconductors, 30.1%; and information and communications equipment, 43.3%.

INFRASTRUCTURE

Transport

Until quite recently, the principal means of freight and passenger traffic in South Korea was railway transport. With the rapid expansion of the motorway network, improvements in its quality and extended motor vehicle ownership, roads have now assumed the position previously filled by railways. In 2000, for example, 496.2m. tons of domestic freight were transported by road—12.5% more than in 1995. By contrast, during the same period freight transport by rail fell by 21% to 45.2m. tons. The outcome was that almost three-quarters of all domestic freight was now handled by road transport (ship transport accounting for 20%).

In addition to highways, mass transit rail systems in the largest cities have recently been accorded special priority, as exemplified by the construction of underground railway systems in Seoul, Busan, Daegu, Daejeon, Gwangju and Incheon. With signs of a degree of *rapprochement* with North Korea, work began in September 2000 to rebuild the Seoul–Shinuiju (North Korea) Railway Line and to construct a four-lane highway linking Seoul and the North Korean capital, Pyongyang. Both projects were delayed by the political situation, but were scheduled for completion in 2003.

The capacity of South Korea's ports, including newly-constructed facilities at Bukbyong on the east coast, has also expanded rapidly, reaching 295m. metric tons per annum in 1996 (compared with almost 100m. tons in 1986). In line with this expansion, the national merchant fleet has greatly increased: in 2001 its 2,426 vessels had a total displacement of 6.4m. grt.

Air transport capacity, both internal and external, has also expanded markedly. Until Asiana Airlines began operations on domestic routes in December 1988, Korean Air was the only airline company to operate in and from South Korea. However, by 1995 Asiana operated international flights to destinations in Japan, China, South-East Asia and the USA. A new international airport opened in 2001 at Incheon. In 2000 the total number of air passengers using South Korean airports exceeded 27m.

Energy

Between 1990 and 1997 South Korea's commercial energy use rose from 91.4m. metric tons of oil equivalent to 176.4m. tons (the implied average growth of per caput use being 8.9% per annum). Between 1990 and 1997 net energy imports, expressed as a percentage of commercial energy use, rose from 76% to 86%. The country's energy constraint is further highlighted by figures which show that in 2000, in addition to having to import all its oil requirements, it suffered deficits (production minus consumption) of –62.4m. tons of coal, and –35,600m. kWh of electricity.

Until 1977 South Korea relied predominantly on oil and coal for electric power generation. In that same year, as part of an effort to minimize dependence on imported petroleum, the first nuclear power station came into operation. Twenty years later, the share of nuclear power as a source of electricity had reached 34.3% of the total, while hydroelectric and thermal power provided 2.4% and 63.2%. Looking further ahead, there is an expectation that longer-term energy requirements will be met by rationalizing the distribution of petroleum-, nuclear- and coal-derived energy sources. For example, plans for 1991–2006 foresaw the construction of 14 new nuclear power plants (with a combined generating capacity of 12,800 MW), in order to help fulfil the increase in targeted generating capacity from 24,120 MW in 1992 to 58,669 MW in 2006.

In order to diversify its sources of energy, South Korea also sought to encourage the production of liquefied natural gas (LNG) for both domestic and industrial consumption. The first LNG terminal, in Pyeongtaek, was completed in April 1987 and has an annual processing capacity of 1m. metric tons. The Korean Gas Corpn (KGC), which operates the terminal, has signed a 20-year agreement with Indonesia, providing for the import of 2m. tons of LNG annually from 1986 until 2006. In 1987 KGC began to supply LNG to the Seoul metropolitan area, making South Korea the seventh nation in the world to use LNG. Meanwhile, KGC plans to construct a second LNG terminal in the centre of the country, with a capacity three times that of the original facilities.

Finally, in an effort to minimize energy dependence, South Korea has recently begun to develop its own petroleum and coal fields in Indonesia through the implementation of joint-venture schemes. It is, however, a salutary reminder of the magnitude of the task facing South Korea that oil consumption continued to rise steadily throughout the 1990s, leaving the economy increasingly exposed to rising international prices for crude petroleum.

INTERNATIONAL TRADE

Although South Korea lacks natural resources and is constrained by its small domestic market, it enjoys the benefits of a hard-working and highly-educated labour force, which the Government and private sector have exploited in order to facilitate the expansion of exports that has sustained the high economic growth rate. In every single year between 1953 to 1985, imports exceeded exports, although accelerating export growth facilitated a sharp contraction in the trade deficit as a share of exports—from 772.2% in 1953 to 137.5% in 1970, then to a mere 2.8% in 1985. In 1986 South Korea recorded a trade surplus of US $4,210m.—the first to be achieved since the end of the Korean War—and by 1988 the corresponding figure had reached US $11,440m. This surplus was virtually eliminated in 1989, after which, until 1998, the trade balance moved back into deficit. Among the factors responsible for the rapid rise in import costs during this period were the enormous increase in petroleum prices, following the Iraqi invasion of Kuwait in August 1990, the rising value of the Japanese yen, and the expansion of domestic demand in South Korea itself. According to the Asian Development Bank (ADB), the trade deficit reached almost US $19,700m. in 1996, before narrowing to US $8,450m. in 1997. In 1998, as South Korea's demand for imports declined sharply during the recession, a substantial trade surplus of US $39,030m. re-emerged. Merchandise trade remained in surplus during 1999–2001, although the absolute level declined in successive years (from US $23,900m. to $11,800m.). In these most recent years, export growth has been driven by sales of semiconductors, computers and petrochemical products, although the associated benefits have been partly offset by high international oil prices and increasing import demand for raw material and components.

Exports

Rapid export growth got under way in the 1960s, following a deliberate decision to pursue vigorous export promotion in pursuit of rapid and sustained economic growth. Between 1965 and 1980 exports grew, on average, by an astonishing 27.2% per year—a record unmatched anywhere in the world. In the 1980s the export sector encountered more difficulties and was subject to wide annual fluctuations—compare a nominal rate of increase of 36.2% in 1987 with one of just 2.8% in 1989—whilst also recording a sharp downturn in annual growth (to 12.8% per year).

The 1990s too were a decade of varying fortunes. Between 1990 and 2000 average export growth was a very creditable 10.25% per annum. Yet concealed within this figure were again large annual swings, ranging from 30.3% in 1994 to –2.8% in 1998—the former, reflecting widening international demand for Korean electronic goods (especially semiconductors), cars and ships; the latter, not just a familiar reflection of the impact of the financial crisis, but also of falling international prices for Korean goods and of the weakness of the Japanese yen. In 1999 and 2000 export recovery was swift, the value of overseas sales rising cumulatively by more than 30% during these two years. In 2001, however, the trend was reversed, as the value of exports decreased by 12.7% to US $150,400m.

South Korea continued to face formidable challenges from a variety of sources. One is fierce competition coming from low-wage economies, such as the People's Republic of China and countries in South-East Asia. Another external pressure has been the impact of protectionist measures introduced by advanced countries. Finally, at home, labour unrest and upward pressure on wages have also taken their toll. Nevertheless, South Korean products have competed favourably with goods produced in developed countries, and in some cases (for example, cars, microwave ovens, television receivers, VCRs and personal computers) their brand names have continued to gain international customer recognition.

More than 90% of exports are manufactured goods, headed by information and communications equipment, and semiconductors, and followed by textiles, and chemical and chemical products. Other important export items are passenger cars and spare parts, ships, iron and steel, footwear, rubber tyres and tubes, plywood and fishery products.

The USA remained easily the most important market for South Korean exports. In 2001 the USA accounted for 20.7% of all exports (in value terms). For the first time, the People's Republic of China overtook Japan to take second place, purchasing 12.1%, compared with Japan's 11% of total exports (Hong Kong took a further 6.3%). The growth of shipments to China is the most noteworthy feature of South Korea's export trade in recent years, their value having risen from US $1,000m. in 1991 to US $18,190m. in 2001—an average rate of growth of about 70% per annum. Other important export destinations include (in order of importance), Taiwan, Germany, Singapore, the United Kingdom, Indonesia, Malaysia, and the Philippines.

Imports

Import growth between 1965 and 1980 was 15.2% per annum, falling to 10.8% per year during the 1980s. Between 1990 and 1996 the momentum of rapid growth was maintained, with imports expanding, on average, by almost 12% annually. Thereafter the collapse of domestic demand in the wake of the Asian financial crisis had a dramatic effect, and import growth fell to 4.1% in 1997 before plummeting to –35.5% in 1998. Recovery from the downturn was, however, swift. As demand for industrial raw materials, machinery and high-price petroleum recovered, so imports rose again—by 28.4% in 1999 and by an astonishing 34% in 2000 (by which time, the value of imports was 11% above the previous 1997 peak level). Less favourable conditions in 2001 were reflected in a fall of 12%.

The two most important categories of imports are now mineral fuels (principally petroleum), machinery and transport equipment, and raw materials (excluding fuels). In 2001 these accounted for around two-thirds of the total value of all inward shipments.

Japan and the USA remained the two most important sources of South Korean imports, together accounting for 34.7% of the total in 2001. In particular, import dependence on Japan for machinery and electronic goods has become increasingly strong in recent years. Yet just as China has grown in importance as a destination for its exports, so South Korea has also become an increasingly important customer for Chinese products. Thus, between 1991 and 2001 the value of Chinese imports rose from US $3,400m. to US $13,300m., registering an average increase of over 14% per annum. In 2001 China accounted for 9.4% of all South Korea's imports.

In response to the mounting trade deficit with South Korea in the late 1980s, the US Government began to exert strong pressure for greater US access to South Korean markets. Anxious to avoid the economic sanctions which the USA had already imposed on certain Japanese electronic products, South Korea introduced measures designed to liberalize its import trade, whilst also encouraging voluntary export restraints on selected products. In order to appease US protectionist sentiment, and to counter the effects of the appreciation of the Japanese yen, it began to import from the USA some 100 products which had previously come from Japan. The South Korean Government also sought to placate its US critics by allowing the exchange value of the won to appreciate, thereby enhancing the competitiveness of US imports.

Throughout the 1980s and 1990s South Korea consistently ran a trade deficit *vis-à-vis* Japan (rising from US $3,000m. to US $15,400m. between 1985 and 1996). By contrast, until 1990 it enjoyed a large surplus with the USA, although this was subsequently eliminated, facilitating the attainment of greater balance in bilateral trade—and even, during 1991–92, 1994 and 1996–97, the emergence of a deficit. Liberalization of South Korea's agricultural market and acceptance, in 1993, of rice imports were important contributory factor towards reducing the US deficit. Since 1998, however, the trade balance had moved back towards an increasingly large surplus, reaching US $8,800m. in 2001.

Invisible Trade

With the single exception of 1975, during the period from the end of the Korean War to the end of the 1970s, South Korea consistently enjoyed a surplus in its invisible trade—at times, sufficiently large to offset its merchandise trade deficit and move its current account into surplus. However, between 1980 and 1985 this position was reversed, as construction contracts with Middle Eastern countries declined and interest payments on outstanding foreign debt increased. Since 1986 the current account has moved between periods of surplus and deficit. In 1996 a record deficit of US $23,000m. was recorded, although in 1997 this figure contracted sharply and from 1998 it moved back into surplus (averaging US $21,400m. during 1998–2001.

FINANCE

Fiscal Policy

The South Korean Government has used tax reforms in order to influence resource allocation and guide the direction and pattern of national economic development. Early (pre-1960) measures were primarily designed to limit consumption and promote capital accumulation. By contrast, more comprehensive reforms introduced in the 1960s sought to put in place a more indigenously financed growth strategy, by replacing economic aid with increased domestic savings. Thus, between 1965 and 1975 the savings rate rose sharply (from 7.4% to 19.1% of GDP). By 1986 it had reached 30%, for the first time making it possible to finance investment wholly from domestic sources. Since that time, South Korea has been a net exporter of capital—for example, in 2000 gross domestic savings exceeded gross domestic capital formation by US $19,900m.

South Korea's tax burden (tax receipts as a share of GNP) is relatively low, although between 1995 and 2000 it rose from 16.5% to 21%. Fiscal policy was relaxed in mid-1998, as South Korea's economic recession deepened, in order to facilitate increased expenditure on social security benefits, job creation and financial restructuring. The central Government budget, having been in surplus 1993, during 1997–99 reverted to deficit (peaking at 18,800m. won in 1998, or 4.3% of GNP). In 2000, however, in the wake of more stringent fiscal and monetary policies, it moved once more into surplus to the tune of 6,500m. won—this figure rising to 7,300m.won in 2001.

Foreign Debt

Between 1985 and 1990 South Korea's total outstanding debt was reduced from US $47,100m. to US $35,000m. Subsequently, however, financial liberalization encouraged increasingly large inflows of foreign capital. As a result, total debt rose sharply until, by 1997, it had reached US $139,100m., implying average growth of 18.8% per annum since 1990. Meanwhile, many enterprises continued to finance their industrial expansion by borrowing large amounts of capital from abroad. The seriousness of the situation was highlighted in the fact that by 1996—on the eve of the financial crisis—some 57% of outstanding debt was in the form of short-term debt. This was a dangerously high figure, as shown by the fact that in 1996 interest on short-term debt was US $3,900m., compared with only US $2,800m. on long-term debt. Meanwhile, in 1998 the cost of debt-servicing was equivalent to 12.9% of revenue from exports of goods and services. Against the background of a deterioration in its external debt situation, during 1997–99 South Korea had recourse to IMF credit, totalling over US $34,000m. for the three years.

In 2001 South Korea's foreign-exchange reserves totalled US $102,487.5m. This figure compared with US $19,700m. in 1997, when reserves fell by 39% below the level of the previous year. The implied average rate of increase was 51% per annum (1997–2001).

Monetary Policy and Banking

Through the operations of the Central Bank and by means of direct ownership—or control through equity participation—of most financial institutions, until the 1980s the Government maintained very tight control over interest rate determination, the underwriting of private loans from abroad, and the allocation of financial resources to the private sector and other enterprises. In 1964 a government-sponsored foreign exchange rate initiative involving a major currency devaluation (of about 50%) and the introduction of a unified floating rate system greatly facilitated export expansion. In the wake of subsequent economic growth, the case in favour of financial liberalization became increasingly pressing, and in the 1980s significant monetary reforms took place. Amongst these were denationalization of the commercial banking sector, the first moves towards the freeing of interest rates from government control, and the abolition of credit ceilings and quotas in order to control bank lending. By such means, banks were given new discretion in managing loanable funds in pursuit of profit maximization. More recent evidence of increasing reliance on indirect control is afforded by the Bank of Korea's (BOK) involvement in limited open-market operations.

By 1991 interest rate deregulation had embraced most money market instruments, large certificates of deposits and repurchase agreements. By the end of 1993 lending rates at banks and non-banks had also been freed, while interest rates on policy loans and special credit facilities were scheduled for decontrol during 1994–97. As interest rate liberalization took place, the BOK began to shift from using direct monetary controls, involving the imposition of 'ceiling rates' on bank loans, to reliance on indirect policy instruments and open market operations. Meanwhile, starting in October 1993, the range of permissible daily interbank foreign exchange rate fluctuations was widened. December 1994 saw the introduction of the Foreign Exchange Reform Plan, designed to be implemented in three stages between 1995 and 1999, focusing, in turn, on economic globalization-related issues, the liberalization of cross-border transactions, and improvements in the foreign-exchange system.

A major reform, introduced in August 1993, was the implementation of a 'real-name' system of financial transactions, which replaced the previous system that had allowed financial accounts and property to be recorded under false, assumed or borrowed names. The desired effect was to curb corruption and enhance incentives, as well as to facilitate the emergence of a more equitable tax regime. Following the publication of the findings of a presidential commission on financial reform in mid-1997, the Government also undertook to seek to curb the influence of the powerful Ministry of Finance and the Economy through the creation of a Financial Supervisory Commission. The principal purpose of the new body, which would be directly responsible to the Prime Minister, was to strengthen supervision over the financial sector. Measures to increase the independence of the BOK were also proposed.

During 1986–89 a by-product of an appreciating won was a significant narrowing of the gap between official and black-market rates for foreign currencies. From 1990 until 1994, the value of the won registered a declining trend, although after mid-1994 its value began to rise again. This trend, combined with the depreciation of the Japanese yen in mid-1995, did not bode well for South Korean exports. Following the rapid depreciation of the won in late 1997, the Government adopted tight monetary policies in order to stabilize the currency. This having been achieved, from mid-1998 monetary policy was eased, with interest rates lowered substantially in a bid to stimulate domestic demand.

The stability of the banking system was tested in 1997, following the collapse of the Hanbo Group. Following revelations that, notwithstanding the lack of adequate collateral, several of the country's largest banks had lent money to Hanbo under government pressure, an investigation was launched in an attempt to discover how such loose credit creation could have taken place. Emergency funds were released into the banking system by the Ministry of Finance and the Economy in order to prevent further corporate bankruptcies.

The opening, in 1967, of a branch of the Chase Manhattan Bank was a signal for other foreign banks to establish branches in South Korea. By the end of 1993 some 74 foreign banks had established offices throughout the country. Measures were also introduced to provide foreign access to the domestic securities market, and from January 1992 direct investments by foreigners in South Korea's stock market were permitted, albeit initially with an upper limit of 10% of total shares. In May 1996 it was announced that most restrictions on the entry of foreign firms into the stock market would be removed by the year 2000. Meanwhile, in July 1993 the limit for foreign equity investment had already been eliminated for companies with a 50% or greater foreign ownership, but in December 1997, the IMF insisted, as a condition of its rescue programme, that the limit for foreign equity investment should be abandoned entirely—this was in the hope that foreign investors would purchase stakes in the ailing *chaebol*.

The stock market, the main index of which, under the impact of the regional financial crisis, had declined dramatically at the end of 1997, subsequently rose sharply. By the end of 1999 the stock price index was 173% higher than it had been two years previously. In 2000, however, it lost 50% of its value—not least because of struggling investment trust companies' divestment of their portfolios in order to finance their debts. Substantial recovery took place in 2001, during which the index rose by more than 37%. Indeed, in 2001, with one exception (Russia), the Korean stock market outperformed those of every other country.

In 1998 financial institutions and industrial corporations were radically restructured in accordance with the IMF programme. By mid-2000 the Government had closed 440 failing financial institutions, including five large commercial banks (more than a third of workers in the financial sector lost their jobs). In addition, the Government recapitalized 15 of the 17 remaining commercial banks to internationally required standards, as well as introducing regulatory reforms in order to improve the transparency of banking operations. Such measures notwithstanding, in 1999 the banking sector recorded losses of 5,000,000m. won, principally as a result of huge liabilities resulting from the collapse of the Daewoo Group. In September 1999 agreement was reached to sell Korea First Bank—one of five banks (the others were Hanvit Bank, Cho Hung Bank, Korea Exchange Bank and Seoulbank) which had been nationalized in 1998—to Newbridge Capital, a US investment fund.

Between late 1997 and early 2000 the Korean Government spent some 102,000,000m. won in an attempt to prevent the collapse of the banking sector. In May 2000, in the face of continuing severe difficulties, plans to inject a further 30,000,000m. won were announced. From the perspective of 2002, a consensus view would be that significant progress has been made towards improving the state of South Korea's banking sector, even though the position of some individual institutions remains far from good. It is an essential condition of future sustained economic growth that the benefits of banking reforms in recent years should not be jeopardized. Nor can it be doubted that further progress lies in the direction of privatization. Finally, urgent attention is required in order to address the high level of non-performing loans in the non-bank financial sector (especially investment trust companies).

Wages and Prices

The annual rate of price inflation has fallen significantly in recent years, to below 10%. In the second half of the 1980s, the rate of increase in the urban consumer price index (CPI) averaged 4.1% per annum—a figure which accelerated to 6% annually between 1990 and 1995. Rising prices during this period reflected the award of large wage rises, associated with emerging shortages of labour, growing unionization and a higher incidence of labour disputes. Thus, by 1995, the average monthly manufacturing wage had reached 1,123,895 won (some US $1,500).

The effect of the financial crisis was quickly to exacerbate inflationary pressures. Thus, from an annual CPI increase of 4.5% in 1997, by February 1998 the index had risen to 9.5% (year on year), and although it subsequently moderated, the annual figure for 1998 was still 7.5%. In 1999 inflation fell sharply to 0.8%, although it subsequently increased, rising by 2.2% and 4.1% in 2000 and 2001 respectively.

Increasing labour unionization and the award of higher fringe benefits have combined to undermine South Korea's export competitiveness *vis-à-vis* a number of low-wage industrializing countries. In 2000 there was also a resurgence of strike activity, reflecting growing confidence by the trade unions in their ability to press claims for wage increases and enhanced job security on behalf of their members as the economy achieved rapid recovery from the regional financial crisis of 1997. By February 2001 the unemployment rate had risen from its three-year low of 3.4% in October 2000 to 5%. In the event, this rising trend was not subsequently maintained, the annual rate of employment for 2001 being 3.7%.

Statistical Survey

Source (unless otherwise stated): National Statistical Office, Bldg III, Government Complex-Daejeon 920, Dunsan-dong, Seo-gu, Daejeon 302-701; tel. (42) 481-4114; fax (42) 481-2460; internet www.nso.go.kr.

Area and Population

AREA, POPULATION AND DENSITY*

Area (sq km)	99,313†
Population (census results)‡	
1 November 1995	44,608,726
1 November 2000	
Males	23,068,181
Females	22,917,108
Total	45,985,289
Population (official estimates at mid-year)	
2000	47,008,000
2001	47,343,000
2002	47,640,000
Density (per sq km) at mid-2002	479.7

* Excluding the demilitarized zone between North and South Korea, with an area of 1,262 sq km (487 sq miles).

† 38,345 sq miles. The figure indicates territory under the jurisdiction of the Republic of Korea, surveyed on the basis of land register.

‡ Excluding adjustment for underenumeration, estimated at 1.4% in 1995.

PRINCIPAL TOWNS (population at 1995 census)

Seoul (capital)	10,231,217	Jeonju (Chonju)	563,153
Busan (Pusan)	3,814,325	Jeongju (Chongju)	531,376
Daegu (Taegu)	2,449,420	Masan	441,242
Incheon (Inchon)	2,308,188	Jinju (Chinju)	329,886
Daejeon (Taejon)	1,272,121	Kunsan	266,559
Gwangju (Kwangju)	1,257,636	Jeju (Cheju)	258,511
Ulsan	967,429	Mokpo	247,452
Seongnam (Songnam)	869,094	Chuncheon (Chunchon)	234,528
Suwon	755,550		

2000 census: 9,853,972; Busan 3,655,437; Daegu 2,473,990; Incheon 2,466,338; Daejeon 1,365,961; Gwangju 1,350,948; Ulsan 1,012,110.

BIRTHS, MARRIAGES AND DEATHS*

	Registered live births		Registered marriages		Registered deaths	
	Number	Rate (per 1,000)	Number	Rate (per 1,000)	Number	Rate (per 1,000)
1993	723,924	16.4	402,593	9.0	240,468	5.4
1994	728,515	16.3	393,121	8.7	248,377	5.5
1995	721,074	16.0	398,484	8.7	248,089	5.4
1996	695,825	15.3	434,911	9.4	245,588	5.3
1997	678,402	14.8	388,591	8.4	247,938	5.3
1998	642,972	13.8	375,616	8.0	248,443	5.3
1999	616,322	13.2	362,673	7.7	246,539	5.2
2000	636,780	13.4	334,030	7.0	247,346	5.2

* Owing to late registration, figures are subject to continuous revision. The foregoing data refer to events registered by the end of 2000, tabulated by year of occurrence.

Expectation of life (WHO estimates, years at birth, 2000): Males 70.5; Females 78.3 (Source: WHO, *World Health Report*).

ECONOMICALLY ACTIVE POPULATION*
(annual averages, '000 persons aged 15 years and over)

	1998	1999	2000
Agriculture, forestry and fishing	2,480	2,349	2,288
Mining and quarrying	21	20	18
Manufacturing	3,898	4,006	4,244
Electricity, gas and water	61	61	63
Construction	1,578	1,476	1,583
Trade, restaurants and hotels	5,571	5,724	5,943
Transport, storage and communications	1,169	1,202	1,260
Financing, insurance, real estate and business services	1,856	1,925	2,089
Community, social and personal services	3,339	3,499	3,551
Total employed (incl. others)	19,994	20,281	21,061
Unemployed	1,461	1,353	889
Total labour force	21,456	21,634	21,950
Males	12,893	12,889	12,950
Females	8,562	8,745	9,000

2001 ('000 persons aged 15 years and over): Agriculture, forestry and fishing 2,193; Manufacturing 4,199; Total employed 21,362; Unemployed 819; Total labour force 22,181 (Males 13,012; Females 9,169).

* Excluding armed forces.

Health and Welfare

KEY INDICATORS

Fertility (births per woman, 2000)	1.5
Under-5 mortality rate (per 1,000 live births, 2000)	5
HIV/AIDS (% of persons aged 15–49, 2001)	<0.10
Physicians (per 1,000 head, 1997)	1.36
Hospital beds (per 1,000 head, 1997)	5.1
Health expenditure (1998): US $ per head (PPP)	580
% of GDP	5.1
public (% of total)	46.2
Access to water (% of persons, 2000)	92
Access to sanitation (% of persons, 2000)	63
Human Development Index (2000): ranking	27
value	0.882

For sources and definitions, see explanatory note on p. vi.

Agriculture

PRINCIPAL CROPS ('000 metric tons)

	1998	1999	2000
Rice (paddy)	6,779.3	7,032.8	7,124.8
Barley	256.5	330.6	226.6
Maize	80.2	79.3	614.2
Potatoes	562.0	678.3	704.6
Sweet potatoes	339.1	428.1	344.9
Dry beans	24.1	22.8	21.0
Chestnuts	110.0	95.8	92.8
Soybeans (Soya beans)	140.4	116.1	113.2
Sesame seed	27.7	24.1	31.7
Other oilseeds	41.9	37.3	34.7
Cabbages	2,992.2	2,738.3	3,420.3
Lettuce	142.5	173.7	203.5
Spinach	116.9	105.5	121.0
Tomatoes	231.6	290.7	276.7
Pumpkins, squash and gourds	194.6	217.0	217.0*
Cucumbers and gherkins	408.3	418.8	418.8*
Chillies and green peppers	288.1	436.6	391.3
Green onions and shallots	500.5	606.6	606.6*
Dry onions	872.1	935.8	877.5
Garlic	393.9	483.8	474.4
Carrots	145.5	151.3	155.2
Mushrooms	16.0	19.8	21.8
Other vegetables*	3,498	3,352	3,706
Tangerines, mandarins, clementines and satsumas	511.9	624.2	563.5
Apples	459.0	490.5	490.0
Pears	260.0	259.1	324.2
Peaches and nectarines	151.3	157.2	170.0
Plums	39.0	43.7	51.7
Strawberries	155.5	152.5	180.5
Grapes	397.8	407.1	475.6
Watermelons	807.3	936.7	922.7
Cantaloupes and other melons	298.7	319.4	300.0*
Persimmons	260.7	273.8	288.0
Other fruits	89.8	82.5	82.2*
Tobacco (leaves)	55.5	65.4	68.2

* FAO estimate(s).

Source: FAO.

LIVESTOCK ('000 head)

	1998	1999	2000
Cattle	2,922	2,486	2,134
Pigs	7,544	7,864	8,214
Goats	539	462	449
Rabbits	259	462	550
Chickens	85,488	94,587	102,547
Ducks	3,167	4,787	5,405

LIVESTOCK PRODUCTS ('000 metric tons)

	1998	1999	2000
Beef and veal	375.7	342.4	303.4
Pig meat	939.4	996.3	915.9
Chicken meat	349.7	390.0*	393.0*
Duck meat*	27.0	39.3	44.7
Other meat	8.1*	9.1*	9.8†
Cows' milk	2,027.0	2,243.9	2,253.0
Goats' milk	5.3	3.5	4.6
Butter	49.0	50.1	50.1†
Hen eggs	455.4	461.9	478.8
Other poultry eggs	9.5	20.2	21.3
Honey	7.7	10.6	17.7
Cattle hides (fresh)	61.6	50.4	46.9

* Unofficial figure. † FAO estimate.

Source: FAO.

Forestry

ROUNDWOOD REMOVALS ('000 cubic metres, excl. bark)

	1998	1999	2000
Sawlogs, veneer logs and logs for sleepers	490	621	420*
Pulpwood	406	410	552*
Other industrial wood	532	663	620*
Fuel wood	2,438*	2,444	2,449*
Total	3,866	4,138	4,041

* FAO estimate.

Source: FAO.

SAWNWOOD PRODUCTION ('000 cubic metres, incl. sleepers)

	1997	1998	1999
Coniferous (softwood)	4,059	1,900	3,648
Broadleaved (hardwood)	700	340	652
Total	4,759	2,240	4,300

2000: Production as in 1999 (FAO estimates).

Source: FAO.

Fishing

('000 metric tons, live weight)

	1997	1998	1999
Capture	2,204.0	2,026.9	2,119.7
Alaska (walleye) pollock	223.1	236.3	146.2
Croakers and drums	120.1	105.6	129.5
Japanese anchovy	230.9	249.5	238.5
Skipjack tuna	115.9	143.4	109.8
Yellowfin tuna	61.2	73.4	43.3
Chub mackerel	160.5	172.9	177.6
Largehead hairtail	67.2	74.9	64.4
Argentine shortfin squid	208.2	92.4	271.7
Japanese flying squid	225.0	163.0	249.3
Aquaculture	392.4	327.5	303.1
Pacific cupped oyster	200.9	175.9	177.3
Other molluscs	101.3	63.9	43.8
Total catch	2,596.4	2,354.4	2,422.8

Note: Figures exclude aquatic plants ('000 metric tons): 671.1 (capture 23.2, aquaculture 647.8) in 1997; 481.8 (capture 12.6, aquaculture 469.2) in 1998; 486.6 (capture 12.9, aquaculture 473.7) in 1999. Also excluded are aquatic mammals, recorded by number rather than by weight. The number of whales and dolphins caught was: 156 in 1997; 78 in 1998; 104 in 1999.

Source: FAO, *Yearbook of Fishery Statistics*.

Mining

('000 metric tons, unless otherwise indicated)

	1998	1999	2000
Hard coal (Anthracite)	4,356	4,197	4,174
Iron ore: gross weight	486	410	336
metal content	272	230	188
Lead ore (metric tons)*	3,558	1,822	2,724
Zinc ore (metric tons)*	10,488	9,832	11,474
Kaolin	2,259.8	1,858.4	2,098.5
Feldspar	248.5	409.3	330.4
Salt (unrefined)†	770	750	800
Mica (metric tons)	38,459	24,733	65,249
Talc (metric tons)	24,411	15,313	11,344
Pyrophyllite	843.6	754.7	918.0

* Figures refer to the metal content of ores.

† Estimated production.

Source: US Geological Survey.

Industry

SELECTED PRODUCTS ('000 metric tons, unless otherwise indicated)

	1997	1998	1999
Wheat flour	1,750	1,722	1,834
Refined sugar	1,691	1,132	1,182
Beer (million litres)	1,691	1,408	1,487
Cigarettes (million)	96,725	101,011	95,995
Cotton yarn—pure and mixed (metric tons)	276,411	n.a.	n.a.
Woven cotton fabrics—pure and mixed ('000 sq m)*	328,405	n.a.	n.a.
Plywood ('000 cu m)	995	587	664
Newsprint (metric tons)	1,583,303	1,699,164	1,737,753
Rubber tyres ('000)†	59,281	60,192	67,120
Caustic soda (metric tons)	959,217	1,069,308	1,163,413
Urea fertilizer (metric tons)	903,295	n.a.	n.a.
Liquefied petroleum gas (million litres)	3,897	4,238	4,893
Naphtha (million litres)	21,968	21,767	21,688
Kerosene (million litres)	11,308	9,809	15,071
Distillate fuel oil (million litres)	41,694	37,622	35,157
Bunker C oil (million litres)	43,847	32,625	36,509
Residual fuel oil (million litres)	1,079	710	812
Cement	60,317	46,791	48,579
Pig-iron	22,712	23,093	23,328
Crude steel	42,554	39,856	41,042
Television receivers ('000)	16,407	13,578	16,616
Passenger cars—assembled (number)	2,313,160	1,576,701	2,157,909
Lorries and trucks—assembled (number)	282,127	178,401	256,467
Electric energy (million kWh)	224,445	215,307	239,925

* After undergoing finishing processes.

† Tyres for passenger cars and commercial vehicles.

Shipbuilding (merchant ships launched, '000 grt): 7,156 in 1997; 6,974 in 1998; n.a. in 1999; 9,856 in 2000 (Source: UN, *Monthly Bulletin of Statistics*).

2000 ('000 metric ton): Cement 51,424; Pig-iron 24,938; Crude steel 43,107 (Source: US Geological Survey).

Finance

CURRENCY AND EXCHANGE RATES

Monetary Units

100 chun (jeon) = 10 hwan = 1 won.

Sterling, Dollar and Euro Equivalents (31 May 2002)

£1 sterling = 1,798.6 won;
US $1 = 1,226.3 won;
€1 = 1,151.1 won;
10,000 won = £5.560 = $8.155 = €8.687.

Average Exchange Rate (won per US $)

1999 1,188.82
2000 1,130.96
2001 1,290.99

BUDGET ('000 million won)*

Revenue	1996	1997	1998
Taxation	72,385	78,434	78,310
Taxes on income, profits and capital gains	24,137	24,292	27,975
Income tax	14,767	14,868	17,194
Corporation tax	9,356	9,425	10,776
Social security contributions	7,425	8,506	10,512
Employees	2,804	3,433	n.a.
Employers	4,261	4,864	n.a.
Taxes on property	1,473	1,590	1,379
Domestic taxes on goods and services	27,478	30,650	27,159
Value-added tax	16,790	19,488	15,707
Excises	10,027	10,373	10,530
Import duties	5,309	5,798	3,836
Other current revenue	11,791	13,639	17,480
Entrepreneurial and property income	4,600	5,634	9,854
Administrative fees and charges, non-industrial and incidental sales	1,518	1,394	1,530
Fines and forfeits	3,502	5,032	4,646
Capital revenue	1,352	1,295	883
Total	85,528	93,368	96,673

Expenditure	1996	1997	1998
General public services	7,847	9,039	10,841
Defence	12,553	13,159	13,621
Education	14,435	16,249	17,779
Health	682	777	957
Social security and welfare	7,884	9,632	12,252
Housing and community amenities	7,077	6,677	7,336
Recreational, cultural and religious affairs and services	534	679	788
Economic affairs and services	21,965	24,334	28,453
Interest expenditures	2,241	2,258	3,399
Other	9,211	18,084	20,263
Total	84,429	100,888	115,689
Current	n.a.	62,812	70,631
Capital	n.a.	18,791	20,359
Net lending	n.a.	19,285	23,375
Other expenditures	n.a.	0	1,324

Source: IMF, *Republic of Korea: Statistical Appendix* (February 2000).

1999 ('000 million won)*: Total revenue 107,923 (current 106,523; capital 1,386); Total expenditure (excl. net lending and other expenditures) 101,236 (current 76,798; capital 24,438).

2000 ('000 million won)*: Total revenue 133,584 (current 132,366; capital 1,218); Total expenditure (excl. net lending and other expenditures) 108,259 (current 82,667; capital 25,592).

* Figures refer to the consolidated operations of the central Government, including extrabudgetary accounts.

Source: Bank of Korea.

INTERNATIONAL RESERVES (US $ million at 31 December)

	1999	2000	2001
Gold*	67.1	67.6	68.3
IMF special drawing rights	0.7	3.5	3.3
Reserve position in IMF	286.3	271.8	262.4
Foreign exchange	73,700.3	95,855.1	102,487.5
Total	74,054.4	96,198.1	102,821.6

* National valuation.

Source: IMF, *International Financial Statistics.*

MONEY SUPPLY ('000 million won at 31 December)

	1999	2000	2001
Currency outside banks	19,475	17,636	18,702
Demand deposits at deposit money banks	25,139	29,193	34,918

Source: IMF, *International Financial Statistics.*

COST OF LIVING (Consumer Price Index; base: 2000 = 100)

	1998	1999	2001
Food	96.4	99.1	104.1
Housing	103.9	100.2	103.9
Fuel, light and water	89.4	87.6	111.1
Furniture and utensils	103.3	102.0	102.4
Clothing and footwear	96.8	98.5	103.1
Medical treatment	92.3	93.4	112.3
Education	93.5	95.3	104.4
Culture and Recreation	101.1	100.1	99.7
Transport and communications	95.7	97.2	102.0
All items (incl. others)	97.0	97.8	104.1

NATIONAL ACCOUNTS ('000 million won at current prices)

National Income and Product

	1999	2000	2001*
Compensation of employees	210,411.5	229,605.2	244,898.2
Operating surplus	149,183.2	160,338.7	157,458.2
Domestic factor incomes	359,594.7	389,943.9	402,356.4
Consumption of fixed capital	60,904.2	61,655.9	63,184.5
Gross domestic product (GDP) at factor cost	420,498.9	451,599.8	465,540.9
Indirect taxes	63,552.8	71,811.8	80,938.7
Less Subsidies	1,307.5	1,452.4	1,466.3
GDP in purchasers' values	482,744.2	521,959.2	545,013.3
Factor income from abroad	3,847.5	7,197.6	9,110.7
Less Factor income paid abroad	9,994.1	9,929.4	10,249.4
Gross national product	476,597.6	519,227.4	543,874.6
Less Consumption of fixed capital	60,904.2	61,655.9	63,184.5
National income in market prices	415,693.4	457,571.5	480,690.0
Other current transfers from abroad (net)	2,223.9	644.3	-660.3
National disposable income	417,917.3	458,215.8	480,029.7

* Provisional.

Expenditure on the Gross Domestic Product

	1999	2000	2001*
Government final consumption expenditure	50,089.4	52,479.7	56,785.2
Private final consumption expenditure	271,136.5	299,121.8	324,226.3
Increase in stocks	-5,380.6	-1,033.7	-2,042.5
Gross fixed capital formation	134,151.8	148,202.8	147,497.9
Statistical discrepancy	-352.8	7,241.5	5,740.9
Total domestic expenditure	449,644.3	506,012.1	532,207.8
Exports of goods and services	204,377.6	233,791.7	233,857.1
Less Imports of goods and services	171,277.7	217,844.7	221,051.7
GDP in purchasers' values	482,744.2	521,959.1	545,013.2
GDP at constant 1995 prices	437,709.4	478,532.9	493,025.5

* Provisional.

Source: Bank of Korea.

Gross Domestic Product by Economic Activity

	1999	2000	2001*
Agriculture, forestry and fishing	24,481.5	24,517.6	24,126.7
Mining and quarrying	1,670.0	1,802.2	1,786.0
Manufacturing	148,402.9	163,283.2	163,334.9
Electricity, gas and water	13,014.0	14,374.4	15,845.8
Construction	42,149.3	41,788.0	44,879.3
Trade, restaurants and hotels	54,451.0	63,201.6	68,178.0
Transport, storage and communications	32,976.3	34,901.1	35,039.8
Finance, insurance, real estate and business services	95,276.5	98,977.1	105,967.7
Government services	36,961.5	39,018.5	43,277.2
Other community, social and personal services	24,806.0	27,484.8	32,410.9
Private non-profit services to households	11,470.6	12,320.7	13,514.3
Sub-total	485,659.6	521,669.2	548,360.6
Import duties	15,606.0	19,446.6	20,372.9
Less Imputed bank service charge	18,521.4	19,156.5	23,720.0
GDP in purchasers' values	482,744.2	521,959.2	545,013.3

* Figures are provisional.

BALANCE OF PAYMENTS (US $ million)

	1999	2000	2001
Exports of goods f.o.b.	145,164	175,948	151,371
Imports of goods f.o.b.	-116,793	-159,076	-137,979
Trade balance	28,371	16,872	13,392
Exports of services	26,529	30,534	29,602
Imports of services	-27,180	-33,423	-33,129
Balance on goods and services	27,720	13,982	9,866
Other income received	3,245	6,375	7,040
Other income paid	-8,404	-8,797	-7,926
Balance on goods, services and income	22,561	11,561	8,980
Current transfers received	6,421	6,500	6,548
Current transfers paid	-4,506	-5,820	-6,911
Current balance	24,477	12,241	8,617
Capital account (net)	-389	-615	-443
Direct investment abroad	-4,198	-4,999	-2,600
Direct investment from abroad	9,333	9,283	3,198
Portfolio investment assets	1,282	-520	-5,499
Portfolio investment liabilities	7,908	12,697	11,856
Financial derivatives assets	401	532	272
Financial derivatives liabilities	-915	-711	-378
Other investment assets	-2,606	-2,289	7,458
Other investment liabilities	1,502	-1,268	-11,764
Net errors and omissions	-3,536	-561	2,698
Overall balance	33,260	23,790	13,416

Source: IMF, *International Financial Statistics.*

External Trade

PRINCIPAL COMMODITIES (distribution by SITC, US $ million)*

Imports c.i.f.	1999	2000	2001
Food and live animals	5,551.3	6,496.7	6,789.3
Crude materials (inedible) except fuels	8,413.8	9,912.2	9,052.3
Mineral fuels, lubricants, etc.	22,874.9	38,076.6	34,069.3
Petroleum, petroleum products, etc.	17,906.0	30,535.4	26,485.6
Crude petroleum oils, etc.	14,782.7	25,215.6	21,367.8
Refined petroleum products	2,732.8	4,863.2	4,650.3
Gas (natural and manufactured)	3,003.2	5,355.2	5,236.6
Chemicals and related products	11,332.1	13,517.5	12,941.6
Organic chemicals	3,826.2	4,820.8	4,329.6
Basic manufactures	15,080.0	18,290.9	16,683.8
Iron and steel	4,003.2	5,315.7	4,420.0
Non-ferrous metals	3,770.1	4,449.8	3,894.9

Imports c.i.f. — *continued*	1999	2000	2001
Machinery and transport equipment	43,608.9	59,078.9	47,911.0
Machinery specialized for particular industries	3,370.9	5,510.0	3,713.1
General industrial machinery, equipment and parts	4,000.7	4,942.4	4,594.2
Office machines and automatic data-processing machines	4,330.5	7,711.0	5,640.8
Telecommunications and sound equipment	3,505.7	5,830.1	4,821.5
Other electrical machinery, apparatus, etc.	22,528.8	27,861.3	22,616.5
Thermionic valves and tubes, microprocessors, transistors, etc.	16,892.6	20,470.4	15,865.2
Electronic integrated circuits and microassemblies	13,541.2	16,734.8	13,356.8
Miscellaneous manufactured articles	8,778.3	12,021.5	11,166.6
Total (incl. others)	119,752.3	160,481.0	141,097.8

Exports f.o.b.	1999	2000	2001
Mineral fuels, lubricants, etc.	5,810.9	9,375.5	8,009.1
Petroleum, petroleum products, etc.	5,569.9	9,172.8	7,892.7
Refined petroleum products	5,452.0	9,011.8	7,736.3
Chemicals and related products	10,756.7	13,783.7	12,523.8
Plastics in primary forms	4,173.5	5,147.8	4,633.2
Basic manufactures	27,915.8	30,380.1	26,789.5
Textile yarn, fabrics, etc.	11,617.8	12,710.4	10,940.8
Iron and steel	5,914.0	6,682.3	5,825.8
Machinery and transport equipment	77,953.8	100,275.2	86,694.8
Office machines and automatic data-processing machines	10,572.2	19,633.5	13,498.7
Automatic data-processing machines and units, etc.	7,156.7	9,290.5	7,484.9
Parts and accessories for automatic data-processing equipment	3,158.6	9,950.9	5,640.2
Telecommunications and sound equipment	10,502.8	14,363.9	15,943.6
Transmission apparatus for radio or television	3,756.7	5,672.7	7,483.6
Other electrical machinery, apparatus, etc.	27,678.0	31,836.0	21,694.0
Thermionic valves and tubes, microprocessors, transistors, etc.	21,843.4	24,688.1	14,741.9
Electronic integrated circuits and microassemblies	17,810.3	19,877.2	11,142.3
Road vehicles and parts†	13,424.8	15,436.1	15,363.1
Passenger motor cars (excl. buses)	9,969.0	11,896.0	12,029.4
Other transport equipment and parts†	7,949.6	8,946.1	10,229.9
Ships, boats and floating structures	7,490.3	8,229.4	9,699.2
Miscellaneous manufactured articles	13,918.9	12,432.5	11,247.0
Clothing and accessories (excl. footwear)	4,870.9	5,027.1	4,305.7
Total (incl. others)	143,685.5	172,267.5	150,439.1

* Figures exclude trade with the Democratic People's Republic of Korea (US $ million): Total imports 121.6 in 1999, 152.4 in 2000, 176.2 in 2001; Total exports 211.8 in 1999, 272.8 in 2000, 226.8 in 2001.

† Data on parts exclude tyres, engines and electrical parts.

Source: Korea Trade Information Services.

PRINCIPAL TRADING PARTNERS (US $ '000)*

Imports c.i.f.	1999	2000	2001
Australia	4,672.4	5,958.7	5,534.1
Canada	1,792.9	2,107.8	1,821.3
China, People's Republic	8,886.7	12,798.9	13,302.7
France	1,823.1	2,243.8	2,092.3
Germany	3,826.0	4,624.7	4,473.4
Indonesia	3,986.9	5,286.9	4,473.5
Iran	1,505.8	2,392.8	2,099.3
Italy	1,269.0	1,637.8	1,787.5
Japan	24,142.0	31,827.9	26,633.4
Kuwait	1,416.4	2,716.0	2,250.7
Malaysia	3,155.3	4,878.0	4,125.0
Oman	944.4	1,744.7	2,310.9
Philippines	1,158.7	1,814.7	1,819.0
Qatar	868.4	2,292.1	2,572.1
Russia	1,590.5	2,058.3	1,929.5
Saudi Arabia	5,664.4	9,641.5	8,058.0
Singapore	2,311.7	3,722.9	3,011.5
South Africa	1,275.9	940.2	688.6
Taiwan	2,971.7	4,700.7	4,301.4
Thailand	1,067.8	1,630.9	1,589.2
United Arab Emirates	2,568.1	4,702.6	4,633.0
United Kingdom	2,098.2	2,575.7	2,353.5
USA	24,922.3	29,241.2	22,376.2
Total (incl. others)	119,752.3	160,481.0	141,097.8

Exports f.o.b.	1999	2000	2001
Australia	2,426.0	2,606.2	2,173.2
Brazil	1,209.3	1,724.1	1,611.2
Canada	1,638.5	2,426.7	2,035.7
China, People's Republic	13,684.6	18,454.5	18,190.2
France	1,654.1	1,713.3	1,541.2
Germany	4,184.9	5,153.8	4,321.8
Hong Kong	9,048.2	10,708.1	9,451.7
Indonesia	2,538.7	3,504.0	3,279.8
Italy	1,695.2	1,909.3	2,063.3
Japan	15,862.4	20,466.0	16,505.8
Malaysia	3,647.5	3,514.7	2,628.0
Mexico	2,016.9	2,391.4	2,148.9
Netherlands	2,143.6	2,657.9	2,532.1
Panama	1,812.8	1,247.0	1,719.0
Philippines	3,128.7	3,359.8	2,535.4
Singapore	4,921.8	5,648.2	4,079.6
Spain	1,490.5	1,533.1	1,518.2
Switzerland	1,840.7	515.8	431.9
Taiwan	6,345.5	8,026.6	5,835.3
Thailand	1,734.6	2,015.2	1,848.2
United Arab Emirates	1,550.6	1,991.5	2,169.1
United Kingdom	4,776.1	5,379.8	3,490.0
USA	29,474.7	37,610.6	31,210.8
Viet Nam	1,445.2	1,686.0	1,731.7
Total (incl. others)	143,685.5	172,267.5	150,439.1

* Excluding trade with the Democratic People's Republic of Korea.

Source: Korea Trade Information Services.

Transport

RAILWAYS (traffic)

	1998	1999	2000
Passengers carried ('000)	829,050	823,563	814,472
Freight ('000 metric tons)	43,345	42,081	45,240

ROAD TRAFFIC (motor vehicles in use at 31 December)

	1999	2000	2001*
Passenger cars	7,837,206	8,083,926	8,889,000
Goods vehicles	2,298,116	2,510,992	2,728,000
Buses and coaches	993,169	1,427,221	1,257,000
Motorcycles and mopeds	1,895,675	1,828,529	n.a.

* Figures are provisional.

SHIPPING

Merchant Fleet (registered at 31 December)

	1999	2000	2001
Number of vessels	2,417	2,502	2,426
Total displacement ('000 grt)	5,734.8	6,199.8	6,395.0

Source: Lloyd's Register-Fairplay, *World Fleet Statistics.*

Sea-borne Freight Traffic ('000 metric tons)*

	1998	1999	2000
Goods loaded	254,449	268,728	282,768
Goods unloaded	446,561	506,302	550,811

* Including coastwise traffic loaded and unloaded.

CIVIL AVIATION

	1998	1999	2000
Domestic services			
Passengers ('000)	19,136	20,673	22,289
Freight ('000 metric tons)	356	381	428
International services			
Passengers ('000)	13,541	16,083	18,905
Freight ('000 metric tons)	1,359	1,604	1,865
Mail ('000 metric tons)	19	21	20

Tourism

FOREIGN VISITOR ARRIVALS*

Country of Nationality	1999	2000	2001
China, People's Republic	316,639	442,794	482,227
Hong Kong	234,087	200,874	204,959
Japan	2,184,121	2,472,054	2,377,321
Philippines	198,583	248,737	210,975
Russia	127,892	155,392	134,727
Taiwan	110,563	127,120	129,410
USA	396,286	458,617	426,817
Total (incl. others)	4,659,785	5,321,792	5,147,204

* Including same-day visitors (excursionists) and crew members from ships.
† Including Korean nationals resident abroad: 301,027 in 1999; 277,523 in 2000; 286,585 in 2001.

Source: Korean National Tourism Organization.

Receipts from tourism (US $ million): 6,801.9 in 1999; 6,811.3 in 2000; 6,282.5 (estimate) in 2001 (Source: Bank of Korea).

Communications Media

	1999	2000	2001
Television receivers ('000 in use)	16,896	17,229	n.a.
Telephones ('000 main lines in use)	20,518.1	21,931.7	22,724.7
Mobile cellular telephones ('000 subscribers)	23,442.7	26,816.4	29,045.6
Personal computers ('000 in use)	8,519	11,255	12,000
Internet users ('000)	10,860	19,040	24,380
Book production:			
Titles	25,910	25,632	25,146
Copies ('000)	75,841	68,408	n.a.

1996: Facsimile machines (estimate, '000 in use): 400; Daily newspapers: Number 60, Circulation ('000 copies) 17,700 (estimate).
1997: Radio receivers ('000 in use) 47,500.

Sources: mainly UNESCO, *Statistical Yearbook*; UN, *Statistical Yearbook*; International Telecommunication Union.

Education

(2001)

	Institutions	Teachers	Pupils
Kindergarten	8,407	28,975	545,142
Primary schools	5,332	142,715	4,089,429
Middle schools	2,770	93,385	1,831,152
High schools	1,969	104,314	1,911,173
Junior vocational colleges	158	11,897	952,649
Teachers' colleges	11	710	21,418
Universities and colleges	162	43,309	1,729,638
Graduate schools	905	n.a.	243,270

Source: Ministry of Education, *Statistical Yearbook of Education.*

Adult literacy rate (UNESCO estimates): 97.8% (males 99.1%; females 96.4%) in 2000 (Source: UN Development Programme, *Human Development Report*).

Directory

The Constitution

The Constitution of the Sixth Republic (Ninth Amendment) was approved by national referendum on 29 October 1987. It came into effect on 25 February 1988. The main provisions are summarized below:

THE EXECUTIVE

The President

The President shall be elected by universal, equal, direct and secret ballot of the people for one term of five years. Re-election of the President is prohibited. In times of national emergency and under certain conditions the President may issue emergency orders and take emergency action with regard to budgetary and economic matters. The President shall notify the National Assembly of these measures and obtain its concurrence, or they shall lose effect. He may, in times of war, armed conflict or similar national emergency, declare martial law in accordance with the provisions of law. He shall lift the emergency measures and martial law when the National Assembly so requests with the concurrence of a majority of the members. The President may not dissolve the National Assembly. He is authorized to take directly to the people important issues through national referendums. The President shall appoint the Prime Minister (with the consent of the National Assembly) and other public officials.

The State Council

The State Council shall be composed of the President, the Prime Minister and no more than 30 and no fewer than 15 others appointed by the President (on the recommendation of the Prime Minister), and shall deliberate on policies that fall within the power of the executive. No member of the armed forces shall be a member of the Council, unless retired from active duty.

The Board of Audit and Inspection

The Board of Audit and Inspection shall be established under the President to inspect the closing of accounts of revenue and expenditures, the accounts of the State and other organizations as prescribed by law, and to inspect the administrative functions of the executive agencies and public officials. It shall be composed of no fewer than five and no more than 11 members, including the

Chairman. The Chairman shall be appointed by the President with the consent of the National Assembly, and the members by the President on the recommendation of the Chairman. Appointments shall be for four years and members may be reappointed only once.

THE NATIONAL ASSEMBLY

Legislative power shall be vested in the National Assembly. The Assembly shall be composed of not fewer than 200 members, a number determined by law, elected for four years by universal, equal, direct and secret ballot. The constituencies of members of the Assembly, proportional representation and other matters pertaining to the Assembly elections shall be determined by law. A regular session shall be held once a year and extraordinary sessions shall be convened upon requests of the President or one-quarter of the Assembly's members. The period of regular sessions shall not exceed 100 days and of extraordinary sessions 30 days. The Assembly has the power to recommend to the President the removal of the Prime Minister or any other Minister. The Assembly shall have the authority to pass a motion for the impeachment of the President or any other public official, and may inspect or investigate state affairs, under procedures to be established by law.

THE CONSTITUTIONAL COURT

The Constitutional Court shall be composed of nine members appointed by the President, three of whom shall be appointed from persons selected by the National Assembly and three from persons nominated by the Chief Justice. The term of office shall be six years. It shall pass judgment upon the constitutionality of laws upon the request of the courts, matters of impeachment and the dissolution of political parties. In these judgments the concurrence of six members or more shall be required.

THE JUDICIARY

The courts shall be composed of the Supreme Court, which is the highest court of the State, and other courts at specified levels (for further details, see section on Judicial System). The Chief Justice and justices of the Supreme Court are appointed by the President, subject to the consent of the National Assembly. When the constitutionality of a law is a prerequisite to a trial, the Court shall request a decision of the Constitutional Court. The Supreme Court shall have the power to pass judgment upon the constitutionality or legality of administrative decrees, and shall have final appellate jurisdiction over military tribunals. No judge shall be removed from office except following impeachment or a sentence of imprisonment.

ELECTION MANAGEMENT

Election Commissions shall be established for the purpose of fair management of elections and national referendums. The National Election Commission shall be composed of three members appointed by the President, three appointed by the National Assembly and three appointed by the Chief Justice of the Supreme Court. Their term of office is six years, and they may not be expelled from office except following impeachment or a sentence of imprisonment.

POLITICAL PARTIES

The establishment of political parties shall be free and the plural party system guaranteed. However, a political party whose aims or activities are contrary to the basic democratic order may be dissolved by the Constitutional Court.

AMENDMENTS

A motion to amend the Constitution shall be proposed by the President or by a majority of the total number of members of the National Assembly. Amendments extending the President's term of office or permitting the re-election of the President shall not be effective for the President in office at the time of the proposal. Proposed amendments to the Constitution shall be put before the public by the President for 20 days or more. Within 60 days of the public announcement, the National Assembly shall decide upon the proposed amendments, which require a two-thirds majority of the National Assembly. They shall then be submitted to a national referendum not later than 30 days after passage by the National Assembly and shall be determined by more than one-half of votes cast by more than one-half of voters eligible to vote in elections for members of the National Assembly. If these conditions are fulfilled, the proposed amendments shall be finalized and the President shall promulgate them without delay.

FUNDAMENTAL RIGHTS

Under the Constitution all citizens are equal before the law. The right of habeas corpus is guaranteed. Freedom of speech, press, assembly and association are guaranteed, as are freedom of choice of residence and occupation. No state religion is to be recognized and freedom of conscience and religion is guaranteed. Citizens are protected against retrospective legislation, and may not be punished without due process of law.

Rights and freedoms may be restricted by law when this is deemed necessary for the maintenance of national security, order or public welfare. When such restrictions are imposed, no essential aspect of the right or freedom in question may be violated.

GENERAL PROVISIONS

Peaceful unification of the Korean peninsula, on the principles of liberal democracy, is the prime national aspiration. The Constitution mandates the State to establish and implement a policy of unification. The Constitution expressly stipulates that the armed forces must maintain political neutrality at all times.

The Government

HEAD OF STATE

President: KIM DAE-JUNG (took office 25 February 1998).

STATE COUNCIL
(September 2002)

Prime Minister: KIM SUK-SOO.

Deputy Prime Minister for Finance and the Economy: JEON YUN-CHURL.

Deputy Prime Minister for Education and Human Resources Development: LEE SANG-JOO.

Minister of Unification: JEONG SE-HYUN.

Minister of Foreign Affairs and Trade: CHOI SUNG-HONG.

Minister of Justice: KIM JUNG-KIL.

Minister of National Defence: Gen. (retd) LEE JUN.

Minister of Government Administration and Home Affairs: LEE KEUN-SIK.

Minister of Science and Technology: CHAE YUNG-BOK.

Minister of Culture and Tourism: KIM SUNG-JAE.

Minister of Agriculture and Forestry: KIM DONG-TAE.

Minister of Commerce, Industry and Energy: SHIN KOOK-HWAN.

Minister of Information and Communication: LEE SANG-CHUL.

Minister of Health and Welfare: KIM SUNG-HO.

Minister of the Environment: KIM MYUNG-JA.

Minister of Labour: BANG YONG-SUK.

Minister of Construction and Transportation: LIM IN-TAIK.

Minister of Maritime Affairs and Fisheries: KIM HO-SHIK.

Minister of Planning and Budget: CHANG SEUNG-WOO.

Minister of Gender Equality: HAN MYONG-SOOK.

Chairman of the Civil Service Commission: CHO CHANG-HYUN.

Chairman of the Financial Supervisory Commission: LEE KEUN-YOUNG.

Minister of Government Policy Co-ordination: KIM JIN-PYO.

Minister of the Government Information Agency: SHIN JUNG-SIK.

Chairman of the Korea Independent Commission Against Corruption: KANG CHUL-KYU.

MINISTRIES

Office of the President: Chong Wa Dae (The Blue House), 1, Sejong-no, Jongno-gu, Seoul; tel. (2) 770-0055; fax (2) 770-0344; e-mail president@cwd.go.kr; internet www.bluehouse.go.kr.

Office of the Prime Minister: 77, Sejong-no, Jongno-gu, Seoul; tel. (2) 737-0094; fax (2) 739-5830; internet www.opm.go.kr.

Ministry of Agriculture and Forestry: 1, Jungang-dong, Gwacheon City, Gyeonggi Prov.; tel. (2) 503-7200; fax (2) 503-7238; internet www.maf.go.kr.

Ministry of Commerce, Industry and Energy: 1, Jungang-dong, Gwacheon City, Gyeonggi Prov.; tel. (2) 503-7171; fax (2) 503-3142; internet www.mocie.go.kr.

Ministry of Construction and Transportation: 1, Jungang-dong, Gwacheon City, Gyeonggi Prov.; tel. (2) 503-9405; fax (2) 503-9408; internet www.moct.go.kr.

Ministry of Culture and Tourism: 82-1, Sejong-no, Jongno-gu, Seoul 110-050; tel. (2) 7704-9114; fax (2) 3704-9119; internet www.mct.go.kr.

Note: In 2001–02 the romanization of place-names in South Korea was in the process of change, to be completed by 2005. Names of people and corporations were to remain unchanged for the time being.

Ministry of Education and Human Resources Development: 77, 1-ga, Sejong-no, Jongno-gu, Seoul 110-760; tel. (2) 720-3404; fax (2) 720-1501; internet www.moe.go.kr.

Ministry of Environment: 1, Jungang-dong, Gwacheon City, Gyeonggi Prov.; tel. (2) 2110-6576; fax (2) 504-9277; internet www.moenv.go.kr.

Ministry of Finance and the Economy: 1, Jungang-dong, Gwacheon City, Gyeonggi Prov.; tel. (2) 503-9032; fax (2) 503-9033; internet www.mofe.go.kr.

Ministry of Foreign Affairs and Trade: 77, 1-ga, Sejong-no, Jongno-gu, Seoul; tel. (2) 3703-2555; fax (2) 720-2686; internet www.mofat.go.kr.

Ministry of Gender Equality: 520-3, Banpo-dong, Seocho-gu, Seoul 137-756; tel. (2) 2106-5000; fax (2) 2106-5145; internet www.moge.go.kr.

Ministry of Government Administration and Home Affairs: 77-6, Sejong-no, Jongno-gu, Seoul; tel. (2) 3703-4110; fax (2) 3703-5501; internet www.mogaha.go.kr.

Ministry of Health and Welfare: 1, Jungang-dong, Gwacheon City, Gyeonggi Prov. 427-760; tel. (2) 503-7505; fax (2) 503-7568; internet www.mohw.go.kr.

Ministry of Information and Communication: 100, Sejong-no, Jongno-gu, Seoul 110-777; tel. (2) 750-2000; fax (2) 750-2915; internet www.mic.go.kr.

Ministry of Justice: 1, Jungang-dong, Gwacheon City, Gyeonggi Prov.; tel. (2) 503-7012; fax (2) 504-3337; internet www.moj.go.kr.

Ministry of Labour: 1, Jungang-dong, Gwacheon City, Gyeonggi Prov.; tel. (2) 503-9713; fax (2) 503-8862; internet www.molab.go.kr.

Ministry of Maritime Affairs and Fisheries: 139 Chungjeong-no 3, Seodaemun-gu, Seoul 120-715; tel. (2) 3148-6040; fax (2) 3148-6044; internet www.momaf.go.kr.

Ministry of National Defence: 1, 3-ga, Yonsan-dong, Yeongsan-gu, Seoul; tel. (2) 795-0071; fax (2) 796-0369; internet www.mnd.go.kr.

Ministry of Planning and Budget: 520-3, Banpo-dong, Seocho-gu, Seoul 137-756; tel. (2) 3480-7716; fax (2) 3480-7600; internet www.mpb.go.kr.

Ministry of Science and Technology: 1, Jungang-dong, Gwacheon City, Gyeonggi Prov.; tel. (2) 503-7619; fax (2) 503-7673; internet www.most.go.kr.

Ministry of Unification: 77-6, Sejong-no, Jongno-gu, Seoul 110-760; tel. (2) 720-2424; fax (2) 720-2149; internet www.unikorea.go.kr.

Civil Service Commission: Kolon Bldg, 35-34, Dongui-dong, Jongno-gu, Seoul 110-040; tel. (2) 3703-3633; fax (2) 3771-5027; internet www.csc.go.kr.

Financial Supervisory Commission: 27 Yeouido-dong, Yeongdeungpo-gu, Seoul; tel. (2) 3771-5000; fax (2) 785-3475; internet www.fsc.go.kr.

Korea Independent Commission Against Corruption: Seoul City Tower, 581, 5-ga, Namdaemun-no, Jung-gu, Seoul 100-095; tel. (2) 2126-0114; fax (2) 2126-0310; internet www.kicac.go.kr.

President and Legislature

PRESIDENT

Election, 18 December 1997

Candidate	Votes	% of total
Kim Dae-Jung	10,326,275	40.27
Lee Hoi-Chang	9,935,718	38.75
Rhee In-Je	4,925,591	19.21
Kwon Young-Kil	306,026	1.19
Others	148,828	0.58
Total*	25,642,438	100.00

* In addition, there were 400,195 blank or invalid votes.

KUK HOE
(National Assembly)

1 Yeouido-dong, Yeongdeungpo-gu, Seoul; tel. (2) 788-2786; fax (2) 788-3375; internet www.assembly.go.kr.

Speaker: PARK KWAN-YONG.

General Election, 13 April 2000

Party	Elected Representatives	Proportional Representatives	Total Seats
Grand National Party	112	21	133
Millennium Democratic Party	96	19	115
United Liberal Democrats	12	5	17
Democratic People's Party	1	1	2
New Korea Party of Hope	1	—	1
Independents	5	—	5
Total	227	46	273

Political Organizations

Democratic Labour Party (DLP): DooRay Bldg, 903, Yeouido-dong 24, Yeongdeungpo-gu, Seoul 151-010; tel. (2) 761-1333; fax (2) 761-4115; internet www.kdlp.org; f. 2000; Pres. KWON YOUNG-GHIL.

Grand National Party (GNP) (Hannara Party): 17-7, Yeouido-dong, Yeongdeungpo-gu, Seoul 150-010; tel. (2) 3786-3373; fax (2) 3786-3610; internet www.hannara.or.kr; f. 1997 by merger of Democratic Party and New Korea Party; Chair. SUH CHANG-WON.

Korean Coalition for the Future: c/o National Assembly, Seoul; f. 2002 by defectors from the GNP; Chair. PARK GEUN-HYE.

Millennium Democratic Party (MDP): 15, Gisan Bldg, Yeongdeungpo-gu, Seoul; tel. (2) 784-7007; fax (2) 784-6070; internet www.minjoo.or.kr; f. 2000 following dissolution of National Congress for New Politics (f. 1995); Chair. HAHN HWA-KAP; Sec.-Gen. KIM WON-GIL.

United Liberal Democrats (ULD): Insan Bldg, 103-4, Shinsu-dong, Mapo-gu, Seoul 121-110; tel. (2) 701-3355; fax (2) 707-1637; internet www.jamin.or.kr; f. 1995 by fmr mems of the Democratic Liberal Party; Pres. KIM JONG-PIL.

Civic groups play an increasingly significant role in South Korean politics. These include: the People's Solidarity for Participatory Democracy (Dir JANG HASUNG); the Citizens' Coalition for Economic Justice; and the Citizens' Alliance for Political Reform (Leader KIM SOK-SU).

Diplomatic Representation

EMBASSIES IN THE REPUBLIC OF KOREA

Algeria: 2-6, Itaewon 2-dong, Yeongsan-gu, Seoul 140-202; tel. (2) 794-5034; fax (2) 792-7845; e-mail sifdja01@kornet.net; internet www.algerianemb.or.kr; Ambassador: AHMED BOUTACHE.

Argentina: Chun Woo Bldg, 5th Floor, 534 Itaewon-dong, Yeongsan-gu, Seoul 140-861; tel. (2) 793-4062; fax (2) 792-5820; Ambassador: RODOLFO IGNACIO RODRÍGUEZ.

Australia: Kyobo Bldg, 11th Floor, 1, 1-ga, Jongno-gu, Seoul 110-714; tel. (2) 2003-0100; fax (2) 722-9264; internet www.australia.or.kr; Ambassador: COLIN STUART HESELTINE.

Austria: Kyobo Bldg, Rm 1913, 1-1, 1-ga, Jongno, Jongno-gu, Seoul 110-714; tel. (2) 732-9071; fax (2) 732-9486; e-mail austroam@kornet.net; internet www.austria.or.kr; Ambassador: Dr HELMUT BOECK.

Bangladesh: 7-18, Woo Sung Bldg, Dongbinggo-dong, Yeongsan-gu, Seoul; tel. (2) 796-4056; fax (2) 790-5313; e-mail dootrok@soback.kornet21.net; Ambassador: HUMAYUN A. KAMAL.

Belarus: 432-1636 Shindang 2-dong, Jung-gu, Seoul; tel. (2) 2237-8171; fax (2) 2237-8174; e-mail consul_korea@belembassy.org; Ambassador: ALYAKSANDR VIKTOROVICH SEMESHKO.

Belgium: 1-94, Dongbinggo-dong, Yeongsan-gu, Seoul 140-230; tel. (2) 749-0381; fax (2) 797-1688; e-mail seoul@diplobel.org; Ambassador: KOENRAAD ROUVROY.

Brazil: Ihn Gallery Bldg, 4th and 5th Floors, 141 Palpan-dong, Jongno-gu, Seoul; tel. (2) 738-4970; fax (2) 738-4974; e-mail braseul@soback.kornet21.net; Ambassador: SÉRGIO B. SERRA.

Brunei: Gwanghwamun Bldg, 7th Floor, 211, Sejong-no, Jongnogu, Seoul 110-050; tel. (2) 399-3707; fax (2) 399-3709; e-mail kbnbd_seoul@yahoo.com; Ambassador: Dato' ABD. RAHMAN HAMID.

Bulgaria: 723-42, Hannam 2-dong, Yeongsan-gu, Seoul 140-894; tel. (2) 794-8626; fax (2) 794-8627; e-mail ebdy1990@unitel.co.kr; Chargé d'affaires a.i.: VALERY ARZHENTINSKI

Cambodia: 657-162, Hannam-dong, Yeongsan-gu, Seoul; tel. (2) 3785-1041; fax (2) 3785-1040; e-mail camboemb@korea.com; Ambassador: CHHEANG VUN.

Canada: Kolon Bldg, 10-11th Floors, 45, Mugyo-dong, Jung-gu, Seoul 100-662; tel. (2) 3455-6000; fax (2) 3455-6123; e-mail canada@cec.or.kr; internet www.korea.gc.ca; Ambassador: DENIS COMEAU.

Chile: Heungkuk Life Insurance Bldg, 14th Floor, 226 Shinmun-no 1-ga, Jongno-gu, Seoul; tel. (2) 2122-2600; fax (2) 2122-2601; e-mail echilekr@unitelkr; Ambassador: FERNANDO SCHMIDT.

China, People's Republic: 54, Hyoja-dong, Jongno-gu, Seoul; tel. (2) 738-1038; fax (2) 738-1077; Ambassador: LI BIN.

Colombia: Kyobo Bldg, 13th Floor, 1-ga, Jongno, Jongno-gu, Seoul; tel. (2) 720-1369; fax (2) 725-6959; Ambassador: Dr MIGUEL DURÁN ORDÓÑEZ.

Congo, Democratic Republic: 702, Daewoo Complex Bldg, 167 Naesu-dong, Jongno-gu, Seoul; tel. and fax (2) 6272-7997; e-mail demcongoseoul@yahoo.fr; Chargé d'affaires .: N. CHRISTOPHE NGWEY.

Côte d'Ivoire: Chungam Bldg, 2nd Floor, 794-4, Hannam-dong, Yeongsan-gu, Seoul; tel. (2) 3785-0561; fax (2) 3785-0564; Ambassador: HONORAT ABENI KOFFI.

Czech Republic: 1-121, 2-ga, Shinmun-no, Jongno-gu, Seoul 110-062; tel. (2) 725-6765; fax (2) 734-6452; e-mail seoul@embassy.mzv.cz; Ambassador: IVAN HOTEK.

Denmark: Namsong Bldg, 5th Floor, 260-199, Itaewon-dong, Yeongsan-gu, Seoul 140-200; tel. (2) 795-4187; fax (2) 796-0986; e-mail selamb@um.dk; Ambassador: LEIF DONDE.

Dominican Republic: Taepyeong-no Bldg, 19th Floor, 2-ga, 310 Taepyeong-no, Jung-gu, Seoul; tel. (2) 756-3513; fax (2) 756-3514; Ambassador: JOSÉ M. NUNEZ.

Ecuador: Korea First Bldg, 19th Floor, 100 Gongpyeong-dong, Jongno-gu, Seoul; tel. (2) 739-2401; fax (2) 739-2355; e-mail mecuadorcor1@kornet.net; Ambassador: FRANKLIN ESPINOSA.

Egypt: 46-1, Hannam-dong, Yeongsan-gu, Seoul; tel. (2) 749-0787; fax (2) 795-2588; internet www.mfg.gov.eg; Ambassador: AMR HELMY.

El Salvador: Samsung Life Insurance Bldg, 20th Floor, Taepyeong-no 2-ga, Jung-gu, Seoul 100-716; tel. (2) 753-3432; fax (2) 753-3456; e-mail koembsal@hananet.net; Ambassador: ALFREDO FRANCISCO UNGO.

Ethiopia: 657-26, Hannam-dong, Yeongsan-gu, Seoul; tel. (2) 790-8927; fax (2) 790-8929; Chargé d'affaires a.i.: HAILE GEBRESELASSE.

Finland: Kyobo Bldg, Suite 1602, 1-1, 1-ga, Jongno, Jongno-gu, Seoul 110-714; tel. (2) 732-6737; fax (2) 723-4969; e-mail sanomat.seo@formin.fi; internet www.finlandembasy.or.kr; Ambassador: LAURI KORPINEN.

France: 30, Hap-dong, Seodaemun-gu, Seoul 120-030; tel. (2) 312-3272; fax (2) 393-6108; e-mail ambfraco@elim.net; internet ambassade.france.or.kr; Ambassador: FRANÇOIS DESCOUEYTE.

Gabon: Yoosung Bldg, 4th Floor, 738-20, Hannam-dong, Yeongsan-gu, Seoul; tel. (2) 793-9575; fax (2) 793-9574; e-mail amgabsel@unitel.co.kr; Ambassador: EMMANUEL ISSOZE-NGONDET.

Germany: 308-5, Dongbinggo-dong, Yeongsan-gu, Seoul 140-230; tel. (2) 748-4114; fax (2) 748-4161; e-mail dboseoul@kornet.net; internet www.gembassy.or.kr; Ambassador: HUBERTUS VON MORR.

Ghana: 5-4, Hannam-dong, Yeongsan-gu, Seoul (CPOB 3887); tel. (2) 3785-1427; fax (2) 3785-1428; e-mail ghana3@kornet.net; Ambassador: EDWARD OBENG KUFUOUR.

Greece: Hanwha Bldg, 27th Floor, 1, Janggyo-dong, Jung-gu, Seoul 100-797; tel. (2) 729-1401; fax (2) 729-1402; Ambassador: GEORGE ASSIMACOPOULOS.

Guatemala: 3422, Lotte Hotel, 1, Sogong-dong, Jung-gu, Seoul; tel. (2) 771-7582; fax (2) 771-7584; Ambassador: EMILIO R. MALDONADO.

Holy See: 2, Gungjeong-dong, Jongno-gu, Seoul (Apostolic Nunciature); tel. (2) 736-5725; fax (2) 739-2310; e-mail nunseoul@kornet.net; Apostolic Nuncio: Most Rev. GIOVANNI BATTISTA MORANDINI, Titular Archbishop of Numida.

Honduras: Jongno Tower Bldg, 2nd Floor, 6, Jongno 2-ga, Jongno-gu, Seoul 110-160; tel. (2) 738-8402; fax (2) 738-8403; e-mail hondseul@kornet.net; Ambassador: RENE FRANCISCO UMANA CHINCHILLA.

Hungary: 1-103, Dongbinggo-dong, Yeongsan-gu, Seoul 140-230; tel. (2) 792-2105; fax (2) 792-2109; e-mail huembsel@shinbiron.com; internet www.shinbiro.com/huembsel; Ambassador: BÉLA LÁSZLÓ.

India: 37-3, Hannam-dong, Yeongsan-gu, CPOB 3466, Seoul 140-210; tel. (2) 798-4257; fax (2) 796-9534; e-mail eoiseoul@soback.kornet.nm.kr; Chargé d'affaires: MOHINDER SINGH GROVER.

Indonesia: 55, Yeouido-dong, Yeongdeungpo-gu, Seoul 150-010; tel. (2) 783-5675; fax (2) 780-4280; e-mail bidpen@soback.kornet21.net; Ambassador: ABDUL GHANI.

Iran: 726-126, Hannam-dong, Yeongsan-gu, Seoul; tel. (2) 793-7751; fax (2) 792-7052; e-mail iranssy@chollian.net; internet www.mfa.gov.ir; Ambassador: MOHSEN TALAE'I.

Ireland: Daehan Fire and Marine Insurance Bldg, 15th Floor, 51-1, Namchang-dong, Jung-gu, Seoul; tel. (2) 774-6455; fax (2) 774-6458; e-mail hibernia@bora.dacom.co.kr; Ambassador: PAUL MURRAY.

Israel: Dae-kong Bldg, 15th Floor, 823-21, Yeoksam-dong, Gangnam-gu, Seoul 135-080; tel. (2) 564-3448; fax (2) 564-3449; e-mail israeli@chollian.net; internet www.israelemb.or.kr; Ambassador: UZI MANOR

Italy: 1-398, Hannam-dong, Yeongsan-gu, Seoul 140-210; tel. (2) 796-0491; fax (2) 797-5560; e-mail ambseoul@italyemb.or.kr; Ambassador: FRANCESCO RAUSI.

Japan: 18-11, Junghak-dong, Jongno-gu, Seoul; tel. (2) 2170-5200; fax (2) 734-4528; Ambassador: TOSHIYUKI TAKANO (designate).

Kazakhstan: 13-10, Seongbuk-dong, Seongbuk-gu, Seoul; tel. (2) 744-9714; fax (2) 744-9760; e-mail kazkor@chollian.net; Ambassador: BORLANT K. NURGALIYEV.

Kuwait: 309-15, Dongbinggo-dong, Yeongsan-gu, Seoul; tel. (2) 749-3688; fax (2) 749-3687; Ambassador: FAWZI AL-JASEM.

Laos: 657-93, Hannam-dong, Yeongsan-gu, Seoul; tel. (2) 796-1713; fax (2) 796-1771; e-mail laoseoul@korea.com; Ambassador: THONGSAVATH PRASEUTH.

Lebanon: 1-48, Dongbinggo-dong, Yeongsan-gu, Seoul 140-230; tel. (2) 794-6482; fax (2) 794-6485; e-mail emleb@nuri.net; Ambassador: MOHAMAD NASRAT EL-ASSAAD.

Libya: 4-5, Hannam-dong, Yeongsan-gu, Seoul; tel. (2) 797-6001; fax (2) 797-6007; e-mail libyaemb@kornet.net; Ambassador: AHMED MOHAMED TABULI.

Malaysia: 4-1, Hannam-dong, Yeongsan-gu, Seoul 140-210; tel. (2) 794-0349; fax (2) 794-5488; e-mail mwseoul@kornet.net; Ambassador: Dato' VYRAMUTTU YOOGALINGAM.

Mexico: 33-6, Hannam 1-dong, Yeongsan-gu, Seoul 140-885; tel. (2) 798-1694; fax (2) 790-0939; Ambassador: ROGELIO GRANGUILLHOME.

Mongolia: 33-5, Hannam-dong, Yeongsan-gu, Seoul; tel. (2) 794-1350; fax (2) 794-7605; e-mail monemb@uriel.net; internet www.mongoliaemb.or.kr; Ambassador: URJINLHUNDEV PERENLEYN.

Morocco: S-15, UN Village, 270-3, Hannam-dong, Yeongsan-gu, Seoul; tel. (2) 793-6249; fax (2) 792-8178; e-mail sifamase@bora.dacom.co.kr; internet www.moroccoemb.or.kr; Ambassador: JAAFAR ALJ HAKIM.

Myanmar: 724-1, Hannam-dong, Yeongsan-gu, Seoul 140-210; tel. (2) 792-3341; fax (2) 796-5570; e-mail myanmare@ppp.kornet.net; Ambassador: U NYO WIN.

Netherlands: Kyobo Bldg, 14th Floor, 1-ga, Jongno, Jongno-gu, Seoul 110-714; tel. (2) 737-9514; fax (2) 735-1321; e-mail nlgovseo@bora.dacom.co.kr; Ambassador: HEIN J. DE VRIES.

New Zealand: Kyobo Bldg, 18th Floor, 1, 1-ga, Jongno, Jongno-gu, CPOB 1059, Seoul 100-610; tel. (2) 730-7794; fax (2) 737-4861; e-mail nzembsel@kornet.net; internet www.nzembassy.com/korea; Ambassador: DAVID TAYLOR.

Nigeria: 310-19, Dongbinggo-dong, Yeongsan-gu, Seoul; tel. (2) 797-2370; fax (2) 796-1848; e-mail chancery@nigeriaembassy.or.kr; Ambassador: AKPANG ADE OBI ODU.

Norway: 258-8, Itaewon-dong, Yeongsan-gu, CPOB 355, Seoul 100-603; tel. (2) 795-6850; fax (2) 798-6072; e-mail emb.seoul@mfa.no; internet www.norway.or.kr; Ambassador: ARILD BRAASTAD.

Oman: 309-3, Dongbinggo-dong, Yeongsan-gu, Seoul; tel. (2) 790-2431; fax (2) 790-2430; e-mail omanembs@ppp.kornet.nm.kr; Ambassador: MOOSA HAMDAN AL-TAEE.

Pakistan: 258-13, Itaewon 2-dong, Yeongsan-gu, Seoul 140-202; tel. (2) 796-8252; fax (2) 796-0313; e-mail heamb@pakistan-korea-trade.org; internet www.pakistan-korea-trade.org; Ambassador: TARIQ OSMAN HYDER.

Panama: Hyundai Merchant Marine Bldg, 4th Floor, 66, Jeokseon-dong, Jongno-gu, Seoul; tel. (2) 734-8610; fax (2) 734-8613; e-mail panaemba@kornet.net; Ambassador: FÉLIX PÉREZ ESPINOSA.

Papua New Guinea: 36-1, Hannam 1-dong, Yeongsan-gu, Seoul; tel. (2) 798-9854; fax (2) 798-9856; e-mail pngembsl@ppp.kornet.nm.kr; Ambassador: DAVID ANGGO.

Paraguay: SK Bldg, 2nd Floor, 99 Seorin-dong, Jongno-gu, Seoul; tel. (2) 730-8335; fax (2) 730-8336; e-mail pyemc@nuri.net; Ambassador: LUIS FERNANDO AVALOS GIMÉNEZ.

Peru: Namhan Bldg, 6th Floor, 76-42, Hannam-dong, Yeongsan-gu, Seoul 140-210; tel. (2) 793-5810; fax (2) 797-3736; e-mail ipruseul@uriel.net; Chargé d'affaires: GUSTAVO LEMBCKE.

Philippines: Diplomatic Center, 9th Floor, 1376-1, Seocho 2-dong, Seocho-gu, Seoul; tel. (2) 577-6147; fax (2) 574-4286; e-mail phsk@soback.kornet.net; Ambassador: JUANITO P. JARASA.

Poland: 70 Sagan-dong, Jongno-gu, Seoul; tel. (2) 723-9681; fax (2) 723-9680; e-mail embassy@polandseoul.org; Ambassador: TADEUSZ CHOMICKI.

Portugal: Wonseo Bldg, 2nd Floor, 171, Wonseo-dong, Jongno-gu, Seoul; tel. (2) 3675-2251; fax (2) 3675-2250; e-mail ambport@chollian.net; Ambassador: FERNANDO MACHADO.

Qatar: 1-77, Dongbinggo-dong, Yeongsan-gu, Seoul; tel. (2) 790-1308; fax (2) 790-1027; Ambassador: ABDUL RAZZAK AL-ABDULGHANI.

Romania: 1-42, UN Village, Hannam-dong, Yeongsan-gu, Seoul 140-210; tel. (2) 797-4924; fax (2) 794-3114; e-mail romemb@uriel.net; internet www.uriel.net/~romemb; Ambassador: VIOREL ISTICIOAIA-BUDURA.

Russia: 34-16, Jeong-dong, Jung-gu, Seoul; tel. (2) 318-2116; fax (2) 754-0417; Ambassador: TEYMURAZ. O. RAMISHVILI.

Saudi Arabia: 1-112, 2-ga, Shinmun-no, Jongno-gu, Seoul; tel. (2) 739-0631; fax (2) 732-3110; Ambassador: SALEH BIN MANSOUR AL-RAJHY.

Singapore: Seoul Finance Bldg, 28th Floor, 84, 1-ga, Taepyeong-no, Jung-gu, Seoul 100-102; tel. (2) 774-2464; fax (2) 773-2465; e-mail singemb@unitel.co.kr; Ambassador: CALVIN EU MUN HOO.

Slovakia: 389-1, Hannam-dong, Yeongsan-gu, Seoul 140-210; tel. (2) 794-3981; fax (2) 794-3982; e-mail slovakemb@yahoo.com; Ambassador: PETER SOPKO.

South Africa: 1-37, Hannam-dong, Yeongsan-gu, Seoul 140-210; tel. (2) 792-4855; fax (2) 792-4856; e-mail sae@saembasy.dacom.net; internet saembassy.dacom.net; Ambassador: SYDNEY BAFANA KUBHEKA.

Spain: 726-52 Hannam-dong, Yeongsan-gu, Seoul; tel. (2) 794-3581; fax (2) 796-8207; Ambassador: ENRIQUE PANES CALPE.

Sri Lanka: Kyobo Bldg, Rm 2002, 1-1, 1-ga, Jongno, Jongno-gu, Seoul 110-714; tel. (2) 735-2966; fax (2) 737-9577; e-mail lankaemb@chollian.net; Ambassador: K. C. LOGESWARAN.

Sudan: 653-24, Hannam-dong, Yeongsan-gu, Seoul; tel. (2) 793-8692; fax (2) 793-8693; Ambassador: BABIKER A. KHALIFA.

Sweden: Seoul Central Bldg, 12th Floor, 136, Seorin-dong, Jongno-gu, KPO Box 1154, Seoul 110-110; tel. (2) 738-0846; fax (2) 733-1317; e-mail swedemb@swedemb.or.kr; internet www.swedemb.or.kr; Ambassador: BO LUNDBERG.

Switzerland: 32-10, Songwol-dong, Jongno-gu, Seoul 110-101; tel. (2) 739-9511; fax (2) 737-9392; e-mail swissemb@elim.net; internet www.elim.net/~swissemb/; Ambassador: CHRISTIAN MUEHLETHALER.

Thailand: 653-7, Hannam-dong, Yeongsan-gu, Seoul; tel. (2) 795-3098; fax (2) 798-3448; e-mail rteseoul@elim.net; Ambassador: SOMBOON SANGIAMBUT.

Tunisia: 7-13, Dongbinggo-dong, Yeongsan-gu, Seoul 140-230; tel. (2) 790-4334; fax (2) 790-4333; e-mail tunseoul@att.co.kr; Ambassador: MONDHER JEMAIL.

Turkey: Vivien Corpn Bldg, 4th Floor, 4-52, Seobinggo-dong, Yeongsan-gu, Seoul; tel. (2) 794-0255; fax (2) 797-8546; e-mail tcseulbe@kornet.net; Ambassador: TOMUR BAYER.

Ukraine: Diplomatic Center 905, 1376-1, Seocho 2-dong, Seocho-gu, Seoul; tel. (2) 578-6910; fax (2) 578-5514; e-mail ambassador@ukrembrk.com; Ambassador: VOLODYMYR V. FURKALO.

United Arab Emirates: 5-5, Hannam-dong, Yeongsan-gu, Seoul; tel. (2) 790-3235; fax (2) 790-3238; Ambassador: ABDULLA MOHAMED ALI AL-SHURAFA AL-HAMMADY.

United Kingdom: 4, Jeong-dong, Jung-gu, Seoul 100-120; tel. (2) 3210-5500; fax (2) 725-1738; e-mail bembassy@britain.or.kr; internet www.britain.or.kr; Ambassador: CHARLES HUMFREY.

USA: 82, Sejong-no, Jongno-gu, Seoul; tel. (2) 397-4114; fax (2) 735-3903; internet usembassy.state.gov/seoul/wwwh418f.html; Ambassador: THOMAS C. HUBBARD.

Uruguay: Daewoo Bldg, 1025, 541, 5-ga, Namdaemun, Jung-gu, Seoul; tel. (2) 753-7893; fax (2) 777-4129; e-mail uruseul@kornet.net; Ambassador: JULIO GIAMBRUNO.

Uzbekistan: Diplomatic Center, Rm. 701, 1376-1, Seocho 2-dong, Seocho-gu, Seoul; tel. (2) 574-6554; fax (2) 578-0576; Ambassador: VITALI V. FEN.

Venezuela: Garden Tower Bldg, 18th Floor, 98-78, Wooni-dong, Jongno-gu, Seoul; tel. (2) 741-0036; fax (2) 741-0046; e-mail emvesel@taeback.kornet.nm.kr; Chargé d'affaires: KIDDER SALAZAR.

Viet Nam: 28-58, Samcheong-dong, Jongno-gu, Seoul 140-210; tel. (2) 738-2318; fax (2) 739-2064; e-mail vietnam@elim.net; Ambassador: DUONG CHINH THUC.

Yemen: 11-444, Hannam-dong, Yeongsan-gu, Seoul 140-210; tel. (2) 792-9883; fax (2) 792-9885; e-mail yemensel@ppp.kornet21.net; internet www.gpc.org.ye; Chargé d'affaires: YAHYA AHMED AL-WAZIR.

Judicial System

SUPREME COURT

The Supreme Court is the highest court, consisting of 14 Justices, including the Chief Justice. The Chief Justice is appointed by the President, with the consent of the National Assembly, for a term of six years. Other Justices of the Supreme Court are appointed for six years by the President on the recommendation of the Chief Justice. The appointment of the Justices of the Supreme Court, however, requires the consent of the National Assembly. The Chief Justice may not be reappointed. The court is empowered to receive and decide on appeals against decisions of the High Courts, the Patent Court, and the appellate panels of the District Courts or the Family Court in civil, criminal, administrative, patent and domestic relations cases. It is also authorized to act as the final tribunal to review decisions of courts-martial and to consider cases arising from presidential and parliamentary elections.

Chief Justice: CHOI JONG-YOUNG; 967, Seocho-dong, Seocho-gu, Seoul; tel. (2) 3480-1002; fax (2) 533-1911; internet www.scourt.go.kr.

Justices: SONG JIN-HUN, SUH SUNG, CHO MOO-JEH, BYUN JAE-SEUNG, YOO JI-DAM, YOON JAE-SIK, LEE YONG-WOO, BAE KI-WON, KANG SHIN-WOOK, LEE KYU-HONG, LEE KANG-KOOK, SON JI-YOL, PARK JAE-YOON.

CONSTITUTIONAL COURT

The Constitutional Court is composed of nine adjudicators appointed by the President, of whom three are chosen from among persons selected by the National Assembly and three from persons nominated by the Chief Justice. The Court adjudicates the following matters: constitutionality of a law (when requested by the other courts); impeachment; dissolution of a political party; disputes between state agencies, or between state agencies and local governments; and petitions relating to the Constitution.

President: YUN YOUNG-CHUL; 83 Jae-dong, Jongno-gu, Seoul 110-250; tel. (2) 708-3456; fax (2) 708-3566; internet www.ccourt.go.kr.

HIGH COURTS

There are five courts, situated in Seoul, Daegu, Busan, Gwangju and Daejeon, with five chief, 78 presiding and 145 other judges. The courts have appellate jurisdiction in civil and criminal cases and can also pass judgment on administrative litigation against government decisions.

PATENT COURT

The Patent Court opened in Daejeon in March 1998, to deal with cases in which the decisions of the Intellectual Property Tribunal are challenged. The examination of the case is conducted by a judge, with the assistance of technical examiners.

DISTRICT COURTS

District Courts are established in 13 major cities; there are 13 chief, 241 presiding and 966 other judges. They exercise jurisdiction over all civil and criminal cases in the first instance.

MUNICIPAL COURTS

There are 103 Municipal Courts within the District Court system, dealing with small claims, minor criminal offences, and settlement cases.

FAMILY COURT

There is one Family Court, in Seoul, with a chief judge, four presiding judges and 16 other judges. The court has jurisdiction in domestic matters and juvenile delinquency.

ADMINISTRATIVE COURT

An Administrative Court opened in Seoul in March 1998, to deal with cases that are specified in the Administrative Litigation Act. The Court has jurisdiction over cities and counties adjacent to Seoul, and deals with administrative matters, including taxes, expropriations of land, labour and other general administrative matters. District Courts deal with administrative matters within their districts until the establishment of regional administrative courts is complete.

COURTS-MARTIAL

These exercise jurisdiction over all offences committed by armed forces personnel and civilian employees. They are also authorized to try civilians accused of military espionage or interference with the execution of military duties.

Religion

The traditional religions are Mahayana Buddhism, Confucianism and Chundo Kyo, a religion peculiar to Korea and combining elements of Shaman, Buddhist and Christian doctrines.

BUDDHISM

Korean Mahayana Buddhism has about 80 denominations. The Chogye-jong is the largest Buddhist order in Korea, having been introduced from China in AD 372. The Chogye Order accounts for almost two-thirds of all Korean Buddhists. In 1995 it had 2,426 out of 19,059 Buddhist temples and there were 12,470 monks.

Korean United Buddhist Association (KUBA): 46-19, Soosong-dong, Jongno-gu, Seoul 110-140; tel. (2) 732-4885; 28 mem. Buddhist orders; Pres. SONG WOL-JOO.

Won Buddhism

Won Buddhism combines elements of Buddhism and Confucianism. In 1995 there were 404 temples, 9,815 priests, and 86,823 believers.

CHRISTIANITY

National Council of Churches in Korea: Christian Bldg, Rm 706, 136-46, Yeonchi-dong, Jongno-gu, Seoul 110-736; tel. (2) 763-8427; fax (2) 744-6189; e-mail kncc@kncc.or.kr; internet www.kncc.or.kr; f. 1924 as National Christian Council; present name adopted 1946; eight mem. churches; Gen. Sec. Rev. PAIK DO-WOONG.

The Anglican Communion

South Korea has three Anglican dioceses, collectively forming the Anglican Church of Korea (founded as a separate province in April 1993), under its own Primate, the Most Rev. MATTHEW CHUNG CHUL-BUM.

Bishop of Pusan (Busan): Rt Rev. JOSEPH DAE-YONG LEE, 455-2, Oncheon-1-dong, Dongnae-gu, Busan 607-061; tel. (51) 554-5742; fax (51) 553-9643; e-mail bpjoseph@hanmail.net.

Bishop of Seoul: Most Rev. MATTHEW CHUNG CHUL-BUM, 3, Jeong-dong, Jung-gu, Seoul 100-120; tel. (2) 738-6597; fax (2) 723-2640; e-mail bishop100@hosanna.net.

Bishop of Taejon (Daejeon): Rt Rev. PAUL YOON HWAN, 88-1, Sonhwa 2-dong, POB 22, Daejeon 300-600; tel. (42) 256-9987; fax (42) 255-8918.

The Roman Catholic Church

For ecclesiastical purposes, North and South Korea are nominally under a unified jurisdiction. South Korea comprises three archdioceses, 10 dioceses, and one military ordinate. At 31 December 2001 some 4,228,488 people (8.8% of the population) were adherents of the Roman Catholic Church.

Bishops' Conference: Catholic Bishops' Conference of Korea, 643-1, Junggok-dong, Gwangjin-gu, Seoul 143-912; tel. (2) 460-7500; fax (2) 460-7505; e-mail cbck@cbck.or.kr; internet www.cbck.or.kr; f. 1857; Pres. Most Rev. MICHAEL PAK JEONG-IL, Bishop of Masan.

Archbishop of Kwangju (Gwangju): Most Rev. ANDREAS CHOI CHANG-MOU, Archdiocesan Office, 5-32, Im-dong, Buk-gu, Gwangju 500-886; tel. (62) 510-2838; fax (62) 525-6873; e-mail biseo@kjcatholic.or.kr.

Archbishop of Seoul: Most Rev. NICHOLAS CHEONG JIN-SUK, Archdiocesan Office, 1, 2-ga, Myeong-dong, Jung-gu, Seoul 100-022; tel. (2) 727-2114; fax (2) 773-1947; e-mail ao@seoul.catholic.or.kr.

Archbishop of Taegu (Daegu): Most Rev. PAUL RI MOON-HI, Archdiocesan Office, 225-1, Namsan 3-dong, Jung-gu, Daegu 700-804; tel. (53) 253-7011; fax (53) 253-9441; e-mail taegu@tgcatholic.or.kr.

Protestant Churches

Korean Methodist Church: 64-8, 1-ga, Taepyeong-no, Jung-gu, Seoul 100-101; KPO Box 285, Seoul 110-602; tel. (2) 399-4300; fax (2) 399-4307; e-mail bishop@kmcweb.or.kr; internet www.kmcweb.or.kr; f. 1885; 1,470,042 mems (2001); Bishop CHANG KWANG-YOUNG.

Presbyterian Church in the Republic of Korea (PROK): 1501, Ecumenical Bldg, 136-56, Yeonchi-dong, Jongno-gu, Seoul 110-470; tel. (2) 708-4021; fax (2) 708-4027; e-mail prok3000@chollian.net; internet www.prok.org; f. 1953; 332,915 mems (2001); Gen. Sec. Rev. Dr KIM JONG-MOO.

Presbyterian Church of Korea (PCK): Korean Church Centennial Memorial Bldg; 135, Yeochi-dong, Jongno-gu, Seoul 110-470; tel. (2) 741-4350; fax (2) 766-2427; e-mail e-mail thepck@pck.or.kr; internet www.pck.or.kr; 2,280,802 mems (2000); Moderator Rev. CHOI BYUNG-GON; Gen. Sec. Rev. Dr. KIM SANG-HAK.

There are some 160 other Protestant denominations in the country, including the Korea Baptist Convention and the Korea Evangelical Church.

CHUNDO KYO

A religion indigenous and unique to Korea, Chundo Kyo combines elements of Shaman, Buddhist, and Christian doctrines. In 1995 there were 274 temples, 5,597 priests, and 28,184 believers.

CONFUCIANISM

In 1995 there were 730 temples, 31,833 priests, and 210,927 believers.

TAEJONG GYO

Taejong Gyo is Korea's oldest religion, dating back 4,000 years, and comprising beliefs in the national foundation myth, and the triune god, Hanul. By the 15th century the religion had largely disappeared, but began a revival in the late 19th century. In 1995 there were 103 temples, 346 priests, and 7,603 believers.

The Press

NATIONAL DAILIES

(In Korean, unless otherwise indicated.)

Chosun Ilbo: 61, 1-ga, Taepyeong-no, Jung-gu, Seoul 100-756; tel. (2) 724-5114; fax (2) 724-5059; internet www.chosun.com; f. 1920; morning, weekly and children's edns; independent; Pres. BANG SANG-HOON; Editor-in-Chief KIM DAE-JUNG; circ. 2,470,000.

Daily Sports Seoul: 25, 1-ga, Taepyeong-no, Jung-gu, Seoul; tel. (2) 721-5114; fax (2) 721-5396; internet www.seoul.co.kr; f. 1985; morning; sports and leisure; Pres. LEE HAN-SOO; Man. Editor SON CHU-WHAN.

Dong-A Ilbo: 139-1, 3-ga, Sejong-no, Jongno-gu, Seoul 100-715; tel. (2) 2020-0114; fax (2) 2020-1239; e-mail newsroom@donga.com; internet www.donga.com; f. 1920; morning; independent; Pres. KIM HAK-JOON; Editor-in-Chief LEE HYUN-NAK; circ. 2,150,000.

Han-Joong Daily News: 91-1, 2-ga, Myeong-dong, Jung-gu, Seoul; tel. (2) 776-2801; fax (2) 778-2803; Chinese.

Hankook Ilbo: 14, Junghak-dong, Jongno-gu, Seoul; tel. (2) 724-2114; fax (2) 724-2244; internet www.hankooki.com; f. 1954; morning; independent; Pres. CHANG CHAE-KEUN; Editor-in-Chief YOON KOOK-BYUNG; circ. 2,000,000.

Hankyoreh Shinmun (One Nation): 116-25, Gongdeok-dong, Mapo-gu, Seoul 121-020; tel. (2) 710-0114; fax (2) 710-0210; internet www.hani.co.kr; f. 1988; centre-left; Chair. KIM DOO-SHIK; Editor-in-Chief SUNG HAN-PYO; circ. 500,000.

Ilgan Sports (The Daily Sports): 14, Junghak-dong, Jongno-gu, Seoul 110-792; tel. (2) 724-2114; fax (2) 724-2299; internet www.dailysports.co.kr; morning; f. 1969; Pres. CHANG CHAE-KEUN; Editor KIM JIN-DONG; circ. 600,000.

Jeil Economic Daily: 24-5 Yeouido-dong, Yeongdeungpo-gu, Seoul; tel. (2) 792-1131; fax (2) 792-1130; f. 1988; morning; Pres. HWANG MYUNG-SOON; Editor LEE SOO-SAM.

JoongAng Ilbo (JoongAng Daily News): 7, Soonhwa-dong, Jung-gu, Seoul; tel. (2) 751-5114; fax (2) 751-9709; internet www.joins.com; f. 1965; morning; Pres. LEE JE-HOON; Man. Editor LEE CHANG-KYU; circ. 2,300,000.

Kookmin Ilbo: 12, Yeouido-dong, Yeongdeungpo-gu, Seoul; tel. (2) 781-9114; fax (2) 781-9781; internet www.kukminilbo.co.kr; Pres. CHA IL-SUK.

Korea Daily News: 25, 1-ga, Taepyeong-no, Jung-gu, Seoul; tel. (2) 2000-9000; fax (2) 2000-9659; internet www.kdaily.com; f. 1945; morning; independent; Publr and Pres. SON CHU-HWAN; Man. Editor LEE DONG-HWA; circ. 700,000.

Korea Economic Daily: 441, Junglim-dong, Jung-gu, Seoul 100-791; tel. (2) 360-4114; fax (2) 779-4447; internet www.ked.co.kr; f. 1964; morning; Pres. PARK YONG-JUNG; Man. Dir and Editor-in-Chief CHOI KYU-YOUNG.

The Korea Herald: 1-12, 3-ga, Hoehyeon-dong, Jung-gu, Seoul; tel. (2) 727-0114; fax (2) 727-0670; internet www.koreaherald.co.kr; f. 1953; morning; English; independent; Pres. KIM CHIN-OUK; Man. Editor MIN BYUNG-IL; circ. 150,000.

The Korea Times: 14, Junghak-dong, Jongno-gu, Seoul 110-792; tel. (2) 724-2114; fax (2) 732-4125; internet www.koreatimes.co.kr; f. 1950; morning; English; independent; Pres. CHO BYUNG-PIL; Man. Editor KIM MYONG-SIK; circ. 100,000.

Kyung-hyang Shinmun: 22, Jeong-dong, Jung-gu, Seoul; tel. (2) 3701-1114; fax (2) 737-6362; internet www.khan.co.kr; f. 1946; evening; independent; Pres. HONG SUNG-MAN; Editor KIM HI-JUNG; circ. 733,000.

Maeil Business Newspaper: 51-9, 1-ga, Bil-dong, Jung-gu, Seoul 100-728; tel. (2) 2000-2114; fax (2) 2269-6200; internet www.mk.co.kr; f. 1966; evening; economics and business; Pres. CHANG DAE-WHAN; Editor JANG BYUNG-CHANG; circ. 235,000.

Munhwa Ilbo: 68, 1-ga, Chungjeong-no, Jung-gu, Seoul 110-170; tel. (2) 3701-5114; fax (2) 722-8328; internet www.munhwa.co.kr; f. 1991; evening; Pres. NAM SI-UK; Editor-in-Chief KANG SIN-KU.

Naeway Economic Daily: 1-12, 3-ga, Hoehyon-dong, Jung-gu, Seoul 100; tel. (2) 727-0114; fax (2) 727-0661; www.naeway.co.kr;

f. 1973; morning; Pres. KIM CHIN-OUK; Man. Editor HAN DONG-HEE; circ. 300,000.

Segye Times: 63-1, 3-ga, Hangang-no, Yeongsan-gu, Seoul; tel. (2) 799-4114; fax (2) 799-4520; internet www.segyetimes.co.kr; f. 1989; morning; Pres. HWANG HWAN-CHAI; Editor MOK JUNG-GYUM.

Seoul Kyungje Shinmun: 19, Junghak-dong, Jongno-gu, Seoul 100; tel. (2) 724-2114; fax (2) 732-2140; internet www.sed.co.kr; f. 1960; morning; Pres. KIM YOUNG-LOUL; Man. Editor KIM SEO-WOONG; circ. 500,000.

Sports Chosun: 61, 1-ga, Taepyeong-no, Jung-gu, Seoul; tel. (2) 724-6114; fax (2) 724-6979; internet www.sportschosun.com; f. 1964; Publr BANG SANG-HOON; circ. 400,000.

LOCAL DAILIES

Cheju Daily News: 2324-6, Yeon-dong, Jeju; tel. (64) 740-6114; fax (64) 740-6500; internet www.chejunews.co.kr; f. 1945; evening; Pres. KIM DAE-SUNG; Man. Editor KANG BYUNG-HEE.

Chonbuk Domin Ilbo: 207-10, 2-ga, Deokjin-dong, Deokjin-gu, Jeonju, N Jeolla Prov.; tel. (63) 251-7114; fax (63) 251-7127; internet www.domin.co.kr; f. 1988; morning; Pres. LIM BYOUNG-CHAN; Man. Editor YANG CHAE-SUK.

Chonju Ilbo: 568-132, Sonosong-dong, Deokjin-gu, Jeonju, N. Jeolla Prov.; tel. (63) 285-0114; fax (63) 285-2060; f. 1991; morning; Chair. KANG DAE-SOON; Man. Editor SO CHAE-CHOL.

Chonnam Ilbo: 700-5, Jungheung-dong, Buk-gu, Gwangju, 500–758; tel. (62) 527-0015; fax (62) 510-0436; internet www.chonnamilbo.co.kr; f. 1989; morning; Pres. LIM WON-SIK; Editor-in-Chief KIM YONG-OK.

Chunbuk Ilbo: 710-5, Kumam-dong, Deokjin-gu, Jeonju, N. Jeolla Prov.; tel. (63) 250-5500; fax (63) 250-5550; f. 1950; evening; Pres. SUH JUNG-SANG; Man. Editor LEE KON-WOONG.

Chungchong Daily News: 304, Sachang-dong, Hungduk-gu, Cheongju, N. Chungcheong Prov.; tel. (43) 279-5114; fax (43) 262-2000; internet www.ccnews.co.kr; f. 1946; morning; Pres. SEO JEONG-OK; Editor IM BAIK-SOO.

Halla Ilbo: 568-1, Samdo 1-dong, Jeju; tel. (64) 750-2114; fax (64) 750-2520; internet www.hallailbo.com; f. 1989; evening; Chair. KANG YONG-SOK; Man. Editor HONG SONG-MOK.

Incheon Ilbo: 18-1, 4-ga, Hang-dong, Jung-gu, Incheon; tel. (32) 763-8811; fax (32) 763-7711; internet www.inchonnews.co.kr; f. 1988; evening; Chair. MUN PYONG-HA; Man. Editor LEE JAE-HO.

Jungdo Daily Newspaper: 274-7, Galma-dong, Seo-gu, Daejeon; tel. (42) 530-4114; fax (42) 535-5334; internet www.joongdo.com; f. 1951; morning; Chair. KI-CHANG; Man. Editor SONG HYOUNG-SOP.

Kangwon Ilbo: 53, 1-ga, Jungang-no, Chuncheon, Gangwon Prov.; tel. (33) 252-7228; fax (33) 252-5884; internet www.kwnews.co.kr; f. 1945; evening; Pres. CHO NAM-JIN; Man. Editor KIM KEUN-TAE.

Kookje Daily News: 76-2, Goje-dong, Yeonje-gu, Busan 611-702; tel. (51) 500-5114; fax (51) 500-4274; e-mail jahwang@ms.kookje.co.kr; internet www.kookje.co.kr; f. 1947; morning; Pres. LEE JONG-DEOK; Editor-in-Chief JEONG WON-YOUNG.

Kwangju Ilbo: 1, 1-ga, Geumnam-no, Dong-gu, Gwangju; tel. (62) 222-8111; fax (62) 227-9500; internet www.kwangju.co.kr; f. 1952; evening; Chair. KIM CHONG-TAE; Man. Editor CHO DONG-SU.

Kyeonggi Ilbo: 452-1, Songjuk-dong, Changan-gu, Suwon, Gyeonggi Prov.; tel. (31) 247-3333; fax (31) 247-3349; internet www.kgib.co.kr; f. 1988; evening; Chair. SHIN SON-CHOL; Man. Editor LEE CHIN-YONG.

Kyeongin Ilbo: 1121-11, Ingye-dong, Paldal-gu, Suwon, Gyeonggi Prov.; tel. (31) 231-5114; fax (31) 232-1231; internet www.kyeongin.com; f. 1960; evening; Chair. SUNG BAEK-EUNG; Man. Editor KIM HWA-YANG.

Kyungnam Shinmun: 100-5, Shinwol-dong, Changwon, S. Gyeongsang Prov.; tel. (55) 283-2211; fax (55) 283-2227; internet www.knnews.co.kr; f. 1946; evening; Pres. KIM DONG-KYU; Editor PARK SUNG-KWAN.

Maeil Shinmun: 71, 2-ga, Gyesan-dong, Jung-gu, Daegu; tel. (53) 255-5001; fax (53) 255-8902; internet www.m2000.co.kr; f. 1946; evening; Chair. KIM BOO-KI; Editor LEE YONG-KEUN; circ. 300,000.

Pusan Daily News: 1-10, Sujeong-dong, Dong-gu, Busan 601-738; tel. (51) 461-4114; fax (51) 463-8880; internet www.pusanilbo.co.kr; f. 1946; Pres. JEONG HAN-SANG; Man. Editor AHN KI-HO; circ. 427,000.

Taegu Ilbo: 81-2, Shincheon 3-dong, Dong-gu, Daegu; tel. (53) 757-4500; fax (53) 751-8086; internet www.tgnews.go.kr; f. 1953; morning; Pres. PARK GWON-HEUM; Editor KIM KYUNG-PAL.

Taejon Ilbo: 1-135, Munhwa 1-dong, Jung-gu, Daejeon; tel. (42) 251-3311; fax (42) 253-3320; internet www.taejontimes.co.kr; f. 1950; evening; Chair. SUH CHOON-WON; Editor KWAK DAE-YEON.

Yeongnam Ilbo: 111, Shincheon-dong, Dong-gu, Daegu; tel. (53) 757-5114; fax (53) 756-9009; internet www.yeongnam.co.kr; f. 1945; morning; Chair. PARK CHANG-HO; Man. Editor KIM SANG-TAE.

SELECTED PERIODICALS

Academy News: 50, Unjung-dong, Bundang-gu, Seongnam, Gyeonggi Prov. 463-791; tel. (31) 709-8111; fax (31) 709-9945; organ of the Acad. of Korean Studies; Pres. HAN SANG-JIN.

Business Korea: 26-3, Yeouido-dong, Yeongdeungpo-gu, Seoul 150-010; tel. (2) 784-4010; fax (2) 784-1915; f. 1983; monthly; Pres. KIM KYUNG-HAE; circ. 35,000.

Eumak Dong-A: 139, Sejong-no, Jongno-gu, Seoul 110-715; tel. (2) 781-0640; fax (2) 705-4547; f. 1984; monthly; music; Publr KIM BYUNG-KWAN; Editor KWON O-KIE; circ. 85,000.

Han Kuk No Chong (FKTU News): Federation of Korean Trade Unions, FKTU Bldg, 35, Yeouido-dong, Yeongdeungpo-gu, Seoul; tel. (2) 786-3970; fax (2) 786-2864; e-mail fktuintl@nownuri.net; internet www.fktu.or.kr; f. 1961; labour news; Publr LEE NAM-SOON; circ. 20,000.

Hyundae Munhak: Mokjung Bldg, 1st Floor, 1361-5, Seocho-dong, Seocho-gu, Seoul; tel. (2) 3472-8151; fax (2) 563-9319; f. 1955; literature; Publr KIM SUNG-SIK; circ. 200,000.

Korea Business World: Yeouido, POB 720, Seoul 150-607; tel. (2) 532-1364; fax (2) 594-7663; f. 1985; monthly; English; Publr and Pres. LEE KIE-HONG; circ. 40,200.

Korea Buyers Guide: Rm 2301, Korea World Trade Center, 159, Samseong-dong, Gangnam-gu, Seoul; tel. (2) 551-2376; fax (2) 551-2377; e-mail mkbg@buyersguide.co.kr; internet www.buykorea21.com; f. 1973; monthly, consumer goods; quarterly, hardware; Pres. YOU YOUNG-PYO; circ. 30,000.

Korea Journal: CPOB 54, Seoul 100-022; tel. (2) 776-2804; organ of the UNESCO Korean Commission; Gen. Dir CHUNG HEE-CHAE.

Korea Newsreview: 1-12, 3-ga, Hoehyeon-dong, Jung-gu, Seoul 100-771; tel. (2) 756-7711; weekly; English; Publr and Editor PARK CHUNG-WOONG.

Korean Business Review: FKI Bldg, 28-1, Yeouido-dong, Yeongdeungpo-gu, Seoul 150-756; tel. (2) 3771-0114; fax (2) 3771-0138; monthly; publ. by Fed. of Korean Industries; Publr KIM KAK-CHOONG; Editor SOHN BYUNG-DOO.

Korea and World Affairs: Rm 1723, Daewoo Center Bldg, 5-541, Namdaemun-no, Jung-gu, Seoul 100-714; tel. (2) 777-2628; fax (2) 319-9591; organ of the Research Center for Peace and Unification of Korea; Pres. CHANG DONG-HOON.

Literature and Thought: Seoul; tel. (2) 738-0542; fax (2) 738-2997; f. 1972; monthly; Pres. LIM HONG-BIN; circ. 10,000.

Monthly Travel: Cross Bldg, 2nd Floor, 46-6, 2-ga, Namsan-dong, Jung-gu, Seoul 100-042; tel. (2) 757-6161; fax (2) 757-6089; e-mail kotfa@unitel.co.kr; Pres. SHIN JOONG-MOK; circ. 50,000.

News Maker: 22, Jung-dong, Jung-gu, Seoul 110-702; tel. (2) 3701-1114; fax (2) 739-6190; e-mail hudy@kyunghyang.com; internet www.kyunghyang.com/newsmaker; f. 1992; Pres. JANG JUN-BONG; Editor PARK MYUNG-HUN.

Reader's Digest: 295-15, Deoksan 1-dong, Geumcheon-gu, Seoul 153-011; tel. (2) 866-8800; fax (2) 839-4545; f. 1978; monthly; general; Pres. YANG SUNG-MO; Editor PARK SOON-HWANG; circ. 115,000.

Shin Dong-A (New East Asia): 139, Sejong-no, Jongno-gu, Seoul 110-050; tel. (2) 721-0611; fax (2) 734-7742; f. 1931; monthly; general; Publr KIM BYUNG-KWAN; Editor KWON O-KIE; circ. 308,000.

Taekwondo: Shinmun-no Bldg, 5th Floor, 238 Shinmun-no, 1-ga, Jongno-gu, Seoul 110-061; tel. (2) 566-2505; fax (2) 553-4728; e-mail wtf@unitel.co.kr; internet www.wtf.org; f. 1973; organ of the World Taekwondo Fed.; Pres. Dr KIM UN-YONG.

Vantage Point: 85-1 Susong-dong, Jongno-gu, Seoul, 110-140; tel. (2) 398-3519; fax (2) 398-3539; e-mail kseungji@yna.co.kr; internet www.yna.co.kr; f. 1978; monthly; developments in North Korea; Editor: KWAK SEUNG-JI.

Weekly Chosun: 61, Taepyeong-no 1, Jung-gu, Seoul; tel. (2) 724-5114; fax (2) 724-6199; weekly; Publr BANG SANG-HOON; Editor CHOI JOON-MYONG; circ. 350,000.

The Weekly Hankook: 14, Junghak-dong, Jongno-gu, Seoul; tel. (2) 732-4151; fax (2) 724-2444; f. 1964; Publr CHANG CHAE-KUK; circ. 400,000.

Wolgan Mot: 139, Sejong-no, Jongno-gu, Seoul 110; tel. (2) 733-5221; f. 1984; monthly; fashion; Publr KIM SEUNG-YUL; Editor KWON O-KIE; circ. 120,000.

Women's Weekly: 14, Junghak-dong, Jongno-gu, Seoul; tel. (2) 735-9216; fax (2) 732-4125.

Yosong Dong-A (Women's Far East): 139, Sejong-no, Jongno-gu, Seoul 110-715; tel. (2) 721-7621; fax (2) 721-7676; f. 1933; monthly; women's magazine; Publr KIM BYUNG-KWAN; Editor KWON O-KIE; circ. 237,000.

NEWS AGENCIES

Yonhap News Agency: 85-1, Susong-dong, Jongno-gu, Seoul; tel. (2) 398-3114; fax (2) 398-3257; internet www.yonhapnews.co.kr; f. 1980; Pres. KIM KUN.

Foreign Bureaux

Agence France-Presse (AFP): Yonhap News Agency Bldg, 3rd Floor, 85-1, Susong-dong, Jongno-gu, Seoul; tel. (2) 737-7353; fax (2) 737-6598; e-mail seoul@afp.com; Bureau Chief TIM WITCHER.

Associated Press (AP) (USA): Yonhap News Agency Bldg, 85-1, Susong-dong, Jongno-gu, Seoul; tel. (2) 739-0692; fax (2) 737-0650; Bureau Chief REID MILLER.

Central News Agency (Taiwan): 33-1, 2-ga, Myeong-dong, Jung-gu, Seoul; tel. (2) 753-0195; fax (2) 753-0197; Bureau Chief CHIANG YUAN-CHEN.

Deutsche Presse-Agentur (Germany): 148, Anguk-dong, Jongno-gu, Seoul; tel. (2) 738-3808; fax (2) 738-6040; Correspondent NIKOLAUS PREDE.

Informatsionnoye Telegrafnoye Agentstvo Rossii—Telegrafnoye Agentstvo Suverennykh Stran (ITAR—TASS) (Russia): 1-302, Chonghwa, 22-2, Itaewon-dong, Yeongsan-gu, Seoul; tel. (2) 796-9193; fax (2) 796-9194.

Jiji Tsushin (Jiji Press) (Japan): Joong-ang Ilbo Bldg, 7, Soonhwa-dong, Jung-gu, Seoul; tel. (2) 753-4525; fax (2) 753-8067; Chief Correspondent KENJIRO TSUJITA.

Kyodo News Service (Japan): Yonhap News Agency Bldg, 85-1, Susong-dong, Jongno-gu, Seoul; tel. (2) 739-2791; fax (2) 737-1776; Bureau Chief HISASHI HIRAI.

Reuters (UK): Byuck San Bldg, 7th Floor, 12-5, Dongja-dong, Yeongsan-gu, Seoul 140-170; tel. (2) 727-5151; fax (2) 727-5666; Bureau Chief ANDREW BROWNE.

Rossiiskoye Informatsionnoye Agentstvo—Novosti (RIA—Novosti) (Russia): 14, Junghak-dong, Jongno-gu, Seoul; tel. (2) 737-2829; fax (2) 798-0010; Correspondent SERGEI KUDASOV.

United Press International (UPI) (USA): Yonhap News Agency Bldg, Rm 603, 85-1, Susong-dong, Jongno-gu, Seoul; tel. (2) 737-9054; fax (2) 738-8206; Correspondent JASON NEELY.

Xinhua News Agency (People's Republic of China): B-1, Hillside Villa, 726-111, Hannam-dong, Yeongsan-gu, Seoul; tel. (2) 795-8258; fax (2) 796-7459.

PRESS ASSOCIATIONS

Korean Newspaper Editors' Association: Korea Press Center, 13th Floor, 25, 1-ga, Taepyeong-no, Jung-gu, Seoul; tel. (2) 732-1726; fax (2) 739-1985; f. 1957; 416 mems; Pres. SEONG BYONG-WUK.

Korean Newspapers Association: Korea Press Center, 13th Floor, 25, 1-ga, Taepyeong-no, Jung-gu, Seoul 100-745; tel. (2) 733-2251; fax (2) 720-3291; e-mail ccy73_2000@yahoo.co.kr; f. 1962; 49 mems; Pres. CHOE HAK-RAE.

Seoul Foreign Correspondents' Club: Korea Press Center, 18th Floor, 25, 1-ga, Taepyeong-no, Jung-gu, Seoul; tel. (2) 734-3272; fax (2) 734-7712; f. 1956; Pres. PARK HAN-CHUN.

Publishers

Ahn Graphics Ltd: 260-88, Seongbuk 2-dong, Seongbuk-gu, Seoul 136-012; tel. (2) 763-2320; fax (2) 743-3352; e-mail lbr@ag.co.kr; f. 1985; computer graphics; Pres. KIM OK-CHUL.

Bak-Young Publishing Co: 13-31, Pyeong-dong, Jongno-gu, Seoul; tel. (2) 733-6771; fax (2) 736-4818; f. 1952; sociology, philosophy, literature, linguistics, social science; Pres. AHN JONG-MAN.

BIR Publishing Co Ltd: 506, Shinsa-dong, Gangnam-gu, Seoul 135-120; tel. (2) 515-2000; fax (2) 514-3249.

Bobmun Sa Publishing Co: Hanchung Bldg, 4th Floor, 161-7, Yomni-dong, Mapo-gu, Seoul 121-090; tel. (2) 703-6541; fax (2) 703-6594; f. 1954; law, politics, philosophy, history; Pres. BAE HYO-SEON.

Bumwoo Publishing Co: 21-1, Kusu-dong, Mapo-gu, Seoul 121-130; tel. (2) 717-2121; fax (2) 717-0429; f. 1966; philosophy, religion, social science, technology, art, literature, history; Pres. YOON HYUNG-DOO.

Cheong Moon Gak Publishing Co Ltd: 486-9, Kirum 3-dong, Seongbuk-gu, Seoul 136-113; tel. (2) 985-1451; fax (2) 982-8679; e-mail hanscmg@nownuri.net; f. 1975; science, technology; Pres. KIM HONG-SEOK.

Design House Publishing Co: Paradise Bldg, 186-210, Jangchung-dong, 2-ga, Jung-gu, Seoul 100-392; tel. (2) 2275-6151; fax (2) 2275-7884; f. 1987; social science, art, literature, languages, children's periodicals; Pres. LEE YOUNG-HEE.

Dong-Hwa Publishing Co: 130-4, 1-ga, Wonhyoro, Yeongsan-gu, Seoul 140-111; tel. (2) 713-5411; fax (2) 701-7041; f. 1968; language, literature, fine arts, history, religion, philosophy; Pres. LIM IN-KYU.

Doosan Co-operation Publishing BG: 18-12, Ulchi-ro, 6-ga, Jeong-gu, Seoul 100-196; tel. (2) 3398-880; fax (2) 3398-2670; f. 1951; general works, school reference, social science, periodicals; Pres. CHOI TAE-KYUNG.

Eulyoo Publishing Co Ltd: 46-1, Susong-dong, Jongno-gu, Seoul 110-603; tel. (2) 733-8151; fax (2) 732-9154; e-mail eulyoo@chollian .net; internet www.eulyoo.co.kr; f. 1945; linguistics, literature, social science, history, philosophy; Pres. CHUNG CHIN-SOOK.

Hainaim Publishing Co Ltd: Minjin Bldg, 5th Floor, 464-41, Seokyo-dong, Mapo-gu, Seoul 121-210; tel. (2) 326-1600; fax (2) 333-7543; e-mail hainaim@chollian.net; f. 1983; philosophy, literature, children's; Pres. SONG YOUNG-SUK.

Hakwon Publishing Co Ltd: Seocho Plaza, 4th Floor, 1573-1, Seocho-dong, Seocho-gu, Seoul; tel. (2) 587-2396; fax (2) 584-9306; f. 1945; general, languages, literature, periodicals; Pres. KIM YOUNG-SU.

Hangil Publishing Co: 506, Shinsa-dong, Gangnam-gu, Seoul 135-120; tel. (2) 515-4811; fax (2) 515-4816; f. 1976; social science, history, literature; Pres. KIM EOUN-HO.

Hanul Publishing Company: 201, Hyuam Bldg, 503-24, Changcheon-dong, Seodaemun-gu, Seoul 120-180; tel. (2) 336-6183; fax (2) 333-7543; e-mail newhanul@nuri.net; f. 1980; general, philosophy, university books, periodicals; Pres. KIM CHONG-SU.

Hollym Corporation: 13-13, Gwancheol-dong, Jongno-gu, Seoul 110-111; tel. (2) 735-7554; fax (2) 735-7551; e-mail hollym@chollian .net; internet www.hollym.co.kr; f. 1963; academic and general books on Korea in English; Pres. HAM KI-MAN.

Hyang Mun Sa Publishing Co: 645-20, Yeoksam-dong, Gangnam-gu, Seoul 135-081; tel. (2) 538-5672; fax (2) 538-5673; f. 1950; science, agriculture, history, engineering, home economics; Pres. NAH JOONG-RYOL.

Hyonam Publishing Co Ltd: 627-5, Ahyun 3-dong, Mapo-gu, Seoul 121-013; tel. (2) 365-5056; fax (2) 365-5251; e-mail lawhyun@ chollian.net; f. 1951; general, children's, literature, periodicals; Pres. CHO KEUN-TAE.

Il Ji Sa Publishing Co: 46-1, Junghak-dong, Jongno-gu, Seoul 110-150; tel. (2) 732-3980; fax (2) 722-2807; f. 1956; literature, social sciences, juvenile, fine arts, philosophy, linguistics, history; Pres. KIM SUNG-JAE.

Ilchokak Publishing Co Ltd: 9, Gongpyeong-dong, Jongno-gu, Seoul 110-160; tel. (2) 733-5430; fax (2) 738-5857; f. 1953; history, literature, sociology, linguistics, medicine, law, engineering; Pres. HAN MAN-NYUN.

Jigyungsa Publishers Ltd: 790-14, Yeoksam-dong, Gangnam-gu, Seoul 135-080; tel. (2) 557-6351; fax (2) 557-6352; e-mail jigyung@ uriel.net; www.jigyung.co.kr; f. 1979; children's, periodicals; Pres. KIM BYUNG-JOON.

Jihak Publishing Co Ltd: 180-20, Dongkyo-dong, Mapo-gu, Seoul 121-200; tel. (2) 330-5220; fax (2) 325-5835; f. 1965; philosophy, language, literature; Pres. KWON BYONG-IL.

Jipmoondang: 95, Waryon-dong, Jongno-gu, Seoul 110-360; tel. (2) 743-3098; fax (2) 743-3192; philosophy, social science, Korean studies, history, Korean folklore; Pres. LIM KYOUNG-HWAN.

Jisik Sanup Publications Co Ltd: 35-18, Dongui-dong, Jongno-gu, Seoul 110-040; tel. (2) 738-1978; fax (2) 720-7900; f. 1969; religion, social science, art, literature, history, children's; Pres. KIM KYUNG-HEE.

Jung-Ang Publishing Co Ltd: 172-11, Yomni-dong, Mapo-gu, Seoul 121-090; tel. (2) 717-2111; fax (2) 716-1369; f. 1972; study books, children's; Pres. KIM DUCK-KI.

Kemongsa Publishing Co Ltd: 772, Yeoksam-dong, Gangnam-gu, Seoul 135-080; tel. (2) 531-5335; fax (2) 531-5520; f. 1946; picture books, juvenile, encyclopaedias, history, fiction; Pres. RHU SEUNG-HEE.

Ki Moon Dang: 286-20, Haengdang-dong, Seongdong-gu, Seoul 133-070; tel. (2) 2295-6171; fax (2) 2296-8188; f. 1976; engineering, fine arts, dictionaries; Pres. KANG HAE-JAK.

Korea Britannica Corpn: 117, 1-ga, Jungchung-dong, Seoul 100-391; tel. (2) 272-2151; fax (2) 278-9983; f. 1968; encyclopaedias, dictionaries; Pres. Jang Ho-Sang, Sujan Elen Tapani.

Korea University Press: 1-2, Anam-dong, 5-ga, Seongbuk-gu, Seoul 136-701; tel. (2) 3290-4231; fax (2) 923-6311; f. 1956; philosophy, history, language, literature, Korean studies, education, psychology, social science, natural science, engineering, agriculture, medicine; Pres. Kim Jung-Bae.

Kum Sung Publishing Co: 242-63, Gongdeok-dong, Mapo-gu, Seoul 121-022; tel. (2) 713-9651; fax (2) 718-4362; f. 1965; literature, juvenile, social sciences, history, fine arts; Pres. Kim Nak-Joon.

Kyohak-sa Publishing Co Ltd: 105-67, Gongdeok-dong, Mapo-gu, Seoul 121-020; tel. (2) 717-4561; fax (2) 718-3976; f. 1952; dictionaries, educational, children's; Pres. Yang Cheol-Woo.

Kyung Hee University Press: 1, Hoeki-dong, Dongdaemun-gu, Seoul 130-701; tel. (2) 961-0106; fax (2) 962-8840; f. 1960; general, social science, technology, language, literature; Pres. Choe Young-Seek.

Kyungnam University Press: 28-42, Samchung-dong, Jongno-gu, Seoul 110-230; tel. (2) 370-0700; fax (2) 735-4359; Pres. Park Jae-Kyu.

Minumsa Publishing Co Ltd: 5/F Kangnam Publishing Culture Centre, 506, Shinsa-dong, Gangnam-gu, Seoul 135-120; tel. (2) 515-2000; fax (2) 515-2007; e-mail michell@bora.dacom.co.kr; f. 1966; literature, philosophy, linguistics, pure science; Pres. Park Maeng-Ho.

Munhakdongne Publishing Co Ltd: 6/F Dongsomun B/D 260, Dongsomundong 4-ga, Seongbuk-gu, Seoul 136-034; tel. (2) 924-4736; fax (2) 927-6794; e-mail greenpen@chollian.net; internet www.munhak.com; f. 1993; art, literature, children's, periodicals; Pres. Kang Byung-Sun.

Panmun Book Co Ltd: 923-11, Mok 1-dong, Yangcheon-gu, Seoul 158-051; tel. (2) 653-5131; fax (2) 653-2454; e-mail skliu@panmun.co.kr; internet www.medicalplus.co.kr; f. 1955; social science, pure science, technology, medicine, linguistics; Pres. Liu Sung-Kwon.

Sakyejul Publishing Ltd: 1-181, Shinmun-no-2-ga, Jongno-gu, Seoul 110-062; tel. (2) 736-9380; fax (2) 737-8595; e-mail sakyejul@soback.kornet.nm.kr; f. 1982; social sciences, art, literature, history, children's; Pres. Kang Mar-Xill.

Sam Joong Dang Publishing Co: 261-23, Soke-dong, Yeongsan-gu, Seoul 140-140; tel. (2) 704-6816; fax (2) 704-6819; f. 1931; literature, history, philosophy, social sciences, dictionaries; Pres. Lee Min-Chul.

Sam Seong Dang Publishing Co: 101-14, Non Hyun-dong, Gangnam-gu, Seoul 135-010; tel. (2) 3442-6767; fax (2) 3442-6768; e-mail kyk@ssdp.co.kr; f. 1968; literature, fine arts, history, philosophy; Pres. Kang Myung-Chae.

Sam Seong Publishing Co Ltd: 1516-2, Seocho-dong, Seocho-gu, Seoul 137-070; tel. (2) 3470-6900; fax (2) 597-1507; internet www.howpc.com; f. 1951; literature, history, juvenile, philosophy, arts, religion, science, encyclopaedias; Pres. Kim Jin-Yong.

Segyesa Publishing Co Ltd: Dasan Bldg 102, 494-85, Yeongkan-dong, Mapo-gu, Seoul 121-070; tel. (2) 715-1542; fax (2) 715-1544; f. 1988; general, philosophy, literature, periodicals; Pres. Choi Sun-Ho.

Se-Kwang Music Publishing Co: 232-32, Seogye-dong, Yeongsan-gu, Seoul 140-140; tel. (2) 719-2652; fax (2) 719-2656; f. 1953; music, art; Pres. Park Sei-Won; Chair. Park Shin-Joon.

Seong An Dang Publishing Co: 4579, Shingil-6-dong, Yeongdeungpo-gu, Seoul 150-056; tel. (2) 3142-4151; fax (2) 323-5324; f. 1972; technology, text books, university books, periodicals; Pres. Lee Jong-Choon.

Seoul National University Press: 56-1, Shinrim-dong, Gwanak-gu, Seoul 151-742; tel. (2) 889-0434; fax (2) 888-4148; e-mail snubook@chollian.net; f. 1961; philosophy, engineering, social science, art, literature; Pres. Lee Ki-Jun.

Si-sa-young-o-sa, Inc: 55-1, 2-ga, Jongno, Jongno-gu, Seoul 110-122; tel. (2) 274-0509; fax (2) 271-3980; internet www.ybmsisa.co.kr; f. 1959; language, literature; Pres. Chung Young-Sam.

Sogang University Press: 1, Shinsu-dong, Mapo-gu, Seoul 121-742; tel. (2) 705-8212; fax (2) 705-8612; f. 1978; philosophy, religion, science, art, history; Pres. Lee Han-Taek.

Sookmyung Women's University Press: 53-12, 2-ga, Jongpa-dong, Yeongsan-gu, Seoul 140-742; tel. (2) 710-9162; fax (2) 710-9090; f. 1968; general; Pres. Lee Kyung-Sook.

Tam Gu Dang Publishing Co: 158, 1-ga, Hanggangno, Yeongsan-gu, Seoul 140-011; tel. (2) 3785-2271; fax (2) 3785-2272; f. 1950; linguistics, literature, social sciences, history, fine arts; Pres. Hong Suk-Woo.

Tong Moon Gwan: 147, Gwanhoon-dong, Jongno-gu, Seoul 110-300; tel. (2) 732-4355; f. 1954; literature, art, philosophy, religion, history; Pres. Lee Kyum-No.

Woongjin.com Co. Ltd: Woongjin Bldg, 112-2, Inui-dong, Jongno-gu, Seoul; tel. (2) 3670-1832; fax (2) 766-2722; e-mail lois.kim@email.woongjin.com; internet www.woongjin.com; children's; Pres. Yoon Suck-Keum.

Yearimdang Publishing Co Ltd: Yearim Bldg, 153-3, Samseong-dong, Gangnam-gu, Seoul 135-090; tel. (2) 566-1004; fax (2) 567-9610; e-mail yearim@yearim.co.kr; internet www.yearim.co.kr; f. 1973; children's; Pres. Na Choon-Ho.

Yonsei University Press: 134, Shincheon-dong, Seodaemun-gu, Seoul 120-749; tel. (2) 361-3380; fax (2) 393-1421; e-mail ysup@yonsei.ac.kr; f. 1955; philosophy, religion, literature, history, art, social science, pure science; Pres. Kim Byung-Soo.

Youl Hwa Dang: 506, Shinsa-dong, Gangnam-gu, Seoul 135-120; tel. (2) 515-3141; fax (2) 515-3144; e-mail horang2@unitel.co.kr; f. 1971; art; Pres. Yi Ki-Ung.

PUBLISHERS' ASSOCIATION

Korean Publishers Association: 105-2, Sagan-dong, Jongno-gu, Seoul 110-190; tel. (2) 735-2702; fax (2) 738-5414; e-mail kpa@kpa21.or.kr; internet www.kpa21.or.kr; f. 1947; Pres. Lee Jung-Il; Sec.-Gen. Jung Jong-Jin.

Broadcasting and Communications

TELECOMMUNICATIONS

Dacom Corpn: Dacom Bldg, 706-1, Yeoksam-dong, Gangnam-gu, Seoul 135-610; tel. (2) 6220-0220; fax (2) 6220-0702; internet www.dacom.net; f. 1982; domestic and international long-distance telecommunications services and broadband internet services; CEO. Park Un-Suh.

Daewoo Telecom Co Ltd: 14-34, Yeouido-dong, Yeongdeungpo-gu, Seoul; tel. (2) 3779-7114; fax (2) 3779-7500; internet www.dwt.co.kr; Pres. (vacant).

Hanaro Telecom: Kukje Electronics Center Bldg, 24th Floor, 1445-3, Seocho-dong, Seocho-gu, Seoul 137-728; tel. (2) 6266-4114; fax (2) 6266-4379; internet www.hanaro.com; local telecommunications and broadband internet services; CEO Shin Yun-Sik.

Korea Mobile Telecommunications Corpn: 267, 5-ga, Namdaemun-no, Jung-gu, Seoul; tel. (2) 3709-1114; fax (2) 3709-0499; f. 1984; Pres. Seo Jung-Uk.

Korea Telecom: 206 Jungja-dong, Bundang-gu, Seongnam-shi, Gyeonggi Prov. 463-711-; tel. (2) 727-0114; fax (2) 750-3994; internet www.kt.co.kr; domestic and international telecommunications services and broadband internet services; privatised in Jun. 2002; Pres. Lee Yong-Kyung.

Korea Telecom (KT) Freetel: Seoul; 33% owned by Korea Telecom; 3.17m. subscribers (1999); Pres. Lee Sang-Chul.

KTF: KTF Tower, 890-20, Daechi-dong, Gangnam-gu, Seoul 135-280; tel. (2) 2016-1114; fax (2) 2016-0032; internet www.ktf.com; mobile telecommunications and wireless internet services; merged with KTm.com in May 2001; commenced (code division multiple access) commercial CDMA2000 1x services in May 2001, and (evolution data only) 1x EV-DO services in May 2002; 10m. subscribers (2002); CEO Lee Kyung-Joon.

LG Telecom: LG Gangnam Tower, 19th Floor, 679 Yeoksam-dong, Gangnam-gu, Seoul 135-985; tel. (2) 2005-7114; fax (2) 2005-7505; internet www.lg019.co.kr; mobile telecommunications and wireless internet services; commenced commercial CDMA2000 1x service in May 2001; 4m. subscribers (2002); CEO Nam Yong.

Onse Telecom: 192-2, Gumi-dong, Bundang-gu, Seongnam-shi, Gyeonggi Prov. 463-500; tel. and fax (31) 738-6000; internet www.onse.net; domestic and international telecommunications services; Pres. and CEO Hwang Kee-Yeon.

SK Telecom Co Ltd: 99, Seorin-dong, Jongno-gu, Seoul 110-110; tel. (2) 2121-2114; fax (2) 2121-3999; internet www.sktelecom.com; cellular mobile telecommunications and wireless internet services; merged with Shinsegi Telecom in Jan. 2002; 16m. subscribers (2002); Chair. and CEO Son Kil-Seung.

BROADCASTING

Regulatory Authority

Korean Broadcasting Commission: KBS Bldg, 923-5, Mok-dong, Yangcheon-gu, Seoul 158-715; tel. (2) 3219-5117; fax (2) 3219-5371; Chair. Kang Dae-In.

Radio

Korean Broadcasting System (KBS): 18, Yeouido-dong, Yeongdeungpo-gu, Seoul 150-010; tel. (2) 781-1000; fax (2) 781-4179; internet www.kbs.co.kr; f. 1926; publicly-owned corpn with 26 local broadcasting and 855 relay stations; overseas service in Korean, English, German, Indonesian, Chinese, Japanese, French, Spanish, Russian and Arabic; Pres. PARK KWAN-SANG.

Buddhist Broadcasting System (BBS): 140, Mapo-dong, Mapo-gu, Seoul 121-050; tel. (2) 705-5114; fax (2) 705-5229; internet www.bbsfm.ko.kr; f. 1990; Pres. CHO HAE-HYONG.

Christian Broadcasting System (CBS): 917-1, Mok-dong, Yangcheon-gu, Seoul 158-701; tel. (2) 650-7000; fax (2) 654-2456; internet www.cbs.co.kr; f. 1954; independent religious network with seven network stations in Seoul, Daegu, Busan, Gwangju, Chonbuk, Jeonju and Chuncheon; programmes in Korean; Pres. Rev. KWON HO-KYUNG.

Educational Broadcasting System (EBS): 92-6, Umyeon-dong, Seocho-gu, Seoul 137-791; tel. (2) 526-2000; fax (2) 526-2179; internet www.ebs.co.kr; f. 1990; Pres. Dr PARK HEUNG-SOO.

Far East Broadcasting Co (FEBC): 89, Sangsu-dong, Mapo-gu, MPO Box 88, Seoul 121-707; tel. (2) 320-0114; fax (2) 320-0129; e-mail febcadm@febc.or.kr; internet www.febc.netr; Dir Dr BILLY KIM.

Radio Station HLAZ: MPO Box 88, Seoul 121-707; tel. (2) 320-0114; fax (2) 320-0129; e-mail febcadm@febc.or.kr; internet www.febc.net; f. 1973; religious, educational service operated by Far East Broadcasting Co; programmes in Korean, Chinese, Russian and Japanese; Dir Dr BILLY KIM.

Radio Station HLKX: MPO Box 88, Seoul 121-707; tel. (2) 320-0114; fax (2) 320-0129; e-mail febcadm@febc.or.kr; internet www.febc.net; f. 1956; religious, educational service operated by Far East Broadcasting Co; programmes in Korean, Chinese and English; Dir Dr BILLY KIM.

Munhwa Broadcasting Corpn (MBC): 31, Yeouido-dong, Yeongdeungpo-gu, Seoul 150-728; tel. (2) 784-2000; fax (2) 784-0880; e-mail mbcir@imbc.com; internet www.imbc.com; f. 1961; public; Pres. KIM JOONG-BAE.

Pyong Hwa Broadcasting Corpn (PBC): 2-3, 1-ga, Jeo-dong, Jung-gu, Seoul 100-031; tel. (2) 270-2114; fax (2) 270-2210; internet www.pbc.co.kr; f. 1990; religious and educational programmes; Pres. Rev. PARK SHIN-EON.

Seoul Broadcasting System (SBS): 10-2, Yeouido-dong, Yeongdeungpo-gu, Seoul 150-010; tel. (2) 786-0792; fax (2) 780-2530; internet www.sbs.co.kr; f. 1991; Pres. SONG DO-KYUN.

US Forces Network Korea (AFN Korea): Seoul; tel. (2) 7914-6495; fax (2) 7914-5870; e-mail info@afnkorea.com; internet afnkorea.com; f. 1950; six originating stations and 19 relay stations; 24 hours a day.

Television

In late 1997 almost 40 domestic television channels were in operation.

Educational Broadcasting System (EBS): (see Radio).

Inchon Television Ltd (ITV): 587-46, Hakik-dong, Nam-gu, Incheon; tel. (32) 830-1000; fax (32) 865-6300; internet www.itv.co.kr; f. 1997.

Jeonju Television Corpn (JTV): 656-3, Sonosong-dong, Deokjin-gu, Jeonju, N. Jeolla Prov.; tel. (63) 250-5231; fax (63) 250-5249; e-mail jtv@jtv.co.kr; f. 1997.

Korean Broadcasting System (KBS): 18, Yeouido-dong, Yeongdeungpo-gu, Seoul 150-790; tel. (2) 781-1000; fax (2) 781-4179; f. 1961; publicly-owned corpn with 25 local broadcasting and 770 relay stations; Pres. PARK KWAN-SANG.

Munhwa Broadcasting Corpn (MBC-R/TV): 31, Yeouido-dong, Yeongdeungpo-gu, Seoul 150-728; tel. (2) 789-2851; fax (2) 782-3094; f. 1961; public; 19 TV networks; Pres. NOH SUNG-DAI.

Seoul Broadcasting System (SBS): (see Radio).

US Forces Network Korea (AFN Korea): Seoul; tel. (2) 7914-2711; fax (2) 7914-5870; f. 1950; main transmitting station in Seoul; 19 rebroadcast transmitters and translators; 168 hours weekly.

Finance

(cap. = capital; res = reserves; dep. = deposits; m. = million; brs = branches; amounts in won, unless otherwise indicated)

BANKING

The modern financial system in South Korea was established in 1950 with the foundation of the central bank, the Bank of Korea. Under financial liberalization legislation, adopted in the late 1980s, banks were accorded greater freedom to engage in securities or insurance operations. In March 1999 there were 87 commercial banks in South Korea, comprising 11 nation-wide banks, eight provincial banks and 68 branches of foreign banks. The Financial Supervisory Commission was formed in April 1998 to oversee and reorganize the operations of commercial banks and the financial services sector.

Specialized banks were created in the 1960s to provide funds for sectors of the economy not covered by commercial banks. There are also two development banks: the Korea Development Bank and the Export-Import Bank of Korea.

In late 1997 many merchant banks were forced to cease operations, after incurring heavy losses through corporate bankruptcies. In June 1998 five commercial banks were also required to cease operations.

Regulatory Authority

Financial Supervisory Commission: 27, Yeouido-dong, Yeongdeungpo-gu, Seoul; tel. (2) 3771-5234; fax (2) 3771-5190; internet www.fss.or.kr; Chair. LEE KEUN-YOUNG.

Central Bank

Bank of Korea: 110, 3-ga, Namdaemun-no, Jung-gu, Seoul 100-794; tel. (2) 759-4114; fax (2) 759-4139; e-mail bokdiri@bok.or.kr; internet www.bok.or.kr; f. 1950; bank of issue; res 4,613,900m., dep. 112,868,500m. (Dec. 2000); Gov. PARK SEUNG; Dep. Gov. PARK CHEUL; 16 domestic brs, 7 overseas offices.

Commercial Banks

Chohung Bank: 14, 1-ga, Namdaemun-no, Jung-gu, Seoul 100-757; tel. (2) 733-2000; fax (2) 720-2882; internet www.chb.co.kr; f. 1897; merged with Chungbuk Bank in May 1999 and Kangwon Bank in Sept. 1999; cap. 3,395,400m., dep. 39,225,900m. (Dec. 2001); Pres. and CEO HONG SERCK-JOO; 446 domestic brs, 11 overseas brs.

Hana Bank: 101-1, 1-ga, Ulchi-no, Jung-gu, Seoul 100-191; tel. (2) 2002-1111; fax (2) 775-7472; e-mail webmaster@hanabank.com; internet www.hanabank.co.kr; f. 1991; merged with Boram Bank in Jan. 1999; cap. 853,549m., res 468,602m., dep. 39,139,314m. (Sep. 2002); Chair. and CEO KIM SEUNG-YU; 303 brs.

Kookmin Bank: 9-1, 2-ga, Namdaemun-no, Jung-gu, CPOB 815, Seoul 100-703; tel. (2) 317-2114; fax (2) 769-7229; e-mail kangseok@www.kookmin-bank.com; internet www.kookminbank.com; f. 1963 as Citizen's National Bank, renamed 1995; re-established Jan. 1999, following merger with Korea Long Term Credit Bank; merged with H&CB in November 2001; dep. 139,187.1m. (Jun. 2002); Chair. and Pres. KIM JUNG-TAE; 1,122 domestic brs, 6 overseas brs.

KorAm Bank: 39, Da-dong, Jung-gu, Seoul 100-180; tel. (2) 3455-2114; fax (2) 3455-2966; internet www.goodbank.com; f. 1983; jt venture with Bank of America; cap. 1,071,334m., res 170,871m., dep. 19,226,170m. (Dec. 2001); CEO and Chair. HA YUNG-KU; 222 domestic brs, 4 overseas brs.

Korea Exchange Bank: 181, 2-ga, Ulchi-no, Jung-gu, Seoul 100-793; tel. (2) 729-0114; fax (2) 729-9812; e-mail chan@koexbank.co.kr; internet www.keb.co.kr; f. 1967; merged with Korea International Merchant Bank in Jan. 1999; cap. 1,850,875m., res –168,034m., dep. 32,170,619m. (Dec. 2000); Pres. LEE KANG-WON; 261 domestic brs, 28 overseas brs.

Korea First Bank: 100, Gongpyeong-dong, Jongno-gu, Seoul 110-702; tel. (2) 3702-3114; fax (2) 3702-4901; e-mail master@kfb.co.kr; internet www.kfb.co.kr; f. 1929; 51% owned by Newbridge Capital Ltd (USA); cap. 980,584m., res 64,527m., dep. 17,388,790m. (Dec. 2000); Pres. and CEO ROBERT COHEN; 392 domestic brs, 4 overseas brs.

Seoulbank: 10-1, 2-ga, Namdaemun-no, Jung-gu, Seoul 100-746; tel. (2) 3709-5114; fax (2) 3709-6422; e-mail bos0216@chollian.net; internet www.seoulbank.co.kr; f. 1959; nationalized in Jan. 1998; cap. 554,900m., dep. 13,143,200m. (Dec. 2000); Pres. and CEO KANG CHUNG-WON; 291 domestic brs, 3 overseas brs.

Shinhan Bank: 120, 2-ga, Taepyeong-no, Jung-gu, Seoul 100-102; tel. (2) 756-0505; fax (2) 774-7013; internet www.shinhan.com; f. 1982; cap. 1,599,031m., res 660,995m., dep. 28,319,695m. (Dec. 2000); Pres. and CEO LEE IN-HO; 333 domestic brs, 8 overseas brs.

Woori Bank: 203, 1-ga, Hoehyeon-dong, Jung-gu, Seoul; tel. (2) 2002-3000; fax (2) 2002-5615; internet www.wooribank.com; f. 2002, following the merger of Hanvit Bank and Peace Bank of Korea; 100% owned by Government; cap. 2,764,400m., res 1,762,300m., dep. 51,806,200m. (Dec. 2001); Pres. LEE DUK-HOON; 688 domestic brs, 12 overseas brs.

Development Banks

Export-Import Bank of Korea: 16-1, Yeouido-dong, Yeongdeungpo-gu, Seoul 150-873; tel. (2) 3779-6114; fax (2) 3779-6732; e-mail kexim@koreaexim.go.kr; internet www.koreaexim.go.kr; f. 1976; cap. 2,675,755m., res 5,187m. (Dec. 2000); Chair. and Pres. LEE YOUNG-HOI; 8 brs.

Korea Development Bank: 16-3, Yeouido-dong, Yeongdeungpo-gu, Seoul 150-793; tel. (2) 787-4000; fax (2) 787-6191; internet www.kdb.co.kr; f. 1954; cap. 4,341m., res 66,059m., dep. 6,020m. (Dec. 1999); Gov. JUNG KEUN-YONG; 37 domestic brs, 9 overseas brs.

Specialized Banks

Asian Banking Corpn: Young Poong Bldg, 13th–14th Floors, 33, Seorin-dong, Jongno-gu, Seoul 110-752; tel. (2) 399-5500; fax (2) 399-5400; f. 1977; Pres. CHO KWAN-HAENG.

Industrial Bank of Korea: 50, 2-ga, Ulchi-no, Jung-gu, Seoul 100-758; tel. (2) 729-6114; fax (2) 729-6402; e-mail ifd@ibk.co.kr; internet www.ibk.co.kr; f. 1961 as the Small and Medium Industry Bank; cap. 2,291,385m., res 155,299m., dep. 33,233,163m. (Dec. 2000); Chair. and Pres. KIM JONG-CHANG; 387 domestic brs, 6 overseas brs.

Korea Merchant Banking Corpn: Daewoo Center Bldg, 2nd Floor, 541, 5-ga, Namdaemun-no, Jung-gu, Seoul 100-714; tel. (2) 3788-0114; fax (2) 753-9740; internet www.kmbc.co.kr; f. 1976; cap. 105,370m., dep. 1,904,762m. (March 1999); Pres. KIM IN-JU.

Korean-French Banking Corpn (SogeKo): Marine Center, 118, 2-ga, Namdaemun-no, Jung-gu, CPOB 8572, Seoul 100-092; tel. (2) 777-7711; fax (2) 777-7710; f. 1977; Pres. KIM DOO-BAE.

National Agricultural Co-operative Federation (NACF): 75, 1-ga, Chungjeong-no, Jung-gu, Seoul 100-707; tel. (2) 397-5114; fax (2) 397-5140; e-mail nacfico@nuri.net; internet www.nonghyup.com; f. 1961; cap. 2,564,400m., res 1,395,800m., dep. 64,063,500m. (2002); Chair. and Pres. HYUN EUI-SONG; 2,025 brs and member co-operatives.

National Federation of Fisheries Co-operatives: 11-6, Shincheon-dong, Songpa-gu, Seoul 138-730; tel. (2) 2240-2114; fax (2) 2240-3049; internet www.suhyup.co.kr; f. 1962; cap. 1,158,100m., res 301,900m., dep. 4,371,000m. (2002); Chair. and Pres. CHANG BYUNG-KOO; 120 brs.

National Livestock Co-operatives Federation: 451, Songnaedong, Gangdong-gu, Seoul 134-763; tel. (2) 2224-8753; fax (2) 475-8253; internet www.nlcf.co.kr; f. 1981; cap. 96,718m., dep. 2,813,715m. (Dec. 1997); Chair. and Pres. PARK SOON-YONG; 35 brs.

Saehan Merchant Banking Corpn: Ankuk Insurance Bldg, 87, 1-ga, Ulchi-no, Jung-gu, CPOB 2723, Seoul 100-191; tel. (2) 754-1616; fax (2) 756-6093; internet www.smbc.co.kr; f. 1977; cap. 22,000m., res. 118,581m., dep. 112,894m. (March 1995); Pres. HUR MANN-GUI.

Provincial Banks

Cheju Bank: 1349, Ido-1-dong, Jeju 690-021, Jeju Prov.; tel. (64) 734-1711; fax (64) 720-0183; f. 1969; cap. 55,500m., res. 30,700m., dep. 1,044,100m. (2002); merged with Central Banking Co in 2000; Chair. and Pres. KANG JOON-HONG; 29 brs.

Daegu Bank Ltd: 118, 2-ga, Susong-dong, Susong-gu, Daegu 706-712; tel. (53) 756-2001; fax (53) 740-6902; internet www.dgb.co.kr; f. 1967; cap. 602,100m., res 157,900m., dep. 10,551,500m. (2002); Chair. and Pres. KIM KUK-NYON; 183 brs.

Jeonbuk Bank Ltd: 669-2, Geumam-dong, Deokjin-gu, Jeonju 561-711, N Jeolla Prov.; tel. (63) 250-7114; fax (63) 250-7078; internet www.jbbank.co.kr; f. 1969; cap. 165,300m., res 30,200m., dep. 2,784,100m. (2002); Chair. and Pres. HONG SUNG-JOO; 68 brs.

Kwangju Bank Ltd: 7-12, Daein-dong, Dong-gu, Gwangju 501-730; tel. (62) 239-5000; fax (62) 239-5199; e-mail kbjint1@nuri.net; internet www.kjbank.com; f. 1968; cap. 170,400m., res 72,600m., dep. 4,750,400m. (2002); Chair. and Pres. UM JONG-DAE; 119 brs.

Kyongnam Bank: 246-1, Sokjeon-dong, Hoewon-gu, Masan 630-010, Gyeongsang Prov.; tel. (55) 290-8000; fax (55) 290-8199; internet www.knbank.co.kr; f. 1970 as Gyeongnam Bank Ltd, name changed 1987; cap. 259,000m., res 114,800m., dep. 5,643,700m. (2002); Chair. and Pres. KIM HYUNG-YUNG; 110 brs.

Pusan Bank: 830-38, Beomil 2-dong, Dong-gu, Busan 601-717; tel. (51) 640-4000; fax (51) 640-4099; e-mail psbkint@bora.dacom.co.kr; internet www.pusanbank.co.kr; f. 1967; cap. 475,226m., res –68,601m., dep. 9,284,245m. (Dec. 2000); Pres. HOON SHIM; 143 brs.

Samyang Merchant Bank: 38-3, 3-ga, Gyongwon-dong, Wansan-gu, Jeonju 560-020; tel. (63) 83-7111; fax (63) 84-3056; f. 1979; cap. 30,254m., res 43,487m., dep. 400,426m. (March 1996); Pres. and CEO KIM PAIK-JOON.

Foreign Banks

ABN-AMRO Bank NV (Netherlands): Seoul City Tower Bldg, 11–12th Floors, 581, 5-ga, Namdaemun-no, Jung-gu, Seoul; tel. (2) 2131-6000; fax (2) 399-6554; f. 1979; Gen. Man. CHUNG DUCK-MO.

American Express Bank Ltd (USA): Gwanghwamun Bldg, 15th Floor, 64-8, 1-ga, Taepyeong-no, Jung-gu, CPOB 1390, Seoul 100-101; tel. (2) 399-2929; fax (2) 399-2966; f. 1977; Gen. Man. CHOE JAE-ICK.

Arab Bank PLC (Jordan): Daewoo Center Bldg, 22nd Floor, 541, 5-ga, Namdaemun-no, Jung-gu, CPOB 1331, Seoul 100-714; tel. (2) 317-9000; fax (2) 757-0124; Gen. Man. JO SEUNG-SHIK.

Australia and New Zealand Banking Group Ltd (Australia): Kyobo Bldg, 18th Floor, 1, 1-ga, Jongno, Jongno-gu, CPOB 1065, Seoul 110-714; tel. (2) 730-3151; fax (2) 737-6325; f. 1987; Gen. Man. PHIL MICHELL.

Bank Mellat (Iran): Bon Sol Bldg, 14th Floor, 144-27, Samseong-dong, Gangnam-gu, Seoul; tel. (2) 558-4448; fax (2) 557-4448; f. 2001; Gen. Man. ALI AFZALI.

Bank of America (USA): Hanwha Bldg, 9th Floor, 1, Janggyo-dong, Jung-gu, Seoul 100-797; tel. (2) 729-4500; fax (2) 729-4400; Gen. Man. BANG CHOON-HO.

Bank of Hawaii (USA): Daeyonkak Bldg, 14th Floor, 25-5, 1-ga, Jungmu-no, Jung-gu, Seoul 100-011; tel. (2) 757-0831; fax (2) 757-3516; Man. PARK YONG-SOO.

Bank of Nova Scotia (Canada): KCCI Bldg, 9th Floor, 45, 4-ga, Namdaemun-no, Jung-gu, Seoul 100-094; tel. (2) 757-7171; fax (2) 752-7189; e-mail bns.seoul@scotiabank.com; Gen. Man. HENRY YONG.

Bank of Tokyo-Mitsubishi Ltd (Japan): Young Poong Bldg, 4th Floor, 33, Seorin-dong, Jongno-gu, Seoul; tel. (2) 399-6474; fax (2) 735-4897; f. 1967; Gen. Man. KAZUMASA KOGA.

Bankers Trust Co (USA): Center Bldg, 10th Floor, 111-5, Sokong-dong, Jung-gu, Seoul; tel. (2) 3788-6000; fax (2) 756-2648; f. 1978; Man. Dir LEE KEUN-SAM.

BNP Paribas (France): Dong Yang Chemical Bldg, 8th Floor, 50, Sogong-dong, Jung-gu, Seoul 100-070; tel. (2) 317-1700; fax (2) 757-2530; e-mail bnppseoul@asia.bnparibas.com; f. 1976; Gen. Man. ALAIN PÉNICAUT.

Citibank NA (USA): Citicorp Center Bldg, 89-29, 2-ga, Shinmun-no, Jongno-gu, CPOB 749, Seoul 110-062; tel. (2) 2004-1114; fax (2) 722-3644; f. 1967; Gen. Man. SAJJAD RAZVI.

Crédit Agricole Indosuez (France): Kyobo Bldg, 19th Floor, 1, 1-ga, Jongno, Jongno-gu, CPOB 158, Seoul 110-714; tel. (2) 3700-9500; fax (2) 738-0325; f. 1974; Gen. Man. PATRICE COUVEGNES.

Crédit Lyonnais SA (France): You One Bldg, 8th–10th Floors, 75-95, Seosomun-dong, Jung-gu, Seoul 100-110; tel. (2) 772-8000; fax (2) 755-5379; f. 1978; Gen. Man. GEOFFROY DE LASSUS.

Deutsche Bank AG (Germany): Sei An Bldg, 20th-22nd Floor, 116, 1-ga, Shinmun-no, Jongno-gu, Seoul 110-700; tel. (2) 724-4500; fax (2) 724-4645; f. 1978; Gen. Man. KIM JIN-IL.

Development Bank of Singapore Ltd: Gwanghwamun Bldg, 20th Floor, 64-8, 1-ga, Taepyeong-no, Jung-gu, CPOB 9896, Seoul; tel. (2) 399-2660; fax (2) 732-7953; e-mail jeefun@dbs.com; f. 1981; Gen. Man. LOW JEE FUN.

First National Bank of Chicago (USA): Oriental Chemical Bldg, 15th Floor, 50, Sokong-dong, Jung-gu, Seoul 100-070; tel. (2) 316-9700; fax (2) 753-7917; f. 1976; Vice-Pres. and Gen. Man. MICHAEL S. BROWN.

Fuji Bank Ltd (Japan): Doosan Bldg, 15th Floor, 101-1, 1-ga, Ulchi-no, Jung-gu, Seoul 100-191; tel. (2) 311-2000; fax (2) 754-8177; f. 1972; Gen. Man. IKUO YAMAMOTO.

Hongkong and Shanghai Banking Corpn Ltd (Hong Kong): HSBC Bldg, 1-ga, Bongrae-dong, Jung-gu, CPOB 6910, Seoul 110-161; tel. (2) 2004-0000; fax (2) 381-9100; Gen. Man. G. P. S. CALVERT.

Indian Overseas Bank: Daeyungak Bldg, 3rd Floor, 25-5, 1-ga, Jungmu-no, Jung-gu, CPOB 3332, Seoul 100-011; f. 1977; tel. (2) 753-0741; fax (2) 756-0279; e-mail iobseoul@chollian.net; f. 1977; Gen. Man. K. P. MUNIRATHMAN.

Industrial and Commercial Bank of China (China): Taepyeong Bldg, 17th Floor, 310, 2-ga, Taepyeong-no, Seoul; tel. (2) 755-5688; fax (2) 779-2750; f. 1997; Gen. Man. ZHANG KEXIN.

ING Bank NV (Netherlands): Hungkuk Life Insurance Bldg, 15th Floor, 226, 1-ga, Shinmun-no, Jongno-gu, Seoul 110-061; tel. (2) 317-1800; fax (2) 317-1883; Man. YIM SANG-KYUN.

JP Morgan Chase Bank (USA): Chase Plaza, 34-35, Jeong-dong, Jung-gu, Seoul 100-120; tel. (2) 758-5114; fax (2) 758-5420; f. 1978; Gen. Man. KIM MYUNG-HAN.

Mizuho Bank Ltd (Japan): Nae Wei Bldg, 14th Floor, 6, 2-ga, Ulchi-no, Jung-gu, Seoul 100-192; tel. (2) 756-8181; fax (2) 754-6844; f. 1972; Gen. Man. TSUNEO KIKUCHI.

National Australia Bank Ltd: KDIC Bldg, 16th Floor, 33, Da-dong, Jung-gu, Seoul; tel. (2) 3705-4600; fax (2) 3705-4602; Gen. Man. MARK EDMONDS.

National Bank of Canada: Leema Bldg, 6th Floor, 146-1, Susong-dong, Jongno-gu, Seoul 110-140; tel. (2) 733-5012; fax (2) 736-1508; Vice-Pres. and Country Man. C. N. KIM.

National Bank of Pakistan: Kyobo Bldg, 12th Floor, 1, 1-ga, Jongno, Jongno-gu, CPOB 1633, Seoul 110-121; tel. (2) 732-0277; fax (2) 734-5817; f. 1987; Gen. Man. ABDUL GHAFOOR.

Overseas Union Bank Ltd (Singapore): Kyobo Bldg, 8th Floor, Suite 806, 1, 1-ga, Jongno, Jongno-gu, Seoul 110-714; tel. (2) 739-3441; fax (2) 732-9004; Vice-Pres. and Gen. Man. OOI KOOI KEAT.

Royal Bank of Canada: Kyobo Bldg, 22nd Floor, 1, 1-ga, Jongno, Jongno-gu, Seoul 110-714; tel. (2) 730-7791; fax (2) 736-2995; f. 1982; Gen. Man. THOMAS P. FEHLNER, Jr.

Société Générale (France): Sean Bldg, 10th Floor, 1-ga, Shinmun-no, Jongno-gu, Seoul 110-700; tel. (2) 2195-7777; fax (2) 2195-7700; f. 1984; CEO ERIC BERTHÉLEMY.

Standard Chartered Bank (UK): Seoul Finance Center, 22nd Floor, 84, 1-ga, Taepyeong-no, Jung-gu, Seoul; tel. (2) 750-6114; fax (2) 757-7444; Gen. Man. WILLIAM GEMMEL.

UBS AG (Switzerland): Young Poong Bldg, 10th Floor, 33, Seorin-dong, Jongno-gu, Seoul 110-752; tel. (2) 3702-8888; fax (2) 3708-8714; f. 1999; Gen. Man. LEE JAE-HONG.

UFJ Bank Ltd (Japan): Lotte Bldg, 22nd Floor, 1, 1-ga, Sogong-dong, Jung-gu, Seoul; tel. (2) 752-7321; fax (2) 754-3870; Gen. Man. HIDEKI YAMAUCHI.

Union Bank of California NA (USA): Kyobo Bldg, 12th Floor, 1, 1-ga, Jongno, Jongno-gu, CPOB 329, Seoul 110; tel. (2) 721-1700; fax (2) 732-9526; Gen. Man. KIM TAEK-JOONG.

Union de Banques Arabes et Françaises (France): ACE Tower, 3rd Floor, 1-170, Sunhwa-dong, Jung-gu, CPOB 1224, Seoul 100-742; tel. (2) 3455-5300; fax (2) 3455-5354; f. 1979; Gen. Man. PATRICK OBERREINER.

United Overseas Bank Ltd (Singapore): Kyobo Bldg, 20th Floor, 1, 1-ga, Jongno, Jongno-gu, Seoul 110-714; tel. (2) 739-3916; fax (2) 730-9570; Gen. Man. LIEW CHAN HARN.

Banking Association

Korea Federation of Banks: 4-1, 1-ga, Myeong-dong, Jung-gu, Seoul; tel. (2) 3705-5000; fax (2) 3705-5338; internet www.kfb.or.kr; f. 1928; Pres. CHONG CHUN-TAEK; Chair. LEE SANG-CHUL; Vice-Chair. LEE CHUNG-NYUNG.

STOCK EXCHANGE

Korea Stock Exchange: 33, Yeouido-dong, Yeongdeungpo-gu, Seoul 150-977; tel. (2) 3774-9000; fax (2) 786-0263; e-mail world@kse.or.kr; internet www.kse.or.kr; f. 1956; Chair. and CEO KANG YUNG-JOO.

Kosdaq Stock Market, Inc: 45-2, Yeouido-dong, Yeongdeungpo-gu, Seoul 150-974; tel. (2) 2001-5700; fax (2) 784-4505; e-mail webmaster@kosdaq.or.kr; internet www.kosdaq.or.kr; f. 1996; stock market for knowledge-based venture cos; 828 listed cos (Aug. 2002) with a market capitalization of US $39,945m.; Pres. and CEO SHIN HO-JOO.

INSURANCE

In 2002 there were 22 life insurance companies and 13 non-life insurance companies.

Principal Life Companies

Allianz Jeil Life Insurance Co Ltd: 1303-35, Seocho 4-dong, Seocho-gu, Seoul 137-074; tel. (2) 3481-3111; fax (2) 3481-0960; f. 1954; Pres. LEE TAE-SIK.

Choson Life Insurance Co Ltd: 111, Shincheon-dong, Dong-gu, Daegu 701-620; tel. (53) 743-3600; fax (53) 742-9263; f. 1988; cap. 12,000m.; Pres. LEE YOUNG-TAEK.

Daishin Life Insurance Co Ltd: 395-68, Shindaebang-dong, Dongjak-gu, Seoul 156-010; tel. (2) 3284-7000; fax (2) 3284-7451; internet www.dslife.co.kr; f. 1989; cap. 144,200m. (2002); Pres. PARK BYUNG-MYUNG.

Dong-Ah Life Insurance Co Ltd: Dong-Ah Life Insurance Bldg, 33, Da-dong, Jung-gu, Seoul; tel. (2) 317-5114; fax (2) 771-7561; f. 1973; cap. 10,000m.; Pres. KIM CHANG-LAK; 900 brs.

Dongbu Life Insurance Co Ltd: Dongbu Bldg, 7th Floor, 891-10, Daechi-dong, Gangnam-gu, Seoul 135-820; tel. (2) 1588-3131; fax (2) 3011-4100; internet www.dongbulife.co.kr; f. 1989; cap. 85,200m. (2002); Pres. CHANG KI-JE.

Dongyang Life Insurance Co Ltd: 185, Ulchi-no 2-ga, Jung-gu, Seoul 100-192; tel. (2) 728-9114; fax (2) 771-1347; internet www.myangel.co.kr; f. 1989; cap. 340,325m. (2002); Pres. KU JA-HONG.

Doowon Life Insurance Co Ltd: 259-6, Sokjon-dong, Hoewon-gu, Masan 630-500; tel. (55) 52-3100; fax (55) 52-3119; f. 1990; cap. 10,000m.; Pres. CHOI IN-YONG.

Han Deuk Life Insurance Co Ltd: 878-1, Bumchyun 1-dong, Busanjin-gu, Busan 641-021; tel. (51) 631-8700; fax (51) 631-8809; f. 1989; cap. 10,000m.; Pres. SUH WOO-SHICK.

Hanil Life Insurance Co Ltd: 118, 2-ga, Namdaemun-no, Jung-gu, Seoul 100-770; tel. (2) 2126-7777; fax (2) 2126-7631; internet www.hanillife.co.kr; f. 1993; cap. 115,000m. (2002); Pres. LEE MYUNG-HYUN.

Hankuk Life Insurance Co Ltd: Daehan Fire Bldg, 51-1, Namchang-dong, Jung-gu, Seoul 100-060; tel. (2) 773-3355; fax (2) 773-1778; f. 1989; cap. 10,000m.; Pres. PARK HYUN-KOOK.

Hansung Life Insurance Co Ltd: 3, Sujung-dong, Dong-gu, Busan 601-030; tel. (51) 461-7700; fax (51) 465-0581; f. 1988; Pres. CHO YONG-KEUN.

Hungkuk Life Insurance Co Ltd: 226, Shinmun-no 1-ga, Jongno-gu, Seoul 100-061; tel. (2) 2002-7000; fax (2) 2002-7804; internet www.hungkuk.co.kr; f. 1958; cap. 12,221m. (2002); Pres. RYU SEOK-KEE.

ING Life Insurance Co Korea Ltd: Sean Bldg, 116, Shinmun-no, Jongno-gu, Seoul 110-700; tel. (2) 3703-9500; fax (2) 734-3309; f. 1991; cap. 64,820m. (2002); Pres. JOOST KENEMANS.

Korea Life Insurance Co Ltd: 60, Yeouido-dong, Yeongdeungpo-gu, Seoul 150-603; tel. (2) 789-5114; fax (2) 789-8173; internet www.korealife.com; f. 1946; cap. 3,550,000m. (2002); Pres. LEE KANG-HWAN.

Korean Reinsurance Company: 80, Susong-dong, Jongno-gu, Seoul 110-733; tel. (2) 3702-6000; fax (2) 739-3754; internet www.koreanre.co.kr; f. 1963; Pres. PARK JONG-WON.

Kumho Life Insurance Co Ltd: 57, 1-ga, Shinmun-no, Jongno-gu, Seoul 110-061; tel. (2) 6303-5000; fax (2) 771-7561; internet www.kumholife.co.kr; f. 1988; cap. 211,249m. (2002); Pres. SONG KEY-HYUCK.

Kyobo Life Insurance Co Ltd: 1, 1-ga, Jongno, Jongno-gu, Seoul 110-714; tel. (2) 721-2121; fax (2) 737-9970; internet www.kyobo.co.kr; f. 1958; cap. 92,500m.; Pres. and CEO CHANG HYUNG-DUK; 84 main brs.

Lucky Life Insurance Co Ltd: 3, Sujung-dong, Dong-gu, Busan 601-716; tel. (51) 461-7700; fax (51) 465-0581; internet www.luckylife.co.kr; f. 1988; cap. 139,054m. (2002); Pres. CHANG NAM-SIK

MetLife Insurance Co of Korea Ltd: Sungwon Bldg, 8th Floor, 141, Samseong-dong, Gangnam-gu, Seoul 135-716; tel. (2) 3469-9600; fax (2) 3469-9700; internet www.metlifekorea.co.kr; f. 1989; cap. 97,700m. (2002); Pres. STUART B. SOLOMON.

Pacific Life Insurance Co Ltd: 705-9, Yeoksam-dong, Gangnam-gu, Seoul 135-080; tel. (2) 3458-0114; fax (2) 3458-0392; internet www.pli.co.kr; f. 1989; cap. 10,000m.; Pres. KIM SUNG-MOO.

PCA Life Insurance Co Ltd: 142, Nonhyun-dong, Gangnam-gu, Seoul 135-749; tel. (2) 515-5300; fax (2) 514-3844; f. 1990; cap. 52,100m. (2002); Pres. MIKE BISHOP.

Prudential Life Insurance Co of Korea Ltd: Prudential Bldg, Yeoksam-dong, Gangnam-gu, Seoul; tel. (2) 2144-2000; fax (2) 2144-2100; internet www.prudential.or.kr; f. 1989; cap. 26,400m.; Pres. JAMES C. SPACKMAN.

Samshin All State Life Insurance Co Ltd: Samwhan Bldg, 5th Floor, 98-5, Unni-dong, Jongno-gu, Seoul 110-742; tel. (2) 3670-5000; fax (2) 742-8197; Pres. KIM KYUNG-YOP.

Samsung Life Insurance Co Ltd: 150, 2-ga, Taepyeong-no, Jung-gu, Seoul 100-716; tel. (2) 751-8000; fax (2) 751-8100; internet www.samsunglife.com; f. 1957; cap. 100,000m. (2002); Pres. BAE JUNG-CHOONG; 1,300 brs.

Shinhan Life Insurance Co Ltd: 120, 2-ga, Taepyeong-no, Jung-gu, Seoul 100-102; tel. (2) 3455-4000; fax (2) 753-9351; internet www.shinhanlife.co.kr; f. 1990; Pres. HAN DONG-WOO.

SK Life Insurance Co Ltd: 168, Gongduk-dong, Mapo-gu, Seoul 121-705; tel. (2) 3271-4114; fax (2) 3271-4400; internet www.sklife.com; f. 1988; cap. 246,275m. (2002); Pres. KANG HONG-SIN.

Non-Life Companies

Daehan Fire and Marine Insurance Co Ltd: 51-1, Namchang-dong, Jung-gu, Seoul 100-778; tel. (2) 3455-3114; fax (2) 756-9194; e-mail dhplane@daeins.co.kr; internet www.daeins.co.kr; f. 1946; cap. 19,500m.; Pres. LEE YOUNG-DONG.

Dongbu Insurance Co Ltd: Dongbu Financial Center, 891-10, Daechi-dong, Gangnam-gu, Seoul 135-840; tel. (2) 2262-3450; fax (2) 2273-6785; e-mail dongbu@dongbuinsurance.co.kr; internet www.idongbu.com; f. 1962; cap. 30,000m.; Pres. LEE SU-KWANG.

First Fire and Marine Insurance Co Ltd: 12-1, Seosomun-dong, Jung-gu, CPOB 530, Seoul 100-110; tel. (2) 316-8114; fax (2) 771-

7319; internet www.insumall.co.kr; f. 1949; cap. 17,200m.; Pres. KIM WOO-HOANG.

Green Fire and Marine Insurance Co Ltd: Seoul City Tower, 581, 5-ga, Namdaemun-no, Jung-gu, Seoul 100-803; tel. (2) 1588-5959; fax (2) 773-1214; internet www.greenfire.co.kr; KIM JONG-CHEN.

Haedong Insurance Co Ltd: 1424-2, Seocho-dong, Seocho-gu, Seoul; tel. (2) 520-2114; e-mail webmaster@haedong.co.kr; internet www.haedong.co.kr; f. 1953; cap. p.u. 12,000m.; Chair. KIM DONG-MAN; CEO NAH BOO-WHAN.

Hankuk Fidelity and Surety Co Ltd: 51-1, Namchang-dong, Jung-gu, Seoul; tel. (2) 773-3355; fax (2) 773-1778; e-mail hfs025@unitel.co.kr; f. 1989; cap. 103,000m.; Pres. CHO AM-DAE.

Hyundai Marine and Fire Insurance Co Ltd: 8th Floor, 140-2, Kye-dong, Jongno-gu, Seoul 110-793; tel. (2) 3701-8000; fax (2) 732-5687; e-mail webpd@hdinsurance.co.kr; internet www.hi.co.kr; f. 1955; cap. 30,000m.; Pres. KIM HO-IL.

Korean Reinsurance Co: 80, Susong-dong, Jongno-gu, Seoul 100-733; tel. (2) 3702-6000; fax (2) 739-3754; e-mail service@koreanre.co.kr; internet www.koreanre.co.kr; f. 1963; cap. 34,030m.; Pres. PARK JONG-WON.

Kukje Hwajae Insurance Co Ltd: 120, 5-ga, Namdaemun-no, Jung-gu, Seoul 100-704; tel. (2) 753-1101; fax (2) 773-1214; internet www.directins.co.kr; f. 1947; cap. 10,784m.; Chair. LEE BONG-SUH.

Kyobo Auto Insurance Co Ltd: 76-4, Jamwon-dong, Seocho-gu, Seoul 137-909; tel. (2) 3479-4900; fax (2) 3479-4800; internet www.kyobodirect.com; Pres. SHIN YONG-KIL.

LG Insurance Co Ltd: LG Da-dong Bldg, 85, Da-dong, Jung-gu, Seoul 100-180; tel. (2) 310-2391; fax (2) 753-1002; e-mail webmaster@lginsure.com; internet www.lginsure.com; f. 1959; Pres. KOO CHA-HOON.

Oriental Fire and Marine Insurance Co Ltd: 25-1, Yeouido-dong, Yeongdeungpo-gu, Seoul 150-010; tel. (2) 3786-1910; fax (2) 3886-1940; e-mail webmaster@ofmi.co.kr; internet www.insuworld.co.kr; f. 1922; cap. 42,900m.; Pres. CHUNG KUN-SUB.

Samsung Fire and Marine Insurance Co Ltd: Samsung Insurance Bldg, 87, 1-ga, Ulchi-no, Jung-gu, Seoul 100-191; tel. (2) 758-7948; fax (2) 758-7831; internet www.samsungfire.com; f. 1952; cap. 6,566m.; Pres. LEE SOO-CHANG.

Seoul Guarantee Insurance Co: 136-74, Yeonchi-dong, Jongno-gu, Seoul 110-470; tel. (2) 3671-7459; fax (2) 3671-7480; internet www.sgic.co.kr; Pres. PARK HAE-CHOON.

Shindongah Fire and Marine Insurance Co Ltd: 43, 2-ga, Taepyeong-no, Jung-gu, Seoul; tel. (2) 6366-7000; fax (2) 755-8006; internet www.sdafire.com; f. 1946; cap. 60,220m.; Pres. JEON HWA-SOO.

Ssangyong Fire and Marine Insurance Co Ltd: 60, Doryeom-dong, Jongno-gu, Seoul 110-716; tel. (2) 724-9000; fax (2) 730-1628; e-mail sfmi@ssy.insurance.co.kr; internet www.insurance.co.kr; f. 1948; cap. 27,400m.; Pres. LEE JIN-MYUNG.

Insurance Associations

Korea Life Insurance Association: Kukdong Bldg, 16th Floor, 60-1, 3-ga, Jungmu-no, Jung-gu, Seoul 100-705; tel. (2) 2262-6600; fax (2) 2262-6580; internet www.klia.or.kr; f. 1950; Chair. BAE CHAN-BYUNG.

Korea Non-Life Insurance Association: KRIC Bldg, 6th Floor, 80, Susong-dong, Jongno-gu, Seoul; tel. (2) 3702-8539; fax (2) 3702-8549; internet www.knia.or.kr; f. 1946; 13 corporate mems; Chair. PARK JONG-IK.

Trade and Industry

GOVERNMENT AGENCIES

Fair Trade Commission: 1, Jungang-dong, Gwacheon-shi, Gyeonggi Prov. 427-760; internet www.ftc.go.kr; Chair. LEE NAM-KEE.

Federation of Korean Industries: FKI Bldg, 2nd Floor, 28-1, Yeouido-dong, Yeongdeungpo-gu, Seoul 150-756; tel. (2) 3771-0114; fax (2) 3771-0110; e-mail webmaster@fki.or.kr; internet www.fki.or.kr; f. 1961; conducts research and survey work on domestic and overseas economic conditions and trends; advises the Govt and other interested parties on economic matters; exchanges economic and trade missions with other countries; sponsors business conferences; 380 corporate mems and 65 business asscns; Chair. KIM KAK-CHOONG.

Korea Appraisal Board: 171-2, Samseong-dong, Gangnam-gu, Seoul; tel. (2) 555-1174; Chair. KANG KIL-BOO.

Korea Asset Management Corpn (KAMCO): 814, Yeoksam-dong, Gangnam-gu, Seoul; tel. (2) 3420-5049; fax (2) 3420-5100; internet www.kamco.co.kr; f. 1963; collection and disposal of non-performing loans; appointed following Asian financial crisis as sole institution to manage and dispose of non-performing loans for financial institutions; Pres. CHUNG JAE-RYONG.

Korea Export Industrial Corpn: 33, Seorin-dong, Jongno-gu, Seoul; tel. (2) 853-5573; f. 1964; encourages industrial exports, provides assistance and operating capital, conducts market surveys; Pres. KIM KI-BAE.

Korea Export Insurance Corpn: 33, Seorin-dong, Jongno-gu, Seoul; tel. (2) 399-6800; fax (2) 399-6597; internet www.keic.or.kr; f. 1992; and official export credit agency of Korea; Pres. LIM TAE-JIN.

Korea Institute for Industrial Economics and Trade (KIET): 206-9, Cheongnyangni-dong, Dongdaemun-gu, Seoul; tel. (2) 3299-3114; fax (2) 963-8540; internet www.kiet.re.kr; f. 1976; economic and industrial research; Pres. PAI KWANG-SUN.

Korean Intellectual Property Office: Government Complex-Daejeon, Dunsan-dong, Seo-gu, Daejeon; tel. (42) 481-5027; fax (42) 481-3455; internet www.kipo.go.kr; Commissioner KIM GWANG-LIM.

Korea Industrial Research Institutes: FKI Bldg, 28-1, Yeouido-dong, Yeongdeungpo-gu, Seoul; tel. (2) 780-7601; fax (2) 785-5771; f. 1979; analyses industrial and technological information from abroad; Pres. KIM CHAE-KYUM.

Korea Trade-Investment Promotion Agency (KOTRA): 300-9, Yeomgok-dong, Seocho-gu, Seoul; tel. (2) 3460-7114; fax (2) 3460-7777; e-mail net-mgr@kotra.or.kr; internet www.kotra.or.kr; f. 1962; various trade promotion activities, market research, cross-border investment promotion, etc.; 98 overseas brs; Pres. OH YOUNG-KYO.

CHAMBER OF COMMERCE

Korea Chamber of Commerce and Industry: 45, 4-ga, Namdaemun-no, Jung-gu, Seoul 100-743; tel. (2) 316-3114; fax (2) 757-9475; internet www.korcham.net; f. 1884; over 80,000m. mems; 63 local chambers; promotes development of the economy and of international economic co-operation; Pres. PARK YONG-SUNG.

INDUSTRIAL AND TRADE ASSOCIATIONS

Agricultural and Fishery Marketing Corpn: 191, 2-ga, Hangang-no, Yeongsan-gu, CPOB 3212, Seoul 140; tel. (2) 790-8010; fax (2) 798-7513; internet www.afmc.co.kr; f. 1967; integrated development for secondary processing and marketing distribution for agricultural products and fisheries products; Pres. AHN KYO-DUCK; Exec. Vice-Pres. KIM JIN-KYU.

Construction Association of Korea: Construction Bldg, 8th Floor, 71-2, Nonhyon-dong, Gangnam-gu, Seoul 135-701; tel. (2) 547-6101; fax (2) 542-6264; f. 1947; national licensed contractors' asscn; 2,700 mem. firms (1995); Pres. CHOI WON-SUK; Vice-Pres. PARK KU-YEOL.

Electronic Industries Association of Korea: 648, Yeoksam-dong, Gangnam-gu, CPOB 5650, Seoul 135-080; tel. (2) 553-0941; fax (2) 555-6195; e-mail eiak@soback.kornet.nm.kr; internet www.eiak.org; f. 1976; 328 mems; Chair. JOHN KOO.

Korea Automobile Manufacturers Association: 658-4. Deungchon-dong, Gangseo-gu, Seoul; tel. (2) 3660-1800; fax (2) 3660-1800; internet www.kama.co.kr; f. 1988; Chair. KIM NOI-MYUNG.

Korea Coal Association: 80-6, Susong-dong, Jongno-gu, Seoul; tel. (2) 734-8891; fax (2) 734-7959; f. 1949; 49 corporate mems; Chair. JANG BYEONG-DUCK.

Korea Consumer Goods Exporters Association: KWTC Bldg, Rm 1802, 159, Samseong-dong, Gangnam-gu, Seoul; tel. (2) 551-1865; fax (2) 551-1870; f. 1986; 230 corporate mems; Pres. YONG WOONG-SHIN.

Korea Federation of Textile Industries: 944-31, Daechi-dong, Gangnam-gu, Seoul; tel. (2) 528-4001; fax (2) 528-4069; e-mail kofoti@kofoti.or.kr; internet www.kofoti.or.kr; f. 1980; 50 corporate mems; Pres. PARK SANG-CHUL.

Korea Foods Industry Association: 1002-6, Bangbae-dong, Seocho-gu, Seoul; tel. (2) 585-5052; fax (2) 586-4906; internet www.kfia.or.kr; f. 1969; 104 corporate mems; Pres. CHUN MYUNG-KE.

Korea Importers Association (KOIMA): 218, Hangang-no, 2-ga, Yeongsan-gu, Seoul 140-875; tel. (2) 792-1581; fax (2) 785-4373; e-mail info@aftak.com; internet www.aftak.or.kr; f. 1970; 11,903 mems; Chair. CHIN CHUL-PYUNG.

Korea International Trade Association: 159-1, Samseong-dong, Gangnam-gu, Seoul; tel. (2) 6000-5114; fax (2) 6000-5115; internet www.kita.org; f. 1946; private, non-profitmaking business org. representing all licensed traders in South Korea; provides foreign businessmen with information, contacts and advice; 80,000 corporate mems; Pres. KIM JAE-CHUL.

Korea Iron and Steel Association: 824, Yeoksam-dong, Gangnam-gu, Seoul; tel. (2) 559-3500; fax (2) 559-3508; internet www.kosa.or.kr; f. 1975; 39 corporate mems; Chair. YOO SANG-BOO.

Korea Oil Association: 28-1, Yeouido-dong, Yeongdeungpo-gu, Seoul; tel. (2) 3775-0520; fax (2) 761-9573; f. 1980; Pres. CHOI DOO-HWAN.

Korea Productivity Center: 122-1, Jeokseon-dong, Jongno-gu, Seoul 110-052; tel. (2) 724-1114; fax (2) 736-0322; internet www.kpc.or.kr; f. 1957; services to increase productivity of the industries, consulting services, education and training of specialized personnel; Chair. and CEO LEE HEE-BEOM.

Korea Sericultural Association: 17-9, Yeouido-dong, Yeongdeungpo-gu, Seoul; tel. (2) 783-6072; fax (2) 780-0706; f. 1946; improvement and promotion of silk production; 50,227 corporate mems; Pres. CHOI YON-HONG.

Korea Shipbuilders' Association: 65-1, Unni-dong, Jongno-gu, Seoul; tel. (2) 766-4631; fax (2) 766-4307; internet www.koshipa.or.kr; f. 1977; 9 mems; Chair. KIM HYUNG-BYUK.

Korea Textiles Trade Association: Textile Center, 16th Floor, 944-31, Daechi-dong, Gangnam-gu, Seoul; tel. (2) 528-5158; fax (2) 528-5188; f. 1981; 947 corporate mems; Pres. KANG TAE-SEUNG.

Korean Apparel Industry Association: KWTC Bldg, Rm 801, 159, Samseong-dong, Gangnam-gu, Seoul 135-729; tel. (2) 551-1454; fax (2) 551-1467; f. 1993; 741 corporate mems; Pres. PARK SEI-YOUNG.

Korean Development Associates: Seoul; tel. (2) 392-3854; fax (2) 312-3856; f. 1965; economic research; 25 corporate mems; Pres. KIM DONG-KYU.

Mining Association of Korea: 35-24, Dongui-dong, Jongno-gu, Seoul 110; tel. (2) 737-7748; fax (2) 720-5592; f. 1918; 128 corporate mems; Pres. KIM SANG-BONG.

Spinners and Weavers Association of Korea: 43-8, Gwancheol-dong, Jongno-gu, Seoul 110; tel. (2) 735-5741; fax (2) 735-5749; internet www.swak.org; f. 1947; 20 corporate mems; Pres. SUH MIN-SOK.

EMPLOYERS' ORGANIZATION

Korea Employers' Federation: 276-1 Daeheung-dong, Mapo-gu, Seoul 121-726; tel. (2) 3270-7300; fax (2) 706-1059; e-mail kef@kef.or.kr; internet www.kef.or.kr; f. 1970; 13 regional employers' asscns, 20 economic and trade asscns, and 4,000 major enterprises; Chair. KIM CHANG-SUNG.

UTILITIES

Electricity

Korea Electric Power Corpn (KEPCO): 167, Samseong-dong, Gangnam-gu, Seoul; tel. (2) 3456-3630; fax (2) 3456-3699; internet www.kepco.co.kr; f. 1961; transmission and distribution of electric power, and development of electric power sources; privatization pending; Pres. KANG DONG-SUK.

Gas

Korea Gas Corpn: 215, Jeongja-dong, Bundang-gu, Seongnam, Gyeonggi Prov.; tel. (31) 710-0114; fax (31) 710-0117; internet www.kogas.or.kr; state-owned; proposed transfer to private-sector ownership announced in July 1998; Pres. KIM MYUNG-KYU.

Samchully Co Ltd: 35-6, Yeouido-dong, Yeongdeungpo-gu, Seoul; tel. (2) 368-3300; fax (2) 783-1206; internet www.samchully.co.kr; f. 1966; gas supply co for Seoul metropolitan area and Gyeonggi Prov.; Chair. JIN JU-HWA.

Water

Korea Water Resources Corpn: 6-2, Yeonchuk-dong, Daedeok-gu, Daejeon; tel. (42) 629-3114; fax (42) 623-0963; internet www.kowaco.or.kr.

Office of Waterworks, Seoul Metropolitan Govt: 27-1 Hap-dong, Seodaemun-gu, Seoul; tel. (2) 390-7332; fax (2) 362-3653; f. 1908; responsible for water supply in Seoul; Head SON JANG-HO.

Ulsan City Water and Sewerage Board: 646-4, Shin-Jung 1-dong, Nam-gu, Ulsan; tel. (52) 743-020; fax (52) 746-928; f. 1979; responsible for water supply and sewerage in Ulsan; Dir HO KUN-SONG.

CO-OPERATIVES

Korea Computers Co-operative: Seoul; tel. (2) 780-0511; fax (2) 780-7509; f. 1981; Pres. MIN KYUNG-HYUN.

Korea Federation of Knitting Industry Co-operatives: 586-1, Shinsa-dong, Gangnam-gu, Seoul; tel. (2) 548-2131; fax (2) 3444-9929; internet www.knit.or.kr; f. 1962; Chair. JOUNG MAN-SUB.

Korea Federation of Non-ferrous Metal Industry Co-operatives: Backsang Bldg, Rm 715, 35-2, Yeouido-dong, Yeongdeungpo-gu, Seoul; tel. (2) 780-8551; fax (2) 784-9473; f. 1962; Chair. PARK WON-SIK.

Korea Federation of Small and Medium Business (KFSB): 16-2, Yeouido-dong, Yeongdeungpo-gu, Seoul 150-010; tel. (2) 2124-3114; fax (2) 782-0247; f. 1962; Chair. KIM YOUNG-SOO.

Korea Mining Industry Co-operative: 35-24, Dongui-dong, Jongno-gu, Seoul; tel. (2) 735-3490; fax (2) 735-4658; f. 1966; Chair. JEON HYANG-SIK.

Korea Steel Industry Co-operative: 915-14, Bangbae-dong, Seocho-gu, Seoul; tel. (2) 587-3121; fax (2) 588-3671; internet www.kosic.or.kr; f. 1962; Pres. KIM DUK-NAM.

Korea Woollen Spinners and Weavers Co-operatives: Rm 503, Seawha Bldg, 36, 6-ga, Jongno-gu, Seoul; tel. (2) 747-3871; fax (2) 747-3874; e-mail woollen@woolspd.or.kr; internet www.woolspd.or.kr; f. 1964; Pres. KIM YOUNG-SIK.

National Agricultural Co-operative Federation (NACF): 1, 1-ga, Chungjeong-no, Jung-gu, Seoul; tel. (2) 397-5114; fax (2) 397-5380; internet www.nacf.co.kr; f. 1961; international banking, marketing, co-operative trade, utilization and processing, supply, co-operative insurance, banking and credit services, education and research; Pres. WON CHUL-HEE.

National Federation of Fisheries Co-operatives: 11-6, Shincheon-dong, Songpa-gu, Seoul; tel. (2) 2240-3114; fax (2) 2240-3024; internet www.suhyup.co.kr; f. 1962; Pres. HONG JONG-MOON.

MAJOR COMPANIES

The following are some of South Korea's major industrial groups and companies, arranged by sector (cap. = capital; res = reserves; m. = million; amounts in won, unless otherwise indicated):

Major Industrial Groups

Daelim Group: 23-9 Yeouido-dong, Yeongdeungpo-gu, Seoul; tel. (2) 368-7114; fax (2) 368-7700; internet www.dic.co.kr; mfrs of construction materials, light industrial goods; Chair. LEE YONG-KU.

Daewoo International Corpn: 541, 5-ga, Namdaemun-no, Jung-gu, Seoul; tel. (2) 759-2114; fax (2) 753-9489; internet www.daewoo.com; f. 1967; construction, machinery, shipbuilding, automobiles, electronics, financing, chemicals, light industry, etc.; collapsed with debts of US $50,000m. in 1999; Pres. and CEO LEE TAE-YONG.

Dongbu Group: 21-9, Jeo-dong, Jung-gu, Seoul; tel. (2) 2279-9426; fax (2) 278-3615; f. 1969; mfrs of chemicals, semiconductors, steel and steel products; civil engineering and construction; Pres. KIM CHUN-KI.

Doosan Group: 18-12, 6-ga, Ulchi-no, Jung-gu, Seoul; tel. (2) 3398-1081; fax (2) 3398-1135; internet www.doosan.co.kr; industrial machinery, construction, electro-materials, glass; Chair.and CEO PARK YOUNG-OH.

Haitai Group: 131, Namyong-dong, Yongsan-gu, Seoul; tel. (2) 709-7766; fax (2) 790-8123; f. 1945; food, retailing, electronics; Chair. YANG JONG-SOK.

Hanjin Group: 51, Sogong-dong, Jung-gu, Seoul; tel. (2) 756-7739; fax (2) 757-7478; internet www.hanjin.net; f. 1945; transport, shipping, heavy industries; Chair. CHO CHOONG-HOON.

Hanwha Group: 1, Janggyo-dong, Jung-gu, Seoul; tel. (2) 729-2700; fax (2) 729-3000; e-mail webmaster@hanwha.co.kr; internet www.hanwha.co.kr; f. 1952; chemicals; Chair. KIM SEUNG-YOUN.

Hyosung Group: 17-7, 4-ga, Namdaemun-no, Jung-gu, Seoul; tel. (2) 771-1100; fax (2) 754-9983; internet www.hyosung.co.kr; f. 1957; steel and metals, electronics, industrial equipment, chemicals, fabrics, leather goods; Chair. CHO SOOK-RAE; Pres. HUH CHUNG-WOOK; 25,000 employees.

Hyundai Group: 140-2, Kye-dong, Jongno-gu, Seoul; tel. (2) 746-1873; fax (2) 741-2341; f. 1953; electronics, construction, heavy industry, petrochemicals, automobile manufacture, finance and securities, etc.; Pres. CHOI NAM-CHUL; Chair. (vacant); 180,000 employees.

Kolon Group: Kolon Bldg, 45, Mukyo-dong, Jung-gu, Seoul; tel. (2) 311-8114; fax (2) 754-5314; internet www.kolon.co.kr; f. 1954; chemicals, construction, electric machinery; Chair. LEE WOONG-YEOL.

Kumho Group: 10-1, 2-ga, Hoehyeon-dong, Jung-gu, Seoul; tel. (2) 758-1114; fax (2) 758-1515; internet www.kumho.net; construction, engineering, chemicals, textiles; Chair. PARK JONG-KU.

LG Group: 20, Yeouido-dong, Yeongdeungpo-gu, Seoul 100; tel. (2) 787-1114; fax (2) 785-7762; f. 1947; internet www.lg.co.kr; fmrly Lucky-Goldstar Group; chemicals and energy, electronics and telecommunications, financial services, etc.; Chair. KOO BON MOO.

Lotte Group: 23, 4-ga, Yangpyeong-dong, Yeongdeungpo-gu, Seoul; tel. (2) 670-6114; fax (2) 6672-6600; internet www.lotte.co.kr; f. 1967; foods and beverages, distribution, tourism and leisure, chemicals, construction and machinery; Chair. SHIN KYUK-HO.

Samsung Group: Taepyeong-no Bldg, 310, 2-ga, Taepyeong-no, Jung-gu, Seoul; tel. (2) 751-3355; fax (2) 3706-1212; internet www.samsungcorp.com; f. 1945; electronics, service industries, financial services, etc.; Chair. HYUN MYUNG-KWAN; 174,000 employees.

SK Group: 26-4, Yeouido-dong, Yeongdeungpo-gu, Seoul; tel. (2) 758-5114; fax (2) 788-7001; e-mail info@sk.com; internet www.sk.co.kr; f. 1956; engineering, electronics, petroleum and gas, industry; Chair. SON KIL-SEUNG ; 25,000 employees.

Ssangyong Group: 24-1, 2-ga, Jeo-dong, Jung-gu, Seoul; tel. (2) 270-8155; fax (2) 273-0981; e-mail webadm@www.ssy.co.kr; internet www.ssangyong.co.kr; f. 1954; cement, construction materials, iron and steel, electronic goods, machinery, chemicals, automobiles, garments, textiles, etc.; Chair. KIM SEOK-WON; Pres. SON MYOUNG-WON.

Cement

Asia Cement Manufacturing Co Ltd: 726, Yoksam-dong, Gangnam-gu, CPOB 5278, Seoul; tel. (2) 527-6400; fax (2) 563-5839; e-mail webmaster@asiacement.co.kr; internet www.asiacement .co.kr; f. 1957; manufactures and exports Portland cement, sulphate resistant cement, concrete; cap. and res 418,076m., sales 249,237m. (2001); Chair. LEE BYUNG-MOO; Man. Dir. LEE YUN-MOO; 480 employees.

Hanil Cement Co Ltd: 832-2, Yeoksam-dong, Gangnam-gu, Seoul; tel. (2) 531-7000; fax (2) 531-7115; internet www.hanilcement.co.kr; f. 1961; cap. and res 555,454m., sales 484,913m. (2001); Pres. JEONG HWAN-JIN; 766 employees.

Hyundai Cement Co Ltd: 1424-2, Seocho-dong, Seocho-gu, Seoul; tel. (2) 520-2114; fax (2) 520-2118; internet www.hdcement.co.kr; f. 1970; cap. and res 295,105m., sales 367,822m. (2001); mfrs of Portland cement and various building materials; Pres. KIM KWANG-YONG; 918 employees.

Ssangyong Cement Industrial Co Ltd: 24-1, 2-ga, Jeo-dong, Jung-gu, Seoul 100-748; tel. (2) 270-5114; fax (2) 272-2191; internet www.ssangyongcement.co.kr; f. 1962; cap. and res 175,444m., sales 1,168,167m. (2001); cement mfrs; mine excavating, exporting and importing, civil engineering; Chair. KIM SEOK-WON; Pres. and CEO MYUNG HO-KEUN; 1,464 employees.

Tong Yang Cement Corpn: TYSEC Bldg, 23-8, Yeouido-dong, Yeongdeungpo-gu, Seoul; tel. (2) 3770-3000; fax (2) 3770-3305; e-mail pr@tycement.co.kr; internet www.tycement.co.kr; f. 1957; cap. and res 261,627m., sales 1,440,781m. (2001); mfrs of Portland cement and ready-mixed concrete; Pres. ROH YOUNG-IN; 1,040 employees.

Chemicals

DC Chemical Co Ltd: 50, Sogong-dong, Jung-gu, Seoul 100-718; tel. (2) 727-9500; fax (2) 777-0615; internet www.dcchem.co.kr; f. 1959, as Oriental Chemical Industries; assumed present name in Apr. 2001; absorbed Korea Steel Chemical in Mar. 2000; production of basic chemicals, agrochemicals and fine chemicals; cap. 940,000m., sales 1,639,000m. (2000); Pres. LEE BOK-YOUNG; 1,301 employees.

Hanwha Chemical Corpn: Hanwha Bldg, 1, Changgyo-dong, Jung-gu, Seoul 100-797; tel. (2) 729-2700; fax (2) 729-2997; internet www.hanwha.co.kr. f. 1974 (fmrly Hanyang Chemical Corpn); cap. and res 1,356,437m., sales 3,410,096m. (2001); mfrs of dynamite and other industrial explosives, safety fuses, electric detonators, ammunition, precision machinery and chemicals; Chair. KIM SEUNG-YEON; Pres. PARK WON-BAE; 1,869 employees.

Korea Kumho Petrochemical Co Ltd: 15th–16th Floors, Kumho Bldg, 57, 1-ga, Shinmun-no, Jongno-gu, Seoul; tel. (2) 399-7560; fax (2) 399-9248; internet www.kkpc.co.kr; f. 1976; cap. and res 252,356m. (1999), sales 787,142m. (2001); Chair. PARK CHAN-KOO; 750 employees.

Kumho Industrial Co Ltd: 10-1, 2-ga, Hoehyeon-dong, Jung-gu, Seoul; tel. (2) 6303-7114; fax (2) 758-1515; internet www.kumho .co.kr; cap. and res 1,023,430m., sales 2,768,096m. (2000); industrial materials, tyres; Chair. and CEO PARK SAM-KOO; 6,280 employees.

LG Chemical Ltd: 20, Yeouido-dong, Yeongdeungpo-gu, Seoul; tel. (2) 3773-7223; fax (2) 3773-7899; e-mail chparkb@mail.lgchem .lg.co.kr; internet www.lgchem.co.kr; f. 1947; cap. 365,400m., sales 4,744,500m. (2001); petrochemical products; Pres. and CEO NO KI-HO; 8,183 employees.

Construction

Daewoo Engineering and Construction Co Ltd: 541, 5-ga, Namdaemun-no, Jung-gu, Seoul; tel. (2) 759-2114; fax (2) 753-9489; e-mail webmaster@mail.dwconst.co.kr; internet www.dwconst.co.kr; f. 1973; cap. and res –18,727,099m., sales 22,134,018m. (1999); construction projects; Chair. CHANG YOUNG-SOO; Pres. and CEO NAM SANG-KOOK; 3,050 employees.

Dong Ah Construction Industrial Co Ltd: 120-23, Sosomun-dong, Jung-gu, Seoul; tel. (2) 3709-2114; fax (2) 3709-3000; e-mail webmaster@dongah.co.kr; internet www.dongah.co.kr; cap. and res 250,294m., sales 2,205,741m. (1999); contracting, construction; Chair. CHOI DONG-SUP; 4,956 employees.

Hanjin Heavy Industries and Construction Co Ltd: 546-1, Guui-dong, Seongdong-gu, Seoul; tel. (2) 450-8114; fax (2) 450-8101; e-mail webmaster@hanjinsc.com; internet www.hanjinsc.com; f. 1967; sales 1,834,100m. (2001); construction, electrical work, mining, gas and petroleum transport; Pres. PARK JAE-YOUNG; 5,295 employees.

Hyundai Engineering & Construction Co Ltd: 140-2, Kye-dong, Jongno-gu, Seoul; tel. (2) 746-1114; fax (2) 743-8963; internet www.hec.co.kr; f. 1947; merged with LG Semicon in 1999; cap. and res –885,177m., sales 392,246m. (2000); engineering, manufacture and supply of civil, architectural and industrial plants and electrical works; CEO BANG JUNG-SUP; 4,500 employees.

LG Engineering and Construction Co Ltd: 537, 5-ga, Namdaemun-no, Jung-gu, Seoul; tel. (2) 3777-1114; fax (2) 774-6610; internet www.lgenc.co.kr; f. 1969; cap. and res –2,639,800m., sales 3,153,100m. (2001); contracting, construction; Chair. HUH CHANG-SOO; Pres. and CEOs KIM KAB-RYUL, HAROLD J. SHIN; 3,584 employees.

Samsung Engineering and Construction Corpn: Samsung Plaza Bldg, 263 Seohyon-dong, Bundang-gu, Seongnam-shi, Gyeonggi Prov., 463-721; tel. (2) 2145-6338; fax (2) 2145-6343; e-mail encmaster@samsung.com; internet www.secc.co.kr; f. 1938; cap. and res 3,073,370m., sales 36,289,400m. (2001); electronics, chemicals; Pres. and CEO. LEE SANG-DAE; 5,600 employees.

Electrical and Electronics

Anam Electronics Co Ltd: 280-8, 2-ga, Songsu-dong, Seongdong-gu, Seoul; tel. (2) 460-5114; fax (2) 460-5393; internet www.aname .co.kr; f. 1956; cap. and res 1,156,676m. (2000), sales US $166m. (2001); electronics; Chair. NAM KWI-HYEN; 9,000 employees.

Daewoo Electronics Co Ltd: 541, Daewoo Center Bldg, Namdaemun-no 5-ga, Jung-gu, Seoul; tel. (2) 360-7114; fax (2) 360-7979; internet www.dwe.co.kr; f. 1972; cap. and res 3,088,000m., sales 3,031,000m. (2001); mfrs of computers, TV, hi-fi, microwave ovens, refrigerators and other consumer electronic components; Pres. and CEO CHANG KYU-HWAN; 8,700 employees.

Hynix Semiconductor Inc: San 136-1, Ami-ri, Pubal-up, Ichon-shi, Gyeonggi; tel. (336) 630-4114; fax (336) 630-4101; internet www.hynixco.kr; f. 1949; fmrly Hyundai Electronics Industrial Co Ltd, merged with LG Semiconductor in 1999; cap. and res. 5,242,434m, sales 3,983,461m. (2001); mfr of electronic equipment for industries; Chair. Y. W. JUN; Pres. and CEO PARK SANG-HO; 14,000 employees.

LG Electronics Inc: LG Twin Towers, 20, Yeouido-dong, Yeong-deungpo-gu, Seoul 150-721; tel. (2) 3777-1114; fax (2) 3777-5304; internet www.lge.co.kr; f. 1958; cap. and res 4,265,236m., sales 16,600,971m. (2001); mfrs and exporters of electric and electronic products, incl. computers and communications equipment; merged with LG Information and Communications in 2000; Vice-Chair. and CEO JOHN KOO; Pres. CHUL JUNG-BYUNG; 26,789 employees.

Orion Electric Co Ltd: 165, Gongdan-dong, Gumi-shi, Gyeongsan buk-do; tel. (54) 469-5000; fax (54) 461-8779; internet www.orion .co.kr; f. 1965; cap. and res 507,827m., sales 1,176,107m. (1998); electricals; Pres. KIM YOUNG-NAM; 5,074 employees.

Samsung Electro-Mechanics Co Ltd: 314, Maetan 3-dong, Paldal-gu, Suwon-shi, Gyeonggi; tel. (331) 210-5114; fax (331) 210-5992; internet www.sem.samsung.co.kr; f. 1973; cap. and res 1,587,040m. (2000), sales 3,112,000m. (2001); mfr of electronic components; Pres. and CEO KANG HO-MOON; 8,500 employees.

Samsung Electronics Co Ltd: 11/F Samsung Main Bldg, 250, Taepyeong-no 2-ga, Jung-gu, Seoul; tel. (2) 727-7114; fax (2) 727-7159; internet www.samsungelectronics.com; f. 1969; cap. and res 19,474,000m., sales 46,444,000m. (2001); world's largest producer of dynamic random access memory (DRAM) semiconductor chips; mfrs of wide range of electronic goods, incl. TV, washing machines, hi-fi, refrigerators and industrial electronic equipment; Chair. LEE KUN-HEE; Pres. and CEO YUN JONG-YONG; 55,000 employees.

Samsung SDI Co Ltd: 575 Shin-dong, Paldal-gu, Jung-gu, Suwon-shi, Gyeonggi-do; tel. (331) 210-1114; fax (331) 210-7146; internet www.samsungsdi.co.kr; mfr of colour television tubes; cap. and res 5,631,000m., sales 4,030,000m. (2001); Chair. LEE KUN-HEE; Pres. and CEO KIM SOON-TAEK; 8,207 employees.

Samsung Techwin Co Ltd: 647-9, Yeoksam 1-dong, Gangnam-gu, Seoul; tel. (2) 3467-7114; fax (2) 3467-7050; internet www.samsung-smt.com; fmrly Samsung Aerospace Industries; mfrs of aerospace parts, semiconductors, industrial robots, optical and defence-related products; cap. and res 435,697m., sales 1,430,899m. (2000); Chair. LEE JOONG-KOO.

Engineering

Daewoo Heavy Industries and Machinery Co Ltd: 541, Namdaemun-no 5-ga, Chung-gu, Seoul; tel. (2) 726-3114; fax (2)

726-3307; internet www.dhiltd.co.kr; f. 1937; cap. and res 839,787m., sales 1,540,261m. (2001); mfrs of diesel engines, industrial vehicles, railroad carriages, industrial automated machinery, aircraft components; Pres. YANG JAE-SHIN; 4,377 employees.

Hyundai Heavy Industries Co Ltd: 1, Jeonha-dong, Dong-gu, Ulsan-shi, Gyeonsang nam-do; tel. (52) 230-3899; fax (52) 230-3450; e-mail ir@hhi.co.kr; internet www.hhi.co.kr; f. 1973; cap. and res 2,832,400m., sales 7,404,200m. (2001); industrial and offshore construction and engineering, shipbuilding; Pres. and CEOs CHOI KIL-SEON, MIN KEH-SIK; 26,507 employees.

Hyundai Mobis Co Ltd: 140-2, Kye-dong, Jongno-gu, Seoul 110-793; tel. (2) 746-1114; fax (2) 741-4244; internet www.mobis.co.kr; f. 1977; cap. and res 486,775m. (1998), sales 1,976,200m. (2000); largest container producer in the world; also manufactures heavy machinery, rolling stock, machine tools; Chair. CHUNG MONG-KOO; Pres. PARK JUNG-IN; 7,200 employees.

Samsung Heavy Industries Co Ltd: Samsung Yeoksam, 17th Floor, Bldg 649-7, Yeoksam-dong, Gangnam-gu, Seoul 135-080; tel. (2) 3458-6000; fax (2) 3458-6501; e-mail isnam@samsung.co.kr; internet www.shi.samsung.co.kr; f. 1974; cap. and res 1,715,288m., sales 4,110,559m. (2001); shipbuilding, industrial and construction equipment; Pres. and CEO KIM JING-WAN; 8,533 employees.

Iron and Steel

Dongkuk Steel Mill Co Ltd: 50, Suha-dong, Jung-gu, Seoul; tel. (2) 317-1149; fax (2) 317-1391; internet www.dongkuk.co.kr; f. 1954; cap. and res 440,060m., sales 1,785,169m. (2001); iron and steel mfrs; Pres. and CEO CHANG SAE-JOO; 1,599 employees.

INI Steel Co Ltd: 1, Songhyun-dong, Dong-gu, Incheon; tel. (32) 760-2114; fax (32) 760-2814; internet www.inisteel.co.kr; f. 1953; fmrly Inchon Iron and Steel Co Ltd, assumed present name in Aug. 2001; cap. and res 646,622m., sales 2,608,218m. (2001); mfrs of iron and steel products; Chair. and CEO RYU IN-GYUN; 4,499 employees.

Pohang Iron & Steel Co (POSCO) Ltd: 1, Goedong-dong, Pohang-shi, Gyeongbuk; tel. (562) 220-0114; fax (562) 220-6000; internet www.posco.co.kr; f. 1968; state-owned; proposed transfer to private-sector ownership announced in July 1998; cap. and res 1,301,722m., sales 11,086,119m. (2001); mfr of steel and steel products; CEO YOO SANG-BOO; Pres. LEE KU-TAEK; 19,012 employees.

Sammi Steel Co Ltd: 1004, Daechi-dong, Gangnam-gu, Seoul; tel. (2) 2222-4115; fax (2) 538-3806; e-mail webmaster@sammi.co.kr; internet www.sammi.co.kr; f. 1966; cap. and res 131,311m., sales 312,077m. (1997); mfr of special steel; Pres. KIM DONG-SIK; 3,321 employees.

Motor Vehicles

Daewoo Motor Co Ltd: 199, Chongchon-dong, Bupyeong-gu, Incheon; tel. (32) 520-2001; fax (32) 520-4606; e-mail webmaster@dm.co.kr; internet www.dm.co.kr; f. 1972; absorbed by General Motors (USA) in April 2002; cap. and res. 4,072,950m., sales 5,119,125m. (1998); mfr of buses, passenger cars, heavy-duty trucks; Pres. KIM TAE-KU; 13,555 employees.

Hyundai Motor Co Ltd: 231, Yangjae-dong, Seocho-gu, Seoul; tel. (2) 3464-1114; fax (2) 3464-3453; internet www.hyundai-motor.com; f. 1967; cap. and res 9,097,811m., sales 22,505,100m. (2001); mfrs and assemblers of passenger cars, trucks, buses, etc.; Chair. CHUNG MONG-KOO; Pres. LEE YOO-IL; 48,831 employees.

Renault Samsung Motors: 25, 1-ga, Bongrae-dong, Jung-gu, Seoul; tel. (2) 3707-5000; fax (2) 757-4577; internet www.renault samsung.com; f. 2000; mfr of passenger cars; cap. and res 440,000m., sales 836,300m. (2001); Chair. JEROME STOLL; 3,970 employees.

Ssangyong Motor Co Ltd: 150-3, Chilgoe-dong, Pyeongtaek-shi, Gyeonggi-do; tel. (31) 610-1114; fax (31) 610-3700; internet www.smotor.com; f. 1954; mfrs of passenger cars, minibuses and special-purpose vehicles; cap. and res 252,927m., sales 2,326,694m. (2001); Chair. SO JIN-KWAN; Man. Dir JIN CHANG-KI; 6,126 employees.

Textiles, Silk and Synthetic Fibres

Cheil Industries Inc: 290, Kandan-dong, Gumi-shi, Gyeongbuk; tel. (546) 468-2114; fax (546) 468-2229; internet www.cii.samsung.com; f. 1954; owned by Samsung Corp; mfrs of clothing, textiles and petrochemical products; cap. and res 250,000m., sales 1,736,000m. (2001); Pres. and CEO AHH BOK-HYUN; 1,800 employees.

Hanil Synthetic Fiber Co Ltd: 222, Yangdeok-dong, Hoewon-gu, Masan-shi, Gyeonsangnam-do; tel. (551) 90-3114; fax (551) 90-3114; internet www.hanilsf.com; f. 1964; cap. and res 307,270m., sales 345,027m. (2001); mfrs and exporters of synthetic fibre; Pres. SON BYUNG-SUK; 1,000 employees.

Ilshin Spinning Co Ltd: 15-15, Yeouido-dong, Yeongdeungpo-gu, Seoul; tel. (2) 3774-0114; fax (2) 786-5893; internet www.ilshin.co.kr; f. 1951; cap. and res 311,200m., sales 326,100m. (2001); cotton spinning and production of yarn and fabrics; one subsidiary with dyeing and finishing factories; import and export; Chair. KIM YOUNG-HO; 1,120 employees.

Taekwang Industries: 162-1, Jangchung-dong, Jung-gu, Seoul; tel. (2) 3406-0300; fax (2) 2273-9160; internet www.taekwang.co.kr; f. 1954; miscellaneous household goods and textiles; cap. and res 5,567m., sales 1,079,814m. (2001); Pres. LEE HO-JIN; 6,499 employees.

Miscellaneous

Daelim Industrial Co Ltd: 23-9, Yeouido-dong, Yeongdeungpo-gu, Seoul; tel. (2) 368-7114; fax (2) 368-7700; internet www.daelim.co.kr; f. 1939; cap. and res 1,590,732m., sales 2,516,401m. (2001); general contractor for all construction fields, engineering and petrochemical producer; Chair. LEE YONG-KU; 2,500 employees.

Hankuk Glass Industry Co Ltd: 64-5 Jungmu-no, 2-ga, Jung-gu, Seoul; tel. (2) 3706-9114; fax (2) 771-5340; internet www.hanglas.co.kr; f. 1957; cap. and res 634,889m., sales 333,987m. (2001); mfrs of flat glass, figured glass and tube glass; one subsidiary; Pres. KIM SUNG-MAN; 828 employees.

Korea Coal Corpn: 33, Yeouido-dong, Yeongdeungpo-gu, Seoul; tel. (2) 767-6600; fax (2) 782-4010; internet www.kocoal.or.kr; f. 1950; cap. and res 181,162m., sales 166,259m. (2001); operation and development of coal mines, and related research, sales, import, export, etc.; Chair. YOO SUNG-KYU; 3,204 employees.

Korea Land Corpn: 217, Jeongja-dong, Seongnam-shi, Gyeonggi Prov.; tel. (31) 738-7114; fax (31) 717-5431; internet www.koland.co.kr; f. 1975; land development; Chair. KIM JIN-HO.

Korea National Housing Corpn: 175, Gumi-dong, Bundang-gu, Seongnam-shi, Gyeonggi Prov.; tel. (31) 738-3114; internet www.knhc.co.kr; f. 1962; housing business; Chair. KWON HAE-OK.

Korea Tobacco and Ginseng Corpn: 100, Pyeongchon-dong, Daedeok-gu, Daejeon 306-130; tel. (42) 939-5122; fax (42) 933-5128; internet www.ktg.or.kr; cap. and res 2,615,947m., sales 4,713,340m. (2001); mfr of cigarettes, tobacco, and ginseng products; Pres. and CEO KWAK JOO-YOUNG; 4,430 employees.

Shinsegae Co Ltd: 25-5, 1-ga, Jungmu-no, Jung-gu, Seoul; tel. (2) 727-1449; fax (2) 727-1192; internet www.shinsegae.com; retailing and department stores; cap. and res 901,022m., sales 3,722,092m. (2000); Pres. and CEO KOO HAK-SUH.

SK Corpn: 99 Seorin-dong, Jongno-gu, Seoul; tel. (2) 2121-5114; fax (2) 2121-7001; internet www.skcorp.com; f. 1962 (fmrly Yukong Ltd); production and marketing of petroleum, petrochemical and lubricating oil products; cap. and res 5,648,240m., sales 14,114,861m. (2001); Chair. CHEY TAE-WON; 4,541 employees.

SK Global Co Ltd: 226, 1-ga, Shinmun-no, Jongno-gu, Seoul; tel. (2) 758-2114; fax (2) 754-9414; e-mail webmaster@skglobal.com; internet www.skglobal.com; f. 1953 (fmrly Sunkyong Ltd); cap. and res 2,220,817m., sales 18,036,333m. (2001); provision of services to various sectors, incl. energy, chemicals, telecommunications, engineering and construction; CEO KIM SYNG-JEUNG; 2,485 employees.

S-Oil Corpn: Yeouido POB 758, 60, Yeouido-dong, Yeongdeungpo-gu, Seoul 150-607; tel. (2) 3772-5151; fax (2) 786-4031; internet www.s-oil.com; oil refining and production of petrochemicals and lubricants; cap. and res 1,379,768m., sales 7,623,771m. (2001); Chair. and CEO KIM SUN-DONG; Pres. YOO HO-KI.

Whashin Industrial Co Ltd: 360-1, Magok-dong, Gangseo-gu, Seoul 157-210; tel. (2) 3661-5343; fax (2) 3661-5347; e-mail export@whashin.com; internet www.whashin.com; f. 1962; exporters, importers, domestic sales of stationery, textiles, electrical consumer products, commercial air-conditioning equipment and other merchandise; 8 subsidiaries; Pres. PARK JUNG-KYU; 2,000 employees.

TRADE UNIONS

Federation of Korean Trade Unions (FKTU): FKTU Bldg, 35, Yeouido-dong, Yeongdeungpo-gu, Seoul; tel. (2) 782-3884; fax (2) 784-2864; e-mail fktuintl@nownuri.net; internet www.fktu.org; f. 1941; Pres. LEE NAM-SOON; affiliated to ICFTU; 29 union federations are affiliated with a membership of some 960,000.

Federation of Foreign Organization Employees' Unions: 5-1, 3-ga, Dangsan-dong, Yeongdeungpo-gu, Seoul; tel. (2) 2068-1645; fax (2) 2068-1644; f. 1961; Pres. KANG IN-SIK; 22,450 mems.

Federation of Korean Apartment Workers' Unions: 922-1, Bangbae-dong, Seocho-gu, Seoul; tel. (2) 522-6860; fax (2) 522-4624; f. 1997; Pres. LEE DAE-HYUNG; 3,670 mems.

Federation of Korean Chemical Workers' Unions: Sukchun Bldg, 2nd Floor, 32-100, 4-ga, Dangsan-dong, Yeongdeungpo-gu, Seoul; tel. (2) 738-2441; internet www.fkcu.or.kr; f. 1961; Pres. PARK HUN-SOO; 116,286 mems.

Federation of Korean Metalworkers' Unions: 1570-2, Shinrim-dong, Gwanak-gu, Seoul; tel. (2) 864-2901; fax (2) 864-

0457; e-mail fkmtu@chollian.net; internet www.metall.or.kr; f. 1961; Pres. LEE BYUNG-KYUN; 130,000 mems.

Federation of Korean Mine Workers' Unions: Guangno Bldg, 2nd Floor, 10-4, Karak-dong, Songpa-gu, Seoul; tel. (2) 403-0973; fax (2) 400-1877; f. 1961; Pres. KIM DONG-CHUL; 6,930 mems.

Federation of Korean Printing Workers' Unions: 201, 792-155, 3-ga, Kuro-dong, Kuro-gu, Seoul; tel. (2) 780-7969; fax (2) 780-6097; f. 1961; Pres. LEE KWANG-JOO; 5,609 mems.

Federation of Korean Public Construction Unions: 293-1, Kumdo-dong, Sujong-gu, Seongnam-shi, Gyeonggi-do; tel. (2) 2304-7016; fax (2) 230-4602; f. 1998; Pres. HONG SANG-KI (acting); 9,185 mems.

Federation of Korean Public Service Unions: Sukchun Bldg, 3rd Floor, 32-100, 4-ga, Dangsan-dong, Yeongdeungpo-gu, Seoul; tel. (2) 769-1330; fax (2) 769-1332; internet www.fkpu.or.kr; f. 1997; Pres. LEE KWAN-BOO; 15,641 mems.

Federation of Korean Rubber Workers' Unions: 830-240, 2-ga, Bumil-dong, Dong-gu, Busan; tel. (51) 637-2101; fax (51) 637-2103; f. 1988; Pres. CHO YUNG-SOO; 6,600 mems.

Federation of Korean Seafarers' Unions: 544, Donhwa-dong, Mapo-gu, Seoul; tel. (2) 716-2764; fax (2) 702-2271; e-mail fksu@chollian.net; internet www.fksu.or.kr; f. 1961; Pres. KIM PIL-JAE; 60,037 mems.

Federation of Korean State-invested Corporation Unions: Sunwoo Bldg, 501, 350-8, Yangjae-dong, Seocho-gu, Seoul; tel. (2) 529-2268; fax (2) 529-2270; internet www.publicunion.or.kr; f. 1998; Pres. JANG DAE-IK; 19,375 mems.

Federation of Korean Taxi & Transport Workers' Unions: 415-7, Janan 1-dong, Dongdaemun-gu, Seoul; tel. (2) 2210-8500; fax (2) 2247-7890; internet www.ktaxi.or.kr; f. 1988; Pres. KWAN OH-MAN; 105,118 mems.

Federation of Korean Textile Workers' Unions: 274-8, Yeomchang-dong, Gangseo-gu, Seoul; tel. (2) 3665-3117; fax (2) 3662-4373; f. 1954; Pres. OH YOUNG-BONG; 6,930 mems.

Federation of Korean United Workers' Unions: Sukchun Bldg, 32-100, 4-ga, Dangsan-dong, Yeongdeungpo-gu, Seoul; internet www.fkuwu.or.kr; f. 1961; 51,802 mems.

Federation of Korean Urban Railway Unions: Urban Railway Station, 3-ga, Yeouido-dong, Yeongdeungpo-gu, Seoul; tel. (2) 786-5163; fax (2) 786-5165; f. 1996; Pres. HA WON-JOON; 9,628 mems.

Korea Automobile & Transport Workers' Federation: 678-27, Yeoksam-dong, Gangnam-gu, Seoul; tel. (2) 554-0890; fax (2) 554-1558; f. 1963; Pres. KANG SUNG-CHUN; 84,343 mems.

Korea Federation of Bank & Financial Workers' Unions: 88, Da-dong, Jung-gu, Seoul; tel. (2) 756-2389; fax (2) 754-4893; internet www.kfiu.org; f. 1961; Pres. LEE YUNG-DUK; 113,994 mems.

Korea Federation of Communication Trade Unions: 10th Floor, 106-6, Guro 5-dong, Guro-gu, Seoul; tel. (2) 864-0055; fax (2) 864-5519; internet www.ictu.co.kr; f. 1961; Pres. OH DONG-IN; 18,810 mems.

Korea Federation of Food Industry Workers' Unions: 106-2, 1-ga, Yanpyeong-dong, Yeongdeungpo-gu, Seoul; tel. (2) 679-6441; fax (2) 679-6444; f. 2000; Pres. BAEK YOUNG-GIL; 19,146 mems.

Korea Federation of Port & Transport Workers' Unions: Bauksan Bldg, 19th Floor, 12-5, Dongja-dong, Yeongsan-gu, Seoul; tel. (2) 727-4741; fax (2) 727-4749; f. 1980; Pres. CHOI BONG-HONG; 33,347 mems.

Korea National Electrical Workers' Union: 167, Samseong-dong, Gangnam-gu, Seoul; tel. (2) 3456-6017; fax (2) 3456-6004; internet www.knewu.or.kr; f. 1961; Pres. KIM JU-YOUNG; 16,741 mems.

Korea Professional Artist Federation: Hanil Bldg, 43-4, Donui-dong, Jongno-gu, Seoul; tel. (2) 764-5310; fax (2) 3675-5314; f. 1999; Pres. PARK IL-NAM; 2,395 mems.

Korea Tobacco & Ginseng Workers' Unions: 100, Pyeongchon-dong, Daedeok-gu, Daejeon; tel. (42) 932-7118; fax (42) 931-1812; f. 1960; Pres. KANG TAE-HEUNG; 6,008 mems.

Korea Unions of Teaching and Educational Workers: Dongin Bldg, 7th Floor, 65-33, Shingil 1-dong, Yeongdeungpo-gu, Seoul; tel. (2) 849-1281; fax (2) 835-0556; internet www.kute.or.kr; f. 1999; Pres. SON KYUNG-SOON; 18,337 mems.

Korean Communications Workers' Unions: 154-1, Seorin-dong, Jongno-gu, Seoul; tel. (2) 2195-1752; fax (2) 2195-1761; internet www.kpwu.or.kr; f. 1958; Pres. JEONG HYUN-YOUNG; 26,071 mems.

Korean Postal Workers' Union: 154-1, Seorin-dong, Jongno-gu, Seoul 110-110; tel. (2) 2195-1773; fax (2) 2195-1761; e-mail cheshin@chol.com; internet www.kpwu.or.kr; f. 1958; Pres. JUNG HYUN-YOUNG; 23,500 mems.

Korean Railway Workers' Union: 40, 3-ga, Hangang-no, Yeongsan-gu, Seoul; tel. (2) 795-6174; f. 1947; Pres. KIM JONG-WOOK; 31,041 mems.

Korean Tourist Industry Workers' Federation: 749, 5-ga, Namdaemun-no, Jung-gu, Seoul 100-095; tel. (2) 779-1297; fax (2) 779-1298; f. 1970; Pres. JEONG YOUNG-KI; 27,273 mems.

National Medical Industry Workers' Federation of Korea: 134, Shincheon-dong, Seodaemun-gu, Seoul; tel. (2) 313-3900; fax (2) 393-6877; f. 1999; Pres. LEE YONG-MOO; 5,610 mems.

Korean Confederation of Trade Unions: 139, 2-ga, Yeouido-dong, Yeongdeungpo-gu, Seoul; tel. (2) 635-1133; fax (2) 635-1134; internet www.kctu.or.kr; f. 1995; legalized 1999; Chair. DAN PYONG-HO; c. 600,000 mems.

Transport

RAILWAYS

At the end of 2001, there were 6,819 km (including freight routes) of railways in operation. Construction of a new high-speed rail system connecting Seoul to Busan (412 km) via Cheonan, Daejeon, Daegu, and Gyungju, was underway in 2001. The first phase, Seoul–Daejeon, was scheduled for completion in 2004. The second phase, Daejeon–Busan, was scheduled for completion in 2010. Construction work on the reconnection of the Kyongui (West coast, Shinuiju (North Korea)–Seoul) and East Coast Line (Wonsan (North Korea)–Seoul) began in September 2002; the former was expected to be completed by the end of that year, and the latter by September 2003. Eventually the two would be linked to the Trans-China and Trans-Siberian railways respectively, greatly enhancing the region's transportation links.

Korean National Railroad: 920, Dunsan-dong, Seo-gu, Daejeon 302-701; tel. (42) 1544-7788; fax (42) 481-373; internet www.korail.go.kr; f. 1963; operates all railways under the supervision of the Ministry of Construction and Transportation; total track length of 6,819 km (2001); Admin. SON HAK-LAE.

City Underground Railways

Busan Subway: Busan Urban Transit Authority, 861-1, Bumchun-dong, Busan 614-021; tel. (51) 633-8783; e-mail ipsubway@buta.or.kr; internet subway.busan.kr; f. 1988; length of 71.6 km (2 lines, with a further 3rd line under construction); Pres. LEE HYANG-YEUL.

Daegu Metropolitan Subway Corpn: 1500 Sangin 1-dong, Dalseo-gu, Daegu; tel. (53) 640-2114; fax (53) 640-2229; e-mail webmaster@daegusubway.co.kr; internet www.daegusubway.co.kr; length of 28.3 km (1 line, with a further five routes totalling 125.4 km planned or under construction); Pres. YOON JIN-TAE.

Incheon Rapid Transit Corpn: 67-2, Gansok-dong, Namdong-gu, Incheon 405-233; tel. (32) 451-2114; fax (32) 451-2160; internet www.irtc.co.kr; length of 24.6 km (22 stations, 1 line), with two further lines planned; Pres. CHOUNG IN-SOUNG.

Seoul Metropolitan Rapid Transit Corporation: Seoul; internet www.smrt.co.kr; operates lines 5-8.

Seoul Metropolitan Subway Corpn: 447-7, Bangbae-dong, Seocho-gu, Seoul; tel. (2) 520-5020; fax (2) 520-5039; internet www.seoulsubway.co.kr; f. 1981; length of 134.9 km (115 stations, lines 1-4); Pres. KIM JUNG-GOOK.

Underground railways were also under construction in Daejeon and Gwangju.

ROADS

At the end of 2001 there were 91,396 km of roads, of which 76.7% were paved. A network of motorways (2,637 km) links all the principal towns, the most important being the 428-km Seoul–Busan motorway. Improvements in relations with North Korea resulted in the commencement of work on a four-lane highway to link Seoul and the North Korean capital, Pyongyang, in September 2000; construction of the road was scheduled for completion in 2003.

Korea Highway Corpn: 293-1, Kumto-dong, Sujong-gu, Seongnam, Gyeonggi Prov.; tel. (822) 2230-4114; fax (822) 2230-4308; internet www.freeway.co.kr; f. 1969; responsible for construction, maintenance and management of toll roads; Pres. OH JUM-LOCK.

SHIPPING

In December 2001 South Korea's merchant fleet (2,426 vessels) had a total displacement of 6,394,994 grt. Major ports include Busan, Incheon, Donghae, Masan, Yeosu, Gunsan, Mokpo, Pohang, Ulsan, Jeju and Gwangyang.

Korea Maritime and Port Authority: 112-2, Inui-dong, Jongno-gu, Seoul 110; tel. (2) 3466-2214; f. 1976; operates under the Ministry of Maritime Affairs and Fisheries; supervises all aspects of shipping and port-related affairs; Admin. AHN KONG-HYUK.

Korea Shipowners' Association: Sejong Bldg, 10th Floor, 100, Dangju-dong, Jongno-gu, Seoul 110-071; tel. (2) 739-1551; fax (2) 739-1565; e-mail korea@shipowners.or.kr; internet www.shipowners .co.kr; f. 1960; 40 shipping co mems; Chair. HYUN YUNG-WON.

Korea Shipping Association: 66010, Dungchon 3-dong, Gangseo-gu, Seoul 157-033; tel. (2) 6096-2024; fax (2) 6096-2029; e-mail kimny@haewoon.co.kr; internet www.haewoon.co.kr; f. 1962; management consulting and investigation, mutual insurance; 1,189 mems; Chair. PARK HONG-JIN.

Principal Companies

Cho Yang Shipping Co Ltd: Chongam Bldg, 85-3, Seosomun-dong, Jung-gu, CPOB 1163, Seoul 100; tel. (2) 3708-6000; fax (2) 3708-6926; internet www.choyang.co.kr; f. 1961; Korea–Japan, Korea–China, Korea–Australia–Japan, Asia–Mediterranean–America liner services and world-wide tramping; Chair. N. K. PARK; Pres. J. W. PARK.

DooYang Line Co Ltd: 166-4, Samseong-dong, Gangnam-gu, Seoul 135-091; tel. (2) 550-1700; fax (2) 550-1777; internet www.dooyang .co.kr; f. 1984; world-wide tramping and conventional liner trade; Pres. CHO DONG-HYUN.

Hanjin Shipping Ltd: 25-11, Yeouido-dong, Yeongdeungpo-gu, Seoul; tel. (2) 3770-6114; fax (2) 3770-6740; internet www.hanjin .com; f. 1977; marine transportation, harbour service, warehousing, shipping and repair, vessel sales, harbour department and cargo service; Pres. CHOI WON-PYO.

Hyundai Merchant Marine Co Ltd: 66, Jeokseon-dong, Jongno-gu, Seoul 110-052; tel. (2) 3706-5114; fax (2) 723-2193; internet www.hmm.co.kr; f. 1976; Chair. HYUN YUNG-WON.

Korea Line Corpn: Dae Il Bldg, 43, Insa-dong, Jongno-gu, Seoul 110-290; tel. (2) 3701-0114; fax (2) 733-1610; f. 1968; world-wide transportation service and shipping agency service in Korea; Pres. JANG HAK-SE.

Pan Ocean Shipping Co Ltd: 51-1, Namchang-dong, Jung-gu, CPOB 3051, Seoul 100-060; tel. (2) 316-5114; fax (2) 316-5296; f. 1966; transportation of passenger cars and trucks, chemical and petroleum products, dry bulk cargo; Pres. CHIANG JIN-WON.

CIVIL AVIATION

There are seven international airports in Korea; at Incheon (Seoul), Gimpo (Seoul), Busan, Cheongju, Daegu, Gwangju, Jeju, and Yangyang. The main gateway into Seoul is Incheon International Airport, which opened for service in March 2001. It is used by 30m. passengers annually, and has a capacity for 240,000 aircraft movements annually. The second phase began construction in 2002, with completion due by 2008. When complete, the airport will handle 44m. passengers and 4.5m. tons of cargo annually. The airport is located 52 km from Seoul. A new airport, Yangyang International Airport, opened in Gangwon province in April 2002.

Asiana Airlines Inc: 47, Osae-dong, Gangseo-gu, Seoul; tel. (2) 758-8114; fax (2) 758-8008; e-mail asianacr@asiana.co.kr; internet www.asiana.co.kr; f. 1988; serves 14 domestic cities and 36 destinations in 16 countries; CEO PARK SAM-KOO.

Korean Air: 1370, Gonghang-dong, Gangseo-gu, Seoul; tel. (2) 656-7092; fax (2) 656-7289; internet www.koreanair.com; f. 1962 by the Govt, privately owned since 1969; fmrly Korean Air Lines (KAL); operates domestic and regional services and routes to the Americas, Europe, the Far East and the Middle East, serving 73 cities in 26 countries; Pres. and CEO SHIM YI-TAEK.

Seoul Air International: CPOB 10352, Seoul 100-699; tel. (2) 699-0991; fax (2) 699-0954; operates domestic flights and routes throughout Asia.

Tourism

South Korea's mountain scenery and historic sites are the principal attractions for tourists. Jeju Island, located some 100 km off the southern coast, is a popular resort. In 2001 there were 5,147,204 visitors to South Korea, of whom about 46% came from Japan. Receipts from tourism in 2000 amounted to US $6,811m.

Korea National Tourism Organization: KNTO Bldg, 10, Da-dong, Jung-gu, CPOB 903, Seoul 100; tel. (2) 729-9600; fax (2) 757-5997; internet www.knto.or.kr; f. 1962 as Korea Tourist Service; Pres. LEE DEUK-RYUL.

Korea Tourism Association: Saman Bldg, 11th Floor, 945, Daechi-dong, Gangnam-gu, Seoul; tel. (2) 556-2356; fax (2) 556-3818; f. 1963; Pres. CHO HANG-KYU, KIM JAE-GI.

Defence

In August 2001 there were armed forces with a total strength of 683,000 (including an estimated 159,000 conscripts): army 560,000, navy 60,000 (including 25,000 marines), air force 63,000. There is also a civilian defence corps totalling about 3.0m. Military service is compulsory and lasts for 26 months in the army, for 28 months in the navy and for 30 months in the air force. In August 2001 36,520 US troops were stationed in South Korea.

Defence Expenditure: 15,300,000m. won in 2001.

Chairman of the Joint Chiefs of Staff: Gen. LEE NAM-SHIN.

Chief of Staff (Army): Gen. KIM PAN-KYU.

Chief of Staff (Air Force): Gen. KIM DAE-WOOK.

Chief of Naval Operations: Adm. CHANG CHUNG-KIL.

Education

Education, available free of charge, is compulsory for nine years between the ages of six and 15 years. Primary education begins at six years of age and lasts for six years. In 2001 enrolment at primary schools included 98.2% of children in the appropriate age-group. Secondary education begins at 12 years of age and lasts for up to six years, comprising two cycles of three years each. Enrolment at secondary schools in 2001 included 96.7% of children (middle schools 98.0%, high schools 95.3%). A five-day school week was to be gradually introduced during 2003–05. In 2002 there were 194 university-level institutions with a student enrolment of 2.3m. There were 945 graduate schools in 2002. In 2000, according to UNESCO estimates, the rate of adult literacy averaged 97.8% (males 99.1%, females 96.5%). Expenditure on education by the central Government in 2002 was projected at 22,278,358m. won, representing 16.3% of total spending.

Bibliography

(Democratic People's Republic of Korea and Republic of Korea)

GENERAL

Akaha, Tsuneo (Ed.). *The Future of North Korea*. London, Routledge, 2002.

Armstrong, Chalres. K. *Korean Society: Civil Society, Democracy, and the State*. London, Routledge, 2002.

Australian National Korean Studies Centre. *Korea to the Year 2000*. Canberra, East Asia Analytical Unit, Department of Foreign Affairs and Trade, 1992.

Bedeski, Robert E. *The Transformation of South Korea*. London, Routledge, 1994.

Belke, Thomas J. *Juche: A Christian Study of North Korea's State Religion*. Bartlesville OK, Living Sacrifice Book Co, 1999.

Bermudez, Joseph S., Jr. *The Armed Forces of North Korea*. London and New York, I. B. Tauris, 2001.

Breen, Michael. *The Koreans: Who They Are, What They Want, Where Their Future Lies*. London, Orion, 1999.

Chamberlain, Paul F. and Kim Kihwan. *Korea 2010: The Challenges of the New Millennium*. Washington, DC, Center for Strategic and International Studies, 2001.

Clark, Donald (Ed.). *Korea Briefing 1993*. Boulder, CO, Westview Press for the Asia Society, 1993. (Also other years.)

Connor, Mary. E. *The Koreas: A Global Studies Handbook*. Santa Barbara, CA, ABC-Clio, 2002.

Cornell, Erik. *North Korea Under Communism: Report of an Envoy to Paradise*. London, RoutledgeCurzon, 2002.

Cotton, James (Ed.). *Politics and Policy in the New Korean State: from Roh Tae-woo to Kim Young-sam*. Melbourne, Longman, and New York, St Martin's Press, 1995.

Covell, Jon C. *Korea's Cultural Roots*. Seoul, Moth House/Hollym, 1981.

De Mente, Boye. *NTC's Dictionary of Korea's Business and Cultural Code Words*. Chicago, NTC, 1998.

Dong Wonmo (Ed.). *The Two Koreas and the United States—Issues of Peace, Security, and Economic Cooperation.* Armonk, NY, M. E. Sharpe, 2000.

Eberstadt, Nicholas and Ellings, Richard J (Eds). *Korea's Future and the Great Powers.* Seattle and London, University of Washington Press, 2001.

Eder, Norman R. *Poisoned Prosperity—Development, Modernization, and the Environment in South Korea.* Armonk, NY, M. E. Sharpe, 1995.

Eder, Norman R., and Hong, Wuk-hee (Eds). *Re-inventing Han—Continuity and Change in Modern South Korea.* Armonk, NY, M. E. Sharpe, 1999.

European Union Chamber of Commerce in Korea. *A Practical Business Guide on the Democratic People's Republic of Korea.* Seoul, EUCCK, 1998.

Foster-Carter, Aidan. *Korea's Coming Reunification: Another East Asian Superpower?* London, Economist Intelligence Unit, 1992.

Grinker, Roy Richard. *Korea and Its Futures: Unification and the Unfinished War.* New York, St Martin's Press, 1998.

Harrison, Selig S. *Korean Endgame: A Strategy for Reunification and US Disengagement.* Princeton, NJ, Princeton University Press, 2002.

Henriksen, Thomas H., and Lho, Kyongsoo (Eds). *One Korea? Challenges and Prospects for Reunification.* Stanford, CA, Hoover Institution Press, 1994.

Hoare, James E., and Pares, Susan. *Conflict in Korea: An Encyclopedia.* Santa Barbara, ABC-Clio, 1999.

Kang Chol Hwan—, and Rigoulot, Pierre. *The Aquariums of Pyongyang: Ten Years in the North Korean Gulag.* New York, Basic Books, 2001.

Kihl Young Whan. *Politics and Policies in Divided Korea: Regimes in Contrast.* Boulder, CO, and London, Westview Press, 1984.

(Ed.). *Korea and the World: Beyond the Cold War.* Boulder, CO, Westview Press, 1994.

Kim Byung-Lo Philo. *Two Koreas in Development.* NJ, Transaction Books, 1992.

Kim Dae Hwan, and Kong Tat Yan (Eds). *The Korean Peninsula in Transition.* London, Macmillan, 1997.

Kim, Samuel S (Ed.). *The North Korean System in the Post-Cold War Era.* New York, Palgrave Macmillan, 2001.

Koo, Hagen (Ed.). *State and Society in Contemporary Korea.* Ithaca, NY, Cornell University Press, 1993.

Lee Hyangjin. *Contemporary Korean Cinema: Identity, Culture, and Politics.* Manchester, Manchester University Press, 2001.

Lewis, James. B., and Sesay, Amadu (Eds). *Korea and Globalization: Politics, Economics, and Culture.* RoutledgeCurzon, 2002.

Macdonald, Donald S. (Clark, Donald, Ed.). *The Koreans: Contemporary Politics and Society.* Boulder, CO, Westview Press (3rd edn), 1996.

Mack, Andrew (Ed.). *Asian Flashpoint: Security and the Korean Peninsula.* St Leonards, NSW, Allen and Unwin, 1993.

McCune, Shannon. *Korea's Heritage: A Regional and Social Geography.* Tokyo and Rutland, VT, Charles E. Tuttle, 1966.

Moltz, James Clay, and Mansourov, Alexandre Y. (Eds). *The North Korean Nuclear Program: Security, Strategy, and New Perspectives from Russia.* New York and London, Routledge, 2000.

Moon, Chung-In (Ed.). *Understanding Regime Dynamics in North Korea.* Seoul, Yonsei University Press, 1998.

Nahm, Andrew C. (Ed.). *Studies in the Developmental Aspects of Korea.* Kalamazoo, The Center of Korean Studies, Western Michigan University, 1969.

North Korea: Her Past, Reality, and Impression. Kalamazoo, The Center for Korean Studies, Western Michigan University, 1978.

Natsios, Andrew S. *The Great North Korean Famine.* Washington, DC, United States Institute of Peace, 2001.

Oh, Kongdan, and Hassig, Ralph C. (Eds). *North Korea Through the Looking Glass.* Washington, DC, Brookings Institution, 2000.

Korea Briefing 2000–01: First Steps Toward Reconciliation and Reunification. Armonk, NY, M. E. Sharpe, 2002.

Park, Han S. *North Korea: The Politics of Unconventional Wisdom.* Boulder, CO, Lynne Rienner, 2002.

Park Kyung-Ae (Ed.). *Korean Security Dynamics in Transition.* New York, Palgrave Macmillan, 2001.

Pollack, Jonathan D., and Lee, Chung Min. *Preparing for Korean Unification: Scenarios and Implications.* Santa Monica, CA, RAND, 1999.

Potrzeba Lett, Denise. *In Pursuit of Status: The Making of South Korea's 'New' Urban Middle Class.* Cambridge, MA, Harvard University Press, 2002.

Ryang, Sonia. *North Koreans in Japan: Language, Ideology and Identity.* Boulder, CO, Westview Press, 1997.

Savada, Andrea Matles (Ed.). *North Korea: A Country Study.* Washington, DC, Library of Congress for Department of the Army, 1994.

Scalapino, Robert, and Kim, Jun-Yop (Eds). *North Korea Today: Strategic and Domestic Issues.* Los Angeles, University of California Press, 1984.

Sigal, Leon V. *Disarming Strangers: Nuclear Diplomacy with North Korea.* Princeton, NJ, Princeton University Press, 1998.

Smith, Hazel, et al (Eds). *North Korea in the New World Order.* London, Macmillan, 1996.

Snyder, Scott. *Negotiating on the Edge: North Korean Negotiating Behavior.* US Institute of Peace, 1999.

Soh, Chunghee Sarah. *Women in Korean Politics.* Boulder, CO, Westview Press, 1993.

Steinberg, David. *The Republic of Korea: Economic Transformation and Social Change.* Boulder, CO, Westview Press, 1991.

Won Dal Yang. *Korean Ways, Korean Mind.* Seoul, Tamgu Dang Book Centre, 1983.

Yang Sung-Chul. *The North and South Korean Political Systems: A Comparative Analysis.* Elizabeth, NJ, Hollym, 2001 (revised edition).

Yoon Chang-Ho, and Lau, Lawrence J. *North Korea in Transition.* Cheltenham, Edward Elgar, 2001.

Yu Chai-Shin. *The Founding of Catholic Tradition in Korea.* Berkeley, CA, Asian Humanities Press, 2002.

HISTORY

Bandow, Doug, and Galen Carpenter, Ted (Eds). *The US-South Korean Alliance.* New Brunswick, NJ, and London, Transaction Publishers, 1993.

Bateman, Robert. *No Gun Ri: A Military History of the Korean War Incident.* Mechanicsburg, PA, Stackpole, 2002.

Breuer, William B. *Shadow Warriors.* New York, John Wiley and Sons, 1996.

Bridges, Brian. *Korea and the West.* London, Routledge and Kegan Paul, 1986.

Buzo, Adrian. *The Guerrilla Dynasty: Politics and Leadership in North Korea.* Boulder, CO, Westview Press, 1999.

The Making of Modern Korea: A History. London, Routledge, 2002.

Catchpole, Brian. *The Korean War 1950–1953.* London, Robinson, 2001.

Cho Soo-Sung. *Korea in World Politics 1940–1950.* Berkeley, CA, University of California Press, 1967.

Choy Bong-Youn. *Korea: A History.* Rutland, VT, Charles E. Tuttle.

Chung, Chin O. *Pyongyang Between Peking and Moscow: North Korea's Involvement in the Sino-Soviet Dispute 1958–75.* University of Alabama Press, 1978.

Conroy, F. H. *The Japanese Seizure of Korea, 1868–1910.* Philadelphia, University of Pennsylvania Press, 1960.

Cumings, Bruce. *Korea's Place in the Sun: A Modern History.* New York, W. W. Norton and Co, 1997.

The Origins of the Korean War. Princeton, NJ, Princeton University Press, Vol. 1, 1981, Vol. 2, 1990.

(Ed.). *Child of Conflict: The Korean-American Relationship 1943–53.* Seattle and London, University of Washington Press, 1983.

Deuchler, Martina. *Confucian Gentlemen and Barbarian Envoys: The Opening of Korea 1875–1885.* Seattle, University of Washington Press, 1978.

Diamond, Larry, and Kim, Byung-Kook (Eds). *Consolidating Democracy in South Korea.* Boulder, CO, Lynne Rienner, 1999.

Downs, Chuck. *Over the Line: North Korea's Negotiating Strategy.* Washington, DC, American Enterprise Institute, 1999.

Duus, Peter. *The Abacus and the Sword: The Japanese Penetration of Korea, 1895–1910.* Berkeley, CA, University of California Press, 1995

Eberstadt, Nicholas. *The End of North Korea.* Washington, DC, American Enterprise Institute, 1999.

Eckert, Carter, et al. *Korea Old and New: a History.* Cambridge, MA, Harvard University Press, 1990.

Gibney, Frank. *Korea's Quiet Revolution: From Garrison State to Democracy.* New York, Walker and Co, 1994.

Gills, Barry. *Korea versus Korea—A Case of Contested Legitimacy.* London, Routledge, 1998.

Gragent, Edwin H. *Land Ownership under Colonial Rule—Korea's Japanese Experience, 1900–1935.* Honolulu, HI, University of Hawaii Press, 1994.

Grayson, James H. *Korea: A Religious History*. London, Routledge-Curzon, 2002.

Halliday, Jon, and Cumings, Bruce. *Korea: The Unknown War*. London, Viking, 1988.

Hamm, Taik-Young. *Arming the Two Koreas—State, Capital and Military Power*. London, Routledge, 1999.

Han Sungjoo. *The Failure of Democracy in South Korea*. Berkeley, CA, University of California Press, 1974.

Hanley, Charles J, Choe Sang-Hun, and Mendoza, Martha. *The Bridge at No Gun Ri*. New York, Henry Holt and Co, 2001.

Helgesen, Geir. *Democracy and Authority in Korea: The Cultural Dimension in Korean Politics*. Richmond, Surrey, Curzon Press, 1998.

Henderson, Gregory. *Korea: The Politics of the Vortex*. Cambridge, MA, Harvard University Press, 1968.

Henthorn, William E. *A History of Korea*. New York, NY, The Free Press, 1971.

Hickey, Michael. *The Korean War: The West Confronts Communism 1950–1953*. London, John Murray, 1999.

Hicks, George. *The Comfort Women: Japan's Brutal Regime of Enforced Prostitution in the Second World War*. New York, W. W. Norton, 1995.

Howard, Keith (Ed.). *True Stories of the Korean Comfort Women*. London, Cassell, 1995.

Hulbert, Homer B. *History of Korea*. London, Routledge, 1998 (reissue).

Hunter, Helen-Louise. *Kim Il-song's North Korea*. Westport, CT, Praeger, 1999.

Kim, C. I. Eugene, and Ki, Han-Kyo. *Korea and the Politics of Imperialism, 1876–1910*. Berkeley, CA, University of California Press, 1970.

Kim, C. I. Eugene, and Mortimore, D. E. (Eds). *Korea's Response to Japan: The Colonial Period 1910–45*. Kalamazoo, MI, The Center for Korean Studies, Western Michigan University, 1977.

Kim, Ilpyong J. (Ed.). *Two Koreas in Transition*. Rockville, MD, Paragon House, 1998.

Kim, Samuel S. (Ed.). *North Korean Foreign Relations in the Post-Cold War Era*. Oxford, Oxford University Press, 1999.

Kim Se Jin. *The Politics of Military Revolution in Korea*. Chapel Hill, NC, University of North Carolina Press, 1971.

Kwak Tae-Hwan. *US-Korean Relations 1882–1982*. Seoul, Kyungnam University Press.

Lee Chang-Soo (Ed.). *Modernization of Korea and the Impact of the West*. Los Angeles, CA, University of Southern California Press, 1981.

Lee Chong-Sik. *The Politics of Korean Nationalism*. Berkeley, CA, University of California Press, 1963.

Lee Jong-Sup, and Heo Uk. *The US-South Korean Alliance, 1961–88: Free-riding or Bargaining?* New York, Edwin Mellen Press, 2002.

Lee Ki-Baik. *A New History of Korea*. (trans. by Edward W. Wagner and Edward J. Shultz). Cambridge and London, Harvard University Press, 1984.

Lee, Peter H. (Ed.). *Sourcebook of Korean Civilization: From Early Times to the Sixteenth Century (Vol. I)*. New York, Columbia University Press, 1993.

Sourcebook of Korean Civilization: From the Seventeenth Century to the Modern Period (Vol. II). New York, Columbia University Press, 1996.

Lewis, Linda Sue. *Laying Claim to the Memory of May: A Look Back at the 1980 Kwangju Uprising*. Honolulu, University of Hawaii Press, 2002.

Lim, Un. *The Founding of a Dynasty in North Korea*. Tokyo, Jiyusha, 1982.

Lone, Stewart, and McCormack, Gavan. *Korea Since 1850*. Melbourne, Longman Cheshire Pty, 1993.

Lowe, Peter. *The Origins of the Korean War*. Harlow, Longman, 1986.

McCann, David R. (Ed.) *Korea Briefing—Toward Reunification*. Armonk, NY, M. E. Sharpe, 1996.

Myers, Ramon H., and Peattie, Mark R. (Eds). *The Japanese Colonial Empire, 1895–1914*. Princeton, NJ, Princeton University Press, 1984.

Nahm, Andrew C. (Ed.). *Korea Under Japanese Colonial Rule*. Kalamazoo, MI, The Center for Korean Studies, Western Michigan University, 1973.

The United States and Korea—American-Korean Relations 1866–1976. Kalamazoo, MI, The Center for Korean Studies, Western Michigan University.

A Panorama of 5,000 Years: Korean History. Seoul and Elizabeth, NJ, Hollym International Corpn, 1983.

Oberdorfer, Don. *The Two Koreas: A Contemporary History*. New York, Basic Books, 2002 (2nd edition).

Oh, Bonnie. B. C. *Korea Under the American Military Government, 1945–48*. Westport, CT, Praeger, 2002.

Oh, John K. C. *Korea: Democracy on Trial*. Ithaca, NY, Cornell University Press, 1968.

Park, Tong Whan (Ed.). *The U.S. and the Two Koreas: A New Triangle*. Boulder, CO, Lynne Rienner, 1998.

Robinson, M. *Cultural Nationalism in Colonial Korea, 1920–25*. Seattle, University of Washington Press, 1989.

Rutt, Richard. *James Scarth Gale and his History of the Korean People*. Seoul, Royal Asiatic Society, Korea Branch, Seoul, 1972.

Scalapino, Robert A., and Lee, Chong-Sik. *Communism in Korea*. Berkeley, CA, University of California Press, 1972.

Shin, Doh C. *Mass Politics and Culture in Democratizing Korea*. Cambridge, UK, Cambridge University Press, 1999.

Stueck, William. *The Korean War: An International History*. Princeton, NJ, Princeton University Press, 1996.

Suh Dae-Sook. *The Korean Communist Movement 1918–1948*. Princeton, NJ, Princeton University Press, 1967.

Kim Il Sung: The North Korean Leader. New York, Columbia University Press, 1989.

Suh Dae-Sook, and Lee Chae-Jin (Eds). *North Korea after Kim Il-Sung*. Boulder, CO, Lynne Rienner, 1998.

Summers, Harry. G. *Korean War Almanac*. Replica Books, 2001.

Toland, John. *In Mortal Combat: Korea, 1950–53*. New York, William Morrow, 1991.

Wells, Kenneth M. (Ed.) *South Korea's Minjung Movement—The Culture and Politics of Dissidence*. Honolulu, HI, University of Hawaii Press, 1996.

Wickham, Gen. (retd) John A. *Korea on the Brink: A Memoir of Political Intrigue and Military Crisis*. Dulles, VA, Brassey's, 2001.

Wright, Edward R. (Ed.). *Korean Politics in Transition*. Seattle, University of Washington Press, 1975.

Yang Sung-Chul. *Korea and Two Regimes*. Cambridge, MA, Schenkman Publishing Co, 1981.

Young, Whan Kihl, and Hayes, Peter (Eds). *Peace and Security in Northeast Asia—The Nuclear Issue and the Korean Peninsula*. Armonk, NY, M. E. Sharpe, 1996.

ECONOMY

Amsden, Alice H. *Asia's Next Giant: South Korea and Late Industrialization*. New York, Oxford University Press, 1990.

Cho Lee-Jay, and Kim Yoon-Hyung. *Economic Development in the Republic of Korea: A Policy Perspective*. Honolulu, HI, East-West Center, University of Hawaii Press, 1991.

(Eds). *Economic Systems in North and South Korea: The Agenda for Economic Integration*. Seoul, Korea Development Institute, 1995.

Choi Young-Back, and Merrill, Yesook (Eds). *Perspectives on Korean Unification and Economic Integration*. Cheltenham, Edward Elgar, 2001.

Chung Jae-Yong, and Kirkby, Richard J. *The Political Economy of Development and Environment in Korea*. London, Routledge, 2000.

Chung, Joseph Sang-Hoon. *The North Korean Economy: Structure and Development*. Stanford, CA, Hoover Institution Press, 1974.

Clifford, Mark L. *Troubled Tiger: The Unauthorised Biography of Korea, Inc*. Singapore, Butterworth-Heinemann Asia, 1994, reissued 1998.

Cyhn, Jin W. *Technology Transfer and International Production: The Development of the Electronics Industry in Korea*. Cheltenham, Edward Elgar, 2002.

Eberstadt, Nicholas. *Korea Approaches Reunification*. Armonk, NY, M. E. Sharpe, for National Bureau of Asian Research, 1995.

Eberstadt, Nicholas, and Banister, Judith. *The Population of North Korea*. Berkeley, CA, Institute of East Asian Studies, University of California, 1992.

Frank, Charles R., Kim, Kwang Suk, and Westphal, Larry. *Foreign Trade Régimes and Economic Development: South Korea*. New York, Columbia University Press (for the National Bureau of Economic Research), 1977.

Hillebrand, Wolfgang. *Shaping Competitive Advantages: Conceptual Framework and the Korean Approach*. London, Frank Cass, 1996.

Hwang Eui-Gak. *The Korean Economies: A Comparison of North and South*. London, Clarendon Press, 1993.

International Business Publications. *North Korea Business and Investment Opportunities Yearbook*. USA, International Business Publications, 2002.

International Business Publications. *North Korea–US Political and Economic Co-operation Handbook*. USA, International Business Publications, 2002.

Janelli, Roger, with Yim, Dawnhee. *Making Capitalism: The Social and Cultural Construction of a South Korean Conglomerate*. Stanford, CA, Stanford University Press, 1995.

Jwa Sung-Hee. *The Evolution of Large Corporations in Korea*. Cheltenham, Edward Elgar, 2002.

Kim Dong Ki, and Kim Linsu. *Management Behind Industrialization: Readings in Korean Business*. Seoul, Korea University Press, 1990.

Kirk, Donald. *Korean Dynasty: Hyundai and Chung Ju Yung*. Hong Kong, Asia 2000, 1995.

Korean Crisis, Unraveling of the Miracle in the IMF Era. New York, NY, St Martin's Press, 2000.

Kong Tat Yan. *The Politics of Economic Reform in South Korea—A Fragile Miracle*. London, Routledge, 2000.

Kuznets, Paul W. *Economic Growth and Structure in the Republic of Korea*. New Haven, CT, Yale University Press, 1977.

Kwon Seung-Ho, and O'Donnell, Michael. *The Chaebol and Labour in Korea*. London, Routledge, 2001.

Lee, Chung H., and Yamazawa, Ippei (Eds). *The Economic Development of Japan and Korea: A Parallel with Lessons*. New York, Praeger Publishers, 1990.

Lee Yeon-Ho. *The State, Society and Big Business in South Korea*. London, Routledge, 1997.

Lee, You Il. *The Political Economy of Korean Crisis: A Turning Point or the End of the Miracle?* London, Ashgate Publishing, 2001.

Lie, John. *Han Unbound—The Political Economy of South Korea*. Cambridge, Cambridge University Press, 1998.

McNamara, Dennis L. (Ed.). *Corporatism and Korean Capitalism*. London, Routledge, 1999.

Market and Society in Korea: Interest, Institution, and the Textile Industry. London, RoutledgeCurzon, 2002.

Michell, T. *From a Developing to a Newly Industrialised Country: The Republic of Korea, 1961–82*. Geneva, International Labour Office, 1989.

Mo, Jongryn, and Moon, Chung Il (Eds). *Democracy and the Korean Economy*. Stanford, CA, Hoover Institute Press, 1999.

Noland, Marcus. *Avoiding the Apocalypse: The Future of the Two Koreas*. Washington, DC, Institute for International Economics, 2000.

Noland, Marcus (Ed.) *Economic Integration of the Korean Peninsula*. Washington, DC, Institute for International Economics, 1998.

O Yul-Kwon (Ed.). *Korea's Economic Prospects: From Financial Crisis to Prosperity*. Cheltenham, Edward Elgar, 2001.

Ogle, George E. *South Korea: Dissent Within the Economic Miracle*. London, Zed Books, 1991.

Sakong, Il. *Korea in the World Economy*. Washington, DC, Institute for International Economics, 1994.

Sakong, Il, and Kim, Kwang Suk (Eds). *Policy Priorities for the Unified Korean Economy*. Seoul, Institute for Global Economics, 1998.

Song Byung-Nak. *The Rise of the Korean Economy*. Oxford, Oxford University Press, 1997 (2nd edition).

Steers, Richard M., et al. *The Chaebol: Korea's New Industrial Might*. New York, Harper and Row, 1990.

Steers, Richard M. *Made in Korea—Chung Ju Yung and the Rise of Hyundai*. London, Routledge, 1999.

Suh Sang-Chul. *Growth and Structural Changes in the Korean Economy, 1910–40*. Cambridge, MA, Harvard University Press, 1978.

Woo Jung-En. *Race to the Swift: State and Finance in Korean Industrialization*. New York, Columbia University Press, 1993.

LAOS

Physical and Social Geography

HARVEY DEMAINE

The Lao People's Democratic Republic is a land-locked state in South-East Asia, bordered by the People's Republic of China to the north, by Viet Nam to the east, by Cambodia to the south, by Thailand to the west and by Myanmar (formerly Burma) to the north-west. Covering an area of 236,800 sq km (91,400 sq miles), Laos consists almost entirely of rugged upland, except for the narrow floors of the river valleys. Of these rivers, by far the most important is the Mekong, which forms the western frontier of the country for much of its length.

In the northern half of Laos, the deeply-dissected plateau surface is more than 1,500 m above sea-level over wide areas. The average altitude of the Annamite chain, which occupies most of the southern half of the country, is somewhat lower, but its rugged and more densely-forested surface makes it equally inhospitable. Temperatures on the plateau and in the Annamite chain are mitigated by altitude, but the more habitable lowlands experience tropical conditions throughout the year, and receive a total annual rainfall of about 1,250 mm, most of which falls between May and September. In Vientiane, the capital, temperatures range between 23°C and 38°C in April, the hottest month, and from 14°C to 28°C in January, the coolest month.

The natural resources of Laos have not been fully surveyed. In 2000 it was estimated by the World Bank that some 54% of the country was still covered with forest, but there was continuing concern about deforestation. Laos has considerable mineral resources: tin and gypsum are the principal minerals that are exploited and exported. Other mineral deposits include lead, zinc, coal, potash, iron ore and small quantities of gold, silver and precious stones. The Mekong River offers substantial potential for fisheries, irrigation and hydroelectricity. The Nam Ngum dam and power complex, built on the Mekong 80 km north of Vientiane, began operations in 1971. In 1991 a second major hydroelectric project, the Xeset dam in southern Laos, was completed.

Laos had an enumerated population of 3,584,803 at the census of 1 March 1985, although the migration of refugees, as a result of problems of internal security and government policies, may well have rendered this figure an overestimate. The population was enumerated at 4,581,258 at the census of 1 March 1995. According to official estimates, the population of Laos reached 5,240,000 at mid-2000, with an average density of 22.1 per sq km. About 60% of the population are ethnic Lao, residing mainly in the western valleys. A further 35% belong to various hill tribes, although the important Hmong group has been affected by fighting. The remainder are either Vietnamese or Chinese. The urban population is an estimated 20% of the total; Vientiane, the capital, is the only large town. Its population was 176,637 in 1973, but had increased to 528,109 at the census of 1995. According to UN estimates, the population of Vientiane was 663,000 at mid-2001.

History

MARTIN STUART-FOX

EARLY HISTORY: THE KINGDOM OF LAN XANG

More than 60 different ethnic groups inhabit present-day Laos. Officially, they are divided into three broad categories on the basis of settlement patterns, culture and language. The earliest inhabitants were those minorities now known as 'Lao of the mountain slopes' (Lao Thoeng) who spoke Austro-Asiatic languages akin to Cambodian and farmed using slash-and-burn methods. From perhaps the 10th century they began to be displaced by speakers of Tai languages who entered Laos from the north-east. These included the now politically dominant lowland (or ethnic) Lao, along with other Tai groups, which together comprised the 'Lao of the plains' (Lao Lum). All practised wet-rice cultivation and most became Theravada Buddhists. The 'Lao of the mountain tops' (Lao Sung) were the last to arrive, from southern China, in the 19th century. They spoke either Hmong-Mien or Tibeto-Burman languages, followed their own various religions, and often cultivated opium as a cash crop.

Very early human remains have been discovered in northern Laos, but the first culture to have been archaeologically investigated was centred on the Plain of Jars, and was an iron-age megalithic culture which built both underground burial chambers and massive stone mortuary urns to hold the ashes of the dead. Some of these 'jars' (after which the plain was named) were more than 2 m high and weighed some 10 tons. Who these people were, however, and what became of them remains a mystery.

By the eighth or ninth century, north-eastern Thailand and Laos had begun to be influenced by the early Indianized kingdoms in mainland South-East Asia. Laos was situated at an important crossroads of trade routes along which travelled not only merchants, but also Buddhist monks. In the areas of Thakhaek in central Laos, Vientiane (Viang Chan) and Luang Prabang small principalities were formed, which at first owed allegiance to more powerful states. By the late 12th century the Cambodian Angkorian empire had begun to expand north to include not only southern Laos, but most of the Mekong basin perhaps as far north as Luang Prabang. Khmer power was short-lived, however, and as the Khmer empire contracted, Tai-speaking peoples established their own kingdoms in northern Laos and northern and central Thailand. By the late 13th century it is known that there was an established Lao principality in the region of Luang Prabang, and others in the central Mekong basin. By the mid-14th century an enterprising ruler, King Fa Ngum—subsequently revered by the Lao—had incorporated the Lao principalities into the powerful kingdom of Lan Xang Hom Khao ('A Million Elephants and the White Parasol'), a title indicating both military might and royal kingship. Many of the symbols of the modern Laotian state originate in the Kingdom of Lan Xang. For two centuries Luang Prabang (then known as Xieng Dong Xieng Thong) served as the capital of the kingdom. Lan Xang was loosely organized as a tributary state comprising several *meuang* (semi-feudal principalities of variable extent), each of which not only paid an annual tribute of gold or other valuable products, but was also expected to raise an army in time of conflict.

The kings of Lan Xang were ardent Buddhists and, as in the other Tai states and Burma (now Myanmar) and Cambodia, Theravada Buddhism served to legitimize their rule. In return for his patronage of the *Sangha* (the monastic order), monks taught that the King ruled because he possessed superior *karma* (moral merit accumulated during previous lifetimes). The image of Buddha known as the *Phra Bang* became the much revered palladium of the kingdom. The kingdom of Lan Xang was the equal of other states in mainland South-East Asia at the time, and defeated and expelled invaders from Viet Nam and Burma. Lao settlers advanced south down the Mekong valley as far as Champasak and beyond, and on to the Korat plateau (now north-eastern Thailand). As they did so, the centre of Lao population shifted south. When Burmese armies threatened Luang Prabang in the mid-16th century, King Xetthathirat decided to re-establish the capital at the more strategically situated and less vulnerable site of Vientiane.

Lan Xang was at its apogee in the 17th century during the long reign of King Surinyavongsa (1637–94). It was then that the first European merchants and missionaries arrived in Vientiane. Their descriptions of the wealth of the city and the brilliance of its court were the first independent accounts, and portray a centre of art, culture and religion attracting scholars and artists from throughout the region. Surinyavongsa's death was followed by one of the periodic successional disputes that served to weaken the kingdom. Within two decades the kingdom had split into three parts, centred on Luang Prabang in the north, Vientiane in the centre with control over much of the Korat plateau, and Champasak in the south. Xiangkhouang, on the Plain of Jars, reluctantly acknowledged the suzerainty of Vientiane, but took every opportunity to assert its autonomy. The weakened Lao kingdoms could no longer match their powerful neighbours. Even before the disintegration of Lan Xang, the maritime states of mainland South-East Asia had been much better placed than the inland states to benefit from increased seaborne trade, particularly with the recently-arrived Europeans. Their greater wealth enabled them to purchase new weapons and to equip larger armies; thus, well before all three Lao kingdoms were reduced to tributaries of Siam in the late 18th century, the balance of power had begun shifting against the Lao.

In 1827 Anuvong, the last King of Vientiane, made a desperate bid to free himself and his kingdom from Siamese hegemony. The war that followed was a disaster: Vientiane was captured and sacked, its people were forcibly resettled, and the king was removed to Bangkok where he subsequently died. Appeals by local Lao rulers to the Vietnamese were unsuccessful, except in Xiangkhouang where Viet Nam had an historic interest. In the 1870s the Laotian territories were ravaged by marauding bands of Chinese and, despite appeals for assistance, the Siamese—themselves hard-pressed by encroaching European powers—were slow to respond. The court in Bangkok was nevertheless determined to assert Siamese suzerainty even over the remote Tai highlands in what is now north-western Viet Nam. It was there in the late 1880s that they encountered the French.

LAOS UNDER FRENCH RULE

French interest in Laos derived initially from a belief that the Mekong River would provide a 'river road' to southern China. When the Mekong expedition of 1867–68 proved that the river was unnavigable, interest waned. However, French commercial interests in Saigon still hoped to tap the wealth of the Mekong basin and, with the annexation of central and northern Viet Nam as a French protectorate in 1884, French interest in Laos was revived. French control of the Mekong was deemed essential to the strategic defence and economic prosperity of the new possession; at a minimum, the Laotian territories east of the Mekong had to be annexed to 'round out' French Indo-China.

Attempts to assert Vietnamese claims to these Laotian lands were hardly convincing, and were contested by Siam. The creation of a French presence through exploration and commerce, however, was more successful. Eventually the determined efforts of Auguste Pavie, the French consul appointed to Luang Prabang, and gunboat diplomacy in Bangkok, forced the Siamese in 1893 to cede all territories east of the Mekong to France. Subsequent treaties in 1904 and 1907 established the present borders that both Cambodia and Laos share with Thailand.

For half a century Laos was ruled as a French colony, although the former kingdom of Luang Prabang nominally enjoyed the status of a protectorate. The French rebuilt Vientiane as the administrative capital of French Laos, and extended a minimal presence throughout the rest of the country. Their first priority in Laos was to cover the cost of administration. However, the depleted population that had escaped Siamese resettlement provided an insufficient tax base. Although taxes were high and all had to perform unpaid *corvée* labour, Laos was always dependent on a subsidy from the federal budget for Indo-China. The French devised various schemes designed to 'open up' Laos to economic exploitation, which required construction of a railway from the Vietnamese coast to the Mekong, and mass immigration of Vietnamese to provide an adequate work-force. From the beginning, the middle ranks of the civil service in Laos were largely filled by Vietnamese; the Great Depression in the 1930s, however, prevented construction of the railway, and relatively few Vietnamese migrated. Had the Second World War not intervened, however, the French might well have succeeded in their intention to reduce the Lao to a minority in their own country.

In 1939 Siam was renamed Thailand as part of a policy designed to appeal to all Tai-speaking peoples, including notably the Lao. To counter this appeal, for the first time the French administration began to encourage a weak Laotian nationalism among the small and educated élite. Thai seizure of Laotian territories west of the Mekong provoked Lao anger against both the Thai and the French for failing to protect the borders.

Under an agreement between the Japanese Government and Vichy France, administration of French Indo-China remained the responsibility of the French, while the Japanese had the right to move and station troops throughout the region. Not until 9 March 1945 did the Japanese forces stage a lightning pre-emptive attack to neutralize and intern all French military and civilian personnel. Only in Laos did a few French officers and men escape the Japanese net, their survival in jungle hideouts being due to the support they received from loyal Laotians.

As in other parts of South-East Asia, the élite in Laos was divided between opposition to the Japanese and opposition to colonialism. While some fought for the Allies, others collaborated. In Laos King Sisavang Vong, though pro-French, was forced on 8 April 1945 to declare the independence of his country, while, less reluctantly, Prince Phetsarath served as Prime Minister under the Japanese. The surrender of Japan in August left a political vacuum throughout Indo-China, which nationalists in all three countries moved to exploit: in Viet Nam the communist Viet Minh seized power; in Laos the nationalist Lao Itsara, or Free Laos movement. On 1 September Prince Phetsarath in Vientiane reaffirmed the independence of Laos, even though the King in Luang Prabang had welcomed the return of the French. When the King repudiated Phetsarath's actions, the Prince declared the reunification of the protectorate of Luang Prabang with the rest of the country. In October the King dismissed Phetsarath as Prime Minister but, in response, a newly-constituted Lao Itsara Government deposed the King shortly after, thereby initiating a struggle for power.

Under the terms of the Potsdam Agreement between the Allies, the Japanese surrender in Indo-China was accepted by the Chinese Nationalists north of the 16th parallel and by the British to the south. While the British facilitated the return of the French to southern Laos, the Chinese favoured the Lao Itsara. Not until the Chongqing Agreement had been concluded between France and China did the Chinese withdraw, thus allowing French forces to reoccupy central and northern Laos. In March 1946 French forces and their Laotian allies moved north. Lao Itsara volunteers supported by local Vietnamese countered the incursion at Thakhaek, but the French successfully reoccupied Vientiane on 24 April and Luang Prabang on 13 May. Some 2,000 Lao Itsara supporters and thousands of Vietnamese crossed the Mekong to Thailand, where Phetsarath established a government-in-exile in Bangkok. The French, meanwhile, set about reasserting their control. Prince Bunum of Champasak, who had aided the French, renounced his claim to a separate southern kingdom, and Laos was unified under the royal house of Luang Prabang. The nominally independent Kingdom of Laos was incorporated into the French Union, but was still closely tied (in terms of, *inter alia*, defence, currency and customs regulations) to Viet Nam and Cambodia.

By early 1947 the new Kingdom of Laos had begun to take shape. The territories west of the Mekong seized by Thailand in 1940 had been returned, elections for a Constituent Assembly had been held, and in May a new Constitution was proclaimed.

The Government, which was both conservative and pro-French, was acutely aware of its nationalist opponents in Bangkok. Its members, drawn from the powerful families of the élite that had benefited most from the French presence, reflected a judicious balance from northern, central and southern Laos. While some attempt was made, with French support, to improve woefully neglected services such as education, health and agricultural extension, much of the politicking was between influential leaders who sought to obtain regional or family advantage. Perhaps the most serious shortcoming of the new Government, however, was its failure to generate any real sense of national unity or purpose. The country was still deeply divided, with regional and family loyalties counting for more than national allegiance. The only unifying symbol might have been the monarchy, as in Thailand or Cambodia, but the King remained in Luang Prabang, and the political opportunity to unify the royal and administrative capitals and overcome regionalism by moving to Vientiane was lost.

The outbreak of the First Indo-China War in December 1946 between the Viet Minh and their allies and the French, and the activities of the Lao Itsara, both served to complicate the establishment of governmental authority. The radical anti-French nationalism of the Viet Minh provided an example for the like-minded elements of the Lao Itsara, led by Phetsarath's younger half-brother, Prince Souphanouvong. Lao Itsara guerrilla raids targeting the French in Laos were co-ordinated by and carried out with the Viet Minh. The proximity of the alliance between Souphanouvong and the Viet Minh, however, caused divisions within the Lao Itsara. Criticism of Souphanouvong eventually led him to resign from the organization in March 1949, and two months later the moderate majority responded by formally relieving him of all his ministerial functions.

In July 1949 a Franco-Lao Convention was signed giving the Laotian Government much greater powers and sufficient independence to meet the demands of the moderates in the Lao Itsara. In October, led by Phetsarath's younger brother, Souvanna Phouma, the Lao Itsara was dissolved, and its members returned to Laos. Only Phetsarath himself remained in Bangkok. Souphanouvong went to Viet Nam where he made contact with the Viet Minh. While the moderate Lao Itsara joined the new Royal Lao Government (RLG) in August 1950, Souphanouvong established his own government of the 'Land of Laos' (Pathet Lao, the name by which the communist movement in Laos became known). Over the next four years, as communist Chinese military support flowed to the Viet Minh and the USA supported France, the First Indo-China War engulfed the region. Twice Laos was subjected to major Viet Minh invasions, during which large areas of the country were seized and turned over to the Pathet Lao. The French responded by granting Laos formal independence in October 1953. The defeat of French forces at Dien Bien Phu, located in a mountain valley close to the border with Laos, represented the end of French military involvement in Viet Nam. Meetings were already under way in Geneva to seek an end to the conflict, and with respect to Laos, the Geneva Conference agreed in July 1954 to an armistice and a regrouping of opposing forces, leading to elections within two years. The Pathet Lao were allotted the two north-eastern provinces of Phongsali and Xam Neua, while the RLG administered the rest of the country. By the end of 1954 Lao independence was reinforced by the abrogation of all agreements linking Laos with the other states of Indo-China.

THE QUEST FOR UNITY AND NEUTRALITY

For the Royal Lao Government in Vientiane, the first priority was to regain administrative control of the two Pathet Lao provinces so that elections could be held in accordance with the Geneva Agreement. As a *quid pro quo*, however, the Pathet Lao insisted on changes to the electoral law and on freedom for its front organization—the Lao Patriotic Front (behind which stood the secret Lao People's Party)—to operate as a political party. Negotiations continued throughout 1955, but failed to bring results. In December 1955 the Government proceeded with elections in the provinces that it controlled. These resulted in the formation of a new Government under the leadership, once again, of Souvanna Phouma, who immediately entered into new negotiations with his half-brother, Souphanouvong.

By early 1956 the USA had replaced France as the dominant Western power in Indo-China. As of early 1955 a US Operations Mission (USOM) was functioning in Vientiane and the USA was financing not only much of the Lao budget, but also meeting the entire cost of the Lao National Army (LNA). Under the terms of the Geneva Agreement, a French Military Mission continued to train the LNA, but growing numbers of US military personnel in civilian guise were attached to the US embassy. Both the US Information Service and the Central Intelligence Agency (CIA) were also active. From 1955 to 1962 US aid to Laos, the overwhelming majority of it military, was in per caput terms the highest for any country in South-East Asia, including South Viet Nam. In the context of the Cold War the USA aimed to prevent Laos from becoming communist and thus was strongly opposed to the inclusion of communists in the Government. Souvanna Phouma's agreement with the Pathet Lao to include two of their members in a coalition government as the price for reintegration of the two provinces under their control met strenuous opposition from the USA. Souvanna Phouma pushed ahead, however, in the belief that national unity and a policy of neutrality were essential for the preservation of the Laotian state. An agreement was signed with the Pathet Lao in November 1957. Supplementary elections held the following May gave leftist candidates 21 seats in the National Assembly, much to the alarm of the USA.

With the active support of the US embassy and the CIA, right-wing politicians and army officers formed the Committee for the Defence of National Interests (CDNI). When US aid was withheld in July 1958, Souvanna Phouma's first coalition collapsed, and was replaced by a right-wing Government led by Phuy Sananikon. In January 1959, on the basis of fabricated reports of a North Vietnamese invasion, Phuy received emergency powers to govern for a year without reference to the National Assembly. Gen. Phoumi Nosavan, a powerful military figure, was appointed Vice-Minister of Defence in the new Government. The Pathet Lao watched these events with mounting concern. Negotiations to integrate two Pathet Lao battalions into the LNA stalled, and in May one battalion absconded to Xam Neua. As insurgent activity resumed, the Government responded by imprisoning Pathet Lao members of the National Assembly in Vientiane. However, the conservative Government was internally divided by personal and political differences, and in December 1959 Gen. Phoumi, with the support of the CDNI, mounted a coup. Although Gen. Phoumi failed to gain the premiership, the coup resulted in the formation of a new Government dominated by the military. New elections were held in April and, owing to malpractice, all left-wing candidates lost their seats, much to US satisfaction. As the country moved towards civil war, however, even elements of the military became concerned at the turn of events. In August 1960 a young army captain, Kong Lae, unexpectedly seized control of Vientiane under the banner of neutrality and an end to 'Lao killing Lao'. Souvanna Phouma was again invited to form a Government, which Gen. Phoumi refused to join. With the support of the CIA, but in defiance of the US embassy, Phoumi built up his forces in central Laos. In mid-December, after his efforts to prevent a civil war had failed, Souvanna flew to Phnom-Penh and Gen. Phoumi seized control of Vientiane. Kong Lae's neutralist force staged an orderly withdrawal to the Plain of Jars, where they were welcomed by the Pathet Lao. As Gen. Phoumi failed to follow up his victory, large areas of the country fell to the combined neutralist and Pathet Lao forces.

Following the undermining and collapse of Souvanna's Government in 1957, the communists made impressive gains. US policy, having clearly failed in this respect, took a new course. In March 1961, as a renewed neutralist and Pathet Lao offensive got under way, President Kennedy declared US support for a political settlement involving the neutralization of Laos. The communist response was conciliatory and a cease-fire came into effect in early May, followed by the convening of a second conference of interested powers at Geneva. It took more than a year, however, for the feuding Laotian factions to reach agreement on the formation of a second coalition Government of National Union, and then only after renewed fighting had resulted in a decisive defeat for the LNA at the battle of Nam Tha in northern Laos. The new Government, including two full ministers and two vice-ministers from the Pathet Lao, eventually signed the final document in Geneva, proclaiming the neutralization of Laos on 21 July 1962.

The second coalition, however, failed to achieve either of its two objectives: to reunify the country and, through neutralization, to insulate Laos from the gathering war in Viet Nam. Of the three factions comprising the coalition, the neutralists were the weakest and under the greatest political pressure. While the Pathet Lao and the right-wing elements enjoyed military and economic support from their principal supporters, North Viet Nam and the USA respectively, the neutralists enjoyed only diplomatic backing, principally from France. Neutralist armed forces were dependent for supplies on either the Pathet Lao or the LNA. As both the left and right wings attempted to absorb the neutralist centre, divisions developed between the neutralists themselves. Only a façade of coalition government and neutrality remained, as Laos was drawn increasingly into the Second Indo-China war. The Government lasted less than a year and after the assassination in April 1963 of the neutralist Minister of Foreign Affairs, Kinim Phonsena, Pathet Lao ministers left Vientiane, fearing their own assassination or arrest. Thereafter, both the USA and North Viet Nam subverted Laotian neutrality for their own purposes in pursuing the war in Viet Nam. The North Vietnamese had two strategic aims in Laos: to prevent northern Laos, particularly the Plain of Jars, from being used by the USA to threaten North Viet Nam, and to control the Ho Chi Minh trail in the mountainous east of Laos down which combatants and weapons flowed to communist forces in South Viet Nam. US policy sought to challenge communist control of both areas: on the Plain of Jars by building up a clandestine army recruited mainly from the Hmong ethnic minority and commanded by the Hmong General, Vang Pao; and on the Ho Chi Minh trail through the (initially secret) massive use of air power. For a decade, until the cease-fire of February 1973 brought fighting to an end, the country was caught up in the Viet Nam War. The war in Laos was of much greater strategic significance to both sides than the war in Cambodia, and in the north the Hmong suffered considerable casualties against North Vietnamese regular forces and had to be reinforced by Thai 'volunteers'. A great number of North Vietnamese and their Pathet Lao allies were killed in the US bombing in both northern and southern Laos (200,000 killed and more than 400,000 wounded is a conservative estimate); by 1973 2m. tons of bombs had been dropped, making Laos the most heavily bombed country per caput in the history of warfare. A quarter of the entire population of the country was displaced by the war.

The Lao people themselves were unable to prevent the use of their territory by opposing forces. While the North Vietnamese were nominally 'aiding' the Pathet Lao, the US embassy was directing bombing 'in defence of Laotian neutrality'. Souvanna Phouma attempted to preserve a minimum freedom of action, but only retained office in the face of attempted right-wing coups with the support of foreign ambassadors. Not until peace talks got under way did the Laotians regain some influence over their own affairs. Negotiations lasting over a year eventually led to the formation in April 1974 of a third coalition Government, the composition of which reflected the gains made by the Pathet Lao during a decade of war: half the ministerial portfolios went to communists or left-leaning 'neutralists' and the remainder to right-wing figures. The only real neutralist left was Souvanna Phouma, who once again presided as Prime Minister. Souphanouvong headed the National Political Consultative Council (NPCC), a policy-making body which met in the royal capital of Luang Prabang.

The NPCC agreed upon a relatively moderate 18-point programme, and it seemed initially that Laos might gradually work towards its own form of mild socialism, preserving both the monarchy and traditional Buddhist values. However, events in other parts of Indo-China had repercussions for Laos. In April 1975 first Phnom-Penh, then Saigon, fell to Cambodian and Vietnamese communist forces. In Laos, Pathet Lao forces advanced towards Vientiane. As towns in southern Laos were progressively 'liberated', demonstrations were mounted in Vientiane against both the continuing US presence (in the form of the US Agency for International Development—USAID) and right-wing political and military figures. Five ministers and several generals fled the country, but even as power shifted to the Pathet Lao the facade of the third coalition was retained. On 23 August Vientiane was symbolically 'liberated' by the arrival of a contingent of 50 women soldiers of the Pathet Lao. Fearing Pathet Lao reprisals, some families fled to Thailand at this time, but many more elected to stay and to serve the new regime. Thousands of civil servants and military officers went willingly to re-education 'seminars' in the remote north-east of the country, which they were assured would last only a few weeks. The Pathet Lao took advantage of the absence of their opponents, however, to press ahead with the final stage of their takeover of power. On 2 December 1975 a National Congress of People's Representatives accepted the abdication of King Savang Vatthana and proclaimed the Lao People's Democratic Republic (LPDR). While Souphanouvong was named President, real power lay with the little-known Secretary-General of the (renamed) Lao People's Revolutionary Party (LPRP) and Chairman of the Council of Ministers (Prime Minister), Kaysone Phomvihane.

THE LAO PEOPLE'S DEMOCRATIC REPUBLIC

The leaders of communist Laos saw their task as building and defending socialism through 'bypassing' the capitalist stage of development through three simultaneous revolutions: in production, through nationalizing industry and collectivizing agriculture; in science and technology, through their application to the economy; and in ideology and culture, in order to create new Lao 'socialist men and women' devoted to the regime. Laos was seen by its new leaders as the vanguard of socialism in South-East Asia, and as such they believed the country was a prime target for destabilization by its principal opponents, the USA and Thailand. Support for both building and defending socialism in Laos came from the communist bloc countries, notably the USSR, Viet Nam and China, but also from East European states and even Mongolia and Cuba, all of which established embassies in Vientiane.

The steady progress towards modernization expected by the new regime almost immediately encountered difficulties, however, largely owing to unimaginative and dogmatic policies. The end of US aid and Thailand's closure of its border with Laos, which curtailed the supply of consumer goods, both contributed to the collapse of the urban economy; new government restrictions also limited internal trade. Shops closed as their owners fled to Thailand and factories, deprived of imported inputs, had to cease production. An unpopular tax on agricultural production, introduced when much of the country was suffering from drought and poor harvests, further reduced the availability of food supplies as farmers withheld produce from markets. The new Government's policies, which sought to reduce religious expenditure and placed restrictions on freedom of movement because of security fears, further lost it support. However, the principal concern of the educated middle class, which had been prepared to co-operate with the new Government, was the latter's refusal to allow the return of those undergoing political re-education. Terms of imprisonment (in 're-education' camps), frequently extending into years, deprived many families of their principal income-earner and forced them to sell their possessions in order to survive. Many crossed the Mekong River into Thailand. Most of those eventually released also fled the country at the first opportunity. In a decade Laos lost 10% of its population, comprising an estimated 90% of its educated class, a loss that probably set the country back a generation in its development.

Increasing domestic disillusionment and the growing numbers of refugees in camps in Thailand created ideal conditions for the recruitment of opponents of the regime; a 'Lao National Revolutionary Front' was consequently established in Thailand to send anti-Government propaganda and sabotage teams into Laos. When in March 1977 rebel remnants of the Hmong 'secret army' in northern Laos briefly captured a village not far from Luang Prabang, the regime feared that the former King might instigate a revolt. The royal family was arrested and banished to a remote region of Xam Neua, where the elderly King and Queen subsequently both died, as did the crown prince, reportedly of malaria. Vietnamese forces assisted in putting down the Hmong revolt, and in July Laos and Viet Nam signed a 25-year Treaty of Friendship and Co-operation to formalize Vietnamese political, economic and military assistance, including the stationing of 30,000–40,000 Vietnamese troops in Laos over the next decade. Relations with Viet Nam and the USSR were close over these years, but increasingly difficult with the People's Republic of China and Cambodia. As hundreds of Soviet technicians and Vietnamese advisers drew Laos firmly into the Soviet sphere of influence, Chinese aid was limited to projects in the north of the country, in an area where Chinese influence had always been strong. Though the Government tried hard to maintain good relations with both sides in the Sino-Soviet dispute, the Vietnamese invasion of Cambodia in January 1979 and China's response in invading northern Viet Nam eventually forced Laos to take sides. China was asked politely to terminate its aid projects and reduce the size of its embassy staff. Subsequent Chinese warnings of the risk that the Laotian regime was taking and the acceptance of several thousand Lao refugees from Thailand for settlement in China led to charges by Laos of a Chinese-supported insurgency. Not until the mid-1980s did Laotian-Chinese relations begin to improve.

As relations with China were becoming more strained, those with Thailand improved, and an exchange of prime ministerial visits in January and April 1979 took place. Both sides agreed to suppress insurgent activity aimed at the other and to encourage bilateral trade. Relations with Thailand were variable, however, and it was not long before the Government in Vientiane was accusing Bangkok of collusion with Beijing in attempts to destabilize the regime. Security concerns were an important reason for the decision in July 1979 to suspend further co-operativization of agriculture. This unpopular programme had been pursued over two years leading to the theoretical formation by highly-motivated cadres of some 2,500 co-operatives. In fact, most were inadequately organized and the benefits promised did not materialize, not least because the Government had so few economic resources. Moreover, peasants objected to pooling their land and working for 'work points' rather than wages. Some peasants, mostly in the south, slaughtered their livestock and left for Thailand, whilst others joined the anti-Government resistance. By 1979 both the Soviet and Vietnamese Governments were advising that the programme be halted.

The external and internal threats by then confronting the regime forced a reappraisal of government policy. By the end of 1979 the decision had been taken to reform the currency (a new National Bank kip replaced the former 'liberation kip'), and to adopt a less rigid form of socialism. The change in direction was justified by reference to Lenin's 'new economic policy' of the early 1920s, but the regime could barely disguise the fact that earlier policies had been a failure. The economy of Laos was recognized as comprising a mix of modes of production, including subsistence farming and a capitalist sector, all of which were to be officially encouraged. Profit was introduced as a criterion of efficiency, economic decision-making was decentralized, and controls on the circulation and marketing of goods and produce were eliminated, preparing for the successful return of a market economy. On these new economic foundations the LPDR launched its first five-year economic development plan (1981–85), to coincide with those of other Soviet bloc countries. The plan's targets were over-ambitious, however, and partly owing to a shortage of trained personnel and to structural inadequacies, virtually none was met. Both party and governmental organization was weak, and cadres lacked training and commitment. At the Third Party Congress held in April 1982, the first since the formation of the LPDR, there was considerable criticism of the reforms. While the same seven-member Politburo was re-elected, the Central Committee was more than doubled in size to include new members from the provinces, the military and the Government. Provinces were given the right to trade directly with foreign countries and to determine their own development strategies in conformity with central government planning, a measure which considerably strengthened the political power of the Party's provincial secretaries. Party reform extended to the expulsion of members on the basis of ideological shortcomings or for corruption. In the early 1980s solidarity with Viet Nam was the measure of ideological orthodoxy and anyone questioning the proximity of relations with Viet Nam could expect to be purged for being 'pro-Chinese'. Meanwhile, the easing of economic restrictions together with the patronage exercised by powerful party leaders encouraged corruption. In 1983 and 1984 a number of officials, including six vice-ministers, were arrested on charges that were never made public but which were understood to include corruption and criticism of the Party. Several officials were subsequently reinstated, but tensions remained, in part from jealousy at the promotion of Western-trained technocrats over those with 'revolutionary credentials'.

Early in 1984 relations with Thailand deteriorated following the outbreak of fighting in the vicinity of three villages on the border of Sayabouri Province claimed by both Laos and Thailand. In June a full-scale attack by 1,500 Thai troops failed to take the disputed area. A cease-fire was agreed upon, but subsequent negotiations failed to resolve the problem, and border demarcation remained a matter of dispute, which four years later again erupted in border fighting. Relations with both China and the USA, however, improved. Border trade resumed with China, and an agreement in February 1985 with the USA led to the first excavation at the crash site of a US aircraft to determine the fate of US servicemen missing-in-action (MIA) during the Viet Nam War.

In March 1985 the LPRP celebrated 30 years of 'correct and creative' leadership of the revolution, and in December the regime celebrated both its first decade in power and the completion of the first Five-Year Plan. However, relatively little had been accomplished. The country remained desperately poor, and dependent as ever on foreign aid. The per caput income of the country's 3.5m. people was estimated at just over US $100 a year, making Laos one of the poorest countries in the world. However, the country was more or less self-sufficient in rice—given favourable weather conditions—although only a tiny fraction of paddy land was irrigated. Industrial production stood at little more than 5% of gross domestic product (GDP), a figure low even for the least developed countries. Most state-owned enterprises continued to make losses. Claims of 100% literacy were manifestly false, and both educational and health standards had actually declined through loss of trained personnel. Moreover, according to the human rights organization, Amnesty International, some 6,000 political prisoners remained in detention in remote internment camps. The feeling grew within the Party that a change of direction was necessary—especially given the possible reduction in aid from the USSR and Viet Nam.

For some time the LPRP Secretary-General, Kaysone Phomvihane, had been warning of a 'two-line struggle' being waged, although between which factions and in pursuit of which policies remained unclear at the time. Only subsequently was it revealed that the struggle was between those who wanted to introduce more radical economic reforms, led by Kaysone himself, and those who resisted them in the name of socialist orthodoxy, led by Kaysone's deputy in charge of the economy, Nouhak Phoumsavanh. Kaysone eventually succeeded in securing his policy orientation, but only after intense debate within the Party had led to the postponement of the Fourth Party Congress and of the introduction of the second Five-Year Plan until November 1986. The Congress eventually endorsed what was called the 'new economic mechanism', the essence of which allowed the operation of a market economy. State-owned enterprises were granted greater autonomy and expected to make a profit, food subsidies were progressively eliminated and the civil service was reduced in size.

Economic difficulties in 1987, brought on by drought and a decrease in electricity production, most of which was sold to Thailand, served to strengthen the position of the reformers. As the currency continued to depreciate and revenue consistently failed to cover expenditure, so dependency on foreign aid increased. Pressure for further reform came from the IMF, from foreign aid donors, and even from the USSR and Viet Nam, which were then undertaking their own programmes of reform. Measures were subsequently taken to dismantle the remaining elements of the centralized socialist economy. Over the next two years, as communism began to collapse in Eastern Europe and the USSR, and as Viet Nam withdrew its forces from both Laos and Cambodia, the LPDR strengthened ties with Thailand (following border fighting early in 1988) and with capitalist states, notably Japan, Sweden and Australia. At the same time, the Government passed a liberal foreign investment law, and began to lay the necessary legal foundations to attract foreign capital.

In April 1988 the first local elections since 1975 were held, followed in November by district, municipal and provincial elections. In March 1989 national elections took place to replace the Supreme People's Assembly appointed in 1975. The new 79-member Assembly met in June and elected Nouhak Phoumsavanh as Chairman, an indication that it would no longer be a powerless institution. Its first task was to appoint a Constitution Drafting Committee to draw up the long-delayed Constitution. Even though all candidates were carefully screened by the Party, these elections did provide some popular legitimacy for the regime at a time when, in response to the collapse of communism in Eastern Europe and events in Cambodia, anti-communist opposition to the regime had increased. Bolstered by the possibility of international support, both Hmong and right-wing Lao guerrillas operating from Thailand intensified their activities, though never sufficiently to threaten the Party's hold on power. In May 1988 Laos and China re-established full diplomatic relations. The following October Kaysone led a high-ranking Laotian delegation to Beijing to reinforce the much-improved relations with China, a visit reciprocated in December 1990 when the Chinese Premier, Li Peng, arrived in Vientiane. Relations with Thailand also rapidly improved after the Thai Prime Minister, Gen. Chatichai Choonhavan, exchanged visits with Kaysone in November 1988 and February 1989. Thai businessmen led foreign investment in Laos, and Princess Maha Chakri Sirindhorn became the first member of the Thai royal family to visit the LPDR. At the same time the Laotian Government continued to proclaim its special, if somewhat weakened, relationship with Viet Nam. By the early 1990s, therefore, Laos had succeeded in developing good relations with all its neighbours, as the country reverted to its more traditional role as a buffer state between contending powers.

Although not all problems with neighbouring states have been solved, in 1990 the diplomatic efforts of the Government led to an agreed delineation of the Laotian-Vietnamese frontier. Border agreements were also signed with China and Myanmar. Only the Laotian-Thai border remained a matter of contention. In June 1991 an agreement was concluded with Thailand in conjunction with the United Nations High Commissioner for Refugees (UNHCR) for the repatriation or resettlement in third countries of the 60,000 Laotian refugees, the majority of them Hmong, remaining in Thai camps. Although the programme moved more slowly than envisaged, owing mainly to Hmong resistance, the closure of several camps proceeded with a corresponding reduction in support for anti-Government insurgents operating in Laos. Laotian and Thai Governors of provinces along the common border began to meet regularly to discuss border issues. Co-operation with the USA on the control of drugs and the search for missing US servicemen resulted in 1992 in the re-establishment of full ambassadorial relations. The resumption of US aid to Laos followed three years later, when an exception was made to the restrictions imposed by the US administration on granting aid to communist states. In mid-1998 US officials agreed to extend financial and logistical support for the ongoing programme to clear unexploded ordnance from the Viet Nam War (supported by the USA since 1996).

The broadening of diplomatic and economic relations that followed the Government's 'open-door' approach reflected both increased confidence on the part of the regime and a series of important political initiatives. By 1991 the LPRP had sufficiently recovered from the impact of events in the former USSR to hold its own Fifth Congress. During the previous year the Party had orchestrated debate on the new Constitution, which subsequently underwent three separate drafts. It had also indicated that it would permit no challenge to its monopoly hold on political power when it arrested and subsequently imprisoned three critics whom it accused of 'activities aimed at overthrowing the regime'. All three were members of a group of intellectuals who advocated greater democracy. The Fifth Congress not only endorsed the draft Constitution but also introduced major changes in Party structure and in relations between the Party and government. The Party Secretariat was abolished, and Kaysone was named Party President. Three members of the Politburo retired, one had died, while another, Sisavat Keobounphan, was demoted for alleged corruption while mayor of Vientiane. Changes were also made to the membership of the Central Committee, with a number of younger members gaining election, several of whom were closely related to senior members of the Party. Equally important, the Party endorsed the direction of economic reform in accordance with free-market principles, symbolically replacing the communist red star in the national crest by an outline of the That Luang stupa and simultaneously eliminating the word 'socialism' from the national motto.

On 14 August 1991, more than 15 years after the formation of the LPDR, the Supreme People's Assembly finally adopted a Constitution that referred to the 'Party' only once (as the 'leading nucleus' of the political system), and formally established Laos as a 'people's democracy' in the Marxist sense. The Constitution also guaranteed basic freedoms and the right to private ownership of property. The SPA was renamed the National Assembly, the title used by the former Royal Lao Government, and its powers were enunciated. The executive powers of the President of the State were greatly enhanced, and provision was made for the appointment of a Vice-President, though none was named. Kaysone was appointed President of the LPDR, replacing both Souphanouvong and Phoumi Vongvichit as President and Acting President respectively, while the former Minister of Defence, Khamtay Siphandone, took Kaysone's place as Prime Minister, so entitled in preference to Chairman of the Council of Ministers.

The internal cohesion of the Party and the strength of the new institutions were tested in November 1992 by the death of Kaysone. He had led the Lao communist movement since the formation of the Lao People's Party in 1955, and his power as President of both the State and Party had been unchallenged. On his death, power was divided between the Chairman of the National Assembly, Nouhak Phoumsavanh, who became State President, and Khamtay Siphandone who added the Presidency of the Party to his post as Prime Minister. The transition had clearly been worked out in advance and was remarkably smooth, thereby ensuring continued political stability. Within a month scheduled elections for the National Assembly went ahead as planned. The 85 seats were contested by 154 candidates, all endorsed by the Party-controlled Lao Front for National Construction. At its initial sitting in February 1993, the new Assembly confirmed the appointments of Nouhak and Khamtay, elected Saman Vignaket as its President in place of Nouhak, and endorsed a new ministry based on an extensively reorganized structure of government.

The new Government undertook to continue the economic reform programme, to extend the rule of law, to limit the worst excesses resulting from earlier decentralization of power, and to curb corruption. Reforms to the tax system sought to increase revenue collection, and further to liberalize conditions for foreign investment. Thailand continued to be the largest source of investment (inflows having reached US $1,940m. by the end of 1995), followed by the USA, with Australia, France and China also being prominent. Inflation and the chronic underlying trade deficit continued to cause concern, although it was hoped that the future completion of major hydroelectricity and mining projects would improve the balance-of-payments situation.

In March 1996 the LPRP's Sixth Congress revealed the concern felt by senior members of the party over the pace and implications of economic change. Secret political discussions prior to the Congress led to an outcome that was unexpected by most observers: the ruling Politburo was reduced from 11 to nine members, six of whom were military generals; Khamtay Siphandone remained President of the Party, but Deputy Prime Minister Khamphoui Keoboualapha, widely identified as a leading proponent of economic reform, was excluded from both the Politburo and the Central Committee (itself reduced from 55 to 49 members), while Sisavat Keobounphan (a close associate of Khamtay) not only regained his membership of the Politburo, but was also named as the country's first Vice-President. As expected, Nouhak Phoumsavanh stepped down from the Politburo, leaving the Party firmly under the control of the army.

In July 1997 Laos formally joined the Association of South East Asian Nations (ASEAN); membership of ASEAN entails costs as well as benefits for Laos, not the least of which is the financial burden of participating in the organization's many regional forums. Relations with neighbouring states continue to be friendly; Laos has developed particularly close ties with Myanmar and Cambodia, both of which share a degree of suspicion of Thai ambitions in the region. Relations between Vientiane and Beijing remain cordial: delegations are frequently exchanged, and China provides not only economic and technical assistance to Laos, but also some military aid. Vientiane has been careful, however, to balance its foreign relations. Historically close political ties with Viet Nam mean that Hanoi still wields considerable influence: links between Vietnamese and Lao parties and military establishments are strong, and a large memorial on the Plain of Jars has been dedicated to Vietnamese troops who died in Laos during the Viet Nam War. Japan, meanwhile, remained the largest foreign aid donor, followed by Germany, Sweden, France and Australia; a total of US $1,200m. in foreign aid was pledged for the period 1998–2000. Cordial relations with the USA have been maintained through continued co-operation over the issues of drugs and of US servicemen missing-in-action since the Viet Nam War; the USA remains critical, however, of Laos's human rights record. Full diplomatic relations have been established with the Republic of Korea and several Central Asian republics.

In December 1997 elections were held for the 99-seat National Assembly. Seventeen of the candidates elected were army officers, while only one was not a member of the ruling Party. At the first session of the Assembly in February 1998, Nouhak relinquished the presidency to Khamtay Siphandone, while Vice-President Sisavat replaced Khamtay as Prime Minister and Oudom Khattigna was appointed Vice-President. (Oudom, however, subsequently died in office in December 1999.) Political developments since the Sixth Party Congress confirmed both the dominance of the army and its desire to exercise closer control over the economy, although political appointments still reflected family and clan influence, regionalism and the country's ethnic diversity. The military was determined to gain a substantial share of the benefits to be derived from resource exploration and developing projects. Three military-controlled companies have divided the country among them to develop commercial agriculture, logging, mining and tourism; contracts for construction projects constitute another profitable source of income. As corruption has become more blatant, however, so political influence has increasingly been used to gain lucrative appointments for family members or clients, a development that the Prime Minister's Anti-Corruption Commission seems unable to prevent.

The strategic position of Laos makes it a key state in the economic integration of mainland South-East Asia. An Australian-financed bridge across the Mekong River, some 30 km downstream from Vientiane, was opened in April 1994, and was the first in a series of infrastructure projects, including roads and bridges, that will eventually link Thailand, Viet Nam and southern China via Laos. The construction of a second, Japanese-financed bridge at Paksé in southern Laos was completed in 2000, and an agreement has been reached to build a third bridge at Savannakhet, to be completed by 2005. The railhead at Nong Khai, on the Thai side, will be extended as far as Vientiane, although a feasibility study for a proposed rail link through northern Laos into southern China has indicated that the project is not commercially viable. Meanwhile, airports have been upgraded to cope with increasing tourist arrivals, a new air traffic control system has been installed, and a telecommunications satellite has been launched.

Particular attention is being given to the development of the road network. The last stretch of the southbound Route 13, the highway following the Mekong River from Vientiane to the Cambodian border, is being surfaced, while several roads linking Laos with Viet Nam are being upgraded. These include Route 7, linking Houaphanh to the Laotian–Vietnamese border in the north, Route 9, which will connect with the bridge at Savannakhet, and a new road from Sekong across the southern highlands of Viet Nam to Danang to be constructed at a cost of US $33m. by Malaysian timber interests. Meanwhile Laos, Thailand and China have agreed to contribute equally to a US $45m. road project, to be mainly constructed in Laos, to link the three countries. The project will be co-ordinated by the Asian Development Bank (ADB) and will be completed by 2006.

Some Lao, however, are becoming increasingly concerned over the threat that rapid regional integration poses to their society and culture, as well as over the effects that such integration may have on the environment. There exists a growing awareness of the importance of environmental issues such as the impact of dam construction, the rate of timber extraction and the diminution of the country's natural biodiversity. Dam construction slowed in the late 1990s as a result of the Asian economic crisis: in 1999 it appeared unlikely that the series of hydroelectric projects planned to follow the completion of the major Nam Theun 2 project would go ahead, and some doubt surrounded the completion of even the Nam Theun 2 project itself. It was not until February 2002 that protracted negotiations between the Laotian and Thai authorities and the consortium of companies building the massive dam resulted in the signing of a contract committing Thailand to the purchase of sufficient Laotian electricity to make the project viable. Hydropower seemed unlikely to provide a major source of government income for some time. Substantial levels of foreign aid are thus likely to continue to be crucial to Laos for the foreseeable future. In May 2000 the Government imposed a ban on all timber exports, in an attempt to reduce the endemic over-exploitation and smuggling of the country's dwindling timber reserves. Whether the measure would have any effect, given the voracious demand of foreign timber interests and the level of official corruption, remained to be seen.

Related government attempts to reduce swidden ('slash-and-burn') farming and encourage reafforestation have so far proved only partially successful. (In 1993, in an initiative to preserve unique Laotian flora and fauna, the Government set aside 17 'national biodiversity conservation areas', which together constituted just over 10% of Laos's total land area. However, these areas are not national parks; they are inhabited, and some timber extraction is permitted.) Illicit trade in exotic Lao wildlife, mainly to China, is a serious problem. Tourism is also likely to have an increasing impact on the Laotian environment (although environmental and ethnological tourism in the country is as yet at an early stage): for example, it is expected that the fragile beauty of the city of Luang Prabang, approved by UNESCO in February 1998 as a World Heritage site, will come under serious threat in the new millennium, as a result of the sheer numbers of tourists visiting the city (expected to attract more than one-third of the annual total of 0.6m. tourists travelling to the country). Tourism, however, is viewed by the Government as an expandable source of national income, particularly in a time of economic crisis.

Another area of concern is that of the potential social impact of consumerism, drugs, HIV/AIDS and prostitution, as the country's boundaries become more porous. Despite the imposition of relatively strict controls by the Government, prostitution has flourished. Laos has not been unaffected by the growing HIV/AIDS epidemic in the region, and HIV/AIDS awareness campaigns are now part of the national public health programme. Of equal concern in the spread of the disease is intravenous drug use. Despite the fact that the cultivation of opium was outlawed in Laos in 1997 as a result of pressure from foreign governments, and that the Lao authorities aimed to eradicate opium production by 2008, the drug is still readily available. Meanwhile, heroin and amphetamines also flood in across the border from neighbouring Myanmar, attracting Western 'drug tourists' and increasing numbers of young Lao. (An estimated 15% of Lao students aged between 15 and 20 are reported to be addicted.) In 2001 the Government introduced the death penalty for drug trafficking and launched an intensive anti-drug campaign aimed at the country's youth. As an indication of the Government's mounting concern, a Central Committee for Drug Control has been established, chaired by the Prime Minister, and Laos has entered into drug control agreements with neighbouring states.

In August 1999 the Asian financial crisis resulted in the removal from their posts of two leading economic officials, the Governor of the Central Bank of Laos, Cheuang Sombounkhan, and the Deputy Prime Minister and Minister of Finance, Khamphoui Keoboualapha, for alleged mismanagement of fiscal and banking policy. Economic conditions were subsequently slow to improve, however, and popular dissatisfaction continued to increase. On 26 October students staged a rare anti-Government protest in Vientiane. A number of the demonstrators were promptly arrested, whilst others suspected of involvement in the protest fled across the border to Thailand. The Government refused even to acknowledge that either the incident or the arrests had ever taken place but, according to informed sources, some of the leaders of the demonstration remained in detention in 2002.

In June 1999 Hmong insurgent groups in north-eastern Laos renewed their anti-Government activities. It was speculated that the unrest had been fomented from abroad by Hmong activists linked to former Gen. Vang Pao. In March 2000 a bomb exploded in a restaurant in Vientiane, injuring a number of people, several of them foreigners. This attack was followed by a series of further explosions over subsequent months. Although no organization claimed responsibility, a government spokesperson attributed the explosions to Hmong insurgents and other 'bad elements'. The Hmong denied responsibility, however, and the incidents appeared instead to have been organized by Lao dissidents operating from abroad, with the aim of discrediting the Government by showing it to be incapable of maintaining security. A more serious attack took place in July 2000, when about 50 suspected royalist insurgents seized customs and immigration offices on the Laotian–Thai border, near the southern town of Paksé. At least six of the dissidents were subsequently killed by government troops, some were captured, while a further 28 were arrested by Thai authorities. This incident was generally perceived to be an attempt to exploit more widespread discontent within the country. With the exception of one small explosion in January 2001 at the Lao end of the Friendship Bridge over the Mekong River, however, security was soon restored. One positive outcome was the subsequent signing of an extradition treaty with Thailand.

The principal response of the Laotian Government, both to the risk posed to national security by the bomb attacks and to the ongoing economic crisis, was to seek to consolidate relations with its communist neighbours. Both Viet Nam and the People's Republic of China offered to increase economic assistance to Laos. Cross-border trade was stimulated in order to reduce Laotian dependency on Thai imports and the country's substantial negative trade balance with Thailand, while Chinese and Vietnamese investment accordingly increased. China agreed to provide Laos with technical assistance and emergency loans, partly for the purchase of military equipment. In July 2000 President Khamtay made an official visit to China, and in November President Jiang Zemin became the first Chinese Head of State to visit Laos. Senior Laotian and Vietnamese officials also exchanged visits. Relations with Thailand, meanwhile, remained friendly, although Vientiane was dissatisfied with Bangkok's trade policy. The process of the demarcation of the Laotian–Thai border was extended for two years to the end of 2002, and work also commenced on the Laotian border with Cambodia.

Laos entered the new millennium with some trepidation. Short-term economic prospects were unfavourable, with little likelihood of any reduction of either the budgetary or trade deficits. However, the value of the currency had stabilized by the end of 2000, and some growth in the economy was evident. Security was a renewed concern, however, and both the Government and the Party feared continuing popular dissatisfaction, precipitated by growing social and regional disparities and endemic corruption. Nevertheless, these continual problems did not delay the Seventh Congress of the LPRP, which took place in March 2001. The outcome was as expected, with the military retaining control of the Politburo. All eight surviving members of the previous Politburo were re-elected, together with three new members (thereby increasing the total number to 11). Of these, eight were either retired or serving military officers (seven generals and one colonel). Of the other three, two were senior Party officials in charge of mass mobilization and Party organization, while the other was the new first Deputy Prime Minister, Thongloun Sisolit. The only unexpected omission from the new Politburo was that of the second Deputy Prime Minister and Minister of Foreign Affairs, Somsavat Lengsavat. Twelve new members were appointed to the Central Committee, increasing total membership to 53, including all 16 provincial governors. Party membership was reported to have increased by 28%, to 100,000.

Barring unforeseen circumstances, this LPRP leadership, which was perceived to be both cautious and conservative with respect to political liberalization and economic reform, was to remain in power for the next five years. The Party Congress stated its opposition to a multi-party system, and proclaimed ambitious targets for economic growth (see Economy). The Congress endorsed a reduction in tariffs in accordance with its commitment to the ASEAN Free Trade Area (AFTA), and reiterated its aim to join the World Trade Organization (WTO). A projected improvement in living standards was likely to be assisted by funds amounting to US $40m. promised to Laos under the IMF Poverty Reduction and Growth Facility.

Following the Congress in March 2001, the National Assembly convened to endorse a change of government. Boungnang Volachit, hitherto Deputy Prime Minister and Minister of Finance, replaced the elderly Sisavat Keobounphan as Prime Minister, with Thongloun Sisolit as the new first Deputy Prime Minister and President of the State Planning Committee. Lt-Gen. Choummali Saignason, hitherto the Minister of Defence, was elected the country's Vice-President (following the death of Oudom Khattigna in December 1999). Nevertheless, most government ministers retained their portfolios, thereby reinforcing the conservative continuity demonstrated by the LPRP Congress. If the Party's intention was to perpetuate existing policies, however, it still faced significant popular discontent, mainly over poor economic performance and increasing levels of corruption and crime (especially in Vientiane).

In an apparent attempt to reinforce its legitimacy, the Government advanced the date of elections to the National Assembly to 24 February 2002, several months ahead of schedule. The Assembly was enlarged from 99 to 109 members, elected from provincial lists numbering 166 candidates, all of whom were endorsed by the Lao Front for National Construction. Of those elected, only one was not a member of the LPRP. A total of 25 were women, while 39 were members of minority ethnic groups (including six from Tai minorities). The remaining 70 were ethnic Lao. Overall, the members of the new Assembly were younger (with an average age of 51) and better educated (63% had received some tertiary education) than their predecessors.

In the conduct of its foreign relations Laos maintained an even balance between Viet Nam and China. Prime Minister Boungnang Volachit visited first Hanoi and then Beijing shortly after the elections of early 2002, as did the new Minister of Defence, Gen. Douangchai Phichit. On each occasion new bilateral agreements were signed, including one concerning security ties with Viet Nam. The month of July 2002 marked both the 40th anniversary of the establishment of diplomatic relations between Laos and Viet Nam, and the 25th anniversary (and expiration) of the Treaty of Friendship and Co-operation signed by the two countries in 1977. President Khamtay paid an official four-day visit to Hanoi in May, during which both sides agreed to hold joint celebrations and to protect and develop their 'traditional relations'. No mention was made of an extension of the Treaty, which seemed unnecessary as both states had now acceded to ASEAN membership.

Relations with Cambodia were relaxed as border demarcation progressed. Plans were announced for a new development zone in the border area shared by Laos, Cambodia and Viet Nam. Demarcation of the border between Laos and Thailand also progressed; the land frontier was due for completion by the end of 2002 and the Mekong River frontier by the end of 2003. However, relations with Thailand continued to be uneasy, despite the visit of Thai Prime Minister Thaksin Shinawatra to Vientiane in June 2001. Tensions centred upon river works being undertaken by both countries, Thai naval patrols, drug and people trafficking, the activities of Lao anti-government insurgents in Thailand, and even a Thai film that the Lao considered insulting to the 19th-century King of Viang Chan, Chao Anou. While production of the film was halted, other matters were expected to prove more intractable.

In 2002 the Government could congratulate itself on the apparent attainment of political stability, demonstrated by the Seventh Congress and the National Assembly elections, and for restoring security. However, although the LPRP faced no overt political opposition, with the collapse of its Marxist ideology its legitimacy was more than ever dependent on its ability to manage the economy and to improve the performance of its own cadres. This perhaps explained an apparent increase in official support for Buddhist ceremonies and celebrations in the new millennium.

Economy

NICK FREEMAN

The establishment of the Lao People's Democratic Republic (Lao PDR) in December 1975 marked the end of a lengthy civil war in Laos. Caught within the vortex of Cold War rivalry and the more intensive conflict being waged in neighbouring Viet Nam, Laos's civil war was primarily fought between pro-communist Pathet Lao forces and anti-communist Royal Lao Government (RLG) forces. The chaos and division caused by the civil war had excluded the possibility of any significant economic development occurring in Laos following the end of French colonial rule in 1953. The preceding 70 years of French administration had resulted in very little economic development in the country. Having been regarded as little more than a colonial backwater within the French empire, Laos had been governed by France on a low budget. Compared with the relatively significant investment enacted in Viet Nam, French entrepreneurs identified few commercial projects in Laos, other than a limited number of isolated agriculture-related and mining operations. Rather, landlocked Laos's primary role was deemed to be strategic, with the country acting as a buffer between France's more lucrative occupation of Viet Nam and British interests in colonial Burma (now Myanmar) and the independent Kingdom of Siam (now Thailand).

Following the Pathet Lao victory in 1975, senior members of the political leadership, the Lao People's Revolutionary Party (LPRP), descended from their headquarters in the remote north-east of the country and took power in the capital, Vientiane. In its assumption of the role of national Government, the LPRP was immediately obliged to address a number of significant issues. In addition to the social, political and security challenges confronting the new Government, the LPRP rapidly had to contend with an economy that was suddenly having to function without the massive levels of US assistance that had effectively financed the RLG regime, and grossly distorted Laos's economy for much of the previous decade. The immense damage inflicted on the country during the Viet Nam War, most notably as a result of US 'carpet bombing' of areas along Laos's eastern border with Viet Nam, needed to be addressed, in order that refugees could be resettled and agricultural activity could re-commence. Furthermore, areas of upland Laos that had previously been under LPRP control now had to be integrated with the newly-liberated lowland parts of the country. With Soviet-inspired central planning techniques, and under the guidance of fraternal sponsors, the LPRP leadership set about addressing these challenges with a degree of zeal (and insensitivity) perhaps to be expected of those still flush with victory. The Government's aim was to create a centrally-planned economy in Laos, based on the notion of collective ownership. Most private companies in the nascent industry and service sectors were nationalized, as was the entire banking sector; the latter was also consolidated into a single mono-bank structure. It is estimated that up to 80% of Laos's small industrial sector was placed under direct state ownership during this period, and most companies found that market forces were replaced as the leading influence on business by output targets set by the State Planning Committee.

A state marketing board to which peasants were obligated to sell their surplus agricultural goods was established in 1976, setting prices for staple goods, including rice. The marketing board issued coupons in payment for agricultural products, which peasants could then use to buy goods in state-run stores. Adverse weather conditions in the period 1976–78, compounded by ill-conceived policies, resulted in a marked decline in agricultural output. The mass collectivization of agriculture was also attempted by the LPRP, albeit relatively briefly. Initially at least, the number of agricultural collectives was low, but by 1978 the total had exceeded 1,000. Although mandatory directives on collectivization were abandoned as early as 1979, the subsequent introduction of various inducements—such as privileged access to cheap credit, and lower tax rates—resulted in an increase in the number of collectives to almost 4,000 by 1986. Some of these collectives, however, were little more than quasi-formal groups of peasants providing mutual assistance, content to be classified as collectives in order to receive the privileges granted by the Government. Collectivization was particularly strong in areas that had previously been under the control of the Pathet Lao prior to 1975, or where the provincial Government's socialist vigour was most ardent, and weak in areas where swidden (shifting) cultivation was practised. For example, over 80% of the cultivated area of Champasak Province was under collectivization in 1984, compared with 8.5% in Vientiane and less than 6% in Luang Prabang. State-owned trading companies enjoyed a monopoly on both external and inter-provincial trading activity. A broad policy of import-substitution was introduced by Laos's policy-makers, despite the very obvious limitations of the domestic industrial sector.

The scale of the challenge confronting the relatively inexperienced leadership, together with the inappropriate use of economic planning methods and the lack of sensitivity shown to those who had previously lived in areas controlled by the RLG, cumulatively served to create an economic crisis. The exodus (primarily across the Mekong River to Thailand) of those Lao who had been directly associated with the RLG Government, its regular armed forces or irregular ethnic minority forces, was followed by the departure of those entrepreneurs and professionals who did not relish the prospect of living under a communist regime, where property rights were no longer respected and where business assets were arbitrarily seized. Within a few years, Laos thus lost a substantial proportion of its already small educated middle and entrepreneurial classes, and the resulting paucity of human resources has been a significant factor in the slow pace of the country's economic development ever since.

Prior to 1975, Laos had been heavily dependent upon trade with neighbouring Thailand for a wide range of goods. However, tension between Vientiane and Bangkok (particularly over the fate of the Laotian royal family) led to a disruption of border trade in the late 1970s. High inflation soon developed, exacerbated by an expansive monetary and fiscal policy implemented by the new leadership. The scale and vehemence of popular resistance to the leadership's attempt at the collectivization of lowland agriculture, as well as opposition to its efforts to halt swidden upland agriculture, along with various other elements of the country's 'socialist transformation', appear to have surprised the LPRP. Far from showing signs of the development of a vigorous new economy, and deriving the anticipated benefits of the peace dividend and central planning methods, the first years of the Lao PDR were characterized by declining output, lower living standards for the urban Lao (no longer supported by US aid), and stubborn rural resistance to the policies of the new leadership. Quite clearly, attempts to create a centrally-planned economy, in accordance with the model advocated by the Soviet Union and other fraternal socialist allies, were not generating the required results in Laos. Consequently, in 1979 the LPRP was obliged to signal a less zealous approach to the socialist transformation of the Laotian economy, following a similar decision taken in neighbouring Viet Nam in that same year. The concept of obligatory collectivization was abandoned, and the limited role of the private sector was formally recognized. State enterprises were slowly granted a greater degree of independence over day-to-day decision-making. The local currency, the kip, was effectively devalued in late 1979, with the 'liberation kip' being replaced by the 'national bank kip'. The Third Congress of the LPRP, held in 1982, witnessed the affirmation by the leadership that Laos's transition to a socialist system could not be conducted according to the rapid pace envisaged after the party's military victory in 1975. Instead, it was decided that a more gradual and incremental approach would be pursued, although the ultimate goal of the socialist transformation of the economy was still very clearly envisaged by the LPRP. While these partial reforms helped withstand the economic crisis facing Laos in the late 1970s, they were insufficient in bringing about a sustained economic revival, and by the mid-1980s it had become clear that a more substantive programme of economic liberalization measures would be needed. The decision to press ahead with a second series of economic reforms, in a bid to revive the Laotian economy, was made in the approach to the Fourth Party Congress in 1986, and was actively supported by the party's foremost leader, Kaysone Phomvihane.

A more radical and comprehensive programme of reforms, referred to as the New Economic Mechanism (NEM), was endorsed by the Fourth Party Congress in November 1986. The NEM involved a transition of the economy from a broadly centrally-planned economic system to a more market-orientated system, albeit with many socialist elements remaining in place, and from an economy striving towards collective ownership to one based on private ownership. The NEM principally entailed the introduction of a Constitution and a legal regime, the recognition of property rights, the privatization of most state enterprises, price reform, the creation of factor markets and the end of state distribution systems, financial and macro-economic reforms, and the opening of the economy to foreign trade and investment. As the period of central planning in Laos had endured for less than a decade, it was possible to dismantle much of the socialist economic system within the first five years of the reform programme. The collapse of the socialist bloc in the late 1980s also influenced Laos's economic reform programme, as aid from fraternal allies contracted sharply. The country was thus obliged to seek alternative sources of external assistance: in order to attract funding from the international donor community, the Laotian leadership had little choice but to make changes to its economic management methods. In 1987 the state marketing board was closed, allowing the prices and distribution of items like rice to be dictated by the market. The policy of import-substitution was also abandoned, in favour of greater external trade, and state-owned trading enterprises slowly began to lose their monopoly on import and export activities. One year later, the tax and credit privileges granted to agricultural collectives were halted. The local currency was again devalued in 1987, and the fixed exchange rate system was abandoned in the following year. Subsequently, the official exchange rate was adjusted to correspond to the unofficial market rate, ultimately allowing for a managed 'float' of the kip to be formally adopted in 1995. Today, the margin between the official bank and unofficial parallel exchange rate rarely exceeds 2%.

The first, and long overdue, Constitution of the Lao PDR was promulgated in August 1991, 16 years after the LPRP took power, and heralded the leadership's belated recognition that genuine economic reform and sustained development could not proceed without the rule of law and some respect for property rights. Foreign investors, in particular, who were perceived as an important source of both financial and non-financial contributions to the economic development of the country, had been unwilling to commit substantial sums of investment capital into Laos without some recognition for property rights and a legal process, however vague and untested. A property law (albeit based more on user rights than private ownership as such), contract law and inheritance law were all passed in 1990. A number of other reforms were enacted in 1990–91, including the reintroduction of central government control over regional bank branches and state enterprises (responsibility for these agencies had previously been with the relevant provincial authorities). The provincial authorities also lost control over the collection of revenues and the allocation of state expenditure. A minimum wage was introduced in 1991. A second foreign investment law was approved in 1994, along with a business law and customs law, and the remaining restrictions on internal movement were removed. A domestic investment law and tax law were passed one year later, with the latter undergoing slight revision in 1998.

In the late 1990s the average per caput gross national product (GNP) in Laos remained low, at US $320 in 1998, albeit measuring more than double the figures recorded at the commencement of the economic reform programme. Some upland provinces, however, have average per caput incomes of less than US $60. Having registered annual growth rates of between 5.9% and 8.1% in 1992–97 (according to the Asian Development Bank—ADB), gross domestic product (GDP) increased by just 4.0% in 1998 and 5.2% in 1999, owing in part to the impact on Laos of the regional economic crisis. (The GDP growth rates for 1998–99 might actually have shown a contraction, had it not been for the commissioning of the Theun Hinboun power project.) According to the IMF, GDP growth in 2001 was around 5.2%. According to UNDP, in 2000 average life expectancy at birth in Laos was just 53.5 years; the country had an adult illiteracy rate of 51.3%; and in 1999 only 46% used adequate sanitation facilities. Of a total population of around 5.2m. in 2000, only about 22% live in urban areas. The distribution of the population in Laos is far from uniform, with 45% of the country's population living in just four of Laos's 18 provinces (Vientiane, Savannakhet, Champasak and Luang Prabang) in 1995; 18% of the population resides within Vientiane Province alone. Population density in Laos as a whole is very low, at 22.1 people per sq km in 2000. The total work-force in Laos is around 2.2m., of whom about 10% are salaried. Approximately 130,000 people work in some element of government administration.

AGRICULTURE AND FORESTRY

Agriculture remains the primary source of income and employment in Laos, although much agricultural activity continues to be conducted on a subsistence basis, and productivity levels are relatively low. While the economy as a whole achieved relatively high average annual rates of growth during much of the 1990s, the agricultural sector generally recorded more modest growth rates over the decade. According to the ADB, agricultural GDP grew by 5.0% in 1999 and 4.4% in 2000. Yet despite the relatively rapid growth of the industrial and service sectors under the economic reform programme, the agricultural sector continues to dominate the Laotian economy, accounting for approximately 51% of the country's GDP in 2001, and around 80% of all employment. Indeed, this was the case during much of the second half of the 20th century. Consequently, weather conditions have the potential to cause a marked impact on the country's overall economic performance, as witnessed during the drought of 1987–88 and the floods of 1995–96 and 2000. This is particularly true with reference to the upland areas of Laos, where subsistence farming dominates, most households are poor, there is a lack of capital for the upgrading of technology, environmental degradation appears to be accelerating, and transport to the limited number of markets remains wholly inadequate. The lowland areas of Laos began to show signs of greater vitality in the 1990s, however, with households able to sell a proportion of their increased output, as the revival of market forces began to generate benefits. Lowland farmers are now able to invest in new technology and to buy pesticides and fertilizer and have better access to markets to sell surplus output, thereby benefiting from a conducive spiral of improved income and living standards. The change is particularly evident in the lowland 'Mekong corridor', where the creation of all-weather roads and the development of increased border trade are identified as the main catalysts behind the achievement of improved productivity and income levels. This divergence between the two agro-economic zones—the uplands and the lowlands—warrants some concern, as all indicators suggest that the disparity between the two areas continued to widen throughout the 1990s.

In 2000 crop production in Laos accounted for 59% of total agricultural output, followed by livestock and fishery activities (35%), and forestry (6%). The dominant crop by far is rice, with almost 2.2m. metric tons of paddy harvested in 2000 (compared with 1.8m. tons in 1999). However, rice output declined in 2001, as a result of widespread flooding in the south and central regions of the country. The Government set a production target of 2.4m. tons of rice for 2002. Vientiane municipality has tended to be the most productive province for growing paddy, followed by Bokeo, Xiangkhouang, Saravan and Champasak Provinces. Sekong, Phongsali and Luang Prabang Provinces, by contrast, have tended to be the least productive. Factors influencing the level of productivity in each province include the quality of transport available, the level of foreign assistance provided, the presence of unexploded ordnance, and the extent to which swidden cultivation methods are still being used. Laos has tended to have only one main rice harvest per year, during the wet season, with a much smaller dry season harvest. Although the Lao population continued to increase during the 1990s, at a rate of about 2.5% per year, rice output has remained broadly static, resulting in a fairly substantial deficit that had to be offset through imports. However, in recent years the Government has sought to increase the size of the dry season rice crop substantially through a series of measures in a bid to make the country self-sufficient in rice. In 1999, for example, it was reported that the dry season rice crop totalled 300,000 tons, compared with less than 50,000 tons in 1995. The area being harvested during the 1999 dry season was reported to total 92,000 ha, more than double that harvested in the previous year, and a dramatic increase from only 15,500 ha in 1994. In 1997–98 the Laotian Government took a risk when it spent a considerable proportion of its foreign-exchange reserves on the purchase of a substantial number of diesel-powered water pumps to help farmers irrigate the dry season paddy fields in lowland areas. This purchase was followed up with training courses on dry season cultivation techniques for both paddy and other cash crops. The initiative constituted part of a wider 'strategic vision' for the agricultural sector, announced by the Ministry of Agriculture and Forestry in late 1999. This vision was reported to include the extension of policies and initiatives that had previously worked well in the lowland areas (including transport upgrading, access to micro-financing for farmers, and guidance on diversifying crop production) to the upland areas. Aid donors have noted the omission of some important aspects from the 'strategic vision'; little attention is focused on, for example, the fishery sub-sector (despite fish being an important source of protein in Laos), the use of livestock (one of the few consistent growth areas in upland agriculture), and forestry.

Other crops grown in relatively substantial quantities in Laos include corn, sweet potatoes, cassava, peanuts, soybeans, coffee and tobacco, as well as some tea and sugar cane. Although total coffee production remains quite small (24,000 metric tons were harvested in 2000, up from 10,000 tons in 1996), Laos has significant potential in this area, and it is likely that coffee will become a more prominent source of foreign-exchange earnings in the future, if the international price of coffee stabilizes. The development of a dry season harvest of cash crops should also result in an increase in the output of other agricultural products, providing a useful addition to farmers' incomes and increasing the foreign-exchange earnings of the country as a whole.

Swidden cultivation remains common in some upland provinces, despite the Government's attempts to halt this form of activity. (In 1998 it was estimated that more than 155,000 households continued this practice, compared with 280,000 in the mid-1990s.) Many practitioners of swidden cultivation tend to be from ethnic minorities that resist what they perceive as lowland Lao interference. However, under the Government's new 'strategic vision' for the agricultural sector, a renewed attempt to convert swidden farmers to more sedentary forms of cultivation was to be attempted through the introduction of feeder roads to allow improved market access, better rural savings mobilization and credit techniques, the development of land entitlement and land use zoning practices, support for crop diversification, and so on.

With assistance from UNDP, the Laotian Government has sought to clear substantial areas of southern and eastern Laos of unexploded ordnance, most of which was dropped by the USA during the Viet Nam War. Approximately one-half of Laos remains contaminated by over 0.5m. tons of unexploded ordnance, resulting in about 120 casualties per year, and effectively rendering parts of 15 provinces unsafe for habitation or cultivation. (The USA dropped a massive quantity of ordnance on Laos, partly in a covert bid to support the RLG Government, but also in an attempt to destroy the 'Ho Chi Minh trail', a supply route between North and South Viet Nam, which ran through large parts of eastern Laos.) This unexploded ordnance—and small anti-personnel devices known as 'bombies', in particular—has also hindered the expansion of agriculture in certain areas.

The Laotian Government has also sought to eradicate the cultivation of opium in remote upland areas of the country; opium is grown mostly by small-scale subsistence farmers both for use as a medicine and as a cash crop. The US Department of State alleged that in 2001 Laos was the second largest opium producer in the world, after neighbouring Myanmar. Most opium cultivated in Laos is produced by small-scale subsistence farmers, and the country is believed to have the world's second highest opium addiction rate, after Iran. According to the US Department of State, total opium production in 2001 was estimated to be 210 metric tons (a considerable increase from 140 tons in 1999), cultivated across 11 northern provinces of Laos, particularly Phongsali and Houaphanh provinces. The potential harvest area for opium has declined from 28,150 ha in 1997 to 22,000 ha in 2001. Most opium addicts live in remote upland areas, making it difficult for detoxification programmes to reach the estimated 60,000 addicts in Laos. The Government has pledged to eradicate opium production by 2005, and all other drugs by 2015. It thus sought US $80m. from foreign donors in early 2002 to fund a three-year programme to rid Laos of opium.

About 42% of Laos is covered in natural forestland, a reduction from about 50% in 1985. In 2000, according to official figures, the production of logs totalled 378,000 cu m, compared with 819,000 cu m in 1995. A small number of companies connected to the Laotian military dominate the logging industry in Laos, and have been particularly active in those areas identified for eventual flooding under proposed hydropower projects. An Environment Protection Law, which is retroactive in effect, was passed in 1999, although it remains to be seen whether Laos's legal institutions have the capacity to enforce this law properly, particularly with regard to powerful vested interests.

INDUSTRY

The industrial sector (comprising all manufacturing, mining, construction, and electricity-generating activity) has recorded a faster rate of growth since the enactment of the NEM economic reforms than either the agriculture or service sectors. Between 1993 and 1996 the rate of growth of the industrial sector was in double figures, although this subsequently declined to 8% in 1999, and remained at about the same level in 2000, owing in part to the impact of the regional economic crisis on foreign investment inflows. Foreign investment participation in the industrial sector—most notably in the energy, mining and garment sub-sectors—played a critical role in the sector's relatively impressive performance during the 1990s. Yet, despite commendable growth during that decade, in 2000 industry accounted for less than 23% of GDP in Laos, a large proportion of which is light industry and handicrafts.

The manufacturing sector accounted for around 75% of industrial activity in 2000, and includes a relatively substantial export-orientated garment sector, which enjoyed improved performance following the reinstatement by the European Union (EU) of its Generalized System of Preferences (GSP) for Laos in late 1997. The principal products of the manufacturing sector include beer and soft drinks, wood products, plastic products, tobacco and cigarettes. The industrial sector is not evenly distributed within Laos: roughly 63% of all enterprises are located in Vientiane, Savannakhet, Champasak, and Luang Prabang Provinces, and two-thirds of all Laos's large-scale manufacturing companies are to be found within Vientiane Province alone. Similarly, the vast majority of Laos's garment, footwear and textiles companies are located within municipal Vientiane. An Industry Processing Law, which governs the actions of all companies involved in the manufacture of garments, textiles, and products made from wood, paper and coal, was passed in 1999. The construction sector failed to prosper in the late 1990s, owing in large part to the suspension of most of the country's planned hydropower projects and a steep decline in foreign investment inflows.

Despite having been granted partial managerial autonomy in the late 1970s, state enterprises continued to perform poorly during much of the 1980s. The Government responded by introducing a programme of privatization for all non-strategic state firms in 1989. The privatization programme has entailed a number of different forms of divestment, including leasing arrangements, management buy-outs, transfer to provincial authorities, outright sales to local or foreign enterprises, partial equity sales into joint-venture companies with foreign investors, and several liquidations. However, the programme has also faced a number of difficulties and criticisms relating to the methods used to value state assets, the opacity of sales procedures, resistance to the initiative from civil servants, state enterprise employees and powerful vested interests, and the rather inconclusive terms of fixed-term leasing arrangements. Nevertheless, by the late 1990s most state enterprises (including the state telecommunications company) had been partially or fully disposed of, with the exception of those strategic state organizations that the Government does not wish to see divested. Although the size of its state sector is much smaller than those of Viet Nam and the People's Republic of China, Laos appears to have been more successful in its efforts towards privatization than either of those two countries. By the late 1990s only about 65 state companies remained from among the 800 or so that had existed less than a decade earlier, prompting the IMF to describe the country's privatization programme as 'one of the most successful parts of Laos's structural reforms thus far'. Of the 65 companies that remain, approximately one-half are strategic enterprises that will remain state-owned, whilst the remainder are non-strategic companies that have proven impossible to divest and will ultimately face liquidation. Since 1997 the strategic state enterprises—such as Electricité du Laos, Postes du Laos, the National Tourism Authority of Lao PDR, Nam Papa Lao (Lao Water Supply Authority), and the Banque pour le Commerce Extérieur Lao—have been undergoing a process of 'commercialization', entailing financial and managerial restructuring, in order that they might be better able to compete with their private-sector equivalents.

ENERGY

In 2000 Laos's total electricity generation was slightly over 3,000m. kWh (up from 1,085m. kWh in 1995), and electricity accounted for around 10% of the value of the country's total industrial output. However, this was expected to increase in 2001–02, with the commissioning of a number of new power stations. The vast majority of Laos's energy supplies are derived from hydroelectric generators, with a relatively small amount of electricity also being sourced from diesel-powered installations. About 60% of the electricity generated by Laos is exported to Thailand, providing much-needed foreign-exchange earnings. Despite the presence of a growing number of major power installations in Laos, the country does not yet have a national power grid, and only about 20% of the Lao population has access to electricity, with firewood remaining the dominant source of energy for those living in non-urban areas. Large parts of the country remain completely without access to electricity supplies; indeed, some border provinces import small quantities of electricity from neighbouring provinces in Viet Nam and Thailand. Three regional transmission sub-systems serve Vientiane and Luang Prabang, Savannakhet and Thakhaek, and Champasak and Saravan. Domestic consumers of electricity in Laos enjoy low electricity prices, cross-subsidized from power export earnings.

Laos's potential power-generating capabilities are considerable, with the country's hydropower potential alone being estimated at approximately 18,000 MW (although only 623 MW has been harnessed to date). The Government aspires, in consequence, for Laos to become the 'battery of Asia'. Although there have been plans for the construction of a substantial number of hydropower plants on rivers feeding into the Mekong (a total of 24 projects were at, or beyond, the advanced planning stage in 1997), only seven of these had received investment licences, and just two had been realized by late 1999. Finance appears to have been the principal obstacle for a number of the projects, including the 920-MW Nam Theun 2 project located 250 km east of Vientiane which—if it goes ahead—was to be the single biggest investment project ever undertaken in Laos, at US $1,200m. It had initially been intended that construction of Nam Theun 2 would commence in 1996 and be completed by 2000, but construction was subsequently expected to commence in 2003, with the commissioning of the project envisaged for 2008. The World Bank agreed to provide partial risk cover for the project in 2000, and a revised power-purchasing agreement between Vientiane and Bangkok was signed in February 2002. Thailand is committed to buy electricity generated by the power plant, at an agreed price, for 25 years. With Thailand expected to take 95% of the power generated by Nam Theun 2, the project was expected to raise more than US $200m. in revenue for Laos per year. A reservoir extending about 450 sq km was to be created, necessitating the relocation of 16 villages. Since its commissioning in 1971, the ageing Nam Ngum hydropower plant, located 80 km north of Vientiane, has been the primary source of electricity in Laos, with an installed capacity of 150 MW. (Japan has agreed to overhaul the power plant's turbines by 2005, at a cost of US $9.5m.) A 45-MW plant located at Xeset was completed in 1991, and generates power solely for export purposes. In April 1998 the 187-MW Thuen Hinboun hydropower project became operational, raising export earnings through the sale of the electricity generated to neighbouring Thailand. The 126-MW power project at Huay Ho and the 60-MW Nam Leuk power plant in north-western Laos were both commissioned in 2000.

Although Laos and Thailand had earlier signed a non-binding power purchase agreement, which envisaged the purchase by Thailand of 3,000 MW of Laotian electricity per year by 2006, the sharp economic downturn in Thailand following the onset of the regional economic crisis in 1997 prompted the Electricity Generating Authority of Thailand (EGAT) to revise downwards its future power demand forecasts. In 2001 EGAT intended to purchase just 1,880 MW of power per year from Laos by 2006, and 3,200 MW by 2008, with a new pricing formula that was no greater than the cost of purchasing power from independent power producers in Thailand (4.2 US cents per kWh). The revised pricing was to have a significant impact on the viability of Laos's proposed power projects, as their funding is calculated in US dollars. In addition, both Cambodia and Myanmar are also keen to export power to Thailand; indeed, Myanmar is already piping natural gas from its offshore Yadana field to a 3,645-MW power station at Ratchaburi. China is also seeking to supply electricity to Thailand, using a power transmission line that will run across Laos.

MINING

Although Laos is rich in mineral resources, the mining sector accounted for just 2.4% of industrial sector output in 2000 (compared with 10% for the construction sector). Substantial deposits of such natural resources as lignite, tin, gypsum, potash, iron ore, coal, gold, copper, silver, manganese, zinc and lead are believed to be present, along with some precious stones. However, the lack of supporting physical and legal infrastructure, together with the remote location of many of the deposits, has meant that mining has represented a challenging proposition for foreign investors. During the period of French colonial rule, tin mining was the largest single area of industry in Laos, accounting for roughly 40% of total export earnings in the years prior to the Second World War. In 1986 Laos's tin reserves were estimated at 70,000 metric tons, although some reports suggest that this may be a conservative figure. Gypsum production is centred on mines in Savannakhet Province. Potentially viable coal seams have been identified in Saravan Province and north of Vientiane, whilst high-quality iron-ore reserves are located on the Plain of Jars, 170 km north-east of the capital. The Newmont Mining Corporation of the USA signed a joint-venture agreement in 1993 to mine for gold in Vientiane Province. Rio Tinto, meanwhile, began exploration in 1992 at a wholly-owned copper and gold mine at Sepon, east of Savannakhet, under a 36-year exploration and production agreement with the Government. The mine is believed to contain 1m. tons of high grade copper, more than 3.5m. ounces of gold, and some silver, all of which can be extracted using open-pit mining techniques. In 2000 Rio Tinto sold an 80% stake in this mine, for US $22m., to Oxiana Resources of New Zealand, which conducted exploratory work and feasibility studies during 2001, prior to investing US $150m. in the mine. Construction of the mine began in late 2001, and it was scheduled to commence gold production in late 2002. Other ongoing mining projects in Laos include a granite and limestone mine in Bolikhamsai Province (awarded to a Lao-Taiwanese joint venture), a tin mine in Khammouane Province (awarded to a Lao-South Korean joint venture), a gypsum mine, also in Khammouane Province (awarded to a Thai company), and several copper and gold mines at various locations across the country. In late 2001 two Chinese companies jointly signed a US $1m. agreement to mine for zinc and copper in Oudomxay province.

Three production-sharing contracts for the exploration and production of petroleum have been signed between the Laotian Government and a number of foreign energy companies, relating to substantial concessions in the southern panhandle of the country and Vientiane Province. The first of these contracts was signed in 1989 between the Laotian Government and a consortium led by Enterprise Oil of the United Kingdom, and related to a 20,000-sq-km area in the Savannakhet basin. However, the contract was halted after initial surveying work was completed. Hunt Oil of the USA had a 28,000-sq km concession around Paksé, and undertook exploratory drilling work in the mid-1990s, whilst Monument Oil of the United Kingdom took a controlling stake in a 37,000-sq km concession in Vientiane Province, originally issued to Shlapak Development. Survey work in the southern provinces was hampered, however, by the considerable quantities of unexploded ordnance that remain scattered over large parts of the country, necessitating intensive land clearance in advance of any exploration activity. Despite fairly extensive surveys and limited exploratory drilling, no commercial reserves of petroleum or gas have yet been identified in Laos.

TRANSPORT AND COMMUNICATIONS

In 2001 transport, storage and communications accounted for almost 24% of the service sector, or nearly 6% of total GDP. In the period 1995–97 about 40% of the Government's capital expenditure budget was allocated to transport and communications, compared with 9% for education and 7% for public health. Despite this, the road and communications networks remain inadequate. Laos's national highway system is composed of about 22,300 km of roads, although a large proportion of these are in poor condition, and some can be used only during the dry season. It is estimated that about one-third of all villages in Laos, and 22% of the population, are located in areas that are not accessible by vehicles. About 4,500 km of roads have a metalled surface, while a further 7,600 km have a gravel surface. The country's river network constitutes an important element of the transport system, with a total of about 4,600 km of navigable waterways available along stretches of the Mekong and its tributaries. A number of dock facilities were constructed or upgraded during the 1980s and 1990s, and improvements were also made to some river routes through the dynamiting of rapids.

Only one of Laos's 18 provinces does not have a border with a neighbouring country, and for some of the more outlying towns, transport and trading links with the neighbouring country are often better than those with Vientiane. Laos's poor transport infrastructure continues to keep most transaction costs high, to prevent the establishment of a more integrated national economy, and to hinder regions in their attempts at the development of specialized inputs. In 1994 the Friendship Bridge (also referred to as the Mitraphab Bridge)—the first bridge to span the Mekong River, linking Laos with Thailand—was completed. This road bridge connects Nong Khai in Thailand with Tha Naleng (a relatively short distance east of Vientiane) in Laos, and was funded by the Australian Government. A second Mekong road bridge (a 1.4-km suspension bridge, costing US $50m. and funded largely by Japan), linking Paksé with Thailand's Phongthong district, was opened in August 2000. A third road bridge across the Mekong, extending 2 km and linking Savannakhet with Mukdahan in Thailand (costing US $45m., and largely funded by the Japan Bank for International Cooperation—JBIC) is scheduled for completion in 2006. The ADB envisage this third road bridge forming part of an east–west arterial road, often referred to as Route 9, which will run from the coastal port of Da Nang in Viet Nam right across Laos's southern panhandle and the Annamite cordillera into north-eastern Thailand. The main purpose of the road is to enable companies in both north-eastern Thailand and land-locked Laos to use the port at Da Nang as a conduit for exports, with the aid of favourable customs agreements at the various border crossing points. Indeed, an east–west economic corridor is being considered for the territory on either side of Route 9, in a bid to create a conducive business environment for new investment in these relatively neglected provinces of all three participating countries. A feasibility study of the east–west corridor proposal was completed by the ADB in 2001. The Governments of Laos, Thailand and China are also seeking to construct, by 2004, a trans-national highway linking Kunming, in Yunnan Province, China, with Bangkok. Whilst the sections of the road in both Thailand and China are likely to meet this deadline, by 2001 little progress had been made on the 250-km stretch of road in Laos.

In May 2000 Laos signed a pact on the navigation of the Mekong River with China, Myanmar and Thailand. After more than five years of protracted negotiations, this pact, which took effect in 2001, finally allowed for the cross-border commercial navigation of an 886-km stretch of the upper Mekong, from Simao in China's Yunnan Province to Luang Prabang in Laos. Of the 14 river ports designated under the pact, six are in Laos. Authorized vessels using this stretch of the river are no longer obliged to pay transit fees, and it is therefore anticipated that the use of the river for both goods and passenger traffic will increase substantially. It is possible that attempts will be made to widen the course of this stretch of the Mekong River, which at present can take vessels of only 50 tons during the wet season (and vessels of just 15 tons during the dry season).

In 1997 the Laotian Government announced plans to develop a comprehensive railway network in the country. However, whilst a contract was awarded to a Thai company, no timetable for the implementation of the scheme was announced. The only railway line as yet completed in Laos was a short, narrow-gauge line near the Khone waterfalls, built and operated during the colonial period, as a means to transport goods around an unnavigable part of the Mekong River. More recently, the Friendship Bridge was designed to take a single railway track, in addition to a two-lane road. Although a railway track from the Thai rail terminus at Nong Khai to the centre of the Friendship Bridge was laid in 1996, the planned continuation of the track a further 14 km into Vientiane has not occurred. The company given the concession for the railway line, Lao Railway Transportation Corpn—a joint venture between the Laotian Government (with a 25% stake) and the Sahaviriya Group of Thailand—announced in mid-1999, after having substantially revised downward its forecasts of passenger demand, that the project had been suspended. A far more ambitious plan to extend the railway line 1,000 km further north, via Luang Prabang and across the border into China (as part of a scheme ultimately to link Singapore with Europe by rail), is unlikely to be implemented in the foreseeable future. On a much more modest level, the commencement of a bus service linking Vientiane with Nong Khai and Udon Thani provinces in Thailand was agreed to by the Lao and Thai Governments in May 2002.

Given Laos's challenging terrain and poor road system, there is a significant role for a domestic airline service. With the assistance of various bilateral donors, the country's airports were steadily upgraded during the 1990s. Domestic flights provided by Lao Aviation link Vientiane with Luang Prabang, Xiangkhouang, Luang Namtha, Oudomxay, Houeisay, Sam Neua, Sayabouri, Phongsali, Xaysomboune, Savannakhet and Paksé. International flights provided by Lao Aviation currently link Vientiane with Bangkok, Chiang Mai (via Luang Prabang), Kunming, Hanoi, Ho Chi Minh City, and Phnom-Penh (via Paksé). The airline carried about 51,000 passengers on international flights in 2000. A small number of foreign airlines also fly to Vientiane, including Viet Nam Airlines, Yunnan Airlines of China and Thai Airways International. (Malaysia Airlines and SilkAir of Singapore both suspended their flights to Vientiane in 1998, as a result of low passenger volumes.) Lao Aviation's previous attempts to expand have not proved very successful, having been hampered by various financial and managerial constraints, including subsidized prices for domestic flights. The upgrading of Luang Prabang airport, including an extension of the runway, in order to permit international flights, was largely funded by Thailand and was completed in 1998. Meanwhile, the upgrading of Vientiane's Wattai airport in the late 1990s, incorporating improvements to the runway and the construction of a new terminal building, received funding from Japan. With some 70 foreign airlines transiting Lao airspace, there are about 150 flights over Laotian territory each day, generating revenue of about US $10m. per year for the Government.

Improvements to both Luang Prabang and Vientiane airports were completed in anticipation of 'Visit Laos Year', which actually spanned both 1999 and 2000. In support of this tourism campaign, visas were for the first time made available on entry at both airports and at the Friendship Bridge crossing. In 2000 Laos attracted around 480,000 tourists, which was an increase from the previous year, but below the Government's target of 600,000. Aggregate earnings from tourism in 2000 were estimated at US $23m. Having previously been very cautious in the development of its tourism industry, Laos began to place greater emphasis on tourism receipts in the late 1990s. However, this attempt to attract more tourists was not helped by a spate of bomb attacks carried out in Vientiane during 2000, nor by ongoing concerns about Lao Aviation's safety record. (In 2000 two aircraft belonging to Lao Aviation crashed, in Sam Neua and Xieng Khuang.) Even prior to 2000, tourists had been cautioned against travelling on roads traversing areas known to be occupied by anti-Government elements and bandits, including parts of Xiangkhouang, Xaysomboune and Bolikhamsai Provinces, and Route 13, which links Vientiane and Luang Prabang. Tourist numbers in Laos are also constrained by a shortage of hotel accommodation, with only about 7,000 hotel rooms available in the country.

In 1994 the Laotian Government urged the involvement of foreign investors in the country's relatively primitive telephone network. Shortly after this, Vientiane licensed a joint-venture agreement between Enterprises des Postes et Télécommunications de Laos (a state-owned enterprise) and the Shinawatra Group of Thailand, the joint venture being known as Lao Télécommunications. The company has a 25-year concession to operate all telecommunications services in Laos, including pagers, mobile phones and internet services. In a partial privatization of the telecommunications system, Lao Télécommunications has been upgrading both the fixed-line and mobile telephone networks. Although the system encompasses the whole country, in 2000 there was less than one fixed-line telephone per 100 people. Lao Télécommunications aimed to have 80,000 telephones installed by the end of 2001. The number of mobile phone users was expected to reach 25,000 in 2002, from about 12,000 in 2000. In early 2002 it was reported that Millicom International had been awarded a licence to provide a national GSM wireless network in Laos, in collaboration with the Government. Laos's two internet service providers (Globnet and Lao Télécommunications) reportedly had a combined client base of no more than 2,000 users in 2001. An ambitious international joint venture to launch a satellite—'Lao Star'—did not survive the impact of the Asian financial crisis, and in late 1999 Bangkok-based United Communications Industry (Ucom) announced that it was cancelling investment in the 'Lao Star' satellite project.

BANKING

Laos's small banking sector has experienced a number of transformations since economic reforms commenced in the late 1980s, yet it remains undeveloped. Prior to 1988, the two principal banks in Laos were the Banque d'Etat de la RDP Lao and its subsidiary, the Banque pour le Commerce Extérieur Lao (BCEL). The former was responsible for all domestic banking, including local currency issuance and public-sector accounts, and subsidized lending to state enterprises. The latter's remit extended to all foreign-trade financing, foreign-exchange reserves, foreign loans and debt. The standard format for banking in command economies was revised in 1988, in order to conform with reforms being implemented in other areas of the economy. The Banque d'Etat de la RDP Lao lost its monopoly status and became a more conventional central bank, subsequently renamed the Bank of the Lao PDR. The BCEL became one of several state-owned commercial banks, losing its monopoly over all international currency transactions. However, in 2000 BCEL continued to be the principal participant in the area of trade financing, and remained the largest of Laos's new commercial banks. Between 1988 and 1991 a further six state-run commercial banks came into operation (two in Vientiane, and one each in Luang Prabang, Savannakhet, Champasak and Xiangkhouang), formed from various branches of the former central bank. These banks were joined by an eighth state-run commercial bank in 1993, the Agricultural Promotion Bank, which was designed to provide low-cost loans to farmers and to administer micro-financing credit schemes (funded by external donors) through its substantial branch network. In 1999 six of the eight state-run commercial banks were merged back into just two entities. The three banks in the northern half of the country were merged to form Lane Xang Bank, while their three counterparts in the south were merged to form Lao May Bank. In 2001 it was further decided that these two banks should also be merged into a single entity. As a result, the Bank of the Lao PDR will govern three state-owned commercial banks (which accounted for about 70% of total bank assets in 1999), three foreign joint-venture banks (9% of total bank assets) and seven foreign bank branches (with 21% of total bank assets). One joint-venture bank (Joint Development Bank) has Thai investor participation, having commenced operations as early as 1989. Another joint-venture bank, Vientiane Commercial Bank Ltd, was established in 1993 and includes Taiwanese, Thai and Australian equity partners. The newest bank in Laos is a US $10m. joint venture between BCEL and the Bank for Investment and Development of Vietnam—one of Viet Nam's four state-run commercial banks—which commenced operations in 2000 as Lao-Viet Bank. Based in Vientiane, this bank's primary aim is to help finance burgeoning trade flows between Laos and Viet Nam, and it has opened branch offices in Champasak and Hanoi. In 2002 it was also granted permission to open a branch in Ho Chi Minh City. Both BCEL and Lao-Viet Bank joined the Worldwide Interbank Financial Telecommunications (SWIFT) payment system in late 2001, marking the entry of SWIFT into Laos for the first time. Six of the seven foreign bank branch licences issued in Laos during the early 1990s are held by Thailand's major commercial banks, with the Public Bank of Malaysia holding the remaining one. Standard Chartered Bank has operated a representative office in Vientiane since 1996.

In the view of the IMF, Laos's banking sector remains largely insolvent, despite the fairly considerable efforts of both the ADB and the World Bank to recapitalize the country's state-run commercial banks in 1994. According to the IMF, these commercial banks remained deeply insolvent, with reported aggregate non-performing loan levels of 52% (the real figure was probably markedly higher). A four-year recapitalization programme for these banks was to be implemented between 2002 and 2005, funded by the Government, in a bid to raise the capital adequacy levels of these banks to 12%. It was estimated that around US $50m. would be required for this purpose, equivalent to 3% of GDP. Most Laotian citizens do not have bank accounts, preferring instead to keep their savings in gold, foreign currency, or even livestock in rural areas. The local currency is also unwieldy for transactions, with the highest denomination note (5,000 kip) worth about 50 US cents, although the central bank announced its intention to issue new 10,000 and 20,000 kip notes during 2002. These factors explain in part why the Lao economy is highly 'dollarized', with over 75% of broad money in the form of foreign currency deposits (mostly US dollars and Thai baht), much of which is held outside the formal banking sector. Urban Lao remain generally reluctant to use bank savings accounts, owing in part to recent depreciations in the value of the local currency, the fragility of the banks themselves, and the fact that interest rates have not kept pace with high inflation in recent years. Laos has yet to develop a capital market, although it has experimented with bond issues in recent years in a bid to improve the mobilization of domestic savings and to absorb excess liquidity. In 1998 Laos issued its first retail-orientated bonds, which, in addition to providing a fixed rate of interest, also comprised a lottery component.

FOREIGN TRADE AND INVESTMENT

During the 1990s Laos consistently recorded a trade deficit of more than US $200m. In 2000 Laos's exports amounted to US $393m. (equivalent to about one-quarter of Laos's GDP). Major export-earners include wood products (30% of total exports), coffee and other agricultural products (7%), garments (20%), electricity (30%) and motorcycles (10%). Most data pertaining to Laos's external trade tend to be rather inaccurate, however, given the relatively substantial amount of smuggling and informal trading that is conducted across the country's five porous land borders.

Laos commenced garment exports in the late 1980s, and this sector of export activity developed into a major source of foreign-exchange earnings—as well as a major source of urban employment—in the 1990s, offsetting in part the decline in the export of wood-related items. Under the Generalized System of Preferences (GSP), a large proportion of garment exports are directed to EU countries. Laos's GSP status was briefly revoked in the mid-1990s, after an EU delegation found that the country was not complying with the minimum 60% local content required for goods exported under the GSP programme; however, Laos subsequently regained its GSP privileges. Thailand has traditionally been the destination for about one-quarter of Laos's total exports, ahead of all other countries in the Asia-Pacific region and beyond. However, since the mid-1990s it appears that Viet Nam may have become the leading recipient of Laos's exports, reflecting the development of closer relations between the two countries since the onset of the Asian economic crisis: exports from Laos to Viet Nam (at US $135m.) were almost double those to Thailand (US $70m.) in 1997. In 2001, according to the ADB, Laos's imports were valued at US $859.7m., compared with US $689.6m. in 1996. Major import items include consumption goods (which accounted for about 38% of total imports in 2000), fuels (13%), materials for the garment industry (11%), construction and electrical equipment (9%), and motorcycle parts (7%). According to the ADB, Thailand provided more than one-half of Laos's total imports in 2001, followed by Viet Nam, China (including Hong Kong), Singapore, Japan and France.

Having participated as an observer at meetings of the Association of South East Asian Nations (ASEAN) since 1992, Laos applied for full membership of the Association in 1993 and was inducted into the grouping in mid-1997. As part of its commitments to ASEAN, Laos must comply with a wide range of tariff reductions under the ASEAN Free Trade Area (AFTA) agreement; these include reducing tariff rates for most products imported from other ASEAN member countries to below 5% by 2005. The reduction of tariff rates will have some impact on government revenues, as around 20% of Laos's total budgetary revenues are derived from import duties. However, Laos's tariff rates have traditionally tended not to be particularly high (with the exception of cars and luxury items), and the country should be able to meet its deadline for complying with the agreement. Laos continues to seek normal trading relations (NTR) status—formerly known as 'most favoured nation' (MFN) status—with the USA, although increasing concerns in the USA regarding Laos's record on human rights and religious freedom are proving to be an obstacle in this regard.

Since the onset of the regional economic crisis, Laos's heavy reliance on Thailand as a source of investment and trade has been diminished by a reorientation towards the country's other immediate neighbours, particularly Viet Nam and China. Even relations with Myanmar have been intensified. While Vientiane's close ties with Hanoi and Beijing are most apparent in the political realm, they are also evident in the economic sphere, as exemplified by burgeoning cross-border investment and trading activity, and various other business-related initiatives. This development has been motivated in part by a shortage of foreign currency, obliging Laotian companies to enact barter and countertrade deals with other countries. Trade and investment relations between Laos and Yunnan Province in China also developed rapidly in the late 1990s, as exemplified by the construction of a number of new cement plants by Yunnan companies, in Vientiane and Saravan provinces. The Laotian and Thai Governments have been working on an economic co-operation ageement (similar to those Thailand already has with Cambodia and Myanmar)—focusing on the areas of electricity, agriculture, telecommunications and transport, and investment—since 1997. It had been hoped that the agreement would be signed during the Thai Prime Minister's visit to Vientiane in May 2000, but this did not occur. Trade relations between Laos and Thailand have not always been straightforward, partly as a result of various differences of opinion between the two Governments on non-trade issues (such as border demarcation), but also because of a perception in Vientiane that Thailand has taken unfair advantage of Laos's land-locked state to exact onerous transhipment costs on the country's exports.

Foreign direct investment (FDI) activity in Laos is regulated under the Law on the Promotion and Management of Foreign Investment, promulgated in June 1994; this law replaced a 1989 foreign investment law that heralded the opening up of the Laotian economy to foreign capital. The 1994 law outlines a relatively liberal foreign investment regime, at least in theory, with wholly foreign-owned projects permitted and an efficient licensing process in place. However, this law lacks the necessary supporting implementing regulations, and elements of it are not wholly compatible with various other Laotian laws (including the country's mining and domestic investment laws). The Foreign Investment Management Committee (FIMC) is the government agency that approves, monitors and promotes all FDI activity in Laos and reports directly to the Prime Minister's office. By early 2000 Laos had signed bilateral investment treaties with 17 countries, primarily from East Asia and Europe. By late 2001 Laos had approved 860 foreign investment projects, with an aggregate registered capital of more than US $7,000m., sourced from over 35 countries. Of these, one-half were wholly foreign-owned, and two-thirds were small-scale projects with registered capital of less than US $1m. However, only around 25%–30% of approved FDI has actually been invested in Laos, and it is likely that many projects will never be implemented. None the less, it is estimated that the country's aggregate stock of FDI increased from virtually nil in the late 1980s to around US $500m. in 1998. In terms of FDI inflows, in 1996 a peak inflow of around US $1,300m. was recorded, compared with just US $122m. in 1998. In the first nine months of 2000, however, it was reported that just 26 investment projects were licensed, with a cumulative capitalization of only US $25m. Not surprisingly perhaps, in recent years the largest single investor in Laos by far has been neighbouring Thailand (accounting for 268 projects and 74% of total FDI inflows), followed by the USA (47 projects), the Republic of Korea (42 projects), and Malaysia. (A proportion of Laos's US-sourced investment is likely to be relatively small-scale FDI projects enacted by overseas Lao now residing in the USA.) Laos's heavy dependence on Thailand for FDI inflows became apparent in 1997, when new investment pledges declined to almost nil and actual flows contracted by more than 40%, as Thailand's corporate sector was overwhelmed by the country's economic crisis.

In terms of sectoral distribution, the energy sector has witnessed the largest proportion of total FDI inflows by far, as a spectrum of foreign companies have sought to develop power generation (primarily hydropower) projects in Laos. While Laos's energy needs are small, anticipated demand from Thailand for additional electricity supplies has stimulated business interest in generating power for export from Laos. As at late 1998, about 65% of total approved foreign investment in Laos pertained to the hydropower sector (in connection with just seven projects, only two of which had been completed by 2000); the telecommunications and transport sector accounted for 9% of total approved foreign investment at that date, followed by the hotel and tourism sector (9%), and industry and handicrafts (7%). As measured by the number of foreign investment project licences issued, the industry and handicrafts sector has received 160 projects, while the services sector has secured 153 projects (with 124 projects in trade, 89 in agriculture, 87 in garments, 76 in processing and construction, 45 in hotels and tourism, 39 in consulting, 31 in petroleum and mining, and 17 in communications). As a percentage of gross fixed capital formation, FDI inflows in Laos have averaged 18.7% between 1995 and 1999. As a member of ASEAN, Laos will be expected to comply with the ASEAN Investment Area (AIA) initiative, which was launched in 1998. Under this agreement, Laos must provide all ASEAN investors with both 'national treatment' and access to most of the country's business sectors by 2010. Laos is also committed to an unrestricted flow of foreign investment activity, including national treatment and open access to all business sectors for foreign investors beyond ASEAN member countries, by 2020.

INTERNATIONAL AID AND DEBT

The economy is heavily dependent on external assistance and aid, both from multilateral agencies and bilateral donors. International donations account for around 17%–18% of the country's total GDP. In particular, external grants fund both Laos's current-account deficit and a proportion of the country's public finances, with budget revenues rarely exceeding more than 50% of government expenditure. In 1998 the current-account deficit and the budget deficit were each equivalent to around 10% of total GDP. In the case of the latter, of the total tax revenue collected by the Government in 2000, about 10% was from taxes on trade (import duties), 20% from turnover tax, 22% from profit and income tax, 23% from excise duties, 8% from timber royalties, and 7% from overflight fees (collected from airlines using Laotian airspace). Thus, overseas grants amounted to more than the aggregate tax revenues collected from trade, excise duties, timber royalties and overflight fees combined. Indeed, tax revenues have generally been decreasing since 1996, owing in part to a weakening tax administration. Laos was expected to introduce a new value-added tax in 2003. As at the end of 1998, Laos's aggregate debt obligations (excluding Russian debt) amounted to US $1,040m., equivalent to about 85% of the country's GDP. This compared with estimated foreign-exchange reserves (including gold) of US $133m. in 2001 (equivalent to around 2.4 months of import cover), up from US $106m. in 1999. Laos's debt-servicing ratio, as a ratio of total goods and services exports, was estimated to be 10.4% in 2001. Whilst much of this debt is on concessional terms to various multilateral agencies, it also includes some commercial debt (for example, US $160m. incurred during the construction of the Theun Hinboun power plant). External debt statistics produced by the World Bank, the IMF, the OECD and the Bank for International Settlements indicate that Laos's total bank loans stood at US $79m. at the end of 1999, and that multilateral claims amounted to US $1,020m. In 1998 Laos's total external debt-service burden was US $52m. (compared with US $25m. in 1996), of which about one-half was interest payments and the other half amortization of principal. Of the principal, 28% was to bilateral lenders, 44% was to multilateral agencies, and 28% to former socialist bloc countries (primarily Russia). Of the interest, none had been paid to the former socialist countries for several years, 69% was owed to bilateral lenders and 31% to multilateral agencies. Vientiane continues to discuss with Moscow the renegotiation of Laos's considerable debt to Russia, around US $1,300m., having suspended rouble debt payments in 1997.

Given the importance of the agricultural sector to the whole economy, it is not surprising that a significant proportion of total external assistance is focused on this sector. In 1999 there were reported to be around 80 agriculture-orientated aid projects active in Laos, with aggregate funds of US $140m. The ADB's GMS programme has also contributed to Laos's economic development plans since its commencement in 1993. The GMS programme—which also encompasses Cambodia, Myanmar, Thailand, Viet Nam, and Yunnan Province in China—has sought to bring private-sector participants together with external assistance agencies to conduct a series of economic and business initiatives in the participant countries. These initiatives have ranged from broader tourism, trade and investment and human resource development projects to very specific power generation, road and rail projects. Meanwhile, in addition to supporting the unexploded ordnance clearing programme in Laos, the USA has also contributed to attempts to eradicate the production and trafficking of opium in the country. The USA continues to assist in the establishment of counter-narcotics enforcement units in each of the relevant provinces, as well as crop control and development projects in Houaphanh and Phongsali Provinces.

In recent years both multilateral agencies and bilateral donors have expressed their disappointment at the evident deceleration in the pace of economic reform in Laos. The IMF, in particular, has urged an increase in the pace of financial reform and business liberalization initiatives in the country, after deciding not to enact a new loan programme after the 1993–96 'enhanced structural adjustment facility' came to an end. Even Japan has been withholding lending until more stringent economic reforms are implemented. In 2000 Tokyo sent a delegation to assist the Laotian Government in devising a macro-economic development strategy for the country. Japanese grant aid—including support for the new National University of Laos—continues, however. A report by the ADB cited 'inadequate government capacity and commitment to pushing forward economic reforms', as well as 'insufficient transparency and accountability', as factors contributing to the undeveloped state of the economy of Laos. Furthermore, a recent UNDP survey of donor perceptions noted that the 'burdensome government decision-making process and the lack of transparency' are becoming 'matters of serious concern'. Since the external assistance agencies and donors play such an important role in supporting the Laotian economy, providing official development assistance that is equivalent to between 15% and 25% of GDP, their increasing disenchantment with the Government's lack of progress in instituting new reforms could, if not arrested, pose significant problems for Vientiane. In the same context, mounting concern over Laos's human rights record and the Government's treatment of political protesters could also indirectly prompt a further contraction in external assistance to the country. Notwithstanding this stance adopted by multilateral lending agencies and donors, the IMF announced in April 2001 that it was to implement a new three-year US $40.2m. Poverty Reduction and Growth Facility for Laos, which was generally designed to strengthen macro-economic stability and reduce poverty 'through growth with equity'. More specifically, the programme attached to the loan provided for 'continued fiscal and monetary restraint and is centred on the implementation of revenue enhancement, restraining credit of the central bank, restructuring state-owned commercial banks, commercializing large enterprises, and developing the enterprise sector'.

PROBLEMS AND PROSPECTS

There are clear indications that the pace of economic reform in Laos decelerated considerably after 1996–97, although there were some signs of a possible return of reforming momentum in 2001. This slowdown was attributable in part to the impact on the country of the regional economic crisis, which has led to apparent indecision within the Laotian leadership over whether further economic liberalization represents the correct way to proceed. It may also stem, however, from recent changes in the profile of the leadership and the development of much greater military representation in the senior ranks of the LPRP: by 2000, all but one of the eight members of the Politburo were serving or retired military men. The removal of one of the leadership's most ardent advocates of economic liberalization, Khamphoui Keoboualapha, from both the LPRP's Politburo and Central Committee in 1996 indicated the extent to which the Government's drive towards economic reform was beginning to lose momentum by the mid-1990s, even prior to the regional economic crisis. Khamphoui returned to the Government a few years later, as Deputy Prime Minister and Minister of Finance, but was removed from the latter post in August 1999 after having failed to prevent the collapse of the currency; the Governor of the central bank, Cheuang Sombounkhan, was also removed from his post. A parallel deceleration in the pace of the economic reform programme in Viet Nam indicated that, while both countries had achieved relative success in the enactment of the first two stages of economic reforms (in 1979 and 1986, respectively), both Governments found it more difficult to proceed with the third stage of reform measures.

The sharp economic deterioration in neighbouring Thailand in 1997 undoubtedly had an adverse impact on Laos, most notably through a very sharp downturn in the value of the kip against both the US dollar and the Thai baht. Relative to the US dollar, the kip lost 80% of its value in the two years following the onset of the regional economic crisis in July 1997. Not all of the depreciation in the value of the kip can be attributed directly to contagion from Thailand, however: a fairly large spending programme was implemented by Vientiane at this time in a bid substantially to increase the amount of dry season paddy through a mass acquisition of water pumps. Under this programme, funding from the central bank was directed both to state enterprises to enable them to import the pumps, and as credit to farmers to permit them to buy the imported pumps. Thus, at a time when fiscal restraint might have been most appropriate in order to restore confidence in the Laotian currency and economy, the Government embarked upon an expansionary monetary programme to fund the (off-budget) dry season irrigation programme. This, together with the Government's issuing of higher-denomination currency notes and a vigorous campaign against unlicensed foreign-exchange dealers (which prompted some Lao to fear an impending revaluation of the currency), served further to erode popular confidence in the local currency. The resulting panic exacerbated the precipitous decline in the kip, as Lao citizens and companies alike sought to convert into foreign currency or gold. Even though Laos did not suffer the massive political upheaval witnessed in Indonesia following the onset of the regional economic crisis, the damage done to the value of the kip in 1998–99 was even greater than that inflicted on the rupiah, and the Laotian currency depreciated from around 1,500 to more than 7,500 to the US dollar within just a few years. This decline in the value of the currency resulted in triple-digit inflation in 1998–99, as the price of imported goods rose sharply. Consequently, the spending power of the urban populace decreased considerably, forcing the Government to reduce the length of the working week for civil servants in order that they could devote more time to the pursuit of secondary incomes. After having fallen to as low as 10,000 to the US dollar at one point in 1999, the exchange rate for the kip stabilized at around 7,500–8,000 to the US dollar. By late 2001 the kip was trading at around 9,500 to the US dollar. According to the ADB, the rate of inflation declined from 128.4% in 1999 to 23.2% in 2000, and was just 7.5% by the end of 2001. Such a commendable contraction in the inflation rate has allowed the Government to embark on upward price adjustments for heavily subsidized water (by 100%), electricity and domestic aviation tariffs, as well as a 25% increase in salaries for state employees (partially to offset the decline in their real income during 1998–99) at the beginning of 2002.

Since the mid-1990s, Laos's post-socialist economic development has been focused less on the transition of the economy from one guided by central planning to one led by market forces, and more on the straightforward challenge of general economic progress for one of Asia's least developed countries. While the leadership of the Lao PDR remains the LPRP, and it articulates its policies in the vernacular of an avowedly-socialist state, in the economic sphere little evidence remains of the initial post-1975 socialist zeal. The economic challenges currently facing Laos are those commonly experienced by numerous less-developed countries in Asia and beyond: namely, the identification of policy prescriptions to address the problem of economic under-achievement; the coherent and competent enactment of those policies; the tackling of bureaucracy and corruption; and the radical improvement of the human development level of the country. Widening disparities in income between rural and urban Lao—and even between those living in rural upland and lowland areas—need to be addressed, particularly where they are congruent with ethnic divisions. The better integration of the activities of subsistence farmers into the national economy, the diversification of crops, the creation of specialized markets and the improvement of agricultural output levels in general are also required if the living standards of the Lao populace as a whole are to be improved. To date, the benefits of the economic reform process in Laos have mostly been witnessed in the urban areas of the country, largely through advances made in the service and industry sectors. There is, however, a need to ensure that the effects of future development initiatives are extended to the rural areas, both upland and lowland, through parallel advances in the agricultural sector. The challenges facing Laos in the construction of a more effective domestic transport system and communications infrastructure—and thereby the reduction of the high transaction costs faced by the agricultural sector—across a sparsely-populated (an average of just 22 people per sq km) and topographically-demanding country do not make this an easy task. Furthermore, economic development will also require a strengthening of the capacities of numerous state institutions, a move towards good governance, improved macro-economic management, and the enforcement of a relatively new legislative regime. The need to improve the education and skills levels of the country's populace remains a particularly critical issue in relation to the sustained economic development of Laos (which produces around 3,000 higher education graduates per year). In the foreseeable future, however, it appears that the Laotian economy will continue to depend in large part on external assistance.

At the LPRP's Seventh Party Congress, held in March 2001, the Government announced its next five-year plan and its socio-economic development strategy to 2020. By that year Laos aimed to progress from its current status as a less developed country. Under the five-year plan, the Government aimed to record GDP growth of 7.0%–7.5% per year, to keep inflation in single figures, to restrain the budget deficit to below 5% of GDP, and to increase average per caput income to US $500–US $550. Targets of 4%–5% growth per year for the agricultural sector, 10%–11% for the industrial and handicrafts sector, and 8%–9% for the services sector were presented under the plan. Both opium production and swidden activity were to be eradicated, the latter by 2003. Whether these commendable targets can be achieved, however, remains to be seen. In 2001 the Government also embarked on a decentralization initiative, granting more autonomy to the provinces, and placing greater budgetary planning responsibilities at the district level. A similar decentralization scheme had been attempted in 1986, but was subsequently reversed in 1991 after a sharp contraction in tax revenues. It will be interesting to see whether this second attempt at decentralization proves more successful, or results in another dramatic downturn in tax receipts. The Government is also considering amending the 1991 Constitution in ways that should make it adhere more closely to the new socio-economic development strategy. However, the pace of economic reform in Laos will remain gradual and relatively cautious, as the Government remains mindful of the social and political consequences.

Statistical Survey

Source (unless otherwise stated): Service National de la Statistique, Vientiane.

Area and Population

AREA, POPULATION AND DENSITY

Area (sq km)	236,800*
Population (census results)	
1 March 1985	3,584,803
1 March 1995	
Males	2,265,867
Females	2,315,391
Total	4,581,258
Population (official estimate at mid-year)	
2000	5,218,000
Density (per sq km) at mid-2000	22.0

* 91,400 sq miles.

PROVINCES (official estimates, mid-1995)

	Area (sq km)	Population	Density (per sq km)
Vientiane (municipality)	3,920	531,800	135.6
Phongsali	16,270	153,400	9.4
Luang Namtha	9,325	115,200	12.4
Oudomxay	15,370	211,300	13.7
Bokeo	6,196	114,900	18.5
Luang Prabang	16,875	367,200	21.8
Houaphanh	16,500	247,300	15.0
Sayabouri	16,389	293,300	17.9
Xiangkhouang	15,880	201,200	12.7
Vientiane	15,927	286,800	18.0
Bolikhamsai	14,863	164,900	11.1
Khammouane	16,315	275,400	16.9
Savannakhet	21,774	674,900	31.0
Saravan	10,691	258,300	24.2
Sekong	7,665	64,200	8.4
Champasak	15,415	503,300	32.7
Attopu	10,320	87,700	8.5
Special region	7,105	54,200	7.6
Total	236,800	4,605,300	19.4

PRINCIPAL TOWNS (population in 1985)

Vientiane (capital)	377,000	Luang Prabang	68,000
Savannakhet	97,000	Paksé	47,000

Source: Statistisches Bundesamt, Wiesbaden, Germany.

1995 (at census of March): Vientiane 528,109.

Mid-2001 (UN estimate, including suburbs): Vientiane 663,000 (Source: UN, *World Urbanization Prospects: The 2001 Revision*).

BIRTHS AND DEATHS (UN estimates, annual averages)

	1985-90	1990–95	1995–2000
Birth rate (per 1,000)	44.6	41.3	38.2
Death rate (per 1,000)	18.2	15.8	14.1

Source: UN, *World Population Prospects: The 2000 Revision*.

Birth rate (1999): 38.8 per 1,000.
Death rate (1999): 13.0 per 1,000.

Source: UN, *Statistical Yearbook for Asia and the Pacific*.

Expectation of life (WHO estimates, years at birth, 2000): Males 52.2; Females 56.1 (Source: WHO, *World Health Report*).

ECONOMICALLY ACTIVE POPULATION
(ILO estimates, '000 persons at mid-1980)

	Males	Females	Total
Agriculture, etc.	717	675	1,393
Industry	79	51	130
Services	193	123	316
Total labour force	990	849	1,839

Source: ILO, *Economically Active Population Estimates and Projections, 1950–2025*.

Mid-2000 (estimates in '000): Agriculture, etc. 2,007; Total labour force 2,625 (Source: FAO).

Health and Welfare

KEY INDICATORS

Fertility (births per woman, 2000)	5.1
Under-5 mortality rate (per 1,000 live births, 2000)	105
HIV/AIDS (% of persons aged 15–49, 2001)	<0.10
Physicians (per 1,000 head, 1996)	0.24
Hospital beds (per 1,000 head, 1990)	2.57
Health expenditure (1998): US $ per head (PPP)	50
% of GDP	4.1
public (% of total)	37.1
Access to adequate water (% of persons, 2000)	90
Access to adequate sanitation (% of persons, 2000)	46
Human Development Index (2000): ranking	143
value	0.485

For sources and definitions, see explanatory note on p. vi.

Agriculture

PRINCIPAL CROPS ('000 metric tons)

	1998	1999	2000
Rice (paddy)	1,675	2,103	2,202
Maize	110	96	117
Potatoes*	33	33	35
Sweet potatoes	108	81	118
Cassava (Manioc)*	70	71	71
Sugar cane	170	174	297
Pulses*	13	13	13
Soybeans	4	6	5
Groundnuts (in shell)	15	13	13
Sesame seed	4	5	5*
Vegetables and melons	150	269	288*
Fruit (excl. melons)	171	173	173*
Coffee (green)	17	18	24
Cotton (lint)	8	4	11
Tobacco (leaves)	26	23	33

* FAO estimate(s).

Source: FAO.

LIVESTOCK ('000 head, year ending September)

	1998	1999	2000
Horses*	27	28	28
Cattle	1,127	944	1,145
Buffaloes	1,093	992	1,008
Pigs	1,432	1,036	1,326
Goats	122	94	112
Chickens	12,176	11,215	13,095
Ducks	1,040	1,351	1,630*

* FAO estimate(s).

Source: FAO.

LIVESTOCK PRODUCTS ('000 metric tons)

	1998	1999	2000
Beef and veal	15	19	16
Buffalo meat	16	19	17
Pig meat	31	32	33
Poultry meat	11	11	13
Cows' milk	6	6	6
Hen eggs	8	9	10
Cattle and buffalo hides (fresh)	4	4	4

Source: FAO.

Forestry

ROUNDWOOD REMOVALS ('000 cubic metres, excl. bark)

	1997	1998	1999
Sawlogs, veneer logs and logs for sleepers	560	442	734
Other industrial wood	125	129	132
Fuel wood	3,803	3,902	4,003
Total	4,488	4,473	4,869

2000: Production as in 1999 (FAO estimates).

Source: FAO.

SAWNWOOD PRODUCTION
('000 cubic metres, incl. railway sleepers)

	1997	1998	1999
Coniferous (softwood)	209	100	150
Broadleaved (hardwood)	351	150	200
Total	560	250	350

2000: Production as in 1999 (FAO estimates).

Source: FAO.

Fishing

('000 metric tons, live weight)

	1997	1998	1999
Capture	26.0	26.8	30.0
Cyprinids*	4.0	4.0	4.5
Other freshwater fishes*	22.0	22.8	25.5
Aquaculture*	14.0	14.1	30.4
Common carp*	1.8	1.8	3.9
Roho labeo*	1.8	1.8	3.8
Mrigal carp*	1.8	1.8	3.8
Bighead carp*	1.8	1.8	3.8
Catla*	1.8	1.8	3.8
Grass carp (White amur)*	1.8	1.8	3.8
Silver carp*	1.8	1.8	3.8
Nile tilapia*	1.8	1.8	3.8
Total catch	40.0	40.9	60.4

* FAO estimates.

Source: FAO, *Yearbook of Fishery Statistics*.

Mining

('000 metric tons, unless otherwise indicated)

	1999	2000	2001*
Coal (all grades)	78.8	121.3	125.0
Gemstones ('000 carats)	4,013.3	150.0*	100.0
Gypsum	134.7	147.7	150.0
Salt	1.7	1.5	1.6
Tin (metric tons)†	404	414	400

* Estimated production.

† Figures refer to metal content.

Source: US Geological Survey.

Industry

SELECTED PRODUCTS

	1998	1999	2000
Beer ('000 hectolitres)	332	356	399
Soft drinks ('000 hectolitres)	125	123	117
Cigarettes (million packs)	55	38	41
Clothing ('000 pieces)	23,000	n.a.	n.a.
Wood furniture (million kips)	7,155	12,725	13,800
Plastic products (metric tons)	3,225	3,900	4,225
Detergent (metric tons)	912	879	800
Agricultural tools ('000)	4	4	4
Nails (metric tons)	624	691	825
Bricks (million)	53	n.a.	n.a.
Electric energy (million kWh)	1,996	2,436	3,036
Tobacco (metric tons)	1,000	757	1,190
Plywood ('000 sheets)	n.a.	2,086	2,125

Source: IMF, *Lao People's Democratic Republic: Selected Issues and Statistical Appendix* (March 2002).

Finance

CURRENCY AND EXCHANGE RATES

Monetary Units

100 at (cents) = 1 new kip.

Sterling, Dollar and Euro Equivalents (31 May 2002)

£1 sterling = 14,092.1 new kips;
US $1 = 9,608.0 new kips;
€1 = 9,019.0 new kips;
100,000 new kips = £7.096 = $10.408 = €11.088.

Average Exchange Rate (new kips per US $)

1999 7,102.03
2000 7,887.64
2001 8,954.58

Note: In September 1995 a policy of 'floating' exchange rates was adopted, with commercial banks permitted to set their rates.

GENERAL BUDGET ('000 million new kips, year ending 30 September)*

Revenue†	1998/99	1999/2000‡	2000/01§
Tax revenue	745	1,323	1,742
Profits tax	80	172	316
Income tax	70	116	182
Agricultural/land tax	5	7	13
Turnover tax	160	252	379
Taxes on foreign trade	123	182	254
Import duties	99	138	192
Export duties	24	44	62
Excise tax	157	211	336
Timber royalties	89	288	115
Hydro royalties	17	22	21
Other revenue	184	293	452
Payment for depreciation or dividend transfers	22	43	212
Leasing income	11	15	20
Overflight	40	122	125
Interest or amortization	89	80	40
Total	929	1,615	2,194

Expenditure	1998/99	1999/2000‡	2000/01§
Current expenditure	539	1,031	1,417
Wages and salaries	182	348	419
Transfers	58	142	269
Materials and supplies	132	197	306
Interest	68	103	196
Timber royalty-financed expenditure	89	184	115
Capital expenditure and net lending	1,270	1,623	1,965
Local	297	506	805
Loan-financed projects	478	792	780
Grant-funded projects	519	403	420
Onlending (net)	–24	–78	–40
Total (incl. others)	1,809	2,655	3,382

* Since 1992 there has been a unified budget covering the operations of the central Government, provincial administrations and state enterprises.

† Excluding grants received ('000 million new kips): 532 in 1998/99; 403 in 1999/2000‡; 420 in 2000/01§.

‡ Estimates.

§ Budget forecasts.

Source: IMF, *Lao People's Democratic Republic: Selected Issues and Statistical Appendix* (March 2002).

INTERNATIONAL RESERVES (US $ million at 31 December)

	1999	2000	2001
Gold*	4.10	0.59	2.42
IMF special drawing rights	0.07	0.10	3.42
Foreign exchange	101.12	138.87	127.51
Total	105.29	139.56	133.35

* National valuation.

Source: IMF, *International Financial Statistics*.

MONEY SUPPLY (million new kips at 31 December)

	1999	2000	2001
Currency outside banks	77,785	67,830	113,080
Demand deposits at commercial banks	141,193	272,230	256,880
Total (incl. others)	218,981	344,351	371,840

Source: IMF, *International Financial Statistics*.

COST OF LIVING (Consumer Price Index for Vientiane; base: 1995 = 100)

	1999	2000	2001
All items	628.7	786.4	847.8

Source: IMF, *International Financial Statistics*.

NATIONAL ACCOUNTS

Expenditure on the Gross Domestic Product
(million new kips at current prices)

	1989	1990	1991
Government final consumption expenditure	34,929	61,754	69,499
Private final consumption expenditure	414,639	558,437	647,826
Increase in stocks / Gross fixed capital formation	55,560	75,572	91,435
Total domestic expenditure	505,128	695,763	808,760
Exports of goods and services	49,421	69,411	73,359
Less Imports of goods and services	128,613	150,154	156,550
GDP in purchasers' values	425,936	615,020	725,569
GDP at constant 1987 prices	213,769	228,105	237,098

Source: World Bank, *Historically Planned Economies: A Guide to the Data.*

Gross Domestic Product by Economic Activity
(million new kips at current prices)

	1999	2000	2001
Agriculture, hunting, forestry and fishing	5,507,539	7,127,372	7,974,629
Mining and quarrying	53,625	67,033	73,150
Manufacturing	1,744,051	2,305,848	2,772,616
Electricity, gas and water	246,919	423,331	450,414
Construction	276,090	309,341	376,985
Wholesale and retail trade, restaurants and hotels	991,694	1,283,970	1,502,018
Transport, storage and communications	590,780	794,024	929,723
Finance, insurance, real estate and business services	57,478	105,170	134,618
Public administration	219,394	392,690	496,698
Other services	566,056	756,786	820,392
GDP at factor cost	10,253,626	13,565,564	15,531,241
Indirect taxes *less* subsidies	74,990	105,728	138,747
GDP in purchasers' values	10,328,616	13,671,292	15,669,988

Source: Asian Development Bank, *Key Indicators of Developing Asian and Pacific Countries.*

BALANCE OF PAYMENTS (US $ million)

	1997	1998	1999
Exports of goods f.o.b.	318.3	342.1	338.2
Imports of goods f.o.b.	–601.3	–506.8	–527.7
Trade balance	–283.0	–164.7	–189.5
Exports of services	105.8	145.0	130.0
Imports of services	–110.5	–95.5	–51.8
Balance on goods and services	–287.7	–115.2	–111.3
Other income received	11.1	6.9	10.5
Other income paid	–28.9	–41.8	–49.9
Balance on goods, services and income	–305.5	–150.1	–150.7
Current transfers received	—	—	80.2
Current transfers paid	—	—	–50.6
Current balance	–305.5	–150.1	–121.1
Capital account (net)	33.4	43.1	—
Other investment assets	39.5	–22.8	–43.2
Other investment liabilities	–36.0	–20.6	–3.7
Net errors and omissions	–100.5	–103.8	–165.1
Overall balance	–369.1	–254.2	–333.1

Source: IMF, *International Financial Statistics*.

External Trade

PRINCIPAL COMMODITIES (US $ million)

Imports c.i.f.	1998	1999	2000
Investment goods	277	184	153
Machinery and equipment	44	21	9
Vehicles*	39	36	14
Fuel*	62	37	79
Construction/electrical equipment	81	91	51
Consumption goods	234	253	226
Materials for garments industry	67	67	67
Motorcycle parts for assembly	17	38	42
Gold and silver†	1	2	0
Electricity	6	9	9
Fuel purchased abroad by Lao carriers	2	2	2
Total	553	554	591

* Estimates based on the assumption that 50% of total are consumption goods.

† Including gold for re-export.

Exports f.o.b.	1998	1999	2000
Wood products	115.4	105.6	119.9
Logs	10.5	n.a.	69.0
Timber	87.4	n.a.	41.3
Others*	17.5	n.a.	9.6
Coffee	48.0	15.2	15.1
Other agricultural products	8.4	8.3	12.7
Manufactures†	10.1	27.9	11.0
Garments	70.2	72.0	76.9
Motorcycles	17.8	38.4	41.0
Electricity	66.5	90.5	111.6
Fuel purchases by foreign carriers	0.6	0.8	0.9
Total (incl others)	337.0	362.8	393.0

* Including semi-finished and finished products.

† Excluding garments and wood products.

Source: IMF, *Lao People's Democratic Republic: Selected Issues and Statistical Appendix* (March 2002).

PRINCIPAL TRADING PARTNERS (US $ million)

Imports	1999	2000	2001
China, People's Republic	24.4	37.9	49.4
France	7.6	27.5	8.4
Germany	9.5	3.6	2.7
Hong Kong	11.0	7.9	9.8
Japan	24.9	23.6	12.6
Korea, Republic	11.9	4.9	8.4
Singapore	37.0	33.6	28.9
Thailand*	452.0	419.0	451.7
United Kingdom	8.7	6.1	3.6
Viet Nam	181.8	209.1	230.8
Total (incl. others)	807.6	816.8	859.7

Exports	1999	2000	2001
Belgium	13.5	13.6	12.4
China, People's Republic	8.7	6.7	—
France	18.2	27.1	33.7
Germany	27.0	20.8	23.4
Italy	5.9	9.2	11.1
Japan	12.3	10.9	6.6
Netherlands	8.9	10.0	9.0
Thailand*	51.6	68.9	81.0
United Kingdom	12.5	7.2	8.4
USA	12.6	8.8	3.6
Viet Nam	179.4	206.4	227.0
Total (incl. others)	320.6	502.5	544.9

* Trade with Thailand may be overestimated, as it may include goods in transit to and from other countries.

Source: Asian Development Bank, *Key Indicators of Developing Asian and Pacific Countries*.

Transport

ROAD TRAFFIC (motor vehicles in use at 31 December, estimates)

	1994	1995	1996
Passenger cars	18,240	17,280	16,320
Buses and coaches	440	n.a.	n.a.
Lorries and vans	7,920	6,020	4,200
Motorcycles and mopeds	169,000	200,000	231,000

Source: International Road Federation, *World Road Statistics*.

SHIPPING

Inland Waterways (traffic)

	1993	1994	1995
Freight ('000 metric tons)	290	876	898
Freight ton-kilometres (million)	18.7	40.8	98.8
Passengers ('000)	703	898	652
Passenger-kilometres (million)	110.2	60.6	24.3

Source: Ministry of Communications, Transport, Post and Construction.

Merchant Fleet (registered at 31 December)

	1999	2000	2001
Number of vessels	1	1	1
Displacement ('000 grt)	2.4	2.4	2.4

Source: Lloyd's Register-Fairplay, *World Fleet Statistics*.

CIVIL AVIATION (traffic on scheduled services)

	1996	1997	1998
Kilometres flown (million)	1	1	1
Passengers carried ('000)	125	125	124
Passenger-kilometres (million)	48	48	48
Total ton-kilometres (million)	5	5	5

Source: UN, *Statistical Yearbook*.

Tourism

FOREIGN VISITOR ARRIVALS (incl. excursionists)

Country of Nationality	1998	1999	2000
China, People's Republic	15,802	20,269	28,215
France	17,863	19,960	24,534
Japan	12,936	14,860	20,687
Thailand	273,095	356,105	442,564
United Kingdom	8,902	12,298	15,204
USA	20,174	24,672	32,869
Viet Nam	78,216	71,748	68,751
Total (incl. others)	500,200	614,278	737,208

Source: World Tourism Organization: *Yearbook of Tourism Statistics*.

Tourism receipts (US $ million): 80 in 1998; 97 in 1999; 114 in 2000 (Source: World Bank).

Communications Media

	1999	2000	2001
Television receivers ('000 in use) .	51	52	n.a
Telephones ('000 main lines in use)	35.1	40.9	52.6
Mobile cellular telephones ('000 subscribers)	12.1	12.7	29.5
Personal computers ('000 in use)	12	14	16
Internet users ('000)	2.0	6.0	10.0

Radio receivers ('000 in use): 730 in 1997.
Facsimile machines (number in use): 500 in 1994*.
Book production (1995): Titles 88; copies ('000) 995.
Daily newspapers (1996): 3 (average circulation 18,000).
Non-daily newspapers (1988, estimates): 4 (average circulation 20,000).

* Estimate (Source: UN, *Statistical Yearbook*).

Sources (unless otherwise specified): International Telecommunication Union; UNESCO, *Statistical Yearbook*.

Education

(1996/97)

	Institu-tions	Teachers	Students		
			Males	Females	Total
Pre-primary . . .	695	2,173	18,502	19,349	37,851
Primary. . . .	7,896	25,831	438,241	348,094	786,335
Secondary					
General . . .	n.a.	10,717	108,996	71,164	180,160
Vocational* . .	n.a.	808	3,731	1,928	5,659
Teacher training .	n.a.	197	960	780	1,740
University level . .	n.a.	456	3,509	1,764	5,273
Other higher . .	n.a.	913	5,378	2,081	7,459

* Data for 1995/96.

Source: UNESCO, *Statistical Yearbook*.

Adult literacy rate (UNESCO estimates): 48.7% (males 64.1%; females 33.2%) in 2000. (Source: UN Development Programme, *Human Development Report*).

Directory

The Constitution

The new Constitution was unanimously endorsed by the Supreme People's Assembly on 14 August 1991. Its main provisions are summarized below:

POLITICAL SYSTEM

The Lao People's Democratic Republic (Lao PDR) is an independent, sovereign and united country and is indivisible.

The Lao PDR is a people's democratic state. The people's rights are exercised and ensured through the functioning of the political system, with the Lao People's Revolutionary Party as its leading organ. The people exercise power through the National Assembly, which functions in accordance with the principle of democratic centralism.

The State respects and protects all lawful activities of Buddhism and the followers of other religious faiths.

The Lao PDR pursues a foreign policy of peace, independence, friendship and co-operation. It adheres to the principles of peaceful co-existence with other countries, based on mutual respect for independence, sovereignty and territorial integrity.

SOCIO-ECONOMIC SYSTEM

The economy is market-orientated, with intervention by the State. The State encourages all economic sectors to compete and co-operate in the expansion of production and trade.

Private ownership of property and rights of inheritance are protected by the State.

The State authorizes the operation of private schools and medical services, while promoting the expansion of public education and health services.

FUNDAMENTAL RIGHTS AND OBLIGATIONS OF CITIZENS

Lao citizens, irrespective of their sex, social status, education, faith and ethnic group, are equal before the law.

Lao citizens aged 18 years and above have the right to vote, and those over 21 years to be candidates, in elections.

Lao citizens have freedom of religion, speech, press and assembly, and freedom to establish associations and to participate in demonstrations which do not contradict the law.

THE NATIONAL ASSEMBLY

The National Assembly is the legislative organ, which also oversees the activities of the administration and the judiciary. Members of the National Assembly are elected for a period of five years by universal adult suffrage. The National Assembly elects its own Standing Committee, which consists of the Chairman and Vice-Chairman of the National Assembly (and thus also of the National Assembly Standing Committee) and a number of other members. The National Assembly convenes its ordinary session twice annually. The National Assembly Standing Committee may convene an extraordinary session of the National Assembly if it deems this necessary. The National Assembly is empowered to amend the Constitution; to endorse, amend or abrogate laws; to elect or remove the President of State and Vice-Presidents of State, as proposed by the Standing Committee of the National Assembly; to adopt motions expressing 'no confidence' in the Government; to elect or remove the President of the People's Supreme Court, on the recommendation of the National Assembly Standing Committee.

THE PRESIDENT OF STATE

The President of State, who is also Head of the Armed Forces, is elected by the National Assembly for a five-year tenure. Laws adopted by the National Assembly must be promulgated by the President of State not later than 30 days after their enactment. The President is empowered to appoint or dismiss the Prime Minister and members of the Government, with the approval of the National Assembly; to appoint government officials at provincial and municipal levels; and to promote military personnel, on the recommendation of the Prime Minister.

THE GOVERNMENT

The Government is the administrative organ of the State. It is composed of the Prime Minister, Deputy Prime Ministers and Ministers or Chairmen of Committees (which are equivalent to Ministries), who are appointed by the President, with the approval of the National Assembly, for a term of five years. The Government implements the Constitution, laws and resolutions adopted by the National Assembly and state decrees and acts of the President of State. The Prime Minister is empowered to appoint Deputy Ministers and Vice-Chairmen of Committees, and lower-level government officials.

LOCAL ADMINISTRATION

The Lao PDR is divided into provinces, municipalities, districts and villages. Provincial governors and mayors of municipalities are appointed by the President of State. Deputy provincial governors, deputy mayors and district chiefs are appointed by the Prime Minister. Administration at village level is conducted by village heads.

THE JUDICIARY

The people's courts comprise the People's Supreme Court, the people's provincial and municipal courts, the people's district courts and military courts. The President of the People's Supreme Court and the Public Prosecutor-General are elected by the National Assembly, on the recommendation of the National Assembly Standing Committee. The Vice-President of the People's Supreme

Court and the judges of the people's courts at all levels are appointed by the National Assembly Standing Committee.

The Government

HEAD OF STATE

President of State: Gen. KHAMTAY SIPHANDONE (took office February 1998).

Vice-President: Lt-Gen. CHOUMMALI SAIGNASON.

COUNCIL OF MINISTERS
(September 2002)

Prime Minister: BOUNGNANG VOLACHIT.

Deputy Prime Minister and President of the State Planning Committee: THONGLOUN SISOLIT.

Deputy Prime Minister and Minister of Foreign Affairs: SOMSAVAT LENGSAVAT.

Deputy Prime Minister: Maj.-Gen. ASANG LAOLI.

Minister of Defence: Maj.-Gen. DOUANGCHAI PHICHIT.

Minister of Finance: SOUKANH MAHALATH.

Minister of the Interior: Maj.-Gen. SOUDCHAI THAMMASITH.

Minister of Justice: KHAMOUANE BOUPHA.

Minister of Agriculture and Forestry: SIANE SAPHANTHONG.

Minister of Communications, Transport, Post and Construction: BOUATHONG VONGLOKHAM.

Minister of Industry and Handicrafts: SOULIVONG DARAVONG.

Minister of Commerce and Tourism: PHOUMI THIPPHAVON.

Minister of Information and Culture: PHANDOUANGCHIT VONGSA.

Minister of Labour and Social Welfare: SOMPHAN PHENGKHAMMI.

Minister of Education: PHIMMASONE LEUANGKHAMMA.

Minister of Public Health: Dr PONEMEKH DARALOY.

Minister to the Office of the President: SOUBANH SRITHIRATH.

Ministers to the Prime Minister's Office: BOUNTIEM PHITSAMAI, SOULI NANTHAVONG, SAISENGLI TENGBIACHU, SOMPHUNG MONGKHUNVILAI.

MINISTRIES

Office of the President: rue Lane Xang, Vientiane; tel. (21) 214200; fax (21) 214208.

Office of the Prime Minister: Ban Sisavat, Vientiane; tel. (21) 213653; fax (21) 213560.

Ministry of Agriculture and Forestry: Ban Phonxay, Vientiane; tel. (21) 412359; fax (21) 412344.

Ministry of Commerce and Tourism: Ban Phonxay, Muang Saysettha, Vientiane; tel. (21) 412436; fax (21) 412434; internet www.moc.gov.la.

Ministry of Communications, Transport, Post and Construction: Ban Phonxay, Vientiane; tel. (21) 412251; fax (21) 414123.

Ministry of Education: rue Lane Xang, Ban Sisavat, Vientiane; tel. (21) 216005; fax (21) 212108.

Ministry of Finance: rue That Luang, Ban Phonxay, Vientiane; tel. (21) 412401; fax (21) 412415.

Ministry of Foreign Affairs: rue That Luang 01004, Ban Phonxay, Vientiane; tel. (21) 413148; fax (21) 414009; e-mail sphimmas@laonet.net; internet www.mfa.laogov.net.

Ministry of Industry and Handicrafts: rue Nongbone, Ban Phai, Vientiane; tel. (21) 413007; fax (21) 413005.

Ministry of Information and Culture: rue Sethathirath, Ban Xiengnheun, Vientiane; tel. (21) 210409; fax (21) 212408.

Ministry of the Interior: rue Nongbone, Ban Hatsady, Vientiane; tel. (21) 212500.

Ministry of Justice: Ban Phonxay, Vientiane; tel. (21) 414105.

Ministry of Labour and Social Welfare: rue Pangkham, Ban Sisaket, Vientiane; tel. (21) 213003.

Ministry of National Defence: rue Phone Kheng, Ban Phone Kheng, Vientiane; tel. (21) 412803.

Ministry of Public Health: Ban Simeuang, Vientiane; tel. (21) 214002; fax (21) 214001; e-mail cabinet.fr@moh.gov.la.

Legislature

At the election held on 23 February 2002 166 candidates, approved by the Lao Front for National Construction, contested the 109 seats in the National Assembly.

President of the National Assembly: Lt-Gen. SAMAN VIGNAKET.

Vice-President: PANY YATHOTU.

Political Organizations

Lao Front for National Construction—LFNC: POB 1828, Vientiane; f. 1979 to replace the Lao Patriotic Front; comprises representatives of various political and social groups, of which the LPRP (see below) is the dominant force; fosters national solidarity; Pres. PHENG LASOUKANH; Vice-Chair. SIHO BANNAVONG, KHAMPHOUI CHANTHASOUK, TONG YEUTHOR.

Phak Pasason Pativat Lao (Lao People's Revolutionary Party—LPRP): Vientiane; f. 1955 as the People's Party of Laos; reorg. under present name in 1972; Cen. Cttee of 53 full mems elected March 2001; Pres. Gen. KHAMTAY SIPHANDONE.

Political Bureau (Politburo)

Full members: Gen. KHAMTAY SIPHANDONE, Lt-Gen. SAMAN VIGNAKET, Lt-Gen. CHOUMMALI SAIGNASON, THONGSIN THAMMAVONG, Gen. OSAKAN THAMMATHEVA, BOUNGNANG VOLACHIT, Gen. SISAVAT KEOBOUNPHAN, Maj.-Gen. ASANG LAOLI, THOUNGLONG SISOLIT, Maj.-Gen. DOUANGCHAI PHICHIT, BOUSONE BOUPAVANH.

Numerous factions are in armed opposition to the Government. The principal groups are:

Ethnics' Liberation Organization of Laos: Leader PA KAO HER.

Free Democratic Lao National Salvation Force: based in Thailand.

United Front for the Liberation of Laos: Leader PHOUNGPHET PHANARETH.

United Front for the National Liberation of the Lao People: f. 1980; led by Gen. PHOUMI NOSAVAN until his death in 1985.

United Lao National Liberation Front: Sayabouri Province; comprises an estimated 8,000 members, mostly Hmong (Meo) tribesmen; Sec.-Gen. VANG SHUR.

Diplomatic Representation

EMBASSIES IN LAOS

Australia: rue Pandit J. Nehru, quartier Phonxay, BP 292, Vientiane; tel. (21) 413600; fax (21) 413601; e-mail lynne.hunt@dfat.gov.au; internet www.laos.embassy.gov.au; Ambassador: MICHAEL JONATHAN THWAITES.

Brunei: Unit 12, Ban Thoungkang, rue Lao-Thai Friendship, Muang Sisattanak, Xaysettha District, Vientiane; tel. (21) 352294; fax (21) 352291; e-mail embdlaos@laonet.com; Ambassador: Pengiran Haji HAMDAN BIN Haji ISMAIL.

Cambodia: rue Thadeua, Km 2, BP 34, Vientiane; tel. (21) 314952; fax (21) 314951; e-mail recamlao@laotel.com; Ambassador: HUOT PHAL.

China, People's Republic: rue Wat Nak, Muang Sisattanak, BP 898, Vientiane; tel. (21) 315100; fax (21) 315104; e-mail embassyprc@laonet.net; Ambassador: LIU ZHENGXIU.

Cuba: Ban Saphanthong Neua 128, BP 1017, Vientiane; tel. (21) 314902; fax (21) 314901; e-mail embacuba@laonet.net; Ambassador: MARÍA AIDA NOGALES JIMÉNEZ.

France: rue Sethathirath, Vientiane; tel. (21) 215253; fax (21) 215250; e-mail contact@ambafrance-laos.org; internet www.ambafrance-laos.org; Ambassador: BERNARD POTTIER.

Germany: rue Sok Paluang 26, BP 314, Vientiane; tel. (21) 312110; fax (21) 314322; e-mail germemb@laotel.com; Ambassador: CHRISTIAN K. G. BERGER.

India: rue That Luang, BP 225, Vientiane; tel. (21) 412640; fax (21) 412768; e-mail indiaemb@laotel.com; internet www.indianembassylaos.com; Ambassador: LAVANYA PRASAD.

Indonesia: ave Phone Keng, BP 277, Vientiane; tel. (21) 413909; fax (21) 214828; Ambassador: ZAINUDDIN NASUTION.

Japan: rue Sisangvone, Vientiane; tel. (21) 414401; fax (21) 414406; Ambassador: YOSHINORI MIYAMOTO.

Korea, Democratic People's Republic: quartier Wat Nak, Vientiane; tel (21) 315261; fax (21) 315260; Ambassador: CHOE PYONG KWAN.

Korea, Republic: 13 Phonesa-Ath Village, Saysettha District, Vientiane; tel. (21) 415833; fax (21) 415831; Ambassador: CHANG CHUL-KYOON.

Malaysia: rue That Luang, quartier Pholxay, POB 789, Vientiane; tel. (21) 414205; fax (21) 414201; e-mail mwvntian@laonet.net; Ambassador: MOHAMMED DAUD MOHAMMED YUSOF.

Mongolia: rue Wat Nak, Km 3, BP 370, Vientiane; tel. (21) 315220; fax (21) 315221; e-mail embmong@pan-laos.net.la; Ambassador: N. ALIASUREN.

Myanmar: Ban Thong Kang, rue Sok Palaung, BP 11, Vientiane; tel. (21) 314910; fax (21) 314913; e-mail mev@loxinfo.co.th; Ambassador: U TIN OO.

Philippines: Ban Phonsinuane, Sisattanak, BP 2415, Vientiane; tel. (21) 452490; fax (21) 452493; e-mail pevntianlaonet.net; Ambassador MARIO I. GALMAN.

Poland: 263 Ban Thadeua, Km 3, quartier Wat Nak, BP 1106, Vientiane; tel. (21) 312940; fax (21) 312085; e-mail vieampol@laotel.com; Chargé d'affaires: Dr TOMASZ GERLACH.

Russia: Ban Thadeua, quartier Thaphalanxay, BP 490, Vientiane; tel. (21) 312219; fax (21) 312210; e-mail ruscons@pan-laos.net.la; Ambassador: VALENTIN EREMCHENKO.

Singapore: Unit 12, Ban Naxay, rue Nong Bong, Muang Sat Settha, Vientiane; tel. (21) 416860; fax (21) 416855; e-mail sinemvte@laotel.com; Ambassador HOY CHENG SEETOH.

Sweden: rue Sok Paluang, BP 800, Vientiane; tel. (21) 313772; fax (21) 315001; e-mail embassy.vientiane@sida.se; Chargé d'affaires a.i.: CHRISTER HOLTSBERG.

Thailand: ave Phone Keng, Vientiane; tel. (21) 214581; fax (21) 4110017; e-mail thaivtn@mfa.go.th; Ambassador: SUVIDHYA SIMASKUL.

USA: 19 rue Bartholonie, BP 114, Vientiane; tel. (21) 212581; fax (21) 212584; internet www.usembassy.state.gov/laos; Ambassador: DOUGLAS A. HARTWICK.

Viet Nam: 85 rue That Luang, Vientiane; tel. (21) 413409; fax (21) 413379; e-mail dsqvn@laotel.com; Ambassador: HUYNH ANH DUNG.

Judicial System

President of the People's Supreme Court: KHAMMY SAYAVONG.

Vice-President: DAVON VANGVICHIT.

People's Supreme Court Judges: NOUANTHONG VONGSA, NHOTSENG LITTHIDETH, PHOUKHONG CHANTHALATH, SENGSOUVANH CHANTHALOUNNAVONG, KESON PHANLACK, KONGCHI YANGCHY, KHAMPON PHASAIGNAVONG.

Public Prosecutor-General: KHAMPANE PHILAVONG.

Religion

The 1991 Constitution guarantees freedom of religious belief. The principal religion of Laos is Buddhism.

BUDDHISM

Lao Unified Buddhists' Association: Maha Kudy, Wat That Luang, Vientiane; f. 1964; Pres. (vacant); Sec.-Gen. Rev. SIHO SIHAVONG.

CHRISTIANITY

The Roman Catholic Church

For ecclesiastical purposes, Laos comprises four Apostolic Vicariates. At 31 December 2000 an estimated 0.7% of the population were adherents.

Episcopal Conference of Laos and Cambodia: c/o Mgr Pierre Bach, Paris Foreign Missions, 254 Silom Rd, Bangkok 10500, Thailand; f. 1971; Pres. Mgr JEAN KHAMSÉ VITHAVONG (Titular Bishop of Moglaena), Vicar Apostolic of Vientiane.

Vicar Apostolic of Luang Prabang: Mgr BANCHONG THOPAYONG, Evêché, BP 74, Luang Prabang.

Vicar Apostolic of Paksé: Mgr LOUIS-MARIE LING MANGKHANEKHOUN (Titular Bishop of Proconsulari), Centre Catholique, BP 77, Paksé, Champasak; tel. (31) 212879.

Vicar Apostolic of Savannakhet: Mgr JEAN SOMMENG VORACHAK (Titular Bishop of Muzuca in Proconsulari), Centre Catholique, BP 12, Thakhek, Khammouane; tel. (51) 212184; fax (51) 213070.

Vicar Apostolic of Vientiane: Mgr JEAN KHAMSÉ VITHAVONG (Titular Bishop of Moglaena), Centre Catholique, BP 113, Vientiane; tel. (21) 216219; fax (21) 215085.

The Anglican Communion

Laos is within the jurisdiction of the Anglican Bishop of Singapore.

BAHÁ'Í FAITH

National Spiritual Assembly: BP 189, Vientiane; tel. (21) 216996; fax (21) 217127; e-mail nsalaos@laotel.com.

The Press

Aloun Mai (New Dawn): Vientiane; f. 1985; theoretical and political organ of the LPRP.

Heng Ngan: 87 ave Lane Xang, BP 780, Vientiane; tel. (21) 212750; fortnightly; organ of the Federation of Lao Trade Unions; Editor BOUAPHENG BOUNSOULINH.

Lao Dong (Labour): 87 ave Lane Xang, Vientiane; f. 1986; fortnightly; organ of the Federation of Lao Trade Unions; circ. 46,000.

Laos: 80 rue Sethathirath, BP 3770, Vientiane; tel. (21) 21447; fax (21) 21445; internet www.laolink.com; quarterly; published in Lao and English; illustrated; Editor V. PHOMCHANHEUANG; English Editor O. PHRAKHAMSAY.

Meying Lao: rue Manthatoarath, BP 59, Vientiane; e-mail chansoda@hotmail.com; f. 1980; monthly; women's magazine; organ of the Lao Women's Union; Editor-in-Chief VATSADY KHUTNGOTHA; Editor CHANSODA PHONETHIP; circ. 7,000.

Noum Lao (Lao Youth): Vientiane; f. 1979; fortnightly; organ of the Lao People's Revolutionary Youth Union; Editor DOUANGDY INTHAVONG; circ. 6,000.

Pasason (The People): 80 rue Setthathirath, BP 110, Vientiane; f. 1940; daily; organ of the Cen. Cttee of the LPRP; Editor BOUABAN VOLAKHOUN; circ. 28,000.

Pathet Lao: 80 rue Setthathirath, Vientiane; tel. (21) 215402; fax (21) 212446; f. 1979; monthly; Lao and English; organ of Khao San Pathet Lao (KPL); Dep. Dir SOUNTHONE KHANTHAVONG.

Sciences and Technics: Dept of Science and Technology, Science, Technology and the Environment Agency (STEA), POB 2279, Vientiane; f. 1991 as Technical Science Magazine; quarterly; organ of the Dept of Science and Technology; scientific research and development.

Siang Khong Gnaovason Song Thanva (Voice of the 2nd December Youths): Vientiane; monthly; youth journal.

Sieng Khene Lao: Vientiane; monthly; organ of the Lao Writers' Association.

Suksa Mai: Vientiane; monthly; organ of the Ministry of Education.

Valasan Khosana (Propaganda Journal): Vientiane; f. 1987; organ of the Cen. Cttee of the LPRP.

Vientiane Mai (New Vientiane): rue Setthathirath, BP 989, Vientiane; tel. (21) 2623; fax (21) 5989; f. 1975; morning daily; organ of the LPRP Cttee of Vientiane province and city; Editor SICHANE (acting); circ. 2,500.

Vientiane Times: BP 5723, Vientiane; tel. (21) 216364; fax (21) 216365; internet www.vientianetimes.com; f. 1994; 2 a week; English; emphasis on investment opportunities; Editor SOMSANOUK MIXAY; circ. 3,000.

Vientiane Tulakit (Vientiane Business-Social): rue Setthathirath, Vientiane; tel. (21) 2623; fax (21) 6365; weekly; circ. 2,000.

There is also a newspaper published by the Lao People's Army, and several provinces have their own newsletters.

NEWS AGENCIES

Khao San Pathet Lao (KPL): 80 rue Setthathirath, Vientiane; tel. (21) 215402; fax (21) 212446; e-mail kpl@laonet.net; internet www.kplnet.net; f. 1968; organ of the Cttee of Information, Press, Radio and Television Broadcasting; news service; daily bulletins in Lao, English and French; teletype transmission in English; Gen. Dir KHAMSÈNE PHONGSA.

Foreign Bureaux

Rossiiskoye Informatsionnoye Agentstvo—Novosti (RIA—Novosti) (Russia): Vientiane; tel. (21) 213510; f. 1963.

Viet Nam News Agency (VNA): Vientiane; Chief DO VAN PHUONG.

Reuters (UK) is also represented in Laos.

PRESS ASSOCIATION

The Journalists' Association of the Lao PDR: BP 122, Vientiane; tel. (21) 212420; fax (21) 212408; Pres. BOUABANE VORAKHOUNE; Sec.-Gen. KHAM KHONG KONGVONGSA.

Publishers

Khoualuang Kanphim: 2–6 Khoualuang Market, Vientiane.

Lao-phanit: Ministry of Education, Bureau des Manuels Scolaires, rue Lane Xang, Ban Sisavat, Vientiane; educational, cookery, art, music, fiction.

Pakpassak Kanphin: 9–11 quai Fa-Hguun, Vientiane.

State Printing: 314/C rue Samsemthai, BP 2160, Vientiane; tel. (21) 213273; fax (21) 215901; Dir Nouphay Kounlavong.

Broadcasting and Communications

TELECOMMUNICATIONS

Entreprises des Postes et Télécommunications de Laos: ave Lane Xang, 0100 Vientiane; tel. (21) 215767; fax (21) 212779; state enterprise, responsible for the postal service and telecommunications; Dir-Gen. Soulikhan Luangsena.

Lao Télécommunications Co Ltd: ave Lane Xang, BP 5607, 0100 Vientiane; tel. (21) 216465; fax (21) 213493; e-mail hpinthar@laotel.com; internet www.laotel.com; f. 1996; a joint venture between a subsidiary of the Shinawatra Group of Thailand and Entreprises des Postes et Télécommunications de Laos; awarded a 25-year contract by the Government in 1996 to undertake all telecommunications projects in the country; Dir-Gen. Houmphanh Intharath.

BROADCASTING

Radio

In addition to the national radio service, there are several local stations.

Lao National Radio: rue Phangkham, Km 6, BP 310, Vientiane; tel. (21) 212432; fax (21) 212430; e-mail natradio@laonet.net; f. 1951; state-owned; programmes in Lao, French, English, Thai, Khmer and Vietnamese; domestic and international services; Dir-Gen. Bounthanh Inthaxay.

In 1990 resistance forces in Laos established an illegal radio station, broadcasting anti-Government propaganda: **Satthani Vithayou Kachai Siang Latthaban Potpoi Sat Lao** (Radio Station of the Government for the Liberation of the Lao Nation): programmes in Lao and Hmong languages; broadcasts four hours daily.

Television

A domestic television service began in December 1983. In May 1988 a second national television station commenced transmissions from Savannakhet. In December 1993 the Ministry of Information and Culture signed a 15-year joint-venture contract with a Thai firm on the development of broadcasting services in Laos. Under the resultant International Broadcasting Corporation Lao Co Ltd, IBC Channel 3 was inaugurated in 1994 (see below).

Lao National Television (TVNL): rue Chommany Neua, Km 6, BP 5635, Vientiane; tel. (21) 412183; fax (21) 412182; f. 1983; colour television service; Dir-Gen. Bouasone Phongphavanh.

Laos Television 3: Vientiane; operated by the International Broadcasting Corpn Lao Co Ltd; f. 1994 as IBC Channel 3; 30% govt-owned, 70% owned by the International Broadcasting Corpn Co Ltd of Thailand; programmes in Lao.

Finance

(cap. = capital; dep. = deposits; br.(s) = branch(es); m. = million)

BANKING

The banking system was reorganized in 1988–89, ending the state monopoly of banking. Some commercial banking functions were transferred from the central bank and the state commercial bank to a new network of autonomous banks. The establishment of joint ventures with foreign financial institutions was permitted. Foreign banks have been permitted to open branches in Laos since 1992. In 1998 there were nine private commercial banks in Laos, most of them Thai. In March 1999 the Government consolidated six state-owned banks into two new institutions—Lane Xang Bank Ltd and Lao May Bank Ltd: these merged in 2001.

Central Bank

Banque de la RDP Lao: rue Yonnet, BP 19, Vientiane; tel. (21) 213109; fax (21) 213108; f. 1959 as the bank of issue, became Banque Pathetlao 1968, took over the operations of Banque Nationale du Laos 1975; known as Banque d'Etat de la RDP Lao from 1982 until adoption of present name; Gov. Chansy Phosikham.

Commercial Banks

Agriculture Promotion Bank: 58 rue Hengboun, Ban Haysok, BP 5456, Vientiane; tel. (21) 212024; fax (21) 213957; e-mail apblaopdr@laonet.net; Man. Dir Bounsong Sommalavong.

Banque pour le Commerce Extérieur Lao (BCEL): 1 rue Pangkham, BP 2925, Vientiane; tel. (21) 213200; fax (21) 213202; e-mail bcelhovt@laotel.com; f. 1975; 100% state-owned; Chair. Bounthong Keomahavong; Man. Dir Somphao Phaysith.

Joint Development Bank: 75/1–5 ave Lane Xang, BP 3187, Vientiane; e-mail jdb@jdbbank.com; internet www.jdbbank.com; f. 1989; the first joint-venture bank between Laos and a foreign partner; 30% owned by Banque de la RDP Lao, 70% owned by Thai company, Phrom Suwan Silo and Drying Co Ltd; cap. US $4m.

Lao May Bank Ltd: 39 rue Pangkam, BP 2700, Vientiane; tel. (21) 213300; fax (21) 213304; f. 1999 as a result of the consolidation by the Government of ParkTai Bank, Lao May Bank and NakornLuang Bank; merged with Lane Xang Bank Ltd in 2001.

Lao-Viet Bank (LVB): 5 ave Lane Xang, Vientiane; tel. (21) 251418; fax (21) 212197; e-mail lvb@laonet.net; internet www.laovietbank.com; f. 1999; joint venture between BCEL and the Bank for Investment and Development of Vietnam.

Vientiane Commercial Bank Ltd: 33 ave Lane Xang, Ban Hatsady, Chanthaboury, Vientiane; tel. (21) 222700; fax (21) 213513; f. 1993; privately-owned joint venture by Laotian, Thai, Taiwanese and Australian investors; Man. Dir Sop Sisomphou.

Foreign Banks

Bangkok Bank Public Co Ltd (Thailand)**:** 38/13–15 rue Hatsady, BP 5400, Vientiane; tel. (21) 213560; fax (21) 213561; f. 1993; Man. Tossatis Rodprasert.

Bank of Ayudhya Public Co Ltd (Thailand): 79/6 Unit 17, ave Lane Xang, BP 5072, Vientiane; tel. (21) 213521; fax (21) 213520; e-mail baylaos@laotel.com; internet www.bay.co.th; f. 1994; Man. Suwat Tantipatanasakul.

Krung Thai Bank Public Co Ltd (Thailand): Unit 21, 80 ave Lane Xang, Ban Xiengngeuanthong, Chanthaboury, Vientiane; tel. (21) 213480; fax (21) 222762; e-mail ktblao@laotel.com; internet www.ktb.co.th; f. 1993; Gen. Man. Somchai Kanokpetch.

Public Bank Berhad (Malaysia): 100/1-4 rue Talat Sao, BP 6614, Vientiane; tel. (21) 216614; fax (21) 222743; e-mail pbbvte@laotel.com; Gen. Man. Tay Hong Heng.

Siam Commercial Bank Public Co Ltd (Thailand): 117 ave Lane Xang-Samsenethai, BP 4809, Ban Sisaket Mouang, Chanthaboury, Vientiane; tel. (21) 213500; fax (21) 213502; Gen. Man. Charanya Dissamarn.

Thai Military Bank Public Co Ltd: 69 rue Khoun Boulom, Chanthaboury, BP 2423, Vientiane; tel. (21) 217174; fax (21) 216486; the first foreign bank to be represented in Laos; Man. Amnat Kosktpon.

INSURANCE

Assurances Générales du Laos (AGL): Vientiane Commercial Bank Bldg, ave Lane Xang, BP 4223, Vientiane; tel. (21) 215903; fax (21) 215904; e-mail agl@agl-allianz.com; Dir-Gen. Philippe Robineau.

Trade and Industry

GOVERNMENT AGENCY

National Economic Research Institute: rue Luang Prabang, Sithanneua, Vientiane; govt policy development unit; Dir Souphan Keomisay.

DEVELOPMENT ORGANIZATIONS

Department of Livestock and Fisheries: Ministry of Agriculture and Forestry, BP 811, Vientiane; tel. (21) 416932; fax (21) 415674; public enterprise; imports and markets agricultural commodities; produces and distributes feed and animals.

State Committee for State Planning: Vientiane; Pres. Bouathong Vonglokham.

CHAMBER OF COMMERCE

Lao National Chamber of Commerce and Industry: rue Sihom, Ban Haisok, BP 4596, Vientiane; tel. and fax (21) 219223; e-mail ccilcciv@laotel.com; f. 1990; executive board comprising 11 mems and five advisers; Acting Pres. Chanhpheng Bounnaphol.

INDUSTRIAL AND TRADE ASSOCIATION

Société Lao Import-Export (SOLIMPEX): 43-47 ave Lane Xang, BP 278, Vientiane; tel. (21) 213818; fax (21) 217054; Dir Kanhkeo Saycocie; Dep. Dir Khemmani Pholsena.

UTILITIES

Electricity

Electricité du Laos: rue Nongbonc, BP 309, Vientiane; tel. (21) 451519; fax (21) 416381; e-mail edlgmo@laotel.com; responsible for production and distribution of electricity; Gen. Man. Viraphonh Viravong.

Lao National Grid Co: Vientiane; responsible for Mekong hydroelectricity exports.

Water

Nam Papa Lao (Lao Water Supply Authority): rue Phone Kheng, Thatluang Neua Village, Sat Settha District, Vientiane; tel. (21) 412880; fax (21) 414378; f. 1962; responsible for the water supply of the entire country; Gen. Man. Dr SOMPHON DETHOUDON.

STATE ENTERPRISES

Agricultural Forestry Development Import-Export and General Service Co: trading co of the armed forces.

Bolisat Phatthana Khet Phoudoi Import-Export Co: Lak Sao; f. 1984; trading co of the armed forces.

Dao-Heuang Import-Export Co: 38/2 Ban Hatsadi, POB 384, Vientiane; tel. (21) 213790; fax (21) 216317; internet www.dao-heuang.com; imports and distributes whisky, beer, mineral water and foodstuffs.

Luen Fat Hong Lao Plywood Industry Co: BP 83, Vientiane; tel. (21) 314990; fax (21) 314992; internet www.luenfathongyada.laopdr.com; development and management of forests, logging and timber production.

CO-OPERATIVES

Central Leading Committee to Guide Agricultural Co-operatives: Vientiane; f. 1978 to help organize and plan regulations and policies for co-operatives; by the end of 1986 there were some 4,000 co-operatives, employing about 74% of the agricultural labour force; Chair. (vacant); Chief KHAMSEN VONONOKEO.

TRADE UNION ORGANIZATION

Federation of Lao Trade Unions: 87 ave Lane Xang, BP 780, Vientiane; tel. (21) 313682; e-mail kammabanlao@pan-laos.net.la; f. 1956; 21-mem. Cen. Cttee and five-mem. Control Cttee; Chair. KHAMPAN PHILAVONG; Vice-Chair. BOUNPHON SANGSOMSAK; 70,000 mems.

Transport

RAILWAYS

The construction of a 30-km rail link between Vientiane and the Thai border town of Nong Khai began in January 1996; the rail link was scheduled for completion in 1998, but was indefinitely postponed in February of that year as an indirect consequence of a severe downturn in the Thai economy. In 1997 the Government announced plans to develop a comprehensive railway network, and awarded a contract to a Thai company, although no timetable for the implementation of the scheme was announced.

ROADS

The road network provides the country's main method of transport, accounting for about 90% of freight traffic and 95% of passenger traffic in 1993 (according to the Asian Development Bank—ADB). In 1999 there were an estimated 21,716 km of roads, of which 9,664 km were paved. The main routes link Vientiane and Luang Prabang with Ho Chi Minh City in southern Viet Nam and with northern Viet Nam and the Cambodian border, Vientiane with Savannakhet, Phong Saly to the Chinese border, Vientiane with Luang Prabang and the port of Ha Tinh (northern Viet Nam), and Savannakhet with the port of Da Nang (Viet Nam). In 2002 Laos, Thailand and China agreed to a US $45m. road project intended to link the three countries; most of the road construction would be carried out in Laos. The project was to be completed by 2006.

The Friendship Bridge across the Mekong river, linking Laos and Thailand between Tha Naleng (near Vientiane) and Nong Khai, was opened in April 1994. In early 1998 construction work began in Paksé on a second bridge across the Mekong river. The project was granted substantial funding from the Japanese Government, and was completed in August 2000. An additional bridge, linking Savannakhet and Mukdahan, is also planned and is scheduled for completion by 2005.

INLAND WATERWAYS

The Mekong River, which forms the western frontier of Laos for much of its length, is the country's greatest transport artery. However, the size of river vessels is limited by rapids, and traffic is seasonal. In April 1995 Laos, Cambodia, Thailand and Viet Nam signed an agreement regarding the joint development of the lower Mekong, and established a Mekong River Commission. There are about 4,600 km of navigable waterways.

CIVIL AVIATION

Wattai airport, Vientiane, is the principal airport. Following the signing of an agreement in 1995, the airport was to be upgraded by Japan; renovation work commenced in 1997, and a new passenger terminal was opened in 1998. The development of Luang Prabang airport by Thailand, at a cost of 50m. baht, began in May 1994 and the first phase of the development programme was completed in 1996; the second phase was completed in 1998. In April 1998 Luang Prabang airport gained formal approval for international flights. The airports at Paksé and Savannakhet were also scheduled to be upgraded to enable them to accommodate wide-bodied civilian aircraft; renovation work on the airport at Savannakhet was completed in April 2000. Construction of a new airport in Oudomxay Province was completed in the late 1990s.

Lao Civil Aviation Department: POB 119, Vientiane; tel. and fax (21) 512163; e-mail laodca@laotel.com; Dir-Gen. YAKUA LOPANGKAO.

Lao Aviation (International): National Air Transport Co, 2 rue Pangkham, BP 6441, Vientiane; tel. (21) 212057; fax (21) 212056; e-mail pothong@lao-aviation.com; internet www.lao-aviation.com; f. 1975; state airline, fmrly Lao Aviation; operates internal and international passenger and cargo transport services within South-East Asia; Gen. Man. Dir POTHONG NGONPHACHANH.

Tourism

Laos boasts spectacular scenery, ancient pagodas and abundant wildlife. However, the development of tourism remains constrained by the poor infrastructure in much of the country. Western tourists were first permitted to enter Laos in 1989. In 1994, in order to stimulate the tourist industry, Vientiane ended restrictions on the movement of foreigners in Laos. Also in 1994 Laos, Viet Nam and Thailand agreed measures for the joint development of tourism. Luang Prabang was approved by UNESCO as a World Heritage site in February 1998. The number of visitors reached 614,278 in 1999, when receipts from tourism were estimated at US $97m. Tourist arrivals increased further, to 737,208, in 2000, when receipts from tourism totalled an estimated US $114m. 1999–2000 were designated as Visit Laos Years.

National Tourism Authority of Lao PDR: ave Lane Xang, BP 3556, Vientiane; tel. (21) 212251; fax (21) 212769; internet www.visit-laos.com; 17 provincial offices; Dir CHENG SAYAVONG.

Defence

In August 2001 the total strength of the armed forces was estimated at 29,700: army 25,600; navy an estimated 600; air force 3,500. Conscription lasts a minimum of 18 months. Paramilitary forces comprise militia self-defence forces numbering about 100,000 men. Defence expenditure for 2000 was an estimated 150,000m. kips.

Supreme Commander of the Lao People's Army (Commander-in-Chief): Lt-Gen. CHOUMMALI SAIGNASON.

Chief of the General Staff: Maj.-Gen. KHEN KHAMSENG LATHON.

Education

Education was greatly disrupted by the civil war, causing a high illiteracy rate, but educational facilities have since improved significantly. Lao is the medium of instruction. A comprehensive educational system is in force.

Education is officially compulsory for nine years, between six and 15 years of age. Primary education begins at six years of age and lasts for five years. Secondary education, beginning at the age of 11, lasts for six years, comprising two cycles of three years each (the second being a senior high school course). In 1996 enrolment at primary schools included 72% of the primary school-age population (males 76%; females 68%). Total enrolment at secondary schools in the same year was equivalent to 28% of the relevant age-group (males 34%; females 23%). The total enrolment at primary and secondary schools was equivalent to 72% of the school-age population (males 80%; females 63%) in 1996, compared with 68% in 1987. There are several regional technical colleges. The National University of Laos was founded in 1995. Enrolment in tertiary education in 1996 was equivalent to 3% of the relevant age-group (males 4%; females 2%). Government expenditure on education in 1997/98 was budgeted at 37,400m. kips, representing 6.9% of total budgetary expenditure.

In 1990 it was reported that the Government had permitted the establishment of five private primary schools.

Bibliography

See also Cambodia and Viet Nam

Anderson, Kym. *Lao Economic Reform and WTO Accession: Implications for Agriculture and Rural Development.* Singapore, Institute of Southeast Asian Studies, 1999.

Asian Development Bank. *Lao PDR and the Greater Mekong Subregion: Securing Benefits from Economic Cooperation.* Manila, 1996.

Reforming the Financial Sector in the Lao PDR. Manila, 1996.

Bourdet, Yves. *The Economics of Transition in Laos: From Socialism to ASEAN Integration.* Cheltenham, Edward Elgar, 2000.

Brahm, Laurence, and Macpherson, Neill. *Investment in the Lao People's Democratic Republic.* Hong Kong, Longman, 1992.

Brown, M., and Zasloff, J. *Apprentice Revolutionaries: The Communist Movement in Laos, 1930–1985.* Stanford, CA, Hoover Institution Press, 1986.

Castle, Timothy N. *A War in the Shadow of Vietnam.* New York, Columbia University Press, 1995.

Chazee, Laurent (Ed.). *The People of Laos.* Bangkok, White Lotus, 2001.

Conroy, Paul. *10 Months in Laos: A Vast Web of Intrigue, Missing Millions and Murder.* Melbourne, Vic, Crown Content, 2002.

Cooper, R., Tapp, N., Yia Lee, G., and Schwoer-Kohl, G. *The Hmong.* Bangkok, Artasia Press, 1992.

Deuve, J. *La Royaume de Laos, 1949–1965.* Paris, 1984.

Dommen, A. J. *Conflict in Laos: The Politics of Neutralization.* London, Pall Mall Press, 2nd Edn, 1971.

Evans, G. *Lao Peasants Under Socialism.* New Haven, CT, Yale University Press, 1991.

The Politics of Ritual and Remembrance: Laos since 1975. Chiang Mai, Silkworm Books, 1998.

Evans, Grant (Ed.). *Laos: Culture and Society.* Chiang Mai, Silkworm Books, 1999.

Evans, G., and Rowley, K. *Red Brotherhood at War.* London, Verso, Revised Edn, 1990.

Freeman, Nick, J. 'Laos: No Safe Haven from the Regional Tumult' in *Southeast Asian Affairs, 1998.* Singapore, Institute of Southeast Asian Studies, 1998.

Gunn, G. C. *Political Struggles in Laos (1930–1954).* Bangkok, Editions Duang Kamol, 1988.

Rebellion in Laos. Boulder, CO, Westview Press, 1990.

Hamilton-Merritt, Jane. *Tragic Mountains: The Hmong, the Americans, and the Secret Wars for Laos, 1942–1992.* Bloomington, IN, Indiana University Press, 1993.

Hannah, Norman. *The Key to Failure.* New York, Madison Books, 1987.

Kremmer, Christopher. *Stalking the Elephant Kings.* St Leonards, NSW, Allen and Unwin, 1998.

Lancaster, D. *The Emancipation of French Indo-China.* London, Oxford University Press, 1961.

Langer, P. F., and Zasloff, J. J. *North Vietnam and the Pathet Lao.* Cambridge, MA, Harvard University Press, 1970.

McCoy, A. W. *The Politics of Heroin in Southeast Asia.* New York, Harper and Row, 1972.

Matelas, S. *Laos: A Country Report.* Washington, DC, US Government Printing Office, 1995.

Menon, Jayant. *Laos in the ASEAN Free Trade Area: Trade, Revenue and Investment Implications.* Pacific Economic Papers, No. 276, Canberra, Australia-Japan Research Centre, 1998.

Murphy, Dervla. *One Foot In Laos.* London, John Murray, 2000.

Ngaosyvathn, Mayoury. *Lao Women Yesterday and Today.* Vientiane, State Publishing Enterprise, 1993.

Ngaosyvathn, Mayoury and Pheuiphanh. *Kith and Kin Politics: The Relationship Between Laos and Thailand.* Manila, Journal of Contemporary Asia Publishers, 1994.

Pham, Chi Do (Ed.). *Economic Development in Lao P.D.R.: Horizon 2000.* Vientiane, 1994.

Program for South-East Asian Studies. *New Laos, New Challenges.* Tempe, Arizona State University Press, 1998.

Quincy, Keith. *Harvesting Pa Chay's Wheat: The Hmong and America's Secret War in Laos.* Washington, DC, University of Washington Press, 2000.

Sagar, D. J. *Major Political Events in Indochina 1945–1990.* Oxford, Facts on File, 1991.

Simms, Peter and Sanda. *The Kingdoms of Laos: Six Hundred Years of History.* Richmond, Surrey, Curzon Press, 1998.

Sisouphanthong, Bounthavy and Taillard, Christian. *Atlas of Laos.* Copenhagen, Nordic Institute of Asian Studies, 2000.

Stuart-Fox, Martin. *Laos: Politics, Economics and Society.* London, Francis Pinter, 1986.

'Laos: Towards Subregional Integration' in *Southeast Asian Affairs,* 1995. Singapore, Institute of Southeast Asian Studies, 1995.

Buddhist Kingdom, Marxist State: The Making of Modern Laos. Bangkok, White Lotus, 1996.

A History of Laos. Cambridge, Cambridge University Press, 1997.

The Lao Kingdom of Lan Xang: Rise and Decline. Bangkok, White Lotus, 1998.

Historical Dictionary of Laos. Metuchen, NJ, Scarecrow Press, 2nd Edn, 2000.

Stuart-Fox, Martin (Ed.). *Contemporary Laos.* University of Queensland Press, 1982.

Taillard, Christian. *Le Laos, stratégie d'un Etat-tampon.* Montpellier, Reclus, 1989.

Than, Mya, and Tan, Joseph L. H. (Eds). *Laos' Dilemmas and Options: The Challenge of Economic Transition in the 1990s.* Singapore, Institute of Southeast Asian Studies, 1996.

Toye, H. *Laos—Buffer State or Background.* London, Oxford University Press.

United Nations Development Programme. *Micro-finance in Rural Lao PDR: A National Profile.* Vientiane, UNDP, 1997.

Warner, Roger. *Back Fire: The CIA's Secret War in Laos.* New York, Simon & Schuster, 1995.

Zasloff, J. J. *The Pathet Lao: Leadership and Organisation.* Lexington, MA, Heath, 1973.

Zasloff, J. J., and Unger, L. (Eds). *Laos: Beyond the Revolution.* Basingstoke, Macmillan, 1991.

MALAYSIA

Physical and Social Geography

HARVEY DEMAINE

Malaysia covers a total area of 329,847 sq km (127,355 sq miles), comprising the 11 states of Peninsular Malaysia, with an area of 131,686 sq km (50,845 sq miles), together with the two states of Sarawak and Sabah (with the Federal Territory of Labuan), in northern Borneo, with areas of, respectively, 124,450 sq km (48,051 sq miles) and 73,711 sq km (28,460 sq miles). Peninsular Malaysia includes a number of islands, the largest being Langkawi and Pulau Pinang (Penang).

While Peninsular Malaysia, Sabah and Sarawak lie in almost identical latitudes between 1° N and 7° N of the Equator, and have characteristic equatorial climates with uniformly high temperatures and rain in all seasons, there is nevertheless a fundamental difference in their geographical position. Peninsular Malaysia forms the southern tip of the Asian mainland, bordered by Thailand to the north and by the island of Singapore at its southernmost point. On its western side, facing the sheltered and calm waters of the Straits of Melaka (Malacca), Peninsular Malaysia flanks one of the oldest and most frequented maritime highways of the world, whereas Sabah and Sarawak lie off the main shipping routes, along the northern fringe of the remote island of Borneo, bordered by Indonesia and, in north-eastern Sarawak, by Brunei.

PHYSICAL FEATURES

Structurally, both parts of Malaysia form part of the old stable massif of Sunda-land, though whereas the dominant folding in the Malay peninsula is of Mesozoic age, that along the northern edge of Borneo dates from Tertiary times. In Peninsular Malaysia the mountain ranges, whose summit levels reach 1,200 m–2,100 m, run roughly north to south and their granitic cores have been widely exposed by erosion. The most continuous is the Main Range, which, over most of the peninsula, marks the divide between the relatively narrow western coastal plain draining to the Straits of Melaka, and the much larger area of mountainous interior and coastal lowland which drains to the South China Sea.

Because of the much greater accessibility of the western lowlands to the main sea-routes, and also of the existence of extensive areas of alluvial tin in the gravels deposited at the break of slope in the western foothills of the Main Range, the strip of country lying between the latter and the western coast of Peninsular Malaysia has been much more intensively developed than the remaining four-fifths of the country. The planting of rubber became concentrated in the vicinity of roads, railways and other facilities originally developed in connection with the tin industry. In contrast to the placid waters of the west coast, the east coast is open to the full force of the north-east monsoon during the period from October to March.

In many respects Sabah and Sarawak display similar basic geographical characteristics to eastern Peninsular Malaysia, but in a more extreme form. Thus, the lowlands are mostly wider, the rivers longer and even more liable to severe flooding, the coastline exposed to the north-east monsoon and avoided by shipping, and the equatorial forest cover even denser and more continuous than that of the peninsula. Moreover, while in general the mountains of Sabah and Sarawak are of comparable height to those in Peninsular Malaysia, there is one striking exception in Mt Kinabalu, a single isolated horst, which towers above the Croker Range of Sabah to an altitude of 4,101 m.

Throughout Malaysia, average daily temperatures range from about 21°C to 32°C, although in higher areas temperatures are lower and vary more widely. Rainfall averages about 2,540 mm throughout the year, although this is subject to regional variation.

NATURAL RESOURCES

Malaysia is endowed with an extremely rich natural resource base. The country has extensive tin deposits, and geophysical surveys in the eastern part of the peninsula's Main Range have suggested the presence of substantial deposits of other important minerals such as copper and uranium. Significant deposits have also been identified in East Malaysia, with copper mining established in Sabah, and bauxite and coal exploited in Sarawak.

East Malaysia's main wealth, however, remains the coastal and offshore deposits of hydrocarbons. Petroleum production from the original Miri field, in onshore Sarawak, has ceased, but discoveries off shore, made in the 1960s, have maintained production. In 2001 Malaysia's crude and condensate petroleum reserves totalled 5,000m. barrels (compared with 5,500m. barrels in 1996), and natural gas reserves 81,700,000m. cu ft. Malaysia's production of crude petroleum and natural gas liquids was estimated at 36.6m. tons in 1999. Petroleum production in 2000 averaged 679,610 barrels per day from Malaysia's 33 oilfields.

Until the rise of petroleum, Malaysia's main economic resource was the agricultural potential of the peninsula. This derived not so much from the inherent superiority of its soils—indeed, those of Sarawak and Sabah are similar—but rather from its accessibility for commercial enterprise. Rubber and, more recently, oil palm have flourished in this environment. Sabah and Sarawak rely heavily upon their vast wealth in tropical timbers. However, the rate of extraction of timber has been so rapid since the late 1970s that serious efforts are now having to be made to conserve resources, particularly in the peninsula.

POPULATION AND CULTURE

The total population of Malaysia, including adjustments for underenumeration, was 23,274,690 at the census of July 2000 (compared with the August 1991 census total of 18,379,655), of whom 18,523,632 resided in Peninsular Malaysia (the most urbanized part of the country, where the average density was 140.7 per sq km), 2,679,552 were in Sabah and Labuan (36.4 per sq km) and 2,071,506 in Sarawak (16.6 per sq km). In Peninsular Malaysia the indigenous population, apart from some 50,000 or so aboriginal peoples, consists mainly of Muslim Malays, who, according to the census of 1991, form 57.0% of the total population, which also includes 28.7% Chinese and a further 9.3% Indians (an ethnic term which applies to people from India, Pakistan or Bangladesh). In Sabah and Sarawak, on the other hand, Malays and other Muslim peoples are confined mainly to the coastal zone, while various other ethnic groups occupy the interior. There is also a large Chinese element, amounting to 27.7% of the population in Sarawak and 11.7% in Sabah in 1991. According to the census of July 2000, Muslim Malays comprised 65.1%, Chinese 26.0% and Indians 7.7% of the total population.

History

ROBERT CRIBB

Based on an earlier article by IAN BROWN

The founding of the Melaka (Malacca) sultanate in c. 1400 AD conventionally marks the beginning of the modern history of the territory that constitutes present-day Malaysia. Until its capture by the Portuguese in 1511, Melaka was not only the dominant trading centre in the region, and arguably the greatest emporium in the Asia of that period, but also a vigorous centre of Malay culture, influential in shaping the political institutions and traditional culture of the Malays through the succeeding centuries.

The Portuguese were unable to maintain Melaka's dominance in regional trade and in 1641 they lost control of the city to the Dutch. The Dutch were principally interested in Java, however, and during the 17th and 18th centuries local and outside influences vied for power in the Malay peninsula. Johor (Johore) inherited some of the prestige of Melaka, but it was rivalled in influence by the Dutch, the Aceh and Siak in Sumatra, and the Siamese. Refugees and explorers from southern Sulawesi (in what is now Indonesia) took control of some regions, including Johor, and Minangkabau migrants from Sumatra became a strong presence in Negeri Sembilan (Negri Sembilan). By the mid-18th century the peninsula was divided into a number of small Malay states, which had various links with outside powers.

Britain (subsequently the United Kingdom) began its territorial advance in the late 18th century, aiming to expand its commercial activities east of India, and, in particular, to secure the trade route to China through the Straits of Melaka. Pinang (Penang) was acquired in 1786 and Melaka in 1795, and a trading settlement was founded on the island of Singapore in 1819. In 1826 Pinang, Melaka and Singapore became a single administrative unit, the Straits Settlements, which remained under the authority of British India until 1867, when administrative responsibility was transferred to the colonial office in London. British interest in the peninsula was further secured by an Anglo-Dutch treaty of 1824, which established the Straits as the boundary of their respective spheres of influence. The treaty contained no reference to Borneo, but in 1841 an English adventurer, James Brooke, was installed by the Sultan of Brunei as Raja of Sarawak, thus founding a dynasty of 'white rajas' which was to rule the territory for over a century (see History of Brunei); in 1847 Brunei ceded the small island of Labuan to the United Kingdom as a coaling station. In the north-east corner of Borneo concessions granted by the Sultans of Brunei and Sulu were eventually acquired by the British North Borneo Co, formed in 1881 as a chartered company under the British crown. Brunei itself was reduced to two small enclaves under British protection.

Through the middle decades of the 19th century, British policy (formulated in Calcutta and London) sought to avoid involvement in the Malay states, but important economic developments in the west coast states of the peninsula gradually drew the Straits Settlements into a closer commercial, and then political, relationship with its hinterland.

The discovery of major tin deposits in Larut (Perak) in the 1840s led to a substantial expansion of mining activity on the west coast, financed in large part by mercantile interests in the Straits, and dependent on a very considerable influx of Chinese immigrant labour. Rival Chinese secret societies, frequently in alliance with factions within the Malay ruling houses, fought for control of this important new source of wealth. By the late 1860s Perak and Selangor, in particular, were approaching anarchy, and the British administration in the Straits Settlements was urged by local merchants, Chinese as well as European, to intervene to restore order.

Eventually, in 1873, the British Government itself agreed to intervene, possibly because it feared that a rival European power, imperial Germany, might take advantage of the disorder in the peninsula to establish a base which would threaten the British strategic domination of the Straits, but more fundamentally in order to secure wider British commercial interests in the east. With the Pangkor Treaty of January 1874, British administration was accepted in Perak; it was then rapidly extended to Selangor, Negeri Sembilan and, in 1888, to Pahang. In 1896 these four states were brought together as the Federated Malay States (FMS), with the federal capital at Kuala Lumpur. In 1909 the four northern states of Kedah, Perlis, Kelantan and Terengganu (Trengganu), long within the influence of Siam, were transferred to British authority and accepted British advisers; the northern Malay states, including Pattani and Singgora (Songkhla), remained under Siamese hegemony. In 1914 a permanent adviser was appointed to Johor, the one remaining independent Malay state. However, these five states did not enter the centralized administration of the FMS, but became collectively known as the Unfederated Malay States (UMS). Thus, by 1914 British authority had been extended throughout the Malay Peninsula, except for the Siamese north, but with considerable variation in both constitutional form and administrative practice.

BRITISH RULE IN THE MALAY STATES

The basis of British administration in the Malay states, until the Japanese invasion in 1941, was a short phrase in the Pangkor Treaty which required the Sultan to accept a British Resident whose advice 'must be asked and acted upon on all questions other than those touching Malay religion and custom'. Consequently, as the residential system evolved in the FMS, government was in the name of the Sultan but executive authority lay very firmly with the Resident. Although there was a brief Malay uprising in Perak in 1875, in general the Malay ruling families found little difficulty in reconciling themselves to their loss of political powers. Acceptance was eased by the fact that the British administration, eager to sustain the fiction of Malay rule with British advice, not only maintained the full splendour of Malay court ceremonial but also treated the Malay rulers in public with the deference due to royalty. In the UMS, particularly in Johor and Kedah, the appointed British official, here called the Adviser, in general carried significantly less executive authority than his counterpart, the Resident, in the FMS. The more assertive Sultans here could exercise independence of British advice.

Malaya emerged as a major world producer of tin and, from the early 20th century, of rubber. Both the tin industry and the plantation rubber interests were heavily dependent on immigrant labour, from the southern coastal provinces of China in the case of the former, and from southern India in the case of the latter. By 1931 Chinese constituted 39% of the population of British Malaya, compared with 45% Malays. Moreover, Chinese clearly outnumbered Malays in the states of the west coast, and in the main urban centres: it was only in the four northern unfederated states that the Malays maintained their numerical superiority. Chinese (and Indians) were dominant in the production of tin and rubber for the world market, in internal trade and in money-lending. The Malays were predominantly subsistence rice farmers, although they did develop a considerable rubber smallholding production by the inter-war years, despite strong opposition from a colonial administration which sought to reinforce the self-sufficiency of their *kampung* economy and to encourage their cultivation of food crops for the immigrant labouring populations.

In the inter-war period Malay nationalism began to develop, fostered principally by a vocal generation of village teachers trained at the Malay-medium Sultan Idris Training College (founded in 1922), by English-educated Malay civil servants and by religious figures who drew on the Islamic reformist ideas then emanating from the Middle East. The political concerns of the Chinese and Indians in this period lay primarily outside Malaya. From the 1920s the Kuomintang Government in China sought political support and financial contributions from among the Malayan Chinese, and, as China itself fell victim to Japanese aggression in the following decade, there was an upsurge of patriotism among the community in Malaya, which manifested itself most clearly in a series of boycotts of Japanese trade. Similarly, the Malayan Indians focused their attention on the gathering independence struggle in the subcontinent. With the important exception of the Communist Party of Malaya (CPM), formally organized in 1930, no radical party emerged to secure significant support among the Malayan peoples. The colonial order, founded on accommodation with both the Malay aristocracy and the wealthy Chinese mercantile class, appeared unshakeable.

OCCUPATION AND INDEPENDENCE

The Japanese invasion and occupation of Malaya swept aside that order and made its full restoration impossible. The rapid collapse of British power in Malaya and Singapore in the early weeks of 1942 did much to destroy the myth of white superiority which had sustained colonial rule in Malaya, as elsewhere, while the three years of Japanese administration which followed the British surrender greatly heightened the political sensibilities and racial antagonisms of the diverse elements in the Malayan population. The Malay rulers, who had refused to evacuate with the retreating British administration, largely collaborated with the Japanese, but did not receive the deference which had been theirs in the pre-war colonial order. Moreover, through the organization of mass demonstrations, Pan-Malayan conferences and paramilitary youth groups, the Japanese sought to weaken the established allegiance of the Malays to their individual state and sultan, and to encourage loyalty to a peninsula-wide entity. In August 1943, however, Japan transferred the four northern states, which were predominantly Malay, to Thailand, giving the immigrant communities overwhelming numerical dominance in the remaining states. The Indian community fared less well. Many Indian estate workers were forcibly conscripted for Japanese projects, including work on the Siam–Burma railway, and never returned. However, substantial enlistment into the Indian National Army, which was supported by Japan, helped to protect the community from the most harsh treatment. It was the Chinese who offered the only serious resistance to Japanese rule, for the anti-Japanese patriotism of the community had been strongly fuelled by the aggression of the 1930s, and it was they who suffered most brutally during the occupation. Chinese comprised by far the largest component in the Malayan People's Anti-Japanese Army, the main resistance force, which was dominated by the CPM. When the Japanese administration suddenly collapsed in mid-August 1945, the CPM was left as the only effective political-military organization in the peninsula in advance of the returning British.

During the Japanese occupation, British officials in London, isolated from the Malayan reality, drew up proposals for major post-war constitutional reforms. Previous attempts to simplify the peninsula's complex constitutional and administrative structures had been largely unsuccessful, but the perceived need to promote rapid economic recovery in the post-war years gave greater urgency to centralized direction. It was proposed to incorporate the FMS, the UMS, Pinang and Melaka into a unified administrative unit, the Malayan Union, while making Singapore a separate crown colony. It was also proposed that citizenship of the Malayan Union be extended to all, irrespective of race or origin, and that all citizens would have equal rights. Sovereignty was to be transferred from the Malay rulers to the British crown. The opening of liberal citizenship provisions for Chinese and Indians reflected, in part, an awareness that both populations had now taken on the character of a predominantly settled community, and, in part, a recognition that they had, in general, remained loyal to the United Kingdom during the occupation. It also seriously challenged, however, the long-established privileged position and rights of the Malays, who considered themselves to be the indigenous people of the country, despite the long history of migration from other parts of South-East Asia.

When the Malayan Union was announced by the restored colonial administration in January 1946, and formally introduced in April, the usually quiescent Malay community was angered, not only by the actual provisions, but also by the overbearing manner in which the new constitutional form had been introduced. Malay opposition was brought together in a new political force, the United Malays National Organization (UMNO), inaugurated in May. The provisions of the Union could not be brought into effect in the face of determined Malay opposition. The British then began negotiations with the Malay rulers and UMNO for a new constitutional arrangement. This was the Federation of Malaya, which was eventually inaugurated in February 1948. The Federation maintained the Malayan Union concept of a unified administrative unit (embracing the FMS, the UMS, Pinang and Melaka), but it also reaffirmed the sovereignty of the Sultans, preserved the special privileges of the Malays, and introduced citizenship provisions which, for Chinese and Indians, were markedly more restrictive than those contained in the abortive Malayan Union.

Many Chinese saw in the Federation a betrayal of the loyalty which they had shown towards the colonial power during the Japanese invasion and occupation, and in this sense its introduction undoubtedly strengthened the position of those within the CPM who sought an armed confrontation with the British. For the three years from the re-establishment of British administration in 1945, the CPM had pursued the 'open and legal' struggle, which principally had involved organizing and radicalizing the labour movement in Malaya. The immediate post-war years thus saw a high level of labour unrest, notably on the estates and in the public services. In late 1947 the Government introduced stringent controls over the organization and structure of trade unions. With its legal position thus threatened, in early 1948 the CPM inevitably moved towards an armed struggle. A spate of murders of European planters signalled to the authorities the change in CPM strategy, and on 18 June 1948 the Government proclaimed a state of emergency throughout Malaya.

The communist insurrection posed a severe military challenge to the colonial Government. The guerrilla forces secured considerable initial success against European plantation and mining personnel, and in October 1951 they assassinated the British High Commissioner, Sir Henry Gurney. The CPM received only limited support from the Malayan population at large, for its overwhelmingly Chinese membership denied it access to the Malay community, while its ideology found little acceptance among wealthy Chinese. Moreover, from the early 1950s the colonial Government undertook a resettlement of the Chinese squatter communities which had sustained the CPM with food, information and recruits, relocating them into secured, military-protected 'new villages'. By the mid-1950s the communist insurrection had collapsed, although the state of emergency officially remained in force until 1960. The CPM finally abandoned its armed struggle in December 1989, when the long-term leader, Chin Peng, signed agreements with the Malaysian and Thai Governments.

The CPM's strength in the mid-1950s was also undermined by a British announcement that Malaya would move quickly to political independence. From the late 1940s the colonial administration had sought to encourage a non-communal Malayan leadership, and in this context placed its faith largely in Dato' Onn Ja'afar, President of UMNO; however, Onn's inability to persuade his party to open its membership to all races, and the subsequent electoral failure of his non-communal, but élite, Independence of Malaya Party, closed that avenue. An alternative approach to securing a viable political leadership for an independent Malaya emerged from within the Malayan communities themselves. In the Kuala Lumpur municipal elections of February 1952, the local branches of UMNO and the Malayan Chinese Association (MCA) successfully contested seats as a united front. From this grew a national alliance (into which the Malayan Indian Congress (MIC) was incorporated in 1954) in which each party retained its separate identity and policies, while the Alliance acted as a single organization in selecting the candidates and party to contest each particular seat. In the 1955 federal elections the UMNO-MCA-MIC Alliance secured 51 of the 52 contested seats and 81% of the vote.

As Malaya now approached self-government, a new Constitution was prepared, providing for a single nationality, with citizenship open to all those in Malaya who qualified either by birth or by fulfilling requirements of residence and language. In order to meet Malay unease that these provisions were too liberal, the Constitution also provided for an unusual elective monarchy. The Yang di-Pertuan Agong (paramount ruler) was to be selected for a five-year term by, and from among, the nine ruling Sultans of the Malay states. He held a special responsibility for safeguarding the privileged position of the Malays, who were designated *bumiputra* ('sons of the soil'). Islam was made the official religion, but the degree to which Islamic law might be implemented remained under the control of the states. Independence (*merdeka*) was proclaimed on 31 August 1957, with Tunku Abdul Rahman, President of UMNO, as the first Prime Minister.

FORMATION OF MALAYSIA

Singapore, excluded from the unified Malaya created in 1948, followed a separate path to political independence. Internal self-government was secured in 1959, with the prospect of full independence being achieved in 1963. This prospect, however, caused considerable concern in independent Malaya, for it was feared that Singapore, whose politics had been notably radical in the 1950s, might soon be in a position to encourage and aid the remnants of Chinese left-wing elements in the peninsula. It was therefore proposed from 1961, notably by Tunku Abdul Rahman, that an independent Singapore be incorporated into a federation with Malaya: this would not only enable the latter to restrain the more volatile political forces in Singapore, but would also reinforce the natural economic relationship between the island entrepôt and its peninsular hinterland. However, federation with overwhelmingly Chinese Singapore threatened the numerical superiority of the Malays, and it was therefore further proposed that the northern Borneo territories also be brought within the new alignment. Sarawak and North Borneo both had significant Chinese communities, but the Muslim Malays and the often Christian indigenous peoples (principally Dayak in Sarawak and Kadazan in North Borneo) together outnumbered the immigrant communities in Malaysia.

Since 1946 both Sarawak and North Borneo had been crown colonies, following the respective terminations of Brooke rule and the administration of the British North Borneo Co, while Brunei remained a British protectorate. In none of these territories, however, had the United Kingdom made significant preparations for self-government, and there were strong local doubts regarding the prospect of being ruled from distant Kuala Lumpur. The Sultan of Brunei considered himself senior to the Sultans of the peninsula and, in view of Brunei's petroleum resources, the federation had few economic attractions for the protectorate. A basic nationalist movement thus emerged, with the aim of establishing an independent northern Borneo. However, the United Kingdom exploited disunity within the movement and concern that neighbouring Indonesia might seek to annex a small independent state. The British Government consequently proceeded with the creation of the federation, although the Sultan of Brunei finally decided not to join the grouping. In September 1963 both Sarawak and North Borneo (now renamed Sabah) joined Singapore and the Federation of Malaya to form the independent Federation of Malaysia. Within this federation, Sarawak and Sabah retained a higher degree of autonomy than the peninsular states, including the right to control immigration from the peninsula.

Indonesia, for reasons that derived primarily from its own internal political tensions, sought from the first to break up the Federation. In addition, the Philippines pursued a claim to the territory of Sabah. In September 1963 Indonesia and the Philippines broke off diplomatic relations with Malaysia, and Indonesia launched a series of military raids into Sarawak and Sabah from Indonesian Borneo (Kalimantan). However, this military challenge was successfully contained by Malaysian and Commonwealth forces and, following the fall from power of President Sukarno, a *rapprochement* between the two countries was achieved in August 1966.

An internal challenge to Malaysia arose from the determination of the People's Action Party (under Lee Kuan Yew), the governing party in Singapore, to campaign for the Chinese vote in peninsular elections, and so, in effect, oppose the MCA. This strategy threatened to undermine the Alliance consensus, and Malaysian leaders accused Singapore of provoking inter-communal animosity. In August 1965 Singapore was effectively expelled from Malaysia, despite protests from the island's leaders.

RESHAPING THE POLITICAL ORDER

The 1957 Constitution envisaged a multi-ethnic Malaysia in which the political and administrative dominance of the Malays would be balanced by the continuing economic pre-eminence of the Chinese and, to a lesser extent, the Indians. Within the parliamentary system, it was assumed, the interests of these groups would be represented by their respective élites, UMNO, the MCA and the MIC, who would negotiate policies aimed primarily at preserving the status quo and then at gradually achieving a convergence in the social standing of the three communities. Thus, it was expected that the Malays would achieve a steadily greater share of the economy, while the Chinese and Indians would gradually obtain more political influence, although there was no model for the kind of society this process might eventually produce and there was no prospect of any kind of ethnic or cultural fusion. The expulsion of Singapore from the Federation appeared to ensure that Malays would take part in this system from a position of numerical dominance, and would thus enjoy perpetual political pre-eminence, as long as they remained disciplined in their support of UMNO. The planners of the 1950s, however, had not allowed for the rapidity of social change in the new country. Amongst Malays, the impact of modernization contributed to a growing responsiveness to Islam and to political support for the Parti Islam se Malaysia (PAS—Islamic Party of Malaysia). The Islamic party had its political base amongst rural Islamic teachers and scholars, who were generally unsympathetic to the Malay aristocracy dominating UMNO. The Chinese for their part grew increasingly dissatisfied with political subordination, and in the federal election of May 1969 the MCA lost considerable ground among the Chinese voters to opposition parties, notably Gerakan Rakyat Malaysia (GERAKAN—Malaysian People's Movement) and the Democratic Action Party (DAP), which had demanded a more rapid end to Malay political predominance. Subsequent communal violence in the federal capital left many hundreds dead. To restore order, the Constitution was suspended and a national emergency declared.

The May 1969 riots forced a major readjustment both in the terms upon which communal interests and aspirations were accommodated, and in the manner by which the details of that accommodation were negotiated between the principal communities. The New Economic Policy (NEP), to be implemented over the 20 years to 1990, had as its primary objectives the eradication of poverty (irrespective of race) and of the identification of race with economic function. The latter objective implied securing for the Malays not only a far greater share in the wealth of the country but also a much wider range of educational and employment opportunities. It was intended that by 1990 30% of commercial and industrial share capital would be in *bumiputra* ownership (the ownership of Malays and other indigenous communities, or public enterprises acting on their behalf). Immediately after the 1969 riots, new legislation removed from public discussion such sensitive issues as the powers and status of the Sultans, Malay special rights, the status of Islam as the official religion and citizenship rights. At the same time the structure of coalition politics changed. The tripartite UMNO-MCA-MIC alliance was replaced by a broader coalition, registered in 1974 and called the Barisan Nasional (BN—National Front), which aimed to draw as many parties as possible into the Government under the leadership of UMNO. This strategy had the aim not only of giving the Government a broader electoral base but also of muting criticism by involving potential opposition parties in government policy. The BN has governed Malaysia ever since, and all significant parties except the DAP and Semangat '46 (dissolved in October 1996) have joined it in government at least for a time.

A major complicating factor in Malaysian politics is the position of the state Governments. The states vary greatly in their ethnic composition, their socio-economic structure and even their constitutional relationship to the federal Government. Politics, for instance, has a very different character in Pinang (urbanized, mainly Chinese), Kelantan (rural, predominantly Malay and ruled by a Sultan) and Sabah (Malays, Chinese and mainly Christian indigenous Borneans in roughly equal proportions). The nine peninsular states with reigning Sultans have greater political influence in the Conference of Rulers than the four states that do not (Pinang, Melaka, Sabah and Sarawak), but the two Borneo states have maintained the distinct status which allows them to control immigration from the peninsula as well as to exercise greater economic and cultural autonomy than any peninsular state. Most of Malaysia's politicians, therefore, work from a power base within just one state, and build their national political careers by means of alliances with politicians from other regions. Movement between the state and federal legislatures and Governments is also quite common. Although the political role of the Sultans is constitutionally limited, individual Sultans have had considerable influence within their own states from time to time.

Under the rule of the BN, the idiom of politics changed from one of national coalition between ethnic groups to one of Malay dominance as *bumiputra* (indigenes). The term *bumiputra* has always been problematic: not only does the Malay community include the descendants of 17th and 18th century immigrants to the peninsula from Sumatra and Sulawesi in what is now Indonesia, but more recent migrants from Indonesia and the Philippines, and even Muslim Cham refugees from Cambodia, have sometimes found it possible to acquire 'indigenous' status, even though their ties to the country are much more recent than those of some Chinese communities. Whereas on the peninsula *bumiputra* status, moreover, is closely linked to Islam, the indigenous peoples of the Borneo states are mostly Christian. Because of the sedition laws governing discussion of the rights of Malays and the position of Islam, however, such issues have seldom received more than tangential mention in Malaysian political discourse. None the less, the growing influence of the Malays was unmistakable. Bahasa Malaysia was adopted as the language of education and administration at all levels, racial quotas gave advantages to Malays, especially in the education system, and the cultural heritages of Chinese and Indian Malaysians were given clearly subordinate standing. UMNO patronage became increasingly important in the allocation of government posts, and Chinese and Indians appeared to be losing ground in the administration. Malays began to take a greater share of the economy, both through private firms receiving significant support from the Government and through state-owned enterprises. A steady trickle of educated Chinese and Indian Malaysians to Singapore and other destinations contributed to Malay dominance. In 1995 official policy on the use of Bahasa Malaysia was partially reversed, with a decision to reintroduce English as a language of instruction at tertiary level for the sake of international business and technological connections.

THE MAHATHIR YEARS 1981–

Within UMNO itself, however, important changes were in progress. Malaysia's first Prime Minister, Tunku Abdul Rahman (1963–70), was a royal prince, and his successors, Tun Abdul Razak (1970–76) and Dato' Hussein bin Onn (1976–81), were both Malay aristocrats. In 1981, however, Hussein Onn was succeeded by Dr Mahathir Mohamad, a professional and a commoner, who was widely seen as representing a new generation of modern Malays who were in thrall neither to the old aristocratic élite nor to the Islamic teachers of the countryside. Mahathir, who had earlier written a controversial defence of Malay interests (*The Malay Dilemma*, 1970), also represented a generation determined to consolidate the dominant position of the Malays in Malaysia. Mahathir's rule was characterized by a determined modernizing drive, based on both industrialization and the exploitation of raw materials (especially timber). In the early 1980s the Government was widely commended for its forceful insistence on efficiency and honesty, but by the late 1980s accusations of corruption and of abuse of power for economic advantage had become increasingly common. Business figures linked with UMNO appear to have prospered greatly from their connections, though legal restrictions have hampered detailed investigation of these allegations. In June 1991 the New Development Policy (NDP) was launched to succeed the NEP. The NDP shifted the emphasis from the NEP's racial economic restructuring to overall economic growth and the eradication of poverty. Racial quotas were retained, but no specific date was set for achieving the NEP's target of 30% *bumiputra* control of the country's corporate assets. An important part of this programme was the so-called 'Vision 2020', which Mahathir outlined in February 1991, embodying an ambition to turn Malaysia into a 'fully developed' country by the year 2020. Under this vision, Malaysia was not just to enjoy the material benefits of being fully developed (health care, public transport, education and general infrastructure) but was to be self-confident, harmonious, just, dynamic and democratic. Inevitably, however, progress towards the more material signs of development was easier to achieve than the less tangible goals.

The UMNO leadership faced two main challenges to its dominance over the Malays. PAS, whose main base was in rural Kelantan and Terengganu, also had some following amongst urban Malays who continued to resent Chinese economic influence and who wished to see Malaysia become more Islamic. The old Malay élite also resented Mahathir's drive for a more meritocratic society (at least amongst the Malays), and were shocked in 1983 by his proposals to restrict the power of the hereditary rulers by effectively removing the rulers' right to withhold assent from legislation. The Government and Sultans later reached a compromise on the proposals, but the conflict lingered on in a growing rift between Mahathir and his Minister of Trade and Industry, Tunku Razaleigh Hamzah, an aristocrat from Kelantan. Razaleigh narrowly failed in a challenge to Mahathir's party leadership in April 1987. Mahathir then removed Razaleigh supporters from most of the significant positions in both the Government and the party, but was given an unexpected opportunity to consolidate his dominance in February 1988, when the High Court ruled that, because of irregularities in the UMNO elections of 1987, the party was in breach of the Societies Act and was technically illegal. To regularize the party's position, Mahathir created a new party, UMNO Baru (New UMNO), later in February, which inherited the property of the 'old' UMNO. All members of the former party, however, were required to apply anew for registration. In this way, Razaleigh and other opponents were excluded without the difficulty of going through expulsion proceedings. A number of dissidents subsequently accepted Mahathir's dominance and joined UMNO Baru (henceforth referred to as UMNO), but in October 1989 Razaleigh announced the creation of a new movement called Semangat '46 (Spirit of 1946, the year of founding of the original UMNO).

Although the ideas and social groups represented by Razaleigh still had considerable support amongst Malays, the electoral prospects of the new party (which was registered in May 1990) were hampered by its lack of access to government patronage and by its need to seek allies amongst the forces outside the BN. Semangat '46 quickly developed an alliance with PAS (although PAS and the Razaleigh group had been bitter rivals in Kelantan state politics and Razaleigh himself had engineered the expulsion of PAS from the BN in 1978), under the name Angkatan Perpaduan Ummah (APU—Muslim Unity Movement). As the 1990 elections approached, however, Semangat '46 also developed an alliance, called the Gagasan Rakyat (People's Concept), with the overwhelmingly Chinese DAP. Although PAS and the DAP each shared interests and concerns with Semangat '46, they had virtually nothing in common with each other, and the coalition looked implausible as an alternative government. The elections of October 1990 thus returned the Mahathir Government. The BN won slightly fewer seats (127 of the 180 seats in the extended House of Representatives), but retained the two-thirds majority required to amend the Constitution. The opposition did well in the DAP stronghold of Pinang and won overwhelmingly in Kelantan, but for the most part performed poorly elsewhere. Semangat '46 in fact won only six of the 61 seats it contested. This victory gave Mahathir a platform from which to pursue his campaign to reduce the authority of the Sultans. In July 1992 he oversaw the introduction of a code of conduct for the rulers, which restricted their ability to intervene in the political process. In January 1993 Parliament passed legislation removing the Sultans' personal legal immunity. When the rulers withheld assent from the bill, the Government orchestrated a campaign of public revelations of excesses and abuses of position on the part of various Sultans until the Sultans capitulated. The Government also rescinded the traditional privileged treatment which the rulers had enjoyed from government officials and which some of them had used to develop significant business interests. In May 1994 the House of Representatives approved a constitutional amendment definitively removing the rulers' power to block legislation by withholding assent. In September 1997 Mahathir continued his attack on state power by convening a conference to centralize the administration of Islamic law, previously a state matter. His target in this case, however, was not so much state politicians as state religious authorities whose conservative *fatwa*, he alleged, were impeding national development. At the UMNO assembly in September, he accused many Muslims of being more concerned with form (beards, clothing, etc.) than with the substance of Islamic teaching.

During the late 1980s the Mahathir Government came into increasing conflict with the judiciary after a number of cases in which government decisions were overturned, although the Malaysian courts have traditionally been rather conservative. In May 1987, just before one of the crucial court hearings over the legal status of UMNO, the Yang di-Pertuan Agong suspended the Lord President of the Supreme Court, Tun Salleh Abbas, from his post. A tribunal of judges then concluded he was guilty of 'misbehaviour' in the form of bias against the Government and he was dismissed in August. Five of the remaining Supreme Court judges were also suspended at this time, and two were dismissed, in connection with the legal proceedings surrounding the dismissal of Salleh Abbas. These measures were followed in March 1988 by constitutional amendments limiting the power of the judiciary to interpret laws. In 1994 the Government restyled the Supreme Court as the Federal Court and the Lord President as the Chief Justice, as well as introducing a mandatory code of ethics for judges.

The Government was also willing to use its extensive security powers against opposition groups. In October 1987 the appointment of more than 100 non-sinophone teachers to Chinese schools provoked mass public protests by the Chinese community. These led, in turn, to counter-demonstrations by UMNO youth organizations. To restore order, the Government invoked its security powers to detain more than 100 people without trial. As well as politicians from all parties, journalists, lawyers and leaders of pressure groups, the detainees included Lim Kit Siang, the Secretary-General of the DAP. (All were released by the following April.) Three newspapers were closed by government order and political rallies were banned. In November and December the Government introduced legislation to impose stringent penalties on editors and publishers if they published what the Government regarded as 'false' news, and empowering the Minister of Information to monitor all radio and television broadcasts, and to revoke the licence of any private broadcasting company not conforming with 'Malaysian values'. In June 1988 the Government introduced legislation removing the right of persons being detained under the Internal Security Act (ISA) to have recourse to the courts. At the end of December 1991 the High Court upheld a ruling by the Ministry of Home Affairs to ban the public sale of party newspapers. This was widely interpreted as an attempt to undermine further the potential effectiveness of the opposition parties, because it mainly affected opposition journals, including *The Rocket* (DAP), *Harakah* (PAS) and *Berita Rakyat* (Parti Rakyat Malaysia), all of which were henceforth allowed to be distributed only to party members. The extent of BN dominance of the media became apparent in March 1995, when the leader of Semangat '46, Razaleigh, won a court case in Hong Kong against the *South China Morning Post* newspaper, which had blamed him for huge losses incurred by a subsidiary of the state-owned Bank Bumiputra Malaysia Bhd in 1983, an accusation which raised questions over his integrity. The settlement included a promise by the newspaper to publish an apology in Malaysia, but the country's two largest newspapers, which were close to UMNO, refused to accept the advertisement.

Although the BN under Mahathir found perennial difficulty in dominating Kelantan and Pinang on the peninsula, its greatest difficulties came in Borneo, especially in Sabah. The main parties in Sabah when the BN was formed in 1974 were the ruling Muslim United Sabah National Organization (USNO) and the multi-ethnic Bersatu Rakyat Jelata Sabah (Berjaya—Sabah People's Union). Both joined the BN at national level, but were rivals within Sabah. Berjaya won state elections in 1976 and remedied many of the abuses associated with USNO rule, but by 1985 it too had become corrupt and authoritarian, and was displaced by the new multi-ethnic Parti Bersatu Sabah (PBS—Sabah United Party). The PBS joined the BN in 1986, but its relations with Mahathir were cool, and in October 1990 the party abruptly withdrew from the BN prior to the general election, allying itself with Semangat '46. After the BN's electoral victory Mahathir largely excluded the Sabah Chief Minister, Joseph Pairin Kitingan, from government meetings to discuss federal/state issues and withheld development funds from the state. In January 1991 the Government arrested Pairin Kitingan on corruption charges; he was subsequently released on bail, and although he was convicted in early 1994 he was fined less than the minimum RM 2,000 that was required to disqualify him from office. The case was widely seen in Sabah as victimization by the federal Government. Meanwhile, in February 1991 UMNO established its first branch in Sabah; in August 1992 the Government arranged the deregistration of its former ally USNO, which had joined a coalition with the PBS. Although the PBS narrowly won the state election in 1994, UMNO managed to engineer numerous defections from Pairin Kitingan to new splinter parties and to construct its own coalition with Tan Sri Sakaran Dandai as Chief Minister. The coalition agreement included a promise that the post of Chief Minister would rotate among Sabah's three main ethnic groups, the Malays, the Kadazan and the Chinese. In March 1996 Mahathir supported the Malay incumbent, Salleh Tun Said Keruak, to stay on 'provisionally', but this suggestion so angered the other ethnic groups that Salleh was forced to stand down in May and the Chinese leader of the Sabah Progressive Party, Datuk Yong Teck Lee, was installed in his place. In Sarawak, meanwhile, the High Court ruled that the government victory in the Bukit Begunan constituency in the September 1996 state election was null and void on the grounds of vote-buying by BN campaigners. The BN, however, won the subsequent by-election.

The general election of 24–25 April 1995 approached, with few observers believing that the opposition Gagasan Rakyat had any chance of victory. Malaysia's rapid economic growth had led to a widespread feeling that the administration was performing well. The uneasy alliance between Semangat '46, the DAP and PAS, moreover, had been made still more uncomfortable by an announcement from the PAS state Government in Kelantan in 1992 that it intended to introduce the Islamic criminal code (*hudud*) in the state. Unlike the laws on Islamic religious practice which the state already applied to Muslims in Kelantan, this would have subjected non-Muslims to Islamic law. It also prescribed the death sentence for apostasy, although the implementation of the penalty required federal consent, which was not forthcoming. The legislation was adopted in 1993, despite claims that it contravened the Constitution's guarantee of freedom of religion. This and related issues sowed such discord in opposition ranks that the DAP withdrew from the Gagasan in January 1995. The opposition also had to cope with a lack of media coverage and an official campaign period limited by the Government to just nine days. In fact, the only issues that seemed likely to detract significantly from the Government's electoral support were the persistent allegations of corruption that emerged against its senior figures. In September 1994 the Chief Minister of Melaka and leader of the powerful UMNO youth wing, Tan Sri Datuk Rahim Thamby Chik, was forced to resign following allegations that he had had sexual relations with a minor, an offence constituting statutory rape. The charges were later abandoned. The DAP youth leader, Lim Guan Eng, was subsequently tried for sedition for remarks he had made suggesting that the authorities had not been even-handed in the case, and in April 1997 he was convicted and fined RM 15,000 (Lim was released in August 1999 following the failure of an appeal against his conviction—the judgment automatically disqualified him from holding a parliamentary seat).

The 1995 election results were a triumph for Mahathir. The BN's share of the vote rose to 64%, from 53% in 1990, and it won 162 of the 192 seats in the extended House of Representatives, as well as all the seats in the State Legislative Assemblies in Perlis and Johor, and a majority in every other state except Kelantan. The PAS-Semangat '46 coalition retained power in Kelantan and lost only two seats nationally, but the DAP lost 11 of its 20 seats in the House of Representatives and all but one of its 14 state seats in Pinang. The PBS, led by Pairin Kitingan, won eight of Sabah's 20 federal seats. The election defeat led to a crisis of confidence in Semangat '46. The party's coalition with PAS in Kelantan began to break down and in October 1996 the party was formally dissolved, with its 200,000 members joining UMNO.

At the UMNO party congress in late 1993 there had been considerable speculation over likely successors to Mahathir, who was born in 1925. Attention focused then on the Minister of Finance and former UMNO youth leader, Dato' Seri Anwar Ibrahim, who was elected Deputy President of the party (normally a stepping stone to the leadership) and whose self-styled 'Vision Team' won all three vice-presidential positions. The 1995 election results briefly ended such speculation, but by the end of the year it had resurfaced as signs of jostling for power grew at all levels of the UMNO organization. Observers were far from certain that Mahathir supported Anwar as his successor, and in the aftermath of the election the Prime Minister appeared to shift the balance of power in the Cabinet slightly against Anwar and his allies. In particular, Dato' Seri Najib Tun Razak was moved from the defence to the education portfolio, a significant post because the last three Malaysian Prime Ministers had all served in that department before acceding to power. Najib had been one of Anwar's 'Vision Team' vice-presidents, but was now seen as having shifted to the Mahathir camp. In November 1995 the annual UMNO assembly decided not to allow any challenge to Mahathir or Anwar at the triennial party congress scheduled for October 1996, thus postponing the battle for succession until 1999. The contest, however, continued by proxy over the several junior leadership positions that were at stake, although in July 1996 the party's Supreme Council banned open campaigning by or for any candidate. The return of Semangat '46 members to UMNO took place too late to affect the outcome of the congress, but most observers believed that their presence strengthened the position of Mahathir, whose relations with Razaleigh were surprisingly cordial. The vice-presidential elections saw the return to office of Najib and of Anwar loyalist Mohammad Taib, and the election of a Mahathir supporter, the Minister of Foreign Affairs, Abdullah Ahmad Badawi. On the other hand, two Mahathir allies who had been damaged by corruption accusations, Rafidah Aziz (head of the UMNO women's wing) and Rahim Thamby Chik, were defeated by Anwar supporters, Dr Siti Zaharah Sulaiman and Ahmad Zahid Hamidi. Both were thus victims, in part, of Mahathir's increasing outspokenness against what is commonly called 'money politics', which he described in October 1995 as the only factor that could destroy UMNO. Taib, a prominent Anwar supporter, fell victim to the same affliction in December 1996, when he was arrested at the airport in Brisbane, Australia, carrying the equivalent of more than RM 2.3m., thus contravening an Australian law requiring the declaration of amounts greater than about RM 10,000 being taken into or out of the country. Taib subsequently resigned as Chief Minister of Selangor, and in May 1997 he was forced to resign as Vice-President of UMNO; however, he was later acquitted of all charges. New Chief Ministers in Selangor and Melaka announced strict standards of probity for politicians and senior officials within their states, but appeared to find it difficult to distinguish clearly between legitimate business interests and corrupt behaviour. Throughout 1996–98 many lesser figures were charged or otherwise disciplined for alleged financial irregularities, but public opinion did not interpret these moves as a genuine attempt to eliminate corrupt practices. The weakening of Anwar's position that Taib's disgrace implied, however, was counterbalanced by a period of two months from mid-May 1997, during which Mahathir took leave to travel, write and promote Malaysia abroad, leaving Anwar as acting Prime Minister in his place.

Mahathir returned to office in time to face a growing political challenge arising from the Asian financial crisis. In mid-July 1997 the ringgit began to depreciate, placing sudden pressure on the many firms and investors who had borrowed in foreign currency, making foreign credits suddenly much more difficult to obtain and forcing down prices on the Malaysian stock exchange. The Malaysian crisis was precipitated by simple contagion from events in Thailand, but the markets soon focused on what were seen as structural problems in the Malaysian system, notably overexpenditure on prestige infrastructure projects and opacity in the economy, partly a result of corruption, partly a result of the formal policy of promoting the economic development of the Malay community. The ringgit's decline became catastrophic in October, when it lost 40% of its previous value within a month. Mahathir's public response, however, was to portray the crisis as a selfish, and perhaps malevolent, attack on Malaysia's economic achievements by a small group of foreign speculators and Western media, possibly in league with unfriendly governments. Remarks made by Mahathir, which were widely interpreted as showing that the Prime Minister did not understand the issues that concerned the financial markets, placed still further pressure on the ringgit.

Unlike Thailand, Indonesia and the Republic of Korea, Malaysia declined to accept IMF intervention, which would almost certainly have required the abandonment of most of the major infrastructure projects favoured by Mahathir and might have condemned the policy of preference for Malays. None the less, Anwar, as Minister of Finance, was able to persuade Mahathir to abandon several large projects. In early December 1997 all federal and state ministers took a 10% cut in salary and smaller reductions were imposed on parliamentarians and senior bureaucrats. Most observers agreed that Anwar's standing as Mahathir's likely successor had been strengthened by his measured response to the crisis, but he personally showed no keenness to displace Mahathir and thus to assume prime responsibility for the continuing difficulties.

The atmosphere of crisis in 1997 was exacerbated by a heavy pall of smoke (generally referred to as 'haze') from forest fires in Indonesia, which drifted over large areas of peninsular Malaysia and Sarawak, reaching its worst in September. Air pollution levels were dangerous to public health for several weeks and hundreds of airline flights were cancelled, causing massive business losses, especially in the tourist industry. The problem was worst in Sarawak, where at times visibility dropped to a few metres in the capital, Kuching. In November the Government banned the country's academics from making public statements about the smoke, on the grounds that commentators had been alarmist and had been 'manipulated' by foreign media.

In November 1997 Anwar moved a parliamentary motion of confidence in Mahathir in order to defuse the growing speculation about a possible change of leadership. Internal elections for divisional committee members in UMNO in March 1998 left most of Mahathir's supporters in place, leaving Anwar with no clear power base from which to launch a challenge. None the less, the resignation of the Indonesian President, Suharto, in May revived speculation that the economic crisis might also bring down Mahathir. In a reflection of the Indonesian resentment of the business interests of Suharto's children, there was increased public attention in Malaysia to the business activities of Mahathir's three sons. The Prime Minister's eldest son, Mirzan Mahathir, received government assistance to save his businesses from bankruptcy under circumstances which some Malaysians regarded as favouritism, although several other prominent business executives had also received assistance as part of a programme intended to keep the local corporate sector relatively intact until the economy improved.

Although Anwar was careful not to give any indication of a challenge to Mahathir, he spoke out publicly against corruption and political restriction in a way that clearly laid out a case for a change of leadership. Then, at the UMNO annual conference in June 1998, one of Anwar's supporters launched a strong attack on the party leadership over the same issues. Mahathir's supporters responded with a brochure entitled 'Fifty Reasons Why Anwar Cannot Become Prime Minister', in which Anwar was accused of conspiracy and sexual offences. Information on Anwar associates who appeared to have benefited from 'cronyism' was also released. During the following weeks, Mahathir systematically dismantled Anwar's power base, appointing Dato' Paduka Daim Zainuddin to oversee the economy, dismissing newspaper editors close to Anwar, and ordering the arrest of a close associate of Anwar on firearms charges carrying the death penalty under Malaysian law. Increasingly lurid accounts of Anwar's alleged sexual misdemeanours began to circulate, and Mahathir reportedly pressed his deputy to resign or to face dismissal and criminal charges. Anwar declined to resign and was dismissed on 2 September.

The rift between the two men appeared to be based partly on their very different responses to the economic crisis: Mahathir blamed foreign speculators and believed that Malaysia's economic salvation lay in protection and in continued economic expansion, whereas Anwar, as Minister of Finance, supported austerity measures close in spirit to IMF prescriptions. Anwar's dismissal was preceded by an announcement from Mahathir imposing tight currency and stock-market controls in direct opposition to global pressures, and Anwar's preference, for greater liberalization. Many observers believed that Mahathir wished to forestall the possibility that Anwar might succeed to the premiership and reverse such measures. Mahathir himself formally denied that policy divisions had prompted his action, and stated that Anwar's lifestyle made him unsuited to lead a conservative, religious country; further underlining this point, on 3 September 1998 the UMNO Supreme Council voted unanimously in favour of Anwar's expulsion from the party.

Anwar responded to his dismissal by denying the rumours of impropriety, alleging that there was a conspiracy against him and denouncing Mahathir as 'paranoid'. He forecast that a popular movement would bring Mahathir down, as had toppled President Suharto in Indonesia. His supporters held daily demonstrations, bearing portraits of Anwar and banners with the word *'reformasi'* (reform), which had been the rallying cry of the opposition to Suharto in April and May 1998. Although government officials were quick to accuse Anwar of hypocrisy in attacking the system of which, until recently, he had himself been a part, the authorities in turn had difficulty explaining why a minister so central to the Mahathir team should be suddenly so ferociously vilified. As well as arousing his own considerable following, Anwar's dismissal crystallized broader resentment of the autocratic methods of the Mahathir Government. As the demonstrations in support of Anwar gathered momentum, Anwar and 16 supporters were arrested by riot police on 20 September, under the ISA. Foreign television reports of the arrest were reported to have been jammed by the Malaysian authorities. Anwar's wife, Dr Wan Azizah Wan Ismail was summoned for questioning by police. A restriction order was issued, banning her from holding rallies at her house, which had become a focus for the *reformasi* movement. Anwar appeared in court on 29 September and was charged with five counts of corruption and five of unnatural sexual acts. He appeared badly bruised and claimed to have been assaulted while in custody. Anwar's allegations provoked expressions of extreme concern from foreign governments—in particular from the Presidents of the Philippines and Indonesia—and prompted the UN Secretary-General, Kofi Annan, to urge the Malaysian Government to ensure humane treatment for Anwar. Although the Malaysian Government initially dismissed Anwar's claims of assault, it was subsequently announced that a special investigation was to be established. In December the Inspector-General of the Malaysian police force, Tan Sri Abdul Rahim Noor, resigned after an initial inquiry blamed the police for the injuries Anwar had sustained. Malaysia's Attorney-General publicly admitted in January 1999 that Anwar had been assaulted while in police custody, and an official inquiry completed in March found Tan Sri Rahim Noor to be personally responsible for the beating. He was later sentenced to two months' imprisonment and a fine of RM 2,000.

Meanwhile, popular demonstrations demanding the reform of the ISA, Mahathir's resignation and Anwar's release continued to take place, but were ignored by the local media. In October 1998, however, the influential Malaysian Bar unanimously adopted resolutions condemning detention without trial and demanding that independent inquiries be held into allegations of police brutality; on the same day several thousand people marched in Kuala Lumpur in support of similar reforms. It was subsequently announced that Anwar was no longer to be detained under the ISA, but would be transferred to a regular prison. (The last of the supporters of Anwar also detained under the ISA in September were released in November.) The trial of Anwar on four charges of corruption (which referred to efforts allegedly made by Anwar in 1997 to use his position to suppress an investigation of his alleged sexual misconduct) began on 2 November 1998. During the trial the credibility of the prosecution was undermined by a number of factors, including the professed willingness of a principal witness to lie under oath, the withdrawal by two witnesses for the prosecution of their claims to have engaged in illegal homosexual activity with Anwar, and the retraction by Anwar's adoptive brother and his speech-writer of their confessions, which they claimed had been obtained through police coercion. Also during the trial, a former head of the police Special Branch testified that he had used special police techniques to intimidate Anwar's accusers into withdrawing their statements; although this testimony reflected badly on Anwar, it also indicated in a more general way that political leaders were able to subvert criminal procedure for their own interests. Meanwhile, the defence suffered a number of set-backs during the trial. In November the judge sentenced one of Anwar's lawyers to three months' imprisonment for contempt of court.

In January 1999 the charges against Anwar were unexpectedly amended, with the emphasis being shifted from sexual misconduct to abuse of power; the amendment meant that the prosecution would no longer have to prove that Anwar had committed sexual offences, but only that he had attempted to use his position to influence the police to quash the investigation into the allegations, effectively making it easier for a conviction to be obtained. The judge subsequently ruled that further testimony relating to the earlier allegations of sexual misconduct was irrelevant, leading the defence to claim that it had been denied the opportunity to refute the damaging and by now widely-publicized accusations. (The ruling also meant that the defence would no longer be able to carry out its planned cross-examination of Mahathir and Daim Zainuddin on the issue of whether the allegations of sexual misconduct in particular were part of a political conspiracy against Anwar.) The trial, the longest-running criminal trial in Malaysia's history, was ended abruptly in late March, and the verdict was delivered in mid-April: Anwar was found guilty on each of the four charges of corruption and was sentenced to six years' imprisonment. (Under Malaysian law, a sentence of this length is automatically followed by a five-year period of disqualification from political office.) Following the delivery of the verdict, supporters of Anwar clashed with security forces outside the court in demonstrations of protest that were later violently dispersed.

Meanwhile, Mahathir sought to confirm his dominance by appointing a new Deputy Prime Minister, Abdullah Badawi, in a major reorganization of the Cabinet effected in January 1999. Also in the reshuffle, Mahathir relinquished the home affairs portfolio to Badawi and the finance portfolio to Daim Zainuddin, thus restoring a 'normal' distribution of portfolios in the Cabinet. Mahathir also postponed for up to one year internal party elections which had been due in June. Badawi's background as Minister of Foreign Affairs made him a useful foil to the continuing allegations of UMNO corruption, while his subdued political style meant that he was unlikely to become a political threat to Mahathir. Within UMNO, a wide-ranging purge removed many known Anwar supporters, while a prominent academic supporter of Anwar, Chandra Muzaffar, was effectively dismissed from the University of Malaya in February 1999. With Mahathir preparing the ground for UMNO's campaign in the forthcoming general election (which was to be held by June 2000), Anwar's supporters countered by founding a new political party, the Parti Keadilan Nasional (PKN, National Justice Party), in early April under the leadership of Wan Azizah; the new party reportedly aimed to establish itself as a multi-ethnic and multi-religious party (although its initial membership appeared to be predominantly Muslim), and declared that, should it come to power, it would seek a royal pardon for Anwar. At mid-1999 the level of support for the new party was difficult to establish, but it seemed likely that in the forthcoming election the party would share with PAS the votes of former supporters of UMNO alienated by the Anwar affair. PAS membership reportedly grew by 25% to 600,000 between September 1998 and mid-1999, while the PKN claimed to have 150,000 members. PAS also sought to broaden its appeal by opening a dialogue with non-Muslims, courting local businessmen and opening social welfare centres which provided legal and medical assistance to those Malaysians suffering the effects of the regional financial crisis. In June 1999 PAS, the PKN, the predominantly Chinese Democratic Action Party (DAP) and the Malaysian People's Party (PRM) formed a coalition, the Barisan Alternatif (BA—Alternative Front), to contest the elections, prompting Mahathir to accuse them of being supported by foreigners who wished to undermine the Malaysian economy. The BA was a disparate group united mainly by hostility to Mahathir, whom Wan Azizah described as a 'once respected leader who has lost all sense of perspective, all sense of right and wrong and all sense of reality'. The coalition subsequently selected Anwar as its prime ministerial candidate, but quarrelled over electoral strategy and experienced difficulty in its attempts to avoid misgivings over the differences in the long-term aims of the individual parties within the coalition.

The Government responded to this wave of dissent by accusing its opponents of deliberately seeking chaos and by issuing numerous civil laws suits in which ruling politicians sued journalists and opposition figures for defamation. The Attorney-General warned that those who alleged selective prosecution would themselves be prosecuted for contempt of court.

In late April 1999 Anwar was further charged with one count of illegal homosexual activity, to which he pleaded not guilty; it was announced that four other similar charges and one additional corruption charge against him had been 'suspended'. In the same month three of Anwar's associates (including his adoptive brother) who had earlier retracted statements they had made accusing Anwar of illegal homosexual activity and other sexual misdemeanours, claiming that the statements had been extracted by the police under duress, were charged with perjury; Anwar's adoptive brother was additionally charged with one count of illegal homosexual activity and one count of assisting Anwar to commit such an activity. The second trial of Anwar began on 7 June. On the first day of the trial the prosecution amended the wording of its charge, changing the month and year in which the alleged crimes were supposedly committed; the defence claimed that the change was made because the building in which the alleged activity occurred had not yet been constructed at the time specified in the original wording of the charge. Meanwhile, at the UMNO General Assembly in mid-May, Mahathir made it clear that there was no prospect of any reconciliation with Anwar. In a long speech delivered to delegates, he accused Anwar of being the stooge of racist foreign Governments whose aim was to recolonize Malaysia. Anwar responded from prison with accusations that Mahathir and his colleagues were guilty of corruption and nepotism and claimed that he had been removed from the Government because of his commitment to ending such practices. (In October the Government responded with accusations that Anwar himself had accumulated RM 780m. in illicit funds.) In September the trial was adjourned and Anwar was sent for medical examination, following claims by the defence that Anwar had proven high levels of arsenic in his blood and was quite possibly the victim of deliberate poisoning. In the same month Anwar lost a defamation suit that he had filed against Mahathir following his arrest. In a report released in early October, doctors concluded that Anwar 'showed no clinical signs of acute or chronic arsenic poisoning'; the High Court subsequently ordered that the trial of the former Deputy Prime Minister resume. In mid-October Mahathir was subpoenaed by the defence to give evidence in the trial, but on 21 April 2000 the High Court finally ruled that the Prime Minister was not required to give evidence. On 29 April, the Court of Appeal upheld Anwar's original conviction on charges of abuse of power, and the former Deputy Prime Minister and Minister of Finance was finally convicted of sodomy on 8 August, receiving a sentence of nine years' imprisonment to commence after the expiry of his earlier sentence, meaning that he could remain imprisoned until 2014. In May 2001 the prosecution abandoned the five remaining charges against Anwar. In July 2002 Anwar's appeal against his corruption conviction was finally rejected by the High Court.

In November 1999 the Government unexpectedly announced that a general election was to be held later the same month. The opposition expressed dissatisfaction at the limited period of time allowed for the election campaign. During this brief official campaign period, the opposition focused on what it claimed was corruption and arrogance on the part of the Government, while the BN attacked the character of Anwar and emphasized the incompatibility of the four opposition parties. Constituencies were threatened with the loss of federal government funds if they failed to return BN candidates at the election, and Mahathir warned of the prospect of an outbreak of violence if the Government were not returned to office.

The national elections held on 29 November 1999 returned the BN to government, the coalition winning 148 of the 193 seats in the House of Representatives. Although the BN retained the two-thirds majority required to allow the Government to amend the Constitution, the coalition's share of the national vote declined from 64.1% (at the previous general election) to 56.5%, while UMNO's representation in the legislature decreased to 72 members. There was a substantial swing against UMNO in the states of Kedah and Pahang, and even Mahathir's winning margin in his own constituency fell from 17,000 to 10,000 votes. PAS, by contrast, increased its number of seats from seven to 27 and the PAS leader, Fadzil Nor, was officially appointed parliamentary leader of the opposition. The party also retained power in the state of Kelantan and took office in Terengganu. PAS's partners in the BA, however, performed poorly. The DAP won 11 seats, as it had in 1995, but its Secretary-General, Lim Kit Siang, lost his seat as did its Deputy Chairman, Karpal Singh (who was also Anwar's legal representative). Wan Azizah retained Anwar's former seat for the PKN, but the party won only four other seats, all of them in regions that otherwise would probably have returned a PAS candidate. The distribution of votes suggested that 70% of Chinese voters and 90% of Indians had votes for the BN, whereas only about 50% of Malays had done so. For the first time in a federal election, there were widespread allegations of malpractice, including claims that eligible voters had been denied a ballot (especially newly-registered young voters who were considered likely to be hostile to Mahathir) and that the names of opposition candidates on the ballot papers had been tampered with using wax or resin, so that they could not be marked with pen or pencil. An unusually large number of ballot papers were reported spoiled. There were also rumours of vote-buying and the use of 'phantom' voters on behalf of UMNO.

Mahathir made few changes in his cabinet after the election, although former Minister of Education, Najib Tun Razak, who only narrowly retained his seat in the House of Representatives, was demoted from the education portfolio to that of defence. There was much interest, however, in the policies of the new PAS state legislature in Terengganu. The new Chief Minister, Abdul Hadi Awang, had pledged to ban gambling, restrict alcohol sales and make Friday a public holiday, and had also suggested the introduction of both strict Islamic criminal law and a religious income tax, called *kharaj*, on non-Muslims. Once in office, however, Awang banned *karaoke* and gambling but postponed more radical proposals and concentrated on winning business confidence and establishing for himself a reputation for efficiency and honesty. Expensive prestige projects were cancelled, and a new openness was introduced into the allocation of government tenders and licences. In early September 2000 the federal Government, alarmed by Terengganu's successes, announced that it would no longer pay Terengganu a royalty percentage on petroleum production in the state, but would instead channel the revenue into a federally-controlled development fund. (Royalty payments amounted to about RM 1,000m. per year and accounted for 90% of Terengganu state revenues.)

In January 2000 the authorities arrested five prominent opposition leaders, including Karpal Singh and the editor and publisher of the popular PAS newspaper, *Harakah*, most of them on charges of sedition. *Harakah* itself was threatened with closure, as a result of the newspaper's illegal sale to the public. In March the Ministry of Home Affairs announced that it would permit *Harakah* to be published only twice a month, rather than twice a week, but later emphasized Mahathir's insistence that Malaysian internet websites, including opposition news websites, such as that of *Harakah* itself, would not be censored. A small demonstration, which took place in Kuala Lumpur in mid-April on the first anniversary of Anwar's sentencing, was dispersed. Other opposition figures faced charges, which had apparently been brought with the aim of removing them from political life. In April and May 2001 16 opposition figures, most of them members of the PKN, were arrested under the ISA. Both courts and the Malaysian Human Rights Commission criticized the Government for using legislation that was intended to combat communist insurrection as a means of suppressing its political opponents. With increasing restrictions on the print media, an internet newspaper, *Malaysiakini,* established in mid-2000, became an increasingly important alternative source of information for the Malaysian public.

Contrary to many expectations, the BA did not disintegrate after the election, but continued to function as a coalition in opposition, creating a form of shadow cabinet in March 2000, maintaining pressure on the BN in parliamentary debates and continuing to minimize the fundamental policy differences between its members on the issue of the place of Islam in Malaysian politics and society. As PAS broadened its appeal to Muslim professionals and younger, urban voters, the party's Islamic character became steadily less intimidating to non-Malay groups. The PAS Government in Terengganu further sought the favour of non-Muslims by allowing a Chinese cultural festival to take place, and issuing permits for non-Muslim places of worship, which had been continually refused by the BN Government. The PKN, by contrast, grew increasingly uncertain of itself, divided over the extent to which it should continue to focus on the treatment of Anwar and over whether to promote public demonstrations against the Government, even though these actions appeared to be attracting fewer supporters. On 10 June, however, the party achieved increased support in a by-election, although it still failed to win the seat, and was further boosted when the Malaysian People's Party agreed in principle to merge with it. In November 2000 the BA defeated the BN in a by-election for the Lunas seat in Kedah, which had been won by the BN one year earlier. The victory was significant, since Kedah was Mahathir's home state and since the result deprived the BN of its symbolic former two-thirds' majority in the state legislature. The UMNO leadership was also concerned by resistance within the party to a proposal to extend the term of UMNO officials from three to five years. In addition, the MCA faced corruption scandals, including revelations that some of the beneficiaries of a fund that had been administered by the association for victims of the 1999 Japanese encephalitis outbreak were, in fact, party members and staff, who had not been affected by the virus. UMNO's response to this pressure was to make efforts to improve its Islamic credentials. In March 2000 the BN state Government of Perlis introduced legislation prescribing detention at a Faith Rehabilitation Centre for those found guilty of 'deviationism' and apostasy, while Johor activated 1997 legislation, whereby lesbianism, pre-marital sex, prostitution, pimping and incest would be punishable by whipping and terms of imprisonment. The federal Government envisaged legislation to make misuse of religion a criminal offence. In May 2000 the Government introduced a requirement for all Muslim civil servants to attend classes in religion twice weekly. The Government also continued to emphasize long-term reforms, such as the introduction of Islamic banking and insurance. A proposal, presented in late 1999, for the inclusion of a statement of religious affiliation on identity cards (which must be carried by all Malaysians), was, however, suspended. The measure was widely criticized as likely to exacerbate religious differences and to hinder the emergence of the shared Malaysian identity, which formed an integral part of Mahathir's 'Vision 2020'. In September 2000 the Government charged 29 members of the al-Ma'unah cult with treason, following a robbery of weapons in Perak in July, in which two hostages were killed. Government attempts to attribute the incident to PAS were received with considerable scepticism.

Controversy continued over the random destruction of Chinese cultural heritage in Malaysia. During 2000 the federal Government began to develop a new 10-year plan, provisionally known as the Vision Development Policy, which was to replace the National Development Policy. Although the new plan maintained affirmative action policies for Malays, speculation that the extent of these policies would be reduced prompted Malay demonstrations against Chinese organizations, and fierce condemnation of alleged Chinese extremism. Chinese and Indian communities, in turn, criticized government plans for multi-ethnic so-called 'Vision Schools', which they viewed as a means of ending the separate Chinese and Indian educational systems.

As the result of a decision of the UMNO Supreme Council, the post of President, held by Mahathir, was not contested at the UMNO General Assembly on 11–13 May 2000, and Badawi stood as the sole candidate for the post of Deputy President, vacant since Anwar's dismissal. There was strong competition, however, for three positions of Vice-President. The Minister of Defence, Najib Tun Razak, an incumbent Vice-President, was re-elected along with a former Chief Minister of Selangor, Mohammad Taib, and the Minister of Domestic Trade and Consumer Affairs, Muhyiddin Mohd Yassin. Although all three had formerly been members of Anwar's 'Vision Team' in 1993, they were nominated by Mahathir's own Kubang Pasu faction in UMNO. Hints from the Prime Minister that he was not happy with the outcome of the ballot seemed to be ingenuous, as none of the defeated candidates, including three state Chief Ministers, had Mahathir's favour. At the conclusion of the Assembly, Mahathir announced that he had not decided when to retire but that he intended to relinquish greater responsibility to Badawi in preparation for the eventual transfer of office.

During 2001 Mahathir continued his public attacks on corruption within UMNO, urging party officials to declare their assets and suggesting that the very rich should not hold principal posts. Six division-level UMNO leaders were dismissed for having used bribery to win party elections in April, and the Minister of Information and UMNO Secretary-General, Khalil Yacoob, was charged with misuse of public funds. Many observers, however, considered the Minister of Finance, Daim Zainuddin, who was one of Malaysia's most wealthy men, to be Mahathir's main target. Daim took two months' leave of absence from his post from 19 April, and formally resigned in June 2001. Mahathir assumed the finance portfolio, in addition to carrying out his duties as Prime Minister. Daim had been widely criticized for using public funds to assist Malay business associates, but was also known to have policy differences with Mahathir. Daim's former significant role in fund-raising for UMNO cast further uncertainty on the issue of whether Badawi would be able to defeat leadership challenges from Razaleigh and Najib Tun Razak, in the event of Mahathir's departure from politics.

During the second half of 2000 PAS became less concerned to downplay its intention to introduce an Islamic state, while the BN seemed to disengage from its campaign to match PAS in the promotion of Islam. In September 2000 Datuk Haji Nik Abdul Aziz Nik Mat, spiritual leader of PAS, declared that the revealing clothes worn by some women encouraged rape; in October he urged women to be banned from competitions in the reading of the Koran because their voices might seduce men. In July 2001 a senior Islamic leader, Hashim Yahya, ruled that a man might divorce his wife by sending her a text message from a mobile cellular telephone. Women's groups called on the Government to reject the finding and to insist that divorce cases continue to be heard in the courts. Fadzil Nor assured PAS's partners in the BA that his party would not seek to impose an Islamic state without fully discussing the topic with other groups; he was, however, unable to dissuade the DAP from leaving the BA over the issue in September of that year. The opposition was further weakened when the Parti Bersatu Sabah (PBS), which had withdrawn from the BN in 1990, applied in late 2001 to rejoin the Government. In contrast, the continuation of serious infighting within the MCA did not seem to affect the BN. The BA's Islamic character was reinforced when the uncompromising Chief Minister of Terengganu, Abdul Hadi Awang, became leader of PAS after Fadzil Nor's death in June 2002.

The Government responded to the developments of October 2000 by suspending proposed legislation that would have authorized punishment for Muslims who abandoned their faith. Addressing a conference on Islamic law, Mahathir condemned Islamic intolerance and urged flexibility and tolerance in the observance of Islam. The Government tightened its control over Islamic groups in August 2001, detaining Nik Adli Nik Abdul Aziz, son of Nik Abdul Aziz Nik Mat, and 16 others on charges of planning to overthrow the Government. They were ordered to be detained for two years without trial under the ISA. In the same month the Government banned public political meetings and passed legislation formally outlawing discrimination against women and making it possible for women to sue in cases where they had suffered discrimination. In September measures were also announced against religious leaders who raised political themes in sermons and, later in the same month, Mahathir declared that Malaysia was in fact already an Islamic state, apparently implying that further Islamization, as proposed by PAS, was unnecessary (although this declaration caused consternation in non-Muslim circles). In December the High Court sentenced three members of the radical al-Ma'unah cult to death for attempting to overthrow the Government and establish an Islamic state, owing to their involvement in the police shootings of July 2000. The court itself had recovered its reputation for independence significantly under a new Chief Justice, Tan Sri Dato' Mohamed Dziaddin bin Haji Abdullah, and had opposed the Government in prominent cases in which contempt proceedings and defamation charges had been used against opposition figures.

The terrorist attacks of 11 September 2001 on the USA gave the Government a further opportunity to suppress Islamic extremism. In October six people were arrested under the ISA on suspicion of membership of the Kumpulan Mujahidin Malaysia (KMM), which was suspected of having connections with the al-Qa'ida international terrorist network. A further 65 people were arrested during 2002. The Government implied openly that the KMM and the related Jemaah Islamiah terrorist group were connected with PAS. Nik Abdul Aziz Nik Mat encouraged these perceptions by demanding a *jihad* ('holy war') against the USA and urging Malaysians to support the Taliban regime of Afghanistan by providing money, warriors and prayers. During campaigning for a by-election in January 2002, propaganda produced by the Government explicitly linked PAS with the Taliban, drawing particular attention to the subordinate position of women under Taliban rule. In February 2001 UMNO had established Puteri UMNO, an organization aimed at women under the age of 35. This group was generally perceived to hold more modern views and to be opposed to radical Islamic practices.

In July 2002 the PAS-controlled Government of Terengganu followed Kelantan in formally introducing state Islamic law, which included penalties such as that of stoning for adultery and amputation for theft. As in Kelantan, the law could not be implemented because criminal law remained under federal control and, on this occasion, the police force announced publicly that it would not participate in the enforcement of the new laws. None the less, the legislation was widely seen to constitute a statement of PAS's intentions if it secured victory in the national elections due to be held in 2004. Women's groups were incensed that the new laws required the testimony of four male witnesses to prove that a rape had occurred. A provision that a woman who could not prove her accusation could be whipped as punishment for slander appeared in the draft legislation, but was omitted from the final version. The law also prescribed the death penalty for apostasy and whipping for the consumption of alcohol.

On 22 June 2002 Mahathir threw Malaysian politics into confusion by abruptly announcing his resignation during a speech to the annual congress of UMNO. Within an hour, however, party officials announced that the Prime Minister had been persuaded to withdraw his resignation. Although opposition figures immediately described the incident as a pre-election ploy to rally support for Mahathir, others believed that the Prime Minister was increasingly keen to relinquish power after 21 years in office, and that the speech was intended to prepare the ground for an orderly transfer of power to his deputy and heir apparent, Minister of Home Affairs Abdullah bin Ahmad Badawi. At the congress Badawi had already sought to strengthen his position by adopting as a theme the cleansing of UMNO of corruption, which was widely seen to be a major reason for the party's electoral set-backs. During the approach to the congress, six senior party officials had been dismissed on corruption charges. In September 2002 Mahathir announced that he would not contest the general election scheduled for 2004.

INTERNATIONAL RELATIONS

Malaysia effected a major realignment of its external alliances after it achieved independence in 1957. Whereas the country formerly enjoyed a strong relationship with the Western powers, notably the United Kingdom, it began, in the years following independence, to show a greater commitment towards its neighbours in South-East Asia and to develop closer ties with the emerging powers of eastern Asia.

In the early and middle years of the 1960s the newly-formed Federation faced major challenges from Indonesia and the Philippines: in surmounting those challenges, Malaysia was assisted by commonwealth military forces, composed mainly of British troops. Malaysia's pro-Western orientation was illustrated by its support of US involvement in Viet Nam, and by the absence of formal diplomatic relations with any communist countries, including the USSR and the People's Republic of China. The shift in Malaysia's foreign policy occurred in 1970, following the British Government's decision to withdraw British military forces 'east of Suez', including those in the Malaysia-Singapore area, and the reduction, and subsequent complete withdrawal, of US land forces from Viet Nam. The Western withdrawal was accompanied in the early 1970s by the emergence of China and Japan as major political and economic influences in South-East Asia. Diplomatic relations between Malaysia and the People's Republic of China were established in 1974, when the latter undertook not to interfere in Malaysia's internal affairs.

The most important development in this period was the formation of a strong regional grouping in South-East Asia in 1967, the Association of South East Asian Nations (ASEAN), whose founder-members were Malaysia, Indonesia, the Philippines, Thailand and Singapore; Brunei joined in January 1984. ASEAN was primarily concerned with economic development, although co-operation in foreign policy issues increased rapidly. The organization represented its members' political solidarity in opposing the Vietnamese occupation of Cambodia (then Kampuchea), and played a significant role in negotiations prior to the Vietnamese withdrawal from Cambodia, effected in 1989. Following the admission of Viet Nam to ASEAN in 1995, there was a general expectation that Laos, Cambodia and Myanmar (formerly Burma) would follow in due course. Initially, Malaysia preferred to make admission dependent on stable and reasonably democratic conditions in the candidate countries, but by mid-1996 it had come to favour rapid and unconditional admission, partly because Malaysian firms had become major investors in Myanmar. This policy led to verbal clashes with the USA and other Western countries, which wished to see Myanmar excluded until its observance of human rights improved. In the event, Myanmar and Laos were admitted to ASEAN in July 1997. Malaysia then pressed to have Myanmar accepted as a participant at the 1998 Asia-Europe Meeting (ASEM) in London, threatening to boycott the meeting if Myanmar were excluded, as the British Government announced would be the case. By the time the summit took place, however, the Asian financial crisis had intervened and the issue of Myanmar's participation was postponed. Myanmar joined ASEAN in 1999. In July 2002 Malaysia offered to host a permanent secretariat for 'ASEAN + 3', the informal grouping linking ASEAN with China, Japan and the Republic of Korea. At a meeting of ASEAN foreign ministers in Brunei, however, the proposal was rejected on the grounds that it might weaken ASEAN as an institution.

In January 1992, at the Fourth ASEAN Summit, the member-states agreed to establish an ASEAN Free Trade Area (AFTA) within 15 years. (AFTA was finally formally established on 1 January 2002.) In July 1994 the first ASEAN Regional Forum (ARF) was convened in Bangkok, Thailand; ARF was expected to provide a platform for the discussion of political and security issues. Malaysia's and Mahathir's role within ASEAN and within groupings of developing nations over trade and security issues continued to expand. Mahathir's articulation of his proposal to establish an East Asia Economic Caucus (EAEC), a trade group which was to exclude the USA, Australia and New Zealand, angered both the US Government (which was concerned to continue to promote the US-inspired Asia-Pacific Economic Co-operation—APEC) and other nations. In July 1993, at the ASEAN ministerial meeting, a consensus was reached on the EAEC. It was agreed, despite the continuing reluctance of Japan to participate, that the EAEC should operate as an East Asian interest group within APEC. The EAEC formally came into existence at an ASEAN informal summit in November 2000. Its economic significance was limited by the aftermath of the Asian economic crisis, but it provided an opportunity for Malaysia's proposal for the establishment of a trans-Asian railway, which would promote economic integration in the region. In May 1994 relations with the USA improved significantly as Mahathir visited the US President, Bill Clinton, in Washington and invited him to visit Kuala Lumpur. However, relations deteriorated in 1997 after Mahathir demanded a review of the UN Declaration on Human Rights and paid a state visit to Cuba. Mahathir also speculated publicly that international pressure on the ringgit might be part of a Jewish plot to undermine the progress of Muslim countries. Members of the US Congress threatened a resolution urging him formally to apologize or resign. Relations worsened again after the Malaysian oil and gas corporation, Petroleum National Bhd (PETRONAS), joined a consortium to develop an offshore gas field in Iran. Under the US Iran-Libya Sanctions Act, directed against alleged terrorist countries, PETRONAS was thus liable to sanctions in the USA; Mahathir described this legislation as an unacceptable intrusion into Malaysia's affairs.

In the early 1990s international attention focused on the issues surrounding the logging of the rain forest and its effect on the lives and land of indigenous communities. Prior to the UN Conference on Environment and Development in Rio de Janeiro, Brazil, in June 1992, this issue received much attention both within Malaysia and internationally. Mahathir became the effective international spokesperson for the developing countries against those of the industrialized North. In April 1992 he chaired a meeting on the environment attended by the developing nations, in Kuala Lumpur, in which he led demands for a withdrawal of international criticism on such issues as logging in developing nations, and appealed to the countries of the North to stop their 'imperialist agendas' and to adjust their own consumption and production patterns to avoid environmental pollution. This message, in the form of the Kuala Lumpur Declaration, which also included a rejection of the linking of development aid with human rights improvements, was taken to the Rio Conference. Prior to the 1995 election, Mahathir also offered sharp criticism of what he termed the continuing racism, hedonism and immorality of Western countries. Malaysia, however, also hosted an annual 'International Dialogue' between heads of state of developing countries and senior international business executives, which acted as a forum for seeking practical solutions to the problems of globalization. During 2000 Mahathir argued that the next meeting of the World Trade Organization (WTO) should be postponed until problems arising from existing agreements had been solved. He strongly attacked the West over what he called its abandonment of the Muslims in Bosnia and Herzegovina and sought, without conspicuous success, to co-ordinate a more vigorous response by the international Muslim community to the crisis. Although Mahathir formally wrote to the Indonesian President, Suharto, to protest against the smoke that disrupted commerce and daily life in much of Malaysia in September 1997, Malaysia's public criticism of Indonesia was muted, perhaps because its own environmental record was vulnerable to criticism.

Relations with Singapore underwent some strain in mid-1996, when Singapore's former Prime Minister, Lee Kuan Yew, stated that a reunification of Singapore and Malaysia might be possible and desirable if Malaysia abandoned its policy of preference for *bumiputra*. Then, in March 1997, Lee poured scorn on a Singaporean opposition figure, who claimed to have fled to the Malaysian city of Johor Bahru for safety, alleging that Johor Bahru was 'notorious for shootings, muggings and car-jackings'. Malaysia delivered a formal protest note to Singapore, following which Lee apologized and retracted his remarks. The first volume of Lee's memoirs, published in September 1998, however, contained criticisms of Malaysian leaders of the 1950s and 1960s, and thus provoked a further deterioration in relations. Relations were further strained in 1998 when Singapore unilaterally transferred its immigration officials from Tanjong Pagar railway station in Singapore to a modern facility near the Malaysian border. Other bilateral problems included Malaysia's failure to provide a formal agreement on water supply to Singapore and Singapore's refusal to allow Peninsular Malaysians to withdraw mandatory savings until the age of 55 even if they leave Singapore, a rule that does not apply to other foreign workers. Most of these issues were resolved in a treaty signed on 4 September 2001. However, during 2002 the two sides clashed again over allegations that land reclamation work being carried out by Singapore was impeding access to Malaysian ports, and over rival plans for replacing the causeway linking the two countries with one or more bridges. Partly as a result of the regional economic crisis that began in 1997, in 1998 Malaysia withdrew its participation in military exercises under the Five-Power Defence Arrangements (FPDA), in which Singapore, the United Kingdom, Australia and New Zealand were also involved; however, the Government expressed its intention to rejoin the exercises in 1999.

In May 1997 the Malaysian and Indonesian Governments agreed to refer to the International Court of Justice (ICJ) their conflicting claims to the sovereignty of two small islands off the coast of Borneo, Sipadan and Ligitan. A judgment in the case was due to be reached in November 2002. Another territorial claim being pursued through negotiation was the dispute with Singapore over the island of Batu Putih (Pedra Branca), which the two countries had agreed to refer to the ICJ in September 1994. In March 1998 Malaysia began to construct a building on Investigator Shoal, a part of the disputed Spratly Islands to which Malaysia, the Philippines and China maintained overlapping claims; Malaysia's move was probably prompted by China's construction of substantial facilities on Mischief Reef further to the north.

During the early 1990s, as economic growth fuelled the demand for labour, Malaysia became an increasingly attractive destination for illegal immigrants from nearby countries, especially the Philippines, Indonesia and Bangladesh. About 1m. illegal immigrants were believed to be living in Malaysia in the mid-1990s. By 1995 both the number of illegal immigrants and their treatment (by employers and, if they were apprehended, by the Government) had become an issue of increasing public concern. In June 1996 642 Indonesian illegal immigrants, held in a detention camp at Triang for more than five months, went on hunger strike to demand early repatriation. In the same month the Malaysian and Indonesian authorities agreed on joint measures to limit the flow of illegal workers into Malaysia. Malaysia repatriated the remaining Vietnamese refugees from its territory by the UN-imposed deadline of June 1996; some had been held in camps since 1975. The financial crisis led Malaysia to prepare plans for the large-scale repatriation of both illegal and now unemployed legal immigrant workers. By March 1998 17,000 Indonesians had been arrested as part of 'Operation Nyah (Go Away)' and naval patrols of the coastline were increased.

The restriction of illegal immigration to Malaysia became more stringent during 2001, and an estimated 120,000 illegal immigrants were expelled from the country. In early 2002 the Government ended the legal recruitment of labourers from Indonesia and began a campaign of bulldozing squatter settlements; sea patrols to interdict people smugglers also increased in number. The Malaysian authorities routinely expelled illegal immigrants from Myanmar across its northern border into Thailand, despite compelling evidence that some were being captured by criminal gangs and held for ransom, sold into slavery or smuggled back into Malaysia. In April the Government announced that it would take yet firmer action against illegal immigrants, who were estimated to number between 300,000 and 1m. The move was prompted by several factors. Malaysia's economic difficulties (see Economy) had led to increased rates of unemployment and public pressure for a 'Malaysians First' policy. Members of the public also perceived the illegal workers as being responsible for rising crime levels; the perception of the immigrants as being unruly was reinforced when clashes occurred between police and Indonesian illegal immigrants in a detention centre in December 2001, and in a textile factory in January 2002. Moreover, especially after the 11 September terrorist attacks on the USA, the Government feared that the immigrants might include political and religious militants. Under new legislation which entered into force from 1 August 2002, illegal immigrants faced punishments of fines, whipping or prison terms, although an amnesty was granted to those with confirmed tickets to leave the country by the end of the month. For the first time the employers of illegal immigrants also faced strict penalties. Many of the immigrants came from Indonesia and the Philippines, and both countries sent ships to assist in the repatriation of their citizens. Bangladeshis and Muslim Rohingyas from Myanmar were also affected. Government officials estimated that about 300,000 people, mainly Indonesians, had left the country prior to 1 August. On the eve of the deadline imposed for departure, hundreds of illegal immigrants, mainly Acehnese from Indonesia and Rohingyas, sought certification of refugee status from the office of the United Nations High Commissioner for Refugees (UNHCR) in Kuala Lumpur, claiming that they would suffer discrimination if they returned to their own countries. Malaysia, however, was not a signatory of the 1951 UN Convention on Refugees, and seemed unlikely to accept any immigrants on these grounds. An estimated 1.7m. foreign workers remained legally in Malaysia.

Relations with Thailand were strained in early 1996 by Malaysia's construction of a wall along its border with Thailand to stem the arrival of illegal immigrants. Thailand accused Malaysia of arbitrarily expelling illegal immigrants to Thai territory and of making insufficient effort to prevent Muslim separatists in southern Thailand from using Malaysian territory as a sanctuary. However, in January 1998 three Thai Muslim separatists were arrested by the Malaysian authorities and deported to Thailand, and in April an agreement was signed jointly to develop a huge offshore gas and oilfield in a disputed area of the Gulf of Thailand.

The arrest of the former Deputy Prime Minister and Minister of Finance, Anwar Ibrahim, in September 1998 prompted critical reactions from President B. J. Habibie of Indonesia and President Estrada of the Philippines, both of whom had enjoyed good relations with Anwar; for the most part, however, Malaysia was able to invoke the ASEAN custom that implicitly prohibited interference in the internal affairs of fellow member countries. The Malaysian Government reacted indignantly in November when the US Vice-President, Al Gore, expressed support for the *reformasi* movement while attending an APEC summit meeting in Malaysia. Relations with the Philippines were further strained in 2000 after Muslim separatists from the southern Philippines kidnapped 21 tourists, 12 of them foreigners, from the island of Sipadan, off Sabah, in late April. Malaysia complained that lack of security in the Philippines had damaged its interests. Meanwhile, Malaysia's relations with China became closer during May 1999, when the two countries signed a 12-point co-operation agreement. Mahathir and the Chinese Prime Minister, Zhu Rongji, exchanged state visits later in the year. The *rapprochement* partly reflected the countries' shared suspicion of economic liberalization. Criticism from Western countries over the conviction of Anwar on sodomy charges in August 2000, however, left Malaysia temporarily somewhat isolated in world affairs.

The terrorist attacks on New York and Washington, DC, on 11 September 2001 initially prompted speculation that the USA would identify Malaysia as a country that harboured terrorists, especially after Mahathir described the attacks as a retaliation for Israel's 'state terrorism'; evidence was also discovered revealing that two of those who had perpetrated the September attacks had stayed in the home of a former Malaysian army captain in 2000. Malaysia also criticized the USA for killing innocent people during its attacks on the Taliban Government in Afghanistan. In the event, however, the Government's swift suppression of the KMM allowed it to be perceived as clearly opposing Islamic extremism. Malaysia also promised to co-operate with the USA in tracing al-Qa'ida funds in Malaysia. In May 2002 Mahathir visited the USA to reinforce the improved bilateral relationship and to sign a formal agreement to co-operate in combating terrorism, but he warned the West against becoming 'impatient' with Malaysia over democratization and human rights issues, stating that a transition to democracy was likely to be slow. The two sides later announced plans for the establishment of a joint anti-terrorism training centre in Malaysia. The Malaysian Government also initiated a major expansion of the country's military capacity, purchasing both submarines and F/A-18 fighter jets. Malaysia also signed an anti-terrorism agreement with Australia in August 2002. In June Mahathir met the Pope to discuss peace initiatives in the Middle East.

Economy

CHRIS EDWARDS

Revised by ROKIAH ALAVI

INTRODUCTION

From the mid-1970s Malaysia had one of the most dynamic and fastest-growing economies in Asia, and between 1985 and 1995 it was the eighth fastest-growing economy in the world. In the quarter of a century following the adoption of the New Economic Policy (NEP) in 1971, Malaysia's gross domestic product (GDP) grew at an annual average rate of about 7%. Between 1985 and 1995 GDP growth averaged over 8% per annum, which, with the population expanding at a little over 2.5% annually, gave an average growth in per caput income of 5.7% per annum. During the 1980s real GDP growth averaged 5% annually, but the growth rate was uneven. Between 1981 and 1983 growth had faltered, and then accelerated in 1984 only to decline sharply in 1985 and 1986, when there was a recession with a GDP growth rate of zero. In 1987 and 1988 the growth in GDP averaged over 7% annually, stimulated by an increase in external demand, and by a real devaluation of the Malaysian ringgit of 16% in 1986 and by a further 4% in 1987. The year-by-year GDP growth rate was particularly spectacular until the mid-1990s. However, Malaysia's economy decelerated drastically in 1997, owing to the regional economic crisis, which started in July of that year. In the second half of the year GDP growth declined to 7.1%, compared with growth of 8.5% in the first half of the year. The impact of the crisis became more evident in 1998, in which year GDP contracted by 7.5%. However, various government policies helped the economy to recover to the extent that GDP grew by 5.8% in 1999 and by 8.5% in 2000. The performance of the Malaysian economy in 2001 was adversely affected by the global economic slowdown, particularly in the USA. This was reflected in the modest rate of economic expansion; GDP grew by only 0.4% in 2001.

The unemployment rate increased from 2.5% in 1996 to 2.7% in 1997, and further to 3.2% in 1998. Official estimates indicated that the number of workers retrenched increased to 83,865 in 1998, compared with 18,863 workers in 1997 and 7,773 workers in 1996. As the economy strengthened, the unemployment rate declined to 3.4% in 1999, and to 3.1% in 2000. The rate increased slightly to 3.7% in 2001, owing to the slowdown in the economy. The inflation rate, which showed a significant upward trend in late 1997 and in the first half of 1998 (owing to the impact of the depreciation of the ringgit), declined progressively after June 1998. For 1998 as a whole, inflation rose by 5.3%. The recovery of the economy contributed to a decline in the rate of inflation to 2.7% in 1999, and further, to 1.5% in 2000. Inflationary pressures remained subdued, and the CPI experienced a modest increase of only 1.4% in 2001. Bank Negara reported in 2001 that this was mainly due to the prevalence of excess capacity in several sectors of the economy, the moderate appreciation of the ringgit in relation to non-US dollar currencies, and lower imported inflation.

The Sectoral Growth Pattern

During 1971–90 the manufacturing sector registered the highest rate of output growth, expanding at an annual average of 10.3%. The sector grew at a higher rate of 11.3% per annum in the 1970s, compared with 9.4% annually in the 1980s. However, during the second half of the 1980s, the sector expanded at an average annual rate of 13.7%. Between 1990 and 1995 the sector experienced growth of an average annual rate of 13.3%. Manufacturing output subsequently grew at a slightly slower pace of 12.2% in 1996 and 12.5% in 1997. In 1998 the output of the manufacturing sector contracted by 10.2%, the first decline since 1985; this was due mainly to the economic slowdown in the Asia-Pacific region as a whole. The effects of the regional financial crisis had been less severe in the first quarter of 1998, in which period the output of the manufacturing sector contracted by only 1.8%; the impact of the crisis became evident in the second quarter of the year, however, when production fell by 8.9%, and the situation subsequently worsened in the third and fourth quarters when the sector contracted sharply by 14.5% and 14.7%, respectively. However, the sector experienced a strong positive growth of 13.5% in 1999. The sector grew further by 21.0% in 2000, as a result of significant increase in external demand as well as sustained strong domestic requirements. However, the slowdown in major industrial countries and the downturn in the global electronics cycle adversely affected the overall performance of Malaysia's manufacturing sector in 2001, leading to a deceleration of 5.1%. The sector's share of GDP increased significantly from 16.9% in 1975 to 33.7% in 1997; in 1998 its share increased further to 34.4%, despite the regional economic crisis, indicating the sector's considerable importance in the context of the economy as a whole. The manufacturing sector's share of GDP was 30% in 1999, 33% in 2000 and 32% in 2001.

The services sector also expanded rapidly, growing at an average annual rate of 7.6% during 1971–90, 9.3% between 1990–95, and 9.7% and 8.7% in 1996 and 1997 respectively; however, following the contraction of the economy in 1997–98, this sector experienced a slow growth rate of 1.5% in 1998. In accordance with the overall strong expansion of the economy, the sector grew at a faster rate of 3.2% in 1999, 4.8% in 2000 and 4.9% in 2001. The intermediate services group (comprising transport, storage and communications and finance, insurance, real estate and business services) expanded more rapidly, at a rate of 6.5% in 2001 (compared with a rate of 5.9% in 2000), than the final services group (comprising electricity, gas and water, wholesale and retail trade, hotels and restaurants and government services), which grew at 3.9% in 2001 (compared with a rate of 4.1% in 2000). The strong expansion in the transport, storage and communications sub-sector could primarily be attributed to the rapid growth of the mobile cellular telephone and internet services segment of the telecommunications industry and to the increase in the transhipment activities of local ports. In the final services group sector, the utilities sub-sector recorded a higher rate of growth owing to higher demand by domestic industries and the commercial sector. The strong growth of the sector contributed to its increasing share of GDP (from 38.3% in 1970 to 55.8% in 2001).

The construction sector had a lower growth rate during 1971–90 (6.4% annually) but this accelerated to 13.3% per annum during 1990–95, and 14.2% and 9.5% in 1996 and 1997, respectively. In 1998 the sector experienced a contraction in output of 24.5%, mainly as a result of lower aggregate demand. In 1999, however, the sector strengthened as a result of various policy measures introduced by the Government, recording a rate of contraction of only 5.6%. In 2000 and 2001, however, the sector recorded positive growth rates of 1.1% and 2.3% respectively. The agricultural sector, which traditionally provided the impetus for growth in the economy, experienced a continued deceleration in growth rates, from an average of 5% per annum in the 1970s to 3.8% in the 1980s, 2.0% per annum during 1990–95, 2.2% in 1996 and 3.5% in 1997. In 1998 the sector experienced a contraction of 3.3%, before recording a rate of growth of about 3.8% in 1999. In 2000 and 2001 the sector expanded at rates of only 0.6% and 2.5% respectively, owing to slower growth in the production of crude palm oil. This led to a reduction in its contribution to GDP from 29% in 1970 to about 8% in 2001. The change in the sectoral growth pattern clearly demonstrates the change in development strategy, moving from an economy based on agriculture to one based on industry.

Regional and Rural-Urban Divisions

Regional development strategies implemented since independence have resulted in improved living standards and a higher quality of life for the inhabitants of all states, as well as the reduction of regional disparities. The population of Malaysia in 2001 was approximately 23.8m. An estimated 43% of the population resided in the less developed states, with Sabah and Sarawak populated by more than 2m. people. Based on the composite index of development in 2000, the states of Johor, Perak, Pulau Pinang (Penang), Melaka (Malacca), Negeri Sembilan (Negri Sembilan), Selangor and the Federal Territory of Kuala Lumpur were categorized as more developed states, while Kedah, Kelantan, Pahang, Perlis, Sabah, Sarawak and Terengganu (Trengganu) were categorized as less developed states. The average per caput income of those living in the more developed states was RM 17,410 in 2000, compared with RM 10,893 for the inhabitants of the less developed states. The national average per caput income was RM 14,584. However, the average growth of per caput GDP between 1995 and 2000 in the less developed states was slightly higher (6.3%) than in the more developed states (6.1%). This indicated that the income gap between the more developed and less developed states was narrowing. The overall incidence of poverty in Malaysia declined from 8.7% in 1995 to 7.5% in 1999. In the more developed states the incidence of poverty declined slightly, from 4.2% in 1995 to 3.9% in 1999. In the less developed states the incidence declined from 15.6% in 1995 to 13.2% in 1999, with Terengganu experiencing the most significant decline, from 23.4% in 1995 to 14.9% in 1999. In terms of access to infrastructure and social amenities, 100% of rural areas in Peninsular Malaysia had access to electricity supply, while Sabah and Sarawak had 80% and 70% access respectively.

Malaysia is a rapidly-urbanizing society. In 1980 just over one-third of the Malaysian population lived in urban areas, but by 1991 this had increased to 51% and by 2000 to 62%. In the decade to 1995 the urban population increased at an average annual rate of 4%, much faster than the 2.5% increase in the population as a whole. Between 1990 and 1995 the average incomes of urban households grew faster (at 8.1% per annum) than those of rural households (at 5.3%).

Employment and Income Distribution

The economically active population accounted for 62.9% of the whole in 2000. The Labour Force Survey indicated that 55.3% of the labour force was concentrated in urban areas. The creation of new jobs took place mainly in the services sector, where 217,300 persons found employment in 2000. The manufacturing sector registered a decline in the number of new jobs created in 2000, while the construction sector witnessed the establishment of 55,500 new jobs, owing to an increase in residential housing and public infrastructure projects.

Malaysia began to experience persistent labour shortage problems from the second half of the 1990s. The Eighth Malaysia Plan, for the 2001–05 period, estimated that the number of registered foreign workers in the labour force had risen from 650,000 in 1995 to 749,200 in 2000, but these figures were widely thought to be underestimates. The number of foreign workers in Malaysia was probably close to 2m. in 2000. In connection with the Eighth Malaysia Plan, it was also calculated that, from a total of 749,200 foreign employees holding work permits in the year 2000, 31.3% were engaged in manufacturing, 22.9% in agriculture, 8.7% in construction and 7.4% in services, while 20.3% worked as maids. In 2001 the majority (73.7%) originated from Indonesia. About 16% of foreigners recruited in the first half of 2001 were skilled workers. India accounted for the largest number of approved skilled workers, followed by Japan and the People's Republic of China. In terms of occupational groups, directors accounted for the largest number, followed by managers and engineers.

Malaysia planned to deport 110,000 illegal Indonesian workers who were being held in detention in early 2001, but it intended to do so in phases to avoid overburdening Indonesia with returned migrants. It was reported that 97,147 illegal migrants were deported in 2000, including 83,190 Indonesians. In Sabah there were 600,000 foreign workers, of whom about 100,000–150,000 were believed to be illegally employed; they were mainly from the Philippines and Indonesia. In Sarawak there were about 60,000 foreign workers, mainly of Indonesian origin.

By 2002 Malaysia had announced that it would admit foreign workers from Myanmar and Nepal to be employed in the manufacturing, construction and plantation sectors. The Federation of Malaysian Manufacturers stated that, although it welcomed the decision, it should only be regarded as a temporary measure to address the labour shortage and not as a means of reducing labour costs.

In 2001 unemployment in Malaysia was estimated at 3.7% of the labour force, compared with a rate of 8.7% in 1987. The average rate conceals quite considerable disparities among states. For example, Terengganu and Kelantan, in the east of the peninsula, and Sabah and Sarawak all had unemployment rates of 4.5% or more, whereas the federal capital, Selangor and Pulau Pinang had rates of 1.1% and below.

The impact of the slowdown in economic activity was experienced by the labour market, and was most acutely reflected by the number of retrenched workers in the manufacturing sector. In 2001 a total of 38,116 workers were retrenched (compared with 25,236 in 2000); 75.6% of these had been engaged in manufacturing activities. The electronics and electrical products sub-sector accounted for almost one-half (45.7%) of the total number of workers made redundant. The main reason for the retrenchments was a decline in the demand for manufactured products. Local workers accounted for the majority (86.9%) of retrenched workers, and 96.9% of all retrenchments were made in West Malaysia.

The avowed aims of the NEP were to bring about (over a 20-year period from 1971 to 1990) a redistribution of income and wealth, particularly in favour of the *bumiputra* (indigenous population, mostly Malays), since in 1971 Malays were disproportionately poor. In 1995 about 58% of the total population possessed *bumiputra* status. In terms of reducing absolute poverty, the NEP was successful since, whereas in 1970 almost one-half of the households in Peninsular Malaysia were classified as poor, by 1990 less than one-sixth of Malaysian households were so classified. Furthermore, by 1995 the proportion of households that were classified as 'poor' had declined to less than 9%. In 1997 the overall incidence of poverty declined to 6.1%. However, the regional economic crisis led to an increase in this index to 8.5% in 1998, before the level declined to 7.5% in 1999. Both rural and urban households recorded reductions in poverty between 1995 and 1999. The incidence of rural poverty decreased fron 14.9% in 1995 to 12.4% in 1999, while urban poverty declined from 3.6% in 1995 to 3.4% in 1999. The incidence of poverty amongst agricultural workers was highest, at 16.4% in 1999. The proportion of households classified as very poor (defined as having less than one-half of the poverty line income and known as 'hardcore' poverty) has also fallen in recent years, from 3.9% in 1990 to 1.4% in 1999. The incidence of rural 'hardcore' poverty declined from 3.6% in 1995 to 2.4% in 1999, while in the urban areas it decreased from 0.9% to 0.5% in these years.

In terms of reducing relative poverty, the NEP was less successful. Between 1970 and 1999 the 'Gini coefficient' (a commonly-used measure of inequality) had improved only slightly, and in 1999 the average monthly income of *bumiputra* households was RM 1,984, compared with an average for Chinese households of RM 3,456. Thus, in 1999 the gap in incomes between the two major ethnic groups remained substantial. A major cause of this was the higher proportion of *bumiputra* households living in rural areas. In both rural and urban areas the gap between the ethnic groups was less but, in general, rural households were worse off, with the average rural household income (RM 1,718) being less than the average urban household income (RM 3,103). Income distribution in Malaysia in general has remained unequal, with the 'Gini coefficient' of 0.446 in 1990 declining marginally to 0.443 in 1999. At the beginning of the 21st century the NEP's original objective to achieve 30% *bumiputra* ownership had yet to be realized. In 1999 the proportion of corporate equity owned by *bumiputra* was 19.1%, compared with 37.9% under Chinese ownership. The highest proportion of equity controlled by the *bumiputra* was in the transport (32.2%), construction (27.1%) and agriculture sectors (24.3%). In comparison, the proportion of equity of non-*bumiputra* controlled companies was high in almost all sectors, ranging from 41% to 57%, except in the manufacturing sector, which was 60% under foreign control.

In 1991 the NEP was replaced by the National Development Policy (NDP). Under the NDP, there is less rhetorical emphasis on *bumiputra* preferences, but the consensus is that there has been a continuation of the NEP's strategy of encouraging the emergence of a sizeable core of Malay entrepreneurs. Furthermore, there is a widespread belief that the beneficiaries of preferences consist disproportionately of prominent politicians and their close contacts.

AGRICULTURE, FORESTRY AND FISHING

Land Use

In 1995 it was officially reported that a little under 19m. ha of land in Malaysia was under forest, compared with about 20.5m. in 1980. This 19m. represented just under 60% of Malaysia's total land area (of 33m. ha). The area used for cultivation of agricultural commodities in 2000 was 6m. ha or about 18% of the total land area, of which 8% was under oil palm cultivation, 5% rubber, 2% paddy and 1% each under cocoa, coconuts and fruit. An increase in the area under cultivation was recorded for oil palm, pepper, tobacco, vegetables and fruits. However, about 430,800 ha of land used for the cultivation of rubber and cocoa was converted to oil palm cultivation and other uses.

Contribution to Export Revenue

Agriculture and forestry's share of total export earnings have declined rapidly, from 53% in 1973 to 13.3% in 2001. The traditional dominance of rubber, which provided almost one-half of Malaysia's export earnings in 1961, continues to be eroded. In 2001 rubber accounted for only 4.1% of total agriculture exports, compared with 10% of all exports in 1988. In 1989 palm oil replaced rubber as the second largest commodity export-earner after petroleum; it contributed 52.4% of total agriculture exports in 2001. Sawlog exports are the other major primary commodity export, but they accounted for only 24.2% of total agriculture exports in 2001. The export performance of the latter commodity and of the agriculture and forestry sectors in general was strong in 1998, despite the ongoing regional financial crisis; export earnings from these two sectors increased by 17.4% and 30.4%, respectively, during that year. Owing to a decline in international commodity prices, however, export earnings for the sector fell by 8.4% in 1999, and by 17.2% and 13.2% in 2000 and 2001 respectively.

Rubber

Rubber, a principal export of Malaysia since colonial times, has experienced a relative decline over the past few decades. Since the 1960s there has been considerable replanting of rubber land with other crops, especially oil palm. As a result, the area under rubber declined from 2m. ha in 1980 to 1.66m. in 1997 and further to 1.52m. in 1999. Over 85% of the land under rubber is in Peninsular Malaysia and only 15% in East Malaysia. Similarly, over 80% of all Malaysian rubber land is under smallholdings, although the statistics can be quite misleading since the area under the Federal Land Development Authority (FELDA) is classified as smallholdings, even though these might be more appropriately labelled as state-run, profit-sharing estates.

The trend in the real price of rubber has been a downward one. However, in 1994 and in the first half of 1995 there was a sharp rise in the price compared with 1993. Then, in the period from the end of 1995 to the third quarter of 1996 the price dropped by one-quarter. Such volatility in the rubber price has been common, resulting in the formation of the International Natural Rubber Organization (INRO) in 1980, which aimed to stabilize prices through a buffer stock system. However, in spite of the efforts by INRO, prices have continued to be volatile. The free on board (f.o.b.) price of rubber peaked in 1988 (at 310 sen per kg), mainly owing to an increased global demand for latex condoms and gloves because of the AIDS epidemic, but declined to 227 sen per kg in 1991, in spite of the efforts of the buffer stock manager. Prices did not recover in 1992 and 1993, but rose in 1994 (to 293 sen per kg). By the end of 1995 the price had further risen to 400 sen per kg, but it declined to just over 300 sen per kg in late 1996. The industry continued to be affected by depressed prices, labour shortages and the reduction in cultivated area. Slackening external demand, combined with ample global supplies, depressed the price further in 1998 and 1999, in which years the price of natural rubber declined to 274.50 sen and 240 sen per kg, respectively. The continuing low price of natural rubber also adversely affected rubber producers, particularly smallholders, leading the Government to introduce a temporary scheme in mid-1999 in accordance with which it purchased rubber directly from smallholders and rationalized the stock of latex in the country. The scheme was discontinued in February 2000 when the rubber prices improved. Owing to the continuing decline in rubber prices, Malaysia withdrew from INRO with effect from 15 October 1998. In the same month the International Rubber Agreement (INRA) was terminated following the withdrawal of Malaysia and Thailand from the pact. However, the two countries signed a joint memorandum of understanding (MoU) with the objective of working together and sharing resources in order to achieve an equitable rubber price for smallholders. Malaysia and Thailand also established a US $43m. fund to purchase rubber stocks held by INRO to avoid a large build-up of stock in the international rubber market.

Rubber prices, which recovered somewhat in 2000, were unsustainable in 2001 as global supply exceeded consumption. The average price of rubber fell to 227 sen per kg. Prolonged low international prices, amidst an excess of supply in the international rubber markets, prompted the three major rubber-producing countries, namely Thailand, Indonesia and Malaysia (which together accounted for 85% of the world's total natural rubber output), to co-operate in order to revive rubber prices through supply management. This trilateral co-operation initiative culminated in the establishment of the International Tripartite Rubber Organisation (ITRO) in July 2001. Among the initial arrangements made by the ITRO were the reduction of annual natural rubber production by 4% and a 10% decrease in exports, to commence in January 2002.

In 1980 Malaysia was the world's biggest producer of natural rubber, accounting for 1.5m. metric tons or almost two-fifths of the world's total output. The second biggest producer at that time was Indonesia, with an output of 1m. tons. By 1991 Malaysia's rubber production had fallen to under 1.26m. tons, and in that year Malaysia was overtaken in production volume by Thailand (1.34m. tons) and Indonesia (1.28m. tons). By 1994 Malaysia's production had fallen to 1.10m. tons (less than 20% of total world production), and it declined further in 1995 and 1996 to 1.09m. tons and 1.08m. tons, respectively. In 1998 production fell by a further 8.8%, to 885,400 tons, representing the fourth consecutive year of decline in production. The sector continued to experience contraction, with production decreasing further, by 13.2% in 1999, and by 19.9% in 2000. The decrease was due mainly to continuing low prices, as well other factors, such as labour constraints, conversion of rubber land to other crops or to other economic activities. Despite the continued decline in production, Malaysia remained the world's third largest producer and net exporter of natural rubber.

Palm Oil

Since the early 1960s, when the Government and the private sector began to diversify agriculture away from rubber, palm oil production has increased spectacularly, with an average annual growth rate in production of 19.6% between 1970 and 1980. As a result, Malaysia has become the largest producer and exporter of palm oil, accounting for 50% of world production in 1998, and for almost two-thirds of international trade in palm oil. An average annual increase in production of more than 8% over the period 1986–94 was due to improvements in planting, harvesting techniques, the increase in mature oil palm trees and the introduction of the Cameroon weevil to stimulate production. Representing the fastest-growing sub-sector within agriculture, the palm oil sub-sector contributed substantially to the value-added of the agricultural sector as a whole in the late 1990s, and in 2001 grew by 8.9% compared with the rate of growth of 2.5% of the agricultural sector overall.

The bulk of crude palm oil comes from Peninsular Malaysia, which accounted for an estimated 67.5% of the country's production (or 7.96m. tons) in 2001. Sarawak produced 0.54m. tons or 4.6% of the total in that year, while Sabah produced 3.29m. tons or 27.9% of the total. Total area planted with oil palm in 2001 was estimated at 3.5m. ha, of which 3.1m. ha were matured holdings. In terms of ownership, the industry is dominated by private estates, which constituted 59.9% of the total planted area of 3.5m. ha in 1995. Of the rest, smallholders organized under FELDA, the Federal Land Consolidation and Rehabilitation Authority (FELCRA) and the Rubber Industry Smallholders Development Authority (RISDA), and various state land schemes accounted for 30.6%, with independent smallholders owning 9.5%.

After 1975 the Government attempted to change the emphasis of the industry from planting and exporting crude palm oil to producing, refining, manufacturing and selling oil-based products. Consequently, by the early 1990s there were 264 operational palm oil mills, 54 palm oil refineries and a growing oleochemical industry. By 1996 there were 290 mills in the country. In 1998 a total of 19 new palm oil mill licences were issued by the Palm Oil Registration and Licensing Authority (PORLA). The average rate of capacity utilization among these mills showed a significant improvement, rising from 74% in 1992 to 86% in 1996. Research into improved production techniques is carried out both in the private sector and by the Palm Oil Research Institute of Malaysia (PORIM). In the 1990s research aimed to address the shortage of labour experienced by the industry, by studying mechanization in harvesting and the transportation of oil palm fruits, as well as in the fertilization of crops and the maintenance of estates. The Malaysian Palm Oil Promotional Council and PORIM provided valuable promotional activities that were intended to extend the use of palm oil in food preparation in diverse parts of the world, including the People's Republic of China, Africa and Latin America. The need to find new export markets was partly due to the problems of the former USSR, which had been a major importer of Malaysian palm oil, but also to the threat posed by the rapid expansion of palm oil production in Indonesia. The palm oil industry seemed likely to prosper in the 1990s. However, labour shortages were becoming a serious problem as workers moved to urban areas for higher wages; on some estates migrant foreign labour accounted for up to 70% of the work-force. Malaysian plantation workers were, however, paid more than three times the amount earned by their Indonesian counterparts in 1993, and Indonesian labour remained a cheaper option despite a government levy payable for every foreign worker. Another way in which Malaysian companies were able to take advantage of cheaper Indonesian labour was by investing in projects in Indonesia. In recent years 27 joint-venture agreements and MoUs have been co-signed by Malaysian and Indonesian firms to develop 1.5m. ha of oil palm, but in early 1997 the Indonesian Government imposed a freeze on Malaysian investment in the oil palm sector, stating that it had reached an unacceptably high level.

In 1980 exports of palm oil totalled RM 2,500m., but they had risen to RM 4,300m. by 1990 and to RM 10,466m. by 2001. Like rubber, however, palm oil faced a declining real price. In the 1980s the average price of crude palm oil in the Rotterdam market was US $459 per metric ton, whereas the average price for the first half of the 1990s was US $395 per ton. In real terms the price had fallen by about one-half. In mid-1996 the price was slightly greater than US $400 per ton. In 1996 export earnings from palm oil decreased by 8.8%, owing to lower export volume and weak export prices. However, the decline in the global supply of palm oil contributed to a sharp increase in Malaysian palm oil exports in both 1997 and 1998, in which years exports of the commodity increased by 14.6% and 64.4%, respectively, thus making palm oil the single largest export earner within the commodities sector. Owing to lower export prices, the value of exports of Malaysian palm oil declined sharply, by 18.6% in 1999, and by 31.3% in 2000. In 2001 the contraction in palm oil exports moderated to 0.7% owing to the higher volume of exports (18.1%) and a more moderate decline in export prices (15.9%).

In May 2000 the Malaysian Palm Oil Board (MPOB) was established, following the merger of the Palm Oil Registration and Licensing Authority and the Palm Oil Research Institute of Malaysia. The objective of establishing the MPOB was to strengthen the role of agricultural agencies; the Board was expected to undertake research and development, licensing and enforcement of regulations for the industry, and to disseminate information related to palm oil.

Forestry

The production of timber is an important sector of the Malaysian economy. Total sawlog production in 1994 was 36m. cu m, but declined in 2001 to 19.5m. cu m. Output in Peninsular Malaysia and Sabah fell by 28.0% and 13.5%, respectively, and Sarawak accounted for over one-half of Malaysia's total production, reflecting the large-scale clearance of forests to make way for the Bakun hydroelectric dam (see below). Production of sawlogs declined sharply in 1998, decreasing by 27.2% to 22.7m. cu m. The central bank reported that the decline was principally a result of weaker demand from traditional buyers (mainly from within the Asia-Pacific region). In the same year, production in Sarawak and Sabah was affected by adverse weather conditions. Overall production was also affected by the Government's conservation policy and commitment to the achievement of sustainable forest management by the year 2000, in compliance with the requirements of the International Tropical Timber Organization.

In 2001 Sarawak was the principal producer of sawlogs, accounting for 62% of total production, with Sabah accounting for 12% and Peninsular Malaysia 26%. The principal markets for Malaysian logs in 2001 were Japan (28.2%), China (22.1%), India (20.3%), Taiwan (13.7%) and Hong Kong (8.6%). To ensure sustainable forest management, the Government initiated a National Forestry Policy in 1978, aimed at encouraging sustainable development of Malaysia's timber resources through forest conservation, the promotion of under-utilized species and the reduction of waste. Successive five-year plans reduced logging targets from 223,000 ha per year for the Fourth Plan (1981–86) to 152,140 ha per year for the 1986–90 period. The annual permissible logging area in permanent forests was reduced to 46,000 ha in Peninsular Malaysia, 60,000 ha in Sabah and 170,000 ha in Sarawak during the Seventh Malaysia Plan (1996–2000) period. In addition, logging companies in Sarawak were required to allocate 50% of their output to local processors. This was to increase the domestic value-added of the sector. Further evidence of the government policy of encouraging downstream activity in the forestry sector was apparent in 1993, when the Government introduced for the first time export levies on selected species of timber and veneer, in furtherance of its policy to provide adequate cheap resources for the expanding downstream wood-processing activities. From 1 January 1994 the export of rubberwood was banned to encourage local furniture and panel manufacturing activities.

As a result of these measures, the production of sawlogs declined by 5.6% per annum, from 31.8m. cu m in 1995 to about 24m. cu m in 2000. Accordingly, the production of sawn timber decreased from 7.5m. cu m in 1995 to 5.2m. cu m in 2000. However, rubber wood became a major source of raw material in the furniture and other wood-based industries, with total exports increasing from RM 1,900m. in 1995 to RM 4,300m. in 2000. Rubber wood furniture exports increased by 11.1% to RM 3,900m. in 2001 (compared to RM 3,500m. in 2000).

Although the Government has promoted conservation, Malaysia has still attracted international and domestic criticism from anti-tropical hardwood campaigners for its forestry policies. In 1992 the Government responded by providing up to RM 10m. for a joint study by the Malaysian and Sarawak Timber Industry Development Councils which was to attempt to redress allegedly biased reporting on logging activities. The Forest Research Institute announced that it would support only sustainable management practices, and the 1995 Economic Report of the Ministry of Finance stated that 3,000 ha of forest would be planted in that year, bringing the total area under the forest plantation programme to 57,000 ha. In 1996 a total of 15,985 ha was reafforested, while 13,000 ha was designated for reafforestation in both 1997 and 1998.

Subsistence and Other Agriculture

The principal subsistence crop in Malaysia is rice. Malaysia was about 75% self-sufficient in rice in 1995, compared with about 80% self-sufficiency in 1990. The self-sufficiency level reduced further, to 71%, in 2000. In real terms, the world price of rice declined particularly sharply from the mid-1980s, so that in spite of government incentives and subsidies for the sector, production and area under paddy are declining. Poverty is high in the paddy-producing areas, and there is little prospect of reversing this through paddy production itself. The trend of youths leaving the paddy-producing areas is likely to continue, exacerbating the existing labour shortages. However, rice production increased from about 2.1m. metric tons in 1995 to about 2.2m. tons in 2000. In 2000 the value of rice exports was RM 1.5m., while the value of imports was RM 500.7m. Between 1996 and 2000 exports of rice declined by 4.8% and imports rose by 7.1%. This provided an indication of Malaysia's increasing dependency on imported rice.

Cocoa production expanded rapidly during the late 1980s to become Malaysia's fourth most important agricultural subsector after palm oil, timber and rubber. Cocoa production increased from 88,000 metric tons in 1984 to 235,000 tons in 1991, making Malaysia the world's fourth largest producer of cocoa, accounting for around 7% in 1991, after Côte d'Ivoire, Brazil and Ghana (a position Malaysia was subsequently unable to maintain). In 1991 the Malaysian Cocoa Board introduced compulsory grading to control the quality of exports. However, low cocoa prices, the conversion of cocoa-cultivated land to other crops, increasing labour costs and the rising cost of agricultural inputs together resulted in a decrease in Malaysian cocoa production and exports throughout the 1990s. In 2001 total cocoa production was about 58,000 tons.

Pepper production, 99% of which is located in Sarawak, rapidly increased in the late 1980s to reach 31,000 metric tons in 1990. However, production declined by one-half to about 15,000 tons in 1995. The decline in output was partly due to substantial hectarage being replanted to replace old and diseased pepper plants, as well as a marginal decrease in the area under cultivation. Pepper production increased, however, to 28,500 tons in 2001, as a result of efforts to promote low-cost planting and enhanced efficient fertilizer application, as well as increased demand. Malaysia accounted for 11.1% of the world's supply (ranking the fifth-largest producer) in 2000.

By contrast, fruit production has expanded in Malaysia and has more than kept pace with consumption. As a result, Malaysia was 91.3% self-sufficient in fruits and 88.5% self-sufficient in vegetables in 2000; it is a net importer of both fruits and vegetables. The value of fruit and vegetable exports in 2000 was RM 701.2m., while the value of imports was RM 1,913.6m. A total of 15 different types of fruit were promoted for commercial cultivation, including banana, papaya, pineapple, watermelon, starfruit, mango, durian, rambutan, guava and citrus fruits. The principal local fruits are durians and bananas, and these account for over two-thirds of fruit output. Fruit production registered an annual increase of 6.2%, from 1m. metric tons in 1995 to 1.4m. tons in 2000, while vegetable production recorded a growth rate of 7.2% per annum during the same period.

In 1990 Malaysia was more than self-sufficient in poultry, pork and egg production, and remained a net exporter in 1995, with the principal market being Singapore. However, the self-sufficiency level for pork had declined from 104% in 1995 to 80% in 2000. In beef and mutton production, Malaysia was 22.7% (compared to 19.2% in 1995) and 6.4% (compared with 6% in 1995) respectively self-sufficient in 2000.

In 1995 Malaysia was about 91% self-sufficient in fishery products, the same percentage as in 1990. However, the level had declined to 89% in 2000. The country's total fish production for 2000 amounted to 1.5m. metric tons (equivalent to RM 5,500m.) and a total value of RM 1,000m. of fish was imported in that year, reflecting insufficient domestic production to meet the increase in per caput consumption. Malaysia's per caput consumption of fish, totalling 49 kg in 1999, was one of the highest in ASEAN. Although aquaculture production has expanded rapidly, more than 85% of the value of fisheries production comes from the sea. In 2000 1.3m. tons of fish were produced from capture fisheries and 147,000 tons from aquaculture. Under the Third National Agricultural Policy, aquaculture production was envisaged to increase fourfold, to 600,000 tons, by 2010.

MINING

Mineral output accounts for over 40% of Malaysia's industrial production and for about 7% of total GDP, with about four-fifths of this being accounted for by petroleum. The mining sector's contribution to GDP declined to 9.5% in 2000, compared with 10% in 1980.

Tin

Tin production was once one of Malaysia's leading industries, but between 1980 and 2000 the annual output of tin-in-concentrates declined substantially, from 61,000 metric tons to 6,686 tons. In 1980 Malaysia was the largest producer in the world, accounting for 31% of global output. By contrast, in 1997 Malaysia was the eighth largest producer of tin in the world, providing only an estimated 2.4% of total output.

The decline in Malaysian production reflected a fall in the tin price. In 1980 the price was RM 35.7 per kg, but it had collapsed to RM 15.5 by 1986. Prices (and Malaysian production) experienced a mild recovery until 1989, as the Supply Rationalization Scheme (SRS) of the Association of Tin Producing Countries (ATPC) managed to limit the supply of tin through the imposition of export controls on member countries. However, the international recession, the political turmoil in Eastern Europe and the unpredictable release of tin stocks by the United States Defence Logistics Agency caused a further decline in tin prices, from RM 23.1 per kg in 1989 to less than RM 15 in late 1996. In 2000 only 40 mines were in production, compared with 847 in 1980. Employment in 2000 was down to 1,700 workers, compared with almost 50,000 in 1970 and 39,000 in 1980. In mid-1998 only 15 mines remained in production, although there were plans to revive 10 small dormant tin mines mainly in the states of Perak and Selangor.

Despite the sharp decline in tin production, Malaysia remained the world's fourth largest centre of tin smelting in 1997. The Malaysia Smelting Corporation, the world's largest tin smelter, is the only tin smelter in Malaysia, following the closure of the Escoy tin smelter in March 1998. As domestic production of tin-in-concentrates declined, Malaysia was obliged to import supplies in order to keep its smelters working at near capacity.

Petroleum and Gas

Malaysian petroleum production is not significant in international terms: in 1997 Malaysia's production of crude petroleum accounted for 1.0% of world output. However, Malaysia is more than self-sufficient in primary commercial energy, and the surplus over self-sufficiency increased from 176 petajoules in 1990 to 511 petajoules in 1995.

Average production of domestic crude petroleum declined from 663,000 barrels per day (b/d) in 1995 to 606,000 b/d in 2000. The bulk of the total output was from Peninsular Malaysia (about 63%), with Sarawak and Sabah accounting for 23.2% and 13.8% respectively. At the end of 1998 there were 37 oilfields in production, including two new oilfields in Peninsular Malaysia and one in Sabah: of these 37 oilfields, 16 were in Peninsular Malaysia, while 13 were in Sabah and eight were in Sarawak. By 2000 the number of oilfields in production had declined to 33.

Petroleum and gas production is the responsibility of Petroliam Nasional Bhd (PETRONAS), which operates mainly through production-sharing contracts. In 1995 PETRONAS was partially privatized by the Government. By the end of 1991 a total of 29 production-sharing contracts had been signed under the revised terms introduced in 1985.

In 1997 reserves of crude petroleum in Malaysia were estimated at 534,247,000 metric tons, compared with 397,260,000 tons in 1990. In 1980 the Government implemented the National Depletion Policy, in order to slow exploitation rates and hence conserve the country's reserves. However, during the recession of the early 1980s the Government became increasingly dependent on revenue from petroleum exports, and the policy was allegedly abandoned. However, the Seventh Malaysia Plan stated that production throughout the Sixth Plan period was in line with the National Depletion Policy. Between 1995 and 2000 Malaysia's reserves of crude petroleum declined by 17%, from 4,100m. barrels to 3,400m. barrels. The decline was mainly due to sustained production and the maturity of existing fields. To increase reserves, PETRONAS ventured into upstream activities abroad by securing the rights to several exploration areas in Algeria, Angola, Chad, Gabon, Indonesia, Iran, Libya, Myanmar, Pakistan, Sudan, Syria, Tunisia, Turkmenistan and Viet Nam. Domestic crude petroleum in Malaysia, which has a low sulphur content and is therefore considered to be of premium quality, was largely exported. In 2000 natural gas produced off the east coast state of Terengganu was processed to produce several components for use as fuel by petrochemical industries, while gas produced off the coast of Sabah was utilized by the methanol and hot briquette iron plants there. Gas from Sarawak was used to produce liquid natural gas (LNG) for export to Japan and South Korea. The LNG complex in Bintulu, Sarawak, was to become the world's largest, upon the completion of its third plant at the end of 2002. Malaysia's oil and gas exports amounted to RM 25,500m. (US $6,700m.) in 2000, equivalent to 6.8% of the country's total export earnings. In the downstream sector, domestic crude petroleum-refining capacity increased by 72% to 356,000 b/d, as a result of a 100,000 b/d-capacity PETRONAS refinery in Melaka coming on stream in 1994 and the expansion of existing refineries. In 1997 Malaysia had a refining capacity of 18.5m. metric tons, representing 0.5% of world refining capacity.

In 1995 Malaysia's reserves of natural gas were estimated at 2,200m. tons of oil equivalent (TOE) or 85,000,000m. cu ft. This constituted an increase of 700m. TOE compared with 1990. Extraction of natural gas in 1995 was 3,500m. cu ft per day, almost double the 1990 extraction level. Thus, on the basis of 1995 figures, the reserves were sufficient to maintain production levels for 65 years. In 2001 natural gas reserves were estimated at 81,700,000m. cu ft.

During the Sixth Plan period (1991–95) there was a marked increase in the utilization of gas in Malaysia, particularly for electricity generation. To diversify gas utilization in the country and to encourage greater use of cleaner transportation fuels, gas was promoted as a fuel for vehicles. Under the natural gas for vehicles (NGV) promotion programme, the fuel was exempted from excise duty, making its retail price at the pump half that of premium petrol. In addition, conversion kits that allowed petrol engines to use gas were exempted from import duty and sales tax. With the implementation of the NGV programme, a total of 18 public NGV refuelling stations and two private NGV outlets were built, while 3,700 vehicles were converted to operate on natural gas. In 1998 PETRONAS was given approval to import, in stages, 1,000 monogas taxis, of which 300 were already in operation. The Gas District Cooling (GDC) system was introduced to further diversify the use of gas. The GDC, which utilizes gas to produce chilled water for air-conditioning and waste heat for power generation, helps to lower peak load demand and reduces investment for peaking capacity. Three GDC plants—at the Kuala Lumpur City Centre (KLCC), Kuala Lumpur's international airport and Putrajaya—have started operations.

To ensure the sustainable development of gas resources, a long-term utilization limit of 2,000m. cu ft of processed gas was adopted for Peninsular Malaysia in 1993. Of this, 1,300m. cu ft was reserved for electricity generation, with most of the rest set aside for use as a feedstock by the petrochemical industries.

Other Minerals

The production of other minerals in Malaysia generally declined in the 1990s. In 1996 production of bauxite was an estimated 218,680 metric tons, compared with 376,418 tons in 1991. In 1996 production of copper totalled an estimated 87,220 tons, compared with 111,593 tons in 1992. In 1996 production of iron ore increased by an estimated 60.7%, compared with the previous year, but was still below production in 1991, which totalled 375,869 tons.

INDUSTRY AND INDUSTRIAL POLICY

The Manufacturing Sector

Following independence in 1957, Malaysia, like many developing countries, had only a rudimentary manufacturing sector, with the majority of national income coming from the exploitation of its primary resources. However, successive five-year plans focused on developing Malaysia's industrial base, producing a rapid expansion in manufacturing output, which culminated in manufacturing superseding agriculture as the largest contributor to GDP in 1987, providing 22.3%, compared with 8.7% in 1960. Since the Second Malaysia Plan (1971–75) an additional aim of the industrialization policy has been to increase the participation by indigenous Malays in non-agricultural activities. During the 1960s industrialization proceeded through an import substitution strategy, which focused on increasing domestic processing of natural products and on producing basic consumer goods for domestic consumption. However, during the 1970s the emphasis changed to export-orientated, labour-intensive industries such as textiles and electronics, which were predominantly financed by foreign investment. During the first half of the 1980s there was a second phase of import substitution focusing on heavy industries, such as steel and car production, and led by the public sector, particularly the Heavy Industries Corporation of Malaysia (HICOM). This was the period when the national (Perusahaan Otomobil Nasional—PROTON) car project was launched. However, these large investments were likely to be slow to develop, given the small size of the domestic market for industries that are subject to considerable economies of scale.

A major study of the Malaysian manufacturing sector, the Industrial Master Plan (IMP), was completed in 1986. The IMP drafted policy recommendations to cover the period 1986–95. It emphasized 12 key industries and gave details of how linkages and diversification of the manufacturing base could be achieved. The general thrust of the IMP was that Malaysia should target certain industries for development and that these should be high value-added, high-skill industries. In November 1996 the second IMP was published, proposing strategies to develop a more competitive manufacturing sector in the period to 2005. It emphasized the enhancement of manufacturing productivity and competitiveness, built upon the foundation laid by the previous industrial plan and placed particular focus on developing dynamic industry groups and industrial clusters, strengthening industrial linkages and expanding value-added activities. Eight industrial clusters or groups of related industries were identified for further development. These clusters included the electrical and electronics industry group, the transport industry group, the chemical industry group, the textiles and apparel industry group, the resource-based industry group, the materials and advanced materials industry group, and the agro-based and food products industry group. Under this cluster-based approach, attention is also paid to 'downstream' activities such as distribution, packaging and marketing to move the focus of industries from original equipment manufacturing (OEM) to higher value-added activities including indigenous design and branding.

The manufacturing sector has played an important role in the economic growth of Malaysia since the country's independence. The sector's share of GDP grew from 8.6% in 1960 to 14.8% in 1970, and further to 21% in 1988; by 2000 the sector accounted for 33.1% of GDP. The contribution of manufactured exports to overall export earnings increased significantly from 12% in 1970 to 22% in 1980, and sharply to 59% in 1990 and 86% in 2000. During the period 1988–99, both the value-added and exports of the manufacturing sector grew strongly by an average annual rate of 13.9% and 24.3%, respectively. Manufactured exports have been concentrated mainly in one industrial sub-sector since the mid-1970s, that is, in the electrical and electronics manufacturing industries. Its share of total manufactured exports increased rapidly from 9% in 1970 to 48% in 1980, and further increased to 57% and 66% in 1990 and 1997, respectively; this share increased further to 71% in 2000. Manufactured goods exports experienced a strong recovery, growing by 14.7% in 1999, and by 15.9% in 2000, after having recorded a contraction of 4.6% in 1998. This strong growth was led mainly by increased demand from industrial countries and economic recovery in the region.

Foreign Direct Investment

Since independence in 1957 the Malaysian Government has striven to attract foreign direct investment into the manufacturing sector. It is estimated that in 1970 foreign investors owned something like 60% of the manufacturing sector. The statistics on ownership in Malaysia are crude, but it is clear that the flow of foreign direct investment into Malaysia has been exceptionally high, amounting to just under 5% of GDP between 1967 and 1986—not as high as the flow into Singapore (at 7% of GDP), but well above the flows into Indonesia and the Republic of Korea over the same period (less than 1% of GDP). Between 1989 and 1994 inflows of foreign direct investment into Malaysia totalled US $22,500m., equivalent to 5% of GDP. The comparable figures for Singapore and Thailand were US $26,300m. (7% of GDP) and US $10,700m. (1%), respectively. Bank Negara reported that despite the currency crisis, net inflows of foreign investment remained strong at RM 19,200m. in 1997, compared with RM 19,400m. in 1996. Inflows of foreign direct investment declined to below 4% of GDP in 1998, owing to the financial crisis that adversely affected the region in 1997. However, the stability and certainty accorded by the selective exchange control rules and the fixed exchange rates, together with the Government's commitment to maintain a pro-business environment, contributed to a significant increase in foreign direct investment. In 2000 applications received for manufacturing investment rose to RM 29,700m., compared with RM 9,000m. in 1999.

During 1990–97 most of the inflows of foreign direct investment were channelled to the manufacturing sector, which accounted for about 65% of total inflows. The oil and gas sector received 18% of foreign investment inflows, while services acquired 10% and the property sector 7%. Following the financial crisis, however, the share of foreign direct investment in the manufacturing sector declined to about 43% of the total inflows in 1998–2000. The share of foreign direct investment in the oil and gas sector remained at about the same level (19%). The services sector received a higher share of 35%, reflecting increased investment interests in the financial services, trading and marketing, communication and services related to information technology. Prior to the crisis, the major investing countries were Japan, Singapore, the USA, Taiwan and the United Kingdom. During the period following the Asian financial crisis some significant changes in terms of major investing countries took place. Of the countries that increased their share of investment in Malaysia, the most notable was the USA, followed by Japan, Germany and Singapore.

Malaysia has continued to strive to attract foreign direct investment on an ever-increasing scale, by improving investment conditions and by creating a more attractive destination for the relocation of overseas firms. Prior to 1994, companies that had been granted pioneer status were given tax exemption on 70% of statutory income for a period of five years. After that date, companies granted the Income Tax Allowance (ITA) enjoyed a concession of 60% of qualifying capital expenditure, with the amount to be given exemption for any year of assessment not to exceed 70% of statutory income. These percentages were subsequently raised to 80% and 85%, respectively. As a result, during the Sixth Plan period (1991–95) the inflow of foreign direct investment continued. In this period approved private investment in the manufacturing sector totalled RM 116,000m., of which foreign direct investment accounted for 53%. Foreign investment was particularly important in petroleum products, textiles and electronic products. To encourage greater domestic investment, in 1993 the Government launched the Domestic Investment Initiative, and in that year approved domestic investment exceeded the approvals for foreign investment for the first time since 1987. The Government had taken steps to promote high technology, knowledge-based and capital-intensive industries, and foreign investment into these areas was highly encouraged. Among various initiatives undertaken by the Government was the establishment in 1996 of the Multimedia Super Corridor (MSC) project, in accordance with which companies with approved MSC status enjoy attractive benefits under a 10-point guarantee plan. At July 2000 there were 347 companies with MSC status. Approvals for foreign investment in the MSC almost trebled, to RM 9,400m., in 2000, compared with RM 3,200m. in 1999.

Overseas investment by Malaysian-owned companies had risen rapidly since 1991. However, overseas investment declined in 1997, owing to the uncertainty in the region. Net overseas investment declined to RM 8,100m. in 1998, compared with RM 11,500m. in 1997. In 2000 overseas investment by Malaysian companies totalled RM 7,700m. The significant decrease in overseas investment was attributable to various factors; these included the domestic economic deceleration, the Government's directive to defer overseas investments that do not have direct linkages with the domestic economy, the tightening of exchange control regulations on overseas investment since 1 September 1998 and liquidation of the overseas assets of Malaysian companies. Major overseas investments have been made by the state-controlled hydrocarbon company, PETRONAS (with investments in Algeria, Iran and Sudan), and by the private sector. Both the private and public corporations have invested particularly heavily in South Africa since 1994, and in early 1996 PROTON, the national car-maker, acquired a prestigious British car company, Lotus. The major recipient countries of Malaysian overseas investment in 1998 were Singapore (28%), the USA (22%), the United Kingdom (11%), Thailand (7%) and the Netherlands (4%). Investment in Singapore was concentrated principally in the finance and business services sector (mainly in investment holding companies) and in the manufacturing sector.

Regional Co-operation

Malaysia has pursued regional links at the sub-regional, South-East Asian and East Asian levels. At the sub-regional level, following the success of the first Association of South East Asian Nations (ASEAN) growth triangle (the Southern Growth Triangle—SGT), initiated by Malaysia, Singapore and Indonesia in the late 1980s, other intra-ASEAN economic activities have been initiated. In July 1993 the Indonesia-Malaysia-Thailand Growth Triangle, encompassing northern Sumatra, southern Thailand and the northern states of Peninsular Malaysia, was established. The East ASEAN Growth Area (EAGA) was formed in March 1994, covering Sarawak, Sabah and Labuan in East Malaysia; Brunei; East and West Kalimantan, together with North Sulawesi in Indonesia; and Mindanao in the southern Philippines.

At country level, attempts have been made to promote integration through ASEAN, which celebrated its 30th anniversary in June 1997. In order to enhance intra-ASEAN trade, in 1992 ASEAN member countries endorsed the Framework Agreement on Enhancing ASEAN Economic Co-operation. A significant outcome of this agreement was the decision to establish an ASEAN Free Trade Area (AFTA) by the year 2008. This was subsequently brought forward to the year 2003 and then to 2002, when AFTA was formally implemented. The main mechanism for the realization of AFTA was the Common Effective Preferential Tariff scheme through which tariff barriers in ASEAN would be gradually reduced to 5% or less. The scheduled time frame for the realization of AFTA is 2002/03 for the original six member countries, 2006 for Viet Nam and 2008 for Laos and Myanmar. ASEAN has also agreed to eliminate duties on all products by 2010 for the original six members, and by 2015 for the newer members of the grouping. Total intra-ASEAN trade in 1999 accounted for 22.0% of total ASEAN global trade in that year. Malaysia accounted for 25.4% of total intra-ASEAN trade (US $35,500m.) in 1999.

Development at the level of ASEAN has been slow, but integration at the wider level of East Asia has been even slower. There have been conflicts of interest concerning the Malaysian-inspired East Asia Economic Caucus (EAEC), a trade group that was to include the People's Republic of China and Japan but exclude the USA, Australia and New Zealand. Some Governments regarded it as a potential counterweight to the European Union and the North American Free Trade Agreement (NAFTA), whilst others, notably Japan, saw the EAEC as a way of integrating the region across the Pacific to North America and Australasia. China, Japan and certain members of ASEAN, however, were reluctant to jeopardize trade relations with the USA, which opposed the new grouping. In July 1993, at an ASEAN ministerial meeting, agreement was reached for the EAEC to operate as a regional grouping within the broader forum of Asia-Pacific Economic Co-operation (APEC).

The 1997–98 financial and economic crisis resulted in greater efforts towards regional co-operation. For example, in March 1999 Ministers of Finance of the association's member nations established the ASEAN Surveillance Process, which was to monitor current economic and financial sector developments and their impact on the region, and required the submission of information by member states. Subsequently, in March 2000 ASEAN agreed to expand the foreign-exchange repurchasing arrangement (which had been initially established in August 1997 by five member countries) to include the remaining ASEAN countries. In addition, ASEAN, together with China, Japan and the Republic of Korea (designated 'ASEAN + 3'), agreed to enhance existing co-operation among the region's central banks and monetary authorities, with the pronouncement of the Chiang Mai Initiative in May 2000. The initiative involved the establishment of a network of bilateral foreign-exchange repurchase agreements among East Asian countries.

An informal summit meeting of ASEAN + 3 leaders, which took place in Singapore in November 2000, further demonstrated closer co-operation within the group and the region. At the meeting a 'Protocol Regarding the Implementation of the Common Effective Preferential Tariff (CEPT) Scheme Temporary Exclusion List' was approved. This agreement provided the mechanism for member countries to delay temporarily the transfer of products into the 'Inclusion List', or to suspend concessions on products already transferred onto the list. This protocol made it possible to accommodate Malaysia's request to defer the inclusion of automotive products into the CEPT Scheme. At the end of 2000 98.3% of all products were already on the Inclusion List, with 92.7% of the products having tariffs of less than 5%. The average ASEAN tariff rate for the original six countries was 3.5%, and it was expected to decline progressively to 2.4% by 1 January 2003.

The summit meeting also accepted the formation of an East Asian study group, which was to recommend measures to enhance co-operation between ASEAN and the North-East Asian countries. Two main areas identified for the study were the possibility of expanding the ASEAN + 3 summit meeting into an East Asian grouping, and the establishment of an East Asian free trade zone. In order to narrow the disparity within ASEAN and to enhance the competitiveness of the organization, there was an initiative whereby the more developed ASEAN member countries would assist the less-developed through education and training projects, and the construction and improvement of rail, road and air links. One of the projects approved was that of the Singapore–Kunming rail connection, which had been initiated by Malaysia to link countries in the region. The route will connect eight countries: Thailand, Laos, Cambodia, Myanmar, Viet Nam, China, Malaysia and Singapore.

TOURISM

Tourism was not identified as a potential area for growth until 1986. In 1987 the Ministry of Tourism was formed and in 1990 the Government sponsored Visit Malaysia Year 1990, which comprised an international promotion and advertising campaign. The approach was so successful that a similar campaign was launched in 1994, which led to an increase of 12% in tourist arrivals compared with the previous year. However, in 1996 the number of tourist arrivals declined for the first time since 1991, by 3.4% to 7.2m. (from 7.5m. in 1995). In 1997 the performance of the tourism industry was particularly affected by the prolonged haze in the South-East Asian region, and this problem persisted in 1998. Furthermore, the regional economic downturn exacerbated the situation. Tourist arrivals in 1997 and 1998 declined to 6.2m. and 5.6m., respectively. However, in 1999 there was a 41.0% increase in the number of tourist arrivals, to 7.9m., and in 2000 arrivals exceeded 10.2m. To provide for these higher tourist arrivals, there has been much investment in hotel accommodation in recent years. The hotel occupancy rate in Kuala Lumpur increased, by more than 55% in 2000, compared with 49% in 1999. Several tourist destinations in the island resorts of Langkawi, Pangkor, Redang Island and highland resorts also recorded a hotel occupancy rate of more than 70%. In 2000 70.3% of tourists came from ASEAN countries, Japan (4.5%), and China (4.2%). The most rapid increase in the number of tourist arrivals was from emerging markets such as India and China, with annual average growth rates of 34.6% and 32.4% respectively. Domestic tourism expanded significantly in the late 1990s as a result of aggressive promotional activities such as 'Cuti-cuti Malaysia', 'Visit Perak Year', 'Visit Selangor Year' and other similar campaigns. In addition, the declaration of holidays for those employed in public services on the first Saturday of the month, effective from 1 January 1999, and also the third Saturday of the month, effective from 1 February 2000, had a positive effect on domestic tourism. The number of domestic tourist excursions increased by 89.9%, to 15.8m. trips, in 1999, compared with 8.32m. trips between August 1997 and July 1998.

INFRASTRUCTURE AND THE CONSTRUCTION INDUSTRY

Energy

In the early 1990s there was a shortage of electricity in Malaysia, and five independent power producers (IPPs) were licensed to build and operate electricity-generating plants. By 1996 the power shortage had been transformed into a significant surplus, as the IPPs established more than 4,000 MW of capacity. In March 1997, in this context of over-supply, the 77% state-owned monopoly, Tenaga Nasional Bhd (TNB), submitted proposals to the Government for the restructuring of its operations. It proposed a separation of its generating and distribution facilities, a diversification of investments into other sectors and a revised consumer tariff formula. By the end of 1996 a wholly-owned subsidiary had been established, with responsibility for managing the 7,621 MW of installed capacity. The revised tariff formula proposed that more of the burden of buying high-priced electricity from the five IPPs be passed on to consumers. Between 1995 and 2000 the other two major utilities—Sabah Electricity Board (SEB) and Sarawak Electricity Supply Company (SESCO)—were also restructured. In 2000 TNB's share of total generation in Peninsular Malaysia was at 63%, with the remainder contributed by the IPPs. The IPPs contributed 40% in Sabah and 36% in Sarawak. The average electricity tariff for domestic consumers in Peninsular Malaysia increased by 17.3%, from 20.03 sen per kWh in 1995 to 23.5 sen per kWh in 2000. Sabah maintained its tariff at 24.4 sen per kWh during this period, while that in Sarawak was reduced to 27.1 sen from 28.5 sen per kWh. At the same time, TNB has been seeking a lower price for gas feedstock purchased from PETRONAS, and the IPPs are now bearing some of the cost of subsidizing supplies to rural areas. In 2000 rural electricity coverage in Malaysia was 93%. Malaysia is not expected to need any more new plants until 2004, although the excess supply was scheduled to decline from 50% in 1996 to 30% by 2000. No more IPPs are expected to be licensed in the near future.

In the longer term some 2,400 MW of additional capacity should be provided upon the completion of the controversial Bakun hydroelectric dam in Sarawak. The six shareholders in the company that is to manage the plant formally committed themselves to the project in April 1997. The main shareholder (with a 32% holding) is Ekran, a private company chaired by Tan Sri Dato' Paduka Dr Ting Pek Khing. Five government institutions hold a further 43% of the shares. The huge project, which is expected to cost RM 13,600m. to complete, has been slow to attract foreign investors and was deferred in December 1997, owing to the economic crisis. At the end of the 1990s the Government revived the project; Sarawak Hidro Sdn Bhd, a company operating under the control of the Ministry of Finance, has been appointed to act as the project's implementing agency.

Telecommunications

The telecommunications sector continues to develop, following its partial liberalization in mid-1994, which allowed for the establishment of several new operators. However, Telekom Malaysia (in which the Government holds a controlling interest) maintains a dominant share of the market, precisely because the liberalization remains partial, with the Government deciding to defer equal access for other operators to Telekom's network from July 1996 to January 1999. Competition has been keener in the more liberalized, and rapidly-expanding, mobile telephone market. In 1996 this market grew by 49% to reach 1.5m. subscribers, with foreign investors gaining sizeable stakes (of between 20% and 30%) in three domestic companies. In February 1998 the Government decided to raise the permitted ceiling on foreign ownership of telecommunications companies from 30% to 49%, and increased it further to 61% in April. However, foreign companies were required to reduce their stake to 49% again within five years.

The communication sub-sector also grew strongly in 2000, benefiting from the increased level of economic activity, as well as the rapid expansion in the mobile phone industry. The number of cellular phone subscribers increased to 5.1m. (compared with 2.9m. in 1999). New services were introduced over the cellular network, such as Short Messaging Services (SMS), Voice Mail and Calling Line Identification, as well as internet access with Wireless Application Protocol (WAP). Subscription for internet services also increased, with Jaring subscribers rising to 326,930 (compared with 255,100 in 1999), while TMNet's subscription base increased to 712,000 (compared with 405,300 subscribers in 1999).

Transport

In general, road, rail and port communications are well-developed in Malaysia, and are more highly developed in Peninsular than in East Malaysia.

The total network of main roads in 1996 was an estimated 94,500 km, of which about three-quarters was paved. During the Sixth Plan period (1991–95) road development was based on a three-pronged strategy, to improve inter-urban links, to alleviate capacity constraints and to open new growth areas. As well as the 848-km North–South Highway down the western corridor of the peninsula (which opened in September 1994), three major projects were undertaken along the east–west corridor. In addition, various projects were initiated along the Klang valley between Kuala Lumpur and Port Klang, the main seaport. However, congestion in the major urban areas grew rapidly in the Sixth Plan period. It was particularly bad in Johor Bahru, Georgetown and Kuala Lumpur. Traffic entering the capital city increased by 17% per annum, and it was clear that new road improvements would do little to alleviate congestion. As a result, the Government embarked on the construction of an integrated public transport system, in which a major part was to be played by a Light Rail Transit (LRT) system. LRT System I (LRT STAR) began its commercial operations in December 1996, followed by LRT System II (LRT PUTRA) in September 1998. By June 1999 the LRT System in the Klang Valley encompassed a total route length of 56 km. Use of the LRT STAR increased from an initial average of 46,853 passengers per day in 1997 to an average of 77,803 passengers per day by the end of 2000. The LRT PUTRA also experienced a high growth rate, with the number of passengers increasing from an average of 12,532 per day to 121,950 per day by the end of 2000. The KL Monorail and the Express Rail Link (ERL) to Kuala Lumpur International Airport (KLIA, see below) from Kuala Lumpur Sentral, a privatized intra-city light rail network of 8.6 km in length, have been in operation since April 2001. In addition, the eight existing Kuala Lumpur-based bus companies were amalgamated into two consortia in 1994.

The railway development programme during the Sixth Plan period was aimed at increasing haulage capacity, enhancing operational safety and improving commuter train services, but more ambitious railway schemes were announced in early 1997. In April the Government announced that approval had been given to a diversified transport group (DRB-HICOM) to build a RM 1,800m. high-speed tilting-train service between Rawang, on the outskirts of Kuala Lumpur, and Ipoh, 175 km to the north. It was also announced that the Government might authorize the construction of a RM 8,300m. high-speed rail link between Kuala Lumpur and Singapore, which has been proposed by Renong. The latter, a Malaysian conglomerate, has a 50% stake in the consortium (in which DRB-HICOM also has a 30% stake) which is scheduled to assume control of Keretapi Tanah Melayu (KTP), the state railway corporation. Other projects that were completed included: a 180-km inter-city electrified double track railway linking Rawang and Ipoh; a 32-km rail link from Kempas to the Port of Tanjung Pelepas; a 14-km rail link to Port Klang; a 3-km rail link to the North Butterworth Container Terminal; and a rail link to the Segamat Inland Port.

Malaysia's five main seaports handled 112m. metric tons of cargo in 1996, an increase of 19% on 1995. Port Klang (the main port, west of Kuala Lumpur) handled 49m. tons, almost one-half of the total, while Johor Bahru handled just under 20% of the total. Port Klang is now one of the world's leading container terminals, having risen from 57th to 26th in the rankings between 1980 and 1995. As a result of the increase in the volume of cargo handled by the major ports in Malaysia (an increase of 9.5% in 1999), in 2000 various expansion plans were being undertaken by the Government to enhance port facilities and services. Bank Negara reported that at West Port in Pulau

Indah, for example, work had begun on the construction of a new 600-m terminal which would increase the capacity of the port to 1.8m. 20-foot equivalent units (TEUs) annually. The construction of 12 new berths at the Kuantan Port Consortium (KPC) was expected to raise the port's capacity by 9m. tons. In the south a new port, the Port of Tanjung Pelepas (PTP), commenced operations in 2000. During the Seventh Malaysia Plan, more than 90% of Malaysia's international trade was conducted through seaports.

As part of the expansion of infrastructural facilities, in 1991 the Government laid out plans for a new airport at Sepang, 70 km south of Kuala Lumpur, to ease congestion at the existing main airport at Subang (renamed the Sultan Abdul Aziz Shah Airport in 1996). The first phase of the new KLIA, costing RM 9,000m., began operations in June 1998. The airport, consisting of two 4-km runways and a four-winged satellite building with monorail, was able to handle 25m. passengers a year initially, and ultimately 45m., compared with the previous airport's 14m. passengers.

The major airline is Malaysia Airlines (formerly the Malaysian Airline System—MAS), which operates an extensive domestic and international service. In 1992 Malaysia Airlines announced a comprehensive aircraft modernization programme at an estimated eventual cost of US $5,000m. The number of international destinations to which it operated services increased from 66 in 1995 to 81 in 2000, while the number of domestic destinations was reduced from 36 to 33. In late 1994 a second national carrier, Air Asia Sdn Bhd, was launched to operate both domestic and regional flights. Pelangi Airways Sdn Bhd and Transmile Air Sdn Bhd were established later and provide air services to selected domestic and regional destinations, particularly tourist resorts such as Tioman, Pangkor and Medan in Indonesia.

Megaprojects and the Construction Industry

There was considerable concern in Malaysia that the very large infrastructure projects initiated in the 1990s would overheat the economy. Major projects included the hydroelectric dam at Bakun in Sarawak (at an estimated cost of RM 13,600m.), the world's tallest twin towers in Kuala Lumpur (RM 2,000m.), the new airport (RM 9,000m.) and the new administrative capital at Putrajaya (RM 20,000m.), south of Kuala Lumpur. In 1997 several of the projects were deferred, in an attempt to reduce the trade deficit and restore confidence in the financial markets, following the significant decline in the value of the ringgit and concomitant turmoil in the stock exchange.

The construction sector experienced a contraction in output in 1998, principally as a result of lower aggregate demand. In the same year the value-added component of the sector declined by 24.5%, following growth of 9.5% in 1997. The contraction moderated in 1999, however, to just 5.6%. The growth impetus for this sub-sector was derived from the higher allocation of funds in the 1999 budget to infrastructure projects and the resumption of construction work on the new Pantai Expressway, the express rail link connecting central Kuala Lumpur and the new Kuala Lumpur International Airport, and the People-Mover Rapid Transit System. In 2000 growth in the construction industry emanated largely from four privatized road projects (the Kajang Ring Road, Ipoh–Lumut Highway, Guthrie Corridor expressway and the Butterworth Outer Ring Road) and one independent power plant (the Technology Tenaga in Perlis).

Several measures were introduced in 1998 and 1999 to support the construction industry. Emphasis was placed upon the construction of low- and medium-cost houses, for which import content was low and sectoral linkages were high whilst the underlying demand remained strong. In May 1998 a RM 2,000m. fund for the Special Scheme for Low and Medium Cost Houses was established, of which RM 1,000m. was made available for bridging finance and another RM 1,000m. for end-financing. Other measures introduced included the liberalization of lending for the construction or purchase of residential properties costing RM 250,000 and below; the removal of the RM 100,000 levy on foreign purchases (effective from August 1997); and a reduction of the Real Property Gains Tax to 5%. With effect from late April 1998, foreigners were permitted to purchase any type of residential units, shop-houses, commercial and office space costing above RM 250,000 per unit, provided that the financing for any such purchase was not obtained from within Malaysia and also that purchases remained confined to newly-completed projects or to those which were at least 50% completed. To help reduce excess stocks, the Government assisted the First and Second Home Ownership campaigns. Incentives offered during the campaigns included an exemption of stamp duties and a minimum price discount of 5% on properties costing RM 100,000 or less (and of 10% on properties costing above RM 100,000). As a result of these efforts, the value-added of the residential sub-sector grew by 32.8% in 1999, a marked improvement on 1998, in which year the sector contracted by 16.5%. However, the residential sub-sector continued to be faced with the problem of excess supply. As at the end of June 1999, the number of unsold units was estimated at 93,599. House prices continued their downward trend in 1999, with the Malaysian House Price Index having declined by 12% in the first half of that year following a contraction of 9.4% in 1998. Depressed house prices stimulated purchases by foreign buyers, which increased by 18.7% in 1999. However, from the second half of 1999 into 2000, prices of residential properties rose by 15.4%. In 2001 prices increased only marginally (by 0.9% in the first half of 2001). Meanwhile, the non-residential sub-sector remained weak, owing to the continued excess supply of office and retail space. The overall occupancy rate for purpose-built office space in the Klang Valley declined from 79.8% in 1998 to 76.2% in 1999. However, the occupancy rate of the retail space sub-sector improved substantially (by 76.6%) in 1999, compared with an increase of 59.5% in 1998. According to Bank Negara, the main reasons for this improvement were improved business and consumer sentiments and lower levels of new supply.

In 2001 the construction sector recovered to record growth of 2.3%, owing primarily to government spending under the fiscal stimulus programme, privatized infrastructure projects and residential housing development. However, the non-residential sector continued to experience excess capacity, owing to an increased surplus of both office and retail space.

PRIVATIZATION

In 1991 the Privatization Master Plan (PMP) was introduced, and during the Sixth Malaysia Plan period a total of 204 projects were privatized. It is in the area of transport and infrastructure that the main thrust of privatization has taken place in Malaysia. Principal projects included the LRT system in Kuala Lumpur, the National Sports Complex, PROTON, the ports of Klang and Johor, the Second Causeway Link to Singapore and TNB, the electricity supply company.

During the Seventh Malaysia Plan (1996–2000), 98 projects were privatized, of which 47 were existing projects and 51 new projects. Of the total number of new projects, 49 were in the construction, transport, and electricity and gas sectors. Five of the projects were completed, while 25 were in various stages of implementation and the remainder in the planning stage. The completed projects were: the Damansara–Puchong Highway; the upgrading of the Sungei Besi Road; and the three IPPs in Sandakan, Karambunai and Batu Sapi in Sabah.

The privatization programme as embodied in the PMP had the following main objectives: to relieve the financial and administrative burden of the Government; to improve efficiency and productivity; to reduce the size of the public sector; and to help restructure the economy. However, considerable doubt remained as to whether all or even most of these objectives have been realized.

TRADE, THE BALANCE OF PAYMENTS AND THE EXCHANGE RATE

Malaysia is an extremely open economy in the sense that in 1995 exports of goods and non-factor services were slightly greater than GDP. At the end of the 1980s the current account of the balance of payments was in surplus, but by the early 1990s it had moved sharply into deficit. According to Malaysian sources, the merchandise account remained in surplus. Exports of goods and services grew by an annual average of 9.2% during 1971–90, 18.4% during 1990–95 and 13.3% in 1997. In 2000 exports of manufactured goods recorded an increased growth of 17% (compared with 14.3% in 1999). However, exports of manufactured goods declined by 10.3% in 2001. In 1997 the merchandise account registered a surplus of RM 11,300m. compared with a surplus of RM 933m. in 1996. The performance of the account was even better in 1998 and 1999, in which years it recorded a surplus of more than RM 69,300m. and RM 83,000m., respectively. However, the trade account surplus decreased to RM 60,900m. in 2000 and RM 53,700m. in 2001. Growth in gross exports, which had remained positive since 1997, declined by 10.4% in 2001. Imports also declined, by 9.9%.

However, the high merchandise growth in exports was accompanied by rapid import growth. Imports grew by an annual average of 10.0% during 1971–90, compared with 19.7% during 1990–95, and 9.9% in 1999. The majority of imports were intermediate goods, which accounted for 73.3% of total imports in 1999, while imports of capital goods accounted for 13.3% and imports of consumption goods 6.1% of total imports in the same year. The primary cause of the overall growth in imports was the increase in imports of intermediate goods (which recorded a rate of growth of 17.3% in 1999) and, to a lesser extent, the increase in imports of consumption and dual-use goods (imports of which increased by 21.3% in 1999). Imports of capital goods experienced a decline of 6.7% in 1999, reflecting the more gradual recovery of private investment and the low import content of public investment. However, imports of capital goods recorded a 47.7% increase in 2000, reflecting the recovery in investment activities particularly in new growth areas, such as information and communications technology.

The services account has been in deficit since the late 1970s, and the deficit widened in the 1980s largely owing to high outflows of investment income, freight and insurance and other services. It was this rapid growth in the services deficit that caused the deficits in the current account from 1990. According to the Bank Negara Report 1997, prior to 1980 Malaysia had not experienced prolonged periods of deficit on the current account of the balance of payments. The first period of sustained current-account deficit occurred in 1980–86, when the deficits averaged 6.5% of GNP. However, following voluntary structural adjustment policies undertaken by the Government, surpluses were recorded in the period 1987–89. The current-account deficit re-emerged during the period 1990–97, averaging 6.2% of GNP. There was a significant improvement in the current-account position in 1998, however, when a surplus of RM 36,100m. was recorded, following a deficit of RM 14,200m. in 1997; this constituted the first surplus on the current account of the balance of payments since 1989. In terms of GNP, the surplus increased to 13.7% of GNP in 1998 from 5.4% in 1997, surpassing the previous high of 8.9% achieved in 1987 after the last recession. The current account improved further in 1999, recording an increased surplus of RM 47,381m. or 16.9% of GNP (compared with a surplus of RM 36,800m. in 1998). However, the surplus declined to RM 31,959m. in 2000 and further, to RM 25,070m., in 2001.

Large inflows of long-term capital into Malaysia, however, were more than sufficient to finance the current-account deficit. Net inflows of long-term capital were moderate in the 1960s and 1970s. In the late 1970s and early 1980s the Government relied on external loans to sustain public-sector investments, leading to higher net inflows in the long-term official capital account (reaching a peak of RM 6,300m. in 1983). The net long-term official capital account was in deficit during 1987–92, indicating repayment for the large external debt incurred in the early 1980s. However, increasing net long-term private capital inflows from 1988 onwards caused an overall surplus on the balance of payments. This was due to the new incentives introduced in 1986, combined with the buoyant domestic economy and the lower exchange rate of the ringgit. This led to large inflows of foreign direct investment mainly into the manufacturing and petroleum sectors, with smaller amounts accruing to the agricultural and property sector. It increased from RM 1,100m. in 1987 to total more than RM 10,000m. throughout the 1990s. In 1997 the net inflow of long-term capital increased by 27.7% in real terms to RM 18,800m. (compared with RM 13,600m. in 1996). This consisted of RM 13,200m. (RM 12,800m. in 1996) of net long-term private investment and RM 5,600m. (RM 800m. in 1996) of net official long-term capital. Thus, a surplus of RM 5,700m. was recorded on the capital account in 1997, compared with a surplus of RM 1,300m. in 1996.

In 1998 the surplus on the current account was higher than the surplus on the capital account, and from 1999 the current-account surplus began to offset the deficit on the capital account. In 1998 the surplus on the current account was RM 37,394m. while that on the long-term capital account declined to RM 10,900m. as a result of the weakened global economy and of a risk-averse attitude among the investors. Since the first quarter of 2001 Malaysia's balance-of-payment accounts have been estimated in accordance with the guide-lines prescribed by the fifth edition of the Balance-of-Payments Manual (BPM5). In this new format, the capital account has become known as the 'financial account', recording direct, portfolio and other investments. Using this format, the current-account surplus for 2000 was RM 31,959m., and for 2001 was RM 25,070m., while the financial account displayed deficits of RM 23,848m. and RM 17,948m. in 2000 and 2001 respectively. However, the overall balance showed a huge deficit of RM 10,900m. in 1997 (compared with RM 6,200m. in 1996), which led to a decline in external reserves from RM 70,020m. to RM 59,120m. The large deficit was a result of substantial outflows of short-term portfolio investment from the country. Movement of private short-term capital only became significant in 1989. Net short-term capital inflows increased from RM 1,600m. in 1989 to RM 13,000m. in 1993, owing to an increase in the net external liabilities of the commercial banks and large inflows of portfolio funds into the booming stock market. In 1994 Malaysia experienced a high net outflow, totalling RM 7,900m., for speculative reasons. In 1995 the net inflow of short-term capital improved, and there was a small surplus of RM 734m. before increasing rapidly to RM 11,200m. in 1996. However, the short-term capital account recorded a large outflow of RM 14,000m. and RM 21,700m. in 1997 and 1998, respectively, in the wake of the currency turmoil in the region. The short-term capital account recorded a further substantial net outflow of RM 36,000m. in 1999. The bulk of the net outflow of funds in 1997 was due to the liquidation of portfolio investment as well as intervention to support the ringgit exchange rate. This resulted in a huge deficit in the overall balance of the balance of payments. In 1998 the overall balance of payments reverted to a surplus of RM 40,300m., following a deficit in 1997. Net international reserves of Bank Negara increased to RM 99,400m. by the end of 1998 from RM 59,100m. at the end of 1997; this level of reserves was sufficient to finance 5.7 months of retained imports. In 1999 larger outflows of short-term capital, together with exchange revaluation losses of RM 5,400m., led to a decline in the overall balance of payments to RM 17,819m. (reduced from RM 40,301m. in 1998). In the same year, external reserves increased to RM 117,244m., or US $30,854m. The level of reserves for 2000 and 2001 were RM 113,500m. and RM 112,934m., or US $29,900m. and US $29,720m., respectively.

Commentators argued that deficits in the 1990s were largely driven by the private sector, unlike the deficits in the 1980s which were led by the government sector. Large-scale investment projects undertaken by the private sector in the 1990s resulted in deficits in the resource balance. Prior to the 1980s there had been no serious deficit in the savings-investment position. However, in the first half of the 1980s the savings-investment gap widened to 8.8%, mainly owing to large-scale investment by the Government. Following the voluntary adjustment programme undertaken by the Government, in the latter half of the 1980s savings were higher than investment. However, the national resource position reverted to a deficit in 1990. For the first half of the 1990s, the deficit widened further as investment growth continued to accelerate. The deficit in the resource balance in the 1990s was mainly due to a significant growth in private-sector investment activities, despite the high rate of domestic savings in the country by international standards. In terms of GNP, the share of gross national savings was 38.5% and 40.0% in 1996 and 1997, respectively. Meanwhile, the gross domestic capital formation as a share of GNP was 45.1% in 1997, compared with 43.6% in 1996. This led to a deficit in the savings-investment position of RM 14,200m. in 1997 (compared with RM 12,300m. in 1996). However, the situation was reversed in 1998, in which year gross national savings increased by 5.1% in spite of the ongoing regional financial crisis, and thereby increased its share of GNP to 41.2%. This increase, combined with a decline in gross capital formation of 38.4%, resulted in a surplus in the savings-investment position of RM 36,100m., or 13.7% of GNP. The country's resource balance position recorded an increased surplus of RM 47,900m. (or 17.1% of GNP) in 1999 A smaller total resource surplus of RM 31,200m., accounting for 10% of GNP, was recorded for 2000.

Bank Negara reported that total medium- and long-term external debt at the end of 1998 had increased by 3% on the previous year to RM 131,300m. In US dollar terms, the debt increased by 5.5% to US $34,500m. in 1998 from US $32,700m. in 1997. Owing to prudent management and an efficient debt-monitoring system, however, total external debt outstanding declined by 1.4% to RM 159,000m. in 1999. Short-term debt, comprising mainly the external borrowings of commercial banks and the non-bank private sector, had declined by 34% to RM 28,500m. at the end of 1998, and further by 29% to RM 22,800m. at the end of 1999. For the first time since 1989, in 1999 the private sector recorded a net repayment of external loans of RM 1,800m. However, this was offset by higher net borrowing by the Federal Government and non-financial public enterprises (NFPEs) totalling RM 6,800m. in 1999. The Federal Government's external debt, which accounted for 9.3% of total external debt in 1998, had increased by 15.2% to RM 14,900m. at the end of 1998 from RM 12,900m. in 1997. This debt had increased further by 23% to RM 18,400m. at the end of 1999, accounting for an increased share of 12.0% of total external debt. Meanwhile, the outstanding debt of the NFPEs increased by 10.2% to RM 58,600m. in the same year. Private-sector external debt declined by 37.4% to RM 9,600m. in 1998 from RM 15,400m. in 1997, owing mainly to a slowdown of the economy resulting from the financial crisis. Total outstanding external debt declined by 3% to RM 157,000m. at the end of 2000, principally owing to the reduction in short-term debt and, to a lesser extent, the revaluation gains resulting from the stronger ringgit. In 2001 the total debt was RM 169,800m. and the ratio of external debt to GNP was 55.4% (the ratio had been 64% in 1997 following the regional financial crisis). The new loans were mainly drawn by the public sector (RM 7,200m.) and private sector, with new external borrowing totalling RM 2,800m.

FINANCE AND BANKING

Monetary policy has emerged as an important aspect of economic management in Malaysia, with the rapid expansion in the external reserves held by the central bank and the commercial banks, and with the growth in the money and capital markets. Since the inflationary problems experienced in the early 1980s, Bank Negara has attempted to exercise strict control over commercial and merchant banks, in order to control the growth in the money supply. However, following an apparently successful period of low inflation and high growth in the mid- to late 1980s, the inflation rate (up to 4.4% in 1991 and 4.8% in 1992, compared with less than 1% during 1985–87) and the growth in the money supply (11% in 1991, compared with 3.6% in 1987) increased during the early 1990s. The renewed inflationary pressures were a consequence of the strong domestic demand for credit and the sharp increase in liquidity caused by inflows of foreign capital, which were related to Malaysia's rapid economic growth. In August 1991 Bank Negara introduced a strict monetary policy to curb inflation and restrict the growth in the money supply. During 1992 high interest rates and restrictions on credit resulted in a slowing of consumer spending. These high interest rates attracted funds from abroad, however, accelerating the appreciation of the ringgit. In December 1992 the dollar notation was abandoned, and the official currency denomination became ringgit Malaysia (RM).

In 1993 the Government continued its cautious, restrained monetary policy that sought to reduce excess liquidity in the banking system, so as to restrict inflation to a minimum level. In the mid-1990s Bank Negara has increasingly resorted to direct action to control the monetary sector. In 1994, 1995 and 1996 it attempted to stabilize liquidity by changing reserve requirements, and in March 1997 it imposed limits on the composition of lending. In early 1998 monetary policy was tightened in order to contain inflation and restore stability in the foreign-exchange market. There was some disagreement between the Prime Minister, Mahathir Mohamad, and the then Minister of Finance, Anwar Ibrahim, over the interest rate policy: Mahathir believed that lowering the interest rate would stimulate the weakening economy and constituted a politically-favourable option, while Anwar insisted on a tight monetary policy, arguing that it was necessary that the interest rate remain high in order to restore confidence in the economy and to avoid a deterioration of the exchange rate as well as capital flight. However, the appointment of Dato' Paduka Daim Zainuddin as Minister of Special Functions in charge of economic development by Mahathir in June 1998 severely undermined Anwar's position as Minister of Finance, and signalled a change of direction in the interest rate policy. In early August 1998 the three-month intervention rate was reduced from 11% to 10.5%. This rate was subsequently reduced further to 10% and 9.5% on 10 and 27 August, respectively, and was reduced again to 8% in early September following the introduction of new exchange-control measures on 1 September 1998. By 9 November, the rate had been reduced to 7%. Through a combination of monetary and fiscal policy, together with a rapidly-expanding economy, the Government was also quite successful in controlling inflation.

A more influential central role for Bank Negara was part of the wide-ranging Banking and Financial Institutions Act of 1989, which also aimed to bring greater competition to the money and capital markets. As part of the legislation, foreign banks operating in Malaysia were required to incorporate locally and transfer more than 50% of equity to local ownership by October 1994 or face expulsion.

In the 1990s the banking sector flourished. In 1995 its pre-tax profit was RM 6,900m. In 1996 the sector's pre-tax profits rose by 26%, to RM 8,700m., with commercial banks accounting for RM 6,200m. In March 1993 Bank Negara attracted strong criticism when it was revealed that it had incurred losses of about US $3,570m. in 1992, mostly in speculation on the foreign-exchange markets. This scandal was compounded by further losses of US $2,100m. in foreign-currency trading in 1993. Since May 1998, however, the Government has placed priority on strengthening the financial system in an effort to stimulate the country's economic recovery. One of the measures adopted was a comprehensive plan to restructure the banking sector which included a merger programme; the creation of an asset management company, Pengurusan Danaharta Nasional Berhad (Danaharta); and the establishment of a special-purpose vehicle (SPV), Danamodal Nasional Berhad (Danamodal), and of the Corporate Debt Restructuring Committee (CDRC). In 1998 eight finance companies were absorbed or merged. Bank Negara reported that the merger programme would eventually result in the creation of six large domestic financial groups, reducing the number of domestic commercial banks, finance companies and merchant banks to six each, respectively (one for each group), from the existing 21 domestic commercial banks, 25 finance companies and 12 merchant banks. A consolidation programme for the domestic banking sector was announced in July 1999. Subsequently, however, objections were raised with regard to certain aspects of the programme, especially issues relating to the number and composition of the banking groups and the scheduled time frame for the programme. By the end of October the Government had announced that the number of anchor banking institutions was to be increased from six to 10, that all banking institutions were to be given flexibility to form their own merger groups and to choose their own leader within each group. The merger programme was concluded in 2000, although three banks missed the December deadline and were granted extensions. By August 2001 51 banks had merged under the terms of the programme.

According to the Bank Negara Report 1998, Danaharta had purchased and managed non-performing loans (NPLs) amounting to RM 21,700m. from the financial system, of which RM 15,100m. was from the banking system. It was reported that the exercise had succeeded in reducing the net NPL ratio of the banking system based on the six-month classification from 8.1% as at end-September 1998 to 7.6% as at December 1998. By the end of December 1999 the NPLs of the banking sector had been reduced to 6.6%, with loans to the value of RM 34,000m. having been removed from the banking system. Bank Negara also reported that Danamodal had injected capital into 10 banking institutions in the form of Exchangeable Subordinated Capital Loans (ESCL) amounting to RM 6,150m., thus increasing the risk-weighted capital ratio of the banking system from 11.2% as at end-June 1998 to 11.9% as at end-January 1999 and resulting in an increased new lending capacity of local banks. The recapitalization exercise undertaken by Danamodal helped to strengthen the position of these institutions from 9.9% as at end-September 1998 to 12.3% as at end-December 1999. On 9 August 1998 the Government announced the creation of the CDRC under the auspices of Bank Negara. The purpose of the committee is to aid negotiations of mutually satisfactory repayment schedules between businesses and their creditors, and the establishment of the committee was intended partly to discourage businesses from seeking temporary court protection from their lenders. By mid-1999 the CDRC had received 48 applications for debt restructuring, involving debt of RM 22,700m. As at 30 June 2000 the CDRC had succeeded in resolving the debts of 25 companies, amounting to RM 18,350m., out of a total of 71 applications received with debts totalling RM 39,640m. At mid-2000 the outstanding value of debts to be resolved amounted to RM 15,660m., representing 39.5% of the value of total applications. In 2001 11 cases were resolved by the CDRC, involving debts amounting to RM 11,900m. In March 2002 12 cases, with debts totalling RM 18,800m., remained outstanding. These included one case that had previously been resolved but had to be reviewed. The target was to complete the restructuring of the remaining cases by July 2002.

In 1990 the Government declared the island of Labuan an international offshore financial centre, as part of an attempt to stimulate Malaysia's financial sector. By 1993, however, only 13 banks were licensed to establish offshore units in Labuan. Its failure to attract significant investment was largely due to a lack of basic infrastructure and telecommunications systems. In mid-1993 Malaysia banned Singapore-based offshore banks from financing Malaysian business ventures in an attempt to promote Labuan. By September 1998 Labuan had issued 64 licences.

In November 1994 Bank Negara introduced a two-tier regulatory system, separating larger banks from those less well-capitalized. The 11 commercial banks in the Tier One league at the end of 1996 were required to have shareholders' funds of at least RM 1,000m. by the end of 1998, and a similar level of paid-up capital by the end of 2000 to retain the status. The Tier One designation entitled these banks to privileges that lesser banks do not enjoy, such as the rights to issue negotiable instruments, to participate in the derivatives market and to expand overseas. However, this system was abolished on 10 April 1999, and incentives that had previously been accorded only to Tier One banking institutions were made available to all institutions (subject to the approval of Bank Negara). In April 1996 it was announced that foreign state-owned banks would be permitted to establish offices in Malaysia, but a ban on new privately-owned foreign banks (except in the offshore centre of Labuan) would remain in place to protect the financial markets. However, in the late 1990s the domestic financial system moved towards greater liberalization, as evidenced by the significant foreign presence in the Malaysian financial sector by 2000. In the banking sector at mid-2000, there were 13 wholly foreign-owned commercial banks, with foreign interests in the aggregate, accounting for about 30% of the total assets of the country's commercial banks. In the insurance sector, meanwhile, the foreign market share amounted to 74% of life insurance premiums and 35% of general insurance premiums. However, foreign banks are conditioned to operate as locally-owned subsidiaries and are required to obtain 60% of their local credit from Malaysian banks.

Other developments since the mid-1980s include the establishment of an Islamic bank, the formation of a secondary mortgage market, the establishment of property unit trusts and, in 1991, of the country's first credit rating company, the Rating Agency of Malaysia. In April 1994 the Government announced the establishment of Khazanah Nasional to manage government assets. Khazanah, which was based on the highly successful state-run investment agency in Singapore, Temasek Holdings, unified all government corporate holdings, and was able to invest in industries considered important for the country's economic development.

Since the early 1980s the Government has also focused on decreasing its budget deficit, primarily through a reduction in public expenditure and the privatization of publicly-owned companies. In every year between 1993 and 1996 there was a surplus on government finances, with the surplus of operating revenue over operating expenditure being more than RM 14,000m. in each of the three years 1994–96. Owing to the economic crisis, the 1997 budget aimed for an increase in the overall fiscal surplus to 1.6% of GNP in 1997, compared with the surplus of 0.8% of GNP achieved in 1996. A budgetary surplus of 2.7% of GNP was initially forecast for 1998. However, the severe deflationary impact of the regional financial crisis on the domestic economy resulted in a revision of policy: additional budgetary funds were allocated from mid-1998, mainly for infrastructure development, and this contributed to a fiscal deficit equivalent to 3.7% of GDP in 1998. According to the IMF, the budget deficit amounted to US $9,488m. in 1999 (equivalent to 3.2% of GDP). The budget deficits for 2000 and 2001 were estimated at 4.0% and 5.1% of GDP respectively.

The Kuala Lumpur Stock Exchange (KLSE) was established in 1973 but assumed an independent existence only after the traditional links with the Stock Exchange of Singapore were severed in December 1989. Confidence in the exchange was eroded in the first half of 1990, leading the Government to introduce higher capital requirements for licensed brokerage firms from June of that year, which caused many companies to merge. Owing to the Government's privatization policy, the KLSE's market capitalization was higher than that of its regional competitors in Bangkok and Singapore. In 1995 the Government announced a series of measures that aimed to liberalize the capital market, including permission for the full foreign ownership of fund-management companies, in anticipation of a future role as a major regional capital market. In May 1996 the Government granted an operating licence for the country's second financial futures exchange, the Malaysia Monetary Exchange. An additional exchange, the Malaysian Exchange of Securities Dealings and Automated Quotations (MESDAQ), which was aimed at technology companies, began operating at the end of 1998. (In March 2002, however, MESDAQ merged with the KLSE and ceased to operate as a stock exchange.) In 1996 new funds tapped from the KLSE grew by 37%, to a record RM 15,900m., with rights issues accounting for about one-third of these funds and with initial public offers accounting for a further quarter. In 1996 the KLSE's daily turnover almost doubled to 268m. shares, worth RM 1,900m. In 1999 positive market sentiment, driven mainly by the country's strong economic performance and improved corporate earnings, led to an increase in the KLSE composite index by 38.6% (from a low of about 420 in July 1998, owing to the regional financial crisis) to end the year at 812.33 points. The composite index failed to return to its pre-crisis level, however. In 2000 the KLSE composite index fell by 16.3%, to end the year at 679.64 points, while the market capitalization declined by 19.6%, to RM 444,350m. The index improved by 2.4% in 2000, while the market capitalization rose by 4.6%, to RM 465,000m. The central bank reported that the KLSE performed quite favourably compared with the regional bourses. The contributing factors to this positive development were: strong economic fundamentals; the completion of the restructuring of several large corporations; and favourable changes in corporate governance.

In February 2000 multilateral trade negotiations conducted under the auspices of the World Trade Organization (WTO) concerning the services sector commenced. At the Fourth WTO Ministerial Conference, which was held in Doha, Qatar, on 9–14 November 2001, it was agreed that member countries should submit initial requests for specific commitments by 30 June 2002, with initial offers to be entered by 31 March 2003. It was also agreed that negotiations relating to the services sector were to be completed by no later than 1 January 2005. Malaysia had committed, under the General Agreement on Trade in Services (GATS), to allow an aggregate maximum foreign equity limit in the domestic banking institutions of 30%. A commitment was also made to allow existing, original, foreign shareholders to own up to 51% of companies within the insurance sector. Foreign ownership in the financial sector is quite substantial. Of the 27 commercial banks (including two Islamic banks), 14 are wholly foreign-owned and foreigners own an average of 18% of the total equity of five domestically-owned banks. Twenty five out of 63 insurance companies are completely under foreign ownership.

DEVELOPMENT AND PLANNING

Malaysia has launched 10 development plans since independence: the First Malaya Plan (1956–60), the Second Malaya Plan (1961–65) and the eight five-year Malaysia Plans covering the period 1966–2005.

In the 1950s a basic feature of the Malaysian economy was the concentration of Malays and other indigenous people in the 'traditional', subsistence agriculture sector of the economy with other races, notably the Chinese, having the major role in the modern rural and urban sectors. In order to redress the balance, the Second Malaysia Plan and, to some extent, the Third Plan were based on the New Economic Policy (NEP), which was inaugurated in 1970 in the aftermath of the 1969 racial riots. The two main aims of the NEP (and of the Second Malaysia Plan) were to reduce and eventually eradicate poverty by increasing income levels and employment opportunities for all Malaysians, irrespective of race; and to accelerate the process of restructuring Malaysian society in order to correct economic and geographical imbalances, thereby reducing, and eventually eliminating, the identification of race with economic function. The period 1971–80 represented the first decade of the Outline Perspective Plan (OPP) 1971–90, within which the objectives of the NEP were to be realized.

Over the period covered by the NEP, the controversial target of 30% *bumiputra* equity ownership was not achieved. However, the *bumiputras'* share of the corporate sector increased from 2.4% to 20.3% between 1970 and 1990. Chinese and Indian equity ownership increased from 32% to 46% over the same period, while that of foreigners was reduced from 63% to 25%. The proportion not accounted for was held by nominee companies which were not classified by race, promoting conflicting claims about the accuracy of the declared share of *bumiputra* ownership. However, the transfer of state assets to *bumiputra* ownership resulted in the creation of a wealthy élite within the Malay community, where income disparity was now greater than in other ethnic groups.

In June 1991 the New Development Policy (NDP), the successor to the NEP, was announced. This formed the basis of the Prime Minister's 'Vision 2020', the date by which he intended Malaysia to become an industrialized country. The focus of the NDP differed slightly from that of the NEP; racially-based economic and social engineering was relaxed in favour of national unity. The 30% target for *bumiputra* corporate ownership was retained, but there was no deadline set for its achievement. The emphasis was placed on the development of skills to promote the consolidation of *bumiputra* wealth. In the early 1990s there were too few Malays with relevant management qualifications; this shortage of suitable personnel hindered government efforts to broaden *bumiputra* participation at a high level. The NDP's macroeconomic and social targets were contained in the OPP for 1991–2000. Real GDP was projected to grow at an average rate of 7% per year, while development expenditure was to total RM 224,000m. Manufacturing's share of exports was projected to increase to more than 80%, while average annual growth in imports was to be restrained to 11.8%, compared with the average 15.7% increase that occurred under the NEP. The level of unemployment was to be reduced from 6% of the labour force in 1991 to 4% by the year 2000, and the poverty rate was to decrease from 17% to 7%.

In May 1996 the Seventh Malaysia Plan (1996–2000) was introduced. Under this, the average annual GDP growth target was set at 8.6%, with the manufacturing sector expected to grow at an annual average of just under 11%. Exports of manufactures were expected to increase at an average of 17% annually. The major thrust of the Seventh Malaysia Plan was to upgrade the economy and to achieve a strategic shift from low-skill, low value-added output to high-skill, high value-added output. A major aspect of this was an emphasis on improved vocational training, which was to be stimulated by the Human Resources Development Council and the provision of greater opportunities within tertiary education under a commercialized and partly-privatized university system.

However, one of the major obstacles to this restructuring, which the Seventh Plan did not address in detail, was the increasing reliance of the Malaysian economy on imported unskilled labour. There is also a growing caucus that is concerned about the increasing pollution and congestion problems, which are seen as being related to the rapid rate of growth that Malaysia achieved in the late 1980s and early 1990s and which was projected to continue under the Seventh Malaysia Plan. However, these concerns were superseded by the economic crisis of 1997–98, which transformed the economic situation and delayed by at least 10 years attainment of industrialized status, the Prime Minister's 'Vision 2020', put forward in 1991. ('Vision 2020' had predicted, on the basis of forecasts of the country's future average income per head, that Malaysia would be classified as a high-income or developed country by 2020.)

In early 2001 the Malaysian Government introduced the Third Outline Perspective Plan, a 10-year development programme for 2001–10, which focused on creating a resilient and competitive economy. In addition, the Eighth Malaysia Plan (2001–2005) was announced on 23 April 2001. The main aims of the plan were to shift the growth strategy from input-driven to one that is knowledge-driven; accelerate structural transformation within manufacturing and services sector; and strengthen socio-economic stability through equitable distribution of income and wealth. The plan laid emphasis on nine principal strategies: maintaining macroeconomic stability; eradicating poverty and restructuring society; enhancing productivity-driven growth; increasing competitiveness in key sectors; expanding usage of information and communications technology; enhancing human resource development; achieving sustainable development; ensuring quality of life; and strengthening moral and ethical values. Under the plan, the Government aimed to achieve economic growth averaging 7.5% per year, with low inflation and sustainable budgetary and external accounts. It was envisaged that the manufacturing and services sectors would continue to provide the greatest contribution to the economic growth of Malaysia.

Statistical Survey

Sources (unless otherwise stated): Department of Statistics, Blok C6, Parcel C, Pusat Pentadbiran Kerajaan Persekutuan, 62514 Putrajaya, tel. (3) 88857000; fax (3) 88889248; e-mail jpbpo@stats.gov.my; internet www.statistics.gov.my; Departments of Statistics, Kuching and Kota Kinabalu.

Note: Unless otherwise indicated, statistics refer to all states of Malaysia.

Area and Population

AREA, POPULATION AND DENSITY

Area (sq km)	
Peninsular Malaysia	131,686
Sabah (incl. Labuan)	73,711
Sarawak	124,450
Total	329,847*
Population (census results)†	
14 August 1991	17,566,982
5–20 July 2000‡	
Males	11,212,525
Females	10,990,089
Total	22,202,614
Population (official estimates at mid-year)	
1998	22,180,000
1999	22,712,000
2000	23,266,000
Density (per sq km) at mid-2000	70.6

* 127,355 sq miles.

† Excluding adjustments for underenumeration. The adjusted totals were 18,379,655 and 23,274,690 in 2000.

‡ Based on Preliminary Count Report.

PRINCIPAL ETHNIC GROUPS (at census of August 1991)*

	Peninsular Malaysia	Sabah†	Sarawak	Total
Malays and other indigenous groups	8,433,826	1,003,540	1,209,118	10,646,484
Chinese	4,250,969	218,233	475,752	4,944,954
Indians	1,380,048	9,310	4,608	1,393,966
Others	410,544	167,790	10,541	588,875
Non-Malaysians	322,229	464,786	18,361	805,376
Total	14,797,616	1,863,659	1,718,380	18,379,655

* Including adjustment for underenumeration.

† Including the Federal Territory of Labuan.

Mid-1997 (estimates, '000 persons): Malays 10,233.2; Other indigenous groups 2,290.9; Chinese 5,445.1; Indian 1,541.7; Others 685.7; Non-Malaysians 1,468.9; Total 21,665.5.

STATES (census of 5–20 July 2000)

	Area (sq km)	Population*	Density (per sq km)	Capital
Johor (Johore)	18,987	2,740,625	144.3	Johore Bahru
Kedah	9,425	1,649,756	175.0	Alor Star
Kelantan	15,024	1,313,014	87.4	Kota Bahru
Melaka (Malacca)	1,652	635,791	384.9	Malacca
Negeri Sembilan (Negri Sembilan)	6,644	859,924	129.4	Seremban
Pahang	35,965	1,288,376	35.8	Kuantan
Perak	21,005	2,051,236	97.7	Ipoh
Perlis	795	204,450	257.2	Kangar
Pulau Pinang (Penang)	1,031	1,313,449	1,274.0	George Town
Sabah	73,619	2,603,485	35.4	Kota Kinabalu
Sarawak	124,450	2,071,506	16.6	Kuching
Selangor	7,960	4,188,876	526.2	Shah Alam
Terengganu (Trengganu)	12,955	898,825	69.4	Kuala Trengganu
Federal Territory of Kuala Lumpur	243	1,379,310	5,676.2	—
Federal Territory of Labuan	92	76,067	826.8	Victoria
Total	329,847	23,274,690	70.6	

* Including adjustment for underenumeration.

PRINCIPAL TOWNS (population at 2000 census)

Kuala Lumpur (capital)*	1,297,526	Shah Alam	319,612
Ipoh	566,211	Kuantan	283,041
Kelang (Klang)	563,173	Kuala Terengganu (Kuala Trengganu)	250,528
Petaling Jaya	438,084	Seremban	246,441
Selayang	426,951	Kota Bahru	233,673
Subang Jaya	423,338	Taiping†	183,320
Johor Baharu (Johore Bahru)	384,613	George Town (Penang)	180,573
Melaka Bandaraya Bersejarah	369,222	Kuching Utara	152,310
		Ampang Jaya	126,459
Kota Kinabalu	354,153	Alor Setar	114,949

* The new town of Putrajaya is being developed as the future administrative capital.

† Excluding a part of Pondok Tanjong, which is in the District of Kerian.

Mid-2001 (UN estimate, incl. suburbs): Kuala Lumpur 1,410,000 (Source: UN, *World Urbanization Prospects: The 2001 Revision*).

BIRTHS AND DEATHS

	Registered live births		Registered deaths	
	Number	Rate (per 1,000)	Number	Rate (per 1,000)
1993	541,760	27.7	87,594	4.5
1994	537,611	26.7	90,051	4.5
1995	539,234	24.9	95,025	4.4
1996	540,866	25.5	95,520	4.5
1997	537,104	24.8	97,042	4.5
1998	554,573	25.0	97,906	4.4

Source: UN, mainly *Demographic Yearbook*.

1999 (rates per 1,000): Births 25.4; Deaths 4.6.

2000 (provisional, rates per 1,000): Births 24.5; Deaths 4.4.

2001 (provisional, rates per 1,000): Births 23.5; Deaths 4.4.

Source: Ministry of Health, Kuala Lumpur.

Expectation of life (WHO estimates, years at birth, 2000): Males 68.3; Females 74.1 (Source: WHO, *World Health Report*).

ECONOMICALLY ACTIVE POPULATION*

(sample surveys, ISIC Major Divisions, '000 persons aged 15 to 64 years)

	1998	1999	2000
Agriculture, forestry and fishing	1,401	1,389	1,408
Mining and quarrying	42	42	41
Manufacturing	2,277	2,379	2,559
Electricity, gas and water	70	72	75
Construction	810	804	755
Trade, restaurants and hotels	1,437	1,449	1,584
Transport, storage and communications	435	442	462
Finance, insurance, real estate and business services	418	420	509
Government services	875	877	981
Other services	832	867	899
Total employed	8,597	8,741	9,271
Unemployed	284	269	302
Total labour force	8,881	9,010	9,573

* Excluding members of the armed forces.

Source: IMF, *Malaysia: Statistical Appendix* (October 2001).

Health and Welfare

KEY INDICATORS

Fertility (births per woman, 2000)	3.1
Under-5 mortality rate (per 1,000 live births, 2000)	9
HIV/AIDS (% of persons aged 15–49, 2001)	0.35
Physicians (per 1,000 head, 1996)	2.01
Health expenditure (1998): US $ per head (PPP)	168
% of GDP	2.5
public (% of total)	57.7
Human Development Index (2000): ranking	59
value	0.782

For sources and definitions, see explanatory note on p. vi.

Agriculture

PRINCIPAL CROPS ('000 metric tons)

	1998	1999	2000
Rice (paddy)	1,944	2,037	2,037*
Maize	50†	57†	57*
Sweet potatoes*	40	41	41
Cassava (Manioc)*	400	380	380
Other roots and tubers*	48	48	48
Sugar cane*	1,600	1,600	1,600
Groundnuts (in shell)*	6	5	5
Coconuts	711†	683†	683*
Palm kernels	2,428	3,026	3,175†
Vegetables and melons*	559	488	488
Mangoes*	23	19	19
Pineapples*	143	134	134
Bananas*	535	545	545
Other fruit (excl. melons)*	373	368	368
Coffee (green)*	12	13	13
Cocoa beans	90	84	98†
Tea (made)*	6	5	5
Tobacco (leaves)	11	10*	10*
Natural rubber	886	769	769*

* FAO estimate(s). † Unofficial figure.

Source: FAO.

LIVESTOCK ('000 head, year ending September)

	1998	1999	2000*
Cattle	714	723	723
Buffaloes	160	155	155
Goats	236	232	232
Sheep	166	175	175
Pigs	2,934	1,829	1,829
Chickens*	115,000	118,000	120,000
Ducks*	13,000	13,000	13,000

* FAO estimates.

Source: FAO.

LIVESTOCK PRODUCTS ('000 metric tons)

	1998	1999	2000
Beef and veal	18	20	20
Buffalo meat	4	4	4
Pig meat	262	250*	250
Poultry meat*	789	810	810
Cows' milk	40*	41†	42†
Buffaloes' milk	7	7	7
Hen eggs*	390	398	413
Other poultry eggs*	14	14	14
Cattle and buffalo hides	3	4	4

* FAO estimate(s). † Unofficial figure.

Source: FAO.

Forestry

ROUNDWOOD REMOVALS (FAO estimates, '000 cubic metres, excl. bark)

	1998	1999	2000
Sawlogs, veneer logs and logs for sleepers	20,207	20,288	21,442
Pulpwood	700	703	743
Other industrial wood	828	847	895
Fuel wood	3,414	3,382	3,346
Total	25,149	25,220	26,426

Source: FAO, *Yearbook of Forest Products*.

SAWNWOOD PRODUCTION
('000 cubic metres, incl. railway sleepers)

	1998	1999	2000
Coniferous (softwood)*	150	150	150
Broadleaved (hardwood)	5,091	5,237	5,590
Total	5,241	5,387	5,740

* FAO estimates.

Source: FAO, *Yearbook of Forest Products*.

Fishing

('000 metric tons, live weight)

	1997	1998	1999
Capture	1,172.9	1,153.7	1,251.8
Threadfin breams	30.1	40.3	39.7
Indian scad	71.2	53.4	70.2
Marine clupeoids	62.3	72.3	68.8
Kawakawa	48.5	49.5	57.3
Indian mackerels	86.8	102.1	111.4
Prawns and shrimps	91.4	47.2	90.5
Squids	38.5	38.7	40.3
Jellyfishes	53.8	11.8	7.2
Aquaculture	108.0	133.6	155.1
Blood cockle	58.4	81.7	79.9
Total catch	1,280.9	1,287.3	1,406.9

Note: Figures exclude crocodiles, recorded by number rather than by weight. The number of estuarine crocodiles caught was: 120 in 1997; 320 in 1998; 120 in 1999. Also excluded are shells and corals. Catches of turban shells (FAO estimates, metric tons) were: 90 in 1997; 80 in 1998; 80 in 1999. Catches of hard corals (FAO estimates, metric tons) were: 4,000 in 1997; 4,000 in 1998; 4,000 in 1999.

Source: FAO, *Yearbook of Fishery Statistics*.

Mining

PRODUCTION (metric tons, unless otherwise indicated)

	1998	1999	2000*
Tin-in-concentrates	5,754	7,340	6,307
Copper concentrates	13,907	4,600	n.a.
Bauxite	160,271	222,724	123,000
Iron ore†	376,009	337,462	259,000
Kaolin	198,930	208,187	225,139
Gold (kg)	3,394	3,449	4,026
Silver (kg)	7,285	2,744	4
Barytes	1,580	13,506	7,274
Hard coal	349,849	308,502	382,942
Crude petroleum ('000 barrels)	264,641	252,115	248,737
Natural gas (million cu m)‡	48,388	51,376	56,009
Ilmenite†	124,689	127,695	124,801
Zirconium†	3,057	1,763	3,642

* Data are preliminary.

† Figures refer to the gross weight of ores and concentrates.

‡ Including amount reinjected, flared and lost.

§ Including condensate.

Sources: Minerals and Geoscience Dept; US Geological Survey; UN, *Statistical Yearbook for Asia and the Pacific*.

Industry

SELECTED PRODUCTS
('000 metric tons, unless otherwise indicated)

	1999	2000	2001
Canned fish, frozen shrimps/ prawns	34.8	35.8	40.1
Palm oil (crude)	10,553	10,839	11,804
Refined sugar	1,225.8	1,234.1	1,210.4
Soft drinks ('000 litres)	351.3	403.1	501.7
Cigarettes (metric tons)	15,504	27,271	25,618
Woven cotton fabrics (million metres)	181.1	187.5	177.4
Veneer sheets ('000 cu metres)	1,370.3	1,468.0	1,173.8
Plywood ('000 cu metres)	3,700.8	3,739.8	3,940.2
Gasoline (motor spirit)*	3,000	2,612	n.a.
Kerosene and jet fuel	2,057.5	2,533.1	3,293.8
Gas-diesel (distillate fuel) oil*	5,861	7,716	n.a.
Residual fuel oil*	1,798	1,864	n.a.
Liquefied petroleum gas	1,572.5	1,918.8	2,307.0
Inner tubes and pneumatic tyres ('000)	24,984	26,208	26,507
Rubber gloves (million pairs)	10,906.6	11,598.0	12,233.9
Clay building bricks (million)	873.3	1,036.3	1,198.5
Cement	10,104	11,445	13,820
Iron and steel bars and rods	2,260.6	2,583.6	2,712.2
Refrigerators for household use ('000)	194.3	215.3	190.5
Television receivers ('000)	7,610.9	10,550.5	9,612.9
Radio receivers ('000)	32,957	36,348	29,184
Semiconductors (million)	9,959	16,373	16,324
Electronic transistors (million)	13,230	17,519	19,989
Integrated circuits (million)	14,902	21,424	17,470
Passenger motor cars ('000)†	258.1	300.8	390.8
Lorries, vans and buses ('000)†	45.0	55.7	63.4
Motorcycles and scooters ('000)	271.8	273.6	235.9

* Source: UN, *Monthly Bulletin of Statistics*.

† Vehicles assembled from imported parts.

Tin (smelter production of primary metal, metric tons): 28,913 in 1999; 27,200 (estimate) in 2000 (Source: US Geological Survey).

Source (unless otherwise indicated): Bank Negara Malaysia, Kuala Lumpur.

Finance

CURRENCY AND EXCHANGE RATES

Monetary Units

100 sen = 1 ringgit Malaysia (RM—also formerly Malaysian dollar).

Sterling, US Dollar and Euro Equivalents (31 May 2002)

£1 sterling = RM 5.5735;
US $1 = RM 3.8000;
€1 = RM 3.5671;
RM 100 = £17.94 = US $26.32 = €28.03.

Exchange Rate

A fixed exchange rate of US $1 = RM 3.8000 has been in effect since September 1998.

FEDERAL BUDGET (RM million)

Revenue	1999	2000	2001*
Tax revenue	45,346	47,173	61,492
Taxes on income and profits	27,246	29,156	42,097
Companies (excl. petroleum)	15,742	13,905	20,770
Individuals	6,419	7,015	9,436
Petroleum	2,856	6,010	9,858
Export duties	670	1,032	867
Import duties	4,720	3,599	3,193
Excises on goods	4,723	3,803	4,130
Sales tax	4,488	5,968	7,356
Service tax	1,459	1,701	1,927
Other revenue	13,329	14,692	18,076
Total	58,675	61,864	79,567

Expenditure	1999	2000	2001*
Defence and security	6,108	6,958	8,310
Economic Services	4,213	6,637	5,150
Agriculture and rural development	1,222	1,323	1,366
Trade and industry	1,596	3,761	1,870
Transport	1,156	1,286	1,672
Social services	16,612	18,784	21,757
Education	11,458	12,923	14,422
Health	3,626	4,131	4,680
Transfer payments	2,542	2,524	5,561
Debt service charges	7,941	9,055	9,634
Pensions and gratuities	3,793	4,187	4,711
General administration	5,490	8,401	8,636
Total	46,699	56,547	63,757

* Preliminary.

Source: Bank Negara Malaysia, Kuala Lumpur.

FEDERAL DEVELOPMENT EXPENDITURE (RM million)

	1999	2000	2001*
Defence and security	3,122	2,332	3,287
Social services	6,936	11,077	15,384
Education	3,865	7,099	10,363
Health	836	1,272	1,570
Housing	1,081	1,195	1,268
Economic services	8,969	10,412	12,724
Agriculture and rural development	1,088	1,183	1,395
Public utilities	1,850	1,517	1,092
Trade and industry	2,798	3,667	4,829
Transport	2,893	3,636	5,042
General administration	3,587	4,122	3,839
Total	22,614	27,942	35,235

* Estimates.

Source: Bank Negara Malaysia, Kuala Lumpur.

INTERNATIONAL RESERVES (US $ million at 31 December)

	1999	2000	2001
Gold*	57	53	51
IMF special drawing rights	83	105	125
Reserve position in IMF	835	792	764
Foreign exchange	29,670	28,625	29,585
Total	30,645	29,576	30,526

* Valued at SDR 35 per troy ounce.

Source: IMF, *International Financial Statistics.*

MONEY SUPPLY (RM million at 31 December)

	1999	2000	2001
Currency outside banks	24,757	22,263	22,148
Demand deposits at commercial banks	46,841	54,520	57,791
Total money (incl. others)	75,602	80,656	83,882

Source: IMF, *International Financial Statistics.*

COST OF LIVING (Consumer Price Index; base: 2000 = 100)

	1998	1999	2001
Food	93.8	98.1	100.7
Beverages and tobacco	90.1	97.2	104.8
Clothing and footwear	103.9	101.8	97.4
Rent and other housing costs, heating and lighting	97.0	98.6	101.4
Furniture, domestic appliances, tools and maintenance	98.7	100.0	100.1
Medical care	95.1	98.0	102.9
Transport and communications	97.5	98.0	103.6
Education and leisure	97.0	99.5	99.9
Other goods and services	97.6	99.1	100.7
All items	95.8	98.5	101.4

Source: Bank Negara Malaysia, Kuala Lumpur.

NATIONAL ACCOUNTS (RM million at current prices)

Expenditure on the Gross Domestic Product

	1999	2000	2001
Government final consumption expenditure	33,044	36,231	42,859
Private final consumption expenditure	125,056	144,726	150,555
Change in stocks	1,476	4,998	-3,660
Gross fixed capital formation	65,841	87,729	83,345
Total domestic expenditure	225,417	273,684	273,099
Exports of goods and services	364,861	427,003	389,256
Less Imports of goods and services	289,514	358,529	327,765
GDP in purchasers' values	300,764	342,157	334,589
GDP at constant 1987 prices	193,422	209,538	210,480

Source: Bank Negara Malaysia, Kuala Lumpur.

Gross Domestic Product by Economic Activity

	1999	2000	2001
Agriculture, forestry and fishing	32,610	29,730	28,461
Mining and quarrying	23,081	37,428	35,969
Manufacturing	93,045	112,755	102,276
Electricity, gas and water	9,619	10,928	11,794
Construction	13,987	14,080	14,273
Trade, restaurants and hotels	44,378	47,113	47,914
Transport, storage and communications	20,290	22,880	24,296
Finance, insurance, real estate and business services	38,326	39,085	39,187
Government services	20,184	22,695	24,157
Other services	20,837	21,644	22,568
Sub-total	316,357	358,337	350,895
Import duties	6,459	5,826	5,841
Less Imputed bank service charges	22,052	22,006	22,147
GDP in purchasers' values	300,764	342,157	334,589

Source: Bank Negara Malaysia, Kuala Lumpur.

BALANCE OF PAYMENTS (US $ million)

	1998	1999	2000
Exports of goods f.o.b.	71,883	84,098	98,429
Imports of goods f.o.b.	-54,378	-61,453	-77,576
Trade balance	17,505	22,644	20,854
Exports of services	11,517	11,919	13,775
Imports of services	-13,127	-14,736	-16,726
Balance on goods and services	15,895	19,829	17,903
Other income received	1,542	2,003	2,098
Other income paid	-5,446	-7,499	-9,612
Balance on goods, services and income	11,991	14,332	10,388
Current transfers received	728	801	720
Current transfers paid	-3,190	-2,529	-2,699
Current balance	9,529	12,606	8,409
Direct investment abroad	—	-1,422	-2,026
Direct investment from abroad	2,163	3,895	3,788
Portfolio investment liabilities	283	-1,156	-2,472
Other investment assets	-5,269	-7,936	-5,565
Other investment liabilities	272	—	—
Net errors and omissions	3,039	-1,273	-3,142
Overall balance	10,018	4,712	-1,009

Source: IMF, *International Financial Statistics.*

External Trade

PRINCIPAL COMMODITIES (RM million)

Imports c.i.f.	1999	2000	2001
Food and live animals	10,873	11,393	12,310
Beverages and tobacco	682	709	925
Crude materials (inedible) except fuels	6,225	7,096	6,911
Mineral fuels, lubricants, etc.	7,489	14,973	14,697
Animal and vegetable oils and fats	1,056	604	794
Chemicals	18,790	22,371	20,725
Basic manufactures	28,467	32,596	29,642
Machinery and transport equipment	153,971	195,728	169,964
Miscellaneous manufactured articles	12,873	17,659	16,075
Other commodities and transactions	8,050	8,330	8,649
Total	248,477	311,459	280,691

Exports f.o.b.	1999	2000	2001
Food and live animals	6,229	6,470	6,596
Beverages and tobacco	1,047	1,215	1,307
Crude materials (inedible) except fuels	9,910	10,288	7,563
Mineral fuels, lubricants, etc.	22,480	35,903	32,505
Animal and vegetable oils and fats	18,280	12,937	12,323
Chemicals	10,353	14,278	14,376
Basic manufactures	24,243	25,788	24,194
Machinery and transport equipment	200,072	233,379	202,734
Miscellaneous manufactured articles	26,188	29,925	29,263
Other commodities and transactions	2,758	3,088	3,559
Total	321,560	373,270	334,420

Source: Asian Development Bank, *Key Indicators of Developing Asian and Pacific Countries*.

PRINCIPAL TRADING PARTNERS (RM million)

Imports c.i.f.	1999	2000	2001
Australia	5,670	6,052	5,943
China, People's Republic	8,125	12,321	14,457
France	4,150	5,139	4,340
Germany	7,704	9,282	10,415
Hong Kong	6,250	8,557	7,191
India	2,014	2,748	2,935
Indonesia	6,677	8,623	8,517
Ireland	3,259	2,611	3,802
Italy	2,027	2,092	2,864
Japan	51,803	65,513	54,002
Korea, Republic	12,974	13,926	11,240
Philippines	6,213	7,562	6,989
Singapore	34,817	44,696	35,313
Taiwan	13,259	17,511	15,932
Thailand	9,377	11,987	11,121
United Kingdom	5,611	6,080	6,872
USA	43,318	51,744	44,841
Total (incl. others)	248,477	311,459	280,691

Exports f.o.b.	1999	2000	2001
Australia	7,711	9,210	7,798
Belgium	3,431	3,526	2,536
China, People's Republic	8,808	11,507	14,520
France	3,231	2,752	3,572
Germany	7,692	9,336	7,767
Hong Kong	13,344	16,854	15,299
India	7,745	7,312	5,993
Indonesia	4,679	6,484	5,940
Japan	37,289	48,770	44,503
Korea, Republic	9,498	12,464	11,157
Netherlands	16,233	15,616	15,429
Philippines	4,929	6,558	4,893
Singapore	53,106	68,574	56,669
Taiwan	14,600	14,188	12,117
Thailand	10,481	13,485	12,768
United Kingdom	12,067	11,566	8,779
USA	70,391	76,579	67,672
Total (incl. others)	321,560	373,270	334,420

Source: Bank Negara Malaysia, Kuala Lumpur.

Transport

RAILWAYS (traffic, Peninsular Malaysia and Singapore)

	1997	1998	1999
Passenger-km (million)	1,492	1,397	1,313
Freight ton-km (million)	1,336	992	908

Source: UN, *Statistical Yearbook*.

ROAD TRAFFIC (registered motor vehicles at 31 December)

	1998*	1999*	2000
Passenger cars	3,517,484	3,852,693	4,212,567
Buses and coaches	45,643	47,674	48,662
Lorries and vans	599,149	642,976	665,284
Road tractors	286,898	304,135	315,687
Motorcycles and mopeds	4,692,183	5,082,473	5,356,604

* Source: International Road Federation, *World Road Statistics*. Data for 1999 are estimates.

SHIPPING

Merchant Fleet (registered at 31 December)

	1999	2000	2001
Number of vessels	828	865	882
Total displacement ('000 grt)	5,244.7	5,328.1	5,207.1

Source: Lloyd's Register-Fairplay, *World Fleet Statistics*.

Sea-borne Freight Traffic*
(Peninsular Malaysia, international and coastwise, '000 metric tons)

	1998	1999	2000
Goods loaded	35,206	39,755	42,547
Goods unloaded	48,314	54,854	56,537

* Including transhipments.

Source: UN, *Monthly Bulletin of Statistics*.

CIVIL AVIATION (traffic on scheduled services)

	1996	1997	1998
Kilometres flown (million)	173	183	189
Passengers carried ('000)	15,118	15,592	13,654
Passenger-km (million)	26,862	28,698	29,372
Total ton-km (million)	3,620	3,777	3,777

Source: UN, *Statistical Yearbook*.

Tourism

TOURIST ARRIVALS BY COUNTRY OF RESIDENCE*

	1999	2000	2001
Australia	134,311	236,775	222,340
Brunei	187,704	195,059	309,529
China, People's Republic	190,851	425,246	453,246
Indonesia	307,373	545,051	777,449
Japan	286,940	455,981	397,639
Singapore	4,900,084	5,420,200	6,951,594
Taiwan	136,863	213,016	249,811
Thailand	498,578	940,215	1,018,797
United Kingdom	136,398	237,757	262,423
Total (incl. others)	7,932,149	10,221,582	12,775,073

* Including Singapore residents crossing the frontier by road through the Johore Causeway.

Tourism receipts (RM million): 12,321 in 1999; 17,335.4 in 2000; 24,221.5 in 2001.

Source: Malaysia Tourism Promotion Board.

Communications Media

	1999	2000	2001
Television receivers ('000 in use)*	3,800	3,900	n.a.
Telephones ('000 main lines in use)	4,430.8	4,634.3	4,738.0
Mobile cellular telephones ('000 subscribers)	2,990.0	4,960.8	7,128.0
Personal computers ('000 in use)*	1,500	2,400	3,000
Internet users ('000)*	2,500	3,700	5,700

Radio receivers ('000 in use, 1997): 9,100.

Facsimile machines ('000 in use): 175.0* in 1998.

Book production (1996): 5,843 titles (29,040,000 copies)†.

Newspapers (1996): 42 dailies (average circulation 3,345,000 copies); 44 non-dailies (average circulation 1,424,000 copies).

Periodicals (1992): 25 titles (average circulation 996,000 copies).

* Estimate(s).

† Including pamphlets (106 titles and 646,000 copies in 1994).

Sources: International Telecommunication Union; UNESCO, *Statistical Yearbook*; UN, *Statistical Yearbook*.

Education

(January 1997, unless otherwise indicated)

	Institutions	Teachers	Students
Primary	7,084	150,681	2,870,667
Secondary	1,561	97,401	1,804,519
Academic	1,460	91,659	1,767,946
Vocational	47	3,007	14,211
Technical	31	1,857	12,358
MARA Junior Science College	23	878*	10,004*
Tertiary†	48	14,960	210,724
Universities†	9	7,823	97,103
Teacher-training†	31	3,220	46,019
MARA Institute of Technology†	1	2,574	42,174

* As at 30 July 1997.

† 1995 figures.

Pre-primary: 9,743 schools (1994); 20,352 teachers (1994); 459,015 pupils (1995) (Source: UNESCO, *Statistical Yearbook*).

Adult literacy rate (UNESCO estimates): 87.5% (males 91.4%; females 83.4%) in 2000 (Source: UN Development Programme, *Human Development Report*).

Directory

The Constitution

The Constitution of the Federation of Malaya became effective at independence on 31 August 1957. As subsequently amended, it is now the Constitution of Malaysia. The main provisions are summarized below.

SUPREME HEAD OF STATE

The Yang di-Pertuan Agong (King or Supreme Sovereign) is the Supreme Head of Malaysia.

Every act of government is derived from his authority, although he acts on the advice of Parliament and the Cabinet. The appointment of a Prime Minister lies within his discretion, and he has the right to refuse to dissolve Parliament even against the advice of the Prime Minister. He appoints the Judges of the Federal Court and the High Courts on the advice of the Prime Minister. He is the Supreme Commander of the Armed Forces. The Yang di-Pertuan Agong is elected by the Conference of Rulers, and to qualify for election he must be one of the nine hereditary Rulers. He holds office for five years or until his earlier resignation or death. Election is by secret ballot on each Ruler in turn, starting with the Ruler next in precedence after the late or former Yang di-Pertuan Agong. The first Ruler to obtain not fewer than five votes is declared elected. The Deputy Supreme Head of State (the Timbalan Yang di-Pertuan Agong) is elected by a similar process. On election the Yang di-Pertuan Agong relinquishes, for his tenure of office, all his functions as Ruler of his own state and may appoint a Regent. The Timbalan Yang di-Pertuan Agong exercises no powers in the ordinary course, but is immediately available to fill the post of Yang di-Pertuan Agong and carry out his functions in the latter's absence or disability. In the event of the Yang di-Pertuan Agong's death or resignation he takes over the exercise of sovereignty until the Conference of Rulers has elected a successor.

CONFERENCE OF RULERS

The Conference of Rulers consists of the Rulers and the heads of the other states. Its prime duty is the election by the Rulers only of the Yang di-Pertuan Agong and his deputy. The Conference must be consulted in the appointment of judges, the Auditor-General, the Election Commission and the Services Commissions. It must also be consulted and concur in the alteration of state boundaries, the extension to the federation as a whole, of Islamic religious acts and observances, and in any bill to amend the Constitution. Consultation is mandatory in matters affecting public policy or the special position of the Malays and natives of Sabah and Sarawak. The Conference also considers matters affecting the rights, prerogatives and privileges of the Rulers themselves.

FEDERAL PARLIAMENT

Parliament has two Houses—the Dewan Negara (Senate) and the Dewan Rakyat (House of Representatives). The Senate has a membership of 70, comprising 30 elected and 40 appointed members. Each state legislature, acting as an electoral college, elects two Senators; these may be members of the State Legislative Assembly or otherwise. The remaining four Senators represent the two Federal Territories, Kuala Lumpur and the island of Labuan. The Yang di-Pertuan Agong appoints the other 40 members of the Senate. Members of the Senate must be at least 30 years old. The Senate elects its President and Deputy President from among its members. It may initiate legislation, but all proposed legislation for the granting of funds must be introduced in the first instance in the House of Representatives. All legislative measures require approval by both Houses of Parliament before being presented to the Yang di-Pertuan Agong for the Royal Assent in order to become law. A bill originating in the Senate cannot receive Royal Assent until it has been approved by the House of Representatives, but the Senate has delaying powers only over a bill originating from and approved by the House of Representatives. Senators serve for a period of three years, but the Senate is not subject to dissolution. Parliament can, by statute, increase the number of Senators elected from each state to three. The House of Representatives consists of 193 elected members (see Amendments). Of these, 144 are from Peninsular Malaysia (including seven from Kuala Lumpur), 28 from Sarawak and 21 from Sabah (including one from Labuan). Members are returned from single-member constituencies on the basis of universal adult franchise. The term of the House of Representatives is limited to five years, after which time a fresh general election must be held. The Yang di-Pertuan Agong may dissolve Parliament before then if the Prime Minister so advises.

THE CABINET

To advise him in the exercise of his functions, the Yang di-Pertuan Agong appoints the Cabinet, consisting of the Prime Minister and an unspecified number of Ministers (who must all be Members of Parliament). The Prime Minister must be a citizen born in Malaysia and a member of the House of Representatives who, in the opinion of the Yang di-Pertuan Agong, commands the confidence of that House. Ministers are appointed on the advice of the Prime Minister. A number of Deputy Ministers (who are not members of the Cabinet) are also appointed from among Members of Parliament. The Cabinet meets regularly under the chairmanship of the Prime Minister to formulate policy.

PUBLIC SERVICES

The Public Services, civilian and military, are non-political and owe their loyalty not to the party in power but to the Yang di-Pertuan Agong and the Rulers. They serve whichever government may be in power, irrespective of the latter's political affiliation. To ensure the impartiality of the service, and its protection from political interference, the Constitution provides for a number of Services Commissions to select and appoint officers, to place them on the pensionable establishment, to determine promotion and to maintain discipline.

THE STATES

The heads of nine of the 13 states are hereditary Rulers. The Ruler of Perlis has the title of Raja, and the Ruler of Negeri Sembilan that of Yang di-Pertuan Besar. The rest of the Rulers are Sultans. The heads of the States of Melaka (Malacca), Pinang (Penang), Sabah and Sarawak are each designated Yang di-Pertua Negeri and do not participate in the election of the Yang di-Pertuan Agong. Each of the 13 states has its own written Constitution and a single Legislative Assembly. Every state legislature has powers to legislate on matters not reserved for the Federal Parliament. Each State Legislative Assembly has the right to order its own procedure, and the members enjoy parliamentary privilege. All members of the Legislative Assemblies are directly elected from single-member constituencies. The head of the state acts on the advice of the State Government. This advice is tendered by the State Executive Council or Cabinet in precisely the same manner in which the Federal Cabinet tenders advice to the Yang di-Pertuan Agong.

The legislative authority of the state is vested in the head of the state in the State Legislative Assembly. The executive authority of the state is vested in the head of the state, but executive functions may be conferred on other persons by law. Every state has its own Executive Council or Cabinet to advise the head of the state, headed by its Chief Minister (Ketua Menteri in Melaka, Pinang, Sabah and Sarawak and Menteri Besar in other states), and collectively responsible to the state legislature. Each state in Peninsular Malaysia is divided into administrative districts, each with its District Officer. Sabah is divided into four residencies: West Coast, Interior, Sandakan and Tawau, with headquarters at Kota Kinabalu, Keningua, Sandakan and Tawau, respectively. Sarawak is divided into five Divisions, each in charge of a Resident—the First Division, with headquarters at Kuching; the Second Division, with headquarters at Simanggang; the Third Division, with headquarters at Sibu; the Fourth Division, with headquarters at Miri; the Fifth Division, with headquarters at Limbang.

AMENDMENTS

From 1 February 1974, the city of Kuala Lumpur, formerly the seat of the Federal Government and capital of Selangor State, is designated the Federal Territory of Kuala Lumpur. It is administered directly by the Federal Government and returns five members to the House of Representatives.

In April 1981 the legislature approved an amendment empowering the Yang di-Pertuan Agong to declare a state of emergency on the grounds of imminent danger of a breakdown in law and order or a threat to national security.

In August 1983 the legislature approved an amendment empowering the Prime Minister, instead of the Yang di-Pertuan Agong, to declare a state of emergency.

The island of Labuan, formerly part of Sabah State, was designated a Federal Territory as from 16 April 1984.

The legislature approved an amendment increasing the number of parliamentary constituencies in Sarawak from 24 to 27. The amendment took effect at the general election of 20–21 October 1990. The total number of seats in the House of Representatives, which had increased to 177 following an amendment in August 1983, was thus expanded to 180.

In March 1988 the legislature approved two amendments relating to the judiciary (see Judicial System).

In October 1992 the legislature adopted an amendment increasing the number of parliamentary constituencies from 180 to 192. The Kuala Lumpur Federal Territory and Selangor each gained three seats, Johor two, and Perlis, Kedah, Kelantan and Pahang one. The amendment took effect at the next general election (in April 1995).

In March 1993 an amendment was approved which removed the immunity from prosecution of the hereditary Rulers.

In May 1994 the House of Representatives approved an amendment which ended the right of the Yang di-Pertuan Agong to delay legislation by withholding his assent from legislation and returning it to Parliament for further consideration. Under the amendment, the Yang di-Pertuan Agong was obliged to give his assent to a bill within 30 days; if he failed to do so, the bill would, none the less, become law. An amendment was simultaneously approved restructuring the judiciary and introducing a mandatory code of ethics for judges, to be drawn up by the Government.

In 1996 an amendment was approved, increasing the number of parliamentary constituencies from 192 to 193.

In 2001 an amendment was approved banning all discrimination on grounds of gender.

The Government

SUPREME HEAD OF STATE
(HM the Yang di-Pertuan Agong)

HM Tuanku Syed Sirajuddin ibni Al-Marhum Syed Putra Jamalullail (Raja of Perlis) (took office 13 December 2001).

Deputy Supreme Head of State
(Timbalan Yang di-Pertuan Agong)

HRH Sultan Mizan Zainal Abidin (Sultan of Terengganu).

THE CABINET
(September 2002)

Prime Minister and Minister of Finance and of Special Functions: Dato' Seri Dr Mahathir bin Mohamad.

Deputy Prime Minister and Minister of Home Affairs: Dato' Seri Abdullah bin Haji Ahmad Badawi.

Minister of Housing and Local Government: Dato' Ong Kah Ting.

Minister of Foreign Affairs: Datuk Seri Syed Hamid bin Syed Jaafar Albar.

Minister of International Trade and Industry: Dato' Seri Paduka Rafidah binti Aziz.

Minister of Domestic Trade and Consumer Affairs: Tan Sri Dato' Haji Muhyiddin bin Haji Mohd Yassin.

Minister of Defence: Dato' Seri Najib bin Tun Abdul Razak.

Minister of Transport: Dato' Seri Dr Ling Liong Sik.

Minister of National Unity and Social Development: Dato' Dr Siti Zaharah binti Sulaiman.

Minister of Primary Industries: Dato' Seri Dr Lim Keng Yaik.

Minister of Energy, Communications and Multimedia: Datuk Leo Moggie Anak Irok.

Minister of Works: Dato' Seri S. Samy Vellu.

Minister of Youth and Sports: Dato' Hishamuddin bin Tun Hussein.

Minister of Education: Tan Sri Musa bin Mohamad.

Minister of Information: Tan Sri Mohd Khalil bin Yaacob.

Minister of Human Resources: Datuk Dr Fong Chan Onn.

Minister of Land and Co-operative Development: Tan Sri Datuk Kasitah bin Gaddam.

Minister of Culture, Arts and Tourism: Datuk Abdul Kadir bin Haji Sheikh Fadzir.

Minister of Science, Technology and the Environment: Datuk Law Hieng Ding.

Minister of Health: Dato' Chua Jui Meng.

Minister of Agriculture: Datuk Mohamed Effendi bin Norwawi.

Minister of Rural Development: Dato' Amzi bin Khalid.

Minister of Entrepreneur Development: Datuk Mohamed Nazri bin Tan Sri Dato' Abdul Aziz.

Minister of Women's Affairs: Datuk Shahrizat bte Abdul Jalil.

Ministers in the Prime Minister's Department: Brig.-Gen. Senator Datuk Abdul Hamid bin Zainal Abidin, Tan Sri Datuk Seri Panglima Bernard Giluk Dompok, Dato' Rais bin Yatim, Datuk Pandikar Amin Mulia.

MINISTRIES

Prime Minister's Department (Jabatan Perdana Menteri): Blok Utama, Tingkat 1–5, Pusat Pentadbiran Kerajaan Persekutuan, 62502 Putrajaya; tel. (3) 88888000; fax (3) 88883424; e-mail ppm@smpke.jpm.my; internet www.smpke.jpm.my.1

Ministry of Agriculture (Kementerian Pertanian): Tingkat 4, Wisma Tani, Jalan Sultan Salahuddin, 50624 Kuala Lumpur; tel. (3) 26982011; fax (3) 26913758; e-mail admin@moa.my; internet www.agrolink.moa.my.

Ministry of Culture, Arts and Tourism (Kementerian Kebudayaan, Kesenian dan Pelancongan): Menara Dato' Onn, 34th–36th Floors, POB 5–7, Putra World Trade Centre, 45 Jalan Tun Ismail, 50694 Kuala Lumpur; tel. (3) 26937111; fax (3) 26941146; e-mail mocat@tourism.gov.my; internet www.mocat.gov.my.

Ministry of Defence (Kementerian Pertahanan): Wisma Pertahanan, Jalan Padang Tembak, 50634 Kuala Lumpur; tel. (3) 26921333; fax (3) 26914163; e-mail cpa@mod.gov.my; internet www.mod.gov.my.

Ministry of Domestic Trade and Consumer Affairs (Kementerian Perdagangan Dalam Negeri Dan Hal Ehwal Pengguna):

Note: in 2002 the telephone and fax numbers of Malaysia were in the process of change. See www.telekom.com.my for further details.

Tingkat 33, Menara Dayabumi, Jalan Sultan Hishamuddin, 50632 Kuala Lumpur; tel. (3) 22742100; fax (3) 22745260; e-mail menteri@kpdnhq.gov.my; internet www.kpdnhq.gov.my.

Ministry of Education (Kementerian Pendidikan): Block J, Tingkat 7, Pusat Bandar Damansara, 50604 Kuala Lumpur; tel. (3) 2586900; fax (3) 2543107; e-mail webmaster@moe.gov.my; internet www.moe.gov.my.

Ministry of Energy, Communications and Multimedia (Kementerian Tenaga, Telekom dan Pos): Wisma Damansara, 3rd Floor, Jalan Semantan, 50668 Kuala Lumpur; tel. (3) 20875000; fax (3) 20957901; e-mail ZainalAbidin@ktkm.gov.my; internet www.ktkm.gov.my.

Ministry of Entrepreneur Development (Kementerian Pembangunan Usahawan): Tingkat 22–26, Medan MARA, Jalan Raja Laut, 50652 Kuala Lumpur; tel. (3) 26985022; fax (3) 26917623; e-mail nazri@kpun.gov.my; internet www.kpun.gov.my.

Ministry of Finance (Kementerian Kewangan): Kompleks Kementerian Kewangan, Precinct 2, Pusat Pentadbiran Kerajaan Persekutuan, 62592 Putrajaya; tel. (3) 88823000; fax (3) 88823892; e-mail mk1@treasury.gov.my; internet www.treasury.gov.my.

Ministry of Foreign Affairs (Kementerian Luar Negeri): Wisma Putra, 1 Jalan Wisma Putra, 62602 Putrajaya; tel. (3) 88874000; fax (3) 88891717; e-mail webmaster@kln.gov.my; internet www.kln.gov.my.

Ministry of Health (Kementerian Kesihatan): Jalan Cenderasari, 50590 Kuala Lumpur; tel. (3) 26985077; fax (3) 26985964; e-mail CJM@moh.gov.my; internet www.moh.gov.my.

Ministry of Home Affairs (Kementerian Dalam Negeri): Blok D1, Parcel D, Pusat Pentadbiran Kerajaan Persekutuan, 62546 Putrajaya; tel. (3) 88868000; e-mail irg@kdn.gov.my; internet www.kdn.gov.my.

Ministry of Housing and Local Government (Kementerian Perumahan dan Kerajaan Tempatan): Paras 4 and 5, Blok K, Pusat Bandar Damansara, 50782 Kuala Lumpur; tel. (3) 2547033; fax (3) 2547380; e-mail menteri@kpkt.gov.my; internet www.kpkt.gov.my.

Ministry of Human Resources (Kementerian Sumber Manusia): Level 6–9, Block D3, Parcel D, Pusat Pentadbiran Kerajaan Persekutuan, 62502 Putrajaya; tel. (3) 88865000; fax (3) 88893381; e-mail mhr@po.jaring.my; internet www.jaring.my/ksm.

Ministry of Information (Kementerian Penerangan): 5th Floor, Wisma TV, Angkasapuri, 50610 Kuala Lumpur; tel. (3) 2825333; fax (3) 2821255; e-mail webmaster@kempen.gov.my; internet www.kempen.gov.my.

Ministry of International Trade and Industry (Kementerian Perdagangan Antarabangsa dan Industri): Block 10, Kompleks Pejabat Kerajaan, Jalan Duta, 50622 Kuala Lumpur; tel. (3) 62033022; fax (3) 62031303; e-mail mitiweb@miti.gov.my; internet www.miti.gov.my/.

Ministry of Land and Co-operative Development (Kementerian Tanah dan Pembangunan Koperasi): Wisma Tanah, 11th Floor, Jalan Semarak, 50574 Kuala Lumpur; tel. (3) 26921566; fax (3) 26919426; e-mail kasitah@ktpk.gov.my; internet www.ktpk.gov.my.

Ministry of National Unity and Social Development (Kementerian Perpaduan Negara dan Pembangunan Masyarakat): Tingkat 19–21, Wisma Bumi Raya, Jalan Raja Laut, 50562 Kuala Lumpur; tel. (3) 26925022; fax (3) 26937353; e-mail adminkpn@kempadu.gov.my; internet www.kempadu.gov.my.

Ministry of Primary Industries (Kementerian Perusahaan Utama): Menara Dayabumi, 6th–8th Floors, Jalan Sultan Hishamuddin, 50654 Kuala Lumpur; tel. (3) 22747511; fax (3) 22745014; e-mail webeditor@kpu.gov.my; internet www.kpu.gov.my.

Ministry of Rural Development (Kementerian Pembangunan Luar Bandar): Aras 5–9, Blok D9, Parcel D, Pusat Pentadbiran Kerajaan Persekutuan, 62606 Putrajaya; tel. (3) 88863500; fax (3) 88892096; e-mail info@kplb.gov.my; internet www.kplb.gov.my.

Ministry of Science, Technology and Environment (Kementerian Sains, Teknologi dan Alam Sekitar): Level 4, Blok C5, Parcel C, Federal Government Administrative Centre, 62662 Putrajaya; tel. (3) 88858000; fax (3) 88892980; e-mail mastic@mastic.gov.my; internet www.mastic.gov.my.

Ministry of Transport (Kementerian Pengangkutan): Wisma Perdana, Level 5–7, Block D5, Parcel D, Federal Government Administrative Centre, 62502 Putrajaya; tel. (3) 88866000; fax (3) 88892537; e-mail LeeLC@mot.gov.my; internet www.mot.gov.my.

Ministry of Works (Kementerian Kerja Raya): Ground Floor, Block A, Kompleks Kerja Raya, Jalan Sultan Salahuddin, 50580 Kuala Lumpur; tel. (3) 27111100; fax (3) 27116612; e-mail menteri@kkr.gov.my; internet www.kkr.gov.my.

Ministry of Youth and Sports (Kementerian Belia dan Sukan): Block G, Jalan Dato' Onn, 50570 Kuala Lumpur; tel. (3) 26932255; fax (3) 26932231; e-mail webmaster@kbs.gov.my; internet www.kbs.gov.my.

Legislature

PARLIAMENT

Dewan Negara
(Senate)

The Senate has 70 members, of whom 30 are elected. Each State Legislative Assembly and Federal Territory elects two members. The Supreme Head of State appoints the remaining 40 members.

Speaker: Tan Sri MOHAMED YAACOB.

Dewan Rakyat
(House of Representatives)

The House of Representatives has a total of 193 members: 144 from Peninsular Malaysia (including seven from Kuala Lumpur), 28 from Sarawak and 21 from Sabah (including one from the Federal Territory of Labuan).

Speaker: Tan Sri MUHAMMAD ZAHIR ISMAIL.

Deputy Speaker: ONG TEE KEAT.

General Election, 29 November 1999

Party	Seats
Barisan Nasional (National Front)	148
United Malays National Organization	72
Malaysian Chinese Association	28
Parti Pesaka Bumiputera Bersatu	10
Sarawak United People's Party	7
Malaysian Indian Congress	7
Parti Gerakan Rakyat Malaysia	7
Parti Bansa Dayak Sarawak	6
Sarawak National Action Party	4
UPKO	3
Sabah Progressive Party	2
Liberal Democratic Party	1
Direct BN	1
Barisan Alternatif (Alternative Front)	42
Parti Islam se Malaysia	27
Democratic Action Party	10
Parti Keadilan Nasional	5
Parti Bersatu Sabah	3
Total	193

The States

JOHOR
(Capital: Johor Bahru)

Sultan: HRH Tuanku MAHMOOD ISKANDAR IBNI AL-MARHUM Sultan ISMAIL.

Menteri Besar: Datuk Haji ABDUL GHANI OTHMAN.

State Legislative Assembly: 40 seats: Barisan Nasional 40; elected November 1999.

KEDAH
(Capital: Alor Star)

Sultan: HRH Tuanku Haji ABDUL HALIM MU'ADZAM SHAH IBNI AL-MARHUM Sultan BADLISHAH.

Menteri Besar: Datuk SYED RAZAK SYED ZAIN BARAKBAH.

State Legislative Assembly: 36 seats: Barisan Nasional 24; Parti Islam se Malaysia 12; elected November 1999.

KELANTAN
(Capital: Kota Bahru)

Sultan: HRH Tuanku ISMAIL PETRA IBNI AL-MARHUM Sultan YAHAYA PETRA.

Menteri Besar: Tuan Guru Haji Nik ABDUL AZIZ BIN Nik MAT.

State Legislative Assembly: 43 seats: Parti Islam se Malaysia 41; Barisan Nasional 2; elected November 1999.

MELAKA (MALACCA)
(Capital: Melaka)

Yang di-Pertua Negeri: HE Tun Datuk Sri UTAMA SYED AHMAD Al-Haj BIN SYED MAHMUD SHAHABUDIN.

Ketua Menteri: Datuk WIRA MOHAMED ALI RUSTAM.

State Legislative Assembly: 25 seats: Barisan Nasional 21; Democratic Action Party 4; elected November 1999.

NEGERI SEMBILAN
(Capital: Seremban)

Yang di-Pertuan Besar: Tuanku JA'AFAR IBNI AL-MARHUM Tuanku ABDUL RAHMAN.

Menteri Besar: Tan Sri MOHAMMED ISA BIN Datuk Haji ABDUL SAMAD.

State Legislative Assembly: 32 seats: Barisan Nasional 32; elected November 1999.

PAHANG
(Capital: Kuantan)

Sultan: HRH Haji AHMAD SHAH AL-MUSTA'IN BILLAH IBNI AL-MARHUM Sultan ABU BAKAR RI'AYATUDDIN AL-MU'ADZAM SHAH.

Menteri Besar: Dato' ADNAN BIN YAAKOB.

State Legislative Assembly: 38 seats: Barisan Nasional 30; Parti Islam se Malaysia 6; Democratic Action Party 1; Parti Keadilan Nasional 1; elected November 1999.

PERAK
(Capital: Ipoh)

Sultan: HRH Sultan AZLAN SHAH.

Menteri Besar: Dato' Seri DiRaja MOHAMAD TAJOL ROSLI.

State Legislative Assembly: Pejabat Setiausaha Kerajaan Negeri, Perak Darul Ridzuan, Bahagian Majlis, Jalan Panglima Bukit Gantang Wahab, 30000 Ipoh; tel. (05) 2410451; fax (05) 2552890; e-mail master@perak.gov.my; internet www.perak.gov.my; 52 seats: Barisan Nasional 44; Democratic Action Party 4; Parti Islam se Malaysia 3; Parti Keadilan Nasional 1; elected November 1999.

PERLIS
(Capital: Kangar)

Regent: Tuanku SYED FAIZUDDIN PUTRA IBNI Tuanku SYED SIRAJUDDIN PUTRA JAMALULAIL.

Menteri Besar: Dato' Seri SHAHIDAN KASSIM.

State Legislative Assembly: internet www.perlis.gov.my; 15 seats: Barisan Nasional 12; Parti Islam se Malaysia 3; elected November 1999.

PINANG (PENANG)
(Capital: George Town)

Yang di-Pertua Negeri: HE Datuk ABDUL RAHMAN Haji ABBAS.

Ketua Menteri: Tan Sri Dr KOH TSU KOON.

State Legislative Assembly: 33 seats: Barisan Nasional 30; Democratic Action Party 1; Parti Islam se Malaysia 1; Parti Keadilan Nasional 1; elected November 1999.

SABAH
(Capital: Kota Kinabalu)

Yang di-Pertua Negeri: HE Tan Sri SAKARAN DANDAI.

Ketua Menteri: Datuk CHONG KAH KIAT.

State Legislative Assembly: Dewan Undangan Negeri Sabah, Aras 4, Bangunan Dewan Undangan Negeri Sabah, Peti Surat 11247, 88813 Kota Kinabalu; tel. (88) 427533; fax (88) 427333; e-mail pejduns@sabah.gov.my; internet www.sabah.gov.my; 48 seats: Barisan Nasional 31, Parti Bersatu Sabah 17; elected March 1999.

SARAWAK
(Capital: Kuching)

Yang di-Pertua Negeri: HE Tun Datuk Patinggi Abang Haji MUHAMMED SALAHUDDIN.

Ketua Menteri: Datuk Patinggi Tan Sri Haji ABDUL TAIB BIN MAHMUD.

State Legislative Assembly: Bangunan Dewan Undangan Negeri, 93502 Petra Jaya, Kuching, Sarawak; tel. (82) 441955; fax (82) 440790; e-mail mastapaj@sarawaknet.gov.my; internet www.dun.sarawak.gov.my; 62 seats: Barisan Nasional 60; Democratic Action Party 1; Independents 1; elected September 2001.

SELANGOR
(Capital: Shah Alam)

Sultan: Tuanku IDRIS SALAHUDDIN ABDUL AZIZ SHAH.

Menteri Besar: MOHAMAD KHIR TOYO.

State Legislative Assembly: 48 seats: Barisan Nasional 42; Parti Islam se Malaysia 4; Democratic Action Party 1; Parti Keadilan Nasional 1; elected December 1999.

TERENGGANU
(Capital: Kuala Terengganu)

Sultan: HRH Sultan MIZAN ZAINAL ABIDIN.

Menteri Besar: ABDUL HADI AWANG.

State Legislative Assembly: 32 seats: Parti Islam se Malaysia 28; Barisan Nasional 4; elected November 1999.

Political Organizations

Barisan Nasional (BN) (National Front): Suite 1–2, 8th Floor, Menara Dato' Onn, Pusat Dagangan Dunia Putra, Jalan Tun Ismail 50480 Kuala Lumpur; tel. (3) 2920384; fax (3) 2934743; e-mail info@bn.org.my; internet www.bn.org.my; f. 1973; the governing multiracial coalition of 15 parties; Sec.-Gen. Dato' Datuk Sri MOHAMMED RAHMAT. Comprises:

Angkatan Keadilan Rakyat (AKAR) (People's Justice Movement): Tingkat 2, No. 16, Lot 8, Blok B, Nountun Light Industrial Estate, Lorong Perindustrian Nountun, Kota Kinabalu, 88450 Sabah; tel. (88) 437485; fax (88) 434716; Dusun-based breakaway faction of the PBS; Leaders Dato' MARK KODING, KALAKAU UNTOL, PANDIKAR AMIN MULIA.

Liberal Democratic Party: Tingkat 2, Lot 1, Wisma Jasaga, POB 1125, Sandakan, 90712 Sabah; tel. (89) 271888; fax (89) 288278; e-mail ldpkk@tm.net.my; Chinese-dominated; Pres. Datuk CHONG KAH KIAT; Sec.-Gen. Datuk ANTHONY LAI VAI MING.

Malaysian Chinese Association (MCA): Wisma MCA, 8th Floor, 163 Jalan Ampang, POB 10626, 50720 Kuala Lumpur; tel. (3) 21618044; fax (3) 21619772; e-mail info@mca.org.my; internet www.mca.org.my; f. 1949; c. 1,033,686 mems; Pres. Dato' Seri Dr LING LIONG SIK; Sec.-Gen. Dato' Seri Dr TING CHEW PEH.

Malaysian Indian Congress (MIC): Menara Manickavasagam, 6th Floor, 1 Jalan Rahmat, 50350 Kuala Lumpur; tel. (3) 4424377; fax (3) 4427236; internet www.mic.malaysia.org; f. 1946; 401,000 mems (1992); Pres. Dato' Seri S. SAMY VELLU; Sec.-Gen. Dato' G. VADIVELOO.

Parti Bansa Dayak Sarawak (PBDS) (Sarawak Native People's Party): 622 Jalan Kedandi, Tabuan Jaya, POB 2148, Kuching, Sarawak; tel. (82) 365240; fax (82) 363734; f. 1983 by fmr mems of Sarawak National Party; Pres. Datuk LEO MOGGIE ANAK IROK; Vice-Pres. Datuk DANIEL TAJEM.

Parti Bersatu Rakyat Sabah (PBRS) (United Sabah People's Party): POB 20148, Luyang, Kota Kinabalu, 88761 Sabah; tel. and fax (88) 269282; f. 1994; breakaway faction of PBS; mostly Christian Kadazans; Leader Datuk JOSEPH KURUP.

Parti Bersatu Sabah (PBS) (Sabah United Party): Block M, Lot 4, 2nd and 3rd Floors, Donggongon New Township, Penampang, Kota Kinabalu, Sabah; POB 13066, 88834 Kota Kinabalu, Sabah; tel. (88) 714891; fax (88) 718067; internet www.pbs-sabah.org; f. 1985; multiracial party, left the BN in 1990 and rejoined in January 2002; Pres. Datuk Seri JOSEPH PAIRIN KITINGAN; Sec.-Gen. RADIN MALLEH.

Parti Gerakan Rakyat Malaysia (GERAKAN) (Malaysian People's Movement): Tingkat 5, Menara PGRM, 8 Jalan Pudu Ulu Cheras, 56100 Kuala Lumpur; tel. (3) 92876868; fax (3) 92878866; e-mail gerakan@gerakan.org.my; internet www.gerakan.org.my; f. 1968; 300,000 mems; Pres. Dato' Seri Dr LIM KENG YAIK; Sec.-Gen. CHIA KWANG CHYE.

Parti Pesaka Bumiputera Bersatu (PBB) (United Traditional Bumiputra Party): Lot 401, Jalan Bako, POB 1953, 93400 Kuching, Sarawak; tel. (82) 448299; fax (82) 448294; f. 1983; Pres. Tan Sri Datuk Patinggi Amar Haji ABDUL TAIB MAHMUD; Dep. Pres. Datuk ALFRED JABU AK NUMPANG.

Parti Progresif Penduduk Malaysia (PPP) (People's Progressive Party): 27–29a Jalan Maharajalela, 50150 Kuala Lumpur; tel. (3) 2441922; fax (3) 2442041; e-mail info@ppp.com.my; internet www.jaring.my/ppp; f. 1953 as Perak Progressive Party; joined the BN in 1972; Pres. Datuk M. KAYVEAS.

Sabah Progressive Party (SAPP) (Parti Maju Sabah): Lot 23, 2nd Floor, Bornion Centre, 88300 Kota Kinabalu, Sabah; tel. (88) 242107; fax (88) 254799; e-mail sapp@po.jaring.my; internet www.jaring.my/sapp/; f. 1994; non-racial; Pres. Datuk YONG TECK LEE.

Sarawak National Action Party (SNAP): 304–305 Bangunan Mei Jun, 1 Jalan Rubber, POB 2960, 93758 Kuching, Sarawak; tel. (82) 254244; fax (82) 253562; internet www.snap.org.my; f. 1961; Pres. Datuk Amar JAMES WONG KIM MIN; Sec.-Gen. PETER GANI AK KIAI.

Sarawak United People's Party (SUPP): 7 Jalan Tan Sri Ong Kee Hui, POB 454, 93710 Kuching, Sarawak; tel. (82) 246999; fax (82) 256510; e-mail supp@po.jaring.my; internet www.sarawak.com.my/supp/; f. 1959; Sarawak Chinese minority party; Pres. Datuk Dr GEORGE CHAN HONG NAM; Sec.-Gen. SIM KHENG HUI.

United Kadazan People's Organization (UPKO): Penampang Service Centre, Km 11, Jalan Tambunan, Peti Surat 420, 89507 Penampang, Sabah; tel. (88) 718182; fax (88) 718180; f. 1994 as the Parti Demokratik Sabah (PDS—Sabah Democratic Party); formed after collapse of PBS Govt by fmr leaders of the party, represents mostly Kadazandusun, Rungus and Murut communities; Pres. Tan Sri BERNARD GILUK DOMPOK.

United Malays National Organization (Pertubuhan Kebangsaan Melayu Bersatu)—**UMNO Baru** (New UMNO): Menara Dato' Onn, 38th Floor, Jalan Tun Dr Ismail, 50480 Kuala Lumpur; tel. (3) 40429511; fax (3) 40412358; e-mail email@umno.net.my; internet www.umno.org.my; f. 1988 to replace the original UMNO (f. 1946) which had been declared an illegal organization, owing to the participation of unregistered branches in party elections in April 1987; Supreme Council of 45 mems; 2.5m. mems; Pres. Dato' Seri Dr MAHATHIR BIN MOHAMAD; Dep. Pres. Dato' Seri ABDULLAH BIN Haji AHMAD BADAWI; Sec.-Gen. Tan Sri MOHD KHALIL BIN YAACOB.

Angkatan Democratic Liberal Sabah (Adil): Sabah; intended primarily to attract Malay Muslims.

Angkatan Keadilan Insan Malaysia (AKIM) (Malaysian Justice Movement): f. 1995; founded by fmr members of PAS and Semangat '46; Pres. CHE GU MUSA SALIH.

Barisan Alternatif (Alternative Front): Kuala Lumpur; f. June 1999 to contest the general election; opposition electoral alliance originally comprising the PAS, the DAP, the PKN and the PRM; the DAP left in Sept. 2001.

Barisan Jama'ah Islamiah Sa-Malaysia (Berjasa) (Front Malaysian Islamic Council—FMIC): Kelantan; f. 1977; pro-Islamic; 50,000 mems; Pres. Dato' Haji WAN HASHIM BIN Haji WAN ACHMED; Sec.-Gen. MAHMUD ZUHDI BIN Haji ABDUL MAJID.

Bersatu Rakyat Jelata Sabah (Berjaya) (Sabah People's Union): Natikar Bldg, 1st Floor, POB 2130, Kota Kinabalu, Sabah; f. 1975; 400,000 mems; Pres. Haji MOHAMMED NOOR MANSOOR.

Democratic Action Party (DAP): 24 Jalan 20/9, 46300 Petaling Jaya, Selangor; tel. (3) 7578022; fax (3) 7575718; e-mail dap.Malaysia@pobox.com; internet www.malaysia.net/dap; f. 1966; main opposition party; advocates multiracial society based on democratic socialism; 12,000 mems; Chair. LIM KIT SIANG; Sec.-Gen. KERK KIM HOCK.

Democratic Malaysia Indian Party (DMIP): f. 1985; Leader V. GOVINDARAJ.

Kongres Indian Muslim Malaysia (KIMMA): Kuala Lumpur; tel. (3) 2324759; f. 1977; aims to unite Malaysian Indian Muslims politically; 25,000 mems; Pres. AHAMED ELIAS; Sec.-Gen. MOHAMMED ALI BIN Haji NAINA MOHAMMED.

Malaysian Solidarity Party: Kuala Lumpur.

Parti Hisbul Muslimin Malaysia (Hamim) (Islamic Front of Malaysia): Kota Bahru, Kelantan; f. 1983 as an alternative party to PAS; Pres. Datuk ASRI MUDA.

Parti Ikatan Masyarakat Islam (Islamic Alliance Party): Terengganu.

Parti Islam se Malaysia (PAS) (Islamic Party of Malaysia): Pejabat Agung PAS Pusat, Lorong Haji Hassan, off Jalan Batu Geliga, Taman Melewar, 68100 Batu Caves, Selangor Darul Ehsan; tel. (3) 61895612; fax (3) 61889520; e-mail pas@po.jaring.my; internet www.parti-pas.org; f. 1951; seeks to establish an Islamic state; 700,000 mems; Pres. ABDUL HADI AWANG (acting); Sec.-Gen. NASHARUDIN MAT ISA.

Parti Keadilan Masyarakat (PEKEMAS) (Social Justice Party): Kuala Lumpur; f. 1971 by fmr mems of GERAKAN; Chair. SHAHARYDDIN DAHALAN.

Parti Keadilan Nasional (PKN) (National Justice Party): Kuala Lumpur; internet www.partikeadilan.org; f. 1999 to unite the supporters of Anwar Ibrahim's *reformasi* movement; due to merge with the PRM before 2004; Pres. WAN AZIZAH WAN ISMAIL; Dep. Pres. ABDUL RAHMAN OTHMAN; Sec.-Gen. ANUAR TAHIR.

Parti Nasionalis Malaysia (NasMa): f. 1985; multiracial; Leader ZAINAB YANG.

Parti Rakyat Jati Sarawak (PAJAR) (Sarawak Native People's Party): 22A Jalan Bampeylde, 93200 Kuching, Sarawak; f. 1978; Leader ALI KAWI.

Parti Rakyat Malaysia (PRM) (Malaysian People's Party): 42 Jalan Masjid, 46000 Petaling Jaya, Selangor; tel. (3) 77812151; fax (3) 77818704; e-mail p_rakyat@hotmail.com; internet www.partirakyat.org; f. 1955; named Parti Sosialis Rakyat Malaya from 1970–90; due to merge with the PKN before 2004; Pres. Prof. SYED HUSIN ALI; Sec.-Gen. SANUSI OSMAN.

Persatuan Rakyat Malaysian Sarawak (PERMAS) (Malaysian Sarawak Party): Kuching, Sarawak; f. March 1987 by fmr mems of PBB; Leader Haji BUJANG ULIS.

Pertubuhan Bumiputera Bersatu Sarawak (PBBS) (United Sarawak National Association): Kuala Lumpur; f. 1986; Chair. Haji WAN HABIB SYED MAHMUD.

Pertubuhan Rakyat Sabah Bersatu (United Sabah People's Organization—USPO): Kota Kinabalu, Sabah.

Sabah Chinese Party (PCS): Kota Kinabalu, Sabah; f. 1986; Pres. Encik FRANCIS LEONG.

Sabah Chinese Consolidated Party (SCCP): POB 704, Kota Kinabalu, Sabah; f. 1964; 14,000 mems; Pres. JOHNNY SOON; Sec.-Gen. CHAN TET ON.

Setia (Sabah People's United Democratic Party): Sabah; f. 1994.

United Malaysian Indian Party: aims to promote unity and economic and social advancement of the Indian community; Sec. KUMAR MANOHARAN.

Diplomatic Representation

EMBASSIES AND HIGH COMMISSIONS IN MALAYSIA

Afghanistan: Suite 606, 6th Floor, North Block, The Amp Walk, 218 Jalan Ampang, 50450 Kuala Lumpur; tel. (3) 21628897; fax (3) 21628924; e-mail muradl@tm.net.my; Chargé d'affaires a.i.: ABDUL SATTAR MURAD.

Albania: 2952 Jalan Bukit Ledang, off Jalan Duta. 50480 Kuala Lumpur; tel. (3) 2537808; fax (3) 2537359; Chargé d'affaires a.i.: AHMET LALA.

Algeria: 5 Jalan Mesra, off Jalan Damai, 55000 Kuala Lumpur; tel. (3) 21488159; fax (3) 21488154; Ambassador: RACHID BLADEHANE.

Argentina: 3 Jalan Semantan Dua, Damansara Heights, 50490 Kuala Lumpur; tel. (3) 2550176; fax (3) 2552706; e-mail emsia@po.jaring.my; Ambassador: ARMANDO J. J. MAFFEI.

Australia: 6 Jalan Yap Kwan Seng, 50450 Kuala Lumpur; tel. (3) 21465555; fax (3) 21415773; e-mail info@australia.org.my; internet www.australia.org.my; High Commissioner: PETER VARGHESE.

Austria: MUI Plaza, 7th Floor, Jalan P. Ramlee, POB 10154, 50704 Kuala Lumpur; tel. (3) 21484277; fax (3) 21489813; e-mail austria@ppp.nasionet.net; Ambassador: Dr OSWALD SOUKOP.

Bangladesh: Block 1, Lorong Damai 7, Jalan Damai, 55000 Kuala Lumpur; tel. (3) 21487490; fax (3) 21413381; e-mail bddoot@pc.jaring.my; High Commissioner: MUHAMMAD KAMALUDDIN.

Belgium: 8A Jalan Ampang Hilir, 55000 Kuala Lumpur; tel. (3) 42525733; fax (3) 42527922; e-mail kualalumpur@diplobel.org; Ambassador: ROLAND VAN REMOORTELE.

Bosnia and Herzegovina: JKR 854, Jalan Bellamy, 50460 Kuala Lumpur; tel. (3) 21440353; fax (3) 21426025; e-mail hsomun@hotmail.com; Ambassador: HAJRUDIN SOMUN.

Brazil: 22 Pesiaran Damansara Endah, Damansara Heights, 50490 Kuala Lumpur; tel. (3) 2548607; fax (3) 2555086; e-mail brazil@po.jaring.my; Ambassador: GERALDO AFFONSO MUZZI.

Brunei: Tingkat 19, Menara Tan & Tan, Jalan Tun Razak, 50400 Kuala Lumpur; tel. (3) 21612800; fax (3) 2631302; High Commissioner: Pengiran Setia Negara Pengiran Haji MOHD YUSOF BIN Pengiran Haji ABDUL RAHIM.

Cambodia: 83 Lingkungan U Thant, 55000 Kuala Lumpur; tel. (3) 42573711; fax (3) 42571157; Ambassador: KEO PUTH REASMEY.

Canada: POB 10990, 50732 Kuala Lumpur; tel. (3) 27183333; fax (3) 27183399; e-mail klmpr@dfait-maeci.gc.ca; internet www.dfait-maeci.gc.ca/kualalumpur; High Commissioner: JEAN C. MCCLOSKEY.

Chile: 8th Floor, West Block 142-C, Jalan Ampang, Peti Surat 27, 50450 Kuala Lumpur; tel. (3) 21616203; fax (3) 21622219; e-mail eochile@ppp.nasionet.net; internet www.chileembassy-malaysia.com.my; Ambassador: ROBERTO IBARRA GARCÍA.

China, People's Republic: 229 Jalan Ampang, 50450 Kuala Lumpur; tel. (3) 2428495; fax (3) 2414552; e-mail cn@tm.net.my; Ambassador: HU ZHENGYUE.

Colombia: Level 26, UOA Centre, 19 Jalan Pinang, 50450 Kuala Lumpur; tel. (3) 2645488; fax (3) 2645487; Ambassador: ARTURO ALBERTO INFANTE VILLARREA.

Croatia: 3 Jalan Menkuang, off Jalan Ru Ampang, 55000 Kuala Lumpur; tel. (3) 42535340; fax (3) 42535217; e-mail croemb@tm.net.my; Ambassador: DAMIR PERINČIĆ.

Cuba: 20 Lingkungan U Thant, off Jalan U Thant, 55000 Kuala Lumpur; tel. (3) 42516808; fax (3) 42520428; e-mail malacub@po.jaring.my; Ambassador: TERESITA FERNÁNDEZ DÍAZ.

Czech Republic: 32 Jalan Mesra, off Jalan Damai, 55000 Kuala Lumpur; tel. (3) 21427185; fax (3) 21412727; e-mail kualalumpur@embassy.mzv.cz; Ambassador: Dr VÍTĚZSLAV GREPL.

Denmark: POB 10908, 50728 Kuala Lumpur; tel. (3) 20322001; fax (3) 20322012; e-mail denmark@denmark.com.my; internet www.denmark.com.my; Ambassador: LEIF MOGENS REIMANN.

Ecuador: 8th Floor, West Block, Wisma Selangor Dredging, 142-C Jalan Ampang, 50450 Kuala Lumpur; tel. (3) 2635078; fax (3) 2635096; e-mail embecua@po.jaring.my; Chargé d'affaires a.i.: Dr MARCO TULIO CORDERO ZAMORA.

Egypt: 28 Lingkungan U Thant, POB 12004, 55000 Kuala Lumpur; tel. (3) 4568184; fax (3) 4573515; e-mail egyembkl@tm.net.my; Ambassador: ALI EL-NAGGARY.

Fiji: Level 2, Menara Chan, 138 Jalan Ampang, 50450 Kuala Lumpur; tel. (3) 27323335; fax (3) 27327555; e-mail fhckl@pd.jaring.my; High Commissioner: Adi SAMANUNU Q. TALAKULI CAKOBAU.

Finland: Wisma Chinese Chamber, 258 Jalan Ampang, POB 10909, 50728 Kuala Lumpur; tel. (3) 42577746; fax (3) 42577793; e-mail sanomat.kul@formin.fi; Ambassador: UNTO JUHANI TURUNEN.

France: 196 Jalan Ampang, 50450 Kuala Lumpur; tel. (3) 20535500; fax (3) 20535501; e-mail france@france.org.my; internet www.france.org.my; Ambassador: XAVIER DRIENCOURT.

Germany: 3 Jalan U Thant, POB 10023, 50700 Kuala Lumpur; tel. (3) 21169666; fax (3) 21413943; e-mail contact@german-embassy.org.my; Ambassador: JUERGEN A. R. STAKS.

Ghana: 14 Ampang Hilir, off Jalan Ampang, 55000 Kuala Lumpur; tel. (3) 42526995; fax (3) 42578698; e-mail ghcomkl@tm.net.my; High Commissioner: JOHN BENTUM-WILLIAMS.

Guinea: 5 Jalan Kedondong, off Jalan Ampang Hilir, Kuala Lumpur; tel. (3) 42576500; fax (3) 42511500; Ambassador: MAMADOU TOURÉ.

Hungary: City Square Centre, 30th Floor, Empire Tower, Jalan Tun Razak, 50400 Kuala Lumpur; tel. (3) 21637914; fax (3) 21637918; e-mail huembkl@tm.net.my; Ambassador: LÁSZLÓ VÁRKONYI.

India: 2 Jalan Taman Duta, off Jalan Duta, 50480 Kuala Lumpur; tel. (3) 2533510; fax (3) 2533507; e-mail information@po.jaring.my; High Commissioner: VEENA SIKRI.

Indonesia: 233 Jalan Tun Razak, POB 10889, 50400 Kuala Lumpur; tel. (3) 2452011; fax (3) 2417908; internet www.kbrikl.org.my; Ambassador: HADI A. WARAYABI ALHADAR.

Iran: 1 Lorong U Thant Satu, off Jalan U Thant, 55000 Kuala Lumpur; tel. (3) 42514824; fax (3) 42562904; e-mail ir_emb@tm.net.my; Ambassador: MOHAMMAD GHASEM MOHEB ALI.

Iraq: 2 Jalan Langgak Golf, off Jalan Tun Razak, 55000 Kuala Lumpur; tel. (3) 2480555; fax (3) 2414331; Ambassador: ADNAN MALIK AL-GHAZALI.

Ireland: Ireland House, the Amp Walk, 218 Jalan Ampang, POB 10372, 50450 Kuala Lumpur; tel. (3) 21612963; fax (3) 21613427; e-mail ireland@po.jaring.my; Ambassador: DANIEL MULHALL.

Italy: 99 Jalan U Thant, 55000 Kuala Lumpur; tel. (3) 42565122; fax (3) 42573199; e-mail embassyit@italy-embassy.org.my; internet www.italy-embassy.org.my; Ambassador: ANACLETO FELICANI.

Japan: 11 Pesiaran Stonor, off Jalan Tun Razak, 50450 Kuala Lumpur; tel. (3) 21427044; fax (3) 21672314; internet www.embjapan.org.my; Ambassador: MASAKI KONISHI.

Jordan: 2 Jalan Kedondong, off Jalan Ampang Hilir, 55000 Kuala Lumpur; tel. (3) 42521268; fax (3) 42528610; Ambassador: MAZEN JUMA.

Kazakhstan: Suite 607, 6th Floor, North Block, The Amp Walk, 218 Jalan Ampang, 50540 Kuala Lumpur; tel. (3) 21664144; fax (3) 21668553; e-mail klkazemb@po.jaring.my; Ambassador: BOLATKHAN K. TAIZHAN.

Kenya: 7A Gerbang Ampang Hilir, 55000 Kuala Lumpur; tel. (3) 42572431; fax (3) 42572059; e-mail kenya@po.jaring.my; High Commissioner: JAMES K. KARUGA.

Korea, Democratic People's Republic: 9 Jalan Madge, off Jalan U Thant, 55000 Kuala Lumpur; tel. (3) 4569913; fax (3) 4569933; Ambassador: KIM JA RYONG.

Korea, Republic: Lot 968 & 3112, Jalan Nipah, off Jalan Ampang, 55000 Kuala Lumpur; tel. (3) 4512336; fax (3) 4521425; e-mail korem-my@mofat.go.kr; Ambassador: RHEE YOUNG-MIN.

Kuwait: 229 Jalan Tun Razak, 50400 Kuala Lumpur; tel. (3) 21410033; fax (3) 21426126; Ambassador: SHAMLAN ABDUL AZIZ MOHAMMAD SHAMLAN AL-ROOMI.

Kyrgyzstan: 1 Lorong Damai 10, 55000 Kuala Lumpur; tel. (3) 21649862; fax (3) 21632024; e-mail kyrgyz@tm.net.my; Ambassador: MAMBETJUNUS ABYLOV.

Laos: 12A Pesiaran Madge, off Jalan Ampang Hilir, 55000 Kuala Lumpur; tel. (3) 42511118; fax (3) 42510080; Ambassador: CHALEUNE WARINTHRASAK.

Libya: 6 Jalan Madge, off Jalan U Thant, 55000 Kuala Lumpur; tel. (3) 21411035; fax (3) 21413549; Chargé d'affaires a.i.: (vacant).

Luxembourg: Menara Keck Seng Bldg, 16th Floor, 203 Jalan Bukit Bintang, 55100 Kuala Lumpur; tel. (3) 21433134; fax (3) 21433157; e-mail emluxem@po.jaring.my; Chargé d'affaires a.i.: CHARLES SCHMIT.

Mauritius: Lot W17-B1 and C1, 17th Floor, West Block, Wisma Selangor Dredging, Jalan Ampang, 50450 Kuala Lumpur; tel. (3) 21636306; fax (3) 21636294; e-mail maur@tm.net.my; High Commissioner: S. K. S. DUSOWOTH.

Mexico: Menara Tan & Tan, 22nd Floor, 207 Jalan Tun Razak, 50400 Kuala Lumpur; tel. 21646362; fax (3) 21640964; e-mail embamex@po.jaring.my; internet www.embamex.org.my; Ambassador: ALFREDO PÉREZ BRAVO.

Morocco: Wisma Selangor Dredging, 3rd Floor, East Block, 142B Jalan Ampang, 50450 Kuala Lumpur; tel. (3) 21610701; fax (3) 21623081; e-mail sifmakl@po.jaring.my; Ambassador: BADR EDDINE ALLALI.

Myanmar: 10 Jalan Mengkuang, off Jalan Ru, 55000 Kuala Lumpur; tel. (3) 4560280; fax (3) 4568320; e-mail mekl@tm.net.my; Ambassador: U HLA MAUNG.

Namibia: 11 Jalan Mesra, off Jalan Damai, 55000 Kuala Lumpur; tel. (3) 2433595; fax (3) 2417803; e-mail namhckl@po.jaring.my; High Commissioner: NDEUTAPO AMAGULU.

Netherlands: The Amp Walk, 7th Floor, 218 Jalan Ampang, POB 10543, 50450 Kuala Lumpur; tel. (3) 21686200; fax (3) 21686240; e-mail nlgovkl@netherlands.org.my; Ambassador: J. C. F. VON MÜHLEN.

New Zealand: Menara IMC, 21st Floor, 8 Jalan Sultan Ismail, 50250 Kuala Lumpur; tel. (3) 20782533; fax (3) 20780387; e-mail nzhckl@po.jaring.my; High Commissioner: MAC PRICE.

Nigeria: 85 Jalan Ampang Hilir, 55000 Kuala Lumpur; tel. (3) 42517843; e-mail nighcomm@tm.net.my; High Commissioner: IBRAHIM YARIMA ABDULLAH.

Norway: Suite CD, 53rd Floor, Empire Tower, Jalan Tun Razak, 50400 Kuala Lumpur; tel. (3) 21637100; fax (3) 21637108; e-mail emb.kualalumpur@mfa.no; Ambassador: ARILD EIK.

Oman: 6 Jalan Langgak Golf, off Jalan Tun Razak, 55000 Kuala Lumpur; tel. (3) 21452827; fax (3) 21452826; e-mail omanemb@jaring.my; Ambassador: (vacant).

Pakistan: 132 Jalan Ampang, 50450 Kuala Lumpur; tel. (3) 21618877; fax (3) 21645958; e-mail parepklumpur@po.jaring.my; internet www3.jaring.my/pakistanhc/; High Commissioner: Gen. (retd) NASIM RANA.

Papua New Guinea: 46 Jalan U Thant, 55000 Kuala Lumpur; tel. (3) 42532400; fax (3) 42532411; e-mail pnghckl@tm.net.my; High Commissioner: EMILY DAVID (acting).

Peru: Wisma Selangor Dredging, 6th Floor, South Block 142-A, Jalan Ampang, 50450 Kuala Lumpur; tel. (3) 21633034; fax (3) 21633039; e-mail info@embperu.com.my; internet www.embperu.com.my; Ambassador: JAVIER GONZALES.

Philippines: 1 Changkat Kia Peng, 50450 Kuala Lumpur; tel. (3) 21484233; fax (3) 21483576; e-mail philgov@tm.net.my; internet www.philembassykl.org.my; Ambassador: JOSE S. BRILLANTES.

Poland: 495 Bt 4½ Jalan Ampang, 68000 Ampang; tel. (3) 42576733; fax (3) 42570123; e-mail polamba@tm.net.my; Ambassador: MAREK PASZUCHA.

Romania: 114 Jalan Damai, off Jalan Ampang, 55000 Kuala Lumpur; tel. (3) 21423172; fax (3) 21448713; e-mail romemb@tm.net.my.

Russia: 263 Jalan Ampang, 50450 Kuala Lumpur; tel. (3) 42567252; fax (3) 42576091; e-mail consulrf@tm.net.my; Ambassador: VLADIMIR NIKOLAEVICH MOROZOV.

Saudi Arabia: 7 Jalan Kedondong, off Jalan Ampang, POB 12002, 55000 Kuala Lumpur; tel. (3) 42579433; fax (3) 42578751; Ambassador: HAMED MOHAMMED YAHYA.

Seychelles: 12th Floor, West Block, Wisma Selangor Dredging, POB 24, 142C Jalan Ampang, 50450 Kuala Lumpur; tel. (3) 21635726; fax (3) 21635729; e-mail seyhicom@po.jaring.my; High Commissioner: LOUIS SYLVESTRE RADEGONDE.

Singapore: 209 Jalan Tun Razak, 50400 Kuala Lumpur; tel. (3) 21616277; fax (3) 21616343; e-mail shckl@po.jaring.my; internet www.mfa.gov.sg/kl; High Commissioner: KRISHNASAMY KEVASAPANY.

South Africa: 12 Lorong Titiwangsa, Taman Tasik Titiwangsa, Setapak, 53200 Kuala Lumpur; tel. (3) 40244456; fax (3) 40249896; e-mail sahcpol@tm.net.my; internet www.afrikaselatan.com; High Commissioner: Dr ABRAHAM SOKHAYA NKOMO.

Spain: 200 Jalan Ampang, 50450 Kuala Lumpur; tel. (3) 21484868; fax (3) 21424582; e-mail embespmy@mail.mae.es; Ambassador: ALVARO IRANZO GUTIÉRREZ.

Sri Lanka: 116 Jalan Damai, off Jalan Ampang, 55000 Kuala Lumpur; tel. (3) 21612199; fax (3) 21612219; e-mail slhicom@putra.net.my; internet www.kuala-lumpur.mission.gov.lk; High Commissioner: DAYACHANDRA YASASIRI LIYANAGE.

Sudan: 2A Persiaran Ampang, off Jalan Ru, 55000 Kuala Lumpur; tel. (3) 42569104; fax (3) 42568107; e-mail sudanikuala@hotmail.com; Ambassador: MOHAMED ADAM ISMAIL.

Swaziland: Suite 22.03 & 03 (A), Menara Citibank, 165 Jalan Ampang, 50450 Kuala Lumpur; tel. (3) 21632511; fax (3) 21633326; e-mail swazi@tm.net.my; High Commissioner: MABILI D. DLAMIMI.

Sweden: Wisma Angkasa Raya, 6th Floor, 123 Jalan Ampang, POB 10239, 50708 Kuala Lumpur; tel. (3) 21485433; fax (3) 21486325; e-mail ambassaden.kuala-lumpur@foreign.ministry.se; internet www.embassyofswedenmy.org; Ambassador: BRUNO BEIJER.

Switzerland: 16 Persiaran Madge, 55000 Kuala Lumpur; tel. (3) 21480622; fax (3) 21480935; e-mail vertretung@kua.rep.admin.ch; Ambassador: RUDOLF STAUB.

Thailand: 206 Jalan Ampang, 50450 Kuala Lumpur; tel. (3) 21488222; fax (3) 21486527; e-mail thaikul@mfa.go.th; Ambassador: CHAISIRI ANAMARN.

Turkey: 118 Jalan U Thant, 55000 Kuala Lumpur; tel. (3) 42572225; fax (3) 42572227; e-mail turkbe@tmnet.my; Ambassador: KORAY TARGAY.

United Arab Emirates: 1 Gerbang Ampang Hilir, off Persiaran Ampang Hilir, 55000 Kuala Lumpur; tel. (3) 42535221; fax (3) 42535220; Ambassador: MOHAMMED ALI AL-OSAIMI.

United Kingdom: 185 Jalan Ampang, 50450 Kuala Lumpur; POB 11030, 50732 Kuala Lumpur; tel. (3) 21702200; fax (3) 21442370; e-mail political.kualalumpur@fco.gov.uk; internet www.britain.org.my; High Commissioner: BRUCE CLEGHORN.

USA: 376 Jalan Tun Razak, POB 10035, 50700 Kuala Lumpur; tel. (3) 21685000; fax (3) 21422207; internet www.usembassymalaysia.org.my; Ambassador: MARIE T. HUHTALA.

Uruguay: 6 Jalan 3, Taman Tun Abdul Razak, 68000 Ampang, Selangor Darul Bhsan; tel. (3) 42518831; fax (3) 42517878; e-mail urukual@po.jaring.my; Ambassador: ROBERTO PABLO TOURINO TURNES.

Uzbekistan: Suite 6.03, 6th Floor, North Block, The Amp Walk, 218 Jalan Ampang, 50450 Kuala Lumpur; tel. (3) 21618100; fax (3) 21618102.

Venezuela: Suite 20–05, 20th Floor, Menara Tan & Tan, 207 Jalan Tun Razak, 50400 Kuala Lumpur; tel. (3) 21633444; fax (3) 21636819; e-mail venezuela@po.jaring.my; Ambassador: Maj.-Gen. (retd) NOEL ENRIQUE MARTÍNEZ OCHOA.

Viet Nam: 4 Pesiaran Stonor, 50450 Kuala Lumpur; tel. (3) 2484036; fax (3) 2483270; e-mail daisevn@putra.net.my; Ambassador: TRAN TRONG TOAN.

Yemen: 6 Jalan Kedondong, off Jalan Ampang Hilir, 55000 Kuala Lumpur; tel. (3) 42511793; fax (3) 42511794; Ambassador: MOHAMED TAHA MUSTAFA.

Zimbabwe: 124 Jalan Sembilan, Taman Ampang Utama, 68000 Ampang, Selangor Darul Ehsan; tel. (3) 4516779; fax (3) 4516782; High Commissioner: CHITSAKA CHIPAZIWA.

Judicial System

The two High Courts, one in Peninsular Malaysia and the other in Sabah and Sarawak, have original, appellate and revisional jurisdiction as the federal law provides. Above these two High Courts is the Court of Appeal, which was established in 1994; it is an intermediary court between the Federal Court and the High Court. When appeals to the Privy Council in the United Kingdom were abolished in 1985 the former Supreme Court became the final court of appeal. Therefore, at that stage only one appeal was available to a party aggrieved by the decision of the High Court. Hence, the establishment of the Court of Appeal. The Federal Court (formerly the Supreme Court) has, to the exclusion of any other court, jurisdiction in any dispute between states or between the Federation and any state; and has special jurisdiction as to the interpretation of the Constitution. The Federal Court is headed by the Chief Justice (formerly the Lord President); the other members of the Federal Court are the President of the Court of Appeal, the two Chief Judges of the High Courts and the Federal Court Judges. Members of the Court of Appeal are the President and the Court of Appeal judges, and members of the High Courts are the two Chief Judges and their respective High Court judges. All judges are appointed by the Yang di-Pertuan Agong on the advice of the Prime Minister, after consulting the Conference of Rulers. In 1993 a Special Court was established to hear cases brought by or against the Yang di-Pertuan Agong or a Ruler of State (Sultans).

The Sessions Courts, which are situated in the principal urban and rural centres, are presided over by a Sessions Judge, who is a member of the Judicial and Legal Service of the Federation and is a qualified barrister or a Bachelor of Law from any of the recognized universities. Their criminal jurisdiction covers the less serious indictable offences, excluding those that carry the death penalty. Civil jurisdiction of a Sessions Court is up to RM 250,000. The Sessions Judges are appointed by the Yang di-Pertuan Agong.

The Magistrates' Courts are also found in the main urban and rural centres and have both civil and criminal jurisdiction, although of a more restricted nature than that of the Sessions Courts. The Magistrates consist of officers from the Judicial and Legal Service of the Federation. They are appointed by the State Authority in which they officiate on the recommendation of the Chief Judge.

There are also Syariah (Shariah) courts for rulings under Islamic law. In July 1996 the Cabinet announced that the Syariah courts were to be restructured with the appointment of a Syariah Chief Judge and four Court of Appeal justices, whose rulings would set precedents for the whole country.

Prior to February 1995 trials for murder and kidnapping in the High Courts were heard with jury and assessors, respectively. The amendment to the Criminal Procedure Code abolished both the jury and the assessors systems, and all criminal trials in the High Courts are heard by a judge sitting alone. In 1988 an amendment to the Constitution empowered any federal lawyer to confer with the Attorney-General to determine the courts in which any proceedings, excluding those before a Syariah court, a native court or a court martial, be instituted, or to which such proceedings be transferred.

Federal Court of Malaysia: Bangunan Sultan Abdul Samad, Jalan Raja, 50506 Kuala Lumpur; tel. (3) 26939011; fax (3) 26932582; internet www.kehakiman.gov.my.

Chief Justice of the Federal Court: Tan Sri Dato' MOHAMED DZAIDDIN BIN Haji ABDULLAH.

President of the Court of Appeal: (vacant).

Chief Judge of the High Court in Peninsular Malaysia: Dato' AHMAD FAIRUZ BIN Dato' SHEIKH ABDUL HALIM.

Chief Judge of the High Court in Sabah and Sarawak: Datuk STEVE SHIP LIM KIONG.

Attorney-General: ABDUL GANI PATAIL.

Religion

Islam is the established religion but freedom of religious practice is guaranteed. Almost all ethnic Malays are Muslims, representing 53% of the total population in 1985. In Peninsular Malaysia 19% followed Buddhism (19% in Sarawak and 8% in Sabah), 7% were Christians (29% in Sarawak and 24% in Sabah), and Chinese faiths, including Confucianism and Daoism, were followed by 11.6%. Sikhs and other religions accounted for 0.5%, while 2%, mostly in Sabah and Sarawak, were animists.

Malaysian Consultative Council of Buddhism, Christianity, Hinduism and Sikhism (MCCBCHS): 528 Jalan Bukit Nanas, 50250 Kuala Lumpur; tel. (3) 2324193; fax (3) 2308608; f. 1981; a non-Muslim group.

ISLAM

President of the Majlis Islam: Datuk Haji MOHD FAUZI BIN Haji ABDUL HAMID, Kuching, Sarawak.

Jabatan Kemajuan Islam Malaysia (JAKIM) (Department of Islamic Development Malaysia): Aras 4–9, Block D7, Pusat Pentadbiran Persekutuan, 62502 Putra Jaya; tel. (3) 88864000; e-mail faizal@islam.gov.my; internet www.islam.gov.my.

Istitut Kefahaman Islam Malaysia (IKIM) (Institute of Islamic Understanding Malaysia): 2 Langgak Tunku, off Jalan Duta, 50480 Kuala Lumpur; tel. (3) 62010889; fax (3) 62014189; internet www.ikim.gov.my.

BUDDHISM

Malaysian Buddhist Association (MBA): MBA Building, 113, 3¼ Miles, Jalan Klang, 58000 Kuala Lumpur; tel. (3) 7815595; e-mail mbapg@po.jaring.my; internet www.jaring.my/mba; f. 1959; the national body for Chinese-speaking monks and nuns and temples from the Mahayana tradition; Pres. Venerable CHEK HUANG.

Young Buddhist Association of Malaysia (YBAM): 10 Jalan SS2/75, 47300 Petaling Jaya, SelangorPinang; tel. (3) 78764591; fax (3) 78762770; e-mail ybamhq@po.jaring.my; internet www.ybam.org.my; f. 1970.

Buddhist Missionary Society Malaysia (BMSM): 123 Jalan Berhala, off Jalan Tun Sambanthan, 50470 Brickfields, Kuala Lumpur; tel. (3) 22730150; fax (3) 22740245; e-mail president@bmsm.org.my; internet www.bmsm.org.my; f. 1962 as Buddhist Missionary Society; Pres. ANG CHOO HONG.

Malaysian Fo Kuang Buddhist Association: 2 Jalan SS3/33, Taman University, 47300 Petaling Jaya, Selangor.

Buddhist Tzu-Chi Merit Society (Malaysia): 24 Jesselton Ave, 10450 Pinang; e-mail mtzuchi@po.jaring.my; internet www.tzuchi.org.my.

Sasana Abhiwurdhi Wardhana Society: 123 Jalan Berhala, off Jalan Tun Sambanthan, 50490 Kuala Lumpur; f. 1894; the national body for Sri Lankan Buddhists belonging to the Theravada tradition.

CHRISTIANITY

Majlis Gereja-Gereja Malaysia (Council of Churches of Malaysia): 26 Jalan Universiti, 46200 Petaling Jaya, Selangor; tel. (3) 7567092; fax (3) 7560353; e-mail cchurchm@tm.net.my; internet www.ccmalaysia.org; f. 1947; 16 mem. churches; 8 associate mems; Pres. Most Rev. Datuk YONG PING CHUNG (Anglican Bishop of Sabah); Gen. Sec. Rev. Dr HERMEN SHASTRI.

The Anglican Communion

Malaysia comprises three Anglican dioceses, within the Church of the Province of South East Asia.

Primate: Most Rev. Datuk YONG PING CHUNG (Bishop of Sabah).

Bishop of Kuching: Rt Rev. MADE KATIB, Bishop's House, POB 347, 93704 Kuching, Sarawak; tel. (82) 240187; fax (82) 426488; e-mail bkg@pc.jaring.my; has jurisdiction over Sarawak, Brunei and part of Indonesian Kalimantan (Borneo).

Bishop of Sabah: Most Rev. Datuk YONG PING CHUNG, Rumah Bishop, Jalan Tangki, POB 10811, 88809 Kota Kinabalu, Sabah; tel. (88) 247008; fax (88) 245942; e-mail pcyong@pc.jaring.my.

Bishop of West Malaysia: Rt. Rev. Tan Sri Dr LIM CHENG EAN, Bishop's House, 14 Pesiaran Stonor, 50450 Kuala Lumpur; tel. (3) 20312728; fax (3) 20313225; e-mail diocese@tm.net.my.

The Baptist Church

Malaysia Baptist Convention: 2 Jalan 2/38, 46000 Petaling Jaya, Selangor; tel. (3) 77823564; fax (3) 77833603; e-mail mbcpj@tm.net.my; Chair. Dr TAN ENG LEE.

The Methodist Church

Methodist Church in Malaysia: 69 Jalan 5/31, 46000 Petaling Jaya, Selangor; tel. (3) 79541811; fax (3) 79541788; e-mail methmas@tm.net; 140,000 mems; Bishop Dr PETER CHIO SING CHING.

The Presbyterian Church

Presbyterian Church in Malaysia: Joyful Grace Church, Jalan Alsagoff, 82000 Pontian, Johor; tel. (7) 711390; fax (7) 324384; Pastor TITUS KIM KAH TECK.

The Roman Catholic Church

Malaysia comprises two archdioceses and six dioceses. At 31 December 2000 approximately 3.3% of the population were adherents.

Catholic Bishops' Conference of Malaysia, Singapore and Brunei: Xavier Hall, 133 Jalan Gasing, 46000 Petaling Jaya, Selangor; tel. and fax (3) 79581371; e-mail cbcmsb@pc.jaring.my; Pres. Most Rev. A. SOTER FERNANDEZ (Archbishop of Kuala Lumpur).

Archbishop of Kuala Lumpur: Most Rev. ANTHONY SOTER FERNANDEZ, Archbishop's House, 528 Jalan Bukit Nanas, 50250 Kuala Lumpur; tel. (3) 2388828; fax (3) 2013815; e-mail archbishop@archway.org.my.

Archbishop of Kuching: Most Rev. PETER CHUNG HOAN TING, Archbishop's Office, 118 Jalan Tun Abang Haji Openg, POB 940, 93718 Kuching, Sarawak; tel. (82) 242634; fax (82) 425724.

BAHÁ'Í FAITH

Spiritual Assembly of the Bahá'ís of Malaysia: 4 Lorong Titiwangsa 5, off Jalan Pahang, 53200 Kuala Lumpur; tel. (3) 40235183; fax (3) 40226277; e-mail nsa-sec@bahai.org.my; internet www.bahai.org.my; mems resident in 800 localities.

The Press

PENINSULAR MALAYSIA

DAILIES

English Language

Business Times: Balai Berita 31, Jalan Riong, 59100 Kuala Lumpur; tel. (3) 2822628; fax (3) 2825424; e-mail bt@nstp.com.my; internet www.btimes.com.my; f. 1976; morning; Editor HARDEV KAUR; circ. 15,000.

Malay Mail: Balai Berita 31, Jalan Riong, 59100 Kuala Lumpur; tel. (3) 2822829; fax (3) 2821434; e-mail malaymail@nstp.com.my; internet www.malaymail.com.my; f. 1896; afternoon; Editor FAUZI OMAR; circ. 75,000.

Malaysiakini: 2–4 Jalan Bangsa-Utang 9, 59000 Kuala Lumpur; tel. (3) 22835567; fax (3) 22892579; e-mail editor@malaysiakini.com; internet www.malaysiakini.com; Malaysia's first on-line newspaper; English and Malay; Editor STEVEN GAN.

New Straits Times: Balai Berita 31, Jalan Riong, 59100 Kuala Lumpur; tel. (3) 2823322; fax (3) 2821434; e-mail mishar@nstp.com.my; internet www.nstpi.com.my; f. 1845; morning; Exec. Dir ABDULLAH AHMAD; Group Editor (vacant); circ. 190,000.

The Edge: G501–G801, Levels 5–8, Block G, Phileo Damansara I, Jalan 16/11, off Jalan Damansara, 46350 Petaling Jaya, Selangor; tel. (3) 76603838; fax (3) 76608638; e-mail eeditor@bizedge.com; internet www.theedgedaily.com; f. 1996; weekly, with daily internet edition; business and investment news.

The Star: 13 Jalan 13/6, 46200 Petaling Jaya, POB 12474, Selangor; tel. (3) 7581188; fax (3) 7551280; e-mail msd@thestar.com.my; internet www.thestar.com.my; f. 1971; morning; Group Chief Editor NG POH TIP; circ. 192,059.

The Sun: Sun Media Corpn Sdn Bhd, Lot 6, Jalan 51/217, Section 51, 46050 Petaling Jaya, Selangor Darul Ehsan; tel. (3) 7946688; fax (3) 7952624; e-mail editor@sunmg.po.my; f. 1993; Editor-in-Chief HO KAY TAT; Man. Dir TAN BOON KEAN; circ. 82,474.

Chinese Language

China Press: 80 Jalan Riong, 59100 Kuala Lumpur; tel. (3) 2828208; fax (3) 2825327; circ. 206,000.

Chung Kuo Pao (China Press): 80 Jalan Riong, 59100 Kuala Lumpur; tel. (3) 2828208; fax (3) 2825327; f. 1946; Editor POON CHAU HUAY; Gen. Man. NG BENG LYE; circ. 210,000.

Guang Ming Daily: 19 Jalan Semangat, 46200 Petaling Jaya, Selangor; tel. (3) 7582888; fax (3) 7575135; circ. 87,144.

Kwong Wah Yit Poh: 19 Jalan Presgrave, 10300 Pinang; tel. (4) 2612312; fax (4) 2615407; e-mail editor@kwongwah.com.my; internet www.kwongwah.com.my; f. 1910; morning; Chief Editor TAN AYE CHOO; circ. 72,158.

Nanyang Siang Pau (Malaysia): 1 Jalan SS7/2, 47301 Petaling Jaya, Selangor; tel. (3) 78776000; fax (3) 78776855; e-mail editor@nanyang.com.my; internet www.nanyang.com.my; f. 1923; morning and evening; Editor-in-Chief WONG KAM HOR; circ. 185,000 (daily), 223,000 (Sunday).

Shin Min Daily News: 31 Jalan Riong, Bangsar, 59100 Kuala Lumpur; tel. (3) 2826363; fax (3) 2821812; f. 1966; morning; Editor-in-Chief CHENG SONG HUAT; circ. 82,000.

Sin Chew Jit Poh (Malaysia): 19 Jalan Semangat, POB 367, Jalan Sultan, 46200 Petaling Jaya, Selangor; tel. (3) 7582888; fax (3) 7570527; internet www.sinchew-i.com; f. 1929; morning; Chief Editor LIEW CHEN CHUAN; circ. 227,067 (daily), 230,000 (Sunday).

Malay Language

Berita Harian: Balai Berita 31, Jalan Riong, 59100 Kuala Lumpur; tel. (3) 2822323; fax (3) 2822425; e-mail bharian@bharian.com.my; internet www.bharian.com.my; f. 1957; morning; Group Editor AHMAD REJAL ARBEE; circ. 350,000.

Metro Ahad: Balai Berita 31, Jalan Riong, 59100 Kuala Lumpur; tel. (3) 2822328; fax (3) 2824482; e-mail metahad@nstp.com.my; internet www.metroahad.com.my; circ. 132,195.

Mingguan Perdana: 48 Jalan Siput Akek, Taman Billion, Kuala Lumpur; tel. (3) 619133; Group Chief Editor KHALID JAFRI.

Utusan Malaysia: 46M Jalan Lima, off Jalan Chan Sow Lin, 55200 Kuala Lumpur; tel. (3) 2217055; fax (3) 2220911; e-mail corpcomm@utusan.com.my: internet www.utusan.com.my; Editor-in-Chief (vacant).

Watan: 23–1 Jalan 9A/55A, Taman Setiawangsa, 54200 Kuala Lumpur; tel. (3) 4523040; fax (3) 4523043; circ. 80,000.

Tamil Language

Malaysia Nanban: 11 Jalan Murai Dua, Batu Kompleks, off Jalan Ipoh, 51200 Kuala Lumpur; tel. (3) 6212251; fax (3) 6235981; circ. 45,000.

Tamil Nesan: 28 Jalan Yew, Pudu, 55100 Kuala Lumpur; tel. (3) 2216411; fax (3) 2210448; f. 1924; morning; Editor V. VIVEKANANTHAN; circ. 35,000 (daily), 60,000 (Sunday).

Tamil Osai: 19 Jalan Murai Dua, Batu Kompleks, Jalan Ipoh, Kuala Lumpur; tel. (3) 671644; circ. 21,000 (daily), 40,000 (Sunday).

Tamil Thinamani: 9 Jalan Murai Dua, Batu Kompleks, Jalan Ipoh, Kuala Lumpur; tel. (3) 66719; Editor S. NACHIAPPAN; circ. 18,000 (daily), 39,000 (Sunday).

SUNDAY PAPERS

English Language

New Sunday Times: Balai Berita 31, Jalan Riong, 59100 Kuala Lumpur; tel. (3) 2822328; fax (3) 2824482; e-mail news@nstp.com.my; f. 1932; morning; Group Editor (vacant); circ. 191,562.

Sunday Mail: Balai Berita 31, Jalan Riong, 59100 Kuala Lumpur; tel. (3) 2822328; fax (3) 2824482; e-mail smail@nstp.com.my; f. 1896; morning; Editor JOACHIM S. P. NG; circ. 75,641.

Sunday Star: 13 Jalan 13/6, 46200 Petaling Jaya, POB 12474, Selangor Darul Ehsan; tel. (3) 7581188; fax (3) 7551280; f. 1971; Editor DAVID YEOH; circ. 232,790.

Malay Language

Berita Minggu: Balai Berita 31, Jalan Riong, 59100 Kuala Lumpur; tel. (3) 2822328; fax (3) 2824482; e-mail bharian@bharian.com.my; f. 1957; morning; Editor Dato' AHMAD NAZRI ABDULLAH; circ. 421,127.

Mingguan Malaysia: 11A The Right Angle, Jalan 14/22, 46100 Petaling Jaya; tel. (3) 7563355; fax (3) 7577755; f. 1964; Editor-in-Chief JOHAN JAAFAR; circ. 493,523.

Utusan Zaman: 11A The Right Angle, Jalan 14/22, 46100 Petaling Jaya; tel. (3) 7563355; fax (3) 7577755; f. 1939; Editor MUSTAFA FADULA SUHAIMI; circ. 11,782.

Tamil Language

Makkal Osai: 11 Jalan Murai Dua, Batu Kompleks, off Jalan Ipoh, 51200 Kuala Lumpur; tel. (3) 6212251; fax (3) 6235981; circ. 28,000.

PERIODICALS

English Language

Her World: Berita Publishing Sdn Bhd, Balai Berita, 31 Jalan Riong, 59100 Kuala Lumpur; tel. (3) 2824322; fax (3) 2828489; monthly; Editor ALICE CHEE LAN NEO; circ. 35,000.

Malaysia Warta Kerajaan Seri Paduka Baginda (HM Government Gazette): Percetakan Nasional Malaysia Berhad, Jalan Chan Sow Lin, 50554 Kuala Lumpur; tel. (3) 92212022; fax (3) 92220690; e-mail pnmb@po.jaring.my; fortnightly.

Malaysian Agricultural Journal: Ministry of Agriculture, Publications Unit, Wisma Tani, Jalan Sultan Salahuddin, 50624 Kuala Lumpur; tel. (3) 2982011; fax (3) 2913758; f. 1901; 2 a year.

Malaysian Forester: Forestry Department Headquarters, Jalan Sultan Salahuddin, 50660 Kuala Lumpur; tel. (3) 26988244; fax (3) 26925657; e-mail skthai@forestry.gov.my; f. 1931; quarterly; Editor THAI SEE KIAM.

The Planter: Wisma ISP, 29–33 Jalan Taman U Thant, POB 10262, 50708 Kuala Lumpur; tel. (3) 21425561; fax (3) 21426898; e-mail isphq@tm.net.my; internet www.isphq.com; f. 1919; publ. by Isp Management (M); monthly; Editor W. T. PERERA; circ. 4,000.

Young Generation: 11A The Right Angle, Jalan 14/22, 46100 Petaling Jaya, Selangor; tel. (3) 7563355; fax (3) 7577755; monthly; circ. 50,000.

Chinese Language

Mister Weekly: 2A Jalan 19/1, 46300 Petaling Jaya, Selangor; tel. (3) 7562400; fax (3) 7553826; f. 1976; weekly; Editor WONG AH TAI; circ. 25,000.

Mun Sang Poh: 472 Jalan Pasir Puteh, 31650 Ipoh; tel. (5) 3212919; fax (5) 3214006; bi-weekly; circ. 77,958.

New Life Post: 80M Jalan SS21/39, Damansara Utama, 47400 Petaling Jaya, Selangor; tel. (3) 7571833; fax (3) 7181809; f. 1972; bi-weekly; Editor LOW BENG CHEE; circ. 231,000.

New Tide Magazine: Nanyang Siang Pau Bldg, 2nd Floor, Jalan 7/2, 47301 Petaling Jaya, Selangor; tel. (3) 76202118; fax (3) 76202131; e-mail newtidemag@hotmail.com; f. 1974; monthly; Editor NELLIE OOI; circ. 39,000.

Malay Language

Dewan Masyarakat: Dewan Bahasa dan Pustaka, POB 10803, 50926 Kuala Lumpur; tel. (3) 2481011; fax (3) 2484211; f. 1963; monthly; current affairs; Editor ZULKIFLI SALLEH; circ. 48,500.

Dewan Pelajar: Dewan Bahasa dan Pustaka, Jalan Wisma Putra, POB 10803, 50926 Kuala Lumpur; tel. (3) 2481011; fax (3) 2484211; f. 1967; monthly; children's; Editor ZALEHA HASHIM; circ. 100,000.

Dewan Siswa: POB 10803, 50926 Kuala Lumpur; tel. (3) 2481011; fax (3) 2484208; monthly; circ. 140,000.

Gila-Gila: 38-1, Jalan Bangsar Utama Satu, Bangsar Utama, 59000 Kuala Lumpur; tel. (3) 22824970; fax (3) 22824967; fortnightly; circ. 70,000.

Harakah: Jabatan Penerangan dan Penyelidikan PAS, 28A Jalan Pahang Barat, Off Jalan Pahang, 53000 Kuala Lumpur; tel. (3) 40213343; fax (3) 40212422; e-mail hrkh@pc.jaring.my; internet www.harakahdaily.com; two a month; Malay; organ of the Parti Islam se Malaysia (PAS—Islamic Party of Malaysia); Editor ZULKIFLI SULONG.

Jelita: Berita Publishing Sdn Bhd, 16–20 Jalan 4/109E, Desa Business Park, Taman Desa, off Jalan Klang Lama, 58100 Kuala Lumpur; tel. (3) 7620811; fax (3) 76208015; e-mail jelita@com.my; internet www.jelita.com.my; monthly; fashion and beauty magazine; Editor ROHANI PA' WAN CHIK; circ. 80,000.

Mangga: 11A The Right Angle, Jalan 14/22, 46100 Petaling Jaya, Selangor; tel. (3) 7563355; fax (3) 7577755; monthly; circ. 205,000.

Mastika: 11A The Right Angle, Jalan 14/22, 46100 Petaling Jaya, Selangor; tel. (3) 7363355; fax (3) 7577755; monthly; Malayan illustrated magazine; Editor AZIZAH ALI; circ. 15,000.

Utusan Radio dan TV: 11A The Right Angle, Jalan 14/22, 46100 Petaling Jaya, Selangor; tel. (3) 7363355; fax (3) 7577755; fortnightly; Editor NORSHAH TAMBY; circ. 115,000.

Wanita: 11A The Right Angle, Jalan 14/22, 46100 Petaling Jaya, Selangor; tel. (3) 7563355; fax (3) 7577755; monthly; women; Editor NIK RAHIMAH HASSAN; circ. 85,000.

Punjabi Language

Navjiwan Punjabi News: 52 Jalan 8/18, Jalan Toman, Petaling Jaya, 46050 Selangor; tel. (3) 7565725; f. 1950; weekly; Assoc. Editor TARA SINGH; circ. 9,000.

SABAH

DAILIES

Api Siang Pau (Kota Kinabalu Commercial Press): 24 Lorong Dewan, POB 170, Kota Kinabalu; f. 1954; morning; Chinese; Editor Datuk LO KWOCK CHUEN; circ. 3,000.

Borneo Mail (Nountan Press Sdn Bhd): 1 Jalan Bakau, 1st Floor, off Jalan Gaya, 88999 Kota Kinabulu; tel. (88) 238001; fax (88) 238002; English; circ. 14,610.

Daily Express: News House, 16 Jalan Pasar Baru, POB 10139, 88801 Kota Kinabalu; tel. (88) 256422; fax (88) 238611; e-mail sph@tm.net.my; internet www.dailyexpress.com.my; f. 1963; morning; English, Bahasa Malaysia and Kadazan; Editor-in-Chief SARDATHISA JAMES; circ. 30,000.

Hwa Chiaw Jit Pao (Overseas Chinese Daily News): News House, 16 Jalan Pasar Baru, POB 10139, 88801 Kota Kinabalu; tel. (88) 256422; e-mail sph@tm.net.my; internet www.dailyexpress.com.my; f. 1936; morning; Chinese; Editor HII YUK SENG; circ. 30,000.

Merdeka Daily News: Lot 56, BDC Estate, Mile 1½ North Road, POB 332, 90703 Sandakan; tel. (89) 214517; fax (89) 275537; e-mail merkk@tm.net.my; f. 1968; morning; Chinese; Editor-in-Chief FUNG KON SHING; circ. 8,000.

New Sabah Times: Jalan Pusat Pembangunan Masyarakat, off Jalan Mat Salleh, 88100 Kota Kinabalu; POB 20119, 88758 Kota Kinabalu; tel. (88) 230055; fax (88) 241155; internet www.newsabahtimes.com.my; English, Malay and Kadazan; Editor-in-Chief EDDY LOK; circ. 30,000.

Syarikat Sabah Times: Kota Kinabalu; tel. (88) 52217; f. 1952; English, Malay and Kadazan; circ. 25,000.

Tawau Jih Pao: POB 464, 1072 Jalan Kuhara, Tawau; tel. (89) 72576; Chinese; Editor-in-Chief STEPHEN LAI KIM YEAN.

SARAWAK

DAILIES

Berita Petang Sarawak: Lot 8322, Lorong 7, Jalan Tun Abdul Razak, 93450 Kuching; POB 1315, 93726 Kuching; tel. (82) 480771; fax (82) 489006; f. 1972; evening; Chinese; Chief Editor HWANG YU CHAI; circ. 12,000.

Borneo Post: 40 Jalan Tuanku Osman, POB 20, 96000 Sibu; tel. (84) 332055; fax (84) 321255; internet www.borneopost.com.my; morning; English; Man. Dir LAU HUI SIONG; Editor NGUOI HOW YIENG; circ. 60,000.

Chinese Daily News: Lot 164–165, Jalan Sungei Padungan, Kuching; tel. (82) 233888; fax (82) 233399; internet www.chinesedaily.com.my; f. 1945; Chinese; Editor T. T. CHOW; circ. 10,406.

International Times: Lot 2215, Jalan Bengkel, Pending Industrial Estate, POB 1158, 93724 Kuching; tel. (82) 482215; fax (82) 480996; e-mail news@intimes.com; internet www.intimes.com.my; f. 1968; morning; Chinese; Editor LEE FOOK ONN; circ. 37,000.

Malaysia Daily News: 7 Island Rd, POB 237, 96009 Sibu; tel. (84) 330211; tel. (84) 320540; f. 1968; morning; Chinese; Editor WONG SENG KWONG; circ. 22,735.

Miri Daily News: Lot 88, Piasau Industrial Estate, POB 377, 98007 Miri; tel. (85) 656666; fax (85) 655655; internet www.miridaily.com.my; f. 1957; morning; Chinese; Editor KU KIANG FAH; Man. HWANG JUN HIEN; circ. 22,431.

Sarawak Tribune and Sunday Tribune: Lot 231, Jalan Nipah, off Jalan Abell, 93100 Kuching; tel. (82) 424411; fax (82) 420358;

internet www.jaring.my/tribune; f. 1945; English; Editor FRANCIS SIAH; circ. 29,598.

See Hua Daily News: 40 Jalan Tuanku Osman, POB 20, 96000 Sibu; tel. (84) 332055; fax (84) 321255; f. 1952; morning; Chinese; Man. Editor LAU HUI SIONG; circ. 80,000.

PERIODICALS

Pedoman Rakyat: Malaysian Information Dept, Mosque Rd, 93612 Kuching; tel. (82) 240141; f. 1956; monthly; Malay; Editor SAIT BIN Haji YAMAN; circ. 30,000.

Pembrita: Malaysian Information Services, Mosque Rd, 93612 Kuching; tel. (82) 247231; f. 1950; monthly; Iban; Editor ALBAN JAWA; circ. 20,000.

Sarawak Gazette: Sarawak Museum, Jalan Tun Abang Haji Openg, 93566 Kuching; tel. (82) 244232; fax (82) 246680; e-mail museum@po.jaring.my; f. 1870; 2 a year; English; Chief Editor Datuk Dr Haji HATTA SOLHEE.

Utusan Sarawak: Lot 231, Jalan Nipah, off Jalan Abell, POB 138, 93100 Kuching; tel. (82) 424411; fax (82) 420358; internet www.tribune.com.my/tribune; f. 1949; Malay; Editor Haji ABDUL AZIZ Haji MALIM; circ. 32,292.

NEWS AGENCIES

Bernama (Malaysian National News Agency): Wisma Bernama, 28 Jalan 1/65A, off Jalan Tun Razak, POB 10024, 50700 Kuala Lumpur; tel. (3) 2945233; fax (3) 2941020; e-mail sjamil@bernama.com; internet www.bernama.com; f. 1968; general and foreign news, economic features and photo services, public relations wire, screen information and data services, stock market on-line equities service, real-time commodity and monetary information services; daily output in Malay and English; in June 1990 Bernama was given the exclusive right to receive and distribute news in Malaysia; Gen. Man. SYED JAMIL JAAFAR.

Foreign Bureaux

Agence France-Presse (AFP): 26 Hotel Equatorial, 1st Floor, Jalan Treacher, 2610520 Kuala Lumpur; tel. (3) 2691906; fax (3) 2615606; Correspondent MERVIN NAMBIAR.

Associated Press (AP) (USA): Wisma Bernama, 28 Jalan 1/65A, off Jalan Tun Razak, POB 12219, Kuala Lumpur; tel. (3) 2926155; Correspondent HARI SUBRAMANIAM.

Inter Press Service (IPS) (Italy): 32 Jalan Mudah Barat, Taman Midah, 56000 Kuala Lumpur; tel. (3) 9716830; fax (3) 2612872; Correspondent (vacant).

Press Trust of India: 114 Jalan Limau Manis, Bangsar Park, Kuala Lumpur; tel. (3) 940673; Correspondent T. V. VENKITACHALAM.

United Press International (UPI) (USA): Room 1, Ground Floor, Wisma Bernama, Jalan 1/65A, 50400 Kuala Lumpur; tel. (3) 2933393; fax (3) 2913876; Rep. MARY LEIGH.

Reuters (UK) and Xinhua (People's Republic of China) are also represented in Malaysia.

PRESS ASSOCIATION

Persatuan Penerbit-Penerbit Akhbar Malaysia (Malaysian Newspaper Publishers' Asscn): 17 Jalan Wan Kadir 2, Taman Tun Dr Ismail, 60000 Kuala Lumpur; tel. (3) 7198195; fax (3) 7197394; Chair. AZIZI MEOR NGAH.

Publishers

KUALA LUMPUR

Arus Intelek Sdn Bhd: Plaza Mont Kiara, Suite E-06-06, Mont Kiara, 50480 Kuala Lumpur; tel. (3) 62011558; fax (3) 62018698; e-mail arusintelek@po.jaring.my; Man. Datin AZIZAH MOKHZANI.

Berita Publishing Sdn Bhd: Balai Berita, 31 Jalan Riong, 59100 Kuala Lumpur; tel. (3) 2824322; fax (3) 2821605; internet www.jelit-a.com.my; education, business, fiction, cookery; Man. ABDUL MANAF SAAD.

Dewan Bahasa dan Pustaka (DBP) (Institute of Language and Literature): POB 10803, 50926 Kuala Lumpur; tel. (3) 21481011; fax (3) 21444460; e-mail aziz@dbp.gov.my; internet www.dbp.gov.my; f. 1956; textbooks, magazines and general; Chair. Dato' Haji ABDUL RAHIM BIN BAKAR; Dir-Gen. Dato' Haji A. AZIZ DERAMAN.

International Law Book Services: Lot 4.1, Wisma Shen, 4th Floor, 149 Jalan Masjid India, 50100 Kuala Lumpur; tel. (3) 2939864; fax (3) 2928035; e-mail gbc@pc.jaring.my; Man. Dr SYED IBRAHIM.

Jabatan Penerbitan Universiti Malaya (University of Malaya Press): University of Malaya, Lembah Pantai, 50603 Kuala Lumpur; tel. (3) 79574361; fax (3) 79574473; e-mail a8shaab@umcsd.um.edu.my; internet www.um.edu.my; f. 1954; general fiction, literature, economics, history, medicine, politics, science, social science, law, Islam, engineering, dictionaries; Chief Editor Dr HAMEDI MOHD ADNAN.

Malaya Press Sdn Bhd: Kuala Lumpur; tel. (3) 5754650; fax (3) 5751464; f. 1958; education; Man. Dir LAI WING CHUN.

Pustaka Antara Sdn Bhd: Lot UG 10–13, Upper Ground Floor, Kompleks Wilayah, 2 Jalan Munshi Abdullah, 50100 Kuala Lumpur; tel. (3) 26980044; fax (3) 26917997; e-mail pantara@tm.net.my; textbooks, children's, languages, fiction; Man. Dir Datuk ABDUL AZIZ BIN AHMAD.

Utusan Publications and Distributors Sdn Bhd: 1 & 3 Jalan 3/91A, Taman Shamelin Perkasa, Cheras, 56100 Kuala Lumpur; tel. (3) 9856577; fax (3) 9846554; e-mail rose@utusan.com.my; internet www.upnd.com.my; school textbooks, children's, languages, fiction, general; Exec. Dir ROSELINA JOHARI.

JOHOR

Penerbitan Pelangi Sdn Bhd: 66 Jalan Pingai, Taman Pelangi, 80400 Johor Bahru; tel. (7) 3316288; fax (7) 3329201; e-mail ppsb@po.jaring.my; internet www.pelangibooks.com; children's books, guidebooks and reference; Man. Dir SAMUEL SUM KOWN CHEEK.

Textbooks Malaysia Sdn Bhd: 49 Jalan Tengku Ahmad, POB 30, 85000 Segamat, Johor; tel. (7) 9318323; fax (7) 9313323; school textbooks, children's fiction, guidebooks and reference; Man. Dir FREDDIE KHOO.

NEGERI SEMBILAN

Bharathi Press: 166 Taman AST, POB 74, 70700 Seremban, Negeri Sembilan Darul Khusus; tel. (6) 7622911; f. 1939; Mans M. SUBRAMANIA BHARATHI, BHARATHI THASAN.

Minerva Publications: 96 Jalan Dato, Bandar Tunggal, 70000 Seremban, Negeri Sembilan; tel. and fax (6) 7634439; f. 1964; English, business, religion; Man. Dir TAJUDDIN MUHAMMED.

PINANG

Syarikat United Book Sdn Bhd: 187–189 Lebuh Carnarvon, 10100 Pulau Pinang; tel. (4) 61635; fax (4) 615063; textbooks, children's, reference, fiction, guidebooks; Man. Dir CHEW SING GUAN.

SELANGOR

SNP Panpac (Malaysia) Sdn Bhd: Lot 3, Jalan Saham, s3/3 Kawasan MIEL, Phase 8, 40675 Shah Alam, Selangor; tel. (3) 55481088; fax (3) 55481080; f. 1980; fmrly Eastview Publications Sdn Bhd; school textbooks, children's, fiction, reference, general; Man. Dir IVAN HOE.

Federal Publications Sdn Bhd: Lot 46, Subang Hi-Tech Industrial Park, Batu Tiga, 40000 Shah Alam, Selangor; tel. (3) 56286888; fax (3) 56364620; e-mail fpsb@tpg.com.my; f. 1957; computer, children's magazines; Gen. Man. STEPHEN K. S. LIM.

FEP International Sdn Bhd: 6 Jalan SS 4C/5, POB 1091, 47301 Petaling Jaya, Selangor; tel. (3) 7036150; fax (3) 7036989; f. 1969; children's, languages, fiction, dictionaries, textbooks and reference; Man. Dir LIM MOK-HAI.

Mahir Publications Sdn Bhd: 39 Jalan Nilam 1/2, Subang Sq., Subang Hi-Tech Industrial Park, Batu Tiga, 40000 Shah Alam, Selangor; tel. (3) 7379044; fax (3) 7379043; e-mail mahirpub@tm.net.my; Gen. Man. ZAINORA BINTI MUHAMAD.

Pearson Education Malaysia Sdn Bhd: Lot 2, Jalan 215, off Jalan Templer, 46050 Petaling Jaya, Selangor; tel. (3) 77820466; fax (3) 77818005; e-mail inquiry@pearsoned.com.my; internet www.pearsoned.com.my; textbooks, mathematics, physics, science, general, educational materials; Dir WONG WEE WOON; Man. WONG MEI MEI.

Pelanduk Publications (M) Sdn Bhd: 12 Jalan SS 13/3E, Subang Jaya Industrial Estate, 47500 Subang Jaya, Selangor; tel. (3) 7386885; fax (3) 7386575; e-mail pelpub@tm.net.my; internet www.pelanduk.com; Man. JACKSON TAN.

Penerbit Fajar Bakti Sdn Bhd: 4 Jalan U1/15, Sekseyen U1, Hicom-Glenmarie Industrial Park, 40150 Shah Alam, Selangor; tel. (3) 7047011; fax (3) 7047024; e-mail edes@pfb.po.my; school, college and university textbooks, children's, fiction, general; Man. Dir EDDA DE SILVA.

Penerbit Pan Earth Sdn Bhd: 11 Jalan SS 26/6, Taman Mayang Jaya, 47301 Petaling Jaya, Selangor; tel. (3) 7031258; fax (3) 7031262; Man. STEPHEN CHENG.

Penerbit Universiti Kebangsaan Malaysia: Universiti Kebangsaan Malaysia, 43600 UKM, Selangor; tel. (3) 8292840; fax (3) 8254375; Man. HASROM BIN HARON.

Pustaka Delta Pelajaran Sdn Bhd: Wisma Delta, Lot 18, Jalan 51A/22A, 46100 Petaling Jaya, Selangor; tel. (3) 7570000; fax (3) 7576688; e-mail dpsb@po.jaring.my; economics, language, environment, geography, geology, history, religion, science; Man. Dir LIM KIM WAH.

Pustaka Sistem Pelajaran Sdn Bhd: Lot 17–22 and 17–23, Jalan Satu, Bersatu Industrial Park, Cheras Jaya, 43200 Cheras, Selangor; tel. (3) 9047558; fax (3) 9047573; Man. T. THIRU.

Sasbadi Sdn Bhd: 103A Jalan SS 21/1A, Damansara Utama, 47400 Petaling Jaya, Selangor; tel. (3) 7182550; fax (3) 7186709; Man. LAW KING HUI.

Times Educational Sdn Bhd: 22 Jalan 19/3, 46300 Petaling Jaya, Selangor; tel. (3) 7571766; fax (3) 7573607; textbooks, general and reference; Man. FOONG CHUI LIN.

GOVERNMENT PUBLISHING HOUSE

Percetakan Nasional Malaysia Bhd (Malaysia National Printing Ltd): Jalan Chan Sow Lin, 50554 Kuala Lumpur; tel. (3) 2212022; fax (3) 2220690; fmrly the National Printing Department, incorporated as a company under govt control in January 1993.

PUBLISHERS' ASSOCIATION

Malaysian Book Publishers' Association: 306 Block C, Glomac Business Centre, 10 Jalan SS 6/1 Kelana Jaya, 47301 Petaling Jaya, Selangor; tel. (3) 7046628; fax (3) 7046629; e-mail mabopa@po.jaring.my; internet www.mabopa.com.my; f. 1968; Pres. NG TIEH CHUAN; Hon. Sec. KOW CHING CHUAN; 95 mems.

Broadcasting and Communications

TELECOMMUNICATIONS

Celcom (Malaysia) Sdn Bhd: Menara TR, 161B Jalan Ampang, 50450 Kuala Lumpur; tel. (3) 2623900; fax (3) 2625900; internet www.celcom.com.my; private co licensed to operate mobile cellular telephone service; Pres. ROSLI BIN MAN; Group Exec. Vice-Pres. WAN AISHA WAN HAMID.

DiGi Telecommunications Sdn Bhd: Lot 30, Jalan Delima 1/3, Subang Hi-Tech Industrial Park, 40000 Shah Alam, Selangor; tel. (3) 57211800; fax (3) 57211857; internet www.digi.com.my; private co licensed to operate mobile telephone service; Chair. Tan Sri Dato' Seri VINCENT TAN CHEE YIOUN.

Jabatan Telekomunikasi Malaysia (JTM): c/o Ministry of Energy, Communications and Multimedia, Wisma Damansara, 3rd Floor, Jalan Semantan, 50668 Kuala Lumpur; tel. (3) 2575000; fax (3) 2557901; internet www.ktkm.gov.my.

Maxis Communications Bhd: Menara Maxis, Kuala Lumpur City Centre, 50088 Kuala Lumpur; tel. (3) 3807802; fax (3) 3807010; internet www.maxis.com.my; provides mobile, fixed line and multimedia services; 800,000 subscribers in 1999; CEO JAMALUDIN IBRAHIM.

Telekom Malaysia Bhd: Ibu Pejabat Telekom Malaysia, 1st Floor, Jalan Pantai Baru, 50672 Kuala Lumpur; tel. (3) 2082103; fax (3) 7574747; internet www.telekom.com.my; public listed co responsible for operation of basic telecommunications services; 74% govt-owned; 4.22m. fixed lines (95% of total); Chair Haji MUHAMMAD RADZI BIN Haji MANSOR; Chief Exec. Dr MD KHIR ABDUL RAHMAN.

Technology Resources Industries Bhd (TRI): Menara TR, 23rd Floor, 161B Jalan Ampang, 50450 Kuala Lumpur; tel. (3) 2619555; fax (3) 2632018; operates mobile cellular telephone service; Chair. and Chief Exec. Tan Sri Dato' TAJUDIN RAMLI.

Time dotCom Bhd: Wisma Time, 1st Floor, 249 Jalan Tun Razak, 50400 Kuala Lumpur; tel. (3) 27208000; fax (3) 27200199; internet www.time.com.my; f. 1996 as Time Telecommunications Holdings Bhd; name changed as above in Jan. 2000; state-controlled co licensed to operate trunk network and mobile cellular telephone service; Exec. Chair. Dato' Prof. ZAIDIN Haji OTHMAN.

BROADCASTING

Regulatory Authority

Under the Broadcasting Act (approved in December 1987), the Minister of Information is empowered to control and monitor all radio and television broadcasting, and to revoke the licence of any private company violating the Act by broadcasting material 'conflicting with Malaysian values'.

Radio Televisyen Malaysia (RTM): Dept of Broadcasting, Angkasapuri, Bukit Putra, 50614 Kuala Lumpur; tel. (3) 22825333; fax (3) 2824735; e-mail helpdesk@rtm.net.my; internet www.rtm.net.my; f. 1946 (television introduced 1963); supervises radio and television broadcasting; Dir-Gen. JAAFAR KAMIN; Dep. Dir-Gen. TAMIMUDDIN ABDUL KARIM.

Radio

Radio Malaysia: Radio Televisyen Malaysia (see Regulatory Authority), POB 11272, 50740 Kuala Lumpur; tel. (3) 2823991; fax (3) 2825859; f. 1946; domestic service; operates six networks; broadcasts in Bahasa Malaysia, English, Chinese (Mandarin and other dialects), Tamil and Aborigine (Temiar and Semai dialects); Dir of Radio MADZHI JOHARI.

Suara Islam (Voice of Islam): Islamic Affairs Division, Prime Minister's Department, Jalan Dato' Onn, 50502 Kuala Lumpur; f. 1995; tel. (3) 2321957; fax (3) 2388374; Asia-Pacific region; broadcasts in Bahasa Malaysia on Islam.

Suara Malaysia (Voice of Malaysia): Wisma Radio, Angkasapuri, POB 11272, 50740 Kuala Lumpur; tel. (3) 22887824; fax (3) 22847594; f. 1963; overseas service in Bahasa Malaysia, Arabic, Myanmar (Burmese), English, Bahasa Indonesia, Chinese (Mandarin/Cantonese), Tagalog and Thai; Controller of Overseas Service STEPHEN SIPAUN.

Radio Televisyen Malaysia—Sabah: Jalan Tuaran, 88614 Kota Kinabalu; tel. (88) 213444; fax (88) 223493; f. 1955 (television introduced 1971); a dept of RTM; broadcasts programmes over two networks for 280 hours a week in Bahasa Malaysia, English, Chinese (two dialects), Kadazan, Murut, Dusun and Bajau; Dir of Broadcasting JUMAT ENGSON.

Radio Televisyen Malaysia—Sarawak: Broadcasting House, Jalan P. Ramlee, 93614 Kuching; tel. (82) 248422; fax (82) 241914; e-mail pvgrtmsw@tm.net.my; f. 1954; a dept of RTM; broadcasts 445 hours per week in Bahasa Malaysia, English, Chinese, Iban, Bidayuh, Melanau, Kayan/Kenyah, Bisayah and Murut; Dir of Broadcasting NORHYATI ISMAIL.

Rediffusion Sdn Bhd: Rediffusion House, 17 Jalan Pahang, 53000 Kuala Lumpur; tel. (3) 4424544; fax (3) 4424614; f. 1949; two programmes; 44,720 subscribers in Kuala Lumpur; 11,405 subscribers in Pinang; 6,006 subscribers in Province Wellesley; 20,471 subscribers in Ipoh; Gen. Man. ROSNI B. RAHMAT.

Time Highway Radio: Wisma Time, 10th Floor, Jalan Tun Razak, 50400 Kuala Lumpur; tel. (3) 27202993; fax (3) 27200993; e-mail chief@thr.fm; internet www.thr.fm; f. 1994; serves Kuala Lumpur region; broadcasts in English; CEO ABDUL AZIZ HAMDAN.

Television

Measat Broadcast Network Systems Sdn Bhd: Kuala Lumpur; internet www.astro.com.my; nation-wide subscription service; Malaysia's first satellite, Measat 1, was launched in January 1996; a second satellite was launched in October of that year; Chair. T. ANANDA KRISHNAN.

Mega TV: Kuala Lumpur; internet www.megatv.com.my; subscription service; began broadcasting in November 1995; 5 foreign channels; initially available only in Klang Valley; 40%-owned by the Govt.

MetroVision: 33 Jalan Delima, 1/3 Subang Hi-Tech Industrial Park, 40000 Shah Alam, Selangor; tel. (3) 7328000; fax (3) 7328932; e-mail norlin@metrovision.com.my; internet www.metrovision.com.my; began broadcasting in July 1995; commercial station; operates only in Klang Valley; 44%-owned by Senandung Sesuria Sdn Bhd, 56%-owned by Metropolitan Media Sdn Bhd; Man. Dr SABRI ABDUL RAHMAN.

Radio Televisyen Malaysia—Sabah: (see Radio).

Radio Televisyen Malaysia—Sarawak: (see Radio).

Sistem Televisyen Malaysia Bhd (TV 3): 3 Persiaran Bandar Utama, Bandar Utama, 47800 Petaling, Selangor Darul Ehsan; tel. (3) 77266333; fax (3) 77261333; internet www.tv3.com.my; f. 1983; Malaysia's first private television network, began broadcasting in 1984; Chair. Dato' MOHD NOOR YUSOF; Man. Dir HISHAM Dato' ABD. RAHMAN.

Televisyen Malaysia: Radio Televisyen Malaysia (see Regulatory Authority); f. 1963; operates two national networks, TV1 and TV2; Controller of Programmes ISMAIL MOHAMED JAH.

Under a regulatory framework devised by the Government, the ban on privately-owned satellite dishes was ended in 1996.

Finance

(cap. = capital; auth. = authorized; res = reserves; dep. = deposits; m. = million; brs = branches; amounts in ringgit Malaysia)

BANKING

In July 2002 there were 47 domestic commercial banks, merchant banks and finance companies. In February 2000 the Government announced that it had approved plans for the creation of up to 10 banking groups to be formed through the merger of existing institutions. By August 2001 51 banks had merged under the terms of these plans. In February 1998 59 banks held offshore licences in Labuan.

Central Bank

Bank Negara Malaysia: Jalan Dato' Onn, 50480 Kuala Lumpur; tel. (3) 26988044; fax (3) 2912990; e-mail info@bnm.gov.my; internet www.bnm.gov.my; f. 1959; bank of issue; financial regulatory authority; cap. 100m., res 23,904.5m., dep. 76,772.0m. (April 2001); Gov. Datuk Dr ZETI AKHTAR AZIZ; 12 brs.

Regulatory Authority

Labuan Offshore Financial Services Authority (LOFSA): Level 17, Main Office Tower, Financial Park Labuan, Jalan Merdeka, 87000 Labuan; tel. (87) 408188; fax (87) 413328; e-mail communication@lofsa.gov.my; internet www.lofsa.gov.my; regulatory body for the International Offshore Financial Centre of Labuan established in October 1990; Chair. Gov. of Bank Negara Malaysia; Dir-Gen. NOORAZMAN AZIZ.

Commercial Banks

Peninsular Malaysia

ABN Amro Bank Bhd: Level 1, 25–27 MNI Twins Tower II, 11 Jalan Pinang, 50450 Kuala Lumpur; tel. (3) 21627888; fax (3) 21625692; internet www.abnamromalaysia.com; f. 1963.

Affin Bank Bhd: Menara AFFIN, 17th Floor, Jalan Raja Chulan, 50200 Kuala Lumpur; tel. (3) 20559000; fax (3) 2061415; e-mail head.ccd@affinbank.com.my; internet www.affinbank.com.my; f. 1975 as Perwira Habib Bank Malaysia Bhd; name changed to Perwira Affin Bank Bhd 1994; merged with BSN Commercial Bank (Malaysia) Bhd Jan. 2001, and name changed as above; cap. 650.0m., res 424.6m., dep. 12,350.0m. (Dec. 1999); Chair. Gen. Tan Sri Dato' ZAIN HASHIM; Deputy Chair. and CEO Raja Dato' AMAN AHMAD; 110 brs.

Alliance Bank Malaysia Bhd: Menara Multi-Purpose, Ground Floor, Capital Square, 8 Jalan Munshi Abdullah, 50100 Kuala Lumpur; POB 10069, 50704 Kuala Lumpur; tel. (3) 26948800; fax (3) 26946727; e-mail multilink@alliancebg.com.my; internet www.alliancebank.com.my; f. 1982 as Malaysian French Bank Berhad; name changed to Multi-Purpose Bank Bhd 1996; name changed as above Jan. 2001, following acquisition of six merger partners; cap. 230.0m., res 183.7m., dep. 7,907.2m. (Dec. 1999); Chair. Tan Sri ABU TALIB OTHMAN; Chief Exec. Dir NG SIEK CHUAN; 73 brs.

AmBank Bhd: Level 18, Menara Dion, Jalan Sultan Ismail, 50250 Kuala Lumpur; POB 10980, 50732 Kuala Lumpur; tel. (3) 2063939; fax (3) 2066855; internet www.ambg.com.my; f. 1994; fmrly Arab-Malaysian Bank Bhd; cap. 348.0m., res 337.9m., dep. 9,902.2m. (March 1999); Chair. Tan Sri Dato' AZMAN HASHIM; Man. Dir AZLAN ZAINOL.

Bangkok Bank Bhd (Thailand): 105 Jalan Tun H. S. Lee, 50000 Kuala Lumpur; POB 10734, 50923 Kuala Lumpur; tel. (3) 2324555; fax (3) 2388569; e-mail bbb@tm.net.my; f. 1958; cap. 88.5m., res 41.2m., dep. 508.7m. (Dec. 2000); Chair. ALBERT CHEOK SAYCHUAN; CEO CHALIT TAYJASANANT; 1 br.

Bank of Tokyo-Mitsubishi (Malaysia) Bhd (Japan): 1 Leboh Ampang, 50100 Kuala Lumpur; POB 10959, 50931 Kuala Lumpur; tel. (3) 2389100; fax (3) 2308340; f. 1996, following merger of the Bank of Tokyo and Mitsubishi Bank; cap. 200m., res 300m., dep. 1,718m. (1998); Chair. AKIRA OKUHATA.

Bank Pembangunan & Infrastruktur Malaysia Bhd: Menara Bank Pembangunan, POB 12352, Jalan Sultan Ismail, 50774 Kuala Lumpur; tel. (3) 26152020; fax (3) 26928520; e-mail bpimb-pr@bpimb.com.my; internet www.bpimb.com.my; f. 1973; cap. 1,000m. (Dec. 1999); dep. 2,190m. (Dec. 2000); Exec. Chair. Tan Sri Datuk Dr ARIS OTHMAN; Man. Dir Datuk Nik IBRAHIM ABDULLAH; 13 brs.

Bumiputra Commerce Bank Bhd: 6 Jalan Tun Perak, 50050 Kuala Lumpur; POB 10753, 50724 Kuala Lumpur; tel. (3) 2931722; fax (3) 2986628; internet www.bcb.com.my; f. 1999, following merger of Bank Bumiputra Malaysia Bhd with Bank of Commerce Bhd; cap. 1,708.3m., res 1,773.2m., dep. 48,969.3m. (Dec. 2000); Chair. Tan Sri RADIN SOENARNO AL-HAJ; Man. Dir and CEO Dr ROZALI MOHAMED ALI; 249 brs.

Citibank Bhd (USA): 165 Jalan Ampang, POB 10112, 50904 Kuala Lumpur; tel. (3) 2325334; fax (3) 2328763; internet www.citibank.com.my; f. 1959; cap. 121.7m., res 519.2m., dep. 10,683.3m. (1998); CEO ROBERT MATTHEWS; 3 brs.

Deutsche Bank (Malaysia) Bhd (Germany): 18–20 Menara IMC, 8 Jalan Sultan Ismail, 50250 Kuala Lumpur; tel. (3) 2021163; fax (3) 2019822; f. 1994; cap. 124.0m., res 144.1m., dep. 1,328.4m. (Dec. 2000); Man. Dir ERDMANN R. G. VOGT.

EON Bank Bhd: Wisma Cyclecarri, 11th Floor, 288 Jalan Raja Laut, 50350 Kuala Lumpur; POB 12996, 50796 Kuala Lumpur; tel. (3) 26941188; fax (3) 26949588; e-mail eontsy@tm.net.my; internet www.eonbank.com.my; f. 1963; fmrly Kong Ming Bank Bhd; merged with Oriental Bank Bhd, Jan. 2001; cap. 1,168.2m., res 137.1m., dep. 6,906.2m. (Dec. 2000); Chair. Tan Sri Dato' Seri MOHAMED SALEH BIN SULONG; Dir and CEO KOK NAM SOON; 46 brs.

Hong Leong Bank Bhd: Wisma Hong Leong, Level 3, 18 Jalan Perak, 50450 Kuala Lumpur; POB 12372, 50776 Kuala Lumpur; tel. (3) 21642828; fax (3) 27156365; internet www.hlb.hongleong.com.my; f. 1905; fmrly MUI Bank Bhd; merged with Wah Tat Bank Bhd, Jan. 2001; cap. 577.2m., res 1,152.4m., dep. 15,568.6m. (June 2000); Chair. Tan Sri QUEK LENG CHAN; Man. Dir JAMES LIM CHENG POH; 72 brs.

HSBC Bank Malaysia Bhd (Hong Kong): 2 Leboh Ampang, POB 10244, 50912 Kuala Lumpur; tel. (3) 2300744; fax (3) 2302678; e-mail manager.public.affairs@hsbc.com.my; internet www.hsbc.com.my; f. 1860; fmrly Hongkong Bank Malaysia Bhd; adopted present name in 1999; cap. 304.5m., res 828.4m., dep. 20,502.8m. (Dec. 1999); Chair. ARMAN MEHTA

Malayan Banking Bhd (Maybank): Menara Maybank, 100 Jalan Tun Perak, 50050 Kuala Lumpur; POB 12010, 50936 Kuala Lumpur; tel. (3) 2308833; fax (3) 2302611; e-mail maybank@po.jaring.my; internet www.maybank.com.my/maybank; f. 1960; acquired Pacific Bank Bhd, Jan. 2001; merged with PhileoAllied Bank (Malaysia) Bhd, March 2001; cap. 2,308m., res 5,588m., dep. 57,581m. (Dec. 1999); Chair. Tan Sri MOHAMED BASIR BIN AHMAD; Man. Dir Datuk AMIRSHAM A. AZIZ; 264 domestic brs, 30 overseas brs.

OCBC Bank (Malaysia) Bhd: Tingkat 1–8, Wisma Lee Rubber, Jalan Melaka, 50100 Kuala Lumpur; POB 10197, 50100 Kuala Lumpur; tel. (3) 26920344; fax (3) 26926518; f. 1932; cap. 287.5m., res 1,438.5m., dep. 17,108.8m. (Dec. 2000); Chair. Tan Sri Dato' NASRUDDIN BAHARI; CEO ALBERT YEOH BEOW TIT; 25 brs.

Public Bank Bhd: Menara Public Bank, 146 Jalan Ampang, 50450 Kuala Lumpur; POB 12542, 50947 Kuala Lumpur; tel. (3) 21638888; fax (3) 21639917; internet www.publicbank.com.my; f. 1965; merged with Hock Hua Bank Bhd, March 2001; cap. 1,195.1m., res 2,429.6m., dep. 27,777.3m. (Dec. 2000); Chair. Tan Sri Dato' THONG YAW HONG; Pres. and CEO Tan Sri Dato' Dr TEH HONG PIOW; 213 domestic brs, 3 overseas brs.

RHB Bank Bhd: Towers Two and Three, RHB Centre, 426 Jalan Tun Razak, 50400 Kuala Lumpur; tel. (3) 9878888; fax (3) 9879000; e-mail md_ceo@rhbbank.com; internet www.rhbbank.com; formed in 1997 by a merger between DCB Bank Bhd and Kwong Yik Bank Bhd; officially took over Sime Bank Bhd in mid-1999; cap. 3,318.1m., res 1,218.6m., dep. 38,854.9m. (June 2000); Chair. Dato' ALI HASSAN; CEO YVONNE CHIA; 148 brs.

Southern Bank Bhd: 83 Medan Setia 1, Plaza Damamsara, Bukit Damansara, 50490 Kuala Lumpur; POB 12281, 50772 Kuala Lumpur; tel. (3) 2637000; fax (3) 2017305; e-mail info@sbbgroup.com.my; internet www.sbbgroup.com.my; f. 1963; merged with Ban Hin Lee Bank Bhd, July 2000; cap. 1,122.8m., res 765.7m., dep. 19,149.6m. (Dec. 2000); Chair. Tan Sri OSMAN S. CASSIM; CEO Dato' TAN TEONG HEAN; 105 domestic brs, 1 overseas br.

Standard Chartered Bank Malaysia Bhd: 1st Floor, 2 Jalan Ampang, 50450 Kuala Lumpur; tel. (3) 20726555; fax (3) 2010621; internet www.standardchartered.com.my.

United Overseas Bank (Malaysia) Bhd: Menara UOB, Jalan Raja Laut, POB 11212, 50738 Kuala Lumpur; tel. (3) 26927722; fax (3) 26981228; e-mail uobmtre@uobgrp.po.my; f. 1920; merged with Chung Khiaw Bank (Malaysia) Bhd in 1997; cap. 470m., res 785.4m., dep. 7,239.5m. (Dec. 1999); Chair. WEE EE CHEONG; Dir and CEO FRANCIS LEE CHIN YONG; 25 brs.

Sarawak

Bank Utama (Malaysia) Bhd: Lot 363, Jalan Kulas, POB 2049, 93400 Kuching; tel. (82) 419294; fax (82) 424954; e-mail utamab@tm.net.my; internet www.cmsb.com.my/ubg; f. 1976; cap. 800.0m., res 142.9m., dep. 4,657.5m. (Dec. 1999); Chair. Tan Sri Datuk AMAR MOHD JEMURI BIN SERJAN; Pres. and CEO ABDULLAH MAT NOH; 35 brs.

Merchant Banks

Affin Merchant Bank Bhd: Menara Boustead, 27th Floor, 69 Jalan Raja Chulan, POB 1124, 50200 Kuala Lumpur; tel. (3) 2423700; fax (3) 2424982; f. 1970 as Permata Chartered Merchant Bank Bhd; name changed as above March 2001; cap. 187.5m., res 168.9m., dep. 1,732.1m. (Dec. 2000); Chair. Tan Sri YAACOB MOHAMED ZAIN; CEO HASSAN HUSSEIN.

Alliance Merchant Bank Bhd: Menara Multi-Purpose, 20th Floor, Capital Sq., 8 Jalan Munshi Abdullah, 50100 Kuala Lumpur; tel. (3) 26927788; fax (3) 26928787; e-mail amanah@amanahb.po.my; f. 1974 as Amanah-Chase Merchant Bank Bhd; name changed as above Jan. 2001, following merger with Bumiputra Merchant Bankers Bhd; cap. 125.0m., res 42.5m., dep. 1,685.1m. (Dec. 1997); Chair. Dato' ABDUL KHALID BIN IBRAHIM; CEO AZMAN BIN YAHYA.

AmMerchant Bank Bhd: Bangunan Arab-Malaysian, 22nd Floor, 55 Jalan Raja Chulan, 50200 Kuala Lumpur; POB 10233, 50708 Kuala Lumpur; tel. (3) 2382633; fax (3) 2382842; e-mail jida@ammb.com.my; internet www.ambg.com.my; f. 1975; fmrly Arab-Malaysian Merchant Bank Bhd; cap. 292.5m., res 333.0m., dep. 13,423.9m. (March 2000); Chair. Tan Sri Dato' AZMAN HASHIM; Man. Dir CHEAH TEK KUANG; 4 brs.

Aseambankers Malaysia Bhd: Menara Maybank, 33rd Floor, 100 Jalan Tun Perak, 50050 Kuala Lumpur; POB 11057, 50734 Kuala Lumpur; tel. (3) 20591888; fax (3) 2384194; e-mail faudziah@aseam.com.my; f. 1973; cap. 50.1m., res 236.0m., dep. 2,616.6m. (June 2000); Man. Dir Encik AGIL NATT; Snr Gen. Mans ROZIDIN MASARI, WONG YOKE NYEN; 2 brs.

Commerce International Merchant Bankers Bhd: Commerce Sq., 10th–12th Floors, Jalan Semantan, Damansara Heights, 50490 Kuala Lumpur; tel. (3) 2536688; fax (3) 2535522; f. 1974; cap. 250.2m., res 544.3m., dep. 4,492.2m. (Dec. 2000); Chair. Dato' MOHAMED NOR BIN MOHAMED YOUSOF.

Malaysian International Merchant Bankers Bhd: Wisma Cyclecarri, 21st Floor, 288 Jalan Raja Laut, 50350 Kuala Lumpur; POB 12250, 50772 Kuala Lumpur; tel. (3) 26910200; fax (3) 26948388; f. 1970; cap. 75.0m., res 163.3m., dep. 1,887.0m. (March 2000); Chair. Tan Sri Dato' Ir WAN A. RAHMAN YAACOB; CEO YANG SHU-YIN; 2 brs.

RHB Sakura Merchant Bankers Bhd: 9th–13th Floors, RHB Centre, 426 Jalan Tun Razak, 50400 Kuala Lumpur; tel. (3) 9873888; fax (3) 9878000; f. 1974; cap. 60.0m., res 81.0m., dep. 4,045.4m. (Dec. 1996); Chair. Tan Sri Dato' ABDUL RASHID HUSSAIN; Man. Dir GEORGE RATILAL.

Southern Investment Bank Bhd: POB 10491, 50714 Kuala Lumpur; tel. (3) 20594188; fax (3) 20722964; e-mail sibb@sibb.com.my; internet www.sibb.com.my; f. 1988; fmrly Perdana Merchant Bankers Bhd; cap. 77.9m., res 47.7m., dep. 449.3m. (Dec. 1998); Chair. Dato' Nik IBRAHIM KAMIL; CEO YAP FAT (acting).

Utama Merchant Bank Bhd: Central Plaza, 27th Floor, Jalan Sultan Ismail, 50250 Kuala Lumpur; POB 12406, 50776 Kuala Lumpur; tel. (3) 2438888; fax (3) 2430357; e-mail umbb@umbb.po.my; internet www.cmsb.com.my; f. 1975 as Utama Wardley Bhd, name changed 1996; cap. 223.0m., res 63.6m., dep. 992.6m. (Dec. 1999); Chair. Nik HASHIM BIN Nik YUSOFF; CEO DONNY KWA SOO CHUAN; 1 br.

Co-operative Bank

Bank Kerjasama Rakyat Malaysia Berhad: Bangunan Bank Rakyat, Jalan Tangsi, Peti Surat 11024, 50732 Kuala Lumpur; tel. (3) 2985011; fax (3) 2985981; f. 1954; 83,095 mems. of which 823 were co-operatives (Dec. 1996); Chair. Dr YUSUF YACOB; Man. Dir Dato' ANUAR JAAFAR; 67 brs.

Development Banks

Bank Industri & Teknologi Malaysia Bhd (Industrial Development Bank of Malaysia): Level 28, Bangunan Bank Industri, Bandar Wawasan, 1016 Jalan Sultan Ismail, POB 10788, 50724 Kuala Lumpur; tel. (3) 26929088; fax (3) 26985701; e-mail pru@bankindustri.com.my; internet www.bankindustri.com.my; f. 1979; govt-owned; finances long-term, high-technology projects, shipping and shipyards and engineering (plastic, electrical and electronic); cap. 320.5m., res 10.1m., dep. 3,368.4m. (Dec. 1998); Chair. Tan Sri Datuk WIRA ABDUL RAHMAN ARSHAD; Man. Dir Encik MD NOOR YUSOFF.

Sabah Development Bank Bhd: SDB Tower, Wisma Tun Fuad Stephens, POB 12172, 88824 Kota Kinabalu, Sabah; tel. (88) 232177; fax (88) 261852; e-mail sdbank@po.jaring.my; internet www.borneo-online.com.my/sdb; f. 1977; wholly owned by State Government of Sabah; cap. 350m., res 152.1m., dep. 607.3m. (Dec. 2000); Chair. Datuk Haji HASSAN IBRAHIM; Man. Dir and CEO JIMMY DUIS.

Islamic Banks

Bank Islam Malaysia Bhd: Darul Takaful, 10th Floor, Jalan Sultan Ismail, 50250 Kuala Lumpur; POB 11080, 50734 Kuala Lumpur; tel. (3) 26935842; fax (3) 26922153; e-mail bislam@po.jaring.my; internet www.bankislam.com.my; f. 1983; cap. 500m., res 478.5m., dep. 7,350.5m. (June 2000); Chair. Dato' MOHAMED YUSOFF BIN MOHAMED NASIR; Man. Dir Dato' Haji AHMAD TAJUDIN ABDUL RAHMAN; 82 brs.

Bank Muamalat Malaysia Bhd: 21 Jalan Melaka, 50100 Kuala Lumpur; tel. (3) 26988787; e-mail webmaster@muamalat.com.my; internet www.muamalat.com.my; f. 1999; CEO TUAN Haji MOHD SHUKRI HUSSIN; 40 brs.

'Offshore' Banks

Abn Amro Bank, Labuan Branch: Level 9 (A), Main Office Tower, Financial Park Labuan, Jalan Merdeka, 87000 Labuan; tel. (87) 423008; fax (87) 421078; Man. WILLIAM YAP KIM SEONG.

AMInternational (L) Ltd: Level 12 (B), Block 4, Office Tower, Financial Park Labuan, Jalan Merdeka, 87000 Labuan; tel. (87) 413133; fax (87) 425211; e-mail felix-leong@ambg.com.my; internet www.ambg.com.my; CEO PAUL ONG WHEE SEN.

Asahi Bank Ltd, Labuan Branch: Level 12 (D), Main Office Tower, Financial Park Labuan, Jalan Merdeka, 87000 Labuan; tel. (87) 422516; fax (87) 422517; Gen. Man. SHINICHI HAYASHI.

Bank Islam (L) Ltd: Level 15, Block 4, Financial Park Labuan, Jalan Merdeka, 87000 Labuan; tel. (87) 451802; fax (87) 451800; e-mail bislamln@tm.net.my; CEO Y. M. Raja ZAINAL ALAM SHAH BIN Raja ABDULLAH OMAR.

Bank of America, National Trust and Savings Association, Labuan Branch: Level 13 (D), Main Office Tower, Financial Park Labuan, Jalan Merdeka, 87000 Labuan; tel. (87) 411778; fax (87) 424778; Man. IBRAHIM BIN NASIR.

Bank of Commerce (L) Ltd: Level 13 (A), Main Office Tower, Financial Park Labuan, Jalan Merdeka, 87000 Labuan; tel. (87) 410305; fax (87) 410313; Gen. Man. HARI PRASAD.

Bank of East Asia Ltd, Labuan Offshore Branch: Level 10 (C), Main Office Tower, Financial Park Labuan, Jalan Merdeka, 87000 Labuan; tel. (87) 451145; fax (87) 451148; e-mail bealbu@hkbea.com.my; Gen. Man. THOMAS WONG WAI YIP.

Bank of Nova Scotia, Labuan Branch: Level 10 (C2), Main Office Tower, Financial Park Labuan, Jalan Merdeka, 87000 Labuan; tel. (87) 451101; fax (87) 451099; Man. M. S. SEVILLA.

Bank of Tokyo-Mitsubishi Ltd, Labuan Branch: Level 12 (A & F), Main Office Tower, Financial Park Labuan, Jalan Merdeka, 87000 Labuan; tel. (87) 410487; fax (87) 410476; Gen. Man. SEITA TSUSHIMA.

Banque Nationale de Paris, Labuan Branch: Level 13 (C2), Main Office Tower, Financial Park Labuan, Jalan Merdeka, 87000 Labuan; tel. (87) 419103; fax (87) 419105; Gen. Man. CHUA PIN.

Barclays Bank PLC: Level 5A, Main Office Tower, Financial Park Labuan, Jalan Merdeka, 87000 Labuan; tel. (87) 425571; fax (87) 425575; e-mail barclay@tm.net.my; Man. MIAW SIAW LOONG.

Bayerische Landesbank Girozentrale, Labuan Branch: Level 14 (C), Block 4, Office Tower, Financial Park Labuan, Jalan Merdeka, 87000 Labuan; tel. (87) 422170; fax (87) 422175; e-mail blblab@tm.net.my; Exec. Vice-Pres., CEO and Gen. Man. LOUISE PAUL.

BNP Paribas, Labuan Branch: Level 9 (E), Main Office Tower, Financial Park Labuan, Jalan Merdeka, 87000 Labuan; tel. (3) 2458068; fax (3) 2458066; e-mail bnpkul@tm.net.my; Gen. Man. YAP SIEW YING.

Bumiputra Commerce International Trust: Level 14B, Main Office Tower, Financial Park Labuan, Jalan Merdeka, 87000 Labuan; tel. (87) 414252; fax (87) 411855; e-mail bumitrst@tm.net.my; Trust Officer NOR AZLI MOHD NOOR.

Chase Manhattan Bank, Labuan Branch: Level 5 (F), Main Office Tower, Financial Park Labuan, Jalan Merdeka, 87000 Labuan; tel. (87) 424384; fax (87) 424390; e-mail fauziah.hisham@chase.com; Gen. Man. PUAN FAUZIAH HISHAM.

Citibank Malaysia (L) Ltd: Level 11 (F), Main Office Tower, Financial Park Labuan, Jalan Merdeka, 87000 Labuan; tel. (87) 421181; fax (87) 419671; Gen. Man. CLARA LIM AI CHENG.

Commerzbank AG, Labuan Branch: Level 6 (E), Main Office Tower, Financial Park Labuan, Jalan Merdeka, 87000 Labuan; tel. (87) 416953; fax (87) 413542; Gen. Man. DENIS POO.

Crédit Agricole Indosuez, Labuan Branch: Level 11 (C), Main Office Tower, Financial Park Labuan, Jalan Merdeka, 87000 Labuan; tel. (87) 425118; fax (87) 424998; Gen. Man. BOON EONG TAN.

Crédit Lyonnais, Labuan Branch: Level 6 (B), Main Office Tower, Financial Park Labuan, Jalan Merdeka, 87000 Labuan; tel. (87) 408331; fax (87) 439133; Man. CLEMENT WONG.

Crédit Suisse First Boston, Labuan Branch: Level 10 (B), Main Office Tower, Financial Park Labuan, Jalan Merdeka, 87000 Labuan; tel. (87) 425381; fax (87) 425384; Gen. Man. TAN BOON EONG.

Dai-Ichi Kangyo Bank Ltd, Labuan Branch: Level 9 (B and C), Main Office Tower, Financial Park Labuan, Jalan Merdeka, 87000 Labuan; tel. (87) 419418; fax (87) 419424; Gen. Man. RYOICHI SHIMIZU.

Deutsche Bank AG, Labuan Branch: Level 14 (C), Main Office Tower, Financial Park Labuan, Jalan Merdeka, 87000 Labuan; tel. (87) 439811; fax (87) 439866; Gen. Man. GRACE WONG.

Development Bank of Singapore Ltd, Labuan Branch: Level 12 (E), Main Office Tower, Financial Park Labuan, Jalan Merdeka, 87000 Labuan; tel. (87) 423375; fax (87) 423376; Gen. Man. TAN CHEE CHEONG (acting).

Dresdner Bank AG, Labuan Branch: Level 13 (C), Main Office Tower, Financial Park Labuan, Jalan Merdeka, 87000 Labuan; tel. (87) 419271; fax (87) 419272; Gen. Man. JAMALUDIN NASIR.

First Commercial Bank, Labuan Branch: Main Office Tower, 6th Floor, Financial Park Labuan, Jalan Merdeka, 87000 Labuan; tel. (87) 451699; fax (87) 451366; Gen. Man. JAN REN-WEN.

Fuji Bank Ltd, Labuan Branch: Level 10 (A), Main Office Tower, Financial Park Labuan, Jalan Merdeka, 87000 Labuan; tel. (87) 417766; fax (87) 419766; Gen. Man. KEN UEDA.

Hongkong & Shanghai Banking Corporation, Offshore Banking Unit: Level 11 (D), Main Office Tower, Financial Park Labuan, Jalan Merdeka, 87000 Labuan; tel. (87) 417168; fax (87) 417169; Man. ROSLI RAHMAT.

Industrial Bank of Japan Ltd, Labuan Branch: Level 11 (A), Main Office Tower, Financial Park Labuan, Jalan Merdeka, 87000 Labuan; tel. (87) 419115; fax (87) 419121; Gen. Man. KOHEI OHGAKI.

ING Bank N.V.: Level 8 (B2), Main Office Tower, Financial Park Labuan, Jalan Merdeka, 87000 Labuan; tel. (87) 425733; fax (87) 425734; e-mail Jean-Francois.Gillard@Asia.ING.com; Gen. Man. JEAN-FRANCOIS GILLARD.

International Commercial Bank of China: Level 7 (E2), Main Office Tower, Financial Park Labuan, Jalan Merdeka, 87000 Labuan; tel. (87) 581688; fax (87) 581668; Gen. Man. YU CHENG HSIUNG.

J. P. Morgan Malaysia Ltd: Level 9 (G2), Main Office Tower, Financial Park Labuan, Jalan Merdeka, 87000 Labuan; tel. (87) 459000; fax (87) 451328; Gen. Man. RAMESH RAMANKUTTY NAIR.

KBC Bank N.V., Labuan Branch: Main Office Tower, 3rd Floor, Financial Park Labuan, Jalan Merdeka, 87000 Labuan; tel. (87) 581778; fax (87) 583787; Gen. Man. KONG KOK CHEE.

Lloyds TSB Bank PLC: Lot B, 11th Floor, Wisma Oceanic, Jalan OKK Awang Besar, 87007 Labuan; tel. (87) 418918; fax (87) 411928; e-mail labuan@lloydstsb; Dir and Gen. Man. BARRY FRANCIS LEA.

Maybank International (L) Ltd: Level 16 (B), Main Office Tower, Financial Park Labuan, Jalan Merdeka, 87000 Labuan; tel. (87) 414406; fax (87) 414806; e-mail millmit@tm.net.my; Gen. Man. RIDZUAN SALLEH.

Merrill Lynch Capital Markets Bank Ltd, Labuan Branch: Unit 4G, Level 4, Main Office Tower, Financial Park Labuan, Jalan Merdeka, 87000 Labuan; tel. (87) 453800; fax (87) 453808; Gen. Man. Dato' KAMARUDIN ABU.

Morgan Guaranty Trust Co of New York, Labuan Branch: Level 9 (G2), Main Office Tower, Financial Park Labuan, Jalan Merdeka, 87000 Labuan; tel. (87) 459000; fax (87) 451328; Gen. Man. RAMESH RAMANKUTTY NAIR.

Natexis Banque Populaires: Level 9 (G), Main Office Tower, Financial Park Labuan, Jalan Merdeka, 87000 Labuan; tel. (87) 581009; fax (87) 583009; Gen. Man. RIZAL ABDULLAH.

National Australia Bank, Labuan Branch: Level 12 (C2), Main Office Tower, Financial Park Complex, Jalan Merdeka, 87008 Labuan; tel. (87) 443286; fax (87) 443288; e-mail natausm@po.jaring.my; Gen. Man. GREG WARD.

Oversea-Chinese Banking Corporation Ltd: Level 8 (C), Main Office Tower, Financial Park Labuan, Jalan Merdeka, 87000 Labuan; tel. (87) 423381; fax (87) 423390; Gen. Man. BRYAN LO.

Overseas Union Bank Ltd, Labuan Branch: Level 13 (B), Main Office Tower, Financial Park Labuan, Jalan Merdeka, 87000 Labuan; tel. (87) 418909; fax (87) 411909; Gen. Man. DANIEL LOW THIEN SU.

Public Bank (L) Ltd: Level 8 (A and B), Main Office Tower, Financial Park Labuan, Jalan Merdeka, 87000 Labuan; tel. (87) 411898; fax (87) 413220; Man. ALEXANDER WONG.

Rabobank Nederland, Labuan Branch: Lot C, Level 7, Wisma Oceanic, Jalan OKK Awang Besar, 87007 Labuan; tel. (87) 423603; fax (87) 423607; Man. RICARDO BABA.

RHB Bank (L) Ltd: Level 15 (B), Main Office Tower, Financial Park Labuan, Jalan Merdeka, 87000 Labuan; tel. (87) 417480; fax (87) 417484; Gen. Man. TOH AY LENG.

Sanwa Bank Ltd, Labuan Branch: Level 10 (D), Main Office Tower, Financial Park Labuan, Jalan Merdeka, 87000 Labuan; tel. (87) 419200; fax (87) 419202; Gen. Man. YASUSHI ONUKI.

Sime International Bank (L) Ltd: Level 16 (A), Main Office Tower, Financial Park Labuan, Jalan Merdeka, 87000 Labuan; tel. (87) 417475; fax (87) 417470; CEO TEO KENG LEE.

Société Générale, Labuan Branch: Level 11 (B), Main Office Tower, Financial Park Labuan, Jalan Merdeka, 87000 Labuan; tel. (87) 421676; fax (87) 421669; Man. CHOW YING HOONG.

Standard Chartered Bank Offshore Labuan: Level 10 (F), Main Office Tower, Financial Park Labuan, Jalan Merdeka, 87000 Labuan; tel. (87) 417200; fax (87) 417202; Gen. Man. THOMAS LEE OY BENG.

Sumitomo Mitsui Banking Corpn, Labuan Branch: Level 12 (B & C), Main Office Tower, Financial Park Labuan, Jalan Merdeka, 87000 Labuan; tel. (87) 410955; fax (87) 410959; Gen. Man. TAKAYA LIDA.

Tat Lee Bank Ltd: Level 8 (D), Main Office Tower, Financial Park Labuan, Jalan Merdeka, 87000 Labuan; tel. (87) 451292; fax (87) 442292; Gen. Man. LIM TENG HO.

Tokai Bank Ltd, Labuan Branch: Level 7 (D), Main Office Tower, Financial Park Labuan, Jalan Merdeka, 87000 Labuan; tel. (87) 408025; fax (87) 419193; Gen. Man. SUSUMU ARAKI.

Union Bank of Switzerland, Labuan Branch: Level 5 (E), Main Office Tower, Financial Park Labuan Complex, Jalan Merdeka, 87000 Labuan; tel. (87) 421743; fax (87) 421746; Man. ZELIE HO SWEE LUM.

Union Européenne de CIC, Labuan Branch: Level 11 (C2), Main Office Tower, Financial Park Labuan, Jalan Merdeka, 87000 Labuan; tel. (87) 452008; fax (87) 452009; Gen. Man. YEOW TIANG HUI.

United Overseas Bank Ltd, Labuan Branch: Level 6A, Main Office Tower, Financial Park Labuan, Jalan Merdeka, 87000 Labuan; tel. (87) 424388; fax (87) 424389; Gen. Man. NG KEOK HU.

United World Chinese Commercial Bank: Level 3 (C), Main Office Tower, Financial Park Labuan, Jalan Merdeka, 87000 Labuan; tel. (87) 452168; fax (87) 453678; Gen. Man. THOMAS TANG TOR-TSAI.

Banking Associations

Association of Banks in Malaysia: UBN Tower, 17th Floor, 10 Jalan P. Ramlee, 50250 Kuala Lumpur; tel. (3) 2388041; fax (3) 2388004; Chair. AMIRSHAM A. AZIZ; Exec. Dir WONG SUAN LYE.

Institute of Bankers Malaysia: Wisma IBI, 5 Jalan Semantan, Damansara Heights, 50490 Kuala Lumpur; tel. (3) 20956833; fax (3) 20952322; e-mail ibbm@ibbm.org.my; internet www.ibbm.org.my; Chair. Tan Sri Dato' Dr ZETI AKHTAR AZIZ.

Malayan Commercial Banks' Association: POB 12001, 50764 Kuala Lumpur; tel. (3) 2983991.

Persatuan Institusi Perbankan Tanpa Faedah Malaysia (Association of Islamic Banking Institutions Malaysia—AIBIM): Tingkat 9, Menara Tun Razak, Jalan Raja Laut, 50350 Kuala Lumpur; tel. (3) 26932936; fax (3) 26910453; e-mail secretariat@aib-im.com.my; internet www.aibim.com.my.

STOCK EXCHANGES

Commodity and Monetary Exchange of Malaysia: Citypoint, Dayabumi Complex, 5th Floor, Jalan Sultan Hishamuddin, 50050 Kuala Lumpur; tel. (3) 2936822; fax (3) 2738057; e-mail inquiry@commex.com.my; internet www.commex.com.my; f. 1998 as a result of the merger of the Kuala Lumpur Commodity Exchange and the Malaysia Monetary Exchange Bhd; multi-product futures exchange trading mainly in palm oil (crude palm oil futures); Exec. Chair. Dato' SYED ABDUL JABBAR SHAHABUDIN; Gen. Man. RAGHBIR SINGH BHART.

Kuala Lumpur Stock Exchange (KLSE): Exchange Sq., Bukit Kewangan, 50200 Kuala Lumpur; tel. (3) 2067099; fax (3) 2063684; internet www.klse.com.my; f. 1973; in 1988 KLSE authorized the ownership of up to 49% of Malaysian stockbroking companies by foreign interests; 112 mems; 727 listed cos (June 1998); merged with Malaysian Exchange for Securities Dealing and Automated Quotation Bhd (MESDAQ) in March 2002; Chair. MOHAMAD AZLAN HASHIM; Pres. Dato' MOHD SALLEH BIN ABDUL MAJID.

Regulatory Authority

Securities Commission (SC): 3 Sri Semantan Satu, 50490 Kuala Lumpur; tel. (3) 2539988; fax (3) 2536184; e-mail cau@seccom.com.my; internet www.sc.com.my; f. 1993; Chair. Datuk ALI ABDUL KADIR.

INSURANCE

From 1988 onwards, all insurance companies were placed under the authority of the Central Bank, Bank Negara Malaysia. In 1997 there were 69 insurance companies operating in Malaysia; nine reinsurance companies, 11 composite, 40 general and life and two takaful insurance companies.

Principal Insurance Companies

Allianz Life Insurance Malaysia Bhd: Wisma UOA II, Floors 23 and 23A, 21 Jalan Pinang, 50450 Kuala Lumpur; tel. (3) 27166848; fax (3) 21633596; fmrly MBA Life Assurance Sdn Bhd; Chief Financial Officer CHARLES ONG ENG CHOW.

Asia Insurance Co Ltd: Bangunan Asia Insurance, 2 Jalan Raja Chulan, 50200 Kuala Lumpur; tel. (3) 2302511; fax (3) 2323606; f. 1923; general.

Capital Insurance Bhd: 38 Jalan Ampang, POB 12338, 50774 Kuala Lumpur; tel. (3) 2308033; fax (3) 2303657; Gen. Man. MOHD YUSOF IDRIS.

John Hancock Life Insurance (Malaysia) Bhd: Bangunan John Hancock, 6th Floor, Jalan Semantan, Damansara Heights, 50490 Kuala Lumpur; tel. (3) 2548055; fax (3) 2556291; life and non-life insurance; fmrly British American Life and General Insurance Bhd; Chair. Tun AZMI BIN Haji MOHAMED; Man. Dir ALEX FOONG SOO HAH.

Hong Leong Assurance Sdn Bhd: Wisma Hla, 18th Floor, Jalan Raja Chulan, 50200 Kuala Lumpur; tel. (3) 2421267; fax (3) 2414022; Man. CHIA AH KOW.

Jerneh Insurance Corpn Sdn Bhd: Wisma Jerneh, 12th Floor, 38 Jalan Sultan Ismail, POB 12420, 50788 Kuala Lumpur; tel. (3) 2427066; fax (3) 2426672; f. 1970; general; Gen. Man. GOH CHIN ENG.

Malaysia National Insurance Sdn Bhd: Tower 1, 26th Floor, MNI Twins, 11 Jalan Pinang, 50450 Kuala Lumpur; tel. (3) 2645000; fax (3) 2641010; internet www.mni.com.my; f. 1970; life and general; CEO SULAIMAN SALLEH.

Malaysian Co-operative Insurance Society Ltd: Wisma MCIS, Jalan Barat, 46200 Petaling Jaya, Selangor; tel. (3) 7552577; fax (3) 7571563; e-mail info@mcis.po.my; internet www.mcis.com.my/mcis; f. 1954; CEO L. MEYYAPPAN.

Mayban Assurance Bhd: 27 Lorong Medan Tuanku Satu, 50300 Kuala Lumpur; tel. (3) 2918777; fax (3) 2914930; e-mail mayassur@tm.net.my; internet www.maybangen.com.my; Man. KASSIM ZAKARIA.

MBf Insurans Sdn Bhd: Plaza MBf, 5th Floor, Jalan Ampang, POB 10345, 50710 Kuala Lumpur; tel. (3) 2613466; fax (3) 2613466; Man. MARC HOOI TUCK KOK.

Multi-Purpose Insurans Bhd: Menara Multi-Purpose, 9th Floor, Capital Square, 8 Jalan Munshi Abdullah, 50100 Kuala Lumpur; tel. (3) 26919888; fax (3) 26945758; e-mail info@mpib.com.my; fmrly Kompas Insurans Bhd; Man. LIUNG CHEONG POH.

Overseas Assurance Corpn Ltd: Wisma Lee Rubber, 21st Floor, Jalan Melata, 50100 Kuala Lumpur; tel. (3) 2022939; fax (3) 2912288; Gen. Man. A. K. WONG.

Progressive Insurance Sdn Bhd: Plaza Berjaya, 9th, 10th and 15th Floors, 12 Jalan Imbi, POB 10028, 50700 Kuala Lumpur; tel. (3) 2410044; fax (3) 2418257; Man. JERRY PAUT.

RHB Insurance Bhd: Tower 1, 4th Floor, RHB Centre, Jalan Tun Razak, 50450 Kuala Lumpur; tel. (3) 9812731; fax (3) 9812729; Man. MOHAMMAD ABDULLAH.

Sime AXA Assurance Bhd: Wisma Sime Darby, 15th Floor, Jalan Raja Laut, 50350 Kuala Lumpur; tel. (3) 2937888; fax (3) 2914672; e-mail hkkang@simenet.com; Gen. Man. HAK KOON KANG.

South-East Asia Insurance Bhd: Tingkat 9, Menara SEA Insurance, 1008 Jalan Sultan Ismail, 50250 Kuala Lumpur; POB 6120 Pudu, 55916 Kuala Lumpur; tel. (3) 2938111; fax (3) 2930111; internet www.sea.com.my; CEO HASHIM HARUN.

UMBC Insurans Sdn Bhd: Bangunan Sime Bank, 16th Floor, Jalan Sultan Sulaiman, 50000 Kuala Lumpur; tel. (3) 2328733; fax (3) 2322181; f. 1961; CEO ABDULLAH ABDUL SAMAD.

United Oriental Assurance Sdn Bhd: Wisma UOA, 36 Jalan Ampang, 50450 Kuala Lumpur; tel. (3) 2302828; fax (3) 2324250; e-mail uoa@uoa.po.my; f. 1976; CEO R. NESARETNAM.

Zürich Insurance (Malaysia) Bhd: Wisma Selangor Dredging, 4th Floor, South Block, 142A Jalan Ampang, 50450 Kuala Lumpur; tel. (3) 27133838; fax (3) 27133833; CEO MICHAEL WONG TECK KAT.

Trade and Industry

GOVERNMENT AGENCIES

Corporate Debt Restructuring Committee (CDRC): Kuala Lumpur; f. 1998 to restructure corporate and financial debt; Chair. C. RAJANDRAM.

Danamodal Nasional Bhd (Danamodal): Level 11 & 12, Block C, Bank Negara Malaysia, Jalan Dato' Onn, POB 10922, 50929 Kuala Lumpur; tel. (3) 2943954; fax (3) 2948632; e-mail dmodal2@tm.net.my; internet www.bnm.gov.my/danamodal/main2bck.htm; f. 1998 to recapitalize banks and restructure financial institutions, including arranging mergers and consolidations; Man. Dir MARIANUS VONG SHIN TZOI.

Federal Agricultural Marketing Authority (FAMA): Fama Point Bldg, Lot 17304, Jalan Persiaran 1, Bandar Baru Selayang, 68100 Batu Caves, Selangor Darul Ehsan; tel. (3) 61389622; fax (3) 61365597; f. 1965 to supervise, co-ordinate and improve existing markets and methods of marketing agricultural produce, and to seek and promote new markets and outlets for agricultural produce; Chair. SHAHIDAN KASSIM; Dir-Gen. Dr ABDUL AZIZ MOHAMED YAACOB.

Federal Land Development Authority (FELDA): Jalan Maktab, 54000 Kuala Lumpur; tel. (3) 2935066; fax (3) 2920087; f. 1956; govt statutory body formed to develop land into agricultural smallholdings to eradicate rural poverty; 893,150 ha of land developed (1994); involved in rubber, oil palm and sugar-cane cultivation; Chair. RAJA Tan Sri MUHAMMAD ALIAS; Dir-Gen. MOHAMED FADZIL YUNUS.

Khazanah Nasional: 21 Putra Place 100, Ilu Putra, 50350 Kuala Lumpur; e-mail knb@po.jaring.my; f. 1994; state-controlled investment co; assumed responsibility for certain assets fmrly under control of the Minister of Finance Inc.; holds 40% of Telekom Malaysia Bhd, 40% of Tenaga Nasional Bhd, 6.6% of HICOM Bhd and 17.8% of PROTON; Chair. Datuk Seri Dr MAHATHIR MOHAMAD.

Malaysia Export Credit Insurance Bhd: Bangunan Bank Industri, 17th Floor, Bandar Wawsan, 1016 Jalan Sultan Ismail, POB 11048, 50734 Kuala Lumpur; tel. (3) 26910677; fax (3) 26910353; e-mail mecib@mecib.com.my; internet www.mecib.com.my; f. 1977; wholly-owned subsidiary of Bank Industri Malaysia Technologi Bhd; provides insurance, financial guarantee and other trade-related services for exporters of locally manufactured products and for banking community; cap. RM 150m., exports declared RM 740m. (2001); Gen. Man. EN. AMINURRASHID ZULKIFLY; 67 employees.

Malaysia External Trade Development Corpn (MATRADE): Wisma Sime Darby, Jalan Raja Laut, 50350 Kuala Lumpur; tel. (3) 26947259; fax (3) 26947362; e-mail info@hq.matrade.gov.my; internet www.matrade.gov.my; f. 1993; responsibility for external trade development and promotion; CEO MERLYN KASIMIR.

Malaysian Institute of Economic Research: Menara Dayabumi, 9th Floor, Jalan Sultan Hishamuddin, POB 12160, 50768 Kuala Lumpur; tel. (3) 22725897; fax (3) 22730197; e-mail Admin@mier.po.my; internet www.mier.org.my; Exec. Dir MOHAMED ARIFF.

Malaysian Palm Oil Board (MPOB): Lot 6, SS6, Jalan Perbandaran, 47301 Kelana Jaya, Selangor; tel. (3) 7035544; fax (3) 7033533; internet porla.gov.my; f. 2000 by merger of Palm Oil Registration and Licensing Authority and Palm Oil Research Institute of Malaysia; Dir-Gen. Dato' MOHD YUSOF BASIR.

Malaysian Timber Industry Board (Lembaga Perindustrian Kayu Malaysia): 13-17 Menara PGRM, Jalan Pudu Ulu, POB 10887, 50728 Kuala Lumpur; tel. (3) 9822235; fax (3) 9851477; e-mail mtib@po.jaring.my; internet www.gov.my; f. 1968 to promote and regulate the export of timber and timber products from Peninsular Malaysia; Chair. Dato' Dr Haji ABDULLAH BIN MOHD TAHIR; Dir-Gen. Dato' Haji ABDUL RASHID MAT AMIN.

Muda Agricultural Development Authority (MADA): MADA HQ, Ampang Jajar, 05990 Alor Setar, Kedah; tel. (4) 7728255; fax (4) 7722667; internet www.mada.gov.my; Chair. Dato' Seri SYED RAZAK BIN SYED ZAIN.

National Economic Action Council: NEAC-MTEN, Office of the Minister of Special Functions, Level 2, Block B5, Federal Government Administrative Centre, 62502 Putrajaya, Selangor Darul Ehsan; tel. (88) 883333; internet www.neac.gov.my/; Exec. Dir Dato' MUSTAPA MOHAMED.

National Information Technology Council (NITC): Kuala Lumpur; Sec. Datuk Tengku Dr MOHD AZZMAN SHARIFFADEEN.

National Timber Certification Council: Kuala Lumpur; Chair. CHEW LYE TENG.

Pengurusan Danaharta Nasional Bhd (Danaharta): Tingkat 10, Bangunan Setia 1, 15 Lorong Dungun, Bukit Damansara, 50490 Kuala Lumpur; tel. (3) 2531122; fax (3) 2537482; internet www.danaharta.com.my; f. 1998 to acquire non-performing loans from the banking sector and to maximize the recovery value of those assets; Man. Dir Dato' AZMAN YAHYA.

Perbadanan Nasional Bhd (PERNAS): Kuala Lumpur; tel. (3) 2935177; f. 1969; govt-sponsored; promotes trade, banking, property and plantation development, construction, mineral exploration, steel manufacturing, inland container transportation, mining, insurance, industrial development, engineering services, telecommunication equipment, hotels and shipping; cap. p.u. RM 116.25m.; 10 wholly-owned subsidiaries, over 60 jointly-owned subsidiaries and 18 assoc. cos; Chair. Tunku Dato' SHAHRIMAN BIN Tunku SULAIMAN; Man. Dir Dato' A. RAHMAN BIN HAMIDON.

DEVELOPMENT ORGANIZATIONS

Fisheries Development Authority of Malaysia: Tingkat 7, Wisma PKNS, Jalan Raja Laut, Peti Surat 12630, 50784 Kuala Lumpur; tel. (3) 2924044; fax (3) 2911931; e-mail info@kim.moa.my.

Johor Corporation: 13th Floor, Menara Johor Corporation, Kotaraya, 80000Johor Bahru; tel. (7) 2232692; fax (7) 2233175; e-mail pdnjohor@jcorp.com.my; internet www.jcorp.com.my; development agency of the Johor state govt; Chief Exec. Dato' H. MUHAMMAD ALI.

Kumpulan FIMA Bhd (Food Industries of Malaysia): Kompleks FIMA, International Airport, Subang, Selangor; tel. (3) 7462199; f. 1972; fmrly govt corpn, transferred to private sector in 1991;

promotes food and related industry through investment on its own or by co-ventures with local or foreign entrepreneurs; oil palm, cocoa and fruit plantation developments; manufacturing and packaging, trading, supermarkets and restaurants; Man. Dir Dato' MOHD NOOR BIN ISMAIL; 1,189 employees.

Majlis Amanah Rakyat (MARA) (Trust Council for the People): MEDAN MARA Bldg, 13th Floor, Jalan Raja Laut, 50609 Kuala Lumpur; tel. (3) 2915111; fax (3) 2913620; f. 1966 to promote, stimulate, facilitate and undertake economic and social development; to participate in industrial and commercial undertakings and jt ventures; Chair. Tan Sri NAZRI AZIZ.

Malaysian Industrial Development Authority (MIDA): Wisma Damansara, 6th Floor, Jalan Semantan, POB 10618, 50720 Kuala Lumpur; tel. (3) 2553633; fax (3) 2557970; e-mail promotion@mida.gov.my; internet www.mida.gov.my; f. 1967; Chair. Tan Sri Datuk ZAINAL ABIDIN BIN SULONG; Dir-Gen. Dato' ZAINUN AISHAH AHMAD.

Malaysian Industrial Development Finance Bhd: 195A Jalan Tun Razak, POB 12110, 50939 Kuala Lumpur; tel. (3) 2610066; fax (3) 2615973; f. 1960 by the Govt, banks, insurance cos; industrial financing, advisory services, project development, merchant and commercial banking services; Chair. Tan Sri Dato' Seri AHMAD SARJI BIN ABDUL HAMID; CEO and Dir DARWIS BIN MOHD DAEK.

Malaysian Pepper Marketing Board: Tanah Putih, POB 1653, 93916 Kuching; tel. (82) 331811; fax (82) 336877; e-mail pmb@pepper.po.my; internet www.sarawakpepper.gov.my/sarawakpepper; f. 1972; responsible for the statutory grading of all Sarawak pepper for export, licensing of pepper dealers and exporters, trading and the development and promotion of pepper grading, storage and processing facilities; Gen. Man. ANANDAN ABDULLAH.

Pinang Development Corporation: Pinang; development agency of the Pinang state government; Gen. Man. SITI BALKISH BIN SHARIFF.

Sarawak Economic Development Corpn: Menara SEDC, 6th–11th Floors, Sarawak Plaza, Jalan Tunku Abdul Rahman, POB 400, 93902 Kuching; tel. (82) 416777; fax (82) 424330; f. 1972; statutory org. responsible for commercial and industrial development in Sarawak either solely or jtly with foreign and local entre preneurs; responsible for the development of tourism infrastructure; Chair. Haji TALIB ZULPILIP.

Selangor State Development Corporation (PKNS): f. 1964; partially govt-owned; Corporate Man. YUSOF OTHMAN.

CHAMBERS OF COMMERCE

The Associated Chinese Chamber of Commerce: Wisma Chamber, 4th Floor, Lot 214, Jalan Bukit Mata, 93100 Kuching; tel. (82) 428815; fax (82) 429950; e-mail kcjong@pc.jaring.my; f. 1965; Pres. TIONG SU KOUK; Sec. Gen. LEE KHIM SIN.

Associated Chinese Chambers of Commerce and Industry of Malaysia: 8th Floor, Office Tower, Plaza Berjaya, 12 Jalan Imbi, 55100 Kuala Lumpur; tel. (3) 2452503; fax (3) 2452562; e-mail acccim@mol.net.my; internet www.acccim.org.my; Pres. Dato' LIM GUAN TEIK; Exec. Sec. ONG KIM SENG.

Malay Chamber of Commerce and Industry of Malaysia: Plaza Pekeliling, 17th Floor, Jalan Tun Razak, 50400 Kuala Lumpur; tel. (3) 4418522; fax (3) 4414502; Pres. Tan Sri Dato' TAJUDIN RAMLI; Sec.-Gen. ZAKI SAID.

Malaysian Associated Indian Chambers of Commerce and Industry: 116 Jalan Tuanku Abdul Rahman, 2nd Floor, 50100 Kuala Lumpur; tel. (3) 26931033; fax (3) 26911670; e-mail klsicci@po.jaring.my; internet www.maicci.com; f. 1950; Pres. Dato' K. KENNETH ESWARAN; Hon. Sec.-Gen. MUTHUSAMY V. V. M. SAMY; 8 brs.**Malaysian International Chamber of Commerce and Industry (MICCI)** (Dewan Perniagaan dan Perindustrian Antarabangsa Malaysia): C-8-8, 8th Floor, Block C, Plaza Mont' Kiara, 50480 Kuala Lumpur; tel. (3) 62017708; fax (3) 62017705; e-mail micci@micci.com; internet www.micci.com; f. 1837; brs in Pinang, Perak, Johor, Melaka and Sabah; 1,100 corporate mems; Pres. P. J. DINGLE; Exec. Dir STEWART J. FORBES.

National Chamber of Commerce and Industry of Malaysia: 37 Jalan Kia Peng, 50450 Kuala Lumpur; tel. (3) 2419600; fax (3) 2413775; e-mail nccim@po.jaring.my; internet www.nccim.org.my/nccim; f. 1962; Pres. Tan Sri TAJUDIN RAMLI; Sec.-Gen. Dato' ABDUL HALIM ABDULLAH.

Sabah Chamber of Commerce and Industry: Jalan Tiga, Sandakan; tel. (89) 2141; Pres. T. H. WONG.

Sarawak Chamber of Commerce and Industry (SCCI): POB A-841, Kenyalang Park Post Office, 93806 Kuching; tel. (82) 237148; fax (82) 237186; e-mail phtay@pc.jaring.my; internet www.cmsb.com.my/scci; f. 1950; Chair. Datuk Haji MOHAMED AMIN Haji SATEM; Dep. Chair. Datuk ABANG Haji ABDUL KARIM Tun ABANG Haji OPENG.

South Indian Chamber of Commerce of Sarawak: 37C India St, Kuching; f. 1952; Pres. HAJA NAZIMUDDIN BIN ABDUL MAJID; Vice-Pres. SYED AHMAD.

INDUSTRIAL AND TRADE ASSOCIATIONS

Federation of Malaysian Manufacturers: Wisma FMM, 3 Persiaran Dagang, PJU 9 Bandar Sri Damansara, 52200 Kuala Lumpur; tel. (3) 6361211; fax (3) 6341266; e-mail webmaster@fmm.org.my; internet www.fmm.org.my; f. 1968; 2,036 mems (Feb. 2000); Pres. JEN (B.) Tan Sri Dato' ZAIN HASHIM; CEO LEE CHENG SUAN.

Federation of Rubber Trade Associations of Malaysia: 138 Jalan Bandar, 50000 Kuala Lumpur; tel. (3) 2384006.

Malayan Agricultural Producers' Association: Kuala Lumpur; tel. (3) 42573988; fax (3) 42573113; f. 1997; 464 mem. estates and 115 factories; Pres. Tan Sri Dato' Haji BASIR BIN ISMAIL; Dir MOHAMAD BIN AUDONG.

Malaysian Iron & Steel Industry Federation: 28E, 30E, 5th Floor, Block 2, Worldwide Business Park, Jalan Tinju 13/50, Section 13, 40675 Shah Alam, Selangor; tel. (3) 55133970; fax (3) 55133891; e-mail misif@po-jaring.my; Chair. Tan Sri Dato' SOONG SIEW HOONG; 125 mems.

Malaysian Oil Palm Growers' Council: Bangunan Getah Asli I, 3rd Floor, 148 Jalan Ampang, POB 10747, 50724 Kuala Lumpur; tel. (3) 2615088; fax (3) 2612504; f. 1953.

The Malaysian Pineapple Industry Board: Wisma Nanas, 5 Jalan Padi Mahsuri, Bandar Baru UDA, 81200 Johor Bahru; tel. (7) 2361211; fax (7) 2365694; e-mail mpib@tm.net.my; Dir Gen. Tuan Haji ISMAIL BIN ABD JAMAL.

The Malaysian Rubber Products Manufacturers' Association: 1 Jalan USJ 11/1J, Subang Jaya, 47620 Petaling Jaya, Selangor; tel. (3) 56316150; fax (3) 56316152; e-mail mrpma@po.jaring.my; internet www.mrpma.com; f. 1952; Pres. Tan Sri Datuk ARSHAD AYUB; 144 mems.

Malaysian Rubber Board: 20 Jalan Ampang, 50450 Kuala Lumpur; tel. (3) 4567033; fax (3) 4573512; f. 1998; implements policies and development programmes to ensure the viability of the Malaysian rubber industry; regulates the industry (in particular, the packing, grading, shipping and export of rubber); Dir-Gen. Datuk Dr ABDUL AZIZ BIN S. A. KADIR.

National Tobacco Board Malaysia (Ibu Pejabat Lembaga Tembakau Negara): Kubang Kerian, POB 198, 15720 Kota Bharu, Kelantan; tel. (9) 7652933; fax (9) 7655640; e-mail ltnm@ltn.gov.my; Dir-Gen. TEO HUI BEK.

Northern Malaya Rubber Millers and Packers Association: 22 Pitt St, 3rd Floor, Suites 301–303, 10200 Pinang; tel. (4) 620037; f. 1919; 153 mems; Pres. HWANG SING LUE; Hon. Sec. LEE SENG KEOK.

Palm Oil Refiners' Association of Malaysia (PORAM): Kuala Lumpur; tel. (3) 2488893; f. 1975 to promote the palm oil refining industry; Chair. Datuk ROBERT W. K. CHAN; 27 mems.

Rubber Industry Smallholders' Development Authority (RISDA): 4½ Miles, Jalan Ampang, 50450 Kuala Lumpur; tel. (3) 4564022; Dir-Gen. MOHD ZAIN BIN Haji YAHYA.

Timber Trade Federation of Malaysia: 19d, 19th Floor, Menara PGRM, 8 Jalan Pudu Ulu, Cheras, 56100 Kuala Lumpur; tel. (3) 9872152; fax (3) 9811985; e-mail mpma@tm.net.my.

Tin Industry Research and Development Board: West Block, 8th Floor, Wisma Selangor Dredging, Jalan Ampang, POB 12560, 50782 Kuala Lumpur; tel. (3) 21616171; fax (3) 21616179; e-mail mcom@po.jaring.my; Chair. SUKOR BIN SHAHAR; Sec. MUHAMAD NOR MUHAMAD.

EMPLOYERS' ORGANIZATIONS

Malaysian Employers' Federation: 3A06–3A07, Block A, Pusat Dagangan Phileo Damansara II, 15 Jalan 16/11, off Jalan Damansara, 46350 Petaling Jaya, Selangor; tel. (3) 79557778; fax (3) 79559008; e-mail mef-hq@mef.po.my; internet www.mef.org.my; f. 1959; Pres. JAFAR ABDUL CARRIM; private-sector org. incorporating 10 employer organizations and 3,447 individual enterprises, including:

Association of Insurance Employers: c/o Royal Insurance (M) Sdn Bhd, Menara Boustead, 5th Floor, 69 Jalan Raja Chulan, 50200 Kuala Lumpur; tel (3) 2410233; fax (3) 2442762; Pres. NG KIM HOONG.

Commercial Employers' Association of Peninsular Malaysia: c/o The East Asiatic Co (M) Bhd, 1 Jalan 205, 46050 Petaling Jaya, Selangor; tel. (3) 7913322; fax (3) 7913561; Pres. HAMZAH Haji GHULAM.

Malayan Commercial Banks' Association: see Banking Associations, above.

Malaysian Chamber of Mines: West Block, Wisma Selangor Dredging, 8th Floor, Jalan Ampang, 50350 Kuala Lumpur; tel. and fax (3) 21616171; e-mail mcom@po.jaring.my; internet www.mcom.com.my; f. 1914; promotes and protects interests of Malaysian mining industry; Pres. Ir ABDUL RAHMAN DAHAN; Exec. Dir MUHAMAD NOR MUHAMAD.

Malaysian Textile Manufacturers' Association: Wisma Selangor Dredging, 9th Floor, West Block, 142C Jalan Ampang, 50450 Kuala Lumpur; tel. (3) 21621587; fax (3) 21623953; e-mail textile@po.jaring.my; internet www.fashion-asia.com; Pres. BAHAR AHMAD; Exec. Dir CHOY MING BIL; 230 mems.

Pan Malaysian Bus Operators' Association: 88 Jalan Sultan Idris Shah, 30300 Ipoh, Perak; tel. (5) 2549421; fax (5) 2550858; Sec. Datin TEOH PHAIK LEAN.

Sabah Employers' Consultative Association: Dewan SECA, No. 4, Block A, 1st Floor, Bandar Ramai-Ramai, 90000 Sandakan, Sabah; tel. and fax (89) 272846; Pres. E. M. KHOO.

Stevedore Employers' Association: 5 Pengkalan Weld, POB 288, 10300 Pinang; tel. (4) 2615091; Pres. ABDUL RAHMAN MAIDIN.

UTILITIES

Electricity

Electricity Supply Department: Kuala Lumpur; regulatory body supervising electricity supply.

Tenaga Nasional Bhd: 129 Jalan Bangsar, POB 11003, 50732 Kuala Lumpur; tel. (3) 2825566; fax (3) 2823274; e-mail webadmin @tnb.com.my; internet www.tnb.com.my; f. 1990 through the corporatization and privatization of the National Electricity Board; 53% govt-controlled; generation, transmission and distribution of electricity in Peninsular Malaysia; generating capacity of 7,573 MW (65% of total power generation); also purchases power from 12 licensed independent power producers; Chair. JAMALUDDIN JARIS; CEO Dato' FUAD B. JAAFAR (acting).

Sabah Electricity Board (SEB): Wisma Lembaga Letrik Sabah, 88673 Kota Kinabalu; tel. (88) 211699; generation, transmission and distribution of electricity in Sabah.

Sarawak Electricity Supply Corpn (SESCO): POB 149, Kuching, Sarawak; tel. (82) 441188; fax (82) 444434; generation, transmission and distribution of electricity in Sarawak.

Gas

Gas Malaysia Sdn Bhd: West Block, Wisma Selangor Dredging, 1st Floor, 142C Jalan Ampang, POB 12968, 50794 Kuala Lumpur; tel. (3) 2632333; fax (3) 2633208; f. 1992; Chair. Tan Sri Dato' IBRAHIM MENUDIN; CEO AHMAD DAMANHURI ABDUL RAHIM.

Water

Under the federal Constitution, water supply is the responsibility of the state Governments. In 1998, owing to water shortages, the National Water Resources Council was established to co-ordinate management of water resources at national level. Malaysia's sewerage system is operated by Indah Water Konsortium, owned by Prime Utilities.

National Water Resources Council: c/o Ministry of Works, Jalan Sultan Salahuddin, 50580 Kuala Lumpur; tel. (3) 2919011; fax (3) 2986612; f. 1998 to co-ordinate management of water resources at national level through co-operation with state water boards; Chair. Dato' Seri Dr MAHATHIR BIN MOHAMAD.

Regulatory Authorities

Johor State Regulatory Body: c/o Pejabat Setiausaha Kerajaan Negeri Johor, Aras 1, Bangunan Sultan Ibrahim, Jalan Bukit Timbalan, 80000 Johor Bahru; tel. (7) 223850; Dir Tuan Haji OMAR BIN AWAB.

Kelantan Water Department: Tingkat Bawah Blok 6, Kota Darul Naim, 15503 Kota Bahru, Kelantan; tel. (9) 7475240; Dir Tuan Haji WAN ABDUL AZIZ BIN WAN JAAFAR.

Water Supply Authorities

Kedah Public Works Department: Bangunan Sultan Abdul Halim, Jalan Sultan Badlishah, 05582 Alor Setar, Kedah; tel. (4) 7334041; fax (4) 7341616; Dir Dr NORDIN BIN YUNUS.

Kelantan Water Sdn Bhd: 14 Beg Berkunci, Jalan Kuala Krai, 15990 Kota Bahru, Kelantan; tel. (10) 9022222; fax (10) 9022236; Dir PETER NEW BERKLEY.

Kuching Water Board: Jalan Batu Lintang, 93200 Kuching, Sarawak; tel. (82) 240371; fax (82) 244546; Dir DAVID YEU BIN TONG.

Labuan Public Works Department: Jalan Kg. Jawa, POB 2, 87008 Labuan; tel. (87) 414040; fax (87) 412370; Dir Ir ZULKIFLY BIN MADON.

LAKU Management Sdn Bhd: Soon Hup Tower, 6th Floor, Lot 907, Jalan Merbau, 98000 Miri; tel. (85) 442000; fax (85) 442005; e-mail chuilin@pd.jaring.my; serves Miri, Limbang and Bintulu; CEO YONG CHIONG VAN.

Melaka Water Corpn: Tingkat Bawah, 1 10–13, Graha Maju, Jalan Graha Maju, 75300 Melaka; tel. (6) 2825233; fax (6) 2837266; Ir ABDUL RAHIM SHAMSUDI.

Negeri Sembilan Water Department: Wisma Negeri, 70990 Seremban; tel. (6) 7622314; fax (6) 7620753; Ir Dr MOHD AKBAR.

Pahang Water Supply Department (Jabatan Bekalan Air Pahang): 9–10 Kompleks Tun Razak, Bandar Indera Mahkota, 25582 Kuantan, Pahang; tel. (9) 5721222; fax (9) 5721221; e-mail p-jba@pahang.gov.my; Dir Ir Haji ISMAIL BIN Haji MAT NOOR.

Pinang Water Supply Department: Level 29, KOMTAR, 10000 Pinang; tel. (4) 6505462; fax (4) 2645282; e-mail lyc@sukpp.gov.my; f. 1973; Gen. Man. Datuk Ir LEE YOW CHING.

Perak Water Board: Jalan St John, Peti Surat 589, 30760 Ipoh, Perak; tel. (5) 2551155; fax (5) 2556397; Dir Ir SANI BIN SIDIK.

Sabah Water Department: Wisma MUIS, Blok A, Tingkat 6, Beg Berkunci 210, 88825 Kota Kinabalu; tel. (88) 232364; fax (88) 232396; Man. Ir BENNY WANG.

SAJ Holdings Sdn Bhd: Bangunan Ibu Pejabat, SAJH, Jalan Garuda, Larkin, 80350 Johor Bahru; tel. (7) 2244040; fax (7) 2234060; internet www.saj.com.my; f. 1999; Exec. Chair. Dir Dato' Haji HAMDAN BIN MOHAMED.

Sarawak Public Works Department: Wisma Seberkas, Jalan Tun Haji Openg, 93582 Kuching; tel. (82) 244041; fax (82) 429679; Dir MICHAEL TING KUOK NG.

Selangor Water Department: POB 5001, Jalan Pantai Baru, 59990 Kuala Lumpur; tel. (3) 2826244; fax (3) 2827535; f. 1972; Dir Ir LIEW WAI KIAT.

Sibu Water Board: Km 5, Jalan Salim, POB 405, 96007 Sibu, Sarawak; tel. (84) 211001; fax (84) 211543; e-mail pengurus @swb.po.my; Man. DANIEL WONG PARK ING.

Terengganu Water Department: Tkt 3, Wisma Negeri, Jalan Pejabat, 20200 Kuala Terengganu; tel. (9) 6222444; fax (9) 6221510; Ir Haji WAN NGAH BIN WAN.

MAJOR COMPANIES

The following are among the major industrial undertakings in Malaysia (cap. = capital; res = reserves; m. = million; amounts in ringgit Malaysia):

Aluminium Co of Malaysia Bhd: Lot 8, Jalan Universiti, 46200 Petaling Jaya, Selangor Darul Ehsan; POB 1096, 46870 Petaling Jaya, Selangor Darul Ehsan; tel. (3) 79561588; fax (3) 79564940; e-mail kok-heng.chan@alcan.com; f. 1960; mfrs of aluminium sheet, foil and extruded and fabricated products; cap. and res 214.0m., sales 283.7m. (1999); Man. Dir TSUYOSHI NAKAJIMA; 820 employees.

Amsteel Corpn Bhd: Menara Lion, 46th Floor, 165 Jalan Ampang, 50450 Kuala Lumpur; tel. (3) 21622155; fax (3) 21641036; internet www.lion.com.my; f. 1974; mfrs of steel and steel products, assembly of motor cycle engines, etc.; cap. and res 105.2m., sales 5,134.7m. (1998/99); Chair. Gen. Tan Sri Dato' ZAIN HASHIM; Man. Dir WILLIAM H. J. CHENG; 14,649 employees.

Arab-Malaysian Development Bhd: Bangunan AMDB, 20th Floor, 1 Jalan Lumut, 50400 Kuala Lumpur; tel. (3) 4432311; fax (3) 4430311; e-mail amdb@po.jaring/my; internet www.ambg.com.my; f. 1965; mfrs and exporters of cotton and finished fabrics; cap. and res 367.3m., sales 343.4m. (1998/99); Chair. Tan Sri Dato' AZMAN HASHIM; Man. Dir FOONG WING LING; 2,028 employees.

Asiatic Development Bhd: Wisma Genting, 24th Floor, Jalan Sultan Ismail, 50250 Kuala Lumpur; tel. (3) 2612288; fax (3) 2616149; internet www.asiatic.com.my; plantation and property development, food production; cap. and res 1,048.8m., sales 446.8m. (1999); Chair. Tan Sri MOHD AMIN BIN OSMAN; Chief Execs Tan Sri LIM KOK THAY, Dato' BAHARUDDIN BIN MUSA; 4,544 employees.

Berjaya Group Bhd: Menara Shahzan Insas, 17th Floor, 30 Jalan Sultan Ismail, 50250 Kuala Lumpur; tel. (3) 9358888; fax (3) 2432246; e-mail judytan@berjaya.com.my; internet www.berjaya .com.my; f. 1967; mfg, commercial and residential property, insurance and finance; cap. and res –156.8m., sales 7,272.5m. (1998/99); Chair. and CEO Tan Sri Dato' VINCENT TAN CHEE YIOUN; Man. Dir Dato' DANNY TAN CHEE SING; 22,300 employees.

British American Tobacco (Malaysia) Bhd: Virginia Park, Jalan Universiti, 46200 Petaling Jaya, Selangor Darul Ehsan; tel. (3) 79566899; fax (3) 79558416; internet www.batmalaysia.com; cigarette and other tobacco products mfrs; cap. and res 405.8m., sales 3,010m. (2001); Chair. Tan Sri ABU TALIB BIN OTHMAN; 1,400 employees.

Carlsberg Brewery Malaysia Bhd: 55 Persiaran Selangor, Section 15, 40000 Shah Alam, Selangor; POB 10617, Kuala Lumpur; tel. (3) 55191621; fax (3) 55191931; e-mail info@carlsberg.com.my; internet www.carlsberg.com.my; brewers of beer and stout; cap. and res 380.9m., sales 842m. (1999); Chair. MICHAEL IUUL; Man. Dir Dato' JORGEN BORNHOFT; 650 employees.

Cement Industries of Malaysia Bhd: Bukit Ketri, Mukim of Chuping, 02450 Kangar, Perlis; tel. (4) 9382006; fax (4) 9382722; e-mail coo@pc.jaring.my; internet www.cima.com.my; f. 1975; mfrs of cement and investment holding; cap. and res 642.9m., sales 224.7m. (1999); Chair. Dato' Dr YAHA BIN ISMAIL; Man. Dir Dato' BADARUDIN KHALID; 500 employees.

Chocolate Products (Malaysia) Bhd: Menara Lion, 46th Floor, 165 Jalan Ampang, 50450 Kuala Lumpur; tel. (3) 2622155; fax (3) 7033104; internet www.lion.com.my; mfrs of chocolate and related products, cocoa butter, cocoa powder and snacks, property development and investment holding; cap. and res 586.5m., sales 683.5m. (1998/99); Chair. Tan Sri WILLIAM H. J. CHENG; Man. Dir WONG YOKE LIN; 700 employees.

CSM Corpn Bhd: Menara Cold Storage, 10th Floor, Jaya Shopping Centre, Jalan Semangat, 46100 Petaling Jaya, Selangor; tel. (3) 79588888; fax (3) 79581289; f. 1903; mfrs of ice cream, UHT and non-carbonated drinks, butter and dairy spreads, ghee, margarine, squashes, cordials, ice and meat products; operates retail supermarkets, pharmacies and shopping arcades; imports and distributes refrigerated and non-refrigerated foods, beverages and pharmaceuticals; cap. and res 322.8m., sales 218.7m. (1998); Chair. Dato' ABDUL RAHMAN BIN HAMZAH; Chief Exec. GAN GWO CHYANG; 700 employees.

Cycle and Carriage Bintang Bhd: Lot 9, Jalan 219, Federal Highway, 46100 Petaling Jaya, Selangor; tel. (3) 79572422; fax (3) 79560593; internet www.cyclecarriage.com.my; f. 1967; franchise holders for Mercedes Benz and Mazda commercial and passenger vehicles; cap. and res 546.8m., sales 661.1m. (2000); Chair. Tan Sri Dato' ABDUL BIN ALI; Man. Dir MOHAMAD Haji HASAN; 1,264 employees.

DMIB Bhd: 4 Jalan Tandang, 46050 Petaling Jaya, POB 66, Selangor; tel. (3) 7918833; fax (3) 7925414; e-mail info@dmi.com.my; internet www.dmi.com.my; f. 1961; mfrs of a complete range of Dunlop tyres, chemical products, industrial gloves, mattresses and golf balls; cap. and res 270.5m., sales 615.6m., (1999/2000); Chair. Tunku Tan Sri Dato' Seri AHMAD BIN Tunku YAHAYA; Man. Dir JAFAR BIN ABDUL CARRIM; 1,800 employees.

Esso Malaysia Bhd: Menara Esso, 28th Floor, off Jalan Kia Peng, 50450 Kuala Lumpur; tel. (3) 2033000; fax (3) 2033401; f. 1960; refines and markets all classes of petroleum products, lubricating oils, gas and ammonia; cap. and res 392.5m., sales 2,257.3m. (1998); Chair. PHILIP J. DINGLE; Man. Dir OOI POH KHENG; 666 employees.

FCW Holdings Bhd: Jalan 222, Lot 2, Section 51A, 46100 Petaling Jaya, Selangor Darul Ehsan; tel. (3) 79561711; fax (3) 79568968; provision of management services and the trading of telecommunications equipment; cap. and res 138.6m., sales 251.9m. (1998/99); Chair. TAN HUA CHOON; Sec. WONG YAN YAN; 206 employees.

Federal Flour Mills Bhd: Wisma Jerneh, 16th Floor, 38 Jalan Sultan Ismail, 50250 Kuala Lumpur; tel. (3) 2424077; fax (3) 2414059; internet www.ffmb.com.my; f. 1962; flour-milling, soya bean-processing, maize, wheat, palm oil refining and animal feed; cap. and res 1,250.1m., sales 3,952.6m. (1999); Chair. Dato' Haji MOHD SHAMSUDDIN BIN MOHD YAACOB; Man. Dir OH SIEW NAM; 2,119 employees.

General Corpn Bhd: Plaza Ampang City, 19th Floor, 332A-19 Jalan Ampang, 50450 Kuala Lumpur; tel. (3) 42564599; fax (3) 42578197; quarrying, construction, property management and manufacturing; cap. and res 471.6m., sales 551.5m. (1998/99); Chair. Tun MOHAMED HANIFF BIN OMAR; Man. Dir LOW KENG BOON.

Goodyear (Malaysia) Bhd: POB 7049, 40914 Shah Alam, Selangor; tel. (3) 5592411; fax (3) 5595729; mfrs of passenger car, truck and tractor tyres and tubes; Chair. Dato' SHAHRIMAN BIN TUNKU SULAIMAN; Man. Dir HARISH KHOSIA; 720 employees.

Guinness Anchor Bhd: Sungei Way Brewery, POB 144, 46710 Petaling Jaya, Selangor Darul Ehsan; tel. (3) 78614688; fax (3) 78740986; mfrs of beer and stout; cap. and res 309.3m., sales 1,042.4m. (1998/99); Chair. Tan Sri SAW HUAT LYE; Man. Dir T. A. CHALLENOR; 1,057 employees.

HICOM Diecastings Sdn Bhd: Wisma HICOM, 5th Floor, 2 Jalan Usahawan U1/8, 4050 Shah Alam, Selangor; tel. (3) 2028000; fax (3) 2028118; e-mail hicom@hicom.drb-hicom.com.my; internet www.drb-hicom.com; frmly HICOM Holdings Bhdindustrial projects incl. building materials, commercial vehicles and welded pipes; cap. and res 2,082.0m., sales 1,703.3m. (1998/99); Chair. Dato' MOHD SALEH BIN SULONG.

Highlands and Lowlands Bhd: Wisma Guthrie, 21 Jalan Gelenggang, Bukit Damansara, 50490 Kuala Lumpur; tel. (3) 2541644; fax (3) 2557934; internet www.kumpulanguthrie.com; f. 1975; cultivation and processing of rubber, oil palm, coconut and cocoa; property investment and devt; cap. and res 2,291.1m., sales 544.0m. (1999); Chair. Dato' ABDUL KHALID BIN IBRAHIM.

Hume Industries (Malaysia) Bhd: Wisma Hong Leong, 8th Floor, 18 Jalan Perak, 50450 Kuala Lumpur; tel. (3) 2642300; fax (3) 2642513; e-mail hcm@himb.hongleong.com.my; internet www .hongleong.com; f. 1961; mfrs of asbestos cement products, steel and concrete pipes, pre-stressed concrete beams and piles, tanks, electrical conduits and other moulded products, pressure vessels, autoclaves and lift gates; cap. and res -65.1m., sales 5,281.3m. (1998/99); Chair. Tan Sri QUEK LENG CHAN; CEO ROGER TAN KIM HOCK; 10,000 employees.

IOI Corpn Bhd: No. 7–10, 5 Jalan Kenari, Bandar Puchong Jaya, off Jalan Puchong, 47100 Puchong, Selangor Darul Ehsan; tel. (3) 5752288; fax (3) 5753997; e-mail corp@ioigroup.com; internet www.io.group.com; cultivation and processing of oil palm, rubber and cocoa, property devt, production of industrial and medical gases; cap. and res 1,914.1m., sales 1,411.9m. (1998/99); Chair. Dato' Haji IBRAHIM BIN ABDUL RAHMAN.

Keck Seng (Malaysia) Bhd: 2-G Foh Chong Bldg, Jalan Ibrahim, Johor Baru, Johor; tel. (7) 3555866; fax (7) 3540827; f. 1958; cultivation and processing of oil palm, cocoa, housing devt, property investment; cap. and res 805.7m., sales 937.9m. (1998); Chair. HO KIAN GUAN; 1,500 employees.

Kemayan Corpn Bhd: Foh Chong Bldg 5E, 66 Jalan Ibrahim, Johor Baru, Johor; tel. (7) 2225714; fax (7) 2230387; f. 1965; cultivation and processing of oil palm and cocoa; cap. and res 150.0m., sales 486.7m. (1997/98); Chair. Dato' ONG KIM HOAY; 1,500 employees.

Kuala Lumpur Kepong Bhd: Wisma Taiko, 1 Jalan S. P. Seenivasagam, 30000 Ipoh; POB 626, 30770 Ipoh, Perak; tel. (5) 2417844; fax (5) 2555466; f. 1973; plantations cover 145,967 ha; cap. and res 3,263.3m., sales 2,224.1m. (1999/2000); Chair. Dato' LEE OI HIAN.

Kumpulan Guthrie Bhd: Wisma Guthrie, 21 Jalan Gelenggang, Damansara Heights, 50490 Kuala Lumpur; tel. (3) 2541644; fax (3) 2557934; internet www.kumpulanguthrie.com; production, processing, export and distribution of rubber, palm oil, palm kernel, cocoa and coconut; cap. and res 2,141.6m., sales 1,580.2m. (1998); Chair. Tan Sri Dato' MOHD GHAZALI Haji CHE MAT; 16,096 employees.

Lion Land Bhd: Menara Lion, 17th Floor, 165 Jalan Ampang, 50450 Kuala Lumpur; tel. (3) 21622155; fax (3) 21613166; internet www.lion.com.my; f. 1924; mfrs of computer components, property development, construction, steel-mill operations; cap. and res 1,149.5m., sales 1,020,4m. (1998/99); Chair. Tan Sri Dato' MUSA BIN HITAM; Man. Dir Datuk CHENG YONG KIM.

Malakoff Bhd: 8th Floor, Blok B, Wisma Semantan, 12 Jalan Gelenggang, Damansara Heights, 50490 Kuala Lumpur; tel. (3) 20923388; fax (3) 20922288; e-mail malakoff@malakoff.com.my; internet www.malakoff.com.my; f. 1975; cultivation and processing of natural rubber and oil palm, generation and sale of electrical energy and generating capacity; cap. and res 1,835.6m., sales 1,473.2m. (1999/2000); Chair. Tan Sri IBRAHIM MENUDIN; Man. Dir AHMAD JAUHARI YAHYA.

Malaysia Mining Corpn Bhd (MMCB): Menara PNB, 32nd Floor, 201A Jalan Tun Razak, 50400 Kuala Lumpur; tel. (3) 21616000; fax (3) 21612951; e-mail corpsec@mol.net.my; f. 1981 by merger of Malayan Tin Dredging Co and Malaysia Mining Corpn; the world's largest tin-mining group (active in the exploration, mining, smelting and marketing of tin) until April 1993, when it ceased tin-mining operations, owing to depressed tin prices; plantations and diamond exploration, property and financial services; cap. and res 1,592.9m. (1998/99), sales 276.0m. (1999/2000); Chair. Tan Sri Datuk IBRAHIM MENUDIN; 2,211 employees.

Malaysian Oxygen Bhd: 13 Jalan 222, 46100 Petaling Jaya, Selangor Darul Ehsan; tel. (3) 79554233; fax (3) 79566389; f. 1960; mfrs of industrial and medical gases and electrodes, supplies welding, safety, marine, medical and fire-fighting equipment; cap. and res 491.2m., sales 434.7m. (1999/2000); Chair. Tun Dato' Haji OMAR YOKE LIN ONG; Man. Dir DAVID JOHN FULLER; 643 employees.

Malaysian Tobacco Co Bhd: 178–3 Jalan Sungai Besi, POB 10187, 50910 Kuala Lumpur; tel. (3) 2213066; fax (3) 2213130; f. 1956; cigarette mfrs; cap. and res 789.4m., sales 420.2m. (1999); Chair. GHAUS BIN BADIOZE ZAMAN; 560 employees.

Maruichi Malaysia Steel Tube Bhd: Lot 53, Persiaran Selangor, POB 7018, 40700 Shah Alam, Selangor Darul Ehsan; tel. (3) 55192455; fax (3) 55192033; e-mail maruichi@tm.net.my; internet www.maruichi.com.my; f. 1969; steel pipes and tubes, steel wire, engineering services and share registration services; cap. and res 389.4m., sales 300.9m. (1998/99); Chair. ZAIN AZAHARI BIN ZAINAL ABIDIN; Man. Dir YANG YEN FANG; 370 employees.

Mitsubishi Electric (Malaysia) Bhd: Senai Industrial Area, Lot 32, Senai, 81400 Johor; tel. (607) 5996060; fax (607) 5996076; f. 1989; mfr of audio and video equipment; sales 2,259m. (1995); Gen. Man. T. TAKEDA; 2,250 employees.

Motorola Malaysia Sdn Bhd: 2 Jalan SS8/2, 47300 Petaling Jaya, Selangor Darul Ehsan; tel. (3) 2583095; fax (3) 2533771; e-mail f10339@email.mot.com; internet www.mot.com; mfr of electronic components and telecommunications equipment; sales 3,310m. (1995); Vice-Pres. RAMLI ABBAS; 8,300 employees.

Multi-Purpose Holdings Bhd: 38th Floor, Menara Multi-Purpose, Capital Square, 8 Jalan Munshi Abdullah, 50100 Kuala Lumpur; tel. (3) 26948333; fax (3) 26941380; e-mail info@mphb.com.my; internet www.mphb.com.my; financial services, property development and investment, gaming and leisure and utilities; cap. p.u. 781.6m., sales 548.6m. (2000); Chair. Dr CHAN CHIN CHEUNG.

Nylex (Malaysia) Bhd: Persiaran Selangor, Shah Alam Industries, POB 7033, 40910 Shah Alam, Selangor Darul Ehsan; tel. (3) 55191706; fax (3) 55107264; e-mail nylex@nylex.com; internet www.nylex.com; mfr of vinyl coated fabrics, calendered film, and sheeting and plastic products; cap. and res 300.6m., sales 530.2m. (1999); Chair. GRAHAM CHARLES PEARSON; Man. Dir HEAH KOK SOON; 2,035 employees.

Shell Refining Co (FOM) Bhd: Bangunan Shell Malaysia, off Jalan Semantan, Damansara Heights, POB 11027, 50490 Kuala Lumpur; tel. (3) 2559144; fax (3) 7556398; f. 1960; refining and manufacture of all classes of petroleum products; cap. and res 2,178.0m., sales 2,433m. (1998); Chair. Datuk MEGAT ZAHARUDDIN BIN MEGAT MOHD NOR; Man. Dir C. E. MARIE BALMES; 335 employees.

Sime Darby Bhd: Wisma Sime Darby, 21st Floor, Jalan Raja Laut, 50350 Kuala Lumpur; tel. (3) 26914122; fax (3) 26987398; e-mail enquiries@simenet.com; internet www.simenet.com; plantation management, manufacturing tyres and trucks, commodity trading, insurance services, oil and gas; cap. and res 6,457.9m., sales 11,959.9m. (2000/01); Chair. Dato' Seri AHMAD SARJI BIN ABDUL HAMID; Chief Exec. Datuk Nik MOHAMED BIN Nik YAACOB; 26,842 employees.

STMicroelectronics Sdn Bhd: POB 28, Tanjung Agas Industrial Estate, 84007 Muar, Johor; tel. (6) 9521801; fax (6) 9524401; mfr of electronic components; sales 1,495m. (1995); Gen. Man. EUGENIO RE; 3,800 employees.

Tan Chong Motor Holdings Bhd: 62–68 Jalan Ipoh, 51200 Kuala Lumpur; tel. (3) 40427644; fax (3) 40427198; e-mail tcmh@ tanchong.com.my; internet www.nissan.com.my; assembly and distribution of motor vehicles, provision of after-sales services and related financial services; cap. and res 750.9m., sales 1,183.6m. (2000); Chair. Dato' Tan KIM HOR; Man. Dir Tan ENG SOON; 5,700 employees.

Tasek Corporation Bhd: 31st Floor, Menara Promet, Jalan Sultan Ismail, 50250 Kuala Lumpur; tel. (5) 2428668; fax (3) 2423318; fmrly Tasek Cement Bhd; mfr of building materials; cap. and res 546.7m., sales 178.7m. (1998/99); Chair. Tan Sri QUEK LENG CHAN.

United Engineers (Malaysia) Bhd: UE Complex, 5 Jalan 217, 46700 Petaling Jaya, Selangor Darul Ehsan; tel. (3) 7922600; fax (3) 7910381; internet www.uem.com.my; iron, steel and non-ferrous founders; mechanical, electrical, civil, structural and telecommunication engineers for contract and project schemes; cap. and res –10,974.7m., sales 3,239.2m. (1999); Chair. Tan Sri RADIN SOENARNO AL-HAJ; Man. Dir Dato' Dr RAMLI BIN MOHAMAD; 8,500 employees.

United Plantations Bhd: Jendarata Estate, 36009 Teluk Intan; tel. (5) 6411411; fax (5) 6411876; e-mail upnet@tm.net.my; cultivation and processing of oil palm, copra and cocoa; cap. and res 539.6m., sales 276.7m. (2000); Chair. Tan Sri Dato' Haji BASIR BIN ISMAIL; 6,413 employees.

MAJOR INVESTMENT HOLDING COMPANIES

AMMB Holdings Bhd: Bangunan Arab-Malaysian, 22nd Floor, 55 Jalan Raja Chulan, 50200 Kuala Lumpur; tel. (3) 2382633; fax (3) 2382842; e-mail gpa@ambg.com.my; internet www.ambg.com.my; f. 1991; investment holding; cap. and res 940m., sales 4,372m. (March 1999); Chair. Tan Sri Dato' AZMAN HASHIM; 6,009 employees.

Arab-Malaysian Corpn Bhd: Lot 271, 1st Floor, Jalan Dua, off Jalan Chan Sow Lin, 55200 Kuala Lumpur; tel. (3) 2228870; fax (3) 2217793; e-mail amcorp@amcorp.com.my; internet www.amcorp.com.my; investment holding, operation of rubber and oil palm plantations, management services; cap. and res 1,671.1m., sales 119.5m. (2000/01); Chair. Tan Sri Dato' AZMAN HASHIM; Man. Dir SOO KIM WAI.

Batu Kawan Bhd: Wisma Taiko, 1 Jalan S.P. Seenivasagam, 30000 Ipoh, Perak Darul Ridzuan; tel. (5) 2417844; fax (5) 2548054; e-mail bkawan@pd.jaring.my; investment holding, manufacture of chemicals, and stockbroking activities; sales 158.2m. (1999/2000; Group Man. Dir Dato' LEE HAU HIAN.

Berjaya Capital Bhd: Menara Shahzan Insas, 16th Floor, 30 Jalan Sultan Ismail, 50250 Kuala Lumpur; tel. (3) 9358888; fax (3) 9358054; e-mail judytan@berjaya.com.my; internet www.berjaya.com.my; investment holding, property investment and development, hotels, development of resorts and recreational facilities, travel, gaming and lottery management; cap. and res 1,685.8m., sales 2,669.3m. (1998/99); Chair. Dato' SULAIMAN BIN MOHAMED AMIN.

Cahya Mata Sarawak Bhd: Wisma Mahmud, 6th Floor, Jalan Sungai Sarawak, POB 2710, 93754 Kuching, Sarawak; tel. (82) 238888; internet www.cmsb.com.my; investment holding, management services, property development; cap. and res 898.6m., sales 1,177.0m. (2000); Chair. Dato' Haji ONN BIN MAHMUD; Chief Exec. DAYAN WAZIR BERRY; 2,589 employees.

Chemical Co of Malaysia Bhd: 9th Floor, Wisma Sime Darby, 14 Jalan Raja Laut, 50350 Kuala Lumpur; tel. (3) 26919366; fax (3) 26919901; internet www.jaring.my/com; f. 1963; subsidiaries engaged in mfr of fertilizers, chlor-alkali products pharmaceuticals and healthcare products; cap. and res 500.0m., sales 545.0m. (1999); Chair. Tan Sri Dato' MOHD SHERIFF BIN MOHD KASSIM; Man. Dir LIM SAY CHONG; 1,200 employees.

Commerce Asset-Holding Bhd: Tingkat 12, Commerce Square, Jalan Semantan, Damansara Heights, 50490 Kuala Lumpur; tel. (3) 2535333; fax (3) 2533335; internet www.commerz.com.my; f. 1924; investment holding; property management; cap. and res 4,695.3m. (1999); Chair. Dato' MOHD DESA PACHI; approximately 10,000 employees.

Ekran Bhd: Wisma Ting Pek Khing, 16th Floor, 1 Jalan Padungan, 93100 Kuching; tel. (82) 236908; fax (82) 236922; investment holding and management services; cap. and res 1,334.3m., sales 43.8m. (1998/99); Chair. Tan Sri Dato' Paduka Dr TING PEK KHING.

Genting Bhd: Wisma Genting, 24th Floor, Jalan Sultan Ismail, 50250 Kuala Lumpur; tel. (3) 21612288; fax (3) 21615304; internet www.genting.com.my; gaming operations, hotels and plantations, property development, manufacturing and trading in paper and related products, electricity generation and supply; cap. and res 788.9m., sales 3,077.4m. (1999); Chair. and Exec. Dir Tan Sri LIM GOH TONG; Man. Dir Dato' LIM KOK THAY; 14,000 employees.

Golden Hope Plantations Bhd: Menara PNB, 13th Floor, 201A Jalan Tun Razak, 50400 Kuala Lumpur; tel. (3) 2619022; fax (3) 2618221; production and processing of rubber, palm oil, palm kernels, cocoa and copra; cap. and res 3,608.4m., sales 1,946.8m. (1998/99); plantations cover 116,811 ha; Chair. Tan Sri Dato' Seri AHMAD SARJI BIN ABDUL HAMID.

Golden Plus Holdings Bhd: Level 13, Wisma Idris, 17 Jalan Sultan Ismail, 52200 Kuala Lumpur; tel. (3) 2523311; fax (3) 2547788; property development and construction; cap. and res 210.8m., sales 130.9m. (1999); Chair. Dato' Haji Dr ZAINAL ABIDIN BIN HAJI MOHD ALI; Man. Dir TEH SOON SENG.

Hong Leong Industries Bhd: Wisma Hong Leong, 9th Floor, 18 Jalan Perak, 50450 Kuala Lumpur; tel. (3) 2642631; fax (3) 2642591; f. 1982; subsidiaries engaged in investment and property holding, property management, manufacture of mosaic and ceramic tiles, steel products, PVC flooring, office products; cap. and res 469.3m., sales 1,961.9m. (1998/99); Chair. Tan Sri QUEK LENG CHAN; Man. Dir QUEK LENG SENG; 3,929 employees.

Innovest Bhd: Suite 201, 20th Floor, Menara Haw Par, Jalan Sultan Ismail, 50250 Kuala Lumpur; tel. (3) 2633633; fax (3) 2633033; investment holding and management services; cap. and res 11.7m., sales 51.4m. (1999); Chair. Dato' AZRAT GULL BIN AMIRZAT GULL.

Jaya Tiasa Holdings Bhd: 17th Floor, Shahzan Prudential Tower, 30 Jalan Sultan Ismail, 50250 Kuala Lumpur; tel. (3) 2422622; fax (3) 2484866; investment holding and management services, manufacture and sales of veneer plywood and sawn timber; cap. and res 545.4m., sales 425.6m. (1998/99); Chair. Tan Sri ABDUL RAHMAN BIN ABDUL HAMID; Man. Dir TIONG CHIONG HOO.

Leader Universal Holdings Bhd: Wisma Leader, 8 Jalan Larut, 10050 Pinang; POB 923, 10810 Pinang; tel. (4) 2292888; fax (4) 2292333; internet www.leaderuniversal.com; mfr and sale of telecommunication and power cables, copper and aluminium rods and conductors, cable installation and engineering services, power generation and property development; cap. and res 430.1m., sales 1,137.2m. (2001); Chair. Tan Sri RAZALI ISMAIL; Dep. Chair and CEO Dato' Seri HING BOK SAN.

Malayan Cement Bhd: Level 12, Bangunan TH Uptown 3, 3 Jalan SS21/39, 47400 Petaling Jaya, Selangor Darul Ehsan; tel. (3) 77238200; fax (3) 77224100; e-mail info@my.lafarge.com; mfg and marketing of cement, ready-mixed concrete and allied products; cap. and res 3,083m., sales 1,657m. (2001); Chair. Tunku ABDULLAH IBNI AL-MARHUM Tunku ABDUL RAHMAN; Pres. and CEO QUAH THAIN KHAN; 2,300 employees.

Malayan United Industries Bhd: MUI Plaza, 14th Floor, Jalan P Ramlee, 50250 Kuala Lumpur; tel. (3) 21482566; fax (3) 21445209; internet www.mui-global.com; activities include retailing, hotels, food and confectionery, financial services, property, and travel and tourism; cap. and res 7,750m., sales 2,130m. (2001); Chair. and Chief Exec. Tan Sri Dato' Dr KHOO KAY PENG.

Malaysian Pacific Industries Bhd: Wisma Hong Leong, 9th Floor, 18 Jalan Perak, 50450 Kuala Lumpur; tel. (3) 2642631; fax (3) 2644801; f. 1962; subsidiaries engaged in manufacture of cartons, semiconductors and electronic components; cap. and res 615.6m., sales 1,006.6m. (1998/99); Chair. Tan Sri QUEK LENG CHAN; Man. Dir DAVID E. COMLEY; 6,800 employees.

Malaysian Resources Corpn Bhd: Menara MRCB, 2 Jalan Majlis, Seksyen 14, 40000 Shah Alam, Selangor Darul Ehsan; tel. (3) 55138080; fax (3) 55122608; e-mail info@mrcb.com.my; internet www.mrcb.com.my; f. 1968; property development, construction and civil engineering, telecommunications; cap. and res 1,141.6m., sales 248.6m. (1999/2000); Chair. Datuk Seri SYED ANWAR JAMALULLAIL; 160 employees.

Metroplex Bhd: Level 10, Grand Seasons Ave, 72 Jalan Pahang, 53000 Kuala Lumpur; tel. (3) 26931828; fax (3) 26912798; investment holding, hotel and casino operations, property development, quarry operations; cap. and res 1,114.1m., sales 343.3m. (2000/01); Chair. LIM SIEW KIM; Man. Dir CHAN TEIK HUAT.

Minho (M) Bhd: 31C Jalan Satu Kaw 16, Berkeley Town Centre, off Federal Highway, Klang, 41300 Selangor; tel. (3) 3911300; fax (3) 3912100; activities include manufacture, export and dealing in moulded timber and timber products; cap. and res 146.2m., sales 308.1m. (1999); Chair. Tunku Tan Sri IMRAN IBNI JA'AFAR.

MNI Holdings Bhd: Tower 1, 26th Floor, MNI Twins, 11 Jalan Pinang, 50450 Kuala Lumpur; tel. (3) 21645000; fax (3) 21641010; internet www.mni.com.my; investment holding, insurance, takaful, manufacturing and marketing of welding supplies, tin mining; cap. and res 743.6m. (1996/97); Chair. Tan Sri Dato' Seri Dr AHMAD SARJI ABDUL HAMID; CEO Dato' Dr SHAMSUDDIN BIN KASSIM.

Nestlé (Malaysia) Bhd: Nestlé House, 4 Lorong Pesiaran Barat, 46918 Petaling Jaya; tel. (3) 79554466; fax (3) 79550992; subsidiaries engaged in manufacture and marketing of milk products and halal food and beverage products; cap. and res 307.7m., sales 2,107.2m. (1998); Chair. Tan Sri Dato' MOHD GHAZALI SETH; Man. Dir AJIT SARAN; 2,426 employees.

Oriental Holdings Bhd: Wisma Pinang Garden, 1st Floor, 42 Jalan Sultan Ahmad Shah, 10050 Pinang; tel. (4) 2294390; fax (4) 2265860; subsidiaries engaged in manufacture of plastic articles, etc.; cap. and res 2,344.2m., sales 2,204.3m. (1999); Chair. LOH CHENG YEAN; Man. Dir WONG LUM KONG.

PacificMas Bhd: 2nd Floor, Wisma Genting, Jalan Sultan Ismail, 50250 Kuala Lumpur; tel. (3) 21761000; fax (3) 2066868; e-mail jlcphuah@pacificmas.com.my; internet www.pacbanc.com.my/pacific/; f. 1919; frmly The Pacific Bank Bhd, acquired by Malayan Banking Bhd and became investment holding company in Jan. 2001; cap. 342.0m. (Dec. 2000), res 470.4m. (Dec. 1998), dep. 913.1m. (Dec. 2000); Pres. and CEO LAI WAN; 69 brs.

Palmco Holdings Bhd: Wisma Palmex, Lorong Perusahaan Satu, Prai Industrial Complex, 13600 Prai, Pinang; tel. (4) 3906766; fax (3) 3900067; e-mail tkwok@pc.jaring.my; f. 1976; subsidiaries engaged in production of palm kernel oil, manufacture of fatty acids and glycerine, bulk cargo warehousing, property devt and oil palm plantations; cap. and res 356.6m., sales 838.5m. (1998/99); Exec. Chair. LIM KENG KAY; 860 employees.

Perlis Plantations Bhd: Wisma Jerneh, 17th Floor, 38 Jalan Sultan Ismail, 50250 Kuala Lumpur; tel. (3) 2412077; fax (3) 2418242; e-mail ppb@po.jaring.my; internet www.ppbgroup.com; sugar, flour and feed milling, film distribution, edible oils processing and marketing and computer services; cap. and res 2,421.7m., sales 6,737.0m. (1999); Chair. KUOK KHOON EAN; Man. Dir OH SIEW NAM; 16,000 employees.

Perusahaan Otomobil Nasional Bhd (PROTON): Kawasan Perindustrian HICOM, Batu Tiga, 40000 Shah Alam, Selangor; tel. (3) 5111055; fax (3) 5111252; f. 1983; manufacture, assembly and sale of motor vehicles; cap. and res 2,732.2m., sales 4,075.0m. (1998/99); Chair. Dato' MOHD SALEH BIN SULONG; Chief Exec. Tengku MAHALEEL BIN Tengku ARIFF; 5,400 employees.

Petroliam Nasional Bhd (PETRONAS): Tower 1, Petronas Twin Towers, Persiaran KLCC, 50088 Kuala Lumpur; tel. (3) 20515000; fax (3) 2065055; e-mail webmaster@petronas.com.my; internet www.petronas.com.my; f. 1974; national oil co engaged in exploration, production, refining and marketing; total assets 121,555m. (March 2000); Chair. Tan Sri Datuk Seri AZIZAN ZAINUL ABIDIN; Pres. and CEO Tan Sri Dato' MOHD HASSAN BIN MARICAN; 18,578 employees.

Petronas Dagangan Bhd: Tower 1, Petronas Twin Towers, Persiaran KLCC, 50088 Kuala Lumpur; tel. (3) 2615500; fax (3) 2605505; domestic marketing of petroleum products, operation of service stations and distribution of lubricants; cap. and res 1,497.6m., sales 4,002.5m. (March 1999); Chair. Tan Sri Dato' MOHD HASSAN BIN MARICAN; Chief Exec. ABDUL RAHIM BIN ABU BAKAR.

Petronas Gas Bhd: Menara Dayabumi, Kompleks Dayabumi, Jalan Sultan Hishamuddin, 50050 Kuala Lumpur; tel. (3) 2613355; fax (3) 2617161; separates natural gas into components, and stores, transports and distributes them; cap. and res 4,839.7m., sales 1,605.7m. (March 1999); Chair. Tan Sri Dato' MOHD HASSAN BIN MARICAN; Chief Exec. ABDUL RAHIM BIN ABU BAKAR.

Promet Bhd: 3rd Floor, Plaza Kelanamas, 19 Lorong Dungun, Damansara Heights, 50490 Kuala Lumpur; tel. (3) 2521919; fax (3) 2521911; internet www.promet.com.my; steel fabrication, civil engineering and construction; cap and res –377.6m., sales 161.9m. (1998/99); Chair. Tan Sri MOHD NGAH SAID; Pres. and CEO SOH CHEE WEN.

Rashid Hussain Bhd: Tower 1, 9th Floor, RHB Centre, Jalan Tun Razak, 50400 Kuala Lumpur; tel. (3) 9852233; fax (3) 9855522; internet www.rhb.com.my; commercial banking, securities, merchant banking, financial and management services, insurance; cap. and res –1,113.4m., sales 3,894.5m. (1998/99); Chair. Tan Sri Dato' ABDUL RASHID HUSSAIN; 800 employees.

Renong Bhd: Bangunan MCOBA, 2nd Floor, 42 Jalan Syed Putra, 50460 Kuala Lumpur; tel. (3) 22742166; fax (3) 22743979; internet www.renong.com.my; f. 1982; engineering, construction and infrastructure project procurement and management, strategic investment; cap. and res –4,618.9m., sales 757.1m. (1998/99); Chair. Tan Sri Dato' SERI HALIM SAAD.

Resorts World Bhd: Wisma Genting, 24th Floor, Jalan Sultan Ismail, 50250 Kuala Lumpur; tel. (3) 21612288; fax (3) 21615304; e-mail roomrsv@genting.po.my; internet www.mol.net.my/genting; hotels, restaurants, theme parks, gaming, time-share ownership, tours and travel-related services; cap. and res 4,025.8m., sales 2,178.5m. (1999); Chair. and Chief Exec. Tan Sri LIM GOH TONG; Man. Dir Dato' LIM KOK THAY.

RHB Capital Bhd: Level 8 Tower 3, RHB Centre, 426 Jalan Tun Razak, 50400 Kuala Lumpur; tel. (3) 92806777; fax (3) 92806507; internet www.rhb.com.my; f. 1994; investment holding, banking; cap. and res 3,608.2m., sales 3,238.2m. (2001/02); Exec. Chair. Tan Sri Dato' ABDUL RASHID HUSSAIN.

R. J. Reynolds Bhd: Menara John Hancock, 6th Floor, 6 Jalan Gelenggang, Damansara Heights, 50490 Kuala Lumpur; tel. (3) 2549011; fax (3) 2550230; manufacture, marketing and sale of tobacco products; cap. and res 406.5m., sales 583.0m. (2000); Chair. Dato' MOHD NADZMI BIN MOHD SALLEH; 931 employees.

Road Builder (M) Holdings Bhd: Menara John Hancock, Level 16, 6 Jalan Gelenggang, Damansara Heights, 50490 Kuala Lumpur; tel. (3) 2539888; fax (3) 2525498; building, civil construction, quarry operations; cap. and res 114.6m., sales 449.3m. (1998/99); Chair. Tengku Tan Sri Dato' Seri AHMAD RITHAUDEEN BIN Tengku ISMAIL; Man. Dir Dato' CHUA HOCK CHIN.

Sarawak Enterprise Corpn Bhd (SECB): Custodev Twin Tower, 1st Floor, 2679 Rock Rd, 93200 Kuching, Sarawak; tel. (82) 244000; fax (82) 248588; e-mail info@secb.com.my; internet www.jaring.my/mphb/secb; fmrly Dunlop Estates Bhd; investment holding; power generation, transmission and distribution; property development and investment; manufacture and trading of plastic packaging products; cap. and res 2,865m., sales 157.5m. (2000); Chair. Dato' MOHAMAD TAHA BIN ARIFFIN; CEO Datuk WAN ALI TUANKU YUBI.

Sports Toto Malaysia Sdn Bhd: Menara Prime, Levels 8–10, 30 Jalan Sultan Ismail, 50250 Kuala Lumpur; tel. (3) 21489888; fax (3) 21419581; e-mail webmaster@sportstoto.com.my; internet www.sportstoto.com.my; investment holding, management services, betting services, property development; cap. and res 708.6m., sales 2,195.4m. (1998/99); Chair. Tan Sri Dato' Seri VINCENT TAN CHEE YIOUN.

Technology Resources Industries Bhd: Menara Technology Resources, 21st Floor, 161B Jalan Ampang, 50450 Kuala Lumpur; tel. (3) 2619555; fax (3) 2632018; f. 1966; telecommunications and transport services; mfr of consumer electricals and electronics; cap. and res 178.3m., sales 1,701.4m. (1999); Chair. and Chief Exec. Tan Sri Dato' TAJUDIN RAMLI.

UMW Holdings Bhd: The Corporate, 3rd Floor, 15/7 Jalan Utas, POB 7052, 40915 Shah Alam, Selangor; tel. (3) 55191911; fax (3) 55102282; internet www.umw.com.my; automotive, heavy equipment, industrial equipment, manufacturing and engineering, parts, services, energy; cap. and res 350,881m., sales 129,859m. (2000); Chair. Haji ASMAT BIN KAMALUDIN; Chief Exec. Haji ABDUL HALIM BIN HARUN.

YTL Corpn Bhd: Yeoh Tiong Lay Plaza, 11th Floor, 55 Jalan Bukit Bintang, 55100 Kuala Lumpur; tel. (3) 2426633; fax (3) 2412703; e-mail ctrl@ytl.com.my; property devt, manufacture of industrial products; cap. and res 3,740.0m., sales 1,897.3m. (1998/99); Chair Tan Sri Dato' Dr YEOH TIONG LAY; Man. Dir Tan Sri Dato' FRANCIS YEOH SOCK PING.

TRADE UNIONS

In 1995 there were 502 trades unions, 56% of which were from the private sector. About 8.2% of the Malaysian work-force of 7.9m. belonged to unions.

Congress of Unions of Employees in the Public Administrative and Civil Services (CUEPACS): a nat. fed. with 53 affiliates, representing 120,150 govt workers (1994).

Malaysian Trades Union Congress: Wisma MTUC, 10–5, Jalan USJ 9/5T, 47620 Subang Jaya, Selangor; POB 3073, 46000 Petaling

Jaya, Selangor; tel. (3) 80242953; fax (3) 80243224; e-mail mtuc@tm.net.my; internet www.mtuc.org.my; f. 1949; 230 affiliated unions; Pres. ZAINAL RAMPAK; Sec.-Gen. G. RAJASEKARAN.

Principal affiliated unions:

All Malayan Estates Staff Union: POB 12, 46700 Petaling Jaya, Selangor Darul Ehsan; tel. 7249533; e-mail mes@po.jaring.my; 2,654 mems; Pres. TITUS GLADWIN; Gen. Sec. D. P. S. THAMOTHARAM.

Amalgamated Union of Employees in Government Clerical and Allied Services: 32A Jalan Gajah, off Jalan Yew, Pudu, 55100 Kuala Lumpur; tel. (3) 9859613; fax (3) 9838632; 6,703 mems; Pres. IBRAHIM BIN ABDUL WAHAB; Gen. Sec. MOHAMED IBRAHIM BIN ABDUL WAHAB.

Chemical Workers' Union: Petaling Jaya, Selangor; 1,886 mems; Pres. RUSIAN HITAM; Gen. Sec. JOHN MATHEWS.

Electricity Industry Workers' Union: 55-2 Jalan SS 15/8A, Subang Jaya, 47500 Petaling Jaya, Selangor; tel. (3) 7335243; 22,000 mems; Pres. ABDUL RASHID; Gen. Sec. P. ARUNASALAM.

Federation of Unions in the Textile, Garment and Leather Industry: c/o Selangor Textile and Garment Manufacturing Employees Union, 9D Jalan Travers, 50470 Kuala Lumpur; tel. (3) 2742578; f. 1989; four affiliates; Pres. ABDUL RAZAK HAMID; Gen. Sec. ABU BAKAR IBRAHIM.

Harbour Workers' Union, Port Kelang: 106 Persiaran Raja Muda Musa, Port Kelang; 2,426 mems; Pres. MOHAMED SHARIFF BIN YAMIN; Gen. Sec. MOHAMED HAYAT BIN AWANG.

Kesatuan Pekerja Tenaga Nasional Bhd: 30 Jalan Liku Bangsar, POB 10400, 59100 Kuala Lumpur; tel. (3) 2745657; 10,456 mems; Pres. MOHAMED ABU BAKAR; Gen. Sec. IDRIS BIN ISMAIL.

Kesatuan Pekerja-Pekerja FELDA: 2 Jalan Maktab Enam, Melalui Jalan Perumahan Gurney, 54000 Kuala Lumpur; tel. (3) 26929972; fax (3) 26913409; 3,111 mems; Pres. INDERA PUTRA Haji ISMAIL; Gen. Sec. JAMALLUDIN BIN LIMUN.

Kesatuan Pekerja-Pekerja Perusahaan Membuat Tekstil dan Pakaian Pulau Pinang dan Seberang Prai: 23 Lorong Talang Satu, Prai Gardens, 13600 Prai; tel. (4) 301397; 3,900 mems; Pres. ABDUL RAZAK HAMID; Gen. Sec. KENNETH STEPHEN PERKINS.

Malayan Technical Services Union: 3A Jalan Menteri, off Jalan Cochrane, 55100 Kuala Lumpur; tel. (3) 92851778; fax (3) 92811875; 6,500 mems; Pres. Haji MOHAMED YUSOP Haji HARMAIN SHAH; Gen. Sec. SAMUEL DEVADASAN.

Malaysian Rubber Board Staff Union: POB 10150, 50908 Kuala Lumpur; tel. (3) 4565102; 1,108 mems; Pres. JUDE MICHAEL; Gen. Sec. NG SIEW LAN.

Metal Industry Employees' Union: Metalworkers' House, 5 Lorong Utara Kecil, 46200 Petaling Jaya, Selangor; tel. (3) 79567214; fax (3) 79550854; e-mail mieum@tm.net.my; 15,491 mems; Pres. KAMARUSZAMAN BIN MANSOR; Gen. Sec. JACOB ENGKATESU.

National Union of Commercial Workers: Bangunan NUCW, 98A-D Jalan Masjid India, 50100 Kuala Lumpur; POB 12059, 50780 Kuala Lumpur; tel. (3) 2927385; fax (3) 2925930; f. 1959; 11,937 mems; Pres. TAIB SHARIF; Gen. Sec. C. KRISHNAN.

National Union of Plantation Workers: 428 A, B, Jalan 5/46, Gasing Indah, POB 73, 46700 Petaling Jaya, Selangor; tel. 77827622; fax (3) 77815321; e-mail sangkara@mail.tm.net.my; f. 1990; 41,000 mems; Pres. AWI BIN AWANG; Gen. Sec. G. SANKARAN.

National Union of PWD Employees: 32B Jalan Gajah, off Jalan Yew, 55100 Kuala Lumpur; tel. (3) 9850149; 5,869 mems; Pres. KULOP IBRAHIM; Gen. Sec. S. SANTHANASAMY.

National Union of Telecoms Employees: Wisma NUTE, 17A Jalan Bangsar, 59200 Kuala Lumpur; tel. (3) 2821599; fax (3) 2821015; 15,874 mems; Pres. MOHAMED SHAFIE B. P. MAMMAL; Gen. Sec. MOHD JAFAR BIN ABDUL MAJID.

Non-Metallic Mineral Products Manufacturing Employees' Union: 99A Jalan SS 14/1, Subang Jaya, 47500 Petaling Jaya, Selangor; tel. (3) 56352245; fax (3) 56333863; e-mail nonmet@tm.net.my; 10,000 mems; Pres. ABDULLAH ABU BAKAR; Sec. S. SOMAHSUNDRAM.

Railwaymen's Union of Malaya: Bangunan Tong Nam, 1st Floor, Jalan Tun Sambathan (Travers), 50470 Kuala Lumpur; tel. (3) 2741107; fax (3) 2731805; 5,500 mems; Pres. ABDUL GAFFOR BIN IBRAHIM; Gen. Sec. S. VEERASINGAM.

Technical Services Union—Tenaga Nasional Bhd: Bangunan Keselamatan, POB 11003, Bangsar, Kuala Lumpur; tel. (3) 2823581; 3,690 mems; Pres. RAMLY YATIM; Gen. Sec. CLIFFORD SEN.

Timber Employees' Union: 10 Jalan AU 5C/14, Ampang, Ulu Kelang, Selangor; 7,174 mems; Pres. ABDULLAH METON; Gen. Sec. MINHAT SULAIMAN.

Transport Workers' Union: 21 Jalan Barat, Petaling Jaya, 46200 Selangor; tel. (3) 7566567; 10,447 mems; Pres. NORASHIKIN; Gen. Sec. ZAINAL RAMPAK.

Independent Federations and Unions

Kongres Kesatuan Guru-Guru Dalam Perkhidmatan Pelajaran (Congress of Unions of Employees in the Teaching Services): Johor; seven affiliates; Pres. RAMLI BIN MOHD JOHAN; Sec.-Gen. KASSIM BIN Haji HARON.

Malaysian Medical Association: MMA House, 4th Floor, 124 Jalan Pahang, 53000 Kuala Lumpur; tel. (3) 40420617; fax (3) 40418187; e-mail mma@tm.net.my; internet www.mma.org.my; 10 affiliates; Pres. Datuk Dr N. ATHIMULAM.

National Union of Bank Employees: NUBE Bldg, 61 Jalan Ampang, POB 12488, 50780 Kuala Lumpur; tel. (3) 20789800; fax (3) 20703800; e-mail nubehq@pd.jaring.my; internet www.nube.org.my; 27,000 mems; Gen. Sec. J. SOLOMON.

National Union of Journalists: 30B Jalan Padang Belia, 50470 Kuala Lumpur; tel. (3) 2742867; fax (3) 2744776; f. 1962; 1,700 mems; Gen. Sec. ONN EE SENG.

National Union of Newspaper Workers: 11B Jalan 20/14, Paramount Garden, 46300 Petaling Jaya, Selangor; tel. (3) 78768118; fax (3) 78751490; e-mail nunwl@tm.net.my; 3,000 mems; Pres. GAN HOE JIAN; Exec. Sec. MOHD SHAH DANIEL.

Sabah

Sabah Banking Employees' Union: POB 11649, 88818 Kota Kinabalu; internet sbeukk@tm.net.my; 729 mems; Gen. Sec. LEE CHI HONG.

Sabah Civil Service Union: Kota Kinabalu; f. 1952; 1,356 mems; Pres. J. K. K. VOON; Sec. STEPHEN WONG.

Sabah Commercial Employees' Union: Sinsuran Shopping Complex, Lot 3, Block N, 2nd Floor, POB 10357, 88803 Kota Kinabalu; tel. (88) 225971; fax (88) 213815; e-mail sceu-kk@tm.net.my; f. 1957; 980 mems; Gen. Sec. REBECCA CHIN.

Sabah Medical Services Union: POB 11257, 88813 Kota Kinabalu; tel. (88) 242126; fax (88) 242127; e-mail smsu@hotmail.com; 3,000 mems; Pres. VISVALINGAM SUPPIAH; Gen. Sec. LAURENCE VUN.

Sabah Petroleum Industry Workers' Union: POB 1087, Kota Kinabalu; 168 mems; Gen. Sec. THIEN FOOK SHIN.

Sabah Teachers' Union: POB 10912, 88810 Kota Kinabalu; tel. (88) 420034; fax (88) 431633; f. 1962; 3,001 mems; Pres. KWAN PING SIN; Sec.-Gen. PATRICK Y. C. CHOK.

Sarawak

Kepak Sarawak (Kesatuan Pegawai-Pegawai Bank, Sarawak): POB 62, Bukit Permata, 93100 Kuching, Sarawak; tel. (19) 8549372; e-mail kepaksar@tm.net.my; bank officers' union; 1,430 mems; Gen. Sec. DOMINIC CH'NG YUNG TED.

Sarawak Commercial Employees' Union: POB 807, Kuching; 1,636 mems; Gen. Sec. SONG SWEE LIAP.

Sarawak Teachers' Union: 139A Jalan Rock, 1st Floor, 93200 Kuching; tel. (82) 245727; fax (82) 245757; e-mail swktu@po.jaring.my; internet www.geocities.com/swktu; f. 1965; 12,110 mems; Pres. WILLIAM GHANI BINA; Sec.-Gen. THOMAS HUO KOK SEN.

Transport

RAILWAYS

Peninsular Malaysia

The state-owned Malayan Railways had a total length of 1,672 km in Peninsular Malaysia in 1996. The main railway line follows the west coast and extends 782 km from Singapore, south of Peninsular Malaysia, to Butterworth (opposite Pinang Island) in the north. From Bukit Mertajam, close to Butterworth, the Kedah line runs north to the Thai border at Padang Besar where connection is made with the State Railway of Thailand. The East Coast Line, 526 km long, runs from Gemas to Tumpat (in Kelantan). A 21-km branch line from Pasir Mas (27 km south of Tumpat) connects with the State Railway of Thailand at the border station of Sungei Golok. Branch lines serve railway-operated ports at Port Dickson and Telok Anson as well as Port Klang and Jurong (Singapore). An express rail link connecting central Kuala Lumpur and the new Kuala Lumpur International Airport (KLIA) opened in 2001.

Keretapi Tanah Melayu Bhd (KTMB) (Malayan Railways): KTMB Corporate Headquarters, Jalan Sultan Hishamuddin, 50621 Kuala Lumpur; tel. (3) 22757142; fax (3) 27105706; e-mail pro@ktmb.com.my; internet www.ktmb.com.my; f. 1885; incorporated as a co under govt control in Aug. 1992; privatized in Aug.

1997; managed by the consortium Marak Unggal (Renong, DRB & Bolton); Chair. Tan Sri Dato' THONG YAW HONG.

Sabah

Sabah State Railway: Karung Berkunci 2047, 88999 Kota Kinabalu; tel. (88) 254611; fax (88) 236395; 134 track-km of 1-m gauge (1995); goods and passenger services from Tanjong Aru to Tenom, serving part of the west coast and the interior; diesel trains are used; Gen. Man. Ir BENNY WANG.

ROADS

Peninsular Malaysia

Peninsular Malaysia's road system is extensive, in contrast to those of Sabah and Sarawak. In 1999 the road network in Malaysia totalled an estimated 65,877 km, of which 16,206 km were highways and 31,777 km secondary roads; 75.8% of the network was paved.

Sabah

Jabatan Kerja Raya (Public Works Department): 88582 Kota Kinabalu, Sabah; tel. (88) 244333; fax (88) 237234; e-mail pos@jkr.sabah.gov.my; maintains a network totalling 10,878 km, of which 1,230 km were trunk roads in 1997; the total included 4,007 km of sealed roads; Dir DAVID CHIU SIONG SENG.

Sarawak

Jabatan Kerja Raya (Public Works Department): 88582 Kota Kinabalu, Sabah; tel. (88) 244333; fax (88) 237234; e-mail pos@jkr.sabah.gov.my; road network totalling 10,979 km, of which 3,986 km were sealed roads; Dir DAVID CHIU SIONG SENG.

SHIPPING

The ports in Malaysia are classified as federal ports, under the jurisdiction of the federal Ministry of Transport, or state ports, responsible to the state ministries of Sabah and Sarawak.

Peninsular Malaysia

The federal ports in Peninsular Malaysia are Klang (the principal port), Pinang, Johor and Kuantan.

Johor Port Authority: POB 66, 81707 Pasir Gudang, Johor; tel. (7) 2517721; fax (7) 2517684; e-mail jport@lpj.com.my; internet www.lpj.gov.my; f. 1973; Gen. Man. MOHD ROZALI BIN MOHD ALI..

Johor Port Bhd: POB 151, 81707 Pasir Gudang, Johor; tel. (7) 2525888; fax (7) 2522507; e-mail joport@silicon.net.my; internet www.joport.com.my; Exec. Chair. Dato' MOHD TAUFIK ABDULLAH.

Klang Port Authority: POB 202, Jalan Pelabuhan, 42005 Port Klang, Selangor; tel. (3) 31688211; fax (3) 31670211; e-mail pka_admin@pka.gov.my; f. 1963; Gen. Man. Datin Paduka O. C. PHANG.

Kuantan Port Authority: Tanjung Gelang, POB 161, 25720 Kuantan, Pahang; tel. (9) 5833201; fax (9) 5833866; e-mail lpk@po.jaring.my; internet www.1pktn.gov.my; f. 1974; Gen. Man. KHAIRUL ANUAR BIN ABDUL RAHMAN.

Penang Port Commission: POB 143, 10710 Pinang; tel. (4) 2633211; fax (4) 2626211; e-mail sppp@po.jaring.my; internet www.penangport.gov.my; f. 1956; Gen. Man. Dato' Capt. Haji ADBUL RAHIM ABDUL AZIZ.

Sabah

The chief ports are Kota Kinabalu, Sandakan, Tawau, Lahad Datu, Kudat, Semporna and Kunak and are administered by the Sabah Ports Authority. Many international shipping lines serve Sabah. Local services are operated by smaller vessels. The Sapangar Bay oil terminal, 25 km from Kota Kinabalu wharf, can accommodate oil tankers of up to 30,000 dwt.

Sabah Ports Authority: Bangunan Ibu Pejabat LPS, Jalan Tun Fuad, Tanjung Lipat, 88617 Kota Kinabalu, Sabah; tel. (88) 256155; fax (88) 223036; e-mail sabport@po.jaring.my; internet www.infosabah.com.my/spa.

Sarawak

There are four port authorities in Sarawak: Kuching, Rajang, Miri and Bintulu. Kuching, Rajang and Miri are statutory ports, while Bintulu is a federal port. Kuching port serves the southern region of Sarawak, Rajang port the central region, and Miri port the northern region.

Kuching Port Authority: Jalan Pelabuhan, Pending, POB 530, 93710 Kuching, Sarawak; tel. (82) 482144; fax (82) 481696; e-mail kuport@po.jaring.my; f. 1961; Gen. Man. CHOU CHII MING.

Rajang Port Authority: 96000 Sibu, Sarawak; tel. (84) 319009; fax (84) 318754; e-mail RAJANG@po.jaring.my; f. 1970; Gen. Man. CHONG SIEW YANG.

Principal Shipping Companies

Achipelego Shipping (Sarawak) Sdn Bhd: Lot 267/270, Jalan Chan Chin Ann, POB 2998, 93758 Kuching; tel. (82) 412581; fax (82) 416249; Gen. Man. MICHAEL M. AMAN.

Malaysia Shipping Corpn Sdn Bhd: Office Tower, Plaza Berjaya, Suite 14C, 14th Floor, 12 Jalan Imbi, 55100 Kuala Lumpur; tel. (3) 2418788; fax (3) 2429214; e-mail mscsb@po.jaring.my; Chair. Y. C. CHANG.

Malaysian International Shipping Corpn Bhd (National Shipping Line of Malaysia): Suite 3–8, Tingkat 3, Wisma MISC, 2 Jalan Conlay, 50450 Kuala Lumpur; tel. (3) 2428088; fax (3) 2486602; e-mail zzainala@miscnote1.miscbhd.com; internet www.misc-bhd.com; f. 1968; regular sailings between the Far East, South-East Asia, Australia, Japan and Europe; also operates chartering, tanker, haulage and warehousing and agency services; major shareholder, Petroliam Nasional Bhd (PETRONAS); Chair. Tan Sri Dato' MOHD HASSAN BIN MARICAN; Man. Dir Dato' Haji MOHD ALI BIN Haji YASIN.

Perbadanan Nasional Shipping Line Bhd (PNSL): Kuala Lumpur; tel. (3) 2932211; fax (3) 2930493; f. 1982; specializes in bulk cargoes; Chair. Tunku Dato' SHAHRIMAN BIN Tunku SULAIMAN; Exec. Dep. Chair. Dato' SULAIMAN ABDULLAH.

Persha Shipping Agencies Sdn Bhd: Bangunan Mayban Trust, Penthouse Suite, Jalan Pinang, 10200 Pinang; tel. (4) 2612400; fax (4) 2623122; Man. Dir MOHD NOOR MOHD KAMALUDIN.

Syarikat Perkapalan Kris Sdn Bhd (The Kris Shipping Co Ltd): 3AO7 Block A, Kelana Centre Point, 3 Jalan SS7/19, Kelana Jaya; POB 8428, 46789 Petaling Jaya, Selangor; tel. (3) 7046477; fax (3) 7048007; domestic services; Chair. Dato' Seri SYED NAHAR SHAHABUDIN; Gen. Man. ROHANY TALIB; Dep. Gen. Man. THO TEIT CHANG.

Trans-Asia Shipping Corpn Sdn Bhd: Unit 715–718, Block A, Kelana Business Centre, 97 Jalan SS7/2, Kelana Jaya, 47301 Petaling Jaya, Selangor; tel. (3) 78802020; fax (4) 78802200; e-mail ahmad@tasco.com.my; internet www.tasco.com.my; Man. Dir LEE CHECK POH.

CIVIL AVIATION

The new Kuala Lumpur International Airport (KLIA), situated in Sepang, Selangor (50 km south of Kuala Lumpur) began operations in June 1998, with an initial capacity of 25m.–30m. passengers a year, rising to 45m. by 2020. It replaced Subang Airport in Kuala Lumpur (which was renamed the Sultan Abdul Aziz Shah Airport in 1996). An express rail link between central Kuala Lumpur and KLIA opened in early 2001. There are regional airports at Kota Kinabalu, Pinang, Johor Bahru, Kuching and Pulau Langkawi. In addition, there are airports catering for domestic services at Alor Star, Ipoh, Kota Bahru, Kuala Terengganu, Kuantan and Melaka in Peninsular Malaysia, Sibu, Bintulu and Miri in Sarawak and Sandakan, Tawau, Lahad Datu and Labuan in Sabah. There are also numerous smaller airstrips.

Department of Civil Aviation (Jabatan Penerbangan Awam Malaysia): Aras B1, 1,2 and 3, Block D5, Parcel D, Pusat Pentadbiran Kerajaan Persekutuan, 62502 Putrajaya; tel. (3) 88866000; fax (3) 88891541; Dir-Gen. (vacant).

Air Asia Sdn Bhd: Wisma HICOM, 6th Floor, 2 Jalan Usahawan, U1/8, Seksyen Ul, 40150 Shah Alam, Selangor; tel. (3) 2028007; fax (3) 2028137; f. 1993; internet www.airasia.com; f. 1993; a second national airline, with a licence to operate domestic, regional and international flights; 85%-owned by HICOM.

Berjaya Air: Apprentice Training Bldg, 1st Floor, Mas Complex B (Hangar 1), Lapangan Terbang Sultan Abdul Aziz Shah, Shah Alam, Selangor, 47200 Kuala Lumpur; tel. (3) 7476828; fax (3) 7476228; e-mail berjayaa@tm.net.my; f. 1989; scheduled and charter domestic services; Pres. Dato TENGKU ADNAN MANSOR.

Malaysia Airlines: 32nd Floor, Bangunan MAS, Jalan Sultan Ismail, 50250 Kuala Lumpur; tel. (3) 21655140; fax (3) 21633178; e-mail grpcomm@malaysiaairlines.com.my; internet www.malaysiaairlines.com.my; f. 1971 as the Malaysian successor to the Malaysia Singapore Airlines (MSA); known as Malaysian Airline System (MAS) until Oct. 1987; services to 33 domestic points and to 79 international destinations; Chair. Tan Sri Datuk Seri AZIZAN ZAINUL ABIDIN.

Pelangi Air: Kuala Lumpur; tel. (3) 2624453; fax (3) 2624515; internet www.asia123.com/pelangi/home.htm; f. 1988; domestic scheduled passenger services; Chair. Tan Sri SAW HWAT LYE.

Transmile Air: Wisma Semantan, Mezzanine 2, Block B, 12 Jalan Gelenggang, Bukit Damansara, 50490 Kuala Lumpur; tel. (3) 2537718; fax (3) 2537719; f. 1992; scheduled and charter regional and domestic services for pasengers and cargo; Chair. Tan Sri ZAINOL MAHMOOD.

Tourism

Malaysia has a rapidly-growing tourist industry, and tourism remains an important source of foreign-exchange earnings. In 2001 some 12.8m. tourists visited Malaysia. In that year tourist receipts totalled RM 24,221.5m.

Malaysia Tourism Promotion Board: Menara Dato' Onn, 17th, 24th–27th, 30th Floors, Putra World Trade Centre, Jalan Tun Ismail, 50480 Kuala Lumpur; tel. (3) 26935188; fax (3) 26935884; e-mail tourism@tourism.gov.my; internet www.tourism.gov.my; f. 1972 to co-ordinate and promote activities relating to tourism; Chair. Datuk ABDUL KADIR Haji Sheikh FADZIR; Dir-Gen. Datuk ABDULLAH JONID.

Sabah Tourist Association: Kota Kinabalu; tel. (88) 211484; f. 1962; 55 mems; parastatal promotional org.; Chair. THOMAS MORE WILLIE; Exec. Sec. CHRISTINE NGUI.

Sarawak Tourist Association: Sarawak Tourist Information Centre, Main Bazaar, 93000 Kuching; POB 887, 93718 Kuching; tel. (82) 240620; fax (82) 427151; f. 1963; Chair. PHILIP YONG KHI LIANG; Hon. Sec. AUDRY WAN ULLOK.

Defence

In August 2001 the total strength of the armed forces was 100,500; army 80,000, navy 12,500, air force 8,000; military service is voluntary. Paramilitary forces included the General Operations Force of 18,000 and the People's Volunteer Corps of 240,000. Malaysia is a participant in the Five-Power Defence Arrangements with Singapore, Australia, New Zealand and the United Kingdom.

Defence Budget: The budget for 2001 allocated RM 7,300m. (excluding procurement allowance) to defence.

Chief of the Defence Forces: Gen. Tan Sri Dato' Seri MOHD ZAHIDI BIN Haji ZAINUDDIN.

Chief of Army: Gen. Dato' Seri MD HASHIM BIN HUSSEIN.

Chief of Navy Staff: Adm. Dato' Seri ABU BAKAR BIN ABDUL JAMAL.

Chief of Air Force Staff: Gen. Dato' Haji SULEIMAN BIN MAHMUD.

Education

Under the Malaysian education system, free schooling is provided at government-assisted schools for children between the ages of six and 18. There are also private schools, which receive no government financial aid. Education is compulsory for 11 years between the ages of six and 16 years. Government expenditure on education was estimated at RM 14,422m. in 2001 (22.6% of total expenditure). Total enrolment in primary and secondary education in 1997 was equivalent to 82% of children in the relevant age group (males 80%; females 85%). Scholarships are awarded at all levels and there are many scholarship-holders studying at universities and other institutes of higher education at home and abroad.

PRIMARY EDUCATION

The national language, Bahasa Malaysia, is the main medium of instruction, although English, Chinese and Tamil are also used. Two-thirds of the total primary school enrolment is in National Schools where Malay is used and the remainder in National-Type Primary Schools where Tamil or Chinese is used. A place in primary school is now assured to every child from the age of six onwards, and parents are free to choose the language of instruction. Enrolment in primary education was equivalent to 101% (males 101%; females 101%) of children in the relevant age group in 1997. The primary school course lasts for six years.

SECONDARY EDUCATION

Bahasa Malaysia is the only medium of instruction in secondary schools, while English is taught as a second language and Chinese and Tamil are taught as pupils' own languages. There are, however, private Chinese secondary schools. Secondary education lasts for seven years, comprising a first cycle of three years and a second of four. In 1997 enrolment at the secondary level was equivalent to 64% of pupils of the relevant age (males 56%; females 69%).

HIGHER EDUCATION

In 1997 there were nine universities, including the International Islamic University. In the same year there were eight polytechnics and colleges including the MARA Institute of Technology. In 1995 enrolment in tertiary education was equivalent to 12% of those in the relevant age-group.

Malaysia's universities adhere to a quota system (55% of entrants should be Malays and 45% non-Malays), which, in practice, makes it considerably more difficult for non-Malays to gain a place at university. The Government was attempting to encourage foreign universities to establish campuses in Malaysia to improve standards and reduce the cost of sending Malaysian students abroad to study. In 1994 the Prime Minister announced that from 1995, contrary to previous policy, English would be used to teach scientific and technological subjects at university. In 1995 the Government announced that, from 1996, basic university degree courses would be reduced in length from four to three years, in order to increase the number of graduates entering the employment market.

Bibliography

GENERAL

Brown, Ian, and Ampalavanar, Rajeswary. *Malaysia* (World Bibliographical Series, vol. 12), Oxford, Clio Press, 1986.

Hodder, B. W. *Man in Malaya*. London, University of London Press, 1959.

Purcell, V. *Malaysia*. London, Thames and Hudson, 1965.

Smith, T. E., and Bastin, J. *Malaysia*. London, Oxford University Press, 1967.

PEOPLES OF MALAYSIA

Ackerman, S. E., and Lee, R. *Heaven in Transition: Non-Muslim Religious Innovation and Ethnic Identity in Malaysia*. Kuala Lumpur, Forum, 1990.

Ali, H. S. *Peasant Society and Leadership*. London, Oxford University Press, 1977.

The Malays. Their Problems and Future. Kuala Lumpur, Heinemann, 1981.

Arasaratnam, S. *Indians in Malaysia and Singapore*. Singapore, Oxford University Press, 1979.

Breman, J. *Taming the Coolie Beast*. Delhi, Oxford University Press, 1987.

Chandra, Muzaffar. *Islamic Resurgence in Malaysia*. Kuala Lumpur, Penerbit Fajar Bakti, 1987.

Hew Cheng Sim. *Women Workers, Migration and Family in Sarawak*. London, RoutledgeCurzon, 2002.

Hong, Evelyne. *The Natives of Sarawak*. Pinang Institut Masyarakat, 1987.

Ibrahim, Zawawi. *The Malay Labourer: by the Window of Capitalism*. Singapore, Institute of Southeast Asian Studies, 1998.

Jones, L. W. *The Population of Borneo*. London, Athlone Press, 1966.

King, Victor T. *The Peoples of Borneo*. Oxford, Blackwell, 1993.

de Koninck, Rodolphe. *Malay Peasants Coping with the World: Breaking the Community Circle?* Singapore, Institute of Southeast Asian Studies, 1992.

Loh Kok, Francis, and Khoo Boo Teik. *Democracy in Malaysia. Discourses and Practices*. Richmond, Surrey, Curzon Press, 2001.

Pillai, P. *People on the Move—An Overview of Recent Immigration and Emigration in Malaysia*. Kuala Lumpur, Institute of Strategic and International Studies, 1992.

Purcell, V. *The Chinese in South East Asia*. London, Oxford University Press, 1965.

The Chinese in Malaya. Oxford, Oxford University Press, 1971.

Sandhu, Kernial Singh. *Indians in Malaya 1786–1957*. Cambridge, Cambridge University Press, 1969.

Sellato, Bernard. *Nomads of the Borneo Rainforest: The Economics, Politics and Ideology of Settling Down*. Honolulu, HI, University of Hawaii Press, 1994.

Wong, Diana. *Peasants in the Making: Malaysia's Green Revolution*. Singapore, Institute of Southeast Asian Studies, 1987.

HISTORY

Amin, Mohamad, and Caldwell, M. (Eds). *Malaya: The Making of a Neo-Colony*. Nottingham, Spokesman, 1979.

Andaya, Barbara Watson, and Andaya, Leonard. *A History of Malaysia,* London, Macmillan, 1982.

A History of Malaysia. Second Edition. Honolulu, HI, University of Hawaii Press, 2001.

Bastin, J., and Winks, R. W. *Malaysia—Selected Historical Readings.* London, Oxford University Press, 1979.

Black, Ian. *A Gambling Style of Government. The Establishment of the Chartered Company's Rule in Sabah, 1878–1915.* Kuala Lumpur, Oxford University Press, 1983.

Blythe, W. *The Impact of Chinese Secret Societies in Malaya.* London, Oxford University Press, 1969.

Cheah Boon Kheng. *Red Star over Malaya. Resistance and Social Conflict during and after the Japanese Occupation of Malaya, 1941–46.* Singapore, Singapore University Press, 1983.

Malaysia: The Making of a Nation. Singapore, Institute of Southeast Asian Studies, 2002.

Comber, Leon. *13 May 1969: A Historical Survey of Sino-Malay Relations.* Singapore, Graham Brash, 2001.

Cowan, C. D. *Nineteenth Century Malaya.* London, Oxford University Press, 1961.

Emerson, R. *Malaysia, a Study in Direct and Indirect Rule.* Kuala Lumpur, University of Malaya Press, 1964.

Goh Cheng Teik. *The May Thirteenth Incident and Democracy in Malaysia.* Kuala Lumpur, Oxford University Press, 1971.

Gullick, J. M. *Malay Society in the Late Nineteenth Century: The Beginnings of Change.* Singapore, Oxford University Press, 1987.

Rulers and Residents: Influence and Power in the Malay States 1870–1920. Singapore, Oxford University Press, 1992.

Jackson, Robert. *The Malayan Emergency: The Commonwealth's Wars 1948–66.* London, Routledge, 1991.

Kratoska, Paul H. *The Japanese Occupation of Malaya: a Social and Economic History.* London, Hurst, 1998.

Kaur, Amarjit, and Metcalfe, Ian (Eds.). *The Shaping of Malaysia.* Basingstoke, Macmillan, 1999.

Milner, Anthony. *The Invention of Politics in Colonial Malaya.* Cambridge, Cambridge University Press, 1995.

Parkinson, C. N. *British Intervention in Malaya 1867–77.* Kuala Lumpur, University of Malaya Press, 1960.

Pringle, R. *Rajahs and Rebels: the Iban of Sarawak under Brooke Rule 1841–1941.* London, Macmillan, 1971.

Rahman, Abdul Embong. *State-led Modernization and the New Middle Class in Malaysia.* New York, Palgrave Macmillan, 2001.

Rashid, Rehman. *A Malaysian Journey.* Kuala Lumpur, Rehman Rashid, 1993.

Reece, R. H. W. *The Name of Brooke. The End of White Rajah Rule in Sarawak.* Kuala Lumpur, Oxford University Press, 1982.

Riddell, Peter G. *Islam and the Malay-Indonesian World: Transmission and Responses.* Honolulu, HI, University of Hawaii Press, 2001.

Rimmer, Peter J., and Allen, Lisa M. (Eds). *The Underside of Malaysian History: Pullers, Prostitutes, Plantation Workers.* Singapore, Singapore University Press, 1990.

Roff, W. *The Origins of Malay Nationalism.* New Haven, CT, Yale University Press, 1967.

Runciman, S. *The White Rajahs.* Cambridge, Cambridge University Press, 1960.

Sandhu, Kernial Singh, and Wheatley, Paul (Eds). *Melaka: The Transformation of a Malay Capital c. 1400–1980.* Kuala Lumpur, Oxford University Press, 1983.

Shennan, Margaret. *Out In The Midday Sun: The British in Malaya 1880–1960.* London, John Murray, 2000.

Short, A. *The Communist Insurrection in Malaya 1948–1960.* London, Frederick Muller, 1975.

Simandjuntak, B. *Malayan Federalism 1945–63.* Kuala Lumpur, Oxford University Press, 1969.

Stockwell, A. J. *British Policy and Malay Politics during the Malayan Union Experiment 1942–48.* Kuala Lumpur, Malaysian Branch of the Royal Asiatic Society, 1979.

British Documents on the End of Empire, Series B, Vol. 3. Malaya. London, HMSO, 1995.

Stubbs, R. *Hearts and Minds in Guerilla Warfare: The Malayan Emergency 1948–1960.* Singapore, Oxford University Press, 1989.

Swettenham, F. A. *British Malaya.* London, Allen and Unwin, 1948.

Tregonning, K. G. *A History of Modern Sabah 1881–1963.* Oxford, Oxford University Press, 1965.

Turnbull, C. M. *The Straits Settlements 1826–67.* London, Athlone Press, 1972.

White, Nicholas. *Business, Government and the End of Empire: Malaya 1942–1957.* Kuala Lumpur, Oxford University Press, 1996.

Yong, C. F., and McKenna, R. F. *The Kuomintang Movement in British Malaya 1912–1949.* Singapore, Singapore University Press, 1990.

Weiss, Meredith, and Saliha, Hassan (Eds). *Social Movements in Malaysia: From Moral Communities to NGOs.* London, RoutledgeCurzon, 2002.

POLITICS

ALIRAN. *Reflections on the Malaysian Constitution.* Pinang, ALIRAN, 1987.

Ariff, M. O. *The Philippines Claim to Sabah.* Singapore, Oxford University Press, 1970.

Atkins, William. *The Politics of Southeast Asia's New Media.* Richmond, Surrey, Press, 2001.

Bowie, Alasdair. *Crossing the Industrial Divide: State, Society, and the Politics of Economic Transformation in Malaysia.* New York, Columbia University Press, 1991.

CARPA. *Tangled Web: Dissent, Deterrence and the October 1987 Crackdown.* Australia, Collins/Angus and Robertson Publishers Australia, 1988.

Cheong Mei Sui, and Amin, Adibah. *Daim: The Man Behind the Enigma.* Petaling Jaya, Pelanduk Publications, 1995.

Clutterbuck, Richard. *Conflict and Violence in Singapore and Malaysia 1945–83.* Singapore, Graham Brash, 1985.

Crouch, Harold. *Government and Society in Malaysia.* Ithaca, NY, Cornell University Press, 1996.

Crouch, H., Lee, K. H., and Ong, M. *Malaysian Politics and the 1978 Election.* 1980.

Esman, M. J. *Administration and Development in Malaysia.* Ithaca, NY, Cornell University Press, 1972.

Goh Cheng Teik. *Malaysia: Beyond Communal Politics.* Petaling Jaya, Pelanduk Publications, 1994.

Gomez, Edward Terence. *Money Politics in the Barisan Nasional.* Kuala Lumpur, Forum, 1990.

UMNO's Corporate Investments. Kuala Lumpur, Forum, 1990.

Political Business: Corporate Involvement in Malaysian Political Parties. Townsville, James Cook University of North Queensland, 1994.

The 1995 Malaysian General Elections: a Report and Commentary. Singapore, Institute of Southeast Asian Studies, 1996.

Gould, J. W. *The United States and Malaysia.* Cambridge, MA, Harvard University Press, 1969.

Hefner, Robert W. (Ed.). *The Politics of Multiculturalism: Pluralism and Citizenship in Malaysia, Singapore, and Indonesia.* Honolulu, HI, University of Hawaii Press, 2001.

Heng Pek Koon. *Chinese Politics in Malaysia: A History of the Malaysian Chinese Association.* Kuala Lumpur, Oxford University Press, 1988.

Hilley, John. *Malaysia: Mahathirism, Hegemony and the New Opposition.* London, Zed Books, 2001.

Hua Wu Yin. *Class and Communalism in Malaysia: Politics in a Dependent Capitalist State.* London, Zed Books, 1983.

International Bar Association. *Justice in Jeopardy: Malaysia in 2000—Report of a Mission (17–27 April 1999) on behalf of the International Bar Association, the ICJ Centre for the Independence of Judges and Lawyers, the Commonwealth Lawyers' Association, the Union Internationale des Avocats.* London, International Bar Association, 2000.

Kahn, Joel S., and Loh Kok Wah, Francis (Eds). *Fragmented Vision: Culture and Politics in Contemporary Malaysia.* Sydney, Asian Studies Association of Australia, 1993.

Khoo Boo Teik. *Paradoxes of Mahathirism: An Intellectual Biography of Mahathir Mohamad.* Kuala Lumpur, Oxford University Press, 1995.

Lee, H. P. *Constitutional Conflicts in Contemporary Malaysia.* Kuala Lumpur, Oxford University Press, 1995.

Mahathir Mohamad. *The Malay Dilemma.* Singapore, Asia Pacific Press, 1970, republished 1981.

A New Deal for Asia. Kuala Lumpur, Pelanduk Publications, 1999.

Mauzy, Diane K. Barisan Nasional. *Coalition Government in Malaysia, Kuala Lumpur, Singapore, Marican, 1983.*

Means, G. P. *Malaysian Politics.* London, Hodder and Stoughton, 1976.

Milne, R. S., and Mauzy, Diane K. *Politics and Government in Malaysia.* Singapore, Federal Publications, 1978.

Malaysian Politics under Mahathir. London, Routledge, 1999.

Munro-Kua, Anne. *Authoritarian Populism in Malaysia.* New York, St Martin's Press, 1997.

Mutalib, Hussin. *Islam and Ethnicity in Malay Politics.* Singapore, Oxford University Press, 1990.

Nair, Shanti. *Islam in Malaysian Foreign Policy.* London, Routledge, 1997.

Pathmanathan, Murugesu, and Lazarus, David. *Winds of Change: The Mahathir Impact on Malaysia's Foreign Policy.* Petaling Jaya, Eastview Productions Sdn Bhd, 1984.

Ratnam, K. J. *Communalism and the Political Process in Malaya.* Kuala Lumpur, University of Malaya Press, 1965.

Roff, M. C. *The Politics of Belonging: Political Change in Sabah and Sarawak.* London, Oxford University Press, 1975.

Said, Ikmal, and Saravanamuttu, J. (Eds). *Images of Malaysia.* Kuala Lumpur, Persatuan Sosial Sains Malaysia, 1991.

Salleh Abas, Tun, and Das, K. *May Day for Justice.* Kuala Lumpur, Magnus Books, 1990.

Shome, Tony. *Malay Political Leadership.* Richmond, Surrey, Curzon Press, 2001.

Tan Liok Ee. *The Politics of Chinese Education in Malaya 1945–61.* Kuala Lumpur, Oxford University Press, 1998.

Teng, Fan Yew. *The UMNO Drama.* Kuala Lumpur, Egret Books, 1989.

ECONOMY

Alavi, Rokiah. *Industrialization in Malaysia: Import Substitution and Infant Industry Performance.* London, Routledge, 1996.

Ariffin, Jamilah. *Women and Development in Malaysia.* Petaling Jaya, Pelanduk Publications, 1992.

Athukorala, Prema-chandra. *Crisis and Recovery in Malaysia: The Role of Capital Controls.* Cheltenham, Edward Elgar Publishing, 2001.

Barlow, C. *The Natural Rubber Industry.* Kuala Lumpur, Oxford University Press, 1978.

Modern Malaysia in the Global Economy. Political and Social Change into the 21st Century. Cheltenham, Edward Elgar Publishing, 2001.

Chai, H. C. *The Development of British Malaya 1896–1909.* Kuala Lumpur, Oxford University Press, 1964.

Cho, George. *The Malaysian Economy: Spatial Perspectives.* London, Routledge, 1990.

Cooke, Fadzillah M. *The Challenge of Sustainable Forests: Forest Resource Policy in Malaysia, 1970–1995.* St Leonards, NSW, Allen and Unwin, 1999.

Drabble, J. H. *Rubber in Malaya 1876–1922.* London, Oxford University Press, 1973.

An Economic History of Malaysia, c.1800–1990: The Transition to Modern Economic Growth. Basingstoke, Palgrave Macmillan, 2000.

Faaland, J., Parkinson, J. R., and Saniman R. *Growth and Ethnic Inequality; Malaysia's New Economic Policy.* London, Hurst and Company, 1990.

Fisk, E. K., and Osman-Rani, H. (Eds). *The Political Economy of Malaysia.* Kuala Lumpur, Oxford University Press, 1982.

Ghani, Mohamed Nor Abdul, et al. *Malaysia Incorporated and Privatization: Towards National Unity.* Petaling Jaya, Pelanduk Publications, 1984.

Gomez, E. T. *Political Business; Corporate Involvement of Malaysian Political Parties.* Townsville, James Cook University of North Queensland, 1994.

Chinese Business in Malaysia: Accumulation, Ascendance, Accommodation. Honolulu, HI, University of Hawaii Press, 1999.

Gomez, E. T., and Jomo, K. S. *Malaysia's Political Economy: Politics, Patronage and Profits.* Cambridge, Cambridge University Press, 1997.

Gullick, John. *Malaysia: Economic Expansion and National Unity.* London, Ernest Benn, 1981.

Heyzer, N. (Ed.). *Women Farmers and Rural Change in Asia.* Kuala Lumpur, Asian Pacific Development Centre, 1987.

Hill, R. D. *Rice in Malaya: A Study in Historical Geography.* Kuala Lumpur, Oxford University Press, 1977.

Hoffman, Lutz, and Tan, Siew Ee. *Review of Industrial Growth, Employment and Foreign Investment in Peninsular Malaysia.* Kuala Lumpur, Oxford University Press, 1980.

Jesudason, J. *Ethnicity and the Economy; The State, Chinese Business and Multinationals in Malaysia.* Kuala Lumpur, Oxford University Press, 1989.

Jomo, K. S. *Growth and Structural Change in the Malaysian Economy.* London, MacMillan, 1990.

U-Turn? Malaysian Economic Development Policies after 1990. Townsville, James Cook University of North Queensland, 1994.

Jomo, K. S. (Ed.). *A Question of Class: Capital, the State and Uneven Development in Malaysia.* Singapore, Oxford University Press, 1986.

Mahathir's Economic Policies. Petaling Jaya, INSAN, 1989.

Industrializing Malaysia; Policy, Performance, Prospects. London, Routledge, 1993.

Privatizing Malaysia: Rents, Rhetoric and Reality. Boulder, CO, Westview Press, 1994.

Japan and Malaysian Development: In the Shadow of the Rising Sun. London, Routledge, 1995.

Rethinking Malaysia. Hong Kong, Asia 2000, 1999.

Malaysian Eclipse: Economic Crisis and Recovery. London, Zed Books, 2001.

Jomo, K. S., Felker, Greg, and Rajah, Rasiah. *Industrial Technology Development in Malaysia.* London, Routledge, 1999.

Kanpathy, V. (Ed.). *Managing Industrial Transition in Malaysia.* Kuala Lumpur, Institute of Strategic and International Studies, 1995.

Kanpathy, V., and Ismail Salleh (Eds). *Malaysian Economy; Selected Issues and Policy Directions.* Kuala Lumpur, Institute of Strategic and International Studies, 1994.

Khera, H. S. *The Oil Palm Industry of Malaysia: An Economic Study.* Kuala Lumpur, University of Malaya Press, 1976.

King, Victor T. *Tourism in Borneo: Issues and Perspectives.* Williamsburg, Borneo Research Council, 1994.

Lee, H. L. *Household Saving in West Malaysia and the Problem of Financing Economic Development.* Kuala Lumpur, Faculty of Economics and Administration, University of Malaya Press, 1971.

Public Policies and Economic Diversification in West Malaysia, 1957–70. Kuala Lumpur, University of Malaya Press, 1978.

Lee Kiong Hock, and Shyamala, Nagaraj (Eds). *The Malaysian Economy beyond 1990.* Kuala Lumpur, Persatuan Ekonomi Malaysia, 1991.

Lim, David. *Further Readings on Malaysian Economic Development.* Oxford University Press, 1982.

Lim, T. G. *Peasants and their Agricultural Economy in Colonial Malaya 1874–1941.* Kuala Lumpur, Oxford University Press, 1977.

McGee, T. G. *The Urbanization Process in the Third World.* London, Bell, 1971.

Malaysia: Economic Planning Unit.

Second Malaysia Plan 1971–75. Kuala Lumpur, Government Press, 1971.

Third Malaysia Plan 1976–80. Kuala Lumpur, Government Press, 1976.

Fourth Malaysia Plan 1981–85. Kuala Lumpur, Government Press, 1981.

Fifth Malaysia Plan 1986–90. Kuala Lumpur, Government Press, 1986.

Sixth Malaysia Plan 1991–95. Kuala Lumpur, Government Press, 1991.

Seventh Malaysia Plan 1996–2000. Kuala Lumpur, Government Press, 1996.

Mehmet, Ozay. *Development in Malaysia: Poverty, Wealth and Trusteeship.* London, Croom Helm, 1986.

Nyland, Chris, Smith, Wendy, Smyth, Russell, and Vicziany, Marika (Eds). *Malaysian Business in the New Era.* Cheltenham, Edward Elgar Publishing, 2001.

Rao, V. V. Bhanoji. *Malaysia: Development Pattern and Policy, 1947–71.* Singapore University Press, 1980.

Searle, Peter. *The Riddle of Malaysian Capitalism—Rent-seekers or Real Capitalists?* Honolulu, HI, University of Hawaii Press, 1998.

Sieh Lee Mei Ling. *Taking on the World: Globalization Strategies in Malaysia.* Kuala Lumpur, McGraw Hill, 2000.

Silcock, T. H., and Fisk, E. K. (Eds). *The Political Economy of Independent Malaya.* Singapore, Eastern Universities Press, 1963.

Snodgrass, D. R. *Inequality and Economic Development in Malaysia.* Kuala Lumpur, Oxford University Press, 1980.

Sundaram, Jomo (Ed.). *Malaysian Eclipse—Economic Crisis and Recovery.* London, Zed Books, 2001.

World Bank. *Malaysia: Selected Issues in Rural Poverty.* Washington, DC, World Bank, 1980.

Yip, Y. H. *The Development of the Tin Mining Industry in Malaya.* Singapore, University of Malaya Press, 1969.

Young, Kevin, Bussink, Willem C. F., and Hasan, Parvez (Eds). *Malaysia: Growth and Equity in a Multiracial Society.* Baltimore and London, Johns Hopkins University Press, 1980.

THE MALDIVES

Physical and Social Geography

B. H. FARMER

With additions by the editorial staff

The Republic of Maldives (commonly referred to as 'the Maldives') comprises a chain of 1,190 small coral islands in the Indian Ocean, lying about 675 km south-west of Sri Lanka, and extending from just north of the Equator to about 8° N. Of these islands, which cover a land area of 298 sq km (115 sq miles), 200 are inhabited. According to the results of the census held in March–April 2000, the population totalled 270,101 (with an average density of 906.4 per sq km). According to census figures, an estimated 74,069 people resided in the capital, Malé.

The Maldives rests on a submarine ridge, which may be volcanic in origin. The islands are grouped into 26 natural atolls (rings of coral islands, each ring encircling a lagoon: the word *atoll* is itself, in fact, Maldivian); but are divided, for administrative purposes, into 20 atolls. All of the islands consist entirely of coral, coral sand and other coral detritus, and none exceeds a land area of 13 sq km. The average daily temperature ranges from 25° C to 31° C. The average annual rainfall is 2,143mm. Most of the islands are covered with coconut palms.

The lack of suitable land for construction purposes and attendant population pressures have become major problems, particularly on Malé, where, until the 1990s, buildings were traditionally restricted to one storey. The Malé land-reclamation project was begun in 1979 and completed in 1986. As a result of this US $6m. project, about 600,000 sq m of land was reclaimed, adding around 50% to the total land area of the capital. Another land-creation programme, involving the addition of an island extending to 4 sq km in area, was scheduled for completion in 2002. The new island of Hulhumale was projected to accommodate 125,000 people. The first settlements were scheduled to begin in 2003.

The Maldivians are thought to be of mixed descent, deriving from South Indians (Dravidians), Sinhalese and Arabs. The Maldivians' language, Dhivehi, is related to Sinhala. Islam is the state religion, and the Maldivians are Sunni Muslims.

History

Revised by the editorial staff

The people of the Maldives adopted the Islamic faith in the 12th century. The earliest known description of conditions in the islands was recorded by Ibn Batutah, an Arab traveller and historian, in the 14th century. The ruler was then a sultan of the Somavansa dynasty, one of the six great dynasties that, for the most part, ruled the country following its conversion to Islam. The Portuguese, in their rapid and widespread colonization during the 16th century, established themselves on the islands in 1558, but were driven out in 1573. In the 17th century the islands came under the protection of the Dutch rulers of Ceylon (now Sri Lanka). When the British took possession of Ceylon in 1795–96, they extended their protection to the Maldive Islands, and this was formally recorded in an agreement in 1887. The sultanate was made elective in 1932, and the islands remained a British crown protectorate until January 1953, when a Republic was inaugurated. In February 1954, however, the sultanate was restored under a new Constitution.

In 1948, when Ceylon became independent, a new agreement between the United Kingdom and the Maldive Islands provided that the UK should control the foreign affairs of the islands but should not interfere internally. The Sultan undertook to provide necessary facilities to British forces for the defence of the islands.

In 1956 the Maldivian and British Governments agreed to the establishment of a British air force staging post on Gan, an island in the southernmost atoll, Addu. The Maldivian Government accorded free and unrestricted use by the UK Government of Gan Island and of 44.5 ha of Hittadu Island, for radio facilities. Another agreement was signed in 1960, under which the Maldivian Government permitted the continued use by the UK of Gan and the demarcated area on Hittadu, together with the Addu atoll and the adjacent territorial waters, for a term of 30 years. This period was to be extendable by agreement.

INDEPENDENCE

The Maldive Islands achieved full independence on 26 July 1965, becoming a full sovereign state with all rights to conduct its own defence and external relations. The British Government, however, retained those facilities in Addu atoll that had been accorded to it in 1960 for purposes of Commonwealth defence. It also undertook to pay the Maldivian Government £100,000, with a further £750,000 spread over five years or more, for economic development. In 1975, however, the UK decided to close the air force base. With the evacuation of Gan by the British forces completed in March 1976, the 30-year agreement was terminated, creating a large commercial and military vacuum.

In October 1977 the Maldives Government rejected a US $1m. offer from the USSR to lease the former base on Gan, on the grounds that it did not want to lease the island for military purposes, nor to a superpower. In 1981 plans were announced for the establishment of an industrial zone on Gan. By 1990 there were two factories (producing ready-made garments) operating on Gan. The airport on Gan is now fully operational. It links the capital, Malé, with the south, and is due to become an international airport in the near future.

The Maldives seeks to maintain and develop strong and varied foreign relations in order to obtain more aid and to ensure a peaceful Indian Ocean area. The country participates in numerous international organizations; it has been a member of the Colombo Plan since 1963 and of the UN since 1965. It joined the IMF, the World Bank and the Asian Development Bank (ADB) in 1978, and has been a full member of the Commonwealth since 1985. The Maldives is also a founder member of the South Asian Association for Regional Co-operation (SAARC), which was formally constituted in December 1985. The Maldives' international standing was enhanced in November 1990 and again in May 1997, when it successfully hosted the fifth and ninth SAARC summit meetings respectively, which were held in Malé. The Maldives' international profile was further heightened in February 1997, when it hosted the Asia-Pacific Ministers' Conference on Tourism and Environment. In January 2000 the Maldives hosted the fourth SAARC Economic Co-operation Conference. In July 2002 the Maldives had diplomatic relations with 135 countries. In October 1995 the Maldives opened its third resident diplomatic mission (in addition to those in Sri Lanka and at the UN headquarters in New York, USA) in London, in the United Kingdom.

POLITICAL DEVELOPMENTS

In a national referendum in March 1968, over 80% of voters approved a proposal to establish a republic in place of the sultanate. The Republic of the Maldive Islands was proclaimed on 11 November 1968. Amir Ibrahim Nasir, who had been Prime Minister since 1957, was elected President. The country was renamed the Maldives in April 1969.

A new Constitution, promulgated in 1968, vested considerable powers in the President, including the right to appoint and dismiss the Prime Minister and the Cabinet of Ministers. In March 1975, following rumours of a coup conspiracy, President Nasir invoked emergency powers and dismissed the Prime Minister, Ahmed Zaki, who was banished to a remote atoll, and the office of Prime Minister was abolished. In June 1978 Nasir announced that, for health reasons, he would not seek re-election at the end of his second five-year term, and in November, following a national referendum, Maumoon Abdul Gayoom, the erstwhile Minister of Transport in Nasir's Cabinet and a former permanent representative of the Maldives to the UN, succeeded Nasir as President. Nasir subsequently left the Maldives to take up residence in Singapore.

Gayoom's Government made the development of poor rural regions a priority, and claimed to have restored freedom to the Republic, such as freedom of the press. It also pursued investigations into the activities of former government officials, notably Nasir's Minister of Public Safety, Amir Abdul Hannan, who had been accused of human rights violations. Nasir himself, who was reputed to have amassed a substantial fortune while in office, was to face trial for misuse of government funds if he returned to the Maldives, and in November 1980 it was announced that the Government intended to try him *in absentia* on a number of charges.

In April 1980 President Gayoom confirmed the discovery of an attempted coup against the Government, and implicated Nasir in the alleged plot. In April 1981 Ahmed Naseem, former Deputy Minister of Fisheries and brother-in-law of Nasir, was sentenced to life imprisonment for plotting to overthrow President Gayoom. Nasir himself vigorously denied any involvement in the plot, and attempts to extradite him from Singapore were unsuccessful. (In July 1990, however, President Gayoom officially pardoned Nasir *in absentia* in recognition of the role that he had played in winning national independence.) In 1983 another unsuccessful plot against President Gayoom was reported. In September he was re-elected as President, for a further five years, by a national referendum in which he obtained 95.6% of the popular vote. In September 1988 Gayoom was again re-elected unopposed, for a third five-year term, obtaining a record 96.4% of the popular vote.

A third, and more serious, attempt to depose President Gayoom took place in November 1988, when a force of sea-borne mercenary troops, numbering about 80 men, landed in Malé and attempted to seize control of important government installations. A number of senior officials, including the Minister of Transport and Shipping, were captured, but the President, who went into hiding, successfully appealed for help to the Indian Government, which dispatched an emergency contingent of 1,600 troops. Although the insurrection was suppressed within a matter of hours, 19 people were reported to have died in the fighting. In their flight from the Indian forces, the mercenaries took a number of hostages, several of whom were subsequently killed. Most of the mercenary force was reported to have been captured as it attempted to escape by sea. The mercenaries were stated to be Sri Lankan members of the Tamil separatist group, the People's Liberation Organization of Tamil Eelam (PLOTE), allegedly recruited by a disaffected Maldivian businessman, Abdullah Luthufi, who was believed to have been acting in concert with the leader of PLOTE, Kadirkamam Uma Maheswaran. The Sri Lankan Government, however, was in no way implicated in the affair. In September 1989 the President commuted to life imprisonment the death sentences imposed on 12 Sri Lankans and four Maldivians, who took part in the aborted coup. The Indian Government withdrew its remaining 160 troops from the Maldives in early November.

In February 1990, despite alleged opposition from powerful members of the privileged élite, President Gayoom announced that, as part of proposals for a broad new policy of liberalization and democratic reform, he was planning to introduce legislation, in the near future, enabling him to distribute powers, currently enjoyed by the President alone, amongst other official bodies. A further sign of growing democratization in the Maldives was the holding of discussions by the President's Consultative Council, in early 1990, concerning freedom of speech (particularly in the local press). In April, however, it became apparent that some Maldivians opposed political change, when three pro-reform members of the Majlis (legislature) received anonymous death threats. A few months later, following the emergence of several politically outspoken magazines, including *Sangu* (The Conchshell), there was an abrupt reversal of the Government's policy regarding the liberalization of the press. All publications not sanctioned by the Government were banned, and a number of leading writers and publishers were arrested.

As part of a major cabinet reshuffle in late May 1990, President Gayoom dismissed the Minister of State for Defence and National Security, Ilyas Ibrahim (who also held the Trade and Industries portfolio and headed the State Trading Corporation), from his post, following the latter's abrupt and unannounced departure from the country. The Government later disclosed that Ibrahim (Gayoom's brother-in-law) was to have appeared before a presidential special commission investigating alleged embezzlement and misappropriation of government funds. On his return to the Maldives in August, Ibrahim was placed under house arrest. In March 1991, however, the special commission concluded that there was no evidence of involvement, either direct or indirect, by Ibrahim in the alleged financial misdeeds; in the same month the President appointed Ilyas Ibrahim as Minister of Atolls Administration. In April the President established an anti-corruption board, which was to investigate allegations of corruption, bribery, fraud, misappropriation of government funds and property, and misuse of government office.

In early August 1993, a few weeks before the Majlis vote on the presidential candidate, Gayoom was informed that Ilyas Ibrahim, whose position as Minister of Atolls Administration had afforded him the opportunity to build a political base outside Malé (where he already enjoyed considerable popularity), was seeking the presidency and attempting to influence members of the Majlis (at that time, the legislature nominated and elected by secret ballot a single candidate, who was presented to the country in a referendum). In the Majlis vote, held in late August, the incumbent President, who had previously been unanimously nominated for the presidency by the legislature, obtained 28 votes, against 18 for his brother-in-law. For his allegedly unconstitutional behaviour, however, Ibrahim was charged with attempting to 'influence the members of the Majlis' and he promptly left the country. Ibrahim was subsequently tried *in absentia* and sentenced to 15 years' imprisonment. In addition, his brother, Abbas Ibrahim, was removed from his post as Minister of Fisheries and Agriculture. (Ilyas Ibrahim returned to the Maldives in 1996 when he was placed under house arrest; this restriction was lifted in 1997.)

In October 1993 Gayoom was re-elected as President, for a further five years, by a national referendum in which he obtained 92.8% of the popular vote. Following his re-election, the President carried out an extensive cabinet reshuffle and a far-reaching reorganization of government bodies, including the establishment of two new ministries (that of Youth, Women's Affairs and Sports and that of Information and Culture) and the appointment of the country's first female government minister.

In November 1994, at an official ceremony marking Republic Day, President Gayoom outlined various measures intended to strengthen the political system and to advance the process of democratization. These included the granting of greater autonomy and responsibilities to members of the Cabinet of Ministers, the introduction of regulations governing the conduct of civil servants (in order to increase their accountability), the introduction of democratic elections to island development committees and atoll committees, and the establishment of a Law Commission to carry out reforms to the judicial system.

Although the possibility of a direct, multi-candidate presidential election and the drafting of a new constitution were much discussed in 1995, no actual changes were carried out.

In November 1996 President Gayoom effected an extensive cabinet reshuffle and a reorganization of government bodies, including the establishment of a Supreme Council for Islamic Affairs, which was to be under direct presidential control and was to advise the Government on matters relating to Islam. In early 1997 President Gayoom announced that the Citizens' Special Majlis (which was established in 1980 with the specific task of amending the Constitution) had resolved to complete the revision of the Constitution during that year and to implement the amended version by 1 January 1998. The Citizens' Special Majlis finished its 17-year-long task in early November 1997 (passing the amendments by 88 votes to two votes). The revised Constitution was ratified by the President on 27 November and came into effect, as planned, on 1 January 1998. Under the new 156-article Constitution, a formal, multi-candidate contest was permitted for the legislature's nomination for the presidency; no restriction was placed on the number of terms a president may serve; for administrative purposes, the number of atolls was increased from 19 to 20; the Majlis, which was henceforth known as the People's Majlis, was enlarged from 48 to 50 seats; the Citizens' Special Majlis was renamed the People's Special Majlis; the rights of the people were expanded; parliamentary immunity was introduced; the office of auditor-general was created; the post of commissioner of elections was constitutionalized; ministers were afforded greater power; public officers were made more accountable; parliamentary questions were allowed; and judges and magistrates were obliged to take special oaths of loyalty.

In September 1998 five individuals declared their candidacy for the presidency; the People's Majlis unanimously voted by secret ballot for the incumbent President to go forward to the national referendum. In the referendum, which was held in mid-October, Gayoom was re-elected as President for a fifth term in office, obtaining 90.9% of the popular vote. Following his re-election, the President carried out an extensive cabinet reorganization, including the establishment of two new ministries (that of Communications, Science and Technology and that of Human Resources, Employment and Labour). In an unexpected move, Ilyas Ibrahim was appointed to hold the new portfolio of transport and civil aviation.

In November 1999 elections for 42 members of the 50-seat People's Majlis were conducted (on a non-partisan basis). In an attempt to strengthen and develop the Maldivian system of public administration, the President established an Advisory Committee on Public-Sector Reform and Modernization and a Network of Senior Government Officials in November 1999 and February 2000, respectively. At the end of May 2000 the Minister of State for Finance and Treasury, Arif Hilmy, resigned owing to ill health, and was replaced by Mohamed Jaleel. As part of a government initiative to promote the advancement of women in public life, President Gayoom appointed a woman as the new Island Chief of Himmafushi in June 2001. In December a woman was appointed as Atoll Chief of Vaavu atoll (the first woman to be assigned a senior executive position of an atoll). In October the President announced his support for the US-led military campaign against the al-Qa'ida (Base) organization, held principally responsible for the 'suicide attacks' in New York and Washington, DC, USA in September.

In early September 2002 an armed passenger attempted to hijack an Air Seychelles aircraft en route from Mumbai (India) to the Seychelles, via Malé. Airline staff managed to overpower the suspect, who was arrested in Malé; no other passengers were injured. It was reported that the passenger wanted to divert the aeroplane to another destination.

In November 1989, meanwhile, the Maldives hosted an international conference, with delegates from other small island nations, to discuss the threat posed to low-lying island countries by the predicted rise in sea-level caused by heating of the earth's atmosphere as a result of pollution (the 'greenhouse effect'—see Environmental Issues of Asia and the Pacific, p. 29). In June 1990 an Environmental Research Unit, which was to operate under the Ministry of the Environment, was established in the Maldives. The Maldives again expressed its serious concern with regard to problems of world-wide environmental pollution when it hosted the 13th conference of the UN's Intergovernmental Panel on Climate Change in September 1997. In September 1999 a special session of the UN General Assembly was convened in New York to address the specific problems faced by the 43-member Alliance of Small Island States (including the Maldives), notably climate change, rising sea levels and globalization. At the UN Millennium Summit meeting in September 2000 the President of the Maldives again took the opportunity to urge leaders to address environmental issues. The Government expressed its grave disappointment and concern at the USA's decision in April 2001 to reject the Kyoto Protocol to the UN's Framework Convention on Climate Change. The rest of the international community adopted the protocol in July after many of the targets had been reduced. The USA proposed an alternative in February 2002; however, most nations dismissed it as ineffective. In early March the Maldives, Kiribati and Tuvalu announced their decision to take legal action against the USA for refusing to sign the Kyoto Protocol, thus contributing to global warming which has produced the rising sea levels that threaten to submerge the islands. At the World Summit on Sustainable Development held in September 2002 in Johannesburg, South Africa, President Gayoom warned the international community that low-lying islands were at greater risk than ever before. He called for urgent action, including the universal ratification and implementation of the Kyoto Protocol, to prevent a global environmental catastrophe. On his return to the Maldives, the President stated that some progress had been made in certain areas, although the decisions were not as far-reaching as desired by small island nations. In September 2000, meanwhile, the Comprehensive Nuclear Test Ban Treaty was ratified by the Maldives.

Economy

Revised by the editorial staff

The population is dispersed over 200 coral islands, with individual islands' populations ranging from 100 to more than 5,000 (the population of the capital, Malé, however, totalled 74,069 at the 2000 census). Tourism, fishing, agriculture and transport services provide the main income in the atolls. Arable land is minimal and, while small amounts of coconuts, millet, sorghum, maize and yams are grown, virtually all the main food staples, such as rice, wheat flour and sugar, have to be imported. A large proportion of the coconut crop is regularly destroyed by rats: eradication programmes are carried out every few years. During the 1970s the growth rate of the Maldivian economy failed to keep pace with the increase in the country's population, which averaged 3% annually. In 1979, according to estimates by the World Bank, the Maldives' gross national product (GNP) per head was US $220 (at average 1978–80 prices), having declined by 0.7% per year, in real terms, since 1970. However, despite the constraints imposed by geography, sparse agricultural resources and a narrowly based economy, the Maldives achieved an average annual economic growth of 9.5% between 1978 and 1982. During 1990–99, it was estimated, GNP per head increased, in real terms, at an average annual rate of 3.8%. The World Bank estimated the country's GNP for 2000 to be US $541m. (at average 1998–2000 prices), equivalent to about US $1,960 per head (or US $4,240 per head on an international purchasing-power parity basis). The Maldives' gross domestic product (GDP) increased, in real terms, by an annual average of 5.4% in 1990–2000. According to the Asian Development Bank (ADB), the Maldives' GDP increased, in real terms, by

7.4% in 1999, by 4.6% in 2000 and by 2.1% in 2001. The economy fared well in the first eight months of 2001; however, the 'suicide attacks' on the USA in September and the subsequent US-led military action in Afghanistan led to a decline in tourism and a deceleration in economic growth. The trade, fisheries and financial sectors were also adversely affected by security fears and a global economic slowdown. During 1990–99 the population increased at an average annual rate of 2.6%. The working population at the 2000 census was 86,245 (31.9% of the total population). Less than 8% of the workforce were farmers in 1990, producing less than 10% of the GDP. The Government has successfully diversified the economy by developing the shipping and tourist industries.

FISHING

The fishing industry remains a vital sector of the Maldivian economy, although its contribution to GDP has declined in recent years. It is still the principal source of livelihood for the majority of the population, providing direct employment to almost 10,000 people. The catch consists mainly of tuna, 90% of which was traditionally exported to Sri Lanka in a dried form known as 'Maldive fish'. However, from 1972 the Sri Lankan Government gradually reduced its quota, and by 1978 had ceased importing 'Maldive fish'. This led to a change in the fisheries sector from dried fish to wet fish production, and in 1978, through an agreement with the Marubeni Corporation of Japan, the Maldive Nippon Corporation was formed and the first factory outside Malé for canning and processing fresh fish opened in the Faadhippolhu atoll. Although Sri Lanka resumed imports of 'Maldive fish' in 1979, it imported much less than before, and in the same year the Government announced the formation of the Maldives Fisheries Corporation, 'to exploit the fisheries resources in the most profitable manner for the benefit of the country'. Raw and fresh fish (whether frozen or canned) now constitute the bulk of fish exports.

There are several thousand fishing boats built in the country out of coconut wood, each boat taking about a dozen fishermen. In 1991 the fishing fleet comprised 1,258 pole and line fishing boats (*masdhoani*) and 352 trawling boats (*vadhudhoani*). Since 1974, when the Government introduced a major modernization programme, with the help of a 50-year loan of US $3.2m. from the International Development Association, about 90% of the fishing fleet has been mechanized, diesel engines replacing sails, and more maintenance and repair centres have been built. In 2001 the number of mechanized *masdhoani* totalled 1,647. Although a long-term investment, this has had the unfortunate effect of increasing the cost of fuel imports, but it also helped to increase the output of the fishing industry by more than 100% between 1982 and 1985. The total catch of fish increased from 56,992 metric tons in 1987 to a record 133,000 tons in 1999, before declining to 119,000 tons in 2000, and rising again to 127,200 tons in 2001. The Second Fisheries Development Project, which was carried out during the 1980s and early 1990s at an estimated total cost of US $12.6m., with the help of the World Bank and other international organizations, aimed to improve productivity in the fishing industry. Substantial progress was made. Earnings from the export of canned fish from Felivaru increased from US $230,000 in 1983 to US $1.6m. in 1985. In 1986 the State Trading Organization invested 60m. rufiyaa in the extension and upgrading of the harbour and refrigeration facilities at the Felivaru Fish Canning Factory in the Faadhippolhu atoll. As a result of improvements to the factory, the Maldives' production of canned fish increased by 400%, and the export market expanded. In 1993 two new refrigeration plants (with a total cold storage capacity of 1,000 metric tons) were being constructed, with Japanese and Kuwaiti aid, on Maamendhoo Island in the Laamu atoll, and a new refrigeration plant was being built in the Gaafu Alif atoll. The Third Fisheries Development Project was drawn up in 1992 and was expected to cost about US $30.5m. The Project was completed in February 1999, with the official opening of the Kooddoo Fisheries Complex in the South Huvadhu atoll. The Project incorporated the construction of a refrigeration complex with a capacity of 1,900 tons, a quay for collector vessels (four of which were purchased as part of the project) and an ice plant. In 2001 revenue from exports of marine products reached 538.3m. rufiyaa, thus accounting for 57.4% of total export earnings.

In 1985 the Government issued fishing licences to foreign countries, principally France and Spain, enabling them to catch up to 40,000 metric tons of tuna per year within the Maldives' exclusive economic zone (with a range of about 120 km), in return for a 10% royalty on the total catch, based on US landing prices. In 1992 the fishing industry employed about 22.4% of the labour force and provided around 15% of total GDP. In the same year, fishing was the Maldives' second largest source of foreign exchange, after tourism. The GDP of the fisheries sector grew by 15% in 1994, compared with 1993. Poor fish catches in the early part of 1995, however, combined with large stock levels in the frozen fish export market, resulted in depressed fisheries activity in 1995. In mid-1997 the Minister of Fisheries and Agriculture stated that, partly owing to the Government's successful efforts in improving the quality of Maldivian fish exports, the price of fish from the Maldives on the world market had become markedly stronger. In January 2001 the fresh fish export market was opened to the private sector.

SHIPPING

Another important commercial sector is the shipping industry, which was established in 1958; two ships were then in operation. By reinvesting the profits, the country was able to develop a sizeable fleet of ships, and in 1980 the profits of the state-owned Maldives Shipping Ltd (later renamed Maldives National Ship Management Ltd and, again, Maldives National Shipping Ltd), with 40 ships, provided 9% of government revenue. The Government tried to develop the shipping industry as much as possible by the training of technical personnel, to replace the foreigners engaged in this activity, and by increasing the total displacement of the fleet. In June 1981 the ADB approved a loan of US $1m. to the Maldives to assist in providing the country's first reliable scheduled shipping services between Malé and the atolls. During the 1980s, however, the shipping sector, which is dependent on third-country trade for more than 90% of its cargo earnings, suffered from the world-wide shipping recession as well as from the effects of the Iran–Iraq war; moreover, the UNCTAD code of conduct (effective from 1983), limiting third-country carriers to 20% of international sea freight, curtailed the lucrative trade of Maldivian vessels from Colombo. Because of the heavy losses incurred during 1982–84, the Maldivian shipping industry was reorganized, and both its fleet size and its level of operations were substantially reduced. The Maldives' international shipping sector, however, made a small profit in 1987 and 1988. In 1999 Maldives National Shipping Ltd operated a fleet of seven general cargo vessels and one container vessel.

TOURISM

The Maldives, with its white sandy beaches, clear water and multi-coloured coral formations, offers an ideal setting for the development of a thriving tourist industry. Following the decline of the shipping industry in the 1980s, tourism rapidly gained in importance as an economic sector, and by 1989 it had overtaken the fishing industry as the Maldives' largest source of foreign exchange. Since 1972 tourist facilities have been developed by local private enterprises. According to the Second Tourism Master Plan, which was approved by the Government in May 1996, the number of tourist beds was to be increased by 10,000 within the next 10 years, and tourism was to be introduced in new areas, based on the existing transport and communications facilities. Bidding for the 14 islands to be developed for tourism under the Master Plan opened in June 1997. In 1996 the Government declared 1997 'Visit Maldives Year' and launched an intense promotional campaign. By mid-2001 a total of 87 island resorts had been developed for tourists, with 16,428 hotel beds (compared with 11,400 in 1996). In late 2001 a four-year plan was under way to convert 12 islands into holiday resorts and to increase the number of hotel beds by 4,000. There is no tourist accommodation on Malé, on the grounds that it would interfere with the traditional Islamic way of life pursued by the island's inhabitants.

The number of tourists visiting the Maldives rose from 3,789 in 1972/73 to 467,154 in 2000 (the majority of whom were from Europe). This figure decreased in 2001 to 461,063, despite promotional campaigns conducted in the previous year, largely due to concerns over travel safety and stability in the South

Asian region after the terrorist attacks on the USA in September. In 2000 receipts from tourism provided an estimated US $344m., compared with US $325m. in 1999. In an effort to boost tourism, the Government has introduced ways to improve the infrastructure. Telephones were installed on several resort islands for the first time in 1977, and a Tourist Advisory Board was established in 1981 to expand the industry yet further. Tourism was, initially, seriously affected by the civil disturbances in Sri Lanka, the usual embarkation point for the Maldives. However, the inauguration of direct charter flights carrying tourists from Europe to Malé, as well as the establishment of three new domestic airports (in 1986, 1990 and 1993), increased the Maldives' share of the market and ensured that revenue from tourism was sustained.

FINANCE

In 1981 the country's first central bank, the Maldives Monetary Authority (MMA), was established, and the currency was changed from rupees to rufiyaa. In 1982 the first commercial bank, The Bank of Maldives Ltd, was opened as a joint venture between the Government and the International Finance Investment and Credit Bank of Bangladesh. Import controls, obliging foreign business executives to use banking facilities in the Maldives, were also announced in 1982. In 1985, aiming to reduce the deficit on the balance-of-payments current account and to remedy a serious shortage of foreign exchange, the Government imposed controls on the supply of bank credit, restricted capital expenditure on development projects, and 'pegged' the exchange rate of the rufiyaa to the currencies of the Maldives' principal trading partners. In 1986 it introduced an import-licensing system, which successfully curtailed expenditure on imports, but this was revoked in March 1987, when the rufiyaa was devalued by 30% and allowed to 'float'.

In September 1992 the MMA introduced a range of restrictive measures, including an increase in bank reserve requirements to 35%, a rise in the ceiling on bank loan rates, the imposition of a minimum deposit rate of 5%, and an increase in bank capital requirements.

In 1993 the Government sold 15% of its shares in the Bank of Maldives Ltd to public companies and 25% to private individuals. The MMA periodically reviews quantitative credit limits for commercial banks and imposes new limits in an attempt to maintain the level of domestic credit expansion. The rate of domestic credit expansion decreased from more than 50% in 1993 to 8.8% in 1997, owing to a sharp reduction in credit to the Government and to public non-financial bodies.

OTHER ECONOMIC ACTIVITIES

The harvesting of coconuts forms another significant commercial activity in the Maldives. Coir yarn weaving, in which only women are engaged, is also a major occupation. In spite of several centuries of continued production of this commodity, the methods in use have not undergone much change; the women do the work in their own homes.

Collecting cowries is another occupation in which only women take part. Cowries and other varieties of shells are a natural product meant solely for export, and not generally used for any domestic purpose. Many varieties of shells in demand by collectors are found in the Maldives, including some of the rarest in the world.

Other small-scale cottage industries include mat-weaving, mostly in the three southernmost atolls of the archipelago, and applying lacquer designs on vases and containers. The highly-coloured mats have some commercial value abroad. Cadjan weaving is also common on the islands, and cadjan is much in demand because of its value for roofing: the heat of the tropical sun is considerably reduced by its use.

Although these small-scale activities employ nearly one-quarter of the total labour force, there has been little scope for expansion, owing to the limited size of the domestic market. In the late 1980s and 1990s, however, there was a substantial increase in demand for traditional handicrafts, such as lacquer work and shell craft, as a result of the expansion of the tourist market. There are only a small number of 'modern' industries in the Maldives, including fish-canning, garment-making (in early 1998 there were eight garment factories operating in the Maldives) and soft-drink bottling. In 1998 the Foreign Investment Services Bureau announced that seven new garment factories were to be built over the next two years (creating about 7,000 new jobs). In mid-1999 the opening of a cement-packing factory on Thilafushi Island in Malé atoll was expected to bring considerable economic benefits to the Maldives. In an attempt to improve and diversify the domestic socio-economy, particularly in the less advanced outlying atolls, the Government has, since the late 1970s, begun to establish a more modern infrastructure (including better communications systems, sanitation and water supply). One of the major infrastructural projects was the Malé land-reclamation project, completed in 1986 (see above). In 1987 the ADB granted a loan of US $6.1m. for the construction of a 4,000-kW power plant, which commenced operations in 1991, on an area of this reclaimed land. In 1987 the Government also announced plans to provide telephone facilities and postal services to all the inhabited islands over the next few years. By 1993 postal services were available to all the inhabited islands, telephone facilities were provided in the major islands of seven of the southern atolls and three of the northern atolls and facsimile (fax) services were available to some islands. By mid-1999 the Maldives telecommunications company, DHIRAAGU, had provided telephone facilities to all of the inhabited islands. In mid-1999 DHIRAAGU signed a contract worth 47m. rufiyaa with a French telecommunications company for the supply and implementation of a mobile cellular telephone system for the Maldives. By March 2002 22,800 inhabitants had subscribed to mobile cellular telephones. In mid-2000 DHIRAAGU launched its 'Instant Internet Access'. In May 2000 the ADB agreed to provide a grant of US $600,000 for the purposes of the Maldives' development of a science and technology master plan, with particular reference to the tourism and fisheries industries. In early 1996, in an effort to combat deforestation, the Government instituted a three-year afforestation programme, which aimed to plant 1m. trees (the target was later increased to 2m. trees, owing to the rapid success of the programme).

In February 1989 the Government and the Netherlands company, Royal Dutch Shell, signed a contract permitting exploration for petroleum in the Maldives. Despite the drilling of an offshore test well in 1991, no reserves of petroleum or natural gas have, as yet, been discovered in Maldivian waters. Owing to a surge in commercial activities and a significant increase in construction projects in Malé, demand for electricity in the capital grew rapidly in the late 1980s and early 1990s. Accordingly, plans were formulated in late 1991 to augment the generating capacity of the power station in Malé and to improve the distribution network. By early 1998 20 islands had been provided with electricity (equivalent to about 60% of the total population). In 2001 the third phase of the Malé power project, further to increase the capital's power supply, was under way; the project was scheduled for completion at the end of 2002.

The economy as a whole was adversely affected by the world recession in the early 1980s. The fishing and tourism industries made a rapid recovery, however, and helped to reduce the country's economic deficits. In the first half of the 1990s the trade deficit steadily increased, as fish exports declined and imports grew. The decrease in fish exports reflected the slump in global demand, more intense competition from foreign producers and falling prices in the principal European markets. At the same time, imports were boosted by import liberalization measures and by expansionary monetary and fiscal policies. Despite the relative strength of the fisheries sector and buoyant tourist receipts in the latter half of the 1990s, the current-account deficit persisted (rising from 6.8% of GDP in 1998 to 11.1% in 1999) and the trade deficit continued to grow (largely owing to a surge in imports associated with development investment in the tourism sector). However, in 2000 the trade deficit decreased, as exports increased and imports declined. The current-account deficit decreased to 9.5% of GDP. The trade deficit increased again in 2001 and the current-account deficit grew to 10.9% of GDP. In 2001 total merchandise imports were valued at US $348.8m., while exports totalled only US $106.8m. Owing to the dearth of manufacturing industries, the Maldives has to import most essential consumer and capital goods. In 2001 the principal source of imports was Singapore (25%); other major sources were Sri Lanka, India and Malaysia. In 2001 the principal market for exports (41%) was the USA; other major purchasers were Sri Lanka, the United Kingdom and Thailand. The principal exports in 2001 were marine products (tuna being the largest export commodity) and clothing. The principal imports were machinery and mechanical appliances and electrical equipment, mineral products and textile and textile articles.

Reflecting an improvement in the country's general economic condition (aided by the fact that the Maldives was not significantly affected by the Asian financial crisis that began in mid-1997), the overall budgetary deficit, including grants, was reduced from 5% of GDP in 1997 to about 3% in 1998. However, the country's fiscal deficit grew from 4.9% in 2000 to 5.3% in 2001, largely owing to an increase in government expenditure. The Maldives' total external debt was an estimated US $206.7m. at the end of 2000, of which US $185.3m. was long-term public debt. In that year the cost of debt-servicing was equivalent to 4.3% of revenue from exports of goods and services. Foreign grant aid in 1998 was projected to total an estimated US $20.2m.; Japan is the Maldives' largest aid donor (disbursing US $11.9m. in 1997). During 1990–98 the average annual rate of inflation was 8.8%; consumer prices rose by 7.6% in 1997. In 1998, however, consumer prices declined sharply, the rate of deflation reaching –1.4%. An inflation rate of 3.0% was recorded in 1999, which declined in 2000 to a deflation rate of –1.1%. Consumer prices increased by only 0.7% in 2001. The numerous development projects undertaken during the 1980s and 1990s resulted in a shortage of labour, which was partly alleviated by employing workers from abroad and by the establishment of vocational training courses. In 2001 about 29,201 expatriate workers (mainly from India, Sri Lanka and Bangladesh) were employed in the Maldives, and it was estimated that in 1999 almost 20% of the country's GDP went to non-Maldivians.

Overall economic performance in the late 1990s was favourable, with greater private-sector participation in the economy, a rise in foreign investment (helped by the recently-established Foreign Investment Promotion Advisory Board), a considerable increase in exports (aided by the expansion of the garment industry), and continued expansion in the tourism sector. In 2000, according to the *Human Development Report 2002,* published by the United Nations Development Programme (UNDP), the Maldives continued to be classified within the Medium Human Development Category, ranking 84th on a list of 173 countries. Three notable areas of investment in the late 1990s were commercial seaweed farming, pearl cultivation and horticulture (in an attempt to reduce reliance on expensive imports of fruit and vegetables). The Maldives was still, however, confronted with the problem of serious macroeconomic imbalances, which have resulted in rising debt, low levels of foreign-exchange reserves and an overvalued nominal exchange rate. In April 2000 Air Maldives, a joint venture between the Government and a Malaysian company, permanently ceased operating international flights owing to estimated losses of US $50m.–$70m. This outcome adversely affected the tourist industry and business confidence in 2000. Furthermore, allegations of mismanagement and corruption at the airline were made public. Development in the private sector has been constrained by the dominant role still played by the highly regulated public sector in economic activity. In early 2001, however, the Government opened up the export of fresh and canned fish to the private sector. This measure was expected to encourage competition and improve efficiency, as well as increase export earnings and the industry's contribution to GDP. Reforms are required in the banking and financial sectors. In June 2000 the Maldives was one of more than 30 countries and territories named by the Organisation for Economic Co-operation and Development (OECD) as unfair tax havens. In 2000–01 the Government introduced measures to curtail public expenditure in an attempt to strengthen the economy. According to UN projections, the Maldives' population was expected to double between 1995 and 2025. The high average annual rate of population growth (estimated at 2.7% in 1990–95), which has placed a heavy burden on the economy in general, is effectively being addressed (according to the results of the March 2000 census, the rate of increase had fallen to 1.96% in 1995–2000). From 2000, in an attempt to solve the problem of overcrowding in Malé, a nearby island was being developed as a suburb to relieve congestion in the capital. In February 2002 the ADB endorsed a three-year country strategy and programme for the Maldives, designed to assist the Maldives in improving living conditions, the education system and access to social infrastructure in the remote islands. In March the Maldives and the ADB signed a poverty reduction partnership agreement with the intention of reducing the incidence of absolute poverty from 43% in 1998 to 25% by 2015 and promoting involvement of local communities in public-sector decision-making. Three other key issues that require prompt attention are: the protection of the fragile environment to ensure sustainable economic growth; the encouragement of greater regional development (particularly in the remote outer atolls) to foster more equitable growth; and an improvement in Maldivian teaching standards in order to upgrade the national skills base.

Statistical Survey

Sources (unless otherwise stated): Ministry of Planning and National Development, Ghaazee Bldg, 4th Floor, Ameer Ahmed Magu, Malé 20-05; tel. 322919; fax 327351; internet www.planning.gov.mv.

AREA AND POPULATION

Area: 298 sq km (115 sq miles).

Population: 244,814 at census of 25 March 1995; 270,101 (males 137,200, females 132,901) at census of 31 March–7 April 2000; 276,000 (official estimate) at mid-2001.

Density (mid-2001): 926 per sq km.

Principal Town: Malé (capital), population 74,069 (2000 census).

Births and Deaths (provisional, 2001): Registered live births 4,882 (birth rate 17.7 per 1,000); Registered deaths 1,079 (death rate 3.9 per 1,000).

Expectation of Life (WHO estimates, years at birth, 2000): Males 64.6; Females 64.6. Source: WHO, *World Health Report*.

Economically Active Population (persons aged 12 years and over, census of April 2000): Agriculture, hunting and forestry 2,495; Fishing 9,294; Mining and quarrying 473; Manufacturing 11,081; Electricity, gas and water 1,132; Construction 3,691; Trade, restaurants and hotels 15,606; Transport, storage and communications 7,873; Financing, insurance, real estate and business services 1,690; Community, social and personal services 18,089; Activities not adequately defined 14,821; Total employed 86,245 (males 57,351; females 28,894); Unemployed 1,742 (males 928, females 814); Total labour force 87,987 (males 58,279; females 29,708).

HEALTH AND WELFARE

Key Indicators

Fertility (births per woman, 2000): 5.6.

Under-5 Mortality Rate (per 1,000 live births, 2000): 80.

HIV/AIDS (% of persons aged 15–49, 2001): 0.06.

Physicians (per 1,000 head, 1996): 0.40.

Hospital Beds (per 1,000 head, 1996): 0.76.

Health Expenditure (1998): US $ per head (PPP): 211.
% of GDP: 7.2.
public (% of total): 72.3.

Access to Water (% of persons, 2000): 100.

Access to Sanitation (% of persons, 2000): 56.

Human Development Index (2000): ranking: 84.
value: 0.743.

For sources and definitions, see explanatory note on p. vi.

AGRICULTURE, ETC.

Principal Crops (metric tons, 1992): Coconuts (number of nuts) 13,442,737, Finger millet 5.7, Maize 1.6, Cassava 31.6, Sweet potatoes 13.8, Taro (Colocasia) 141.7, Alocasia 522.3, Onions 0.1, Chillies 40.3, Sorghum 2.0.

Coconuts (number): 13.2m in 1999; 18.9m. in 2000; 27.2m. in 2001.

Sea Fishing ('000 metric tons, 1999): Skipjack tuna (Oceanic skipjack) 92.9; Yellowfin tuna 13.7; Sharks, rays, skates, etc. 6.9; Total catch (incl. others) 133.5. Source: FAO, *Yearbook of Fishery Statistics*.

2000 ('000 metric tons): Skipjack tuna (Oceanic skipjack) 79.7; Yellowfin tuna 15.7; Total catch (incl. others) 119.0.

2001 ('000 metric tons): Skipjack tuna (Ocean skipjack) 88.0; Yellowfin tuna 15.2; Total catch (incl. others) 127.2.

INDUSTRY

Selected Products ('000 metric tons, unless otherwise indicated, 1999): Frozen fish 9.5; Salted, dried or smoked fish 6.5; Canned fish 4.6. Source: UN, *Industrial Commodity Statistics Yearbook*.

Electric Energy (million kWh): 107 in 1999; 117 in 2000. Source: Asian Development Bank, *Key Indicators of Developing Asian and Pacific Countries*.

2001 (million kWh): Electric energy 130.

FINANCE

Currency and Exchange Rates: 100 laari (larees) = 1 rufiyaa (Maldivian rupee). *Sterling, Dollar and Euro Equivalents* (31 May 2002): £1 sterling = 18.774 rufiyaa; US $1 = 12.800 rufiyaa; €1 = 12.015 rufiyaa; 1,000 rufiyaa = £53.27 = $78.13 = €83.23. *Average Exchange Rate* (rufiyaa per US dollar): 11.770 in 1999; 11.770 in 2000; 12.242 in 2001. Note: Between October 1994 and July 2001 the mid-point rate of exchange was maintained at US $1 = 11.77 rufiyaa. In July 2001 a new rate of $1 = 12.80 rufiyaa was introduced.

Budget (forecasts, million rufiyaa, 2002): *Revenue*: Tax revenue 1,100.3; Other current revenue 1,528.2; Capital revenue 12.3; Total 2,640.8, excl. grant received (99.5). *Expenditure*: General public services 785.0, Defence 449.2, Education 597.2, Health 314.6, Social security and welfare 80.2, Community programmes 500.0, Economic services 467.7 (Agriculture 31.0, Trade and industry 5.6, Electricity, gas and water 61.7, Transport and communications 339.5, Tourism 29.9); Total (incl. others) 3,320.8 (Current 2,113.0, Capital 1,207.8), excl. net lending (–41.5).

International Reserves (US $ million at 31 December 2001): IMF special drawing rights 0.31; Reserve position in IMF 1.95; Foreign exchange 90.80; Total 93.07. Source: IMF, *International Financial Statistics*.

Money Supply (million rufiyaa at 31 December 2001): Currency outside banks 566.52; Demand deposits at commercial banks 1,022.15; Total money (incl. others) 1,655.91. Source: IMF, *International Financial Statistics*.

Cost of Living (Consumer price index; base: 1995 = 100): All items 116.0 in 1999; 114.7 in 2000; 115.4 in 2001. Source: IMF, *International Financial Statistics*.

Gross Domestic Product by Economic Activity (revised estimates, million rufiyaa at constant 1995 prices, 2001): Agriculture 181.4; Fishing 383.6; Coral and sand mining 36.6; Manufacturing, electricity and water supply 772.6; Construction 176.4; Wholesale and retail trade, tourism 2,366.7; Transport and communications 1,048.6; Finance, real estate and business services 897.7; Public administration 814.7; Education, health and social services 138.6; *Sub-total* 6,816.9; *Less* Financial intermediation services indirectly measured 422.9; *Total* 6,393.9.

Balance of Payments (US $ million, 2000): Exports of goods f.o.b. 108.7; Imports of goods f.o.b. –342.0; *Trade balance* –233.3; Exports of services 348.5; Imports of services –109.7; *Balance on goods and services* 5.5; Other income received 10.3; Other income paid –40.4; *Balance on goods, services and income* –24.6; Current transfers received 17.7; Current transfers paid –46.2; *Current balance* –53.1; Direct investment from abroad 13.0; Other investment assets 22.8; Other investment liabilities 4.2; Net errors and omissions 8.8; *Overall balance* –4.3. Source: IMF, *International Financial Statistics*.

Official Development Assistance (US $ million, 1998): Bilateral 15.9, Multilateral 9.1; Total 25.0 (Grants 20.2, Loans 4.8); Per caput assistance (US $) 93.5. Source: UN, *Statistical Yearbook for Asia and the Pacific*.

EXTERNAL TRADE

Principal Commodities (million rufiyaa, 2001): *Imports:* Live animals; animal products 272.7 (Dairy produce, eggs, honey and edible products 158.2); Vegetable products 375.5 (Edible vegetables 130.2, Edible fruits and nuts, peel of citrus or melons 98.2); Prepared food, beverages, spirits and tobacco 411.8 (Beverages, spirits and vinegar 111.7); Mineral products 704.0 (Salt, sulphur, earth and stone, lime and cement 142.9; Mineral fuels, oils, waxes, bituminous substances 559.5); Chemicals and allied industries 262.8; Plastics, rubber and articles thereof 112.6 (Plastics and articles thereof 99.7); Wood, wood charcoal, cork, straw, plaiting materials and articles thereof 163.5 (Wood and articles of wood; wood charcoal 161.9); Paper-making material, paper and paperboard and articles thereof 118.9; Textile and textile articles 506.6 (Cotton incl. yarns and woven fabrics thereof 175.9); Articles of stone, plaster, cement, asbestos, mica or similar materials, glass and glassware 80.0; Base metal and articles of base metal 260.3; Machinery and mechanical appliances; electrical equipment, parts and accessories 884.6 (Nuclear reactors, boilers, machinery and mechanical appliances, computers 447.9; Electrical machinery and equipment and parts thereof, telecommunications equipment, sound recorders, television recorders 436.7); Vehicles, aircraft, vessels and associated transport equipment 293.1 (Vehicles other than railway or tramway rolling stock 105.4; Aircraft, spacecraft and parts thereof 81.3); Miscellaneous manufactured articles 151.8 (Furniture, bedding, cushions, lamps and light fittings, illuminated signs, nameplates, prefabricated buildings 105.7); Total (incl. others) 4,741.0. *Exports*: Marine products 538.3 (Fresh or chilled tuna 64.8; Fresh or chilled reef fish 23.1; Frozen tuna 88.9; Dried tuna 136.3; Sea cucumber 34.3; Canned fish 120.2; Live reef fish 37.1; Other marine products 12.8); (Apparel and clothing accessories 396.7); Total (incl. others) 937.3.

Principal Trading Partners (million rufiyaa, 2001): *Imports:* Australia 106.1, Canada 68.1, Denmark 141.7, France 58.1, Germany 63.6, Hong Kong 53.9, India 502.4, Indonesia 176.1, Italy 52.9, Japan 107.7, Malaysia 421.2, Netherlands 96.7, New Zealand 67.9, Singapore 1,204.3, Sri Lanka 619.7, Thailand 148.8, United Arab Emirates 397.5, United Kingdom 129.2, USA 99.8; *Total* (incl. others) 4,741.0. *Exports*: Canada 11.9, Germany 56.8, Hong Kong 38.7, Japan 43.0, Singapore 25.0, Sri Lanka 180.9, Thailand 80.3, United Kingdom 84.7, USA 381.4; *Total* (incl. others) 937.3.

TRANSPORT

Road Traffic (estimates, 1996): Passenger cars 1,080, Buses and coaches 200, Lorries and vans 1,060, Road tractors 320, Motorcycles and mopeds 5,640, Bicycles 49,026 (1994). Source: mainly International Road Federation, *World Road Statistics*.

1999: Passenger cars 3,037, Commercial vehicles 1,003. Source: UN, *Statistical Yearbook for Asia and the Pacific*.

Merchant Shipping Fleet (displacement, '000 gross registered tons at 31 December): 89.9 in 1999; 78.4 in 2000; 66.6 in 2001. Source: Lloyd's Register-Fairplay, *World Fleet Statistics*.

International Shipping (freight traffic, '000 metric tons, 1990): Goods loaded 27; Goods unloaded 78. Source: UN, *Monthly Bulletin of Statistics*.

Civil Aviation (traffic on scheduled services, 1998): Passengers carried 247,000; Passenger-km (million) 355. Source: UN, *Statistical Yearbook*.

TOURISM

Foreign Visitors by Country of Nationality (2001): Austria 10,476, France 30,542, Germany 65,956, Italy 115,327, Japan 41,895, Switzerland 28,313, United Kingdom 77,151; Total (incl. others) 461,063. Source: Ministry of Tourism, Malé.

Tourism Receipts (US $ million): 303 in 1998; 325 in 1999; 344 in 2000 (estimate) (Source: World Tourism Organization).

COMMUNICATIONS MEDIA

Radio Receivers (July 2000): 29,724 registered.

Television Receivers (July 2000): 10,701 registered.

Telephones (main lines in use): 22,179 in 1999; 24,432 in 2000; 27,242 in 2001.

Mobile Cellular Telephones (March 2002): 22,800 subscribers.

Personal Computers (2001): 6,000 in use.

Internet users (2001): 10,000.

Sources: Ministry of Planning and National Development, Malé; International Telecommunication Union.

EDUCATION

Pre-primary: 148 schools (2000); 12,809 pupils (2001); 411 teachers (2000).

Primary: 230 schools (2000); 46,229 pupils (2000); 2,221 teachers (2000).

Middle (2000): 222 schools; 27,293 pupils; 1,025 teachers.

Lower Secondary: 74 schools (2000); 21,644 pupils (2001); 1,134 teachers (2000).

Higher Secondary: 2 schools (2000); 824 pupils (2001); 53 teachers (2000).

Teacher-training (1999): 171 students.

Vocational: 11 schools (1986); 151 students (2000); 54 teachers (1986).

Source: mainly Ministry of Education, Malé.

Adult literacy rate (UNESCO estimates): 96.7% (males 96.6%; females 96.8%) in 2000 (Source: UN Development Programme, *Human Development Report*).

Directory

The Constitution

Following a referendum in March 1968, the Maldive Islands (renamed the Maldives in April 1969) became a republic on 11 November 1968. On 27 November 1997 the President ratified a new 156-article Constitution, which was to replace the 1968 Constitution; the new Constitution came into effect on 1 January 1998. The main constitutional provisions are summarized below:

STATE, SOVEREIGNTY AND CITIZENS

The Maldives shall be a sovereign, independent, democratic republic based on the principles of Islam, and shall be a unitary State, to be known as the Republic of Maldives. In this Constitution, the Republic of Maldives shall hereinafter be referred to as 'the Maldives'.

The powers of the State of the Maldives shall be vested in the citizens. Executive power shall be vested in the President and the Cabinet of Ministers, legislative power shall be vested in the People's Majlis (People's Council) and the People's Special Majlis, and the power of administering justice shall be vested in the President and the courts of the Maldives.

The religion of the State of the Maldives shall be Islam. The national language of the Maldives shall be Dhivehi.

FUNDAMENTAL RIGHTS AND DUTIES OF CITIZENS

Maldivian citizens are equal before and under the law and are entitled to the equal protection of the law. No Maldivian shall be deprived of citizenship, except as may be provided by law. No person shall be arrested or detained, except as provided by law. Any Maldivian citizen subjected to oppressive treatment shall have the right to appeal against such treatment to the concerned authorities and to the President.

The following are guaranteed: inviolability of residential dwellings and premises; freedom of education; inviolability of letters, messages and other means of communication; freedom of movement; the right to acquire and hold property; protection of property rights; the right to work; and freedom of expression, assembly and association.

Loyalty to the State and obedience to the Constitution and to the law of the Maldives shall be the duty of every Maldivian citizen, irrespective of where he may be.

THE PRESIDENT

The President shall be the Head of State, Head of Government and the Commander-in-Chief of the Armed Forces and of the Police.

The President shall be elected by secret ballot by the People's Majlis (more than one candidate may be nominated for election) and endorsed in office for five years by a national referendum.

In addition to the powers and functions expressly conferred on or assigned to the President by the Constitution and law, the President shall have the power to execute the following: appointment to and removal from office of the Vice-President, Chief Justice, Speaker and Deputy Speaker of the People's Majlis, Ministers, Attorney-General, Atoll Chiefs, judges, Auditor-General and Commissioner of Elections; appointment and dissolution of the Cabinet of Ministers; presiding over meetings of the Cabinet of Ministers; making a statement declaring the policies of the Government at the opening session of the People's Majlis every year; promulgating decrees, directives and regulations, as may be required from time to time for the purposes of ensuring propriety of the affairs of the Government and compliance with the provisions of the Constitution and law; holding public referendums on major issues; the declaration of war and peace.

While any person holds office as President, no proceedings shall be instituted or continued against him in any court or tribunal in respect of anything done or omitted to be done by him either in his official or private capacity.

A motion to remove the President from office may be considered in the People's Majlis only when one-third of the members of the Majlis have proposed it and two-thirds of the Majlis have resolved to consider it.

In the event that the presidency becomes vacant by reason of death, resignation or removal from office, the Speaker of the People's Majlis shall discharge the functions as Acting President from the time of occurrence of such vacancy. He shall continue to discharge these functions until a three-member Council is elected by a secret ballot of the People's Majlis to administer the State.

The President shall have the right to appoint at his discretion a Vice-President to discharge the duties and responsibilities assigned by the President.

THE CABINET OF MINISTERS

There shall be a Cabinet of Ministers appointed by the President, and the Cabinet shall be presided over by the President. The Cabinet of Ministers shall consist of the Vice-President (if any), Ministers charged with responsibility for Ministries and the Attorney-General.

The Cabinet of Ministers shall discharge the functions assigned to it by the President. The following shall be included in the said functions: to assist the President in formulating government policy on important national and international matters and issues; to advise the President on developing the Maldives economically and socially; to assist the President in the formulation of the annual state budget and government bills to be submitted to the People's Majlis; and to advise the President on the ratification of international treaties and agreements signed by the Maldivian Government with foreign administrations that require ratification by the State.

The President may, at his discretion, remove any Minister or the Attorney-General from office.

In the event of a vote of no confidence by the People's Majlis in a member of the Cabinet of Ministers, such member shall resign from office.

The President may dissolve the Cabinet of Ministers if, in his opinion, the Cabinet of Ministers is unable effectively to discharge its functions. Upon dissolution of the Cabinet of Ministers, the President shall inform the People's Majlis of the fact, specifying the reasons thereof, and shall appoint a new Cabinet of Ministers as soon as expedient.

THE PEOPLE'S MAJLIS

Legislative power, except the enactment of the Constitution, shall be vested in the People's Majlis. The People's Majlis shall consist of 50 members, of whom eight members shall be appointed by the President, two members elected from Malé and two members elected from each of the atolls. The duration of the People's Majlis shall be five years from the date on which the first meeting of the People's Majlis is held after its election. The Speaker and Deputy Speaker of the People's Majlis shall be appointed to and removed from office by the President. The Speaker shall not be a member of the People's Majlis, whereas the Deputy Speaker shall be appointed from among the members of the People's Majlis.

There shall be three regular sessions of the People's Majlis every year. The dates for the commencement and conclusion of these sessions shall be determined by the Speaker. An extraordinary sitting of the People's Majlis shall only be held when directed by the President. With the exception of the matters that, in accordance with the Constitution, require a two-thirds' majority for passage in the People's Majlis, all matters proposed for passage in the People's Majlis shall be passed by a simple majority.

Prior to the commencement of each financial year, the Minister of Finance shall submit the proposed state budget for approval by the People's Majlis.

A bill passed by the People's Majlis shall become law and enter into force upon being assented to by the President.

A motion expressing want of confidence in a member of the Cabinet of Ministers may be moved in the People's Majlis.

THE PEOPLE'S SPECIAL MAJLIS

The power to draw up and amend the Constitution of the Maldives shall be vested in the People's Special Majlis. The People's Special Majlis shall consist of: members of the Cabinet of Ministers, members of the People's Majlis, 42 members elected from Malé and the atolls, and eight members appointed by the President.

Any article or provision of the Constitution may be amended only by a law passed by a majority of votes in the People's Special Majlis and assented to by the President.

THE JUDICIARY

The High Court shall consist of the Chief Justice and such number of Judges as may be determined by the President. The Chief Justice and the Judges of the High Court shall be appointed by the President.

All appeals from the courts of the Maldives shall, in accordance with regulations promulgated by the President, be heard by the High Court. The High Court shall hear cases determined by the President to be filed with the High Court from among the proceedings instituted by the State.

There shall be in the Maldives such number of courts at such places as may be determined by the President. The judges of the courts shall be appointed by the President.

PROCLAMATION OF EMERGENCY

Where the President has determined that the security of the Maldives or part thereof is threatened by war, foreign aggression or civil unrest, the President shall have the right to issue a Proclamation of Emergency. While the Proclamation is in force, the President shall have the power to take and order all measures expedient to protect national security and public order. Such measures may include the suspension of fundamental rights and laws. A Proclamation of Emergency shall initially be valid for a period of three months. The Proclamation may be extended, if approved by the People's Majlis, for a period determined by the People's Majlis.

GENERAL PROVISIONS

No bilateral agreement between the Government of the Maldives and the government of a foreign country and no multilateral agreement shall be signed or accepted by the Government of the Maldives unless the President has authorized in writing such signature or acceptance. In the event that such agreement requires ratification by the Maldives, such agreement shall not come into effect unless the President has ratified the same on the advice of the Cabinet of Ministers.

The Government

President and Head of State: Maumoon Abdul Gayoom (took office 11 November 1978; re-elected 30 September 1983, 23 September 1988, 1 October 1993 and 16 October 1998).

THE CABINET OF MINISTERS

(September 2002)

President, Minister of Defence and National Security, and of Finance and Treasury: Maumoon Abdul Gayoom.

Minister of Fisheries, Agriculture and Marine Resources: Abdul Rasheed Hussain.

Minister of Foreign Affairs: Fathulla Jameel.

Minister of Women's Affairs and Social Security: Rashida Yoosuf.

Minister of Education: Dr Mohamed Latheef.

Minister of Trade and Industries: Abdulla Yameen.

Minister of Health: Ahmed Abdulla.

Minister of Justice: Ahmed Zahir.

Minister of Tourism: Hassan Sobir.

Minister of Transport and Civil Aviation: Ilyas Ibrahim.

Minister of Planning and National Development: Ibrahim Hussain Zaki.

Minister of Home Affairs, Housing and Environment: Ismail Shafeeu.

Minister of Construction and Public Works: Umar Zahir.

Minister of Atolls Administration: Abdulla Hameed.

Minister of Youth and Sports: Mohamed Zahir Hussain.

Minister of Information, Arts and Culture: Ibrahim Manik.

Minister of Human Resources, Employment and Labour: Abdulla Kamaluddeen.

Minister at the President's Office: Abdulla Jameel.

Minister of State for Presidential Affairs: Mohamed Hussain.

Minister of State for Defence and National Security: Maj.-Gen. Anbaree Abdul Sattar.

Minister of State for Finance and Treasury: Mohamed Jaleel.

Minister of State and Auditor-General: Ismail Fathy.

Attorney-General: Dr Mohamed Munavvar.

MINISTRIES

The President's Office: Boduthakurufaanu Magu, Malé 20-05; tel. 323701; fax 325500; internet www.presidencymaldives.gov.mv.

The Attorney-General's Office: Huravee Bldg, Malé 20-05; tel. 323809; fax 314109.

Ministry of Atolls Administration: Faashana Bldg, Boduthakurufaanu Magu (North), Malé 20-05; tel. 323070; fax 327750.

Ministry of Communication, Science and Technology: 5th Floor, Bank of Maldives Bldg, Boduthakurufaanu Magu, Malé 20-05; tel. 331695; fax 331694; e-mail secretariat@mcst.gov.mv; internet www.mcst.gov.mv.

Ministry of Construction and Public Works: Izzuddeen Magu, Malé 20-01; tel. 323234; fax 328300; e-mail mcpw@dhivehinet.net.mv.

Ministry of Defence and National Security: Bandaara Koshi, Ameer Ahmed Magu, Malé 20-05; tel. 322607; fax 332689; e-mail admin@defence.gov.mv.

Ministry of Education: Ghaazee Bldg, 2nd Floor, Ameer Ahmed Magu, Malé 20-05; tel. 323262; fax 321201; e-mail educator@dhivehinet.net.mv; internet www.thauleem.net.

Ministry of Finance and Treasury: Block 379, Ameenee Magu, Malé 20-03; tel. 317590; fax 324432; e-mail minfin@dhivehinet.net.mv.

Ministry of Fisheries, Agriculture and Marine Resources: Ghaazee Bldg, Ground Floor, Ameer Ahmed Magu, Malé 20-05; tel. 322625; fax 326558; internet www.fishagri.gov.mv.

Ministry of Foreign Affairs: Boduthakurufaanu Magu, Malé 20-05; tel. 323400; fax 323841; e-mail admin@foreign.gov.mv.

Ministry of Health: Ameenee Magu, Malé 20-03; tel. 328887; fax 328889; e-mail moh@dhivehinet.net.mv; internet www.health.gov.mv.

Ministry of Home Affairs, Housing and Environment: Huravee Bldg, 3rd Floor, Ameer Ahmed Magu, Malé 20-05; tel. 323820; fax 324739; e-mail env@environment.gov.mv.

Ministry of Human Resources, Employment and Labour: Ghaazee Bldg, 4th Floor, Ameer Ahmed Magu, Malé 20-05; e-mail info@manpowermaldives.org; internet www.manpowermaldives.org.

Ministry of Information, Arts and Culture: Buruzu Magu, Malé 20-04; tel. 323836; fax 326211; e-mail informat@dhivehinet.net.mv; internet www.maldivesinfo.gov.mv.

Ministry of Justice: Justice Bldg, Orchid Magu, Malé 20-05; tel. 322303; fax 325447.

Ministry of Planning and National Development: Ghaazee Bldg, 4th Floor, Ameer Ahmed Magu, Malé 20-05; tel. 322919; fax 327351; internet www.planning.gov.mv.

Ministry of Trade and Industries: Ghaazee Bldg, 1st Floor, Ameer Ahmed Magu, Malé 20-05; tel. 323668; fax 323840; e-mail trademin@dhivehinet.net.mv; internet www.investmaldives.com.

Ministry of Transport and Civil Aviation: Huravee Bldg, Ameer Ahmed Magu, Malé 20-05; tel. 323992; fax 323994; e-mail admin@transport.gov.mv; internet www.transport.gov.mv.

Ministry of Women's Affairs and Social Security: Umar Shopping Arcade, 2nd and 4th Floors, Chaandhanee Magu, Malé 20-02; tel. 323687; fax 316237.

Ministry of Youth and Sports: Ghaazee Bldg, Ameer Ahmed Magu, Malé 20-05; tel. 326986; fax 327162.

Legislature

PEOPLE'S MAJLIS

The People's Majlis (People's Council) comprises 50 members, of whom eight are appointed by the President, two elected by the people of Malé and two elected from each of the 20 atolls (for a five-year term). The most recent election was held on 19 November 1999.

Speaker: Abdulla Hameed.

Deputy Speaker: Abdul Rasheed Hussain.

Political Organizations

There are no political parties in the Maldives.

Diplomatic Representation

HIGH COMMISSIONS IN THE MALDIVES

Bangladesh: H. High Grove, 6, Hithaffinivaa Magu, Malé; tel. 315541; fax 315543; e-mail bdootmal@dhivehinet.net.mv; High Commissioner: Abdul Latif (acting).

India: H. Athireege-Aage, Ameeru Ahmed Magu, Malé; tel. 323015; fax 324778; High Commissioner: N. T. Khankup (acting).

Pakistan: G. Penta Green, Majeedhee Magu, Malé; tel. 322024; fax 321832; Chargé d'affaires: Muhammad Nasar Hayat.

Sri Lanka: H. Sakeena Manzil, Medhuziyaaraiyh Magu, Malé 2005; tel. 322845; fax 321652; e-mail highcom@dhivehinet.net.mv; High Commissioner: ZAROOK SAMSUDEEN.

Judicial System

The administration of justice is undertaken in accordance with Islamic (Shari'a) law. In 1980 the Maldives High Court was established. There are four courts in Malé, and 200 island courts, one in every inhabited island. All courts, with the exception of the High Court, are under the control of the Ministry of Justice.

In January 1999 the Government declared that the island court of each atoll capital would thenceforth oversee the administration of justice in that atoll. At the same time it was announced that arrangements were being made to appoint a senior magistrate in each atoll capital.

HIGH COURT

Chief Justice: MOHAMED RASHEED IBRAHIM.

Judges: IBRAHIM NASEER, AHMED HAMEED FAHMY, ALI HAMEED MOHAMED.

In February 1995 the President established a five-member Advisory Council on Judicial Affairs. The Council was to function under the President's Office (equivalent, in this respect, to a Supreme Court) and was to study and offer counsel to the President on appeals made to the President by either the appellant or the respondent in cases adjudicated by the High Court. The Council was also to offer such counsel as and when requested by the President on other judicial matters.

ADVISORY COUNCIL ON JUDICIAL AFFAIRS

Members: MOOSA FATHY, ABDULLA HAMEED, DR MOHAMED MUNAWWAR, Prof. MOHAMED RASHEED IBRAHIM, AL-SHEIKH HASSAN YOOSUF.

Religion

Islam is the state religion, and the Maldivians are Sunni Muslims. In mid-1991 there were 724 mosques and 266 women's mosques throughout the country.

In late 1996 a Supreme Council for Islamic Affairs was established, under the authority of the President's Office. The new body was to authorize state policies with regard to Islam and to advise the Government on Islamic affairs.

Musthashaaru of the Supreme Council for Islamic Affairs: MOOSA FATHY.

President of the Supreme Council for Islamic Affairs: MOHAMED RASHEED IBRAHIM.

Deputy President of the Supreme Council for Islamic Affairs: AHMED FAROOG MOHAMED.

The Press

In 1993 the Government established a National Press Council to review, monitor and further develop journalism in the Maldives.

DAILIES

Aafathis Daily News: Feerpaz Magu, Maafannu, Malé 20-02; tel. 318609; fax 312425; e-mail aafathis@dhivehinet.net.mv; internet www.aafathisnews.com.mv; f. 1979; daily; Dhivehi and English; Editor ABDUL SATTAR MANADHOO; circ. 3,000.

Haveeru Daily: Ameenee Magu, POB 20103, Malé; tel. 325671; fax 323103; e-mail haveeru@haveeru.com.mv; internet www.haveeru.com.mv; f. 1979; Dhivehi and English; Chair. MOHAMED ZAHIR HUSSAIN; Editor ALI RAFEEQ; circ. 4,500.

Miadhu News: G. Mascot, Koimalaa Hingun, Malé 20-02; tel. 320700; fax 320500; e-mail miadhu@dhivehinet.net.mv; internet www.miadhu.com; daily newspaper; Propr IBRAHIM RASHEED MOOSA; Chair. AHMED ABDULLA.

PERIODICALS

Adduvas: Malé; f. 2000; weekly; news, entertainment, health issues and social affairs.

Dheenuge Magu (The Path of Religion): The President's Office, (Mulee-aage) Boduthakurufaanu Magu, Malé 20-05; tel. 323701; fax 325500; e-mail info@presidencymaldives.gov.mv; f. 1986; weekly; Dhivehi; religious; publ. by the President's Office; Editor President MAUMOON ABDUL GAYOOM; Dep. Editor MOHAMED RASHEED IBRAHIM; circ. 7,500.

Dhivehingetharika (Maldivian Heritage): National Centre for Linguistic and Historical Research, Soasun Magu, Malé 20-05; tel. 323206; fax 326796; e-mail nclhr@dhivehinet.net.mv; f. 1998; Dhivehi; Maldivian archaeology, history and language.

Faiythoora: National Centre for Linguistic and Historical Research, Soasun Magu, Malé 20-05; tel. 323206; fax 326796; e-mail nclhr@dhivehinet.net.mv; f. 1979; monthly magazine; Dhivehi; Maldivian history, culture and language; Editor UZ. ABDULLA HAMEED; circ. 800.

Furadhaana: Ministry of Information, Arts and Culture, Buruzu Magu, Malé 20-04; tel. 321749; fax 326211; e-mail informat@dhivehinet.net.mv; internet www.maldives-info.com; f. 1990; monthly; Dhivehi; Editor IBRAHIM MANIK; circ. 1,000.

Jamaathuge Khabaru (Community News): Non-Formal Education Centre, Salahudeen Bldg, Malé 20-04; tel. 328772; fax 322231; monthly; Dhivehi; Editor AHMED ZAHIR; circ. 1,500.

Maldives Marine Research Bulletin: Marine Research Centre, Ministry of Fisheries, Agriculture and Marine Resources, H. White Waves, Malé 20-06; tel. 322328; fax 322509; e-mail marine@fishagri.gov.mv; f. 1995; biannual; fisheries and marine research.

Maldives News Bulletin: Maldives News Bureau, Ministry of Information, Arts and Culture, Buruzu Magu, Malé 20-04; tel. 323836; fax 326211; e-mail informat@dhivehinet.net.mv; internet www.maldives-info.com; weekly; English; Editor ALI SHAREEF; circ. 350.

Monday Times: H. Neel Villa, Boduthakunufaanu Magu, Malé; tel. and fax 315084; e-mail info@mondaytimes.com.mv; internet www.mondaytimes.com.mv; f. 2000; weekly; Editor MOHAMED BUSHRY.

Our Environment: Forum of Writers on the Environment, c/o Ministry of Planning and National Development, Ghaazee Bldg, Ameer Ahmed Magu, Malé 20-05; tel. 324861; fax 327351; f. 1990; monthly; Dhivehi; Editor FAROUQ AHMED.

Rasain: Ministry of Fisheries, Agriculture and Marine Resources, Ghaazee Bldg, Ameer Ahmed Magu, Malé 20-05; tel. 322625; fax 326558; e-mail fishagri@dhivehinet.net.mv; f. 1980; annual; fisheries development.

Samugaa: Malé; f. 1995; publ. by the Government Employees' Club.

NEWS AGENCIES

Haveeru News Service (HNS): POB 20103, Malé; tel. 313825; fax 323103; e-mail haveeru@dhivehinet.net.mv; internet www.haveeru.com; f. 1979; Chair. MOHAMED ZAHIR HUSSAIN; Man. Editor AHMED ZAHIR.

Hiyama News Agency: H. Navaagan, Malé 20-05; tel. 322588.

Maldives News Bureau (MNB): Ministry of Information, Arts and Culture, Buruzu Magu, Malé 20-04; tel. 323836; fax 326211; e-mail informat@dhivehinet.net.mv; internet www.maldives-info.com.

PUBLISHERS

Corona Press: Faamudheyri Magu, Malé; tel. 314741.

Cyprea Print: Raiydhebai Magu, Malé 20-03; tel. 328381; fax 328380; f. 1984; Man. Dir ABDULLA SAEED.

Loamaafaanu Print: POB 20103, Malé 20-04; tel. 317209; fax 313815; e-mail haveeru@netlink.net.mv.

Novelty Printers and Publishers: Malé 20-01; tel. 318844; fax 327039; e-mail novelty@dhivehinet.net.mv; general and reference books; Man. Dir ASAD ALI.

Ummeedhee Press: M. Aasthaanaa Javaahirumagu, Malé 20-02; tel. 325110; fax 326412; e-mail ummpress@dhivehinet.net.mv; f. 1986; printing and publishing; Principal Officers ABDUL SHAKOOR ALI, MOHAMED SHAKOOR.

Broadcasting and Communications

TELECOMMUNICATIONS

Ministry of Communication, Science and Technology: Post and Telecommunication Section, Telecom Bldg, Husnuheena Magu, Malé 20-04; tel. 323344; fax 320000; e-mail telecom@dhivehinet.net.mv; regulatory authority; Dir-Gen. (Post and Telecommunication Section) HUSSAIN SHAREEF; Dir MOHAMED AMIR.

Dhivehi Raajjeyge Gulhun Ltd (DHIRAAGU): Medhuziyaaraiy Magu, Malé 20-03; tel. 322802; fax 322800; e-mail info@dhiraagu.com.mv; internet www.dhiraagu.com.mv; f. 1988; jointly-owned by the Maldivian Government (55%) and by Cable and Wireless PLC of the UK (45%); functions under Ministry of Communication, Science and Technology; operates all national and international telecommunications services in the Maldives (incl. internet service–Dhivehinet); Chair. ISMAIL SHAFEEU; CEO and Gen. Man. KEITH WILSON.

RADIO

Radio Eke: Malé.

Voice of Islam: Malé.

Voice of Maldives (VOM) (Dhivehi Raajjeyge Adu): Moonlight Higun, Malé 20-06; tel. 325577; fax 328357; radio broadcasting began in 1962 under name of Malé Radio; name changed as above in 1980; three channels; home service in Dhivehi (0530 hrs–2245 hrs daily) and English (1700 hrs–1900 hrs daily); Dir-Gen. IBRAHIM MANIK.

TELEVISION

Television Maldives: Buruzu Magu, Malé 20-04; tel. 323105; fax 325083; television broadcasting began in 1978; two channels: TVM broadcasts for an average of 6–7 hrs daily and TVM Plus (f. 1998) broadcasts for 10 hrs daily; covers a 40-km radius around Malé; Dir-Gen. HUSSAIN MOHAMED; Dep. Dirs MOHAMED NASHID, ABDUL MUHUSIN.

Finance

(cap. = capital; brs = branches; amounts in US dollars unless otherwise stated)

BANKING

Central Bank

Maldives Monetary Authority (MMA): Umar Shopping Arcade, 3rd Floor, Chandhanee Magu, Maafannu, Malé 20-01; tel. 323783; fax 323862; e-mail mail@mma.gov.mv; internet www.mma.gov.mv; f. 1981; bank of issue; supervises and regulates commercial bank and foreign exchange dealings and advises the Govt on banking and monetary matters; authorized cap. 4m. rufiyaa (2001); Gov. President MAUMOON ABDUL GAYOOM; Vice-Gov. MOHAMED JALEEL; Gen. Man. ABDUL GHAFOOR.

Commercial Bank

Bank of Maldives (PLC) Ltd (BML): 11 Boduthakurufaanu Magu, Malé 20-05; tel. 322948; fax 328233; e-mail bmlho@dhivehinet.net.mv; internet www.bml.com.mv; f. 1982; 75% state-owned, 25% privately-owned; cap. 36.5m., res 102.7m., dep. 1,027m. (Dec. 1999); Chair. ABDULLA HAMEED; Asst Gen. Man. KEITH L. BROWN; 14 brs.

Foreign Banks

Bank of Ceylon (Sri Lanka): 'Meedhufaru', 2 Orchid Magu, Malé; tel. 323045; fax 320575; e-mail bcmale@dhivehinet.net.mv; internet www.bankofceylon.net; Sr Exec. ARTHUR PERERA; 1 br.

Habib Bank Ltd (Pakistan): Ground Floor, Ship Plaza, 1/6 Orchid Magu, POB 20121, Malé; tel. 322051; fax 326791; e-mail hblmale@dhivehinet.net.mv; Vice-Pres. and Chief Man. MUHAMMAD ASAF SHAIKH.

Hong Kong and Shanghai Banking Corpn Ltd (Hong Kong): MTCC Bldg, 1st Floor, Boduthakurufaanu Magu, Malé; CEO MARK HUMBLE.

State Bank of India: Boduthakurufaanu Magu, Malé; tel. 320860; fax 323053; e-mail sbimale@dhivehinet.net.mv; CEO G. N. DASH.

INSURANCE

Allied Insurance Co of the Maldives (Pte) Ltd: 04–06 STO Trade Centre, Orchid Magu, Malé; tel. 324612; fax 325035; e-mail allied@dhivehinet.net.mv; www.alliedmaldives.com; f. 1985; all classes of non-life insurance; operated by State Trading Organisation (see below); Chief Exec. MOHAMED MANIKU; Gen. Man. ISMAIL RIZA.

Trade and Industry

GOVERNMENT AGENCIES

Foreign Investment Services Bureau (FISB): Malé; tel. 323890; fax 323756; e-mail trademin@dhivehinet.net.mv; internet www.investmaldives.com; under administration of Ministry of Trade and Industries; Dir-Gen. AHMED NASEEM.

Maldives Housing and Urban Development Board: Malé; Dir ABDUL AZEEZ; Dep. Dir ABDULLAH SODIQ.

CHAMBER OF COMMERCE AND INDUSTRY

Maldives National Chamber of Commerce and Industry (MNCCI): G. Viyafaari Hiyaa, Ameenee Magu, POB 92, Malé 20-04; tel. 310234; fax 310233; e-mail mncci@dhivehinet.net.mv; f. 1994; merged with the Maldivian Traders' Association in 2000; Pres. AHMED MUJUTHABA; Chair. GASIM IBRAHIM.

INDUSTRIAL AND TRADE ASSOCIATIONS

Sri Lanka Trade Centre: 3rd Floor, Girithereyege Bldg, Hithaffinivaa Magu, Malé; tel. 315183; fax 315184; e-mail dirsltc@avasmail.com.mv; f. 1993 to facilitate and promote trade, tourism, investment and services between Sri Lanka and the Maldives; Dir G. V. CHANDRASENA.

State Trading Organisation (STO): STO Bldg, 7 Haveeree Higun, Malé 20-02; tel. 323279; fax 325218; e-mail sto@dhivehinet.net.mv; internet www.stomaldives.com; f. 1964 as Athirimaafannuge Trading Account, renamed as above in 1976; became private limited company in 2001; state-controlled commercial organization; under administration of independent Board of Directors; imports and distributes staple foods, fuels, pharmaceuticals and general consumer items; acts as purchaser for govt requirements; undertakes long-term development projects; Man. Dir MOHAMED MANIKU; Dir ISMAIL IBRAHIM.

UTILITIES

Electricity

Maldives Electricity Bureau: Malé; tel. 328753; fax 323840; e-mail trademin@dhivehinet.net.mv; f. 1998; under administration of Ministry of Trade and Industries; regulatory authority.

State Electric Co (STELCO) Ltd: Malé; e-mail admin@stelco.com.mv; internet www.stelco.com.mv; f. 1997 to replace Maldives Electricity Board; under administration of Ministry of Trade and Industries; provides electricity, consultancy services, electrical spare parts service, etc.; operates 22 power stations; installed capacity 32,921 kW (Dec. 2000); Chair. ABDULLAH YAMEEN; Man. Dir ABDUL SHAKOOR.

Gas

Maldive Gas Pvt Ltd: Thilafushi, Malé Atoll; f. 1999 as a jt venture between State Trading Organisation and Champa Gas and Oil Co; Chair. MOHAMED MANIK.

Water

Maldives Water and Sanitation Authority (MWSA): Malé; f. 1973; Dir FAROOQ MOHAMED HASSAN.

Malé Water and Sewerage Co: Ameenee Magu, Machangolhi, POB 20148, Malé; tel. 323209; fax 324306; e-mail mwsc@dhivehinet.net.mv; f. 1995; 70% govt-owned; produces approximately 5,000 cubic metric tons of fresh, desalinated water daily; provides water and sewerage services to the islands of Malé and Villingili; Chair. HASSAN SOBIR; Gen. Man. MOHAMED AHMED DIDI.

MAJOR COMPANIES

Donad Garments Industries: M. Feeroaz Lodge, Muranga Magu, Malé; tel. 322176; fax 321615; f. 1987; manufacture of ready-made garments; cap. 5.3m. rufiyaa, sales 3.9m. rufiyaa (1999); CEO DHON ADAM FULHU; 85 employees.

E-Biz Maldives (Pvt) Ltd: M. Nirolhu, Malé; tel. 326062; fax 326014; e-mail info@ebizmaldives.com; internet www.ebizmaldives.com; f. 2000; provides computer services, software and training.

Fuel Supplies Maldives Private Ltd: Malé; f. 2001; supplies diesel and petroleum to Malé and neighbouring atolls.

Grey Rose Maldives (Pvt) Ltd: Gan, Addu Atoll; tel. 326746; f. 1987; manufactures textiles; CEO MILTON JOHN.

IMD and Sons: tel. 323352; f. 1961; manufacture of marine products; CEO IBRAHIM MOHAMED DIDI.

Leniar Clothing Maldives Pvt Ltd: Gan, Addu Atoll; f. 1996; jointly-owned by a US co and a Sri Lankan co; manufactures garments.

Maldives Industrial Fisheries Co Ltd (MIFCO): 04-02 STO Trade Centre, 4th Floor, Malé 20-02; tel. 323932; fax 323955; e-mail mifco@dhivehinet.net.mv; f. 1993 to replace the Fisheries Projects Implementation Department (f. 1984); 80% owned by Govt, 20% owned by STO; under administration of Ministry of Fisheries and Agriculture; commercial enterprise engaged in fish purchasing, processing, canning and export; operates Felivaru Tuna Processing Plant; Chair. and Man. Dir IBRAHIM SHAKEEB; Dir (Admin.) HASSAN HALEEM.

Felivaru Tuna Processing Plant: Felivaru, Lhaviyani Atoll; tel. 230376; fax 230375; f. 1978; capacity to produce 50 metric tons of canned fish per day; Gen. Man. IBRAHIM WASEEM; Dep. Dir (Operations) ADNAN ALI.

MIFCO Boatyard Ltd: Malé; f. 1997; builds and repairs all types of small craft and vessels in wood and fibreglass, especially fishing boats; Gen. Man. Ahmed Wajeeh.

Maldives Marine Cement Pvt Ltd: Thilafushi; jt venture between State Trading Organisation and Marine Cement of Switzerland.

Malé Aerated Water Co (Pvt) Ltd: 70 Boduthakurufaanu Magu, POB 7, Malé; tel. 326701; fax 326703; e-mail info@mawc.com.mv; f. 1987; production of soft drinks; bottlers for Coca-Cola in the Maldives; Man. Hassan Habeeb.

MUK Apparels: Foammulah; manufactures garments; Chair. Mohamed Umar Manik.

Multicoral Handicrafts Co (Pvt) Ltd: tel. 325287; f. 1987; CEO Abdulla Mohamed.

Multifarm (Pvt) Ltd: tel. 322365; f. 1985; poultry; CEO Dr Ahmed Didi.

Multilinx (Maldives) Pvt Ltd: 2 Fadiyaru Magu, POB 20123, Malé 20–02; tel. 323113; fax 323006; e-mail multlnx@dhivehinet.net.mv; f. 1983; manufacture of detergents, wood glue, plastic bottles and containers, corrugated boards and cartons, and candles; exports marine products; CEO Mohamed Zahir.

PVC Maldives (Pvt) Ltd: f. 1984; manufacture of PVC pipes; CEO Mohamed Umar Manik.

Rococo Maldives Pvt Ltd: Foammulah; f. 1999; manufactures garments.

Trans Ocean Pvt Ltd: exports marine products.

Transport

Maldives Transport and Contracting Co Ltd (MTCC): MTCC Bldg, 4th Floor, Boduthakurufaanu Magu, POB 2063, Malé 20-02; tel. 326822; fax 323221; e-mail mtcc@dhivehinet.net.mv; internet www.mtccmaldives.com; f. 1980; 60% state-owned, 40% privately-owned; marine transport, civil and technical contracting, harbour development, shipping agents for general cargo, passenger liners and oil tankers; Man. Dir Bandhu Ibrahim Saleem; Dirs Umar Zahir, Abdullah Majeed, Mohamed Nazeer.

SHIPPING

Vessels operate from the Maldives to Sri Lanka and Singapore at frequent intervals, also calling at points in India, Pakistan, Myanmar (formerly Burma), Malaysia, Bangladesh, Thailand, Indonesia and the Middle East. In 1998 the merchant shipping fleet of the Maldives numbered 68 vessels. Smaller vessels provide services between the islands on an irregular basis. Malé is the only port handling international traffic. In 1986 a new commercial harbour was opened in Malé. The Malé Harbour Development Project was implemented during 1991–97, and improved and increased the capacity and efficiency of Malé Port.

Maldives Ports Authority (MPA): Commercial Harbour, Malé 20-02; tel. 329339; fax 325293; e-mail maldport@dhivehinet.net.mv; f. 1986; under administration of Ministry of Transport and Civil Aviation; Man. Dir Ismail Shafeeq.

Island Enterprises Pvt Ltd: Lhoheege, 2nd Floor, Majeedhee Magu, Henveiru, POB 20169, Malé 20-05; tel. 323531; fax 325645; e-mail fiberbot@dhivehinet.net.mv; internet www.pmlboatyard.com.mv; f. 1978; fleet of two vessels (capacity 22,003 dwt); shipping agents, chandlers, cruising agents, surveyors and repairs; Man. Dir Omar Maniku.

Precision Marine Pvt Ltd: Lhoheege, 2nd Floor, Majeedhee Magu, Henveiru, POB 20169, Malé 20-05; tel. 323531; fax 325645; e-mail fiberbot@dhivehinet.net.mv; internet www.pmlboatyard.com.mv; subsidiary of Island Enterprises Pvt Ltd; mfrs and repairers of fibreglass boats, launches, yachts, marine sports equipment, etc.; Dir Omar Maniku.

Madihaa Co (Pvt) Ltd: 1/40 Shaheed Ali Higun, Malé; tel. 327812; fax 322251; e-mail madicom@dhivehinet.net.mv; f. 1985; imports and exports fresh fruit and vegetables, construction raw materials, confectionary items and soft drinks; Man. Dir Moosa Ahmed.

Maldives National Shipping Ltd: Ship Plaza, 2nd Floor, 1/6 Orchid Magu, POB 2022, Malé 20-02; tel. 323871; fax 324323; e-mail mns@dhivehinet.net.mv; f. 1965; 100% state-owned; fleet of seven general cargo vessels and one container vessel; br. in Mumbai (India); Gen. Man. Mohamed Hilmy; Man. Dir Ali Umar Manik.

Matrana Enterprises (Pvt) Ltd: 97 Majeedhee Magu, Malé; tel. 321733; fax 322832; Sr Exec. Mohamed Abdulla.

Villa Shipping and Trading Co (Pvt) Ltd: Villa Bldg, POB 2073, Malé; tel. 325195; fax 325177; e-mail villa@dhivehinet.net.mv; Man. Dir Qasim Ibrahim.

CIVIL AVIATION

The existing airport on Hululé Island near Malé, which was first opened in 1966, was expanded and improved to international standard with financial assistance from abroad and, as Malé International Airport, was officially opened in 1981. Charter flights from Europe subsequently began. In addition, there are four domestic airports covering different regions of the country: one on Gan Island, Addu Atoll, another on Kadhdhoo Island, Hadhdhummathi Atoll, another on Hanimaadhoo Island, South Thiladhummathi Atoll, and another on Kaadedhdhoo Island, South Huvadhu Atoll. The airport on Gan Island was expected to be capable of servicing international flights in the near future. Construction of a fifth domestic airport, in Raa Atoll Dhuvaafaru, was scheduled to begin in 1994. In early 1995 there were 10 helipads in use in the Maldives.

Maldives Airport Co Ltd: Malé International Airport, Hulhule; tel. 323506; fax 325034; e-mail enquiry@airports.com.mv; internet www.airports.com.mv; f. 2000; 100% govt-owned; under administration of Ministry of Transport and Civil Aviation; Man. Dir Mohamed Ibrahim.

Air Maldives Ltd: 26 Ameer Ahmed Magu, Henveyru, POB 2049, Malé 20-05; tel. 328454; fax 318757; e-mail airmldvs@dhivehinet.net.mv; f. 1974; 51% govt-owned, 49% owned by Naluri Bhd (Malaysia); under administration of Ministry of Transport and Civil Aviation; domestic flights; operated international flights until March 2000; national carrier.

Island Aviation Services Ltd: Malé; e-mail info@island.com.mv; internet www.island.com.mv; f. 2000; 100% govt-owned; operates domestic flights (suspended by Air Maldives Ltd in April 2000); Chair. Abdulla Yameen; Man. Dir Bandhu Ibrahim Saleem.

Maldivian Air Taxi: Malé International Airport, POB 2023, Malé; tel. 315201; fax 315203; e-mail mat@mat.com.mv; internet www.mataxi.com; f. 1993; seaplane services between Malé and outer islands; operates 15 aircraft; Chair. Lars Erik Nielsen; Gen. Man. Aum Fawzy.

Ocean Air (Pvt) Ltd: Malé; scheduled domestic flights between Malé and Gan.

Trans Maldivian Airways (Pvt) Ltd: POB 2079, Malé; tel. 325708; fax 323161; e-mail mail@tma.com.mv; internet www.tma.com.mv; f. 1989 as Hummingbird Island Airways Pvt Ltd, name changed as above in 2000; operates 12 floatplanes; Man. Dir Capt. Ernst-Ulrich Maas.

Tourism

The tourism industry brings considerable foreign exchange to the Maldives, and receipts from tourism amounted to an estimated US $344m. in 2000. The islands' attractions include white sandy beaches, excellent diving conditions and multi-coloured coral formations. By April 2001 there were 87 island resorts in operation, and 16,428 hotel beds were available. The annual total of foreign visitors increased from only 29,325 in 1978 to 467,154 in 2000, and decreased to 461,063 in 2001. A plan was implemented in late 2001 to convert 12 islands into resorts and to increase the number of hotel beds by some 4,000 by 2005.

Maldives Association of Tourism Industry (MATI): Gadhamoo Bldg, 3rd Floor, Henveyru, Malé; tel. 326640; fax 326641; e-mail mati@dhivehinet.net.mv; f. 1984; promotes and develops tourism; Chair. M. U. Maniku; Sec.-Gen. S. I. Mohamed.

Maldives Tourism Promotion Board: Bank of Maldives Bldg, 4th Floor, Boduthakurufaanu Magu, Malé 20-05; tel. 323228; fax 323229; e-mail mtpb@visitmaldives.com.mv; internet www.visitmaldives.com; f. 1998.

Air Maldives Travel Bureau/Tourist Information: Arrival Hall, Malé International Airport, Hululé Island; f. 1997; tel. 325511 (Ext. 8240); fax 325056.

Defence

There is no army, navy or air force. A voluntary National Security Service, which was founded in 1892 and has about 2,000 members, undertakes paramilitary security duties (including coast-guard duties). The first female recruits were sworn into the National Security Service in February 1989.

Commander-in-Chief of the National Security Service: President Maumoon Abdul Gayoom.

Deputy Commander-in-Chief of the National Security Service: Maj.-Gen. Anbaree Abdul Sattar.

Chief of Staff of the National Security Service: Brig. Mohamed Zahir.

Deputy Chief of Staff of the National Security Service: Brig. Adam Zahir.

Education

Until the late 1970s, education was centred largely on the capital, Malé. In 1976 the 16 schools in existence were all in Malé and catered mainly for children of primary school age. In 1977 the Government established a teacher-training institute (which had produced more than 400 qualified teachers by the end of 1986). UNICEF, in particular, has contributed to provincial development, and in 1978 the first primary school outside Malé opened, on Baa atoll. The construction of the first secondary school outside Malé was completed, on Addu atoll, in 1992. By 2001 there were 21 schools in Malé and 293 schools in the rest of the Maldives.

Education is not compulsory. There are three types of formal education: traditional Koranic schools (*Makthab*), Dhivehi-medium primary schools (*Madhrasa*) and English-medium primary and secondary schools. Primary education begins at six years of age and lasts for five years. Secondary education, beginning at the age of 11, lasts for up to seven years, comprising a first cycle of five years and a second of two years. In 1997 the total enrolment at primary and secondary schools was equivalent to 96% of the school-age population. Primary enrolment in 1997 was equivalent to 128% of children in the relevant age-group (boys 130%; girls 127%); the comparable ratio for secondary enrolment was 69% (boys 67%; girls 71%).

In January 1989 the Government established a National Council on Education, under the chairmanship of the President, to oversee the development of education in the Maldives. The Maldives' higher education establishments include a College of Higher Education (which was opened in October 1998 and which incorporates an Institute of Shari'a and Law), a full-time vocational training centre, a teacher-training institute, an Institute of Hotel and Catering Services, an Institute of Management and Administration, a Science Education Centre, an Institute of Health Sciences, an Institute for Islamic Studies, and a Non-formal Education Centre. The Maldives Centre for Social Education was constructed in 1991 with US $8.5m. of grant aid from Japan. The Maldives Institute of Technical Education, which was completed in late 1996, was expected to alleviate the problem of the lack of local skilled labour.

The Asian Development Bank's 2003–05 Country Strategy and Program, endorsed in 2002, pledged to assist improvements in the Maldives' education system. Projected budgetary expenditure on education by the central Government in 2001 was 597.2m. rufiyaa, representing 18.0% of total spending.

Bibliography

Adeney, M., and Carr, W. K. 'The Maldives Republic', in *The Politics of the Western Indian Ocean Islands.* London, Praeger Publishers.

Agassiz, A. 'The Coral Reefs of the Maldives', in *Memoirs of the Museum of Comparative Zoology at Harvard College.* Cambridge, MA, 1903.

Bell, H. C. P. *The Maldive Islands: An Account of the Physical Features, Climate, History, Inhabitants, Production and Trade.* Colombo, Government Printer, 1883.

Butany, W. T. *Report on Agricultural Survey and Crop Production.* Rome, United Nations Development Programme, 1974.

Gayoom, Maumoon Abdul. *The Maldives: A Nation in Peril.* Malé, Ministry of Planning and National Development, 1998.

Government Printer. *The Maldive Islands: Monograph on the History, Archaeology and Epigraphy.* Colombo, 1940.

Heyerdahl, Thor. *The Maldive Mystery.* London, George Allen and Unwin, 1986.

Lateef, K. *An Introductory Economic Report.* Washington, DC, World Bank, 1980.

Maloney, C. 'The Maldives: New Stresses in an Old Nation', in *Asian Survey,* University of California Press, 1976.

People of the Maldive Islands. New Delhi, Orient Longman, 1980.

Maniku, Hassan Ahmed. *The Maldives: A Profile.* Malé, Department of Information and Broadcasting, 1977.

Changes in the Topography of the Maldives. Maldives, Forum of Writers on the Environment, 1990.

Munch-Peterson, N. F. *Background Paper for Population Needs Mission.* Rome, United Nations Development Programme, 1981.

Reynolds, C. H. B. *The Maldive Islands.* London, Royal Central Asian Society, 1974.

Linguistic Strands in the Maldives. London, School of Oriental and African Studies, 1978.

Smallwood, C. *A Visit to the Maldive Islands.* London, Royal Central Asian Society, 1961.

Webb, Paul. A. *Maldives: People and Environment.* Malé, Department of Information and Broadcasting, 1989.

Young, I. A., and Christopher, W. *Memoir on the Inhabitants of the Maldive Islands.* Mumbai, Bombay Geographical Society, 1844.

MONGOLIA

Physical and Social Geography

ALAN J. K. SANDERS

Mongolia occupies an area of 1,564,116 sq km (603,909 sq miles) in east-central Asia. It is bordered by only two other states: the Russian Federation, along its northern frontier (extending for 3,543 km according to a new survey completed in December 2001), and the People's Republic of China, along the considerably longer southern frontier (4,676 km).

PHYSICAL ENVIRONMENT

For the purpose of geographical description Mongolia may be divided into five regions. In the west is the Altai area, where peaks covered with eternal snow rise to more than 4,300 m above sea-level. To the east of this lies a great depression dotted with lakes, some of salt water and some of fresh. Some of these, such as Uvs *nuur* (3,350 sq km) and Khövsgöl *nuur* (2,760 sq km), the latter being quite important for navigation, reach a considerable size. The north-central part of the country is occupied by the Khangai-Khentii mountain complex, enclosing the relatively fertile and productive agricultural country of the Selenge-Tuul basin. This has always been the focus of what cultural life existed in the steppes of north Mongolia: the imperial capital of Karakorum lay here and the ruins of other early settlements are still to be seen. To the east again lies the high Mongolian plateau reaching to the Chinese frontier, and to the south and east stretches the Gobi or semi-desert.

Water is unevenly distributed. In the mountainous north and west of the country large rivers originate, draining into either the Arctic or the Pacific. A continental watershed divides Mongolia, and the much smaller rivers of the south drain internally into lakes or are lost in the ground.

CLIMATE

The climate shows extremes of temperature between the long, cold, dry winter and the short, hot summer during which most of the year's precipitation falls. In Ulan Bator (Ulaanbaatar) the July temperature averages 17.0°C and the January temperature -26.1°C. Annual precipitation is variable but light. Ulan Bator's average is 233 mm, with 72.6 mm of rain in July. Rain is liable to fall in sudden, heavy showers or more prolonged outbursts in mid-summer, with severe flooding and damage to towns and bridges. Average snowfall in Ulan Bator in October–March is 16.9 mm. The bitter winter weather is relieved by the almost continuous blue sky and sunshine. Mongolia occasionally suffers severe earthquakes, especially in mountainous regions, but the population is too widely scattered for heavy losses to be caused.

POPULATION

Mongolia is mostly sparsely inhabited. The January 2000 census indicated a population of 2,373,493, or 1.5 persons per sq km. It is not correct to regard the Mongols as essentially nomadic herdsmen, although stock-movement (*otor*), sometimes covering large distances, has been a regular feature of rural life. Of the total population, more than 58% live in towns, with more than one-half of these, 813,500 in 2002, residing in the capital, Ulan Bator. There are over 300 rural settlements, inhabited by about 22% of the population. The population is, relatively speaking, homogenous. Some 90% of the people are Mongols, and of these the overwhelming majority belong to the Khalkha (Halh) group. The only important non-Mongol element in the population is that of the Kazakhs, a Turkic-speaking people dwelling mostly in the far west, and representing approximately 4.3% (in 2000) of the whole. The population had grown steadily over recent years: between 1963 and 1983 it increased by 74%, but the annual growth rate peaked at 2.6% in 1990 and has declined since then to between 1.2% and 1.4%. As a result, there is a preponderance of young people: according to the January 2000 census, 66% of the population were less than 30 years of age. Infant mortality declined from 64.4 per 1,000 births in 1990 to 32.8 in 2000. The official language is Mongol, written in a native vertical script or for everyday purposes in modified Cyrillic. Mongol is quite different from both Russian and Chinese, its geographic neighbours, but does show certain similarities, perhaps fortuitous, to Turkish, Korean and Japanese. Several Mongol dialects beside the dominant Khalkha are spoken, and in the Kazakh province of Bayan-Ölgiy the first language is Kazakh, most people being bilingual in Mongol.

History

ALAN J. K. SANDERS

EARLY HISTORY

Today only a minority of ethnic Mongols live in Mongolia, the sole independent Mongol state. Besides the related Buryat and Kalmyk peoples who are to be found within the Russian Federation in their own republics (near Lake Baikal and on the lower Volga, respectively), many true Mongols dwell outside Mongolia, most of them in the Inner Mongolia Autonomous Region of the People's Republic of China and adjacent areas—Heilongjiang, Jilin, Liaoning, Gansu, Ningxia and Xinjiang.

This division came about in the following way: in the early 17th century the Manchus, expanding southwards from Manchuria towards their ultimate conquest of all China, passed through what came to be called Inner Mongolia, which lay across their invasion routes. Many of the Mongol princes allied themselves with the Manchus (sometimes reinforcing such alliances by marriage), others submitted voluntarily to them, while yet others were conquered. In 1636, after the death of Ligdan Khan (the last Mongol Emperor), the subordination of these princes to the new, rising dynasty was formalized. The princes of Khalkha or Outer Mongolia maintained a tributary relationship towards the Manchus for a further half-century but, in their turn, lost their independence at the Convention of Dolonnor in 1691. The Manchus had, in 1688, entered Khalkha to expel Galdan, the ruler of the West Mongol Oirats, who was both terrorizing the Khalkhas and challenging the Manchus for supremacy in this area. With Galdan defeated, the three great princes of Khalkha and the Javzandamba Khutagt, or Living Buddha of Urga, the head of the lamaist church in Mongolia, had to accept Manchu overlordship. The 1728 Treaty of Kyakhta (Khiagt) defined the western borders between the Russian and Manchu empires, and confirmed Manchu rule in Outer Mongolia and Tannu Tuva (Uriankhai).

Outer Mongolia was administered by the Manchus as a separate area from Inner Mongolia. A fourth princedom (*aimag*) was created in addition out of the existing three in 1725, and soon afterwards the princedoms were renamed leagues and removed from the jurisdiction of the hereditary princes, to be administered instead by Mongol league heads, appointed by the imperial

Government in Beijing. Within the league organization Mongolia was divided into about 100 banners and a number of temple territories, while the Living Buddha owned a huge number of widely dispersed serfs. This state structure survived the fall of the Manchus in 1911 and lasted until the foundation of the Mongolian People's Republic (MPR) in 1924. In spite of their dependence on Beijing, however, the Mongols always considered themselves allies of the Manchus, not subjects on the same level as the Chinese, and made good use of this distinction when the Manchu (Qing) dynasty lost the throne of China.

AUTONOMOUS MONGOLIA

The beginnings of the existence of modern Mongolia can be traced back to 1911. In that year the fall of the Manchus enabled the Mongols to terminate their association with China. With some political and military support from Russia, a number of leading nobles proclaimed Mongolia an independent monarchy, and the throne was offered to the Living Buddha. The new Government, in an unrealistic excess of euphoria, invited all Mongols everywhere to adhere to the new state, but this involved them in conflict with China, which retained control of Inner Mongolia. Nor did they obtain much useful support from Russia, which was bound by secret treaties with Japan not to obstruct the latter's interests in Inner Mongolia, and which in any case was reluctant to engage in a doubtful pan-Mongolist adventure. In 1915 Russian, Chinese and Mongol representatives, meeting at Kyakhta on the Russo-Mongol border, agreed to the reduction of Mongolia's would-be independence to autonomy under Chinese suzerainty. At this time autonomous Mongolia consisted more or less of the territory of present-day Mongolia, the only substantial difference being the accession of Dariganga in the south-east at the time of the 1921 revolution. Inner Mongolia, Barga and the Altai district of Xinjiang were to remain under Chinese control. Tannu Tuva, after a brief period of autonomy as a 'people's republic', was absorbed by the USSR in 1944.

Autonomous Mongolia was a theocratic monarchy and during the few years of its existence very little happened to change the conditions inherited from Manchu times. Russian advisers began to modernize the Mongol army and to bring some sort of order into the fiscal system. Several primary schools and a secondary school were opened, some children (including the future dictator, Khorloogiin Choibalsan) were sent to study in imperial Russia, and the first newspaper appeared; but the state structure, the feudal organization of society and the administration of justice remained more or less as they had been, while the Buddhist clergy managed to consolidate and enhance its position of privilege. While legally subject to Chinese suzerainty, Mongolia was, in fact, a Russian protectorate. When Russian power and prestige in Central Asia were sapped by the collapse of the tsarist regime and the outbreak of revolution in 1917, this dependence of Mongolia became very apparent, and China lost no time in reasserting its authority. By mid-1919 the abrogation of autonomy was being discussed by the Mongol Government and the Chinese resident in Urga, the capital, but the process was brutally accelerated by the arrival in Mongolia of Gen. Xu Shuzeng who, with a large military force at his disposal, forced the Mongols to relinquish all authority to the Chinese in February 1920.

THE REVOLUTIONARY MOVEMENT

Towards the end of 1919 two revolutionary groups had been founded in Urga; the next year these amalgamated to form the Mongolian People's Party (MPP). There was no long-standing revolutionary tradition in Mongolia, which perhaps explains how it was that the Mongol revolution fell so completely under Soviet control. The members of the groups were men of varied social origin, including lamas (such as Dogsomyn Bodoo, the premier of 1921, who was liquidated in 1922), government servants, workers, soldiers (such as Damdiny Sükhbaatar) and students who had returned from Russia (such as Khorloogiin Choibalsan). They had the sympathy of several prominent nobles through whom they were able to approach the King, while at the same time they acquired some knowledge of Marxism from their acquaintance with left-wing Russian workers in Urga.

The first real contacts with Soviet Russia took place in early 1920 when a Comintern agent, Sorokovikov, came to Urga to assess the situation. It is therefore not surprising to find that the aims of the revolutionaries were at this time fairly moderate. First of all they desired national independence from the Chinese, then an elective government, internal administrative reforms, improved social justice, and the consolidation of the Buddhist faith. With Sorokovikov's approval they planned to send a delegation to Russia to seek help against the Chinese. They obtained the sanction of the King and carried with them a letter authenticated with his seal. They were, in fact, authorized only to obtain advice from Russia, not to negotiate actual intervention.

In their absence from Mongolia the situation was complicated by the incursion into the country of White Russian forces under Baron von Ungern-Sternberg. At first the Mongol authorities and the people welcomed the White Russians who dislodged the oppressive Chinese, and with the help of Ungern, the King was restored to the throne. However, Ungern's brutalities soon turned the Mongols against him. More important, the Soviet agents dealing with the Mongol delegation were able to use Ungern's apparent ascendancy over the Urga regime to extract far-reaching concessions. They made the offer of help conditional upon the establishment in Urga later of a new government friendly to them.

In March 1921 the first Congress of the MPP was held at Kyakhta on Soviet territory, and a provisional revolutionary Government was formed there, in opposition to the legal authorities in Urga who had sponsored the delegates who now abandoned them. This provisional Government gathered a small band of partisans who, with substantial Soviet forces, entered Mongolia, defeated Ungern and then marched on Urga. Here, in July 1921, a new Government was proclaimed, under the restored King. The monarchy existed now, however, in name only. Mongolia came more and more under Soviet direction. A secret police force was set up and in 1922 the first of a long series of political purges took place. In 1924 the King died. The MPP was officially renamed the Mongolian People's Revolutionary Party (MPRP); and a People's Republic, with a Soviet-style Constitution, was proclaimed.

THE MONGOLIAN PEOPLE'S REPUBLIC

Mongolia was now, in name, a people's republic, the second socialist state in the world, but its primitive stage of development posed daunting problems. Buddhism, which commanded deep loyalty from the people, weighed heavily on the economy and was a powerful ideological opponent of communism. Local separatism, especially in the far west, took years to overcome and in some outlying parts local government could not be established until 1928 or 1929. Moreover, it was easy for disillusioned herdsmen to trek with their herds over the frontiers into China and there were considerable losses of population by emigration. There was widespread illiteracy and many of those who could read and write were lamas whose skill was in Tibetan rather than Mongol.

The country's economy depended exclusively on extensive animal herding. Trade and crafts were in the hands of foreigners, almost all of them Chinese. There was no banking system, no national currency, no industry and no medical service in the modern sense. Finally, most of those men who were politically experienced and capable of running the local administration were lamas or nobles, two classes at whose eventual annihilation the revolutionary regime aimed.

Thus, the stage of economic, social and intellectual development which Mongolia had reached was far below that of the USSR and its capacity for independent action was extremely limited against its one international partner, the immeasurably more powerful USSR. Mongolia was ineluctably involved with Soviet interests and developments, and its history over the next two decades shows the same progression of events as characterized Stalin's USSR.

At first, until 1928, there was some measure of semi-capitalist development, during which the privileges of the nobility and clergy were not seriously curtailed. In international contacts, too, the Mongols reached out to France and Germany. However, parallel with the rise of Stalin and the swing to the left in the USSR there developed in Mongolia what came to be known as the 'leftist deviation'. All foreign contacts other than with the USSR were terminated. The USSR monopolized Mongolia's trade, in which it had hitherto had only a modest share. Between

1929 and 1932 an ill-prepared programme of collectivization ruined the country's economy, stocks of cattle falling by at least one-third. A rigorous anti-religious campaign did much to turn people against the MPRP, and in 1932 uprisings broke out which, particularly in West Mongolia, reached the proportions of civil war and necessitated the intervention of the Soviet army. Thousands of Mongols deserted the country with their herds. This disastrous course was reversed only on the direct instructions of the Comintern in June 1932. Leaders who until then had been enthusiastic leftists, such as Peljidiin Genden, who became Chairman of the Council of Ministers (Prime Minister) and was later 'unmasked' as a 'Japanese spy' and liquidated by Choibalsan, now adopted a more moderate line; and, under what was termed the 'New Turn Policy', private ownership of cattle and private trade were again encouraged, and Buddhism was treated more leniently.

However, from 1936 onwards, Mongolia fell under the dictatorship of Marshal Choibalsan (died 1952), whose methods were indistinguishable from those of Stalin. Buddhism was largely destroyed, with much loss of life and property, and most of the former leadership of revolutionaries, politicians, high military officers and intellectuals were liquidated on charges, usually of treasonable plotting with the Japanese, which have since been acknowledged to have been quite false. Thus, Choibalsan declared in 1940 that Mongolia could begin the transition from the 'democratic stage' of the revolution to the socialist stage.

The progress made by 1940 had been mostly negative, consisting in the elimination of old social groupings and the redistribution of wealth confiscated from the former nobles, liquidated in and after 1929, and the clergy. A certain amount of reconstruction had been achieved, in the fields of education, medical services, communications and industry, but it was not until well after the Second World War that any extensive programme of modernization was to be attempted in Mongolia. One reason for this tardiness was the threat posed by the Japanese in Manchuria, which meant that most of the Soviet expenditure in Mongolia was devoted to a military build-up. It is significant that the only railway to be built in pre-war years served the town of Bayantümen, renamed Choibalsan, in eastern Mongolia. Only after the war was Mongolia's main economic region, the area around Ulan Bator, to be connected with the Trans-Siberian railway line.

POLITICAL DEVELOPMENTS SINCE 1945

Mongolia escaped the worst of the Second World War, though not without suffering some effects. The Japanese in Manchuria had for some years been probing the defences of Mongolia, and in mid-1939 they provoked a series of battles on the Khalkha River (Khalkhyn Gol) in which they were heavily defeated by Soviet and Mongol troops. From then on a truce reigned until August 1945, when Mongolia followed the USSR in declaring war on Japan. Mongol forces advanced as far as the Pacific coast of China, but were soon afterwards withdrawn, and the only advantage Mongolia drew from its belated participation in the war was the labour of a number of Japanese prisoners. Imports from the USSR almost ceased during the war years, and Mongolia made a heavy contribution to the Soviet war effort, although it was never at war with Germany. As a result, there was practically no economic progress.

Following the allied Powers' agreement in Yalta to preserve the *status quo* in Mongolia, a plebiscite in October 1945 confirmed the country's wish for independence, which was recognized by China in January 1946. However, Mongolia's international position of isolation, in sole dependence on the USSR, did not change until the communization of Eastern Europe and the success of the communists in China provided it with a new and ready-made field of diplomatic activity. Between October 1948 and March 1950 it exchanged diplomatic recognition with all the then existing communist states except Yugoslavia, and thereafter with a number of non-aligned countries such as India, Burma (Myanmar) and Indonesia. The United Kingdom was the first Western European state to recognize Mongolia (1963). Mongolia was admitted to the United Nations in 1961.

Mongolia continued to look mainly to the USSR for guidance and help in its affairs, in spite of its widening international contacts. In 1946 the traditional alphabet was abandoned in favour of a form of the Cyrillic script. Mongolia's alignment with the USSR in the Sino-Soviet dispute was predictable, and the official press continued to adopt an uncompromising anti-Beijing line. China was accused, among other things, of carrying out a colonialist policy in its minority areas, including Inner Mongolia, and of openly preparing for war with the USSR and Mongolia. Soviet troops were stationed in the MPR at the Mongolian Government's request, because of the 'real threat' of Chinese 'great-power expansion'.

By 1986, however, Mongolia's relations with China appeared to have improved significantly, with a visit to Ulan Bator by the Chinese Vice-Minister of Foreign Affairs and the subsequent signing of an agreement on consular relations between the two countries. Mongolia's position as a 'buffer' state between China and the USSR was illustrated in July, when the Soviet leader, Mikhail Gorbachev, offered to withdraw some of the Soviet troops stationed in Mongolia, as a step towards the normalization of relations between Moscow and Beijing. A partial withdrawal (of about 20% of the estimated total) took place between April and June 1987, and a second stage began in May 1989. Following a series of high-level Mongolian-Chinese negotiations, Mongolia and China subsequently declared the normalization of relations, and in May 1990 the Mongolian Head of State, Punsalmaagiin Ochirbat, paid a short visit to Beijing. The final stage of Soviet troop withdrawals was completed in September 1992.

The partial *détente* which was initiated in the USSR by Nikita Khrushchev in the 1950s and 1960s was imitated in Mongolia, where several of the leaders who had been executed in the 1930s were 'rehabilitated'. Contacts with non-communist foreigners were permitted, a small tourist industry was developed and controls on publications were slightly relaxed. A feature of this period was the reassertion of feelings of Mongolian nationalism, which for 20 years had been repressed. Since 1936 the existence of pre-revolutionary culture in Mongolia had been systematically denied. Nothing of ancient Mongol literature was taught in schools, no old books were reprinted and manuscripts considered to be contrary to contemporary ideology were destroyed. After 1956 this policy was modified. School curricula, while still insisting that children be given a communist education, were liberalized to the extent that they included the study of extracts from ancient literature once more. The Committee (later Academy) of Sciences was able to begin a programme of research and publication in the fields of literature, history and linguistics, and to organize in 1959 the First International Congress of Mongolists. This was the first occasion on which scholars from the Western world, the Soviet bloc and China conferred together in Mongolia.

This renascence of national sentiment was rebuffed from time to time when it clashed with Soviet requirements of greater international communist conformity, as in 1962 when the Mongols celebrated the 800th anniversary of the birth of Genghis Khan. The enthusiasm provoked in Mongolia was regarded by Moscow, and in more orthodox quarters in Mongolia itself, as manifesting excessive feelings of nationalism at the expense of 'proletarian internationalism' and the celebrations were abruptly cancelled. In early 1963 an ideological conference was held in Ulan Bator with the participation of a strong Soviet delegation, in order to reassert the correct political line. It was not until the early 1990s that Genghis Khan was officially rehabilitated; President Ochirbat referred to him in 1992 as 'a national hero and the pride of the country'.

In June 1974 Yumjaagiin Tsedenbal, the Chairman of the Council of Ministers since 1952, became Chairman of the Presidium of the People's Great Khural (Head of State), succeeding Jamsrangiin Sambuu, who had died in May 1972. The new Chairman of the Council of Ministers, Jambyn Batmönkh, was a comparative newcomer to political life. Tsedenbal was concurrently First Secretary of the MPRP Central Committee from 1958 (from 1981 General Secretary), and had been General Secretary of the party in 1940–54.

In August 1984, following an extraordinary session of the MPRP Central Committee, Tsedenbal, who was on holiday in the USSR, was unexpectedly replaced as General Secretary of the Central Committee by Jambyn Batmönkh. He was also removed from the Politburo and relieved of the post of Chairman of the Presidium of the People's Great Khural—ostensibly owing to ill health and with his full agreement. In December 1984 Batmönkh was elected to the post of Chairman of the Presidium of the People's Great Khural, while Dumaagiin Sodnom was elected to membership of the Politburo and the post of Chairman of the Council of Ministers.

In late 1986 government ministries responsible for agriculture, water supply and construction were reorganized, and more extensive restructuring took place in late 1987–early 1988, with the aim of improving the efficiency and productiveness of the country's economy.

In November 1988 the MPRP Politburo, obliged to admit that economic renewal was not succeeding because of the need for social reforms, proposed wide-ranging improvements in procedures for elections to party and legislative offices, and other changes in the name of 'democratization', *il tod* (openness) and *öörchlön shinechlelt* (renewal). The proposals were reported to have received widespread public approval.

THE BIRTH OF DEMOCRACY

Between December 1989 and March 1990 there was a great upsurge in public political activity, as several newly-formed opposition movements organized a series of peaceful demonstrations in Ulan Bator, demanding political and economic reforms. The most prominent of these groups was the Mongolian Democratic Association (MDA), which was founded in December 1989. In January 1990 dialogue was initiated between MPRP officials and representatives of the MDA, including its chief co-ordinator, Sanjaasürengiin Zorig (a lecturer at the Mongolian State University).

The emergence of further opposition groups, together with escalating public demonstrations (involving as many as 20,000 people), led to a crisis of confidence within the MPRP. At a party plenum, held in mid-March 1990, Batmönkh announced the resignation of the entire Politburo as well as of the Secretariat of the Central Committee. Gombojavyn Ochirbat, a former head of the Ideological Department of the Central Committee and a former Chairman of the Central Council of Mongolian Trade Unions, was elected the new General Secretary of the party, replacing Batmönkh. A new five-member Politburo was formed. Delegates at the plenum voted to expel the former MPRP General Secretary, Yumjaagiin Tsedenbal, from the party and to rehabilitate several prominent victims of Tsedenbal's purges of the 1960s.

At a session of the People's Great Khural, which was held shortly after the MPRP plenum, the senior positions in the Presidium were reorganized. The People's Great Khural also adopted amendments to the Constitution, including the removal of references to the MPRP as the 'guiding force' in Mongolian society, approved a new electoral law and brought forward the date of the next general election from 1991 to 1990.

In April 1990 an extraordinary congress of the MPRP was held, at which more than three-quarters of the membership of the Central Committee was renewed. General Secretary Gombojavyn Ochirbat was elected to the restyled post of Chairman of the party. The Politburo was renamed the Presidium, and a new four-member Secretariat of the Central Committee was appointed.

In May 1990 the People's Great Khural approved a law on political parties, which legalized the new 'informal' movements through official registration; it also adopted further amendments to the Constitution, introducing a presidential system with a standing legislature called the State Little Khural, elected by proportional representation of parties.

At the July 1990 general election and subsequent re-elections, 430 deputies were elected to serve a five-year term: 357 from the MPRP (in some instances unopposed), 16 from the Mongolian Democratic Party (MDP, the political wing of the MDA), nine from the Mongolian Revolutionary Youth League, six from the Mongolian National Progress Party (MNPP), four from the Mongolian Social-Democratic Party (MSDP) and 39 without party affiliation. Under the constitutional amendments adopted in May, the People's Great Khural was required to convene at least four times in the five years of its term.

In September 1990 the People's Great Khural elected Punsalmaagiin Ochirbat to be the country's first President, with a five-year term of office; the post of Chairman of the Presidium lapsed and Jambyn Gombojav was elected Chairman (speaker). Radnaasümbereliin Gonchigdorj of the MSDP was subsequently elected Chairman of the State Little Khural, *ex officio* becoming Vice-President of Mongolia. Dashiin Byambasüren was appointed Prime Minister (formerly the post of Chairman of the Council of Ministers) and began consultations on the formation of a multi-party government. The newly-restyled Cabinet was elected by the State Little Khural in September and October. Under the amended Constitution, the President, Vice-President and Ministers were not permitted to remain concurrently deputies of the People's Great Khural; therefore, re-elections of deputies to the People's Great Khural took place in mid-November.

The 20th Congress of the MPRP, which was held in February 1991, elected a new 99-member Central Committee, which, in turn, appointed a new Presidium. The Central Committee also elected a new Chairman, Büdragchaagiin Dash-Yondon, the Chairman of the Ulan Bator City Party Committee, who had become a Presidium member in November 1990.

A new Constitution was adopted by an almost unanimous vote of the Great Khural in January 1992 and entered into force in the following month. It provided for a unicameral Mongolian Great Khural, comprising 76 members, to replace the People's Great Khural following legislative elections, to be held in June. The State Little Khural was abolished. The country's official name was changed from the Mongolian People's Republic to Mongolia and the communist gold star was removed from the national flag.

At the elections to the Mongolian Great Khural in June 1992, a total of 293 candidates stood in 26 constituencies, comprising the 18 *aimag* (provinces), the towns of Darkhan and Erdenet, and Ulan Bator City (six). The constituencies had two, three or four seats, according to the size of the local electorate. The MPRP presented 82 candidates, compared with 51 put forward by an alliance of the MDP, the MNPP and the United Party (UP), and 30 by the MSDP; six other parties and another alliance also took part, although with fewer candidates.

A total of 1,037,392 voters (95.6% of the electorate) participated in the elections, although 62,738 ballots were declared invalid. Candidates were elected by a simple majority, provided that they obtained the support of at least 50% of the electorate in their constituency. The MPRP candidates received altogether 1,719,887 votes (some 57%), while the candidates of the other parties (excluding independents) achieved a combined total of 1,205,350 votes (40%), of which the MDP-MNPP-UP alliance won 521,883 votes and the MSDP 304,548. The outcome of the election was disproportionate, however, the MPRP taking 70 seats (71, if a pro-MPRP independent is included). The remaining seats went to the MDP (two, including an independent), the MSDP, the MNPP and the UP (one each).

The first session of the Mongolian Great Khural opened in July 1992 with the election of officers, the nomination of Puntsagiin Jasrai (who had been a Deputy Chairman of the Council of Ministers and a candidate member of the MPRP Politburo at the end of the communist period) to the post of Prime Minister, and the approval of his Cabinet. Natsagiin Bagabandi, a Vice-Chairman of the MPRP Central Committee, was elected Chairman of the Great Khural. Jambyn Gombojav (Chairman of the People's Great Khural from late 1990 to late 1991) was elected Vice-Chairman of the new Khural. Meanwhile, in June, a National Security Council was established, with the country's President as its Chairman, and the Prime Minister and Chairman of the Great Khural as its members.

In October 1992 the MDP, the MNPP, the UP and the Mongolian Renewal Party amalgamated to form the Mongolian National Democratic Party (MNDP), with a General Council headed by the MNPP leader, Davaadorjiin Ganbold, and including Sanjaasürengiin Zorig and other prominent opposition politicians. In the same month the MPRP Central Committee was renamed the MPRP Little Khural, and its membership was increased to 169 (subsequently to 198). The Presidium was replaced by a nine-member Party Leadership Council.

Political life in Mongolia during the first half of 1993 was dominated by the country's first direct presidential election, held on 6 June. Apparently dissatisfied with the increasingly independent line adopted by the incumbent President, Punsalmaagiin Ochirbat, and angered by presidential vetoes on legislation proposed by the Government, the MPRP Little Khural decided not to support Ochirbat, who had been an MPRP member, and nominated Lodongiin Tüdev as its candidate. Meanwhile, Ochirbat received the nomination of the organizationally weaker opposition coalition of the MNDP and the MSDP. The MPRP expected to win by imposing party discipline on its more numerous supporters, but miscalculated. The outcome of the election was a victory for Ochirbat: 57.8% of the vote, as against 38.7% for Tüdev.

Amendments to the Election Law introduced in early 1996 increased the number of constituencies for election to the Great Khural from 24 to 76; all would be single-seat constituencies, with representatives elected by the majority vote system. The parliamentary opposition parties, the MNDP and MSDP, supported by the Mongolian Green Party and the Mongolian Believers' (Buddhist) Democratic Party, formed a coalition, the Democratic Alliance, to contest the general election of June 1996.

THE END OF COMMUNIST RULE

In the general election held on 30 June 1996 the Democratic Alliance confounded most observers by winning 50 of the 76 seats in the Great Khural. The ruling MPRP took only 25 seats, while one seat went to a candidate of the pro-MPRP United Heritage Party (UHP). A total of 1,057,182 voters (officially 92.15% of the electorate) participated in the elections (47,022 ballots were spoiled). Although official nation-wide totals were not published, it can be calculated from constituency returns that the Democratic Alliance polled 469,586 votes (46.67%), the MPRP 408,977 (40.64%), and other parties and independents 127,684 (12.69%); the last figure included nearly 4,000 ballots which were blank but ruled as valid votes for no candidate.

The first session of the newly-elected Great Khural opened in mid-July 1996 amidst confusion. The election of the MSDP leader, Radnaasümbereliin Gonchigdorj (who had been Vice-President of Mongolia during 1990–92), to the post of Chairman of the Great Khural passed without incident. The Democratic Alliance's choice of Prime Minister, Mendsaikhany Enkhsaikhan (head of the presidential secretariat), was nominated by President Ochirbat and voted into office by the Great Khural. However, the MPRP had issued a list of demands, including the allocation of the vice-chairmanship of the Khural and two important standing committee chairmanships to MPRP members, and when these demands were rejected by the Democratic Alliance, MPRP members walked out of the Great Khural, leaving it inquorate and unable to function.

The boycott of the Great Khural by the MPRP lasted three days. The Khural elected the MNDP leader, Tsakhiagiin Elbegdorj, to be its Vice-Chairman; thereafter, the political confrontation focused on the six standing committees, whose chairmen were all members of the Democratic Alliance. Moreover, the Democratic Alliance declared that it intended to remove MPRP officials from all important posts in the administration.

Eight members of Prime Minister Enkhsaikhan's Government were presented to the Great Khural on 30 July 1996 and voted into office. The selection process had been delayed by a ruling of the Constitutional Court (MPRP appointees) that no member of the Government could remain a member of the Great Khural; the ruling was later overturned by the Great Khural. In late July 1996 the MPRP Little Khural elected a new General Secretary, Nambaryn Enkhbayar, the former Minister of Culture, and a new Leadership Council.

In local government elections, held in October 1996, the Democratic Alliance won 208 seats at provincial council level, while the MPRP achieved 142. However, the Democratic Alliance failed to gain control of Ulan Bator City Council (MPRP 23 seats, MNDP nine, MSDP six, Mongolian Green Party one). At rural and urban district council level, the MPRP won 3,660 seats, the Democratic Alliance secured 3,169 and other parties 29 seats.

It became clear that the Democratic Alliance was losing support to the MPRP in its efforts to promote privatization and the development of a market economy in the face of industrial stagnation, increasing poverty and unemployment. For the presidential election of 18 May 1997 the Democratic Alliance nominated the incumbent President, Punsalmaagiin Ochirbat, as its candidate. The MPRP put forward the former Chairman of the Great Khural (1992–96), Natsagiin Bagabandi, who had been elected MPRP Chairman in February. The third party in the Mongolian Great Khural, the UHP, nominated Jambyn Gombojav, who had defected from the MPRP after Bagabandi's election, altering the balance of power in the Great Khural. The election was won by Bagabandi, with 60.8% of the votes, compared with 29.8% for Ochirbat and 6.6% for Gombojav, a result which many observers saw as an expression of popular dissatisfaction with the Democratic Alliance. Meanwhile, the chairmanship of the MPRP reverted to Nambaryn Enkhbayar, who, in mid-August, won the by-election for Bagabandi's seat in the Great Khural.

A CRISIS OF CONFIDENCE

In April 1998 the Democratic Alliance decided that the Cabinet would be headed by the Alliance's leader and, unlike the Enkhsaikhan Cabinet, would comprise members of the Great Khural. Thus, Tsakhiagiin Elbegdorj, leader of the MNDP, was appointed Prime Minister, although the formation of the new Cabinet took a month. The policies of the Elbegdorj Cabinet did not differ much from those of its predecessor, although it sought to project a reformist image.

Soon afterwards the Government became embroiled in a dispute over its amalgamation of the state-owned Reconstruction Bank (which had been declared bankrupt after having overextended its credit) with the private Golomt Bank. Although various authorities, including the IMF and the Asian Development Bank (ADB), approved this amalgamation, some Democratic Alliance members of the Great Khural were unsure about it, while the opposition MPRP bitterly opposed it. Amidst accusations that Democratic Alliance leaders and ministers had obtained loans from the Bank just before it collapsed, the MPRP resorted to another boycott of the Great Khural. When the spring session closed (in August 1998), although the Khural had sat for 103 days, 20 working days had been lost, thus delaying important legislation, including finance bills.

Insisting that the Democratic Alliance Cabinet should resign, the MPRP refused to accept a government compromise but returned to the Great Khural to pursue a vote of 'no confidence' in the Government. The vote of 'no confidence' was carried on 24 July 1998 by 42 votes to 33, with 15 members of the Democratic Alliance 'crossing the floor'. The three-month-old Elbegdorj Government resigned, leaving the Democratic Alliance 30 days to choose a new Prime Minister.

Meanwhile, a new altercation arose over the management of the Mongolian-Russian copper-mining joint venture at Erdenet. In February 1998 the Enkhsaikhan Government had become embroiled in a dispute over the reappointment of the Mongolian director-general of the Erdenet enterprise, Shagdaryn Otgonbileg. For many years a member of the MPRP Little Khural, he had been in charge of the enterprise from its inception. The Russians wanted him to be maintained in the post, but Enkhsaikhan refused to reappoint him on the grounds that he had attempted to privatize part of the enterprise illegally. However, President Bagabandi intervened on the Russian side and Otgonbileg's contract was extended.

When Otgonbileg's contract finally ended, he refused to attend the ceremony marking the official hand-over to his successor—the former Minister of Defence, Dambyn Dorligjav—but sought a court ruling that his 'dismissal' was illegal. The court's decision in his favour was overturned on appeal by the State Property Committee.

The Elbergdorj Cabinet established a government commission and imposed a 'special regime' on the Erdenet enterprise. President Bagabandi then stated that the Government could not impose such a 'special regime' on the enterprise unilaterally, without consulting the Russian co-directors. The government commission accused Otgonbileg of criminal negligence and appealed to the President to withdraw his support for the Russian position. President Bagabandi retorted that the 'special regime' had been imposed in disregard of his opinion, and he issued a statement criticizing anti-Russian reports in the 'official media'. Various MPRP leaders joined him in condemning the 'politicization' of the Erdenet affair as harmful to relations with the 'northern neighbour'. Later in the year a meeting of the full board of Erdenet approved Dorligjav's appointment and the 'special regime' was terminated.

In mid-August 1998 the Democratic Alliance nominated as their choice for the next Prime Minister Davaadorjiin Ganbold, the Chairman of the Economic Standing Committee of the Great Khural, who had served as First Deputy Chairman of the Government in 1990–92 and President of the MNDP in 1992–96. However, President Bagabandi refused to accept Ganbold's nomination, on the grounds that he had done nothing as Chairman of the Economic Standing Committee to resolve the bank merger crisis. Ganbold was nominated a second time, but the President rejected him again. The Democratic Alliance protested that the President had no constitutional right to reject its nomination, but he did so yet again and put forward his own nominee, Dogsomyn Ganbold, whom the Democratic Alliance ignored. After Davaadorjiin Ganbold's nomination had been rejected a sixth time by the President, the Democratic Alliance presented a new nominee, the acting Minister of External Relations, Rinchinnyamyn Amarjargal. His nomination was accepted by President Bagabandi on 31 August 1998 but rejected by the Great Khural on the following day by a majority of only one vote. After a further period of delay, the Democratic Alliance nominated a new candidate, Galsangiin Gankhuyag, who was rejected by the President on the grounds that he might face charges of drunken driving. In late September Bagabandi rejected a further nominee, Erdeniin Bat-Üül, who had been replaced as Vice-President of the MNDP by Davaadorjiin Ganbold in August. On 2 October Sanjaasürengiin Zorig, the Minister of Infrastructure Development, was murdered at his home. Zorig, the founder of the Mongolian democratic movement, had been widely seen as a potential candidate for the post of Prime Minister, although he had not been nominated.

After Zorig's state funeral, President Bagabandi issued the names of six more candidates of his own, including Dogsomyn Ganbold and the Mayor of Ulan Bator, Janlavyn Narantsatsralt. The Democratic Alliance ignored the presidential list and, for the seventh time, nominated Davaadorjiin Ganbold. Although the nomination was supported by all 48 Democratic Alliance members of the Great Khural, the President again rejected him. Later the same month the political crisis was deepened by the Constitutional Court's latest ruling, reaffirming that members of the Great Khural could not serve concurrently in the Government. The ruling overturned an amendment to the Law on the Status of Great Khural Members adopted in January 1998. Two months later the Democratic Alliance finally nominated Bagabandi's candidate, Janlavyn Narantsatsralt, who was appointed Prime Minister in early December. The formation of his Government was completed with the appointment of the last four ministers in mid-January 1999.

Narantsatsralt's Government remained in power for just over six months. In July 1999 the Prime Minister was challenged in the Great Khural over a letter that he had written in January to Yurii Maslyukov, First Deputy Chairman of the Russian Government, in which he seemingly acknowledged Russia's right to privatize its share in the Erdenet joint venture without reference to the Mongolians. Unable to offer a satisfactory explanation, in late July Narantsatsralt lost a vote of confidence, in which MSDP members of the Great Khural voted with the opposition MPRP. The Democratic Alliance nominated Rinchinnyamyn Amarjargal for the post of Prime Minister, but the proposal was immediately challenged by President Bagabandi. The President insisted that, following the Constitutional Court ruling of late 1998, he could consider Amarjargal's suitability for nomination in the Great Khural only after the candidate had resigned his seat. After several days of arguments, representatives of the Democratic Alliance and the President adopted a formula that allowed the Great Khural's approval of the prime ministerial nomination and the nominee's resignation of his Great Khural seat to take place simultaneously. Amarjargal was elected Prime Minister at the end of July. The ministers of Narantsatsralt's Government remained in office in an acting capacity until early September, when all but one (the Minister of Law) were reappointed. In November Amarjargal replaced Narantsatsralt as President of the MNDP.

The 1992 Constitution was amended for the first time in December 1999 by a Mongolian Great Khural decree, supported by all three parliamentary parties, which *inter alia* simplified the procedure for the appointment of the Prime Minister and allowed members of the Great Khural to serve as government ministers while retaining their seats in the legislature. However, the President vetoed the decree, stating that the amendments (due to come into force from 15 July) could not be approved by the Great Khural alone, without public consideration of his opinion and that of the Constitutional Court. The presidential veto was rejected by the Great Khural in January 2000, but in March a five-member session of the Constitutional Court ruled that the decree had been unconstitutional. When the Great Khural opened its spring session in April, members rejected the ruling and refused to discuss it. The Constitutional Court's demand for a statement on the issue was disregarded by the Great Khural.

As the general election approached, party political activity increased dramatically. A breakaway grouping of the MNDP re-constituted the Mongolian Democratic Party, and a faction of the MSDP founded the Mongolian New Social Democratic Party. Sanjaasürengiin Oyuun, the sister of the murdered minister, Zorig, established the Civil Courage Party (CCP, or Irgenii Zorig Party) drawing away from the MNDP several more members of the Great Khural, and formed an electoral alliance with the Green Party. The MNDP, unable to reconstitute the previously-successful Democratic Alliance with the MSDP, therefore formed a new Democratic Alliance with the Mongolian Believers' Democratic Party. A grand alliance of nine non-parliamentary parties was quickly reduced to three—the Democratic Renewal Party, Mongolian Traditional United Party (UHP) and For Mongolia Party—following a decision by the Mongolian Democratic New Socialist Party (MDNSP) and the Mongolian Republican Party (the latter headed by wealthy businessmen, a new feature of Mongolian politics) to present their own candidates.

At the election, held on 2 July 2000, three coalitions and 13 parties were represented by a total of 603 candidates, including 27 independents. The MPRP took 72 of the 76 seats in the Great Khural. Prime Minister Rinchinnyamyn Amarjargal and his entire Cabinet lost their seats. The MPRP received 50.2% of the votes cast, the level of participation being 82.4% of the electorate. The party's victory was attributed to widespread popular support for its platform of social welfare and poverty reduction, and to the disintegration of the MNDP-MSDP coalition. Moreover, in the more numerous rural constituencies, where its main support lay, the MPRP was widely seen as willing and able to put an end to the economic and social stagnation of the countryside.

The four seats not taken by the MPRP went to Sanjaasürengiin Oyuun (President of the CCP); Badarchiin Erdenebat (Chairman of the MDNSP); Lamjavyn Gündalai (Independent), a businessman from Khövsgöl Province; and ex-Prime Minister Janlavyn Narantsatsralt (MNDP). The Democratic Alliance, which presented 71 candidates, received 13% of the votes cast; the MDNSP, with 73 candidates, received 10.7% of the votes cast. The 67 MSDP candidates received 8.9% of votes cast, but won no seats.

When the new Great Khural opened, Lkhamsürengiin Enebish, the MPRP General Secretary, was elected to the post of Chairman (Speaker). However, the nomination of the MPRP Chairman, Nambaryn Enkhbayar, for the post of Prime Minister was rejected by President Natsagiin Bagabandi, on the grounds that priority be given to the constitutional amendments. After a week of discussion a compromise was reached whereby Enkhbayar's nomination was presented to the Great Khural, while the amendments remained in force pending a Great Khural debate and a full nine-member session of the Constitutional Court. On 26 July 2000 the Great Khural approved Prime Minister Enkhbayar's appointment by 67 MPRP members' votes to three. It approved the membership of Enkhbayar's Cabinet on 9 August.

Reflecting the MPRP's emphasis on social issues, Enkhbayar divided the former Ministry of Health and Social Welfare into two separate ministries, the Ministry of Health and the Ministry of Social Protection and Welfare. The Ministry of Law became the Ministry of Justice and Home Affairs and took charge of the Border Troops. Furthermore, the MSDP alleged that the new Government was acting in violation of the spirit of the Constitution, by dismissing large numbers of civil servants because of their party affiliation. On 28 September 2000 Rinchinnyamyn Amarjargal, leader of the MNDP, and Radnaasümbereliin Gonchigdorj, leader of the MSDP, signed a joint declaration announcing that a conference of the parties would be held on 6 December, to formalize the merging of the two parties. This was done with a view to ensuring the necessary parliamentary basis for Gonchigdorj's nomination in the 2001 presidential election. The two parties formed a new Coalition of Democratic Forces (together with four smaller parties) to contest the provincial and Ulan Bator local government elections held on 1 October. None the less, the MPRP won 552 of the 695 seats available in the city and *aimag* (provincial) khurals, a voter participation rate of 60.75% being recorded.

At a conference held on 6 December 2000, altogether five democratic parties—the MNDP, MSDP, Mongolian Democratic Party, Believers' Democratic Party, and Democratic Renewal Party—resolved to dissolve themselves and form a new Democratic Party (DP). Dambyn Dorligjav, a former Minister of Defence and director of the Erdenet copper combine, was elected Chairman, while ex-Prime Minister Janlavyn Narantsatsralt and former Minister of the Environment Sonomtserengiin Mendsaikhan were elected Vice-Chairmen. When registered on 26 December the DP claimed a membership of 160,000. Lamjavyn Gündalai, elected to the Great Khural as an Independent, joined the DP. After the formation of the DP's primary organizations nationwide in February 2001, they elected the party's National Advisory Committee, comprising two members from each of the Great Khural's 76 constituencies. They included many of the former leaders of the MNDP and MSDP who in the Great Khural elections of July 2000 had failed to be elected. In July 2001 the DP's Secretary-General, Zandaakhüügiin Enkhbold, was released to attend a study course in the USA, and his duties were taken over by the former Mongolian ambassador to the United Kingdom, Tsedenjavyn Sükhbaatar. A new Secretary-General, Norovyn Altankhuyag, was elected in September 2001.

On 14 December 2000 the Great Khural readopted unchanged the decree of December 1999 amending the 1992 Constitution for immediate implementation. The decree was vetoed by the President, and his veto was rejected, but the Constitutional Court was unable to meet in full session because the election of replacements for time-expired members was delayed in the Great Khural. Finally, President Bagabandi sealed the amendments in May.

The MPRP's 23rd Congress was held at the end of February 2001. The Chairman, Nambaryn Enkhbayar, and General Secretary, Lkhamsürengiin Enebish, were re-elected. Two of the three party secretaries, Taukein Sultaan and Baldangiin Enkhmandakh, were released for diplomatic duties, while Sanjbegziin Tömör-Ochir and Luvsandagvyn Amarsanaa joined the secretariat, although Amarsanaa was soon nominated to be the next Mongolian ambassador to China. The membership of the Party Leadership Council was increased from 11 to 15.

The presidential election on 20 May 2001 was won by the MPRP's Natsagiin Bagabandi, who received 574,553 votes (57.95% of the total ballot), as against 362,684 votes for Radnaasümbereliin Gonchigdorj of the DP (36.58%) and 35,139 votes for Luvsandambyn Dashnyam of the Civil Courage Party (3.54%).

In January 2001, meanwhile, a member of the Great Khural and former director of the Erdenet copper combine, Shagdaryn Otgonbileg, was killed when an Mi-8 helicopter carrying 23 passengers and crew investigating the *zud* in western Mongolia crashed in Malchin district of Uvs *aimag*. The eight dead included several UN staff. Otgonbileg was given a state funeral, and in May his widow, Tuyaa, was elected unopposed as Great Khural MPRP member for his Zavkhan 22 constituency. The Chairman of the Great Khural, Lkhamsürengiin Enebish, died in September 2001, and was succeeded by Sanjbezgiin Tömör-Ochir. He was replaced as General Secretary of the MPRP by Doloonjingiin Idevtkhen, and Byambajavyn Övgönhüü was elected for the MPRP in Enebish's constituency. In March 2002 Sanjaasürengiin Oyuun's Civil Courage Party merged with Bazarsadyn Jargalsaikhan's Mongolian Republican Party to form the Civil Courage Republican Party under Oyuun's leadership. A member of the Great Khural for the MPRP, Mendiyn Zenee, died in June 2002. At the beginning of August the CCRP and DP signed a partnership agreement for an electoral alliance to contest the September by-election in Töv province, to elect a successor to Zenee. The partnership was expected to continue to the general election scheduled for 2004.

EXTERNAL RELATIONS

The collapse of the USSR in December 1991 had far-reaching effects on Mongolia, which was obliged to negotiate separate treaties with the USSR's former constituent parts to ensure the continuation of aid and trade, on which Mongolia remained largely dependent. In January 1993 President Ochirbat visited Moscow, where he signed with President Yeltsin a new 20-year Mongolian-Russian Treaty of Friendly Relations and Co-operation to replace the defunct Mongolian-Soviet treaty of 1986. Ochirbat and Yeltsin also issued a joint statement expressing regret at the imprisonment and execution of Mongolian citizens in the USSR during the Stalinist purges. Similar treaties of friendly relations and co-operation were concluded with Kazakhstan and Ukraine.

Relations between Mongolia and China had improved by April 1994, when a new Treaty of Friendship and Co-operation was concluded during a visit to Ulan Bator by the Chinese Premier, Li Peng. An agreement on cultural, economic and technical co-operation was also signed.

In July 1994 two important documents outlining Mongolian foreign policy objectives were published, the *National Security Concept* and the *Foreign Policy Concept*. While emphasizing 'complete equality' in its co-operation with Russia and China, Mongolia also focused on the development of relations with its 'third neighbour'—primarily the USA, Japan, Western Europe, the Asia-Pacific region, the UN and international financial bodies.

In May 1995 the US Congress issued a statement of support for Mongolia, and in August President Clinton authorized the provision of US military aid to Mongolia. Hillary Clinton paid a brief visit to Mongolia in September and announced further aid of US $4.5m. In the same month President Ochirbat flew to Germany and then to the headquarters of the European Union in Brussels for aid talks. Ochirbat returned to Europe in April 1996 for official visits to France and the United Kingdom; in London he promoted bilateral trade, and was received by the Queen. Prime Minister Jasrai had paid an official visit to China at the end of March.

Relations with China were consolidated in 1997 by the visits to Ulan Bator of Qiao Shi, the Chairman of the Standing Committee of the National People's Congress (in April), and of the Minister of Foreign Affairs, Qian Qichen (in August). The Malaysian Prime Minister, Mahathir Mohamad, visited Mongolia in September, but various aid and co-operation projects discussed during his visit were postponed owing to the financial crisis affecting Malaysia.

Prime Minister Enkhsaikhan travelled to Switzerland (Davos) and Hungary in January 1998. President Bagabandi paid official visits to Kazakhstan, Kuwait and Turkey in March, and in May he went to Japan, where he was received by Emperor Akihito. The US Secretary of State, Madeleine Albright, paid a very brief visit to Ulan Bator in May. In July Mongolia was admitted to the Association of South East Asian Nations (ASEAN) Regional Forum (ARF) at its ministerial meeting in Manila. Mongolia received three important foreign visitors in mid-1999: President Kim Dae-Jung of the Republic of Korea visited in May, and in July official visits were paid by Prime Minister Keizo Obuchi of Japan and President Jiang Zemin of China. In November Prime Minister Amarjargal visited the Democratic People's Republic of Korea, China and the Republic of Korea, and in March 2000 he paid an official visit to the United Kingdom. He was followed a fortnight later by a delegation of 10 members of the Mongolian Great Khural. In May Amarjargal attended a conference in Riga, Latvia, where Mongolian membership of the European Bank for Reconstruction and Development (EBRD) was approved. In June 2000 President Bagabandi paid official visits to Italy and Bulgaria. In that month Mongolia became the 24th member of the Parliamentary Union of the Countries of Asia and the Pacific.

In November 2000 Russian President Vladimir Putin made an overnight stop in Ulan Bator on his way to the Asia-Pacific Economic Co-operation (APEC) conference in Brunei. He was the first senior-level Moscow visitor to Mongolia since Soviet Communist Party General Secretary Leonid Brezhnev's visit in

1974. Presidents Putin and Bagabandi issued a joint declaration which pledged Mongolia and Russia 'not to join any military-political alliances against one another, nor conclude any treaty or agreement with third countries harmful to the interests of the other's sovereignty or independence. Neither side will allow its territory to be used by a third state for purposes of aggression or other acts of violence harmful to the sovereignty, security and public order of the other'. Russia confirmed its adherence to the five nuclear powers' declaration of guarantees for Mongolia's security in connection with its nuclear-weapons-free status.

President Bagabandi visited the Philippines and also travelled to the USA, visiting New York in September 2000. In January 2001 he paid a state visit to India, and in February visited Seoul, the South Korean capital. Enkhbayar travelled abroad as Prime Minister for the first time to the Davos international economic forum in Switzerland in January 2001, then Japan. The Chinese Minister of Foreign Affairs, Tang Jiaxuan, visited Ulan Bator in July 2001. Russian Premier Mikhail Kasyanov's brief visit to Mongolia in March 2002 raised once more the dispute between Moscow and Ulan Bator over Mongolia's repayment to Russia of the large debt for Soviet aid (see Economy).

Economy

ALAN J. K. SANDERS

Between 1948 and 1990 the Mongolian economy was developed under a series of Five-Year Plans, with large-scale assistance from the USSR and other communist countries, principally those that formed the Council for Mutual Economic Assistance (CMEA, dissolved in mid-1991). The two salient features of development during this period were the completion of the transition to the socialist system of production and a rate of economic expansion very much faster than was achieved in the first 30 years of the republic.

In the early 1990s, parallel with the political developments taking place in Mongolia, the Government initiated a series of far-reaching reforms aimed at achieving a market economy and privatization. Mongolia was faced with a rapidly-growing population and an increasing demand for foodstuffs and consumer goods. During 1980–91 the population increased by an annual average of 2.7%, but, with the population of working age rising by 3.4% per year, it was feared that unemployment would increase considerably. (The population rose by an annual average of 1.2% in 1992–2000.) A high rate of infant mortality was disclosed after decades of concealment. (According to the UN Development Programme (UNDP), this stood at 62 deaths per 1,000 births in 2000.) Poor living conditions were reported to be responsible for 50% of infant deaths in the 1980s, genetic and ecological conditions for 30% and inadequate medical services for 20%. During the 1980s there was also a severe shortage of convertible currency, necessary to acquire new technology, to stimulate production and export earnings, and to reduce Mongolia's foreign debt. In an attempt to revitalize the economy, Mongolia planned to promote the tourist industry and to secure a relatively small medium-term loan in convertible currency. This was to be used to buy small, mobile mining machinery, to exploit the country's deposits of gold and silver, and modern technology for the improvement of livestock-breeding and the associated processing industry.

In 1989, according to official sources, gross national product (GNP) per head was US $473. Reflecting the dislocation of the economy in the transition to a free market, GNP per head had declined to US $112 by 1991. Large devaluations of the tögrög since then have made the exact figure uncertain, but the World Bank estimated GNP per head to be US $390 in 1997 and US $380 in 1998. In July 2001 the President of Mongolbank estimated average annual per caput income at US $360–380.

AGRICULTURE

After the catastrophe of the period of 'leftist deviation' (1929–32), animal herding, the mainstay of Mongolia's economy, reverted to private enterprise, and, apart from taking compulsory deliveries of produce during the period of the Second World War, the Government did not interfere with herding activity. Small-scale mutual help in carrying out certain tasks was practised, and some herdsmen joined together in small producers' associations, but under the 'New Turn Policy' the formation of co-operatives was discouraged. By 1952 the existing co-operatives contained only 280,000 animals out of a national stock of nearly 23m. However, collectivization of herding had by 1957 again become a matter of policy. Although collectivization was said to have been carried out voluntarily by the herdsmen, the initiative came from the MPRP, and propaganda and economic compulsion were widely used to persuade people to join. Thus, state loans were granted to newly-formed co-operatives, discriminatory rates of taxation were imposed on individuals who owned large herds and similarly differential norms of compulsory deliveries of produce were set.

The collectivization programme reached its height in 1958 and by April 1959 all but a tiny minority of herdsmen had been collectivized. The herdsmen's associations (*negdel*) were quite different in character from the earlier producers' associations. They were of considerable size, and were units of local administration as well as economic units. Labour was regulated by means of work-books issued to each member, who received pay according to his work. All families were allowed to retain a certain number of private animals. Produce was purchased by the State which also granted loans to the co-operatives. Internally, each co-operative was organized into a number of permanent brigades, each with its own territory and headquarters and its own special tasks. The brigade in its turn contained a number of sections (*heseg*) comprising several bases, each of usually two households living in felt tents and looking after a number of animals.

An innovation in the Mongolian rural economy has been the development of large-scale agriculture. This did not affect any previous pattern of economic activity and from the start was organized as a direct state venture. Ten state farms existed in 1940 and 52 state farms in 1988. In and after 1959 the area under cultivation increased sharply as large tracts of virgin land were opened, but the sown area was smaller in 1970 than in 1965. By 1978 1m. ha of virgin land had been put to the plough. It was reported that the 1985 grain harvest reached a record 889,400 tons, enabling Mongolia to meet its own grain requirements and to export surplus wheat to Siberia. Production amounted to 798,600 tons in 1989, but it subsequently declined annually and by 2000 totalled only 142,066 tons.

Increasing attention was paid to mechanization and the introduction of scientific methods of farming. The division of activity between the 255 *negdel* and the 52 state farms was not a strict one. Co-operatives also engaged in field work, especially fodder growing, while state farms were expected to supply good breeding animals. The principal crops produced by the state farms were cereals, potatoes and other vegetables. An apparently successful innovation was the establishment of 17 inter-co-operative production enterprises, in which neighbouring co-operatives combined resources to specialize in particular farm-related activities. A new law on co-operatives came into force in January 1990. This law controlled co-operative activity in small-scale industry, trade and services and transformed the *negdel* into proper co-operatives. In 1991, however, following the new Government's initiation of political and economic reforms, these were privatized and mostly divided into smaller units. All restrictions on private livestock ownership were removed in 1990. Some state farms became joint stock companies, others were broken up.

At the annual year-end livestock census in 1995, Mongolia had a record total of 28.6m. head of sheep, goats, horses, cows and camels. This was largely due to a 2m. head increase in the number of goats, encouraged by the growth in the cashmere industry. In 1996 the rise in livestock numbers continued, reaching 29.3m., but this was also a reflection of low levels of industrial consumption of meat and hides.

In early 1996 Mongolia experienced unusually large-scale and widespread forest and steppe fires, which burned out of control for several weeks. The fires killed 25 people and 7,800 livestock, and caused damage estimated at more than US $2,000m.; 2.4m. ha of forest and 7.8m. ha of steppe were destroyed. In mid-1996 several people were drowned when heavy rains caused flash floods in Ulan Bator and other areas of northern Mongolia; meanwhile, in scattered regions across Mongolia, herdsmen were concerned about prolonged drought. A survey of the herding community at the end of 1996 revealed that, of the 517,700 families in Mongolia, 170,100, or 32.8%, were herding families, with 395,400 herdsmen (16.8% of the population) engaged in livestock raising. Only 9.3% of these families had electricity.

Mongolia's livestock herds increased in 1999 to a new record of 33.6m. (compared with 31.3m. in 1997). However, serious drought in late 1999 was followed in early 2000 by several months of severe cold, snow and frost. In consequence, by mid-2000 an estimated 2.5m. head of livestock had died from starvation and cold. In response to government appeals, international donors offered financial aid, and relief teams of the International Committee of the Red Cross (ICRC) were mobilized to take food and medicine to isolated herding families. Almost 2,500 families were believed to have lost all their animals by late June, when survivals of new-born stock numbered 8.4m. head, compared with 10.2m. in 1999.

The December 2000 livestock census recorded a fall in the herds to 30,096,400 head, and in the following months the weakened animals faced even more severe conditions, with deep snow and very low temperatures. It was reported at the end of June 2001 that 3,312,000 head had died, 26.7% more than the year before, and that 7,364 households had lost all their animals. The hardest-hit provinces were Zavkhan (28.9% of stock lost), Arkhangai (18.9%) and Khövsgöl (18.3%). Eastern provinces were affected by foot-and-mouth disease. Newborn stock thriving in the summer of 2001 numbered 7.6 m., 762,800 fewer than in 2000.

Prime Minister Enkhbayar expressed concern about the state of the nomadic herding economy, stating that it was important to improve the quality of stock, raise yields and invigorate product processing. The key was the intensification of livestock raising to meet the growing needs of large towns, especially Ulan Bator. The capital's population was estimated at more than 813,500 in 2002, with some 100,000–150,000 people commuting into the city daily.

INDUSTRY

Large-scale industry has developed only since the 1960s. Before the Revolution most manufactured requisites were imported or were made locally, chiefly by Chinese craftsmen. In the 1920s technicians from Western Europe were engaged to help develop Mongolia's infant industry. In particular they built a power station and a brickworks. After the swing to the left in 1929, however, only Soviet aid and expertise were welcome, and in the years prior to the Second World War industrial growth was slow. Only one enterprise of any size was commissioned, the Industrial Combine in Ulan Bator, which in 1934 commenced production of leather goods and felts. Industry developed in two channels. Co-operative industry had a much smaller output than state industry, producing many items needed for domestic use, as well as providing repair services. After the Second World War state-operated industry expanded rapidly and many new enterprises were commissioned.

Mongolia received enormous aid from its political allies—some 10,000m. roubles from the USSR alone between 1945 and 1990—without which its industrial advance, modest though it is in world terms, could not have been envisaged. For a time, in the 1950s, it seemed as if China was hoping to challenge the USSR's leading position in Mongolia, using the weapon of economic aid. A first gift of 160m. roubles in 1955 was followed by the dispatch of Chinese labourers to help Mongolia's inadequate and undertrained labour force. Exact numbers are not available, but in the peak years of 1959 and 1960 several thousand Chinese labourers were working on diverse projects, such as building apartment blocks, laying roads and installing irrigation systems. Many had their families with them. As the Sino-Soviet rift widened, the Chinese workers began to leave Mongolia, until by mid-1964 most had returned home. To some extent the loss of these workmen was made good by the supply of Soviet construction labourers and engineers (some 50,000 at their peak), working principally in Ulan Bator, the Darkhan area and Choibalsan, where a third industrial area was planned. However, the break with China had other adverse effects. Chinese consumer goods, in particular silk and cloth, which were plentiful in 1959, were, by 1968, no longer available. The drastic fall in railway through-goods traffic between the USSR and China also meant a considerable loss of state revenue.

The principal centres of industry are in the central economic region, at Ulan Bator and Darkhan, half-way between the capital and the Russian frontier. Both centres are situated in the area of densest population and have direct road and rail communication with Russia. Both have their own coal supplies also, Darkhan at an open-cast mine at Sharyn Gol, to which it is linked by a new rail spur, and Ulan Bator at a large, new, open-cast mine at Baganuur, linked to the Trans-Mongolian railway. The two centres account for most of Mongolia's production in terms of electric power, capital materials such as cement, bricks and wall panels, and consumer goods—food, drink, leather goods, china, sweets, soap and so on. A large new cement and lime complex at Khötöl, between Darkhan and Erdenet, was expected to produce 100,000 metric tons of lime and 500,000 tons of cement per year, enough to satisfy the country's total requirements. In the mid-1990s, however, the construction industry was working at only some 20% of its capacity. Many of Mongolia's industrial enterprises were not viable in market conditions and ceased production, being in effect bankrupt. A factory producing disposable syringes, financed by the Republic of Korea, began production in the mid-1990s. At the end of the 1990s there was an improvement in the output of the knitwear and garment industry.

One of the most important developments in Mongolia's economy has been the joint Soviet-Mongolian exploitation of copper and molybdenum deposits at Erdenet in Orkhon province. The deposits are located near Khangal *sum*, about two hours' journey by road to the west of Darkhan, and thus accessible to transport routes. The Salkhit–Erdenet railway line, linking the new complex with the main rail system, went into operation in October 1975, and the ore concentrator in December 1978. The combine attained its full capacity in November 1983. In the 1990s the Erdenet copper enterprise became Mongolia's largest source of foreign exchange, while Erdenet town emerged as an industrial centre in its own right, with a large carpet factory and other enterprises.

In 1995 copper concentrate exports were sufficient to finance more than 67% of Mongolia's imports. However, in 1995–96 fluctuating world copper prices and the declining metal content of exported concentrate underlined Mongolia's vulnerability as a one-asset economy. There was a continuing slow decline in the share of copper in Mongolia's total exports, falling from 53.0% in 1995 to 33.3% in 1999. In 2000–01 the concern operated at a loss, unable to reduce production costs, and unable to pay government taxes, set too high on world copper price forecasts.

Output of fluorspar declined by 200,000 metric tons in 1994, when only 88,000 tons were exported, owing to the lack of a steady market; production increased again from 1995, reaching 597,100 tons in 1999. A new open-cast phosphate mine with an annual capacity of 50,000 metric tons was due to go into production in 1996 at Bürenkhaan, close to the freshwater Lake Khövsgöl. Its western European equipment was reportedly 'environment friendly', but Mongolian scientists and lawyers expressed concern about pollution, and the mine's future was uncertain. The most successful industry was that of gold-mining, with production rising from 4.5 tons in 1995 to 11.8 tons in 2000, and 13.7 tons in 2001.

In 1997 exploratory drilling at Tamsag, in eastern Mongolia, began to yield crude petroleum, at a rate of 1,500 barrels per day. The first consignment was delivered to China for analysis and refining. A clear sign of long-term improvement in government revenues appeared in July 1997, with income of 500m. tögrög from petroleum exploitation included for the first time. The number of wells was scheduled to reach eight in 1998 and 17 in 1999. Production of crude petroleum rose from 44,791 barrels in 1998 to 71,914 barrels in 1999, then fell slightly to 65,522 barrels in 2000. The SOCO oil company had suffered a severe fire at its Tamsag base in eastern Mongolia, but restarted extraction at its three production wells for export to China (73,700 barrels in 2001).

The 1990s witnessed a resurgence of Chinese business activity in Mongolia. By 2001 companies with Chinese investment accounted for 35% of all companies with foreign investment, and companies benefiting from Hong Kong investment for a further 13.7%, while the Republic of Korea accounted for 23.7%.

Mongolia's hopes of benefiting from the oil and gas pipelines to be built from Russia to China finally expired in mid-2001 when it emerged that they would bypass Mongolia on the way to the refineries at Daqing in the Chinese province of Heilongjiang.

FOREIGN TRADE

Trade was traditionally almost entirely with the countries formerly constituting the 'socialist bloc': in 1989 93.1% of Mongolia's exports went to socialist countries (CMEA 90.3%), which were also the source of 95.6% of imports (CMEA 92.5%). However, the share of Mongolia's total foreign trade conducted with former socialist states had declined to some 74% by 1992. In 1999 the principal source of imports (supplying 29.2%) was Russia, followed by Japan (22.4%) and China (15.1%). The principal markets for exports were China (taking 58.1%), Russia (13.5%) and the USA (12.9%).

In 2000 Mongolian exports to China were worth US $274.3m. (58.9% of all exports) and imports from China US $125.8m. (20.5%), compared with US $208.2m. (58.1%) and US $77.6m. (15.1%) the previous year. Exports to Russia and imports from Russia were worth US $45.1m (9.7%) and US $206.2m. (33.6%) respectively, as against US $48.2m. (13.5%) and US $149.8m. (29.2%) in 1999.

Mongolia exports mainly primary products and imports industrial goods and equipment. In 1989 some 42.8% of its exports consisted of fuels, minerals and metals, while raw materials, including foodstuffs, accounted for a further 35.7%. In that year industrial consumer goods accounted for 17.5% of total exports. In 1993 industrial goods accounted for 75.4% of total imports, while consumer goods comprised the remaining 24.6%. Fuel and petroleum accounted for 32.6% of industrial imports.

In 1993 59.9% of imports were conducted by general (convertible currency) trade, 29.5% by barter and 10.6% by other kinds of trade. The breakdown of exports was as follows: 51.6% general trade, 35.2% barter and 13.2% other kinds of trade. In 1994–95 Mongolia aimed to achieve a trade surplus for the first time, reducing petroleum imports and promoting the export of cashmere goods. Mongolia's international trade recorded a deficit of US $87.4m. in 1996. With world copper prices low, the trade deficit in 1998 was US $155.6m., compared with a surplus of US $30.2m. in 1997. The trade deficit was estimated at US $90.2m. in 1999, and US $148.4m. in 2000.

In 1996 the principal imports were machinery (22.4%), mineral products (20.0%) and transport equipment (17.2%). Capital goods accounted for 31.7% of imports in 1997. The principal exports in 1997 were copper concentrate (35.0%), cashmere (8.4%) and gold (20.6%). In 1999 exports of copper concentrate were worth US $111.7m., combed cashmere US $43m. and sawn timber US $4.8m., as against US $124.8m., US $33m. and US $31.1m. respectively in 1998. Textile exports in 1999 were worth US $45.7m., 58.7% more than in 1998. In 1999 minerals constituted 40% of exports by value, textiles 38% and leather and furs 8%. Machinery accounted for 26% of imports by value, minerals 20% and foodstuffs 14%.

In 2001 Mongolia's exports were worth US $385.2m. and imports US $554.8m. The main export destinations were China (US $212.4m.—55.1%), the USA (US $84.7m.—22.0%), and Russia (US $39.7m.—10.3%). The main exports by value were copper concentrate (US $145.0m.—37.6%) and cashmere (US $39.5m.—10.3%), both mostly to China, and textiles (US $138.4m.—35.9%). Copper concentrate exports rose by 6.3% by volume but their value fell by 9.5%. Renewed exports of frozen beef to Russia were worth US $10.4m. (2.7%), down slightly on 2000 (US $14.3m.). The chief sources of imports were Russia (US $201.9m.—36.4%), China (US $121.4m.—21.9%), the Republic of Korea (US $53.6m.—9.7%), and Japan (US $52.8m.—9.5%). Mineral products (essentially refined petroleum from Russia) accounted for US $131.7m. (23.7%) of imports, and machinery US $102.1m. (18.4%).

POWER AND TRANSPORT

Fuel of many types is used in Mongolia. At one end of the scale is the Ulan Bator No. 4 power station, built with Soviet assistance, which went into operation in 1985. Its capacity of 380 MW doubled the country's generating capacity. The station is fuelled by coal from Baganuur. Provincial (*aimag*) centres may have thermal power stations or diesel generators, and in rural centres small diesel generators are common. Domestic heating in apartment blocks in Ulan Bator is by central town-heating from the power station. Elsewhere wood, roots, bushes and dried animal dung are used for domestic firing. In 1998 plans were revealed for a US $120m. petroleum refinery project in the former coal-mining town of Nalaikh. Part of the projected annual output of 1.4m. tons of petroleum products was to be fuel oil for a new 70-MW power station nearby.

Transport shows a similar range of sophistication. Ulan Bator is linked with Beijing and Höhhot (China), Ulan-Ude and Irkutsk (Russian Federation), as well as provincial centres by An-24 turbo-prop aircraft. The airline's one Airbus flies to Moscow and Berlin and also to Seoul, two Boeing 727s also fly the shorter international routes, and a Boeing 737-800 was delivered in mid-2002. Mongolian railways connect the Trans-Siberian main line with the Chinese railway system, providing a direct route from Moscow to Beijing and an eastern link with the town of Choibalsan. Because the Mongolian and Chinese gauges are different, goods are transhipped at the border stations Zamyn-Üüd or Erenhot. In order to encourage foreign investment, Mongolia is planning long-term road improvements. To mark the millennium the Government launched the building of a road running from west to east across the country, linking Siberian Russia with northern China, and improving communications with Ulan Bator from outlying parts of Mongolia. The route was from Kosh-Agach in the Altai Republic to Ölgii, the Zavkhan valley and through Arkhangay to Ulan Bator, then via Öndörkhaan in Khentii to Sümber (Khalkhyn Gol) and into Inner Mongolia. The project was expected to take about 10 years to complete, but because of the cost the road was not planned to be hardtopped for the whole length. Meanwhile, long-distance transport is mainly cross-country by lorry or Soviet-built UAZ (jeep-type vehicle). Horse, ox and camel carts are still widely used, even in Ulan Bator, and camels are employed as beasts of burden. Water transport is not of great significance.

In the mid-1990s the decline in rail and road freight traffic continued. Only 150,000 of the scheduled 670,000 metric tons of transit freight were carried from Russia to China in 1994 and 3,000 of the scheduled 300,000 tons from China to Russia. The amount of freight transported by rail rose steadily in the late 1990s, however, reaching almost 8.2m. tons in 1999. Rail passenger traffic also increased steadily. In September 1995 there were new concerns over the state of Mongolia's ageing aviation equipment after a MIAT Antonov An-24 twin turboprop crashed into a mountain 17 km from Mörön airport in Khövsgöl province, killing 41 people. Although pilot error was blamed, the civil aviation authority decided to acquire ground position indicators for the fleet. The crash of a MIAT Yu-12 in June 1997, which killed eight passengers, appeared to have been caused by freak weather conditions. In May 1998 a Chinese-built Yu-12 belonging to MIAT crashed in the mountains of southern Khövsgöl province, while on an internal flight from Erdenet to Tosontsengel, killing the 28 crew and passengers. Although, the crash was attributed to 'pilot error', MIAT's remaining Yu-12 aircraft were to be returned to China.

REFORM AND RECENT DEVELOPMENTS

The regular pattern of Five-Year Plans and CMEA-orientated trade was disrupted in 1990–91 by the collapse of command economies in the USSR and Eastern Europe, by the transition to payments in convertible currencies, and by the first steps towards privatization and a market economy in Mongolia itself. There was a rapid decline in Mongolia's foreign trade, which, with traditional partners, was largely reduced, by the shortage of convertible currencies, to barter transactions. Petroleum, medicines, and some imported foodstuffs and consumer goods were in particularly short supply, owing to Mongolia's inability to pay for all its requirements at prevailing world prices. Industrial production also declined sharply. The rationing of basic foodstuffs, such as flour, pasta, sugar, tea, vodka and meat, was introduced for the urban population. In January 1991 the Government doubled wages and private savings in order to compensate for the expected doubling of retail prices.

The Government initiated a programme for the privatization of state property in two stages. The first, involving small-scale enterprises, began in May 1991 with the auctioning of several shops and restaurants in Ulan Bator to private individuals. The privatization of large state industrial enterprises began haltingly in early 1992. However, the Government prohibited the privatization of railways, roads, the airline, the state oil company, gold mines, hunting and forestry enterprises, and large irrigation systems. The State also retained a 51% interest in power stations and transmission lines, mines producing coal and metalliferous ores, communications links, some flour mills, meat-packing plants and cement works, motor transport depots, the brewery, distillery, etc. Although it had been claimed that the members of the *negdel* did not wish them to be dissolved, it was announced in mid-1991 that at least some of the members would leave with their stock, and an Association of Individual Herdsmen was established. The privatization of livestock farming and of internal trade and services had been 80% and 90% completed, respectively, by mid-1993.

In June 1991 a massive devaluation of the tögrög changed the official exchange rate from US $1 = 7.10 tögrög at the end of May to US $1 = 40.00 tögrög. A devaluation of the currency on 1 January 1993 from US $1 = 40.00 tögrög to 150.00 was followed at the end of May by its flotation at US $1 = 400.00 tögrög, stabilizing at 395.00. This policy had the support of the IMF, whose confidence in the Government's economic programme ensured the continuation of international aid for Mongolia. The first signs of economic growth and a sharp fall in inflation emerged in 1994. While the World Bank welcomed these developments, it estimated that Mongolia would still need aid worth US $150m.–$200m. per year for the foreseeable future. Among the Government's immediate priorities were to minimize the social impact of the transition to a market economy, to reduce the government sector in agriculture and to improve the environment.

A UNDP report, completed in June 1994, stated that privatization in Mongolia had failed to create an environment in which the market mechanism could operate efficiently. Many supposedly privatized enterprises were still partially owned by the State. The report declared that 'the problem is not a low volume of credit but an allocation of credit that responds to political interference and personal private connections rather than to commercial criteria', and stated that the Mongolian Government should have promoted new private-sector enterprises, creating additional wealth, rather than simply redistributing assets through the voucher scheme. Substantial aid was forthcoming, the report added, but it was not to be used to sustain consumption rather than investment. The UNDP urged price stabilization, lower interest rates, bank regulation and a system of commercial law, as well as a mechanism for the enforcement of contracts.

In November 1994 an IMF report criticized state interference in the allocation of bank credits, which the Government had directed to agriculture and strategic public-sector projects without consultation with Mongolbank, the central bank. This practice had 'adverse consequences for monetary management', constraining private-sector activity. Prime Minister Jasrai's address to Mongolia's first convention of industrialists and business representatives, held in April 1995, was not successful. Delegates complained about government bureaucracy, and criticized middle- and low-ranking officials who were hindering the growth of private businesses with their excessive administrative procedures.

Following the establishment of a Securities Committee in November 1994, under the chairmanship of Jigjidsürengiin Yadamsüren, former Chairman of Ulan Bator City Council, the Mongolian Securities Exchange opened in late August 1995. The annual rate of inflation declined from 183% in 1993 to 66% in 1994. However, the tögrög declined from its 1993 flotation value of US $1=400 to US $1=534 at the official rate of exchange by July 1996. New 5,000 and 10,000 tögrög notes and coins of 20, 50, 100 and 200 tögrög, recycled from older demonetized coins, were put into circulation. GDP growth in 1995 was estimated at 7.0%; forecasts for 1996 and 1997 were 3.0% and 3.7%, respectively.

One of the first actions of the Enkhsaikhan Government, which took office in mid-1996, was to remove the ban on the export of raw cashmere. The ban had been imposed in March 1994, to protect the cashmere garment industry's 'added value'. The lifting of the ban was welcomed by the IMF, the World Bank and the Asian Development Bank (ADB), which had opposed it on the grounds that it interfered with trade. The Government subsequently abolished customs duty on almost all imports, on the grounds that the imports were needed to boost the country's export production capacity. To protect domestic garment production, a new tax was levied on raw cashmere and camel wool exports.

Prime Minister Enkhsaikhan urged public support for the Democratic Alliance's proposals to transform the state executive and to reform government agencies so as to meet the demands of the market system. The Democratic Alliance's rationalization programme began with the establishment of 'sectoral ministries' which combined (and in some cases relocated and co-sited) ministries of the previous Government. The Democratic Alliance Government's first year in office produced no real achievements in its efforts to stimulate the free-market economic revival it had hoped for. With GDP growth at 2.4% in 1996, inflation, at 44.6%, was lower than in the previous year. Consumer prices increased at an average annual rate of 20.5% in 1997.

The restructuring of the social security 'net', without extra revenue, was not well received by those most in need of financial support, i.e. pensioners, the very poor and the unemployed. The number of registered unemployed reached 64,200 at the end of June 1997, but several estimates put the true figure at around 227,000, if school-leavers, ex-servicemen and others who had never been employed were included. The number of unemployed declined to 49,800 in 1998 and to 39,800 in 1999, the latter figure representing a rate of 4.6% of the economically active population. Unemployment continued to decline, to 38,600 in 2000 (4.6%), but increased to 40,300 in 2001.

Privatization continued to make slow progress, with attention focused on the free disposal of state housing stock and the auction of small businesses, rather than the dispersal of large state-owned enterprises, such as the department store in central Ulan Bator, for which there were no bidders. By the beginning of 1996 more than 91% of trade enterprises had been privatized, as well as 88% of agricultural assets, but over 50% of industrial enterprises remained wholly under state ownership. In September 1997 a radical privatization programme was revealed by the Government, under which it was proposed to sell by auction to the highest bidder the entire state sector except some assets such as the railway.

The country's external currency reserves had increased to US $128m. by mid-1997, declining to US $107m. at the end of the year. The value of the tögrög declined by 13% in the first half of 1997, falling to around US $1 = 830 tögrög in March/April before stabilizing and standing at an average rate of US $1 = 840.83 in 1998. In 1999, however, the average rate of exchange declined to US $1 = 1,021.87 tögrög. The tögrög continued to decline during 2000 and 2001, to US $1 = 1,076.67 and US $1 = 1,097.70 respectively.

Real GDP growth in 1998 was estimated at 3.5%, compared with 4.0% in 1997. Consumer prices, meanwhile, rose by only 6.0% in 1998. Industrial production increased slightly in terms of value but declined in terms of unit output in 1998. In 1999 GDP registered growth of 3.5%, to reach 873,700m. tögrög or 359,583 tögrög (US $335) per caput. GDP growth in 2000 was 1.4%. The annual rate of inflation rose to 10.0% in 1999 and by mid-2000 had reached 17.4%, before declining to 12.6% in mid-2001 and 11.2% for the year as a whole. According to official sources, foreign-exchange reserves increased from US $116.9m.

(11.1 weeks' imports) at the end of 1999 to US $140m. (12.6 weeks' imports) at mid-2000, and US $173.3m. in May 2002.

Substantial deficits were incorporated into the budgets for 1996–2000. The 2001 draft budget, presented to the Great Khural in October 2000, envisaged revenue of 380,600m. tögrög and expenditure of 469,300m. tögrög. The budget deficit in 2002 was expected to rise to 6.9% of GDP, having fallen from 12.9% in 1999 to 6.8% in 2000 and 5.3% in 2001.

According to the World Bank, Mongolia's foreign debt at the end of December 1998 amounted to US $710.6m. The external debt rose to US $890.9m. in December 1999, decreasing to US $858.8m. at the end of 2000. In 2002 total debt reached the equivalent of 84% of GDP.

EXTERNAL AID

In the early 1990s, in response to an appeal by the Mongolian Government for foreign aid, the USA offered grain credits and, during his visit to Ulan Bator in July 1991, the US Secretary of State, James Baker, pledged further US aid to the value of US $10.6m. Japan also provided wheat, and in August, on the occasion of Prime Minister Kaifu's visit to Mongolia, the Japanese Government announced economic assistance worth US $15m. and development aid of US $7m. for improvements to communications. In September a conference of representatives of the IMF, the ADB (which two bodies Mongolia had joined in February 1991), the European Community (now European Union—EU) and Japan approved emergency aid totalling US $155m. to Mongolia. Another donors' conference, held in Tokyo in September 1993, pledged US $250m. to Mongolia for 1993–94.

The next international donors' conference, held in Tokyo in November 1994, pledged US $210m. to Mongolia in grants and credits for 1994–95. Apart from the international banks, Japan continued to be the biggest donor, with US $82.5m. in grants and US $87m. in credits pledged for 1993–95. The next donors' conference, held in Tokyo in February 1996, followed up with new pledges totalling US $212.5m. The outgoing Jasrai Government was criticized by Japan for not taking up aid quickly enough. In 1997 there was continued support for Mongolia at the Tokyo international aid donors' conference, held in October, which pledged Mongolia US $256.1m. (the ADB and Japan US $60m. each, Russia US $30m., the World Bank US $25m., the Republic of Korea US $21m., Germany US $17m. and the IMF US $15m.).

Convening in Ulan Bator for the first time, the aid donors at the seventh Mongolia Assistance Group Meeting, held in June 1999, pledged a record US $320m. in aid for banking-sector reform, poverty relief and privatization. The Assistance Group urged the Mongolian Government to strengthen the financial sector by increasing transparency and improving conditions for private enterprise, including the privatization of state-owned banks and a legal framework for other financial institutions. Future Assistance Group meetings were to take the form of Consultative Group meetings chaired by the World Bank, the venue rotating between Ulan Bator, Tokyo and Paris.

In February 2000, following several months of drought and continuing severe cold, an appeal by the Mongolian Government for international aid was supported by the UN. The climatic conditions of 1999–2000 were believed to have killed millions of livestock (see Agriculture) and directly or indirectly affected the livelihood of at least 500,000 people. Most of the US $5m. received in aid was donated by the Japanese, German, US and British Governments, and the World Bank pledged the balance of US $1.3m. from its Poverty Alleviation Programme to Mongolia's relief measures. By mid-2000 a total of US $7.4m. had been pledged in relief assistance. Mongolia's membership of the European Bank for Reconstruction and Development (EBRD) was approved in May 2000.

The eighth meeting of the Mongolia Consultative Group took place in Paris at the end of May 2001, attended by representatives of 11 countries, the EU, UN, ADB, IMF and World Bank, and three Mongolian ministers. Prime Minister Enkhbayar announced the outcome of the Paris meeting at a press conference in Ulan Bator: Mongolia would receive US $330m. in loans and donations for the coming year, compared with the 1999 meeting's provision of US $320m. over 18 months.

On returning to Ulan Bator the Minister of Finance and Economics, Chültemiin Ulaan, explained that US $1,900m. of the US $2,600m. of Mongolia's development aid 1991–2000 had been implemented. Interest was payable on 47.6% of this sum; 37% of the money had been allocated to infrastructure, 16.5% to social services, 10.8% to industry and agriculture, and 23% to financial and economic management sectors; 40% of the money came from the ADB, 26% from Japan, 18% from the World Bank, and 6% from Germany.

About 1,700 companies from 65 countries had invested around US $420m. in Mongolia as of June 2001. The leading investors were China, the Republic of Korea, Japan, the USA and Russia. The main sectors of investment were mining, light industry and agricultural processing. Foreign investment had created 50,000 jobs and accounted for 14.2% of Mongolia's tax revenue.

The ninth meeting of the Mongolia Consultative Group took place in Ulan Bator at the beginning of July 2002, attended by representatives of 11 countries, the EU, EBRD, ADB, IMF, World Bank and various UN bodies. The meeting pledged US $333m. in aid for the next year, but the IMF and other donors suspended some measures and complained about Mongolia's budget deficits, bureaucracy and the slow pace of reform. The Mongolian Deputy Minister of Finance and Economics, Luvsandagvyn Enkhtaivan, told the press that some US $2,300m. of the US $2,800m. in aid pledged by the previous eight meetings had been implemented, 83% of loans totalling US $1,300m., and US $1,100m. of grants totalling US $1,400m. Most of the loans were for 30–40 years at an interest rate of 0.5–0.75%.

Russian Premier Mikhail Kasyanov's brief visit to Ulan Bator in March 2002 and the signing of routine co-operation agreements passed in the usual cordial atmosphere. However, the Russian media reported that he and Mongolian Prime Minister Enkhbayar had discussed Mongolia's repayment to Moscow of its Soviet-era aid debt 'amounting to US $11,600m.'. Enkhbayar said later that only the terms of repayment had been discussed, not the exact amount, but the Mongolian media and opposition fiercely disputed the equivalence of the defunct transferable Soviet rouble to the US dollar. The issue remained unresolved, although it had been raised at many inter-governmental meetings over the past decade.

Statistical Survey

Unless otherwise indicated, revised by Alan J. K. Sanders.

Area and Population

AREA, POPULATION AND DENSITY

Area (sq km)	1,564,116*
Population (census results)	
5 January 1989	2,043,400
5 January 2000	
Males	1,177,981
Females	1,195,512
Total	2,373,493
Population (official estimates at mid-year)	
2000	2,390,000
2001	2,425,000
Density (per sq km) at mid-2001	1.5

* 603,909 sq miles.

ADMINISTRATIVE DIVISIONS (January 2000 census)

Province (Aimag)	Area ('000 sq km)	Estimated population ('000)	Provincial Centre
Arkhangai	55.3	97.1	Tsetserleg
Bayankhongor	116.0	84.8	Bayankhongor
Bayan-Ölgii	45.7	91.1	Ölgii
Bulgan	48.7	61.8	Bulgan
Darkhan-Uul	3.3	83.3	Darkhan
Dornod (Eastern)	123.6	75.4	Choibalsan
Dornogobi (East Gobi)	109.5	50.6	Sainshand
Dundgobi (Central Gobi)	74.7	51.5	Mandalgobi
Gobi-Altai	141.4	63.7	Altai
Gobi-Sümber	5.5	12.2	Choir
Khentii	80.3	70.9	Öndörkhaan
Khovd	76.1	86.8	Khovd
Khövsgöl	100.6	119.1	Mörön
Orkhon	0.8	71.5	Erdenet
Ömnögobi (South Gobi)	165.4	46.9	Dalanzadgad
Övörkhangai	62.9	111.4	Arvaikheer
Selenge	41.2	100.0	Sükhbaatar
Sükhbaatar	82.3	56.2	Baruun Urt
Töv (Central)	74.0	99.3	Zuun mod
Ulaanbaatar (Ulan Bator)*	4.7	760.1	(capital city)
Uvs	69.6	90.0	Ulaangom
Zavkhan	82.5	90.0	Uliastai
Total	1,564.1	2,373.5	

* Ulaanbaatar, including Nalaikh, and Bagakhangai and Baganuur districts beyond the urban boundary, has special status as the capital city.

ETHNIC GROUPS (January 2000 census)

	Number	%
Khalh (Khalkha)	1,934,700	81.5
Kazakh (Khasag)	103,000	4.3
Dörvöd (Durbet)	66,700	2.8
Bayad (Bayat)	50,800	2.1
Buryat (Buriat)	40,600	1.7
Dariganga	31,900	1.3
Zakhchin	29,800	1.3
Uriankhai	25,200	1.1
Other ethnic groups	82,600	3.5
Foreign citizens	8,100	0.3
Total	2,373,500	100.0

PRINCIPAL TOWNS (estimated population, December 1999)

Ulan Bator (capital)	813,500*	Erdenet	65,700
Darkhan	72,600	Choibalsan	40,900†

* March 2002.

† January 2000 census.

BIRTHS, MARRIAGES AND DEATHS

	Registered live births		Registered marriages		Registered deaths	
	Number	Rate (per 1,000)	Number	Rate (per 1,000)	Number	Rate (per 1,000)
1995	54,293	24.3	15,106	6.8	16,794	7.5
1996	51,806	22.9	14,188	6.3	17,550	7.7
1997	49,488	21.5	14,421	6.3	16,980	7.4
1998	49,256	21.2	13,908	6.0	15,799	6.8
1999	49,461	21.0	13,722	5.8	16,105	6.8
2000	48,721	20.4	12,601	5.3	15,472	6.5
2001	49,685	20.5	12,393	5.1	15,999	6.6

Source: mainly *Mongolian Statistical Yearbook*.

Expectation of life (WHO estimates, years at birth, 2000): Males 61.2; Females 66.9 (Source: WHO, *World Health Report*).

EMPLOYMENT

('000 employees at 31 December)

	1998	1999	2000
Agriculture and forestry	394.1	402.6	393.5
Industry*	97.9	98.8	91.0
Transport and communications	33.4	34.9	34.1
Construction	27.5	27.6	23.4
Trade	n.a.	83.1	83.9
Public administration	n.a.	31.5	34.7
Education Science, research and development	42.5	43.2	54.4
Health	35.6	34.8	33.5
Total (incl. others)	809.5	813.6	809.0

* Comprising manufacturing (except printing and publishing), mining and quarrying, electricity, water, logging and fishing.

Unemployed ('000 registered at 31 December): 49.8 in 1998; 39.8 in 1999; 38.6 in 2000.

Source: *Mongolian Statistical Yearbook*.

2001 ('000 persons at 31 December): Registered unemployed 40.3.

Health and Welfare

KEY INDICATORS

Fertility (births per woman, 2000)	2.5
Under-5 mortality rate (per 1,000 live births, 2000)	78
HIV/AIDS (% of persons aged 15–49, 2001)	<0.10
Physicians (per 1,000 head, 2001)	2.7
Hospital beds (per 1,000 head, 2001)	7.4
Health expenditure (1998): US $ per head (PPP)	88
% of GDP	6.2
public (% of total)	65.4
Access to water (% of persons, 2000)	60
Access to sanitation (% of persons, 2000)	30
Human Development Index (2000): ranking	113
value	0.655

For sources and definitions, see explanatory note on p. vi.

Agriculture

PRINCIPAL CROPS (metric tons)

	1999	2000	2001
Cereals*	169,500	142,100	150,900
Potatoes	63,800	58,900	58,000
Other vegetables	39,000	44,000	44,500
Hay	715,200	689,400	802,600

* Mostly wheat, but also small quantities of barley and oats.

LIVESTOCK (at 31 December)

	1999	2000	2001
Sheep	15,191,300	13,876,400	11,938,100
Goats	11,033,900	10,077,500	9,683,700
Horses	3,163,500	2,660,700	2,190,800
Cattle	3,824,700	3,097,600	2,069,600
Camels	355,600	322,900	285,500
Pigs	21,900	14,684	n.a.
Poultry	78,100	89,122	n.a.

LIVESTOCK PRODUCTS ('000 metric tons, unless otherwise indicated)

	1998	1999	2000
Meat	268.3	289.0	310.6
Beef and veal	99.3	104.6	113.4
Mutton, lamb and goat meat	120.2	128.9	120.0
Sheep's wool: greasy	20.1	20.9	21.7
Raw cashmere	n.a.	3.3	3.3
Milk	430.8	467.0	375.6
Eggs (million)	8.5	9.6	6.7

Source: Mongolian Statistical Directorate.

Forestry

ROUNDWOOD REMOVALS
('000 cubic metres, excl. bark)

	1998	1999	2000
Total	631	631	631

Source: FAO.

SAWNWOOD PRODUCTION
('000 cubic metres, incl. railway sleepers)

	1999	2000	2001
Total	31.7	30.5	39.7

Source: National Statistical Office, *Monthly Bulletin of Statistics*.

Fishing

(metric tons, live weight)

	1997	1998	1999
Total catch (freshwater fishes)	180	311	524

Source: FAO, *Yearbook of Fishery Statistics*.

Mining

(metric tons, unless otherwise indicated)

	1999	2000	2001
Coal	4,952,800	5,019,300	5,134,200
Fluorspar (Fluorite)	597,100	733,500	584,700
Fluorspar concentrate	184,200	210,000	209,000
Copper concentrate*	361,900	357,800	381,400
Molybdenum concentrate*	4,157	2,843	3,028
Gold (kilograms)	10,246	11,808	13,674
Crude petroleum (barrels)	71,914	65,522	73,700

* Figures refer to the gross weight of concentrates. Copper concentrate has an estimated copper content of 25%, while the metal content of molybdenum concentrate is 47%.

Source: National Statistical Office, *Monthly Bulletin of Statistics*.

Industry

SELECTED PRODUCTS

	1999	2000	2001
Flour ('000 metric tons)	67.3	40.2	37.7
Bread ('000 metric tons)	14.7	20.2	23.3
Confectionery ('000 metric tons)	8.0	7.6	7.2
Vodka ('000 litres)	5,510.9	6,595.7	8,626.5
Beer ('000 litres)	1,852.7	3,247.2	4,267.8
Soft drinks ('000 litres)	6,860.8	8,644.7	11,082.7
Cashmere (combed) (metric tons)	612.5	450.9	608.4
Woollen cloth ('000 metres)	18.5	21.0	n.a.
Felt ('000 metres)	102.0	113.9	110.5
Camelhair blankets ('000)	21.2	28.5	43.1
Spun thread (metric tons)	14.3	40.8	45.6
Knitwear ('000 garments)	696.8	1,233.5	2,315.7
Carpets ('000 sq metres)	628.6	704.8	614.8
Leather footwear ('000)	6.6	5.6	16.7
Felt footwear ('000 pairs)	11.9	34.0	33.4
Surgical syringes (million)	15.4	16.3	17.7
Bricks (million)	17.0	17.3	21.0
Lime ('000 metric tons)	49.6	37.0	30.1
Cement ('000 metric tons)	103.5	91.7	67.7
Ferroconcrete ('000 cu metres)	14.7	14.8	17.0
Steel blanks ('000 metric tons)	21.8	20.4	17.2
Copper (metric tons)	1,545.2	641.1	1,475.9
Electricity (million kWh)	2,842	2,239.1	2,367.0

Sources: *Mongolian Statistical Yearbook* 2000, and *Monthly Bulletin of Statistics*.

Finance

CURRENCY AND EXCHANGE RATES

Monetary Units
100 möngö = 1 tögrög (tughrik).

Sterling, Dollar and Euro Equivalents (31 May 2002)
£1 sterling = 1,617.8 tögrög;
US $1 = 1,103.0 tögrög;
€1 = 1,035.4 tögrög;
10,000 tögrög = £6.181 = $9.066 = €9.658.

Average Exchange Rate (tögrög per US $)
1999 1,021.87
2000 1,076.67
2001 1,097.70

BUDGET (million tögrög)

Revenue	1999	2000
Tax revenue	181,232.6	274,109.2
Income tax	39,044.3	74,088.8
Customs duty	26,731.3	35,741.3
Taxes on goods and services	93,923.5	117,562.3
Value-added tax	60,360.1	74,974.5
Social insurance	29,784.9	38,691.7
Other current revenue	66,626.7	65,555.7
Foreign aid (grants)	6,890.6	3,067.6
Capital revenue (privatization)	11,744.8	7,469.8
Total	266,494.6	350,202.2

Expenditure	1999	2000
General public services	32,986.0	39,350.5
Education	64,811.4	78,814.7
Health	35,658.3	43,579.5
Social security and welfare	59,929.4	77,168.1
Housing and community services	4,728.7	6,997.4
Recreation, culture, art and sport	11,476.6	13,595.1
Fuel and energy	4,830.4	6,512.1
Agriculture and forestry	5,039.3	7,491.0
Industry, construction and mining	1,250.4	1,411.3
Transport and communications	6,836.2	8,649.5
Other economic affairs and services	4,453.0	4,730.7
Total (incl. others)	364,693.9	412,926.6

Source: Mongolian Statistical Directorate.

2001 (million tögrög): Total revenue 424,544.3 (Tax revenue 319,419.2, Other current revenue 95,984.6, Grants 9,140.5); Total expenditure 470,064.7 (Source: Mongolbank, *Monthly Bulletin*).

2002 (forecasts, million tögrög): Total revenue 356,035.9; Total expenditure 435,727.7 (Source: *Töriin Medeelel*).

INTERNATIONAL RESERVES (US $ million at 31 December)

	1999	2000	2001
Gold*	0.40	23.31	50.91
IMF special drawing rights	0.16	0.01	0.02
Reserve position in IMF	0.03	0.05	0.08
Foreign exchange	136.30	178.70	205.60
Total	136.89	202.08	256.61

* Valued at 4,300 tögrög per gram.

Source: IMF, *International Financial Statistics*.

MONEY SUPPLY (million tögrög at 31 December)

	1999	2000	2001
Currency outside banks	87,281	100,910	109,131
Demand deposits at deposit money banks	27,544	29,842	46,995
Total money	114,826	130,751	156,126

Source: IMF, *International Financial Statistics*.

COST OF LIVING (Consumer Price Index for Ulan Bator at December; base: December 1995 = 100)

	1996	1997	1998
Food and beverages	133.7	148.8	150.1
Clothing and footwear	146.0	193.4	213.8
Rent and utilities	172.7	260.1	284.2
All items (incl. others)	144.6	174.2	184.7

Source: National Statistical Office.

All items: 203.1 in 1999; 219.6 in 2000.

December 2001 (base: December 2000 = 100): All items 108.0.

Source: Mongolbank, *Monthly Bulletin*.

NATIONAL ACCOUNTS (million tögrög at current prices)

Expenditure on the Gross Domestic Product

	1996	1997	1998
Government final consumption expenditure	96,406.8	132,867.3	153,515.0
Private final consumption expenditure	373,466.0	459,922.8	486,201.8
Increase in stocks	12,281.0	17,055.3	18,078.6
Gross fixed capital formation	135,250.9	180,300.0	208,017.5
Total domestic expenditure	617,404.7	790,145.4	865,812.9
Exports of goods and services *Less* Imports of goods and services	−11,616.6	−19,764.4	−50,568.2
Sub-total	605,788.1	770,381.0	815,244.7
Statistical discrepancy*	−19,259.2	−11,454.3	60,614.3
GDP in purchasers' values	586,528.9	758,926.7	875,859.0
GDP at constant 1993 prices	185,047.9	192,508.3	199,205.2

* Referring to the difference between the sum of the expenditure components and official estimates of GDP, compiled from the production approach.

Source: Asian Development Bank, *Key Indicators of Developing Asian and Pacific Countries*.

Gross Domestic Product by Economic Activity

	1998	1999	2000
Agriculture	306,240.5	342,127.6	348,821.0
Mining	68,346.1	79,780.0	88,582.5
Manufacturing	47,493.8	54,970.8	58,342.0
Electricity, heating and water supply	33,221.5	33,711.1	34,621.3
Construction	20,074.1	22,984.1	24,317.2
Trade	172,241.0	191,672.1	244,723.9
Transport and communications	71,977.0	84,690.5	99,402.0
Finance	−605.4	4,121.7	12,026.3
Public administration	30,578.5	33,621.7	42,289.7
Other services	67,826.3	77,666.1	91,454.7
GDP in purchasers' values	817,393.4	925,345.8	1,044,580.6

Source: *Mongolian Statistical Yearbook* 2000.

BALANCE OF PAYMENTS (US $ million)

	1997	1998	1999
Exports of goods f.o.b.	568.5	462.4	454.3
Imports of goods f.o.b.	−453.1	−524.2	−510.7
Trade balance	115.4	−61.8	−56.4
Exports of services	52.7	77.8	75.8
Imports of services	−105.1	−146.8	−145.7
Balance on goods and services	63.0	−130.8	−126.3
Other income received	6.1	10.1	6.7
Other income paid	−18.1	−9.7	−6.6
Balance on goods, services and income	51.0	−130.4	−126.2
Current transfers received	4.2	5.5	17.6
Current transfers paid	—	−3.6	−3.6
Current balance	55.2	−128.5	−112.2
Direct investment from abroad	25.0	18.9	30.4
Other investment assets	−108.1	−54.8	−51.8
Other investment liabilities	110.1	162.1	91.0
Net errors and omissions	−75.6	−50.2	23.6
Overall balance	6.6	−52.5	−19.0

Source: IMF, *International Financial Statistics*.

External Trade

PRINICIPAL COMMODITIES (US $ million)

Imports c.i.f.	2000	2001
Vegetable products	46.4	29.6
Prepared foodstuffs; beverages, spirits and vinegar; tobacco and manufactured substitutes	47.2	43.4
Mineral products	120.3	131.7
Products of chemical or allied industries	28.1	30.4
Textiles and textile articles	79.9	57.0
Base metals and articles thereof	22.7	27.3
Machinery and mechanical appliances; electrical equipment; sound and television apparatus	133.3	102.1
Vehicles, aircraft, vessels and associated transport equipment	67.0	65.3
Optical, photographic, measuring, precision and medical apparatus; clocks and watches; musical instruments	21.1	16.0
Total (incl. others)	614.5	554.8

Exports f.o.b.	1999	2000	2001
Copper concentrate	111.7	160.3	145.0
Fluorite concentrate	n.a.	19.3	17.1
Cashmere (dehaired)	43.0	54.5	39.5
Cashmere (greasy/raw)	n.a.	21.8	0.7
Textiles	127.4	192.3	138.4
Knitwear	n.a.	25.9	16.9
Hides and skins	28.2	33.8	11.6
Beef (frozen)	n.a.	14.3	10.4
Total (incl. others)	335.6	432.3	385.2

Exports of Gold (US $ million): 117.2 in 1998.

Sources: IMF, *Mongolia: Statistical Annex* (March 2000); National Statistical Office, *Monthly Bulletin of Statistics*.

PRINCIPAL TRADING PARTNERS (US $ million)

Imports c.i.f.	1999	2000	2001
Belarus	2.4	4.2	6.1
Belgium	1.9	2.4	6.0
China, People's Republic	77.6	125.8	121.4
Czech Republic	4.9	3.5	5.6
Denmark	3.0	4.4	7.5
France	8.5	8.3	4.8
Germany	23.6	29.7	28.4
Japan	115.0	73.3	52.8
Kazakhstan	0.6	6.8	3.3
Korea, Republic	36.2	55.6	53.6
Russia	149.8	206.2	201.9
Singapore	9.1	10.6	8.5
USA	31.5	28.4	13.9
Total (incl. others)	512.8	614.5	554.8

Exports f.o.b.	1999	2000	2001
China, People's Republic	208.2	274.3	212.4
Italy	14.6	14.5	11.5
Japan	10.9	8.1	12.6
Russia	48.2	45.1	39.7
United Kingdom	13.6	11.2	6.7
USA	46.3	92.9	84.7
Total (incl. others)	358.3	466.1	385.2

Source: National Statistical Office, *Monthly Bulletin of Statistics*.

Transport

FREIGHT CARRIED ('000 metric tons)

	1999	2000	2001
Rail	8,199.0	9,158.2	10,147.4
Road	1,330.4	1,480.4	1,658.2
Air	2.8	2.9	2.9
Water	1.8	1.9	2.0
Total	9,534.0	10,643.4	11,810.5

Source: Mongolian Statistical Directorate.

PASSENGERS CARRIED (million)

	1999	2000	2001
Rail	4.2	4.3	4.5
Road	83.3	88.4	94.1
Air*	0.2	0.2	0.2
Total	87.7	92.9	98.8

* MIAT only.

Source: Mongolian Statistical Directorate.

RAILWAYS (traffic)

	1999	2000	2001
Passengers carried ('000)	4,119.1	4,282.5	4,556.1
Freight carried ('000 metric tons)	8,199.3	9,158.5	10,147.7
Freight ton-km (million)	3,491.7	4,282.5	5,427.3

Source: Mongolian Statistical Directorate.

ROAD TRAFFIC (motor vehicles in use)

	1998	1999	2000
Passenger cars	37,795	39,921	44,100
Buses and coaches	4,579	6,012	8,500
Lorries, special vehicles and tankers	29,116	28,907	29,100

Source: mainly Mongolian Statistical Directorate.

CIVIL AVIATION (traffic on scheduled services)

	1999	2000	2001
Passengers carried ('000)	223.4	252.4	254.5
Freight carried (tons)	2,882.5	2,877.0	2,970.0

Source: Mongolian Statistical Directorate.

Tourism

FOREIGN ARRIVALS BY NATIONALITY

Country	1998	1999*	2000
China, People's Republic	92,789	58,346	57,546
France	1,819	1,983	1,841
Germany	3,388	3,506	4,206
Japan	11,846	11,775	11,392
Korea, Republic	3,073	5,171	8,039
Russia	63,532	55,782	49,456
United Kingdom	2,251	2,221	2,800
USA	4,622	5,381	6,451
Total (incl. others)	197,424	158,734	158,205

* Figures are provisional. The revised total is 159,745.

Source: *Mongolian Statistical Yearbook*.

2001: Total arrivals 192,051 (Source: National Statistical Office, *Monthly Bulletin of Statistics*).

Tourism receipts (US $ million): 33 in 1998; 28 in 1999 (Source: World Bank).

Communications Media

	1999	2000	2001
Television receivers ('000 in use)	168.8	169.1	n.a.
Telephones ('000 main lines in use)	104.1	112.2	123.0
Mobile cellular telephones ('000 subscribers)	48.2	75.1	195.0
Personal computers ('000 in use)	24	n.a.	35
Internet users ('000)	12.0	30.0	40.0
Newspapers printed (million copies)	22.2	18.0	19.2

Radio receivers ('000 in use): 360 in 1997.
Facsimile machines (number in use): 7,963 in 1999.
Book production (1994): 128 titles; 640,000 copies.
Non-daily newspapers (titles): 80 in 1998.
Other periodicals (titles): 24 in 1998.

Sources: UNESCO, *Statistical Yearbook*; UN, *Statistical Yearbook*; International Telecommunication Union; Mongolian Statistical Directorate.

Education

(2000/01)

	Institutions	Teachers	Students
General education schools:			
Primary (grades 1–3)	133	19,200	494,500
Incomplete secondary (grades 4–8)	219		
Complete secondary (grades 9–10)	351		
Vocational schools	36	865	97,100
Higher education:			
Universities and colleges			
State-owned	38	3,455	56,906
Private	134	1,465	28,064

* Excluding those studying abroad (152 in 1999/2000).

Pre-school institutions (2000): 27 crèches (1,900 pupils) and 653 kindergartens (79,300 pupils).

Source: Mongolian Statistical Directorate.

2002: Schools 700; General education students 515,200; Vocational school students 105,700 (Source: National Statistical Office, *Monthly Bulletin of Statistics*).

Adult literacy rate (UNESCO estimates): 98.9% (males 99.1%; females 98.8%) in 2000 (Source: UN Development Programme, *Human Development Report*).

Directory

The Constitution

The Constitution was adopted on 13 January 1992 and came into force on 12 February of that year. It proclaims Mongolia (*Mongol Uls*), with its capital at Ulan Bator (Ulaanbaatar), to be an independent sovereign republic which ensures for its people democracy, justice, freedom, equality and national unity. It recognizes all forms of ownership of property, including land, and affirms that a 'multi-structured economy' will take account of 'universal trends of world economic development and national conditions'.

The 'citizen's right to life' is qualified by the death penalty for serious crimes, and the law provides for the imposition of forced labour. Freedom of residence and travel within the country and abroad may be limited for security reasons. The citizens' duties are to respect the Constitution and the rights and interests of others, pay taxes, and serve in the armed forces, as well as the 'sacred duty' to work, safeguard one's health, bring up one's children and protect the environment.

Supreme legislative power is vested in the Mongolian Great Khural (Assembly), a single chamber with 76 members elected by universal adult suffrage for a four-year term, with a Chairman and Vice-Chairman elected from amongst the members. The Great Khural recognizes the President on his election and appoints the Prime Minister and members of the Cabinet. A presidential veto of a decision of the Great Khural can be overruled by a two-thirds majority of the Khural. Decisions are taken by a simple majority.

The President is Head of State and Commander-in-Chief of the Armed Forces. He must be an indigenous citizen at least 45 years old who has resided continuously in Mongolia for the five years before election. Presidential candidates are nominated by parties with seats in the Great Khural; the winning candidate in general presidential elections is President for a four-year term.

The Cabinet is the highest executive body and drafts economic, social and financial policy, takes environmental protection measures, strengthens defence and security, protects human rights and implements foreign policy for a four-year term.

The Supreme Court, headed by the Chief Justice, is the highest judicial organ. Judicial independence is protected by the General Council of Courts. The Procurator General, nominated by the President, serves a six-year term.

Local administration in the 21 *aimag* (provinces) and Ulan Bator is effected on the basis of 'self-government and central guidance', comprising local khurals of representatives elected by citizens and governors (*zasag darga*), nominated by the Prime Minister to serve four-year terms.

The Constitutional Court, which guarantees 'strict observance' of the Constitution, consists of nine members nominated for a six-year term, three each by the Great Khural, the President and the Supreme Court.

The first amendments to the Constitution, adopted by the Mongolian Great Khural in December 2000, despite opposition over procedure from the Constitutional Court, were finally approved by President Bagabandi in May 2001. The main effects of the amendments were to clarify the method of appointment of Prime Ministers, enable decision-making by a simple majority vote, and shorten the minimum length of sessions of the Khural from 75 days to 50.

The Government

PRESIDENCY

President and Commander-in-Chief of the Armed Forces: NATSAGIIN BAGABANDI (elected President of Mongolia 18 May 1997; re-elected 20 May 2001).

Head of Presidential Secretariat: BADAMDORJIIN BATKHISHIG.

Director of the Presidential Information Service: DALANTAIN KHALIUN.

NATIONAL SECURITY COUNCIL

The President heads the National Security Council; the Prime Minister and the Chairman of the Mongolian Great Khural are its members (the Secretary is the President's national security adviser).

Chairman: NATSAGIIN BAGABANDI.

Members: NAMBARYN ENKHBAYAR, SANJBEGZIIN TÖMÖR-OCHIR.

Secretary: RAVDANGIIN BOLD.

CABINET
(September 2002)

Prime Minister: NAMBARYN ENKHBAYAR.

General Ministries

Minister of Foreign Affairs: LUVSANGIIN ERDENECHULUUN.

Minister of Finance and Economics: CHÜLTEMIIN ULAAN.

Minister of Justice and Home Affairs: TSENDIIN NYAMDORJ.

Sectoral Ministries

Minister of Nature and Environment: ULAMBAYARYN BARSBOLD.

Minister of Defence: JÜGDERDEMIDIIN GÜRRAGCHAA.

Minister of Education, Culture and Science: AYUURZANYN TSANJID.

Minister of Infrastructure: BYAMBYN JIGJID.

Minister of Social Protection and Labour: SHIILEGIIN BATBAYAR.

Minister of Industry and Trade: CHIMIDZORIGIIN GANZORIG.

Minister of Food and Agriculture: DARJAAGIIN NASANJARGAL.

Minister of Health: PAGVAJAVYN NYAMDAVAA.

Head of Government Affairs Directorate: ÖLZIISAIKHANY ENKHTÜVSHIN.

GOVERNMENT DEPARTMENTS

(September 2002)

Basic Structure Directorates

Head of the Chief Direcorate of Intelligence: MANDAAKHÜÜGIN BATSAIKHAN

Head of the Chief Directorate of Police: DANZANGIIN SANDAG-OCHIR.

Head of the Radio and Television Affairs Directorate: BAASANJAVYN GANBOLD.

Head of the Statistical Directorate: CHÜLTEMJAMTSYN DAVAASÜREN.

Head of the Montsame News Agency: TUGALKHÜÜGIIN BAASANSÜREN.

Infrastructure Directorates

Head of the Chief Directorate of Customs: KHORLOOGIIN BAATAR.

Head of the Chief Directorate of Taxation: LUVSANDORJIIN ZORIG.

Head of the Border Troops Directorate: Maj.-Gen. PALAMYN SÜNDEV.

Head of the Civil Defence Directorate: ODKHÜÜGIIN ÜRJIN.

MINISTRIES AND GOVERNMENT DEPARTMENTS

All Ministries and Government Departments are in Ulan Bator. Some were in the process of restructuring in 2001–02.

Ministry of Agriculture and Industry: Government Bldg 2, Ulan Bator 210646; tel. 325250; fax 323442; e-mail mag@magicnet.mn; internet www.pmis.gov.mn/agriculture.

Ministry of Defence: Government Bldg 7, Ulan Bator; tel. 451248; internet www.pmis.gov.mn/mdef/defense.html.

Ministry of Education, Culture and Science: Government Bldg 3, Ulan Bator; tel. 322011; internet med.pmis.gov.mn.

Ministry of Finance and Economics: Government Bldg 5, Ulan Bator; tel. 329947; internet www.pmis.gov.mn/mof.

Ministry of Foreign Affairs: Enkh Taivny Gudamj Bldg 7a, Ulan Bator; tel. 311311; fax 322127; e-mail mongmer@magicnet.mn; internet www.extmin.mn.

Ministry of Health and Social Welfare: Government Bldg 8, Olimpiin Gudamj 2, Ulan Bator; tel. and fax 321485; e-mail mhsw@magicnet.mn; internet www.pmis.gov.mn/health.

Ministry of Infrastructure: Government Bldg 2, Ulan Bator; tel. 329196; internet mid.pmis.gov.mn.

Ministry of Justice and Home Affairs: Government Bldg 5, Khudaldaany Gudamj 6/1, Ulan Bator 210646; tel. and fax 325225; e-mail forel@moj.pmis.gov.mn; internet www.pmis.gov.mn/mjus.

Ministry of Nature and the Environment: Khudaldaany 5, Ulan Bator 11; tel. 326649; fax 329968; internet www.env.pmis.gov.mn.

President and Legislature

PRESIDENT

Office of the President: Ulan Bator; internet www.mongol.net/president.

Election, 20 May 2001

Candidate	Votes	%
Natsagiin Bagabandi (MPRP)	574,553	57.95
Radnaasümbereliin Gonchigdorj (Democratic Party)	362,684	36.58
Luvsandambyn Dashnyam (Civil Courage Party)	35,139	3.54

MONGOLIAN GREAT KHURAL

Under the fourth Constitution, which came into force in February 1992, the single-chamber Mongolian Great Khural is the State's supreme legislative body. With 76 members elected for a four-year term, the Great Khural must meet for at least 50 working days in every six months. Its Chairman may act as President of Mongolia when the President is indisposed.

Chairman: SANJBEGZIIN TÖMÖR-OCHIR.

Vice-Chairman: JAMSRANGIIN BYAMBADORJ.

General Secretary: DAADANKHÜÜGIIN BATBAATAR.

General Election, 2 July 2000

Party	Seats
Mongolian People's Revolutionary Party (MPRP)	72
Civil Courage Party*	1
Mongolian Democratic New Socialist Party (MDNSP)	1
Mongolian National Democratic Party (MNDP)†	1
Independent	1
Total	76

* In coalition with the Mongolian Green Party.

† In coalition with the Mongolian Believers' Democratic Party.

Political Organizations

Civil Courage Republican Party: Rm 3, Mongolian University of Knowledge, Huvisgalchdyn Gudamj, Chingeltei District, Ulan Bator; (CPO 13, Box 37); tel. and fax 313297; e-mail oyun@mail.parl.gov.mn; f. 2002 by merger of the Civil Courage Party and Mongolian Republican Party; c. 140,000 mems. (May 2002); Chair. SANJAASÜRENGIIN OYUUN; First Deputy Chair. BAZARSADYN JARGALSAIKHAN.

Democratic Party: f. 2000 by amalgamation of the Mongolian National Democratic Party, Mongolian Social-Democratic Party, Mongolian Democratic Party, Mongolian Democratic Renewal Party and the Mongolian Believers' Democratic Party; c. 170,000 mems. (May 2002); Chair. DAMBYN DORLIGJAV; Sec.-Gen. NOROVYN ALTANKHUYAG.

Mongolian Civil Democratic New Liberal Party: f. 1999; ruling body Little Khural of 90 mems with Leadership Council of nine; Chair. DORJIIN YAVUUKHULAN; Sec.-Gen. DARIIN DANZAN.

Mongolian Communist Party: f. 1999; Chair. L. SHIITER.

Mongolian Democratic New Socialist Party (MDNSP): Erel Co, Bayanzürkh District, Ulan Bator; internet www.mongol.net/mdnsp; f. 1998; amalgamated with Mongolian Workers' Party 1999; 110,000 mems (May 2002); Chair. BADARCHIIN ERDENEBAT; Sec. DASHJAAGIIN ZORIGT.

Mongolian Democratic Party: Ulan Bator; f. 1990; merged in Oct. 1992 with other parties to form the Mongolian National Democratic Party (MNDP); reconstituted in Jan. 2000, the party won no seats in the 2000 elections, and in Dec. 2000 most members merged with the MDNP and other parties to form the Democratic Party; a splinter group opposed to the merger tried unsuccessfully to challenge the legal status of the DP and then elected a new MDP leadership; Chair. DAMINDORJIIN NINJ.

Mongolian Democratic Socialist Party: State Property Bldg No. 5, Ulan Bator; 947 mems (1998); Chair. DASHDORJIIN MANDAKH.

Mongolian Green Party: POB 51, Erkh Chölöönii Gudamj 11, Ulan Bator 38; tel. 323871; fax 458859; f. 1990; political wing of the Alliance of Greens; 5,000 mems (March 1997); Chair. DAVAAGIIN BASANDORJ.

Mongolian Liberal Democratic Party: POB 470, Ulan Bator 44; tel. 151030; fax 310076; e-mail mldp@magicnet.mn; internet www.mldp.mn; f 1998 as Mongolian Socialist Democratic (Labour) Party; ruling body Political Council; 848 mems (1998); Chair. TÜVSHINBATYN TÖMÖRMÖNKH.

Mongolian New Social Democratic Party: f. 2000 by MSDP dissidents; Chair. LANTUUGIIN DAMDINSÜREN.

Mongolian Party of Tradition and Justice: f. 1999; fmrly Mongolian National Democratic Socialist Party; Sec.-Gen. GANTÖMÖRIIN GALINA.

Mongolian People's Party: Ulan Bator; tel. 311083; f. 1991; forestalled any MPRP plans to revert to its original name, MPP; 2,000 mems (June 1995); in March 2000 some mems (led by Chairman Dembereliin Ölziibaatar) claimed to have merged the MPP with the MPRP; others reaffirmed the MPP's independence at a party congress in April; Chair. Lama DORLIGJAVYN BAASAN.

Mongolian People's Revolutionary Party (MPRP): Baga Toiruu 37/1, Ulan Bator 11; tel. 322745; fax 320368; f. 1921 as Mongolian People's Party; c. 122,000 mems (May 2002); ruling body Party Little Khural (183 mems in March 2000), which elects the

Leadership Council; Chair. NAMBARYN ENKHBAYAR; Gen. Sec. DOLOONJINGIIN IDEVKHTEN.

Mongolian Rural Development Party: f. 1995 as the Mongolian Countryside Development Party, reorganized in December 1999; Pres. L. CHULUUNBAATAR.

Mongolian National Solidarity Party: 'Ikh Zasag' Institute Bldg, 4th Horoo, Bayanzürkh district, Ulan Bator; tel. and fax 455736; f. 1994, as Mongolian Solidarity Party; 15,480 mems (March 2002); Chair. NAMSRAIN NYAM-OSOR.

Mongolian Traditional United Party: Huvisgalchdyn Örgön Chölöö 26, Ulan Bator; tel. 325745; fax 342692; also known as the United Heritage (conservative) Party; f. 1993 as an amalgamation of the United Private Owners' Party and the Independence Party; 14,000 mems (1998); ruling body General Political Council; Chair. ÜRJINGIIN KHÜRELBAATAR.

Society of Russian Citizens: Ulan Bator; represents local Russian long-term residents; Chair. LYUDMILA G. MASLOVA.

United Socialist Party of Mongols: Ulan Bator; f. 2000; nationalist party; Chair. (vacant).

Diplomatic Representation

EMBASSIES IN MONGOLIA

Bulgaria: Olimpiin Gudamj 8, Ulan Bator (CPO Box 702); tel. and fax 322841; e-mail posolstvobg@magicnet.mn; Ambassador: NIKOLAI MARIN.

China, People's Republic: Zaluuchuudyn Örgön Chölöö 5, Ulan Bator (CPO Box 672); tel. 320955; fax 311943; Ambassador: HUANG JIAKUI.

Cuba: Negdsen Ündestnii Gudamj 18, Ulan Bator (CPOB 710); tel. 323778; Ambassador: PEDRO ARNALDO MORÁN TAPENES.

Czech Republic: POB 665, Olimpiin Gudamj 14, Ulan Bator; tel. 321886; fax 323791; e-mail czechemb@mongol.net; Chargé d'affaires: ADAM PIÑOS.

France: Diplomatic Corps Bldg, Apartment 48, Ulan Bator 6 (CPO Box 687); tel. 324519; fax 329633; e-mail ambafrance@magicnet.mn; Ambassador: JACQUES-OLIVIER MANENT.

Germany: Negdsen Ündestnii Gudamj 7, Ulan Bator (CPO Box 708); tel. 323325; fax 323905; e-mail germanemb_ulanbator@mongol.net; Ambassador: MICHAEL VORWERK.

Hungary: Enkh Taivny Gudamj 1, Ulan Bator (CPO Box 668); tel. 323973; fax 311793; e-mail hunamb@magicnet.mn; Ambassador: ISTVÁN BALOGH.

India: Zaluuchuudyn Örgön Chölöö 10, Ulan Bator (CPO Box 691); tel. 329522; fax 329532; e-mail indembmongolia@magicnet.mn; Ambassador: KARMA TOPDEN.

Japan: Zaluuchuudyn Gudamj 12, Ulan Bator 13 (CPO Box 1011); tel. 320777; fax 313332; e-mail eojmongol@magicnet.mn; internet www.eojmongolia.mn; Ambassador: TATSUO TODA.

Kazakhstan: Diplomatic Corps Bldg, Apartment 11, Chingeltei District, Ulan Bator (CPO Box 291); tel. 312240; fax 312204; e-mail kzemby@magicnet.mn; Chargé d'affaires: KAYRAT ISAGALIYEV.

Korea, Republic: Olimpiin Gudamj 10, Ulan Bator (CPO Box 1039); tel. 321548; fax 311157; Ambassador: CHOI YOUNG-CHUL.

Laos: Ikh Toiruu 59, Ulan Bator (CPO Box 1030); tel. 322834; fax 321048; e-mail laoemb@mongol.net; Ambassador: VANHEUANG VONGVICHIT.

Poland: Diplomatic Corps Bldg, 95, Apartment 66–67, Ulan Bator 13; tel. 320641; fax 320576; Ambassador: KRZYSZTOF DEBNICKE.

Russia: Enkh Taivny Gudamj A-6, Ulan Bator (CPO Box 661); tel. 327071; fax 324425; Ambassador: OLEG DERKOVSKII.

Turkey: Enkh Taivny Örgön Chölöö 5, Ulan Bator (CPO Box 1009); tel. 313992; fax 313992; e-mail turkemb@mongol.net; Ambassador: MEHMET NURI YILDIRIM.

United Kingdom: Enkh Taivny Gudamj 30, Ulan Bator 13 (CPO Box 703); tel. 458133; fax 458036; e-mail britemb@magicnet.mn; Ambassador: PHILIP ROUSE.

USA: Ikh Toiruu 59/1, Ulan Bator (CPO Box 1021); tel. 329606; fax 320776; e-mail webmaster@us-mongolia.com; Ambassador: JOHN R. DINGER.

Viet Nam: Enkh Taivny Örgön Chölöö 47, Ulan Bator (CPO Box 670); tel. 458917; fax 458923; Ambassador: NGUYEN THI DUC.

Judicial System

Under the fourth Constitution, judicial independence is protected by the General Council of Courts, consisting of the Chief Justice (Chairman of the Supreme Court), the Chairman of the Constitutional Court, Procurator General, Minister of Law and others. The Council nominates the members of the Supreme Court for approval by the Great Khural. The Chief Justice is chosen from among the members of the Supreme Court and approved by the President for a six-year term. Civil, criminal and administrative cases are handled by Ulan Bator City court, the 21 *aimag* (provincial) courts, *sum* (rural district) and urban district courts, while the system of special courts (military, railway, etc.) is still in place. The Procurator General and his deputies, who play an investigatory role, are nominated by the President and approved by the Great Khural for six-year terms. The Constitutional Court safeguards the constitutional legality of legislation. It consists of nine members, three nominated each by the President, Great Khural and Supreme Court, and elects a Chairman from among its number.

Chief Justice: CHIMEDLKHAMYN GANBAT.

Procurator General: MONGOLYN ALTANKHUYAG.

Chairman of Constitutional Court: NAVAANPERENLEIN JANTSAN.

Religion

The 1992 Constitution maintains the separation of Church and State but forbids any discrimination, declaring that 'the State shall respect religion and religion shall honour the State'. During the early years of communist rule Mongolia's traditional Mahayana Buddhism was virtually destroyed, then exploited as a 'show-piece' for visiting dignitaries (although the Dalai Lama himself was not permitted to visit Mongolia until the early 1980s). The national Buddhist centre is Gandantegchinlen Khiid (monastery) in Ulan Bator, with about 100 lamas and a seminary; it is the headquarters of the Asian Buddhist Conference for Peace. In the early 1990s some 2,000 lamas established small communities at the sites of 120 former monasteries, temples and religious schools, some of which were being restored. These included two other important monasteries, Erdene Zuu and Amarbayasgalant. The Kazakhs of western Mongolia are nominally Sunni Muslims, but their mosques, also destroyed in the 1930s or closed subsequently, are only now being rebuilt or reopened. Traces of shamanism from the pre-Buddhist period still survive. In recent years there has been a new upsurge in Christian missionary activity in Mongolia. However, the Law on State-Church Relations (of November 1993) sought to make Buddhism the predominant religion and restricted the dissemination of beliefs other than Buddhism, Islam and shamanism. The law was challenged by human rights campaigners and Mongolian Christians as unconstitutional.

BUDDHISM

Living Buddha: The Ninth Javzandamba Khutagt (Ninth Bogd), JAMBALNAMDOLCHOIJINJALTSAN (resident in Dharamsala, India).

Buddhist Believers' Association: Pres. S. BAYANTSAGAAN.

Gandantegchinlen Monastery: Ulan Bator 58; tel. 360023; Centre of Mongolian Buddhists: Khamba Lama (Abbot) DEMBERELIIN CHOIJAMTS.

Mongolian Buddhist Association: Pres. G. ENKHSAIKHAN.

CHRISTIANITY

Roman Catholic Church

The Church is represented in Mongolia by a single mission. At 7 July 1999 there were 85 baptized Mongolian Catholic Christians in the country.

Catholic Mission: POB 694, Ulan Bator; tel. 452575; fax 458027; e-mail ccmvatican@magicnet.mn; f. 1992; Superior Rev. Fr WENS PADILLA.

Protestant Church

Association of Mongolian Protestants: f. 1990; Pastor M. BOLDBAATAR.

Russian Orthodox Church

Holy Trinity Church: Jukovyn Gudamj 55, Ulan Bator; opened in 1870, closed in 1930; services recommenced 1997 for Russian community; Father ANATOLII FESECHKO.

ISLAM

Muslim Society: f. 1990; Hon. Pres. K. SAIRAAN; Chair. of Central Council M. AZATKHAN.

BAHÁ'Í FAITH

Bahá'í Community: Ulan Bator; f. 1989; tel. 321867; Leader A. ARIUNAA.

The Press

PRINCIPAL NATIONAL NEWSPAPERS

State-owned publications in Mongolia were denationalized with effect from 1 January 1999, although proper privatization could not proceed immediately.

MN-Önöödör (Today): Mongol News Co, Ikh Toiruu 20, Ulan Bator; tel. 352504; fax 352501; e-mail mntoday@mobinet.mn; f. 1996; 304 a year; Editor-in-Chief Ts. BALDORJ; circ. 5,500.

Mongolyn Medee (Mongolian News): Erel Group, 13th District, Bayanzürkh Düüreg, Ulan Bator; tel. 453169; fax 453816; e-mail news-of-mon@magicnet.mn; 256 a year; Editor-in-Chief D. SANDAGSÜREN; circ. 2,900.

Ödriin Sonin (Daily News): Ikh Toiruu, Ulan Bator 20; tel. 99263536; fax 352499; e-mail daily_news@mbox.mn; f. 1924, restored 1990; fmrly Ardyn Erkh, Ardyn Ündesnii Erkh, Ündesnii Erkh and Ödriin Toli; 312 a year; Editor-in-Chief JAMBALYN MYAGMARSÜREN; circ. 14,200.

Ünen (Truth): Baga Toiruu 11, Ulan Bator; tel. 323847; fax 321287; e-mail unen@magicnet.mn; internet www.unen.mn; f. 1920; publ. by MPRP; 256 a year; Editor-in-Chief TSERENSODNOMYN GANBAT; circ. 8,330.

Zuuny Medee (Century's News): Amaryn Gudamj 1, Ulan Bator 20; tel. 320940; fax 321279; e-mail zuunii_medee@yahoo.com; internet www.zm.mongolmedia.com; f. 1991 as *Zasgiin Gazryn Medee*; 312 a year; Editor-in-Chief TSERENDORJIIN TSETSEGCHULUUN; circ 8,000.

PRINCIPAL PERIODICALS

Anagaakh Arga Bilig (Health Yin and Yang): POB 1053/13, Ulan Bator; tel. 321367; e-mail arslny7144@magicnet.mn; monthly; Editor YA. ARSLAN.

Ardyn Elch (People's Envoy): St. Petersburgh Centre, 2nd Floor, Rm 36, Sükhbaataryn Örgön Chölöö; tel. 95252346; fax 314580; monthly; Editor-in-Chief B. TSEDEN.

Business Times: Chamber of Commerce and Industry, Government Bldg 1, Rm 806, Erkh Chölöönii Talbai, Ulan Bator; tel. 325374; fax 324620; e-mail bis_times@usa.net; 48 a year; Editor B. SARANTUYAA.

Deedsiin Amidral (Elite's Life): Bldg 6, Rm 207, A. Amaryn Gudamj, POB 536/13, Ulan Bator; tel. 91189399; fax 323847; e-mail elitslife@mongolmedia.com; internet www.elitslife.mongolmedia.com; Editor-in-Chief TSEGMIDIIN CHIMIDDONDOG.

Deedsiin Khüreelen (Elite's Forum): CPO Box 1114, Ulan Bator; tel. 325687; 48 a year; Editor NYAMBUUGIIN BILGÜÜN; circ. 12,000.

Dorno-Örnö (East-West): POB 17/48, Ulan Bator; fax 322613; f. 1978; publ. by Institute of Oriental and International Studies of Acad. of Sciences; scientific and socio-political journal; history, culture, foreign relations; articles in Mongolian; two a year; Editor-in-Chief Dr N. ALTANTSETSEG.

Erüül Mend (Health): Ulan Bator; fax 321278; publ. by Ministry of Health; monthly; Editor-in-Chief SH. JIGJIDSÜREN; circ. 5,600.

Il Tovchoo (Openness): Mongol Nom Co Bldg, Rm 8, Ulan Bator; POB 234, Ulan Bator 46; tel. 325517; e-mail iltovchoo@magicnet.mn; f. 1990; current affairs and cultural news; 36 a year; Editor-in-Chief G. AKIM.

Khani (Spouse): POB 600/49, National Agricultural Co-operative Members' Association Bldg, Rm 103, Enkh Taivny Gudamj 18A-1, Bayanzürkh Düüreg, Ulan Bator; women and family issues; 36 a year; Editor-in-Chief D. OTGONTUYAA; circ. 64,920.

Khöldömör (Labour): Sükhbaataryn Talbai 3, Ulan Bator 210664; tel. 323026; f. 1928; publ. by the Confederation of Mongolian Trade Unions; 36 a year; Editor-in-Chief TSOODOLYN KHULAN; circ. 64,920.

Khökh Tolbo (Blue Spot): POB 306/24; Mon-Azi Co Bldg, Ulan Bator; tel. and fax 313405; 48 a year; Editor-in-Chief BATYN ERDENEBAATAR; circ. 3,500.

Khuuli Züin Medeelel (Legal Information): Ministry of Justice and Home Affairs, Ulan Bator; f. 1990; 24 a year.

Khuviin Amidral (Private Life): POB 429/44, Ulan Bator 44; tel. 329926; fax 310181; 36 a year; Editor-in-Chief T. AMARDAVAA; circ. 2,900.

Khuviin Soyol (Personal Culture): CPOB 1254, Rm 2, Block 39, behind No. 5 School, Baga Toiruu, Ulan Bator; Editor BEKHBAZARYN BEKHSÜREN.

Khümüün Bichig (People and Script): Montsame, Ulan Bator; tel. 329486; fax 327857; e-mail montsame@pop.mn; current affairs in Mongolian classical script; 36 a year; Editor T. GALDAN; circ. 15,000.

Khümüüs (People): POB 411, Ulan Bator 46; tel. 328732; fax 318363; e-mail khumuus@mongol.net; 48 a year; Editor D. BADAMGARAV; circ. 21,500.

Khümüüsiin Amidral (People's Life): POB 411, Ulan Bator 46; tel. 328732; fax 318363; e-mail khumuus@mongol.net; 48 a year; Editor B. KHULAN.

Mash Nuuts (Top Secret): POB 113/49, Ulan Bator 49; 24 a year; Editors N. BATDELGER, TS. MÖNKHTUYAA.

Mongol Taims (Mongol Times): Jamyangiin Gudamj 9, Ulan Bator; tel. and fax 458802; 40 a year; Editor CHONOIN KULANDA.

Mongol Törkh (Mongolian Style): POB 418/46, MPRP Bldg, Rm 102, Sükhbaatar Düüreg, Ulan Bator; tel. and fax 311406; 36 a year; Editor D. BADAMGARAV.

Mongoljin Goo (Mongolian Beauty): POB 717/44, Mongolian Women's Federation, Ulan Bator; tel. 320790; fax 367406; e-mail monwofed@magicnet.mn; f. 1990; monthly; Editor J. ERDENECHIMEG; circ. 3,000.

Mongolyn Anagaakh Ukhaan (Mongolian Medicine): CPOB 696/13, Ulan Bator 13; tel. 112306; fax 451807; e-mail nymadawa@hotmail.com; publ. by Scientific Society of Mongolian Physicians, Sub-assembly of Medical Sciences and Mongolian Academy of Sciences; quarterly; Editor-in-Chief Prof. PAGVAJAVYN NYAMDAVAA.

Mongolyn Khödöö (Mongolian Countryside): Ulan Bator; tel. 455577; publ. by Ministry of Agriculture and Industry, and Academy of Agricultural Sciences; monthly; Editor-in-Chief TS. MÖNKHBAATAR.

Montsame Medee (Montsame News): CPOB 1514, Montsame, Ulan Bator; tel. 99136081; daily news digest primarily for government departments; Editor B. NAMINCHIMED.

Notstoi Medee (Important News): POB 359/20, Maximum Press Co, Ulan Bator; tel. 99133270; Editor B. MONKHZUL.

Oroin Medee (Evening News): Bayangol Düüreg, Ulan Bator; tel. 90151080; e-mail e_news@hotmail.com; Editor-in-Chief S. BADAMRAGCHAA.

Sain Baina Uu? (Hello!): CPOB 1085, Chingisiin Örgön Chölöö 1, Ulan Bator; tel. 310757; fax 372810; internet sain.mongolmedia.com; publ. by the Democratic Party; weekly; Editor SH. BATBAYAR.

Serüüleg (Alarm Clock): POB 1094/13, Flat 2, Entrance 1, Block A4, 1-40 Myangat, Ulan Bator; tel. and fax 318006; 40 a year; Editor-in-Chief SENGEEGIIN BAYARMÖNKH; circ. 28,600.

Setgüülch (Journalist): POB 600/46, Ulan Bator; tel. 325388; fax 313912; f. 1982; publ. by Union of Journalists; journalism, politics, literature, art, economy; quarterly; Editor TSENDIIN ENKHBAT.

Shar Sonin (Yellow Newspaper): POB 76/20A, Ulan Bator; tel. 313984; 48 a year; Editor B. ODGEREL.

Shinjlekh Ukhaany Akademiin Medee (Academy of Sciences News): Sükhbaataryn Talbai 3, Ulan Bator; f. 1961; publ. by Academy of Sciences; quarterly; Editor-in-Chief T. GALBAATAR.

Shuurkhai Zar (Quick Advertisement): POB 151/46A, Ulan Bator Bank Bldg, Rm 104, 1st Floor, Ulan Bator; tel. 313778; e-mail shirevger@mobinet.mn; Editor E. TSEYENKHORLOO.

Tavan Tsagarig (Five Rings): National Olympic Committee, Ikh Toiruu 20, Ulan Bator; tel. 352487; fax 352462; e-mail t_ts_sport@yahoo.com; Editor-in-Chief SODNOMDARJAAGIIN BATBAATAR.

Töriin Medeelel (State Information): Secretariat of the Mongolian Great Khural, State Palace, Ulan Bator 12; tel. 329612; fax 322866; e-mail elbegsaihan@maild.parl.gov.mn; internet www.parl.gov.mn; f. 1990; presidential and governmental decrees, state laws; 48 a year; Editor R. ENKHTAIVAN; circ. 5,000.

Tsenkher Delgets (Light Blue Screen): Ulan Bator; tel. 312010; fax 311850; e-mail bsnews@magicnet.mn; weekly guide to TV and radio programmes; Editor-in-Chief GALIGAAGIIN BAYARSAIKHAN.

Tsonkh (Window): CPOB 1085, Chingisiin Örgön Chölöö 1, Ulan Bator; tel. 310717; publ. by the Democratic Party's Political Department; monthly.

Ug (Word): CPOB 680, Rm 2, Block 8B, 1 Döchin Myangat, Ulan Bator; tel. 321165; fax 329795; e-mail ugsonin@mol.mn; fmrly the journal of the Mongolian Social Democratic Party (until 2000); Editor B. KHANDOLGOR.

Ulaanbaatar Times (Ulan Bator Times): A. Amaryn Gudamj 1, Ulan Bator 20; tel. and fax 311187; f. 1990 as *Ulaanbaatar*; publ. by Ulan Bator City Govt; weekly; Editor-in-Chief JÜMPERELIIN SARUULBUYAN; circ. 2,000.

Utga Zokhiol Urlag (Literature and Art): Union of Writers, Sükhbaataryn Gudamj 11, Ulan Bator 46; tel. 321863; f. 1955; monthly; Editor-in-Chief Ü. KHÜRELBAATAR; circ. 3,000.

Zar Medee (Advertisement News): State Property Bldg 5, 1st Floor, Rm 130, Chingeltei Düüreg, Ulan Bator; tel. and fax 324885; e-mail advertisement-news@yahoo.com; personal and company advertisements; 122 a year; Editor D. BAYASGALAN.

Zindaa (Ranking): Kyoküshyuzan Development Fund Bldg, Chingeltei Düüreg, Ulan Bator; tel. 312008; internet www.zindaa

.mongolmedia.com; wrestling news; 36 a year; Editor-in-Chief KH. MANDAKHBAYAR.

FOREIGN LANGUAGE PUBLICATIONS

Email Daily News: Ulan Bator; e-mail ganbold@magicnet.mn; press and media summaries in English; Editor CHULUUNY GANBOLD.

Menggu Xiaoxi Bao (News of Mongolia): Montsame News Agency, CPOB 1514, Ulan Bator; e-mail mgxxbao@yahoo.com; f. 1929, as Ajilchny Zam; closed 1991, reopened 1998; 48 a year; in Chinese; Sec. B. MÖNKHTUUL.

Mongolia This Week: Ulan Bator; tel. and fax 318339; e-mail mongoliathisweek@mobinet.mn; internet www.mongoliathisweek .mn; weekly in English, online daily; Editor-in-Chief D. NARANTUYAA; English Editor ERIC MUSTAFA.

The Mongol Messenger: Montsame News Agency, CPOB 1514, Ulan Bator; tel. 325512; fax 327857; e-mail monmessenger@ mongolnet.mn; internet www.mongolmessenger.mn; f. 1991; weekly newspaper in English; Exec. Editor B. INDRA; circ. 2,000.

Montsame Daily News: CPOB 1514, Montsame, Ulan Bator; tel. 314574; fax 327857; daily English news digest for embassies, etc.

Novosti Mongolii (News of Mongolia): CPOB 1514, Montsame, Ulan Bator; tel. 310157; fax 327857; e-mail montsame@pop .magicnet.mn; f. 1942; weekly; in Russian; Editor-in-Chief ENKHBAYARYN RAVDAN.

The UB Post: Mongol News Co, Ikh Toiruu 20, Ulan Bator; tel. 352480; fax 352495; e-mail info@theubpost.mn; internet www.theubpost.mn; f. 1996; weekly; in English; Editor-in-Chief NAMSRAIN OYUUNBAYAR; circ. 1,700.

NEWS AGENCIES

Montsame (Mongol Tsakhilgaan Medeenii Agentlag) (Mongolian News Agency): Jigjidjavyn Gudamj 8, Ulan Bator 13 (CPO Box 1514); tel. 314502; fax 327857; e-mail montsame@magicnet.mn; internet www.montsame.mn; f. 1921; govt-controlled; Gen. Dir TUGALKHÜÜGIIN BAASANSÜREN; Editor-in-Chief GIVAANDONDOGIIN PÜREVSAMBUU.

Mongolyn Medee (Mongolian News): operated by Mongolteleviz; Dir S. MÖNKHTSEREN.

Foreign Bureaux

Informatsionnoye Telegrafnoye Agentstvo Rossii—Telegrafnoye Agentstvo Suverennykh Stran (ITAR—TASS) (Russia): October 4, Rm 323, Ulan Bator; Bureau Chief V. B. IONOV; Correspondent ALEKSANDR DENISOVICH.

Rossiiskoye Informatsionnoye Agentstvo—Novosti (RIA—Novosti) (Russia): POB 686, Ulan Bator; tel. 327384; Correspondent ALEKSANDR ALTMAN.

Xinhua (New China) News Agency (People's Republic of China): Ulan Bator; tel. 322718; Correspondent LI REN.

Publishers

Mongolian Book Publishers' Association: Ulan Bator; Exec. Dir S. TSERENDORJ.

Mongolian Free Press Publishers' Asociation: POB 306, Ulan Bator 24; tel. and fax 313405; Pres. BATYN ERDENEBAATAR.

The Government remains the largest publisher, but the ending of the state monopoly has led to the establishment of several small commercial publishers, including Shuvuun Saaral (Ministry of Defence), Mongol Khevlel and Soyombo Co, Mongolpress (Montsame), Erdem (Academy of Sciences), Süülenkhüü children's publishers, Sudaryn Chuulgan, Interpress, Sükhbaatar Co, Öngöt Khevlel, Admon, Odsar, Khee Khas Co, etc. Newspaper publishing fell from 134.1m. copies in 1990 to 21.1m. copies in 1999. Book printing likewise declined, from 96.3m. printer's sheets (each of 16 pages) in 1990 to 19.2m. in 1993. In 1994 128 book titles appeared, with a total of 640,000 copies. The two main press, periodical and book subscription agencies are Mongol Shuudan and Gurvan Badrakh Co.

Broadcasting and Communications

TELECOMMUNICATIONS

Digital exchanges have been installed in Ulan Bator, Darkhan, Erdenet, Sükhbaatar, Bulgan and Arvaikheer, while radio-relay lines have been digitalized between: Ulan Bator–Darkhan–Sükhbaatar; Ulan Bator–Darkhan–Erdenet; and Dashinchilen–Arvaikheer. Mobile telephone companies operate in Ulan Bator and other central towns, in addition to Arvaikheer, Sainshand and Zamyn-Üüd.

Datakom: Negdsen Ündestnii Gudamj 49, Ulan Bator 46; tel. 315544; fax 320210; e-mail info@magicnet.mn; service provider for Magicnet connection to internet; Dir DANGAASÜRENGIIN ENKHBAT.

Micom: Mongol Tsakhilgaan Kholboo Co Bldg, 3rd Floor, Ulan Bator; tel. 313229; fax 325412; e-mail info@micom.mng.net; internet service provider.

MobiCom: Amaryn Gudamj 2, Ulan Bator 210620 (CPO Box 20A); tel. 312222; fax 310411; e-mail mobicom@mobicom-corp.com; mobile telephone service provider.

Moncom: 51 Post Office, Box 207, Ulan Bator; tel. 329409; e-mail ch.enkhmend@hotmail.com; pager services.

Mongolia Telecom: Sükhbaataryn Talbai 1, Ulan Bator 210611 (CPO Box 1166); tel. 320597; fax 325412; e-mail mt@mtcone.net; internet www.mongol.net; 54.6% state-owned, 40.0% owned by Korea Telecom; Pres. and CEO OONOI SHAALUU.

Skytel: Montel Co Bldg, 4th Floor, 1st Khoroo, I. Chingeltei District, Ulan Bator 13; Tel. 318488; fax 318487; e-mail skytel@mtcone.net; mobile telephone and voice mail service provider; Mongolia-Republic of Korea joint venture.

BROADCASTING

A 1,900-km radio relay line from Ulan Bator to Altai and Ölgii provides direct-dialling telephone links as well as television services for western Mongolia. New radio relay lines have been built from Ulan Bator to Choibalsan, and from Ulan Bator to Sükhbaatar and Sainshand. Most of the population is in the zone of television reception, following the inauguration of relays via satellites operated by the International Telecommunications Satellite Organization (INTELSAT).

All provincial centres receive two channels of Mongolian national television; and all district centres can receive television, although only a third can receive Mongolian television.

Head of Mongolian Radio and Television Affairs Directorate: BAASANJAVYN GANBOLD.

Radio

Mongolradio: Khuvisgalyn Zam 3, Ulan Bator 11; tel. 323096; f. 1934; operates for 17 hours daily on three long wave and one medium-wave frequency, and VHF; programmes in Mongolian (two) and Kazakh; Dir BAARANGIIN PÜREVDASH.

Voice of Mongolia: Ulan Bator; e-mail radiomongolia@magicnet .mn; external service of Mongolradio; broadcasts in Russian, Chinese, English and Japanese on short wave; Dir B. NARANTUYAA.

Khökh Tenger (Blue Sky Radio): broadcasts for 12 hours Monday to Saturday and for shorter hours on Sundays on 100.9 MHz and 4850 kHz; Dir L. AMARZAYAA.

The BBC World Service is relayed on 103.1 MHz in Ulan Bator.

AE and JAAG Studio: Amryn Gudamj 2, Ulan Bator 210620, POB 126, Ulan Bator; tel. 310631; fax 326545; e-mail aejaag@magicnet .mn; f. 1996; broadcasts for 4.5–5 hours daily; CEO Z. ALTAI.

FM 106.6: Ulan Bator; f. 2001; Voice of America news and information in Mongolian; English lessons and music.

FM 107: Ulan Bator; local entertainment; also relays Voice of America broadcasts in English and Russian; Dir M. BUYANBADRAKH.

Info Radio: Youth Palace, Ulan Bator; tel. 329353; e-mail inforadio @mongol.net; broadcasts on 105.5 MHz.

Puls-Misheel: Ulan Bator; f. 2001 by Mongolradio and Buryat Puls radio; Russian-language broadcaster on 102.5 MHz, 24 hours; hourly news in Russian and Mongolian.

Radio Ulaanbaatar: Ulan Bator; f. 1995; fmrly *Dörvön Uul* (Four Mountains); broadcasts on 101.6 MHz; Dir U. BULGAN.

There are seven long and shortwave radio transmitters and 49 FM stations in 23 towns (13 in Ulan Bator).

Television

Mongolteleviz: Khuvisgalyn Zam 3, Ulan Bator 11 (CPO Box 365); tel. 326663; fax 327234; e-mail mrtv@magicnet.mn; f. 1967; daily morning and evening transmissions of locally-originated material relayed by land-line and via INTELSAT satellites; Dir TSENDIIN ENKHBAT.

MN Channel 25: AE and JAAG Studio, Ulan Bator; broadcasts entertainment in the evening from Tuesday to Sunday; CEO Z. ALTAI.

Eagle (Bürged) TV: Ulan Bator; tel. 458657; fax 458505; e-mail eagle@eagletvmongolia.com; broadcasts for nine hours daily, carrying Mongolian news, cartoons, films, educational programmes, sports and relays of CNN; News Editor TSAGAANY OYUUNDARI; Gen. Man. PAUL SWARTZENDRUBER.

Sansar: Ikh Toiruu 46, Ulan Bator; tel. 313752; fax 313770; cable television equipment and services; Dir-Gen. TS. ELBEGZAYAA.

UBSTV: Ulaanbaatar Broadcasting System (operated by Ulan Bator City Government); evening broadcasts repeated the following morning except Mondays; Dir-Gen. L. BALKHJAV.

Cable TV companies (29 in total) operate in 19 towns. There are local TV stations in Ulan Bator (three), Darkhan, Sükhbaatar and Baganuur. ORT and RTR may be received via Russian satellites, and Kazakh television is received in Bayan-Ölgii. NHK, Deutsche Welle, RTF and Inner Mongolia (China) Television programmes are relayed in Ulan Bator on Channel 10.

Finance

(cap. = capital; res = reserves; dep. = deposits; m. = million; brs = branches; amounts in tögrög)

BANKING

Before 1990 the State Bank was the only bank in Mongolia, responsible for issuing currency, controlling foreign exchange and allocating credit. With the inauguration of market reforms in Mongolia in the early 1990s, the central and commercial functions of the State Bank were transferred to the newly-created specialized commercial banks: the Bank of Capital Investment and Technological Innovation and the State Bank International. In May 1991 the State Bank became an independent central bank, and the operation of private, commercial banks was permitted. By the end of 1996 there were 15 commercial banks. The performance of these banks was poor, owing to high levels of non-performing loans, inexperienced management and weak supervision. Loss of confidence in the sector resulted in the implementation of extensive restructuring: in November 1996 amendments were made to banking legislation to improve the regulation and supervision of commercial banks, and two major insolvent banks were liquidated. Restructuring continued in the late 1990s.

Central Bank

Bank of Mongolia: Baga Toiruu 9, Ulan Bator 46; tel. 322169; fax 311471; e-mail ad@mongolbank.mn; internet www.mongolbank.mn; f. 1924 as the State Bank of the Mongolian People's Republic; cap. 1,000m., res. 132,932m. (Dec. 2000), dep. 176,043m. (Dec. 1999); Gov. OCHIRBATYN CHULUUNBAT; 20 brs.

Other Banks

AG Bank—Agricultural Bank (KhAAN Bank): Enkh Taivny Gudamj 51, Ulan Bator 240149 (POB 185, Ulan Bator 51); tel. and fax 458670; e-mail www.haanbank@magicnet.mn; f. 1991; plans for privatization in 2003; cap. 4,945m. (Dec. 1999); CEO PETER MORROW; 352 brs.

Anod Bank: Khudaldaany Gudamj 18, Ulan Bator 211238 (POB 361, Ulan Bator 13); tel. 315315; fax 313070; e-mail anod@magicnet.mn; internet www.anod.mn; cap. 1,000m., dep. 8,722m. (Dec. 2000); Dir-Gen. D. ENKHTÖR.

Avtozam Bank (Motor Roads Bank): Bridge-Building Office, Ulan Bator; tel. 381744; fax 368094; f. 1990; cap. 95m.; Dir-Gen. Ts. SANGIDORJ.

Aziin Khöröngö Oruulaltyn Bank (Asian Capital Investment Bank): Khölög Group Bldg, Eastern entrance, 2nd Floor, Bayangol District, Ulan Bator; tel. 367386; Dir-Gen. TSEDENGIIN BATBOLD.

Bayanbogd Bank: Sambuugiin Gudamj 11, Ulan Bator; tel. and fax 329942; privately owned; cap. 423.7m., dep. 795.5m. (June 1999); Owner D. ADYAA.

Capitron Bank: Enkhtaivny Örgön Chölöö, Ulan Bator 210648; tel. 327550; fax 315635; e-mail info@capitronbank.mn.

Chingis Khan Bank: Ulan Bator; f. 2001 by Millennium Securities Management Ltd (British Virgin Islands); cap. US $4.5m.

Ediin Tenger Bank: Barilgachdyn Talbai 13, Ulan Bator; tel. 458601; Dir-Gen. D. DANZAN; licence withdrawn, Oct. 1998.

Erel Bank: 'Erel' Co No 2 Bldg, Chingisiin Örgön Chölöö, 3rd Khoroo, Ulan Bator (POB 500, Ulan Bator 36); tel. and fax 343567; e-mail erelbank@mongol.net; f. 1997; cap. 2,600m., res 34.0m., dep. 849.2m. (Aug. 2002); Owner BADARCHIIN ERDENEBAT; CEO GOMBOJAVYN DORJ.

Export Import Bank: Zamchny Gudamj 1, Bayangol District, Ulan Bator (CPO Box 28/52); tel. 311693; fax 311323; f. 1993 as Ulaanbaatar Bank; cap. 506.8m.; CEO L. SARANGEREL.

Golomt Bank of Mongolia: Sükhbaataryn Talbai 3, 4th Floor, Ulan Bator 210620A; tel. 311530; fax 312307; e-mail mail@golomtbank.com; f. 1995 by Mongolian-Portuguese IBH Bodi International Co Ltd; cap. 2,716m. dep. 25,851m. (Dec. 2001); Chair. of Bd LUVSANVANDANGIIN BOLD; Dir-Gen. D. BAYASGALAN; 10 brs.

Khadgalamjiin Bank (Savings Bank): Khudaldaany Gudamj 6, Ulan Bator 11; tel. 312043; fax 310621; e-mail savbank@mongol.net; f. 1996 as Ardyn Bank; cap. 1,268m. (Dec. 1999); Dir-Gen. G.TSERENPÜREV; 37 brs.

KhAS Bank: Yörönkhii said Amaryn Gudamj, Sükhbaatar District, Ulan Bator 210646 (POB 46/721); tel. (11) 318185; fax (11) 328701; e-mail bank@xacbank.or; cap. 3,700m.

Khöröngö Oruulalt Tekhnologiin Shinechleltiin Bank (Bank of Capital Investment and Technological Innovation, ITIBank of Mongolia): Khudaldaany Gudamj 11, Ulan Bator 46; tel. 381933; fax 381115; e-mail itibank2@magicnet.mn; f. 1991; licence withdrawn 2000; cap. 3,306m., res 2,108m., dep. 2,694m.; Pres. N. CHULUUNBAATAR; 32 brs.

Kredit Bank: Ulan Bator; cap. 1,117m. (March 2000).

Mongol Khorshoo Bank (Mongolian Co-operative Bank): Olimpiin Gudamj 4, Ulan Bator 48; tel. 325239; f. 1990; cap. 95.8m.; Chair. of Board MIJIDIIN TERBISH; 5 brs.

Mongol Post Bank: Kholboochdiin Gudamj 4, Ulan Bator 13; tel. 311270; fax 328501; e-mail post_bank@mongol.net; internet www.postbank.mn; f. 1993; cap. 2,002.3m., res 582.4m., dep. 14,899.7m., equity 18,566.5m. (Dec. 2001); 100% in private ownership; Exec. Dir D. OYUUNJARGAL.

SB Bank–Restoration Bank: Sükhbaataryn Talbai 20A, Ulan Bator 11; tel. 310827; fax 323614; f. 1990 as Mongol Daatgal Bank; licence withdrawn 2000; cap. 1,121m.; Dir-Gen. S. NASANJARGAL (acting); 22 brs.

Teever Khögjliin Bank (Transport and Development Bank): Amarsanaagiin Gudamj 2, Bayanzürkh District, Ulan Bator; tel. 458617; cap. 1,072m.

Trade and Development Bank of Mongolia (Khudaldaa Khögjliin Bank): Khudaldaany Gudamj 7, Ulan Bator 11; tel. 321171; fax 325449; e-mail tdbank@tdbm.mn; internet www.tdbm.mn; f. 1991; carries out Mongolbank's foreign operations; cap. 1,500m., res. 3,153m., dep. 83,031m. (Dec. 2000); 76% equity bought by Banca Commerciale (Lugano) and Jerald Metals (Stanford, CT), May 2002.

Tülsh-Erchim Bank (Fuel and Power Bank): Baga Toiruu, Ulan Bator; tel. 310605; fax 310981; f. 1992; Dir M. MYAGMARSÜREN.

Ulaanbaatar Bank: Baga Toiruu 15, Ulan Bator (PO 370, Ulan Bator 46); tel. 312155; fax 311067; e-mail ubbank@magicnet.mn; f. 1998 by Capital City with assistance from the Bank of Taipei (Taiwan); cap. 4,800m; Dir-Gen. G. BUYANBAT.

Üildveriin Huvi Niilüülsen Bank (Industrial Shares Bank, 'Shinechlel' Innovation Bank): Ulan Bator 120646; tel. 310833; f. 1990; cap. 418m.; Dir-Gen. SÜKHRAGCHAAGIIN MÖNKHTÖR.

Zoos Bank: 'Oi Mod' Co Bldg, Choimbolyn Gudamj 6, 2nd Khoroo, Chingeltei District, Ulan Bator (POB 314, Ulan Bator 44); tel. 312107; fax 324450; e-mail zoosbank@mongol.net; f. 1999; cap. 1,073m.; Exec. Dir SH. CHUDANJII.

Banking Associations

Bankers' Association: Ulan Bator; Pres. D. NYAMTSEREN; Chair. of Bd S. ORGODOL.

Mongolian Bankers Association: Ulan Bator; e-mail monba@mongolnet.mn; Pres. LUVSANVANDANGIIN BOLD; Exec. Dir JIGJIDIIN ÜNENBAT.

STOCK EXCHANGE

Stock Exchange: Sükhbaataryn Talbai 2, Ulan Bator; tel. 310501; fax 325170; e-mail mse@magicnet.mn; internet www.mse.com.mn; f. 1991; Dir DULAMSÜRENGIIN DORLIGSÜREN.

INSURANCE

Agricultural Insurance Co: Nairamdal District, Ulan Bator; f. 1992; insurance of farm stock, equipment and buildings.

Mongol Daatgal (National Insurance and Reinsurance Co): Ikh Toiruu 11, Ulan Bator 28; tel. 313641; fax 310347; e-mail daatgal@magicnet.mn; internet www.mol.mn/insurance; f. 1934; Chair. and CEO B. JARGALSAIKHAN; Gen. Man. U. BYAMBASÜREN.

Trade and Industry

GOVERNMENT AGENCIES

Labour Co-ordination Directorate: Khuvisgalchdyn Gudamj 14, Ulan Bator; tel. and fax 327906; Dir D. GANKHÜÜ.

Mineral Resources Authority; Government Bldg 5, Barilgachdyn Talbai 13, Ulan Bator 211238; tel. and fax 310370; e-mail mram@magicnet.mn; Dir D. JARGALSAIKHAN.

Mongol Gazryn Tos: Üildverchnii Gudamj, Ulan Bator 37; tel. 61584; e-mail petromon@magicnet.mn; supervises petroleum exploration and development; Dir O. DAVAASAMBUU.

State Industry and Trade Control Service: POB 38/66, Barilgachdyn Talbai, Ulan Bator 38; tel. and fax 328049; e-mail chalkhaa javd@mongolnet.mn; f. 2000; enforces laws and regulations relating to trade and industry, services, consumer rights, and geology and mining; Dir DAMBADARJAAGIIN CHALKHAAJAV.

State Property Committee: Government House 4, Ulan Bator 12; tel. 328790; fax 312798; internet zorigt@spc.gov.mn; supervision and privatization of state property; Chair. LKHANAASÜRENGIIN PÜREVDORJ.

State Resources Agency: Ulan Bator; management of reserves of agricultural produce; Dir JADAMBYN BYAMBANOROV.

DEVELOPMENT ORGANIZATIONS

Economics and Market Research Center: Government Bldg 11, J. Sambuugiin Gudamj 11, Ulan Bator 38; tel. 324258; fax 324620; e-mail emrc@mongolchamber.mm; internet www.mongolchamber .mn; Dir J. BOZKHUUHEN.

Foreign Investment and Foreign Trade Agency (FIFTA): Government Bldg 1, J. Sambuugiin Gudamj 11, Ulan Bator; tel. 326040; fax 324076; e-mail fifta@investnet.mn; internet www.investnet.mn; Chair. BAASANKHÜÜGIIN GANZORIG.

Mongolian Business Development Agency: Yörönkhii said Amaryn Gudamj, Ulan Bator; CPO Box 458, Ulan Bator 13; tel. 311094; fax 311092; e-mail mbda@mongol.net; internet www.mbda-mongolia .org; f. 1994; Gen. Man. D. BAYARBAT.

CHAMBERS OF COMMERCE

Central Asian Chamber of Commerce: PO Box 470, Ulan Bator 44; tel. 38970; fax 311757; Chair. G. TÖMÖRMÖNKH.

Junior Chamber of Commerce: Youth Union Bldg, Ulan Bator; tel. 328694; Chair NATSAGDORJ.

Mongolian National Chamber of Commerce and Industry: Sambuugiin gudamj 11, Ulan Bator 38; tel. 312501; fax 324620; e-mail chamber@mongolchamber.mn; internet www.mongolchamber .mn; f. 1960; responsible for establishing economic and trading relations, contacts between trade and industrial organizations, both at home and abroad, and for generating foreign trade; organizes commodity inspection, press information, and international exhbns and fairs at home and abroad; registration of trademarks and patents; issues certificates of origin and of quality; Chair. SAMBUUGIIN DEMBEREL.

INDUSTRIAL AND TRADE ASSOCIATIONS

Association of Private Herders' Co-operatives: POB 21/787, Ulan Bator 211121; tel. 633601; fax 325935; e-mail mongolherder@ magicnet.mn; f. 1991; Pres. R. ERDENE.

Mongolian Farmers and Flour Producers' Association: AgroPro Business Centre, 19th Khoroo, Bayangol District, Ulan Bator 24; tel. 300114; fax 362875; e-mail agropro@magicnet.mn; f. 1997; research and quality inspection services in domestic farming and flour industry; Pres. SHARAVYN GUNGAADORJ.

Mongolian Franchising Council of the Mongolian National Chamber of Commerce and Industry: Ulan Bator; tel. 327178; fax 324620; e-mail tecd@mongolchamber.mn; Pres. BAATARYN CHADRAA.

Mongolian Marketing Association: Ulan Bator; Pres. D. DAGVADORJ.

Mongolian National Mining Association: PO Box 46/994, Ulan Bator 210646; tel. 328898; fax 326849; Exec. Dir N. ALGAA.

Mongolian Printing Works Association: Ulan Bator; Pres. G. KHAVCHUUR.

Mongolian Wool and Cashmere Federation: Khan-Uul District, Ulan Bator; tel. 341871; fax 342814; Pres. G. YONDONSAMBUU.

EMPLOYERS' ORGANIZATIONS

Employers' and Owners' United Association: Ulan Bator; Exec. Dir. B. SEMBEEJAV.

Federation of Business Professional Women of Mongolia: Ulan Bator 20B; tel. and fax 315638; e-mail mbpw@mongolnet.mn; f. 1992; provides education, training, and opportunities for women to achieve economic independence, and the running of businesses; Pres. OCHIRBATYN ZAYAA; 7,000 mems, 14 brs.

Free Labour Managers' Association: Ulan Bator; Pres. N. PÜREVDORJ.

Immovable Property (Real Estate) Business Managers' Association: Ulan Bator; Pres. J. BYAMBADORJ.

Mongolian Management Association: Ulan Bator; Chair. Exec. Council DAGVADORJIIN TSERENDORJ.

Private Business Owners' Association: Ulan Bator; Pres. T. NYAMDORJ.

Private Employers' Association: Ulan Bator; Pres. O. NATSAGDORJ.

Private Industry Owners' Association: Ulan Bator; f. 1990 with 39 mems; Pres. LUVSANBALDANGIIN NYAMSAMBUU.

UTILITIES

Electricity

TsShSG: Ulan Bator; tel. 41294; supervision of electric power network in Ulan Bator; Dir D. BASSAIKHAN.

Water

DShSG: Ulan Bator; tel. 343047; supervision of hot water district heating network in Ulan Bator; Dir SHARAVYN BAASANJAV.

USAG: Khökh Tengeriin Gudamj 5, Ulan Bator 49; tel. 455055; fax 450120; e-mail usag@magicnet.mn; supervision of water supply network in Ulan Bator; Chair. OSORYN ERDENEBAATAR.

IMPORT AND EXPORT ORGANIZATIONS

Agrotekhimpeks: Ulan Bator 32; imports agricultural machinery and implements, seed, fertilizer, veterinary medicines and irrigation equipment.

Arisimpex: Ulan Bator 52; tel. 343007; fax 343008; exports hides and skins, fur and leather goods; imports machinery, chemicals and accessories for leather, fur and shoe industries; Pres. A. TSERENBALJID.

Avtoimpeks: Sonsgolon-2, Ulan Bator (POB 37, Ulan Bator 211137); tel. 331860; fax 331383; f. 1934; privatization pending 1999; imports of vehicles and spare parts, vehicle servicing; Exec. Dir TS. TOGTMOL.

Barter and Border: Khuvisgalchdyn Örgön Chölöö, Ulan Bator 11; tel. 324848; barter and border trade operations.

Böönii Khudaldaa: Songinokhairkhan District, Ulan Bator; wholesale trader; privately-owned; Dir-Gen. OCHBADRAKHYN BALJINNYAM.

Khorshoololimpeks: Tolgoit 37, Ulan Bator (PO Box 262); tel. 332926; fax 331128; f. 1964; exports sub-standard skins, hides, wool and furs, handicrafts and finished products; imports equipment and materials for housing, and for clothing and leather goods; Dir L. ÖLZIIBUYAN.

Kompleksimport: Enkh Taivny Gudamj 7, Ulan Bator; tel. and fax 382718; f. 1963; imports consumer goods, foodstuffs, sets of equipment and turnkey projects; training of Mongolians abroad; state-owned pending privatization in 1999; cap. 3,500m. tögrög.

Makhimpeks: 4th Khoroo, Songinokhairkhan District, Ulan Bator; tel. 63247; fax 632517; e-mail makhimpex@mongol.net; f. 1946; abattoir, meat processing, canning, meat imports and exports; 51% share privatized in 1999; cap. 7,800m. tögrög; Dir H. BATTULGA.

Materialimpex: Teeverchdiin Gudamj 35, Ulan Bator 35; tel. 365125; fax 367904; e-mail miehnco@magicnet.mn; f. 1957; exports cashmere, wool products, animal skins; imports glass, roofing material, dyes, sanitary ware, metals and metalware, wallpaper, bitumen, wall and floor tiles; privatized Feb. 1999 (most shares state-owned); Gen. Dir B. ZORIG; 126 employees.

Mongoleksport Co Ltd: Government Bldg 7, 8th Floor, Erkh Chölöönii Talbai, Ulan Bator 11; tel. 329234; fax 324848; exports wool, hair, cashmere, mining products, antler, skins and hides; Dir-Gen. D. CHIMEDDAMBAA.

Mongolemimpex: Ikh Toiruu 39, Ulan Bator 28; tel. 323961; fax 323877; e-mail moemim@magicnet.mn; procurement and distribution to hospitals and pharmacies of drugs and surgical appliances; Dir-Gen. R. BYAMBAA.

Mongolimpeks: Khuvisgalchdyn Örgön Chölöö, Ulan Bator 11; tel. 326081; exports cashmere, camels' wool, hair, fur, casings, powdered blood and horn, antler, wheat gluten, alcoholic drinks, cashmere and camels' wool knitwear, blankets, copper concentrate, souvenirs, stamps and coins; imports light and mining industry machinery, scientific instruments, chemicals, pharmaceuticals and consumer goods; state-owned; Dir-Gen. DORJPALAMYN DÖKHÖMBAYAR.

Mongol Safari Co: Ulan Bator 38; tel. 360267; fax 360067; e-mail monsafari@magicnet.mn; exports hunting products; imports hunting equipment and technology; organizes hunting and trekking tours; Dir-Gen. U. BUYANDELGER.

Monos Cosmetics: Sonsgolon Toiruu 5, Songinokhairkhan District 20, POB 62, Ulan Bator 211137; tel. 633257; fax 633117; e-mail monospharma@mongol.net; f. 1994; production, export and import of cosmetics.

Monospharma Co Ltd: Chingünjavyn gudamj 9, Bayangol District 2, Ulan Bator 210526; tel. and fax 361419; e-mail monospharma@ mongol.net; f. 1990; production, export and import of medicine and medical equipment; Dir-Gen. L. KHÜRELBAATAR.

MTT (Mongol Transport Team): POB 582, Ulan Bator 21; tel. 689000; fax 684953; e-mail mtteam@mtteam.mn; internet www.mtteam.mn; international freight forwarders by air, sea, rail and road; offices in Beijing, Berlin, Moscow and Prague.

NIK: Yörönkhii said Amaryn Gudamj, Ulan Bator 210620; POB B20 'A', Ulan Bator; tel. 321277; fax 327288; e-mail otgongerel@nic.com.mn; imports oil and oil products; Dir-Gen. P.TÜVSHINBAATAR.

Noosimpeks: Ulan Bator 52; tel. 342611; fax 343057; exports scoured sheep's wool, yarn, carpets, fabrics, blankets, mohair and felt boots; imports machinery and chemicals for wool industry.

Nüürs: Ulan Bator 21; tel. 327428; exports and imports in coal-mining field; Man. D. DÜGERJAV.

Packaging: Tolgoit, Ulan Bator; tel. 31053; exports raw materials of agricultural origin, sawn timber, consumer goods, unused spare parts and equipment, and non-ferrous scrap; imports machinery and materials for packaging industry, and consumer goods.

Raznoimpeks: 3rd Khoroo, Bayangol District, Ulan Bator 36; tel. 329465; fax 329901; f. 1933; exports wool, cashmere, hides, canned meat, powdered bone, alcoholic drinks, macaroni and confectionery; imports cotton and woollen fabrics, silk, knitwear, shoes, fresh and canned fruit, vegetables, tea, milk powder, acids, paints, safety equipment, protective clothing, printing and packaging paper; state-owned pending planned privatization of 51% share in 1999; cap. 6,100m. tögrög; Exec. Dir TS. BAT-ENKH.

Tekhnikimport: Ulan Bator; tel. 32336; imports machinery, instruments and spare parts for light, food, wood, building, power and mining industries, road-building and communications; state-owned; Dir-Gen. ERDENIIN GANBOLD.

Tushig Trade Co Ltd: Peace Ave, Ulan Bator 44, PO Box 481; tel. 314062; fax 314052; e-mail d.ganbaatar@mongol.net; exports sheep and camel wool, and cashmere goods; imports machinery for small enterprises, foodstuffs and consumer goods; Dir-Gen. D. GANBAATAR.

Tuushin Co Ltd: Yörönkhii said Amaryn Gudamj 2, Ulan Bator 210620; tel. 320064; fax 325909; e-mail tuushin@magicnet.mn; f. 1990; international freight forwarders; transport and forwarding policy and services, warehousing, customs agent; tourism; offices in Beijing, Moscow and Prague; Dir-Gen. N. ZORIGT.

CO-OPERATIVES

Central Association of Consumer Co-operatives: Ulan Bator 20; tel. and fax 329025; f. 1990; wholesale and retail trade; exports animal raw materials; imports foodstuffs and consumer goods; Chair. G. MYANGANBAYAR.

Individual Herdsmen's Co-operatives Association: Ulan Bator; Pres. R. ERDENE.

Mongolian Co-operatives Development Centre: Ulan Bator; Dir DANZANGIIN RADNAARAGCHAA.

Mongolian Producer Co-operatives Central Association: Ulan Bator; Pres. CHOGSOMJAVYN BURIAD.

Mongolian United Association of Savings and Credit Co-operatives: Ulan Bator; Pres. TSERENDORJIIN GANKHUYAG.

National Association of Mongolian Agricultural Co-operatives: Enkh Taivny Gudamj 11, Ulan Bator; tel. and fax 358671; Pres. N. NADMID.

Union of Mongolian Production and Services Co-operatives: POB 470, Ulan Bator 210646; tel. 328446; fax 329669; f. 1990; Pres. of Supreme Council (vacant).

MAJOR COMPANIES

Ajnay (Mongol Savkhi): Chingis Khaany Örgön Chölöö, Khan-Uul District, Ulan Bator 52; tel. 343237; fax 342356; leather processing and garment manufacture; Dir-Gen. S. HÜNIIHÜÜ.

Altai Holdings: CPOB 513, Ulan Bator; tel. and fax 358067; subsidiaries include Altai Petroleum, Altai Mining, Altai Trading and Altai Travel; Pres. S. BATBOLD.

Altan Taria: Songinokhairkhan District, Ulan Bator 211125; tel. and fax 632057; e-mail altantaria@magicnet.mn; flour milling and retailing; 51% owned by Mongolian-Czech Credit Co; Dir-Gen. P. TSENGÜÜN.

APU: Chingis Khaany Örgön Chölöö 14, Khan-Uul District, Ulan Bator; tel. 342434; fax 343063; e-mail apu@magicnet.mn; vodka, beer and non-alcoholic drinks; privatized in 2002; Dir SANDAGDORJIIN JAMYANSÜREN.

Baganuur: Baganuur town (130 km from Ulan Bator); Ulan Bator office tel. 457717; fax 457715; coal-mining co, main supplier of Ulan Bator's power stations; 75% state-owned; Dir D. DAMBAPELJEE

Bayangol Zochid Buudal: Chingis Khaany Örgön Chölöö, Ulan Bator; tel. 328869; fax 326880; 418-bed hotel and restaurants; CEO Ü. OTGONBAYAR.

Berkh-Uul: Berkh, Khentiy Province; fluorspar mining and concentrating; part of Mongolrostsvetmet jt enterprise; state-owned.

Betonarmatur: Chingis Khaany Örgön Chölöö, Khan-Uul District, Ulan Bator 52; tel. and fax 342622; ferro-concrete structures.

Biokombinat: Khan-Uul District, Ulan Bator 210131; tel. and fax 326642; medicines, drugs, veterinary medicines; state-owned; Dir LUVSANGIIN DORJSAMBUU.

Bodi International: Sükhbaataryn Talbai 3, 4th Floor, Ulan Bator; POB 11/20A, Ulan Bator; tel. 311971; fax 329057; financial services, trade, property, gold-mining; Pres. L. BOLDKHUYAG.

Bolovsrol: POB 982, Surguuliin Gudamj 8, Ulan Bator 210646; tel. and fax 320674; e-mail bolovsrol@magicnet.mn; f. 1990; educational and medical services, food and industrial goods production; Dir-Gen. S. BYAMBADORJ.

Bor-Öndör: Bor-Öndör, Khentii Province; fluorspar mining enterprise under Mongolrostsvetmet; Dir B. A. KUTMIN.

Buligaar: Ulan Bator; tanning, shoemaking; exporting shoes to India and China; Exec. Dir OCHIRBATYN RAGCHAA.

Buyan: Khan-Uul District, Ulan Bator; tel. 325413; fax 326755; cashmere and camel-wool processing and garment manufacture; Dir-Gen. B. JARGALSAIKHAN.

Chinggis Khan Hotel: Tokiogiin Gudamj, Ulan Bator 49 (CPO Box 513, Ulan Bator); tel. 458076; fax 458067; e-mail altaiholdings@magicnet.mn; 186 rooms and 400 beds; trade, conference and shopping centres and a casino.

Darkhan Nekhii: POB 901, Darkhan Nekhii JSC, Industrial Zone, Darkhan-Uul Province; tel. (137) 227025; fax (137) 223149; f. 1972; cap. US $3,055,891; sheepskin processing and garment manufacture; Exec. Dir. E. BATSAIKHAN, 300 employees.

Em Hangamj: Barilgachdyn Talbai, Ulan Bator; tel. and fax 324504; distribution of pharmaceuticals to Ulan Bator retail pharmacies.

Emiin Üildver: Ulan Bator; state-owned pharmaceuticals co; Dir O. DAMBA.

Erchim Khüchnii Zasvaryn Üildver: next to No. 4 Power Station, Bayangol District, Ulan Bator; tel. and fax 332626; production, repair and service of equipment and spares for electric power generation; state-owned; Dir CH. TÖMÖR.

Erdenet: Erdenet, Orkhon Province; tel. (35) 73505; fax (35) 23002; copper mining and concentrating; jt-stock co with Russia (24% owned by Russian State, 25% owned by Russian businesses), 51% state-owned by Mongolia; Jt Chair. of Board LKHANAASÜRENGIIN PÜREVDORJ (Mongolia) and A. S. LADYGO (Russia); Dir-Gen. KHALZHÜÜGIIN NARANHKÜÜ.

Erdenet Hivs: Nairamdal District, Erdenet; tel. (35) 20111; fax (35) 21617; wool spinner and woollen carpet manufacturer; Dir-Gen. J. DELGER-TSETSEG.

Erdes: Mardai, Dornod Province; uranium mining; former Soviet concession, transferred to Mongolia June 1999; state-owned pending planned establishment of a Mongolian-US-Canadian jt venture.

Erdmin: POB 631 Erdenet, Orkhon Province; tel. (35) 72176; Mongolian-US jt venture f. 1994 between Erdenet Concern (51%) and Armada Copper (49%) production since 1997 of pure (A grade) copper cathodes by chemical leaching of low-grade ore from Erdenet mine's waste dump; most sold to Marubeni Corpn; Dir-Gen. J. DAMDINJAV.

Erel Group: POB 88, Ulan Bator 51; tel. 341714; fax 341739; mining, geological research, construction, banking, financial services, investment; Dir-Gen. BADARCHIIN ERDENEBAT.

Gobi: Khan-Uul District, Ulan Bator 52; tel. 342713; fax 343081; e-mail gobimon@magicnet.mn; f. 1981; cashmere processing and knitwear production; cashmere and camel-wool processing, yarn, knitted and woven production; jt stock company; Dir-Gen. BADARCHIIN YONDONJAMTS.

Gurvan Saikhan: Khairkhan, Dundgobi Province; uranium mining; jt venture by Mongolia, USA and Russia; Exec. Dir ALEKSANDR V. RUDCHENKO; Mongolian Dir DASHIIN BAT-ERDENE.

Jagar International: CPO Box 9, Ulan Bator 13; tel. 322823; fax 313289; e-mail jagar@magicnet.mn; transport and storage of wholesale household goods, foodstuffs and cosmetics, production of soft drinks; leasing of retail premises; Dir J. ERDENETSOGT.

Khünstreyd: Songinokhairkhan District, Tolgoyt 37, Ulan Bator; tel. 631846; fax 631891; domestic and foreign food trader and wholesaler; state-owned; Dir-Gen. ÜRDEEGIIN TÖMÖRBAATAR.

Monel: Science and Culture Bldg, 8th Floor, Sükhbaataryn Talbai, Ulan Bator 11; tel. 327546; tel 79311; electronics manufacturer and trader; 40% state-owned.

Monenzym: Research and Production Association of Enzymology and Microbiology, Tolgoyt 25, Ulan Bator; tel. 32431; research, testing and production of enzymes and microbiological products.

Mongol-Amikal: Ulan Bator; joint venture (USA 55%, Mongolia 45%) producing cashmere, goathair and camelhair; annual capacity 450 metric tons; Exec. Dir RONNY LAMB.

Mongol Energy Service: PO Box 193, Ulan Bator 28; tel. 320468; fax 327146; e-mail mes@magicnet.mn; installation and maintenance of electricity generation equipment and district heating pipelines; Mongolian-Russian joint venture; Dir-Gen. B. SHATAR.

Mongolrostsvetmet: Jukovyn Gudamj, Bayanzürkh District, Ulan Bator 51; tel. 458072; fax 458380; e-mail mrtsvetmet@Mongol.net; fluorspar mining at Bor Öndör, Airag and Örgön, gold mining at Zaamar Placer; joint venture with Russia; Joint Chair. of Board L. PÜREVDJORJ (Mongolia) and A. S. LADYGO (Russia); Dir-Gen. KHOOKHORYN BADAMSÜREN.

Mongol Shuudan: CPO Box 1106, Ulan Bator 13; tel. 320137; fax 328413; e-mail shuudan@magicnet.mn; handling of letters, parcels, subscriptions to periodicals, book and newspaper retail sales, counter services, printing of postage stamps, rural transport services; Dir-Gen. JASRAYN JANTSAN.

Mongol Tamga: Sükhbaatar district, Ulan Bator; tel. 310667; fax 310571; official seals and stamps; state-owned; Dir Col SANGIDORJIIN SODNOMBALJIR.

Mongolyn Alt Corpn: POB 287, Ulan Bator 21; tel. 750199; fax 758075; e-mail mglgold@magicnet.mn; gold-mining, coal mining, agriculture, geology exploration; Pres. B. NYAMTAISHIR.

Mongolyn Nüürs: POB 147, Ulan Bator 13; tel. and fax 682570; association of Mongolian coal-mines; state-owned; Pres. DORJIIN DONDOV; Exec. Dir TOSHOONY SAMBASANCHIR.

Mongolyn Ünet Tsaasny Khevlekh Üildver (Mongolian Securities Printing Works): POB 613, Ulan Bator 13; tel. 327101; fax 328555; e-mail mnspc@magicnet.mn; jt venture with British company De La Rue; Exec. Dir CH. CHULUUNBAATAR.

Monmap: Sükhbaataryn Talbai 3, 4th Floor, Ulan Bator 46; tel. and fax 320728; e-mail monmap@magicnet.mn; surveying and remote sensing; Chair. M. SAANDAR.

Monnoos: Khan-Uul District, Ulan Bator; tel. 342591; fax 342592; wool-washing and spinning; Dir-Gen. NOROV.

Monsam: Ulan Bator; tel. 351069; fax 351068; f. 1995; jt venture with Samsung; surgical syringes and needles; Dr B. DOYODDORJ.

Monsan: Baga Toiruu 5, Chingeltei District, Ulan Bator; tel. 310775; fax 320810; electrical and plumbing installation; Dir M. BATBAATAR.

Naran Trade Co Ltd: POB 46/568, Ulan Bator 46; tel 322758; fax 320396; e-mail narantrade@mongol.net; f. 1990; retail and wholesale trade, media, real estate; Man. Dir SEREETERIIN BOLDKHET.

Petroleum Production Co: Orkhon Province; f. 2001 as Mongolia-Kyrgyzstan joint venture; oil refinery producing petrol, diesel and furnace oil from imported Russian gas condensate; annual capacity 50,000 metric tons.

Oyuuny Undraa: POB 867, Ulan Bator 46; tel. 325496; fax 325495; printing, sale and service of cars and aviation equipment; Dir-Gen. S. OTGONBAYAR.

Shijir Alt: Jukovyn Gudamj 18/6, Bayanzürkh District, POB 244, Ulan Bator 51; tel. 453521; f. 1995; gold mining in the Tuul river valley; CEO N. JANCHIV.

Spirt Bal Buram: Mandal District, Züünkharaa, Selenge Province; tel. Züünkharaa 397; producer of alcohol and treacle; Dir. L. ELDEV-OCHIR.

Süü: Üildverchnii Gudamj 13, Songinokhairkhan District, Ulan Bator; tel. 331950; fax 331901; milk and dairy produce; Dir T. BAYARKHÜÜ.

Talkh Chikher: Songinokhairkhan District, Ulan Bator 57; tel. 633383; fax 631580; bread, confectionery; state-owned; Exec. Dir D. PÜREVSÜREN.

TAS Group: POB 142, Ulan Bator 46; tel. 312223; fax 311753; mining, trade and retail services, tourism, light and food industry, banking and investment services; Pres. J. BATBAATAR.

Tsement: Darkhan; tel. (37) 4770; fax (37) 4570; output of Portland cement; Dir-Gen. I. DORJGOTOV.

Tsement Shokhoi: Khötöl, Selenge Province; producer of cement and lime; state-owned; Dir-Gen. R. SHIILEGJAMBAL.

Ulaanbaatar Barilga: POB 52, Ulan Bator; fax 342806; building materials, construction; Dir-Gen. B. JÜGDER.

Ulaanbaatar Khivs JSC: Khan-Uul District, Ulan Bator 36; tel. 342559; fax 343311; e-mail ubk@magicnet.mn; internet www.mongolia-carpet.com; woollen carpet manufacturer; Exec. Dir D. MUNKHJARGAL.

Ulaanbaatar Zochid Buudal: Baga Toiruu, Ulan Bator; tel. 320230; fax 324485; 280-bed hotel and restaurants; Exec. Dir. CH. OCHIRSÜKH.

Ulsyn Ikh Delgüür: Enkh Taivny Gudamj, Chingeltei District, Ulan Bator; tel. 325720; fax 320792; department store retailing household goods, foodstuffs, clothing, etc; state-owned.

XL-TA Holding: POB 981 Ulan Bator 13; fax 310133; f. 1990; investment, tourism, banking, trade, security services; Pres. BATDELGERIIN BATBOLD.

TRADE UNIONS

Confederation of Mongolian Trade Unions: Sükhbaataryn Talbai 3, Ulan Bator 11; tel. 327253; fax 322128; brs throughout the country; Chair. GORCHINSÜRENGIIN ADYAA; International Relations Adviser TS. NATSAGDORJ; 450,000 mems (1994).

'Khökh Mongol' (Blue Mongolia) Free Trade Unions: Ulan Bator; f. 1991 by Mongolian Democratic Union; Leader SH. TÖMÖRBAATAR.

United Association of Free Trade Unions: f. 1990; Pres. SH. DORJPAGMA.

Transport

RAILWAYS

In 1999 the Mongolian Railway had a total track length of 1,815 km. In 1990 it carried 2.6m. passengers and 14.5m. tons of freight (about 70% of total freight traffic). However, traffic by rail later declined, owing to fuel shortages; in 1991 rail freight carriage was 10.3m. tons, falling to 8.6m. tons in 1992. In 2001 the railway carried 4.5m. passengers, and 10.1m. tons of freight (about 86% of total freight traffic) was transported by rail.

Ulan Bator Railway: POB 376, Ulan Bator 13; tel. 944401; fax 328360; e-mail slc-mr@magicnet.mn; internet www.mtz.mn; joint-stock co with Russian Federation; Dir RADNAABAZARYN RAASH; First Dep. Dir N. BATMÖNKH.

External Lines: from the Russian frontier at Naushki/Sükhbaatar (connecting with the Trans-Siberian Railway) to Ulan Bator and on to the Chinese frontier at Zamyn-Üüd/Erenhot, connecting with Beijing (total length 1,110 km).

Branches: from Darkhan to Sharyn Gol coalfield (length 63 km); branch from Salkhit near Darkhan, westwards to Erdenet (Erdenetiin-ovoo open-cast copper mine) in Bulgan Province (164 km); from Bagakhangai to Baganuur coal-mine, south-east of Ulan Bator (96 km); from Khar Airag to Bor-Öndör fluorspar mines (60 km); from Sainshand to Züünbayan oilfield (63 km).

Eastern Railway, linking Mongolia with the Trans-Siberian and Chita via Borzya; from the Russian frontier at Solovyevsk to Choibalsan (238 km), with branch from Chingis Dalan to Mardai uranium mine near Dashbalbar (110 km).

IFFC (International Freight-forwarding Centre): 2/F Ulan Bator Railway Building, Ulan Bator, CPO Box 376; tel. 312509; fax 313165; e-mail iffc@magicnet.mn; international freight forwarding.

Mongoltrans: Khan-Uul District, Ulan Bator; POB 373, Ulan Bator 211121; tel. 312281; fax 320185; e-mail montrans@magicnet.mn; internet www.magicnet.mn/montrans; rail freight forwarding; offices in Beijing and Moscow; Dir-Gen. B. MYAGMAR.

ROADS

Main roads link Ulan Bator with the Chinese frontier at Zamyn üüd/Erenhot and with the Russian frontier at Altanbulag/Kyakhta. A road from Chita in Russia crosses the frontier in the east at Mangut/Onon (Ölzii) and branches for Choibalsan and Öndörkhaan. In the west and north-west, roads from Biisk and Irkutsk in Russia go to Tsagaannuur, Bayan-Ölgii aimag, and Khankh, on Lake Khövsgöl, respectively. The total length of 'improved' roads was 3,453.5 km in 2000, and the total length of asphalted roads was 1,567.4 km. The first section of a hard-surfaced road between Ulan Bator and Bayankhongor was completed in 1975. The road from Darkhan to Erdenet was also to be surfaced. Mongolia divides its road system into state-grade and country-grade roads. State-grade roads run from Ulan Bator to provincial centres and from provincial centres to the border. There are 11,200 km of state-grade roads, of which 10% are hard-surfaced and a further 13% gravel-surfaced. Country-grade roads (also 13% gravel-surfaced) account for the remaining 38,000 km, but they are mostly rough cross-country tracks.

To mark the millennium, the Government decided to construct a new east–west road, linking the Chinese and Russian border regions via Ölgii, Lake Khar Us, Zavkhan and Arkhangai provinces, Dashinchilen, Lün, Ulan Bator, Nailakh, Baganuur, and Öndörkhaan and Sümber. Construction was expected to take about 10 years, but because of the cost, the road was not expected to be surfaced for the whole length.

According to a vehicle census reported in December 2000, Mongolia had 81,693 motor vehicles, including 24,671 goods vehicles,

1,683 tankers, 2,740 specialized vehicles (such as ambulances and fire engines), 8,548 buses and trolleybuses, and 44,051 cars. Of these vehicles, 57,814 were privately-owned.

There are bus services in Ulan Bator and other large towns, and road haulage services throughout the country on the basis of motor transport depots, mostly situated in provincial centres. However, in some years services have been truncated, owing to fuel shortages.

INLAND WATERWAYS

Water transport plies Lake Khövsgöl and the River Selenge (397 km navigable) in the northern part of the country. Tugs and barges on Lake Khövsgöl transport goods brought in by road to Khankh from Russia to Khatgal on the southern shore.

CIVIL AVIATION

Civil aviation in Mongolia, including the provision of air traffic control and airport management, is the responsibility of the Civil Aviation Directorate of the Ministry of Infrastructure Development. It supervises the Mongolian national airline (MIAT) and smaller operators such as Khangarid and Tengeriin Ulaach, which operate local flights. There are scheduled services to Ulan Bator (Buyant-Ukhaa) by Aeroflot (Russia) and Air China.

Director-General of Civil Aviation: MANJIIN DAGVA.

Khangarid: Room 210, MPRP Bldg, Baga Toiruu 37/1, Ulan Bator; tel. 379935; fax 379973; domestic and international passenger and freight services; Dir L. SERGELEN.

Mongolian Civil Air Transport (MIAT): Buyant-Ukhaa, Ulan Bator; tel. 379935; fax 379919; internet www.miat.com; f. 1956; scheduled services to Moscow, Irkutsk, Beijing, Seoul, Osaka, Berlin, Höhhot, and to some Mongolian provincial centres; in 2000 MIAT carried some 250,000 passengers and 3,000 tons of freight, and operated 10 aircraft on scheduled services; Dir LUTYN SANDAG.

Tengeriin Ulaach Shine: Buyant-Ukhaa 34-17, Khan-Uul District, Ulan Bator; tel. 983043; fax 379765; internal transport for tourists and businesspeople; Dir L. TÖMÖR.

Tourism

A foreign tourist service bureau was established in 1954, but tourism is not very developed. There are 12 hotels for foreign tourists in Ulan Bator, with some 1,500 beds, and the outlying tourist centres (Terelj, South Gobi, Öndör-Dov and Khujirt) have basic facilities. The country's main attractions are its scenery, wildlife and historical relics. There were 192,051 foreign visitors to Mongolia in 2001. Tourist receipts totalled US $28m. in 1999.

Juulchin Tourism Corporation of Mongolia: Chingis Khaan Avenue 5B, Ulan Bator 210543; tel. 328428; fax 320246; e-mail juulchin@Mongol.net; internet www.mongoljuulchin.mn; f. 1954; offices in Berlin, New Jersey, Beijing, Tokyo, Osaka and Seoul; Exec. Dir S. NERGÜI; Chair. B. DELGERSÜREN.

National Centre for Tourism: Ulan Bator; supervises 57 camps in the main tourist areas; Dir D. KHALIUN.

National Travel and Tourism Agency: Ministry of Infrastructure, Ulan Bator; Dir GANKHUYAGIIN SHIILEGDAMBA.

Defence

Under the 1992 Constitution, the President of Mongolia is *ex officio* Commander-in-Chief of the Armed Forces. The defence roles of the President, the Mongolian Great Khural, the Government and local administrations are defined by the Mongolian Law on Defence (November 1993). Mongolia's Military Doctrine, a summary of which was issued by the Great Khural in July 1994, defines the armed forces as comprising general purpose troops, air defence troops, construction troops and civil defence troops. The border troops and internal troops, which are not part of the armed forces, are responsible for protection of the borders and of especially important installations, respectively. The general purpose troops comprise rear services, communications, artillery, etc. The Ministry of Defence has departments in charge of personnel, foreign relations and contracts, etc. In August 2001, according to Western estimates, the army totalled 9,100, including the air defence of 800. There was also a paramilitary force of 7,200, comprising 6,000 border guards and 1,200 internal troops, as well as 300 construction troops and 500 civil defence troops. (The internal troops are under the command of the Chief of Police.) Military service is for 12 months (for males aged 18–28 years). Transport aircraft and helicopters for support of the ground forces have been authorized to carry civilian passengers, thus blurring the distinction between military and civil air transport operations.

Defence Expenditure: Estimated at 25,286.1m. tögrög for 2001 (5.9% of total government expenditure under revised budget, and 2.1% of GDP).

Chief of Staff of the Mongolian Armed Forces: Maj.-Gen. TSEVEGSÜRENGIIN TOGOO.

Education

Ten-year general education is compulsory. In the 2000/01 school year there were 703 general education schools with a total teaching staff of 19,200 and 494,500 pupils. Many of these schools provide instruction in two shifts. Vocational schools (36), which had 12,177 pupils in 2000/01, train personnel for the service industries, and vehicle drivers and machine operators for industry and agriculture. There were 40 private schools with 2,000 pupils.

In 2000/01, 56,906 students (excluding those studying abroad) were enrolled at institutes of higher education. The Mongolian National University comprises four faculties (mathematics, natural sciences, physics and social sciences), four institutes (biology, economics, law and Mongol studies) and the School of Foreign Service (diplomatic training). In 2000/2001 there were five other universities (medicine, agriculture, art, technology and defence) as well as 38 state-owned and 134 private higher schools and colleges. About 28,064 students attended the private higher schools and colleges. Many Mongolian students continue their academic careers at universities and technical schools in Russia and Germany.

Bibliography

GENERAL AND ECONOMY

Allen, Benedict. *Edge of Blue Heaven—A Journey through Mongolia*. London, BBC Books, 1998.

Asian Development Bank. *Mongolia: A Centrally Planned Economy in Transition*. Manila, 1992.

Badarch, Dendevin, and Zilinskas, Raymond A. *Mongolia Today—Science, Culture, Environment and Development*. London, RoutledgeCurzon, 2002.

Batbayar, Bat-Erdene (trans Ed. Kaplonski, C.). *Twentieth Century Mongolia*. Cambridge, White Horse Press, 1999.

Batbayar, Tsedendambyn (Ed.). *Renovation of Mongolia on the Eve of the XXI Century and Future Development Patterns*. Ulan Bator, Mongolian Development Research Centre, 2000.

Bawden, Charles. *Mongolian–English Dictionary*. London, Kegan Paul International, 1997.

Becker, Jasper. *The Lost Country: Mongolia Revealed*. London and Sydney, Hodder and Stoughton, 1992.

Bruun, Ole, and Odgaard, Ole (Eds). *Mongolia in Transition: Old Patterns, New Challenges*. Richmond, Curzon Press, 1996.

Bulag, Uradyn E. *Nationalism and Hybridity in Mongolia*. Oxford, Clarendon Press, 1998.

Butler, William E. *The Mongolian Legal System*. The Hague, Martinns Nijhoff, 1982.

Damdinsuren, H. (Ed.) *Ulaanbaatar Capital of Mongolia*. Ulan Bator, Mongolian Business Press and Information Bureau and Montsame News Agency, 2000.

Doing Business in Mongolia: A Guide for European Companies: Ulan Bator, Mongolian Business Development Agency and European Union Tacis Programme for Mongolia, 1996.

Enkhtuvshin, A. (Ed.) *Reference Book on Mongolian Investment (National Almanac 98–99)*. Ulan Bator, Board of Foreign Investment and Hamag Mongol National Advertising Agency, 1999.

Ganbold, D. (Ed.). *Facts about Mongolia*. Ulan Bator, Admon, 2000.

Goldstein, Melvyn C., and Beall, Cynthia M. *The Changing World of Mongolia's Nomads*. Hong Kong, The Guidebook Company, 1994.

Griffin, Keith (Ed.). *Poverty and the Transition to a Market Economy in Mongolia*. Basingstoke, Macmillan Press, 1995.

Hansen, Henny Harald. *Mongol Costumes*. London, Thames and Hudson, 1993.

Humphrey, Caroline, and Onon, Urgunge. *Shamans and Elders*. Oxford, Clarendon Press, 1996.

Jagchid, S., and Hyer, P. *Mongolia's Culture and Society*. Folkestone, Wm Dawson and Sons Ltd, 1979.

Kotkin, Stephen, and Elleman, Bruce A. (Eds). *Mongolia in the Twentieth Century: Landlocked Cosmopolitan*. London, M. E. Sharpe, 1999.

Krouchkin, Yuri. *Mongolia Encyclopedia*. Ulan Bator, Edmon Publishing House, 1998. (A business-orientated collection of laws and regulations.)

Kullman, Rita, and Tserenpil, D. *Mongolian Grammar*. Hong Kong, Jensco Ltd, 1996.

Lawless, Jill. *Wild East: Travels in the New Mongolia*. Toronto, ECW Press, 2000.

Man, John. *Gobi: Tracking the Desert*. London, Weidenfeld and Nicolson, 1997.

Mayhew, Bradley. *Mongolia: Discover a Land without Fences*. Hawthorn, Vic, Lonely Planet, 2001.

Mongolian Business Directory. Ulan Bator, Mongolian Chamber of Commerce and Industry, 1994.

Mongolian Economy and Society in 1996. Ulan Bator, State Statistical Office, 1997.

Mongolian National Security and Defense Policy Handbook. USA, International Business Publications, 2002.

Mongolian Statistical Yearbook 2000. Ulan Bator, State Statistical Office, 2001.

MPR Academy of Sciences. *Information Mongolia*. Oxford, Pergamon, 1990.

Myagmarsuren, D. (Ed.). *Special Protected Areas of Mongolia*. Ulan Bator, Environmental Protection Agency, 2000.

Nixson, Frederick, Walters, Bernard, Suvd, B., and Luvsandorj, P. *The Mongolian Economy*. Cheltenham, Edward Elgar, 2000.

Nordby, Judith. *Mongolia*. World Bibliographical Series Vol. 156, Oxford, Clio Press, 1993.

Pegg, Carole. *Mongolian Music, Dance, and Oral Narrative*. Seattle and London, University of Washington Press, 2001.

Sanders, A. J. K. *Mongolia: Politics, Economics and Society*. London, Frances Pinter, 1987.

Historical Dictionary of Mongolia. Lanham, MD, and London, Scarecrow Press, 2002 (2nd edition).

Sanders, A. J. K., and Bat-Ireedüy, J. *Colloquial Mongolian*. London, Routledge, 2002 (reprint).

Sermier, Claire. *Mongolia: Empire of the Steppes*. Hong Kong, Odyssey/Airphoto International, 2002.

Severin, Tim. *In Search of Genghis Khan*. London and Sydney, Hutchinson, 1992.

Stewart, Stanley. *In the Empire of Genghis Khan—A Journey among Nomads*. London, HarperCollins, 2000.

Thevenet, Jacqueline. *Les Mongols de Genghis Khan et d'aujourd'hui*. Paris, Armand Colin, 1986.

Traders' Manual for Asia and the Pacific: Mongolia. New York, UN Economic and Social Commission for Asia and the Pacific, 1995.

Worden, Robert L., and Savada, Andrea Matles (Eds). *Mongolia: A Country Study*. Washington, DC, Library of Congress, 1991, 2nd edn.

HISTORY

Akiner, Shirin (Ed.). *Mongolia Today*. London, Kegan Paul International, 1992.

Allsen, Thomas T. *Mongol Imperialism*. University of California, 1987.

Barkmann, Udo. *Geschichte der Mongolei* (History of Mongolia). Bonn, Bouvier, 1999.

Bat-Ochir, Bold. *Mongolian Nomadic Society—A Reconstruction of the 'Medieval' History of Mongolia*. Richmond, Curzon Press, 1999.

Bawden, C. R. *The Modern History of Mongolia*. (2nd edn, with afterword by A. J. K. Sanders). London, Kegan Paul International, 1989.

Biran, Michal. *Qaidu and the Rise of the Independent Mongolian State in Central Asia*. Richmond, Surrey, Curzon Press, 1997.

Brown, W. A., and Onon, U. *History of the Mongolian People's Republic*. Cambridge, MA, Harvard University Press, 1976. English trans., with extensive footnotes, of Vol. III of Mongolia's official history.

Colvin, John. *Nomonhan*. London, Quartet Books, 1999.

Dashpurev, D., and Soni, S. K. *Reign of Terror in Mongolia 1920–1990*. New Delhi, South Asian Publishers, 1992.

Dashpurev, D., and Prasad, Usha. *Mongolia: Revolution and Independence 1911–1992*. New Delhi, Subhash and Associate, 1993.

de Rachewiltz, I. *Papal Envoys to the Great Khans*. London, Faber and Faber, 1971.

Ewing, E. E. *Between the Hammer and the Anvil? Chinese and Russian Policies in Outer Mongolia 1911–21*. Bloomington, IN, Indiana University, 1980.

Heissig, W. *A Lost Civilisation*. London, Thames and Hudson, 1964.

Lattimore, Owen. *Nationalism and Revolution in Mongolia*. Leiden, E. J. Brill, 1955. English trans. of the official life of the revolutionary leader, Sühbaatar, with introduction.

Nomads and Commissars. London, Oxford University Press, 1962.

Studies in Frontier History, Collected Papers 1929–58. London, Oxford University Press, 1962.

Marshall, Robert. *Storm from the East*. London, BBC Books, 1993.

Morgan, D. *The Mongols*. Oxford, Blackwell, 1986.

Murphy, G. G. S. *Soviet Mongolia*. University of California, 1966.

Musée National des Arts Asiatiques. *Trésors de Mongolie XVIIe-XIXe siècles*. Paris, Guimet, 1993.

Onon, Urgunge. *The Secret History of the Mongols—The Life and Times of Chinggis Khan*. London, RoutledgeCurzon, 2001.

Onon, Urgunge (Trans.). *Mongolian Heroes of the 20th Century*. New York, AMS Press, 1976.

Onon, Urgunge, and Pritchatt, D. *Asia's First Modern Revolution*. Leiden, E. J. Brill, 1989.

Ratchnevsky, Paul (trans. Thomas Haining). *Genghis Khan: His Life and Legacy*. Oxford, Blackwell, 1991.

Rupen, R. A. *Mongols of the Twentieth Century, Vol. 1 (History), Vol. 2* (Bibliography). The Hague, Indiana University and Mouton and Co, 1964.

Sabloff, Paula (Ed.). *Modern Mongolia: Reclaiming Genghis Khan*. Philadelphia, University of Pennsylvania Museum of Archaeology and Anthropology, 2001.

Sandag, Shagdariin, and Kendall, Harry H. *Poisoned Arrows: The Stalin-Choibalsan Mongolian Massacres 1921–1941*. Oxford, Westview Press, 2000.

Saunders, J. J. *The History of the Mongol Conquests*. London, Routledge and Kegan Paul, 1971.

The Mongolia Society Inc, of Indiana University, Bloomington, IN, publishes historical and contemporary studies (see Part Three, Regional Information—Research Institutes, USA).

MYANMAR

(BURMA)

Physical and Social Geography

HARVEY DEMAINE

The Union of Myanmar (until 1989 the Socialist Republic of the Union of Burma), which covers a total area of 676,552 sq km (261,218 sq miles), lies to the east of India and Bangladesh and to the south-west of the People's Republic of China, and has a long coastline facing the Bay of Bengal and the Andaman Sea. Much the greater part of its territory, lying between latitudes 28° 50′ and 16° N, forms a compact unit surrounded on three sides by a great horseshoe of mountains and focusing on the triple river system of the Ayeyarwady, Chindwinn and Sittoung (or Irrawaddy, Chindwin and Sittang, respectively). In addition, Tanintharyi (Tenasserim), consisting of a narrow coastal zone backed by steep mountains, extends south from the Gulf of Martaban to Victoria Point, only 10° N of the Equator.

PHYSICAL FEATURES

Structurally, the topography of Myanmar falls into three well-marked divisions, of which the first comprises the mid-Tertiary fold mountains of the west. These ranges, swinging in a great arc from the Hukwang valley to Cape Negrais, appear to represent a southward continuation of the eastern Himalayan series. From north to south these western ranges are known successively as the Patkai, Naga, and Chin Hills, and the Arakan Yoma, though hills is a misleading description of ranges with summits exceeding 3,650 m in the case of the Patkai and reaching 1,800 m–2,400 m in the case of the Chin and Naga Hills. Further south, in the Arakan Yoma, the summit levels gradually decrease to 900 m–1,500 m.

The second major structural unit consists of the eastern mountain ranges, of Mesozoic or earlier origin, which, beginning as a continuation of the Yunnan plateau of China across the Myanma border into the north-eastern corner of Kachin State, extend thence through the Shan and Kayinni (or Karenni) plateaux into more subdued but still rugged upland, which forms the divide between Tanintharyi and peninsular Thailand. In the far north, where this system adjoins the western mountain system, the general plateau level is of the order of 1,800 m, with higher ridges frequently attaining 3,000 m. The corresponding altitudes in the Shan area, however, are only about one-half as great, though here also the surface is dissected, with the main rivers, notably the great Thanlwin (Salween), rushing southwards in deeply incised gorges.

Between the two main mountain systems lies the third major structural unit, namely the vast longitudinal trough of central Myanmar, containing the great alluvial lowlands which form the cultural and economic heart of the country. Throughout the length of these lowlands the Ayeyarwady provides the central artery, both of drainage and of communication. To the north it is paralleled by its largest tributary, the Chindwinn, which joins it near the centre of the Dry Zone, and further south by the Sittoung, which flows separately to the sea on the opposite side of the recent volcanic uplands of the Pegu Yoma. Central Myanmar is a zone of crustal instability; a severe earthquake in July 1975 caused extensive damage. Altogether, the Ayeyarwady drains a total area of some 400,000 sq km, and its huge delta potentially provides one of the greatest 'rice bowls' of the world.

CLIMATE

Apart from the highest uplands in the far north of the country, the climate of practically the whole of Myanmar may be classified as tropical monsoonal, although important regional variations nevertheless occur within that overall category. In all parts of the country the main rains come during the period of the south-west monsoon, i.e. between May and October, and those areas, notably Rakhine (or Arakan) and Tanintharyi, which face the prevailing winds and are backed by steep and high ranges, receive some of the heaviest rainfall in the world (Sittwe, or Akyab, 5,180 mm annually; Kyaikkami, or Amherst, 4,980 mm). Moreover, even the flat and low-lying Ayeyarwady delta receives an annual rainfall of about 2,500 mm, and in all of these three areas mean annual temperatures are around 27°C, though the seasonal range varies from 6.5°C in Sittwe to 3.5°C in Kyaikkami.

A considerable portion of the interior of the central lowland constitutes a rain-shadow area relative to the south-west monsoon, and here the total annual precipitation is less than 1,000 mm. In some places it is even below 640 mm. Although in this Dry Zone the seasonal incidence is similar to that of other areas, the spectacular difference in total amount is reflected in a major change of vegetation, from the heavy tropical monsoon forest prevailing elsewhere, to a much more open cover and, in places, a mere thorny scrub. Moreover, the relative aridity is also responsible for a wider range of temperature, as is shown by Mandalay's 21°C in January and 32°C in April, immediately before the onset of the rains. Finally, in the eastern plateaux, rainfall is above that of the Dry Zone, but much less than along the western coastal margins, and this fact, combined with temperatures some 6°–8°C below those of the torrid plains, gives the Shan plateau the most equable climate of any part of the country.

NATURAL RESOURCES

Myanmar's natural resources are closely related to the salient features of its physical geography. Thus, the greatest wealth of the humid mountain slopes lies in timber, particularly teak, and while the young folded mountains of the west are not noted for mineral wealth, the older plateaux of the east have long been noted for a variety of metallic minerals, including the silver, lead and zinc of Bawdwin and the tungsten of Mawchi. Further south, Tanintharyi forms a minor part of the South-East Asian tin zone, though its resources in this respect are very small compared with those of Malaysia and Thailand. More important than any of these metals, or the sub-bituminous coal deposits at Kalewa, near the Chindwinn/Myittha confluence, are the petroleum and natural gas deposits which occur in the Tertiary structures underlying the middle Ayeyarwady lowlands. Prospects for the petroleum industry, which remained small by world standards, were much improved by the early 1990s, owing to foreign participation in onshore exploration, and to expectations of future foreign participation in offshore exploration.

It is in agricultural resources that Myanmar is potentially most richly endowed, and the Ayeyarwady delta should eventually fulfil its potential as a 'rice bowl' under the stimulus of higher prices, higher-yielding varieties and improved water control. The Dry Zone is also well suited for the production of oil-seeds and cotton, especially under irrigation, and in Tanintharyi conditions are appropriate, though not ideal, for the cultivation of rubber and fruit crops.

POPULATION AND ETHNIC GROUPS

At mid-2001, according to UN estimates, Myanmar's population had reached 48,360,000: a density of only 71.5 per sq km. The greatest concentration of population occurs in the delta. In the lowlands, including Rakhine and Tanintharyi, the Bamar (Burmans) form the majority element in the population. The uplands are more sparsely inhabited by a series of minority groups at varying levels of development. The Bamar, whose ancestors came from the Sino-Tibetan borders and supplanted all but a fraction of the earlier Mon population of lowland Burma, formed some 68% of the total population of Myanmar in 1992. A further 7% were Shan, the ethnic kinsfolk of the Thai and Lao, who follow the Theravada form of Buddhism, like the Bamar and the Mon (2.3%), while the Arakanese constituted a further 3.8% of the population.

Of the non-Buddhist indigenous groups, who are often referred to collectively as hill peoples, the Kayin (Karen) are the most numerous (6% of the total population in 1992). Their homeland occupies the uplands between the Shan plateau and Tanintharyi, but many have migrated into the lowlands around Mawlamyine (Moulmein) and to the Ayeyarwady delta, and considerable numbers have discarded animism and adopted Christianity. Other upland peoples include the Kachin (2.3%), Chin (2.3%), Wa-Palaung, Lolo-Muhso and Naga, who are still mostly animists.

Myanmar has remained below the South-East Asian average in respect of urbanization, with Yangon (Rangoon), the capital, having a population of 2,513,023 at the census of 31 March 1983, and only seven other towns exceeding 100,000 inhabitants. By mid-2001, according to UN estimates, the population of Yangon had increased to 4,504,000.

History

ROBERT CRIBB

Based on an earlier article by JOSEF SILVERSTEIN

EARLY HISTORY

Modern Myanmar falls into three distinct geo-political zones: the valley of the Ayeyarwady (Irrawaddy), the hill country that surrounds the valley, and the coastal areas of Rakhine (Arakan) and Tanintharyi (Tenasserim). The long, fertile valley of the Ayeyarwady, which is navigable for 1,400 km from Bhamo to the sea, has witnessed a succession of powerful kingdoms based on both agriculture and trade; only for brief periods, however, were those kingdoms able to unite the entire valley in a single polity. The earliest kingdoms were founded by the Mon, ethnically close to today's Cambodians, and the Pyus. However, from about the 10th century a Tibeto-Burmese people, the Burmans (now Bamars), entered the valley and eventually conquered the Mon and Pyus, absorbing many elements of those earlier cultures in the process. The hill country, which surrounds the valley in a broad horseshoe of territory, is inhabited by smaller ethnic groups—the Shan (who are closely related to the Thai), the Karen (now Kayin), the Kachin, the Chin and the Naga—which sometimes briefly established kingdoms extending into the valley, but which were more often subject or tributary to the kingdoms of the Mon and Burmans. The third zone, which comprises the coastal strips of Rakhine and Tanintharyi, has remained relatively isolated from the country's heartland and has a long history of maritime engagement with the outside world.

The first large Burman kingdom, Pagan, was founded in the 11th century and it was in the context of this kingdom that Theravada Buddhism was established as the religion of the Burmans. Pagan was destroyed by a Mongol invasion in 1287. Its successor kingdom, Ava, was weakened by fighting with the Mon and the Shan. In the mid-16th century the Toungoo dynasty created an empire which extended briefly from Rakhine in the west to Laos in the east. However, spread over too wide an area, the Toungoo empire was unable to defeat counter-attacks from Rakhine and Siam, and subsequently collapsed at the end of the 16th century. Only in the late 18th century did a new dynasty, the Konbaung, unite the country and resume Burma's expansion. In doing so, however, it came into conflict with British power in India, and in three wars between 1824 and 1885 Burma lost first Rakhine and Tanintharyi, then the lower reaches of the Ayeyarwady, and finally the north of the country. The British abolished the Burman monarchy and annexed Burma to British India, inheriting at the same time the Konbaung dynasty's contested claims to the hill regions. The Kachin region in the far north was not fully subdued until 1915, and the British also faced continuing resistance in the countryside of the Ayeyarwady valley.

BRITISH AND JAPANESE RULE

British rule (which lasted from 1896 to 1948) transformed Burma socially, economically, and administratively. The power of the court was removed and that of the aristocracy greatly diminished, while village headmen were included in a new centralized administrative system, leaving the Buddhist monastic establishment (*sangha*) as the country's most powerful indigenous institution and a centre of hostility to foreign rule. Indians began to migrate to Burma in large numbers, as traders and labourers, to the extent that the capital, Rangoon (now Yangon), became a predominantly Indian city. The establishment of Rangoon University in 1920 made Western learning accessible to a new generation of Burmese and with the growth of exports of rice, oil, teak, tin, rubies and cotton, Burma became more integrated than ever before in the global economy. This integration led to serious hardship in Burma during the Depression, and discontent was expressed in the Saya San uprising of 1930–31.

As part of British India, Burma was included in the gradual development of democratic institutions. In 1923 the British introduced a partly-elected Legislative Council and, under the system known as 'dyarchy', devolved political power in several fields to ministers responsible to the Council. In 1937 the administration of Burma was separated from that of India and Burmese cabinet ministers responsible to an elected parliament took over all areas of government except defence, foreign relations and monetary policy. The influence of Burman parliamentarians, however, was circumscribed by the existence of separate, more generously represented electorates for several minorities (Karen, Indians, Anglo-Indians, Chinese and Europeans), so that the four successive Governments that served in office between 1937 and 1942 were all coalitions between Burman and minority representatives. These constitutional arrangements, however, excluded most of the hill regions, which remained under direct British rule.

The modern Burmese nationalist movement that arose in the context of these developments was strongly dominated by ethnic Burmans. The Young Men's Buddhist Association (YMBA), founded in 1906, campaigned initially on religious issues, but subsequently developed into the General Council of Buddhist Associations (GCBA), which pursued a more political agenda. In contrast, the Thakin (master) movement, founded by members of the young intelligentsia in Rangoon in 1930, emphasized a more secular Burmese nationalism which incorporated Marxist elements but which drew strongly on the Burman language, culture and traditions. This movement provided the new generation of leaders who guided the nation through the war and into independence. Throughout the 1930s, while the British tried to lead Burma towards full self-government, the nationalist movement sought the country's independence. Believing that only armed force could overthrow the British, 30 Thakins, including Aung San, went to Japan in 1940 and returned in 1942 with invading Japanese forces and a small but symbolic Burma Independence Army (BIA).

The Japanese advanced rapidly, driving the British out of most of Burma by mid-1942; however, they were unable to press more than a few kilometres beyond Burma's borders into India. The Japanese ruled Burma with a combination of conciliation and repression. In August 1943, for example, they granted 'puppet' independence to a state headed by the pre-war Burman leader, Dr Ba Maw, and also expanded the BIA into the Burma National Army (BNA). However, they demanded labour and materials for the war effort and were brutal in their repression of the growing resistance movement, especially amongst the Karen and other hill peoples. In August 1943 the Japanese transferred part of the Shan region to Thailand. In late 1944, with Japan in retreat on its Indian front, Aung San and leaders of the growing Communist movement founded the Anti-Fascist People's Freedom League (AFPFL), turning the BNA against the Japanese in March 1945 and launching a revolt which hastened the Allied victory in Burma.

The British announced in May 1945 that they were willing to grant Burma independence within the British Commonwealth. Following the end of Allied military administration in October, however, this promise was suspended in favour of a period of economic reconstruction. Concerned that such a delay would allow British economic domination to continue, Aung San and other nationalist leaders led a campaign of unrest which forced the British to appoint AFPFL members to the governor's Executive Council and to call elections in April 1947 for a constituent assembly to draft a new constitution. The AFPFL won 171 of the 182 seats contested, and the assembly drafted a constitution, which gave Burma full independence outside the Commonwealth. In July 1947 Aung San and six other members of the Executive Council were assassinated; however, the governor appointed Thakin Nu (later U Nu) as Aung San's successor and allowed the movement towards independence to continue. Burma thus became independent on 4 January 1948.

CONSTITUTIONAL GOVERNMENT, 1948–62

At independence in 1948, the governing party was the socialist AFPFL. Throughout independence negotiations, the United Kingdom had preferred to deal with the non-communist wing of the AFPFL. As a consequence, the communist wing, with strong popular support both in the Ayeyarwady delta and amongst former members of the BIA, perceived itself to be excluded from power in the new Government. In March 1948, after Government incursions against them, the communist element went into revolt, taking significant sections of the army and the militia with it. In 1949 the situation became more complicated when the Karen also launched a revolt. The independent Union of Burma was an unequally balanced federation: alongside the Burman heartland, it included the hill regions as states with varying degrees of autonomy. The Shan and Kayah states had the formal right to secede from the Union; the Kachin and Karen states had autonomy but no right to secede; the Chin Special Division had only limited autonomy, while a separate status for Arakan was only foreshadowed. The army was also constructed federally, with each unit drawn primarily from one or other of the ethnic groups. From the outset, however, the Government in Rangoon tended to concentrate power in its own hands, and the Karen, who were generally well-educated and who had prospered on the whole under British rule, grew increasingly discontented. In time, revolts were to break out amongst almost all the country's minorities. Also, during 1949, the eastern Shan region was occupied by Chinese Nationalist armies in retreat after the victory of the Chinese Communist Party.

For several months the central government controlled only Rangoon and a few other centres. Burma's formal unity survived partly because the rebels fought amongst themselves, partly because they had no significant external support, and partly because U Nu's Government responded vigorously to the crisis. U Nu reformed the army, placing Gen. Ne Win in charge. Ne Win subsequently centralized and enlarged the military, eliminating the ethnic units and placing Burman officers in most command positions. He also operated ruthlessly against the rebels, developing for the army a reputation for brutality against civilian opponents. Meanwhile, U Nu campaigned energetically in the country's heartland, winning support as a charismatic proponent of state Buddhism. By 1951 the Government was once again in control of the Burman heartland and was well-established in parts of the hill country, although perhaps 10% of the country remained outside its control.

The AFPFL won national elections in 1951–52 and 1956, with an overwhelming but decreasing share of the vote, and in 1958 the party split into 'Clean' and 'Stable' rival factions. To avert renewed civil war, U Nu invited Gen. Ne Win to form a 'caretaker' government to prepare the country for new elections which were to be held in 1960. The 18-month interlude of military rule was generally welcomed as a period of law and order, economic growth and the implementation of serious measures against corruption. Although the U Nu-led 'Clean' faction of the AFPFL, renamed the Union Party, won the elections, U Nu soon alienated minorities by declaring Buddhism as the state religion, which provoked a revolt in the Shan and Kachin regions and exacerbated discontent amongst the Mon and Karen. With corruption and administrative mismanagement plaguing the country once more, the armed forces under Gen. Ne Win carried out a *coup d'état* on 2 March 1962, arresting members of the Government, suspending the Constitution and appointing a Revolutionary Council (RC) to govern Burma by decree.

MILITARY RULE, 1962–74

Following the *coup d'état*, Gen. Ne Win quickly rescinded U Nu's declaration of Buddhism as the state religion; in other respects, however, his regime paid little attention to public opinion. The democratic institutions of the 1950s were dismantled and power was concentrated in the hands of the RC, which comprised a small group of senior officers led by Gen. Ne Win. In form and theory, Burma remained a federal state; however, for all practical purposes the new leadership treated the country as a unitary state. At the local level, authority was placed under the control of new Security and Administration Committees (SACs), headed by local military commanders. For the next decade, however, the Ne Win Government continued to fight ethnic and communist insurgents in almost all the hill country outside the Burman heartland. In 1969–71 U Nu tried unsuccessfully to create a coalition of rebel forces under his leadership; his lack of popularity among the ethnic minorities, however, rendered this impossible. A more serious threat to the Government came from the Communist Party of Burma (CPB), which received substantial support from the People's Republic of China, especially during the latter's Cultural Revolution. From 1970, however, relations between Burma and China improved, and Chinese support for the CPB was reduced. Ne Win's long-term political aim was to reshape Burma into a Socialist one-party state, and to this end he created the Burma Socialist Programme Party (BSPP, also known as Lanzin, from its Burmese name) in June 1962. The party adopted as its doctrine a manifesto issued two months earlier by the RC entitled *The Burmese Way to Socialism*, which took a Marxist approach to capitalism, but which incorporated doctrinal elements from Theravada Buddhism, in particular the concept of impermanence. At the same time, the Government sought to prevent the Buddhist *sangha* (order of monks) from becoming a focus of political opposition, and in 1965 an attempt was made by the Government to require all Buddhist monks to register and to carry identity cards. The manifesto adopted by the BSPP also included the notion that human greed needs to be kept under control by state intervention. The BSPP refrained from becoming involved in international conflicts, emphasizing the need for Burma to follow its own path and keeping the country remarkably isolated from the outside world. In 1966, in order to ensure that these ideas were widely disseminated throughout society, the RC launched a thorough reform of the education system, bringing schools (including monastic schools) under the closer control of the Ministry of Education and adding an ideological element to the curriculum. Ne Win's Government also sought to 'Burmanize' the economy, nationalizing land, the banking sector, oil wells, foreign trade, the insurance sector, shipping, wholesale trade, cinemas, and much of the publishing, mining and saw-milling industries in the years between 1963 and 1971. In so doing, they displaced the European, Indian and Chinese business interests which had previously dominated these sectors and caused an exodus of technical and managerial personnel. The economy gradually began to show signs of stagnation, including the emergence of a 'black market'. Formerly a major exporter of rice, Burma ceased to produce rice surpluses. Meanwhile, the reputation of the regime was not helped by growing indications of corruption and the abuse of power by members of the RC itself. The competence of the administration was further diminished by the exclusion of civilians from the Government: whereas Gen. Ne Win had made considerable use of highly qualified civilians in his administration during the 'caretaker' Government of 1958–60, the Government that held office from 1962 to 1974 was thoroughly dominated by a small group of senior military officers. In those 12 years, only three civilians achieved ministerial rank, while the Council of Ministers—Burma's Cabinet—was reshuffled only twice.

In its early stages, the BSPP was a cadre party with a small membership: when the party held its first Congress in 1971 it had only 73,369 members, more than half of whom were drawn from the military. At the party's inaugural Congress Gen. Ne Win was formally elected as leader. The party identified its mission as twofold: to transform itself from a cadre party into a mass party in order to replace centralism with democratic centralism; and to transform the nation into a socialist democratic state under a new constitution. In July 1971 the military leaders announced their intention to draft a new constitution and to transfer power to a civilian government. A recruitment campaign for the party subsequently began in 1972, and within a decade its membership had expanded to 1.5m. Meanwhile, in April 1972, to accord with the move toward constitutionalism, Gen. Ne Win and 20 of his senior commanders retired from the army and became civilian members of the Government. The RC began to prepare the way for its own dissolution, proclaiming the end of the revolutionary Government and its replacement by the Government of the Union of Burma. Gen. Ne Win became Prime Minister, heading a Cabinet of nine retired officers, three serving officers and two civilians. This 'civilianization' of Gen. Ne Win's rule was completed in early 1974, in which year elections were held, the new Constitution came into effect and the RC was dissolved. Ne Win was elected Chairman of the Council of State and thus became President under the new Constitution. Eleven of the 29 members of the Council of Ministers were carried over from the now-defunct RC.

BSPP RULE, 1974–88

Civilian rule was not merely intended to make military dominance appear more acceptable. Ne Win hoped that the one-party state would provide a format for engaging the public in government and national development without, however, permitting the political turmoil and drift which had blighted the parliamentary system. In January 1978 and October 1981, therefore, the Government held national elections, although only BSPP candidates were permitted to stand. The BSPP Government also presented itself as the protector of Burmese national identity in 1982, by formalizing a citizenship law, which created three categories of citizen—national, associated and naturalized. Resident Indians and Chinese were consigned to the latter categories, under which they had restricted rights in politics and the economy and were not permitted to join the armed forces. The Government also reversed the RC's previous antagonism towards the Buddhist *sangha*: rather than confronting organized Buddhism, the regime provided it with financial and administrative support, establishing a Ministry of Religious Affairs and acknowledging the importance of Buddhist tradition to the history and culture of the nation. In May 1980 the regime sponsored a nation-wide congregation for the purification, propagation and perpetuation of Buddhism. At this convention, representatives created a centralized authority to control the *sangha* throughout the nation and finally approved the introduction of identification cards for monks and nuns. In 1981 the religious courts, which had been inactive for years, were revived. Two sects were brought before them and charged with teaching heretical doctrines. After an extended trial, both sects were found guilty and ordered to be dissolved. Monks belonging to the two orders were to recant publicly or cease to be monks. These measures seemed to eliminate the potential of the *sangha* to serve as a base for opposition, and gave the Government the confidence to declare an extensive amnesty for U Nu and his followers, who were permitted to return to the country. Thousands of political prisoners were also released.

In December 1974, less than one year after the new civilian Government had been installed, riots broke out in Rangoon and other centres over food shortages, corruption and generally declining economic conditions. (The immediate catalyst for the riots had, however, been the perceived lack of proper honour accorded by the Government to the funeral of U Thant, a former Secretary-General of the UN and a friend of U Nu.) Students in Rangoon were particularly angry at declining standards and conditions at the universities, and further demonstrations broke out in March 1976. The BSPP responded initially by modifying its socialist programme, approving the idea of foreign aid and investment. The complaints about official corruption were met by new regulations requiring leaders at all levels to disclose their assets, so that corruption amongst those in power could be more easily detected. These signs of independent initiative on the part of the BSPP appear to have alarmed Ne Win, who launched a series of purges of the party. In October 1976 some 50,000 party members were expelled, the party's structure was reformed and more than half the Central Committee resigned, followed by several members of the national Cabinet, including the Prime Minister, U Sein Win. Further purges took place in September 1977 and February 1978, leaving the upper ranks of the BSPP and much of the Cabinet under the control of serving or retired military officers. In 1977 the Pyithu Hluttaw (People's Assembly) adopted a Private Enterprises Law, which firmly rejected the economic liberalization proposed by the BSPP. The law prohibited private foreign investment in Burma, and only grudgingly permitted local private investment in sectors not yet taken over by the State or the co-operatives. In 1981 Ne Win, who had by that time taken the honorific title U, announced that he would retire as President of the Socialist Republic of the Union of Burma (as the country had been redesignated), while continuing to lead the party. Formal procedures for Ne Win's succession were put in place, and San Yu took over formally as President, although U Ne Win in fact continued to control Burmese politics from behind the scenes.

The return to socialism under a remilitarized BSPP led to continuing economic decline in Burma. Unfavourable weather, mismanagement in agricultural production and distribution, and growing inflation caused increasing hardship throughout the country. In August 1987 U Ne Win finally admitted publicly to 'failures and faults' in his Government's past management of the economy and announced major reforms. The Government freed the purchase, sale, transport and storage of basic food items from state control, hoping that farmers would increase production to meet local market demands. In early 1988 the Government also terminated its 25-year monopoly on rice exports. These measures were popular, but they were followed by a regulation demonetizing the 25, 35 and 75 kyat currency notes, intended to strike at the wealth of black marketeers. This action, which effectively confiscated money from the public, was deeply resented, and student protests broke out in Rangoon and elsewhere. In March 1988 the police responded with violence to the demonstrations, beating several students to death and allowing others to suffocate in police vans. At least 50 people were killed, leading to mass public demonstrations against the regime. The Government closed the universities, and briefly quelled the dissent by promising to investigate the students' grievances. By mid-1988, however, public impatience with the Government had returned and the demonstrations resumed. In June security forces brutally suppressed a demonstration by about 5,000 students and others demanding the release of persons detained in March. The Government responded by imposing a curfew and closing universities and schools indefinitely. The regional cities of Tanggyi, Pegu and Prome were also placed under curfew as unrest spread throughout the country. In an atmosphere of crisis, U Ne Win called an extraordinary meeting of the BSPP in July, at which he and San Yu resigned from their posts. Sein Lwin, a close military associate of U Ne Win and a known advocate of harsh repressive measures, took over as both BSPP Chairman and State President. Although U Ne Win warned in his resignation speech that the army would shoot to kill if the demonstrations continued, the public sensed that the regime had been placed on the defensive, and preparations began for massive strikes and demonstrations to begin on the supposedly auspicious date, 8 August 1988 (8-8-88), at 8.08 a.m. The protests proceeded peacefully until late in the evening of that day, when security forces responded with violence to the demonstrations. During the following five days, some 2,000 to 3,000 demonstrators are believed to have been killed as the reform movement was violently suppressed. On 13 August, however, with unrest continuing, Sein Lwin resigned and was replaced by the more moderate Dr Maung Maung, hitherto the Attorney-General. Maung Maung ended martial law, released political prisoners and offered political reforms, which implied that the BSPP was willing to surrender power to the opposition in a peaceful transition. An emergency meeting of the BSPP held in September 1988 agreed to hold free elections within three months and decided that members of the armed forces, police and civil service could no longer be affiliated to a political party. New political groups—including the All Burma Students Union (ABSU) and the National United Front for Democracy, later renamed the National League for Democracy (NLD)—were permitted to form in preparation for the election. The NLD quickly emerged as the main opposition group, its leaders including Brig.-Gen. Aung Gyi (formerly an associate of U Ne Win, but subsequently an outspoken critic of the regime, who was briefly detained under Sein Lwin), Gen. U Tin Oo (a former chief of staff and Minister of Defence) and Aung San Suu Kyi, daughter of the assassinated nationalist leader Aung San, whose portraits had been particularly prominent during the demonstrations of 8 August. Even though she had been out of the country since 1960, Aung San Suu Kyi increasingly came to represent the peaceful, prosperous country which people imagined Burma might have become but for her father's death. Amid general expectations that the NLD would resoundingly win the coming elections, and with Buddhist monks already taking over municipal administrations in many parts of the country, the military under Gen. Saw Maung launched a coup on 18 September 1988, ostensibly to maintain public order in the approach to the elections. Saw Maung, however, immediately created a new ruling body, the State Law and Order Restoration Council (SLORC), comprising 19 senior military officers, with himself as Chairman. All state organs, including the Pyithu Hluttaw, the State Council and the Council of Ministers, were abolished, demonstrations were banned and a nation-wide dusk to dawn curfew was imposed. In the first days after the military coup, more than 1,000 demonstrators were killed by security forces, and thousands of students and others then fled to areas along the border with Thailand, where they sought the protection and help of ethnic insurgents.

THE SLORC, 1988–97

The SLORC announced the formation of a nine-member Government, with Saw Maung as Minister of Defence and of Foreign Affairs and subsequently also Prime Minister. It was widely believed, however, that U Ne Win, although in retirement, retained a controlling influence over the new leaders, all of whom, including Saw Maung, were known to be his supporters. The new Government changed the official name of the country to the Union of Burma (as it had been before 1974). The law maintaining the BSPP as the sole party was abrogated, and new parties were encouraged to register for the forthcoming elections. By February 1989 a total of 233 parties had registered. Most were small and based on ethnicity, religion or location. Beyond registering, the new parties had little influence; under the Government's martial law regulations, group gatherings were limited to five persons, a curfew existed, and there were restrictions on travel, publication and public meetings. The BSPP was re-established under a new name, the National Unity Party (NUP), with U Tha Kyaw, the former Minister of Transport, as Chairman. Although the NLD registered, it was uncertain whether it would contest elections, which, it asserted, could not be held fairly under military rule. In December 1988, owing to disagreements with Aung San Suu Kyi, Aung Gyi was expelled from the NLD and founded the Union National Democracy Party (UNDP). In May 1989 the Government ratified electoral legislation, which had been promulgated in March. It provided for the holding of multi-party elections in May 1990, and permitted campaigning only in the three months prior to the election date. Stringent campaign regulations were imposed by the SLORC, including restrictions on public rallies and official censorship of speeches. In June 1989 the SLORC reiterated that martial law was still in force, and that it would retain power after the elections until the resulting legislative assembly drafted a new constitution and formed a civilian government. In the same month 3,000 people demonstrated on the anniversary of the student protests of 1988. Troops fired on the crowd and one person was killed.

On 18 June 1989 the name of the country was changed to the Union of Myanmar (Myanma Naing-ngan). The SLORC explained that the change had been made to avoid the racial connotation of the previous name, Union of Burma, which implied that the population were all Burmans, while, in fact, it included many racial groups. The Roman transliteration of many towns, divisions, states, rivers and nationalities was changed (although the pronunciation remained the same in Burmese). Thus, Rangoon was changed to Yangon, Pegu to Bago and the Irrawaddy River became the Ayeyarwady. The race known as the Burmans was renamed the Bamars, and the Karen and Karenni were restyled Kayin and Kayinni, respectively.

Tension between the SLORC and the opposition groups increased in July 1989. In an attempt to crush political dissent, the SLORC established five military tribunals (and a further six in August) to try persons violating martial law regulations (e.g. by failing to observe the curfew or participating in gatherings of more than five people). The tribunals could impose penalties ranging from three years' imprisonment to death. On 19 July, the anniversary of the 1947 assassination of her father, Aung San Suu Kyi planned to lead a protest march through the capital with members of more than 100 of the country's political parties. Suu Kyi cancelled the rally, however, fearing that troops deployed by the Government would fire on the marchers, as they had done in September 1988. The next day she and Tin Oo (the Chairman of the NLD) were placed under house arrest. They were accused of attempting to create disunity within the army and 'nurturing public hatred for the military'. In December 1989 Tin Oo was tried and sentenced to three years' imprisonment, with hard labour. Former Prime Minister U Nu was placed under house arrest for refusal to disband a parallel government which he had proclaimed during the uprising in 1988. Other leaders, especially amongst the student parties, were either arrested or went 'underground'. When the NLD sought to nominate Suu Kyi as an election candidate, an opposition candidate challenged the nomination and the committee responsible for certifying candidates upheld the challenge on the grounds of her marriage to a British citizen. In March 1990 reports began to circulate abroad that the armed forces were forcibly moving people out of certain areas in Yangon, Mandalay and elsewhere to distant new living quarters. Since most of the people moved were believed to be supporters of the NLD, this was seen as an effort by the army to weaken support for the opposition in the cities.

The 1990 Election and its Aftermath

Despite SLORC efforts to weaken opposition leaders and eliminate dissidents, 93 parties presented a total of 2,297 candidates to contest the 492 constituencies. In every constituency there were at least two candidates. Prior to the election, it was widely believed that the armed forces favoured certain parties, particularly the NUP but also Aung Gyi's UNDP. No single party was expected to win a clear majority. Two days before the election, the SLORC unexpectedly issued visas to 61 foreign journalists to observe and report on proceedings. The voting, which took place on 27 May 1990, was orderly, quiet and free. The NLD won an overwhelming victory, taking 392 of the 485 seats that were, in the event, contested, while the NUP won only 10. The remainder of the seats were allocated to 23 other parties. Parties representing ethnic groups achieved considerable success: the Shan Nationalities League for Democracy (SNLD) won 23 seats, and the Arakan (Rakhine) League for Democracy 11. Following the election, nearly all the parties representing non-Bamar nationalities formed a coalition known as the United Nationalities League for Democracy (UNLD), including 65 elected representatives. The total representation in the assembly of anti-SLORC forces—the NLD, the UNLD, the Party for National Democracy (PND, led by Dr Sein Win, a cousin of Suu Kyi; which had secured three seats) plus one other elected deputy—was thus 461 of 485 seats, or some 95%.

Following the NLD's electoral victory, its leaders demanded immediate talks with the SLORC, and movement towards popular rule. However, the SLORC announced that the election was intended only to produce a constituent assembly, which was to draft a constitution under the direction of a national convention to be established by the SLORC. In July 1990 the SLORC issued Order 1/90, which stated: that the SLORC had international legitimacy because it was recognized by the UN and individual countries; that it was incumbent on the SLORC to prevent the disintegration of the Union and of national solidarity and to ensure the perpetuity of state sovereignty; and that the SLORC would continue as the *de facto* Government until a new constitution was accepted by all the races of Myanmar. The elected membership of the NLD responded (independently of their leadership) with the 'Gandhi Hall Declaration'. This proclaimed that the NLD was ready to hold discussions with the SLORC and to convene the national assembly, according to the electoral law; that the national assembly was the highest authority in the State and not simply a constituent assembly; that the NLD had drafted a provisional Constitution by which it could govern and that this provisional Constitution would bring about the transfer of power in accordance with the law, pending the drafting of a new Constitution; finally, it demanded the immediate restoration of democratic rights.

In early August 1990 at an anti-Government protest in Mandalay, commemorating the deaths of thousands of demonstrators at the hands of the armed forces in 1988, troops killed four protesters. This led to a decision by various Buddhist orders to withhold their services from members of the military. Later in the same month the NLD, with the support of other parties, announced plans to convene a national assembly in September. In early September, however, the SLORC arrested six members of the NLD, including its acting leader, Kyi Maung, and its acting General Secretary, Chit Hlaing, on charges of passing state secrets to unauthorized persons. Both were tried in the special tribunals and given 10-year prison sentences. Also in September, NLD representatives discussed plans to declare a provisional government in Mandalay, without the support of the party's central executive committee. Influential monks agreed to support the declaration which was to take place in October. However, the plan was abandoned after government troops surrounded the monasteries; the SLORC subsequently banned all but nine Buddhist sects and empowered military commanders to impose death sentences on rebellious monks. More than 50 senior members of the NLD were arrested, and in late October and early November members of all political parties were required to endorse Order 1/90. In acquiescing, the NLD effectively nullified its demand for an immediate transfer of power.

Leaders of other parties were also arrested, disappeared or went 'underground' to avoid arrest. Reports of political prisoners being tortured and dying while in detention circulated widely. In the face of the steady repression and threats to the elected members of the national assembly, many of those in the NLD, not under arrest, assembled secretly in Mandalay in November 1990 and agreed to send some of their members to the border to create a provisional government. In early December eight opposition politicians arrived at Manerplaw, the Kayin (Karen) headquarters, and entered into discussions with the Democratic Alliance of Burma (DAB—a 21-member organization uniting ethnic rebel forces with student dissidents and monks). They subsequently agreed to form the National Coalition Government of the Union of Burma (NCGUB). The aims of the NCGUB were: to wage war against the military rulers; to convene a national conference of all elected leaders, representatives of the DAB, democratic forces and other notable individuals; to draft a new federal constitution; and to form a true democratic government. On 18 December the NCGUB was constituted with Sein Win, the leader of the PND, as its President. The remainder of his cabinet consisted of six elected NLD representatives and one independent. Other elected members of the national assembly made their way to Manerplaw and gave their support to this rival government. The SLORC quickly denounced the NCGUB and compelled the NLD to do likewise.

Members of the NCGUB agreed to form a Supreme Council of Burma Democratic Forces, known as the Burma Front, in partnership with the minority party leaders. It was to be the policy-making body during the interim period. It consisted of six Bamars and five minority members under the leadership of Gen. Bo Mya, then leader of the Karen (Kayin) National Union (KNU). In February 1991 the NCGUB sent a small delegation to Switzerland to address the UN Commission on Human Rights during its consideration of the issue of human rights violations in Myanmar. Later, the delegation visited other European countries to discuss conditions inside Myanmar and possible measures to bring about change. Although the NCGUB did not receive any official recognition by foreign states, it received funds from non-governmental organizations in Canada, Switzerland and Norway.

In April 1991, following intense pressure from the army, the NLD central executive committee was restructured. Suu Kyi and Tin Oo, both still under house arrest, were deprived of their former posts of General Secretary and Chairman. Suu Kyi was replaced by U Lwin, a little-known political figure, and Tin Oo by the former Acting Chairman, U Aung Shwe. In the same month Lt-Gen. (later Senior Gen.) Than Shwe, the Vice-Chairman of the SLORC and the Deputy Commander-in-Chief of the Armed Forces, officially ruled out a transfer of power to those elected in May 1990, condemning the political parties that had taken part in the elections as subversive. In May 1991 34 opposition politicians (25 of them elected representatives) were sentenced to prison terms of up to 25 years, for alleged treason and attempting to establish an alternative government. Suu Kyi, who was under increasing pressure from the army to leave the country, was systematically attacked in the state-controlled press. At the end of May a military tribunal extended the sentences of Kyi Maung and Chit Hlaing to 20 years' imprisonment.

In October 1991 Aung San Suu Kyi was awarded the Nobel Peace Prize. The award ceremony, which took place in Oslo, Norway, in December, was attended by the leader of the NCGUB, Sein Win. In Myanmar students staged the first demonstrations since 1989 to coincide with the ceremony. The students were dispersed, and universities and colleges, which had reopened in May 1991, were closed. The now-compliant NLD leadership expelled Suu Kyi from the party.

On 23 April 1992 the SLORC announced the resignation of its Chairman, Saw Maung, on the grounds of ill health (Saw Maung later died in July 1997), and his replacement by Than Shwe (who had already replaced Saw Maung as Minister of Defence in March 1992). On the following day Than Shwe was named as Prime Minister, although Maj.-Gen. (later Lt-Gen.) Khin Nyunt, the First Secretary of the SLORC and the head of the intelligence service, was still widely regarded as the most powerful member of the SLORC, owing to U Ne Win's patronage. The SLORC permitted Suu Kyi to receive visits from her husband and sons. The SLORC also announced that political prisoners who were no longer a threat to the regime would be released. By mid-May about 100 prisoners had been released, including U Nu and numerous NLD representatives. Shortly thereafter, the SLORC announced that it would convene a co-ordinating meeting for a national convention (the first meeting between representatives of political parties, ethnic groups and members of the SLORC) to develop the principles for a new constitution and to determine who would participate in drawing up the future basic law. In June the co-ordinating meeting convened with 43 delegates, comprising 15 representatives from the SLORC, 15 from the NLD, six from the SNLD, three from the NUP, four from separate ethnic minority parties and one independent.

In August 1992 universities and colleges were reopened, and in September the night curfew, imposed four years previously, was repealed. In the same month a reorganization of the Cabinet included the appointment of two Deputy Prime Ministers and the promotion to ministerial posts of six regional commanders of the armed forces who were known to oppose Khin Nyunt. These appointments, which ended the first overt power struggle under the SLORC, strengthened Khin Nyunt's position by effectively depriving the commanders of their regional power. Following the government reshuffle, the SLORC revoked two martial law decrees, which had been in force for three years, although the ban on gatherings of more than five people remained in place. In late September further political prisoners were granted amnesties, bringing the total released to 534. It was estimated, however, that a further 1,600 prisoners remained in detention.

The National Convention

In January 1993 the National Convention finally assembled. From the outset the Convention was under the firm control of the SLORC: of the initial 702 delegates, only 93 were NLD members (elected as legislators in 1990), while some 80% of all delegates were appointed by the SLORC. The first session was swiftly adjourned, owing to the objections of the opposition members to the SLORC's demand that the armed forces be allocated a leading role in government under the new Constitution. When the National Convention reconvened at the beginning of February, the NLD issued a statement opposing military dominance and proposing a national referendum on whether it should be incorporated in the new Constitution. The Convention was again adjourned. The SLORC reacted to opposition intransigence by suspending its conciliatory gestures; many arrests were reported during January and February. Following several meetings and adjournments of the Convention between March and September, the Chairman of the National Convention's Convening Committee, U Aung Toe (the Chief Justice), subsequently announced (seemingly without grounds) that consensus existed in favour of the SLORC's demands, which included: the representation, in both the lower and upper chambers of a proposed parliament, of military personnel (to be appointed by the Commander-in-Chief of the Defence Services); the independent self-administration of the armed forces; and the right of the Commander-in-Chief to exercise state power in an emergency (effectively granting legitimate status to a future coup).

In September 1993 an alternative mass movement to the NUP (which had lost credibility through its election defeat) was formed to establish a civilian front through which the armed forces could exercise control. The Union Solidarity and Development Association (USDA), whose aims were indistinguishable from those of the SLORC, was not officially registered as a political party, thus enabling civil servants to join the organization, with the incentive of considerable privileges.

In January 1994 the National Convention's discussions on the draft Constitution resumed. In that month large numbers of people were coerced into joining USDA rallies to demonstrate support for the constitutional proposals presented by the SLORC. In February a delegation led by a member of the US Congress was granted permission to visit Suu Kyi (the first time that she had received visitors, other than family members, during the period of her detention). Suu Kyi sent an encouraging message to the democracy movement and appealed for a meeting with the SLORC, expressing her willingness to negotiate on all issues except her exile. On the following day the SLORC announced that Suu Kyi would be detained until at least 1995 (despite the legal maximum of five years under house arrest, whereby Suu Kyi would be released in July 1994), since her first year in detention had only been an 'arrest period'.

The National Convention adjourned in April 1994, having determined three significant chapters of the future Constitution. According to these, Myanmar was to be renamed the Republic of the Union of Myanmar (Pyidaungsu Thammada Myanmar Naingandaw). The Republic's territorial organization was to preserve the existing seven *taing* or divisions in central and southern Myanmar (Yangon, Bago, Ayeyarwady, Tanintharyi, Magway, Sagaing and Mandalay), inhabited mainly by Bamars, and seven *pyinay* or states, associated with minority ethnic groups (Rakhine, Chin, Kachin, Shan, Kayinni, Kayin and Mon). The Republic would be headed by an executive president, elected by the legislature for five years; a number of conditions, including one disqualifying any candidate with a foreign spouse or children, were clearly designed to prevent Suu Kyi from entering any future presidential election (her husband and children were British citizens).

The Convention, which reconvened in early September 1994, again stressed that the central role of the military (as 'permanent representatives of the people') be enshrined in the new Constitution. Proposals by six smaller ethnic minority groups—Naga, Wa, Pa-O, Danu, Kokang and Palaung—for their own self-administered 'national zones' were considered favourably, although comparable demands by several other minority groups were rejected. The establishment of the six 'national zones' was agreed in April 1995, by which time agreement had also been reached on key chapters of the Constitution, covering the legislature, judiciary and Government, at Union, state and regional level. It was determined that legislative power be shared between a bicameral Pyidaungsu Hluttaw (Union Assembly) and regional and state hluttaws, all of which were to include representatives of the military. The Pyidaungsu Hluttaw was to comprise the Pyithu Hluttaw (People's Assembly) and the Amyotha Hluttaw (Assembly of Nationalities). The former would comprise 330 elected deputies and 110 members of the Tatmadaw (armed forces) and would be elected for five years. The latter would comprise 224 members: 12 elected from each of the 14 divisions and states, as well as 56 members of the Tatmadaw.

In late November 1995 the National Convention reconvened. Under instructions from their party, all 86 NLD delegates boycotted this session and were expelled after two days, leaving only a few small elected parties, mainly representing minorities, among the 545 delegates present. The proportion of delegates representing elected parties had declined from over 20% at the start of the Convention to less than 10%; the rest were various categories of SLORC appointees. In late March 1996 30 delegates from five of these remaining parties, the largest of which was the SNLD, protested publicly about the proposed military appointments to the People's Assembly. Not surprisingly, the protest had no effect. The 104 'basic principles' remained in place, and more of the 15 draft chapters continued to be produced. When the NLD representatives who had been expelled in late 1995 asked to rejoin the convention in 1997, their requests were rejected. However, observers representing various ethnic groups who had signed truces with the SLORC were permitted to join. The Convention was described in *The Nation*, a major Bangkok newspaper, as 'the world's slowest-operating rubber-stamp body', but in fact it ceased to operate at all after going into recess in 1996, though official statements commonly implied that it would reassemble one day.

The Opening of Dialogue with Aung San Suu Kyi

In July 1994 Khin Nyunt announced what appeared to be a major change of policy: that the SLORC was prepared to hold talks with Suu Kyi. In the same month the Minister of Foreign Affairs, U Ohn Gyaw, attending a meeting of the Association of South East Asian Nations (ASEAN) in Bangkok, stated that his Government would accept the invitation of the UN Secretary-General, Dr Boutros Boutros-Ghali, to discuss issues of democratization, national reconciliation and human rights in Myanmar. Following mediation by a senior Buddhist monk between Suu Kyi and leading members of the SLORC, in mid-September Suu Kyi was permitted to leave her house for the first time during her five-year detention to meet Than Shwe and Khin Nyunt. Parts of the meeting were broadcast on state television, although no specific details of the talks were actually reported. In late October Suu Kyi was invited to a second meeting with senior members of the SLORC, and in November she was permitted to meet Tin Oo and Kyi Maung, who were still imprisoned. In the same month, however, a delegation led by the US Deputy Assistant Secretary of State for East Asian and Pacific Affairs was not permitted to visit Suu Kyi. In February 1995 the fourth round of talks was held in Yangon between leading members of the SLORC and UN Assistant Secretary-General Alvaro de Soto on the range of issues agreed in mid-1994. However, de Soto was prevented from visiting Suu Kyi. Nevertheless, in March 1995 the Government released 31 political prisoners, including Tin Oo and Kyi Maung.

A reorganization of the Cabinet was carried out in June 1995, in which a new Ministry of Immigration and Population was created specifically for Lt-Gen. Maung Hla, a member of the SLORC, who had led the successful campaign against the Kayins earlier in the year (see below). As in the 1992 reshuffle, several regional military commanders were appointed ministers, in an apparent attempt to prevent them from developing a local power base.

On 10 July 1995, after almost six years under house arrest, Suu Kyi was released by the SLORC. No dialogue had taken place between Suu Kyi and the military regime since October 1994, and thus her release had not been expected at this time. Some observers suggested that the SLORC had finally yielded to international pressure, while others indicated that the regime could afford to release Suu Kyi at a time when it considered its position stronger than before (largely owing to the defeat or surrender of virtually all the ethnic insurgent groups, see below). Suu Kyi immediately began to re-establish contact with those remaining NLD leaders who had not been imprisoned or exiled, as well as with the party leadership which had compromised with the SLORC. Despite the continuing official ban on gatherings of more than five persons, crowds of up to 1,000 supporters of Suu Kyi assembled daily outside her house in Yangon; they were not dispersed by the police. However, there was no announcement in the official media of Suu Kyi's release until 19 July, when state television covered the annual Martyrs' Day ceremony in Yangon, at which Suu Kyi was permitted to lay a wreath on her father's grave. Than Shwe and Khin Nyunt were noticeably absent from the ceremony.

In public statements and extensive interviews with the foreign media, Suu Kyi emphasized that her release was only an initial step in a very long process and that pressure for democratic reforms should be maintained. She appealed to the SLORC for the release of all political prisoners, the gradual easing of martial-law restrictions, the recognition of the 1990 election result, and the holding of talks on national reconciliation. In August 1995 de Soto revisited Myanmar, and urged the military leaders to initiate dialogue with Suu Kyi. In the following month Dr Madeleine Albright, then US Permanent Representative to the UN, visited Yangon (the most senior US official to do so since 1988). During talks with leading members of the SLORC she stated that any change in US policy towards Myanmar would depend on fundamental changes in the regime's treatment of Myanmar's people. Dr Albright also met Suu Kyi. By mid-November, however, there appeared to be no indication of willingness by the SLORC to resume dialogue with Suu Kyi. Indeed, in late October the authorities decreed illegal the NLD's reinstatement of Suu Kyi as its General Secretary (with Aung Shwe re-elected as Chairman, and Tin Oo and Kyi Maung as Vice-Chairmen).

In November 1995 23 retired political and military leaders, including Bohmu Aung (one of the 'Thirty Comrades' together with Gen. Aung San and Gen. Ne Win), issued an open letter urging dialogue between the SLORC and the NLD. They were severely reprimanded and threatened by the SLORC. Later that month the remaining NLD delegates boycotted the National Convention and were expelled. The SLORC continued to harass the NLD and arrest its members and supporters throughout 1996, and Suu Kyi's activities were progressively restricted. Although no longer under house arrest, Suu Kyi was often warned by the military surrounding her home not to go out 'for her own safety'. On one occasion in 1996, she was prevented from travelling to Mandalay when the train carriage that she had booked was suddenly found to be unserviceable and removed. NLD colleagues who assisted her visit to a Kayin New Year celebration were subsequently imprisoned, and several well-known comedians who told anti-SLORC jokes at an NLD rally were sent to a labour camp. In September 1996 the military blocked off the area around Suu Kyi's house in University Avenue, rendering impossible the delivery of her regular weekend speeches from her garden. In November the car in which Suu Kyi was travelling was attacked by a 200-strong mob and severely damaged. Also, in August, Win Htein, Suu Kyi's personal assistant, was arrested and sentenced to seven years' imprisonment (subsequently doubled) for allegedly conspiring with groups in India to destabilize the country. Many foreigners, especially journalists, politicians and any groups communicating with the NLD before arrival in the country, or with intentions to meet with Suu Kyi during their visit, found their visas refused or revoked, their aircraft inexplicably delayed and their other scheduled meetings cancelled, while most local people were unable even to get near her house, let alone to see or hear her.

In May 1996 the NLD held its first party congress. Prior to its opening, 262 delegates, including 238 of those elected in 1990, were arrested and held until the congress was over; up to 20 remained political prisoners in July. However, the congress proceeded with the attendance of hundreds of NLD members, as well as foreign diplomats and journalists; the main outcome of the congress was the adoption of a resolution to draft an alternative constitution. In early June 1996 the SLORC intensified pressure on the NLD by issuing an order authorizing the Ministry of Home Affairs to ban any organization holding unlawful gatherings or obstructing the drafting of a new constitution by the National Convention; it was announced that members of a proscribed party could be sentenced to between five and 20 years' imprisonment. Each time the NLD attempted to hold a large meeting, hundreds of those planning to attend were arrested or detained until after the proposed date.

Harassment, detention, arrests, imprisonment and deaths in prison of the middle and lower level NLD leadership also continued in 1997, while government propaganda vilifying the party grew more frequent. In August three relatives of Suu Kyi were each sentenced to 10 years' imprisonment, having been found guilty of accepting funding for NLD activities from the USA (allegations which were strongly denied); in a separate trial, a fourth NLD member was sentenced to life imprisonment for allegedly importing explosives. Further harsh sentences were imposed on seven NLD members in December. In July 1997 SLORC First Secretary Khin Nyunt held a meeting with the NLD Chairman, Aung Shwe; however, the leaders of the ruling military junta had not met Suu Kyi since her 'release' from house arrest in July 1995. A further meeting with the SLORC leadership scheduled to take place in September was cancelled by the NLD because the military junta refused to allow Suu Kyi to participate. The SLORC media continued to assert that the NLD (to which they referred as the 'notorious league for demons') was funded from overseas, although this appeared not to be the case.

THE SPDC

Following the circulation during 1997 of rumours anticipating changes in the membership of the SLORC, on 15 November the leadership unexpectedly announced the dissolution of the SLORC and its immediate replacement by a new State Peace and Development Council (SPDC). The four most senior members of the SLORC retained their positions at the head of the new council: Gen. Than Shwe, despite his deteriorating health, was appointed Chairman of the SPDC (and also remained Prime Minister and Minister of Defence); the Commander-in-Chief of the Army, Gen. Maung Aye, was nominated Vice-Chairman; Lt-Gen. Khin Nyunt, head of military intelligence, was appointed First Secretary and Lt-Gen. Tin Oo Second Secretary (as opposed to the former NLD chairman, also called Tin Oo). Lt-Gen. Win Myint, the Adjutant-General, was appointed Third Secretary. Unlike the SLORC, the 19-member SPDC was composed entirely of serving military commanders from central and regional levels. Moreover, only the SPDC Chairman, Gen. Than Shwe, concurrently held posts in the Cabinet, of which about half the members were new appointments, many of them younger civilians from the USDA. The formation of the SPDC therefore appeared to be part of the military's slowly-developing strategy to outflank the NLD by creating 'safe' political institutions. The USDA in particular expanded rapidly under the sponsorship and funding of the Ministry of Education; its Secretary-General was the Minister of Education, Than Aung, while Gen. Than Shwe was its chief patron. By late 1996 the USDA claimed 5m. members (more than 10% of the population), with a further 1m. in affiliated youth organizations. Government employees were under heavy pressure to join the USDA, and there were strong indications that the regime was seeking to model the organization on Indonesia's then state-supported Golkar party. Lt-Gen. Khin Nyunt subsequently emerged as the chief strategist in this process. He was identified as a protégé of the ageing Gen. Ne Win, and in 1994 had established an Office of Strategic Studies (OSS) within the Ministry of Defence which took over responsibility for formulating policy on problematic issues, such as the drug trade and ethnic minorities, and on the delicate issue of corruption in the upper echelons of the political administration. (In November 1997 several ministers were arrested on corruption charges.) Khin Nyunt also appeared to be the influential force behind the work of a committee responsible to the National Convention which, in the late 1990s, was said by the Government to be close to completing the draft of a new Constitution; in September 1998 he created a Political Affairs Committee (PAC), including both civilian and military figures, to oversee this process. A cabinet reorganization effected in November 1998 also indirectly further strengthened the position of Khin Nyunt: in the reshuffle, Ohn Gyaw was replaced as

Minister of Foreign Affairs by Win Aung, hitherto the Myanma ambassador to the United Kingdom and reportedly a close ally of Khin Nyunt.

Faced with the gradual stalling of their 1990 democratic mandate, the NLD held a congress in May 1998 and subsequently issued an ultimatum to the SPDC to convene the Pyithu Hluttaw, in accordance with the results of the 1990 election, by 21 August 1998, announcing that it would convene the Assembly itself if the SPDC failed to comply. The SPDC, however, both rejected the demand and began a series of arrests of NLD MPs and members. By November about 850 MPs and members were reported to be in detention; about half of these were released after they agreed not to take part in an NLD-convened Assembly, but some 270 were given prison sentences. By mid-1999 at least three NLD MPs, including NLD founder member Tin Shwe, had died in prison since 1990. The Government claimed that only 129 of the original 392 NLD parliamentarians still held an electoral mandate; the remainder were reported variously to have died, resigned, left the party or been disqualified. Furthermore, the regime allegedly began a systematic campaign of coercion and intimidation in an attempt to secure the involuntary resignation of vast numbers of NLD members and the closure of a number of regional party headquarters; by the end of 1998 some 40,000 members were reported to have left the party. The junta also began to orchestrate calls for the party to be declared illegal, thus exposing its members to the risk of imprisonment. Rather than convening the Pyithu Hluttaw under such circumstances, in September 1998 the NLD instead created a Committee Representing the People's Parliament (CRPP) to issue statements on behalf of the Pyithu Hluttaw and to develop policy. Meanwhile, speculation continued on the subject of whether there were elements within the regime that might be interested in opening a dialogue with the NLD. The SPDC Vice-Chairman, Gen. Maung Aye, was said to be the most vehement opponent of dialogue. It was reported in September 1998 that 15 senior military officers had been arrested for seeking contact with Suu Kyi. In late 1998 the UN reportedly raised the possibility of providing US $1,000m. in aid and assistance to Myanmar if the Government would release political prisoners and begin a dialogue with the NLD, which in turn was to be requested to abandon its demand that the Pyithu Hluttaw convene on the basis of the results of the 1990 election. However, when news of the proposal emerged, both the SPDC and the NLD angrily rejected the suggestion of any possible compromise. The establishment of genuine dialogue was rendered unlikely by the SPDC's continuation of the SLORC's campaign of attrition against Suu Kyi, and also by its refusal to allow her involvement in any discussions. The validity of Suu Kyi's Myanma nationality was repeatedly questioned on the grounds of her marriage to a British citizen, Dr Michael Aris, and in mid-1998 the regime repeatedly used road-blocks to prevent her from attending NLD meetings, leading to prolonged confrontations between Suu Kyi and the military. In early 1999 Dr Aris, who had been diagnosed with terminal cancer, was refused permission to enter Myanmar to see Suu Kyi for the last time; he died in March. (Although the junta had encouraged Suu Kyi to visit Aris in the United Kingdom, she declined to do so for fear that she would not be permitted to return to Myanmar.) In many other respects also, the regime seemed far from conciliatory. After student riots against the Government in December 1996, universities and some high schools were closed indefinitely. Further large-scale anti-Government demonstrations were staged by students in September 1998. In January 1999 four medical schools were reopened, but other areas of the higher education sector remained closed, and plans were announced to move several campuses to remote regions before they would be permitted to open again. In July 2000 the ruling junta reportedly allowed some 60,000 university students to resume their education in a further step in the phased reopening of Myanmar's universities and colleges; all returning students were reportedly required to sign an oath, pledging not to engage in political activity. It was estimated that many thousands more students, however, remained excluded from education. In August 2001 the Government announced plans for a major expansion in distance education, apparently intended to develop the human capital needed for Myanmar's economic development, while avoiding the political risks associated with campus-based education. In the late 1990s reports emerged from Arakan, the Kayin State, the Chin State and elsewhere of deliberate harassment of religious minorities by government forces, and of the destruction by soldiers, local government officials, and even Buddhist monks, of mosques and churches to make way for Buddhist temples. In urban areas, the cemeteries of non-Buddhists were reportedly targeted for redevelopment, and relatives were told to move remains of the deceased at short notice and at their own expense; some remains were moved more than once. In 2001 communal riots between Buddhists and Muslims were reported in Taungoo, north of Yangon, and in Rakhine.

Meanwhile, the army, or Tatmadaw, increased in size from 175,000 to 400,000 in 1999, according to one estimate (with perhaps an additional 100,000 in the police force and militia groups). The age of recruitment, officially 17, was reportedly lowered in order to increase numbers. According to further reports, villages were given quotas to fill, young boys were persuaded to falsify their age and to enlist, boys were picked up from the street, and orphans were placed in Ye Nyunt paramilitary training centres. Some opponents of the regime also reported that units of boys under 18 were sometimes given amphetamines and used for 'human wave' attacks across minefields against fortified positions, although such accounts cannot be confirmed. There is no doubt, however, that the army used local forced labour extensively for portering and logistical support work. In addition, army units were placed in charge of development projects, such as the building of roads, railways and dams, which again relied mainly on forced labour and the labour of prisoners. In principle, non-prison labour was remunerated, but often much of the payment was retained by the military officer in charge. A report published by the International Labour Organization (ILO) in August 1998 confirmed that the use of forced labour was 'pervasive' throughout Myanmar and accused the military junta of using beatings, torture, rape and murder in the implementation of its forced labour policy (see below).

In April 1999 Suu Kyi was reported to have sent a videotaped appeal to the Office of the UN High Commissioner for Human Rights in Geneva, Switzerland, requesting that the organization make a 'firm resolution' to protect human rights in Myanmar. In the same month the UN adopted a unanimous resolution deploring the escalation in the persecution of the democratic opposition. Nevertheless, the harassment and intimidation of NLD members continued throughout 1999 and early 2000, with the resignations from the party of nearly 300 members reported in July 1999; further resignations were reported in November and January 2000, and in December 1999 it was reported that an elected representative of the People's Assembly, U Maung Maung Myint, had been forced to resign by the ruling SPDC. The NLD's failure to make any progress against the regime in 1999 led to increasing tensions within the opposition itself and even, among some elements of the party, to growing dissatisfaction with the uncompromising policy of Suu Kyi. In April three senior NLD members wrote to the party Chairman, Aung Shwe, and to Khin Nyunt, urging both the NLD and the Government to be more conciliatory; Aung San Suu Kyi publicly rejected their suggestion, however, and the three were suspended from party membership. In early August a series of protests was staged by supporters of the democratic opposition to mark the anniversary of the massacre of thousands of pro-democracy demonstrators by the military Government in 1988. Local and overseas opposition groups attempted to force a confrontation with the Government on 9 September 1999 (9-9-99), designated an auspicious date by analogy with 8-8-88; government forces were well prepared for the protests, however, and there were no more than small disturbances in several centres. In October 1999 Myanmar's Supreme Court issued a decision rejecting a claim by the NLD that its activities had been 'continuously disrupted, prevented and destroyed' and that hundreds of its members had been illegally detained; the NLD, however, subsequently expressed its intention to resubmit the claim.

In February 2000 senior Buddhist monks called for renewed dialogue between the regime and the opposition, evidently irritating the Government and Suu Kyi to equal degrees. By September, however, all indications were that attitudes on both sides had hardened. In late August the regime engaged in a stand-off with Suu Kyi when she attempted to travel from her home in Yangon to conduct party business at other centres. After nine days, troops eventually forcibly removed Suu Kyi from an informal camp she had established at a road-block and returned her to her home. Following the conclusion of the stand-off, the ruling junta continued to restrict the movements of Suu Kyi and a number of other NLD leaders, holding them under effective house arrest at Suu Kyi's Yangon home and denying diplomatic access to Suu Kyi. Although the restrictions were lifted in mid-September, later the same month Suu Kyi was prevented from leaving Yangon by train. Tin Oo and eight other NLD workers, who were planning to accompany Suu Kyi, were detained in a 'government guest house', while Suu Kyi herself was again placed under house arrest. Meanwhile, the NLD lost its lease over the building housing its headquarters, while an estranged brother of Suu Kyi, resident in the USA, began legal proceedings to take possession of her home in Yangon. Both the NLD and its leader thus faced the prospect of homelessness. In September 2000 the NLD-dominated CRPP announced that it would proceed with developing its own constitution for the country. On the other hand, in October, Gen. Khin Nyunt held talks with Suu Kyi, although no results from the discussions were announced. In January 2001 the regime released from detention 85 NLD members, including Tin Oo, while a court dismissed the case brought by Suu Kyi's brother. Another NLD leader, Maung Wuntha, was released in June 2001, and both sides became noticeably more restrained in their comments about the other. Talks continued without publicity throughout 2001, mediated by the special envoy of the UN Secretary-General, Malaysian diplomat Tan Sri Razali Ismail. By the end of 2001 some 174 NLD detainees had been released and the party had been permitted to reopen some offices in Yangon. Following the downfall of Indonesia's President Suharto in 1998, there was speculation that the SPDC was seeking an alternative model for political stability and economic development, and that it was attracted by the example of Malaysia.

In a reorganization of the Cabinet announced on 29 October 1999 the Minister of Commerce, Maj.-Gen. Kyaw Than, and the Minister of Sports, Brig.-Gen. Sein Win, were both replaced. In early December the Minister at the Office of the Chairman of the SPDC, Brig.-Gen. Maung Maung, was forced to resign his portfolio and was also removed from his position as Chairman of the Myanmar Investment Commission; Maung Maung was reportedly dismissed as a result of the ruling junta's displeasure at the sharp decline in foreign investment in the country. In mid-August 2000 it was reported that the Deputy Minister for National Planning and Economic Development, Brig.-Gen Zaw Tun, had been forced to resign from the SPDC as a result of his criticism of the Government's economic policies. It was further reported that a number of other senior government officials and military officers had recently been dismissed or forced into retirement; amongst these individuals was former Commander-in-Chief of the Navy and SPDC member, Vice-Adm. Nyunt Thein. A further set of retirements took place in November 2001, some of them allegedly prompted by private warnings from Malaysia's Prime Minister, Mahathir Mohamad, that the SPDC needed to take action against corruption if it was to create an attractive business climate in Myanmar. There was much speculation over the implications of these changes for the political fortunes of the rival factions headed by Gen. Maung Aye—widely perceived as a hard-liner in the context of his dealings with the NLD—and Gen. Khin Nyunt, but there was no clear indication that either faction would predominate.

In February 2001 the death in a helicopter crash of Lt-Gen. Tin Oo, who had been SPDC Second Secretary and Army Chief of Staff, led to speculation as to whether the crash was an accident or an assassination. Also ambiguous was the arrest in March 2002 of the son-in-law and three grandsons of U Ne Win, on charges of plotting a coup. The heads of the air force and the national police were both dismissed shortly before the arrests took place. Since there was little evidence of any coup-planning, speculation focused on whether the detentions were related to U Ne Win's hostility to any *rapprochement* with Suu Kyi, or whether they were prompted by his family's reputed involvement in a criminal gang. There was some suggestion that their real target was U Ne Win's unpopular daughter, Sandar Win. In September 2002 those arrested were convicted on charges of treason and sentenced to death. The significance of these events in Yangon was uncertain, however, because of the increasing power of Myanmar's regional military commanders. In practice, the SPDC devolved much administrative and economic decision-making to these commanders, who were therefore able to develop strong regional economic interests and to build powerful local political bases, sometimes approaching those of regional warlords. In November 2001 10 of the 12 regional commanders were recalled to Yangon to assume senior positions in the central Government, but only two appeared to have accepted this removal from regional power.

On 6 May 2002 Aung San Suu Kyi was, at last, released unconditionally from detention. There was no expectation that the SPDC would recognize the 1990 election result and relinquish power to the NLD, but the release did lead to increasing speculation that members of the NLD might be included in a transitional government preceding the holding of new elections. Talks between Suu Kyi and the SPDC, however, ceased after she was freed and Razali, who was seen as having played a key role in negotiating her release, continued to seek a dialogue between the two sides on political progress.

Meanwhile, the ready availability of heroin for injecting within Myanmar, and the social disruption caused by the civil wars, created an environment in which HIV/AIDS spread rapidly. A survey in Kachin state indicated that 90% of heroin users were HIV-positive, and observers have suggested that as many as 1m. people may be infected. The rapid rate of uncontrolled logging in Myanmar's forests seems likely to have serious long-term ecological consequences for the country.

INSURGENTS AND DISSIDENTS

The Communist Party of Burma (CPB), located on the Chinese border in the northern part of the Shan State, posed the most serious military challenge to the Burmese armed forces until 1989. The party was well armed and supported by anti-Government, pro-CPB broadcasts from its China-based secret radio transmitter, the 'Voice of the People of Burma'. In 1984 China's policy changed, and the supply of weapons to the CPB diminished. Faced with declining fortunes, the CPB allegedly began exporting illicit drugs through Viet Nam and Laos, using the proceeds to purchase Soviet weapons. In early 1989 the CPB was split by internal dissent; certain ethnic factions of the party, critical of its 'narrow racial policies', challenged the central leadership. In April the Wa hill tribesmen and Kokang Chinese, who had served as cadres for the party, mutinied and forced the ageing CPB leaders across the border into China. Thus, the CPB was effectively defunct; its various regional armies divided into ethnic groupings, the most prominent being the Wa, Shan, Kokang Chinese, and Kachin.

Apart from the CPB, several groups of ethnic insurgents have been engaged in low-level warfare against the authorities since 1948, when Burma's independence was achieved. Despite the Government's efforts to eliminate and destroy the various insurgent groups, they survived and united to form the National Democratic Front (NDF) in 1975. The political objective of the NDF was the creation of a truly federal union (as envisaged by the original Constitution of 1947), based on the principles of self-determination, equality and democracy. The NDF hoped to achieve its objective through negotiations with the central Government, but fighting would continue until such talks could be arranged. The NDF formed three commands (northern, central and southern) to co-ordinate the military effort. In 1988 the NDF numbered 10 groups, representing Karen (Kayin), Arakanese (Rakhine), Mon, Karenni (Kayinni), Shan, Kachin, Palaung, Pa-O and Wa. In May 1986 the NDF formed a political and military anti-Government alliance with the CPB, following an NDF conference at Pa Jau in January. This alliance was maintained despite opposition from the Karen (Kayin) National Union (KNU), one of the largest ethnic insurgent groups in the NDF. The Government initially responded with renewed attacks on Karen guerrillas, although this resulted in early victories for the combined forces. By May 1987, however, government forces had gained control of 60 km of border areas previously controlled by the CPB, and had reasserted control over 500 sq km of territory in the north-east. Also in the same month, the Government launched a major assault against the Kachin, temporarily capturing their military and political headquarters.

In 1988 the unity of the minorities was tested as the Karen and Mon openly fought over control of the 'black-market' trade at the Three Pagoda Pass area on the Thai-Burmese border. Through the mediation of the NDF, the fighting ended in August. In April a prominent human rights organization, Amnesty International, issued two long reports documenting human rights violations committed by the Burmese Army in its war against the minorities. These reports drew world attention, but were ignored by the Burmese Government.

The insurgent groups were sympathetic to the anti-Government movements in Rangoon and other major cities in 1988. After the armed forces seized power, an estimated 7,000–10,000 students fled to the border areas to seek refuge and arms in order to continue their struggle against the Government. Despite shortages of weapons and supplies, units of the NDF gave them refuge and some training. At the same time, units of the NDF and the CPB launched attacks on government outposts. During 1989 and 1990 the armed forces' assault against the KNU continued, with the capture of six river enclaves, although the KNU retained their headquarters at Manerplaw. During the same period, the Kachin continued to engage the armed forces in their area. The Kachin held most of the countryside in their state, while government forces controlled the two major cities, Bhamo and Myitkyina, and their rail and road connections with the rest of Myanmar.

In the light of the changes in Rangoon, the NDF created a new political grouping, the Democratic Alliance of Burma (DAB), to include Burman students, monks and expatriates in a broad coalition which would, it hoped, eventually incorporate the peoples in the Burmese heartland, on the model of the original post-war nationalist movement, the AFPFL. Maj.-Gen. Bo Mya, the KNU leader, was elected President of the DAB, and Brang Seng, the Kachin leader, was named first Vice-President. At its first convention, in November 1988, 23 separate groups participated. It declared as its main objectives the overthrow of the military Government, the establishment of democratic rule, the ending of the civil war, the restoration of internal peace and national reconciliation, and the creation of a genuine federal union. Student forces within the DAB united to form the All-Burma Student Democratic Front (ABSDF), which operated in border regions and received weapons and training from the KNU and from Kayin rebels. The DAB did not replace the NDF, however; the latter continued to exist and control its own areas and armed forces. In late 1988 it admitted its 11th member, the Chin National Front.

The collapse of the CPB in 1989 provided the SLORC with an opportunity to divide its ethnic opposition and cause some groups to end their participation in the civil war. The Government successfully approached first the Kokang Chinese, and later the Wa, and offered much-needed rice in exchange for support in the government campaign against the NDF and Chang Chi Fu, known as Khun Sa, the 'opium warlord' and leader of the rebel Mong Tai Army (MTA, formerly the Shan United Army), in the Shan State. It was reported that the armed forces promised, in addition to food, to allow the Wa to continue to trade opium, the major crop of their area. The SLORC also pledged to initiate a border development programme (including the construction of roads, hospitals and schools) in the former CPB areas. The SLORC also approached members of the NDF, and was successful in securing agreements with the Shan State Progressive Party in September 1989, the Pa-O National Organization in February 1991 and the Palaung State Liberation Organization in April. In July 1991, at its third Congress, the NDF responded by expelling these three organizations, thus reducing the NDF membership to eight.

Following the establishment of the 'parallel' government (the NCGUB, see above) in Manerplaw in December 1990, the SLORC intensified its attacks on KNU positions. In particular, the use of newly-acquired jet fighters from the People's Republic of China resulted in tens of thousands of villagers fleeing across the Thai border. In October 1991 the KNU surprised the government armed forces by infiltrating the Ayeyarwady (Irrawaddy) delta area and launching an attack with local support at Bogale, 200 km south-west of Rangoon, now Yangon. Until the attack, the SLORC had considered the area secure. Government forces responded with air and land attacks, and, after nearly one month of fighting, they regained control. In December the SLORC launched a major military campaign to defeat the KNU. Employing four divisions and many of its newly-purchased aircraft, it attacked Manerplaw and Kawmoora. It aimed to capture the KNU and DAB headquarters, which was also the seat of the NCGUB, before Armed Forces Day on 27 March 1992. Its failure either to defeat the KNU in the field or capture its headquarters (owing, in part, to Thailand's actions, see below) led directly to the announcement in April that it was halting its war against the KNU. In October, however, government troops resumed hostilities.

In February 1993 the Kachin Independence Organization (KIO) agreed to attend peace talks with the Government in the Kachin capital, Myitkyina. The discussions, which took place during February and March, were the result of pressure exerted by China and Thailand. The Kachin (who were the second largest ethnic insurgent force, after the KNU) reportedly demanded a nation-wide cease-fire and that further talks include other rebel groups. However, the KIO finally appeared to have agreed to a bilateral cease-fire with the Government, prior to comprehensive peace talks with all ethnic rebels. The KIO were suspended from the DAB in October for negotiating separately with the SLORC, and the DAB reiterated its conditions for discussions with the SLORC in a series of open letters. The DAB stipulations included: the recognition of the DAB as a single negotiating body (the SLORC insisted on meeting each ethnic group separately); an immediate end to the forcible mass relocation of villages; a new body to draft a constitution; and the release of all political detainees, beginning with Suu Kyi. The cease-fire agreement between the KIO and the Government was announced in October.

The process of reconciliation continued with the return to the 'legal fold' in May 1994 of the Karenni (Kayinni) National People's Liberation Front, the 11th insurgent group to conclude a cease-fire agreement with the SLORC. This was followed, in July, by the declaration of a cease-fire by the Kayan New Land Party, and in October by the Shan State Nationalities Liberation Organization. In late December government forces launched a new offensive against the KNU, capturing its headquarters at Manerplaw in January 1995 and forcing many hundreds of KNU fighters to retreat across the border into Thailand. The virtual defeat of the KNU forces, after almost 50 years of military resistance, was attributed to their reportedly severe lack of ammunition and funds and to the defection from the Christian-led KNU in December 1994 of a mainly Buddhist faction, which established itself as the Democratic Karen (Kayin) Buddhist Organization (DKBO). The DKBO, which had comprised an estimated 10% of the strength of the KNU's military wing, the Karen (Kayin) National Liberation Army (KNLA), allegedly supported the government forces in their offensive. In February 1995 the Myanma army captured another major KNU stronghold, at Kawmoora, and in the following month Bo Mya resigned as the commander-in-chief of the KNLA (although he remained the leader of the KNU and was re-elected to the post in August 1995). The SLORC and their proxies, the Democratic Karen (Kayin) Buddhist Army (DKBA, the military wing of the DKBO) continued to attack KNU bases as well as refugee camps inside Thai territory. Discussions between the KNU and the SLORC began in early 1994. Despite the KNU's participation in a series of formal cease-fire negotiations with the SLORC between late 1995 and late 1996, as well as its request for further discussions, the SLORC attacked the KNU in February 1997 and drove its forces from nearly all of their remaining fixed bases. The KNU 16th Battalion Commander, Thamu Hae, surrendered, and it was rumoured that he might be given some position of authority in the SLORC Government of the Karen State. Unlike the previous offensive, few, if any, DKBA Karen troops were used in 1997. Because the rains were very late in 1997, this offensive continued beyond the middle of the year. It also displaced most of the ABSDF and other forces who co-operate with the KNU. From 1995 the DKBA made frequent incursions into Thai territory, abducting KNU members, attempting to coerce refugees into returning, robbing, raping and destroying villages (including two large Karen refugee villages, Huay Kaloke and Mawker, in March 1998). In late March 1998 the DKBA also abducted an Australian aid worker and his Thai counterpart from Thailand and held the pair hostage for five days. In March 1999 it was reported that

Kayin rebels had executed at least 13 government officials whom they had abducted the previous month.

In the Shan region, after extensive battles with government forces between late 1993 and late 1995, there was great tension within the 20,000-strong MTA between the genuine Shan nationalists among the field officers and the Chinese leaders, who were more interested in the drugs trade. In attempts to prevent a split, the Chinese/Shan leader Khun Sa, long a prominent figure in the drugs trade, proclaimed an independent Shan State in May 1994, and in mid-1995 established a new Shan State National Congress Party as the political wing of the MTA, with Khun Kan Chit, a Shan, as its nominal leader. This did not prevent a substantial revolt of some northern MTA units led by Karn Yord, who formed the Shan State National Army in July, taking nearly one-quarter of the MTA forces with him. Weakened by this division, as well as by major government attacks, desertions and, reportedly, by his own ill health, Khun Sa, who remained the real MTA leader, agreed to a cease-fire with the SLORC in January 1996. The MTA headquarters at Homong, some other MTA troops at Mong Hsat and a few other locations in the southern Shan State surrendered later in January. Most Shan commanders and soldiers of the MTA disapproved of the surrender and continued their resistance, linking up with other Shan groups. This alliance was formalized in September 1997 when three major groups, including the Shan State National Army (SSNA), remnants of the MTA, and the Shan State Peace Council (SSPC) and its military wing, the Shan State Army (SSA), joined together in an enlarged SSA. As a result, the truce between the Government and the SSPC/SSA broke down, and SSA elements resumed guerrilla activity in various parts of the Shan State. Khun Sa subsequently moved to Yangon, like the Kokang drugs-trafficker, Lo Hsing-han, and started a number of businesses, including a bus service and an overseas trading company. Having previously referred to Khun Sa as a 'narco-terrorist' until late 1995, the SLORC Government subsequently used the honorific prefix, U, before his name and refused to extradite him to the USA for prosecution on drugs-trafficking charges (he had been indicted by the USA in 1989 and 1992). Clashes between SSA units and government forces were reported in December. In March 2000, however, following the group's announcement that it wished to seek a peaceful settlement with the ruling junta, the SSA issued a statement outlining cease-fire terms.

The Karenni (Kayinni) National Progress Party (KNPP) cease-fire with the SLORC, which was signed in March 1995, collapsed almost immediately, and government offensives on the KNPP area continued. These attacks intensified from January 1996 after Khun Sa's surrender at Homong, to the north-east of the KNPP area. In that month the KNPP and the KNU agreed to fight together again against the SLORC and both groups continued to exist as guerrilla armies along much of the Myanma border with western Thailand. Following negotiations begun in December 1993, however, the New Mon State Party (NMSP) signed a cease-fire with the SLORC in June 1995. This truce was particularly significant as the NMSP had controlled part of the area where a major gas pipeline to Thailand was under construction. The last members of the NMSP surrendered in May 1997, and the KNU was virtually eliminated from this area.

The SLORC regularly reported that all ethnic groups except the KNU had ceased armed resistance; however, various small groups in other areas (which were not often mentioned) continued their struggle: several Rohingya Muslim and Rakhine Buddhist groups in the Rakhine State, the Chin National Army in the Chin State, the National Socialist Council of Nagaland (various factions) in the Naga areas of western Sagaing Division, and a number of breakaway groups from the MTA, which continued resistance after the MTA surrender in January 1996 and formed a substantial Shan alliance in June. Many of the groups with which truces continued to hold were restive; clashes between SLORC forces and KIA forces were reported in early 1996, and further tension was caused in April 1996 when the authorities forced the Kachin to take down a *Manau* (ceremonial dance) pole erected for a Kachin celebration. In December 1995 the United Wa State Party (UWSP) was reportedly very discontented by the replacement of MTA forces by Myanma army troops in some areas adjacent to them and by the restrictions that were placed on their movements from early 1996.

ABSDF students in areas controlled by various groups, such as the KIA and KNU, experienced difficulties following the various cease-fires and offensives; the SLORC also attacked them directly, capturing their bases in Myanmar. For years they were also divided by factionalism. With the development of closer relations between Thailand and Myanmar, the Thai security forces increased their harassment, detention, and deportation of the thousands of Myanma refugee students in Thailand; some were moved to a remote camp in western Thailand known as the 'Safe Area.' In September 1996 the ABSDF reunited, with Dr Naing Aung as Chairman and Moe Thee Zun as Vice-Chairman. However, it continued to lose ground militarily: for example, Battalion 203 in Mergui surrendered in early 1997, reportedly because the SLORC had located and was threatening the family of its commander. In March 1998 the SPDC (which had replaced the SLORC) detained 40 members of the ABSDF whom it accused of planning terrorist attacks on government buildings and embassies and the assassination of national leaders; the allegations were rejected by the ABSDF.

Various other groups who had signed cease-fires with the SLORC also expanded their involvement in the drugs trade; these included the Wa UWSP and its armed wing, the United Wa State Army (UWSA, reported to have a major amphetamine factory near the Thai border, in addition to its opium and heroin interests) and other former CPB groups in the eastern Shan State, as well as several Chinese groups in the Kokang area of the north-eastern Shan State, notably the Eastern Shan State Army of Lin Min Shin (Sai Lin). The surrender of Khun Sa and the break-up of the MTA did not in any way reduce opium production. Despite the truces, many of the former members of the DAB continued to be in contact; a meeting was held in January 1996, and a DAB congress in April. According to the SLORC, all groups that had signed cease-fire agreements were invited to send observers to the National Convention; apparently few did so.

Following the cease-fires with most ethnic rebels, the Tatmadaw was able to move into many areas where it had had no presence for 20–30 years or more. In some areas, the Tatmadaw forced groups of ethnic soldiers to relocate, contrary to the agreed cease-fire terms. In many zones, especially around the remaining active ethnic rebellions, there was a massive forced movement of villages away from rebel areas and into relocation areas in the plains. Hundreds of thousands of people were displaced from their homes in the south-western Shan State, the eastern Kayah State and the eastern Karen State in 1996 and 1997. In May 1999 it was reported that at least 300,000 Shan had been forced from their villages into resettlement camps by government troops. This population movement severely affected the local support base of the Karen KNU, Karenni KNPP, Pa-O and former MTA, which did not participate in the surrender of early 1996. Many of the villagers who did not wish to relocate in the plains became refugees, especially in Thailand but also in Bangladesh, India and China: the Tatmadaw offensive in the Karen State which started in February 1997, for example, drove an estimated 20,000 additional Karen refugees into Thailand. In many cases, potential refugees were turned back at the Thai, Indian and Chinese borders; in others, people were persuaded to return to Myanmar. Most such people ended up in relocation areas, which some non-governmental organizations working along the Thai-Myanma border termed 'concentration camps'. In 1996 Myanmar announced that the local population would be removed from a large tract of land in Tanintharyi (Tenasserim) to create a major nature reserve. Since the gas pipeline to Thailand was to pass through this region, however, the announcement was widely interpreted as a security measure, rather than a gesture towards nature conservation. In 2001 it was reported that government agents were fomenting tension between Buddhists and Muslims in Rakhine.

On 12–14 December 1998 23 ethnic groups met to issue a statement of support for the NLD and for the convening of the elected National Assembly. The SSA and the KNPP announced that they would co-operate to fight the regime. In January 2000 Gen. Bo Mya was succeeded as the leader of the KNU by the former Secretary-General of the organization, Saw Ba Thin.

Following his appointment as leader, Ba Thin announced that, while the KNU intended to continue its struggle against the ruling SPDC, the movement was prepared to negotiate a political settlement with the military regime. It was subsequently reported by both government and independent sources that an initial but inconclusive round of talks between the KNU and the SPDC was held in February, followed by further discussions in March.

The *rapprochement* between the SPDC and the NLD in 2001 aroused alarm among many ethnic groups, which feared that the two sides in Yangon would reach an agreement that gave no place to greater regional autonomy. In September 2001 several ethnic groups formed the National Solidarity and Co-operation Committee to press for a tripartite dialogue.

REFUGEES AND OTHER MIGRANTS

As a result of SLORC policies since 1988, large numbers of ethnic minority refugees have flooded into every neighbouring country. This includes at least 288,000 (or nearly one-half) of the Muslim Rohingya population of Rakhine State, who fled to Bangladesh between 1989 and 1991. In Thailand there were about 70,000 Kayins from the KNU areas, about 10,000 Kayinnis from the KNPP area, and some 18,000 Mon from the former NMSP areas in the south; most of these fled Myanmar in the early 1990s, but more Kayin and Kayinni continued to arrive from 1996 onwards. There were also many Kachin refugees (estimated at as many as 15,000) in the People's Republic of China, and Chin and Naga refugees (up to 10,000) in north-eastern India. The most recent group of refugees were the Shan from the former MTA area, who arrived in Thailand following the MTA surrender at Homong in January 1996; their number was estimated at up to 100,000, but this was probably an exaggeration. These Shan refugees were not placed in camps but dispersed around northern Thailand. The office of the UN High Commissioner for Refugees (UNHCR) was involved in sending more than 200,000 Rohingya back into Myanmar between 1992 and 1997 as they did in 1976–78. In July 1999, however, about 20,000 Rohingya refugees remained in camps in Bangladesh, despite the expiry of the official deadline for their repatriation in August 1997. In April 2000 the International Federation of Human Rights Leagues (FIDH) issued a report condemning the treatment of Rohingya Muslims by the Myanma Government, including forced labour, punitive taxes and extra-judicial killings. The FIDH claimed that the regime was attempting to force the exodus of Rohingyas from their native Rakhine and criticized UNHCR for its effective complicity with the Myanma regime in designating the more recent refugees as economic migrants. The Mon were repatriated in early 1996. Japan offered humanitarian aid to support the repatriation of the Kayin on a similar basis. Returning refugees were often concentrated in camps rather than being allowed to return to their homes, or were unable to recover their homes and land.

In addition to these recognized refugees, there were many economic migrants working in Thailand, estimated by some Thai sources to number hundreds of thousands or even 1m.; they provided much of the menial and seasonal labour needs of northern, western and southern Thailand and supplied the Thai sex industry. There were also many more who were internally displaced, either because they had obeyed SLORC demands to move from remote areas and urban centres to relocation zones, or because they had moved away from SLORC-controlled areas. Nearly all such people were undergoing severe hardship, deprived of their traditional homes, land and crops.

Large numbers of people were conscripted into forced labour squads, used by the SLORC to complete infrastructure projects (roads, railways, irrigation systems, etc.) or to carry weapons and supplies for the army, thus also undergoing temporary displacement. The SLORC defended this kind of labour as traditional in Myanmar; but the scale of the works undertaken was the greatest in recent history, and inadequate provision was made for feeding and accommodating the workers, who were required to bring their own tools and sometimes even to feed themselves, while neglecting their own crops or other work for weeks or months at a time. It was usually possible to pay to avoid this labour, but this option was too expensive for many people and only further enriched the local military commanders, who also sometimes received payment for the work done. The mortality rate among such labourers was high, but lower than that for gangs of prisoners (criminal and some political) engaged in such work full time.

In the first half of 1996 an estimated 70,000–75,000 Kayah were relocated within the Kayah State, while about 80,000 Shan were relocated in the former MTA area of south-western Shan State. Similar numbers of Karen were relocated away from the KNU in the first half of 1997. With each relocation, thousands more refugees appeared at the Thai border. Although many, especially Shan, were absorbed into local villages and the local work-force in Thailand, Thai police conducted occasional raids and deported those without Thai documentation. Some, particularly Karen, were placed in refugee camps along the western border. The SLORC on a number of occasions sent DKBA soldiers to burn these camps and kidnap KNU leaders. After the Asian economic crisis began in Thailand in July 1997, Thai soldiers increasingly turned back newly-arrived refugees, and also repatriated some existing refugees. Nevertheless, about 98,000 Karen remained in western Thailand, living in camps which they could no longer leave for work, as well as a similar number of more widely-dispersed Shan refugees. In December 1999 Thailand expelled tens of thousands of refugees who had been working in the country illegally. In January 2000 it was reported that 800–1,000 Karen had fled across the border into Thailand following clashes between government forces and the KNU.

There has always been considerable population movement in both directions across Myanmar's long border with China, but during the 1990s many observers reported a substantial increase in the Chinese population of the Myanma border regions and in northern cities, including Mandalay.

FOREIGN RELATIONS

After attaining independence in 1948, Burma pursued a policy of neutrality and non-alignment in world affairs. Burma declined to join the British Commonwealth and was the first non-communist country to recognize the People's Republic of China in 1949. Cordial relations with China were consolidated by a 1960 agreement to settle outstanding border disagreements, but relations were suspended between 1967 and 1970 over what Burma perceived as attempts to promote the Cultural Revolution amongst Burmese of Chinese descent. Burma supported the UN, and in 1961 became a founder member of the Non-aligned Movement (it subsequently withdrew from the Movement for a number of years, but was readmitted in 1992). Burma's foreign policy following the military seizure of power in 1962 continued to emphasise independence and non-alignment. Although Ne Win's Government was initially rather isolationist and sought to exclude foreign influences, governments from the 1970s onwards were aware of the importance of foreign contacts and investment for development. They sought to open the country to the West to the extent that this could be done without undermining government authority. Western interest in Burma was prompted especially by the country's importance in the drug trade. In 1976 Burma began to participate in drug enforcement programmes of the UN and the USA, in an attempt to suppress the cultivation of opium in north-eastern Burma which, together with northern Thailand and north-western Laos, was known as the 'Golden Triangle'. Substantial anti-narcotics assistance, including funds and equipment, failed to halt drug production, as many of the areas cultivated for opium were under the control of insurgent groups which relied on the proceeds of drugs-trafficking to support their anti-Government campaign. The military coup in 1988 prompted the USA to suspend all assistance, and the annual crop increased significantly. The Myanma authorities continued to express willingness to co-operate with the outside world in controlling the trade, arguing that international isolation over human rights issues made this co-operation unnecessarily difficult. In June 1989 Myanmar ratified the 1988 UN Vienna Convention against trafficking in illegal drugs. During the 1990s, however, Myanmar became increasingly important as a regional source of amphetamines and metamphetamines, which were traded especially across the border with China and increasingly through India and Sri Lanka, as well as along more traditional routes through Thailand and the countries of Indo-China. It has been estimated that 50% of the heroin consumed in the USA is of Myanma origin, while earnings from drug exports are believed to exceed the value of all Myanmar's other exports. Weak supervision of the Myanma banking system facilitates this trade. Although allegations were persistently heard that the SLORC and later the SPDC were themselves involved in drugs-trafficking (with particular attention being given to claimed links between Gen. Khin Nyunt and Wa producers), regional military commanders appeared to be the most important local figures in the trade. Opium production appeared to increase in Myanmar in 2000 after the Taliban Government in Afghanistan restricted production there (see the chapter on Afghanistan), but statistics were unreliable and the growing importance of the industrial production of amphetamines and metamphetamines meant that the cultivation of opium itself constituted only a small part of the problem.

The assumption of power by the armed forces in September 1988, and the subsequent brutal suppression of demonstrations by the opposition movement, provoked widespread international censure. Many creditor nations, including Japan, the Federal Republic of Germany, the USA, the United Kingdom and Australia, suspended economic aid, pending an improvement in Burma's human rights record. Among Burma's immediate neighbours, India was most vocal in its criticism of the military repression; it closed Indian trade routes to Burma and established refugee camps near the border. In March 1993, however, the Indian Minister of External Affairs visited Myanmar and signed bilateral agreements on the suppression of separatist movements and drugs-trafficking along the common border. In 1995–96 two border crossings between India and Myanmar were opened and, in 2002, India agreed with Myanmar to begin the construction of a network of roads linking the two countries; there were also joint military operations against Naga rebel groups. This closer relationship was widely believed to be India's reaction to the growing influence of China in Myanmar. Relations with Bangladesh, with which Myanmar shares a short border, were strained both by the presence of an estimated 21,000 Muslim refugees from Myanmar in camps in Bangladesh and by Myanma plans to dam the shared Naf river.

In response to the events of 1988, the USA halted all non-humanitarian assistance, barred Burma from trade benefits under its Generalized System of Preferences, decertified Burma on narcotics and opposed loans from the World Bank, the IMF and other international financial institutions. It blocked all sales of arms from the USA to Burma and urged other nations to do the same. In 1990 the US Congress passed, and the President signed into law, the Customs and Trade Act, which empowered the President to restrict trade with Myanmar if it failed to comply with certain conditions, which were to be monitored twice annually. These were: the protection of human rights; an end to martial law and the introduction of democracy; and adherence to the requirements of the 1986 Narcotics Trade Control Act. In conformity with the law, in July 1991 the President invoked economic sanctions by declining to renew a bilateral textile agreement. (In 1990 textile exports to the USA amounted to nearly one-half of total Myanma exports.) The US administration retained its tough stance towards the SLORC, and subsequently the SPDC, throughout the 1990s, and continued to condemn the widespread abuse of human rights in Myanmar and to demand the release of all political detainees. In mid-1996 the US Congress passed a law prohibiting new investment and trade with Myanmar; an official ban was announced in April 1997. During 1998 the US administration criticized the military junta in Myanmar for its treatment of Suu Kyi and, once again, demanded the release of hundreds of political prisoners. In March 1999 the US Secretary of State, Madeleine Albright, publicly criticized the regime for taking insufficient action to combat the production of, and trade in, narcotics within Myanmar. During the 1990s the European Union (EU) also maintained a common position of refusing to deal with the Myanma authorities, and in October 1998 an existing ban on visas for members of the Myanma Government and their families was extended to cover Myanma citizens working in the tourism industry.

At the end of 1991 the UN General Assembly passed a resolution, without opposition, which expressed 'grave concern' at the human rights situation in Myanmar and drew attention to the continued detention of Suu Kyi. In March 1992 the UN Commission on Human Rights adopted a resolution calling for a permanent representative to monitor developments in Myanmar.

Japan was also critical of the ruling military junta in Myanmar, but like other donors it completed existing aid projects after 1988. Japanese investment and business activities never ceased, and intensified since a Japan Federation of Economic Organizations (KEIDANREN) visit in June 1994. Substantial new Japanese aid started in mid-1995 after the release of Suu Kyi, and in April 2001 Japan agreed to provide US $28m. for the rehabilitation of a hydroelectric dam. Other countries, including Australia, Norway and Switzerland, have provided humanitarian aid to refugees outside Myanmar, and more limited humanitarian aid for projects within the country. After resistance to its attempts to observe and reduce human rights abuses, the International Committee of the Red Cross (ICRC) withdrew from Myanmar in July 1995. However, the ICRC subsequently regained permission to visit a limited number of prisons in Myanmar in 1999. Although she was initially critical of the ICRC for reaching an agreement with the SPDC, Suu Kyi was reported subsequently to have expressed her support for the Committee's work with political prisoners. Despite visits in 1995 and subsequently, the Asian Development Bank (ADB), IMF and World Bank had not resumed loans by mid-1998. Relations with the USA, the EU, Australia and many other non-Asian countries continue to be difficult. The US Secretary of State denounced Myanmar publicly for its human rights abuses and lack of progress towards democracy at the ministerial meeting that followed the ASEAN meeting in July 1997. Myanmar was vigorously defended, however, by Prime Minister Mahathir of Malaysia; and, earlier in 1997, former Prime Minister Lee Kuan Yew of Singapore was widely reported as having said that Suu Kyi would not be capable of ruling Myanmar. Suu Kyi continued to advocate a diplomatic, economic and tourist boycott of Myanmar under the SLORC (and, subsequently, the SPDC).

Facing such consistent hostility from the West, the Government of Ne Win placed great emphasis on fostering its relations with its immediate neighbours, especially Thailand. From about 1988, during the boom years before the Asian economic crisis of 1997, Thailand became a major source of foreign investment in Myanmar. The SLORC granted licences to Thai business interests to exploit raw materials in Burma, especially teak and other timber, in return for much-needed foreign exchange, while the Thai Government offered technical training and other assistance. Plans have been made for a bridge across the Sai river, which would improve communications between Myanmar and Thailand, for a gas pipeline to Thailand from reserves off the Ayeyarwady delta and for a dam in the Shan states to supply water to Thailand.

Although there was no announcement of any official Thai-Burmese agreement, offensives by government forces against rebel groups, particularly the KNU, achieved unprecedented success, with Myanma troops frequently entering Thai territory and attacking insurgent bases from the rear. Partly because of deep-seated historical suspicion between the two countries, these operations led to tension. In early 1992 the Thai Government warned Myanma soldiers not to cross into Thailand in their attempts to capture the KNU headquarters at Manerplaw. Following repeated border violations, there were clashes between Myanma and Thai forces in March as the Thai military forced hundreds of Myanma troops out of entrenched positions that they had taken up to attack the KNU base from the rear. In October, however, government troops resumed hostilities and made several incursions into Thai territory. In December the Thai and Myanma Governments reached agreement to relocate the Myanma armed forces, and in February 1993 they resolved to delineate their common border. However, incursions by Myanma forces into Thai territory continued in early 1995, leading to a further deterioration in bilateral relations. In June 1997 Myanma and Thai troops confronted each other on a disputed island in the Moei river, and a battle was only narrowly averted. Tatmadaw shelling of, and incursions into, Thai territory in pursuit of KNU and KNPP rebels occurred frequently, and Thai soldiers, police, paramilitary force members and local Thai villagers were occasionally killed. In December 1998 two Thai naval officers were killed during a clash between two fishing vessels, and in January 1999 a confrontation between naval patrols from the two countries occurred near the Thai city of Ranong. Clashes between Myanma and Thai troops along Thailand's northern border took place between February and May 2001. Thailand also became increasingly concerned at the inflow of drugs, including metamphetamines, from Myanmar.

Myanmar's relations with Thailand were further strained by the large number of Myanma refugees in Thailand. Refugees began reaching Thailand in significant numbers following the military suppression of the pro-democracy movement in 1988, though Thailand was then reluctant to grant them refugee status and in 1990 forcibly repatriated 1,000 Myanma dissidents. By mid-1998 the number of Myanma refugees in Thailand had increased to an estimated 300,000–500,000 (including many economic refugees). Many of these, it was believed, were seeking to escape conscription into forced labour squads used by the Myanma Government for the construction of roads, railways and other infrastructure projects. Others were members of various ethnic or insurgent groups which had been defeated by, or had capitulated to, the SLORC. In early November 1999 Myanma government troops threatened to shoot at least one group of Myanma illegal labourers whom Thai officials were attempting to deport from Thailand. In October 1999 a group of armed Myanma student activists seized control of their country's embassy in Bangkok, demanding the release of all political prisoners in Myanmar and the opening of dialogue between the Government and the opposition. More than 30 hostages, including tourists as well as diplomats, were taken. They were released by the gunmen within 24 hours, in exchange for the Thai Government's provision of helicopter transport to the Thai–Myanma border. Myanmar closed its border with Thailand immediately after the incident. In January 2000 Thai troops shot dead 10 armed Myanma rebels who had taken control of a hospital in Ratchaburi, holding hundreds of people hostage. The rebels, who were reported by some sources to be linked to the Kayin insurgent group, God's Army (a small breakaway faction of the KNU—the KNU itself denied any connection with the rebels), had issued several demands, including that the shelling of their base on the Thai–Myanma border by the Thai military be halted, that co-operation between the Thai and Myanma armies against the Kayins should cease, and that Kayin tribespeople be allowed to seek refuge in Thailand. Whilst the Thai Government denied reports that the perpetrators had been summarily executed after handing over their weapons, the brutal resolution of the incident was praised by the military Government in Myanmar.

None the less, shared economic interests helped to keep Thailand's relations with Myanmar close, despite these strains. Border crossings, which had been closed due to fighting in 1995, were reopened in early 1996, including those at Tachilek and at Myawaddy. Senior Gen. Than Shwe, the head of the SLORC, visited Thailand in December 1995 and his visit was reciprocated in 1996 and 1997. Thai Prime Minister Thaksin Shinawatra made a visit to Yangon in June 2001 during which both sides made it clear that they wished to improve relations, and in September 2001 Gen. Khin Nyunt paid a three-day visit to Thailand, which was hailed as establishing a new basis for closer co-operation. In particular, Thailand began to work closely with the Myanma authorities to control the flow of drugs by launching military operations against drug organizations and by promoting crop substitution programmes in production areas. In January 2002, at a meeting of a joint Thai-Myanma commission (the first to have been held since 1999), the two countries also agreed to establish a task force to aid in the repatriation of illegal workers. In April 2002 Gen. Maung Aye paid a visit to Bangkok, during which he promised to help reduce the flow of drugs between the two countries. However, relations deteriorated in the following month when fighting began between Myanma government troops, allied with the UWSA, and the SSA, who had seized four posts on the border. Thai troops were alleged to have fired shells into the country, claiming that the fighting had encroached upon Thai territory. In response the Myanma Government accused Thailand of supporting the SSA. Shortly afterwards the Thai–Myanma border was closed in response to the escalating tensions, which were compounded by reports that the SPDC had expelled hundreds of Thai workers from the country. Border incursions continued throughout June 2002 as relations worsened. Early in that month masked gunmen, thought to be members of the KNU, opened fire on a Thai school bus travelling close to the border, resulting in the deaths of three children. The KNU denied responsibility for the attack and Thai Prime Minister Thaksin subsequently stated that he did not believe the KNU or Myanma soldiers to have been responsible. However, in August the Thai Minister of Foreign Affairs, Surakiart Sathirathai, met with SPDC leaders in an effort to resolve the tensions. Talks were reported to have been fruitful, and in October 2002 the border reopened.

From 1988, as Burma's international isolation intensified, China assumed an increasingly important role. In August 1988 the two countries signed a broad cross-border trade agreement, which opened the Burmese market and resources to Chinese exploitation. By 1990 China had become the major supplier of consumer goods, which had previously been purchased mainly from Thailand. In 1991 China also became the SLORC's chief arms supplier, with the sale of weapons valued at more than US $1,000m. It was believed that many of the fighter aircraft that Myanmar purchased from China in the early 1990s were used in the suppression of anti-Government rebel groups. China played a significant role in delaying the passage (both in the UN Commission on Human Rights in Geneva in 1989 and 1990 and at the UN General Assembly in 1990) of strong resolutions criticizing the SLORC's human rights violations. China also improved road and bridge links with northern Myanmar, and Chinese firms became important in the timber industry. In the late 1990s several border towns became the centre of a tourist industry based on gambling, drugs and prostitution. It was reported that in some towns the Myanma kyat had been displaced by the Chinese yuan for virtually all transactions. The Chinese President, Jiang Zemin, visited Myanmar in December 2001, and agreements for economic co-operation in several fields were concluded. During the late 1990s, however, Chinese authorities became increasingly concerned by the flow of drugs from Myanmar into the newly affluent coastal regions of China and began to co-operate more closely with the Myanma Government in attempting to control the trade. In 2000 the Myanma army reportedly began to develop closer ties with the army of Pakistan.

From the 1980s, relations with ASEAN were central to Myanmar's efforts to avoid international isolation. As relatively developed economies, both Malaysia and Thailand were interested in the emerging economic opportunities in Myanmar, while ASEAN as a whole, and Indonesia in particular, was keen to ensure that Myanmar did not fall into China's orbit. In 1991 ASEAN denied a US request to use its influence with Myanmar to help persuade it to end human rights violations and allow democratic government to be restored. ASEAN declared that it pursued a policy of 'constructive engagement' with the SLORC and that it would not interfere in Myanmar's internal affairs. Trade between Myanmar and ASEAN continued to expand, and in July 1994 U Ohn Gyaw, then Myanma Minister of Foreign Affairs, travelled to Bangkok to attend the opening and closing ceremonies of the annual meeting of ASEAN ministers responsible for foreign affairs (the first time that Myanmar had been invited to attend as a guest). Myanmar's links with ASEAN became steadily closer from this time. It signed a treaty of friendship and co-operation with ASEAN members in 1995, and was granted full observer status at the July 1996 ASEAN meeting in Jakarta, also becoming a full member of the ASEAN Regional Forum (ARF). Myanmar applied to join ASEAN in October 1996 and was admitted as a full member on 1 July 1997. It also joined the BISTEC (Bangladesh-India-Sri Lanka-Thailand Economic Forum) in 1997. However, the country was not allowed to participate in the second ASEM (Asia-Europe Meeting) in early 1998, at the insistence of various European states. In early 1999 a meeting between ASEAN and the EU scheduled to take place in February was postponed indefinitely as a result of continued disagreement over the representation of Myanmar at the meeting. ASEAN objected that the EU should not attempt to dictate ASEAN membership and defended its approach of 'constructive engagement'. The Minister of Foreign Affairs for Singapore commented, 'In Asia, we marry first and expect the bride to adapt her behaviour after the marriage.' As EU governments would not permit Myanma senior officials to enter their territory, ASEAN hosted a two-day ministerial summit in Vientiane in Laos in December 2000, but only junior ministers attended from the European side. The meeting ended with an agreement that an EU delegation would visit Myanmar for discussions with both the Government and Aung San Suu Kyi. The visit took place in January 2001, but produced no formal outcome. In April 1996 James Leander (Leo) Nichols, a businessman, honorary consul of Norway and Denmark and local representative for Sweden, was arrested and imprisoned for having an unauthorized fax machine and additional telephone lines. Despite many vigorous but polite requests for his release on the grounds of old age and ill health, including a visit by the Norwegian, Danish and Swedish diplomatic representatives in Thailand and Singapore, Nichols was kept at Insein Jail, where he died in June. The SLORC autopsy reported the cause of death as a stroke; Insein Jail is notorious for the ill-treatment and torture of prisoners, many of whom have died in custody. Observers believed that the real reason for Nichols' arrest was his close relationship with Suu Kyi. Strong protests about his death were made by Australia (where much of his family lived) as well as Norway, Denmark and Sweden, and Myanmar's hopes for better relations with the EU suffered a major set-back.

In September 1999 a diplomatic dispute began between Myanmar and the United Kingdom, after British consular staff were refused permission to visit two Britons, James Mawdsley and Rachel Goldwyn, being held in prison in Myanmar for their separate involvement in pro-democracy protest action. The British Government expressed its grave concern over the treatment of the pair. Rachel Goldwyn was released in November; James Mawdsley was sentenced to 17 years' imprisonment by the ruling junta in September for illegal entry into the country and sedition, however, and served more than 400 days in solitary confinement before being released in October 2000 as a result of pressure from the UN, the British and US Governments and other international bodies.

In mid-1997 the ILO began a major investigation of forced labour and the suppression of trade unions in Myanmar. The findings of the investigation were subsequently published in late August 1998: in its report, the ILO found the use of forced labour to be 'pervasive' throughout the whole of the country (and to include women, children, the sick and the elderly), and accused the regime of using beatings, torture, rape and murder in the enforcement of its forced labour policy, constituting a 'gross denial of human rights'. In June 1999 a resolution condemning Myanmar for its widespread use of forced labour was adopted by the member countries of the ILO, and the country was barred from participating in any ILO activities. At the organization's annual conference in Geneva on 14 June 2000, its members voted by an overwhelming majority to adopt measures against Myanmar if the military Government did not halt the practice of forced labour within four months. The sanctions came into effect in November 2000, though their implementation depended on the co-operation of individual countries. The Myanma Government responded by describing the sanctions as 'unfair', 'unreasonable' and 'unjust' and announcing that it would cease to co-operate with the ILO. In May 2001 ASEAN labour ministers issued a joint communiqué noting what they described as concrete actions by Myanmar to eradicate forced labour and calling on the ILO to end its campaign against Myanmar. The ILO sent a delegation to Myanmar in October 2001 to investigate the claims of improvement; it reported, however, that forced labour was still widespread in areas controlled by the military.

Myanmar has also been condemned annually since 1991 by the UN for human rights violations within the country, with increasingly strong resolutions having been passed by the General Assembly each year. As a result, companies operating in Myanmar may find themselves subject to boycotts and other protest activity, such as that which persuaded Pepsi, Texaco and many others to withdraw completely from the country. Various national governments now encourage companies not to invest in Myanmar, and several local governments, such as that of New York City in the USA, have selective purchasing policies and will not do business with companies that operate in Myanmar. (In June 1998, however, a US court ruled that state and local governments could not impose a boycott on Myanmar by law, since such actions infringed the right of the Federal Government to conduct foreign policy.) In late November the Republic of Korea became the first Asian country to co-sponsor a UN General Assembly resolution criticizing human rights abuses in Myanmar. In January 2002 the European lingerie manufacturer Triumph decided to close its factory in Myanmar in response to a long campaign in Europe claiming that it was exploiting forced labour.

From late 1998, however, Myanmar's international isolation began, in some respects, to diminish, and Western diplomats began to speak approvingly of the possibility of effecting change in Myanmar through the employment of policies of engagement, rather than isolation, towards its Government. In October 1998 the British Government convened a low-key meeting at Chilston Park in the United Kingdom at which ministers of foreign affairs and ambassadors from several countries, together with UN and World Bank officials, began to develop a strategy of engaging with the Myanma Government. These meetings gave rise to the proposal, quickly rejected by the ruling junta, that Myanmar should receive US $1,000m. in aid in return for significant political concessions. A follow-up meeting in Seoul in March 2000, nicknamed Chilston-2, failed to come up with further strategies. None the less, in February 2000 Myanmar hosted a major Interpol conference addressing drug-related crime. Although the United Kingdom and the USA boycotted the meeting, the military junta convinced some of those attending that it was interested in attacking the trade. The Australian, Japanese and South Korean Governments all made official contact with the Myanma Government to explore possibilities for political change in Myanmar. In November 1999 the Japanese Prime Minister, Keizo Obuchi, met with Senior Gen. Than Shwe during an ASEAN summit meeting in Manila; the meeting was the first between the leader of a major world power and a senior member of the military Government since the junta's suppression of the democratic opposition in 1988. Also in November 1999 the former Japanese Prime Minister, Ryutaro Hashimoto, visited Yangon. In April 2000 the EU announced the introduction of increased sanctions against Myanmar, but in the second half of 2001, in response to increasing indications that dialogue was taking place between the SPDC and Aung San Suu Kyi, it agreed to allow Myanmar to take part in future ASEAN-EU dialogues and to sponsor a variety of aid programmes, while keeping the sanctions in place. The removal of restrictions on Suu Kyi in May 2002 was welcomed in international circles, although it was widely described as being only the first step towards change. The first diplomatic benefit of the release came in August 2002, when the Japanese Minister of Foreign Affairs, Yoriko Kawaguchi, visited Myanmar. The USA also signalled its willingness to lift sanctions in return for political progress.

Economy

RICHARD VOKES

Revised for this edition by CHRISTOPHER TORRENS

INTRODUCTION

In November 1997 Myanmar's military junta renamed the ruling State Law and Order Restoration Council (SLORC) the State Peace and Development Council (SPDC). Within a year several powerful regional commanders who had recently been promoted to the Council were replaced, and the Cabinet doubled in size to consolidate around two key generals, Maung Aye and Khin Nyunt (see below), who competed for control, but who both favoured economic privatization. However, sanctions imposed by Western democracies severely hindered this policy, so attention was turned to agriculture, where the expansion of cultivated land became the focus of a revitalized Ministry of Agriculture and Irrigation. Whereas high-yielding rice and double cropping were emphasized during the period of economic expansion between 1993 and 1996, the priority shifted to expanding acreage by means of awarding benefits to new agri-corporations for the purchase and cultivation of unused land. The SPDC's goal was to achieve self-sufficiency in food grains and to re-enter the global rice market.

Myanmar's economic growth rate was negative or low throughout the late 1980s, but the situation improved in the 1990s owing to a recovery in the level of exports resulting from foreign direct investment (FDI). In 1996/97, according to the Asian Development Bank (ADB), real GDP increased by 6.4%, compared with a growth rate of 6.9% in 1995/96, but real GDP growth declined to 5.7% in 1997/98, before increasing to 5.8% in 1998/99. GDP growth was officially declared to be 10.9% in 1999/2000 and 13.6% in 2000/01. In the latter year the ADB suggested that that a growth rate of 6.2% was more likely. This decrease in the rate of growth was forecast to continue in 2001/02 as a result of adverse global economic conditions, declining Japanese investment, the effect of sanctions and the severe flooding of agricultural regions in 2001. The Government confirmed this when it issued a rare statement predicting 5%–6% growth for 2001/02, followed by a progressive slowdown over the succeeding four years. Furthermore, it was thought that power shortages would have a negative effect on manufacturing GDP. Compared with the previous year, the GDP of the manufacturing sector increased by 5.3% in 1997/98 and by 9.3% in 1998/99. Growth in manufacturing GDP was reportedly 15% in 1999/2000, although foreign investment in the manufacturing sector declined sharply.

While the Government attracted foreign investment in several natural resource sectors, particularly energy development, after the Foreign Investment Law came into effect in December 1988, by 1999 investment had declined to one-tenth of the 1992 level. Meanwhile, the agricultural sector grew at an average annual rate of 5.0% from 1992 to 1996, as foreign capital flowed into a number of large corporate farming ventures, but then entered a brief period of decline as the Ministry of Agriculture and Irrigation tried to manipulate the market by means of quotas and price controls. However, in 1999/2000 real growth in agriculture was reported to have exceeded 11%, following good weather and an extension of the area under cultivation, reversing the downward trend of the previous years. Between 1996 and 1999 overall FDI declined from US $2,814m. to a mere US $29.5m. This sharp decline abated slightly in 1999/2000, when investment increased to US $55.6m., owing to a shift in capital flow, according to Myanmar's Central Statistical Organization (CSO). The USA and France had invested heavily in petroleum and natural gas in the early 1990s, but US sanctions took effect in 1998, following which the source of capital flow shifted to Asian sources, primarily Japan, Thailand, Hong Kong, Singapore, and the Republic of Korea. FDI resumed its steep decline in 2001/02, totalling just US $17.5m and US $3.3m. in the oil and gas sectors respectively, and US $14.2m. in manufacturing. The six principal investors in Myanmar remained: the Republic of Korea (US $5m.); Japan (US $4.7m.); China (US $3.3m.); Hong Kong (US $1.5m.); Indonesia (US $1.5m); and Malaysia (US $1.5m.). By 2002 FDI in Myanmar from ASEAN countries had fallen to 17.1% (US $3m.) of the total, from 39% in 2000. The decrease in FDI resulted from the impact of the 1997 Asian financial crisis, the terrorist attacks on the USA of 11 September 2001, the overall global economic slowdown and a unfavourable environment for domestic investment. According to official statistics, in the period between 1988 and March 2002 FDI reached a total of US $7,400m.

Official data ignore a large influx of 'black money' earned from narcotics and smuggling, estimated at between US $1,000m. and US $2,000m. annually. The highway between China and Mandalay provides extensive evidence of substantial unrecorded expenditures on elaborate new pagodas and monasteries, palatial houses, expensive cars and construction equipment, and upmarket resorts. A small but affluent new class of officials, merchants and farmers deals in this illicit hard currency. While urban property prices have decreased sharply in recent years, the volume of highway traffic remains unaffected; indeed, one multifaceted corporation owned by a retired trader in narcotics contracted to expand and maintain this key highway near China, to be financed by levying tolls. In addition, several small private airlines and upmarket bus companies apparently capitalized by 'black money' opened in the mid-1990s, hoping to serve Myanmar's new rich and an expected influx of foreign tourists. Energy shortages reflect unwillingness by the members of Myanmar's new class to invest their wealth in long-term projects such as hydroelectric dams or thermal plants, and a failure by the Government under the *Burmese Way to Socialism* (see below) and the military regimes since 1988, to implement a comprehensive programme of economic reform. In particular, at the official exchange rate, the currency continued to be highly overvalued; at the end of 2001 the unofficial exchange rate had risen to nearly 720 kyats = US $1, while the official rate remained at 6.7 kyats = US $1. Moreover, the limited inflow of foreign assistance prevented major structural problems, such as the overvalued exchange rate, from being addressed. This failure undermined the pattern of growth recorded in the first half of the 1990s, as suggested by the deceleration between 1996/97 and 1998/99 and that forecast to occur from 2001/02 onwards. Meanwhile, a high annual rate of inflation continued to prevail, owing largely to the constantly expanding budget deficit and to a decline in the rice harvest in 2001. Although actual economic data are unavailable, it has been estimated that consumer price inflation (CPI) averages around 20%–30% per annum. With no prospect of a substantial increase in external assistance, development opportunities remain poor. The resumption of both aid and investment depends on greater political stability, which in turn depends on some reasonable transition to democracy. By mid-2001 the SPDC had taken its first tentative steps towards liberalization, but combating poverty remained its most pressing problem. Per caput income was estimated at US $97 (at the free-market exchange rate) in 2000, confirming that Myanmar remained one of the poorest countries in Asia.

ECONOMIC POLICY AND PLANNING SINCE 1962

Until the reforms of 1988, Myanmar had been ruled consistently by Governments that espoused an essentially socialist path to development. The military coup in March 1962 and the subsequent publication, in April, of the new Government's economic policy document, *The Burmese Way to Socialism,* signified a turning-point in Myanmar's post-war economic development.

The document outlined the military Government's commitment to the establishment of a 'socialist democratic state'. The four principal objectives of the Government's economic policy were: the elimination of foreign control of the economy; a reduction in the country's dependence on foreign markets; a restructuring of the economy away from its dependence on primary production towards a more balanced industrial condition; and, finally, the centralization of economic power in the hands of the State, in order to reduce the power of the private market. These objectives were to be realized through the nationalization of all vital means of production, including those in agriculture, industry, commerce, transport, communications and external trade. Ownership of the means of production was to be vested either in the State, or in co-operatives or unions. While the importance of the role of agriculture in the economy was recognized, priority was given to the development of industry and the improvement of social services.

Implementation of these policies initially brought some benefit to the population, especially in rural areas. However, the country soon faced a growing economic crisis. As a result of the priority given to building a modern industrial sector, agriculture was neglected and, coupled with low procurement prices, this led to a decline in the production of rice, the country's principal export as well as staple food, thus resulting in a severe shortage of foreign exchange. The industrial sector also failed to perform well, despite the priority it received in terms of investment. This was due to the bias towards continued investment in new plants, despite the fact that existing capacity was being used inefficiently, and to inadequate managerial capacity. Growth in the output of the state-owned industrial sector was insufficient to compensate for the decline in the private sector; as a result, shortages and rationing developed, leading to the growth of a 'black market', which continues to exist.

As the country's economic crisis worsened, the Government was forced to introduce its first programme of economic reform. This involved: increased priority for the production and export of primary products; the decentralization of management and greater use of commercial incentives, in an effort to improve efficiency within state enterprises; an enhanced role for the private sector; and a new willingness to seek and accept external assistance, in an effort to gain access to both capital and technology. After 1972 there was a rapid growth in foreign assistance, particularly from Japan, and from the World Bank and the ADB. Foreign assistance, which had totalled only US $21.7m. in 1970/71, grew rapidly, reaching a peak of US $512m. in 1979/80. All these policies were to be implemented within the framework of a 20-Year Plan. This represented the country's first real attempt at long-term planning, and provided only broad guidelines with respect to goals and priorities: it was to be divided up into five Four-Year Plans.

While economic performance did improve after 1972, and particularly after 1976, by 1982 the country was once more facing serious economic problems, caused by slow growth in the agricultural sector, a significant decline in the price of both teak and rice, the two principal exports, and growing debt-service payments. In response to the worsening crisis, further economic reforms were introduced by the Government of the Burma Socialist Programme Party (BSPP) between August 1987 and July 1988. The implementation of these reforms was disrupted by widespread political unrest, which resulted, finally, in the establishment of the SLORC in September 1988.

The economic reform programme followed since then, based on the earlier reforms introduced by the BSPP, implies the complete abandonment of the policy of self-sufficiency and the adoption of an 'open-door policy' on foreign investment, which is now accepted as crucial to the country's economic development. Under the Foreign Investment Law published in November 1988, 100% foreign-owned companies were allowed, in addition to joint ventures where foreign capital had to form at least 35% of total capital. The law also offered exemption from tax for at least three years and a range of other incentives, as well as guarantees against nationalization. In seeking foreign investment, priority was to be given to the promotion and expansion of exports, the exploitation of natural resources requiring large investment, the acquisition of advanced technology, employment generation, energy conservation and regional development. By 1991 the Government had had some success in attracting foreign investment, particularly into the energy sector. However, Myanmar's ability to absorb a major inflow of foreign investment was limited in the short term, most notably by its poor infrastructure, inefficient banking sector and shortages of skilled labour.

In 1996 the Government embarked upon its second Five-Year Plan. This was intended to achieve a 6% rise in the GDP growth rate. According to the SPDC, it had succeeded in reaching an annual growth rate of 8.4% by 2001. The previous Four-Year Plan (1992–96) had apparently achieved an average annual growth rate of 7.5%. Overall, economic growth had more than doubled since the end of the 1980s as the Government's short-term economic plans took effect, creating favourable conditions for Myanmar's economic development.

In March 2001 the Government implemented its third Five-Year Plan. The plan beginning in 2001 projected average GDP growth rates in excess of 8% until 2005/06. The main aims of the plan were: to promote the establishment of agro-based industries; to develop the power and energy sectors; to expand the agriculture, meat and fish sectors in order to meet local demand and provide a surplus for export; to establish forest reserves; to extend the health and education sectors; and to develop the rural areas.

AGRICULTURE, FORESTRY AND FISHING

Agriculture (including livestock, forestry and fishing) remains a key sector in the Myanma economy, contributing 57.1% of GDP in 2000/01, according to the ADB. Approximately 70% of the population are engaged in farming. Exports from this sector accounted for more than three-quarters of total exports in 1995/96. Agriculture is thus central to the performance of the whole economy. The performance of the sector improved markedly after it was accorded increased priority in the economic reforms of 1971/72, although the sector has still frequently failed to achieve the targets set. The agricultural sector expanded at an average annual rate of 6.6% over the period 1973–83, but it subsequently advanced more slowly, achieving a growth rate of 4.7% under the Fourth Plan (1982/83–1985/86). The sector was seriously affected by the economic and political disruptions of 1988 and 1989, with production declining significantly. Between 1990/91 and 1995/96 agricultural output increased in all but one year, and in the years from 1992/93 to 1996/97 the sector averaged annual growth of 5.0%. However, whilst the improvement of irrigation systems has been a central part of the Government's economic policy, other factors (such as continued vulnerability to adverse weather and pests, a shortage of agricultural inputs such as fertilizers, and government rice procurement policies of doubtful wisdom) have continued to constrain the sector; another major factor previously undermining agricultural development was the Government's failure to provide adequate incentives, in the form of higher prices and support services, to farmers, although these have been improved. In 1997/98, compared with the previous year, agricultural GDP expanded by 3.7%; the rate of growth slowly increased to 4.5% in 1998/99 before benefiting from favourable climatic conditions to reach 11.5% in 1999/2000 and 10.9% in 2000/01, according to the ADB.

Until the mid-1970s growth in agricultural production was achieved largely through a gradual increase in the area under cultivation. Since then, greater emphasis has been given to raising productivity through the use of improved seeds and modern inputs. Owing to a lack of funds for maintenance and the shortage of fuel to operate pumps, the area under irrigation actually declined by 7.4% between 1986/87 and 1991/92. A further expansion in irrigation was vital to efforts to promote greater use of modern inputs, especially fertilizer and pesticides. Between 1988 and 2002, according to the Ministry of Agriculture and Irrigation, the Government built 127 new dams at a cost of US $140.2m., bringing to 265 the total number of dams in the country. Some 1.92m. ha (19%) of Myanmar's arable land is cultivated through irrigation.

In 1995/96 an estimated 9.1m. ha of land were under cultivation, representing about 13.1% of the land area, and slightly less than one-half of the land available for cultivation. By 2002 this figure had risen to 15.0m. ha. While this suggests that there is ample scope for expanding the land frontier, much virgin land is remote from the major centres of population and would require considerable investment in infrastructure to bring it into production. The increase of area under cultivation has not kept pace with population growth, resulting in a decline in the availability of cultivated land per caput, from 0.56 ha in 1940/41 to only 0.20 ha in 1992/93. However, there has been a rapid increase in the cultivation of non-paddy crops, such as pulses and beans (which by 1997 occupied 14% of cultivable land), sesame (10%) and sugar (0.7%).

Rice

Rice dominates Myanmar's economy. It is the main source of employment as well as the principal export earner. It is also the staple food, providing the bulk of the calorie and protein intake for the population. The total area under paddy in 1995/96 was estimated at 6.2m. ha, 47.5% of all land under cultivation. Of this, some 1.3m. ha were planted with summer paddy, and 4.9m. ha with the monsoon crop. It was not until 1964 that the area under paddy reached the level attained immediately prior to the Second World War. Paddy production, which was only 8.4m. metric tons in 1964/65, increased significantly to 14.1m. tons in 1986/87. Following a decline in 1987/88 and 1988/89, production had increased to 20.1m. tons by 1999/2000. According to official statistics, in 2001/02 Myanmar produced 22.3m. tons of rice. The Government intended to cultivate 6.8m. ha of paddy with the aim of producing 28.2m. tons of rice in 2002; rice exports were forecast to reach 1m. tons.

The increase in production was particularly marked from the late 1970s, reflecting the success of government efforts to promote the use of high-yielding varieties (HYV). An experimental 'Whole Township Special High Yield Variety Paddy Cultivation Programme', introduced in 1975/76, was gradually extended, and by 1987 the programme covered 82 townships. While extension and other support services are concentrated in these areas, the use of HYV has also spread to areas outside the programme. Government data record the use of HYV on 60% of the total paddy area, providing 70% of production, in 1992/93. The average yield of HYV paddy in 1991/92 was 3,300 kg per ha, compared with 2,900 kg per ha for paddy as a whole; both figures, however, are low by regional standards. Paddy accounted for an estimated 74.8% of the irrigated area, 82.9% of fertilizer use in Myanmar and most of the pesticide use in 1995/96.

Until 1986 the State, working through the Agricultural and Farm Produce Trade Corporation (AFPTC—renamed the Myanma Agricultural Products Agency in 1989), was responsible for procurement and distribution of paddy and rice. After 1986 the Government began to liberalize the marketing of paddy and rice, first by allowing co-operative societies to operate alongside the AFPTC and then, in September 1987, by opening the trade to the private sector. This was followed in January 1988 by the ending of the State's monopoly on rice exports. These policies were intended to increase both production and exports. However, their introduction coincided with a decline in production and a period of rapidly rising rice prices that helped to fuel the growing unrest in urban areas during 1988. As a result, after 1988, state procurement, albeit in competition with the private sector, was reintroduced. Although state procurement prices were increased, they were still below those offered by private traders. However, because the state marketing organizations were able to provide fertilizer and credit at subsidized prices, they were still able to attract supplies from farmers. In 1990/91 it was estimated that the State purchased around 15% of total paddy production, while co-operatives purchased a further 7%. In 1997 a quota system, under which state agencies procured paddy from farmers at low prices, was still in operation. However, in late 1997, prices paid to farmers by the Government were raised, and a relaxation of the state monopoly on rice exports was attempted.

Given the country's acute shortage of foreign exchange, the SLORC sought to boost the level of rice exports, although priority was still being given to ensuring an adequate domestic supply of rice in an attempt to reduce pressure on rice prices. Owing to unreliable harvests, however, the Government achieved varying degrees of success in its attempt to raise rice exports. In seeking to expand its exports of rice, Myanmar was also faced with strong competition from other exporters, especially Thailand and the USA and, since 1989, from Viet Nam; Myanmar was also hampered by the low quality of its rice, although this had improved as a result of a programme, completed in 1985, to modernize the country's facilities for the storage and processing of rice. Exports of rice dwindled from late 1997 onwards, owing to a burgeoning population which consumed the majority of the domestic supply, and also because of ongoing smuggling through Yunnanese traders. In December 2000 rice prices declined to an estimated 50% of their 1999 value, owing to unfavourable market conditions, causing a further fall in rice exports. In late 2002 a massive increase in rice prices, precipitated by a production shortage, threatened to contribute to rising levels of starvation amongst the Myanma population.

Other Crops

Besides paddy, Myanmar produces a wide range of other crops including maize, pulses, groundnuts, sesame seed and the so-called 'industrial crops', jute, cotton, sugar cane and tobacco. These are produced primarily for domestic use, although pulses and sesame seeds are important export commodities, and small quantities of maize, rubber, jute and tobacco have been exported in recent years. Both the area and production of these crops have increased steadily since the mid-1970s, with the exception of rubber. In 1995/96 an estimated 102,465 ha of land was under cultivation for rubber. In 1998/99 rubber production was 27,000 tons, in 1999/2000 output was 23,000 tons and, according to FAO estimates, production was 23,000 tons in 2000/01, most of which was exported. In 2001, according to official statistics, Myanmar exported 18,400 tons of raw rubber, a 29.2% decrease in comparison with 2000. Export earnings reached US $9.0m., a decline of 33.4% from 2000. In the same year the country imported rubber goods worth US $34.8m., 13.0% less than 2000. In an attempt to raise production levels, the Government increased the size of the area under rubber plantation from 81,000 ha in 1994 to 182,250 ha by the end of 2001. A total of 2.6m. ha are reportedly suitable for rubber cultivation.

The Government is trying to encourage the use of improved varieties on all non-paddy crops; during the Fourth Plan, the 'Whole Township Programme' was extended to include 20 other crops, and particular attention was given to those crops with export potential, or to those crops which could be substituted for imports. After paddy, sesame seed, groundnuts, maize, sugar cane and beans and pulses are the most important crops in terms of the area cultivated. The prospects for exports of maize, beans and pulses in the 1990s were favourable as demand for these commodities remained high in neighbouring countries and Japan. Jute production increased in the early 1990s, from 12,363 tons in 1990/91 to an estimated 43,000 tons in 1995/96. Jute production totalled 33,000 tons in 1998/99 and 1999/2000, and remained at the same level in 2000/01, according to FAO estimates. Tobacco is produced primarily for the local market, but small quantities of Virginia are exported. Production of tobacco was 57,000 tons in 1998/99, 42,000 tons in 1999/2000 and was estimated at 46,000 tons in 2000/01. Since the Government does not seek to control the prices of non-rice crops, decisions with respect to the planted area of such crops have been determined more by relative prices on the private market than by government plans and targets; efforts are now being made, however, to design cropping patterns that are beneficial to both farmers and the State, as well as being suited to local conditions.

Livestock and Fisheries

The livestock and fisheries sector has increased rapidly in recent years, achieving an annual growth rate of 6.4% under the Fourth Plan. Following a poor performance between 1986/87 and 1990/91, the sector recorded a growth rate of 72% in 1991/92, and a further average annual increase of 5.8% between 1991/92 and 1995/96. In 1996/97 the sector achieved a growth rate of 9.7%. Continued growth is regarded by the Government as an important means of expanding domestic consumption, thereby improving nutrition, and, in the case of fisheries, expanding exports. In addition, the livestock sector is vital to the development of agriculture, since the vast majority of farmers continue to rely on animal draught power. The number of draught animals was estimated at 6.8m. in 1995/96.

Fish is the major source of animal protein in the Myanma diet. In 1985/86 consumption per caput amounted to 11.02 viss (1 viss = 1.63 kg or 3.60 lb). By contrast, meat consumption was only 3.32 viss per caput. Owing to shortages, meat prices are high, and meat is therefore regarded as a 'luxury' food. There was, however, a particularly rapid increase in chicken and duck production from the late 1970s; meat production from these sources increased by 70% and 95% respectively between 1979/80 and 1985/86. There was a further increase of 35.4% in the production of chicken meat between 1992/93 and 1995/96. Total meat production increased by an estimated 27.2% between 1992/93 and 1995/96 from 1.2m. viss to 1.5m. viss, while milk production increased by only 4% over the same period, having doubled between 1979/80 and 1986/87. In 1998/99 total meat production (including the production of poultry meat, output of which reached an estimated 144,000 tons) increased to an estimated 390,000 tons. In the same year the production of cows', buffaloes' and goats' milk totalled an estimated 588,000 tons. In 1999/2000 total meat production was approximately 437,000 tons (of which poultry meat constituted an estimated 177,000 tons) and milk output was 604,000 tons. In 2000/01, according to FAO estimates, 444,000 tons of meat were produced (including 208,000 tons of poultry meat), and 744,000 tons of milk. Since the mid-1970s significant efforts have been made to promote the fisheries sector, particularly offshore marine fisheries. Considerable donor assistance has been given to off-shore fisheries, and production has increased significantly since 1976/77. In contrast to the livestock sector, a primary development objective of the fisheries sector is to increase exports. Export earnings from the fisheries sector have increased rapidly, and the prospects for further expansion in the sector are favourable. In 1993/94 government figures suggested that the total fish catch was 922,500 tons, of which 75% came from the sea. In 1994/95 output of marine products increased by 1.7%, compared with 1993/94, although export earnings from the fisheries sector increased by 57%. Although exports of fish and fish products declined in 1995/96, exports of fresh and dried prawns continued to show strong growth, reaching an estimated 392.3m. kyats (equivalent to 9.7% of the value of total exports). Exports of fish and fish products recovered in 1996/97, totalling an estimated 227.8m. kyats in that year. According to FAO, the total fish catch rose from 917,700 tons in 1997/98 to 958,200 tons in 1998/99 and 945,800 tons in 1999/2000.

From early 1989 several agreements were signed allowing foreign trawlers, including those from Thailand, Malaysia, Japan and the Republic of Korea, access to Myanma waters. Future development prospects could now be adversely affected by overfishing. In mid-1993 the SLORC announced the cancellation of fishing rights granted to Thai firms. A fresh attempt to revitalize the fisheries sector was made by the Government in August 1994, when it announced the dissolution of the state-owned Myanma Fisheries Enterprise, whose work was assumed by the Department of Fisheries. The aim was to attract greater private-sector participation.

Forestry

Prior to the Second World War, teak was the third most important export commodity after rice and petroleum. Production was severely disrupted by the war, and, after the attainment of independence in 1948, by insurgency. Teak production in 1970/71, at 291,000 cu tons (each of 50 cu ft or 1.416 cu m), was still below pre-war levels (447,000 tons in 1939/40), while teak exports were almost one-half of their pre-war level. None the less, teak exports still accounted for 25% of export earnings in that year, and, with rice exports continuing to decline, the development of the forestry sector was identified as one of the most important means of increasing foreign-exchange earnings. Increased investment resulted in a rise in teak production to 436,000 tons in 1981/82, but production declined to 291,000 tons in 1988/89 before rising to a post-war peak of 440,000 tons in 1990/91. Owing to conservation measures (see below), teak production declined steadily thereafter to an estimated 220,000 tons in 1996/97. Production of other hardwoods totalled 1,840,000 tons in 1992/93 (most of which was for domestic consumption), but subsequently declined to an estimated 1,109,000 tons in 1995/96. Forest products accounted for an estimated 22% of exports in 1994/95, compared with 32.1% in 1993/94. Nearly 70% of such exports were derived from teak. In 1994/95 forestry contributed around 5% to GDP. The value of exports of teak and other hardwood was estimated to have declined from 1,060.9m. kyats in 1994/95 to 1,048.5m. kyats in 1995/96, but increased to an estimated 1,140.9m. kyats in 1996/97. Timber production declined by an annual average of 4.9% between 1992/93 and 1996/97. According to FAO, roundwood removals totalled 22.25m. cu m in 1998. In that year exports of roundwood were estimated at US $137.2m., compared with US $98.1m. in 1997. Roundwood removals were estimated at 22.57m. cu m in both 1999/2000 and 2000/01.

Today, Myanmar's forest covers 50 percent of its total land area, 7% less than that in 1962. To overcome teak shortages, Myanmar launched a special plantation plan five years ago and has been able to grow more than 32,400 ha of teak. Of the total forest area, 18.6% is protected with the target due to increase to 30%. Myanmar has since planted more than 32,400 hectares of teak.

The illegal felling of teak, and its smuggling into Thailand, has been a major problem. In an effort to ease the country's acute shortage of foreign exchange, the then BSPP Government announced an end to the 40-year ban on cross-border trade in teak in early 1988. From September 1988 onwards the SLORC made strenuous efforts to boost foreign-exchange earnings and its foreign reserves by signing a series of logging contracts with Thai companies. This resulted in a significant increase in the rate of felling, particularly for hardwoods other than teak, mainly in areas along the Myanmar–Thailand border. The increase in the rate of timber extraction gave rise to growing concern about over-felling and likely adverse environmental impacts. This led to the announcement in January 1990 of an 80% reduction in the level of timber exports allowed by the Thai companies and a statement that no new timber contracts would be allowed. In June 1990 export fees on teak and other hardwoods were increased by more than 100%. However, policing such regulations was difficult. Many of the concessions awarded to Thai companies were in areas affected by the long-running insurgency. Measures taken to prevent rapid deforestation were undermined by the SLORC's initiation of agreements with insurgent groups in border areas, which provided for the rebels' cross-border trade to be legalized in exchange for truce arrangements with government forces. A logging ban was reimposed in 1994. Deforestation was held to be partly responsible for the serious flooding that affected the country in mid-1997.

In the more medium term there is a crucial need to reduce the export of raw logs and to increase the value added from local processing both as a means of increasing export earnings from forestry and ensuring a more sustainable development of the sector. At 1990 felling rates, it was estimated that the country's teak resources could be exhausted in as little as 15 years. In mid-1993 the SLORC cancelled 47 Thai timber-logging concessions in an attempt to slow the pace of deforestation. It also launched a new, three-year reafforestation programme (with an annual target of some 50,000 ha). In 1996/97 an estimated 48% of Myanmar was still under forest cover. The area of reserved forest increased from 10.2m. ha in 1992/93 to 10.4m. ha in 1995/96.

MINING AND PETROLEUM

Myanmar has a rich natural resource base which offers considerable potential for long-term developments. Mining was another sector accorded a higher priority under the 20-Year Plan. This primarily reflected the need to increase petroleum production to meet the country's development needs. Emphasis was, however, also given to expanding the supply of mineral raw materials for local industry, and to raising the level of mineral exports. Although production targets were not always achieved, the sector grew rapidly from the mid-1970s onwards, recording an annual growth rate of 8.2% under the Third Plan and 12.8% under the Fourth Plan (the latter representing the second-highest growth rate of any sector during the Plan period). In the final year of the Fourth Plan, output was provisionally estimated to have risen by 21.9%, but the increase was later adjusted to 9.9%. Since then the value of production has often declined in real terms, owing to a lack of capital and technology and the continuing shortage of fuel. In 1991/92 production was about 20% below the level of 1985/86. However, mining output has increased considerably since the introduction of the Myanmar Mining Law in 1994, which granted concessions to foreign mining companies. By mid-1998 12 foreign mining companies had signed joint-venture agreements, and the production of oil, gas, zinc, lead, gold and gems had increased substantially. In 1998/99 the mining sector provided 0.9% of GDP, decreasing to 0.5% in 1999/2000 before increasing marginally to 0.6% in 2000/01, and in 1997/98 it accounted for 0.7% of employment. In 1996/97 the output of the sector expanded by 13%, largely as a result of foreign investment (which totalled US $178.3m. in that year). By 2002 total foreign investment in Myanmar's mining sector had amounted to US $522.5m. since 1988. The Lepadaung project in Monywa, the country's north-western Sagaing division, is expected to become one of the world's largest sources of copper production. US firm Ivanhoe, which has invested US $150m. in a joint venture with the Myanma Mining Enterprise to operate the mine, estimates that Lepadaung is about five times larger than the other two deposits at Sabetaung and Kyinsintaung.

Although petroleum was a principal export commodity prior to the Second World War, the industry was all but destroyed by the hostilities. While efforts were made to rehabilitate the industry in the post-war period, these proceeded only slowly, and petroleum imports were still required during the 1970s. An independent study carried out in 1995 estimated that (contrary to official statistics) Myanmar is still able to meet only some 50% of domestic fuel requirements. Once it had acquired improved access to both capital and foreign technology, the Government was successful in increasing annual production from the 6.8m. barrels recorded in 1974/75, to 11m. barrels in 1979/80; in that year 1m. barrels of petroleum were exported to Japan. In 1995/96 production was estimated at only 6.9m. barrels, decreasing to 4.4m. barrels in 1997/98, 3.4m. in 1998/99 and a preliminary US Geological Survey figure of 3.39m. in 1999/2000. In 2001, according to the CSO, Myanmar produced a total of 4.7m. barrels of petroleum. During that year petroleum imports totalled US $217.6m. Since 1988 total foreign investment in the oil and gas sector has reached US $2,600m. from at least 34 contracts, which include exploration projects being conducted in 47 inland blocks and 15 joint-venture contracts in the same undertakings at 25 offshore blocks in the Mottama, Tanintharyi and Rakhine coastal areas. Growth continued in 2002; Myanmar produced a total of 820,000 barrels of petroleum in the first two months of the year, an increase of 12% compared with the corresponding period of 2001. The BSPP Government followed a policy of not allowing petroleum imports. However, this was only possible as a result of severe restrictions on consumption; petrol was rationed and there was a thriving 'black market', a situation that continued under the SLORC. The rationing of petrol was relaxed in August 1997, however, in an attempt to limit the 'black market'. Foreign involvement in the petroleum and natural gas sector has been problematic. The difficult operating environment, combined with the failure to locate commercially viable deposits, has prompted a number of foreign companies to cease exploration, notably the US oil company, Amoco, in March 1994. In 1995–96 new production-sharing contracts, both off shore and on shore, were awarded to Australian, Japanese and US companies, amongst others. However, the Myanma Oil and Gas Enterprise, a state corporation established to deal with foreign investors, proved to be a weak and inexperienced ally for the new shareholders, causing them to abandon their expectations of reasonable profits. Baker Hughes, the largest operator in Central Myanmar, was among seven companies that withdrew from the country or became inactive in 2000.

Prospects for natural gas exports to Thailand were excellent throughout the 1990s until the sharp decline in the value of the kyat in 1998. In 1994/95 and 1995/96 natural gas production was 45,599m. cu ft and 69,540m. cu ft respectively; in 1996/97 production declined slightly to 65,700m. cu ft. Production in 2000/01 reached 8,804.1m. cu m, while 5,608.6m. cu m of natural gas was exported, generating US $523.1m. in foreign exchange. Most of the output came from wells on the west bank of the Ayeyarwady (Irrawaddy) river in central Myanmar. A further major impetus to natural gas production and exports of liquefied natural gas (LNG) was anticipated, following the discovery, in 1982 and 1983, of major offshore fields in the Gulf of Martaban. In September 1994 the Myanma and Thai Governments concluded an agreement, under which Thailand was to purchase around US $400m. worth of natural gas annually from Myanmar for a period of 30 years, starting in 1998. To this end construction of a 670-km pipeline to transport natural gas from the Gulf of Martaban to Thailand began in 1996. Partners in the project included Total of France and Unocal of the USA, as well as the Petroleum Authority of Thailand and the Myanma Oil and Gas Enterprise. In 1997 the project accounted for about one-third of all foreign investment committed in Myanmar. Production was scheduled to start in July 1998, but was delayed owing to environmental and human rights protests on the Thai side of the border. Production delays on the Thai side from 1998 delayed natural gas purchases until 2000, when the first gas began to flow into the Ratchaburi power station, and sales were only US $50m., instead of the expected level of US $400m.

A major impetus to economic growth in 2002/03 was expected to be the additional exploitation of the Yadana and Yetagun offshore gas fields, which were approaching their targeted production levels in 2002. The main destinations for Myanmar's gas are neighbouring Thailand and other South-East Asian destinations. In February 2002 Daewoo International of the Republic of Korea announced that it would begin exploration on its Block A-1 offshore concession near the north-west coast, where estimates place reserves at 10,000 cu ft of gas. In the following month the Petroleum Exploration and Production Company of Thailand (PTTEP) announced that its Yetagun II offshore gas project in the Adaman Sea's Gulf of Martaban would go on stream in October 2002 at approximately 215,000m. cu ft per day. A sub-sea pipeline was to carry the gas produced to Myanmar for processing. Yadana, a second Myanma gas project in the Adaman Sea to provide output to Thailand, was expected to produce 525,000m. cu ft per day within five years.

There was also scope for expanding onshore gas production and this was to receive increased priority. In the late 1990s total onshore reserves were estimated to be 1,100,000m. cu ft. To ease fuel shortages, the Government has sought to encourage greater use of natural gas as an alternative fuel, and production of compressed natural gas increased by over 50% between 1988/89 and 1991/92. Although further foreign investment in this sector is crucial, its realization is not secure, particularly following the decision by the USA in 1997 to ban new investment by its nationals in the country. Indeed, in late 1997 the US company, Texaco, sold its gas interests in Myanmar, in response to shareholder and other pressure linked to the issue of human rights in the country. In late 1996 a lawsuit was brought against Unocal, the major company involved in pipeline construction in Yadana, because of its alleged direct responsibility for human rights abuses in Myanmar. In July 2000 a US federal judge agreed to hear the case against Unocal but, following a trial in September 2000, the company was exonerated of all charges of unlawful conduct. In September 2002 the British company, Premier Oil, announced that it was to dispose of all its interests in Myanmar. While claiming that its decision was made purely for commercial reasons, the company was thought to have been influenced by a campaign against it led by human rights activists.

Myanmar possesses a range of other important minerals that are commercially exploited. These include coal, tin, tungsten, gold, copper, lead, zinc, silver, barytes and gypsum. Following increases during the early 1980s, the production of many of these minerals declined after 1985/86, again largely owing to the shortage of fuel, foreign exchange and new technology. Gold production, however, has increased significantly since 1988/89, following the completion of a new gold-mining and -processing centre at Bawdwin, north-east of Mandalay. Myanmar also possesses commercially exploitable quantities of jade and gems. In the first half of 2001 Myanmar's sapphire production reached 2.643m. carats, a decline of 5.2% compared with the corresponding period of 2000. Ruby production increased by 13.2%, to 1.184m. carats, during the same period, while production of jade reached 69.645 metric tons.

While the production of gems has increased significantly, owing to the discovery of new gem tracts, smuggling of these high-value items has remained a problem. In 1993/94 coal production increased by 58% to 128,000 tons. Exports of minerals and gems accounted for 8.6% of total exports in 1993/94, but declined to an estimated 4.1% in 1994/95. Production remained largely in the state sector, which produced 76% of the output in 1991/92, while the co-operatives produced 2% and the private sector 22%. There has, however, been a steady growth in the share of the private sector since 1988/89.

INDUSTRY AND ENERGY

In spite of the priority given to the development of the agricultural, forestry and mining sectors under the 20-Year Plan, the share of public investment allocated to the industrial sector actually increased after 1972. From an average allocation of around 13% during the 1960s, the share increased to around 30% in the 1970s, with the industrial sector receiving the largest single share in all but a few years. Although industry's share subsequently declined, it still continued to receive one of the largest allocations of public investment through the 1980s. However, since 1990/91 its share has declined significantly and in 1992/93 the sector received only 5.7% of estimated public investment expenditure, reflecting the increased priority being given by the Government to construction, transport and communications and social services. In contrast to earlier policies, which aimed to promote the development of heavy industry, after 1972 emphasis was placed on the development of agro-based and resource-based industries, ensuring an effective link between industry and primary production, and on light consumer goods industries. At the same time, greater emphasis was given to improving the rate of utilization and efficiency of existing plants. While these remain key elements of industrial policy, after the mid-1980s greater emphasis was given to the development of export-orientated manufacturing industries. The increased level of investment after 1972, as well as reforms in management and accounting practices, and the introduction of incentives, meant that the industrial sector grew at a far greater rate than in the period 1962–1972 (when growth of 2.8% was recorded), although it has still generally failed to reach plan targets. Since the mid-1980s the performance of the sector has been seriously affected by the shortage of foreign exchange and energy (see below), production being further disrupted by the unrest of 1987/88 and 1988/89. The estimated value of production in 1991/92 (in constant prices) was still some 18% below that of 1985/86. Between 1992/93 and 1996/97 production increased by an annual average of 9.8% per year. Compared with the previous year, industrial GDP rose by an estimated 6.1% in 1998/99, by 13.7% in 1999/2000 and by 20.1% in 2000/01. In 2000/01 the industrial sector (including mining and quarrying, manufacturing, utilities and construction) contributed an estimated 10.4% of GDP, and in 1997/98 it accounted for about 12.1% of total employment.

Despite the nationalization of all major industries after 1962, the private sector retained an important role in industry, and this has been increasing since the reforms of 1988. In 1992/93 the private sector accounted for 69% of industrial output, 94% of all industrial establishments and as much as 80% of employment. However, the majority of these establishments (over 90%) are small enterprises employing fewer than 10 persons. In 1995/96, of a total of 474 factories employing more than 100 workers, 399 were state-owned, 68 were privately-owned and seven were run by co-operatives. In 1995, according to the ADB, state-owned enterprises accounted for about one-third of public investment but contributed only one-fifth of government receipts. Subsequent assessments suggest that there has been little, if any, improvement in the management and productivity of state-owned enterprises.

The economic reforms of 1971 recognized the role that the private sector could play in the development of the industrial sector, and some efforts were subsequently made to encourage increased private investment. A Rights of Private Enterprise Law was passed in 1977, which provided for guarantees against nationalization, but only until 1994. In mid-1994 the SLORC introduced new procedures for private investment, particularly in the manufacturing sector. The publication of a foreign investment law in December 1988, under which both 100% foreign-owned and joint-venture companies were allowed, was expected to lead to a significant expansion in industrial investment and production in the medium term. The sector remained dominated by food and beverage processing, which accounted for an estimated 85.0% of gross manufacturing output in 1995/96. Other principal activities included the production of industrial raw materials (5.4%), mineral and petroleum products (2.5%) and the manufacture of textiles and clothing (2.3%). While growth in agro-based industry has slowed, the rate of growth of the manufacturing sector has increased. However, the development of the manufacturing sector was hindered by the shortage of foreign exchange (which restricted the imports required by the sector) and by the country's poor infrastructure. While deficiencies in the sector, along with international concern over the abuse of human rights in the country, have discouraged foreign investment to some extent, foreign investment in light manufacturing increased in 1996/97.

Shortages of energy supply are a major constraint on the long-term development of the industrial sector. While energy reserves were more than adequate in the late 1980s, supply fell well short of demand, despite a 20% increase in generating capacity between 1985/86 and 1991/92. The average annual growth of energy production was 3.9% in 1980–89, compared with an average annual increase in consumption of 4.2%. Although 18 new steam and gas turbines were installed during the Fourth Plan period, the Government has continued to stress the expansion of hydroelectric power, and in 1985/86 a 56-MW hydroelectric plant was commissioned at the Kinda dam near Mandalay, and seven small-scale hydroelectric plants were constructed. In June 1989 the Sedawgyi hydroelectric power plant near Mandalay was commissioned. Thailand's National Energy Administration proposed the construction of seven dams on rivers along the border with Myanmar. At the end of 1989 Thai and Myanma officials agreed on the construction of the first two of these dams which would provide water for irrigation, as well as increasing hydroelectric power output. In April 1990 two new power projects, including a 6,000-MW hydropower plant near Yangon, were announced, with assistance provided by the Japanese private sector. Following an agreement with Thailand in May 1994, a number of smaller hydropower plants were to be constructed, including one on the Mae Sai river.

In 1994/95 the state-owned Myanma Electric Power Enterprise (MEPE) had an installed capacity of 845 MW, of which 48% was generated by natural gas, 35% by hydroelectric power, 9% by diesel generators and the remaining 7% by thermal energy. Power shortages in 1991/92 were aggravated by renovation work on one of the generators at the Lawpita hydroelectricity station and by low water levels in a number of other major hydroelectric dams. Lawpita, built in the 1950s by the Japanese, provided some 40% of Myanmar's electricity in 1990. Shortages of power continued to be a major problem in the 1990s, with the result that industry rarely operated at more than 50% of full capacity. In 1996 hydroelectric power projects were estimated to have the potential to add 1,000 MW to installed capacity, but it was not clear when this would be realized and some projects were unlikely to receive financial support. In 1998/99 total installed electrical capacity was 1,055 MW, compared with 1,042 MW in 1997/98. By the end of 1999 total electricity generating capacity was 1,058 MW. In 1999/2000 total installed electrical capacity was 1,162 MW. In December 2000 63.00% of electricity was generated by gas, 21.27% from hydroelectric power, 14.49% from thermal energy and 1.24% from diesel generators. The increase in capacity was due mainly to the commissioning of three new hydroelectricity plants, designed to extend electrification to areas not previously served by the national grid. Electricity prices, however, were reportedly increased 10-fold in March 1999. In September 2000 the Export and Import Bank of China announced a US $120m. low-interest loan for the completion of a plant near Pyinmana, which had been partially built by MEPE. The Yunnan Machinery and Equipment Import and Export Corporation was to supply equipment, design and construction supervision for the project, which would have a generating capacity of 105 MW and would increase power generation by as much as 30% upon completion in 2003.

A total of 2,225m. kWh of electricity was distributed in 1988/89. Thirty two new power plants—26 hydroelectric power stations and six gas-fired and combined recycle power plants—have been built in Myanmar since 1988, and power generation in 2000/01 exceeded 5,024m. kW hrs of electricity. Since 1988 the country's total installed electrical power generating capacity (IGC) had increased by 509 MW. The nation's IGC, according to the MEPE, remained at 1,172 MW at the end of June 2001. In May 2002 the Japanese Government announced a US $5m. loan for the Baluchaung No. 2 hydroelectric power plant. In the same month the MEPE announced plans for the construction of its first coal-burning electric power station, a 120-MW unit to be built in partnership with the Myanma Mining Enterprise in Pinlaung. In 2002 the MEPE launched plans to build five hydroelectric power plants—three of them with Chinese assistance—at Paunglaung, Zaungtu, Mone, Thaphanseik and Maipan. These were expected to help to generate a further 2,000 MW of electricity within the next five years.

TRANSPORT AND COMMUNICATIONS

The poor state of the country's transport infrastructure was another factor undermining development efforts in the late 1980s and 1990s. Roads provide the most important means of transport for both freight and passenger traffic. In 2001/02 there were 28,598 km of roads accessible to motor vehicles in Myanmar, compared with 21,816 km in 1988/89. Many more roads linking the northern and southern regions or eastern and western sectors of the nation were under construction in 2002. These include: the Mandalay–Myitkyina highway on the west bank of the Ayeyarwady (Irrawaddy) River; the Mandalay–Bhamo highway on the east bank of the Ayeyarwady; the Myitkyina–Putao highway; the Pa-an–Zathabyin–Moulmein highway; the Taunggyi–Ywangan–Hanmyintmo highway; the Pyinmana–Pinlaung highway; the Sittwe–An–Minbu highway; the Kawthoung–Bokpyin–Tavoy–Moulmein highway; the Taungup–Maei–Kyaukpru highway; and the Monywa–Hkamti highway. Most road freight is handled by the private sector and there has also been a significant increase in the number of privately-owned passenger buses since 1988/89. Private haulage trucks increased from 23,753 in 1992/93 to an estimated 29,318 in 1995/96, whereas state-owned trucks declined from 2,044 to an estimated 1,969. Similarly, private passenger buses increased from 108,815 in 1992/93 to an estimated 154,853 in 1995/96, while state-owned buses declined from 1,082 to 951.

In 1996/97 Myanma Railways operated a network of 3,955 km, most of which was single-track. In the same year the network carried an estimated 53.4m. passengers and 3.3m. long tons of freight. As a result of the acquisition of new locomotives and rolling stock from abroad, both passenger and freight traffic has expanded since 1988/89. The SLORC oversaw some upgrading and expansion of the rail network, including the construction of a new 160-km line from Ye in Mon State to Tavoy in the south of Tanintharyi Division. The latter project received widespread condemnation by international human rights organizations, which claim that forced labour squads were being used in its construction. Financial aid from the People's Republic of China and the involvement in projects of Chinese engineers have been of great importance in various projects undertaken to repair and extend both railways and roads. By 2002 the Government had spent more than US $398m. on railways since 1988 and had constructed new rail routes linking the following towns: Prome, Aunglan and Taungdwingyi, passing through the central Yoma mountain range; Pakokku and Kyaw, cutting through the Pondaung–Ponnya mountain range; and Shwenyaung, Taunggyi and Hsaik-kaung, which traverses the Shan–Yoma mountain ranges.

Air transport has been particularly affected by the shortage of foreign exchange, necessary for the purchase of spare parts and aviation fuel. As a result, both passenger and freight traffic declined in the early 1980s. Since 1988/89 there has been some recovery, at least in passenger traffic. Work on upgrading the country's one international airport, near Yangon, began in 1988, but was suspended, owing to aid restrictions. However, a new international airport opened near Mandalay in 2000. In April 1993 Myanma Airways International (MAI) was formed to operate international routes, leaving Myanma Airways as the domestic carrier. In September a private consortium took control of 70% of MAI in Myanmar's first large-scale privatization. In 1995 Myanma Airways formed a joint-venture airline, Air Mandalay, with Air Mandalay Holdings of Singapore, to cater for the anticipated increase in foreign tourist demand. In 1995/96 the two airlines carried an estimated total of 719,000 and 138,000 passengers and 2,800 short tons and 3,000 short tons of freight on internal and external flights respectively. By January 2002 Myanmar had 12 airports capable of handling jet aircraft; a further six airports were under construction.

In the mid-1990s inland water transport continued to provide an important link in north–south communications. There are some 12,800 km of inland waterways in Myanmar, including approximately 8,000 km of navigable rivers, of which the Ayeyarwady (Irrawaddy), the Chindwin (Chindwinn) and the delta creeks are the principal arteries. By January 2002 nine bridges spanned the Ayeyarwady (at Magwe, Dedaye and Mandalay), the Chindwin (at Monywa), the Sittang (at Shwekyin-Madauk), and the Salween (at Moulmein). The state-owned Inland Water Transport carried an estimated 3.2m. tons of freight in and 24.5m. passengers in 1995/96. However, like road transport, most river transport was controlled by the private sector. In an attempt to overcome transport delays and to improve internal distribution and export trade, controls on the transport of goods to ports were removed, with effect from 1 June 1988.

Efforts were being made to upgrade other forms of communications, especially telecommunications. In 1992/93 there were an estimated 89,318 telephones in Myanmar, approximately equivalent to one for every 474 persons. This had increased to 197,026 telephones by 1996/97, and by 2001 there were 281,200 main line telephones in use. In 1996 cellphone equipment was installed in Mandalay and Yangon, and a digital telephone system was in place in a number of towns. The completion of a satellite ground station in March 1994 resulted in Myanmar having international direct dialling with 40 other countries. In 1996/97 there were 227 telex services and 1,503 licensed fax machines in Myanmar. In 2002 there were 351,000 telephones in operation in Myanmar (11,000 of them CDMA mobile cellular phones) with 569 exchange stations, compared with 67,000 in 1988. In March 2002 the China National Electronics Import and Export Shenzhen Company signed an agreement with Myanma Posts and Telecommunications (MPT) to construct digital auto-telephone exchanges with a capacity of 13,500 lines in 12 towns across the country over the following 18 months, at a cost of US $6.5m.

The transport, storage and communications sector contributed an estimated 5.9% of GDP in 2000/01. The Government has given increasing priority to the sector, which was allocated 13.3% of public investment expenditure under the 1989/90 plan, although this declined to only 9.5% in 1992/93. In 1992/93 the private sector owned 58% of the transport facilities, while 40% was controlled by the state sector and the balance by co-operatives.

TOURISM

The exploitation of tourism potential has been regarded in recent years as one way of increasing foreign-exchange earnings. During the unrest of 1988 the Government stopped the issuing of tourist visas. The new Government began issuing visas again in May 1989, allowing tourists on 'package' tours to remain for as long as two weeks in the country, compared with the previous one-week limit. However, tourist arrivals, estimated at 11,430 in 1992, were substantially fewer than in the period prior to 1988 (arrivals had totalled 41,904 in 1987), although foreign-exchange earnings from tourism were at a record high (nearly double the 1990 figure). This was due to the higher cost of package tours and the related higher incomes and expenditure of recent tourist arrivals. The SLORC's aim was to attract some 250,000 tourists in 1996/97, which was officially declared 'Visit Myanmar Year'; however, this target was widely regarded as over-ambitious, particularly in view of the opposition's demands for an international boycott of Myanmar. The actual number of tourist arrivals in 1996/97, as reported by Myanmar Hotels and Tourism Services, was 179,594. According to the World Tourism Organization, tourist arrivals rose to 189,000 in 1997/98 and to 201,000 in 1998/99, before declining slightly to 198,210 in 1999/2000. However, arrivals rose to 206,243 in 2000/01. According to official statistics, this figure declined to 119,027 in 2001/02. Of these, 7,167 were US visitors (6%) and only 2.5% were from China. The country hopes eventually to raise the annual number of foreign tourist arrivals to roughly 500,000. Revenue from tourism totalled a reported US $35m. in 1999/2000. Since the late 1980s a number of agreements for the construction of new 'five-star' hotels and tourist-related facilities have been concluded with foreign investors. However, in recent years a combination of Western sanctions, Asian financial problems, stringent visa procedures and restricted air access has caused a huge downturn in the hotel trade. Hotels have been forced to implement drastic price reductions in order to survive, and several planned developments have been abandoned. In early 2001, in an effort to combat the decline, the tourism industry announced a new advertising campaign with a 'Mystical Myanmar' theme and lobbied the Government to make Myanmar more accessible to visitors. Funding issues, however, continued to create problems. By 2002, according to the Ministry of Information, total foreign investment in the country's hotel projects had reached US $585.3m. Twenty-five new hotel projects were completed between 1993 and 2001. These included 19 in Yangon, three in Mandalay, and one each in Bagan, Kawthaung and Tachilek. Leading these investments were three hotels built with investment from Singapore: the 450-room Sedona Hotel, with an investment of US $103.3m. from the Straits Steamship Land (Keppel Land Group); the 496-room Traders Hotel, using US $84m. from the Kuok and Shangri-La; and the 359-room Hotel Equatorial, with US $50m. provided by Yangon Investment Ltd.

DOMESTIC COMMERCE AND PRICES

Much of the country's internal trading network was nationalized after 1963 as part of the military Government's programme of 'Burmanization' of the economy. However, a considerable proportion of the country's internal trade remained officially in private hands. In 1985/86 the State controlled 46.5% of the internal trade sector, while the private sector controlled 41.3% and co-operatives 12.2%. Owing to the moves to liberalize both internal and foreign trade begun by the BSPP in 1987 and 1988 and continued by the SLORC, the share of internal trade controlled by the private and co-operative sectors has been increasing, particularly since the legalization after 1988 of many of the trading activities (including border trade) previously associated with the 'black market'. Thus, while the volume of internal trade handled by the state sector more than doubled between 1988/89 and 1992/93, the State's share declined to only 14% in the latter year. In July 1994 the Government announced that 3,815 registered limited companies, 311 foreign companies and 974 'partnerships' had been registered since 1988, with the majority involved in the retail trade. The continued shortage of consumer goods, including some basic necessities, resulted in the continuation of some 'black market' activities, with prices based on the free-market exchange rate. One method that the Government periodically employed to combat the 'black market' was the demonetization of large-denomination currency notes. This occurred twice in the second half of the 1980s: in November 1985 and September 1987. While these actions did cause some temporary disruption to 'black market' activity, their main effect was to undermine still further the population's faith in the Myanma currency and to increase the degree of dissatisfaction with the Government's management of the economy. Indeed, the demonetization measures of September 1987, which resulted in 60% of the currency in circulation being declared worthless with almost no compensation, set off the chain of unrest that culminated in the military coup of September 1988. In an effort to restore confidence in the currency, the SLORC strongly emphasized that there would be no further demonetizations. From April 1994 local private banks were permitted for the first time to deal in foreign exchange. In February 1993 the Government introduced foreign-exchange certificates (FECs) for use by overseas visitors. Since December 1995 Myanma citizens have been legally allowed to hold these FECs, which can be exchanged for kyat at a rate close to the unofficial rate of around 350 kyats = US $1; by 2000 SPDC policy obliged most private companies to pay for imported goods in FECs, and confiscated US dollars for the settlement of government foreign accounts.

Since 1962 the Government has placed considerable emphasis on the maintenance of price stability; procurement prices for crops, especially for paddy, have thus been kept low. Inflation was officially put at only 2% per year in the 1960s, but increased significantly in the 1970s. The Yangon Consumer Price Index (CPI) more than doubled between 1972 and 1975. It was subsequently more stable; the index stood at 132.28 in 1985 (base: 1978 = 100), while the annual rate of inflation was officially around 10% in 1986. After 1986 the rate of inflation increased significantly. Rice prices increased rapidly following the liberalization of rice marketing in November 1987, and the unrest during 1988 aggravated the already widespread shortages of food and consumer goods. Further increases in rice prices were reported throughout 1989. Rice prices in mid-1989 were double the level of mid-1988 and similar increases for other basic commodities were also reported. On a new base of 1986 = 100, the Yangon CPI stood at 349.3 by 1992 and at 455.3 in 1993. Officially inflation was estimated at around 22% for 1992, but official figures took no account of price movements in the 'black market'. Inflation continued to be fuelled by the rapid growth in money supply to enable the SLORC to fund the budget deficit, which was estimated to be equivalent to about 8% of GDP in 1990/91. The budget deficit was subsequently reduced, to approximately 2.5% of GDP in 1994/95, although monetization of the deficit continued. The budget deficit increased to 3.3% of GDP in 1995/96, but declined to 2.2% and 1.0% of GDP in 1996/97 and 1997/98, respectively, before increasing to 4.0% of GDP in 1998/99. Inflation reached an annual average of 23.8% between 1992 and 1996. According to official data, inflation stood at 30%–35% in 1995/96, rising to 40% in 1996/97; some analysts, however, estimated it to be considerably higher. As a result of harvest failure and increases in the prices of fuel and electricity, inflationary pressure remained strong in the late 1990s. According to the ADB, consumer prices in Yangon increased by 34.0% in 1997/98 and by 49.0% in 1998/99, before prices steadied somewhat, registering a smaller increase of 11.4% in 1999/2000. In 2000/01 consumer prices were estimated by the ADB to have fallen by 1.7% in comparison with the previous year. The budget deficit for 1999/2000 was 20,200m. kyats. With total expenditure originally projected to decline by some 37% compared with the previous year, from 591,200m. kyats in 1998/99 to 430,400m. kyats in 1999/2000, the budget reflected the need for fiscal retrenchment in the context of the deceleration in economic growth.

FOREIGN TRADE

The adoption of a more liberal policy towards foreign investment and trade in 1987 and 1988 represented a major shift in the country's economic policy which, since independence, had been designed to reduce the country's dependence on foreign markets, in an effort to minimize its exposure to fluctuations in commodity markets and to protect domestic industry. After 1962 the military Government sought, with renewed determination, as far as possible to pursue a policy of self-sufficiency, with minimum foreign contacts. A government monopoly was extended to embrace all foreign trade. However, the neglect of the trade sector, and the resultant dramatic fall in export earnings, meant that the country's economic performance was subsequently undermined by a shortage of foreign exchange. Thus, from 1972, rather than seeking to minimize foreign trade, the Government was compelled to give it first priority, by placing particular emphasis on expanding the level of the country's traditional primary exports.

Measures introduced by the SLORC after September 1988 to liberalize foreign trade contributed to the recovery in export earnings. These measures included an end to the state's monopoly on foreign trade, except for teak, petroleum, natural gas, pearls and gems. In addition, the Government legalized much of the previous 'black market' border trade. In November 1988 official border trade was initiated with China, with three trading points opened. In 1988–90 exporters were permitted to retain an increasing share of their export earnings. In 1989–95 the cross-border trade carried out by certain groups of insurgents was legalized in exchange for peace agreements with the SLORC.

Rice exports, amounting to over 3m. metric tons in 1940/41, had declined to a mere 262,000 tons by 1972/73. Rice exports subsequently increased in line with the Government's policy of promoting traditional exports, totalling 646,000 tons in 1985/86. In the three years from 1994/95 rice exports decreased in volume terms from 675,000 tons to 250,000 tons. Revenue from rice exports, meanwhile, declined sharply from US $198m. to US $47m. Teak and other hardwoods have constituted a major source of foreign exchange since 1985. By the mid-1980s teak exports had increased to a level similar to the overall levels attained in the immediate pre-war years. In 1992/93 the sale of forest products temporarily eclipsed rice, accounting for 32% of the value of total exports. In 1994/95 rice and rice products accounted for 21.6% of total exports, while pulses and beans accounted for 14.8%, teak and other hardwood 19.6% and rubber 2.3%. However, the contribution to total exports made by rice and rice products declined to 8.8% in 1995/96, to 2.4% in 1996/97, and to a mere 0.6% in 1997/98. Rice provided 2.4% of total exports in 1998/99. Meanwhile, the contribution of pulses and beans to total exports increased to 27.1% in 1995/96 but declined to 24.2% in 1996/97, to 22.3% in 1997/98 and to 16.3% in 1998/99. Exports of both rubber and teak and other hardwood increased in 1995/96 (to 20.9% and 3.6% of total exports, respectively); the export of teak and other hardwood continued to increase in 1996/97 (representing 21.8% of total exports in that year) but declined to just 13.6% of total exports in 1997/98 and to 11.3% in 1998/99. The export of rubber declined in both 1996/97 (when it constituted 3.2% of total exports) and 1997/98 (to 2.1% of total exports). In 2000/01 rice exports increased by 389%, to 692,700 tons. Moreover, the CSO stated that Myanmar exported 230,000 tons of rice in the first two months of 2002—an increase of more than 220% compared with the corresponding period of 2001. Timber, including teak and hardwood, has become Myanmar's second largest export after agricultural products, with the country accounting for some 85% of the world's teak. In 2001/02 Myanmar exported 283,707 cu m of teak, a decline of 8.1% from 308,753 cu m in the previous year. In 2001/02 Myanmar also exported 404,407 cu m of hardwood, a reduction of 13.2% from 466,101 cu m in 2000/01. Timber export earnings totalled US $280m. The industry received a boost in May 2002 when Myanmar signed a US $1m. agreement to export 1,000 tons of teak to India—the largest timber deal ever concluded. In recent years garment exports have increased, although the USA's decision in 1996 to cease purchasing from Myanmar had a serious, negative impact on exports from within this sector. Myanmar conducts the majority of its external trade with neighbouring Asian countries. In 2001 Thailand was the principal destination (accounting for 26.0% of the total) for exports; other major markets were the USA, India, the People's Republic of China and Singapore.

Despite the rising trend in the volume of exports after 1972, the country experienced acute problems in the trade sector from 1981/82, largely as a result of falling prices for export commodities, increased import prices and, more recently, the decline in export volumes. Government figures show that prices for rice, teak, hardwoods and minerals fell by over 30% between 1981/82 and 1986/87. Export prices continued to fall subsequently. In contrast, the prices of imports, which consisted mainly of capital goods, equipment and industrial raw materials, have risen sharply since 1981/82, and particularly since 1985/86, increasing by about 35% between 1985/86 and 1991/92. As a result, Myanmar suffered a steady decline in its terms of trade. In 1994/95 the value of imports increased to an estimated US $1,414.2m., and by 1999/2000 this figure stood at US $2,400m., according to official estimates. In terms of local currency, the cost of imports continued to rise in 1995/96, 1996/97 and 1997/98 to an estimated 10,302m. kyats, 11,779m. kyats and 14,257m. kyats respectively, while the value of exports declined from 5,405m. kyats in 1994/95 to an estimated 5,044m. kyats in 1995/96, before increasing to an estimated 5,488m. kyats in 1996/97 and to an estimated 6,290m. kyats in 1997/98. The principal source of imports in 2001 was the People's Republic of China (accounting for 21.8% of all imports); other major suppliers were Singapore, Thailand, the Republic of Korea and Malaysia. In 1999/2000, according to the CSO, Myanmar's foreign trade, including cross-border legal trade, totalled US $3,800m., having declined by 6.9% compared with 1998/99. In 1999/2000 imports were valued at US $2,600m. (of which 69.6% was accounted for by the private sector). Exports in that year amounted to US $1,180m. (the value of the private sector was 72.4% of the total). Myanmar's principal trading partners in 1999/2000 were Singapore, the People's Republic of China and Thailand. In 2001/02, according to the Ministry of National Planning and Economic Development, Myanmar's imports and exports increased by 21.9% in comparison to the previous fiscal year to reach US $5,299.7m. Imports rose by 16.4%, to US $742.9m., while exports surged by 28.4%, to US $2,556.8m. The trade deficit declined by 49% from its 2000 level to US $186.1m. During this period, the import value of intermediate goods, capital goods and consumer goods accounted for 40.3%, 30.2% and 29.5% of total imports, respectively. The private sector accounted for some US $1,800m., or 64.9%, of the total value of imports.

China has become Myanmar's third largest trading partner after Singapore and Thailand; during the first 10 months of 2001 bilateral trade reached US $499m., a 3.1% year-on-year increase according to China's Ministry of Foreign Trade and Economic Co-operation (MOFETC). Trade levels with neighbouring countries were expected to increase following an announcement by the Ministry of Commerce in July 2002 that it had opened a total of 10 border trade points with China (at Muse, Lweje and Laizar), Thailand (at Tachilek, Myawaddy, Kawthoung and Myeik), Bangladesh (at Maungtaw and Sittwe) and India (at Tamu).

From January 1993 private banks were permitted to operate, in a move designed to facilitate private business. Moreover, in the early 1990s the SLORC issued licences to foreign banks, particularly from Thailand and Singapore, to open representative offices in Myanmar. In 1996 there were about 20 foreign banks with representative offices in Yangon. However, many restrictions remained regarding their activities, with the Government giving priority to the development of domestic private banks. Most foreign representative offices are primarily involved with arranging short-term trade finance.

A major obstacle to increased exports remained the country's exchange rate, which favoured imports at the expense of exports. While the official exchange rate was just over 6 kyats = US $1 in 1997–98, the 'black market' rate declined to 250–300 kyats in July 1997. The Government indicated that the exchange rate would not be adjusted, as this would have an inflationary effect. In June 1996, in order to increase revenue from customs duties and to simplify the tariff system, a new customs valuation rate of 100 kyats = US $1 was introduced. In January 1998, in an attempt to stabilize the currency, the Government revoked the licences of Myanmar's 30 foreign-exchange dealers. In March the Central Bank suspended the rights of the 10 part-state-owned and private banks to engage in foreign-exchange transactions. In mid-2000 the 'black market' rate was around 400 kyats = US $1, and by mid-2001 the rate was closer to 550 kyats = US $1. In April 2002 the kyat reached an all-time low of 1,004 kyats = US $1, prompting the Government to begin targeting 'black market' currency traders.

Myanmar developed increasingly close relations with the Association of South East Asian Nations (ASEAN) during the 1990s, and in July 1997 the country was admitted as a full member of the Association; Myanmar's trading position appeared likely to improve as a result of its membership of ASEAN, although the country's external trade has suffered as a result of the loss of trade privileges with a number of Western countries. While the Government had imposed new restrictions on imports in 1998, hoping thereby to curb the outflow of foreign currency from the country, by 2000 the SPDC had relaxed those controls but imposed the use of FECs in order to achieve the same objective.

FOREIGN AID, INVESTMENT AND DEBT

After the 1972 economic reforms, foreign assistance increased rapidly, from only US $21.7m. in 1971 to US $511.8m. in 1979/80. Between 1980/81 and 1985/86, the Myanma Government found that it was increasingly difficult to maintain the flow of aid and concessionary loans, and this was a major factor contributing to balance-of-payments problems from 1981 onwards. In 1986 total foreign assistance amounted to US $413.8m., with commitments of US $306.1m. from bilateral donors and US $107.7m. from multilateral donors. Japan was by far the largest bilateral donor, providing some 73% of all bilateral aid in 1986 in the form of both extensive project and programme aid. The World Bank and the ADB accounted for the bulk of multilateral lending, providing 41% and 25% of multilateral aid in 1986 respectively. At the Burma Aid Group meeting in Tokyo in January 1986, donors agreed to provide approximately US $500m. a year over the period of the Fifth Plan (1986/87–1989/90), with about one-half of this sum donated by Japan. In 1988 Japan provided some US $250m. in grant aid, equivalent to 60% of the country's total aid receipts in that year. Since the Government had come to rely heavily on foreign aid to maintain the level of imports and public investment, the economy was severely affected by the boycott on aid, introduced by Japan and Western donors, following the political unrest in 1988. While Japan did recognize the new military Government in February 1989, it indicated that aid payments would be made only for existing projects. This was still considerable, however, as Japan was involved in five grant projects, their cost totalling 9,200m. yen (US $66m.), of which 65% had been disbursed, and 19 loan projects totalling 125,000m. yen, of which only 20% had been disbursed. As a result of the aid boycott, the country received virtually no other aid in 1989–95. Following the release of opposition leader Aung San Suu Kyi from house arrest in July 1995, Japan reinstituted some limited aid programmes; in 1998 the Japanese Government agreed partially to resume official development assistance to Myanmar. In general, however, there were severe problems with regard to foreign investment in the country: according to the IMF, of the US $3,200m. of investment approved since the first reforms of 1989, only US $1,300m. had been invested by 31 March 2000.

Despite the aid boycott, the Government continued to receive private credit, which increased the external debt burden. Concessionary loans accounted for almost 80% of disbursed debt in 1986, reflecting the Government's reliance on official development assistance rather than commercial borrowing. Even so, the debt-service ratio rose to almost 60% in 1987; in 1965 it had been only 4.5%. The status of 'least developed country', granted at the end of 1987, brought some relief to Myanmar's debt problems; most of the new aid that was announced during the first six months of 1988 was in the form of grants rather than loans. Following the suspension of aid payments, Myanmar stopped repayments on debt to its major creditors, Japan and Germany. While arrears have accumulated, the debt-service ratio, based on actual as opposed to contractual debt-service payments, declined to 11.1% in 1991/92. By May 1989 Myanmar was 11,600m. yen in arrears on repayments to Japan. In March 1990 Myanmar made a debt repayment of 3,500m. yen to Japan, which Japan later returned to Myanmar in the form of a debt-relief grant. In May 1991 Myanmar repaid 3,000m. yen, which was also subsequently returned as a debt-relief grant, under which Myanmar could purchase raw materials, machinery or spare parts from any country. In June 1991 the French Government announced that it would waive debts incurred by the country's Government in 1976. Myanmar's debt to China at the end of 1993/94 totalled US $73m., excluding several hundred million dollars worth of credits that had helped pay for imports of military equipment. In 1995 the USA secured an agreement with 'Paris Club' donors that a debt settlement with Myanmar would have to be reached via a multilateral route on the basis of an agreement with the IMF. Total external debt was US $5,063m. in 1997, compared with US $5,184m. in 1996 and US $5,771m. in 1995. In 1999 Myanmar's external debt rose to US $5,999m., of which long-term public debt accounted for US $5,333m. In 2000, according to the ADB, outstanding external debt amounted to US $6,046.1m.

The BSPP Government had been forced to deplete its foreign-exchange reserves to finance its balance-of-payments deficit. By the end of 1987, they had fallen to less than US $30m., sufficient for only about three weeks' imports. By 1990 reserves had recovered and stood at US $560.7m., owing mostly to the revenue gained from granting concessions for timber, fisheries and minerals. Foreign-exchange reserves reached a record US $674m. in May 1995 but subsequently declined, falling to US $229m. in December 1996 before increasing to US $250m. in December 1997. Foreign-exchange reserves rose from US $314.6m. in December 1998 to US $398.5m. at the end of 1999. In March 2000 foreign-exchange reserves were reported to stand at US $240m. By July 2000, however, as had been the case in September 1998, it was reported that foreign-exchange reserves were sufficient to finance only one month's imports. An improvement in Myanmar's export performance and a resumption of aid from its Western donors remained vital to a long-term improvement in the balance of payments.

The previous Government's sensitivity over foreign interference and its refusal to be bound by 'conditionality' were reasons why Myanmar made little use of the IMF in the past; however, a decline in export earnings and increasing debt-service obligations caused the Government to negotiate a US $250m. loan with the IMF in 1986. In addition, Myanmar was one of 62 poor, commodity-dependent countries with serious debt-repayment problems that were eligible for special concessionary loans under the IMF's Enhanced Structural Adjustment Facility, introduced in December 1987. However, more extensive reform, including a devaluation of the kyat, was likely to be a condition of any significant new assistance from the IMF. In 2000 the USA was still opposing Myanma requests for loans from the IMF, the World Bank and other international lending institutions, and supported the World Bank's unusual decision, in September 1998, to sever financial ties with Myanmar on account of the country's failure to make repayments on earlier loans, arrears being estimated at US $14m. The International Labour Organization (ILO) passed a resolution regarding Myanmar in June 2000, which was expected to affect adversely the provision of international assistance to the country. However, the decision, made at the annual summit of the IMF and the World Bank in Prague in September 2000, to provide debt relief for debtor developing countries appeared likely to benefit Myanmar in the near future.

Foreign investment in Myanmar since the promulgation of legislation in 1988 has been largely limited to petroleum, gas and mining concerns. South-East Asian investors have also tended to concentrate on US dollar-earning sectors, such as hotels and tourism. In 1996 cumulative foreign investment approvals totalled almost US $3,800m., although the disbursement rate is poor. Singapore was the largest investor in Myanmar in 1996/97, followed by the United Kingdom, France, Thailand and Malaysia. In the same year, foreign direct investment approvals totalled US $2,800m.; however, in 1997/98 approved foreign direct investment declined to about US $1,000m. In 1996 there was an increasing consumer boycott, particularly in the USA and Europe, of companies investing in Myanmar in protest at the SLORC's abuses of human rights. This led to the withdrawal from the country in that year of a number of large investors, including the drinks manufacturers PepsiCo (which withdrew in April), Carlsberg and Heineken (both of which withdrew in July); US garment manufacturers such as Oshkosh, Madison Avenue and Levi Strauss have also ceased operations in Myanmar, although a number of other well-known companies (for example, the Australian brewing company, Foster's, and the German car manufacturer, BMW) continue to operate and to expand in the country. Inflows have slowed further following the imposition by the USA in early 1997 of sanctions on new investment in Myanmar by US companies, although in June 1998 a US court ruled that state and local governments could not by law impose a boycott on Myanmar. While the Asian economic crisis of 1997–98 reduced the inflow of foreign direct investment into Myanmar, by mid-2000 China, Thailand and Singapore had committed themselves with renewed vigour to investments in both the public and private sectors. There was a gradual relaxation of international attitudes towards Myanmar from 2001. Various ASEAN members, most notably Malaysia, proclaimed their interest in making investments in Myanmar, and in April 2001 Japan agreed to fund a US $28m. bilateral aid programme intended to facilitate the rehabilitation of a hydroelectric dam, a direct result of a liberalization of the SPDC stance. In October 2001 the European Union (EU) voted to ease its sanctions, having extended them for a six-month period in April of that year, although most Western countries awaited more substantial concessions from the SPDC. In February 2002 the US Government issued a report offering the possibility of an easing of sanctions, but only if the country made further tangible progress towards democracy. Following the release of Aung San Suu Kyi in May 2002, it was thought that more international concessions would be forthcoming. However, a lack of further substantive political progress in the country during subsequent months meant that Myanmar continued to await full reintegration into the global economic and political community.

Statistical Survey

Source (unless otherwise stated): Ministry of National Planning and Economic Development, 653–691 Merchant St, Yangon; tel. (1) 272009; fax (1) 282101.

Area and Population

AREA, POPULATION AND DENSITY

Area (sq km)	676,552*
Population (census results)	
31 March 1973	28,885,867
31 March 1983†	
Males	17,507,837
Females	17,798,352
Total	35,306,189
Population (UN estimates at mid-year)‡	
1999	47,114,000
2000	47,749,000
2001	48,364,000
Density (per sq km) at mid-2001	71.5

* 261,218 sq miles.
† Figures exclude adjustment for underenumeration. Also excluded are 7,716 Myanma citizens (5,704 males; 2,012 females) abroad.
‡ Source: UN, *World Population Prospects: The 2000 Revision*.

PRINCIPAL TOWNS (population at census of 31 March 1983)

Yangon (Rangoon)	2,513,023	Pathein (Bassein)	144,096
Mandalay	532,949	Taunggyi	108,231
Mawlamyine (Moulmein)	219,961	Sittwe (Akyab)	107,621
Bago (Pegu)	150,528	Manywa	106,843

Source: UN, *Demographic Yearbook*.

Mid-2001 (UN estimate, incl. suburbs): Yangon 4,504,000 (Source: UN, *World Urbanization Prospects: The 2001 Revision*).

BIRTHS AND DEATHS (UN estimates, annual averages)

	1985–90	1990–95	1995–2000
Birth rate (per 1,000)	31.4	29.9	26.5
Death rate (per 1,000)	13.2	12.2	11.8

Source: UN, *World Population Prospects: The 2000 Revision*.

Birth rate (1998): 27.5 per 1,000.
Death rate (1998): 8.2 per 1,000.

Source: UN, *Statistical Yearbook for Asia and the Pacific*.

Expectation of life (WHO estimates, years at birth, 2000): Males 56.2; Females 61.1 (Source: WHO, *World Health Report*).

EMPLOYMENT (estimates, '000 persons aged 15 to 59 years)

	1995/96	1996/97	1997/98
Agriculture, hunting, forestry and fishing	11,848	11,960	12,093
Mining and quarrying	116	132	121
Manufacturing	1,481	1,573	1,666
Electricity, gas and water	19	21	26
Construction	354	378	400
Trade, restaurants and hotels	1,715	1,746	1,781
Transport, storage and communications	441	470	495
Community, social and personal services (excl. government)	563	577	597
Administration and other services	776	835	888
Activities not adequately defined	274	272	270
Total employed	17,587	17,964	18,359

Unemployed ('000 persons aged 18 years and over): 425.3 registered in 1998/99.

Source: mainly UN, *Statistical Yearbook for Asia and the Pacific*.

Health and Welfare

KEY INDICATORS

Fertility (births per woman, 2000)	3.1
Under-5 mortality rate (per 1,000 live births, 2000)	110
HIV/AIDS (% of persons aged 15–49, 1999)	1.99
Physicians (per 1,000 head, 1999)	0.30
Hospital beds (per 1,000 head, 1999)	0.30
Health expenditure (1998): US $ per head (PPP)	32
% of GDP	1.5
public (% of total)	15.1
Access to water (% of persons, 2000)	68
Access to sanitation (% of persons, 2000)	46
Human Development Index (2000): ranking	127
value	0.552

For sources and definitions, see explanatory note on p. vi.

Agriculture

PRINCIPAL CROPS ('000 metric tons)

	1998	1999	2000
Wheat	93	117	94
Rice (paddy)	17,077	20,125	21,324
Maize	308	349	365
Millet	150	169	169
Potatoes	237	245	255
Sweet potatoes	25*	31	38
Cassava	81	88	77
Sugar cane	5,137	5,429	5,449
Other sugar crops	237	240*	240*
Dry beans	1,078	1,235	1,285
Dry peas	27	38†	46†
Chick-peas	89	68	84
Dry cow peas	58	80*	100*
Pigeon peas	176	160	189
Soybeans (Soya beans)	75	85	99
Groundnuts (in shell)	540	562	634
Sunflower seed	90	189	160
Sesame seed	296	210	296
Cottonseed	109†	106	118
Coconuts	246	263	263*
Dry onions	225	476	476
Garlic	53	53	67
Other vegetables (incl. melons)*	2,700	2,800	2,800
Plantains	394	423	354
Other fruits (excl. melons)*	895	930	930
Areca (Betel) nuts	36	38	39
Tea (made)	20	18	19*
Pimento and allspice	40	40	40*
Tobacco (leaves)	57	42	47
Jute	33	33	33
Cotton (lint)	55	53	59
Natural rubber	27	23	27

* FAO estimate(s). † Unofficial figure.
Source: FAO.

LIVESTOCK ('000 head, year ending September)

	1998	1999	2000
Horses*	120	120	120
Cattle	10,493	10,740	10,964
Buffaloes	2,337	2,391	2,441
Pigs	3,501	3,715	3,914
Sheep	369	379	390
Goats	1,319	1,353	1,392
Chickens	36,132	39,529	43,522
Ducks	5,300	5,600*	5,800*
Geese*	450	500	500

* FAO estimate.

Source: FAO.

LIVESTOCK PRODUCTS ('000 metric tons)

	1998	1999	2000
Beef and veal	100.7	100.8	102.0
Buffalo meat	19.9	20.2	20.4
Goat meat	6.7	6.8	8.8
Pig meat	91.3	133.1	103.9
Poultry meat	154.2	176.5	208.6
Cows' milk	477.0	488.2	611.9
Buffaloes' milk	106.2	108.7	124.9
Goats' milk	6.8	7.1	7.3
Butter	10.5	10.7	13.5
Cheese	29.9	30.6	38.4
Hen eggs	61.2	69.9	82.7
Other poultry eggs	9.2	9.6	10.1
Cattle hides (fresh)	20.5	20.5	20.5*

* FAO estimate.

Source: FAO.

Forestry

ROUNDWOOD REMOVALS ('000 cubic metres, excl. bark)

	1998*	1999	2000
Sawlogs, veneer logs and logs for sleepers	2,264	2,085	2,299
Other industrial wood	1,000	1,263	1,275
Fuel wood	18,250	19,226*	19,226*
Total	22,250	22,574	22,800

* FAO estimate(s).

Source: FAO.

SAWNWOOD PRODUCTION ('000 cubic metres, incl. railway sleepers)

	1998	1999	2000
Coniferous (softwood)*	38	38	38
Broadleaved (hardwood)	299	298	343
Total	337	336	381

* FAO estimates.

Source: FAO.

Fishing

('000 metric tons, live weight, year ending 30 June)

	1996/97	1997/98	1998/99
Capture	830.3	873.0	851.6
Freshwater fishes	157.4	153.6	129.7
Marine fishes	647.5	693.9	695.9
Aquaculture*	87.3	85.3	94.2
Roho labeo	87.0	85.0	93.9
Total catch	917.7	958.2	945.8

* FAO estimates.

Source: FAO, *Yearbook of Fishery Statistics*.

Mining

(metric tons, unless otherwise indicated)

	1998	1999	2000*
Coal and lignite	27,766	40,309	49,500
Crude petroleum ('000 barrels)	3,423	3,394	3,600
Natural gas (million cu m)†	1,750	1,674	3,600
Copper ore‡	6,700*	26,736	26,711
Lead ore*‡	2,200	2,000	2,000
Zinc ore‡	474	279	220
Tin concentrates‡	221	149	220
Chromium ore (gross weight)	4,059§	3,200*	3,000
Tungsten concentrates‡	178	87	82
Silver ore (kilograms)‡	3,359	4,168	2,500
Gold ore (kilograms)‡‖	172	242	250
Feldspar*‖	12,000	12,000	12,000
Barite (Barytes)	22,004	24,651	29,200
Salt (unrefined, excl. brine)*	35,000	35,000	35,000
Gypsum (crude)	36,411	44,857	46,300
Rubies, sapphires and spinel ('000 metric carats)‖	14,447	5,475¶	7,740
Jade	1,526	2,342	8,970

* Estimated production.

† Marketed production.

‡ Figures refer to the metal content of ores and concentrates (including mixed concentrates).

§ Reported figure.

‖ Twelve months beginning 1 April of year stated.

¶ Excluding production of rubies from Mine-Shu.

Source: US Geological Survey.

Industry

SELECTED PRODUCTS ('000 metric tons, unless otherwise indicated)

	1997	1998	1999
Raw sugar*	52	61	53
Refined sugar†	53	53	43
Cigarettes (million)†	1,991	n.a.	n.a.
Cotton yarn†	3.7	3.9	4.8
Plywood ('000 cu m)	10	n.a.	n.a.
Printing and writing paper	11	n.a.	n.a.
Nitrogenous fertilizers‡	74	54	52
Petroleum refinery products ('000 barrels)§‖	5,414	5,815	5,605
Clay building bricks (million)	67	68	n.a.
Cement§	515,682	364,959	339,025
Tin—unwrought (metric tons)§	228	150	150
Electric energy (million kWh, net)¶	4,261	4,377	4,813

Beer (hectolitres): 13,000 in 1994.

Woven cotton fabrics (million sq m): 16 in 1995.

* Data from FAO.

† Production by government-owned enterprises only.

‡ Production in terms of nitrogen during twelve months ending 30 June of stated year.

§ Twelve months beginning 1 April of year stated. Data from US Geological Survey.

‖ Figure includes gasoline, jet fuel, kerosene, diesel, distillate fuel oil and residual fuel oil.

¶ Data from Energy Information Administration, US Department of Energy.

Source (unless otherwise specified): UN, *Statistical Yearbook for Asia and the Pacific*.

Finance

CURRENCY AND EXCHANGE RATES

Monetary Units

100 pyas = 1 kyat.

Sterling, Dollar and Euro Equivalents (31 May 2002)

£1 sterling = 9.7717 kyats;
US $1 = 6.6624 kyats;
€1 = 6.2540 kyats;
1,000 kyats = £102.34 = $150.10 = €159.90.

Average Exchange Rate (kyats per US $)

1999 6.2858
2000 6.5167
2001 6.7489

Note: Since January 1975 the value of the kyat has been linked to the IMF's special drawing right (SDR). Since May 1977 the official exchange rate has been fixed at a mid-point of SDR 1 = 8.5085 kyats. On 1 June 1996 a new customs valuation exchange rate of US $1 = 100 kyats was introduced. In September 2001 the free market exchange rate was $1 = 450 kyats.

CENTRAL GOVERNMENT BUDGET
('000 million kyats, year ending 31 March)

Revenue*	1996/97	1997/98	1998/99
Tax revenue	28.9	45.9	52.9
Taxes on income and profits	9.2	15.3	20.9
Commercial tax	9.5	18.1	22.7
Customs duties	7.8	8.6	5.2
Other revenue	24.2	40.7	63.5
Transfers from State Economic Enterprises	15.4	26.9	43.7
Mechanized Agricultural Department receipts	2.2	1.0	2.7
State Lottery	2.2	3.7	4.2
Total	53.2	86.7	116.4

Expenditure	1996/97	1997/98	1998/99
Current expenditure	39.0	48.0	49.3
General services	3.3	5.1	4.1
Home affairs	2.4	2.7	2.8
Defence	13.1	14.7	16.2
Economic services	7.2	10.0	10.1
Agriculture and forestry	4.3	5.0	5.7
Transport and communications	0.2	0.3	0.3
Public works and housing	1.9	3.8	3.1
Social services	7.8	8.9	9.2
Education	4.9	5.3	5.7
Health	1.1	1.6	1.3
Pensions and gratuities	1.6	1.7	1.8
Interest payments	6.1	7.8	9.0
Capital expenditure†	37.6	49.9	22.8
General services	1.5	1.4	0.8
Defence	11.3	15.5	8.3
Economic services	15.3	24.5	9.6
Agriculture and forestry	7.0	8.2	3.9
Transport and communications	1.4	2.2	2.2
Public works and housing	6.6	13.9	3.2
Social services	7.4	6.6	3.3
Education	5.4	4.7	2.3
Health	2.0	1.9	1.0
Total	76.6	97.9	72.1

* Excluding grants received from abroad ('000 million kyats): 0.6 in 1996/97; 1.6 in 1997/98; 0.6 in 1998/99.

† Including net lending.

Source: IMF, *Myanmar: Statistical Appendix* (January 2001).

INTERNATIONAL RESERVES (US $ million at 31 December)

	1999	2000	2001
Gold*	11.1	10.6	10.2
IMF special drawing rights	0.2	0.1	0.6
Foreign exchange	265.3	222.8	399.9
Total	276.6	233.5	410.7

* Valued at SDR 35 per troy ounce.

Source: IMF, *International Financial Statistics*.

MONEY SUPPLY (million kyats at 31 December)

	1999	2000	2001
Currency outside banks	296,471	378,001	551,343
Demand deposits at deposit money banks	72,707	119,746	206,349

Source: IMF, *International Financial Statistics*.

COST OF LIVING
(Consumer Price Index for Yangon; base: 1990 = 100)

	1997	1998	1999
Food (incl. beverages)	548.2	834.6	997.0
Fuel and light	457.3	590.2	632.3
Clothing (incl. footwear)	366.0	620.3	700.4
Rent	405.1	568.9	624.1
All items (incl. others)	498.1	754.6	893.4

Source: ILO.

All items (base: 1995 = 100): 270.5 in 1999; 270.2 in 2000; 327.2 in 2001 (Source: IMF, *International Financial Statistics*).

NATIONAL ACCOUNTS

(million kyats at current prices, year ending 31 March)

National Income and Product

	1995/96	1996/97	1997/98
Compensation of employees	282,758	370,522	506,706
Operating surplus	291,782	380,175	512,517
Domestic factor incomes	574,540	750,697	1,019,223
Consumption of fixed capital	15,339	18,040	21,512
Gross domestic product (GDP) at factor cost	589,879	768,737	1,040,735
Indirect taxes, *less* subsidies	14,850	22,140	26,787
GDP in purchasers' values	604,729	790,877	1,067,522
Net factor income from abroad	−689	−116	−139
Gross national product	604,040	790,761	1,067,383
Less Consumption of fixed capital	15,339	18,040	21,512
National income in market prices	588,701	772,721	1,045,871

Source: UN, *National Accounts Statistics.*

Expenditure on the Gross Domestic Product

	1997/98	1998/99	1999/2000
Final consumption expenditure	987,513	1,419,709	1,906,136
Increase in stocks	−10,276	−7,604	48,325
Gross fixed capital formation	150,240	206,912	241,694
Total domestic expenditure	1,127,477	1,619,017	2,196,155
Exports of goods and services	6,290	7,700	9,394
Less Imports of goods and services	−14,258	−16,941	−15,248
GDP in purchasers' values	1,119,509	1,609,776	2,190,301
GDP at constant 1985/86 prices	75,123	79,460	88,134

Source: IMF, *International Financial Statistics.*

Gross Domestic Product by Economic Activity

	1998/99	1999/2000	2000/01
Agriculture, hunting, forestry and fishing	950,574	1,312,285	1,458,270
Mining and quarrying	7,895	10,842	15,234
Manufacturing	112,774	143,244	195,876
Electricity, gas and water	991	2,558	3,445
Construction	37,034	40,425	50,263
Wholesale and retail trade	377,595	524,403	601,690
Transport, storage and communications	80,031	105,669	149,669
Finance	1,945	2,215	2,587
Government services	14,622	16,505	40,260
Other services	26,315	32,174	35,429
GDP in purchasers' values	1,609,776	2,190,320	2,552,723

Source: Asian Development Bank, *Key Indicators of Developing Asian and Pacific Countries.*

BALANCE OF PAYMENTS (US $ million)

	1998	1999	2000
Exports of goods f.o.b.	1,065.1	1,281.1	1,618.8
Imports of goods f.o.b.	−2,451.2	−2,159.6	−2,134.9
Trade balance	−1,386.1	−878.5	−516.1
Exports of services	626.1	507.1	526.5
Imports of services	−364.8	−288.2	−514.4
Balance on goods and services	−1,124.7	−659.7	−504.1
Other income received	10.9	51.1	30.0
Other income paid	−11.3	−54.0	−66.1
Balance on goods, services and income	−1,125.1	−662.6	−540.1
Current transfers received	631.2	381.0	297.3
Current transfers paid	−0.3	−0.3	−0.1
Current balance	−494.2	−281.9	−243.0
Direct investment from abroad	314.5	253.1	254.8
Other investment liabilities	220.7	−4.3	−94.7
Net errors and omissions	18.8	−12.3	59.6
Overall balance	59.7	−45.4	−23.3

Source: IMF, *International Financial Statistics.*

External Trade

PRINCIPAL COMMODITIES*

(distribution by SITC, million kyats, year ending 31 March)

Imports c.i.f.	1998/99	1999/2000	2000/01
Food and live animals	453	620	586
Mineral fuels, lubricants, etc.	941	1,654	1,145
Animal and vegetable oils, fats and waxes	689	488	412
Chemicals and related products	1,672	1,871	1,924
Basic manufactures	4,436	4,125	4,401
Machinery and transport equipment	6,348	4,868	3,754
Miscellaneous manufactured articles	574	643	1,000
Total (incl. others)	16,872	16,265	14,900

Exports f.o.b.†	1998/99	1999/2000	2000/01
Food and live animals	2,543	2,237	3,206
Dried beans, peas, etc. (shelled)	1,135	1,179	1,658
Crude materials (inedible) except fuels	1,233	1,819	1,081
Teak and other hardwood	789	925	803
Basic manufactures	690	602	1,559
Miscellaneous manufactured articles	527	176	116
Total (incl. others)	6,756	8,947	12,262

* Totals include, but distribution by commodities excludes, border trade, mainly with the People's Republic of China, Thailand and Bangladesh. In 1998/99 the total value of such trade (in US $ million) was: Imports 253.1; Exports 301.6 (Source: IMF, *Myanmar: Statistical Appendix* (January 2001).

† Excluding re-exports.

Source: Asian Development Bank, *Key Indicators of Developing Asian and Pacific Countries.*

PRINCIPAL TRADING PARTNERS
(US $ million)

Imports	1999	2000	2001
China, People's Republic	447.2	546.1	611.3
Germany	61.5	44.7	25.3
Hong Kong	70.7	97.9	79.8
India	58.4	67.1	73.9
Indonesia	81.8	71.2	70.9
Japan	203.5	215.6	199.6
Korea, Republic	205.9	318.2	255.3
Malaysia	257.7	254.1	224.5
Singapore	460.2	479.7	465.6
Thailand	435.3	554.7	390.5
Total (incl. others)	2,549.7	3,027.8	2,806.2

Exports	1999	2000	2001
China, People's Republic	92.3	113.5	141.1
France	56.3	71.3	71.8
Germany	54.4	77.8	99.4
Hong Kong	34.0	33.5	n.a.
India	227.3	261.3	288.5
Japan	92.2	108.4	96.5
Malaysia	52.2	63.2	74.7
Singapore	90.3	99.8	102.1
Thailand	102.6	233.0	735.4
United Kingdom	35.0	67.3	87.8
USA	222.2	442.7	456.2
Total (incl. others)	1,474.0	2,116.2	2,823.9

Source: Asian Development Bank, *Key Indicators of Developing Asian and Pacific Countries*.

Transport

RAILWAYS (traffic, million)

	1997	1998	1999
Passenger-kilometres	3,784	3,948	4,112
Freight ton-kilometres	674	988	1,043

Source: UN, *Statistical Yearbook*.

ROAD TRAFFIC (registered motor vehicles at 31 March)

	1994	1995	1996
Passenger cars	119,126	131,953	151,934
Trucks	39,939	36,728	42,828
Buses	19,183	14,624	15,639
Motorcycles	71,929	82,591	85,821
Others	8,377	6,251	6,611
Total	258,554	272,147	302,833

Source: Department of Road Transport Administration.

INLAND WATERWAYS (traffic by state-owned vessels)

	1993/94	1994/95*	1995/96†
Passengers carried ('000)	36,003	26,582	24,491
Passenger-miles (million)	617	531	544
Freight carried ('000 tons)	3,172	3,194	3,158
Freight ton-miles (million)	353	346	351

* Provisional. † Estimates.

SHIPPING

Merchant Fleet (registered at 31 December)

	1999	2000	2001
Number of vessels	127	123	124
Displacement (grt)	540,232	445,583	379,819

Source: Lloyd's Register-Fairplay, *World Fleet Statistics*.

International Sea-Borne Traffic
(state-owned vessels)

	1993/94	1994/95*	1995/96†
Passengers carried ('000)	69	77	60
Passenger-miles (million)	23	26	20
Freight carried ('000 metric tons)	773	1,213	1,030
Freight ton-miles (million)	2,655	2,765	2,807

* Provisional. † Estimates.

CIVIL AVIATION (traffic on scheduled services)

	1996	1997	1998
Kilometres flown (million)	8	9	8
Passengers carried ('000)	676	575	522
Passenger-km (million)	392	385	345
Total ton-km (million)	44	46	40

Source: UN, *Statistical Yearbook*.

Tourism

TOURIST ARRIVALS BY COUNTRY OF NATIONALITY

	1998	1999	2000
China, People's Republic	n.a.	12,148	14,336
France	15,410	13,594	13,313
Germany	8,492	9,039	9,920
Japan	28,672	25,319	21,623
Malaysia	n.a.	7,583	9,938
Singapore	n.a.	11,074	11,074
Taiwan	n.a.	32,977	32,098
Thailand	18,840	19,392	19,070
United Kingdom	9,494	9,267	9,020
USA	10,700	10,270	11,554
Total (incl. others)	201,000	198,210	206,243

Source: World Tourism Organization, *Yearbook of Tourism Statistics*.

Tourism receipts (US $ million): 35 in 1998; 35 in 1999 (Source: World Bank).

Communications Media

	1999	2000	2001
Television receivers ('000 in use)	323.3	344.3	n.a.
Telephones ('000 main lines in use)	249.1	266.2	281.2
Facsimile machines (number in use)	2,540	n.a.	n.a.
Mobile cellular telephones ('000 subscribers)	11.4	29.3	13.8
Personal computers ('000 in use)	50	50	55
Internet users ('000)	0.5	1.0	10.0

Book production (1993): 3,660 titles.

Newspapers (1996): 5 dailies (average circulation 449,000).

Radio receivers (1997): 4,200,000 in use.

Sources: International Telecommunication Union; UNESCO, *Statistical Yearbook*.

Education

(provisional, 1994/95)

	Institutions	Teachers	Students
Primary schools*	35,856	169,748	5,711,202
Middle schools	2,058	53,859	1,390,065
High schools	858	18,045	389,438
Vocational schools	86	1,847	21,343
Teacher training	17	615	4,031
Higher education	45	6,246	247,348
Universities	6	2,901	62,098

* Excluding 1,152 monastic primary schools with an enrolment of 45,360.

1997/98 (provisional): Primary: Institutions 35,877, Teachers 167,134, Students ('000) 5,145.4; General Secondary: Institutions 2,091, Teachers 56,955, Students ('000) 1,545.6; Tertiary: Institutions 923, Teachers 17,089, Students ('000) 385.3 (Source: UN, *Statistical Yearbook for Asia and the Pacific*).

Adult literacy rate (UNESCO estimates): 84.7% (males 89.0%; females 80.5%) in 2000 (Source: UN Development Programme, *Human Development Report*).

Directory

The Constitution

On 18 September 1988 a military junta, the State Law and Order Restoration Council (SLORC), assumed power and abolished all state organs created under the Constitution of 3 January 1974. The country was placed under martial law. The state organs were superseded by the SLORC at all levels with the Division, Township and Village State Law and Order Restoration Councils. The SLORC announced that a new constitution was to be drafted by the 485-member Constituent Assembly that was elected in May 1990. In early 1993 a National Convention, comprising members of the SLORC and representatives of opposition parties, met to draft a new constitution; however, the Convention was adjourned in March 1996 and remained in recess in 2002. In November 1997 the SLORC was dissolved and replaced by the newly-formed State Peace and Development Council (SPDC).

The Government

HEAD OF STATE

Chairman of the State Peace and Development Council: Field Marshal THAN SHWE (took office as Head of State 23 April 1992).

STATE PEACE AND DEVELOPMENT COUNCIL
(September 2002)

Field Marshal THAN SHWE (Chairman), Dep. Senior Gen. MAUNG AYE (Vice-Chairman), Gen. KHIN NYUNT (First Secretary), (Second Secretary—vacant), (Third Secretary—vacant), Rear-Adm. KYI MIN, Lt-Gen. KYAW THAN, Maj.-Gen. AUNG HTWE, Maj.-Gen. YE MYINT, Maj.-Gen. KHIN MAUNG THAN, Maj.-Gen. KYAW WIN, Maj.-Gen. THEIN SEIN, Maj.-Gen. THURA SHWE MANN, Maj.-Gen. MYINT AUNG, Maj.-Gen. MAUNG BO, Maj.-Gen. THIHA THURA TIN AUNG MYINT OO, Maj.-Gen. SOE WIN, Maj.-Gen. TIN AYE.

CABINET
(September 2002)

Prime Minister and Minister of Defence: Field Marshal THAN SHWE.

Deputy Prime Ministers: (vacant).

Minister of Military Affairs: (vacant).

Minister of Agriculture and Irrigation: Maj.-Gen. NYUNT TIN.

Minister of Industry (No. 1): U AUNG THAUNG.

Minister of Industry (No. 2): (vacant).

Minister of Foreign Affairs: U WIN AUNG.

Minister of National Planning and Economic Development: U SOE THA.

Minister of Transport: Maj.-Gen. HLA MYINT SWE.

Minister of Labour: U TIN WIN.

Minister of Culture: Maj.-Gen. KYI AUNG.

Minister of Co-operatives: Lt-Gen. TIN NGWE.

Minister of Rail Transportation: U PAN AUNG.

Minister of Energy: Brig.-Gen. LUN THI.

Minister of Education: U THAN AUNG.

Minister of Health: Maj.-Gen. KET SEIN.

Minister of Commerce: Brig.-Gen. PYI SONE.

Minister of Communications, Posts and Telegraphs and Minister of Hotels and Tourism: Brig.-Gen. THEIN ZAW.

Minister of Finance and Revenue: U KHIN MAUNG THEIN.

Minister of Religious Affairs: U AUNG KHIN.

Minister of Construction: Maj.-Gen. SAW TUN.

Minister of Science and Technology: U THAUNG.

Minister of Immigration and Population and Minister of Social Welfare, Relief and Resettlement: Maj.-Gen. SEIN HTWA.

Minister of Information: Brig.-Gen. KYAW HSAN.

Minister of Progress of Border Areas, National Races and Development Affairs: Col THEIN NYUNT.

Minister of Electric Power: Maj.-Gen. TIN HTUT.

Minister of Sports: Brig.-Gen. THURA AYE MYINT.

Minister of Forestry: U AUNG PHONE.

Minister of Home Affairs: Col TIN HLAING.

Minister of Mines: Brig.-Gen. OHN MYINT.

Minister of Livestock and Fisheries: Brig.-Gen. MAUNG MAUNG THEIN.

Ministers at the Office of the Chairman of the State Peace and Development Council: Lt.-Gen. MIN THEIN, Brig.-Gen. DAVID ABEL.

Minister at the Office of the Prime Minister: U THAN SHWE.

MINISTRIES

Office of the Chairman of the State Peace and Development Council: 15–16 Windermere Park, Yangon; tel. (1) 282445.

Prime Minister's Office: Ministers' Office, Theinbyu Rd, Botahtaung Township, Yangon; tel. (1) 283742.

Ministry of Agriculture and Irrigation: Thiri Mingala Lane, Kaba Aye Pagoda Rd, Yangon; tel. (1) 665587; fax (1) 664493.

Ministry of Commerce: 228–240 Strand Rd, Yangon; tel. (1) 287034; fax (1) 280679; e-mail com@mptmail.net.mm; internet www.myanmar.com/Ministry/commerce.

Ministry of Communications, Posts and Telegraphs: cnr of Merchant and Theinbyu Sts, Yangon; tel. (1) 292019; fax (1) 292977; internet www.mptp.gov.mm.

Ministry of Construction: 39 Nawaday St, Dagon Township, Yangon; tel. (1) 283938; fax (1) 289531.

Ministry of Co-operatives: 259–263 Bogyoke Aung San St, Yangon; tel. (1) 277096; fax (1) 287919.

Ministry of Culture: 131 Kaba Aye Pagoda Rd, Bahan Township, Yangon; tel. (1) 543235; fax (1) 283794; internet www.myanmar.com/Ministry/culture.

Ministry of Defence: Ahlanpya Phaya St, Yangon; tel. (1) 281611.

Ministry of Education: Theinbyu St, Botahtaung Township, Yangon; tel. (1) 285588; fax (1) 285480.

Ministry of Electric Power: Yangon.

Ministry of Energy: 23 Pyay Rd, Yangon; tel. (1) 221060; fax (1) 222964; e-mail myanmoe@mptmail.net.mm; internet www.energy.gov.mm.

Ministry of Finance and Revenue: 26(A) Setmu Rd, Yankin Township, Yangon; tel. (1) 284763; internet www.myanmar.com/Ministry/finance.

Ministry of Foreign Affairs: Pyay Rd, Dagon Township, Yangon; tel. (1) 222844; fax (1) 222950; e-mail mofa.aung@mptmail.net.mm; internet www.myanmar.com/Ministry/mofa.

Ministry of Forestry: Thirimingala Lane, Kaba Aye Pagoda Rd, Yangon; tel. (1) 289184; fax (1) 664459; internet www.myanmar.com/Ministry/Forest.

Ministry of Health: Theinbyu Rd, Botahtaung Township, Yangon; tel. (1) 277334; fax (1) 282834; internet www.myanmar.com/Ministry/health.

Ministry of Home Affairs: cnr of Saya San St and No. 1 Industrial St, Yankin Township, Yangon; tel. (1) 549208; internet www.myanmar.com/Ministry/Moha.

Ministry of Hotels and Tourism: 77–91 Sule Pagoda Rd, Kyauktada Township, Yangon; tel. (1) 282705; fax (1) 287871; e-mail mtt.mht@mptmail.net.mm; internet www.myanmar.com/Ministry/Hotel_Tour.

Ministry of Immigration and Population: cnr of Mahabandoola Rd and Thein Phyu Rd, Botahtaung Township, Yangon; tel. (1) 249090; internet www.myanmar.com/Ministry/imm&popu.

Ministry of Industry (No. I): 192 Kaba Aye Pagoda Rd, Yangon; tel. (1) 566066; internet www.myanmar.com/Ministry/MOI-1.

Ministry of Industry (No. II): 56 Kaba Aye Pagoda Rd, Yankin Township, Yangon; tel. (1) 666134; fax (1) 666135; e-mail dmip@mptmail.net.mm; internet www.myanmar.com/Ministry/moi2.

Ministry of Information: 365–367 Bo Sung Kyaw St, Yangon; tel. (1) 245631; fax (1) 289274.

Ministry of Labour: Theinbyu St, Botahtaung Township, Yangon; tel. (1) 278320; fax (1) 256185.

Ministry of Livestock and Fisheries: Theinbyu St, Botahtaung Township, Yangon; tel. (1) 280398; fax (1) 289711.

Ministry of Military Affairs: Yangon.

Ministry of Mines: 90 Kanbe Rd, Yankin Township, Yangon; tel. (1) 577316; fax (1) 577455; internet www.myanmar.com/Ministry/Mines.

Ministry of National Planning and Economic Development: Theinbyu St, Botahtaung Township, Yangon; tel. (1) 254667; fax (1) 243791.

Ministry of Progress of Border Areas, National Races and Development Affairs: Ministers' Office, Theinbyu St, Botahtaung Township, Yangon; tel. (1) 280032; fax (1) 285257.

Ministry of Rail Transportation: 88 Theinbyu St, Yangon; tel. (1) 292769.

Ministry of Religious Affairs: Kaba Aye Pagoda Precinct, Mayangone Township, Yangon; tel. (1) 665620; fax (1) 665728; internet www.myanmar.com/Ministry/religious.

Ministry of Science and Technology: 6 Kaba Aye Pagoda Rd, Yankin Township, Yangon; tel. (1) 665686.

Ministry of Social Welfare, Relief and Resettlement: Theinbyu St, Botahtaung Township, Yangon; tel. (1) 665697; fax (1) 650002; e-mail social-wel-myan@mptmail.net.mm; internet www.myanmar.com/Ministry/social-welfare.

Ministry of Sports: Ministers' Office, Botahtaung Township, Yangon; tel. (1) 553958.

Ministry of Transport: 363–421 Merchant St, Botahtaung Township, Yangon; tel. (1) 296815; fax (1) 296824; internet www.myanmar.com/Ministry/Transport.

Legislature

CONSTITUENT ASSEMBLY

Following the military coup of 18 September 1988, the 489-member Pyithu Hluttaw (People's Assembly), together with all other state organs, was abolished. A general election was held on 27 May 1990. It was subsequently announced, however, that the new body was to serve as a constituent assembly, responsible for the drafting of a new constitution, and that it was to have no legislative power. The next legislative election was provisionally scheduled for September 1997, but did not take place.

General Election, 27 May 1990

Party	% of Votes	Seats
National League for Democracy	59.9	392
Shan Nationalities League for Democracy	1.7	23
Arakan (Rakhine) League for Democracy	1.2	11
National Unity Party	21.2	10
Mon National Democratic Front	1.0	5
National Democratic Party for Human Rights	0.9	4
Chin National League for Democracy	0.4	3
Kachin State National Congress for Democracy	0.1	3
Party for National Democracy	0.5	3
Union Pa-O National Organization	0.3	3
Zomi National Congress		2
Naga Hill Regional Progressive Party		2
Kayah State Nationalities League for Democracy		2
Ta-ang (Palaung) National League for Democracy		2
Democratic Organization for Kayan National Unity		2
Democracy Party		1
Graduates' and Old Students' Democratic Association		1
Patriotic Old Comrades' League	12.8	1
Shan State Kokang Democratic Party		1
Union Danu League for Democracy Party		1
Kamans National League for Democracy		1
Mara People's Party		1
Union Nationals Democracy Party		1
Mro (or) Khami National Solidarity Organization		1
Lahu National Development Party		1
United League of Democratic Parties		1
Karen (Kayin) State National Organization		1
Independents		6
Total	100.0	485

Political Organizations

A total of 93 parties contested the general election of May 1990. By October 1995 the ruling military junta had deregistered all except nine political parties:

Kokang Democracy and Unity Party: Yangon.

Mro (or) Khami National Solidarity Organization: f. 1988; Leader U San Tha Aung.

National League for Democracy (NLD): 97B West Shwegondine Rd, Bahan Township, Yangon; f. 1988; initially known as the National United Front for Democracy, and subsequently as the League for Democracy; present name adopted in Sept. 1988; central exec. cttee of 10 mems; Gen. Sec. Daw Aung San Suu Kyi; Chair. U Aung Shwe; Vice-Chair. U Tin Oo, U Kyi Maung.

National Unity Party (NUP): 93C Windermere Rd, Kamayut, Yangon; tel. (1) 278180; f. 1962 as the Burma Socialist Programme Party; sole legal political party until Sept. 1988, when present name was adopted; 15-mem. Cen. Exec. Cttee and 280-mem. Cen. Cttee; Chair. U Tha Kyaw; Jt Gen. Secs U Tun Yi, U Than Tin.

Shan Nationalities League for Democracy: f. 1988; Leader Khun Htun Oo.

Shan State Kokang Democratic Party: 140 40 St, Kyauktada; f. 1988; Leader U Yankyin Maw.

Union Karen (Kayin) League: Saw Toe Lane, Yangon.

Union Pa-O National Organization: f. 1988; Leader U San Hla.

Wa National Development Party: Byuhar St, Yangon.

The following parties contested the general election of March 1990 but subsequently had their legal status annulled:

Anti-Fascist People's Freedom League: Bo Aung Kyaw, Bahan Township, Yangon; f. 1988; assumed name of wartime resistance movement which became Myanmar's major political force after independence; Chair. Bo Kyaw Nyunt; Gen. Sec. Cho Cho Kyaw Nyein.

Democracy Party: f. 1988; comprises supporters of fmr Prime Minister U Nu; Chair. U Thu Wai; Vice-Chair. U Khun Ye Naung.

Democratic Front for National Reconstruction: Yangon; f. 1988; left-wing; Leader Thakin Chit Maung.

Lahu National Development Party: f. 1988; deregistered 1994; Leader U Daniel Aung.

League for Democracy and Peace: 10 Wingaba Rd, Bahan Township, Yangon; f. 1988; Gen. Sec. U Thein Sein.

Party for National Democracy: Yangon; f. 1988; Chair. Dr Sein Win.

Union National Democracy Party (UNDP): 2–4 Shin Saw Pu Rd, Sanchaung Township, Yangon; f. 1988 by Brig.-Gen. Aung Gyi (fmr Chair. of the National League for Democracy); Chair. U Kyaw Myint Lay.

United League of Democratic Parties: 875 Compound 21, Ledauntkan St, Sa-Hsa Ward, Thingangyun Township, Yangon; f. 1989.

United Nationalities League for Democracy: Yangon; an alliance of parties representing non-Bamar nationalities; won a combined total of 65 seats at the 1990 election.

Other deregistered parties included the Arakan (Rakhine) League for Democracy, the Mon National Democratic Front, the National Democratic Party for Human Rights, the Chin National League for Democracy, the Kachin State National Congress for Democracy, the Zomi National Congress, the Naga Hill Regional Progressive Party, the Kayah State Nationalities League for Democracy, the Ta-ang (Palaung) National League for Democracy, the Democratic Organization for Kayan National Unity, the Graduates' and Old Students' Democratic Association, the Patriotic Old Comrades' League, the Union Danu League for Democracy, the Kamans National League for Democracy, the Mara People's Party and the Karen (Kayin) State National Organization.

The following groups are, or have been, in armed conflict with the Government:

Chin National Army: Chin State.

Chin National Front: f. 1988; forces trained by Kachin Independence Army 1989–91; first party congress 1993; conference in March 1996; carried out an active bombing campaign in 1996–97, mainly in the Chin State; Pres. Thomas Tang No.

Communist Party of Burma (CPB): f. 1939, reorg. 1946; operated clandestinely after 1948; participated after 1986 in jt military operations with sections of the NDF; in 1989 internal dissent resulted in the rebellion of about 80% of CPB members, mostly Wa hill tribesmen and Kokang Chinese; the CPB's military efficacy was thus completely destroyed; Chair. of Cen. Cttee Thakin Ba Thein Tin (exiled).

Democratic Alliance of Burma (DAB): Manerplaw; f. 1988; formed by members of the NDF to incorporate dissident students, monks and expatriates; Pres. Maj.-Gen. Bo Mya; Gen. Sec. U Tin Maung Win. Remaining organizations include:

All-Burma Student Democratic Front (ABSDF): Dagwin; f. 1988; in 1990 split into two factions, under U Moe Thi Zun and U Naing Aung; the two factions reunited in 1993; Leader U Naing Aung; Sec.-Gen. Aung Thu Nyein.

Karen (Kayin) **National Union (KNU):** f. 1948; Chair. Saw Ba Thin; Vice-Chair. Maj.-Gen. Bo Mya; Sec.-Gen. Mahn Sha. (Military wing: **Karen** (Kayin) **National Liberation Army (KNLA),** c. 6,000 troops; Chief of Staff Gen. Tamalabaw.)

Karenni (Kayinni) **National Progressive Party:** agreement with the SLORC signed in March 1995 but subsequently collapsed; resumed fighting in June 1996; Chair. Gen. Aung Than Lay. (Military wing: **Karenni** (Kayinni) **Revolutionary Army.**)

God's Army: breakaway faction of the KNU; Leaders Johnny Htoo, Luther Htoo (surrendered to the Thai authorities in Jan. 2001).

National Democratic Front (NDF): f. 1975; aims to establish a federal union based on national self-determination; largely defunct.

National Socialist Council of Nagaland: Sagaing Division; comprises various factions.

Shan State Army (SSA): enlarged in Sept. 1997 through formal alliance between the following:

Shan State National Army (SSNA): Shan State; f. 1995; breakaway group from Mong Tai Army (MTA); Shan separatists; 5,000–6,000 troops; Leaders Karn Yord, Yee.

Shan State Peace Council (SSPC): fmrly Shan State Progressive Party; Pres. Hso Hten; Gen. Sec. Karn Yord; cease-fire agreement signed in Sept. 1989, but broken by SSA elements following establishment of above alliance in Sept. 1997. (Military wing: original **Shan State Army**; 5,000 men; Leaders Sai Nong, Kai Hpa, Pang Hpa.)

Other MTA remnants also participated in the alliance.

Vigorous Burmese Student Warriors: f. 1999.

Most of the following groups have signed cease-fire agreements, or reached other means of accommodation, with the ruling military junta (the date given in parentheses indicates the month in which agreement with the junta was concluded):

Democratic Karen (Kayin) **Buddhist Organization:** Manerplaw; breakaway group from the KNU. (Military wing: Democratic Karen (Kayin) Buddhist Army.)

Kachin Democratic Army: (Jan. 1991); formerly the 4th Brigade of the Kachin Independence Army; Leader U Zaw Maing.

Kachin Independence Organization (KIO): (Oct. 1993); Chair. Maj.-Gen. Zau Mai. (Military wing: Kachin Independence Army.)

Karen (Kayin) **Solidarity Organization (KSO):** f. 1997; fmrly All Karen Solidarity and Regeneration Front; breakaway group from the KNU; 21-mem. exec. cttee; advocates nation-wide cease-fire and the settlement of all national problems through negotiations; Pres. Saw W. P. Ni; Sec.-Gen. Mahn Aung Htay.

Karenni (Kayinni) **National People's Liberation Front:** (May 1994); Leader U Tun Kyaw.

Kayan National Guard: (Feb. 1992).

Kayan New Land Party: (July 1994); Leader U Than Soe Naing.

Myanmar National Democracy Alliance: (March 1989).

National Democracy Alliance Army: (June 1989).

New Democratic Army: (Dec. 1989); Kachin.

New Mon State Party: (June 1995); Chair. Nai Shwe Kyin. (Military wing: Mon National Liberation Army.)

Palaung State Liberation Organization: (April 1991). (Military wing: Palaung State Liberation Army; 7,000–8,000 men.)

Pa-O National Organization: (Feb. 1991); Chair. Aung Kham Hti. (Military wing: Pa-O National Army.)

Shan State Nationalities Liberation Organization: (Oct. 1994); Chair. U Tha Kalei.

United Wa State Party: (May 1989); formerly part of the Communist Party of Burma. (Military wing: United Wa State Army; 10,000-15,000 men; Leaders Chao Ngi Lai, Pao Yu Chang.)

Since 1991 the National Coalition Government of the Union of Burma, constituted by representatives elected in the general election of 1990, has served as a government-in-exile:

National Coalition Government of the Union of Burma (NCGUB): Washington Office, 1319 F St NW, Suite 303, Washington, DC 20004, USA; tel. (202) 393-7342; fax (202) 393-7343; e-mail ncgub@ncgub.net; internet www.ncgub.net; Prime Minister Dr Sein Win.

Diplomatic Representation

EMBASSIES IN MYANMAR

Australia: 88 Strand Rd, Yangon; tel. (1) 251810; fax (1) 246159; Ambassador: Trevor Wilson.

Bangladesh: 11B Thanlwin Rd, Yangon; tel. (1) 515275; fax (1) 515273; e-mail bdootygn@mptmail.mm; Ambassador: Ahmed Rahim.

Brunei: 51 Golden Valley, Bahan, Yangon; tel. (1) 510422; fax (1) 512854; Ambassador: Pehin Datu Pekerma Dato' Paduka Haji Hussin bin Haji Sulaiman.

Cambodia: 34 Kaba Aye Pagoda Rd, Yangon; tel. (1) 546157; fax (1) 546156; e-mail recyangon@mptmail.net.mm.

China, People's Republic: 1 Pyidaungsu Yeiktha Rd, Yangon; tel. (1) 221281; fax (1) 227019; Ambassador: Li Jinjun.

Egypt: 81 Pyidaungsu Yeiktha Rd, Yangon; tel. (1) 222886; fax (1) 222865; Ambassador: Mohamed El Meneissy.

France: 102 Pyidaungsu Yeiktha Rd, POB 858, Yangon; tel. (1) 212523; fax (1) 212527; Ambassador: Bernard Amaudric du Chaffaut.

Germany: 32 Nat Mauk St, POB 12, Yangon; tel. (1) 548951; fax (1) 548899; e-mail germemb@mptmail.net.mm; Ambassador: Dr Klaus Wild.

India: 545–547 Merchant St, POB 751, Yangon; tel. (1) 82550; fax (1) 89562; e-mail amb.indembygn@mptmail.net.mm; Ambassador: Vivek Katju.

Indonesia: 100 Pyidaungsu Yeiktha Rd, POB 1401, Yangon; tel. (1) 254465; fax (1) 254468; Ambassador: Nasaruddin M. Koro.

Israel: 15 Khabaung St, Hlaing Township, Yangon; tel. (1) 515115; fax (1) 515116; e-mail yangon@israel.org; Ambassador: Yaakov Avrahami Meron.

Italy: 3 Inya Myaing Rd, Golden Valley, Yangon; tel. (1) 527100; fax (1) 514565; e-mail capitani@mptmail.net.mm; Ambassador: Raffaele Miniero.

Japan: 100 Natmauk Rd, Yangon; tel. (1) 549644; fax (1) 549643; e-mail embassyofjapan@mptmail.net.mm; Ambassador: Shigeru Tsumori.

Korea, Republic: 97 University Ave, Yangon; tel. (1) 527142; fax (1) 513286; e-mail KoreaEmb.Myanmar@mtpt400.stems.com; Ambassador: Chung Jung-Gum.

Laos: A1 Diplomatic Quarters, Franser Rd, Yangon; tel. (1) 222482; fax (1) 227446; Ambassador: Ly Bounkham.

Malaysia: 82 Diplomatic Quarters, Pyidaungsu Yeiktha Rd, Yangon; tel. (1) 220249; fax (1) 221840; e-mail mwyangon@mweb .com.na; Ambassador: Dato' Cheah Sam Kip.

Nepal: 16 Natmauk Yeiktha Rd, POB 84, Tamwe, Yangon; tel. (1) 545880; fax (1) 549803; e-mail rnembygn@datseco.com.mm; Ambassador: Dibya Dev Bhatta.

Pakistan: A4 Diplomatic Quarters, Pyay Rd, Yangon; tel. (1) 222881; fax (1) 221147; Ambassador: (vacant).

Philippines: 50 Saya San Rd, Bahan Township, Yangon; tel. (1) 558149; fax (1) 558154; e-mail phyangon@mptmail.net.mm; Ambassador: Phoebe Abaya Gomez.

Russia: 38 Sagawa Rd, Yangon; tel. (1) 241955; fax (1) 241953; e-mail rusinmyan@mptmail.net.mm; Ambassador: Gleb A. Ivashentsov.

Singapore: 326 Pyay Rd, Yangon; tel. (1) 525688; fax (1) 525734; e-mail SingEmb@mptmail.net.mm; Ambassador: Simon Tensing de Cruz.

Sri Lanka: 34 Taw Win Rd, POB 1150, Yangon; tel. (1) 222812; fax (1) 221509; e-mail srilankaemb@mpt.net.mm; Ambassador: Ubhayasekera Mapa.

Thailand: 437 Pyay Rd, 8 Ward, Kamayut Township, Yangon; tel. (1) 512018; fax (1) 527792; e-mail thaiygn@mfa.go.th; Ambassador: Oum Maolanon.

United Kingdom: 80 Strand Rd, POB 638, Yangon; tel. (1) 295300; fax (1) 289566; e-mail chancery@Rangoon.mail.fco.gov.uk; Ambassador: John Jenkins.

USA: 581 Merchant St, POB 521, Yangon; tel. (1) 282055; fax (1) 280409; e-mail rangooninfo@state.gov; Chargé d'affaires: Priscilla Clapp.

Viet Nam: 36 Wingaba Rd, Bahan Township, Yangon; tel. (1) 548905; fax (1) 549302; e-mail vinaemb.myr@mptmail.net.mm; Ambassador: Pham Quang Khon.

Yugoslavia: 114A Inya Rd, POB 943, Yangon; tel. (1) 515282; fax (1) 504274; Chargé d'affaires a.i.: Vladimir Stamenović.

Judicial System

A new judicial structure was established in March 1974. Its highest organ, composed of members of the People's Assembly, was the Council of People's Justices, which functioned as the central Court of Justice. Below this Council were the state, divisional, township, ward and village tract courts formed with members of local People's Councils. These arrangements ceased to operate following the imposition of military rule in September 1988, when a Supreme Court with five members was appointed. A chief justice, an attorney-general and a deputy attorney-general were also appointed.

Office of the Supreme Court: 101 Pansodan St, Kyauktada Township, Yangon; tel. (1) 280751.

Chief Justice: U Aung Toe.

Attorney-General: U Tha Tun.

Religion

Freedom of religious belief and practice is guaranteed. In 1992 an estimated 87.2% of the population were Buddhists, 5.6% Christians, 3.6% Muslims, 1.0% Hindus and 2.6% animists or adherents of other religions.

BUDDHISM

State Sangha Maha Nayaka Committee: c/o Dept of Promotion and Propagation of the Sasana, Kaba Aye Pagoda Precinct, Mayangone Township, Yangon; tel. (1) 660759.

CHRISTIANITY

Myanmar Naing-ngan Khrityan Athin-dawmyar Kaung-si (Myanmar Council of Churches): Myanmar Ecumenical Sharing Centre, 601 Pyay Rd, University PO, Yangon 11041; tel. (1) 533957; fax (1) 296848; f. 1974 to succeed the Burma Christian Council; 13 mem. churches; Pres. Rev. Saw Mar Gay Gyi; Gen. Sec. Rt Rev. Smith N. Za Thawng.

The Roman Catholic Church

Myanmar comprises three archdioceses and nine dioceses. At 31 December 2000 an estimated 1.1% of the total population were adherents.

Catholic Bishops' Conference of Myanmar: 292 Pyi Rd, POB 1080, Sanchaung PO, Yangon 11111; tel. (1) 237198; f. 1982; Pres. Rt Rev. Charles Maung Bo, Bishop of Pathein.

Archbishop of Mandalay: Most Rev. Alphonse U Than Aung, Archbishop's House, 82nd and 25th St, Mandalay 05071; tel. (2) 36369.

Archbishop of Taunggyi: Most Rev. Matthias U Shwe, Archbishop's Office, Bayint Naung Rd, Taunggyi 06011; tel. (81) 21689; fax (81) 22164.

Archbishop of Yangon: Most Rev. Gabriel Thohey Mahn Gaby, Archbishop's House, 289 Theinbyu St, Botataung, Yangon; tel. (1) 246710.

The Anglican Communion

Anglicans are adherents of the Church of the Province of Myanmar, comprising six dioceses. The Province was formed in February 1970, and contained an estimated 45,000 adherents in 1985.

Archbishop of Myanmar and Bishop of Yangon: Most Rev. Samuel San Si Htay, Bishopscourt, 140 Pyidaungsu Yeiktha Rd, Dagon PO (11191), Yangon; tel. (1) 285379; fax (1) 251405.

Protestant Churches

Lutheran Bethlehem Church: 181–183 Theinbyu St, Mingala Taung Nyunt PO 11221, POB 773, Yangon; tel. (1) 246585; Pres. Rev. Jenson Rajan Andrews.

Myanmar Baptist Convention: 143 Minye Kyawswa Rd, POB 506, Yangon; tel. (1) 223231; fax (1) 221465; e-mail mbc<mbc@mptmail.net.mm; f. 1865 as Burma Baptist Missionary Convention; present name adopted 1954; 550,104 mems (1994); Pres. Rev. U Tha Din; Gen. Sec. Rev. Dr Simon Pau Khan En.

Myanmar Methodist Church: Methodist Headquarters, 22 Signal Pagoda Rd, Yangon; Bishop Zothan Mawia.

Presbyterian Church of Myanmar: Synod Office, Falam, Chin State; 22,000 mems; Rev. Sun Kanglo.

Other denominations active in Myanmar include the **Lisu Christian Church** and the **Salvation Army**.

The Press

DAILIES

Botahtaung (The Vanguard): 22–30 Strand Rd, Botahtaung PO, POB 539, Yangon; tel. (1) 274310; daily; Myanmar.

Guardian: 392–396 Merchant St, Botahtaung PO, POB 1522, Yangon; tel. (1) 270150; daily; English.

Kyehmon (The Mirror): 77 52nd St, Dazundaung PO, POB 819, Yangon; tel. (1) 282777; daily; Myanmar.

Myanmar Alin (New Light of Myanmar): 58 Komin Kochin Rd, Bahan PO, POB 21, Yangon; tel. (1) 250777; f. 1963; fmrly Loktha Pyithu Nezin (Working People's Daily); organ of the SPDC; morning; Myanmar; Chief Editor U Soe Myint; circ. 400,000.

New Light of Myanmar: 22–30 Strand Rd, Yangon; tel. (1) 297028; f. 1963; fmrly Working People's Daily; internet www.myanmar.com/nlm; organ of the SPDC; morning; English; Chief Editor U Kyaw Min; circ. 14,000.

PERIODICALS

A Hla Thit (New Beauty): 46 90th St, Yangon; tel. (1) 287106; international news.

Dana Business Magazine: 72 8th Street, Lanmadaw Township, Yangon; tel. and fax (1) 224010; e-mail dana@mptmail.net.mm; economic; Editor-in-Chief William Chen.

Do Kyaung Tha: Myawaddy Press, 184 32nd St, Yangon; tel. (1) 274655; f. 1965; monthly; Myanmar and English; circ. 17,000.

Gita Padetha: Yangon; journal of Myanma Music Council; circ. 10,000.

Guardian Magazine: 392/396 Merchant St, Botahtaung PO, POB 1522, Yangon; tel. (1) 296510; f. 1953; nationalized 1964; monthly; English; literary; circ. 11,600.

Kyee Pwar Yay (Prosperity): 296 Bo Sun Pat St, Yangon; tel. (1) 278100; economic; Editor-in-Chief U MYAT KHINE.

Moethaukpan (Aurora): Myawaddy Press, 184 32nd St, Yangon; tel. (1) 274655; f. 1980; monthly; Myanmar and English; circ. 27,500.

Myanma Dana (Myanmar's Economy): 210A, 36th St, Kyauktada PO, Yangon; tel. (1) 284660; economic; Editor-in-Chief U THIHA SAW.

Myanmar Morning Post: Yangon; f. 1998; weekly; Chinese; news; circ. 5,000.

Myanmar Times & Business Review: Level 1, 5 Signal Pagoda Rd, Dagon Township, Yangon; tel. (1) 242711; fax (1) 242669; e-mail myanmartimes@mptmail.net.mm; internet www.myanmar.com/myanmartimes; f. 2000; Editor-in-Chief ROSS DUNKLEY.

Myawaddy Journal: Myawaddy Press, 184 32nd St, Yangon; tel. (1) 274655; f. 1989; fortnightly; news; circ. 8,700.

Myawaddy Magazine: Myawaddy Press, 184 32nd St, Yangon; tel. (1) 274655; f. 1952; monthly; literary magazine; circ. 4,200.

Ngwetaryi Magazine: Myawaddy Press, 184 32nd St, Yangon; tel. (1) 274655; f. 1961; monthly; cultural; circ. 3,400.

Pyinnya Lawka Journal: 529 Merchant St, Yangon; tel. (1) 283611; publ. by Sarpay Beikman Management Board; quarterly; circ. 18,000.

Shwe Thwe: 529 Merchant St, Yangon; tel. (1) 283611; weekly; bilingual children's journal; publ. by Sarpay Beikman Management Board; circ. 100,000.

Taw Win Journal (Royal Journal): 149 37th St, Yangon; news; Editor-in-Chief SOE THEIN.

Teza: Myawaddy Press, 184 32nd St, Yangon; tel. (1) 274655; f. 1965; monthly; English and Myanmar; pictorial publication for children; circ. 29,500.

Thwe Thauk Magazine: Myawaddy Press, 185 48th St, Yangon; f. 1946; monthly; literary.

Ya Nant Thit (New Fragrance): 186 39th St, Yangon; tel. (1) 276799; international news; Editor-in-Chief U CHIT WIN MG.

NEWS AGENCIES

Myanmar News Agency (MNA): 212 Theinbyu Rd, Botahtaung, Yangon; tel. (1) 270893; f. 1963; govt-controlled; Chief Editors U ZAW MIN THEIN (domestic section), U KYAW MIN (external section).

Foreign Bureaux

Agence France-Presse (AFP) (France): 12L Pyithu Lane, 7th Mile, Yangon; tel. (1) 661069; Correspondent U KHIN MAUNG THWIN.

Agenzia Nazionale Stampa Associata (ANSA) (Italy): POB 270, Yangon; tel. (1) 290039; fax (1) 290804; Rep. (vacant).

Associated Press (AP) (USA): 283 U Wisara Rd, Sanchaung PO 11111, Yangon; tel. (1) 527014; Rep. AYE AYE WIN.

Xinhua (New China) News Agency (People's Republic of China): 105 Leeds Rd, Yangon; tel. (1) 221400; Correspondent ZHANG YUHFEI.

Reuters (UK) and **UPI** (USA) are also represented in Myanmar.

Publishers

Hanthawaddy Press: 157 Bo Aung Gyaw St, Yangon; f. 1889; textbooks, multilingual dictionaries; Man. Editor U ZAW WIN.

Knowledge Publishing House: 130 Bo Gyoke Aung San St, Yegyaw, Yangon; art, education, religion, politics and social sciences.

Kyipwaye Press: 84th St, Letsaigan, Mandalay; tel. (2) 21003; arts, travel, religion, fiction and children's.

Myawaddy Press: 184 32nd St, Yangon; tel. (1) 285996; journals and magazines; CEO U THEIN SEIN.

Sarpay Beikman Management Board: 529 Merchant St, Yangon; tel. (1) 283611; f. 1947; encyclopaedias, literature, fine arts and general; also magazines and translations; Chair. AUNG HTAY.

Shumawa Press: 146 West Wing, Bogyoke Aung San Market, Yangon; mechanical engineering.

Shwepyidan: 12A Haiaban, Yegwaw Quarter, Yangon; politics, religion, law.

Smart and Mookerdum: 221 Sule Pagoda Rd, Yangon; arts, cookery, popular science.

Thu Dhama Wadi Press: 55–56 Maung Khine St, POB 419, Yangon; f. 1903; religious; Propr U TIN HTOO; Man. U PAN MAUNG.

Government Publishing House

Printing and Publishing Enterprise: 228 Theinbyu St, Yangon; tel. (1) 294645; Man. Dir U MYINT THEIN.

PUBLISHERS' ASSOCIATION

Myanma Publishers' Union: 146 Bogyoke Market, Yangon.

Broadcasting and Communications

TELECOMMUNICATIONS

Posts and Telecommunications Department: Ministry of Communications, Posts and Telegraphs, 125 Ground Floor, Pansodan St, Yangon; tel. (1) 292019; fax (1) 292977; internet www.mptp.gov.mm; Dir-Gen. of Posts and Telecommunications Dept U KHIN SOE.

Myanma Posts and Telecommunications (MPT): 43 Bo Aung Gyaw St, Kyauktada Township, Yangon; tel. (1) 285840; fax (1) 290429; internet www.mpt.net.mm; Man. Dir Col MAUNG MAUNG TIN.

BROADCASTING

Radio

Myanma TV and Radio Department (MTRD): 426 Pyay Rd, Kamayut 11041, Yangon; POB 1432, Yangon 11181; tel. (1) 531850; fax (1) 530211; radio transmissions began in 1937; broadcasts in Bamar, Arakanese (Rakhine), Shan, Karen (Kayin), Kachin, Kayah, Chin, Mon and English; Dir-Gen. U KYI LWIN; Dir of Radio Broadcasting U KO KO HTWAY.

In 1992 the National Coalition Government of the Union of Burma (NCGUB) began broadcasting daily to Myanmar from Norway under the name Democratic Voice of Burma (DVB). In 1995 it was believed that the DVB was being operated by Myanma student activists from the Norway-Burma Council, without any formal control by the NCGUB.

Television

Myanma TV and Radio Department (MTRD): Pyay Rd, Kamayut 11041, Yangon; POB 1432, Yangon 11181; tel. (1) 531014; fax (1) 530211; colour television transmissions began in 1980; Dir-Gen. U KYI LWIN; Dir of Television Broadcasting U PHONE MYINT.

TV Myawaddy: Hmawbi, Hmawbi Township, Yangon; tel. (1) 620270; f. 1995; military broadcasting station transmitting programmes via satellite.

Finance

(cap. = capital; res = reserves; dep. = deposits; m. = million; brs = branches; amounts in kyats)

BANKING

In July 1990 new banking legislation was promulgated, reorganizing the operations of the Central Bank, establishing a state-owned development institution, the Myanma Agricultural and Rural Development Bank, and providing for the formation of private-sector banks and the opening of branches of foreign banks.

Central Bank

Central Bank of Myanmar: 26A Settmu Rd, POB 184, Yankin Township, Yangon; tel. (1) 543511; fax (1) 543621; f. 1968; bank of issue; cap. 350m., dep. 13,545m.; Gov. U KYI AYE; 37 brs.

State Banks

Myanma Economic Bank (MEB): 1–19 Sule Pagoda Rd, Yangon; tel. (1) 289345; fax (1) 283679; provides domestic banking network throughout the country; Man. Dir U KYAW KYAW.

Myanma Foreign Trade Bank: 80–86 Maha Bandoola Garden St, POB 203, Yangon; tel. (1) 284911; fax (1) 289585; e-mail mftbhoygn@mptmail-net.mm; f. 1976; cap. 110m., res 483.9m., dep. 2,425.9m. (March 1999); handles all foreign exchange and international banking transactions; Chair. U KO KO GYI; Sec. U TIN MAUNG AYE.

Development Banks

Myanma Agricultural and Rural Development Bank (MARDB): 1–7 cnr of Latha St and Kanna Rd, Yangon; tel. (1) 226734; f. 1953 as State Agricultural Bank, reconstituted as above 1990; state-owned; cap. 60.0m., dep. 615.6m. (Sept. 1993); Man. Dir U CHIT SWE.

Myanma Investment and Commercial Bank (MICB): 170/176 Bo Aung Kyaw St, Botataung Township, Yangon; tel. (1) 250509;

fax (1) 281775; f. 1989; state-owned; cap. 400m., dep. 4,778m. (March 1999); Chair. and Man. Dir U TUN CHUN; 2 brs.

Private Banks

By February 1996 16 private banks were established, 14 in Yangon and one each in Mandalay and Taunggyi.

Asia Wealth Bank: 638 cnr of Maha Bandoola St and 22nd St, Latha Township, Yangon; tel. (1) 243700; fax (1) 245456; Chair. WIN MAUNG; Vice-Chair. AIK HTUN; 38 brs.

Asian Yangon International Bank Ltd: 319/321 Maha Bandoola St, Botataung Township, Yangon; tel. (1) 245825; fax (1) 245865.

Co-operative Bank Ltd: 334–336 Kanna Rd, Yangon; tel. (1) 272641; fax (1) 283063; Gen. Man. U NYUNT HLAING.

First Private Bank Ltd (FPB): 619–621 Merchant St, Pabedan Township, Yangon; tel. (1) 289929; fax (1) 242320; e-mail fpb.hq@mptmail.net.mm; f. 1992 as the first publicly-subscribed bank; fmrly the Commercial and Development Bank Ltd; provides loans to private business and small-scale industrial sectors; cap. 654.06m. (March 2001); Chair. Dr SEIN MAUNG; 15 brs.

Myanma Citizens Bank Ltd (MCB): 383 Maha Bandoola St, Kyauktada Township, Yangon; tel. (1) 273512; fax (1) 245932; f. 1991; Chair. U HLA TIN.

Myanma Oriental Bank Ltd: 166–168 Pansodan St, Kyauktada Township, Yangon; tel. (1) 246594; fax (1) 253217; e-mail mobl.ygn@mptmail.net.mm; Chair. U TIN U.

Myanma Universal Bank: 81 Theinbyu Rd, Yangon; tel. (1) 297339; fax (1) 245449; f. 1995.

Myanmar Industrial Development Bank Ltd: 26–42 Pansodan St, Kyauktada Township, Yangon; tel. (1) 249536; fax (1) 249529; f. 1996; cap. US $335m.

Myanmar May Flower Bank Ltd: 1B Yadanar Housing Project, 9 Mile Pyay Rd, Mayangone Township, Yangon; tel. (1) 666112; fax (1) 666110; e-mail mmb-hq@mptmail.net.mm; Chair. U KYAW WIN.

Myawaddy Bank Ltd: 24–26 Sule Pagoda Rd, Kyauktada Township, Yangon; tel. (1) 283665; fax (1) 250093; e-mail mwdbankygn@mtpt400.stems.com; Gen. Mans U TUN KYI, U MYA MIN.

Prime Commercial Bank Ltd: 437 Pyay Rd, Kamayut Township, Yangon; tel. (1) 525990; fax (1) 522420; f. 1994; cap. 122.5m., dep. 358m.; Chair. Dr AUNG KHIN; Man. Dir U MAUNG MAUNG HAN; 2 brs.

Tun Foundation Bank Ltd: 165–167 Bo Aung Gyaw St, Yangon; tel. (1) 270710; Chair. U THEIN TUN.

Yadanabon Bank Ltd: 26th St, cnr of 84th and 85th St, Mandalay; tel. (2) 23577.

Yangon City Bank Ltd: 12–18 Sepin St, Kyauktada Township, Yangon; tel. (1) 289256; fax (1) 289231; f. 1993; auth. cap. 500m.; 100% owned by the Yangon City Development Committee; Chair. Col MYINT AUNG.

Yoma Bank Ltd: 1 Kungyan St, Mingala Taung Nyunt Township, Yangon; tel. (1) 242138; fax (1) 246548; Chair. SERGE PUN.

Foreign Banks

By late 1996 more than 20 foreign banks had opened representative offices in Yangon. These included the Bank of Tokyo-Mitsubishi (Japan), the Development Bank of Singapore, Keppel Bank of Singapore, the Standard Chartered Bank (UK), the Thai Military Bank (Thailand), Fuji Bank (Japan), Sumitomo Bank (Japan), Tokai Bank (Japan) and Sanwa Bank (Japan).

STOCK EXCHANGE

Myanmar Securities Exchange Centre: 1st Floor, 21–25 Sule Pagoda Rd, Yangon; tel. (1) 283984; f. 1996; joint venture between Japan's Daiwa Institute of Research and Myanma Economic Bank; Man. Dir EIJI SUZUKI.

INSURANCE

Myanma Insurance: 627–635 Merchant St, Yangon; tel. (1) 283376; fax (1) 289596; e-mail MYANSURE@mptmail.net.com; f. 1976; govt-controlled; Man. Dir Col THEW LWIN.

Trade and Industry

GOVERNMENT AGENCIES

Inspection and Agency Service: 383 Maha Bandoola St, Yangon; tel. (1) 276048; fax (1) 284823; works on behalf of state-owned enterprises to promote business with foreign companies; Man. Dir U OHN KHIN.

Myanmar Investment Commission: Yangon; Chair. U THAUNG; Vice-Chair. Maj.-Gen. TIN HTUT.

Union of Myanmar Economic Holdings: 72–74 Shwadagon Pagoda Rd, Yangon; tel. (1) 78905; f. 1990; public holding co; auth. cap. 10,000m. kyats; 40% of share capital subscribed by the Ministry of Defence and 60% by members of the armed forces.

CHAMBER OF COMMERCE

Chamber of Commerce and Industry: 504–506 Merchant St, Kyauktada Township, Yangon; tel. (1) 243151; fax (2) 248177; f. 1919; Gen. Sec. ZAW MIN WIN.

UTILITIES

Electricity

Myanma Electric Power Enterprise (MEPE): 197–199 Lower Kyimyindine Rd, Yangon; tel. (1) 220918; Man. Dir U THAUNG SEIN.

Water

Mandalay City Development Committee (Water and Sanitation Dept): cnr of 26th and 72nd St, Mandalay; tel. (2) 36173; f. 1992; Head of Water and Sanitation Dept U TUN KYI.

Yangon City Development Committee (Water and Sanitation Dept): City Hall, Yangon; tel. (1) 289781; fax (1) 284910; f. 1992; Head of Water and Sanitation Dept U ZAW WIN.

CO-OPERATIVES

In 1993/94 there were 22,800 co-operative societies, with a turnover of 23,603m. kyats. This was estimated to have increased to 24,760 societies, with a turnover of 20,927m. kyats, in 1994/95.

Central Co-operative Society (CCS) Council: 334/336 Strand Rd, Yangon; tel. (1) 274550; Chair. U THAN HLANG; Sec. U TIN LATT.

Co-operative Department: 259–263 Bogyoke Aung San Rd, Yangon; tel. (1) 277096; Dir-Gen. U MAUNG HTI.

MAJOR COMPANIES

State Enterprises

Livestock Feedstuff and Milk Products Enterprise: Station Rd, Insein Township, Yangon; tel. (1) 642019; fax (1) 642023; Man. Dir U KHIN MAUNG AYE.

Myanma Agricultural Produce Trading (MAPT): 70 Pansodan St, Yangon; tel. (1) 254018; fax (1) 285578; e-mail mapt.hr@mptmail.net.mm; Man. Dir U THEIN MYINT.

Myanma Agriculture Service: Kanbe, Yankin, Yangon; tel. (1) 663541; fax (1) 283651; Man. Dir Dr MYA MAUNG.

Myanma Ceramic Industries: 192 Kaba Aye Pagoda Rd, Bahan Township, POB 11201, Yangon; tel. (1) 566077; fax (1) 578226; e-mail MMI1MCI@mtmail.net.mm; produces cement, glass, pottery, marble, asbestos sheets and bricks; Man. Dir U THAN SHWE.

Myanma Export-Import Services: 622–624 Merchant St, Yangon; tel. (1) 550661; fax (1) 289587; Man. Dir U THAUNG SEIN.

Myanma Farms Enterprise: Pyi Rd, 9th Mile, Yangon; tel. (1) 665631; Man. Dir Col U NYUNT MG.

Myanma Foodstuff Industries: 192 Kaba Aye Pagoda Rd, Bahan Township, POB 11201, Yangon; tel. (1) 566533; fax (1) 566053; produces foodstuffs, incl. soft drinks, biscuits, lagers and distillled spirits; Man. Dir U KYAW MYINT.

Myanma Gems Enterprise: 23–25 Myanmar Gems Museum, Mayangan Township, Yangon; tel. (1) 665169; fax (1) 665092; Man. Dir U KHIN OO.

Myanma General Industries: 192 Kaba Aye Pagoda Rd, Yangon; tel. (1) 640411; fax (1) 56053; Gen. Man U MYINT SWE.

Myanma Heavy Industries: 56 Kaba Aye Pagoda Rd, POB 370, Yangon; tel. (1) 662880; fax (1) 660465; f. 1960; mfr of vehicles, electrical appliances, electronic goods and agricultural machinery; Man. Dir U SOE THEIN.

Myanma Jute Industries: 257 Yangon-Insein Rd, Yangon; tel. (1) 578946; Man. Dir U MYINT MG.

Myanma Metal Industries: 192 Kaba Aye Pagoda Rd, Yangon; tel. (1) 566842; Man. Dir THEIN TAN.

Myanma Oil and Gas Enterprise: 604 Merchant St, Yangon; tel. (1) 282266; fax (1) 222964; fmrly Myanma Oil Corpn (previously Burma Oil Co); nationalized 1963; Man. Dir U PE KYI.

Myanma Paper and Chemical Industries: 192 Kaba Aye Pagoda Rd, PO 11201, Yangon; tel. (1) 565776; fax (1) 577744; Man. Dir U NGWE THAW.

Myanma Petrochemical Enterprise: 23 Minye Kyawswa Rd, Yangon; tel. (1) 222822; fax (1) 221723; f. 1975; Man. Dir HLAING MYINT SAN.

Myanma Petroleum Products Enterprise: 7A Thanlyetsun Rd, Yangon; tel. (1) 222153; Man. Dir U AUNG HLAING.

Myanma Pharmaceutical Industries: 192 Kabu Aye Pagoda Rd, Bahan Township, POB 11201, Yangon; tel. (1) 566740; fax (1) 566722; Man. Dir U TIN HLAING.

Myanma Textile Industries: 192 Kaba Aye Pagoda Rd, Bahan Township, POB 11201, Yangon; tel. (1) 579495; fax (1) 573373; produces wide range of fabrics and yarns; sales 23,365,040m. kyats (1998); Man. Dir U SAN KYI.

Myanma Timber Enterprise: POB 206, Ahlone, Yangon; tel. (1) 220637; fax (1) 221816; f. 1948; extraction, processing, and main exporter of teak and other timber, veneers, plywood and other forest products; Gen. Man. U MYINT KYU PE.

No. 1 Mining Enterprise: 90 Kanbe Rd, Yankin, Yangon; tel. (1) 577457; fax (1) 577309; development and mining of non-ferrous metals; Man. Dir U KO KO.

No. 2 Mining Enterprise: Kanbe Rd, Yankin, Yangon; tel. (1) 551421; fax (1) 552615; development and mining of tin, tungsten and antimony; Man. Dir Col TIN WIN.

No. 3 Mining Enterprise: 90 Kanbe Rd, Yankin, Yangon; tel. (1) 577444; fax (1) 566224; e-mail mines@mpt; govt-controlled; production of pig iron, carbon steel, steel grinding balls, coal, barytes, gypsum, limestone, chromite, antimony, various clays and granite, etc.; Man. Dir U SAN TUN.

Private Companies

Daewoo Electronics: 139 MHI Compound, Kaba Aye Pagoda Rd, POB 737, Yangon; tel. (1) 64886; fax (1) 62870; f. 1990; South Korean company in joint venture with Myanma Heavy Industries; mfr of televisions, refrigerators and audio systems; Man. Dir KIM CHANG HUN.

Myanmar Inctech: Yangon; f. 1991; auth. cap. 50m. kyats; joint venture between Inctech (Singapore); import, export and leasing of finished and semi-finished construction-related products.

Myanmar International Hotels: 77/91 Sule Pagoda Rd, Yangon; tel. (1) 62857; joint venture between Strand Hotels International and Myanmar Hotels and Tourism Services; construction and renovation of hotels.

Myanmar Natsteel Hardware Centre: 262 Seikkantha St, Yangon; tel. (1) 84985; f. 1991; joint venture between Natsteel Trade International (Singapore) and the local Construction and Electrical Stores Trading; mfg and marketing of building materials and steel products.

WORKERS' AND PEASANTS' COUNCILS

Conditions of work are stipulated in the Workers' Rights and Responsibilities Law, enacted in 1964. Regional workers' councils ensure that government directives are complied with, and that targets are met on a regional basis. In January 1985 there were 293 workers' councils in towns, with more than 1.8m. members. They are co-ordinated by a central workers' organization in Yangon, formed in 1968 to replace trade union organizations which had been abolished in 1964. The Myanma Federation of Trade Unions operates in exile.

Peasants' Asiayone (Organization): Yangon; tel. (1) 82819; f. 1977; peasants' representative org.; Chair. Brig.-Gen. U THAN NYUNT; Sec. U SAN TUN.

Workers' Unity Organization: Central Organizing Committee, 61 Thein Byu St, Yangon; tel. (1) 284043; f. 1968; workers' representative org.; Chair. U OHN KYAW; Sec. U NYUNT THEIN.

Transport

All railways, domestic air services, passenger and freight road transport services and inland water facilities are owned and operated by state-controlled enterprises.

RAILWAYS

The railway network comprised 3,955 km of track in 1996/97, most of which was single track.

Myanma Railways: Bogyoke Aung San St, POB 118, Yangon; tel. (1) 280508; fax (1) 284220; f. 1877; govt-operated; Man. Dir U AUNG THEIN; Gen. Man. U THAUNG LWIN.

ROADS

In 1996 the total length of the road network in Myanmar was an estimated 28,200 km, of which an estimated 3,440 km were paved. In 2001/02 the total length of road accessible to motor vehicles was 28,598 km.

Road Transportation Department: 375 Bogyoke Aung San St, Yangon; tel. (1) 284426; fax (1) 289716; f. 1963; controls passenger and freight road transport; in 1993/94 operated 1,960 haulage trucks and 928 passenger buses; Man. Dir U OHN MYINT.

INLAND WATERWAYS

The principal artery of traffic is the River Ayeyarwady (Irrawaddy), which is navigable as far as Bhamo, about 1,450 km inland, while parts of the Thanlwin and Chindwinn rivers are also navigable.

Inland Water Transport: 50 Pansodan St, Yangon; tel. (1) 222399; fax (1) 286500; govt-owned; operates cargo and passenger services throughout Myanmar; 36m. passengers and 3.1m. tons of freight were carried in 1993/94; Man. Dir U KHIN MAUNG.

SHIPPING

Yangon is the chief port. Vessels with a displacement of up to 15,000 tons can be accommodated.

In 2001 the Myanma merchant fleet totalled 124 vessels, with a combined displacement of 379,819 grt.

Myanma Port Authority: 10 Pansodan St, POB 1, Yangon; tel. (1) 280094; fax (1) 295134; f. 1880; general port and harbour duties; Man. Dir U TIN OO; Gen. Man. U HLAING SOON.

Myanma Five Star Line: 132–136 Theinbyu Rd, POB 1221, Yangon; tel. (1) 295279; fax (1) 297669; e-mail mfsl.myr@mptmail.net.mm; f. 1959; cargo services to the Far East and Australia; Man. Dir U KHIN MAUNG KYI; Gen. Man. U KYAW ZAW; fleet of 26 coastal and ocean-going vessels.

CIVIL AVIATION

Mingaladon Airport, near Yangon, is equipped to international standards. The newly-built Mandalay International Airport was inaugurated in September 2000. In December 1993 Kyauktheingan in Bago (Pegu) was selected as the location of the proposed Hanthawaddy international airport.

Department of Civil Aviation: Mingaladon Airport, Yangon; tel. (1) 662700; Dir-Gen. U TIN AYE.

Air Mandalay: 146 Dhammazedi Rd, Bahan Township, Yangon; tel. (1) 525488; fax (1) 525937; e-mail airmandalay@myanmars.net; internet www.airmandalay.com; f. 1994; Myanmar's first airline; joint venture between Air Mandalay Holding and Myanma Airways; operates domestic services and regional services to Chiang Mai and Phuket, Thailand, and Siem Reap, Cambodia; Chair. THURA U WIN MYINT; Man. Dir ERIC KANG; 242 employees.

Myanmar Airways (MA): 123 Sule Pagoda Rd, Yangon; tel. (1) 80710; fax (1) 255305; e-mail 8mpr@maiair.com.mm; internet www.maiair.com; f. 1993; govt-controlled; internal network operates services to 21 airports; Chief Operating Officer PRITHPAL SINGH.

Myanmar Airways International (MAI): 08–02 Sakura Tower, 339 Bogyoke Aung San Rd, Yangon; tel. (1) 255260; fax (1) 255305; e-mail 8mpr@maiair.com.mm; internet www.maiair.com; f. 1993; govt-owned; established by Myanmar Airways in jt venture with Highsonic Enterprises of Singapore to provide international services; operates services to Bangkok, Dhaka, Hong Kong, Kuala Lumpur and Singapore; Man. Dir GERARD DE VAZ.

Tourism

Yangon, Mandalay, Taunggyi and Pagan possess outstanding palaces, Buddhist temples and shrines. The number of foreign visitors to Myanmar declined severely following the suppression of the democracy movement in 1988. In the early 1990s, however, the Government actively promoted the revival of the tourism industry, and between 1995 and 1998 alone the number of hotel rooms almost doubled, reaching a total of nearly 14,000. In 2000 there were 206,243 foreign tourist arrivals (compared with only 5,000 in 1989). In 1999 revenue from tourism totalled an estimated US $35m.

Myanmar Hotels and Tourism Services: 77–91 Sule Pagoda Rd, Yangon 11141; tel. (1) 282013; fax (1) 254417; e-mail mtt.mht@mptmail.net.mm; govt-controlled; manages all hotels, tourist offices, tourist department stores and duty-free shops; Man. Dir U KYI HTUN.

Myanmar Tourism Promotion Board: 5 Signal Pagoda Rd, Yangon; tel. (1) 243639; fax (1) 245001; e-mail mtpb@mptmail.net.mm; internet www.myanmar-tourism.com.

Myanmar Travels and Tours: 77–91 Sule Pagoda Rd, POB 559, Yangon 11141; tel. (1) 287993; fax (1) 254417; e-mail mtt.mht@mptmail.net.mm; govt tour operator and travel agent; handles all travel arrangements for groups and individuals; Gen. Man. U HTAY AUNG.

Defence

In August 2001 the total strength of the armed forces was reported to be some 444,000; army some 325,000, navy 10,000, air force 9,000. Military service is voluntary. Paramilitary forces comprise a people's police force (65,000 men) and a people's militia (35,000 men). As Myanmar maintains a policy of neutrality and has no external defence treaties, the armed forces are engaged mainly in internal security duties.

Defence Expenditure: Budgeted at US $1,700m. for 2001.

Commander-in-Chief of the Defence Services: Field Marshal THAN SHWE.

Commander-in-Chief of the Army: Dep. Senior Gen. MAUNG AYE.

Commander-in-Chief of the Navy: Rear-Adm. KYI MIN.

Commander-in-Chief of the Air Force: Lt-Gen. KYAW THAN.

Education

The organization and administration of education is the responsibility of the Ministry of Education. Education is compulsory for five years between five and 10 years of age. Pre-school education begins at four years of age. Primary education lasts for five years between the ages of five and 10. Education in lower secondary, or middle, schools lasts four years from the age of 10 to 14, when pupils take the external government examination. Upper secondary, or high, school lasts for a further two years. In 1995 the total enrolment at secondary level was equivalent to 32% of children in the relevant age-group. In the same year enrolment at primary and secondary levels was equivalent to 65% of the school-age population.

In 1994/95 there were 45 institutes of higher education and six universities. Student enrolment in tertiary education totalled 245,317 in that year (not including students enrolled in medical science courses), including 89,717 university students.

In 1998/99 government expenditure on education was 5,700m. kyats (7.9% of total expenditure).

Bibliography

GENERAL

Aung San Suu Kyi. *Freedom from Fear and Other Writings.* Harmondsworth, Penguin, 1991.

Aung San Suu Kyi: Letters From Burma. London, Penguin, 1997.

Aung San Suu Kyi: The Voice of Hope. Conversations with Alan Clements. London, Penguin, 1997.

Becka, Jan. *Historical Dictionary of Myanmar.* Metuchen, NJ, Scarecrow Press, 1995.

Bradley, David. *Myanmar, A Comparative Study.* Canberra, Australian Government Publishing Service, 1992.

Donnison, F. S. V. *Burma.* London, Benn, 1970.

Evans, Grant, Hutton, Chris, and Kuah Khun Eng (Eds). *Where China meets Southeast Asia: Social and Cultural Change in the Border Regions.* New York, St Martin's Press, 2000.

Hall, D. G. E. *Burma.* 2nd Edn, London, Hutchinson, 1956.

Herbert, Patricia M. *Burma (World Bibliographical Series).* Oxford and Denver, Clio Press, 1991.

The Life of the Buddha. London, British Library Board, 1993.

Images Asia. *No Childhood At All: A Report about Child Soldiers in Burma.* Chiang Mai, Images Asia, 1996.

Mawdsley, James. *The Heart Must Break: The Fight for Democracy and Truth in Burma.* London, Century, 2001.

Mi Mi Khaing. *Burmese Family.* London, Longman, Green, 1946.

The World of Burmese Women. London, Zed Books, 1984.

Nash, Manning. *The Golden Road to Modernity: Village Life in Contemporary Burma.* Chicago, University of Chicago Press, 1965.

Open Society Institute. *Country in Crisis: a Burma Handbook.* New York, Soros Foundation, 1997.

Rodrigues, Yves. *Nat-Pwe: Burma's Supernatural Sub-Culture.* Gartmore, Kiscadale, 1993.

Shulman, Frank Joseph. *Burma: An Annotated Bibliographical Guide to International Doctoral Dissertation Research 1898–1985.* Lanham, MD, University Press of America, 1986.

Shwe Yoe (Sir George Scott). *The Burman: His Life and Notions.* London, 1982.

Spiro, Melford E. *Buddhism and Society: A Great Tradition and its Burmese Vicissitudes.* London, Allen and Unwin, 1971.

Kinship and Marriage in Burma. Berkeley, University of California Press, 1977.

Anthropological Other or Burmese Brother? Studies in Cultural Analysis. New Brunswick, NJ, Transaction Publishers, 1992.

Steinberg, David I. *Burma: A Socialist Nation of South-East Asia.* Boulder, CO, Westview Press, 1982.

Tinker, H. *The Union of Burma.* 4th Edn, London, Oxford University Press, 1967.

Tucker, Shelby. *Among Insurgents: Walking through Burma.* London, Flamingo, 2001.

Yegar, Moshe. *Between Integration and Secession: The Muslim Communities of the Southern Philippines, Southern Thailand, and Western Burma/Myanmar.* Lanham, MD, Lexington Books, 2002.

HISTORY

Allen, Louis. *Burma: The Longest War 1941–45.* London, Dent, 1985.

Apple, Betsy. *School for Rape: The Burmese Military and Sexual Violence.* Bangkok, EarthRights, 1998.

Aung San Suu Kyi. *Aung San of Burma.* Edinburgh, Kiscadale Publications, 1991.

Burma and India: Some Aspects of Intellectual Life Under Colonialism. Shimla, Indian Institute of Advanced Study, Allied Publishers Pvt. Ltd, 1990.

Aung-Thwin, Michael. *Pagan: The Origins of Modern Burma.* Honolulu, HI, University of Hawaii Press, 1985.

Myth and History in the Historiography of Early Burma: Paradigms, Primary Sources, and Prejudices. Athens, OH, Ohio University Center for International Studies, 1998.

Aye Kyaw. *The Voice of Young Burma.* New York, Cornell University Press, 1993.

Ba Maw. *Breakthrough in Burma.* New Haven, CT, Yale University Press, 1968.

Bachoe, Ralph, and Stothard, Debbie (Eds). *From Consensus to Controversy: ASEAN's Relationship with Burma's SLORC.* Bangkok, Altsean, 1997.

Becka, J. *The National Liberation Movement in Burma during the Japanese Occupation Period (1941–45).* Prague, Oriental Institute of Academia, Publishing House of the Czechoslovak Academy of Sciences, 1983.

Blackburn, Terence. *The British Humiliation of Burma.* Bangkok, Orchid Press, 2001.

Bless, R. *'Divide et impera?' Britische Minderheitenpolitik in Burma 1917–1948.* Stuttgart, Franz Steiner Verlag, 1990.

Cady, J. F. A. *History of Modern Burma.* Ithaca, NY, Cornell University Press, 1958.

The United States and Burma. Cambridge, MA, Harvard University Press, 1976.

Clements, Alan. *Burma: The Next Killing Fields?* Berkeley, CA, Odonian Press, 1992.

Clements, Alan, and Kean, Leslie. *Burma's Revolution of the Spirit: The Struggle for Democratic Freedom and Dignity.* New York, Aperture, 1995.

Falla, Jonathan. *True Love and Bartholomew: Rebels on the Burmese Border.* Cambridge, Cambridge University Press, 1991.

Fink, Christina. *Living Silence: Burma under Military Rule.* London, Zed Books, 2001.

Furnivall, John S. *The Fashioning of Leviathan: The Beginnings of British Rule in Burma.* Canberra, Department of Anthropology Occasional Paper, Research School of Pacific Studies, Australian National University, 1991.

Ghosh, Parimal. *Brave Men of the Hills: Resistance and Rebellion in Burma, 1825–1932.* London, Hurst & Co, 2000.

Gooden, Christian. *Three Pagodas: A Journey down the Thai-Burmese Border.* Halesworth, Jungle Books, 1996.

Hall, D. G. E. *Early English Intercourse with Burma 1587–1743.* London, Frank Cass, 1968.

Images Asia. *Nowhere To Go: A Report on the 1997 SLORC Offensive against Duplaya District (KNU 6th Brigade), Karen State, Burma.* Chiang Mai, Images Asia, 1997.

A Question of Security: A Retrospective on Cross-border Attacks on Thailand's Refugee and Civilian Communities along the Burmese Border since 1995. Chiang Mai, Images Asia, 1998.

All Quiet on the Western Front? The Situation in Chin State and Sagaing Division, Burma. Chiang Mai, Images Asia, 1998.

Khin Yi. *The Dobama Movement in Burma.* Vol. 2. Ithaca, NY, Cornell University Press, 1988.

Kin Oung. *Who Killed Aung San?* Bangkok and Cheney, White Lotus, 1993.

Koenig, William J. *The Burmese Polity, 1752–1819: Politics, Administration, and Social Organization in the Early Kon-baung Period.* Ann Arbor, MI, Michigan Papers on South and Southeast Asia, Center for South and Southeast Asian Studies, University of Michigan, Number 34, 1990.

Lehman, F. K. (Ed.). *Military Rule in Burma since 1962.* Maruzen Asia, Singapore, Institute of Southeast Asian Studies, 1981.

Liberman, Victor B. *Burmese Administrative Cycles: Anarchy and Conquest 1580–1760.* Princeton, NJ, Princeton University Press, 1984.

Lintner, Bertil. *Outrage: Burma's Struggle for Democracy.* Hong Kong, Review Publishing Co Ltd, 1989.

Land of Jade: A Journey Through Insurgent Burma. Edinburgh, Kiscadale Publications, 1990.

The Rise and Fall of the Communist Party of Burma. Ithaca, NY, Cornell University Press, 1990.

Burma in Revolt: Opium and Insurgency Since 1948. Boulder, CO, Westview Press, 1994.

Marshall, Andrew. *The Trouser People: A Story of Burma in the Shadow of the Empire.* Boulder, CO, Counterpoint Press, 2002.

Maung Htin Aung. *A History of Burma.* New York, Columbia University Press, 1968.

Maung Maung. *Burmese Nationalist Movements: 1940–1948.* Honolulu, HI, University of Hawaii Press, 1990.

The 1988 Uprising in Burma. New Haven, CT, Yale University Southeast Asia Studies, 1999.

McRae, Alister. *Scots in Burma: Golden Times in a Golden Land.* Edinburgh, Kiscadale Publications, 1990.

Ministry of Information, Government of the Union of Myanmar. *The Conspiracy of Treasonous Minions Within the Myanmar Naing-ngan and Traitorous Cohorts Abroad.* Yangon, 1989.

Mirante, Edith T. *Burmese Looking Glass: A Human Rights Adventure.* New York, Grove Press, 1992.

Naw, Angelene. *Aung San and the Struggle for Burmese Independence.* Chiang Mai, Silkworm Books, 2001.

Ni Ni Myint. *Burma's Struggle Against British Imperialism.* Yangon, Universities Press, 1983.

Nu, Thakin. *Burma under the Japanese.* London, Macmillan,1954.

O'Brien, Harriet. *Forgotten Land: A Rediscovery of Burma.* London, Michael Joseph, 1991.

Pollak, Oliver B. *Empires in Collision: Anglo-Burmese Relations in the Mid-Nineteenth Century.* Westport, CT, Greenwood Press, 1979.

Selth, Andrew. *Death of a Hero: The U Thant Disturbances in Burma, December 1974.* Nathan, Queensland, Australia-Asia Papers, No. 49, April 1989, Griffith University.

Transforming the Tatmadaw: The Burmese Armed Forces since 1988. Canberra, Strategic and Defence Studies Centre, Australian National University, 1996.

Burma's Intelligence Apparatus. Canberra, Strategic and Defence Studies Centre, Australian National University, 1997.

The Burma Navy. Canberra, Strategic and Defence Studies Centre, Australian National University, 1997.

Burma's Secret Military Partners. Canberra, Strategic and Defence Studies Centre, Australian National University, 2000.

Silverstein, Josef. *The Political Legacy of Aung San.* New York, Cornell University Press, 1993.

Singh, Balwant. *Independence and Democracy in Burma, 1945–1952: The Turbulent Years.* Ann Arbor, MI, University of Michigan Press, 1993.

Stewart, A. T. Q. *The Pagoda War: Lord Dufferin and the Fall of the Kingdom of Ava, 1885–86.* London, Faber and Faber, 1972.

Tatsuro, Izumiya. *The Minami Organ.* Yangon, Universities Press, 1981.

Thant, Myint U. *The Making of Modern Burma.* New York, Cambridge University Press, 2001.

Tinker, Hugh (Ed.). *Burma: The Struggle For Independence 1944–1948.* 2 vols, London, HMSO, 1984.

Trager, Frank. *Burma: From Kingdom to Republic.* New York, Praeger, 1966.

Trager, Frank, and Koenig, William. *Burmese Sit-tans 1764–1826: Records of Rural Life and Administration.* Tucson, AZ, University of Arizona Press, 1979.

Tucker, Shelby. *Burma: The Curse of Independence.* London, Pluto Press, 2001.

Win Naing Oo. *Human Rights Abuse in Burmese Prisons.* Sydney, ACFOA, 1996.

ECONOMY AND POLITICS

Andrus, J. R. *Burmese Economic Life.* Stanford, CA, Stanford University Press, 1948.

Aung-Thwin, Michael. *Irrigation in the Heartland of Burma: Foundations of the Pre-Colonial Burmese State.* DeKalb, IL, Center for Southeast Asian Studies, Occasional Paper No. 15, 1990.

Ball, Desmond. *Burma and Drugs: the Regime's Complicity in the Global Drug Trade.* Canberra, Strategic and Defence Studies Centre, Australian National University, 1999.

Ball, Desmond, and Lang, Hazel. *Factionalism and the Ethnic Insurgent Organisations.* Canberra, Strategic and Defence Studies Centre, Australian National University, 2001.

Boucaud, André and Louis. *Burma's Golden Triangle: On the Trail of the Opium Warlords.* Bangkok, Asia Books, 1988.

Carey, Peter (Ed.). *Burma: The Challenge of Change in a Divided Society.* Basingstoke, Macmillan, 1997.

Chakravarti, N. *The Indian Minority in Burma: The Rise and Decline of an Immigrant Community.* London, Oxford University Press, 1971.

Chao Tzang Yawnghwe. *The Shan of Burma; Memoirs of a Shan Exile.* Singapore, Institute of Southeast Asian Studies, 1987.

Cheng Siok-Hwa. *The Rice Industry of Burma, 1852–1940.* London, University of Malaya Press, Kuala Lumpur, and Oxford University Press, 1969.

Collignon, Stefan, and Taylor, Robert H. (Eds). *Burma: Political Economy Under Military Rule.* Basingstoke, Palgrave Macmillan, 2001.

Fleischmann, Klaus. *Die Kommunistische Partei Birmas: Von den Anfangen bis zur Gegenwart.* Hamburg, Mitteilungen des Instituts für Asienkunde, 1989.

Furnivall, J. S. *Colonial Policy and Practice: A Co-operative Study of Burma and Netherlands India.* London, Cambridge University Press, 1957.

The Governance of Modern Burma. New York, Institute of Pacific Relations, 1960.

Gravers, Mikael. *Nationalism as Political Paranoia in Burma: An Essay on the Historical Practice of Power.* Richmond, Surrey, Curzon, 1999.

Houtman, Gustaaf. *Mental Culture in Burmese Crisis Politics: Aung San Suu Kyi and the National League for Democracy.* Tokyo, Tokyo University of Foreign Studies, Institute for the Study of Languages and Cultures of Asia and Africa, 1999.

International Commission of Jurists. *The Burmese Way to Where? Report of a Mission to Myanmar (Burma).* Geneva, 1991.

Ismael Khin Maung. *The Myanmar Labour Force: Growth and Change, 1973–83.* Singapore, Institute of Southeast Asian Studies, 1997.

Johnstone, W. C. *Burma's Foreign Policy: A Study in Neutralism.* Cambridge, MA, Harvard University Press, 1963.

Khin Maung Gyi. *Memoirs of Oil Industry in Burma: 905 AD—1980 AD.* Yangon, 1989.

Khin Maung Nyunt. *Foreign Loans and Aid in the Economic Development of Burma, 1974/75 to 1985/86.* Bangkok, Institute of Asian Studies, Chulalongkorn University Paper, No. 46, 1990.

Lang, Hazel J. *Fear and Sanctuary: Burmese Refugees in Thailand.* New York, Cornell University Press, 2002.

Leach, E. R. *Political Systems of Highland Burma—A Study of Kachin Social Structure.* Cambridge, MA, Harvard University Press, 1954.

Lehman, F. K. *The Structure of Chin Society.* Urbana, IL, University of Illinois, 1963.

Liang Chi-sha. *Burma's Foreign Relations: Neutralism in Theory and Practice.* New York, Praeger, 1990.

Lissak, Moshe. *Military Roles in Modernization: Civil-Military Relations in Thailand and Burma.* Beverly Hills, CA, Sage Publications, 1976.

Mason, Jana M. *No Way Out, No Way In: The Crisis of Internal Displacement in Burma.* Washington, DC, US Committee for Refugees, 2000.

Maung Maung. *Burma's Constitution.* 2nd Edn, The Hague, Nijhoff, 1961.

Burma and General Ne Win. London, Asia Publishing House, 1969.

Maung Maung Gyi. *Burmese Political Values: The Socio-Political Roots of Authoritarianism.* New York, Praeger, 1983.

Mendelson, E. Michael, and Ferguson, John (Eds). *Sangha and State in Burma.* Ithaca, NY, Cornell University Press, 1975.

Mi Mi Khine. *The World of Burmese Women.* London, Zed Books, 1984.

Moscotti, Albert D. *Burma's Constitution and the Elections of 1974.* Singapore, Institute of Southeast Asian Studies, 1977.

Mya Maung. *The Burma Road to Poverty.* New York, Praeger, 1991.

Totalitarianism in Burma: Prospects for Economic Development. New York, Paragon House, 1992.

Mya Than. *Growth Pattern of Burmese Agriculture: A Productivity Approach.* Singapore, Institute of Southeast Asian Studies, Occasional Paper No. 81, 1988.

Myanmar's External Trade: An Overview in the Southeast Asian Context. Singapore, Institute of Southeast Asian Studies, 1992.

Mya Than and Joseph L. H. Tan. *Myanmar Dilemmas and Options: The Challenge of Economic Transition in the 1990s.* Singapore, Institute of Southeast Asian Studies, 1990.

Mya Than and Myat Thein (Eds.). *Financial Resources for Development in Myanmar: Lessons from Asia.* Singapore, Institute of Southeast Asian Studies, 1999.

Mya Than and Gates, Carolyn L. (Eds). *ASEAN Enlargement: Impacts and Implications.* Singapore, Institute of Southeast Asian Studies, 2001.

Nishizawa, Nobuyoshi. *Economic Development of Burma in Colonial Times.* Hiroshima, Institute for Peace Science, Hiroshima University, 1991.

Nu, U. *U Nu—Saturday's Son.* New Haven, CT, Yale University Press, 1975.

Pedersen, Morten B., Rudland, Emily, and May, Ronald J. *Burma-Myanmar: Strong Regime, Weak State?* Adelaide, Crawford House Publishing, 2000.

Pradhan, M. V. *Burma, Dhamma and Democracy.* Mumbai, Mayflower Publishing House, 1992.

Pye, L. W. *Politics, Personality, and Nation Building.* New Haven, CT, Yale University Press, 1962.

Sarkisyanz, E. *Buddhist Backgrounds of the Burmese Revolution.* The Hague, Martinus Nijhoff, 1965.

Saito, Teruko, and Lee Kin Kiong (Eds). *Statistics on the Burmese Economy: The 19th and 20th Centuries.* Singapore, Institute of Southeast Asian Studies, 1999.

Schendel, Willem van. *Three Deltas: Accumulation and Poverty in Rural Burma, Bengal and South India.* Newbury Park, CA, Sage, 1991.

Seekins, Donald M. *The Disorder in Order: The Army-State in Burma since 1962.* Bangkok, White Lotus Press, 2002.

Shwe Lu Maung. *Burma—Nationalism and Ideology.* Dhaka University Press, 1989.

Silverstein, Josef. *Burma: Military Rule and the Politics of Stagnation.* Ithaca, NY, Cornell University Press, 1977.

Burmese Politics: The Dilemma of National Unity. New Brunswick, NJ, Rutgers University Press, 1980.

Independent Burma at Forty Years: Six Assessments. Ithaca, NY, Cornell Southeast Asia Program, 1989.

Smith, D. E. *Religion and Politics in Burma.* Princeton, NJ, 1965.

Smith, Martin. *Burma: Insurgency and the Politics of Ethnicity.* London, Zed Books, 1999.

State of Fear: Censorship in Burma. London, Article 19, Country Report, 1991.

South, Ashley. *Mon Nationalism and Civil War in Burma: The Golden Sheldrake.* London, RoutledgeCurzon, 2002.

Steinberg, David I. *Burma's Road toward Development: Growth and Ideology under Military Rule.* Boulder, CO, Westview Press, 1981.

The Future of Burma: Crisis and Choice in Myanmar. Lanham and New York, Asia Society/University Press of America, 1990.

Crisis in Burma: Stasis and Change in a Political Economy in Turmoil. Bangkok, Institute of Security and International Studies, Chulalongkorn University, 1989.

Burma, the State of Myanmar. Washington, DC, Georgetown University Press, 2001.

Stewart, Whitney. *Aung San Suu Kyi: Fearless Voice of Burma.* Minneapolis, MN, Lerner Publications, 1996.

Taylor, Robert H. *Marxism and Resistance in Burma 1942–45: Thein Pe Myint's Wartime Traveler.* Athens, Ohio University Press, 1984.

The State in Burma, 1987. London, Hurst & Co, 1988.

Taylor, Robert H. (Ed.). *Burma: Political Economy under Military Rule.* London, St Martin's Press, 2000.

Thanakha Team (Eds). *Burma: Voices of Women in the Struggle.* Bangkok, Altsean, 1998.

Thaw Han, Daw. *Common Vision: Burma's Regional Outlook.* Washington, Institute for the Study of Diplomacy, 1988.

Walinsky, Louis. *Economic Development in Burma 1951–1960.* New York, Twentieth Century Fund, 1962.

NEPAL

Physical and Social Geography

B. H. FARMER

The Kingdom of Nepal is situated between the high Himalayas and the Ganges plains, between India and Tibet (the Xizang Autonomous Region) in the People's Republic of China. It occupies an area of 147,181 sq km (56,827 sq miles) and extends from 26° 20′ to 30° 10′ N, and from 80° 15′ to 88° 15′ E.

PHYSICAL FEATURES

Nepal's southernmost physical region is the Terai which, like the similar region in India, is a belt of low-lying plain, highly liable to flooding during the monsoon. To the north rises the Himalaya system, the world's greatest mountain range. With the associated Karakoram, Hindu Kush and Pamir ranges, the Himalaya system contains all but two of the 86 mountains over 7,500 m above sea-level. The world's highest peak, Mt Everest (known as Sagarmatha to the Nepalese), rises to 8,848 m and lies on Nepal's frontier with Tibet. A series of transverse or more complex valleys breaks up the simple pattern of parallel ranges, and one of these, the Valley of Nepal, contains the capital, Kathmandu.

CLIMATE

It is difficult to be at all precise about the climate in the absence of accurate data. It would seem, however, that it exemplifies two main tendencies. In the first place, temperatures, for obvious reasons, decrease as one moves from the Terai through the foothills and internal valleys to higher Himalayan ranges. At Kathmandu, 1,337 m above sea-level, monthly temperatures average 10°C in January and 23°C in May. In January the average daily maximum is 18°C and the average minimum 2°C. In the highest Himalaya, air temperatures are always below freezing point. In the second place, rainfall tends to decrease from east to west, as it does in the Indian plains below. Eastern Nepal receives about 2,500 mm per year; Kathmandu 1,420 mm; and western Nepal about 1,000 mm.

SOILS AND NATURAL RESOURCES

There is little reliable scientific information on soils. As in corresponding parts of the Indian Himalayas, soils are likely to be skeletal, thin and poor on steep slopes (except where improved artificially under terraced cultivation); and better soils are probably confined to valley bottoms and interior basins, and to the Terai.

There has been a great deal of clearing for cultivation in the Terai, in interior valleys like the Valley of Nepal, and on lower hillsides. Yet in some areas textbook examples of altitudinal zonation may be seen: tropical moist deciduous forests to some 1,200 m; moist hill pine forests from 1,200 to some 2,600 m; coniferous forests at 2,600–3,350 m, alpine vegetation beginning at the latter altitude.

The only mineral so far discovered in significant quantities is mica, mined east of Kathmandu. There are local workings of lignite in the outermost range of mountains, and small deposits of copper, cobalt and iron ore. Raw materials exist for cement manufacture. In 1986 an agreement was signed allowing two foreign oil companies to explore for petroleum in the area adjoining the borders with India.

POPULATION AND ETHNIC GROUPS

According to the provisional results of the census of June 2001, Nepal had a total population of 23,214,681. The population is unevenly distributed (average density at mid-2001 was 157.7 per sq km), with fairly dense clusters and ribbons along the valleys and in the Terai, a scatter of isolated upland settlements, and great empty spaces at high altitude.

Nepal is populated by a mixture of Indo-Aryan peoples, who originally migrated from India, and a range of Mongoloid tribes, including the Gurungs, Magars, Rai and Limbu, who speak Tibeto-Burman languages. The Kathmandu valley is the home of the Newar community, while small communities of indigenous peoples and Muslim immigrants are found in the Terai. Large-scale migration from Bangladesh has resulted in a notable demographic transformation in Nepal, with the Muslim population increasing from around 4% of the total in the early 1990s to about 10% by the end of the decade.

History

LOK RAJ BARAL

Revised by T. LOUISE BROWN and JOHN McGUIRE

Nepal's history has been dictated by its position, located in the Himalayas on the north-east frontier of India, and forming the only practicable gateway to the Indo-Gangetic plains from Tibet (the Xizang Autonomous Region) in the People's Republic of China.

The word 'Nepal', which appeared for the first time in AD 879, means 'the beginning of a new era'. Although ancient Nepalese history is still only partially documented, it is assumed that from about the year 700 BC the Kirantis ruled. Mentioned in Vedic literature and the Mahabharata, they are the ancestors of ancient Nepalese groups including the Newars, Rais, Limbus, Tamangs and Sunwars. In 560 BC, during the rule of the Kirantis, Buddha was born in the small town of Lumbini in the Terai, near the Indian border. It remains a centre of pilgrimage for Buddhists from all over the world. Between the ninth and the 14th centuries AD, the Valley of Nepal, then, as now, the most important part of the country, was invaded from India until Jaya Sthithi Malla, a southern Indian, began the Malla dynasty. Jaksha Malla, the most able of the Malla kings, extended his power far beyond the Valley. He divided his kingdom among his four heirs in 1488; Kathmandu, Bhatgaon, Patan and Banepa remained intact until the Gurkha conquest. The Gurkhas were originally a warlike tribe of the Rajput Kshatriyas who were expelled from India in 1303 by the Sultan, Ala-ud-din. They escaped into the hills of central Nepal and gradually spread out into the region of Gorakhnath, where they settled in about 1559. At this time the country was divided into small principalities and was thus later vulnerable to the adventurous and energetic Gurkha, Prithvinarayan Shah.

THE GURKHAS

Prithvinarayan Shah, the acknowledged founder of modern Nepal, conceived the idea of creating a viable kingdom in the Himalayas by conquering neighbouring territories and assimilating them in socio-political terms. His plan was to conquer the Valley of Nepal and from there to expand in all directions. By a series of campaigns ending in 1767, he gained control of the territories that today constitute Nepal. Just before his death in 1775, he was planning to annex Sikkim in order to establish a continuous boundary with Bhutan.

In addition to providing Nepal with a territorial identity, Prithvinarayan Shah preserved it in its earliest days from foreign intrusion. He was excessively anti-foreign; he wanted to encourage local enterprise and he advised his countrymen to support native industries. Opposing British efforts to open up trade with Tibet and China, he prohibited the entry of certain British traders to Kathmandu and advised the authorities in Lhasa not to be tempted by a British offer of establishing new relations between Bengal and Tibet. In short, had he been a less determined man, Nepal might well have become just another princely state of British India. As it is, the Shah dynasty which he founded remains to this day.

During the years 1786–94 the armies of his successor, Bahadur Shah, occupied states of the Baisis and Chaubisis and Kumaon and Garhwal in the west and Sikkim in the east. A portion of Tibetan Kachhar was also captured. His policy was even more vigorously pursued when his nephew, Rana Bahadur, then aged only 20, assumed power in 1796. He outraged public sentiment by marrying a Brahmin, and subsequently the country split between two warring families, the Pandes and Thapas. A revolt on the part of the Brahmins and hostile courtiers forced Rana Bahadur to abdicate. When he regained the throne in 1804, he dismissed his Prime Minister, Damodar Pande, who had signed a treaty with the East India Co allowing it the right to appoint a British Resident in Nepal.

The next Prime Minister, Bhim Sen Thapa, continued an expansionist policy, which was largely aimed at consolidating his position by keeping his rivals occupied in warfare rather than in manoeuvring for power at court. This policy brought him into conflict with British India, and led to the Anglo-Nepalese War of 1814–16. Bhim Sen Thapa sued for peace in March 1816. The Treaty of Segauli (4 March 1816) gave Britain the right to appoint a Resident and to occupy the hills of Kumaon, Garhwal, Nainital Simla, and a great portion of the Terai. In return, the British agreed to withdraw from Sikkim.

THE RANA SYSTEM

Bhim Sen Thapa's authority remained virtually unchallenged until the young King Rajendra Vikram Shah came of age and decided to take control himself. The Prime Minister was dismissed and imprisoned in 1837; he committed suicide two years later. From the confusion, massacres and intrigues that followed, another powerful figure emerged—Jung Bahadur Rana. He proclaimed himself Prime Minister and Commander-in-Chief of the army, assumed the family name of Rana and, independently of the ruling monarchy, distributed power among his own relations and made his own and their positions hereditary. The Rana family thus attained a complete monopoly of power in every department of Nepalese life; from birth a kinsman could be appointed to high military rank.

Jung Bahadur Rana also reversed the policy of his predecessors by allying himself with Britain and offering support in its war against the Sikhs. The British encouraged the Ranas to pursue an isolationist policy. Nepal became a recruiting ground for the British armies in which Gurkha regiments became famous for their toughness and loyalty. At the outbreak of the First World War, the British Government received permission for the free recruitment of Gurkha soldiers. The Rana Chandra Shamsher (who ruled from 1901 to 1929) had his reward in 1923 when the Treaty of Segauli was revised. The Nepalese sought an unequivocal declaration of their independence, but the British Government insisted on retaining those clauses that limited Nepal's external relations to those with the UK. An annual contribution of 1m. rupees was arranged to be remitted by the Indian exchequer to the Nepalese ruler.

A treaty of 1792 had placed Nepal in an undefined position of vassalage to China, and, until 1900, the Nepalese had sent a goodwill mission to Beijing every 12th year. In 1911, when the revolution in China created confusion in the area's relations, the time came for the next mission; on the advice of the Delhi authorities, however, Chandra Shamsher refused to send a mission. By implication, Nepal thus unilaterally repudiated the 1792 treaty. Chandra Shamsher allowed a lessening of Nepal's isolation in terms of social ideas, and in 1926, under external pressure, he abolished slavery, freeing some 60,000 people at a cost of 3.7m. rupees.

As long as British rulers remained in India, the Ranas felt secure. However, the new ideas which swept across India in the 1930s, and which were realized in 1947 with the coming of Indian independence, influenced the 3m. Nepalese residing in the frontier provinces of Bengal, Bihar and Uttar Pradesh, and, in turn, spread into the Valley of Nepal.

In 1950 the Nepali National Congress was merged with the Nepali Democratic Congress, which had a similar programme, to form the Nepali Congress Party (NCP). With covert encouragement from the monarch, King Tribhuvan, the NCP proceeded with its plans to overthrow the Rana regime, and an armed struggle was organized under the direction of the President of the NCP, Matrika Prasad (M.P.) Koirala.

The Chinese occupation of Tibet in October 1950 undoubtedly influenced the timing of King Tribhuvan's dramatic challenge to the position of the Ranas; in November 1950 he refused to sign death warrants of alleged plotters against the Rana regime and took political asylum in the Indian diplomatic mission. The Indian Government sent aircraft to transport him to Delhi. Along the border the insurgents attacked, captured Nepal's second largest town, Birganj, and proclaimed a rival Government.

The Nepalese army remained loyal to the Rana regime, but the Prime Minister of India, Jawaharlal Nehru, and his colleagues stood firm in their support for the King, and the Nepalese Government finally accepted India's proposals on 7 January 1951. They provided for the King's reinstatement, an amnesty for the insurgents if they surrendered their weapons, elections by 1952, and the formation of an interim government of 14 ministers on the basis of parity between the Ranas and popular representatives. The royal family and the NCP leaders made a triumphal return to Kathmandu on 15 February 1951. Three days later, the new Council of Ministers was sworn in, with the membership reduced from 14 to 10. Mohun Shumshere Jung Bahadur Rana became the Prime Minister, while Bisweswor Prasad (B.P.) Koirala (half-brother of M. P. Koirala) was appointed to the vital Ministry of Home Affairs. The formation of the new Government represented the end of Rana domination, and the beginning of an experiment in democracy.

PARLIAMENTARY GOVERNMENT

The experiment soon ran into difficulty. The Ranas were not reconciled to the loss of their century-old absolute power. Personal and ideological differences caused factionalism to emerge within the leadership of the NCP. King Tribhuvan declared a state of emergency in the country in January 1952 and armed the Prime Minister with emergency powers. Extreme parties of right and left (the Rashtravadi Gorkha Parishad and the Communist Party of Nepal—CPN—respectively) were declared illegal and political meetings banned indefinitely. The King made two attempts to establish an advisory assembly, in July 1952 and May 1954, but internal rivalries and corruption prevented the success of either. The communists, working in 'front' organizations since their party was illegal, made considerable headway, especially among the younger generation of disillusioned intellectuals in Kathmandu.

King Tribhuvan died in March 1955. His heir, Mahendra Bir Bikram Shah Dev, was resolute, immensely hard-working and pragmatic. He made no pretence of believing in parliamentary democracy. Nevertheless, in December 1957 he announced that elections would be held in February 1959. They were held a week after the King had given Nepal its first Constitution providing for a Mahasabha (senate), consisting of 36 members, of whom 18 would be elected by the Pratinidhi Sabha (lower house) and 18 nominated by the King. The lower house would consist of 109 members elected from single-member territorial constituencies. In a country where 96% of the population were illiterate, the elections were held with surprising success. Most candidates gave priority to the abolition of the *birta* system, by which landlords, mostly Ranas, held land tax-free; to the nationalization of the *zamindari* system; to irrigation; to co-operative farming; to cottage industries, and to government-supported medium-sized industries. Most parties subscribed to this programme, though the NCP seemed the most likely to carry it out, if elected; the party's top echelons had subscribed to socialist ideas for many years.

The NCP won 38% of the total votes cast, securing 74 seats out of the 109 in the lower house. The right-wing Gorkha Parishad won 19 seats, or 17.1% of the votes cast, while communist supporters secured 4 seats, or 7.4%. When the King appointed B. P. Koirala as Prime Minister and the first popularly-elected legislature was opened in July 1959, it seemed as if the long road towards democracy was firmly established. Yet the Constitution providing for a parliamentary government and civil rights left sovereignty in fact, not only in form, with the King. He could, for example, force the Prime Minister to resign; he could suspend the Government and rule directly or with newly-appointed ministers; he could prorogue the legislature or call for a special sitting; and he had a veto over all legislation and constitutional amendments. This fundamental limitation of the democratic process was a source of frustration for B. P. Koirala, whose electoral majority, nevertheless, allowed him to proceed with his schemes for land reform. He gave greater security to tenants and redistributed some of the large estates owned by the Ranas. The Ranas maintained their campaign of obstruction, which Koirala could still have defeated but for a growing tension between himself and the young King. This clash of personalities came to a head on 15 December 1960, when King Mahendra staged a coup, and imprisoned B. P. Koirala and most of the senior leadership of the NCP. He suspended rights guaranteed by the Constitution and dissolved Parliament, substituting his own hand-picked Council of Ministers. Political parties were banned by royal decree in January 1961. The royal *coup d'état* demonstrated the loyalty of the army to the King.

THE PANCHAYAT SYSTEM

King Mahendra, who profoundly distrusted party politics and politicians, sought to create a 'non-party Panchayat (village council) democracy'. This Panchayat system, proclaimed in 1961 and promulgated under a new Constitution in the following year, comprised a four-tier administrative structure. At its head was the King, who appointed the Prime Minister. This office was filled successively by Dr Tulsi Giri (1962–65), Surya Bahadur Thapa (1965–69) and Kirti Nidhi Bista (1969–70). The King himself was also Prime Minister from April 1970 to April 1971, when Bista was reappointed. Bista resigned in July 1973 and was succeeded as Prime Minister by Nagendra Prasad Rijal.

In September 1967 the Rashtriya Panchayat (National Assembly) adopted a far-reaching programme based on a 'Back to the Village' campaign, and a detailed scheme for Panchayat administration. The decision of NCP leaders in May 1968 to co-operate with the King in the Panchayat system led to the release of B. P. Koirala and his colleagues in October; they subsequently went into self-exile in India. The King and his Council of Ministers introduced well-known royalist supporters into the Government and reiterated the ban on political activity outside the Panchayat system.

King Mahendra died in January 1972, and was succeeded by his son, Birendra Bir Bikram Shah Dev, whose coronation eventually took place in February 1975. King Birendra had been educated in the United Kingdom and the USA, and there were short-lived hopes that he might relax the late King's somewhat autocratic style of government.

In December 1975 Dr Tulsi Giri was again appointed Prime Minister. During 1976 Giri nominated supporters of the banned NCP and ex-communists as members of the Rashtriya Panchayat and there was renewed demand for political change. Numerous amendments to the Constitution were adopted which allowed for a widening of the franchise and more frequent elections to the Rashtriya Panchayat, but the King's powers were not eroded.

In December 1976 B. P. Koirala returned to Nepal from exile in India, but was immediately arrested and charged with treason. However, six months later, under pressure from India, he was released and left the country. In September 1977 Giri resigned as Prime Minister, primarily because of differences with the King over Koirala's detention. Giri had also been accused of corrupt practices and a number of Rashtriya Panchayat members had put pressure on him to resign in order to save Nepal from economic chaos and political disorder. Kirti Nidhi Bista was reappointed Prime Minister.

By late 1977 Koirala had been acquitted of five charges of treason and in March 1978 he returned to Nepal to spearhead a renewed campaign for political change. He claimed to have the support of other banned opposition groups, including the CPN. He also had the open sympathy of certain elements in the Rashtriya Panchayat, which resulted in its purge by the King and a strengthening of the Raj Sabha (State Council), the King's personal advisory body.

However, rioting and student unrest continued and some members of the NCP lost patience with Koirala's insistence on co-operation with the King and urged a nationwide 'non-violent movement' against the authorities. But this was clearly out of the question while the King retained the support of the army and police force. In February 1979 two NCP activists were executed for 'sedition and treason'; in April Koirala was put under house arrest and numerous other NCP members were reported to have been detained. Demonstrations in April and May were suppressed with considerable violence by the police: five people were reported to have been killed. In April Bista submitted his resignation as Prime Minister, and King Birendra announced, at the end of May, that a national referendum would be held to choose between the Panchayat system and a multi-party system. In June a new Government was formed by the liberal former Prime Minister, Surya Bahadur Thapa. A national election committee was set up to supervise the referendum and a general amnesty was granted to political prisoners and exiles so that all eligible adults could vote in the May 1980 poll. Out of 4,813,486 voters, 54.8% supported the Panchayat system, with reforms, whereas 45.2% favoured a multi-party system.

On 15 December 1980 King Birendra issued a decree under which amendments to the Constitution were made, including the proviso that the appointment of the Prime Minister by the King would henceforth be on the recommendation of the Rashtriya Panchayat. Under the new provisions, legislative elections were held on 9 May 1981, the first of their kind since 1959, although still on a non-party basis. Despite calls by Koirala to boycott the polling on the grounds that it was 'inadequate and undemocratic', 1,096 candidates contested the 112 elective seats in the Rashtriya Panchayat. Only 35 of the 93 pro-Government candidates obtained seats, while newcomers, who pledged to eliminate corruption, improve the economy and reduce unemployment, won a majority. Surya Bahadur Thapa was unanimously re-elected by the Rashtriya Panchayat as Prime Minister on 14 June 1981 and the King installed a 28-member Council of Ministers (on the recommendation of the Prime Minister).

In May 1982 elections to more than 4,000 village and town Panchayats were held—the first time that such elections had taken place on the basis of direct adult suffrage since 1959. The results strengthened Thapa's position. Koirala died in July 1982, leaving a political void in the unofficial opposition. In October there was an extensive ministerial reshuffle to combat growing criticism of bad economic management and corruption. A late monsoon led to droughts and severe food shortages, and the economic situation worsened. Mounting criticism of the Government continued, and Thapa's ministry fell to a vote of 'no confidence' on 11 July 1983, as he had lost the King's support. This was the first time in the 23-year history of the Panchayat system that an incumbent Prime Minister had been removed. His successor as Prime Minister, Lokendra Bahadur Chand, a former speaker of the National Assembly and effective leader of the opposition, formed a new Council of Ministers.

In March 1985 the NCP held a convention in Kathmandu, and in May embarked upon a campaign of civil disobedience aimed at restoring a multi-party political system and parliamentary rule under a constitutional monarchy. This was followed in June by a series of bomb explosions, resulting in loss of life and apparently orchestrated by two newly-formed groups, the Janawadi Morcha (Democratic Front), led by Ram Raja Prasad Singh, and the Samyukta Mukti Bahini (United Liberation Torch-bearers). These bombings united an otherwise seriously divided Parliament against the terrorists and forced the predominantly moderate opposition to abandon its campaign of civil disobedience.

In January 1986 the Government announced that a general election would be held in May. The banned NCP stated that it would take part in the election if the Government would release all political prisoners and abolish the rule requiring all candidates to be members of one of the six Panchayat class organizations. The King announced in the following month that the electoral laws would not be changed, and, consequently, the NCP decided to boycott the election. Only 40 of the 112 pre-election members retained their seats. Members of the Marxist-Leninist faction of the banned CPN competed as independent candidates, winning 16 seats. A further 28 parliamentary members were nominated by the King. Official reports stated that over 60% of the electorate had participated in the voting, in spite of threats from the Indian-based Janawadi Morcha to disrupt the election. The Rashtriya Panchayat elected Marich Man Singh Shrestha as Prime Minister and an unofficial parliamentary group, in opposition to the Government, was formed.

The NCP planned a new campaign of passive resistance against the Panchayat system for 1987, but the party later announced that it would contest the local elections that were scheduled to be held in March of that year. (The party was to present candidates as members of class organizations.) The Marxist-Leninist faction of the CPN declared that it would also contest the elections. To counter the growing influence of the communist faction in the Rashtriya Panchayat, several senior figures (including Jog Meher Shrestha, a former government minister, and Chand) established a 'Democratic Panchayat Forum' in support of the non-party system. Pro-Government candidates won 65% of the votes in the local elections.

In June 1987, in an apparent attempt to improve the image of the Panchayat system, the Government launched an anti-corruption campaign, and in December it announced plans to reorganize government ministries and departments, in an effort to increase efficiency and to curb administrative malpractices: more than 160 officials were dismissed from their posts. In March 1988 the Prime Minister announced a major reshuffle of the Council of Ministers, which included the dismissal of six ministers and the establishment of a new Ministry of Housing and Physical Planning.

During 1988 opposition to the Government continued to be actively discouraged. In January the President of the NCP was arrested, and in February more than 100 people, who were planning to demonstrate in support of the NCP Mayor of Kathmandu (who had been suspended from office for his anti-Panchayat stance), were also detained. In October there was another major reshuffle of the Council of Ministers, which involved the dismissal of 11 ministers.

THE TRANSITION TO DEMOCRACY

By 1989 the Panchayat system was approaching a crisis. Political instability was exacerbated by a deteriorating economic situation. Indo-Nepalese relations were severely strained and, owing to the failure of the vital Trade and Transit Treaty to be renegotiated (see below), trade between the two countries was greatly restricted. Thirteen of the usual 15 transit points on the border were closed. As the Nepalese economy was so heavily dependent upon India, these closures had a serious impact, particularly in urban areas where there were shortages of basic commodities. Against this background political tensions mounted and opposition political forces manoeuvred to take advantage of the regime's economic difficulties and to capitalize on the Panchayat system's internal weaknesses. Considerable inspiration was also derived from pro-democracy movements in Eastern Europe. Consequently, by the end of 1989 a process of accommodation was under way between Nepal's hitherto divided opposition parties.

In early January 1990 six factions of the CPN together with a labour group, founded the United Left Front (ULF), with Sahana Pradhan as its President. The aim of the alliance was to work for the restoration of democracy. In mid-January the NCP held a party meeting at the Kathmandu residence of its Supreme Leader, Ganesh Man Singh, to discuss the establishment of an official democracy movement. At the end of the month the NCP and the ULF formed a co-ordination committee to conduct the Jana Andolan (People's Movement), and in mid-February the pro-democracy forces launched their campaign. Demonstrations and *bandhs* (general strikes) were held throughout February and March. The Government responded by censoring the media and by suppressing the movement with force. Leaders of the opposition parties and political activists were arrested but the Government's acts of repression did not halt the agitation.

Initially, the Jana Andolan drew much of its support from the professional middle class, but towards the end of March 1990 the complexion of the movement changed as it began to attract mass support. In response to the rapidly-expanding challenge to his regime, King Birendra dismissed Marich Man Singh Shrestha's Government on 6 April and appointed the more moderate Chand as Prime Minister. This minor concession, however, served only to incense the participants in the movement and incited them to greater radicalism. On the same day, more than 100,000 people marched towards the royal palace in Kathmandu. The police dispersed the demonstrators with tear gas, baton charges and then opened fire upon them, killing around 50 people. A curfew was subsequently imposed upon the capital. During the curfew, negotiations began between the palace and sections of the Jana Andolan, and on 8 April the King announced that the 30-year ban on political parties was to be ended. At the same time, the leadership of the movement suspended its campaign. For many of the political activists, however, the cessation of the campaign was a betrayal, since although political parties had been legalized, the formal structures of the Panchayat system remained in place. As a result, the agitation continued, and a week later the King agreed to dissolve all Panchayat organs, including the Rashtriya Panchayat, to dismiss the Chand Government and to appoint an interim government. On 19 April an 11-member coalition Council of Ministers was appointed under the premiership of the President of the NCP, Krishna Prasad (K.P.) Bhattarai. The members of the Government comprised four representatives of the NCP, three from the ULF, two independents and two nominees of the King.

The new Prime Minister announced that a general election would be held, on a multi-party basis, within a year. The principal task of the interim Government was to prepare a new constitution in accordance with the spirit of multi-party democracy and constitutional monarchy. King Birendra stated that he was committed to transforming his role into that of a constitutional monarch, and following further violent clashes in Kathmandu between anti-royalists and police, he ordered the army and the police to comply with the orders of the interim Government in order to facilitate a smooth transition to democracy.

The new Constitution proved a subject of great controversy. The palace manoeuvred in order to preserve as much of the King's power as possible but, owing to the concerted action of multi-party supporters, the Constitution that was finally promulgated on 9 November 1990 was, in general, a democratic one. The King was reduced to the role of a constitutional monarch, and sovereignty was vested not in the monarchy but in the people. King Birendra did, however, retain some significant authority. For instance, he retained emergency powers so that in the event of an unspecified national crisis he could suspend articles of the Constitution relating to civil liberties and then assume executive authority. Such powers, nevertheless, had to be approved after a period of three months by a majority of the House of Representatives, whereupon they could be granted for another three months.

The 1990 Constitution made provision for the election, by universal adult suffrage, of a 205-seat House of Representatives (Pratinidhi Sabha) for a five-year term. The Prime Minister was to be drawn from the party that won a majority in the legislature, and the King was to act on the advice and only with the consent of the Prime Minister and his Council of Ministers. In addition, the Constitution made provision for the establishment of a 60-seat National Council (Rashtriya Sabha), which was to be elected by members of the House of Representatives on the basis of proportional representation for a six-year term.

Political parties were legalized by the 1990 Constitution and the civil liberties associated with a democratic state were enshrined in law. Nepal, however, remained a Hindu nation and the Constitution made few concessions to Nepal's multi-ethnic, multi-lingual and multi-cultural population. In particular, the Constitution prohibited the formation of parties based on regional, communal or ethnic lines.

A large number of political parties emerged in the aftermath of the Jana Andolan and stated their intention to participate in the general election scheduled for May 1991. The two most important parties were the NCP and the CPN (Unified Marxist-Leninist), more commonly known as the UML. The UML developed from the ULF, which began to disintegrate following the success of the Jana Andolan. In December 1990 four of the seven constituent parts of the ULF broke away from the front, and in January 1991 the two principal communist factions, the CPN (Marxist) and the CPN (Marxist-Leninist), merged to form the UML. Another party that emerged was the Nepali Sadbhavana Party (NSP), which, despite the constitutional prohibition against regional-based parties, was a plains- or Terai-based party. There were also two parties of former Panchayat stalwarts, both headed by ex-Prime Ministers—the National Democratic Party (Chand) and the National Democratic Party (Thapa). The extreme left was represented by the United People's Front (UPF), which was an amalgam of radical, Maoist groups.

The general election, which was held on 12 May 1991, was not only peaceful, but was also characterized by a good turnout (65.2% of the electorate). Of the 20 contending parties, 12 did not win a single seat in the House of Representatives and lost their deposits. The National Democratic Party (Chand) and the National Democratic Party (Thapa), fared badly in the election, winning only four seats—the latter one and the former three. The NCP won a comfortable majority (110 seats), but it was soundly defeated by the UML in the eastern hill districts and in some parts of the Terai. In Kathmandu, supposedly an NCP stronghold, the party lost all of the seats but one. By winning 69 seats, the UML established itself as the second largest party in the House of Representatives, followed by the UPF, with nine seats. Two other communist organizations—the Nepal Workers' and Peasants' Party and a faction of the CPN—gained two seats each, thus making a total communist tally in the House of Representatives of 82 seats. The NSP obtained six seats, all of which were in the Terai. All of the three independent candidates who won seats subsequently joined the NCP. The acting Prime Minister, K. P. Bhattarai, lost his seat in the capital, and was replaced in the premiership by Girija Prasad (G.P.) Koirala, the General Secretary of the NCP and brother of the late B. P. Koirala. The results of the general election did not reveal any substantive communal or regional trends, since the main-line national parties, particularly the NCP and the UML, were more successful in winning the support of various ethnic groups than those parties whose main vote-winning tactic was to woo directly certain groups.

The aftermath of the May 1991 general election was marked by a clarification of the political positions of the various parties that had emerged after the demise of the Panchayat system. On the right of the political spectrum, the two wings of the former Panchayat politicians, the National Democratic Party (Chand) and the National Democratic Party (Thapa), which had contested the general election separately, merged in February 1992 to form the National Democratic Party (NDP). Within the communist camp, the UML moderated its ideological position in favour of a mixed economy, under the twin influences of the collapse of the USSR and the prospect of eventually gaining power through electoral means. Despite widespread discrimination against citizens from the Terai and from Mongoloid tribes, no significant political movements representing these ethnic groups (apart from the NSP) emerged.

Under the leadership of G. P. Koirala, the centrist NCP Government shifted to the right. The public image of the monarchy and leading members of the former Panchayat regime were rehabilitated with government support. No efforts were made to reform the hierarchy of the armed forces or police, and the secluded staff of the palace secretariat remained largely unchanged. No charges were brought against leading officials of the former Panchayat administration for corruption or human rights violations, and no action was taken in response to the Mallick Commission Report into contraventions of human rights committed during the pro-democracy movement. Replicating the patronage system of the Panchayat regime, the NCP rapidly began to dominate the public administration system. In June 1993 the NDP held its first national conference in Kathmandu, an event that would have been unthinkable three years previously, when its leaders were forced underground by the democracy movement.

The local government elections held in May–June 1992 were seen as a key test of support for the new Government. In the run-up to the elections, growing left-wing agitation in the Kathmandu valley was fuelled by popular discontent over the rapid rise in prices of basic commodities and over water shortages. However, despite strikes staged by the opposition and the rising cost of living, the NCP surprised many observers by performing well in the elections, especially in the Kathmandu valley where it had performed so badly in the 1991 general election. However, the NCP electoral victories were marred by widespread reports of vote-purchasing and ballot-rigging, features that had apparently been absent from the 1991 general election.

In the year following the May/June 1992 local elections there was continued and increasing rivalry within the senior leadership of the NCP, with the ageing party leader, Ganesh Man Singh, emerging as a radical challenge to the authority of the conservative Prime Minister, G. P. Koirala, who also retained the important posts of Minister of Foreign Affairs, of Defence and of Royal Palace Affairs.

In addition to opposition from the leadership of his own party, G. P. Koirala was confronted by growing criticism from the opposition parties of the UML and UPF, which focused on a December 1991 agreement, made by Koirala in New Delhi granting the Indian Government access to water from the Tanakpur barrage on the Mahakali River, the terms of which were only subsequently revealed to the Nepalese House of Representatives. Arguing that the agreement amounted to a treaty affecting national sovereignty, and therefore requiring a two-thirds' majority in the House of Representatives, the opposition mounted a vigorous extra-parliamentary campaign calling for the resignation of Koirala on the grounds of unconstitutional behaviour. An indeterminate Supreme Court ruling in mid-December 1992 on Koirala's action only intensified the protest.

In late 1992 two distinct factions emerged within the UML. One of these, advocating 'multi-party people's democracy' and led by Madan Bhandari, recognized the need to jettison much of the party's Marxist dogma, while the faction advocating 'new people's democracy', headed by C. P. Mainali, adhered to a Leninist concept of the role of the communist party. The national UML congress, which was held in January/February 1993, adopted the former policy, tacitly acknowledging the UML's commitment to working within a democratic multi-party system. However, the untimely deaths of Madan Bhandari and Politburo member Jiv Raj Ashrit, following a mysterious road accident in mid-May, threw the party into disarray, leading to fears of an open split. The rejection by the UML of the findings of a government inquiry, which concluded that Bhandari's death had been accidental, provoked nation-wide protests in support of demands for an independent inquiry. In late May Madhav Kumar Nepal replaced Bhandari as the General Secretary of the UML. The UML and radical opposition parties launched a rolling programme of protests demanding, amongst many other things, an impartial inquiry into Bhandari's death, an end to the 'congressization' of public life and the resignation of G. P. Koirala over the Tanakpur controversy. The Kathmandu Valley was brought to a standstill by frequent *bandhs* and demonstrations; the agitation was suspended, however, during the disastrous 1993 monsoon. On 18–19 July heavy rains caused extensive flash floods, affecting 21 of the country's 75 districts, particularly the Terai districts of Sarlahi, Rautahat and Chitwan. Tens of thousands were left homeless and around

2,000 people died. The Kathmandu Valley was cut off for several weeks from the south, necessitating the airlift of vital supplies.

The G. P. Koirala Government was criticized from all sides during late 1993 and early 1994. Its failure to address the deteriorating economic situation and its alleged involvement in corruption were amongst the most serious complaints. The NCP administration was attacked not only by the opposition but also by its own party organization. Factionalism in the NCP, and in particular the Koirala–Ganesh Man Singh split, continued to dominate political life in Nepal throughout the first half of 1994. Other political events also followed trends established after the Jana Andolan: the extreme left continued its agitation; the Government was accused of corruption; procedures in the legislature remained rather confused; and the main opposition group, the UML, continued to be divided between radical and conservative camps.

The split in the ruling party widened further during April and May 1994. There was doubt over G. P. Koirala's ability to retain the support of NCP parliamentary members. Thirty-six members associated with the Ganesh Man Singh camp threatened to withdraw their support for the Government if the Prime Minister failed to institute radical changes. On 10 July the dissidents abstained from an official motion of thanks on the Royal Address, resulting in a vote of 74 for and 86 against the motion, thereby stripping Koirala of his majority. The Prime Minister consequently tendered his resignation, and on the following day King Birendra dissolved the House of Representatives. Koirala was then appointed as interim Prime Minister pending elections, which were hastily brought forward from mid-1996 to 15 November 1994.

The elections did not produce a clear majority. The UML emerged as the largest party, winning 88 of the 205 seats in the House of Representatives. As a result of continued feuding within the party, the NCP did not contest the elections as a united body. Consequently, it performed relatively badly, and its legislative representation was reduced from 110 seats in 1991 to 83 seats in 1994. In a dramatic reversal of fortune, the NDP, which was founded by supporters of the former, discredited Panchayat regime, won 20 seats. It thus held the balance of power in the House of Representatives. By contrast, support for the Terai-based NSP declined, and it obtained only three seats. Support for the divided UPF was even less apparent, and it failed to win any seats. Attempts were made to establish a coalition government, but when these proved unsuccessful the UML formed a minority Government headed by the party President, Man Mohan Adhikari. The new Government was supported by the other parties because no party was prepared, either financially or organizationally, to fight another general election. The realities of holding power forced the communist Government to abandon many of its more radical election pledges. The hostility that the UML had expressed towards India during the election campaign was quickly moderated, and the party's long-standing opposition to Gurkha recruitment to the British army was abandoned. More importantly, in order to calm the Nepalese business élites and anxious aid donors, the UML committed itself to a mixed economy and the Government's programme appeared to approximate that of a socialist rather than a communist party. Yet, at the same time, communist cadres were insisting that the party follow a radical agenda. This situation created severe tensions within the party as the Government sought to reconcile its communist tradition with the pragmatic considerations of power.

In December 1994 the Government launched an ambitious supplementary budget. The centre-piece of this was the 'Build Your Village Yourself' campaign, which aimed to decentralize the development process by granting villages substantial funds so that the community could finance its own development programmes. The Government's critics, however, insisted that the UML was simply buying votes in order to win an outright majority in another mid-term poll.

A commission was established in January 1995 to investigate the land reform issue. Like its NCP predecessor, the UML Government was censured for assigning the majority of posts to its own supporters and replicating the NCP Government's monopolization of public life. It was also damaged by an unverified corruption scandal over the import of sugar and by the World Bank's decision to withdraw support for the Arun III hydropower project.

The consensus between the political parties began to break down when it was widely related that the communists were preparing for a general election and that the UML would increase its electoral support as a result of implementing populist policies. The NCP established an informal alliance with the NDP and the NSP, and tabled a vote of 'no confidence' in the Government. In order to avert the passage of this vote, on 13 June 1995 the UML recommended to the King that the legislature be dissolved and fresh elections called. Adhikari therefore became caretaker Prime Minister pending the holding of a general election scheduled for November. Although it was an interim administration, the UML nevertheless announced a new budget under royal ordinance in July. The budget increased expenditure by 27.5% over that of the supplementary budget passed in December 1994, and was characterized by an expansion of the 'Build Your Village Yourself' campaign and the implementation of various welfare programmes. This outraged the opposition because the budget was interpreted as a communist 'spending spree' and a cynical attempt to win support in advance of the forthcoming general election. The dissolution of the House of Representatives was challenged in the Supreme Court. It was argued that the legislature could not be dissolved on the advice of a Prime Minister who headed a minority administration, when a majority coalition, formed by the NCP, the NDP and the NSP, was ready to assume power. Amidst great controversy, the Supreme Court ruled on 28 August that the dissolution was unconstitutional. Consequently, the House of Representatives was reconvened, and the elections were postponed. The UML Government was then defeated in a vote of 'no confidence' on 10 September by 107 votes to 88. On 12 September a coalition Government led by the NCP, and headed by the party's parliamentary leader, Sher Bahadur Deuba, was formed. The coalition was fragile because the three parties that formed it—the NCP, the NDP and the NSP—had differing outlooks, especially regarding foreign policy matters. Its short-term prospects, however, were encouraging, since the main objective of the coalition was to avoid legislative elections in which the communists were predicted to perform well.

The coalition consolidated itself under Prime Minister Deuba's leadership. Paradoxically, Deuba's lack of a powerful political support base or of significant influence over the coalition allies contributed to his strength as head of the Government, since he antagonized few of the competing factions and posed a threat to no-one. Long-standing political and personal antagonisms, however, continued to unsettle the coalition and to lead to incessant rumours that the Government was about to collapse. In March 1996 the UML almost succeeded in enticing a section of the NDP, led by Lokendra Bahadur Chand, away from the coalition. The Government faced a parliamentary vote of 'no confidence' and, although the motion was defeated and the NDP dissidents did not ultimately defect to the opposition, the potential schism, nevertheless, undermined both the coalition and the NDP. In order to keep his coalition partners quiescent and to humour rebels within his own party, Deuba responded by exercising his powers of patronage and vastly increasing the number of ministers in the Government. By the end of March there were 48 members in the Council of Ministers, ridiculed as the 'jumbo cabinet' and the largest in Nepalese history.

In 1996 G. P. Koirala, the principal architect of the divisions that had led to the NCP's humiliating defeat in the 1994 general election, began to re-establish his authority over the party. The process by which power had begun to be transferred from the elderly NCP leaders to a new generation of politicians (most notably Deuba himself) was interrupted when Koirala was elected (with an overwhelming majority of votes) as President of the NCP at the party conference in May. By gaining this important position within the party Koirala was able to extend his control over its members. Critics alleged that his aim was to establish firm authority over the organizational wing of the NCP and then to usurp Deuba and replace him as Prime Minister following the next general election.

Nepal's other main political parties continued to be debilitated by internecine divisions. The UML had been afflicted throughout its period in office by a power struggle within the party between the 'majority' faction, which advocated less radical policies, and the 'minority' faction, which supported a more dogmatic interpretation of communism. These divisions continued into 1996. The NDP was also weakened by a simmering internal conflict and the extreme left was, in time-honoured fashion, wracked by defections and schisms. In February 1996 a splinter group, the Communist Party of Nepal (Maoist), launched a 'people's revolutionary war' in the hills of Nepal, demanding the abolition of the constitutional monarchy and the establishment of a republic. Although this was small in scale and did not pose a real threat to the political system, it nevertheless disturbed the left and in particular the UML, which in recent years has consistently adopted a more conservative line. The 'war' reminded the UML that its position as Nepal's leading revolutionary party was not guaranteed.

As a result of the divisions within the coalition, the Government's performance was criticized as 'lacklustre'. The administration remained mired in dishonesty, and investigative bodies were denied the requisite instruments and authority with which to tackle the problem. Of major importance, none -the less, was the signing of the Mahakali Treaty between Nepal and India in February 1996, which made provision for the construction of a massive hydroelectric power (HEP) plant and for the exploitation of the water resources of the Mahakali River. The costs and benefits of the project were to be divided between Nepal and India, although not, some critics claimed, to Nepal's benefit. The treaty also made provision for the ending of the controversy surrounding the 1991 Tanakpur Agreement. Ratification of the treaty was not, however, a foregone conclusion. Despite anti-Government demonstrations and protests by left-wing opposition parties, the Mahakali Treaty was ratified by the House of Representatives on 20 September 1996.

The coalition Government was undermined both by corruption scandals and by feuding within the two main parties in the alliance. G.P. Koirala and his supporters conducted a campaign against Prime Minister Deuba in an attempt to oust the latter and place Koirala in the premiership. The NDP also remained seriously divided between the Chand and Thapa factions; a power struggle developed between the two rival groups when it appeared that Thapa was set to gain outright control over the party as a whole. In an attempt to prevent this from happening, Chand renewed his efforts to forge an alliance with the communists. This resulted in the UML presenting another legislative vote of 'no confidence' against the Government in late December 1996. Although the motion was defeated, the Government did not win a majority of votes and was consequently obliged to seek a confidence motion. The securing of the confidence vote was widely thought to be simply a formality, but to great surprise on 6 March 1997 the Deuba coalition lost the vote. It received the support of 101 members of the legislature—two fewer than the 103 required to secure a majority. Significantly, two NCP members abstained from voting. Their decision to withdraw support for Deuba was interpreted by some observers as the direct result of the Koirala faction's undermining of the Prime Minister. Deuba resigned and a period of frantic bargaining began as parties sought to negotiate the formation of a new coalition. On 10 March Chand of the NDP announced that he would form a government with the support of the UML, two members of the NSP and one from the Nepal Workers' and Peasants' Party. Chand was appointed Prime Minister (for the fourth time), in the process thus creating a de facto split in the NDP, since the Thapa wing remained close to its former coalition partner, the NCP.

The NDP-UML alliance was an unlikely one and was essentially the product of political opportunism. Chand wanted to gain power at any cost—even when this entailed an alliance with a party that was at the opposite end of the political spectrum. Likewise, the UML, in its quest for power (and looking ahead to the next general election in particular), was willing to join an alliance with the man who had been the last Prime Minister under the Panchayat system. Although Chand held the premiership, the communists, as the larger partner in the coalition, were responsible for a higher proportion of ministerial posts than the NDP. Furthermore, significant power was believed to be wielded by Bam Dev Gautam, the Deputy Prime Minister and a leader of the UML.

The communists won resounding successes in by-elections in January 1997 and in May and June they triumphed in local elections, thus replacing the NCP as the country's dominant force in local government. The local elections were marred, however, by violent clashes between supporters of the main political parties in which about 30 people were killed. The series of electoral successes enjoyed by the UML created a degree of panic within the coalition Government as the NDP grew fearful of its allies. The NCP, which had not performed well in the local elections, was also alarmed by the communists' popularity. Indications were that the UML would win a substantial majority in the next general election. Both the NDP and the NCP were therefore keen to avoid the prospect of early polls, and there were constant rumours that the unstable coalition was on the verge of collapsing.

On 4 October 1997 the Government lost a parliamentary vote of 'no confidence' (by 107 votes to 94) tabled by the NCP. A few days later King Birendra appointed Surya Bahadur Thapa, the President of the NDP, to replace Lokendra Bahadur Chand as Prime Minister. A new coalition Government, comprising members of the NDP and the NSP, took office on the following day. On 9 October the new coalition administration won a parliamentary vote of confidence (by 109 votes to two—the UML abstained). In early December Prime Minister Thapa expanded the Council of Ministers in a reshuffle that introduced members of the NCP and a number of independents into the coalition. Thapa's Government, however, was wracked by the same instability as its predecessors. Fearing that Chand's faction of the NDP was about to form a new alliance with disgruntled elements of the NCP, on 8 January 1998 the Prime Minister recommended to the King that he dissolve the legislature and set a date for mid-term elections. In response, the UML and dissident members of the NDP (including Chand) decided to introduce a parliamentary vote of 'no confidence' against the Government. Uncertain as to how to act in this political impasse, the King referred the matter to the Supreme Court (the first time a Nepalese monarch had ever done so). In early February the Court advised King Birendra to convene a special session of the House of Representatives to discuss a 'no confidence' motion against Thapa's Government. Although the Supreme Court's advice was not binding, the King called the parliamentary session. The 'no confidence' motion, which was presented on 20 February, was, however, defeated, by 103 votes to 100. Meanwhile, in mid-January Chand and nine other rebel deputies were expelled from the NDP; they immediately re-established a breakaway faction known as the NDP (Chand). In March the UML suffered a serious set-back when about one-half of the party's parliamentary deputies formed a breakaway faction entitled the Communist Party of Nepal (Marxist-Leninist) (ML). Bam Dev Gautam was unanimously elected as the new party's leader. The creation of the new party left the UML with 49 parliamentary deputies, while the ML claimed the support of 40 deputies. The emergence of the ML had a dramatic impact on Nepal's political system—firstly, it meant that the NCP was the party with by far the largest representation in the House of Representatives, and, secondly, it ensured that the two factions of the NDP no longer held the parliamentary balance of power, thus rendering them minor players on the political stage.

Under an agreement reached in October 1997 when Thapa assumed power, the Prime Minister was to transfer the leadership of the coalition Government to the NCP within an agreed time frame. By early April 1998, however, Thapa appeared reluctant to relinquish his post and the NCP threatened to withdraw support for the Government unless the Prime Minister resigned immediately. Thapa tendered his resignation on 10 April and the President of the NCP, G. P. Koirala, was appointed Prime Minister on 12 April. Koirala took office on 15 April with only two other ministers. After obtaining a parliamentary vote of confidence (as required by the Constitution), by 144 votes to four, on 18 April, the Prime Minister substantially expanded his Council of Ministers a few days later. Koirala stated that amongst the top priorities of the one-party minority Government would be the tackling of the Maoist insurgency (which had escalated in recent months).

The NCP found itself in the ascendant essentially by default: it had not really prospered because of its own merits and the structural weakness and internal divisions that had led to its defeat in the 1994 general election had still to be addressed.

Consequently, G. P. Koirala's Government remained vulnerable despite its ability to play the two hostile communist parties (the UML and the ML) off against one another. Moreover, the UML still retained significant popular support and the prospect of a UML victory in the general elections that Koirala promised to hold in April–May 1999 could not be ruled out. Therefore, in an attempt to buttress his own precarious administration and to encourage the UML's communist rivals, in August 1998 the Prime Minister invited the ML to ally itself with the NCP and to form a coalition government. A new coalition administration was consequently formed on 26 August (with the NCP retaining the key ministries), giving Prime Minister Koirala a comfortable parliamentary majority.

The alliance of a radical communist party with the centre-ground NCP was a good indication of the ideological contortions that Nepalese politicians are willing to undergo in order to stay in power. The coalition Government was simply a holding mechanism designed to keep the UML out of power in the run-up to the next general election. Corruption flourished amidst the political opportunism, and the general cynicism regarding the political system, coupled with the latter's utter failure to address the country's economic troubles, continued to encourage extremism. As a result, the 'people's war' waged by the Maoist activists in the hills of Nepal continued to gather momentum. In May 1998 the Government launched a major police operation in an attempt to curb the guerrilla violence, and in July the Minister of Home Affairs claimed that a total of 257 people had died as a result of the insurgency (a figure that had risen to more than 900 by September 1999).

In mid-October 1998 the Speaker of the House of Representatives, Ram Chandra Poudel, a member of the ruling NCP, survived a parliamentary motion introduced by opposition parties, charging him with dereliction of duty in an attempt to oust him (earlier in the month the Deputy Speaker had been forced to resign as a result of the ongoing confrontation between the ruling and opposition parties). In early December 1998 the ML withdrew from the coalition Government, alleging that its ruling partner, the NCP, had failed to implement a number of agreements drawn up between the two parties and other political groups in August. On 21 December Prime Minister G. P. Koirala tendered his resignation, but was asked to head a new coalition Council of Ministers, which was to govern in an acting capacity pending the holding of a general election. On the recommendation of the Prime Minister, the King appointed a new coalition administration, composed of members of the NCP, the UML and the NSP, and, for the first time in eight years, a nominee of the King, on 25 December. In mid-January 1999 the acting Government won a convincing vote of confidence in the House of Representatives, which it required in order to continue in power, and the following day the King dissolved the legislature in preparation for the general election, which was to be held in May.

In late April 1999 the UML suffered a reverse when its veteran leader and former Prime Minister, Man Mohan Adhikari, died during the electoral campaign. The NCP won an outright majority in the general election, which was held over two rounds on 3 and 17 May, gaining 110 of the 205 legislative seats; the UML obtained 68 seats and the NDP (Thapa) took 11 seats, while the ML and the NDP (Chand) both failed to win a single seat. Voting was conducted relatively peacefully, according to government sources, despite threats by the Maoist insurgents to disrupt the electoral proceedings. A new Council of Ministers, headed by the veteran NCP leader K. P. Bhattarai and composed solely of NCP members, was appointed at the end of the month. (G. P. Koirala had offered Bhattarai—a long-standing party rival—the post-poll premiership months before the election, in an effort to heal dissension within the NCP). In late June the UML won all six seats in elections to the National Council.

In mid-December 1999 the ruling NCP, despite a number of by-election victories, was once again beset by internecine strife when about 80 pro-Koirala legislators launched an attempt to oust (by means of a petition) the Prime Minister from his position as the NCP's parliamentary party leader (which would automatically lead to his removal from the premiership). Koirala had initially been supportive of Bhattarai's premiership, but had since become a vociferous critic of his rival's administration. The resignation of the Minister of Finance, Mahesh Acharya, following a disagreement with K. P. Bhattarai, led to a minor reorganization of the Council of Ministers at the beginning of February 2000. The former Speaker of the House of Representatives, Ram Chandra Poudel, was appointed Deputy Prime Minister. His nomination prompted the Minister of Education, Yog Prasad Upadhyaya, to resign in protest. The political unrest culminated in the presentation of a vote of 'no confidence' against the Prime Minister in mid-February and, subsequently, the resignation of 11 government ministers. K. P. Bhattarai resigned on 16 March, before the vote of 'no confidence' was scheduled to take place. G. P. Koirala replaced him six days later.

G. P. Koirala's succession to the premiership constituted his fourth occupancy of the position since the establishment of competitive party politics in Nepal almost 10 years previously. Koirala's reason for bringing down the Government was that it had failed in its principal tasks, foremost of which was the suppression of the Maoist insurgency. The new Prime Minister pledged to defeat the insurgency, curb corruption and improve the performance of the bureaucracy. At the beginning of April 2000 G. P. Koirala instructed the former NCP Prime Minister, Sher Bahadur Deuba, to resume negotiations with the CPN (Maoist) insurgents. Koirala also announced his intention to activate the National Defence Council which, according to the Constitution, comprised the Prime Minister, Minister of Defence and Commander-in-Chief of the Royal Nepal Army, to resolve the Maoist crisis. In November 1999 the CPN (Maoist) had stated that it required the withdrawal of arrest warrants issued against its leaders, an official investigation into alleged extra-judicial killings of suspected militants by the police and the release of imprisoned activists before it entered into serious peace negotiations. The Government responded in late 1999 and 2000 by releasing a number of Maoist leaders. However, despite some indication of willingness on the part of the Maoist leadership to enter dialogue, by September 2000 it seemed to have concluded that the Government had failed to create the conditions conducive to serious negotiations. Indeed, until October there was little evidence that the Government regarded the insurgency as a political problem, rather than as a security problem to be countered by ever harsher action by armed police.

In the mean time, the former NCP Prime Minister, Sher Bahadur Deuba, challenged G. P. Koirala, claiming that he should step aside for a younger leader. He attacked Koirala for failing to address the question of peace and security in Nepal, in particular, the perceived problems with the Maoist insurgency. Tension remained high at this time; the police force's use of violence to suppress a strike held by jute mill workers prompted the opposition UML to force the adjournment of parliament at the beginning of July 2000. In late August a prolonged strike, which led to the closure of banks and other 'essential' services, caused the Government to ban strikes by workers employed in this sector.

In an attempt to deal with a continuous conflict within the Government, in August 2000 G. P. Koirala dismissed the Minister for Water Resources, Khum Bahadur Khadka, for his involvement in the Deuba-led faction. Later that month the Prime Minister was under pressure from his party and the opposition to prosecute Prince Paras Shah, the only son of the brother of King Birendra, who was alleged to have driven a vehicle that hit, and killed, Prabin Gurung, a popular local singer and musician. The CPN (ML) held a demonstration in protest at the Government's inaction and demanded that the Prime Minister remove the Prince's title. At the same time the royal family encountered pressure to relinquish its right to immunity from prosecution. This event drew attention again to the complex role of the monarchy in Nepal's political affairs. Koirala, who held the portfolio for the royal palace affairs, was criticized for failing to address the issue seriously and for what was considered an attempt to support his weakening position, through forging closer links with the monarchy. His response to the criticism was to prorogue the legislature, two weeks ahead of the due date.

The CPN (Maoist) continued to wage a 'People's War' against the state, a process through which it hoped to replace the constitutional monarchy with a communist state. As part of an overall strategy, militants targeted village and district police stations outside Kathmandu. By mid-2000 the number of people who had died during the four-and-a-half years of insurgency appeared to be approaching 1,500. In the latter half of 2000 the situation worsened when G. P. Koirala sought the support of the Indian Government to suppress the activities of the rebels in locations based in India, particularly in the state of Bihar, a move that provoked the militants to widen their attacks.

The Maoist insurgency was socially detrimental. According to human rights organizations, whereas the police were indiscriminate in their use of force, in many cases either killing or injuring people not connected with the rebel movement, the Maoist militants were guilty of kidnapping children and using them as shields to attack the police. The question regarding the most effective way to deal with the militants required the fullest attention at the end of September, when hundreds of Maoist insurgents were reported to have attacked a police station in Dunai, the district headquarters of Dolpa, and Lamjung, killing 24 police officers and injuring 44. The Royal Nepal Army was criticized for failing to intervene to protect the police from the insurgents. It was, in fact, awaiting permission from the King, who, according to the 1990 Constitution, was required to endorse any action decided by the National Defence Council (see above). Although the Government was keen to use the army to establish a paramilitary force that could control the rebels, the King was reluctant to sanction a decision that could lead to civil war. As the army refused to take orders from anyone but the monarch, the Government was placed in a position of considerable weakness. The Minister of Home Affairs, Govinda Raj Joshi, resigned after admitting his failure to 'maintain law and order in the country'. The Prime Minister responded to the confusion over the command and control structure of the army by giving Mahesh Acharya, the Minister of Finance, the additional portfolio of defence. G. P. Koirala had hitherto always retained this portfolio personally, but it had become clear that the Government and army required an independent defence minister, clarification of the army's ambiguous role and the development of a procedure for mobilizing the army, absent from the 1990 Constitution.

This event was yet another example of the Government's inability to assert its authority in the context of the prevailing political system. To complicate issues further, left-wing parties urged the Government to engage in dialogue rather than use the army, suggesting that the latter move could lead to civil war. The first direct unofficial negotiations between the Government and the CPN (Maoist) began at the end of October; however, they were short-lived, and the violent campaign soon resumed. Clashes with police occurred in late November after Maoist students in Kathmandu held a meeting on the university and set fire to the principal's office. Shortly afterwards, schools in Kathmandu closed down after insurgents attacked them for charging fees and for apparently denying students' rights in other ways. The militants argued that the Government had failed to deliver free primary and secondary education to the people, despite having promised to do so in 1990. The Government responded to these and other attacks by moving to set up a special court to try cases of crime against the state.

Tension remained high at the end of 2000. In late December rumours that an Indian film actor had made derogatory remarks about Nepal and the Nepalese public in a television interview provoked an outburst of anti-Indian sentiment and a week of violent street protests in Kathmandu. Once it became known that the television station had no knowledge of such an interview and that the allegations were false, the violence ceased. At the same time 56 of the ruling NCP's 113 legislators registered a no-confidence motion against the Prime Minister. However, doubts began to emerge among the dissidents, partly owing to the fear of potential consequences should the government fall, especially given that eight governments had collapsed since 1990. Consequently, on 4 January 2001 the no-confidence motion was defeated after most of the supporters of the motion boycotted the vote. Shortly afterwards, Deuba began a nation-wide campaign to remove the Prime Minister from the NCP leadership and announced his candidacy for the party presidency, to be determined in mid-January. Nevertheless, at the party's general convention, held in Pokhara, G. P. Koirala was convincingly re-elected NCP President. This result was reflected in the election of members to the Central Working Committee, in which Koirala's faction won 12 of the 18 seats, and Deuba's faction gained the remainder. Although Koirala subsequently attempted to unite the feuding party, he failed to resolve the underlying differences and the Deuba faction continued to refuse to join the Council of Ministers. During the struggle to maintain control of the legislature, the Government was suspected of corruption following a controversial agreement to lease an Austrian aircraft to the Royal Nepal Airlines Co-operation, without putting the contract out to a competitive tender. Consequently, the Minister of Culture, Tourism and Civil Aviation, Tarani Datta Chataut, resigned at the end of January. The parliamentary Public Accounts Committee and an anti-corruption agency investigating the alleged misuse of powers by government members, including the Prime Minister, instructed the Government not to deliver the aircraft to Nepal until the investigation was complete. However, the directive was ignored and the transaction was performed. In early February leading opposition parties issued a memorandum to the Prime Minister, demanding his resignation over the aircraft deal and also the worsening security situation. Koirala strongly denied his involvement in the leasing of the Austrian aircraft and the receipt of a large payment. In May the Prime Minister was exonerated of involvement in the case; however, the anti-corruption commission filed cases against 10 other people, including the former minister, Chataut.

It had become increasingly difficult to operate the National Assembly and House of Representatives and maintain stability, owing to continuous protests from within the governing NCP and from opposition parties. Consequently, parliament was frequently adjourned; in fact, since the legislature was convened in early February, it had not completed one working day until it was prorogued in early April. Meanwhile, the Maoist insurgency continued to be a growing problem. In the first week of April alone, militants reportedly killed more than 60 police officers. By this time the insurgency had spread to 73 of the 75 districts of Nepal. Finally, in mid-April, the Prime Minister requested King Birendra to permit the mobilization of the army, suggesting that the country was in a state of emergency. The King appeared reluctant to support such a development.

In April–May 2001 the situation remained tense: the Maoist insurgents maintained their attacks on police stations, strikes closed down businesses and educational institutions across the country, opposition parties continued to criticize the Government, and the ruling party remained beset by internecine divisions. It is clear, thus, that the prevailing political atmosphere in Nepal was highly unstable. However, what was to follow was completely unanticipated and will undoubtedly claim its place as a watershed in Nepal's history.

On the evening of 1 June 2001 King Birendra, Queen Aishwarya and six other members of the royal family were shot dead. The youngest brother of the King was also shot and died later in hospital. The heir to the throne, Crown Prince Dipendra, was gravely wounded. Initial reports suggested that Prince Dipendra had shot members of his family before shooting himself, following a dispute between himself and his mother, regarding his plans to marry Devyani Rani (the daughter of a leading Nepalese politician), of whom the Queen disapproved. An official statement by the King's brother, Prince Gyanendra, claimed that the deaths were the result of an accidental discharge from an automatic weapon. Immediately after the incident Prince Dipendra was pronounced King, and Prince Gyanendra was appointed regent. However, on 4 June King Dipendra died and was succeeded by Prince Gyanendra. In the mean time, rumours about the incident began to spread. Questions were asked as to why the Commander-in Chief of the Nepalese armed forces did not attend the funeral of the royal family, why there was a delay in an official statement, and why the Prime Minister had not been immediately informed of the deaths. There were rumours that Gyanendra, who was not present and whose immediate family (wife, son and daughter) emerged unharmed from the event, had plotted a conspiracy against the deceased King Birendra. Some suggested that the deaths were the result of actions by Maoists, while others claimed that India was the perpetrator. These events caused unrest in Kathmandu, and a curfew was imposed. However, it failed to suppress the protests. Some five days after the incident, three journalists of Nepal's largest daily newspaper, *Kantipur*, were arrested on charges of sedition for publishing an article written by a Maoist leader supporting the conspiracy theory and calling on the army to overthrow the Government. Following his accession, King Gyanendra established a two-member commission to investigate the killings. The commission, comprising Chief Justice K. P. Upadhaya, and Speaker of the House of Representatives, T. Ranabhat, published their report on 14 June. It confirmed that Prince Dipendra was responsible for the killings and that at the time he had been under the influence of drugs and alcohol. Prior to the shooting, he had telephoned his girlfriend, Devyani Rani, three times. He then changed into battle dress, returned to the gathering and with three guns shot members of the royal family, before shooting himself.

Meanwhile, concerns continued to mount as the CPN (Maoist) refused to engage in dialogue. Following the killings, a Maoist leader was reported to have appealed to all nationalists, left-wing supporters and republicans to unite to form an interim government. Maoist leaders appeared to be taking advantage of the discontent in Nepal by intensifying the insurgency. In mid-July 2001 the Deputy Prime Minister, Ram Chandra Poudel, resigned in protest at the Prime Minister's failure to deal with the discontent and to end the country's political paralysis. Nearly one week later G. P. Koirala resigned, largely owing to the opposition's increasing criticism of his approach towards the Maoist insurgency and of his handling of the royal family killings, and because of long-standing corruption allegations.

Thus, 16 months after he had returned to power, G. P. Koirala was forced to relinquish his control to Deuba. Like Koirala, Deuba had served previously as leader of the NCP and Prime Minister of Nepal. This underlined the highly factional nature of the NCP and the inability of both leaders to address the fundamental problems facing Nepal. Indeed, while Koirala had just completed his third period as Prime Minister, Deuba was about to begin his second. Moreover, although Maoist leaders declared a cease-fire immediately after the appointment of Deuba as Prime Minister in mid-July 2001, the new Government's capacity to achieve a satisfactory solution to the problem that had troubled Nepal since 1996 remained highly questionable.

It was not long before the 'temporary truce' collapsed. After three rounds of talks in August, September and November 2001, in which the Maoists sought substantial changes in Nepal's political system, including, ultimately, a republic, in contrast to the much more limited changes that the Government was prepared to offer, the Maoists ended negotiations. In late November the insurgents resumed their violent campaign: army barracks and other locations throughout Nepal were attacked. The Government responded by declaring a state of emergency and seeking, successfully, King Gyanendra's authorization to mobilize the army.

Significantly, for the first time since 1996, the army appeared committed to confronting the Maoist insurgents. It had been suggested that the army sought the formal declaration of emergency rule as a condition to it mobilizing its forces. An ongoing struggle between the security forces (the army and police) and the Maoists ensued, during which the detention of teachers, journalists and others known to have Maoist connections quickly brought the question of civil rights into public discussion. Furthermore, human rights organizations, such as Amnesty International, claimed that the Government had exceeded its authority in suspending Article 23 of the Constitution, thereby allowing it to refuse people the right to judicial representation. The promulgation of an anti-terrorist ordinance, whereby people engaged in what were perceived to be 'terrorist' acts by making political statements could be detained for 90 days, without charge, was also heavily criticized. Concerns were raised that the police and the army were firing at villages indiscriminately in a supposed attempt to suppress the Maoists. At the same time the Maoists' contravention of human rights caused alarm. The insurgents were accused of killing innocent victims, torturing those who refused to obey their instructions and recruiting children into their fighting units.

Despite government statements that the Maoists were on the retreat, the hostilities intensified. In mid-February 2002 the Maoists attacked and overthrew the Mangalsen army barracks, in Achham district, killing more than 100 soldiers, police officers and civilians. This major victory drew attention to the political crisis beleaguering Nepal. Firstly, there was the issue of the emergency, and whether it should be extended and for how long. Secondly, the relationship between the new King and the army, in other words the relationship in terms of the Constitution and to what extent it marginalized the Government, was questioned. Finally, there was the issue of the army itself and whether it had the capacity to subdue the Maoist uprising. The debate that ensued raised into question the global issue of 'terrorism' and the delicate matter of inviting foreign forces to support the national armed forces. What had previously been a domestic question, therefore, was now rapidly becoming an international one.

The legislature decided to extend the emergency for three months from 21 February 2002. The Government also introduced more stringent anti-terrorist legislation in an effort to curb the Maoist insurgency. The bill, which included clauses regarding life imprisonment, loss of property and the right to search and arrest without warrant, was passed into law in April for a period of two years. At the same time the Government sought talks with foreign governments. In particular, it initiated dialogue with the Indian Government on the matter of the insurgency. Deuba's and then G. P. Koirala's visit to New Delhi in April was followed by the Chief of the Indian Army's visit to Nepal in May, where he promised military aid to the Nepalese Government. In the mean time, Nepal was engaged in discussions with the USA. The US Secretary of State Gen. Colin Powell's visit to Kathmandu in January was the first of a series of meetings between the two countries that gradually led to Nepal's incorporation into the USA's global strategy against terrorism. The internationalization of Nepal's internal security problems was broadened in May when, during his meeting with the British Prime Minister, Tony Blair, in London, Deuba requested military aid from the United Kingdom.

Alongside these attempts to secure Nepal's political system was the perception that the Constitution on which the system was based was being undermined. Consequently, when Deuba tabled a parliamentary motion proposing a six-month extension of the emergency in mid-May 2002, members of his own party, as well as the opposition, voiced strong opposition to such a proposal. After the Central Working Party of the governing NCP directed him not to extend the emergency, Deuba consulted the Council of Ministers and then recommended King Gyanendra to dissolve the House of Representatives. King Gyanendra, thus, dissolved parliament on 22 May; an election was scheduled to take place on 13 November. Deuba also sought and gained permission from the King to continue as the caretaker Prime Minister until the election was held. The King then issued a royal ordinance to extend the emergency by three months on 27 May. Although Deuba and his allies had achieved victory in the short term, they faced enormous difficulties in the longer term. By shifting control away from parliament and its underlying constitutional constraints, they had allowed the King and the army to exert much greater influence, on the one hand, and granted access to foreign intervention, on the other.

In the period that immediately followed, these difficulties became increasingly evident. Fears of Deuba's close links to the army and royal palace, for example, led to suggestions that he was part of an attempt to undermine parliamentary democracy in favour of the monarchy. Deuba's actions had already caused a rift in the governing NCP: three ministers resigned on 23 May 2002; on the same day Deuba was suspended from the party and three days later was expelled. The NCP officially split at the party's general convention in mid-June after Deuba's supporters expelled party President G. P. Koirala from the party for three years (Koirala's supporters had boycotted the convention, which had been convoked by Deuba). Deuba, who had been reinstated as a party member by the convention, was elected President of the NCP the next day. Koirala's faction immediately denounced the meeting as illegal, since Deuba had already been expelled by the party and therefore had no right to summon such a gathering. After weeks of legal dispute, in mid-September the Election Commission refused to recognize Deuba's breakaway faction as the official NCP; Koirala's faction retained this status. Deuba could either reunite with the Koirala faction or establish a new party. In June the Federation of Nepalese Journalists again accused the Government of condoning the torturing and killing of a local journalist while under arrest by security forces for protesting against political issues.

A month later Deuba was accused of acting unconstitutionally when he presented the 2002/03 budget as an ordinance passed by the King. His critics argued that he had undermined a Supreme Court precedent endorsed in 1995, which defined the way in which interim governments could introduce budgets. In early October Deuba requested King Gyanendra to postpone the national elections, which were scheduled to take place in November, owing to the worsening security situation. However, King Gyanendra dismissed the Prime Minister and the interim Council of Ministers for reportedly failing to organize the general election. The King postponed the general election indefinitely and assumed executive power; he was expected to form a new non-elected interim government.

Underlying the political instability that has characterized Nepal since 1996 has been a fragile economy. In a country where almost 50% of the 23m.-strong population live below the poverty line and only 27% are literate, the difficulties confronting the Government are formidable. A significant number of bonded labourers in the western districts, widespread use of child labour—involving more than 2.5m. children—and a female population that is largely deprived in terms of education, health and civil rights, reflect a society that is economically underdeveloped. Furthermore, the Madhesias, who represent more than one-half the population of Nepal and who provide the basis of agricultural labour, remain largely without rights, even though they have resided in Nepal for most of the 20th century and continue to stay, having originally migrated from the Indian states bordering Nepal.

In terms of the economy, agriculture remained the most important sector, providing work for more than 80% of the working population and representing around 40% of GDP. However, while carpet and textile production were successful export-orientated industries, tourism and hydroelectricity, potentially the two most powerful areas of growth, remained unable to deliver the economic benefits that the country could expect. The tourist sector in 2001/02 was adversely affected by the political uncertainties and the fear of civil war. In the case of hydroelectricity, the need to rely on multilateral international aid to fund the majority of the large development projects, as well as more than one-quarter of the general budgetary expenditure, which increasingly was being overtaken by a deficit budget, created difficulties. In particular, the Government had to attempt to meet demands set by international aid agencies regarding financial sector reforms in an environment distinguished by economic backwardness and growing political violence. Although there was a concerted attempt in 2001/02 to address problems relating to development by increasing development expenditure by approximately 26%, by the end of the fiscal year, the economy had decelerated as a result of the prevailing political instability—the targeting of infrastructure developments by Maoists, for example. The country's development suffered another setback when the interim Government reduced the allocated development expenditure in the 2002/03 budget. Development previously had been the Government's principal policy in achieving a transformation in the economy.

FOREIGN RELATIONS

Nepal's relations with India have traditionally been very close. At least geographically, Nepal is a South Asian nation, and the Nepalese Terai is an extension of India's gangetic plains. The long, open, porous border between the two countries has ensured that the Nepalese economy has become almost an adjunct to the much larger Indian economy. This has had a profound effect upon relations between the two countries, and Nepal has continually struggled to emphasize both its political and economic independence from its huge southern neighbour. On many occasions Nepal has vociferously asserted its national sovereignty. In 1978 the old Trade and Transit Treaty between the two countries was replaced by two treaties (renewed in the mid-1980s), the one concerning bilateral trade between India and Nepal, the other allowing Nepal to develop trade with other countries via India. Relations between Nepal and India deteriorated in December 1987, however, when the Chief Minister of the Indian state of West Bengal accused Nepal of providing sanctuary for activists of the Gurkha National Liberation Front (GNLF), campaigning for separate status for the Gurkha-populated area of the state. This accusation was strongly denied by the Government of Nepal. In July 1988 Nepal claimed that Indian security personnel were violating Nepalese territory. In March 1989 India decided not to renew the two treaties determining trade and transit, insisting that a common treaty covering both issues be negotiated. Nepal refused, stressing the importance of keeping the treaties separate, on the grounds that trade issues are negotiable, whereas the right of transit is a recognized right of land-locked countries. India responded by closing 13 of the 15 transit points through which most of Nepal's trade is conducted. Severe shortages of food and fuel ensued and the prices of basic products increased significantly. It was widely believed that a major issue aggravating the dispute was Nepal's acquisition (in 1988) of Chinese-made military equipment (including anti-aircraft guns) which, according to India, violated the Treaty of Peace and Friendship concluded by India and Nepal in 1950, by the terms of which successive Indian Governments have traditionally considered the entire region south of the Himalayas as belonging to the Indian security system. Diplomatic relations between Nepal and India remained strained throughout 1989, with trade at a virtual standstill. Following several rounds of senior-level talks, a joint communiqué was signed by the two countries during a visit by Prime Minister Bhattarai to India in June 1990, restoring trade relations and reopening the transit points, and assuring mutual consultations on matters of security. A few days earlier, as an apparent gesture of goodwill to India, the Nepalese Government had told the Chinese Government to defer indefinitely the delivery of the final consignment of arms destined for Nepal. A return visit to Nepal was made by the Indian Prime Minister, Chandra Shekhar, in February 1991 (the first official visit by an Indian Premier since 1977), shortly after it was announced that the first free elections there were to be held in May. Separate trade and transit treaties (valid for five and seven years respectively) were signed during a visit by Prime Minister G. P. Koirala to India in December 1991; these treaties were both subsequently renewed on expiry. Koirala's signing of the Tanakpur Agreement with India in December 1991 (see above) became a matter of great domestic political controversy in 1992. The issue acquired such importance because water resources and the control of Nepal's rivers have become a subject of acrimony between Nepal and India. Critics of the agreement argued that India was anxious to lay claim to Nepal's water resources in order to irrigate its northern states and because it was keen to purchase cheap electricity from proposed Nepalese hydroelectric plants.

Indo-Nepalese relations were further strained by the election of the minority UML Government in November 1994. Nepal's communist movement has traditionally been hostile towards India, but, once in power, the UML was forced to be more accommodating towards India, as no Nepalese Government can afford to remain on bad terms with its huge southern neighbour.

Indo-Nepalese relations have improved considerably since 1995. In January 1996 the Indian Minister of External Affairs, Pranab Mukherjee, made an official visit to Nepal during which he signed a treaty for the Integrated Development of the Mahakali River. This treaty, which was formalized during Prime Minister Deuba's visit to New Delhi in February, made provision for the joint exploitation of the water resources of the Mahakali and effectively superseded the Tanakpur Agreement. At the same time India also made some trade concessions to Nepal. In particular, India agreed to waive the 50% (material cum labour) content requirement for Nepali products to be granted preferential access to the Indian market. Also of importance was the signing of a Power Trade Agreement between India and Nepal, which allowed for private-sector participation in the implementation of (HEP) projects. The Chand coalition Government, which came to power in March 1997, maintained close relations with New Delhi. During a visit to Nepal by the Indian Prime Minister, Inder Kumar Gujral, in June, the Mahakali Treaty was formally endorsed and India granted Nepal access to Bangladeshi ports through a new transit facility across Indian territory via the Karkavita–Phulbari road (this facility was extended and improved in 1998). Some tension in Indo-Nepalese relations, nevertheless, remained; this centred on border demarcation disputes and, in particular, on the Indian border police's use of territory that Nepal claims as its own in the far west of the country. Since the Sino-Indian war in 1962, an Indian paramilitary force has been stationed at the strategic Kalapani junction between India, Nepal and China. Nepal asserts that this 35 sq km area of territory lies in the Nepalese district of Darchula, while New Delhi claims that it is part of India. The controversy rests on different interpretations of 19th century maps and the 1816 Treaty of Sugauli between Nepal and the United Kingdom. An Indo-Nepalese team is currently working on the border demarcation problem, but in mid-1998 the controversy was accentuated as it became further mired in the competition between Nepal's political parties and the hardline attitude adopted by India's ruling nationalist Bharatiya Janata Party. In June 2000 the Nepalese Government announced that the border would be delineated by 2003.

In early August 2000, less than four months after his accession to the premiership, G. P. Koirala embarked on a 'goodwill visit and confidence-building mission' to India. This was only the Prime Minister's second official visit to India in some eight years of office, and around four years after the previous visit by any head of government, a circumstance that reflected the continuing unease felt by Nepal towards India. The visit was deemed a success on both sides, but it did not dispel the basis of Nepalese ambivalence in relation to its most influential neighbour. Although the nations share many religious, linguistic, political and general cultural features, the vast difference in size and international power inevitably cast India occasionally into the role of an oppressive authority. Nepal was keen to renegotiate the Treaty of Peace and Friendship concluded by India and Nepal in 1950, because of the adverse effect of this kind of patronizing attitude. India, however, viewed any sign of deterioration of its fundamental relations with Nepal in the context of Nepal's relationship with its other powerful neighbour—China. India agreed to discuss the treaty at foreign secretary level; therefore it appeared highly unlikely that such a significant political matter would be solved in the foreseeable future. Koirala's visit did, however, help dispel India's lingering discontent caused by the hijacking of an Indian Airlines aircraft from Kathmandu in 1999. Indian Airlines resumed its flights to Kathmandu in June 2000. The two leaders also agreed on common action in relation to the control of terrorism, the reduction of trade barriers, dams and irrigation.

Relations between Nepal and India were temporarily disrupted in December 2000 and early 2001, owing to false allegations that an Indian actor had made derogatory remarks about Nepal (see above). The extending influence of Maoist militants to Nepalese communities located in India became a matter of concern to the Indian Government. It was claimed that, in a number of cases, especially in the state of Bihar, Maoist insurgents were being trained in camps. Furthermore, in December 2000 the Indian Prime Minister expressed his concerns to his Nepalese counterpart about the anti-Indian sentiment propagated in Nepal by the Maoists. The following year began more positively: in mid-January 2001 Nepal and India announced their agreement to widen the exchange of electricity and to increase the rate at which Nepal charged India for this energy. Although efforts were made to review the Treaty of Peace and Friendship in early February, effective negotiations were not under way until April. The main issue discussed was India's concern about imports from other countries, especially the People's Republic of China, being routed through Nepal. By repackaging these goods in Nepal, it was possible to export them as Nepalese goods and thus avoid custom duties, which, according to the treaty, Nepal was not obliged to pay.

In June 2001 India, like the rest of the world, turned its attention to the royal family killings. Owing to the growing fear that the Maoist militants would expand their base following this incident, the Indian Government dispatched paramilitary forces to patrol the Indian side of the Nepalese-Indian border. At the same time the forces joined the Nepalese army, which had been patrolling the Nepalese side of the border since March, in an effort to contain the illegal import and export of arms and drugs. The Indian Government was especially concerned to curb the perceived infiltration into Nepal of Pakistan's Inter-Services Intelligence (ISI), which it claimed was responsible for the illegal trade and which allegedly supported the Maoist movement. In addition, Nepal and India issued complaints against each other's use of common waterways. Whereas Nepal feared that construction works in Uttar Pradesh, India, would lead to the flooding of Nepalese villages, India pointed out that the Nepalese Government had failed to provide adequate safety for Indian engineers who had crossed the Nepalese border to inspect sites that were threatening water projects in the Indian state of Bihar. By early 2002, however, attention on both sides had turned to what was emerging as a major threat to the Government of Nepal: the civil disorder that had worsened since the Nepalese army had been deployed to curb the insurgency in November 2001. Nepal viewed India as a necessary ally in addressing this problem, especially as close links existed between the Maoists in Nepal and those in Bihar and other parts of north-east India. Equally, India was anxious to contain the expansion of this movement. Consequently, both Governments held talks, and the Indian Government promised to provide the necessary support.

The People's Republic of China has contributed a considerable amount to the Nepalese economy, and the first meeting of a joint Sino-Nepalese committee on economic co-operation took place in December 1984. This committee met for a second time (and thenceforth annually) in Kathmandu in March 1986, when China agreed to increase its imports from Nepal in order to minimize trade imbalances. Relations between Nepal and China improved further in November 1989, when the Chinese Premier, Li Peng, paid an official three-day visit to Kathmandu. This visit was viewed with some misgiving by India as emphasizing Nepal's increasingly friendly relations with China. In March 1992 the Nepalese Prime Minister, G. P. Koirala, paid an official goodwill visit to Beijing, as did Prime Minister Deuba in April 1996. Although Deuba did not succeed in gaining any major new concessions during his visit, he reiterated Nepal's continuing commitment to the 'One China' policy. Sino-Nepalese relations were further strengthened in December 1996 by a state visit by the Chinese President, Jiang Zemin, to Nepal.

In 1985 it was agreed that Nepal's border with Tibet (the Xizang Autonomous Region) should be opened; the border was closed indefinitely, however, following the outbreak of ethnic violence in Tibet in March 1989. In February 1991 the interim Government of Nepal cancelled a visit by the Dalai Lama, the Tibetan leader in exile, on 'technical grounds'. The cancellation followed Chinese protests made to the Nepalese Government against the proposed visit. The Nepalese authorities have been consistent in their efforts to repatriate refugees fleeing from Tibet and banned a proposed peace march by Tibetans through Nepalese territory in 1995.

In August 2000 the Nepalese Minister of Foreign Affairs visited China where an agreement was reached to allow Nepal greater use of a new road in Tibet, which offered favourable access to Nepal's own north-western regions. Greater technological and economic co-operation was also achieved, thus significantly increasing bilateral trade. Each nation continued to avoid taking any stance that might lead to conflict. Thus, Nepal consistently declined to be critical of China with regard to the Tibet issue and supported the 'One China' policy, by not recognizing Taiwan. For its part, China made no criticism of the Nepalese monarchy, nor gave any support to communist groups in Nepal. At the end of 2000, Nepal and China concluded initial negotiations with regard to proposals to abolish dual tariffs and to promote trade.

In 2001 relations were further improved. In January Chinese and Nepalese government representatives met in Nepal to strengthen ties between the two governing political parties. Shortly after this meeting, the Chinese Government issued what had become a regular invitation to the King and Queen of Nepal to visit China. Having previously visited China nine times, King Birendra was a strong advocate of close relations between the two countries. In February Nepal's Minister of Foreign Affairs assured the Chinese defence minister of his full support in suppressing anti-Chinese activities among Tibetans in Nepal. During a visit to Nepal by a Chinese delegation in March the Nepalese Prime Minister remarked on China's assistance towards Nepal's economic development and reaffirmed Nepal's support for the 'One China' policy and for China's approach to Tibet. Similar sentiments were again expressed in May, when King Birendra met the visiting Chinese Premier, Zhu Rongji.

In 2001/02, China continued to pursue the policy of strengthening ties with Nepal. As well as other matters, it agreed to make the Chinese yuan convertible with the Nepalese rupee in order to facilitate trade between the two countries and to increase the number of Chinese tourists visiting Nepal. In July 2002 the Chinese Government hosted a visit by King Gyanendra, which endorsed his position within Nepalese society. However, while the Chinese Government supported the Nepalese authorities in their struggle against the Maoists, unlike India, it made no attempt to become involved further, preferring to observe the unfolding of events from a distance.

Ties with Bangladesh are also important, particularly regarding the utilization of joint water resources. Nepal and Pakistan have attempted to facilitate trade and tourism through a joint economic commission and a regular air link. However, Bhutan has occupied most of its attention. In late 1991 thousands of Bhutanese of Nepalese origin began to flee to east Nepal, following the outbreak of political and ethnic violence in Bhutan. By the end of July 1994 more than 85,000 refugees were living in seven camps (later increased to eight) in the districts of Jhapa and Morang; by early 1996 the total number of refugees had risen to about 100,000.

In the first half of 1993 talks were held between officials of the Nepalese and Bhutanese Governments in an attempt to resolve the refugee crisis. The Nepalese Government steadfastly refused to consider any solution other than the resettlement in Bhutan of all ethnic Nepalese living in the camps. The Bhutanese Government countered by claiming that the majority of the refugees were not actually Bhutanese and that they had no documentation to prove otherwise. The issue was further clouded by the question of which role India should play in the crisis: first, because India was deemed by the Nepalese to exercise considerable influence over Bhutan's foreign policy; and, second, because the refugees had crossed Indian territory before seeking sanctuary in Nepal, thus requiring India to assume some responsibility for the refugee problem. The apparent deadlock was broken when, in mid-July 1993, the Nepalese and Bhutanese Governments agreed to establish a high-level committee to work towards a settlement. This resulted in an agreement, drawn up in October, to categorize the refugees into four groups, in only one of which were the refugees to be acknowledged as 'legitimate'. Yet, even despite this first step towards a resolution of the crisis, the Bhutanese refugee problem still remained unresolved following the failure of numerous rounds of talks. Nepal and Bhutan finally achieved a breakthrough at the 10th round of negotiations in December 2000. Both countries agreed that nationality would be verified on the basis of the head of the refugee family for those over 25 years of age. Refugees under 25 years of age would be verified on an individual basis. By the end of January 2001 joint teams had concluded the inspection of refugee camps; verification began at the end of March. Inevitably, this process has to date proved to be very slow.

Nepal (with six other countries) is a founder-member of the South Asian Association for Regional Co-operation (SAARC), formally established in 1985: the Association's permanent secretariat was officially inaugurated in Kathmandu in January 1987. Since that time, it has met regularly in this forum to discuss questions relating to development and joint projects that could be funded with support from the UN and other agencies.

Economy

MARIKA VICZIANY

Following the tragedy that decimated the Nepalese royal family on 1 June 2001, the economy of Nepal entered a period of unprecedented precariousness. Despite the modest economic growth reported in previous years, the Maoist insurgency, which began in 1996, has grown in strength; some estimates suggested that the Maoists controlled about 60% of Nepal's administrative regions in mid-2002. The economic and political instability is not limited to Nepal, but has serious implications for the region as a whole. In particular, since the terrorist attacks on New York and Washington, DC, USA on 11 September 2001, for which the USA held the Islamist militant al-Qa'ida (Base) organization responsible, the Chinese Government has demanded the extradition of Uygur separatists who had fled from China's often brutal campaign to control the Islamist separatist movement in the Xinjiang Autonomous Region. Although it is difficult to imagine Maoist insurgents in Nepal harbouring or joining Uygur separatists, civil disorder in Nepal has provided an undesirably volatile environment not only on the border of the People's Republic of China, but also India and Pakistan. The divided and factious nature of the Communist Party of Nepal—Maoist (commonly referred to as the Maoists) has not reduced these concerns and, in fact, has added to the apprehension of neighbouring states. The fact that the Nepalese Maoist insurgency is one of the few remaining Maoist movements in the world has not allayed fears for regional security either. For all these reasons, this economic review begins with an analysis of the economics of the Maoist insurgency and then proceeds to review the general economic indicators. In the aftermath of the September 2001 attacks on the USA, the Maoists' militant campaign was universally condemned. US Secretary of State Gen. Colin Powell's assurances of support against the insurgency as part of the USA's global campaign against terrorism, during a meeting with King Gyanendra in January 2002, indicated the rising concern over Nepal's instability. Gen. Powell also promised to develop the two countries' trade links by, for example, reducing trade barriers and reviewing the textile quotas restricting Nepal's exports.

THE ECONOMICS OF THE MAOIST INSURGENCY

The number of people killed during the Maoist insurgency has risen steadily since the movement began in 1996. Between 1996 and 2000 about 1,600 people died, from late November 2001 to May 2002 a further 2,000 were killed; more recent figures suggest that 3,021 people died in January–August 2002. Thus, in 1996–2002 Nepal experienced one of the highest death rates of any struggles between insurgents and a state in the world at that time. According to the Nepalese Informal Sector Service Centre (INSEC), the majority of those killed were Maoists, followed by police officers and soldiers. The death toll in the first half of 2002 equalled the estimated death toll resulting from the insurgency movement during the 1990s. The number of people taken hostage by the Maoists also caused concern. In rural areas, farmers not only faced poverty, but were also at risk of being killed in the conflict as Maoists and security forces fought for local control. By late November 2001 the law and order situation had deteriorated to such an extent that a state of emergency was declared. The temporary reconciliation that followed lasted only briefly before fundamental disagreements about land reform legislation destroyed any possibility of co-operation between the governing Nepali Congress Party (NCP) and Maoist representatives. The state of emergency was still in place in September 2002.

According to one observer, a direct correlation existed between the extent of poverty and the successes of the Maoist insurgency, which explained why the Maoist movement was most active in the poor mid-western region of Nepal. He also suggested that the state was on the verge of defeat by insurgents numbering some 2,000 core fighters and another 10,000 militia. Land reform was not the only Maoist demand. The insurgents also wanted the monarchy to be replaced by a republic and an end to foreign aid and the historically important relationship with India. The Maoists' main strategy in 2001–02 was targeting police officers and police stations, more recently they attacked infrastructure. By attacking infrastructure that was funded largely by foreign aid, Maoists intended to discourage international expectations that the constitutional monarchy would survive in the 12-year-old democracy.

It was also noted that the recent increased death toll compared with earlier periods of political compromise probably indicated the new low-caste leadership of the Maoist movement, which was socially remote from the high-caste, left-wing representation in parliament. The number of women who joined the movement reflected the growing social acceptability of the insurgency. The remoteness of the new leadership was itself a testimony to the growing disaffection between the Nepalese Government and the situation at the grass-roots level.

An important development of the insurgency movement has been its proximity to the capital, Kathmandu. According to one observer, in August 2001 the town of Kirtipur, only 15 km from Kathmandu, openly expressed its allegiance to the Maoists. Earlier in July the Maoists launched an audacious bomb attack outside the home of the Chief Justice. In April 2002 the Maoists set fire to the country residence of the Nepalese Prime Minister, after a spate of similar attacks on other politicians' houses.

It appeared in 2002 that the Maoist insurgency had not only survived, but had grown in strength and popularity, against a background of deep-rooted social and economic problems. In particular, the country's failure to facilitate a more rapid transition to a developed state able to deliver sufficient economic growth and a better standard of living for previously disadvantaged sections of society, encouraged disillusionment in the Government. Ironically, draconian measures to combat the Maoists, for example, the Government's decision to track down Maoists and imprison all politicians who had any connection with the militants, provoked further public opposition to government policy. By mid-2002 the situation had deteriorated to such an extent that the insurgency itself had negatively affected the Nepalese Government's capacity to reform and deliver significant economic growth. Government funds were diverted from development projects to the procurement of supplies and salaries for internal security. In early 2002 all the ministries were directed to reduce non-foreign aid-related development expenditure by 25% and routine expenditure by a further 10%. These extra financial burdens coincided with rapidly declining state revenues generated, in part, by the impact of the insurgency on income from tourism. The Maoist movement adversely affected all sections of the economy. Foreign investment, tourism and infrastructure development have declined or slowed down since 2000. One of the most damaging consequences has been the dramatic decline in inflow (from 25% to 10% in 2000/01) of private foreign direct investment (FDI) as a proportion of approved projects.

KEY ECONOMIC TRENDS

In the 1990s the Nepalese economy experienced persistent growth; in the early 2000s, however, the rate of growth declined. The Asian Development Bank (ADB) reported gross domestic product (GDP) growth of 4.4% in 1999, 6.1% in 2000, 5.0% in 2001 and 3.5% in 2002. This broadly matches other reports; however, ADB projections of 5% GDP growth in 2003 were questioned, owing to the domestic political turmoil that has overtaken Nepal.

Until mid-2002, growth had been facilitated by economic diversification. It was this diversification into the recently declining tourism sector, for example, that had begun to threaten Nepal's economic prospects. Nevertheless, the structure of the Nepalese economy had changed. By the late 1990s Nepal was no longer primarily an agricultural economy. In fact, the agriculture sector's share of GDP declined from 49% in the 1980s to 40% in the late 1990s, while that of service increased to 40%. This structural shift was accompanied by growing overseas remittances that brought prosperity to some sections of the population. Although these structural changes were welcome, Nepal continued to be restrained by the lack of industrialization. Industrial GDP remained at 20% for a lengthy period of time; within this aggregate, manufacturing accounted for about 10%. In 2002 the manufacturing sector remained problematic and had again entered a period of contraction (see below).

The economic diversification that occurred was insufficient to reduce widespread poverty and economic backwardness. Indeed, the number of people living in absolute poverty in Nepal grew rather than diminished during the 1990s. The causes of poverty include ill health, poor hygiene, low education, underemployment and unemployment, and very low wages. Mortality figures in Nepal have declined, yet serious illnesses persist (especially among women and children) and have a detrimental impact on productivity. WHO placed Nepal 150th out of 190 countries in its ranking of the health status of nations. One powerful index of the nature of the problem is that 47% of children under the age of five years are underweight and about 11% are wasting. Women in Nepal have also suffered disproportionately as a result of backwardness: the maternal mortality rate of 540 deaths per 100,000 live births is amongst the highest in the region. At the same time, the average number of hours worked by women exceeds that of men in both rural and urban areas by, on average, two hours. Economic growth has also been hindered by the combined effects of geography, topography, political instability, lack of investment and incentives in agriculture, and the difficulties of competing with other countries in industrial manufacturing. A fall in international confidence in the future of Nepal has meant that the country continues to be heavily dependent on foreign aid as its main source of investment capital. This dependency has encouraged bureaucratic corruption and contributed to the lack of political will to secure the passage of land reform and economic liberalization. Corruption together with administrative inefficiency encouraged Maoist criticisms that the Nepalese Government had been grossly incompetent as well as unwilling to deal with the fundamental question of mass poverty. A comprehensive anti-corruption strategy was being planned in mid-2002 and was scheduled to be implemented in October; however, scepticism was widespread regarding the capacity to change entrenched habits. The country's economic trends were adversely affected by the escalating costs of international trade in the aftermath of the attacks on the USA in September 2001. Nepal, a land-locked nation, depends heavily on freight, insurance and other long distance transport, the costs of which have increased dramatically since the September attack. In summary, the forecasts for Nepal's economy in the short to medium term are no longer optimistic, despite the achievements of the previous decade. Economic growth has been decelerating and it has been widely predicted that the economy will contract while the country experiences serious political instability.

POVERTY AND SOCIO-ECONOMIC BACKWARDNESS

In January 2002 the World Bank ranked Nepal as the 12th poorest country in the world. Although the 2.2% annual average GDP per caput growth in 1980–2000 was recognized as a long-term positive trend, the World Bank concluded that Nepal's medium-term prospects are bleak. According to the UN Development Programme's (UNDP's) *Human Development Report 2002*, in 2000 Nepal was classed as a 'low human development' country and ranked 142nd out of 173 countries. It was less developed than Pakistan (ranked 138th) and more developed than Bangladesh (ranked 145th). According to AusAID (the Australian aid agency) the per caput gross national product (GNP) of Nepal is the lowest in South Asia: US $210 in 2000 compared with US $490 in Pakistan, US $800 in Sri Lanka, US $390 for India, US $400 in Bhutan and US $270 in Bangladesh. An estimated 42% of the population live below the poverty line of US $77 per caput; another 30% just above it. According to the ADB, the poverty indicators for Nepal have remained static since 1991. This figure has been disputed by the Nepalese Government. It insists that poverty has fallen from 42% to 38% of the population. Official estimates, however, have little credibility.

Poverty in Nepal has distinct regional characteristics: 56% of people living in the Himalayas are very poor as well as 42% living in the Terai and 41% living in the Hill regions. An average 44% of rural and 23% of urban people are very poor. These people are always at risk of falling back below the poverty line, owing to minor illnesses, accidents or loss of income. Social and economic inequality remained a major problem in Nepal, thus giving a rational basis to the arguments of the Maoist insurgents. The poorest 20% of households received less than 8% of total income, whilst the richest 20% received about 45%. The Gini index (a measurement of the extent to which the distribution of income among individuals or households deviates from an equal distribution) for Nepal was 36.7 in 1995–96. Chronic seasonal food deficits affected 50% of the population, and in the 1990s there was little improvement in major health indicators. The Ninth Five-Year Plan (1998–2002) seeks to reduce the poverty level to 30%. Nepal remains heavily dependent upon the agricultural sector. At the same time, the capacity for the physical expansion of agriculture is limited by the fact that much of Nepal's land is unsuitable for cultivation. The Himalayan region covers 79% of the landmass, and the Terai, which is an extension of the Gangetic plain, comprises 21%. This small area, the Terai, accounts for the greater part of agricultural output. It also supports the largest proportion of the Nepal population—about 47.7% in 1996, having increased by almost 4% since the early 1980s. Agricultural production needs to move in the direction of intensive technologies, but this is hampered by the lack of many modern inputs. For example, in 2000 the Government continued its attempts to reform the fertilizer industry, but farmers remained reluctant to use fertilizers while they did not have guaranteed access to irrigation water.

The poverty and income disparities of Nepal are reflected in massive community differences, ranging from the prosperous Newars to the extreme poverty of the underprivileged 'untouchable' castes. Vast regional disparities accentuate the uneven nature of development in Nepal: the human development indicators for Kathmandu, for instance, are four times higher than those for the most backward district of Mugu. One significant index of Nepal's economic backwardness is to be found in the demographic data. Nepal's population of about 23.2m. (provisional 2001 census figure) was growing at an annual average of 2.24%. Like other less developed countries, the population is very youthful: some 39% are 14 years or younger. The high population growth rate is likely to persist since mortality remains very high and consequently couples have more babies, in the belief that most will not survive. According to WHO, in 2000 life expectancy at birth was only 58.5 years for males and 58.0 years for women. According to UNDP, in the same year infant mortality was 72 per 1,000 live births and the under-five mortality rate was 100 per 1,000 live births. About 23% of the cohort born in 1997 will not survive to the age of 40 years and about 14% will not survive to the age of 15 years. A comparison of the poverty indicators for 90 developing countries placed Nepal in 77th position, just ahead of Cambodia. In the remote district of Mugu, life expectancy at birth was only 37 years on average. Despite this, between 1980 and 2000 life expectancy increased by a total of about 14 years. As the rate of mortality declined, attention was increasingly focused on morbidity in Nepal. About one-half of the population suffered from iodine deficiency, which causes goitre, and about one-half of the population under 14 years of age had TB/leprosy. The World Bank attempted to summarize the inter-relationship between death and morbidity in a new Disability Adjusted Life Years (DALYs) indicator. This index shows that DALYs lost per 1,000 population in Nepal (366) is higher than in China (117) and India (344), but lower than Sub-Saharan Africa (574). According to an IMF review of recent economic developments in Nepal, social expenditure as a percentage of Nepal's GDP increased from 3.5% to about 6% between 1985 and 2000, but the allocation was still insufficient to lift people out of poverty.

Addressing these aspects of Nepal's poverty is not easy, given the great socio-cultural diversity of the population. In addition to some 60 ethnic groups and castes and 18 official language groups, in 2001 Nepal had about 130,900 refugees, of whom 110,800 were from Bhutan and lived in seven camps in eastern Nepal. The number of displaced persons from Bhutan had decreased to approximately 100,000 by the end of 2001. According to the *Nepal Human Development Report 1998*, Nepal's 'physical ruggedness, the relative salience of feudal and subsistence modes of production and weak articulation of markets within the national space have historically led to the enduring resilience of the localized cultures'. These localized cultures make it very difficult to persuade families to resort to any preventive and curative medical treatments other than traditional ones. The lack of a health-hygiene infrastructure also forces people to fall back on traditional knowledge. According to UNDP, in 1990–98 71% had access to safe water and only 16% to sanitation.

Across the border in India, the information technology 'revolution' is generating enormous opportunities for employment, export earnings and joint ventures with foreign companies. Nepal's capacity to respond to similar opportunities, by contrast, is severely hindered by the lack of educational infrastructure. India shares Nepal's problems of illiteracy, but its universities and institutes of technology annually produce vast numbers of highly trained and skilled labour. In 2000 Nepal's adult literacy rate was only 41.8%. The average length of schooling amongst adults was 1.6 years. Great gender inequalities persisted, with 59.6% of men literate but only 24.0% of women. These estimates remained the same in 2002. The next generation of adults might not be at a greater advantage, in view of the fact that by 2000 compulsory education had been implemented in only seven of Nepal's 40 districts. According to UNICEF, about 48% of school children left the education system before reaching Grade 5. Official figures on secondary-school enrolments are probably exaggerated, but even these figures show that they are equivalent to only about one-third of enrolments in primary schools. Nepal has five universities with about 130,000 students. Moreover, between 1993/94 and 1996/97 the number of diplomas and certificates awarded by the leading university (which enrols about 97% of all university students in Nepal) decreased by 42%, at a time when the country needed more, not fewer, qualified young people.

All these difficulties are perhaps most effectively summarized in the figures depicting unemployment and underemployment in Nepal. Nepal's adult workforce reached some 12m., of which about 5% were unemployed in the late 1990s and about 50% of the population were underemployed and worked for less than 40 hours a week. The level of remuneration also emerged as a major issue, particularly in 1998/99 when the inflation rate rose sharply. Between 1995 and 2000 real wages in both industry and agriculture declined, forcing the Nepalese Government to declare a minimum agricultural wage of NRs 70 (US $1) per day in the Kathmandu valley. A minimum industrial wage was also declared, to little avail. Implementation of minimum wages in other parts of South Asia has been extraordinarily difficult, owing to a lack of political will. It is likely that Nepal will record a similar failure. Not surprisingly, poor families have been compelled to send children to work. According to estimates by the International Labour Organization (ILO), almost one-third of Nepal's children between the ages of five and 14 work, and this child labour accounts for about 10% of the 12m. in Nepal's labour force. According to AusAID, the number of Nepalese children unable to attend school, owing to work obligations, is 5m.

Women in particular, suffer from the burden of poverty and neglect. According to UNDP, in 2000 Nepal was ranked 119th out of 173 countries in the gender-related development index. Gender disadvantages are reflected in all indicators, especially maternal mortality. International donors have reported great difficulties in making gender-based programmes work successfully in Nepal. The gender bias is said to be so acute that externally funded projects are able to make little difference. Women have limited participation in the decision-making process at the highest level; for example, only 3.4% of parliamentary seats are held by women. In fact, many development projects have increased the social and economic burden on women; dam construction has been particularly onerous. The extent of gender bias varies from community to community. Indo-Aryan women, for example, have greater opportunities to assume entrepreneurial roles than the Tibeto-Burmese. Nepalese women are also the victims of people-trafficking, especially across the border into India. It has been estimated that about 250,000 Nepalese girls work in Indian brothels.

In early February 2002 the Nepalese Government presented its new Poverty Reduction Strategy Paper to an assembly of aid donors in Kathmandu. The meeting accepted the paper's recommendations, despite the fact that the new policy would place the Nepalese Government under unprecedented financial pressure. One estimate reckoned that the fiscal deficit would rise to US $400–$500m. The size of the deficit, as well as all the other structural problems, suggest that Nepal will remain dependent on aid for the foreseeable future, as it has done since 1950. At an informal level, there is also the growing conviction that Nepal should be absolved of all its debt commitments and begin anew. However, the discussions about aid and the debt burden are themselves flawed, as they appear not to take into account the problem that the corrupt disbursement of aid funds was one of the reasons that the insurgency grew in strength.

AGRICULTURE AND FORESTRY

Although the services sector has emerged as equally productive, agriculture continues to define the lives of the Nepalese public. Despite diversification, Nepal's economy remains primarily one of subsistence. The majority of the population lives in villages, depends on agriculture for survival and only intermittently finds employment in the services sector. Some 76% of the workforce depends on agriculture for their living. This persistent dependency, notwithstanding the population growth, that since 1983 has increased by at least 6.7m. or 43%, has placed intense pressure on land resources. Limited urbanization and technological stagnation have led to the subdivision and fragmentation of landholdings, leaving 50% of Nepal's farms less than 0.5 ha in size. The pressure of population would be a less serious problem if Nepal could expand agricultural production in the direction of intensive technologies. However, technological innovation has been stagnant and the country's vast water resources have not been harnessed. Only one-third of the land is irrigated, and the incentives to production remain hindered by primitive land tenure arrangements, which have also become the focus of protest by Maoist groups. These structural constraints on agricultural output are more important reasons for the limited success of Nepalese agriculture, than population pressure and the fragmentation of landholdings. Nevertheless, the fragmentation of land has provided Maoists with a growing support base. Between 1981 and 1991, the number of farms of less than 0.5 ha in size increased by 81% and farms between 0.5 and 1 ha grew by 89%. These farmers, pressured by land fragmentation, find the Maoists' arguments appealing.

Long-term trends show that the Nepalese economy has been moving towards the commercialization of agriculture. Taking 1984/85 as the base year, the index of agricultural production in 1999/2000 was 208 for cash crops, 152 for food grains, 186 for other crops, 155 for livestock and 162 overall. On its own, the commercialization of agriculture might be regarded as a positive indicator for change; however, considering the isolated nature of much of Nepal's population and its continued dependence on agriculture, the relative stagnation of food production is not necessarily a sign of progress. Moreover, agricultural production has only just managed to keep up with population growth. Commercialization could contribute towards the development of agri-industries; however, for this to occur the rate of reform of crop production must be greatly accelerated.

To promote agriculture, the Government introduced the Agricultural Perspective Plan which, with the support of the ADB, aims to rationalize inputs into agriculture. The distribution of fertilizers is to be restructured by abolishing subsidies, liberalizing imports and encouraging domestic trade. Privatization of trade in fertilizers has, however, given rise to serious problems with adulteration. Despite all these plans, government spending on agricultural development (measured as a proportion of GDP) declined from 2.8% in 1993/94 to 1.6% in 1997/98.

The budget for 2002/03 recognized the need to assist farmers who were in serious debt to the Agricultural Development Bank for loans issued before 1994. Special arrangements were made to encourage loan repayments with interest at such a rate that would not put the farmers under intense financial pressure. A Special Agricultural Production Program has also begun to meet the needs of farmers in hilly and isolated areas, while a Special Agriculture Development Program has been introduced into a third of Nepal's districts. Although these initiatives display some effort to address the needs of agriculture, they do not supply enough of the expenditure required to develop a comprehensive irrigation system. With government expenditure increasingly focusing on the country's internal security, the capacity to accelerate development is even more constrained.

One index of Nepal's dependence on agriculture is the economic instability caused by the failure of the monsoon. Years of accelerated economic growth typically reflect good and timely rains, whilst declines in economic growth rates are usually, in part, caused by inclement weather, flooding, poor timing or the lack of rain, as in 1990/91, 1994/95, 1996/97 and 1997/98. However, despite the constraints, Nepal possesses much agricultural potential. The climate and topography are suitable for growing tea and jute but unlike its neighbours, Nepal produces neither in large volume. Nepal used to produce jute in abundance, and research in Bangladesh has suggested that modern processing of jute can again turn this fibre into a commodity of great importance to the world economy. Instead, Nepal's agriculture has been concentrated on a narrow range of food and cash crops. The contrast with neighbouring India is dramatic, considering the latter's revolution in dairy produce and a wide range of horticultural goods. Food grains accounted for about 67% of agricultural output in Nepal in 1998/99. The principal crops are rice, maize, wheat, millet and barley. Cash crops constituted about one-third of agricultural production, and consisted of sugar cane, potato, oil-seeds, jute and tobacco, in descending order of importance. Jute, once a major crop, accounted for 0.4% of the output of cash crops in 2000. Since 1975 foodgrain production has expanded very slowly, at the average annual rate of about 2.2%. Growth in cash-crop production has been much better—about 6.5% per annum during the same period—but unremarkable, in view of the new agricultural technologies that have become available in South Asia.

The principal problem of Nepalese agriculture has been that of low yields. This is a relatively new problem. During the 1960s Nepal had the highest yields in South Asia and met its own needs for food grains. By 2000 its productivity was between 10% and 30% below that of other South Asian countries. This clearly reflects the lack of investment in agriculture. As a result, since 1980 Nepal has been a food-importing country, in a region largely characterized by food self-sufficiency. In 1998 the Government of Nepal signed the Second Agricultural Program with the ADB in order to address the problem of agricultural reform across a broad front. The strategy focused largely on market-orientated solutions and some institutional reforms, but did not address the problem of land reform or land tenure and so would be unlikely to curb the activities of the Maoist insurgents or to provide sufficient incentives to increase agricultural yields. In late 2001 the NCP introduced new legislation that promised to address the problem of rural inequality. The limits imposed on landholdings, however, undermined popular support for the programme. In the Terai, for example, the limit was a generous 6.9 ha, compared with the Maoist demand of 2.7 ha.

Forestry is a major contributor to national income, despite the long-term destruction of Nepal's forests. Between 1950 and 1980 almost 50% of the forests were destroyed. Poverty itself led to deforestation, as wood and its residues are the primary source of fuel for the poor. Deforestation in turn increased poverty, as the time taken to forage grows with the depletion of natural resources. Fuelwood collection, taking as much as 4.7 hours per headload in some parts of Nepal, is arduous work performed by women and children. The poorest families do not collect or use fuelwood; instead they forage for residues left on the ground. The result is a reduction of the amount of humus, leading to poorer soil quality. At the upper end of the economic scale, families grow their own fuelwood or substitute fuelwood with alternatives. Hence, any decline in the incidence of poverty in Nepal would contribute to conserving residues and fuelwood by encouraging the poor to change their fuel consumption patterns.

Traditional energy sources accounted for 87.3% of total energy consumption in 1998/99, most of this being fuelwood (90%). Forest cover was reduced from 60% of the total land area in the early 1950s to about 30% (8m. ha) in the early 1980s. In the period 1979–91 the annual rate of deforestation continued at 1.5% and resulted in the destruction of 99,000 ha. Some of the worst deforestation occurred on the fragile ecologies of the Himalayan slopes. Forest cover was also lost on the plains where land was colonized rapidly from the early 1960s by migrants from the overpopulated hills and from India. In the hills themselves, large tracts of land were cleared many decades ago, and the remaining forests have been thinned and degraded.

The Forest Act of 1992 was introduced to encourage people to own and use their own forest rather than national or state-owned forests. In 1994 the Forest Regulation Act fixed the prices of timber, fruits and other produce and introduced a cess on animals grazing on forest lands. The 1992 Act encouraged the establishment of Forest User Groups to manage 3.5m. ha of community forest. However, the exclusion of the poorest families from these groups and new prices and cesses on forest products hindered environmental protection and gave rise to community discord and resentment. During 1996/97 reforestation was carried out on 2,799 ha of land. Under the community forestry programme, 8.25m. saplings were planted in 1997/98 and 7.76m. were planted in the first nine months of 1998/99. The cultivation of herbs in forest areas was also actively encouraged in an attempt to develop non-timber products and mixed forestry. However, these initiatives have not had a significant impact, owing to poor implementation and the lack of involvement of local people, who are heavily dependent upon forests for the supply of energy, honey, medicinal herbs and fodder.

INDUSTRY

An estimated of 21.9% GDP was derived from industry, making Nepal one of the least industrialized countries in the world. During the 1990s industrial growth was unremarkable, and since then has been declining in response to a significant downturn in global demand for Nepalese products. By early 2002 this unimpressive record had been confirmed by an estimated 30% to 50% decline in the value of total manufactures. One-third of Nepal's industrial output was produced by the garments and woollen carpet industries. The carpet industry remains far more important to the Nepalese economy than the garments industry because it provides employment for more than 2m. people, compared with the 30,000 employed in the garments sector.

Nepalese industry is seriously constrained by many factors. Production is highly concentrated in a few areas and takes place mainly in small factories. Small-scale cottage industries, which produce baskets, textiles and edible oils, account for around 60% of total industrial output. The remaining 40% of industrial production is derived from modern industries, but at the lower level of the technological scale: brick and tile manufacturing, cement and other construction materials, paper, carpet-making, foodgrain processing, vegetable-oil extraction, sugar-refining and breweries. Labour-intensive industries, such as carpet and garment production, also have serious underlying difficulties with European buyers who are under intense consumer pressure not to purchase goods made by child labour. On the other hand, the potential for large-scale, heavy industry is greatly constrained by the lack of mineral resources and modern entrepreneurship, together with the strong competition from Indian industries across the border. Indian manufacturers have traditionally established factories in Nepal to avoid US import quotas on Indian shipments, but then close the factories down when this strategy is no longer required. Furthermore, the doubts surrounding the implications of Nepal joining the World Trade Organization (WTO) contributes to the uncertainty in export orientation. Nepal has applied for membership of the WTO, but it is too soon to determine whether membership would help or hinder Nepal's development. Given the trend towards growing corporate power within the WTO, it is unlikely that Nepal will find membership particularly beneficial.

Thus, it could indeed be the case that Nepal's comparative advantage exists in other areas, such as tourism (in particular eco-tourism and winter sports) and energy exports. However, in the early 21st century the option of expanding revenues from tourism had collapsed dramatically, largely in response to international perceptions of Nepal as an unsafe tourist destination, owing to the Maoist insurgency.

TOURISM

The Government diversified into the tourism sector in order to develop Nepal's sources of economic growth and small-scale employment opportunities. In the period 1988–99, this strategy appeared to be working: the number of tourists visiting Nepal each year increased greatly from about 163,000 foreign tourists in 1980, to almost 500,000 in 1999. From 1994, tourist arrivals in Nepal grew annually by between 6% and 11% and by the late 1990s the industry employed some 300,000 people. The Government aimed to attract 1m. tourists by 2010. This strategy, however, started to founder in 2000 when tourist arrivals declined by 6%. By November 2001 income from tourism had fallen by 50% compared with the previous year. Despite Nepal's extraordinary beauty and the growing interest in eco-tourism, domestic and international political instability have had a negative impact on Nepal's appeal as a holiday destination. The September 2001 terrorist attacks on the USA have discouraged people from taking holidays abroad, while the global efforts against terrorism have focused international attention more sharply on Nepal's domestic problems, namely the insurgency and the associated bomb attacks. Tourist arrivals into Nepal in 2001 decreased by about one-third compared with the previous year and the downward trend is expected to continue indefinitely.

The expanded tourist facilities developed during the 1990s now face the serious risk of significant under-utilization. By 1999 there were 785 hotels and 32,214 beds in Nepal and tourism had become the third major source of foreign-exchange earnings, although the percentage decreased from 26.6% in 1986/87 to 12.9% in 1999/2000. In 1999/2000 this sector contributed only 3.1% of GDP. Even at its peak, the Nepalese tourist industry has been unable to attract high-spending visitors. The majority of tourists do not spend much money in Nepal, preferring to trek and stay in low-budget accommodation. At the height of the tourist campaign in 1998, the average spending per foreign tourist in Nepal remained relatively low. In 1999, however, earnings from tourism increased by a dramatic 12%, and, according to IMF figures, the average tourist spent US $470. The country of origin of tourists has remained relatively static. The figures for 2000 are roughly indicative of the long-term situation: about 10% of tourists come from the USA and Canada, 37% from Europe, and between 21% and 28% from India. The latter are less wealthy than the rest. Also, there is concern that a large proportion of the tourist revenue does not remain within Nepal because of the high import content of expenditure by foreign tourists; even the less affluent visitor requires goods of a quality that can only be imported. Finally, the Government's tourist policy has been too heavily focused on the Kathmandu valley, with the result that the number of hotels in that area now exceeds demand. From March 2001 the tourist industry faced a new problem when workers organized strikes, insisting that hotel bills include a 10% service charge to be paid to employees instead of tipping, which is a far less reliable way of augmenting personal income. The Government and Supreme Court declared that these strikes were illegal and a threat to the country's competitiveness. The Kathmandu valley has since become a less popular tourist destination, owing to the proximity of the Maoist insurgency.

The Government has adopted a number of initiatives to increase the flow of foreign visitors and to change the composition of the tourists. New training centres were established in order to provide the tourism sector with the requisite skilled workforce. Special promotional efforts were also undertaken, such as the designation of 1998 as 'Visit Nepal Year'. The latter, however, was not very successful in attracting high-spending visitors, although it did increase the number of tourists from within Nepal and neighbouring countries. In 2002 the Government undertook the tourist promotional effort 'Destination Nepal Year'. A whole range of measures was taken to reduce visa fees and other tourist cesses, to open more peaks for mountaineering and to relax the regulations controlling the activities of tourists. Nepal also signed a special agreement with China to facilitate Chinese tourism to Nepal, the only new tourist market to be developed in recent years.

On balance, Nepal has not managed to utilize its tourist potential, despite the growing demand for eco-tourism and the location of eight out of 10 of the world's highest peaks within its borders. In 1999 the Government replaced the Department of Tourism with the Nepal Tourism Board, which includes representatives from the public and private sectors charged with the task of developing a long-term strategy for promoting Nepal as a tourist destination. The International Finance Corporation (the private-sector affiliate of the World Bank) recorded its approval of these changes by investing some US $60m. in tourist and hydroelectric power (HEP) projects in the country.

Despite its contribution to the diversification of Nepal's economy away from agriculture, and towards the development of a service sector, the tourist industry remains problematic. Regular strikes, the Maoist rebellion, the massacre of most of the royal family and the terrorist attacks on the USA, have all contributed to a negative perception of Nepal's tourist potential. It is unlikely that this opinion will recede in the short to medium term.

ENERGY

Energy is another resource that has yet to be fully exploited. Nepal is surrounded by energy-deficient economies, in particular India and China, and has enormous quantities of domestic energy locked in its hydroelectricity potential. Even after allowing for a range of environmental concerns about hydroelectricity, Nepal's capacity to export energy to its neighbours is inestimable. Despite this, the economic wealth of hydroelectricity is only now being slowly exploited. In 2000/01 Nepal's total energy consumption was estimated at 8.0m. metric tons of oil equivalent. Traditional sources provided 86% of total energy consumption (fuelwood 78%, farm residue 4% and livestock residue 6%). Only 14% was supplied by the modern commercial sector (petroleum products 9%, coal 2.6% and hydroelectricity 1%). Nepal has the highest per caput HEP generation potential in the world, which is estimated to be 83,000 MW. At the end of 1999 only 300 MW of hydroelectricity was actually being harnessed (equivalent to only 0.3% of the total potential). The demand for power within Nepal has been growing by about 10% annually, but this has not been sufficient to compel the economy to utilize its remaining capacities. Paradoxically, despite increasing domestic demand, only 16% of the Nepalese population have access to electrical power, and throughout the 1990s industrial growth was hampered by power shortages.

Urbanization and the associated increase in the number of vehicles contributed to a growing demand for imported petroleum products, which reached 509,000 kilolitres in the first nine months of 1997/98—an increase of 14.5% over the corresponding period in the previous year—at a cost of NRs 7,418.1m. (about US $119m.). Of these imports in the first nine months of 1997/98, diesel accounted for 41.5%, kerosene 41.1%, petrol 6.7%, aviation fuel 6.6% and furnace oil 4.0%.

Recognition of the export potential of Nepal by the Government led to the 1993 Nepal Electricity Act, which opened the power sector to private investment, including foreign capital. This Act was supported by the Power Trade Agreement between Nepal and India, and the Nepalese Government's decision to prioritize 15 projects for foreign investment. There were also indications that China was considering ways of handling the energy shortage in its western, border provinces by importing energy from neighbouring countries. Nepal could be involved in any such future arrangements. Foreign aid was also vital in developing Nepal's hydroelectricity, but growing concerns by international environmental groups about ecological damage rendered this an uncertain source of support. In 1995, for example, the World Bank withdrew its support from the controversial 402-MW Arun III project.

The development of Nepal's power potential was also hindered by the lack of agreement on the implementation of various international treaties and opposition from environmental groups. In June 1997, for example, India and Nepal endorsed the Mahakali Treaty, which was supposed to facilitate joint development and sharing of hydroelectricity, irrigation and flood control. However, implementation was slow, owing to disputes about the size of the project, disagreements about the use of the waters and opposition from environmental lobbies. Foreign private investment in hydroelectricity was also problematic. The US Enron Renewable Energy Corporation, for instance, withdrew its US $6,000m. investment application for a project in April 1998. Paradoxically, the events leading to Enron's withdrawal brought stern criticism from the Nepalese communists who would have preferred Enron to stay. In retrospect, it was suggested that Nepal was shielded from the economic damage that other countries experienced, owing to the collapse of Enron in 2002. Unlike Enron, in 2000 the Australian company, SMEC, continued with its construction of the 750-MW West Seti hydroelectric dam in West Nepal, at a cost of US $1,000m. Some 10% of the electricity produced will be given free of charge to Nepal and the rest exported to the energy-deficient states of northern India. India would also benefit, as the dam would help to regulate the flow of water into the parts of northern India susceptible to floods. Export arrangements with India had not yet been finalized, owing to continued disagreements over the price of power and the rate of supply. The dam will be not only the largest hydroelectric project, but also Nepal's single biggest ever foreign investment project, and the country's first experiment with a build-own-operate-transfer (BOOT) development strategy. In 1997, at the time of the signing of the contract, the export value of energy from this project to India was estimated at US $380m. and was considered an acceptable strategy to counterbalance Nepal's trade deficit with India. Although there is great economic pressure for hydroelectric development in Nepal, this option remains very controversial, owing to the ongoing debate about the environmental impact of dams and the risks they pose. Furthermore, hydroelectricity is not an approach that can solve all Nepal's energy problems. In an effort to improve efficiency, Nepal has concentrated on the privatization of hydroelectricity. In July 2000 the first privately-owned generator began production; however, by April 2001 power failures had begun to recur. This is due to the fact that most hydroelectricity in Nepal is generated by 'run-of-river' projects that depend on good rainfall or melting snow. Dry weather is a constant threat to production, affecting both private and state facilities. Privatization of the state-controlled power plants has also been proceeding slowly. In March 2002 the Government decided to privatize the Butwal Power Company; however, privatization is likely to be delayed, owing to the damage caused to some of the infrastructure when Maoists attacked parts of the Jhimruk power station.

TRANSPORT, COMMUNICATIONS AND TRADE TREATIES

Nepal is a land-locked country, which shares 1,236 km of its border with China and 1,690 km with India. Nepal's location has produced many obstacles to the development of its international trade, much of which depends on the goodwill of neighbouring countries. The topography of Nepal has exacerbated the problems of communication, both on the international and domestic front. Given the difficult terrain, Nepal should have more roads to compensate for the difficulties of building railways and the lack of navigable rivers. However, according to the World Bank's 'normalized roads index', which measures the actual road mileage compared with what one would expect to find given a country's socio-economic variables, Nepal is ranked low amongst the poorer countries: 70 out of 119 nations in the late 1990s. Moreover, Nepal's roads are in poor condition and hard to reach. In mid-2001 Nepal had 15,458 km of roads of which only 30% were black-topped, and the rest temporary. However, as a World Bank report noted, a more serious problem than the quality of the roads was the complete lack of roads in many parts of rural Nepal. The average walking time to a dirt road that would allow a vehicle to pass was 3 hours and 29 minutes in 1999. The average walking time to a paved road was 5 hours and 39 minutes. Despite having 45 airports, Nepal has only one international airport and only five airports with tarred runways. Telephone and telegraphic communications are also poor. There were only an estimated 298,100 telephones in 2001, 170,000 television receivers in 2000 and an estimated 840,000 radios in 1997. Although the modern system of communications is poor, traditional trade and transport are very effective, as shown by Nepal's role in the international drug-trading system. Nepal itself is an illicit producer of cannabis and a transit route for opium derivatives from South-East Asia to Europe, the USA and Australia.

Since the 1973 Non-Aligned Summit in Algiers, Algeria, Nepal has considered itself a neutral buffer between India and China. Despite this, Nepal's foreign relations and trade have tended to be dominated by the influence of India, beginning in the 1950s with the Treaty of Trade and Commerce and the Citizenship Act. The former established Nepal's right to import and export through Indian territory without customs being imposed on the goods in transit, and the latter allowed Indians to migrate to the Nepalese Terai and become Nepalese citizens. More recently, however, Nepal has developed stronger relations on its northern borders with China. In 1989 Nepal decided to buy weapons from China, and China decided to build a road infrastructure linking the two countries. These developments displeased India, which immediately retaliated by suspending trade with Nepal. The restoration of democracy in Nepal from the early 1990s again improved relations with India. However, the relationship with China continued to grow in importance, especially given China's decision to prioritize the development of Great Western China, namely the border regions, many of which lie adjacent to Nepal.

In addition to transit trade, China is exploring ways of encouraging more bilateral trade. The recent acceleration of infrastructure development in Tibet, Hingham and Xinjiang by China promises to boost demand for Nepalese products, especially energy. Moreover, a considerable domestic trade has developed between eastern and north-western Nepal via a transit trade which takes Nepal's goods along a Chinese highway running parallel to the Nepal–China border on the Tibetan side. By 2000 four border crossings were open at Yari, Timureghadi, Tatopanii and Olangchunggola, and another 200 could be brought into operation. These border crossings are rapidly proving an important economic addition to the main Kodari highway from Kathmandu to Lhasa, a link that was built in 1960. Plans to build a superhighway between Lhasa and Shanghai also open up the possibility of exporting commodities via a new sea outlet in China rather than through India, although the long distances suggest that the freight costs will be prohibitive. New agreements were reached in 1999 for direct flights between Kathmandu and Lhasa and Kathmandu and Shanghai. In 2000 China and Nepal celebrated 45 years of bilateral relations with mutual visits by ministers to discuss, among other issues, common interests in the development of tourism in Tibet and Nepal. China has encouraged these developments in many ways, including the provision of aid. China has been a major bilateral aid donor to Nepal. China has also emerged as one of the largest foreign investors in Nepal, especially in the tourist sector. In February–March 2001, links were further strengthened by the visit to Nepal by the Chinese Minister of National Defence followed by King Birendra's visit to China. The Chinese Minister pointedly did not meet Nepal's communist leaders.

Despite the improvement of Nepal-China relations, India remains Nepal's primary partner, as demonstrated by the frequent amendments to the Trade and Transit Treaty (TTT), first signed in 1960. Following amendments in 1971, the treaty provided road transport facilities, warehouse space and port facilities in Calcutta (now known as Kolkata). In 1976 the treaty was extended, and then replaced in 1978 by two separate treaties, one dealing with bilateral Indo-Nepalese trade and the other allowing Nepal to expand its trade with other countries. In March 1989 India decided not to extend these treaties in response to Nepal's weapons deal with China, and closed 13 of the 15 transit points through which most of Nepal's foreign trade was conducted. In April Nepal announced a new customs tariff system, whereby imports from India no longer received privileged treatment. Uniform import duties were imposed on all imports, regardless of country of origin. In the short term, Nepal's foreign trade deteriorated until trade relations with India were normalized in June 1990 and the transit points reopened. In January 1996 the Trade and Transit Treaty was replaced by two separate agreements: the Nepal-India Trade Agreement and the Nepal-India Transit Agreement. With few exceptions, the trade agreement gave Nepal preferential access to the Indian market by allowing imports of all manufactures without incurring Indian duty. The Nepal-India Transit Agreement, automatically renewed after seven years, made it easier for Nepal to access Indian ports. Prior to reaching this agreement in June 1997, the Indian Government extended a further courtesy to Nepal by providing a new transit route to Bangladesh through Indian territory (see History). As a result of the 1996 agreement, bilateral trade between Nepal and India has grown significantly: exports increased by 475% and imports by 67% in the period 1995/96 to 2000/01. In that time, India's share of Nepal's total trade grew from 30% to 40%. The trade links between India and Nepal will be further increased when the dry port at Birgunj becomes operational. Construction of this dry port was completed in December 2000, but was not yet functioning in mid-2002, owing to ongoing disagreements between Nepal and India on a range of issues, including the Customs Tariff Agreement. Expenses incurred by transactions in cross-border trade are expected to reduce by about 40%, owing to the new dry port facility. A more recent factor that has brought Nepal closer to India has been the Maoist insurgency, common to Nepal and north-eastern India. In March 2002 Nepal and India agreed to collaborate in controlling cross-border militant activity and to conduct joint initiatives in trade facilitation and flood control. In the same month the 1996 trade treaties between Nepal and India were reconfirmed and extended for a further five years, but with some revisions, including the imposition of tariffs on Nepalese exports made from non-Nepalese inputs, and quotas on ghee, yarn, copper wire and zinc oxide. These relatively modest changes are likely, nevertheless, to place great pressure on Nepal's competitive position at a time when its industrial capacity has been limited by the disruption to infrastructure and transport, caused by the Maoist insurgency. Moreover, Nepal's status within the US market as a provider of clothing and textiles will also be challenged by new WTO rules. The only factor likely that has made the US market more lenient in its attitude towards Nepal's exports is the US Government's concern over Nepal's domestic instability. Anything that penalises the Nepalese economy contributes to even greater support for the Maoists.

Nepal's participation in the South Asian Association for Regional Co-operation (SAARC), the regional headquarters of which is located in Kathmandu, demonstrates the country's stronger links with South Asia, rather than China. Although SAARC was not particularly active in the first decade or so after its establishment in 1983, from the mid-1990s it emerged as a regional economic grouping of growing significance. That growth, however, was thwarted by rising hostility between India and Pakistan. The result was that SARRC did not meet for three years from 1999 to January 2002. It remains to be seen what impact the South Asia Free Trade Agreement (SAFTA) of 2001 will have. The accelerated level of hostility between India and Pakistan suggests that SAARC is destined to play a mute role in the development of Nepal. Perhaps the clearest indication of the strong link between Nepal and India is that the Nepalese currency was pegged to the Indian rupee in February 1993, at the value of NRs 1.6 per Rs 1. The Indian rupee continues to be the international standard against which Nepal values its national currency. SAARC might have helped Nepal increase its exports to Bangladesh. During a visit to Bangladesh in January 2001 by Nepal's Minister of Foreign Affairs, Bangladesh agreed to implement zero tariffs on Nepali imports. Bangladesh is also keen to promote cross-border trade and provide Nepal with trade routes to South and South-East Asia.

FOREIGN TRADE

In recent years India has re-emerged as Nepal's dominant trading partner. In 2001 30% of Nepal's exports went to India and India accounted for 37% of Nepal's imports. Nepal's imports were also derived from Argentina, China, the United Arab Emirates (UAE) and Singapore, but neither partner was considered a serious threat to India's trading status, accounting for only 16%, 13%, 6% and 5% of imports, respectively. The largest market for exports in 2001 was the USA, accounting for 31% of total exports. Germany was also an important export market, accounting for 12%, but Nepal's neighbour, China, was a fairly minor partner. There has been a noticeable change in the geographical composition of Nepal's total trade (imports plus exports) since the early 1970s when India's trade share was 82%. However, the degree of diversification has been disappointing and India is set to remain Nepal's largest market into the foreseeable future.

An analysis of the commodity composition of Nepal's foreign trade suggests a similar history to that of diversification, in other words a period of growth followed by decline. In the early 1980s agricultural products, such as rice, timber, maize and jute accounted for some 75% of total exports. By 1990 this had changed dramatically, with manufactured goods and handicrafts, such as garments and carpets, together accounting for 75% of exports. Since then, garments and carpets have declined in their relative importance: in 2000/01 they represented 24% and 15% of total export earnings, respectively. In the intervening period, another manufactured product, toothpaste, emerged as the fourth most important export item, accounting for 5% of exports. More traditional agri-products such as ghee and jute still played a role by contributing 6.5% and 2.6%, respectively, to foreign-exchange earnings.

The main threat to Nepal's export income in the early 2000s was not diversification, but the decline in global demand for carpets and garments. Apart from the occasional short-term opportunities, for example following the imposition of sanctions on India by some of its major partners, in protest against the nuclear tests in 1998, Nepal is struggling with the long-term trend of rising global competition. In 2001/02 there was a massive decline in Nepal's garment exports and, consequently, two-thirds of Nepal's garment factories ceased production. Nepal has begun to face competition from Africa and even western China. Even the export of pashmina shawls, in 1999/2000 the third largest group of exported goods, has since been adversely affected by declining demand. Only Indian pashmina appears to have retained its value on global markets. In January 2002 the USA recognized the urgency of assisting Nepal's foundering textile industry, in order to help prevent a domestic fiscal crisis that would have a negative impact on the state's capacity to deal with domestic terrorism and, hence, cross-border terrorism. As a result, the USA promised to review US trade regulations against Nepal in order to give Nepal a greater chance to increase its export earnings and, consequently, manage the economy more effectively.

Government statistics, however, may not give an accurate picture of Nepal's trade. In particular, there is extensive smuggling across the open Indo-Nepalese border. In 1998 the President of the Federation of Nepalese Chambers of Commerce and Industry estimated that this unofficial trade accounted for as much as 65% of the country's entire trade. Smuggling has also prevented the Nepalese Government from increasing revenues from customs duties. During the first eight months of 2000/01, however, customs collections increased by 18% partly as a result of increased surveillance of the borders by the Royal Nepal Army.

Equally poorly documented is the contribution that the export of human labour makes to the Nepalese economy. This export trade dates back to the first Anglo-Ghurkha War of 1814–16. In early 2000 Nepalese citizens were still serving in foreign armies: an estimated 48,000 in the Indian army and another 3,400 in the British army. Nepal also has an estimated 26,000 British army pensioners and 105,000 retired Nepalese Indian servicemen. In addition to the earnings of currently employed soldiers, the pensions alone brought some NRs 6,200m. into Nepal in the first eight months of 1998/99. Beyond these remittances, there are the extra earnings of at least another 392,000 non-military Nepalis working in about 20 foreign countries, including Brunei, Hong Kong, India, Japan, Singapore and the UAE. Although figures on the exact number of these overseas workers and their remittances are not reliable, it has been estimated that there might be about 1m. people working abroad. Nepalese workers in India alone, send NRs 40,000m. each year back to Nepal. Malaysia has become the most recent overseas market for Nepalese workers. According to IMF estimates, in 1999 there was a great increase in the inflows of foreign remittances: pension payments rose by 44% to US $80m. and earnings of overseas Nepalese labourers increased by 29% to US $315m. In the first eight months of 2000/01 an additional 26,000 Nepalis went abroad on short-term contracts. Nepal's overseas diplomatic missions have played an important role in encouraging overseas employment and have negotiated with some 17 countries for the easier passage of Nepalese contract workers. According to 2002 World Bank estimates, overseas remittances increased by 145% in 1999–2001. In 2001 remittances reached an estimated US $400m., equivalent to the total official foreign aid received by Nepal. Indeed, remittances in recent years have been one of the few areas of economic growth. They are such a source of national and personal prosperity, that as part of the Government's fight against Maoist insurgents, some 100,000 young people from the regions most affected by the insurgency will be sent abroad to find work in 2002/03.

In summary, Nepal is having great difficulty in promoting an export-orientated growth strategy, largely because freight costs are so high for such a land-locked country, and because certain important trade markets important have not been very sympathetic to Nepal's development needs. For example, the Indian Government often opposes Nepalese imports, claiming that products, such as ghee, do not meet India's health regulations. In 2001/02 Indian ghee producers opposed ghee imports from Nepal into India, claiming unfair competition. It was known that Nepal imports duty-free palm oil from Malaysia and processes it for re-export to India. The Indian Government insists that it will not treat Nepalese imports generously unless the constituents of those imports 'originate' in Nepal. In mid-2002 there remained an impasse in the trade dispute over tariffs and the certificate of origin. Nepal's dependency on imports from India, on the other hand, is pertinently displayed by its import of gold, which is later re-exported to India. Gold and silver together account for 12% of commodity imports, exceed only marginally by imports of petroleum. Other imported items of note are basic manufactures and machinery and transport equipment. Textiles represent some 7% of imports, which is surprising given that Nepal is also an exporter of textiles.

The volume of imports and exports into Nepal fluctuates from year to year, but the underlying pattern has been a persistent trade deficit that in 1999/2000 represented some 60% of the total value of exports. Nevertheless, in 2001/02 the trade deficit declined in value by 7.3%. Since 1997 Nepal has had a persistent current-account deficit. In 1998, however, the current-account deficit decreased significantly from US $388m. to US $67m. Thereafter, the deficit increased again to US $256m. and US $277m. in 1999 and 2000, respectively. The deficit continued to enlarge in 2001/02. Overall, the balance of payments remained in surplus, owing largely to foreign aid, in the form of both grants and loans from bilateral and multilateral agencies. In 1998/99, however, the surplus declined for various reasons, including a decrease in private and official capital inflows, less aid from India, and a reduction by US $9m. of FDI. By mid-2002 the balance-of-payments surplus achieved in 2000/01 had been converted into a deficit, largely owing to the continued decline of capital imports.

There is, however, reason for optimism. There has been a slight, long-term decline in Nepal's debt ratio. In 1998/99 despite a slight increase in external debt (to US $2,700m.) the total debt of Nepal as a proportion of GDP decreased to under 54%. According to the ADB, in 2000/01 it had declined further to less than 47%. Nepal's capacity to finance the debt increased in 1995–2001: the debt-revenue relationship in 2001 decreased from 459% to 410% and the debt-export ratio declined from 644% to 350%. These modest but positive developments were under serious threat in 2002/03 by the economic impact of the Maoist insurgency. Revenue collection during the latter half of 2001 reached only 37% of the 2001/02 target. This has had an adverse effect on Nepal's capacity to pay its debt; some 13% of the total budget for 2001/02 was allocated for debt repayments. In mid-April 1997 foreign-currency reserves stood at NRs 45,409m., having increased by NRs 971.1m., compared with the level of reserves at the corresponding period in 1995/96. This was sufficient to cover imports for six months. By mid-2000 Nepal's foreign-currency reserves had increased to NRs 92,061.8m., which was enough to sustain imports for 10.5 months. In 2002 reserves were sufficient to sustain imports for one year.

Economic reform of Nepal's trade regime has proceeded very rapidly in contrast to the reform of the domestic industrial sector. According to the IMF, Nepal has one of the most liberal trade regimes in the world. Its average tariff rate is 14%, but the effective rate is about one-half of that. Hardly any import restrictions, such as in the form of quotas apply to Nepal, and the country intends to maintain this liberal regime as part of its strategy to join the WTO.

FOREIGN AID

Foreign aid plays a vital role in the Nepalese economy. In 1998 total aid reached US $404.3m., of which 54% came from donor countries and 46% from multilateral organizations, while 37% was in the form of loans. These proportions remained virtually unchanged throughout the 1990s. The country's balance-of-payments position remained positive because of the inflow of aid. However, it is widely acknowledged that despite massive amounts of aid, the structural difficulties that plague Nepal's economy have not been solved by foreign aid. External aid has also increased the foreign indebtedness of Nepal. In 1975 the ratio of total external debt to GDP was only 2%, but by the mid-1990s this had increased to 57.5%. In 1997 the debt ratio declined to 48.6%, reflecting the Government's new policy of reducing the level of dependency, and rose to 54.2% in 1998. In 2000/01 it declined further to less than 47%. Foreign-aid dependence increased in 2000/01, with foreign assistance funding 58% of all development projects, a significant rise from the 47% level maintained during the previous five years. Recent inflows of foreign aid typically reflect the international community's desire to encourage democracy in the region. Historically, however, US aid has been primarily motivated by the foreign policy objective of preventing Nepal from falling into China's sphere of influence. The advent of multi-party democracy in 1990 led to increased aid flows to Nepal, especially from multilateral donors. However, Nepal's capacity to absorb foreign aid remained extremely low, mainly because of the inefficiency of public administration and widespread corruption. Of total aid commitments in 1995/96, 86% was utilized, although this figure declined significantly to 38% of total commitments in 1996/97.

According to official estimates, more than 65% of total government development expenditure was financed by foreign aid in the Eighth Plan of 1992–97. The Ninth Plan (1997–2002) sought to reduce this to 58%. The most important bilateral donors are China, Denmark, Germany, India, the United Kingdom and the USA, while the most important multilateral lenders are the World Bank, the ADB, and various UN agencies. The USA was the largest source of aid in the early 1960s, but India quickly superseded it. At about the same time, China began to provide Nepal with aid. By the mid-1970s a new pattern began to establish itself. This persisted into the 1990s with Indian aid leading the way, and US and Chinese aid following in roughly equal proportions. US interest in Nepal declined after 1970, but the economic liberalization of Nepal and the opportunities in hydroelectricity are changing this. However, the dangers of the Maoist campaign could provoke a reassessment of Nepal as an aid receiver.

The ADB commenced its aid programme in Nepal in 1966. A total of 102 loans worth US $1,300m. have been funded since then, of which 27 were in operation at the end of 2001. The strategic situation of Nepal and its status as one of the least developed countries in the world resulted in an element of competition among the donors as regards aid to Nepal, and this aggravated the problem of poor utilization and corruption in the management of aid resources. In 1999 the ADB introduced a revised aid policy for Nepal that stressed the importance of governance, the involvement of the private sector in development projects and principles of gender equity, sub-regional development and decentralization of development objectives and programmes. Dealing with many of these difficulties, however, also requires economic growth; for example, it was difficult to eliminate corruption among civil servants below the rank of officer, when in 1996 their salaries and allowances were lower, in real terms, than in 1985. Stability was considered particularly important from late 2001, with the result that the ADB gave Nepal a loan of US $30m. to address the administrative problems that hinder good governance.

An important aid project, implemented by the ADB, was the Small Farmers' Development Program. In 1997/98 about 170,000 families were involved in this programme which sought, among other aims, to assist farmers with small plots located in Nepal's hills to combat deforestation, soil erosion and landslides. In recent years, however, foreign aid has also paid attention to the needs of landless labourers and urban squatters. An ADB-financed Microcredit Project for Women provides small loans to enable women to repay debts by founding small enterprises to keep milk buffaloes, establishing snack-food businesses or other micro-business concerns. Alternative credit schemes of this kind are the only alternative to the informal loans market that accounts for 80% of rural loans, typically at exorbitant rates of interest. Rural indebtedness, in turn, fostered the maintenance of *kamaiya* or bonded labour. Although bonded labour was formally abolished in July 2000 (see History), many government departments were unaware of the proposed change and were ill-prepared to implement it. In the mean time, landlord resistance was mounted in the form of a writ to the Supreme Court of Nepal in August 2000.

FOREIGN DIRECT INVESTMENT

In contrast to Nepal's dependence on external aid, FDI has been minimal and its share of total available FDI has been declining. Between 1995 and 1998 FDI averaged merely NRs 900m. a year, equivalent to about 0.006% of foreign aid. Given that FDI is regarded throughout Asia as one of the most effective instruments for bringing in new technology, management and capital for development, the lack of FDI in Nepal is a powerful indicator of the country's deeply entrenched problems of economic backwardness. Since the early 1990s 399 FDI projects worth NRs 53,300m. have been approved, but only a proportion of these have converted into actual investment inflows. In 1999/2000 another 66 foreign companies received approval for a total investment of NRs 2,527m. New investment was expected to generate 81,536 jobs by March 2001.

The flow of foreign investment into Nepal in recent years has been in response to the Foreign Investment and Technology Act of 1992. Between 1992 and 1997 about 250 foreign investment projects by Indian, Japanese and US investors were started, largely in industry. This was a significant increase over the 150 foreign projects initiated in the previous 15 years. The 1992 act superseded the structural adjustment programmes of the 1980s (1985–87), which first introduced the idea of five–10 years tax 'holidays' for foreign investors. In 1996 the act was amended and the threshold of NRs 20m. removed. In September 1997 the Industrial Enterprises Act was introduced further to improve tax incentives to foreign investors. In theory, it also opened all economic sectors to foreign investment up to 25% equity. However, the list of exceptions was very long: some 23 industrial sectors remained without access to foreign equity, and the level of foreign equity itself was very low compared with the percentages offered by other countries in the region. The creation of four new industrial zones for emerging industries financed by overseas capital did not prove sufficient to overcome these disincentives. Many of the new foreign investment guidelines remain uncompetitive in relation to those that other countries have introduced, especially considering the general shortage of international investment capital.

Nepal's foreign investment history also links it more closely to the Indian market. Most FDI in Nepal has traditionally involved small manufacturing concerns from India, rather than Indian or other foreign multinationals. The primary motive of Indian investors has been the market opportunities afforded by Nepal, in particular the chance to diversify business portfolios in a country very close to Indian headquarters. Indian firms have reported that Nepal has been a profitable market for them, and the returns to Nepal have also been beneficial except for the loss of revenue caused by the long tax 'holidays'. The bilateral investment relationship, however, has on occasion become caught up with trade disputes between India and Nepal. In September 1999, for example, Kodak Nepal, a joint venture between an Indian company and a US multinational, built a factory in Nepal in 1999 and invested some US $4.8m. Production, however, ceased because of Nepal's reluctance to allow the duty-free export of Kodak products into India and the impasse regarding the implementation of India's revised Harmonized Commodity Description and Coding System. In 2001 Kodak applied for permission to withdraw from its venture in Nepal, a request that conveyed a powerful warning to the global economy.

According to the Nepal-India Chamber of Commerce and Industry, foreign investment opportunities in Nepal are not very attractive when compared to neighbouring countries, especially India. The Maoist insurgency movement has been only one factor; another has been the inability of the Nepalese Government to develop a package of incentives that can compete with others in the region. For example, Nepal gives no tax 'holidays' for new ventures, whereas even Bangladesh gives tax breaks of between five and 12 years.

ECONOMIC REFORM

For many years, Nepal followed the Indian example of generating modern industry through import substitution. This changed in 1992 with the introduction of a New Industrial Policy, which sought to encourage increased foreign and domestic private investment in industry. Policies were also implemented to facilitate the disinvestment of public-sector enterprises, abolish industrial licences and quotas, lower tariffs and establish the convertibility of Nepal's currency in all current-account transactions. In view of the constraints on agriculture, Nepal's development strategy emphasizes industrial growth. Therefore the Government also regulated against industrial pollution by passing the Environmental Protection Act and the Environment Protection Regulation of 1997 and the Industrial Enterprises Act of 1999. The latter reduces by 50% taxes on businesses that invest in anti-pollution strategies.

The growth of the private sector, however, will depend critically on the ability of firms to utilize private savings and capital. Unfortunately, the poverty and lack of economic diversification in Nepal are also reflected in the low savings rate and poor capital base. Moreover, state controls over the financial sector persist, despite the announced deregulation of that sector in the 1980s. A further constraint on private-sector growth was the lack of any institutional structure to pool capital, but this was remedied in 1993/94 with the establishment of the Securities Exchanges Board of Nepal (SEBO) and the Nepal Stock Exchange Ltd (NEPSE). These institutions replaced the highly inadequate Securities Exchange Centre Ltd that dated from 1976. However, the market capitalization to GDP ratio in Nepal remained low: between 8% and 5% from 1994 to 1996, compared with 64% in USA and 16% in India. The number of companies listed and traded on the NEPSE also remained low: 62 and 23 in February 1994 and only 90 and 47 respectively in December 1996. Hence, the first three years of NEPSE's existence were disappointing. Nevertheless, the establishment of the NEPSE signified an important departure from the pattern of past dependency on public-sector investment.

An important part of economic and industrial reform has been the reorganization of Nepal's financial sector. The banking sector of Nepal has been open to foreign investment since the 1980s. In 1987 Grindlays Bank established a joint venture with Standard Chartered, the Nepal Bank and Nepalese public. The bank inaugurated its 11th branch office in Bhairawa in September 2000. However, the reform of the domestic banking sector had yet to begin. A strategy was designed and foreign consultants were to be employed to evaluate Nepal's two major commercial banks, Nepal Bank Limited (NBL) and the Rastriya Banija Bank (RBB), and their capacity to provide finance to the private sector, given the extent of the non-performing loans, which are estimated at between 20% and 30% of total loans. The latter has unwillingly converted the NBL and RBB into Nepal's largest owners of real estate. New loans appear to have the same ratio of non-performing funds. Nevertheless, in contrast to the situation that prevailed in the early 1990s when there were the only two commercial banks operating within Nepal, the reforms at least created a more diversified banking sector. By the end of 2001 Nepal had 15 commercial banks, 14 development banks, five rural development banks, one postal savings bank, 49 finance companies, 34 financial co-operatives, 17 insurance companies and 16 financial non-governmental organizations. This growth has been important but not large enough to increase the ability of the banking sector to meet the needs of Nepal. The NBL (41% state-owned) and the RBB (100% state-owned) continued to dominate all aspects of commercial banking, lending and deposits. The other 11 commercial banks are mainly foreign joint ventures which specialize in financing trade. The remainder of the banking system is less sound than the numbers suggest, because of the small scale of their operations and their inability to compete with the two big domestic banks. Combined, the RBB and NBL employ about 10,000 and control some 60% of banking in Nepal. Hence, reform would have an impact on both domestic entrepreneurship and employment. Management of the banking system was undermined in 2000/01 by a leadership struggle over the governorship of the Nepal Rastra Bank (the country's central bank). The issue was finally settled when the Supreme Court of Nepal ordered the reinstatement of Dr Tilak Bahadur Rawal, who had been displaced in August 2000. Rawal reaffirmed his determination to proceed with reforming the NBL and RBB, in particular the instalment of new management. Further aid from the IMF's Poverty Reduction Growth Fund is contingent on banking reform.

Despite these changes, by January 2002 the World Bank had concluded that Nepal's financial problems were seriously exacerbated by the weak performance of the two state-controlled banks. In March 2002 the Nepal Rastra Bank, in a dramatic move to contain the damage within Nepal's banking system, declared the NBL insolvent, dismissed its managers and transferred control to a committee of three government appointees. This followed auditor reports in 2001 that the NBL was 'technically insolvent', owing to the advance of large sums of money to a small number of big Nepalese companies who were also shareholders in the NBL. The move by the Nepal Rastra Bank was in response to international pressure to 'clean up' the banking sector. The World Bank and the British Department for International Development agreed to provide a total aid package of US $35m. to Nepal on the understanding that the NBL and RBB both be handed over to international management companies in a desperate attempt to introduce accountability, transparency and an effective loan recovery programme. This complies with the Nepal Government's stated objective of curbing corruption and introducing transparency throughout the economic system.

Another aspect of the Government's reform programme has been the introduction of market mechanisms into the production and retailing system. Subsidies have been slowly abolished and the prices of essential commodities increased to more realistic levels that reflect market prices. During the late 1990s all fertilizer subsidies were removed and the prices of petroleum, kerosene, diesel and electricity increased. These reversals in government policy gave rise to popular protests and a parliamentary inquiry. However, the policy has remained in place, and there is some evidence to show that the reforms are working, albeit very slowly.

Privatization has been another element in the reform programme. In 1991–2001 18 out of the 60 state-owned enterprises in Nepal were privatized. The privatization process since then appears to have slowed down, despite the Ninth Five-Year Plan (1997–2002) naming 30 more state-owned enterprises for privatization. Privatization in Nepal has proceeded by various means. Of the 18 companies, three were liquidated, the assets of three were sold, 10 companies' shares were floated, one was tendered to private-sector management and one was leased out. On its own, however, privatization is no guarantee of success and of the 18 privatized enterprises, three reverted to state control within a short period of time, owing to private mismanagement.

Privatization has also encouraged entrepreneurs to establish new industries, especially in the power sector. However, private-sector initiatives have been adversely affected by the Maoist insurgency. At least five HEP stations (Jhhimruk, Andhikhola, Bajhhang, Khandbari and Piluwa) have been attacked by Maoists. The privatization process has also been unpopular with workers, partly because it has meant downsizing the labour force by an average of about 50%. One observer argued that privatization made middle-level workers insecure about their futures and that industrial disputes have increased commensurately: complaints between 1993 and 1997 doubled (from 434 to 854) and lock-outs increased from one to 16. Strikes have regularly taken place: as many as 25 in any given year. To facilitate the growth of the private sector, the Government also established industrial estates, encouraged the development of cottage and small-scale industries, and provided business and management training through the Industrial Enterprise Development Institute. Assessments about the success of these policy measures are not available but a survey of Nepalese business attitudes towards privatization in August 2000 revealed that 79% of the respondents thought that the reform process was too slow and that Government was no more 'business friendly' than the previous administration.

The remaining public-sector enterprises in Nepal have reported considerable difficulties. Financial accounts for 34 of these were made public in 1999: 14 reported persistent losses. To keep these enterprises afloat, the equivalent of 6% of government revenue was transferred to them in the three years 1997–99. The three largest loss-making enterprises were Nepal Food Company, AIC and the Udayapur Cement Factory; their losses together equalled 0.5% of GDP. As in India, the losses incurred by public-sector firms were caused by poor bureaucratic management, the lack of accountability, the lack of financial autonomy, and the absence of modern managerial practice. In an effort to assist Nepal's failing industries, the Government began to buy supplies for clothing, shoes, cement, iron, furniture and drugs from Nepalese producers. Government buying power, however, is limited and unlikely to make public-sector enterprises more efficient. Other government initiatives, such as the requirement that all public-sector companies provide audited accounts to the Government by mid-April 2002, are, perhaps, more important. Without proper auditing, the actual extent of profits and losses cannot be ascertained. More than one-half of the public-sector companies were to be transferred to the private sector in the short to medium term. The 22 enterprises that were to remain under government ownership included electricity and water utilities, financial institutions and trading companies. The target in 1998/99 was to privatize five large firms: Himal Cement, Nepal Tea Development Corporation, Butwal Power Company, Nepal Telecommunications Corporation (NTC) and the Royal Nepal Airlines Corporation (RNAC). The NTC, meanwhile, is being privatized even though it is the most profitable state enterprise in Nepal. The privatization process has, however, been fraught with difficulties and delays. Private bids for these firms have been disappointing and unacceptable to the Government for a range of financial reasons. A review by the IMF in March 2000 summarized the slow progress towards privatization: in 1992 three public-sector firms were sold to the public; in 1993 another three; in 1994 two; in 1995 none; in 1996 three; in 1997 three; in 1998–99 none; in 2000 three sales dating back to 1998 were expected to be finalized.

Considering the slow rate and difficulties of the privatization process, the Government has needed to adopt special measures to support failing industries. In March 2002 the Nepal Banker's Association announced new banking support to the foundering industries. Special financial concessions are to be extended to industries, including hotels, which are in difficulty but might recover. However, it is difficult to envisage how these measures might provide genuine relief, particularly with regard to the hotel industry, as the substantial decline in tourism seems irreversible. The privatization process itself has been inexplicably delayed by the Nepal Rastra Bank. When the French Crédit Agricole Indosuez (CAI) demanded its right to sell its share of Nepal Indosuez Bank Ltd, the central bank responded only after the CAI warned that the consequences would be disastrous if there were further delays. The recent stage of privatization has been adversely affected by the devaluation of assets as a result of damage caused by the insurgency movement.

GOVERNMENT REVENUE AND FINANCE

Like the rest of South Asia, the Nepalese Government has faced a persistent fiscal crisis caused by the growth of total government expenditure well beyond the increase in government revenues. Total revenue as a percentage of GDP increased throughout the 1990s, from 8.6% in 1990/91 to 10.7% in 1997/98. Revenue from taxes also increased in this period, from 6.7% to 8.7% of GDP. Despite this, the revenue of the Government of Nepal was well below the average for Asian countries by almost 5% in the case of the total revenue to GDP ratio and 4.2% in the case of tax revenue to GDP ratio. The burden of servicing foreign and domestic loans increased greatly, absorbing 14% of total government expenditure in 1995/96. There are major constraints on increasing government income in Nepal. Taxes yielded about 82% of government revenue, with the rest coming from duties, cesses, etc. The capacity to increase revenues from other sources is limited because of the need to provide private and foreign firms with production incentives in the form of low import duties and easy access to foreign markets. Tax income is equally difficult to increase, owing to the scale of the illegal economy and bureaucratic inefficiency that hampers the implementation of value-added tax (VAT) collection. VAT was fully implemented by mid-August 1999, despite the opposition of business lobbies, but problems of efficient collection remain. Moreover, the VAT threshold was too high and hence did not apply to many businesses. The budget for 2000/01 lowered the tax-paying threshold.

Despite the constraints on Nepal's fiscal system, there is some capacity for revenue reform by reallocating expenditures. The fiscal deficit was not caused by expenditure on social welfare; only 3.4% of the Government's budget was allocated to this area, compared with the internationally accepted norm of 5%. Although Nepal does not spend heavily on the military (it is ranked 120 out of 150 nations on this index) the US $44m. a year spent on weapons could be reallocated to more pressing needs. The insurgency movement, however, has placed new pressures on the budget, with the growing need to allocate funds to the police and army. In early 2002 about 10% of the total budget was spent on security. This is widely regarded as an underestimate. Considering this new financial pressure, the Government's introduction of the Voluntary Declaration of Income Scheme (VDIS) in November 2001 was a very modest step in the direction of fiscal reform.

The first budget of the majority NCP Government, announced in July 1999, was welcomed as indicative of the strong, reformist tendency of the new administration. It was regarded as the most reform-orientated budget of the 1990s. A significant part of the budget addressed the need for better governance of banks, public expenditure management, and the administrative machinery charged with implementing development policies. The budget also targeted the very poorest, women and the question of how to promote employment. Closer analysis of the budget, however, revealed some very disturbing facts, suggesting that the reform programme was no more realistic than its predecessors. The budget projected a revenue increase of NRs 7,300m.: NRs 4,400m. from taxes and NRs 2,900m. from aid funds. Both these estimates were much larger than the record of the previous five years suggested were possible, yet the budget optimistically assumed that this money would be available to finance its development objectives, and targets were formulated accordingly. By 2002 the budgetary constraints on development had become clearer. Of the total budget estimates for 2002/03, 56% of government expenditure would be based on revenue, 16% on foreign grants and 13% on foreign loans, leaving a deficit equivalent to 15% of the budget. In the mean time, no serious suggestion appeared to have been put forward by the international community for a special programme of financial aid to assist Nepal.

PROSPECTS

While Nepal's economy has diversified into one that is outward-looking and export-orientated, the failure to address mass poverty has encouraged a Maoist insurgency, which, in turn, threatens lives, political stability and the capacity of Nepal to continue to grow in the way that it has done over the last decade. The growth that did occur, however, did not bring about sufficient development at a fast enough rate, owing to the social structures that constrain a proper distribution of the benefits of growth. The Government is regarded as corrupt and uncommitted to fundamental reforms that would dismantle the power of landlords and big business. The developments achieved recently appear to be unravelling, accelerated by the new cautious international environment following the terrorist attacks on the USA in September 2001. The collapse of the tourist trade, the fall in demand for Nepalese handicraft exports and the bombing by Maoists of HEP projects are the most fundamental constraints on the development of Nepal, exacerbated by the limitations of Nepal's resource base and its land-locked nature. In 2002 the Nepalese Government faced a most serious fiscal crisis. In contemplating the potential consequences of this, one should remember that the disastrous history of Afghanistan in recent years could be traced back to a serious fiscal crisis experienced by the Afghan state in the late 1970s.

Other persistent problems in Nepal are potentially solvable with accelerated growth and the proper distribution of its benefits. However, distribution in Nepal is hampered by the social and political structures that continue to privilege established families, landlords and high castes. The radicalization of Nepalese politics extends beyond the Maoist insurgency. Students from 'untouchable' castes in Kathmandu have formed Dalit associations along the Indian pattern and demanded that the school textbooks be rewritten in order to remove passages offensive to the low castes. Assuming that the Maoist insurgency can be contained, Nepal is still destined to witness major political changes of the kind that India has experienced since the 1980s. In particular, the needs and aspirations of previously disadvantaged groups will play a growing role in national politics, provided that Nepal's constitutional monarchy begins to represent a genuine devolution of power.

To make change possible, greater international aid is required. In the short term, any attempt to redress poverty will require financial assistance from rich nations. Without significant intervention, the number of people living in absolute poverty is predicted to increase to 20m. by the year 2010. In the absence of any significant industrialization, most of these poor will be marginal farmers or labourers. Clearly, poverty alleviation will require major agricultural change, in addition to a range of programmes to address those in most dire need.

Projections by the World Bank give little cause for optimism about Nepal's short-term future. If average annual GDP were to increase by 4.5% in 2000–01 and then rise to 5% in 2002–05, the percentage of the population living below the poverty line could decline by 20%. This decline may be too modest to deliver political stability, however. World Bank projections also assume that inequality will not worsen during this period. That assumption, however, requires the anti-poverty strategies to penetrate to the families below the poverty line, which means that government funds and programmes need to extend well beyond the margins of Nepal's urban areas into the rural parts where poverty prevails. Owing to inadequate infrastructure, lack of political will and poor governance, there is a genuine risk that these development strategies will not reach the intended beneficiaries. If growth, development and the new prosperity touch only the lives of urban dwellers, inequality will increase and social discord intensify, with serious consequences for the long-term viability of Nepal's experiment with a constitutional monarchy.

To some extent the advancement in information technology can be utilized to bring improvements to rural areas, including remote regions. Nepal is a participant in the Healthnet Project, which is accessible to about 500 health professionals, through 150 contact points. Information by this means can be disseminated more widely, but in order for that information to be used, investment in health delivery systems is essential. This experiment apart, Nepal has been classified as a country which has been 'marginalized' by the information technology 'revolution' and the country's inadequate infrastructure will continue to constrain developments in this area. The monthly internet access charge as a percentage of average monthly income in Nepal is about 278% compared with the next highest proportion of 191% in Bangladesh. In the USA the monthly charge stands at only 1.2%. Low levels of education are related to the lack of technology development in Nepal; with an estimated 2.4 mean years of schooling for those above the age of 15 years, Nepal ranks lower than some African nations such as Senegal and Tanzania.

The solution to Nepal's problems lies in political reform. Since the early 1990s the focus has been on decentralization and local participation in governance, and the administration of poverty alleviation programmes through the establishment of district development committees. The critical question is whether decentralization will achieve its objectives and whether and how the people below the poverty line will be empowered to have a greater say in the allocation of national resources. Unless the Government can develop a direct rapport with the ordinary people in the villages of Nepal, the Maoist insurgency will continue to be more popular at the local level and Nepal's growth will be seriously compromised. That rapport depends critically on social reforms to reduce the power of vested interests represented by landlords and privileged urban families.

Statistical Survey

Source (unless otherwise stated): National Planning Commission Secretariat, Singha Durbar, POB 1284, Kathmandu; tel. 225879; fax 226500; e-mail npcs@wlink.com.np; internet npc.gov.np:8080.

Area and Population

AREA, POPULATION AND DENSITY

Area (sq km)	147,181*
Population (census results)	
22 June 1991	18,491,097
22 June 2001†‡	
Males	11,563,921
Females	11,587,502
Total	23,151,423
Population (official estimates at mid-year)	
1998	21,843,068
1999	22,367,048
2000	22,904,000
Density (per sq km) at June 2001	157.3

* 56,827 sq miles.

† Population is *de jure*.

‡ Includes estimates for certain areas in 12 districts where the census could not be conducted, owing to violence and disruption.

Capital: Kathmandu, population 1,081,845 at 2001 census.

BIRTHS AND DEATHS (UN estimates, annual averages)

	1985–90	1990–95	1995–2000
Birth rate (per 1,000)	38.6	37.9	36.3
Death rate (per 1,000)	14.5	12.9	11.2

Source: UN, *World Population Prospects: The 2000 Revision*.

Expectation of life (WHO estimates, years at birth, 2000): Males 58.5; Females 58.0 (Source: WHO, *World Health Report*).

2001 (estimates): Birth rate 33.1 per 1,000; Death rate 9.6 per 1,000.

ECONOMICALLY ACTIVE POPULATION (1999 Labour Force Survey)

Agriculture, hunting, forestry and fishing	7,203,000
Mining and quarrying	8,000
Manufacturing	552,000
Electricity, gas and water	26,000
Construction	344,000
Trade, restaurants and hotels	522,000
Transport, storage and communications	135,000
Financing, insurance, real estate and business service	51,000
Community, social and personal services	614,000
Activities not adequately defined	8,000
Total employed	9,463,000

Source: Central Bureau of Statistics.

Health and Welfare

KEY INDICATORS

Fertility (births per woman, 2000)	4.7
Under-5 mortality rate (per 1,000 live births, 2000)	100
HIV/AIDS (% of persons aged 15–49, 2001)	0.49
Physicians (per 1,000 head, 1995)	0.04
Hospital beds (per 1,000 head, 1997)	0.17
Health expenditure (1998): US $ per head (PPP)	58
% of GDP	5.4
public (% of total)	23.5
Access to water (% of persons, 2000)	81
Access to sanitation (% of persons, 2000)	27
Human Development Index (2000): ranking	142
value	0.490

For sources and definitions, see explanatory note on p. vi.

Agriculture

PRINCIPAL CROPS ('000 metric tons)

	1998	1999	2000
Wheat	1,001	1,086	1,184
Rice (paddy)	3,641	3,710	4,030
Barley	37	32	31
Maize	1,367	1,346	1,445
Millet	285	291	295
Potatoes	935	1,091	1,183
Other roots and tubers	145*	103	105*
Sugar cane	1,718	1,972	2,103
Beans, dry	23	24	25
Lentils	114	132	137
Other pulses	59	55	58
Mustard seed	110	120	123
Linseed*	27	28	28
Vegetables and melons	1,414	1,252	1,490
Fruit (excl. melons)	415	457	447
Spices*	34	34	35
Jute and jute-like fibres	16	15	15
Tobacco (leaves)	5	4	4

* FAO estimate(s).

Source: FAO.

LIVESTOCK ('000 head, year ending September)

	1998	1999	2000
Cattle	7,049	7,031	7,023
Buffaloes	3,389	3,471	3,526
Pigs	766	825	878
Sheep	870	855	852
Goats	6,080	6,205	6,325
Chickens	15,800*	17,797	18,620

* FAO estimate.

Source: FAO.

LIVESTOCK PRODUCTS ('000 metric tons)

	1998	1999	2000
Beef and veal	47.9	47.8	48.0
Buffalo meat	117.4	119.6	121.8
Mutton and lamb	2.9	2.9	2.9
Goat meat	35.6	36.2	36.9
Pig meat	13.1	13.9	14.6
Poultry meat	11.7	12.4	13.0
Cows' milk	318.7	328.9	337.5
Buffaloes' milk	729.4	744.0	759.6
Goats' milk	57.5	59.0	60.5
Ghee	18.2	19.0	19.2
Poultry eggs	22.4	24.2	23.4
Wool: greasy	0.6	0.6	0.6

Source: FAO.

Forestry

ROUNDWOOD REMOVALS (estimates, '000 cubic metres, excluding bark)

	1998	1999	2000
Sawlogs, veneer logs and logs for sleepers*	620	620	620
Fuel wood	12,597	12,678	12,763
Total	13,217	13,298	13,383

* Output assumed to be unchanged since 1991.

Source: FAO.

SAWNWOOD PRODUCTION
('000 cubic metres, including railway sleepers)

	1989*	1990	1991
Coniferous (softwood)	10	20	20
Broadleaved (hardwood)	210	550	600
Total	220	570	620

* FAO estimates.

1992–2000: Annual production as in 1991 (FAO estimates).

Source: FAO.

Fishing

('000 metric tons, live weight)

	1997	1998	1999
Capture	11.2	12.0	12.8
Freshwater fishes	11.2	12.0	12.8
Aquaculture	12.0	12.9	13.0
Common carp	3.0	2.6	2.6
Bighead carp	1.2	1.9	2.0
Grass carp (White amur)	0.6	0.7	0.7
Silver carp	3.6	3.9	3.9
Other cyprinids	3.6	3.8	3.8
Total catch	23.2	24.9	25.8

Source: FAO, *Yearbook of Fishery Statistics*.

Industry

SELECTED PRODUCTS
('000 metric tons, unless otherwise indicated, year ending 15 July)

	1997/98	1998/99	1999/2000
Cement	276.5	190.6	248.0
Steel rods	125.3	106.6	144.9
Jute goods	51.4	49.3	49.7
Raw sugar	67.2	75.5	77.2
Tea	2.3	2.3	3.6
Vegetable ghee	28.9	87.0	91.3
Beer and liquor (million litres)	17.0	22.1	28.9
Soft drinks (million litres)	24.0	29.1	n.a.
Paper	16.2	19.5	18.6
Cigarettes (million)	8,127	7,315	7,125
Cotton textiles (million sq metres)	3.2	3.3	26.3*
Synthetic textiles (million sq metres)	18.7	17.8	15.6*
Soap	39.1	47.7	73.7

* Million metres.

Sources: National Planning Commission Secretariat, Kathmandu, and *Far Eastern Economic Review*, *Asia 2001 Yearbook*.

Finance

CURRENCY AND EXCHANGE RATES

Monetary Units

100 paisa (pice) = 1 Nepalese rupee (NR).

Sterling, Dollar and Euro Equivalents (31 May 2002)

£1 sterling = NRs 114.33
US $1 = NRs 77.95;
€1 = NRs 73.17;
1,000 Nepalese rupees = £8.747 = $12.829 = €13.666.

Average Exchange Rate (rupees per US $)

1999 68.239
2000 71.094
2001 74.961

BUDGET (NRs million, year ending 15 July)*

Revenue†	2000/01‡	2001/02§	2002/03‖
Taxation	38,865	40,397	45,928
Taxes on income, profits and capital gains	9,114	9,248	9,863
Taxes on property	616	929	1,101
Domestic taxes on goods and services	16,583	16,580	19,205
Taxes on international trade and transactions	12,552	13,641	15,760
Other revenue	7,971	8,199	9,675
Charges, fees, fines, etc.	1,931	1,879	2,556
Sales of goods and services	1,184	1,052	1,239
Dividends	2,336	2,676	2,885
Interest receipts	1,440	860	1,066
Total	46,837	48,596	55,603

Expenditure	2000/01‡	2001/02§	2002/03‖
Regular expenditure	37,079	44,079	49,104
General administration	8,027	10,961	11,225
Defence	3,813	5,785	7,228
Social services	10,692	13,454	14,130
Education	8,226	10,413	10,968
Health	1,547	2,115	2,151
Economic services	2,533	2,965	3,260
Agriculture-related	544	575	774
Infrastructure	924	1,055	1,132
Interest payments	4,698	5,720	8,006
Other purposes	7,315	5,194	5,255
Development expenditure	35,009	30,210	37,132
Social services	12,873	11,108	16,860
Education	2,784	2,402	3,318
Health	1,972	1,702	2,748
Provision of drinking water	2,407	2,077	3,773
Economic services	22,136	19,102	20,273
Agriculture-related	6,624	5,716	5,413
Infrastructure	12,779	11,028	12,800
Total	72,087	74,289	86,236

* Figures refer to the regular and development budgets of the central Government.

† Excluding grants received (NRs million, estimates): 6,800 in 2000/01; 8,700 in 2001/02; 14,600 in 2002/03.

‡ Revised figures.

§ Estimates.

‖ Forecasts.

Source: IMF, *Nepal: Selected Issues and Statistical Appendix* (September 2002).

INTERNATIONAL RESERVES (US $ million at mid-December)

	1998	1999	2000
Gold*	48.3	48.1	45.5
IMF special drawing rights	—	0.3	—
Reserve position in IMF	8.1	7.9	7.5
Foreign exchange	748.2	834.9	937.9
Total	804.6	891.2	990.9

* Valued at US $315 per troy oz in 1998 and 1999, and at $297 per oz in 2000.

Source: IMF, *International Financial Statistics.*

MONEY SUPPLY (NRs million at mid-December)*

	1999	2000	2001
Currency outside banks	36,929	44,526	51,699
Private sector deposits with monetary authorities	4,346	3,160	3,570
Demand deposits at commercial banks	13,832	15,343	16,891
Total money	55,107	63,028	72,161

* Excluding Indian currency in circulation.

Source: IMF, *International Financial Statistics.*

COST OF LIVING (National Consumer Price Index; base: 1990 = 100)

	1997	1998	1999
Food (incl. beverages)	198.9	229.5	247.1
Fuel and light	196.5	204.6	215.4
Clothing (excl. footwear)	187.7	200.3	211.5
Rent	227.2	237.8	242.0
All items (incl. others)	197.7	220.5	235.8

Source: ILO, *Yearbook of Labour Statistics.*

2000: Food 240.9; All items 241.4.

2001: Food 244.1; All items 248.1.

Source: UN, *Monthly Bulletin of Statistics.*

NATIONAL ACCOUNTS

(NRs million at current prices, year ending 15 July)

National Income and Product

	1995/96	1996/97	1997/98
Domestic factor incomes*	228,991	256,891	270,641
Consumption of fixed capital	4,465	5,670	7,182
Gross domestic product (GDP) at factor cost	233,456	262,561	277,823
Indirect taxes, *less* subsidies	15,457	17,952	18,724
GDP in purchasers' values	248,913	280,513	296,547
Factor income from abroad / *Less* Factor income paid abroad	3,566	4,661	6,025
Gross national product (GNP)	252,479	285,174	302,572
Less Consumption of fixed capital	4,465	5,670	7,182
National income in market prices	248,014	279,504	295,390
Other current transfers from abroad (net)†	900	1,009	1,157
National disposable income	248,914	280,513	296,547

* Compensation of employees and the operating surplus of enterprises.

† Excluding official grants.

Source: UN, *National Accounts Statistics.*

Expenditure on the Gross Domestic Product

	1999/2000	2000/01	2001/02*
Government final consumption expenditure	34,579	40,973	45,387
Private final consumption expenditure	287,947	309,107	326,108
Increase in stocks	18,376	21,480	16,965
Gross fixed capital formation	73,314	78,017	84,165
Total domestic expenditure	414,216	449,577	472,625
Exports of goods and services	88,360	91,821	77,796
Less Imports of goods and services	123,055	131,403	123,143
GDP in purchasers' values	379,521	410,194†	428,033†
GDP at constant 1994/95 prices	277,751	291,139	293,595

* Provisional figures.

† Including adjustments.

Source: Central Bureau of Statistics, Kathmandu.

Gross Domestic Product by Economic Activity

	1999/2000	2000/01	2001/02*
Agriculture, forestry and fishing	144,644	149,040	156,384
Mining and quarrying	1,815	1,981	2,091
Manufacturing	33,550	35,566	34,616
Electricity, gas and water	5,942	6,989	9,339
Construction	37,373	39,571	43,984
Trade, restaurants and hotels	42,895	45,381	42,817
Transport, storage and communications	29,336	33,050	34,800
Finance and real estate	36,919	41,835	43,636
Community and social services	33,810	40,060	42,826
Sub-total	366,284	393,473	410,493
Less Imputed bank service charges	10,708	11,912	12,269
Indirect taxes, *less* subsidies	23,945	28,633	29,809
GDP in purchasers' values	379,521	410,194	428,033

* Provisional figures.

Source: Central Bureau of Statistics, Kathmandu.

BALANCE OF PAYMENTS (US $ million)

	1998	1999	2000
Exports of goods f.o.b.	482.0	612.3	785.7
Imports of goods f.o.b.	−1,239.1	−1,494.2	−1,578.3
Trade balance	−757.1	−881.9	−792.7
Exports of services	565.1	655.1	505.9
Imports of services	−196.2	−212.5	−199.9
Balance on goods and services	−388.1	−439.2	−486.7
Other income received	45.4	55.8	72.2
Other income paid	−26.5	−28.4	−35.2
Balance on goods, services and income	−369.2	−411.9	−449.7
Current transfers received	326.0	182.3	189.0
Current transfers paid	−24.1	−26.9	−16.7
Current balance	−67.2	−256.5	−277.4
Direct investment from abroad	12.0	—	—
Other investment assets	90.8	48.2	128.6
Investment liabilities	110.0	−72.8	−52.6
Net errors and omissions	134.0	58.3	124.6
Overall balance	279.7	−222.7	−76.8

Source: IMF, *International Financial Statistics*.

OFFICIAL DEVELOPMENT ASSISTANCE (US $ million)

	1996	1997	1998
Bilateral donors	235.0	233.7	215.0
Multilateral donors	155.4	167.0	189.3
Total	390.4	400.7	404.3
Grants	282.4	271.0	253.9
Loans	108.0	129.7	150.4
Per caput assistance (US $)	18.7	18.8	18.5

Source: UN, *Statistical Yearbook for Asia and the Pacific*.

External Trade

PRINCIPAL COMMODITIES (NRs million, year ending 15 July)

Imports c.i.f.	1998/99*	1999/2000*	2000/01
Food and live animals	7,619	10,839	5,994
Crude materials (inedible) except fuels	6,247	7,012	7,560
Mineral fuels and lubricants	8,737	9,098	11,269
Animal and vegetable oils and fats	3,329	4,446	5,589
Chemicals and pharmaceuticals	12,476	14,474	12,942
Basic manufactures	25,638	34,420	41,188
Machinery and transport equipment	18,064	20,548	23,028
Miscellaneous manufactured articles	4,302	6,683	7,210
Total (incl. others)	87,525	108,505	115,687

Exports f.o.b.	1998/99*	1999/2000*	2000/01
Food and live animals	3,724	4,240	4,777
Animal and vegetable oils and fats	3,597	3,230	4,104
Chemicals and pharmaceuticals	2,804	3,933	4,042
Basic manufactures	13,540	15,839	18,909
Miscellaneous manufactured articles	11,393	21,509	22,651
Total (incl. others)	35,676	49,823	55,654

* Revised figures.

Exports of carpets (NRs million, year ending 15 July): 9,802 in 1998/99; 9,842 in 1999/2000; 8,592 in 2000/01.

Exports of garments (NRs million, year ending 15 July): 9,702 in 1998/99; 13,942 in 1999/2000; 13,125 in 2000/01.

Source: Asian Development Bank, *Key Indicators of Developing Asian and Pacific Countries*.

PRINCIPAL TRADING PARTNERS (US $ million)

Imports	1999	2000	2001
Argentina	196.3	225.8	248.4
China, People's Republic	227.7	216.8	213.2
Hong Kong	96.1	107.5	65.3
India	464.7	534.5	587.9
Japan	29.1	34.1	24.8
Korea, Republic	29.0	21.0	16.0
Saudi Arabia	30.5	37.8	40.7
Singapore	95.5	108.4	81.6
Thailand	17.2	31.9	33.0
United Arab Emirates	69.2	85.9	92.6
Total (incl. others)	1,480.3	1,626.4	1,600.1

Exports	1999	2000	2001
Argentina	37.8	43.5	48.0
Bangladesh	8.1	3.6	4.7
France	11.7	14.2	7.8
Germany	92.4	87.3	74.8
India	153.8	176.9	195.3
Italy	4.5	8.4	8.9
Japan	4.7	25.7	14.8
Switzerland	6.5	11.6	12.7
United Kingdom	16.3	16.2	12.5
USA	174.7	220.2	198.2
Total (incl. others)	565.1	679.5	645.8

Source: Asian Development Bank, *Key Indicators of Developing Asian and Pacific Countries*.

Transport

ROAD TRAFFIC (vehicles registered at 30 June)

	2000
Cars, jeeps and vans	53,073
Buses and minibuses	12,054
Trucks and tankers	20,011
Motorcycles	147,157
Tractors	20,469

CIVIL AVIATION

Royal Nepal Airlines Corporation (traffic on scheduled services)

	1996	1997	1998
Kilometres flown (million)	11	11	11
Passengers carried ('000)	755	755	754
Passenger-km (million)	908	908	908
Total ton-km (million)	99	99	99

Source: UN, *Statistical Yearbook*.

Communications Media

	1998	1999	2000
Television receivers ('000 in use)	85	150	170
Telephones ('000 main lines in use)	208.4	253.0	266.9
Facsimile machines (number in use)*	5,000	8,000	n.a.
Mobile cellular telephones ('000 subscribers)	—	5.5	10.2
Personal computers ('000 in use)	50	60	70
Internet users ('000)	15.0	35.0	50.0
Daily newspapers (titles)*	n.a.	n.a.	189
Non-daily newspapers (titles)*	n.a.	n.a.	2,554

1997: Radio receivers ('000 in use) 840.

2001: Telephones ('000 main lines in use) 298.1; Mobile cellular telephones ('000 subscribers) 17.3; Personal computers ('000 in use) 80; Internet users ('000) 60.0.

* Year ending 15 July.

Sources: UNESCO, *Statistical Yearbook*; International Telecommunication Union.

April 2001: Daily newspapers 193.

Tourism

FOREIGN TOURIST ARRIVALS

Country of residence	1998	1999	2000
Australia	11,227	11,997	12,138
Bangladesh	6,677	10,003	9,365
France	21,610	23,942	24,028
Germany	23,584	25,990	25,907
India	143,627	140,672	96,995
Italy	12,571	12,656	11,384
Japan	37,069	38,566	40,841
Netherlands	14,131	16,872	15,878
Sri Lanka	10,995	12,413	16,628
United Kingdom	32,628	34,281	35,080
USA	34,968	38,681	39,377
Total (incl. others)	463,684	491,504	463,646

Tourism receipts (US $ million): 153 in 1998; 168 in 1999.

Source: World Tourism Organization, *Yearbook of Tourism Statistics*.

Visitor arrivals: 298,066 in 2001 (Source: Nepal Tourism Board, Kathmandu).

Education

(2000)

	Institutions	Teachers	Students
Primary	25,927	97,879	3,623,150
Lower Secondary	7,289	25,375	957,446
Secondary	4,350	19,498	372,914
Higher	n.a.	4,925*	129,174†

* 1991 figure (Source: UNESCO, *Statistical Yearbook*).

† Year ending 30 June.

Adult literacy rate (UNESCO estimates): 41.8% (males 59.6%; females 24.0%) in 2000 (Source: UN Development Programme, *Human Development Report*).

Directory

The Constitution

The main provisions of the Constitution, which was promulgated by the King on 9 November 1990, are summarized below:

The preamble to the Constitution envisages the guarantee of the fundamental rights of every citizen and the protection of his liberty, the consolidation of parliamentary government, the constitutional monarchy and the multi-party system, and the provision of an independent judicial system. Sovereignty resides in the Nepalese people. The Constitution is the fundamental law of the land.

Nepal is a multi-ethnic, multi-lingual, democratic, independent, indivisible, sovereign, Hindu and constitutional monarchical kingdom. Nepali is recognized as the national and official language.

FUNDAMENTAL RIGHTS

Part Three of the Constitution provides for the fundamental rights of the citizen: all citizens are equal before the law; no discrimination is to be practised on the basis of religion, race, sex, caste, tribe or ideology; no person can be deprived of his liberty except in accordance with the law; capital punishment remains abolished; freedom of expression, freedom to assemble peaceably and without arms, freedom to form trade unions and associations, and freedom of movement are also guaranteed. Similarly, pre-censorship of publications is prohibited and, thus, the right to press and publications is ensured. In the sphere of criminal justice, the following rights are specified in the Constitution: no person is to be punished unless made punishable by law; no person may be tried more than once for the same offence; no one is compelled to testify against himself; no one is to be given punishment greater than that which the law at the time of the offence has prescribed; cruelty to detainees is prohibited; no person is to be detained without having first been informed about the grounds for such an action; and the detainee must appear before the judicial authorities within 24 hours of his arrest. In addition, provision has also been made to compensate any person who is wrongfully detained. A person's right to property is ensured, and the right to protect and promote one's own language, script and culture, as well as the right to education up to primary level in the child's mother tongue, have been safeguarded. Similarly, the right to practise religion and to manage and protect religious places and trusts has been granted to the country's various religious groups. The right to secrecy and inviolability of the person, residence, property, documents, letters and other information is also guaranteed.

GOVERNMENT AND LEGISLATURE

His Majesty the King is the symbol of Nepalese nationality and of the unity of the people of Nepal. The expenditures and the privileges relating to His Majesty and the royal family are determined by law. His Majesty's income and property are exempt from tax.

The executive powers of the country are vested in His Majesty and the Council of Ministers. The direction, supervision and conduct of the general administration of the Kingdom of Nepal are the responsibility of the Council of Ministers. All official duties undertaken by His Majesty, except those which are within his exclusive domain or which are performed on the recommendation of some other institutions or officials, are discharged only on the advice of, and with the consent of, the Council of Ministers. His Majesty appoints the leader of the party that commands a majority in the House of Representatives as Prime Minister, while other Ministers are appointed, from among the members of Parliament, on the recommendation of the Prime Minister. The Council of Ministers is answerable to the House of Representatives. In the event that no single party holds an outright majority in the House, the member who commands a working majority on the basis of the support of two or more parties shall be asked to form the Government. Should this also not be the case, His Majesty may ask a member of the party with the largest number of deputies to form the Government. In the event of these exceptional circumstances, the leader forming the Government must obtain a vote of confidence in the House within 30 days. If such confidence is lacking, His Majesty is to dissolve the House and to order a fresh election to be held within six months. The Parliament is bicameral, comprising the House of Representatives and the National Assembly. His Majesty, the House of Representatives and the National Assembly together form the Parliament of the country. The House of Representatives has 205 members, and all persons who have attained the age of 18 years are eligible to vote for candidates, on the basis of adult franchise. The National Assembly has 60 members, consisting of 10 nominees of His Majesty, 35 members, including three female members, elected by the House of Representatives, and 15 members elected by the electoral college, which includes the heads of the local committees of various development regions. The tenure of office of the members of the House of Representatives is five years, and that of the members of the National Assembly six years.

THE JUDICIARY

The judicial system has three tiers: the Supreme Court, the Appellate Courts and the District Courts. The Supreme Court is the principal Court and is also a Court of Record. The Supreme Court consists of a Chief Justice and 14 other Judges. The appointment of the Chief Justice is made on the recommendation of the Constitutional Council, while other Judges of the Supreme Court, the Appellate Courts and the District Courts are nominated on the recommendation of the Judicial Council. All Judges are appointed by His Majesty on such recommendations.

OTHER INSTITUTIONS

The Constitution also makes provisions for the establishment of a Council of State (Raj Parishad) and its standing committee, a Public Service Commission, Auditor General, Election Commission, Attorney-General, Abuse of Authority Investigation Commission, etc.

POLITICAL PARTIES

Political parties are required to register with the Election Commission, and, to be officially recognized, at least 5% of the candidates presented by a party must be female and the party should obtain at least 3% of the total votes cast at the election to the House of Representatives. It has been specifically provided that no law that bans, or imposes restrictions on, political parties may be enacted.

EMERGENCY PROVISIONS

If and when there is a grave emergency in the country, caused by threat to the sovereignty, indivisibility or security of the country (owing to war, foreign aggression, armed revolt or extreme economic depression), His Majesty may declare a state of emergency in the country. Such a declaration must obtain the approval of the House of Representatives within three months. During the period of emergency, fundamental rights, with the exception of the right of recourse to *habeas corpus*, may be suspended.

AMENDMENTS

The Constitution may be amended by a two-thirds majority in each House of Parliament. No changes, however, would be allowed to alter the spirit of the preamble.

DEFENCE

His Majesty is the Supreme Commander-in-Chief of the Royal Nepal Army. The Royal Nepal Army is administered and deployed by His Majesty on the recommendation of the National Defence Council. The Commander-in-Chief is appointed on the recommendation of the Prime Minister. The National Defence Council consists of the Prime Minister, as Chairman, the Minister of Defence and the Commander-in-Chief.

Official matters that involve, *inter alia*, the subjects of defence and strategic alliance, the boundaries of the Kingdom of Nepal, agreements on peace and friendship, and treaties concerning the utilization and distribution of natural resources, have to be approved by a two-thirds majority of the members of both Houses in a joint session of Parliament.

The Government

HEAD OF STATE

HM King Gyanendra Bir Bikram Shah Dev (succeeded to the throne 4 June 2001).

INTERIM COUNCIL OF MINISTERS

(October 2002)

Prime Minister and Minister of Royal Palace Affairs, of Defence, of Forest and Soil Conservation, of General Administration, of Land Reforms and Management, of Physical Planning and Works, of Culture, Tourism and Civil Aviation, of Water Resources, of Information and Communications, of Population and the Environment, of Industries, Commerce and Supplies, and of Labour and Transport Management: Lokendra Bahadur Chand.

Deputy Prime Minister and Minister of Agriculture and Co-operatives, and of Local Development: Badri Prasad Mandal.

Minister of Finance and of Education and Sports: Dr Badri Prasad Shrestha.

Minister of Foreign Affairs: Narendra Bikram Shah.

Minister of Home Affairs and of Law, Justice and Parliamentary Affairs: Dharma Bahadur Thapa.

Minister of Women, Children and Social Welfare: Gore Bahadur Khapangi.

Minister of Health and of Science and Technology: Dr Upendra Devkota.

MINISTRIES

All Ministries are in Kathmandu.

Ministry of Agriculture: Singha Durbar, Kathmandu; tel. 225108; fax 225825; e-mail moa@fert.mos.com.np.

Ministry of Culture, Tourism and Civil Aviation: Singha Durbar, Kathmandu; tel. 225579; fax 227758; e-mail vny@mos.com.np.

Ministry of Defence: Singha Durbar, Kathmandu; tel. 228089; fax 228204.

Ministry of Education and Sports: Keshar Mahal, Kanti Path, Kathmandu; tel. 411599; fax 412460.

Ministry of Finance: Foreign Aid Co-ordination Division, POB 12845, Kathmandu; tel. 259837; internet www.facd.gov.np.

Ministry of Foreign Affairs: Shital Niwas, Maharajganj, Kathmandu; tel. 416011; fax 416016; e-mail mofa@mos.com.np.

Ministry of Home Affairs: Singha Durbar, Kathmandu; tel. 226996; fax 227186; e-mail moha@mos.com.np; internet www.southasia.com/hmg_home.

Ministry of Industry, Commerce and Supplies: Singha Durbar, Kathmandu; tel. 251174; fax 220319.

Ministry of Information and Communications: Singha Durbar, Kathmandu; tel. 220150; fax 221729.

Ministry of Labour and Transport Management: Singha Durbar, Kathmandu; tel. 228291; fax 256877.

Ministry of Law, Justice and Parliamentary Affairs: Babar Mahal, Kathmandu.

Ministry of Population and the Environment: Singhadurbar, Kathmandu; tel. 245367; fax 242138; e-mail info@mope.gov.np; internet www.mope.gov.np.

COUNCIL OF STATE

The Council of State (Raj Parishad) has a standing committee headed by a royal appointee. The 15-member committee is composed of eight royal appointees and seven other members, including the Prime Minister, the Ministers of Defence and Foreign Affairs, the Chief Justice of the Supreme Court and the Chief of Army Staff.

Chairman of Standing Committee: Dr Keshar Jung Rayamajhi.

Legislature

NATIONAL ASSEMBLY

The National Assembly (Rashtriya Sabha) has 60 members, consisting of 10 nominees of the King, 35 members (including three women) elected by the House of Representatives, and 15 members elected by the electoral college, which includes the heads of the local committees of various development regions. The tenure of office of the members of the National Assembly is six years.

Chairman: Dr MOHAMMAD MOHASIN.

HOUSE OF REPRESENTATIVES

The 205-member House of Representatives (Pratinidhi Sabha) is elected, on the basis of adult franchise, for five years.

Speaker: TARANATH RANABHAT.

Deputy Speaker: CHITRA LEKHA YADAV.

General Election, 3 and 17 May 1999

Party	Seats
Nepali Congress Party (NCP)	111
Communist Party of Nepal (Unified Marxist-Leninist—UML)	71
National Democratic Party (NDP)	11
Rashtriya Jana Morcha	5
Nepali Sadbhavana Party	5
Nepal Workers' and Peasants' Party	1
Samyukta Janmorcha Nepal	1
Total	205

Notes: Polling was deferred until 8 and 23 June 1999 in four constituencies, owing to the deaths of candidates. The House of Representatives was dissolved on 22 May 2002. A general election, originally scheduled for 13 November, was postponed indefinitely on 4 October.

Political Organizations

According to the 1990 Constitution, political parties are required to register with the Election Commission, and, in order to be officially recognized, 5% of the candidates presented by a party must be female and the party should obtain at least 3% of the total votes cast in the election to the House of Representatives. The Constitution also specifies that no law may be adopted that bans, or imposes restrictions on, political parties.

Communist Party of Nepal (Maoist): underground political movement; orchestrates 'people's war' in hills of west Nepal (1996–); advocates abolition of constitutional monarchy and establishment of people's republic; Leaders PUSPA KAMAL DAHAL ('PRACHANDRA'), Dr BABURAM BHATTARAI.

Communist Party of Nepal (Mashal): Kathmandu; Leader CHITRA BAHADUR.

Communist Party of Nepal (Unified Marxist-Leninist—UML): Madan Nagar Balkhu, POB 5471, Kathmandu; tel. 278081; fax 278084; e-mail uml@mos.com.np; internet www.south-asia.com/uml/; f. 1991, when two major factions of the Communist Party of Nepal (CPN; f. 1949; banned 1960; legalized 1990)—the Marxist and Marxist-Leninist factions—merged; the Communist Party of Nepal (Marxist-Leninist—ML) seceded in 1998 and rejoined the UML in 2002; Chair. (vacant); Gen. Sec. MADHAV KUMAR NEPAL.

Communist Party of Nepal (United): Dillibazar, POB 2737, Kathmandu; tel. 430869; fax 411642; Leader BISHNU B. MANANDHAR.

Communist Party of Nepal (Verma): Dillibazar, Kathmandu; tel. 414997; Leader KRISHNA RAJ VERMA.

Green Nepal Party: Kalikasthan, POB 890, Kathmandu; tel. 411730; fax 419497; e-mail greennp@wlink.com.np; Leader KUBER SHARMA.

Janawadi Morcha: Indrachowk, Itumbahal, Kathmandu; tel. 211033; Leader PIRUDDHIN MIR.

National Democratic Party (NDP) (Rashtriya Prajatantra Party—RPP): Naxal, Kathmandu; tel. 437057; fax 434441; right-wing; Pres. SURYA BAHADUR THAPA; Vice-Pres. PRAKASH CHANDRA LOHANI; Gen. Sec. PASHUPATI SHUMSHER J. B. RANA.

National Democratic Party (NDP) (Chand) (Rashtriya Prajatantra Party—RPP): Maitighar, Kathmandu; tel. 223044; fax 223628; right-wing; Leader LOKENDRA BAHADUR CHAND.

National People's Council (Rashtriya Janata Parishad): Dillibazar, Kathmandu; tel. 415150; f. 1992; royalist; aims to defend democracy, nationalism and sovereignty; Pres. MAITRIKA PRASAD KOIRALA; Vice-Pres. KIRTI NIDHI BISTA.

National People's Front (Rashtriya Jana Morcha): Mahaboudha, Kathmandu; tel. 224226; Leader CHITRA BAHADUR.

National People's Liberation Forum: Kathmandu; left-wing; rejects 1990 Constitution as reactionary; Chair. M. S. THAPA.

Nepal Praja Parishad: Battisputali, Kathmandu; tel. 471616; f. 1936; banned 1961; legalized 1990; Pres. RAM HARI SHRESTHA; Gen. Secs Dr MEENA ACHARYA, MAHESWOR SHARMA.

Nepal Workers' and Peasants' Party: Golmadhi Tole, 7-Bhaktapur, Kathmandu; tel. 610974; fax 613207; Chair. NARAYAN MAN BIJUKCHHE (ROHIT).

Nepali Congress Party (NCP): Bhansar Tole, Teku, Kathmandu; tel. 227748; fax 227747; e-mail ncparty@mos.com.np; internet www.nepalicongress.org.np; f. 1947; banned 1960; legalized 1990; Pres. GIRIJA PRASAD KOIRALA; Gen. Sec. SUSHIL KOIRALA; 135,000 active members, 500,000 ordinary members.

Nepali Janata Dal: Samakhusi, Kathmandu; tel. 352476; f. 1990; advocates the consolidation of the multi-party democratic system and supports the campaign against corruption; Leader KESHAR JUNG RAYAMAJHI.

Nepali National Congress: Lazimpat, Kathmandu; tel. 411090; Pres. DILLI RAMAN REGMI.

Nepali Sadbhavana Party (NSP) (Nepal Goodwill Party): Shantinagar, New Baneshwor, Kathmandu; tel. 488068; fax 470797; f. 1990; promotes the rights of the Madhesiya community, who are of Indian origin and reside in the Terai; demands that the Government recognize Hindi as an official language, that constituencies in the Terai be allocated on the basis of population, and that the Government grant citizenship to those who settled in Nepal before April 1990; Pres. GAJENDRA NARAYAN SINGH; Gen. Sec. HRIDAYESH TRIPATHI.

Samyukta Janmorcha Nepal: c/o House of Representatives, Kathmandu.

United People's Front (UPF): Koteshwar, Kathmandu; tel. 479159; fax 470457; Maoist; involved in 'people's war' in hills of west Nepal (1996–); Chair. AMIK SHERCHAN; Leaders Dr BABURAM BHATTARAI, LILAMANI POKHAREL.

Diplomatic Representation

EMBASSIES IN NEPAL

Australia: Bhat Bhateni, POB 879, Kathmandu; tel. 411578; fax 417533; Ambassador: B. DORAN.

Bangladesh: Maharajgunj Ring Rd, POB 789, Kathmandu; tel. 372843; fax 373265; e-mail bdootktm@wlink.com.np; Chargé d'affaires a.i.: GOLAM SARWAR.

China, People's Republic: Baluwatar, POB 4234, Kathmandu; tel. 415383; fax 411388; Ambassador: WU CONGYONG.

Denmark: Baluwatar, Lalita Niwas Rd, POB 6332, Kathmandu; tel. 413010; fax 411409; e-mail danemb@wlink.com.np; Chargé d'affaires: GERT MEINECKE.

Egypt: Pulchowk, Lalitpur, POB 792, Kathmandu; tel. 524844; fax 522975; Ambassador: ABD EL-HAMID MOHAMED TABAK.

Finland: Lazimpat, POB 2126, Kathmandu; tel. 416636; fax 416703; e-mail finembka@mos.com.np; internet www.south-asia.com/embassy-Finland; Chargé d'affaires a.i.: ASKO LUUKKAINEN.

France: Lazimpat, POB 452, Kathmandu; tel. 412332; fax 418288; e-mail ambafr@mos.com.np; Ambassador: CLAUDE ABROSINI.

Germany: Gyaneshwar, POB 226, Kathmandu; tel. 412786; fax 416899; e-mail gerembnp@mos.com.np; Ambassador: Dr KLAUS BARTH.

India: Lainchaur, POB 292, Kathmandu; tel. 411940; fax 413132; e-mail eipi@mos.com.np; internet www.south-asia.com/embassy-India; Ambassador: KRISHNA V. RAJAN.

Israel: Bishramalaya House, Lazimpat, POB 371, Kathmandu; tel. 411811; fax 413920; e-mail israelem@mos.com.np; Ambassador: AVRAHIM NIR.

Japan: Panipokhari, POB 264, Kathmandu; tel. 426680; fax 414101; Ambassador: MITSUAKI KOJIMA.

Korea, Democratic People's Republic: Jhamsikhel, Lalitpur, Kathmandu; tel. 521084; Ambassador: KIM THAE JONG.

Korea, Republic: Himshail, Red Cross Marg, Tahachal, POB 1058, Kathmandu; tel. 270172; fax 272041; e-mail koreasamb@mos.com.np; Ambassador: HWANG BOO-HONG.

Myanmar: Chakupath, Patan Gate, Lalitpur, POB 2437, Kathmandu; tel. 523734; fax 523402; Ambassador: U TIN LATT.

Norway: Surya Court, Pulchowk, Lalitpur, POB 20765, Kathmandu; tel. 545307; fax 545226; e-mail emb.kathmandu@norad.no.

Pakistan: Panipokhari, POB 202, Kathmandu; tel. 411421; Ambassador: MUHAMMAD NASSER MIAN.

Russia: Baluwatar, POB 123, Kathmandu; tel. 412155; fax 416571; Ambassador: VLADIMIR V. IVANOV.

Sri Lanka: Maharajgunj, POB 8802, Chundevi, Kathmandu; tel. 413623; fax 418128; e-mail embassy@srilanka.info.com.np; Ambassador: PAMELA J. DEEN.

Thailand: Jyoti Kendra, Thapathali, POB 3333, Kathmandu; tel. 213912; fax 420408; Ambassador: POWTHEP VANACHINDA.

United Kingdom: Lainchaur, POB 106, Kathmandu; tel. 410583; fax 411789; e-mail britemb@wlink.com.np; internet www.britain.gov.np; Ambassador: KEITH BLOOMFIELD.

USA: Panipokhari, POB 295, Kathmandu; tel. 411179; fax 419963; Ambassador: MICHAEL E. MALINOWSKI.

Judicial System

According to the 1990 Constitution, the judicial system is composed of three tiers: the Supreme Court (which is also a Court of Record), the Appellate Courts and the District Courts. The Supreme Court consists of a Chief Justice and up to 14 other judges. The Chief Justice, whose tenure of office is seven years, is appointed by the King on the recommendation of the Constitutional Council, while all other judges are appointed on the recommendation of the Judicial Council.

Chief Justice: KESHAV PRASAD UPADHYAYA.

Attorney-General: BADRI BAHADUR KARKI.

Religion

At the 2001 census, an estimated 80.6% of the population professed Hinduism (the religion of the Royal Family), while 10.7% were Buddhists and 4.2% Muslims. There were an estimated 101,976 Christians in Nepal in 2001.

BUDDHISM

All Nepal Bhikkhu Council: Vishwa Shanti Vihara (World Peace Temple), 465 Ekadantamarga, Minbhawan, New Baneshwar, POB 8973, Kathmandu; tel. 482984; fax 482250; e-mail vishwa@ntc.net.np; internet www.vishwavihara.org.

Nepal Buddhist Association: Kathmandu; tel. 5214420; Sec. Rev. BHIKKHU AMRITANANDA, Ananda Kuti, Kathmandu.

CHRISTIANITY

Protestant Church

Presbyterian Church of the Kingdom of Nepal: POB 3237, Kathmandu; tel. and fax 524450.

The Roman Catholic Church

The Church is represented in Nepal by a single apostolic prefecture. At December 2000 there were an estimated 6,195 adherents in the country.

Apostolic Prefecture: Church of the Assumption, Everest Postal Care P. Ltd, POB 8975 EPC-343, Kathmandu; tel. 542802; fax 521710; e-mail anath@wlink.com.np; f. 1983 as Catholic Mission; Prefect Apostolic Fr ANTHONY FRANCIS SHARMA.

ISLAM

All Nepal Muslim Society: Durbar Marg, Kathmandu; tel. 220534.

The Press

PRINCIPAL DAILIES

The Commoner: Naradevi, POB 203, Kathmandu; tel. 228236; f. 1956; English; Publr and Chief Editor GOPAL DASS SHRESTHA; circ. 7,000.

Daily News: Bhimsensthan, POB 171, Kathmandu; tel. 279147; fax 279544; e-mail manju-sakya@hotmail.com; f. 1983; Nepali and English; Chief Editor MANJU RATNA SAKYA; Publr SUBHA LAXMI SAKYA; circ. 20,000.

Dainik Nirnaya: Bhairawa; tel. 20117; Nepali; Editor P. K. BHATTACHAN.

Gorkhapatra: Dharma Path, POB 23, Kathmandu; tel. 221478; fax 222921; f. 1901; Nepali; govt-owned; Editor-in-Chief KRISHNA BHAKTA SHRESTHA; circ. 75,000.

Himalaya Times: Kathmandu; Exec. Editor KUMAR PRASAD SAPKOTA.

Janadoot: Ga-2, 549, Kamal Pokhari (in front of the Police Station), Kathmandu; tel. 412501; f. 1970; Nepali; Editor GOVINDA BIYOGI; circ. 6,500.

Kantipur: Shantinagar, Naya Baneswor, POB 8559, Kathmandu; tel. 473798; fax 470178; Nepali; internet www.kantipuronline.com; Chief Exec. HEM RAJ GYAWALI; Editor YUBARAJ GHIMIRE.

The Kathmandu Post: Subidhnagar, Naya Baneshwor, POB 8559, Kathmandu; tel. 480100; fax 470178; e-mail kpost@kantipur.com.np; internet www.kantipuronline.com; f. 1993; English; Chief Editor SHYAM BAHADUR; Editor SUMAN PRADHAN; circ. 30,000.

The Motherland: POB 1184, Kathmandu; English; Editor MANINDRA RAJ SHRESTHA; circ. 5,000.

Nepal Samacharpatra: Sagarmatha Press, Ramshah Path, Kathmandu; e-mail sadhana@mail.com.np; f. 1945; Nepali; Editor NARENDRA BILAS PANDEY; circ. 1,000.

Nepali Hindi Daily: Maitidevi Phant, Shantinagar 32, Kathmandu; tel. 436584; fax 435931; e-mail das@ntc.net.np; f. 1954; evening; Hindi; Publr UMA KANT DAS; Chief Editor VIJOY KUMAR DAS; circ. 65,000.

Rising Nepal: Dharma Path, POB 1623, Kathmandu; tel. 227493; fax 224381; internet www.south-asia.com/news-ktmpost.html; f. 1965; English; Editor-in-Chief GYAN BAHADUR RAI (acting); circ. 20,000.

Samaj: National Printing Press, Dilli Bazar, Kathmandu; f. 1954; Nepali; Editor MANI RAJ UPADHYAYA; circ. 5,000.

Samaya: Kamal Press, Ramshah Path, Kathmandu; f. 1962; Nepali; Editor MANIK LAL SHRESTHA; circ. 18,000.

Swatantra Samachar: Vina Bhandranalya, Chhetrapati, Kathmandu; f. 1957; Editor MADAN DEV SHARMA; circ. 2,000.

SELECTED PERIODICALS

Agricultural Credit: Agricultural Training and Research Institute, Agricultural Development Bank, Head Office, Ramshah Path, Panchayat Plaza, Kathmandu; tel. 220756; fax 225329; 2 a year; publ. by the Agricultural Development Bank; Chair. Dr NARAYAN N. KHATRI; Editor RUDRA PD. DAHAL.

Arpan: Bhimsensthan, POB 285, Kathmandu; tel. 244450; fax 279544; e-mail manju-sakya@hotmail.com; f. 1964; weekly; Nepali; Publr and Chief Editor MANJU RATNA SAKYA; circ. 18,000.

Commerce: Bhimsensthan, POB 171, Kathmandu; tel. 279636; fax 279544; e-mail manju-sakya@hotmail.com; f. 1971; monthly; English; Publr and Chief Editor MANJU RATNA SAKYA; Editor SUBHA LAXMI SAKYA; circ. 12,000.

Current: Kamalpokhari, POB 191, Kathmandu; tel. 413554; f. 1982; weekly; Nepali; Publr and Editor DEVENDRA GAUTAM; Foreign Editor UPENDRA GAUTAM; circ. 7,000.

Cyber Post: Kathmandu; fortnightly; computers, electronics.

Foreign Affairs Journal: 5/287 Lagon, Kathmandu; f. 1976; 3 a year; articles on Nepalese foreign relations and diary of main news events; Publr and Editor BHOLA BIKRUM RANA; circ. 5,000.

Himal, The South Asian Magazine: POB 7251, Kathmandu; tel. 543333; fax 521013; e-mail info@himalmag.com; internet www.himalmag.com; f. 1987; monthly; political, business, social and environmental issues throughout South Asia; Editor-in-Chief KANAK MANI DIXIT; Marketing Man. SUMAN SHAKYA.

The Independent: Shankher Deep Bldg, Khichhapokhari, POB 3543, Kathmandu; tel. 249256; fax 226293; e-mail independ@mos.com.np; internet www.nepalnews.com/independent.htm; f. 1991; weekly; English; Editor SUBARNA B. CHHETRI.

Janadharana: Kathmandu; e-mail dharana@mail.com.np; internet www.nepalnews.com.np/dharana.htm; weekly; left-wing; Editor NEEMKANT PANDEY.

Janmabhumi: Janmabhumi Press, Tahachal, Kathmandu; tel. 280979; e-mail sirishnp@hotmail.com; internet www.catmando.com; weekly; Nepali; Publr and Editor SHIRISH BALLABH PRADHAN.

Koseli: Kathmandu; weekly.

Madhuparka: Dharma Path, POB 23, Kathmandu; tel. 222278; f. 1986; monthly; Nepali; literary; Editor-in-Chief KRISHNA BHAKTA SHRESTHA; circ. 20,000.

Mulyankan: Kathmandu; monthly, left-wing; Editor SHYAM SHRESTHA.

Matribhoomi (Nepali Weekly): GA 2-549, Kamal Pokhai (in front of the Police Station), Kathmandu; tel. 412501; weekly; Nepali; Editor GOVINDA BIYOGI.

Nepal Chronicle: Maruhiti; weekly; English; Publr and Editor CHANDRA LAL JHA.

Nepal Overseas Trade Statistics: Trade Promotion Centre, Pulchowk, Lalitpur, POB 825, Kathmandu; tel. 532642; fax 525464; e-mail tpcnep@mos.com.np; internet www.tpcnepal.org.np; annual; English.

Nepal Trade Bulletin: Trade Promotion Centre, Pulchowk, Lalitpur, POB 825, Kathmandu; tel. 532642; fax 525464; e-mail tpcnep@mos.com.np; internet www.tpcnepal.org.np; 3 a year; English; Editors NABIN RAJ SHARMA.

Nepali Times: Himalmedia Pvt Ltd, POB 7251, Kathmandu; tel. 543333; fax 521013; e-mail editors@nepalitimes.com; internet www.nepalitimes.com; f. 1955; weekly; Nepali; Publr and Editor CHANDRA LAL JHA; circ. 9,000.

People's Review: Pipalbot, Dillibazar, POB 3052, Kathmandu; tel. 417352; fax 438797; e-mail preview@ntc.net.np; internet www.peoplesreview.com.np; weekly; English; Editor-in-Chief PUSHPA RAJ PRADHAN; circ. 15,000.

Rastrabani: Kathmandu; weekly.

Sanibariya: Kathmandu; weekly.

Sanghu Weekly: Kathmandu; weekly; Editor GOPAL BUDHATHOKI.

Saptahik: Kathmandu; weekly.

Spotlight: POB 7256, Kathmandu; tel. 410772; e-mail spotlight@mos.com.np; f. 1991; weekly; English; Editor MADHAV KUMAR RIMAL.

Swatantra Manch Weekly: POB 49, Kathmandu; tel. 436374; fax 435931; e-mail das@ntc.net.np; f. 1985; weekly; Nepali; Publr and Chief Editor V. K. DAS; circ. 30,000.

The Telegraph: Ghattekulo, Dillibazar, POB 4063, Kathmandu; tel. 419370; e-mail tgw@ntc.net.np; weekly; English; Chief Editor NARENDRA P. UPADHYAYA.

Vashudha: Makhan, Kathmandu; monthly; English; social, political and economic affairs; Publr and Editor T. L. SHRESTHA.

Weekly Chronicle: Kathmandu.

NEWS AGENCIES

Rastriya Samachar Samiti (RSS): Prithivi Path, POB 220, Kathmandu; tel. 227912; fax 227698; f. 1962; state-operated; Gen. Man. MUKUNDA PARAJULI.

Foreign Bureaux

Agence France-Presse (AFP): Bhote Bahal-South, Hansa Marg, POB 402, Kathmandu; tel. 253960; fax 222998; e-mail afpresse@mos.com.np; Chief of Bureau KEDAR MAN SINGH.

Associated Press (AP) (USA): Thapathli Panchayan, POB 513, Kathmandu; tel. 212767; Correspondent BINAYA GURACHARYA.

Deutsche Presse-Agentur (dpa) (Germany): KH 1-27 Tebahal Tole, POB 680, Kathmandu 44601; tel. 224557; Correspondent K. C. SHYAM BAHADUR.

Inter Press Service (IPS) (Italy): c/o Nepal Press Institute, POB 4128, Kathmandu; tel. and fax 228943; Correspondent DHRUBA ADHIKARY.

Kyodo News (Japan): GA 2-502, Battisputali, POB 3772, Kathmandu; tel. 470106; fax 480571; e-mail macharya@kyodo.mos.com.np; Correspondent MADHAV ACHARYA.

Reuters (UK): POB 3341, Kathmandu; tel. 372152; fax 373814.

United Press International (UPI) (USA): POB 802, Kathmandu; tel. 215684; Correspondent BHOLA BIKRAM RANA.

PRESS ASSOCIATIONS

Federation of Nepalese Journalists (FNJ): Kathmandu.

Nepal Journalists' Association (NJA): Maitighar, POB 285, Kathmandu; tel. 262426; fax 279544; e-mail manju-sakya@hotmail.com; 5,400 mems; Pres. MANJU RATNA SAKYA; Gen. Sec. NIRMAL KUMAR ARYAL.

Press Council: RSS Bldg, Prithvipath, POB 3077, Kathmandu; tel. 262829; fax 262894; e-mail prescoun_mdf@wlink.com.np; f. 1970; Chair. HARIHAR BIRAHI; Admin. Officer BISHNU PRASAD SHARMA.

Publishers

Educational Enterprise (Pvt) Ltd: Mahankalsthan, POB 1124, Kathmandu; tel. 223749; e-mail ishwarbshrestha@yahoo.com; educational and technical.

International Standards Books and Periodicals (Pvt) Ltd: Bhotatity Bazaar, Chowk Bhitra, POB 3000, Kathmandu 44601; tel. 262815; fax 264179; e-mail u2@ccsl.com.np; f. 1991; Sr Man. Dir SUINDRA LALL CHHIPA; Chief Exec. and Man. Dir GANESH LALL SINGH CHHIPA.

Lakoul Press: Palpa-Tansen, Kathmandu; educational and physical sciences.

Mahabir Singh Chiniya Main: Makhan Tola, Kathmandu.

Mandass Memorials Publications: Kamabakshee Tole, Gha 3-333, Chowk Bitra, Kathmandu; tel. 212289; fax 223036; Man. BASANT RAJ TULADHAR.

Pilgrims Book House: Thamel, POB 3872, Kathmandu; tel. 425919; fax 424943; e-mail pilgrims@wlink.com.np; internet www.pilgrimsbooks.com; f. 1986; Asian studies, religion and travel; Propr PUSHPA TIWARI.

Pilgrims Publishing Nepal (Pvt) Ltd: Thamel, POB 21646, Kathmandu; tel. 428919; fax 424943; e-mail johnsnepal@wlink.com.np; internet www.pilgrimsbooks.com; f. 2000; Exec. Dir JOHN SNYDER.

Ratna Pustak Bhandar: Bhotahity Tole, POB 98, Kathmandu; tel. 223026; fax 248421; e-mail rpb@wlink.com.np; f. 1945; textbooks, general, non-fiction and fiction; Propr RATNA PRASAD SHRESTHA.

Royal Nepal Academy: Kamaladi, Kathmandu; tel. 221241; fax 221175; f. 1957; languages, literature, social sciences, art and philosophy; Dep. Admin. Chief T. D. BHANDARI.

Sajha Prakashan: Pulchowk, Lalitpur, Kathmandu; tel. 521023; fax 544236; f. 1966; educational, literary and general; Chair. BISHNU PRASAD GHIMIRE; Gen. Man. NETRA PRASAD ADHIKARI.

Trans Asian Media Pvt Ltd: Thapathali Crossing, POB 5320, Kathmandu; tel. 242895; fax 223889; Man. Editor SHYAM GOENKA.

Government Publishing House

Department of Information: Ministry of Information and Communications, Singha Durbar, Kathmandu; tel. 220150; fax 221729.

Broadcasting and Communications

TELECOMMUNICATIONS

Nepal Telecommunications Authority: Singha Durbar, Kathmandu; tel. 221944; fax 260400; e-mail ntra@mos.com.np; internet www.nta.gov.np; telecommunications regulatory body; Chair. BHOOP RAJ PANDEY.

Nepal Telecommunications Corpn: Bhadrakali Plaza, POB 11803; Kathmandu; tel. 246034; fax 222424; e-mail rkt@ntc.net.np; internet www.ntc.com.np; f. 1975; monopoly provider; scheduled for transfer to private sector; Man. Dir CHET PRASAD BHATTARAI.

BROADCASTING

Radio

In 1992 radio broadcasts reached about 90% of Nepal's population.

Radio Nepal: Radio Broadcasting Service, HM Government of Nepal, Singha Durbar, POB 634, Kathmandu; tel. 223910; fax 221952; e-mail radio@rne.wlink.com.np; internet www.catmando.com./news/radio-nepal/radionp.htm; f. 1951; broadcasts on short and medium wave in Nepali and English for 17 hours daily (incl. two hours of regional broadcasting in the evening); short-wave station at Khumaltar and medium-wave stations at Bhaisepati, Pokhara, Surkhet, Dipayal, Bardibas and Dharan; Exec. Dir SHAILENDRA RAJ SHARMA; Dep. Exec. Dir M. P. ADHIKARI.

Television

In 1986 Nepal's first television station began broadcasting within the Kathmandu valley.

Nepalese Television Corporation: Singha Durbar, POB 3826, Kathmandu; tel. 228447; fax 228312; broadcasts 32 hours a week; programmes in Nepali (50%), English (25%) and Hindi/Urdu (25%); regional stations at Pokhara, Biratnagar and Hetuada; Gen. Man. TAPA NATH SHUKLA; Dep. Gen. Man. (Technical) RAVINDRA S. RANA; Dep. Gen. Man. (Productions) DURGA NATH SHARMA.

Shangri-La Channel (Pvt) Ltd: Sangharsh Chamber, Gyaneshwor, POB 5852, Kathmandu; tel. 415299; fax 416333; Chief Exec. NEER SHAH.

Space-Time Network: Iceberg Bldg, 3rd Floor, Putali Sadak, Kathmandu; tel. 419133; fax 419504; f. 1994; satellite transmission service.

Finance

(auth. = authorized; cap. = capital; p.u. = paid up; m. = million; dep. = deposits; res = reserves; brs = branches; amounts in Nepalese rupees)

BANKING

Central Bank

Nepal Rastra Bank: Central Office, Baluwatar, POB 73, Kathmandu; tel. 419804; fax 414553; e-mail nrb@mos.com.np; internet www.nrb.org.np; f. 1956; bank of issue; 100% state-owned; cap. 10m., res 23,623.5m., dep. 19,241.2m. (July 2000); Gov. Dr TILAK RAWAL; 9 brs.

Domestic Commercial Banks

Kumari Bank Ltd: Putalisadak, POB 21128, Kathmandu; tel. 232112; fax 231960; e-mail kumaribank@info.com.np; f. 2001; auth. cap 1,000m. (April 2001); Chair. NOOR PRATAP RANA.

Nepal Bank Ltd: Nepal Bank Bldg, Dharmapath, New Rd, POB 36, Kathmandu; tel. 221185; fax 222383; e-mail arbnbl@wlink.com.np; f. 1937; 40% state-owned, 60% owned by Nepalese public; cap. 378m., res 489.6m., dep. 21,570.5m. (July 1997); Chair. SHAMBHU SHARAN PRASAD KAYASTHA; 165 brs.

Nepal Industrial and Commercial Bank Ltd (NIC Bank): Main Rd, Koshi Zone, Morang District, POB 232, Biratnagar; tel. 21921; fax 22748; e-mail nicb@brt.wlink.com.np; internet www.nicbank.com.np; f. 1998; privately-owned; cap. 499.8m., res 16.3m., dep. 3,575.8m. (July 2001); Chair. JAGDISH PRASAD AGRAWAL; CEO K. R. IYER; 6 brs.

Rastriya Banijya Bank (National Commercial Bank): Singha Durbar Plaza, Kathmandu; tel. 252595; fax 252931; f. 1966; 100% state-owned; cap. 1,172m., res 268m., dep. 33,329m. (July 1999); Pres. PANYA PRASAD DAHAL; 212 brs, 4 regional offices.

Joint-venture Banks

Bank of Kathmandu Ltd: Kamal Pokhari, POB 9044, Kathmandu; tel. 418068; fax 418990; e-mail info@bok.com.np; f. 1993; 55% owned by Nepalese public, 45% by local promoters; cap. 90m., res 10.6m., dep. 2,564.8m. (July 1999); Chair. DAMBAR BAHADUR MALLA.

Everest Bank Ltd: New Baneshwor, POB 13384, Kathmandu; tel. 481017; fax 482263; e-mail ebl@mos.com.np; internet www.ebl.com.np; f. 1994; 50% owned by directors, 20% by Punjab National Bank (India), 30% by the Nepalese public; cap. 235.5m., res 159.6m., dep. 4,482.1m. (Jan. 2002); Exec. Dir S. S. DABAS; 22 brs.

Himalayan Bank Ltd: Karmachari Sanchaya Kosh Bldg, Tridevi Marg, Thamel, POB 20590, Kathmandu; tel. 227749; fax 222800; e-mail hbl@hbl.com.np; internet www.hbl.com.np; f. 1993; 20% owned by Habib Bank Ltd (Pakistan); cap. 300m., res 200.6m., dep. 14,237.5m. (July 2000); Chair. HIMALAYA S. J. B. RANA; CEO PRITHIVI BAHADUR PANDEY; 8 brs.

Nepal Arab Bank Ltd (Nabil): Nabil House, Kamaladi, POB 3729, Kathmandu; tel. 429546; fax 429548; e-mail nabil@nabilbank.com.np; internet www.nabilbankltd.com; f. 1984; 50% owned by National Bank of Bangladesh, 30% by the Nepalese public and 20% by Nepalese government financial institutions; cap. 491.7m., res 623.1m., dep. 15,839.0m. (July 2001); Chair. LOK BAHADUR SHRESTHA; Vice-Chair. DAYA RAM AGRAWAL; 16 brs.

Nepal Bangladesh Bank Ltd: Bijulibazar, New Baneswor, POB 9062, Kathmandu; tel. 490767; fax 490824; e-mail nbblho@nbbl.com.np; f. 1994; 50% owned by International Finance Investment and Commerce Bank Ltd (Bangladesh), 20% by Nepalese promoters and 30% public issue; cap. 238.2m., res 211.2m., dep. 8,610.4m. (July 2001); Man. Dir NARENDRA BHATTARAI; Chair. JEET BAHADUR SHRESTHA; 10 brs.

Nepal Bank of Ceylon Ltd: Bagh Bazar, POB 12559, Kathmandu; tel. 246105; fax 244610; Man. Dir D. V. K. JAYSURYA.

Nepal Investment Bank Ltd: Durbar Marg, POB 3412, Kathmandu; tel. 228229; fax 226349; e-mail info@nibl.com.np; f. 1986; 50% owned by a consortium of Nepalese investors, 20% by general public, 15% by Rastriya Banijya Bank and 15% by Rastriya Beema Sansthan; cap. 170m., res 249m., dep. 4,256m. (July 2001); Chair. TIRTHA MAN SHAKYA; Chief Exec. Dir PRITHIVI B. PANDE; 6 brs.

Nepal SBI Bank Ltd: Corporate Office, Hattisar, POB 6049, Kathmandu; tel. 435516; fax 435612; e-mail nsblco@mos.com.np; f. 1993; 50% owned by State Bank of India, 30% by Nepalese public, 15% by Employees' Provident Fund (Nepal) and 5% by Agricultural Development Bank (Nepal); Chair. B. P. ACHARYA; Man. Dir B. B. DAS.

Nepal Sri Lanka Merchant Bank Ltd: N.B. Bldg, Bagh Bazar, POB 12248, Kathmandu; tel. 227555; fax 240674; Man. Dir ARJUNA HERATH.

Standard Chartered Bank Nepal Ltd: Grindlays Bhavan, Nayabaneshwor, POB 3990, Kathmandu; tel. 246753; fax 226762; f. 1986; 50% owned by Standard Chartered Grindlays, 33% by Nepal Bank Ltd and 17% by the Nepalese public; cap. 340m., res 502m., dep. 14,997m. (July 2000); Chair. B. N. NEPAL; CEO R. J. COX; 8 brs.

Development Finance Organizations

Agricultural Development Bank: Ramshah Path, Kathmandu; tel. 262885; fax 262616; e-mail info@adbn.gov.np; www.adbn.gov.np; f. 1968; 93.6% state-owned, 2.1% owned by the Nepal Rastra Bank, and 4.3% by co-operatives and private individuals; specialized agricultural credit institution providing credit for agricultural development to co-operatives, individuals and asscns; receives deposits from individuals, co-operatives and other asscns to generate savings in the agricultural sector; acts as Government's implementing agency for small farmers' group development project, assisted by the Asian Development Bank and financed by the UN Development Programme; operational networks include 14 zonal offices, 37 brs, 92 sub-brs, 52 depots and 160 small farmers' development projects, 3 Zonal Training Centres, 2 Appropriate Technology Units; Chair. SHYAM PRASAD MAINALI.

Nepal Development Bank: Heritage Plaza, POB 11017, Kamaladi, Kathmandu; tel. 245753.

Nepal Housing Development Finance Co Ltd: POB 5624, Kathmandu; tel. 223390; Chief Exec. INDRA PRASHAD KARMACHARYA.

Nepal Industrial Development Corporation (NIDC): NIDC Bldg, Durbar Marga, POB 10, Kathmandu; tel. 228322; fax 227428; e-mail nidc@wlink.com.np; f. 1959; state-owned; holds investments of 5,609.9m. in 1,125 industrial enterprises (2000/01); offers financial and technical assistance to private-sector industries; in 2000/01 approved a total of 9.41m. in loans and working capital, and disbursed 8.17m.; Gen. Man. UTTAM NARAYAN SHRESTHA.

STOCK EXCHANGE

Nepal Stock Exchange Ltd: Singh Durbar Plaza, POB 1550, Kathmandu; tel. 250735; fax 262538; e-mail nepse@stock.mos.com.np; internet www.nepalstock.com; f. 1976, reorg. 1984; converted in 1993 from Securities Exchange Centre Ltd to Nepal Stock Exchange Ltd; 118 listed cos, 120 scripts; Gen. Man. MUKUNDA NATH DHUNGEL; Man. (Admin. and Market Operations) M. P. SHARMA; Man. (Information, Planning and Development) P. BHATTARAI.

INSURANCE

Alliance Insurance Co Ltd: Durbar Marg, POB 10811, Kathmandu; tel. 222836; fax 241411; e-mail sk@aic.wlink.com.np.

Everest Insurance Co: Kantipath, POB 8857, Kathmandu; tel. 243631; fax 240083.

Himalayan General Insurance Co Ltd: Durbar Marg, POB 148, Kathmandu; tel. 226634; fax 223906; Chief Exec. RAJ KRISHNA SHRESTHA.

National Insurance Co Ltd: Tripureswor, POB 376, Kathmandu; tel. 250710; fax 261289; e-mail natinsur@ccsl.com.np; Man. A. S. KOHLI.

National Life and General Insurance Co Ltd: Lazimpat, POB 4332, Kathmandu; tel. 412625; fax 416427; Chief Exec. S. K. SINGH.

Neco Insurance Ltd: Hattisar, POB 12271, Kathmandu; tel. 427354; fax 418761.

Nepal Insurance Co Ltd: Kamaladi, POB 3623, Kathmandu; tel. 221353; fax 225446.

The Oriental Insurance Co Ltd: Jyoti Bhavan, POB 165, Kathmandu; tel. 221448; fax 223419; e-mail oriental@wlink.com.np.

Premier Insurance Co (Nepal) Ltd: 1988 Ram Rukmani Sadan, Kamaladi Marg, POB 9183, Kathmandu; tel. 417765; fax 420554; e-mail premier@picl.com.np; internet www.premier-insurance.com.np; Man. Dir SURESH LAL SHRESTHA.

Rastriya Beema Sansthan (National Insurance Corpn): RBS Bldg, Ramshah Path, POB 527, Kathmandu; tel. 213882; fax 262610; e-mail beema@wlink.com.np; f. 1967; Gen. Man. BIR BIKRAM RAXAMAJHI.

Sagarmatha Insurance Co Ltd: Kathmandu Plaza, Block Y, Kamaladi, POB 12211, Kathmandu; tel. 240896; fax 247941; e-mail sagarmatha@insurance.wlink.com.np; Exec. Dir K. B. BASNYAT.

United Insurance Co (Nepal) Ltd: Durbar Marg, POB 9075, Kathmandu; tel. 246686; fax 246687.

Trade and Industry

GOVERNMENT AGENCY

National Planning Commission (NPC): Singha Durbar, POB 1284, Kathmandu; tel. 225879; fax 226500; e-mail npcs@npcnepal.gov.np; internet npc.gov.np:8080; Vice-Chair. Dr NARAYAN KHADKA.

DEVELOPMENT ORGANIZATIONS

Agriculture Inputs Corporation: Teku, Kuleshwar, POB 195, Kathmandu; tel. 279715; fax 278790; f. 1966; govt-owned; sole supplier of inputs for agricultural development (procuring and distribution of chemical fertilizers, improved seeds, agricultural tools and plant protection material) at national level; operates seeds multiplication programme (paddy, wheat, maize and vegetable); seed processing plants at Dang, Hetauda, Itahari, Janakpur, Nepalgunj and Sidharthanagar; Chair. MOHANDEV PANT; Gen. Man. ARJUN KUMAR THAPA.

National Trading Ltd: Teku, POB 128, Kathmandu; tel. 227683; fax 225151; e-mail natreli@mos.com.np; f. 1962; govt-owned; imports and distributes construction materials and raw materials for industry; also machinery, vehicles and consumer goods; operates bonded warehouse, duty-free shop and related activities; brs in all major towns; Chair. SONAFI YADAV; Gen. Man. MADHAV JUNG RANA.

Nepal Foreign Trade Association: Bagmati Chamber, 1st Floor, Milanmarg, Teku, POB 541, Kathmandu; tel. 223784; fax 247159; e-mail nfta@mos.com.np; Pres. ASHOK KUMAR AGRAWAL; Vice-Pres. AKHIL K. CHAPAGAIN.

Nepal Productivity and Economic Development Centre: Balaju, POB 1318, Kathmandu; tel. 350566; fax 350530; e-mail npedc@wlink.com.np; internet www.panasia.org.sg/nepalnet/npedc/html; functions as secretariat of National Productivity Council; provides services for industrial promotion and productivity improvement through planning research, consultancy, training, seminars and information services; Dir-Gen. VIJAY S. SHRESTHA.

Nepal Resettlement Co: Kathmandu; f. 1963; govt-owned; engaged in resettling people from the densely-populated hill country to the western Terai plain.

Nepal Tea Development Corporation: Kathmandu.

Trade Promotion Centre (TPC): Pulchowk, Lalitpur, POB 825, Kathmandu; tel. 525348; fax 525464; e-mail tpcnep@mos.com.np; internet www.tpcnepal.org.np; f. 1971 to encourage exports; govt-owned; Exec. Dir DEB BAHADUR ROKAYA.

CHAMBERS OF COMMERCE

Federation of Nepalese Chambers of Commerce and Industry (FNCCI): Pachali Shahid Shukra FNCCI Milan Marg, Teku, POB 269, Kathmandu; tel. 262061; fax 261022; e-mail fncci@mos.com.np; internet www.fncci.org; f. 1965; comprises 86 District Municipality Chambers (DCCIs), 50 Commodity Associations, 424 leading industrial and commercial undertakings in both the public and private sector, and nine Bi-national Chambers; Pres. RAVI BHAKTA SHRESTHA; Sec.-Gen. BADRI PRASAD OJHA.

Birgunj Chamber of Commerce: Birgunj; Pres. BABU LAL CHACHAN.

Lalitpur Chamber of Commerce and Industry: Mangal Bazar, POB 26, Lalitpur; tel. 521740; fax 530661; e-mail lcci@mos.com.np; internet www.lcci.org.np.

Nepal Chamber of Commerce: Chamber Bhavan, Kantipath, POB 198, Kathmandu; tel. 230947; fax 229998; e-mail chamber@wlink.com.np; internet www.nepalchamber.com; f. 1952; non-profit organization promoting industrial and commercial development; 8,000 regd mems and 16,000 enrolled mems; Pres. RAJESH KAZI SHRESTHA; Sec.-Gen. SURESH KUMAR BASNET.

Nepal-German Chamber of Commerce and Industry: Putalisadak, POB 201, Kathmandu; tel. 228733; fax 244417.

Nepal-India Chamber of Commerce and Industry: Shahid Shukra Brikshya, Teku, POB 13245, Kathmandu; tel. 250607; fax 250642.

INDUSTRIAL AND TRADE ASSOCIATIONS

Association of Craft Producers: Ravi Bhavan, POB 3701, Kathmandu; tel. 275108; fax 272676; e-mail craftacp@mos.com.np; f. 1984; local non-profit organization providing technical, marketing and management services for craft producers, manufacturer, exporter and retailer of handicraft goods; Programme Co-ordinator REVITA SHRESTHA.

Association of Forest-based Industries and Trade: Thapathali, POB 2798, Kathmandu; tel. 216020.

Association of Nepalese Rice and Oil Industries: Ganabahal, POB 363, Kathmandu; tel. 250001; fax 249723; e-mail ktm@golchha.com; Pres. PASHUPATI GIRI; Gen. Sec. HULASCHAND GOLCHHA.

Association of Pharmaceutical Producers of Nepal: 63/284, Chhetrapati, POB 4506, Kathmandu; tel. 415330; fax 436395; e-mail vaidya@vpharma.wlink.com.np.

Cargo Agents Association of Nepal: Thamel, POB 5355, Kathmandu; tel. 419019.

Central Carpet Industries Association of Nepal: Bijulee Bazar, POB 2419, Kathmandu; tel. 496108; fax 475291; e-mail ccia@enet.com.np; internet www.nepalcarpet.org; Pres. A. G. SHERPA.

Computer Association of Nepal: Putalisadak, POB 4982, Kathmandu; tel. 432700; fax 424043; e-mail info@can.org.np; internet www.canorg.np; f. 1992; Pres. LOCHAN LAL AMATYA.

Footwear Manufacturers' Association of Nepal: Khichapokhari, POB 648, Kathmandu; tel. 228131; fax 416576.

Garment Association of Nepal: Shankhamul Rd, New Baneshwor, POB 21332, Kathmandu; tel. 482691; fax 482173; e-mail gan@asso.wlink.com.np; internet www.ganasso.org; Pres. KIRAN P. SAAKHA.

Handicrafts Association of Nepal: Maitighar, POB 784, Thapathali; tel. 243015; fax 222940; e-mail han@wlink.com.np; internet www.nepalhandicraft.com.np.

Nepal Association of Travel Agents: Gairidhara Rd, Goma Ganesh, Naxal, POB 362, Kathmandu; tel. 418661; fax 418684; e-mail info@nata.org.np; internet www.nata.org.np; f. 1966; 165 active mems, 14 allied mems.

Nepal Cottage and Small Industries Association: Teku, Kathmandu; tel. 212876.

Nepal Forest Industries Association: Gyaneshwor, POB 1804, Kathmandu; tel. 411865; fax 413838; e-mail padmasri@ccsl.com.np.

Nepal Leather Industry and Trade Association: Baghbazar, POB 4991, Kathmandu; tel. 410315.

Nepal Plastic Manufacturers' Association: Kupondol, Kathmandu; tel. 211981.

Nepal Tea Planters' Association: Bhadrapur; tel. 20183.

Nepal Textile Industries Association: Kupondol, Lalitpur; tel. 523693; Pres. MAHESH LAL PRADHAN.

Nepal Trans-Himalayan Trade Association: Kantipath, Kathmandu; tel. 223764; Vice-Chair. NIL KANTHA CHAULAGAIN.

UTILITIES

Electricity

Butwal Power Co Ltd: POB 126, Kathmandu; tel. 525732; fax 527898.

Chilime Hydropower Co Ltd: Kathmandu; 51% owned by Nepal Electricity Authority; Dir DAMBER BAHADUR NEPALI.

Electricity Development Centre: Exhibition Rd, POB 2507, Kathmandu; tel. 227262; fax 227537; f. 1993; under Ministry of Water Resources; Dir-Gen. VIJAY SHANKER SHRESTHA.

Nepal Electricity Authority: Ratna Park, Kathmandu; tel. 227725; fax 227035; e-mail neamd@mos.com.np; internet www.nea.org.np; f. 1985 following merger; govt-owned; Man. Dir Dr J. L. KARMACHARYA.

Water

Nepal Water Supply Corpn: Tripureswor Marg, Kathmandu; tel. 253656; fax 223484; f. 1990; govt-owned; Exec. Chair. ARUN KUMAR RANJITKAR.

MAJOR COMPANIES

Breweries and Distilleries

Gorkha Brewery Ltd: Bijuli Bazar, POB 4140, Kathmandu; tel. 492080; fax 491464; e-mail gbpl@wlink.com.np; CEO C. P. KHETAN.

Himalayan Brewery Ltd: 1448 Dillibazar, Kathmandu; tel. 419196; fax 412847; Chief Exec. KUMAR MOHAN BAHADUR SHAHI.

Jawalakhel Distillery Pvt Ltd: Jawalakhel, Lalitpur, POB 423, Kathmandu; tel. 538549; fax 538236; e-mail jd@hdpl.mos.com.np; Chair. VIJAYA KUMAR SHAH.

Mount Everest Brewery (Pvt) Ltd: 1213 Bina Chambers, Exhibition Rd, POB 1480, Kathmandu; tel. 225912; fax 225785; Chief Exec. PIYUSH BAHADUR AMATYA.

Nepal Brewery Co (Pvt) Ltd: 2/24 Baneshwor Heights, POB 595, Kathmandu; tel. 471705; fax 473831; Chief Exec. JAGADISH PD AGRAWAL.

Nepal Distilleries (Pvt) Ltd: Balaju, POB 45, Kathmandu; tel. 271988; fax 271971; Chief Exec. SHEOROO SOLI MANEKSHAW.

Shree Distillery (Pvt) Ltd: Naxal, Chardhunge, Kathmandu; tel. and fax 419617; Chief Exec. MATHURA PD MASKEY.

Carpets

Abhijit Carpet Industries (Pvt) Ltd: Kantipath, POB 3263, Kathmandu; tel. 226603; fax 227392; Chief Exec. ASHIS K. SEN GUPTA.

Boudha Designer Carpets (Pvt) Ltd: Jorpathi, Ward 4, POB 9165, Kathmandu; tel. 470905; fax 242553; e-mail bdesigner@wlink.com.np; Chief Exec. SONAM TSERING GURUNG.

Carpet Creation Nepal (Pvt) Ltd: Sinamangal, POB 1244, Kathmandu; tel. 474747; fax 419385; f. 1992; Chief Exec. RAVI KANTA AGRAWAL; 500 employees.

Nepal Carpet Industries: POB 10308, Kathmandu; tel. 220406; fax 523685; Chief Exec. PURNA MAN SAKYA.

Shambala Carpet Industries (Pvt) Ltd: Jorpathi, Besi Gaun, Ward No. 9, Bouddha, POB 5256, Kathmandu; tel. 471502; fax 471758; Chief Exec. HIRAKAJI SHAKYA.

Snowlion Carpets (Pvt) Ltd: POB 596, Kathmandu; tel. 227130; fax 225487; Chief Exec. BIJAYA BAHADUR SHRESTHA.

Srijana Carpet Industry: POB 939, Kathmandu; tel. 212080; fax 220267; Chief Exec. SITA RAM PRASAI.

Tara Thimi Carpets: Bhaktapur, Pithu Thimi, Ward No. 1, Kathmandu; tel. 224412; Chief Exec. NAMGYAL SHRESTHA.

Cement

Hetaunda Cement Industries Ltd: Hetaunda, POB 24, Makawanpur; tel. 20352; fax 21023; f. 1976; sales NRs 434m. (2001); Chief Exec. SHREE KRISHNA PRASAD ACHARYA.

Himal Cement Co Ltd: Chovar, POB 321, Kathmandu; tel. 214958; Chief Exec. RAMAKANTA MAINALI.

Food and Food Products

Annapurna Vegetable Products (Pvt) Ltd: Indra Chowk, POB 772, Kathmandu; tel. 224074; fax 224037; Chief Exec. GOPAL RAI SANGHAI.

Birgunj Sugar Factory Ltd: Pipra, Birgunj 17; tel. 22299; fax 21391; Chief Exec. BALARAM BASKOTA.

General Food Industries (Pvt) Ltd: Pulchowk, POB 148, Lalitpur; tel. 526907; fax 523501; Chief Exec. RAJENDRA LAL SHRESTHA.

Gyan Food Products: Kantipath, POB 1991, Kathmandu; tel. 221602; fax 225099; Chief Exec. KUMUD KUMAR DUGAR.

Hukam Foods Nepal (Pvt) Ltd: Balaju, POB 6661, Kathmandu; tel. 421149; fax 421396; Chief Exec. HUKAMCHAND DUGAR.

Nepal Vegetable Ghee Industries Ltd: Hetauda Industrial Estate, POB 8, Hetauda; tel. 20369; fax 20751; Chief Exec. ANANGMAN SHERCHAN.

Salt Trading Corporation Ltd: Kalimati, POB 483, Kathmandu; tel. 271208; fax 271704; e-mail saltkath@mos.com.np; f. 1963 as a joint venture of the public and private sectors (30% and 70% respectively) to manage the import and distribution of salt; also deals in sugar, edible oils, cereals, pulses and spices; deals in the export of tyres, inner tubes and spinning yarn; Chair. K. M. DIXIT; Chief Exec. R. P. JOSHI.

Shiva Shakti Ghee Udyog (P) Ltd: Milan Marg, Teku, Kathmandu; tel. 224762; fax 225406; Chief Exec. RAJ KUMAR AGRAWAL.

Shree Ganesh Biscuit Udyog (Pvt) Ltd: Kamal Pokhari, POB 1906, Kathmandu; tel. 410003; fax 418653; Chief Exec. BHAMA RAJKARNIKAR.

Shree Mahalaxmi Sugar Ltd: POB 1073, Lalitpur; tel. 525039; fax 523818; Chief Exec. M. D. AGRAWAL.

Footwear

Bansbari and Shoe Factory Ltd: Gaidakot, Nawalparasi, Lumbini Zone; Chief Exec. IDRIS AHMAD.

Birat Shoe Co Ltd: POB 1887, Kathmandu; tel. 418429; fax 418907; Chief Exec. BIR BAHADUR THAPA.

Naveen Footwear (Pvt) Ltd: POB 4045, Kathmandu; tel. 222258; fax 225249; Chief Exec. NAVEEN KUMAR PODDAR.

Pashupati Footwear Industries (Pvt) Ltd: Main Rd, POB 34, Biratnagar; tel. 26271; fax 224461; Chief Exec. DAMODAR PRASAD AGRAWAL.

Relaxo Footwear Industries (Pvt) Ltd: Shanker Deep Bldg, Khichapokhari, POB 1275, Kathmandu; tel. 250066; fax 249105; e-mail lg@wlink.com.np; Chief Exec. MAHESH KUMAR AGRAWAL.

Universal Footwear Products: POB 497, Kathmandu; tel. 225414; fax 225974; e-mail unigroup@nepalnetwork.com; Chief Exec. NOOR PRATAP J. B. RANA.

Metals

Agrani Aluminium (Pvt) Ltd: Simra, Bara; tel. 20070; Chief Exec. DIWAKAR GOLCHHA.

Bhagawati Steel Industries (Pvt) Ltd: Jhhonche Tole, Layakusal, POB 556, Kathmandu; Chief Exec. SHASHI KANTA AGRAWAL.

Everest Iron and Steel (Pvt) Ltd: Dhakhwa Bldg, Dharmapath, POB 386, Kathmandu; tel. 220870; Chief Exec. RAVI BHAKTA SHRESTHA.

Hetaunda Iron and Steel (Pvt) Ltd: Tripureswor, POB 2544, Kathmandu; tel. 226058; fax 229124; Chief Exec. SHIVA RATAN SHARDA.

Pancha Kanya Iron Industries (Pvt) Ltd: 3/42 Krishna Galli, POB 2743, Lalitpur; tel. 526551; fax 526529; Chief Exec. PRADEEP SHRESTHA.

Plastics

Jayant Plastics: POB 1275, Kathmandu; tel. 228539; fax 222105; Chief Exec. KAMLESH KUMAR AGRAWAL.

Laxmi Plastics Ltd: POB 650, Lalitpur; tel. 523559; fax 526837; e-mail npgroup@mos.com.np; f. 1985; production of pipes and fittings; Chief Exec. LAXMI SHRESTHA.

Narayani Plastics Udyog (Pvt) Ltd: Bagbazar, POB 1978, Kathmandu; tel. 224460; Chief Exec. JAGADISH PRASAD CHAUDHARY.

Nepal Plastics (Pvt) Ltd: Kupondole, POB 650, Kathmandu; tel. 535473; fax 526837; e-mail npgroup@mos.com.np; f. 1979; production of pipes and fittings; Dir KRISHNA GOPAL SHRESTHA.

Nepal Polythene and Plastic Industries (Pvt) Ltd: Tripureswor, POB 1015, Kathmandu; tel. 261749; fax 261828; Man. Dir ARUN KUMAR KHANAL.

Pioneer Plastics Industries (Pvt) Ltd: POB 5009, Kathmandu; tel. 272509; fax 279877; e-mail lucky@ccsl.com.np; Chief Exec. RAM PRASHAD SHRESTHA.

Sanghai Plastic Industries (Pvt) Ltd: Indrachowk, Kathmandu; tel. 221236; fax 221003; Chief Exec. RATAN LAL SANGHAI.

Tea

Bansal Tea Estate (Pvt) Ltd: Bhadrapur, Jhapa; tel. 20210; Chief Exec. BANSIDHAR BANSAL.

Chandragadhi Tea Estate (Pvt) Ltd: Chandragadhi 2; tel. 20119; Chief Exec. VISNU RAJ POKHAREL.

Guranse Tea Estate (Pvt) Ltd: Voith House, Tinkune Complex, Sinamangal, Tinkune, POB 2640, Kathmandu; tel. 478301; fax 471195; e-mail business@voith.com.np; internet www.guransetea.com; f. 1990; Chair. V. G. VAIDYA; 250 employees.

Haldibari Tea Industries (Pvt) Ltd: Haldibari 2, Jhapa, Mechi Zone; tel. 20092; Chief Exec. BABURAM PARAJULI.

Mittal Tea Estate (Pvt) Ltd: Bhadrapur, Jhapa; tel. 20072; Chief Exec. MOHAN LAL AGRAWAL.

Textiles and Garments

Ami Apparels (Pvt) Ltd: New Baneshwor, POB 1147, Kathmandu; tel. 473812; Chief Exec. PRASANT POKHAREL.

Annapurna Textile Ltd: 6/31 New Rd, POB 2515, Kathmandu; tel. 221536; fax 221403; Chief Exec. A. K. JATIA.

Arun Textile (Pvt) Ltd: POB 4297, Kathmandu; tel. 228992; Chief Exec. SURESH KUMAR STHAPIT.

Ashok Textile Industries (Pvt) Ltd: Mills Area, Rani Biratnagar; tel. 26798; fax 30221; e-mail atibrt@ecomail.com.np; Chief Exec. K. DARBARI.

Contilex Garment Industries: Kamaladi, POB 2740, Kathmandu; tel. 414987; fax 419020; Chief Exec. ARUNA KHETAN.

Eastern Textile Industries Ltd: 8/324 Pyukha Tole, Kathmandu; tel. 222729; fax 221295; Chief Exec. SITARAM LOHIYA.

Gangadharam Cotton and Terry Fabrics (P) Ltd: GD Bldg, Suite 100, Jhamsikhel, POB 5953, Lalitpur; tel. 5967; fax 5510; e-mail gctf@yahoo.com; Chief Exec. TOYA NATH LAMICHHANE.

Gaylord Garments Industries (Pvt) Ltd: POB 1329, Kathmandu; tel. 224703; fax 248112; e-mail makharia@wlink.com.np; Chief Exec. RAMESH KUMAR AGRAWAL.

Girja Garment Industries: POB 6258, Kathmandu; tel. 224185; fax 421258; Chief Exec. SAVITRI DEVI INNANI.

Global Garments (Pvt) Ltd: Gyaneswor, POB 1036, Kathmandu; tel. 417001; fax 416496; Chief Exec. B. L. AGRAWAL.

Global Trading Concern Ltd: Khichapokhari, POB 3127, Kathmandu; tel. 242855; fax 247088; e-mail gtc@ntc.net.np; Chief Exec. ANIL KUMAR AGRAWAL.

Hetauda Textile Industries Ltd: Hetauda Industrial District, POB 36, Hetauda; tel. 20015; fax 20016; Chief Exec. YADAV P. SHARMA.

Imperial Garments Udyog: POB 40, Kathmandu; tel. 226870; fax 226134; Chief Exec. SANJAYA AGRAWAL.

KTM Quality Fashion Industries (Pvt) Ltd: Ga-2/205 Old Baneshwor, Kathmandu; tel. 470423; fax 474727; Chief Exec. ANANDA BHADARI.

Mahalaxmi Garment Industries Group: V. Narsing Kunj, New Plaza, Putali Sadak, POB 4206, Kathmandu; tel. 421048; fax 421258; e-mail mgigroup@inani.com.np; f. 1980; Chair. O. P. INNANI; 2,500 employees.

Momento Apparels (Pvt) Ltd: Tinkune, POB 6431, Kathmandu; tel. 473219; Chief Exec. CHANDI RAJ DHAKAL.

Pragati Textiles Industries (Pvt) Ltd: Ga-1-684 Gyaneshwor, POB 4482, Kathmandu; tel. 418378; fax 418332; Chief Exec. BHAGWAN DAS LOHIA.

Shree Gopi Textile Industries (Pvt) Ltd: 10/268 Indrachowk, Kathmandu; tel. 221081; Chief Exec. RADHE SHYAM AGRAWAL.

Shree Textiles Pvt Ltd: Patan Industrial Estate, Lagankhel, Lalitpur; tel. 522313; Chief Exec. MAHESH LAL PRADHAN.

Surya Silks (Pvt) Ltd: POB 159, Lalitpur; tel. 521341; fax 525136; Chief Exec. MAGGIE SHAH.

Swastic Textile Products (Pvt) Ltd: Koteshwor, POB 584, Kathmandu; tel. 473234; Chief Exec. MURALI DHAR AGRAWAL.

Vishakha Garments (Pvt) Ltd: POB 1962, Kathmandu; tel. 526831; fax 527015; Chief Exec. MADAN PRASHAD SARAWAGI.

Vishal Garments Industries: Jhonchen Tole, POB 2740, Kathmandu; tel. 411484; fax 419020; Chief Exec. PREM KUMAR KHETAN.

Wood and Wood Products

Decor Doors and Wood Products (Pvt) Ltd: Bhosiko Tole, Kathmandu; tel. 221412; Chief Exec. ASHOK KUMAR AGRAWAL.

Everest Paper Mills (Pvt) Ltd: POB 8, Janakpurdham; tel. 20512; fax 20317; e-mail epm@col.com.np; f. 1981; Chief Exec. GOVIND SARRAFF; 400 employees.

Pumori Agro Forestry Industries (Pvt) Ltd: POB 4045, Kathmandu; tel. 222258; fax 225249; Chief Exec. SATYA PRAKASH PODDAR.

Shree Padma Furniture Factory (Pvt) Ltd: Gyaneshwor, POB 1804, Kathmandu; tel. 411865; fax 413838; Chief Exec. PADMA THAPALIYA.

Sundar Furniture Industries (Pvt) Ltd: POB 50, Birgunj; tel. 21412; fax 22086; e-mail kedia@atcnet.com.np; Chief Exec. BIMAL KEDIA.

Miscellaneous

Aarti Soap and Chemical Industries (Pvt) Ltd: Ramshah Path, POB 5161, Kathmandu; tel. 430997; fax 431211; e-mail aarti@mos.com.np; Chief Exec. SHYAM KUMAR LOHIYA.

Cottage Industries and Handicrafts Emporium Ltd: New Road Gate, POB 3775, Kathmandu; tel. 225619; fax 222672; Chief Exec. RAM CHANDRA NAINA BAST.

Exotic Oriental Crafts (Pvt) Ltd: POB 4228, Kathmandu; tel. 220109; fax 526816; Chief Exec. P. THAKUR.

Gorkhali Rubber Udyog Ltd: Kalimati, POB 1700, Kathmandu; tel. and fax 270367; e-mail grul@wlink.com.np; Chief Exec. SHER BAHADUR PANDEY.

Himalaya Auto Industries (Pvt) Ltd: Tankisinwari, POB 42, Biratnagar; tel. 27654; Chief Exec. SHYAM SUNDHAR RATHI.

Jai Nepal Auto Industries (Pvt) Ltd: Balaju Industrial District, Balaju, POB 2350, Kathmandu; tel. 412634; fax 419137; Chief Exec. GAURI LAL SHRESTHA.

Janakpur Cigarette Factory Ltd: POB 5, Janakpurdham; tel. 20127; fax 21004; Chief Exec. PADMA PRASHAD SHARMA.

Mahashakti Soap and Chemical Industries (Pvt) Ltd: Ramshahpath, POB 534, Kathmandu; tel. 226638; fax 225178; e-mail msci@puja.mos.com.np; Chair. ASHOK KUMAR LOHIA; Man. Dir ROHIT LOHIA.

Nepal Battery Co Ltd: BID, Ring Rd, Balaju, POB 3194, Kathmandu; tel. 350954; fax 350913; e-mail eveready@mos.com.np; cap. and res NRs 48.5m., sales NRs 95m. (1999); Chair. A. ROY; 105 employees.

Nepal Coal Ltd: POB 6321, Kathmandu; tel. 474464; fax 473272; Chief Exec. URMILA ARYAL.

Nepal Ekarat Engineering Co (Pvt) Ltd: POB 1939, Kathmandu; tel. 213436; fax 227564; Chief Exec. PRAKASH KUMAR SHRESTHA.

Nepal Jute Industries (Pvt) Ltd: Teenpaini, POB 86, Biratnagar 2; tel. and fax 27657; Chief Exec. G. P. RIJAL.

Nepal Lube Oil Ltd: Thapathali, POB 1916, Kathmandu; tel. 241917; fax 244736; e-mail cggulf@mos.com.np; sales NRs 107.4m. (1999); privatized in 1994; Chief Exec. SAMBHU SARAN PD KAYASTHA.

Nepal Oil Corpn Ltd: Babar Mahal, Kathmandu; tel. 263481; fax 263499; e-mail supp-noc@ccsl.com.np; govt-owned; Chief Exec. NARAYAN PRASHAD BHATTARAI.

Premier Electrical Industries (Pvt) Ltd: POB 5226, Kathmandu; tel. 419087; fax 417784; Chief Exec. MADAN K. SHRESTHA.

Surya Tobacco Co (Pvt) Ltd: Shree Bal Sadan Gha 2-513, Kantipath, POB 1864, Kathmandu; tel. 248260; fax 227585; e-mail stc@mos.com.np; Chair. PRABHAKAR S. J. B. RANA; 400 employees.

Xian Electrical (Nepal) (Pvt) Ltd: Kamalpokhari, Lal Durbar, POB 6450, Kathmandu; tel. 417939; fax 414882; Chief Exec. DEEPMANI RAJBHANDARI.

TRADE UNIONS

Trade unions were banned in Nepal in 1961, but were legalized again in 1990, following the success of the pro-democracy movement and the collapse of the Panchayat system.

Nepal Trade Union Centre: Tinkune Koteshower, POB 9667, Kathmandu; tel. 480551; fax 419148; f. 1986; Sec.-Gen. LAXMAN PRASAD PANDEY.

Democratic Confederation of Nepalese Trade Unions (DECONT): Kathmandu; Chair. KHILANATH DAHAL.

General Federation of Nepalese Trade Unions (GEFONT): Kathmandu, POB 10652; tel. 248072; fax 248073; e-mail info@gefont.org; internet www.gefont.org; f. 1989; Chair. MUKUNDA NEUPANE.

Transport

Ministry of Labour and Transport Management: Babar Mahal, Kathmandu; tel. 226537; Sec. MUKTI PRASAD KAFLE.

Nepal Transport Corpn (Napal Yatayat Sansthan): Kathmandu; tel. 222547; f. 1966; scheduled for transfer to private ownership; controls the operation of road transport facilities, railways, ropeway, trucks, trolley buses and container services; Gen. Man. A. B. SHRESTHA.

Interstate Multi-Modal Transport (Pvt) Ltd: Sabitri Sadan, Red Cross Marg, Tahachal, Kalimati, Kathmandu; tel. 271473; fax 271570; e-mail rauniar@mos.com.np; internet www.rauniar.com; f. 1975; provides freight forwarding, customs clearance, warehousing and shipping services, transport consultancy; Gen. Man. ANAND S. RAUNIAR.

RAILWAYS

Janakpur Railway: Khajuri; tel. 2082; HQ Jayanagar, India; f. 1937; 53 km open, linking Jayanagar with Janakpur and Bijalpura; narrow gauge; 11 steam engines, 25 coaches and vans, and 20 wagons; Man. J. B. THAPA.

Nepal Government Railway: Birganj; f. 1927; 48 km linking Raxaul in India to Amlekhganj, of which the 6 km between Raxaul and Birganj are used for goods traffic; 7 steam engines, 12 coaches and 82 wagons; Man. D. SINGH (acting).

ROADS

In mid-2001 there were 15,458 km of roads, of which 4,577 km were black-topped. Around Kathmandu there are short sections of roads suitable for motor vehicles, and there is a 28-km ring road round the valley. A 190-km mountain road, Tribhuwana Rajpath, links the capital with the Indian railhead at Raxaul. The Siddhartha Highway, constructed with Indian assistance, connects the Pokhara valley, in mid-west Nepal, with Sonauli, on the Indian border in Uttar Pradesh. The 114-km Arniko Highway, constructed with Chinese help, connects Kathmandu with Kodari, on the Chinese border. In the early 1990s the final section of the 1,030-km East–West Highway was under construction. A number of north–south roads were also being constructed to connect the district headquarters with the East–West Highway. In November 1999 the World Bank agreed to provide Nepal with a loan of US $54.5m. for the construction and maintenance of roads (particularly in the far west of the country).

A fleet of container trucks operates between Kolkata and Raxaul and other points in Nepal for transporting exports to, and imports from, third countries. Trolley buses provide a passenger service over the 13 km between Kathmandu and Bhaktapur.

ROPEWAY

A 42-km ropeway links Hetauda and Kathmandu and can carry 22 tons of freight per hour throughout the year. Food grains, construction goods and heavy goods on this route are transported by this ropeway.

CIVIL AVIATION

Tribhuvan international airport is situated about 6 km from Kathmandu. In 2001 Nepal had an estimated 44 airports, five of which were tarred.

Royal Nepal Airlines Corporation (RNAC): RNAC Bldg, Kanti Path, POB 401, Kathmandu 711000; tel. 220757; fax 225348; internet www.royalnepal.com/; f. 1958; 100% state-owned (scheduled for transfer to private ownership); scheduled services to 37 domestic airfields and international scheduled flights to Europe, the Middle East and the Far East; Chair. BAL KRISHNA MAN SINGH; Dir (Operations) Capt. D. M. S. RAJBHANDARI.

The monopoly of the RNAC in domestic air services came to an end in 1992. By 1999 there were about 12 private airlines in Nepal serving internal routes.

Buddha Air: Jawalakhal, Lalitpur, POB 2167, Kathmandu; tel. 521015; fax 537726; e-mail buddhaair@wlink.com.np; internet www.buddhaair.com; f. 1997; domestic passenger services; Man. Dir BIRENDRA BASNET.

Gorkha Airlines: New Baneshwor, POB 9451, Kathmandu; tel. 487033; fax 471136; e-mail gorkha@mos.com.np; internet www.yomari.com/gorkha/; f. 1996; scheduled and charter passenger and cargo flights to domestic destinations; Exec. Chair. PRAJJWAAL SHRESTHA.

Lumbini Airways (Pvt) Ltd: Kamaladi, Kathmandu; tel. 255936; fax 483380; e-mail lumbini@resv.wlink.com.np; f. 1996; scheduled passenger and cargo flights to domestic destinations; Man. Dir R. K. SAKYA.

Necon Air Ltd: Kalimatidole, Necon Hamlet, Airport Area, POB 10038, Kathmandu; tel. 473860; fax 471679; e-mail info@necon.mos.com.np; internet www.neconair.com; f. 1992; scheduled and charter flights to domestic destinations and to India; Chair./Man. Dir NARAYAN SINGH PUN.

Tourism

Tourism is being developed through the construction of new tourist centres in the Kathmandu valley, Pokhara valley and Chitwan. Regular air services link Kathmandu with Pokhara and Chitwan. Major tourist attractions include Lumbini, the birthplace of Buddha, the lake city of Pokhara, and the Himalaya mountain range, including Mt Everest, the world's highest peak. In 1989, in an effort to increase tourism, the Government abolished travel restrictions in 18 areas of north-western Nepal that had previously been inaccessible to foreigners. As expected, following the restoration of parliamentary democracy in 1990, tourist arrivals in Nepal rose considerably. Further travel restrictions in the remote areas of the kingdom were abolished in 1991, and efforts have been made to attract foreign investment in the Nepalese tourism industry. Nepal received an estimated 463,646 tourists in 2000. The number of visitor arrivals reportedly declined to 298,066 in 2001. Tourism receipts rose from US $153m. in 1998 to $168m. in 1999. Hotel bed capacity increased from 32,214 in 1999 to an estimated 34,958 in 2000. The Government granted access to a further 103 mountains, raising the total number of mountains open to climbers to 263, in an effort to promote tourism.

Nepal Tourism Board: Tourist Service Centre, Bhrikuti Mandap, Kathmandu; tel. 256909; fax 256910; e-mail info@ntb.wlink.com.np; internet www.welcomenepal.com.

Association of Tourism: Thamel, Kathmandu; tel. 424740.

Hotel Association of Nepal: Kathmandu; tel. 412705.

Tourist Guide Association of Nepal: Durbar Marg, POB 4344, Kathmandu; tel. 225102.

Trekking Agents Association of Nepal: Naxal, POB 3612, Kathmandu; tel. 419245.

Defence

In August 2001 Nepal's total armed forces numbered 46,000 (to be increased to 50,000 in the near future). Military service is voluntary.

Defence Budget: NRs 7,228m. in 2002/03.

Commander-in-Chief of the Royal Nepal Army: Gen. PRAJWALLA SHAMSHER JUNG BAHADUR RANA.

Education

Primary education, beginning at six years of age and lasting for five years, is officially compulsory and is provided free of charge in government schools. Secondary education, beginning at the age of 11, lasts for a further five years, comprising a first cycle of three years (lower secondary) and a second of two years (secondary). In 1996 the total enrolment at primary and secondary schools was equivalent to 80% of the school-age population. Primary enrolment in that year was equivalent to 113% of children in the relevant age-group (boys 129%; girls 96%), while the comparable ratio for secondary enrolment was 42% (boys 51%, girls 33%). Some 8,000 pupils attended the country's 321 primary schools in 1950; in 2000 there were an estimated 25,927 primary schools, with a total of 3,623,150 pupils. The number of secondary schools rose from two in 1950 to 11,639 in 2000. In that year there were an estimated 1,330,360 pupils enrolled at secondary schools.

In 1975 the Government began to provide free primary education for five years and to use Nepali as the medium of instruction. Vernacular schools give secular education to villagers in local dialects, while, in addition to Buddhist and Hindu religious establishments, there are a number of Basic schools, on the pattern set in India, which concentrate on handicrafts and agriculture.

The Ministry of Education supervises the finance, administration, staffing and inspection of government schools, and makes inspection of private schools receiving government subsidies. In other respects, private schools are autonomous. The National Educational Planning Commission recommends educational curricula, and in some cases these have been adopted by the private schools.

The oldest of the colleges of higher education in Nepal is Tri Chandra School in Kathmandu, founded in 1918, which provides four-year arts courses. The only other advanced college in existence before the 1951 Revolution was the Sanskrit College in Kathmandu, founded in 1948. A single college of education was established in 1956 for the training of secondary school teachers and other educational personnel. There are also nine primary teacher-training centres. The first 300-bed teaching hospital for 500 pupils, built with Japanese government assistance, was opened in 1984. There are four state universities. The Tribhuvan University in Kathmandu had 115,608 students in 2001/02. The second state university, the Mahendra Sanskrit Viswavidyalaya in Beljhundi, Dang, was founded in 1986. In 2000/01 the university had an enrolment of 3,252 students. The Purbanchal University, which was opened in 1995, had 2,840 students in 2001/02, and the Pokhara University, which was opened in 1997, had 2,946 students. In addition, there is one private university—the Kathmandu University in Banepa, Kavrepalanchok, which was opened in 1992. In 2001/02 the university had an enrolment of 1,783 students.

Proposed expenditure on education by the central Government in the 2002/03 budget was NRs 14,286m. (16.6% of total spending). The Eighth Five-Year Plan (1992–97) included proposals to introduce free compulsory secondary education in phases over the next 10 years. By 2000 compulsory education had been implemented in only seven of Nepal's 40 districts.

In 1990 (to coincide with the UN-designated International Literacy Year) the Government launched a 12-year literacy programme, directed at 8m. people between the ages of six and 45 years.

Bibliography

Agrawal, H. N. *Administrative System of Nepal: From Tradition to Modernity.* New Delhi, Vikas Publishing House, 1976.

Baral, L. R. *Oppositional Politics in Nepal.* New Delhi, Abhinav, 1977.

Bhooshan, B. S. *The Development Experience of Nepal.* Delhi, Concept Publishing, 1979.

Bista, Dor Bahadur. *Fatalism and Development in Nepal.* Kolkata, Orient Longman, 1991.

Blaikie, Piers, et al. *Nepal in Crisis.* Delhi, Oxford University Press, 1980.

Blaikie, Piers, and Seddon, D. *Peasants and Workers in Nepal.* New Delhi, Viking Publishing House, 1979.

Brown, T. Louise. *The Challenge to Democracy in Nepal: A Political History.* London, Routledge, 1995.

Caplan, Lionel. *Land and Social Change in East Nepal.* London, Routledge and Kegan Paul, 1970.

Administration and Politics in a Nepalese Town. London, Oxford University Press, 1971.

Warrior Gentlemen: Gurkhas in the Western Imagination. Berghahn Books, 1995.

Chattopadhyay, K. P. *An Essay on the History of Newar Culture.* Kathmandu, Educational Enterprise, 1980.

Chauhan R. S. *Political Development in Nepal.* Delhi, Associated Publishing House, 1970.

Connell, Monica. *Against a Peacock Sky.* London and New York, NY, Viking, 1991.

Fisher, James F. *Trans-Himalayan Traders: Economy, Society and Culture in Northwest Nepal.* New Delhi, Motilal Banarsidass Publishers Ltd, 1987.

Living Martyrs: Individuals and Revolution in Nepal. Delhi, Oxford University Press, 1997.

Gaige, Frederick H. *Regionalism and National Unity in Nepal.* Berkeley, CA, University of California Press, 1975.

Gould, Tony. *Imperial Warriors.* London, Granta Books, 2000.

Gregson, Jonathan. *Blood Against the Snows.* London, Fourth Estate, 2002

Gupta, Anirudha. *Politics in Nepal.* Mumbai, Allied Publishers, 1964.

Hagen, Toni, Wahlen, F. T., and Corti, W. R. *Nepal: The Kingdom in the Himalayas.* Berne, Kummerly and Frey, 1961.

Haimendorf, C. von F. (Ed.). *Caste and Kin in Nepal, India and Ceylon.* London, East-West Publications, 1966.

Himalayan Traders. London, Murray, 1975.

Hamilton, F. *An Account of the Kingdom of Nepal.* Edinburgh, Constable, 1819.

Hofer, A. *The Caste Hierarchy and the State in Nepal: A Study of the Muluki Ain of 1854.* Innsbruck, Universitätsverlag, Wagner, 1979.

Hoftun, M., and Raeper, W. (Eds). *Spring Awakening: An Account of the 1990 Revolution in Nepal.* New Delhi, Penguin Books India, 1992.

Husain, Asad. *British India's Relations with the Kingdom of Nepal.* London, George Allen and Unwin, 1970.

Hutt, Michael J. *Nepali: A National Language and its Literature.* New Delhi, Sterling Publishers Ltd, 1988.

Nepal in the Nineties: Versions of the Past, Visions of the Future. New Delhi, Oxford, 1994.

Ives, J. D., and Messerli, B. *The Himalayan Dilemma: Reconciling Development and Conservation.* London, Routledge, 1989.

Joshi, B. L., and Rose, L. E. *Democratic Innovations in Nepal: A Study of Political Acculturation.* Berkeley, CA, University of California Press, 1986.

Justice, J. *Politics, Plans and People: Culture and Health Development in Nepal.* Berkeley, CA, University of California Press, 1986.

Karan, Pradyumna P. *Nepal: A Cultural and Physical Geography.* Lexington, KY, University of Kentucky Press, 1960.

Karan, Pradyumna P., and Ishii, Hiroshi. *Nepal: A Himalayan Kingdom in Transition.* New York/London, United Nations University Press, 1996.

Karan, Pradyumna P., and Jenkins, W. M. *The Himalayan Kingdoms: Bhutan, Sikkim and Nepal.* Princeton, NJ, Van Nostrand, 1963.

Khadka, Narayan. *Foreign Aid, Poverty and Stagnation in Nepal.* New Delhi, Vikas Publishing House, 1991.

Kumar, Satish. *Rana Polity in Nepal: Origin and Growth.* Asia Publishing House for the Indian School of International Studies, 1968.

Landon, Percival. *Nepal.* London, Constable, 1928.

Macfarlane, A. *Resources and Population: A Study of the Gurungs of Nepal.* Cambridge, Cambridge University Press, 1976.

Malla, Kamal P. (Ed.). *Nepal: Perspectives on Continuity and Change.* Kathmandu, Centre for Nepal and Asian Studies, 1989.

Messerschmidt, D. A. *The Gurungs of Nepal: Conflict and Change in a Village Society.* Warminster, Aris and Philips, 1976.

Metz, J. J. *A Reassessment of the Causes and Severity of Nepal's Environmental Crisis.* World Development, Vol. 19, No. 7 (1991), pp. 805–820.

Mihaly, Eugene Bramer. *Foreign Aid and Politics in Nepal.* London, Oxford University Press for Royal Institute of International Affairs, 1965.

Mojumdar, Kanchanmoy. *Political Relations between India and Nepal.* New Delhi, Munshiram Manoharlal Publishers Ltd, 1973.

Muni, S. D. *Foreign Policy of Nepal.* Delhi, National Publishing House, 1973.

Nickson, R. A. *Foreign Aid and Foreign Policy: The Case of British Aid to Nepal.* Birmingham, University of Birmingham, Development Administration Group, Papers in the Administration of Development No. 48, 1992.

Panday, Devendra Raj (Ed.). *Foreign Aid and Development in Nepal: Proceedings of a Seminar.* Kathmandu, Integrated Development Systems, 1983.

Pant, Y. P. *Development of Nepal.* Allahabad, Kitab Mahal, 1968.

Parajulee, R. P. *Democratic Transition in Nepal.* Lanham, MD, University Press of America, 2000.

Petech, Luciano. *Medieval History of Nepal.* Rome, Istituto Italiano per il Medio ed Estremo Oriente, 1984.

Pradhan, B. B. *Rural Development in Nepal—Problems and Prospects.* Kathmandu, 1982.

Pradhan, Kumar. *The Gorkha Conquests.* Kolkata, Oxford University Press, 1991.

Pye-Smith, C. *Travels in Nepal.* London, Penguin Books, 1988.

Raeper, William, and Hoftun, Martin (Eds). *Spring Awakening: An Account of the 1990 Revolution in Nepal.* New Delhi, Penguin Books India, 1992.

Ramakant. *Nepal, China and India.* Delhi, Abhinar, 1976.

Ramakant and Upreti, B. C. (Eds). *Indo-Nepal Relations.* New Delhi, South Asian Publishers, 1992.

Rana, Pashupati Shumshere J. B. *Kathmandu: A Living Heritage.* The Perennial Press, IBD, 1990.

Regmi, D. R. *Ancient Nepal.* Kolkata, Mukhopadhyay, 1960.

Modern Nepal: Rise and Growth in the Eighteenth Century. Kolkata, Mukhopadhyay, 1961.

Regmi, M. C. *Land Ownership in Nepal.* Berkeley, CA, University of California Press, 1976.

Land Tenure and Taxation System in Nepal. Kathmandu, Ratna Pustak Bhandar, 1978.

Rehnstrom J. *Development Co-operation in Practice: The United Nations Volunteers in Nepal.* Washington, DC, Brookings Institution, 2000.

Roberts, Patricia, and Kelly, Thomas L. *Kathmandu: City on the Edge of the World.* London, Weidenfeld and Nicolson, 1990.

Rose, Leo E. *Nepal: Strategy for Survival.* Berkeley, University of California Press, 1971.

Rose, Leo E., and Scholz, J. T. *Nepal: Profile of a Himalayan Kingdom.* Boulder, CO, Westview Press, 1980.

Seddon, D. *Nepal—A State of Poverty.* New Delhi, Vikas Publishing House, 1987.

Shaha, Rishikesh. *Nepali Politics: Retrospect and Prospect.* Oxford University Press, 1977.

Modern Nepal: A Political History, 1769–1955. 2 vols. New Delhi, Manohar Publications, 1990.

Politics in Nepal, 1980–1990. New Delhi, Manohar Publications, 1990.

Ancient and Medieval Nepal. New Delhi, Manohar Publications, 1992.

Sharma, Pitamber. *Urbanization in Nepal.* Honolulu, HI, East-West Center, 1989.

Shrestha, N. R. *Landlessness and Migration in Nepal.* Boulder, CO, Westview Press, 1990.

Sill, M., and Kirkby, J. *Atlas of Nepal in the Modern World.* London, Earthscan, 1991.

Sitwell, Sacheverell. *Great Temples of the East.* New York, Oblensky, 1962.

Snellgrove, D. *Himalayan Pilgrimage.* Oxford, Bruno Cassirer, 1961.

Stewart, Frank, Upadhyay, Samrat, and Thapa, Manjushree (Eds). *Secret Places.* Honolulu, HI, University of Hawaii Press, 2002.

Tucker, Francis. *Gorkha: The Story of the Gurkhas of Nepal.* London, Constable, 1957.

Uprety, Prem. *Political Awakening in Nepal.* New Delhi, Commonwealth Publishers, 1992.

Watkins, Joanne. *Spirited Women: Gender, Religion and Cultural Identity in the Nepal Himalayas.* New York, NY, Columbia University Press, 1996.

Whelpton, J. *Nepal: World Bibliographical Series.* Oxford, Clio Press, 1990.

Kings, Soldiers and Priests: Nepalese Politics, 1830–57. New Delhi, Manohar Publications, 1992.

Zivetz, L. *Private Enterprise and the State in Modern Nepal.* Chennai, Oxford University Press, 1992.

NEW ZEALAND

Physical and Social Geography

A. E. McQUEEN

New Zealand lies 1,600 km south-east of Australia. It consists of two main islands, North Island with an area of 115,777 sq km (44,702 sq miles) and South Island with an area of 151,215 sq km (58,384 sq miles), plus Stewart Island (or Rakiura) to the south, with an area of 1,746 sq km (674 sq miles), and a number of smaller islands. North and South Islands are separated by Cook Strait, which is about 30 km wide at the narrowest point. The total area of New Zealand is 270,534 sq km (104,454 sq miles).

CLIMATE

There are three major factors affecting the climate of New Zealand, particularly as regards pasture growth. The first is the country's situation in the westerly wind belt which encircles the globe. The main islands lie between 34°S and 47°S, and are therefore within the zone of the eastward moving depressions and anti-cyclones within this belt. The second factor is the country's location in the midst of a vast ocean mass, which means that extremes of temperature are modified by air masses passing across a large expanse of ocean. It also means that abundant moisture is available by evaporation from the ocean, and rainfall is considerable and fairly evenly distributed throughout the year. The mean annual rainfall varies from 330 mm east of the Southern Alps to more than 7,500 mm west of the Alps, but the average for the whole country is between 600 mm and 1,500 mm. The third factor is more of local significance: the presence of a chain of mountains extending from south-west to north-east through most of the country. The mountains provide a barrier to the westward moving air masses, and produce a quite sharp climatic contrast between east and west. The rain shadow effect of the mountains produces in certain inland areas of the South Island an almost continental climate, although no part of New Zealand is more than 130 km from the sea.

The annual range of mean monthly temperatures in western districts of both islands is about 8°C, while elsewhere it is 9°C–11°C, except in inland areas of the South Island, where it may be as high as 14°C. The mean temperatures for the year vary from 15°C in the far north to 12°C about Cook Strait and 9°C in the south. With increasing altitude, mean annual temperatures fall about 1°C per 180 m. Snow is rare below 600 m in the North Island, and falls for only a few days a year at lower altitudes in the South Island. Rainfall and temperature combine to give a climate in which it is possible to graze livestock for all the year at lower altitudes in all parts of the country, and at higher altitudes, even in the South Island, for a considerable part of each year. Pasture growth varies according to temperature and season, but ranges from almost continual growth in North Auckland to between eight and 10 months in the South Island.

PHYSICAL FEATURES

Altitude and surface configuration are important features affecting the amount of land which is readily available for farming. Less than one-quarter of the land surface lies below 200 m; in the North Island the higher mountains, those above 1,250 m, occupy about 10% of the surface, but in the South Island the proportion is much greater. The Southern Alps (or Ka Tiriti o te Moana), a massive chain including 16 peaks over 3,100 m, run for almost the entire length of the island. The economic effect of the Southern Alps as a communications barrier has been considerably greater than that of the North Island mountains; their rain-shadow effect is also significant for land use, as the lower rainfall, while giving a reduced growth rate, also produces the dry summers of the east coast plains which are major grain-growing areas. In addition, the wide expanses of elevated open country have led to the development of large-scale pastoral holdings, and it is the South Island high country that produces almost all New Zealand's fine wools, particularly from the Merino sheep.

New Zealand rivers are of vital importance for hydroelectric power production, with their high rate of flow and reliable volume of ice-free water. Many of the larger lakes of both islands, most of which are situated at quite high altitudes, are also important in power production, acting as reservoirs for the rivers upon which the major stations are situated. Earthquakes are a particular risk along a zone west of the Southern Alps, through Wellington and thence north-east to Napier and Wairoa.

NATURAL RESOURCES

In general geological terms, New Zealand is part of the unstable circum-Pacific mobile belt, a region where, in parts, volcanoes are active and where the earth's crust has been moving at a geologically rapid rate. Such earth movements, coupled with rapid erosion, have formed the sedimentary rocks which make up about three-quarters of the country. New Zealand also includes in its very complex geology schist, gneiss, and other metamorphic rocks, most of which are hundreds of millions of years old, as well as a number of igneous rocks. In such a geologically mobile country the constant exposure of new rock has led to young and generally fertile soils.

Within this broad pattern a variety of minerals has been found, many of them, however, in only very small deposits. Non-metallic minerals, such as coal, clay, limestone and dolomite are today both economically and industrially more important than metallic ores; but new demands from industry, and a realization that apparently small showings of more valuable minerals may well indicate much larger deposits, have led to a surge of prospecting since the early 1960s. One of the most successful results so far has been the proving of iron sand deposits on the west coast of the North Island. This development, along with the discovery of a satisfactory method of processing the sands, has paved the way to the founding of an iron and steel industry which began production in 1969. However, knowledge of New Zealand's economic geology is still far from complete; in many respects the concentration upon farming had led to the belief that there were no economically attractive mineral resources. Exploration and prospecting carried out by both local and overseas firms has only recently shown that the nation has other worthwhile natural resources than its climate and soil. A notable discovery in 1970 was a large natural gas field, off the South Taranaki coast. The construction of pipelines to bring the gas to major centres, and of plants to convert this gas into synthetic petrol and methanol, had been completed by 1985.

When the first European settlers came to New Zealand they found two-thirds of the land's surface covered by forest. In 1995 about 29% of the area was forested, most of it kept as reserve or as national parks. The rest has been felled, much of it with little regard for land conservation principles. Of today's total forested area of 7.9m. ha, 6.4m. are still indigenous forest, much of it (some 4.9m. ha) unmillable protected forest. The 1.5m. ha of man-made exotic forest provide building timber and raw material for well-established pulp and paper and other forest product industries. These activities are based largely on the extensive exotic forests of the Bay of Plenty–Taupo region, near the centre of the North Island, but widespread planting has taken place in other regions for eventual use in newly-developed processing plants.

POPULATION

The majority of the population is of European origin. At the census of March 1996, 523,374 persons (14.5% of the usually resident population) were enumerated as indigenous Maori; New Zealand's total population stood at 3,681,546. At the census of March 2001 the total population was enumerated at 3,737,277. In terms of international comparison, the population is small, the density (14.2 per sq km in mid-2001) and growth rate are low and the degree of urbanization is high. Some 85% of the population reside in cities, boroughs or townships with populations greater than 1,000.

Between 1926 and 1945 an average annual increase in population of 1.1% was recorded, one of the lowest rates in the country's history. Between 1945 and 1970, however, the rate of population growth was maintained at a high level—a trend supported by a significant level both of natural increase and of immigration. The high post-war birth rate reached a peak of 27.0 per 1,000 in 1961. The birth rate declined steadily to 15.7 per 1,000 in 1983, before gradually rising to 17.9 in 1990, then decreasing to 15.8 in 1995 and to 14.5 in 2001. This contrasted with death rates of 8.1 per 1,000 in 1983, 7.6 in 1995 and 7.0 in 2001, among the lowest in the world. The high rate of increase was complemented by a steady influx of immigrants, some of them assisted by the New Zealand Government. The total number of immigrants increased annually until 1952/53, since when there have been large variations in both the immigration and emigration rates. In the year to August 2001 immigrants totalled 72,699 and emigrants 77,090. The net decrease in the year to June 1999 was 11,370, compared with a net increase of 16,770 in 1996/97 and 460 in 1997/98. In the year to June 1996 Taiwan displaced the United Kingdom as the leading source of immigrants.

The processes of economic development have dictated a steadily increasing concentration of population, farm products processing, and industrial output in the major cities, especially within the North Island. Larger towns contain more of the population than other urban areas. In 1996 69% of the population resided in urban areas with populations of over 30,000.

History

JEANINE GRAHAM

THE COLONIAL ERA

New Zealand's earliest migrant population was well established in coastal settlements by the 12th century. Oral tradition tells of voyages from Hawaiiki, the islands of eastern Polynesia, and of subsequent migrations within New Zealand waters. The Maori culture, which was to be of such interest to early European explorers and observers, developed in isolation as one variant of Polynesian culture.

Although the Dutch navigator, Abel Tasman, sailed in 1642–43 along part of the western coastline of the country that he called Staten Landt, it was the three scientific expeditions led by Capt. James Cook (in 1769, 1773 and 1774) that brought New Zealand into prominence. During his first voyage Cook spent more than six months circumnavigating the islands and produced a chart remarkable for its detail and accuracy. Scientists and artists with the expedition recorded their impressions of the nature and habits of the indigenous Maori and New Zealand's unique flora and fauna. Voyages by other 18th and early 19th century European explorers were peripheral. The traders, missionaries, scientists and settlers who followed in Cook's wake built on the secure foundations of his achievements.

Sealers, whalers and traders sought to exploit New Zealand's natural resources for economic advantage. Christian missionaries aimed to evangelize the *tangata whenua* (people of the land). The consequences of cultural encounter for the Maori people were varied. Against such diseases as influenza, measles, tuberculosis and whooping cough, the indigenous inhabitants had no immunity. Death rates remained high throughout the 19th century. Tribal receptiveness to new technology, literacy and Christianity was selective. Although the lifestyle of the Maori people was disrupted, it was not, especially in the case of those tribes in locations away from the coast, necessarily undermined. The early Europeans were, in fact, heavily dependent upon Maori co-operation and goodwill, a pattern that persisted during the first two decades after New Zealand became part of the British Empire in 1840.

The New Zealand Co and related organizations founded the settlements of Wellington, Nelson, Wanganui, New Plymouth, Christchurch and Dunedin. Until 1864, the colonial administration was based in Auckland, the character of this town being influenced by its strong links with the Australian colonies. A steady stream of assisted or independent immigrants flowed into New Zealand until the 1880s, with a dramatic influx during the gold rushes of the 1860s and large numbers of labouring-class settlers arriving during the era of public-works expansion in the 1870s. A minority in their own land by the late 1850s, the Maori population had declined to 42,000 by 1896, while Pakeha (non-Maori) settlers numbered some 700,000.

The insatiable demand of European settlers for land was a major cause of conflict between Maori and European during the 19th century. Settlers south of the Cook Strait region scarcely felt the impact of racial tension, for relatively few Maori lived there, but many North Island communities were affected. Sporadic and localized fighting in the 1840s was followed by a major outbreak in central and west-coast areas of the North Island in the early 1860s. The Treaty of Waitangi, signed on 6 February 1840 by the Lieutenant-Governor-elect, Capt. William Hobson, and subsequently by many—but by no means all—of the major Maori chiefs, had acknowledged Maori ownership of land, and accorded *tangata whenua* the status of British subjects. However, post-conflict confiscation of much tribal land and the introduction of a system of individualized land tenure, to replace the traditional communal form of ownership, caused major cultural upheaval during the last decades of the 19th century and effectively undermined the socio-economic base of those tribes most affected. Only since the 1970s have New Zealanders of European origins begun to appreciate that Maori understandings of the treaty's guarantees had largely been ignored by successive Governments for more than a century.

British legislation provided a constitution for New Zealand in 1852. A bicameral General Assembly and six Provincial Councils were functioning by 1854, but responsible government was not granted until 1856. Improved internal and coastal communications, returns from wool and gold exports and the need to co-ordinate loan applications undermined the rationale for separate provincial development. The provincial governments were abolished in 1876 and were replaced by a plethora of local bodies which dominated local government for more than a century and, as with central government, took little cognizance of bicultural values. The granting of the vote to Maori men in 1867 and the establishment of four Maori seats in the House of Representatives in the same year were not sufficient measures to ensure that Maori interests were articulated at parliamentary level and that their needs were satisfied. Inter-tribal initiatives to set up complementary political forums met with no parliamentary support.

The economic crises of the 1880s caused many recent immigrants to leave New Zealand for the Australian colonies. Social distress and revelations of 'sweated labour' in the clothing industry fostered a sense of radicalism and protest against the apparently ineffectual conservative 'continuous ministry'. Politicians espousing a liberal ideology came to form a coherent grouping and took office under the leadership of John Ballance in January 1891. During the ensuing 18 months, a hostile, nominated Legislative Council continually blocked reforms, a situation resolved only when the Governor was instructed by the British Secretary of State for the Colonies not to reject the advice of his responsible ministers in making new appointments. Ballance died in early 1893 and was succeeded as Premier by Richard John Seddon. For the next 13 years 'King Dick' Seddon dominated New Zealand life and politics. Assisted initially by some very able colleagues, Seddon carried through legislation that provided for industrial conciliation and arbitration, better factory conditions, accident compensation, shorter working hours and old-age pensions. Maori leaders found Seddon sympathetic to their people's plight, but the initiatives for urgent health reform came from a small group of Maori university graduates. Liberal policy towards Maori needs remained ambivalent, however: increased pressure for the further alienation of Maori land in the North Island resulted from measures that were implemented during the 1890s to foster the expansion of small farming, especially dairying. The technology of refrigeration had provided the key to resolving New Zealand's export difficulties. Such was the new sense of accomplishment and colonial pride that few in New Zealand were disposed to entertain seriously the idea of federation with the Australian colonies. New Zealanders entered the 20th century firmly committed to the ideal of the British Empire, a loyalty that cost the country and its people dearly during the First World War.

THE INTER-WAR PERIOD

After 1918, under conditions of general prosperity and full employment, New Zealand resumed a selective, assisted migration policy, which had increased the population by nearly 70,000 by 1928 when the intake temporarily ceased. As trade conditions worsened, the Government increasingly intervened to control the nation's economy. Efforts to borrow in the face of the oncoming depression proved fruitless, and a coalition Government of United and Reform parties took office in September 1931. Orthodox financial solutions were tried. Railway construction was halted and expenditure on defence reduced. Emergency taxes were imposed. Incomes fell by an average of 20%. The depression worsened, and with it the social distress suffered by the growing number of unemployed. An estimated 80,000 people—12% of the labour force—were out of work. Employment schemes, including state forestry planning, provided relatively little relief. Labour unrest was rife throughout the country and short-lived bouts of rioting occurred in the major cities. A noted Maori politician, Sir Apirana Ngata, nevertheless succeeded in promoting a cultural revival amongst Maori and addressing issues of Maori poverty through consolidation of fragmented land titles and the establishment of Maori-owned incorporations to develop unproductive land.

The election of 1935 marked a radical political change. Small farmers combined with urban workers to return the Labour Party to power with a substantial majority. Under its leader, Michael Joseph Savage, the prices of essential commodities were fixed. Dairy farmers were given a guaranteed price for their butter and cheese, which were marketed by the Government both at home and abroad. Unemployment was tackled by the introduction of large-scale public works such as road and railway construction. The State offered the right to work at a fixed basic wage and made trade-union membership compulsory. Salary and wage cuts were restored, and a 40-hour week was introduced to increase the demand for labour. An ambitious housing programme was launched. These various undertakings were financed by means of increased taxation and public loans. A political alliance forged in 1936 between Savage and a Maori spiritual leader, Tahupotiki Wiremu Ratana, resulted in Ratana candidates being elected to all four Maori seats; the Ratana movement continued to support Labour until 1979.

In 1938 the Labour Government was re-elected with an increased majority and immediately began to build upon the social legislation of the 1890s. A Social Security Act provided for free general practitioner services, medicines, hospital treatment and maternity benefits, and for family allowances and increased old-age pensions. To finance such comprehensive insurance a special tax was levied on all incomes and supplemented by grants from ordinary revenue. Such measures were possible because these were years of prosperity and prices for exports were high. By 1939, however, heavy withdrawals to meet overseas commitments, together with the flight of private capital, forced the Government to restrict imports and control the export of capital.

The British declaration of war in 1939 was felt to be as binding on New Zealand as that of 1914, even though the two countries had differed publicly in their attitude to League of Nations' policy initiatives during the 1930s. A special war cabinet was formed on the basis of a coalition of all parties. The Prime Minister, Peter Fraser, concentrated economic policy around the objective of stabilization, and in this regard he was largely successful. Conscription was introduced for overseas service, essential commodities were rationed and the country's resources were mobilized for the war effort. However, the rationalizing of manpower in 1942 provoked a crisis in the coal-mining industry and led the Government to assume control of the mines. Incensed at what it regarded as the Government's capitulation to the coal miners, the National Party withdrew from the war cabinet. When Japan entered the war, New Zealand responded to meet the threat of invasion, but, even after the attack on Pearl Harbor in December 1941, it did not recall its troops from the Middle East. The 40-hour week was suspended, and in 1943 thousands of men were released from the armed forces in order to increase food and factory production and thereby to assist the USA in its Pacific campaign. Employment opportunities, together with the difficulty of providing for a growing population on fragmented landholdings, prompted significant numbers of rural Maori to leave their subsistence lifestyle and migrate to the cities.

THE POST-WAR YEARS

The Labour Party won the election held in November 1946, but by a narrow majority; shortages, rationing, high food prices, poor housing and a reaction against wartime bureaucratic control all undermined the Labour vote. The subsequent introduction of compulsory military training in peacetime further alienated Labour supporters. The National Party, led by Sidney (later Sir Sidney) Holland, capitalized on public dissatisfaction with government regulation, and won a decisive victory at the 1949 election.

With the full approval of the Labour opposition, the Government abolished the Legislative Council, which, as a council of review, had gradually declined in importance. Subsidies on certain commodities were withdrawn, but attempts to 'freeze' prices failed to prevent inflation. In a climate marked by Cold War fears of communism, the Government severely restricted civil liberties during a prolonged strike by dock workers, and eventually dispatched troops to end the unrest. Among the public there were strong feelings concerning the Prime Minister's handling of the crisis, but in the election called at short notice in 1951 the Government secured an increased parliamentary majority. Growing dissatisfaction with the performance of both parties was reflected three years later in the 1954 election, when the newly-formed Social Credit League won 11% of the votes cast. While support for its economic policies was always problematic, as a third party Social Credit continued to benefit from tactical and protest voting until the mid-1980s. Electoral legislation in 1956 entrenched the franchise and electoral system and made enrolment compulsory for Maori, as it had been for Europeans since 1924.

Two months before the 1957 election, Holland retired from office because of ill health. Under his successor, Keith (later Sir Keith) Holyoake, the National Party narrowly lost the election. Labour's marginal victory was attributed to its espousal of a new Pay As You Earn (PAYE) system of collecting income tax. Almost immediately the Labour Government, with 75-year-old Walter Nash as Prime Minister, was embarrassed by pressing economic problems. Falling prices for meat and dairy produce led to an adverse balance of trade and to an alarming depletion of the country's overseas reserves. The Government reimposed import licensing and exchange control and thereby raised over £30m. in London and Australia and another £20m. internally. These measures arrested the decline, but the Government's fate was sealed by the 'black budget' of 1958, which, while introducing 3% loans for housing, increasing pensions, countering a balance-of-payments problem and encouraging industry, also increased taxes on beer, spirits, cigarettes and petrol. At the election in 1960 the National Party, led by Holyoake, was returned to power. Among the more important changes that followed was the appointment in 1962 of a Parliamentary Commissioner (ombudsman) to inquire into public complaints arising from governmental administrative decisions. The National Party retained office in an election in 1963. Labour's new leader, Arnold Nordmeyer, had tried unsuccessfully to revive the Labour Party's popularity by denying the social need for class struggle. The formation in 1966 of the small Socialist Unity Party, many of whose 60 adherents were former members of the New Zealand Communist Party, indicated the persistence of more radical views on the subject of class conflict. Meanwhile, in 1965 Nordmeyer was ousted as Labour's leader by a former Party President, Norman Kirk.

Although economic policy was the issue most frequently debated in the 1966 election, attitudes to New Zealand's involvement in Viet Nam cut across party lines and secured a further victory for the National Party. Holyoake's consensus style of politics continued to have electoral appeal, but he retired in February 1972, to be succeeded by John (later Sir John) Marshall, a leader whose urbane demeanour was challenged by ambitious and aggressive younger politicians within the party. Labour gained a sweeping victory in November 1972 in an election that had been contested by National, Labour, Social Credit and a newly-formed Values Party, one of the world's first 'Green' parties, which, by emphasizing the importance of environmental issues, appealed to many younger voters. As Labour's leader, Kirk was vigorous and forthright, especially in the field of foreign policy, but his leadership was cut short by his untimely death in August 1974. His successor, Wallace (later Sir Wallace) Rowling, opposed by a new leader of the National Party, Robert (later Sir Robert) Muldoon, continued Kirk's policy, but conducted it less forcefully.

In the post-war world, New Zealand's first major step in pursuing a policy independent of British interests was made in 1944 with the signing of the Canberra Pact, a mutual security agreement with Australia. In 1947 New Zealand finally adopted the Statute of Westminster, which gave it complete autonomy and freedom of action in international affairs. As a strong supporter of the United Nations, in 1950 the Government sent troops to join the UN Command in the Republic of Korea. Despite official misgivings about the exclusion of the United Kingdom, in 1952 it signed the Australia, New Zealand and the USA (ANZUS) defence treaty, and two years later New Zealand became a member of the South-East Asia Treaty Organization (SEATO). New Zealand sent a military unit to Malaya in 1955, and combined with Australia in an ANZAC unit in Viet Nam. Along with Australia, it also sent troops to Singapore and Malaysia to combine with remaining British forces in safeguarding the political status quo of the region. In 1971 New Zealand joined Australia, Malaysia, Singapore and the United Kingdom in establishing new arrangements for the defence of Malaysia and Singapore, and maintained a presence there until the last troops were withdrawn in 1990.

New Zealand played an increasingly important role in the Pacific after joining the South Pacific Commission (now Pacific Community) as a founder member in 1947. It administered the UN Trust Territory of Western Samoa until 1962, when those islands became independent, and in 1965 it assisted the Cook Islands to achieve self-government in free association with New Zealand. When Fiji became independent in 1970, New Zealand helped to establish the University of the South Pacific in Suva, and in 1971 it joined the South Pacific Forum (now Pacific Islands' Forum), which was founded to promote economic and political co-operation in the region.

RECENT DEVELOPMENTS

Political Affairs

Playing on public fears of national economic disaster consequent on the inflationary effects of Labour's policy of heavy overseas borrowing, the opposition leader, Robert Muldoon, campaigned on the promise of a more attractive and egalitarian pensions system than that offered by the Government. At the November 1975 general election a revitalized National Party won 55 of the 87 seats in the House of Representatives. Labour lost 23 seats, including those of five cabinet members.

The National Party retained office in the 1978 election, although its share of the total vote fell, largely owing to the abrasive style of leadership practised by Muldoon as Prime Minister. The Labour Party received more votes than the National Party but won fewer seats, while the Social Credit Party secured only one seat. The Values Party, with no firm base of appeal, fared poorly (in 1989 it changed its name to the Green Party of Aotearoa). To stabilize the parliamentary representation of the South Island (as its share of the country's population in proportion to that of the North Island had been—and is still—declining), its number of seats was fixed at 25. In 1981 public opinion was highly polarized by the Government's failure to discourage a South African Springbok rugby tour of New Zealand. The National Party narrowly retained office in November. The Social Credit Party lost political credibility, but in August 1983 a new third party was founded: the right-wing New Zealand Party, led by a wealthy property-owner, Robert (later Sir Robert) Jones. Meanwhile, in February 1983, the Labour Party had replaced its much respected but publicly unimpressive leader, Wallace Rowling, with David Lange, a lawyer with a more vigorous style and greater charisma, who became Prime Minister in July 1984 when Labour capitalized on Muldoon's unpopularity and poor tactics in calling an early general election. The New Zealand Party gained no representation but attracted 12% of the total number of votes cast. The high turn-out of eligible voters (86%) was an indication of public dissatisfaction with the Muldoon administration.

In November 1984 Muldoon was replaced as leader of the National Party by James McLay, the deputy leader and a former Attorney-General. The transfer was not effected smoothly, as Muldoon made no pretence of co-operation and maintained a high political profile, working to destabilize the leadership of his successor. In March 1986 McLay was ousted by his deputy leader, James (Jim) Bolger, a farmer from King Country.

Initially, the Labour Government benefited considerably from the opposition's disarray, for the programme of economic restructuring along free-market lines was alienating many of Labour's traditional urban-based supporters. The social cost of New Zealand's high level of inflation and worsening balance-of-payments difficulties, and of Labour's policy initiatives, bore most heavily upon low-income earners and welfare beneficiaries, in which group Maori and Pacific Islanders were heavily represented.

At the general election of August 1987, popular support for the Government's anti-nuclear defence policy, a stance then opposed (but later endorsed) by the National Party, enabled Lange's administration to become the first Labour Government since 1946 to be elected for two successive terms of office. Labour's political euphoria was short-lived, however. Policy disagreements emerged between Finance Minister Roger Douglas, the architect of Labour's deregulation and free market economics, and David Lange, who wished to prevent the extension of market principles into social policy. Douglas lost his portfolio, but in August 1989 Lange resigned as Prime Minister, his position having been consistently undermined by the continued internal political intriguing of Roger Douglas, and by the formation of the NewLabour Party (led by a former President of the New Zealand Labour Party, Jim Anderton), which aimed to appeal to erstwhile Labour supporters who had become disillusioned with the Government's continued advocacy of privatization. The new Deputy Prime Minister, Helen Clark, a former lecturer in political science, became the first woman to hold such office in New Zealand's parliamentary history. Geoffrey (later Sir Geoffrey) Palmer, previously a professor of law, came to the Prime Minister's position with a reputation for cautious and careful administration and did not find it easy to project a more personable image. In September 1990, less than eight weeks before the next election, Palmer resigned from his position. Michael Moore, the Minister of External Relations and Trade (who had contested the August 1989 leadership election), replaced Palmer as Prime Minister.

The National Party secured 67 of the 97 seats in the House of Representatives in the October 1990 election, the Labour Party won 29 seats, and the NewLabour Party one seat. The NewLabour Party provided one option for protest votes, while disenchanted voters with environmental concerns supported the Green Party. Non-voting increased again, and the incoming National Government actually received fewer votes than had Labour in 1987. Maori voters still had the choice of registering on either the general or the Maori electoral roll, but the Mana Motuhake party, founded in November 1979 by the former member for Northern Maori, Matiu Rata, did not have the resources to contest more than a few seats.

Jim Bolger thus became the country's fourth Prime Minister within 15 months, and the new National Party Government immediately signalled a series of cost-cutting measures (see Economy), designed essentially to reduce the welfare burden, which was to consume 60% of total government spending in the 1991/92 financial year. Under the direction of the Minister of Finance, Ruth Richardson, 'user pays' initiatives in health and education undermined long-cherished principles of a welfare state, while a crisis over pensions funding, with which the Minister of Social Welfare, Jenny Shipley, had to contend, was essentially a result of political decisions made by the National Party at the time of the 1975 general election. The passing of the Employment Contracts Act in 1991 promoted the rapid deregulation of the labour market and further undermined a trade union movement already weakened by high unemployment. More than 10% of the labour force was out of work in 1992, with the Maori unemployment rate being significantly greater than that of Pakeha (those of predominantly British origin). By 1992 there was a new political alignment, the Alliance, made up of a coalition of minor parties, including the Greens, NewLabour, Mana Motuhake and the New Zealand Democratic Party (descended from the former Social Credit Party). It also included another new party, the Liberal Party, formed by two dissident ex-National Party MPs. The maverick political behaviour of the former National and subsequently Independent member for Tauranga, Winston Peters, resulted in his expulsion from the National Party; he subsequently formed New Zealand First, a political grouping to which a number of prominent Alliance members defected once it became apparent that Peters would not support the coalition.

Such political manoeuvrings were presented as an argument against electoral reform, for which strong support had been expressed by voters during a referendum in September 1992; but at a second, binding referendum, held in conjunction with the general election on 6 November 1993, the electorate voted in favour of the introduction of a mixed member proportional representation (MMP) system. The close election results (National 50 seats, Labour 45, Alliance two, New Zealand First two) led to some weeks of political uncertainty, but Bolger continued to govern with his marginal majority because the Alliance rejected Labour proposals that it form a coalition to bring down the Government. The snap by-election held in August 1994 in the Canterbury constituency of Selwyn, following the resignation from politics of the former Minister of Finance, Ruth Richardson, confirmed National's position. Labour's poor third-place rating in the polls reflected public reaction to the internecine wrangling that dominated party affairs after Helen Clark replaced Michael Moore as Labour's leader following the November 1993 election.

As a result of opposition disunity, National was able to continue to govern effectively; no key policy issue faced a unified challenge, not even the ongoing sale of state assets. The growing appeal (in particular among Maori and the elderly) of New Zealand First, the leadership of which was openly critical of overseas investment, Asian immigration and government policies affecting the elderly, continued to erode support for both National and Labour. The increasing dogmatism of both individuals and political parties in the months preceding the 1996 election caused many New Zealanders, desirous of more responsive government, to view the forthcoming change to MMP with considerable scepticism (which was little assuaged by subsequent events).

At the general election held on 12 October 1996, the National Party won 44 of the 120 parliamentary seats, the Labour Party 37, New Zealand First 17 and the Alliance 13. An increased number of Maori and women were returned as MPs: 15 and 36 respectively. As no party had secured an outright majority, prolonged negotiations ensued, with both Labour and National endeavouring to establish an alliance with New Zealand First. Eventually, on 10 December, a coalition Government was formed comprising National and New Zealand First (which together represented 47% of the votes cast). Winston Peters, as well as being appointed Deputy Prime Minister, was assigned the post of Treasurer, giving him substantial control over economic policy. However, Bill Birch, a National MP, remained Minister of Finance.

Older voters, many of whom had supported New Zealand First in protest at National's health and pensions policies, were highly critical of the new coalition, which for National was essentially an arrangement of political convenience. The political inexperience of many New Zealand First MPs and factionalism within that party contributed to its steady decrease in popularity. The leadership change effected by Jenny Shipley and her supporters during Jim Bolger's absence overseas in November 1997 was an indication of National's growing concern that its own standing was being undermined by the reputation and performance of its coalition partner. Differences of economic and social policy, including the continuing privatization of state assets, culminated in Shipley's dismissal of Winston Peters as Deputy Prime Minister and Treasurer on 14 August 1998. The engagement of both parties in an agreed disputes resolution process was a formality. The coalition Government was dissolved four days later. Jenny Shipley subsequently led a minority Government that was dependent for its survival upon dissident ex-New Zealand First MPs, independents and the right-wing ACT New Zealand, a party founded by Sir Roger Douglas and led by a former Labour cabinet minister, Richard Prebble. During 1999 Shipley's political reputation was not enhanced by her Government's handling of various controversies concerning substantial severance payments to senior officers within the departments of tourism, the fire service, and work and income support services: the appropriateness of trying to imbue the public service with a corporate ethos continued to be widely debated. In August the withdrawal of the IBM corporation from further software development of the much-vaunted new police computer system, already $NZ30m. beyond its original $NZ100m. budget and remaining incomplete after five years of effort, was a further political embarrassment for a Government that had pledged a strong policy on law enforcement but appeared to have left its 'front-line' police officers inadequately resourced to cope with the growing rates of drug- and gang-related crime.

At the election conducted on 27 November 1999, the opposition Labour Party won the largest share of votes cast. A recount of votes in one constituency, where the Green Party candidate then unexpectedly took the seat from the incumbent National MP, combined with the incorporation of 'special votes' (which included those cast by New Zealanders overseas), led to a substantial modification of the initial results. Having secured 38.7% of the votes cast, the Labour Party was finally allocated 49 of the 120 seats in the House of Representatives, while the National Party, which had won 30.5% of the votes, received 39 seats. The Alliance was allocated 10 seats and ACT New Zealand nine seats. Under the recently-introduced system of proportional representation, the Green Party's victory in the one constituency automatically entitled the movement to a further six seats in the legislature. New Zealand First's representation declined to five; the party's leader, Winston Peters, only narrowly retained his seat. United New Zealand took the one remaining seat. Having previously discounted any co-operation with the Green Party, the Labour Party was thus obliged to seek the support not only of the Alliance but also of the seven Green MPs. The leader of the Labour Party, Helen Clark, therefore became the first woman politician to win a New Zealand general election. On 4 April 2001 Dame Silvia Cartwright took office as Governor-General, leading to an unprecedented situation: five important public roles in the country—that of Prime Minister, Leader of the Opposition, Attorney-General, Chief Justice and Governor-General—were all occupied by women. In October, however, Bill English replaced Jenny Shipley as leader of the National Party.

Clark's minority Government, which incorporated several members of the Alliance, including Jim Anderton as Minister for Regional Development, took office in December 1999, and in 2001 continued to function relatively harmoniously under the Prime Minister's strong control, although progress on initiatives to address the disparities between Maori and non-Maori communities, particularly in the socio-economic indicators of health, housing, income, education, criminality and domestic violence, was slow. In March 2001 the Government announced *ex gratia* payments of $NZ30,000 per person to survivors of military and civilian Japanese prison camps in the Second World War, or to surviving spouses. In conservation and environmental issues the political influence of the Green Party became apparent, notably in debates over research involving genetic modification.

The disintegration of the Alliance and the clear differences between Labour and the Greens over the continuation of a moratorium banning the commercial release of genetically modified organisms (due to expire in October 2003) contributed to Helen Clark's decision to call an early election for 27 July 2002. The Government hoped to take advantage of its popularity and secure sufficient electoral support to function without the need for coalition partners. Only 77% of registered voters participated on election day. Labour polled 41% of the party votes and secured 52 of the 120 in the House of Representatives, three more than in 1999. New Zealand First won 10% (13 seats); ACT New Zealand 7% (nine seats); the Greens 7% (also nine seats) and United Future New Zealand 7% (eight seats). The Alliance failed to win any parliamentary representation but Jim Anderton's Progressive Coalition party, a personal grouping formed after the disintegration of the Alliance, won two seats, despite securing only 1.7% of the party votes. The final outcome was disastrous for the National Party, and its leader, Bill English, was clearly dissatisfied with the campaign strategies of the President of the party, Michelle Boag. National lost 12 of its sitting MPs and recorded the worst result of its 66-year history as a major force in New Zealand politics, winning just 21% of the party vote and only 27 seats.

Subsequent negotiations enabled Clark to announce that her minority coalition Government, comprising Labour and the Progressive Coalition, had enlisted United Future New Zealand's support on matters of confidence and supply. Formed in 1995 by its leader Peter Dunne, this centrist party appealed to many middle-class voters with its emphasis on family values. By remaining outside the Government, Dunne's party hoped to avoid the fate of the junior coalition partners (New Zealand First and the Alliance respectively) in the previous two governments elected under the system of proportional representation. Yet in meeting the expectations of its centre-left supporters, Labour would need to maintain good working relationships with the Greens, the co-leader of which, Jeanette Fitzsimons, lost her electorate seat but was returned to Parliament as a party list MP.

Other Domestic Affairs

Official immigration policies continued to be a source of electoral concern (exploited most obviously by New Zealand First). The 2001 census revealed a continuing trend towards ethnic diversity in the country's population: Pacific Peoples comprised 6.5% of the total population, while those identifying as Asian totalled 6.6% (compared with 3% in 1991), despite the imposition in October 1996 of a $NZ20,000 fee on immigrants lacking competence in the English language. Adequate support services are still not in place to assist new migrants. Highly-skilled professionals, admitted to New Zealand because of their qualifications, are frequently unable to work in their area of expertise owing to language difficulties, administrative barriers or racial prejudice. According to the 2001 census, Maori totalled 14.7% of the population, while those identifying as European accounted for 80%. An increase in South African and Croatian immigrants was noticeable within the European category. The median age varied widely across the different ethnic groups; that of Europeans being considerably older (36.8 years) than that of Maori (21.9) and Pacific Peoples (21.0). The ageing of the post-1945 'baby boomers' was expected to have a major impact on the social services, health and superannuation policies in due course.

More than 80% of Maori continue to be urban dwellers, a situation that has caused many to become alienated from their tribal background and traditions, though sustained and vigorous efforts are now being made to arrest this decline in Maoritanga. In 1985 the Lange Government enabled the Waitangi Tribunal (established in 1975) to consider retrospectively Maori grievances dating back to 1840. The evidence presented by claimants to the Tribunal is enabling Maori perspectives on the colonial past to be aired in a public forum, and the findings of the Tribunal, while not binding on the Government, have already contributed significantly towards changing public perceptions on this issue. The strengthening cultural renaissance initially encountered a mixed reception from Pakeha. While the status of Maori as an official language and the establishment of the *Kohanga Reo* ('language nest') early childhood programmes were soon accepted, the need for affirmative action to redress educational and social disadvantage, much of which is the unforeseen consequence of past policies, was more contentious. National Government promotion of a $NZ2,000m. 'fiscal envelope' scheme as a means of resolving outstanding claims was soundly rejected by Maori at a series of consultative *hui* (gatherings) held throughout the country in 1995. Direct negotiation with the Crown remains an option, however, and a 1995 agreement, which included the return of assets and a formal apology by the Crown, with the powerful North Island Tainui tribes met with a mixed reception from other claimants. In October 1996 a similar settlement was reached with the Ngai Tahu tribes of South Island. The government-initiated Sealord deal, whereby fishing quotas were allocated to coastal tribes, caused dissension about the fairest method of distributing returns within Maoridom. Urban Maori authorities argue that payments according to *iwi* (tribal) affiliation deny them a share of the resources to which their urban-born membership is entitled. Costly legal action has resulted, nevertheless, in an affirmation that an urban Maori authority cannot be defined as an *iwi* even if it serves that purpose for its members: affiliation based on *whakapapa* (descent), not on residential location, must be the basis upon which payments are made. Efforts continue to resolve the issue without further redress to the courts.

Relatively few New Zealanders are well-informed about their country's history, although the overwhelming public response to Te Papa, the new national museum opened in Wellington in 1998, indicated a high level of interest. Yet for citizens adversely affected by recent social and economic policy, the problems of the present assume much greater significance than any knowledge of the past. The conspicuous rise in poverty, violent crime, youthful offending, gang association and drug-trafficking, and the persistence of a significant level of unemployment, do not augur well for social harmony, particularly when the country's youth, Maori and Polynesians are over-represented in statistics for the above. High rates of teenage pregnancy, alcohol abuse and youth suicide are also matters of social concern. Despite political rhetoric concerning the need for a more skilled work-force in a knowledge-based economy, escalating costs for tertiary education have created extremely high levels of indebtedness amongst the student population, an increasing number of whom have been forced to rely upon bank loans to fund their training. Shortages of trained staff in the health, education and information technology sectors especially, reflect the trend of recent graduates to seek higher-paid employment abroad in an effort to reduce their burden of debt. Successive governments have fostered the notion of community responsibility for social welfare, but have yet to provide adequate resourcing, particularly in mental health, and many church leaders, social workers, and voluntary agencies are critical of policies that suggest a market-led abandonment of a long-held national commitment to the principles of a welfare state. The Labour Government took measures to redress the previous administration's policies of reducing the number of state houses and charging market value rents for such properties. These practices were perceived to have contributed to the plight of urban low-income families, and to the poor health of their children, particularly in the South Auckland area, with its high concentration of unskilled and unemployed Pacific Island Polynesians. Evoking the precedent of the influential Maori Land March of 1975, in September 1998 the Anglican Church organized an ecumenical Hikoi of Hope in which marchers from both northern and southern ends of the country converged on Parliament to protest against the trends in social policy. The closure of rural hospitals, increased privatization and a continual and expensive restructuring of the health service have yet to be perceived by the public at large as improvements on the previous public health care system. Campaigns against smoking, which initially had considerable success in the creation of smoke-free work environments, have still to meet targets amongst youth (young women and Maori, in particular); entrenched attitudes that equate heavy drinking with masculinity are proving to be difficult to change, despite the obvious link between alcohol consumption and a high incidence of driving accidents, domestic violence and homicides. Many New Zealanders entered the 21st century with a strong conviction that the individualism and ideology of market forces that prevailed in the last two decades of the 20th century are not serving the country and its people well.

International Relations

Continuing the more independent foreign policy initiated by Norman Kirk, from 1984 the Lange Government made a determined effort to foster Pacific unity and to build closer relations with New Zealand's Asian neighbours. Strong diplomatic and trading links were established with Japan, the Republic of Korea and the People's Republic of China. The Lange Government was also the first foreign power to give diplomatic recognition to the Aquino administration in the Philippines. Support for the policy of creating a nuclear-free zone in the Pacific—in 1972 the Kirk Government sent a frigate into the testing zone near Mururoa Atoll, in French Polynesia, in an effort to force French testing to be conducted underground—led to a strengthening of ties between New Zealand and the other island nations of the Pacific. Long-term strategies to promote Pacific unity were seriously impeded, however, by the successful military coups in Fiji in May and September 1987. During 1989 New Zealand endeavoured to give leadership on other issues of mutual concern to South Pacific nations. For example, at a meeting of the South Pacific Forum in Vanuatu in July, New Zealand stated its intention to ban fishing by drift gill-nets from its territorial waters and to refuse permission for vessels using such nets to enter its ports. In 1990 the Japanese decision to cease drift gill-net fishing in Pacific waters received general approval. There have been similar small-power initiatives concerning measures to protect the ozone layer in the atmosphere and to conserve Antarctica's special status. New Zealand's initiative to broker a peace agreement between Bougainville separatists and the Government of Papua New Guinea led to a cessation of hostilities and to the presence of a New Zealand peace-keeping mission on the island of Bougainville throughout 1998. The Labour Government strongly condemned the hostage-taking and eventual overthrow of the Indian-dominated elected Government of Fiji in May 2000.

Despite the common heritage of British Commonwealth membership, New Zealand had little diplomatic contact with the African continent, but following Lange's visit there in April 1985, a High Commission was established in Harare, Zimbabwe. Limited promises of aid were also made. The offence caused to the Indian Government by the Muldoon administration's closure of the New Zealand High Commission in New Delhi was redressed by the appointment of the world-famous mountaineer, Sir Edmund Hillary, as High Commissioner in India in 1985. In the mid-1990s the National Government sought to strengthen relations with South Africa, which had been severely weakened by controversy over the apartheid system, and the ill-conceived and government-supported Springbok Rugby Tour of New Zealand in 1981. The success of President Mandela's visit to New Zealand in November 1995 was consolidated when Bolger opened an embassy in Pretoria in August 1996. While in South Africa, New Zealand's Prime Minister acknowledged that the 1981 Tour had been a costly mistake.

In July 1985 the trawler *Rainbow Warrior*, the flagship of the anti-nuclear environmentalist group, Greenpeace (which was to have led a flotilla to Mururoa Atoll, in French Polynesia, to protest against French testing of nuclear weapons in the Pacific), was blown up and sunk in Auckland harbour. The vessel's photographer died in the explosion. Alain Mafart and Dominique Prieur, two agents of the French External Security Division, the Direction générale de la sécurité extérieure (DGSE), were subsequently arrested and, after being convicted of manslaughter at a court hearing in November, were imprisoned in Auckland. In July 1986, despite pressure from France (including the imposition of trade sanctions) that they be released or returned to France, the two agents were transferred to the atoll of Hao in French Polynesia, where they were scheduled to be detained for the remainder of their 10-year sentence. The French Government made a formal apology for the sabotage operation, and paid the New Zealand Government $NZ7m. in compensation. Relations deteriorated in late 1987 when Mafart was returned to Paris, ostensibly for medical treatment, and in May 1988 a pregnant Prieur was airlifted back to France immediately prior to the French presidential election. Prieur's promotion to the rank of major on the fourth anniversary of the sinking of the *Rainbow Warrior* and the public decoration of Mafart in July 1991, together with the continuation of French nuclear testing in the Pacific, showed that protests by New Zealand had little real impact on French policy. President Chirac's resumption of underground nuclear testing at Mururoa Atoll in September 1995, however, outraged world opinion and was vehemently opposed by countries in the South Pacific. In response to public pressure within New Zealand, the National Government sent a naval research vessel to Mururoa. New Zealand's attempt to reopen its 1973 case against France at the International Court of Justice in The Hague was unsuccessful.

New Zealand's relationship with Australia was strengthened by the implementation of the Closer Economic Relations (CER) agreement. Inaugurated on 1 January 1983 and taking full effect on 1 July 1990, the arrangement was not without local critics, who pointed to a disparity of access, maintaining that Australian manufacturers had a competitive advantage owing to their unrestricted entry into the open New Zealand market. Meanwhile, defence links between the two countries were seriously undermined by dissension that developed within the ANZUS alliance as a consequence of the Labour Government's opposition to nuclear testing and weaponry in the Pacific region. In February 1985 the Lange Government upheld its popular election manifesto by imposing a ban on the entry of any nuclear-capable ships into New Zealand ports. The US Government maintained that such a standpoint rendered the ANZUS Treaty inoperable as, for security reasons, it was policy neither to confirm nor to deny that any US vessel was nuclear-propelled or nuclear-armed. New Zealand's access to intelligence-sharing and military co-operation was withheld, and in August 1986 security guarantees to New Zealand under the ANZUS Treaty were suspended. In November Lange reaffirmed his Government's decision to impose the ban on nuclear-capable ships. The US Government responded with the announcement, in February 1987, of its decision not to renew a 1982 memorandum of understanding (due to be renegotiated in June of that year), whereby New Zealand was able to purchase military equipment from the USA at concessionary prices.

The New Zealand Government subsequently proposed a new defence strategy, based on increased self-reliance for the country's military forces, in conjunction with continuing co-operation with Australia and greater involvement in the affairs of the South Pacific region. US military aircraft which, by the nature of their operations, did not need to carry nuclear missiles, were nevertheless permitted to continue using the US Antarctic supply base at Christchurch (income from which is some $NZ20m. annually). In June 1987 the ban on nuclear-capable vessels became law, with the enactment of the New Zealand Nuclear Free Zone, Disarmament and Arms Control Bill. The Labour Government's anti-nuclear policy continued to command widespread support within the country, although the National Government, which took office in 1990, appeared to be uncomfortable with such a commitment, as was evidenced by the diplomatic overtures extended towards the USA by the Minister of External Relations, Don McKinnon. By 1992 the Government was signalling that it wished to amend the anti-nuclear law to allow for the entry of nuclear-powered vessels, but the National Party could not risk its slender majority by initiating such a change. The ban on nuclear arms is still supported by all parties: only the removal of nuclear weapons from the vessels of the US Pacific fleet would enable the Government to contemplate visits by US warships.

McKinnon's successful campaign to obtain for New Zealand a seat on the United Nations Security Council for a two-year term from January 1993 increased the country's international profile and encouraged a greater domestic awareness of foreign policy issues, as did his accession to the position of Commonwealth Secretary-General. Members of the armed forces joined the UN Peace-keeping Force in Bosnia, and the National Government agreed to continue involvement despite the escalation of the conflict in former Yugoslavia. New Zealand's UN role and increasing global support for an international Nuclear Test Ban led to some easing of tension with the USA. Bolger was received in Washington by President Bill Clinton in early 1995. The US President joined other world leaders at the 'summit' meeting of the Asia-Pacific Economic Co-operation forum (APEC) held in Auckland in September 1999. President Clinton announced the end of the 14-year ban on New Zealand's participation in military exercises with the USA, in preparation for the dispatch of a multinational peace-keeping force to East Timor, of which New Zealand troops continued to form part throughout

2000. Subsequent—and controversial—government decisions concerning defence expenditure indicated nevertheless a continuing commitment to such roles in the future. (In December 2001 New Zealand announced that, at the request of the UN transitional administration, its 660 peace-keeping troops were to remain in East Timor until November 2002.) The USA also supported former Labour leader Michael Moore's protracted bid to become head of the World Trade Organization, a position he assumed in September 1999 but relinquished in September 2002 after a half-term in office, in favour of his Thai rival for the post.

The need for export markets has been a major influence on New Zealand's recent foreign policy. New Zealand has sought access to the markets of the European Union (EU), Eastern Europe and the Middle East, and has also become a member of the Organisation for Economic Co-operation and Development (OECD). Responses to international crises have been tempered by trade considerations. As part of the general protest against the Soviet intervention in Afghanistan, New Zealand temporarily severed diplomatic relations with the USSR and supported the US appeal for a boycott of the Moscow Olympic Games in 1980. In 1982, with considerable swiftness, the Muldoon Government offered aid to the United Kingdom during the crisis over the Falkland Islands, and imposed a boycott on Argentine goods. The government-authorized massacre of students in Tiananmen Square, Beijing, in June 1989 received only diplomatic condemnation, as trade with China, especially in wool, has assumed significant proportions since the late 1970s. An official visit to China by Prime Minister Helen Clark in April 2001 was intended to improve New Zealand's trading position with that country prior to its accession to the World Trade Organization (WTO). Prime Minister Bolger's state visits to the Republic of Korea and Japan in the 1990s, and the accompanying public insistence that New Zealand's trading future was to be found in Asia, led to economic initiatives that were to prove unsustainable by that market. In 1998 the tourism and forestry sectors were particularly badly affected by the Asian economic crisis, thus further exposing the social costs of New Zealand's vulnerable position within the global economy.

Responses to world events during 2001 and 2002 reflected New Zealand's non-isolationist stance. The Government was quick to express support for the USA in the aftermath of the terrorist attacks of 11 September 2001 and committed special combat force troops to service in Afghanistan, without full parliamentary debate on the decision. The nature of US policies in the ongoing 'war against terrorism' were a source of debate and concern among many New Zealanders. In 2001, for humanitarian reasons, the Government accepted 141 of the Afghan refugees rescued at sea by a Norwegian vessel but denied access to the Australian mainland (see the chapter on Christmas Island). The New Zealand Prime Minister's presence at a meeting of the Pacific Islands Forum held in Fiji in early 2002 indicated a renewal of closer relationships following Fiji's return to democracy. New Zealand expressed disquiet about the level of ongoing violence and civil disorder in Solomon Islands and about the political unrest that surrounded the election in Papua New Guinea in mid-2002, concerns that were shared by other Pacific nations. At the meeting of Commonwealth heads of government in March 2002, New Zealand officials joined in the condemnation of President Robert Mugabe's controversial policies of farm seizures and land redistribution. At the World Summit on Sustainable Development, held in Johannesburg, South Africa, in September 2002, New Zealand delegates continued to uphold the principles of the Kyoto Protocol regarding the limitation of carbon dioxide emissions.

Economy

KENNETH E. JACKSON

Based on an earlier article by J. W. ROWE

New Zealand is best described as a small, open economy centred on two main islands. At July 2002 its estimated population was 3.94m. The country's renowned advocacy for, and implementation of, a regime of deregulation, free trade and liberalized investment remained in place, although the policy was no longer followed with the same zeal as previously. In fact, most of the liberalization efforts were concentrated in the mid 1980s and the early 1990s, during the respective first terms of the Labour administration (1984–87) and the successor National Party (1990–93).

New Zealand is far distant from its traditional markets and relatively distant from its nearest major market, Australia. Export receipts continue to be concentrated upon a very narrow range of primary products. These are subject to considerable fluctuations in their prices, which are largely determined externally. Market access for agricultural products has improved, particularly since the successful conclusion of the 'Uruguay Round' of the General Agreement on Tariffs and Trade (GATT) in December 1993, and the subsequent establishment of the World Trade Organization (WTO). Restrictions on New Zealand exports remain an occasional problem on the demand side, whilst drought and other constraints on output affect supply from time to time. The internal market is constrained by physical obstacles and by the low density of population over much of the land surface.

Debate continued over the causes of New Zealand's relatively poor macro-economic performance compared with the average of the other member countries of the Organisation for Economic Co-operation and Development (OECD) and with the Australian experience in particular. Some commentators, including the former Governor of the Reserve Bank of New Zealand (RBNZ), Don Brash, took issue with this assessment, arguing that from 1990 the New Zealand average annual per caput increase in real GDP of some 2.5% had set the country behind only Ireland, Australia, Norway, the USA and the Netherlands. Judicious choice of other start and end dates of course gave an entirely different outcome. The average growth rate in the long run (since 1900) was of the order of 1.6% and more in line with Argentina than with the countries normally thought of as being in the same 'club', such as Australia, Canada or the United Kingdom. Australia generally outperforms New Zealand, despite its castigation from time to time in the media and elsewhere for its lack of micro-economic reform on the New Zealand pattern. New Zealand incomes had declined from their 1995 peak of 87% of the OECD average to 84% by 2001, when that organization estimated the Australian figure to be 108% of the OECD average.

Migration figures moved from negative to positive in the 12 months to mid-2002. For the year to June 2002 the net inflow of immigrants was 32,800, compared with the net loss of 9,300 experienced in the preceding 12-month period. The factors of both fewer departures and more arrivals combined to produce the change. The RBNZ appeared concerned that this inflow, largely settling in the Auckland region, would add to income rises in producing a boost to house prices in that region specifically and would compound inflationary pressures in the country generally. The central bank subsequently pursued an aggressive policy, according preference to controlling inflation rather than to encouraging growth. Following the repercussions of the terrorist attacks on the USA on 11 September 2001, New Zealand interest rates declined, but by a smaller margin than elsewhere and with a slight delay. In the three months to 31 July 2002, rates rose again, by one percentage point to reach 5.75%, in advance of any such movement overseas. How such action would correspond to the Government's desire to encourage growth and innovation and to the emergence of some universal concerns over the possibility of deflation as a problem rather than inflation, remained to be seen.

The development of the New Zealand economy since the initiation of the 1984 reform programme has incorporated a continuation of many of the previous characteristic features, such as relatively slow growth rates and comparatively high real interest rates, along with a propensity to import, which inclines the economy towards a deficit on the current account of the balance of payments. Unemployment, as indicated by conventional measures, was virtually non-existent in 1970, but subsequently increased to a significant level, with major peaks in 1983 and 1992. The employment rate subsequently fluctuated around a slowly declining trend, and was estimated at 5.3% in mid-2002. Inflation also rose in the 1970s, but slowed to an annual average of 8.5% in 1995–98, was negligible by 1999 and in 2002 remained below the 3% upper limit of the target set by the RBNZ. Past difficulties were partly attributable to external factors, in the guise of prolonged periods of international recession. Restricted market access for some agricultural exports has continued from time to time, but the country's economic problems have been aggravated, even where not originally induced, by the slow pace of domestic adjustment to external market changes.

The New Zealand of the reform era has been described by Don Brash as ' a model for change' from an economic perspective. Outcomes, however, have failed to match expectations. Apart from the period of 1991–96, from 1970 through to the early 21st century, New Zealand has performed below the OECD average and fallen well behind not only Australia (see above), but also the United Kingdom and the USA in terms of gross domestic product (GDP) per caput. This has occurred despite the post-1984 campaign for extensive deregulation of the economy, involving deregulation of financial institutions, liberalization of shopping hours and liquor-licensing laws, delicensing of the internal transport system and the meat-processing industry and the removal of the last vestiges of import licensing. Farm subsidies were discontinued, and many state trading activities were corporatized if not privatized. The model still has its critics, but whether other models and prescriptions would have performed any better is a moot point.

The policy measures adopted from 1984, starting with the deregulation of financial and foreign-exchange sectors of the New Zealand economy, were part of a broader range of policies avowedly intended to promote more rapid economic adjustment. Not all the desirable aims were in fact achieved immediately. Fiscal balance and then a fiscal surplus were accomplished, but only in the longer run. The taxation system was radically altered with the introduction of a goods and services tax (GST) and the reduction of marginal income tax rates on higher incomes. The Government attempted to take a secondary role in economic matters, regarding its function as one of encouraging the efficient operation of markets, competition and an economy able to respond quickly and flexibly to changing circumstances and demands. Initially, a burgeoning fiscal deficit emerged, as taxation revenue stagnated while welfare spending rose. Restructuring involved excessive unemployment, at least in the short term. Regional, age and skill disparities appeared in the unemployment figures.

In October 1990, when the National Party returned to power, a second spate of enthusiasm for deregulation occurred. Greater emphasis was placed on decreasing the fiscal deficit and further reducing inflation. In addition, from early 1991 legislation was introduced with the aim of deregulating the labour market. The Employment Contracts Act (ECA) marked a major shift in negotiating power. It reintroduced voluntary unionism and enhanced the employer's bargaining power. Union membership halved. The ECA was claimed to have produced greater flexibility in the labour market, resulting in a significant stimulus to employment and production, notably for export. The exact outcome was difficult to assess, as the figures were confusing and the choice of benchmark for comparison was an important determinant of the result. Amendments to the employment law were made from October 2000 through the Employment Relations Act (ERA), which among other measures, restored a greater role for collective agreements.

In 1991 the Government also moved to reduce the cost of the welfare state and to contain the rising bill for national superannuation. The ensuing outcry led to some reversal, but the main features of the cut-backs remained. Measures were also put in place to curb the increasing public costs of health and education, along with institutional changes intended to improve service delivery and accountability. For a while, in the early 1990s, external income and expenditure were approximately balanced for the first time in two decades, annual inflation had declined to around 1% and, temporarily, strong growth in production and employment was apparent. From 1993 to 1996 the economy continued to perform strongly, with unemployment declining and fiscal balance being achieved by mid-1994, largely owing to buoyant tax revenues, but also to spending restraint. A policy of allocating priority to the repayment of overseas public debt from these fiscal surpluses was then implemented, thus improving the country's international credit rating.

Economic problems re-emerged in 1996–97, albeit less serious than those of the 1970s and 1980s. The strength of the New Zealand dollar in the mid-1990s and high interest rates curbed the growth of exports and production generally, whilst inflation had risen slightly. Some decline in the exchange rate gave exporters a boost. Parliamentarians conducted the new electoral system of mixed member proportional representation (MMP, see History) in an unstable manner, and one not highly conducive to economic growth. Economic instability was exacerbated in 1998 by the adverse effects of the Asian financial crisis, which was particularly damaging to the tourism and forestry sectors. These factors combined with New Zealand's high propensity to demand imports, resulting in a balance-of-payments deficit equivalent to some 7% of GDP. Any recovery in 1998 and 1999 was somewhat slow and hesitant, as well as uneven, both geographically and sectorally. A revision of some of the previous reforms emerged following the 1999 election of a new Government, with further review likely following the election of July 2002. The methods and targets of the RBNZ remained under question. The changes from a quantity type control to an interest rate control developed during 1999 and 2000, with the original target band of price inflation being set at 0%–2%, and subsequently amended to 0%–3%. The major monetary control variable, the official cash rate (OCR), stood at 5.75% in August 2002. Fears of New Zealand moving into recession were seen as related more to external than to internal events, with internal expansionary effects dominating. Any significant break in the strong growth being experienced in primary product export receipts by New Zealand farmers in 2001, however, was viewed with some trepidation.

PRIMARY INDUSTRY

Agriculture

Farming and associated processing industries play a greater part in the New Zealand economy than in most developed countries. The historic concentration on pastoral products for export income, arose partly from preferential access to a large market, the United Kingdom, but production was also favoured by a benign climate. Since soil fertility is not generally high, a scientific approach to the improvement of soil productivity and of stock-breeding and management has been necessary, together with a heavy reliance on (imported) phosphatic fertilizers. Diversification into manufacturing and service industries has taken place in recent decades, although traditionally these have been limited to the small domestic market with its protection by distance and by government intervention. The agricultural sector remains of fundamental importance for external trade (although wool receipts are not as prominent a contributor to export earnings as previously), and, of necessity, farming is highly efficient by world standards. Capital intensity in the guise of large farm size and a high degree of mechanization, have been major factors in maintaining the international competitiveness of agricultural and pastoral production.

Dairying is now the most important sector of farming in New Zealand. Favourable factors have been product and market diversification, increasing average farm size and concentration of processing in a few very large plants. The New Zealand Dairy Board, which in earlier years had played a vital role in improving efficiency in dairying, both on-farm and off-farm, was replaced in 2001 by a new organization, Globalco, which subsequently began trading under the new name of Fonterra, one of the biggest such concerns in the world. Issues relating to fears of cross-subsidization of export production and long-term implications for efficiency and competition were expressed at the time of its introduction, but farmers largely supported the move. New Zealand domestic dairy prices generally have remained below world levels, rather than above them, allaying overseas competitors' suspicions of cross-subsidization, and some measures to ensure domestic competition have been put in place. Domestic dairy prices, however, have been rising overall since the new organization was established. Declines in the world price for dairy products in the first half of 2002 were not matched by any significant fall in domestic prices.

Pastoral farming is still of major significance and is also predominantly export-orientated. Problems of access to some overseas markets and limited progress in the processing of products have restricted profitability. In recent years livestock diversification has occurred, such as moves to expand the number of deer and goats, whilst reducing sheep numbers. Cropping, fruit-growing and horticulture are also of increasing importance, and latterly there has been a major expansion of viticulture, with significant exports of wine. Consistent quantity production capacity problems have proven something of a difficulty for this industry in the past, but the development of major producers in newer regions has contributed to an improvement in the situation.

The agricultural sector as a whole faced major reorganization when support prices were abandoned in 1985/86 as part of the programme of economic reform. The sector withstood the restructuring surprisingly well. Despite diversification elsewhere in the economy, exports of farm products of all kinds still account for a substantial percentage of total exports and for much of the growth in exports witnessed since 1999. Meat and dairy products together accounted for some 30% of total export earnings in 2001. About 90% of the June 2001 quarter's seasonally-adjusted 6.6% rise in export values was derived from meat and dairy products.

New Zealand welcomed the successful conclusion in December 1993 of the 'Uruguay Round' of GATT negotiations, and has actively participated in subsequent bilateral negotiations, which on the whole have been reasonably successful. Agricultural protectionism in Japan, the European Union (EU) and elsewhere, however, remains a problem. In 1999 a dispute with the USA led to that country's imposition of safeguard measures against lamb imports from New Zealand, along with those from Australia. Despite a ruling in favour of New Zealand and Australia by the disputes tribunal, some problems continued into 2001. New Zealand's membership of the influential Cairns Group of agricultural traders, notwithstanding, the prospects of further trade liberalization in the next round of trade negotiations remain uncertain, with effective implementation of existing agreements being as big an issue as the obtaining of new ones.

Forestry

Most parts of New Zealand were still heavily forested when European settlers arrived, although substantial areas had been deforested during the centuries of Maori occupation. Today large tracts remain in indigenous forest, although mainly in rugged terrain. Large-scale clearance of forest cover was needed for pastoral expansion. Timber from forest clearance was originally used for ships' masts, then as inputs into farming through fencing and construction, a process that extended to urban construction and later export to Australia, to supply Melbourne in its late 19th century building boom for dwellings. In the last decades of the 19th century, clearance was so rapid that much of the timber was burnt rather than used.

Today plantation-grown *Pinus radiata*, along with other introduced species, has largely replaced indigenous timber. *Pinus radiata*, which in New Zealand produces logs suitable for milling within 25–30 years, also provides the raw material for a widening range of manufactured products—pulp and paper, paperboard and compressed boards of various sorts, as well as exports of sawlogs on a considerable scale. The forestry industry's contribution to export earnings has increased, and by 2001 the value of exports of wood and wood articles reached $NZ2,219m., representing almost 7% of total export earnings. In the year to October 2000 logs, wood and wood articles had been the third major commodity contributor, behind dairy products and meat. Major plantings in the late 1960s and 1970s were reaching maturity in the early 21st century. A 74% increase in wood available for export was anticipated between 1996 and 2010, assuming 60,000 ha of new plantings every year, but processing expansion requires heavy investment. There has also been extensive planting of *Pinus radiata* for land stabilization and environmental, as well as for production, purposes. These developments point to forestry becoming markedly more important in the years ahead, with the amount of land used for farming continuing to decline, whilst that allocated to forestry production continues to increase.

Acts relating to native forests have increased the level of protection of old growth forests so that the felling of indigenous trees has been reduced, mainly for heritage and conservation reasons. Restrictions on indigenous forest use on the west coast of the South Island and the 2001 conflict over a proposed extension to gold-mining in the same area continue to cause tension between advocates of conservation and those espousing the economic exploitation of such resources. Farm forestry combining both aesthetic and economic considerations, has reduced the vulnerability of pastoral farming to fluctuations in meat and wool prices. It has also made better use of marginal land and has been instrumental in protecting some hill farms from erosion problems. Forestry development is one of the few areas where tax advantages are to be found in New Zealand's deregulated, non-interventionist atmosphere , but the long-term nature of the investment tends to deter many would-be participants.

Fishing

New Zealand has a wide variety of fish in waters around its long coastline, and many of these are now recognized to be commercially valuable species. The Territorial Sea and Exclusive Economic Zone Act of 1978 gave New Zealand control over the fisheries resources in more than 4m. sq km. (1.3m. nautical sq miles) of sea surrounding New Zealand territory, or approximately 13 times the land mass of New Zealand. Joint ventures with foreign partners have contributed substantially to the development of the industry, especially in the trawl fisheries of deeper waters. There has also been continuing growth in the domestic finfish industry. Exports of fish, crustaceans and molluscs were valued at $NZ1,463.6m. and accounted for almost 4.5% of total exports in 2000/01. Poaching and organized smuggling of paua (abalone) has emerged as a serious threat to the sustained development of such activity.

In the 1980s a promising start was made in fish and shellfish farming and in processing eels, the only commercially significant indigenous fish. Production is directed primarily to the export market. Trout, introduced from the northern hemisphere, have not so far been commercially exploited, but salmon are farmed, as well as fished recreationally, in parts of the country. Aquaculture, principally involving the production of mussels, salmon and Pacific oysters, has become a significant part of total fisheries output. By 2000 its value was estimated at some $NZ200m. Transferable quota arrangements have been developed as a way of dealing with issues relating to the long-term sustainability of common property rights to fish stocks. Allocation of quota to Maori has also been undertaken as part of the Treaty of Waitangi process (see History).

Mining

Mining of metallic minerals is limited except for titanomagnetic ironsands from the west coast of the North Island, originally for export but later also for local steel production. Recent efforts to revive mining for precious metals have been remarkably successful, although they are capital-intensive and face problems with meeting environmental protection requirements in many cases. The Resource Management Act (RMA) covering environmental requirements has made compliance a more expensive undertaking for the mining sector, as well as for many other industries.

Coal production is limited and mainly for use in thermal power stations. Household consumption is insignificant. New Zealand has substantial coal reserves, but their economic utilization has not been high. Japan, Chile, India and China are the principal export markets. Natural gas has become increasingly important, especially since the onshore supply has been supplemented by offshore gas from the large Maui field, and a considerable amount is utilized in the production of synthetic petrol and in thermal power stations. For many years drilling companies failed to make any significant petroleum discoveries, but there are now several onshore producing wells, which together make a small, yet significant, contribution to meeting New Zealand's oil demands.

SECONDARY INDUSTRY

Most of the country's larger industrial enterprises are export-orientated and process pastoral products (milk, livestock and wool), natural gas, logs or ironsand, but there is also a large aluminium smelter using imported alumina. Other large enterprises based on imported raw materials have faced increasing import competition, and some enterprises have closed down as border protection has been reduced or removed. The WTO, the Asia-Pacific Economic Co-operation group (APEC) and the Closer Economic Relations agreement (CER) have all played a part in this process, but successive New Zealand Governments have moved more generally towards a progressive reduction in tariffs. This has included a unilateral programme aimed at increasing the competitive environment in the domestic market. It has also led many manufacturers to relocate their operations off shore. Others have become more specialized, while diversification is evident in the expansion of non-traditional manufactured exports.

Some manufacturers have called for a deceleration of liberalization. In 2000 the Government acted to curb the rate of tariff reduction, as well as to promote the need for more involvement in regional development. New Zealand already has fewer non-tariff barriers to imports than is the case in many other countries. Of equal importance are the issues of the exchange rate and the prevailing relatively high interest rates, which have tended to curb manufactured exports. In the first six months of 2002 the currency strengthened as interest rates moved upwards. Greater trans-Tasman integration has continued, with common food regulations being implemented, and some calls for a common currency and stock market. Achieving easier access to the greater Australian market, combined with improved efficiency, remain the key factors for New Zealand secondary industrial development.

TERTIARY INDUSTRY

Construction

The construction industry in New Zealand has three distinct sectors: the residential construction sector, largely timber-framed in single units; commercial and industrial construction, which also employs timber framing as well as steel and concrete; and civil engineering. Since the mid-1960s the industry as a whole, and especially its residential component, has been subject to marked cyclical fluctuations arising from demographic trends (including sharp fluctuations in migration) and economic vicissitudes. The reversal from a net migration outflow to a net inflow in 2001–02 led to some recovery in activity levels and prices in the residential sector in particular. More generally, the Building Activity Survey recorded some strong increases during 2000 and into 2001.

Transport and Communications

Historically, the central Government was heavily and directly involved in transport, as with other areas of infrastructure, through its ownership of NZ Rail, Air New Zealand and the Shipping Corporation. All were privatized, although Air New Zealand was renationalized in October 2001, following the collapse of Ansett, its Australian subsidiary carrier. In 2002 the Government held an 82% stake in Air New Zealand. QANTAS operations in New Zealand were being managed by the airline directly, following the Australian carrier's own problems with an associated operator flying New Zealand domestic routes. Aggressive competition has emerged on the main domestic routes.

The Government remains involved in transport regulation, notably through Transit New Zealand, which has responsibility for main highways, road safety, etc. and in part for urban passenger subsidies. Since mid-1998 debates concerning how to apply 'user pays' principles to land transport, and how to restructure it, have continued. Proposals have involved active consideration of private-public partnership schemes and toll roads. In other areas of transport, major airports have been privatized or corporatized, with Auckland and Christchurch airports being the focus of investigations by the Commerce Commission over allegations of their overcharging airlines. The prospect of price controls over Auckland International Airport was thus raised. Reform of the port operations was largely complete by the mid-1990s, a period during which transport became more efficient and competitive. In the early 21st century, however, shipping and air services across the Tasman Sea remained far from totally liberalized.

Equally dramatic changes have taken place in communications, with the privatization of telecommunications and the corporatization of postal services. Historically, the Post Office in New Zealand, as a government department, handled postal services and various collections on behalf of other government agencies, as well as telecommunications. It also operated a savings bank catering mainly for small depositors. The Government re-established banking operations in the guise of 'Kiwibank'. NZ Post remains a 'stand-alone' state-owned enterprise, but its monopoly of mail services has been removed. National Post and other competitors initially appeared, offering household delivery and separate on-street mail collection boxes. but National Post subsequently withdrew from the market, following financial difficulties, and its owners were unable to find a buyer.

ENERGY

New Zealand has substantial hydroelectric generating potential, although the limited storage capacity is a weakness, revealed by substantial rises in the spot price in the winter of early 2001 and calls for a voluntary savings campaign. The winter of 2002 passed without any such crisis. Electricity output is more than 112.40 petajoules per year, with hydroelectricity contributing approximately two-thirds of the total. The main thermal stations are fired by a variety of fuels. There are two large geothermal stations with a capacity comparable to that of both the main thermal stations. Two-way direct current cables link the two main islands, so virtually the whole country is served by the grid; even relatively remote areas, as the result of the previous subsidized extensions to rural networks.

In a major departure from tradition, generation of electricity was separated from the operation of the grid to encourage non-state generation. Until the 1980s such private involvement had been hampered, if not prohibited directly, by government regulation. These changes at the wholesale level have been accompanied by the corporatization and some privatization of 'power boards', which used to handle the retail distribution of most electricity. With the development of a wholesale electricity market, electricity retail companies are now in apparent competition with one another, although the reality is that this is difficult to make effective for small consumers with existing technology. In an attempt to control the abuse of monopoly power in the retail market, separate transmission line companies and retail energy companies have been formed. Further refinements to the regulatory system now allow some vertical integration, whilst attempting to ensure the separating out of the natural monopoly elements of the wholesale and retail distribution networks, from generation and retail supply.

Since 1973 considerable efforts have been made to reduce the country's dependence on petroleum products, both crude and refined, through measures such as the expansion and modification of the existing petroleum refinery, the conversion of natural gas to methanol as feed stock for the refinery and moves towards more efficient energy use. Such developments, together with increasing production from onshore and offshore gas and petroleum wells, and the switch from oil to coal and gas in thermal power stations, greatly increased energy self-sufficiency. Not all of the 1970s efforts made economic sense, with some developments failing to be subjected to adequate project appraisal in the rush to save on imported energy. More recently, energy policy debates have placed a greater emphasis on the reduction of carbon dioxide emissions and their offset by large-scale afforestation in line with predictions of global warming, and on the need to address carbon emission issues. In 2002 discussion continued as to the merits or otherwise of ratifying the Kyoto Protocol on the reduction of the emission of 'greenhouse gases'.

SERVICE INDUSTRIES

The increase in complexity of the economy has been accompanied by a steady growth in the proportion of the labour force in service industries, some of which render specialist services to primary and secondary industries as well as to the community in general. This growth has been at the expense of manufacturing in particular, but also of the service-like activities of building and construction and also transport and communications.

Tourist business is a major component of economic activity, providing jobs for around 10% of the population. Economic expansion in industrial countries generated a significant increase in international tourism, from which New Zealand benefited considerably. In 1987/88 tourism, as officially defined, became the single largest source of foreign-exchange earnings, its expansion said to have been aided by the increased competitiveness of the industry following the freeing up of the labour market. As might be expected, given its proximity, Australia remains the main source of overseas visitors, followed by Japan, the USA and the United Kingdom. As a result of the Asian economic crisis, however, the total number of visitor arrivals declined from 1,551,341 in 1996/97 to 1,464,766 in 1997/98, the number of South Korean tourists showing the sharpest decrease (44%). Total receipts from tourism declined to $NZ3,068m. in 1998. A recovery in the tourist sector subsequently became evident, with visitor numbers reaching record levels by mid-2001 and being only briefly affected by the repercussions of the terrorist attacks on the USA in September of that year. Growth continued in 2002. In the quarter to March 2002 both the numbers of visitors and the average amount they spent per head rose strongly, adding a further $NZ116m. to the receipts of the last quarter of 2001. The service sector is notoriously difficult to assess in terms of labour productivity, but its expansion is an essential part of modern economic development, and New Zealand exhibits much the same trend as other developed economies.

PUBLIC SECTOR

Until 1991/92 the public sector's claim on national resources was inexorably rising. Within the public sector itself, the central Government was increasingly obliged to transfer resources to territorial and other local authorities because the latter lack the automatically-increasing flow of funds that a relatively fixed and progressive (personal) income tax structure so conveniently provides in an era of rising wages and salaries. At the same time, there was a tendency for local or regional authorities to assume responsibility for a greater proportion of total public sector expenditure. This was given further impetus by the extensive reform of local government undertaken in 1989. As in many other countries, deficit-financing was adopted in the early 1980s, deficits averaging 7% of GDP. Despite efforts by successive Governments, public-sector expenditure, including transfers, was equivalent to more than 40% of GDP by the end of 1990, when the National Party took office. By 2001 the proportion was approximately 35%, a level similar to the previous three–four years, although about one-third of payments represented transfers rather than direct expenditure. Between 1984 and 1990 the Labour Government initiated wide-ranging reforms in the public sector, notably by corporatizing many enterprises and privatizing others. This process was continued by the National Party Government. Some of the apparent decline in share of GDP represented by government expenditure was due to the shifting of these enterprises off the government account. Fiscal surpluses were achieved in the early 1990s (even excluding the proceeds of asset sales). Net public sector debt as a percentage of GDP also declined during this period, down to an estimated 16%. Household indebtedness, however, increased consistently through to 2000 to a level comparable with that of other developed countries.

INTERNATIONAL TRADE

Exports and imports of goods and services are usually roughly equivalent, at a little under 30% of GDP, although a persistent balance-of-payments deficit was recorded in the 28 years to 2000/01, with the current-account deficit reaching the equivalent of some 2.2% of GDP. The merchandise trade deficit has been reduced in recent times, and in the year to June 2002 a further improvement compared with the previous 12 months was recorded. Forestry, agriculture and pastoral exports remained a major component of foreign-exchange earnings (some 65%), whilst fish are of increasing relative importance. Exports of manufactures (other than processed primary products) are also growing steadily, and earnings of New Zealand companies operating overseas are now becoming appreciable. Half of New Zealand's foreign exchange comes from the exports of just 30 companies, a reflection of the small size of the economy. Meanwhile, 96% of companies do not export.

Exports have been diversified, as regards both commodity composition and market destination. In 1950 the United Kingdom purchased nearly two-thirds of New Zealand's exports. By the 1980s it had been overtaken by Australia, Japan and the USA, which remained the three principal export markets in 2001. For imports the pattern was similar. The increasing interdependence of the Australian and New Zealand economies led their respective Governments to implement the CER agreement, signed by the two countries on 14 December 1982, following three years of negotiations. The bilateral trade agreement took effect on 1 January 1983. Its main objective was to encourage the development of economically-strong productive structures in both countries. Two basic mechanisms were set in place by the CER agreement: the phasing out of tariffs both ways and the progressive elimination of import-licensing and tariff quotas between Australia and New Zealand. By and large, CER has benefited both countries, perhaps more so New Zealand, and mutual undertakings have generally been respected. CER was larger in impact than the preceding agreement, which had required items for liberalization to be included in the list rather than the CER approach, which stipulates the listing of exceptions.

The New Zealand dollar's fixed relationship with the US dollar was ended in July 1973, when the authorities introduced a trade-weighted managed daily 'float' involving weighting against the currencies of New Zealand's main trading partners. In July 1984, immediately following the election of a Labour Government, the currency was devalued by 20%. In March 1985 the New Zealand dollar was freely 'floated' in response to fears of a renewed 'run' on the currency, which had been caused by a sharp upsurge in inflation following devaluation and the end of a 'freeze' of wages and prices. By mid-1986, contrary to the expectation of many people, the currency had remained very close to its average value at the time of the 'float', and it continued to fluctuate around this level until 1991, when the trade-weighted index fell appreciably, giving exporters a welcome boost. In 1993 the New Zealand dollar strengthened again, and in particular appreciated markedly vis-a-vis the Australian dollar. It also proved remarkably resilient in the face of turbulence in the exchange-rate mechanism of the EU. These phenomena reflected improvement in the economy as well as relatively high real interest rates. The new-found strength of the New Zealand dollar at that time no doubt also owed something to the independence enjoyed by the RBNZ and confidence in the fiscal stance of the National Party Government. Thereafter, the New Zealand dollar appreciated further, against the US dollar and the Australian dollar in particular. This helped to contain inflationary pressures, but rendered New Zealand's exports less competitive internationally. To the relief of exporters, the New Zealand dollar depreciated slightly against the US dollar in 1997. There was a continuation and increase in this trend through to early 2001, with a decline to the low 40s in terms of US cents against the New Zealand dollar, although the cross rate against the Australian currency was rising. The New Zealand dollar stood at 0.82 Australian cents by August 2001. Relief in terms of additional export revenue was somewhat slower to appear than expected, and there were even calls for the introduction of a common trans-Tasman currency in order to obtain a reduction in transaction costs for traders. Further rises against both the US dollar (to 47 cents) and the Australian dollar (to 87 cents) occurred in the first half of 2002.

DOMESTIC ECONOMY

Throughout the 1950s and 1960s the average rate of growth of real GDP was more than 4%, which was not much less than the average for OECD countries. New Zealand's performance in the 1970s, particularly after the first oil shock with its sharp rises in international petroleum prices in 1973 and 1974, was comparatively worse than the OECD average, with the terms of trade deteriorating substantially. Between 1975 and 1982 there was virtually no real growth in GDP. Between 1982 and 1987 there was modest growth, but this improvement was not sustained. Large fiscal deficits emerged in the late 1970s and, together with increasing external imbalance, acted to create a mounting burden of debt in which the external component was increasingly important. By the early 1980s economic performance—as measured by a wide range of indicators including growth, unemployment, inflation, external deficit, budgetary imbalance and debt—had deteriorated substantially. In real terms GDP grew by an average annual rate of 2.5% over the 1990s, but this covers a wide range of economic activities. In 1998 GDP contracted by 0.3%. Signs of a recovery from the recession had emerged by mid-1999 when GDP expanded by an estimated 3.5%. Growth of 1.8% was achieved for 2000, with a similar figure recorded in 2001 and projections for the year to March 2003 running at 3.1%. The external sector appeared strongest in 2001; domestic sources were being looked to as important sources of sustained activity levels in 2002–03.

In the early 1980s unemployment emerged for the first time since the 1930s as a serious problem. There had effectively been full employment in New Zealand throughout most of the post-war period. It was only in 1978 that the unemployment rate first rose above 1% of the labour force. It then increased steadily, reaching a peak in 1983, and, despite declining in 1984 and 1985 owing to renewed growth in the economy, rose to 6% at the end of 1988, and to over 10% in 1992. Subsequently, unemployment levels appeared to stabilize, growth in employment having more than offset rising labour force participation. In the 1998 recession the average rate of unemployment increased to 7.5% of the work force. In 1999 unemployment decreased to 6.8% of the labour force; with a further decline to a mid-2002 rate of 5.3%.

The average annual rate of inflation was 4.8% in 1985–95. Lower rates set in thereafter: consumer prices increased by an annual average of 2.3% in 1996, by only 1.2% in 1997 and by 1.3% for 1998. By 1999 some commentators had declared inflation to be defunct. In the first quarter of 1999 the consumer price index (CPI) was negative compared with 12 months previously. In mid-2002, however, the CPI stood at an annual rate of 2.8%, and the RBNZ at least appeared unconvinced that inflation was defunct

Until May 1991 wage bargaining was based on national awards, covering broad occupational groups, and took little or no account of regional considerations or of the economic well-being of individual industries and enterprises. The wage-bargaining process had had a long history of inflexibility, regarded as out of place in the more competitive, less regulated environment of recent times.

In its efforts to liberalize the economy from 1984 to 1990s, the Labour Government 'floated' the currency on international exchange markets, maintained a non-accommodating monetary policy and embarked on a programme of taxation reform in an effort to increase economic efficiency and competitiveness on a medium to long-term basis. Debate on the moves towards increased deregulation and exposure to market forces focused mainly on the pace and sequence of change, rather than on the need for it. From 1990 the National Party Government maintained the momentum, particularly in containing spending and introducing a greater element of 'user pays' in health and education.

Attempts to reduce the budget deficit without increasing the money supply led to high real interest rates in the 1980s, and these, in turn, sustained the exchange rate. In accordance with a programme of tax reform that was initiated in 1984, a 10% tax on all goods and services became effective from late 1986, and the GST rate was raised to 12.5% in July 1989. This was followed by a reduction in the rate of corporate tax, from 45% to 33%, and the introduction of a basically two-tier rate of personal income tax at 24% and 33%, compared with the former 30% and 48% respectively. Between mid-1996 and mid-1998 the lower rate of personal income tax was reduced further. From April 2000 this trend was reversed, with a higher rate of 39% being imposed on income in excess of $NZ60,000. Budget surpluses have in the past been used not only to fund tax reductions, but also to decrease public debt levels. The 2002 budget estimated a surplus of $NZ2,636m., with a rising trend leading to a projected $NZ4,242m. by 2006.

The position in New Zealand with regard to social welfare expenditure is similar to that in most other OECD countries. Benefit payments account for about two-fifths of the Government's total health, education and welfare budget, while health and education each account for about one-quarter. The rate of increase in expenditure in all sectors tends to outstrip economic growth. Following its election in late 1990, the National Party Government made a determined effort to curb welfare spending, as well as to reduce expenditure in other areas. At the same time it placed more emphasis on relevant education, recognizing that education and vocational training play a pivotal role in the drive to improve overall economic performance. The indigenous Maori population is making explicit claims for a greater influence over the way in which the country is administered, as well as for ownership of a higher proportion of its output. In 1999 the incoming Labour administration regarded a strong economy as necessary to achieve success in its varied goals. External economic problems and the changes currently taking place in New Zealand, together with major demographic and social developments (in common with many other countries), are being accompanied by changes in political philosophy and traditional affiliations. The July 2002 election resulted in the formation of a three-party coalition led by the Labour Party, to replace the previous two-party administration. The inclusion of the United Future New Zealand party in the coalition Government appeared unlikely to result in any immediate or dramatic change in economic policy.

Statistical Survey

Source (unless otherwise stated): Statistics New Zealand, Aorangi House, 85 Molesworth St, POB 2922, Wellington 1; tel. (4) 495-4600; fax (4) 472-9135; e-mail info@stats.govt.nz; internet www.stats.govt.nz.

Area and Population

AREA, POPULATION AND DENSITY

Area (sq km)	270,534*
Population (census results)†	
5 March 1996	3,618,303
6 March 2001	
Males	1,823,004
Females	1,914,273
Total	3,737,277
Population (official estimates at mid-year)	
2000	3,830,800
2001	3,850,000
2002	3,940,000
Density (per sq km) at mid-2002	14.6

* 104,454 sq miles.

† Figures refer to the population usually resident. The total population (including foreign visitors) was: 3,681,546 in 1996; 3,820,749 in 2001.

PRINCIPAL CENTRES OF POPULATION

(population at census of 6 March 2001)

Auckland	1,074,507	Palmerston North	72,681
Wellington (capital)	339,747	Hastings	58,139
Christchurch	334,107	Napier	54,534
Hamilton	166,128	Nelson	53,685
Dunedin	107,088	Rotorua	52,608
Tauranga	95,694		

BIRTHS, MARRIAGES AND DEATHS

	Live births*		Marriages†		Deaths*	
	Number	Rate (per '000)	Number	Rate (per '000)	Number	Rate (per '000)
1993	58,866	16.9	20,802	5.9	27,243	7.8
1994	57,435	16.3	20,587	5.7	27,092	7.7
1995	57,671	15.8	20,452	5.6	27,813	7.6
1996	57,280	15.4	20,453	5.5	28,255	7.6
1997	57,604	15.3	19,953	5.3	27,471	7.3
1998	57,251	15.1	20,135	5.3	26,206	6.9
1999	57,053	15.0	21,085	5.5	28,117	7.4
2000	56,605	14.7	20,655	5.4	26,660	7.0
2001	55,790	14.5	19,972	5.1	27,827	7.0

* Data for births and deaths are tabulated by year of registration rather than by year of occurrence.

† Based on the resident population concept, replacing the previous *de facto* concept.

Expectation of life (WHO estimates, years at birth, 2000): Males 75.9; Females 80.9 (Source: WHO, *World Health Report*).

IMMIGRATION AND EMIGRATION (year ending 31 August)*

	1998/99	1999/2000	2000/01
Long-term immigrants	56,880	62,051	72,699
Long-term emigrants	68,003	72,083	77,090

* Figures refer to persons intending to remain in New Zealand, or New Zealand residents intending to remain abroad, for 12 months or more.

ECONOMICALLY ACTIVE POPULATION

('000 persons aged 15 years and over, excl. armed forces)

	1998	1999	2000
Agriculture, hunting, forestry and fishing	146.9	165.6	155.5
Mining and quarrying	4.2	3.6	3.9
Manufacturing	289.7	278.4	281.3
Electricity, gas and water	10.1	8.9	8.5
Construction	111.1	109.5	118.4
Trade, restaurants and hotels	370.1	371.5	388.4
Transport, storage and communications	103.2	110.4	110.9
Finance, insurance, real estate and business services	221.9	228.6	229.5
Community, social and personal services	462.4	469.5	473.8
Activities not adequately defined	5.3	4.4	8.8
Total employed	1,725.0	1,750.3	1,779.0
Unemployed	139.1	127.8	113.4
Total labour force	1,864.1	1,878.1	1,892.4
Males	1,024.9	1,029.0	1,036.1
Females	839.3	849.1	856.3

Source: ILO, *Yearbook of Labour Statistics.*

Health and Welfare

KEY INDICATORS

Fertility (births per woman, 2000)	2.0
Under-5 mortality rate (per 1,000 live births, 2000)	6
HIV/AIDS (% of persons aged 15–49, 2001)	0.06
Physicians (per 1,000 head, 1997)	2.18
Hospital beds (per 1,000 head, 1998)	6.2
Health expenditure (1998): US $ per head (PPP)	1,469
% of GDP	8.1
public (% of total)	77.0
Human Development Index (2000): ranking	19
value	0.917

For sources and definitions, see explanatory note on p. vi.

Agriculture

PRINCIPAL CROPS ('000 metric tons)

	1998	1999	2000
Wheat	302	320	326
Barley	340	304	302
Maize	176	197	181
Oats	42	42	35
Potatoes	500	500	500
Dry peas	66	52	49
Cabbages	38	39	36
Lettuce	36	37	37
Tomatoes	68	87	87
Cauliflower	63	63	56
Pumpkins, squash and gourds	148	155	155
Green onions and shallots	190	220	240
Green peas	52	57	60
Carrots	110	70	77
Green corn	100	95	101
Other vegetables*	132	106	106
Grapes	78	80	80
Apples	501	504	620
Pears	41	44	42
Kiwi fruit	240	252	254
Other fruits (excl. melons)*	96	106	98

* FAO estimate(s).

Source: FAO.

LIVESTOCK ('000 head at 30 June)

	1998	1999	2000
Cattle	8,873	8,960	9,217
Sheep	45,956	45,680	45,379
Goats	228	186	183
Pigs	351	369	369
Horses†	85	80	80
Chickens	12,000	12,700†	13,000
Ducks†	160	200	240
Geese†	65	65	65
Turkeys†	60	60	60

* Unofficial figure. † FAO estimate(s).

Source: FAO.

LIVESTOCK PRODUCTS ('000 metric tons)

	1998	1999	2000
Beef and veal*	634.1	561.3	571.8
Mutton and lamb*	545.1	516.9	539.0
Pig meat*	49.7	50.0	46.2
Poultry meat*	98.3	100.7	109.0†
Game meat*	21.9	26.3	26.3‡
Cows' milk§	11,380	10,881	12,235
Butter§	343.7	317.0	344.0
Cheese§	265.6	238.5	296.7
Hen eggs	42.3	51.1	68.0
Other poultry eggs	2.4	2.4	2.4
Honey	8.1	9.1	9.6
Wool: greasy	265.8	252.0	257.3
scoured	218.6	220.3	223.6
Cattle hides (fresh)‡	55	51	51
Sheepskins (fresh)‡	106	100	100

* Twelve months ending 30 September of year stated.

† Unofficial figure.

‡ FAO estimate(s).

§ Twelve months ending 31 May of year stated.

Source: FAO.

Forestry

ROUNDWOOD REMOVALS
('000 cubic metres, year ending 31 March)

	1999/2000	2000/01	2001/02
Sawlogs	7,043	7,273	7,268
Pulp logs	3,049	3,566	3,455
Export logs and chips	6,030	6,428	7,759
Other	2,074	2,206	2,265
Total	18,196	19,473	20,747

Source: Forestry Statistics Section, Ministry of Agriculture and Forestry, Wellington.

SAWNWOOD PRODUCTION ('000 cu m, year ending 31 March)

Species	1998/99	1999/2000	2000/2001
Radiata pine	2,996	3,583	3,625
Other introduced pines	27	28	32
Douglas fir	143	134	136
Rimu and miro	30	22	17
Total (incl. others)	3,226	3,806	3,848

Source: Forestry Statistics Section, Ministry of Agriculture and Forestry, Wellington.

Fishing*

('000 metric tons, live weight)

	1997	1998	1999
Capture	596.0	636.2	594.1
Southern blue whiting	10.2	35.1	39.0
Blue grenadier (Hoki)	229.9	267.6	236.7
Pink cusk-eel	22.6	22.2	21.4
Orange roughy	20.5	21.5	23.8
Oreo dories	21.9	21.1	22.6
Jack and horse mackerels	34.1	36.1	34.0
Snoek (Barracouta)	22.0	26.0	20.6
Wellington flying squid	44.8	42.5	27.3
Aquaculture	76.9	93.8	91.7
New Zealand mussel	65.5	75.0	71.0
Total catch	672.9	730.0	685.7

Note: Figures exclude aquatic plants ('000 metric tons, capture only): 0.0 in 1997; 7.4 in 1998; 0.7 in 1999. Also excluded are aquatic mammals (recorded by number rather than by weight) and sponges. The number of whales and dolphins caught was: 9 in 1997; 16 in 1998; 19 in 1999. The catch of sponges (in metric tons) was: 4.1 in 1998; 14.0 in 1999.

* Excluding catches made by chartered vessels and landed outside New Zealand.

Source: FAO, *Yearbook of Fishery Statistics*.

Mining

('000 metric tons, unless otherwise indicated)

	1999	2000	2001
Coal (incl. lignite)	3,505.7	3,586	3,911
Gold (kg)	8,577	9,880	9,850
Crude petroleum	1,931.9	n.a.	n.a.
Gross natural gas (terajoules)	252,390	n.a.	n.a.
Liquid petroleum gas (terajoules)	12,030	11,970	n.a.
Iron sands	2,303.4	2,692	1,636
Silica sand	25.0	47.4	36.0
Limestone	2,050	4,159	4,746

Source: mainly Ministry of Commerce, Wellington.

Industry

SELECTED PRODUCTS

(metric tons, unless otherwise indicated)

	1997	1998	1999
Wine ('000 hectolitres)	458	606	602
Beer (sales, '000 hectolitres)	3,214	3,206	3,148
Wool yarn (pure and mixed)	20,900	n.a.	23,500
Knitted fabrics*	4,900	4,200	3,700
Footwear ('000 pairs)†	2,222	1,484	1,650
Chemical wood pulp‡§	652,308	675,453	645,032
Mechanical wood pulp‡§	724,956	736,712	755,707
Newsprint‡§	384,147	393,545	383,372
Other paper and paperboard‡§	493,005	486,031	430,942
Fibre board (cu m)‡§	536,831	613,345	600,673
Particle board (cu m)‡§	233,988	196,395	169,569
Veneer (cu m)‡§	300,648	292,171	285,825
Plywood (cu m)‡§	180,713	189,447	192,445
Jet fuels ('000 metric tons)	829	812	839
Motor spirit—petrol ('000 metric tons)	1,518	1,578	1,360
Gas-diesel (Distillate fuel) oils ('000 metric tons)	1,564	1,751	1,686
Residual fuel oils ('000 metric tons)	451	455	431
Cement ('000 metric tons)‖	976	950	900
Aluminium—unwrought ('000 metric tons)			
Primary¶	310.2	317.5	300
Secondary¶	8.0	8.0	n.a.
Electric energy (million kWh)‡	34,225	36,219	33,994

* Twelve months ending 30 September of year stated.
† Twelve months ending 30 June of year stated.
‡ Twelve months ending 31 March of year stated.
§ Source: Ministry of Agriculture and Forestry, Wellington.
‖ Data from US Geological Survey, Washington, DC.
¶ Data from *World Metal Statistics* (London).

Source (unless otherwise stated): mainly UN, *Industrial Commodity Statistics Yearbook* and *Monthly Bulletin of Statistics*.

1999/2000 (year ending 31 March): Chemical wood pulp (metric tons) 753,885; Mechanical wood pulp (metric tons) 773,680; Newsprint (metric tons) 360,623; Other paper and paperboard (metric tons) 469,189; Fibre board (cu m) 744,879; Particle board (cu m) 188,054; Veneer (cu m) 378,282; Plywood (cu m) 239,947.

2000/01 (year ending 31 March): Chemical wood pulp (metric tons) 744,991; Mechanical wood pulp (metric tons) 827,286; Newsprint (metric tons) 380,614; Other paper and paperboard (metric tons) 490,993; Fibre board (cu m) 801,493; Particle board (cu m) 204,524; Veneer (cu m) 401,590; Plywood (cu m) 243,702.

Source (for 1999/2000 and 2000/01): Ministry of Agriculture and Forestry, Wellington.

Finance

CURRENCY AND EXCHANGE RATES

Monetary Units

100 cents = 1 New Zealand dollar ($NZ).

Sterling, US Dollar and Euro Equivalents (31 May 2002)

£1 sterling = $NZ3.0858;
US $1 = $NZ2.1039;
€1 = $NZ1.9750;
$NZ100 = £32.41 = US $47.53 = €50.63.

Average Exchange Rate (US $ per New Zealand dollar)

1999 0.5295
2000 0.4574
2001 0.4206

BUDGET ($NZ million, year ending 30 June)

Revenue	1998/99	1999/2000	2000/01
Direct taxation	19,963	21,192	23,520
Individuals	14,618	15,470	16,780
Companies	3,693	4,158	4,831
Withholding taxes	1,651	1,563	1,905
Indirect taxation	11,216	11,738	12,026
Goods and services	7,321	7,735	7,927
Excise duties	1,949	2,027	2,010
Other receipts	2,085	2,239	2,304
Interest, profits and dividends	1,307	1,281	1,284
Total	33,264	35,169	37,850

Expenditure	1998/99	1999/2000	2000/01
Public administration	2,401	1,939	2,078
Defence	1,163	1,803	1,261
Law and order	1,430	1,388	1,478
Education	5,540	5,825	6,097
Health	6,085	6,247	6,761
Social welfare	12,977	13,259	13,644
Economic services	4,478	4,403	4,582
Total (incl. others)	34,202	35,020	36,024

INTERNATIONAL RESERVES (US $ million at 31 December)

	1999	2000	2001
IMF special drawing rights	7	13	16
Reserve position in IMF	424	320	387
Foreign exchange	4,025	2,996	2,605
Total	4,455	3,329	3,008

Source: IMF, *International Financial Statistics*.

MONEY SUPPLY ($NZ million at 31 December)

	1999	2000	2001
Currency outside banks	2,077	2,069	2,241
Demand deposits at banking institutions	12,528	13,460	15,463
Total money (incl. others)	14,649	15,568	17,753

Source: IMF, *International Financial Statistics*.

COST OF LIVING

(Consumer Price Index; base: 1990 = 100)

	1998	1999	2000
Food (incl. beverages)	110.2	111.3	112.7
Fuel and light	147.3	149.9	151.8
Clothing (incl. footwear)	103.4	105.2	105.8
Rent	147.8	146.0	146.4
All items (incl. others)	116.2	116.0	119.1

Source: ILO, *Yearbook of Labour Statistics*.

2001 (base: 2000 = 100): All items 102.6 (Source: IMF, *International Financial Statistics*).

NATIONAL ACCOUNTS

($NZ million at current prices, year ending 31 March)

National Income and Product

	1998/99	1999/2000	2000/01
Compensation of employees	43,183	44,462	46,756
Operating surplus	30,617	33,117	35,934
Domestic factor incomes	73,800	77,579	82,690
Consumption of fixed capital	13,928	14,262	15,205
Gross domestic product (GDP) at factor cost	87,728	91,841	97,895
Indirect taxes	13,466	14,129	14,775
Less Subsidies	298	330	353
GDP in purchasers' values	100,897	105,641	112,316
Net factor income from abroad	-4,977	-6,603	-7,736
Gross national product	95,920	99,038	104,580
Less Consumption of fixed capital	13,928	14,262	15,205
National income in market prices	81,992	84,776	89,375

Expenditure on the Gross Domestic Product

	1998/99	1999/2000	2000/01
Government final consumption expenditure	18,924	20,109	20,248
Private final consumption expenditure	61,775	64,471	67,224
Increase in stocks	-114	1,480	1,143
Gross fixed capital formation	20,016	20,926	21,389
Total domestic expenditure	100,601	106,984	110,005
Exports of goods and services	30,378	33,151	41,065
Less Imports of goods and services	30,144	34,448	39,209
GDP in purchasers' values	100,835	105,687	111,861
GDP at constant 1995/96 prices	97,585	101,612	104,975

Gross Domestic Product by Economic Activity

(at constant 1995/96 prices)

	1998/99	1999/2000	2000/01
Agriculture	5,479	5,767	6,019
Hunting and fishing; Forestry and logging; Mining and quarrying	2,786	2,845	2,879
Manufacturing	15,643	16,329	16,731
Electricity, gas and water	2,152	2,084	2,192
Construction	3,702	4,160	3,776
Trade, restaurants and hotels	14,603	15,772	16,151
Transport, storage and communications	8,767	9,695	10,476
Finance, insurance, real estate and business services; Ownership of dwellings	25,133	25,356	25,881
Government administration and defence	4,201	4,137	4,175
Other personal and community services	11,476	12,003	12,553
Sub-total	93,942	98,168	100,833
Goods and services tax on production; Import duties; Other indirect taxes; *Less* Imputed bank service charge	3,740	4,083	4,142
Total	97,682	102,251	104,975

BALANCE OF PAYMENTS (US $ million)

	1999	2000	2001
Exports of goods f.o.b.	12,595	13,484	13,918
Imports of goods f.o.b.	-13,028	-12,848	-12,447
Trade balance	-433	636	1,471
Exports of services	4,286	4,326	4,230
Imports of services	-4,575	-4,511	-4,263
Balance on goods and services	-722	452	1,437
Other income received	919	590	590
Other income paid	-4,036	-4,018	-3,727
Balance on goods, services and income	-3,840	-2,976	-1,700
Current transfers received	622	646	584
Current transfers paid	-413	-404	-472
Current balance	-3,632	-2,734	-1,587
Capital account (net)	-218	-182	439
Direct investment abroad	-803	-963	-369
Direct investment from abroad	1,412	3,209	2,012
Portfolio investment assets	-666	-2,184	-1,079
Portfolio investment liabilities	-2,285	2,261	-1,730
Other investment assets	-1,282	-836	-3,260
Other investment liabilities	5,597	1,848	5,191
Net errors and omissions	2,065	-564	197
Overall balance	188	-144	-187

Source: IMF, *International Financial Statistics*.

External Trade

(Source: Statistics New Zealand, Overseas Trade, Wellington)

PRINCIPAL COMMODITIES ($NZ million)

Imports (value for duty)	1999	2000	2001
Food and live animals	1,523.7	1,716.3	1,939.1
Mineral fuels, lubricants, etc.	1,532.6	2,976.5	2,879.0
Petroleum, petroleum products, etc.	1,528.9	2,971.1	2,872.0
Chemicals and related products	3,116.8	3,512.7	3,811.0
Medicinal and pharmaceutical products	717.5	758.7	796.7
Basic manufactures	3,553.1	3,943.1	4,013.9
Machinery and transport equipment	11,179.6	11,543.9	11,565.5
Machinery specialized for particular industries	777.2	974.3	1,127.3
General industrial machinery, equipment and parts	1,007.3	1,092.6	1,211.1
Office machines and automatic data-processing machines	1,361.1	1,587.9	1,516.1
Telecommunications and sound equipment	1,321.2	1,739.7	1,380.1
Other electrical machinery, apparatus, etc.	1,098.7	1,310.0	1,305.2
Road vehicles (incl. air-cushion vehicles) and parts*	2,980.1	3,104.8	3,449.1
Other transport equipment and parts*	2,042.4	1,183.2	1,066.4
Miscellaneous manufactured articles	3,522.3	3,962.9	4,099.2
Clothing and accessories (excl. footwear)	725.7	847.3	889.6
Total (incl. others)	25,435.7	28,851.1	29,612.7

* Excluding tyres, engines and electrical parts.

Total imports c.i.f. ($NZ million): 27,113.6 in 1999; 30,735.7 in 2000; 31,682.7 in 2001.

Exports f.o.b	1999	2000	2001
Food and live animals	10,361.4	12,298.3	14,951.4
Meat and meat preparations	3,022.7	3,745.3	4,380.3
Dairy products and birds' eggs	3,714.2	4,618.4	6,379.4
Fish (not marine mammals), crustaceans, molluscs, etc., and preparations	1,314.1	1,410.6	1,463.6
Vegetables and fruit	1,593.6	1,634.0	1,639.0
Crude materials (inedible) except fuels	3,249.9	4,180.2	4,143.8
Cork and wood	1,304.9	1,659.5	1,679.2
Textile fibres (excl. wool tops) and waste	740.6	899.3	856.0
Chemicals and related products	1,785.1	2,583.0	2,537.1
Basic manufactures	3,365.7	4,015.8	3,945.6
Non-ferrous metals	985.0	1,244.5	1,221.8
Machinery and transport equipment	2,421.3	3,074.0	3,015.4
Miscellaneous manufactured articles	1,079.6	1,204.2	1,387.6
Total (incl. others)*	23,582.9	29,257.1	32,666.5

* Including re-exports ($NZ million): 974.8 in 1999; 1,154.6 in 2000; 1,094.1 in 2001.

PRINCIPAL TRADING PARTNERS
($NZ million)

Imports (value for duty)*	1999	2000	2001
Australia	6,238.7	6,483.0	6,564.0
Belgium	196.3	222.8	296.3
Canada	342.9	443.7	429.0
China, People's Republic	1,339.9	1,803.0	2,067.2
France	633.9	552.1	573.2
Germany	1,051.2	1,226.6	1,431.4
Indonesia	245.0	267.5	387.4
Italy	511.7	566.2	677.0
Japan	3,066.3	3,186.3	3,220.8
Korea, Republic	592.1	630.8	676.2
Malaysia	572.7	756.0	912.7
Saudi Arabia	307.1	715.3	363.2
Singapore	509.0	491.1	584.6
Sweden	323.9	362.8	327.0
Taiwan	544.9	642.4	625.9
Thailand	361.0	412.7	469.6
United Arab Emirates	116.7	453.0	260.2
United Kingdom	1,039.3	1,101.2	1,144.4
USA	4,259.4	5,035.4	4,777.7
Total (incl. others)	25,435.7	28,851.1	29,612.7

* Excluding specie and gold.

Exports*	1999	2000	2001
Australia	5,133.3	5,960.4	6,180.6
Belgium	408.5	469.6	546.5
Canada	308.3	439.6	631.4
China, People's Republic	649.4	929.6	1,349.4
France	293.9	394.5	367.3
Germany	620.5	690.8	838.7
Hong Kong	610.8	790.9	786.0
Indonesia	254.7	495.4	550.5
Italy	396.3	490.1	548.5
Japan	2,979.9	3,951.8	4,083.3
Korea, Republic	995.9	1,315.1	1,440.2
Malaysia	432.9	598.3	697.7
Mexico	209.4	320.2	535.9
Philippines	276.7	403.1	564.7
Singapore	418.8	487.4	398.4
Taiwan	610.7	701.9	710.9
Thailand	250.8	336.8	412.0
United Kingdom	1,470.9	1,522.7	1,558.2
USA	3,203.7	4,241.7	4,850.6
Viet Nam	109.5	169.0	371.2
Total (incl. others)	23,582.9	29,257.1	32,666.5

* Including re-exports. Excluding specie and gold.

Transport

RAILWAYS (traffic, year ending 30 June)

	1996/97	1997/98	1998/99
Freight ('000 metric tons)	11,525	11,706	12,899
Passengers ('000)	11,572	11,751	n.a.

Source: Tranz Rail Ltd, Wellington.

ROAD TRAFFIC (vehicles licensed at 31 March)

	2000	2001	2002
Passenger cars	1,877,850	1,909,480	1,960,503
Goods service vehicles	368,964	364,928	366,639
Taxis	7,479	7,181	7,366
Buses and service coaches	12,264	12,667	13,339
Trailers and caravans	359,400	368,994	381,914
Motorcycles and mopeds	48,722	47,670	47,423
Tractors	20,526	21,377	22,914

Source: Ministry of Transport, Wellington.

SHIPPING

Merchant Fleet (registered at 31 December)

	1999	2000	2001
Number of vessels	164	163	159
Displacement (grt)	264,988	180,049	174,942

Source: Lloyd's Register-Fairplay, *World Fleet Statistics*.

Vessels Handled (international, '000 grt)

	1993	1994	1995
Entered	37,603	39,700	48,827
Cleared	35,128	37,421	42,985

Source: UN, *Statistical Yearbook*.

International Sea-borne Freight Traffic
('000 metric tons, year ending 30 June)

	1998/99	1999/2000	2000/01
Goods loaded	19,500	22,038	22,077
Goods unloaded	12,646	13,507	14,074

CIVIL AVIATION
(domestic and international traffic on scheduled services)

	1996	1997	1998
Kilometres flown (million)	156	173	174
Passengers carried ('000)	9,597	9,435	8,655
Passenger-km (million)	22,052	20,983	19,014
Total metric ton-km (million)	2,841	2,816	2,700

Source: UN, *Statistical Yearbook*.

Tourism

VISITOR ARRIVALS (year ending 28 February)

Country of residence	1999/2000	2000/01	2001/02
Australia	534,710	584,212	629,003
Canada	32,882	34,474	38,476
Germany	47,726	53,265	49,460
Japan	145,743	154,960	147,554
Korea, Republic	50,871	69,811	91,578
Taiwan	39,980	40,914	36,022
United Kingdom	173,927	208,685	217,638
USA	186,473	193,640	194,024
Total (incl. others)	1,644,282	1,824,375	1,929,202

1999/2000: Total tourist receipts (year ending 31 March; excl. international air fares): $NZ4,260m.

Source: New Zealand Tourism Board.

Communications Media

	1999	2000	2001
Television receivers ('000 in use)	1,975	2,000	n.a.
Telephones ('000 main lines in use)	1,889	1,915	1,834
Mobile telephones ('000 subscribers)	1,395	2,158	2,417
Personal computers ('000 in use)	1,250	1,380	1,500
Internet users ('000)	700	830	1,092

Radio receivers ('000 in use, 1997): 3,750.
Facsimile machines ('000 in use, year ending 31 March 1996): 65.
Daily newspapers: 26 (circulation 850,000 copies, 2002).
Non-daily newspapers: 2 (circulation 311,380 copies, 2002).
Book production (1999): 4,800 titles.

Sources: partly International Telecommunication Union; UNESCO, *Statistical Yearbook*; UN, *Statistical Yearbook*.

Education

(July 2001)

	Institutions	Teachers (full-time equivalent)	Students
Early childhood services	4,213	11,701[1]	171,333[2]
Primary schools[3]	2,209	25,578[4]	449,491
Composite schools[5]	126	1,496[4]	42,701
Secondary schools[6]	336	16,596[4]	239,481
Special schools	47	613[4]	2,248
Polytechnics	22	3,999	87,965
Colleges of education	4	475	10,884
Universities	8	6,103	125,668
Wananga[7]	3	237	11,278
Private training establishments receiving government grants	455	3,753	51,666

[1] Excludes teaching staff of the 562 Kohanga Reo (responsible for Maori 'Language Nests' and 503 playcentres).

[2] Includes children on the regular roll of the Correspondence School, kindergartens, playcentres, Te Kohanga Reo, Early Childhood Development Unit funded playgroups, Early Childhood Development Unit funded Pacific Islands language groups, education and care centres (incl. home-based childcare).

[3] Primary schools include Full Primary Years 1–8, Contributing Years 1–6, Intermediate Years 7–8.

[4] Teachers employed in state schools at 1 March 1999.

[5] Composite schools provide both primary and secondary education (includes area schools and the Correspondence School).

[6] Secondary schools include Years 7–15, Years 9–15.

[7] Tertiary institutions providing polytechnic and university level programmes specifically for Maori students, with an emphasis on Maori language and culture.

Source: Ministry of Education, Wellington.

Directory

The Constitution

New Zealand has no written constitution. The political system is closely modelled on that of the United Kingdom (with an element of proportional representation introduced to the legislature in 1996). As in the United Kingdom, constitutional practice is an accumulation of convention, precedent and tradition. A brief description of New Zealand's principal organs of government is given below:

HEAD OF STATE

Executive power is vested in the monarch and is exercisable in New Zealand by the monarch's personal representative, the Governor-General.

In the execution of the powers and authorities vested in him or her, the Governor-General must be guided by the advice of the Executive Council.

EXECUTIVE COUNCIL

The Executive Council consists of the Governor-General and all the Ministers. Two members, exclusive of the Governor-General or the presiding member, constitute a quorum. The Governor-General appoints the Prime Minister and, on the latter's recommendation, the other Ministers.

HOUSE OF REPRESENTATIVES

Parliament comprises the Crown and the House of Representatives. At the 1996 general election, a system of mixed member proportional representation was introduced. The House of Representatives comprises 120 members: 67 electorate members (five seats being reserved for Maoris) and 53 members chosen from party lists. They are designated 'Members of Parliament' and are elected for three years, subject to the dissolution of the House before the completion of their term.

Everyone over the age of 18 years may vote in the election of members for the House of Representatives. Since August 1975 any person, regardless of nationality, ordinarily resident in New Zealand for 12 months or more and resident in an electoral district for at least one month is qualified to be registered as a voter. Compulsory registration of all electors except Maoris was introduced at the end of 1924; it was introduced for Maoris in 1956. As from August 1975, any person of the Maori race, which includes any descendant of such a person, may enrol on the Maori roll for that particular Maori electoral district in which that person resides.

By the Electoral Amendment Act, 1937, which made provision for a secret ballot in Maori elections, Maori electors were granted the same privileges, in the exercise of their vote, as general electors.

In local government the electoral franchise is the same.

The Government

Head of State: HM Queen ELIZABETH II (acceded to the throne 6 February 1952).

Governor-General and Commander-in-Chief: Dame SILVIA CARTWRIGHT (took office 4 April 2001).

CABINET
(September 2002)

A coalition of the Labour Party and the Progressive Coalition.

Prime Minister and Minister for Arts, Culture and Heritage: Helen Clark.

Deputy Prime Minister, Minister of Finance, Minister of Revenue and Leader of the House: Dr Michael Cullen.

Minister for Economic Development and Minister for Industry and Regional Development: Jim Anderton*.

Minister of Social Services and Employment and of Broadcasting: Steve Maharey.

Minister of Foreign Affairs and Trade and of Justice: Phil Goff.

Minister of Health and for Food Safety: Annette King.

Minister of Agriculture, for Biosecurity, of Forestry and for Trade Negotiations: Jim Sutton.

Minister of Education, of State Services and for Sport and Recreation: Trevor Mallard.

Minister of Energy, of Fisheries, of Research, Science and Technology and for Crown Research Institutes: Pete Hodgson.

Attorney-General and Minister for Courts, Minister of Labour and in Charge of Treaty of Waitangi Negotiations: Margaret Wilson.

Minister of Maori Affairs: Parekura Horomia.

Minister of Commerce, Immigration and for Senior Citizens: Lianne Dalziel.

Minister of Police, of Internal Affairs, of Civil Defence and of Veteran's Affairs: George Hawkins.

Minister of Defence, for State Owned Enterprises and of Tourism: Mark Burton.

Minister of Transport, of Communications and for Information Technology: Paul Swain.

Minister for the Environment and of Disarmament and Arms Control: Marian Hobbs.

Minister of Corrections, of Housing and of Pacific Island Affairs and for Racing: Mark Gosche.

Minister for Accident Compensation and of Women's Affairs: Ruth Dyson.

Minister of Youth Affairs, for Land Information and of Statistics: John Tamihere.

Minister of Conservation and of Local Government: Chris Carter.

* Denotes member of the Progressive Coalition.

In addition, there are six Ministers outside the Cabinet.

MINISTRIES AND GOVERNMENT DEPARTMENTS

Department of the Prime Minister and Cabinet: Executive Wing, Parliament Bldgs, Wellington; tel. (4) 471-9700; fax (4) 473-2508; internet www.dpmc.govt.nz.

Ministry of Agriculture and Forestry: POB 2526, Wellington; tel. (4) 474-4100; fax (4) 474-4111; internet www.maf.govt.nz.

Ministry of Civil Defence and Emergency Management: POB 5010, Wellington; tel. (4) 473-7363; fax (4) 473-7369.

Department of Conservation: POB 10-420, Wellington; tel. (4) 471-0726; fax (4) 471-1082; e-mail tsmith@doc.govt.nz; internet www.doc.govt.nz.

Ministry for Culture and Heritage: POB 5364, Wellington; tel. (4) 499-4229; fax (4) 499-4490; e-mail info@mch.govt.nz; internet www.mch.govt.nz.

Ministry of Defence: POB 5347, Wellington; tel. (4) 496-0999; fax (4) 496-0859; internet www.defence.govt.nz.

Ministry of Economic Development: POB 1473, 33 Bowen St, Wellington; tel. (4) 472-0030; fax (4) 473-4638; e-mail info@med.govt.nz; internet www.med.govt.nz.

Ministry of Education: Level 7, St Paul's Square, 45–47 Pipitea St, Thorndon, Wellington; tel. (4) 463-8000; fax (4) 463-8001; e-mail communications@minedu.govt.nz; internet www.minedu.govt.nz.

Ministry for the Environment: POB 10-362, Wellington; tel. (4) 917-7400; fax (4) 917-7523; e-mail library@mfe.govt.nz; internet www.mfe.govt.nz.

Ministry of Fisheries: POB 1020, Wellington; tel. (4) 470-2600; fax (4) 470-2601; internet www.fish.govt.nz.

Ministry of Foreign Affairs and Trade: Private Bag 18901, Wellington; tel. (4) 494-8500; fax (4) 472-9596; e-mail enquiries@mfat.govt.nz; internet www.mfat.govt.nz.

Ministry of Health: POB 5013, Wellington; tel. (4) 496-2000; fax (4) 496-2340; internet www.moh.govt.nz.

Ministry of Housing: POB 10729, Level 12, Vogel Bldg, Aitken St, Wellington; tel. (4) 472-2753; fax (4) 499-4744; e-mail info@minhousing.govt.nz; internet www.minhousing.govt.nz.

Department of Internal Affairs: POB 805, Wellington; tel. (4) 495-7200; fax (4) 495-7222; e-mail webmaster@dia.govt.nz; internet www.dia.govt.nz.

Ministry of Justice: POB 180, Wellington; tel. (4) 494-9700; fax (4) 494-9701; e-mail reception@justice.govt.nz; internet www.justice.govt.nz.

Department of Labour: POB 3705, Wellington; tel. (4) 915-4444; fax (4) 915-0891; e-mail info@dol.govt.nz; internet www.dol.govt.nz.

Ministry of Maori Development: POB 3943, Wellington 6015; tel. (4) 922-6000; fax (4) 922-6299; e-mail tpkinfo@tpk.govt.nz; internet www.tpk.govt.nz.

Ministry of Pacific Island Affairs: POB 833, Wellington; tel. (4) 473-4493; fax (4) 473-4301; e-mail contact@minpac.govt.nz; internet www.minpac.govt.nz.

Ministry of Research, Science and Technology: POB 5336, Wellington; tel. (4) 917-2900; fax (4) 471-1284; e-mail talk2us@morst.govt.nz; internet www.morst.govt.nz.

Ministry of Social Policy: Private Bag 39993, Wellington 1; tel. (4) 916-3860; fax (4) 916-3910; internet www.mosp.govt.nz.

State Services Commission: POB 329, Wellington; tel. (4) 495-6600; fax (4) 495-6686; e-mail commission@ssc.govt.nz; internet www.ssc.govt.nz.

Statistics New Zealand: POB 2922, Wellington; tel. (4) 495-4600; fax (4) 495-4610; e-mail info@stats.govt.nz; internet www.stats.govt.nz.

Ministry of Tourism: POB 5640, Wellington; tel. (4) 498-7440; fax (4) 498-7445; e-mail info@tourism.govt.nz; internet www.tourism.govt.nz.

Ministry of Transport: POB 3175, Wellington; tel. (4) 472-1253; fax (4) 473-3697; e-mail reception@transport.govt.nz; internet www.transport.govt.nz.

Treasury: POB 3724, Wellington; tel. (4) 472-2733; fax (4) 473-0982; e-mail information@treasury.govt.nz; internet www.treasury.govt.nz.

Ministry of Women's Affairs: POB 10-049, Wellington; tel. (4) 473-4112; fax (4) 472-0961; e-mail mwa@mwa.govt.nz; internet www.mwa.govt.nz.

Legislature

HOUSE OF REPRESENTATIVES

Speaker: Jonathan Hunt.

General Election, 27 July 2002

Party	Number of votes	% of votes	Party seats	List seats	Total seats
NZ Labour Party	838,219	41.26	45	7	52
NZ National Party	425,310	20.93	21	6	27
New Zealand First	210,912	10.38	1	12	13
ACT New Zealand	145,078	7.14	—	9	9
Green Party	142,250	7.00	—	9	9
United Future NZ	135,918	6.69	1	7	8
Progressive Coalition	34,542	1.70	1	1	2
Total (incl. others)	2,031,617	100.00	69	51	120

Political Organizations

In June 2002 21 parties were registered.

ACT New Zealand: Level 1, Block B, Old Mercury Bldg, Nuffield St, POB 99-651, Newmarket, Auckland; tel. (9) 523-0470; fax (9) 523-0472; e-mail info@voteact.org.nz; internet www.act.org.nz; f. 1994; supports free enterprise, tax reform and choice in education and health; Pres. Catherine Judd; Leader Richard Prebble.

The Green Party of Aotearoa—New Zealand: POB 11-652, Wellington; tel. (4) 801-5102; fax (4) 801-5104; e-mail greenparty@greens.org.nz; internet www.greens.org.nz; f. 1989 (fmrly Values Party, f. 1972); Co-Leaders Rod Donald, Jeanette Fitzsimons.

Mana Motuhake o Aotearoa (New Zealand Self-Government Party): Private Bag 68-905, Newton, Auckland; f. 1979; pro-Maori; promotes bicultural policies; Leader Willie Jackson.

The New Zealand Democratic Party Inc: 414 Glenfield Rd, POB 40364, Glenfield, North Shore City; tel. (9) 442-2364; fax (9) 442-

2438; e-mail nzdp.inc@xtra.co.nz; internet www.geocities.com/CapitolHill/Senate/2550; f. 1953 as Social Credit Political League; adopted present name 1985; liberal; Pres. PETER KANE; Leader JOHN WRIGHT.

New Zealand First: c/o House of Representatives, Wellington; fax (4) 472-8557; e-mail nzfirst@parliament.gov.nz; f. 1993 by fmr National Party mems; Leader WINSTON PETERS; Pres. DOUG WOOLERTON.

New Zealand Labour Party: POB 784, 160–162 Willis St, Wellington; tel. (4) 384-7649; fax (4) 384-8060; f. 1916; e-mail nzlpho@labour.org.nz; internet www.labour.org.nz; advocates an organized economy guaranteeing an adequate standard of living to every person able and willing to work; Pres. MIKE WILLIAMS; Parl. Leader HELEN CLARK; Gen. Sec. MIKE SMITH.

New Zealand New National Party: 14th Floor, Willbank House, 57 Willis St, POB 1155, Wellington 60015; tel. (4) 472-5211; fax (4) 478-1622; e-mail hq@national.org.nz; internet www.national.org.nz; f. 1936; centre-right; supports private enterprise and competitive business, together with maximum personal freedom; Pres. MICHELLE BOAG; Parl. Leader BILL ENGLISH.

Progressive Coalition: c/o House of Representatives, Wellington; f. 2002 to contest the general election; Leader JIM ANDERTON.

United Future New Zealand (UNZ): c/o House of Representatives, Wellington; e-mail united.nz@parliament.govt.nz; internet www.united.org.nz; f. 1995 by four mems of National Party, two mems of Labour Party and leader of Future New Zealand; joined by New Zealand Conservative Party in 1998; Leader PETER DUNNE.

Other parties that contested the 2002 election included the Alliance, the Aotearoa Legalise Cannabis Party, the Christian Heritage Party, Mana Maori Movement, NMP, One New Zealand Party and Outdoor Recreation New Zealand.

Diplomatic Representation

EMBASSIES AND HIGH COMMISSIONS IN NEW ZEALAND

Argentina: Sovereign Assurance House, 14th Floor, 142 Lambton Quay, POB 5430, Lambton Quay, Wellington; tel. (4) 472-8330; fax (4) 472-8331; e-mail enzel@arg.org.nz; internet www.arg.org.nz; Ambassador: ENRIQUE J. DE LA TORRE.

Australia: 72–78 Hobson St, Thorndon, POB 4036, Wellington; tel. (4) 473-6411; fax (4) 498-7118; High Commissioner: ROBERT L. COTTON.

Brazil: Wool House, 10 Brandon St, POB 5432, Wellington; tel. (4) 473-3516; fax (4) 473-3517; e-mail brasemb@ihug.co.nz; Ambassador: EDGARD TELLES RIBEIRO.

Canada: 61 Molesworth St, POB 12049, Wellington 1; tel. (4) 473-9577; fax (4) 471-2082; High Commissioner: VALERIE RAYMOND.

Chile: 19 Bolton St, POB 3861, Wellington; tel. (4) 471-6270; fax (4) 472-5324; e-mail embchile@ihug.co.nz; Ambassador: CARLOS APPELGREN BALBONTÍN.

China, People's Republic: POB 17257, Karori, Wellington; tel. (4) 472-1382; fax (4) 499-0419; internet www.chinaembassy.org.nz; Ambassador: CHEN MINGMING.

Fiji: 31 Pipitea St, Thorndon, POB 3940, Wellington; tel. (4) 473-5401; fax (4) 499-1011; e-mail viti@paradise.net.nz; internet www.fiji.org.nz; High Commissioner: BAL RAM.

France: 34–42 Manners St, Open Networks Building, 12th Floor, POB 11-343, Wellington; tel. (4) 802-7787; fax (4) 384-2579; e-mail laurence.oxenberg@diplomatic.gouv.fr; internet www.ambafrance-nz.org; Ambassador: JACKY MUSNIER.

Germany: 90–92 Hobson St, POB 1687, Wellington; tel. (4) 473-6063; fax (4) 473-6069; e-mail germanembassywellington@xtra.co.nz; Ambassador: GUIDO HEYMER.

Greece: 10th Floor, 5–7 Willeston St, POB 24-066, Wellington; tel. (4) 473-7775; fax (4) 473-7441; e-mail info@greece.org.nz; Ambassador: CHRISTOS KARAPANOS.

Holy See: Apostolic Nunciature, 112 Queen's Drive, Lyall Bay, POB 14-044, Wellington 6041; tel. (4) 387-3470; fax (4) 387-8170; e-mail nuntius@ihug.co.nz; Apostolic Nuncio: Most Rev. PATRICK COVENEY, Titular Archbishop of Satriano.

India: 180 Molesworth St, POB 4045, Wellington 1; tel. (4) 473-6390; fax (4) 499-0665; e-mail hicomind@clear.org.nz; internet www.hicomind.org.nz; High Commissioner: BAL ANAND.

Indonesia: 70 Glen Road, Kelburn, POB 3543, Wellington; tel. (4) 475-8699; fax (4) 475-9374; e-mail kbriwell@ihug.co.nz; internet www.indonesianembassy.org.nz; Ambassador: H. E. SUTOYO.

Iran: POB 10-249, The Terrace, Wellington; tel. (4) 386-2983; fax (4) 386-3065; e-mail embassy.of.iran@xtra.co.nz; Ambassador: MOHAMMAD ALI KORMI NOURI.

Israel: Equinox House, 13th Floor, 111 The Terrace, POB 2171, Wellington; tel. (4) 472-2368; fax (4) 499-0632; e-mail israel-ask@israel.org.nz; internet www.webnz.co.nz/israel; Ambassador: RUTH KAHANOFF.

Italy: 34–38 Grant Rd, Thorndon, POB 463, Wellington 1; tel. (4) 473-5339; fax (4) 472-7255; e-mail ambwell@xtra.co.nz; internet www.italy-embassy.org.nz/em_well.html; Ambassador: ROBERTO PALMIERI.

Japan: Levels 18–19, The Majestic Centre, 100 Willis St, POB 6340, Wellington 1; tel. (4) 473-1540; fax (4) 471-2951; Ambassador: KOICHI MATSUMOTO.

Korea, Republic: ASB Bank Tower, Level 11, 2 Hunter St, POB 11-143, Wellington; tel. (4) 473-9073; fax (4) 472-3865; e-mail korembec@world-net.co.nz; Ambassador: CHONG WOO-SEONG.

Malaysia: 10 Washington Ave, Brooklyn, POB 9422, Wellington; tel. (4) 385-2439; fax (4) 385-6973; e-mail mwwelton@xtra.co.nz; High Commissioner: Dato' ZULKIFLY ABDUL RAHMAN.

Mexico: Perpetual Trust House, Level 8, 111–115 Customhouse Quay, POB 11-510, Manners St, Wellington; tel. (4) 472-0555; fax (4) 496-3559; e-mail mexico@xtra.co.nz; internet www.mexico.org.nz; Ambassador: JORGE ALVAREZ FUENTES.

Netherlands: Investment House, 10th Floor, Cnr Featherston and Ballance Sts, POB 840, Wellington; tel. (4) 471-6390; fax (4) 471-2923; e-mail wel@minbuza.nl; internet www.netherlandsembassy.co.nz; Ambassador: A. E. DE BIJLL NACHENIUS.

Papua New Guinea: 279 Willis St, POB 197, Wellington; tel. (4) 385-2474; fax (4) 385-2477; e-mail pngnz@globe.net.nz; High Commissioner: LUCY BOGARI.

Peru: Cigna House, Level 8, 40 Mercer St, POB 2566, Wellington; tel. (4) 499-8087; fax (4) 499-8057; e-mail embperu@xtra.co.nz; Ambassador: JAVIER LEÓN.

Philippines: 50 Hobson St, Thorndon, POB 12-042, Wellington; tel. (4) 472-9848; fax (4) 472-5170; e-mail embassy@wellington-pe.co.nz; Ambassador: FRANCISCO F. SANTOS.

Poland: 17 Upland Rd, Kelburn, POB 10211, Wellington; tel. (4) 475-9453; fax (4) 475-9458; Chargé d'affaires: ANDRZEJ SOŁTYSIŃSKI.

Russia: 57 Messines Rd, Karori, Wellington; tel. (4) 476-6113; fax (4) 476-3843; e-mail eor@netlink.co.nz; Ambassador: GENNADII SHABANNIKOV.

Samoa: 1A Wesley Rd, Kelburn, POB 1430, Wellington; tel. (4) 472-0953; fax (4) 471-2479; e-mail samoahicom@clear.net.nz; High Commissioner: FEESAGO SIAOSI FEPULEA'I.

Singapore: 17 Kabul St, Khandallah, POB 13140, Wellington; tel. (4) 479-2076; fax (4) 479-2315; e-mail shcwlg@xtra.co.nz; High Commissioner: TAN KENG JIN.

Switzerland: Panama House, 22 Panama St, Wellington; tel. (4) 472-1593; fax (4) 499-6302; e-mail vertretung@wel.rep.admin.ch; Ambassador: SYLVIE MATTEUCCI.

Thailand: 2 Cook St, Karori, POB 17-226, Wellington; tel. (4) 476-8618; fax (4) 476-3677; e-mail thaiembassynz@xtra.co.nz; Ambassador: ANUCHA OSATHANOND.

Turkey: Level 8, 15–17 Murphy St, POB 12-248, Wellington; tel. (4) 472-1292; fax (4) 472-1277; e-mail turkem@xtra.co.nz; Ambassador: ÜNAL MARASLI.

United Kingdom: 44 Hill St, POB 1812, Wellington; tel. (4) 924-2888; fax (4) 473-4982; e-mail bhc.wel@xtra.co.nz; internet www.britain.org.nz; High Commissioner: RICHARD FELL.

USA: 29 Fitzherbert Terrace, POB 1190, Wellington; tel. (4) 462-6000; fax (4) 472-3537; internet usembassy.state.gov/wellington; Ambassador: CHARLES SWINDELLS.

Judicial System

The Judicial System of New Zealand comprises a Court of Appeal, a High Court and District Courts, all of which have civil and criminal jurisdiction, and the specialist courts, the Employment Court, the Family Court, the Youth Court and the Maori Land Court. Final appeal is to the Judicial Committee of the Privy Council in the United Kingdom. In civil cases parties have an appeal to the Privy Council from the Court of Appeal as a matter of right if the case involves $NZ5,000 or more; leave to appeal is not automatically granted for criminal cases.

The Court of Appeal hears appeals from the High Court and from District Court Jury Trials, although it does have some original jurisdiction. Its decisions are final, except in cases that may be appealed to the Privy Council. Appeals regarding convictions and sentences handed down by the High Court or District Trial Courts are by leave only.

The High Court has jurisdiction to hear cases involving crimes, admiralty law and civil matters. It hears appeals from lower courts and tribunals, and reviews administrative actions.

District Courts have an extensive criminal and civil law jurisdiction. They hear civil cases up to $NZ200,000, unless the parties agree to litigate a larger sum (up to $NZ62,500 per year for rent and up to $NZ500,000 for real estate). Justices of the Peace can hear minor criminal and traffic matters if less than $NZ5,000. The Family Court, which is a division of the District Courts, has the jurisdiction to deal with dissolution of marriages, adoption, guardianship applications, domestic actions, matrimonial property, child support, care and protection applications regarding children and young persons, and similar matters.

The tribunals are as follows: the Employment Tribunal (administered by the Department of Labour), Disputes Tribunal, Complaints Review Tribunal, Residential Tenancies Tribunal, Waitangi Tribunal, Environment Court, Deportation Review Tribunal and Motor Vehicles Disputes Tribunal. The Disputes Tribunal has the jurisdiction to hear civil matters involving sums up to $NZ7,500. If the parties agree, it can hear cases involving sums up to $NZ12,000.

In criminal cases involving indictable offences (major crimes), the defendant has the right to a jury. In criminal cases involving summary offences (minor crimes), the defendant may elect to have a jury if the sentence corresponding to the charge is three months or greater.

In early 2002 the Government announced its intention to replace the system of final appeal to the Privy Council with a local Supreme Court.

Attorney-General: MARGARET WILSON.

Chief Justice: Dame SIAN ELIAS.

THE COURT OF APPEAL

President: THOMAS MUNRO GAULT.

Judges: Dame SIAN ELIAS (*ex officio*), JOHN STEELE HENRY, JOHN J. MCGRATH, Sir KENNETH KEITH, PETER BLANCHARD, ANDREW PATRICK CHARLES TIPPING, SUSAN GLAZEBROOK.

THE HIGH COURT

Permanent Judges: Dame SIAN ELIAS (*ex officio*), RICHARD ALEXANDER HERON, ANTHONY ARTHUR TRAVERS ELLIS, ROBERT ANDREW MCGECHAN, JOHN ANTHONY DOOGUE, NOEL CROSSLEY ANDERSON, JAMES BRUCE ROBERTSON, ROBERT LLOYD FISHER, PETER GEORGE SPENSER PENLINGTON, ROBERT GRANT HAMMOND, DAVID STEWART MORRIS, JOHN W. HANSEN, HUGH WILLIAMS, DAVID BARAGWANATH, LOWELL GODDARD, GRAHAM PANCKHURST, LESTER H. CHISHOLM, PETER M. SALMON, BARRY J. PATERSON, J. WARWICK GENDALL, JUDITH M. POTTER, JOHN A. LAURENSON, TONY RANDERSON, WILLIE YOUNG, Justice NICHOLSON, Justice WILD, E. T. DURIE, Justice CHAMBERS, RODNEY HANSEN.

Religion

CHRISTIANITY

Conference of Churches in Aotearoa New Zealand: POB 22-652, Christchurch; tel. (3) 377-2702; fax (3) 377-6634; e-mail ccanz@clear.net.nz; internet www.ccanz.godzone.net.nz; f. 1987 to replace the National Council of Churches in New Zealand (f. 1941); 12 mem. churches, 1 assoc. mem.; Gen. Sec. MICHAEL EARLE.

Te Runanga Whakawhanaunga i Nga Hahi o Aotearoa (Maori Council of Churches in New Zealand): Private Bag 11903, Ellerslie, Auckland, Aotearoa-New Zealand; tel (9)525 4179; fax (9) 525 4346; f. 1982; four mem. churches; Administrator TE RUA GRETHA.

The Anglican Communion

The Anglican Church in Aotearoa, New Zealand and Polynesia comprises Te Pihopatanga o Aotearoa and eight dioceses (one of which is Polynesia). In 1996 the Church had an estimated 631,764 members in New Zealand.

Primate of the Anglican Church in Aotearoa, New Zealand and Polynesia, and Bishop of Auckland: Rt Rev. JOHN CAMPBELL PATERSON, POB 37-242, Parnell, Auckland; tel. (9) 302-7201; fax (9) 377-6962.

General Secretary and Treasurer of the Anglican Church in Aotearoa, New Zealand and Polynesia: ROBIN NAIRN, POB 885, Hastings; tel. (6) 878-7902; fax (6) 878-7905; e-mail gensec@hb.ang.org.nz; internet www.anglican.org.nz.

The Roman Catholic Church

For ecclesiastical purposes, New Zealand comprises one archdiocese and five dioceses. At 31 December 2000 there were an estimated 456,947 adherents.

Bishops' Conference: New Zealand Catholic Bishops' Conference, POB 1937, Wellington; tel. (4) 496-1747; fax (4) 496-1746; e-mail t.oliver@wn.catholic.org.nz; f. 1974; Pres. Rt Rev. PETER CULLINANE, Bishop of Palmerston North; Sec. Bishop JOHN DEW, Auxiliary Bishop of Wellington; Executive Officer TERENCE OLIVER.

Archbishop of Wellington: Cardinal THOMAS STAFFORD WILLIAMS, POB 1937, Wellington 6015; tel. (4) 496-1795; fax (4) 496-1728; e-mail bishop.tsw@xtra.co.nz.

Other Christian Churches

Baptist Churches of New Zealand: 8 Puhinui Rd, Manukau City, POB 97543, South Auckland; tel. (9) 278-7494; fax (9) 279-7499; e-mail info@Baptist.org.nz; internet www.baptist.org.nz; f. 1882; 22,456 mems; Pres. JUDY HARVEY; Nat. Leader Rev. BRIAN WINSLADE.

Congregational Union of New Zealand: 10 The Close, 42 Arawa St, New Lynn, Auckland; tel. and fax (9) 827-3708; e-mail cunz@xtra.co.nz; f. 1884; 786 mems, 15 churches; Gen. Sec. BOB FRANKLYN; Chair. BARBARA KENNETT.

Methodist Church of New Zealand: Connexional Office, POB 931, Christchurch; tel. (3) 366-6049; fax (3) 366-6009; e-mail info@methodist.org.nz; 16,995 mems; Gen. Sec. Rev. JILL VAN DE GEER.

Presbyterian Church of Aotearoa New Zealand: 100 Tory St, POB 9049, Wellington; tel. (04) 801-6000; fax (04) 801-6001; e-mail assemblyoffice@pcanz.org.nz; internet www.presbyterian.org.nz; 50,000 mems; Moderator Rt Rev. MICHAEL THAWLEY; Assembly Exec. Sec. Rev. Dr KERRY M. ENRIGHT.

There are several Maori Churches in New Zealand, with a total membership of over 30,000. These include the Ratana Church of New Zealand, Ringatu Church, Church of Te Kooti Rikirangi, Absolute Maori Established Church and United Maori Mission. The Antiochian Orthodox Church, the Assemblies of God, the Greek Orthodox Church of New Zealand, the Liberal Catholic Church, and the Society of Friends (Quakers) are also active.

BAHÁ'Í FAITH

National Spiritual Assembly of the Bahá'ís of New Zealand: POB 21-551, Henderson, Auckland 1231; tel. (9) 837-4866; fax (9) 837-4898; e-mail natsec@nsa.org.nz; internet www.bahai.org.nz; CEO SUZANNE MAHON.

The Press

NEWSPAPERS AND PERIODICALS

Principal Dailies

In 1999 there were 29 daily newspapers in New Zealand (eight morning, 21 evening).

Bay of Plenty Times: 108 Durham St, Private Bag TG12002, Tauranga; tel. (7) 578-3059; fax (7) 578-0047; e-mail news@boptimes.co.nz; internet www.mytown.co.nz/bayofplenty; f. 1872; evening; Gen. Man. JOHN WOOD; Editor BRUCE MORRIS; circ. 22,920.

The Daily News: Currie St, POB 444, New Plymouth; tel. (6) 758-0559; fax (6) 758-6849; e-mail editor@dailynews.co.nz; f. 1857; morning; Gen. Man. KEVIN NIELSEN; Editor (vacant); circ. 27,316.

The Daily Post: 1143 Hinemoa St, POB 1442, Rotorua; tel. (7) 348 6199; fax (7) 346 0153; e-mail daily@dailypost.co.nz; f. 1885; evening; Gen. Man. ALAN SAMPSON; Editor R. G. MAYSTON; circ. 13,421.

The Dominion: 40 Boulcott St, POB 1297, Wellington; tel. (4) 474-0000; fax (4) 474-0350; internet www.wnl.co.nz; f. 1907; morning; Gen. Man. I. D. WELLS; Editor RICHARD LONG; circ. 70,000.

Evening Post: Press House, 40 Boulcott St, POB 3740, Wellington; tel. (4) 474-0444; fax (4) 474-0237; e-mail editor@evpost.co.nz; internet www.stuff.co.nz; f. 1865; Gen. Man. I. D. WELLS; Editor TIM PANKHURST; circ. 59,055.

Evening Standard: POB 3, Palmerston North; tel. (6) 356-9009; fax (6) 350-9836; e-mail editor@msl.co.nz; f. 1880; evening; Gen. Man. TREVOR HOWES; Editor TONY CURRAN; circ. 21,367.

Gisborne Herald: 64 Gladstone Rd, POB 1143, Gisborne; tel. (6) 868-6655; fax (6) 867-8048; e-mail editorial@gisborneherald.co.nz; f. 1874; evening; Man. Dir M. C. MUIR; Editor IAIN GILLIES; circ. 9,587.

Hawke's Bay Today: 113 Karamu Rd, POB 180, Hastings; tel. (6) 873-0800; fax (6) 873-0805; e-mail hb–2>news@hbtoday.co.nz; f. 1999; evening; conservative; Gen. Man. RON D. HALL; Editor LOUIS PIERARD; circ. 33,000.

Marlborough Express: 62–64 Arthur St, POB 242, Blenheim; tel. (3) 578-6059; fax (3) 578-0497; e-mail Brendonb@marlexpress.co.nz; f. 1866; Gen. Man. ROGER G. ROSE; Editor BRENDON BURNS; circ. 10,321.

The Nelson Mail: 15 Bridge St, POB 244, Nelson; tel. (3) 548-7079; fax (3) 546-2802; f. 1866; evening; Business Man. MARK HUGHES; Editor DAVID J. MITCHELL; circ. 18,555.

New Zealand Herald: 46 Albert St, POB 32, Auckland; tel. (9) 379-5050; fax (9) 373-6421; f. 1863; morning; Man. Dir J. C. SANDAS; Editor STEPHEN DAVIS; circ. 215,000.

Northern Advocate: 36 Water St, POB 210, Whangarei; tel. (9) 438-2399; fax (9) 430-5669; e-mail daily@northernadvocate.co.nz; internet www.wilsonandhorton.co.nz; f. 1875; evening; Gen. Man. JOHN T. WOOD; Editor G. A. BARROW; circ. 14,602.

Otago Daily Times: Lower Stuart St, POB 517, Dunedin; tel. (3) 477-4760; fax (3) 474-7422; e-mail odt.editor@alliedpress.co.nz; internet www.odt.co.nz; f. 1861; morning; Man. Dir JULIAN C. S. SMITH; Editor ROBIN CHARTERIS; circ. 44,500.

The Press: Cathedral Sq., Private Bag 4722, Christchurch; tel. (3) 379-0940; fax (3) 364-8492; e-mail editorial@press.co.nz; internet www.press.co.nz; f. 1861; morning; Gen. Man. PETER O'HARA; Editor PAUL THOMPSON; circ. 92,000.

Southland Times: 67 Esk St, POB 805, Invercargill; tel. (3) 218-1909; fax (3) 214-9905; e-mail editor@stl.co.nz; f. 1862; morning; Gen. Man. BLAIR BURR; Editor FRED TULETT; circ. 33,300.

Timaru Herald: 52 Bank St, POB 46, Timaru; tel. (3) 684-4129; fax (3) 688-1042; e-mail editor@timaruherald.co.nz; f. 1864; morning; Gen. Man. BARRY APPLEBY; Editor DAVE WOOD; circ. 14,141.

Waikato Times: Private Bag 3086, Hamilton; tel. (7) 849-6180; fax (7) 849-9603; f. 1872; evening; independent; Gen. Man. P. G. HENSON; Editor VENETIA SHERSON; circ. 42,000.

Wanganui Chronicle: 59 Taupo Quay, POB 433, Wanganui; tel. (6) 349-0710; fax (6) 349-0722; e-mail wc_editorial@wilsonandhorton.co.nz; f. 1856; morning; Gen. Man. R. A. JARDEN; Editor J. MASLIN; circ. 14,000.

Weeklies and Other Newspapers

Best Bets: POB 1327, Auckland; fax (9) 366-4565; Sun. and Thur.; horse-racing, trotting and greyhounds; Editor MIKE BROWN; circ. 10,000.

Christchurch Star: 293 Tuam St, POB 1467, Christchurch; tel. (3) 379-7100; fax (3) 366-0180; f. 1868; 2 a week; e-mail bob_cotton@christchurch.co.nz; Chief reporter BOB COTTON; circ. 118,170.

MG Business: 8 Sheffield Crescent, Christchurch 8005; tel. (3) 358-3219; fax (3) 358-4490; f. 1876; fmrly *Mercantile Gazette*; fortnightly; Mon.; economics, finance, management, stock market, politics; Editor BILL HORSLEY; circ. 16,300.

The National Business Review: Level 26, Bank of New Zealand Tower, 125 Queen St, POB 1734, Auckland; tel. (9) 307-1629; fax (9) 307-5129; e-mail editor@nbr.co.nz; f. 1970; weekly; Editor NEVIL GIBSON; circ. 14,328.

New Truth and TV Extra: News Media (Auckland) Ltd, 155 New North Rd, POB 1327, Auckland; tel. (9) 302-1300; fax (9) 307-0761; f. 1905; e-mail editor@truth.co.nz; Friday; local news and features; TV and entertainment; sports; Editor CLIVE NELSON; circ. 22,000.

New Zealand Gazette: Dept of Internal Affairs, POB 805, Wellington; tel. (4) 470-2930; fax (4) 470-2932; e-mail gazette@parliament.govt.nz; internet www.gazette.govt.nz; official government publication; f. 1840; weekly; Man. JANET GOOTJES; circ. 1,000.

North Shore Times Advertiser: POB 33-235, Takapuna, Auckland 9; tel. (9) 489-4189; fax (9) 486-1950; 3 a week; Editor I. DUNN; circ. 59,000.

Sunday Star-Times: POB 1409, Auckland; tel. (9) 302-1300; fax (9) 309-0258; f. 1994 by merger; Editor SUZANNE CHETWIN; circ. 207,375.

Sunday News: POB 1327, Auckland; tel. (9) 302 1300; fax (9) 358 3003; e-mail editor@Sunday-news.co.nz; Editor CLIVE NELSON; circ. 108,869.

Taieri Herald: POB 105, Mosgiel; tel. (3) 489-7123; fax (3) 489-7668; f. 1962; weekly; Man. Editor LEE HARRIS; circ. 10,700.

Waihi Gazette: Seddon St, Waihi; tel. (7) 863-8674; fax (7) 863-8103; weekly; Editor FRITHA TAGG; circ. 8,650.

Wairarapa News: POB 87, Masterton; tel. (6) 370-5690; fax (6) 379-6481; f. 1869; Editor ERIC TURNER; circ. 18,200.

Other Periodicals

AA Directions: AA Centre, cnr Albert and Victoria Sts, Auckland; tel. (9) 356-6444; fax (9) 357-9975; e-mail editor@nzaa.co.nz; internet www.aa.co.nz/online; quarterly; official magazine of the The New Zealand Automobile Association; Editor JOHN CRANNA; circ. 542,219.

Air New Zealand Inflight Magazine: Private Bag 47-920, Ponsonby, Auckland; tel. (9) 379-8822; fax (9) 379-8821; e-mail nzsales@pol.net.nz; monthly; in-flight magazine of Air New Zealand; circ. 61,000.

Architecture New Zealand: AGM Publishing Ltd, Private Bag 99-915, Newmarket, Auckland; tel. (9) 846-4068; fax (9) 846-8742; e-mail johnw@agm.co.nz; f. 1987; every 2 months; Editor JOHN WALSH; circ. 10,000.

Australian Women's Weekly (NZ edition): Private Bag 92512, Wellesley St, Auckland; tel. (9) 308-2735; fax (9) 302-0667; monthly; Editorial Dir LOUISE WRIGHT; circ. 100,550.

Computer Buyer New Zealand: 246 Queen St, Level 8, Auckland; tel. (9) 377-9902; fax (9) 377-4604; every 2 months; Man. Editor DON HILL; circ. 120,968.

Dairying Today: POB 3855, Auckland; tel. (9) 307-0399; fax (9) 307-0122; e-mail rural_news@clear.net.nz; monthly; Editor ADAM FRICKER; circ. 25,979.

Farm Equipment News: POB 4233, Auckland; tel. (9) 520-9451; fax (9) 520-9459; e-mail ruralprs@iconz.co.nz; 17 a year; Editor BARRY LEADER; circ. 88,700.

Fashion Quarterly: ACP Media Centre, Private Bag 92512, Auckland; tel. (9) 308-2735; fax (9) 302-0667; e-mail fq@acpmedia.co.nz; f. 1982; 5 a year; Editor LEONIE DALE; circ. 31,500.

Grapevine: Private Bag 92124, Auckland; tel. (9) 624-3079; fax (9) 625-8788; monthly; family magazine; Editor JOHN COONEY; circ. 149,658.

Info-Link: AGM Publishing Ltd, Private Bag 99-915, Newmarket, Auckland; tel. (9) 846-4068; fax (9) 846-8742; e-mail pengelly@agm.co.nz; internet www.info-link.co.nz; quarterly; Editor STEVEN PENGELLY; circ. 22,000.

Landfall: University of Otago Press, POB 56, Dunedin; tel. (3) 479-8807; fax (3) 479-8385; e-mail landfall@otago.ac.nz; f. 1947; 2 a year; literary; Editor JUSTIN PATON; circ. 1,200.

Mana Magazine: POB 1101, Rotorua; tel. (7) 349-0260; fax (7) 349-0258; e-mail editor@manaonline.co.nz; internet www.manaonline.co.nz; Maori news magazine; Editor DEREK FOX.

Management: POB 5544, Wellesley St, Auckland; tel. (9) 630-8940; fax (9) 630-1046; e-mail editor@management.co.nz; internet www.profile.co.nz; f. 1954; monthly; business; Editor REG BIRCHFIELD; circ. 12,000.

New Idea New Zealand: 48 Greys Ave, 4th Floor, Auckland; tel. (9) 979-2700; fax (9) 979-2721; weekly; women's interest; Editor ANATHEA JOHNSTON; circ. 59,039.

New Truth: 155 New North Rd, Auckland 1; tel. (9) 302-1300; fax (9) 307-0761; e-mail editor@truth.co.nz; weekly; Editor CLIVE NELSON; circ. 22,000.

New Zealand Dairy Exporter: POB 299, Wellington; tel. (4) 499-0300; fax (4) 499-0330; e-mail lance@dairymag.co.nz; f. 1925; monthly; Man. Editor L. MCELDOWNEY; circ. 22,739.

The New Zealand Farmer: Great South Rd, POB 4233, Auckland; tel. (9) 520-9451; fax (9) 520-9459; f. 1882; weekly; Editor HUGH STRINGLEMAN; circ. 18,000.

New Zealand Forest Industries: POB 5544, Auckland; tel. (9) 630-8940; fax (9) 630-1046; e-mail info@nzforest.co.nz; internet www.nzforest.co.nz; f. 1960; monthly; forestry; Publr REG BIRCHFIELD; circ. 2,500.

New Zealand Gardener: POB 6341, Wellesley St, Auckland; tel. (4) 293-4495; f. 1944; monthly; Editor P. MCGEORGE; circ. 77,077.

New Zealand Geographic: POB 37291, Parnell, Auckland; tel. (9) 303-0126; fax (9) 303-0127; e-mail editor@nzgeographic.co.nz; f. 1988; 6 a year; people, places and wildlife of New Zealand; Editor KENNEDY WARNE; circ. 24,612.

New Zealand Horse & Pony: POB 12965, Auckland; tel. (9) 634-1800; fax (9) 634-2918; e-mail editor@horse-pony.co.nz; f. 1959; monthly; Editor JOAN E. GILCHRIST; circ. 9,252.

New Zealand Medical Journal: Department of Medicine, Christchurch Hospital, POB 4345, Christchurch; tel. (3) 364-0640; fax (3) 364-0752; e-mail frank.frizell@chmeds.ac.nz; internet www.nzma.org.nz; 2 a month; Editor Prof. FRANK A. FRIZELL; circ. 5,000.

New Zealand Science Review: POB 1874, Wellington; fax (4) 389-5095; e-mail mberridge@malaghan.org.nz; internet www.rsnz.govt.nz/clan/nzmss; f. 1942; 4 a year; reviews, policy and philosophy of science; Editor M. V. BERRIDGE.

New Zealand Woman's Day: Private Bag 92512, Wellesley St, Auckland; tel. (9) 308-2700; fax (9) 357-0978; e-mail wdaynz@acp.nz.co.nz; weekly; Editor in Chief LOUISE WRIGHT; circ. 143,420.

New Zealand Woman's Weekly: NZ Magazines Ltd, POB 90-119, Auckland Mail Centre, Auckland; tel. (9) 360-3820; fax (9) 360-3826; e-mail editor @nzww.co.nz; internet www.on-line.co.nz; f. 1932; Mon.; women's issues and general interest; Editor ROWAN DIXON; circ. 130,706.

Next: Level 4, Cnr Fanshawe and Beamont Sts, Westhaven, Private Bag 92512, Auckland 1036; tel. (9) 308-2773; fax (9) 377-6725; e-mail next@acpmedia.co.nz; f. 1991; monthly; home and lifestyle; Editor LIZ PARKER; circ. 63,000.

North & South: 100 Beaumont St, Private Bag 92512, Wellesley St, Auckland; tel. (9) 308-2700; fax (9) 308-9498; e-mail northsouth@acpmedia.co.nz; f. 1986; monthly; current affairs and lifestyle; Editor ROBYN LANGWELL; circ. 35,959.

NZ Catholic: POB 147000, Ponsonby, Auckland 1034; tel. (9) 378-4380; fax (9) 360-3065; e-mail catholic@iconz.co.nz; f. 1996; fortnightly; Roman Catholic; Editor PAT MCCARTHY; circ. 7,700.

NZ Home and Entertaining: ACP Media Centre, Cnr Fanshawe and Beaumont Sts, Private Bag 92512, Auckland; tel. (9) 308 2700; e-mail cmcall@acpmedia.colnz; f. 1936; bi-monthly, design, architecture, lifestyle; Editor CLARE MCCALL; circ. 21,298.

NZ Listener: NZ Magazines Ltd, POB 90-119, Auckland Mail Centre, Auckland; tel. (9) 360-3820; fax (9) 360-3831; f. 1939; weekly; general features, politics, arts, TV, radio; Editor FINLAY MACDONALD; circ. 96,000.

NZ Turf Digest: News Media (Auckland) Ltd, 155 New North Rd, POB 1327, Auckland; tel. (9) 302-1310; fax (9) 366-4565; Sun./Thur.; Editor MIKE BROWN; circ. 10,000.

Otago Southland Farmer: POB 805, Invercargill; tel. (3) 211-1051; fax (3) 214-3713; fortnightly; Editor REX TOMLINSON; circ. 19,000.

Pacific Wings: NZ Wings Ltd, POB 120, Otaki; tel. (6) 364-6423; fax (6) 364-7797; e-mail editor@nzwings.co.nz; internet www.nzwings.co.nz; f. 1932; monthly; Editor CALLUM MACPHERSON; circ. 20,000.

Prodesign: AGM Publishing Ltd, Private Bag 99-915, Newmarket, Auckland; tel. (9) 846-4068; fax (9) 846-8742; e-mail agm.publishing@xtra.co.nz; f. 1993; every 2 months; Man. Editor STEVE BOHLING; circ. 9,000.

PSA Journal: PSA House, 11 Aurora Terrace, POB 3817, Wellington 1; tel. (4) 917-0333; fax (4) 917-2051; e-mail enquiries@psa.org.nz; internet www.pas.org.nz; f. 1913; 8 a year; journal of the NZ Public Service Asscn; circ. 52,000.

Reader's Digest: L5/235 Broadway, Newmarket, Auckland 1015; tel. (9) 522-9777; fax (9) 522-9778; f. 1950; monthly; Editor TONY SPENCER-SMITH; circ. 105,000.

RSA Review: 181 Willis St, POB 27248, Wellington; tel. (4) 384-7994; fax (4) 385-3325; e-mail rsareview@paradise.net.nz; every 2 months; magazine of the Royal New Zealand Returned Services' Asscn; circ. 106,000.

Rural News: POB 3855, Auckland; tel. (9) 307-0399; fax (9) 307-0122; e-mail rural_news@clear.net.nz; fortnightly; Editor ADAM FRICKER; circ. 85,813.

She Magazine: Private Bag 92512, Wellesley St, Auckland; tel. (9) 308-2735; fax (9) 302-0667; e-mail she@acpmedia.co.nz; Editor LEONIE DALE.

Spanz: POB 9049, Wellington; tel. (4) 801-6000; fax (4) 801-6001; e-mail marym@pcanz.org.nz; internet www.presbyterian.org.nz; f. 1987; bi-monthly; magazine of Presbyterian Church; Editor MARY MACPHERSON; circ. 24,000.

Straight Furrow: c/o Rural Press, POB 4233, Auckland; tel. (9) 520-9451; fax (9) 520-9459; e-mail straightfurrow@ruralpress.com; f. 1933; fortnightly; Editor SEAN STEPHENS; circ. 90,000.

Time New Zealand: Tandem House, 18 St Martins Lane, POB 198, Auckland; fax (9) 366-4706; weekly; circ. 42,765.

TV Guide (NZ): POB 1327, Auckland; tel. (9) 302-1300; fax (9) 373-3036; e-mail editor@tv-guide.co.nz; f. 1986; weekly; Editor ANTHONY PHILLIPS; circ. 225,648.

UNANewZ: UN Asscn of NZ, POB 12324, Wellington; tel. (4) 473-0441; fax (4) 473-2339; e-mail unanz@xtra.co.nz; internet www.converge.org.nz/unanz; f. 1945; quarterly; Editor (vacant).

NEWS AGENCIES

New Zealand Press Association: Newspaper House, 93 Boulcott St, POB 1599, Wellington; tel. (4) 472-7910; fax (4) 473-7480; e-mail news@nzpa.co.nz; internet www.nzpa.co.nz; f. 1879; non-political; Chair. RICK NEVILLE.

South Pacific News Service Ltd (Sopacnews): POB 5026, Lambton Quay, Wellington; tel. and fax (3) 472-8329; f. 1948; Man. Editor NEALE MCMILLAN.

Foreign Bureaux

Agence France-Presse (AFP): POB 11-420, Manners St, Wellington; tel. (021) 688438; fax (021) 471085; e-mail afpnz@clear.net.nz; Correspondent MICHAEL FIELD.

Reuters (UK): POB 11-744, Wellington; tel. (4) 471-4277; e-mail wellington.newsroom@reuters.com; Correspondent RODNEY JOYCE.

United Press International (UPI) (USA): Press Gallery, Parliament Bldgs, Wellington; tel. (4) 471-9552; fax (4) 472-7604; Correspondent BRENDON BURNS.

Xinhua (New China) News Agency (People's Republic of China): 136 Northland Rd, Northland, Wellington; tel. (4) 475-7607; fax (4) 475-7607; e-mail xinhua@ihug.co.nz; Correspondent ZHOU CIPU.

PRESS COUNCIL

New Zealand Press Council: POB 10879, The Terrace, Wellington; tel. (4) 473-5220; fax (4) 471-1785; e-mail presscouncil@asa.co.nz; internet www.presscouncil.org.nz; f. 1972; Chair. Sir JOHN JEFFRIES; Sec. M. E. MAJOR.

PRESS ASSOCIATIONS

Commonwealth Press Union (New Zealand Section): POB 1066, Wellington; tel. (4) 472-6223; fax (4) 471-0987; Chair. G. ELLIS; Sec. L. GOULD.

Newspaper Publishers' Association of New Zealand (Inc): Newspaper House, POB 1066, 93 Boulcott St, Wellington 1; tel. (4) 472-6223; fax (4) 471-0987; e-mail npa@npa.co.nz; f. 1898; 31 mems; Pres. J. SANDERS; CEO L. GOULD; Corporate Affairs Man. H. SOUTER.

Publishers

Auckland University Press: Private Bag 92019, University of Auckland, Auckland; tel. (9) 373-7528; fax (9) 373-7465; e-mail aup@auckland.ac.nz; internet www.auckland.ac.nz/aup; f. 1966; scholarly; Dir ELIZABETH P. CAFFIN.

Lexis-Nexis NZ Ltd: 205–207 Victoria St, POB 472, Wellington; tel. (4) 385-1479; fax (4) 385-1598; e-mail Customer.Relations@lexisnexis.co.nz; internet www.lexisnexis.co.nz; legal; Man. Dir R. W. GRAY.

Christchurch Caxton Press Ltd: 113 Victoria St, POB 25-088, Christchurch 1; tel. (3) 366-8516; fax (3) 365-7840; f. 1935; human and general interest, gardening, craft, local and NZ history, tourist publs; Man. Dir BRUCE BASCAND.

Dunmore Press Ltd: POB 5115, Palmerston North; tel. (6) 358-7169; fax (6) 357-9242; e-mail dunmore@xtra.co.nz; internet www.dunmore.co.nz; f. 1975; non-fiction, educational; Publrs MURRAY GATENBY, SHARMIAN FIRTH.

HarperCollins Publishers (New Zealand) Ltd: 31 View Rd, Glenfield, Auckland; tel. (9) 443-9400; fax (9) 443-9403; f. 1888; general and educational; Man. Dir BARRIE HITCHON.

Hodder Moa Beckett Publishers Ltd: POB 100–749, North Shore Mail Centre, Auckland 1330; tel. (9) 478-1000; fax (9) 478-1010; e-mail admin@hoddermoa.co.nz; f. 1971; Man. Dir KEVIN CHAPMAN.

Learning Media Ltd: POB 3293, Wellington; tel. (4) 472-5522; fax (4) 472-6444; e-mail info@learningmedia.co.nz; internet www.learningmedia.com; f. 1947 as School Publications; became Crown-owned company in 1993; general and educational books, audio cassettes, videos and computer software in English, Spanish, Maori, etc.; International Man. TRISH STEVENSON.

Legislation Direct: Bowen State Bldg, Bowen St, POB 12-418, Wellington; tel. (4) 496-5655; fax (4) 496-5698; e-mail idenquiries@legislationdirect.co.nz; internet www.gplegislation.co.nz; general publishers and leading distributor of government publs; fmrly Govt Printing Office/GP Publications; Man. DOUGAL CABLE.

McGraw-Hill Book Co, New Zealand Ltd: 2nd Floor, Westfield Tower, Westfield Shopping Town, Manukau City, POB 97082, Wiri; tel. (9) 262-2537; fax (9) 262-2540; e-mail cservice_auckland@mcgraw-hill.com; f. 1974; educational; Man. FIRGAL ADAMS.

New Zealand Council for Educational Research: POB 3237, Wellington; tel. (4) 384-7939; fax (4) 384-7933; e-mail sales@nzcer.org.nz; internet www.nzcer.org.nz; f. 1934; scholarly, research monographs, educational, academic, periodicals; Chair. Prof. RUTH MANSELL; Dir ROBYN BAKER.

Pearson Education New Zealand Ltd: Private Bag 102908, North Shore Mail Centre, Glenfield, Auckland 10; tel. (9) 444-4968; fax (9) 444-4957; e-mail rosemary.stagg@pearsoned.co.nz; f. 1968; fmrly Addison Wesley Longman; educational; Dirs ROSEMARY STAGG, A. HARKINS, P. FIELD, E. IMPEY.

Penguin Books (NZ) Ltd: Cnr Airborne and Rosedale Rds, Albany, Private Bag 102902, North Shore Mail Centre, Auckland; tel. (9) 415-4700; fax (9) 415-4701; e-mail geoff.walker@penguin.co.nz; internet www.penguin.co.nz; f. 1973; Publ. Dir GEOFF WALKER; Man. Dir TONY HARKINS.

Wendy Pye Ltd: Private Bag 17-905, Greenlane, Auckland; tel. (9) 525-3575; fax (9) 525-4205; e-mail admin@sunshine.co.nz; children's fiction and educational; Man. Dir WENDY PYE.

Random House New Zealand Ltd: Private Bag 102950, North Shore Mail Centre, Glenfield, Auckland; tel. (9) 444-7197; fax (9) 444-7524; e-mail admin@randomhouse.co.nz; internet www.randomhouse.co.nz; f. 1977; general; Man. Dir MICHAEL MOYNAHAN.

Reed Publishing (NZ) Ltd: Private Bag 34901, Birkenhead, Auckland 10; tel. (9) 441 2960; fax (9) 480-4999; e-mail info@reed.co.nz; internet www.reed.co.nz; children's and general non-fiction; Heinemann Education primary, secondary tertiary and library; Man. Dir ALAN L. SMITH.

University of Otago Press: POB 56, Dunedin; tel. (3) 479-8807; fax (3) 479-8385; e-mail university.press@otago.ac.nz; f. 1958; academic, trade publs; Man. Editor WENDY HARREX.

Whitcoulls Ltd: 3rd Floor, 210 Queen St, Private Bag 92098, Auckland 1; tel. (9) 356-5410; fax (9) 356-5423; NZ, general and educational; Gen. Man. S. PRESTON.

PUBLISHERS' ASSOCIATION

Book Publishers' Association of New Zealand Inc: POB 36477, Northcote, Auckland 1309; tel. (9) 480-2711; fax (9) 480-1130; e-mail bpanz@copyright.co.nz; internet www.bpanz.org.nz; f. 1977; Pres. KEVIN CHAPMAN.

Broadcasting and Communications

TELECOMMUNICATIONS

Asia Pacific Telecom (NZ) Ltd: POB 331214, Takapuna, Auckland.

Clear Communications: Clear Centre, Cnr Northcote and Taharoto Rds, Takapuna, Private Bag 92-143, Auckland; tel. (9) 912-4200; fax (9) 912-4442; e-mail webmaster@clear.co.nz; internet www.clear.co.nz; f. 1990; business solutions, local and toll services, enhanced internet, etc.; owned by British Telecommunications; CEO PETER KALIAROPOLOUS.

Compass Communications Ltd: POB 2533, Auckland.

Global One Communications Ltd: Level 15, Phillips Fox Tower, 209 Queen St, Auckland; tel. (9) 357-3700; fax (9) 357-3737.

NewCall Communications Ltd: Box 8703, Symonds St, Auckland; Man. Dir NORMAN NICHOLLS.

Singtel Optus Ltd: Level 14, ASB Centre, 135 Albert St, Auckland; tel. (9) 356 2660; fax (9) 356 2669.

Telecom Corpn of New Zealand Ltd: Telecom Networks House, 68 Jervois Quay, POB 570, Wellington; tel. (4) 801-9000; fax (4) 385-3469; internet www.telecom.co.nz; Chair. RODERICK DEANE; Chief Exec. THERESA GATTUNG.

Telecom Mobile Telecommunications: Midcity Tower, 141 Willis St, Wellington 6001; tel. (4) 801-9000; internet www.telecom.co.na; f. 1987; Gen. Man. LORRAINE WITTEN.

Telstra Saturn Ltd: Telstra Business Centre, Level 9, 191 Queen St, Auckland; tel. (9) 980-8800; fax (9) 980-8801; e-mail enquiries@telstra.co.nz; internet www.telstra.co.nz; f. 2000 through merger of Telstra New Zealand and Saturn Communications.

Vodafone New Zealand Ltd: 21 Pitt St, Private Bag 92-161, Auckland; tel. (9) 357-5100; fax (9) 357-4836; internet www.vodafone.co.nz; fmrly Bell South; cellular network; CEO LARRY CARTER; Man. Dir GRAHAME MAHER.

WorldxChange Communications Ltd: 55 Shortland St, POB 3296, Auckland; tel. (9) 308-1300.

Regulatory Authority

Telecommunications Policy Section, Ministry of Economic Development: 33 Bowen St, POB 1473, Wellington; tel. (4) 472-0030; fax (4) 473-7010; e-mail info@med.govt.nz; internet www.med.govt.nz/pbt/telecom.html.

BROADCASTING

In December 1995 Radio New Zealand Commercial (RNZC) and New Zealand Public Radio Ltd (NZPR) became independent entities, having assumed responsibility for, respectively, the commercial and non-commercial activities of Radio New Zealand. RNZC was sold to the New Zealand Radio Network Consortium in 1996, and NZPR, which remained a Crown-owned company, assumed the name of its now-defunct parent company, to become Radio New Zealand Ltd. In late 1999 there were 190 radio stations broadcasting on a continuous basis, of which 170 were operating on a commercial basis.

Radio

Radio Broadcasters' Association (NZ) Inc: POB 3762, Auckland; tel. (9) 378-0788; fax (9) 378-8180; e-mail rba@xtra.co.nz; represents commercial radio industry; Exec. Dir D. N. G. INNES; Sec. JANINE BLISS; 142 mems.

Radio New Zealand Ltd: RNZ House, 155 The Terrace, POB 123, Wellington; tel. (4) 474-1999; fax (4) 474-1459; e-mail rnz@radionz.co.nz; internet www.radionz.co.nz; f. 1936; Crown-owned entity, operating non-commercial national networks: National Radio and Concert FM; parliamentary broadcasts on AM Network; Radio New Zealand News and Current Affairs; the short-wave service, Radio New Zealand International; and archives; Chief Exec. SHARON CROSBIE.

The Radio Network of New Zealand Ltd: 54 Cook St, Private Bag 92198, Auckland; tel. (9) 373-0000; e-mail enquiry@radionetwork.co.nz; operates 87 commercial stations, reaching 1.3m. people; Chief Exec. JOHN MCELHINNEY.

Television

Television New Zealand (TVNZ) Ltd: Television Centre, Cnr Hobson and Victoria Sts, POB 3819, Auckland; tel. (9) 916-7000; fax (9) 379-4907; internet www.tvnz.co.nz; f. 1960; the television service is responsible for the production of programmes for two TV networks, TV One and 2; networks are commercial all week and transmit in colour; both channels broadcast 24 hours a day, seven days a week, and reach 99.9% of the population; Chair. Dr ROSS ARMSTRONG; CEO RICK ELLIS; Gen. Man. ALAN BROOKBANKS.

Private Television

Auckland Independent Television Services Ltd: POB 1629, Auckland.

Bay Satellite TV Ltd: Hastings; tel. (6) 878-9081; fax (6) 878-5994; Man. Dir JOHN LYNAM.

Broadcast Communications Ltd: POB 2495, Auckland; tel. (9) 916-6400; fax (9) 916-6404; Man. Dir GEOFF LAWSON.

Sky Network Television Limited: 10 Panorama Rd, POB 9059, Newmarket, Auckland; tel. (9) 579-9999; fax (9) 579-0910; internet www.skytv.co.nz; f. 1990; UHF service on six channels, satellite service on 18 channels; Chief Exec. NATE SMITH.

TV3 Network Services Ltd: Private Bag 92624, Symonds St, Auckland; tel. (9) 377-9730; fax (9) 366-5999; internet www.tv3.co.nz; f. 1989; owned by CanWest Global Corpn; Man. Dir RICK FRIESEN.

TV4 Network Ltd: Private Bag 92624, Symonds St, Auckland; tel. (9) 377-9730; fax (9) 302-2321; 'free-to-air' entertainment channel; Head of Programming BETTINA HOLLINGS.

Finance

(cap. = capital; res = reserves; dep. = deposits; m. = million; amounts in New Zealand dollars)

BANKING

Central Bank

Reserve Bank of New Zealand: 2 The Terrace, POB 2498, Wellington; tel. (4) 472-2029; fax (4) 473-8554; e-mail rbnz-info@rbnz.govt.nz; internet www.rbnz.govt.nz; f. 1934; res 400.1m., dep. 7,123.3m. (June 2000); Gov. Dr R. M. CARR (acting); Dep. Gov. M. A. SHERWIN, Dr R. M. CARR.

Registered Banks

As a result of legislation which took effect in April 1987, several foreign banks were incorporated into the domestic banking system.

ANZ Banking Group (New Zealand) Ltd: Private Bag 92-210 AMSC, Auckland; tel. (9) 374-4040; fax (9) 374-4038; internet www.nz.anz.com; f. 1979; subsidiary of Australia and New Zealand Banking Group Ltd of Melbourne, Australia; cap. 406.5m., res. 0.45m., dep. 23047.3m. (Sept 2000); Chair. R. S. DEANE; Man. Dir Dr M. J. HORN; 150 brs and sub-brs.

ASB Bank Ltd: ASB Bank Centre, Cnr Wellesley and Albert Sts, POB 35, Auckland 1; tel. (9) 377-8930; fax (9) 358-3511; e-mail helpdesk@asbbank.co.nz; internet www.asbbank.co.nz; f. 1847 as Auckland Savings Bank, name changed 1988; cap. 373.1m., res 473.8m., dep. 16,187.0m. (June 2000); Chair. G. J. JUDD; Man. Dir R. J. NORRIS; 118 brs.

Bank of New Zealand (BNZ): BNZ Centre, 1 Willis St, POB 2392, Wellington; tel. (4) 474-6999; fax (4) 474-6861; f. 1861; internet www.bnz.co.nz; owned by National Australia Bank; cap. 1,511m., dep. 29,801m. (Sept. 2000); Chair. T. K. McDONALD; Man. Dir P THODEY; 241 brs and sub-brs.

Citibank NA (USA): POB 3429, 23 Customs Street East, Auckland; tel. (9) 307-1902; fax (9) 307-1983; internet www.citibank.com; CEO ANDREW AU; 2 brs.

Deutsche Bank AG: POB 6900, Wellesley St, Auckland; tel. (9) 351-1000; fax (9) 351-1001; internet www.deutsche-bank.co.nz; f. 1986; fmrly Bankers Trust New Zealand; CEO BRETT SHEPHERD.

Hongkong and Shanghai Banking Corporation Ltd (Hong Kong): POB 5947, Level 9, 1 Queen St, Auckland; tel. (9) 308-8888; fax (9) 308-8997; e-mail hsbcplb@clear.net.nz; internet www.asiapacific.hsbc.com; CEO S. EDWARDS; 6 brs.

National Bank of New Zealand Ltd: 1 Victoria St, POB 1791, Wellington 6000; tel. (4) 494-4000; fax (4) 494-4023; internet www.nationalbank.co.nz; f. 1873; merged with Countrywide

Banking Corpn in 1999; cap. 472m., res 1,066m., dep. 28,881m. (Dec. 1999); Chair. Sir WILSON WHINERAY; Dir and CEO Sir JOHN ANDERSON; 164 brs.

Rabobank (New Zealand): POB 1069, Auckland; tel. (9) 375-3700; fax (9) 375-3710; f. 1996; full subsidiary of Rabobank Nederland.

TSB Bank Ltd: POB 240, New Plymouth; tel. (6) 757-92700; fax (6) 759-2768; f. 1850; dep. 1,400m. (March 2001); Man. Dir K. W. RIMMINGTON; 15 brs.

Westland Bank Ltd: 99 Revell St, POB 103, Hokitika; tel. (3) 755-8680; fax (3) 755-8277; full subsidiary of ASB Bank Ltd; cap. and res 6,176m., dep. 108m. (June 1992); Man. Dir K. J. BEAMS; 9 brs.

WestpacTrust: 318 Lambton Quay, POB 691, Wellington; tel. (4) 498-1000; fax (4) 498-1350; acquired Trust Bank New Zealand; New Zealand division of Westpac Banking Corpn (Australia); Chief Exec. D. T. GALLAGHER.

Other Banks

Postbank: 58–66 Willis St, Wellington 1; tel. (4) 729-809; f. 1987; owned by Australia and New Zealand Banking Corpn; 550 brs.

Association

New Zealand Bankers' Association: POB 3043, Wellington; tel. (4) 472-8838; fax (4) 473-1698; e-mail acopland@nzba.org.nz; f. 1891; CEO ERROL LIZAMORE.

STOCK EXCHANGES

Dunedin Stock Exchange: POB 298, Dunedin; tel. (3) 477-5900; Chair. E. S. EDGAR; Sec. R. P. LEWIS.

New Zealand Stock Exchange: ASB Tower, Level 9, 2 Hunter St, POB 2959, Wellington 1; tel. (4) 472-7599; fax (4) 473-1470; e-mail nzse@nzse.co.nz; internet www.nzse.co.nz; Chair. SIMON ALLEN; Man. Dir M. WELDON.

Supervisory Body

New Zealand Securities Commission: POB 1179, Wellington; tel. (4) 472-9830; fax (4) 472-8076; e-mail seccom@sec-com.govt.nz; internet www.sec-com.govt.nz; f. 1979; Chair. JANE DIPLOCK.

INSURANCE

ACE Insurance NZ Ltd: POB 734, Auckland; tel. (9) 377-1459; fax (9) 303-1909; e-mail grant.simpson@ace-ina.com; Gen. Man. GRANT SIMPSON.

AMI Insurance Ltd: 29–35 Latimer Sq., POB 2116, Christchurch; tel. (3) 371-9000; fax (3) 371-8314; e-mail amichch@es.co.nz; f. 1926; Chair. K. G. L. NOLAN; CEO JOHN B. BALMFORTH.

AMP General Insurance Ltd: 86/90 Customhouse Quay, POB 1093, Wellington; tel. (4) 498-8000; fax (4) 471-2312; f. 1958; fire, accident, marine, general; Chair. J. W. UTZ; Mans (NZ) L. ROSS, R. CUFF.

AMP General Insurance (NZ) Ltd: 86/90 Customhouse Quay, POB 1093, Wellington; tel. (4) 498-8000; fax (4) 471-2312; f. 1958; fire, accident, marine, general; Chair. GRAEME W. VALENTINE; Man. K. SHAW.

ANZ Life Assurance Co Ltd: POB 1492, Wellington; tel. (4) 496-7000; fax (4) 470-5100; Man. R. A. DEAN.

BNZ Life Insurance Ltd: POB 1299, Wellington; tel. (4) 382-2577; fax (4) 474-6883; e-mail rodger-murphy@bnz.co.nz; Gen. Man. R. J. MURPHY.

Colonial Life (NZ) Ltd: 117 Customhouse Quay, POB 191, Wellington 6000; tel. (4) 470-4700; fax (4) 470-4701; e-mail servicecentre@colonialfs.co.nz; life, accident, investment, sickness and disability, staff superannuation; expected to adopt the name Sovereign during 2001, following its merger with Sovereign group; Man. Dir DAVID MAY.

Commercial Union General Insurance Co Ltd: 142 Featherston St, POB 2797, Wellington; tel. (4) 473-9177; fax (4) 473-7424; fire, accident, travel, engineering; Gen. Man. T. WAKEFIELD.

Farmers' Mutual Group: 68 The Square, POB 1943, Palmerston North 5330; tel. (6) 356-9456; fax (6) 356-4603; e-mail enquiries@fmg.co.nz; internet fmg.co.nz; comprises Farmers' Mutual Insurance Asscn, Farmers' Mutual Insurance Ltd and other cos; fire, accident, motor vehicle, marine, life; CEO G. SMITH.

Gerling NCM EXGO: POB 3933, Wellington 6015; tel. (4) 474-0901; fax (4) 472-6966; trade credit insurance services; division of Gerling NZ Ltd since December 2001; e-mail info@gerlingEXGO; Gen. Man. ARTHUR DAVIS.

Metropolitan Life Assurance Co of NZ Ltd: Sovereign Assurance House, 33–45 Hurstmere Rd, Takapuna, Auckland 1; tel. (9) 486-9500; fax (9) 486-9501; f. 1962; life; Man. Dir PETER W. FITZSIMMONS.

New Zealand Insurance: NZI House, 151 Queen St, Private Bag 92130, Auckland 1; tel. (9) 309-7000; fax (9) 309-7097; internet www.nzi.co.nz; Chief Exec. M. HANNAN.

The New Zealand Local Government Insurance Corporation Ltd (Civic Assurance): Local Government Bldg, 114–118 Lambton Quay, POB 5521, Wellington; tel. (4) 470-0037; fax (4) 471-1522; e-mail rod.mead@civicassurance.co.nz; internet www.civicassurance.co.nz; f. 1960; fire, motor, all risks, accident; Chair. K. N. SAMPSON; Gen. Man. R. D. MEAD.

QBE Insurance (International) Ltd: POB 44, Auckland; tel. (9) 366-9920; fax (9) 366-9930; e-mail gevans@qbe.co.nz; f. 1890; Gen. Man. GRAEME EVANS.

State Insurance Ltd: Microsoft House, 3–11 Hunter St, POB 5037, Wellington 1; tel. (4) 496-9600; fax (4) 476-9664; internet www.state.co.nz; f. 1905; mem. NRMA Insurance Group; Man. Dir T. C. SOLE.

Tower Insurance Ltd: 67–73 Hurstmere Rd, POB 33-144, Takapuna; tel. (9) 486-9340; fax (9) 486-9368; f. 1873; fmrly National Insurance Co of New Zealand; Chair. Sir C. J. MAIDEN; Man. Dir P. R. HUNT.

Associations

Insurance Council of New Zealand: POB 474, Wellington; tel. (4) 472-5230; fax (4) 473-3011; e-mail icnz@icnz.org.nz; internet www.icnz.org.nz; CEO CHRISTOPHER RYAN.

Investment Savings and Insurance Association of New Zealand Inc: POB 1514, Wellington; tel. (4) 473-8730; fax (4) 471-1881; e-mail isi@isi.org.nz; f. 1996 from Life Office Asscn and Investment Funds Asscn; represents cos that act as manager, trustee, issuer, insurer, etc. of managed funds, life insurance and superannuation; Chief Exec. VANCE ARKINSTALL; Exec. Officer DEBORAH KEATING.

Trade and Industry

GOVERNMENT AGENCY

New Zealand Trade Development Board (Trade New Zealand): POB 10-341, Wellington; tel. (4) 499-2244; fax (4) 473-3193; internet www.tradenz.govt.nz; f. 1988; CEO FRAN WILDE; Chair. JOE POPE.

CHAMBERS OF COMMERCE

Auckland Regional Chamber of Commerce and Industry: POB 47, Auckland; tel. (9) 309-6100; fax (9) 309-0081; e-mail mbarnett@chamber.co.nz; internet www.chamber.co.nz; CEO MICHAEL BARNETT; Pres. DAVID TRUSCOTT.

Canterbury Employers' Chamber of Commerce: 57 Kilmore St, POB 359, Christchurch; tel. (3) 366-5096; fax (3) 379-5454; e-mail info@cecc.org.nz; internet www.cecc.org.nz; CEO PETER TOWNSEND.

Otago Chamber of Commerce and Industry Inc: Level 7, Westpac Trust Bldg, 106 George St, POB 5713, Dunedin; tel. (3) 479-0181; fax (3) 477-0341; e-mail office@otagochamber.co.nz; f. 1861; CEO J. A. CHRISTIE; Pres. BEVAN RICKERBY.

Wellington Regional Chamber of Commerce: 9th Floor, 109 Featherston St, POB 1590, Wellington; tel. (4) 914-6500; fax (4) 914-6524; e-mail info@wgtn-chamber.co.nz; internet www.wgtn-chamber.co.nz; f. 1856; Chief Exec. PHILIP LEWIN; Pres. BARRIE SAUNDERS; 1,000 mems.

INDUSTRIAL AND TRADE ASSOCIATIONS

Canterbury Manufacturers' Association: POB 13-152, Armagh, Christchurch; tel. (3) 353-2540; fax (3) 353-2549; e-mail cma@cma.org.nz; internet www.cma.org.nz; f. 1879; CEO JOHN WALLEY; 500 mems.

Employers' and Manufacturers' Association (Central Inc): Federation House, 95–99 Molesworth St, POB 1087, Wellington; tel. (4) 473-7224; fax (4) 473-4501; e-mail ema@emacentral.org.nz; f. 1997 by merger of Wellington Manufacturers' Asscn and Wellington Regional Employers' Asscn; Pres. R. KERR-NEWELL; 2,200 mems.

Employers' and Manufacturers' Association (Northern Inc): 159 Khyber Pass Rd, Grafton, Private Bag 92066, Auckland; tel. (9) 367-0900; fax (9) 367-0902; e-mail ema@ema.co.nz; internet www.emacentral.org.nz; f. 1886; fmrly Auckland Manufacturers' Asscn; Pres. R. KERR-NEWELL; 2,200 mems.

ENZAFRUIT: POB 279, Hastings; tel. (6) 878-1898; fax (6) 878-1850; e-mail info@enza.co.nz; fmrly New Zealand Apple and Pear Marketing Board; Man. Dir MICHAEL DOSSOR; Chair. B BIRNIE.

Federated Farmers of New Zealand (Inc): 6th Floor, Agriculture House, 12 Johnston St, Wellington 1; POB 715, Wellington; tel. (4) 473-7269; fax (4) 473-1081; e-mail wellingtonoffice@fedfarm.org.nz;

internet www.fedfarm.org.nz; f. 1946; Pres. ALISTAIR POLSON; CEO TONY ST CLAIR; 16,000 mems.

Kiwifruit New Zealand: POB 4246, Mt Maunganui South; tel. (7) 574-7139; fax (7) 574-7149; Chair. PETER TRAPSKI.

National Beekeepers' Association of New Zealand (Inc): Agriculture House, 12 Johnston St, POB 715, Wellington 6015; tel. (4) 473-7269; fax (4) 473-1081; e-mail tleslie@fedfarm.org.nz; internet www.nba.org.nz; f. 1913; 1,500 mems; Pres. DON BELL; Sec. TIM LESLIE.

New Zealand Animal By-Products Exporters' Association: POB 12-222, 11 Longhurst Terrace, Christchurch; tel. (3) 332-2895; fax (3) 332-2825; 25 mems; Sec. J. L. NAYSMITH.

New Zealand Berryfruit Growers' Federation (Inc): POB 10-050, Wellington; tel. (4) 473-5387; fax (4) 473-6999; e-mail berryfed@xtra.co.nz; 530 mems; Pres. JOHN GARELJA; Executive Officer PETER ENSOR.

New Zealand Council of Wool Exporters Inc: POB 2857, Christchurch; tel. (3) 353-1049; fax (3) 374-6925; e-mail cwe@xtra.co.nz; www.woolexport.net; f. 1893; Exec. Man. R. H. F. NICHOLSON; Pres. C. HALL.

The New Zealand Forest Industries Council: POB 2727, Wellington; tel. (4) 473-9220; fax (4) 473-9330; e-mail griffithsj@nzfic.org.nz; internet www.nzfic.nzforestry.co.nz; CEO JAMES GRIFFITHS.

The New Zealand Forest Owners' Association: POB 1208, Wellington; tel. (4) 473-4769; fax (4) 499-8893; e-mail robmcl@nzfoa.org.nz; internet www.nzfoa.nzforestryco.nz/; CEO ROB MCCLAGAN.

New Zealand Fruitgrowers' Federation: Huddart Parker Bldg, POB 2175, Wellington, 6015; tel. (4) 472-6559; fax (4) 472-6409; e-mail hans@fruitgrowers.org.nz; www.fruitgrowers.org.nz; f. 1928; 5,000 mems; CEO P. R. SILCOCK.

New Zealand Fruit Wine & Cider Makers: 81 Branch Rd, New Plymouth, Taranaki; tel. and fax (6) 758-6910; e-mail admin@fruitwines.co.nz; internet www.fruitwines.co.nz; 30 mems; Chair. BRIAN SHANKS; Exec. Officer CHRIS GARNHAM.

New Zealand Meat Board: Wool House, 10 Brandon St, POB 121, Wellington; tel. (4) 473-9150; fax (4) 474-0800; e-mail help@meatnz.co.nz; internet www.meatnz.co.nz; f. 1922; Chair. JEFF GRANT; Sec. A. DOMETAKIS; 13 mems.

New Zealand Pork Industry Board: POB 4048, Wellington; tel. (4) 385-4229; fax (4) 385-8522; e-mail info@pork.co.nz; internet www.pork.co.nz; f. 1937; Chair. C. TRENGROVE; CEO A DAVIDSON.

New Zealand Seafood Industry Council: Private Bag 24-901, Wellington; tel. (4) 385-4005; fax (4) 384-2727; e-mail info@seafood.co.nz; internet www.seafood.co.nz; CEO JOHN VALENTINE; Chair. DAVID SHARP.

New Zealand Timber Industry Federation: 2–8 Maginnity St, POB 308, Wellington; tel. (4) 473-5200; fax (4) 473-6536; e-mail enquiries@nztif.co.nz; 350 mems; Exec. Dir W. S. COFFEY.

New Zealand Vegetable and Potato Growers' Federation (Inc): POB 10232, Wellington 1; tel. (4) 472-3795; fax (4) 471-2861; e-mail information@vegfed.co.nz; internet www.vegfed.co.nz; 4,000 mems; Pres. B. GARGIULO; CEO P. R. SILCOCK.

New Zealand Wool Board: 10 Brandon St, Box 3225, Wellington; tel. (4) 472-6888; fax (4) 473-7872; e-mail info@woolboard.co.nz; internet www.woolboard.co.nz; assists research, development, production and marketing of NZ wool; Chair. B. C. MUNRO; CEO MARK O'GRADY.

NZMP: 25 The Terrace, POB 417, Wellington; tel. (4) 462-8096; fax (4) 471-8600; internet www.nzmp.com; f. 2001 through merger of New Zealand Dairy Board and Fonterra Co-operative.

Registered Master Builders' Federation (Inc): Level 6, 234 Wakefield St, POB 1796, Wellington; tel. (4) 385-8999; fax (4) 385-8995; internet www.masterbuilder.org.nz; Chief Exec. C. PRESTON.

Retail Merchants' Association of New Zealand (Inc): 8th Floor, Willbank House, 57 Willis St, Wellington; tel. (4) 472-3733; fax (4) 472-1071; e-mail bhellberg@retail.org.nz; f. 1920 as the NZ Retailers' Fed. (Inc); present name adopted in 1987, following merger with the NZ Wholesale Hardware Fed.; direct membership 3,500; Pres. TERENCE DELANEY; CEO JOHN ALBERTSON.

EMPLOYERS' ORGANIZATION

Business New Zealand: Level 6, Microsoft House, 3–11 Hunter St, Wellington; tel. (4) 496-6555; fax (4) 496-6550; e-mail admin@businessnz.org.nz; internet www.businessnz.org.nz; Chief Exec. SIMON CARLAW.

UTILITIES

Energy Efficiency and Conservation Authority (EECA): Level 1, Simpson Grierson Bldg, 44 The Terrace, Wellington; tel. (4) 470-2200; fax (4) 499-5330; e-mail eecainfo@eeca.govt.nz; internet www.eeca.govt.nz.

Electricity

Bay of Plenty Electricity Ltd: 52 Commerce St, POB 404, Whakatane; tel. (7) 307-2700; fax (7) 307-0922; f. 1995; generation of electricity, operation of distribution network; Chair. C. G. HOLMES; CEO ROB BALDEY.

Contact Energy Ltd: Level 1, Harbour City Tower, 29 Brandon St, Wellington; tel. (4) 449-4001; fax (4) 499-4003; internet www.contactenergy.co.nz; generation of electricity, wholesale and retail of energy; transferred to the private sector in 1999; Chair. PHIL PRYKE.

The Marketplace Co Ltd (M-CO): Level 2, Wool House, 10 Brandon St, POB 5422, Wellington; tel. (4) 473-5240; fax (4) 473-5247; e-mail info@m-co.co.nz; internet www.m-co.co.nz; administers wholesale electricity market; Chief Exec. CHRIS RUSSELL.

Powerco: New Plymouth; operates power networks in Wairarapa, Manawatu, Wanganui and Taranaki; Chair. BARRY UPSON.

TransAlta New Zealand Ltd: 10 Hutt Rd, Petone, Wellington; tel. (4) 576-8700; fax (4) 576-8600; e-mail transalta@transalta.co.nz; internet www.transalta.co.nz; f. 1993; retailer of electricity and gas; Chair. R. H. ARBUCKLE: Chief Exec. MURRAY NELSON.

Transpower New Zealand Ltd: Unisys House, 56 The Terrace, POB 1021, Wellington; tel. (4) 495-7000; fax (4) 495-7100; internet www.transpower.co.nz; manages national grid; Chair. Sir COLIN MAIDEN; Chief Exec. BOB THOMSON.

TrustPower Ltd: Private Bag 12023, Tauranga, Auckland; tel. (7) 574-4800; fax (7) 574-4825; e-mail trustpower@trustpower.co.nz; internet www.trustpower.co.nz; f. 1920 as Tauranga Electric Power Board; independent generator; Chair. HAROLD TITTER.

Vector Ltd: POB 99882, Newmarket, Auckland; tel. (9) 978-7788; fax (9) 978-7799; internet www.vector-network.co.nz; fmrly Mercury Energy Ltd; Chair. WAYNE BROWN; CEO Dr PATRICK STRANGE.

Wairarapa Electricity Ltd: 316–330 Queen St, Masterton, Auckland; tel. (6) 377-3773; fax (6) 378-2347; f. 1993; owned by South Eastern Utilities Ltd; distribution of electric power; Chair. JOHN MATHESON; CEO A. LODGE.

Gas

Natural Gas Corpn: Natural Gas Corpn House, 22 The Terrace, POB 1818, Lambton, Wellington; (4) 499-0136; fax (4) 499-0993; f. 1992; purchase, processing and transport of natural gas; wholesale and retail sales; Chair. LEONARD BLEASEL; CEO RICHARD BENTLEY.

Nova Gas Ltd: POB 10-141, Wellington; tel. (4) 472-6263; fax (4) 472-6264; e-mail hansv@novagas.co.nz; internet www.novagas.co.nz.

Water

Waste Management NZ Ltd: 86 Lunn Ave, Mt Wellington, Auckland; tel. (9) 527-8044; fax (9) 570-5595; f. 1985; water and waste water services; Chair. J. A. JAMIESON; Man. Dir K. R. ELLIS.

MAJOR COMPANIES

Construction and Cement

Golden Bay Cement Co Ltd: POB 1359, 2nd Floor, 308 Great South Rd, Greenlane, Auckland; tel. (9) 523-3050; fax (9) 520-2163; f. 1909; mfrs of cement; Gen. Man. C. BADGER; employees: 210.

Milburn New Zealand Ltd: POB 6040, Christchurch; tel. (3) 348-8509; fax (3) 348-3442; internet www.milburn.co.nz; f. 1888; cap. and res $NZ137.5m., sales $NZ195.3m. (1998); mfrs of cement and concrete, aggregate lime and associated products; Chair. J. L. R. MAYCOCK; Man. Dir R. R. WILLIAMS.

Food and Drink

DB Group Ltd: Citibank Centre, 23 Customs St East, Auckland 1; tel. (9) 377-8990; fax (9) 377-3871; f. 1966; cap. and res $NZ226.9m., sales 530.2m. (1999/2000); mfrs and distributors of beer, wine, brewers, and bottlers; Chair. DAVID G. SADLER; Man. Dir BRIAN JAMES BLAKE.

Lion Nathan Ltd: Level 17, Tower 2, Shortland Centre, 55–65 Shortland St, Auckland; tel. (9) 303-3388; fax (9) 303-3307; internet www.lion-nathan.co.nz; f. 1923; cap. and res $NZ –334m., sales $NZ1,612m. (1999/2000); brewers, bottlers, wine and spirits merchants; Chair. DOUGLAS MYERS; CEO GORDON CAIRNS; 3,792 employees.

New Zealand Dairy Group: 80 London St, POB 459, Hamilton; tel. (7) 839-8398; fax (7) 839-8123; internet www.nzdairy.co.nz; f. 1918; cap. and res $NZ875.0m., sales $NZ2,451.0m. (1998/99);

collecting and processing of milk, production of dairy products, etc.; Chair. HENRY VAN DER HEYDEN; CEO JOHN SPENCER.

Sanford Ltd: 22 Jellicoe St, Auckland 1001; tel. (9) 379-4720; fax (9) 309-1190; e-mail info@sanford.co.nz; internet www.sanford.co.nz; cap. and res $NZ382.9m., sales $NZ341.9m. (1999/2000); processing and distribution of seafood; Chair W. D. GOODFELLOW; Man. Dir E. F. BARRATT.

Forestry, Pulp and Paper

Carter Holt Harvey Ltd: Private Bag 92-106, 640 Great South Rd, Manukau City, Auckland; tel. (9) 262-6000; fax (9) 262-6099; internet www.chh.com; f. 1971; cap. and res $NZ4,700m., sales $NZ3,755m. (2000/01); activities include sawmilling, pulp forestry, tissue, paperboard and plastic packaging; Chair. W. J. WHINERAY; CEO CHRIS LIDDELL.

Steel

BHP-New Zealand Steel Ltd: PB 92 121, Auckland 1; tel. (9) 375-8999; fax (9) 375-8959; internet www.bhp.com.au; f. 1966; cap. p.u. $NZ650m. (1998); suppliers of iron-sand concentrate; mfrs of hot- and cold-rolled steel, hollow sections, galvanized flat sheet and coil and pre-painted flat sheet and coil; Man. Dir J. HOWARD.

Steel and Tube Holdings Ltd: 15–17 Kings Cres., Lower Hutt; tel. (4) 570-5000; fax (4) 569-4218; internet www.steelandtube.co.nz; cap. and res $NZ69.3m.. sales NZ$403m. (1999/2000); holding company; 20 subsidiary companies; Chair. R. L. EVERY; CEO N. CALAVRIAS.

Miscellaneous

Cavalier Corporation Ltd: 7 Grayson Ave, Papatoetoe, POB 97–040, South Auckland; tel. (9) 277-6000; fax (9) 279-4756; cap. and res $NZ80.1m., sales $NZ218.4m. (1999/2000); wool merchants and carpet mfrs; Chair. A. C. TIMPSON; CEO and Man. Dir A. M. JAMES.

Ceramco Corporation Ltd: POB 1134, Auckland; tel. (9) 273-0850; fax (9) 273-0851; e-mail info@bendon.co.nz; internet www.ceramco.co.nz; f. 1987; cap. and res $NZ52.5m., sales $NZ89.2m. (1998/99); mfrs of china clay, underwear, lingerie; Chair. D. R. APPLEBY; CEO H. VENTER; 744 employees.

Donaghys Ltd: Donaghys House, 123 Crawford St, POB 209, Dunedin; tel. (3) 349-1735; fax (3) 349-1736; e-mail donaghys@deepsouth.co.nz; cap. and res $NZ55.5m., sales $NZ116.4m. (1998/99); building materials; Chair. GRAEME J. MARSH.

Fernz Corporation Ltd: Level 38, Coopers and Lybrand Tower, 23–29 Albert St, Auckland; tel. (9) 379-3001; fax (9) 366-1394; internet www.fernz.com; f. 1916; fmrly NZ Farmers' Fertilizer Co; cap. and res $NZ283.4m., sales 1,363.8m. (1997/98); mfrs and distributors of fertilizers, sulphuric acid, sulphate of alumina, chrome sulphate, agricultural chemicals, animal health products; 16 subsidiaries; Chair. W. WILSON; Man. Dir KERRY M. HOGGARD; employees: 1,194.

Fisher & Paykel Industries Ltd: POB 58550, Greenmount, Auckland; tel. (9) 273-0600; fax (9) 273-0538; e-mail customer.care@fp.co.nz; internet www.fisherpaykel.co.nz; cap. and res $NZ382.6m., sales $NZ833.2m. (1999/2000); electricals; Chair. Sir COLIN MAIDEN; Man. Dir and CEO G. A. PAYKEL.

Fletcher Challenge Ltd: 810 Great South Rd, Penrose, Auckland; tel. (9) 525-9000; fax (9) 525-0559; internet www.fcl.co.nz; f. 1981, reorganized as holding co in 1996; cap. and res $NZ6,475m., sales $NZ7,837m. (1999/2000); operations in building, energy, forestry and paper; manufacture and distribution of building materials, incl. concrete, steel, plasterboard, wood-based panel products and aluminium extrusion, also commercial, industrial, civil and residential construction; petroleum exploration, production and distribution; plantation forest ownership and management, wood processing and distribution; manufacture of communications papers and speciality pulps; international company, with major operations in New Zealand, Australia, Canada, the USA, South America, Asia; Chair Dr MICHAEL DEANE; CEO MICHAEL ANDREWS; employees: 16,000.

ICI Industrial Group: 8 Pacific Rise, Mt Wellington, Auckland 1006; tel. (9) 573-2700; fax (9) 573-2710; f. 1935; manufacturers and suppliers of industrial chemicals and explosives, synthetic resins, pharmaceuticals, plastics, dyestuffs, agricultural chemicals, polythene films and packaging, industrial and domestic paints; Chair. T. SILVERSON; Man. Dir D. P. PIKE; employees: 840.

Montana Group (New Zealand) Ltd: Level 15, Tower II, The Shortland Centre, 55-65 Shortland St, Auckland; tel. (9) 307-2660; fax (9) 366-1579; fmrly Corporate Investments Ltd; cap. and res $NZ278.1m., sales $NZ449.6m. (1999/2000); production and export of wine; Chair. P. H. MASFEN.

New Zealand Refining Co Ltd: Marsden Point, Private Bag 9024, Whangarei; tel. (9) 432-3811; fax (9) 432-8035; e-mail gsmith@nzrc.co.nz; f. 1961; cap. and res $NZ302.3m., sales $NZ206.3m. (2000); refines petrol, diesel oils, fuel oils and bitumen; Chair. IAN FARRANT; employees: 280.

Richina Pacific Ltd: 11th Floor, 385 Queen St, Auckland; tel. (9) 375-2188; fax (9) 375-2104; e-mail richina@richinapacific.co.nz; internet www.richinapacific.com.nz; cap. and res $NZ95m., sales $NZ725m. (2000); construction, leather; Chair. Sir ALASTAIR MCCORMICK; CEO RICHARD C. L. YAN.

Sealord Group Ltd: Sealord House, Trafalgar St, Nelson 7001; tel. (3) 548-3069; fax (3) 546-0966; e-mail corporate@sealord.co.nz; internet www.sealord.co.nz; f. 1973; 50% owned by Treaty of Waitangi Fisheries Commission, 50% owned by Brierley Investments; catching, processing and marketing of seafood; sales $NZ384m. (1998); Chair Sir TIPENE O'REGAN; 1,600 employees.

TRADE UNIONS

In December 1998 a total of 83 unions were in operation; 306,687 workers belonged to a union.

The New Zealand Council of Trade Unions: Education House, West Block, 178–182 Willis St, POB 6645, Wellington 1; tel. (4) 385-1334; fax (4) 385-6051; e-mail ctu@nzctu.org.nz; internet www.union.org.nz; f. 1937, present name since 1987; affiliated to ICFTU; 25 affiliated unions with 250,000 mems; Pres. ROSS WILSON; Sec. PAUL GOULTER.

Principal Affiliated Unions

Association of Staff in Tertiary Education (ASTE)/Te hau Takitini O Aotearoa: POB 27141, Wellington; tel. (4) 801-5098; fax (4) 385-8826; e-mail national.office@aste.ac.nz; 3,500 mems; Nat. Sec. SHARN RIGGS.

Association of University Staff (AUS): POB 11-767, Wellington; tel. (4) 915-6690; fax (4) 915-6699; e-mail national.office@aus.ac.nz; internet www.aus.ac.nz; 6,000 mems; Gen. Sec HELEN KELLY.

Central Amalgamated Workers Union (AWUNZ): POB 27-291, 307 Willis St, Wellington; tel. (4) 384-4049; fax (4) 801-7306; e-mail centralawunz@xtra.co.nz; Sec. JACKSON SMITH.

FinSec Finance and Information Workers Union: POB 27-355, Wellington; tel. (4) 385-7723; fax (4) 385-2214; e-mail union@finsec.org.nz; internet www.finsec.org.nz/; Pres. ROBYN WOLLER; Sec. DONALD FARR.

Meat and Related Trades Workers Union of Aotearoa: POB 17056, Greenlane, Auckland; tel. (9) 520-0034; fax (9) 523-1286; e-mail meat.union@xtra.co.nz; Sec. GRAHAM COOKE.

New Zealand Dairy Workers Union, Inc: POB 9046, Hamilton; tel. (7) 839-0239; fax (7) 838-0398; e-mail nzdwu@wave.co.nz; internet www.nzdwu.org.nz f. 1992; 5,900 mems; Sec. RAY POTROZ; Pres. J. SMITH.

New Zealand Educational Institute/Te Riu Roa: POB 466, Wellington; tel. (4) 384-9689; fax (4) 385-1772; e-mail nzei@nzei.org.nz; internet www.nzei.org.nz; f. 1883; Pres. AMANDA COULSTON; Sec. LYNNE BRUCE.

New Zealand Engineering, Printing & Manufacturing Union (EPMU): POB 31-546, Lower Hutt; tel. (4) 568-0086; fax (4) 576-1173; e-mail epmunion@epmunion.org.nz; internet www.epmunion.org.nz; Sec. REX JONES.

New Zealand Meat Workers and Related Trades Union: POB 13-048, Armagh, Christchurch; tel. (3) 366-5105; fax (3) 379-7763; e-mail nzmeatworkersunion@clear.net.nz; 7,629 mems; Pres. D. WILSON; Gen. Sec. R. G. KIRK.

New Zealand Nurses' Organization: POB 2128, Wellington; tel. (4) 385-0847; fax (4) 382-9993; e-mail nurses@nzno.org.nz; internet www.nzno.org.nz; 32,000 mems; CEO GEOFF ANNALS.

New Zealand Post Primary Teachers' Association: POB 2119, Wellington; tel. (4) 384-9964; fax (4) 382-8763; e-mail gensec@ppta.org.nz; internet www.ppta.org.nz; Pres. JEN MCCUTCHEON; Gen. Sec. KEVIN BUNKER.

New Zealand Waterfront Workers Union: POB 27004, Wellington; tel. (4) 385-0792; fax (4) 384-8766; e-mail nzwwu@paradise.net.nz; 1,200 mems; Sec. TREVOR HANSON.

NZ PSA (New Zealand Public Service Association): PSA House, 11 Aurora Terrace, POB 3817, Wellington 1; tel. (4) 917-0333; fax (4) 917-2051; e-mail enquiries@psa.org.nz; internet www.psa.org.nz; 40,000 mems; Pres. IAN BAMBER.

Rail & Maritime Transport Union Inc: POB 1103, Wellington; tel. (4) 499-2066; fax (4) 471-0896; e-mail postmaster@rmtunion.org.nz; internet rmtunion.intra.net.nz; 3,497 mems; Pres. J. KELLY; Sec. W. BUTSON.

Service and Food Workers' Union: Private Bag 68–914, Newton, Auckland; tel. (9) 375-2680; fax (9) 375-2681; e-mail darien@sfwu.org.nz; 19,000 mems; Pres. SUE WETERE; Sec. DARIEN FENTON.

Other Unions

Manufacturing & Construction Workers Union: POB 11-123, Manners St, Wellington; tel. (4) 385-8264; fax (4) 384-8007; e-mail M.C.Union@TradesHall.Org.NZ; Gen. Sec. GRAEME CLARKE.

National Distribution Union (NDU): Private Bag 92-904, 120 Church St, Onehunga, Auckland; tel. (9) 622-8355; fax (9) 622-8353; e-mail ndu@nduunion.org.nz; 18,500 mems; Pres. BILL ANDERSEN; Sec. MIKE JACKSON; **Wood Sector:** e-mail jjones@ndunion.org.nz; Pres. DENNIS DAWSON.

New Zealand Building Trades Union: POB 11-356, Manners St, Wellington; tel. (4) 385-1178; fax (4) 385-1177; e-mail nzbtu@tradeshall.org.nz; Pres. P. REIDY; Sec. ASHLEY RUSS.

New Zealand Seafarers' Union: POB 9288, Marion Square, Wellington; tel. (4) 385-9288; fax (4) 384-9288; e-mail admin@seafarers.org.nz; f. 1993; Pres. DAVE MORGAN.

Transport

RAILWAYS

There were 3,904 km of railways in New Zealand in 2000, of which more than 500 km were electrified.

Tranz Rail Ltd: Wellington Station, Private Bag, Wellington 1; tel. (4) 498-3000; fax (4) 498-3259; e-mail info@tranzrail.co.nz; internet www.tranzrail.co.nz; f. 1990; transferred to private ownership in 1993; fmrly New Zealand Rail; 3,904 km of railway; also provides road and ferry services; Man. Dir MICHAEL BEARD.

ROADS

In June 1999 there were a total of 92,075 km of maintained roads in New Zealand, including 10,605 km of state highways and motorways.

Transfund New Zealand: POB 2331, Customhouse Quay, Wellington; tel. (4) 916 4220; fax (4) 916 0028; e-mail reception@transfund.govt.nz; internet www.transfund.gout.nz; f. 1996; Crown agency responsible for purchasing a safe and efficient road system and efficient alternatives; Chair. MICHAEL GROSS; Chief Exec. MARTIN GUMMER.

Transit New Zealand: POB 5084, 20–26 Ballance St, Wellington; tel. (4) 499-6600; fax (4) 496-6666; e-mail deborah.willett@transit.govt.nz; internet www.transit.govt.nz; Crown agency responsible for management and development of the state highway network; Chair. ALAN BICKERS; CEO Dr ROBIN DUNLOP.

SHIPPING

There are 13 main seaports, of which the most important are Auckland, Tauranga, Wellington, Lyttleton (the port of Christchurch) and Port Chalmers (Dunedin). In December 2001 the New Zealand merchant fleet comprised 159 vessels, with a total displacement of 174,942 grt.

Principal Companies

P & O Nedlloyd Ltd: 2–10 Customhouse Quay, POB 1699, Wellington; tel. (4) 462-4000; fax (4) 462-4162; e-mail g.f.quirke@ponl.com; internet www.ponl.com; worldwide shipping services; Man. Dir GARY F. QUIRKE.

Sofrana-Unilines New Zealand Ltd: 101 Customs St, CPOB 3614, Auckland; tel (9) 377 3279; fax (9) 377 8629; internet www.sofrana.co.nz; Chair DIDIER LEROUX; Man. Dir HANS ASSARSSON.

Other major shipping companies operating services to New Zealand include Blue Star Line (NZ) Ltd and Columbus Line, which link New Zealand with Australia, the Pacific Islands, South-East Asia and the USA.

CIVIL AVIATION

There are international airports at Auckland, Christchurch and Wellington.

Civil Aviation Authority of New Zealand: Aviation House, 1 Market Grove, POB 31441, Lower Hutt; tel. (4) 560-9400; fax (4) 569-2024; e-mail info@caa.govt.nz; internet www.caa.govt.nz; Dir of Civil Aviation: JOHN JONES.

Principal Airlines

Air Nelson: Private Bag 32, Nelson 7030; tel. (3) 547-8700; fax (3) 547-8788; f. 1979; e-mail john.hambleton@airnewzealand.co.nz; internet www.airnewzealand.com; owned by Air New Zealand; changed to present name 1986; operates services throughout New Zealand; Gen. Man. JOHN HAMBLETON.

Air New Zealand: Quay Tower, 29 Customs St West, Private Bag 92007, Auckland 1; tel. (9) 366-2400; fax (9) 366-2401; internet www.airnz.co.nz; f. 1978 by merger; privatized in 1989, in process of return to state sector in late 2001; services to Australia, the Pacific Islands, Asia, Europe and North America, as well as regular daily services to 26 cities and towns in New Zealand; Chair. JOHN PALMER; Man. Dir and CEO RALPH NORRIS

Tourism

New Zealand's principal tourist attractions are its high mountains, lakes, forests, volcanoes, hot springs and beaches. In 2001/02 New Zealand received 1,929,202 visitors. Receipts from tourism totalled almost $NZ4,260m. in 1999/2000.

Tourism New Zealand: POB 95, Wellington; tel. (4) 917-5400; fax (4) 915-3817; internet www.tourisminfo.govt.nz; f. 1901; responsible for marketing of New Zealand as a tourism destination; offices in Auckland, Wellington and Christchurch; 13 offices overseas; Chair. PETER ALLPORT; Chief Exec. GEORGE HICKTON.

Defence

In August 2001 the total strength of the regular forces was 9,230: army 4,450, navy 1,980 and air force 2,800. In addition, there were 2,410 regular reserves (army 1,550, navy 850, air force 10) and 3,080 territorial reserves (army 1,550, navy 850, air force 10). Military service is voluntary. New Zealand is a participant in the Five-Power Defence Arrangements with Australia, Malaysia, Singapore and the United Kingdom.

Defence Expenditure: Budgeted at $NZ1,600m. for 2001.

Chief of Defence Force: Air-Marshal JERRY MATEPARAE.

Chief of General Staff: Maj.-Gen. BRUCE FERGUSON.

Chief of Naval Staff: Rear-Adm. PETER M. MCHAFFIE.

Chief of Air Staff: Air Vice-Marshal J. H. S. HAMILTON.

Commander Joint Forces New Zealand: Maj-Gen. MARTYN J. DUNNE.

Education

Education in New Zealand is free and secular in state schools. It is compulsory for all children aged six to 16 years, although in practice almost 100% start at the age of five years. Budgetary expenditure on education by the central Government in 2000/01 was $NZ6,097m., and was projected at $NZ7,041m for 2001/02.

In October 1989 the central administrative body, the Department of Education, and the education boards were disestablished and replaced by six agencies, assigned responsibility for the administration of early childhood and compulsory education: the Early Childhood Development Unit, the Education Review Office, the Ministry of Education, the Special Education Service, the Parent Advocacy Council (later disestablished) and the Teacher Registration Board. In July 1990 three agencies to administer the post-compulsory sector were established: the Education and Training Support Agency, the New Zealand Qualifications Authority and Quest Rapuara, the Career Development and Transition Education Service. The most significant change in the delivery and administration of primary and secondary education consists in the participation of parents and the community, in partnership with teachers. Responsibility for the administration of primary and secondary schools, previously controlled by education boards and the regional offices of the Department of Education, was decentralized to boards of trustees of individual schools. Boards of trustees are accountable for attaining the objectives declared in their charter, and for expenditure made from bulk grants received from Government to administer institutions. Boards are required to report to the Education Review Office, which, in turn, reports directly to the Minister of Education.

PRE-SCHOOL PRIMARY AND SECONDARY EDUCATION

Local early childhood centres are maintained and controlled by voluntary associations to which the Government gives substantial assistance including grants and subsidies. Since 1 July 1990 all early childhood centres wishing to receive government funding have been required to hold a charter. Those not holding a charter must still be licensed. In July 2001 there were 171,333 children enrolled in early childhood education services.

In July 2001 there were 449,491 pupils enrolled in primary classes at 2,209 schools. Pupils may complete the eight-year primary course at a full primary school (or, in rural areas, an area school) or, as is the case for most pupils, they may proceed to an intermediate school for the final two years. An intermediate school is a centrally-located school, usually instructing 300–600 pupils between the ages of 11 and 13 years. In July 2000 58,852 pupils were enrolled at 133 of these schools, which, because of economies of scale, can provide specialist teachers and facilities not normally within the reach of primary schools.

All children are entitled to free secondary education until the end of their 19th year. In mid-2000 a total of 239,481 pupils received secondary education. The majority of pupils leave school at the end of their fourth year. The School Certificate examination is taken at the end of the third or fourth year of secondary school. Pupils who pass subjects in this examination may go on to a year in the sixth form. At the end of the sixth-form year they may obtain the Sixth Form Certificate. Pupils intending to go on to university usually spend a further year in the seventh form to obtain a Higher School Certificate which is awarded without examination and provides a higher bursary. They may also sit examinations for university bursaries and entrance scholarships.

RURAL EDUCATION

In order to give children in country districts the advantage of special equipment and the more specialized teaching of larger schools, the consolidation of the smaller rural schools has been undertaken wherever this is practicable. In certain cases boarding allowances are granted to pupils living in areas where there are no convenient transport services enabling them to attend school. In small rural districts area schools provide primary and secondary education for all pupils in the immediate vicinity, and education from the first to the seventh form is provided in larger districts in separate schools.

CORRESPONDENCE SCHOOL

This school, which had an enrolment of 8,119 in July 2000, serves students who cannot attend school because they live in remote areas, because of illness or for other reasons. It also provides courses for pupils who wish to study subjects not offered at their local school, and adults who do not have access to secondary-school classes.

POLYTECHNICS AND TEACHER TRAINING

Since the early 1980s vocational education and training has moved away from the secondary to the continuing education sector, with training formerly provided by technical high schools now provided by polytechnics. Polytechnics provide a diverse range of vocational education resources and cover an increasing number of subjects at various levels of specialization.

In 2001 there were 22 polytechnics, including the Open Polytechnic of New Zealand. This last is the largest polytechnic in the country, with 17,322 students in July 1998. In mid-2001 there were a total of 3,999 full-time equivalent staff and 87,965 students in the polytechnic system.

In mid-2001 there were 10,884 full-time and part-time students undergoing kindergarten, primary and secondary teacher training in four colleges of education. Most pre-school primary teacher trainees follow a three-year course. University graduates take a course lasting one or two years.

UNIVERSITIES

The eight universities are autonomous bodies with their own councils. Eighty per cent of the universities' funds are state-provided. About 20% of pupils leaving secondary school go to university. In mid-2001 there were 125,668 students enrolled at the universities. There was a teaching staff of 6,103 full-time equivalent teachers.

EDUCATION OF MAORI AND PACIFIC ISLAND STUDENTS

There has been a steady increase in the number of Maori children attending pre-school institutions, and Maori students make up about 20% of the primary and secondary school roll. The period of stay of Maori secondary pupils, however, remains considerably shorter than that for other pupils. In July 2000 there were 146,913 Maori children receiving primary and secondary education. Recognized play centres provided for 1,832 Maori and 324 Pacific Island children out of a total enrolment of 15,808 in July 2000, and kindergartens for 7,048 Maori and 3,437 Pacific Island children out of a total of 45,869. In addition, 8,921 Maori and 3,890 Pacific Island children regularly attended licensed childcare centres. Te Kohanga Reo ('Language Nests') were established by Maori in the early 1980s to provide an educational environment in which children can learn Maori language and Maori cultural values. Kohanga Reo are special-purpose childcare centres under the control of Te Kohanga Reo Trust (Inc.), and licences are approved by the trust. Small non-profit-making pre-school groups and Pacific Island play-groups receive special funding support from the Government, but are exempt from the need to hold a charter or licence. Pacific Island communities operate early childhood centres with an emphasis on language development, both in their indigenous language and in English, increasing parental knowledge in early childhood care and education and assisting a child's transition into the formal education system. Home-based programmes are also linked to these centres. In July 1999 there were 11,859 pupils enrolled at licensed Te Kohanga Reo, 524 children at developing Te Kohanga Reo and 2,948 at developing Pacific Island language groups.

There is a renaissance in the learning and teaching of Maori language and culture, in recognition of the reality that New Zealand is the only place in the world where the Maori culture can be preserved. In-service training courses are run for teachers of Maori students, universities and colleges of education offer Maori Studies courses, and advisers and teachers throughout the country are developing Maori Studies programmes for all pupils. There are increasing numbers of bilingual classes in primary and secondary schools, and 'total immersion' Maori language schools (Kura Kaupapa Maori) have also been established. By 1998 the Kura Kaupapa Maori totalled 60. The three wananga, tertiary institutions providing polytechnic and university level programmes with an emphasis on Maori language and culture, had an enrolment of 11,278 students in mid-2001.

In 1961 the Maori Education Foundation was set up to provide financial assistance to Maori students, and it has also been active in other areas, notably pre-school education. A Pacific Island Polynesian Education Foundation was also established in 1972.

Bibliography

GENERAL

The Dictionary of New Zealand Biography, Vols 1–5, 1769–1960, 1990–2000; internet www.dnzb.govt.nz.

Jackson, Keith, and McRobie, Alan. *Historical Dictionary of New Zealand.* Auckland, Longman, 1996.

Kirkpatrick, Russell. *Bateman Contemporary Atlas: New Zealand: The Shapes of Our Nation.* Auckland, Bateman, 1999.

McKinnon, Malcolm (Ed.). *New Zealand Historical Atlas: Papatuanuku e Takoto Nei.* Wellington, David Bateman in association with Historical Branch, Department of Internal Affairs, 1997.

McLintock, A. H. (Ed.). *An Encyclopaedia of New Zealand.* Wellington, Government Printer, 1966.

Patterson, Brad and Kathryn (Eds). *World Bibliographical Series, Vol. 18, New Zealand.* Oxford, Clio Press, 1998.

Statistics New Zealand. *New Zealand Official Yearbook*, 1990, 1993 and 2000 editions especially. Wellington, annually.

Sturm, Terry (Ed.) *The Oxford History of New Zealand Literature in English*, 2nd edn, Auckland, Oxford University Press, 1998

Thorns, David and Sedwick, Charles. *Understanding Aotearoa/ New Zealand: Historical Statistics.* Palmerston North, Dunmore Press, 1997.

HISTORY

Bassett, Michael, and King, Michael. *Tomorrow Comes the Song: A Life of Peter Fraser.* Auckland, Penguin, 2000.

Belich, James. *Making Peoples: a History of the New Zealanders from Polynesian Settlement to the End of the Nineteenth Century.* Auckland, Allen Lane, the Penguin Press, 1996.

Paradise Reforged: A History of the New Zealanders from the 1880s to the Year 2000. Auckland, Allen Lane, Penguin Press, 2001.

Binney, Judith, Bassett, Judith, and Olssen, Erik. *The People and the Land: Te Tangata me Te Whenua: an illustrated history of New Zealand, 1820–1920.* Wellington, Allen and Unwin, 1990.

Binney, Judith (Ed.). *The Shaping of History: Essays from the New Zealand Journal of History 1967–1999.* Wellington, Bridget Williams Books, 2001.

Chapman, Robert. *New Zealand Politics and Social Patterns.* Victoria University Press, 2001.

Gustafson, Barry. *His Way: A Biography of Robert Muldoon.* Auckland, Auckland University Press, 2000.

Ihimaera, Witi. (Ed.). *Growing Up Maori.* Auckland, Tandem Press, 1998.

Kawharu H. (Ed.). *Waitangi: Contemporary Maori and Pakeha Perspectives on the Treaty.* Auckland, Oxford University Press, 1989.

King, M. *Death of the Rainbow Warrior.* Harmondsworth, Penguin, 1986.

King, M. *Maori: A Photographic and Social History.* Auckland, Heinemann, 1983.

McGibbon, Ian. (Ed.). *The Oxford Companion to New Zealand Military History*. Auckland, Oxford University Press, 2000.

Oliver, W. H. *Claims to the Waitangi Tribunal*. Wellington, Daphne Brassell Associates, 1991.

Orange, C. *The Treaty of Waitangi*. Wellington, Allen and Unwin/ Port Nicholson Press, 1987.

Owen, Alwyn. (Ed.). *Snapshots of the Century*. Auckland, Tandem Press, 1998

Reader's Digest. *New Zealand Yesterdays*. Auckland, David Bateman, 2001.

Rice, G. R. (Ed.). *The Oxford History of New Zealand*, 2nd Edn. Auckland, Oxford University Press, 1992.

Rollo, Arnold. *New Zealand's Burning*. Wellington, Victoria University Press, 1994.

Salmond, Anne *Two Worlds: first meetings between Maori and Europeans 1642 - 1772*. Auckland, Viking, 1991.

Sinclair, K. (Ed.). *The Oxford Illustrated History of New Zealand*. Auckland, Oxford University Press, 1990.

Sinclair, Keith *A History of New Zealand*, revised edn with additional material by Raewyn Dalziel. Auckland, Penguin, 2000.

Trapeznik, Alexander. *Common Ground: Heritage and Public Places in New Zealand*. University of Otago Press, 2000.

Walker, Ranginui. *Ka Whawhai Tonu Mataou: Struggle without end*. Auckland, Penguin Books, 1990.

Ward, Alan. *An Unsettled History: Treaty Claims in New Zealand Today*. Wellington, Bridget Williams Books, 1999.

Wilson, J. (Ed.). *From the Beginning: the Archaeology of the Maori*. Auckland, Penguin Books, 1987.

Websites: www.nz.history.net.nz; and www.timeframes .natlib.govt.nz.

ECONOMY

Birks, Stuart. *The New Zealand Economy, Issues and Policies* (3rd edn). Palmerston North, Dunmore Press, 1997.

Bollard, Alan. *Economic Liberalization in New Zealand*. Wellington, Allen and Unwin, 1987.

Dalziel, Paul, and Lattemore, Ralph. *New Zealand Macroeconomy* (3rd edn). Auckland, Oxford University Press, 1999.

Davey, Judith (Ed.). *Economic Policy, Social Aspects*. Wellington, New Zealand Institute of Policy Studies.

Douglas, Roger. *Unfinished Business*. Auckland, Random House, 1993.

Duncan, Ian, and Bollard, Alan. *Corporatisation and Privatisation: Lessons from New Zealand*. Auckland, Oxford University Press, 1994.

Easton, Brian. *In Stormy Seas—The New Zealand Economy since 1945*. Dunedin, University of Otago Press, 1997.

The Whimpering of the State: Policy after MMP. Auckland, Auckland University Press, 1999.

Fryer, Glenda, and Oldfield, Yvonne. *New Zealand Employment Relations*. Auckland, Addison Wesley Longman New Zealand Ltd, 1994.

Gould, J. *The Rake's Progress? The New Zealand Economy since 1945*. Auckland, Hodder and Stoughton, 1983.

Goldfinch, Shaun. *Remaking New Zealand and Australian Economic Policy: Ideas, Institution and Policy Communities*. Georgetown University Press, 2000.

The Muldoon Years. Auckland, Hodder and Stoughton, 1985.

Hawke, G. R. *The Making of New Zealand, An Economic History*. Cambridge University Press, 1985.

Hazledine, Tim. *Taking New Zealand Seriously: The Economics of Decency*. Auckland, Harper Collins, 1998.

Henderson, David. *Economic Reform, New Zealand in International Perspective*. Wellington, New Zealand Business Roundtable, 1996.

Kelsey, Jane. *The New Zealand Experiment—A World Model for Structural Adjustment*. Auckland, Auckland University Press/ Bridget Williams Books, 1995.

Reclaiming the Future: New Zealand and the Global Economy. University of Toronto Press, 2000.

Massey, Patrick. *New Zealand—Market Liberalisation in a Developed Economy*. New York, St Martin's Press, 1995.

Organisation for Economic Co-operation and Development. *New Zealand*. Paris, OECD, annual country surveys, 1985 and subsequent years.

Roper, B., and Rudd, Chris (Eds.). *State and Economy in New Zealand (Oxford Readings in New Zealand Politics)*. Oxford University Press, 1993.

Sandrey, R., and Reynolds, R. *Farming Without Subsidies*. Wellington, Government Printer, 1990.

Savage, J., and Bollard, A. *Turning It Around: Closure and Revitalization in New Zealand Industry*. Auckland, Oxford University Press, 1990.

THE PACIFIC ISLANDS

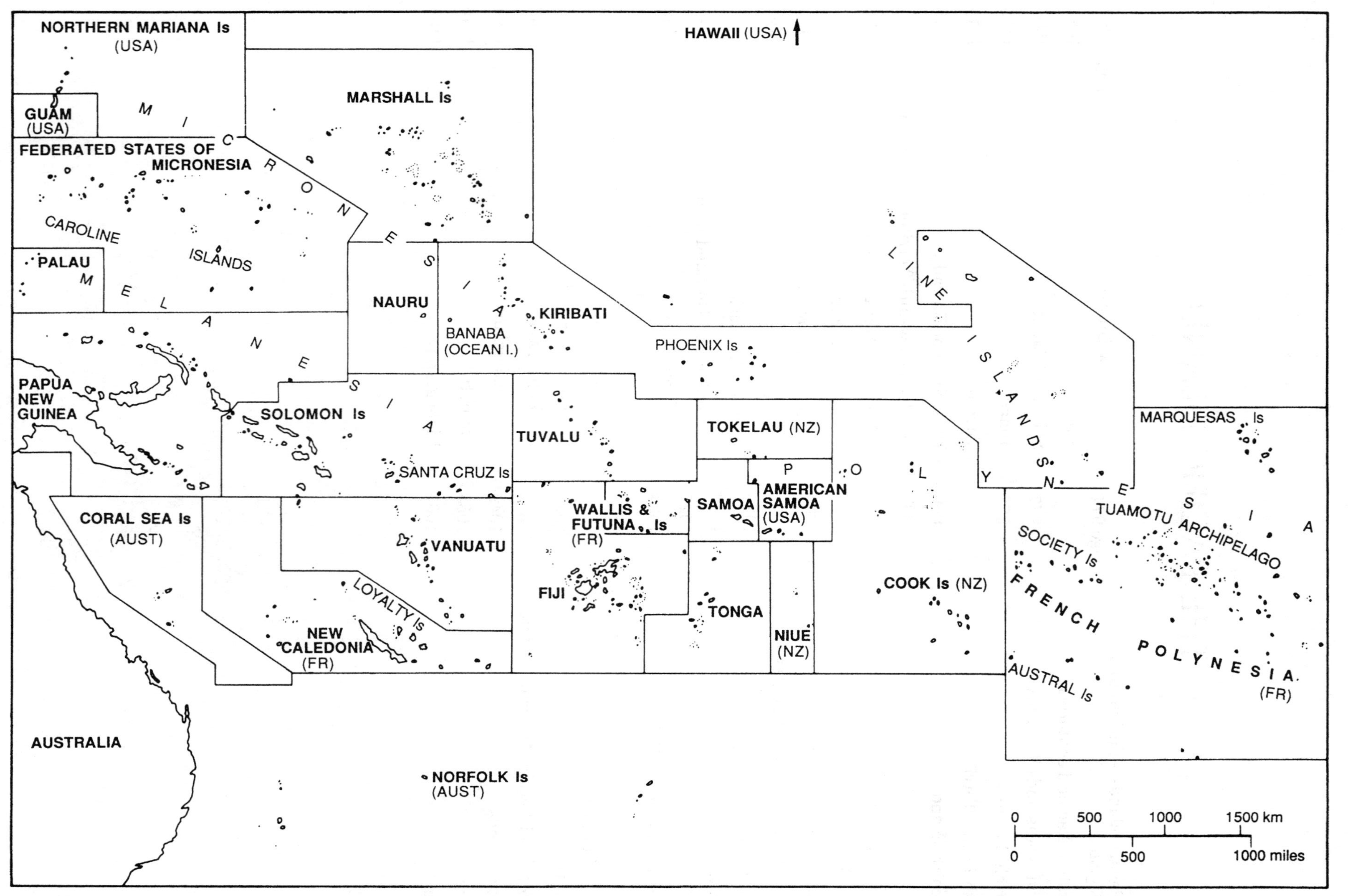

The Pacific Islands

THE PACIFIC ISLANDS

Background to the Region

BRYANT J. ALLEN

With subsequent revisions by JENNY J. BRYANT and the editorial staff

PHYSICAL AND SOCIAL GEOGRAPHY

The Pacific Ocean occupies a third of the earth's surface. Within it are located many thousands of islands, more than in all the rest of the world's seas combined. The large number of the Pacific islands, and their widespread distribution, gives rise to a great variety of physical, social and economic environments. Their location relative to the continents and larger islands that border the Pacific, which include North and South America, Japan, China, the Philippines, Indonesia, Australia and New Zealand, continues to influence political and economic conditions in them. Their small size and physical isolation have rendered them vulnerable to influences from the rest of the world. Rapid and often traumatic ecological, social, economic and political changes have occurred throughout the Pacific following penetration by European and Asian explorers and colonists, a process that is still under way, as improved communications and the neo-colonialism of mining, investment and tourism bring the area closer to the modern world.

A number of broad classifications of Pacific islands exist. The islands may be divided into continental islands, high islands, low islands and atolls. The people of the Pacific may be divided into Melanesians, Polynesians and Micronesians. Melanesians occupy the larger islands in the south-west, Papua (formerly Irian Jaya) and Papua New Guinea, Solomon Islands, Vanuatu, Fiji and New Caledonia. Polynesians live on islands that are located over an immense area from Hawaii in the north to Easter Island in the south-east to New Zealand in the south-west. In the central Pacific, Polynesians occupy the major groups of Tonga, Samoa, the Society Islands including Tahiti, and the Cook Islands, as well as numerous small atolls. The Micronesians live in the north, central and west Pacific in the Mariana, Caroline, Marshall, Gilbert (Tungaru), Phoenix and Line groups.

Physical Features

No agreement exists on the origin of the Pacific basin. One hypothesis suggests that the basin is the result of shrinkage and depression of the earth's crust, while another argues that the gradual expansion of the earth, the emergence of new rocks on the ocean floors and the drift of continental land masses on great plates, has created the great oceans of the world, of which the Pacific is the largest.

The physical features of the Pacific basin are better known. The basin is 4–6 km deep and roughly circular in shape. The boundary is, in most places, the continental margin, but elsewhere it is obscured in a jumble of island arcs and fragmented continental blocks. The northern half of the basin forms one relatively deep unit measuring 5–6 km deep, and the southern half another shallower one. The north is characterized by a number of enormous volcanoes and numerous clusters of smaller ones. The crust here is broken by very long faults. The south is deformed by a series of very long broad arches or rises with associated block and wrench faulting. Island arcs and deep trenches occur along the margins of the basins and parallel to them, archipelagos of volcanic islands and clusters of submarine volcanoes occur in all parts of the basins but most are in the west and south-west.

These structures give rise to a number of characteristic island types. West of the so-called 'andesite-line', representing the furthest eastward limit of the continental blocks of Asia and Australia, are islands formed on the broken edges of the continental blocks. These continental islands have foundations of ancient folded and metamorphosed sediments which have been intruded by granites. Vulcanism has overlaid these rocks with lavas, tuff and ash, and transgressions by the ocean have laid down softer and younger marine sediments. Erosion has resulted in plains, deltas and swamps along the modern coastline. New Guinea (comprising Papua New Guinea, Papua and surrounding islands) is the best example of these continental islands; it is dominated by a massive central cordillera within which lie dissected and flat-floored montane valleys. The highest peak in the island is over 5,000 m. Active volcanoes exist along the north coast and in the New Guinea islands. North and south of the central mountains are broken hills and vast swamps. The coastal pattern is one of small coastal plains alternating with low river terraces, high marine terraces, coastal hills and steep mountain slopes plunging straight into the sea. The largest rivers of all the Pacific islands are found here. The River Fly is navigable by motorized vessels for about 800 km and the Sepik for 500 km. Other continental islands are Fiji, Solomon Islands, Vanuatu and New Caledonia.

The high islands of the central Pacific are composed almost entirely of volcanic materials, together with reef limestone and recent sediments. The islands are the peaks of the largest volcanoes in the world. The Hawaiian volcano of Mauna Loa, for example, rises 9 km from the ocean floor and is over 200 km in diameter. Characteristic landforms of the high islands are striking peak and valley forms, with old volcanic cores often eroded to form fantastic skylines. Waterfalls, cliff faces and narrow beaches, with fringing coral reefs, complete the pattern. High islands in the Pacific include Hawaii, the Samoas, Tahiti and the Marquesas, Rarotonga in the Cook Islands, Pohnpei in the Eastern Carolines and the Northern Mariana Islands.

Low islands are of two types: some are volcanic islands which have been eroded, while others are raised atolls, which resemble sea-level reefs, but which are now elevated above modern sea-level. Caves and sinkholes occur widely. Small pockets of soil occur within the limestone rocks. Surface water is uncommon. Examples of low volcanic islands include Aitutaki, in the Cook Islands, and Wallis Island. Raised coral islands include some of the islands of the Tuamotu, Society, Cook, Line, Tokelau, Marshall, Caroline and Kiribati groups. Low islands with raised reefs are also common. One of the best examples is Mangaia in the Southern Cook group, which has a central core of volcanic rock 180 m high surrounded by an unbroken 1 km-wide band of coral limestone raised 70 m above the present sea-level. A new fringing reef now surrounds the island.

The atolls are the fourth island form, roughly circular reefs of coral limestone, partly covered by sea water, on which there are small islands made up of accumulations of limestone debris, and within each of which there occurs a lagoon of calm water. Atoll islets are commonly less than 3 m above the high-tide level. It is generally agreed that atolls have developed on the tops of volcanoes, which now no longer protrude above sea-level. Atolls vary in size from Rose Island (American Samoa), an atoll about 3 km by 3 km, to the Kwajalein Atoll in the Marshall Islands which is over 60 km long. Sources of fresh water are rain and a freshwater lens which is frequently found floating on salt groundwater beneath the islets. Hurricanes and typhoons frequently sweep over atolls, partially or completely submerging islets.

Climate

Five atmospheric circulation regions have been identified in the Pacific. A middle latitude area is characterized by the occurrence of extra-tropical cyclones with characteristic distinctive frontal weather systems. The Marianas and the western Hawaiian Islands sometimes receive this type of weather in the northern winter. The trade winds regions, where at least 60% of prevailing winds are from the north-west in the northern hemisphere and the south-east in the southern hemisphere, lie in an arc from the west coast of Mexico through Hawaii to the Marshall Islands in the north, and from the west coast of South America across the Marquesas and Tuamotus to the Society Islands. In these areas distinct wet and dry zones appear on larger islands, Hawaii being a good example. The monsoon area occurs to the far west and influences few of the Pacific Islands. The weather of Papua New Guinea is influenced, however, and a wet season and a dry season are distinguishable, although they are by no means as sharp as the term 'monsoon' implies. A doldrums area occurs in a poorly-defined band south of the Equator in an arc extending east from Solomon Islands to the Phoenix Islands. Finally, a hurricane zone exists in the northern Pacific in an arc extending west from Panama and including the Marshall, Caroline and Mariana Islands. A similar zone occurs in the south extending from the Tuamotus west across the Cooks, the Samoas, Tonga and Fiji to the north-east Australian coast. Serious cyclonic storm damage is sometimes incurred. Cyclone Ofa, one of the most severe of the century, occurred in February 1990, causing devastation in Niue, Samoa, Tokelau and Tuvalu.

Rainfall in the Pacific is geographically most variable; some islands are semi-arid while others are very wet. In the northern Pacific, for example, Midway receives a mean annual rainfall of 1,194 mm and Honolulu 550 mm. Further south Yap receives 3,023 mm, Palau 3,900 mm, Pohnpei 4,700 mm and Fanning 2,054 mm. Islands in the eastern Pacific near the Equator are frequently barren. Rainfall decreases from west to east along the Equator: Nauru receives 2,050 mm, Ocean Island (Banaba) 1,930 mm and Christmas Island (Kiritimati) 950 mm. Further south in an arc extending east from New Guinea to the Society Islands in the Central Pacific average annual rainfall varies from between 3,500 mm in the west to 2,000 mm in the east. In Papua New Guinea altitude and local relief influence climate. Areas exposed to the north-west and south-east winds receive over 5,000 mm of rain, while inland areas cut off from moist air masses may receive less than 1,500 mm. On the south-eastern coast, east and west of Port Moresby, average annual rainfall is less than 1,000 mm.

The predictions of climate change and the possibility of rising sea-levels could have devastating consequences for the low-lying islands of the Pacific. Even a half-a-metre rise in sea-level would mean the flooding of territories such as the Tokelau group of atolls, Tuvalu, the Marshall Islands and parts of Kiribati. On high islands, arable low-lying land would also be lost. The effects of this on population migration, both within and outside the Pacific, need to be planned for. In addition, the salinization of soil and drinking water, the changing environment for the practice of subsistence agriculture, the likelihood of more frequent and intense cyclones, the pressure on land, and consequently the political implications for the region, constitute major threats to the Pacific islands.

Soils, Minerals, Vegetation

Geology, soil, altitude, land-forms, location and climate are all combined in the creation of the widely varying physical environments of Pacific islands. Continental islands exhibit the widest range of environments, from high alpine grasslands, through montane forest and lowland rain forest to savannah and mangrove swamps. They also contain the richest deposits of minerals: nickel, chrome and manganese are mined in New Caledonia, gold and copper in New Guinea. The high volcanic islands contain no known minerals of commercial value. A rich source of minerals with potential for future exploitation are the deep-sea manganese nodules (containing copper, nickel and cobalt), which have been found in the north and south-west Pacific. Terrain is frequently a limit to cultivation, although soils are in general heavily leached and of low fertility, with low mineral and humus content. Raised coral islands lack groundwater and soils are shallow and often scattered in pockets. Phosphate deposits are mined from the coralline limestone on Nauru and Banaba (Ocean Island), and were formerly mined on Makatea in the Society Islands. The atolls contain only sparse resources. Soil development is often nil, fresh water difficult to obtain and foodplants other than coconuts and pandanus nuts difficult to cultivate. Special techniques are used to cultivate taro, but storms or high sea-levels frequently destroy gardens. The atolls provide the most tenuous existence for man in the Pacific.

The flora and fauna of the Pacific islands are unbalanced in comparison with those of the continents in that many major categories of plants have not reached the islands. A few ancestral immigrants have given rise to the entire endemic biota. Lack of ecological competition appears to have resulted in genera developing many more species than plants on continental land masses have been able to produce.

Prehistory, Culture and Early Society

The continental and oceanic Pacific islands were never linked by land bridges to the Asian continent and the Indonesian islands east of Bali and west of New Guinea form a frontier zone between a realm of placental mammals and marsupial mammals, the Wallace Line. Many palaeanthropologists argue therefore that man, a placental mammal, is an intruder in the Pacific. The first men to immigrate across the Wallace Line are believed to have been *Homo sapiens* approaching the modern form. The people of the interior of New Guinea are classified as Australoid populations, which are thought to have begun moving into the area more than 40,000 years ago. Recent archaeological discoveries in Papua New Guinea have been dated as 38,000 years old, and evidence of agricultural activity more than 9,000 years ago exists in the central highlands. Archaeological evidence indicates that the Pacific islands east of the Bismarck Archipelago were devoid of human settlement until about 3000 BC. Between 4,000 and 2,000 years ago, people who are thought to have lived in north-eastern Indonesia and the Philippines, and who had descended from a Mongoloid stock, spread into the Pacific and along the coasts of the continental islands, intermarrying with the existing Australoid populations of eastern Indonesia and New Guinea. Modern Melanesians, Polynesians and Micronesians are thus, to varying degrees, the outcome of the mixing of these early Australoid and Mongoloid stocks.

Therefore, the Melanesians who inhabit the island chains from Solomon Islands eastwards to Fiji are basically an Australoid group, while the Fijians are a more intermediate group. Polynesians tend towards the Mongoloid end of the continuum and Micronesians more so. The actual pattern, however, is far more complex than this simple description.

Origins of the three groups may also be evidenced in their cultures. The Polynesians are culturally and linguistically the most homogenous. Polynesian societies are basically patrilineal and genealogically ranked, with elaborate hierarchical systems of rank and class, best developed on the Hawaiian, Tongan and Society Islands. Micronesian societies are mainly matrilineal, with the exception of those in Yap and Kiribati. Melanesia is culturally the most diverse area of all. Hereditary ranking occurs in Fiji, but in many areas, especially in Papua New Guinea, status is achieved rather than inherited. Most groups are patrilineal, but matrilineal societies occur in New Guinea, Solomon Islands and Vanuatu.

Throughout the Pacific, the pre-contact subsistence economy was based on the vegetative propagation of root and tree crops, together with fishing and some pig husbandry and hunting. The only domesticated animals were dogs, pigs and fowls, but all three were not present everywhere in the region. The major root crops, taro and yam, have Asian origins, but one, the sweet potato, which was grown in New Guinea and in the Hawaii, Marquesas, Society and Easter Island groups prior to European contact, has a South American origin. Shifting cultivation was the main agricultural technique in most areas, although the intensity of land use and the periodicity of cycles varied widely in relation to population densities. In New Caledonia and parts of Polynesia, notably Hawaii, Tahiti and the Cook Islands, taro was cultivated in relatively elaborate, terraced, irrigated gardens.

Short-distance ocean voyaging was well-established in Polynesia and Micronesia before European contact, with large double-hulled canoes and navigation based on stars, wave patterns, bird flights and inherited geographical knowledge. Large ocean-going and coastal canoes were also used in Papua New Guinea and Fiji.

About 1,200 different languages, and many more dialects, are spoken in the Pacific islands, some 750 being found in Papua

New Guinea alone. They belong to two groups, the non-Austronesian phyla found in Papua New Guinea (and in scattered pockets in Indonesia), and the Austronesian phyla, which are spoken in coastal Papua New Guinea, most of island Melanesia, all of Polynesia and Micronesia (as well as in parts of Indonesia, the Philippines, South-East Asia and Madagascar).

To summarize, existing evidence suggests that Papua New Guinea was already settled over 30,000 years ago by ancestral Australoid populations who were followed about 3,000 years ago by Austronesian speakers of Mongoloid stock who probably brought pottery, horticulture and pigs to Papua New Guinea. Intermixing occurred, followed by further movements east to New Caledonia and Vanuatu. Fiji was then settled by people who carried with them a pottery technology previously established in Papua New Guinea and islands to the east, and further movements into the Pacific Ocean took place. During the last 2,500 years further intermixing has occurred in Melanesia while Polynesian and Micronesian populations have had less interaction.

Population and Socio-Economic Characteristics

The 22 countries and territories of the region encompassed by the Pacific Community had an estimated population of 7,605,100 at mid-2000; some 63% of that total were found in Papua New Guinea, which includes the eastern part of New Guinea, the second largest island in the world. Of the remaining 2,814,300, some 74% resided in Fiji, Solomon Islands, French Polynesia, New Caledonia, Samoa and Vanuatu. The remaining 15 states together had less than 10% of the region's inhabitants. The 22 countries and territories occupy about 550,000 sq km of land in 30m. sq km of ocean.

The rate of increase in the population of Pacific nations is near the average for developing countries (around 2.0% per year), but there are variations among states. For example, in the mid-1990s Solomon Islands and the Marshall Islands had population growth rates of more than 3.5% per year. In islands with apparently lower growth rates, natural increase is partly offset by out-migration to the Pacific rim nations of New Zealand, Australia and the USA. A feature of the Polynesian Pacific, in particular, is that about 300,000 islanders reside in the metropolitan rim countries, where they seek employment, education and generally better standards of living.

Pacific countries are becoming increasingly urbanized, with, for example, 46% of Fiji's population in mid-2000, and more than 24% of the population in most other countries, residing in urban areas. The associated problems of overcrowding, housing shortages, the widening economic gap between rural and urban areas, environmental pressures and the need for economic diversification are facing all Pacific nations in the 1990s.

Many of the Pacific countries have a narrow resource base and limited arable land. Those that do possess more diverse resources, such as minerals and the possibilities of plantation agriculture, have frequently suffered over-exploitation of resources, political turmoil and dislocation of the populations. The susceptibility of the small island nations to cyclones, droughts or the possible impacts of climatic change and rising sea-levels make them particularly vulnerable. Future sustainable and carefully-managed development of the Pacific nations will need to involve a considerable degree of regional co-operation and co-ordinated policy, particularly as regards access to land and resources. Cordial relations with the metropolitan powers on the Pacific rim, to mitigate the impact of international economic and political changes, will also need to be maintained if the countries are to succeed as economically-viable nations. Although many of the countries are very small, some have extremely large exclusive economic zones (EEZs). For example, the EEZ of Kiribati, with a population of about 92,000 in 2000, covers 3,550,000 sq km of ocean, which, although used for fishing by local people, is also subject to major and lucrative fishing agreements with Pacific rim powers. Throughout the Pacific the ocean floor is being explored for mineral resources (fuel and manganese).

Agriculture and Employment

Most Pacific countries have depended on mixed subsistence cultivation of coconuts, root crops (taro, sweet potatoes and cassava) and a large number of other tree and leaf crops. Cash-cropping has become a major part of the agricultural sector, with the introduction of oil palm, coffee, cocoa, rice, sugar cane, pumpkins, ginger and nuts, as well as commercial exploitation of crops that are also grown for subsistence purposes, such as taro, pineapples and papayas (pawpaws). Pacific island nations are increasingly dependent upon imported foodstuffs, and the declining nutritional levels of the population reflect this change.

The majority of the Pacific islands' labour force continues to be employed in the agricultural sector, with the next largest employer being the government/administrative sector. Service employment is increasing, particularly in Fiji, where tourism is second to sugar in the provision of the nation's gross domestic product. Manufacturing employs only a small proportion of the Pacific labour force, although this is increasing as countries move to industrialize.

Income, Education and Literacy

The average annual income per caput of Pacific islanders in the mid-1990s was around US $1,000. The phosphate island of Nauru, however, has an average of some US $7,000, and in Kiribati and Tuvalu the annual income per caput is only about US $700. French and US territories are generally more prosperous and well provided with services, although they are experiencing increasing social problems (annual average income per head in French Polynesia and New Caledonia was some US $16,000 in 1992). While levels of primary school enrolment and literacy appear to be high in the Pacific (mostly more than 90% of the adult population being literate and more than 80% of the relevant group attending primary school), there is evidence that these ratios have been declining in recent years, with increasing inequalities appearing, partly as a result of rapid urban development, the decreases in world commodity prices, the shift towards more industrial-based economies and the declining ability of governments to satisfy demands for more urban services.

POLITICAL DEVELOPMENTS

The islands may be divided into politically dependent and independent states. Dependent states governed wholly or partially by colonial administrations include the Pitcairn Islands (the United Kingdom); Wallis and Futuna (France); and Hawaii, a state of the USA. Other dependent states are internally self-governing and include Tokelau, the Cook Islands and Niue (New Zealand); Norfolk Island (Australia); French Polynesia (France); and the Northern Mariana Islands, Guam and American Samoa (USA).

Former dependencies that have achieved full political independence are Samoa, formerly Western Samoa (from New Zealand in 1962); Nauru (from the United Nations and Australia in 1968); Tonga (from the UK in 1970); Fiji (from the UK in 1970); Papua New Guinea (from Australia in 1975); Tuvalu (from the UK in 1978); Solomon Islands (from the UK in 1978); Kiribati (from the UK in 1979); and Vanuatu (from the UK and France in 1980). The Federated States of Micronesia and the Marshall Islands achieved independence from the USA when the Compact of Free Association took effect in 1991. Palau, the last remaining component of the Trust Territory of the Pacific Islands, achieved independence under a similar agreement in October 1994. The political future of the region's dependent territories was considered in a UN report on decolonization, compiled in 1996, which particularly focused on the status of New Caledonia, Tokelau and Guam. In the late 1990s there were moves towards full autonomy by both New Caledonia and French Polynesia. In 1998 France and New Caledonia signed the Nouméa Accord, which provided for the gradual transfer of powers to local authorities over the next 15 to 20 years. As part of these changes, in 1999 New Caledonia acquired the status of an 'overseas country'. Papua (formerly Irian Jaya), the western half of the island of New Guinea, is a province of Indonesia and is not considered in this section; New Zealand and the Philippines are also excluded.

REGIONAL ORGANIZATIONS

In 1947 the South Pacific Commission (SPC) was established by the United Kingdom, France, the USA, New Zealand, Australia and the Netherlands. Its aim was to 'promote the economic and social welfare and advancement of the peoples of the region', although commentators feel that it was more a move by Australia and New Zealand to extend their power and to deter others from obtaining a foothold, and it was obvious that organizations such as the SPC served the interests of the metropolitan powers.

In 1950 the South Pacific Conference was established as a separate body for the island nations. The moves towards independence for the island nations in the 1960s and 1970s challenged the role of the South Pacific Conference, which was still controlled by the metropolitan powers. This was most evident in the debates over nuclear testing in the Pacific during 1970, when the French delegation walked out of a meeting of the South Pacific Commission. In 1971 the South Pacific Forum (SPF) was established.

In May 1997 members of the South Pacific Commission voted to change the name of the organization to reflect the expanded membership of the group. The change to Pacific Community was approved at a meeting of the South Pacific Conference which took place in October 1997, and became effective in February 1998.

Pacific Islands Forum

The Pacific Islands Forum (PIF—which changed its name from the South Pacific Forum in 2000) has become the most important regional organization in the Pacific region, enabling Pacific nations to work towards and foster regional responses to a number of economic, social and political issues which, because of the isolation, distance and small populations of the Pacific nations, might otherwise be ineffectively managed. The PIF comprises the heads of government of the independent and self-governing island countries, as well as Australia and New Zealand. The Forum is a political body, which can raise and discuss any issue. The organization has an administrative, research and development arm, the Pacific Islands Forum Secretariat (called the South Pacific Bureau for Economic Co-operation (SPEC) until 1988 and the South Pacific Forum Secretariat until 2000). There are 16 members, the most recent entrant being Palau, which joined in September 1995. In addition, there are nine dialogue partners, including Malaysia, which acquired the status in January 1997. In October 1994 the South Pacific Forum (SPF—as it then was) was granted observer status at the UN General Assembly. In July 1997 the first annual SPF economy ministers' meeting was convened in Cairns, Australia, to provide a specific forum for the discussion of regional economic issues, and particularly of proposals for increased trade liberalization (a process begun in late 1995). However, relations between the host country and other SPF members were seriously damaged when a confidential briefing paper intended for Australian ministers attending the conference was unofficially disclosed. The Australian Government tried to distance itself from the document, which contained insulting remarks about numerous Pacific island leaders, by stating that it had been written by junior officials. Relations between Australia and the other SPF members were further undermined at the SPF summit meeting in the following month over the issue of climate change (see below). At the following year's meeting ministers further discussed trade liberalization and the impact of the Asian economic crisis on the region.

The 31st summit in October 2000 in Kiribati saw the official launch of the organization's new title of 'Pacific Islands Forum', which aimed to reflect the group's expanding membership. At this meeting negotiations for a Pacific regional trade agreement, which had been the subject of discussions for several years, were formally initiated. Convening in Nauru in August 2001 for the 32nd summit meeting, nine regional leaders signed the newly-drafted Pacific Island Countries Trade Agreement. Leaders expressed environmental concerns regarding the delay in the implementation of the Kyoto Protocol and also the shipment of radioactive materials. The problem of international 'money-laundering' was also addressed. The 33rd summit meeting, held in Fiji in August 2002, focused on security issues. (See Regional Organizations for further details.)

Other Agreements

In 1981 a trade agreement was signed by Australia, New Zealand and the SPF countries. Known as the South Pacific Regional Trade and Economic Co-operation Agreement (SPARTECA), it was designed to ease import restrictions on island goods into Australia and New Zealand, in an attempt to adjust the massive trade imbalance that exists. On 1 January 1987 new terms of trade came into effect, whereby all duties and quotas on island imports were abolished, with the exception of those on garments, footwear, sugar, steel and motor vehicles. The disparities in size and economic power have presented an obstacle to SPARTECA. Fiji is generally considered to be benefiting from regional trade agreements to a greater extent than other, smaller nations which have fewer export resources.

Accusations of too great a role by New Zealand and Australia in the region's affairs have been an ongoing problem, particularly as Australia, in particular, did not assume a high profile in the workings of the SPF until the fourth meeting, when its Prime Minister attended for the first time.

In 1986 a five-year fisheries treaty was signed between the USA and members of the South Pacific Forum Fisheries Agency, bringing to a close a long-running dispute which had involved the capture and confiscation of US fishing boats by Papua New Guinea and Solomon Islands. The treaty guaranteed royalties of some US $60m., to be paid over a five-year period, and was renegotiated for a further 10 years in 1992. The fisheries treaty developed out of the lack of return Pacific countries were receiving for tuna taken by distant nations from their waters. The total access fees paid to all countries by the fishing nations were on average less than 3% of the annual market value of tuna caught in the region (which in the early 1990s was valued at some US $1,200m.). In June 1997 the members of the South Pacific Forum Fisheries Agency, together with representatives from several major fishing nations, signed the Majuro Declaration, which contained a commitment to introduce measures for the conservation and management of the region's migratory fish stocks. The South Pacific region was thought to be the only major fishing area in the world not to have adopted such an agreement already. The measures were to be implemented by June 2000. In mid-1999 plans by SPF countries to establish a fisheries commission were announced, in an effort to conserve tuna resources which, according to experts, could be depleted if not properly managed. These fears were confirmed by a report by the World Bank, which claimed that over-fishing posed a serious threat to many Pacific Island countries. In April of that year Micronesian countries announced that they were to sign an agreement which would provide for the joint monitoring of their EEZs, in an attempt to end illegal fishing.

During 1986 and 1987 continued discussions were held on the implications of the South Pacific Nuclear-Free Zone (SPNFZ) treaty, signed in 1985 by Australia, New Zealand, the Cook Islands, Fiji, Kiribati, Niue, Tuvalu and Western Samoa (now Samoa). (Vanuatu and Solomon Islands had refused to sign, on the grounds that the treaty's provisions were not far-reaching enough.) The treaty designates a 'nuclear-free zone' in the South Pacific, and imposes a ban on the manufacture, testing, storage and use of nuclear weapons, and the dumping of nuclear waste, in the region. Both the USSR and the People's Republic of China signed protocols attached to the treaty, but in 1987 the Governments of the USA and the United Kingdom rejected the South Pacific signatories' request for their endorsement of the treaty, a decision that provoked expressions of anger and concern from member countries of the SPF. Widespread protests against the French Government's programme of nuclear testing on Mururoa Atoll, in French Polynesia, continued in the early 1990s. In 1993 the French Government decided to continue the moratorium on testing, introduced in the previous year, for an indefinite period. However, shortly after his election in May 1995, President Chirac announced that France would resume nuclear testing, with a programme of eight tests (subsequently curtailed to six) commencing in September 1995. The decision provoked almost universal outrage in the international community, and was condemned for its apparent disregard for regional opinion, as well as for undermining the considerable progress made by Western nations towards a world-wide ban on nuclear testing. After its final test in January 1996, France signed the SPNFZ treaty, together with the United Kingdom and the USA, and was reinstated as a dialogue partner to the SPF (following its earlier suspension). In August 1998, at the annual summit meeting of the SPF, leaders urged former nuclear-testing nations (notably the United Kingdom, France and the USA) to accept liability for their actions in the region, and to award compensation to those affected.

The establishment of the Joint Commercial Commission in Hawaii in 1992 created greater opportunities for private-sector trade between the USA and the countries of the Pacific region.

In March 1993 several Pacific island nations with important tuna reserves signed the Palau Agreement, aimed at limiting the number of fishing vessels licensed to operate in the region.

Parties to the Nauru Agreement (a sub-group of the South Pacific Forum Fisheries Agency, comprising eight island nations) endorsed proposals for a comprehensive regional fisheries management policy in May 1996.

At a meeting in Hawaii in early 1996 representatives of the countries and territories of Micronesia formed the Council of Micronesian Government Executives. The new body aimed to facilitate discussion on economic developments in the region and to examine possibilities for reducing the considerable cost of shipping essential goods between the islands. In early 1997 the Council established a technical working group on fisheries management in the region.

Under the Cotonou Agreement, concluded in June 2000 by the EU and ACP states as a successor arrangement to the Lomé Convention, the eight Pacific ACP countries and the EU were to commence negotiations in September 2002 on a regional economic partnership agreement; this was to enter into effect by 2008 at the latest and would allow the EU increased access to the Pacific markets. However, representatives of the island nations were concerned that this could have implications for their countries' economies, as many of them are dependent on custom duties for their internal revenue.

At a meeting in Hawaii in mid-2000 a group of Pacific island nations began discussions on the possible establishment of a regional tuna commission.

SPREP and Other Environmental Issues

Of increasing significance in the region is the South Pacific Regional Environment Programme (SPREP). SPREP grew out of concern over environmental problems in the region voiced by the South Pacific Conference in the 1960s. In 1982 the South Pacific Commission, with support from the United Nations Environment Programme's Regional Seas Programme and the regional Governments, established SPREP at an intergovernmental conference held in Rarotonga, Cook Islands. SPREP operates on the basis of a Convention and several protocols, which required several rounds of meetings and conferences before they were adopted and ratified. In 1990 the SPREP Convention came into force when ratified by 10 countries. The Convention addresses the threat to marine and coastal environments from all types of pollution (including mining, oil spillages, dumping of toxic wastes and hazardous materials) and the need for co-operation to ensure sustainable resource management. The island Governments have remained firm in their demand for a prohibition of nuclear dumping and testing, but the final convention excludes a prohibition clause which is dealt with in the separate Nuclear-Free Zone Treaty (NFZT) banning radioactive waste dumping and testing. The SPREP Convention then allowed for full regional participation, including that of France and its territories.

The ratification of the Programme's Convention meant that SPREP became the recipient of a great deal of aid and assistance from bilateral funding agreements. The regional Governments participating in SPREP took the environmental concerns of the Pacific to the UN Conference on Environment and Development (UNCED), held in Brazil in June 1992, and to the third Conference of the Parties (COP) to the UN Framework Convention on Climate Change (UNFCCC), held in Kyoto, Japan, in December 1997. Prior to the fourth COP of the UNFCCC, held in Buenos Aires, Argentina, in November 1998, the SPREP published a report detailing the effects of global warming and climate change in the Pacific. The South Pacific delegations at the conference emphasized the need to ensure compliance with the Kyoto Protocol on the reduction of the emission of 'greenhouse gases'. A Pacific Islands Conference on Climate Change, Variability and Sea Level Rise was convened by SPREP in April 2000 at Rarotonga; the participating governments aimed to develop a regional strategic framework for action on climate change.

The South Pacific Sea Level and Climate Monitoring Project was launched in 1991 with Australian aid and aimed to allow 11 Pacific island nations to monitor the effects of climate change on their territory. In 2000 it was announced that the programme would be extended until 2006.

Controversy over Japan's hunting of whales for the purposes of 'scientific research' continued. At a meeting of the International Whaling Commission (IWC) in May 2002, for the fourth consecutive year Japan succeeded in defeating a proposal to establish a South Pacific Whale Sanctuary. Presented by Australia and New Zealand, the proposal was also supported by the PIF. A number of PIF members, however, including the Cook Islands, Niue and Papua New Guinea, had meanwhile established their own whale sanctuaries within their respective EEZs.

RECENT DEVELOPMENTS

Major social and political changes swept through the Pacific in the late 1980s and 1990s. In 1987 and 1988 violence in New Caledonia, by Melanesian Kanaks seeking independence from France, and two successful military coups in Fiji suggested fundamental political changes in the future of the Pacific. Racial tensions in Fiji, exacerbated by the success of an ethnic-Indian-led Government, culminated in violence and a coup in April 2000. In March 1988 Papua New Guinea, Solomon Islands and Vanuatu formed a 'Melanesian Spearhead Group', stressing that this was in no way a threat to the SPF. It has been seen, however, as a reaction to both the informal formation of a 'Polynesian Community', which has received overt and covert support from France, and to Australian and New Zealand disapproval of Vanuatu's links with Libya, now discontinued. The Melanesian group also supported more radical efforts on the part of the SPF towards the decolonization of French territories in the Pacific. In 1994 the group concluded a trade agreement regarded as a first step towards the establishment of a free-trade area by the three countries. In 1996 a fourth country, Fiji, was admitted to the group. In April 1991 Western Samoa (now Samoa) held its first election based on universal suffrage. In Papua New Guinea charges of major corruption in the forestry industry and the closure of the Bougainville copper mine, in addition to a major social crisis manifested in a breakdown of law and order, have made the future of the country as a resource-rich nation less stable. In Tonga, where demands for political reform were increasing, in the nine years to 1991 the country earned millions of dollars from the sales of its passports. Some of the sales proved to be illegal, and the money from those sales was missing.

Political and economic events in the region in the 1990s were increasingly influenced by environmental concerns. A sudden increase in unsustainable logging activity in the islands (most notably in Solomon Islands, Papua New Guinea and Vanuatu) led to the introduction of legislation aimed at restricting the number of licences issued to logging companies and the volume of timber exported. However, by 1995 many of the new regulations had been removed or relaxed, and logging had again reached unsustainable levels. At the SPF summit meeting in 1994 the exploitation of the region's natural resources, particularly its tropical forests, was the principal topic of debate. A draft code of conduct on logging was prepared in late 1994 by representatives from those member countries with a forestry industry. The proposed regulations were considered at the SPF summit in the following year, but the code was not signed until the 1996 meeting. In 1994 the World Bank had joined various environmental and political organizations in criticizing the Pacific islands, particularly Papua New Guinea and Solomon Islands, for placing insufficient importance on the conservation of their environment, particularly their tropical forests.

Meanwhile, proposals to establish a large-scale nuclear waste storage facility in the Marshall Islands provoked considerable controversy among environmentalists and neighbouring Pacific islands during 1994. Moreover, Japanese shipments of plutonium, which passed within the maritime boundaries of several Pacific islands during the 1990s, caused widespread concern in the region. Most controversial, however, was President Chirac's decision in mid-1995 to resume France's nuclear-testing programme on Mururoa Atoll, French Polynesia. The announcement led to angry demonstrations throughout the region, which intensified when French commandos violently seized *Rainbow Warrior II*, the flagship of the environmentalist group Greenpeace, and its crew, which had been protesting peacefully near the test site. Following the sixth and final test in early 1996, the French Government, which had attracted almost universal criticism for its actions, initiated a series of measures aimed at improving relations with the Pacific islands, including the doubling of its aid budget to the region.

The increasing impact of the 'greenhouse effect' (the heating of the earth's atmosphere as a consequence of pollution) on the Pacific islands has continued to cause concern in the region. As well as the rise in sea-levels, with its implications for the continued habitability of many low-lying atolls, the phenomenon was also thought to be responsible for a dramatic increase in the frequency of cyclones, tidal waves and other associated natural disasters in the region. The issue dominated the 28th SPF summit meeting in August 1997 and provoked an unprecedented rift within the group when Australia refused to support recommended reductions in the emission of pollutant gases known to contribute to the 'greenhouse effect'. In mid-1999 the SPREP announced that two uninhabited islands in Kiribati had disappeared beneath the sea as a result of rising sea-levels. This followed severe flooding and coastal erosion in Kiribati, Tuvalu and the Marshall Islands. Following the USA's decision in April 2001 to reject the Kyoto Protocol, in March 2002 Kiribati and Tuvalu announced their decision to take legal action against the USA.

Tourism remains vitally important to the Pacific islands' economy. In 1993, when 745,000 tourists visited the region, the industry earned US $658.4m. (equivalent to 24.6% of the value of total regional exports) and employed some 50,000 people directly and indirectly. By 1998 the annual total of tourists visiting the region had increased to 967,600, and tourism earned the region some US $1,100m. However, the growth of the industry on many islands is restricted by limited infrastructure and inadequate transport facilities, whereas in those countries that have experienced a rapid expansion in tourist arrivals, damage to the environment has often resulted. Consequently, in many islands the development of 'eco-tourism', which encourages the conservation and appreciation of the natural environment, is being explored as a more sustainable alternative to traditional tourism. The South Pacific Tourism Organization (formerly the Tourism Council of the South Pacific) has focused attention on the problems affecting the industry, including the shortage of hotel accommodation in the region and the paucity of regular air services. The industry was seriously affected by the Asian economic crisis of the late 1990s and again by the repercussions of the terrorist attacks on the USA in September 2001.

The economic development of much of the region, particularly the smaller islands, has been impeded by the lack of efficient communications. Regional airlines have often suffered from problems relating to the islands' small size and populations, their remoteness and the frequent inability of their Governments to subsidize unprofitable routes. In an attempt to address this problem, SPF member nations commissioned a report in 1995 on the possible rationalization of regional air services and established a regular Forum Aviation Policy Meeting. At a meeting of the group in May 1998 representatives adopted a policy framework to manage the region's airspace as a unified area and to replace the numerous bilateral agreements between countries with an integrated regional aviation plan, with the possible establishment of a single aviation market among SPF members.

The development of 'offshore' financial services throughout the region during the 1990s represented an important new source of revenue for the islands. However, repeated accusations that these services were being targeted by criminal organizations for the processing of funds from their illegal activities (most significantly the illicit drugs trade) led to problems in the establishment of the industry and prompted the introduction of new legislation throughout much of the region from 2000. In 2002 a number of Pacific islands remained on the list of non co-operative countries and territories drawn up the Paris-based Financial Action Task Force (FATF) on Money Laundering (established in 1989 on the recommendation of the Group of Seven (G-7) industrialized nations) or on the list of unco-operative tax havens maintained by the Organisation for Economic Co-operation and Development (OECD). The licensing of internet services and the sale of website domain names was also becoming an increasingly important source of revenue for the Pacific islands in the late 1990s and early 2000s.

Australian Pacific Territories

There are two external dependencies or Territories of the Commonwealth of Australia in the Pacific Ocean: the Coral Sea Islands Territory and Norfolk Island. The Minister for Territories is responsible for the administration of the dependencies, which lie within the jurisdiction of the Commonwealth Government.

Head of State: HM Queen ELIZABETH II (succeeded to the throne 6 February 1952).
Governor-General: Dr PETER J. HOLLINGWORTH (assumed office 29 June 2001).
Department of Transport and Regional Services with responsibility for Territories and Local Government: GPOB 594, Canberra, ACT 2601, Australia; tel. (2) 6274-7612; fax (2) 6274-7706; internet www.dotrs.gov.au.
Minister for Regional Services, Territories and Local Government: WILSON TUCKEY.

CORAL SEA ISLANDS TERRITORY

The Coral Sea Islands became a Territory of the Commonwealth of Australia under the Coral Sea Islands Act of 1969. The Territory lies east of Queensland, between the Great Barrier Reef and longitude 156° 06′E, and between latitude 12°S and 24°S, and comprises several islands and reefs. The islands are composed largely of sand and coral, and have no permanent fresh water supply, but some have a cover of grass and scrub. The area has been known as a notorious hazard to shipping since the 19th century, the danger of the reefs being compounded by shifting sand cays and occasional tropical cyclones. The Coral Sea Islands have been acquired by Australia by numerous acts of sovereignty since the early years of the 20th century.

Spread over a sea area of approximately 780,000 sq km (300,000 sq miles), all the islands and reefs in the Territory are very small, totalling only a few sq km of land area. They include Cato Island, Chilcott Islet in the Coringa Group, and the Willis Group. In 1997 the Coral Sea Islands Act was amended to include Elizabeth and Middleton Reefs. A meteorological station, operated by the Commonwealth Bureau of Meteorology and with a staff of four, has provided a service on one of the Willis Group since 1921. The other islands are uninhabited. There are eight automatic weather stations (on Cato Island, Flinders Reef, Frederick Reef, Holmes Reef, Lihou Reef, Creal Reef, Marion Reef and Gannet Cay) and several navigation aids distributed throughout the Territory.

The Act constituting the Territory did not establish an administration on the islands, but provides means of controlling the activities of those who visit them. The Lihou Reef and Coringa-Herald National Nature Reserves were established in 1982 to provide protection for the wide variety of terrestrial and marine wildlife, which include rare species of birds and sea turtles (one of which is the largest, and among the most endangered, of the world's species of sea turtle). The Australian Government has concluded agreements for the protection of endangered and migratory birds with Japan and the People's Republic of China. The Governor-General of Australia is empowered to make ordinances for the peace, order and good government of the Territory and, by ordinance, the laws of the Australian Capital Territory apply. The Supreme Court and Court of Petty Sessions of Norfolk Island have jurisdiction in the Territory. The Territory is administered by a parliamentary secretary appointed by the Minister for Regional Services, Territories and Local Government, and the area is visited regularly by the Royal Australian Navy.

NORFOLK ISLAND

Physical and Social Geography

Norfolk Island lies off the eastern coast of Australia, about 1,400 km east of Brisbane, to the south of New Caledonia and 640 km north of New Zealand. The Territory also comprises uninhabited Phillip Island and Nepean Island, 7 km and 1 km south of the main island respectively. Norfolk Island is hilly and fertile, with a coastline of cliffs and an area of 34.6 sq km (13.4 sq miles). It is about 8 km long and 4.8 km wide. The climate is mild and subtropical, and the average annual rainfall is 1,350 mm, most of which occurs between May and August. The resident population numbered 2,037 at the census of August 2001, and consists of 'islanders' (descendants of the mutineers from HMS *Bounty*, evacuated from Pitcairn Island, who numbered 824 in 1996) and 'mainlanders' (originally from Australia, New Zealand or the United Kingdom). English is the official language, but a Norfolk Island dialect (a mixture of old English and Tahitian) is also spoken. The capital of the Territory is Kingston.

History

The island was uninhabited when discovered in 1774 by a British expedition, led by Capt. James Cook. Norfolk Island was used as a penal settlement from 1788 to 1814 and again from 1825 to 1855, when it was abandoned. In 1856 it was resettled by 194 emigrants from Pitcairn Island, which had become overpopulated. Norfolk Island was administered as a separate colony until 1897, when it became a dependency of New South Wales. In 1913 control was transferred to the Australian Government.

Under the Norfolk Island Act 1979, Norfolk Island is progressing to responsible legislative and executive government, enabling it to manage its own affairs to the greatest practicable extent. Wide powers are exercised by the nine-member Legislative Assembly and by the Executive Council, comprising the executive members of the Legislative Assembly who have ministerial-type responsibilities. The Act preserves the Australian Government's responsibility for Norfolk Island as a Territory under its authority, with the Minister for Territories as the responsible minister. The Act indicated that consideration would be given within five years to an extension of the powers of the Legislative Assembly and the political and administrative institutions of Norfolk Island. In 1985 legislative and executive responsibility was assumed by the Norfolk Island Government for public works and services, civil defence, betting and gaming, territorial archives and matters relating to the exercise of executive authority. In 1988 further amendments empowered the Legislative Assembly to select a Norfolk Island Government Auditor (territorial accounts were previously audited by the Commonwealth Auditor-General). The office of Chief Minister was replaced by that of the President of the Legislative Assembly. David Ernest Buffett was reappointed to this post following the May 1992 general election. A lack of consensus among members of the Executive Council on several major issues prompted early legislative elections in April 1994. The newly-elected Legislative Assembly was remarkable in having three female members. Following elections in April 1997, in which 22 candidates contested the nine seats, George Smith was appointed President (subsequently reverting to the title of Chief Minister) of the eighth Legislative Assembly. At legislative elections in February 2000 three new members were elected to the Assembly, and Ronald Nobbs was subsequently appointed Chief Minister. Geoffrey Gardner, hitherto Minister for Health, replaced Nobbs as Chief Minister following the elections of November 2001. The incoming Assembly included four new members.

In December 1991 a referendum took place at which a proposal by the Australian Government to include Norfolk Island within the Australian federal electorate was overwhelmingly rejected by the islanders. The outcome of the poll led the Australian Government, in June 1992, to announce that it had abandoned the plans. Similarly, in late 1996 a proposal by the Australian Government to combine Norfolk Island's population with that of Canberra for record-keeping purposes was strongly opposed by the islanders.

In late 1997 the Legislative Assembly debated the issue of increased self-determination for the island. Pro-independence supporters argued that the Territory could generate sufficient income by exploiting gas- and oilfields in the island's exclusive economic zone.

In August 1998 a referendum proposing that the Norfolk Island electoral system be integrated more closely with that of mainland Australia (initiated by the Minister for Regional Development, Territories and Local Government) was rejected by 78% of the Territory's electorate. A similar referendum in May 1999 was opposed by 73% of voters.

Frustration with the Australian Government's perceived reluctance to facilitate the transfer of greater powers to the Territory (as outlined in the Norfolk Island Act of 1979, see above) led the island's Legislative Assembly in mid-1999 to vote by seven members to one in favour of full internal self-government. Negotiations regarding the administration of crown land on the island, which continued in 2000, were seen as indicative of the islanders' determination to pursue greater independence from Australia.

In April 2002 a hotel worker from Sydney, Australia, was murdered. This was the first murder to occur on Norfolk Island in more than 150 years. As part of its investigation, the police force took fingerprints of the entire adult population in August. In the same month a referendum was due to be held as to whether to allow the operation of mobile telephones on the island.

Economy

Despite the island's natural fertility, agriculture is no longer the principal economic activity. About 400 ha of land are arable. The main crops are Kentia palm seed, cereals, vegetables and fruit. Cattle and pigs are farmed for domestic consumption. Development of a fisheries industry is restricted by the lack of a harbour. Some flowers and plants are grown commercially. The administration is increasing the area devoted to Norfolk Island pine and hardwoods. Seed of the Norfolk Island pine is exported. Potential oil- and gas-bearing sites in the island's waters may provide a possible future source of revenue. A re-export industry has developed to serve the island's tourist industry. In early 1999 the Norfolk Island Legislative Assembly announced plans to seek assistance from the Australian Government to establish an offshore financial centre on the island.

In 2000/01 the cost of the island's imports totalled almost $A41.3m. (compared with $A59.1m. in 1999/2000), while revenue from exports amounted to $A2.7m. (compared with almost $A2.8m. in the previous year). Norfolk Island's trade is conducted mainly with Australia and New Zealand. Imports from Australia in 2000/01 cost $A19 (compared with almost $A23m. in the previous year). In 1999/2000 exports to Australia earned $A1m. but were negligible in 2000/01. In 1999/2000 imports from New Zealand totalled $A9.3m. (compared with $A9.0m. in 1998/99). The authorities receive revenue from customs duties (some $A3.9m., equivalent to 34.3% of total revenue in 2000/01) and the sale of postage stamps, but tourism is the island's main industry. In 2000/01 there were 40,221 tourist arrivals on the island. In 1985 and 1986 the Governments of Australia and Norfolk Island jointly established the 465-ha Norfolk Island National Park. This was to protect the remaining native forest, which is the habitat of several unique species of flora (including the largest fern in the world) and fauna (such as the Norfolk Island green parrot, the guavabird and the boobook owl). Conservation efforts include the development of Phillip Island as a nature reserve.

Statistical Survey

Source: The Administration of Norfolk Island, Administration Offices, Kingston, Norfolk Island 2899; tel. 22001; fax 23177; internet www.norfolk.gov.nf.

AREA AND POPULATION

Area: 34.6 sq km (13.3 sq miles).

Population: 2,181, including 409 visitors, at census of 6 August 1996; 2,601 (males 1,257, females 1,344), including 564 visitors, at census of 7 August 2001.

Density (2001): 75.2 per sq km.

Births, Marriages and Deaths (2000/01): Live births 17; Marriages 32 (1999/2000); Deaths 28.

Economically Active Population (persons aged 15 years and over, 2001 census): 1,609 (males 849, females 760).

FINANCE

Currency and Exchange Rates: Australian currency is used (see p. 118).

Budget (year ending 30 June 2001): Revenue $A11,499,600 (Customs duties $A3,948,541); Expenditure $A10,199,300 (Education $A1,846,000).

EXTERNAL TRADE

2000/01 (year ending 30 June): *Imports*: $A41,260,213, mainly from Australia and New Zealand. *Exports*: $A2,708,120.

Trade with Australia ($A million, 2000/01): *Imports* 19.

Trade with New Zealand ($NZ million, 2000/01): *Imports* 6.7; *Exports* 0.04.

TOURISM

Visitors (year ending 30 June): 36,514 in 1998/99; 38,298 in 1999/2000; 40,221 in 2000/01.

COMMUNICATIONS MEDIA

Radio Receivers (1996): 2,500 in use.

Television Receivers (1996): 1,200 in use.

Non-daily Newspaper (2002): 1 (estimated circulation 1,400).

EDUCATION

Institution (2002): 1 state school incorporating infant, primary and secondary levels.

Teachers (2001/02): 20.

Students (1999/2000): Infants 79; Primary 116; Secondary 119.

Directory

The Constitution

The Norfolk Island Act 1979 constitutes the administration of the Territory as a body politic and provides for a responsible legislative and executive system, enabling it to administer its own affairs to the greatest practicable extent. The preamble of the Act states that it is the intention of the Australian Parliament to consider the further extension of powers.

The Act provides for an Administrator, appointed by the Australian Government, who shall administer the government of Norfolk Island as a territory under the authority of the Commonwealth of Australia. The Administrator is required to act on the advice of the Executive Council or the responsible Commonwealth Minister in those matters specified as within their competence. Every proposed law passed by the Legislative Assembly must be effected by the assent of the Administrator, who may grant or withhold that assent, reserve the proposed law for the Governor-General's pleasure or recommend amendments.

The Act provides for the Legislative Assembly and the Executive Council, comprising the executive members of the Assembly who have ministerial-type responsibilities. The nine members of the Legislative Assembly are elected for a term of not more than three years under a cumulative method of voting: each elector is entitled to as many votes (all of equal value) as there are vacancies, but may not give more than four votes to any one candidate. The nine candidates who receive the most votes are declared elected.

The Government

The Administrator, who is the senior representative of the Commonwealth Government, is appointed by the Governor-General of Australia and is responsible to the Minister for Regional Services, Territories and Local Government. A form of responsible legislative and executive government was extended to the island in 1979, as outlined above.

Administrator: Anthony J. Messner (assumed office on 4 August 1997).

EXECUTIVE COUNCIL

(September 2002)

Chief Minister and Minister for Intergovernment Relations: Geoffrey R. Gardner.

Minister for Finance: Graeme Donaldson.

Minister for Tourism and Community Services: George Smith.

Minister for Land and the Environment: Ivens Buffett.

MINISTRIES

All Ministries are located at: Old Military Barracks, Kingston, Norfolk Island 2899; tel. 22003; fax 23378; e-mail executives@assembly.gov.nf.

GOVERNMENT OFFICES

Office of the Administrator: New Military Barracks, Norfolk Island 2899; tel. 22152; fax 22681.

Administration of Norfolk Island: Administration Offices, Kingston, Norfolk Island 2899; tel. 22001; fax 23177; e-mail rmurdoch@admin.gov.nf; all govt depts; CEO Robyn Murdoch.

Legislature

LEGISLATIVE ASSEMBLY

Nine candidates are elected for not more than three years. The most recent general election was held on 29 November 2001.

Speaker: DAVID ERNEST BUFFETT.

Deputy Speaker: CHLOE NICHOLAS.

Other Members: RONALD C. NOBBS, GEOFFREY R. GARDNER, IVENS BUFFETT, GEORGE SMITH, GRAEME DONALDSON, VICKY JACK, JOHN T. BROWN.

Judicial System

Supreme Court of Norfolk Island: Kingston; appeals lie to the Federal Court of Australia.

Chief Magistrate: RON CAHILL.

Judges: BRYAN ALAN BEAUMONT (Chief Justice), MURRAY RUTLEDGE WILCOX.

Religion

The majority of the population professes Christianity (70.4%, according to the census of 1996), with the principal denominations being the Church of England (38%), the Uniting Church (14%) and the Catholic Church (11%).

The Press

Norfolk Island Government Gazette: Kingston, Norfolk Island 2899; tel. 22001; fax 23177; weekly.

Norfolk Islander: Greenways Press, POB 150, Norfolk Island 2899; tel. 22159; fax 22948; f. 1965; e-mail news@islander.nf; weekly; Co-Editors TOM LLOYD, TIM LLOYD; circ. 1,350.

Broadcasting and Communications

TELECOMMUNICATIONS

Norfolk Telecom: Kingston; internet www.telecom.gov.nf; Man. KIM DAVIES.

BROADCASTING

Radio

Norfolk Island Broadcasting Service: New Cascade Rd, POB 456, Norfolk Island 2899; tel. 22137; fax 23298; e-mail 2niradio@ni.net.nf; internet www.users.nf/nfradio/; govt-owned; non-commercial; broadcasts 112 hours per week; relays television and radio programmes from Australia; Broadcast Man. MARGARET MEADOWS.

Radio VL2NI: New Cascade Rd, POB 456, Norfolk Island 2899; tel. 22137; fax 23298; e-mail 2niradio@ni.net.nf; internet www.users.nf/nfradio/.

Television

Norfolk Island Broadcasting Service: (see Radio).

Norfolk Island Television Service: f. 1987; govt-owned; relays programmes of Australian Broadcasting Corpn, Special Broadcasting Service Corpn and Central Seven TV by satellite.

TV Norfolk (TVN): locally-operated service featuring programmes of local events and information for tourists.

Finance

BANKING

Commonwealth Bank of Australia (Australia): Taylors Rd, Norfolk Island 2899; tel. 22144; fax 22805.

Westpac Banking Corpn Savings Bank Ltd (Australia): Burnt Pine, Norfolk Island 2899; tel. 22120; fax 22808.

Trade

Norfolk Island Chamber of Commerce Inc: POB 370, Norfolk Island 2899; tel. 22317; fax 23221; e-mail photopress@ni.net.nf; f. 1966; affiliated to the Australian Chamber of Commerce; 60 mems; Pres. GARY ROBERTSON; Sec. MARK MCGUIRE.

Transport

ROADS

There are about 100 km of roads, including 85 km of sealed road.

SHIPPING

Norfolk Island is served by the three shipping lines, Neptune Shipping, Pacific Direct Line and Roslyndale Shipping Company Pty Ltd. A small tanker from Nouméa (New Caledonia) delivers petroleum products to the island and another from Australia delivers liquid propane gas.

CIVIL AVIATION

Norfolk Island has one airport, with two runways (of 1,900 m and 1,550 m), capable of taking medium-sized jet-engined aircraft. Air New Zealand operates a twice-weekly direct service between Christchurch and Norfolk Island (via Auckland). Charter flights from Lord Howe Island and occasionally from New Caledonia also serve the island. The cessation of scheduled services from Australia by Ansett Australia in 1997 had an adverse effect on the island's important tourist industry. As a consequence, Norfolk Jet Express was established to provide a weekly service to Australia. In February 1999 Air Nauru began to operate a weekly charter flight service to Norfolk Island from Sydney, under contract with Norfolk Jet Express. In mid-2002 services from Brisbane and Sydney were also being provided by Alliance Airlines.

Tourism

Visitor arrivals totalled 40,221 in 2000/01.

Norfolk Island Visitors Information Centre: Taylors Rd, Burnt Pine, POB 211, Norfolk Island 2899; tel. 22147; fax 23109; e-mail info@norfolkisland.com.au; internet www.norfolkisland.com.au; Gen. Man. JOANNE LIBLINE.

Education

Education is free and compulsory for all children between the ages of six and 15. Pupils attend the one government school from infant to secondary level. In 2000/01 a total of 79 pupils were enrolled at infant level, 116 at primary level and 119 at secondary levels. Students wishing to follow higher education in Australia are eligible for bursaries and scholarships. The budgetary allocation for education was $A1,846,000 in 2000/01 (equivalent to 18.1% of total expenditure).

British Pacific Territory

There is only one British Dependent Territory remaining in the Pacific, which is the Crown Colony of Pitcairn, Henderson, Ducie and Oeno Islands. Until the end of 1995 the United Kingdom maintained membership of the South Pacific Commission (now Pacific Community) in respect of the Pitcairn Islands. The British Minister responsible for overseas possessions is the Secretary of State for Foreign and Commonwealth Affairs.

Head of State: HM Queen ELIZABETH II (succeeded to the throne 6 February 1952).
Foreign and Commonwealth Office: Whitehall, London, SW1A 2AH, United Kingdom; tel. (20) 7270-3000; internet www.fco.gov.uk.
Secretary of State for Foreign and Commonwealth Affairs: JOHN (JACK) STRAW.

PITCAIRN ISLANDS

Physical and Social Geography

The British Dependent Territory of Pitcairn, Henderson, Ducie and Oeno Islands is commonly known as Pitcairn (after the one inhabited island) or the Pitcairn Islands. Pitcairn Island is situated at 25°04′ S and 130°06′ W, about midway between Panama and New Zealand and 2,172 km (1,350 miles) east-south-east of Tahiti (French Polynesia). It is a rugged and fertile island of volcanic origin, which rises to a height of some 330 m (1,100 ft) and has an area of 4.35 sq km (1.75 sq miles). Even at the only landing place, access from the sea is difficult. The climate is equable, with mean monthly temperatures ranging from 19°C (66°F) in August to 24°C (75°F) in February, and average annual rainfall of 2,000 mm. The resident population has been in decline since 1937 (when it peaked at 233), and in August 2002 numbered 43. There is a large population of some 1,500 descendants of Pitcairn Islanders, most of whom live in New Zealand (an estimated 171 in 2002) and Australia. It was estimated in 1990, however, that fewer than 500 people had been born on Pitcairn since 1790. The official language is English, but most of the islanders use Pitcairnese or Pitkern, a dialect based on 18th-century seafarers' English and Tahitian. The islanders are adherents of the Seventh-day Adventist Church. The chief settlement is Adamstown on Pitcairn Island.

The other three islands of the Territory are uninhabited, although the islanders regularly visit Henderson and Oeno Islands, the former being a large, raised atoll of 30 sq km (11.6 sq miles), 169 km east-north-east of Pitcairn, which provides miro wood, and the latter an atoll of less than 1 sq km and 121 km north-west of Pitcairn. Ducie Island (471 km east of Pitcairn) is the smallest of the four islands, and is largely inaccessible.

History

Pitcairn Island was discovered in 1767, when it was uninhabited, although there is evidence of previous occupation by Polynesian peoples. The island was first settled by the British in 1790, when it was occupied by nine mutineers of HMS *Bounty* (led by Fletcher Christian), accompanied by 12 women and six men from Tahiti. Despite the violence of the first decade (by 1800 the only surviving adult male was John Adams, who led the community until his death in 1829), the population increased steadily. Concern about the size of the population led to a temporary evacuation to Tahiti in 1831 and, when numbers reached 194 in 1856, the entire community was evacuated to a new home, provided by the British Government, on Norfolk Island. By 1864 43 Pitcairners had returned to the island, which has been permanently settled ever since. Pitcairn officially became a British settlement in 1887. In 1893 a parliamentary form of government was adopted, and in 1898 responsibility for administration was assumed by the High Commissioner for the Western Pacific. Pitcairn came under the jurisdiction of the Governor of Fiji in 1952, and, from 1970 onwards, of the British High Commissioner in New Zealand acting as Governor, in consultation with the Island Council, presided over by the Island Magistrate (who is elected triennially) and comprising one *ex-officio* member (the Island Secretary), five elected and three nominated members.

In 1987 the British High Commissioner in Fiji, acting on behalf of Pitcairn, the United Kingdom's last remaining dependency in the South Pacific, joined representatives of the USA, France, New Zealand and six South Pacific island states in signing the South Pacific Regional Environment Protection Convention, the main aim of which is to prevent the disposal of nuclear waste in the region.

In 1989 uninhabited Henderson Island was included on the UNESCO 'World Heritage List'. The island, 169 km east-north-east of Pitcairn, was to be preserved as a bird sanctuary. As well as many endemic plants, there are five species of bird unique to the island: the flightless rail or Henderson chicken, the green Henderson fruit dove, the Henderson crake, the Henderson warbler and the Henderson lorikeet. However, concern was expressed in 1994, following claims by scientists studying the island that its unique flora and fauna were threatened by the accidental introduction of foreign plant species by visitors, and by an increase in the rat population.

In April 1993, during an official visit to Pitcairn, the Governor was presented with a document expressing dissatisfaction with British policy towards the islands, and raising the question of a transfer of sovereignty.

Following some structural changes in the local government of Pitcairn, Steve Christian was elected to the position of Mayor in December 1999, presiding over the Island Council (a role previously fulfilled by the Island Magistrate).

In early 2000 British detectives began an investigation into an alleged rape case on the island. The British team was joined by the New Zealand police force in early 2001, when the case was widened to include 15 alleged sexual assaults, amid reports claiming that sexual abuse, particularly of children, was commonplace on the island. The trial, which was expected to take place either on Pitcairn or in Wellington, New Zealand, would represent the first significant criminal case on Pitcairn since a murder trial in 1897. In November 2000 Auckland's Crown Solicitor, Simon Moore, was appointed Pitcairn's first Public Prosecutor, with the task of deciding whether to bring charges against 20 Pitcairn islanders. His decision was delayed by the fact that many of the complainants now lived in New Zealand and by the logistical problems of a trial that could potentially involve the entire populace. In late July 2002, however, the British High Commission in Wellington confirmed that charges would be brought. It was reported that the prosecution was hoping to bring charges before the end of the year, and that fewer than 20 men were likely to be charged. The trial was expected to be conducted in New Zealand, via a video link to Pitcairn.

The British Overseas Territories Act, which entered into effect in May 2002, granted citizenship rights in the United Kingdom to residents of the Overseas Territories, including Pitcairn. The legislation also entitled Pitcairn Islanders to hold British passports and to work in the United Kingdom and elsewhere in the European Union.

Economy

The economy has been based on subsistence gardening, fishing, handicrafts and the sale of postage stamps. Attempts to increase revenue from the island's agricultural output by producing dried fruits (notably bananas, mangoes and pineapples) began in 1999. Diversification of this sector to include production of jam, dried fish and coffee was subsequently under consideration. In early 1999 the Pitcairn Island police and customs office requested that no honey or beeswax be sent to the Island in order to protect from disease the island's growing honey industry, which was being developed as a source of foreign exchange. Pitcairn honey, which was pronounced to be 'exceptionally pure' by the New Zealand Ministry of Agriculture, began to be exported, largely through internet sales, in late 1999. A new stamp was issued to commemorate the launch of the industry.

A reafforestation scheme, begun in 1963, concentrated on the planting of miro trees, which provide a rosewood suitable for handicrafts. In 1987 the Governor of the islands signed a one-year fishing agreement with Japan, whereby the Japan Tuna Fisheries Co-operative Association was granted a licence to operate vessels within Pitcairn's EEZ. The agreement was subsequently renewed but lapsed in 1990. In 1992 an exclusive economic zone (EEZ), designated in 1980 and extending 370 km (200 nautical miles) off shore, was officially declared.

In early 1992 it was reported that significant mineral deposits, formed by underwater volcanoes, had been discovered within the islands' EEZ. The minerals, which were believed to include manganese, iron, copper, zinc, silver and gold, could (if exploited) dramatically affect the Territory's economy.

New Zealand currency has been in everyday use since 1967. There is no taxation, except for small licensing fees on guns and vehicles, and government revenue has been derived from philatelic sales (one-half of current revenue in 1992/93), and from interest earned on investments. In 1998/99 revenue totalled $NZ492,000 and expenditure $NZ667,000. Capital assistance is received from the United Kingdom. In 2000/01 exports from Pitcairn to New Zealand were worth $NZ134,000, while imports from New Zealand totalled NZ$32,000. Exports to Australia totalled $A21,000 and imports $A7,000, consisting mainly of food. In 2001 Pitcairn's imports from the USA totalled US $5.5m., while exports to the USA were worth US $0.2m.

Hopes that Pitcairn might find an additional source of revenue through the sale of website addresses were boosted in early 2000 when the island won a legal victory to gain control of its internet domain name suffix, '.pn'.

Development projects have been focused on harbour improvements, power supplies, telecommunications and road-building. Pitcairn's first radio-telephone link was established in 1985, and a modern telecommunications unit was installed in 1992. A new health clinic was established, with British finance, in 1996.

A steady decline in the population, owing mainly to emigration to New Zealand, is the island's main problem. In March 2001 a New Zealand company, Wellesley Pacific, expressed an interest in acquiring development rights on Pitcairn with the aim of establishing fishing and tourism projects. The company claimed that if the islands achieved self-sufficiency through the proposals within five years, then Pitcairn could eventually become an independent state within the Commonwealth. In May 2002 the company's director reportedly announced that the development would begin within the next 12 months, describing plans for a lodge on Pitcairn Island and for a floating hotel off Oeno Island. The British High Commission in Wellington, however, emphasized that any such developments remained subject to the approval of Pitcairn Island Council, but that the company was welcome to submit proposals.

Statistical Survey

Source: Office of the Governor of Pitcairn, Henderson, Ducie and Oeno Islands, c/o British Consulate-General, Pitcairn Islands Administration, Private Box 105-696, Auckland, New Zealand; tel. (9) 366-0186; fax (9) 366-0187; e-mail pitcairn@iconz.co.nz.

AREA AND POPULATION

Area: 35.5 sq km. *By island:* Pitcairn 4.35 sq km; Henderson 30.0 sq km; Oeno is less than 1 sq km and Ducie is smaller.

Population: 43 (August 2002).

Density (Pitcairn only, August 2002): 9.9 per sq km.

Employment (able-bodied men, 2002): 9.

FINANCE

Currency and Exchange Rates: 100 cents = 1 Pitcairn dollar. The Pitcairn dollar is at par with the New Zealand dollar ($NZ). New Zealand currency is usually used (see p. 953).

Budget ($NZ, 1998/99): Revenue 492,000; Expenditure 667,000.

TRANSPORT

Road Traffic (motor vehicles, 2002): Passenger vehicles 29 (two-wheeled 1, three-wheeled 6, four-wheeled 23); Tractors 3; Bulldozer 1; Digger 1.

Shipping: *Local vessels* (communally-owned open surf boats, 2000): 3. *International Shipping Arrivals* (visits by passing vessels, 1996): Ships 51; Yachts 30.

COMMUNICATIONS

Telephones (2002): a party-line service with 15 telephones in use; 2 public telephones; 2 digital telephones. Most homes also have VHF radio.

Directory

The Constitution and Government

Pitcairn is a British settlement under the British Settlements Act 1887, although the islanders reckon their recognition as a colony from 1838, when a British naval captain instituted a Constitution with universal adult suffrage and a code of law. That system served as the basis of the 1904 reformed Constitution and the wider reforms of 1940, effected by Order in Council. The Constitution of 1940 provides for a Governor of Pitcairn, Henderson, Ducie and Oeno Islands (who, since 1970, is concurrently the British High Commissioner in New Zealand), representing the British monarch. A Mayor is elected every three years to preside over the Island Council. The Local Government Ordinance 1964 constituted an Island Council of 10 members: in addition to the Mayor, five members are elected annually; three are nominated for terms of one year (the Governor appoints two of these members at his own discretion); and the Island Secretary is an *ex-officio* member. In addition to the Island Council there is an Island Magistrate who presides over the Magistrate's Court of Pitcairn, and is appointed by the Governor. Liaison between the Governor and the Island Council is conducted by a Commissioner, usually based in the Office of the British Consulate-General in Auckland, New Zealand.

Customary land tenure provides for a system of family ownership (based upon the original division of land in the 18th century). Alienation to foreigners is not forbidden by law, but in practice this is difficult. There is no taxation, and public works are performed by the community.

Governor of Pitcairn, Henderson, Ducie and Oeno Islands: RICHARD FELL (British High Commissioner in New Zealand—took office December 2001).

Office of the Governor of Pitcairn, Henderson, Ducie and Oeno Islands: c/o British High Commission, 44 Hill St, POB 1812, Wellington, New Zealand; tel. (4) 924-2888; fax (4) 473-4982; e-mail bhc.wel@xtra.co.nz; internet www.britain.org.nz; Gov. RICHARD FELL; Deputy Gov. MATTHEW FORBES; Commissioner LEON SALT.

Pitcairn Islands Administration: Private Box 105-696, Auckland, New Zealand; tel. (9) 366-0186; fax (9) 366-0187; e-mail admin @pitcairn.gov.pn; internet www.government.pn.

ISLAND COUNCIL
(September 2002)

Mayor: STEVE CHRISTIAN.

Island Secretary (*ex officio*): BETTY CHRISTIAN.

Government Treasurer: OLIVE CHRISTIAN.

Island Auditor: MIKE CHRISTIAN.

Chairman of Internal Committee: JAY WARREN.

Other Members: LEA BROWN, BRENDA CHRISTIAN, TOM CHRISTIAN, ROBERT MCDONALD, JOHN O'MALLEY, MERALDA WARREN, NOLA WARREN.

Elections to the Island Council take place each December. Meetings are held at the Court House in Adamstown.

Office of the Island Secretary: The Square, Adamstown.

Judicial System

Chief Justice: CHARLES BLACKIE.

Island Magistrate: LEA BROWN.

Public Prosecutor: SIMON MOORE.

Public Defender: PAUL DACRE.

Religion

CHRISTIANITY

Since 1887 many of the islanders have been adherents of the Seventh-day Adventist Church.

Pastor: JOHN O'MALLEY, SDA Church, The Square, POB 24, Adamstown; fax 872-7620/9763.

The Press

Pitcairn Miscellany: monthly four-page mimeographed news sheet; f. 1959 and edited by the Education Officer; circulation 1,400 in 2002; Editor P. FOLEY.

Finance, Trade and Industry

There are no formal banking facilities. A co-operative trading store was established in 1967. Industry consists of handicrafts, honey and dried fruit.

Transport

ROADS

There are approximately 14 km (9 miles) of dirt road suitable for two-, three- and four-wheeled vehicles. In 2002 there was one conventional motor cycle, six three-wheelers and 22 four-wheeled motor cycles, one four-wheel-drive motor car, three tractors, a five-ton digger and a bulldozer; traditional wheelbarrows are used occasionally. In late 1995 a total of £79,000 was received from individual donors for work to improve the road leading to the jetty at Bounty Bay. Additional funding from the United Kingdom and the European Union was suspended in 2001, and the project remained incomplete.

SHIPPING

No passenger ships have called regularly since 1968, and sea communications are restricted to cargo vessels operating between New Zealand and Panama, which make scheduled calls at Pitcairn three times a year, as well as a number of unscheduled calls. There are also occasional visits by private yachts. The number of cruise ships calling at Pitcairn increased in the late 1990s, and 10 such vessels visited the island in 2000 (compared with just two or three annually in previous years). Bounty Bay, near Adamstown, is the only possible landing site, and there are no docking facilities. In 1993 the jetty derrick was refitted with an hydraulic system. The islanders have three aluminium open surf boats.

Education

Free primary education is provided on the island under the direction of a qualified schoolteacher, recruited in New Zealand. Scholarships, provided by the Pitcairn Government, are available for post-primary education or specialist training in New Zealand. In July 2001 there were five children being educated on Pitcairn.

Fiji

Physical and Social Geography

The Republic of Fiji lies in the south-west Pacific Ocean, south of the Equator, 1,770 km north of Auckland (New Zealand) and 2,730 km north-east of Sydney (Australia). To the west lies Melanesia: Solomon Islands in the north-west, Vanuatu and New Caledonia. East of Fiji is Tonga and, in the north-east, other Polynesian islands, those of Wallis and Futuna and Western Samoa. Tuvalu is to the north. The Fiji group comprises four main islands, Viti Levu (where 70% of the population lives), Vanua Levu, Taveuni and Kadavu and some 840 smaller islands, atolls and reefs, of which fewer than 100 are inhabited. The island of Rotuma, 386 km (240 miles) north of Vanua Levu, and the eight smaller islands of the group also constitute part of the Republic. The total area of the Republic of Fiji is 18,376 sq km (7,095 sq miles). The climate is tropical, with temperatures ranging from 16° to 32°C (60° to 90°F). Rainfall is heaviest between November and April, but is more constant on the windward side.

Fiji is characterized by racial diversity. The indigenous Fijian population declined sharply during the 1850s, owing to epidemics of measles and influenza in which thousands died, and only in the 1950s did it begin to rise. The Indian population was originally brought to Fiji as labour for the canefields from 1879. The population at the census of August 1986 was 715,375, of whom 48.7% were Indians and 46.1% Fijians. Following the coups of 1987, there was emigration on a large scale, particularly from among the Indian community. In 1989 official statistics claimed that ethnic Fijians again formed the largest part of the population; and by 1996 it was estimated that ethnic Fijians comprised 51.1% of the population, Indians 43.6% and others 5.3%. In 1986 53% of the population were Christian (mainly Methodist), 38% were Hindus and 8% Muslim. Fiji's population totalled 844,330 in mid-2001. English is the official language, but Fijian (the principal dialect being Bauan) and Hindi (the locally developed dialect being known as Hindustani) are widely spoken. The capital is Suva on Viti Levu.

History

The Fijian islands were settled some 3,500 years ago, by Melanesian and Polynesian peoples. The first Europeans to settle on the islands were sandalwood traders, missionaries and shipwrecked sailors. Under their influence, local fighting and jealousies reached unprecedented heights until, by the 1850s, one Ratu (chief), Thakombau, had gained a tenuous influence over the whole of the western islands. Thakombau ran foul of US interests during the 1850s and turned to the British for assistance, unsuccessfully at first, but in 1874 Britain agreed to a second offer of cession, and Fiji was proclaimed a British possession. The island of Rotuma and its dependencies were added to the territory in 1881. Fiji became independent on 10 October 1970.

The racial diversity, compounded by actions of the past colonial administrations, presents Fiji with one of its most difficult problems. The colonial Government consistently favoured the Fijian population, protecting them from exploitation and their land from alienation, but allowed the importation of foreign labour. Approximately 80% of the islands were owned by Fijian communities, but over 90% of the sugar crop, Fiji's largest export, was produced by Indians, usually on land leased from Fijians. Until the mid-20th century Indians were poorly represented politically, while Fijians had their own administrative and judicial systems. The army is comprised almost entirely of ethnic Fijians.

After independence, Fijian politics were, for a long time, dominated by Ratu Sir Kamisese Mara, leader of the Alliance Party (AP). In a general election in 1977, the Indian-led opposition won a majority of seats in the House of Representatives, but failed to form a government because its leaders were uncertain whether Fijians would accept an Indian leadership. At elections in 1982 the AP won 28 seats, while the National Federation Party (NFP) won 22 seats.

Following tension between the Government and its opposition in Parliament (supported by the labour movement), a meeting of union leaders in May 1985 represented the start of discussions which culminated in the founding of the Fiji Labour Party (FLP), officially inaugurated in Suva in July 1985. Sponsored by the Fijian Trades Union Conference (FTUC), and under the presidency of Dr Timoci Bavadra, the new party was formed with the aim of presenting a more effective parliamentary opposition, and announced the provision of free education and a national medical scheme to be among its priorities.

At a general election in April 1987 a coalition of the FLP and the NFP won 28 seats in the House of Representatives, thereby defeating the ruling AP, which won 24 seats. Bavadra subsequently took office as Prime Minister, leading the first Fijian Government to be dominated by MPs of ethnic Indian, rather than ethnic Fijian (i.e. Melanesian), origin. Bavadra, a commoner, announced the formation of a new Cabinet, comprising seven Indians and five Fijians (including Bavadra himself). However, on 14 May 1987 the Government was removed from power by a military coup, led by Lt-Col (later Maj.-Gen.) Sitiveni Rabuka, who forcibly abducted and imprisoned Bavadra and the other 27 members of the coalition Government, seeking to justify his unconstitutional action by claiming that the militant ethnic Fijian Taukei Movement had been planning to attack Bavadra and his Government. Rabuka immediately formed a 17-member interim ruling Council (which included Mara, the former Prime Minister), of which he declared himself the Chief Minister. The Governor-General, Ratu Sir Penaia Ganilau, refused to recognize Rabuka's administration (although he subsequently swore in Rabuka as its Chief Minister), and declared a state of emergency. In an attempt to resolve the crisis, Ganilau appointed a 19-member Advisory Council, comprising Rabuka and seven other members of his intended Council of Ministers, together with members of Fiji's Great Council of Chiefs or Bose Levu Vakaturaga (a traditional body comprising every hereditary chief, or Ratu, of a Matagali, or Fijian clan) and a number of public servants. Bavadra, one other member of the elected Government (all of whose members had been released from detention), and another Indian were offered posts on the Advisory Council, but declined to participate, on the grounds that the Council was unconstitutional and biased in its composition. Of the remaining 16 appointed members, most were supporters of Mara's AP and only one was an ethnic Indian.

Widespread racial violence, continuing demonstrations of protest against the interim administration and public demands for Bavadra's reinstatement as Prime Minister led to increased civil tension and political uncertainty. In July 1987 the Great Council of Chiefs approved proposals for constitutional reform, including an increase in the number of seats in the House of Representatives, more than one-half of which were to be held by ethnic Fijians. According to the proposals, the Prime Minister was invariably to be of Melanesian origin, and was to be appointed only by Fijian MPs. Negotiations, between delegations led by Bavadra and Mara, took place in September, despite violence perpetrated (allegedly by the radical Taukei Movement) against one of Bavadra's spokesmen, and it was announced that the two factions had agreed to form an interim bipartisan Government.

The implementation of this compromise plan was, however, forestalled on 25 September 1987 by a second *coup d'état*, again led by Rabuka, who announced his intention of declaring a republic. Ganilau, who refused to recognize Rabuka's seizure of power, sought to reconcile the opposing factions. Negotiations between Ganilau, Rabuka, Bavadra and Mara took place on 29–30 September, but collapsed on 1 October, when Rabuka formally revoked the Constitution and deposed Queen Elizabeth II as Head of State. Further efforts were made to seek a new arrangement whereby Ganilau would remain in office at the head of a constitutional government, but these were abandoned on 7 October, when Rabuka installed an interim Council of Ministers, of which more than one-half of the members were drawn from the Taukei Movement. Rabuka, who became Minister for Home Affairs and the Public Service (with control of the armed forces), stated that the Council would remain in power for at least one year, during which time a new constitution, guaranteeing the dominance of ethnic Fijians, would be promulgated. On 15 October Ganilau, who had refused to accept the presidency of a Republic of Fiji, resigned as Governor-General, and Fiji was deemed to have left the Commonwealth. The Chief Justice and senior judges, who had opposed the coup, were removed from office, and Rabuka declared himself Head of State. While the new Government received recognition from France, the Governments of Australia and New Zealand condemned the Rabuka regime. On 6 December Rabuka resigned as Head of State, and Ganilau, the former Governor-General, was appointed the first President of the Fijian Republic, although he had earlier refused to accept the post. Mara was reappointed Prime Minister, and Rabuka became Minister of Home Affairs. The new Cabinet contained no member of Bavadra's deposed Government.

In February 1988 Rotuma (the only Polynesian island in the country), which lies to the north-west of Vanua Levu, attempted to declare independence from Fiji, announcing that it did not recognize

Fiji's newly-declared status as a republic and affirming its continued loyalty to the Commonwealth. However, Fijian troops were dispatched to the island and soon quelled the dissent. In the constitutional settlement of 1990, however, Rotumans received a special status, with one seat in each of the houses of Parliament.

A new draft Constitution was approved by the interim Government in September 1988. A constitutional committee, which was multiracial but included no member of the former Bavadra Government, received submissions during the following year and published a revised draft in September 1989. Bavadra and the FLP-NFP coalition, however, continued to condemn the proposals.

In January 1989 statistical information, released by the interim Government, indicated that the islands' ethnic Fijians were the largest group in the population for the first time since 1946. Some 9,500 ethnic Indians and 2,800 others had emigrated since the coup of May 1987.

In November 1989 Bavadra died and was succeeded as leader of the FLP by his widow, Adi (a female honorific corresponding to the chiefly title of Ratu) Kuini Bavadra. In October Mara agreed to remain as Prime Minister only if Rabuka left the Cabinet and returned to his military duties. Rabuka and two other army officers duly left the Cabinet in January 1990.

In June 1990 the Great Council of Chiefs approved the draft Constitution. It also initiated the formation of a new party, the Soqosoqo ni Vakavulewa ni Taukei (SVT) or Fijian Political Party, to advocate the cause of ethnic Fijians. The new Constitution was promulgated on 25 July 1990 by President Ganilau. This was reported to have been prompted by fears of another coup. The FLP-NFP coalition immediately condemned the Constitution and announced that it would not participate in any elections held under it. The opposition criticized the legislative majority of ethnic Fijians, who were reserved 37 of the 70 elective seats, compared with 27 Indian seats. Furthermore, the Great Council of Chiefs was to nominate ethnic Fijians to 24 of the 34 seats in the Senate and to appoint the President of the Republic.

In July 1991 Rabuka resigned as Commander of the Armed Forces in order to join the Cabinet as Deputy Prime Minister and Minister of Home Affairs, but later that year he relinquished the post to assume the leadership of the SVT.

Disagreements between the Government and the FTUC re-emerged at the beginning of 1991. In February a strike by more than 900 members of the Fijian Miners' Union over union recognition, pay and poor working conditions led to the dismissal of some 400 of the workers. In May the Government announced a series of reforms to the labour laws, including the abolition of the minimum wage, restrictions on strike action and derecognition of unions that did not represent at least two-thirds of the work-force. A significant announcement by the Government in late 1992 was the official recognition of the FTUC (withheld since 1986) as the sole representative of workers in Fiji.

At legislative elections held in May 1992 the SVT secured 30 of the 37 seats reserved for ethnic Fijians, while the NFP won 14 and the FLP 13 of the seats reserved for Indian representatives. Following the election, the FLP agreed to participate in Parliament and to support Rabuka in his campaign for the premiership, in return for a guarantee from the SVT of a full review of the Constitution and of trade union and land laws. Rabuka was, therefore, appointed Prime Minister, and formed a coalition Government (consisting of 14 members of the SVT and five others).

In July 1992 a report was published, detailing the findings of a corruption inquiry, undertaken following the military coups of 1987. Rabuka aroused some controversy by ordering that the report remain 'classified'. Nevertheless, in December Rabuka formally invited the opposition leaders, Jai Ram Reddy of the NFP and Mahendra Chaudhry of the FLP, to form a government of national unity. The move was largely welcomed, but Indian politicians expressed reluctance to take part in a government whose political control remained fundamentally vested with ethnic Fijians. Rabuka was criticized equally by nationalist extremists of the Taukei Solidarity Movement, who accused him of conceding too much political power to Fijian Indians. Following the appointment of a new Cabinet in June 1993, all 13 of the FLP members began an indefinite boycott of Parliament, in protest at Rabuka's failure to implement the reforms, which he had agreed to carry out in return for their support for his election to the premiership in June 1992.

In December 1993 President Ganilau died, following a long illness, and was replaced by Ratu Sir Kamisese Mara, who took office in January 1994 (re-elected on 18 January 1999). At legislative elections held in February 1994 the SVT increased the number of its seats in the House of Representatives to 31, while the Fijian Association Party (FAP, formed in January by former members of the SVT) secured only five seats, of a total of 37 reserved for ethnic Fijians. Of the 27 seats reserved for ethnic Indian representatives, 20 were secured by the NFP. The SVT subsequently formed a governing coalition with the General Voters' Party (GVP) and an independent member, under the premiership of Rabuka, who announced the formation of a new Cabinet composed entirely of ethnic Fijians. In response to international concern regarding the continued existence of Fiji's racially-biased Constitution, Rabuka announced in June 1994 that the Constitutional Review Commission had been established, which, it was hoped, would have completed a review of the Constitution by 1997.

In January 1995 the Government announced that it was to recommend that Parliament vote to repeal the Sunday observance law (imposed after the coups of 1987), which prohibited work and organized entertainment and sport on that day. The announcement aroused intense opposition from nationalist politicians and Methodist church leaders, who organized demonstrations in three cities, attended by more than 12,000 people. In February, however, the House of Representatives voted in favour of removing the regulations. The Senate narrowly rejected the proposal (by 15 votes to 14), thus effectively delaying the implementation of any changes. The Sunday observance law was finally repealed in November 1995.

The issue of independence for the island of Rotuma was raised again in September 1995 with the return of the King of Rotuma from exile in New Zealand. King Gagaj Sa Lagfatmaro, who had fled to New Zealand following death threats made against him during the military coups of 1987, appeared before the Constitutional Review Commission to petition for the island's independence within the Commonwealth, reiterating his view that Rotuma remained a British colony rather than a part of Fiji.

In September 1995 the Government decided to transfer all state land (comprising some 10% of Fiji's total land area), hitherto administered by the Government Lands Department, to the Native Land Trust Board. The decision was to allow the allocation of land to indigenous Fijians on the basis of native custom. However, concern among the Fijian Indian population increased following reports in early 1996 that many would not be able to renew their land leases (most of which were due to expire between 1997 and 2024 under the Agricultural Landlords and Tenants Act—ALTA). The reports were strongly denied by the Government, despite statements by several Fijian land-owning clans that Indians' leases would not be renewed. Moreover, a recently-formed sugar cane growers' association solely for ethnic Fijians, the Taukei Cane-Growers' Association, announced its intention to campaign for ethnic Fijian control of the sugar industry, largely by refusing to renew land leases to ethnic Indians (who held some 85% of sugar farm leases). In mid-1999 a government survey indicated that at least 70% of leases were likely to be renewed under ALTA, although there were continuing reports that ethnic Fijian landowners were unwilling to sign new contracts under the act. Concern was expressed that mounting tensions between landowners and tenants might lead to violence, and that the situation was affecting investor confidence. The Government announced that it was considering alternative proposals, including the transferral of land to the Native Land Trust Board, under which leases were subject to more frequent renewal than under ALTA.

Meanwhile racial tension intensified in October 1995, following the publication of the SVT's submission to the Constitutional Review Commission. In its report the party detailed plans to abandon the present multiracial form of government, recommending instead the adoption of an electoral system based on racial representation, in which each ethnic group selects its own representatives. The expression of numerous extreme anti-Indian sentiments in the document was widely condemned as offensive. Josefata Kamikamica of the FAP was one of several political leaders to describe the submission as disgraceful and insulting to Fijian, as well as to Indian, sensibilities.

A rift within the GVP in early 1996, which resulted in two of the four GVP members of the House of Representatives withdrawing their support for the Government, prompted Rabuka to seek alternative coalition partners from among the opposition, in an attempt to establish a more secure majority. However, the Prime Minister was unsuccessful in persuading parliamentary members of the FAP to join the Government. The administration's troubles during 1996 contributed to the defeat of the SVT in virtually every municipality at local elections, which took place in September.

Existing divisions within the Government were further exacerbated by the presentation to the House of Representatives, in September 1996, of the Constitutional Review Commission's report. The report included recommendations to enlarge the House of Representatives to 75 seats, with 25 seats reserved on a racial basis (12 for ethnic Fijians, 10 for Fijian Indians, two for General Electors and one for Rotuma Islanders), and also proposed that the Prime Minister should be a Fijian of any race, while the President should continue to be an indigenous Fijian. Rabuka and Mara both endorsed the findings of the report, while several nationalist parties, including the Vanua Independent Party, the Fijian Nationalist United Front Party (FNUFP) and the Taukei Solidarity Movement, expressed extreme opposition to the proposals, and formed a coalition in an attempt to further their influence within Parliament. In addition, a number of SVT members of the House of Representatives aligned themselves with the nationalists, and in early 1997 were reported to be responsible for a series of political manoeuvres within the

Cabinet, aimed at undermining Rabuka's position. The parliamentary committee reviewing the report agreed on a majority of the 700 recommendations, but proposed that the House of Representatives be enlarged to only 71 seats, with 46 seats reserved on a racial basis (23 for ethnic Fijians, 19 for Indians, three for General Electors and one for Rotuma Islanders) and 25 seats open to all races. The committee's modified proposals were presented in May to the Great Council of Chiefs, which endorsed the recommendations on constitutional change, but demanded that the number of lower chamber seats reserved for ethnic Fijians be increased from 23 to 28. However, the Council approved the proposal to reduce the number of nominated senators to 15 (from 24). The reforms, as proposed by the committee, were officially endorsed by the Great Council of Chiefs in early June. The Constitution Amendment Bill was approved unanimously by the House of Representatives and the Senate in the following month. Rabuka was anxious to reassure extremist nationalist Fijians, who had vociferously opposed the reforms throughout the debate, that their interests would be protected under the amended Constitution and that indigenous Fijians would continue to play a pre-eminent role in the government of the country.

Despite opposition from both the FLP and the nationalist parties, Fiji was readmitted to the Commonwealth at a meeting of member states in October 1997. In the same month Rabuka was granted an audience with Queen Elizabeth II in London, at which he formally apologized for the military coups of 1987. (Rabuka subsequently apologized to the Indo-Fijian community, in April 1999, for the events of 1987.)

Events in early 1998 were dominated by political reaction to the reformed Constitution. An extremist nationalist group of former SVT supporters, including senior church, military and police officials were rumoured to be planning to overthrow Rabuka's Government. Meanwhile, it was reported that opponents of the Constitution were discussing the establishment of several new political parties, the most significant of which was the Christian Fellowship Party, formed in March under the leadership of Rev. Manasa Lasaro. Nevertheless, the new Constitution came into effect on 27 July 1998.

Following a period of severe drought, nation-wide water restrictions were introduced in early 1998. The sugar industry was drastically affected by the drought, resulting in an annual crop some 60% lower than predicted, with exporters unable to meet commitments to foreign buyers. By September of that year more than one-quarter of the population were dependent on emergency food and water rations. Devastating floods in the west of the country in early 1999, in which seven people died, destroyed the drought rehabilitation programme and that year's sugar crop.

A dispute between tribal landowners and the Government over compensation payments for land flooded by the Monosavu hydroelectric power station erupted into violence in July 1998. Landowners, who had been demanding compensation worth some $A30m. since the plant was constructed in 1983, seized control of the station (which supplies 90% of Fiji's electricity) and carried out a series of arson attacks on Fiji Electricity Authority property. In October the Government agreed to pay the landowners compensation totalling some $A12m., although many involved in the dispute rejected the offer and announced their intention of pursuing a legal claim against the Government. In late 1998 the Government was also believed to be considering a claim for compensation by landowners whose land was compulsorily acquired during the Second World War and now occupies the site of Nadi airport.

The prospect of a general election, to be held in early May 1999, prompted reports of political manoeuvring as parties sought to increase their influence by forming alliances. In addition, a number of changes in the country's political organizations occurred in late 1998. Following the death of Josefata Kamikamica, Adi Kuini Speed (widow of ex-President Bavadra) was elected leader of the Fijian Association Party. Meanwhile, the General Voters' Party and the General Electors' Party merged to form the United General Party under the leadership of the Minister for Tourism, Transport and Civil Aviation, David Pickering, and Rabuka was re-elected leader of the SVT (despite the party being required to amend its constitution in order for this to be possible). The formation of a new party, the Veitokani ni Lewenivanua Vakarisito (Christian Democratic Alliance—VLV), by several senior church and military leaders and former members of the nationalist Taukei Movement, was widely criticized for its extremist stance and refusal to accept the newly-formed, multiracial Constitution. In April 1999 Poesci Bune defeated former army commander Ratu Epeli Ganilau to become leader of the party.

At legislative elections held on 8–15 May 1999, the first to be held under the new Constitution, Rabuka's coalition Government was defeated by Mahendra Chaudhry, leader of the Indian-dominated FLP, who thus became Fiji's first ethnic Indian Prime Minister. Chaudhry's broad-based Government (a coalition of the FLP, FAP and the Party of National Unity—PANU) seemed initially threatened by the reluctance of FAP members to serve under an Indian Prime Minister. The leaders were persuaded to remain in the coalition in the interests of national unity, after the intervention of President Mara. However, in June there were renewed demands for the FAP to withdraw from the coalition because of the alleged discontent of party members at the lack of representation afforded to the party in the Senate nominations put forward by Chaudhry. Political stability after the elections was marred by demands for Chaudhry's resignation by the Fijian Nationalist Vanua Takolavo Party, and by a number of arson attacks, allegedly linked to the outgoing SVT party (although these allegations were denied by Rabuka).

Following the SVT's decisive defeat in the elections, Rabuka resigned as party leader; he was replaced by Ratu Inoke Kubuabola, the former Minister for Communications, Works and Energy. Rabuka was subsequently appointed the first independent Chairman of the newly-autonomous Great Council of Chiefs. In August 1999 three bombs exploded in Suva. A member of the Nationalist Vanua Takolavo Party was subsequently arrested. In the same month a parliamentary vote of 'no confidence' against Prime Minister Chaudhry was overwhelmingly defeated. In the latter half of 1999 there were persistent demands by various nationalist groups (including the SVT) that Chaudhry be replaced by a leader of indigenous Fijian descent, and a number of demonstrations were organized expressing disillusionment with the Government. In October the opposition coalition was successful in gaining control of a majority of councils in local elections, while the FLP won control of four municipal councils (having previously been in charge of none).

The Government's decision to disband the Fiji Intelligence Service from December 1999 was criticized by the opposition as 'foolish' and racially motivated. An announcement by the Chief Justice in December of a project to amend a number of laws that did not comply with the terms of the new Constitution, together with reports that the Government was planning to withdraw state funds previously provided to assist indigenous Fijian business interests, prompted further accusations of racism by the Government against ethnic Fijians. Consequently, the SVT and the VLV held talks to discuss ways of consolidating the ethnic Fijian political base. Proposed legislation, which would alter the distribution of power between the President and the Prime Minister, attracted further criticism from the opposition, and in February 2000 a faction of the FAP announced its withdrawal from the governing coalition, citing dissatisfaction with Chaudhry's leadership. Of greater significance, however, was the announcement in April that the extreme nationalist Taukei Movement (which had been inactive for several years) had been revived with the sole intention of removing the Prime Minister from office. The group subsequently publicized a campaign of demonstrations and civil disobedience, prompting the army to issue a statement distancing itself from any anti-Government agitation and pledging loyalty to Chaudhry. The campaign attracted considerable popular support, however, and culminated in a march through Suva by some 5,000 people in early May.

On 19 May 2000 a group of armed men, led by businessman George Speight, invaded the parliament building and ousted the Government, taking hostage Chaudhry and 30 other members of the governing coalition. President Mara condemned the coup and declared a state of emergency as Speight's supporters rampaged through the streets of Suva, looting and setting fire to Indian businesses. Speight declared that he had reclaimed Fiji for indigenous people and had dissolved the Constitution. Moreover, he threatened to kill the hostages if the military intervened. On 22 May Mara formally invited Rabuka, in his role as chairman of the Great Council of Chiefs, to seek a resolution of the crisis. In the following days the Great Council of Chiefs convened to discuss the situation and proposed the replacement of Chaudhry's Government with an interim administration, an amnesty for Speight and the rebels, and the amendment of the Constitution. Speight rejected the proposals, demanding that Mara also be removed from office. Meanwhile, violent clashes erupted at the headquarters of Fiji Television when the rebels stormed the building following the broadcast of an interview with an opponent of the coup. A police officer was shot dead, television equipment was destroyed and the station's employees were taken hostage. On 29 May Mara resigned, and the Commander of the Armed Forces, Frank Bainimarama, announced the imposition of martial law and a curfew, in an attempt to restore calm and stability to the country. In an expression of his apparent reluctance to assume the role, Bainimarama gave Mara a whale's tooth, a traditional Fijian symbol of regret.

Negotiations between the Military Executive Council and the Great Council of Chiefs continued throughout June 2000. Failure to reach a conclusive outcome seemed to be the result of inconsistencies in Speight's demands and an ambivalent attitude on the part of the military towards the coup. Regular patrols by the security forces curbed rioting in Suva, although outbreaks of violence in rural areas (mostly in the form of attacks on Indian Fijians, the looting and burning of Indian-owned farms and the occupation of several tourist resorts) were reported. On 25 June the four female hostages were released from the parliament building. The Military Executive Council announced its intention to appoint an interim government without consulting Speight and demanded that the rebel leader release the remaining hostages. Speight reiterated his threat to kill all those held if any rescue attempts were made.

An interim administration of 19 indigenous Fijians led by Laisenia Qarase (the former managing director of the Merchant Bank of Fiji) was sworn in on 4 July 2000. Minutes after the ceremony a gun battle erupted outside the parliament building in which four civilians and one rebel were injured; the rebel subsequently died. Speight announced that he did not recognize the interim authority, and most of Fiji's mainstream political parties similarly denounced it, although the Methodist Church declared its support for the body. On 12 July a further nine hostages were released, and on the following day the remaining 18, including Chaudhry, were liberated. In accordance with Speight's wishes, Ratu Josefa Iloilo, hitherto the First Vice-President, was then installed as President. In the same month Chandrika Prasad, a farmer, quickly brought a legal challenge to the abrogation of the 1997 Constitution in the High Court of Fiji. Chaudhry launched an international campaign to reinstate both the Constitution and the People's Coalition Government.

Incidents of civil unrest (including the occupation of the hydroelectric dam at Monasavu and of the army barracks on Vanua Levu) continued throughout July 2000 as Speight sought to manipulate existing grievances, particularly disputes over land ownership, in order to mobilize additional support. On 29 July, however, Speight was finally arrested, along with dozens of his supporters, for breaking the terms of his amnesty by refusing to relinquish weapons. Armed rebels responded violently to the arrest, and in Labasa Indian Fijians were rounded up and detained in army barracks by supporters of Speight. In early August more than 300 rebels appeared in court on a variety of firearms and public order offences. Speight was similarly charged with several minor offences. On 11 August Speight and 14 of his supporters were formally charged with treason. On 15 November the High Court ruled that the existing Constitution remained valid and that the elected Parliament, ousted in the coup, remained Fiji's legitimate governing authority. Laisenia Qarase responded by declaring that the interim authority, of which he was leader, would continue as the country's national government until new elections could be organized and a new constitution drafted within 18 months.

In mid-December 2000 Chaudhry's campaign to re-establish his Government suffered a significant reversal when the ministers of foreign affairs of Australia and New Zealand announced that they were abandoning their appeal for its reinstatement, although they would continue to support a return to the 1997 Constitution. However, within Fiji supporters of a return to democracy formed the Fiji First Movement, which aimed to consolidate opposition to the post-coup regime. The group organized a series of protests across the country in late 2000 and early 2001.

In February 2001 an international panel of judges at the Court of Appeal began the hearing against the November 2000 ruling, which found the abrogation of the 1997 Constitution to be illegal. In its final judgment the court ruled that the 1997 Constitution remained the supreme law of Fiji, that the interim civilian government could not prove that it had the support of a majority of Fijian people and was therefore illegal and that, following Mara's resignation, the office of President remained vacant. The ruling was welcomed by many countries in the region, including Australia and New Zealand, and appeared to be accepted by the interim authority, which announced that it would organize elections as soon as possible. However, on 14 March Iloilo informed Chaudhry in a letter that he had been dismissed as Prime Minister, claiming that by advising Iloilo to dissolve the authority in preparation for elections he had accepted that he no longer had the mandate of Parliament. Chaudhry rejected the decision as unconstitutional and unlawful. Ratu Tevita Momoedonu—Labour and Industrial Relations Minister in Qarase's Government—was appointed Prime Minister on the same day. On the following day, however, Iloilo dismissed Momoedonu, on the advice of the Great Council of Chiefs, and reinstated Laisenia Qarase as head of the interim authority, with a mandate to prepare the country for general elections. The Great Council of Chiefs had reconfirmed Iloilo as President and agreed to accept the 1997 Constitution. It was announced that a general election would be held in August–September 2001, and would be conducted under the preferential voting system, similar to that of Australia, as used in Fiji's 1999 election.

There followed a period of factionalism and fragmentation among Fiji's political parties. George Speight had already been appointed President of the new Matanitu Vanua (MV—Conservative Alliance Party) party, despite facing the charge of treason for his part in the 2000 coup. On 9 May 2001 Qarase formed the Soqosoqo Duavata ni Lewenivanua (SDL—Fiji United Party), a new contender for the indigenous Melanesian vote, thus rivalling the established SVT. Another indigenous party, the Bai Kei Viti, was launched on 28 June. In the same month Tupeni Baba, former Deputy Prime Minister in Chaudhry's Government, left the FLP and formed the New Labour United Party. The election took place between 25 August and 1 September. Qarase's SDL was victorious, but failed to obtain an overall majority. The SDL secured 31 seats in the House of Representatives (increasing to 32 of the 71 seats after a by-election on 25 September). The FLP won 27 seats, the MV six seats and the NLUP two seats. International monitors were satisfied that the election had been contested fairly.

Following the election, however, by refusing to allow the FLP any representation in his new Cabinet, Qarase was accused of contravening a provision of the Constitution whereby a party winning more than 10% of the seats in the House of Representatives was entitled to a ministerial post. Two members of George Speight's MV were included in the Cabinet. Qarase claimed that Mahendra Chaudhry had not accepted that the Government should be based fundamentally on nationalist Fijian principles. In October 2001, when members of the House of Representatives were sworn in, Chaudhry refused to accept the position of Leader of the Opposition, a title that consequently fell to Prem Singh, leader of the NFP. In December Parliament approved the Social Justice Bill, a programme of affirmative action favouring Fijians and Rotumans in education, land rights and business-funding policies.

The Prime Minister defended himself against demands for his resignation in January 2002. The former Minister for Agriculture had alleged that Qarase had broken the Electoral Act after it was revealed that more than F$25m. had been misused by the interim Government's Ministry of Agriculture during the 2001 election campaign. The money was supposedly to have assisted impoverished indigenous Fijian farmers, yet Fijian businesses and, more significantly, their owners were alleged to have received the majority. In February 2002, furthermore, an appeal court ruled that the Prime Minister had violated the Constitution by failing to incorporate any member of the FLP in his Cabinet. Qarase had previously declared that he would resign if the legal challenge against him were to be successful and contested this ruling. (The newly appointed Chief Justice, Daniel Fatiaki, was himself under scrutiny in mid-2002; the Chief Justice being appointed on the advice of the Prime Minister and the Leader of the Opposition, and being responsible for assembling the Supreme Court.) In September the High Court ruled that Prem Singh, the NFP leader, was not entitled to retain his parliamentary seat (the validity of certain votes cast at the 2001 election having been questioned). The disputed seat was therefore allocated to a member of the FLP. Also in September, in advance of the ruling by the Supreme Court on the issue of the inclusion of the FLP in the Cabinet, the Prime Minister effected a ministerial reorganization, assuming personal responsibility for a number of additional portfolios.

Meanwhile, in June 2002 the Prime Minister and the FLP leader co-operated briefly in addressing the issue of expiring land leases that were threatening Fiji's sugar industry. A committee, comprising members of both the SDL and FLP, was established to try to negotiate land leases that would satisfy both Indo-Fijian tenants and their predominantly ethnic Fijian landowners. Most of the 30-year leases drawn up under the ALTA (see above) were expiring, and both tenants and the FLP were opposed to its replacement by the Native Land Trust Act (NLTA), which they saw as disproportionately favouring landowners. Two parliamentary bills had been approved by the Senate in April, reducing the land under state control to around 1% of the total and increasing the amount under the Native Land Trust Board to over 90%.

In August 2002, however, the FLP abandoned a second round of land lease discussions and announced that it would boycott most of the proceedings in the current session of Parliament. Chaudhry accused the Government of attempting to accelerate the passage of six bills through Parliament without regard for the mandatory 30 days' notice of a bill being tabled. He also complained that the Government had not given the FLP the full details of the proposed NLTA. The Prime Minister protested that this would compel the Government to accept the decision of the Great Council of Chiefs regarding the leases. Tensions between the ruling SDL and the FLP and, furthermore, between Fijians and Indo-Fijians had been further exacerbated by anti-Indian comments made by the Minister for Women, Social Welfare and Land Resettlement, Asenaca Caucau, which the Prime Minister had not denounced.

Justice for both the perpetrators and the victims of Fiji's military coup of 2000 remained a slow process. The trial of George Speight and his accomplices on charges of treason opened in May 2001. (Speight was refused bail that would have enabled him to occupy the seat that he won in the legislative election later in the year.) All the accused pleaded guilty to their involvement in the coup of May 2000, and at the conclusion of the trial in February 2002 Speight was sentenced to death. Within hours of the verdict, however, President Iloilo signed a decree commuting the sentence to life imprisonment (Fiji being in the process of abolishing the death penalty). Prison sentences of between 18 months and three years were imposed on 10 of Speight's accomplices, the charges of treason having been replaced by lesser charges of abduction. The trial of two other defendants began in July, following the rejection of protests from the defendants that they were protected by an Immunity Decree promulgated by the Commander of the Fiji Military Forces, Frank Bainimarama.

Fiji's foreign relations had been severely compromised by the coups of 1987. Its traditional links with the Commonwealth, particularly India, Australia and New Zealand, deteriorated markedly, most notably in terms of military co-operation, which Fiji sought instead from France and several Asian nations. India remained a consistent critic of the new regime, and tension increased after the fire-bombing of Indian places of worship in Fiji in October 1989. Comments by the Indian ambassador resulted in his expulsion from Fiji and the redesignation of the embassy as a consulate. In May 1990 the Fijian Government ordered the complete closure of the diplomatic post. In May of the following year the Secretary-General of the Commonwealth stated that Fiji would not be readmitted to the organization until it changed its Constitution. Following the approval of major constitutional reforms in July 1997, therefore, Fiji applied for readmission to the Commonwealth and rejoined the organization at a meeting of member states in October 1997. Diplomatic relations were resumed between Fiji and India in 1998, and in May 1999 India reopened its High Commission in Suva. However, Fiji's relations with the international community suffered a major reversal following the coup of May 2000, which was condemned by the UN, the Commonwealth, the United Kingdom, Australia, New Zealand and several other nations in the region. In June Fiji was partially suspended from the Commonwealth, and a delegation of ministers of foreign affairs from the organization visited the islands to demand the reinstatement of the 1997 Constitution. Following the democratic elections of August–September 2001, both Australia and New Zealand removed the bilateral sanctions they had imposed. The sanctions imposed by the European Union (EU) remained in place until early 2002. In December 2001, the Commonwealth Ministerial Action Group recommended that Fiji be readmitted to meetings of the Commonwealth. The decision by the French Government in June 1995 to resume nuclear testing in the region was widely condemned by the Pacific island nations and, in protest at the announcement, Fiji cancelled its annual military exercise with France. A demonstration by some 5,000 people in July against the tests typified the reaction of Pacific islanders throughout the region. In June 1999 the Pacific Concerns Resources Centre announced that it had filed a case with the European Court of Human Rights to establish British responsibility for the alleged exposure of Fijian soldiers to radioactive material on Christmas Island (now part of Kiribati) in the 1950s. Earlier that year the Fijian Government announced that it had decided to grant pensions to Fijian soldiers and sailors involved in the United Kingdom's nuclear testing in the Pacific.

Economy

Traditionally the Fijian economy is agricultural and dominated by the sugar industry, althoughboth tourism and exports of garments have also become valuable sources of foreign exchange. In 2000, according to estimates by the World Bank, Fiji's gross national product (GNP), measured at average 1998–2000 prices, was US $1,480m., and GNP per head was US $1,830 (or US $4,500 on an international purchasing-power parity basis). In 1990–99 GNP per head was estimated to have increased by an annual average of 1.0%. According to the Asian Development Bank (ADB), Fiji's gross domestic product (GDP) increased, in real terms, by an average of 1.6% during 1990–2000. Compared with the previous year, real GDP was provisionally estimated to have contracted by 9.3% in 2000. This figure, however, was subsequently revised to a decrease of only 2.8% in 2000, and the ADB then estimated that Fiji's GDP had increased by 2.6% in 2001. In 1990–2000 the population increased by an annual average of 1.0%.

Agriculture (including forestry and fishing) contributed 15.9% of GDP in 2000. According to FAO, agriculture engaged 39.8% of the economically active population in 2000. During 1990–2000, according to ADB estimates, agricultural GDP rose by an average annual rate of 0.5%. The sector's GDP was provisionally estimated to have declined by 0.6% in 2000. In mid-2002, however, the ADB estimated the decline to have been 1.2%, with a further contraction, of 2.4%, being recorded in 2001. According to FAO, in 1999 less than 16% of Fiji's land area was used for permanent crops or as arable land.

Sugar cane is the principal cash crop. Following a successful crop rehabilitation programme in the late 1990s, sugar cane production increased by 81% in 1999. However, the stability of the industry was disrupted by the May 2000 coup, and by the consequences of ongoing uncertainty surrounding the expiry of land leases. In 2001 sugar accounted for an estimated 21.0% of total export earnings. Sugar production declined by 25.9% in 2001 and was expected to remain at a similar level in 2002.

Other important export crops are coconuts and ginger, although production levels of both crops declined in the early 1990s. Vegetables and fruit are grown for domestic consumption, and paddy rice has been particularly encouraged as a subsistence crop. Plans to begin producing cotton for export were announced in 1996. The most important livestock products are beef and poultry meat.

Fiji has extensive timber reserves, but forestry has become important as an export trade only since the mid-1980s. Pulpwood and pine timber accounted for most of the increase in log production. Overall timber production increased by 4.3% in 2001. Lumber accounted for 4.2% of exports in 2000, worth $F44.9m.

Fishing is an important activity in Fiji, both for export and for domestic consumption. Commercial fish-farming became a significant sector in the 1990s. In 2001 fish products earned some $F98.3m in export revenue (8.0% of export receipts). Fiji also benefits from the sale to foreign interests of licences to fish in the islands' exclusive economic zone. Some 50 vessels operated in 1996, providing $F80m. in licence fees. However, plans to increase the number of licences permitted from 80 to 150 promised to augment revenue from this source.

Industry (including mining, manufacturing, power and construction) contributed 24.2% of GDP in 2000. In 1998 the sector engaged 33.8% of those in paid employment. The GDP of the industrial sector, according to the ADB's provisional figures, increased at an average rate of 2.2% per year during 1990–2000. According to subsequent figures from the ADB, the industrial sector's GDP was estimated to have contracted by 7.4% in 2000, before declining by 2.3% in 2001.

Mining and quarrying contributed 2.4% of GDP in 2000 and employed 1.8% of the paid labour force in 1999. Gold and silver are the major mineral exports. Gold exploration activity increased in the mid-1990s (with the number of prospecting licences totalling 49 in late 1998). The Vatukoula mine exported 3,655 kg of gold, worth $F56m. in 1997. Gold production at Mount Kasi began in 1996, and in the following year output reached 944 kg, which earned $F17m. in export revenue. However, operations at the mine were suspended in mid-1998, prompted by the installation's adverse impact on the environment. A large copper-mining project in Namosi, central Viti Levu, began operations in 1997. Fiji's production of gold declined from 3,794 kg in 2000 to an estimated 2,823 kg in 2001, when exports earned $F85.4m., equivalent to 7.0% of total export earnings. The mining sector's GDP, however, declined in real terms at an average annual rate of 0.8% between 1990 and 2000, a sharp decrease of 14.1% being recorded in 2000. Other mineral reserves include marble. In addition, 20 potential petroleum-bearing sites were identified in early 1993.

Manufacturing contributed an estimated 13.7% of GDP in 2000. The sector employed 26.0% of those in paid employment in 1999. Manufacturing GDP increased at an average rate of 2.4% per year during 1990–2000. Compared with the previous year, manufacturing GDP rose by 9.6% in 1999 but decreased by 12.1% in 2000. The most important activity is food processing, notably sugar, molasses, coconut oil and fish-canning. Manufacturing has received particular encouragement since 1987, when the Government established a register for factories which, provided 95% of their products were exported, would be exempt from any taxation. By 1997 there were 156 tax-free factories in operation (compared with 44 in 1988), including 96 garment factories. Output from the garment industry increased by 10% in 1999, owing to the introduction of preferential trade arrangements with Australia and New Zealand, but declined in the following year as a result of sanctions imposed by those countries in protest at the May 2000 coup. Garment exports none the less reached $F332.9m. in 2000, before declining to $F313.9m. in 2001, in which year they represented 25.6% of total export earnings.

Hydroelectricity is the principal source of power, providing some 90% of Fiji's electricity in the late 1990s. Electricity and water contributed 4.1% of GDP in 2000. Mineral fuels accounted for 15.0% of total imports in 2001.

The service industries contributed 59.9% of GDP in 2000, and in 1996 engaged 66.8% of those in paid employment. During 1990–2000 the sector's GDP rose by an average annual rate of 1.7%, according to the ADB. The ADB subsequently estimated that the GDP of the services sector had decreased by an estimated 1.1% in 2000 before rising by 4.2% in 2001. Tourist arrivals declined sharply to 294,070 in 2000, owing to the repercussions of coup in May of that year, but increased to 348,014 in 2001. The industry earned $F495.5. in foreign exchange in 2001, compared with $F413.5m. in 2000. Most visitors are from Australia (28.2% of total arrivals in 2001), followed by New Zealand (19.1%), the USA (16.6%), the United Kingdom (8.8%) and Japan (5.9%). The trade, restaurants and hotels sector engaged 18.8% of those in paid employment in 1996 and contributed 17.7% of GDP in 2000.

Fiji consistently records a trade deficit. According to the IMF, this amounted to US $115.6m. in 1999, although in that year the country recorded a surplus of US $12.7m. on the current account of the balance of payments. According to the ADB, export earnings decreased from $F672.0m. in 2000 to $F650m. in 2001. Imports rose from $F755.5m. 2000 to $F812.3m. in 2001. The principal sources of imports in 2001 were Australia (47.7%), New Zealand (13.8%) and Singapore (7.8%). The principal markets for exports were Australia (20.5%), the USA (27.8%) and the United Kingdom (12.1%). The principal imports are basic manufactures (23.1% of total imports in 2001) and machinery and transport equipment (22.9%). Fiji's principal domestic exports are clothing, sugar, gold and fish. Fiji also re-exports mineral fuels (including bunkers for ships and aircraft).

In 2002 there was a projected budgetary deficit equivalent to 6% of GDP. Fiji's total external debt was US $135.9m. at the end of 2000, of which US $101.2m. was long-term public debt. In that year the cost of debt-servicing was equivalent to 2.5% of the revenue from goods and services. The average annual rate of inflation was 3.4% in 1990–2000, decreasing to 1.1% in 2000. According to the ADB, the inflation rate increased to 4.3% in 2001. Of the total labour force, some 12.1% was unemployed in 2000. Since 1987 Fiji has suffered a very high rate of emigration, particularly of skilled and professional personnel. Between January 1987 and December 1995 72,688 citizens emigrated from Fiji, of whom some 90% were Fijian Indians, with an estimated 30% described as professional or semi-professional workers. Emigration of professional and technical workers decreased by 2.8% in 2001, although the number of emigrants from the services sector increased by 28.2%.

The overthrow of the Government during a coup in May 2000 had a severe impact on Fiji's economy, resulting in the first contraction in GDP since 1997. The previous year had witnessed strong economic growth, attributed to a buoyant tourist industry, an increase in garment production and a recovery in the sugar industry, despite problems relating to the land tenure issue, poor industrial relations and the prospect of losing preferential access to European markets. In 2000, however, it was estimated that 6,700 people lost their jobs in the second half of the year, the overwhelming majority of these having been engaged either in tourist-related activities or in manufacturing. A significant amount of that year's excellent sugar crop was not harvested, and a large proportion of tourist bookings was cancelled. In addition, the islands lost a considerable sum of revenue owing to cancellation of foreign aid and investment, and the Government was unable to collect taxes, worth more than $F90m.

In response to the economic difficulties following the coup, the Government introduced an emergency interim budget in July 2000. The budget decreased government spending, reducing the salaries of public officials by 12.5%. The austerity measures were successful in keeping government debt at a manageable level. The 2001 budget, announced in November 2000, reduced business taxes as a way of stimulating investment in the economy. The Government signalled a yet more interventionist policy in the 2002 budget, which substantially reduced customs tariffs on construction materials and capital goods. It announced that all income derived from exports in the 2001/02 financial year would be tax-exempt, with the percentage of export income taxed set to rise gradually to 100% during 2003–09. Budgeted expenditure for 2002 was F$1,255m. This included $F283m. in capital expenditure for investment; the Government established the Fiji Investment Corporation to manage and promote investment in Tourism, Forestry, Fisheries and Inter-island Shipping Services. The budget projected an increase in economic growth to 3.5% in 2002, which the Reserve Bank later revised to 4.4% in April 2002. In the same month the sale of Amalgamated Telecom Holdings earned over $F64m., the first of the Government's proposed major privatization plans.

In June 2002, for the third time since the announcement of the annual budget in November 2001, the Senate approved additional funding, this time of $F24m., for the purposes of government expenditure. Civil servants' salaries had been increased in April 2002, and losses of $F30m. from abuse of the Government's agriculture assistance scheme (see above) had been alleged. The Reserve Bank of Fiji predicted an increase in economic growth to 6% in 2003. Many Fijian observers, including the former Governor of the Reserve Bank, claimed that this was an unrealistic prediction.

Fiji is a member of the Pacific Islands Forum (formerly the South Pacific Forum), the Pacific Community (formerly the South Pacific Commission), the UN's Economic and Social Commission for Asia and the Pacific (ESCAP), the Asian Development Bank, the Colombo Plan for Co-operative Economic and Social Development in Asia and the Pacific, and the International Sugar Organization. Fiji is a signatory to the South Pacific Regional Trade and Economic Co-operation Agreement (SPARTECA) and also to the Lomé Conventions and successor Cotonou Agreement with the European Union (EU). In 1996 Fiji was admitted to the Melanesian Spearhead Group.

Statistical Survey

Sources (unless otherwise stated): Bureau of Statistics, POB 2221, Government Bldgs, Suva; tel. 315144; fax 303656; internet www.statsfiji.gov.fj; Reserve Bank of Fiji, POB 1220, Suva; tel. 3313611; fax 3301688; e-mail rbf@reservebank.gov.fj; internet www.reservebank.gov.fj.

AREA AND POPULATION

Area (incl. the Rotuma group): 18,376 sq km (7,095 sq miles). Land area of 18,333 sq km (7,078 sq miles) consists mainly of the islands of Viti Levu (10,429 sq km—4,027 sq miles) and Vanua Levu (5,556 sq km—2,145 sq miles).

Population: 715,375 at census of 31 August 1986; 775,077 (males 393,931, females 381,146) at census of 25 August 1996; 844,330 (estimate) at mid-2001.

Density (mid-2001): 45.9 per sq km.

Principal Towns (population at 1996 census): Suva (capital) 77,366; Lautoka 36,083; Nadi 9,170; Labasa 6,491; Ba 6,314.

Ethnic Groups (1996 census): Fijians 393,575; Indians 338,818; Part-European 11,685; European 3,103; Rotuman 9,727; Chinese 4,939; Other Pacific Islanders 10,463; Others 2,767; Total 775,077.

Births, Marriages and Deaths (registrations, 1998): Live births 17,944 (birth rate 22.5 per 1,000); Marriages 8,058 (marriage rate 10.1 per 1,000); Deaths 5,241 (death rate 6.6 per 1,000). Source: UN, *Demographic Yearbook*.

Expectation of Life (WHO estimates years at birth, 2000): Males 66.9; Females 71.2. (Source: WHO, *World Health Report*).

Economically Active Population (persons aged 15 years and over, census of 31 August 1986): Agriculture, hunting, forestry and fishing 106,305; Mining and quarrying 1,345; Manufacturing 18,106; Electricity, gas and water 2,154; Construction 11,786; Trade, restaurants and hotels 26,010; Transport, storage and communications 13,151; Financing, insurance, real estate and business services 6,016; Community, social and personal services 36,619; Activities not adequately defined 1,479; Total employed 222,971 (males 179,595, females 43,376); Unemployed 18,189 (males 10,334, females 7,855); Total labour force 241,160 (males 189,929, females 51,231).

1999 (total labour force, provisional): 330,800 (unemployed 25,100). *2000* (total labour force, provisional): 341,700 (unemployed 41,700).

HEALTH AND WELFARE

Key Indicators

Fertility (births per woman, 2000): 3.1.

Under-5 Mortality Rate (per 1,000 live births, 2000): 22.

HIV/AIDS (% of persons aged 15–49, 2001): 0.07.

Physicians (per 1,000 head, 1997): 0.48.

Health Expenditure (1998): US $ per head (PPP): 170.
% of GDP: 4.1.
public (% of total): 65.4.

Access to Water (% of persons, 2000): 47.

Access to Sanitation (% of persons, 2000): 43.

Human Development Index (2000): ranking: 72.
value: 0.758.

For sources and definitions, see explanatory note on p. vi.

AGRICULTURE, ETC.

Principal Crops (mostly FAO estimates, '000 metric tons, 2000): Sugar cane 2,250; Coconuts 215; Copra 13; Cassava 30; Rice (paddy) 18; Sweet potatoes 8; Bananas 7; Yams 4; Taro 27. Source: FAO.

Livestock (FAO estimates, '000 head, year ending September 2000): Cattle 350; Pigs 115; Goats 235; Horses 44; Chickens 4,000. Source: FAO.

Livestock Products (mostly FAO estimates, metric tons, 2000): Poultry meat 8,270; Beef and veal 9,500; Goat meat 935; Pig meat 3,600; Hen eggs 3,600; Cows' milk 57,600; Butter and ghee 1,800; Honey 65. Source: FAO.

Forestry ('000 cubic metres, 2000): *Roundwood removals* (excl. bark): Sawlogs and veneer logs 199; Fuel wood 37; Pulpwood 250; Total 486. *Sawnwood production* (incl. sleepers): 112. Source: FAO, *Yearbook of Forest Products*.

Fishing ('000 metric tons, live weight, 1999): Capture 36.7 (Groupers 1.6, Snappers 1.7, Emperors 3.0, Barracudas 3.0, Mullets 3.1, Narrow-barred Spanish mackerel 2.3, Albacore 2.3, Freshwater molluscs 5.0, Anadara clams 3.0, Other marine molluscs 3.3); Aquaculture 1.8; Total catch 38.5. Figures exclude aquatic plants ('000 metric tons): 1.6 (Capture 0.1, Aquaculture 1.5). Also excluded are trochus shells (165 metric tons), pearl oyster shells (12 tons) and corals (1,000 tons). Source: FAO, *Yearbook of Fishery Statistics*.

MINING

Production (kg, 2001): Gold 3,865; Silver 1,934.

INDUSTRY

Production (metric tons, 2001): Sugar 310,000; Molasses 142,000*; Flour 59,569; Soap 5,341; Cement 98,000; Paint 2,789 ('000 litres); Beer 18,000 ('000 litres); Soft drinks 24,160 ('000 litres); Cigarettes

442; Matches 128 ('000 gross boxes); Electric energy 535† (million kWh); Ice cream 1,257 ('000 litres); Toilet paper 20,225 ('000 rolls).

* 1997 figure.

† 1998 estimate (Source: UN, *Industrial Commodity Statistics Yearbook*).

FINANCE

Currency and Exchange Rates: 100 cents = 1 Fiji dollar ($F). *Sterling, US Dollar and Euro Equivalents* (31 May 2002): £1 sterling = $F3.1454; US $1 = $F2.1445; €1 = $F2.0131; $F100 = £31.79 = US $46.63 = €49.68. *Average Exchange Rate* ($F per US $): 1.9696 in 1999; 2.1286 in 2000; 2.2766 in 2001.

General Budget (provisional, $F million, 2000): *Revenue:* Current revenue 894 (Taxes 713, Non-taxes 181); Capital revenue 16; Total 910. *Expenditure:* General public services 125.1; Defence 60.2; Education 123.1; Health 72.8; Social security and welfare 1.6; Housing and community amenities 6.3; Economic services 109.4 (Agriculture 9.1, Industry 27.6, Electricity, gas and water 9.0, Transport and communications 21.4); Other purposes 583.5; Total 1,082 (Current 936, Capital 146. Source: Asian Development Bank, *Key Indicators of Developing Asian and Pacific Countries*.

2001 ($F million): Total revenue 921.7; Total expenditure 935.7.

International Reserves (US $ million at 31 December 2001): Gold (valued at market-related prices) 0.23; IMF special drawing rights 6.04; Reserve position in IMF 18.85; Foreign exchange 341.64; Total 366.54. Source: IMF, *International Financial Statistics*.

Money Supply ($F million at 31 December 2001): Currency outside banks 181.7; Demand deposits at commercial banks 434.2; Total money (incl. others) 620.9. Source: IMF, *International Financial Statistics*.

Cost of Living (Consumer Price Index; base: 1995 = 100): 114.8 in 1999; 116.1 in 2000; 121.0 in 2001. Source: IMF, *International Financial Statistics*.

Expenditure on the Gross Domestic Product ($F million at current prices, 1999): Government final consumption expenditure 588.2; Private final consumption expenditure 2,105.3; Increase in stocks 40.0; Gross fixed capital formation 390.2; *Total domestic expenditure* 3,123.7; Exports of goods and services 2,062.8; *Less* Imports of goods and services 1,818.5; Statistical discrepancy 220.4; *GDP in purchasers' values* 3,588.4. Source: IMF, *International Financial Statistics*.

Gross Domestic Product by Economic Activity ($F million at constant 1989 prices, 2000, preliminary): Agriculture, forestry and fishing 342.1; Mining and quarrying 51.1; Manufacturing 295.9; Electricity, gas and water 87.6; Building and construction 88.4; Wholesale and retail trade 331.8; Hotels and restaurants 50.2; Transport and communications 270.0; Finance, real estate, etc. 248.3; Community, social and personal services 376.4; Other services 16.3; Sub-total 2,158.1; *Less* Imputed bank service charges 125.8; GDP at factor cost 2,032.2. Source: Fiji Islands Trade and Investment Bureau.

Balance of Payments (US $ million, 1999): Exports of goods f.o.b. 537.7; Imports of goods f.o.b. –653.3; *Trade balance* –115.6; Exports of services 525.1; Imports of services –389.8; *Balance on goods and services* 19.7; Other income received 47.3; Other income paid –82.8; *Balance on goods, services and income* –15.8; Current transfers received 42.7; Current transfers paid –14.2; *Current balance* 12.7; Capital account (net) 14.0; Direct investment abroad –53.0; Direct investment from abroad –33.2; Other investment assets –62.2; Other investment liabilities 44.4; Net errors and omissions 32.5; *Overall balance* –44.9. Source: IMF, *International Financial Statistics*.

EXTERNAL TRADE

Principal Commodities ($F million, 2001): *Imports c.i.f.* (distribution by SITC): Food and live animals 310.8; Mineral fuels, lubricants, etc. 271.7; Chemicals and related products 143.3; Basic manufactures 417.4; Machinery and transport equipment 414.0; Miscellaneous manufactured articles 200.2; Total (incl. others) 1,807.9. *Exports f.o.b.:* Food and live animals 398.9; Beverages and tobacco 29.3; Crude materials (inedible) except fuels 52.2; Basic manufactures 65.8; Miscellaneous manufactured articles 354.1; Total (incl. others) 1,007.8. Source: Fiji Islands Trade and Investment Bureau.

Principal Trading Partners (US $ million, 2001): *Imports c.i.f.:* Australia 387.3; China, People's Republic 27.3; Hong Kong 25.8; India 16.2; Japan 29.1; Malaysia 12.0; New Zealand 112.1; Singapore 63.6; Thailand 16.2; USA 21.3; Total (incl. others) 812.3. *Exports:* Australia 133.0; Hong Kong 10.9; Japan 32.0; Kiribati 9.3; New Zealand 22.0; Portugal 16.4; Samoa 31.0; Tonga 15.0; United Kingdom 79.0; USA 181.0; Total (incl. others) 650.0. Source: Asian Development Bank, *Key Indicators of Developing Asian and Pacific Countries*.

TRANSPORT

Road Traffic (motor vehicles registered at 31 December 1998): Passenger cars 47,053; Goods vehicles 34,182; Buses 1,801; Taxis 2,956; Rental vehicles 4,714; Motorcycles 4,409; Tractors 5,404; Total (incl. others) 104,760.

Shipping: *Merchant Fleet* (registered at 31 December 2001): Vessels 50; Total displacement ('000 grt) 28.7. Source: Lloyd's Register-Fairplay, *World Fleet Statistics*. *International Freight Traffic* ('000 metric tons, 1990): Goods loaded 568; Goods unloaded 625. Source: UN, *Monthly Bulletin of Statistics*.

Civil Aviation (traffic on scheduled services, 1998): Passengers carried 516,000; Passenger-kilometres 2,000 million; Total ton-kilometres 200 million. Source: UN, *Statistical Yearbook*.

TOURISM

Foreign Visitors by Country of Residence (excluding cruise-ship passengers, 2001): Australia 98,213, Canada 10,752, Japan 20,411, New Zealand 66,472, Pacific Islands 23,608, United Kingdom 30,508, USA 57,711; Total (incl. others) 348,014.

Tourism Receipts ($F million): 558.6 in 1999; 413.5 in 2000; 495.5 in 2001.

COMMUNICATIONS MEDIA

Radio Receivers (1997): 500,000 in use*.

Television Receivers (2000): 92,000 in use†.

Telephones (2001): 90,400 main lines in use†.

Facsimile Machines (1999): 2,815 in use†.

Mobile Cellular Telephones (2001): 76,000 subscribers†.

Personal Computers (2001): 50,000 in use†.

Internet Users (2001): 15,000†.

Book Production (1980): 110 titles (84 books, 26 pamphlets); 273,000 copies (229,000 books, 44,000 pamphlets).

Daily Newspaper (2001): 3 (estimated combined circulation 49,124)‡.

Non-daily Newspapers (provisional, 1988): 7 (combined circulation 99,000)*.

* Source: UNESCO, *Statistical Yearbook*.

† Source: International Telecommunication Union.

‡ Source: Audit Bureau of Circulations, Australia.

EDUCATION

Primary (2000): 709 schools (1995); 5,082 teachers; 142,912 pupils.

General Secondary (2000): 146 schools (1995); 3,696 teachers; 66,905 pupils.

Vocational and Technical (2000): 31 institutions (1994); 1,024 teachers (including special schools); 1,730 students.

Teacher Training (2000): 4 institutions (1994); 97 teachers; 1,003 students.

Medical (1989): 2 institutions; 493 students.

University (1999): 1 institution; 277 teachers (1991); 9,208 students.

Source: mainly UNESCO, *Statistical Yearbook*, and UN, *Statistical Yearbook for Asia and the Pacific*.

Adult literacy rate (UNESCO estimates): 92.9% (males 94.9%, females 90.8%) in 2000 (Source: UN Development Programme, *Human Development Report*).

Directory

The Constitution

On 1 March 2001 President Iloilo reinstated the 1997 Constitution, after the Great Council of Chiefs (Bose Levu Vakaturaga—a traditional body, with some 70 members, consisting of every hereditary chief or Ratu of each Fijian clan) had approved the draft. The Constitution Amendment Bill that was approved in July 1997 included provisions to ensure of a multi-racial Cabinet. The following is a summary of the main provisions:

The Constitution, which declares Fiji to be a sovereign, democratic republic, guarantees fundamental human rights, a universal, secret and equal suffrage and equality before the law for all Fijian citizens. Citizenship may be acquired by birth, descent, registration or naturalization and is assured for all those who were Fijian citizens before 6 October 1987. Parliament may make provision for the deprivation or renunciation of a person's citizenship. Ethnic Fijians, and the Polynesian inhabitants of Rotuma, receive special constitutional consideration. The Judicial and Legal Services Commission, the Public Service Commission and the Police Service Commission are established as supervisory bodies.

THE GREAT COUNCIL OF CHIEFS

The Great Council of Chiefs (Bose Levu Vakaturaga) derives its authority from the status of its members and their chiefly lineage.

The Great Council appoints the President of the Republic and selects the 14 nominees for appointment to the Senate, the upper chamber of the Parliament.

The Great Council became fully independent of the Government in mid-1999.

THE EXECUTIVE

Executive authority is vested in the President of the Republic, who is appointed by the Great Council of Chiefs, for a five-year term, to be constitutional Head of State and Commander-in-Chief of the armed forces. The Presidential Council advises the President on matters of national importance. The President, and Parliament, can be empowered to introduce any necessary measures in an emergency or in response to acts of subversion which threaten Fiji.

In most cases the President is guided by the Cabinet, which conducts the government of the Republic. The Cabinet is led by the Prime Minister, who is a Fijian of any ethnic origin and is appointed by the President from among the members of Parliament, on the basis of support in the legislature. The Prime Minister selects the other members of the Cabinet (the Attorney-General, the minister responsible for defence and security and any other ministers) from either the House of Representatives or the Senate on a multi-party and multiracial basis. The Cabinet is responsible to Parliament.

THE LEGISLATURE

Legislative power is vested in the Parliament, which comprises the President, the appointed upper house or Senate and an elected House of Representatives. The maximum duration of a parliament is five years.

The Senate has 32 members, appointed by the President of the Republic for the term of the Parliament. A total of 14 senators are nominated by the Great Council of Chiefs, nine are appointed on the advice of the Prime Minister, eight on the advice of the Leader of the Opposition, and one on the advice of the Rotuma Island Council. The Senate is a house of review, with some powers to initiate legislation, but with limited influence on financial measures. The Senate is important in the protection of ethnic Fijian interests, and its consent is essential to any attempt to amend, alter or repeal any provisions affecting ethnic Fijians, their customs, land or tradition.

The House of Representatives has 71 elected members, who themselves elect their presiding officials and the Speaker from outside the membership of the House, and Deputy Speaker from among their number (excluding ministers). Voting is communal, with universal suffrage for all citizens of the Republic aged over 21 years. Seats are reserved on a racial basis: 23 for ethnic Fijians, 19 for Indians, three for other races (General Electors), one for Rotuma Islanders and 25 open seats. Elections must be held at least every five years and are to be administered by an independent Supervisor of Elections. An independent Boundaries Commission determines constituency boundaries.

THE JUDICIARY

The judiciary is independent and comprises the High Court, the Fiji Court of Appeal and the Supreme Court. The High Court and the Supreme Court are the final arbiters of the Constitution. The establishment of Fijian courts is provided for, and decisions of the Native Lands Commission (relating to ethnic Fijian customs, traditions and usage, and on disputes over the headship of any part of the Fijian people, with the customary right to occupy and use any native lands) are declared to be final and without appeal.

The Government

HEAD OF STATE

President: Ratu JOSEFA ILOILO (appointed 12 July 2000 by an interim authority established following the coup of 19 May 2000).

Vice-President: Ratu JOPE SENILOLI.

THE CABINET

(September 2002)

Prime Minister, Minister for Fijian Affairs, Culture and Heritage, National Reconciliation and Unity, Information and Media Relations: LAISENIA QARASE.

Minister for Foreign Affairs and External Trade: KALIOPATE TAVOLA.

Minister for Finance, National Planning and Communications: Ratu JONE KUBUABOLA.

Attorney-General and Minister for Justice: QORINIASI BALE.

Minister for Lands and Mineral Resources: Ratu NAIQAMA LALABALAVU.

Minister for Works and Energy: SAVENACA DRAUNIDALO.

Minister for Education: RO TEIMUMU VUIKABA KEPA.

Minister for Tourism: PITA NACUVA.

Minister for Transport and Civil Aviation: JOSEFA VOSANIBOLA.

Minister for Labour, Industrial Relations and Productivity: KENNETH ZINCK.

Minister for Commerce, Business Development and Investment: TOMASI VUETILOVONI.

Minister for Local Government, Housing, Squatter Settlement and Environment: MATAIASI VAVE RAGIGIA

Minister of Health: SOLOMONE NAIVALU.

Minister for Agriculture, Sugar and Land Resettlement: JONETANI GALUINADI.

Minister for Regional Development: ILAITIA TUISESE.

Minister for Women, Social Welfare and Poverty Alleviation: ASENACA CAUCAU.

Minister for Youth, Employment Opportunities and Sports: ISIRELI LEWENIQILA.

Minister for Home Affairs and Immigration: JOKETANI COKANASIGA.

Minister for Fisheries and Forests: KONISI YABAKI.

Minister for Public Enterprises and Public Sector Reform: IRAMI MATAIRAVULA.

Minister for Multi-Ethnic Affairs: GEORGE SHIU RAJ.

MINISTRIES

Office of the President: Government Bldgs, POB 2513, Suva; tel. 3314244; fax 3301645.

Office of the Prime Minister: Government Bldgs, POB 2353, Suva; tel. 3211201; fax 3306034; e-mail pmsoffice@is.com.fj; internet www.fiji.gov.fj.

Office of the Attorney-General and Ministry of Justice: Government Bldgs, Victoria Parade, POB 2213, Suva; tel. 3309866; fax 3305421.

Ministry of Agriculture, Sugar and Land Resettlement: PMB, POB 358, Raiwaqa; tel. 3384233; fax 3385048; e-mail maffinfo@is.com.fj.

Ministry of Commerce, Business Development and Investment: Government Bldgs, POB 2118, Suva; tel. 3305411; fax 3302617.

Ministry of Education: Marela House, Thurston St, PMB, Suva; tel. 3314477; fax 3303511.

Ministry of Fijian Affairs: Government Bldgs, POB 2100, Suva; tel. 3304200; fax 3302585.

Ministry of Finance and National Planning: Government Bldgs, POB 2212, Suva; tel. 3307011; fax 3300834.

Ministry of Fisheries and Forests: POB 2218, Government Bldgs, Suva; tel. 3301611; fax 3301595; e-mail forestry-hq@msd.gov.fj.

Ministry of Foreign Affairs and External Trade: Government Bldgs, POB 2220, Suva; tel. 3211458; fax 3301741; e-mail info@foreignaffairs.gov.fj; internet www.foreignaffairs.gov.fj.

Ministry of Health: Government Bldgs, POB 2223, Suva; tel. 3306177; fax 3306163; e-mail info@health.gov.fj.

Ministry of Home Affairs and Immigration: Government Bldgs, POB 2349, Suva; tel. 3211401; fax 3300346.

Ministry of Labour, Industrial Relations and Productivity: Government Bldgs, POB 2216, Suva; tel. 3211640 and fax 3304701; e-mail minlabour@is.com.fj.

Ministry of Lands and Mineral Resources: Government Bldgs, POB 2222, Suva; tel. 3211556; fax 330437; e-mail mbaravilala@lands.gov.fj.

Ministry of Local Government, Housing, Squatter Settlement and Environment: *National Planning:* Government Bldgs, POB 2351, Suva; tel. 3313411; fax 3304809; *Local Government:* Government Bldgs, POB 2131; tel. 3211310; fax 3303515; *Environment:* Government Bldgs, POB 2131; tel. 3311069; fax 3312879; e-mail msovaki@govnet.gov.fj.

Ministry of National Reconciliation, Information and Media Relations: Government Bldgs, POB 2645, Suva; tel. 3211250; fax 3303146; e-mail info@fiji.gov.fj.

Ministry of Public Enterprise and Public Sector Reform: Government Bldgs, POB 2278, Suva; tel. 3315577; fax 3315035; e-mail achandoo2@govnet.gov.fj.

Ministry of Regional Development: Government Bldgs, POB 2219, Suva; tel. 3313400; fax 3313035.

Ministry of Tourism: Third Floor, Civic Tower, POB 1260, Suva; tel. 3312788; fax 3302060; e-mail infodesk@fijivb.gov.fj; internet www.bulafiji.com.

Ministry of Transport and Civil Aviation: POB 1260, Suva; tel. 3312788; fax 3302060; e-mail infodesk@fijifvb.gov.fj; internet www.bulafiji.com.

Ministry of Women, Social Welfare and Poverty Alleviation: POB 14068, Suva; tel. 3312199; fax 3303829; e-mail slomaloma@govnet.gov.fj.

Ministry of Works and Energy: POB 2493, Government Bldgs, Suva; tel. 3384111; fax 3383198.

Ministry of Youth, Employment Opportunities and Sports: Government Bldgs, POB 2448, Suva; tel. 3315960; fax 3305348.

Legislature

PARLIAMENT

Senate

The Senate is also known as the House of Review. The upper chamber comprises 32 appointed members (see The Constitution).

House of Representatives

The lower chamber comprises 71 elected members: 23 representing ethnic Fijians, 19 representing ethnic Indians, three representing other races (General Electors), one for Rotuma Islanders and 25 seats open to all races.

Speaker: Ratu EPELI NAILATIKAU.

General Election, 25 August–1 September 2001

	Communal Seats			Open Seats	Total Seats
	Fijian	Indian	Other*		
Fiji United Party (SDL)	18	—	1	13	32
Fiji Labour Party (FLP)	—	19	—	8	27
Conservative Alliance Party (MV)	5	—	—	1	6
New Labour Unity Party (NLUP)	—	—	1	1	2
National Federation Party (NFP)	—	0	—	1	1
United General Party (UGP)	—	—	1	—	1
Independents	—	—	1	1	2
Total	23	19	4	25	71

* One Rotuman and three General Electors' seats.

Notes: The total includes one seat won by the Fiji United Party in a by-election held on 25 September 2001. In September 2002, following a court ruling, the one NFP seat was awarded to the FLP, thus bringing the latter's representation to 28 seats.

Political Organizations

Bai Kei Viti: Suva; f. 2001; Sec. Ratu TEVITA MOMOEDONU.

Fiji Indian Congress: POB 3661, Samabula, Suva; tel. 3391211; fax 3340117; f. 1991; Gen. Sec. VIJAY RAGHWAN.

Fiji Indian Liberal Party: Rakiraki; f. 1991; represents the interests of the Indian community, particularly sugar-cane farmers and students; Sec. SWANI KUMAR.

Fiji Labour Party (FLP): POB 2162, Government Bldgs, Suva; tel. 3305811; fax 3305317; e-mail flp@connect.com; internet www.flp.org.fj; f. 1985; Pres. JOKAPECI KOROI; Sec.-Gen. MAHENDRA PAL CHAUDHRY.

Fijian Association Party (FAP): Suva; f. 1995 by merger of Fijian Association (a breakaway faction of the SVT) and the multiracial All Nationals Congress; Leader Ratu TU'UAKITAU COKANAUTO (acting); Pres. Ratu VILIAME DREUNIMISIMISI.

Fijian Conservative Party: Suva; f. 1989 by former mems of the Fiji Nationalist Party and the Alliance Party; Leader ISIRELI VUIBAU.

Fijian Nationalist United Front Party (FNUFP): POB 1336, Suva; tel. 3362317; f. 1992 to replace Fijian Nationalist Party; seeks additional parliamentary representation for persons of Fijian ethnic origin, the introduction of other pro-Fijian reforms and the repatriation of ethnic Indians; Leader SAKEASI BAKEWA BUTADROKA.

Janata Party: Suva; f. 1995 by former mems of NFP and FLP.

Matanitu Vanua (MV) (Conservative Alliance Party): c/o House of Representatives, Suva; f. 2001; Leader GEORGE SPEIGHT.

National Federation Party (NFP): POB 13534, Suva; tel. 3305811; fax 3305317; f. 1960 by merger of the Federation Party, which was multiracial but mainly Indian, and the National Democratic Party; Leader PREM SINGH; Pres. SHIU CHARAN; Gen. Sec. ATTAR SINGH.

Nationalist Vanua Takolavo Party (NVTLP): c/o House of Representatives, Suva; Leader SAULA TELAWA.

New Labour Movement: Suva; Gen. Sec. MICHAEL COLUMBUS.

New Labour United Party (NLUP): Suva; f. 2001 by TUPENI BABA.

Party of National Unity (PANU): Ba; f. 1998 to lobby for increased representation for the province of Ba; Leader MELI BOGILEKA.

Soqosoqo Duavata ni Lewenivanua (SDL) (Fiji United Party): c/o House of Representatives, Suva; f. 1990; Leader LAISENIA QARASE.

Soqosoqo ni Vakavulewa ni Taukei (SVT) (Fijian Political Party): Suva; f. 1990 by Great Council of Chiefs; supports constitutional dominance of ethnic Fijians but accepts multiracialism; Pres. Ratu EPELI MATAITIUI.

Taukei Movement: POB 505, Lautoka; f. 1987, following merger of Taukei Liberation Front and Domo Ni Taukei group; right-wing indigenous Fijian nationalist group; Pres. Ratu TEVITA BOLOBOLO; Vice-Pres. Ratu INOKE KUBUABOLA; Gen. Sec. APISAI TORA.

United General Party (UGP): Suva; f. 1998 by the merger of the General Electors' Party and the General Voters' Party (fmrly the General Electors' Association, one of the three wings of the Alliance Party—AP, the ruling party 1970–87); represents the interests of the minority Chinese and European communities and people from other Pacific Islands resident in Fiji, all of whom are classed as General Electors under the 1998 Constitution; Pres. DAVID PICKERING.

Vanua Independent Party: Leader ILIESA TUVALOVO; Sec. URAIA TUISOVISOVI.

Veitokani ni Lewenivanua Vakarisito (VLV) (Christian Democratic Alliance): c/o House of Representatives, Suva; f. 1998 in opposition to constitutional reforms and to defend Christian and Melanesian interests; Leader POESCI WAQALEVU BUNE; Sec. TANIELA TABU.

Other minor parties that contested the 2001 election included the Justice and Freedom Party, the Dodonu ni Taukei Party, the Girmit Heritage Party, the General Voters Party, the Lio'on Famor Rotuma Party and the Party of the Truth.

Supporters of secession are concentrated in Rotuma.

Diplomatic Representation

EMBASSIES AND HIGH COMMISSIONS IN FIJI

Australia: 37 Princes Rd, POB 214, Suva; tel. 3382211; fax 3382065; e-mail public-sffairs-suva@dfat.gov.au; High Commissioner: SUSAN BOYD.

China, People's Republic: 147 Queen Elizabeth Dr., PMB, Nasese, Suva; tel. 3300215; fax 3300950; e-mail chinaemb@is.com.fj; Ambassador: ZHANG JUNSAI.

France: Dominion House, 7th Floor, Thomson St, Suva; tel. 3312233; fax 3301894; e-mail vidon@ambafrance.org.fj; Ambassador: JEAN-PIERRE VIDON.

India: POB 471, Suva; tel. 3301125; fax 3301032; e-mail hicomind suva@is.com.fj; High Commissioner: ISHWAR SINGH CHAUHAN.

Japan: Dominion House, 2nd Floor, POB 13045, Suva; tel. 3304633; fax 3302984; e-mail eojfiji@is.com.fj; Ambassador: HISATO MURAYAMA.

Korea, Republic: Vanua House, 8th Floor, PMB, Suva; tel. 3300977; fax 3303410; Ambassador: LIM DAE-TAEK.

Malaysia: Pacific House, 5th Floor, POB 356, Suva; tel. 3312166; fax 3303350; e-mail mwsuva@is.com.fj; High Commissioner: MOHAMMED TAKWIR DIN.

Marshall Islands: 41 Borron Rd, Government Bldgs, POB 2038, Suva; tel. 3387899; fax 3387115; Ambassador: MACK KAMINAGA.

Micronesia, Federated States: 37 Loftus St, POB 15493, Suva; tel. 304566; fax 3300842; e-mail fsmsuva@sopacsun.sopac.org.fj; Ambassador: KODARO MARTIN GALLEN.

Nauru: Ratu Sukuna House, 7th Floor, Government Bldgs, POB 2420, Suva; tel. 3313566; fax 3302861; High Commissioner: CAMILLA SOLOMON.

New Zealand: Reserve Bank of Fiji Bldg, 10th Floor, Pratt St, POB 1378, Suva; tel. 3311422; fax 3300842; e-mail nzhc@is.com.fj; High Commissioner: ADRIAN SIMCOCK.

Papua New Guinea: Credit Corporation House, 3rd Floor, Government Bldgs, POB 2447, Suva; tel. 3304244; fax 3300178; e-mail kundufj@is.com.fj; High Commissioner: BABANI MARAGA.

Tuvalu: 16 Gorrie St, POB 14449, Suva; tel. 3301355; fax 3308479; High Commissioner: TAUKELINA FINIKASO.

United Kingdom: Victoria House, 47 Gladstone Rd, POB 1355, Suva; tel. 3311033; fax 3301406; e-mail ukinfo@bhc.org.fj; internet www.ukinthepacific.bhc.org.fj; High Commissioner: CHARLES MOCHAN.

USA: 31 Loftus Rd, POB 218, Suva; tel. 3314466; fax 3300081; e-mail usembsuva@is.com.fj; internet www.amembassy-fiji.gov; Chargé d'affaires: RONALD K. MCMULLEN.

Judicial System

Justice is administered by the Supreme Court, the Fiji Court of Appeal, the High Court and the Magistrates' Courts. The Supreme Court of Fiji is the superior court of record presided over by the Chief Justice. The 1990 Constitution provided for the establishment of Fijian customary courts and declared as final decisions of the Native Lands Commission in cases involving Fijian custom, etc.

Supreme Court: Suva; tel. 3211524; fax 3300674.

Chief Justice: DANIEL FATIAKI.

President of the Fiji Court of Appeal: JAI RAM REDDY.

Director of Public Prosecutions: PETER RIDGWAY.

Solicitor-General: NAINENDRA NAND.

Religion

CHRISTIANITY

Most ethnic Fijians are Christians. Methodists are the largest Christian group, followed by Roman Catholics. In the census of 1986 about 53% of the population were Christian (mainly Methodists).

Fiji Council of Churches: POB 2300, Government Bldgs, Suva; tel. (1) 3313798; f. 1964; seven mem. churches; Pres. Most Rev. APIMELEKI QILIO; Gen. Sec. BENJAMIN BHAGWAN.

The Anglican Communion

In April 1990 Polynesia, formerly a missionary diocese of the Church of the Province of New Zealand, became a full and integral diocese. The diocese of Polynesia is based in Fiji but also includes Wallis and Futuna, Tuvalu, Kiribati, French Polynesia, Cook Islands, Tonga, Samoa and Tokelau.

Bishop of Polynesia: Rt Rev. Jabez Leslie Bryce, Bishop's Office, 8 Desvoeux Rd, Suva; e-mail episcopus@is.com.fj; tel. 3304716; fax 3302687.

The Roman Catholic Church

Fiji comprises a single archdiocese. At 31 December 1999 there were an estimated 86,141 adherents in the country.

Bishops' Conference: Episcopal Conference of the Pacific Secretariat (CEPAC), 14 Williamson Rd, POB 289, Suva; tel. 3300340; fax 3303143; e-mail cepac@is.com.fj; f. 1968; 17 mems; Pres. Most Rev. MICHEL MARIE CALVET, Archbishop of Nouméa, New Caledonia; Gen. Sec. (vacant); Admin. Officer THOMAS TAVUTONIVALU

Regional Appeal Tribunal for CEPAC: 14 Williamson Rd, POB 289, Suva; tel. 300340; fax 3303143; e-mail cepac@is.com.fj; f. 1980; 17 mems; Judicial Vicar Rev. THEO KOSTER.

Archbishop of Suva: Most Rev. PETERO MATACA, Archdiocesan Office, Nicolas House, Pratt St, POB 109, Suva; tel. 3301955; fax 3301565.

Other Christian Churches

Methodist Church in Fiji (Lotu Wesele e Viti): Epworth Arcade, Nina St, POB 357, Suva; tel. 3311477; fax 3303771; f. 1835; autonomous since 1964; 215,416 mems (1999); Pres. Rev. TOMASI KANAILAGI; Gen. Sec. Rev. LAISIASA RATABACACA.

Other denominations active in the country include the Assembly of God (with *c.* 7,000 mems), the Baptist Mission, the Congregational Christian Church and the Presbyterian Church.

HINDUISM

Most of the Indian community are Hindus. According to the census of 1986, 38% of the population were Hindus.

ISLAM

In 1993 some 8% of the population were Muslim. There are several Islamic organizations:

Fiji Muslim League: POB 3990, Samabula, Suva; tel. 3384566; fax 3370204; f. 1926; e-mail fijimuslim@is.com.fj; Nat. Pres. HAFIZUD DEAN KHAN; Gen. Sec. NISAR AHMAD ALI; 26 brs and 3 subsidiary orgs.

SIKHISM

Sikh Association of Fiji: Suva; Pres. HARKEWAL SINGH.

BAHÁ'Í FAITH

National Spiritual Assembly: National Office, POB 639, Suva; tel. 3387574; fax 3387772; e-mail nsafijiskm@suva.is.com.fj; mems resident in 490 localities; national headquarters for consultancy and co-ordination.

The Press

NEWSPAPERS AND PERIODICALS

Coconut Telegraph: POB 249, Savusavu, Vanua Levu; f. 1975; monthly; serves widely-scattered rural communities; Editor LEMA LOW.

Fiji Calling: POB 12095, Suva; tel. 3305916; fax 3301930; publ. by Associated Media Ltd; every 6 months; English; Publr YASHWANT GAUNDER.

Fiji Cane Grower: POB 12095, Suva; tel. 3305916; fax 3305256.

Fiji Daily Post: 10–16 Toorak Rd, POB 2071, Govt Bldgs, Suva; f. 1987 as *Fiji Post*, daily from 1989; English; 45% govt-owned; Gen. Man. ANURA BANDARA (acting); Editor JALE MOALA.

Fiji Magic: POB 12095, Suva; tel. 3305916; fax 3301930; e-mail review@is.com.fj; publ. by The Review Ltd; monthly; English; Publr YASHWANT GAUNDER.

Fiji Republic Gazette: Printing Dept, POB 98, Suva; tel. 3385999; fax 3370203; f. 1874; weekly; English.

Fiji Sun: Suva; re-established 1999; daily; Editor MARK GARRET.

Fiji Times: 20 Gordon St, POB 1167, Suva; tel. 3304111; fax 3301521; f. 1869; publ. by Fiji Times Ltd; daily; English; Man. Dir TONY IANNI; Editor SAMISONI KAKAIUALU; circ. 34,000.

Fiji Trade Review: The Rubine Group, POB 12511, Suva; tel. 3313944; monthly; English; Publr GEORGE RUBINE; Editor MABEL HOWARD.

Islands Business Magazine: 46 Gordon St, POB 12718, Suva; tel. 3303108; fax 3301423; e-mail editor@ibi.com.fj; internet www.pacificislands.cc; fmrly *Pacific Magazine;* regional monthly news and business magazine featuring the Fiji Islands Business supplement; English; Publr ROBERT KEITH-REID; Editor-in-Chief LAISA TAGA; circ. 8,500.

Na Tui: 422 Fletcher Rd, POB 2071, Govt Bldgs, Suva; f. 1988; weekly; Fijian; Publr TANIELA BOLEA; Editor SAMISONI BOLATAGICI; circ. 7,000.

Nai Lalakai: 20 Gordon St, POB 1167, Suva; tel. 3304111; fax 3301521; e-mail fijitimes@is.com.fj; f. 1962; publ. by Fiji Times Ltd; weekly; Fijian; Editor SAMISONI KAKAIVALU; circ. 18,000.

Pacific Business: POB 12095, Suva; tel. 3305916; fax 3301930; publ. by Associated Media Ltd; monthly; English; Publr YASHWANT GAUNDER.

Pacific Telecom: POB 12095, Suva; tel. 3300591; fax 3302852; e-mail review@is.com.fj; publ. by Associated Media Ltd; monthly; English; Publr YASHWANT GAUNDER.

Pactrainer: PMB, Suva; tel. 3303623; fax 3303943; e-mail pina@is.com.fj; monthly; newsletter of Pacific Journalism Development Centre; Editor PETER LOMAS.

PINA Nius: Pacific Islands News Association, 46 Gordon St, PMB, Suva; tel. 3303623; fax 3303943; e-mail pina@is.com.fj; internet www.pinarius.org; monthly newsletter of Pacific Islands News Association; Editor NINA RATULELE.

The Review: POB 12095, Suva; tel. 3305916; fax 3301930; e-mail review@is.com.fj; publ. by Associated Media Ltd; monthly; English; Publr YASHWANT GAUNDER.

Sartaj: John Beater Enterprises Ltd, Raiwaqa, POB 5141, Suva; f. 1988; weekly; Hindi; Editor S. DASO; circ. 15,000.

Shanti Dut: 20 Gordon St, POB 1167, Suva; f. 1935; publ. by Fiji Times Ltd; weekly; Hindi; Editor NILAM KUMAR; circ. 12,000.

Top Shot: Suva; f. 1995; golf magazine; monthly.

Volasiga: 10–16 Toorak Rd, POB 2071, Suva; f. 1988; weekly; Fijian; Gen. Man. ANURA BANDARA (acting); Editor SAMISONI BOLATAGICI.

The Weekender: 2 Dension Rd, POB 15652, Suva; tel. 3315477; fax 3305346; publ. by Media Resources Ltd; weekly; English; Publr JOSEFATA NATA.

PRESS ASSOCIATIONS

Fiji Islands Media Association: c/o Vasiti Ivaqa, POB 12718, Suva; tel. 3303108; fax 3301423; national press asscn; operates Fiji Press Club and Fiji Journalism Training Institute; Sec. NINA RATULELE.

Pacific Islands News Association: 46 Gordon St, PMB, Suva; tel. 3303623; fax 3303943; e-mail pina@is.com.fj; internet www.pinarius.org; regional press asscn; defends freedom of information and expression, promotes professional co-operation, provides training and education; Administrator NINA RATULELE; Pres. JOHNSON HONIMAE.

Publishers

Fiji Times Ltd: POB 1167, Suva; tel. 3304111; fax 3302011; f. 1869; e-mail tyianni@fijitimes.com.fj; Propr News Corpn Ltd; largest newspaper publr; also publrs of books and magazines; Man. Dir TONY IANNI.

Lotu Pasifika Productions: POB 2401, Suva; tel. 3301314; fax 3301183; f. 1973; cookery, education, poetry, religion; Gen. Man. SERU L. VEREBALAVU.

University of the South Pacific: University Media Centre, POB 1168, Suva; tel. 3313900; fax 3301305; e-mail austin_l@usp.ac.fj; f. 1986; education, natural history, regional interests.

Government Publishing House

Printing and Stationery Department: POB 98, Suva; tel. 3385999; fax 3370203.

Broadcasting and Communications

TELECOMMUNICATIONS

Fiji International Telecommunicatons Ltd (FINTEL): 158 Victoria Parade, POB 59, Suva; tel. 3312933; fax 3300750; e-mail prichards@fintelfiji.com; 51% govt-owned; 49% C&W plc; CEO PHILIP RICHARDS.

Telcom Fiji Ltd: Private Mail Bag, Suva; tel. 3304019; fax 3301765; internet www.tfl.com.fj/; Chair. LIONEL YEE; CEO WINSTON THOMPSON.

Vodafone Fiji Ltd: Private Mail Bag, Suva; tel. 3312000; fax 3312007; e-mail aslam.khan@vodafone.com.fj; 51% owned by Telecom Fiji, 49% by Vodafone International Holdings BV; Man. Dir ASLAM KHAN.

BROADCASTING

Radio

Fiji Broadcasting Commission—FBC (Radio Fiji): Broadcasting House, POB 334, Suva; tel. 3314333; fax 3301643; f. 1954; statutory body; jointly funded by govt grant and advertising revenue; Chair. DANIEL WHIPPY; CEO SIRELI KINI.

Radio Fiji 1 broadcasts nationally on AM in English and Fijian.

Radio Fiji 2 broadcasts nationally on AM in English and Hindi.

Radio Fiji Gold broadcasts nationally on AM and FM in English.

104 FM and Radio Rajdhani 98 FM, mainly with musical programmes, broadcast in English and Hindi respectively, but are received only on Viti Levu.

Bula FM, musical programmes, broadcasts in Fijian, received only on Viti Levu.

Communications Fiji Ltd: 231 Waimanu Rd, PMB, Suva; tel. 3314766; fax 3303748; e-mail cfl@fm96.com.fj; f. 1985; operates three commercial stations; Man. Dir WILLIAM PARKINSON; Gen. Man. IAN JACKSON.

FM 96, f. 1985, broadcasts 24 hours per day, on FM, in English.

Navtarang, f. 1989, broadcasts 24 hours per day, on FM, in Hindi.

Viti FM, f. 1996, broadcasts 24 hours per day, on FM, in Fijian.

Radio Light: Shop 11B, Pacific Harbour Culture Centre, POB 319, Pacific Harbour; tel. and fax 3450007; e-mail radiolight@connect .com.fj; f. 1990; non-profit religious organization; broadcasts on FM 106 and FM 93.6; Station Man. and Programmes Dir DOUGLAS ROSE.

Radio Pasifik: POB 1168, University of the South Pacific, Suva; tel. 3313900; fax 3312591; e-mail schuster@usp.ac.fj; Gen. Man. ALFRED SCHUSTER.

Television

Film and Television Unit (FTU): c/o Ministry of Information and Communications, Govt Bldgs, POB 2225, Suva; tel. 3314688; fax 3300196; video library; production unit established by Govt and Hanns Seidel Foundation (Germany); a weekly news magazine and local documentary programmes.

Fiji Television Ltd: 20 Gorrie St, POB 2442, Govt Bldgs, Suva; tel. 3305100; fax 3305077; e-mail fijitv@is.com.fj; internet www .fijitv.com; f. 1994; operates two services, Fiji 1, a free channel, and Sky Fiji, a three-channel subscription service; Chair. OLOTA ROKOVUNISEI; CEO KEN CLARK; Head of Programming RICHARD BROADBRIDGE.

Fiji Vision Ltd: Suva; f. 1997; subscription television; jointly-owned by Yasana Holdings Ltd and a Hawaiian consortium.

In 1990 two television stations were constructed at Suva and Monsavu, with aid from the People's Republic of China. A permanent television station became operational in July 1994.

Finance

In 1996 the Ministry of Finance announced that it had secured financial assistance for the undertaking of a study to investigate the possibility of developing an 'offshore' financial centre in Fiji.

BANKING

(cap. = capital; res = reserves; dep. = deposits; m. = million; brs = branches; amounts in Fiji dollars)

Central Bank

Reserve Bank of Fiji: Pratt St, PMB, Suva; tel. 3313611; fax 3301688; e-mail rbf@reservebank.gov.fj; internet www.reservebank .gov.fj; f. 1984 to replace Central Monetary Authority of Fiji; bank of issue; administers Insurance Act; cap. and res 32.1m., dep. 143.1m. (Dec. 2000); Chair. and Gov. SAVENACA NARUBE.

Commercial Bank

National Bank of Fiji Ltd: 3 Central St, POB 1166, Suva; tel. 3314400; fax 3302190; f. 1974; 51% acquired from Fiji Govt by Colonial Ltd in 1999; cap. 11.5m., dep. 145.1m. (June 1998); Chair. LIONEL YEE; Man. Dir KENNETH R. MCARTHUR; 13 brs; 66 agencies.

Development Bank

Fiji Development Bank: 360 Victoria Parade, POB 104, Suva; tel. 3314866; fax 3314886; f. 1967; finances the development of natural resources, agriculture, transportation and other industries and enterprises; statutory body; cap. 50.8m., res 14.0m., dep. 182.6m. (June 1993); Chair. CHARLES WALKER; 9 brs.

Merchant Banks

Merchant Bank of Fiji Ltd: 231 Waimanu Rd, POB 14213, Suva; tel. 3314955; fax 3300026; e-mail merchantbk@is.com.fj; f. 1986; owned by the Fijian Holdings Ltd; Man. Dir S. WETEILAKEBA; 3 brs.

National MBf Finance (Fiji) Ltd: Burns Philp Bldg, 2nd Floor, POB 13525, Suva; tel. 302232; fax 3305915; e-mail mbf@is.com.fj; f. 1991; 51% owned by the National Bank of Fiji, 49% by MBf Asia Capital Corpn Holding Ltd (Hong Kong); Chief Operating Officer SIEK KART; 4 brs.

Foreign Banks

Agence Française de Développement (ADF) (France): Suva; licensed to operate in Fiji in 1997.

Australia and New Zealand (ANZ) Banking Group Ltd: ANZ House, 25 Victoria Parade, POB 179, Suva; tel. 3213000; fax 3312527; bought Bank of New Zealand in Fiji (8 brs) in 1990; Gen. Man. (Fiji) DAVID BELL; 17 brs; 9 agencies.

Bank of Baroda (India): Bank of Baroda Bldg, Marks St, POB 57, Suva; tel. 3311400; fax 3302510; f. 1908; CEO S. K. BAGCHI; 7 brs; 2 agencies.

Bank of Hawaii (USA): 67–69 Victoria Parade, POB 273, Suva; tel. 3312144; fax 3312464; f. 1993; Gen. Man. BRIAN BLISS; 3 brs.

Habib Bank (Pakistan): Narsey's Bldg, Renwick Rd, POB 108, Suva; tel. 3304011; fax 3304835; Chief Man. (Fiji) ABDUL MATIN; licensed to operate in Fiji 1990; 3 brs.

Westpac Banking Corporation (Australia): 1 Thomson St, Suva; tel. 3300666; fax 3301813; Chief Man. (Pacific Islands region) TREVOR WISEMANTEL; 12 brs; 9 agencies.

STOCK EXCHANGE

South Pacific Stock Exchange: Level 2, Plaza One, Provident Plaza, 33 Ellery St, POB 11689, Suva; tel. 3304130; fax 3304145; e-mail suvastockex@is.com.fj; internet www.suvastockex.com; formerly Suva Stock Exchange; name changed as above in 2000; Chair. FOANA T. NEMANI; Man. MESAKE NAWARI.

INSURANCE

Blue Shield (Pacific) Ltd: Parade Bldg, POB 15137, Suva; tel. 3311733; fax 3300318; Fijian co; subsidiary of Colonial Mutual Life Assurance Society Ltd; medical and life insurance; Chief Exec. SIALENI VUETAKI.

Colonial Mutual Life Assurance Society Ltd: Colonial Bldg, PMB, Suva; tel. 314400; fax 3303448; f. 1876; inc in Australia; life; Gen. Man. SIMON SWANSON.

Dominion Insurance Ltd: Civic House, POB 14468, Suva; tel. 3311055; fax 3303475; partly owned by Flour Mills of Fiji Ltd; general insurance; Man. Dir GARY S. CALLAGHAN.

FAI Insurance (Fiji) Ltd: Suva.

Fiji Reinsurance Corpn Ltd: RBF Bldg, POB 12704, Suva; tel. 3313471; fax 3305679; 20% govt-owned; reinsurance; Chair. Ratu JONE Y. KUBUABOLA; Man. PETER MARIO.

Fijicare Mutual Assurance: 41 Loftus St, POB 15808, Suva; tel. 3302717; fax 3302119; f. 1992; CEO JEFF PRICE.

Insurance Trust of Fiji: Loftus St, POB 114; Suva; tel. 3311242; fax 3302541; Man. SAMUEL KRISHNA.

National Insurance Co of Fiji Ltd: McGowan Bldg, Suva; tel. 3315955; fax 3301376; owned by New Zealand interests; Gen. Man. GEOFF THOMPSON.

New India Assurance Co Ltd: Harifam Centre, POB 71, Suva; tel. 3313488; fax 3302679; Man. MILIND A. KHARAT.

Queensland Insurance (Fiji) Ltd: Queensland Insurance Center, Victoria Parade, POB 101, Suva; tel. 3315455; fax 3300285; owned by Australian interests; Gen. Man. PETER J. NICHOLLS.

There are also two Indian insurance companies operating in Fiji.

Trade and Industry

GOVERNMENT AGENCIES

Fiji National Training Council (FNTC): Beaumont Rd, POB 6890, Nasinu; tel. 3392000; fax 3340184; e-mail gen-enq@fntc.ac.fj; internet www.fntc.ac.fj; Dir-Gen. NELSON DELAILOMALOMA.

Fiji Trade and Investment Board: Civic House, 6th Floor, Victoria Parade, Suva; tel. 3315988; fax 3301783; e-mail ftibinfo@ftib.org.fj; internet www.ftib.org.fj; f. 1980, restyled 1988, to promote and stimulate foreign and local economic development investment; Chair. JAMES DATTA; CEO JESONI VITUSAGAVULU.

Mineral Resources Department: Private Mail Bag; Suva; tel. 3381611; fax 3370039; internet www.mrd.gov.fj/index.html.

DEVELOPMENT ORGANIZATIONS

Fiji Development Company Ltd: POB 161, FNPF Place, 350 Victoria Parade, Suva; tel. 3304611; fax 3304171; e-mail hfc@is.com.fj; f. 1960; subsidiary of the Commonwealth Development Corpn; Man. F. KHAN.

Fiji-United States Business Council: CI-FTIB; POB 2303; Suva; f. 1998 to develop and expand trade links between the two countries; Pres. RAMENDRA NARAYAN.

Fijian Development Fund Board: POB 122, Suva; tel. 3312601; fax 3302585; f. 1951; funds derived from payments of $F20 a metric ton from the sales of copra by indigenous Fijians; deposits receive interest at 2.5%; funds used only for Fijian development schemes; Chair. Minister for Fijian Affairs; CEO VINCENT TOVATA.

Land Development Authority: c/o Ministry for Agriculture, Sugar and Land Resettlement, POB 5442, Raiwaqa; tel. 33384900; fax 33384058; f. 1961 to co-ordinate development plans for land and marine resources; Chair. JONETANI GALUINADI.

CHAMBERS OF COMMERCE

Ba Chamber of Commerce: POB 99, Ba; tel. 6670134; fax 6670132; Pres. DIJENDRA SINGH.

Labasa Chamber of Commerce: POB 121, Labasa; tel. 8811262; fax 8813009; Pres. SHIVLAL NAGINDAS.

Lautoka Chamber of Commerce and Industry: POB 366, Lautoka; tel. 6661834; fax 6662379; e-mail vaghco@is.com.fj; Pres. NATWARLAL VAGH.

Levuka Chamber of Commerce: POB 85, Levuka; tel. 3440248; fax 3440252; Pres. ISHRAR ALI.

Nadi Chamber of Commerce: POB 2735, Nadi; tel. 6701704; fax 6702314; e-mail arunkumar@is.com.fj; Pres. VENKAT RAMANI AIYER.

Nausori Chamber of Commerce: POB 228, Nausori; tel. 3478235; fax 3400134; Pres. ROBERT RAJ KUMAR.

Sigatoka Chamber of Commerce: POB 882, Sigatoka; tel. 6500064; fax 6520006; Pres. NATWAR SINGH.

Suva Chamber of Commerce and Industry: 37 Viria Rd, Vatuwaqa Industrial Estate, POB 337, Suva; tel. 3380975; fax 3380854; f. 1902; Joint Sec. VERONIKA HANSRAJ; 150 mems.

Tavua-Vatukoula Chamber of Commerce: POB 698, Tavua; tel. 6680390; fax 6680390; Pres. SOHAN SINGH.

INDUSTRIAL AND TRADE ASSOCIATIONS

Fiji Forest Industries (FFI): Suva; Deputy Chair. Ratu SOSO KATONIVERE.

Fiji National Petroleum Co Ltd: Suva; f. 1991; govt-owned, distributor of petroleum products.

Fiji Sugar Corporation Ltd: Western House, 2nd and 3rd Floors, Cnr of Bila and Vidilo St, PMB, Lautoka; tel. 6662655; fax 6664685; nationalized 1974; buyer of sugar-cane and raw sugar mfrs; Chair. HAFIZUD D. KHAN; Man. Dir JONETANI K. GALUINADI.

Fiji Sugar Marketing Co Ltd: Dominion House, 5th Floor, Thomson St, POB 1402, Suva; tel. 3311588; fax 3300607; Man. Dir JONETANI GALUINADI.

Mining and Quarrying Council: 42 Gorrie St, Suva; tel. 33313188; fax 3302183; e-mail employer@is.com.fj; Chief Exec. K. A. J. ROBERTS.

National Trading Corporation Ltd: POB 13673, Suva; tel. 3315211; fax 3315584; f. 1992; a govt-owned body set up to develop markets for agricultural and marine produce locally and overseas; processes and markets fresh fruit, vegetables and ginger products; CEO APIAMA CEGUMALINA.

Native Lands Trust Board: Suva; manages holdings of ethnic Fijian landowners; Gen. Man. MAIKA QARIKAU.

Pacific Fishing Co: Suva; fish-canning; govt-owned.

Sugar Cane Growers' Council: Canegrowers' Bldg, 3rd Floor, 75 Drasa Ave, Lautoka; tel. 6650466; fax 6650624; e-mail canegrower@is.com.fj; f. 1985; aims to develop the sugar industry and protect the interests of registered growers; CEO JAGANNATH SAMI; Chair. RUSIATE MUSUDROKA.

Sugar Commission of Fiji: POB 5993, Lautoka; tel. 6664866; fax 6664051; e-mail scof@is.com.fj; Chair. GERALD BARRACK.

EMPLOYERS' ORGANIZATIONS

Fiji Employers' Federation: 42 Gorrie St, POB 575, Suva; tel. 3313188; fax 3302183; e-mail employer@fef.com.fj; represents 206 major employers; Pres. D. Y. AIDNEY; CEO KENNETH A. J. ROBERTS.

Fiji Manufacturers' Association: POB 1308, Suva; tel. 9212223; fax 3302567; e-mail volau-m@usp.ac.fj; internet www.fijibusiness.com; f. 1902; Pres. DESMOND WHITESIDE; 55 mems.

Local Inter-Island Shipowners' Association: POB 152, Suva; fax 3303389; Pres. VITI G. WHIPPY.

Textile, Clothing and Footwear Council: POB 10015, Nabua; tel. 3384777; fax 3370446; Sec. R. DUNSTAN.

UTILITIES

Electricity

Fiji Electricity Authority (FEA): PMB, Suva; e-mail ceo@fea.com.fj; tel. 3311133; fax 3311882; f. 1966; govt-owned; responsible for the generation, transmission and distribution of electricity throughout Fiji; CEO NIZAM UD-DEAN.

Water

Water and Sewerage Section: Public Works Dept, Ministry of Works and Energy, Nasilivata House, Kings Rd, PMB, Samabula; tel. 3384111; fax 3383013; e-mail rsshandil@fijiwater.gov.fj; Dir RAM SUMER SHANDIL.

MAJOR COMPANIES

BPT (South Sea) Co Ltd: POB 355, Suva; tel. 3384888; fax 3370309; f. 1920; importers and distributors of motor vehicles, machinery and outboard motors; Gen. Man. ALMA MAHARAJ.

Carlton Brewery (Fiji) Ltd: POB 696, Suva; f. 1957; a subsidiary of Foster's Brewing Group Ltd (Australia); Gen. Man. J. PICKERING.

Carter Holt Harvey (Fiji) Ltd: POB 427, Suva; tel. 3410011; fax 3410808; f. 1965; mfrs of polythene bags and paper products; Gen. Man. C. D. BOSSLEY.

Central Manufacturing Co Ltd: POB 560, Suva; tel. 3381144; fax 3370080; f. 1955; mfrs and distributors of cigarettes and tobacco; Gen. Man. JOHN J. NELSON.

Crest Chicken Ltd: POB 83, Nausori; tel. 3478400; fax 3400061; f. 1965; mfrs of animal food; Gen. Man. DON MACLELLAN.

Eddie Hin Industries Ltd: Marine Drive, POB 98, Lautoka; tel. 6661433; fax 6665886; f. 1947; mfrs of non-alcoholic beverages; Man. Dir EDDIE WONG.

Emperor Gold Mining Co Ltd: Vatukoula; tel. 6680477; fax 6680779; f. 1935; gold mining and processing; assoc. cos: Jubilee Mining and Koula Mining; 2,000 employees; Chair. GEORGE DRYSDALE.

Fiji Motor Works Ltd: Namaka, Nadi; f. 1997; assembly of cars and small commercial vehicles; Man. Dir RICHARD BRETNAL.

Fiji National Petroleum Co Ltd: Suva; f. 1991; govt-owned; distributor of petroleum products.

Fiji Pine Ltd: 85 Drasa Ave, Lautoka; tel. 6661511; fax 6661784; e-mail fijipine@connect.com.fj; internet www.fijipine.com; f. 1991 to replace Fiji Pine Commission; owned by Govt and Fiji Pine Trust; Chair. SEMI TABAKANALAGI; CEO DEO SARAN (acting).

Flour Mills of Fiji Ltd: POB 977, Suva; fax 3300944; f. 1971; Man. Dir HARI PUNJA; CEO SANJAY PUNJA.

Homecentres (Fiji) Ltd: GPOB 15278, Rodwell Rd, Suva; e-mail hcmerchandise@courts.com.fj; Dir of Merchandise DHARMA NAND.

Ika Corporation Ltd: POB 1371, Suva; tel. 3361922; fax 3351194; incorporated 1990; govt-owned; tuna-fishing co; exporter of fresh fish; leasing of vessels; Gen. Man. MITIELI BALEIVANUALALA.

Natural Waters of Viti Ltd: Civic House, Ground Floor, POB 14128, Suva; tel. 3302654; fax 3302714; mineral water bottling.

P. A. Lal & Co Ltd: POB 1242, Suva; f. 1946; builders of buses, trucks, trailers, coaches, furniture and fibreglass work; Dir RICHARD LAL.

Pacific Fishing Company (PAFCO): Fiji's largest fish-processing factory.

Pacific Green Industries (Fiji) Ltd: Sigatoka; exports furniture made from coconut wood; Man. BRUCE CLAY.

Rewa Co-operative Dairy Company: Ratu Mara Rd, Suva; processes, packages and supplies dairy produce; Chair RAM CHAND.

Shell Fiji Ltd: POB 168, Suva; tel. 3313933; fax 3302279; f. 1928; petrol stations and distribution of petroleum products; Gen. Man. KEVIN DWYER.

Shipbuilding Fiji Ltd: POB 16695, Sannergren Drive, Korovou, Walu Bay, Suva; tel. 3314699; fax 3303500; e-mail sfl@is.com.fj; 49% govt-owned, 51% owned by MCI/Carpenters; builds and services ocean-going vessels; CEO WAYNE SHAW.

South Pacific Distilleries Ltd of Fiji: Lautoka; Gen. Man. JOE RODAN; Chair. NUNO D'AQUINO.

Voko Industries: Suva; fish canners.

TRADE UNIONS

Fiji Trades Union Congress (FTUC): 32 Des Voeux Rd, POB 1418, Suva; tel. 3315377; fax 3300306; e-mail ftucl@is.com.fj; f. 1951; affiliated to ICFTU and ICFTU—APRO; 35 affiliated unions; more than 42,000 mems; Pres. DANIEL URAI; Gen. Sec. FELIX ANTHONY.

Principal affiliated unions:

Association of USP Staff: POB 1168, Suva; tel. 3313900; fax 3301305; f. 1977; Pres. GANESH CHAND; Sec. D. R. RAO.

Federated Airline Staff Association: Nadi Airport, POB 9259, Nadi; tel. 6722877; fax 6790068; Sec. RAM RAJEN.

Fiji Aviation Workers' Association: FTUC Complex, 32 Des Voeux Rd, POB 5351, Raiwaqa; tel. 3303184; fax 3311805; Pres. VALENTINE SIMPSON; Gen. Sec. ATTAR SINGH.

Fiji Bank and Finance Sector Employees' Union: 101 Gordon St, POB 853, Suva; tel. 3301827; fax 3301956; e-mail fbeu@is.com.fj; Nat. Sec. DIWAN C. SHANKAR.

Fiji Electricity and Allied Workers Union: POB 1390, Lautoka; tel. 6666353; e-mail feawu@is.com.fj; Pres. LEONE SAKETA; Sec. J. A. PAUL.

Fiji Garment, Textile and Allied Workers' Union: c/o FTUC, Raiwaqa; f. 1992.

Fiji Nursing Association: POB 1364, Suva; tel. 333305855; Gen. Sec. KUINI LUTUA.

Fiji Public Service Association: 298 Waimanu Rd, POB 1405, Suva; tel. 3311922; fax 3301099; e-mail fpsa@is.com.fj; f. 1943; 3,434 mems; Pres. AISEA BATISARESARE; Gen. Sec. RAJESHWAR.SINGH.

Fiji Sugar and General Workers' Union: 84 Naviti St, POB 330, Lautoka; tel. 6660746; fax 664888; 25,000 mems; Pres. SHIU LINGAM; Gen. Sec. FELIX ANTHONY.

Fiji Teachers' Union: 1–3 Berry Rd, Govt Bldgs, POB 2203, Suva; tel. 3314099; fax 3305962; e-mail ftn@is.com.fj; f. 1930; 3,200 mems; Pres. BALRAM; Gen. Sec. AGNI DEO SINGH.

Fijian Teachers' Association: POB 14464, Suva; tel. 3315099; fax 3304978; e-mail fta@.com.fj; Pres. TARITA KOREI; Gen. Sec. MAIKA NAMUDU.

Insurance Officers' Association: POB 71, Suva; tel. 3313488; Pres. JAGDISH KHATRI; Sec. DAVID LEE.

Mineworkers' Union of Fiji: POB 876, Tavua; f. 1986; Pres. HENNESY PETERS; Sec. KAVEKINI NAVUSO.

National Farmers' Union: POB 522, Labasa; tel. 8811838; 10,000 mems (sugar-cane farmers); Pres. DEWAN CHAND; Gen. Sec. M. P. CHAUDHRY; CEO MOHAMMED LATIF SUBEDAR.

National Union of Factory and Commercial Workers: POB 989, Suva; tel. 3311155; 3,800 mems; Pres. CAMA TUILEVEUKA; Gen. Sec. JAMES R. RAMAN.

National Union of Hotel and Catering Employees: Nadi Airport, POB 9426, Nadi; tel. 670906; fax 6700181; Pres. EMOSI DAWAI; Sec. TIMOA NAIVAHIWAQA.

Public Employees' Union: POB 781, Suva; tel. 3304501; 6,752 mems; Pres. SEMI TIKOICINA; Gen. Sec. FILIMONE BANUVE.

Transport and Oil Workers' Union: POB 903, Suva; tel. 3302534; f. 1988; following merger of Oil and Allied Workers' Union and Transport Workers' Union; Pres. J. BOLA; Sec. MICHAEL COLUMBUS.

There are several independent trade unions, including Fiji Registered Ports Workers' Union (f. 1947; Pres. JIOJI TAHOLOSALE).

Transport

RAILWAYS

Fiji Sugar Corporation Railway: Rarawai Mill, POB 155, Ba; tel. 6674044; fax 670505; for use in cane-harvesting season, May–Dec.; 595 km of permanent track and 225 km of temporary track (gauge of 600 mm), serving cane-growing areas at Ba, Lautoka and Penang on Viti Levu and Labasa on Vanua Levu; Gen. Man. ADURU KUVA.

ROADS

At the end of 1996 there were some 3,440 km of roads in Fiji, of which 49.2% were paved. A 500-km highway circles the main island of Viti Levu.

SHIPPING

There are ports of call at Suva, Lautoka, Levuka and Savusavu. The main port, Suva, handles more than 800 ships a year, including large passenger liners. Lautoka handles more than 300 vessels and liners and Levuka, the former capital of Fiji, mainly handles commercial fishing vessels. In 1996 a feasibility study into the possible establishment of a free port at Suva was commissioned. In May 1997 the Government approved 14 new ports of entry in the northern, western and central eastern districts of Fiji.

Maritime and Ports Authority of Fiji (MPAF): Administration Bldg, Princes Wharf, POB 780, Suva; tel. 3312700; fax 3300064; corporatized in 1998; Chair. DANIEL ELISHA; Port Master Capt. GEORGE MACOMBER.

Ports Terminals Ltd: POB S13, Suva; tel. 3304725; fax 3304769; f. 1998, e-mail herbert@suv.ptl.com.fj; stevedore, pilotage, storage and warehousing; CEO H. HAZELMAN; Port Manager E. KURUSIGA.

Burns Philp Shipping (Fiji) Ltd: Rodwell Rd, POB 15832, Suva; tel. 3315444; fax 3302754; e-mail burshipfiji@is.com.fj; shipping agents, customs agents and international forwarding agents; Gen. Man. DANNY REES.

Consort Shipping Line Ltd: Muaiwalu Complex, Rona St, Walubay, POB 152, Suva; tel. 3313344; fax 3303389; CEO HECTOR SMITH; Man. Dir JUSTIN SMIT.

Fiji Maritime Services Ltd: c/o Fiji Ports Workers and Seafarers Union, 36 Edinburgh Drive, Suva; f. 1989 by PAF and the Ports Workers' Union; services between Lautoka and Vanua Levu ports.

Inter-Ports Shipping Corpn Ltd: 25 Eliza St, Walu Bay; POB 152, Suva; tel. 3313638; f. 1984; Man. Dir JUSTIN SMITH.

Transcargo Express Fiji Ltd: POB 936, Suva; f. 1974; Man. Dir LEO B. SMITH.

Wong's Shipping Co Ltd: Suite 647, Epworth House, Nina St, POB 1269, Suva; tel. 3311867.

CIVIL AVIATION

There is an international airport at Nadi (about 210 km from Suva), a smaller international airport at Nausori (Suva) and 15 other airfields. Nadi is an important transit airport in the Pacific and in 1990 direct flights to Japan also began.

Airports Fiji Ltd: Nadi International Airport, Nadi; tel 6725777; fax 6725 161; e-mail info@afl.com.fj; Chair. VILIAME S. J. GONELEVU; CEO JONE KOROITAMANA.

Air Fiji Ltd: 219 Victoria Parade, POB 1259, Suva; tel. 3314666; fax 3300771; internet www.airfiji.net; operates 65 scheduled services daily to 15 domestic destinations; daily service to Tonga and Tuvalu and direct flights to Auckland and Sydney commenced in 1999; charter operations, aerial photography and surveillance also conducted; partly owned by the Fijian Govt, which was expected to sell a majority of its shares in 2001; Chair. DOUG HAZARD; CEO KEN MACDONALD.

Air Pacific Ltd: Air Pacific Centre, POB 9266, Nadi International Airport, Nadi; tel. 6720777; fax 6720512; internet www.airpacific.com; f. 1951 as Fiji Airways, name changed in 1971; domestic and international services from Nausori Airport (serving Suva) to Nadi and international services to Tonga, Solomon Islands, Cook Islands, Vanuatu, Samoa, Japan, Australia, New Zealand and the USA; 51% govt-owned, 46.05% owned by Qantas (Australia); Chair. GERALD BARRACK; Man. Dir and CEO MICHAEL MCQUAY.

Fijian Airways International: POB 10138, Nadi International Airport, Nadi; tel. 6724702; fax 6724654; f. 1997; service to London via Singapore and Mumbai (India) planned; Chair. NEIL UNDERHILL; CEO ALAN LINDREA.

Hibiscus Air Ltd: Nadi International Airport, Nadi; domestic airline operating charter and non-scheduled flights around Fiji.

Sunflower Airlines Ltd: POB 9452, Nadi International Airport, Nadi; tel. 6723555; fax 6720085; e-mail sun@is.com.fj; internet www.fiji.to; f. 1980; scheduled flights to domestic destinations, also charter services; Man. Dir DON IAN COLLINGWOOD.

Vanua Air Charters: Labasa; f. 1993; provides domestic charter and freight services; Proprs Ratu Sir KAMISESE MARA, CHARAN SINGH.

Tourism

Scenery, climate, fishing and diving attract visitors to Fiji, where tourism is an important industry. The number of foreign tourist arrivals increased from 294,070) in 2000 to 348,014 in 2001 (excluding cruise-ship passengers who numbered 6,858 in 2001). In 2001 some 28.2% of visitors came from Australia, 19.1% from New Zealand, 16.6% from the USA, 8.8% from the United Kingdom and 5.9% from Japan. A total of 5,542 rooms in 187 hotels were available in 2001. Receipts from tourism increased from $F413.5m. in 2000 to $F495.5m. in 2001. The South Pacific Tourism Organization (formerly the Tourism Council of The South Pacific) is based in Suva. In 1998 the Government announced its intention further to develop the tourist industry in Fiji through the establishment of the Fiji Tourism Development Plan: 1998–2005. In April 1999 construction began on a new luxury resort at Korotoga, situated half-way between Suva and Nadi. The industry was severely affected by the coup of May 2000.

Fiji Hotel Association (FHA): 42 Gorrie St, GPOB 13560, Suva; tel. 3302980; fax 3300331; e-mail fha@connect.com.fj; represents 76 hotels; Pres. DIXON SEETO; Chief Exec. OLIVIA PARETI.

Fiji Visitors' Bureau: POB 92, Suva; tel. 3302433; fax 3300986; e-mail infodesk@fijifvb.gov.fj; internet www.bulafiji.com; f. 1923; Chair. SITIVENI WELEILAKEBA; Chief Exec. VILIAME GAVOKA; Dir of Tourism ERONI LUVENIYALI.

Defence

The Fiji Military Forces consist of men in the regular army, the Naval Squadron, the conservation corps and the territorials. The defence budget for 2001 was an estimated $F58m. At 1 August 2001 the total armed forces numbered 3,500 (3,200 in the army and 300 in the navy), supported by about 6,000 reservists. The Republic of Fiji has co-operated militarily with France, Taiwan, the People's Republic of China and Malaysia. Defence co-operation with New Zealand and Australia, which ceased following the coups of 1987, was resumed in 1992 and 1993. Collaboration was again interrupted by the coup of May 2000.

Commander-in-Chief: President of the Republic.

Commander of the Armed Forces: Cdre FRANK BAINIMARAMA.

Deputy Commander of the Armed Forces: Col IOANE NAIVALARUA.

Education

Education in Fiji is not compulsory, but in 1992 about 97% of children of school age were enrolled at the country's schools, and the Government provided free education for the first eight years of schooling. Primary education begins at six years of age and lasts for six years. Secondary education, beginning at the age of 12, lasts for a further six years. State subsidies are available for secondary and tertiary education in cases of hardship. In 1995 there were 709 state primary schools (with a total enrolment of 142,912 pupils in 2000) and 146 state secondary schools (with an enrolment of 66,905 pupils in 2000). In 1994 there were 31 vocational and technical institutions, a school of medicine and a nursing school and, in that year, four teacher-training colleges. There were 200 holders of Fiji government scholarships at the University of the South Pacific in Fiji in 1989. In 1996 university students on campus totalled about 4,000 and extension students totalled 6,000. Fiji has experienced a shortfall in the number of trained teachers, as a result of increased emigration prompted by the political upheavals. Budgetary proposals for 2000 allocated an estimated $F123.1m. for education. The adult literacy rate in 2000 averaged an estimated 92.9% (males 94.9%; females 90.8%).

French Pacific Territories

There are two French Overseas Territories, territoires d'outre-mer, in the Pacific Ocean, French Polynesia and Wallis and Futuna (the third being the French Southern and Antarctic Territories). They are integral parts of the French Republic. Each is administered by a High Commissioner or Chief Administrator, who is the representative of the State and appointed by the French Government. Each permanently-inhabited Territory has a Territorial Assembly or Congress (elected by universal adult suffrage) and representation in the National Assembly and Senate of the Republic in Paris. They have varying degrees of autonomy. The High Commissioner of French Polynesia is also directly responsible for Clipperton Island, although it is not part of the Territory. French policy in the Pacific region, particularly as regards development and relations with other Pacific countries and territories, is mooted by the Council of the South Pacific (Conseil du Pacifique Sud). This body, chaired by the President of the Republic, was established in 1985 and revived in 1990, following a period of inactivity. The French Republic has membership of the Pacific Community (formerly the South Pacific Commission) in respect of its Pacific Territories. The French Government includes a Minister Delegate with responsibility for Overseas France.

Head of State: President JACQUES CHIRAC (took office 17 May 1995; re-elected 5 May 2002).

Council of the South Pacific: Conseil du Pacifique Sud, 57 blvd des Invalides, 75700 Paris, France; regional consultative and development body; mems: French ambassadors in the region and representatives of the French Govt, of the French State High Commissioners, etc.) and of the territorial legislatures; Chair. President of the Republic.

Ministry of Overseas Departments and Territories: 27 rue Oudinot, 75358 Paris 07 SP, France; tel. 1-53-69-20-00; fax 1-43-06-60-30; internet www.outre-mer.gouv.fr.

Minister of Overseas Departments, Territories and Country: BRIGITTE GIRARDIN.

FRENCH POLYNESIA

Revised by FRÉDÉRIC ANGLEVIEL

Physical and Social Geography

French Polynesia is an Overseas Territory of France, covering an area of 4,167 sq km (1,609 sq miles—land area of 3,521 sq km), including 35 volcanic islands and about 183 low-lying coral atolls in five archipelagos: Society, Austral (or Tubuai), Tuamotu, Gambier and Marquesas. The Society Islands, in the west of the Territory, comprise a Windward Islands group (Iles du Vent—including Tahiti and Moorea) and, about 160 km to the north-west, a Leeward Islands group (Iles Sous le Vent—including the islands of Raiatea and Bora Bora). The five Austral Islands proper lie some 160 km to the south of Tahiti and include Tubuai itself; 770 km to the south-east of Tubuai is the separate island of Rapa. The Tuamotu Archipelago is a chain of about 80 atolls stretching from the north of Tahiti, south-east for about 1,500 km, from the islands around Rangiroa (the largest in the Territory) towards those beyond Mururoa Atoll, which is over 1,000 km from Tahiti. The chain is continued in the south-east by the small group of the Gambier Islands, including Mangareva, which is some 1,700 km from Tahiti. In the north-east, 1,500 km from Tahiti, are the Marquesas Islands, which comprise a southern and a northern group around the chief island of Nuku Hiva. The Territory's nearest neighbours are Kiribati to the north-west and the Cook Islands to the west. The small, uninhabited island of Clipperton, located far to the north-east of the Territory, some 600 km off the coast of Mexico, is administered from French Polynesia, being under the direct jurisdiction of the High Commissioner.

The average monthly temperature throughout the year varies between 20°C (68°F) and 29°C (84°F), and most rainfall occurs between November and April, the average annual precipitation being 1,625 mm (64 ins). The more mountainous volcanic islands (notably the Society Islands) receive the most rainfall, and the south of the Territory is cooler than the north.

The official languages are French and Tahitian. Polynesian languages are spoken by the indigenous population. Christianity is the principal religion, and the Protestant Evangelical Church the largest denomination. The population, which is predominantly Polynesian, includes minorities of French and other Europeans, Chinese (a small but economically significant community) and 'Demis' (persons of mixed race—Polynesian with others). In 1990 it was estimated that 82.8% of the population were Polynesian or of Polynesian descent and 11.9% were European. At the census of 3 September 1996 the population totalled 219,521, and was estimated at 238,800 at 1 January 2002. Some 86% of the inhabitants live in the Society Islands, which constitute about one-half of the land area. The population of the capital, Papeete (on Tahiti), was 25,553 in 1996.

History

The islands of French Polynesia were already inhabited by the Maohi, a Polynesian people, when first visited by Spanish explorers during the 16th century. Dutch, French, and British explorers followed during the 1700s. Descriptions of Tahiti and other Society Islands by Wallis, who first visited in 1767, Bougainville in 1768 and Capt. James Cook in 1769 gave rise in Europe to a Utopian concept of the South Pacific, a romantic view which drew Europeans to the islands. In fact, European discovery dealt the Tahitian and other island groups' populations a severe blow. Disease caused rapid declines in population, and many more were killed in inter-island and inter-group warfare.

The Tahitian-based kingdom of the Pomare monarchs was made a French protectorate in 1842 and a colony in 1880. All the islands that now constitute French Polynesia had been annexed by the end of the 19th century. Clipperton Island, which is administered as a distinct entity, was first claimed by France in 1857. After disputes with the USA and Mexico, the island was restored to France by the arbitration of the King of Italy in February 1931.

The islands were governed from France under a decree of 1885 until 1946, when the French signed a new decree allowing the Polynesians to manage their domestic affairs while maintaining institutional control through a Governor in Papeete, the capital, on Tahiti. The Territorial Assembly was established in 1957 to assist the Governor. Moves towards increased local autonomy began in 1977, and new statutes creating a fully elected local executive were approved in Paris in May 1977.

Following elections to the Territorial Assembly in May 1982, the Gaullist Tahoeraa Huiraatira party (led by Gaston Flosse) formed successive ruling coalitions, first with the Ai'a Api party, and in September with the Pupu Here Ai'a Te Nunaa Ia Ora party, which advocates territorial autonomy. Seeking self-government, especially in economic matters, elected representatives of the Assembly held discussions with the French Government in Paris in 1983, and in September 1984 a new statute was approved by the French National Assembly. This allowed the Territorial Government greater powers, mainly in the sphere of commerce and development; the Council of Government was replaced by a Council of Ministers, whose President was to be elected from among the members of the Territorial Assembly. Gaston Flosse became the first President of the Council of Ministers.

At elections held in March 1986, the Tahoeraa Huiraatira gained the first outright majority to be achieved in the Territory, winning 24 of the 41 seats in the Territorial Assembly. Leaders of opposition parties subsequently expressed dissatisfaction with the election result, claiming that the Tahoeraa Huiraatira victory had been secured only as a result of allocating a disproportionately large number of seats in the Territorial Assembly to one of the five constituencies. The constituency at the centre of the dispute comprised the Mangareva and Tuamotu islands, where the two French army bases at Hao and Mururoa constituted a powerful body of support for Flosse and the Tahoeraa Huiraatira, which, in spite of winning a majority of seats, had obtained a minority of individual votes in the election (30,571, compared with the opposition parties' 43,771). At the concurrent elections for French Polynesia's two seats in the National Assembly in Paris, Flosse and Alexandre Léontieff, the candidates of the Rassemblement pour la République (RPR—to which party the Tahoeraa Huiraatira is affiliated), were elected, Flosse subsequently ceding his seat to Edouard Fritch. Flosse was later appointed as Secretary of State for Pacific Affairs in the French Council of Ministers.

In April 1986 Flosse was re-elected President of the Territory's Council of Ministers. However, he faced severe criticism from leaders of the opposition for his allegedly inefficient and extravagant use of public funds. He was accused, in particular, of corrupt electoral practice, having distributed government-financed gifts of construction materials, food and clothing, in an attempt to influence voters during his election campaign. Finally, in February 1987 Flosse resigned as President of the Council of Ministers, and was replaced by Jacques Teuira.

Unrest among dock-workers in Papeete led to serious rioting in October 1987 and the declaration of a state of emergency by the authorities. In December a coalition of opposition parties and a breakaway faction of Tahoeraa Huiraatira, the Te Tiarama party, led by Alexandre Léontieff, took power from Tahoeraa.The Léontieff Government survived several challenges in the Territorial Assembly to its continuation in office during 1988 and 1989. Amendments to the Polynesian Constitution, which were enacted by July 1990, augmented the powers of the President of the Territorial Government and increased the competence of the Territorial Assembly. Furthermore, five consultative Archipelago Councils were established, comprising Territorial and municipal elected representatives. The main purpose of these amendments was to clarify the areas of responsibility of the State, the Territory and the judiciary, which was considered particularly necessary following various disputes about the impending single market of the European Community (EC, now European Union—EU). In June 1989, in protest, 90% of the electorate refused to vote in the elections to the European Parliament.

At territorial elections in March 1991 the Tahoeraa Huiraatira won 18 of the 41 seats. Flosse then formed a coalition with the Ai'a Api, resulting in a majority of 23 seats in the Territorial Assembly. Emile Vernaudon, leader of the Ai'a Api, was elected President of the Assembly, and Flosse was elected President of the Council of Ministers. In September Flosse announced the end of the coalition between his party and the Ai'a Api, accusing Vernaudon of disloyalty, and signed a new alliance with the Pupu Here Ai'a Te Nunaa Ia Ora, led by Jean Juventin (a former political rival of Flosse).

In April 1992 Flosse was found guilty of fraud (relating to an illegal sale of government land to a member of his family), and there were widespread demands for his resignation. In November Juventin and Léontieff were charged with 'passive' corruption, relating to the construction of a golf course by a Japanese company. In the following month the French Court of Appeal upheld the judgment against Flosse, who received a six-month suspended prison sentence. The case provoked a demonstration by more than 3,000 people in January 1993, demanding the resignation of Flosse and Juventin. In September 1994 Flosse succeeded in having the conviction overruled, in a second court of appeal, on a procedural matter. In October 1997 Léontieff was found guilty of accepting substantial bribes in order to facilitate a business tenure and was sentenced to three years in prison (half of which was to be suspended). In May 1998 Léontieff was sentenced to a further three years' imprisonment (two of which were to be suspended) for corruption.

French presidential elections took place in April/May 1995. During the second round of voting in the Territory, the socialist candidate, Lionel Jospin, received 39% of the total votes, while the RPR candidate, Jacques Chirac, won 61%. (Chirac was elected to the presidency with 52.6% of votes cast throughout the republic.)

In November 1995 the Territorial Assembly adopted a draft statute of autonomy, which proposed the extension of the Territory's powers to areas such as fishing, mining and shipping rights, international transport and communications, broadcasting and the offshore economic zone. France, however, would retain full responsibility for defence, justice and security in the islands. Advocates of independence for French Polynesia criticized the statute for promising only relatively superficial changes, while failing to increase the democratic rights of the islanders. The statute was approved by the French National Assembly in December and came into force in April 1996.

On 13 May 1996 the Gaullist Tahoeraa Huiraatira achieved an outright majority at the territorial elections, although the principal pro-independence party, Tavini Huiraatira/Front de Libération de la Polynésie (FLP), made considerable gains throughout the Territory (largely owing to increased popular hostility towards France since the resumption of nuclear-weapons tests at Mururoa Atoll—see below). Tahoeraa Huiraatira secured 22 of the 41 seats in the Territorial Assembly, with 38.7% of total votes cast, while Tavini Huiraatira won 10 seats, with 24.8% of votes. Other anti-independence parties won a total of eight seats and an additional pro-independence grouping secured one seat. Flosse defeated the independence leader, Oscar Temaru, by 28 votes to 11 to remain as President of the Council of Ministers later in the month, and Justin Arapari was elected President of the Territorial Assembly. Allegations of voting irregularities led to legal challenges, which overturned the results in 11 constituencies. Following by-elections in May 1998 for the 11 seats, Tahoeraa Huiraatira increased its representation by one seat. Tavini Huiraatira again claimed that the elections had not been fairly conducted.

At elections for French Polynesia's two seats in the French National Assembly in May 1997, Michel Buillard and Emile Vernaudon, both supporters of the RPR, were elected, with 51.6% and 58.9% of total votes cast, respectively. However, the pro-independence leader, Oscar Temaru, was a strong contender for the western constituency seat, securing 41.6% of the votes. Flosse was elected as the Territory's representative to the French Senate in September 1998. In March 1999 proposals to increase French Polynesia's autonomy, as part of constitutional reforms, were announced in Paris. The proposed changes would allow the Territory to draft its own laws and negotiate its own international treaties. These proposals followed an initial agreement between the Territory and the French Government in late 1998, on the future of French Polynesia. In October 1999 the French Senate adopted a constitutional amendment granting French Polynesia a greater degree of autonomy. According to the bill (which had also been approved by the National Assembly in June), the status of the islands was to be changed from that of overseas territory to overseas country, and a new Polynesian citizenship was to be created. Although France was to retain control over areas such as foreign affairs, defence, justice and electoral laws, French Polynesia would have the power to negotiate with other Pacific countries, and sign its own international treaties. The constitutional amendment was presented to a joint session of the French Senate and National Assembly for final ratification in late January 2000. However, no decision was taken on the matter, and the issue was unlikely to be addressed again in the near future.

In November 1999 Flosse was found guilty of corruption, on charges of accepting more than 2.7m. French francs in bribes from the owner of an illegal casino, allegedly to help fund his party. Flosse was sentenced to a two-year suspended prison term, a large fine, and a one-year ban on seeking office. Demonstrations, organized by the pro-independence FLP, took place in Tahiti, in protest at Flosse's refusal to resign from his post as President of the Territorial Council of Ministers. In October Flosse lodged an appeal with the High Court, which reversed the ruling in May 2001.

In December 2000 some 2,000 workers went on strike in Papeete, protesting against low wages, and demanding that their pay be raised to a level commensurate with the prosperous state of the Territory's economy. In that month provision was made for the number of seats in the Territorial Assembly to be increased from 41 to 49, in an attempt to reflect demographic changes in the Territory more accurately. On 6 May 2001 elections to the Assembly took place. Tahoeraa Huiraatira won 28 seats, securing a fifth successive term in office. The pro-independence Tavini Huiraatira took 13 seats. Gaston Flosse was subsequently re-elected President of the Territorial Assembly, and a government reorganization ensued.

In December 2001 the President of the Employers Council made a complaint about the lack of consultation over the Government's budget for 2002, particularly criticizing the significant increase in fiscal pressures on citizens, companies and employees (see Economic Affairs). Following the Territorial Assembly's approval of the controversial budget, trade unions and employers joined forces to stage a demonstration on 11 December; shops were closed, and 4,000 people participated in a protest march in Tahiti.

In January 2002 representatives of state and local government met to review the first five years of the Restructuring Fund, an agreement implemented in 1996 to further the economic autonomy of Polynesia and to regulate financial subsidies to the Territory following the cessation of nuclear testing. The President and Prime Minister of France took part in further such meetings in June and July. It was agreed that funding would be extended for a further 10 years after 2006. The French delegation supported the proposal for a new autonomy statute to grant more powers of self-government to French Polynesia. The Territory's status, however, was to remain unchanged. In early June 2002 elections for the Territory's two seats in the French National Assembly were won by the Tahoeraa'a Huiraatira candidates, Michel Buillard and Béatrice Vernaudon. The FLP did not present a candidate.

The testing of nuclear devices by the French Government at Mururoa Atoll, in the Tuamotu Archipelago, began in 1966. In July 1985 the trawler, *Rainbow Warrior*, the flagship of the anti-nuclear environmentalist group, Greenpeace, which was to have led a flotilla to Mururoa Atoll to protest against the French nuclear-test programme, was blown up and sunk in Auckland Harbour, New Zealand. One member of the crew was killed. Two agents of the French secret service, the Direction Générale de la Sécurité Extérieure (DGSE), were found responsible, and relations between France and New Zealand were seriously affected by the resulting dispute, especially over the treatment of the two agents.

France, however, continued to perform tests in the islands despite growing local opposition and the protests of the South Pacific Forum nations. Between 1975 and 1992 France conducted 135 underground and 52 atmospheric nuclear tests. In May 1991, during a visit to New Zealand, the French Prime Minister, Michel Rocard, formally apologized for the bombing of the *Rainbow Warrior*. However, in July 1991 tension between France and the region was exacerbated by the French Government's decision to award a medal for 'distinguished service' to one of the agents convicted for his role in the bombing.

In April 1992 the French Government announced that nuclear tests would be suspended until the end of the year. Although the decision was welcomed throughout the South Pacific, concern was expressed in French Polynesia over the economic implications of the move, because of the Territory's dependence on income received from hosting the nuclear-test programme. Similarly, it was feared that unemployment resulting from the ban would have a serious impact on the economy. A delegation of political leaders subsequently travelled to Paris to voice its concerns, and in January 1993 accepted assistance worth 7,000m. francs CFP in compensation for lost revenue and in aid for development projects. It was subsequently confirmed that the suspension of tests would continue for an indefinite period.

However, shortly after his election in May 1995, President Jacques Chirac announced that France would resume nuclear testing, with a programme of eight tests between September 1995 and May 1996. The decision provoked almost universal outrage in the international community, and was condemned for its apparent disregard for regional opinion, as well as for undermining the considerable progress made by Western nations towards a world-wide ban on nuclear testing. Scientists also expressed concern at the announcement; some believed that further explosions at Mururoa could lead to the collapse of the atoll, which had been weakened considerably. Large-scale demonstrations and protest marches throughout the region were accompanied by boycotts of French products and the suspension of several trade and defence co-operation agreements. Opposition to the French Government intensified in July 1995, when French commandos violently seized the flagship of Greenpeace, *Rainbow Warrior II*, together with its crew, who had been protesting peacefully near the test site. Chirac continued to defy mounting pressure from the EU, Japan and Russia, as well as Australia, New Zealand and the South Pacific community, all of which urged him to reverse the decision to carry out the tests.

French Polynesia became the focus of world attention when the first test was carried out in September 1995. The action attracted further statements of condemnation from Governments around the world, and provoked major demonstrations in many countries. In Tahiti hitherto peaceful protests soon developed into full-scale riots, as several thousand demonstrators, enraged by the French authorities' intransigent stance, rampaged through the capital demanding an end to French rule. Meanwhile, violent clashes with police, and the burning of dozens of buildings in Papeete during the riots, left much of the capital in ruins. In defiance of world opinion, a further five tests were carried out, the sixth and final one being conducted in January 1996. In September 1998 the trial of more than 60 people charged with offences relating to the riots and protests of September 1995 began in Papeete. Hiro Tefaare, a pro-independence member of the Territorial Assembly and former police officer, was found guilty of instigating the riots and sentenced to three years' imprisonment (of which 18 months were to be suspended). Furthermore, in September 1999 the French Government was ordered by the Administrative Tribunal to pay 204m. francs CFP in compensation for failing to maintain law and order.

Meanwhile, in early 1996 the French Government confirmed reports by a team of independent scientists that radioactive isotopes had leaked into the waters surrounding the atoll, but denied that they represented a threat to the environment. However, following the election of a new socialist administration in France in mid-1997, the French Minister of the Environment demanded in August 1998 that the matter be investigated further, stating that she had not been reassured by the initial reports. Work to dismantle facilities at the test site began in 1997 and was completed in July 1998.

In early 1999 a study by the French Independent Research and Information Commission reported that there was serious radioactive leakage into underground water, lagoons and the ocean at Mururoa and Fangataufa atolls. These claims were dismissed by a New Zealand scientist who had taken part in an earlier study by the International Atomic Energy Agency, which had claimed that radiation levels were nearly undetectable. In May 1999 a French government official admitted that fractures had been found in the coral cone at the Mururoa and Fangataufa nuclear testing sites. The reports by Greenpeace that the atoll was in danger of collapsing had always been previously denied by France. However, France's claim that no serious long-term damage had been done was contested by Greenpeace, which also suggested the need for an urgent independent study of the test sites. In January 2000, in what was considered to be a significant development, the commander of the French armed forces in French Polynesia admitted that there were significant cracks in the coral reef surrounding Mururoa, and that these could lead to the occurrence of a tsunami.

The French Government is responsible for conducting the external affairs of the Territory although, by the constitutional settlement of 1990, the Territorial Government was enabled to enter into treaties with other Pacific countries and territories concerning matters in which it has competence. An agreement settling the delimitation of the conflicting exclusive economic zones claimed by the Cook Islands and French Polynesia was signed in August 1990.

Economy

The economy of French Polynesia is dominated by income from the French State and especially, from 1966, by the presence of the Centre d'Expérimentation du Pacifique (CEP) and the Commission d'Energie Atomique (CEA). In 2000, according to World Bank estimates, French Polynesia's gross national product (GNP), measured at average 1998–2000 prices, was US $4,063m., equivalent to US $17,370 per head (or US $23,510m. per head on an international purchasing-power parity basis). During 1990–2000, it was estimated, GNP per head increased, in real terms, at an average annual rate of 0.6%. Over the same period, the population increased at an average annual rate of 1.7%. French Polynesia's gross domestic product (GDP) increased, in real terms, at an average annual rate of 2.3% in 1990–2000. Real GDP increased by 4.0% in both 1999 and 2000. One of French Polynesia's main problems has been the rapid rate of population growth (although this has shown signs of declining because of a fall in the birth rate) which, between 1990 and 2000, was estimated at an annual average of 1.7%. At the census of 1996, 43% of the population were estimated to be under 20 years of age.

Agriculture, forestry and fishing contributed only 4.7% of GDP in 2000, but provided most of French Polynesia's exports. The sector engaged 14.6% of the employed labour force in 1996. Coconuts are the principal cash crop, and in 2000 the estimated harvest was 77,000 metric tons. Most coconut trees are grown in the Tuamotu-Gambier region. Monoï oil is produced by macerating tiaré flowers in cononut oil, and in 1998 187 metric tons were exported, earning some 128m. francs CFP. Vegetables, fruit (especially citrus fruit), vanilla and coffee are also cultivated. The most important livestock products are dairy produce, eggs and honey. The forestry sector is still being developed.

Most commercial fishing, principally for tuna, is conducted, under licence, by Japanese and Korean fleets. The total catch by French Polynesian vessels in 1998 was 9,016 metric tons. The aquaculture sector produced only 43 metric tons of shrimps in 1999. The most important of the marine industries (which include the farming of shrimps and mussels) is the production of cultured black pearls, of which the quantity exported increased from about 50 kg in 1978 to 8,182 kg in 1999; it accounted for 54.8% of total exports in 2001. In the latter year the Territory's exports of black pearls earned some 14,244m. francs CFP (compared with 17,328m. francs CFP and 20,934m. francs CFP in 1999 and 2000 respectively). During the mid-1990s French Polynesia was estimated to have produced more than 95% of the world's cultured black pearls. Japan is the biggest importer of black pearls from the Territory, and in 1998 purchased an estimated 65% of black pearls produced in that year (9,600m. francs CFP). In 2000 French Polynesia's pearl producers embarked on a 'clean-up' operation aimed at preserving high standards and deterring the sale of cheaper, poor-quality pearls. However, the black pearl industry continued to decline in 2001. Auctions early in the year raised less revenue than expected, with a marked reduction in the number of buyers from Japan in particular, largely owing to the downturn in that country's economy, as well as in Europe and the USA. In December the industry lowered prices to maintain the level of sales, while at the same time it formed a centralized buying syndicate, to ensure minimum prices and quality control. Meanwhile, the Territory's largest producer of black pearls had suspended operations at five farms and reduced staff levels, in the hope that pearl prices would rise.

Industry (including construction) engaged 16.6% of the employed labour force in 1998 and provided 15.5% of GDP in 1997. There is a small manufacturing sector, which is heavily dependent on agriculture. Coconut oil and meal or oilcake (for animal feed) are produced from copra, as are soap and monoï. There are breweries, fruit juice and soft drinks factories and some textile and handicraft manufacturers. The manufacturing sector engaged 8.2% of all employees in 1998 and contributed 7.0% of GDP in 1997. Construction is an important industrial activity, contributing 5.3% of GDP in 1997 and engaging 8.4% of the employed labour force in 1998.

Hydrocarbon fuels are the main source of energy in the Territory, with the Papeete thermal power station providing about three-quarters of the electricity produced. Hydroelectric dams with the capacity to generate 36% of Tahiti's electricity requirements have been constructed. Solar energy is also increasingly important, especially on the less-populated islands.

The services sector engaged 69.8% of the employed labour force in 1996 and provided 80.4% of GDP in 1997. Tourism remains the primary source of revenue, and receipts from tourism totalled an estimated 49,900m. francs CFP in 2000. The Territory received some 227,658 tourists in 2001. As hotel occupancy was low in late 2001, the prices of various services were reduced. In June 2002 P&O agreed to operate two luxury cruise liners, which had been abandoned in Papeete harbour when their former owners, Renaissance Cruises, went bankrupt in 2001. Corsair, a French airline company, announced in August 2002 that it was to cease its twice-weekly service from Paris to Papeete, which had carried some 61,000 passengers to and from French Polynesia in 2001. The President of French Polynesia, Gaston Flosse, and the Chairman of Air Tahiti Nui attempted to persuade Corsair to continue the service until April 2003.

In 2000, according to the Institut d'Émission d'Outre-Mer (IEOM—the French overseas reserve bank), French Polynesia recorded a visible trade deficit of 81,052m. francs CFP. The Territory's recurring deficit is partly offset by receipts from tourism, but mainly by transfers from the French treasury. On the current account of the balance-of payments there was a surplus of 45,660m. francs CFP, equivalent to 11% of GDP and an increase of 75.8% compared with the previous year. In 2001 imports reached 140,939.3m. francs CFP and exports totalled 25,979.3m. francs CFP. France is traditionally the principal trading partner, accounting for 36.0% of imports and 13.8% of exports in 2000. The USA was next in importance that year, supplying 13.9% of imports and receiving 13.1% of exports. Australia, New Zealand and Hong Kong are also significant trading partners. The principal imports in 2001 included road vehicles (12.1%) and machinery and mechanical appliances (9.9%). The principal commodity exports in that year were cultured black pearls (which provided 58.8% of total export revenue). Coconut oil, vanilla, fish and cut flowers were also important exports in the 1990s.

A budgetary deficit of 44,579m. francs CFP was projected in 2000 (the recorded deficit in 1999 was 28,990m. francs CFP). In that year expenditure by the French State in the Territory totalled 124,800m. francs CFP, 28.4% of which was on the military budget. In 2002 France allocated budgetary aid of €929,682m., compared with €905,545m. in 2001. The total external debt was estimated at US $390m. in 1992. The annual rate of inflation averaged 1.2% in 1990–2000, standing at 1.1% in 2000.

The Territory suffers from a high rate of unemployment, recorded at 13.2% of the labour force in 1996. Problems are accentuated by the marked predominance of young people in the population, as well as by the migration from the countryside and the outer islands to the urban centres since the 1960s, and the consequent housing difficulties and loss of subsistence skills.

French Polynesia is an Overseas Territory in association with the EU. The Territory is part of the Franc Zone (an association of countries with currencies linked to the French franc), and has membership in its own right of the Pacific Community (formerly the South Pacific Commission). French Polynesia is also an associate member of the UN's Economic and Social Commission for Asia and the Pacific (ESCAP).

The Territory enjoys a very high standard of living, compared with its island neighbours. However, despite one of the region's highest incomes per head in statistical terms, French Polynesia has considerable disparities of wealth. Perhaps the most significant, if distorting, economic factor in French Polynesia has been the presence of the CEP and the CEA. Polynesian opinion was caught in a dichotomy: the fear of adverse environmental consequences from the nuclear tests and apprehension of an economic disaster if the French were to withdraw from the islands. The changes brought about by the nuclear-testing programme effectively transformed the islands from a state of self-sufficiency to one of import-dependency within less than a generation. Prior to the establishment of the CEP and the CEA and the start of nuclear testing in 1966, French Polynesia exported commodities to the value of 80% of its imports and the primary sector provided 54% of employment (1962). It was estimated that, in 1989, the CEP alone provided 12.5% of local jobs and accounted for 55% of all the Territory's external financial aid, 22% of GDP and 28% of total imports. With the help of revenues from the programme of nuclear testing, the economy of French Polynesia has been dominated by the large number of semi-public companies—such as the Société de Financement du Développement de la Polynésie Francaise, and Air Tahiti Nui.

In 1993 the Governments of French Polynesia and metropolitan France concluded an agreement, the 'pacte de progrès', which was to provide the Territory with aid worth some 26,000m. francs CFP over five years. This financial arrangement was extended following the conclusion of a further series of nuclear tests to some 28,300m. francs CFP annually over 10 years (1996–2006). It was hoped that the arrangement would enable French Polynesia to establish an economy that was more reliant upon local resources and would consequently create greater employment, thereby enhancing the Territory's potential for durable independence. In an attempt to supplement revenue provided by the Contribution de Solidarité Territoriale (an income tax introduced in 1993), the Territorial Government announced the introduction of a value-added tax (VAT) from October 1997. French Polynesia's steady economic growth partly resulted from the development of the services sector, notably in hotel construction and other tourism-related services, which led to significant employment creation. Other sectors of the economy, such as pearl farming, however, have not expanded as rapidly, principally because of regional economic conditions (notably the recession in Japan, one of the largest importers of black pearls). In 2001 customs duties were decreased, while VAT rates were maintained at similar levels, as the Government continued the anti-inflationary policy that it had instigated in 1996. The principal aim of the 2002 budget, however, was to avoid recession and to counter the repercussions of the deteriorating global economic situation. VAT rates were increased by an average of 3.3%, and total VAT receipts for the year were expected to reach 36,600m. francs CFP. The 2002 budget also introduced new taxes on alcohol, soft drinks, sugar and new road vehicles. The Government defended the introduction of these new taxes by citing the 'economic uncertainties' faced by French Polynesia. Of total budgetary expenditure of 139,000m. francs CFP, some 50,000m. francs CFP were allocated for investment purposes. The tourism sector, meanwhile, proved vulnerable in the wake of the terrorist attacks on the USA on 11 September 2001. The number of visitor arrivals declined sharply in late 2001, and by early 2002 many of French Polynesia's hotels were reporting occupancy rates as low as 35%.

Statistical Survey

Source (unless otherwise indicated): Institut Statistique de la Polynésie Française, Immeuble UUPA, rue Edouard Ahne, BP 395, 98713 Papeete; tel. 473434; fax 427252; e-mail ispf@ispf.pf; internet www.ispf.pf.

AREA AND POPULATION

Area: Total 4,167 sq km (1,609 sq miles); Land area 3,521 sq km (1,359 sq miles).

Population: 188,814 at census of 6 September 1988; 219,521 (males 113,934, females 105,587) at census of 3 September 1996; 238,800 (provisional estimate) at 1 January 2002.

Population by island group (1996 census): Society Archipelago 189,524 (Windward Islands 162,686, Leeward Islands 26,838); Marquesas Archipelago 8,064; Austral Islands 6,563; Tuamotu-Gambier Islands 15,370.

Density (January 2002): 57.3 per sq km.

Ethnic Groups (census of 15 October 1983): Polynesian 114,280; 'Demis' 23,625 (Polynesian-European 15,851, Polynesian-Chinese 6,356, Polynesian-Other races 1,418); European 19,320; Chinese 7,424; European-Chinese 494; Others 1,610; Total 166,753. *1988 census* ('000 persons): Polynesians and 'Demis' 156.3; Others 32.5.

Principal Towns (population at 1996 census): Papeete (capital) 25,553; Faaa 25,888; Punaauía 19,524; Pirae 13,974; Moorea-Maiao 11,965; Mahina 11,640; Paea 10,281.

Births, Marriages and Deaths (1999, provisional): Registered live births 4,580 (birth rate 20.0 per 1,000); Marriages (1997) 1,176 (marriage rate 5.3 per 1,000); Registered deaths 1,003 (death rate 4.4 per 1,000).

Expectation of Life (years at birth, 1999, provisional): 72.5 (males 70.0; females 75.0). Source: UN, *Statistical Yearbook for Asia and the Pacific*.

Economically Active Population (persons aged 14 years and over, 1996 census): Agriculture, hunting, forestry and fishing 10,888; Mining and manufacturing 6,424; Electricity, gas and water 459; Construction 4,777; Trade, restaurants and hotels 9,357; Transport, storage and communications 3,788; Financial services 1,482; Real estate 383; Business services 3,710; Private services 9,033; Education, health and social welfare 10,771; Public administration 13,475; Total employed 74,547 (males 46,141, females 28,406); Persons on compulsory military service 1,049 (all males); Unemployed 11,525 (males 6,255, females 5,270); Total labour force 87,121 (males 53,445, females 33,676).

HEALTH AND WELFARE

Key Indicators

Physicians (per 1,000 head, 2001): 1.8.

For definitions, see explanatory note on p.vi.

AGRICULTURE, ETC.

Principal Crops (metric tons, 2000): Roots and tubers 11,500*; Vegetables and melons 6,550*; Pineapples 3,200*; Other fruit 3,460*; Coconuts 77,000*; Vanilla 40; Coffee (green) 18. Source: FAO and Service du Développement Rural.

* FAO estimate.

Livestock (FAO estimates, year ending September 2000): Cattle 10,000; Horses 2,200; Pigs 37,000; Goats 16,500; Sheep 440; Chickens 180,000; Ducks 32,000. Source: FAO.

Livestock Products (metric tons, 2000): Beef and veal 180*; Pig meat 1,200*; Goat meat 75; Poultry meat 638; Cows' milk 1,000*; Hen eggs 1,800*; Other poultry eggs 85.

* FAO estimate.

Source: FAO.

Fishing ('000 metric tons, live weight, 1999): Capture 12.3 (Common dolphinfish 0.4, Skipjack tuna 1.4; Albacore 2.6, Yellowfin tuna 1.2, Marlins and sailfishes 0.7, Sharks, rays, skates, etc. 0.4); Aquaculture 0.0; Total catch 12.4. Note: Figures exclude trochus shells (FAO estimate, metric tons): 35. Source: FAO, *Yearbook of Fishery Statistics*.

INDUSTRY

Production: Copra 8,262 metric tons (sales, 2001); Coconut oil 5,000* metric tons (2001); Oilcake 2,500* metric tons (2001); Beer 129,000 hectolitres (1992); Printed cloth 200,000 m (1979); Japanese sandals 600,000 pairs (1979); Electric energy 495.2m. kWh (2001).

* FAO estimate.

FINANCE

Currency and Exchange Rates: 100 centimes = 1 franc de la Communauté française du Pacifique (franc CFP or Pacific franc). *Sterling, Dollar and Euro Equivalents* (31 May 2002): £1 sterling = 186.45 francs CFP; US $1 = 127.12 francs CFP; €1 = 119.33 francs CFP; 1,000 francs CFP = £5.363 = $7.866 = €8.380. *Average Exchange Rate* (francs CFP per US $): 112.01 in 1999; 129.52 in 2000; 133.35 in 2001. Note: Until 31 December 1998 the value of the franc CFP was fixed at 5.5 French centimes (1 French franc = 18.1818 francs CFP). Since the introduction of the euro, on 1 January 1999, an official exchange rate of 1,000 francs CFP = €8.38 (€1 = 119.332 francs CFP) has been in operation. Accordingly, the value of the franc CFP has been adjusted to 5.4969 French centimes (1 French franc = 18.1920 francs CFP), representing a 'devaluation' of 0.056%.

Territorial Budget (million francs CFP, 2001): *Revenue:* Current 108,036 (Indirect taxation 59,523). *Expenditure:* Current 95,796, Capital 44,913; Total 140,709.

French State Expenditure (million francs CFP, 1996): Civil budget 61,706 (Current 56,564, Capital 5,142); Military budget 46,119 (Current 37,160, Capital 8,959); Pensions 10,458; Total (incl. others) 123,774 (Current 109,060, Capital 14,714).

1998 (million francs CFP): 121,788 (incl. military budget 37,982).

1999 (million francs CFP): 120,631 (incl. military budget 34,343).

2000 (million francs CFP): 124,800 (incl. military budget 35,400).

2001 (million francs CFP): 128,480 (incl. military budget 36,774).

Money Supply (million francs CFP at 31 December 2001): Currency in circulation 9,366; Demand deposits 100,617; Total money 109,983. Source: Institut d'Emission d'Outre-Mer.

Cost of Living (Consumer Price Index; base: 1990 = 100): All items 111.7 in 1999; 112.9 in 2000; 114.0 in 2001. Source: UN, *Monthly Bulletin of Statistics*.

Gross Domestic Product (million francs CFP at current prices): 378,501 in 1997; 404,886 in 1998; 412,100 in 1999; 446,100 in 2000.

Expenditure on the Gross Domestic Product (million francs CFP at current prices, 1993): Government final consumption expenditure 126,127; Private final consumption expenditure 202,563; Increase in stocks –536; Gross fixed capital formation 53,494; *Total domestic expenditure* 381,648; Exports of goods and services 34,523; *Less* Imports of goods and services 86,905; *GDP in purchasers' values* 329,266. Source: UN, *National Accounts Statistics*.

Gross Domestic Product by Economic Activity (million francs CFP at current prices, 1997): Agriculture, forestry and fishing 15,534; Manufacturing 26,360*; Electricity, gas and water 12,221*; Construction 20,104; Trade 81,854; Transport and telecommunications 27,832. Other private services 96,714; Government services 97,238; Domestic services 646; *GDP in purchasers' values* 378,503. *Manufacturing of energy-generating products is included in electricity, gas and water. Source: UN, *National Accounts Statistics*.

EXTERNAL TRADE

Principal Commodities (million francs CFP, 2001): *Imports c.i.f.:* Live animals and animal products 9,617.3 (Meat and edible meat offal 6,188.0); Prepared foodstuffs; beverages, spirits and vinegar; tobacco and manufactured substitutes 13,890.5; Mineral products 13,257.9 (Mineral fuels, mineral oils and products of their distillation; bituminous substances; mineral waxes 11,725.0); Products of chemical or allied industries 9,871.5 (Pharmaceutical products 4,675.7); Plastics, rubber and articles thereof 5,313.2; Paper-making materials; paper and paperboard and articles thereof 4,266.3; Textiles and textile articles 4,751.3; Base metals and articles thereof 8,177.2; Machinery and mechanical appliances; electrical equipment; sound and television apparatus 24,524.1 (Nuclear reactors, boilers, machinery, mechanical appliances and parts 14,007.9, Electrical machinery, equipment, etc. 10,516.2); Vehicles, aircraft, vessels and associated transport equipment 24,955.2 (Road vehicles, parts and accessories 17,087.7); Miscellaneous manufactured articles 5,689.9; Total (incl. others) 140,939.3. *Exports f.o.b.:* Live animals and animal products 1,627.9 (Fish and crustaceans, molluscs and other aquatic invertebrates 1,458.2); Prepared foodstuffs; beverages, spirits and vinegar; tobacco and manufactured substitutes 950.1 (Preparations of vegetables, fruit, nuts or other parts of plants 862.8); Natural or cultured pearls, precious or semi-precious stones, precious metals and articles thereof; imitation jewellery; coin 15,281.3; Machinery and mechanical appliances; electrical equipment; sound and television apparatus 1,746.1 (Nuclear reactors, boilers, machinery, mechanical appliances and parts 1,213.2); Vehicles, aircraft, vessels and associated transport equipment 4,851.8 (Aircraft, spacecraft and parts 4,324.3); Total (incl. others) 25,979.3.

Principal Trading Partners (million francs CFP, 2000): *Imports:* Australia 11,763; Belgium 6,004; China, People's Republic 3,566; France 45,531; Germany 1,775; Italy 3,828; Japan 5,116; Korea, Republic 1,544; New Zealand 9,338; Singapore 2,445; Spain 1,707; Taiwan 1,634; United Kingdom 2,447; USA 17,594; Total (incl. others) 126,407. *Exports:* France 3,989; Germany 499; Hong Kong 6,010; Japan 349; New Caledonia 1,440; New Zealand 297; USA 3,768; Total (incl. others) 28,829. Source: ISPF—Service des Douanes.

TRANSPORT

Road Traffic (1987): Total vehicles registered 54,979; (1996 census): Private cars 47,300.

Shipping (1990): *International traffic:* Passengers carried 47,616; Freight handled 642,314 metric tons. *Domestic traffic:* Passengers carried 596,185; Freight handled 261,593 metric tons. (2001): Goods unloaded 904,727 metric tons; Goods loaded 32,658 metric tons.

Civil Aviation (2001): *International traffic:* Passengers carried 560,701; Freight handled 8,717 metric tons. *Domestic traffic:* Passengers carried 833,086; Freight handled 2,992 metric tons.

TOURISM

Visitors (excluding cruise passengers and excursionists): 210,800 in 1999; 252,000 in 2000; 227,658 in 2001.

Tourist Arrivals by Country of Residence (2001): Australia 6,420; Canada 3,648; France 50,466; Germany 5,448; Italy 9,351; Japan 19,031; New Zealand 5,435; United Kingdom 6,496; USA 93,363; Total (incl. others) 227,658.

Tourism Receipts (US $ million) 359 in 1997; 354 in 1998; 394 in 1999. Source: World Tourism Organization.

2000: 49,900m. francs CFP.

Source: Ministère du Tourisme.

COMMUNICATIONS MEDIA

Radio Receivers (1997): 128,000 in use*.

Television Receivers (2000): 44,000 in use†.

Telephones (2001): 52,600 main lines in use)†.

Facsimile Machines (1998): 3,000 in use†.

Mobile Cellular Telephones (subscribers, 2001): 67,000†.

Internet Users (2001): 16,000†.

Daily Newspapers (2000): 2.

* Source: UNESCO, *Statistical Yearbook*.

† Source: International Telecommunication Union.

EDUCATION

Pre-primary (2000/01): 54 schools; 408 teachers (1996/97); 13,720 pupils.

Primary (2000/01): 173 schools; 2,811 teachers (1996/97); 26,249 pupils.

General Secondary (2000/01): 2,035 teachers (1998/99); 24,743 pupils.

Vocational (1992): 316 teachers; 3,730 students.

Tertiary (1993): 34 teachers; 892 students.

Source: partly UNESCO, *Statistical Yearbook*.

Directory

The Constitution

The constitutional system in French Polynesia is established under the aegis of the Constitution of the Fifth French Republic and specific laws of 1977, 1984 and 1990. The French Polynesia Statute 1984, the so-called 'internal autonomy statute', underwent amendment in a law of July 1990. A further extension of the Territory's powers under the statute was approved by the French National Assembly in December 1995. A constitutional amendment granting French Polynesia a greater degree of autonomy was presented to a joint session of the French Senate and National Assembly for final ratification in January 2000 (see History). By early 2002, however, no decision had been taken on the matter.

French Polynesia is declared to be an autonomous Territory of the French Republic, of which it remains an integral part. The High Commissioner, appointed by the French Government, exercises the prerogatives of the State in matters relating to defence, foreign relations, the maintenance of law and order, communications and citizenship. The head of the local executive and the person who represents the Territory is the President of the Territorial Government, who is elected by the Territorial Assembly from among its own number. The Territorial President appoints and dismisses the Council of Ministers and has competence in international relations as they affect French Polynesia and its exclusive economic zone, and is in control of foreign investments and immigration. The Territorial Assembly, which has financial autonomy in budgetary affairs and legislative authority within the Territory, is elected for a term of up to five years on the basis of universal adult suffrage. There are 49 members: 32 elected by the people of the Windward Islands (Iles du Vent—Society Islands), seven by the Leeward Islands (Iles Sous le Vent—Society Islands), four by the Tuamotu Archipelago and the Gambier Islands and three each by the Austral Islands and by the Marquesas Archipelago. The Assembly elects a Permanent Commission of between seven and nine of its members, and itself meets for two ordinary sessions each year and upon the demand of the majority party, the Territorial President or the High Commissioner. Local government is conducted by the municipalities. There is an Economic, Social and Cultural Council (composed of representatives of professional groups, trade unions and other organizations and agencies which participate in the economic, social and cultural activities of the Territory), a Territorial Audit Office and a judicial system which includes a Court of the First Instance, a Court of Appeal and an Administrative Court. The Territory, as a part of the French Republic, also elects two deputies to the National Assembly and one member of the Senate, and may be represented in the European Parliament.

The Government

(September 2002)

High Commissioner: MICHEL MATHIEU (appointed October 2001).

Secretary-General: CHRISTIAN MASSIMON.

COUNCIL OF MINISTERS

President and Minister for Foreign Affairs, the Pearl Culture Industry and Urban Development: GASTON FLOSSE.

Vice-President and Minister for Employment and Training, Outer Island Development, New Technologies and Post: EDOUARD FRITCH.

Minister for Economy and Finance: GEORGES PUCHON.

Minister for Housing, Land Use, Urban Affairs, Town Humanization and Government Spokesman: JEAN-CHRISTOPHE BOUISSOU.

Minister for Lands, Land Redistribution and Valuation: GASTON TONG SANG.

Minister for Education and Technical Training: NICOLAS SANQUER.

Minister for Ports and Utilities: JONAS TAHUAITU.

Minister for Environment and City Policy: BRUNO SANDRAS.

Minister for Tourism and Transport: BRIGITTE VANIZETTE.

Minister for Fisheries, Industry and Small and Medium Businesses: NINA VERNAUDON.

Minister for Agriculture and Livestock: FRÉDÉRIC RIVETA.

Minister for Solidarity and Family: PIA FAATOMO.

Minister for Youth and Sports, Youth Opportunities and Associative Affairs, responsible for Relations with the Territorial Assembly and the Economic, Social and Cultural Council: REYNALD TEMARII.

Minister for Health, Public Service and Administrative Decentralization: ARMELLE MERCERON.

Minister for Culture and Higher Education, responsible for the Promotion of Women's Affairs and Polynesian Languages: LOUISE PELTZER.

Minister for Arts and Crafts: PASCALE HAITI.

GOVERNMENT OFFICES

Office of the High Commissioner of the Republic: Bureau du Haut Commissaire, ave Bruat, BP 115, 98713, Papeete; tel. 468686; fax 468689; e-mail courrier@haut-commissariat.pf.

Office of the President of the Territorial Government: BP 2551, 98713 Papeete; tel. 472000; fax 419781; e-mail presid@mail.pf; internet www.presidence.pf.

Territorial Government of French Polynesia: BP 2551, Papeete; tel. 472000; fax 419781; e-mail presid@mail.pf; all ministries; Delegation in Paris: 28 blvd Saint-Germain, 75005 Paris, France; tel. 1-55-42-65-10; fax 1-55-42-64-09.

Economic, Social and Cultural Council: ave Bruat, BP 1657, 98716 Papeete; tel. 416500; fax 419242; e-mail cesc@cesc.gov.pf; Pres. BRUNO SANDRAS.

Ministry of the Pearl Industry: Papeete; internet www.perle.gov.pf.

Ministry of the Economy and Finance: Papeete; e-mail cabinet@economie.gov.pf; internet www.finances.gov.pf.

Ministry of Housing: Papeete; internet www.logement.gov.pf.

Ministry of Land Affairs: Papeete; internet www.foncier.gov.pf.

Ministry of Education: Papeete; internet www.education.gov.pf.

Ministry of Public Works and Harbours: Papeete; internet www.equipement.gov.pf.

Ministry of Health: Papeete; internet www.sante.gov.pf.

Ministry of Environment: Papeete.

Ministry of Tourism: Papeete; internet www.tourisme.gov.pf.

Ministry of Fisheries: Papeete; internet www.mer.gov.pf.

Ministry of Agriculture: Papeete; internet www.agriculture.gov.pf.

Ministry of Solidarity and Family Affairs: Papeete; internet www.solidarite.gov.pf.

Ministry of Youth: Papeete; internet www.jeunesse.gov.pf.

Ministry of Culture: Papeete; internet www.culture.gov.pf.

Ministry of Craft Industry: Papeete; internet www.artisanat.gov.pf.

Legislature

ASSEMBLÉE TERRITORIALE

President: LUCETTE TAERO.

Territorial Assembly: Assemblée Territoriale, BP 28, Papeete; tel. 416100; fax 416160.

Election, 6 May 2001

Party	Seats
Tahoeraa Huiraatira/RPR	28
Tavini Huiraatira	13
Fe'tia Api	7
Tapura Amui No Tuhaa Pae	1
Total	49

PARLEMENT

Deputies to the French National Assembly: MICHEL BUILLARD (Tahoeraa Huiraatira/RPR), BÉATRICE VERNAUDON (Tahoeraa Huiraatira/RPR)

Representative to the French Senate: GASTON FLOSSE (Tahoeraa Huiraatira/RPR).

Political Organizations

Ai'a Api (New Land): BP 11055, Mahina, Tahiti; tel. 481135; f. 1982 after split in Te E'a Api; Leader EMILE VERNAUDON.

Alliance 2000: c/o Assemblée Territoriale, BP 28, Papeete; pro-independence grouping.

Fe'tia Api (New Star): c/o Assemblée Territoriale, BP 140 512, Arue; Leader BORIS LÉONTIEFF.

Haere i Mua: Leader ALEXANDRE LÉONTIEFF.

Heiura-Les Verts: BP 44, Borabora; tel. and fax 677174; e-mail heiura@mail.pf.

Ia Mana Te Nunaa: rue du Commandant Destrémau, BP 1223, Papeete; tel. 426699; f. 1976; advocates 'socialist independence'; Sec.-Gen. JACQUES DROLLET.

Polynesian Union Party: Papeete; Leader JEAN JUVENTIN.

Pupu Here Ai'a Te Nunaa Ia Ora: BP 3195, Papeete; tel. 420766; f. 1965; advocates autonomy; 8,000 mems.

Te Hono e Tau I te Honu Hui: Papeete; f. 2002; Leader STANLEY CROSS.

Te Tiaraama: Papeete; f. 1987 by split from the RPR; Leader ALEXANDRE LÉONTIEFF.

Pupu Taina/Rassemblement des Libéraux: rue Cook, BP 169, Papeete; tel. 429880; f. 1976; seeks to retain close links with France; associated with the French Union pour la Démocratie Française (UDF); Leader MICHEL LAW.

Taatiraa No Te Hali: BP 2916, Papeete; tel. 437494; fax 422546; f. 1977; Pres. ROBERT TANSEAU.

Tahoeraa Huiraatira/Rassemblement pour la République—RPR: rue du Commandant Destrémeau, BP 471, Papeete; tel. 429898; fax 450004; f. 1958; supports links with France, with internal autonomy; Pres. GASTON FLOSSE; Hon. Pres. JACQUES TEUIRA.

Tapura Amui No Tuhaa Pae: c/o Assemblée Territoriale, BP 28, Papeete; represents the Austral Islands; Leader CHANTAL FLORES.

Tavini Huiraatira/Front de Libération de la Polynésie (FLP): independence movement; anti-nuclear; Leader Oscar Temaru.

Te Avei'a Mau (True Path): c/o Assemblée Territoriale, BP 28, Papeete; Leader TINOMANA EBB.

Te e'a No Maohi Nui: Leader JEAN-MARIUS RAAPOTO.

Te Henua Enata Kotoa: c/o Assemblée Territoriale, BP 28, Papeete; Leader LUCIEN KIMITETE.

Judicial System

Court of Appeal: Cour d'Appel de Papeete, BP 101, 98713 Papeete; tel. 415553; fax 424416; Pres. PATRICK MICHAUX; Attorney-General JACK GAUTHIER.

Court of the First Instance: Tribunal de Première Instance de Papeete, BP 101, Papeete; tel. 415500; fax 454012; internet www.polynesie-francaise.gouv.fr; e-mail pr.tpi-papeete@justice.pf; Pres. JEAN-LOUIS THIOLET; Procurator MICHEL MAROTTE; Clerk of the Court CAROLE VAIRAAROA.

Court of Administrative Law: Tribunal Administratif, BP 4522, Papeete; tel. 509025; fax 451724; e-mail tapapeete@mail.pf; Pres. ALFRED POUPET; Cllrs RAOUL AUREILLE, MARIE-CHRISTINE LUBRANO, ALAIN LEVASSEUR, HÉLÈNE ROULAND.

Religion

About 54% of the population are Protestants and 30% are Roman Catholics.

CHRISTIANITY

Protestant Church

L'Eglise évangélique en Polynésie française (Etaretia Evaneria i Porinetia Farani): BP 113, Papeete; tel. 460600; fax 419357; e-mail eepf@mail.pf; f. 1884; autonomous since 1963; c. 95,000 mems; Pres. of Council Rev. JACQUES TERAI IHORAI; Sec.-Gen. (vacant).

The Roman Catholic Church

French Polynesia comprises the archdiocese of Papeete and the suffragan diocese of Taiohae o Tefenuaenata (based in Nuku Hiva, Marquesas Is). At 31 December 1999 there were an estimated 83,000 adherents in the Territory, representing about 37% of the total population. The Archbishop and the Bishop participate in the Episcopal Conference of the Pacific, based in Fiji.

Archbishop of Papeete: Most Rev. HUBERT COPPENRATH, Archevêché, BP 94, Vallée de la Mission, 98713 Papeete; tel. 502351; fax 424032; e-mail catholic@mail.pf.

Other Churches

There are small Sanito, Church of Jesus Christ of Latter-day Saints (Mormon), and Seventh-day Adventist missions.

The Press

La Dépêche de Tahiti: Société Océanienne de Communication, BP 50, Papeete; tel. 464343; fax 464350; e-mail journalistes@france-antilles.pf; internet www.ladepechedetahiti.com; f. 1964; daily; French; Editor-in-Chief DANIEL PARDON; Dir-Gen. PASCAL HEEMS; circ. 15,000.

Les Nouvelles de Tahiti: place de la Cathédrale, BP 629, Papeete; tel. 508100; fax 508109; e-mail nouvelles@mail.pf; f. 1956; daily; French; Editor MURIEL PONTAROLLO; Dir-Gen. PASCAL HEEMS; Publr PHILIPPE HERSANT; circ. 6,500.

Le Semeur Tahitien: BP 94, 98713 Papeete; tel. 420251; e-mail catholic@mail.pf; f. 1909; monthly; French; publ. by the Roman Catholic Church.

Tahiti Beach Press: BP 887, 98713 Papeete; tel. 426850; fax 423356; e-mail tahitibeachpress@mail.pf; f. 1980; weekly; English; Publr G. WARTI; circ. 3,500.

Tahiti Pacifique Magazine: BP 368, Maharepa, Moorea; tel. 562894; fax 563007; e-mail tahitipm@mail.pf; internet www.tahiti-pacifique.com; monthly; French; Editor ALEX DU PREL; circ. 5,000.

Tahiti Rama: Papeete; weekly.

Tahiti Today: BP 887, 98713 Papeete; tel. 426850; fax 423356; f. 1996; quarterly; Publr G. WARTI; circ. 3,000.

La Tribune Polynésienne: place du Marché, BP 392, Papeete; tel. 481048; fax 481220; weekly; Dir LOUIS BRESSON.

Ve'a Katorika: BP 94, 98713 Papeete; f. 1909; monthly; publ. by the Roman Catholic Church.

Ve'a Porotetani: BP 113, Papeete; tel. 460623; fax 419357; e-mail eepf@mail.pf; f. 1921; monthly; French and Tahitian; publ. by the Evangelical Church; Dir IHORAI JACQUES; circ. 5,000.

NEWS AGENCIES

Tahitian Press Agency (ATP): Papeete; f. 2001; bilingual French and English news service providing pictures and radio reports.

Foreign Bureaux

Agence France-Presse (AFP): BP 629, Papeete; tel. 508100; fax 508109; e-mail international@france-antilles.pf; Correspondent CHRISTIAN BRETAULT.

Associated Press (AP) (USA): BP 912, Papeete; tel. 437562; Correspondent AL PRINCE.

Reuters (UK): BP 50, Papeete; tel. 464340; fax 464390; e-mail danielpardon@mail.pf; Correspondent DANIEL PARDON.

Publishers

Haere Po No Tahiti: BP 1958, Papeete; fax 582333; f. 1981; travel, history, botany, linguistics and local interest.

Scoop/Au Vent des Îles: BP 5670, 98716 Pirae; tel. 435456; fax 426174; e-mail scooptah@mail.pf; f. 1992; Gen. Man. ROBERT CHRISTIAN.

Government Printer

Imprimerie Officielle: 43 rue des Poilus-Tahitiens, BP 117, 98713 Papeete; tel. 425067; fax 425261; f. 1843; printers, publrs; Dir CLAUDINO LAURENT.

Broadcasting and Communications

TELECOMMUNICATIONS

Office des Postes et Télécommunications: 8 rue de la Reine Pomare IV, Papeete; tel. 414242; fax 436767; Dir-Gen. GEFFRY SALMON.

France Cables et Radio (FCR): Télécommunications extérieures de la Polynésie française, BP 99, Papeete; tel. 415400; fax 437553; e-mail fcr@mail.pf.

BROADCASTING

Radio

RFO Polynésie: 410 rue Dumont d'Urville, POB 60, Pamatai; tel. 861616; fax 861611; e-mail jrbodin@mail.pf; internet www.rfo.fr.html; public service radio and television station operated by Réseau France Outre-Mer (RFO), Paris; daily programmes in French and Tahitian; Area Man. WALLES KOTRA; Communications Man. JEAN-RAYMOND BODIN.

Private Stations

NRJ Radio: Papeete; tel. and fax 464346; e-mail nrj@mail.pf; French.

Radio Bleue: Papeete; tel. 483436; fax 480825; e-mail redaction@radiobleue.pf; affiliated to the political party Ai'a Api; French.

Radio Maohi: Maison des Jeunes, Pirae; tel. 819797; fax 825493; e-mail tereo@mail. pf; owned by the political party Tahoeraa Huiraatira; French and Tahitian.

Radio One: Fare Ute, BP 3601, Papeete; tel. 434100; fax 423406; e-mail infos@radio1.pf.

Radio Tefana: Papete; tel. 819797; fax 825493; e-mail tereo@mail.pf; affiliated to the political party Tavini Huiraatira; French and Tahitian.

Radio Tiare: Fare Ute, Papeete; tel. 434100; fax 423406; e-mail contact@tiarefm.pf.

Television

Radio-Télé-Tahiti: (see Radio).

Canal Plus Polynésie: Immeuble Pomare, blvd Paofai, BP 20051, 98713 Papeete; tel. 540754; fax 540755; e-mail classagne@cplus.pf; privately-owned; Dir Christophe Lassagne.

Telefenua: Centre Commercial Le Lotus, Punaauia 98717; tel. 461111; fax 501275; internet www.telefenua.com; paying cable channel broadcasting in French, Tahitian and English; Pres. Yoshiko Payne.

TNTV (Tahiti Nui Television): BP 348 98713, Papeete; tel. 473636; e-mail tntv@tntv.pf; internet www.tntv.pf; broadcasts in French and Tahitian; Gen. Man. Daniel Franco.

TNS (Tahiti Nui Satellite): (see TNTV); French.

Finance

(cap. = capital; res = reserves; dep. = deposits; m. = million; brs = branches; amounts in CFP francs)

BANKING

Commercial Banks

Banque de Polynésie SA: 355 blvd Pomare, BP 530, 9713 Papeete; tel. 466666; fax 466664; e-mail sec.gen@sg-bdp.pf; internet www.sg-bdp.pf; f. 1973; 80% owned by Société Générale (France); cap. and res 5,210.5m., dep. 65,456.4m. (Dec. 1999); Pres. Jean-Louis Mattei; Dir-Gen. Roger Munoz; 19 brs.

Banque de Tahiti SA: rue François Cardella, BP 1602, Papeete; tel. 417000; fax 423376; e-mail dirgene@bt.pf; internet www.banque-tahiti.pf; f. 1969; owned by Caisse Nationale (96%); merged with Banque Paribas de Polynésie, Aug. 1998; cap. 1,336.5m., res 4,600.5m., dep. 78,738.1m. (Dec. 2000); Pres. J. C. Irrmann; Exec. Vice-Pres. Michel Dupieux; 16 brs.

Banque SOCREDO—Société pour le Crédit et le Développement en Océanie: 115 rue Dumont d'Urville, BP 130, 98713 Papeete; tel. 415123; fax 433661; f. 1959; public body; affiliated to Banque Nationale de Paris (France); cap. 7,000m. (Dec. 1993), dep. 76,610m. (Dec. 1995); Pres. Jean Vernaudon; Dir Eric Pommier; 24 brs.

Trade and Industry

DEVELOPMENT ORGANIZATIONS

Agence pour l'Emploi et la Formation Professionnelle: BP 540, Papeete; tel. 426375; fax 426281.

Agence Française de Développement (ACFD): BP 578, Papeete; tel. 544600; fax 544601; public body; development finance institute.

Conseil Economique, Social et Culturel: ave Bruat, BP 1657, 98716 Papeete; tel. 416500; fax 419242; e-mail cesc@cesc.gov.pf; Dir Bruno Sandras.

Service de l'Artisanat Traditionnel: BP 4451, Papeete 98713; tel. 423225; fax 436478; e-mail teura.iriti@artisanat.gov.pf; Dir Teura Iriti.

Service du Développement de l'Industrie et des Métiers: BP 9055, 98713 Papeete; tel. 502880; fax 412645; e-mail self.service@industrie.gov.pf; industry and small business development administration.

Société pour le Développement de l'Agriculture et de la Pêche: BP 1247, Papeete; tel. 836798; fax 856886; agriculture and marine industries.

SODEP—Société pour le Développement et l'Expansion du Pacifique: BP 4441, Papeete; tel. 429449; f. 1961 by consortium of banks and private interests; regional development and finance co.

CHAMBERS OF COMMERCE

Chambre de Commerce, d'Industrie, des Services et des Métiers de Polynésie Française: 41 rue du Docteur Cassiau, BP 118, Papeete 98713; tel. 472700; fax 540701; e-mail info@cci.pf; internet www.ccism.pf; f. 1880; 36 mems; Pres. Stéphane Chin Loy.

Chambre d'Agriculture et de la Pêche Lagonaire: route de l'Hippodrome, BP 5383, Pirae; tel. 425393; fax 438754; f. 1886; 10 mems; Pres. Claude Hauata.

Jeune Chambre Economique de Tahiti: BP 2576, Papeete; tel. 454542; fax 466070; internet www.jce.pf; Pres. Cathy Gourbault.

EMPLOYERS' ORGANIZATIONS

Chambre Syndicale des Entrepreneurs du Bâtiment et des Travaux Publics: BP 2218, Papeete; tel. 438898; fax 423237; Pres. Georges Tramini.

Conseil des Employeurs: Immeuble Farnham, rue Clappier, BP 972, Papeete; tel. 541040; fax 423237; f. 1983; internet cepf@cepf.pf; Pres. Antonima Mambridge; Sec.-Gen. Cédric Vidal.

Fédération Générale du Commerce (FGC): angle rue Albert Leboucher et rue Clappier, BP 1607, 98713 Papeete; tel. 541042; fax 422359; Pres. Gilles Yau.

Fédération Polynésienne de l'Agriculture et de l'Elevage: Papara, Tahiti; Pres. Michel Lehartel.

Union Interprofessionnelle du Tourisme de la Polynésie Française: BP 4560, Papeete; tel. 439114; f. 1973; 1,200 mems; Pres. Paul Maetz; Sec.-Gen. Jean Corteel.

Union Patronale: BP 317, Papeete; tel. 438898; fax 423237; f. 1948; 63 mems; Pres. Didier Chomer.

UTILITES

Electricity

Electricité de Tahiti: route de Puurai, BP 8021, Faaa-Puurai; tel. 867777.

Water

Société Polynésienne des Eaux et Assainissements: Papeete, Tahiti.

Syndicat Central de l'Hydraulique: Tahiti.

TRADE UNIONS

Confédération Syndicale A Tia I Mua: Immeuble la Ora, BP 4523, Papeete; tel. 544010; fax 450245; e-mail atiaimua@ifrance.com; affiliated to CFDT (France); Gen. Sec. Tu Yan.

Fédération des Syndicats de la Polynésie Française: BP 1136, Papeete; Pres. Marcel Ahini.

Syndicat Territorial des Instituteurs et Institutrices de Polynésie: BP 3007, Papeete; Sec.-Gen. Willy Urima.

Union des Syndicats Affiliés des Travailleurs de Polynésie/Force Ouvrière (USATP/FO): BP 1201, Papeete; tel. 426049; fax 450635; Pres. Coco Teraiefa Chang; Sec.-Gen. Pierre Frébault.

Union des Syndicats de l'Aéronautique: Papeete; Pres. Joseph Conroy.

Union des Travailleurs de Tahiti et des Iles: BP 3366, Papeete.

Transport

ROADS

French Polynesia has 792 km of roads, of which about one-third are bitumen-surfaced and two-thirds stone-surfaced.

SHIPPING

The principal port is Papeete, on Tahiti.

Port Authority: Port Autonome de Papeete, Motu Uta, BP 9164, 98715 Papeete; tel. 505454; fax 421950; e-mail portppt@mail.pf; internet www.portoftahiti.com; Harbour Master Commdt Claude Vigor; Port Man. Béatrice Chansin.

Agence Maritime Internationale de Tahiti: BP 274, Papeete, Tahiti; tel. 428972; fax 432184; e-mail amitahiti@mail.pf; services from Asia, Australia, New Zealand, American Samoa and Europe.

CGM Tour du Monde SA: 80 rue du Général de Gaulle, BP 96, Papeete; tel. 420890; fax 436806; shipowners and agents; freight services between Europe and many international ports; Dir Henri C. Ferrand.

Compagnie de Développement Maritime des Tuamotu (CODEMAT): POB 1291, Papeete.

Compagnie Française Maritime de Tahiti: 2 rue de Commerce, POB 368, Papeete; tel. 426393; fax 420617; Man. M. Garbutt.

Compagnie Maritime des Iles Sous le Vent: BP 9012, Papeete.

Compagnie Polynésienne de Transport Maritime: BP 220, Papeete; tel. 426240; fax 434889; e-mail aranui@mail.pf; internet www.aranui.com; Dir Jean Wong.

Leprado Valere SARL: POB 3917, Papeete; tel. 450030; fax 421049.

Richmond Frères SARL: POB 1816, Papeete.

Société de Navigation des Australes: BP 1890, Papeete; tel. 509609; fax 420609.

Société de Transport Insulaire Maritime (STIM): BP 635, Papeete; tel. 452324.

Société de Transport Maritime de Tuamotu: BP 11366, Mahina; tel. 422358; fax 430373.

CIVIL AVIATION

There is one international airport, Faaa airport, 6 km from Papeete, on Tahiti, and there are about 40 smaller airstrips. International services are operated by Air France, Air New Zealand, LAN-Chile, Air Outre Mer, Air Calédonie International, Corsair and Hawaiian Airlines (USA).

Service d'État de l'Aviation Civile: Papeete; internet www.seac.pf; Dir Guy Yeung.

Air Moorea: BP 6019, Faaa; tel. 864100; fax 864269; f. 1968; operates internal services between Tahiti and Moorea Island and charter flights throughout the Territory; Pres. Marcel Galenon; Dir-Gen. Freddy Chanseau.

Air Tahiti: BP 314, 98713 Papeete; tel. 864000; fax 864009; e-mail direction.generale@airtahiti.pf; f. 1953, Air Polynésie 1970–87; operates domestic services to 39 islands; Chair. Christian Vernaudon; Gen. Man. Marcel Galenon.

Air Tahiti Nui: BP 1673, Papeete; tel. 460200; fax 460290; e-mail fly@airtahitinui.pf; internet www.airtahitinui-usa.com; f. 1996; commenced operations 1998; scheduled services to the USA, France, Japan and New Zealand; Chair. and CEO Nelson Levy.

Tourism

Tourism is an important and developed industry in French Polynesia, particularly on Tahiti, and 227,658 people visited the Territory in 2001. In that year some 22.2% of arrivals were from France and 41.0% from the USA. There were a total of 3,650 hotel rooms in Tahiti in 2000. In 1999 the tourism industry earned an estimated 47,300m. francs CFP.

GIE Tahiti Tourisme: Immeuble Paofai, bâtiment D, blvd Pomare, BP 65, 98713 Papeete; tel. 505700; fax 436619; e-mail tahiti-tourisme@mail.pf; internet www.tahiti-tourisme.com; f. 1966 as autonomous public body, transformed into private corpn in 1993; tourist promotion; CEO (vacant).

Service du Tourisme: Fare Manihini, blvd Pomare, BP 4527, Papeete; tel. 476200; fax 476201; govt dept; manages Special Fund for Tourist Development; Dir Clarisse Godefroy.

Syndicat d'Initiative de la Polynésie Française: BP 326, Papeete; Pres. Piu Bambridge.

Defence

In August 2001 France maintained a force of 3,100 military personnel in the Territory, as well as a gendarmerie of 600. France began testing nuclear weapons at Mururoa Atoll, in the Tuamotu Archipelago, in 1966. The military presence has been largely connected with the Centre d'Expérimentation du Pacifique (CEP) and the Commission d'Energie Atomique (CEA). An indefinite suspension of tests was announced in mid-1993. In June 1995, however, the French Government announced its decision to resume nuclear testing at Mururoa Atoll. The final test was conducted in January 1996. The defence budget for 2001 was 36,774m. francs CFP.

Education

Education is compulsory for eight years between six and 14 years of age. It is free of charge for day pupils in government schools. Primary education, lasting six years, is financed by the territorial budget, while secondary and technical education are supported by state funds. In 2000/01 there were 54 kindergartens and 173 primary schools; there were 13,720 children enrolled at kindergarten and 26,249 pupils in the primary sector. Secondary education is provided by two public lycées, 14 public high schools and four private or church high schools. A total of 24,743 pupils attended general secondary schools in 2000/01, while 3,730 secondary pupils were enrolled at vocational institutions in 1992. The Territorial Government assumed responsibility for secondary education in 1988. Technical and professional education includes eight technical institutions, a tourism training programme, preparation for entrance to the metropolitan Grandes Écoles, a National Conservatory for Arts and Crafts and training centres for those in the construction industry, health services, traditional handicrafts, primary school teaching and social work. The French University of the Pacific was established in French Polynesia in 1987. In 1999 it was divided into two separate branches, of which the University of French Polynesia is now based in Papeete. In 1995 the Papeete branch had 50 teachers and, in 1997, some 1,500 students. Total public expenditure on education in the Territory was 40,300m. francs CFP in 1999.

WALLIS AND FUTUNA ISLANDS

Revised by FRÉDÉRIC ANGLEVIEL

Physical and Social Geography

The self-governing French Overseas Territory of the Wallis and Futuna Islands comprises two groups: the Wallis Islands, including Uvea (Wallis Island) and 19 islets (*motu*) on the surrounding reef, and, 230 km to the south-west, the volcanic and mountainous Futuna (Horn) Islands, comprising the two small islands of Futuna and Alofi (the latter being uninhabited owing to lack of water). The islands are located some 600 km to the north-east of Fiji, south-east of Tuvalu and west of Samoa. The total area is 160.5 sq km. Uvea rises to 151 m at Mt Lulu, and Futuna to 524 m at Mt Puke. Temperatures are generally between 23°C (73°F) and 30°C (86°F), and there is a cyclone season between December and March.

The inhabitants, who are nearly all nominally Roman Catholic, are mainly Polynesian. French is an official language and widely spoken, but the indigenous languages of Uvean (Wallisian) and Futunian are generally used. In 2000 the population of the islands totalled 14,600, the majority living on Uvea. The capital is the town of Mata'Utu on Uvea in the Wallis Islands.

History

The Wallis and Futuna Islands were originally settled by proto-Polynesian peoples, Wallis from Tonga in around 1200 BC, and Futuna from Samoa and northern Fiji in around 800 BC. Futuna was subsequently discovered by the Dutch navigators, Schouten and Le Maire, in 1616, and Uvea was discovered by Samuel Wallis in 1767. Three kingdoms later emerged, and in 1837 the first Marist missionaries arrived. By 1842 the majority of the population of the two archipelagos had been converted to Christianity. In April 1842 the authorities in Wallis requested French protection, coinciding with a similar proclamation in Tahiti (now French Polynesia). In 1851 a *fakauvea* war between the Catholic majority and Methodist minority assisted by Tonga (which had commenced in 1843) came to an end when 500 Wallisians left for Tonga. Protectorate status was formalized in 1887 for Wallis and in 1888 for the two kingdoms of Futuna, but domestic law remained in force. The islands were never formally annexed; French law or representative institutions were never introduced, although Wallis and Futuna were treated as a dependency of New Caledonia. The economy was based on family-run agriculture and the export of copra to Fiji. During the Second World War, Wallis was used as an airforce base by the USA. The mountainous Futuna remained isolated. After the war, many of its youth began to migrate to New Caledonia and the New Hebrides. In 1959 the traditional Kings and chiefs requested integration into the French Republic. The islands formally became an Overseas Territory in July 1961, following a referendum in December 1959, in which 94.4% of the electorate requested this status (almost all the opposition was in Futuna, which itself recorded dissent from only 22.2% of the voters; Wallis was unanimous in its acceptance). Government is conducted by the Chief Administrator, the representative of the French State, with the advice of the Territorial Council (including the three Kings) and the Territorial Assembly, elected for the first time in 1961. The Territory also has representation in the French National Assembly.

Although there is no movement in Wallis and Futuna seeking secession of the Territory from France (in contrast with the situation in the other French Pacific Territories, French Polynesia and New Caledonia), in November 1983 the two Kings whose kingdoms share the island of Futuna first requested that the island groups of Wallis and Futuna become separate Overseas Territories of France. It was argued that the administration and affairs of the Territory had become excessively concentrated on Uvea (Wallis Island).

At elections to the 20-member Territorial Assembly in March 1982, the conservative Rassemblement pour la République (RPR) and its allies won 11 seats, while the remaining nine went to candidates affiliated to the Union pour la Démocratie Française (UDF), a metropolitan, moderate right-wing party. Later that year one member of the Lua kae tahi, a group affiliated to the metropolitan UDF, defected to the RPR group. In November 1983, however, three of the 12 RPR members joined the Lua kae tahi, forming a new majority. In the subsequent election for President of the Territorial Assembly, this 11-strong block of UDF-associated members supported the ultimately successful candidate, Falakiko Gata, even though he had been elected to the Territorial Assembly in 1982 as a member of the RPR.

In 1985 the RPR's majority in the Territorial Assembly was restored, following Falakiko Gata's formation of a new political party, the Union Populaire Locale (UPL), a conservative party which was committed to giving priority to local, rather than metropolitan, issues.

In 1987 a dispute broke out between two families both laying claim to the throne of Sigave, the northern kingdom on the island of Futuna. The conflict arose following the deposition of the former King, Sagato Keletaona, and his succession by Sosefo Vanaï. The intervention of the island's administrative authorities, who attempted to ratify Vanaï's accession to the throne, was condemned by the Keletaona family as an interference in the normal course of local custom, according to which such disputes are traditionally settled by a fight between the protagonists.

At elections to the Territorial Assembly, held in March 1987, the UDF (together with affiliated parties) and the RPR each won seven seats. However, by forming an alliance with the UPL, the RPR was able to maintain its majority, and Falakiko Gata was subsequently re-elected President. At the elections for the French National Assembly in June 1988, Benjamin Brial was re-elected Deputy. However, when the result was contested by an unsuccessful candidate, the Futunian and left-wing Kamilo Gata, the election was investigated by the French Constitutional Council and the result declared invalid, owing to electoral irregularities. When the election was re-contested in January 1989, Kamilo Gata, with the help of Michel Hoatau and Gaston Lutui, was elected Deputy, obtaining 57.4% of the total vote. Brial was dismissed from the Territorial Assembly.

Statistical information, gathered in 1990, showed that the emigration rate of Wallis and Futuna islanders had risen to over 50%. In October of that year 13,705 people (of whom 97% were Wallisians and Futunians) lived in the Territory, while 14,186 were resident in New Caledonia. At the 1996 census the number of Wallisians and Futunians resident in New Caledonia had increased to 17,563. According to the results, a proportion of the islanders had chosen to emigrate to other French Overseas Possessions or to metropolitan France. The principal reason for the increase was thought to be the lack of employment opportunities in the islands.

At elections to the Territorial Assembly in March 1992, the newly founded Taumu'a Lelei secured 11 seats, while the RPR won nine. The new Assembly was remarkable in being the first since 1964 in which the RPR directed now by Clovis Logologofalau and Basile Tui did not hold a majority. At elections to the French National Assembly in March 1993, Kamilo Gata was re-elected Deputy, obtaining 52.4% of total votes cast to defeat Clovis Logologofolau. In the same month an earthquake on Futuna resulted in the death of five people and the destruction of many buildings and roads. In 1994 the socialist French Government nominated Clovis Logologofalau of the RPR as the islands' the Social and Economic Adviser.

In June 1994 the Union Locale Force Ouvrière, directed by Soane Uhila, organized a general strike in protest at the increasing cost of living in the Territory and the allegedly inadequate education system. It was reported that demonstrations continued for several days, during which the Territorial Assembly building was damaged in an arson attack.

In October 1994 it was reported that the King of Sigave, Lafaele Malau, had been deposed by a unanimous decision of the chiefs of the northern kingdom of Sigave on Futuna. The action followed the appointment of two customary leaders to represent the Futunian community in New Caledonia, which had led to unrest among the inhabitants of Sigave. He was succeeded by Esipio Takasi.

At elections to the Territorial Assembly in December 1994, the RPR secured 10 seats, while the coalition group of Kamilo Gata, Union Populaire pour Wallis et Futuna (UPWF), won seven, and independent candidates three. Mikaele Tauhavili of the RPR was subsequently elected President of the Assembly.

The refusal by 10 of the 20 members of the Territorial Assembly to adopt budgetary proposals, in January 1996, led to appeals for the dissolution of the Territorial Assembly by France and the holding of new elections. The budget (which, at US $20m., was some US $4.5m. lower than the previous year) aroused opposition for its apparent lack of provision for development funds, particularly for the islands' nascent tourist industry.

Elections to the Territorial Assembly took place on 16 March 1997. A participation rate of 87.2% was recorded at the poll, in which RPR candidates secured 14 seats and left-wing candidates (including independents and members of various political groupings) won six seats. Victor Brial, a representative of the RPR, was elected President of the Territorial Assembly. At elections to the French National Assembly in May–June 1997 Victor Brial defeated the socialist candidate, Kamilo Gata, obtaining 3,241 votes in the second round, equivalent to 51.3% of the total.

Allegations that electoral irregularities had occurred in the elections to the Territorial Assembly of March 1997 were investigated and upheld for 11 of the seats. As a result, new elections were organized for the 11 seats on 6 September 1998, at which the RPR's representation in the Assembly was reduced to 11 seats overall, while the left-wing UPWF and the independents increased their share of the seats to six and three respectively. Also in September 1998, in a second round of voting, Fr Robert Laufoaulu was elected to the French Senate, defeating Kamilo Gata in a vote by the Territorial Assembly. Laufoaulu, a priest and director of Catholic education in the islands, stood as a left-wing candidate, nominated by Victor Brial in preference to other RPR candidates, and was elected with the reluctant support of right-wing politicians.

In late March 1999 festivities were held to commemorate the 40th anniversary of the accession of the King of Wallis Island, Lavelua Tomasi Kulimoetoke. An estimated 10,000 people paid homage to the King, who was crowned in 1959. In late 1999 Kamilo Gata was appointed Social and Economic Adviser by the French Government. From March 2000 delegations from Wallis and Futuna made regular visits to New Caledonia to discuss mutual arrangements concerning bilateral free trade and employment rights.

In January 2001 two candidates of the RPR contested the presidency of the Territorial Assembly. Patalione Kanimoa was elected by the majority of the RPR (eight votes) and of the UPWF (four votes). Soane Muni Uhila, the previous President of the Territorial Assembly, then formed a new party, La Voix des Peuples Wallisiens et Futuniens, along with five other RPR dissidents. The new majority RPR-UPWF grouping elected Albert Likuvalu (of the UPWF) president of the permanent commission.

In June 2001 senior officials from Wallis and Futuna and from New Caledonia agreed on a project to redefine their bilateral relationship under the Nouméa Accord on greater autonomy, signed in 1998. Following decades of migration, the population of Wallis and Futuna was 15,000, while the number of migrants and descendants from the islands in New Caledonia had risen to 20,000. In exchange for controlling immigration, New Caledonia stated that it would make a financial contribution to economic development in Wallis and Futuna. The Nouméa Accord also called for a separate arrangement providing for open access to New Caledonia for residents of Wallis and Futuna. The French State was to address the issue of financial aid before the two territories' assemblies, under the arrangement.

In January 2002 a delegation from Wallis and Futuna met President Jacques Chirac in Paris to discuss the status of members of their community living in New Caledonia. Under the Nouméa Accord, New Caledonia was to have signed a separate agreement with Wallis and Futuna better to define their status, with particular regard to the job market.

A general election was held on 10 March 2002 for the 20 seats of the Territorial Assembly. The RPR won 12 of the seats, whilst socialist candidates, or affiliated independents, won eight. Patalione Kanimoa of the RPR was re-elected President of the Assembly. An unprecedented 82.7% of some 9,500 registered voters cast their vote; there were 32 lists with 134 candidates. The election campaign was the first to give parties coverage on television and radio, provided by the national broadcasting company

At elections to the National Assembly in June, Victor Brial was re-elected as the Territory's deputy to the French legislature, winning 50.4% of the votes cast and thus defeating Penisio Tialetagi, a local merchant. For the first time, the extreme right-wing Front National presented a candidate in the islands, Gaston Lutui, a Wallisian socialist politician and former member of the RPR. Meanwhile, Christian Job replaced Alain Waquet as the islands' Chief Administrator in 2002.

Economy

In 1995 it was estimated that Wallis and Futuna's gross domestic product (GDP) was US $28.7m., equivalent to some US $2,000 per head. Most monetary income on the islands is derived from government employment (60% in 2000) and remittances sent home by islanders employed in New Caledonia and also in metropolitan France.

Agricultural activity is of a subsistence nature. Yams, taro, bananas, cassava and other food crops are also cultivated. Tobacco is grown for local consumption. In 1998 almost all the cultivated vegetation on the island of Wallis, notably the banana plantations, was destroyed by a cyclone. In response to the cyclone damage, the

French Government provided exceptional aid of 80m. francs CFP to alleviate the situation. An estimated 25,000 pigs a year are reared on the islands. Three units rear 800, 500 and 450 hens a year respectively, which are used principally for eggs, and meet an estimated 80% of the territory's commercial needs. Apiculture was revived in 1996, and in 2000 honey production was sufficient to meet the demands of the local market. Copra, which formerly provided the main cash income for the islands, has been seriously affected by rhinoceros beetle. Fishing activity in the Territory's exclusive economic zone increased during the 1990s; the total catch was estimated at 206 metric tons in 1999, compared with 70 tons in 1991. The Territorial Assembly accorded Japan, and also the Republic of Korea, deep-water fishing rights to catch 3,000 tons of fish a year in the islands' exclusive economic zone, a broad area of 200 miles (370 km) around Wallis and Futuna over which France exerts sovereignty.

The only industry is the manufacture of handicrafts (traditional artefacts). Traditional food products, mother of pearl (from the Trochus shell) for sale to Italy, sea cucumber and handicrafts are the only significant export commodities. In 2000 the cost of the islands' imports reached 4,735.7m. francs CFP. Road vehicles, parts and accessories accounted for 10.0% of the total value of imports, followed by mineral fuels and products (9.8%), electrical machinery and sound and television apparatus (7.4%) and meat products (6.4%). Exports totalled only 22.4m. francs CFP. Traditional food products, mother of pearl (from the Trochus shell) and handicrafts are the only significant export commodities. The principal market is New Caledonia and the large Wallisian community there. Exports of copra from Wallis ceased in 1950, and from Futuna in the early 1970s. The principal sources of imports in 2000 were France, which supplied 28.7% of the total, and Australia (22.6%). Most of the islands' exports were purchased by Italy. In August 2001 the frequency of supplies to Wallis and Futuna was significantly improved when the Sofrana shipping company, based in Auckland, began operating a new route linking New Zealand, Tonga and the Samoas to Wallis and Futuna.

Mineral fuels are the principal source of electric energy, although it is hoped that hydroelectric power can be developed, especially on Futuna. There is a 4,000-kW thermal power station on Wallis, and a 2,600-kW thermal power station was built on Futuna in 2000. The hydroelectric power station on Futuna (Vainifao) provided 10% of the production needed. Total electricity output in 2001 reached 14.6m. kWh on Wallis and 3.0m. kWh on Futuna.

There were 291 businesses in the Territory in 2000, of which 24 were in the industrial and artisanal sector, 68 in construction and 199 in the service and commercial sectors; 47 of those businesses were located on Futuna. In 2002 a new commercial centre was to open in Wallis. The tourism sector is very limited. In 2002 Wallis had four hotels and Futuna two.

The islands' principal source of revenue is taxation. French aid to Wallis and Futuna totalled 7,048m. francs CFP in 1999, increasing to 10,329m. francs CFP in 2002. The islands' budgetary expenditure in 2001 totalled an estimated US $25.0m. Budgetary aid from France was to rise from €83,178m. in 2001 to €86,610m. in 2002.

The annual rate of inflation in 1989–2000 averaged 1.2%. In July 2001 the Chief Administrator, Alain Waquet, acknowledged that the minimum wage (of 58,178 francs CFP per month) had not been revised since July 1998. He therefore announced that the monthly minimum wage was to be raised to 70,000 francs CFP by July 2002; the increase was to be implemented in three stages. A rise in the cost of living was expected to follow.

During his visit to Paris in June 1985, the President of the Territorial Assembly informed the French Government of his belief that the policies relating to agricultural and fisheries development since 1960 had failed completely. It was hoped that these areas of the economy could be improved through new administrative arrangements, whereby development funding would be channelled through traditional chiefs. In August 1989 the visiting French Prime Minister, Michel Rocard, announced an additional 55m. francs CFP in aid, for social and economic development, and in June 1991 Clovis Logologofolau, the President of the Territorial Assembly, and Kamilo Gata, the Territory's Deputy to the French National Assembly, travelled to Paris to renegotiate funding for further development projects. The Territory is very dependent upon metropolitan financial assistance.

In early 1995 the Territory signed a convention with the French Government, which provided for 2,800m. francs CFP in funding for development projects over five years. Projects to be undertaken included the renovation of school buildings and the construction of a technical college on Uvea, a training scheme for young agricultural workers, the rebuilding of the wharf at Sigave on Futuna, a road-improvement scheme and the construction of low-cost housing.

In 2001 a delegation from the Institut de Recherche pour le Développement was sent to the islands to assess the possibilities of self-development. In January 2002 an economic orientation document was signed between the French Government and the Territorial Assembly, with the participation of the three kingdoms. Meanwhile, discussions continued regarding reform of the 1961 statute, to give increased responsibilities to local representatives; particular emphasis was placed on issues of youth employment.

Although France is also a member, the Territory has membership in its own right of the Pacific Community (formerly the South Pacific Commission), which is based in New Caledonia.

Statistical Survey

Source (unless otherwise indicated): Service Territorial de la Statistique et des Etudes Economiques, Centre de Havelu, Mata' Utu, 98600 Uvea, Wallis Islands, Wallis and Futuna, via Nouméa, New Caledonia; tel.and fax 722403; e-mail stats@wallis.co.nc; internet www.wallis.co.nc/stats.

AREA AND POPULATION

Area (sq km): 160.5. *By island:* Uvea (Wallis Island) 77.5, Other Wallis Islands 18.5; Futuna Island 45, Alofi Island 19.5.

Population (census of 15 February 1983): 12,408: Wallis Islands 8,084, Futuna Island 4,324, Alofi Island uninhabited; (October 1990 census): 13,705 (males 6,829, females 6,876): Wallis Islands 8,973, Futuna Island 4,732 (Alo 2,860, Sigave 1,872); 14,186 Wallisians and Futunians resided in New Caledonia. Total population 14,166 (males 6,984, females 7,182) at census of 1996; 17,563 Wallisians and Futunians resided in New Caledonia. Total population 14,600 (estimate) at mid-2000.

Density (estimate, mid-2000): 91.0 per sq km.

Principal Town: Mata'Utu (capital), population 1,137 at 1996 census.

Births and Deaths (estimates, 2000): Birth rate 21.7 per 1,000; Death rate 5.6 per 1,000.

Expectation of Life (estimates, years at birth, 1998): 73.8 (males 73.2; females 74.4).

AGRICULTURE, ETC.

Principal Crops (FAO estimates, '000 metric tons, 2000): Cassava 2.4; Taro (coco yam) 1.6; Yams 0.5; Other roots and tubers 1.0; Coconuts 2.3; Vegetables 0.5; Bananas 4.1; Other fruits (excl. melons) 4.6. Source: FAO.

Livestock (FAO estimates, '000 head, year ending September 2000): Pigs 25; Goats 7; Poultry 63. Source: FAO.

Livestock Products (metric tons, 2000): Pig meat 315; Goat meat 15; Poultry meat 46; Cows' milk 30; Hen eggs 33 (FAO estimate); Honey 11 (FAO estimate). Source: FAO.

Fishing (FAO estimates metric tons, live weight, 1999): Total catch 206 (Marine fishes 200). Note: Figures exclude trochus shells (FAO estimate, metric tons); 25. Source: FAO, *Yearbook of Fishery Statistics*.

INDUSTRY

Electricity Production (million kWh, 2001): 14.6 in Wallis; 3.0 in Futuna.

FINANCE

Currency and Exchange Rates: see French Polynesia.

Territorial Budget (million francs CFP): 2,444.2 in 2000; 3,271.1 in 2001.

Aid from France (million francs CFP, 2002): 10,329. Source: Institut d'Emission d'Outre-Mer.

Money Supply (million francs CFP at 30 Sept. 2001): Currency in circulation 759; Demand deposits 1,595; Total money 2,355. Source: Institut d'Emission d'Outre-Mer.

Cost of Living (Consumer Price Index; base: July–Sept. 1989 = 100): All items 114.3 in 2000; 119.9 in 2001.

EXTERNAL TRADE

Principal Commodities (million francs CFP, 2000): *Imports c.i.f.:* Meat and edible meat offal 302.1; Preparations of meat, of fish or of crustaceans, molluscs or other aquatic invertebrates 178.2; Beverages, spirits and vinegar 199.0; Mineral fuels, mineral oils and products of their distillation; bituminous substances; mineral waxes 462.5; Articles of iron or steel 153.9; Boilers, machinery, mechanical appliances and parts 281.2; Electrical machinery, equipment and parts; sound and television apparatus 350.4; Road vehicles, parts and accessories 474.2; Total (incl. others) 4,735.7. *Exports f.o.b.:* Total 22.4.

Principal Trading Partners (million francs CFP, 2000): *Imports c.i.f.:* Australia 1,068.9; China, People's Republic 84.5; Fiji 174.3; France (incl. Monaco) 1,360.5; Japan 270.1; New Caledonia 307.2; New Zealand 643.2; Singapore 107.0; United Kingdom 76.1; USA

99.9; Total (incl. others) 4,735.7. *Exports f.o.b.:* French Polynesia 0.6; Italy 21.6; Total (incl. others) 22.4.

TRANSPORT

Shipping: *Merchant Fleet* (31 December 2001): Vessels registered 7; displacement ('000 grt) 183.0. Source: Lloyd's Register-Fairplay, *World Fleet Statistics*.

Civil Aviation (2001): aircraft arrivals and departures 1,310; freight handled 131.1 metric tons; passenger arrivals and departures 32,445; mail loaded and unloaded 58.3 metric tons.

TOURISM

Visitors: 400 in 1985.

COMMUNICATIONS MEDIA

Telephones (2000): 1,705 main lines in use (Source: International Telecommunication Union).

Facsimile Machines (1993): 90 in use (Source: UN, *Statistical Yearbook*).

Internet Users (2001): 268.

EDUCATION

Pre-primary (2002/03): 3 institutions.

Primary (2002/03): 14 institutions; 2,938 students (incl. pre-primary); 271 teachers.

Secondary (2002/03): 7 institutions (2 vocational); 2,293 students; 191 teachers.

Source: Vice-Rectorat de Wallis & Futuna.

Directory

The Constitution

The Territory of the Wallis and Futuna Islands is administered according to a statute of 1961, and subsidiary legislation, under the Constitution of the Fifth Republic. The Statute declares the Wallis and Futuna Islands to be an Overseas Territory of the French Republic, of which it remains an integral part. The Statute established an administration, a Council of the Territory, a Territorial Assembly and national representation. The administrative, political and social evolution envisaged by, and enacted under, the Statute is intended to effect a smooth integration of the three customary kingdoms with the new institutions of the Territory. The Kings are assisted by ministers and the traditional chiefs. The Chief Administrator, appointed by the French Government, is the representative of the State in the Territory and is responsible for external affairs, defence, law and order, financial and educational affairs. The Chief Administrator is required to consult with the Council of the Territory, which has six members: three by right (the Kings of Wallis, Sigave and Alo) and three appointed by the Chief Administrator upon the advice of the Territorial Assembly. This Assembly assists in the administration of the Territory; there are 20 members elected on a common roll, on the basis of universal adult suffrage, for a term of up to five years. The Territorial Assembly elects, from among its own membership, a President to lead it. The Territory elects national representatives (one Deputy to the National Assembly, one Senator and one Economic and Social Councillor) and votes for representatives to the European Parliament in Strasbourg.

The Government

(September 2002)

Chief Administrator (Administrateur Supérieur): CHRISTIAN JOB (appointed 2002).

CONSEIL DU TERRITOIRE

Chair: Chief Administrator.

Members by Right: King of Wallis, King of Sigave, King of Alo.

Appointed Members: MIKAELE HALAGAHU (Faipule), ATOLOTO UHILA (Kulitea), KELETO LAKALAKA (Sous réserves).

GOVERNMENT OFFICE

Government Headquarters: Bureau de l'Administrateur Supérieur, Havelu, BP 16, Mata'Utu, 98600 Uvea, Wallis Islands, Wallis and Futuna; tel. 722727; fax 722324; all departments.

Legislature

ASSEMBLÉE TERRITORIALE

The Territorial Assembly has 20 members and is elected for a five-year term. The most recent general election took place on 10 March 2002, at which RPR candidates secured a total of 12 seats and various left-wing candidates (including independents) won eight seats.

President: PATALIONE KANIMOA (RPR).

Territorial Assembly: Assemblée Territoriale, Havelu, BP 31, Mata'Utu, 98600 Uvea, Wallis Islands, Wallis and Futuna; tel. 722504; fax 722054.

PARLEMENT

Deputy to the French National Assembly: VICTOR BRIAL (RPR).

Representative to the French Senate: Fr ROBERT LAUFOAULU.

Social and Economic Adviser: KAMILO GATA (UPWF).

The Kingdoms

WALLIS

(Capital: Mata'Utu on Uvea)

Lavelua, King of Wallis: TOMASI KULIMOETOKE.

Council of Ministers: Prime Minister (Kivalu) and five other ministers. Kivalu: TISIMASI HEAFALA.

The Kingdom of Wallis is divided into three districts (Hihifo, Hahake, Mua), and its traditional hierarchy includes three district chiefs (Faipule) and 20 village chiefs (Pule).

SIGAVE

(Capital: Leava on Futuna)

Keletaona, King of Sigave: PASILIO KELETAONA.

Council of Ministers: six ministers, chaired by the King.

The Kingdom of Sigave is located in the north of the island of Futuna; there are five village chiefs.

ALO

(Capital: Ono on Futuna)

Tuigaifo, King of Alo: SAGATO ALOFI.

Council of Ministers: five ministers, chaired by the King.

The Kingdom of Alo comprises the southern part of the island of Futuna and the entire island of Alofi. There are nine village chiefs.

Political Organizations

Rassemblement pour la République (RPR): c/o Assemblée Territoriale; Gaullist; Territorial Leader CLOVIS LOGOLOGOFOLAU.

Taumu'a Lelei (Bright Future): c/o Assemblée Territoriale; f. 1992; Leader SOANE MUNI UHILA.

Union pour la Démocratie Française (UDF): c/o Assemblée Territoriale; centrist; based on Uvean (Wallis) support.

Union Populaire pour Wallis et Futuna (UPWF): c/o Assemblée Territoriale; affiliated to the Parti Socialiste of France in 1998; f. 1994; Leader KAMILO GATA.

La Voix des Peuples Wallisiens et Futuniens: c/o Assemblée Territoriale; f. 2001 by dissident RPR mems.

Religion

Almost all of the inhabitants profess Christianity and are adherents of the Roman Catholic Church.

CHRISTIANITY

The Roman Catholic Church

The Territory comprises a single diocese, suffragan to the archdiocese of Nouméa (New Caledonia). The diocese estimated that there were 14,192 adherents (99.0% of the population) at 31 December 1999. The Bishop participates in the Catholic Bishops' Conference of the Pacific, currently based in Fiji.

Bishop of Wallis and Futuna: Mgr LOLESIO FUAHEA, Evêché Lano, BP G6, 98600 Mata'Utu, Uvea, Wallis Islands, Wallis and Futuna; tel. 722932; fax 722783; e-mail eveche.wallis@wallis.co.nc.

The Press

Te-Fenua Fo'ou: BP 435, 98600 Mata'Utu, Uvea, Wallis Islands, Wallis and Futuna; tel. 721746; e-mail tff@wallis.co.nc; f. 1995; weekly; French, Wallisian and Futurian; ceased publication in April 2002.

Broadcasting and Communications

TELECOMMUNICATIONS

France Telecom—FCR: Télécommunications extérieures de Wallis et Futuna, BP 54, 98600 Mata'Utu, Uvea, Wallis Islands,

Wallis and Futuna; tel. 722436; fax 722255; e-mail admin@wallis.co.nc.

Service des Postes et Télécommunications: Administration Supérieure des Iles Wallis et Futuna, BP 00, 98600 Mata'Utu, Uvea, Wallis Islands, Wallis and Futuna; tel. 722121; fax 722500; e-mail adminspt.get@wallis.co.nc.

BROADCASTING

Radio and Television

Radio Wallis et Futuna: BP 102, 97911 Mata'Utu, Uvea, Wallis Islands, Wallis and Futuna; tel. 722020; fax 722346; internet www.rfo.fr; fmrly Radiodiffusion Française d'Outre-mer (RFO); transmitters at Mata'Utu (Uvea) and Alo (Futuna); programmes broadcast 24 hours daily in Uvean (Wallisian), Futunian and French; a television service on Uvea, transmitting for 12 hours daily in French, began operation in 1986; a television service on Futuna was inaugurated in December 1994; satellite television began operation in March 2000; Man. JOSEPH BLASCO; Head of Information BERNARD JOYEUX.

Finance

BANKING

Bank of Issue

Institut d'Emission d'Outre-Mer: 98600 Mata'Utu, Uvea, Wallis Islands, Wallis and Futuna; tel. 722505; f. 1998.

Other Banks

Agence Française de Développement: 98600 Mata'Utu, Uvea, Wallis Islands, Wallis and Futuna; tel. 722505; fmrly Caisse Française de Développement; development bank.

Banque de Wallis et Futuna: BP 59, 98600 Mata'Utu, Uvea, Wallis Islands, Wallis and Futuna; tel. 722124; fax 722156; f. 1991; 51% owned by BNP Paribas (New Caledonia).

Paierie de Wallis et Futuna: 98600 Mata'Utu, Uvea, Wallis Islands, Wallis and Futuna, via Nouméa, New Caledonia.

Trade and Industry

GOVERNMENT AGENCY

Economie Rurale et Pêche: BP 05, 98600 Mata'Utu, Uvea, Wallis Islands, Wallis and Futuna; tel. 720400; fax 720404; e-mail ecoru@wallis.co.nc; Antenne de Futuna, BP 05, 98620 Sigave, Futuna, Wallis and Futuna; tel. 723214; fax 723402.

UTILITIES

Electricité et Eau de Wallis et Futuna: 98600 Mata'Utu, Uvea, Wallis Islands, Wallis and Futuna; 32.3% owned by the territory and 66.64% owned by EEC of New Caledonia.

TRADE UNIONS

Union Interprofessionnelle CFDT Wallis et Futuna (UI CFDT): BP 178, 98600 Mata'Utu, Uvea, Wallis Islands, Wallis and Futuna; tel. 721880; Sec. Gen. KALOLO HANISI.

Union Territoriale Force Ouvrière: BP 325, Mata-Utu, 98600 Wallis and Futuna; tel. 721732; fax 720132; Sec.-Gen. CHRISTIAN VAAMEI.

Transport

ROADS

Uvea has a few kilometres of road, one route circling the island, and there is also a partially surfaced road circling the island of Futuna; the only fully surfaced roads are in Mata'Utu.

SHIPPING

Mata'Utu serves as the seaport of Uvea and the Wallis Islands, while Sigave is the only port on Futuna. A total of 45 general freight ships and 17 gas and petroleum tankers docked in Wallis in 1999.

Services des Douanes et Affaires Maritimes: Aka'aka, 98600 Mata'Utu, Uvea, Wallis Islands, Wallis and Futuna; tel. 722571; fax 722986.

AMACAL (General Agent): POB 1080, Nouméa, New Caledonia; tel. 232910; fax 287388; e-mail amb.noumea@offratel.nc.

CIVIL AVIATION

There is an international airport in Hihifo district on Uvea, about 5 km from Mata'Utu. Air Calédonie International (New Caledonia) operates five flights a week from Wallis to Futuna, one flight a week from Wallis to Tahiti (French Polynesia) and two flights a week from Wallis to Nouméa (New Caledonia). The airport on Futuna is at Vele, in the south-east, in the Kingdom of Alo.

Tourism

Tourism remains undeveloped. There are four small hotels on Uvea, Wallis Islands. In 1985 there were some 400 tourist visitors, in total, to the islands. There are two small guest-houses for visitors on Futuna.

Education

In 2002/03 there were 19 state-financed primary schools (including three pre-primary, 14 primary and two homecraft centres), and seven secondary schools (including two vocational schools) in Wallis and Futuna. Primary and pre-primary pupils totalled 2,938 and secondary students numbered 2,293. In 1999/2000, 361 students attended various universities overseas.

French Pacific Overseas Country

New Caledonia was formerly an Overseas Territory of France. The Nouméa Accord, concluded in 1998, provides for a gradual transfer of powers to New Caledonia. The Territory became an Overseas Country of France in 1999.

Head of State: President JACQUES CHIRAC (took office 17 May 1995; re-elected 5 May 2002).

NEW CALEDONIA

Revised by FRÉDÉRIC ANGLEVIEL

Physical and Social Geography

New Caledonia is a French Overseas Country located in the Pacific Ocean, lying south and slightly west of Vanuatu, some 1,500 km east of Australia and 1,700 km north of New Zealand. It comprises one large island and several smaller islands, with a total land area of 18,575 sq km (7,172 sq miles). The main island, New Caledonia (la Grande-Terre), is long and narrow, and has a total area of 16,372 sq km (6,321 sq miles); its island chain is continued by the Bélep Archipelago at the north end of the island, the Isle of Pines and the Huon Islands, a group of four barren coral islets, in the south. The coralline Loyalty Islands (including Lifou, Maré and Ouvéa) lie to the north-east of Nouméa in a chain that runs parallel to the main island. The third main group of islands is the uninhabited, well-wooded Chesterfield Islands, which lie about 400 km north-west of the main island. The isolated island of Walpole, a limestone coral island, is to the west of the main island of New Caledonia and the Loyalty Islands. The sporadically active volcanic Matthew and Hunter islands lie east of Walpole island. Rugged mountains, rising to 1,628 m at Mt Panie, divide the west of the main island from the east, and there is little flat land. The climate is generally a mild one, with an average temperature of about 24°C (75°F) and a rainy season between December and March. The average rainfall in the east of the main island is about 2,000 mm (80 ins) per year, and in the west about 1,000 mm (40 ins). French is the official language and the mother tongue of the Caldoches (French settlers). There are some 28 Melanesian languages spoken by the indigenous Kanaks, divided into four main groups. The four most widely spoken and taught forms are Drehu (Lihou), Nengone (Maré), Aji'e (Houaïlou) and Paicï (Poindimié). Other immigrants speak Polynesian and Asian languages.

The population was 196,836 at the 1996 census, comprising Melanesians (44%), Europeans, mainly French (43%), Wallisians and Tahitians (Polynesian) (9%), and others, mainly Indonesians and Vietnamese (3%). In 1996 some 68% of the population lived in the Province of the South, 21% in the Province of the North and 11% in the Province of the Loyalty Islands. At the 1996 census there were 341 tribes (which have legal status under a high chief—living in reserves which covered 21% of total land), representing about 28.7% of the population. An estimated 59% of the population are Roman Catholics, and there is a substantial Protestant minority. The capital is Nouméa, on the main island of New Caledonia. The total population was estimated at 215,904 in January 2002.

History

New Caledonia became a French possession in 1853, when the island was annexed as a dependency of Tahiti. In 1860 a separate administration was established, and in 1885 a Conseil Général was elected to defend the local interests before metropolitan France. From 1887 two separate administrations existed, for Melanesian Kanaks and expatriates, until New Caledonia became an Overseas Territory of the French Republic in 1946. A Territorial Assembly was established in 1956, comprising 30 members elected by universal adult suffrage. There is a governor, the High Commissioner, who retains control of all French national departments and the gendarmerie, but otherwise there is substantial self-government.

Early European settlers on New Caledonia quickly set about acquiring Kanak land, which involved iniquitous legislation and numerous rebellions by Kanaks, the last of which took place in 1917. Further seizures of land followed as punishment. Cattle grazing, practised by the Europeans, disrupted indigenous agriculture, and today large areas of formerly irrigated taro terraces lie abandoned.

The French Government dismissed the Council of Government in March 1979, following its failure to support a proposal for a 10-year contract between France and New Caledonia because the plan did not acknowledge the possibility of New Caledonian independence. The Territory was then placed under the direct authority of the High Commissioner. A new electoral law, recommended by the French Minister for Overseas Departments and Territories, ensured that minor political parties were not represented in the Assembly following the July 1979 general election. Consequently, the numerous small pro-independence groups with largely Kanak supporters were excluded, and the elections resulted in the two new 'national' federations of parties loyal to France (Rassemblement pour la Calédonie dans la République—RPCR—and Fédération pour une Nouvelle Société Calédonienne—FNSC) winning 22 of the 36 seats in the Assembly.

Following the election of François Mitterrand as President of France, tension grew sharply after the assassination in September 1981 of Pierre Declercq, Secretary-General of the pro-independence party, Union Calédonienne (UC). In December, recognizing the need for major reforms, the French authorities outlined their most immediate aims, including equal access for all New Caledonians to positions of authority, land reforms and the fostering of Kanak cultural institutions. To help effect these reforms, the French Government simultaneously announced that it would rule by decree for a period of a year. In 1982 the FNSC joined with the recently-established Front Indépendantiste (FI) in an attempt to form a government that was more favourable to the proposed reforms. In November 1983 the French Government proposed a five-year programme, which provided for an Act of self-determination in 1989, with independence as one of the options to be offered. The French proposals were opposed in New Caledonia, both by parties in favour of independence and by those against, and it was rejected by the Territorial Assembly in April 1984. Sittings of the Territorial Assembly had meanwhile been boycotted by the FI, rendering the Assembly unable to function. Nevertheless, a Statute of Autonomy was approved by the French National Assembly in September 1984. Under the provisions of the Statute, the Territorial Council of Ministers was responsible for many internal matters of government, its President henceforth being an elected member instead of the French High Commissioner; a second legislative chamber, with the right to be consulted on development planning and budgetary issues, was created at the same time.

All of the main parties seeking independence (except the Libération Kanake Socialiste (LKS) party, which left the FI) boycotted elections for a new Territorial Assembly in November 1984. Following the subsequent dissolution of the FI, these parties formed a new movement, the Front de Libération Nationale Kanake Socialiste (FLNKS), whose congress instituted a 'provisional government', headed by Jean-Marie Tjibaou (of the UC, the dominant party in the FLNKS), on 1 December. The elections to the Territorial Assembly attracted only 50.12% of the electorate, and the anti-independence RPCR won 34 of the 42 seats. An escalation of violence by both Kanaks and Caldoches (French settlers) began in November. In December this culminated in the burning of farms belonging to French settlers, the murder of three settlers by pro-independence activists and the deaths of 10 Kanak activists (two of whom were Tjibaou's brothers), who were shot dead by *métis* settlers at Hienghène, in the far north of the Territory.

In January 1985 Edgard Pisani, the new High Commissioner, presented a plan by which the Territory might become independent 'in association with' France, subject to the result of a referendum. Kanak groups opposed the plan, insisting that the indigenous population be allowed to determine its own fate. At the same time, the majority of the population, which backed the RPCR, demonstrated against the plan and in favour of remaining within the French Republic. A resurgence of violence followed Pisani's announcement, and a state of emergency was declared after two incidents in which a leading member of the FLNKS was shot dead by the Groupe d'Intervention de la Gendarmerie Nationale (GIGN) and the son of a French settler was killed by Kanak activists.

In April 1985 the French Prime Minister, Laurent Fabius, announced a new plan for the future of New Caledonia, whereby the referendum on independence, formerly scheduled for July 1985, was deferred until an unspecified date not later than the end of 1987. Meanwhile, the Territory was to be divided into four Regions, each to be governed by its own elected autonomous Council, which would have extensive powers in the spheres of planning and development, education, health and social services, land rights, transport and housing. The elected members of all four Councils together would serve as regional representatives in a Territorial Congress (to replace the Territorial Assembly). The new set of proposals (known as the 'Fabius plan') was well received by the FLNKS, which voted in favour of participating in the regional elections. The RPCR, however, condemned the plan, and the proposals were rejected by the predominantly anti-independence Territorial Assembly in May 1985. Nevertheless, the necessary legislation was approved by the National Assembly in Paris in July, and the Fabius plan came into force.

The parties opposing independence eventually agreed to participate in the elections, which were held in September 1985. As expected, only in the Southern Region around Nouméa, where most of the population are non-Melanesian, was an anti-independence majority returned. However, the Kanaks, in spite of their majorities in the three non-urban Regions, would be in a minority in the Territorial Congress.

The FLNKS boycotted the French legislative elections of March 1986, in which only about 50% of the New Caledonia electorate participated. In May the French Council of Ministers approved a draft law providing for a referendum to be held in New Caledonia within 12 months, whereby a choice would be offered between independence and a further extension of regional autonomy. In December the French Government announced that all those who had been resident in New Caledonia for at least three years would be eligible to participate in the referendum. This concession was rejected by FLNKS leaders, who maintained that, unless eligibility were confined to the Kanak community, the result of such a referendum would be unfairly weighted in favour of the French and other non-indigenous groups (who together outnumbered the Melanesians), and would be unrepresentative of the wishes of the indigenous population.

In December 1986, despite vigorous French diplomatic opposition, the UN General Assembly voted to reinstate New Caledonia on the UN list of non-self-governing territories, thereby affirming the population's right to self-determination. In January 1987 the French Government expelled the Australian Consul-General from New Caledonia, in retaliation against the allegedly central role that he had played in determining the UN decision.

In March 1987 the UN Committee on Decolonization issued a declaration in support of the FLNKS, urging France to make preparations for New Caledonia 'freely and truly' to exert its right to independence. However, in April, despite continuing opposition from President Mitterrand, the French Government's legislation providing for a referendum was approved in the National Assembly. In May, Tjibaou denounced the referendum and urged a boycott of it. The South Pacific Forum also condemned the referendum, maintaining that it did not satisfy the UN code of principles and practices for decolonization. In June the leader of the LKS, Nidoïsh Naisseline (a high chief of Maré island), stated that his party had also decided to recommend that its supporters boycott the referendum.

The referendum was held on 13 September 1987. Votes cast in favour of New Caledonia's continuation as part of the French Republic numbered 48,611 (98.3% of the total), while those in favour of independence numbered only 842 (1.7%). The level of participation, at 58.9% of the registered electorate, was higher than had been expected. The rate of abstention in constituencies inhabited by a majority of Kanaks (where, in most cases, at least 90% of the electorate abstained) was significantly higher than in those inhabited chiefly by the Caldoches.

In October 1987 seven pro-French loyalists were acquitted on a charge of murdering 10 Kanak separatists in 1984. Tjibaou, who reacted to the ruling by declaring that his followers would have to abandon their stance of pacifism, and his deputy, Yeiwéné Yeiwéné, were indicted for 'incitement to violence'. In April 1988 four gendarmes were killed, and 27 held hostage in a cave on the island of Ouvéa, by supporters of the FLNKS. Two days later Kanak separatists prevented about one-quarter of the Territory's polling stations from opening, when local elections, scheduled to coincide with the French presidential elections, were held. The elections were boycotted by the FLNKS. Although 12 of the gendarmes taken hostage were subsequently released, six members of a French anti-terrorist squad were also captured. When negotiations to release those held were unsuccessful, French security forces stormed the cave, freeing the hostages but leaving 19 Kanaks and two gendarmes dead. In the aftermath of the siege, it was alleged that three Kanaks had been executed or left to die after being arrested.

In June 1988 talks were convened between the French Prime Minister, Michel Rocard, the leader of the RPCR, Jacques Lafleur, and the leader of the FLNKS, Jean-Marie Tjibaou. Agreement was reached to transfer the administration of the Territory to Paris for 12 months and to separate it into three Provinces, prior to a territorial plebiscite to be held in 1998. This agreement became known as the Matignon Accord. The programme was presented to the French electorate in a referendum, held on 6 November 1988, and approved by a majority (of 80%), although an abstention rate of 63% was recorded. The programme was approved by a 57% majority in New Caledonia, where the rate of abstention was 37%. In November, under the terms of the agreement, 51 separatists were released from prison, including 26 Kanaks implicated in the incident on Ouvéa.

An increase in support for the pro-independence parties was demonstrated in the municipal elections of March 1989, in which they gained control of 20 out of 32 municipal districts (communes). On 4 May, however, Jean-Marie Tjibaou and Yeiwéné Yeiwéné were assassinated by Djubelly Wéa, a former pastor and a member of the Front Uni de Libération Kanake (FULK), a party that had opposed the participation of the FLNKS in the Matignon Accord with France. In June elections were held for the three provincial councils. The FLNKS gained control of the North Province and the Province of the Loyalty Islands, while the RPCR won control in the South Province. In accordance with the Matignon Accord, direct rule by France over New Caledonia was discontinued on 14 July 1989 and the Provincial Councils gained a degree of limited autonomy.

In April 1991 the LKS announced its intention to withdraw from the Matignon Accord, accusing the French Government, as well as several Kanak political leaders, of seeking to undermine Kanak culture and tradition. The RPCR's policy of encouraging the immigration of skilled workers from mainland France and other European countries continued to be a source of conflict between the conservative coalition and the FLNKS.

At elections for the Representative to the French Senate in September 1992, the RPCR's candidate, Simon Loueckhote, narrowly defeated Roch Wamytan, the Vice-President of the FLNKS.

Debate concerning the political future of the Territory continued in 1994. In October the RPCR leader, Jacques Lafleur, proposed that New Caledonia abandon the planned 1998 referendum on self-determination, in favour of a 30-year agreement with France, similar to the Matignon Accord, but with provision for greater autonomy in judicial matters. The UC, however, rejected the proposal and reiterated its demand for a gradual transfer of power from France to New Caledonia, culminating in a return to sovereignty in 1998.

French presidential elections took place in April/May 1995. During the second round of voting in the Territory (in which only 35% of the electorate participated), the socialist candidate, Lionel Jospin, received 25.9% of the total votes, while the candidate of the Gaullist Rassemblement pour la République (RPR), Jacques Chirac, won 74.1%. (Chirac was elected to the presidency with 52.6% of votes cast throughout the republic.)

At provincial elections in July 1995 the RPCR remained the most successful party, although its dominance was reduced considerably. The FLNKS remained in control of the Provinces of the North and the Loyalty Islands, while the RPCR retained a large majority in the Province of the South. The RPCR retained an overall majority in the Territorial Congress, while the FLNKS remained the second largest party. Considerable gains were made by a newly-formed party led by a Nouméa businessman, Une Nouvelle-Calédonie pour Tous (UNCT), which secured seven seats in the Territorial Congress and seven seats in the Provincial Assembly of the South. An estimated 67% of the electorate participated in the elections. However, a political crisis subsequently arose as a result of the UNCT's decision to align itself with the FLNKS, leaving the RPCR with a minority of official positions in the congressional committees. Lafleur would not accept a situation in which the UNCT appeared to be the dominant party in Congress, and Pierre Frogier, the RPCR's President of Congress, refused to convene a congressional sitting under such circumstances. The deadlock was broken only when the FLNKS released a statement in October, reiterating the importance of the relationship between the FLNKS and the RPCR as signatories of the Matignon Accord, and proposing the allocation of congressional positions on a proportional basis.

Negotiations between the French Prime Minister, Alain Juppé, the Minister for Overseas Territories and delegations from the FLNKS and the RPCR were held in Paris in late 1995. It was agreed that further discussions would take place in early 1996, involving representatives from numerous interest groups in the Territory, to examine the possibility of achieving a consensus solution on the future of the islands. Thus, the major political groups in New Caledonia sought to achieve a consensus solution on the Territory's future, which could be presented to the electorate for approval in the 1998 referendum. It was widely believed that this was preferable to a simple 'for' or 'against' vote on independence, which would necessarily polarize the electorate and create a confrontational political climate.

Elections to the French National Assembly in May–June 1997 were boycotted by the pro-independence FLNKS and LKS, resulting in a relatively low participation rate among the electorate. Jacques Lafleur and Pierre Frogier, both candidates of the RPCR, were elected to represent the Territory.

Intensive negotiations involving the RPCR, the FLNKS and the French Government took place throughout early 1996. The process, however, was disrupted by a dispute over the disclosure of confidential information regarding the talks to the French press (responsibility for which was later admitted by Jacques Lafleur) and the belief by pro-independence leaders that France had apparently reneged on its promise to consider all available options for the Territory's political future by discounting the possibility of outright independence. France's refusal to grant final approval for a large-scale nickel smelter project in the North Province (see Economy) until the achievement of consensus in the discussions on autonomy prompted accusations of blackmail from several sources within the Territory and fuelled suspicions that metropolitan France would seek to retain control of the islands' valuable mineral resources in any settlement on New Caledonia's future status. The issue proved to be a serious obstacle in the negotiations and resulted in the virtual cessation of discussions between the two sides during the remainder of 1996. The FLNKS argued that the smelter project should be administered by local interests, consistent with the process of reallocating responsibility for the economy from metropolitan France to the Territory as advocated in the Matignon Accord. Their demands were supported by widespread industrial action in the mining sector during late 1996.

In February 1997 the French Minister for Overseas Territories travelled to the Territory in an attempt to achieve an exchange agreement on nickel between the Société Minière du Sud-Pacifique (SMSP), controlled by the North Province, and the French-owned company, with numerous interests in the islands, Société Le Nickel (SLN). The minister failed to resolve the dispute during his visit; however, at the end of the month, in a complete reversal of its previous position, the French Government announced its decision not to compensate SLN for any losses incurred. The decision provoked strong criticism from SLN and Eramet, the French mining conglomerate, of which SLN is a subsidiary, and attracted protests from shareholders and employees of the company. During March large-scale demonstrations were held by the UC and the pro-independence trade union, USTKE, in support of the SMSP's acquisition of the smelter. Meanwhile, another trade union, USOENC (which represents a high proportion of SLN employees), organized a protest rally against the unequal exchange of mining sites. Frustrated at SLN's seemingly intransigent position in the negotiations, the FLNKS organized protests and blockades at all the company's major mining installations. Supporters of the pro-independence organization also restricted shipments of ore around the Territory. Consequently, four mines were forced to close, while a 25% reduction in working hours was imposed on 1,500 mine workers, prompting protests by SLN employees and demands from USOENC that the blockades be removed. In January 1998 the FLNKS leader, Roch Wamytan, urged the French Prime Minister, Lionel Jospin, to settle the dispute by the end of the month in order that official negotiations on the political future of the Territory, in preparation for the referendum, might begin. The position of the FLNKS had been somewhat undermined by the decision, in the previous month, of a breakaway group of pro-independence politicians (including prominent members of the UC, Parti de Libération Kanak—PALIKA, the UMP and the LKS) to begin negotiations with the RPCR concerning the dispute. These moderate supporters of independence formed the Fédération des Comités de Coordination des Indépendantistes (FCCI) in 1998. A draft agreement on the exchange of deposits was signed by SLN and the SMSP on 1 February, and in April a deal between the SMSP and a Canadian company for the establishment of the nickel smelter was concluded. Unless construction of the smelter had begun by the end of 2005, control of the nickel deposits transferred to the SMSP was to revert to SLN. Meanwhile, the French Government agreed to pay compensation of about 1,000m. French francs to Eramet for the reduction in the company's reserves. Following the signing of the nickel agreement, tripartite talks on the constitutional future of New Caledonia resumed in Paris in late February 1998. Discussions between representatives of the French Government, the FLNKS and the RPCR continued in March, despite a temporary boycott of the talks by the RPCR delegation, which requested the inclusion of various other minor political groups at the negotiations, including the FCCI. On 21 April, following a final round of talks in Nouméa, an agreement was concluded by the three sides. The agreement, which became known as the Nouméa Accord, postponed the referendum on independence for a period of between 15 and 20 years but provided for a gradual transfer of powers to local institutions. The document also acknowledged the negative impact of many aspects of French colonization on the Territory and emphasized the need for greater recognition of the importance of the Kanak cultural identity in the political development of the islands. The Nouméa Accord was signed on 5 May during the two-day inauguration of the Centre Culturel Tjibaou, a centre for Kanak art.

On 6 July 1998 the French Parliament (the National Assembly and the Senate) voted in favour of adopting the proposed changes regarding the administration of New Caledonia, which were to be incorporated in an annex to the French Constitution. In the following month the French Minister for Overseas Territories returned to New Caledonia for discussions on draft legislation for the devolution process. In September a new political group, called the Comité Provisoire pour la Défense des Principes Républicains de la Nouvelle-Calédonie Française, was formed in opposition to the Nouméa Accord, with support from members of the Front National and other right-wing parties. The UNCT, which was dissatisfied with several aspects of the accord, also urged its supporters to vote against the agreement.

The Nouméa Accord was presented to the electorate of New Caledonia in a referendum on 8 November 1998, when it was decisively approved, with 71.9% of votes cast in favour of the agreement. A participation rate of 74.24% was recorded. The Province of the North registered the strongest vote in favour of the accord (95.5%), while the Province of the South recorded the most moderate level of approval (62.9%). In late December the French National Assembly unanimously approved draft legislation regarding the definitive adoption of the accord. The Senate similarly approved the legislation in February 1999. In March of that year, however, the French Constitutional Council declared its intention to allow any French person who had resided in New Caledonia for 10 years or more to vote in provincial elections. This decision was criticized by Roch Wamytan, leader of the FLNKS, as well as by politicians in the French National Assembly and Senate, who claimed that this was in breach of the Nouméa Accord, whereby only those residing in New Caledonia in 1998 would be permitted to vote in provincial elections. Pro-independence groups threatened to boycott the elections (to be held in May). In response to this, the French Government announced that the Accord would be honoured, claiming that the Constitutional Council had breached the Nouméa Accord, and stating that this contravention would be rectified. In June the French Council of Ministers announced that it had drafted legislation restricting eligibility for voting in provincial elections and in any future referendums on sovereignty, to those who had been eligible to vote in the November 1998 referendum on the Nouméa Accord, and to their children upon reaching the age of majority. This decision was condemned by the right-wing Front National, and the leader of the RPCR. Constitutional amendments on the matter were still to be passed into law.

In compliance with the Nouméa Accord, an agreement was concluded in February 1999 to enable the transfer of 30% of SLN's share capital (and 8% of Eramet's capital) to a newly-created company representing local interests, the Société Territoriale Calédonienne de Participation Industrielle (STCPI), to be owned by the development companies of the three New Caledonian provinces. In this way, it was hoped, the islands' people would be more closely associated with the management of New Caledonia's principal source of wealth. However, agreement on the establishment of the STCPI was repeatedly delayed, owing to disagreements between the FLNKS and the RPCR. Finally, in July 2000, after two years of negotiations, New Caledonia's political leaders signed an agreement on the formation of the STCPI. The new company was to be owned equally by PROMOSUD (representing the South Province) and NORDIL (combining the interests of the North Province and the Loyalty Islands). The French Government welcomed the agreement and announced its commitment of 1,040m. French francs to fund the transfer of shares in SLN and Eramet by means of a loan to the provinces from the Agence Française de Développement. In August the assemblies of the three provinces endorsed the plan, and in early September the STCPI was formally established. At its first meeting the new company confirmed Raphaël Pidjot, the Managing Director of the SMSP, as chairman. Later in September shares in SLN and Eramet were transferred to the STCPI, thus reducing Eramet's interest in SLN from 90% to 60%. Representatives of the STCPI joined SLN's board of directors in October 2000. In November, however, Raphaël Pidjot and other officials of the SMSP and Falconbridge mining companies died in a helicopter accident, but these companies were to continue their joint project for a nickel operation in the North, to open in 2004.

At the general election held on 9 May 1999, no party gained an absolute majority. However, Lafleur's anti-independence RPCR won 24 of the 54 seats in the Territorial Congress, and formed a coalition with the recently-established FCCI and, on an informal level, with the Front National, thus creating an anti-independence block of 31 seats in the Territorial Congress. The pro-independence FLNKS won 18 seats. Simon Loueckhote was re-elected as President of the Territorial Congress in late May. Results of the elections in the Loyalty Island Province were officially challenged by the moderate independence LKS and FCCI parties, as well as by the RPCR, following the issue by the electoral commissioner for the Province of a report claiming that a large number of irregularities had occurred. A new election was held in June 2000, at which a coalition of the RPCR, FCCI, LKS and FULK obtained 44.8% of votes and six seats. The FLNKS obtained 37.3% of votes and six seats, and PALIKA 17.8% of votes and two seats. The composition of the Congress therefore remained unchanged. Robert Xowie was re-elected as President of the Province.

On 28 May 1999 the Territorial Congress elected Jean Lèques as the first President of the Government of New Caledonia, under the increased autonomy terms of the Nouméa Accord. The new Government was elected on the basis of proportional representation and replaced the French High Commissioner as New Caledonia's executive authority. The election of Léopold Jorédié, leader of the FCCI, as Vice-President, was denounced by the FLNKS which argued that, as the second largest party in Congress and as joint negotiators in the Nouméa Accord, the post should have gone to its leader, Roch Wamytan. In the formation of the Government the RPCR-FCCI coalition was awarded seven positions and the FLNKS four.

In October 1999 Wamytan threatened to withdraw from the Government, in protest at the lack of co-operation among parties. He claimed that sections of the Nouméa Accord requiring power to be distributed among the various political parties had not been observed (see above). In December Vice-President Léopold Jorédié received a one-year suspended prison sentence following accusations of misuse of public funds. Jorédié was charged with illegally obtaining grants totalling an estimated 5.5m. francs CFP, for the benefit of his son.

In July 2000 concern was expressed by the French Government over the implementation of the 'collegiality' clause in the Nouméa Accord, which provides for greater political co-operation among parties. Repeated threats by the FLNKS to withdraw from the Government because of its discontent with the RPCR's lack of power-sharing led to the establishment of an agreement between New Caledonia and the French State detailing the role of the two Governments in areas such as education and foreign policy; the role of the traditional chiefs in legal matters was also specified. In August Lafleur threatened to resign from his seat in the French National Assembly, following the upholding of a ruling convicting him of slander against Bruno Van Peteghem, an activist opposing construction plans for a complex near Nouméa. However, in early September Lafleur retracted his threat following pleas by RPCR members.

In August 2000 the Government introduced a 'social pact', aimed at addressing social issues and ongoing industrial conflicts. It proposed an increase in the minimum wage and suggested local employment priorities, subject to ratification by employers' unions in September.

At the FLNKS's annual conference, held in November 2000, Wamytan was re-elected president of the party (Wamytan was also narrowly re-elected leader of the UC); at the same time a new pro-independence party, the group UC du Congrès, formed by a breakaway faction of the UC, was officially recognized by both the UC and the FLNKS.

In March 2001 the municipal elections confirmed the predominance of the RPCR in the south, when it took 39 of the 49 seats in Nouméa. However, in the country as a whole the RPCR controlled only 14 of the 33 municipalities in New Caledonia, against the 19 held by pro-independence parties, principally the UC, PALIKA, LKS and FLNKS. The FLNKS won a majority in the north and took all three communes in the Loyalty Islands. Jean Lèques resigned as President in early April and was replaced by fellow RPCR politician, Pierre Frogier. Déwé Gorodey of the FLNKS was elected Vice-President. The election to the two most senior posts took place after the Congress had elected an 11-member Government, consisting of seven RPCR/FCCI coalition members, three from the FLNKS and one from the UC.

In June 2001, as a result of the failure to resolve industrial action over the dismissal of 12 employees from public works company Lefèbvre Pacifique, the Union Syndicale des Travailleurs Kanak et des Exploités (USTKE) extended its strike to 24-hour blockades of supermarkets, petrol stations, state radio and television companies, schools, the port and airport. In July 2001 a 100,000 francs CFP monthly minimum wage (as provided for in the 'social pact' brokered by Jacques Lafleur in September 2000) was implemented. Further strike action affected the tourist industry when, in December, USTKE launched a strike and occupation of the Château Royal complex, following Club Med's announcement of the Nouméa holiday resort's closure. The USTKE was demanding compensation for the 92 members of staff who were to be made redundant.

In October 2001 the French Council of State ruled that the 11th seat in the New Caledonian Government had been incorrectly allocated to the FLNKS following the local elections of April 2001. As a result, FCCI leader Raphaël Mapou replaced Aukusitino Manuohalalo of the FLNKS as Minister for Social Security and Health. The leader of the FLNKS, Roch Wamytan, threatened to resign from the Government in protest. In the same month, however, Wamytan was replaced as President of the UC by his deputy, Pascal Naouna; many members believed that Wamytan's dual role as President of both the UC and FLNKS was weakening the party. Then, in November, Wamytan lost the presidency of the FLNKS following a leadership struggle between its two main factions, the UC and PALIKA. The political bureau of the FLNKS was to lead the party until its internal disputes were resolved. Wamytan was subsequently replaced as Minister for Customary Affairs and Relations with the Senate by Mapou, necessitating a minor cabinet reshuffle; Manuohalalo became Minister for Social Security and Health.

Meanwhile, a long-standing dispute over the ownership of a Wallisian settlement—Ave Maria, near Nouméa—had led to intense fighting between Wallisian and Kanak communities in December 2001, resulting in one Kanak fatality in February 2002. The Kanak community in neighbouring Saint Louis had demanded the departure of all Wallisians from Ave Maria by March. The French High Commissioner mediated at several meetings in January 2002 to attempt to resolve the issue, leading to the Wallisian spokesman's suggestion that his community might be prepared to leave Ave Maria, provided it was offered an alternative 25 ha of land in which to resettle. Four working groups were established in April to rehouse Wallisians, to improve the area's public facilities, and to help reintegrate youths who had abandoned the education system. In early June a Wallisian man was ambushed by gunmen and shot dead in Ave Maria. Of a total of 127 families, some 60 had been relocated to social housing by June.

Elections to the French National Assembly were held in June 2002. The UC and PALIKA had yet to agree upon their choice of President for the FLNKS. The UC therefore refused to take part in the elections and urged its supporters to abstain from the poll, thereby depriving the President of PALIKA, Paul Néaoutyine, of any chance of election to the National Assembly. Jacques Lafleur was thus re-elected as New Caledonia's representative in the French legislature, winning 55.74% of the votes cast in the second round of polling, and Pierre Frogier, who won 55.71%, was thus returned as New Caledonia's second deputy to the National Assembly in Paris.

Following two resignations in July 2002, a series of ministerial reorganizations took place. The Minister for Labour, Public Service and Educational Training resigned, citing personal reasons and was replaced by a fellow RPCR member, Georges Naturel. In late July Raphaël Mapou resigned, following his outspoken criticism of the tendering of mining and prospecting rights in the Southern Province to a Canadian mining company. He was replaced by Corinne Fuluhea of the RPCR. Shortly afterwards, her portfolio was altered to that of Professional Training.

In August 2001 the Government hosted the 14th Melanesian Spearhead Group (MSG) summit. The organization was established in 1988 as a support movement for the independence of New Caledonia and has developed into a body promoting economic and cultural exchange in the Melanesian archipelago; members are Fiji, Papua New Guinea, Solomon Islands, Vanuatu and the FLNKS. Discussions were held regarding eventual New Caledonian membership.

Economy

In 2000, according to World Bank estimates, New Caledonia's gross national product (GNP) at average 1998–2000 prices totalled US $3,203m., equivalent to $15,060 per head (or $21,880m. per head on an international purchasing-power parity basis). During 1990–2000 it was estimated that GNP per head increased, in real terms, at an average annual rate of 0.7%. Over the same period the population rose by an average annual rate of 2.4%. During 1990–2000 New Caledonia's gross domestic product (GDP) increased, in real terms, at an average annual rate of 1.6%. GDP declined by 3.2% in 1998, but increased by 0.9% in 1999 and by 2.1% in 2000.

Since the first local discovery of nickel ore in 1864, and of cobalt and chromium ore in 1875, New Caledonia has been strongly influenced by the presence of large-scale mining enterprises. Large numbers of New Hebrideans (ni-Vanuatu), Japanese, Vietnamese and Javanese were imported to work the mines. After 1946, the indigenous Melanesian Kanaks began to move into the towns and to the mines, where heavy capitalization increased productivity. Further expansion absorbed more labour from rural areas, and the high level of earnings by nickel workers threatened all forms of rural production and eliminated chromium and cobalt mining, removing almost all forms of non-urban employment, particularly in the northern part of the island. Chromium mining was revived in the mid-1980s at Tiebaghi in the North Province; however, the exhaustion of reserves resulted in the closure of the mine in 1990. The discovery of large deposits of chromium in the South Province in 1992 prompted suggestions of a revival of the industry.

New Caledonia possesses the fifth largest nickel deposits, accounting for about 8% of the world's reserves. It has the fourth largest nickel production in the world. In 1999 some 56,481 metric tons of ferro-nickel and nickel matte were produced and these products, together with nickel ore, accounted for 89.3% of New Caledonia's export income in 1999 (of which 56.2% was ferro-nickel), the main customers being France and Japan. Production of nickel ore (metal content) rose from 110,100 tons in 1999 to 127,500 tons in 2000. Output of ferro-nickel and nickel matte reached 58,973 tons in 2001. France has declared nickel a strategic material and maintains strict control over mining. Mining and quarrying accounted for some 10.0% of GDP in 1999 (compared with 24% in 1989). Considerable growth was experienced in the industry in the mid-1990s. In 1998, however, the industry was adversely affected by the Asian financial crisis, which resulted in a dramatic decline in demand for nickel, a period of unrest among workers at the most severely affected mines and the consequent announcement by Société Le Nickel (SLN) of the loss of some 300 jobs.

Compared with the previous year, metallurgical production increased by 3.9% in 2001. The introduction of the single European currency, effected in January 2002, provided a boost to the nickel industry. (Both the one and two-euro coins used New Caledonian nickel.) In November 2001, however, in response to a decline in world nickel prices, the Société Minière du Sud Pacifique (SMSP) announced plans to reduce its mining activity by 50%, entailing the redundancy of 600 workers. Nevertheless, this did not affect the SMSP's joint project with a Canadian company: the construction of a new nickel-smelting plant in the North Province, subject to feasibility studies to be conducted during 2002. Construction of facilities at two nickel mines was expected to commence in 2002–04.

A major nickel mine at Kopeto, near Nepoui, in the North Province, which had been closed since the 1970s, was reopened in mid-1994. Moreover, in 1999 a Canadian company inaugurated a pilot smelter at Goro, in the South Province, to test new technology for nickel processing. If the testing proved successful, it was hoped that a full-scale commercial plant, producing nickel oxide and cobalt, would be constructed. The project, which would cost an estimated US $1,060m., envisaged the construction of a deep-water port, international airport, power station and associated infrastructure, and was expected to provide 2,000 jobs.

In late 1999 a joint French and Australian research mission made an offshore discovery of what was believed to be the world's largest gas deposit, measuring an estimated 18,000 sq km. It was hoped that this indicated the presence of considerable petroleum reserves.

Agriculture and fishing contributed only 1.9% of GDP in 1999, although the sector engaged 7.2% of the employed labour force in 1996. Some 94% of agriculturally productive land was used for pasture or fodder in 1992, mainly for cattle and pigs. New Caledonia also began to export deer, principally to Thailand, in 1994. In 1998 an Australian company announced major investment in a chicken-farming project in the North Province, increasing the number of chickens from 1,000 in 1995 to 330,000 in 2000. Maize, yams, sweet potatoes and coconuts have traditionally been the principal crops. However, pumpkins (squash) became an exclusive export crop for the Japanese market during the 1990s, and 2,200 metric tons were exported in 2001. Lychees became a new, albeit as yet minor, export in 2001, with Japan, New Zealand and French Polynesia each purchasing 8 metric tons in that year. The main fisheries products are tuna and shrimps (most of which are exported to Japan). A total of 1,651 metric tons of shrimps were produced in farms in 2001 (compared with 632 tons in 1993), and a giant clam project was undertaken in 1996. Exports of fisheries and aquaculture products were worth 2,973m. francs CFP in 2001, some 5.0% of total exports.

The manufacturing sector provided 4.0% of GDP in 1997 and (together with electricity, gas and water services) accounted for 10.9% of total employment in 1995. The sector consists mainly of small and medium-sized enterprises, most of which are situated around the capital, Nouméa, producing building materials, furniture, salted fish, fruit juices and perishable foods.

Electric energy is provided by thermal power stations (71.0% in 1999) and by hydroelectric plants. Solid fuels and mineral products accounted for 9.4% of total imports in 1998. In 1996 construction began on a plant producing wind-generated electricity near Nouméa, at a cost of US $7m., which provides some 4.5m. kWh of energy per year. In 2001 nine windmills were installed on Lifou, one of the Loyalty Islands, to deliver more than 800,000 kWh through the island's electricity network, as part of the Government's attempt to reduce expensive imports of diesel fuel.

Service industries together contributed 73.7% of GDP in 1999 and engaged 69.4% of the employed labour force in 1996. Tourism in New Caledonia, however, has failed to witness similar expansion to that experienced in many other Pacific islands. Tourist arrivals were seriously affected by political unrest and outbreaks of violence in the late 1980s between the Caldoches and Kanaks. Several luxury tourist resorts were under construction in the mid-1990s in an attempt to attract more visitors to the islands. Having increased from 99,735 in 1999 to 109,587 in 2000, the number of tourist arrivals declined to 100,515 in 2001. Receipts from tourism declined from US $140m. in 1997 to US $112m. in 1998. Air France planned to cease operations in New Caledonia in 2003; the route to Tokyo, where Air France would provide connections to Paris, was to be taken over by Air Calédonie International (AirCalin), which was given a tax concession by the French Government on 75% of the cost of two new aircraft.

New Caledonia's external trade is dominated by its chief commodity export, nickel. New Caledonian commerce benefits from its status as an Overseas Country in association with the EU. In 2000 New Caledonia recorded a visible trade deficit of some 42,490m. francs CFP, and there was a surplus of 25,242m. francs CFP, equivalent to 7.2% of that year's GDP, on the current account of the balance of payments (a deficit of 3,000m. francs CFP was registered in 1999). In 2001, however, the trade deficit increased to an estimated 64,526m. francs CFP. The principal imports in 1999 were mineral fuels, foodstuffs, and machinery and transport equipment. France is the main trading partner, providing some 40.3% of imports and purchasing 26.1% of exports in 2001. Other major trading partners in that year included Japan, Taiwan, Australia and Singapore.

The budget for 1999 envisaged a surplus of 3,529m. francs CFP. Budgetary expenditure for 2002 was set at 86,400m. francs CFP. In 1998 the islands received official development assistance totalling US $338.4m., nearly all of which was from France. In 2001 budgetary aid from France totalled the equivalent of €755,317m., increasing to €777,965 in 2002. The average annual rate of inflation in Nouméa was 2.0% in 1990–2000, rising to 2.3% in 2001. Some 11.2% of the labour force were unemployed in 1999. In December 2001 there were 8,259 job-seekers, a rise of 10.1% compared with the corresponding month of the previous year. A total of 10,325 were registered as unemployed in June 2002.

New Caledonia is a member of the Franc Zone (an association of countries and territories with currencies linked to the French franc), an associate member of the UN's Economic and Social Commission for Asia and the Pacific (ESCAP) and, in its own right, of the Pacific Community (formerly the South Pacific Commission—based in Nouméa). Following the adoption of the Nouméa Accord in mid-1998 (see History), New Caledonia obtained observer status at the South Pacific Forum (now Pacific Islands Forum) in September 1999.

New Caledonia's economy is vulnerable to factors affecting the islands' important nickel industry, which included political unrest during the 1980s and fluctuations in international prices for the commodity in the 1990s. The Nouméa Accord, approved by referendum in November 1998 (see Recent History), aimed to improve the economic conditions of the Kanak population and to increase their participation in the market economy and in public administration. Despite previous attempts to redress the balance of New Caledonian society (most importantly in the Matignon Accord of 1988), the indigenous population remained largely excluded from New Caledonia's economic and political administration, and a considerable proportion continued to experience economic hardship in the late 1990s. In mid-1999 the RPCR leader, Jacques Lafleur, revealed proposals for the creation of an inter-provincial committee for economic development, which would allow the comparatively wealthy South Province to assist the economic development of the other Provinces. Moreover, it was hoped that the development of those sectors generally considered not to have reached their full potential (notably tourism, aquaculture, fishing and farm agriculture) would alleviate the economic uncertainty created by the need to reduce dependency on France. In an effort to encourage investment in New Caledonia, legislation to replace the system of tax deductions with one of tax credits was expected to be adopted in 2002. In the tourism sector, visitor arrivals declined by 8.4% in 2001 compared with the previous year. The effect of the decline in world nickel prices during 2001 was compounded by the downturn in the aviation industry that followed the terrorist attacks on the USA in September (aeronautical companies normally being significant consumers of special nickel alloys). Nickel prices, however, appeared to be recovering in early 2002.

Statistical Survey

Source (unless otherwise stated): Institut Territorial de la Statistique et des Etudes Economiques, BP 823, 98845 Nouméa; tel. 275481; fax 288148; internet www.itsee.nc.

AREA AND POPULATION

Area (sq km): New Caledonia island (Grande-Terre) 16,372; Loyalty Islands 1,981 (Lifou 1,207, Maré 642, Ouvéa 132); Isle of Pines 152; Belep Archipelago 70; Total 18,575 (7,172 sq miles).

Population: 164,173 (males 83,862, females 80,311) at census of 4 April 1989; 196,836 (males 100,762, females 96,074) at census of 16 April 1996; 215,904 (official estimate) at 1 January 2002. *Population by province* (1996 census): Loyalty Islands 20,877, North Province 41,413, South Province 134,546.

Density (1 January 2002): 11.6 per sq km.

Ethnic Groups (census of 1996): Melanesians 86,788; French and other Europeans 67,151; Wallisians and Futunians (Polynesian) 17,763; Indonesians 5,003; Tahitians (Polynesian) 5,171; Others 14,960.

Principal Town (1 January 2002): Nouméa (capital), population 83,266.

Births, Marriages and Deaths (2001): Registered live births 4,326 (birth rate 20.2 per 1,000); Registered marriages 925 (marriage rate 4.3 per 1,000); Registered deaths 1,131 (death rate 5.3 per 1,000).

Expectation of Life (years at birth, 2001): Males 70.5; Females 76.1.

Employment (persons aged 14 years and over, 1995, provisional): Agriculture, hunting, forestry and fishing 2,489; Mining and quarrying 1,651; Manufacturing and Electricity, gas and water 5,583; Construction 6,824; Trade, restaurants and hotels 8,477; Transport, storage and communications 2,754; Financing, insurance, real estate and business services 5,676; Community, social and personal services 9,710; Activities not adequately defined 7,920; Total employed 51,260; Unemployed 7,410; Total labour force 58,670. Source: UN, *Statistical Yearbook for Asia and the Pacific*.

1996 (census results, excluding military conscripts): Agriculture 4,663; Industry 8,177; Construction 6,890; Services 44,647; Total employed 64,377; Unemployed 15,048.

1999: Total employed 58,698; Unemployed 7,390; Total labour force 66,088. Source: Institut d'Emission d'Outre-Mer, *Annual Report*.

AGRICULTURE, ETC.

Principal Crops (FAO estimates, '000 metric tons, 2000): Maize 2.1; Potatoes 1.4; Sweet potatoes 3.0; Cassava 2.8; Taro (Coco yam) 2.3; Yams 11.0; Coconuts 15.0; Vegetables 3.7; Bananas 0.9; Other fruits 2.4. Source: FAO.

Livestock (FAO estimates, '000 head, year ending September 2000): Horses 11.5; Cattle 122; Pigs 40; Sheep 0.5; Goats 1.5; Poultry 500. Source: FAO.

Livestock Products ('000 metric tons, 2000): Beef and veal 3.9; Pig meat 1.4; Poultry meat 0.8*; Cows' milk 3.7; Hen eggs 1.6*; Cattle hides (fresh) 0.5*. * FAO estimate. Source: FAO.

Forestry: ('000 cubic metres, 1994): *Roundwood removal:* Sawlogs, veneer logs and logs for sleepers 2.8; Other industrial wood 2.0 (FAO estimate); Total 4.8. *Sawnwood production:* 3.3 (all broadleaved). *1995–2000:* Annual output as in 1994 (FAO estimates). Source: FAO.

Fishing (metric tons, live weight, 1999): Capture 3,152 (Albacore 690, Yellowfin tuna 373, Bigeye tuna 553, Sea cucumbers 493); Aquaculture 1,936 (Shrimps and prawns 1,906); Total catch 5,088. Note: Figures exclude trochus shells (98 metric tons). Source: FAO, *Yearbook of Fishery Statistics*.

MINING

Production ('000 metric tons): Nickel ore (metal content) 125.3 in 1998; 110.1 in 1999; 127.5 in 2000. Source: US Geological Survey.

INDUSTRY

Production (2001): Ferro-nickel and nickel matte 58,973 metric tons (nickel content); Electric energy 1,729m. kWh.

Cement: 84,000 metric tons in 1997 (Source: UN, *Statistical Yearbook for Asia and the Pacific*).

FINANCE

Currency and Exchange Rates: see French Polynesia.

Territorial Budget (million francs CFP, 2001): *Revenue:* 81,337; *Expenditure:* 81,337. French government transfers 86,344.

Aid from France (US $ million): 392.0 in 1996; 336.6 in 1997; 336.3 in 1998. Source: UN, *Statistical Yearbook for Asia and the Pacific*.

Money Supply (million francs CFP at 31 December 2001): Currency in circulation 10,473; Demand deposits 94,525; Total money 104,998. Source: Institut d'Emission d'Outre-Mer.

Cost of Living (Consumer Price Index for Nouméa; base: December 1992 = 100): 111.4 in 1999; 113.1 in 2000; 115.7 in 2001.

Gross Domestic Product (million francs CFP at current prices): 347,303 in 2000. Source: *Bank of Hawaii, An Update on New Caledonia*.

Expenditure on the Gross Domestic Product (million francs CFP at current prices, 1992): Government final consumption expenditure 94,770; Private final consumption expenditure 159,514; Increase in stocks 416; Gross fixed capital formation 66,818; *Total domestic expenditure* 321,518; Exports of goods and services 47,246; *Less* Imports of goods and services 88,403; *Sub-total* 280,361; Statistical discrepancy 1,066; *GDP in purchasers' values* 281,427. Source: UN, *National Accounts Statistics*.

Gross Domestic Product by Economic Activity (million francs CFP at current prices, 1997): Agriculture and food processing 12,835; Energy, mining and metallurgy 37,232; Other manufactures 13,815; Construction and public works 17,447; Transport and communication 23,415; Services and commerce 152,659; Salaries 91,857; Total 349,260. Source: Bank of Hawaii, *An Update on New Caledonia*.

Balance of Payments (million francs CFP, 2000): Trade balance −42,490; Services (net) −5,161; *Balance on goods and services* −47,651; Other income (net) 33,394; *Balance on goods, services and income* −14,257; Current transfers (net) 39,500; *Current balance* 25,242; Capital account (net) 179; Direct investment (net) −5,492; Portfolio investment (net) −15,367; Other capital (incl. charges in reserves) −4,738; Net errors and omissions 176. Source: Institut d'Emission d'Outre-Mer.

EXTERNAL TRADE

Principal Commodities (million francs CFP, 1999): *Imports:* Prepared foodstuffs, beverages, spirits and vinegar, tobacco and manufactured substitutes 18,233; Mineral products 10,579; Products of chemical or allied industries 8,860; Plastics, rubber and articles thereof 4,526; Paper-making material, paper and paperboard and articles thereof 3,115; Textiles and textile articles 3,967; Base metals and articles thereof 8,048; Machinery and mechanical appliances, electrical equipment, sound and television apparatus 22,617; Vehicles, aircraft, vessels and associated transport equipment 17,613; Total (incl. others) 112,808. *Exports:* Ferro-nickel 29,445; Nickel matte 8,764; Nickel ore 8,583; Prawns 1,868; Total (incl. others) 52,388.

2001: Imports c.i.f. 124,400; Exports c.i.f. 59,700. Source: Direction Régionale des Douanes.

Principal Trading Partners (million francs CFP, 2001): *Imports:* Australia 20,666.6; Belgium 1,659.9; China, People's Republic 2,977.9; France (metropolitan) 50,046.6; Germany 3,996.6; Italy 3,619.7; Japan 3,868.5; Korea, Republic 1,445.0; New Zealand 6,131.5; Singapore 7,551.4; Spain 2,485.9; United Kingdom 2,812.1; USA 4,910.6; Total (incl. others) 124,037.8. *Exports:* Australia 4,492.4; Belgium 1,236.2; Finland 1,422.2; France (metropolitan) 15,523.2; Italy 1,370.8; Japan 13,733.0; Korea, Republic 2,612.7; Spain 4,355.3; Taiwan 10,455.8; USA 1,446.4; Total (incl. others) 59,511.9. Source: Direction Régionale des Douanes.

TRANSPORT

Road Traffic (motor vehicles in use, 2001): Total 85,499.

Shipping (2001): Vessels entered 478; Goods unloaded 1,298,829 metric tons, Goods loaded 210,197 metric tons. *Merchant Fleet* (vessels registered, '000 grt, at 31 December 1992): 14.

Civil Aviation (La Tontouta airport, Nouméa, 2001): Passengers arriving 173,913, Passengers departing 172,854; Freight unloaded 3,661 metric tons, Freight loaded 1,401 metric tons.

TOURISM

Foreign Tourist Arrivals (arrivals by air): 99,735 in 1999; 109,587 in 2000; 100,515 in 2001.

Tourist Arrivals by Country of Residence (2000): Australia 18,012, France 30,702, French Polynesia 3,676, Japan 31,051, New Zealand 9,576, Vanuatu 2,606, Wallis and Futuna Islands 4,420; Total (incl. others) 109,587.

Receipts (US $ million): 140.0 in 1997; 111.8 in 1998.

Source: partly World Tourism Organization, *Yearbook of Tourism Statistics*.

COMMUNICATIONS MEDIA

Radio Receivers (1997): 107,000 in use*.

Television Receivers (2000): 106,000 in use†.

Telephones (2000): 51,005 main lines in use†.

Facsimile Machines (1994): 2,200 in use‡.

Mobile Cellular Telephones (2000): 49,948 subscribers†.

Internet Users (estimate, 2000): 24,000†.

Daily Newspapers (1999): 1.

* Source: UNESCO, *Statistical Yearbook*.

† Source: International Telecommunication Union.

‡ Source: UN, *Statistical Yearbook*.

EDUCATION

Pre-primary (2000): 81 schools; 13,033 pupils.

Primary (2001): 289 schools; 1,837 teachers (incl. pre-primary); 36,996 pupils.

Secondary (2001): 64 schools; 2,371 teachers; 29,036 pupils.

Higher (2000): 55 teachers; 2,069 students.

Source: Vice-Rectorat de Nouvelle-Calédonie.

Adult Literacy Rate: Males 94.0%; Females 92.1% in 1989.

Directory

The Constitution

The constitutional system in New Caledonia is established under the Constitution of the Fifth French Republic and specific laws, the most recent of which were enacted in July 1989 in accordance with the terms agreed by the Matignon Accord. A referendum on the future of New Caledonia (expected to be conducted in 1998) was postponed for a period of between 15 and 20 years while a gradual transfer of power from metropolitan France to local institutions is effected under the terms of the Nouméa Accord, concluded in 1998. Under the terms of the Nouméa Accord, the islands are declared to be an Overseas Country of the French Republic, of which they remain an integral part. The High Commissioner is the representative of the State in the Territory and is appointed by the French Government. The High Commissioner is responsible for external relations, defence, law and order, finance and secondary education. New Caledonia is divided into three Provinces, of the South, the North and the Loyalty Islands. Each is governed by a Provincial Assembly, which is elected on a proportional basis and is responsible for local economic development, land reform and cultural affairs. Members of the Assemblies (40 for the South, 22 for the North and 14 for the Loyalty Islands) are subject to re-election every five years. A proportion of the members of the three Provincial Assemblies together form the Congress of New Caledonia (32 for the South, 15 for the North, and seven for the Loyalty Islands), which is responsible for the territorial budget and fiscal affairs, infrastructure and primary education. The Assemblies and the Congress each elect a President to lead them. The Government of New Caledonia is elected by the Congress, and comprises between seven and 11 members. Under the terms of the Nouméa Accord, it replaces the French High Commissioner as the Territory's executive authority. Provision is also made for the maintenance of Kanak tradition: there are eight custom regions, each with a Regional Consultative Custom Council. These eight Councils, with other appropriate authorities, are represented on the Customary Senate, which is composed of 16 members (two elected from each regional council for a six-year period); the Senate is consulted by the Congress and the Government. Local government is conducted by 33 communes. New Caledonia also elects two deputies to the National Assembly in Paris and one Senator, on the basis of universal adult suffrage. One Economic and Social Councillor is also nominated. New Caledonia may be represented in the European Parliament.

The Government

(August 2002)

STATE GOVERNMENT

High Commissioner: DANIEL CONSTANTIN (took office August 2002).

Secretary-General: ALAIN TRIOLLE.

Deputy Secretary-General: CAMILLE PUTOIS.

LOCAL GOVERNMENT

Secretary-General: PATRICK JAMIN.

Deputy Secretary-General: ARMAND LEDER.

Deputy Secretary-General: JULES HMALOKO.

COUNCIL OF MINISTERS

President: PIERRE FROGIER (RPCR).

Vice-President and Minister for Culture, Youth and Sports: DÉWÉ GORODEY (FLNKS).

Minister for Agriculture and Fishing: MAURICE PONGA (RPCR).

Minister for Education: LÉOPOLD JORÉDIÉ (FCCI).

Minister for Employment and Public Services: GEORGES NATUREL (RPCR).

Minister for Transport and Communications and Social Dialogue: PIERRE MARESCA (RPCR).

Minister for Economic Affairs, Relations with the Economic and Social Council and Relations with Congress: ALAIN LAZARE (RPCR).

Minister for Finance and the Budget, responsible for the Development of New Caledonia: HERVÉ CHATELAIN (RPCR).

Minister for Customary Affairs and Relations with the Senate and the Custom Consultative Council: (vacant).

Minister for Professional Training: CORINNE FULUHEA (RPCR).

Minister for Social Security and Health: AUKUSITINO MANUOHALALO (FLNKS).

Minister for Infrastructure: GÉRALD CORTOT (UC).

GOVERNMENT OFFICES

Office of the High Commissioner: Haut-commissariat de la République en Nouvelle-Calédonie, 1 ave Maréchal Foch, BP C5, 98848 Nouméa Cédex; tel. 266300; fax 272828; internet www.etat.nc.

New Caledonian Government: *Présidence du Gouvernement:* 19 ave Maréchal Foch, BP M2, 98849 Nouméa Cédex; tel. 246565; fax 246550; *Congrès de la Nouvelle-Calédonie:* 1 blvd Vauban, BP 31, 98845 Nouméa Cédex; tel. 273129; fax 276219.

Office of the Secretary-General of the Government of New Caledonia: Immeuble administratif Jacques Iekawe, 18 ave Paul Doumer, BP M2, 98844 Nouméa Cédex; tel. 256000; fax 286848; e-mail lmoprini@gouv.nc; internet www.gouv.nc.

Government of the Province of the Loyalty Islands: Gouvernement Provincial des Iles Loyauté, BP 50, 98820 Wé, Lifou, Loyalty Islands; tel. 455100; fax 455100; e-mail loyalty@loyalty.nc; internet www.loyalty.nc.

Government of the Province of the North: Gouvernement Provincial du Nord, BP 41, 98860 Koné, Grande-Terre; tel. 477100; fax 355475.

Government of the Province of the South: Hôtel de la Province Sud, 9 Route des Artifices Artilleries, Port Moselle, BP 4142, 98846 Nouméa Cédex; tel. 258000; fax 274900; internet www.province-sud.nc.

GOVERNMENT DEPARTMENTS

Department of Administrative Services and Computer Technology: 3 rue Gustave Flaubert, Baie de l'Orphelinat, BP 8231, 98807 Nouméa Cédex; tel. 275858; fax 281919; e-mail smai@territoire.nc; internet www.gouv.nc/smai.

Department of Agriculture, Forestry and the Environment: 209 rue Anatole Bénébig, BP 180, 98845 Nouméa Cédex; tel. 255100; fax 255129; e-mail dafe@offratel.nc; internet sfdnouvelle-caledonie@educagri.fr.

Department of Civil Aviation: 179 rue Gervolino, BP H1, 98849 Nouméa Cédex; tel. 265200; fax 265202; e-mail brigitte.pasqualini@aviation-civile.gouv.fr; internet www.dgac.fr.

Department of Culture: 75 rue Sébastopol, BP C5, Nouméa; tel. 242181; fax 242180; e-mail mac@hc.culture.nc; supports and subsidises artists, collectives and educational programmes; Dir JEAN-JACQUES GARNIER.

Department of Education: Vice-Réctorat, 22 rue J. B. Dézarnaulds, BP G4, 98848 Nouméa Cédex; tel. 266100; fax 273048; internet www.ac-nouméa.nc.

Department of Employment: 12 rue de Verdun, BP 141, 98845 Nouméa Cédex; tel. 275572; fax 270494; e-mail dt@gouv.nc; internet www.gouv.nc/dtnc.

Department of Finance: 4 rue Monchovet, BP E4, 98848 Nouméa Cédex; tel. 279200; fax 272675; e-mail tg162.contact@cpfinances.gouv.fr; internet www.finances.gouv.fr.

Department of Human Resources and Civil Service: Nouméa.

Department of Infrastructure, Topography and Transport: 1 bis rue Unger, 1ère vallée du Tir, BP A2, 98848 Nouméa Cédex; tel. 280300; fax 281760; e-mail dittt@gouv.nc; internet www.gouv.nc/dittt.

Department of Maritime Affairs: 2 bis rue Russeil, BP 36, Nouméa Cédex; tel. 272626; fax 287286; e-mail affmar@gouv.nc; internet www.mer.gouv.fr.

Department of Mines and Energy: 1 ter, rue Edouard Unger, 1ère Vallée du Tir, BP 465, 98845 Nouméa Cédex; tel. 273944; fax 272345; e-mail mines@gouv.nc; internet www.gouv.nc/sme.

Department of Social Security and Health: 5 rue Général Galliéni, BP 3278, 98846 Nouméa Cédex; tel. 243700; fax 243702; e-mail dtass@territoire.nc; internet www.gouv.nc/dtass.

Department of Youth and Sports: 23 ave Jean Jaurès, BP810, 98845 Nouméa Cédex; tel. 252384; fax 254585; e-mail djsnc@gouv.nc; internet www.gouv.nc/djsnc; Dir ROMAIN MARCET.

Legislature

ASSEMBLÉES PROVINCIALES

Members of the Provincial Assemblies are elected on a proportional basis for a five-year term. Each Provincial Assembly elects its President. A number of the members of the Provincial Assemblies sit together to make up the Territorial Congress. The Assembly of the Northern Province has 22 members (including 15 sitting for the Territorial Congress), the Loyalty Islands 14 members (including seven for the Congress) and the Southern Province has 40 members (including 32 for the Congress).

Election, 9 May 1999 (results by province)

Party	North	South	Loyalty Islands
Rassemblement pour la Calédonie dans la République (RPCR)	4	25	2
Front de Libération Nationale Kanak Socialiste (FLNKS)	6	6	6
Union Nationale pour l'Indépendance (UNI—PALIKA)	8	—	—
Fédération des Comités de Coordination des Indépendantistes (FCCI)	4	—	2
Front National (FN)	—	5	—
Alliance pour la Calédonie (APLC)	—	4	—
Libération Kanak Socialiste (LKS)	—	—	2
Parti de Libération Kanak (PALIKA)	—	—	2
Total	22	40	14

Province of the North: President PAUL NÉAOUTYINE (UNI—PALIKA).

Province of the South: President JACQUES LAFLEUR (RPCR).

Province of the Loyalty Islands: President ROBERT XOWIE (FLNKS).

Note: following allegations of irregularities in the Loyalty Islands poll, a second election in that province was held on 25 June 2000, following which the distribution of seats remained unchanged.

CONGRÈS

A proportion of the members of the three Provincial Assemblies sit together, in Nouméa, as the Congress of New Caledonia. There are 54 members (out of a total of 76 sitting in the Provincial Assemblies).

President: SIMON LOUECKHOTE (RPCR).

Election, 9 May 1999 (results for the Territory as a whole)

Party	Votes	%	Seats
RPCR	30,774	38.80	24
FLNKS	13,824	17.43	12
UNI	4,831	6.09	5
FCCI	7,515	9.48	4
FN	5,374	6.78	4
APLC	4,830	6.09	3
LKS	2,046	2.58	1
PALIKA	1,335	1.68	1
Others	8,789	11.08	1
Total	79,321	100.00	54

PARLEMENT

Deputies to the French National Assembly: JACQUES LAFLEUR (RPCR), PIERRE FROGIER (RPCR).

Representative to the French Senate: SIMON LOUECKHOTE (RPCR).

Political Organizations

Alliance pour la Calédonie (APLC): 40, rue de la République, BP 14534, 98803 Nouméa Cédex; tel 273367; fax 273370; e-mail courier@alliance.nc; internet www.alliance.nc; Leader DIDIER LEROUX.

Fédération des Comités de Coordination des Indépendantistes (FCCI): f. 1998 by breakaway group from FLNKS; Leaders LÉOPOLD JORÉDIÉ, RAPHAËL MAPOU, FRANÇOIS BURCK.

Front Calédonien (FC): extreme right-wing; Leader M. SARRAN.

Front de Libération Nationale Kanak Socialiste (FLNKS): Nouméa; tel. 272599; f. 1984 (following dissolution of Front Indépendantiste); pro-independence; Pres. (vacant); a grouping of the following parties:

Groupe UC du Congrès: Nouméa; f. 2000 by breakaway faction of the UC.

Parti de Libération Kanak (PALIKA): f. 1975; 5,000 mems; Leader PAUL NÉAOUTYINE.

Rassemblement Démocratique Océanien (RDO): Nouméa; f. 1994 by breakaway faction of UO; supports Kanak sovereignty; Pres. ALOISIO SAKO.

Union Calédonienne (UC): f. 1952; 11,000 mems; Pres. PASCAL NAOUNA; Sec.-Gen. DANIEL YEIWÉNÉ.

Union Nationale pour l'Indépendence (UNI): c/o Congrès de la Nouvelle-Calédonie; Leader PAUL NÉAOUTYINE.

Union Progressiste Mélanésienne (UPM): f. 1974 as the Union Progressiste Multiraciale; 2,300 mems; Pres. VICTOR TUTUGORO; Sec.-Gen. RENÉ POROU.

Front National (FN): BP 4198, Nouméa 98846; tel 258068; fax 258064; e-mail sariman@province-sud.nc; extreme right-wing; Leader GUY GEORGE.

Génération Calédonienne: f. 1995; youth-based; aims to combat corruption in public life; Pres. JEAN RAYMOND POSTIC.

Libération Kanak Socialiste (LKS): Maré, Loyalty Islands; moderate, pro-independence; Leader NIDOÏSH NAISSELINE.

Rassemblement pour la Calédonie dans la République (RPCR): 19 ave du Maréchal Foch, BP 306, 98845 Nouméa; tel. 282620; fax 284033; f. 1977; affiliated to the metropolitan Rassemblement pour la République (RPR); in favour of retaining the status quo in New Caledonia; Leader JACQUES LAFLEUR; a coalition of the following parties:

Centre des Démocrates Sociaux (CDS): f. 1971; Leader JEAN LÈQUES.

Parti Républicain (PR): Leader PIERRE MARESCA.

Union Océanienne (UO): Nouméa; f. 1989 by breakaway faction of RPCR; represents people whose origin is in the French Overseas Territory of Wallis and Futuna; conservative; Leader MICHEL HEMA.

Other political organizations participating in the elections of May 1999 included: **Développer Ensemble pour Construire l'Avenir (DECA), Renouveau, Citoyens Ensemble, La Calédonie Autrement, Front Uni de Libération Kanak (FULK), Groupe Alliance Multiraciale (GAM)** and **Indépendance et Progrès**.

Judicial System

Court of Appeal: Palais de Justice, BP F4, 98848 Nouméa; tel. 279350; fax 269185; e-mail pp.ca-noumea@justice.fr; First Pres. GÉRARD FEY; Procurator-Gen. GÉRARD NÉDELLEC.

Court of the First Instance: 2 blvd Extérieur, BP F4, 98848 Nouméa; fax 276531; e-mail p.tpi-noumea@justice.fr; Pres. JEAN PRADAL; Procurator of the Republic ROBERT BLASER. There are two subsidiary courts, with resident magistrates, at Koné (Province of the North) and Wé (Province of the Loyalty Islands).

Customary Senate of New Caledonia: Conseil Consultatif Coutumier, 68 ave J. Cook, POB 1059, Nouville; tel. 242000; fax 249320; f. 1990; consulted by Local Assembly and French Govt on matters affecting land, Kanak tradition and identity; mems: 40 authorities from eight custom areas; Pres. BERGE KAWA; Vice-Pres. JOSEPH PIDJOT.

Religion

The majority of the population is Christian, with Roman Catholics comprising about 55% of the total in 1998. About 3% of the inhabitants, mainly Indonesians, are Muslims.

CHRISTIANITY

The Roman Catholic Church

The Territory comprises a single archdiocese, with an estimated 110,000 adherents in 1999. The Archbishop participates in the Catholic Bishops' Conference of the Pacific, based in Fiji.

Archbishop of Nouméa: Most Rev. MICHEL-MARIE-BERNARD CALVET, Archevêché, BP 3, 4 rue Mgr-Fraysse, 98845 Nouméa; tel. 265353; fax 265352; e-mail archeveche@ddec.nc.

The Anglican Communion

Within the Church of the Province of Melanesia, New Caledonia forms part of the diocese of Vanuatu (q.v.). The Archbishop of the Province is the Bishop of Central Melanesia (resident in Honiara, Solomon Islands).

Protestant Churches

Eglise évangélique en Nouvelle-Calédonie et aux Iles Loyauté: BP 277, Nouméa; f. 1960; Pres. Rev. SAILALI PASSA; Gen. Sec. Rev. TELL KASARHEROU.

Other churches active in the Territory include the Assembly of God, the Free Evangelical Church, the Presbyterian Church, the New

Apostolic Church, the Pentecostal Evangelical Church and the Tahitian Evangelical Church.

The Press

L'Avenir Calédonien: 10 rue Gambetta, Nouméa; organ of the Union Calédonienne; Dir Paita Gabriel.

La Calédonie Agricole: BP 111, 98845 Nouméa Cédex; tel. 243160; fax 284587; every 2 months; official publ. of the Chambre d'Agriculture; Pres. André Mazurier; Man. Georges Roucou; circ. 3,000.

Eglise de Nouvelle-Calédonie: BP 3, 98845 Nouméa; fax 265352; f. 1976; monthly; official publ. of the Roman Catholic Church; circ. 450.

Les Nouvelles Calédoniennes: 41–43 rue de Sébastopol, BP G5, 98848 Nouméa; tel. 272584; fax 281627; internet www.nouvelles-caledoniennes.nc; f. 1971; daily; Publr Philippe Hersant; Dir Bruno Franceschi; Editor Marc Spisser; circ. 18,500.

Télé 7 Jours: route de Vélodome, BP 2080, 98846 Nouméa Cédex; tel. 284598; weekly.

NEWS AGENCY

Agence France-Presse (AFP): 15 rue Docteur Guégan, 98800 Nouméa; tel. 263033; fax 278699; Correspondent Franck Madoeuf.

Publishers

Editions d'Art Calédoniennes: 3 rue Guynemer, BP 1626, Nouméa; tel. 277633; fax 281526; art, reprints, travel.

Editions du Santal: 5 bis rue Emile-Trianon, 98846 Nouméa; tel. and fax 262533; e-mail santal@offratel.nc; history, art, travel, birth and wedding cards; Dir Paul-Jean Stahl.

Grain de Sable: BP 577, Nouméa; tel. 273057; fax 285707; e-mail lokisa@canl.nc; literature, travel.

Île de Lumière: BP 8401, Nouméa Sud; tel. 289858; history, politics.

Savannah Editions SARL: BP 3086, 98846 Nouméa; e-mail savannahmarc@hotmail.com; f. 1994; sports, travel, leisure.

Société d'Etudes Historiques de Nouvelle-Calédonie: BP 63, Nouméa; tel. 263662.

Broadcasting and Communications

TELECOMMUNICATIONS

France Cables et Radio (FCR): Télécommunications extérieures de la Nouvelle-Calédonie, BP A1, 98848 Nouméa Cédex; tel. 266600; fax 266666; Dir Philippe Dupuis.

Offices des Postes et Télécommunications: Le Waruna, 2 rue Monchovet, Port Plaisance, 98841 Nouméa Cédex; tel. 268210; fax 262927; e-mail direction@opt.nc; Dir Jean-Yves Ollivaud.

BROADCASTING

Radio

NRJ Nouvelle-Calédonie: 41–43 rue Sebastopol, BP G5, 98848 Nouméa; tel. 279446; fax 279447.

Radio Djiido: 29 rue du Maréchal Juin, BP 1671, 98803 Nouméa Cédex; tel. 253515; fax 272187; f. 1985; community station; broadcasts in French; pro-independence.

Radio Nouvelle Calédonie: Mont Coffin, BP 93, Nouméa Cédex; tel. 274327; fax 281252; f. 1942; fmrly Radiodiffusion Française d'Outre-mer (RFO); 24 hours of daily programmes in French; Dir Alain Le Garrec; Editor-in-Chief Francis Orny.

Radio Rythme Bleu: BP 578, Nouméa; tel. 254646; fax 284928; e-mail RRB@lagoon.nc; Dir Christian Prost.

Television

RFO-Télé Nouvelle-Calédonie: Radio Télévision Française d'Outre Mer (RFO), Mont Coffin, BP 93, Nouméa; tel. 274327; fax 281252; f. 1965; transmits 10 hours daily; Dir Alain Le Garrec.

Canal Calédonie: 30 rue de la Somme, BP 1797, 98845 Nouméa; subscription service.

Canal Outre-mer (canal+): Nouméa; f. 1995; cable service.

Finance

(cap. = capital; res = reserves; dep. = deposits; m. = million; brs = branches; amounts in CFP francs unless otherwise stated)

BANKING

Agence Française de Développement: 5 Rue Barleux, BP JI, 98849 Nouméa Cédex; tel. 282088; fax 282413.

Banque de Nouvelle-Calédonie: 25 ave de la Victoire, BP L3, 98849 Nouméa Cédex; tel. 257400; fax 274147; internet www.boh.nc; f. 1974; adopted present name Jan. 2002; owned by Bank of Hawaii (USA—94.5%) and Crédit Lyonnais (France—3%); cap. 3,617.7m., res 940.2m. dep. 55,133.1m. (Dec. 1999); Pres. Michael Bauer; Gen. Man. Gilles Therry; 7 brs.

Banque Calédonienne d'Investissement (BCI): BP K5, 50 ave de la Victoire, 98849 Nouméa; tel. 256565; fax 274035; internet www.bci.nc.

BNP Paribas Nouvelle-Calédonie (France): 37 ave Henri Lafleur, BP K3, 98849 Nouméa Cédex; tel. 258400; fax 258459; e-mail bnp.nc@bnpparibas.com; f. 1969 as Banque Nationale de Paris; present name adopted in 2001; cap. 28.0m. euros, res 315.6m. euros (Dec. 2001); Gen. Man. Gérard D'Here; 10 brs.

Société Générale Calédonienne de Banque: 44 rue de l'Alma, Siège et Agence Principale, 98848 Nouméa Cédex; tel. 256300; fax 276245; e-mail sgcb@canl.nc; f. 1981; cap. 1,068.4m., res 4,843.0m., dep. 80,096.6m. (Dec. 2000); Gen. Man. Dominique Poignon; 12 brs.

Trade and Industry

DEVELOPMENT ORGANIZATIONS

New Caledonia Economic Development Agency (ADECAL): 15 rue Guynemer, BP 2384, 98846 Nouméa Cédex; tel. 249077; fax 249087; e-mail adecal@offratel.nc; internet www.adecal.nc/; f. 1995; promotes investment within New Caledonia; Dir Jean-Michel Arlie.

Agence de Développement de la Culture Kanak: Centre Tjibaou, rue des Accords de Matignon BP 378, 98845 Nouméa Cédex; tel. 414545; fax 414546; e-mail adck@adck.nc; internet www.adck.nc. Pres. Marie-Claude Tjibaou; Dir-Gen. Octave Togna; Dir of Culture Emmanuel Kasarherou.

Agence de Développement Rural et d'Aménagement Foncier (ADRAF): 1 rue de la Somme, BP 4228, 98847 Nouméa Cédex; tel. 258600; fax 258604; e-mail dgadraf@offratel.nc; f. 1986, reorganized 1989; acquisition and redistribution of land; Chair. Daniel Constantin; Dir-Gen. Louis Mapou.

Agence pour l'Emploi de Nouvelle Calédonie: 3 rue de la Somme, BP 497, 98845 Nouméa Cédex; tel. 281082; fax 272079; internet www.apenc.nc.

Conseil Economique et Social: 14 ave Georges Clemenceau, BP 4766, 98847 Nouméa Cédex; tel. 278517; fax 278509; e-mail ces@gouv.nc; represents trade unions and other organizations that are involved in the economic, social and cultural life of the Territory; Pres. Bernard Paul; Gen. Sec. Yolaine Elmour.

Institut Calédonien de Participation: Nouméa; f. 1989 to finance development projects and encourage the Kanak population to participate in the market economy.

CHAMBERS OF COMMERCE

Chambre d'Agriculture: 3 rue A. Desmazures, BP 111, 98845 Nouméa Cédex; tel. 243160; fax 284587; e-mail canc-gr@canl.nc; f. 1909; 33 mems; Pres. André Mazurier.

Chambre de Commerce et d'Industrie: 15 rue de Verdun, BP M3, 98849 Nouméa Cédex; tel. 243100; fax 243131; e-mail cci@cci.nc; internet www.cci.nc; f. 1879; 29 mems; Pres. Michel Quintard; Gen. Sec. Michel Merzeau.

Chambre des Métiers: 10 ave James Cook, BP 4186, 98846 Nouméa Cédex; tel. 282337; fax 282729.

STATE-OWNED INDUSTRIES

Société Minière du Sud Pacifique (SMSP): Nouméa; 87% owned by SOFINOR, 5% owned by SODIL; nickel-mining co; subsidiaries: Compagnie Maritime Calédonienne (CMC) (stevedoring), Nouméa Nickel, Nord Industrie Services, Nickel Mining Corporation (NMC), Bienvenue, San 3; Man. Dir André Dang Van Nha.

Société Le Nickel (SLN): Doniambo; tel. 245300; fax 275989; 60% owned by the Eramet group, privatized in 1999; nickel mining, processing and sales co; CEO Yves Rambaud; Man. Dir Philippe Vecten.

EMPLOYERS' ORGANIZATION

MEDEF Nouvelle-Calédonie/Fédération Patronale: Immeuble Jules Ferry, 1 rue de la Somme, BP 466, 98845 Nouméa Cédex; tel.

273525; fax 274037; e-mail fedepat@canl.nc; f. 1936; represents the leading companies of New Caledonia in the Defence of professional interests, co-ordination, documentation and research in socio-economic fields; Pres. OLIVIER RAZAVET; Sec.-Gen. FRANÇOIS PERONNET.

TRADE UNIONS

Confédération des Travailleurs Calédoniens: Nouméa; Sec.-Gen. R. JOYEUX; grouped with:

Fédération des Fonctionnaires: Nouméa; Sec.-Gen. GILBERT NOUVEAU.

Syndicat Général des Collaborateurs des Industries de Nouvelle Calédonie: Sec.-Gen. H. CHAMPIN.

Union Syndicale des Travailleurs Kanak et des Exploités (USTKE): BP 4372, Nouméa; tel. 277210; fax 277687; Leader LOUIS KOTRA UREGEÏ.

Union des Syndicats des Ouvriers et Employés de Nouvelle-Calédonie (USOENC): BP 2534, Vallée du Tir, Nouméa; tel. and fax 259640; e-mailc1vr@canl.nc; Sec.-Gen. DIDIER GUENANT-JEANSON.

Union Territoriale Force Ouvrière: 13 rue Jules Ferry, BP 4773, 98847 Nouméa; tel. 274950; fax 278202; e-mail utfonc98@ifrance.com; internet www.ifrance.com.fo98000; f. 1982; Sec.-Gen. JEAN-CLAUDE NÉGRE.

Transport

ROADS

In 1983 there was a total of 5,980 km of roads on New Caledonia island; 766 km were bitumen-surfaced, 589 km unsealed, 1,618 km stone-surfaced and 2,523 km tracks in 1980. The outer islands had a total of 470 km of roads and tracks in 1980.

SHIPPING

Most traffic is through the port of Nouméa. Passenger and cargo services, linking Nouméa to other towns and islands, are regular and frequent. There are plans to develop Nepoui, in the Province of the North, as a deep-water port and industrial centre.

Port Autonome de la Nouvelle-Calédonie: BP 14, 98845 Nouméa Cédex; tel. 255000; fax 275490; e-mail noumeaportnc@canl.nc; Port Man. PHILIPPE LAFLEUR; Harbour Master EDMUND MARTIN.

Compagnie Wallisienne de Navigation: BP 1080, Nouméa; tel. 283384; fax 287388; Chair. ARMAND BALLANDE; Man. Dir JEAN-YVES BOILEAU.

Somacal: BP 2099, 98846 Nouméa; tel. 273898; fax 259315.

CIVIL AVIATION

There is an international airport, Tontouta, 47 km from Nouméa, and an internal network, centred on Magenta airport, which provides air services linking Nouméa to other towns and islands. Air France operates a service four times a week between Nouméa and Paris via Tokyo, Air Calédonie International (AirCalin) operates two flights weekly from Nouméa to Osaka, two weekly flights to Sydney and Brisbane, and one weekly flight to Auckland and Papeete (French Polynesia) and AOM two flights weekly, from Paris to Nouméa via Sydney. Other airlines providing services to the island include Air New Zealand, Air Vanuatu and Qantas.

Air Calédonie: BP 212, Nouméa; tel. 250300; fax 254869; e-mail commercial@air-caledonie.nc; internet www.air-caledonie.nc; f. 1954; services throughout New Caledonia; 283,593 passengers carried in 1999/2000; Pres. and CEO OLIVIER RAZAVET.

Air Calédonie International (Aircalin): 8 rue Frédéric Surleau, BP 3736, 98846 Nouméa Cédex; tel. 265546; fax 272772; e-mail dg.aci@canl.nc; internet www.aircalin.nc/aci.htm; f. 1983; 62% owned by Territorial Govt; services to Sydney and Brisbane (Australia), Auckland (New Zealand), Nadi (Fiji), Papeete (French Polynesia), Wallis and Futuna Islands, Port Vila (Vanuatu) and Osaka and Tokyo (Japan); Chair. CHARLES LAVOIX; CEO JEAN-MICHEL MASSON.

Tourism

An investment programme was begun in 1985 with the aim of developing and promoting tourism. A total of 2,388 hotel rooms were available in 1999. In that year there were 99,735 visitors to New Caledonia, of whom 31.1% came from Japan, 29.6% from France, 14.6% from Australia and 7.1% from New Zealand. Tourist arrivals declined from 109,587 in 2000 to 100,515 in 2001. The industry earned US $111.8m. in 1998.

New Caledonia Tourism: Immeuble Nouméa-Centre, 20 rue Anatole France; BP 688, 98845 Nouméa Cédex; tel. 242080; fax 242070; e-mail tourisme@nouvellecaledonie-sud.com; internet www.newcaledoniatourism-sud.com; f. 1990; international promotion of tourism in New Caledonia; Chair. GABY BRIAULT; Dir JEAN-MICHEL FOUTREIN.

Defence

In August 2001 France was maintaining a force of 3,100 military personnel in New Caledonia, including a gendarmerie of 1,050.

Education

Education is compulsory for 10 years between six and 16 years of age. Schools are operated by both the State and churches, under the supervision of three Departments of Education: the Provincial department responsible for primary level education, the New Caledonian department responsible for primary level inspection, and the State department responsible for secondary level education. The French Government finances the state secondary system. Primary education begins at six years of age, and lasts for five years; secondary education, beginning at 11 years of age, comprises a first cycle of four years and a second, three-year cycle. In 2000 there were 81 pre-primary schools, and in 2001 there were 289 primary schools, and 64 secondary schools. In 1999 there were 19 technical and higher institutions (of which 11 were private). Some 400 students attend universities in France. In 1987 the French University of the Pacific (based in French Polynesia) was established, with a centre in Nouméa, and in 1999 it was divided into two universities. In 2000 the University of New Caledonia had 60 teachers and 1,600 students. Several other vocational tertiary education centres exist in New Caledonia. In 1989 the rate of adult illiteracy averaged 6.9% (males 6.0%, females 7.9%). According to UNESCO, total public expenditure on education in 1993 was 1,652m. French francs.

Kiribati

Physical and Social Geography

The Republic of Kiribati (pronounced 'Kir-a-bas') comprises one island and 32 atolls, in three principal groups, scattered over about 5m. sq km of ocean along the Equator and extending about 3,780 km from east to west and 2,050 km from north to south. The island of Banaba (Ocean Island), a solid coral outcrop 306 km to the east of Nauru, and the 16 Gilbert Islands lie in the west of Kiribati, with Tuvalu to the south and the Marshall Islands to the north. The eight Phoenix Islands, which are largely uninhabited, lie some 1,300 km south-east of the Gilbert group and to the north of Tokelau. In the east, Kiribati also comprises eight of the Line Islands (three others are uninhabited dependencies of the USA), including Kiritimati (Christmas Island), the largest coral atoll in the world, which covers 388 sq km (150 sq miles), or more than half of the total 717 sq km (277 sq miles) of dry land in Kiribati. Tahiti, French Polynesia, lies some 900 km to the south-east of the Line Islands.

Most of Kiribati has a maritime equatorial climate, the northern and southern islands being in the tropical zone. Temperature varies very little through the year, and the mean annual temperature ranges from 29°C (84°F) in the southern Gilberts to 27°C (81°F) in the Line Islands. There is a season of north-westerly trade winds from March to October and a season of rains and gales from October to March. Average annual rainfall varies greatly, averaging about 3,000 mm in the islands north of Tarawa, about 1,500 mm on Tarawa and for most of the Gilberts group, and 700 mm in the Line Islands. All the islands can suffer severe drought.

The population, which is mainly Micronesian and Christian, is concentrated in the Gilbert Islands. The principal languages are I-Kiribati (Gilbertese) and English. At the census of November 1995 there were 77,658 people in Kiribati. The total population increased to an estimated 91,985 at mid-2000. The capital is located on Bairiki island in Tarawa.

History

The I-Kiribati people first settled the islands of the Gilberts (or Tungaru) group between 1000 and 1300 AD. European contact began in the 16th century. In 1892 the United Kingdom established a protectorate over the 16 atolls of the Gilbert Islands and the nine Ellice Islands (now Tuvalu). The two groups were administered together under the jurisdiction of the Western Pacific High Commission (WPHC), which was based in Fiji until its removal to the British Solomon Islands (now Solomon Islands) in 1953. Phosphate-rich Ocean Island (Banaba), west of the Gilbert group, was annexed by the United Kingdom in 1900. The Gilbert and Ellice Islands were annexed in 1915, effective from January 1916, when the protectorate was declared a colony. Later in 1916 the new Gilbert and Ellice Islands Colony (GEIC) was extended to include Ocean Island and two of the Line Islands, far to the east. Christmas Island (now Kiritimati), another of the Line Islands, was added in 1919 and the eight Phoenix Islands (then uninhabited) in 1937. A joint British-US administration for two of the Phoenix group, Kanton (Canton) and Enderbury, was agreed in April 1939.

During the Second World War the GEIC was invaded by Japanese forces, who occupied the Gilbert Islands in 1942–43. Tarawa Atoll, in the Gilbert group, was the scene of some of the fiercest fighting in the Pacific between Japan and the USA.

As part of the British Government's programme of developing its own nuclear weapons, the first test of a British hydrogen bomb was conducted near Christmas Island in May 1957, when a device was exploded in the atmosphere. Two further tests took place in the same vicinity later that year.

Preparations for self-government in the GEIC began in 1963, and there were new Constitutions in 1967 (when an assembly containing elected representatives was first introduced) and in 1970. In January 1972 a Governor of the GEIC was appointed to assume almost all the functions previously exercised in the colony by the High Commissioner. At the same time the five uninhabited Central and Southern Line Islands, previously administered directly by the High Commissioner, became part of the GEIC. In May 1974 a House of Assembly, with 28 elected members and three official members, replaced the previous legislature. The House elected Naboua Ratieta as Chief Minister.

On 1 October 1975 the Ellice Islands were allowed to separate from the GEIC to form a distinct territory, named Tuvalu. The remainder of the GEIC was renamed the Gilbert Islands and the House of Assembly's membership was reduced.

In 1975 the British Government refused to recognize as legitimate a demand for independence by the people of Banaba, or Ocean Island, who had been in litigation with the British Government since 1971 over revenues derived from exports of phosphate. The discovery of the guano deposits on the 600 ha island was a prime motive in Britain's annexation of the island. Between 1920 and 1979 the British Phosphate Commission (BPC), a consortium of the British, Australian and New Zealand Governments, mined phosphate for use as a fertilizer in Australia and New Zealand. Open-cast mining so adversely affected the island's environment that most Banabans were removed from the island during the Second World War and resettled on Rabi Island, 2,600 km away in the Fiji group, becoming citizens of Fiji in 1970. Banabans remain the landowners of Banaba.

The Banabans rejected the British Government's argument that phosphate revenues should be distributed over the whole Gilbert Islands group and in 1973, despite winning 50% of the revenues, continued with litigation. They claimed unpaid royalties from the British Government and damages for the destruction of the island's environment against both the Government and the BPC. The Banabans took these two cases to the British High Court in London. In 1976, after a lengthy hearing, their claim for royalties was dismissed but that for damages upheld. In May 1977 the British Government offered them an *ex gratia* payment of $A10m. without admitting liability for damages and on condition that no further judicial appeal would be made. The offer was not accepted.

The Gilbert Islands obtained internal self-government on 1 January 1977. Later that year the number of elected members in the House of Assembly was increased to 36. This was subsequently adjusted to 35, with the remaining seat to be filled by a nominee of the Rabi Council of Leaders. Following a general election in February 1978, Ieremia Tabai, Leader of the Opposition in the previous House of Assembly, was elected Chief Minister in March. On 12 July 1979 the Gilbert Islands became an independent republic, within the Commonwealth, under the name of Kiribati. The country did not become a member of the UN (owing to financial considerations). The House of Assembly was renamed the Maneaba ni Maungatabu, and Ieremia Tabai became the country's first President (Beretitenti). In September Kiribati signed a treaty of friendship with the USA, which relinquished its claim to the Line and Phoenix Islands, including Kanton and Enderbury. In April 1981 the Banaban community on Rabi accepted the British Government's earlier *ex gratia* offer of $A10m. in compensation together with the interest accrued ($A14.58m. in total), although they continued to seek self-government.

The first general election since independence began in March 1982, with a second round of voting in April. The members of the new Maneaba all sat as independents. President Tabai was re-elected in May. However, the Government resigned in December, following the Maneaba's second rejection of proposals to increase salaries for civil servants. As a result, the Maneaba was dissolved, and another general election took place in January 1983. President Tabai was again re-elected in February 1983. Following a general election in March 1987, Tabai was re-elected for a fourth term in May. At a general election in May 1991 eight incumbent members of the Maneaba lost their seats. A presidential election was held in July, when the former Vice-President, Teatao Teannaki, narrowly defeated Roniti Teiwaki to replace Tabai, who had served the maximum period in office permitted by the Constitution.

In January 1992 the Maneaba approved an opposition motion urging the Government to seek compensation from Japan for damage caused during the Second World War. The motion, which had been presented to previous sessions of the legislature, was thought to have been prompted by the success of a similar claim by the Marshall Islands. The intention to pursue a compensation claim against the Japanese was reiterated by President Teburoro Tito in late 1994.

In May 1994 the Government was defeated on a motion of confidence, following opposition allegations that government ministers had misused travel allowances. As a result of the vote, the Maneaba was dissolved, and at legislative elections in July five cabinet ministers lost their seats. Thirteen of the newly-elected members were supporters of the opposition Maneaban Te Mauri, while only eight were known to support the previously dominant National Progressive Party grouping. At the presidential election in September Teburoro Tito was the successful candidate, receiving 51.1% of the total votes. The new President declared that reducing Kiribati's dependence on foreign aid would be a major objective for his Government. He also announced his intention to pursue civil and criminal action against members of the previous Government for alleged misuse of public funds while in office.

In 1995 a committee was created with the aim of assessing public opinion regarding possible amendments to the Constitution. In March 1998 more than 200 delegates attended a Constitutional Review Convention in Bairiki to consider the committee's recommendations, which included equalizing the status of men and women regarding the citizenship rights of foreigners marrying I-Kiribati and changing to the structure of the Council of State. Leaders of the Banaban community in Rabi, Fiji, were also consulted during 1998 as part of the review process.

A general election, held on 23 September 1998 and contested by a record 191 candidates, failed to produce a conclusive result, necessitating a second round of voting, at which the Government and opposition each lost seven seats. At a presidential election on 27 November Tito was re-elected with 52.3% of total votes cast, defeating Dr Harry Tong, who obtained 45.8% of votes, and Ambreroti Nikora, with 1.8%.

In late 1999 concerns were expressed by a Pacific media organization after a New Zealand journalist working for Agence France-Presse was banned from entering Kiribati. The Kiribati Government claimed that a series of articles by the correspondent, unfavourable to Kiribati, which had been published in a regional magazine, were biased and sensationalist. In December former President Ieremia Tabai and Atiera Tetoa, a former member of the Maneaba, were fined, having been convicted of importing telecommunications equipment without a permit. They had launched Newair FM, an independent commercial radio station, 12 months previously; it had been immediately suspended and a criminal investigation was instigated by the police. Tabai subsequently established Kiribati's first private newspaper, the *Kiribati Newstar*, in an attempt to reduce the Government's control over the media in the islands. Its first published edition appropriately coincided with Media Freedom Week in May 2000.

In November 2000 the Vice-President and Minister for Home Affairs and Rural Development, Tewarika Tentoa, collapsed while addressing the Maneaba and died. The post of Vice-President was subsequently combined with the cabinet portfolio of finance and economic planning.

Reports that Palmyra Atoll (an uninhabited US territory some 200 km north of Kiribati's northern Line Islands) was to be sold and used by a US company for the storage of nuclear waste led the Maneaba to pass a unanimous resolution in May 1996 urging the Government to convey the islanders' concerns over the proposals to the US Government. The islanders' anxieties centred largely on Palmyra's geographical proximity to Kiribati, coupled with the belief that the atoll's fragility and porous structure make it an unstable environment for the storage of highly toxic materials. In June Kiribati formally requested that the US Government veto the proposals. In November 2000 Palmyra was purchased by The Nature Conservancy, a conservation group that planned to preserve the natural state of the atoll.

In April 1999 the Kiribati Government announced its desire to acquire Baker, Howland, and Jarvis Islands (see p. 1143) from the USA, because of the economic value of their fish resources. In mid-1999 there was some controversy over the renamed Millennium island (previously Caroline Island). The island had been renamed in 1997 in an attempt to market it as a tourist destination for the coming year 2000. In 1994 Kiribati moved the international date-line to incorporate the Line and Phoenix Island groups (including Millennium Island) in the same time zone as the Gilbert group, thus creating a large eastward projection in the date-line. Millennium Island's position as the first place to celebrate the New Year was subsequently confirmed. In early 2000, however, opposition politicians severely criticized the Government for failing to attract the predicted number of tourists to the islands' millennium celebrations, despite expenditure of more than $A1m.

In 1995 Kiribati suspended its diplomatic relations with France in protest at the French Government's decision to renew nuclear-weapons testing at Mururoa Atoll. Kiribati was admitted to the UN in September 1999.

Owing to the territory's high rate of population growth (more than 2% per year) and, in particular, the situation of over-population on South Tarawa and its associated social and economic problems, it was announced in 1988 that nearly 5,000 inhabitants were to be resettled on outlying atolls, mainly in the Line Islands. The migration began in 1989. A further programme of resettlement from South Tarawa to five islands in the Phoenix group was initiated in 1995.

A Chinese satellite-tracking station was opened on South Tarawa in late 1997. Sea Launch, a US consortium led by the Boeing Commercial Space Company, also announced plans to undertake a rocket-launching project from a converted oil-rig near the islands. The facility began operations in March 1999, when a prototype satellite was launched. It seemed unlikely, however, that Kiribati would benefit financially from the proposed project, as the consortium had controversially sought to carry out its activities in international waters near the outer limits of the islands' exclusive economic zone. The US authorities dismissed environmental concerns about the negative impact of the site (particularly the dumping of large quantities of waste fuel in the islands' waters), which were expressed both by the Government of Kiribati and the South Pacific Regional Environmental Programme in mid-1998. These fears were compounded in March 2000 after a rocket launched from the site crashed and, furthermore, Sea Launch refused to disclose where it had landed. In November 1999 it was announced that the Government of Kiribati and the National Space Development Agency of Japan had reached agreement on the proposed establishment of a space-vehicle launching and landing facility on Kiritimati. In the following year the Japanese organization was also given permission by the Kiribati Government to use land and runway facilities on the island, free of charge, until 2020 and to construct a 100–150-room hotel.

Kiribati is a member of the Pacific Islands Forum (formerly the South Pacific Forum), which expressed concern about the threat of the 'greenhouse effect' (the heating of the earth's atmosphere and a resultant rise in sea-level, as a consequence of pollution) in 1988. In 1989 a UN report on the 'greenhouse effect' listed Kiribati as one of the countries that would completely disappear in the 21st century unless drastic action were taken. None of the land on the islands is more than two metres above sea-level. A rise in sea-level would not only cause flooding, but would also upset the balance between sea and fresh water (below the coral sands), rendering water supplies undrinkable. In mid-1999 it was announced that two uninhabited coral reefs had sunk beneath the sea as a result of the 'greenhouse effect'. In late 1997 President Tito strongly criticized the Australian Government's refusal, at the Conference of the Parties to the Framework Convention on Climate Change (see UN Environment Programme) in Kyoto, Japan, to reduce its emission of gases known to contribute to the 'greenhouse effect'.

As a result of discussions held at the Pacific Islands Forum summit meeting in Kiribati in October 2000, Japan announced that it was willing to negotiate compensation claims with the islanders for damage caused during the Second World War. Furthermore, a six-day visit by President Tito to Japan in February 2001 resulted in a number of informal agreements aimed at enhancing relations between the two countries. These included a decision to try to resolve a dispute over tuna fishing, caused by Japan's refusal to sign a convention aimed at protecting tuna stocks in the central and western Pacific Ocean and agreements to address their differences over whaling and nuclear-fuel shipments. Tito also appeared to modify his position on nuclear energy following the visit to Japan, stating that emissions of harmful 'greenhouse gases' could be reduced by replacing fossil with nuclear fuel. In April 2001 the USA's decision to reject the Kyoto Protocol to the UN's Framework Convention on Climate Change was widely criticized. In March 2002 Kiribati, Tuvalu and the Maldives announced their decision to take legal action against the USA for its refusal to sign the Kyoto Protocol.

In September 2001 Kiribati discussed with the Australian Government the possibility of establishing an offshore refugee-processing centre, in exchange for financial aid (see the chapter on Nauru). It was envisaged that Kanton Atoll might house up to 500 asylum-seekers; however negotiations collapsed in late November, reportedly owing to logistical reasons.

Economy

Until 1979 phosphate rock, derived from rich deposits of guano, was mined on Banaba by the British Phosphate Commission for export to Australia and New Zealand, where it was used for fertilizer. The ending of phosphate production had a devastating effect on the economy, as receipts from phosphates had accounted, on average, for about 80% of total export earnings and 50% of government taxation revenue. The investment of some phosphate earnings from 1956 did result in a considerable fund of foreign reserves, which have been maintained since 1979. In May 1998 the value of the Revenue Equalization Reserve Fund (RERF) was $A511m. The RERF has provided the Government with investment income equivalent to around 33% of gross domestic product (GDP) per year. In 2001 the Asian Development Bank (ADB) estimated that the value of the RERF was such that Kiribati had sufficient foreign reserves for 10 years' worth of imports. It was estimated that, owing to the cessation of phosphate mining, the country's gross domestic product (GDP) per head was halved between the late 1970s and early 1980s.

In 2000, according to estimates by the World Bank, Kiribati's gross national product (GNP), measured at average 1998–2000 prices, was US $85.9m., equivalent to US $950 per head. During 1990–2000, it was estimated, GNP per head decreased, in real terms, at an average annual rate of 1.0%. Over the same period the population increased by an average of 2.3% per year. Kiribati's GDP increased, in real terms, by an estimated average of 2.4% per year in 1990–2000. Real GDP, according to revised estimates by the ADB, expanded by 6.2% in 1999 and by 0.2% in 2000.

Most islanders participate in subsistence activities, although agriculture and fishing engaged only 6.2% of those in paid employment in 1995. Apart from Banaba, Kiribati is composed of coral atolls with poor quality soil. Most of them are covered with coconut palms, which provide the only agricultural export in the form of copra. A government-owned company operates a coconut plantation on Kiritimati, and there are commercial plantations on two other atolls in the Line Islands. Production of copra, however, declined to 6,133 metric tons in 2000 from 11,776 tons in 1999. In the latter year, according to the ADB, exports of the commodity earned almost $A9.0m. (equivalent to 63.9% of total domestic export revenue). According to official figures, agriculture (including fishing), which employs the majority of the working population, contributed an estimated 8.2% of monetary GDP in 2000. Bananas, screw-pine (*Pandanus*), breadfruit and papaya are cultivated as food crops. The cultivation of seaweed began on Tabuaeran in the mid-1980s: seaweed provided an estimated 8.5% of domestic export earnings in 1999. Pigs and chickens are kept. According to the ADB, agricultural GDP rose by an estimated 8.8% in 1999 and by 7.9% in 2000.

As a result of various development projects, the fishing sector's contribution to the country's GDP trebled between 1979 and 1984. The significance of fishing to the economy, however, drastically declined thereafter, and the closure of the state fishing company was announced in 1991. Fish provided only 2.4% of export earnings in 1999 (compared with 46.2% in 1990). Nevertheless, pet fish have become a significant commodity, contributing 13.6% of export earnings in 1999. The sale of fishing licences to foreign fleets (notably from South Korea, Japan, Taiwan and the USA) provides an important source of income. Spain purchased a 12-month licence for 14 vessels in early 2000, and in the same year the European Union (EU) indicated its interest in negotiating a bilateral tuna agreement with Kiribati. An agreement was signed with the People's Republic of China in September 2001 licensing four vessels belonging to a Chinese company to fish in Kiribati waters. Revenue from the sale of fishing licences increased from 1996, when the Government increased their cost in response to the continued illegal operations of foreign vessels, which was noticeable in the following year's fishing licence revenues of $A28m. Income from this source rose from an estimated $A12.8m. in 1999 (uncharacteristically low as a result of unfavourable climatic conditions) to reach US $22m. in 2001. According to official figures, GDP of the agriculture, fishing and seaweed sectors increased at an average annual rate of 0.8% in 1991–2000.

Industry (including manufacturing, construction and power) contributed an estimated 6.0% of monetary GDP in 2000. The sector employed 38.9% of the work-force in 1995. Industrial GDP increased by an average of 0.5% per year in 1991–2000. Compared with the previous year, industrial GDP was estimated by the ADB to have expanded by 38.0% in 1999, but declined by 32.4% in 2000. The production of solar-evaporated salt for export to Hawaii, Fiji, Guam, American Samoa and Samoa (for use on fishing vessels with brine refrigeration systems) began on Kiritimati in 1985. A small industrial centre was established on Betio, with British aid, in 1990. Manufacturers based there produce garments, footwear, furniture, leather goods and kamaimai (a toddy condensed from coconut). Construction of a new copra mill, near Betio port, began in March 2002. The project, in partnership with Australian company Techso, was to extend copra production to the outer islands and produce oils and soaps for both local and international markets. Manufacturing contributed an estimated 1.0% of monetary GDP in 2000. Manufacturing GDP increased by an annual average of 5.6% in 1991–2000. In 2000, compared with the previous year, the GDP of the manufacturing sector contracted by an estimated 42.1%, in contrast to the 51.2% increase recorded in 1999.

Production of electrical energy declined from 14.5m. kWh in 2000 to 12.6m. kWh in 2001. Mineral fuels accounted for an estimated 10.3% of total import costs in 1999. In August 2001 the EU announced that it planned to fund the introduction of 1,500 new solar energy systems, valued at more than $A6m., to Kiribati.

Services provided 85.8% of monetary GDP in 2000. Tourism makes a significant contribution to the economy: the trade and hotels sector provided an estimated 16.6% of GDP in 2000. The GDP of the trade and hotels sector increased by an annual average of 4.2% in 1990–98. The services sector employed 87.4% of the workforce in 1995. Tourist arrivals at Tarawa and Kiritimati rose from 3,112 in 1999 to 4,829 in 2000, in which year receipts from tourism reached $A2.2m. Kiribati's tourist sector was boosted in February 2001 when the Government signed an agreement with a major cruise line, which agreed to include the island in its cruise ship itinerary. Up to 10 ships per year were expected to visit the island, with each visit generating around US $15,000 for the local economy. In December 2001 the Government announced its decision to lease an aircraft which it intended to operate from Tarawa to the Marshall Islands, Tuvalu and Fiji. Air Nauru, meanwhile, provided Kiribati's only air links to Nauru and Fiji, but suspended its services in June, July and November 2001. The GDP of the services sector increased at an annual average rate of 5.1% in 1991–2000. According to revised estimates from the ADB, the services sector's GDP increased by 3.9% in 1999 and by 2.4% in 2000.

Kiribati recorded a trade deficit of an estimated $A44.3m., and a surplus of $A29.5m. on the current account of the balance of payments in 2000. In that year Kiribati's trade deficit narrowed to 56.7% of GDP, as a decline in income from copra exports was more than offset by a fall in imports. The major imports in 1999 were food and live animals, machinery and transport equipment, manufactures, mineral fuels, beverages and tobacco, and chemicals. The major domestic exports were copra, pet fish and seaweed. In 2001 the value of exports rose to US $39.7m., while imports increased to US $65.7m. In that year the principal sources of imports were Australia (25.1%), Poland (16.4%) and Fiji (15.5%). The principal recipients of exports in that year were Japan (44.4%) and Thailand (24.0%).

In 2000 Kiribati recorded an overall budget deficit of $A3.0m. In 2001 the fiscal deficit increased sharply, to reach the equivalent of 37.5% of GDP. Budgetary expenditure for 2002, announced in December 2001, was projected at $A77.9m., 15% less than the revised estimates for 2001, and required a drawdown of $A16.7m. from the RERF. Kiribati's total external debt in 1999 was estimated by the ADB at US $9m., and the cost of debt-servicing was equivalent to 7.6% of revenue from exports of goods and services. The annual rate of inflation averaged 3.1% in 1990–2000. Consumer prices increased by an annual average of only 0.4% in 2000, but rose by 8.8% in 2001. About 2.8% of the labour force were unemployed in 1990. Only around 8,600 people, equivalent to less than 20% of the working-age population, were formally employed in 2001.

Kiribati became a member of the Asian Development Bank (ADB) in 1974. In 1986 Kiribati joined the International Monetary Fund (IMF). Following negotiations held in the same year at the Government's request, Kiribati was placed on the UN list of least developed countries, a status that attracts concessional loans from the World Bank and the IMF, and renders the country's exports eligible for special tariff rates. Kiribati is an associate member of the UN Economic and Social Commission for Asia and the Pacific (ESCAP). The republic is also a member of the South Pacific Forum and of the Pacific Community (formerly the South Pacific Commission). It is a signatory of the South Pacific Regional Trade and Economic Co-operation Agreement (SPARTECA) and of the Lomé Conventions and successor Cotonou Agreement with the EU. In early 1996 Kiribati joined representatives of the other countries and territories of Micronesia at a meeting in Hawaii, at which a new regional organization, the Council of Micronesian Government Executives, was established. The new body aimed to facilitate discussion on economic developments in the region and to examine possibilities for reducing the considerable cost of shipping essential goods between the islands.

According to UN criteria, Kiribati is one of the world's least-developed nations. The islands' vulnerability to adverse climatic conditions was illustrated in early 1999 when a state of national emergency was declared following a prolonged period of severe drought. Kiribati's extremely limited export base and dependence on imports of almost all essential commodities result in a permanent (and widening) trade deficit, which is in most years only partially offset by revenue from fishing licence fees, interest earned on the RERF and remittances from I-Kiribati working overseas. Although the value of the RERF had trebled within 10 years, the fund then declined in value in 2001 as a result of the downturn in world stock markets (its assets being invested in offshore markets). The country is reliant on foreign assistance for its development budget. Grants from principal donors amounted to an estimated $A31.0m. in 1998, of which $A8.5m. was from Japan, $A6.8m. from Australia, and $A6.5m. from New Zealand. In 2001/02 New Zealand provided $NZ3.1m. and Australia $A10.7m. in development assistance. Dependence on external finance is widely regarded as having left Kiribati vulnerable to foreign exploitation. Moreover, concern has been expressed that, although foreign companies specializing in advanced technology (particularly telecommunications and satellite systems) are seeking to establish operations in the islands, Kiribati will not benefit significantly from the major investment involved in such projects. In 2000 the Government generated some US $400,000 of revenue through the sale of I-Kiribati passports to investors in the islands. Further passport sales in 2001 were worth US $375,000 and, combined with sales of Kiribati Residential Permits, produced more than $A2.5m. in revenue. The Government's policy of subsidizing copra producers following a fall in world prices of the commodity, however, had a negative impact on the economy; in 2001 these subsidies totalled $A2m. Having contracted in 2000, the economy recovered in 2001, largely as a result of a substantial increase in recurrent government expenditure, an improvement in copra production and the implementation of various development projects. The Government's National Development Strategy for 2000–03 sought to reform the public sector and promote private-sector development. Investors have in the past been deterred by the country's weak banking system and shortage of investment opportunities. It was estimated in 2001 that around 75% of capital belonging to Kiribati's companies and private citizens was invested abroad. The new proposals were intended to encourage greater investment in the country's private sector, which would allow the creation of jobs and the broadening of the islands' narrow base of exports.

Statistical Survey

Source (unless otherwise stated): Statistics Office, Ministry of Finance and Economic Planning, POB 67, Bairiki, Tarawa; tel. 21082; fax 21307.

AREA AND POPULATION

Area: 810.5 sq km (312.9 sq miles). *Principal atolls* (sq km): Banaba (island) 6.29; Tarawa 31.02 (North 15.26, South 15.76); Abemama 27.37; Tabiteuea 37.63 (North 25.78, South 11.85); Total Gilbert group (incl. others) 285.52; Kanton (Phoenix Is) 9.15; Teraina (Fanning) 33.73; Kiritimati (Christmas—Line Is) 388.39.

Population: 77,658 at census of 7 November 1995; 84,494 (males 41,646, females 42,848) at census of 7 November 2000. *Principal atolls* (2000): Banaba (island) 276; Abaiang 5,794; Tarawa 41,194 (North 4,477, South—including Bairiki, the capital—36,717); Tabiteuea 4,582 (North 3,365, South 1,217); Total Gilbert group (incl. others) 78,158; Kanton (Phoenix Is) 61; Kiritimati 3,431; Total Line and Phoenix Is (incl. others) 6,336.

Density (November 2000): 104.2 per sq km.

Ethnic Groups (census of 2000): Micronesians 83,452; Polynesians 641; Europeans 154; Others 247; Total 84,494.

Births, Marriages and Deaths: Registered live births (1996) 2,299 (birth rate 29.5 per 1,000); Marriages (registrations, 1988) 352 (marriage rate 5.2 per 1,000); Death rate (estimate, 1995) 7 per 1,000.

Expectation of Life (WHO estimates, years at birth, 2000): Males 60.4; Females 64.5. Source: WHO, *World Health Report*.

Employment (paid employees, 1995, provisional): Agriculture, hunting, forestry and fishing 487; Manufacturing 104; Electricity, gas and water 182; Construction 215; Trade, restaurants and hotels 1,026; Transport, storage and communications 710; Financing, insurance real estate and business services 349; Community, social and personal services 4,778; Total employed 7,848. Source: UN, *Statistical Yearbook for Asia and the Pacific*.

HEALTH AND WELFARE

Key Indicators

Fertility (births per woman, 2000): 4.6.

Under-5 Mortality Rate (per 1,000 live births, 2000): 70.

Physicians (per 1,000 head, 1998): 0.30.

Hospital Beds (per 1,000 head, 1990): 4.27.

Health Expenditure (1998): US $ per head (PPP): 138.
% of GDP: 8.4.
public (% of total): 99.2.

Access to Water (% of persons, 2000): 47.

Access to Sanitation (% of persons, 2000): 48.

For sources and definitions, see explanatory note on p. vi.

AGRICULTURE, ETC.

Principal Crops ('000 metric tons, 2000): Taro (Coco yam) 1.6*; Other roots and tubers 7.2*; Coconuts 76.8; Vegetables 5.5*; Bananas 4.5; Other fruits 1.2*. * FAO estimate.

Livestock ('000 head, year ending September 2000): Pigs 12 (FAO estimate); Poultry 365 (unofficial figure). Source: FAO.

Livestock Products (metric tons, 2001): Pig meat 1,360; Poultry meat 391; Hen eggs 210 (FAO estimate). Source: FAO.

Fishing ('000 metric tons, live weight, 1999): Capture 48.2 (Snappers 1.5; Percoids 24.6, Flyingfishes 2.5, Jacks and crevalles 1.9, Skipjack tuna 3.1, Sharks, rays, skates, etc. 3.0); Aquaculture 0.0; Total catch 48.2. Figures exclude aquatic plants ('000 metric tons): 9.4 (all aquaculture). Source: FAO, *Yearbook of Fishery Statistics*.

INDUSTRY

Copra Production (metric tons): 11,368 in 1998; 11,776 in 1999; 6,133 in 2000.

Electric Energy (million kWh): 12.9 in 1999; 14.5 in 2000; 12.6 in 2001.

FINANCE

Currency and Exchange Rates: Australian currency: 100 cents = 1 Australian dollar ($A). *Sterling, US Dollar and Euro Equivalents* (31 May 2002): £1 sterling = $A2.5849; US $1 = $A1.7624; €1 = $A1.6544; $A100 = £38.69 = US $56.74 = €60.45. *Average Exchange Rate* (US $ per Australian dollar): 0.6453 in 1999; 0.5823 in 2000; 0.5176 in 2001.

Budget ($A million, 2000): *Revenue:* Tax revenue 18.7 (Corporate tax 4.7, Import duties 13.9); Other current revenue 42.6 (Fishing licence fees 31.2, Fees and incidental sales 5.8); Capital revenue 0.0; Total 61.3. *Expenditure:* General public services 7.0; Public order and safety 4.7; Education 12.8; Health 8.8; Welfare and environment 1.1; Community amenities 1.5; Agriculture and fishing 2.3; Construction 1.9; Communication 1.7; Commerce 0.7; Labour affairs 1.7; Others 20.0; Total 64.3 (Current 53.9, Capital 10.4).

Cost of Living (Consumer Price Index for Tarawa; base: 1996 = 100): 107.5 in 1999; 107.9 in 2000; 114.3 in 2001.

Expenditure on the Gross Domestic Product ($A '000 at current prices, 1992): Government final consumption expenditure 25,039; Private final consumption expenditure 31,592; Increase in stocks 250; Gross fixed capital formation 25,750; *Total domestic expenditure* 82,631; Exports of goods and services 5,798; *Less* Imports of goods and services 52,625; Statistical discrepancy 10,456; *GDP in purchasers' values* 46,260. Source: UN, *Statistical Yearbook for Asia and the Pacific*.

Gross Domestic Product by Economic Activity ($A million at current prices, 2000): Agriculture 2.4; Fishing 2.6; Manufacturing 0.6; Electricity 0.9; Construction 2.2; Trade, hotels and bars 10.1; Transport and communications 8.5; Finance 3.5; Real estate 1.9; Government administration 25.6; Community and social services 2.6; *Sub-total* 60.8; *Less* Imputed bank service charge 3.1; *GDP at factor cost* 57.7; Indirect taxes *less* subsidies 14.0; *GDP in purchasers' values* 71.7. Figures exclude non-monetary GDP (6.4).

Balance of Payments (estimates, US $ million, 2001): *Trade balance* –27.6; Exports of services and income 39.3; Imports of services and income –21.5; *Balance on goods, services and income* –9.8; Current transfers received 13.0; Current transfers paid –1.4; *Current balance* 1.7; Capital account (net) 3.6; Direct investment (net) –0.5; Portfolio investment –5.7; *Overall balance* –0.9. Source: Asian Development Bank, *Key Indicators of Developing Asian and Pacific Countries*.

EXTERNAL TRADE

Principal Commodities (estimates, $A million, 1999): *Imports f.o.b.:* Food and live animals 18.0; Beverages and tobacco 4.9; Mineral fuels, lubricants, etc. 6.6; Chemicals 2.8; Basic manufactures 9.6; Machinery and transport equipment 14.4; Miscellaneous manufactured articles 4.6; Total (incl. others) 63.7. *Exports f.o.b.:* Copra 9.0; Seaweed 1.1; Pet fish 1.8; Total (incl. others) 13.0 (excl. re-exports 1.0).

Principal Trading Partners (US $ million, 2001): *Imports:* Australia 16.5; China, People's Republic 1.4; Cyprus 3.7; Fiji 10.2; Japan 5.5; New Zealand 1.4; Poland 10.8; USA 6.5; Total (incl. others) 65.7. *Exports* (incl. re-exports): Bangladesh 3.6; Brazil 1.2; Japan 17.6; Korea, Republic 4.1; Poland 0.8; Thailand 9.5; USA 1.1; Total (incl. others) 39.7. Source: Asian Development Bank, *Key Indicators of Developing Asian and Pacific Countries*.

TRANSPORT

Road Traffic (motor vehicles registered on South Tarawa, 2000): Motor cycles 702; Passenger cars 477; Buses 10; Trucks 267; Minibuses 392; Others 13; Total 1,861.

Shipping: *Merchant Fleet* (registered, at 31 December 2001): 8 vessels; total displacement 4,198 grt. Source: Lloyd's Register-Fairplay, *World Fleet Statistics*. *International sea-borne freight traffic* ('000 metric tons, 1990): Goods loaded 15; Goods unloaded 26. Source: UN, *Monthly Bulletin of Statistics*.

Civil Aviation (traffic on scheduled services, 1998): Passengers carried 28,000; Passenger-km 11 million. Source: UN, *Statistical Yearbook*.

TOURISM

Foreign Tourist Arrivals (at Tarawa and Kiritimati): 5,683 in 1998; 3,112 in 1999; 4,829 in 2000.

Tourism Receipts ($A million): 2.0 in 1998; 2.1 in 1999; 2.2 in 2000.

COMMUNICATIONS MEDIA

Radio Receivers (1997): 17,000 in use.

Television Receivers (1997): 1,000 in use.

Telephones (main lines in use, 2000): 3,353.

Facsimile Machines (1996): 200 in use.

Mobile Cellular Telephones (subscribers, 2000): 395.

Personal Computers ('000 in use, 2001): 2.

Internet Users ('000, 2001): 2.

Non-daily Newspapers (2002): 2; estimated circulation 3,600.

Sources: UNESCO, *Statistical Yearbook*; UN, *Statistical Yearbook*; International Telecommunication Union; Australian Press Council.

EDUCATION

Primary (2001): 88 schools; 16,096 students; 627 teachers.

Junior Secondary (2001): 19 schools; 5,743 students; 324 teachers.

Secondary (2001): 14 schools; 5,743 students; 324 teachers.

Teacher-training (2001): 198 students; 22 teachers.

Vocational (2001): 1,303 students; 17 teachers.

Adult literacy rate (UNESCO estimates): 92.5% (males 93%; females 92%) in 2001. Source: UNESCO, *Assessment of Resources, Best Practices and Gaps in Gender, Science and Technology in Kiribati.*

Directory

The Constitution

A new Constitution was promulgated at independence on 12 July 1979. The main provisions are as follows:

The Constitution states that Kiribati is a sovereign democratic Republic and that the Constitution is the supreme law. It guarantees protection of all fundamental rights and freedoms of the individual and provides for the determination of citizenship.

The President, known as the Beretitenti, is Head of State and Head of the Government and presides over the Cabinet which consists of the Beretitenti, the Kauoman-ni-Beretitenti (Vice-President), the Attorney-General and not more than eight other ministers appointed by the Beretitenti from an elected parliament known as the Maneaba ni Maungatabu. The Constitution provided that the pre-independence Chief Minister became the first Beretitenti, but that in future the Beretitenti would be elected. After each general election for the Maneaba, the chamber nominates, from among its members, three or four candidates from whom the Beretitenti is elected by universal adult suffrage. Executive authority is vested in the Cabinet, which is directly responsible to the Maneaba ni Maungatabu. The Constitution also provides for a Council of State consisting of the Chairman of the Public Services Commission, the Chief Justice and the Speaker of the Maneaba.

Legislative power resides with the single-chamber Maneaba ni Maungatabu, composed of 39 members elected by universal adult suffrage for four years (subject to dissolution), one nominated member (see below) and the Attorney-General as an *ex-officio* member if he is not elected. The Maneaba is presided over by the Speaker, who is elected by the Maneaba from among persons who are not members of the Maneaba.

One chapter makes special provision for Banaba and the Banabans, stating that one seat in the Maneaba is reserved for a nominated member of the Banaban community. The Banabans' inalienable right to enter and reside in Banaba is guaranteed and, where any right over or interest in land there has been acquired by the Republic of Kiribati or by the Crown before independence, the Republic is required to hand back the land on completion of phosphate extraction. A Banaba Island Council is provided for, as is an independent commission of inquiry to review the provisions relating to Banaba.

The Constitution also makes provision for finance, for a Public Service and for an independent judiciary (see Judicial System).

The Government

HEAD OF STATE

President (Beretitenti): TEBURORO TITO (elected 30 September 1994; re-elected 27 November 1998).

Vice-President (Kauoman-ni-Beretitenti): BENIAMINA TIINGA.

THE CABINET
(September 2002)

President and Minister of Foreign Affairs: TEBURORO TITO.

Vice-President and Minister of Finance and Economic Planning: BENIAMINA TIINGA.

Minister of Home Affairs and Rural Development: NATANAERA KIRATA.

Minister of Education, Training and Technology: TEAMBO KEARIKI.

Minister of Information, Communications and Transport: WILLIE TOKATAAKE.

Minister of Commerce, Industry and Tourism: MOTETI KAKOROA.

Minister of Labour, Employment and Co-operatives: TEIRAOI TETABEA.

Minister of Works and Energy: TEAIWA TENIOU.

Minister of the Environment and Social Development: KATAOTIKA TEKEE.

Minister of Health and Family Planning: BARANIKO MOOA.

Minister of Line and Phoenix Development: MANRAOI KAIEA.

Minister of Natural Resources Development: TIIM TAEKITI.

Attorney-General: MICHAEL TAKABWEBWE.

MINISTRIES

Office of the President (Beretitenti): POB 68, Bairiki, Tarawa; tel. 21183; fax 21145.

Ministry of Commerce, Industry and Tourism: POB 510, Betio, Tarawa; tel. 26158/26157; fax 26233; e-mail commerce@tskl.net.ki.

Ministry of Education, Training and Technology: POB 263, Bikenibeu, Tarawa; tel. 28091/28033; fax 28222.

Ministry of the Environment and Social Development: POB 234, Bikenibeu, Tarawa; tel. 28211/28071; fax 28334.

Ministry of Finance and Economic Planning: POB 67, Bairiki, Tarawa; tel. 21802/21805; fax 21307.

Ministry of Foreign Affairs: POB 68, Bairiki, Tarawa; tel. 21342; fax 21466; e-mail mfa@tskl.net.ki.

Ministry of Health and Family Planning: POB 268, Bikenibeu, Tarawa; tel. 28100; fax 28152.

Ministry of Home Affairs and Rural Development: POB 75, Bairiki, Tarawa; tel. 21092; fax 21133; e-mail homeaffairs@tskl.net.ki.

Ministry of Information, Communications and Transport: POB 487, Betio, Tarawa; tel. 26003/26435; fax 26193.

Ministry of Labour, Employment and Co-operatives: POB 69, Bairiki, Tarawa; tel. 21068/21071; fax 21452.

Ministry of Line and Phoenix Development: Kiritimati Island; tel. 21449/81213; fax 81278.

Ministry of Natural Resources Development: POB 64, Bairiki, Tarawa; tel. 21099; fax 21120.

Ministry of Works and Energy: POB 498, Betio, Tarawa; tel. 26192; fax 26172.

President and Legislature

PRESIDENT

Election, 27 November 1998

Candidate	Votes	%
Teburoro Tito	13,309	52.33
Harry Tong	11,658	45.84
Ambreroti Nikora	465	1.83
Total	25,432	100.0

MANEABA NI MAUNGATABU
(House of Assembly)

This is a unicameral body comprising 39 elected members (most of whom formally present themselves for election as independent candidates), and one nominated representative of the Banaban community. A general election was held on 23 and 30 September 1998.

Speaker: TEKIREE TAMUERA.

Political Organizations

There are no organized political parties in Kiribati. However, loose groupings of individuals supporting similar policies do exist, the most prominent being the Maneaban Te Mauri (Protect the Maneaba), led by TEBURORO TITO, the National Progressive Party, led by TEATAO TEANNAKI, the Liberal Party, led by TEWAREKA TENTOA, and the Boutokan Te Koaua (Pillars of Truth), led by Dr HARRY TONG.

Diplomatic Representation

EMBASSY AND HIGH COMMISSIONS IN KIRIBATI

Australia: POB 77, Bairiki, Tarawa; tel. 21184; fax 21440; e-mail AHC_Tarawa@dfat.gov.au; High Commissioner: COLIN HILL.

China, People's Republic: POB 30, Bairiki, Tarawa; tel. 21486; fax 21110; e-mail prcembassy@tskl.net.ki; Ambassador: YANG ZHIKUAN.

New Zealand: POB 53, Bairiki, Tarawa; tel. 21400; fax 21402; e-mail nzhc.tar@mfat.govt.nz; High Commissioner: NEIL ROBERTSON.

United Kingdom: POB 5, Bairiki, Tarawa; tel. 22501; fax 22505; e-mail ukrep@tskl.net.ki; internet www.ukinthepacific.bhc.org.fj; Dep. High Commissioner: VERNON SCARBOROUGH.

Judicial System

There are 24 Magistrates' Courts (each consisting of one presiding magistrate and up to eight other magistrates) hearing civil, criminal and land cases. When hearing civil or criminal cases, the presiding magistrate sits with two other magistrates, and when hearing land cases with four other magistrates. A single magistrate has national jurisdiction in civil and criminal matters. Appeal from the Magistrates' Courts lies, in civil and criminal matters, to a single judge of the High Court, and, in matters concerning land, divorce and inheritance, to the High Court's Land Division, which consists of a judge and two Land Appeal Magistrates.

The High Court of Kiribati is a superior court of record and has unlimited jurisdiction. It consists of the Chief Justice and a Puisne Judge. Appeal from a single judge of the High Court, both as a Court of the First Instance and in its appellate capacity, lies to the Kiribati Court of Appeal, which is also a court of record and consists of a panel of three judges.

All judicial appointments are made by the Beretitenti (President).

High Court: POB 501, Betio, Tarawa; tel. 26007; fax 26149; e-mail highcourt@tskl.net.ki.

Chief Justice: ROBIN MILLHOUSE.

Judges of the Kiribati Court of Appeal: RICHARD LUSSICK (President), Sir HARRY GIBBS (Vice-President), PETER DAVID CONNOLLY, KEVIN WILLIAM RYAN.

Religion

CHRISTIANITY

Most of the population are Christians: 53.4% Roman Catholic and 39.2% members of the Kiribati Protestant Church, according to the 1990 census.

The Roman Catholic Church

Kiribati forms part of the diocese of Tarawa and Nauru, suffragan to the archdiocese of Suva (Fiji). At 31 December 2000 the diocese contained an estimated 49,456 adherents. The Bishop participates in the Catholic Bishops' Conference of the Pacific, based in Suva (Fiji).

Bishop of Tarawa and Nauru: Most Rev. PAUL EUSEBIUS MEA KAIUEA, Bishop's House, POB 79, Bairiki, Tarawa; tel. 21279; fax 21401; e-mail cathchurch@tskl.net.ki.

The Anglican Communion

Kiribati is within the diocese of Polynesia, part of the Anglican Church in Aotearoa, New Zealand and Polynesia. The Bishop in Polynesia is resident in Fiji.

Protestant Church

Kiribati Protestant Church: POB 80, Bairiki, Tarawa; tel. 21195; fax 21453; f. 1988; Moderator Rev. BAITEKE NABETARI; Gen. Sec. Rev. TIAONTIN ARUE; 29,432 mems in 1998.

Other Churches

Seventh-day Adventist, Church of God and Assembly of God communities are also represented, as is the Church of Jesus Christ of Latter-day Saints (Mormon).

BAHÁ'Í FAITH

National Spiritual Assembly: POB 269, Bikenibeu, Tarawa; tel. and fax 28074; e-mail emi@tskl.net.ki; 2,400 mems resident in 100 localities in 1995.

The Press

Butim'aea Manin te Euangkerio: POB 80, Bairiki, Tarawa; tel. 21195; e-mail kpc@tskl.net.ki; f. 1913; Protestant Church newspaper; weekly; a monthly publication Te Kaotan te Ota is also produced; Editor Rev. TOOM TOAKAI.

Kiribati Business Link: Bairiki, Tarawa; English.

Kiribati Newstar: POB 10, Bairiki, Tarawa; tel. 21652; fax 21671; e-mail newstar@tskl.net.ki; internet www.users.bigpond.com/kiribati_newstar; f. 2000; independent; weekly; English and I-Kiribati; Editor-in-Chief NGAUEA UATIOA.

Te Itoi ni Kiribati: POB 231, Bikenibeu, Tarawa; tel. 28138; fax 21341; f. 1914; Roman Catholic Church newsletter; monthly; circ. 2,300.

Te Uekera: Broadcasting and Publications Authority, POB 78, Bairiki, Tarawa; tel. 21162; fax 21096; f. 1945; weekly; English and I-Kiribati; Editor TIBWERE BOBO; circ. 5,000.

Broadcasting and Communications

TELECOMMUNICATIONS

Telecom Kiribati Ltd: Bairiki, Tarawa; Gen. Man. ENOTA INGINTAU.

Telecom Services Kiribati Ltd: POB 72, Bairiki, Tarawa; tel. 21446; fax 21424; e-mail ceo@tskl.net.ki; internet www.tski.net.ki; owned by Govt of Kiribati; Gen. Man. STUART EASTWARD; CEO CLIFF MACALPINE.

BROADCASTING

Regulatory Authority

Broadcasting and Publications Authority: POB 78, Bairiki, Tarawa; tel. 21187; fax 21096.

Radio

Radio Kiribati: Broadcasting and Publications Authority, POB 78, Bairiki, Tarawa; tel. 21187; fax 21096; f. 1954; statutory body; station Radio Kiribati broadcasting on SW and MW transmitters; programmes in I-Kiribati (90%) and English (10%); some advertising; Man. BILL REIHER.

Television

Television Kiribati: Broadcasting and Publications Authority, POB 78, Bairiki, Tarawa; tel. 21187; fax 21096; in process of establishing services.

Finance

(cap. = capital; dep. = deposits; res = reserves)

BANKING

The Bank of Kiribati Ltd: POB 66, Bairiki, Tarawa; tel. 21095; fax 21200; e-mail bankofkiribati@tskl.net.ki; f. 1984; 75% owned by ANZ Bank, 25% by Govt of Kiribati; dep. $A42.8m., res $A1.3m., total assets $A46.3m. (Sept. 1999); Chair. ALAN WALTER; Gen. Man. BOB COWLEY; 3 brs.

Development Bank of Kiribati: POB 33, Bairiki, Tarawa; tel. 21345; fax 21297; e-mail dbk@tskl.net.ki; f. 1986; took over the assets of the National Loans Board; identifies, promotes and finances small-scale projects; auth. cap. $A2m.; Gen. Man. KIETAU TABWEBWEITI; 5 brs.

A network of lending entities known as 'village banks' operates throughout the islands, as do a number of credit unions under the management of the Credit Union League. In August 1995 there were 26 credit unions operating in Tarawa and seven in the outer islands with a total membership of 1,808 people.

INSURANCE

Kiribati Insurance Corpn: POB 38, Bairiki, Tarawa; tel. 21260; fax 21426; e-mail kirins@tskl.net.ki; f. 1981; govt-owned; only insurance co; reinsures overseas; Gen. Man. TEAIRO TOOMA.

Trade and Industry

GOVERNMENT AGENCIES

Kiribati Housing Corporation: Bairiki, Tarawa; tel. 21092; operates the Housing Loan and Advice Centre; Chair. TOKOREAUA KAIRORO.

Kiribati Provident Fund: POB 76, Bairiki, Tarawa; tel. 21300; fax 21186; f. 1977; total equity $A56.8m. (Dec. 1998); Gen. Man. TOKAATA NIATA.

CHAMBER OF COMMERCE

Kiribati Chamber of Commerce: POB 550, Betio, Tarawa; tel. 26351; fax 26351; Pres. WAYSANG KUM KEE; Sec.-Gen. TIARITE KWONG.

UTILITIES

Public Utilities Board: POB 443, Betio, Tarawa; tel. 26292; fax 26106; e-mail pub@tskl.net.ki; f. 1977; govt-owned; provides electricity, water and sewerage services in Tarawa; CEO TOKIA GREIG.

Solar Energy Company: Tarawa; e-mail sec@tskl.net.ki; a co-operative administering and implementing solar-generated electricity projects in North Tarawa and the outer islands.

CO-OPERATIVE SOCIETIES

Co-operative societies dominate trading in Tarawa and enjoy a virtual monopoly outside the capital, except for Banaba and Kiritimati.

The Kiribati Copra Co-operative Society Ltd: POB 489, Betio, Tarawa; tel. 26534; fax 26391; f. 1976; the sole exporter of copra; seven cttee mems; 29 mem. socs; Chair. RAIMON TAAKE; CEO RUTIANO BENETITO.

Bobotin Kiribati Ltd: POB 485, Betio, Tarawa; tel. 26092; fax 26224; replaced Kiribati Co-operative Wholesale Society; govt-owned; Gen. Man. AKAU TIARE.

MAJOR COMPANIES

Abamakoro Trading Ltd: POB 492, Betio, Tarawa; tel. 26568; fax 26415; e-mail abamakoro@tskl.net.ki; importer and wholesaler of general merchandise.

Atoll Seaweed Co Ltd: POB 528, Betio, Tarawa; tel. 26442; fax 26442; e-mail atoll.seaweed@tskl.net.ki; CEO KEVIN ROUATU.

Betio Shipyard Ltd: POB 468, Betio, Tarawa; tel. 26282; fax 26064; e-mail shipyard@tskl.net.ki; Gen. Man. TEMAIA EREATA.

Coconut Products Ltd: POB 280, Betio, Tarawa; manufacturer of coconut oil soap and cosmetics.

Kiribati Oil Co Ltd: Betio, Tarawa.

Kiribati Supplies Co Ltd: POB 71, Bairiki, Tarawa; tel. 21185; fax 21104; e-mail kscl@tskl.net.ki.

Marine Export Ltd: Betio, Tarawa.

Tarawa Biscuit Co Ltd: Betio, Tarawa.

Te Mautari Ltd: POB 508, Betio, Tarawa; govt-owned; fishing co; operates five vessels.

TRADE UNIONS

Kiribati Trades Union Congress (KTUC): POB 502, Betio, Tarawa; tel. 26277; fax 26257; f. 1982; unions and asscns affiliated to the KTUC include the Fishermen's Union, the Co-operative Workers' Union, the Seamen's Union, the Teachers' Union, the Nurses' Asscn, the Public Employees' Asscn, the Bankers' Union, Butaritari Rural Workers' Union, Christmas Island Union of Federated Workers, the Pre-School Teachers' Asscn, Makim Island Rural Workers' Org., Nanolelei Retailers' Union, the Plantation Workers' Union of Fanning Island and the Overseas Fishermen's Union (formed in 1998); 2,500 mems; Pres. TATOA KAITEIE; Gen. Sec. TAMARETI TAAU.

Transport

ROADS

Wherever practicable, roads are built on all atolls, and connecting causeways between islets are also being built as funds and labour permit. A programme to construct causeways between North and South Tarawa was completed in the mid-1990s. Kiribati has about 670 km of roads that are suitable for motor vehicles; all-weather roads exist in Tarawa and Kiritimati. In 2000 there were about 1,468 motor vehicles registered in the islands, of which some 48% were motorcycles.

SHIPPING

A major project to rehabilitate the port terminal and facilities at Betio, with finance totalling some US $22m. from Japan, was completed in May 2000. There are other port facilities at Banaba, Kanton and English Harbour.

Kiribati Shipping Services Ltd: POB 495, Betio, Tarawa; tel. 26195; fax 26204; e-mail kssi@tskl.net.ki; operates five passenger/freight vessels on inter-island services; govt-owned; Man. Capt. MAKERAN KWONG.

MATS Shipping and Transport: POB 413, Betio, Tarawa; tel. 26355; operates a fortnightly passenger and cargo service to the outer islands and occasional longer journeys.

CIVIL AVIATION

There are five international airports (Bonriki on South Tarawa, Cassidy on Kiritimati, Antekana on Butaritari, as well as others on Kanton and Tabuaeran) and several other airfields in Kiribati. The airport at Bonriki was enlarged in the early 1990s, using a loan from the Bank of China. Air Nauru and Air Marshall Islands also operate international services to Tarawa, and Aloha Airlines operates a charter flight service between Kiritimati Island and Honolulu, Hawaii. In December 2001 the Government announced its decision to lease a prop-jet, which it intended to operate from Tarawa to the Marshall Islands, Tuvalu and Fiji.

Air Kiribati Ltd: POB 274, Bonriki, Tarawa; tel. 28088; fax 28216; e-mail airkiribati.admin@tsklnet.ki; f. 1977; fmrly Air Tungaru; national airline; operates scheduled services to 15 outer islands; Chair. TAKEI TAOABA; CEO TANIERA TEIBUAKO.

Tourism

Previous attempts to establish tourism have been largely unsuccessful, owing mainly to the remoteness of the islands. There were 14,211 visitor arrivals in 1998 (of whom fewer than 40% were tourists). Of total tourist arrivals in 1998, some 58.3% came from Asia and Oceania, and 26.9% came from the Americas. The number of tourist arrivals rose from 3,112 in 1999 to 4,829 in 2000. In 2000 the industry earned some $A2.2m. In 1996 there were 201 hotel rooms in the islands. In 1989 the Government adopted a plan to develop hotels in the Line Islands and to exploit sites of Second World War battles. A further Tourism Development Action Plan was introduced in 1997. Game-fishing and 'eco-tourism', particularly bird-watching, were promoted in the late 1990s in an attempt to increase tourist arrivals to Kiritimati. Kiribati also exploited the location of some of its islands in the Line and Phoenix group by marketing the area as a destination for tourists wishing to celebrate the year 2000. In 1997 Caroline Island, situated close to the recently-realigned international date-line, was renamed Millennium Island in an attempt to maximize its potential for attracting visitors. In late 2000 an agreement was signed with the Norwegian Shipping Line company allowing large cruise ships to make weekly calls to the Line Islands from the end of 2001.

Kiribati Visitors Bureau: Ministry of Commerce, Industry and Tourism, POB 510, Betio, Tarawa; tel. 26157; fax 26233; e-mail commerce@tskl.net.ki; internet www.spto.com; Sec. TINIAN REIHER; Senior Tourist Officer TARATAAKE TEANNAKI.

Education

Education is compulsory for children between six and 15 years of age. This generally involves six years at a primary school and at least three years at a secondary school. Every atoll is provided with at least one primary school. An estimated 92% of children aged six to 12 receive primary education. In 2001 there were 88 primary schools, three government and six private secondary schools. There were 17,594 primary students and 4,403 general secondary students enrolled in 1997. The tertiary sector is based on Tarawa, except for one of the two private colleges which is based on Abemama. The Government administers a technical college and training colleges for teachers, nurses and seamen. There were 568 students enrolled in total in 1988. An extra-mural centre of the University of the South Pacific (based in Fiji) is also located on South Tarawa. In mid-1999 plans for the establishment of a college of advanced education were announced. In 2000 government expenditure on education totalled $A12.8m. (equivalent to 19.9% of total recurrent budgetary expenditure).

The Marshall Islands

Physical and Social Geography

The Republic of the Marshall Islands consists of two groups of islands, the Ratak ('sunrise') and Ralik ('sunset') chains, comprising 29 atolls (some 1,225 islets) and covering about 180 sq km (70 sq miles) of land. The islands lie within the area of the Pacific Ocean known as Micronesia, some 3,200 km south-west of Hawaii (USA) and about 2,100 km south-east of Guam. The nearest neighbours are Kiribati to the south and the Federated States of Micronesia to the west. Rainfall decreases from south to north, with January, February and March being the driest months, although seasonal variations in rainfall and temperature are generally small. The indigenous population comprises a Micronesian people, whose language is known as Marshallese. Both Marshallese and English are official languages. The traditional society of the Marshall Islands consists of a complex system of matrilineal clans and social stratification. Most of the population are Christian. According to the November 1999 census, the population totalled 50,848, with 23,682 living on Majuro Atoll, where the capital, Dalap-Uliga-Darrit Municipality, is situated.

History

The ancestors of the Micronesians settled the Marshall Islands some 4,000 years ago. The islands were ruled by several, warring, feudal states. The high chiefs, or Iroij, continued to exercise power, following expeditions under the authority of the Spanish Crown (Fernão de Magalhães (Ferdinand Magellan, the Portuguese navigator) in 1521 and Miguel de Saavedra in 1529) and the formal claim to the Marshall Islands by Spain in 1592. The islands received their name from the British explorer, John Marshall, who visited them at the end of the 18th century. Spanish sovereignty over the Marshall Islands was recognized in 1886 by the Papal Bull of Pope Leo XIII, which also gave Germany trading rights there (German trading companies had been active in the islands from the 1850s). In 1899 Germany also acquired, by purchase from Spain, the Caroline Islands and the Northern Mariana Islands (i.e. the Mariana Islands excluding Guam, which was ceded, by Spain, to the USA in 1898). In 1914, at the beginning of the First World War, Japan occupied all of German Micronesia, and received a formal mandate for its administration from the League of Nations in 1920. The territory was intensively colonized. In 1944 the islands were occupied by the US military, and in 1947 the United Nations included the Marshall Islands in the Trust Territory of the Pacific Islands, which was to be administered by the USA. (For the history of the Trust Territory, see the chapter on Palau.)

Following the rejection in a plebiscite, in July 1978, of participation in a federal Micronesian state, the Marshall Islands drafted its own Constitution, which came into effect on 1 May 1979. Negotiations on a Compact of Free Association with the USA continued, and draft agreements were initialled in October and November 1980. In June 1983, after various amendments, the Compact was signed. In September of that year a plebiscite in the Marshall Islands approved the Compact, which was ratified by the US Congress upon the acceptance of some amendments. The Compact of Free Association came into effect on 21 October 1986 and, in November, President Reagan formally ended US administration in Micronesia. The Republic of the Marshall Islands ceased to be part of the Trust Territory, the final dissolution of which occurred on 1 October 1994, when the Compact between the Republic of Palau and the USA came into effect. In December 1990 the UN Security Council finally voted to ratify formally the termination of the Trusteeship Agreement. Under the Compact with the Marshall Islands, the USA was to retain its military bases in the Marshall Islands for at least 15 years and, over the same period, was to provide annual aid of US $30m. The Marshall Islands became a member of the UN in 1991.

The first President of the Republic of the Marshall Islands was Iroijlaplap (paramount chief) Amata Kabua, who was re-elected for further four-year terms of office in 1984, 1988, 1992 and 1995.

Bikini and Enewetak Atolls, in the Marshall Islands, were used by the US Government for experiments with nuclear weapons, Bikini in 1946–58 and Enewetak in 1948–58. A total of 67 such tests were carried out during this period. The indigenous inhabitants of Enewetak were evacuated before tests began, and were allowed to return to the atoll in 1980, after much of the contaminated area had supposedly been rendered safe. The inhabitants of Bikini campaigned for similar treatment, and in 1985 the entire population of Rongelap Atoll (which had been engulfed in nuclear fall-out from the tests at Bikini in 1954) was resettled on Mejato Atoll, following fears that radiation levels were still dangerous. Subsequently, the US administration agreed to decontaminate Bikini Atoll over a period of between 10 and 15 years. Under the terms of the Compact, the US administration consented to establish a US $150m. trust fund to settle claims against the USA resulting from the testing of nuclear devices in the Marshall Islands during the 1940s and 1950s. In 1989 the US Supreme Court ruled that the Compact of 1983 and subsequent US legislation in 1986 prevented the islanders from suing the USA for any additional compensation, but in 1990 further compensation was approved for the islanders. By 1993 US $112m. had been paid to the victims of the nuclear testing out of interest from the trust fund. More than 400 Marshall Islanders received the first nuclear test compensation for personal injury in 1992, from a fund of US $45m., to be paid over 15 years. In 1995 islanders from Enewetak Atoll were campaigning for compensation from the fund for the loss of their land, resulting from the complete or partial vaporization of five islands in the atoll by the tests. Nuclear debris stored in a concrete dome on the atoll was also reported to be leaking.

Another atoll in the Marshall Islands, Kwajalein, is used as a target for the testing of missiles fired from California, USA, and, under the terms of the Compact, the US Government is committed to providing an estimated US $170m. in rent, over a period of 30 years, for land used as the site of a missile-tracking station, and a further US $80m. for development projects. The inhabitants of Kwajalein Atoll were resettled on Ebeye, a small island in the atoll, adjacent to the US base on Kwajalein Island, before testing of the missiles began in 1961. (Consequent overcrowding reportedly led to numerous social problems on Ebeye, including (according to a government report) an increase in crime, suicide and the rate of deaths from malnutrition in children between 1983 and 1989. Violent crime throughout the Marshall Islands increased by 65% between 1988 and 1991.) In 1989 the Marshall Islands Government agreed that the USA could lease a further four islands in the atoll, for five years, for the purpose of military tests. A further lease agreement was signed in 1995 for the use of Biken Island, in Aur Atoll, and Wake Island to be used in the missile-testing programme. In early 1999 the Marshall Islands Government announced plans to increase the rental charges for Kwajalein. (The islands received US $12.76m. in payment from the USA for use of the base in 1998.) In 2001 the Kwajalein Missile Range changed its name to the Ronald Reagan Ballistic Missile Defence Test Site, in response to a resolution adopted by the Nitijela in 1999. In July 2001 the USA tested an intercontinental missile in the Pacific. The missile, launched from California, successfully shot down a target launched from Kwajalein Atoll. An activist belonging to Greenpeace (the environmentalist movement), who had been camping on a nearby island to witness the test was arrested, and the USA unsuccessfully put pressure on the Marshall Islands Government to deport him. The number of scheduled US missile defence missions was increased to six for 2002.

In January 1994 several senior members of the Marshall Islands' legislature, the Nitijela, demanded that the US Government release detailed information on the effects of its nuclear-testing programme in the islands. The Minister of Foreign Affairs, Tom Kijiner, claimed that the fact that information relating to the tests had remained 'classified' had resulted in the payment of inadequate compensation to the islanders. In July documentation released by the US Department of Energy gave conclusive evidence that Marshall Islanders were deliberately exposed to radiation in order that its effects on their health could be studied by US medical researchers. Further evidence emerged during 1995 that the US Government had withheld the medical records of islanders involved in radiation experiments (which included tritium and chromium-51 injections and genetic and bone-marrow transplant experiments). A report by Japanese scientists, published in that year, indicated that some 40% of the former inhabitants of Rongelap Atoll were suffering from cancer. In 1997 the islands' Nuclear Claims Tribunal ruled that compensation from the US Government was not sufficient to meet the health requirements of Marshall Islanders affected by the tests, reiterating its view that the full extent of the problems caused by the tests had not been known when the terms of compensation were agreed in the early 1980s. In late 1998 representatives of the islanders appealed to the US Congress for the immediate payment of compensation to seriously ill victims of the tests; officials claimed that about one-third of islanders eligible for compensation had died before receiving any payment; subsequently it was claimed that the total number of people and the number of islands exposed to fall-out as a result of nuclear testing at Bikini Atoll was far greater than had been acknowledged by the USA. A further study by US scientists concluded in early 1999 that rates of cancer in the Marshall Islands associated with nuclear testing had reached what were termed extreme levels. In October 1999 the Nuclear Claims Tribunal announced that an overall annual compensation payment of US $2.3m. was to be made to victims of nuclear testing, bringing total payments made by the Tribunal to US $39.4m. Also in late 1999 the US Congress confirmed an agreement regarding compensation for the resettled inhabitants of Rongelap Atoll. In May 2000 the Nuclear Claims Tribunal awarded some US $578m. in compensation to the inhabitants of Enewetak Atoll. However, it was reported that the Tribunal did not possess sufficient funds to pay the compensation in full; it subsequently requested that the shortfall be provided by the USA.

In February 1997, meanwhile, a group of Bikini Islanders returned to the atoll for the first time since 1946 to assist in the rehabilitation of the atoll for resettlement, The operation was to involve the removal of radioactive topsoil (although the matter of its disposal presented a serious problem) and the saturation of the remaining soil with potassium, which is believed to inhibit the absorption of radioactive material by root crops. In early 1999 the Nuclear Claims Tribunal demanded the adoption of US Environmental Protection Agency standards in the rehabilitation of contaminated islands, claiming that Marshall Islanders deserved to receive the same treatment as US citizens would in similar circumstances. The US Department of Energy, however, expressed strong resistance to the suggestion.

In 1989 it was announced that Marshall Islands passports were to be offered for sale at a price of US $250,000 (subsequently reduced to US $100,000), in an attempt to stimulate Asian investment. The passport scheme (which earned an estimated US $10m. between 1995 and 1997) was officially suspended in 1997, following a sudden influx of immigrants from the People's Republic of China to the islands.

Following legislative elections in November 1995, at which eight incumbent members of the 33-seat Nitijela were defeated, Kabua was subsequently re-elected for a fifth presidential term. The President died in December 1996. Iroijlaplap Imata Kabua, a cousin of the late President, was elected as his successor on 13 January 1997.

In 1996 the Nitijela approved legislation allowing for the introduction of gambling in the islands, in order to provide an additional source of revenue. However, income earned from the venture did not fulfil expectations and aroused controversy for attracting more local than tourist interest. Moreover, a vociferous campaign by local church leaders in the islands to revoke the legislation led to fierce debate in the Nitijela in early 1998. Divisions within the Cabinet ensued, with three members supporting the President's pro-gambling stance and four others expressing support for the church's position. In April 1998 the Nitijela voted to repeal the law legalizing gambling, following the disqualification from the vote of several influential politicians (including Imata Kabua) known to have major gambling interests. A second bill containing further measures to ensure the prohibition of all gambling activity in the islands was narrowly approved. In August a cabinet reorganization was effected, in which three ministers who had supported the anti-gambling legislation were dismissed. In the following month one of the dismissed ministers proposed a motion of 'no confidence' in Kabua, the first such motion to be presented in the islands' legislature. The President and his supporters boycotted subsequent sessions of the Nitijela, effectively preventing the vote from taking place. The lack of a quorum also resulted in a delay in the approval of the budget for the imminent new financial year. Meanwhile, the opposition claimed that Kabua's continued absence from the Nitijela violated the terms of the Constitution. The motion of 'no confidence' in Kabua was eventually defeated by a margin of one vote on 16 October 1998.

At legislative elections held on 15 November 1999 the opposition United Democratic Party (UDP) secured a convincing victory over the incumbent administration, winning 18 of the 33 seats in the Nitijela (including four of the five seats in Majuro). A total of five senior members of the outgoing Government were defeated, among them the Ministers of Finance and of Foreign Affairs and Trade—both of whom had played a prominent role in the establishment of diplomatic relations with Taiwan in 1998 (see below). The former Nitijela Speaker, Kessai Note, was elected President on 3 January 2000 (the islands' first non-traditional leader to assume the post). The UDP Chairman, Litokwa Tomeing, became Speaker of the legislature. Note subsequently appointed a 10-member Cabinet, and reiterated his administration's intention to pursue anti-corruption policies.In May 2000 a task-force was established by the Government for the purposes of investigating misconduct and corruption. It was hoped that it would help to render Government more accountable.

In November 1998 the Marshall Islands established full diplomatic relations with Taiwan. The action was immediately condemned by the People's Republic of China, which, in December, severed diplomatic ties with the islands, closing its embassy in Majuro and suspending all inter-governmental agreements. The Marshall Islands Government insisted that it wished to maintain cordial relations with both governments and that its decision to recognize Taiwan formally was based solely on economic considerations. The Note administration, which took office in January 2000, emphasized its commitment to the maintenance of diplomatic relations with Taiwan. However, it was subsequently disclosed that a senior-level investigation had begun into allegations of the misappropriation of Taiwanese funds by the previous Government. In February 2001 a proposed visit by a flotilla of Taiwanese vessels to the Marshall Islands was vetoed by the USA, on the grounds that the defence protocol of the Compact of Free Association prohibited such a visit.

In mid-1999 the Government of the Marshall Islands accused the USA of failing to honour its obligations under the terms of the Compact of Free Association, notably regarding a development fund, intended to compensate the islands for certain economic provisions removed from the Compact since its approval in 1983. The Government declared that it had received only US $2m. of a promised US $20m., and that this shortfall was undermining efforts to promote the economic development of the country. Negotiations took place between the US and Marshall Islands Governments in July 2001 to renew the 15-year provisions of the Compact, which was due to expire at the end of September 2001. An extension of up to two years was permitted whilst negotiations were under way, during which time assistance to the Marshall Islands was to increase by some US $5.5m. An agreement was originally scheduled for early 2002 in order to allow adequate time for the US Congress to review it and pass legislation by 1 October 2003 but the procedure was postponed after the Marshall Islands Government submitted a proposal seeking financing of more than $1,000m. over 15 years. The Government had also objected to being allocated 25%–30% less in US grant assistance per caput than that apportioned to the Federated States of Micronesia since 2000. Thus, the Government sought to increase significantly both the level of rental payments charged for the Kwajalein base as well as the level of taxes levied on the employees of the US base. A 20-year funding programme worth more than $800m., including grants and trust-fund contributions, was expected to be signed in October 2002, with a potential 50-year agreement on Kwajalein (the use of which expires in 2016).

Meanwhile, in June 2000 the Marshall Islands was one of more than 30 countries and territories criticized by the Organisation for Economic Co-operation and Development (OECD) for the provision of inappropriate 'offshore' financial establishments. The OECD threatened to implement sanctions against these unfair tax havens unless reforms were introduced before July 2001. In May 2000 the Group of Seven Industrial Nations (G-7) alleged that the Marshall Islands had become a significant centre for the 'laundering' of money generated by international criminal activity. In September the Nitijela passed legislation to ensure the closer regulation of the banking and financial sector, although in October the Marshall Islands was again included in a list of countries judged to be unhelpful in the combating of international crime, which was issued by the Financial Action Task Force (FATF) on Money Laundering, based in Paris, France. The Marshall Islands remained on the list in 2002.

In September 2000 a Marshall Islands High Court judge ruled that a case brought by the Government against US tobacco companies could be heard on the Islands; the tobacco companies had claimed that they would be unable to receive a fair trial. The Government was seeking more than US $14,000m. in damages for health-care costs faced by smokers on the islands. In late February 2001 10 of the 11 charges against the tobacco companies were dismissed by the High Court judge for lack of evidence. The US Government had reportedly warned that its overseas aid flows might be threatened if the trial were to proceed; however, in early April a US judge had ruled that the companies would receive a fair trial in the Marshall Islands and the appeal was filed in June; the trial was expected to begin later in the year.

In November 2000, it was reported that finance officials had discovered that Amata Kabua had used funds granted to the Marshall Islands under the terms of the Compact of Free Association to pay off a personal loan, although the former President denied any wrongdoing. In mid-January 2001 Amata Kabua and former ministers in his Government, including the former Minister of Education, Justin deBrum, presented a 'no confidence' motion against President Note to the Nitijela. Although it was suggested that the vote had been intended to delay the publication of a report into mismanagement and corruption on the part of the former Government, deBrum stated that the motion resulted from a number of failings by the Note Government, including its unwillingness to renegotiate land rental payments with the USA for the use of the military base on Kwajalein Atoll and also the development of an economic relationship between the Note Government and Rev. Sun Myung Moon, the founder of the Unification Church (known as the 'Moonies'). However, the Government was successful in defeating the vote by a margin of 19 to 14. In July 2001 Note announced a cabinet reshuffle.

In 1989 a UN report on the 'greenhouse effect' (a heating of the earth's atmosphere as a result of pollution) predicted a possible rise in sea-level of some 3.7m (12 feet) by the year 2030, which would completely submerge the Marshall Islands. The Marshall Islands

Government has itself, however, given rise to regional concerns over pollution, the most controversial being the possible establishment of large-scale nuclear-waste storage facilities on several of the territory's contaminated islands. Criticism by the US Government of the plans, announced in 1994, was strongly denounced by the Marshall Islands authorities, which claimed that the project constituted the only opportunity for the country to generate sufficient income for the rehabilitation of contaminated islands and the provision of treatment for illnesses caused by the US nuclear-test programme. However, in mid-1997 Iroijlaplap Imata Kabua announced the indefinite suspension of the plans (despite the initiation of a feasibility study into the development of a nuclear-waste storage facility) following criticism of the project from within the Government and from neighbouring island nations. None the less, the Government approved plans for a new feasibility study on the subject in April 1998. The new Minister of Foreign Affairs, Alvin Jacklick (appointed by President Note in January 2000), was known to be strongly opposed to the scheme. In early 2002 the Intergovernmental Panel on Climate Change (IPCC) projected that during the 21st century global sea-level rises would submerge over 80% of Majuro atoll.

In late February 2001 a report published by an eminent Japanese scientist stated that radiation levels on Rongelap Island, according to research conducted in 1999, had now declined to such a level that human habitation of the island was again possible. (However, in October 2000 another scientific report had concluded that islanders had been exposed to more than 20 times as much radiation as had been previously stated.) In March 2001 the Marshall Islands Nuclear Claims Tribunal awarded US $563m. in compensation to former inhabitants of Bikini Atoll; however, as the tribunal had insufficient funds to pay the award, having exhausted a US $45m. compensation fund (part of an overall US $270m. arrangement) on personal injury claims, it was unclear what compensation islanders would in fact receive. In late 2000 the Government had petitioned the US Congress for an additional US $270m. in compensation, although the outcome of this petition remained uncertain, subject to further renegotiation of the Compact of Free Association. The future of the Tribunal after 30 September 2001, when the Compact was to expire, was uncertain, as were compensation payments to Islanders who had received partial payments. In April, following the adoption by the USA of a new standard of radioactivity considered to be acceptable, some six times lower than the previous level, the Tribunal announced that Ailuk Atoll was to be evacuated and environmental studies conducted. In mid-May two Greenpeace members, from the United Kingdom and Denmark, were arrested following a demonstration outside Kwajalein. In July 2002 the Government retained a former US Attorney-General in order to try and restore momentum to the outstanding $200m. claim for compensation against the US Government; claims for Rongelap and Utrik were still pending despite the absence of tribunal funds. In 2002 a working group of representatives from the US Department of Energy and the Marshall Islands Government was established; this was to meet henceforth several times a year.

Economy

In 2000, according to estimates by the World Bank, the Marshall Islands' gross national product (GNP), measured at average 1998–2000 prices, was US $101.9m., equivalent to US $1,970 per head. During 1990–2000 the country's gross domestic product (GDP) decreased, in real terms, at an average annual rate of 1.6%. According to revised figures from the Asian Development Bank (ADB), GDP grew by 1.1% in 1998 and by only 0.1% in 1999. It decreased by 0.9% in 2000, before expanding by 1.7% in 2001. During 1990–98 the population of the Marshall Islands increased by an annual average of 4.2%.

Agriculture (including fishing and livestock-rearing) contributed an estimated 13.7% of GDP in 1999/2000, and (including forestry and fishing) engaged 20.4% of the employed labour force in 2000, According to the ADB, compared with the previous year the GDP of the agricultural sector declined by 13.9% in 1998, but increased by 1.7% in 1999 and by 3.7% in 2000. The sector is mainly on a subsistence level, the principal crops being coconuts, cassava and sweet potatoes. Coconuts are processed into copra (dried coconut meat), some of which is then pressed for coconut oil. In 2000 some 2,706 short tons of copra were produced (a decrease of 19.2% compared with the previous year), and in that year exports of coconut oil and copra accounted for 31.0% of the total value of exports. Low prices, transport problems and an ageing tree stock adversely affected copra production in the late 1990s. There is a commercial tuna-fishing industry, including a tuna-canning factory and transhipment base on Majuro. The cultivation of seaweed was developed extensively in 1992, and in 1994 a project to cultivate blacklip pearl oysters on Arno Atoll was undertaken with US funding. The output of the agriculture and fishing sector declined sharply during 1996–97 and was expected to decrease further in 1998, partly because of poor weather conditions. However, the sale of fishing licences is an important source of revenue and earned the islands some US $3m. in 2000/01. In 2001 the Japanese Government funded the construction of a commercial fishing base at Jaluit atoll, scheduled for completion in 2002.

Industry (including mining, manufacturing, construction and power) contributed some 15.1% of GDP in 1999/2000. Between 1990 and 1999 industrial GDP declined by an average annual rate of 1.5%. According to the ADB, compared with the previous year the sector's GDP rose by 28.3% in 1998, by 1.3% in 1999 and by 3.7% in 2000. There are few mineral resources, although high-grade phosphate deposits exist on Ailinglaplap Atoll. Manufacturing activity, which provided an estimated 1.8% of GDP in 1998/99, and which engaged 7.9% of the employed labour force in 1999, consists mainly of the processing of agricultural products. Tobolar, the Marshall Islands' leading copra-processing company, was unable to process any further supplies of the commodity in 2001, owing to the size of its stockpile of oil and the lack of any additional storage capacity. In April 2002 the Taiwanese Government invested US $1.2m., enabling Tobolar to sell its stockpile, to begin processing again and to open a new oil refinery (hitherto, the Marshall Islands had produced only unrefined oil). Construction activity, which is largely associated with the islands' developing tourist industry, provided some 7.1% of GDP in 1996/97. An estimated 24.4% of the employed population worked in production, transport and labour in 1999, according to census information.

The services sector provided an estimated 71.3% of GDP in 1999/2000. The development of the tourist industry has been hindered by the difficulty of gaining access to the islands and a lack of suitable facilities. There were 5,399 visitors to the islands in 2001, a 3% increase compared with 2000. A short-term tourism development programme focusing on special-interest tourism was established in 2000. Tourist receipts totalled US $4m. in 1999. According to the ADB, compared with the previous year the GDP of the services sector expanded by only 0.2% in 1998 and contracted by 0.5% in 1999 and by 0.8% in 2000.

The international shipping registry experienced considerable expansion following the political troubles in Panama in 1989, and continued to expand in the mid-1990s (largely from US ships reflagging in the islands). The shipping industry also benefited from the construction of a floating dry-dock in Majuro in 1995. An 'offshore' banking system operates.

In the year to September 2000 the Marshall Islands recorded a trade deficit of US $50.9m., but a surplus of US $4.9m. on the current account of the balance of payments. Exports in that year consisted of coconut products and fish. The principal imports included mineral fuels and lubricants, food and live animals and machinery and transport equipment. In 2000 the principal sources of imports were the USA (which provided 61.4% of total imports) and Japan (5.1%).

A budgetary surplus equivalent to 17.5% of GDP was forecast for 2000/01. Financial assistance from the USA (at an annual rate of more than US $65m.), in accordance with the terms stipulated in the Compact of Free Association, contributed a large part of the islands' external revenue. In 2000/2001 budgeted aid from the USA amounted to US $20.7m. (35% of which was provided under the Compact agreement). Aided by an increase in this support, estimates for 2001/02 envisaged a rise in budgetary expenditure to US $74m. (compared with $66m. in the previous year). Recurrent expenditure was projected to increase from $55m. in 2000/01 to $59m. in 2001/02. The islands' external debt was estimated at $67.0m. in 2000/01. In that year the cost of debt-servicing (including repayments) was equivalent to 168.7% of the value of exports of goods and services. The Marshall Islands received $499 of aid per caput in 2000, which increased to $551 budgeted for 2003. The US aid budget for 2002 included a grant of $2.5m. to the Marshall Islands for an extension of the Military Use and Operating Rights Agreement (in addition to its mandatory annual payments of support for Enewetak Atoll and the Compact of Free Association). Aid has also been provided by Japan and Taiwan. The annual rate of inflation in Majuro averaged 5.7% in 1990–99. Consumer prices increased by an annual average of 1.7% in 2000 and by 1.6% in 2001. The unemployment rate stood at 31.5% of the economically active population in 2000.

The introduction, from the mid-1990s, of retrenchment measures in the public sector was welcomed by several international financial organizations and supported by the ADB. However, it was subsequently observed that reform of the public sector, which until the recession of the mid-1990s had employed up to one-half of the economically active population, had been accompanied by a decline in employment in the private sector; business employment declined by 7.4% during 1995–99, leading to a very high rate of unemployment and suggesting that the private sector in the Marshall Islands existed largely as a secondary sector. In 1999 the Government reduced import duties by more than 50% on many items, in an attempt to revitalize the local economy. Later that year reforms to promote the private sector were announced, in the hope that private businesses would assume responsibility for some of the services hitherto administered by the Government. Plans to transfer a number of state-owned companies to the private sector were also under way. A major priority for the administration of Kessai Note, which took office in January 2000, was to be the renegotiation of assistance under the Compact of Free Association with the USA (see History).

During the 1990s the Marshall Islands sought to diversify its economic relations with the international community. This policy achieved most notable success with the People's Republic of China, prior to the Marshall Islands' decision in 1998 to recognize Taiwan (see History). The Marshall Islands have since benefited from numerous economic agreements with Taiwan, worth an estimated US $20m., which have financed numerous projects, including the construction of roads, the acquisition of boats and the development of the agricultural sector. In mid-1999 the two countries signed a commercial co-operation agreement based primarily on the islands' potential as a site for fisheries investment. However, concern was expressed by the ADB in that year that reliance on external aid (notably from the USA and Taiwan) was hampering economic reform in the Marshall Islands. The ADB itself approved a US $12m. low-interest loan in June 2001, urging the Government to use it to improve budgeting and accounting practices. The Japanese Government, however, announced in 2002 that it was to reduce aid by 10%, owing to its own financial difficulties (since 1996 Japan has provided more than $2.2m. in small grants and millions of dollars in infrastructural development assistance). In June 2002 the European Union (EU) rejected a Marshall Islands' country support strategy plan designed to qualify the islands for a five-year $1.5m. annual funding programme. (The proposed strategy focused on education and human resource development. The EU, however, also required emphasis on alternative energy installations.)

The lack of internationally-marketable natural resources and the remote location of the islands present major challenges for the Marshall Islands Government in its efforts to revitalize and expand the economy. Attempts to circumvent these difficulties, including efforts to introduce gambling and 'offshore' financial services (see History) have generated political controversy, both domestically and internationally. As allegations of 'money-laundering' activities continued, in 2002 the Marshall Islands remained on the Financial Action Task Force (FATF) list of Non Co-operative Countries and Territories (NCCT). However, the IMF commended the islands on progress in implementing a comprehensive framework against such fraud, including specific legislation, the establishment of a Domestic Financial Intelligence Unit and joining various international organizations. The Marshall Islands was removed from the list in October of the same year, since their inclusion had been based only on the absence of sufficient preventative measures.

External debt repayments were expected to decline sharply in 2002, leading to the release of substantial resources which the Government planned to channel into the Marshall Islands Intergenerational Trust Fund. In 2001 the Government had transferred a total of $14m. to the Fund, to which it was envisaged future contributions from the USA and financial assistance from other donors would be allocated. It was hoped that within 20 years the Fund might total $750m. and subsequently provide an annual income of $30m.–$40m.

The Marshall Islands is a member of the Pacific Community (formerly the South Pacific Commission), the Pacific Islands Forum (formerly the South Pacific Forum) and the Asian Development Bank (ADB). In 1991 the islands were admitted to the UN (in addition to the UN's Economic and Social Commission for Asia and the Pacific—ESCAP), and in 1992 the Marshall Islands became a full member of the International Monetary Fund and the World Bank. In early 1996 the Marshall Islands joined representatives of the other countries and territories of Micronesia at a meeting in Hawaii, at which a new regional organization, the Council of Micronesian Government Executives, was established. The new body aimed to facilitate discussion of economic developments in the region and to examine possibilities for reducing the considerable cost of shipping essential goods between the islands. In August 2000 it was announced that the Marshall Islands were to participate in the establishment of a tuna commission, along with other Pacific nations.

Statistical Survey

AREA AND POPULATION

Area: 181.4 sq km (70.0 sq miles) (land only); two island groups, the Ratak Chain (88.1 sq km) and the Ralik Chain (93.3 sq km).

Population: 43,380 at census of 13 November 1988; 50,848 (males 26,034, females 24,814) at census of June 1999. *By island group* (1999): Ratak Chain 30,932 (Majuro Atoll 23,682); Ralik Chain 19,916 (Kwajalein Atoll 10,903).

Density (1999 census): 280.3 per sq km.

Births and Deaths (estimates, 1999): Birth rate 41.8 per 1,000; Death rate 4.9 per 1,000.

Expectation of Life (WHO estimates, years at birth, 2000): Males 62.8; Females 67.8. Source: WHO, *World Health Report*.

Economically Active Population (2000): Agriculture, forestry and fishing 2,100; Manufacturing 800; Activities not adequately defined 7,400; Total employed 10,300; Unemployed 4,500; Total labour force 15,000. Source: Asian Development Bank, *Key Indicators of Developing Asian and Pacific Countries*.

HEALTH AND WELFARE

Key Indicators

Fertility (births per woman, 2000): 5.9.

Under-5 Mortality Rate (per 1,000 live births, 2000): 68.

Physicians (per 1,000 head, 1996): 0.42.

Health Expenditure (1998): US $ per head (PPP): 184.
% of GDP: 9.5.
public (% of total): 61.6.

For sources and definitions, see explanatory note on p. vi.

AGRICULTURE, ETC.

Principal Crops, Livestock and Livestock Products: see chapter on the Federated States of Micronesia.

Fishing (FAO estimate, metric tons, live weight): Total catch 400 in 1999. Source: FAO, *Yearbook of Fishery Statistics*.

INDUSTRY

Electric Energy (million kWh)*: 64.1 in 1998; 62.9 in 1999; 63.0 in 2000. Source: Asian Development Bank, *Key Indicators of Developing Asian and Pacific Countries*.

* Figures refer to Majuro only.

FINANCE

Currency and Exchange Rates: United States currency is used: 100 cents = 1 United States dollar (US $). *Sterling and Euro Equivalents* (31 May 2002): £1 sterling = US $1.4667; €1 = 93.87 US cents; US $100 = £68.18 = €106.53.

Budget (estimates, US $ million, year ending 30 September 2000): *Revenue:* Recurrent 27.2 (Tax 17.0, Non-tax 10.2); Grants 46.7; Total 73.9. *Expenditure:* Recurrent 56.2; Capital (incl. net lending) 8.8; Total 65.0. Source: Asian Development Bank, *Key Indicators of Developing Asian and Pacific Countries*.

Cost of Living (Consumer Price Index for Majuro; base: Oct.–Dec. 1982 = 100): All items 190.8 in 1998; 194.0 in 1999, 197.1 in 2000. Source: Asian Development Bank, *Key Indicators of Developing Asian and Pacific Countries*.

Gross Domestic Product by Economic Activity (estimates, US $ million at current prices, year ending 30 September 2000): Agriculture 13.2; Mining 0.3; Manufacturing 1.7; Electricity, gas and water 2.2; Construction 10.4; Trade 17.1; Transport and communications 5.2; Finance 15.7; Other 30.9; *Sub-total* 96.7; Import duties 7.0; *Less* Imputed bank service charges 6.2; *GDP in purchasers' values* 97.5. Source: Asian Development Bank, *Key Indicators of Developing Asian and Pacific Countries*.

Balance of Payments (estimates, US $ million, year ending 30 September 2000): Merchandise exports f.o.b. 7.9; Merchandise imports c.i.f. –58.8; *Trade balance* –50.9; Exports of services 29.4; Imports of services –13.8; *Balance on goods and services* –35.3; Private unrequited transfers (net) 0.6; Official unrequited transfers (net) 39.6; *Current balance* 4.9; Capital account (net) -14.7; Net errors and omissions 5.2; *Overall balance* –4.6. Source: Asian Development Bank, *Key Indicators of Developing Asian and Pacific Countries*.

EXTERNAL TRADE

Principal Commodities (estimates, US $ million, 2000): *Imports:* Food, live animals, beverages and tobacco 7.4; Crude materials, inedible, except fuels 2.9; Mineral fuels, lubricants and related materials 29.7; Animal and vegetable oils and fats 2.9; Chemicals 0.2; Basic manufactures 4.0; Machinery and transport equipment 11.5; Miscellaneous manufactured articles 1.9; Goods not classified by kind 7.7; Total 68.2. *Exports:* Coconut oil (crude) 1.1; Copra cake 1.2; Pet fish 0.5; Total (incl. others) 7.3.

Principal Trading Partners (estimates, US $ million, 2000): *Imports:* Australia 1.4; Hong Kong 1.3; Japan 3.5; New Zealand 0.9; USA 41.9; Total (incl. others) 68.2. *Exports:* USA 5.2; Total (incl. others) 7.3.

Source: mainly Asian Development Bank, *Key Indicators of Developing Asian and Pacific Countries*.

TRANSPORT

Road Traffic (vehicles registered, 1999): Trucks 64; Pick-ups 587; Sedans 1,404; Jeeps 79; Buses 75; Vans 66; Scooters 47; Other motor vehicles 253.

Shipping: *Merchant Fleet* (at 31 December 2001): Vessels 360; Displacement ('000 grt) 11,719 (Source: Lloyd's Register-Fairplay, *World Fleet Statistics*). *International sea-borne freight traffic* (estimates, '000 metric tons, 1990)*: Goods loaded 29; Goods unloaded 123 (Source: UN, *Monthly Bulletin of Statistics*).

* Including the Northern Mariana Islands, the Federated States of Micronesia and Palau.

Civil Aviation (traffic on scheduled services, 1998): Passengers carried 32,000; Passenger-km 20 million. Total ton-km 2 million. Source: UN, *Statistical Yearbook*.

TOURISM

Tourist Arrivals: 4,622 in 1999; 5,246 in 2000; 5,399 in 2001.

Arrivals by Country (2001): Australia 134; Fiji 147; Japan 933; Kiribati 275; Federated States of Micronesia 239; Philippines 180; USA 1,922; Total (incl. others) 5,399.

Tourism Receipts (US $ million): 3 in 1997; 3 in 1998; 4 in 1999.

Sources: World Tourism Organization, *Yearbook of Tourism Statistics*, and Marshall Islands Visitor Authority.

COMMUNICATIONS MEDIA

Telephones (main lines in use): 4,200 in 2001*.

Mobile Cellular Telephones (subscriptions): 500 in 2001*.

Facsimile Machines (number): 160 in 1996†.

Personal Computers: 4,000 in 2001*.

Internet Users: 900 in 2001*.

Non-daily Newspapers: 1 (average circulation 10,000 copies) in 1996‡.

* Source: International Telecommunication Union.

† Source: UN, *Statistical Yearbook*.

‡ Source: UNESCO, *Statistical Yearbook*.

EDUCATION

Primary (1998): 103 schools; 548 teachers; 12,421 pupils*.

Secondary (1998): 16 schools; 162 teachers; 2,667 pupils*.

Higher (1994): 1 college; 25 teachers; 1,149* students.

* by enrolment.

Directory

The Constitution

On 1 May 1979 the locally-drafted Constitution of the Republic of the Marshall Islands became effective. The Constitution provides for a parliamentary form of government, with legislative authority vested in the 33-member Nitijela. Members of the Nitijela are elected by a popular vote, from 25 districts, for a four-year term. There is an advisory council of 12 high chiefs, or Iroij. The Nitijela elects the President of the Marshall Islands (who also has a four-year mandate) from among its own members. The President then selects members of the Cabinet from among the members of the Nitijela. On 25 June 1983 the final draft of the Compact of Free Association was signed by the Governments of the Marshall Islands and the USA, and the Compact was effectively ratified by the US Congress on 14 January 1986. By the terms of the Compact, free association recognizes the Republic of the Marshall Islands as an internally sovereign, self-governing state, whose policy concerning foreign affairs must be consistent with guide-lines laid down in the Compact. Full responsibility for defence lies with the USA, which undertakes to provide regular economic assistance. The economic and defence provisions of the Compact are renewable after 15 years, but the status of free association continues indefinitely.

The Government

HEAD OF STATE

President: KESSAI H. NOTE (took office 10 January 2000).

THE CABINET
(August 2002)

Minister in Assistance to the President: TADASHI LOMETO.

Minister of Education: WILFRED I. KENDALL.

Minister of Finance: MICHAEL M. KONELIOS.

Minister of Transportation and Communication: BRENSON S. WASE.

Minister of Health and Environment: ALVIN JACKLICK.

Minister of Public Works: RIEN R. MORRIS.

Minister of Internal Affairs: NIDEL L. LORA.

Minister of Justice: WITTEN T. PHILIPPO.

Minister of Resources and Development: JOHN M. SILK.

Minister of Foreign Affairs and Trade: GERALD ZACKIOS.

MINISTRIES

Office of the President: Govt of the Republic of the Marshall Islands, POB 2, Majuro, MH 96960; tel. (625) 3445; fax (625) 4021; e-mail presoff@ntamar.com.

Ministry of Education: POB 3, Majuro, MH 96960; tel. (625) 5261; fax (625) 7735/3861; secmoe@ntamar.com.

Ministry of Finance: POB D, Majuro, MH 96960; tel. (625) 7420; fax (625) 3607; e-mail minfin@ntamar.com.

Ministry of Foreign Affairs: POB 1349, Majuro, MH 96960; tel. (625) 3012; fax (623) 4979; e-mail mofatadm@ntamar.com.

Ministry of Health and Environment: POB 16, Majuro, MH 96960; tel. (625) 5660; fax (625) 3432; e-mail mipamohe@ntamar.com.

Ministry of Internal Affairs: POB 18, Majuro, MH 96960; tel. (625) 8240/8718; fax (625) 5353; e-mail rmihpo@ntamar.com.

Ministry of Justice: c/o Office of the Attorney General, Majuro, MH 96960; tel. (625) 3244/8245; fax (625) 5218; e-mail agoffice@ntamar.com.

Ministry of Public Works: POB 1727, Majuro, MH 96960; tel. (625) 8911; fax (625) 3005; e-mail rndadm@ntamar.com.

Ministry of Resources and Development: POB 1727, Majuro, MH 96960; tel. (625) 3206/3277; fax (625) 3821; e-mail rndsec@ntamar.com.

Ministry of Transportation and Communication: POB 1079, Majuro, MH 96960; tel. (625) 3129/8869; fax (625) 3486; e-mail rmimotc@ntamar.com.

Legislature

THE NITIJELA

The Nitijela (lower house) consists of 33 elected members, known as Senators. The most recent election was held on 15 November 1999.

Speaker: Sen. LITOKWA TOMEING.

THE COUNCIL OF IROIJ

The Council of Iroij is the upper house of the bicameral legislature, comprising 12 tribal chiefs who advise the Presidential Cabinet and review legislation affecting customary law or any traditional practice.

Chairman: Iroij KOTAK LOEAK.

Political Organizations

Ralik Ratak Democratic Party: f. 1991; opposed the late Amata Kabua; Founder TONY DEBRUM.

United Democratic Party: Majuro; Chair. LITOKWA TOMEING.

Diplomatic Representation

EMBASSIES IN THE MARSHALL ISLANDS

China (Taiwan): POB 1229, Majuro, MH 96960; tel. (625) 4051; fax (625) 4056; Ambassador: GARY LIN.

Japan: POB 300, Majuro, MH 96960; Ambassador: ATSUO SAEGUSA.

USA: POB 1379, Majuro, MH 96960; tel. (625) 4011; fax (625) 4012; e-mail usembmaj@ntamar.com; internet www.usembassy.state.gov/majuro/; Ambassador: MICHAEL J. SENKO.

Judicial System

The judicial system consists of the Supreme Court and the High Court, which preside over District and Community Courts, and the Traditional Rights Court.

Supreme Court of the Republic of the Marshall Islands: POB 378, Majuro, MH 96960; tel. (625) 3201; fax (625) 3323; e-mail jutrep@ntamar.com; Chief Justice ALLEN P. FIELDS.

District Court of the Republic of the Marshall Islands: Majuro, MH 96960; tel. (625) 3201; fax (625) 3323; Presiding Judge BOKEPOK HELAI.

Traditional Rights Court of the Marshall Islands: Majuro, MH 96960; customary law only; Chief Judge RAILEY ALBERILTAR.

Religion

The population is predominantly Christian, mainly belonging to the Protestant United Church of Christ. The Roman Catholic Church, Assembly of God, Bukot Nan Jesus, Seventh-day Adventists, the Church of Jesus Christ of Latter-day Saints (Mormons), the Full Gospel and the Bahá'í Faith are also represented.

CHRISTIANITY

The Roman Catholic Church

The Apostolic Prefecture of the Marshall Islands included 4,576 adherents at 31 December 2000.

Prefect Apostolic of the Marshall Islands: Rev. Fr JAMES C. GOULD, POB 8, Majuro, MH 96960; tel. (625) 6675; fax (625) 5520; e-mail catholic@ntamar.com.

Protestant Churches

The Marshall Islands come under the auspices of the United Church Board for World Ministries (475 Riverside Drive, New York, NY 10115, USA); Sec. for Latin America, Caribbean and Oceania Dr PATRICIA RUMER.

BAHÁ'Í FAITH

National Spiritual Assembly: POB 1017, Majuro, MH 96960; e-mail nsabaimh@ntamar.com; internet www.mh.bahai.org; mems resident in 50 localities; Sec. Dr IRENE J. TAAFAKI.

The Press

Kwajalein Hourglass: POB 23, Kwajalein, MH 96555; tel. (355) 3539; e-mail jbennett@kls.usaka.smdc.army.mil; internet www.smdc.army.mil/KWAJ/Hourglass/Hourglass.html; f. 1954; 2 a week; Editor JIM BENNETT; circ. 2,300.

Marshall Islands Journal: POB 14, Majuro, MH 96960; tel. (625) 8143; fax (625) 3136; e-mail journal@ntamar.com; f. 1970; weekly; Editor GIFF JOHNSON; circ. 3,700.

Broadcasting and Communications

TELECOMMUNICATIONS

National Telecommunications Authority (NTA): POB 1169, Majuro, MH 96960; tel. (625) 3852; fax (625) 3952; e-mail aefowler@ntamar.com; internet www.ntamar.com; privatized in 1991; sole provider of local and long-distance services in the Marshall Islands; Chair. ALEX C. BING; Pres. and Gen. Man. ALAN FOWLER.

BROADCASTING

Radio

Radio Marshalls V7AB: POB 3250, Majuro, MH 96960; tel. (625) 8411; fax (625) 5353; govt-owned; commercial; programmes in English and Marshallese; Station Man. ANTARI ELBON.

Marshall Islands Broadcasting Co: POB 19, Majuro, MH 96960; tel. (625) 3250; fax (625) 3505; privately-owned; Chief Information Officer PETER FUCHS.

Television

Alele Museum Foundation: POB 629, Majuro, MH 96960; tel. and fax (625) 3226; broadcasts educational programmes.

Marshall Broadcasting Co Television: POB 19, Majuro, MH 96960; tel. (625) 3413; privately-owned; Chief Information Officer PETER FUCHS.

The US Dept of Defense operates a radio station and a television station (24 hours a day) for the military base on Kwajalein Atoll.

Finance

(cap. = capital; res = reserves; dep. = deposits; amounts in US dollars)

BANKING

Bank of Guam (USA): POB C, Majuro, MH 96960; tel. (625) 3322; fax (625) 3444; internet www.bankofguam.com; Man. ROMY ANGEL; brs in Ebeye, Kwajalein and Majuro.

Bank of Hawaii (USA): POB 469, Majuro, MH 96960; tel. (625) 3741; fax (625) 3744; internet www.boh.com; scheduled to close on 30 Nov. 2002; Man. GREG KIM.

Bank of the Marshall Islands: POB 116, Majuro, MH 96960; tel. (625) 3636; fax (625) 3661; e-mail bankmar@ntamar.com; internet www.angelfire.com/ms/bankofMI; f. 1982; 40% govt-owned; dep. 39,202.9m., total assets 48,968.1m. (Dec. 2001); Chair. GRANT LABAUN; Gen. Man. PATRICK CHEN; brs in Majuro and Ebeye.

Marshall Islands Development Bank: POB 1048, Majuro, MH 96960; tel. (625) 3230; fax (625) 3309; f. 1989; total assets 19.5m. (Dec. 1992); Man. Dir AMON TIBON.

INSURANCE

Marshalls Insurance Agency: POB 113, Majuro, MH 96960; tel. (625) 3366; fax (625) 3189; Man. TOM LIKOVICH.

Moylan's Insurance Underwriters (Marshall) Inc: POB 727, Majuro, MH 96960; tel. (625) 3220; fax (625) 3361; e-mail marshalls@moylansinsurance.com; internet www.moylansinsurance.com; Pres. JOEL PHILIP.

Trade and Industry

DEVELOPMENT ORGANIZATIONS AND STATE AUTHORITIES

Marshall Islands Environmental Protection Agency: Majuro, MH 96960; Dir ABRAHAM HICKIN (acting).

Marshall Islands Development Authority: Majuro, MH 96960; Gen. Man. DAVID KABUA.

Marshall Islands Marine Resources Authority: Majuro, MH 96960; Dir DANNY WASE.

Kwajalein Atoll Development Authority (KADA): POB 5159, Ebeye Island, Kwajalein, MH 96970; Dir JEBAN RIKLON.

Tobolar Copra Processing Authority: POB G, Majuro, MH 96960; tel. (625) 3494; fax (625) 7206; e-mail tobolar@ntamar.com; Gen. Man. MIKE SLINGER.

CHAMBER OF COMMERCE

Majuro Chamber of Commerce: Majuro, MH 96960; Pres. KIRTLEY PINHO.

UTILITIES

Electricity

Marshalls Energy Company: POB 1439, Majuro, MH 96960; tel. (625) 3829; fax (625) 3397; Gen. Man. WILLIAM F. ROBERTS.

Kwajalein Atoll Joint Utility Resource (KAJUR): POB 5819, Ebeye Island, Kwajalein, MH 96970; tel. (329) 3799; fax (329) 3722.

Water

Majuro Water and Sewage Services: POB 1751, Majuro, MH 96960; e-mail htakju@ntamar.com; internet www.omip.org/majuro.html; Man. HACKNEY TAKJU.

CO-OPERATIVES

These include the Ebeye Co-op, Farmers' Market Co-operative, Kwajalein Employees' Credit Union, Marshall Is Credit Union, Marshall Is Fishermen's Co-operative, Marshall Is Handicraft Co-operative.

Transport

ROADS

Macadam and concrete roads are found in the more important islands. In 1996 there were 152 km of paved roads in the Marshall Islands, mostly on Majuro and Ebeye. Other islands have stone and coral-surfaced roads and tracks. In early 1997 the Marshall Islands received a grant of some US $0.5m. from Japan for a road-improvement project on Majuro. The project was to form part of an extensive programme costing US $15m., which was due to be completed by 1999.

SHIPPING

The Marshall Islands operates an 'offshore' shipping register. At the end of 2001 the merchant fleet comprised 360 vessels, with a combined displacement of some 11.7m. grt.

Vessel Registry:

Marshall Islands Maritime and Corporate Administrators Inc: 11495 Commerce Park Drive, Reston, VA 20191-1507, USA; tel. (703) 620-4880; fax (703) 476-8522; e-mail info@register-iri.com; internet www.register-iri.com; Senior Deputy Commissioner: DAVID J. F. BRUCE; Local Office: **The Trust Company of the Marshall Islands Inc:** Trust Company Complex, Ajeltake Island, POB 1405,

Majuro, MH 96960; tel. (247) 3018; fax (247) 3017; e-mail tcmi@ntamar.com; Pres. GUY EDISON CLAY MAITLAND.

CIVIL AVIATION

In June 1995 the Marshall Islands, Kiribati, Nauru and Tuvalu agreed to begin discussions on the establishment of a joint regional airline. In May 1997 the Marshall Islands signed a bilateral agreement on international air transport with the Federated States of Micronesia. Continental Micronesia operates three flights a week from Honolulu and Guam, Air Marshall Islands provides a daily domestic service and Aloha Airlines provides a weekly service from Honolulu to Kwajalein and to Majuro.

Air Marshall Islands (AMI): POB 1319, Majuro, MH 96960; tel. (625) 3731; fax (625) 3730; e-mail amisales@ntamar.com; f. 1980; internal services for the Marshall Islands; international operations ceased in early 1999; also charter, air ambulance and maritime surveillance operations; Chair. KUNIO LAMARI; CFO NEIL ESCHERRA.

Tourism

Tourism, which has been hindered by the difficulty of gaining access to the islands and a lack of transport facilities, was expected to develop significantly in the late 1990s, owing to the establishment of major resort complexes on Majuro and on Mili Atoll, funded at an estimated cost of US $1,000m. by South Korean investors. In 1997 the Marshall Islands Visitor Authority was established as a private-sector agency (it had previously existed as a small division within the Ministry of Resources and Development). There were 5,399 tourist arrivals in 2001. In that year some 35.6% of visitors came from the USA and 17.3% from Japan. The islands' attractions include excellent opportunities for diving, game-fishing and the exploration of sites and relics of Second World War battles. The Marshall Islands Visitor Authority has implemented a short-term tourism development programme focusing on special-interest tourism markets. In the long term the Visitor Authority hopes to promote the development of small-island resorts throughout the country.

Marshall Islands Visitor Authority: POB 5, Majuro, MH 96960; tel. (625) 6482/5581; fax (625) 6771; e-mail tourism@ntamar.com; internet www.visitmarshallislands.com; Gen. Man. MARK STEGE.

Defence

Defence is the responsibility of the USA, which maintains a military presence on Kwajalein Atoll. The US Pacific Command is based in Hawaii.

Education

There is a school system, based on that of the USA, operated by the state. However, only 25% of students continue their education beyond a primary level, owing to limited resources and inadequate instruction. In 1999 there were 103 primary schools, with a total enrolment of 12,421 pupils, but only 16 secondary schools, with a total of 2,667 pupils enrolled. The College of the Marshall Islands (which became independent from the College of Micronesia in 1993) is based on Majuro. In 1994 there were 1,149 students enrolled at the College, and in 1991 118 students were enrolled at colleges and universities in the USA. In early 1995 the islands received a grant of US $6m. from Japan to fund projects to improve secondary education, as well as a loan of US $2m. from the People's Republic of China to finance the construction of a new secondary school on Majuro. Government expenditure on education in 1997/98 was budgeted at US $10.0m., equivalent to 23.5% of total budgetary spending.

The Federated States of Micronesia

Physical and Social Geography

The Federated States of Micronesia forms (with Palau, q.v.) the archipelago of the Caroline Islands, about 800 km east of the Philippines. The Federated States of Micronesia includes (from west to east) the states of Yap, Chuuk (formerly Truk, renamed in January 1990), Pohnpei (formerly Ponape, renamed in November 1984) and Kosrae, and consists of some 607 islands and atolls, extending for some 2,900 km. The islands of Yap are in the Western Caroline Islands and are about 870 km south-west of Guam. The remaining islands are in the Eastern Carolines and the easternmost island of Kosrae lies some 4,587 km south-west of Hawaii. The islands are subject to heavy rainfall, although precipitation decreases from east to west. January, February and March are the driest months, although seasonal variations in rainfall and temperature are generally small. Average annual temperature is 27°C (81°F). The indigenous population, which is predominantly Micronesian, consists of various ethno-linguistic groups, the principal ones being Yapese, Ulithian-Woleaian, Chuukese, Pohnpeian, Kosraean and Kapingimarangi-Nukuoroan. English is widely understood. The traditional social structure is based on matrilineal (except in the Polynesian islands of Kapingimarangi and Nukuoro) clans. A considerable degree of social stratification occurred, particularly in Yap, much of which remains. In Pohnpei social status was gained by complex competition for bestowed titles. The erosion of the traditional way of life is a source of considerable social strain. Most of the population, which totalled 107,008 at the census of 2000 according to provisional results, are Christian. The federal capital is at Palikir, on Pohnpei.

History

The Caroline Islands were first settled by the ancestors of the Micronesians some 4,000 years ago. The islands that now constitute the Federated States of Micronesia were then ruled by numerous clan chieftains. A form of tributary empire emerged at one point, initially based in Kosrae, but eventually succumbing to an economic and religious empire dominated by Yap. In 1525 Portuguese navigators first came upon the islands of Yap and Ulithi. Spanish expeditions subsequently reached the other Caroline Islands, and Spain only renounced its sovereignty in 1899, when the Carolines (including Palau) and the Mariana Islands (except the southernmost island of Guam) were sold to Germany, which had already secured the Marshall Islands. In 1914 this territory of German Micronesia was occupied by the Japanese, who acquired a League of Nations mandate to administer it in 1920. The USA conquered the territory in the Second World War and, in 1947, agreed to administer it, on behalf of the UN, as the Trust Territory of the Pacific Islands (TTPI). (For the history of the TTPI, see the chapter on Palau.)

Until 1979 the four districts of Yap, Truk (formerly Hogoleu, now Chuuk), Ponape (now Pohnpei) and Kosrae were governed by a local Administrator, appointed by the High Commissioner of the TTPI. However, on 10 May 1979 the four districts ratified a new Constitution to become the Federated States of Micronesia. The districts of Palau and the Marshall Islands had rejected participation in the federation.

The USA signed a Compact of Free Association with the Federated States of Micronesia in October 1982. The Compact with the Federated States of Micronesia was approved in a plebiscite in June 1983, and the Congress of the Federated States of Micronesia ratified the decision in September. The Compact of Free Association came into effect on 3 November 1986, and the territory was deemed to be subject to the Trusteeship no longer. In November President Reagan issued a proclamation which formally ended US administration in Micronesia. The final dissolution of the TTPI (which, in effect, consisted only of Palau) occurred on 1 October 1994, when the Compact between Palau and the USA came into effect. The UN Security Council formally terminated the Trusteeship Agreement in December 1990. Ponape was renamed Pohnpei in November 1984, when its Constitution came into effect. Truk was renamed Chuuk in January 1990, following the implementation of its new Constitution.

The Federated States of Micronesia has established diplomatic relations with numerous countries world-wide, and was admitted to the UN in September 1991.

The incumbent President, John Haglelgam, was replaced by Bailey Olter, a former Vice-President, in May 1991. At congressional elections in March 1995, Olter was re-elected to the Pohnpei Senator-at-Large seat, and in early May was re-elected to the presidency unopposed. Similarly, Jacob Nena was re-elected as Vice-President. Allegations that financial mismanagement by the Governor of Chuuk, Sasao Gouland, had resulted in state debts of some US $20m. led to his resignation in June 1996, in order to avoid impeachment proceedings. In July Olter suffered a stroke. Jacob Nena served as acting President during Olter's absence from office, and in May 1997 was sworn in as President of the country. Olter died in February 1999.

Congressional elections took place in early March 1997 for the 10 Senators elected on a two-yearly basis, at which all of the incumbents were returned to office. A referendum held concurrently on a proposed amendment to the Constitution (which envisaged increasing the allocation of national revenue to the state legislatures from 50% to 80% of the total budget) was approved in Chuuk and Yap, but rejected in Pohnpei and Kosrae.

Allegations of government interference in the media became widespread when the editor of the country's principal newspaper, *FSM News*, was refused permission to re-enter the islands in June 1997. The Government had sought to deport the editor (who was a Canadian national) following publication in the periodical of reports on government spending, which the authorities claimed were false and malicious. It was also thought that by enforcing the exclusion order, the Government hoped to suppress the publication in the newspaper of information relating to alleged corruption among public officials. The newspaper ceased publication in late 1997.

In February 1998 Congress approved proposals to restructure and reorganize the Cabinet. Several ministerial portfolios were consequently merged or abolished, with the aim of reducing government expenditure. Congressional elections took place on 2 March 1999, at which President Nena was re-elected to the Kosrae Senator-at-Large seat and Vice-President Leo Falcam to the Pohnpei Senator-at-Large seat. On 11 May Congress elected Falcam as President and the Chuuk Senator-at-Large, Redley Killion, as Vice-President.

A first round of renegotiations of the Compact of Free Association (certain terms of which were due to expire in 2001) was completed in late 1999. The USA and the Federated States of Micronesia pledged to maintain defence and security relations. It was also agreed that the USA would continue to provide economic aid to the islands and assist in the development of the private sector, as well as in promoting greater economic self-sufficiency. The Federated States of Micronesia undertook to ensure greater accountability with regard to US funding provided under the Compact. In July 2001 the USA offered assistance of US $61m. and a trust fund of US $13m., and expressed that concern that the US $2,600m. it had given to Micronesia and the Marshall Islands since 1986 had been mismanaged. The provision of the Compact on the funding needs for Micronesia was to expire on 3 November 2001, but negotiations continued in 2002. Provisions guaranteed a funding extension of two years for such an eventuality, during which period US assistance to Micronesia would increase by some $17m. In April 2002 the USA proposed to extend economic assistance for a period of 20 years, commencing with $72m. in 2004, and decreasing gradually each year thereafter. A trust fund of $19m., to increase each year, was established in order to offset the termination of direct financial assistance after 2023. The implementation of these measures required the approval of the US Congress prior to October 2003.

In December 1996 a state of emergency was declared after a typhoon wreaked devastation on the islands of Yap. Moreover, heavy rain which caused flooding and mudslides in Pohnpei in April 1997 resulted in the deaths of more than 20 people; another typhoon in mid-1997 caused considerable damage in Pohnpei and left several people dead. Furthermore, in early 1998 a state of emergency was declared following a prolonged period of severe drought throughout the islands, believed to have been caused by El Niño (a periodic warming of the tropical Pacific Ocean). In mid-1999 11 people in Pohnpei died following an outbreak of cholera on the island. The following May a state of emergency was declared on Pohnpei when cholera struck again. In August 2000 the Government announced a vaccination scheme for the entire population over two years of age. Import restrictions were introduced on the surrounding islands. Pohnpei was officially declared free of cholera on 16 February 2001. During the epidemic some 20 people died and a further 3,525 were estimated to have been infected. At least 49 people lost their lives when a typhoon struck Chuuk in July 2002.

In late 2000 marine biologists issued a warning regarding the erosion of the islands' coastlines, caused by the destruction of the coral reefs by pollution, over-fishing and increasing sea temperatures.

Congressional elections took place on 6 March 2001 for the 10 Senators elected on a two-yearly basis and for the representatives to the Third Constitutional Convention (which was to take place in November 2001). All the incumbents were returned to office, with the exception of the late Senator Nishima Yleizah, whose seat was occupied by Marcellino Umwech. The new Cabinet was confirmed in early April. On 9 April Senator Wagner Moses Lawrence, a member of Congress and the representative of Pohnpei's 2nd Congressional District, Madolenihmw and Kitti, died. His cousin, Onlino Lawrence, won the by-election for the vacant seat, held on 30 June, and was accredited in July. In September 2002 unrest occurred on the Faichuk islands, part of Chuuk, where the Faichuk Commission for Statehood continued its campaign to break away from Chuuk and gain equal status within the federation.

Economy

In 2000, according to estimates by the World Bank, gross national product (GNP) in the Federated States of Micronesia, measured at average 1998–2000 prices, was US $249.7m., equivalent to US $2,110 per head. GNP per head decreased at an average annual rate of 2.3% in 1990–99. Over the same period the population increased by an annual average of 2.1%. Gross domestic product (GDP) increased at an average annual rate of 2.0% in 1999–2000. GDP decreased by 1.6% in 1998, before rising by 2.6% in 1999 and 3.0% in 2000. GDP was estimated at US $205.0m., equivalent to US $1,735 per head, in 2000.

Agriculture is mainly on a subsistence level, although its importance is diminishing. The principal agricultural crops are coconuts (from which some 725 metric tons of copra were produced in 2000), bananas, betel-nuts, cassava and sweet potatoes. White peppercorns are produced on Pohnpei. The sector (including forestry and fishing) engaged 55.3% of the employed labour force in 2000. Exports of bananas accounted for 1.2% of export earnings in 1999. A dramatic increase in the re-export of fish to Japan by foreign vessels operating in the islands' waters in 1994 was responsible for growth of almost 300% in earnings from the fishing industry. In 1996 the islands' share of earnings under the Multilateral Fisheries Treaty with the USA increased from 8% to 20%. Fees from foreign fisheries licensing agreements, mainly with Japan, contributed some 30% of budgetary revenue in 1997. In the same year the Government received a technical assistance grant, worth some $0.9m., for the development and implementation of a national fisheries plan aimed at ensuring the efficient management and conservation of the islands' marine resources. In 1999/2000 fishing access fees totalled $16.8m.

The tourist industry is a significant source of foreign exchange. It was hoped that several projects aimed at improving communications would stimulate tourism, hitherto hindered by the territory's remote situation. The industry was identified in a report by the Asian Development Bank (ADB) in mid-1995 as having the greatest potential for development and thus contribution to the islands' economic growth. Some 32,530 tourists arrived on the islands in 2000.

In the year ending 30 September 2001 there was a visible trade deficit of US $130.8m., but a surplus of $3.3m. on the current account of the balance of payments. The value of exports was estimated at $2m. in 1999, when imports cost some US $12m. The principal imports in 1999 were food and live animals (24.8% of the total), mineral fuels and lubricants (20.3%), machines and transport equipment (19.5%) and basic manufactures (18.9%). Fish is the major export commodity, mainly in the form of re-exports to Japan (accounting for 91.9% of total export earnings in 1999). Other significant exports are garments and buttons (8.4%), handicrafts, bananas, copra, trochus shells and pepper. The USA provided 43.9% of total imports in 1999, when Australia supplied 19.8%. Japan was the principal market for exports in 1999, taking 83.9% of the total.

In 1999/2000 there was an estimated budget surplus of US $0.4m. The Federated States of Micronesia relies heavily on financial assistance, particularly from the USA, which in 2000/01 provided $85m. (equivalent to around 35% of GDP). In April 2001 Japan donated US $7m. to improve the road network in the state of Yap. At the end of the 2000/01 financial year the islands' total external debt was estimated at US $58m. In that year the cost of debt-servicing was projected to be equivalent to 22.0% of the value of exports of goods and services. Consumer prices increased by 2.6% in 1999, by an estimated 3.2% in 2000 and by an estimated 2.6% in 2001. According to the ADB, some 2.6% of the labour force was unemployed in 2000.

The islands are vulnerable to adverse climatic conditions, as was illustrated in late 1997 and early 1998, when a prolonged drought caused problems throughout the islands. An extremely high rate of natural increase in the population has exacerbated certain economic problems, but is partially offset by an annual emigration rate of more than 2%. In 1997 the ADB approved a loan of US $17.68m. for the funding of its so-called Private Sector Development programme, a major structural adjustment of the economy, in preparation for the cessation of US assistance under the Compact of Free Association, the original terms of which expired in September 2001. The reform programme comprised measures to attract new sources of foreign aid and private investment, fiscal reform and the strengthening of the private sector, as well as severe reductions in the number of public-sector employees. In late 1999 an Economic Policy Implementation Council (EPIC) was established in an attempt to monitor the reform process. While commending the successful implementation of certain policies, notably the retrenchment in government expenditure and the development of the private sector, concerns were expressed by the ADB regarding the Federated States of Micronesia's overdependence on foreign aid, and the adverse impact of this on the establishment of economic self-sufficiency. With the renegotiation of several terms of the Compact in late 1999 (see History), the USA emphasized its continued commitment to the economic development of the islands, including the promotion of greater self-sufficiency, in return for improved accountability regarding US funding by the Micronesia Government. In December 2000 the ADB approved a US $8m. loan to fund a six-year reform programme of the health and education sectors. In December 2001 the ADB granted a further loan of $13m. targeted at job creation, increased production for both domestic and export markets and the development of a competitive services sector. The uncertainty surrounding the future of the public sector, meanwhile, had continued to deter investment in the private sector. Furthermore, the private sector was constrained by the disproportionately high cost of domestic labour, rates of pay in the public sector having risen substantially in recent years (to about double those prevailing in the private sector) as a result of the large external inflows. The ADB estimated that GDP expanded by 1.5% in 2001. In June 2002 the ADB and the Micronesian Government agreed to prepare a National Poverty Reduction Strategy.

In early 1996 the Federated States of Micronesia joined representatives of the other countries and territories of Micronesia at a meeting in Hawaii, at which a new regional organization, the Council of Micronesian Government Executives, was established. The new body aimed to facilitate discussion of economic developments in the region and to examine possibilities for reducing the considerable cost of shipping essential goods between the islands. The territory is a member of the Pacific Community (formerly the South Pacific Commission), the Pacific Islands Forum (formerly the South Pacific Forum), the South Pacific Regional Trade and Economic Co-operation Agreement (SPARTECA), the UN and its Economic and Social Commission for Asia and the Pacific (ESCAP), the ADB and from 2000 the Africa, Caribbean and Pacific Group (ACP-EU).

Statistical Survey

Note: Further statistics relating to the Federated States of Micronesia are to be found in the chapter on the Marshall Islands.

AREA AND POPULATION

Area: 700 sq km (270.3 sq miles): Chuuk (294 islands) 127 sq km; Kosrae (5 islands) 110 sq km; Pohnpei (163 islands) 344 sq km; Yap (145 islands) 119 sq km.

Population: 105,506 (53,923 males, 51,583 females) at census of 18 September 1994; 107,008 (males 54,191, females 52,817) at 2000 census (provisional). *By State* (2000): Chuuk 53,595; Kosrae 7,686; Pohnpei 34,486; Yap 11,241.

Density (2000): 153 per sq km. *By State* (per sq km): Chuuk 422.0; Kosrae 70.0; Pohnpei 100.3; Yap 94.5.

Births and Deaths (2000, official estimates): Birth rate 27.1 per 1,000; Death rate 6.0 per 1,000.

Expectation of Life (WHO estimates, years at birth, 2000): Males 63.7; Females 67.7 (Source: WHO, *World Health Report*).

Economically Active Population ('000 persons, 2000): Agriculture, forestry and fishing 17.25; Total employed (incl. others) 31.21; Unemployed 0.82; Total labour force 32.02. Source: Asian Development Bank, *Key Indicators of Developing Asian and Pacific Countries*.

HEALTH AND WELFARE

Key Indicators

Fertility (births per woman, 2000): 5.1.

Under-5 Mortality Rate (per 1,000 live births, 2000): 24.

Physicians (per 1,000 head, 1999): 0.57.

Hospital Beds (per 1,000 head, 1989): 3.47.

Health Expenditure (1998): US $ per head (PPP): 364.
% of GDP: 10.5.
public (% of total): 55.3.

For sources and definitions, see explanatory note on p. vi.

AGRICULTURE, ETC.

Principal Crops:* (FAO estimates, '000 metric tons, 2000): Coconuts 140; Cassava 12; Bananas 2; Sweet potatoes 3. Source: FAO.

Livestock:* (FAO estimates, '000 head, year ending September 2000): Pigs 32; Cattle 14; Goats 4; Poultry 185. Source: FAO.

Livestock Products:* ('000 metric tons, 2000): Beef and veal 245; Pig meat 873; Poultry meat 135; Hen eggs 175; Cattle hides 45. Source: FAO.

* Including the Northern Mariana Islands, the Marshall Islands and Palau.

Fishing ('000 metric tons, live weight, 1999): Skipjack tuna 6.6; Yellowfin tuna 3.1; Bigeye tuna 1.0; Total (incl. others) 11.9 (FAO estimate). Source: FAO, *Yearbook of Fishery Statistics*.

FINANCE

Currency and Exchange Rates: United States currency is used: 100 cents = 1 United States dollar (US $). *Sterling and Euro Equivalents* (31 May 2002): £1 sterling = US $1.4667; €1 = 93.87 US cents; US $100 = £68.18 = €106.53.

Budget (estimates, US $ million, year ending 30 September 2000): *Revenue:* Domestic 56.6 (Tax 26.3, Non-tax 30.3); Grants 96.2; Total 152.8. *Expenditure:* Recurrent 124.4; Capital 28.0; Total 152.4. Source: Asian Development Bank, *Key Indicators of Developing Asian and Pacific Countries*.

Gross Domestic Product by Economic Activity (US $ million at current prices, 1996): Agriculture, forestry and fishing 34.7; Mining and quarrying 0.7; Manufacturing 2.6; Electricity, gas and water 1.9; Construction 1.9; Wholesale and retail trade 39.5; Hotels and restaurants 4.1; Transport, storage and communications 8.5; Finance, real estate and business services 5.5; Government services 76.5; Other services 5.6; GDP in purchasers' values 181.5. Source: IMF, *Federated States of Micronesia: Recent Economic Developments* (August 1998).

Balance of Payments (estimates, US $ million, year ending 30 September 2001): Merchandise exports (incl. re-exports) f.o.b. 23.8; Merchandise imports f.o.b. −154.6; *Trade balance* −130.8; Exports of services 57.9; Imports of services −42.0; *Balance on goods and services* −114.9; Private unrequited transfers 4.2; Official unrequited transfers 107.4; *Current balance* −3.3; Long-term capital (net) −8.9; Short-term capital (net) −2.8; Net errors and omissions 11.0; *Overall balance* −4.0. Source: Asian Development Bank, *Key Indicators of Developing Asian and Pacific Countries*.

EXTERNAL TRADE

Principal Commodities (estimates, US $'000, 1999): *Imports:* Food and live animals 3,053; Beverages and tobacco 738; Crude materials (inedible) except fuel 52; Mineral fuels, lubricants, etc. 2,503; Chemicals 534; Basic manufactures 2,326; Machinery and transport equipment 2,406; Miscellaneous manufactured articles 701; Total (incl. others) 12,328. *Exports:* Fish 1,956; Bananas 25; Total (incl. others) 2,128. Source: Asian Development Bank, *Key Indicators of Developing Asian and Pacific Countries*.

Principal Trading Partners (US $'000, 1999): *Imports:* Australia 2,440; Japan 1,536; USA 5,409; Total (incl. others) 12,328. *Exports:* Japan 1,785; Marshall Islands 23; Total (incl. others) 2,128. Source: Asian Development Bank, *Key Indicators of Developing Asian and Pacific Countries*.

TRANSPORT

Shipping: *Merchant Fleet* (registered at 31 December 2001): Vessels 18; Total displacement ('000 grt) 9.2. Source: Lloyd's Register-Fairplay, *World Fleet Statistics*.

TOURISM

Foreign Tourist Arrivals: 27,222 in 1998; 27,853 in 1999; 32,530 in 2000. Source: World Tourism Organization, *Yearbook of Tourism Statistics*.

Tourist Arrivals by Country of Residence (2000): Australia 895; China, People's Republic 3,639; Japan 6,044; Korea, Republic 2,386; Philippines 2,893; Taiwan 1,197; USA 8,789; Total (incl. others) 32,530. Source: World Tourism Organization, *Yearbook of Tourism Statistics*.

COMMUNICATIONS MEDIA

Telephones ('000 main lines in use, 2001): 10.0*.

Facsimile Machines (number in use, 1998): 539*.

Radio Receivers (1996): 22,000 in use.

Internet Users ('000, 2000): 4.0*.

Television Receivers (1996): 19,800 in use.

* Source: International Telecommunication Union.

EDUCATION

Primary (1995): 174 schools; 1,051 teachers (1984); 27,281 pupils.

Secondary (1995): 24 schools; 314 teachers (1984); 6,898 pupils.

Tertiary (1994): 1,461 students.

Source: UN, *Statistical Yearbook for Asia and the Pacific*.

Directory

The Constitution

On 10 May 1979 the locally-drafted Constitution of the Federated States of Micronesia, incorporating the four states of Kosrae, Yap, Ponape (formally renamed Pohnpei in November 1984) and Truk (renamed Chuuk in January 1990), became effective. Each of the four states has its own Constitution, elected legislature and Governor. The Constitution guarantees fundamental human rights and establishes a separation of the judicial, executive and legislative powers. The federal legislature, the Congress of the Federated States of Micronesia, is a unicameral parliament with 14 members, popularly elected. The executive consists of the President, elected by the Congress, and a Cabinet. The Constitution provides for a review of the governmental and federal system every 10 years.

In November 1986 the Compact of Free Association was signed by the Governments of the Federated States of Micronesia and the USA. By the terms of the Compact, the Federated States of Micronesia is an internally sovereign, self-governing state, whose policy concerning foreign affairs must be consistent with guidelines laid down in the Compact. Full responsibility for defence lies with the USA, which also undertakes to provide regular economic assistance. The security arrangements may be terminated only by mutual agreement. The economic and defence provisions of the Compact are renewable after 15 years (a first round of negotiations was completed in 1999), but the status of free association continues indefinitely.

The Government

HEAD OF STATE

President: Leo Falcam (appointed 11 May 1999).

Vice-President: Redley Killion.

THE CABINET
(September 2002)

Secretary of the Department of Finance and Administration: John Ehsa.

Secretary of the Department of Foreign Affairs: Ieske K. Iehsi.

Secretary of the Department of Economic Affairs: Sebastian Anefal.

Secretary of the Department of Health, Education and Social Services: Dr Eliuel K. Pretrick.

Secretary of the Department of Justice: Paul McIlraith.

Secretary of the Department of Transportation, Communications and Infrastructure: Akilino Susaia.

Public Defender: Beautean C. Worswick.

GOVERNMENT OFFICES

Office of the President: POB PS-53, Palikir, Pohnpei, FM 96941; tel. 320-2228; fax 320-2785.

Department of Economic Affairs: POB PS-12, Palikir, Pohnpei, FM 96941; tel. 320-2646; fax 320-5854; e-mail fsmrd@mail.fm; internet www.fsminvest.fm.

Department of Finance and Administration: POB PS-158, Palikir, Pohnpei, FM 96941; tel. 320-2640; fax 320-2380.

Department of Foreign Affairs: POB PS-123, Palikir, Pohnpei, FM 96941; tel. 320-2641; fax 320-2933; e-mail foreignaffairs@mail.fm.

Department of Health, Education and Social Services: POB PS-70, Palikir, Pohnpei, FM 96941; tel. 320-2872; fax 320-5263.

Department of Justice: POB PS-174, Palikir Pohnpei, FM 96941; tel. 320-2644; fax 320-2234.

Department of Transportation, Communications and Infrastructure: POB PS-2, Palikir, Pohnpei, FM 96941; tel. 320-2865; fax 320-5853.

Office of the Public Defender: POB PS-174, Palikir, Pohnpei, FM 96941; tel. 320-2648; fax 320-5775.

Public Information Office: POB PS-34, Palikir, Pohnpei, FM 96941; tel. 320-2548; fax 320-4356.

Legislature

CONGRESS OF THE FEDERATED STATES OF MICRONESIA

The Congress comprises 14 members (Senators), of whom four are elected for a four-year term and 10 for a two-year term.

Speaker: JACK FRITZ.

STATE LEGISLATURES

Chuuk State Legislature: POB 189, Weno, Chuuk, FM 96942; tel. 330-2234; fax 330-2233; Senate of 10 mems and House of Representatives of 28 mems elected for four years; Gov. ANSITO WALTER.

Kosrae State Legislature: POB 187, Tofol, Kosrae, FM 96944; tel. 370-3002; fax 370-3162; e-mail kosraelc@mail.fm; unicameral body of 14 mems serving for four years; Gov. RENSLEY A. SIGRAH.

Pohnpei State Legislature: POB 39, Kolonia, Pohnpei, FM 96941; tel. 320-2235; fax 320-2505; internet www.fm/pohnpeileg/; 27 representatives elected for four years (terms staggered); Gov. JOHNNY P. DAVID.

Yap State Legislature: POB 39, Colonia, Yap, FM 96943; tel. 350-2108; fax 350-4113; 10 mems, six elected from the Yap Islands proper and four elected from the Outer Islands of Ulithi and Woleai, for a four-year term; Gov. VINCENT A. FIGIR.

Diplomatic Representation

EMBASSIES IN MICRONESIA

Australia: POB S, Kolonia, Pohnpei, FM 96941; tel. 320-5448; fax 320-5449; e-mail australia@mail.fm; internet www.australianembassy.fm; Ambassador: BRENDAN DORAN.

China, People's Republic: Kolonia, Pohnpei, FM 96941; Ambassador: XU JUN.

Japan: Pami Bldg, 3rd Floor, POB 1847, Kolonia, Pohnpei, FM 96941; tel. 320-5465; fax 320–5470; Chargé d'affaires a.i.: SHIGEATSU NAKAJIMA.

USA: POB 1286, Kolonia, Pohnpei, FM 96941; tel. 320-2187; fax 320-2186; e-mail usembassy@mail.fm; internet www.fm/usembassy/index.htm; Ambassador: LARRY DINGER.

Judicial System

Supreme Court of the Federated States of Micronesia: POB PS-J, Palikir Station, Pohnpei, FM 96941; tel. 320-2357; fax 320-2756; Chief Justice ANDON L. AMARAICH.

State Courts and Appellate Courts have been established in Yap, Chuuk, Kosrae and Pohnpei.

Religion

The population is predominantly Christian, mainly Roman Catholic. The Assembly of God, Jehovah's Witnesses, Seventh-day Adventists, the Church of Jesus Christ of Latter-day Saints (Mormons), the United Church of Christ, Baptists and the Bahá'í Faith are also represented.

CHRISTIANITY

The Roman Catholic Church

The Federated States of Micronesia forms a part of the diocese of the Caroline Islands, suffragan to the archdiocese of Agaña (Guam). The Bishop participates in the Catholic Bishops' Conference of the Pacific, based in Fiji. At 31 December 2000 there were 70,185 adherents in the diocese.

Bishop of the Caroline Islands: Most Rev. AMANDO SAMO, Bishop's House, POB 939, Weno, Chuuk, FM 96942; tel. 330-2399; fax 330-4585; e-mail diocese@mail.fm; internet www.diocesecarolines.org.

Other Churches

United Church of Christ in Pohnpei: Kolonia, Pohnpei, FM 96941.

Liebenzell Mission: Rev. Roland Rauchholz, POB 9, Weno, Chuuk, FM 96942; tel. 330-3869.

The Press

Chuuk News Chronicle: POB 244, Wenn, Chuuk, FM 96942; f. 1983; Editor MARCIANA AKASY.

FSM—Job Training Partnership Act News: Pohnpei, FM 96941; f. 1994; monthly; US-funded.

The Island Tribune: Pohnpei, FM 96941; f. 1997; 2 a week.

Micronesia Focus: Pohnpei, FM 96941; f. 1994; Editor KETSON JOHNSON.

The National Union: FSM Public Information Office, POB 490, Kolonia, Pohnpei, FM 96941; tel. 320-2548; f. 1980; 2 a month; Public Information Officer KETSON JOHNSON; circ. 5,000.

Broadcasting and Communications

TELECOMMUNICATIONS

FSM Telecommunication Corporation: POB 1210, Kolonia, Pohnpei, FM 96941; tel. 320-2740; fax 320-2745; e-mail takinaga@mail.fm; internet www.telecom.fm; provides domestic and international services; Gen. Man. TAKURO AKINAGA.

BROADCASTING

Radio

Federated States of Micronesia Public Information Office: POB PS-34, Palikir, Pohnpei, FM 96941; tel. 320-2548; fax 320-4356; e-mail fsmpio@mail.fm; internet www.fsmpio.fm; govt-operated; four regional stations, each broadcasting 18 hours daily; Information Officer TERRY G. THINOM.

Station V6AH: POB 1086, Kolonia, Pohnpei, FM 96941; programmes in English and Ponapean; Man. DUSTY FREDERICK.

Station V6AI: POB 117, Colonia, Yap, FM 96943; tel. 350-2174; fax 350-4426; programmes in English, Yapese, Ulithian and Satawalese; Man. PETER GARAMFEL.

Station V6AJ: POB 147, Tofol, Kosrae, FM 96944; tel. 370-3040; fax 370-3880; e-mail v6aj.@.mail.fm; programmes in English and Kosraean; Man. NENA TOLENNA.

Station V6AK: Wenn, Chuuk, FM 96942; programmes in Chuukese and English; Man. P. J. MAIPI.

Television

Island Cable TV—Pohnpei: POB 1628, Pohnpei, FM 96941; tel. 320-2671; fax 320-2670; e-mail ictv@mail.fm; f. 1991; Pres. BERNARD HELGENBERGER; Gen. Man. DAVID O. CLIFFE.

TV Station Chuuk—TTKK: Wenn, Chuuk, FM 96942; commercial.

TV Station Pohnpei—KPON: Central Micronesia Communications, POB 460, Kolonia, Pohnpei, FM 96941; f. 1977; commercial; Pres. BERNARD HELGENBERGER; Tech. Dir DAVID CLIFFE.

TV Station Yap—WAAB: Colonia, Yap, FM 96943; tel. 350-2160; fax 350-4113; govt-owned; Man. LOU DEFNGIN.

Finance

BANKING

Federated States of Micronesian Banking Board: POB 1887 Kolonia, Pohnpei, FM 96941; e-mail fmbb@mail.fm; f. 1980; Chair. LARRY RAIGETAL; Commissioner WILSON F. WAGUK.

Commercial Banks

Bank of the Federated States of Micronesia: POB 98, Kolonia, Pohnpei, FM 96941; tel. 320-2724; fax 370-5359; e-mail bofsmhq@mail.fm; internet www.fm/BoFSM; brs in Kosrae, Yap, Pohnpei and Chuuk.

Bank of Guam (USA): POB 367, Kolonia, Pohnpei, FM 96941; tel. 320-2550; fax 320-2562; Man. VIDA RICAFRENTE; brs in Chuuk and Pohnpei.

Bank of Hawaii (USA): POB 280, Kolonia, Pohnpei, FM 96941; tel. 320-2543; fax 320-2547; Man. AREN PALIK. POB 309, Yap, Western Caroline Islands FM 96943; tel. 350-2129; Man. CHRISTINA MICHELSON; brs in Kosrae.

Development Bank

Federated States of Micronesia Development Bank: POB M, Kolonia, Pohnpei, FM 96941; tel. 320-2480; fax 320-2842; e-mail fsmdb@mail.fm; f. 1979; total assets US $54m. (Dec. 1994); Chair. WILLIAM IRIARTE; Pres. MANNY MORI; 4 brs.

Banking services for the rest of the islands are available in Guam, Hawaii and on the US mainland.

INSURANCE

Actouka Executive Insurance: POB Q, Kolonia, Pohnpei; tel. 320-5331; fax 320-2331; e-mail mlamar@mail.fm.

Caroline Insurance Underwriters: POB 37, Chuuk; tel. 330-2651; fax 330-2207.

FSM Insurance Group: Kosrae; tel. 370-2294; fax 370-2120.

Moylan's Insurance Underwriters: POB 1448, Kolonia, Pohnpei; tel. 320-2118; fax 320-2519; e-mail moylan90@mail.fm.

Oceania Insurance Co.: POB 1202, Weno, Chuuk, FM 96942; tel. 330-3036; fax 330-3764;/5274; owns Pacific Basin Insurance.

Pacific Basin Insurance: e-mail oceanpac@mail.fm.

Yap Insurance Agency: Yap; tel. 350-2340; fax 350-2341; e-mail tachelioyap@mail.fm.

Trade and Industry

GOVERNMENT AGENCIES

Coconut Development Authority: POB 297, Kolonia, Pohnpei, FM 96941; tel. 320-2892; fax 320-5383; e-mail fsmcda@mail.fm; responsible for all purchasing, processing and exporting of copra and copra by-products in the islands; Gen. Man. Namio Nanpei.

Economic Development Authority: Kolonia, Pohnpei, FM 96941; Chair. President of the Federated States of Micronesia.

FSM National Fisheries Corporation: POB R, Kolonia, Pohnpei, FM 96941; tel. 320-2529; fax 320-2239; e-mail nfcairfreight@mail.fm; internet www.fsmgov.org/nfc/; f. 1984; in 1990 it set up, with the Economic Devt Authority and an Australian co, the Caroline Fishing Co (three vessels); exists to promote fisheries development; Pres. Peter Sitan; Chair. Sebastian Anefal.

Micronesian Fisheries Authority: POB PS-122, Palikir, Pohnpei, FM 96941; tel. 320-2700; fax 320-2383; e-mail fsmfish@mail.fm; fmrly Micronesian Maritime Authority; responsible for conservation, management and development of tuna resources and for issue of fishing licences; Chair. Jesse Raglmar-Subolmar; Vice-Chair. Gerson Jackson; Exec. Dir Bernard Thoulag.

UTILITIES

Chuuk Public Works (CPW): POB 248, Weno, Chuuk, FM 96942; tel. 330-2242; fax 320-4815; e-mail chkpublicworks@mail.fm.

Kosrae Utility Authority: POB 277, Tofol, Kosrae, FM 96944; tel. 370-3799; fax 370-3798; e-mail KUA@mail.fm; corporatized in 1994.

Pohnpei Utility Corporation: POB C, Kolonia, Pohnpei, FM 96941; tel. 320-5606; fax 320-2505; f. 1992; provides electricity, water and sewerage services.

Yap Public Services Corporation: POB 621, Colonia, Yap, FM 96943; tel. 350-2175; fax 350-2331; f. 1996; provides electricity, water and sewerage services.

CO-OPERATIVES

Chuuk: Chuuk Co-operative, Faichuk Cacao and Copra Co-operative Asscn, Pis Fishermen's Co-operative, Fefan Women's Co-operative.

Pohnpei: Pohnpei Federation of Co-operative Asscns (POB 100, Pohnpei, FM 96941), Pohnpei Handicraft Co-operative, Pohnpei Fishermen's Co-operative, Uh Soumwet Co-operative Asscn, Kolonia Consumers' and Producers' Co-operative Asscn, Kitti Minimum Co-operative Asscn, Kapingamarangi Copra Producers' Asscn, Metalanim Copra Co-operative Asscn, PICS Co-operative Asscn, Mokil Island Co-operative Asscn, Ngatik Island Co-operative Asscn, Nukuoro Island Co-operative Asscn, Kosrae Island Co-operative Asscn, Pingelap Consumers' Co-operative Asscn.

Yap: Yap Co-operative Asscn, POB 159, Colonia, Yap, FM 96943; tel. 350-2209; fax 350-4114; e-mail yca@mail.fm; f. 1952; Pres. James Gilmar; Gen. Man. Tony Ganngiyan; 1,200 mems.

Transport

ROADS

Macadam and concrete roads are found in the more important islands. Other islands have stone and coral-surfaced roads and tracks.

SHIPPING

Pohnpei, Chuuk, Yap and Kosrae have deep-draught harbours for commercial shipping. The ports provide warehousing and transhipment facilities.

Truk Shipping Company: POB 669, Weno, Chuuk, FM 96942; tel. 330-2455.

CIVIL AVIATION

The Federated States of Micronesia is served by Continental Micronesia, Air Nauru and Continental Airlines (USA). Pacific Missionary Aviation, based in Pohnpei and Yap, provides domestic air services. There are international airports on Pohnpei, Chuuk, Yap and Kosrae, and airstrips on the outer islands of Onoun and Ta in Chuuk.

Tourism

The tourist industry is a significant source of revenue, although it has been hampered by the lack of infrastructure. Visitor attractions include excellent conditions for scuba-diving (notably in Chuuk Lagoon), Second World War battle sites and relics (many underwater) and the ancient ruined city of Nan Madol on Pohnpei. In 1990 there was a total of 362 hotel rooms. The number of tourist arrivals totalled 32,530 in 2000.

Federated States of Micronesia Visitors Board: Dept of Economic Affairs, National Government, Palikir, Pohnpei, FM 96941; tel. 320-2646; fax 320-5854; internet www.visit-micronesia.fm.

Chuuk Visitors Bureau: POB FQ, Weno, Chuuk, FM 96942; tel. 330-4133; fax 330-4194; e-mail cvb@mail.fm.

Kosrae Visitors Bureau: POB 659, Tofol, Kosrae, FM 96944; tel. 370-2228; fax 370-2187; e-mail kosrae@mail.fm; internet www.kosrae.com.

Pohnpei Department of Tourism and Parks: POB 66, Kolonia, Pohnpei, FM 96941; tel. 320-2421; fax 320-6019; e-mail tourismparks@mail.fm; Deputy Chief Bumio Silbanuz.

Pohnpei Visitors Bureau: POB 1949, Kolonia, Pohnpei, FM 96941; tel. 320-4851; fax 320-4868; e-mail pohnpeiVB@mail.fm; internet www.visit-pohnpei.fm.

Yap Visitors Bureau: POB 36, Colonia, Yap, FM 96943; tel. 350-2298; fax 350-2571; e-mail yvb@mail.fm; internet www.visityap.com.

Defence

Defence and security are the responsibility of the USA. The US Pacific Command is based in Hawaii.

Education

Primary education, which begins at six years of age and lasts for eight years, is compulsory. Secondary education, beginning at 14 years of age, comprises two cycles, each of two years. The education system is based on the US pattern of eight years' attendance at an elementary school and four years' enrolment at a high school. In 1995 there were a total of 27,281 pupils enrolled at 174 primary schools and 6,898 pupils at 24 secondary schools. In 1994 some 1,461 students were involved in tertiary education.

Nauru

Physical and Social Geography

The Republic of Nauru is a small island in the central Pacific Ocean, lying about 4,000 km north-east of Sydney, Australia, and 306 km west of Banaba (Ocean Island), in Kiribati, its nearest neighbour. Covering an area of 21.3 sq km (8.2 sq miles), Nauru is a low-lying island (its highest point is 65 m—213 feet), comprising a narrow, coastal strip of fertile land surrounding coralline cliffs rising to a plateau of phosphatic rock which covers more than three-fifths of the land area. Nauru has a tropical climate, with a westerly monsoon season from November to February, during which time most rainfall occurs. Annual rainfall averages 2,060 mm (80 ins), but there are marked variations from year to year. Indigenous Nauruans are of mixed Polynesian, Micronesian and Melanesian descent, but are predominantly Polynesian. Nauruan is the official language, although English is widely used and generally understood. At the 1992 census the population was 9,919. In July 2001 the population was estimated at 12,088. There is no capital as such, but Parliament House and most government offices are in Yaren district.

History

The first European to discover Nauru was Capt. John Fearn, whose whaling ship, *Hunter*, reached the island in 1798. The territory, which he named Pleasant Island, was described as being inhabited by relatively large numbers of predominantly Polynesian people, organized in 12 clans. The arrival of traders during the 19th century and the subsequent introduction of firearms and alcohol on to the island, however, led to unrest between the tribes and precipitated 'The Ten-Year War': a civil war in which more than one-third of the population were killed. When the island was eventually annexed by Germany in 1888, its inhabitants numbered little more than 900 in total. In 1914, shortly after the outbreak of the First World War, the island was captured by Australian forces. It continued to be administered by Australia under a League of Nations mandate (granted in 1920) which also named the United Kingdom and New Zealand as co-trustees. Between 1942 and 1945 Nauru was occupied by the Japanese, who deported 1,200 islanders to Truk (now Chuuk), Micronesia, where some 500 died as a result of starvation and bombing. In 1947 the island was placed under United Nations Trusteeship, with Australia as the administering power on behalf of the Governments of Australia, New Zealand and the United Kingdom. The UN Trusteeship Council proposed in 1964 that the indigenous people of Nauru be resettled on Curtis Island, off the Queensland coast. This offer was made in anticipation of the progressive exhaustion of the island's phosphate deposits. The Nauruans, however, elected to remain on the island, and studies were initiated in 1966 for the shipping of soil to the island to replace the phosphate rock. Nauru received a considerable measure of self-government in January 1966, with the establishment of Legislative and Executive Councils, and proceeded to independence on 31 January 1968 (exactly 22 years after the surviving Nauruans returned to the island from exile in Micronesia). In early 1998 Nauru announced its intention to seek UN membership and full Commonwealth membership. The decision was largely based on the islanders' desire to play a more prominent role in international policies relating to issues that affect them, most notably climate change (see below). Nauru attained full membership of the Commonwealth in May 1999. The country's bid to seek UN membership was challenged by the People's Republic of China because of Nauru's links with Taiwan. Nevertheless, Nauru became a member of the UN in September 1999.

The Head Chief of Nauru, Hammer DeRoburt, was elected President in May 1968 and re-elected in 1971 and 1973. Dissatisfaction with his increasingly personal rule led to the election of a new President, Bernard Dowiyogo (leader of the informal Nauru Party), in 1976. Dowiyogo was re-elected President after a general election in late 1977. DeRoburt's supporters, however, adopted obstructive tactics in Parliament, and in January 1978 Dowiyogo resigned, in response to a parliamentary impasse over budgetary legislation; he was re-elected shortly afterwards, but was again forced to resign in April, following the defeat of a legislative proposal concerning phosphate royalties. Lagumot Harris, another member of the Nauru Party, succeeded him, but resigned three weeks later, when Parliament rejected a finance measure, and DeRoburt was again elected to the presidency. He was re-elected in December 1980 and again in May and December 1983.

In September 1986, following the Government's defeat on a parliamentary motion proposing an amendment to the annual budget legislation, DeRoburt resigned, and was replaced as President by Kennan Adeang, who was elected in Parliament by nine votes to DeRoburt's eight. However, after holding office for only 14 days, Adeang was, in turn, defeated in a parliamentary vote expressing 'no confidence' and DeRoburt resumed the presidency. Following a general election in December 1986, Adeang was narrowly elected President. However, he was subsequently ousted by another vote of 'no confidence', and DeRoburt was again reinstated as President. The atmosphere of political uncertainty, generated by the absence of a clear majority in Parliament, led DeRoburt to dissolve Parliament in preparation for another general election in January 1987, at which DeRoburt was re-elected to the presidency by 11 votes to six.

In February 1987 Adeang announced the establishment of the Democratic Party of Nauru, thus giving formal status to the first new political grouping in Nauru since 1976. Eight of the 18 members of Parliament subsequently joined the new party, which declared that its aim was to curtail the extension of presidential powers and to promote democracy. In August 1989 a motion of 'no confidence' in DeRoburt (proposed by Adeang) was approved by 10 votes to five, and Kenai Aroi was subsequently elected President. Following a general election, held in December, Bernard Dowiyogo was re-elected President, defeating his only opponent, DeRoburt, by 10 votes to six. The next presidential election, held shortly after a general election in November 1992, resulted in victory for Dowiyogo, who defeated Buraro Detudamo by 10 votes to seven. Following a general election in November 1995, in which all cabinet members were re-elected, Nauru's newly-elected Parliament voted, by nine votes to eight, to replace Dowiyogo with Lagumot Harris in the presidency.

The resignation of the Chairman of Air Nauru, following allegations of misconduct, prompted Parliament to vote on a motion of 'no confidence' in the Government in November 1996. The motion was narrowly approved, and Harris was replaced by Dowiyogo as President. Later that month, however, Dowiyogo's new Government was itself defeated in a parliamentary vote of 'no confidence', and Kennan Adeang was elected to the presidency. A widespread perception that the new Government lacked experience was thought to be a major factor prompting a further motion of 'no confidence' in December, at which Adeang was similarly removed from office. At a subsequent presidential contest Reuben Kun, a former Minister for Finance, defeated Adeang by 12 votes to five, on the understanding that his administration would organize a general election. An election duly took place on 8 February 1997, at which four new members were elected to Parliament, following an apparent agreement between the supporters of Harris and those of Dowiyogo to end the political manoeuvring that had resulted in several months of instability in Nauru. At the election to the presidency on 13 February, Kinza Clodumar (who had been nominated by Dowiyogo) defeated Harris by nine votes to eight.

In early 1998 five members of Parliament (including former President Lagumot Harris) were dismissed by Adeang, the Speaker, for refusing to apologize for personal remarks about him that had been published in an opposition newsletter in late 1997. At the resultant by-elections held in late February 1998 three of the five members were re-elected. A motion expressing 'no confidence' in the President was approved in June, and Dowiyogo was consequently elected to replace Clodumar. In a further vote of 'no confidence', in late April 1999 Dowiyogo was defeated by 10 votes to seven; his replacement was Rene Harris, previously Chairman of the Nauru Phosphate Corporation. Former President Lagumot Harris died in September 1999.

Following legislative elections held on 8 April 2000, Rene Harris was re-elected president, narrowly defeating Dowiyogo by nine votes to eight. Ludwig Scotty was elected Speaker of Parliament. On 18 April, however, Scotty and his deputy, Ross Cain, subsequently resigned, stating only that they were unable to continue under the 'current political circumstances'. Harris tendered his resignation and was replaced by Dowiyogo on 19 April, whereupon Scotty and Cain were re-elected to their posts in the legislature. Observers attributed the manoeuvring to shifting political allegiances within the legislature.

In early 2001, in another reversal to Dowiyogo's leadership, Anthony Audoa, the Minister for Home Affairs, Culture, Health and Women's Affairs, resigned and requested that Parliament be recalled. He claimed that Dowiyogo had squandered Nauru's wealth during his various tenures as President and that in promoting the island as a tax haven he had allowed Nauru to be used by Russian criminal gangs to 'launder' their illegal funds, prompting speculation that he intended to mount a challenge for the presidency. In late March 2001 Dowiyogo was ousted from the presidency in a parliamentary vote of 'no confidence' while he was undergoing hospital treatment in Australia. The motion, which was passed by two votes, led to Rene Harris regaining the presidency. In October, however, Harris was flown to Australia for emergency medical treatment for a diabetes-related illness, during which time Remy Namaduk performed the role of Acting President.

Allegations that Nauru's 'offshore' financial centre was being used extensively by Russian criminal organizations for 'laundering' the proceeds of their illegal activities, led Dowiyogo to order a full review of the industry in March 1999. The Government subsequently stated that it intended to modernize legislation governing the island's financial sector. In early 2000 President Rene Harris announced that Nauru was to suspend its 'offshore' banking services and improve the accountability of existing banks on the island, as part of the Government's efforts to bring Nauru's financial services regulations into conformity with international standards. Dowiyogo similarly reaffirmed his commitment to reform the 'offshore' sector, following his election inu April 2000. However, in February 2001 11 members of Nauru's 18-member legislature signed a petition requesting that Dowiyogo attend a special session of Parliament to answer questions relating to the island's alleged role in 'laundering' significant funds from Russian criminal organizations. The allegations originated in claims by Russia's central bank that some US $70,000m. of illegal funds had been processed in 'offshore' banks in Nauru. It was estimated that 400 such banks existed on the island in early 2001. The Government introduced new legislation designed to deter money-laundering in August 2001, but the Financial Action Task Force (FATF—established in 1989 on the recommendation of the Group of Seven (G-7) industrialized nations) found that the new laws contained several deficiencies, and imposed sanctions in December 2001. Following Islamist attacks on New York and Washington, DC, on 11 September, Nauru's tax system was subject to international scrutiny amid suspicion that it might have been used as a conduit for the terrorists' funds. The Government announced new anti-money-laundering legislation in December, and was considering legal action against the FATF in early 2002. However, in June 2002 Nauru was again listed by the FATF as one of 15 countries that refused to take adequate measures to prevent money-laundering and the financing of terrorist organizations. The FATF was particularly concerned that the existence of about 400 'shell banks', which had no physical presence in the country, was an unacceptable money-laundering risk.

In September 2001 Nauru agreed to accept 310 of 460 predominantly Afghan asylum-seekers who were on board a Norwegian freighter, the *MV Tampa*, unable to disembark on Christmas Island as Australia refused to grant them entry into its territory (see the chapter on Christmas Island). The Australian Government agreed to fund the processing of the asylum-seekers and to pay an undisclosed sum to Nauru, which was to house the asylum-seekers for three months while their claims for asylum were assessed. Those found to be genuine refugees were to be given sanctuary in various nations, including Australia, New Zealand and Norway. Following the interception of another boat carrying asylum-seekers in Australian waters later the same month, Nauru received a pledge of $A20m. from the Australian Government for agreeing to host 800 asylum-seekers. In December 2001 Nauru signed an agreement with Australia's Minister for Foreign Affairs to accommodate a total of 1,200 at any one time, in return for a further $A10m. of aid, to be allocated to education, health and infrastructure programmes. During a brief visit to Australia in January 2002, the President of Nauru declared that the bilateral agreement should end as originally envisaged. However, local residents and owners of the land upon which the camps were located expressed concern over the delays in processing the asylum-seekers' claims. Processing was due to be completed by July 2002, and in May Australia offered monetary assistance to Afghan asylum-seekers as an incentive to return to their homeland. In June the President announced that he anticipated that all the asylum-seekers would have left Nauru within six months. By mid-September more than 1,000 applications from asylum-seekers had been processed with about 100 reviews of failed applications still pending.

In July 2002 a political crisis emerged after President Harris decided unilaterally to recognize the People's Republic of China, thus ending 22 years of diplomatic relations with Taiwan. Several cabinet ministers opposed the shift in policy, and the controversy increased after the President immediately accepted US $60m. in aid and $77m. in debt forgiveness from the People's Republic of China.

In February 1987 the British, Australian and New Zealand Governments officially terminated the functions of the British Phosphate Commissioners, who from 1919 until 1970 had managed the mining of Nauru's phosphate deposits. President DeRoburt subsequently expressed concern over the distribution of the Commissioners' accumulated assets, which were estimated to be worth $A55m. His proposal that part of this sum be spent on the rehabilitation of areas of the island that had been mined before Nauru gained independence in 1968 was rejected by the three Governments involved. The ensuing dispute became known as the 'Matter of Rehabilitation'. In August 1987 DeRoburt established a government commission of inquiry to report on proposals for rehabilitation, and in the following year proposed that the three Governments each provide one-third of the estimated rehabilitation costs of $A216m. (As a result of extensive phosphate mining, 80% of the surface of the island is uninhabitable and impossible to cultivate.) In 1989, because of Australia's refusal to contribute to the rehabilitation of former phosphate mining areas, Nauru appealed to the International Court of Justice (ICJ), at The Hague, for compensation for damage to its environment. (New Zealand and the United Kingdom deposited instruments with the ICJ that prevented them from being sued by Nauru.) Australia agreed to comply with the eventual ruling of the ICJ. However, in 1993, following negotiations between President Dowiyogo and the Australian Prime Minister, Paul Keating, a Compact of Settlement was signed, under which the Australian Government was to pay a total of $A107m. to Nauru. New Zealand and the United Kingdom subsequently agreed to contribute $A12m. each towards the settlement. In 1995 a report commissioned by the Government was published, which gave details of a rehabilitation programme extending over the next 20–25 years and costing $A230m. The success of the rehabilitation scheme, however, was dependent on the co-operation of landowners, some of whom were expected to continue to allow areas to be mined for residual ore once phosphate reserves had been exhausted. In 1997 Parliament approved the Nauru Rehabilitation Corporation Act, providing for the establishment of a corporate body to manage the rehabilitation programme. The programme, which began in May 1999, was expected to transform the mined areas into sites suitable for agriculture and new housing.

Nauru was persistently critical of France's use of the South Pacific region for nuclear-weapons testing, and was one of the most vociferous opponents of the French Government's decision in mid-1995 to resume its nuclear-testing programme. Diplomatic relations between the two countries, suspended in 1995, were formally resumed in early 1998.

In early 2001 Nauru voiced strong opposition to the US Government's plans to develop a missile defence system, in which missiles are deployed to shoot down other missiles in flight. Government officials in Nauru expressed fears that testing of the system in the region could result in missile debris landing on the Pacific islands.

The President of Nauru had discussions with the Cuban Minister of Foreign Affairs in November 2001 at a UN meeting, where they agreed to establish diplomatic relations between their two countries and discussed a proposed technical and economic co-operation agreement whereby Nauru would be provided with health experts from Cuba.

In 1989 a UN report on the 'greenhouse effect' (the heating of the earth's atmosphere and a resultant rise in sea-level, as a consequence of pollution) listed Nauru as one of the countries that might disappear beneath the sea in the 21st century, unless drastic action were taken. Another issue of environmental concern was raised in late 1992, when it was announced that a vessel carrying plutonium would pass close to Nauru *en route* to Japan from France. Dowiyogo travelled to Japan to protest at the proposal. Furthermore, in early 1997 President Kinza Clodumar urged the Japanese Government to ensure that a similar ship (travelling from France to Japan with a cargo of radioactive waste) remain outside its exclusive economic zone, particularly as the vessel had illegally entered the waters of several other countries. The Government of Nauru strongly criticized Australia's refusal, at the December 1997 Conference of the Parties to the Framework Convention on Climate Change, in Kyoto, Japan, to reduce its emission of pollutant gases known to contribute to the 'greenhouse effect'.

In August 2001 Nauru hosted the Pacific Islands Forum summit meeting, despite a problematic shortage of accommodation, caused by the presence of contingents of officials from Australia, refugee agencies, the UN and Eurest (the company subcontracted to operate Nauru's refugee camp). Fiji had been expected to perform this role, but its participation had been opposed owing to its failure to reinstate democratic rule following the coup of the previous year. Japan pledged financial aid for Nauru's hosting of the summit meeting. During the meeting, the Nauruan President urged solidarity among South Pacific states in opposing international demands to restrict financial transactions.

Economy

In 1998, according to UN estimates, Nauru's gross domestic product (GDP), measured at current prices, was US $32m., equivalent to US $2,900 per head. In 1990–98, it was estimated, GDP decreased, in real terms, at an average annual rate of 6.0%. The population increased by an annual average of 2.0% per year in 1990–98. The

UN estimated that GDP declined, in real terms, by 1.9% in 1998. According to official estimates, Nauru's GDP grew in real terms by only 0.8% in 2000 (following growth of 3.2% in 1999) and was in part due to adverse climatic conditions, which affected coffee production, and low international prices for Nauru's coffee, copra and palm oil output. Real GDP growth of around 3% was predicted for 2001.

Agricultural activity comprises mainly the small-scale production of tropical fruit, vegetables, and livestock, although the production of coffee and copra for export is increasingly significant. Coconuts are the principal crop. Bananas, pineapples and the screw-pine (*Pandanus*) are also cultivated as food crops, while the islanders keep pigs and chickens. However, almost all Nauru's requirements (including most of its drinking water) are imported. Increased exploitation of the island's marine resources was envisaged following the approval by Parliament of important fisheries legislation in the late 1990s. Funding for a new harbour for medium-sized vessels was secured from the Government of Japan in 1998, and in 1999 the Marshall Islands Sea Patrol agreed to provide assistance in the surveillance of Nauru's exclusive economic zone. Revenue from fishing licence fees totalled $A8.5m. in 2000.

Until the early 1990s the island's economy was based on the mining of phosphate rock, derived from rich deposits of guano, which constituted about four-fifths of the island's surface area. Phosphate extraction has been conducted largely by indentured labour (with the majority of workers originating from Kiribati and Tuvalu). The annual output of phosphate rock totalled 1,181,000 metric tons in 1989, but declined to 510,000 tons in 1996. Although Nauru accounts for only a small proportion of world phosphate production, the revenue accruing to the island is, in relation to its size, very high; it was estimated to have provided about $A100m.–$A120m. annually since independence. Phosphate exports decreased to an annual average of 0.51m. tons in 1990–97 (compared with 1.58m. tons per year in the 1980s), mainly owing to the collapse of the Australian market. As a result of the Asian financial crisis, exports of phosphate declined by almost 18% in 1998 compared with the previous year. In 2001 phosphate exports were suspended in the second half of the year when a processing plant was blockaded by landowners seeking additional compensation for the use of their land by the plant. Mining production, meanwhile, decreased by 7.9% in 2000. Primary deposits of phosphate are expected to be exhausted by 2005, by which time, it is hoped, Nauru will be able to derive economic security from its shipping and civil aviation services and its position as a tax haven for international business and for 'offshore' banking. Feasibility studies have been conducted into the mining of secondary and residual deposits, although this activity would be less profitable.

The revenue from phosphate exports is shared among the Government (which takes about 50% of the profits), Nauruan landowners, a long-term trust fund (the Nauru Phosphate Royalties Trust—NPRT) and the Nauru Local Government Council. No details concerning receipts of interest on trust fund investments are published, although the book value of investments is estimated at $A1,000m., with returns of 14% per year. Investments by Nauru, using phosphate revenues, have been made in Australia (extensively in Melbourne), London (United Kingdom), the Philippines, New Zealand, Fiji, Guam, Samoa and the USA (Honolulu, Houston, Washington, DC, and Portland, Oregon). Mainly as a result of its phosphate revenues, the Government has been able to provide an extensive welfare system and to maintain an international airline. However, not all investments have been successful, and some Pacific hotel ventures, as well as the staging of a lavish musical production in London, have been described as disastrous. Criticism regarding the inefficient management of Nauru's funds intensified following the conviction, in 1994, of an accountant employed by the NPRT, for the theft of $A1.2m. from the Trust. In the following year a further eight people were charged with, and later convicted of, grand larceny and fraud over the theft of some $A40m. from the NPRT. Moreover, in March 2000 an Australian businessman was found guilty of conspiring to defraud the Trust of some $A100m. Although most of the money was subsequently recovered, a considerable sum remained missing.

The Government is an important employer, engaging 1,138 people in 1989, although this number declined significantly as a result of a series of austerity measures introduced during the 1990s. The rate of unemployment among those aged 15–19 in the late 1990s was estimated by the Asian Development Bank (ADB) to be 33% of males and 52% of females. The national budget for 1998/99 envisaged total revenue of $A38.7m. and expenditure of $A37.2m. (dramatically reduced from expenditure of $A61.8m. in the previous year). According to the ADB, the budgetary deficit was projected at the equivalent of 6.1% of GDP in 1999/2000 and at 10.6% in 2000/01. A fiscal deficit of $A40m.–$A50m. was envisaged in 2001/02. Total public debt was equivalent to 60.8% of GDP in 2000, an improvement on figures in previous years. Development assistance from Australia amounted to $A3.3m. in 1999/2000. Nauru's external debt was estimated at $A280m. in 2000. In that year the cost of debt-servicing was equivalent to an estimated 13% of total revenue from the exports of goods and services. Consumer prices increased by 4.0% in 1998, by 6.7% in 1999 and by 17.9% in 2000; the annual rate of inflation averaged 4.0% in 2001.

The country's trade balance improved significantly in 2001: imports decreased by 5.5%, while exports improved by 7.9%. This resulted in a current-account surplus in that year equivalent to nearly 12% of GDP. The principal imports are food and live animals (which comprised 83.7% of total imports in 1994, while beverages accounted for a further 4.1%), non-metallic mineral manufactures (4.9%) and machinery and transport equipment (2.8%). Phosphates are the most important export, earning $A38.1m. in 1995; exports of crude fertilizers to Australia totalled $A8.5m. in 2001. The principal export markets in 2000 were New Zealand (45.4%), Australia (16.9%), the Republic of Korea (14.9%), the USA (5.4%) and Canada (4.3%); the principal sources of imports were Australia (48.1%), the USA (19.9%), the United Kingdom (10.8%), Indonesia (6.7%) and India (3.7%).

After gaining independence in 1968, Nauru benefited from sole control of phosphate earnings and, as a result, its income per head was among the highest in the world. This, however, had serious repercussions for the country, which became excessively dependent on imported labour, foreign imports and convenience foods, precipitating severe social problems. According to a report on mortality published in 1989, one-third of the adult Nauruan population suffers from diabetes (the worst incidence of the disease anywhere in the world), while obesity, heart-disease, alcoholism and other illnesses attributable to social and dietary problems are also prevalent. It was hoped, however, that, in the long term, some of these problems might be alleviated by the rehabilitation of the damaged areas of the island (which finally began in May 1999), allowing for the cultivation of traditional food crops. By early 1996 the decline in phosphate sales had begun to cause financial difficulties, which led the Government to announce plans to sell a number of its overseas properties and to initiate a corporatization programme in an attempt to reduce external debts of some $A200m. From 1996, furthermore, the Bank of Nauru experienced an ongoing liquidity crisis. The Government's initial failure to address the problem led to a severe crisis of confidence in the bank.

A review of Nauru's economy by the ADB in late 1998 led the organization to devise a programme for major economic and structural adjustment, which aimed to ensure the island's financial security in view of the dramatic decline in revenue from phosphates and from many of its traditional investments. Moreover, in February 1999 President Dowiyogo outlined a series of new policies to stimulate Nauru's economy. The measures included the development of commercial fishing, the development of tourism, new roles for the national airline and shipping line, the establishment of new industries (for example, the cultivation of flowers for export) and increased resources for education to improve the skills of the labour force. In June 1999 the Government announced that it had completed the first phase of the reform programme, funded by the ADB, involving some 434 redundancies in the civil service with a view to reducing personnel expenditure by 35% (although the retrenchment programme was impeded in 2000 by the appointment of some 500 additional employees to the state mining operation).

Measures to reform the financial sector, in response to allegations that Nauru's 'offshore' banking services were being abused for the purposes of 'money-laundering', were announced in early 2000. In September of that year the Government appointed a consultant, who, with the assistance of the ADB, was to conduct a thorough review of operations at the Bank of Nauru. However, serious allegations of 'money-laundering' re-emerged in early 2001, when the Financial Action Task Force (see above) declared Nauru to be one of the worst international offenders. The Government subsequently attempted to implement further stringent reforms of the island's financial regulations.

Nauru received a significant financial windfall in September 2001, in exchange for co-operating with Australia in its 'Pacific Solution' to the problem of asylum-seekers. By the end of 2001, in addition to meeting the costs of caring for the refugees, the Australian Government had committed total aid exceeding $A30m. The aid was allocated to various programmes, including $A10m. towards fuel to power the island's electricity generators and $A3m. towards the purchase of new generators. Australia also offered to refurbish the island's sports stadium, provide scholarships for students to study in Australia and cover the outstanding hospital bills incurred by Nauruans in Australia (where, owing to the shortcomings of Nauru's health service, many of the island's citizens had been obliged to seek treatment).

The decline in GDP growth in 2000 was in part due to adverse climatic conditions, which affected coffee production, and to low international prices for Nauru's coffee, copra and palm oil output. In the medium term, Nauru's economic outlook was poor. It remained unclear how the substantial budgetary deficit (of about A$40m.–A$50m.) envisaged for 2002 would be fully financed; the Government had hitherto relied upon loans from official bilateral sources, overseas corporations or funds from the NPRT, the assets of which had been seriously depleted by 2001. The donation of US $60m. in aid and US $77m. in debt forgiveness from the People's Republic of China in July 2002, however, was expected to help to improve the deficit. The Bank of Nauru, meanwhile, another source of budgetary support and financing of phosphate royalty payments to landowners, was believed to have become practically insolvent. During 2001, furthermore, the repeated suspensions of Air Nauru's operations, owing to lack of funds, had led to serious disruptions in the provision of food, fuel and other essential supplies to the island.

Nauru is a member of the Pacific Islands Forum (formerly the South Pacific Forum), the Pacific Community (formerly the South Pacific Commission) and the UN's Economic and Social Commission for Asia and the Pacific (ESCAP). (Nauru was admitted to the UN itself in September 1999.) In addition, Nauru became a member of the ADB in September 1991.

Statistical Survey

Source (unless otherwise stated): General Statistician, Nauru Government Offices, Yaren.

AREA AND POPULATION

Area: 21.3 sq km (8.2 sq miles).

Population: 8,042 (Nauruan 4,964; Other Pacific Islanders 2,134; Asians 682; Caucasians—mainly Australians and New Zealanders—262) at census of 13 May 1983; 9,919 (5,079 males, 4,840 females) at census of 17 April 1992; 11,845 (official estimate) at mid-2000.

Density (mid-2000): 556 per sq km.

Births, Marriages and Deaths (1995): Registered live births 203 (birth rate 18.8 per 1,000); Registered marriages 57 (marriage rate 5.3 per 1,000); Registered deaths 49 (death rate 4.5 per 1,000).

Expectation of Life (WHO estimates, years at birth, 2000): Males 58.8; Females 66.6. Source: WHO, *World Health Report*.

Economically Active Population (census of 30 June 1966): 2,473 (Administration 845, Phosphate mining 1,408, Other activities 220).

HEALTH AND WELFARE

Key Indicators

Fertility (births per woman, 2000): 4.6.

Under-5 Mortality Rate (per 1,000 live births, 2000): 30.

Physicians (per 1,000 head, 1995): 1.57.

Health Expenditure (1998): US $ per head (PPP): 507.
% of GDP: 4.6.
public (% of total): 97.4.

For sources and definitions, see explanatory note on p. vi.

AGRICULTURE, ETC.

Principal Crop and Livestock (FAO estimates, 2000): Coconuts 1,600 metric tons; Pigs 2,800 head; Chickens 5,000 head. Source: FAO.

Fishing (FAO estimates, metric tons, live weight, 1999): Capture 250; Total catch 250. Source: FAO, *Yearbook of Fishery Statistics*.

MINING

Phosphate Rock ('000 metric tons): 487 in 1998; 600 (estimate) in 1999; 500 (estimate) in 2000. The phosphoric acid content (in '000 metric tons) was: 185 in 1998; 230 (estimate) in 1999; 195 (estimate) in 2000. Source: US Geological Survey.

INDUSTRY

Electric Energy (million kWh): 32 in 1996; 32 in 1997; 32 in 1998. Source: UN, *Industrial Commodity Statistics Yearbook*.

FINANCE

Currency and Exchange Rates: Australian currency: 100 cents = 1 Australian dollar ($A). *Sterling, US Dollar and Euro Equivalents* (31 May 2002): £1 sterling = $A2.5849; US $1 = $A1.7624; €1 = $A1.6544; $A100 = £38.69 = US $56.74 = €60.45. *Average Exchange Rate* (US $ per Australian dollar): 0.6453 in 1999; 0.5823 in 2000; 0.5176 in 2001.

Budget (estimates, $A '000, year ending 30 June 1999): *Revenue:* 38,700. *Expenditure:* 37,200.

EXTERNAL TRADE

Principal Commodities ($A '000, year ending 30 June 1994): *Imports:* Food and live animals 38,420; Beverages 1,890; Non-metallic mineral manufactures 2,268; Non-electrical machinery 758; Transport equipment 534; Total (incl. others) 45,906. *Exports:* Total 45,111. *1995* ($A '000): Total exports 38,081.

Trade with Australia ($A '000, year ending 30 June 2001): *Imports:* 26,000. *Exports:* 9,000. Source: Australian Bureau of Statistics, *Year Book Australia*.

Trade with New Zealand ($NZ '000, 2000): *Imports:* 166; *Exports:* 25,418. Source: Ministry of Foreign Affairs and Trade, Wellington.

TRANSPORT

Road Traffic (1989): 1,448 registered motor vehicles.

Shipping: *Merchant Fleet* (displacement, '000 grt at 31 December): 15 in 1991 (at 30 June); 5 in 1992; 1 in 1993. Source: Lloyd's Register of Shipping. *International Freight Traffic* (estimates, '000 metric tons, 1990): Goods loaded 1,650; Goods unloaded 59. Source: UN, *Monthly Bulletin of Statistics*.

Civil Aviation (traffic on scheduled services, 1998): Kilometres flown (million) 2; Passengers carried ('000) 137; Passenger-km (million) 243; Total ton-km (million) 24. Source: UN, *Statistical Yearbook*.

COMMUNICATIONS MEDIA

Radio Receivers (1997): 7,000 in use*.

Television Receivers (1997): 500 in use*.

Telephones (main lines, 2000): 1,800 in use†.

Mobile Cellular Telephones (2000): 1,200 subscribers†.

* Source: UNESCO, *Statistical Yearbook*.

† Source: International Telecommunication Union.

EDUCATION

Pre-primary (2002): 6 schools; 46 teachers; 634 pupils.

Primary (2002): 5 schools; 64 teachers; 1,566 pupils.

Secondary (2002): 4 schools; 40 teachers; 609 pupils.

Vocational (2001): 6 teachers; 38 students.

Source: Department of Education, Yaren, Nauru.

Nauruans studying at secondary and tertiary levels overseas in 2001 numbered 85.

Directory

The Constitution

The Constitution of the Republic of Nauru came into force at independence on 31 January 1968, having been adopted two days previously. It protects fundamental rights and freedoms, and vests executive authority in the Cabinet, which is responsible to a popularly elected Parliament. The President of the Republic is elected by Parliament from among its members. The Cabinet is composed of five or six members, including the President, who presides. There are 18 members of Parliament, including the Cabinet. Voting is compulsory for all Nauruans who are more than 20 years of age, except in certain specified instances.

The highest judicial organ is the Supreme Court and there is provision for the creation of subordinate courts with designated jurisdiction.

There is a Treasury Fund from which monies may be taken by Appropriation Acts.

A Public Service is provided for, with the person designated as the Chief Secretary being the Commissioner of the Public Service.

Special mention is given to the allocation of profits and royalties from the sale of phosphates.

The Government

HEAD OF STATE

President: RENE HARRIS (elected 30 March 2001).

CABINET

(August 2002)

President, Minister for Finance and Economic Reform, Public Service and Foreign Affairs, Minister of Civil Aviation, Minister of Foreign Affairs, Minister of Home Affairs and Culture, Minister of Industry, Minister of Investments, Minister of Public Service, and Minister of Works, Planning and Housing Development: RENE HARRIS.

Minister of Economic Development, Minister of Education and Vocational Training, Minister of Telecommunications, Minister of Transportation and Minister assisting the President: REMY NAMADUK.

Minister of Finance and Minister of Good Governance: ALOYSIUS AMWANO.

Minister of Health and Minister of Sports: NIMROD BOTELANGA.

Minister of Justice and Minister of Marine Resources: GODFREY THOMA.

MINISTRIES

Office of the President: Yaren, Nauru.

Ministry of Education: Yaren, Nauru; tel. 444-3130; fax 444-3718.

Ministry of Health and Youth Affairs: Yaren, Nauru; tel. 444-3166; fax 444-3136.

Ministry of Finance: Aiwo, Nauru; tel. 444-3140; fax 555-4477.

Ministry of Justice: Yaren, Nauru; tel. 444-3160; fax 444-3108.

Ministry of Works and Community Services: Yaren, Nauru; tel. 444-3177; fax 444-3135.

Legislature

PARLIAMENT

Parliament comprises 18 members. The most recent general election took place on 8 April 2000. All members were elected as independents.

Speaker: LUDWIG SCOTTY.

Political Organizations

Democratic Party of Nauru: c/o Parliament House, Yaren, Nauru; f. 1987; revival of Nauru Party (f. 1975); Leader KENNAN ADEANG.

Naoero Amo (Nauru First): c/o Parliament House, Yaren, Nauru; e-mail visionary@naoeroamo.com; internet www.naoeroamo.com; f. 2001; Co-Leaders DAVID ADEANG, KIERAN KEKE.

Diplomatic Representation

EMBASSY IN NAURU

China, People's Republic: Nauru.

Judicial System

The Chief Justice presides over the Supreme Court, which exercises original, appellate and advisory jurisdiction. The Resident Magistrate presides over the District Court, and he also acts as Coroner under the Inquests Act 1977. The Supreme Court is a court of record. The Family Court consists of three members, one being the Resident Magistrate as Chairman, and two other members drawn from a panel of Nauruans. The Chief Justice is Chairman of the Public Services Appeals Board and of the Police Appeals Board.

SUPREME COURT

tel. 444-3163; fax 444-3104.

Chief Justice: BARRY CONNELL (non-resident).

DISTRICT COURT

Resident Magistrate: G. N. SAKSENA.

FAMILY COURT

Chairman: G. N. SAKSENA.

Religion

Nauruans are predominantly Christians, adhering either to the Nauruan Protestant Church or to the Roman Catholic Church.

Nauruan Protestant Church: Head Office, Nauru; Moderator (vacant).

Roman Catholic Church: POB 16, Nauru; tel. and fax 444-3708; Nauru forms part of the diocese of Tarawa and Nauru, comprising Kiribati and Nauru. The Bishop resides on Tarawa Atoll, Kiribati.

The Press

Central Star News: Nauru; f. 1991; fortnightly.

Nasero Bulletin: Nauru; tel. 444-3847; fax 444-3153; e-mail bulletin@cenpac.net.nr; fortnightly; English; local and overseas news; Editor SEPE BATSIUA; circ. 500.

The Nauru Chronicle: Nauru; Editor RUBY DEDIYA.

Broadcasting and Communications

TELECOMMUNICATIONS

Nauru Telecommunications Service: Nauru; tel. 444-3324; fax 444-3111; Dir EDWARD W. R. H. DEYOUNG.

BROADCASTING

Radio

Nauru Broadcasting Service: Information and Broadcasting Services, Chief Secretary's Department, POB 77, Nauru; tel. 444-3133; fax 444-3153; e-mail ntvdirector@cenpac.net.nr; f. 1968; state-owned and non-commercial; expected to be corporatized in the late 1990s; broadcasts in the mornings in English and Nauruan; operates Radio Nauru; Station Man. RIN TSITSI; Man. Dir GARY TURNER.

Television

Nauru Television (NTV): Nauru; tel. 444-3133; fax 444-3153; e-mail ntvmanager@cenpac.net.nr; began operations in June 1991; govt-owned; broadcasts 24 hrs per day on 3 channels; most of the programmes are supplied by foreign television companies via satellite or on videotape; a weekly current affairs programme is produced locally; Man. MICHAEL DEKARUBE; Dir of Media GARY TURNER.

Finance

(cap. = capital; res = reserves; dep. = deposits; m. = million; amounts in Australian dollars unless otherwise stated)

BANKING

State Bank

Bank of Nauru: Civic Centre, POB 289, Nauru; tel. 444-3238; fax 444-3203; f. 1976; state-owned; cap. 12.0m., res 123.0m., dep. 141.0m. (Dec. 1994); Chair. MARCUS STEPHEN.

Commercial Bank

Hampshire Bank and Trust Inc: Nauru Corporation Bldg, Aiwo Rd, POB 300, Aiwo, Nauru; tel. 444-3283; fax 444-3730; f. 1986; total assets 1,305m., dep. 1,139m. (Dec. 2000); Gen. Man. ROGER VAN ZANTEN.

INSURANCE

Nauru Insurance Corporation: POB 82, Nauru; tel. 444-3346; fax 444-3731; f. 1974; sole licensed insurer and reinsurer in Nauru; Chair. NIMES EKWONA.

Trade and Industry

GOVERNMENT AGENCIES

Nauru Agency Corporation: POB 300, Aiwo, Nauru; tel. 555-4324; fax 444-3730; e-mail nrugrp@cenpac.net.nr; functions as a merchant bank to assist entrepreneurs in the registration of holding and trading corporations and the procurement of banking, trust and insurance licences; Chair. RENE HARRIS; Gen. Man. S. B. HULKAR.

Nauru Corporation: Civic Centre, Yaren, Nauru; f. 1925; operated by the Nauru Council; the major retailer in Nauru; Gen. Man. A. EPHRAIM.

Nauru Fisheries and Marine Resources Authority: POB 449, Nauru; tel. 444-3733; fax 444-3812; e-mail nfmra@cenpac.net.nr; f. 1997.

Nauru Phosphate Corporation: Aiwo, Nauru; tel. 444-3839; fax 444-2752; f. 1970; operates the phosphate industry and several public services of the Republic of Nauru (including provision of electricity and fresh water) on behalf of the Nauruan people; responsible for the mining and marketing of phosphate; Gen. Man. JOSEPH HIRAM.

Nauru Phosphate Royalties Trust: Nauru; e-mail nprtnau@cenpac.net.nr; statutory corpn; invests phosphate royalties to achieve govt revenue; extensive international interests, incl. hotels and real estate; Sec. NIRAL FERNANDO.

Nauru Rehabilitation Corporation—NRC: Nauru; f. 1999; manages and devises programmes for the rehabilitation of those parts of the island damaged by the over-mining of phosphate; Chair. DOGABE JEREMIAH.

UTILITIES

Nauru Phosphate Corporation: Aiwo, Nauru; tel. 555-6481; fax 555-4111; operates generators for the provision of electricity and supplies the island's water; Chair. (vacant); Gen. Man. JOSEPH HIRAM.

Transport

RAILWAYS

There are 5.2 km of 0.9-m gauge railway serving the phosphate workings.

ROADS

A sealed road, 16 km long, circles the island, and another serves Buada District. There were 1,448 registered vehicles in 1989.

SHIPPING

As Nauru has no wharves, passenger and cargo handling are operated by barge. In late 1998 finance was secured from the Japanese Government for the construction of a harbour in Anibare district. Work on the project began in 1999.

Nauru Pacific: Government Bldg, Yaren, Nauru; tel. 444-3133; f. 1969; operates cargo charter services to ports in Australia, New Zealand, Asia, the Pacific and the west coast of the USA; Man. Dir (vacant).

CIVIL AVIATION

Air Nauru: Directorate of Civil Aviation, Government of Nauru Offices, POB 40, Yaren, Nauru; tel. 444-3274; fax 444-3705; e-mail write2us@airnauru.com.au; internet www.airnauru.com.au; f. 1970; corporatized in 1996 and moved to Australian aviation register in mid-1997; operates passenger and cargo services to Kiribati, Fiji, New Caledonia, Solomon Islands, Guam, Palau, the Philippines, the Federated States of Micronesia, Hawaii (USA), Australia and New Zealand; Chair. and CEO KEN MCDONALD.

Defence

The Republic of Nauru has no defence forces. Under an informal agreement, Australia is responsible for the defence of the island.

Education

Education is free and compulsory for children between the ages of six and 16. In 2002 the island had six pre-primary schools, with 634 pupils, five primary schools, with 1,566 pupils, and four secondary schools with 609 pupils. In 2002 Nauruans studying overseas at secondary and tertiary levels numbered 85. An extension centre of the University of the South Pacific, based in Suva, Fiji, was opened in Nauru in the late 1980s.

New Zealand Pacific Territory

Tokelau is the only remaining Island Territory of New Zealand, of which it is an integral part. New Zealand is a member of the Pacific Islands Forum (formerly the South Pacific Forum), both in its own right and in respect of its Pacific dependencies. The cabinet minister responsible is the Minister of Foreign Affairs and Trade; the Secretary of Foreign Affairs and Trade also holds the position of Administrator of Tokelau, unless the Government opts for the offices to be held separately (as at present).

Head of State: HM Queen ELIZABETH II (succeeded to the throne 6 February 1952).

Governor-General: Dame SILVIA CARTWRIGHT (took office 4 April 2001).

Ministry of Foreign Affairs and Trade: Private Bag 18901, Wellington, New Zealand; tel. (4) 494-8500; fax (4) 472-9596; e-mail enquiries@mfat.govt.nz; internet www.mfat.govt.nz.

Minister of Foreign Affairs and Trade, and Minister of Justice: PHIL GOFF.

TOKELAU

Physical and Social Geography

Tokelau is located in the central Pacific Ocean, about 480 km north of Apia in Samoa, its nearest neighbour. Tuvalu lies to the west and Kiribati to the north and east. The Territory consists of three atolls with a total area of 10 sq km (3.9 sq miles). The central atoll of Nukunonu is the largest; Atafu, the smallest, lies 64 km to the north-west and Fakaofo lies 92 km to the south-east of Nukunonu. Each atoll consists of a number of reef-bound islets, or *motu*, encircling a lagoon. The *motu* vary in size but are never wider than 200 m or higher than 5 m, although they can be up to 6 km in length. The average annual temperature is 28°C (82°F), July being the coolest month and May the warmest. Rainfall is heavy but inconsistent, and occasionally there are severe storms. The indigenous inhabitants are a Polynesian people, and Tokelauan is the official language, although English is widely spoken. The population is almost entirely Christian, being either Protestant (just over two-thirds) or Roman Catholic. The total population was 1,487 at the 1996 census, and was estimated at 1,445 in July 2001. Tokelau has no official capital, each atoll having its own administrative centre. However, the seat of Government is recognized as 'the capital' and is rotated on a yearly basis among the three atolls.

History

The islands now comprising Tokelau were inhabited by Polynesians, closely related to the people of Samoa, before becoming a British protectorate in 1877. At the request of the inhabitants, the United Kingdom annexed the territory, then known as the Union Islands, in 1916 and included it within the Gilbert and Ellice Islands Colony. In 1925 the British Government transferred administrative control to New Zealand. In 1946 the group was officially designated the Tokelau Islands, and in 1948 sovereignty was transferred to New Zealand. From 1962 until the end of 1971 the High Commissioner for New Zealand in Western Samoa (now Samoa) was also the Administrator of the Tokelau Islands. In November 1974 the administration of the Tokelau Islands was transferred to the Ministry of Foreign Affairs in New Zealand. In 1976 the Tokelau Islands were officially redesignated Tokelau.

New Zealand has undertaken to assist Tokelau towards increased self-government and economic self-sufficiency. The Territory was visited by the United Nations Special Committee on Decolonization in 1976 and 1981, but on both occasions the missions reported that the people of Tokelau did not wish to change the nature of the existing relationship between Tokelau and New Zealand. This opinion was reiterated by an emissary of the General Fono, the Territory's highest advisory body, in 1987, and by the Official Secretary in 1992. A further survey by the UN in September 2002 found the Tokelauans' sentiments on the issue to be unchanged.

A programme of constitutional change, agreed in 1992 and formalized in January 1994, provided for a more defined role for Tokelau's political institutions, as well as for their expansion. A process of relocating the Tokelau Public Service (hitherto based in Apia, Western Samoa, now Samoa) to the Territory began in 1994, and by 1995 all government departments, except Transport and Communications and part of the Administration and Finance Department, had been transferred to Tokelauan soil. The Tokelau Apia Liaison Office (formerly the Office for Tokelau Affairs) was, however, to remain in Western Samoa (now Samoa), owing to the country's more developed communications facilities.

The development of Tokelau's institutions at a national level has prompted renewed interest in the islands' prospects for greater internal autonomy. In June 1994 the General Fono adopted a National Strategic Plan, which gave details of Tokelau's progression (over the next five to 10 years) towards increased self-determination and, possibly, free association with New Zealand. The executive and administrative powers of the Administrator were formally transferred, in that year, to the General Fono and, when the Fono is not in session, to the Council of Faipule. A draft Constitution was subsequently drawn up. In May 1996 the New Zealand House of Representatives approved the Tokelau Amendment Bill, granting the General Fono the power to enact legislation, to impose taxes and to declare public holidays, effective from 1 August 1996 (although New Zealand was to retain the right to legislate for Tokelau). A visit to the islands by the Prime Minister of Tuvalu in mid-1996, for the signing of a mutual co-operation agreement, was widely interpreted as an indication of Tokelau's increased autonomy.

Elections took place in January 1999, at which two of the Territory's Faipule were re-elected, while the remaining Faipule and three Pulenuku posts were secured by new candidates. Following electoral reforms, delegates were, for the first time, elected to the General Fono for a three-year term; they had previously been nominated by each Taupulega (Island Council). As part of the same reform process, the number of delegates to the General Fono was reduced from 27 to 18. At elections in January 2002, all three incumbent Faipule and one Pulenuku were re-elected to office; two new Pulenuku were elected.

Mounting fears among islanders that, despite their wishes, New Zealand was seeking to loosen its ties with Tokelau led the New Zealand Minister of Foreign Affairs to state in April 2000 that his country would not impose independence on the Territory and that any change in its political status would only occur with the consent of Tokelauans. In early 2001 the head of the Tokelau Public Service Commission, Aleki Silau, reiterated the islanders' reluctance to renounce New Zealand citizenship, and emphasized that both sides have until 2010 to reach a decision. In accordance with legislation approved in 1999, management of the islands' public service was formally transferred to Tokelau in July 2001.

New Zealand is responsible for the external relations of Tokelau. Strong ties are maintained with Samoa, to the people of which the Tokelauans are closely related. There is considerable co-operation in health and education matters.

In December 1980 New Zealand and the USA signed a treaty whereby the US claim to Tokelau, dating from 1856, was relinquished. At the same time, New Zealand relinquished a claim, on behalf of Tokelau, to Swain's Island (Olohenga), administered by the USA since 1925 as part of American Samoa. The treaty was ratified in August 1983, although there was some dissent in Tokelau.

Tokelau is a member of the Pacific Community (formerly the South Pacific Commission) and, as a dependent territory of New Zealand, is represented by that country in the South Pacific Forum and other international organizations. In response to local concern, New Zealand outlawed drift-net fishing within Tokelau's exclusive economic zone (extending to 200 nautical miles (370 km) from the islands' coastline) from November 1989. In 1996 Tokelau signed a memorandum of understanding with Tuvalu which aimed to facilitate co-operation in shipping, trade and fisheries.

A further environmental threat is posed by the possible consequences of the 'greenhouse effect' (the heating of the earth's atmosphere as a result of pollution). A UN report on this subject, published in 1989, listed Tokelau as one of the island groups likely to be completely submerged during the 21st century, owing to a rise in sea-level.

Economy

Tokelau's size, isolation and lack of land-based resources limit economic development. The principal domestic sources of revenue are fees from shipping, fishing licences, radio and telegram excises and customs duties, and exports of copra, handicrafts, postage stamps and souvenir coins (these last are legal tender, although New Zealand currency is in general use). According to estimates by the UN Development Programme, in 1982 Tokelau's gross national product (GNP) was US $1.2m., equivalent to US $760 per head. Gross domestic product (GDP) was estimated at US $1.5m. in 1993 and GDP per caput at US $1,000 in that year.

Tokelau's soil is thin and infertile. Apart from some copra production, agriculture is of a basic subsistence nature. In the year to March 1987 Tokelau exported some 107 metric tons of copra to Western Samoa (now Samoa). Exports were subsequently affected by cyclone damage to the coconut trees. Apart from coconuts, food crops include bananas, breadfruit, pulaka, papaya (pawpaw), and the edible fruit of the screw-pine (*Pandanus*). Livestock consists of pigs, ducks and other poultry. Ocean and lagoon fish and shellfish are staple constituents of the islanders' diet. There is little commercial fishing, but the sale of licences to fish in Tokelau's exclusive economic zone earns some revenue. Tokelau benefited from development assistance and revenue of some US $62,500 per year from the USA, under the treaty negotiated by the Forum Fisheries Agency in 1987. In 2000/01 fisheries licensing provided $NZ1.2m. in revenue, although the Government projected a more modest income of $NZ0.9m. in 2001/02. In 2001 the sum of $NZ0.68m. of the income from fisheries licensing was used to establish the Tokelau Trust Fund.

The only industries of significance are copra production and the manufacture of handicrafts. However, a factory on Atafu, processing highly-priced yellowfin tuna, opened in 1990, providing another important source of income. The factory is supplied by local residents, appointed by Atafu's village council to fish on certain days to provide tuna for the plant. The principal markets for the product are New Zealand and Japan. Construction, mainly public works, is carried out with the help of New Zealand and foreign aid and, often, using the local labour levy. Electricity is provided by diesel generators based in the village of each atoll. Trading relations are dominated by New Zealand and Samoa; there are co-operative stores on each atoll. Most requirements are imported. Imports to the value of $NZ0.5m. were purchased from New Zealand in 1993/94.

Since 1982 the General Fono has levied a tax on the salaries of public servants who are unavailable for the community service labour levy. In the mid-1990s this levy, which was equivalent to 6%–12% of their salaries, was collected from about 160 civil servants. In 1996/97 almost US $0.7m. of total budgetary expenditure (estimated at some US $4m.) was invested in village development projects. In an attempt to enhance the Territory's prospects for increased self-determination, measures were taken during 1996 to augment locally-generated revenue. The measures, which included the expansion of the islands' tax base and the introduction of charges for health and education services, resulted in an increase in Tokelau's contribution to total budgetary revenue from 17% in 1995 to 25% in the following year. The proportion, however, declined to 13.8% in 1997/98. In 1999/2000 there was a budgetary deficit of $NZ0.9m. Tokelau's budget for 2001/02 was to include at least $NZ4.2m. from New Zealand and an estimated $NZ1.7m. to be obtained from local revenues such as fisheries licensing, duty, taxes, philatelic sales, freight charges and interest earned. Official development assistance from New Zealand totalled $NZ8.5m. in 2000/01 and was projected at $NZ7.5m. in 2001/02. Of the latter figure, $NZ4.5m. was allocated towards budgetary support, while $NZ3.0m. was for the purposes of development projects and training, focusing on such areas as health, education, information technology, infrastructure, and financial and economic management. In addition to its links to New Zealand, Tokelau maintains a bilateral development assistance plan with Australia, centred upon human resource development. Australia provides scholarships for Tokelauan students to study in Australia or at regional academic institutions. Development assistance from Australia in 2001/02 was projected at a total of $A100,000.

In 1987 the General Fono decided to delay work on the construction of airstrips and to concentrate resources on the development of shipping links instead. The improvement of these links in the late 1980s and early 1990s, although of general economic benefit, resulted in an increase in imported foods, which, according to a report published in 1992, has contributed to serious social and dietary problems in the islands. In September 2002 the Faipule of Nukunonu, Pio Tuia, announced renewed proposals for the construction of wharves to allow the export of fish and of an airport to enable tourists to visit the islands more easily.

Remittances from Tokelauans working abroad, mainly in New Zealand, are also an important source of private income. At the March 1991 census in New Zealand, it was reckoned that there were 2,802 Tokelauans in that country. The New Zealand budget for 1989 allowed the payment of 50% of retirement income (under a national scheme) to people residing abroad. It was hoped that this would encourage Tokelauans to return to the islands. There is no unemployment as such in the communal system of Tokelau. Emigration has, however, relieved population pressure on the atolls, particularly at the village of Fakaofo (on the *motu* of Fale). A new settlement has been established on the larger *motu* of Fenua Fale nearby. The people of Atafu all live in one village, on the *motu* of Vao. This name is shared by the *motu* on which Nukunonu village is located (a bridge connects it to another islet where some families have settled). There is least population pressure on Nukunonu.

Statistical Survey

Source (unless otherwise indicated): Tokelau Apia Liaison Office, POB 805, Apia, Samoa; tel. 20822; fax 21761.

AREA AND POPULATION

Area: Atafu 3.5 sq km; Nukunonu 4.7 sq km; Fakaofo 4.0 sq km; Total 12.2 sq km (4.7 sq miles).

Population (census of March 1991): Atafu 543; Nukunonu 437; Fakaofo 597; Total 1,577. *Tokelauans resident in New Zealand:* 2,802. (Census of 1996*): Atafu 499; Fakaofo 578; Nukunonu 430; Total 1,507.

* Figures include temporary visitors. Total resident population: 1,487.

Density (resident population, 1996): 121.9 per sq km.

Births and Deaths (1996): Birth rate 33.1 per 1,000; Death rate 8.2 per 1,000.

Expectation of Life (official estimates, years at birth, 1996): Males 68; Females 70. Source: Ministry of Foreign Affairs and Trade, Wellington.

AGRICULTURE, ETC.

Crop Production (FAO estimates, metric tons, 2000): Coconuts 3,000; Copra 45; Roots and tubers 300; Bananas 15. Source: FAO.

Livestock (FAO estimates, year ending September 2000): Pigs 1,000; Chickens 5,000. Source: FAO.

Fishing (FAO estimates, metric tons, live weight, 1999): Capture 200; Total catch 200. Source: FAO, *Yearbook of Fishery Statistics.*

INDUSTRY

Production (estimate, 1990): Electric energy 300,000 kWh.

FINANCE

Currency and Exchange Rates: New Zealand currency is legal tender. Tokelau souvenir coins have also been issued. New Zealand currency: 100 cents = 1 New Zealand dollar ($NZ); *Sterling, US Dollar and Euro Equivalents* (31 May 2002): £1 sterling = $NZ3.0858; US $1 = $NZ2.1039; €1 = $NZ1.9750; $NZ100 = £32.41 = US $47.53 = €50.63. *Average Exchange Rate* (US $ per $NZ): 0.5295 in 1999; 0.4574 in 2000; 0.4206 in 2001.

Budget ($NZ, year ending 30 June 1998): *Revenue:* Local 734,950; New Zealand subsidy 4,600,000; Total 5,334,950. *Expenditure:* Total 5,208,449.

Overseas Aid (projection, $NZ '000, 2001/02): Official development assistance from New Zealand 7,500 (of which Budget support 4,500, Projects and training 3,000). Source: Ministry of Foreign Affairs and Trade, Wellington.

EXTERNAL TRADE

Principal Commodities: *Imports:* Foodstuffs; Building materials WS $104,953 (1983/84); Fuel. *Exports:* Copra $NZ43,542 (1982/83); Handicrafts WS $10,348 (1983/84); there were no other exports.

In 1993/94 imports from New Zealand totalled $NZ500,000.

COMMUNICATIONS MEDIA

Radio Receivers (estimate, 1997): 1,000 in use.

EDUCATION

Schools (1999): 3 (one school for all levels on each atoll).

Teachers (1990): Qualified 43; Aides 8; Adult Learning Centre Co-ordinators 3. (1999): Qualified 30.

Pupils (1991): Pre-primary 133; Primary 361; General secondary 113.

Students Overseas (1990): Secondary 42; Technical and vocational 36; Teacher training 3; University 16. (1999): Secondary 22; Tertiary 20.

Directory

The Constitution

Tokelau is administered under the authority of the Tokelau Islands Act 1948 and subsequent amendments and regulations. The Act declared Tokelau (then known as the Tokelau Islands) to be within the territorial boundaries of New Zealand. The Administrator is the representative of the Crown and is responsible to the Minister of Foreign Affairs and Trade in the New Zealand Government. The office of Administrator is normally held conjointly with that of New Zealand's Secretary of Foreign Affairs and Trade, but provision is made for the offices to be held separately. Most of the powers of the Administrator are delegated to the Tokelau Apia Liaison Office, the General Fono and the Council of Faipule. The chief representative of the Administrator (and the Crown) on each atoll is the highest elected official, the Faipule, who exercises executive, political and judicial powers. The three Faipule, who hold ministerial portfolios and form the Council of Faipule, act as the representatives of the Territory in dealings with the administration and at international meetings, and choose one of their number to hold the title Ulu-O-Tokelau (Head of Tokelau) for a term of one year. The Ulu-O-Tokelau chairs sessions of the territorial assembly, the General Fono. The General Fono is a meeting of 18 delegates (including the Faipule and the Pulenuku—Village Mayor—from each atoll), representing the entire Territory. There are two or three meetings each year, which may take place on any of the atolls. The General Fono is the highest advisory body and the administration must consult it about all policy affecting the Territory. The assembly has responsibility for the territorial budget and has the power to enact legislation, to impose taxes and to declare public holidays. There are a number of specialist committees, such as the Budget Committee and the Law Committee.

Tokelau is an association of three autonomous atoll communities. Local government consists of the Faipule, the Pulenuku and the Taupulega (Island Council or Council of Elders). The Faipule, the Pulenuku and delegates to the General Fono are elected every three years on the basis of universal adult suffrage (the age of majority being 21). The Faipule represents the atoll community, liaises with the administration and the Tokelau Public Service, acts as a judicial commissioner and presides over meetings of the Taupulega. The Pulenuku is responsible for the administration of village affairs, including the maintenance of water supplies and the inspection of plantations, and, in some instances, the resolution of land disputes (practically all land is held by customary title, by the head of a family group, and may not be alienated to non-Tokelauans). The Taupulega is the principal organ of local government. The Taupulega also appoints the Failautuhi (Island Clerk), to record its meetings and transactions. The Taupulega in Atafu consists of the Faipule, the Pulenuku and the head of every family group; in Nukunonu it consists of the Faipule, the Pulenuku, the elders of the community and the nominated heads of extended families; in Fakaofo it consists of the Faipule, the Pulenuku and the elders (meetings of all the heads of family groups take place only infrequently).

The Government

(September 2002)

Administrator: LINDSAY WATT (took office March 1993).

FAIPULE

At elections in January 2002, all three incumbent Faipule were re-elected to office.

Faipule of Fakaofo: KOLOUEI O'BRIEN.

Faipule of Nukunonu: PIO TUIA.

Faipule of Atafu: KURESA NASAU.

PULENUKU

At elections in January 2002, two new Pulenuku were elected to office and one was re-elected.

Pulenuku of Fakaofo: KELI NEEMIA.

Pulenuku of Nukunonu: PANAPA SAKARIA.

Pulenuku of Atafu: PAULO KITONIA.

GOVERNMENT OFFICES

Tokelau Apia Liaison Office/Ofiha o Fehokotakiga Tokelau Ma Apia: POB 865, Apia, Samoa; tel. 20822; fax 21761; responsible for transport, accounting and consular functions; Man. LOGOTASI IOSEFA.

The Tokelau Public Service has seven departments, divided among the three atolls, with a supervising administrative official located in each village. Two departments are established on each atoll, while the seventh department, the Office of the Council of Faipule, rotates on a yearly basis in conjunction with the position of Ulu-O-Tokelau. Management of the Tokelau Public Service was formally transferred to Tokelau in July 2001.

Judicial System

Tokelau's legislative and judicial systems are based on the Tokelau Islands Act 1948 and subsequent amendments and regulations. The Act provided for a variety of British regulations to continue in force and, where no other legislation applies, the law of England and Wales in 1840 (the year in which British sovereignty over New Zealand was established) was to be applicable. New Zealand statute law applies in Tokelau only if specifically extended there. In 1986 legislation formalized the transfer of High Court civil and criminal jurisdiction from Niue to New Zealand. Most cases are judged by the Commissioner established on each atoll, who has limited jurisdiction in civil and criminal matters. Commissioners are appointed by the New Zealand Governor-General, after consultation with the elders of the atoll.

Commissioner of Fakaofo: LUI KELEKOLIO.

Commissioner of Nukunonu: ATONIO EGELIKO.

Commissioner of Atafu: MAKA TOLOA.

Religion

On Atafu almost all inhabitants are members of the Tokelau Congregational Christian Church, on Nukunonu all are Roman Catholic, while both denominations are represented on Fakaofo. In the late 1990s some 70% of the total population adhered to the Congregational Christian Church, and 30% to the Roman Catholic Church.

CHRISTIANITY

Roman Catholic Church

The Church is represented in Tokelau by a Mission, established in 1992. There were an estimated 510 adherents at 31 December 2000.

Superior: Mgr PATRICK EDWARD O'CONNOR, Catholic Mission, Nukunonu, Tokelau (via Apia, Samoa); tel. 4160; fax 4236.

Broadcasting and Communications

Each atoll has a radio station to broadcast shipping and weather reports. Radio-telephone provided the main communications link with other areas until the late 1990s. A new telecommunications system established at a cost of US $2.76m. (US $1m. of which was provided by New Zealand) and operating through an earth station, linked to a communications satellite, on each atoll, became operational in 1997. A new radio station, broadcasting information and music, was to commence operations in 2002.

TELECOMMUNICATIONS

TeleTok: Fenuafala, Fakaofo.

Finance

In 1977 a savings bank was established on each atoll; commercial and other banking facilities are available in Apia, Samoa.

Trade and Industry

A village co-operative store was established on each atoll in 1977. Local industries include copra production, woodwork and plaited craft goods, and the processing of tuna. Electricity is provided by diesel generators based in the village on each atoll.

Transport

There are no roads or motor vehicles. Unscheduled inter-atoll voyages, by sea, are forbidden because the risk of missing landfall is too great. Passengers and cargo are transported by vessels that anchor off shore, as there are no harbour facilities. A scheme to provide wharves (primarily to facilitate the export of fish) was proposed in September 2002. Most shipping links are with Samoa, but a monthly service from Fiji was introduced in 1986. The vessel *Forum Tokelau*, operated by Pacific Forum Line, began a monthly service between Tokelau and Apia, Samoa, in mid-1997. A New Zealand-funded inter-atoll vessel commenced service in 1991, providing the first regular link between the atolls for 40 years. Plans to construct an airstrip on each atoll were postponed in 1987 in favour of the development of shipping links. In late 2002, however, proposals for the construction of an airport were again under consideration.

Education

Education is provided free of charge, and attendance is almost 100%. Kindergarten facilities are available for children from the age of three years, while primary education takes place between the ages of five and 14. The provision of an additional year of schooling, for those aged 15, is rotated among the Territory's three schools every five years. There were 30 qualified teachers, complemented by teacher aides, on the islands in 1999. Pupil enrolment in 1991 at primary and secondary levels totalled 474. In the financial year ending 30 June 1999, government expenditure on education totalled $NZ0.80m., or 18.0% of total budgetary expenditure. The New Zealand Department of Education provides advisory services and some educational equipment. The Education Department of Samoa organizes daily radio broadcasts. Scholarships are awarded for secondary and tertiary education, and for vocational training, in New Zealand, Australia and other Pacific countries. Link arrangements exist between Tokelau and the University of the South Pacific, based in Fiji. There were 97 Tokelauan students at overseas institutions in 1990.

New Zealand Pacific: Associated States

The Associated States of New Zealand, the Cook Islands and Niue, were formerly Island Territories and integral parts of New Zealand. They now enjoy full self-government but continue in free association with New Zealand. New Zealand remains responsible for defence and represents the dependencies at the UN and in whichever external relations not conducted by the local Government.

Head of State: HM Queen Elizabeth II (succeeded to the throne 6 February 1952).
Governor-General: Dame Silvia Cartwright (took office 4 April 2001).

COOK ISLANDS

Physical and Social Geography

The 13 inhabited and two uninhabited islands of the Cook Islands are located in the southern Pacific Ocean. The territory lies between American Samoa, to the west, and French Polynesia, to the east. The total area of all the islands is 237 sq km (91.5 sq miles), but they extend over about 2m. sq km (more than 750,000 sq miles) of ocean, and form two groups: the Northern Cooks, which are all atolls and include Pukapuka (Danger Islands), Rakahanga (Rierson Island) and Manihiki (Humphrey Island), and the Southern Cooks, including Aitutaki, Mangaia and Rarotonga, which are all volcanic islands. From December to March the climate is warm and humid, with the possibility of severe storms; from April to November the climate is mild and equable. The average annual rainfall on Rarotonga is 2,134 mm (84 ins). The official language is English, but Polynesian languages are also spoken. The principal religion is Christianity, with about 58% of the population adhering to the Cook Islands Christian Church. The population was 18,027 in December 2001, according to the provisional results of the census; of these, 12,900 were estimated to be permanent residents. The capital is Avarua, on Rarotonga.

History

The islands were already settled by Polynesian (Maori) clans when the first Europeans, Spaniards, visited the territory. The Cook Islands are named after the leader of a British expedition of 1773, Capt. James Cook. The first islands were proclaimed a British protectorate in 1888. The first British Resident, in 1891, established an Elective Federal Parliament and a Federal Executive Council (the latter comprising Arikis or hereditary chiefs). This system was dissolved when the Cook Islands were annexed to New Zealand in 1901. Subsequent legislation developed government and representative institutions, and a Legislative Assembly was established in 1957. In 1962 the New Zealand Government presented the Assembly with four choices for constitutional development.

Following negotiations on the details and the enactment of the Constitution, the Cook Islands became a self-governing territory in free association with New Zealand on 4 August 1965. The people are New Zealand citizens. Sir Albert Henry, leader of the Cook Islands Party (CIP), was elected Premier in 1965 and re-elected in 1968, 1971, 1974 and March 1978. However, in July 1978, following an inquiry into alleged electoral malpractice, the Chief Justice disallowed votes cast in the elections to the Legislative Assembly by Cook Islands expatriates who had been flown from New Zealand, with their fares paid from public funds. The amended ballot gave a majority to the Democratic Party (DP), and its leader, Dr (later Sir) Thomas Davis, was sworn in as Premier by the Chief Justice. In August 1979 Sir Albert Henry was convicted of conspiracy to defraud, and was stripped of his knighthood.

In May 1981 an Amendment Bill made several changes in the Cook Islands' Constitution, increasing the membership of the Parliament, from 22 to 24, and extending the parliamentary term from four to five years.

In March 1983 Sir Thomas Davis lost power to the CIP, under Geoffrey (later Sir) Henry, cousin of the former Premier. However, with one seat already subject to re-election, Henry's majority of three was eroded by the death of one CIP member of Parliament and the transfer of support to the DP by another, Tupui Henry, son of the late Albert Henry. Geoffrey Henry resigned in August, and a general election in November returned the DP to power under Davis. In August 1984 Davis announced a major reorganization of cabinet portfolios, with three of the seven posts going to members of the CIP, to form a coalition Government, with Geoffrey Henry as Deputy Prime Minister. In mid-1985, however, Davis dismissed Geoffrey Henry, who had endorsed an unsuccessful motion expressing 'no confidence' in the Government, and the CIP withdrew from the coalition. Henry's successor as Deputy Prime Minister was Dr Terepai Maoate, one of four CIP members who continued to support the Davis Government. In July 1987 Davis was ousted as Prime Minister by a vote expressing 'no confidence' in him, following protracted controversy over contentious budget proposals. He was succeeded by Dr Pupuke Robati, a member of the Cabinet and a leading figure in the DP. Geoffrey Henry again became Prime Minister following a general election victory in January 1989.

In mid-1990 the defection of an MP from the DP to the CIP provided the CIP with 15 seats in Parliament and thus the minimum two-thirds' majority support necessary to amend the Constitution. In August 1991 a constitutional amendment was passed, that increased the number of members of Parliament to 25, and at an election to the newly-created seat a CIP candidate was successful. The amendment also provided for an increase in the number of cabinet members from seven to nine (including the Prime Minister).

In mid-1992 Norman George (parliamentary whip of the DP) was dismissed from the party, following a dispute over government spending, and in October he formed the Alliance Party.

At a general election in March 1994 the CIP increased its majority, winning 20 seats in Parliament, while the DP secured three and the Alliance Party two. Davis, who failed to win a seat, subsequently resigned as leader of the DP. A referendum, held simultaneously, revealed that a majority of the electorate favoured retaining the current name (69.8% of voters), national anthem (80.2%) and flag (48.5%) of the Cook Islands. (At subsequent by-elections the CIP lost two seats and the DP and Alliance Party each gained one seat.)

A financial scandal was narrowly averted following reports that during 1994 the Government had issued loan guarantees for foreign companies worth more than $NZ1,200m. (The islands' revenue for 1994/95 was estimated to total $NZ50m.) An investigation into the affair by the New Zealand Reserve Bank found that the Government had not been guilty of fraud, but rather had been coerced into the activity by unscrupulous foreign business interests. However, the affair led many investors to remove their funds from the islands, provoking a financial crisis which resulted in Henry's decision, in mid-1995, to withdraw the Cook Islands dollar from circulation, and to implement a programme of retrenchment measures. The crisis deepened during 1995 as new allegations emerged and Henry's Government was severely criticized by New Zealand for failing to co-operate with an official inquiry into accusations of fraud and tax evasion by several New Zealand companies. Henry maintained that the islands' bank secrecy laws prevented the disclosure of information relating to financial transactions. The situation deteriorated further when it was revealed that the Government had defaulted on a debt of some US $100m. to an Italian bank. In response to pressure from New Zealand and in an attempt to restore a degree of financial stability to the islands. Henry announced a severe restructuring programme in April 1996. The measures included a 50% reduction in the pay of public-sector workers, the closure of almost all diplomatic missions overseas, a 60% reduction in the number of government departments and ministries, and the privatization of the majority of government-owned authorities. A marked increase in 1995/96 in the emigration rate and a decline in the number of Cook Islanders returning to the islands following a period of residency overseas was attributed to the austere economic conditions created by the financial crisis.

Criticism of the Government's management of the austerity programme continued both from within the Government and the opposition in late 1996 and early 1997. However, aid donors praised the Government for the success of the reform programme at a consultative meeting in July 1997.

In August 1997 Parliament approved the Outer Islands Local Government Act, providing for a new budgetary system to allocate funds for projects in the outer islands and for increased powers for local authorities, was expected to result in a significant reduction in central government administration of the outer islands. As part of the plan, three new government bodies were elected in April 1998.

Henry's administration continued to attract controversy, with the announcement in December 1997 of the closure of the Ministry of Public Works, Survey, Housing, Water Supply and Environment Services for exceeding its budget. The minister responsible, Tihina Tom Marsters, resigned in protest at the closure, which resulted in the loss of more than 100 public servants' jobs, problems with the supply of utilities (particularly water) and the suspension of several development projects.

In November 1997 the northern Cook Islands were devastated by Cyclone Martin, which killed at least eight people and destroyed virtually all crops and infrastructure. The islands' important black pearl industry suffered severe losses as a result of extensive damage on Manihiki Atoll.

In April 1999 Chief Justice Sir Peter Quilliam ruled as unconstitutional an electoral amendment, put forward by the ruling CIP, to ban any electoral activity, including the formation of political parties. The amendment was contested by the Democratic Alliance Party (DAP, formerly the Democratic Party) and NAP, which claimed that it contravened fundamental human rights and freedoms.

At legislative elections in June 1999 the CIP won 11 of the 25 seats in Parliament, the DAP 10 seats, and the New Alliance Party (NAP, formerly the Alliance Party) four seats. Sir Geoffrey Henry of the CIP was reappointed Prime Minister and formed a new Cabinet, following the establishment of a political coalition with the NAP. The leader of the NAP, Norman George, became Deputy Prime Minister. With a total of 15 seats in Parliament, it was hoped that the new coalition's accession to power would result in greater political stability. However, three members of the CIP subsequently left the party to form a coalition with the DAP, in protest at the alliance with the NAP, and at the end of July Henry resigned and was replaced by a rebel CIP member, Dr Joe Williams. Williams was confirmed as the new Prime Minister by 13 votes to 12 in a vote of confidence by the Parliament. Williams' appointment provoked a public protest on Rarotonga, exacerbated by general discontent at the nomination of a Prime Minister whose parliamentary constituency was outside the Cook Islands. Electors also voted in a referendum on whether the parliamentary term should be reduced from five years to four. The shorter term was favoured by 63% of voters, and therefore failed to receive the support of the two-thirds' majority required to amend the Constitution. The result of the contest for the Pukapuka seat was challenged by the DAP. The matter was taken to the Court of Appeal, which subsequently declared the result invalid, stripping the Government of its one-seat majority. A by-election was held in late September to decide the Pukapuka seat; however, the result was again deemed to be invalid, and a further by-election was held in November 2000 (although the result of this poll was being disputed in the High Court in late 2000). The Government became a minority administration in mid-October when the Prime Minister dismissed his deputy, Norman George, along with the Minister of Education, following their defection to the opposition. Despite the appointment of three new ministers, Williams failed to regain a majority in Parliament. In November Williams resigned, shortly before a vote of 'no confidence' was to be tabled against him by Dr Terepai Maoate, the leader of the opposition DAP. Maoate won the vote by 14 votes to 11 and was appointed Prime Minister, forming a new coalition Government with the NAP. He subsequently reappointed Norman George to the post of Deputy Prime Minister.

In February 2001 Maoate removed the transport portfolio from among the responsibilities of Dr Robert Woonton (whose other duties included that of Minister of Foreign Affairs). Woonton had vocally upheld the interests of the private sector in the local shipping industry, but the Prime Minister denied that this support had been a factor in the reallocation of the portfolio. Maoate underwent medical treatment in March, prompting speculation that he might stand down as Prime Minister later in the year. In July 2001 Maoate dismissed Norman George alleging that he was working to undermine him; this was the second time that George had lost the position of Deputy Prime Minister. George had allegedly sought to negotiate unacceptably high increases in budgetary resources for the departments encompassed by his own ministerial portfolios. He was replaced by Dr Robert Woonton. Woonton, however, strongly criticized Maoate's leadership in the same month.

In late 2001 the rift between the Prime Minister and his Cabinet widened. Woonton announced his resignation, which Maoate refused to accept. This led to a motion of 'no confidence' in the Prime Minister, which he only narrowly survived. In February 2002 Maoate's leadership was again challenged: 15 of the 25 Members of Parliament voted against him in a second motion of 'no confidence'. He was therefore replaced by Robert Woonton. An extensive ministerial reorganization followed. Sir Geoffrey Henry returned to the Cabinet as Deputy Prime Minister. Woonton declared his priorities to be the encouragement of emigrant workers to return to the islands through income tax incentives and an ambitious redevelopment plan for the capital, Avarua.

In August 2002 it emerged that a senior civil servant in the Prime Minister's office had been arrested and charged with fraud. The authorities insisted that that the individual's name would not be disclosed until the case had been concluded.

The rate of emigration, meanwhile, continued to increase. In late 2000 it was announced that some 1,400 residents had left the islands during that year (compared with 641 in the previous year). This resulted in a reduction in the estimated population of the islands to 14,300 (the lowest level in more than 50 years) and prompted the Government to initiate campaigns in Australia and New Zealand to encourage former residents to return to their homeland. Private sector businesses, many of which had experienced difficulties in recruiting workers in sufficient numbers, were also involved in the campaign. The resident population was estimated to number only 12,900 in December 2001, and the Government feared that it could decrease to just 10,000 by 2006, the majority of the loss being from the outer islands. In August 2002 the Government announced that it would allocate US $23,350 for the campaign.

In early 2000 the islands of Penrhyn, Pukapuka, Rakahanga and Manihiki expressed their desire to become fully devolved and to take sole control over areas such as administration, public expenditure and justice. In response, the Government pledged gradually to phase out the Minister of Outer Islands Development, as well as the post of Government Representative in the outer islands.

A reported increase in the number of Russian nationals opening bank accounts in the Cook Islands led to allegations in early 1999 that the islands' 'offshore' financial centre was being used extensively by criminal organizations for 'laundering' the proceeds of their activities. The claims were vigorously denied by officials in the sector. However, in June 2000 the the islands were named by both the Paris-based Organisation for Economic Co-operation and Development (OECD) and by the Financial Action Task Force (FATF) on Money Laundering as one of a number of countries that had failed to co-operate in international efforts to combat 'harmful' tax havens and the practice of 'money-laundering'. This led to increased pressure on the Government to implement stricter controls over its 'offshore' financial centre. Consequently, legislation was approved in August of that year providing for the creation of the Money Laundering Authority and the introduction of new regulations aimed at reducing criminal activity in the sector. In early 2001, however, the Government announced that it would not be able to meet the July 2001 deadline for the implementation of the reforms recommended and therefore was liable to incur international sanctions. At the end of February 2002 the Government made a conditional commitment to the abolition of harmful tax practices, thus preventing the imposition of financial sanctions by the European Union (EU) and other international organizations. OECD therefore removed the Cook Islands from its list of non-co-operative countries and territories in April. In late 2002, however, the Cook Islands remained on the FATF list, owing to the territory's perceived failure effectively to address the problem of 'money-laundering'.

New Zealand is ultimately responsible for the defence and foreign relations of the Cook Islands, although the territory has progressively assumed control over much of its foreign policy (a Ministry of Foreign Affairs was established in 1983). The Cook Islands is a member of the Pacific Islands Forum (formerly the South Pacific Forum) in its own right. In August 1985 eight members of the South Pacific Forum, including the Cook Islands, signed a treaty on Rarotonga, designating a nuclear-free zone in the South Pacific. The treaty imposed a ban on the manufacture, testing, storage and use of nuclear weapons, and the dumping of nuclear waste, in the region.

In January 1986, after the virtual disintegration of the ANZUS military alliance linking Australia, New Zealand and the USA, Sir Thomas Davis declared the Cook Islands a neutral country, because he considered that New Zealand was no longer in a position to defend the islands. In 1989 and 1990 the Henry Government sought to improve links with the neighbouring territory of French Polynesia (Cook Islanders and Tahitians are related) and secured French co-operation in the policing of the Cook Islands' exclusive economic zone (EEZ). In 1990 an agreement was signed that settled the exact delimitation of the EEZs of the Cook Islands and French Polynesia (the two claims overlapped). In 1991 the Cook Islands signed a treaty of friendship and co-operation with France. The establishment of closer relations with France was widely regarded as an expression of the Cook Islands' Government's dissatisfaction with existing arrangements with New Zealand. However, relations deteriorated considerably when the French Government resumed its programme of nuclear-weapons testing at Mururoa Atoll in September 1995. Henry was fiercely critical of the decision and dispatched a *vaka* (traditional voyaging canoe) with a crew of Cook Islands' traditional warriors to protest near the test site. The tests were concluded in January 1996, and diplomatic relations between the two countries were established in early 2000.

The islands established diplomatic relations at ambassadorial level with the People's Republic of China in July 1997. In November 1998 Henry made an official visit to China, during which the two countries signed a bilateral trade agreement and each conferred the status of 'most favoured nation' on the other. Henry stated that the move constituted a further attempt by his Government to reduce the islands' dependence on New Zealand. During her visit to the islands in June 2001, Helen Clark, the New Zealand Prime Minister, stated that if the Cook Islands desired complete independence and membership of international organizations, the process would not be obstructed by New Zealand. Cook Islanders, however, would then be obliged to renounce their New Zealand citizenship.

Economy

In 2000, according to the Asian Development Bank (ADB), the Cook Islands' gross domestic product (GDP), measured at current prices, totalled an estimated $NZ171.6m. GDP increased, in real terms, at an average annual rate of 2.4% in 1990–2000. According to official figures, GDP rose by 6.1% in 1999/2000 and by 4.3% in 2000/01.

Agriculture has more than subsistence importance on the southern islands, with their fertile volcanic soil. According to estimates by the ADB, agriculture (including hunting, forestry and fishing) contributed 16.1% of GDP in 2000. The sector engaged 11.5% of employees in 1996. In 2000 only 35% of Rarotonga households were classified as being agriculturally active, compared with 74% in the southern outer islands. According to ADB estimates, the real GDP of the agricultural sector contracted by 1.0% per year in 1990–2000. Compared with the previous year, the sector's GDP decreased by 18.1% in 1998 and by 27.5% in 1999, but increased by an estimated 32.4% in 2000. In 2000 the sector provided 3.7% of export earnings (compared with 32.1% in 1995). Papaya is the Cook Islands' most important export crop, and accounted for 24.9% of total export earnings in 1996. Papaya exports were worth some $NZ250,000 in 1998. Most of the produce is sold to New Zealand. Other important cash crops are coconuts and tropical fruits such as mangoes, pineapples and bananas. Aitutaki Island is important for the production of bananas. Cassava, sweet potatoes and vegetables are cultivated as food crops. Pigs and poultry are kept. Plans to develop cattle-ranching, ostrich farming and the cultivation of vanilla, taro, coffee and arrowroot on Atiu, Mangaia and Mauke have been discussed.

Exploitation of the Cook Islands' maritime exclusive economic zone (EEZ) became a major earner of foreign exchange in the 1980s. The Cook Islands' EEZ, extending to 200 nautical miles (370 km) from the territory's shores, is monitored under Australia's regional fisheries programme, and also by the French Government. The sale of fishing licences to foreign fleets provides an important source of income. Aquaculture, in the form of giant clam farming and pearl oyster farming, was developed during the 1980s. The pearl industry expanded considerably during the 1990s. Pearl oyster farming at Manihiki and Penrhyn Island was the islands' most important industry and pearls were the most important export commodity by 2000, earning an estimated $NZ16.3m. in export revenue in 2000/01. The industry was adversely affected, however, by Cyclone Martin which devastated Manihiki Atoll in late 1997, and by a bacterial pearl shell disease in 2000. In response to the infection, the pearl industry agreed to a number of measures designed to protect the environment and reduce overfarming. In early 2001 an Australian fishing company announced plans to invest some US $60m. (including the purchase of 25 long-line fishing vessels and the construction of a fish-processing facility) in a major fishing project in the islands.

According to ADB estimates, industry (comprising mining and quarrying, manufacturing, construction and power) provided 7.5% of GDP in 2000. The sector engaged 12.1% of employees in 1993. Industrial GDP increased, in real terms, at an average rate of 2.7% per year during 1990–2000. Compared with the previous year, the industrial sector's GDP increased by some 7.0% in 1999 and by an estimated 6.8% in 2000.

Manufacturing contributed 4.1% of GDP in 1995, and engaged 4.5% of employees in 1993. The manufacturing and mining sectors together accounted for an estimated 2.2% of GDP in 2000, according to ADB estimates. The real GDP of manufacturing and mining declined at an average rate of 0.5% per year during 1990–2000. Compared with the previous year, however, the two sectors' GDP increased by 6.1% in 1999 and by 6.5% in 2000. The most important industrial activities are fruit-processing, brewing, the manufacture of garments and handicrafts. Construction contributed an estimated 2.8% of GDP in 2000 and engaged 3.4% of the employed labour force in 1993.

The islands depend on imports for their energy requirements. Mineral fuels accounted for 17.6% of total imports in 2000. In September 1997 the Government signed an agreement with a consortium of Norwegian companies to mine cobalt, nickel, manganese and copper by extracting mineral-rich nodules found in the islands' EEZ between Aitutaki and Penrhyn. It was estimated that the deep-sea mining project, which was expected to begin in 2003/04, could earn the islands up to US $15m. per year and US $600m. in total. Trial operations began in 1999.

Service industries contributed an estimated 76.4% to GDP in 2000 and engaged 80.8% of the employed labour force in 1993. According to the ADB, the service sector's GDP expanded by 14.0% in 1999 and by an estimated 6.5% in 2000. Tourism expanded considerably in the late 1980s and early 1990s, and earned an estimated $NZ93.9m. in 2000/01. Visitor arrivals rose from 64,629 in 1999/2000 to an estimated 76,833 in 2000/01. The trade, restaurants and hotels sector contributed 30.2% of GDP in 2000 and engaged 20.9% of the employed labour force in 1993. The withdrawal of Canada 3000's weekly flight from Toronto (following the airline's financial failure in late 2001) and a reduction in Air New Zealand's capacity, combined with the repercussions of the terrorist attacks on the USA in September 2001, had an adverse effect on the Cook Islands' tourism industry. Nevertheless, the islands were expected to retain their appeal as a relatively safe destination.

'Offshore' banking, introduced to the islands in 1982, expanded rapidly, with more than 2,000 international companies registered by 1987. In 1992 the islands were established as an alternative domicile for companies listed on the Hong Kong Stock Exchange. The financial and business services sector provided 9.9% of GDP in 2000 and engaged 3.6% of the employed labour force in 1993. A significant proportion of the islands' revenue is provided by remittances from migrants (who outnumber the residents of the islands).

The Cook Islands suffer from a persistent trade deficit, which increased to more than 70% of GDP in the 1990s, before declining to about 50% in 2000. In 2001 the islands recorded a trade deficit of $NZ95.3m. In 2001 the principal imports were food and live animals (which accounted for 20.6% of total imports), basic manufactures and machinery (15.5%), while basic manufactures were the main export, accounting for over 90% of total exports. In that year New Zealand provided 74.8% of the islands' total imports, while Japan and Australia were the major purchasers of the islands' exports, accounting for 37.5% and 29.1% respectively. Despite the large trade deficit, the islands consistently record a surplus on the current account of the balance of payments. This is primarily due to the role of tourism in generating income for the islands. Remittances sent back by migrant workers account for a large proportion of the islands' income.

According to official estimates, in the financial year ending June 2001 there was an overall budgetary surplus of an estimated $NZ10.8m., a substantial increase on the $NZ2.3m. surplus recorded in 2000. More modest surpluses were projected in 2001/02 and 2002/03. Development assistance from New Zealand totalled $NZ6.2m. in 1999/2000, and was to remain at this level for the following two financial years (New Zealand is the guarantor of the Cook Islands' borrowing from the ADB, which had reached a total of $NZ25m. at 31 October 2001). It was estimated at the end of 2001 that the islands' external debt amounted to some $NZ117m. In mid-2001 net public debt amounted to $NZ128.7m., equivalent to 71.8% of GDP. The annual rate of inflation averaged 2.5% in 1990–98. Average consumer prices rose by 1.7% in 1999/2000 but the inflation rate increased substantially, according to official estimates, to 9.5% in 2000/01. The unemployment rate was 12.9% in 1996, but the employment situation had improved significantly by 2001, owing to increased demand for workers in the tourism and retail sectors.

During the 1980s and 1990s development plans sought to expand the economy by stimulating investment in the private sector and developing the islands' infrastructure. In mid-1995 it was announced that the New Zealand dollar was to become the sole legal currency of the islands, following a financial crisis that led the Government to withdraw the Cook Islands dollar from circulation and to introduce a retrenchment programme. In addition, a radical programme of economic restructuring was announced in 1996, in response to a deepening financial crisis, which had led the Government to default on a US $100m. debt to an Italian bank (see History). Between 1996 and 1998 the number of public-sector workers was reduced from 3,350 to 1,340, and the number of ministries from 52 to 22.

Formal discussions, organized by the ADB, took place between the Cook Islands and its creditors in September 1998, at which a preliminary agreement to reschedule the islands' external debts was reached. The agreement was expected to reduce the total debt from $NZ200m. to $NZ127m. and included an extended repayment period and concessional interest rates. The Government of France (a major creditor to the islands) refused to participate in the arrangement. The external debt remained high in 2000, although it fell as a percentage of GDP due to positive levels of GDP growth in 1999 and 2000. The Government subsequently adopted a policy of accumulating reserves for the purposes of debt-servicing as an annual budgetary allocation. In 2000/01 it set aside $NZ2m. and anticipated reserving at least $NZ1m. for the following financial year. In the longer term the Government aimed to invest these reserves in overseas portfolios in order to reduce the risks arising from currency fluctuations. Plans to restructure the 'offshore' sector, announced in 1998, were expected to increase revenue. However, the islands' financial regulations were severely criticized by the Financial Action Task Force (FATF—see History), which in late 2002 continued to include the Cook Islands on its list of countries and territories, the banking systems of which were allegedly being used for the purposes of 'money-laundering'. Large-scale emigration remained a serious and deepening concern for the Cook Islands' economy in the late 1990s and early 2000s. In August 2002 the Government announced that it would allocate US $23,350 to the campaign to encourage islanders resident abroad to return. The Government was expected to introduce tax incentives in late 2002, raising the limit of tax-free personal income from $NZ6,000 to $NZ12,000 per annum. Meanwhile, the success of the tourist industry and the dramatic increase in arrivals to the islands led to expressions of concern that Rarotonga, in particular, was unable to sustain the growth. Reports indicated that waste disposal and energy provision were inadequate in relation to the demands of large numbers of visitors and that pollution of the lagoon was occurring as a result.

In addition to holding membership of the South Pacific Forum, the Cook Islands is a member of the Pacific Community (formerly the South Pacific Commission), the Asian Development Bank and an associate member of the UN's Economic and Social Commission for Asia and the Pacific (ESCAP). In late 1999 the Cook Islands was granted observer status to the Lomé Convention and successor Cotonou Agreement with the EU.

Statistical Survey

Sources (unless otherwise stated): Statistics Office, POB 125, Rarotonga; tel. 29390; Prime Minister's Department, Government of the Cook Islands, Avarua, Rarotonga; tel. 29300; fax 22856.

AREA AND POPULATION

Area: 237 sq km (91.5 sq miles).

Population: 19,103 (males 9,842; females 9,261) at census of 1 December 1996; 18,027 (males 9,303; females 8,724) at census of December 2001 (provisional); resident population 18,034 (males 9,297; females 8,737) at 1996 census; 12,900 (official estimate) at December 2001. *By island* (resident population, 1996 census): Rarotonga (including the capital, Avarua) 10,337; Aitutaki 2,272; Atiu 942; Mangaia 1,083; Manihiki 656; Mauke 643; Mitiaro 318; Nassau 99; Palmerston (Avarua) 49; Penrhyn (Tongareva) 604; Pukapuka 778; Rakahanga 249; Suwarrow 4. *Cook Island Maoris Resident in New Zealand* (census of 6 March 2001): 52,569.

Density (resident population, December 2001): 54.4 per sq km.

Births and Deaths (1999): Births: 346 (birth rate 21.1 per 1,000); Deaths: 96 (death rate 5.9 per 1,000). Source: UN, *Population and Vital Statistics Report*.

Expectation of Life (WHO estimates, years at birth, 2000): Males 68.7; Females 72.1. Source: WHO, *World Health Report*.

Employment (September 1993): Agriculture, hunting, forestry and fishing 457; Mining and quarrying 16; Manufacturing 290; Electricity, gas and water 254; Construction 215; Trade, restaurants and hotels 1,338; Transport, storage and communications 770; Financing, insurance, real estate and business services 231; Community, social and personal services 2,835; Total employees 6,406 (males 4,069, females 2,337). Source: ILO, *Yearbook of Labour Statistics*.

1996: Agriculture hunting, forestry and fishing 600; Manufacturing, mining and quarrying 300; Activities not adequately defined 4,400; Total employed 5,200; Unemployed 800; Total labour force 6,000. Source: Asian Development Bank, *Key Indicators of Developing Asian and Pacific Countries*.

HEALTH AND WELFARE

Key Indicators

Fertility (births per woman, 2000): 3.3.

Under-5 Mortality Rate (per 1,000 live births, 2000): 24.

Physicians (per 1,000 head, 1997): 0.90.

Health Expenditure (1998): US $ per head (PPP): 419.
% of GDP: 5.3.
public (% of total): 68.3.

Access to Water (% of persons, 2000): 100.

Access to Sanitation (% of persons, 2000): 100.

For sources and definitions, see explanatory note on p. vi.

AGRICULTURE, ETC.

Principal Crops (mainly FAO estimates, metric tons, 2000): Cassava 3,000; Sweet potatoes 1,400; Coconuts 5,000; Vegetables and melons 1,802; Tomatoes 500; Mangoes 2,700; Papayas 908; Pineapples 50; Bananas 230; Avocados 150. Source: FAO.

Livestock (mainly FAO estimates, head, year ending September 2000): Pigs 40,000; Goats 2,500; Poultry 80,000; Horses 300. Source: FAO.

Livestock Products (metric tons, 2000): Hen eggs 250; Goatskins 2; Pigmeat 600; Poultry meat 80. Source: FAO.

Fishing (FAO estimates, metric tons, live weight, 1999): Capture 1,000 (Groupers 120, Flyingfishes 40, Jacks and crevalles 50, Marlins and sailfishes 30, Swordfish 40, Sharks, rays and skates 30, Octopuses 70, Other marine molluscs 200); Total catch 1,000. Figures exclude trochus shells: 25 metric tons (FAO estimate). Source: FAO, *Yearbook of Fishery Statistics*.

INDUSTRY

Electric Energy (million kWh): 21.8 in 1999; 24.7 in 2000; 25.8 in 2001.

FINANCE

Currency and Exchange Rates: New Zealand currency is legal tender. In mid-1995 it was announced that the Cook Islands dollar (formerly the local currency, at par with the New Zealand dollar) was to be withdrawn from circulation. New Zealand currency: 100 cents = 1 New Zealand dollar ($NZ); for details of exchange rates, see Tokelau, p. 1046.

Budget ($NZ '000, year ending 30 June 2001): *Revenue:* Total revenue 65,161 (Tax 54,742, Non-tax 10,419). *Expenditure:* Total expenditure 54,343.

Overseas Aid ($NZ '000): Official development assistance from New Zealand 6,200 in 1999/2000, in 2000/01 and in 2001/02. Source: Ministry of Foreign Affairs and Trade, Wellington.

Cost of Living (Consumer Price Index for Rarotonga; base: 1998 = 100): 102.7 in 2000; 112.4 in 2001.

Gross Domestic Product by Economic Activity (estimates, $NZ '000 in current prices, 2000): Agriculture, forestry and fishing 28,475; Mining, quarrying and manufacturing 4,859; Electricity, gas and water 3,524; Construction 4,940; Trade, restaurants and hotels 53,479; Transport and communications 28,883; Financial and business services 17,605; Public administration 23,156; Other services 12,194; *Sub-total* 177,115; *Less* Imputed bank service charge 5,516; *GDP in purchasers' values* 171,599. Source: Asian Development Bank, *Key Indicators of Developing Asian and Pacific Countries*.

EXTERNAL TRADE

Principal Commodities (distribution by SITC, $NZ '000, 2001): *Imports c.i.f.:* Food and live animals 22,927; Mineral fuels, lubricants, etc. 11,071; Chemicals 6,905; Basic manufactures 17,246; Machinery and transport equipment 29,171; Miscellaneous manufactured articles 16,671; Total (incl. others) 111,437. *Exports f.o.b.:* Food and live animals 861; Basic manufactures 14,612; Miscellaneous manufactured articles 498; Total (incl. others) 16,132. Source: Asian Development Bank, *Key Indicators of Developing Asian and Pacific Countries*.

Principal Trading Partners ($NZ '000, 2001): *Imports:* New Zealand 83,410; Australia 6,737; USA 1,547; Japan 1,382; Fiji 12,453; Total (incl. others) 111,437. *Exports:* Japan 6,057; New Zealand 1,411; Australia 4,698; USA 2,118; Total (incl. others) 16,132. Source: Asian Development Bank, *Key Indicators of Developing Asian and Pacific Countries*.

TRANSPORT

Road Traffic (registered vehicles, April 1983): 6,555. *New motor vehicles registered* (Rarotonga, 2001): 1,698.

Shipping: *Merchant Fleet* (registered at 31 December 2001): 10 vessels, displacement 5,202 grt (Source: Lloyd's Register-Fairplay, *World Fleet Statistics*); *International Sea-borne Freight Traffic* (estimates, '000 metric tons): Goods unloaded 32.6 (2001); Goods loaded 9; Goods unloaded 32 (1990). Source (for 1990): UN, *Monthly Bulletin of Statistics*.

Civil Aviation (2001): *Aircraft Movements:* 559. *Freight Traffic* (metric tons): Goods loaded 290; Goods unloaded 659.

TOURISM

Foreign Tourist Arrivals: 55,599 in 1999; 72,994 in 2000; 74,575 in 2001.

Tourist Arrivals by Country of Residence (2000): Australia 12,128; Canada 5,992; Germany 5,232; New Zealand 22,020; United Kingdom 12,392; USA 6,734; Total (incl. others) 72,994. Source: World Tourism Organization, *Yearbook of Tourism Statistics*).

Visitor Expenditure (estimates, $NZ '000): 73,753 in 1999/2000; 93,929 in 2000/01.

COMMUNICATIONS MEDIA

Radio Receivers (1997): 14,000 in use*.

Television Receivers (1997): 4,000 in use*.

Telephones (main lines, 2000): 5,680 in use†.

Mobile Cellular Telephones (2000): 552 subscribers†.

Facsimile Machines (1990): 230 in use‡.

Daily Newspaper (1996): 1; circulation 2,000*.

Non-daily Newspaper (1996): 1; circulation 1,000*.

* Source: UNESCO, *Statistical Yearbook*.

† Source: International Telecommunication Union.

‡ Source: UN, *Statistical Yearbook*.

EDUCATION

Pre-primary (1998): 26 schools; 30 teachers; 460 pupils.

Primary (1998): 28 schools; 140 teachers; 2,711 pupils.

Secondary* (1998): 23 schools; 129 teachers; 1,779 pupils.

Higher (1980): 41 teachers; 360 pupils†.

* Includes high school education.

† Source: UNESCO, *Statistical Yearbook*.

Directory

The Constitution

On 5 August 1965 a new Constitution was proclaimed, whereby the people of the Cook Islands have complete control over their own affairs in free association with New Zealand, but they can at any time move into full independence by a unilateral act if they so wish.

Executive authority is vested in the British monarch, who is Head of State, and exercised through an official representative. The New Zealand Government also appoints a representative (from 1994 redesignated High Commissioner), resident on Rarotonga.

Executive powers are exercised by a Cabinet consisting of the Prime Minister and between five and seven other ministers including a Deputy Prime Minister. The Cabinet is collectively responsible to Parliament.

Parliament consists of 25 members who are elected by universal suffrage every five years (including one member elected by voters living overseas), and is presided over by the Speaker. The House of Ariki comprises up to 15 members who are hereditary chiefs; it can advise the Government, particularly on matters relating to land and indigenous people but has no legislative powers. The Koutu Nui is a similar organization comprised of sub-chiefs, which was established by an amendment in 1972 of the 1966 House of Ariki Act.

Each of the main islands, except Rarotonga (which is divided into three tribal districts or *vaka*), has an elected mayor and a government representative who is appointed by the Prime Minister. In January 2000 it was announced that the post of Government Representative in the outer islands was to be phased out over two years.

The Government

Queen's Representative: Fred Goodwin.

New Zealand High Commissioner: Kurt Meyer.

THE CABINET
(September 2002)

Prime Minister, Minister of Foreign Affairs and Immigration, Tourism, Marine Resources, House of Ariki, Police, Agriculture, Transport, Airport Authority, Ports Authority and National Disaster Management: Dr Robert Woonton.

Deputy Prime Minister, Minister of Finance, Public Expenditure Review, Committee and Audit, Office of Offshore Financial Services, Bank of the Cook Islands, Cook Islands Investment Corporation, Cook Islands Government Property Corporation, National Research and Development Institute, National Development Council, Revenue Management and Development Investment Board: Sir Geoffrey Henry.

Minister of Outer Islands Development, Attorney-General, Crown Law, Energy and Environment, Natural Heritage, Broadcasting and Communication, Telecom and Information Services, Justice, Ombudsman and National Superannuation: Norman George.

Minister of Education, Culture, Public Service Commission and Human Resources: Jim Marurai.

Minister of Works, Youth, Sports and Recreation: Tihina Tom Marsters.

Minister of Health, Internal Affairs and Non-Government Organizations: Peri Vaevae Pare.

GOVERNMENT OFFICES

Office of the Queen's Representative: POB 134, Titikaveka, Rarotonga; tel. 29311.

Office of the Prime Minister: Government of the Cook Islands, Avarua, Rarotonga; tel. 29300; fax 20856; e-mail pmoffice@cookislands.gov.ck.

Office of the Public Service Commissioner: POB 24, Rarotonga; tel. 29421; fax 21321; e-mail psc@cookislands.gov.ck.

Department of Justice: POB 111, Rarotonga; tel. 29410; fax 29610; e-mail justice@cookislands.gov.ck.

Department of Tourism and Transport: POB 61, Rarotonga; tel. 28810; fax 28816; e-mail tourism@cookislands.gov.ck.

New Zealand High Commission: 1st Floor, Philatelic Bureau Bldg, Takuvaine Rd, POB 21, Avarua, Rarotonga; tel. 22201; fax 21241; e-mail nzhraro@oyster.net.ck.

Ministries

Ministry of Agriculture: POB 96, Rarotonga; tel. 28711; fax 21881; e-mail cimoa@oyster.net.ck.

Ministry of Cultural Development: POB 8, Rarotonga; tel. 20725; fax 23725; e-mail culture1@oyster.net.ck; internet www.cinews.co.ck/culture/index.htm.

Ministry of Education: POB 97, Rarotonga; tel. 29357; fax 28357; e-mail dieducat@oyster.net.uk.

Ministry of Energy: POB 72, Rarotonga; tel. 24484; fax 24485.

Ministry of Finance and Economic Management: POB 120, Rarotonga; tel. 22878; fax 23877; e-mail finsec@oyster.net.ck.

Ministry of Foreign Affairs and Immigration: POB 105, Rarotonga; tel. 29347; fax 21247; e-mail secfa@foraffairs.gov.ck.

Ministry of Health: POB 109, Rarotonga; tel. 22664; fax 23109; e-mail aremaki@oyster.net.ck.

Ministry of Internal Affairs: POB 98, Rarotonga; tel. 29370; fax 23608; e-mail sec1@intaff.gov.ck.

Ministry of Marine Resources: POB 85, Rarotonga; tel. 28721; fax 29721; e-mail rar@mmr.gov.ck.

Ministry of Outer Islands' Development: POB 383, Rarotonga; tel. 20321; fax 24321.

Ministry of Works and Physical Planning: POB 102, Rarotonga; tel. 20034; fax 21134; e-mail herman@mow.gov.ck.

HOUSE OF ARIKI

House of Ariki: POB 13, Rarotonga; tel. 26500; fax 21260.

President: Pa Teariki Upokotini Maire Ariki.

Vice-President: Tinomana Ruta Tuoro Ariki.

KOUTU NUI

Koutu Nui: POB 13, Rarotonga; tel. 29317; fax 21260; e-mail nvaloa@parliament.gov.ck.

President: Tetika Mataiapo Dorice Reid.

Legislature

PARLIAMENT

Parliamentary Service: POB 13, Rarotonga; tel. 26500; fax 21260; e-mail nvaloa@parliament.gov.ck.

Speaker: Pupke Robati.

Clerk of Parliament: Nga Valoa.

General Election, 16 June 1999

Party	Seats
Cook Islands Party (CIP)	11
Democratic Alliance Party (DAP)	10
New Alliance Party (NAP)	4
Total	25

Political Organizations

Cook Islands Labour Party: Rarotonga; f. 1988; anti-nuclear; Leader Rena Ariki Jonassen.

Cook Islands Party (CIP): Rarotonga; f. 1965; Gen. Sec. Tihina Tom Marsters; Leader Dr Joe Williams.

Democratic Alliance Party (DAP): POB 73, Rarotonga; tel. 21224; f. 1971; fmrly the Democratic Party; Leader Dr Terepai Maoate; Pres. Fred Goodwin.

Democratic Tumu Party (DTP): POB 492, Rarotonga; tel. 21224; fax 22520; split from Democratic Party in 1985; Leader Vincent A. K. T. Ingram.

New Alliance Party (NAP): POB 2164, Rarotonga; f. 1992 from split with Democratic Party (Coalition); fmrly the Alliance Party; Leader Norman George.

Judicial System

Ministry of Justice: POB 111, Avarua, Rarotonga; tel. 29410; fax 28610; e-mail offices@justice.gov.ck.

The judiciary comprises the Privy Council, the Court of Appeal and the High Court.

The High Court exercises jurisdiction in respect of civil, criminal and land titles cases on all the islands, except for Mangaia, Pukapuka and Mitiaro, where disputes over land titles are settled according to custom. The Court of Appeal hears appeals against decisions of the High Court. The Privy Council, sitting in the United Kingdom, is the final appellate tribunal for the country in civil, criminal and land matters; since May 1993 the Court of Appeal has been the final appellate tribunal for disputes concerning chiefly titles.

Attorney-General: NORMAN GEORGE.

Solicitor-General: JANET GRACE MAKI.

Chief Justice of the High Court: LAURENCE MURRAY GREIG.

Judges of the High Court: GLENDYN CARTER, NORMAN SMITH, DAVID WILLIAMS, HETA HINGSTON.

Religion

CHRISTIANITY

The principal denomination is the Cook Islands (Congregational) Christian Church, to which about 58% of the islands' population belong, according to figures recorded in the census conducted in 1996.

Religious Advisory Council of the Cook Islands: POB 31, Rarotonga; tel. 22851; fax 22852; f. 1968; four mem. churches; Pres. KEVIN GEELAN; Gen. Sec. TUNGANE POKURA.

The Roman Catholic Church

The Cook Islands form the diocese of Rarotonga, suffragan to the archdiocese of Suva (Fiji). At 31 December 2000 the diocese contained an estimated 3,140 adherents. The Bishop participates in the Catholic Bishops' Conference of the Pacific, based in Suva.

Bishop of Rarotonga: Rt Rev. STUART FRANCE O'CONNELL; Catholic Diocese, POB 147, Rarotonga; tel. 20817; fax 29817; e-mail sbish@oyster.net.ck

The Anglican Communion

The Cook Islands are within the diocese of Polynesia, part of the Church of the Province of New Zealand. The Bishop of Polynesia is resident in Fiji.

Protestant Churches

Cook Islands Christian Church: Takamoa, POB 93, Rarotonga; tel. 26452; 11,193 mems (1986); Pres. Rev. TANGIMETUA TANGA; Gen. Sec. WILLIE JOHN.

Seventh-day Adventists: POB 31, Rarotonga; tel. 22851; fax 22852; e-mail umakatu@oyster.net.ck; 732 mems (1998); Pres. UMA KATU.

Other churches active in the islands include the Assembly of God, the Church of Latter-day Saints (Mormons), the Apostolic Church, the Jehovah's Witnesses and the Baptist Church.

BAHÁ'Í FAITH

National Spiritual Assembly: POB 1, Rarotonga; tel. 20658; fax 23658; e-mail nsacooks@bahai.org.ck; mems resident in eight localities; Sec. JOHNNY FRISBIE.

The Press

Cook Islands Herald: POB 126, Tutakimoa, Rarotonga; e-mail bestread@ciherald.co.ck; internet www.ciherald.co.ck; weekly.

Cook Islands News: POB 15, Avarua, Rarotonga; tel. 22999; fax 25303; e-mail editor@cinews.co.ck; internet www.cinews.co.ck; f. 1954 by Govt, transferred to private ownership 1989; daily; mainly English; Man. Dir PHIL EVANS; Editor MOANA MOEKA'A; circ. 1,800.

Cook Islands Star: POB 798, Rarotonga; tel. 29965; e-mail jason@oyster.net.ck; fortnightly; Chief Reporter JASON BROWN.

Cook Islands Sun: POB 753, Snowbird Laundry, Arorangi, Rarotonga; f. 1988; tourist newspaper; twice a year; Editor WARREN ATKINSON.

Broadcasting and Communications

TELECOMMUNICATIONS

Telecom Cook Islands Ltd: POB 106, Rarotonga; tel. 29680; fax 20990; e-mail stu@telecom.co.ck; internet www.telecom.co.ck; CEO STUART DAVIES.

BROADCASTING

Radio

Cook Islands Broadcasting Corpn (CIBC): POB 126, Avarua, Rarotonga; tel. 29460; fax 21907; f. 1989 to operate new television service, and radio service of former Broadcasting and Newspaper Corpn; state-owned; Gen. Man. EMILE KAIRUA.

Radio Cook Islands: tel. 20100; broadcasts in English and Maori 18 hours daily.

KC Radio: POB 521, Avarua, Rarotonga; tel. 23203; f. 1979 as Radio Ikurangi; commercial; operates station ZK1ZD; broadcasts 18 hours daily on FM; Man. Dir and Gen. Man. DAVID SCHMIDT.

Television

Cook Islands Broadcasting Corpn (CIBC): (see Radio).

Cook Islands TV: POB 126, Rarotonga; tel. 20101; fax 21907; f. 1989; broadcasts nightly, in English and Maori, from 5 p.m. to 10.15 p.m.; 10 hours of local programmes per week; remainder provided by Television New Zealand.

In early 1999 the French Société Nationale de Radio-Télévision Française d'Outre-Mer agreed to operate two or three new television channels in the islands.

Finance

Cook Islands Monetary Board: Rarotonga; tel. 21074; fax 21798; f. 1981; exercises control of currency; controlling body for trade and industry as well as finance; registers companies, financial institutions, etc.; Sec. M. BROWN.

Trustee Companies Association (TCA): Rarotonga; controlling body for the 'offshore' financial sector; Sec. LOU COLVEY.

BANKING

Development Bank

Bank of Cook Islands (BCI): POB 113, Avarua, Rarotonga; tel. 29341; fax 29343; f. July 2001 when Cook Islands Development Bank merged with Cook Island Savings Bank; finances development projects in all areas of the economy and helps islanders establish small businesses and industries by providing loans and management advisory assistance; Gen. Man. UNAKEA KAUVAI; brs on Rarotonga and Aitutaki.

Commercial Banks

Australia and New Zealand (ANZ) Banking Corpn: POB 907, Avarua, Rarotonga; tel. 21750; fax 21760; e-mail lancaster@gatepoly.co.ck; Man. PAUL MURPHY.

Westpac Banking Corpn (Australia): Main Rd, POB 42, Avarua, Rarotonga; tel 22014; fax 20802; e-mail bank@westpac.co.ck; Man. TERRY SMITH.

Legislation was adopted in 1981 to facilitate the establishment of 'offshore' banking operations.

INSURANCE

Cook Islands Insurance: POB 44, Rarotonga.

Trade and Industry

GOVERNMENT AGENCIES

Cook Islands Development Investment Board: Private Bag, Avarua, Rarotonga; tel. 24296; fax 24298; e-mail cidib@cidib.gov.ck; internet www.cookislands-invest.com; f. 1996 as replacement for Development Investment Council; promotes, monitors and regulates foreign investment, promotes international trade, advises the private sector and Government and provides training in business skills; CEO MARK SHORT.

Cook Islands Investment Corporation: Rarotonga; f. 1998; e-mail ciic@oyster.net.ck; manages government assets and shareholding interests; Chair. TAPI TAIO.

Cook Islands Trading Corporation: Avarua, Rarotonga; fax 20857.

CHAMBER OF COMMERCE

Chamber of Commerce: POB 242, Rarotonga; tel. 20925; fax 20969; f. 1956; Pres. EWAN SMITH.

INDUSTRIAL AND TRADE ASSOCIATIONS

Pearl Federation of the Cook Islands, Inc: Manihiki; tel. and fax 43363; f. 1995, following the dissolution of the govt-owned Cook Islands Pearl Authority; oversees the activities and interests of pearl-producers in the northern Cook Islands.

Pearl Guild of the Cook Islands: Rarotonga; e-mail trevon@oyster.net.ck; f. 1994; monitors standards of quality within the pearl industry and develops marketing strategies; Pres. TREVON BERGMAN.

UTILITIES

Electricity

Te Aponga Uira O Tumutevarovaro (TAUOT): POB 112, Rarotonga; tel. 20054; fax 21944.

Water

Water Supply Department: POB 102, Arorangi, Rarotonga; tel: 20034; fax 21134.

TRADE UNIONS

Airport Workers Association: Rarotonga Int. Airport, POB 90, Rarotonga; tel. 25890; fax 21890; f. 1985; Pres. NGA JESSIE; Gen. Sec. (vacant).

Cook Islands Industrial Union of Waterside Workers: Avarua, Rarotonga.

Cook Islands Workers' Association (CIWA): POB 403, Avarua, Rarotonga; tel. 24422; fax 24423; largest union in the Cook Islands; Pres. MIRIAMA PIERRE; Gen. Sec. NGAMETUA ARAKUA.

Transport

ROADS

On Rarotonga a 33-km sealed road encircles the island's coastline. A partly-sealed inland road, parallel to the coastal road and known as the Ara Metua, is also suitable for vehicles. Roads on the other islands are mainly unsealed.

SHIPPING

The main ports are on Rarotonga (Avatiu), Penrhyn, Mangaia and Aitutaki. The Cook Islands National Line operates a three-weekly cargo service between the Cook Islands, Tonga, Samoa and American Samoa. In August 2002 the Government approved proposals to enlarge Avatiu Harbour. The project, work on which was due to start in September 2002, received additional funding from the Ports Authority and from New Zealand.

Apex Maritime: POB 378, Rarotonga; tel. 27651; fax 21138.

Cook Islands National Line: POB 264, Rarotonga; tel. 20374; fax 20855; 30% govt-owned; operates three fleet cargo services between the Cook Islands, Niue, Samoa, Norfolk Island, Tonga and New Zealand; Dirs CHRIS VAILE, GEORGE ELLIS.

Cook Islands Shipping Ltd: POB 2001, Arorangi, Rarotonga; tel. 24905; fax 24906.

Ports Authority: POB 84, Rarotonga and Aitutaki; tel. 21921; fax 21191.

Reef Shipping Company: Rarotonga; operates services between Rarotonga and Aitutaki.

Taio Shipping Ltd: Teremoana Taio, POB 2001, Rarotonga; tel. 24905; fax 24906.

Triad Maritime (1988) Ltd: Rarotonga; fax 20855.

CIVIL AVIATION

An international airport was opened on Rarotonga in 1974. Polynesian Airlines and Air New Zealand operate services linking Rarotonga with other airports in the region. Air Pacific (Fiji) began a twice-weekly service between Nadi and Rarotonga in June 2000, and in August of that year Air New Zealand began a direct service from Rarotonga to Los Angeles, USA.

Airport Authority: POB 90, Rarotonga.

Air Rarotonga: POB 79, Rarotonga; tel. 22888; fax 23288; e-mail bookings@airraro.co.ck; f. 1978; privately-owned; operates internal passenger and cargo services and charter services to Niue and French Polynesia; Man. Dir EWAN F. SMITH.

Tourism

Tourism is the most important industry in the Cook Islands, and there were 72,944 foreign tourist arrivals in 2000, compared with 25,615 in 1984. Of total visitors in 2000, 30.2% came from New Zealand, 16.6% from Australia and 17.0% from the United Kingdom. Visitor arrivals were estimated to have increased to 74,575 in 2001. There were 1,874 beds available at hotels and similar establishments in the islands in 1999. Most of the tourist facilities are to be found on Rarotonga and Aitutaki, but the outer islands also offer attractive scenery. Revenue from tourism was estimated at some $NZ93.9m. in 2000/01.

Cook Islands Tourism Corporation: POB 14, Rarotonga; tel. 29435; fax 21435; e-mail tourism@cookislands.gov.ck; internet www.cook-islands.com; CEO CHRIS WONG.

Education

Free secular education is compulsory for all children between six and 15 years of age. In 1998 there were 28 primary schools, with a total of 2,711 pupils, while the 18 secondary schools had a total enrolment of 1,779 pupils. Under the New Zealand Training Scheme, the New Zealand Government offers overseas scholarships in New Zealand, Fiji, Papua New Guinea, Australia and Samoa for secondary and tertiary education, career-training and short-term in-service training. There is an extension centre of the University of the South Pacific (based in Fiji) in the Cook Islands.

NIUE

Physical and Social Geography

Niue is a coral island of 262.7 sq km (101 sq miles) located about 480 km east of Tonga and 930 km west of the southern Cook Islands. The island is mainly covered with bush and forest and, because of the rocky and dense nature of the terrain, fertile soil is not plentiful. Agriculture is further made difficult because there are no running streams or surface water. Rainfall occurs predominantly during the hottest months, from December to March, when the average temperature is 27°C (81°F). Average annual rainfall is 7,715 mm (298 ins). The restricted nature of local resources has led many islanders to migrate to New Zealand. The population declined from 5,194 in September 1966 to 2,088 at the census of August 1997 and was officially estimated to total 1,489 in October 2001. The official languages are Niuean (a Polynesian language of the indigenous inhabitants) and English. Both are widely spoken. Most of the population are Christian, mainly Protestant. The capital and administrative centre (with a population of some 890 in 1993) is Alofi, on the west coast.

History

The first Europeans to discover Niue, which was inhabited by a Polynesian people related to the Tongans and Samoans, were members of a British expedition, led by Capt. James Cook, in 1774. Missionaries visited the island throughout the 19th century. In 1876 the clans and families of Niue elected a king, and in 1900 the island was declared a British protectorate. In 1901 Niue was formally annexed to New Zealand as part of the Cook Islands, but in 1904 it was granted a separate administration.

In October 1974 Niue attained the status of 'self-government in free association with New Zealand'. Niueans retain New Zealand citizenship, and 14,556 Niueans were resident in New Zealand in 1991. Robert (from 1982, Sir Robert) Rex, who had been Niue's political leader since the early 1950s, was the island's Premier when it became self-governing, and retained the post following three-yearly general elections in 1975–90.

The migration of Niueans to New Zealand has been a cause of increasing concern, and in 1985 the Government of New Zealand announced its intention to review its constitutional relationship with Niue, with the specific aim of preventing further depopulation of the island. In 1987 a six-member committee, comprising four New Zealanders and two Niueans, was formed to examine Niue's economic and social conditions, and to consider the possibility of the island's reverting to the status of a New Zealand-administered territory. It was hoped that the replacement of national superannuation by Guaranteed Retirement Income (GRI) in the July 1989 New Zealand budget would encourage the return of the Niueans resident in New Zealand, since all those eligible for GRI would immediately be able to receive 50% of the entitlement if they resided overseas for more than six months of the year.

At a general election held in March 1987, all except three of the 20 members of the Niue Assembly were re-elected. The newly-founded Niue People's Action Party (NPAP), secured one seat. The NPAP, Niue's only political party, criticized the Government's economic policy, and, in particular, its apparent inability to account for a substantial amount of the budgetary aid received from New Zealand. A declared aim of the party has been to persuade Niueans residing in New Zealand to invest in projects on Niue.

In 1989 Rex survived a vote of 'no confidence' in the Assembly. The dissension was prompted by the New Zealand Auditor-General's report, which was highly critical of the Niuean Government's use of monetary aid from New Zealand. Opponents of the Government accused it of favouring public servants in the allocation of grants, and of insufficient long-term planning. In that year Niue's legislature proposed 37 changes to the island's Constitution. These included the replacement of the New Zealand Governor-General by a Niuean citizen as the British monarch's representative. The implication for relations with New Zealand, however, created a controversy that led the Assembly to withdraw the proposals in November of that year, before a planned referendum could take place.

At a general election in April 1990, the candidates of the NPAP and its sympathizers won 12 of the 20 seats. Earlier disagreements in the NPAP leadership, however, allowed Rex to secure the support of four members previously opposed to his Government. Rex therefore remained Premier.

In September 1990 disagreement within the Cabinet concerning reconstruction policy (following Cyclone Ofa, which had struck the island in February) led two ministers to support a proposal for a change of Premier. Rex dismissed the two, appointing Young Vivian, leader of the NPAP and of the unofficial opposition, and another member of the opposition to the Government.

The announcement in mid-1991 by the New Zealand Government that it was to reduce its aid payments to Niue by about $NZ1m. (a decrease of some 10% on the average annual allocation) caused considerable concern on the island. More than a quarter of the paid labour force on Niue were employed by the Government, and, following the reduction in aid about 150 (some 25%) lost their jobs. Members of the Government subsequently travelled to New Zealand to appeal against the decision and to request the provision of redundancy payments for the dismissed employees. Their attempts failed, however, with the New Zealand Government reiterating its claim that aid had been inefficiently used in the past.

In December 1992 Sir Robert Rex died, and Young Vivian (who had been serving as acting Premier at the time of Rex's death) was unanimously elected Premier by the Government. Legislative elections took place in February 1993, and in the following month the Niue Assembly elected Frank Lui, a former cabinet minister, as Premier. Lui, who defeated Young Vivian by 11 votes to nine, announced a new Cabinet following the election; among the new Premier's stated objectives were the development of tourism and further plans to encourage Niueans resident in New Zealand to return to the island.

In March 1994 Vivian proposed an unsuccessful motion of 'no confidence' in the Government, alleging that too few cabinet meetings had been convened. A further attempt by the opposition to propose a 'no-confidence' motion in the Government was invalidated in the High Court in October on a procedural matter. However, during the ensuing debate, the Minister for National Planning and Economic Development, Sani Lakatani, resigned in order to join the opposition as its deputy leader, thus leaving the Government with only 10 official supporters in the Assembly. Subsequent opposition demands for the intervention of the Governor-General of New Zealand in dissolving the legislature, in preparation for a general election, were rejected, and, despite Lui's assurance that an early election would take place, in order to end the atmosphere of increasing political uncertainty, elections were not held until 16 February 1996. The Premier and his three cabinet ministers were re-elected to their seats, although support among the electorate for candidates of the Niue People's Party (NPP, formerly the NPAP) and independents appeared fairly equally divided; in one village the result was decided by the toss of a coin when both candidates received an equal number of votes. Frank Lui was re-elected by the Niue Assembly as Premier, defeating Robert Rex, Jr (son of Niue's first Premier) by 11 votes to nine.

The issue of Niue's declining population continued to cause concern, particularly when provisional census figures, published in late 1997, revealed that the island's population was at its lowest recorded level. The Government expressed disappointment that its policy of encouraging Niueans resident in New Zealand to return to the island had failed and announced its intention to consider introducing more lenient immigration laws in an attempt to increase the population.

At a general election on 19 March 1999 Lui lost his seat and subsequently announced his retirement from politics. The Minister for Finance also failed to be re-elected. On 29 March Sani Lakatani, leader of the NPP, was elected Premier by the new Assembly, defeating O'Love Jacobsen by 14 votes to six. Lakatani's stated priority as Premier was to increase Niue's population to at least 3,000; he claimed that the sharp decline in the number of residents constituted a threat to the island's self-governing status.

It was reported in May 1999 that New Zealand was to phase out aid to Niue by 2003; New Zealand's aid programme to the island had been reduced by $NZ0.25m. annually over the previous five years. However, doubts were expressed over the legality of the New Zealand Government's action, and it was suggested that New Zealand was required by law to provide financial assistance under the 1974 act that established Niue as a self-governing state.

In December 1999 a motion of 'no confidence' in Lakatani was proposed by a number of opposition ministers, in protest at the Government's plans to fund a new national airline (Coral Air Niue). The result of the vote was inconclusive, with an equal number of votes cast for and against the motion. The proposed airline did not materialize, and the Government lost $NZ400,000 of its initial investment in the project. The New Zealand Government subsequently criticized officials in Niue for failing to secure a business plan or feasibility study for the proposed airline.

In late 1999 allegations made by a foreign news agency that Niue was being used by criminal organizations for 'laundering' the proceeds of their illegal activities were strongly denied by Lakatani. However, in a report published in June 2000, the Financial Action Task Force (FATF) on Money Laundering (established in 1989 on the recommendation of the Group of Seven (G-7) industrialized nations) named the island as one of a number of countries and territories that had 'failed to co-operate' in regional efforts to combat 'money-laundering'. As a result the Government suspended the issue of any further 'offshore' banking licences until stricter regulations governing the financial sector had been introduced. In early 2001 the USA imposed sanctions on Niue (including a ban on transactions with US banks), claiming that the island had not implemented all the recommendations of the report. Lakatani appealed directly to President George W. Bush to end the embargo, which he said was having a devastating effect on Niue's economy. The Government stressed its commitment to meeting international requirements in its financial sector but claimed that it was having difficulty doing so, given its limited legal resources. Moreover, the Premier expressed strong disapproval that a nation as powerful as the USA should choose to inflict such hardship on a small, economically-vulnerable island, and urged other Pacific islands targeted by the report to unite against the forceful tactics of developed nations. In June 2001 the Government engaged a US law firm in an attempt to persuade two banks, Chase Manhattan and Bank of New York, to remove their bans on the transfer of some $NZ1m. to Niue via a business registry in Panama that the Government used for 'offshore' tax activity. Having failed to meet an FATF deadline in August 2001, in February 2002 the Government announced proposals to repeal the 'offshore' banking legislation. Premier Sani Lakatani was also considering closing down international business registrations based in Niue. The presentation of the requisite legislation, however, was delayed by the threat of legal action from one of Niue's 'offshore' banks. Nevertheless, the FATF announced in April 2002 that, in view of the island's commitment to improving the transparency of its tax and regulatory systems, the organization was to remove Niue from its list of non-co-operative territories; the decision was duly implemented in October. The bank licensing legislation was repealed in June.

In December 2001 Frank Lui returned to politics to form a new party, the Alliance of Independents, in order to contest the forthcoming general election. The party's spokesperson, O'Love Jacobsen, announced that the Alliance would campaign for a direct air link to New Zealand and for increased spending on public health.

At the general election, held on 20 April 2002, all 20 incumbent members were returned to the Niue Assembly. Independent candidate Toke Talagi polled the highest number of votes (445), but overall the NPP was victorious. However, despite having polled the second highest number of votes (428), Sani Lakatani did not command the general support of his party, and faced a leadership challenge from his deputy, Young Vivian. Following several days of lobbying within the NPP, Vivian was chosen as Premier. Vivian announced that the party had the support of 10 elected members, having formed a coalition with several independents associated with Toke Talagi. Lakatani was appointed Deputy Premier.

One of the first tasks of the new Government was to draft a budget for 2002/03, which aimed to reduce the territory's deficit by 20%. An initial draft, in which pensions, child allowances and subsidies to village and church councils were reduced, was defeated in the Assembly. A budget that restored these elements but that still aimed to reduce the deficit was approved in late August.

In March 2000 a Niue-New Zealand joint consultative committee met, for the first time, in Alofi to consider the two sides' future constitutional relationship. Later that year the committee proposed to conduct a survey of islanders' views and to consider all options, from reintegration with New Zealand to full independence. A meeting of the joint committee took place in March 2001 in Wellington at which the issues of New Zealand aid and reciprocal immigration laws were discussed, as well as options for Niue's future constitutional status. In early 2001 Hima Takelesi was appointed Niue's first High Commissioner to New Zealand. New Zealand remained committed to annual assistance of $NZ6.3m. in the years 2001–03. At New Zealand's 2001 census, a total of 20,148 Niueans were recorded as resident in New Zealand

Following almost 10 years of technical and political consultations, Niue and the USA signed a maritime boundary treaty in May 1997, delineating the precise boundary between the territorial waters of Niue and American Samoa.

Plans to establish formal diplomatic relations with the People's Republic of China were discussed in early 2001.

Economy

Niue's economic development has been adversely affected by inclement weather, inadequate transport services and the annual migration of about 10% of the population to New Zealand. Two-thirds of the land surface is uncultivable, and marine resources are variable. Until the early 1990s more than 80% of the working population were employed in the public sector on social services and economic development projects, mainly in the agricultural sector. However, significant reductions in aid and budgetary support from New Zealand, which funded the majority of these projects, resulted in a sharp decline in the number of people employed in the sector.

Agricultural activity is mostly of a subsistence nature (according to the census of 1989, some 96% of agricultural holdings were for subsistence; only some 10% of production was exported). The main subsistence crops are coconuts, taro, yams, cassava (tapioca) and sweet potatoes (kumara). Honey is also produced for export, and, until the closure of a processing factory in 1989, coconut cream was the country's leading export. A taro export scheme was introduced in the early 1990s, and production of the crop increased by more than 500% in 1993. Pigs, poultry and beef cattle are reared mainly for local consumption. Fishing is primarily for local consumption, although some fish and coconut crab are exported to Niueans living in New Zealand. Preliminary tests in 1990 revealed the presence of uranium on the island. Further exploration, however, to establish the viability of mining the mineral was delayed by the financial problems of the Australian company concerned. There is no manufacturing industry on Niue.

An increase in the frequency of flights between Niue and Auckland in 1992 enhanced prospects for the island's nascent tourist industry, as did a project to construct 60 hotel rooms and to extend the runway at Hanan airport. A total of 2,010 people visited the island by air in 2000, almost 50% of whom were from New Zealand. Tourism earned some US $1.0m. in 1998. The tourism industry, however, depended upon the twice-weekly service operated by Royal Air Tonga, and the company's decision in March 2001 to suspend flights to the island had a disastrous effect. Niue was forced to rely upon charter flights operated by Air Fiji. The Government of Niue subsequently agreed to subsidize the service and flights resumed in June. In November Kiribati announced plans to operate a 70-seater Airbus service between Niue and Fiji. In late 2002, furthermore negotiations between the Government and Polynesian Airlines for direct flights from the island to New Zealand were also making progress.

Niue records an annual trade deficit, with imports in 1993 exceeding exports by around 1,300%. In that year New Zealand, Niue's main trading partner, provided 86.1% of imports. The principal exports in that year were root crops (which provided 87.1% of total export earnings), coconuts (1.9%), honey and handicrafts. The principal imports were foodstuffs (which cost 28.0% of total imports), electrical goods (11.8%), motor vehicles (10.6%) and machinery (5.4%). In 1999 imports totalled $NZ5.2m., while exports were worth only $NZ0.3m. Taro, honey and vanilla were Niue's most significant exports. The cost of imports from New Zealand reached almost $NZ4.0m. in 2000/01, while exports to that country earned less than $NZ0.7m.

In 1991 the New Zealand Government announced that budgetary aid to Niue was to be reduced considerably, following criticism by the New Zealand Auditor-General that aid had not been used efficiently. By 1993 aid provided by New Zealand was some 30% lower than in 1990, and as a result severe reductions in Niue's public services were made. In mid-1999 the New Zealand Government announced its intention to phase out aid to Niue by 2003. Development assistance from New Zealand was reduced from $NZ6.5m. in 1999/2000 to less than $NZ6.3m. in 2001/02 (compared with $NZ10.0m. in 1994/95). Of the sum granted for 2001/02, $NZ3.8m. was allocated to budgetary support and $NZ2.5m to projects and training, including such areas as human resources, the private sector, health and the development of natural resources. In 2000/01 the budgetary deficit was projected at US $0.75m. In 2002, however, the deficit remained at some NZ$2.0m. The Government aimed to reduce the budget deficit to NZ$1.4m. in the 2002/03 financial year. The annual rate of inflation averaged 2.8% in 1990–95; consumer prices increased by an average of 1.0% in 1995.

In an attempt to diversify Niue's aid sources, efforts were made to improve relations with Australia in the early 1990s. Premier Frank Lui announced further measures in 1993 aimed at encouraging the return to the island of Niueans resident in New Zealand. It was hoped that, by increasing the resident population, Niue's economy could be stimulated, and the island's prospects for self-sufficiency improved. However, the population continued to decline, and in early 1998 the Government was considering measures to ease immigration regulations for non-Niueans. The island's population had fallen to 1,489 by October 2001, compared with 2,321 at the 1994 census. In all, 20,148 Niueans were resident in New Zealand at the March 2001 census.

In 1994 the Niue Assembly approved legislation allowing the island to become an 'offshore' financial centre. The Government predicted that Niue could earn as much as $NZ11m. annually in fees from a financial services industry. By mid-1996 the 'offshore' centre was believed to have attracted some US $280,000. However, following the threat of financial sanctions from the Paris-based Financial Action Task Force (FATF, see History), Niue declared its intention to repeal its 'offshore' banking legislation, despite fears that this would result in annual revenue losses of some US $80,000 in bank licence fees and more than US $500,000 in company registration fees. In June 2002 the Niue Assembly voted to end the issuing of banking licences. A programme of gradual privatization and a reduction in the size of the public sector, in the early 1990s, resulted in a substantial decrease in the number of government employees and a sharp increase in the number of registered businesses in the island (which totalled 144 in 1995). Further attempts to secure additional sources of revenue in Niue included the establishment by an Australian company of a station for the quarantining of up to 500 alpacas, which began operations in 1996, as well as the leasing of the island's telecommunications facilities to foreign companies for use in specialist telephone services. However, the latter enterprise caused considerable controversy when it was revealed that Niue's telephone code had been made available to companies offering personal services considered indecent by the majority of islanders. It seemed likely that further controversy would be aroused by reports in 1998 that the Government was negotiating with a Canadian company to establish a gambling website on the internet. In addition, the island earned some US $0.5m. between 1997 and 2000 from the sale of its internet domain name '.nu'. In November 2001 Premier Sani Lakatani announced that the Government was negotiating a deal with a US company interested in using Nauru as the call-centre of a satellite service. It was hoped that the scheme would create hundreds of new jobs. In 1999, meanwhile, the Premier stated his intention to promote tourism as the island's main source of revenue. Lakatani also announced that he was seeking to gain membership of the Asian Development Bank (ADB) for Niue. It was hoped that Niue might receive a low-interest loan from the ADB, if the New Zealand Government proceeded with its decision to withdraw aid to the island by 2003. In 2001, however, Niue's application was obstructed by the USA. In March 2002 Niue was in the process of concluding a 20-year development programme with the European Union (EU). Initial assistance of €2.6m., to be released in 2003, was to be used to finance renewable energy projects such as wind power generation.

Niue is a member of the Pacific Islands Forum (formerly the South Pacific Forum) and the Pacific Community (formerly the South Pacific Commission) and an associate member of the UN's Economic and Social Commission for Asia and the Pacific (ESCAP). In 2000 Niue became a signatory of the Cotonou Agreement with the EU. In September 2002 Niue joined the Pacific Agreement on Closer Economic Relations, which had earlier been ratified by the Governments of Australia, the Cook Islands, Fiji, New Zealand, Samoa and Tonga.

Statistical Survey

Source (unless otherwise stated): Economics, Planning, Development and Statistics Unit, POB 40, Alofi; tel. and fax 4219.

AREA AND POPULATION

Area: 262.7 sq km (101.4 sq miles).

Population: 2,321 (provisional) at census of October 1994; 2,088 (provisional: males 1,053; females 1,035) at census of 17 August 1997; 1,857 (official estimate: males 944; females 913) in January 2001; 1,489 in October 2001. An estimated 20,148 Niueans lived in New Zealand in March 2001.

Density (October 2001): 5.7 per sq km.

Ethnic Groups (1997): Niueans 1,779; Europeans 115; Tongans 68; Tuvaluans 35; Fijians 22; Samoans 19; Cook Islanders 10; Others 40.

Births, Marriages and Deaths (1998): Births 28 (birth rate 18.3 per 1,000 (1991–97)); Marriages 10; Deaths 17 (death rate 6.6 per 1,000 (1991–97)).

Expectation of Life (WHO estimates, years at birth, 2000): Males 69.5; Females 72.8. Source: WHO, *World Health Report*.

Employment (1991): Agriculture, forestry and fishing 45; Manufacturing 27; Construction 36; Trade 58; Restaurants and hotels 19; Transport 40; Finance 27; Real estate, etc. 43; Public administration 242; Education 66; Health, etc. 61; Total (incl. others) 701.

HEALTH AND WELFARE

Key Indicators

Fertility (births per woman, 2000): 2.6.

Physicians (per 1,000 head, 1996): 1.30.

Health Expenditure (1998): US $ per head (PPP): 328.
% of GDP: 6.7.
public (% of total): 96.7.

Access to Water (% of persons, 2000): 100.

Access to Sanitation (% of persons, 2000): 100.

For sources and definitions, see explanatory note on p. vi.

AGRICULTURE, ETC.

Principal Crops (FAO estimates, metric tons, 2000): Taro 3,200; Other roots and tubers 406; Coconuts 2,000; Bananas 70. Source: FAO.

Livestock (FAO estimates, 2000): Cattle 112; Pigs 1,700; Chickens 10,000. Source: FAO.

Livestock Products (FAO estimates, year ending September 2000): Pigmeat 49; Poultry meat 14; Hens eggs 12; Honey 6. Source: FAO.

Forestry (cu m, 1985): Roundwood removals 613; Sawnwood production 201.

Fishing (FAO estimates, metric tons, 1999): Capture 120; Total catch 120. Source: FAO, *Yearbook of Fishery Statistics*.

INDUSTRY

Production (1998): Electric energy 3 million kWh (estimate).

FINANCE

Currency and Exchange Rates: 100 cents = 1 New Zealand dollar ($NZ). For details, see Tokelau, p. 1046.

Budget ($NZ '000, year ending 30 June 1990): Revenue 11,296 (New Zealand budgetary support 7,625, Niue Govt Revenue 3,671); Expenditure 11,730.6; (year ending 30 June 1993): Revenue 14,927 (New Zealand budgetary support 7,509, Niue Govt Revenue 7,418).

Overseas Aid ($NZ '000, 2001/02): Official development assistance from New Zealand 6,250 (of which Budget support 3,750, Projects and training 2,500). Source: Ministry of Foreign Affairs and Trade, Wellington.

Cost of Living (Consumer Price Index; base: 1990 = 100): 111.6 in 1993; 113.5 in 1994; 114.6 in 1995. Source: ILO, *Yearbook of Labour Statistics*.

Gross Domestic Product ($NZ '000 in current prices): 16,700 in 2000. Source: Ministry of Foreign Affairs and Trade, Wellington.

EXTERNAL TRADE

Principal Commodities ($NZ '000, 1993): *Imports c.i.f.:* Food and live animals 1,949.7; Beverages, spirits and vinegar 334.0; Mineral fuels 228.5; Wood and cork products 345.3; Iron and steel and articles thereof 278.3; Machinery and parts 374.6; Electrical goods 819.1; Motor vehicles 739.0; Total (incl. others) 6,962.1. *Exports f.o.b.:* Taro 450.5; Yams 22.6; Coconuts 10.2; Others (incl. honey and handicrafts) 50.0; Re-exports 10.0; Total 543.2.

1999 ($NZ '000): *Imports:* 5,200; *Exports:* 300. Source: Ministry of Foreign Affairs and Trade, Wellington.

Principal Trading Partners ($NZ '000, 1993): *Imports c.i.f.:* Australia 101.7; Fiji 140.9; Japan 358.3; New Zealand 5,993.8; Samoa 47.2; USA 197.2; Total (incl. others) 6,962.1. *Exports f.o.b.:* Total 543.2.

2001/02 ($NZ '000): Trade with New Zealand: *Imports c.i.f.:* 4,182; *Exports f.o.b.:* 197. Source: Ministry of Foreign Affairs and Trade, Wellington.

TRANSPORT

Road Traffic (registrations, 1992): Passenger cars 130; Motorcycles 301; Vans, etc. 177; Heavy lorries 36; Buses 11; Total motor vehicles 655.

International Shipping: *Ship Arrivals* (1989): Yachts 20; Merchant vessels 22; Total 42. *Freight Traffic* (official estimates, metric tons, 1989): Unloaded 3,410; Loaded 10.

Civil Aviation: *Passengers* (1992): Arrivals 3,500; Departures 3,345; Transit n.a. *Freight Traffic* (metric tons, 1992): Unloaded 41.6; Loaded 15.7.

TOURISM

Foreign Tourist Arrivals (by air): 1,736 in 1998; 2,252 in 1999; 2,010 in 2000.

Tourist Arrivals by Country of Residence (2000): Australia 172; Fiji 58; New Zealand 1,000; Tonga 58; United Kingdom 32; USA 145; Total (incl. others) 2,010.

Tourism Receipts (US $ million): 1 in 1996; 2 in 1997; 1 in 1998.

Source: mainly World Tourism Organization, *Yearbook of Tourism Statistics*.

COMMUNICATIONS MEDIA

Telephones (main lines, 2000): 1,050 in use*.

Radio Receivers (1997): 1,000 in use†.

Television Receivers (1997): 340 in use.

Non-daily Newspapers (1996, estimate): 1, circulation 2,000†.

* Source: International Telecommunication Union.

† Source: UNESCO, *Statistical Yearbook*.

EDUCATION

Pre-primary (1998): 1 facility; 54 pupils.

Primary (1998): 1 school; 12 teachers; 282 pupils.

Secondary (1991): 1 school; 27 teachers; 304 pupils.

Post-secondary (March 1991): 50 students (estimate).

Source: mainly Department of Education, Niue, and UN, *Statistical Yearbook for Asia and the Pacific*.

Directory

The Constitution

In October 1974 Niue gained self-government in free association with New Zealand. The latter, however, remains responsible for Niue's defence and external affairs and will continue economic and administrative assistance. Executive authority in Niue is vested in the British monarch as sovereign of New Zealand but exercised through the government of the Premier, assisted by three ministers. Legislative power is vested in the Niue Assembly or Fono Ekepule, which comprises 20 members (14 village representatives and six elected on a common roll), but New Zealand, if requested to do so by the Assembly, will also legislate for the island. There is a New Zealand representative in Niue, the High Commissioner, who is charged with liaising between the Governments of Niue and New Zealand.

The Government

New Zealand High Commissioner: John Bryan.

Secretary to Government: Bradley Punu.

THE CABINET

(September 2002)

Premier and Minister for External Affairs, International Relations and Aid Co-ordination, the Niue Public Service Commission, the Crown Law Office, Community Affairs, Arts, Culture and Village Councils, Religious Affairs, Population Development and Niueans Abroad, Women's Affairs, Youth and Sport, and Private Sector Development: Young Vivian.

Deputy Premier and Minister for Planning, Economic Development and Statistics, the Niue Development Bank, Post, Telecommunications and Information Computer Technology Development, Philatelic Bureau and Numismatics, Shipping, Investment and Trade, Civil Aviation, and Police, Immigration and Disaster Management: (vacant).

Minister for Education and Language Development, Health, Environment and Biodiversity, Justice, Finance, Customs and Revenue, and Tourism: Toke Talagi.

Minister for Development and Training, Public Works, Water and Utilities, Port Services, the Niue Broadcasting Corporation, and Agriculture, Forestry and Fishing: Bill Vakaafi-Motufou.

GOVERNMENT OFFICES

All ministries are in Alofi.

Office of the New Zealand High Commissioner: POB 78, Tapeu, Alofi; tel. 4022; fax 4173.

Office of the Secretary to Government: POB 40, Alofi; tel. 4200; fax 4232; e-mail secgov.premier@mail.gov.nu.

Legislature

ASSEMBLY

The Niue Assembly or Fono Ekepule has 20 members (14 village representatives and six members elected on a common roll). The most recent general election was held on 20 April 2002.

Speaker: Atapana Siakimotu.

Political Organizations

Alliance of Independents: Alofi; f. 2001; Leader Frank Lui; Spokesperson O'Love Jacobsen.

Niue People's Party (NPP): Alofi; f. 1987 as Niue People's Action Party; name changed in 1995; Leader Young Vivian.

Judicial System

The Chief Justice of the High Court and the Land Court Judge visit Niue quarterly. In addition, lay justices are locally appointed and exercise limited criminal and civil jurisdiction. Appeals against High Court judgments are heard in the Court of Appeal of Niue (created in 1992).

The High Court: exercises civil and criminal jurisdiction.

The Land Court: is concerned with litigation over land and titles.

Land Appellate Court: hears appeals over decisions of the Land Court.

Chief Justice: Norman F. Smith.

Religion

About 66% of the population belong to the Ekalesia Niue, a Protestant organization, which had 1,487 adherents at the time of the 1991 census. Within the Roman Catholic Church, Niue forms part of the diocese of Tonga. The Church of Jesus Christ of Latter-day Saints (Mormon), the Seventh-day Adventists, the Jehovah's Witnesses and the Church of God of Jerusalem are also represented.

Ekalesia Niue: Head Office, POB 25, Alofi; tel. 4195; fax 4352/4010; f. 1846 by London Missionary Society, became Ekalesia Niue in 1966; e-mail ekalesia.niue@niue.nu; Pres. Rev. Matagi Vilitama; Gen. Sec. Rev. Arthur Pihigia.

The Press

Niue Economic review: POB 91, Alofi; tel. 4235; monthly.

Niue Star: POB 151, Alofi; tel. 4207; weekly; Niuean and English; publ. by Jackson's Photography and Video; circ. 600.

Broadcasting and Communications

TELECOMMUNICATIONS

Director of Posts and Telecommunications: Alofi; tel. 4002.

Niue Telecom: Alofi; tel. 4000; internet www.niuenet.com.

BROADCASTING

Radio

Broadcasting Corporation of Niue: POB 68, Alofi; tel. 4026; fax 4217; operates television service and radio service; govt-owned Chair. Sunlou Freddie; CEO Trevor Tiakia; Gen. Man. (vacant).

Radio Sunshine: broadcasts in English and Niuean.

Television

Broadcasting Corporation of Niue: (see Radio).

Television Niue: broadcasts in English and Niuean, six days a week from 5 p.m. to 11 p.m.

Trade and Industry

GOVERNMENT AGENCIES

Business Advisory Service: Alofi; tel. 4228.

Office of Economic Affairs, Planning and Development, Statistics and Trade and Investment: POB 42, Alofi; tel. 4148; e-mail business.epdsu@mail.gov.nu; responsible for planning and financing activities in the agricultural, tourism, industrial sectors, business advisory and trade and investment.

UTILITIES

Niue Power Corporation: POB 198, Alofi; tel. 4119; fax 4385; e-mail gm.npc.@mail.gov.nu.

MAJOR COMPANY

NU Domain Ltd: Alofi; internet www.nunames.nu; f. 1997; responsible for the sale of Niue's internet domain name; Admin. Man. Stafford Guest; Tech. Man. Richard St Clair.

TRADE UNION

Public Service Association: Alofi.

Finance

DEVELOPMENT BANK

Fale Tupe Atihake Ha Niue (Development Bank of Niue): POB 34, Alofi; tel. 4335; fax 4010; f. 1993, began operations July 1994; Gen. Man. Terai McFadzien.

COMMERCIAL BANK

Westpac Banking Corpn: Main St, Alofi; tel. 4221; fax 4043; e-mail westpacniue@sin.net.nu; Man. R. J. Cox.

Transport

ROADS

There are 123 km of all-weather roads and 106 km of access and plantation roads. A total of 655 motor vehicles were registered in 1992.

SHIPPING

The best anchorage is an open roadstead at Alofi, the largest of Niue's 14 villages. Work to extend a small wharf at Alofi began in mid-1998 with US assistance. The New Zealand Shipping Corporation operates a monthly service between New Zealand, Nauru and Niue. Fuel supplies are delivered by a tanker (the *Pacific Explorer*) from Fiji.

CIVIL AVIATION

Hanan International Airport has a total sealed runway of 2,350 m, following the completion of a 700-m extension in 1995, with New Zealand assistance. Air links were seriously affected by the cessation of the Air Nauru service in 1989. In 1995 Royal Tongan Airlines began operating a weekly service between Niue and Tonga, with connections to Auckland, New Zealand, and in 1996 the airline established a twice-weekly direct service between Niue and Tonga. Air Rarotonga (Cook Islands) operates occasional charter flights to Niue. In November 2001 Kiribati announced plans to operate a flight between Niue and Fiji. In late 2002 the Niue Government's negotiations with Polynesian Airlines to introduce direct flights from Niue to Auckland, New Zealand, were also approaching conclusion.

Niue Airways Ltd (NAL): Hanan International Airport; f. 1990; registered in New Zealand; Dir Ray Young.

Tourism

Niue has a small but significant tourism industry (specializing in holidays based on activities such as diving, rock-climbing, caving and game fishing), which was enhanced by an increase in the frequency of flights between the island and New Zealand in the early 1990s. A new 24-room hotel opened in 1996, increasing Niue's tourist accommodation to 158 beds. However, this resort was closed in April 2001 and its 20 staff were made redundant, following numerous cancelled bookings resulting from the cessation of the Royal Tongan Airlines service to the island. A total of 2,210 people arrived by air (about 50%% of whom were from New Zealand) to visit Niue in 2000. The industry earned about US $1m. in 1998.

Niue Tourist Office: POB 42, Alofi; tel. 4224; fax 4225; e-mail niuetourism@mail.gov.nu; internet www.niueisland.com; Dir of Tourism Ida Talagi Hekesi.

Education

Education is free and compulsory between six and 16 years of age (the school-leaving age having been raised from 14 in 1998). In 2000 there was one pre-school education facility, and one bilingual (Niuean/English) primary school on the island, with 12 teachers and an enrolment of 282 pupils in 1998. There was one secondary school, with a teaching staff of 27 and a total enrolment of 304 pupils in 1991. Post-secondary students were estimated to number 50 in March 1991. Higher education takes place at the Niue Extension Centre of the University of the South Pacific (based in Fiji), on government training schemes or by correspondence. Some study overseas, in the Pacific region and New Zealand. A private medical school opened in Niue in 2000. The Government's budget for 1998 allocated $NZ1,190,386 to education.

Palau

Physical and Social Geography

The Republic of Palau (also known as Belau) consists of eight principal and 252 smaller islands, in a chain about 650 km long, stretching from the small groups of islands around Tobi and Sonsorol, north-east to the main group, which extends from Angaur to Kayangel atoll. This latter group includes the main island of Babeldaob (Babelthuap), the second largest island in Micronesia (after Guam). Sometimes referred to by its Japanese name of the *hunto,* it is of volcanic origin and rises to 239 m. Palau lies about 7,150 km south-west of Hawaii and about 1,160 km south of Guam. The territory's nearest neighbour is Yap to the east, one of the Federated States of Micronesia. The Philippines lie to the west and Indonesia to the south and south-west. With the Federated States of Micronesia (q.v.), Palau forms the archipelago of the Caroline Islands. Palau is subject to heavy rainfall, and seasonal variations in precipitation and temperature are generally small. The indigenous population is Micronesian, most of whom speak Palauan, a language with little variation in dialect, although some linguists class Sonsorolese-Tobian (from south-west Palau) as a separate language. English is also an official language, and many people still speak Japanese. Most of the population are Christian, the main denomination being Roman Catholic, but many traditional beliefs persist, even among adherents of the Christian churches. The Modignai church is an indigenous, non-Christian religion. At the April 2000 census the population totalled 19,129, of whom more than 70% resided in Koror, on Koror Island, which is the provisional capital (the Constitution provides for the capital to be established on the less developed island of Babeldaob, in Melekeok state).

History

The earliest settlement of the islands of Palau occurred some 4,500 years ago, probably from Indonesia. A complex society of warring, matrilineal clans emerged. There was a considerable degree of social stratification, with every individual born to a definite rank in society. The clans came to be grouped into two loose confederations, that in the north being presided over by a high chief known as the Reklai and that in the south led by the Ibedul. Palau, as part of the Carolines, was in the Spanish sphere of influence from the 16th century but was not formally annexed to the Spanish Crown until 1886. Until that date, from the late 18th century, the British had dominated trade with the islands. European contacts resulted in the population being devastated by dysentery and influenza. In 1899, following its defeat in the Spanish–American War of 1898, Spain sold the Caroline Islands (including Palau) and the Northern Mariana Islands (i.e. all the Marianas except Guam) to Germany. This area, together with the Marshall Islands, became known as German Micronesia (because of German trading rights in the region) until the First World War began in 1914, when Japan occupied the territory.

Japan's formal administration began in 1920, under a mandate from the League of Nations. The islands were colonized and greatly developed, with over 100,000 permanent Japanese settlers, compared with some 40,000 indigenous inhabitants. In Palau alone, by 1940, there were some 35,000 people, of whom only about 7,500 were Palauan. Micronesia was conquered by the USA in 1944 and the former Japanese territory, removed of its settlers, became the only strategic trusteeship of the 11 trusteeships established by the United Nations in 1947. The USA was named the administering authority of the Trust Territory of the Pacific Islands, which included the Marshall Islands, Ponape (now Pohnpei), Truk (now Chuuk), Yap, Palau and the Northern Mariana Islands; it was also a member of the Trusteeship Council (all permanent members of the UN Security Council, any administering countries and other non-administering countries elected by the UN General Assembly for three-year terms). Within the US federal government, the Secretary of the Navy was responsible for the administration of the Trust Territory until 1951, when it was transferred to the jurisdiction of the Secretary of the Interior.

From 1965 there were increasing demands for local autonomy within the Trust Territory. In that year the Congress of Micronesia was formed, and in 1967 a commission to examine the future political status of the islands was established. In 1970 it declared Micronesians' rights to sovereignty over their own lands, self-determination, the right to form their own constitution and the right to revoke any form of free association with the USA. From the beginning of the negotiations it was clear that the aspirations of the people of the Northern Mariana Islands were different from those of the rest of the Trust Territory. The islands were separated administratively in 1976, as part of a process leading towards the achievement of incorporation within the USA as a commonwealth territory (see p. 1126). In May 1977 President Carter announced that his Administration intended to adopt measures to terminate the Trusteeship Agreement by 1981. In 1978, however, despite the recommendation of both the USA and the UN, the districts of Palau and the Marshall Islands rejected participation in a single federated Micronesian state. Only Yap, Truk (now Chuuk), Ponape (now Pohnpei) and Kosrae proceeded to form the Federated States of Micronesia (FSM). The three jurisdictions that emerged in the Trust Territory, excluding the Northern Mariana Islands, all favoured a similar status of 'free association', a concept with no precise definition in international law. Although recognized under the constitutional treaty or Compact of Free Association between the USA and the respective governments, full sovereignty is generally considered to be precluded by the reservation of defence and security arrangements to the USA.

In the Palau District a referendum in July 1979 approved a proposed local Constitution, which came into effect on 1 January 1981, when the district became known as the Republic of Palau. The USA signed a Compact of Free Association with the Republic of Palau in August 1982, and with the Marshall Islands and the FSM in October. The trusteeship of the islands was due to end after the principle and terms of the Compacts had been approved by the respective peoples and legislatures of the new countries, by the US Congress and by the UN Security Council. Under the Compacts, the three countries (excluding the Northern Mariana Islands) would be independent of each other and would manage both their internal and foreign affairs separately, while the USA would be responsible for defence and security. In addition, the USA was to allocate some US $3,000m. in aid to the islands.

More than 60% of Palauans voted in February 1983 to support their Compact, but fewer than the required 75% approved changing the Constitution to allow the transit and storage of nuclear materials. A revised Compact, which contained no reference to nuclear issues, was approved by 66% of votes cast in a plebiscite in September 1984. A favourable majority of 75% of the votes cast, however, remained necessary for the terms of the Compact to override the provisions of the Palau Constitution in the event of a conflict between the two.

In June 1985 President Haruo Remeliik of Palau was assassinated. (Relatives of a rival candidate in the 1984 presidential election, Roman Tmetuchl, were convicted of the murder, but remained at liberty pending an appeal; this was upheld, on the grounds of unreliable evidence, by Palau's Supreme Court in August 1987.) Alfonso Oiterong assumed office as acting President until elections in September 1985, when he was defeated in the presidential contest by Lazarus Salii.

In January 1986 representatives of the Palauan and US administrations reached a preliminary agreement on a new Compact, whereby the USA consented to provide US $421m. in economic assistance to the islands. The new Compact was approved by only 72% of Palauan voters at a referendum in February, but both Salii and President Reagan of the USA argued that the majority vote was sufficient for the Compact's approval, as the USA had guaranteed that it would observe the constitutional ban on nuclear material.

In May 1986 the UN Trusteeship Council endorsed the US Administration's request for the termination of the existing Trusteeship Agreement with the islands. However, a writ was subsequently submitted to the Palau High Court, in which it was claimed that approval of the Compact with the USA was unconstitutional because it had failed to obtain the requisite 75% of votes. The High Court ruled in favour of the writ, but the Palauan Government appealed against the ruling. In October the Compact was approved by the US Congress, but, at a new plebiscite in December, only 66% of Palauans voted in favour of the Compact. Its ratification, therefore, remained impossible.

The USA's Compacts with the Marshall Islands and with the FSM came into effect in October and November 1986 respectively. In November President Reagan proclaimed the end of US administration in Micronesia and the end of the trusteeship: the Northern Mariana Islands achieved full commonwealth status within the USA, and the Republic of the Marshall Islands and the FSM became Associated States. With the failure to implement the Compact with the Republic of Palau, the USA agreed to continue to administer it as the only remaining part of the Trust Territory of the Pacific Islands.

A fifth plebiscite on Palau's proposed Compact with the USA, held in June 1987, failed to secure the 75% vote in favour required by the Constitution. Under alleged physical intimidation by pro-nuclear supporters of the Compact, the House of Delegates (the lower house of the Palau National Congress) agreed to a further referendum in August of that year. In this referendum an amendment to the Constitution was approved, ensuring that a simple majority would be sufficient to approve the Compact. This was duly achieved in a further referendum in the same month. However, a writ was entered with the Supreme Court challenging the result. The ensuing violence and allegations of corruption and intimidation on the part of the Palau Government resulted, in February 1988, in the opening of an investigation by the US General Accounting Office (GAO). In April Palau's Supreme Court declared invalid the procedure by which the Compact had been approved in the previous August.

Three government employees, including Salii's personal assistant, were imprisoned in April 1988, having been found guilty of firing on the home of Santos Olikong, Speaker of Palau's House of Delegates. The attack was widely considered to have been prompted by Olikong's public opposition to the proposed Compact. In August Salii, who had been the principal subject of bribery allegations, was found dead from a gunshot wound. Rumours to the effect that Salii had committed suicide were confirmed in September.

At elections in November 1988 Ngiratkel Etpison, an advocate of the proposed Compact, narrowly defeated the anti-nuclear candidate, Roman Tmetuchl. Furthermore, Kuniwo Nakamura, another opponent of the Compact, was elected to the vice-presidency by a substantial majority, and the elections also returned opposition majorities in both chambers of the Olbiil era Kelulau (legislature).

A seventh referendum on the issue of the Compact was held in February 1990. The level of participation was low, and only 60% of voters approved the Compact. In July the US Department of the Interior declared its intention to impose stricter controls on the administration of Palau, particularly in financial matters. In the following year the leader of Palau's Council of Chiefs (a presidential advisory body), Yutaka Gibbons, initiated proceedings to sue the US Government. His claim centred on demands for compensation for the extensive damage caused to Palau's infrastructure by US forces during the Second World War and the subsequent retardation of the economy, allegedly as a result of the US administration of the islands.

During 1991 the US authorities reopened investigations into the assassination of Remeliik in 1985. In March 1992 the Minister of State, John Ngiraked, his wife, Emerita Kerradel, and Sulial Heinrick (already serving a prison sentence for another killing) were charged with Remeliik's murder. In April 1993 Ngiraked and Kerradel were found guilty of aiding and abetting the assassination of the President, while Heinrick was acquitted.

Legislative and presidential elections were held in November 1992. The electoral system had been modified earlier in the year to include primary elections, at which two presidential candidates are selected. At secondary elections the incumbent Vice-President, Kuniwo Nakamura, narrowly defeated Johnson Toribiong to become President. A referendum was held concurrently, proposing that in future polls a simple majority be sufficient to approve the adoption of the Compact of Free Association. Some 62% of voters were in favour of the proposal, which was approved in 14 of the territory's 16 states. A further referendum on the proposed Compact took place in November 1993. Some 68.3% of participating voters approved the proposed Compact, giving the Government a mandate to proceed with its adoption. Nevertheless, opposition to the changes remained fierce, and in January 1994 two legal challenges were mounted that questioned the validity of the amendments and stated that the Compact's approval had been procured by coercion. The challenges were not successful, however, and on 1 October 1994 Palau achieved independence under the Compact of Free Association. At independence celebrations, Nakamura appealed to opponents of the Compact to support Palau's new status. He announced that his Government's principal concern was the regeneration of the Palauan economy, which he aimed to initiate with an economic programme financed by funds from the newly-implemented Compact. Palau was admitted to the UN in December 1994, and became a member of the IMF in December 1997.

At a preliminary round of voting in the presidential election in September 1996, Nakamura secured 52.4% of total votes, Toribiong received 33.5%, and Yutaka Gibbons 14.2%. Nakamura and Toribiong were, therefore, expected to proceed to a second election due to take place in November. However, in late September a serious crisis struck Palau when the bridge linking the islands of Koror and Babeldaob collapsed, killing two people and injuring several others. The collapse of the bridge left the capital isolated from the international airport on Babeldaob, with disastrous economic repercussions for Palau, which relies on the route for all domestic and international communications. A state of emergency was declared as the authorities sought to re-establish water and power supplies and to reconnect telephone lines. It was subsequently revealed that major repairs had recently been carried out on the bridge, at a cost of US $3.2m., and several reports implied that inappropriate changes made to its structure were responsible for the disaster. Toribiong was harshly critical of Nakamura, who had commissioned the repair work, and demanded his resignation along with those of the public works officials involved. However, following the revelation that Toribiong's running-mate in the election for the vice-presidency was one of the officials involved in the work, Toribiong withdrew his candidacy from the second round of the presidential election. A new bridge linking Koror to Babeldaob opened in January 2002. Its construction was funded by the Japanese Government.

Legislative elections and the second round of voting were held on 5 November 1996. Nakamura was re-elected with 62.0% of total votes, defeating Yutaka Gibbons (who had re-entered the contest, following the withdrawal of Toribiong in October). Legislation providing for the establishment of an 'offshore' financial centre in Palau was approved by the Senate (the upper house of the Palau National Congress) in October 1998, despite strong opposition by Nakamura, who believed that the new status might attract criminal organizations seeking to 'launder' the proceeds of their illegal activities and that it might compromise the country's ability to enforce corporate law. In December 1999, following discussions with US government officials, President Nakamura signed an executive order establishing a National Banking Review Commission, with the aim of maintaining a legally-responsible banking environment in Palau: both the Bank of New York (of the USA) and Deutsche Bank (of Germany) had alleged that Palau's 'offshore' banks were facilitating 'money-laundering'. The new body was given wide-ranging powers to examine banking operations in the country and to evaluate current banking regulations.

At the presidential election held on 7 November 2000, Thomas E. Remengesau, Jr, hitherto the Vice-President of Palau, was elected with 52% of the votes cast, defeating Senator Peter Sugiyama. Sandra Pierantozzi was elected as Vice-President. Remengesau was officially inaugurated on 19 January 2001, pledging to pursue Nakamura's policies of economic expansion and transparency in government. In July 2001 Remengesau introduced a formal resolution proposing the reduction of the legislature to a single chamber, to replace the existing House of Delegates and the Senate, claiming that a unicameral legislature would reduce bureaucracy. He also proposed that henceforth the President and Vice-President base their election campaign on a common policy, to ensure efficient and cohesive government.

In mid-1999 a delegation from Solomon Islands visited Palau to discuss the possibility of allowing Solomon Islanders to work in Palau, in an attempt to resolve the latter's severe labour shortage. In August 2001 the Government imposed a ban on the hiring of Indian and Sri Lankan workers, citing rising tensions and disputes with local employers which the Government claimed were largely due to religious differences. The ban was to remain in place until legislation to create official recruitment agencies in Palau had been approved. In July 2002 the Senate passed a bill that would amend the islands' immigration law in order to give greater authority over immigration affairs to the President of Palau. (Non-Palauan nationals were estimated to represent about 33% of the islands' population in 2002.)

Diplomatic relations were established, at ambassadorial level, with Taiwan in late 1999; the first Taiwanese Ambassador to Palau was formally appointed in April 2000. Reports in December 2000 that the Palau Government was considering establishing diplomatic relations with the People's Republic of China were denied, and President-elect Remengesau reaffirmed Palau's diplomatic ties with Taiwan. In early 2000, meanwhile, Palau and Taiwan signed an agreement pledging to develop bilateral projects in a number of areas, including agriculture, fisheries and tourism.

In October 2001 the Government sought to establish diplomatic relations with Malaysia and Indonesia, in an attempt to facilitate the resolution of disputes over overlapping territorial boundaries, amid concern over increasing instances of illegal fishing in Palau waters. (Palau introduced more stringent regulations concerning illegal fishing in May 2002.) The Government established diplomatic relations with East Timor in September 2002.

Palau maintains strong diplomatic links with Japan, which was consistently a leading source of tourist revenue throughout the 1980s and 1990s. The Japanese Government provided US $25m. for the construction of the Koror bridge (see above) and was contributing to the construction of a new terminal building at Palau International Airport, upon which work began in February 2002. The President of Palau met travel and tour operators in Japan in November 2001 in an attempt to promote tourism in Palau. In June 2002 President Remengesau undertook his first state visit to the Republic of Korea, during which he was expected to visit a number of infrastructural development projects.

Economy

In 2000, according to the International Monetary Fund (IMF), Palau's gross domestic product (GDP), measured at current prices, totalled US $118.2m., equivalent to $6,179 per head. In nominal terms, GDP increased by an average of 4.4% per year in 1995–2000. Compared with the previous year, real GDP decreased by 5.4% in 1998/99, but increased by 1.1% in 1999/2000 and by an estimated 1.0% in 2000/01. The population increased by an average annual rate of 2.6% in 1990–95 and by 2.1% per year in 1995–2000.

Agriculture (including fishing) is mainly on a subsistence level, the principal crops being coconuts, root crops and bananas. Pigs and chickens are kept for domestic consumption. Eggs are produced commercially, and the introduction of cattle-ranching on Babeldaob was under consideration in the late 1990s. The agricultural sector, together with mining, engaged 2.2% of the employed labour force in 2000. Agriculture and fisheries alone provided an estimated 4.0% of GDP in 2001. Fishing licences are sold to foreign fleets, including those of Taiwan, the USA, Japan and the Philippines. Palau is a signatory of the Multilateral Fisheries Treaty, concluded by the USA and member states of the South Pacific Forum (now Pacific Islands Forum) in 1987. The islands, however, are believed to lose significant amounts of potential revenue through illegal fishing activity. Revenue from the sale of fishing licences totalled US $39,000 in 1999/2000 and an estimated $76,000 in 2000/01, a considerable decline from the total of $230,000 recorded in 1994/95. Fish have traditionally been a leading export, accounting for some $13m. of exports in 1995, but earnings declined to an estimated $7m. in 2001, reportedly owing to adverse weather conditions. The output of the islands' tuna industry declined by more than 35% between 1993 and 1997.

The industrial sector (including mining and quarrying, manufacturing, construction and utilities) provided an estimated 13.0% of GDP in 2001. The only manufacturing activity of any significance is a factory producing garments, which, in 1997, employed some 300 (mostly non-resident) workers. In 2000 the manufacturing sector engaged 3.6% of the employed labour force. In 2001 manufacturing accounted for only about 1.5% of GDP. Construction is the most important industrial activity, contributing an estimated 8.0% of GDP in 2001 and engaging 11.6% of the employed labour force in 2000. Electrical energy is produced by two power plants, at Aimeliik and Malakal. Service industries dominate Palau's economy, providing an estimated 83.0% of GDP in 2001 and (with utilities) engaging 82.6% of the employed labour force in 2000. The Government is an important employer within the sector, with public administration engaging some 33.3% of the total employed labour force in 2000. Tourism is an important source of foreign exchange, with hotels and restaurants contributing an estimated 11.1% of GDP in 1998 and employing 9.4% of paid workers in 1995. In 2000/01 a total of 55,595 visitors (of whom 46,684 were tourists) arrived in the islands. Expenditure by tourists totalled an estimated US $54.3m. in that year.

In the year ending September 2001 the visible trade deficit was estimated at US $80.8m. (equivalent to 66% of GDP). The deficit on the current account of the balance of payments totalled $15.7m. The principal sources of imports were the USA (which supplied 39.3% of the total), Guam (14.0%) and Japan (10.2%). The principal imports in 2000/01 were machinery and transport equipment, manufactured goods and food and live animals.

The islands record a persistent budget deficit, estimated at almost US $18.5m. in the year ending September 2001. Financial assistance from the USA contributes a large part of the islands' external revenue. Furthermore, upon implementation of the Compact of Free Association with the USA in 1994, Palau became eligible for an initial grant of US $142m. and for annual aid of US $23m. over a period of 14 years. Assistance from the USA (including non-Compact funding) totalled $21.0m. in 1999/2000 and an estimated $20.6m. in 2000/01, a respective 28.1% and 33.5% of total budgetary revenue in those years. Compact funding for 2001/02 was projected at $11.8m. in current grants and $2.0m. in capital grants, while non-Compact funding was budgeted at $11.2m. Palau's external debt totalled $20.0m. in 2000/01. The annual rate of inflation was thought to average between 1% and 3% in the mid-1990s. The inflation rate was about 2.5% in 2000/01, according to the IMF. In 2000 2.3% of the total labour force were unemployed.

A period of recession in the early 1990s (caused largely by reductions in government expenditure in an attempt to offset decreases in revenue) was alleviated by substantial aid payments from the US Government, following the implementation of the Compact of Free Association, and by the dramatic expansion of tourism in the country. Subsequent policies to reduce the size of the public sector, to encourage the return of Palauans resident overseas and to attract foreign investment aimed to stimulate economic growth. Particularly strong commercial ties were forged with Taiwan during the mid-1990s, and it was hoped that the establishment of diplomatic relations between Palau and Taiwan in late 1999 would further develop bilateral economic co-operation. Trade between Palau and the Philippines was expected to increase significantly, following the signing of a bilateral agreement in early 1998. The Government announced plans in 1998 for a major expansion of tourism, which had declined in the late 1990s following the Asian financial crisis, and expressed particular interest in developing the country's potential as a destination for visitors of above-average wealth. In December 2001 the Government announced plans to develop a new regional airline to serve Palau and neighbouring Micronesian countries. In August 2002 President Remengesau announced a new five-year plan for the Palauan economy. The principal aim of the economic plan was to develop basic infrastructure in order to permit the further expansion of the tourist sector. Meanwhile, following allegations that Palau's offshore banking system was being used for the purposes of 'money-laundering' (see History), various new banking laws were approved, in an effort to restore the confidence of the international financial community. Although a number of concerns were raised by the Financial Action Task Force on Money Laundering (the FATF having been established in 1989 on the recommendation of the Group of Seven (G-7) industrialized nations), Palau was not included on the FATF's list of non-co-operative countries and territories.

Palau is a member of the Pacific Community (formerly the South Pacific Commission) and of the Pacific Islands Forum (formerly the South Pacific Forum); it is also an associate member of the UN's Economic and Social Commission for Asia and the Pacific (ESCAP). In early 1996 Palau joined representatives of the other countries and territories of Micronesia at a meeting in Hawaii, at which a new regional organization, the Council of Micronesian Government Executives, was established. The new body aimed to facilitate discussion of economic developments in the region.

Statistical Survey

AREA AND POPULATION

Area: 508 sq km (196 sq miles); Babeldaob island 409 sq km (158 sq miles).

Population: 17,225 (males 9,213, females 8,012) at census of 9 November 1995; 19,129 at census of 1 April 2000.

Density (2000): 37.7 per sq km (97.6 per sq mile).

Births and Deaths (2000, estimates): Birth rate 14.5 per 1,000; Death rate 6.5 per 1,000. Source: 2000 Census of Population and Housing, Office of Planning and Statistics, Palau.

Expectation of Life (WHO estimates, years at birth, 2000): Males 64.7; Females 69.3. Source: WHO, *World Health Report*.

Economically Active Population (2000): Agriculture, fishing and mining 215; Construction 1,112; Manufacturing 345; Transport, communications and utilities 765; Trade, hotels and restaurants 2,619; Finance, insurance and real estate 116; Public administration 3,203; Other services 1,246; Total employed 9,621; Unemployed 224; Total labour force 9,845. Source: IMF, *Republic of Palau: Recent Economic Developments* (March 2002).

HEALTH AND WELFARE

Key Indicators

Fertility (births per woman, 2000): 2.8.

Under-5 Mortality Rate (per 1,000 live births, 2000): 29.

Physicians (per 1,000 head, 1998): 1.10.

Health Expenditure (1998): US $ per head (PPP): 437.
% of GDP: 6.4.
public (% of total): 88.0.

Access to Water (% of persons, 2000): 79.

Access to Sanitation (% of persons, 2000): 100.

For sources and definitions, see explanatory note on p. vi.

AGRICULTURE, ETC.

Principal Crops, Livestock and Livestock Products: see Chapter on the Federated States of Micronesia.

Fishing (FAO estimates, metric tons, live weight, 1999): Total catch 1,801 (Marine fishes 1,600). Source: FAO, *Yearbook of Fishery Statistics*.

INDUSTRY

Production (estimate, 1997): Electric energy 208 million kWh. Source: UN, *Statistical Yearbook for Asia and the Pacific*.

FINANCE

Currency and Exchange Rates: United States currency is used:

100 cents = 1 United States dollar (US $). *Sterling and Euro Equivalents* (31 May 2002): £1 sterling = US $1.4667; €1 = 93.87 US cents; US $100 = £68.18 = €106.53.

Budget (estimates, US $'000, year ending Sept. 2001): *Revenue:* Domestic revenue 40,186 (Tax 25,762; Other current revenues 5,907; Local trust fund 1,806; Investment income 6,711); Grants 21,307 (Compact funds 19,128); Total 61,493. *Expenditure:* Current expenditure 63,080 (Wages and salaries 29,863; Purchase of goods and services 25,360; Subsidies and other transfers 7,157); Capital expenditure 14,122; Total 77,202. Note: Figures exclude net errors and omissions (US $ '000): −2,770. Source: IMF, *Republic of Palau: Recent Economic Developments* (March 2002).

Gross Domestic Product by Economic Activity (US $'000 at current prices, 2001, estimates): Agriculture 1,399; Fishing 3,388; Mining and quarrying 245; Manufacturing 1,808; Electricity, gas and water 3,863; Construction 9,621; Trade 25,175; Hotels and restaurants 12,082; Transport and communications 11,272; Finance and insurance 4,828; Real estate and business services 5,108; Public administration 30,816; Other services 10,260; Sub-total 119,867; Import duties 3,842; *Less* Imputed bank service charges 1,250; GDP in purchasers' values 122,459. Source: IMF, *Republic of Palau: Recent Economic Developments* (March 2002).

Balance of Payments (estimates, US $'000, year ending Sept. 2001): Exports of goods f.o.b. 18,267; Imports of goods f.o.b. −99,104; *Trade balance* −80,837; Exports of services 54,307; Imports of services −21,551; *Balance on goods and services* −48,081; Other income (net) 14,028; *Balance on goods, services and income* −34,053; Private current transfers (net) −1,899; Official current transfers (net) 20,267; *Current balance* −15,685; Capital grants received 5,144; Private direct investment 1,000; Net errors and omissions −8,938; *Overall balance* −18,479. Source: IMF, *Article IV Consultation with the Republic of Palau: Staff Report* (March 2002).

EXTERNAL TRADE

Principal Commodities (US $'000, 2000/01): *Imports f.o.b.*: Food and live animals 14,534; Beverages and tobacco 7,954; Mineral fuels, lubricants etc. 9,930; Chemicals 7,134; Basic manufactures 18,203; Machinery and transport equipment 23,179; Miscellaneous manufactured articles 12,744; Total (incl. others) 95,765. *Exports (1996)*: 14,300 (including trochus, tuna, copra and handicrafts). Source: mainly IMF, *Republic of Palau: Recent Economic Developments* (March 2002).

Principal Trading Partners (US $'000, 2000/01) *Imports*: Australia 1,047; China, People's Republic 2,546; Guam 13,379; Hong Kong 3,484; Japan 9,814; Korea, Republic 6,155; Philippines 2,617; Singapore 7,343; Taiwan 5,091; USA 37,611; Total (incl. others) 95,765. *Exports:* Total 18,267. Source: IMF, *Republic of Palau: Recent Economic Developments* (March 2002).

TRANSPORT

International Shipping (1995): *Ship Arrivals:* 280. *Freight Traffic* (metric tons): Goods unloaded 64,034.

TOURISM

Tourist Arrivals: 56,466 in 1998/99; 56,502 in 1999/2000; 55,595 in 2000/01.

Tourist Arrivals by Country of Residence (2000/01): Japan 23,303, Philippines 4,164, Taiwan 14,077, USA 8,456.
Source: IMF, *Republic of Palau: Recent Economic Developments* (March 2002).

COMMUNICATIONS MEDIA

Radio Receivers (1997): 12,000 in use.

Television Receivers (1997): 11,000 in use.

EDUCATION

Elementary (1990): 22 government schools; 172 teachers (1998); 2,125 pupils at government schools; 369 pupils at private schools.

Secondary (1990): 1 government school; 5 private (church-affiliated) schools; 60 teachers (1998); 610 pupils at government schools; 445 pupils at private schools (1989).

Tertiary (1986): 305 students.

2001/02: 20 government schools (19 elementary; 1 secondary) with 3,145 pupils.

Directory

The Constitution

In October 1994 Palau, the last remaining component of the Trust Territory of the Pacific Islands (a United Nations Trusteeship administered by the USA), achieved independence under the Compact of Free Association. Full responsibility for defence lies with the USA, which undertakes to provide regular economic assistance.

From 1986 the three polities of the Commonwealth of the Northern Mariana Islands, the Republic of the Marshall Islands and the Federated States of Micronesia ceased, *de facto*, to be part of the Trust Territory. In December 1990 the United Nations Security Council agreed formally to terminate the Trusteeship Agreement for all the territories except Palau. The agreement with Palau was finally terminated in October 1994.

The islands became known as the Republic of Palau when the locally-drafted Constitution came into effect on 1 January 1981. The Constitution provides for a democratic form of government, with executive authority vested in the directly-elected President and Vice-President. Presidential elections are held every four years. Legislative power is exercised by the Olbiil era Kelulau, the Palau National Congress, which is an elected body consisting of the Senate and the House of Delegates. The Senators represent geographical districts, determined by an independent reapportionment commission every eight years, according to population. There are currently 14 Senators (four from the northern part of Palau, nine from Koror and one from the southern islands). There are 16 Delegates, one elected to represent each of the 16 states of the Republic. The states are: Kayangel, Ngerchelong, Ngaraard, Ngardmau, Ngaremlengui, Ngiwal, Melekeok, Ngchesar, Ngatpang, Aimeliik, Airai, Koror, Peleliu, Angaur, Sonsorol and Tobi. Each state elects its own Governor and legislature.

The Government

HEAD OF STATE

President: THOMAS E. REMENGESAU, Jr (took office 19 January 2001).

Vice-President: SANDRA S. PIERANTOZZI.

THE CABINET
(September 2002)

Vice-President and Minister of Health: SANDRA S. PIERANTOZZI.

Minister of Commerce and Trade: OTOICHI BESEBES.

Minister of Resources and Development: FRITZ KOSHIBA.

Minister of Education: MARIO KATOSANG.

Minister of Justice: MICHAEL ROSENTHAL.

Minister of Community and Cultural Affairs: ALEXANDER R. MEREP.

Minister of State: TEMMY L. SHMULL.

Minister of Administration: ELBUCHEL SADANG.

COUNCIL OF CHIEFS

The Constitution provides for an advisory body for the President, comprising the 16 highest traditional chiefs from the 16 states. The chiefs advise on all traditional laws and customs, and on any other public matter in which their participation is required.

Chairman: Ibedul YUTAKA GIBBONS (Koror).

GOVERNMENT OFFICES AND MINISTRIES

Office of the President: POB 100, Koror, PW 96940; tel. 488-2403; fax 488-1662; e-mail roppresoffice@palaunet.com.

Department of the Interior, Office of Insular Affairs (OIA): OIA Field Office, POB 6031, Koror, PW 96940; tel. 488-2655; fax 488-2649; Field Rep. J. VICTOR HOBSON, Jr.

Ministry of Commerce and Trade: POB 1471, Koror, PW 96940; tel. 488-4343; fax 488-3207.

Ministry of Health: POB 6027, Koror, PW 96940; tel. 488-5552; fax 488-1211; e-mail healthminister@palaunet.com.

Ministry of Resources and Development: POB 100, Koror, PW 96940; tel. 488-2701; fax 488-3380; e-mail mrd@palaunet.com.

All national government offices are based in Koror. Each state has its own administrative headquarters.

President and Legislature

PRESIDENT

At the presidential election held on 7 November 2000, THOMAS E. REMENGESAU, Jr, who won 52% of the votes cast, narrowly defeated Sen. PETER SUGIYAMA.

OLBIIL ERA KELULAU
(Palau National Congress)

President of the Senate: SEIT ANDRES.

Vice-President of the Senate: HARRY R. FRITZ.

Speaker of the House of Delegates: MARIO GULIBERT.

Political Organizations

Palau Nationalist Party: c/o Olbiil era Kelulau, Koror, PW 96940; Leader JOHNSON TORIBIONG.

Ta Belau Party: c/o Olbiil era Kelulau, Koror, PW 96940; Leader KUNIWO NAKAMURA.

Diplomatic Representation

EMBASSIES IN PALAU

China (Taiwan): POB 9087, Koror, PW 96940; tel. 488-8150; fax 488-8151; Ambassador: CLARK K. H. CHEN.

USA: POB 6028, Koror, PW 96940; tel. 488-2920; fax 488-2911; e-mail usembassykoror@palaunet.com; Chargé d'affaires: RONALD A. HARMS.

Judicial System

The judicial system of the Republic of Palau consists of the Supreme Court (including Trial and Appellate Divisions), presided over by the Chief Justice, the National Court (inactive), the Court of Common Pleas and the Land Court.

Supreme Court of the Republic of Palau: POB 248, Koror, PW 96940; tel. 488-2482; fax 488-1597; e-mail a.ngiraklsong@palaunet.com; Chief Justice ARTHUR NGIRAKLSONG.

Religion

The population is predominantly Christian, mainly Roman Catholic. The Assembly of God, Baptists, Seventh-day Adventists, the Church of Jesus Christ of Latter-day Saints (Mormons), and the Bahá'í and Modignai (or Modeknai) faiths are also represented.

CHRISTIANITY

The Roman Catholic Church

Palau forms part of the diocese of the Caroline Islands, suffragan to the archdiocese of Agaña (Guam). The Bishop, who is resident in Chuuk, Eastern Caroline Islands (see Federated States of Micronesia), participates in the Catholic Bishops' Conference of the Pacific, based in Suva, Fiji.

MODIGNAI FAITH

Modignai Church: Koror, PW 96940; an indigenous, non-Christian religion; also operates a high school.

The Press

Palau Gazette: POB 100, Koror, PW 96940; tel. 488-3257; fax 488-1662; e-mail roppresoffice@palaunet.com; newsletter publ. by Govt; monthly.

Palau Horizon: POB 487, Koror, PW 96940; tel. 488-4588; fax 488-4565; weekly; Man. ABED E. YOUNIS; circ. 2,500.

Tia Belau (This is Palau): POB 569, Koror, PW 96940; tel. 488-1461; fax 488-1725; f. 1992; fortnightly; English and Palauan; Publr MOSES ULUDONG.

Broadcasting and Communications

BROADCASTING

Radio

Palau National Communications Corpn (PNCC): Bureau of Domestic Affairs, POB 279, Koror, PW 96940; tel. 587-9000; fax 587-1888; f. 1982; e-mail pncc@palaunet.com; internet www.palaunet.com; mem. of the Pacific Islands Broadcasting Asscn; operates station WSZB; broadcasts American, Japanese and Micronesian music; 18 hrs daily; Gen. Man. ED CARTER.

WSZB Broadcasting Station: POB 279, Koror, PW 96940; tel. 488-2417; fax 488-1932; Station Man. ALBERT SALUSTIANO.

KHBN: POB 66, Koror, PW 96940; tel. 488-2162; fax 488-2163; e-mail hamadmin@palaunet.com; f. 1992; broadcasts religious material; CEO JACKIE MITCHUM YOCKEY.

Television

STV-TV Koror: POB 2000, Koror, PW 96940; tel. 488-1357; fax 488-1207; broadcasts 12 hrs daily; Man. DAVID NOLAN; Technical Man. RAY OMELEN.

Island Cable Television, Inc: POB 39, Koror, PW 96940; tel. 488-1490; fax 488-1499; owned by the United Micronesian Development Asscn and Palau National Communications Corpn.

Finance

(cap. = capital; res = reserves; amounts in US dollars)

BANKING

Bank of Guam: POB 338, Koror, PW 96940; tel. 488-2697; fax 488-1384.

Bank of Hawaii (USA): POB 340, Koror, PW 96940; tel. 488-2428; fax 488-2427; Man. JOAN DEMEI.

Bank Pacific: POB 1000, Koror, PW 96940; tel. 488-5635; fax 488-4752.

Melekeok Government Bank: POB 1711, Koror, PW 96940; tel. 488-2066; fax 488-2065; e-mail mgbank@palaunet.com.

National Development Bank of Palau: POB 816, Koror, PW 96940; tel. 488-2578; fax 488-2579; e-mail ndbp@palaunet.com; f. 1982; cap. and res 9.9m. (Sept. 2000); Pres. TUKANA BOVORO.

Pacific Savings Bank: POB 399, Koror, PW 96940; tel. 488-1859; fax 488-1858; e-mail bank@palaunet.com; internet pnccwg.palaunet.com/bank/index.htm.

In 1990 there were also 22 registered credit unions, with 1,025 members, but they were severely affected by the financial crisis in Palau.

INSURANCE

NECO Insurance Underwriters Ltd: POB 129, Koror, PW 96940; tel. 488-2325; fax 488-2880; e-mail necogroup@palaunet.com.

Poltalia National Insurance: POB 12, Koror, PW 96940; tel. 488-2254; e-mail psata@palaunet.com.

Trade and Industry

CHAMBER OF COMMERCE

Palau Chamber of Commerce: POB 1742, Koror, PW 96940; tel. 488-3400; fax 488-3401; e-mail pcoc@palaunet.com; f. 1984; Pres. (vacant).

CO-OPERATIVES

These include the Palau Fishermen's Co-operative, Palau Boatbuilders' Asscn, Palau Handicraft and Woodworkers' Guild. In 1990, of the 13 registered co-operatives, eight were fishermen's co-operatives, three consumers' co-operatives (only two in normal operation) and two farmers' co-operatives (one in normal operation).

Transport

ROADS

Macadam and concrete roads are found in the more important islands. Other islands have stone and coral-surfaced roads and tracks. The Government is responsible for 36 km (22 miles) of paved roads and 25 km (15 miles) of coral- and gravel-surfaced roads. Most paved roads are located on Koror and are in a poor state of repair. A major project to construct a new 85-km (53-mile) road around Babeldaob began in 1999 and is scheduled for completion in late 2003. The project is being funded with US $150m. from the Compact of Free Association.

SHIPPING

Most shipping in Palau is government-organized. However, the Micronesia Transport Line operates a service from Sydney (Australia) to Palau. A twice-weekly inter-island service operates between Koror and Peleliu. There is one commercial port at Malakal Harbor, which is operated by the privately-owned Belau Transfer and Terminal Company.

CIVIL AVIATION

There is an international airport in the south of Babeldaob island, in Airai state, near Koror. With Japanese assistance, work began on a new terminal building in February 2002. Construction was scheduled for completion in 2003. Domestic airfields (former Japanese military airstrips) are located on Angaur and Peleliu. Continental Micronesia (Northern Mariana Islands and Guam) provides daily flights to Koror from Guam, and twice-weekly flights from Manila (Philippines). Cebu Pacific operates direct flights from Davao (Philippines) to Koror. A civil aviation agreement between Palau and Taiwan was signed in 1997, and direct charter flights between the two countries began in the following year, operated by the Far Eastern Air Transport Corpn. There is one domestic carrier.

Palau Paradise Air, Inc: POB 488, Palau Int. Airport, Airai State, Babeldaob, PW 96940; tel. and fax 488-2348; internal services between Koror, Peleliu and Angaur.

Rock Island Airlines: managed by Aloha Airlines (Hawaii).

Tourism

Tourism is becoming increasingly important in Palau, and plans for a major expansion of the industry were announced in 1998. The islands are particularly rich in their marine environment, and the Government has taken steps to conserve and protect these natural resources. The myriad Rock Islands, now known as the Floating Garden Islands, are a noted reserve in the lagoon to the west of the main group of islands. There were 1,200 hotel rooms in 1998, and a further 558 hotel rooms were expected to be opened by 2001. In 2000/01 there were 55,595 visitor arrivals, of whom 41.9% were from Japan, 25.3% from Taiwan, 15.2% from the USA and 7.5% from the Philippines. Tourist expenditure rose from US $53.2m. in 1999/2000 to $54.3m. in 2000/01.

Belau Tourism Association: POB 9032, Koror, PW 96940; tel. 488-4377; fax 488-1725; e-mail bta@palaunet.com.

Palau Visitors' Authority: POB 256, Koror, PW 96940; tel. 488-2793; fax 488-1453; e-mail pva@palaunet.com; internet www.visit-palau.com; Man. Dir Mary Ann Delemel.

Defence

The USA is responsible for the defence of Palau, according to the Compact of Free Association implemented in October 1994, and has exclusive military access to Palau's waters, as well as the right to operate two military bases on the islands. The US Pacific Command is based in Hawaii.

Education

The educational system is similar to that in the USA. The Government of Palau is now responsible for the state school system, which most children attend. Education is free and compulsory between the ages of six and 14, and secondary education may be obtained at the public High School or one of the five private ones. In 1990 there were 22 public elementary schools with 2,125 pupils (and 369 pupils attending private elementary schools). In the same year there were 610 students enrolled at government high schools, and 445 at private high schools. In 2001/02 3,145 pupils attended 19 public elementary schools and one government high school. The Micronesian Occupational College, based in Koror, provides two-year training programmes. Construction of Palau's first university, as part of a major development project (to include a housing complex for 5,000 people, a commercial centre and leisure facilities), was expected to begin in the late 1990s. The project was to be funded by Taiwanese interests. Government expenditure on education totalled US $9.1m. in 1999/2000, equivalent to 10.7% of total budgetary expenditure.

Papua New Guinea

Physical and Social Geography

Papua New Guinea lies east of Indonesia and north of the north-eastern extremity of Australia. It comprises the eastern part of the island of New Guinea, the western section of which, Papua (formerly Irian Jaya), is part of Indonesia, and some smaller islands including the Bismarck Archipelago (mainly New Britain, New Ireland and Manus) and the northern part of the Solomon Islands (mainly Bougainville and Buka). It covers a total area of 462,840 sq km (178,704 sq miles). The climate is hot and humid throughout the year, with an average maximum temperature of 33°C (91°F) and an average minimum of 22°C (72°F).

A census in July 1990 recorded a population of 3,607,954, and by the date of the next census July 2000 the population had increased to 5,130,365.

History

New Guinea was visited by European navigators from the early 16th century onwards, but exploration and colonial settlement did not begin until the mid-19th century. The western part of New Guinea was administered until 1949 as part of the Netherlands East Indies and from 1949 until 1962 as the Nederlands Nieuw Guinea. In 1963, after military action by Indonesia, the territory was redesignated Daerah Irian Barat and declared a part of Indonesia by an 'act of free choice' in August 1962. It is now known as Papua, a province of Indonesia formerly known as Irian Jaya (or West Papua).

The southern part of eastern New Guinea became British New Guinea in 1906, following the establishment of a British protectorate in 1884 and annexation in 1886. Australia administered what became the Territory of Papua until 1949, when it was joined, under a unified administration, with the Trust Territory of New Guinea (see below).

In 1884 the northern part of eastern New Guinea came under German administration as Schutzgebiet Kaiser-Wilhelmsland und Bismarck-archipel, later becoming known as German New Guinea. In 1914 the Germans were removed from the territory by Australian troops, and Australia subsequently administered the area under a League of Nations mandate until 1942, when much of it fell under Japanese occupation. In 1945 the territory returned to Australian administration under UN trusteeship arrangements. In December 1973 the Territory of Papua New Guinea became internally self-governing, and on 16 September 1975 became the independent nation of Papua New Guinea.

A House of Assembly (renamed the National Parliament at independence) was elected in February 1972. It had 102 members elected by universal adult suffrage. There were 20 ministers including the Prime Minister, Michael Somare, and an inner cabinet of 10 ministers. The Government was formed from a loose coalition of three main political parties with the opposition made up of one main party and a number of independents supporting both sides.

Although broad cultural similarities occur among groups in the Papuan Coastal, New Guinea Highlands, New Guinea Coastal, New Guinea Islands and Bougainville regions, local group sympathies are strong and in rural areas where approximately 80% of the indigenous population live, there is little interest in national issues.

The Papua New Guinea Government inherited from Australia a highly bureaucratic, centralized administration unsuited to a country in which transport is so difficult and national awareness so low. Strong pressure from some provinces during 1975 and 1976 resulted in the Government reintroducing into the Constitution provisions for decentralized provincial governments. In 1976 leaders of a group styling itself the 'Independent Republic of the North Solomons' on Bougainville island threatened to secede from Papua New Guinea. After several months of negotiations, Bougainville was granted provincial government status and became self-governing in July 1976. By 1978 all 20 provinces had been granted provincial government status.

The third national election since independence was held in June 1982. The Pangu Pati won 41 seats in the 102-member National Parliament, which in August elected Michael Somare as Prime Minister. Sir Julius Chan's People's Progress Party (PPP) won only 12 seats. In 1983 the Somare Government effected a constitutional change to provide the central authorities with greater control of the provincial governments as a means of preventing abuse of their powers. As a result, Somare was able to suspend the Enga provincial government in 1984. Several other provincial governments were subsequently suspended for financial mismanagement.

In March 1985 a motion expressing 'no confidence' in Somare's Government was introduced in Parliament by Sir Julius Chan, who nominated Paias Wingti (hitherto Deputy Prime Minister and a member of Somare's Pangu Pati) as alternative Prime Minister. Somare quickly formed a coalition, comprising the ruling Pangu Pati, the National Party (NP) and the Melanesian Alliance (MA), and the 'no confidence' motion was rejected. Fourteen members of Parliament who had supported the motion were expelled from the Pangu Pati, and subsequently formed a new political party, the People's Democratic Movement (PDM), under the leadership of Wingti.

In August 1985 the NP withdrew from Somare's coalition Government, and in November Sir Julius Chan presented another motion of 'no confidence', criticizing Somare's handling of the economy. Somare was defeated, and Wingti took office as Prime Minister, at the head of a new five-party coalition Government (comprising the PDM, the PPP, the NP, the United Party (UP) and the MA), with Chan as Deputy Prime Minister.

At the mid-1987 general election to the National Parliament Somare's Pangu Pati won 26 of the 109 elective seats and Wingti's PDM obtained 18. However, by forming a coalition with four minor parties (the PPP, the UP, the People's Action Party (PAP) and the Papua Party) together with a group of independents, Wingti succeeded in securing a parliamentary majority and was re-elected Prime Minister. In July 1988 Wingti was defeated in a further 'no confidence' motion, and Rabbie Namaliu, who had replaced Somare as leader of the Pangu Pati, took office as Prime Minister.

In June 1990 Namaliu's position was strengthened when Utula Samana, leader of the Melanesian United Front (MUF), and four other members of the party transferred their support to the Government, although they remained members of the MUF. This development gave Namaliu the two-thirds majority in Parliament which he required to pass constitutional amendments. Allegations that Namaliu had paid over K400,000 to four ministers dismissed in a government reorganization in June, in order to secure their support for an aborted 'no confidence' motion, provoked a demonstration of 6,000–7,000 people outside Parliament, calling for its dissolution and for Namaliu's resignation. The increasingly frequent use of the 'no confidence' motion in Parliament prompted the proposal of an amendment to the Constitution, granting incoming Prime Ministers a minimum period of 18 months before such a motion could be presented. In August the proposal was approved by Parliament and was incorporated into the Constitution in July 1991.

Apart from the continued unrest on Bougainville (see below), the principal cause for concern in Papua New Guinea's domestic affairs from the 1980s was the increase in serious crime on the islands. In 1991 the National Parliament approved a programme of severe measures to combat crime, including the introduction of the death penalty and the tattooing of the foreheads of convicted criminals.

In September 1991 a leadership tribunal found Ted Diro, the leader of the PAP, guilty of 81 charges of misconduct in office. However, the Governor-General, Sir Serei Eri, refused to ratify the tribunal's decision and reinstated Diro as Deputy Prime Minister, despite recommendations that he be dismissed. A constitutional crisis subsequently arose, during which a government envoy was sent to London to request that the Queen dismiss Eri. However, on 1 October the resignation of the Governor-General was announced and was followed shortly afterwards by that of Diro.

In 1992 the Government continued to be troubled by allegations of corruption and misconduct (notably bribery and misuse of public funds). The general election campaign began amid serious fighting among the various political factions, which led to rioting, in April 1992, by some 10,000 supporters of rival candidates. At the election, held in June, a total of 59 members of the legislature (including 15 ministers) lost their seats. The final result gave the Pangu Pati 22 of the 109 elective seats, while the PDM secured 15. Independent candidates won a total of 31 seats. Paias Wingti of the PDM was subsequently elected Prime Minister; he subsequently formed a coalition of PDM, PPP and League for National Advancement (LNA) members, as well as several independents. As part of an anti-corruption policy, Wingti suspended six provincial governments for financial mismanagement in October, and announced plans to abolish the entire local government system.

In early 1993 a resurgence of tribal violence, mainly in the Enga province, resulted in the deaths of more than 100 people. This development, together with a continued increase in violent crime throughout the country (despite the severe measures introduced in May 1991), prompted the National Parliament to approve a new Internal Security Act in May 1993. The legislation provided the Government with greatly increased powers, which permitted the introduction of a system of national registration, the restriction of freedom of movement within the country and the erection of permanently-policed gates on all major routes into the capital, Port Moresby. Most significantly, the legal system was to be changed so that defendants accused of serious crimes would be required to prove their innocence, rather than be proved guilty. The measures were criticized by the opposition as oppressive. In May 1994 the Supreme Court nullified six of the 26 sections of the act (most of which concerned the extension of police powers), as unconstitutional.

In September 1993 Prime Minister Wingti announced his resignation to Parliament. The Speaker immediately requested nominations for the premiership, and Wingti was re-elected unopposed with 59 of the 109 votes. According to the Constitution (as amended in July 1991), a motion of 'no confidence' in the Prime Minister could not be presented for at least 18 months, and Wingti claimed that his action had been necessary in order to secure a period of political stability for the country. Opposition members, however, described the events as an abuse of the democratic process, and several thousand demonstrators gathered in the capital to demand Wingti's resignation.

In August 1994 the Supreme Court declared Wingti's re-election in September 1993 invalid. Wingti did not contest the ensuing parliamentary vote for a new Prime Minister, in which Sir Julius Chan of the PPP defeated the Speaker, Bill Skate, by 66 votes to 32. Chris Haiveta, the leader of the Pangu Pati, was appointed Deputy Prime Minister.

In September 1994 a state of emergency was declared following major volcanic eruptions and earthquakes around Rabaul in East New Britain Province. Some 100,000 inhabitants were evacuated from the area, and a programme of rehabilitation was announced in early 1995.

The abolition of the directly-elected provincial government system, as proposed by Wingti, was rejected by Chan's Government. However, there was still considerable support among the opposition for the planned changes, and, as a result, it was decided that Parliament would vote on a series of motions to amend the Constitution accordingly; the first of these was approved in March 1995. However, in June the Pangu Pati withdrew its support for the reforms, and considerable opposition to the proposals was expressed by the provincial governments, particularly in Morobe. Nevertheless, the motion was approved later that month on condition that Chan lent his support to several opposition amendments to be considered later in the year. Chan subsequently dismissed six ministers for failing to vote for the legislation and effected a major reorganization of portfolios. The new regional authorities, comprising national politicians and selected local councillors and led by appointed governors, were appointed in that month. Wingti resigned as leader of the opposition in order to assume the post of Governor in the Western Highlands Province, and was replaced by another PDM member, Roy Yaki.

Meanwhile, the country continued to experience serious problems relating to crime and tribal violence, particularly in Port Moresby and in the form of banditry on the Highlands highway. In November 1996 the Government imposed a nation-wide curfew to combat the increasing lawlessness.

The mercenary affair on Bougainville in early 1997 (see below) led to a period of extreme instability throughout the country, culminating in Chan's resignation and the appointment of John Giheno as acting Prime Minister for about two months. The atmosphere of political uncertainty was exacerbated by serious outbreaks of violence in the weeks preceding the general election (which had been set for mid-June). The Government imposed a dusk-to-dawn curfew and a nation-wide ban on the sale of alcohol, and dispatched security personnel across the country in an attempt to quell the politically-motivated disturbances. Many senior politicians failed to be re-elected in the general election, including Chan, Giheno, and Wingti. Outbreaks of violence were reported in several Highlands constituencies as the results were declared. A period of intense political manoeuvring followed the election, as various members sought to form coalitions and groupings in an attempt to achieve a majority in Parliament. On 22 July Bill Skate of the People's National Congress (PNC), who was the former Speaker and Governor of the National Capital District, was elected Prime Minister, defeating Sir Michael Somare (who had established a new party—the National Alliance in 1996) by 71 votes to 35. Skate was supported by a coalition of the PNC, PDM, PPP, Pangu Pati and independent members. A new Government was appointed in late July, and extensive changes in the functional responsibilities of ministries were announced.

In September 1997 the Government declared a national disaster following a prolonged period of drought believed to have been caused by El Niño (a periodic warming of the tropical Pacific Ocean). By December more than 1,000 people had died, and as many as 1.2m. were threatened by starvation, as a result of the drought, which was the most severe in the country's recorded history. Several countries and organizations that had provided relief funds during the disaster were highly critical of the Government's management of the aid it received. The Minister for Finance, Roy Yaki, was dismissed, in part for his role in the affair, and responsibility for the administration of relief funds was subsequently transferred from the Department of Finance to the Department of Provincial Affairs. In March 1998 (when the drought was deemed to have ended following heavy rainfall) it was revealed that less than one-half of the relief aid received had been deployed to help the victims of the disaster.

On 14 November 1997 Silas (later Sir Silas) Atopare was appointed Governor-General, defeating Sir Getake Gam, head of the Evangelical Lutheran Church, by 54 votes to 44 in the legislature.

A serious political scandal erupted in late November 1997, following allegations of corruption against Skate. The accusations centred on a videotape broadcast on Australian television, which appeared to show Skate arranging bribes and boasting of his strong connections with criminal elements in Port Moresby. The Prime Minister dismissed his recorded comments (and the resultant allegations) saying that he had been drunk at the time of filming. Several senior politicians, including Somare, demanded his resignation over the affair. Meanwhile, Skate dismissed the leaders of the Pangu Pati and the PPP (Haiveta and Baing), his coalition partners, accusing them of conspiring against him. The situation intensified with the resignation of seven Pangu Pati members from the Government in early December, and the announcement that the Pangu Pati and the PPP would join the opposition. However, the PPP rejoined the Government shortly afterwards, having voted to replace Baing as leader of the party with Michael Nali. Similarly, four Pangu Pati ministers rejoined the Government, thereby restoring Skate's majority in the National Parliament. A major ministerial reorganization was subsequently announced, in which Nali was appointed Deputy Prime Minister. In April 1998 Skate announced the formation of a new political grouping, the Papua New Guinea First Party (which absorbed the PNC, the Christian Country Party and several other minor parties), and effected a cabinet reorganization. The Government's majority was subsequently undermined, however, following a series of decisions by the Court of Disputed Returns during mid-1998 which declared the election of seven government MPs (at the 1997 general election) null and void. Furthermore, in June the Pangu Pati officially joined the opposition, thereby reducing the Government's representation to 61 members in the National Parliament.

Rumours of a motion expressing 'no confidence' in the Prime Minister prompted the formation of a new pro-Skate coalition in the National Parliament in late July 1998. In the same month Skate announced a number of major reforms in the structure of the Government, including the merging of several ministerial portfolios, the establishment of new departments for Private Enterprise and Rural Development, a series of new appointments to various public bodies and an extensive ministerial reorganization.

In July 1998 a state of national disaster was declared following a series of tsunami (huge tidal waves caused by undersea earthquakes) which obliterated several villages on the north-west coast of the country and killed an estimated 3,000 people. An estimated K10m. was subsequently received for disaster relief operations, although widespread concern at the apparently inefficient distribution of the funds was expressed in the following months.

In October 1998 the PPP left the governing coalition and, in a subsequent ministerial reorganization, the party's leader, Michael Nali, was replaced as Deputy Prime Minister by Iairo Lasaro.

In late 1998 there was a series of scandals relating to the various serious misdemeanours of a number of provincial governors. Moreover, outbreaks of tribal fighting continued to cause problems. A serious conflict in the Eastern Highlands in early 1999 involved villagers using rocket launchers and grenades, and resulted in numerous deaths. In mid-1999 a state of emergency was declared in the Southern Highlands, following serious disturbances provoked by the death of a former provincial Governor, Dick Mune, in a road accident.

The establishment of a new political party, the PNG Liberal Party (PNGLP), in May 1999 by the Speaker, John Pundari (relaunched in June as the Advance PNG Party—APP), encouraged rumours of a forthcoming vote of 'no confidence' against the Prime Minister. In early June, as part of a government reorganization, Skate dismissed the PDM leader, Sir Mekere Morauta, and three other PDM ministers, replacing them with four Pangu Pati members, including Haiveta. Later that month both the PDM and the United Resource Party (URP) announced their decision to withdraw from the coalition Government, following the resignation of nine government ministers. Both parties were expected to support the APP, in an attempt to subject Skate to a vote of 'no confidence'. On 7 July, however, Skate unexpectedly resigned, but declared that he would remain in power, in an acting capacity, until the appointment of a new Prime Minister. The opposition alliance announced Morauta as their candidate for the premiership. On the day before the National Parliament was due to reconvene, Skate claimed that the APP had pledged support for the Government, thereby ensuring that it would have a sufficient majority to defeat any motion of 'no confidence'. At the opening session of the National Parliament in mid-July, Lasaro, the Prime Minister's nominee, defeated the opposition candidate, Bernard Narokobi of the PDM, by 57 votes to 45 to become Speaker. However, on the next day Morauta was elected Prime Minister with an overwhelming majority, following his nomination by Pundari, who had transferred his allegiance from Skate, having refused to accept the latter's nomination of himself as candidate for the post of Prime Minister. Lasaro immediately resigned as Speaker, and Narokobi was elected unopposed to the position. Morauta subsequently appointed a new Government, with Pundari as Deputy Prime Minister.

In early August 1999 Morauta, a former Governor of the central bank, presented a 'mini-budget', in an attempt to combat various economic problems which, he claimed, were a consequence of the previous Government's mismanagement. As part of a series of measures aimed at stabilizing the political situation in the country, legislation was drafted in October 1999 to prevent ministers transferring political allegiances. In early December Prime Minister Morauta expelled the APP from the coalition Government and dismissed Pundari from his post as Deputy Prime Minister, claiming that this constituted a further move towards the restoration of political stability. (Pundari was rumoured to have conspired with the opposition leader, Skate, to oust the Prime Minister.) Pundari was replaced by the former Minister of Works and deputy leader of the PDM, Mao Zeming. Following Pundari's sudden dismissal, four small political parties within the governing coalition—the National Alliance, the People's National Party, the Melanesian Alliance and the Movement for Greater Autonomy—joined to form the People's National Alliance. Also in that month, Skate (who was faced with a charge of attempted fraud during his term in office as Governor of the National Capital District Commission), announced that his party, the People's National Congress (PNC—which had 10 MPs), was to join the coalition Government; in May 2000 he assumed the leadership of the party. Later in December 1999, the resignation of the Minister of Agriculture and Livestock, Ted Diro, prompted Morauta to carry out a government reshuffle, including the appointment of three new ministers.

In March 2000 Morauta dismissed three ministers on the grounds that they had allegedly conspired to introduce a parliamentary motion of 'no confidence' in the Prime Minister. The parliamentary strength of the ruling coalition was increased to 76 MPs in April, following the readmission of the APP to government, including the appointment of Pundari, to the post of Minister of Lands and Physical Planning. In 2000 Morauta introduced further measures designed to ensure future governmental stability. In August he proposed legislation that would limit the ability of MPs to change their party allegiance within a parliamentary session; he also announced the adjournment of Parliament between January and July 2001, the only period during which votes of 'no confidence' could be tabled. (The Constitution forbids such votes in the 18 months following the election of a Prime Minister, and in the 12 months before a general election.) In November, however, a revolt by 25 government MPs (including six cabinet ministers) prevented a vote on the so-called Political Parties Integrity Bill. The rebellion prompted a major cabinet reshuffle, in which all of the ministers involved in the revolt, including the Deputy Prime Minister, Mao Zeming, were dismissed. Further changes to the composition of the National Executive Council were made in December, notably the dismissal of Sir Michael Somare, the Minister for Foreign Affairs and Trade, following which Morauta secured the parliamentary approval of the bill. The Prime Minister claimed that the introduction of the new legislation represented the most important constitutional change in Papua New Guinea since independence and would greatly enhance the political stability of the country, as it required members of Parliament who wished to change party allegiance to stand down and contest a by-election.

Allegations of corruption and mismanagement resulted in the suspension of four provincial governments (Western Province, Southern Highlands, Enga and the National Capital District—NCD) in late 2000 and early 2001, with the central Government claiming that a failure to deliver services had resulted from the misuse of public funds. Moreover, in January 2001 the Minister for Provincial and Local Government, Iairo Lasaro, was arrested for the alleged misappropriation of public funds, and in mid-March Bill Skate was charged with the same crime, having been acquitted earlier in the month of conspiring to defraud an insurance company (the trial was to be abandoned in December 2001 owing to lack of evidence).

A Commonwealth report into the Papua New Guinea Defence Force published in January 2001 recommended reducing the number of army personnel by one-third. Subsequent plans by the Government to make more than 2,000 soldiers redundant (equivalent to some 50% of the entire Defence Force) resulted in a revolt at the Port Moresby barracks in March. It was believed that senior officers had helped to distribute arms to the rebels, who demanded the resignation of the Prime Minister and the transfer of power to a caretaker administration. The rebellion ended some two weeks later with an amnesty for the soldiers involved, during which hundreds of looted weapons were surrendered. In March 2002 another rebellion by soldiers protesting against the proposed reductions in defence personnel took place at the Moem barracks on the northern coast.

In April 2001 the Advance PNG Party, led by John Pundari, was dissolved and merged with the PDM, led by the Prime Minister. In May, following a minor ministerial reorganization in March, Morauta expelled the National Alliance from the ruling coalition and dismissed the party's ministers (including Bart Philemon, Minister for Foreign Affairs) from the National Executive Council, accusing Somare, its leader, of attempting to destabilize the Government.

In late June, following several days of protests against the Government's economic reforms, police used tear gas to disperse hundreds of demonstrators outside the Prime Minister's office in Port Moresby. In a separate incident, four students were killed and several injured when riot police allegedly entered the premises of the University of Papua New Guinea and opened fire. A temporary curfew was imposed, and a Commission of Inquiry was established; in December relatives of one of the dead students began legal action against the police force.

In October 2001 the Prime Minister effected another reallocation of ministerial portfolios. At the end of the month, furthermore, the Minister for Foreign Affairs, John Pundari, was dismissed. His removal from office followed his criticism of the Government's participation in Australia's 'Pacific Solution', whereby 216 refugees, who had attempted to enter Australia illegally, were being housed on Manus Island. In December negotiations with Australia were under way to accommodate a further 1,000 asylum-seekers, and Australia had requested the Government to hold the refugees for an additional six months, although no formal agreement was made. In January 2002 the Government decided to accept 784 additional asylum-seekers. It was understood that they were to remain only until their asylum claims were processed.

A general election was held in the latter part of June 2002. Voting commenced on 15 June and was to extend over a two-week period. Many polling stations, however, failed to open as scheduled, amid reports of the theft of ballot papers and subsequent strike action by electoral staff. Some 25 people were killed and dozens injured in election-related violence, much of which occurred in the Highlands provinces as a result of disputes between clan-based candidates. A Commonwealth inquiry was subsequently planned to investigate events surrounding the election, which was described as the worst in the country's history. In the final results announced in August six seats in the Highlands provinces remained empty where voting had been unable to proceed. Of the remaining 103 seats Somare's National Alliance Party won 19 and Morauta's People's Democratic Movement secured 12. Independent candidates secured 17 seats with the remainder divided among a large number of minor parties, many of which were formed specifically to contest the election.

On 5 August 2002 Sir Michael Somare was elected Prime Minister with 88 parliamentary votes. No candidates stood against him and Morauta and his supporters abstained from the vote. Bill Skate, who had played an important part in Somare's campaign was elected Speaker. After appointing a 28-member Cabinet (which was dominated by 19 newly-elected MPs), Somare began his third term as Prime Minister with pledges to restore stability, halt the privatization programme and reduce expenditure.

Tribal conflicts, principally between the Ujimap and Wagia tribes, broke out near Mendi, the capital of Southern Highlands province, in December 2001. It was alleged that national and local politicians, along with tribal leaders, had made little effort to end the fighting, which had originated in a dispute over the governorship of the province in 1997; furthermore, many were dissatisfied at the election of Tom Tomiape as Governor, in late November 2001, and at the widespread political corruption and deteriorating public services in the province. Tomiape's election was ruled invalid by the Supreme Court in December, and Wambi Nondi was appointed acting Governor. A brief cease-fire was brokered in early January 2002 and an independent peace commission was formed in February, headed by Francis Awesa, a local businessman. By early 2002 more than 120 people had been killed since the onset of the fighting.

In February 2000 it was announced that about 25,000 inhabitants of the Duke of York Islands, which are situated in East New Britain Province, were expected to be resettled by the Government, following the publication of a UN report indicating that the islands were becoming uninhabitable owing to rising sea levels resulting from the 'greenhouse effect' (the heating of the earth's atmosphere as a consequence of pollution).

The status of the province of Bougainville was increasingly questioned in the late 1980s, a problem that developed into civil unrest and a long-term national crisis. In April 1988 landowners on the island of Bougainville submitted compensation claims, amounting to K10,000m., for land mined by Bougainville Copper Ltd at Panguna since 1972. When no payments ensued, acts of sabotage were perpetrated in late 1988 by the Bougainville Revolutionary Army (BRA), led by Francis Ona, a former miner and surveyor, and the mine was obliged to suspend operations for an initial period of eight days. However, the mine's owners refused to resume operations for fear of further attack, and, following increased violence in January 1989, a curfew was imposed. Operations at the mine resumed but the violence continued. The BRA's demands increasingly favoured secession for the island of Bougainville (and North Solomons Province) from Papua New Guinea, together with the closure of the mine until their demands for compensation and secession had been met. In May, as the violent campaign on the island intensified, the mine was forced once more to suspend production, and in June the Papua New Guinea Government declared a state of emergency on Bougainville, dispatching some 2,000 security personnel to the island. Ted Diro, having been acquitted on a charge of perjury by the Supreme Court but still facing impending charges of corruption, was reinstated to the National Executive Council in May as Minister of State, and was accorded special responsibility for overseeing the Bougainville crisis. In September a minister in the Bougainville provincial Government, who had been negotiating an agreement with landowners to provide them with financial compensation, was shot dead. The signing of the accord, due to take place the following day, was postponed indefinitely, and Diro responded by offering a reward for the capture or killing of Ona and seven of his deputies, including the BRA's military commander, Sam Kauona.

In January 1990 the owners of the Bougainville mine made redundant 2,000 of the remaining 2,300 staff. The escalation of violence on Bougainville prompted the Australian Government to announce plans to send in military forces to evacuate its nationals trapped on the island, and to withdraw the remaining 300 personnel of Bougainville Copper Ltd. Growing criticism of the Government's failure to resolve the Bougainville dispute, the rising death toll among the security forces, rebels and civilians and the worsening economic crisis led the Government to negotiate a cease-fire with the BRA, with effect from the beginning of March 1990. The Government undertook to withdraw its security forces and to release 80 detainees. Bougainville came under control of the BRA in mid-March after the sudden departure of the security forces. The premature withdrawal of the troops was seen as an attempt by Paul Tohian, the police commissioner who had been in charge of the state of emergency on Bougainville, to disrupt the peace process, and was followed by an abortive coup attempt, allegedly led by Tohian, who was summarily dismissed from his post.

In March 1990 the Government imposed an economic blockade on Bougainville; this was intensified in May, when banking, telecommunications and public services on the island were suspended. On 17 May the BRA, allegedly in response to the Government's implementation of economic sanctions, proclaimed Bougainville's independence, renaming the island the Republic of Bougainville. The unilateral declaration of independence, made by Ona, who also proclaimed himself interim President, was immediately dismissed by Namaliu as unconstitutional and invalid. In July negotiations between the BRA and the Government finally began on board a New Zealand naval vessel, *Endeavour*. In the resulting 'Endeavour Accord', the BRA representatives agreed to defer implementation of the May declaration of independence and to hold further discussions on the political status of the island. The Government agreed to end the blockade, and to restore essential services to the island. However, despite assurances from Namaliu that troops would not be sent to the island, the first two ships that left for Bougainville with supplies were found to be carrying 100 security personnel, intending to disembark on the island of Buka, north of Bougainville. The BRA accused the Government of violating the accord, and a week later the security forces and the two ships, together with the supplies, withdrew. In mid-September the Government sent armed troops to take control of Buka, stating that this was in response to a petition for help from Buka islanders. Violent clashes ensued between the BRA and the armed forces on Buka, in which many people were reported to have been killed.

In January 1991 further negotiations took place, in Honiara (the capital of Solomon Islands), between representatives of the Papua New Guinea Government and of Bougainville, which resulted in the 'Honiara Accord'. The agreement stated that the Papua New Guinea Government would not station its security forces on Bougainville if the islanders agreed to disband the BRA and to surrender all prisoners and weapons to a multinational peace-keeping force. The Bougainville secessionists were guaranteed immunity from prosecution. The agreement, however, made no provision for any change in the political status of Bougainville, and by early March it appeared to have failed.

Government troops launched a further attack on Bougainville in April 1991. In June Col Leo Nuia was dismissed from his post as Commander of the Papua New Guinea Defence Force, after admitting that his troops had committed atrocities during fighting on Bougainville in early 1990. Further allegations of human rights abuses and summary executions of BRA members and sympathizers by government troops prompted Namaliu to announce plans for an independent inquiry into the claims.

Fighting continued throughout 1991 and the situation deteriorated further when in early 1992, in an attempt to force the Government to end its economic blockade of the island, the BRA intercepted and burnt a supply ship, and held its crew hostage. As a result, all shipping and air services to Bougainville were suspended.

In October 1992 government troops began a major offensive against rebel-held areas of Bougainville and, later in the month, announced that they had taken control of the main town, Arawa. The BRA, however, denied the claim and began a campaign of arson against government offices and public buildings in Arawa. Violence on the island intensified in early 1993, and allegations of atrocities and violations of human rights, by both sides, were widely reported.

Talks between government representatives and secessionists in Honiara during 1994 led to the signing of a cease-fire agreement in September. Under the terms of the agreement, a regional peace-keeping force, composed of troops from Fiji, Vanuatu and Tonga, was deployed in October (with the Governments of Australia and New Zealand in a supervisory role) and the economic blockade of the island was lifted. In the following month Chan and a group of non-BRA Bougainville leaders signed the Charter of Mirigini, which provided for the establishment of a transitional Bougainville government. The BRA declared its opposition to the proposed authority, reiterating its goal of outright secession. However, in April 1995, following the suspension of the Bougainville provincial government, 27 members of the 32-member transitional administration were sworn in at a ceremony on Buka Island, attended by the Prime Minister and several foreign dignitaries. Theodore Miriong, a former legal adviser to Ona, was elected Premier of the authority. However, the three seats reserved for the BRA leaders, Ona, Kauona and Joseph Kabui (a former Premier of North Solomons Province), remained vacant, as the rebels urged their supporters to reject the new administration and to continue the violent campaign for independence. An amnesty, declared in May by the transitional administration and the Government, for all who had committed crimes during the conflict, was rejected by the BRA. Violence escalated during July and August, and a campaign of arson against public buildings was conducted by BRA rebels. Meanwhile, the Government denied any involvement in a series of attacks on BRA leaders, including an assassination attempt on Kabui. The murder of several more members of the security forces in March 1996 led the Government to abandon all talks with the secessionists, and troops to reimpose a military blockade on Bougainville. An escalation of violence in mid-1996 culminated in a major military offensive against rebel-held areas in June. Civilians on the island were encouraged to seek refuge in government 'care centres', and by August it was estimated that some 67,000 Bougainvilleans were being accommodated in 59 such centres. In the same month defence forces arrested Miriong, accusing him of incitement regarding the killing of 13 government soldiers at an army camp. The incident, in which Miriong was removed from Bougainville and kept under surveillance on Buka, caused the Government considerable embarrassment, particularly as it followed a number of similar cases, in which the security forces had chosen to act independently of government policy. On 12 October Miriong was assassinated at his home in south-west Bougainville by unidentified gunmen. The following month an official inquiry concluded that a group of government soldiers was responsible for the killing, assisted by pro-Government civilians (known as 'resistance fighters'). Meanwhile, Gerard Sinato was elected as the new Premier of the Bougainville Transitional Government.

An apparent deterioration in the situation on Bougainville in late 1996 was characterized by an increase in BRA attacks against civilian targets and a similar escalation in violence by government troops and 'resistance fighters'. The Red Cross temporarily suspended its operations on the island following an attack on one of its vehicles, and human rights organizations repeated demands that observers be allowed to monitor incidents on the island, following a series of attacks on civilians (for which both sides denied responsibility). A report commissioned by the Government and published in late 1996 recommended a thorough reorganization of the country's armed forces. The report identified a number of problems that had contributed to a lack of cohesion and discipline and to a marked decline in morale among troops, which had resulted in many soldiers refusing to serve in Bougainville.

In February 1997 unofficial reports suggested that the Government was planning to engage the services of a group of mercenaries on Bougainville. Chan reacted angrily to the reports, which he claimed were inaccurate; however, he confirmed that a company based in the United Kingdom, Sandline International (a subsidiary of Executive Outcomes, a notorious supplier of private armed forces in Africa), had been commissioned to provide military advice and training for soldiers on Bougainville. Subsequent reports of mercenary activity on the island and of the large-scale purchase of military equipment and weapons provoked expressions of condemnation from numerous interests in the region, including the British High Commission in Port Moresby, and, in particular, from the Government of Australia. The situation developed into a major crisis on 16 March when the Commander of the Defence Force, Brig.-Gen. (later Maj.-Gen.) Jerry Singirok, announced on national radio and television that the country's armed forces were refusing to co-operate with the mercenary programme and demanded the immediate resignation of Chan. He explained that the mercenaries (most of whom were from South Africa) had been captured by the armed forces and were being detained while arrangements were made for their deportation. Singirok denied that his actions constituted a coup attempt. The following day Chan dismissed Singirok, replacing him with Col Alfred Aikung. However, the armed forces rejected the new leadership, remaining loyal to Singirok. Popular support for the army's stance became increasingly vocal as several thousand demonstrators rampaged through the streets of the capital, looting and clashing with security forces. Armed forces in Australia were reported to be prepared for deployment to Papua New Guinea in the event of any worsening of the situation. In view of the escalation in civil unrest, Chan announced the suspension of the contract with Sandline International on 20 March, pending an inquiry into the affair. On the following day the remaining mercenaries left the country, and Aikung was replaced as Commander of the Defence Force by Col Jack Tuat. Despite these attempts at conciliation, however, demands for Chan's resignation intensified, with military, political and religious leaders, as well as the Governor-General, urging him to leave office. Moreover, four government ministers resigned from their posts in an attempt to increase the pressure on Chan to do likewise. On 25 March the National Parliament voted on a motion of 'no confidence' in the Prime Minister. When the vote was defeated protesters laid siege to the parliament building, effectively imprisoning more than 100 members inside the building until the next day, while an estimated 15,000 demonstrators marched on Parliament from across the capital. On the following day Chan announced his resignation, along with that of the Deputy Prime Minister and the Minister for Defence. John Giheno, the erstwhile Minister for Mining and Petroleum, was subsequently elected acting Prime Minister by the Cabinet.

In April 1997 an inquiry was initiated into the mercenary affair. The chief executive of Sandline International, Col (retd) Tim Spicer, was questioned over his alleged acceptance of bribes and in connection with various firearms offences. During the inquiry it was revealed that the company had requested part-ownership of the Panguna copper mine as payment for its military services. Criminal charges against Spicer were withdrawn within several days. The inquiry concluded in early June that Chan had not been guilty of misconduct in relation to the mercenary affair and, as a result (despite Giheno's stated intention to continue as acting Prime Minister until a general election had taken place), Chan announced his immediate resumption of his former position. Shortly after resuming office, Chan again provoked controversy by appointing Col Leo Nuia to the position of Commander of the Defence Force. (Nuia had been dismissed from the post in 1991, following an admission that his troops had committed atrocities during fighting on Bougainville.)

Following the election of a new Government, it was announced in August 1997 that a second inquiry into the mercenary affair, based on broader criteria, would be conducted. Meanwhile, government soldiers reacted angrily to the prosecution of military leaders involved in the operation to oust Sandline mercenaries from Bougainville in March. Nuia was imprisoned in his barracks by members of the Defence Force, while Maj. Walter Enuma, who was being held while awaiting trial on charges of 'raising an illegal force', was freed by rebel soldiers. The second inquiry concluded in September 1998 that Chris Haiveta (the former Deputy Prime Minister) had been the beneficiary of corrupt payments from Sandline and upheld the first inquiry's finding that Chan had not been guilty of any wrongdoing in the affair. In the same month an international tribunal ruled that the Government owed $A28m. to Sandline in outstanding payments under the mercenary contract. In May 1999 the Government agreed to pay this debt and the two parties undertook to end all legal action against each other. The Papua New Guinea Defence Force was to be allowed to retain Sandline military equipment stored on Bougainville.

In July 1997 talks were held in New Zealand (at the Burnham army base) between secessionists and representatives of the Bougainville Transitional Government. As a result of the negotiations, Sinato and Kabui signed the 'Burnham Declaration', which recommended the withdrawal of government troops from Bougainville and the deployment of a neutral peace-keeping force. Persistent reports of internal divisions within the BRA were refuted by the leadership, despite Ona's declared opposition to the 'Burnham Declaration' and to the decision to release the five hostages. However, hopes for a significant improvement in the political climate on Bougainville were encouraged by an official visit by the newly-elected Prime Minister, Bill Skate, in August (the first such visit since 1994) and by the resumption of talks in New Zealand in the following month. Negotiations concluded on 10 October 1997 with the signing of the 'Burnham Truce', in which representatives from both sides agreed to a series of interim measures, which included refraining from acts of armed confrontation pending a formal meeting of government and secessionist leaders in early 1998. Ona (who appeared to be becoming increasingly marginalized within the BRA) refused to be a party to the truce, however, claiming that similar agreements had not been honoured by government troops and 'resistance fighters' in the past, and indirectly threatened the members of an unarmed group of regional representatives, established to monitor the truce. The Prime Ministers of both Papua New Guinea and Solomon Islands made an extended visit to Bougainville in December 1997 to demonstrate their united support for the truce. Further talks held at Lincoln University in Christchurch, New Zealand, in January 1998 resulted in the 'Lincoln Agreement', providing for an extension to the truce, the initiation of a disarmament process and the phased withdrawal of government troops from the island. Skate also issued a public apology for mistakes made by successive administrations during the conflict, which was estimated to have resulted in the deaths of some 20,000 people and to have cost a total of K200m.

In accordance with the provisions of the 'Burnham Truce', a permanent cease-fire agreement was signed in Arawa on 30 April 1998. The occasion was attended by senior government members from Australia, New Zealand, Solomon Islands and Vanuatu, as well as Papua New Guinea government representatives and secessionist leaders. Ona declined to take part in the ceremony, reiterating his opposition to the peace agreement. In the following month he attracted statements of condemnation from Kabui and Kauona for issuing a 'shoot-to-kill' order against the peace-keeping troops on Bougainville to the small band of rebels who remained loyal to him. In June government troops were withdrawn from Arawa under the terms of the agreement and reconstruction projects on Bougainville, financed by funds from various sources, including an aid package of $NZ1m. from the New Zealand Government, were initiated. An increase in crime and arson attacks, however, was reported in the demilitarized zones in the following months.

In August 1998 more than 2,000 representatives from different groups in Bougainville met in Buin (in the south of the island) to discuss their response to the 'Burnham Truce'. The resultant 'Buin Declaration' stated that the islanders were united in their aspiration for independence through peaceful negotiation. In October the National Parliament voted to amend the Constitution to allow the Bougainville Reconciliation Government to replace the Bougainville Transitional Government. The new authority came into existence on 1 January 1999, following the renewed suspension of the Bougainville provincial government, and at its first sitting elected Sinato and Kabui as its co-leaders. In April an agreement signed by Bougainville and Papua New Guinea government representatives (although not acknowledged by the BRA, which threatened to leave the peace process as a result), known as the Matakana and Okataina Understanding, reaffirmed both sides' commitment to the cease-fire, while undertaking to discuss options for the political future of the island.

Elections to the Bougainville People's Congress (BPC, formerly the Bougainville Reconciliation Government) were held in early May 1999, and were reported to have proceeded smoothly. At the first sitting of the BPC, Kabui was elected President by an overwhelming majority, securing 77 of the 87 votes, defeating his former co-leader, Sinato. Kabui subsequently appointed 29 members to the Congressional Executive Council, and Linus Konukong was elected Speaker. Ona refused Kabui's offer to join the BPC, stating that he did not wish to co-operate with the Government. At a subsequent session of the Council, Kabui announced his intention to campaign for independence for Bougainville. In response, Prime Minister Bill Skate stated that, although there was no possibility of independence (as this was not provided for in the Constitution), Parliament would consider terms for greater autonomy for the island. Plans for the disposal of weapons on Bougainville were expected to be drafted by the UN under terms agreed upon at a meeting with the Peace Process Consultative Committee in June. In August the suspension of the Bougainville provincial government was extended for a further six months in an attempt to find a peaceful resolution to the issue of autonomy for Bougainville; the decision was confirmed at a parliamentary session the following month. Following a visit to Bougainville, the Minister for Bougainville Affairs and for Foreign Affairs, Sir Michael Somare (as he had become), stated that the Government was willing to grant the island a greater degree of autonomy. Somare proposed that Bougainville be self-governing in all matters except foreign affairs, defence and policing, all of which would remain the responsibility of the central Government. The proposal was welcomed as an important development by members of the BPC, although they also announced their intention not to surrender their weapons until the Government had agreed to the holding of a referendum on independence. Following further talks between Somare and Kabui, the former reiterated Skate's earlier comments that there was no provision for a referendum on independence in the Constitution.

In October 1999 a Supreme Court ruling declared the suspension of the Bougainville provincial government illegal on technical grounds. On 9 December the provincial government was formally recognized, in theory, despite protests by members of the BPC and concerns that this development would hinder the peace process. In effect, however, the provincial government comprised only four members—the Bougainville Regional Member of Parliament, John Momis, who thus became Governor-elect (although he agreed not to exercise his powers for the mean time) and the three other Bougainville parliamentarians. Following talks in mid-December between Somare and members of the BPC, the BRA and elders of the island, Somare declared, in the consequent agreement, that he would consider the possibility of a referendum on independence for Bougainville. The agreement, known as the Hutjena Accord, stated that the highest possible degree of autonomy should be granted to the island. Further talks regarding the future status of Bougainville commenced in early March 2000. However, following the rejection of an initial proposal on the island's autonomy by secessionist leaders, the talks were suspended. Negotiations resumed in mid-March, and on 23 March an agreement, known as the Loloata Understanding, allowing for the eventual holding of a referendum on independence, once full autonomy had been implemented, and the formal establishment of the Bougainville Interim Provincial Government (BIPG), composed of an Executive Council and a 25-member Provincial Assembly (including the four original members), was signed by Somare and Kabui.

On 30 March 2000 the Provincial Assembly and the Executive Council were sworn in by the Governor-General. Another six seats were left vacant in the Provincial Assembly for other Bougainville officials such as Kabui and Ona; Kabui, however, stated that, rather than joining the BIPG, he would wait until the establishment of a fully autonomous government (which he hoped would be in place by early 2001). Ona and his supporters, who numbered around 8,000, refused to participate in any government that was not completely independent. In May 2000 the Office of Bougainville Affairs was renamed the Office of Peace and Reconstruction. In July Somare approved an allocation of K200,000, as part of a scheme co-ordinated by the United Nations Development Programme (UNDP), to facilitate the collection and disposal of weapons held by dissident groups. Although an initial deadline of 15 September to determine the form and date of a referendum was not met, a further round of negotiations that month was presented as a significant advance in the peace process. Uncertainties regarding the time scale for the island's progression to autonomy continued to delay fulfilment of the peace process; Somare's statement in May that the referendum would be held 15 years hence contradicted a previously-stated deadline of December 2000. Further concerns about renewed Australian funding of the Papua New Guinea Defence Force troops stationed on Bougainville Island, and the failure of the BRA in particular to begin disarmament before the implementation of political autonomy, further impeded progress. In October the BRA commander, Gen. (self-styled) Ishmael Toroama, threatened to abandon the group's cease-fire. Somare was absent from a further, 'final' round of peace talks in October because of illness and a subsequent visit to Australia. At these discussions the conflicting demands for the holding of a referendum on the question of independence, and for prior disarmament, continued to delay the signing of an agreement to implement autonomy in Bougainville. Following a further round of peace talks in November, Kabui confirmed that he had secured an agreement from Somare that a future referendum would include a legally-binding option of independence, although disagreement over how soon the vote should be held persisted. In the following month Somare was abruptly dismissed from his ministerial position and replaced by Bart Philemon; Morauta had apparently believed that Somare was impeding the progress of the Political Parties Integrity Bill.

In February 2001 agreement on the terms of the referendum was finally reached following the intervention of the Australian Minister for Foreign Affairs. The agreement stated that the referendum would be held in 10–15 years' time and would contain the option of independence. In the interim the provincial government was to be granted increased autonomy and the BRA would be expected to disarm. Despite a temporary breakdown in negotiations, in early May commanders of the BRA and the Bougainville Resistance Force (a militia that was allied to the Government during the civil conflict on Bougainville) signed an agreement to surrender their weapons. In the same month, in Port Moresby, the Government and the BPA held negotiations on autonomy for Bougainville. In late June Moi Avei, who had replaced Philemon as Minister for Bougainville Affairs in May, announced that further talks had resulted in a comprehensive agreement on autonomy for the island, with the Government ceding to the BPA's demands that Bougainville be accorded its own system of criminal law and an autonomous police force. It was also agreed that the Papua New Guinea Defence Force's jurisdiction on the island would be strictly limited. On 30 August the Government and island leaders signed the Bougainville peace agreement in Arawa. Although he signed the accord, which was still to be approved by the National Parliament, Toroama stated that the BRA would campaign for the referendum to be held in three–five years' time and would continue to seek full independence. Francis Ona did not attend the signing ceremony.

The weapons disposal process was threatened in late November 2001 when Henry Kiumo, a former commander of the pro-Government Bougainville Resistance Force (BRF) militia, was murdered. However, weapons disposal by the BRA and BRF began in early December, and the UN Observer Mission on Bougainville (UNOMB) formally acknowledged the Bougainville Peace Agreement later in that month. In January 2002 the National Parliament unanimously endorsed the Organic Law enacting the Bougainville peace agreement, along with a bill containing the requisite constitutional amendment. A second vote, held in late March, ratified the legislation, and the Papua New Guinea Defence Force began its withdrawal from Bougainville.

In September 2000 a group of landowners form Bougainville initiated legal action in a US court against Rio Tinto, the operator of the Panguna copper mine between 1972 and 1988. The group was reported to be suing the company for the environmental and social damage caused by its activities, including health problems experienced by workers and islanders living near the mine. Moreover, their case alleged that the company had effectively transformed the Papua New Guinea Defence Force into its own private army and was therefore responsible for the deaths of some 15,000 civilians in military action and a further 10,000 as a result of the economic blockade on the island.

In 1984 more than 9,000 refugees crossed into Papua New Guinea from the Indonesian province of Irian Jaya (officially known as Papua from January 2002), as a consequence of operations by the Indonesian army against Melanesian rebels of the pro-independence Organisasi Papua Merdeka (OPM—Free Papua Movement). For many years, relations between Papua New Guinea and Indonesia had been strained over the conflict in Irian Jaya, not least because the independence movement drew sympathy from many among the largely Melanesian population of Papua New Guinea. A new border treaty was signed in October 1984, and attempts were made to repatriate the refugees, based on assurances by the Indonesian Government that there would be no reprisals against those who returned. However, in 1985 and 1986 more refugees were still crossing into Papua New Guinea than returning to Irian Jaya. By mid-1987 more than 15,000 refugees were living in camps near the border in Papua New Guinea's Western Province, and only a few hundred had taken advantage of the programme of voluntary repatriation. A treaty signed by the two Governments in October 1995, providing for the settlement of disputes by consultation and arbitration, provoked strong criticism among opposition politicians in Papua New Guinea, who claimed that it effectively precluded the censure of any violation of human rights in Irian Jaya. In 1988 Somare (the then Minister for Foreign Affairs) condemned the numerous incursions by Indonesian soldiers into Papua New Guinea, and the resultant violence and killings, as a breach of the treaty, affirming that Papua New Guinea would not support Indonesia in its attempt to suppress the OPM. In late 1995 the Indonesian consulate in Vanimo was attacked by OPM rebels and a subsequent increase in Indonesian troops along the border was reported. Violent confrontations resulted in the killing of several rebels and security personnel and the kidnapping by OPM activists of some 200 villagers. Australia urged the Papua New Guinea Government to accept several thousand refugees living in camps along the border, and in May 1996 the Government announced that 3,500 Irian Jayans would be allowed to remain in Papua New Guinea on condition that they were not involved in OPM activities. In mid-1998, on an official visit to Indonesia, the Prime Minister, Bill Skate, signed a memorandum of understanding on bilateral relations, which was expected to provide the basis for closer co-operation in political, economic and defence matters. Under the terms of the agreement, troop numbers along the border were increased in March 1999. In May of that year 11 Javanese people were taken hostage and three people were reported to have been killed by OPM rebels in the West Sepik province of Papua New Guinea. The hostages were later released as a result of the intervention of the Papua New Guinea security forces. The OPM subsequently demanded an inquiry into the operation leading to the release of the hostages, after its communications director was allegedly shot dead at a border post. During 2000 hundreds of refugees were voluntarily repatriated to Indonesia (including more than 600 in a major operation in early September), although approximately 7,000 were believed to remain in Papua New Guinea in September. In late 2000 it was reported that Indonesian security forces had made some 400 incursions into Papua New Guinea in the previous two months while pursuing separatists. In December the border with Irian Jaya was officially closed, while Morauta reaffirmed his recognition of Indonesia's sovereignty over the region.

Since 1990 relations with Solomon Islands have been overshadowed by the conflict on Bougainville. Solomon Islands (whose inhabitants are culturally and ethnically very similar to Bougainville islanders) has protested against repeated incursions by Papua New Guinea defence forces into Solomon Islands' territorial waters, while the Papua New Guinea Government has consistently accused Solomon Islands of harbouring members of the BRA and providing them with supplies. Despite several attempts during the 1990s to improve the situation between the two countries (including an agreement by Solomon Islands in 1993 to close the BRA office in Honiara), relations remained tense. In April 1997 the Solomon Islands Government announced that it was considering the initiation of proceedings against the Papua New Guinea Government concerning its attempted use of mercenaries on Bougainville. In June 1997 Papua New Guinea and Solomon Islands concluded a maritime border agreement, following several years of negotiations. The purpose of the agreement (which came into effect in January 1998) was not only to delineate the sea boundary between the two countries but also to provide a framework for co-operation in matters of security, natural disaster, customs, quarantine, immigration and conservation. In March 2000 relations between Papua New Guinea and the Solomon Islands were further strengthened following the opening of a Solomon Islands High Commission in Port Moresby.

In March 1988 Papua New Guinea signed an agreement with Vanuatu and Solomon Islands to form the 'Melanesian Spearhead Group' (MSG), dedicated to the preservation of Melanesian cultural traditions and to the achievement of independence for the French Overseas Territory of New Caledonia. In 1989 Papua New Guinea increased its links with South-East Asia, signing a Treaty of Amity and Co-operation with ASEAN, and entering into negotiations with Malaysia on the creation of a Port Moresby Stock Exchange, which started trading in April 1999. The friendly relations between Papua New Guinea and the People's Republic of China which had been jeopardized by a briefly-implemented decision to establish full diplomatic relations with Taiwan in mid-1999, were reconfirmed in 2000 when the Government of Papua New Guinea gave permission for China to construct a new building for the Ministry of Foreign Affairs in Port Moresby, despite fears that this could lead to a breach of national security.

The increasing exploitation of Papua New Guinea's natural resources in the 1990s led to considerable concern over the impact of the activities of numerous foreign business interests on the country's environment. Activity in the forestry sector increased dramatically in the early 1990s, and an official report, published in 1994, indicated that the current rate of logging was three times the sustainable yield of the country's forests. Attempts to introduce new regulations to govern the industry, however, were strongly opposed by several Malaysian logging companies with operations in the country. The exploitation of Papua New Guinea's extensive mineral resources had resulted in considerable environmental damage. In 1989 the Government gave the operators of the Ok Tedi gold and copper mine permission to discharge 150,000 metric tons of toxic waste per day into the Fly River. In 1994 6,000 people living in the region began a compensation claim against the Australian company operating the mine for damage caused by the resultant pollution. A settlement worth some $A110m. was reached in an Australian court in 1995 (and a further settlement worth $A400m. for the establishment of a containment system was concluded in mid-1996), despite opposition from the Papua New Guinea Government, which feared that such action might adversely affect the country's prospects of attracting foreign investment in the future. Similar claims were initiated by people living near the Australian-controlled Porgera gold mine in early 1996 for pollution of the Strickland River system, as well as by landowners near the Kutubu oilfield. The results of an independent study into the effects of mining activities by the Ok Tedi mine, published in mid-1999, showed that damage to the environment might be greater than originally believed, casting doubts over the future of the mine. The Government, however, announced that it would await the findings of an independent review, carried out by the World Bank. The results of this report, which were published in March 2000, found that closure of the mine was necessary on environmental grounds. However, it also emphasized the potentially damaging impact of the mine's early closure on both the local economy and world copper markets. Further talks on the future of the mine were expected to take place later that year. In May BHP, the Australian operator, endorsed the World Bank report and reaffirmed its intention to close the mine. In October 2001 BHP Billiton announced its withdrawal from the Ok Tedi mine and in early 2002 transferred its 52% stake to a development fund called the PNG Sustainable Development Programme Ltd.

Economy

In 2000, according to estimates by the World Bank, Papua New Guinea's gross national product (GNP), measured at average 1998–2000 prices, was US $3,665.4m., equivalent to US $760 per head. During 1990–99, it was estimated, GNP per head increased, in real terms, at an average annual rate of 2.6%. Over the same period the population increased by an annual average of 2.3%. The average annual increase in gross domestic product (GDP) was 4.8% in 1990–2000. According to revised estimates by the Asian Development Bank (ADB), GDP increased by 7.6% in 1999 but decreased by 0.8% in 2000 and by 2.5% in 2001.

More than 70% of the working population are engaged in subsistence agriculture, growing mainly roots and tubers. The principal cash crops are coffee (which accounted for some 3.1% of export earnings in 2001), cocoa (1.8%), coconuts (for the production of copra and coconut oil), palm oil (4.7%), rubber and tea. In 2000–01 agricultural exports were affected by unusual climatic conditions, which particularly affected the coffee harvest, and by low international commodity prices; coffee and copra prices declined by some 30% on the world market in 2001. None the less, cocoa production increased in 2000 as a result of better management practices, and palm oil producion also increased. Shark oil became a significant export in the 1990s. The sale of fishing licences to foreign fleets provides a significant source of revenue (estimated at US $15m. in 1998). In 1999 the ADB approved a loan worth US $9m. for the construction of two fishery wharves, which were expected to generate up to K200m. annually.

In 2001 the agricultural sector contributed 33.1% of GDP and in 2000 it engaged an estimated 73.7% of the employed labour force. During 1990–2000 agricultural GDP rose, in real terms, by an annual average of 4.0%. According to the ADB, it increased by an estimated 9.1% in 2000, by 0.9% in 2001 and was projected to increase by 5.1% in 2002.

The real GDP of the industrial sector (including mining and quarrying, manufacturing, construction and utilities) increased by an annual average of 7.7% in 1990–2000. According to the ADB, industrial GDP decreased by 5.4% in 2000, and by 6.1% in 2001 and was projected to decline by 1.3% in 2002. The sector contributed an estimated 36.0% of GDP in 2001. The manufacturing sector is limited by the small internal market, the low purchasing power of the population and the lack of an integrated transport network. Manufacturing provided 8.5% of GDP in 2000. Measured by the value of output, the principal branches of manufacturing are food products, beverages, wood products, metal products, machinery and transport equipment. Manufacturing GDP increased by an annual average of 5.0% in 1990–2000. Several fish canneries were established in the 1990s. The tertiary sector is large for the size of the economy, a situation that developed during colonial times, and is unlikely to grow in the immediate future.

High rainfall and relief give Papua New Guinea the potential to generate large amounts of hydroelectricity, which is estimated to account for more than 30% of electricity supplies. The sugar industry also provides the raw material for the production of ethyl alcohol (ethanol) as an alternative fuel. In the development of all Papua New Guinea's natural energy resources, foreign investment is of paramount importance. Imports of mineral fuels comprised 8% of the value of total imports in 1992.

Forestry is an important activity. Papua New Guinea is one of the world's largest exporters of unprocessed tropical timber. In 1998 exports of timber provided 13.0% of total export earnings. Low prices for tropical hardwoods on the international market, together with the Asian financial crisis, however, led to a contraction in the industry in the late 1990s. By 2001 timber exports provided only 5.1% of total export earnings. There is serious concern about the environmental damage caused by extensive logging activity in the country, much of which is illegal. Concern regarding the unsustainability of the industry increased in 1999, when tax incentives for logging operators led to a dramatic rise in production. In late 1999 the Government reinstated higher taxes on logging and introduced a moratorium on all new forestry licences in an attempt to control logging activity.

A comparatively new development is the exploitation of Papua New Guinea's extensive mineral resources, chiefly copper, gold and silver, and, more recently, substantial deposits of chromite, cobalt, nickel and quartz have been discovered. Papua New Guinea also has large reserves of natural gas and petroleum. The main source of copper and gold is the island of Bougainville, where copper-mining began in 1972. Operations at the mine ceased indefinitely in 1989, owing to civil unrest (see History). Copper is normally the country's principal export, accounting for 58% of export earnings (K702.8m.) in 1988 (although this figure had fallen to 14.1% by 2001). The development of a new mine in 1984 at Ok Tedi, in the Star mountains on the mainland, placed Papua New Guinea among the world's major gold-producing countries. Production of copper concentrates at Ok Tedi began in 1986, and in 1991 the mine produced the country's entire output of copper; it employed a total of 1,920 people in 1992. In 2000, however, the mine was threatened with closure because of a report indicating that damage to the environment caused by mining activities might be greater than originally believed (see History). The mine, on average, contributes 10% of the country's annual GNP and 20% of export revenues. Large deposits of gold were discovered at several sites during the 1980s (including the largest known deposit outside South Africa at Lihir, which began operations in mid-1997), and annual gold production subsequently rose at a steady rate, reaching an estimated 74.0 metric tons in 2000. Exports of gold provided 34.7% of total export earnings in 2001. Mining and quarrying provided 28.5% of GDP and 77.3% of total export earnings in 2000. Mining GDP fell by 4.0% in 2000, according to ADB figures.

Reserves of natural gas and petroleum were assessed in West Papua New Guinea in the mid-1980s. Recent geological surveys have indicated the presence of a number of large gas reserves. In 1999 plans were under way for the construction of a US $3,500m. gas pipeline to Queensland, Australia, although the agreement between landowners and the oil company involved to begin the project was not signed until June 2002. In 1987 potential recoverable petroleum reserves of an estimated 500m. barrels were discovered at the Iagifu oilfield in the Southern Highlands. Production of petroleum at the Hedinia and nearby Agogo oilfields in the Kutubu joint venture began in 1992, and by 1993 had reached some 130,000 barrels per day, although by early 2000 output had decreased to around 36,400 barrels per day, owing to natural depletion of the field, and an increase in gas production. Production from two new major oilfields (Moran and Gobe), which began in early 1998, was expected to double the volume of exported petroleum. Plans for the construction of several petroleum refineries were approved in the late 1980s. The Napa Napa oil refinery project was initiated in mid-2000 and was expected to begin processing 36,000 barrels per day in 2002. Exports of crude petroleum provided 30.9%% of total export earnings in 2001.

The services sector contributed an estimated 29.6% of GDP in 2000. Tourism is an expanding sector, although political instability and reports of widespread crime have had a detrimental effect on the industry. During the late 1980s and early 1990s annual foreign tourist arrivals barely exceeded 40,000, but the total increased significantly to 67,465 in 1998, before declining slightly to 67,357 in 1999. Tourism receipts were worth an estimated US $76m. in 1999. The GDP of the services sector expanded by an average annual rate of 3.2% in 1990–2000. Having increased by 11.6% in 1999, however, the sector's GDP declined by 5.0% in 2000. According to the ADB, services GDP decreased by 2.6% in 2001.

Government finance is derived from three main sources: internal revenue, loans and overseas aid. Papua New Guinea has received substantial long-term loans from the Asian Development Bank and from the World Bank. In 2001/02 aid from Australia was projected at $A342.9m. in aid-funding for Papua New Guinea. In 2001 there was a budgetary deficit equivalent to around 1.8% of GDP.

In 2001, according to theADB, Australia provided 51.3% of Papua New Guinea's imports and took 25.6% of exports (including gold). Japan supplied 4.5% of imports and purchased 10.4% of exports in that year. Other significant trading partners are the People's Republic of China (7.3% of exports in 2001), the USA, the Republic of Korea, Germany, Singapore (18.3% of imports in that year) and the United Kingdom. In 2000 there was a visible trade surplus of US $712.6m., and a surplus of US $281.6m. on the current account of the balance of payments. Papua New Guinea's total external debt stood at US $2,604m. in 2000, of which US $1,502m. was long-term public debt. In that year the cost of long-term debt-servicing was equivalent to 13.5% of exports of goods and services. At the end of 2001 the external debt stood at an estimated K4,982.1m., of which K4,822.0m. was owed to various international agencies. The annual inflation rate averaged 9.5% in 1990–2000; consumer prices increased by 15.6% in 2000 and by 9.3% in 2001.

Papua New Guinea remains dependent on aid from international donors for its economic development. Foreign investment is sought and encouraged, while fears of neo-colonialism and domination of the economy by overseas interests are frequently expressed. A marked rural–urban migration pattern has developed. The prolonged closure of the Bougainville copper mine from 1989 and the high cost of security operations there coincided with a period of low prices for Papua New Guinea's key agricultural commodities. Strong economic growth in the early 1990s was attributed largely to the success of the new Porgera gold mine and to an increase in petroleum production at the Kutubu oilfield. However, the country's petroleum reserves were likely to be exhausted by 2010, and the Porgera operation planned to cease mining activity by 2007. In 1998 a financial crisis, caused partly by a dramatic decrease in the value of the kina, prompted the Government to reduce expenditure and to introduce increased excises. In the following year expenditure was further reduced and plans for the reduction of the public-service sector by some 7,000 employees were announced. The country is also vulnerable to adverse climatic conditions, as illustrated in mid-1997 when a serious drought resulted in the suspension of operations at the Porgera and Ok Tedi mines (owing to the low water-level in rivers essential for the transport of minerals) as well as in disastrous harvests for cash and subsistence crops. Similarly, a series of tsunami, which struck the north-west of the country in mid-1998, had serious consequences for the country (see History), as did an earthquake and tsunami off the north coast, near Wewak, in September 2002. Growing ethnic and environmental problems (see above), widespread crime and concern over foreign exploitation also continued to threaten Papua New Guinea's economic success. A report published in late 1998 claimed that crime (particularly urban crime, the incidence of which was believed to have increased 20-fold since the 1970s) constituted Papua New Guinea's most serious economic problem.

A 'recovery' budget for 2000 included increased expenditure in areas such as agriculture, health, education and policing, further tax reforms and the privatization of government assets, the proceeds of which were to be used to repay a proportion of the national debt. A joint funding programme, valued at US $500m., was agreed upon by the IMF and the World Bank to assist the Government in the implementation of the economic reforms and Australia pledged a total of US $1,000m. in programme aid over a period of three years. In late 2000 some 1,500 public servants were made redundant as part of ongoing government retrenchment measures. The IMF praised the Government for its structural reform policies and for its intention to effect a major programme of privatizations, recommended by the organization. However, in early 2001 the World Bank expressed concern over the continued high incidence of official corruption in the country, and in February its resident representative (who had been monitoring the implementation of economic reforms) was deported for interfering in domestic politics. In late 2001 the Government established the PNG Business Trust to manage the transfer of state assets to the private sector. It was envisaged that the 2002 budget deficit would be largely financed by revenue from the partial privatization of state-owned organizations, including Air Niugini, Telikom, Elcom and the Harbours Board; K155m. had already been generated by the sale of the Papua New Guinea Banking Corporation to the locally-owned Bank of South Pacific in late 2001. Papua New Guinea received exceptional financing of US $91m. in December 2001 from the World Bank, ADB and the Japan Bank for International Cooperation. The value of the kina, meanwhile continued to decline, losing almost 20% against the US dollar between January and December 2001. The export sector, however, was unable to take advantage of the weak currency, being constrained by declining commodity prices. In April 2002 it was announced that, as part of the ongoing public-sector reforms, more than 3,000 civil servants were to be made redundant by the end of the year. However, the Government suffered a conclusive defeat at a general election held in June 2002 and the newly elected Prime Minister, Sir Michael Somare, announced that one of his Government's most urgent priorities was the immediate cessation of the World Bank-endorsed privatization programme. The new Government also announced plans to reduce expenditure by some K500m. in an attempt to control the budgetary deficit, which was estimated at K800m. for 2002. A potential economic crisis was threatened by the decision of the Supreme Court in September 2002 to rule that a 10% value-added tax, introduced in 1999, was invalid. The Government was reported to be considering the introduction of urgent legislation to reclaim the lost tax (amounting to some US $450m. since 1999) amid warnings of civil unrest, as the likelihood of government services becoming affected by the lack of revenue increased.

Papua New Guinea is a member of the Asian Development Bank, the Asia-Pacific Economic Co-operation (APEC) group, the Pacific Community (formerly the South Pacific Commission), the Pacific Islands Forum (formerly the South Pacific Forum), the International Cocoa Organization and the International Coffee Organization.

Statistical Survey

Source (unless otherwise stated): Papua New Guinea National Statistical Office, POB 337, Waigani, NCD; tel. 3011229; fax 3251869; e-mail nsuvulo@nso.gov.pg; internet www.nso.gov.pg.

Area and Population

AREA, POPULATION AND DENSITY

Area (sq km)	462,840*
Population (census results)	
11 July 1990†	3,607,954
9 July 2000	
Males	2,661,091
Females	2,469,274
Total	5,130,365
Density (per sq km) at July 2000	11.1

* 178,704 sq miles.

† Excluding North Solomons Province (estimated population 154,000).

Administrative Capital: Port Moresby, with a population of 188,089 at the 1990 census.

BIRTHS AND DEATHS (1996 estimates)

Birth rate 32.6 per 1,000; Death rate 10.1 per 1,000).

Expectation of life (WHO estimates, years at birth, 2000): Males 64.7; Females 69.3 (Source: WHO, *World Health Report*).

ECONOMICALLY ACTIVE POPULATION*
(estimates based on 1980 census results)

Agriculture, hunting, forestry and fishing†	564,500
Mining and quarrying	4,300
Manufacturing	14,000
Electricity, gas and water	2,800
Construction	21,600
Trade, restaurants and hotels	25,100
Transport, storage and communications	17,400
Financing, insurance, real estate and business services	4,500
Community, social and personal services	77,100
Others (incl. activities not stated or not adequately described)	1,500
Total labour force†	732,800

* Figures refer to citizens of Papua New Guinea only.

† Excluding persons solely engaged in subsistence agriculture, hunting, forestry and fishing.

1990 census (citizens aged 10 years and over, excl. North Solomons Province): Total employed 1,582,518 (Agriculture, hunting, forestry and fishing 1,269,744); Unemployed 132,812; Total labour force 1,715,330 (males 1,002,891, females 712,439).

Mid-2000 (estimates in '000): Agriculture, etc. 1,704; Total economically active population 2,313 (Source: FAO).

Health and Welfare

KEY INDICATORS

Fertility (births per woman, 2000)	4.5
Under-5 mortality rate (per 1,000 live births, 2000)	112
HIV/AIDS (% of persons aged 15–49, 2001)	0.65
Physicians (per 1,000 head, 1998)	0.07
Hospital beds (per 1,000 head, 1990)	4.02
Health expenditure (1998): US $ per head (PPP)	79
% of GDP	3.9
public (% of total)	91.4
Access to water (% of persons, 1999)	42
Access to sanitation (% of persons, 1999)	82
Human Development Index (2000): ranking	133
value	0.535

For sources and definitions, see explanatory note on p. vi.

Agriculture

PRINCIPAL CROPS ('000 metric tons)

	1998	1999	2000
Maize*	6	7	7
Sorghum*	3	3	3
Sweet potatoes*	460	480	480
Cassava (Manioc)*	112	120	120
Yams	200	220*	220*
Taro (Coco yam)*	160	170	170
Other roots and tubers*	270	270	271
Sugar cane*	400	430	430
Pulses*	2	3	3
Coconuts	695†	826†	826*
Palm kernels*	54	68	68
Vegetables and melons*	386	387	387
Pineapples*	11	12	12
Bananas*	670	700	700
Other fruit (excl. melons)*	489	501	501
Coffee (green)*	81	83	83
Cocoa beans*	29	36	47
Tea (made)	7	9*	9*
Natural rubber (dry weight)	7	7†	7

* FAO estimate(s). † Unofficial figure.

Source: FAO.

LIVESTOCK (FAO estimates, '000 head, year ending September)

	1998	1999	2000
Horses	2	2	2
Cattle	86	87	87
Pigs	1,550	1,550	1,550
Sheep	6	6	6
Goats	2	2	2
Chickens	3,600	3,600	3,700

Source: FAO.

LIVESTOCK PRODUCTS (FAO estimates, '000 metric tons)

	1998	1999	2000
Beef and veal	2	3	3
Pig meat	44	44	44
Poultry meat	5	5	5
Other meat	15	18	18
Poultry eggs	4	4	4

Source: FAO.

Forestry

ROUNDWOOD REMOVALS ('000 cubic metres, excluding bark)

	1997	1998	1999
Sawlogs, veneer logs and logs for sleepers	3,064	3,064	3,064
Pulpwood	175	–	–
Fuel wood	5,533	5,533	5,533
Total	8,772	8,597	8,597

Source: FAO, *Yearbook of Forest Products*.

SAWNWOOD PRODUCTION
('000 cubic metres, including railway sleepers)

	1997	1998	1999
Coniferous (softwood)	43	43	43
Broadleaved (hardwood)	175	175	175
Total	218	218	218

Source: FAO, *Yearbook of Forest Products*.

Fishing

('000 metric tons, live weight)

	1997	1998	1999
Capture*	43.7	67.6	53.7
Mozambique tilapia*	2.3	2.3	2.3
Other freshwater fishes*	8.6	8.6	6.7
Sea catfishes*	1.9	1.9	1.9
Skipjack tuna	11.4	32.0	20.5
Yellowfin tuna	7.1	9.6	5.5
Aquaculture*	0.0	0.0	0.0
Total catch*	43.8	67.7	53.8

* FAO estimates.

Source: FAO, *Yearbook of Fishery Statistics*.

Mining

	1998	1999	2000†
Petroleum ('000 metric tons)	3,800	4,100	3,300
Copper ('000 metric tons)*	152.2	187.9	200.9
Silver (metric tons)*	59	67	53
Gold (metric tons)*	64.1	61.3	74.0

* Figures refer to metal content of ore.
† Estimates.

Source: US Geological Survey.

Industry

SELECTED PRODUCTS

	1996	1997	1998
Palm oil ('000 metric tons)*	230	240	n.a.
Electric energy (estimates, million kWh)	1,790	1,795	1,795
Raw sugar ('000 metric tons)*	43	45	48

* Unofficial figures.

Beer ('000 litres): 39,029 in 1997; 34,826 in 1998.

Sources: FAO, *Production Yearbook*, UN, *Industrial Commodity Statistics Yearbook*, and Papua New Guinea National Statistical Office.

Finance

CURRENCY AND EXCHANGE RATES

Monetary Units

100 toea = 1 kina (K).

Sterling, Dollar and Euro Equivalents (31 May 2002)

£1 sterling = 5.461 kina;
US $1 = 3.723 kina;
€1 = 3.495 kina;
100 kina = £18.31 = $26.86 = €28.61.

Average Exchange Rate (US $ per kina)

1999 0.3939
2000 0.3617
2001 0.2964

Note: The foregoing information refers to the mid-point exchange rate of the central bank. In October 1994 it was announced that the kina would be allowed to 'float' on foreign exchange markets.

BUDGET (million kina)*

Revenue†	1999	2000‡	2001‡
Taxation	1,662	1,917	2,476
Taxes on income, profits, etc.	818	910	1,342
Individual	524	565	650
Corporate	293	345	692
Excises	171	169	185
Taxes on international trade and transactions	551	666	771
Import duties	472	542	636
Export duties	79	124	135
Non-tax revenue	1,148	600	383
Entrepreneurial and property income	1,066	483	111
Total	2,810	2,517	2,859

Expenditure§	1997	1998	1999
Recurrent expenditure	1,768	1,895	2,020
National and statutory	941	994	1,091
National	820	858	970
Salaries and wages	367	384	393
Goods and services	453	475	428
Statutory authorities	120	136	121
Provincial departments	530	566	537
Salaries and wages	288	307	384
Goods and services	73	125	89
Conditional grants	169	135	65
Interest payments	298	335	393
Domestic	206	228	261
External	91	107	132
Development expenditure	428	596	786
National and statutory	318	495	698
Provinces	110	101	88
Total	2,196	2,491	2,806

* Figures refer to the operations of the General Budget and of superannuation and retirement funds. The transactions of other central government units with individual budgets are excluded.
† Excluding grants received from abroad (million kina): 477 in 1999; 555‡ in 2000; 551‡ in 2001.
‡ Estimate(s).
§ Excluding net lending (million kina): -3 in 1997; -5 in 1998; -5 in 1999.

Source: partly IMF, *Papua New Guinea: Recent Economic Developments* (October 2000).

2000 (million kina): *Expenditure:* Recurrent expenditure 2,218.6 (Salaries and wages 836.3; Goods and services 760.4; Interest payments 428.6); Development expenditure 904.7; Total 3,123.3.

Source: IMF, *Papua New Guinea: Recent Economic Developments* (October 2001).

INTERNATIONAL RESERVES (US $ million at 31 December)

	1999	2000	2001
Gold (national valuation)	27.90	27.90	27.90
IMF special drawing rights	0.72	12.17	8.71
Reserve position in IMF	0.07	0.23	0.38
Foreign exchange	204.35	296.07	429.77
Total	233.00	336.37	466.76

Source: IMF, *International Financial Statistics.*

MONEY SUPPLY (million kina at 31 December)

	1999	2000	2001
Currency outside banks	357.49	306.93	308.98
Demand deposits at deposit money banks	982.38	1,061.86	1,104.17
Total money (incl. others)	1,343.56	1,372.69	1,416.95

Source: IMF, *International Financial Statistics.*

COST OF LIVING (Consumer Price Index; base: 1977 = 100)

	1998	1999	2000
Food	390.2	456.5	518.5
Clothing	286.1	324.8	375.9
Rent, fuel and power	216.5	225.6	242.2
All items (incl. others)	411.0	472.4	546.1

Source: National Statistical Office, *Statistical Digest 2000.*

2001 (base: 2000 = 100): All items 109.3 (Source: IMF, *International Financial Statistics*).

NATIONAL ACCOUNTS (million kina at current prices)

National Income and Product

	1997	1998	1999
Compensation of employees	1,778.3	1,751.6	1,852.4
Operating surplus	3,963.2	4,804.6	5,519.4
Domestic factor incomes	5,741.5	6,556.2	7,371.8
Consumption of fixed capital	535.2	539.6	526.5
Gross domestic product (GDP) at factor cost	6,276.7	7,095.8	7,898.3
Indirect taxes / *Less* Subsidies	787.0	692.6	882.4
GDP in purchasers' values	7,063.7	7,788.5	8,780.8
Net factor income from abroad	–310.4	–343.3	–360.1
Gross national product	6,753.3	7,445.2	8,420.7
Less Consumption of fixed capital*	535.2	539.6	526.5
National income in market prices	6,218.1	6,905.6	7,894.2

Expenditure on the Gross Domestic Product

	1997	1998	1999
Government final consumption expenditure	1,361.3	1,406.6	1,488.3
Private final consumption expenditure	4,118.8	4,619.5	6,122.8
Increase in stocks	408.9	306.7	376.6
Gross fixed capital formation	1,079.4	1,088.6	1,062.7
Total domestic expenditure	6,968.3	7,421.4	9,050.4
Exports of goods and services	3,312.0	3,942.3	4,153.2
Less Imports of goods and services	3,216.5	3,575.1	4,422.8
GDP in purchasers' values	7,063.7	7,788.5	8,780.8
GDP at constant 1983 prices	3,674.6	3,536.1	3,803.5

Source: National Statistical Office and Bank of Papua New Guinea.

Gross Domestic Product by Economic Activity

	1999	2000*	2001*
Agriculture, hunting, forestry and fishing	2,520.6	2,638.0	2,847.7
Mining and quarrying	2,086.6	2,662.7	2,745.1
Manufacturing	797.6	793.6	857.9
Electricity, gas and water	100.2	113.1	131.8
Construction	364.1	356.5	349.3
Wholesale and retail trade	834.4	833.6	866.1
Transport, storage and communications	429.6	430.9	430.9
Finance, insurance, real estate and business services	89.7†	321.6	358.1
Community, social and personal services (incl. defence)	1,096.1	1,179.9	1,253.4
Sub-total	8,318.9	9,329.9	9,840.3
Import duties	461.9	320.6‡	237.5‡
GDP in purchasers' values	8,780.8	9,650.5	10,077.8

* Estimates.

† After deducting imputed bank service charge.

‡ After deducting imputed bank service charge and subsidies.

Source: Asian Development Bank, *Key Indicators of Developing Asian and Pacific Countries.*

BALANCE OF PAYMENTS (US $ million)

	1997	1998	1999
Exports of goods f.o.b.	2,160.1	1,773.3	1,927.4
Imports of goods f.o.b.	–1,483.3	–1,078.3	–1,071.4
Trade balance	676.8	695.0	856.0
Exports of services	396.9	318.0	247.8
Imports of services	–923.6	–793.8	–728.1
Balance on goods and services	150.1	219.2	375.6
Other income received	35.1	20.9	18.6
Other income paid	–344.8	–279.7	–291.1
Balance on goods, services and income	–159.5	–39.6	103.1
Current transfers received	69.9	82.4	60.3
Current transfers paid	–102.6	–71.6	–68.7
Current balance	–192.2	–28.9	94.7
Direct investment from abroad	28.6	109.6	296.5
Portfolio investment assets	–25.5	87.0	89.0
Other investment assets	29.6	–55.0	12.8
Other investment liabilities	–24.7	–321.2	–382.3
Net errors and omissions	7.3	–12.5	14.3
Overall balance	–177.0	–221.0	125.0

Source: IMF, *International Financial Statistics.*

2000 (US $ million): Exports of goods f.o.b. 2,214.5; Imports of goods c.i.f. –1,501.9; Trade balance 712.6; Balance on goods and services 103.6; Unrequited transfers 178; Current balance 281.6; Overall balance 70.0.

Source: IMF, *Papua New Guinea: Recent Economic Developments* (October 2001).

External Trade

PRINCIPAL COMMODITIES

Imports f.o.b. (US $ million)*	1998
Food and live animals	220.2
Meat and meat preparations	44.0
Fresh, chilled or frozen meat	40.9
Cereals and cereal preparations	105.3
Rice	75.0
Milled or semi-milled rice	49.1
Chemicals and related products	130.5
Basic manufactures	275.7
Iron and steel	44.1
Iron or steel structures and parts	53.1
Machinery and transport equipment	529.1
Power-generating machinery and equipment	47.8
Machinery specialized for particular industries	71.7
General industrial machinery and equipment	105.2
Electrical machinery, apparatus and appliances, etc.	75.9
Road vehicles and parts†	145.1
Motor vehicles for goods transport	66.8
Other transport equipment and parts†	56.3
Miscellaneous manufactured articles	111.9
Total (incl. others)	1,360.1

* Figures include migrants' and travellers' dutiable effects, but exclude military equipment and some parcel post.

† Data on parts exclude tyres, engines and electrical parts.

Source: UN, *International Trade Statistics Yearbook.*

Total imports (million kina): 3,059.1 in 1999 (Source: UN, *Statistical Yearbook for Asia and the Pacific*); 2,779.0 in 2000 (Source: Treasury, *Budget 2002*).

Exports f.o.b. (million kina)	1999	2000	2001
Coffee	417	295	189
Logs	266	309	310
Copper	574	595	859
Petroleum	1,382	1,922	1,884
Palm oil	338	307	289
Gold	1,546	1,951	2,115
Cocoa	85	85	110
Total (incl. others)	5,006	5,813	6,093

Source: Asian Development Bank, *Key Indicators of Developing Asian and Pacific Countries.*

PRINCIPAL TRADING PARTNERS (US $ million)

Imports f.o.b. (excl. gold)	1999	2000	2001
Australia	607.7	553.2	543.1
China, People's Republic	29.2	24.9	24.6
Hong Kong	15.7	13.8	9.6
Indonesia	33.4	33.5	33.4
Japan	63.6	45.0	48.0
Malaysia	41.0	38.0	30.7
New Zealand	47.1	42.8	40.9
Singapore	146.4	221.9	193.5
Thailand	20.0	19.3	–
USA	41.0	24.0	22.3
Total (incl. others)	1,143.5	1,113.4	1,058.0

Exports f.o.b. (excl. gold)	1999	2000	2001
Australia	733.8	843.3	711.0
China, People's Repub.	77.7	182.5	203.9
Germany	185.4	116.7	120.2
Indonesia	69.8	76.7	–
Japan	324.9	317.3	287.5
Korea, Repub.	132.0	106.8	78.4
Philippines	52.7	17.2	29.2
United Kingdom	96.6	77.6	51.7
USA	127.5	35.5	39.5
Total (incl. others)	2,792.0	2,820.3	2,777.1

Source: Asian Development Bank, *Key Indicators of Developing Asian and Pacific Countries.*

Transport

ROAD TRAFFIC (licensed vehicles)

	1986	1987	1988
Cars and station wagons	16,574	17,121	17,532
Commercial vehicles	26,989	26,061	29,021
Motor cycles	1,246	1,232	1,204
Tractors	1,287	1,313	1,414

1996 (estimates): Passenger cars 31,000; Lorries and vans 85,000.

Source: IRF, *World Road Statistics.*

SHIPPING

Merchant Fleet (registered at 31 December)

	1999	2000	2001
Number of vessels	105	112	114
Total displacement ('000 grt)	64.8	72.5	77.0

Source: Lloyd's Register-Fairplay, *World Fleet Statistics.*

International Sea-borne Freight Traffic

	1997	1998	1999
Cargo unloaded ('000 metric tons)	2,208.6	2,209.0	2,062.8
Cargo loaded ('000 metric tons)	735.9	823.3	788.1

Source: Papua New Guinea Harbours Board, *Monthly Shipping Register Form.*

CIVIL AVIATION (traffic on scheduled services)

	1996	1997	1998
Kilometres flown (million)	14	15	15
Passengers carried ('000)	970	1,114	1,110
Passenger-km (million)	830	735	736
Total ton-km (million)	94	86	87

Source: UN, *Statistical Yearbook.*

Tourism

FOREIGN TOURIST ARRIVALS

Country of Origin	1998	1999	2000
Australia	35,403	33,818	29,285
Canada	912	923	1,762
Japan	1,834	2,427	3,244
New Zealand	3,661	3,712	2,648
United Kingdom	3,087	3,067	2,279
USA	6,101	5,619	5,429
Total (incl. others)	67,465	67,357	58,448

Source: World Tourism Organization, *Yearbook of Tourism Statistics.*

Receipts from tourism (US $ million): 75 in 1998; 76 in 1999.

Source: World Tourism Organization.

Communications Media

	1998	1999	2000
Television receivers ('000 in use)	20	60	80
Telephones ('000 main lines in use)	56.9	59.8	64.8
Mobile cellular telephones ('000 subscribers)	5.6	7.1	8.6
Internet users ('000)	n.a.	2.0	135.0

Daily newspapers (1996): 2 (combined circulation 65,000 copies).
Radio receivers (1997): 410,000 in use.
Facsimile machines (1994): 795 in use.
Personal computers (estimate, 2001): 300,000 in use.

Sources: UNESCO, *Statistical Yearbook*; International Telecommunication Union.

Education

(1999, unless otherwise indicated)

	Institutions*	Teachers	Students
Pre-primary	29	3,816	119,147
Primary	2,790	16,297	594,444
Secondary	n.a.	3,046	74,042
Tertiary	n.a.	815	13,761

* 1995 figures.

Sources: National Department of Education, *The state of education in PNG* (March 2001); UNESCO, *Statistical Yearbook.*

Adult literacy rate (UNESCO estimates): 63.9% (males 70.6%; females 56.8%) in 2000 (Source: UN Development Programme, *Human Development Report*).

Directory

The Constitution

The present Constitution came into effect on 16 September 1975, when Papua New Guinea became independent. The main provisions of the Constitution are summarized below:

PREAMBLE

The national goals of the Independent State of Papua New Guinea are: integral human development, equality and participation in the development of the country, national sovereignty and self-reliance, conservation of natural resources and the environment and development primarily through the use of Papua New Guinean forms of social, political and economic organization.

BASIC HUMAN RIGHTS

All people are entitled to the fundamental rights and freedoms of the individual whatever their race, tribe, place of origin, political opinion, colour, creed or sex. The individual's rights include the right to freedom, life and the protection of the law, freedom from inhuman treatment, forced labour, arbitrary search and entry, freedom of conscience, thought, religion, expression, assembly, association and employment, and the right to privacy. Papua New Guinea citizens also have the following special rights: the right to vote and stand for public office, the right to freedom of information and of movement, protection from unjust deprivation of property and equality before the law.

THE NATION

Papua New Guinea is a sovereign, independent state. There is a National Capital District which shall be the seat of government.

The Constitution provides for various classes of citizenship. The age of majority is 19 years.

HEAD OF STATE

Her Majesty the Queen of the United Kingdom of Great Britain and Northern Ireland is Queen and Head of State of Papua New Guinea. The Head of State appoints and dismisses the Prime Minister on the proposal of the National Parliament and other ministers on the proposal of the Prime Minister. The Governor-General and Chief Justice are appointed and dismissed on the proposal of the National Executive Council. All the privileges, powers, functions, duties and responsibilities of the Head of State may be exercised or performed through the Governor-General.

Governor-General

The Governor-General must be a citizen who is qualified to be a member of Parliament or who is a mature person of good standing who enjoys the respect of the community. No one is eligible for appointment more than once unless Parliament approves by a two-thirds majority. No one is eligible for a third term. The Governor-General is appointed by the Head of State on the proposal of the National Executive Council in accordance with the decision of Parliament by simple majority vote. He may be dismissed by the Head of State on the proposal of the National Executive Council in accordance with a decision of the Council or of an absolute majority of Parliament. The normal term of office is six years. In the case of temporary or permanent absence, dismissal or suspension he may be replaced temporarily by the Speaker of the National Parliament until such time as a new Governor-General is appointed.

THE GOVERNMENT

The Government comprises the National Parliament, the National Executive and the National Judicial System.

National Parliament

The National Parliament, or the House of Assembly, is a single-chamber legislature of members elected from single-member open or provincial electorates. The National Parliament has 109 members elected by universal adult suffrage. The normal term of office is five years. There is a Speaker and a Deputy Speaker, who must be members of Parliament and must be elected to these posts by Parliament. They cannot serve as government ministers concurrently.

National Executive

The National Executive comprises the Head of State and the National Executive Council. The Prime Minister, who presides over the National Executive Council, is appointed and dismissed by the Head of State on the proposal of Parliament. The other ministers, of whom there shall be not fewer than six nor more than a quarter of the number of members of the Parliament, are appointed and dismissed by the Head of State on the proposal of the Prime Minister. The National Executive Council consists of all the ministers, including the Prime Minister, and is responsible for the executive government of Papua New Guinea.

National Judicial System

The National Judicial System comprises the Supreme Court, the National Court, Local Courts and Village Courts. The judiciary is independent.

The Supreme Court consists of the Chief Justice, the Deputy Chief Justice and the other judges of the National Court. It is the final court of appeal. The Chief Justice is appointed and dismissed by the Head of State on the proposal of the National Executive Council after consultation with the minister responsible for justice. The Deputy Chief Justice and the other judges are appointed by the Judicial and Legal Services Commission. The National Court consists of the Chief Justice, the Deputy Chief Justice and no fewer than four nor more than six other judges.

The Constitution also makes provision for the establishment of the Magisterial Service and the establishment of the posts of Public Prosecutor and the Public Solicitor.

THE STATE SERVICES

The Constitution establishes the following State Services which, with the exception of the Defence Force, are subject to ultimate civilian control.

National Public Service

The Public Service is managed by the Department of Personnel Management which is headed by a Secretary, who is appointed by the National Executive Council on a four-year contract.

Police Force

The Police Force is subject to the control of the National Executive Council through a minister and its function is to preserve peace and good order and to maintain and enforce the law.

Papua New Guinea Defence Force

The Defence Force is subject to the superintendence and control of the National Executive Council through the Minister of Defence. The functions of the Defence Force are to defend Papua New Guinea, to provide assistance to civilian authorities in a civil disaster, in the restoration of public order or during a period of declared national emergency.

The fourth State Service is the Parliamentary Service.

The Constitution also includes sections on Public Finance, the office of the Auditor-General, the Public Accounts Commission and the declaration of a State of National Emergency.

The Government

Head of State: HM Queen ELIZABETH II.

Governor-General: Sir SILAS ATOPARE (appointed 14 November 1997).

NATIONAL EXECUTIVE COUNCIL
(September 2002)

Prime Minister: Sir MICHAEL SOMARE.

Deputy Prime Minister and Minister for Trade and Industry: Dr ALLAN MARAT.

Minister for Agriculture and Livestock: MOSES MALADINA.

Minister for Communications and Information: BEN SEMRI.

Minister for Correctional and Institutional Services: PETER ORESI.

Minister for Culture and Tourism: ALOIS KING.

Minister for Defence: YARKA KAPPA.

Minister for Education, Science and Technology: MICHAEL LAIMO.

Minister for Environment and Conservation: SASA ZIBE.

Minister for Finance and Treasury: BART PHILEMON.

Minister for Fisheries: ANDREW BAING.

Minister for Foreign Affairs and Immigration: Sir RABBIE NAMALIU.

Minister for Forestry: PATRICK PRUAITCH.

Minister for Health: MELCHIOR PEP.

Minister for Housing and Urban Resettlement: YUNTUVI BAO.

Minister for Inter-Government Relations: Sir PETER BARTER.

Minister for Internal Security: YAWA SILUPA.

Minister for Justice: MARK MAIPAKAI.

Minister for Labour andIndustrial Relations: PETER O'NEILL.

Minister for Lands and Physical Planning: ROBERT KOPAOL.

Minister for Mining: SAM AKOITAI.

Minister for National Planning and Monitoring: SINAI BROWN.

Minister for Petroleum and Energy: Sir MOI AVEI.

Minister for Privatization: VINCENT AUALI.

Minister for Public Services: Dr PUKA TEMU.

Minister for Science and Technology: ALPHONESE MOROI.

Minister for Transport and Civil Aviation: DON POLYE.

Minister for Welfare and Social Development: Lady CAROL KIDU.

Minister for Works: GABRIEL KAPRIS.

GOVERNMENT DEPARTMENTS AND OFFICES

Office of the Prime Minister: POB 639, Waigani, NCD; tel. 3276544; fax 3277380; e-mail primeminister@pm.gov.pg; internet www.pm.gov.pg/pmsoffice/PMsoffice.nsf.

Department of Agriculture and Livestock: Spring Garden Rd, POB 417, Konedobu 125, NCD; tel. 3231848; fax 3230563; internet www.agriculture.gov.pg.

Department of the Attorney-General: POB 591, Waigani, NCD; tel. 3230138; fax 3230241.

Department of Commerce and Industry: Central Government Offices, Kumul Ave, Post Office, Wards Strip, Waigani, NCD; tel. 3271115; fax 3271750.

Department of Corrective Institution Services: POB 6889, Boroko, NCD; tel. 3214917; fax 3217686.

Department of Defence: Murray Barracks, Free Mail Bag, Boroko 111, NCD; tel. 3242480; fax 3256117; internet www.defence.gov.pg.

Department of Education: POB 446, Waigani, NCD 131, Fin Corp Haus; tel 3013555; fax 3254648; internet www.education.gov.pg.

Department of Environment and Conservation: POB 6601, Boroko 111, Kamul Ave, Waigani, NCD; tel. 3011607; fax 3011691.

Department of Family and Church Affairs: Ori Lavi Haus, Nita St, POB 7354, Boroko, NCD; tel. 3254566; fax 3251230; internet ww3.datec.com.pg/government/famchurch/default.htm.

Department of Finance and Treasury: POB 710, Waigani, Vulupindi Haus, NCD; internet www.treasury.gov.pg.

Department of Fisheries and Marine Resources: POB 2016, Port Moresby; tel. 3271799; fax 3202074; internet www.fisheries.gov.pg.

Department of Foreign Affairs: Central Government Offices, Kumul Ave, Post Office, Wards Strip, Waigani, NCD; tel. 3271311; fax 3254467.

Department of Health: POB 3991, Boroko, Aopi Centre, Waigani Drive, Waigani; tel. 3254648; fax 3013555; internet www.health.gov.pg.

Department of Housing and Urban Resettlement: POB 1550, Boroko, NCD; tel. 3247200; fax 3259918.

Department of Inter-Government Relations: Somare Haus, Independence Drive, Waigani, POB 1287, Boroko, NCD; tel. 3271787; fax 3211623; e-mail paffairs@dalton.com.pg; internet www.dplga.gov.pg.

Department of Justice: Port Moresby; internet www.justice.gov.pg.

Department of Labour and Employment: POB 5644, Boroko, NCD; tel. 3272262; fax 3257092.

Department of Lands and Physical Planning: POB 233, Boroko, NCD; tel. 3013175; fax 3013299; e-mail lubena@lands.gov.pg; internet www.datec.com.pg/government/lands.

Department of Mineral Resources: PMB PO, Konedobu, Port Moresby 121; tel. 3227600; fax 3213701; internet www.mineral.gov.pg.

Department of Mining: Private Mailbag, Port Moresby Post Office; tel. 3227670; fax 3213958.

Department of Personnel Management: POB 519, Wards Strip, Waigani, NCD; tel. 3276422; fax 3250520; e-mail perrtsiamalili@dpm.gov.pg.

Department of Petroleum and Energy: POB 1993, Port Moresby, NCD; tel. 3224200; fax 3224222; e-mail joseph_gabut@petroleum.gov.pg; internet www.petroleum.gov.pg.

Department of Planning and Implementation: POB 710, Waigani 131, Vulupindi Haus, Port Moresby, NCD; tel. 3288302; fax 3288375.

Department of Police: Police Headquarters, POB 85, Konedobu, NCD; tel. 3226100; fax 3226113; internet www.police.gov.pg.

Department of Private Enterprise: Central Government Offices, Kumul Ave, Post Office, Wards Strip, Waigani, NCD.

Department of Social Welfare and Development, Youth and Women: Maori Kiki Bldg, 2nd Floor, POB 7354, Boroko, NCD; tel. 3254967; fax 3213821.

Department of State: Haus To Makala, 5th Floor, Post Office, Wards Strip, Waigani, NCD; tel. 3276758; fax 3214861.

Department of Trade and Industry: Heduru Haus, Waigani Drive, POB 375, Waigani 131, NCD; tel. 3255311; fax 3254482; internet www.trade.gov.pg.

Department of Transport and Civil Aviation: POB 1489, Port Moresby; tel. 3222580; fax 3200236; e-mail dotdirectro@datec.com.pg.

National Forest Authority: POB 5055, Boroko, Frangipani St, Hohola, Port Moresby; tel. 3277800; fax 3254433; internet ww3.datec.com.pg/government/forest/default.htm.

Office of Peace and Reconstruction (fmrly Office of Bougainville Affairs): Morauta Haus, POB 343, Waigani 131, NCD; tel. 3276760; fax 3258038; internet www.oba.gov.pg.

Office of Civil Aviation: POB 684, Boroko 111, NCD; tel. 3257077; fax 3251919; e-mail dgoca@datec.net.pg; internet www.oca.gov.pg.

Office of Information and Communication: Port Moresby; internet www.communication.gov.pg.

Office of Works: POB 1489, Port Moresby 121, cnr Champion Parade and Musgrave St; tel. 3222500; fax 3200236; internet www.works.gov.pg.

Legislature

NATIONAL PARLIAMENT

The unicameral legislature has 109 elective seats: 89 representing open constituencies and 20 representing provincial constituencies. There is constitutional provision for up to three nominated members.

Speaker: Bill Skate.

General Election, 15 June–29 July 2002

Party	Seats
National Alliance	19
People's Democratic Movement	12
People's Progress Party	8
Pangu Pati	6
People's Action Party	5
People's Labour Party	4
Christian Democratic Party	3
Melanesian Alliance	3
National Party	3
United Party	3
National Transformation Party	2
Pan-Melanesian Congress Party	2
People's National Congress	2
People's Solidarity Party	2
Pipol First Party	2
Rural Pipol's Pati	2
Others and undeclared	14
Independents	17
Total	109

Notes: In many cases party affiliations were subject to review in the immediate aftermath of the election.

Autonomous Region

BOUGAINVILLE INTERIM PROVINCIAL GOVERNMENT—BIPG

The BIPG was formally established following the signing of the 'Loloata Understanding' on 23 March 2000, and is responsible for the island's budget, judicial system and local administration. It is composed of an Executive Council and a 25-member Provincial Assembly, which was appointed by the National Executive Council on the recommendation of the four Bougainville Members of Parliament (who themselves joined the Assembly).

BOUGAINVILLE PEOPLE'S CONGRESS

Prior to the establishment of the BIPG, the Bougainville People's Congress (BPC) officially represented the island of Bougainville. Elections to the Congress were held over several days starting on 3 May 1999. Joseph Kabui was elected President, winning 77 of the 87 votes. A Congressional Executive Council, comprising 29 members, was subsequently appointed by Kabui. Although the BPC unanimously endorsed the 'Loloata Understanding', it did not actively participate in the newly-established BIPG.

President: Joseph Kabui.

Vice-President: James Tanis.

Speaker: Linus Konukong.

Political Organizations

Bougainville Revolutionary Army (BRA): demands full independence for island of Bougainville; Leaders Francis Ona, Ismael Toroama.

League for National Advancement (LNA): POB 6101, Boroko, NCD; f. 1986; Leader John Nilkare.

Melanesian Labour Party: Port Moresby; Leader Paul Mondia.

Melanesian United Front: Boroko, NCD; f. 1988; fmrly Morobe Independent Group; Leader Utula Samana.

National Alliance Party: c/o National Parliament, Port Moresby; f. 1996 to combat corruption in public life; Leader Sir Michael Somare.

National Party (NP): Private Bag, Boroko, NCD; f. 1979; fmrly People's United Front; Leader MICHAEL MEL.

Pangu (Papua New Guinea Unity) Pati: POB 289, Waigani, NCD; tel. 3277628; fax 3277611; f. 1968; urban and rural-based; Leader CHRIS HAIVETA.

People's Action Party (PAP): Boroko, NCD; tel. 3251343; f. 1985; Leader TED DIRO.

People's Democratic Movement (PDM): POB 972, Boroko, NCD; f. 1985; merged with Advance PNG Party in 2001; Leader Sir MEKERE MORAUTA.

People's National Alliance (PNA): c/o National Parliament, Port Moresby; f. 1999 by merger of following:

Melanesian Alliance (MA): Port Moresby; tel. 3277635; f. 1978; socialist; Chair. Fr JOHN MOMIS; Gen. Sec. FABIAN WAU KAWA.

Movement for Greater Autonomy: Manus Province; Leader STEPHEN POKAWIN.

People's National Party: Port Moresby.

People's National Congress (PNC): c/o National Parliament, Port Moresby; Leader BILL SKATE.

People's Progress Party (PPP): POB 6030, Boroko, NCD; f. 1970; Leader MICHAEL NALI; Nat. Chair. GLEN KUNDIN.

People's Unity Party: c/o National Parliament, Port Moresby; Leader ALFRED KAIABE.

United Resource Party (URP): Port Moresby; f. 1997; aims to secure greater representation in Government for resource owners; Leader MASKET IANGALIO; Chair. PITA IPATAS.

Diplomatic Representation

EMBASSIES AND HIGH COMMISSIONS IN PAPUA NEW GUINEA

Australia: POB 129, Waigani, NCD; tel. 3259333; fax 3259183; High Commissioner: NICK WARNER.

China, People's Republic: POB 1351, Boroko, NCD; tel. 3259836; fax 3258247; e-mail chnempng@daltron.com.pg; Ambassador: ZHAO ZHENYU.

Fiji: Defence House, 4th Floor, Champion Parade, Port Moresby, NCD; tel. 3211914; fax 3217220; e-mail fiji_high_com@datec .com.pg; High Commissioner: SEVOKE NAQIOLEVU.

France: Pacific Place, 12th Floor, Musgrave St, POB 1155, Port Moresby; tel. 3215550; fax 3215549; e-mail ambfrpom@ global.net.pg; Ambassador: THIERRY BERNADAC.

Holy See: POB 98, Port Moresby; tel. 3256021; fax 3252844; e-mail nunciaturepng@datec.net.pg; Apostolic Nuncio: Archbishop ADOLFO TITO YLLANA.

India: Port Moresby; tel. 3254757; fax 3253138; e-mail hcipom@ datec.net.pg; High Commissioner: BASANT K. GUPTA.

Indonesia: 1-2/410 Kiroki St, Sir John Guise Dr., Waigani, NCD; tel. 3253116; fax 3253544; e-mail kbripom@daltron.com.pg; Ambassador: (vacant).

Japan: Cuthbertson House, Cuthbertson St, POB 1040, Port Moresby; tel. 3211800; fax 3217906; Ambassador: TATSUO TANAKA.

Korea, Republic: Pacific View Apts, Lot 1, sec. 84, Pruth St, Korobosea, Port Moresby; tel. 3254755; fax 3259996; Ambassador: Dr SEO HYUN-SEOP.

Malaysia: POB 1400, Pacific View Apts, Units 1 and 3, 2nd floor, Pruth St, Kovobosea, Port Moresby; tel. 3252076; fax 3252784; e-mail mwpom@datec.com.pg; High Commissioner: MOHAMAD FADZIL AYOB.

New Zealand: Embassy Drive, POB 1051, Waigani, NCD; tel. 3259444; fax 3250565; e-mail nzhc@dg.com.pg; High Commissioner: CHRIS SEED.

Philippines: POB 5916, Boroko, NCD; tel. 3256577; fax 3231803; e-mail pomphpem@datec.com.pg; Ambassador: BIENVENIDO TEJANO.

Solomon Islands: Port Moresby; High Commissioner: PHILIP KAPINI.

United Kingdom: Kiroki St, POB 212, Waigani 131, NCD; tel. 3251677; fax 3253547; e-mail bhcpng@datec.com.pg; High Commissioner: SIMON SCADDAN.

USA: Douglas St, POB 1492, Port Moresby; tel. 3211455; fax 3213423; internet www.altnews.com.au/usembassy; Ambassador: SUSAN S. JACOBS.

Judicial System

The Supreme Court is the highest judicial authority in the country, and deals with all matters involving the interpretation of the Constitution, and with appeals from the National Court. The National Court has unlimited jurisdiction in both civil and criminal matters. All National Court Judges (except acting Judges) are Judges of the Supreme Court. District Courts are responsible for civil cases involving compensation, for some indictable offences and for the more serious summary offences, while Local Courts deal with minor offences and with such matters as custody of children under the provision of Custom. There are also Children's Courts, which judge cases involving minors. Appeal from the District, Local and Children's Courts lies to the National Court. District and Local Land Courts deal with disputes relating to Customary land, and Warden's Courts with civil cases relating to mining. In addition, there are other courts with responsibility for determining ownership of government land and for assessing the right of Customary landowners to compensation. Village Courts, which are presided over by Magistrates with no formal legal qualification, are responsible for all Customary matters not dealt with by other courts.

Supreme Court of Papua New Guinea: POB 7018, Boroko, NCD; tel. 3245700; fax 3234492; Chief Justice Sir MARI KAPI.

Attorney-General: MICHAEL GENE.

Religion

The belief in magic or sorcery is widespread, even among the significant proportion of the population that has adopted Christianity (nominally 97% in 1990). Pantheism also survives. There are many missionary societies.

CHRISTIANITY

Papua New Guinea Council of Churches: POB 1015, Boroko, NCD; tel. 3259961; fax 3251206; f. 1965; seven mem. churches; Chair. EDEA KIDU; Gen. Sec. SOPHIA W. R. GEGEYO.

The Anglican Communion

Formerly part of the Province of Queensland within the Church of England in Australia (now the Anglican Church of Australia), Papua New Guinea became an independent Province in 1977. The Anglican Church of Papua New Guinea comprises five dioceses and had 246,000 members in 2000.

Archbishop of Papua New Guinea and Bishop of Aipo Rongo: Most Rev. JAMES AYONG, POB 893, Mount Hagen, Western Highlands Province; tel. 5421131; fax 5421181; e-mail acpnghgn@global.net.pg.

General Secretary: MARTIN GARDHAM, POB 673, Lae, Morobe Province; tel. 4724111; fax 4721852; e-mail acpng@global.net.pg.

The Roman Catholic Church

For ecclesiastical purposes, Papua New Guinea comprises four archdioceses and 14 dioceses. At 31 December 2000 there were 1,630,289 adherents.

Catholic Bishops' Conference of Papua New Guinea and Solomon Islands: POB 398, Waigani, NCD; tel. 3259577; fax 3232551; e-mail cbc@dg.com.pg; f. 1959; Pres. Most Rev. STEPHEN REICHERT, Bishop of Mendi; Gen. Sec. LAWRENCE STEPHENS.

Archbishop of Madang: Most Rev. WILLIAM KURTZ, Archbishop's Residence, POB 750, Madang; tel. 8522946; fax 8522596; e-mail Kurtz_caom@global.net.pg.

Archbishop of Mount Hagen: Most Rev. MICHAEL MEIER, Archbishop's Office, POB 54, Mount Hagen, Western Highlands Province; tel. 5421245; fax 5422128; e-mail archdios@online.net.pg.

Archbishop of Port Moresby: Most Rev. BRIAN BARNES, Archbishop's House, POB 1032, Boroko, NCD; tel. 3251192; fax 3256731; e-mail archpom@daltron.com.pg.

Archbishop of Rabaul: Most Rev. KARL HESSE, Archbishop's House, POB 357, Kokopo, East New Britain Province; tel. 9828369; fax 9828404; e-mail abkhesse@online.net.pg.

Other Christian Churches

Baptist Union of Papua New Guinea Inc: POB 705, Mount Hagen, Western Highlands Province; tel. 5522364; fax 5522402; f. 1976; Administrator JOSEPH SILIPIN; 36,000 mems.

Evangelical Lutheran Church of Papua New Guinea: Bishop Rt Rev. WESLEY KIGASUNG, POB 80, Lae, Morobe Province; tel. 4723711; fax 4721056; e-mail bishop@elcpng.org.pg; f. 1956; Sec. REUBEN KURE; 815,000 mems.

Gutnius Lutheran Church of Papua New Guinea: Bishop Rev. DAVID P. PISO, POB 111, 291 Wabag, Enga Province; tel. 5471002; f. 1948; Gen. Sec. RICHARD R. MOSES; 95,000 mems.

Papua New Guinea Union Mission of the Seventh-day Adventist Church: POB 86, Lae, Morobe Province 411; tel. 4721488; fax 4721873; Pres. Pastor WILSON STEPHEN; Sec. Pastor BRADLEY RICHARD KEMP; 200,000 adherents.

The United Church in Papua New Guinea: POB 1401, Port Moresby; tel. 3211744; fax 3214930; f. 1968 by union of the Methodist Church in Melanesia, the Papua Ekalesia and United Church, Port Moresby; Moderator Rev. SAMSON LOWA; 600,000 mems; Gen. Sec. DEMAS TONGOGO APELIS.

BAHÁ'Í FAITH

National Spiritual Assembly: Private Mail Bag, Boroko, NCD; tel. 3250286; fax 3236474; e-mail nsapng@datec.net.pg.

ISLAM

In 2000 the Muslim community in Papua New Guinea numbered about 1,500, of whom approximately two-thirds were believed to be expatriates. The religion was introduced to the island in the 1970s. The first mosque there was opened in late 2000 at Poreporena Highway, Hohola, Port Moresby; Imam KHALID ARAI (acting).

The Press

There are numerous newspapers and magazines published by government departments, statutory organizations, missions, sporting organizations, local government councils and regional authorities. They are variously in English, Tok Pisin (Pidgin), Motu and vernacular languages.

Ailans Nius: POB 1239, Rabaul, East New Britain Province; weekly.

Foreign Affairs Review: Dept of Foreign Affairs, Central Government Offices, Kumul Ave, Post Office, Wards Strip, Waigani, NCD; tel. 3271401; fax 3254886.

Hailans Nius: Mount Hagen, Western Highlands Province; weekly.

The Independent: POB 1982, Boroko, NCD; tel. 3252500; fax 3252579; e-mail word@global.net.pg; internet www.niugini.com/independent; f. 1995 to replace the Times of Papua New Guinea; weekly; English; published by Word Publishing Co Pty Ltd; Publr ANNA SOLOMON; Editor DOMINIC KAKAS; circ. 9,000.

Lae Nius: POB 759, Lae, Morobe Province; 2 a week.

The National: POB 6817, Boroko, NCD; tel. 3246731; fax 3246868; e-mail national@thenational.com.pg; internet www.thenational.com.pg; f. 1993; daily; Editor FRANK SENGE KOLMA; circ. 21,036.

Niugini Nius: POB 3019, Boroko, NCD; tel. 3252177; e-mail niusedita@pactok.net; internet pactok.net.au/docs/nius/; daily.

Papua and New Guinea Education Gazette: Dept of Education, PSA Haus, POB 446, Waigani, NCD; tel. 3272413; fax 3254648; monthly; Editor J. OBERLENTER; circ. 8,000.

Papua New Guinea Post-Courier: POB 85, Port Moresby; tel. 3091000; fax 3212721; e-mail postcourier@ssp.com.pg; internet www.postcourier.com.pg; f. 1969; daily; English; published by News Corpn; Gen. Man. TONY YIANNI; Editor OSEAH PHILEMON; circ. 25,044.

PNG Business: POB 1982, Boroko, NCD; tel. 3252500; fax 3252579; e-mail word@global.net.pg; monthly; English; Editor ABBY YADI; circ. 12,000.

Wantok (Friend) Niuspepa: POB 1982, Boroko, NCD; tel. 3252500; fax 3252579; e-mail word@global.net.pg; f. 1970; weekly in New Guinea Pidgin; mainly rural readership; Publr ANNA SOLOMON; Editor LEO WAFIWA; circ. 15,300.

Publishers

Gordon and Gotch (PNG) Pty Ltd: POB 107, Boroko, NCD; tel. 3254855; fax 3250950; e-mail ggpng@online.net.pg; f. 1970; books, magazines and stationery; Gen. Man. PETER G. PORTER.

Scripture Union of Papua New Guinea: POB 280, University, Boroko, NCD; tel. and fax 3253987; f. 1966; religious; Chair. RAVA TAVIRI.

Word Publishing Co Pty Ltd: POB 1982, Boroko, NCD; tel. 3252500; fax 3252579; e-mail word@global.net.pg; f. 1979; 60% owned by the Roman Catholic Church, 20% by Evangelical Lutheran, 10% by Anglican and 10% by United Churches; Gen. Man. (acting) and Publr ANNA SOLOMON.

Broadcasting and Communications

TELECOMMUNICATIONS

Office of Information and Communication: POB 639, Waigani; tel. 3256853; fax 3250412; internet www.communication.gov.pg.

Papua New Guinea Telecommunication Authority (Pangtel): POB 8444, Boroko, NCD; tel. 3258633; fax 3256868; internet www.pangtel.gov.pg; f. 1997; CEO PHILIP AEAVA.

Telikom PNG Pty Ltd: POB 1349, Boroko, NCD; tel. 3004010; fax 3250665; CEO SUNIL ANDRADI; Chair. PILA NININGI.

BROADCASTING

Radio

National Broadcasting Corporation of Papua New Guinea: POB 1359, Boroko, NCD; tel. 3255233; fax 3230404; e-mail md.nbc@global.net.pg; f. 1973; commercial and free govt radio programmes services; broadcasting in English, Melanesian, Pidgin, Motu and 30 vernacular languages; Chair. CHRIS RANGATIN; Man. Dir Dr KRISTOFFA NINKAMA.

Kalang Service (FM): POB 1359, Boroko, NCD; tel. 3255233; commercial radio co established by National Broadcasting Commission; Chair. CAROLUS KETSIMUR.

Nau FM/Yumi FM: POB 774, Port Moresby; tel. 3201996; fax 3201995; internet www.naufm.com.pg; f. 1994; Gen. Mans MARK ROGERS, JUSTIN KILI.

Television

EM TV: POB 443, Boroko, NCD; tel. 3257322; fax 3254450; e-mail emtv@emtv.com.pg; internet www.emtv.com.pg; f. 1988; operated by Media Niugini Pty Ltd; CEO STEPHEN SMITH.

Media Niugini Pty Ltd: POB 443, Boroko, NCD; tel. 3257322; fax 3254450; e-mail emtv@emtv.com.pg; internet www.emtv.com.pg; f. 1987; owned by Nine Network Australia; CEO STEPHEN SMITH.

Finance

(cap. = capital; res = reserves; dep. = deposits; m. = million; brs = branches; amounts in kina unless otherwise stated)

BANKING

Central Bank

Bank of Papua New Guinea: Douglas St, POB 121, Port Moresby; tel. 3227200; fax 3211617; e-mail bpng@datec.com.pg; internet www.datec.com.pg/bpng/bpng.nsf; f. 1973; bank of issue since 1975; sold to Bank of South Pacific in 2002; cap. 62.0m., res 271.5m., dep. 375.8m. (Dec. 1999); Gov. WILSON KAMIT.

Commercial Banks

Australia and New Zealand Banking Group (PNG) Limited: Defens Haus, 3rd Floor, cnr of Champion Parade and Hunter St, POB 1152, Port Moresby; tel. 3223333; fax 3223306; f. 1976; cap. 4.7m., res 1.1m., dep. 494.1m. (Sept. 1998); Chair. R. G. LYON; Man. Dir A. MARLIN; 8 brs.

Bank of Hawaii (PNG) Ltd: Burns House, Champion Parade, POB 1390, Port Moresby; tel. 3213533; fax 3213115; e-mail bohpng@datec.com.pg; f. 1983 as Indosuez Niugini Bank Ltd, name changed in 1997; the bank was expected to cease operations in 2001/02; cap. 3.0m., res 0.8m., dep. 121.1m. (Dec. 1997); Chair. M. BAVER; Man. Dir JOHN SHEATHER; 2 brs.

Bank of South Pacific Ltd: Douglas St, POB 173, Port Moresby; tel. 3212444; fax 3200053; e-mail service@bsp.com.pg; internet www.bsp.com.pg; f. 1974; acquired from National Australia Bank Ltd by Papua New Guinea consortium (National Investment Holdings, now BSP Holdings Ltd) in 1993; cap. 17.9m., res 13.8m., dep. 519.8m. (Dec. 2000); Chair. NOREO BEANGKE; Man. Dir NOEL R. SMITH; 8 brs and 2 sub-brs.

MBf Finance (PNG) Ltd: Elsa Beach Towers, Ground Floor, cnr of Musgrave St, POB 329, Port Moresby; tel. 3213555; fax 3213480; f. 1989.

Maybank (PNG) Ltd: Waigani, NCD; f. 1995.

Papua New Guinea Banking Corporation: cnr of Douglas and Musgrave Sts, POB 78, Port Moresby; tel. 3229700; fax 3211683; f. 1974; corporatized in 2001; cap. 11.3m., res 72.9m., dep. 978.8m. (Dec. 1997); Chair. ROGER PALME; Man. Dir HENRY FABILA; 34 brs.

Westpac Bank—PNG—Ltd: Mogoru Motu Bldg, 5th Floor, Champion Parade, POB 706, Port Moresby; tel. 3220800; fax 3213367; e-mail westpacpng@westpac.com.au; f. 1910 as Bank of New South Wales, present name since 1982; 90% owned by Westpac Banking Corpn, Australia; cap. 5.8m., res 6.1m., dep. 554.7m. (Sept. 1999); Chair. ALAN WALTER; Man. Dir SIMON MILLETT; 15 brs.

Development Bank

Rural Development Bank of Papua New Guinea: Somare Crescent, POB 686, Waigani, NCD; tel. 3247500; fax 3259817; f. 1967; cap. 32.6m., res U17.1m. (Dec. 1992); statutory govt agency; Chair. ROGER PALME; Man. Dir SHEM M. PAKE; 10 brs.

Savings and Loan Societies

Registry of Savings and Loan Societies: Financial System Supervision Dept, POB 121, Port Moresby; tel. 3227200; fax 3214548; 101 savings and loan societies; 125,306 mems (2001); total funds 163.5m., loans outstanding 90.0m., investments 21.4m. (June 2001); CEO ELIZABETH GIMA.

STOCK EXCHANGE

Port Moresby Stock Exchange (POMSoX) Ltd: Level 4, Defens Haus, POB 1531, Port Moresby; tel. 3201980; fax 3201981; e-mail pomsox@datec.com.pg; internet www.pomsox.com.pg; f. 1999; Chair. Sir ANTHONY SIAGURU; Gen. Man. EMILY GEORGE TAULE.

INSURANCE

Niugini Insurance Corporation Ltd: POB 331, Port Moresby; tel. 3214077; fax 3217898; f. 1978; govt-owned; Chair. JACOB POPUNA; Man. Dir DARRYL G. NATHAN.

Pan Asia Pacific Assurance (PNG) Pty Ltd (PAPA): Port Moresby; f. 1993; Chair. BENIAS SABUMEI.

There are branches of several Australian and United Kingdom insurance companies in Port Moresby, Rabaul, Lae and Kieta.

Trade and Industry

GOVERNMENT AGENCIES

Investment Corporation of Papua New Guinea: Hunter St, POB 155, Port Moresby; tel. 3212855; fax 3211240; f. 1971 as govt body to support local enterprise and to purchase shares in foreign businesses operating in Papua New Guinea; partially transferred to private ownership in 1993.

Investment Promotion Authority (IPA): POB 5053, Boroko, NCD 111; tel. 3217311; fax 3212819; e-mail iepd@ipa.gov.pg; internet www.ipa.gov.pg; f. 1992, following reorganization of National Investment and Development Authority; a statutory body responsible for the promotion of foreign investment; the first contact point for foreign investors for advice on project proposals and approvals of applications for registration to conduct business in the country; contributes to planning for investment and recommends priority areas for investment to the Govt; also co-ordinates investment proposals; Man. Dir SIMON PETER (acting).

Privatization Commission: Port Moresby; f. 1999 to oversee transfer of state-owned enterprises to private ownership; Exec. Chair. BEN MICAH.

DEVELOPMENT ORGANIZATIONS

CDC Capital Partners Ltd: CDC Haus, 2nd Floor, POB 907, Port Moresby; tel. 3212944; fax 3212867; e-mail png@cdc.com.pg; internet www.cdcgroup.com; fmrly Commonwealth Development Corpn; Man. Dir ASHLEY EMBERSON-BAIN.

Industrial Centres Development Corporation: POB 1571, Boroko, NCD; tel. 3232913; fax 3231109; promotes foreign investment in non-mining sectors through establishment of manufacturing facilities.

CHAMBERS OF COMMERCE

Papua New Guinea Chamber of Commerce and Industry: POB 1621, Port Moresby; tel. 3213057; fax 3210566; e-mail pngcci@global.net.pg; Pres. MICHAEL MAYBERRY; Vice-Pres. PHILIP FRANKLIN.

Papua New Guinea Chamber of Mines and Petroleum: POB 1032, Port Moresby; tel. 3212988; fax 3217107; e-mail ga@pngchamberminpet.com.pg; internet www.pngchamberminpet.com.pg; Exec. Dir GREG ANDERSON; Pres. PETER BOTTEN.

Port Moresby Chamber of Commerce and Industry: POB 1764, Port Moresby; tel. 3213077; fax 3214203; Pres. CES IEWAGO.

Lae Chamber of Commerce and Industry: POB 265, Lae, Morobe Province.

INDUSTRIAL AND TRADE ASSOCIATIONS

Cocoa Board of Papua New Guinea: POB 1165, Madaney; tel. 8823253; fax 8822198; f. 1974; Chair. SAM TULO.

Coffee Industry Corpn Ltd: POB 137, Goroka, Eastern Highlands Province; tel. 721266; fax 721431; e-mail webmaster@gka.coffeecorp.org.pg; internet www.coffeecorp.org.pg; CEO BADIRA VARI.

Fishing Industry Association (PNG) Inc: POB 2340, Boroko, NCD; e-mail netshop1@daltron.com.pg. Chair. MAURICE BROWNJOHN.

Forest Industries Association: POB 5055, Boroko, NCD; Pres. GARY HONEY; CEO ROBERT TATE.

Higaturu Oil Palms Pty Ltd: POB 28, Popondetta, Oro Province; tel. 3297177; fax 3297137; f. 1976; jtly owned by the Commonwealth Development Corpn (UK) and the Papua New Guinea Govt; major producer of palm oil and cocoa; Gen. Man. RICHARD CASKIE.

Kopra Indasrti Korporesen (KIK): Port Moresby; markets all copra in Papua New Guinea; consists of a chair. and mems representing producers; formerly known as the Copra Marketing Board of Papua New Guinea; Chair. ROBINSON NAMALIU; Gen. Man. TED SITAPAI.

Manufacturers' Council of Papua New Guinea: POB 598, Port Moresby; tel. 3259512; fax 3230199; e-mail pngmadecouncil@datec.com.pg; internet www.pngmade.org.pg; Chair. WAYNE GOLDING; CEO MARYANNE MCDONALD.

National Contractors' Association: Port Moresby; formed by construction cos for the promotion of education, training and professional conduct in the construction industry; Pres. ROY THORPE.

National Fisheries Authority: POB 2016, Port Moresby; tel. 3212643; fax 3202074; Dep. Man. Dir MICHAEL BATTY.

National Housing Corpn (NHC): POB 1550, Boroko NCD; tel. 3247000; fax 3254363; Man. Dir GABRIEL TOVO.

New Britain Palm Oil Ltd: POB 389, Kimbe, West New Britain; tel. 9852177; fax 9852003; e-mail nbpol@nbpol.com.pg; f. 1967; 80% owned by Kulim (Malaysia), 20% owned by Govt, employees and local producers; major producer of palm oil, coffee trader and exporter, supplier of high quality oil palm seed; Man. Dir NICK THOMPSON; Sec. ALLAN MORROW.

Niugini Produce Marketing Pty Ltd: Lae, Morobe Province; f. 1982; govt-owned; handles distribution of fruit and vegetables throughout the country.

Palm Oil Producers Association: Port Moresby; Exec. Sec. ALLAN MAINO.

Papua New Guinea Forest Authority: POB 5055, Boroko, NCD; tel. 3277800; fax 3254433; Man. Dir THOMAS NEN.

Papua New Guinea Growers Association: Port Moresby; Pres. VALENTINE KAMBORI.

Papua New Guinea Holdings Corpn: POB 131, Port Moresby; fax 3217545; f. 1992; responsible for managing govt privatization programme; Chair. MICHAEL MEL; Man. Dir PETER STEELE.

Papua New Guinea Log Carriers Association: f. 1993.

Pita Lus National Silk Institute: Kagamuga, Mount Hagen, Western Highlands Province; f. 1978; govt silk-producing project.

Rural Industries Council: Chair. PETER COLTON.

UTILITIES

Electricity

PNG Electricity Commission (Elcom): POB 1105, Boroko, NCD; tel. 3243200; fax 3214051; plans to privatize the organization were announced in 1999; Chair. PAUL AISA; Chief Exec. SEV MASO.

Water

Eda Ranu (Our Water): POB 1084, Waigani, NCD; tel. 3122100; fax 3122190; e-mail enquiries@edaranu.com.pg; internet www.edaranu.com.pg; fmrly Port Moresby Water Supply Company; Gen. Man. BILLY IMAR.

PNG Waterboard: POB 2779, Boroko, NCD; tel. 3235700; fax 3236317; e-mail pamini@pngwater.com.pg; f. 1986; govt-owned; operates 12 water supply systems throughout the country; Man. Dir PATRICK AMINI.

MAJOR COMPANIES

General

Collins and Leahy Holdings Ltd: ANZ House, Second Floor, Central Avenue, Lae; tel. 4722644; fax 7321946; f.1970; Chair. Sir MICHAEL BROMLEY; Sec. C.I. CUNNIMGHAME.

Kagamuga Natural Products Co Pty Ltd: POB 74, Mount Hagen, Western Highlands Province; tel. 551225; fax 551329; pyrethrum extract and vegetable seeds.

Steamships Trading Co Ltd: POB 1, Port Moresby; tel. 3220222; fax 3213595; hotels, department stores, food and hardware, wholesale and retail; quarrying, manufactures building materials, fibreglass products and UHT products; stevedoring, shipping; road transport, automotive distributors and car rentals; property management; Chair. E. J. R. SCOTT.

Thiess Watkins PNG Ltd: POB 1393, Boroko, NCD; tel. 253466; building contractors, civil engineers, property developers and property management; operates throughout Papua New Guinea.

Food, Drink and Tobacco

Angco Ltd: POB 136, Goroka, Eastern Highlands Province; tel. 7321677; fax 7322154; e-mail angco@global.net.pg; coffee and cocoa exporters; coffee and cocoa plantation managers and developers; CEO DAVID ANDERSON; Chair. THOMAS NEGINTS.

Associated Mills Ltd: POB 1906, Lae, Morobe Province; tel. 4723555; fax 4723424; flour milling; Gen. Man. JIM GREGG.

W. R. Carpenter & Co Estates: POB 94, Mount Hagen, Western Highlands Province; tel. 5422700; fax 5421616; e-mail sales@wrcarpenters.com.pg; internet www.wrcarpenters.com.pg; coffee, cocoa and tea processing; Gen. Man. MARTIN EMSLIE.

Niugini Coffee, Tea and Spice Co Pty Ltd: POB 2531, Lae, Morobe Province; tel. 4725633; fax 4725614; Gen. Man. BRIAN STEVENSON.

Ramu Sugar Ltd: Port Moresby; sugar processing; Gen. Man. ERROL JOHNSTON; Chair. PETER COLTON.

SP Brewery Ltd: POB 6550, Boroko, NCD; tel. 3128200; fax 3250656; f. 1951; beer; Chair. J. TAUVASA; Gen. Man. HEIN VAN DORT.

Star-Kist PNG Pty Ltd: POB 1341, Rabaul, East New Britain Province; fish processing.

Tanubada Dairy Products Pty Ltd: POB 6203, Boroko, NCD; tel. 3212522; fax 3212774; reconstituted milk, ice cream, ice confection, orange drinks; Gen. Man. JOHN GOODWIN.

Tokua Plantation Pty Ltd: POB 65, Kokopo; tel.9839370; fax 9839370; copra and cocoa production; Gen. Man. JOHN CARROLL.

Wills (PNG) Ltd: Modilon Rd, POB 678, Madang; tel. 8523788; fax 8523667; cigarettes and tobacco.

Minerals and Heavy Engineering

Barclay Bros (NG) Pty Ltd: POB 1180, Boroko, NCD; tel. 255711; fax 250094; all types of civil engineering and building construction.

Bishop Bros Engineering Pty Ltd: POB 9081, Hohola; tel. 252900; all types of civil engineering.

Bougainville Copper Ltd: Pacific Place, Level 6, cnr Champion Parade, POB 1274, Port Moresby; tel. 3212044; fax 3213634; e-mail pcoleman-rtm@daltron.com.pg; f.1967; 53.6% owned by Rio Tinto Ltd (Australia), 19.1% state-owned,27.3% owned by public shareholders; Chair. BARRY CUSACK; Sec. PAUL D. COLEMAN.

Hebou Constructions (PNG) Pty Ltd: POB 6207, Boroko, NCD; tel. 3253077; fax 3253441; e-mail info@constant.com.pg; building, civil construction, sand and gravel, timber, hotels.

Highlands Pacific Ltd: Pacific Place, Level 9, cnr Champion Parade, Port Moresby; tel. 3217633; fax 3217551; e-mail info@highlandspacific.com; internet www.highlandspacific.com; exploration for gold, nickel, cobalt, copper and other minerals; Chair. ROBERT BRYAN; Man. Dir IAN R. HOLZBERGER.

Hornibrook NGI Pty Ltd: Spring Garden Rd, Hohola, Port Moresby, NCD; tel. 3253099; fax 3250387; e-mail hngi@datec.com.pg; civil engineering and steel manufacture, pre-fabricated buildings, bridges, tubular fabrications, plant hire; f. 1991; Man. Dir MALCOLM LEWIS.

Lihir Gold Ltd: POB 789, Port Moresby; tel. 3217711; fax 3214705; e-mail anr@lihir.com.pg; internet www.lihir.com.pg; mining; owned by Rio Tinto plc; gold mining on Lihir Island; Chair. ROSS GARNAUT; CEO ALAN ROBERTS.

Mobil Oil New Guinea Ltd: 5th Floor, Credit House, Cuthbertson St, Port Moresby; tel. 3212055; fax 3222100; sale and distribution of fuel; operation of service stations; Area Man. NAMAR T. MAWASON.

Monier (PNG) Ltd: POB 328, Port Moresby; tel. 3253344; fax 3253389; concrete pipes, masonry blocks and roofing tiles, cement supplies, pre-cast concrete, sand and gravel; paints; fibreglass and plastic products; Gen. Man. DUNCAN FRASER.

Naco (NG) Pty Ltd: POB 707, Port Moresby; aluminium windows and sliding doors, louvre windows and metal blades.

Niugini Mining Ltd: developers of the Lihir Island gold project; Chair. GEOFF LOUDON.

Oil Search Ltd: MMI House, POB 1031, Port Moresby; tel. 3213177; fax 3214379; e-mail gmarsden@osl.com.au; internet www.oilsearch.com.au; sales US $90.8m., cap and res US $308.8m. (1998); oil and gas exploration; Chair. TREVOR J. KENNEDY; Man. Dir PETER R. BOTTEN.

Ok Tedi Mining Ltd: POB 1, Tabubil, Western Province; tel. 5483213; fax 5489314; e-mail info@oktedi.com; internet www.oktedi.com; gold and copper mining; 52.6% owned by BHP (Australia), 17.4% owned by Inmet Mining Corpn (Canada), 30% govt.-owned; Man. Dir JOHN GRUBB; CEO CHRISTOPHER M. BROWN; Exec. Man.PAUL JOHNSON.

Orogen Minerals Ltd: Musgrave St, POB 2151, Port Moresby; tel. 3217600; fax 3202209; e-mail sling@datec.com.pg; internet www.orogen.com.au; merged with Oil Search Ltd in March 2002; 18% govt-owned, 82% privately-owned; Chair. LINDSAY MACALISTER; Man. Dir FRANCIS KAUPA.

PNG Oil Refinery Pty Ltd: POB 1071, Boroko, NCD; e-mail hunterd@syd.egis.com; Port Moresby; Chair. SAM PEPENA.

Pacrim Energy Ltd: c/o Sinton Spence Chartered Accountants, POB 6861,Boroko, NCD; tel. 3257611; fax 3259389; e-mail info@pacrimenergy.com.au; f.1988; owned by Pacarc NL; petroleum exploration; Chair. Sir BARRY HOLLOWAY.

Pangpang Development Corpn Pty Ltd: f. 1992 by Lihir Island landowners to participate in business generated by the Lihir gold project.

Uni Group: Boroko, NCD; tel. 260433; civil engineering and building contractors.

United Pacific Drilling (PNG) Pty Ltd: Fikus St, POB 108, Madang; tel. 8522411; fax 8522830; e-mail wkh1@orica.com.au; mineral exploration; Gen. Man. WILLIAM HUGHES.

Timber and Palm Oil

ANG Timbers Pty Ltd: POB 1984, Boroko, NCD; tel. 253966; timber and timber products.

Higaturu Oil Palms Pty Ltd: (see Industrial and Trade Associations, above).

Jant Pty Ltd: POB 714, Madang; wood chips, milled timber.

Milne Bay Estates Pty Ltd: POB 36, Alotau; tel. 6411211; fax 3252959; palm oil production; Gen. Man. JOHN CHESTER.

New Britain Palm Oil Development Ltd: (see Industrial and Trade Associations, above).

Open Bay Timber Pty Ltd: POB 1020, Rabaul, East New Britain Province; tel. 9821633; fax 9821220; e-mail obterry@global.net.pg; milled timber, mouldings, scantlings, log and sawn timber export, reafforestation; Gen. Man TOSHIHARU SHINOHARA; Man. Dir TERRY SAKAKI.

PNG Forest Products Pty Ltd: POB 89, Lae, MP411; tel. 4724944; fax 4726017; plywood, mouldings, milled timber, furniture; Gen. Man. GERRY MASSINGHAM.

Pasis Manua Inland Timber Resources Pty Ltd: f. 1992 by landowners in Kandrian district.

Stettin Bay Lumber Co Pty Ltd: POB 162, Kimbe, West New Britain Province; tel. 983266; fax 9835225; timber merchants; Man. Dir S. FUJIKAWA.

Taway Timbers Pty Ltd: POB 515, Madang; tel. 8523517; fax 8523384; Gen Man. EDDIE FITZGERALD.

Unevulg Development Pty Ltd (UDPL): West New Britain Province; logging; plans to diversify into coconut oil production.

Chemicals

BOC Gases Papua New Guinea: POB 93, Lae, Morobe Province; tel. 4722377; fax 4726177; industrial gases, oxygen, dissolved acetylene, nitrogen, argons, medical gases, pestigas, insectigas and deodour gas; cutting and welding equipment and consumables; Man. Dir BARRY BURKE.

Boral Gas (PNG) Pty Ltd: POB 1468, Boroko, NCD; tel. 3214248; fax 3211570; distribution of LPG; Man. Dir ROY VEERHUIS.

Colgate Palmolive (PNG) Ltd: POB 981, Lae, Morobe Province; tel. 4723166; fax 4726280; soap; Gen. Man. MICHAEL BUBB.

Shell Papua New Guinea Ltd: POB 169, Port Moresby; tel. 3228700; fax 3211840; aviation fuel, other fuels, lubricants and industrial chemicals; Gen. Man. DON MANOA.

TRADE UNIONS

The Industrial Organizations Ordinance requires all industrial organizations that consist of no fewer than 20 employees or four employers to register. In 1977 there were 56 registered industrial organizations, including a general employee group registered as a workers' association in each province and also unions covering a specific industry or profession.

Papua New Guinea Trade Unions Congress (PNGTUC): POB 254, Boroko, NCD; tel. 3212132; fax 3212498; e-mail tucl@daltron.com.pg; Pres. GASPER LAPAN; Gen. Sec. JOHN PASKA; 52 affiliates, 76,000 mems.

The following are among the major trade unions:

Bougainville Mining Workers' Union: POB 777, Panguna, North Solomons Province; tel. 9958272; Pres. MATHEW TUKAN; Gen. Sec. ALFRED ELISHA TAGORNOM.

Central Province Building and Construction Industry Workers' Union: POB 265, Port Moresby.

Central Province Transport Drivers' and Workers' Union: POB 265, Port Moresby.

Employers' Federation of Papua New Guinea: POB 490, Port Moresby; tel. 3214772; fax 3214070; f. 1963; Pres. G. J. DUNLOP; Exec. Dir TAU NANA; 170 mems.

National Federation of Timber Workers: Madang; f. 1993; Gen. Sec. MATHIAS KENUANGI (acting).

Papua New Guinea Communication Workers' Union: Pres. GASPER LAPAN; Gen. Sec. EMMANUEL KAIRU.

Papua New Guinea National Doctors' Association: Pres. Dr Bob Danaya; 225 mems.

Papua New Guinea Teachers' Association: POB 1027, Waigani, NCD; tel. 3262588; f. 1971; Pres. TAINA DAI; Gen. Sec. LEONARD JONLI; 13,345 mems.

Papua New Guinea Waterside Workers' and Seamen's Union: Port Moresby; f. 1979; an amalgamation of four unions; Sec. AUGUSTINE WAVIKI.

Police Association of Papua New Guinea: POB 903, Port Moresby; tel. 3214172; f. 1964; Pres. A. AVIAISA; Gen. Sec. (vacant); 4,596 mems.

Port Moresby Council of Trade Unions: POB 265, Boroko, NCD; Gen. Sec. JOHN KOSI.

Port Moresby Miscellaneous Workers' Union: POB 265, Boroko, NCD.

Printing and Kindred Industries Union: Port Moresby.

Public Employees' Association: POB 965, Boroko, NCD; tel. 3252955; fax 3252186; f. 1974; Pres. NAPOLEON LIOSI; Gen. Sec. JACK N. KUTAL; 28,000 mems.

Transport

There are no railways in Papua New Guinea. The capital city, Port Moresby, is not connected by road to other major population centres. Therefore, air and sea travel are of particular importance.

ROADS

In 1999 there were an estimated 19,600 km of roads in Papua New Guinea, of which 3.5% were paved. In 1995 the Australian Government announced that it was to donate $A155m. over five years for major road-building projects in Papua New Guinea. In 1998 the European Union (EU) committed €24m. over two years to upgrade the Lae–Madang Highway. Japan offered a grant-in-aid in 1998 of 940m. yen for the reconstruction of a bridge on the Highlands Highway. In October 2000 it was announced that this highway was also to be upgraded over six years at a cost of 26.3m. kina financed through a loan negotiated with the Asian Development Bank (ADB).

SHIPPING

Papua New Guinea has 16 major ports and a coastal fleet of about 300 vessels. In early 1999 a feasibility study was commissioned to investigate the possible relocation of port facilities in Port Moresby.

Papua New Guinea Harbours Board: POB 671, Port Moresby; tel. 3211400; fax 3211546; Chair. TIMOTHY BONGA.

Port Authority of Kieta: POB 149, Kieta, North Solomons Province; tel. 9956066; fax 9956255; Port Man. SAKEUS GEM.

Port Authority of Lae: POB 563, Lae, Morobe Province; tel. 4422477; fax 4422543; Port Man. JOSHUA TARUNA.

Port Authority of Madang: POB 273, Madang; tel. 8523381; fax 8523097; Port Man. WILLIE WANANGA.

Port Authority of Port Moresby: POB 671, Port Moresby; tel. 211400; fax 3211546; Gen. Man. T. AMAO.

Port Authority of Rabaul: POB 592, Rabaul, East New Britain Province; tel. 9821533; fax 9821535.

Shipping Companies

Coastal Shipping Pty Co Ltd: Sulphur Creek Rd, POB 423, Rabaul, East New Britain Province; tel. 9828518; fax 9828519.

Lutheran Shipping: POB 1459, Lae, Morobe Province; tel. 4722066; fax 4725806.

Morehead Shipping Pty Ltd: POB 1908, Lae, Morobe Province; tel. 4423602.

New Guinea Australia Line Pty Ltd: POB 145, Port Moresby; tel. 3212377; fax 3214879; e-mail ngal@daltron.com.pg; f. 1970; operates regular container services between Australia, Papua New Guinea, Singapore, Indonesia, Vanuatu, Tuvalu and Solomon Islands; Chair. (vacant); Gen. Man. GEOFFREY CUNDLE.

P & O PNG Ltd: trading as Century Shipping Agencies; MMI House, 3rd Floor, Champion Parade, POB 1403, Port Moresby; tel. 3229200; fax 3229251; e-mail cgcpom@popng.com.pg; owned by P & O (Australia); Gen. Man. ANDREW CRIDLAND.

Papua New Guinea Shipping Corporation Pty Ltd: POB 634, Port Moresby; tel. 3220290; fax 3212815; e-mail shipping@steamships.com.pg; f. 1977; owned by Steamships Trading Co Ltd; provides a container/break-bulk service to Australia and the Pacific islands; Chair. CHRISTOPHER PRATT; Man. Dir JOHN DUNLOP.

South Sea Lines Proprietary Ltd: POB 5, Lae, Morobe Province; tel. 4423455; fax 4424884; Man. Dir R. CUNNINGHAM.

Western Tug & Barge Co P/L: POB 175, Port Moresby; tel. 3212099; fax 3217950; shipowning arm of P & O PNG; operates 24 vessels.

CIVIL AVIATION

There is an international airport at Port Moresby, Jackson's Airport, and there are more than 400 other airports and airstrips throughout the country. International services from Lae and Mount Hagen airports began in March 1999. A programme to upgrade eight regional airports over three years, with finance of $A30m. from the Australian Government, was initiated in mid-1997. New domestic and international terminal buildings were opened at Jackson's Airport in 1998, following a 13-year project financed with K120m. from the Japanese Government. A project to redevelop Tari airport was announced in late 1999. It was expected that, following redevelopment, the airport would receive international flights.

Air Niugini: POB 7186, Boroko, NCD; tel. 3259000; fax 3273482; e-mail airniugini@airniugini.com.pg; internet www.airniugini.com.pg; f. 1973; govt-owned national airline (plans to privatize the airline were announced in 1999); operates scheduled domestic cargo and passenger services within Papua New Guinea and international services to Australia, Solomon Islands, Philippines and Singapore; a new service to Tokyo, Japan, was expected to commence in 2002; Chair. JOSEPH PHILLIP KAPAL; CEO PETER ROBERTS; Man. Dir MICHAEL BULEAU (acting).

MBA Pty Ltd: POB 170, Boroko, NCD; tel. 3252011; fax 3252219; e-mail mba@mbapng.com; internet www.mbapng.com; f. 1984; operates domestic scheduled and charter services; Chair. and CEO JOHN R. WILD; Gen. Man. SIMON D. WILD.

Tourism

Despite Papua New Guinea's spectacular scenery and abundant wildlife, tourism makes only a small contribution to the economy. In 1998 there were 4,280 hotel beds. In 1999 visitor arrivals totalled some 58,000. The industry earned an estimated US $76m. in 1999.

PNG Tourism Promotion Authority: POB 1291, Port Moresby; tel. 3200211; fax 3200223; e-mail tourismpng@dg.com.pg; internet www.paradiselive.org.pg; CEO JOHN KAMBOWA.

Defence

In March 1975 the Papua New Guinea Government assumed responsibility for defence from the Australian Government. In August 2001 the fully integrated Papua New Guinea defence force had a total strength of some 4,400 (army 3,800, navy 400 and air force 200). Military service is voluntary. In mid-1989 the paramilitary border patrol police numbered 4,600. Australian training forces stationed in the country totalled 38. In addition, the 300-strong Bougainville Peace Monitoring Group included 149 Australian troops, the others being from New Zealand, Fiji and Vanuatu. Government expenditure on defence in 2001 was estimated at K90m.

Commander-in-Chief of Papua New Guinea Defence Force: Col CARL MALPO.

Education

Education from pre-school to tertiary level is available in Papua New Guinea, although facilities remain inadequate and unevenly distributed. In 1995 there were 2,790 primary schools, with 516,797 pupils. In 1986 there were 116 secondary schools and 103 technical and vocational schools. Secondary-school pupils totalled 78,759 in 1995. There are two universities.

Children attend school from seven years of age. At the age of 13 they move from community schools to provincial high schools for a further three years and are then eligible to spend another two years at the national high schools, where they are prepared for entrance to tertiary education. Originally schooling was free, but in recent years fees and charges for equipment have been introduced.

In 1995 the total enrolment at public primary schools was equivalent to 82% of that school-age population (males 88%; females 75%). In the same year secondary enrolment was equivalent to only 14% of children in the relevant age-group (boys 17%; girls 11%). In some areas, such as East New Britain and Port Moresby, almost all eligible children attend primary schools, whereas in others, such as the Highlands provinces, attendance is as low as 34%. Access to secondary education ranges from 7% in the Eastern Highlands to almost 50% in East New Britain. In 2000, according to UNESCO estimates, adult illiteracy averaged 63.9% (males 70.6%; females 56.8%).

Budgetary expenditure on education by the central Government in 1994 totalled K286.8m., equivalent to 17.6% of total spending.

Samoa

Physical and Social Geography

The Independent State of Samoa (formerly Western Samoa) comprises the two large islands of Savai'i and Upolu and seven small islands, of which five are uninhabited. Their total area is 2,831 sq km (1,093 sq miles). These high volcanic islands, with rugged interiors and little flat land except along the coasts, lie in the South Pacific, about 2,400 km north of New Zealand. The country's nearest neighbour is American Samoa, to the east. The climate is tropical, with temperatures generally between 23°C (73°F) and 30°C (86°F). The rainy season is from November to April.

At the census of November 2001 the population of Samoa totalled 176,848. About 75% of the population resided on the island of Upolu. The population of Apia, the capital, totalled 34,126 in November 1991.

History

The islands are peopled by Polynesians and are thought to have been the origin of many of the people who now occupy islands further east. The Samoan language is believed to be the oldest extant form of Polynesian speech. Samoan society developed an intricate hierarchy of graded titles comprising titular chiefs and orator chiefs. One of the striking features of modern Samoa is the manner in which these titles and the culture prior to European contact remain a dominant influence. Most of the population have become Christians.

The Samoan islands were first visited by Europeans in the 1700s, but it was not until 1830 that missionaries from the London Missionary Society settled there. The eastern islands (now American Samoa) were ceded to the USA in 1904 but Western Samoa (as it was known until July 1997), a former German colony, was occupied by New Zealand in 1914 and the League of Nations granted a mandate over the territory to New Zealand in 1920. In 1946 the United Nations assumed responsibility for the Territory of Western Samoa through its Trusteeship Council, with New Zealand as the administering power. From 1954 measures of internal self-government were gradually introduced, culminating in the adoption of an independence Constitution in October 1960. This was approved by a UN-supervised plebiscite in May 1961 and the islands became independent on 1 January 1962. The office of Head of State was to be held jointly by two of the paramount chiefs but, upon the death of his colleague in April 1963, Malietoa Tanumafili II became sole Head of State for life.

Samoa has had a Legislative Assembly (Fono) since 1947. Since independence the islands have been governed under a parliamentary system, with a Prime Minister and Cabinet. Until 1991, only two of the 47 seats in the Fono were decided by universal suffrage, the rest being decided by the Matai (elected clan chiefs). The 1973 elections were won by Fiame Mata'afa Fuamui Mulinuu, who was first elected Prime Minister in 1959 but who lost the position in 1970 to Tupua Tamasese Lealofi. Fiame Mata'afa Mulinuu became Prime Minister again in 1973, remaining in office until his death in 1975, when Tupua Tamasese Lealofi was recalled to complete the term of office. Tupuola Taisi Efi was elected Prime Minister in March 1976 and re-elected in February 1979. Elections in February 1982 resulted in a victory for the opposition Human Rights Protection Party (HRPP), which won 24 of the 47 seats in the Fono. Va'ai Kolone was elected Prime Minister but was dismissed in September when a court ruled that he had won his seat improperly. Efi was restored as Prime Minister, but resigned in December 1982 after the Fono had rejected his budget. He was replaced by the new HRPP leader, Tofilau Eti Alesana. At elections in February 1985, the HRPP won 31 of the 47 seats, increasing its majority in the Fono from one to 15 seats. In December Tofilau Eti resigned, following the rejection of the proposed budget by the Fono, and Va'ai Kolone was again appointed Prime Minister. Tupua Tamasese Efi replaced Va'ai Kolone as leader of the ruling coalition in February 1988, immediately prior to a general election, at which both the HRPP and the Samoa National Development Party (SNDP) coalition initially secured 23 seats, with one constituency being tied. When two recounts proved inconclusive, a third was presided over by a New Zealand judge who declared the Christian Democratic Party (CDP) candidate the winner. Before a new government could be formed, however, a member of the SNDP, newly elected to the Fono, transferred allegiance to the HRPP. In April Tofilau Eti was re-elected Prime Minister and a new Government, comprising HRPP members, was formed.

Legislation proposed in early 1990 which would permit local village councils to fine or impose forced labour or exile on individuals accused of offending communal rules was widely perceived as a government attempt to gain the support of the Matai (elected clan chiefs, see above) for the next general election. In the late 1980s and early 1990s the number of Matai titles increased significantly, and this was perceived to have greatly undermined the system of chiefly leadership. A referendum was conducted in October 1990, at which voters narrowly accepted government proposals for the introduction of universal suffrage. A second proposal, to create an upper legislative chamber composed of the Matai, was rejected. A bill to implement universal adult suffrage was approved by the Fono in December 1990, despite strong opposition from the SNDP.

A general election was held in April 1991 (postponed from February, owing to the need to register an estimated 80,000 newly-enfranchised voters). In the following weeks election petitions were filed with the Supreme Court against 11 newly-elected members of the Fono who were accused of corrupt or illegal electoral practices. Moreover, subsequent political manoeuvring resulted in the HRPP increasing its parliamentary representation from an initial 26 to 30 seats, while the SNDP ultimately secured only 16 seats in the Fono, and the remaining seat was retained by an independent. At the first meeting of the new Fono, convened in early May, Tofilau Eti was re-elected for what, he later announced, would be his final term of office as Prime Minister.

In November 1991 the Fono approved legislation to increase the parliamentary term from three to five years and to create an additional two seats in the Fono. These seats were contested in early 1992 and won by the HRPP.

In December 1991 the islands were struck by a devastating cyclone (Cyclone Val), which caused 13 deaths and damage estimated at 662m. tala. This was the second major cyclone to hit Western Samoa in two years, the first being Cyclone Ofa in February 1990, which left an estimated 10,000 islanders homeless. The dramatic increase in the incidence of cyclones occurring in the region was widely attributed to climatic change caused by the 'greenhouse effect' (the heating of the earth's atmosphere as a consequence of pollution).

The introduction of a value-added tax on goods and services in January 1994 (which greatly increased the price of food and fuel in the country) provoked a series of demonstrations and protest rallies, as well as demands for the resignation of the Prime Minister. As a result of overwhelming opposition to the new regulations, the Government agreed, in March, to amend the most controversial aspects of the tax. Meanwhile, four members of the Fono (including three recently-expelled HRPP members), who had opposed the financial reforms, established a new political organization, the Samoa Liberal Party, under the leadership of the former Speaker, Nonumalo Leulumoega Sofara.

In May 1994 treasury officials warned the Government that the financial crisis at the national airline, Polynesian Airlines, was threatening the country's economic stability. It was estimated that the company's debts totalled more than 45m. tala. A report by the Chief Auditor, Tom Overhoff, accused the Government of serious financial mismanagement relating to a series of decisions to commit public funds to the airline, and charged seven cabinet ministers with fraud and negligence in their handling of government resources. An inquiry into the allegations conducted in late 1994 cleared the ministers in question of all the charges, although its findings were harshly criticized by Overhoff, who claimed that the inquiry had been neither independent nor impartial.

Protests against the value-added tax on goods and services continued in early 1995, following the Government's decision to charge two prominent members of the Tumua ma Pule group of traditional leaders and former members of the Fono, with sedition, for organizing demonstrations against the tax during 1994. In March 1995 3,000 people delivered a petition to the Prime Minister, bearing the signatures of 120,000 people (some 75% of the population), that demanded that the tax be revoked. The Prime Minister questioned the authenticity of the signatures and appointed a 14-member committee to investigate the matter. In late June the case against the two members of Tumua ma Pule, which had attracted attention from several international organizations (including the World Council of Churches and Amnesty International) was dismissed on the grounds of insufficient evidence.

In December 1995 the HRPP unanimously re-elected Tofilau Eti as the leader of the party, despite concern over the Prime Minister's deteriorating health, as well as a previous declaration that he would retire from politics upon completion of his current term in office.

In March 1996 one of the two female members of the Fono, Matatumua Naimoaga, left the HRPP in order to form the Samoa

All-People's Party. The formation of the new party, in preparation for the forthcoming general election, was reportedly a result of dissatisfaction with the Government's alleged mismanagement of public assets together with concern over corruption. Legislation was introduced in April, which attempted to distinguish between the traditional Samoan practice of exchanging gifts and acts of bribery, amid numerous reports that voters were demanding gifts and favours from electoral candidates in return for their support.

A general election took place on 26 April 1996. The opposition was highly critical of the delay in the counting of votes (which took some three weeks in total), claiming that the length of time involved allowed the HRPP to recruit successful independent candidates in an attempt to secure a majority of seats in the Fono. It was eventually announced in mid-May that the HRPP had secured a total of 28 seats (with the recruitment of several independent members to their ranks), the SNDP had won 14 seats and independent candidates had secured seven. Tofilau Eti was subsequently re-elected as Prime Minister, defeating the Leader of the Opposition, Tuiatua Tupua Tamasese, with 34 votes to 14.

The issue of government involvement in the media became prominent in early 1997, following Tuiatua Tupua Tamasese's decision to be interviewed on Australian radio. In the interview he urged overseas donors to withhold aid from Western Samoa, alleging widespread mismanagement and corrupt practice within the Government. The opposition leader responded to criticism of his action by denouncing the government policy that denies opposition politicians access to the state-controlled media, and by urging New Zealand to persuade the Western Samoan Government to reform the system.

The strength of traditional religious beliefs among Samoans and resistance to foreign influences on their culture was illustrated in early 1997. In March a member of the Church of Jesus Christ of Latter-day Saints (Mormon the fastest-growing denomination in the country) was tied to a stake surrounded by kindling when he refused to obey a banishment order for criticizing the village council's decision to prevent the construction of a Mormon church in the village. The intended victim was rescued by police officers and church leaders, who negotiated his release from the villagers. A request by the Samoa Council of Churches to impose a ban on the establishment of new churches in the country was refused by the Government as incompatible with the principle of freedom of religion, as guaranteed in the Constitution. The organization was also highly critical of a US religious television channel due to begin operating in the islands in April, claiming that the evangelical style of religion depicted would undermine traditional Samoan Christianity.

In May 1997 the Prime Minister proposed a constitutional amendment in the Fono to change the country's name to Samoa. (The country has been known simply as Samoa at the UN since it was admitted to the organization in 1976.) On 3 July the Fono voted by 41 votes to one to approve the change, which came into effect on the next day when the legislation was signed by the Head of State. The neighbouring US territory of American Samoa, however, expressed dissatisfaction with the change (which was believed to undermine the Samoan identity of its islands and inhabitants), and in September introduced legislation to prohibit the recognition of the new name within the territory. In March 1998 the House of Representatives in American Samoa voted against legislation that proposed not to recognize Samoan passports (thereby preventing Samoans from travelling to the territory), but decided to continue to refer to the country as Western Samoa and to its inhabitants as Western Samoans. Nevertheless, in January 2000 Samoa and American Samoa signed a memorandum of understanding, increasing co-operation in areas including health, trade and education.

A series of reports in *The Samoa Observer* in mid-1997 alleged that a serious financial scandal involving the disappearance of some 500 blank passports, and their subsequent sale to Hong Kong Chinese for up to US $26,000 each, had occurred. The Government refused to comment on the newspaper's allegations, stating only that several senior immigration officials had been suspended pending the outcome of an investigation into the affair. Moreover, the Government subsequently brought charges of defamatory libel against the editor, Savea Sano Malifa, for publishing a letter criticizing the Prime Minister (who was reported to have told the Fono of his intention to change legislation governing business licences, such that publications could have their licences withdrawn for publishing dissenting material). The regional organization, the Pacific Islands News Association, also condemned the Prime Minister's comments as an attack on freedom of information and expression. The continued existence of the newspaper was placed in jeopardy when Savea Sano Malifa was found guilty of defaming the Prime Minister in two libel cases in July and September 1998, and was ordered to pay a total of some US $17,000 in costs. The newspaper had alleged that public funds had been used to construct a hotel owned by the Prime Minister and had criticized the allocation of US $0.25m. in the 1998 budget for Tofilau Eti's legal costs. The Government's increasingly autocratic style, its apparent intolerance of dissent and the perceived lack of accountability of its members, coupled with its poor economic record, resulted in frequent expressions of popular discontent during 1997. These culminated in a series of protest marches in late 1997 and early 1998, organized by the Tumua ma Pule group of chiefs and attended by several thousand people, which aimed to increase pressure on the Prime Minister to resign.

In November 1998 Tofilau Eti Alesana resigned as Prime Minister, owing to ill health. He was replaced by the Deputy Prime Minister, Tuila'epa Sailele Malielegaoi, and, at the same time, the Cabinet was reshuffled. Tofilau Eti Alesana died in March 1999.

In July 1999 the Minister of Public Works, Luagalau Levaula Kamu, was shot dead while attending an event commemorating the 20th anniversary of the foundation of the ruling HRPP. Speculation followed that the killer's intended target had been the Prime Minister, but this was denied both by Tuila'epa Sailele and by the New Zealand police officers sent to the island to assist in the investigation. A man identified as Eletise Leafa Vitale (son of the Minister of Women's Affairs, Leafa Vitale) was arrested and charged with the murder. Eletise Leafa Vitale was convicted of the murder and sentenced to death (subsequently commuted to life imprisonment). Leafa Vitale was also subsequently charged with the murder of Kamu, together with the former Minister of Telecommunications, Toi Akuso, who faced additional charges of incitement to murder Kamu and the Prime Minister, Tuila'epa Sailele. Both of the men were found guilty in April 2000 and were also sentenced to death (which was similarly commuted to life imprisonment; no death sentence had been carried out since Samoa's independence). It later emerged that Kamu had been killed in an attempt to prevent him from uncovering incidences of corruption and bribery in which the two ministers had become involved.

Meanwhile, in November 1999 the ruling HRPP increased its number of seats in the Fono to 34 (out of a possible 49) following the defection of an independent candidate to the HRPP. By-elections for the two imprisoned former ministers' seats were held in June 2000, and HRPP candidates were successful in both constituencies.

In August 2000 a supreme court ruling ordered the Government to allow opposition politicians access to the state-controlled media. For several years the opposition had been denied free access to the media (see above).

At a general election on 2 March 2001 the HRPP won 22 seats, the SNDP secured 13 seats and independent candidates won 14 seats. On 16 March Tuila'epa Sailele won 28 votes in the Fono, after securing the support of six independents, to be re-elected Prime Minister. However, the opposition mounted a number of legal challenges to his election. In August eight elected members of Parliament, including the Deputy Prime Minister, the Minister of Health and the Minister of Internal Affairs, Women's Affairs and Broadcasting, faced charges of electoral malpractice in the Supreme Court. None of the Cabinet Ministers was found guilty, and by-elections for the vacant parliamentary seats were held in October and November. The HRPP won all four contested seats.

An Electoral Commission, established shortly after the March elections, published its recommendations in October 2001, urging the replacement of the two Individual Voters Roll seats with two Urban Seats and that government employees who wished to stand for Parliament should first be obliged to resign from their offices.

Despite independence, Samoa still has strong links with New Zealand, where many Samoans now live and where many others received their secondary and tertiary education. An appeal against attempts to curb the high level of migration to New Zealand led the Privy Council in London to rule in July 1982 that all Western Samoans born between 1924 and 1949, and their male children, were entitled to New Zealand citizenship. The ruling was estimated to affect about 100,000 Western Samoans. However, in August 1982 the New Zealand and Western Samoan Governments agreed to annul the ruling, declaring in its stead that illegal immigrants already in New Zealand would be allowed to apply for citizenship, and that a quota of 1,100 migrants per year would be accepted into New Zealand. In June 2002 New Zealand formally apologized for the mistakes it had committed while administering Samoa during 1914–62. These injustices included New Zealand's poor handling of the 1918 influenza pandemic (which had killed 22% of Samoa's population within a fortnight, the virus having been brought in on a ship from New Zealand); the murder of a Samoan paramount chief and independence leader, Tupua Tamasese Lealofi III, and the killing of nine other supporters of the pacifist Mau movement during a non-violent protest in 1929; and the banishment of native leaders, who were also stripped of their chiefly titles. The apology, while accepted, drew mixed reactions from Samoans, many of whom were more concerned with the issue of the restoration of their rights to New Zealand citizenship, as upheld by the Privy Council in 1982.

The announcement in mid-1995 by the French Government that it was to resume nuclear-weapons testing in the South Pacific provoked large-scale demonstrations in Apia and statements of condemnation by the Government, which introduced an indefinite ban on visits to the islands by French warships and aircraft. The tests were concluded in January 1996.

Economy

In 2000, according to estimates by the World Bank, the country's gross national product (GNP), measured at average 1998–2000 prices, stood at US $246.4m., equivalent to US $1,460 per head (or US $5,090 per head on an international purchasing-power parity basis). During 1990–99 GNP per head increased, in real terms, by an annual average of 0.6%. During 1990–98, the population increased by an annual average of 0.8%. Samoa's gross domestic product (GDP) increased by an average annual rate of 2.5% during 1990–2000. GDP increased, in real terms, by 5.6% in 1999 and by 7.0% in 2000. According to revised figures from the Asian Development Bank (ADB), it was estimated that GDP had increased by 6.5% in 2001.

Agriculture, forestry and fishing engaged 63.6% of the labour force in 1986, but provided only 14.2% of GDP in 2001. Between 1994 and 2000, according to the ADB, agricultural GDP increased, in real terms, at an average annual rate of 5.0%. The principal cash crops are coconuts (in total, coconut oil, cream and copra accounted for 15.0% of exports in 2000, however this declined to just 7.9% in 2001 owing to the fact that the coconut oil mill had remained closed for much of 2000) and taro (also the country's primary staple food). Sales of taro provided 58% of all domestic export earnings in 1993, but an outbreak of taro leaf blight devastated the crop in 1994 and reduced exports to almost nil in that year and subsequently. A campaign to revive the taro industry was launched in mid-2000; exports of taro accounted for 1.6% of total exports in 2001. Small quantities of timber are also exported. Breadfruit, yams, maize, passion fruit and mangoes are cultivated as food crops. Pigs, cattle, poultry and goats are raised, mainly for local consumption. The country's commercial fishing industry expanded considerably in the late 1990s, with export revenues rising from US $4.8m. (33.0% of domestic export earnings) in 1997 to $24.7m. (55.2%) in 2000. The fishing industry it contributed 7.6% of GDP in 2000. In real terms, the GDP of the entire agricultural sector declined by 3.5% in 1999 and increased by 0.3% in 2000, before decreasing by 4.6%% in 2001.

Industry (comprising mining, manufacturing, construction and utilities) provided 25.9% of GDP in 2001 and employed 5.5% of the labour force in 1986. Between 1994 and 2000 manufacturing GDP decreased, in real terms, at an average annual rate of 1.5%, expanding by 11.3% in 2000 and by 11.1% in 2001. Manufacturing provided 16.0% of GDP in 2001 and (with mining) engaged 3.5% of the labour force in 1986. Traditionally, the principal manufactures have been beverages (beer—which accounted for 5.8% of exports in 2001—and soft drinks), coconut-based products and cigarettes. (The coconut oil mill, however, remained closed for much of 2000. The manufacturing sector expanded considerably in the early 1990s with the establishment of a Japanese-owned factory, producing electrical components for road motor vehicles. The Yazaki Samoa factory engaged about 2,500 workers in 1996, making it the largest private-sector employer in the country. The factory assembles wire harnessing systems that are exported to car-manufacturing plants in Australia. Shipments from the Yazaki factory are generally excluded from official statistics for visible (merchandise) exports. Instead, the value added by the plant is recorded as part of 'invisible' trade, in the services account of the balance of payments. Net receipts from the harness assembly trade increased from US $5.7m. in 1995 to US $8.2m. in 1996 and to US $9.7m. in 1997; however, in 1997 the factory's operations were restructured, with output subsequently reduced. Net receipts in the first nine months of 1998 were about US $3.6m., only one-half of the total in the corresponding period of the previous year. Nevertheless, the initial success of the venture, and the availability of government incentives for export processing activities, encouraged further investment in the manufacturing sector. A chocolate factory, processing locally-grown cocoa, has been built with assistance from foreign aid funds. The clothing industry has also expanded, and in 2001 garments accounted for 10.4% of total export earnings.

With the opening of a 3,500-kW hydroelectric power station at Sauniatu in 1985, the country's dependence on imported diesel fuel for electric power generation was reduced from 80% of the total to about 40%. Imports of petroleum accounted for 12.4% of the value of total imports in 2001.

Services engaged 29.5% of the labour force in 1986 and accounted for 59.9% of GDP in 2001. Between 1994 and 2000, according to ADB figures, the sector's GDP increased at an average annual rate of 6.9%. Compared with the previous year, the GDP of the services sector expanded by 7.6% in 2000 and by 8.4% in 2001. Measures to encourage the development of tourism were undertaken during the 1980s, including the expansion of hotel facilities and improvements to the road network and airport. However, financial difficulties within the national airline, Polynesian Airlines, led to the disruption of services in 1994. The tourism sector performed well in 2000, as a result of the completion of new tourist facilities. The sector also benefited from political instability in Fiji and the Solomon Islands. Tourist revenues, including the proportion of international travel credited to carriers based in Samoa, totalled an estimated 133.07m. tala in 2000, compared with 125.80m. tala in 1999.

In 2000 the country recorded a visible trade deficit of US $73.4m., and there was a surplus of $8.9m. on the current account of the balance of payments. In 2001 Australia was Samoa's principal trading partner, providing 21.6% of imports and purchasing 64.7% of exports, while the USA provided 26.6% of imports and purchased 11.7% of exports. Other important trading partners were New Zealand, Indonesia and Fiji. The principal exports are fish, garments, coconut products and beer, and the main imports are food and beverages, industrial supplies and fuels.

In the year ending 30 June 2001 there was an overall budget deficit of 19.2m. tala (equivalent to 2.3% of GDP), reflecting an increase in development spending financed by external borrowing and a decrease in lending to the domestic banking system. At the end of 2000 the country's total external debt stood at US $197.2m., of which $147.0m. was long-term public debt. In that year the cost of debt-servicing was equivalent to 10.8% of total revenue from exports of goods and services. Remittances from Samoans overseas are important to the economy and totalled 150.7m. tala in 2000, equivalent to some 19.5% of GDP in that year (more than three times the value of merchandise exports and, for the first time, exceeding tourist remittances). Official development assistance from Australia totalled $A15.1m. in 2001/02. Aid from New Zealand amounted to $NZ7.7m in 1999/2000 and was projected to remain at that figure for the subsequent two fiscal years. The annual rate of inflation averaged 3.3% in 1990–2000; consumer prices increased by 0.3% in 1999 and by 1.0% in 2000. The ADB estimated that consumer prices increased by 4.0% in 2001. According to the census conducted in late 2001, a total of 2,618 people were unemployed, compared with 1,175 in late 1991.

In 1998 the UN Committee for Development Planning recommended that Samoa be removed from the UN's list of the world's least developed countries (LDCs) and recategorized as a developing country. It appeared likely, however, that Samoa would seek to persuade the UN to defer any decision until a full evaluation of the economy had been carried out. In the early 1990s economic development was adversely affected by cyclones, limited agricultural exports and inadequate transport facilities. A programme of economic reforms, initiated by the Government in the mid-1990s, won the approval of the ADB, the World Bank and other international financial organizations. Strong growth characterized the economy during the mid-1990s, but this slowed considerably in 1997 and 1998, owing to restructuring by the Japanese-owned manufacturing plant, the completion of cyclone reconstruction projects and drought. Nevertheless, by the end of 1998 inflation had been reduced to a low level, foreign reserves had increased and the external debt had fallen. In May 1999 it was announced that Samoa's Post Office and Telecommunications Department was to be privatized as part of a public-sector reform programme. In 2000–01 high rates of GDP growth were maintained (with the construction sector recording particularly strong expansion), while the Samoan currency continued to depreciate against the US dollar. In 2001, however, the increase in consumer prices exceeded the central bank's target of a maximum of 3%. The Government maintained its commitment to private-sector development, including the transfer of the assets of several public enterprises to the corporate and private sectors. The IMF commended the transferral of government-owned land to freehold use in 2001. During 2001 various items of legislation were approved, aiming to raise standards of fiscal and corporate governance and to improve regulation and supervision in the financial sector. The tourism sector, meanwhile, continued to perform well, following the completion of new facilities, and was also well placed to benefit from the political instability in neighbouring Fiji and Solomon Islands. Although the number of arrivals was briefly affected by the repercussions of the terrorist attacks on the USA in September 2001, gross receipts from tourism increased owing to higher individual levels of spending. The Government continued its implementation of the programme of economic and public-sector reform in 2001 and reaffirmed its policies in the Strategy for the Development of Samoa 2002–2004. The document stressed the importance of opportunities for all through sustained economic growth and improvements in health and education. The ADB envisaged a GDP growth rate of 5.0% in 2002.

Samoa is a member of the Pacific Islands Forum (formerly the South Pacific Forum), the Pacific Community (formerly the South Pacific Commission), the UN's Economic and Social Commission for Asia and the Pacific (ESCAP), and the ADB, and is a signatory of the Lomé Conventions and the successor Cotonou Agreement with the EU.

Statistical Survey

AREA AND POPULATION

Area: Savai'i and adjacent small islands 1,708 sq km, Upolu and adjacent small islands 1,123 sq km; Total 2,831 sq km (1,093 sq miles).

Population: Savai'i 44,930, Upolu and adjacent small islands 112,228, Total 157,158 at census of 3 November 1986; Savai'i 45,050, Upolu and adjacent small islands 116,248, Total 161,298 (males 84,601; females 76,697) at census of 3 November 1991; Total 176,848 at census of November 2001.

Density (November 2001): 62.5 per sq km.

Principal Town: Apia (capital), population 34,126 at census of 3 November 1991.

Registered Births and Deaths (1996, provisional): Live births 4,966 (birth rate 29.9 per 1,000); Deaths 352 (death rate 2.1 per 1,000). (1998, provisional): Deaths 531 (death rate 3.2 per 1,000). Source: UN, *Population and Vital Statistics Report*.

Expectation of Life (WHO estimates, years at birth, 2000): Males 70.2; Females 77.8. Source: WHO, *World Health Report*.

Economically Active Population (census of 3 November 1986): Agriculture, hunting, forestry and fishing 29,023; Manufacturing and mining 1,587; Electricity, gas and water 855; Construction 62; Trade, restaurants and hotels 1,710; Transport, storage and communications 1,491; Financing, insurance, real estate and business services 842; Community, social and personal services 9,436; Activities not adequately defined 629; Total labour force 45,635 (males 37,054; females 8,581).

1991 census (persons aged 15 years and over, excluding armed forces): Total labour force 57,142 (males 38,839; females 18,303) (Source: ILO, *Yearbook of Labour Statistics*).

HEALTH AND WELFARE

Key Indicators

Fertility (births per woman, 2000): 4.4.

Under-5 Mortality Rate (per 1,000 live births, 2000): 26.

Physicians (per 1,000 head, 1996): 0.34.

Health Expenditure (1998): US $ per head (PPP): 106.
% of GDP: 3.5.
public (% of total): 68.9.

Access to Water (% of persons, 2000): 99.

Access to Sanitation (% of persons, 2000): 99.

Human Development Index (2000): ranking 101.
value 0.715.

For sources and definitions, see explanatory note on p. vi.

AGRICULTURE, ETC.

Principal Crops (FAO estimates, '000 metric tons, 2000): Taro 15; Yams 1; Other roots and tubers 3; Coconuts 130; Copra 11; Bananas 20; Papayas 10; Pineapples 6; Mangoes 5; Avocados 2; Other fruits 10; Cocoa beans 0.4. Source: FAO.

Livestock (FAO estimates, '000 head, year ending September 2000): Pigs 170; Cattle 28; Horses 1.8; Chickens 440. Source: FAO.

Livestock Products (FAO estimates, '000 metric tons, 2000): Beef and veal 1; Pigmeat 4. Source: FAO.

Forestry (roundwood removals, '000 cubic metres): 131 in 1998; 131 in 1999; 131 in 2000. Source: FAO, *Yearbook of Forest Products*.

Fishing (metric tons, live weight, 1999): Capture 9,750 (Albacore 3,660, Yellowfin tuna 619); Total catch 9,750. Source: FAO, *Yearbook of Fishery Statistics*.

INDUSTRY

Electric Energy (million kWh): 85 in 1999; 91 in 2000; 105 in 2001. Source: Asian Development Bank, *Key Indicators of Developing Asian and Pacific Countries*.

FINANCE

Currency and Exchange Rates: 100 sene (cents) = 1 tala (Samoan dollar). *Sterling, US Dollar and Euro Equivalents* (31 May 2002): £1 sterling = 4.853 tala; US $1 = 3.309 tala; €1 = 3.106 tala; 100 tala = £20.60 = US $30.22 = €32.19. *Average Exchange Rate* (US $ per tala): 0.3320 in 1999; 0.3057 in 2000; 0.2880 in 2001.

Budget (provisional, million tala, year ending 30 June 1998): *Revenue:* Tax revenue 138.2 (Income tax 29.5, Excise tax 25.8, Taxes on international trade 47.1, Value-added gross receipts and services tax (VAGST) 32.2, Other taxes 3.6); Other revenue 33.2 (Fees, service charges, etc. 9.7, Departmental enterprises 19.3, Rents, royalties and international investments 4.2); Total 171.4, excl. external grants received (60.5). *Expenditure:* Current expenditure 142.1 (General administration 39.0, Law and order 11.3, Education 32.0, Health 24.8, Social security and pensions 6.8, Agriculture 9.0, Public works 18.6, Land survey 6.2, Other economic services 4.6, Interest on public debt 4.0, Other purposes (residual) –0.7, Sub-total 155.6, *Less* VAGST payable by government 13.5); Development expenditure 71.3; Total 213.4, excl. net lending (8.2). *1998/99* (projections, million tala, incl. supplementary budget proposals): *Revenue:* Tax revenue 155.4; Other revenue 36.4; Total 191.8, excl. external grants (85.1). *Expenditure:* Current expenditure 172.9; Development expenditure 90.4; Total 263.3, excl. net lending (16.1). Source: IMF, *Samoa: Statistical Appendix* (April 1999).

2000/01 (provisional, million tala, year ending 30 June): *Revenue:* Tax revenue 174.8; Other revenue 22.5; Total 197.4, excl. external grants received (65.1). *Expenditure:* Current expenditure 164.6; Development expenditure 103.1; Capital and net lending 13.9; Total 281.7. Source: Treasury Department.

International Reserves (US $ million at 31 December 2001): IMF special drawing rights 2.95; Reserve position in IMF 0.86; Foreign exchange 52.83; Total 56.64. Source: IMF, *International Financial Statistics*.

Money Supply (million tala at 31 December 2001): Currency outside banks 29.97; Demand deposits at banks 56.87; Total money 86.84. Source: IMF, *International Financial Statistics*.

Cost of Living (Consumer Price Index, excluding rent; base: 1995 = 100): 115.4 in 1999; 116.5 in 2000; 121.0 in 2001. Source: IMF, *International Financial Statistics*.

Gross Domestic Product by Economic Activity (million tala at current prices, 2001): Agriculture and fishing 121.5; Manufacturing 137.0; Electricity and water 25.5; Construction 59.5; Trade 175.8; Transport and communications 116.8; Finance 59.3; Public administration 69.5; Other services 92.4; Sub-total 857.3; *Less* Imputed bank service charges 5.8; Total 851.5. Source: Asian Development Bank, *Key Indicators of Developing Asian and Pacific Countries*.

Balance of Payments (estimates, US $ million, 2000): Exports of goods f.o.b. 17.0; Imports of goods f.o.b. –90.4; *Trade balance* –73.4; Services and other income (net) 19.3; *Balance on goods, services and income* –54.1; Private remittances (net) 38.6; Official transfers (net) 24.5; *Current balance* 8.9; Capital transactions (incl. net errors and omissions) –14.0; *Overall balance* –5.1. Source: IMF Public Information Notice, *IMF Concludes, Article IV Consultation with Samoa* (July 2001).

EXTERNAL TRADE

Principal Commodities (US $'000, 1990): *Imports c.i.f.:* Food and live animals 19,852; Beverages and tobacco 1,753; Mineral fuels 9,345; Chemicals 3,874; Basic manufactures 15,781; Machinery and transport equipment 23,584; Miscellaneous manufactured articles 4,987; Total (incl. others) 81,742. *Exports f.o.b.* (incl. re-exports): Copra 476; Cocoa 219; Coffee 419; Coconuts 2,519; Taro and taamu 512; Beer 402; Cigarettes and tobacco 275; Palm oil 1,745; Total (incl. others) 8,020.

1991 ('000 tala): *Imports c.i.f.* 225,337; *Exports* Taro 6,878; Total (incl. re-exports) 15,515.

1992 ('000 tala): *Imports c.i.f.* 271,325; *Exports* (incl. re-exports) 14,349.

1993 ('000 tala): *Imports c.i.f.* 269,079; *Exports* (incl. re-exports) 16,522.

1994 ('000 tala): *Imports c.i.f.* 206,347; *Exports* (incl. re-exports) 9,121.

1995 ('000 tala): *Imports c.i.f.* 235,353; *Exports* (incl. re-exports) 21,859.

1996 ('000 tala): *Imports c.i.f.* 247,126; *Exports* (incl. re-exports) 24,868.

1997 ('000 tala): *Imports c.i.f.* 247,377; *Exports* (incl. re-exports) 38,531.

1998 ('000 tala): *Imports c.i.f.* 285,652; *Exports* (incl. re-exports) 43,243.

1999 ('000 tala): *Imports c.i.f.* 346,765; *Exports* (incl. re-exports) 61,695.

2000 ('000 tala): *Imports c.i.f.* 348,610; *Exports* (incl. re-exports) 44,800.

Source (for 1991–2000): IMF, *International Financial Statistics*.

2001 ('000 tala): *Imports c.i.f.:* Petroleum 55,780; Total (incl. others) 449,090. *Exports f.o.b.:* Coconut oil 10; Coconut cream 3,390; Fish 36,010; Copra 780; Kava 500; Beer 3,070; Taro 830; Garments 5,490; Total (incl. others) 52,690. Source: Treasury Department, *Quarterly Review*.

Note: The trade data above exclude purchases and sales by the Yazaki car components factory.

Principal Trading Partners (US $ million, 2001): *Imports:* Australia 62.44; Fiji 33.95; Indonesia 4.32; Japan 28.98; Republic of

Korea 3.93; New Zealand 46.64; United Kingdom 7.49; USA 77.11; Total (incl. others) 289.52. *Exports:* American Samoa 1.67; Australia 48.35; Germany 1.85; Indonesia 8.90; New Zealand 1.11; USA 8.73; Total (incl. others) 74.78. Source: Asian Development Bank, *Key Indicators of Developing Asian and Pacific Countries.*

TRANSPORT

Road Traffic (motor vehicles in use, 1993): Private cars 5,000; Commercial vehicles 1,800. Source: UN, *Statistical Yearbook for Asia and the Pacific.*

International Shipping (freight traffic, '000 metric tons, 1998): Goods loaded 50; Goods unloaded 140. Source: UN, *Monthly Bulletin of Statistics. Merchant Fleet* (total displacement, '000 grt at 31 December 2001): 9.7; vessels 7. Source: Lloyd's Register-Fairplay, *World Fleet Statistics.*

Civil Aviation (traffic on scheduled services, 1998): Passengers carried 149,000; Passenger-kilometres 250 million; Total ton-kilometres 24 million. Source: UN, *Statistical Yearbook.*

TOURISM

Visitor Arrivals: 77,926 in 1998; 85,124 in 1999; 87,688 in 2000.

Visitor Arrivals by Country (2000): American Samoa 30,063; Australia 10,954; Fiji 2,032; Germany 1,784; New Zealand 22,818; United Kingdom 2,092; USA 9,032.

Source: World Tourism Organization, *Yearbook of Tourism Statistics.*

Tourism Receipts (million tala)*: 115.2 in 1998; 125.8 in 1999; 133.1 in 2000.

* Includes the proportion of international travel credited to Samoan carriers.

COMMUNICATIONS MEDIA

Telephones (2001): 10,000 main lines in use.*

Facsimile Machines (1999): 500 in use.*

Personal Computers (2001): 1,000.*

Internet Users (2001): 3,000.*

Mobile Cellular Telephones (2001): 3,000 subscribers.*

Radio Receivers (1997): 410,000 in use.†

Television Receivers (1997): 42,000 in use.†

Non-Daily Newspapers (1988): 5 (estimated circulation 23,000).†

* Source: International Telecommunication Union.

† Source: UNESCO, *Statistical Yearbook.*

EDUCATION

Primary (1999): 155 schools (1996); 1,233 teachers; 35,749 pupils.

Intermediate (1983): 8,643 pupils.

General Secondary (1996): 665 teachers; 12,672 pupils.

Universities, etc. (1983): 11 teachers; 136 students.

Other Higher (1996): 71 teachers; 674 students.

Source: partly UNESCO, *Statistical Yearbook.*

Adult Literacy Rate (UNESCO estimates): 80.2% (males 81.2%; females 79.0%) in 2000. Source: UN Development Programme, *Human Development Report.*

Directory

The Constitution

A new Constitution was adopted by a constitutional convention on 28 October 1960. After being approved by a UN-supervised plebiscite in May 1961, the Constitution came into force on 1 January 1962, when Western Samoa became independent. A constitutional amendment adopted in July 1997, shortened the country's name to Samoa. The main provisions of the Constitution are summarized below:

HEAD OF STATE

The office of Head of State is held (since 5 April 1963, when his co-ruler died) by HH Malietoa Tanumafili II, who will hold this post for life. After that the Head of State will be elected by the Fono (Legislative Assembly) for a term of five years.

EXECUTIVE

Executive power lies with the Cabinet, consisting of the Prime Minister, supported by the majority in the Fono, and ministers selected by the Prime Minister. Cabinet decisions are subject to review by the Executive Council, which is made up of the Head of State and the Cabinet.

LEGISLATURE

The Fono consists of 49 members. It has a five-year term and the Speaker is elected from among the members. Beginning at the election of 5 April 1991, members are elected by universal adult suffrage: 47 members of the Assembly are elected from among the Matai (elected clan leaders) while the remaining two are selected from non-Samoan candidates.

The Government

HEAD OF STATE

O le Ao o le Malo: HH MALIETOA TANUMAFILI II (took office as joint Head of State 1 January 1962; became sole Head of State 5 April 1963).

CABINET
(September 2002)

Prime Minister and Minister of Foreign Affairs: TUILA'EPA SAILELE MALIELEGAOI.

Deputy Prime Minister and Minister of Finance: MISA TELEFONI.

Minister of Internal Affairs, Women's Affairs and Broadcasting: TUALA AINIU IUSITINO.

Minister of Education: FIAME NAOMI MATA'AFA.

Minister of Lands, Survey and Environment: TUALA SALE TAGALOA.

Minister of Health and Labour: MULITALO SIAFAUSA.

Minister of Public Works: FAUMUI LIUGA.

Minister of Agriculture, Forestry, Fisheries and Meteorological Services: TUISUGALETAUA SOFARA AVEAU.

Minister of Trade, Commerce and Industry: HANS JOACHIM KEIL.

Minister of Transport: PALUSALUE FAAPO II.

Minister of Youth, Sports and Culture: ULU VAOMALO KINI.

Minister for the Legislative Assembly: TINO GAINA.

Minister of Justice: SEUMANU AITA AH WA.

MINISTRIES AND MINISTERIAL DEPARTMENTS

Prime Minister's Department: POB L 1861, Apia; tel. 63122; fax 21339; e-mail pmdept@ipasifika.net.

Ministry of Agriculture, Forestry, Fisheries and Meteorology: POB 1874, Apia; tel. 22561; fax 24576.

Broadcasting Department: POB 200, Apia; tel. 21420.

Customs Department: POB 44, Apia; tel. 21561.

Economic Affairs Department: POB 862, Apia; tel. 20471.

Education Department: POB 1869, Apia; tel. 21911; fax 21917.

Ministry of Foreign Affairs: POB L 1859, Apia; tel. 25313; fax 21504; e-mail mfa@mfa.gov.ws.

Health Department: Private Bag, Apia; tel. 21212.

Inland Revenue Department: POB 209, Apia; tel. 20411.

Justice Department: POB 49, Apia; tel. 22671; fax 21050.

Lands, Survey and Environment Department: Private Bag, Apia; tel. 22481; fax 23176.

Public Works Department: Private Bag, Apia; tel. 20865; fax 21927; e-mail pwdir@lesamoa.net.

Statistics Department: POB 1151, Apia; tel. 21371; fax 24675.

Department of Trade, Industry and Commerce: POB 862, Apia; tel. 20471; fax 21646; e-mail tipu@tci.gov.ws; internet www.tradeinvestsamoa.ws.

Ministry of Transport: POB 1607, Apia; tel. 23701; fax 21990; e-mail mvnofo@mot.gov.ws.

Treasury Department: Private Bag, Apia; tel. 34333; fax 21312; e-mail treasury@samoa.net.

Ministry of Youth, Sport and Culture: Apia; tel. 23315.

Legislature

FONO
(Legislative Assembly)

The Assembly has 47 Matai members, representing 41 territorial constituencies, and two individual members. Elections are held every five years. At a general election on 2 March 2001, the Human Rights Protection Party (HRPP) won 22 seats, the Samoa National Development Party won 13 seats and independent candidates secured 14 seats. Four by-elections held during October and November 2001 were won by the HRPP.

Speaker: TALEAFOA FAISI.

Political Organizations

Human Rights Protection Party (HRPP): c/o The Fono, Apia; f. 1979; Western Samoa's first formal political party; Leader TUILA'EPA SAILELE MALIELEGAOI; Gen. Sec. LAULU DAN STANLEY.

Samoa All-People's Party: Apia; f. 1996; Leader MATATUMUA NAIMOAGA.

Samoa Liberal Party: Apia; f. 1994; Leader NONUMALO LEULUMOEGA SOFARA.

Samoa Mo Taeao (Samoans for a Better Tomorrow): Apia; Chair. TUIFA'ASISINA MEAOLE KEIL.

Samoa National Development Party (SNDP): POB 1233, Apia; tel. 23543; fax 20536; f. 1988 following general election; coalition party comprising the Christian Democratic Party (CDP) and several independents; Leader Hon. LEMAMEA R. MUALIA; Sec. VALASI TAFITO.

Samoa National Party: Apia; f. 2001; Sec. FETU TIATIA.

Diplomatic Representation

EMBASSIES AND HIGH COMMISSIONS IN SAMOA

Australia: Beach Rd, POB 704, Apia; tel. 23411; fax 23159; e-mail peterhooton@dfat.gov.au; High Commissioner: PETER HOOTON.

China, People's Republic: Private Bag, Vailima, Apia; tel. 22474; fax 21115; Ambassador: GU SICONG.

New Zealand: Beach Rd, POB 1876, Apia; tel. 21711; fax 20086; High Commissioner: PENELOPE RIDINGS.

USA: POB 3430, Apia; tel. 21631; fax 22030; e-mail usembassy@samoa.ws; Chargé d'affaires: FRANKIE REED CALHOUN.

Judicial System

Attorney-General: BRENDA HEATHER.

The Supreme Court is presided over by the Chief Justice. It has full jurisdiction for both criminal and civil cases. Appeals lie with the Court of Appeal.

Chief Justice: TIAVAASUE FALEFATU MAKA SAPOLU.

Secretary for Justice: FAAITAMAI P. F. MEREDITH.

The Court of Appeal consists of the President (the Chief Justice of the Supreme Court), and of such persons possessing qualifications prescribed by statute as may be appointed by the Head of State. Any three judges of the Court of Appeal may exercise all the powers of the Court.

The District Courts: replaced the Magistrates' Court in 1998.

Judges: LESATELE RAPI VAAI, TAGALOA ENOKA FERETI PUNI.

The Land and Titles Court has jurisdiction in respect of disputes over Samoan titles. It consists of the President (who is also a judge of the Supreme Court) and three Deputy Presidents, assisted by Samoan judges and Assessors.

President of The Land and Titles Court: TIAVAASUE FALEFATU MAKA SAPOLU.

Religion

Almost all of Samoa's inhabitants profess Christianity.

CHRISTIANITY

Fono a Ekalesia i Samoa (Samoa Council of Churches): POB 574, Apia; f. 1967; four mem. churches; Sec. Rev. EFEPAI KOLIA.

The Anglican Communion

Samoa lies within the diocese of Polynesia, part of the Church of the Province of New Zealand. The Bishop of Polynesia is resident in Fiji, while the Archdeacon of Tonga and Samoa is resident in Tonga.

Anglican Church: POB 16, Apia; tel. 20500; fax 24663; Rev. PETER E. BENTLEY.

The Roman Catholic Church

The islands of Samoa constitute the archdiocese of Samoa-Apia. At 31 December 2000 there were an estimated 30,336 adherents in the country. The Archbishop participates in the Catholic Bishops' Conference of the Pacific, based in Fiji.

Archbishop of Samoa-Apia: Cardinal PIO TAOFINU'U, Cardinal's Residence, Fetuolemoana, POB 532, Apia; tel. 20400; fax 20402; e-mail archdiocese@samoa.ws.

Other Churches

Church of Jesus Christ of Latter-day Saints (Mormon): Pres. LINI LYON TO'O, Samoa Apia Mission, POB 1865, Apia; tel. 20311; fax 20299; f. 1888; 62,500 mems.

Congregational Christian Church in Samoa: Tamaligi, POB 468, Apia; tel. 22279; fax 20429; e-mail cccsgsec@lesamoa.net; f. 1830; 100,000 mems; Gen. Sec. Rev. MAONE F. LEAUSA.

Congregational Church of Jesus in Samoa: Rev. NAITULI MALEPEAI, 505 Borie St, Honolulu, HI 96818, USA.

Methodist Church in Samoa (Ekalesia Metotisi i Samoa): POB 1867, Apia; tel. 22282; f. 1828; 36,000 mems; Pres. Rev. SIATUA LEULUAIALII; Sec. Rev. FAATOESE AUVAA.

Seventh-day Adventist Church: POB 600, Apia; tel. 20451; f. 1895; covers Samoa and American Samoa; 5,000 mems; Pres. Pastor SAMUELU AFAMASAGA; Sec. UILI SOLOFA.

BAHÁ'Í FAITH

National Spiritual Assembly: POB 1117, Apia; tel. 23348; fax 21363.

The Press

Newsline: POB 2441, Apia; tel. 24216; fax 23623; twice a week.

Samoa News: POB 1160, Apia; daily; merged with the weekly *Samoa Times* (f. 1967) in Sept. 1994; Publr LEWIS WOLMAN.

The Samoa Observer: POB 1572, Apia; tel. 21099; fax 21195; f. 1979; five times a week; independent; English and Samoan; Editor AUMA'AGAOLU ROPETA'ALI; circ. 4,500.

Samoa Weekly: Saleufi, Apia; f. 1977; weekly; independent; bilingual; Editor (vacant); circ. 4,000.

Savali: POB L1861, Apia; publ. of Lands and Titles Court; monthly; govt-owned; Samoan edn f. 1904; Editor FALESEU L. FUA; circ. 6,000; English edn f. 1977; circ. 500; bilingual commercial edn f. 1993; circ. 1,500; Man. Editor (vacant).

South Seas Star: POB 800, Apia; tel. 23684; weekly.

Broadcasting and Communications

TELECOMMUNICATIONS

Samoa Communications Ltd: Apia; tel 23456; fax 24000; corporatized in July 1999; telecommunications and postal services provider; CEO MARK YEOMAN.

BROADCASTING

Radio

Samoa Broadcasting Service: Broadcasting Department, POB 1868, Apia; tel. 21420; fax 21072; f. 1948; govt-controlled with commercial sponsorship; operates Radio 2AP; broadcasts on two channels in English and Samoan for 24 hours daily; Dir J. K. BROWN.

Magik 98 FM: POB 762, Apia; tel. 25149; fax 25147; e-mail magic98fm@samoa.net; f. 1989; privately-owned; operates on FM wavelengths 98.1 and 99.9 MHz; Man. COREY KEIL.

Radio Graceland: Apia; broadcasts gospel music.

Television

Televise Samoa Corporation: POB 3691, Apia; tel. 26641; fax 24789; e-mail ceotvsamoa@samoa.net; f. 1993; govt-owned national television broadcasting service; locally-produced programmes and programmes supplied by Australian Television (ATV); CEO LEOTA UELESE PETAIA.

Finance

(cap. = capital; res = reserves; dep. = deposits; m. = million; brs = branches; amounts in tala, unless otherwise indicated)

BANKING

Central Bank

Central Bank of Samoa: Private Bag, Apia; tel. 34100; fax 20293; e-mail cbs@lesamoa.net; internet www.cbs.gov.ws; f. 1984; cap. 10.0m., res 15.9m., dep. 59.6m. (Dec. 2001); Gov. PAPALI'I TOMMY SCANLAN; Chair. ALOA KOLONE VAAI.

Commercial Banks

ANZ Bank (Samoa) Ltd: Beach Rd, POB L 1885, Apia; tel. 22422; fax 24595; e-mail anz@samoa.ws; internet www.anz.com/samoa; f. 1959 as Bank of Western Samoa, name changed 1997; owned by

ANZ Banking Group Ltd; cap. 1.5m., res 22.8m., dep. 139.2m. (Sept. 1998); Dir R. G. Lyon; Man. Dir G. R. Tunstall; 1 br.

Industrial Bank Inc: POB 3271, Lotemau Centre, Vaea St, Apia; tel. 21878; fax 21869; f. 1995; owned by Industrial Pacific Investments Ltd; cap. US $0.3m., res US $1.9m. (1995); Chair. and Pres. Ian Bystrov.

International Business Bank Corporation Ltd: Chandra House, Convent St, Apia; tel. 20660; fax 23253; e-mail ibb@samoa.net; f. 1991; 46.7% owned by ELECS Investment Ltd, 22.5% by Tidal Funds Co Ltd; cap. US $25.5m., res US $0.8m., dep. US $22.2m. (Jan. 1997); Chair. Ilia Karas; Exec. Dir Serguei Grebelski.

National Bank of Samoa: POB 3047L, Apia; tel. 26766; fax 23477; e-mail info@nationalbanksamoa.com; internet www.nationalbanksamoa.com; f. 1995; owned by consortium of private interests in Samoa, American Samoa and the USA; Chair. Terence Betham; CEO Anne Bonisch; 5 agencies; 1 sub-br.

Westpac Bank Samoa Ltd: Beach Rd, POB 1860, Apia; tel. 20000; fax 22848; e-mail pcb@lesamoa.net; f. 1977 as Pacific Commercial Bank Ltd, current name adopted 2001; first independent bank; 93.5% owned by Westpac Banking Corpn (Australia); cap. 1.2m., res 5.5m., dep. 88.0m. (Dec. 2000); Chair. Alan Walter; Gen. Man. Steve Baker; 3 brs.

Development Bank

Development Bank of Samoa: POB 1232, Apia; tel. 22861; fax 23888; f. 1974 by Govt to foster economic and social development; cap. 12.9m. (1992); Gen. Man. Falefa Lima.

INSURANCE

National Pacific Insurance Ltd: NPF Bldg, Private Bag, Apia; tel. 20481; fax 23374; f. 1977; 30% govt-owned; Gen. Man. Ricky Welch.

Progressive Insurance Company: POB 620, Lotemau Centre, Apia; tel. 26110; fax 26112; e-mail progins@samoa.ws; f. 1993; Gen. Man. I. O. Filemu.

Western Samoa Life Assurance Corporation: POB 494, Apia; tel. 23360; fax 23024; f. 1977; Gen. Man. A. S. Chan Ting.

Trade and Industry

CHAMBER OF COMMERCE

Chamber of Commerce and Industry: Level one, Lotemau Centre, Convent St, POB 2014, Apia; tel. 21237; fax 21578; e-mail info@samoachamber.com; internet www.samoachamber.com; f. 1938; Pres. Norman Wetzell; Vice-Pres. Sala Epa'Tuioti; Sec. John F. Boyle.

INDUSTRIAL AND TRADE ASSOCIATIONS

Samoa Coconut Products: Apia.

Samoa Forest Corporation: Apia.

UTILITIES

Electricity

Electric Power Corporation: POB 2011, Apia; tel. 22261; fax 23748; e-mail epcgm@samoa.ws.

Water

Western Samoa Water Authority: POB 245, Apia; tel. 20409; fax 20376; e-mail swalatu@samoa.ws; Gen. Man. Latu Sauile Toga Kupa.

MAJOR INDUSTRIAL COMPANIES

Wilex CCP Ltd: Apia; operates chocolate factory.

Yazaki Samoa: Apia; manufacturers of automotive components.

TRADE UNIONS

Journalists' Association of Samoa: Apia; Pres. Apulu Lance Polu.

Samoa Manufacturers' Association (SMA): Apia; Pres. Eddie Wilson.

Samoa Nurses' Association (SNA): POB 3491, Apia; Pres. Faamanatu Nielsen; 252 mems.

Samoa Trade Union Congress (STUC): POB 1515, Apia; tel. 24134; fax 20014; f. 1981; affiliate of ICFTU; Pres. Falefata Tuaniu Petaia; Dir Matafeo R. Matafeo; 5,000 mems.

Transport

Public Works Department: see under The Government; Dir of Works Isikuki Punivalu.

ROADS

In 1983 there were 396 km of main roads on the islands, of which 267 km were bitumen surfaced; 69 km of urban roads, of which 32 km were bitumen surfaced; 440 km of unsealed secondary roads and about 1,180 km of plantation roads. The upgrading and expansion of the road network was a priority of the Government during the late 1980s.

SHIPPING

There are deep-water wharves at Apia and Asau. A programme of improvements to port facilities at Apia funded by Japanese aid, was completed in 1991. Regular cargo services link Samoa with Australia, New Zealand, American Samoa, Fiji, New Caledonia, Solomon Islands, Tonga, US Pacific coast ports and various ports in Europe.

Samoa Ports Authority: POB 2279, Apia; tel. 23552; fax 25870; e-mail spa@lesamoa.net; f. 1999.

Samoa Shipping Services Ltd: POB 1884, Apia; tel. 20790; fax 20026.

Samoa Shipping Corporation Ltd: Private Bag, Shipping House Matautu-tai, Apia; tel. 20935; fax 22352; e-mail ssc@samoa.net; internet www.samoashippingcorporation.com; Gen. Man. Oloialii Koki Tuala.

CIVIL AVIATION

There is an international airport at Faleolo, about 35 km from Apia and an airstrip at Fagali'i, 4 km east of Apia Wharf, which receives light aircraft from American Samoa. In mid-1999 US $19.4m. was allocated by the World Bank to improve facilities at Faleolo airport.

Polynesian Airlines (Holdings) Ltd: NPF Bldg, Beach Rd, POB 599, Apia; tel. 21261; fax 20023; e-mail enquiries@polynesianairlines.co.nz; internet www.polynesianairlines.co.nz; f. 1959; govt-owned and -operated; international services to American Samoa, Rarotonga (Cook Islands), Nadi (Fiji), Tonga, Sydney and Melbourne (Australia), Auckland and Wellington (New Zealand) and Hawaii and Los Angeles (USA); domestic services between islands of Upolu and Savai'i; Chair. Tuila'epa Sailele Malielegaoi; CEO Richard Gates.

Samoa Air: tel. 22901; operates local shuttle services between Pago Pago and Apia.

Tourism

Samoa has traditionally maintained a cautious attitude towards tourism, fearing that the Samoan way of life might be disrupted by an influx of foreign visitors. The importance of income from tourism has, however, led to some development, including the expansion of hotel facilities and improvements to the road network and airport. Some 87,688 tourists arrived in 2000, and revenue from the tourist industry totalled 133.1m. tala in that year. In 2000 34.3% of tourists came from American Samoa, 26.0% from New Zealand, 12.5% from Australia and 10.3% from the USA. The principal attractions are the scenery and the pleasant climate.

Samoa Visitors' Bureau: POB 2272, Apia; tel. 26500; fax 20886; e-mail samoa@samoa.net; internet www.samoa.co.nz; f. 1986; Gen. Man. Sonja Hunter; Marketing Man. Alise Faulalo-Stunnenberg.

Defence

In August 1962 Western Samoa (as it was then known) and New Zealand signed a Treaty of Friendship, whereby the New Zealand Government, on request, acts as the sole agent of the Samoan Government in its dealings with other countries and international organizations.

Education

The education system is divided into primary, intermediate and secondary and is based on the New Zealand system. Legislation was passed in 1992 which made education compulsory until the age of 14. In 1997 there were 35,649 pupils at primary schools, and in 1996 12,672 pupils undergoing secondary-level education. Teaching staff at primary and intermediate levels numbered 1,479 in 1996; in that year there were 665 secondary-school teachers. There are also a trades training institute, a teacher-training college and a college for tropical agriculture. About 97% of the adult population are literate in Samoan. The National University of Samoa was founded in 1988, and had an initial intake of 328 students. A new campus for the university, providing accommodation for up to 8,000 students and built at a cost of US $14.4m. with assistance from the Government of Japan, was opened in September 1997. Samoa had joined other governments in the area in establishing the regional University of the South Pacific, based in Fiji, in 1977. Current government expenditure on education in the year ending 30 June 1998 was an estimated 32.0m. tala (20.6% of total current expenditure).

Solomon Islands

Physical and Social Geography

Solomon Islands is a scattered Melanesian archipelago covering a land area of 27,556 sq km (10,639 sq miles) in the south-western Pacific Ocean, east of Papua New Guinea and north of Vanuatu. The country includes most of the Solomon Islands (those to the north-west being part of Papua New Guinea), Ontong Java Islands (Lord Howe Atoll), Rennell Island and the Santa Cruz Islands, about 500 km to the east. There are 21 large islands and numerous small ones. The principal islands, all in the main group, are Choiseul, Santa Isabel (Boghotu), New Georgia, Malaita, Guadalcanal and San Cristobal (Makira). The climate is equatorial, with small seasonal variations governed by the trade winds. Much of the country is mountainous and of volcanic origin, with steep terrain which remains under dense tropical rain forest; extensive tracts of native and introduced grassland cover the northern plains of Guadalcanal. The smaller islands are mainly coralline.

Most of the population are Melanesian, and they speak about 80 dialects and languages. Pidgin English (Pijin—much of the vocabulary is derived from standard English, but used in a Melanesian grammatical form and with different intonations) is the lingua franca and is widely understood, but standard English is the official language. Some 95% of the population are Christian, the largest denomination being the Church of Melanesia (Anglican). The total population at the 1999 census was 409,042, compared with 285,176 at the census of 1986 when some 94% of the population were Melanesian, 4% Polynesian (mainly from the 'outliers' such as Ontong Java), 1% Micronesian (originally resettled from the Gilbert Islands, now Kiribati) and some Europeans and Chinese. Solomon Islands has an extremely high rate of population growth; it increased by an annual average of 2.8% in 1986–99. The capital is Honiara, on the island of Guadalcanal.

History

Solomon Islands, long settled by Melanesian peoples, was named by a Spanish navigator, Alvaro de Mendaña, in 1568. European contacts were intermittent from then, and made little impact on the islanders' lives. It was not until the 19th century that traders, whalers and missionaries began to establish outposts on the main islands. Forcible recruiting of labour ('blackbirding') spread from the New Hebrides (now Vanuatu) to the Solomon Islands during the 1860s. The northern Solomon Islands became a German Protectorate in 1885 and the southern Solomons a British Protectorate in 1893. Rennell Island and the Santa Cruz Islands were added to the British Protectorate in 1898 and 1899. Germany ceded most of the northern Solomons and Ontong Java Islands to the United Kingdom between 1898 and 1900. The whole territory, known as the British Solomon Islands Protectorate, was placed under the jurisdiction of the Western Pacific High Commission (WPHC), with its headquarters in Fiji. The High Commissioner for the Western Pacific was represented locally by a Resident Commissioner.

The Solomon Islands were invaded by Japan in 1942 but, after a fierce battle on Guadalcanal, most of the islands were recaptured by US forces in 1943. After the Second World War the Protectorate's capital was moved from Tulagi, on Ngella (Florida Islands), to Honiara, on Guadalcanal, which was near to a major war-time airfield. In January 1953 the headquarters of the WPHC also moved to Honiara. Meanwhile, elected local councils were established on most of the islands and by 1966 almost the whole territory was covered by such councils. The introduction of responsible local government was initially prompted by the challenge of the Maa'sina (brotherhood) Ruru movement, also known by the anglicized form 'Marching Rule'. This originated in Malaita in 1927, but grew during and after the Second World War. It favoured strictly-controlled, custom-based communities living in large villages and practising a communal agricultural economy and opposed close co-operation with the colonial administration or the dominant churches. The WPHC at first attempted to accommodate the movement, but its influence continued to spread and its suppression took place between 1948 and 1950.

Under a new Constitution, introduced in October 1960, a Legislative Council and an Executive Council were established for the Protectorate's central administration. Initially, all members of both bodies were appointed but from 1964 the Legislative Council included elected members, and the elective element was gradually increased as successive legislative and administrative bodies were created by new Constitutions in March 1970 and April 1974. The Constitution of April 1974 instituted a single Legislative Assembly with 24 members who chose a Chief Minister with the right to appoint his own Council of Ministers. A new office of Governor of the Protectorate was also created to assume almost all the functions previously exercised in the territory by the High Commissioner for the Western Pacific. Solomon Mamaloni, leader of the newly-founded People's Progressive Party (PPP), was appointed the first Chief Minister in August 1974. The territory was officially renamed the Solomon Islands in June 1975, although it retained protectorate status.

In January 1976 the Solomon Islands received internal self-government, with the Chief Minister presiding over the Council of Ministers in place of the Governor. In June elections were held for an enlarged Legislative Assembly and in July the Assembly elected one of its new members, Peter (later Sir Peter) Kenilorea, to the position of Chief Minister. Following a constitutional conference in London in September 1977, Solomon Islands (as it was restyled) became an independent state, within the Commonwealth, on 7 July 1978. The Legislative Assembly became the National Parliament and designated Kenilorea the first Prime Minister.

The main political issue confronting the country was the proposed decentralization of authority to the regions, support for which was particularly strong in the Western District, the most commercially developed part of the country. In 1979 the PPP merged with the Rural Alliance Party to form the People's Alliance Party (PAP), with Solomon Mamaloni as its leader. The first general election since independence was held in August 1980. Independent candidates won more seats than any of the three parties. Parliament again elected Kenilorea as Prime Minister by an overwhelming majority. In August 1981, however, Parliament approved a motion expressing 'no confidence' in Kenilorea, and chose Mamaloni to succeed him as Prime Minister.

After elections to the National Parliament in October 1984, a majority among the minor parties and independent members was decisive in electing Kenilorea to the post of Prime Minister. The new Government consisted of a coalition of nine members of Kenilorea's United Party (UP), three from the newly-formed Solomone Ano Sagufenua (SAS) and three independents. The five provincial ministries, established by Mamaloni, were abolished in line with Kenilorea's declared policy of restoring to central government control some of the powers held by the provincial governments. In October 1985 a new political party, the Nationalist Front for Progress (NFP), was formed, under the leadership of Andrew Nori. However, the SAS subsequently withdrew its support from the coalition, and Kenilorea formed a new Cabinet, comprising nine members of the UP, three of the NFP and three independents. In November 1986 three cabinet ministers (all members of the NFP) resigned, in reaction to allegations that Kenilorea had secretly accepted French aid, amounting to about $A70,000, to repair cyclone damage to his home village. Faced with a third motion expressing 'no confidence' (the previous two having been defeated), Kenilorea himself resigned, and in December he was replaced as Prime Minister by Ezekiel Alebua, the former Deputy Prime Minister. Alebua retained Kenilorea's Cabinet almost in its entirety, with the latter becoming Deputy Prime Minister.

In March 1988 a constitutional review committee, chaired by Mamaloni, recommended that Solomon Islands become a federal republic within the Commonwealth. The next general election was held in February 1989 and the PAP won 11 of the 38 seats, remaining the largest single party by a considerable margin. It had also sponsored several candidates who stood as independents and secured the support of others. Mamaloni was appointed Prime Minister after defeating Bartholomew Ulufa'alu (leader of the Solomon Islands Liberal Party and the parliamentary faction of the Coalition for National Unity) in a parliamentary ballot. The new Government included Sir Baddeley Devesi, the former Governor-General (who had been succeeded by Sir George Lepping in July 1988), and was described as the first since independence solely to comprise the members of a single party.

Dissatisfaction with Mamaloni's leadership was expressed throughout 1990, and, in October, he resigned as leader of the PAP, one week before a party convention. Mamaloni declared that he would remain as an independent Prime Minister and dismissed five members of the Cabinet, replacing them with four members of the opposition and a PAP back-bencher. Persistent demands for Mamaloni's resignation by more than one-half of the country's MPs were defied by the Prime Minister. The PAP subsequently asked the remaining 10 ministers to resign their posts in the interests of party unity, but they refused, and in February 1991 were expelled from the party. By establishing a coalition Government and dividing the opposition and the ruling party, Mamaloni's action was widely interpreted as a return to the political traditions of Solomon Islands, based on personalities rather than on organized parties. The country's economic situation deteriorated throughout 1991, and in November prompted the Solomon Islands Council of Trade Unions to issue an ultimatum demanding Mamaloni's resignation, in order to avert mass industrial action.

At legislative elections in May 1993 the Group for National Unity and Reconciliation, led by Mamaloni, won 21 of the 47 seats in the recently-enlarged National Parliament. As Mamaloni's party had failed to achieve a majority the main opposition parties and independents agreed to form the National Coalition Partners. At elections to the premiership in June the independent member, Francis Billy Hilly (supported by the newly-formed alliance), defeated Mamaloni by a single vote.

In October 1994 a constitutional crisis resulted in several weeks of political confusion, following attempts by the Governor-General to dismiss Hilly on the grounds that he no longer held a parliamentary majority. Hilly remained in office, however, with the support of a High Court ruling, and confusion intensified when the Governor-General appointed the opposition leader, Solomon Mamaloni, to the position of Prime Minister. Hilly finally resigned on 31 October, and the post was declared vacant. In a parliamentary election to the premiership on 8 November Mamaloni defeated the former Governor-General, Sir Baddeley Devesi, by 29 votes to 18. Among the new Government's stated objectives, including several proposed political and constitutional changes, Mamaloni expressed his intention to conduct a thorough review of the country's current logging policy. Consequently, during late 1994 it was announced that many of the regulations introduced by the previous Government, in an attempt to conserve the islands' forestry resources, were to be repealed or relaxed (see Economy).

In April 1995 security forces were dispatched to Pavuvu Island (some 50 km north-west of Honiara), following angry protests by islanders who were resisting a compulsory resettlement programme, which the Government had agreed to implement in return for the sale of logging rights (for some 1m. cu m of timber on the island) to a Malaysian company. Logging began in May, despite continuing protests by the islanders, as well as opposition demands to abandon the programme and a warning from the Solomon Islands Central Bank that the Government's policy of allowing virtually unrestrained logging would seriously undermine the country's long-term economic prospects. An opposition motion to reverse the decision, presented to the National Parliament in July, however, was, defeated by 15 votes to 12. The vote prompted accusations that the Mamaloni Government favoured the protection of foreign business interests over the welfare of its own people.

In late 1995 and early 1996 Mamaloni's Government suffered a series of allegations of corruption and misconduct. In December seven ministers appeared in court accused of accepting payments and other benefits from foreign logging companies between 1993 and 1995. The Prime Minister gave assurances that none of the ministers would be dismissed from their positions, and in February 1996 all were acquitted. In May, moreover, a serious financial scandal at the Ministry of Finance led to the suspension of 25 officials pending an investigation into the disappearance of funds valued at some US $10m.

Meanwhile, the Government's continued reluctance to implement regulations to restrain logging activity in the islands remained a source of controversy. Extensive logging on Mono Island in the Western Province, from early 1996, provoked a series of protests by islanders and landowners. In frustration at the continuation of virtually unchecked logging in the islands, the Australian Government announced that it was to reduce aid to the country by $A2.2m. annually.

Controversy arose in July 1996 when it was reported that members of the National Parliament had begun to present gifts to their constituencies (mostly in the form of canoes and outboard motors) in preparation for the general election scheduled for 1997. This followed the reinstatement of the controversial Constituency Development Fund, which entitled each member to US $66,000, and which had been widely used by members at the previous general election to secure re-election by purchasing gifts for voters in the constituency. Fears that corruption and bribery in the country had reached unacceptable levels were confirmed in September by the regional trades union organization, SPOCTU, which cited the problem as the greatest obstacle to the islands' development, and stated that, with the worst incidence of corruption in the region, investors and aid donors would remain reluctant to make financial commitments to Solomon Islands.

In early August 1996 the National Parliament approved legislation to reform the provincial government system. Under the new system, the legislative and administrative powers of the nine provincial governments were transferred to 75 area assemblies and councils, with financial control vested wholly in the central Government. In February 1997, however, the legislation, which had been vehemently opposed by the larger provinces, was subsequently declared invalid by the High Court.

Concern over foreign exploitation of Solomon Islands resources continued during 1996, and in early 1997 landowners near the proposed Gold Ridge gold mine on Guadalcanal initiated legal proceedings for compensation and greater provision for the protection of the environment against the Australian company involved in the project. Furthermore, incidents in which local people damaged or destroyed equipment belonging to foreign logging companies were reported to have increased throughout the islands during 1997.

In May 1997 Mamaloni announced his intention to hold an early general election, following which he would resign as leader of the Group for National Unity and Reconciliation. Meanwhile, the opposition leader, Ezekiel Alebua, resigned, following accusations of misconduct from fellow opposition members, and was replaced by Edward Hunuehu. A general election took place on 6 August to a legislature that had recently been enlarged to 50 seats (following the creation of three new constituencies). A total of 19 incumbent and 23 new members were successful in the poll, with the Group for National Unity and Reconciliation winning 24 seats and a coalition grouping, Alliance for Change, securing the remainder. A period of intense political manoeuvring followed the election, as groups of successful candidates sought to secure a majority in Parliament. On 27 August Bartholomew Ulufa'alu was elected Prime Minister, defeating the newly-elected leader of the Group for National Unity and Reconciliation, Danny Philip, by 26 votes to 22. The new Government announced a programme of extensive structural reforms (approved in October) which aimed to address many of the country's ongoing problems. The proposals included a review of the public service (involving an expected loss of some 1,000 public servants' jobs) and measures to expand the role of the private sector in the economy and to encourage greater participation of non-governmental organizations in the country's socio-economic development. The measures aimed to restore a degree of economic stability to Solomon Islands and to attract increased foreign investment. Legislation proposing that a politician seeking to change party allegiance would automatically lose his or her seat and be subject to a by-election was similarly intended to increase political stability. The Government also announced plans for major structural changes in the forestry industry, including a sustainable harvesting policy with reduced quotas, greater involvement of local landowners in logging operations and a moratorium on new logging licences (implemented in April 1998).

In early 1998 a shipment of weapons (including a helicopter gunship, two military aircraft and smaller armaments) ordered by the previous administration for use in defending the maritime border with Papua New Guinea, arrived in the country from the USA. Ulufa'alu requested assistance from Australia in impounding the weapons, following widespread concern that unofficial organizations (particularly the Bougainville secessionist rebels within Papua New Guinea) might intercept the shipment. A dispute subsequently arose between Ulufa'alu and the former Prime Minister, Solomon Mamaloni, who had ordered the weapons. Mamaloni accused Ulufa'alu of treason for surrendering sovereign property to a foreign government, while the Prime Minister claimed that serious irregularities had occurred in procuring the arms and cited missing files and apparent overpayment as evidence of this.

In April 1998 Job Dudley Tausinga, whose Coalition for National Advancement (CNA) constituted the largest group outside the Government, was appointed Leader of the Opposition. Following the defection of six government members in July–August 1998, the opposition claimed to hold a majority (with 25 of the 49 sitting members) in the National Parliament and consequently sought to introduce a motion of 'no confidence' in the Prime Minister. The Government effectively delayed the vote for several weeks by lodging an unsuccessful appeal against it in the High Court. A vote took place on 18 September but was deemed to have been defeated as an equal number of votes were cast for and against the motion. Three opposition members subsequently defected to the Government, thus increasing their representation to 27 members. The climate of political instability resulting from the persistent political manoeuvring during mid-1998 prompted the Government to reiterate its proposal for legislation to restrict the rights of elected members to change party allegiance within the National Parliament. In late September Solomon Mamaloni was elected Leader of the Opposition. Mamaloni died in January 2000 and was succeeded by Manasseh Sogavare, under whose leadership the CNA reverted to its original name of the PPP.

From April 1998 violent unrest in Honiara was attributed to ethnic tensions, mainly between the inhabitants of Guadalcanal and Malaita provinces. The previously latent inter-ethnic tensions on Guadacanal island were attributed to the large-scale migration of ethnic Malaitans there in the Second World War period, and their subsequent achievement of status and wealth disproportionate to their numbers, to the perceived detriment of those indigenous to Guadacanal (Isatambu). A specific catalyst of the violent unrest from 1998 was the alienation of land by the Government since independence. Title to some land thus expropriated had been returned to Guadalcanal in late November, but this had not allayed a widespread feeling of resentment in the province at the financial burden imposed by hosting the capital. It was reported that a group styling itself the 'Guadalcanal Revolutionary Army' (GRA) had begun a campaign of militancy to force the Government to relocate the capital. The unrest intensified in early 1999, prompting the Government to establish a peace committee for the province. In mid-1999 talks between the Premier of Guadalcanal Province, Ezekiel Alebua, and the Solomon Islands Prime Minister failed to resolve the ethnic tensions in the province. Riots broke out in the capital, Honiara, and as many as 80 Malaitan immigrants were evacuated following threats by armed GRA militants. Alebua continued to pledge his full commitment to the peace process, and rumours that he was supporting the GRA led him to offer his resignation in an attempt to disprove any connection. Following Ulufa'alu's demands that peace be restored to the province before the implementation of any further measures, the GRA ordered an immediate halt to its activities. The Guadalcanal Provincial Assembly subsequently declared that it had accepted an initial payment of SI $500,000 in compensation for accommodating the national capital. A reconciliation ceremony was held between the two parties, during which Alebua apologized for the recent persecutions of Malaitan immigrants and appealed to the GRA to lay down its arms. However, the Malaitans subsequently demanded that they too be compensated, to the sum of US $600,000, for damage to their property by the GRA militants.

Following an increase in violence during which three Malaitan immigrants were reported to have been killed, and an estimated 10,000 forced to flee their villages, on 15 June 1999 a state of emergency was declared in Guadalcanal, and restrictions on media reporting of the conflict were tightened. A leader of the Isatambu Freedom Movement (IFM, formerly the GRA and also known in 1999 as the Isatambu Freedom Fighters—IFF), Andrew Te'e, announced that the movement was willing to surrender in return for a full amnesty for the militants; however, this was rejected by Ulufa'alu. The former Prime Minister of Fiji, Sitiveni Rabuka, was appointed Commonwealth Special Envoy, following a request for assistance by Ulufa'alu. After meeting with the parties concerned, Rabuka announced on 28 June that a peace agreement had been reached. A UN delegation and police officers from Fiji and Vanuatu were sent to monitor the conflict and help implement the peace plan. As part of the Honiara Peace Accord, the Solomon Islands Government agreed to pay SI $2.5m. into a Reconciliation Trust Fund, which was to be jointly administered by Guadalcanal Province and the national Government, to compensate the victims of the unrest. In return, the IFM agreed to disarm and to abandon their demands for a full amnesty for their supporters. Rabuka also urged the Government to lift the state of emergency and the media restrictions. In August, however, Rabuka and the UN monitoring team returned to the province amid speculation that the Honiara Peace Accord was on the verge of collapse, after four members of the IFM were reported to have been shot by police near Honiara.

On 12 August 1999 a new peace agreement was signed by Rabuka, Alebua and others. The agreement, known as the Panatina Agreement, allowed for a reduction in police activity in the province followed by the eventual revocation of the state of emergency, in return for the surrender of weapons by the IFM. Despite the extension of the disarmament deadline into September, the state of emergency was ended, and media restrictions were lifted in mid-October; following negotiations in the capital, Honiara, and the signing of an agreement in Fiji, a multinational peace-monitoring group from Fiji and Vanuatu, jointly funded by Australia and New Zealand, arrived in Guadalcanal later that month to monitor the disarmament process. In early December the peace-keeping force's mandate was extended into January 2000, and subsequently further extended by three months, following renewed outbreaks of violence and the emergence of a new guerrilla group, the Malaita Eagle Force (MEF), demanding US $40m. in compensation payments for loss of property incurred by Malaitans as a result of the conflict. Among their spokesmen was the former Minister of Finance, Andrew Nori.

Following further outbreaks of violence in the province that led to the death of four people, including two policemen, in February 2000, a decree was issued by the Governor-General outlawing membership of both the IFM and the MEF. Nevertheless, further clashes between the two rebel groups were reported in early March, and later that month riots took place in the capital, Honiara, during which Malaitan immigrants stoned the headquarters of the Guadalcanal Provincial Government. Peace talks took place in May without members of the IFM and the MEF, both of which refused to attend in protest at the decision to outlaw them earlier that year. However, a document known as the Buala Peace Communiqué was issued as the outcome of these talks on 5 May. In an attempt to advance the peace process, the order that outlawed the groups was suspended on 12 May. However, on 5 June members of the MEF, armed with weapons obtained in raids on police armouries, seized control of Honiara, placing Ulufa'alu under arrest. The rebels demanded the immediate resignation of the Prime Minister, claiming that he, himself an ethnic Malaitan, had failed to compensate displaced Malaitans within the established deadline (allegedly set for that day) and also demanded the appointment of a new Commissioner of Police, the de facto head of National Security. In renewed outbreaks of violence, it was alleged that up to 100 people had been killed. The MEF, meanwhile, claimed to have gained control of the Police Force, 98% of the military-style weapons in the territory, broadcasting services and the telecommunications infrastructure. Ulufa'alu was released four days later, following an agreement between the MEF and government negotiators that a special parliamentary sitting would be convened during which Ulufa'alu would be subject to a motion of 'no confidence'. A 14-day ceasefire was also called to guarantee the safe passage of a Commonwealth monitoring team. On 14 June Ulufa'alu resigned, one day before the scheduled 'no confidence' vote; however, he agreed to remain as caretaker Prime Minister for a 14-day transitional period during which negotiations between the MEF, the IFM and a Commonwealth Special Envoy, Prof. Ade Adefuye of Nigeria, were to take place. However, negotiations collapsed following the MEF's refusal to hand over its weapons, pending the appointment of a new Prime Minister. An extraordinary parliamentary session at which a new Prime Minister was to be appointed was set for 28 June. As this session failed to raise the necessary quorum, the election of a new Prime Minister was delayed until 30 June, when the leader of the Opposition, Manasseh Sogavare, defeated Rev. Leslie Boseto, incumbent Minister for Lands and Housing, by 23 votes to 21. (The third candidate, former Premier Francis Billy Hilly, withdrew in support of Boseto.) Sogavare declared that he would seek to establish peace without making significant changes to the policy of the previous Government. None the less, Sogavare announced a comprehensive reallocation of ministerial posts and restructuring of ministries. A new Ministry for National Unity, Reconciliation and Peace was established, and plans to create a Solomon Islands Defence Force and Ministry of Defence were announced. Previously defence issues had fallen within the remit of the police service, which had become compromised because of allegations of MEF infiltration. Sogavare also pledged to examine the issue of an alleged ethnic imbalance within the Solomon Islands Police Force; it was claimed that about 75% of the 900 officers were ethnic Malaitans, and that all 30 of the ethnic Isatambu were deployed outside of their home island of Guadacanal.

New ceasefire negotiations commenced on the Australian naval vessel, *Tobruk*, in early August 2000, resulting in the declaration of a 90-day ceasefire between the IFM and MEF. However, as occurred during the June ceasefire, intermittent violent disorder related to inter-ethnic tension continued across Guadalcanal. In late August IFM dissidents kidnapped the brother of Deputy Prime Minister Allan Kemakeza, demanding SI $6.5m. in compensation for the displaced persons of Guadalcanal. He was released unharmed after 10 days on 31 August without the payment of ransom. Logistical problems delayed the onset of further peace talks on the New Zealand navy frigate, *Te Kana*, until early September. These negotiations produced a communiqué outlining methods by which a lasting peace might be achieved. Meanwhile, in mid-September a breakaway group from the IFM, which reverted to the former name of the GRA and was led by Harold Keke, held an airline pilot hostage with a demand for SI $2m.; he was released unharmed without the demands being acceded to. A further round of peace talks took place in Queensland, Australia, which on 15 October led to the signing of a peace treaty known as the Townsville Agreement. Those party to the agreement were the MEF, the IFM, the Solomon Islands Government, and the Provincial Governments of Malaita and Guadalcanal. The agreement allowed for an amnesty giving immunity to all involved in crimes associated with the ethnic conflict, on condition of a surrender of weaponry within 30 days. It also envisaged the creation of an international peace-monitoring team, and the repatriation to their home villages of all MEF and IFM soldiers at the expense of the Solomon Islands Government. Infrastructure and services in the two provinces would also be restored and developed, within three months of these repatriations. Furthermore, a greater degree of autonomy was to be granted to the two provinces, by devolution of power or the implementation of constitutional amendments, and Malaita Province was to receive additional funding to reflect the demands placed on the region by the influx of 20,000 displaced persons from Guadalcanal. Public displays of forgiveness, reconciliation and confession were to be organized, and a Peace and Reconciliation Committee was to be established.

The implementation of the peace process, overseen by monitors from Australia and New Zealand, was threatened in mid-November 2000, when four people were killed in a shooting in Gizo, Western Province. Among the dead were two members of Papua New Guinea's Bougainville Revolutionary Army. Moreover, delays in the disarmament process involving the MEF and the IFM caused the deadline for the surrender of arms to be extended from 15 November until the end of that month, and then further until 15 December. In mid-November, following an announcement that the Guadalcanal Provincial Government headquarters, which had been occupied by members of the MEF since June, was to be rehabilitated as a symbol of national unity, arsonists, believed to be linked with the MEF, attacked the building. Despite a series of ceremonies in late November and early December, in which members of the IFM and MEF surrendered weapons, it was believed that at least 400 illegally-held weapons remained in circulation at the end of December. The legislation granting immunity to those who had committed crimes during the conflict was passed by Parliament in mid-December, and was criticized by the prominent human rights organization, Amnesty International. In late December one man was wounded in an attack on a motel, in Honiara, in which disarmed former IFM rebels recruited to join the police were resident. Responsibility for the attack was attributed to a group calling itself the Marau Eagle Force, from the eastern Marau region of Guadalcanal, which was subject to separate peace negotiations. The breakaway GLF led by Harold Keke also announced that it had not accepted the cease-fire. In early January 2001 concerns were expressed that, as a result of the ongoing economic crisis and a larger number of rebels having opted to join the police than had been anticipated, the Government might be unable to pay the former rebels, thus precipitating further concerns about security.

In early December 2000 new legislation had permitted the appointment of two further ministers, a Minister of Rehabilitation, Reconstruction and Redirection, and a Minister of Economic Reform and Structural Adjustment. In early January 2001 it was reported that the Government was contemplating an extension of the amnesty. Further violence broke out between Guadalcanal militants and members of the Marau Eagle Force. A peace agreement between the group and the IFM was signed in early February, although the Peace Monitoring Council observed that the infrastructure of the Marau region had been almost entirely destroyed since 1998 and that there was little immediate prospect of recovery. In early March 2001 peace in the Marau region appeared to be threatened following an incident in which police officers, in connection with a drink-driving charge, opened fire on a vehicle owned by a former commander of the Marau Eagle Force. It was also reported that two other former Marau commanders had demanded SI $100,000 from the Government, and that other Marau militants would refuse to surrender their arms, in conformity with the agreement signed in February, unless the GLF were also disarmed. In mid-March tensions heightened following a security operation against the GLF leader, Keke, in which a government patrol boat fired at villages on the western coast of Guadalcanal. In the same month police disarmed and arrested a group of villagers from Munda, Western Provice. Further incidents in early April, in which a boat fired at coastal targets in southern Guadalcanal, led the international peace monitoring force from Australia to state that the cease-fire arrangement reached under the Townsville Agreement might have been breached. The Assistant Commissioner of Police Operations protested that the Townsville Agreement did not require the police to surrender their guns, although a report published in April claimed that some of the weapons used in the security operation should have been surrendered the previous year. In June the Premier of Guadalcanal, Ezekiel Alebua, was shot and seriously injured in an assassination attempt, apparently carried out on the orders of former leaders of the IFM. Harold Keke met the Deputy Prime Minister and the secretary of the Peace Monitoring Council in June and, in October, he voiced his support for the imminent general elections. However, the failure of former militia groups to surrender their guns was the main obstacle to a lasting peace throughout 2001, and officials estimated that there remained some 500 high-powered weapons in the community, in addition to hand-made weapons. The Government declared an 'arms amnesty' in April 2002. Militants surrendered some 2,000 guns with impunity. Weapons disposal began in June, coinciding with the International Peace Monitoring Team's departure from the country.

Meanwhile, in the second half of 2000 Western, Choiseul, and Temutu provinces all declared themselves to be semi-autonomous states within Solomon Islands; on 1 September the legislature of the latter, representing 20,000 inhabitants, approved a bill allowing for a referendum on the province's proposed independence; the worsening economic situation caused by the conflict in Guadalcanal was believed to be a determining factor; additionally, movements in Guadalcanal and Makira provinces demanding greater autonomy were reported to have gained strength at this time. In late November the Minister of Provincial Government and Rural Development Nathaniel Waena announced that legislation to amend the Constitution would be submitted in 2001, in order to institute a federal system of government. Controversy arose following an announcement by the Government, in mid-March 2001, that it intended to introduce legislation to extend the life of Parliament for a further year, to expire in August 2002, stating that the social and economic position of the islands would not facilitate the holding of elections as scheduled in August 2001. This proposal attracted widespread opposition, including that of churches, trade unions, all provincial premiers, and the principal overseas aid donors to Solomon Islands. When it became apparent that he would not possess a parliamentary majority to support the legislation, Sogavare withdrew the bill from Parliament in early May; later that month it was announced that the elections would be held as scheduled, funded wholly from overseas. In September the National Parliament approved a bill to increase national general election fees by 150%; Walter Folotalu, former member of the National Parliament for Baegu, challenged the proposed legislation in the High Court in October. In the same month the High Court also began hearing the case of former Prime Minister Bartholomew Ulufa'alu; he had challenged the legality of the Government, seeking a ruling that the coup and subsequent election that ousted him were unconstitutional. However, Ulufa'alu's challenge was unsuccessful.

In October 2001 public services deteriorated as nation-wide power cuts resulted from the inability of the government-owned Solomon Islands Electricity Authority (SIEA) to pay for its supplies of diesel fuel. The Government announced the introduction of health charges in order to maintain medical services, and was forced to appeal to Australia and New Zealand for assistance in policing, as violent crime became endemic. A storage container holding weapons relinquished under the Townsville peace agreement was broken into and, in November, the revelation that compensation totalling SI $17.4m. had been paid to former members of the MEF for alleged property damage precipitated a violent demonstration by protesters demanding similar recompense. The Prime Minister was prevented from leaving his office (to attend a session of the UN General Assembly in New York), while the house of the Deputy Prime Minister was vandalized.

Accusations and rumours of bribery and intimidation were rife during the campaigning that preceded the general election, held on 5 December 2001. The electoral coalition of the Solomon Islands Alliance for Change Coalition (SIACC) won 12 seats, the PAP secured nine and the PPP six, while 22 seats were won by independent candidates. In the absence of a clear SIACC leader, 11 elected members of the coalition convened with 11 elected independents to decide upon a satisfactory premier. Later that month, following various shifts in allegiances, Sir Allan Kemakeza (as he had become), leader of the PAP and former Deputy Prime Minister, was declared Prime Minister. Despite having been previously accused of misappropriating state funds, the former Minister of Finance, Snyder Rini, was appointed Deputy Prime Minister and Minister of National Planning.

The new Government, however, was unable to improve the increasingly desperate political and economic situation on the islands. A peace summit, organized by the Peace Monitoring Council, scheduled to be held in March 2002 was, in February, postponed until June, and in early March, as the security situation in the country deteriorated further, numerous international peace monitors began withdrawing from the islands. Later in March the New Zealand Deputy High Commissioner to Solomon Islands, Bridget Nichols, was discovered at her home suffering from severe knife wounds, and died shortly afterwards in hospital, in what was initially believed to have been an incident linked to the recent escalation of violence. However, subsequent official investigations by both the New Zealand and Solomon Islands authorities concluded that the diplomat's death had been accidental. Also in March Kemakeza dismissed Michael Maina, the Minister of Finance, after Maina failed to consult the Cabinet prior to announcing a number of drastic budgetary measures, the most significant of which was his decision to devalue the national currency by 25%. Maina was replaced by Laurie Chan, who in early April reversed the devaluation.

There were reports of further disturbances on the western coast of Guadalcanal in early June 2002 during which it was claimed that 11 Malaitans, who were part of a force attempting to capture the GLF leader, Harold Keke, had been killed. In mid-July water and electricity supplies to the capital were interrupted after the SIEA was once again unable to purchase fuel to power its generators, and the Solomon Islands Water Authority had failed to pay rental arrears owed to the landowners of the Kongulai water source. Later that month the Prime Minister effected a reorganization of the Cabinet in which, most notably, Nollen Leni, hitherto Minister for Provincial Government and Rural Development, replaced Alex Bartlett as Minister for Foreign Affairs and Trade Relations; Bartlett was allocated the tourism and aviation portfolio.

The country was further adversely affected by a series of strikes in mid-August 2002 by public sector workers in protest at the non-payment of their salaries. Later that month the Minister for Youth and Sports and Women's Affairs, Rev. Augustin Greve, was assassinated. It was subsequently reported that Harold Keke had claimed responsibility for the murder. In October, in an attempt to address the deteriorating economic situation on the Islands, the Government reduced the number of ministries from 20 to 10.

In 1990 relations between Papua New Guinea and Solomon Islands deteriorated, following allegations by the Solomon Islands' Government that patrol boats from Papua New Guinea were interfering with the traditional crossing between Bougainville Island (Papua New Guinea) and the Shortland Islands, while the Papua New Guinea Government accused Solomon Islands of harbouring members of the rebel Bougainville Revolutionary Army (BRA) and of providing them with supplies. Despite the signing that year of an agreement on joint border surveillance and arrangements to host peace negotiations between the BRA and the Papua New Guinea Government, relations worsened considerably in 1992 when Papua New Guinea forces carried out several unauthorized incursions into the Shortland Islands, in which a fuel depot was destroyed and two Solomon Islanders were killed. Alleging Australian involvement in the incursions, Mamaloni suspended surveillance flights by the Australian air force over its territory, and relations between the two countries deteriorated significantly. Despite the initiation of discussions between Solomon Islands and Papua New Guinea in January 1993, further incursions were reported in April. Following the election of a new Government in May in Solomon Islands, however, relations appeared to improve, and subsequent negotiations between the two countries resulted in an agreement to close the BRA office in Honiara. Tensions with Papua New Guinea, however, increased in 1996 as violence on Bougainville intensified. Numerous incursions by Papua New Guinea defence forces into Solomon Islands' waters were reported, while the Papua New Guinea Government repeated accusations that Solomon Islands was harbouring BRA activists. However, in June 1997 Papua New Guinea and Solomon Islands concluded a maritime border agreement, following several years of negotiations. The purpose of the agreement was not only to delineate the sea boundary between the two countries but also to provide a framework for co-operation in matters of security, natural disaster, customs, quarantine, immigration and conservation. In December 1997 the Prime Ministers of the two countries paid an extended visit to Bougainville to express support for the recently-established truce agreement. Furthermore, the Governor of Bougainville was sympathetic to the problem of increasing numbers of Solomon Islanders from the Western Province crossing to Bougainville in late 2001. Many were trading goods in Bougainville in exchange for food and services. Discussions regarding the border of Papua New Guinea were held in April 2002; both Governments were concerned about the increase of weapons trafficking from Bougainville to the Western Province.

In March 1988 the 'Spearhead Group' was formed after talks between the Governments of Papua New Guinea, Vanuatu and Solomon Islands. The principal aims of the new group were to preserve Melanesian cultural traditions and to campaign for independence for the French Overseas Territory of New Caledonia. In March 1990, at a meeting in Honiara, the Melanesian Spearhead Group (MSG) admitted the FLNKS (the main Kanak, or Melanesian, political group in New Caledonia). In mid-1994 the group concluded an agreement regarded as the first step towards the establishment of a free-trade area by the three countries. Fiji was admitted to the group in mid-1996. Solomon Islands announced its commitment to further economic integration between the MSG countries in late 1997. In 1995 Solomon Islands became a signatory to the Federated States of Micronesia Agreement on Regional Fisheries Access. In early 1997 Solomon Islands and Vanuatu agreed to undertake negotiations on the maritime boundaries between the two countries in an attempt to clarify uncertainty regarding fishing rights.

Solomon Islands is a member of the Pacific Islands Forum (formerly the South Pacific Forum) and supported moves by that organization in 1988 and 1989 to ban drift-net fishing in the region, particularly by Japanese, Taiwanese and Korean fleets. Japan ceased its drift-net operations in 1992.

Relations with Australia, which is one of the principal sources of overseas assistance to Solomon Islands, became increasingly strained in the aftermath of the coup of June 2000. The Australian Minister for Foreign Affairs, Alexander Downer, was notably critical of proposals of Solomon Islands to establish its own defence force. Sogavare, in turn, stated that he regarded the funding of the Solomon Islands peace process by Australia as an attempt by that country to interfere in Solomon Islands' internal affairs, and also accused Australia of failing to alleviate ethnic tensions on Guadalcanal.

Economy

In 2000, according to estimates by the World Bank, Solomon Islands' gross national product (GNP), measured at average 1998–2000 prices, was US $277.5m., equivalent to US $630 per head (or $1,730 on an international purchasing-power parity basis). During 1990–99, it was estimated, GNP per head decreased, in real terms, at an average annual rate of 0.2%. Gross domestic product (GDP) increased in real terms, by an annual average of 1.3% in 1990–2000, but declined by 14.1% in 2000, mainly because of the climate of political uncertainty following an upsurge in civil unrest and ethnic tension. The Asian Development Bank (ADB) estimated that GDP declined by 5.0% in 2001. Solomon Islands has a high rate of population growth, which averaged 3.3% per year in 1990–99.

Agriculture (including hunting, forestry and fishing) contributed 42.1% of GDP (measured at constant 1985 prices) in 2000. The ADB estimated that, compared with the previous year, agricultural GDP declined by 12.0% in 1999 and by 26.4% in 2000. In 2000 an estimated 73.1% of the working population were involved in agriculture. The main subsistence crops are coconuts, sweet potatoes, taro, yams, cassava, rice, garden vegetables and fruit. Livestock development has concentrated on the strengthening of support for cattle, pig and poultry farmers. Spices, particularly chillies, are cultivated for export on a small scale, while in the early 1990s the production of honey became important.

The principal commercial agricultural product was traditionally copra, which was for many years the country's main export. Earnings from copra, however, declined from SI $34.7m. in 2000 to only SI $0.4m. in 2001. The operations of the islands' largest agricultural business, Solomon Islands Plantations Ltd (in which the Government purchased a stake in the late 1970s), were suspended in 2000 as a result of the civil disturbances, seriously affecting the country's palm oil exports.

Besides being a traditional subsistence activity, the fishing sector accounted for 15.0% of total export earnings in 2001 (compared with 11.7% in the previous year). The country's catch of skipjack tuna was estimated at 36,375 metric tons in 1998 and 51,760 tons in 1999. In 1998 earnings from fish exports exceeded US $10m., thus permitting the sector temporarily to regain its position as the country's biggest source of export revenue. By the late 1970s the Solomon Islands Government had been enabled to buy shares in the Japanese skipjack tuna fishing, freezing and canning company, Solomon Taiyo Ltd, operating in the islands. The Government also had its own fishing project, the National Fisheries Development Co (this was sold to Canadian interests in 1990). In 1997 the sale of licences to foreign fishing vessels (mainly from Japan and Taiwan) amounted to some SI $9.5m. Other maritime industries include the culture of marine prawns, seaweed and sea shells. Giant clam farming also became an important activity in the mid-1990s, and by December 1996 a ban on the sale and export of giant clams was introduced in an attempt to conserve stocks. In mid-1999 a grant was secured from the ADB to help develop a sustainable commercial fisheries and aquaculture system. The fishing sector was badly affected from late 1990s by the consequences of civil unrest on the islands and by low international prices for the product. In 2000 and again in 2001 fish export revenue fell to around a quarter of its 1999 level, reaching only SI $37.3m. in 2001.

The forestry sector is an important source of export revenue. However, a dramatic increase in the production of timber in the early 1990s prompted several international organizations, including the World Bank, to express alarm at the current rate of logging in the country. In late 1995 Australia announced the withdrawal of $A2.2m. worth of aid per year, in protest at the Government's refusal to implement a sustainable logging policy. The European Union (EU) reduced its assistance to the islands for similar reasons. By the late 1990s Solomon Islands was one of the few remaining countries in the world to allow the export of round logs. However, a dramatic decline in the price of timber on the international market, together with a decrease in demand for round logs, led to a crisis in the industry in 1997, which the recently-elected Government aimed to address with a new logging policy (including a moratorium on new licences, introduced in April 1998—see History). Roundwood removals were estimated at 872,000 cu m in 1999. Export earnings from roundwood declined from US $130m. in 1997 to US $103m. in 1998. Low international timber prices caused a downturn in the industry's export income in 2001 the value of which amounted to just SI $190,457 (nevertheless contributing 76.6% of total export earnings) in that year, compared with SI $250,658 in 1999.

A heavily mineralized area at Betilonga and in the Sutakiki valley, on Guadalcanal, has been investigated for gold, silver and copper, and there have been surveys of phosphate deposits, estimated at 10m. metric tons, on Bellona Island and of deposits of asbestos at Kumboro, on Choiseul, and high-grade bauxite on Rennell and Vaghena Islands. Deposits of lead, zinc and cobalt, as well as nickel deposits of some 25m. metric tons of ore on San Jorge and Isabel islands, have also been discovered. Research carried out in 1992 revealed several potential petroleum-producing areas in the territory. Small amounts of gold (which is mostly produced by alluvial mining) are exported and earned SI $1.3m., for 50 kg, in 1991. The discovery of significant deposits of gold on Vangunu Island, and of further deposits on Guadalcanal, were reported in 1996. The gold-mining project at Gold Ridge (Guadalcanal) began operations in September 1998, with a projected yield of 100,000 oz per year for 13 years. The forecast output for 1999/2000 was 130,000 oz. However, IFM dissidents (see History) occupied the mine in June 2000, forcing operations to be suspended. In the previous month the mine's owner, Ross Mining (of Australia) was acquired by a larger Australian company, Delta Gold. Inconclusive negotiations regarding the reopening of the mine took place in late 2000; the cost of recommencing operations was expected to be in excess of SI $100m. Further prospecting for gold took place in the late 1990s at Mase, New Georgia. Other (undeveloped) mineral resources include deposits of copper, lead, zinc, silver, cobalt, asbestos, phosphates, nickel and high-grade bauxite. The Government planned to auction nickel deposits of some 43m. metric tons of ore on San Jorge Island, Isabel province, in 2001.

The islands' transport and energy facilities are seriously inadequate, which hampers agricultural and economic development. Energy is derived principally from hydroelectric power, although solar energy is fairly widely, and increasingly, utilized, particularly in rural areas. Solomon Islands policy is to reduce dependence upon imported mineral fuels, which nevertheless accounted for 17.5% of total import costs in 2001.

Tourism remains relatively undeveloped in Solomon Islands. In 2000 an estimated 25,127 tourists visited the islands. Earnings from the sector were estimated at some US $13m. in 1998. Training programmes, investment, airport expansion and the proposed designation of Marovo (New Georgia) and Rennell Island as World Heritage sites (see under UNESCO) were expected to benefit the tourist industry.

In 2000 Solomon Islands recorded a visible trade deficit of SI $223.6m., and a deficit of SI $329.9m. on the current account of the balance of payments. In 2001 the principal source of imports was Australia (providing 29.3% of the total), while the principal market for exports was Japan (purchasing 19.8% of the total). Other major trading partners are the Republic of Korea, Thailand, the Philippines, the People's Republic of China, the USA and Singapore. The principal exports in 2001 were timber, fish and other marine products, and cocoa. The principal imports were foodstuffs, mineral fuels, machinery and transport equipment and basic manufactures.

In 2000 a budgetary surplus of SI $35.4m. was recorded. In 2001, however, a fiscal deficit equivalent to 8% of GDP was anticipated. Overseas aid totalled US $42.6m. in 1998. Aid from Australia totalled $A17.1m. in 1999/2000. In the same year financial assistance from New Zealand totalled $NZ5.3m. The total external debt was US $155.4m. in 2000. In that year debt-service payments were equivalent to 6.7% of the value of exports of goods and services. The annual rate of inflation averaged 10.9% in 1990–99. The rate of inflation in Honiara was estimated by the ADB at 4.8% in 2000 and at 1.8% in 2001.

During the 1990s Solomon Islands' economic development was adversely affected by inadequate transport facilities, inclement weather and by fluctuations in prices on the international market for the major agricultural exports. Successive budget deficits and a substantial current-account deficit were financed by heavy borrowing and foreign aid. Increasing environmental concern over the exploitation of the country's natural resources and its vulnerability to unscrupulous foreign operators continued to threaten the islands' economic stability. Furthermore, from 1999 the economy was severely affected by ethnic unrest in Guadalcanal. Subsequent housing and welfare payments to displaced victims of the unrest became a severe drain on domestic finance, forcing the Government into increased foreign borrowing and unsustainable drawdowns from the Central Bank of Solomon Islands. In July 1999 a US $12m. loan from the World Bank was secured to help stabilize and restructure the economy through a number of measures, including the development of the private sector and the expansion and improved regulation of the forestry sector. In September of that year a local newspaper reported that the Guadalcanal crisis had cost the country SI $18.4m. in lost tourism receipts. Government sources also announced that there had been a significant improvement in the country's financial situation following the repayment of its foreign debt through reductions in government spending and improved revenue collection. In mid-2000, however, government revenue declined sharply, and in August it was announced that 1,000 public servants were to be sent on unpaid leave. By early 2001 a total of 8,000 workers, or 15% of the total workforce, were estimated to have lost their jobs or to have been dispatched on unpaid leave. Youth unemployment, meanwhile, remained a particular problem.

In February 2001 the Central Bank of Solomon Islands reportedly declared that the country faced economic and social disaster, stating that the country's GDP had contracted by 19% within one year, and that exports had declined by 40% in six months, while domestic borrowing, particularly by the Government, had notably increased. The fiscal position deteriorated sharply in 2001. Payments to public servants, along with the transfer of funds to provincial health and education services, were delayed. Moreover, the Government defaulted on various external and domestic debts held by commercial banks and the National Provident Fund (no employee contributions being made to the latter in 2001). Merchandise exports continued to decline in 2001, resulting in a significant rise in the trade deficit. The country's dependence upon forestry—logging being the prime constituent of both taxation and export revenues—rendered the economy vulnerable to the low international prices for round logs prevailing in 2001. Any economic recovery appeared likely to be dependent upon the maintenance of prolonged political stability, necessitating improved inter-ethnic relations, in addition to a settlement of the demands for increased devolution from the provinces. Furthermore, the dramatic rise in crime, which in part had occurred as a result of the alleged infiltration of the police force by rebel groups (see History), appeared to be a deterrent to growth and investment. Among the most serious problems facing the new Government that took office in December 2001 were ongoing security concerns, the need to control expenditure (partly through further reductions in the numbers of public servants) and the restoration of the country's industrial capacity and infrastructure, particularly in the export sector. One of the incoming Government's first decisions related to the termination of duty and tax remissions. The ADB envisaged that GDP would decline by 5.0% in 2002 and subsequently remain stagnant, prior to any recovery in growth. In January 2002 the Central Bank announced that the country's total debt amounted to some US $200m., while its foreign reserves had fallen to below US $18m. The Government subsequently announced plans to reduce the administration's expenditure by up to 50%, which would reportedly result in around one-third of public employees losing their jobs. In April the newly appointed Minister for Finance rescinded the decision to devalue the national currency by 25%, taken in the previous month by his predecessor. However, this action was severely criticized by the Governor of the Central Bank, who also warned the Government that foreign-exchange levels had become critically low and that the country's capacity to trade would thus be severely constrained by the end of 2002, if not before.

Solomon Islands, in addition to being a member of the Pacific Islands Forum (formerly the South Pacific Forum—see above), has membership of the Pacific Community (formerly the South Pacific Commission) and the UN's Economic and Social Commission for Asia and the Pacific (ESCAP). The country is a member of the ADB, and is a signatory of the Lomé Conventions and successor Cotonou Agreement with the EU.

Statistical Survey

Source (unless otherwise stated): Statistics Office, POB G6, Honiara; tel. 23700; fax 20392.

AREA AND POPULATION

Area: 27,556 sq km (10,639 sq miles).

Population: 285,176 at census of 23–24 November 1986; 409,042 (males 211,381; females 197,661) at census of 21–22 November 1999.

Density (November 1999): 14.8 per sq km.

Ethnic Groups (census of November 1986): Melanesians 268,536; Polynesians 10,661; Micronesians 3,929; Europeans 1,107; Chinese 379; Others 564.

Principal Town: Honiara (capital), population 35,288 (official estimate) at mid-1990.

Births and Deaths (provisional, 1998): Birth rate 36.6 per 1,000; Death rate 5.9 per 1,000. Source: UN, *Statistical Yearbook for Asia and the Pacific.*

Expectation of Life (WHO estimates, years at birth, 2000): Males 66.6; Females 71.4. Source: WHO, *World Health Report.*

Employment (employees only, June 1993): Agriculture, hunting, forestry and fishing 8,106; Manufacturing (incl. mining and quarrying) 2,844; Electricity and water 245; Construction 977; Trade, restaurants and hotels 3,390; Transport, storage and communications 1,723; Finance, insurance, real estate and business services 1,144; Community, social and personal services 11,148; Total 29,577. Source: UN, *Statistical Yearbook for Asia and the Pacific.*

In 1993 some 72% of the employed labour force were males.

1996: Total employed 34,200.

HEALTH AND WELFARE

Key Indicators

Fertility (births per woman, 2000): 5.4.

Under-5 Mortality Rate (per 1,000 live births, 2000): 25.

Physicians (per 1,000 head, 1995): 0.14.

Hospital Beds (per 1,000 head, 1992): 2.75.

Health Expenditure (1998): US $ per head (PPP): 92.
% of GDP: 4.4.
public (% of total): 95.8.

Access to Water (% of persons, 2000): 71.

Access to Sanitation (% of persons, 2000): 34.

Human Development Index (2000): ranking: 121.
value: 0.622.

For sources and definitions, see explanatory note on p. vi.

AGRICULTURE, ETC.

Principal Crops (FAO estimates, metric tons, 2000): Coconuts 318,000; Palm kernels 8,000; Rice 4,500; Cocoa beans 3,200; Sweet potatoes 75,000; Yams 24,500; Taro 32,000; Vegetables and melons 6,850; Fruit 16,280. Source: FAO.

Livestock (FAO estimates, '000 head, year ending September 2000): Cattle 12; Pigs 64. Source: FAO.

Livestock Products (FAO estimates, '000 metric tons, 2000): Beef and veal 0.6; Pig meat 2.0. Source: FAO.

Forestry (roundwood removals, '000 cu m): Industrial wood 734 per year in 1996–99; Fuel wood 138 per year in 1996–99. Source: FAO, *Yearbook of Forest Products*.

Fishing (metric tons, live weight, 1999): Capture 82,334* (Skipjack tuna 51,760, Yellowfin tuna 16,076); Aquaculture 13*; Total catch 82,347*. * FAO estimate. Source: FAO, *Yearbook of Fishery Statistics*.

MINING

Production (kilograms, 2000): Gold 338; Silver 200 (estimate). Source: US Geological Survey.

INDUSTRY

Production (metric tons, 2,000, unless otherwise stated): Copra 2,000 (2001); Coconut oil 8,553; Palm oil 28,000 (FAO estimate); Frozen fish 23,100 (1996); Electric energy 32 million kWh (1998).

FINANCE

Currency and Exchange Rates: 100 cents = 1 Solomon Islands dollar (SI $). *Sterling, US Dollar and Euro Equivalents* (31 October 2001): £1 sterling = SI $7.898; US $1 = SI $5.426; €1 = SI $4.906; SI $100 = £12.66 = US $18.43 = €20.38. *Average Exchange Rate* (SI $ per US $): 4.8156 in 1998; 4.8381 in 1999; 5.0889 in 2000.

Budget (SI $ million, 2000): *Revenue:* Taxes 258.8; Other current revenue 18.6; Capital revenue 35.3; Total 312.7; *Expenditure:* Total 277.3 (Current 254.8; Capital 22.5). Source: Asian Development Bank, *Key Indicators of Developing Asian and Pacific Countries*.

Development Expenditure (estimates, SI $ '000, 1990): Human resources and community development 28,125; Natural resources 30,442; Commerce, industry and finance 13,375; Physical infrastructure 18,981; Government and security 6,691; Total 97,614.

2000 (SI $ million): Total 30. Source: Central Bank of Solomon Islands, *Quarterly Review* (June 2001).

Overseas Aid (external grants, US $ million, 1994): Australia 8.5; EU 6.6; Japan 20.5; New Zealand 2.9; Taiwan 2.7; United Kingdom 3.4; USA 0.6; World Health Organization 0.5; Total (incl. others) 54.4.

International Reserves (US $ million at 31 December 2000): IMF special drawing rights 0.002; Reserve position in IMF 0.71; Foreign exchange 31.34; Total 32.05. Source: IMF, *International Financial Statistics*.

Money Supply (SI $ million at 31 December 2000): Currency outside banks 88.27; Demand deposits at deposit money banks 159.35; Total money (incl. others) 248.29. Source: Central Bank of Solomon Islands, *Quarterly Review* (June 2001).

Cost of Living (Consumer Price Index for Honiara; base: 1995 = 100): 120.8 in 1997; 135.7 in 1998; 146.9 in 1999. Source: IMF, *International Financial Statistics*.

Gross Domestic Product by Economic Activity (official estimates, SI $ million at constant 1985 market prices, 2000): Agriculture 116.0; Mining 8.6; Manufacturing 13.4; Electricity, gas and water 3.6; Construction 7.6; Trade 29.7; Transport and communications 15.5; Finance 12.9; Other services 68.0; GDP at factor cost 275.3. Source: Asian Development Bank, *Key Indicators of Developing Asian and Pacific Countries*.

Balance of Payments (US $ million, 1999): Exports of goods f.o.b. 164.57; Imports of goods f.o.b. –110.04. *Trade balance* 54.53; Exports of services 56.30; Imports of services –87.49; *Balance on goods and services* 23.34; Other income received 5.46; Other income paid –22.38; *Balance on goods, services and income* 6.41; Current transfers received 41.54; Current transfers paid –26.48; *Current balance* 21.48; Capital account (net) 9.16; Direct investment from abroad 9.90; Other investment assets 0.04; Other investment liabilities –43.72; Net errors and omissions –1.58; *Overall balance* –4.72. Source: IMF, *International Financial Statistics*.

EXTERNAL TRADE

Principal Commodities (SI $ '000, 2001): *Imports c.i.f.:* Food and live animals 108,448; Beverages and tobacco 9,298; Crude materials (inedible) except fuels, mineral fuels, lubricants, etc., and animal and vegetable oils and fats 75,750; Chemicals 13,745; Basic manufactures 22,577; Machinery and transport equipment 53,320; Miscellaneous manufactured articles and other commodities and transactions 148,799; Total 431,937. *Exports f.o.b.:* Fish 37,336; Copra 432; Timber 190,457; Cocoa 4,536; Palm oil 237; Total (incl. others) 248,685.

Principal Trading Partners (US $ million, 2001): *Imports:* Australia 30.6; Fiji 3.9; Hong Kong 2.6; Japan 3.5; New Zealand 5.1; Papua New Guinea 3.9; Singapore 19.1; Thailand 2.8; USA 7.4; Total (incl. others) 104.3. *Exports:* Australia 1.5; China, People's Republic 8.3; Japan 17.1; Korea, Republic 15.4; Malaysia 1.3; Philippines 9.8; Singapore 0.9; Thailand 7.4; United Kingdom 1.0; Total (incl. others) 86.4.

Source: Asian Development Bank, *Key Indicators of Developing Asian and Pacific Countries*.

TRANSPORT

Road Traffic (motor vehicles in use at 30 June 1986): Passenger cars 1,350; Commercial vehicles 2,026.

Shipping (international traffic, '000 metric tons, 1990): Goods loaded 278; Goods unloaded 349. Source: UN, *Monthly Bulletin of Statistics*; *Merchant Fleet* (registered at 31 December 2001): Vessels 28; Total displacement ('000 grt) 8.4. Source: Lloyd's Register-Fairplay, *World Fleet Statistics*.

Civil Aviation (traffic on scheduled services, 1997): Passengers carried 94,000; Passenger-km 74 million. Source: UN, *Statistical Yearbook*.

TOURISM

Foreign Tourist Arrivals: 13,229 in 1998; 21,318 in 1999; 25,127 in 2000.

Tourist Arrivals by Country (1999): Australia 4,979; China, People's Republic 1,347; Fiji 729; Japan 887; Korea, Republic 1,237; New Zealand 925; Papua New Guinea 1,457; Philippines 2,102; Taiwan 478; United Kingdom 893; USA 1,589; Total (incl. others) 21,318. Source: World Tourism Organization, *Yearbook of Tourism Statistics*.

Tourism Receipts (US $ million): 14 in 1996; 16 in 1997; 13 in 1998. Source: World Bank.

COMMUNICATIONS MEDIA

Non-Daily Newspapers (1996): 3; estimated circulation 9,000.

Radio Receivers (1997): 57,000 in use.

Television Receivers (2000): 10,000 in use.

Telephones (2001): 7,400 main lines in use.

Mobile Cellular Telephones (2001): 1,000 subscribers.

Personal Computers (2001): 22,000 in use.

Internet Users (2001): 2,000.

Facsimile Machines (1999): 764 in use.

Sources: UNESCO, *Statistical Yearbook*; International Telecommunication Union.

EDUCATION

Pre-primary (1994): 12,627 pupils.

Primary (1994): 523 schools (1993); 2,514 teachers; 60,493 pupils.

Secondary: 23 schools (1993); 618 teachers (1994); 7,981 pupils (1995).

Overseas Centres (1988): 405 students.

Source: mainly UNESCO, *Statistical Yearbook*.

Adult Literacy Rate: 76.6% in 2000. Source: UN Development Programme, *Human Development Report*.

Directory

The Constitution

A new Constitution came into effect at independence on 7 July 1978.

The main provisions are that Solomon Islands is a constitutional monarchy with the British sovereign (represented locally by a Governor-General, who must be a Solomon Islands citizen) as Head of State, while legislative power is vested in the unicameral National Parliament composed of 50 members (increased from 47 in 1997), elected by universal adult suffrage for four years (subject to dissolution), and executive authority is exercised by the Cabinet, led by the Prime Minister. The Governor-General is appointed for up to five years, on the advice of Parliament, and acts in almost all matters on the advice of the Cabinet. The Prime Minister is elected by and from members of Parliament. Other ministers are appointed by the Governor-General, on the Prime Minister's recommendation, from members of Parliament. The Cabinet is responsible to Parliament. Emphasis is laid on the devolution of power, and traditional chiefs and leaders have a special role within these arrangements. Legislation approved in August 1996 provided for the abolition of the provincial government system and the transfer of legislative and administrative powers from the nine provincial governments to 75 area assemblies and councils controlled by central Government.

The Constitution contains comprehensive guarantees of fundamental human rights and freedoms, and provides for the introduction of a 'leadership code' and the appointment of an Ombudsman and a Public Solicitor. It also provides for 'the establishment of the underlying law, based on the customary law and concepts of the Solomon Islands people'. Solomon Islands citizenship was automatically conferred on the indigenous people of the islands and on other residents with close ties with the islands upon independence. The acquisition of land is reserved for indigenous inhabitants or their descendants.

In mid-1999 it was announced that two review committees had been established to amend the Constitution. They were expected to examine ways in which the traditions of the various ethnic groups could be better accommodated.

The Government

Head of State: HM Queen ELIZABETH II.

Governor-General: Fr Sir JOHN INI LAPLI (sworn in 7 July 1999).

THE CABINET
(August 2002)

Prime Minister: Sir ALLAN KEMAKEZA.

Deputy Prime Minister and Minister for National Planning and Human Resource Development: SNYDER RINI.

Minister for Agriculture and Livestock: EDWARD HUNUEHU.

Minister for Commerce, Employment and Trade: TREVOR OLAVAE.

Minister for Economic Reform and Structural Adjustment: DANIEL FA'AFUNUA.

Minister for Education and Training: MATHIAS TARO.

Minister for Finance: LAURIE CHAN.

Minister for Fisheries and Marine Resources: NELSON KILE.

Minister for Foreign Affairs and Trade Relations: NOLLEN LENI.

Minister for Forestry, Environment and Conservation: DAVID HOLISIVI.

Minister for Health and Medical Services: BENJAMIN UNA.

Minister for Home Affairs: CLEMENT ROJUMANA.

Minister for Lands and Surveys: SIRIAKO USA.

Minister for Mines and Energy: STEPHEN PAENI.

Minister for National Unity, Reconciliation and Peace: NATHANIEL WAENA.

Minister for Police, Justice and National Security: AUGUSTINE TANEKO.

Minister for Provincial Government and Rural Development: WALTON NAEZON.

Minister for Tourism and Aviation: ALEX BARTLETT.

Minister for Transport, Works and Communication: BERNARD GIRO.

Minister for Youth and Sports and Women's Affairs: (vacant).

MINISTRIES

In October 2002 it was announced that the number of ministries would be reduced from 20 to 10.

Office of the Prime Minister: POB G1, Honiara; tel. 21867; fax 26088

Ministry of Agriculture and Lands: POB G13, Honiara; tel. 21327; fax 21955; e-mail drsteve@solomon.com.sb.

Ministry of Education and Human Resources Development: POB G28, Honiara; tel. 23900; fax 20485.

Ministry of Finance and Treasury: POB 26, Honiara; tel. 22535; fax 20392; e-mail finance@welkam.solomon.com.sb.

Ministry of Foreign Affairs Commerce and Tourism: POB G10, Honiara; tel. 2476; fax 20351; e-mail commerce@commerce.gov.sb; internet www.commerce.gov.sb.

Ministry of Health and Medical Services: POB 349, Honiara; tel. 20830; fax 20085.

Ministry of Infrastructure Development: POB G30, Honiara; tel. 38255; fax 38259; e-mail kudu@mnpd.gov.sb.

Ministry of Natural Resorces: POB G24, Honiara; tel. 25848; fax 21245; e-mail kdfmp@welkam.solomon.com.sb.

Ministry of Police, National Security and Justice: POB 1723/404, Honiara; tel. 22208; fax 25949.

Ministry of Provincial Government, Home Affairs, National Reconciliation and Peace: POB G35, Honiara; tel. 21140; fax 21289.

Legislature

NATIONAL PARLIAMENT

POB G19, Honiara; tel. 21751; fax 23866.

Speaker: PAUL TOVUA.

General Election, 5 December 2001

Party	Seats
Solomon Islands Alliance for Change	12
People's Alliance Party	9
People's Progressive Party	6
Labour Party	1
Independents	22
Total	50

Political Organizations

Parties in the National Parliament can have a fluctuating membership and an influence disproportionate to their representation. There is a significant number of independents who are loosely associated in the amorphous, but often decisive, 'Independent Group'. The following parties represent the main groupings:

National Action Party of Solomon Islands (NAPSI): Honiara; f. 1993; Leader FRANCIS SAEMALA.

National Party: Honiara; f. 1996; Pres. EZEKIEL ALEBUA.

People's Alliance Party (PAP): Honiara; f. 1979 by a merger of the People's Progressive Party (f. 1973) and the Rural Alliance Party (f. 1977); advocates the establishment of a federal republic; Leader Sir ALLAN KEMAKEZA; Sec. EDWARD KINGMELE.

People's Progressive Party (PPP): Honiara; f. 1973; latterly Coalition for National Advancement, reverted to original name in January 2000; Leader MANASSEH SOGAVARE; Pres. JOB DUDLEY TAUSINGA.

Solomon Islands Alliance for Change Coalition (SIACC): Honiara; f. 1997; formed from the previous Solomon Islands Alliance for Change (SIAC); Co-Leaders PATTERSON OTI, FRANCIS BILLY HILLY.

Solomon Islands Labour Party: Honiara; f. 1988; formed from the Solomon Islands Trade Union movement; Leader JOSES TUHANUKU; Gen. Sec. TONY KAGOVAI.

Solomon Islands Liberal Party (SILP): Honiara; f. 1976 as the National Democratic Party (NADEPA); present name adopted in 1986; Leader BARTHOLOMEW ULUFA'ALU.

United Democratic Party (UDP): f. 1980; fmrly United Solomon Islands Party; present name adopted in 2000; Pres. PETER KENILOREA; Chair. JOHN MAETIO.

Diplomatic Representation

EMBASSIES AND HIGH COMMISSIONS IN SOLOMON ISLANDS

Australia: Hibiscus Ave, POB 589, Honiara; tel. 21561; fax 23691; High Commissioner: ROBERT DAVIS.

China (Taiwan): Pantina Plaza, POB 586, Honiara; tel. 38050; fax 38060; Ambassador: PEI Y. TENG.

Japan: National Provident Fund Bldg, Mendana Ave, POB 560, Honiara; tel. 22953; fax 21006; Chargé d'affaires: YUTAKA HIRATA.

New Zealand: Mendana Ave, POB 697, Honiara; tel. 21502; fax 22377; e-mail nzhicom@.solomon.com.sb; High Commissioner: HEATHER RIDDELL.

Papua New Guinea: POB 1109, Honiara; tel. 20561; fax 20562; High Commissioner: PONABE YUWA.

United Kingdom: Telekom House, Mendana Ave, POB 676, Honiara; tel. 21705; fax 21549; e-mail bhc@solomon.com.sb; High Commissioner: BRIAN BALDWIN.

Judicial System

The High Court is a Superior Court of Record with unlimited original jurisdiction and powers (except over customary land) as prescribed by the Solomon Islands Constitution or by any law for the time being in force in Solomon Islands. The Judges of the High Court are the Chief Justice, resident in Solomon Islands and employed by its Government, and the Puisne Judges (of whom there are usually three). Appeals from this Court go to the Court of Appeal, the members of which are senior judges from Australia, New Zealand and Papua New Guinea. The Chief Justice and judges of the High Court are *ex officio* members of the Court of Appeal.

In addition there are Magistrates' Courts staffed by qualified and lay magistrates exercising limited jurisdiction in both civil and criminal matters. There are also Local Courts staffed by elders of the local communities, which have jurisdiction in the areas of established native custom, petty crime and local government by-laws. In 1975 Customary Land Appeal Courts were established to hear land appeal cases from Local Courts, which have exclusive original jurisdiction over customary land cases.

Office of the Registrar: High Court and Court of Appeal, POB G21, Honiara; tel. 21632; fax 22702; e-mail chetwynd@welkam.solomon.com.sb.

President of the Court of Appeal: Sir ANTHONY MASON.

Chief Justice of the High Court: Sir JOHN BAPTIST MURIA.

Puisne Judges: ALBERT ROCKY PALMER, SAM LUNGOLE AWICH, FRANK KABUI.

Registrar and Commissioner of the High Court: DAVID CHETWYND.

Chief Magistrate: DAVID CHETWYND (acting).

Attorney-General: PRIMO AFEAU.

Director of Public Prosecutions: FRANCIS MWANESALUA.

Solicitor-General: RANJIT HEWEGAMA.

Auditor-General: ISAAC VALU.

Public Solicitor: PATRICK LAVERY.

Chair of Law Reform Commission: (vacant).

Religion

More than 95% of the population profess Christianity, and the remainder follow traditional beliefs. According to the census of 1976, about 34% of the population adhered to the Church of Melanesia (Anglican), 19% were Roman Catholics, 17% belonged to the South Seas Evangelical Church, 11% to the United Church (Methodist) and 10% were Seventh-day Adventists. Most denominations are affiliated to the Solomon Islands Christian Association. In many areas Christianity is practised alongside traditional beliefs, especially ancestor worship.

CHRISTIANITY

Solomon Islands Christian Association: POB 1335, Honiara; tel. 23350; fax 26150; e-mail vepsica@welkam.solomon.com.sb; f. 1967; four full mems, one assoc. mem. and eight mem. orgs; Chair. Most Rev. ELLISON L. PAGE; Exec. Sec. PHILIP SOLODIA FUNIFAKA.

The Anglican Communion

Anglicans in Solomon Islands are adherents of the Church of the Province of Melanesia, comprising eight dioceses: six in Solomon Islands (Central Melanesia, Malaita, Temotu, Ysabel, Hanuato'o and Central Solomons, which was established in May 1997) and two in Vanuatu (one of which also includes New Caledonia). The Archbishop is also Bishop of Central Melanesia and is based in Honiara. The Church had an estimated 180,000 members in 1988.

Archbishop of the Province of Melanesia: Most Rev. Sir ELLISON POGO, Archbishop's House, POB 19, Honiara; tel. 21892; fax 21098; epogo@comphq.org.sb.

General Secretary: GEORGE KIRIAU, Provincial Headquarters, POB 19, Honiara; tel. 21892; fax 21098; e-mail gkiriau@comphq.oeg.sb.

The Roman Catholic Church

For ecclesiastical purposes, Solomon Islands comprises one archdiocese and two dioceses. At 31 December 2000 there were an estimated 83,115 adherents in the country. The Bishops participate in the Bishops' Conference of Papua New Guinea and Solomon Islands (based in Papua New Guinea).

Archbishop of Honiara: Most Rev. ADRIAN THOMAS SMITH, Holy Cross, POB 237, Honiara; tel. 21943; fax 26426; e-mail ahonccsi@solomon.com.sb.

Other Christian Churches

Assembly of God: POB 928, Honiara; tel. and fax 25512; f. 1971; Gen. Supt Rev. JERIEL OTASUI.

Christian Fellowship Church: Church, Paradise, Munda, Western Province; f. 1960; over 5,000 mems in 24 villages; runs 12 primary schools in Western Province.

Seventh-day Adventist Mission: POB 63, Honiara; tel. 21191; over 9,000 mems on Guadalcanal and over 6,800 on Malaita (Oct. 2000); Pres. of Western Pacific Region NEIL WATTS; Sec. Pastor J. PIUKI TASA.

South Seas Evangelical Church: POB 16, Honiara; tel. 22388; fax 20302; Pres. ERIC TAKILA; Gen. Sec. CHARLES J. RAFEASI.

United Church of Papua New Guinea and Solomon Islands: POB 82, Munda, Western Province; tel. 61125; fax 61265; a Methodist church; Bishop of Solomon Islands Region: Rev. PHILEMON RITI; Gen. Sec. Rev. ESAU TUZA.

BAHÁ'Í FAITH

National Spiritual Assembly: POB 245, Honiara; tel. 22475; fax 25368: e-mail bahainsa@welkam.solomon.com.sb.

ISLAM

Solomon Islands Muslim League: Honiara; Gen. Sec. Dr MUSTAPHA RAMO; 66 mems. In mid-1997 the organization was still awaiting official registration as a religious group in Solomon Islands.

The Press

Agrikalsa Nius (Agriculture News): POB G13, Honiara; tel. 21211; fax 21955; f. 1986; monthly; Editor ALFRED MAESULIA; circ. 1,000.

Citizens' Press: Honiara; monthly.

Link: Solomon Islands Development Trust, POB 147, Honiara; tel. 21130; fax 21131; pidgin and English; 3 or 4 per year.

Solomon Nius: POB 718, Honiara; tel. 22031; fax 26401; monthly; Dept of Information publication; Editor-in-Chief THOMAS KIVO; monthly; circ. 2,000.

Solomon Star: POB 255, Honiara; tel. 22913; fax 21572; f. 1982; daily; English; Dir JOHN W. LAMANI; Editor OFANI EREMAI (acting); circ. 4,000.

Solomon Times: POB 212, Honiara; tel. 39197; fax 39197; weekly; Chief Editor and Man. Dir EDWARD KINGMELE.

Solomon Voice: POB 1235, Honiara; tel. 20116; fax 20090; f. 1992; daily; circ. 3,000; Editor CAROL COLVILLE.

Broadcasting and Communications

TELECOMMUNICATIONS

Telekom (Solomon Telekom Company Ltd): POB 148, Honiara; tel. 21576; fax 23642; e-mail sales@telekom.com.sb; internet www.solomon.com.sb; 51% owned by Solomon Islands National Provident Fund, 41.9% by Cable and Wireless plc., 7.1% by Govt; operates national and international telecommunications links; Chair. JOHN BEVERLY; Gen. Man. MARTYN ROBINSON.

BROADCASTING

Radio

Solomon Islands Broadcasting Corporation: POB 654, Honiara; tel. 20051; fax 23159; e-mail sibcnews@solomon.com.sb; internet www.sibconline.com; f. 1976; daily transmissions in English and Pidgin; broadcasts total 112 hours per week; Chair. DICKSON WARAKOHIA; Programme Dir DAVID PALAPU; Gen. Man. JOHNSON HONIMAE; Editor WALTER NALAGU.

Finance

The financial system is regulated and monitored by the Central Bank of Solomon Islands. There are three commercial banks and a development bank. Financial statutory corporations include the Home Finance Corpn (which took over from the Housing Authority in 1990), the Investment Corporation of Solomon Islands (the state holding company) and the National Provident Fund. At the end of 1996 there were 142 credit unions, with some 17,000 members and total assets estimated at SI $18m.

BANKING

(cap. = capital; res = reserves; dep. = deposits; brs = branches; amounts in Solomon Islands dollars)

Central Bank

Central Bank of Solomon Islands: POB 634, Honiara; tel. 21791; fax 23513; e-mail cbsi-it@welkam.solomon.com.sb; f. 1983; sole bank of issue; cap. 2.6m., res 93.5m., dep. 26.9m. (Dec. 1997); Gov. RICK HOUWENIPWELA; Deputy Gov. JOHN KAITU.

Development Bank

Development Bank of Solomon Islands: POB 911, Honiara; tel. 21595; fax 23715; e-mail dbsi@welkam.solomon.com.sb; f. 1978; cap.

8.6m., res 4.6m. (Dec. 1998); Chair. JOHN MICHAEL ASIPARA; Man. Dir LUKE LAYMAN ETA; 4 brs; 5 sub-brs.

Commercial Banks

Australia and New Zealand Banking Group Ltd (Australia): Mendana Ave, POB 10, Honiara; tel. 21835; fax 22957; Gen. Man. CECIL BROWNE.

National Bank of Solomon Islands Ltd: Mendana Ave, POB 37, Honiara; tel. 21874; fax 24358; e-mail nbsi@welkam.solomon.com.sb; f. 1982; 51% owned by the Bank of Hawaii; 49% owned by Solomon Islands National Provident Fund; cap. 2.0m., res 20.0m., dep. 221.3m. (Dec. 1999); Chair. W. M. ORD; Gen. Man. E. MURRAY; 11 brs and 6 agencies.

Westpac Banking Corporation (Australia): 721 Mendana Ave, POB 466, Honiara; tel. 21222; fax 23419; e-mail gtaviani@westpac.com.au; Man. GIAN TAVIANI.

INSURANCE

About 10 major British insurance companies maintain agencies in Solomon Islands. In mid-1995 the Government announced a joint venture with an Australian insurance company to establish the Solomon Islands Insurance Company.

Trade and Industry

GOVERNMENT AGENCY

Investment Corporation of Solomon Islands: POB 570, Honiara; tel. 22511; holding company through which the Government retains equity stakes in a number of corporations; Chair. FRANCIS BILLY HILLY.

DEVELOPMENT ORGANIZATIONS

Solomon Islands Development Trust (SIDT): POB 147, Honiara; tel. 21130; fax 21331; e-mail sidt@welkam.solomon.com.sb; f. 1982; development org; Chief Officer ABRAHAM BALANISIA.

CHAMBER OF COMMERCE

Solomon Islands Chamber of Commerce and Employers: POB 650, Honiara; tel. 22643; fax 22907; e-mail chamberc@welkam.solomon.com.sb; 116 member cos (Sept. 2000); Chair. DAVID QUAN; Gen. Sec. HILDA TANGO.

INDUSTRIAL AND TRADE ASSOCIATIONS

Association of Mining and Exploration Companies: c/o POB G24, Honiara; f. 1988; Pres. NELSON GREG YOUNG.

Commodities Export Marketing Authority: POB 54, Honiara; tel. 22528; fax 21262; e-mail cema@solomon.com.sb; sole exporter of copra; agencies at Honiara and Yandina; Chair. HUGO RAGOSO; Gen. Man. MOSES PELOMO.

Livestock Development Authority: Honiara; tel. 29649; fax 29214; f. 1977, privatized 1996; Man. Dir WARREN TUCKER.

Solomon Islands Business Enterprise Centre: POB 972, Honiara; tel. 26651; fax 26650; e-mail simbec@solomon.com.sb.

Solomon Islands Forest Industries Association: POB 1617, Honiara; tel. 26026; fax 20267; Chair. and Sec. KAIPUA TOHI.

EMPLOYERS' ORGANIZATIONS

Chinese Association: POB 1209, Honiara; tel. 22351; fax 23480; asscn of businessmen from the ethnic Chinese community.

Federation of Solomon Islands Business: POB 320, Honiara; tel. 22902; fax 21477.

Solomon Islands Farmers' Association: POB 113, Honiara; tel. 27508; fax 27509; founded a credit union in 1990; Technical Adviser. SRI RAMON JUN QUITALES.

Solomon Islands Chamber of Commerce and Employers: See above.

UTILITIES

Electricity

Solomon Islands Electricity Authority (SIEA): POB 6, Honiara; tel. 21711; fax 21467; e-mail mike@siea.com.sb; f. 1961; Chair. STEPHEN TONAFALEA; CEO M. L. NATION.

Water

Solomon Islands Water Authority (SIWA): POB 1407; Honiara; tel. 23985; fax 20723; f. 1994; Gen. Man. DONALD MAKINI.

CO-OPERATIVE SOCIETIES

In 1986 there were 156 primary co-operative societies, working mostly outside the capital. There are two associations running and aiding co-operative societies in Solomon Islands:

Central Co-operative Association (CCA): Honiara.

Salu Fishing Cooperative Association: POB 1041, Honiara; tel. 26550.

Solomon Islands Consumers Co-operative Society Ltd: Honiara; tel. 21798; fax 23640.

Solomon Islands Farmers and Producers Cooperative Association Ltd: Honiara; tel. 30908.

Western General Co-operative Association (WGCA): Gizo, Western Province.

MAJOR COMPANIES

Evergreen Forest Industries: POB 771, Honiara; tel. 30778.

Gold Ridge Mining: POB 1556, Honiara; tel. 25807; fax 25872; e-mail grml@solomon.com.sb; f. 1998; managed by Delta Gold (Australia), gold mining on Guadalcanal and New Georgia; operations suspended June 2000 due to ethnic tension; Man. DICK BRAIMBRIDGE.

Goodman Fielder (SI) Ltd: Honiara; tel. 30146; fax 30399; e-mail fielders@welkam.solomon.com.sb; flour millers, bakers and biscuit manufacturers; 17% Australian-owned; Gen. Man. PATRICK COTTER.

Honiara Timber Exporters: POB 959, Honiara; tel. 39200; fax 39199.

Kolombangara Forest Products Ltd: POB 382, Honiara; tel. 60230; fax 60020; e-mail office@kfpl.com.sb; internet www.kfpl.com.sb; sustainable forestry; teak, eucalyptus; jt venture of govt of Solomon Islands and Commonwealth Development Corpn; FSC-certified company.

Linkali Timber Development Co Ltd: f. 1988; jtly owned by Xing Ling Timber Co Ltd and the Kalikoqu tribe.

National Fisheries Developments Ltd: Honiara; tel. 21506; fax 21459; f. 1977; sold by Govt in 1990; Singaporean-owned; operates fishing vessels and exports tuna; Gen. Man. PHIL ROBERTS.

Pacific Timbers: POB 201, Honiara; tel. 31100; fax 30062; e-mail movers@welkam.solomon.com.sb.

Russell Islands Plantation Estates Ltd: PO Yandina, Russell Islands, Central Province; tel. 21779; fax 21785; e-mail ripelyan@solomon.com.sb; coconut products; cocoa; livestock.

Solomon Islands Plantations Ltd: POB 350, Honiara; tel. 31121; fax 31188; e-mail sipl@solomon.com.sb; f. 1971; jt venture between Commonwealth Development Corpn, Investment Corpn of Solomon Islands and local landowners; major producer and exporter of palm oil and palm kernels; operations suspended mid-2000; Gen. Man. MIKE WORKMAN.

Solomon Islands Tobacco Co Ltd: Kukum Highway, Ranandi, Honiara; tel. 30127; fax 30463; part-owned by British American Tobacco; Gen. Man. ALLAN FAULDS.

Solomon Soaps Ltd: POB 326, Honiara; Gen. Man. EWALD TISCHLER.

Solomon Taiyo Ltd: POB 965, Honiara; tel. 21664; fax 23462; e-mail gm@stl.com.sb; f. 1972; 51% owned by Govt, 49% by Japanese co; offshore operations suspended Aug. 2000 following hijacking of vessel; Gen. Man. HIDEOTOSHI ITO.

Solrice: Honiara; 100% owned by Ricegrowers' Co-operative of Australia; Gen. Man. (vacant).

Waterking Marine; Gizo Hospital, Gizo, Western Province; tel. 60224; fax 60142; fresh and filleted marine products; Gen. Man. ISACC DAKEI.

TRADE UNIONS

There are 14 registered trade unions in Solomon Islands.

Solomon Islands Council of Trade Unions (SICTU): National Centre for Trade Unions, POB 271, Honiara; tel. 22566; fax 23171; f. 1986; Pres. DAVID P. TUHANUKU; Sec. BENEDICT ESIBAEA; the principal affiliated unions are:

Solomon Islands Media Association: POB 654, Honiara; tel. 20051; fax 23300; e-mail sibcnews@welkam.solomon.com.sb; Pres. GEORGE ATKIN.

Solomon Islands Medical Association: Honiara.

Solomon Islands National Teachers' Association (SINTA): POB 967, Honiara; f. 1985; Pres. K. SANGA; Gen. Sec. BENEDICT ESIBAEA.

Solomon Islands National Union of Workers (SINUW): POB 14, Honiara; tel. 22629; Pres. DAVID P. TUHANUKU.

Solomon Islands Post and Telecommunications Union: Honiara; tel. 21821; fax 20440; Gen. Man. SAMUEL SIVE.

Solomon Islands Public Employees' Union (SIPEU): POB 360, Honiara; tel. 21967; fax 23110; Pres. MARTIN KARANI; Sec.-Gen. CLEMENT WAIWORI.

Solomon Islands Seamen's Association: POB G32, Honiara; tel. 24942; fax 23798.

Transport

ROADS

There are about 1,300 km of roads maintained by the central and provincial governments; in 1976 main roads covered 455 km. In addition, there are 800 km of privately maintained roads mainly for plantation use. Road construction and maintenance is difficult because of the nature of the country, and what roads there are serve as feeder roads to the main town of an island.

Honiara has a main road running about 65 km each side of it along the north coast of Guadalcanal, and Malaita has a road 157 km long running north of Auki and around the northern end of the island to the Lau Lagoon, where canoe transport takes over; and one running south for 35 km to Masa. On Makira a road links Kira Kira and Kakoranga, a distance of 35 km. Before it abandoned mining investigations in 1977, the Mitsui Mining and Smelting Co built 40 km of road on Rennell Island.

SHIPPING

Regular shipping services (mainly cargo) exist between Solomon Islands and Australia, New Zealand, Hong Kong, Japan, Singapore, Taiwan and European ports. In 1994 internal shipping was provided by 93 passenger/cargo ships, 13 passenger-only ships, 61 fishing vessels and 17 tugs. The four main ports are at Honiara, Yandina, Noro and Gizo. The international seaports of Honiara and Noro are controlled by the Solomon Islands Ports Authority.

Solomon Islands Ports Authority: POB 307, Honiara; tel. 22646; fax 23994; e-mail ports@solomon.com.sb; f. 1956; responsible for the ports of Honiara and Noro; Chair. NELSON BOSO; Gen. Man. N. B. KABUI.

Sullivans (SI) Ltd: POB 3, Honiara; tel. 21643; fax 23889; e-mail shipserv@solomon.com.sb; shipping agents, importers, wholesalers.

National Shipping Service of Solomon Islands (NSSI): Honiara; f. 1994; Gen. Man. NELSON KABUI.

Tradco Shipping Ltd: POB 114, Honiara; tel. 22588; fax 23887; e-mail tradco@solomon.com.sb; f. 1984; shipping agents, agents for Lloyd's.

CIVIL AVIATION

Two airports are open to international traffic and a further 25 serve internal flights. Air Niugini (Papua New Guinea), Air Nauru and Qantas (Australia) fly to the principal airport of Henderson, 13 km from Honiara. In March 1998 a new terminal building, built with US $15.5m. of funds from Japan, was opened at Henderson airport.

Director of Civil Aviation: DEMETRIUS T. PIZIKI.

Solomon Airlines Limited: POB 23, Honiara; tel. 20031; fax 20232; e-mail gzoleveke@solair.com.sb; internet solomonairlines.com.au; f. 1968; govt-owned; international and domestic operator; scheduled services between Honiara and Port Moresby (Papua New Guinea), Nadi (Fiji), Brisbane (Australia) and Port Vila (Vanuatu); Chair. STEPHEN TONAFALEA; Gen. Man. GIDEON ZOLEVEKE Jr.

Tourism

Tourism is hindered by the relative inaccessibility of the islands and the inadequacy of tourist facilities. In 2000 tourist arrivals totalled 25,127. The industry earned US $13m. in 1998.

Solomon Islands Visitors Bureau: POB 321, Honiara; tel. 22442; fax 23986; e-mail visitors@solomon.com.sb; internet www.commerce.gov.sb/tourism/index.htm; f. 1980; Gen. Man. MORRIS OTTO NAMOGA; Marketing Man. ANDREW NIHOPARA.

Defence

Before the coup of June 2000, a unit within the Police Force, the Police Field Force, received technical training and logistical support from Australia and New Zealand. The force had two patrol boats and undertook surveillance activities in Solomon Islands' maritime economic zone. Additionally, in 1999–2000 a multinational force consisting largely of officers from Fiji and Vanuatu were deployed to quell inter-ethnic violence. (The officers from Fiji departed in April 2000.) The Solomon Islands Peace Plan of July 2000 (see History) foresaw the creation of separate Ministries of Defence and of Police, Justice and Legal Affairs. The Ministry of Defence would initially be responsible for introducing legislation allowing for the establishment of a Solomon Islands Defence Force. The Solomon Islands National Reconnaissance and Surveillance Force, founded in 1995, would also answerable to this ministry, and it was announced that an air surveillance unit would be established.

Commissioner of Police: MORTON SIRIHETI.

Commissioner of National Reconnaissance and Surveillance Force: Maj. MICHAEL WHEATLEY.

Education

About two-thirds of school-age children receive formal education, mainly in state schools. About 30% of the children who complete a primary school education receive secondary schooling, either in one of eight national secondary schools (at least one of which is run by the Government and the remainder by various Churches) or in one of 12 provincial secondary schools, which are run by provincial assemblies. The provincial secondary schools provide curricula of a practical nature, with a bias towards agriculture, while the national secondary schools offer more academic courses.

In 1993 there were 523 primary schools, with a total of 60,493 pupils in 1994. Also in 1993 there were 23 secondary schools, with a total of 7,981 pupils in 1995. There are two teacher-training schools and a technical institute. According to the 1999 census, 57% of children aged five–14 attended school. Scholarships are available for higher education at various universities overseas. In 1977 the Solomon Islands Centre of the University of the South Pacific (based in Fiji) opened in Honiara. Central government expenditure on education in 1991 was SI $24m., or 7.9% of total spending.

Tonga

Physical and Social Geography

The Kingdom of Tonga, which is located in the central South Pacific about 650 km east of Fiji and south of Samoa, comprises 173 islands, totalling 748 sq km (289 sq miles) in area. The islands consist of two chains, those to the west being volcanic and those to the east being coral islands. They are divided into three groups: Vava'u in the north, Ha'apai and Tongatapu in the south. Only 36 of the islands are permanently inhabited. The climate is mild, with temperatures generally in the range 16°C–21°C (61°F–71°F) for most of the year, although usually hotter (27°C—81°F) in December and January.

The population is predominantly Polynesian, and Tongan is the language of the indigenous inhabitants. English is also widely spoken and is the language of education and administration. Most of the population are Christians, and the leading denomination is Wesleyan. The population of Tonga was estimated at 100,281 in mid-2000. About two-thirds of the population are resident on the largest island, Tongatapu, where the capital, Nuku'alofa, is situated.

History

From about the 10th century Tongan society developed a lineage of sacred chiefs, who gradually became effective rulers. Since European contact the chiefs have become known as kings. The Kingdom of Tonga adopted its first Constitution in 1875, during the reign of King George Tupou I who had reunited the islands. As a result of increasing civil unrest, Tonga negotiated a treaty with the United Kingdom in 1900, whereby it came under British protection.

Queen Salote Tupou III came to the throne in 1918 and ruled Tonga until her death in December 1965. Her son, Prince Tupouto'a Tungi, who had been Prime Minister since 1949, succeeded her. He took the title of King Taufa'ahau Tupou IV and appointed his brother, Prince Fatafehi Tu'ipelehake, to be Prime Minister. In 1958 a treaty of friendship was signed between Tonga and the United Kingdom, providing for the appointment of a British commissioner and consul to be responsible to the Governor of Fiji, who held the office of British Chief Commissioner for Tonga. Tonga gained increased control over internal affairs in 1967 and became fully independent, within the Commonwealth, on 4 June 1970. Tonga was formally admitted to the UN in September 1999.

Elections held in May 1981 resulted in an unexpected defeat for the People's Representatives group, and the new Assembly became dominated by traditionalist conservatives. Further elections to the Legislative Assembly took place in May 1984. Following elections held in February 1987, new members, who were reported to include some of the Government's harshest critics, replaced six of the nine People's Representatives in the Legislative Assembly.

In July 1988 'Akilisi Pohiva, the editor of a local independent magazine, was awarded $T26,500 by the Supreme Court, after the Government had been found guilty of unfairly dismissing him in 1985 from his job in the Ministry of Education, for reporting on controversial issues. The court ruling intensified opposition demands for the abolition of perceived feudal aspects within Tongan society. The King, however, expressed his opposition to majority rule, on the grounds that the monarchy and royal-dominated Government could react to the needs of the people more quickly than the government of a parliamentary democracy. In 1989 the nine commoner members of the Legislative Assembly boycotted the Assembly, leaving it without a quorum, in protest at the absence of the finance minister, Cecil Cocker, when they wished to question him. Upon resuming their seats in the Assembly, in September 1989, the commoners tabled a motion demanding reform of the Assembly to make it more accountable to the people. The motion proposed increasing popular representation to 15 and the reduction of noble representation to three seats (the Cabinet has 12 members who sit in the Assembly). The commoners indicated that, if they were re-elected in the general election of February 1990, they would consider the results as a mandate for change and as a sign of public approval for their attempts to achieve more equitable representation for the Tongan people. Pohiva, the leader of the pro-reform commoners, was the candidate who received the most votes and, with five colleagues, achieved an overwhelming victory. In September 1990 the newly-constituted Appeal Court, comprising judges from other Pacific countries rather than the Privy Council, dismissed allegations of bribery and corruption made against Pohiva by some conservatives. In October 1990 Pohiva initiated a court case against the Government, claiming that its controversial sale of passports to foreign citizens was unconstitutional and illegal. The passports were sold mainly in Hong Kong to citizens of the territory and of the People's Republic of China, for as much as US $30,000 each, allowing the purchasers, in theory, to avoid travel restrictions imposed on Chinese passport-holders. In February 1991, however, a constitutional amendment, to legalize the naturalization of the new passport-holders, was adopted by an emergency session of the Legislative Assembly, and the case was therefore dismissed. In March a large demonstration was held in protest at the Government's actions, and a petition urging the King to invalidate the 426 passports in question, and to dismiss the Minister of Police (who was responsible for their sale), was presented by prominent commoners and church leaders. In the following month the Government admitted that the former President of the Philippines, Ferdinand Marcos, and his family had been given Tongan passports as gifts, after his fall from power in 1986. The events that ensued from the sale of passports were widely viewed as indicative of the growing support for reform and for greater accountability in the government of the country. By 1996, however, most of the 6,600 passports sold under the scheme had expired, as holders had failed to renew them.

In August 1991 the Prime Minister, Prince Fatafehi Tu'ipelehake, retired from office, owing to ill health, and was succeeded by the King's cousin, Baron Vaea, who had previously held the position of Minister of Labour, Commerce and Industries. Tu'ipelehake died in April 1999.

Plans by campaigners for democratic reform to establish a formal political organization were realized in November 1992, when the Pro-Democracy Movement was founded. The group, led by Fr Seluini 'Akau'ola (a Roman Catholic priest), organized a constitutional convention in the same month, at which options for the introduction of democratic reform were discussed. The Government, however, refused to recognize or to participate in the convention, prohibiting any publicity of the event and denying visas to invited speakers from abroad. Nevertheless, the pro-democracy reformists appeared to be enjoying increased public support, and, at elections in February 1993, won six of the nine People's Representative seats in the Legislative Assembly. However, Pohiva's position was undermined when, in December 1993 and February 1994, he lost two defamation cases in the Supreme Court, following the publication of allegations of fraudulent practice in his journal, *Kele'a*. In August 1994 Tonga's first political party was formed when the Pro-Democracy Movement launched its People's Party, under the chairmanship of a local businessman, Huliki Watab.

Elections took place in January 1996, at which pro-democracy candidates retained six of the nine People's Representative seats in the Legislative Assembly.

In July 1996 the Legislative Assembly voted to resume the sale of Tongan passports to Hong Kong Chinese, despite the controversy caused by a similar scheme in the early 1990s. As many as 7,000 citizenships were to be made available for between $T10,000 and $T20,000, granting purchasers all the rights of Tongan nationality, except ownership of land.

In September 1996 a motion to impeach the Minister of Justice and Attorney-General, Tevita Topou, was proposed in the Legislative Assembly. The motion alleged that Topou had continued to receive his daily parliamentary allowance during an unauthorized absence from the Assembly. Moreover, the publication of details of the impeachment motion, which had been reported to *The Times of Tonga* by Pohiva, before it had been submitted to the Legislative Assembly, resulted in the imprisonment of the latter and of the newspaper's editor, Kalafi Moala, and deputy editor, Filakalafi Akau'ola, for contempt of parliament. The three were subsequently released, although in October Moala was found guilty on a further charge of contempt, for critical remarks concerning the justice system in Tonga. In the same month the King closed the Legislative Assembly (which had been expected to sit until mid-November) until further notice. He denied that he had taken this decision in order to prevent further impeachment proceedings against Topou. In September 1997, however, the Legislative Assembly voted to abandon the impeachment proceedings.

The Government rejected accusations in early 1997 from journalists in Tonga and from media organizations throughout the region, that it was attempting to force the closure of *The Times of Tonga*, despite forbidding Moala (who resided in Auckland, New Zealand) to enter Tonga without written permission from the Government and issuing a ban on all government-funded advertising in the publication and on all government employees giving interviews to its journalists.

Parliament reopened in late May 1997. In June Akau'ola was arrested once again and charged with sedition for publishing a letter in *The Times of Tonga* that questioned government policy. However, in the same month the Government suffered a significant reversal when the Court of Appeal ruled that the imprisonment of Pohiva and the two journalists in late 1996 had been unlawful. In August the Prime Minister of New Zealand, James Bolger, paid an official visit to Tonga. Following the visit, Pohiva, who had unsuccessfully sought a meeting with Bolger, criticized New Zealand's relationship with Tonga, claiming that financial assistance from the country hindered democratic reform.

In mid-September 1998 the King closed the Legislative Assembly in response to a petition, signed by more than 1,000 people, which sought the removal from office of the Speaker, Eseta Fusitu'a. A parliamentary committee was forced to conduct an inquiry into the activities of Fusitu'a, who was accused of misappropriating public funds and of abusing his position. Pohiva and other pro-democracy activists commended the King for his decisive action in response to the petition. Legislation presented to the legislature later that month, which proposed that in future the Legislative Assembly should appoint cabinet ministers (a responsibility hitherto reserved for the King) was seen as further evidence of the increasing influence of the pro-democracy lobby in the political life of the country.

At the general election held on 11 March 1999 five members of the reformist Human Rights and Democracy Movement (formerly the People's Party) were returned to the Legislative Assembly, compared with six at the previous election. In April Veikune was appointed as Speaker and Chairman of the Legislative Assembly, replacing Eseta Fusitu'a, who had lost his seat at the general election. In late 1999 the former Minister for Lands, Survey and Natural Resources, Fakafanua, appeared in court on charges of forgery and bribery.

On 3 January 2000 the King appointed Prince 'Ulukalala-Lavaka-Ata as Prime Minister, replacing Baron Vaea who had in 1995 announced his desire to retire. It had been expected that Crown Prince Tupouto'a would take up the position, but his support for constitutional reform in Tonga (notably the abolition of life-time terms for the Prime Minister and Ministers) contrasted with the King's more conservative approach. In March of that year a report published by the US State Department claimed that Tonga's system of government, whereby the Legislative Assembly is not directly elected, was in breach of UN and Commonwealth human rights guide-lines. The report was welcomed by 'Akilisi Pohiva, the leader of the Human Rights and Democracy Movement, who reiterated the party's demands for greater democracy, set out in a draft constitution completed in late 1999.

In November 2000 the Human Rights and Democracy Movement condemned the Government's decision to co-operate with an Australian biotechnology company wishing to carry out research into the genetic causes of a range of diseases. Tonga's extended family structures and the genetic isolation of its ethnically homogenous Polynesian population were cited as providing a rare opportunity for research. In return for its co-operation in the project, Tonga was to receive a share of the royalties from the sale of any drugs developed.

In January 2001 the Prime Minister announced a reallocation of cabinet positions in which he assumed responsibility for the newly created telecommunications portfolio. In the same month claims which appeared in a newspaper report that members of the pro-democracy movement had been involved in a plot to assist a prison break-out, to seize weapons from the army and to assassinate a cabinet minister were vehemently denied by representatives of the group. A spokesperson for the movement stated that the allegations were merely the latest in a series of claims aimed at discrediting the organization. Meanwhile, ongoing concerns for the freedom of the media in Tonga were renewed following the arrest of the deputy editor of *The Times of Tonga* on charges of criminal libel.

In February 2001 the Human Rights and Democracy Movement launched a public petition to amend Tonga's Nationality Act to allow Tongans who had taken up citizenship in other countries to retain Tongan citizenship. Their stated objective in undertaking the petition was to acknowledge Tonga's dependence on remittances from Tongans living overseas.

In September 2000, meanwhile, protests took place in Nuku'alofa, prompted by concerns that Chinese immigrant businesses, encouraged by the Government to establish themselves in Tonga, were creating unfavourable economic conditions for Tongan businesses. The Human Rights and Democracy Movement appealed to the Government to cease issuing work permits to foreign (predominantly Chinese) business people and to end the sale of Tongan passports, which had raised an estimated US $30m. during the 1980s. In order to protect this money from his ministers, whom he feared would squander it on unsuitable public works projects should it enter Tonga, the King requested that the funds be placed in the Tonga Trust Fund, held in a cheque account at the San Francisco, CA, branch of the Bank of America. In June 1999 Jesse Bogdonoff, a Bank of America employee, successfully sought royal approval to invest the money in a company in Nevada called Millennium Asset Management, where Bogdonoff was named as the Fund's Advising Officer. Bogdonoff later claimed that he had made a profit of about $11m., which so impressed the King that he appointed Bogdonoff as Court Jester.

The balance of the Fund and the interest it had accrued (altogether some $40m.) was due to be returned to Tonga on 6 June 2001. Instead the money appeared to have vanished, along with Millennium Asset Management, which had ceased to exist. In September Princess Pilolevu, acting as Regent in the absence of the King and the Crown Prince, dismissed Kinikinilau Tutoatasi Fakafanua, currently Minister of Education, but who at the time of the incident had been Minister of Finance, along with the Deputy Prime Minister and Minister of Justice, Tevita Tupou, both of whom were trustees of the fund. She appointed the Minister of Police, Fire Services and Prisons, Clive Edwards, as Acting Deputy Prime Minister. Parliament created a committee to investigate the crime and tabled a motion to impeach Fakafanua and Tupou. There were no apparent reprisals, or legal action, against Bogdonoff, who claimed that he had been deliberately misled as to the value of the funds. In October the Acting Deputy Prime Minister denied that the Privy Council had directed the transfers from the Fund or that any Ministers were implicated. He stressed that at least $2.1m. of the fund, invested in Tongan banks, was duly accounted for. In June 2002, however, the Government admitted that some $24m. had been lost as a result of Bogdonoff's actions and that legal proceedings had been initiated in the USA.

In January 2002 Pohiva published allegations that the King held a secret offshore bank account containing US $350m., some of which was believed to be the proceeds of gold recovered from an 18th century shipwreck. He claimed to possess a letter written to the King from within the palace referring to the account. The Government dismissed the letter as a forgery. Nevertheless, Pohiva was briefly held in custody in February, whilst police searched the offices of the Human Rights and Democracy Movement and confiscated computer equipment in an attempt to find the source of the allegations. Later that month New Zealand's Minister for Foreign Affairs and Trade condemned Tonga as being endemically corrupt, implying that New Zealand's annual $NZ6m. profited the élite rather than the Tongan people as a whole. In February the King admitted that he did possess an overseas account, with the Bank of Hawaii, but declared that it contained the profits of vanilla sales from his own plantation. Nevertheless, Pohiva was formally charged with the use and publication of a forged document. In May 2002 a court began a preliminary hearing of the charges against him.

A general election was held on 6–7 March 2002, at which 52 candidates competed for the nine commoners' seats in the Legislative Assembly. The Human Rights and Democracy Movement won seven seats.

In late July 2002 it was reported that Pohiva, Moala and Akau'ola were seeking damages from the Tongan Government for wrongful imprisonment, following their incarceration in 1996 on charges of contempt of parliament.

A friendship treaty signed with the USA, in July 1988, provided for the safe transit of US nuclear-capable ships within Tongan waters. Tonga was virtually alone in the region in failing to condemn the French Government for its decision to resume nuclear-weapons tests in the South Pacific in mid-1995. However, in May 1996 it was announced that Tonga was finally to accede to the South Pacific Nuclear-Free Zone Treaty.

In September 1990 Tonga caused some controversy by reserving for itself the last 16 satellite positions in space that are suitable for trans-Pacific communications. Despite the protests of leading member-nations of Intelsat (an international consortium responsible for most of the world's satellite services) and allegations that the move was a profit-making ploy prompted by a US entrepreneur, the International Telecommunication Union was obliged to approve the claim. A dispute with Indonesia, concerning that country's use of satellite positions reserved by Tonga in 1990, was resolved by the signing of an agreement in December 1993. In May of the following year the two countries established diplomatic relations at ambassadorial level.

In January 1997 Tonga pledged its full support for New Zealand's efforts to combat illegal drugs-trafficking in the region. The Government's offer to co-operate with the New Zealand police followed the seizure in late 1996 of a shipment of cocaine which had been smuggled out of Tonga in hollowed yams, prompting fears that the country was becoming a transhipment point for drugs-traffickers operating in the South Pacific region.

In November 1998 Tonga announced that it had decided to terminate its diplomatic links with Taiwan and to establish relations with the People's Republic of China.

In January 2002, in the Red Sea, Israeli commandos seized a ship that was allegedly transporting weapons to Palestinian activists. The ship was flying a Tongan flag of convenience and had been registered in the Kingdom, although its ownership was uncertain. 'Akilisi Pohiva criticized Tonga's policy of international ship registration, which generated income through sales of flags of convenience. (The issue of international shipping registration had never been debated in Parliament.) Following the seizure, the registration system was closed in June. However, in September another Tongan-registered ship was seized off the coast of Italy and its crew arrested on suspicion of plotting an al-Qa'ida-sponsored terrorist attack in Europe. Furthermore, it was reported in early October that the Greek businessman in charge of the Tongan International Registry of Ships, Pelopidas Papadopoulos, had absconded with the proceeds of the operation owed to the Tongan Government, totalling some US $300,000.

Economy

In 2000, according to estimates by the World Bank, Tonga's gross national product (GNP), measured at average 1998–2000 prices, was US $166m., equivalent to US $1,660 per head. During 1990–99, it was estimated, GNP per head increased, in real terms, at an average annual rate of 0.9%. Over the same period, the population increased by an annual average of 4.5%. Tonga's gross domestic product (GDP) increased, in real terms, by 3.1% during 1990–2000. Growth was estimated at 4.7% in 1999 and at 6.1% in 2000. According to Asian Development Bank (ADB) estimates, GDP increased by only 3.0% in the 2000/2001 fiscal year, largely owing to slow growth in the agriculture and tourism sectors. In 2001/02 growth was forecast to decrease further, to 2.9%.

The majority of the islands have an inherently fertile soil. Agriculture (with forestry and fishing) accounted for some 30.0% of GDP in 1999/2000 and engaged 33.8% of the employed labour force in 1996. According to the ADB, agricultural GDP increased at an average annual rate of 0.8% in 1996–2001, rising by 10.8% in 2000 and by 1.3% in 2001. Coconuts and bananas have traditionally accounted for the bulk of Tonga's exports. However, squash have become increasingly important, and exports of the crop provided 48.7% of total export earnings in 1999/2000. Production of vanilla has declined in recent years. Vanilla accounted for just 4.4% of export earnings in 1999/2000, compared with 13.4% in 1995/96. Root crops, breadfruit, watermelons and citrus fruits are also cultivated. Livestock farming consists of pigs, cattle, goats, poultry and bees. The islands are not, however, self-sufficient, and imports of food accounted for some 32% of total import costs in 1999/2000.

The fishing industry was strengthened in 1984 by the opening of a dockyard complex in the Ha'apai group and the construction of a port at Nuku'alofa, together with a fleet of up to 60 fishing-boats. Revenues from fishing improved steadily during the 1990s, and generated income of US$ 4.1m. in 1999/2000. In early 2001 the Australian Government agreed to fund a four-year fishing project on the islands, which was to include the provision of equipment to small-scale fishing operators, improved marketing opportunities and the development of commercial long-line tuna fishing.

Industry (including mining, manufacturing, construction and power) provided some 13.1% of GDP in 1999/2000, and engaged 26.4% of the employed labour force in 1996. Industrial GDP was estimated by the ADB to have increased by 12.4% in 1999, by 3.0% in 2000 and by 5.4% in 2001. Manufacturing contributed 5.1% of GDP in 1999/2000, and (with mining) employed 22.8% of the labour force in 1996. Food products and beverages accounted for 56.8% of total manufactured goods produced in 1999/2000. The food and textile sectors of manufacturing registered the largest increases in 1999/2000, raising the value of their production by 14.6% and 56.8% respectively. The most important industrial activities are the production of concrete blocks, small excavators, clothing, furniture, handicrafts, leather goods, sports equipment (including small boats), brewing and coconut oil. There is also a factory for processing sandalwood.

Service industries contributed some 56.9% of GDP in in 1999/2000. According to the ADB, the GDP of the services sector expanded by 4.1% in 1999, by 5.6% in 2000 and by 3.2% in 2001. Tourism makes a significant contribution to the economy and earned an estimated US $16.5m. in 1999/2000. The trade, restaurants and hotels sector contributed 13.5% of GDP in 1999/2000, and engaged 8.5% of the employed labour force in 1996. Visitor arrivals to totalled 33,868 in 1999/2000, when cruise-ship passengers also accounted for a further 5,151 visitors. The sector saw particularly strong growth in 2000 as Tonga proved a popular location for events held to celebrate the millennium. However, the effects of the suicide attacks on the USA in September 2001 damaged the sector.

The country's visible trade deficit, which increased to US$ 49m. in 2001 is offset by income from tourism and by remittances from the large number of Tongans working overseas. Consequently, the current account of the balance of payments recorded a deficit of US $12m. in the same year. Among Tonga's principal trading partners is New Zealand, accounting for 32.5% of total imports and 5.7% of exports in 2001. In the same year Japan purchased some 42.2% of Tonga's exports. Other important trading partners include Australia, Fiji and the USA. The principal exports in 2001 were foodstuffs. The principal imports were foodstuffs, machinery and transport equipment, basic manufactures and mineral fuels.

Principal donors of aid to Tonga are the United Kingdom, New Zealand, Australia, Germany, Japan, the ADB and the EU. In 1997/98 receipts of development assistance totalled an estimated US $35.7m. Aid from Australia totalled $A9.5m. in 2000/01, in which year assistance from New Zealand totalled $NZ6.0m.

Unemployment and inflation are major problems, which have led to massive temporary migration: between 1974 and 1977 about 10,000 Tongans obtained entry visas to New Zealand. In 1995–2001 the average annual rate of inflation was 4.6%, and stood at 8.4% in 2001, according to IMF figures. Unemployment was 13.3% of the labour force at the time of the 1996 census.

In 2000/01 there was an estimated overall budget deficit of 7.3m. pa'anga. According to preliminary figures from the IMF, Tonga's total external public debt was US $62.3m. in 1999/2000. In that year the cost of debt-servicing was equivalent to 12.1% of the total revenue from exports of goods.

During recent years Tonga's economic development has been adversely affected by inclement weather, inflationary pressures, a high level of unemployment, large-scale emigration and over-reliance on the agricultural sector. Consequently the country has attempted to diversify its sources of income and establish an efficient source of energy, to enable a reduction in fuel imports. In August 2001, following legislative amendments, the country was removed from a list of 'unco-operative tax havens', drawn up by the Organisation for Economic Co-operation and Development, based in Paris. The repercussions of the suicide attacks on the USA in September 2001 not only depressed Tonga's tourism industry in the short term, but were also expected to reduce overseas remittances to the islands, because many emigrant workers were employed in the airline industry in the USA. It was reported in early 2002 that the Tongan Government had reached an agreement with a US company to develop the island of 'Eua as a rocket-launching site for the purposes of space tourism. The first launch was expected to take place in 2005. Meanwhile, the sharp rise in the Government's unbudgeted expenditure continued to cause concern in 2002. In June it was reported that the ADB had approved a US $10m. 24-year loan to support Tonga's public-sector reform programme, which was designed to improve the delivery of public services and balance the islands' finances.

Tonga signed a bilateral trade agreement with the People's Republic of China in 1999, and a trade delegation from that country visited the islands in the following year. It was thought that China was considering using Tonga as a base for the production of export goods (including garments and agricultural products) for the Australian and New Zealand markets.

Tonga is a member of the ADB, of the Pacific Islands Forum (formerly the South Pacific Forum), of the Pacific Community (formerly the South Pacific Commission) and, though not a member of the UN itself until 1999, participated in its Economic and Social Commission for Asia and the Pacific (ESCAP). Tonga gained full UN membership in September of that year. The Kingdom is also a signatory of the Lomé Conventions and successor Cotonou Agreement with the EU, and benefits from their provisions.

Statistical Survey

Source (unless otherwise indicated): Tonga Government Department of Statistics, POB 149, Nuku'alofa; tel. 23300; fax 24303. e-mail statdept@tongatapu.net.to.

AREA AND POPULATION

Area: 748 sq km (289 sq miles).

Population: 94,649 at census of 28 November 1986; 97,784 (males 49,615, females 48,169) at census of 30 November 1996; 100,281 (official estimate) at mid-2000. *By group* (1996 census, provisional): Tongatapu 66,577; Vava'u 15,779; Ha'apai 8,148; 'Eua 4,924; Niuas 2,018.

Density (2000): 134.1 per sq km.

Principal Town: Nuku'alofa (capital): population 22,400 at census of 30 November 1996; population 33,000 (UN estimate, incl. suburbs) at mid-2001. Source: partly UN, *World Urbanization Prospects: The 2001 Revision*.

Births, Marriages and Deaths (1998): Registered live births 2,737 (birth rate 27.0 per 1,000 at 1996 census); Registered marriages 736 (marriage rate 7.7 per 1,000); Registered deaths 498 (death rate 6.5 per 1,000 at 1996 census).

Expectation of Life (WHO estimates, years at birth, 2000): Males 67.4; Females 72.9. Source: WHO, *World Health Report*.

Economically Active Population (persons aged 15 years and over, 1996): Agriculture, forestry and fishing 9,953; Mining and quarrying 43; Manufacturing 6,710; Electricity, gas and water 504; Construction 500; Trade, restaurants and hotels 2,506; Transport, storage and communications 1,209; Financing, insurance, real estate and business services 657; Public administration and defence 3,701; Education 1,721; Health and social work 510; Other community, social and personal services 1,320; Extra-territorial organizations 72; Total employed 29,406 (males 18,402, females 11,004); Total unemployed 4,502 (males 3,293, females 1,209); Total labour force 33,908 (males 21,695; females 12,213).

The totals shown may differ from the sum of the component parts.

AGRICULTURE, ETC.

Principal Crops (metric tons, 2000): Sweet potatoes 8,000; Cassava 9,070; Taro 3,720; Yams 5,040; Copra 4,109*; Coconuts 57,685†; Pumpkins, squash and gourds 17,000*; Bananas 710; Plantains 2,961; Oranges 690; Lemons and limes 2,500*; Other fruits 3,000*. Source: FAO.

* Unofficial figure. † FAO estimate.

Livestock (FAO estimates, '000 head, year ending September 2000): Pigs 81; Horses 11; Cattle 11; Goats 13; Chickens 300. Source: FAO.

Livestock Products (FAO estimates, metric tons, 2000): Pig meat 1,496; Other meat 684; Hen eggs 28; Honey 12; Cattle hides 40; Cow's milk 370. Source: FAO.

Forestry (Roundwood removals, '000 cu m, excluding bark): 4 in 1998; 2 in 1999; 2 in 2000. Source: FAO, *Yearbook of Forest Products*.

Fishing (metric tons, live weight, 1999): Capture 3,663 (Albacore 442, Marine crustaceans 200); Total catch 3,663. Source: FAO, *Yearbook of Fishery Statistics*.

INDUSTRY

Production (1999): Electric energy 29.5 million kWh.

FINANCE

Currency and Exchange Rates: 100 seniti (cents) = 1 pa'anga (Tongan dollar or $T). *Sterling, US Dollar and Euro Equivalents* (31 May 2002): £1 sterling = $T3.151; US $1 = $T2.148; €1 = $T2.017; $T100 = £31.74 = US $46.55 = €49.59. *Average Exchange Rate* (pa'anga per US $): 1.5991 in 1999; 1.7585 in 2000; 2.1236 in 2001.

Budget (estimates, million pa'anga, year ending 30 June 2001): *Revenue:* Taxation 54.0 (Taxes on international transactions 35.4); Other current revenue 20.3; Total 74.3 (excl. grants received from abroad 3.1). *Expenditure:* Current expenditure 75.6 (General public services 17.7, Education 11.9, Health 8.6, Social security and welfare 5.7); Capital expenditure 3.6; Total 79.2 (excl. lending minus repayments 5.5). Source: IMF, *Tonga: Statistical Appendix* (September 2001).

International Reserves (US $ million at 31 December 2001): IMF special drawing rights 0.19; Reserve position in the IMF 2.15; Foreign exchange 23.76; Total 26.10. Source: IMF, *International Financial Statistics*.

Money Supply ('000 pa'anga at 31 December 2001): Currency outside banks 11,355; Demand deposits at deposit money banks 30,389; Total money 41,744. Source: IMF, *International Financial Statistics*.

Cost of Living (Consumer Price Index, excl. rent; base: 1995 = 100): 113.9 in 1999; 120.6 in 2000; 130.7 in 2001. Source: IMF, *International Financial Statistics*.

Gross Domestic Product (million pa'anga at current prices, year ending 30 June): 237.3 in 1998/99; 261.1 in 1999/2000; 277.1 (estimate) in 2000/01. Source: IMF, *Tonga: Statistical Appendix* (September 2001).

Gross Domestic Product by Economic Activity (preliminary figures, million pa'anga at current prices, year ending 30 June 2000): Agriculture, forestry and fishing 69.5; Mining and quarrying 0.9; Manufacturing 11.9; Electricity, gas and water 3.7; Construction 14.0; Trade, restaurants and hotels 31.3; Transport, storage and communications 17.8; Finance and real estate 22.6; Community, social and personal services 50.5; Ownership of dwellings 9.8; *Sub-total* 231.8; *Less:* Imputed bank service charge 12.2; *GDP at factor cost* 219.6; Indirect taxes, *less* subsidies 41.4; *GDP in purchasers' values* 261.1. Source: IMF, *Tonga: Statistical Appendix* (September 2001).

Balance of Payments (US $ million, year ending 30 June 2001): Exports of goods f.o.b. 7; Imports of goods f.o.b. –63; *Trade balance* –56; Exports of services and income 18; Imports of services and income –28; *Balance on goods, services and income* –66; Current transfers (net) 52; *Current balance* –14; Direct investment 4; Portfolio investment 0; Other long-term capital 9; Other short-term capital 2; Net errors and omissions 1; *Overall balance* 2. Source: Asian Development Bank, *Key Indicators of Developing Asian and Pacific Countries*.

2001 (US $ million): Trade balance –49; Current balance –12. Source: Asian Development Bank, *Asian Development Outlook 2002*.

EXTERNAL TRADE

Principal Commodities (US $ million, year ending 30 June 2000): *Imports:* Food and live animals, beverages and tobacco 17.4; Crude materials (inedible) except fuels 2.7; Mineral fuels, lubricants, etc. 8.0; Chemicals 3.9; Basic manufactures 9.4; Machinery and transport equipment 8.5; Miscellaneous manufactured articles 4.2; Total (incl. others) 54.3. *Exports:* Squash 5.5; Root crops 0.5; Vanilla 0.5; Fish 4.1; Manufactured goods 0.8; Total 11.3. Source: IMF, *Tonga: Statistical Appendix* (September 2001).

Principal Trading Partners (US $ million, 2001): *Imports:* Australia 7.8; China, People's Repub. 2.0; Fiji 16.5; France 2.0; Indonesia 1.1; Japan 3.5; New Zealand 24.5; Thailand 6.3; United Kingdom 2.0; USA 5.8; Total (incl. others) 75.3. *Exports:* Australia 0.4; Fiji 0.3; Japan 8.1; New Zealand 1.1; United Kingdom 0.3; USA 7.7; Total (incl. others) 19.2. Source: Asian Development Bank, *Key Indicators of Developing Asian and Pacific Countries*.

TRANSPORT

Road Traffic (registered vehicles in use, 1998): Passenger cars 6,419; Buses and coaches 171; Lorries and vans 9,018.

Shipping (international traffic, '000 metric tons, 1998): Goods loaded 13.8; Goods unloaded 80.4. **1991:** Vessels entered ('000 net registered tons) 1,950. Source: UN, *Statistical Yearbook*. *Merchant Fleet* (registered at 31 December 2001): Vessels 165; Total displacement ('000 grt) 337.6. Source: Lloyd's Register-Fairplay, *World Fleet Statistics*.

Civil Aviation (traffic on scheduled services, 1998): Passengers carried 49,000; Passenger-km 10 million; Total ton-km 1 million. Source: UN, *Statistical Yearbook*.

TOURISM

Foreign Tourist Arrivals: 26,615 (excl. cruise-ship passengers 6,311) in 1997/98; 27,709 (excl. cruise-ship passengers 5,737) in 1998/99; 33,868 (excl. cruise-ship passengers 5,151) in 1999/2000.

Tourist Arrivals by Country (1999/2000): Australia 6,045; New Zealand 10,088; Pacific islands 3,061; USA 6,922; Total (incl. others) 33,868.

Tourism Receipts (million pa'anga): 14.2 in 1997/98; 11.6 in 1998/99; 16.5 in 1999/2000.

Source: IMF, *Tonga: Statistical Appendix* (September 2001).

COMMUNICATIONS MEDIA

Radio Receivers (1997): 61,000 in use.

Television Receivers (1997): 2,000 in use.

Telephones ('000 main lines, 2000): 9.7 in use.

Mobile Cellular Telephones (1999): 140 subscribers.

Internet Users (1999): 1,000.

Facsimile Machines (1996): 250 in use.

Daily Newspapers (1996): 1; estimated circulation 7,000.

Non-Daily Newspapers (2001): 2; estimated circulation 13,000.

Sources: UNESCO, *Statistical Yearbook*; UN, *Statistical Yearbook*; Audit Bureau of Circulations, Australia; and International Telecommunication Union.

EDUCATION

Primary (1999): 117 schools; 745 teachers; 16,206 pupils.

General Secondary (1999): 39 schools; 961 teachers; 13,987 pupils.

Technical and Vocational (1999): 4 colleges; 45 teachers (1990); 467 students.

Teacher-training (1999): 1 college; 22 teachers (1994); 288 students.

Universities, etc. (1985): 17 teachers; 85 students.

Other Higher Education (1985): 36 teachers (1980); 620 students.

In 1990 230 students were studying overseas on government scholarships.

Directory

The Constitution

The Constitution of Tonga is based on that granted in 1875 by King George Tupou I. It provides for a government consisting of the Sovereign; a Privy Council, which is appointed by the Sovereign and consists of the Sovereign and the Cabinet; the Cabinet, which consists of a Prime Minister, a Deputy Prime Minister, eight other ministers and the Governors of Ha'apai and Vava'u; a Legislative Assembly and a Judiciary. Limited law-making power is vested in the Privy Council and any legislation passed by the Executive is subject to review by the Legislative Assembly. The unicameral Legislative Assembly comprises the King, the Cabinet, nine hereditary nobles (chosen by their peers) and nine representatives elected by all adult Tongan citizens. Elected members hold office for three years.

The Government

The Sovereign: HM King TAUFA'AHAU TUPOU IV (succeeded to the throne 15 December 1965).

CABINET
(September 2002)

Prime Minister and Minister of Foreign Affairs, Defence, Agriculture, Forestry and Fisheries and Civil Aviation, responsible for Telecommunications: HRH Prince 'ULUKALALA-LAVAKA-ATA.

Deputy Prime Minister and Minister of Works responsible for Disaster Relief, Environment and Marine Affairs and Ports: CECIL COCKER.

Minister of Finance: SIOSIUA 'UTOIKAMANU.

Minister of Education: PAULA SUNIA BLOOMFIELD.

Minister of Labour, Commerce, Industries and Tourism: Dr MASASO PAUNGA.

Minister of Police, Fire Services and Prisons: CLIVE EDWARDS.

Minister of Lands, Survey and Natural Resources: FIELAKEPA.

Minister of Health: Dr VILIAMI TA'U TANGI.

Attorney-General and Minister of Justice: FRANKIE SUE DEL PAPA.

Governor of Ha'apai: MALUPO.

Governor of Vava'u: S. M. TUITA.

GOVERNMENT MINISTRIES AND OFFICES

Office of the Prime Minister: POB 62, Taufa'ahau Rd, Kolofo'ou, Nuku'alofa; tel. 24644; fax 23888; e-mail fttuita@pmo.gov.to; internet www.pmo.gov.to.

Palace Office: Salote Rd, Kolofo'ou, Nuku'alofa; tel. 21000; fax 24102.

Ministry of Agriculture and Fisheries: Administration Office, Vuna Rd, Kolofo'ou, Nuku'alofa; tel. 23038; fax 23039; e-mail maf-holo@candw.to.

Ministry of Civil Aviation: POB 845, Salote Rd, Nuku'alofa; tel. 24144; fax 24145; e-mail info@mca.gov.to; internet www.mca.gov.to.

Ministry of Education: POB 61, Vuna Rd, Kolofo'ou, Nuku'alofa; tel. 23511; fax 23596; e-mail moe@kalianet.to.

Ministry of Finance: Treasury Building, POB 87, Vuna Rd, Kolofo'ou, Nuku'alofa; tel. 23066; fax 21010; e-mail minfin@candw.to.

Ministry of Foreign Affairs: National Reserve Bank Building, Salote Rd, Kolofo'ou, Nuku'alofa; tel. 23600; fax 23360; e-mail secfo@candw.to.

Ministry of Health: POB 59, Taufa'ahau Rd, Tofoa, Nuku'alofa; tel. 23200; fax 24921.

Ministry of Justice: POB 130, Railway Rd, Kolofo'ou, Nuku'alofa; tel. 21055; fax 23098.

Ministry of Labour, Commerce and Industries: POB 110, Salote Rd, Fasi-moe-afi, Nuku'alofa; tel. 23688; fax 23880; e-mail tongatrade@candw.to.

Ministry of Lands, Survey and Natural Resources: POB 5, Vuna Rd, Kolofo'ou, Nuku'alofa; tel. 23611; fax 23216.

Ministry of Marine and Ports: Fakafanua Centre, Vuna Rd, Ma'ufanga, Nuku'alofa; tel. 22555; fax 26234.

Ministry of Police, Fire Services and Prisons: Mauikisikisi Rd, Longolongo, Nuku'alofa; tel. 23233; fax 23226.

Ministry of Telecommunications: Nuku'alofa.

Ministry of Works and Disaster Relief Activities: 'Alaivahamama'o Rd, Vaololoa, Nuku'alofa; tel. 23100; fax 23102; e-mail mowtonga@kalianet.to.

Department of Civil Aviation: Salote Rd, Fasi-moe-afi; tel. 24144; fax 24145.

Legislative Assembly

The Legislative Assembly consists of the Speaker, the members of the Cabinet, nine nobles chosen by the 33 Nobles of Tonga, and nine representatives elected by all Tongans over 21 years of age. There are elections every three years, and the Assembly is required to meet at least once every year. The most recent election was held on 6–7 March 2002, when seven of the nine elected representatives were members of the reformist Tonga Human Rights and Democracy Movement.

Speaker and Chairman of the Legislative Assembly: TU'IVAKANO.

Political Organization

Kotoa Movement: f. 2001; campaigns in support of monarchy.

Human Rights and Democracy Movement in Tonga (HRDMT): POB 843, Nuku'alofa; tel. 25501; fax 26330; e-mail demo@kalianet.to; f. 1992 (as Tonga Pro-Democracy Movement); campaigns for democratic reform and increased parliamentary representation for the Tongan people; Chair. Rev. SIMOTE VEA; Sec. 'AKILISI POHIVA.

Diplomatic Representation

EMBASSY AND HIGH COMMISSIONS IN TONGA

Australia: Salote Rd, Nuku'alofa; tel. 23244; fax 23243; High Commissioner: COLIN HILL (designate).

China, People's Republic: Nuku'alofa; Ambassador: GAO SHANHAI.

New Zealand: cnr Taufa'ahau and Salote Rds, POB 830, Nuku'alofa; tel. 23122; fax 23487; e-mail nzhcnuk@kalianet.to; High Commissioner: WARWICK A. HAWKER.

United Kingdom: Vuna Rd, POB 56, Nuku'alofa; tel. 24285; fax 24109; e-mail britcomt@kalianet.to; High Commissioner: PAUL NESSLING.

Judicial System

There are eight Magistrates' Courts, the Land Court, the Supreme Court and the Court of Appeal.

Appeal from the Magistrates' Courts is to the Supreme Court, and from the Supreme Court and Land Court to the Court of Appeal (except in certain matters relating to hereditary estates, where appeal lies to the Privy Council). The Chief Justice and Puisne Judge are resident in Tonga and are judges of the Supreme Court and Land Court. The Court of Appeal is presided over by the Chief Justice and consists of three judges from other Commonwealth countries. In the Supreme Court the accused in criminal cases, and either party in civil suits, may elect trial by jury. In the Land Court the judge sits with a Tongan assessor. Proceedings in the Magistrates' Courts are in Tongan, and in the Supreme Court and Court of Appeal in Tongan and English.

Supreme Court: POB 11, Nuku'alofa; tel. 23599; fax 24771.

Chief Justice: TONY FORD.

Puisne Judge: SINILAU KOLOKIHAKAUFISI.

Chief Magistrate: GEORGE FIFITA.

Religion

The Tongans are almost all Christians, and about 36% of the population belong to Methodist (Wesleyan) communities. There are also significant numbers of Roman Catholics (15%) and Latter-day Saints (Mormons—15%). Anglicans (1%) and Seventh-day Adventists (5%) are also represented. Fourteen churches are represented in total.

CHRISTIANITY

Kosilio 'ae Ngaahi Siasi 'i Tonga (Tonga National Council of Churches): POB 1205, Nuku'alofa; tel. 23291; fax 23291; e-mail tncc@kalianet.to; f. 1973; four mem. churches (Free Wesleyan, Roman Catholic, Anglican and Free Constitutional Church of Tonga); Chair. Archdeacon TUINIUA FINAU; Gen. Sec. Rev. SIMOTE M. VEA.

The Anglican Communion

Tonga lies within the diocese of Polynesia, part of the Church of the Province of New Zealand. The Bishop of Polynesia is resident in Fiji.

Archdeacon of Tonga and Samoa: The Ven. SAM KOY, The Vicarage, POB 31, Nuku'alofa; tel. 22136.

The Roman Catholic Church

The diocese of Tonga, directly responsible to the Holy See, comprises Tonga and the New Zealand dependency of Niue. At 31 December 2000 there were an estimated 15,339 adherents in the diocese. The Bishop participates in the Catholic Bishops' Conference of the Pacific, based in Fiji.

Bishop of Tonga: Dr SOANE LILO FOLIAKI, Toutai-mana Catholic Centre, POB 1, Nuku'alofa; tel. 23822; fax 23854; e-mail cathbish@kalianet.to.

Other Churches

Church of Jesus Christ of Latter-day Saints (Mormon): Mission Centre, POB 58, Nuku'alofa; tel. 26007; fax 23763; 40,000 mems; Pres. DOUGLAS W. BANKS.

Church of Tonga: Nuku'alofa; f. 1928; a branch of Methodism; 6,912 mems; Pres. Rev. FINAU KATOANGA.

Free Constitutional Church of Tonga: POB 23, Nuku'alofa; tel. 23966; fax 24458; f. 1885; 15,941 mems (1996); Pres. Rev. SEMISI FONUA; brs in Australia, New Zealand and USA.

Free Wesleyan Church of Tonga (Koe Siasi Uesiliana Tau'a-taina 'o Tonga): POB 57, Nuku'alofa; tel. 23432; fax 24020; e-mail fwc@candw.to; f. 1826; 36,500 mems; Pres. Rev. Dr 'ALIFALETI MONE.

Tokaikolo Christian Fellowship: Nuku'alofa; f. 1978, as break-away group from Free Wesleyan Church; 5,000 mems.

BAHÁ'Í FAITH

National Spiritual Assembly: POB 133, Nuku'alofa; tel. 21568; fax 23120; e-mail patco@kalianet.to; mems resident in 156 localities.

The Press

Eva, Your Guide to Tonga: POB 958, Nuku'alofa; tel. 25779; fax 24749; e-mail vapress@kalianet.to; internet www.matangitonga.to; f. 1989; 4 a year; Editor PESI FONUA; circ. 4,500.

Ko e Kele'a (Conch Shell): POB 1567, Nuku'alofa; tel. 25501; fax 26330; f. 1986; monthly; activist-oriented publication, economic and political; Editor SIOSINA PO'OI POHIVA; circ. 3,500.

Lali: Nuku'alofa; f. 1994; monthly; English; national business magazine; Publr KALAFI MOALA.

Lao and Hia: POB 2808, Nuku'alofa; tel. 14105; weekly; Tongan; legal newspaper; Editor SIONE HAFOKA.

Matangi Tonga: POB 958, Nuku'alofa; tel. 25779; fax 24749; e-mail vapress@kalianet.to; internet www.matangitonga.to; f. 1986; 4 a year; national news magazine; Editor PESI FONUA; circ. 2,000.

'Ofa ki Tonga: c/o Tokaikolo Fellowship, POB 2055, Nuku'alofa; tel. 24190; monthly; newspaper of Tokaikolo Christian Fellowship; Editor Rev. LIUFAU VAILEA SAULALA.

Taumu'a Lelei: POB 1, Nuku'alofa; tel. 26487; fax 27161; e-mail tmlcath@kalianet.to; f. 1931; monthly; Roman Catholic; Editor Dr SOANE LILO FOLIAKI.

The Times of Tonga/Koe Taimi'o Tonga: POB 880, Hala Velingatoni, Kolomotu'a; tel. 23177; fax 23292; e-mail times@kalianet.to; internet www.tongatimes.com; f. 1989; weekly; English edition covers Pacific and world news, Tongan edition concentrates on local news; Editor KALAFI MOALA; Deputy Editor MATENI TAPUELUELU; circ. 8,000.

Tohi Fanongonongo: POB 57, Nuku'alofa; tel. 26533; fax 24020; e-mail fwcfonua@kalianet.to; monthly; Wesleyan; Editor Rev. SIONE HAVEA FONUA.

Tonga Chronicle/Kalonikali Tonga: POB 197, Nuku'alofa; tel. 23302; fax 23336; e-mail chroni@kalianet.to; internet www.netstorage.com/kami/tonga/news; f. 1964; govt-sponsored; weekly; Editor PAUA MANU'ATA; circ. 6,000 (Tongan), 1,200 (English).

Publisher

Vava'u Press Ltd: POB 958, Nuku'alofa; tel. 25779; fax 24749; e-mail vapress@kalianet.to; internet www.matangitonga.to; f. 1980; books and magazines; Pres. PESI FONUA.

Broadcasting and Communications

TELECOMMUNICATIONS

Tonga Communications Corporation: Private Bag 4, Nuku'alofa; tel. 26700; fax 26701; internet www.tcc.to; responsible for domestic and international telecommunications services; Gen. Man. JON E. MORRIS.

Tongasat—Friendly Islands Satellite Communications Ltd: POB 2921, Nuku'alofa; tel. 24160; fax 23322; e-mail kite@tongasat.com; 80% Tongan-owned; private co but co-operates with Govt in management and leasing of orbital satellite positions; Chair. Princess PILOLEVU TUITA; Man. Dir SIONE KITE; Sec. WILLIAM CLIVE EDWARDS.

BROADCASTING

Radio

Tonga Broadcasting Commission: POB 36, Tungi Rd, Fasi-moe-afi, Nuku'alofa; tel. 23555; fax 24417; independent statutory board; commercially operated; manages two stations, A3Z Radio Tonga 1 and Radio Tonga 2, with programmes in Tongan and English; Gen. Man. TAVAKE FUSIMALOHI.

93FM: Pacific Partners Trust, POB 478, Nuku'alofa; tel. 23076; fax 24970; broadcasts in English, Tongan, German, Mandarin and Hindi.

A3V The Millennium Radio 2000: POB 838, Nuku'alofa; tel. 25891; fax 24195; e-mail a3v@tongatapu.net.to; broadcasts on FM; musical programmes; Gen. Man. SAM VEA.

Tonga News Association: Nuku'alofa; Pres. PESI FONUA.

Television

The introduction of a television service has been mooted since 1984. Oceania Broadcasting Inc started relaying US television programmes in 1991. The Tonga Broadcasting Commission was expected to launch the country's first television service in July 2000.

Oceania Broadcasting Network: POB 91, Nuku'alofa; tel 23314; fax 23658.

Finance

(cap. = capital; res = reserves; dep. = deposits; m. = million; amounts in Tongan dollars)

BANKING

Australia and New Zealand Banking Group Ltd: Cnr of Salote and Railway Rds, POB 910, Nuku'alofa; tel. 24944; fax 23870; internet www.candw.to/banks.

Bank of Tonga: POB 924, Nuku'alofa; tel. 23933; fax 23634; e-mail bot-gm@kalianet.to; f. 1974; owned by Govt of Tonga (40%) and Westpac Banking Corpn (60%); cap. 3.0m., res 12.2m., dep. 65.2m. (Sept. 2001); Chair. ALAN WALTER; Gen. Man. BRIAN HARRIS; 4 brs.

MBf Bank Ltd: POB 3118, Nuku'alofa; tel. 24600; fax 24662; e-mail mbfbank@kalianet.to; 93.35% owned by MBf Asia Capital Corpn Holdings Ltd, 4.75% owned by Crown Prince Tupouto'a, 0.95% owned by Tonga Investments Ltd, 0.95% owned by Tonga Co-operative Federation Society.

National Reserve Bank of Tonga: POB 25, Post Office, Nuku'alofa; tel. 24057; fax 24201; e-mail nrbt@kalianet.to; f. 1989 to assume central bank functions of Bank of Tonga; issues currency; manages exchange rates and international reserves; cap. 1.0m., res 0.2m., dep. 41.9m. (June 2000); Gov. SIOSIUA 'UTOIKAMANU. Chair. Prince 'ULUKALALA-LAVAKA-ATA.

Tonga Development Bank: Fatafehi Rd, POB 126, Nuku'alofa; tel. 23333; fax 23775; e-mail tdevbank@tdb.to; f. 1977 to provide credit for developmental purposes, mainly in agriculture, fishery, tourism and housing; cap. 10.5m., res 1.502m. (Dec. 2001); Man. Dir 'OTENIFI AFU'ALO MATOTO; 5 brs.

Westpac Banking Corporation: c/o Bank of Tonga, Railway Rd, Nuku'alofala; tel. 23933; fax 23781.

Trade and Industry

DEVELOPMENT ORGANIZATIONS

Tonga Investments Ltd: POB 27, Nuku'alofa; tel. 24388; fax 24313; f. 1992 to replace Commodities Board; govt-owned; manages five subsidiary companies; Chair. Baron VAEA of Houma; Man. Dir ANTHONY WAYNE MADDEN.

Tonga Association of Small Businesses: Nuku'alofa; f. 1990 to cater for the needs of small businesses; Chair. SIMI SILAPELU.

CHAMBER OF COMMERCE

Tonga Chamber of Commerce and Industries: Tungi Arcade, POB 1704, Nuku'alofa; tel. 25168; fax 26039; e-mail chamber@kalianet.to; Pres. AISAKE EKE.

TRADE ASSOCIATION

Tonga Kava Council: Nuku'alofa; to promote the development of the industry both locally and abroad; Chair. TOIIMOANA TAKATAKA.

UTILITIES

Tonga Electric Power Board: POB 47, Taufa'ahau Rd, Kolofo'ou, Nuku'alofa; tel. 23311; fax 23632; provides electricity via diesel motor generation.

Tonga Water Board: POB 92, Taufa'ahau Rd, Kolofo'ou, Nuku'alofa; tel. 23298; fax 23518; operates four urban water systems, serving about 25% of the population; Man. SAIMONE P. HELU.

MAJOR COMPANIES

Royal Beer Co Ltd: POB 20 Nuku'alofa.

Sea Star Fishing Co Ltd: Faua Wharf Basin, Ma'ufanga, Nuku'alofa; tel. 25458; fax 24779; e-mail seastar@kalianet.to; Financial Man. Tevita Veikoso.

CO-OPERATIVES

In April 1990 there were 78 registered co-operative societies, including the first co-operative registered under the Agricultural Organization Act.

Tonga Co-operative Federation Society: Tungi Arcade, Nuku'alofa.

TRADE UNIONS

Association of Tongatapu Squash Pumpkin Growers: Nuku'alofa; f. 1998.

Tonga Nurses' Association and Friendly Islands Teachers' Association (TNA/FITA): POB 150, Nuku'alofa; tel. 23200; fax 24291; Pres. FINAU TUTONE; Gen. Sec. 'ANA FOTU KAVAEFIAFI.

Transport

ROADS

Total road length was estimated at 680 km in 1996, of which some 27% were all-weather paved roads. Most of the network comprises fair-weather-only dirt or coral roads.

SHIPPING

The chief ports are Nuku'alofa, on Tongatapu, and Neiafu, on Vava'u, with two smaller ports at Pangai and Niuatoputapu.

Shipping Corporation of Polynesia Ltd: Vuna Rd, POB 453, Nuku'alofa; tel. 23853; fax 22334; e-mail shipcorp@kalianet.to; regular inter-islands passenger and cargo services; Chair. Prince 'ULUKALALA-LAVAKA-ATA; Gen. Man. Capt. VOLKER PAHL.

Uata Shipping Lines: 'Uliti Uata, POB 100, Nuku'alofa; tel. 23855; fax 23860.

Warner Pacific Line: POB 93, Nuku'alofa; tel. 21088; services to Samoa, American Samoa, Australia and New Zealand; Man. Dir MA'AKE FAKA'OSIFOLAU.

CIVIL AVIATION

Tonga is served by Fua'amotu International Airport, 22 km from Nuku'alofa, and airstrips at Vava'u, Ha'apai, Niuatoputapu, Niuafo'ou and 'Eua.

Royal Tongan Airlines: Private Bag 9, Royco Building, Fatafehi Rd, Nuku'alofa; tel. 23414; fax 24056; e-mail rta_per@kalianet.to; internet www.candw.to/rta; f. 1985 as Friendly Islands Airways Ltd; govt-owned; operates international service to Auckland (New Zealand), Nadi (Fiji), Niue, Honolulu (Hawaii), Samoa and Sydney (Australia) and internal services to Fua'amotu, Ha'apai, Vava'u, 'Eua, Niuatoputapu and Niuafo'ou; Chair. Prince 'ULUKALALA-LAVAKA-ATA; Gen. Man. LOGAN APPU.

Tourism

Tonga's attractions include scenic beauty and a mild climate. There were 33,868 visitors to the islands in 1999/2000 (an increase of more than 20% compared with the previous year). In addition 5,151 cruise-ship passengers visited the islands in 1999/2000. In that year tourism earned $T16.5m. In 1999/2000 the majority of tourists were from New Zealand, the USA and Australia.

Tonga Tourist Association: POB 74, Nuku'alofa; tel. 23344; fax 23833; e-mail royale@kalianet.to; Pres. JOSEPH RAMANLAL.

Tonga Visitors' Bureau: Vuna Rd, POB 37, Nuku'alofa; tel. 25334; fax 23507; e-mail tvb@kalianet.to; internet www.tongaholiday.com; f. 1978; Dir SEMISI P. TAUMOEPEAU.

Defence

Tonga has its own defence force, the Tonga Defence Services, consisting of both regular and reserve units. The island also has a defence co-operation agreement with Australia. Projected government expenditure on defence in 1999/2000 was $T3.3m. (5.0% of total budgetary expenditure); in the same financial year estimated expenditure on law and order was $T4.6m. (6.9% of total current expenditure).

Education

Free state education is compulsory for children between five and 14 years of age, while the Government and other Commonwealth countries offer scholarship schemes enabling students to go abroad for higher education. In 1999 there were 117 primary schools, with a total of 16,206 pupils, and there was a total of 13,987 pupils in 39 secondary schools. There were also four technical and vocational colleges in 1999, with a total of 467 students, and one teacher-training college, with 288 students. In 1990 there were 230 Tongans studying overseas. Some degree courses are offered at the university division of 'Atenisi Institute. Recurrent government expenditure on education in 1999/2000 was an estimated $T10.9m. (equivalent to 16.5% of total recurrent budgetary expenditure).

Tuvalu

Physical and Social Geography

Tuvalu is a scattered group of nine small atolls, (five of which enclose sizeable lagoons), extending 560 km from north to south and covering a land area of 26 sq km (10 sq miles) in the western Pacific Ocean. Its nearest neighbours are Fiji to the south, Kiribati to the north and Solomon Islands to the west. The climate is warm and pleasant, with a mean annual temperature of 29°C (84°F), and there is very little seasonal variation. The average annual rainfall is 3,000 mm. The inhabitants are a Polynesian people who speak Tuvaluan and English. Almost all profess Christianity, and about 98% are Protestants. The population was estimated to be 10,660 at mid-2001. The capital is on Funafuti Atoll.

History

Tuvalu was formerly known as the Ellice (or Lagoon) Islands. Between about 1850 and 1875 many of the islanders were captured by slave-traders and this, together with European diseases, reduced the population from about 20,000 to 3,000. In 1877 the United Kingdom established the Western Pacific High Commission, with its headquarters in Fiji, and the Ellice Islands and other groups were placed under its jurisdiction. In 1892 a British protectorate was declared over the Ellice Islands and the group was linked administratively with the Gilbert Islands to the north. In 1916 the United Kingdom annexed the protectorate, which was renamed the Gilbert and Ellice Islands Colony (GEIC). During the Japanese occupation of the Gilbert Islands in 1942–43, the administration of the GEIC was temporarily moved to Funafuti in the Ellice Islands. (For more details of the history of the GEIC, see the chapter on Kiribati,)

A series of advisory and legislative bodies prepared the GEIC for self-government. In May 1974 the last of these, the Legislative Council, was replaced by the House of Assembly, with 28 elected members (including eight Ellice Islanders) and three official members. A Chief Minister was elected by the House and chose between four and six other ministers, one of whom had to be from the Ellice Islands.

In January 1972 the appointment of a separate GEIC Governor, who assumed most of the functions previously exercised by the High Commissioner, increased the long-standing anxiety of the Ellice Islanders over their minority position as Polynesians in the colony, dominated by the Micronesians of the Gilbert Islands. In a referendum held in the Ellice Islands in August and September 1974, over 90% of the voters favoured separate status for the group, and in October 1975 the Ellice Islands, under the old native name of Tuvalu ('eight standing together', which referred to the eight populated atolls), became a separate British dependency. The Deputy Governor of the GEIC took office as Her Majesty's Commissioner for Tuvalu. The eight Ellice representatives in the GEIC House of Assembly became the first elected members of the new Tuvalu House of Assembly. They elected one of their number, Toaripi Lauti, to be Chief Minister. Tuvalu was completely separated from the GEIC administration in January 1976. The remainder of the GEIC was renamed the Gilbert Islands and achieved independence, under the name of Kiribati, in July 1979.

Tuvalu's first separate elections were held in August 1977, when the number of elective seats in the House of Assembly was increased to 12. An independence Constitution was finalized at a conference in London in February 1978. After five months of internal self-government, Tuvalu became independent on 1 October 1978, with Lauti as the first Prime Minister. The pre-independence House of Assembly was redesignated Parliament. Tuvalu is a 'special member' of the Commonwealth, taking part in functional activities but not represented at meetings of Heads of Government. Tuvalu was admitted to the UN on 5 September 2000.

In February 1979 Tuvalu signed a Treaty of Friendship with the USA, which renounced its claim, dating from 1856, to the four southernmost atolls. This treaty was ratified in August 1983. Meanwhile, following elections to the Parliament in September 1981, Dr Tomasi Puapua became Prime Minister.

In a general election in 1985 Puapua was re-elected Prime Minister. In February 1986 a nation-wide poll was conducted to establish public sentiment as to whether Tuvalu should remain a constitutional monarchy, with the British monarch at its head, or become a republic. On only one atoll did the community appear to favour republican status. Under a revised Constitution that took effect on 1 October 1986, the Governor-General's ability to veto government measures was abolished. Meanwhile, in March, Tupua (later Sir Tupua) Leupena, a former Speaker of Parliament, had become Governor-General, replacing Sir Penitala Teo, who had occupied the post since independence in 1978.

In September 1989 a general election was held, and in the following month Bikenibeu Paeniu was sworn in as the new Prime Minister. In October 1990 Toaripi Lauti, the former Prime Minister, succeeded Leupena as Governor-General. Legislation approved by Parliament in mid-1991, which sought to prohibit all new religions from the islands and to establish the Church of Tuvalu as the State Church, caused considerable controversy and extensive debate. A survey showed the eight constituencies to be almost equally divided over the matter, although Paeniu firmly opposed the motion, describing it as incompatible with basic human rights.

In 1991 the Government announced that it was to prepare a compensation claim against the United Kingdom for the allegedly poor condition of Tuvalu's economy and infrastructure at the time of the country's achievement of independence in 1979. Moreover, Tuvalu was to seek additional compensation for damage caused during the Second World War when the United Kingdom gave permission for the USA to build airstrips on the islands (some 40% of Funafuti is uninhabitable because of the large pits created by US troops during the construction of an airstrip on the atoll). Relations with the United Kingdom deteriorated further in late 1992 when the British Government harshly criticized the financial policy of Paeniu's Government. Paeniu defended his Government's policies, and stated that continued delays in the approval of aid projects from the United Kingdom meant that Tuvalu would not be seeking further development funds from the British Government.

In mid-1992 a member of Parliament for Funafuti proposed a motion to establish Tuvalu as a republic. It was subsequently reported, however, that (as in 1986) only one of the eight parliamentary constituencies supported the proposal.

At a general election held in September 1993 three of the 12 incumbent members of Parliament lost their seats. At elections to the premiership held in the same month, however, Paeniu and Puapua received six votes each. When a second vote produced a similar result, the Governor-General dissolved Parliament, in accordance with the Constitution. Paeniu and his Cabinet remained in office until the holding of a further general election in November. At elections to the premiership in the following month Kamuta Latasi defeated Paeniu by seven votes to five. Puapua, who had agreed not to challenge Paeniu in the contest in favour of supporting Latasi, was elected Speaker of Parliament. In June 1994 Latasi removed the Governor-General, Toomu Malaefono Sione, from office, some seven months after he had been appointed to the position, and replaced him with Tulaga (later Sir Tulaga) Manuella. Latasi alleged that Paeniu's appointment of Sione had been politically motivated.

In December 1994, in what was widely regarded as a significant rejection of its political links with the United Kingdom, the Tuvaluan Parliament voted to remove Britain's union flag from the Tuvalu national flag. A new design was selected and the new flag was inaugurated in October 1995. Speculation that the British monarch would be removed as Head of State intensified during 1995, following the appointment of a committee to review the Constitution. The three-member committee was to examine the procedure surrounding the appointment and removal of the Governor-General, and, particularly, to consider the adoption of a republican system of government.

In late 1996 the Deputy Prime Minister, Otinielu Tausi, and the parliamentary Speaker, Dr Tomasi Puapua, both announced their decision to withdraw their support for Latasi's Government, thereby increasing the number of opposition members in Parliament from five to seven. This reversal appeared to be in response to increasing dissatisfaction among the population with Latasi. This had been perceived firstly with his unpopular initiative to replace the country's national flag (with a new design that omitted the United Kingdom's union flag), and was exacerbated by revelations that the leasing of Tuvalu's telephone code to a foreign company had resulted in the use of the islands' telephone system for personal services considered indecent by the majority of islanders. (It was announced by the Government in October 2000 that the lease was to cease by the end of the year.) Opponents of the Prime Minister submitted a parliamentary motion of 'no confidence' in his Government in December, which was approved by seven votes to five. Paeniu subsequently defeated Latasi, by a similar margin, to become Prime Minister, and a new Cabinet was appointed. The new premier acted promptly to restore the country's original flag, by proposing a parliamentary motion in February 1997, which was approved by seven votes to five.

A total of 35 candidates contested a general election on 26 March 1998. The period prior to the election had been characterized by a series of bitter disputes between Paeniu and Latasi, in which both had made serious accusations of sexual and financial misconduct against the other. Five members of the previous Parliament were returned to office, although Latasi unexpectedly failed to secure re-election. Paeniu was subsequently re-elected Prime Minister by 10 votes to two. In June the new Government announced a series of development plans and proposals for constitutional reform, including the introduction of a code of conduct for political leaders and the creation of an ombudsman's office. Paeniu stated that his administration intended to consult widely with the population before any changes were implemented. Also in 1998, Puapua was appointed Governor-General, replacing Manuella.

On 13 April 1999 Paeniu lost a parliamentary vote of confidence and was forced to resign. Later in the month Ionatana Ionatana, hitherto the Minister for Health, Education, Culture, Women and Community Affairs, was elected by Parliament as the new Prime Minister. On his appointment Ionatana immediately effected a reshuffle of the Cabinet.

Chronic water shortage on Funafuti led to a state of emergency being declared on the atoll in August 1999. It was hoped that a desalination plant, provided by Japan, would help alleviate the problem.

Potentially the most significant new source of revenue for many years was established in September 1998 when the Government signed an agreement to lease the country's national internet suffix '.tv' to a Canadian information company. The company, which defeated several other business interests to secure the deal, was expected to market the internet address to international television companies. Tuvalu was to receive an initial fee of US $50m. from the arrangement in addition to annual revenue of up to US $100m. However, in July 1999 it was announced that the deal had been abandoned after the company failed to meet its initial agreed payment of US $50m. In February 2000, however, it was announced that a US $50m. deal on the sale of the '.tv' suffix had been concluded with a US company. The sale was expected to generate some US $10m. in revenue annually. The funds generated from the sale enabled Tuvalu officially to join the UN and participate in the 55th annual UN General Assembly Meeting, held in September 2000.

In March 2000 18 schoolgirls and their supervisor were killed in a fire in a school on Vaitupu atoll. A government inquiry was established into the disaster, which was reportedly the worst in independent Tuvalu's history.

In early December 2000 Prime Minister Ionatana Ioantana died unexpectedly. The Deputy Prime Minister, Lagitupu Tuilimu, was immediately appointed as interim Prime Minister, pending the election of a replacement. In late February 2001 Parliament elected as Prime Minister the Minister for Internal Affairs and Rural and Urban Development, Faimalaga Luka; he assumed responsibility for the additional portfolios of foreign affairs, finance and economic planning, and trade and commerce, and immediately named a new cabinet.

A vote of 'no confidence' was upheld against Luka in December 2001 while he was in New Zealand for a medical examination. Kolaoa Talake, a former Minister of Finance, was elected Prime Minister in the same month, winning eight of the 15 votes cast. He appointed an entirely new Cabinet.

Talake announced in March 2002 that lawyers were preparing evidence for legal action against the United Kingdom, seeking compensation for the alleged inequality of the division of assets between Tuvalu and Kiribati when the two nations had achieved independence in the late 1970s. Following general elections held on 25 July 2002, Saufatu Sopoanga replaced Talake as Prime Minister. Sopoanga subsequently announced that a referendum would be held before the end of 2002, on the question of whether the country should become a republic.

Tuvalu is a member of the Pacific Islands Forum (formerly the South Pacific Forum). The 19th Forum, meeting in September 1988, discussed the threat posed to low-lying countries, such as Tuvalu, by the predicted rise in sea-level as a result of the 'greenhouse effect' (the heating of the earth's atmosphere as a consequence of pollution); the highest point of Tuvalu's nine islands is no more than five metres above sea-level. A report published by the UN Environment Programme in late 1989 warned that Tuvalu was one of five island groups that were particularly threatened, and which, unless drastic measures were taken, could be completely submerged by the mid-21st century. At the UN World Climate Conference, held in Geneva in November 1990, Paeniu appealed for urgent action by developed nations to combat the environmental changes caused by the 'greenhouse effect', which were believed to include a 10-fold increase in cyclone frequency (from two in 1940 to 21 in 1990), an increase in salinity in ground water and a considerable decrease in the average annual rainfall. The Government remained critical, however, of the inertia with which it alleged certain countries had reacted to its appeal for assistance, and reiterated the Tuvaluan people's fears of physical and cultural extinction. The subsequent Prime Minister, Kamuta Latasi, was similarly critical of the industrial world's apparent disregard for the plight of small island nations vulnerable to the effects of climate change, particularly when Tuvalu was struck by tidal waves in 1994 (believed to be the first experienced by the islands). Attempts during the mid-1990s to secure approval for resettlement plans for Tuvaluans to other countries, including Australia and New Zealand, were largely unsuccessful. The Government of Tuvalu was strongly critical of Australia's refusal to reduce its emission of pollutant gases (known to contribute to the 'greenhouse effect') at the Conference of the Parties to the Framework Convention on Climate Change (see UN Environment Programme) in Kyoto, Japan, in late 1997. In July 2001 Australia did, however, adopt the Kyoto Protocol, which urged industrialized nations to reduce carbon-dioxide emissions by 5.2% from 1990 levels by 2012. In March 2001 Tuvalu, Kiribati and the Maldives announced their decision to take legal action against the USA for its refusal to sign the Kyoto Protocol. In August Tuvalu was one of six states at the Pacific Islands Forum to demand a meeting with US President George W. Bush to try and enlist his support for the Kyoto Protocol; the USA produced nearly one-third of the industrialized countries' carbon-dioxide emissions and was the only country in the world not to adopt the protocol.

The installation of a new sea-level monitoring station began in December 2001 as part of the South Pacific Sea Level and Climate Monitoring Project administered by the Australian aid agency, Ausaid. In January 2002 it was reported that the Government had engaged a US law firm to prosecute the USA and other nations for failing to meet their commitments to the United Nations Framework Convention on Climate Change (UNFCC). At the September 2002 World Summit for Sustainable Development in Johannesburg, South Africa, government delegates attempted to persuade representatives of other Pacific islands to join their campaign against the USA and Australia.

Economy

In 1998, according to UN estimates, Tuvalu's gross domestic product (GDP), measured at current prices, was US $14m., equivalent to US $1,215 per head. According to provisional estimates by the Asian Development Bank (ADB), in 2000 GDP totalled $A23.4m., equivalent to $A2,236 per head. GDP increased, in real terms, by an annual average rate of 4.9% in 1990–2000. Compared with the previous year, GDP rose by 3.0% in both 1999 and 2000, and by an estimated 4.0% in 2001.

Tuvalu is composed of coral atolls with poor-quality soil. Most of the land is covered with coconut palms, which provide the only export in the form of copra. Exports of copra were worth $A6,000 in 1997. Agriculture (including fishing), which is, with the exception of copra production, of a basic subsistence nature, contributed some 16.8% of GDP in 1998 and engages some 75% of the labour force. According to ADB figures, the GDP of the agricultural sector declined by an average annual rate of 1.8% in 1990–98. Compared with the previous year, agricultural GDP increased by 5.8% in 1997 and by 0.7% in 1998. Pulaka, taro, papayas, the screw-pine (*Pandanus*) and bananas are cultivated as food crops, and honey is produced. There is also subsistence farming of pigs, goats and poultry. Fishing is carried out on a small scale but, with the introduction of an exclusive economic zone covering about 1.3m. sq km (500,000 sq miles) of sea, exploitation of fish resources could be developed to form the basis of the economy. The sale of fishing licences to foreign fleets is an important source of revenue, which was equivalent to an estimated 40% of total government revenue in 1998 and earned US $6.1m. in 2001.

Industry (including mining, manufacturing, construction and utilities) accounted for 24.3% of GDP in 1998. In 1990–98, according to ADB figures, industrial GDP expanded at an average annual rate of 14.0%. Compared with the previous year, the sector's GDP increased by 4.0% in 1997 and by 21.5% in 1998. Manufacturing is confined to the small-scale production of coconut-based products, soap and handicrafts. The manufacturing sector contributed some 4.2% of GDP in 1998.

Energy is derived principally from a power plant (fuelled by petroleum) and, on the outer islands, solar power. In 1989 mineral fuels accounted for almost 13% of total import costs.

The Government is an important employer (engaging almost one-half of the labour force) and consequently the services sector makes a relatively large contribution to Tuvalu's economy (providing some 58.9% of GDP in 1998). In 1990–98, according to ADB figures, the GDP of the services sector increased at an average annual rate of 5.1%. Compared with the previous year, the sector's GDP expanded by 2.7% in 1997 and by 16.0% in 1998. The islands' remote situation and lack of amenities have hindered the development of a tourist industry. In the mid-1990s there was only one hotel (on Funafuti) with 17 rooms. Tourist arrivals totalled only 1,504 in 2000. An important source of revenue, however, has been provided by remittances from Tuvaluans working abroad. In the early 1990s some 1,200 Tuvaluans were working overseas, principally in the phosphate industry on Nauru, although many of these workers were returned to Tuvalu during the late 1990s, as Nauruan phosphate reserves became exhausted. Remittances from Tuvaluan seafarers employed on foreign merchant ships were estimated at US $2.6m. in 2001. In the same year receipts from the leasing of the islands' internet domain address reached US $1.6m., while revenue from telecommunication licence fees totalled US $0.31m.

In 2001 Tuvalu recorded a visible trade deficit of US $13.09m. The cost of imports reached US $14.12m., while export revenue totalled only US $1.03m. In 2001 imports totalling US $9.25m. were purchased from Fiji (which supplied 65.5% of the total) and US $2.51m. from Australia (17.8%). The principal market for exports was Sweden, which purchased 35.0% of the total. In 1997 copra was the sole domestic export of any significance. The principal imports in 1989 were foodstuffs (29.3% of the total), basic manufactures, machinery and transport equipment and mineral fuels. In 2001 total export earnings were equivalent to only 7.3% of the value of imports.

The United Kingdom agreed to continue financial assistance after independence, and in 1990 contributed some £500,000. However, dissatisfaction with British financial provision for Tuvalu led the Government to announce plans for a compensation claim to be brought against the UK in 1991 (see History).

In 1986 the Government drafted plans to establish a $A27m. trust fund to finance Tuvalu's budget requirements. In 1987 the British, Australian and New Zealand Governments signed an agreement whereby the UK pledged to contribute $A8.5m. to the Tuvalu Trust Fund, Australia $A8m. and New Zealand $A8.2m. The value of the Fund stood at some $A32.6m. in 2001 and during the late 1990s contributed some $A7m. towards total annual expenditure. Official development assistance declined from US $10.1m in 1997 to US $5.2m. in 1998. In 2001/02 New Zealand provided bilateral assistance worth $NZ2.05m., while aid from Australia totalled $A3.3m. in 1999/2000. The 2002 budget allowed for operating expenditure of as much as US $11.6m. and for special development spending of US $2.5m., while capital expenditure of US $5.6m. was envisaged. An overall budgetary surplus of US $6.4m. was projected, equivalent to 47% of GDP (compared with a surplus equivalent to 20% in 2001). The annual rate of inflation averaged 3.2% in 1990–99. The average rate was 1.0% in 1999, 5.3% in 2000 and 1.8% in 2001.

According to UN criteria, Tuvalu is one of the world's least developed countries (LDCs), a status that attracts concessionary loans from the World Bank and the IMF, and renders Tuvalu's exports eligible for special tariff rates under provisions of the General Agreement on Tariffs and Trade (GATT, superseded by the World Trade Organization—WTO). Its economic development has been adversely affected by inclement weather (as illustrated by Cyclone Kelo, which devastated the islands of Niulakita and Nukulaelae in mid-1997) and inadequate infrastructure. Tuvalu's vulnerability to fluctuations in the price of copra on the international market and the country's dependence on imports have resulted in a persistent visible trade deficit; it has also remained reliant on foreign assistance for its development budget. In August 1999 a US $4m. loan was secured to establish an outer islands development fund. It was expected that responsibility for development in the outer islands would be transferred from the Government to local communities. The Island Development Programme aimed not only to decentralize administration but also to raise the standards of local public services and to encourage the development of small businesses. The capital assets of the Falekaupule Trust Fund, which was charged with promoting sustainable increases in funding for the development of the outer islands, reached US $8.2m. in 2001. In February 2000, meanwhile, the sale of the '.tv' internet suffix (see History) substantially increased the island's GDP. Government revenues in that year were almost twice the projected budgeted amount. Proceeds from the sale were to be used to develop the country's infrastructure and were channelled largely into improving roads and the education system, also allowing the Government to investigate the possibility of buying land in Fiji, should the resettlement of Tuvalu's population become necessary. In an attempt to ensure the continuity of flights to Tuvalu, the Government committed itself to the purchase of majority shares in Air Fiji in March 2002, using a loan from the National Bank of Tuvalu (although the purchase was subject to parliamentary approval). The ADB envisaged a GDP growth rate of 3.0% in 2002. Tuvalu is a member of the UN's Economic and Social Commission for Asia and the Pacific (ESCAP), of the Pacific Community (formerly the South Pacific Commission) and of the Pacific Islands Forum (formerly the South Pacific Forum). Tuvalu was admitted to the ADB in May 1993.

Statistical Survey

AREA AND POPULATION

Land Area: 26 sq km (10 sq miles).

Population: 8,229 (males 3,902; females 4,327) at mini-census of June 1985; 9,043 (males 4,376; females 4,667) at census of 17 November 1991; 10,450 (official estimate) at mid-2000; 10,660 at 1 July 2001 (Source: Asian Development Bank, *Key Indicators of Developing Asian and Pacific Countries*). *By atoll* (1996): Funafuti 3,836; Vaitupu 1,205; Niutao 749; Nanumea 818; Nukufetau 756; Nanumaga 644; Nui 608; Nukulaelae 370; Niulakita 75.

Density (2001): 410.0 per sq km.

Births and Deaths (1999): Birth rate 20.3 per 1,000; Death rate 7.6 per 1,000. Source: UN, *Statistical Yearbook for Asia and the Pacific.*

Expectation of Life (WHO estimates, years at birth, 2000): Males 63.6; Females 67.6 Source WHO, *World Health Report.*

Economically Active Population: In 1979 there were 936 people in paid employment, 50% of them in government service. In 1979 114 Tuvaluans were employed by the Nauru Phosphate Co, with a smaller number employed in Kiribati and about 255 on foreign ships. At the 1991 census the total economically active population (aged 15 years and over) stood at 2,383 (males 1,605; females 778).

AGRICULTURE, ETC.

Principal Crops (FAO estimates, metric tons, 2000): Coconuts 1,000; Fruit (excl. melons) 520. Source: FAO.

Livestock (FAO estimate, '000 head, year ending September 2000): Pigs 13. Source: FAO.

Livestock Products (FAO estimates, metric tons, 2000): Poultry meat 30, Pig meat 70, Hen eggs 12; Honey 1. Source: FAO.

Fishing (FAO estimates, metric tons, live weight, 1999): Capture 400 (Skipjack tuna 260, Yellowfin tuna 15). Source: FAO, *Yearbook of Fishery Statistics.*

FINANCE

Currency and Exchange Rates: Australian and Tuvaluan currencies are both in use. Australian currency: 100 cents = 1 Australian dollar ($A). *Sterling, US Dollar and Euro Equivalents* (31 May 2002): £1 sterling = $A2.5849; US $1 = $A1.7624; €1 = $A1.6544; $A100 = £38.69 = US $56.74 = €60.45. *Average Exchange Rate* (US $ per Australian dollar): 0.6453 in 1999; 0.5823 in 2000; 0.5176 in 2001.

Budget (provisional, $A '000, 1999): Revenue 22,246; Expenditure 17,709. Source: Asian Development Bank, *Key Indicators of Developing Asian and Pacific Countries.*

Development Budget (provisional capital expenditure, $A '000, 1991): Australia 1,300; New Zealand 1,500; United Kingdom 1,500; Taiwan 2,340; European Development Fund 900; Japan 500; UNDP 900; France 250; USA 200; Total (incl. others) 10,077.

2000: Total development expenditure $A30m.

Cost of Living (Consumer Price Index for Funafuti; base: November 1983 = 100): 161.5 in 1997; 162.5 in 1998; 173.8 in 1999. Source: Asian Development Bank, *Key Indicators of Developing Asian and Pacific Countries.*

Gross Domestic Product by Economic Activity ($A '000 at current prices, 1998): Agriculture 3,484; Mining 638; Manufacturing 881; Electricity, gas and water 574; Construction 2,952; Trade, restaurants and hotels 2,972; Transport storage and communications 1,380; Finance and real estate 2,376; Community, social and personal services 4,806; *Sub-total (incl. others)* 20,769; Indirect taxes, *less* subsidies 1,275; *GDP in purchasers' values* 22,045. Source: Asian Development Bank, *Key Indicators of Developing Asian and Pacific Countries.*

Balance of Payments ($A '000, 1996): Exports of goods f.o.b. 361; Imports of goods f.o.b. -10,740; *Trade balance* –10,379; Exports of services and other income 10,502; Imports of services and other income –8,758; *Balance on goods, services and income* 8,635; Unrequited transfers (net) 9,082; *Current balance* 447; Capital account (net) 2,088; Net errors and omissions –55; *Overall balance* 2,480. Source: Asian Development Bank, *Key Indicators of Developing Asian and Pacific Countries.*

EXTERNAL TRADE

Principal Commodities ($A '000, 1989): *Imports:* Food and live animals 1,514.6; Beverages and tobacco 201.6; Crude materials, inedible, except fuels 239.6; Mineral fuels, lubricants, etc. 660.7; Chemicals 369.1; Basic manufactures 1,001.3; Machinery and transport equipment 631.9; Miscellaneous manufactured articles 455.2; Total (incl. others) 5,170.3. *Exports:* (1990) Copra 29.0; Handicrafts 2.0; Stamps 147.0; Total 178.0; (1997) Copra 6.0.

Principal Trading Partners (US $ million, 2001): *Imports:* Australia 2.51; Fiji 9.25; Japan 0.24; New Zealand 1.09; United Kingdom

0.23; Total (incl. others) 14.12. *Exports:* Belgium 0.01; Fiji 0.11; Poland 0.02; Total (incl. others) 1.03.

Source: Asian Development Bank, *Key Indicators of Developing Asian and Pacific Countries.*

TRANSPORT

Shipping: *Merchant Fleet* (vessels registered, '000 grt at 31 December): 43 in 1999; 59 in 2000; 36 in 2001. Source: Lloyd's Register-Fairplay, *World Fleet Statistics.*

TOURISM

Tourist Arrivals: 1,029 in 1997; 1,077 in 1998; 1,504 in 2000.

Tourist Arrivals by Country of Residence (1998): Australia 163; Germany 35; Japan 71; New Zealand 104; United Kingdom 42; USA 101; Total (incl. others) 1,077.
Source: World Tourism Organization, *Yearbook of Tourism Statistics*, and South Pacific Tourism Organization.

COMMUNICATIONS MEDIA

Non-daily Newspapers (1996): 1; estimated circulation 300*.

Telephones (main lines, 2000): 660 in use†.

Radio Receivers (1997): 4,000 in use*.

Telefax Stations (1993): 10 in use‡.

* Source: UNESCO, *Statistical Yearbook.*
† Source: International Telecommunication Union.
‡ Source: UN, *Statistical Yearbook.*

EDUCATION

Primary (1998): 9 government schools, 3 church schools (1994); 91 teachers; 1,811 pupils.

General Secondary (1990): 1 government school (2000); 31 teachers; 345 pupils.

In 1988 there were 13 kindergartens, three private primary schools, eight community training centres (mainly for the use of primary school leavers) and one maritime school for the training of 25 merchant seamen per year. Education reforms, begun in 1991, resulted in the closure of the largely unsuccessful community training centres and the expansion of the maritime school to offer vocational, technical and commerce-related courses.

Directory

The Constitution

A new Constitution came into effect at independence on 1 October 1978. Its main provisions are as follows:

The Constitution states that Tuvalu is a democratic sovereign state and that the Constitution is the Supreme Law. It guarantees protection of all fundamental rights and freedoms and provides for the determination of citizenship.

The British sovereign is represented by the Governor-General, who must be a citizen of Tuvalu and is appointed on the recommendation of the Prime Minister. The Prime Minister is elected by Parliament, and up to four other ministers are appointed by the Governor-General from among the members of Parliament, after consultation with the Prime Minister. The Cabinet, which is directly responsible to Parliament, consists of the Prime Minister and the other ministers, whose functions are to advise the Governor-General upon the government of Tuvalu. The Attorney-General is the principal legal adviser to the Government. Parliament is composed of 12 members directly elected by universal adult suffrage for four years, subject to dissolution, and is presided over by the Speaker (who is elected by the members). The Constitution also provides for the operation of a Judiciary (see Judicial System) and for an independent Public Service. Under a revised Constitution that took effect on 1 October 1986, the Governor-General no longer has the authority to reject the advice of the Government.

The Government

Head of State: HM Queen ELIZABETH II.

Governor-General: Sir TOMASI PUAPUA (took office June 1998).

CABINET
(September 2002)

Prime Minister, Minister for Foreign Affairs and Labour: SAUFATU SOPOANGA.

Deputy Prime Minister, Minister Works, Communications and Transport: MAATIA TOAFA.

Minister for Education, Sports and Culture, and Health: ALESANA KLIES SELUKA.

Minister for Finance and Economic Planning and and Industries: BIKENIBEU PAENIU

Minister for Home Affairs and Rural Development: OTINIELU T TAUSI

Minister for Natural Resources, Energy, the Environment and Tourism: SAMUELU P TEO.

MINISTRIES

The majority of ministries are situated on Vaiaku, Funafuti; the remainder are on Vaitupu.

Ministry of Tourism, Trade and Industries: see under Tourism.

Ministry of Works, Communications and Energy: PMB, Vaiaku, Funafuti; tel. 20055; fax 20772.

Legislature

PARLIAMENT

Parliament has 12 members who hold office for a term of up to four years. A general election was held on 25 July 2002. There are no political parties.

Speaker: SALOA TAUIA.

Diplomatic Representation

There are no embassies or high commissions in Tuvalu. The British High Commissioner in Fiji is also accredited as High Commissioner to Tuvalu. Other Ambassadors or High Commissioners accredited to Tuvalu include the Australian, New Zealand, US, French and Japanese Ambassadors in Fiji.

Judicial System

The Supreme Law is embodied in the Constitution. The High Court is the superior court of record, presided over by the Chief Justice, and has jurisdiction to consider appeals from judgments of the Magistrates' Courts and the Island Courts. Appeals from the High Court lie with the Court of Appeal in Fiji or, in the ultimate case, with the Judicial Committee of the Privy Council in the United Kingdom.

There are eight Island Courts with limited jurisdiction in criminal and civil cases.

Chief Justice: Sir GAVEN DONNE (non-resident).

Attorney-General: TELETI TEO.

Religion

CHRISTIANITY

Te Ekalesia Kelisiano Tuvalu (The Christian Church of Tuvalu): POB 2, Funafuti; tel. 20755; fax 20651; f. 1861; autonomous since 1968; derived from the Congregationalist foundation of the London Missionary Society; some 98% of the population are adherents; Pres. Rev. ETI KINE; Gen. Sec. Rev. FILOIMEA TELIFO.

Roman Catholic Church: Catholic Centre, POB 58, Funafuti; tel. and fax 20527; e-mail cathcent@tuvalu.tv; 109 adherents (31 December 1999); Superior Fr CAMILLE DESROSIERS.

Other churches with adherents in Tuvalu include the Church of Jesus Christ of Latter-day Saints (Mormons), the Jehovah's Witnesses, the New Apostolic Church and the Seventh-day Adventists.

BAHÁ'Í FAITH

National Spiritual Assembly: POB 48, Funafuti; tel. 20860; mems resident in 8 localities.

The Press

Tuvalu Echoes: Broadcasting and Information Office, Vaiaku, Funafuti; tel. 20731; fax 20732; f. 1984; fortnightly; English; Editor VAIATOA UALE; circ. 250.

Te Lama: Ekalesia Kelisiano Tuvalu, POB 2, Funafuti; tel. 20755; fax 20651; quarterly; religious; Pres. Rev. ETI KINE; Editor Rev. KITIONA TAUSI; circ. 1,000.

Broadcasting and Communications

TELECOMMUNICATIONS

Telecom Tuvalu: Vaiaku, Funafuti; tel. 20010; fax 20002.

BROADCASTING

Tuvalu Media Corporation: PMB, Vaiaku, Funafuti; tel. 20731; fax 20732; govt-owned; Chief Broadcasting and Information Officer PUSINELLI LAAFAI.

Radio

Radio Tuvalu: Broadcasting and Information Office, PMB, Vaiaku, Funafuti; tel. 20138; fax 20732; f. 1975; daily broadcasts in Tuvaluan and English, 43 hours per week; Programme Dir FALAHEA HALETI.

Finance

BANKS

Development Bank of Tuvalu: PMB 9, Vaiaku, Funafuti; tel. 20199; fax 20850; f. 1993 to replace the Business Development Advisory Bureau.

National Bank of Tuvalu: POB 13, Vaiaku, Funafuti; tel. 20803; fax 20802; e-mail nbt@tuvalu.tv; f. 1980; commercial bank; govt-owned; ('000 A$) cap. 471.0, res 1,479.0, dep. 24,808.9 (Dec. 1999); Chair. AFELE PITA; Gen. Man. IONATANA PEIA; brs on all atolls.

Trade and Industry

GOVERNMENT AGENCY

National Fishing Corporation of Tuvalu (NAFICOT): POB 93, Funafuti; tel. 20724; fax 20800; fishing vessel operators; seafood processing and marketing; agents for diesel engine spare parts, fishing supplies and marine electronics; Gen. Man. SEMU SOPOANGA TAAFAKI.

CHAMBER OF COMMERCE

Tuvalu Chamber of Commerce: POB 17, Funafuti; Chair. SEMU TAAFAKI.

UTILITIES

Electricity

Tuvalu Electricity Corporation (TEC): POB 32, Funafuti; tel. 20350; fax 20351; e-mail thomas@tuvalu.tv.

CO-OPERATIVE

Tuvalu Co-operative Society Ltd: POB 11, Funafuti; tel. 20747; fax 20748; f. 1979 by amalgamation of the eight island socs; controls retail trade in the islands; Gen. Man. MONISE LAAFAI; Registrar: SIMETI LOPATI.

Tuvalu Coconut Traders Co-operative: Contact TAAI KATALAKE.

TRADE UNION

Tuvalu Overseas Seamen's Union (TOSU): POB 99, Funafuti; tel. 20609; fax 20610; e-mail tosu@Tuvalu.tv; Sec. TOMMY ALEFAIO.

Transport

ROADS

Funafuti has some impacted-coral roads; elsewhere, tracks exist.

SHIPPING

There is a deep-water lagoon at the point of entry, Funafuti, and ships are able to enter the lagoon at Nukufetau. Irregular shipping services connect Tuvalu with Fiji and elsewhere. The Government operates an inter-island vessel.

CIVIL AVIATION

In 1992 a new runway was constructed with EU aid to replace the grass landing strip on Funafuti. Air Marshall Islands operates three-weekly service between Funafuti, Nadi (Fiji) and Majuro (Marshall Islands). In June 1995 Tuvalu, Kiribati, the Marshall Islands and Nauru agreed to begin discussions on the establishment of a joint regional airline. The Government of Tuvalu planned to purchase a majority shareholding in Air Fiji in 2002.

Tourism

In 1994 there was one hotel, with 17 rooms, on Funafuti. There were an estimated 1,077 tourist arrivals in 1998. In that year 15.1% of tourists came from Australia, 9.4% from the USA, 9.7% from New Zealand, 6.6% from Japan, 3.9% from the United Kingdom and 3.3% from Germany. Tourist arrivals totalled 1,504 in 2000.

Ministry of Tourism, Trade and Commerce: PMB, Vaiaku, Funafuti; tel. 20184; fax 20829.

Tuvalu Tourism Office: PMB, Funafuti; tel. 20184; fax 20829.

Education

Education is provided by the Government, and is compulsory between the ages of six and 15 years. In 1994 there were 12 primary schools, with a total of 1,811 pupils and 91 teachers in 1998. There was one secondary school in 2000. There were 345 secondary pupils and 31 teachers in 1990. The only tertiary institution is the Maritime Training School at Amatuku on Funafuti. Further training or vocational courses are available in Fiji and Kiribati. The University of the South Pacific (based in Fiji) has an extension centre on Funafuti. A programme of major reforms in the education system in Tuvalu, begun in the early 1990s, resulted in the lengthening of primary schooling (from six to eight years) and a compulsory two years of secondary education, as well as the introduction of vocational, technical and commerce-related courses at the Maritime Training School. Total government expenditure on education in 1998 amounted to $A277,813, equivalent to 40.3% of total budgetary expenditure.

USA: State of Hawaii

Physical and Social Geography

The State of Hawaii is one of the 50 federated members of the United States of America. The Hawaiian Islands are located in the central northern Pacific Ocean and comprise a chain of volcanic and coral islands formed by the peaks of huge undersea volcanoes. They cover a total area of 16,636 sq km (6,423 sq miles). There are eight major islands and 124 minor islands, which stretch from Hawaii in the south-east (10,433 sq km), through Maui (1,884 sq km), Molokai (674 sq km), Oahu (1,546 sq km) to Kauai (1,430 sq km) and Niihau (180 sq km) in the north-west. Further west lie a number of small, uninhabited islands, including Nihoa, Necker, Laysan and Lisianski. Kure Atoll and Midway, which lie just east of the International Date Line, complete the chain. The Midway Islands are not part of the territory of the State of Hawaii. Active volcanoes are the outstanding physical feature of the Hawaiian Islands. The climate is tropical with temperatures in Honolulu ranging between 12°C (53°F) and 34°C (94°F) annually. In 1995 annual rainfall varied between 152 mm (6 ins) on Maui island and 2,515 mm (99 ins) on Oahu island.

The Hawaiian population is multiracial. In 2001 22.0% of inhabitants were Caucasian, 16.4% were Japanese and 11.7% were Filipino. Those of mixed race, including part-Hawaiian, accounted for some 44.1% of the population. English is the principal language, but Hawaiian, a Polynesian tongue, is also an official language. Christianity is the main religion, with some 34% of the population claiming to be adherents to various Christian denominations in 1990. At the 2000 census the estimated total resident population of the islands was 1,211,537. Honolulu, on the island of Oahu, is the state capital.

History

The Hawaiian Islands were probably the last of the Pacific Islands to be settled by Polynesians. Oral history suggests that until about AD 1300 contacts were maintained between Tahiti and Hawaii. There followed, however, a long period of isolation during which the Hawaiian Polynesian culture developed its own characteristic features.

Members of a British expedition, led by Capt. James Cook, were the first Europeans known to have visited the islands, which were named the Sandwich Islands. Cook landed at Waimea, on Kauai Island, in 1778, but he was killed at Kealakekua, on Hawaii, during a return visit in 1779. Subsequent Hawaiian history until June 1900, when the islands formally became a US Territory, was one of the virtual destruction of the indigenous Polynesian culture by missionary, commercial and political intervention by outsiders, and the sharp reduction of the indigenous population by disease. The Polynesian population, estimated to be 142,050 in 1823, had fallen to 56,900 by 1872. Organized immigration of non-Polynesian groups into Hawaii began in the 1850s with the arrival of Chinese contract labourers, followed in the 1870s by Portuguese from Madeira and the Azores.

Russian, British, French and US interests all vied for favours with the islands' rulers during the 1800s, while independent traders and entrepreneurs supplied arms to various chiefs in an attempt to gain a foothold for their enterprises. The four chiefdoms in existence in 1782 had been unified under Kamehameha I by 1810. Following the arrival of Protestant missionaries in 1820, Christianity rapidly became a national religion, which accelerated the disintegration of traditional society. Gradually US influence became entrenched. Internal insurrections and unrest in the 1890s led to the overthrow of Queen Lili'uokalani and the end of the monarchy in 1893, the establishment of a US settler-dominated republic in 1894 and outright annexation by the USA in 1898.

Hawaii was admitted to the USA as the 50th State on 21 August 1959. Hawaiians and other native residents are US citizens and may move freely between Hawaii and the mainland.

A resurgence of interest in Polynesian culture has led to an increase in the controversy surrounding the Hawaiian Home Lands (a 187,413-acre Native Hawaiian Land Trust, first established by the US Congress in 1920) and land development generally. During 1983 Hawaiian Polynesians protested at the failure of the US Government to pay reparations for 430,000 ha of land annexed in 1893. Despite the demand for land, there have been several successful attempts to preserve traditional land by Polynesian activists. A principal aim of the Hawaiian 'sovereignty' movement (led by Ka LaHui Hawaii or the Sovereign Hawaiian Nation party) is to secure for Polynesian Hawaiians the same recourse to law and right of self-government enjoyed by other Native Americans, such as Indians and the Inuit (Eskimos). Polynesian Hawaiians generally have lower incomes, and suffer higher unemployment and poorer education, than other ethnic groups in the islands. The 'sovereignty' movement continued to grow in popularity during the early 1990s, and in January 1993 some 16,000 people took part in demonstrations commemorating the 100th anniversary of the overthrow of the monarchy. Supporters of the movement expressed demands for native lands and cultural rights, while a minority of campaigners advocated full independence for the islands. Demonstrations continued in 1994, and during one incident in May of that year 12 sovereignty activists stormed Honolulu's City Hall and attempted to remove the mayor, claiming that, as a non-Hawaiian, he was illegally occupying office. In June 2001 the Federal Court heard a challenge to Article 12 of the Hawaiian Constitution, which gives native Hawaiians, or Kanahele, the right to occupy real estate at heavily discounted prices. The Office of Hawaiian Homelands offers native Hawaiians leases on land statewide for US $1 a year. Opponents who brought the challenge said that the article, introduced in 1978, violated the equal protection clause of the US Constitution, and amounted to racial discrimination.

In a conciliatory move in May 1994 the US Navy returned the island of Kahoolawe, which had formerly been used as a bombing range, to Hawaiian control. The US Congress approved the allocation of US $400m. to rehabilitate the island.

During 1995 the independence movement appeared divided over the subject of a proposed referendum on sovereignty, which was to be organized by the Hawaiian Sovereignty Elections Council (formerly the Sovereignty Advisory Commission), a body created by the State Legislature for the purpose of advising the Government on independence issues. Ka LaHui Hawaii was among the fiercest critics of the proposals, which it claimed were profoundly flawed and impossible to implement, and accused the Government of manipulating the independence issue in order to suppress any serious debate on sovereignty in the future. The referendum, which was open to all persons over 18 years of age claiming indigenous Hawaiian blood regardless of their current nationality, took place over a period of several weeks in mid-1996. Of the estimated 30,000 voters (representing a participation rate of less than 40% of eligible voters), more than 70% registered a vote in favour of the proposal to elect delegates to a convention to consider possibilities for self-government. However, implementation of the result was expected to be delayed following the initiation of legal proceedings by a non-native resident of Hawaii who claimed that, in excluding non-native Hawaiians, the plebiscite was discriminatory and therefore unconstitutional.

Legal proceedings initiated by three homosexual couples in the Hawaii Supreme Court in 1993 were resumed in September 1996. The court's ruling that the prohibition of same-sex marriages constituted an infringement of the civil rights of Hawaiian citizens as defined in the State Constitution was expected to lead to the recognition of such marriages. The US Senate responded by rapidly adopting legislation (the Defense of Marriage Act, which had been approved previously by the House of Representatives) to prevent a similar situation occurring in other states. The issue raised a number of questions regarding Hawaii's independence from federal law, as a result of which the ruling was deferred. In April 1997 the State approved a programme of civil rights laws, which (although not directly addressing the issue of same-sex marriages) granted increased, but not equal, rights to people in homosexual relationships, particularly concerning state benefits and inheritance rights. The validity in other US states, however, of any such marriages conducted in Hawaii under the proposed new law was uncertain. In July 2001 the Legislature voted to raise the age of consent in Hawaii from 14 to 16, overriding a Governor's veto for the first time since Hawaii became a state; the vote ended Hawaii's distinction of having the lowest age of consent in the USA.

In September 1998 the federal and state Governments ordered separate grand-jury investigations into the alleged misuse of political power and investment funds by Bishop Estate, a charitable trust and Hawaii's largest landowner.

Politically, Hawaii is dominated by the Democratic Party, the candidate of which, John Waihee, was elected Governor in November 1986. At the same time, however, Patricia Saiki became the first Republican elected in Hawaii to the US House of Representatives since the islands became a State in 1959. In July 1990 Senator Spark Matsunaga, a Democrat, died four years prior to the expiry of his term in the US Congress. Waihee appointed Daniel Akaka, a Democrat in the US House of Representatives, to the post, pending an election later in the year. The other Hawaiian Representative in

Congress, the Republican, Saiki, also resigned her seat in order to contest the election to the Senate in November. At the elections Waihee was returned as Governor, Akaka confirmed as Senator and two more Democrats were elected to the House of Representatives. At elections in November 1994 the Democratic candidate, Benjamin Cayetano, defeated the Republican, Patricia Saiki, by attaining 55.6% of total votes to become Governor. At elections in November 1996 both Neil Abercrombie and Patsy Mink, the Democratic Representatives in the US Congress, were re-elected. Indications during 1998 appeared to suggest an increase in support for the Republican Party, and it seemed likely that the State might elect its first Republican Governor at gubernatorial elections due to take place in November of that year. The apparent change in public opinion in Hawaii was attributed to a downturn in economic growth (largely as a result of the Asian financial crisis and the consequent withdrawal of Japanese investment) and a desire for increased debate in the political arena. However, at the election on 3 November 1998 incumbent Governor Cayetano narrowly defeated the Republican candidate, Linda Lingle. Cayetano received 49.5% of votes cast, and Lingle 48.2%.

At elections held on 7 November 2000, both the incumbent Senator, Daniel Akaka, and the two Representatives to the US Congress were re-elected to their respective offices. In the presidential election, the Democrat candidate, Al Gore, received 55.3% of votes cast, compared with the 37.1% of votes received by the Republican candidate, George W. Bush.

In March 2002 the House of Representatives approved a bill to legalize the practice of euthanasia. The bill was then transferred to the Senate, which deferred a vote on the proposed legislation indefinitely.

One of the representatives to the US Congress, Patsy Mink, died on 28 September 2002. It was thought unlikely that she would be replaced before the elections scheduled for November of that year.

The USA has supported moves by the South Pacific Forum (now Pacific Islands Forum) to ban drift-net fishing in the region, and in 1989 the State of Hawaii enacted legislation that forbade drift-net fishing vessels in its ports. The USA, however, has provoked criticism in the region, owing to its reluctance to take action on pollution control. There has been considerable controversy over the disposal of toxic wastes and the consequences of the 'greenhouse effect' in Pacific countries. The Pacific states and territories have also expressed concern about the chemical weapons disposal facility on the US territory of Johnston Atoll. In December 2000 President Clinton created the Northwestern Hawaiian Islands Coral Reef Reserve, the largest nature reserve in the USA, covering an area of 99,500 square nautical miles underwater around the north-western Hawaiian Islands. The area, containing nearly 70% of all coral reefs in the USA, was to be protected from oil and gas exploration and the dumping of waste. Local fishermen expressed concerns at limits imposed on fishing in the reserve, which they claimed would lead to the closure of all commercial fisheries and up to one-third of the area's bottom-fishing grounds.

Some controversy ensued in the US Pacific in 1990, when Representative Saiki of Hawaii introduced a measure into the US Congress which would not only incorporate Kingman Reef and the islands of Palmyra, Midway, Jarvis, Baker and Howland into the State of Hawaii, but would also incorporate Wake Island (Enenkio Atoll) into the territory of Guam. The Marshall Islands (then a US Associated State) subsequently laid claim to Wake.

Economy

The economy of the State of Hawaii is very dependent upon tourism and US federal expenditure on defence. Agriculture, once the dominant industry, remains important. The annual income per head of wage and salary earners (US $30,630 in 2000) is somewhat lower than the national average, although the cost of living is higher (an estimated 34% more than the USA as a whole during 1990). This is due to a high level of imports and the inflated price of property. In 2000 the gross state product (GSP), according to official estimates, increased by some 4.6% compared with the previous year, to US $42,364m. GSP per head totalled US $34,946 in 2000.

In 1900 agriculture employed 62.0% of all workers, but this proportion declined steadily through the century: 40.1% in 1930, 7.6% in 1960 and 1.4% in 2000. The agricultural sector contributed 1.2% of GSP in 2000. Agricultural land constituted 47.0% of Hawaii's total land area in 2001. The principal cash crops in 2000 were pineapples, flowers and nursery products, sugar cane and vegetables and melons. Sugar cane, first cultivated commercially in 1802, did not become important until the 1870s, and by 1930 over 1m. metric tons per year were being exported. During the 1980s Hawaii was the USA's second largest producer of sugar cane (after Florida). However, by 1994 there were only 10 sugar mills, compared with 34 in 1940. The value of sales of unprocessed sugar cane declined from US $86.8m. in 1999 to $62.6m. in 2000. Pineapples, first cultivated commercially at the beginning of the 20th century, earned Hawaii US $101.5m. in sales revenue in 2000, compared with $101.4m. in the previous year. The pineapple industry provided employment for some 2,250 people in 1993. However, in 1994 there was only one pineapple cannery, compared with eight in 1940. Diversification is encouraged and other crops include coffee, papayas (pawpaws), oranges, flowers and taro. Hawaii is also one of the world's most important producers of orchids. Sales of flowers and other nursery products reached US $83.4m. in 2000, compared with $75.7m. in 1999. Cattle are the most important livestock, although livestock accounted for only 14.8% of farm incomes in 1998.

Commercial forestry is limited, although the trade in sandalwood was one of the first activities to attract European and American interest in the islands. Commercial fishing, and fish processing, is a well-established and expanding industry. In 2000 the total catch was 26.2m. lb (11,884 metric tons), which earned US $59.3m. Other marine industries include the cultivation of seaweed.

Most industrial activity is dependent upon the principal economic sectors of agriculture and tourism. Industry accounted for 7.5% of GSP in 2000. Manufacturing is dominated by the processing of agricultural products. The sector engaged 3.2% of the employed labour force in 2001. The canning and preserving of fruit and vegetables provide a major source of employment, as does the production of sugar and confectionery. In 1994 Hawaii's principal manufactures, ranked by value added, were food products, apparel and stone, clay and glass products. In 1995 the value of manufacturing shipments from the State totalled US $3,440m. There are also fertilizer plants, two petroleum refineries and a plant for the manufacture of gas. A handicraft industry has developed in response to tourism. Construction is also closely related to the tourist industry. In 1999 the value of new building permits amounted to some US $1,513m. The industry, together with mining, engaged an estimated 4.2% of the employed labour force in 2001. There are no known reserves of fossil fuels and the State's energy requirements must be met by imports (98% of requirements are provided by imported petroleum). Hydroelectric generation is the principal alternative source of energy, although the burning of bagasse (waste from sugar cane) and wood chips from specifically-grown trees, wind machines and water-driven turbines have also been explored. In May 2002 the State Government approved legislation enabling it to regulate motor spirit (petrol) prices in Hawaii; the price regulation was expected to begin in July 2004.

The economy of Hawaii is overwhelmingly service-orientated and dominated by tourism. Service industries accounted for 91.3% of GSP in 2000 and engaged 91.1% of the employed labour force in 2001. Travel and tourism together were estimated to be responsible, directly or indirectly, for more than one-half of the State's jobs in the mid-1990s and about one-third of GSP. The sector's contribution to GSP was estimated at 25% in 1995. The total of tourist visitors increased from 1.3m. in 1968 to almost 7.0m. in 1990, reaching more than 6.9m. in 2000, before declining to 6.3m. in 2001. Most visitors are from the mainland USA (usually the west coast) and Japan, accounting respectively for 62.8% and 24.2% of total arrivals in 2001. According to estimates by the Hawaii Visitors Bureau, the average Japanese tourist spent US $294 per day during 1996 (compared with a daily average of US $138 spent by mainland US tourists). The influx of foreign visitors to the State has, however, precipitated an increase in social problems, particularly in areas where tourism has replaced traditional industries in the local economy. Other services being encouraged include the development of Honolulu as a financial and corporate centre, the maintenance of the islands as a major centre of the regional transport network and the use of Hawaii as the location of film and television productions (seven such productions in 1996, although this had declined from 40 productions in 1994, with expenditure in the State of US $59.7m.). The State has been the beneficiary of increasing investment from overseas and, in 1994, foreign investment totalled US $981m, of which 73% was from Japan. In 1994 some 93% of foreign-owned commercial property was accounted for by the Japanese.

Hawaii is also in receipt of considerable federal funds, much of them expended on the military. The US Pacific Command (USPACOM) based in Hawaii is, in geographical area, the largest of the US unified service commands. Almost one-half of total federal expenditure in the State is on the military, and in 1999 (when total funding was estimated at US $8,568m.) defence spending amounted to US $3,355m. The contribution of federal defence spending to GSP, however, declined from 13.7% in 1983 to some 11% in 1995. In mid-1999 military personnel and their dependants numbered 85,711 (equivalent to 7.2% of the resident population).

Hawaii's visible trade deficit is more than offset by receipts from tourism, other service sectors and federal expenditure. In 1992 imports from the US mainland amounted to US $9,286m. and, from foreign countries, US $2,494m. Total exports were worth US $1,635m. in 1992. Japan is the State's leading foreign trading partner, receiving 41% of Hawaii's exports and providing 23% of imports in 1989. Hawaii benefits from Honolulu's status as a US Foreign Trade Zone (imported goods may be stored, sold wholesale and otherwise utilized or manufactured without being subject to customs duties until withdrawn from the Zone into US customs territory). In 1995 the Zone, with its four sections, accommodated 310 local, US and foreign companies, with 1,702 employees, and processed products worth US $1,952m., of which US $336m.-worth were exported again.

In the financial year ending 30 June 2000, the State recorded a budget surplus of US $336m. In 2000 total taxation raised in the State amounted to US $10,483m., of which some 60% consisted of federal taxes. In 1995–99 the average annual rate of inflation was 0.8%, standing at 2.3% in 2001. The rate of unemployment stood at 4.6% in mid-2001. Unemployment was highest where the traditional sugar and pineapple industries had closed, and ranged from 8.7% on Hawaii to 4.9% on Oahu in 1999. Between 1980 and 1990 net immigration accounted for some 22% of population growth (some 57% of the 7,537 immigrants in 1995 were from the Philippines).

Hawaii's economy, particularly agriculture and tourism, is vulnerable to adverse climatic conditions. The traditional agricultural economy has suffered considerable decline since the Second World War, and the sugar industry, despite being among the most efficient in the world, is dependent upon government subsidies. Moreover, the pressure for development continues to threaten agricultural land. Property in Hawaii is highly valuable, with six landowners accounting for more than one-third of the 62% of land in private ownership in 1990. Tourism is the industry upon which Hawaii has increasingly relied. A programme to redevelop aspects of the tourist industry, initiated in 1994, aimed to promote Hawaiian culture and 'eco-tourism' (which encourages the appreciation of the natural environment) as alternatives to traditional tourism. The nationalist movement among ethnic Hawaiians has consistently opposed the development of tourism on the islands. Moreover, the Asian financial crisis in 1998 led to a decline in tourist arrivals from Japan and to a loss of investment from Japanese interests. Following the terrorist attacks in New York and Washington, DC, of 11 September 2001, there was a sharp decrease in the number of foreign visitors to Hawaii, a trend that was expected to continue well into 2003. This was offset, however, by a corresponding growth in the number of visitors arriving from elsewhere within the USA. In early 1997 a prominent Hawaiian banker urged the USA to expand its economic relations with its Pacific island territories. It was suggested that the Joint Commercial Commission (which was widely believed to have failed to fulfil its proposed role as a body promoting trade and investment between the USA and the region) could be upgraded to act as a regional forum for increased economic co-operation with the USA.

Hawaii is an integral part, and a member State, of the USA, which has membership of the Asia-Pacific Economic Co-operation forum (APEC), the Pacific Community (formerly the South Pacific Commission), the Asian Development Bank (ADB) and the UN's Economic and Social Commission for Asia and the Pacific (ESCAP), and is also a signatory of the Colombo Plan.

Statistical Survey

Source (unless otherwise stated): State Department of Business, Economic Development and Tourism, POB 2359, Honolulu, Hawaii 96804; tel. (808) 586-2423; fax (808) 587-2790; internet www.state.hi.us/dbedt.

Area and Population

AREA, POPULATION AND DENSITY

Area (sq km)	16,635*
Population (census results)†	
1 April 1990	1,108,229
1 April 2000	
Males	608,671
Females	602,866
Total	1,211,537
Population (official estimates at mid-year)†	
1999	1,210,300
2000	1,212,281
2001	1,224,398
Density (per sq km) at mid-2001	73.6

* 6,423 sq miles.

† Figures refer to resident population.

PRINCIPAL ETHNIC GROUPS (sample survey, 2001)*

Hawaiian/part-Hawaiian	267,532
Other unmixed	
Caucasian	258,187
Black	13,040
Japanese	193,197
Chinese	36,113
Filipino	137,953
Korean	7,513
Samoan/Tongan	11,075
Mixed (except Hawaiian)	250,985
Total (incl. others)	1,175,595

* Excludes persons in institutions, military barracks, Niihau, Kalawao, the homeless and households without telephones.

ISLANDS (2000 census)

	Area (sq km)	Resident Population	Density (per sq km)
Hawaii	10,432.5	148,677	14.3
Maui	1,883.5	117,644	62.5
Molokini	0.1	—	—
Kahoolawe	115.5	—	—
Lanai	364.0	3,193	8.8
Molokai	673.4	7,404	11.0
Oahu*	1,553.4	876,156	564.0
Kauai	1,430.4	58,303	40.8
Niihau	179.9	160	0.9
Lehua	1.2	—	—
Kaula	0.6	—	—
Total	16,634.5	1,211,537	72.8

* Including the Northwestern Hawaiian Islands (area 8.1 sq km).

COUNTIES (mid-2001)

	Area (sq km)	Population*	Density (per sq km)
Hawaii	10,432.5	168,524	16.2
Maui†	3,036.5	168,213	55.4
Honolulu	1,553.4	925,250	595.6
Kauai	1,612.1	74,088	46.0
Total	16,634.5	1,336,075	80.3

* Figures refer to *de facto* population, including visitors but excluding residents temporarily absent.

† Figures for Maui include Kalawao, which had a *de facto* population of 135 in 2001.

PRINCIPAL TOWNS (resident population at 2000 census)

Honolulu District (capital)	371,657	Kaneohe	34,970
Hilo	40,759	Pearl City	30,976
Kailua (Oahu)	36,513	Mililani Town	28,608

BIRTHS, MARRIAGES AND DEATHS (resident population)

	Registered live births		Registered marriages		Registered deaths	
	Number	Rate (per 1,000)	Number	Rate (per 1,000)	Number	Rate (per 1,000)
1993	19,567	16.7	9,744	8.3	7,226	6.2
1994	19,438	16.4	9,317	7.8	7,206	6.1
1995	18,552	15.5	9,277	7.8	7,482	6.3
1996	18,378	15.3	9,003	7.5	7,803	6.5
1997	17,326	14.3	8,878	7.3	7,710	6.4
1998	17,567	14.5	8,746	7.2	7,969	6.6
1999	17,032	14.1	9,222	7.6	8,125	6.7
2000	17,514	14.4	9,217	7.6	8,163	6.7

Expectation of life (years at birth, 1990): 78.85 (males 75.90; females 82.06).

EMPLOYMENT (annual averages, '000 persons)*

	1999	2000	2001†
Agriculture, forestry and fishing	7.7	7.9	7.4
Mining and construction	21.7	23.8	23.7
Manufacturing	16.6	17.6	17.9
Transport, communications and utilities	41.2	42.3	42.1
Trade	133.2	137.0	136.3
Finance, insurance and real estate	34.8	33.2	32.7
Government services	112.8	114.6	115.0
Other services	174.9	183.1	186.1
Total	542.8	559.2	562.2‡

* Excluding self-employed persons and unpaid family workers ('000): 37.9 in 1994. Persons with more than one job are counted more than once.
† Provisional figures.
‡ Including 1,250 persons involved in labour disputes.

Agriculture and Fishing

AGRICULTURAL PRODUCTION (value of sales, US $ million)

	1998	1999	2000
Sugar cane (unprocessed)	87.4	86.8	62.6
Pineapple (fresh equivalent)	92.8	101.4	101.5
Vegetables and melons	51.1	56.4	59.8
Fruits (excl. pineapples)	24.5	28.5	31.4
Macadamia nuts (in shell)	37.4	37.9	29.5
Flowers and nursery products	73.2	75.7	83.4
Coffee (parchment)	24.7	21.0	23.1
Seed crops	25.3	30.5	35.4
Taro	3.2	3.6	3.7
Milk	33.3	31.3	28.1
Eggs	11.2	10.8	10.6
Honey	0.7	0.5	0.6

LIVESTOCK ('000 head at 1 December)

	1998	1999	2000
Cattle*	180	173	164
Pigs	29	28	26
Chickens	747	721	722
Bees	8	8	7

* As at 1 January of the following year.

COMMERCIAL FISHING ('000 lb)

	1998	1999	2000
Tunas	15,036	13,203	13,983
Billfishes	5,986	6,703	6.119
Miscellaneous pelagic species	2,124	3,077	3,204
Deep bottom fishes	732	670	776
Akule/opelu	1,545	1,218	1,474
Total catch (incl. others)	26,192	25,959	26,256

Finance

CURRENCY AND EXCHANGE RATES

Monetary Units
100 cents = 1 United States dollar (US $).

Sterling and Euro Equivalents (31 May 2002)
£1 sterling = US $1.4667;
€1 = 93.87 US cents;
US $100 = £68.18 = €106.53.

BUDGET (US $ million, year ending 30 June)

	1998	1999	2000
State Revenue	6,761	6,646	6,941
General revenue	5,474	5,615	5,729
Insurance trust revenue	1,287	1,032	1,212
State Expenditure	5,860	6,266	6,605
General expenditure	5,261	5,651	5,975
Insurance trust expenditure	599	615	629
Federal Tax Revenue	4,691	5,566	6,237
Federal Expenditure	8,442	8,568	9,015
Defence expenditure	3,394	3,356	3,473

CONSUMER PRICE INDEX, HONOLULU (1982–84 average = 100)

	1999	2000	2001
Food and beverages	162.9	164.8	169.5
Housing	175.8	177.9	179.1
Rent*	181.7	180.3	181.6
Fuel and other utilities	133.4	147.4	146.6
Clothing and footwear	105.4	103.5	101.0
Transportation	162.2	169.6	174.5
All items (incl. others)	173.3	176.3	178.4

* Residential, base: December 1982 = 100.

NATIONAL ACCOUNTS
(US $ million at current prices)
Gross State (Domestic) Product by Industry

	1998	1999	2000
Agriculture, forestry and fishing	472	495	509
Mining	41	39	44
Construction	1,618	1,649	1,853
Manufacturing	1,013	1,208	1,296
Transport, communications and utilities	3,963	4,138	4,288
Wholesale and retail trade	5,841	5,910	6,265
Finance, insurance and real estate	9,175	9,349	9,520
Federal government	4,940	5,033	5,301
State and local government	3,686	3,828	3,774
Other services (incl. hotels)	8,622	8,835	9,515
Total	39,371	40,486	42,364

External Trade

(US $ million)

	1995	1996	1997
Imports*	12,398	12,460	12,629
Exports	1,595	1,563	1,531

* Including imports from the US mainland.

Transport

ROAD TRAFFIC (registered motor vehicles)

	1999	2000	2001
Passenger vehicles	725,142	754,840	775,737
Ambulances	59	56	53
Buses	3,028	2,902	2,847
Trucks	161,067	165,104	168,414
Tractors	407	409	405
Cranes	224	270	314
Motorcycles	17,008	17,661	19,268
Total	906,935	941,242	967,148

Tourism

TOURIST ARRIVALS

Country of origin	1999	2000	2001
Canada	252,777	251,843	216,948
Japan	1,825,588	1,817,643	1,528,564
USA	3,910,074	4,145,156	3,960,234
Total (incl. others)	6,741,037	6,948,595	6,303,791

Tourism receipts (US $ million): 10,280 in 1999; 10,918 in 2000; 10,121 in 2001.

Communications Media

	1998	1999	2000
Telephones in use*	731,519	737,653	741,843
Households with television receivers	381,820	385,790	n.a.
Books (number of titles published)	84	83	82

* Figures refer to access lines.

Education

	Pupils		
	1997/98	1998/99	1999/2000
Government schools, primary and secondary	189,887	188,069	185,860
Private schools, primary and secondary	36,723	36,702	36,226
Higher education*	70,450	70,246	71,869

There was a total of 374 educational institutions (including 132 private schools) and 14,045 teaching staff (of whom 11,602 worked in public schools) in Hawaii in 1994/95. There were 11,629 teaching staff working in public schools in 1995/96.

* Excluding Hawaii's three private universities, which had a total enrolment of 13,209 in 1996/97.

Directory

The Constitution

Under Hawaii's State Constitution, drawn up in 1950 and modified in 1968 and 1978, executive powers are vested in a Governor and a Lieutenant-Governor elected for four-year terms. There is a bicameral Legislature which is composed of a House of Representatives, with 51 members elected for two-year terms, and a Senate with 25 members elected for four-year terms. The Legislature meets annually in Honolulu. As a State, Hawaii elects two Senators and two Representatives to the US Congress. Local government is vested in one combined city-county (Honolulu, comprising the island of Oahu and several outlying islets) and three non-metropolitan counties (Hawaii, Kauai and Maui), each with elected mayors and councils, and one area (Kalawao County) administered by the State Department of Health. The islands of Molokai and Lanai are included in the county of Maui, and Niihau in the county of Kauai.

The Government

(October 2002)

HEAD OF STATE

President: George W. Bush (Republican—took office 20 January 2001).

Vice-President: Richard B. Cheney

The State of Hawaii voted for the Democratic candidate in the US presidential election of November 2000.

GOVERNOR OF HAWAII

Governor: Benjamin J. Cayetano (Democrat—re-elected 3 November 1998).

Lieutenant-Governor: Mazie K. Hirono.

GOVERNMENT DEPARTMENTS

Office of the Governor: State Capitol, 415 S. Beretania St, Honolulu, HI 96813; fax (808) 586-0006; e-mail gov@gov.state.hi.us; internet www.gov.state.hi.us.

Department of Accounting and General Services: 1151 Punchbowl St, Honolulu, HI 96813; internet www.state.hi.us/dags.

Department of Agriculture: POB 22159, 1428 South King St, Honolulu, HI 96823-2159; tel. (808) 973-9560; e-mail hdoa_info@exec.state.hi.us; internet www.hawaiiag.org/hdoa.

Department of the Attorney-General: 425 Queen St, Honolulu, HI 96813; internet www.state.hi.us/ag.

Department of Budget and Finance: POB 150, 250 South Hotel St, Room 305, Honolulu, HI 96810; tel.(808) 586-1518; internet www.state.hi.us/budget.

Department of Business, Economic Development and Tourism: POB 2359, Honolulu, HI 96804; tel. (808) 586-2424; fax (808) 587-2790; internet www.hawaii.gov/dbedt.

Department of Commerce and Consumer Affairs: POB 541, Honolulu, HI 96809; internet www.state.hi.us/dcca.

Department of Defense: 3949 Diamond Head Rd, Honolulu, HI 96816-4495; tel. (808) 733-4258; fax (808) 733-4236; internet www.dod.state.hi.us.

Department of Education: POB 2360, Honolulu, HI 96804; e-mail supt–2>doe@notes.k12.hi.us; internet www.k12.hi.us.

Department of Hawaiian Home Lands: POB 1879, Honolulu, HI 96805; tel. (808) 586-3800; fax (808) 586-3899; internet www.state.hi.us/dhhl.

Department of Health: 1250 Punchbowl St, Honolulu, HI 96813; tel. (808) 586-4400; fax (808) 586-4444; internet www.state.hi.us/health.

Department of Human Resources Development: 235 South Beretania St, Honolulu, HI 96813; internet www.state.hi.us/hrd.

Department of Human Services: POB 339, Honolulu, HI 96809; tel. (808) 586-4996; fax (808) 586-4890; internet www.state.hi.us/dhs.

Department of Labor and Industrial Relations: 830 Punchbowl St, Room 321, Honolulu, HI 96813; tel. (808) 586-9099; fax (808) 586-8865; e-mail tjackson@dlir.state.hi.us; internet www.dlir.state.hi.us.

Department of Land and Natural Resources: 1151 Punchbowl St, Room 130, Honolulu, HI 96813; tel. (808) 587-0330; fax (808) 567-0390; internet www.state.hi.us/dlnr/welcome.html.

Department of Public Safety: 919 Ala Moana Blvd, Honolulu, HI 96814; tel. (808) 587-1350; internet www.state.hi.us/icsd/psd/psd.html.

Department of Taxation: POB 259, Honolulu, HI 96809-0259; internet www.state.hi.us/tax.

Department of Transportation: 869 Punchbowl St, Honolulu, HI 96813; tel. (808) 587-2150; e-mail pao@exec.state.hi.us; internet www.state.hi.us/dot.

Federal Departments: 300 Ala Moana Blvd, Honolulu, HI 96850.

Legislature

STATE LEGISLATURE

Senate

Twenty-five elected members; in mid-2002 the Democrats held 22 seats and the Republicans 3 seats.

President: Robert Bunda (Democrat).

Vice-President: Colleen Hanabusa (Democrat).

House of Representatives

Fifty-one elected members; in mid-2002 the Democrats held 32 seats and the Republicans 19 seats.

Speaker: Calvin Say (Democrat).

Clerk: Patricia Mau-Shimizu.

CONGRESS

The State of Hawaii elects two Senators and two Representatives to the US Congress.

Senators: Daniel Kahikina Akaka (Democrat), Daniel K. Inouye (Democrat).

Representatives: Neil Abercrombie (Democrat), (vacant).

Political Organizations

Democratic Party of Hawaii: Suite 111, 770 Kapiolani Blvd, Honolulu, HI 96813; tel. (808) 596-2980; fax (808) 596-2985; e-mail execdir@hawaiidemocrats.org; internet www.hawaiidemocrats.org.

Ka LaHui Hawaii (Sovereign Hawaiian Nation): POB 90417, Honolulu, HI 96835-0417; tel. (808) 386-1363; e-mail kalahui@hotmail.com; advocates self-determination and self-governance under autonomous native government for Kanaka Maoli Hawaiians; Kia'aina (Governor) BLACK HO'OHULI.

Libertarian Party of Hawaii: Honolulu, HI 96814; tel. (808) 597-8008.

Nation of Hawaii: Honolulu, HI 96813; fmrly Ohana Council; advocates independence from the USA; Leader BUMPY KANAHELE.

Republican Party of Hawaii: 725 Kapiolani Blvd, Honolulu, HI 96813; tel. (808) 593-8180; fax (808) 593-7742; e-mail members@gophawaii.com; internet www.gophawaii.com; Chair. DONNA ALCANTARA; Exec. Dir SHANA L. DAVIDSON.

Judicial System

The State Judiciary includes a five-member Supreme Court, an Intermediate Court of Appeals and four Circuit Courts, with judges appointed by the Governor with the consent of the State Senate. The State also has four District Courts whose judges are appointed by the Chief Justice of the State Supreme Court.

Chief Justice: RONALD T. Y. MOON, Supreme Court, 417 South King St, Honolulu, HI 96813; POB 2560, Honolulu, HI 96804.

Associate Justices: SIMEON R. ACOBA, Jr; STEVEN H. LEVINSON; PAULA A. NAKAYAMA; MARIO R. RAMIL.

Attorney-General: EARL I. ANZAI.

Religion

Many different religions are professed. In 1990 an estimated 21.0% of the population were adherents to the Roman Catholic Church, while a further 14.3% of the population claimed affiliation to various other Christian denominations (including the Church of Jesus Christ of Latter-day Saints (Mormon), the United Church of Christ and the Southern Baptist Convention). About 12% of the population are Buddhist (including Japanese Mahayana Buddhism), and Chinese Confucianism, Daoism and Shintoism are also practised. There is a small Jewish community.

CHRISTIANITY

The Roman Catholic Church

Hawaii comprises the single diocese of Honolulu, suffragan to the archdiocese of San Francisco, California. At 31 December 2000 there were an estimated 215,000 adherents in the State.

Bishop of Honolulu: Rt Rev. FRANCIS XAVIER DILORENZO; 1184 Bishop St, Honolulu, HI 96813-2858; tel. (808) 533-1791; fax (808) 521-8428; e-mail bishop@pono.net.

The Anglican Communion

Episcopalians (Anglicans) in Hawaii are adherents of the Episcopal Church in the United States of America. Hawaii comprises a single diocese in Province VIII. In 1998 there were an estimated 10,901 adherents in the State.

Bishop of Hawaii: Rt Rev. RICHARD S. O. CHANG, Office of the Bishop, 229 Queen Emma Sq., Honolulu, HI 96813; tel. (808) 536-7776; fax (808) 538-7194.

Other Churches

Church of Jesus Christ of Latter-day Saints (Mormon): 1500 South Beretania St, Apt 410, Honolulu, HI 96826; tel. (808) 942-0050; fax (808) 946-3738; f. 1830; there were an estimated 53,000 adherents in 1996; Mission Pres. H. ROSS WORKMAN.

Hawaii Pacific Baptist Convention: 2042 Vancouver Drive, Honolulu, HI 96822; tel. (808) 946-9581; fax (808) 941-2309; e-mail 71173.571@compuserve.com; there were an estimated 20,044 adherents in 1997; Head O. W. EFURD.

Hawaii Conference of the United Church of Christ: 15 Craigside Place, Honolulu, HI 96817; tel. (808) 537-9516; fax (808) 521-7196; e-mail hcucc@hcucc.org; there were an estimated 22,852 adherents in 1990; Conference Minister Rev. Dr DAVID HANSEN.

United Methodist Church: 20 South Vineyard Blvd, Honolulu, HI 96813; tel. (808) 536-1864; fax (808) 531-7354; internet www.ilhawaii.net/humu; there were an estimated 8,348 adherents in 1990; Superintendent of Hawaii District Rev. BARBARA GRACE RIPPLE.

BUDDHISM

Honpa Hongwanji Mission of Hawaii: 1727 Pali Highway, Honolulu, HI 96813; tel. (808) 522-9200; fax (808) 522-9209; there were an estimated 10,308 adherents in 1987; Head Bishop THOM T. NAKANISHI.

JUDAISM

Judaism: Temple Emanu-El, 2550 Pali Highway, Honolulu, HI 96817; tel. (808) 595-7521; fax (808) 595-6306; Head Rabbi AVI MAGID.

The Press

In 1990 there were six major English-language daily newspapers, two Japanese/English, one Chinese and one Korean daily newspaper, as well as numerous magazines and other periodicals.

PRINCIPAL DAILIES

The Garden Island: POB 231, Lihue, Kauai, HI 96766; tel. (808) 245-3681; fax (808) 245-5286; f. 1902; weekdays; Publr EDITH TANIMOTO; Editor JULIA NEAL; circ. 10,000.

Hawaii Tribune-Herald: Hilo, HI 96720.

Honolulu Advertiser: 605 Kapiolani Blvd, Honolulu, HI 96813; POB 3110, Honolulu, HI 96802; tel. (808) 525-8000; fax (808) 525-8037; f. 1856; morning; Editor-in-Chief GERRY KEIR; circ. 108,000.

Honolulu Star-Bulletin: 605 Kapiolani Blvd, Honolulu, HI 96813; POB 3080, Honolulu, HI 96882; tel. (808) 525-8000; fax (808) 523-8509; f. 1882; evening Mon.–Sat.; Publr and Editor JOHN FLANAGAN; circ. 67,800.

Maui News: Wailuku, Maui, HI 96793; daily.

PRINCIPAL PERIODICALS

Hawaii Business: Honolulu, HI 96814; tel. (808) 946-3978; monthly magazine.

Honolulu Magazine: 36 Merchant St, Honolulu, HI 96813; tel. (808) 524-7400; fax (808) 531-2306; e-mail honpub@aloha.net; general interest; monthly.

Kauai Times: Kauai, HI 96766; tel. (808) 245-8825; fax (808) 246-9195; f. 1979; 2 a week; Publr and Editor PETER WOLF; circ. 21,000.

Pacific Business News: POB 833, Honolulu, HI 96808; tel. (808) 596-2021; fax (808) 593-2515; e-mail pbn@lava.net; internet www.amcity.com/pacific/; f. 1963; weekly newspaper; Publr LARRY FULLER; Editor BERNIE SILVER.

Sunday Star-Bulletin & Advertiser: 605 Kapiolani Blvd, Honolulu, HI 96813; POB 3110, Honolulu, HI 96802; tel. (808) 525-8000; f. 1962; weekly; Editor-in-Chief GERRY KEIR; circ. 203,762.

Broadcasting and Communications

TELECOMMUNICATIONS

AT & T: Kealakekua, HI 96750; tel. (808) 324-4440.

Digitel: 1000 Bishop St, Honolulu, HI 96813-4212; tel. (808) 547-2500.

Pacific LightNet Inc: 737 Bishop St, Honolulu, HI 96813; tel. (808) 791-1000.

Verizon Hawaii: 1177 Bishop St, Honolulu, HI 96813-2808; tel. (808) 643-3343; internet www.gte.com/HI.

BROADCASTING

In 1996 there were four non-commercial and 65 commercial radio stations, 21 commercial and two non-commercial television stations and seven cable television companies in Hawaii. In 1994 there were some 1m. radio receivers and 379,670 households (some 96.1% of total households) had television sets.

Hawaii Association of Broadcasters: POB 22112, Honolulu, HI 96823-2112; Exec. Dir JAMIE HARTNETT; Pres. MARC HAWORTH.

Television

Hawaii Public Television: 2350 Dole St, Honolulu, HI 96822; tel. (808) 973-1000; fax (808) 973-1090; e-mail e–2>mail@khet.pbs.org; internet www.khet.org; Gen. Man. DONALD ROBBS.

Finance

(cap. = capital; res = reserves; dep. = deposits; m. = million; brs = branches; amounts in US dollars)

The Hawaiian financial sector is mainly based in Honolulu. It consists of six banks, with a total of 190 branches in the State in 1995, six savings and loan associations (159 branches), one trust company (three branches) and 40 industrial or small loan licensees (164 branches). Deposits in all financial institutions totalled some US $22,044.3m. at the end of 1994. Following legislation in the late 1980s, 10 'captive' insurance companies have been established.

BANKING

American Savings Bank: POB 2300, Honolulu, HI 96804-2300; tel. (808) 523-6844; 68 brs.

Bank of Hawaii: 111 South King St, POB 2900, Honolulu, HI 96813; tel. (808) 847-8888; fax (808) 536-9496; e-mail info@boh.com; internet www.boh.com; f. 1897; cap. 14.9m., res 1,071.3m., dep. 8,810.4m. (Dec. 2001); Chair. and CEO MICHAEL E. O'NEILL; Pres. RICHARD J. DAHL; 74 brs, 20 overseas brs.

Central Pacific Bank: 220 South King St, Honolulu, HI 96813; tel. (808) 544-0500; fax (808) 531-2875; 26 brs.

City Bank: 201 Merchant St, POB 3709, Honolulu, HI 96813; tel. (808) 546-2411; fax (808) 523-7458; internet www.citybankhi.com; f. 1959; cap. 10.8m., dep. 1,436.3m., total assets 1,586.7m. (Dec. 2001); Pres. and COO RICHARD C. LIM; CEO RONALD K. MIGITA; 21 brs.

First Hawaiian Bank: 999 Bishop St, POB 3200, Honolulu, HI 96813; tel. (808) 525-7000; fax (808) 525-8708; e-mail gerry.keir@fhwn.com; internet www.fhb.com; f. 1858; cap. 16.2m. (Dec. 2000), dep. 6,268.0m., total assets 8,868.7m. (June 2002); Chair. and CEO WALTER A. DODS, Jr; Pres. and COO JOHN K. TSUI; 61 brs.

Hawaii National Bank: 45 North King St, POB 3740, Honolulu, HI 96812; tel. (808) 528-7711; fax (808) 528-7773; e-mail hnbinfo@hnbhawaii.com; internet www.hnbhawaii.com; f. 1960; cap. 27.1m., dep. 326.4m., total assets 356.0m. (June 2002); Chair, CEO and Pres. WARREN K. K. LUKE; 15 brs.

INSURANCE

Grand Pacific Life Insurance Co: Honolulu, HI 96813; tel. (808) 548-3363; fax (808) 548-5122.

Hawaiian Insurance Group: Honolulu, HI 96813.

Noguchi and Associates Inc: Suite 560, 1341 South King St, Honolulu, HI 96814; tel. (808) 523-7000; Pres. HIDEO NOGUCHI.

Trade and Industry

GOVERNMENT AGENCIES

Joint Commercial Commission (JCC): East-West Center, 1601 East-West Rd, Honolulu, HI 96848; e-mail ewcinfo@eastwestcenter.org; f. 1992; promotes training, investment and increased trade between the USA and the South Pacific region; Pres. CHARLES MORRISON; Dir SITIVENI HALAPUA.

State Department of Business, Economic Development and Tourism: Capitol District Bldg, 250 South Hotel St, POB 2359, Honolulu, HI 96804; tel. (808) 586-2423; fax (808) 586-2452; f. 1963; Dir SEIJI F. NAYA.

State Department of Commerce and Consumer Affairs: POB 3469, Honolulu, HI 96801; Dir AMER KAYANI.

CHAMBER OF COMMERCE

Chamber of Commerce of Hawaii: Suite 402, 1132 Bishop St, Honolulu, HI 96813; tel. (808) 505-4300; e-mail info@cochawaii.org; internet www.cochawaii.com.

UTILITIES

Public Utilities Commission: 465 South King St, Kekuanoa Bldg, Room 103, Honolulu, HI 96813; tel. (808) 586-2020; fax (808) 586-2066; e-mail hipuc@lava-net; internet www.state.hi.us/budget.

Electricity

Hawaiian Electric Industries: POB 730, Honolulu, HI 96808; internet www.hei.com.

Hawaiian Electric Company, Inc: Honolulu.

Maui Electric Company Limited: Wailuku.

Hawaii Electric Light Company, Inc: Honolulu.

TRADE UNIONS

Most of the US trade unions of any size have branches in Hawaii. In 1992 an estimated 29.9% of the employed labour force were union members.

The principal ones represented are:

American Federation of Labor and Congress of Industrial Organisations (AFL-CIO): Honolulu, HI; principal affiliate in the State:

International Brotherhood of Teamsters, Chauffeurs, Warehousemen and Helpers of America: f. 1903; general industrial union.

International Longshoremen's and Warehousemen's Union: Honolulu, HI; independent union.

Transport

Honolulu Department of Transportation Services: Public Transit Division, 650 South King St, 3rd Floor, Honolulu, HI 96813; tel. (808) 523-4138; administers bus contracts and operations of bus service for the disabled.

RAILWAYS

There are no railways in Hawaii.

ROADS

In 1997 there were 4,164 miles (6,701 km) of highways and streets. There were 967,146 registered motor vehicles in 2001, and 733,486 licensed drivers in 1996.

SHIPPING

More than two dozen passenger and cargo steamship companies operate through Honolulu. Hawaii has eight deep-water ports, including the naval shipyard and base at Pearl Harbor (the principal ones being Honolulu and Barbers Point on Oahu, Hilo and Kawaihae on Hawaii, Nawiliwili and Port Allen on Kauai, and Kahului on Maui). The ports have a wide range of services, and terminal facilities are equipped to handle bulk, conventional and container cargo.

CIVIL AVIATION

There were seven commercial airports in the State, with an additional 15 military or semi-private airports and 13 civilian heliports in 1992. Hawaii enjoys extensive international and domestic air links.

Air Molokai: Honolulu Int. Airport, Honolulu, HI 96819; tel. (808) 834-0043; operates passenger and cargo services between Honolulu and the islands of Maui, Molokai and Lanai.

Aloha Airlines Inc: POB 30028, Honolulu, HI 96820; tel. (808) 539-5947; fax (808) 836-0303; internet www.alohaair.com; f. 1946, present name since 1958; operates inter-Hawaiian island services, services to the west coast of the USA and Canada, a weekly service to Kiribati, the Marshall Islands and the Federated States of Micronesia and a twice-weekly service to the Cook Islands; Chair. HAN H. CHING; Pres. and CEO GLENN R. ZANDER.

Aloha IslandAir: Commuter Terminal, Honolulu Int. Airport, Honolulu, HI 96819; tel. (808) 836-7693; fax (808) 833-5498; f. 1980 as Princeville Airways; inter-Hawaiian island services; charter flights; Pres. NEIL TAKEKAWA.

Hawaiian Airlines Inc: POB 30008, Honolulu, HI 96820; tel. (808) 835-3700; fax (808) 835-3690; internet www.hawaiianair.com; f. 1929, present name since 1941; operates scheduled passenger and cargo services between Honolulu and the islands of Kauai, Molokai, Maui, Lanai and Hawaii and scheduled and charter services to the US mainland and to the South Pacific islands; Pres. and CEO PAUL CASEY; Vice-Pres. JOHN HAPP.

Tourism

Tourism is the major industry of the State. Visitors come to Hawaii for its scenery, its climate and the attractions of its cosmopolitan capital, Honolulu. In 1998 there were 71,480 hotel rooms. Tourist arrivals declined from 6,948,595 in 2000 to 6,303,791 in 2001. In the latter year tourism earned US $10,121m.

Hawaii Tourism Authority: Hawaii Tourism Office, POB 2359, Honolulu, HI 96804; tel. (808) 586-2550; fax (808) 586-2549; internet www.state.hi.us/tourism.

Hawaii Visitors and Convention Bureau: Suite 801, 2270 Kalakaua Ave, Honolulu, HI 96815; tel. (808) 923-1811; fax (808) 924-0290; e-mail info@hvcb.org; internet www.gohawaii.com; Pres. and CEO TONY S. VERICELLA.

Defence

Hawaii is the headquarters of the US Pacific Command (USPACOM), which includes two subordinate unified commands: US Forces, Korea and US Forces, Japan. At 1 August 2001 there were 15,500 army, 4,580 air force and 7,500 navy personnel, and 5,680 Marines, based in Hawaii itself. Pearl Harbor, on Oahu, is the headquarters of the Third Fleet and of the entire Pacific Fleet. In 1995/96 expenditure on defence totalled US $3,259m., equivalent to 40.7% of total federal expenditure. A total of 19 finance and accounting operations throughout the US Pacific Command were relocated to Pearl Harbor in 1995, with the creation of 500 jobs.

Commander, US Pacific Command Adm. THOMAS B. FARGO, Pearl Harbor, Oahu, Hawaii.

Education

Hawaii has a state-wide public school system operated by the State Department of Education, and an elected Board of Education formulates school policy and supervises its application. In 1999/2000 185,860 pupils from kindergarten through secondary level attended state schools and 36,226 attended private schools. A total of 71,869 students were enrolled at the University of Hawaii and the seven community colleges in that year. There are also three private universities, with a combined total enrolment of 13,209 in 1996/97. In 1999/2000 Hawaii's expenditure on education totalled US $1,853.8m. (31% of the State's total general expenditure).

United States Commonwealth Territory in the Pacific

There are two US commonwealth territories, the Northern Mariana Islands, in the Pacific Ocean, and Puerto Rico, in the Caribbean Sea. A Commonwealth is a self-governing incorporated territory that is an integral part of, and in full political union with, the USA. The Secretary of the Interior, in the federal government, is responsible for relations with the commonwealth government of the Northern Mariana Islands. Within the Department of the Interior, the Assistant Secretary for Policy, Management and Budget is responsible for the Office of Insular Affairs and exercises authority on behalf of the Secretary in all matters pertaining to the insular governments and territories. The USA maintains membership of the Pacific Community (formerly the South Pacific Commission), the Colombo Plan and the UN's Trusteeship Council and its Economic and Social Commission for Asia and the Pacific (ESCAP).

Head of State: President GEORGE W. BUSH (took office 20 January 2001).

Department of the Interior, Office of Insular Affairs: C St between 18th and 19th Sts, NW, Washington, DC 20240, USA; tel. (202) 208-6816; fax (202) 208-3309.

Secretary of the Interior: GALE A. NORTON.

Director, Office of Insular Affairs: NIKALAO. I. PULA.

Resident Representative to the Government of the Commonwealth of the Northern Mariana Islands: JUAN N. BABAUTA.

THE NORTHERN MARIANA ISLANDS

Physical and Social Geography

The Commonwealth of the Northern Mariana Islands comprises 16 islands (all the Mariana group except Guam), most being of volcanic origin, lying in the western Pacific Ocean. The territory has a land area of 457 sq km (177 sq miles) and is situated about 5,300 km west of Honolulu (Hawaii) and due south of Japan, some 2,300 km from Tokyo. Its nearest neighbours are Guam and the Federated States of Micronesia. The climate is tropical and there is little seasonal variation in temperature, the mean annual temperature being some 28°C (82°F). Mean annual rainfall is some 2,120 mm (84 ins), the driest months being January–May. The Mariana Islands can be affected by monsoons between August and November. English, Chamorro and Carolinian are the official languages of the Commonwealth. Since the evacuation in 1990 of Anatahan, owing to a volcanic eruption, only five islands, including the three largest (Saipan, Tinian and Rota), are inhabited; the chief settlements, and the administrative centre of Capitol Hill, are on Saipan. The population totalled 69,221 at the census of April 2000.

History

The islands, already settled for more than 2,000 years by a Polynesian people now known as the Chamorros, were claimed for Spain by Fernão de Magalhães (Ferdinand Magellan) in 1521. They were known as the Ladrone Islands until 1668, when they were named the Mariana Islands in honour of Mariana of Austria, widow of Philip IV of Spain. Much of the Chamorro population was transferred to Guam in 1698, not to return to the Northern Marianas until the early 19th century. It was only during the Spanish period that the traditional matrilineal organization of Micronesian society changed, for the Chamorros, to a patrilineal system. Meanwhile, some Carolinian peoples, from southern Micronesia, settled in the islands. The Carolinians were primarily a fishing people, the Chamorros mainly agricultural. Spain sold the Northern Mariana Islands to Germany in 1899. In the 20th century the islands have been administered successively by Germany, Japan and the USA, from 1947 as part of the UN Trust Territory of the Pacific Islands. The islands voted for separate status as a US commonwealth territory in June 1975. In March 1976 the US President, Gerald Ford, signed the 'Covenant to Establish a Commonwealth of the Northern Mariana Islands (CNMI) in Political Union with the USA'. In October 1977 President Jimmy Carter approved the Constitution of the Northern Mariana Islands, which provided that, from January 1978, the former Marianas District would become internally self-governing. The CNMI formally entered political union with the USA on 3 November 1986, when President Ronald Reagan issued a proclamation fully effecting the Covenant, after the ending of the Trusteeship in the district. Consequently, the residents of the CNMI became citizens of the USA.

Elections for a bicameral legislature, a Governor and a Lieutenant-Governor were first held in December 1977. Pedro Tenorio, the candidate of the Republican Party, was elected Governor in November 1981, and re-elected in 1985. With a constitutional limit of two consecutive terms as Governor, he did not seek re-election in November 1989, when a Republican, Lorenzo 'Larry' Guerrero, was elected Governor. Democrats retained control of the House of Representatives, but a Republican candidate, Juan Babauta, was elected as the Resident Representative in Washington, DC.

In December 1990 the UN Security Council voted to end the Trusteeship of the Northern Marianas, as well as that of two other Pacific Trust Territories. Although the decision to terminate the relationship had been taken in 1986, voting had been delayed. Guerrero, however, opposed the termination and had requested that the vote be postponed. The new relationship would, he argued, leave the islands subject to US law while remaining unrepresented in the US Congress; moreover, several important sovereignty issues (such as local control of marine resources) would remain unresolved.

At elections to the House of Representatives (which had been enlarged by three seats) in November 1991 Republicans regained a majority. Similarly, the party increased the number of its senators to eight. Republicans retained their majority at elections to the House of Representatives in November 1993. However, in the gubernatorial election a Democrat, Froilan Tenorio, was successful. Similarly, a Democratic candidate, Jesus Borja, was elected as Lieutenant-Governor, while Juan Babauta remained as Washington Representative. The Republicans increased their representation in both the Senate and the House of Representatives in elections in November 1995.

In January 1995 the minimum wage was increased by 12.2%, in accordance with the Governor's stated objectives; however, five days later Tenorio signed legislation that effectively reversed the decision. This prompted several members of the House of Representatives to demand that the US Federal Bureau of Investigation (FBI) conduct an investigation into the incident and the allegations of bribery surrounding the Governor's actions. The territory's reputation deteriorated further in April when the Government of the Philippines introduced a ban on its nationals accepting unskilled employment in the islands, because of persistent reports of abuse and exploitation of immigrant workers. Meanwhile, the US Congress announced that it was to allocate US $7m. towards the enforcement of the islands' labour and immigration laws, following the publication of a report in late 1994, which alleged the repeated violations of these regulations, as well as widespread corruption among immigration officials and business leaders.

At legislative elections in November 1995 Republican candidates won a convincing majority, securing 14 seats in the House of Representatives and six seats in the Senate.

Many of the territory's social and economic problems have been attributed to the dramatic increase in the Northern Marianas' population (from some 17,000 in 1979 to more than 69,000 in 2000). Acknowledging this situation, a US government report, published in mid-1996, recommended the expansion of prison and detention facilities on the islands, and offered further assistance with immigration control.

In May 1997 the US President, Bill Clinton, informed Tenorio of his intention to apply US immigration and minimum wage laws to the territory, stating that labour practices in the islands were inconsistent with US values. Clinton also criticized officials in the territory for failing to address the persistent problems of an inadequate minimum wage and reports of improper treatment of alien workers. In the previous month Democrat Congressman George Miller had proposed legislation in the US House of Representatives (the Insular Fair Wage and Human Rights Act) that would equalize the minimum wage level in the islands with that of the US mainland by 1999. The territory's Government, which denied many of the claims of exploitation of immigrant workers, responded to the proposed legislation by initiating a public relations campaign (at a cost of US $1m.) aimed at persuading the Republican majority in the US

House of Representatives to oppose the bill. A further US $0.5m. was spent funding a visit to the islands by seven Republican members of the US Congress, in an attempt to consolidate their support for Tenorio's stance. The issue dominated the election campaign during late 1997, with Willie Tan (a major entrepreneur who had been fined several million dollars for failing to comply with US Labor Department health and safety standards in his garment factories) providing considerable financial support towards Froilan Tenorio's efforts to remain in office.

At legislative elections on 1 November 1997 Republican candidates won 13 of the 18 seats in the House of Representatives and eight of the nine seats in the Senate. At the gubernatorial election, held concurrently, Pedro Tenorio was successful, securing 46% of total votes. The incumbent Froilan Tenorio secured some 27% of the vote and Jesus Borja (previously the Lieutenant-Governor) won 26%. Opponents of Pedro Tenorio subsequently initiated a legal challenge to his election on the grounds that it constituted his third term as Governor, thereby violating the Constitution, which states that a maximum of two gubernatorial terms may be served by any one individual (although the Constitution had been amended to include this provision only during Pedro Tenorio's second term in office). Following the legislative elections of 6 November 1999, Democrat candidates held two of the nine seats in the Senate and six of the 18 seats in the House of Representatives.

In January 1999 the Office of Insular Affairs (OIA) published a report in which it concluded that the Government's attempts to eradicate abuses of labour and immigration laws had been unsuccessful. In particular, it had failed to reduce the Territory's reliance on alien workers, to enforce US minimum wage laws and to curb evasions of trade legislation governing the export of garments to the USA. In the same month former employees of 18 US clothing retailers initiated legal action against the companies, which were accused of failing to comply with US labour laws in Saipan. In April 2000 a settlement was reached with the garment manufacturers, providing some US $8m. in compensation for the workers. The companies also agreed to conform to regulations established by an independent monitoring system in Saipan. In August 2001 the Saipan Garment Manufacturers' Association (SGMA) denied a claim, made in a report by the US Department of Justice, that factory owners were giving employees methamphetamine to increase productivity.

In February 2000, meanwhile, the US Senate approved a bill granting permanent residency in the Northern Marianas to some 40,000 immigrant workers. However, the bill also included provisions for limiting the stay of all future guest workers. In December 2000 Governor Tenorio announced that he was to oppose the decision by the US Government to bring the Northern Marianas' labour and immigration laws under federal control; Tenorio argued that this could have a negative impact on the Commonwealth's economy. In May 2001, following intense lobbying by the Northern Marianas Government, the US Congress abandoned the bill.

Legislative elections were held on 3 November 2001, at which the Republican Party secured 12 seats in the House of Representatives, the Democratic Party won five and the Covenant Party took one. The Republican Party won six seats in the Senate, the Democratic Party two and the Covenant Party one. Gubernatorial elections were held concurrently, at which Juan Nekai Babauta, the Republican Party candidate and former Representative to Washington, won a convincing victory, securing 42.8% of the votes cast. Benigno Fitial, of the Covenant Party, received 24.4%. Babauta was inaugurated as Governor in January 2002, while Diego Benavente, his running mate and the former Speaker of the House of Representatives, became Lieutenant-Governor.

In January 2002 the Supreme Court suspended deportation proceedings against an immigrant labourer working in the Northern Marianas illegally, after he appealed to the office of the UN High Commissioner for Refugees. The Court warned the Government that it might not be able to order the deportation of up to 10,000 of the Chinese, Sri Lankan and Bangladeshi workers in the Northern Marianas.

In May 2002 the issue of the Northern Marianas' working conditions was raised again by US Senator Edward Kennedy, who proposed a bill that would incrementally increase the minimum wage. The first increase would occur 60 days after the legislation's implementation, should the bill be successful, although Kennedy invited the Northern Marianas to contribute to discussions. In late September 2002 seven further major US clothing retailers agreed to pay US $11.25m. in compensation to employees alleged to have suffered intolerable working conditions for poor rates of pay.

A US court order filed by the Center for Biological Diversity, an environmental group, forced military training on the uninhabited island of Farallon de Medinilla to be suspended for 30 days from early May 2002. Despite environmentalists' concerns about the impact and legality of US military activity, in particular the testing of ordnances, upon the island's wildlife, the Northern Marianas Chamber of Commerce feared that the substantial revenue generated by the visiting US military might be jeopardized.

Also in May the Government 'froze' the assets of the Bank of Saipan, pending auditing of its accounts, after the institution's former Chairman was arrested for allegedly attempting to defraud the bank of more than US $6.6m. The bank ceased all transactions for 20 days, before recommencing operations under close supervision. The Government announced proposals to amend the Territory's banking laws to comply with US federal standards.

In September 2002 Babauta proposed reforms to reduce government expenditure. This and immigration issues were reported to be the subject of tension between the Governor and the Speaker of the House of Representatives, Heinz Hofschneider.

The federal government of the USA is responsible for defence and foreign relations. In 1990 a cause of tension between the federal and insular Governments was removed when the Administration of George Bush, Sr finally appointed its Special Representative, a negotiator on bilateral relations.

In late 1999 it was announced that legal action was to be taken against the US Government following revelations that traces of a toxic chemical had been found in a village near the capital, Saipan. It was alleged that the chemicals had been abandoned by the US army in the 1960s. It was subsequently announced, in November 2000, that the Government of the Northern Marianas was to claim US $1m. from the USA, to repay the costs of a screening programme, established to test the villagers for traces of the chemicals.

Economy

The economy of the Northern Marianas is dominated by the services sector, particularly tourism. In 1999 the Commonwealth's gross national product (GNP) was estimated by the Bank of Hawaii (BOH) to be US $696.3m. GNP per head was estimated at US $8,582. The population increased at an estimated average annual rate of 7.2% in 1990–99.

Agriculture has not contributed significantly to the economy since the devastation of the sugar industry in 1944, during the Second World War (in the late 1980s some 426 acres were used for arable farming, compared with 40,000 acres before the War). Agriculture is now based on smallholdings, important crops being coconuts, breadfruit, tomatoes and melons. Arable farming is particularly important on Rota. Large-scale cattle-ranching is practised on Tinian. Vegetables, beef and pork are important exports. The sector engaged 1.5% of the employed labour force in 2000 and its commercial value is minimal. In 2000 the sector accounted for only 0.1% of gross business revenues (total values generated by business transactions; the Government does not calculate gross domestic product figures).

There is little commercial fishing based on Saipan or the other islands (the total catch was 193 metric tons in 1999); there is, however, a major tuna transhipment facility at Tinian harbour.

Before the Second World War Japan mined phosphate on the islands, but it is estimated that only about 50,000 short tons of low-grade guano phosphate remain on Rota. There is a possibility that mineral resources in Northern Marianan waters (particularly cobalt-rich manganese crusts) might be exploited in the future.

Industry (including manufacturing and construction) engaged 47.2% of the employed labour force in 2000. Manufacturing alone engaged 40.7% of workers, while construction employed 6.5%. The principal manufacturing activity is in the garment factories. Although the garment manufacturing industry was not established until the mid-1980s, it soon accounted for the largest amount of commodity exports from the islands. The manufacturers benefit from US regulations allowing duty-free imports of textiles to the USA from the Commonwealth, and earnings from garment exports to the USA increased from an estimated US $419m. in 1995 to almost $1,000m. in 1998. In that year some 36 garment factories, employing 15,000 Chinese workers, were in operation. Garment manufacturing accounted for 34.7% of gross business revenues in 2000. Overall exports of garments were worth $925.7m. in 2001, compared with $1,017m. in 2000. Other small-scale manufacturing industries include handicrafts and the processing of fish and copra.

The construction industry in the 1980s benefited from the rapid expansion in tourism and government development of the islands' infrastructure. However, the number of building permits sold, both commercial and residential, declined each year during 1997–2001.

In 2000 the services sector (including utilities) engaged 51.3% of the employed labour force, while accounting for 29.2% of gross business revenues. The islands' association with the USA, the availability of foreign investment and the opening of direct air links with Japan encouraged rapid economic development, mainly after 1978. By 1998 there were 3,942 hotel rooms available. In mid-1995 a US company opened the territory's first casino on Tinian. The islands were expected to receive some US $12m. annually in revenue from the casino, which was to be invested in infrastructure projects and health services. However, the Asian financial crisis of the late 1990s had a major impact on the industry, with many hotels reducing charges and employee numbers and others facing closure as a result of the decline in tourist arrivals. Continental Micronesia also significantly reduced its flights to Japan in response to the situation. In September 1998 the hotel and casino complex on Tinian sought the support of several senior politicians in an attempt to secure a loan for US $30m. from a foreign bank. The business, which relied heavily on visitors from Japan, Taiwan and the Republic of Korea, had been particularly badly affected by the economic problems in that region. Visitor arrivals increased by 2.4% in 1999 and by 5.3% in 2000, when a total of 528,597 visitors travelled to the islands. However, the terrorist attacks on the USA on 11 September 2001 adversely affected the tourism industry in the Northern Marianas. The number of visitor arrivals by air decreased sharply, while the hotel occupancy rate declined to only 35% in December 2001. Of the total arrivals of 442,466 in 2001, more than 75% were from Japan. Tourism receipts were worth an estimated US $430m. in 2000. Remittances from overseas workers and investments totalled US $76.7m. in 2001.

The Northern Marianas are very dependent on imports, the value of which totalled US $836.2m. in 1997. The principal imports in that year were foodstuffs (9.6%), petroleum products (8.2% of the total), clothing (7.1%), automobiles and parts (5.0%) and construction materials (4.1%). In 1991 there was a visible trade deficit of US $126.9m. The annual rate of inflation averaged 3.6% in 1990–98. Consumer prices decreased by 0.3% in 1999, but increased by 2.0% in 2000 and declined by 0.8% in 2001. Under the Covenant between the Commonwealth of the Northern Mariana Islands and the USA, the islands receive substantial annual development grants. Budget estimates predicted total revenue of US $297.2m. in the financial year ending 30 September 2000. Total expenditure of $225.5m. was estimated for that year. Loans from the Commonwealth Development Authority totalled more than $0.5m. in 2001.

Rapid economic expansion in the 1980s led to a shortage of local labour and an increase in non-resident alien workers. The number of non-resident alien workers increased by 655% between 1980 and 1989, and by the early 1990s exceeded the permanent population of the islands. Owing to this increase in immigrant workers, wages remained relatively low, and there were widespread complaints of poor working conditions. Increasing concern over the alleged exploitation of foreign workers in the islands' garment factories led to the proposal in April 1997 of legislation in the US House of Representatives to increase the minimum wage to parity with the mainland level by 1999, and in early 1999 a lawsuit was filed against garment manufacturers in Saipan in a further attempt to equalize conditions (see History). In all, 22,560 permits were issued to non-resident workers in the islands in 1994, 67.2% of which were for Filipino nationals. In late 2000 the Northern Marianas' House of Representatives requested that the USA cancel some US $3.2m. in debt, incurred following the drilling of a number of water wells between 1990 and 1997.

The Territory received a total of some US $13m. of US federal funding and development assistance in 2001/02. The islands' Republican administration, inaugurated in 2002, pledged to prioritize economic reform by promoting free, competitive markets with a minimum of government interference. It outlined an environmental rehabilitation programme in an effort to raise the Territory's tourism profile. In May 2002 the assets of the Bank of Saipan were temporarily 'frozen' following the arrest of its chief executive officer on charges of fraud. Meanwhile, in March the Government introduced tax incentives for new businesses and developers, worth a potential 100% abatement of local taxes, or a 95% rebate of federal taxes.

The main restraint on development is the need to expand the islands' infrastructure, coupled with the problem of a labour shortage and the dependence on foreign workers. Many economic problems have been largely attributed to the dramatic increase in the islands' population (from some 17,000 in 1979 to more than 69,000 by 2000). The islands benefit from their political association with the USA and their relative proximity to Japan. The Commonwealth of the Northern Mariana Islands is a member of the Pacific Community (formerly the South Pacific Commission) and also an associate member of the UN's Economic and Social Commission for Asia and the Pacific (ESCAP).

Statistical Survey

Source: (unless otherwise stated): Department of Commerce, Central Statistics Division, POB 10007, Saipan MP, 96950; tel. 664-3000; fax 664-3001; internet www.commerce.gov.mp.

AREA AND POPULATION

Area: 457 sq km (176.5 sq miles). *By island:* Saipan 120 sq km (46.5 sq miles); Tinian 102 sq km (39.2 sq miles); Rota 85 sq km (32.8 sq miles); Pagan 48 sq km (18.6 sq miles); Anatahan 32 sq km (12.5 sq miles); Agrihan 30 sq km (11.4 sq miles).

Population: 43,345 at census of 1 April 1990; 69,221 (males 31,984, females 37,237) at census of 1 April 2000. *By island:* Saipan 62,392; Rota 3,283; Tinian 3,540; Northern Islands 6.

Density (2000 census): 151 per sq km (392 per sq mile).

Ethnic Groups (2000 census): Filipino 18,141; Chinese 15,311; Chamorro 14,749; part-Chamorro 4,383; Total (incl. others) 69,221.

Births and Deaths (2000): Birth rate 20.7 per 1,000; Death rate 2.2 per 1,000.

Employment (2000 census, persons aged 16 years and over): Agriculture, forestry, fisheries and mining 623; Manufacturing 17,398; Construction 2,785; Transport, communication and utilities 1,449; Trade, restaurants and hotels 9,570; Financing, insurance and real estate 1,013; Community, social and personal services 9,915; Total employed 42,753 (males 19,485; females 23,268); Unemployed 1,712 (males 888; females 824); Total labour force 44,465 (males 20,373; females 24,092).

AGRICULTURE, ETC.

Fishing (metric tons, live weight 1999): Total catch 193 (Snappers and jobfishes 16, Emperors 4; Common dolphinfish 6, Skipjack tuna 48, Marine fishes 75). Source: FAO, *Yearbook of Fishery Statistics.*

FINANCE

Currency and Exchange Rates: 100 cents = 1 United States dollar (US $). *Sterling and Euro Equivalents* (31 May 2002): £1 sterling = US $1.4667; €1 = 93.87 US cents; US $100 = £68.18 = €106 53.

Budget (estimates, US $ million, year ending 30 September 2000): Total Revenue 297.2 (Taxes 247.7, Federal Contributions 52.9); Total Expenditure 225.5 (General Government 36.0, Education 49.6, Health and social welfare 43.6, Public safety 21.6, Public works 9.9).

Cost of Living (Consumer Price Index for Saipan; base: 1977, third quarter = 100): 267.8 in 1999; 273.2 in 2000; 271.0 in 2001.

Gross National Product (US $ million in current prices): 696 in 1999. Source: Bank of Hawaii, *Commonwealth of the Northern Mariana Islands: An Economic Report* (August 2001).

EXTERNAL TRADE

Principal Commodities (f.o.b., US $ million, 1997): *Imports:* Food items 80.1; Construction materials 35.1; Automobiles (incl. parts) 42.1; Petroleum products 68.5; Clothing 59.0; Total (incl. others) 836.2; *Exports* (1991): Total 258.4.
Source: partly, UN, *Statistical Yearbook for Asia and the Pacific.*

Principal Trading Partners (US $ million, 1997): *Imports:* Guam 298.0; Hong Kong 200.5; Japan 118.3; Korea, Republic 80.6; USA 63.3; Total (incl. others) 836.2.

TRANSPORT

International Sea-borne Shipping (freight traffic, '000 short tons, 1997): Goods loaded 184.1; Goods unloaded 425.9.

Civil Aviation (Saipan Int. Airport, year ending September 1999): 23,853 aircraft landings; 562,364 boarding passengers. Source: Commonwealth Ports Authority.

Road Traffic (Registered motor vehicles, 2000): 17,616.

TOURISM

Visitor Arrivals: 501,788 in 1999; 528,597 in 2000; 442,466 in 2001.

Visitor Arrivals by Country (2001): Guam 17,989; Japan 333,917; Korea, Republic 54,992; USA 17,229.

Tourism Receipts (US $million)*: 394 in 1998; 407 in 1999; 430 in 2000.

* Source: Bank of Hawaii, *Commonwealth of the Northern Mariana Islands: An Economic Report* (August 2001).

COMMUNICATIONS MEDIA

Radio Receivers (estimate, 1987): 15,350 in use.

Television Receivers (estimate, 1995): 15,460 in use.

Telephones (2001): 25,306 main lines in use.

Mobile Cellular Telephones (2000): 3,000 subscribers†.

Telefax Stations (1996): 1,200 in use*.

* Source: UN, *Statistical Yearbook.*

† Source: International Telecommunication Union.

EDUCATION

Primary (1999/2000, state schools): 11 schools; 279 teachers; 5,651 students; 7,884 students (public and private schools) at 2000 census.

Secondary (1999/2000, state schools): 6 schools; 193 teachers; 3,492 students; 2,750 students (public and private schools) at 2000 census.

Higher (1993/94): 1 college; 3,051 students.

Private schools (1999/2000): 17 schools; 196 teachers; 2,842 students.

Directory

The Government

(September 2002)

Governor: JUAN NEKAI BABAUTA (took office January 2002).

Lieutenant-Governor: DIEGO TENORIO BENAVENTE.

GOVERNMENT OFFICES

Office of the Governor: Caller Box 10007, Capitol Hill, Saipan, MP 96950; tel. 664-2200; fax 664-2211; internet www.cnmi.gov.mp.

Office of the Resident Representative to the USA, Commonwealth of the Northern Mariana Islands: 2121 R St, NW, Washington, DC 20008; tel. (202) 673-5869; fax (202) 673-5873; the Commonwealth Govt also has liaison offices in Hawaii and Guam.

Department of the Interior, Office of Insular Affairs (OIA): Field Office of the OIA, Dept of the Interior, POB 502622, Saipan, MP 96950; tel. 234-8861; fax 234-8814; e-mail jeff.schorr@saipan.com; OIA representation in the Commonwealth; Field Representative JEFFREY SCHORR.

Legislature

Legislative authority is vested in the Northern Marianas Commonwealth Legislature, a bicameral body consisting of the Senate and the House of Representatives. There are nine senators, elected for four-year terms, and 18 members of the House of Representatives, elected for two-year terms. The most recent elections took place on 3 November 2001, following which the Republicans held six of the nine seats in the Senate, the Democratic Party two seats and the Covenant Party one seat. The Republican Party held 12 of the 18 seats in the House of Representatives, the Democrat Party five seats and the Covenant Party one seat.

Senate President: PAUL A. MANGLONA.

Speaker of the House: HEINZ S. HOFSCHNEIDER.

Commonwealth Legislature: Capitol Hill, Saipan, MP 96950; tel. 664-7757; fax 322-6344.

Political Organizations

Covenant Party: c/o Commonwealth Legislature, Capitol Hill, Saipan MP 96950; Leader BENIGNO R. FITIAL; Chair. ELOY INOS.

Democratic Party of the Commonwealth of the Northern Mariana Islands, Inc: POB 500676, Saipan, MP 96950-0676; tel. 234-7497; fax 233-0641; Pres. Dr CARLOS S. CAMACHO; Chair. LORENZO CABRERA.

Republican Party: c/o Commonwealth Legislature, Capitol Hill, Saipan MP 96950; Chair. JOSEPH REYES.

Judicial System

The judicial system in the Commonwealth of the Northern Mariana Islands (CNMI) consists of the Superior Court, the Commonwealth Supreme Court (which considers appeals from the Superior Court) and the Federal District Court. Under the Covenant, federal law applies in the Commonwealth, apart from the following exceptions: the CNMI is not part of the US Customs Territory; the federal minimum wage provisions do not apply; federal immigration laws do not apply; and, the CNMI may enact its own taxation laws.

Religion

The population is predominantly Christian, mainly Roman Catholic. There are small communities of Episcopalians (Anglicans—under the jurisdiction of the Bishop of Hawaii, in the USA) and Protestants.

CHRISTIANITY

The Roman Catholic Church

The Northern Mariana Islands comprise the single diocese of Chalan Kanoa, suffragan to the archdiocese of Agaña (Guam). The Bishop participates in the Catholic Bishops' Conference of the Pacific, based in Fiji. At 31 December 2000 there were 53,066 adherents in the Northern Mariana Islands, including temporary residents.

Bishop of Chalan Kanoa: Most Rev. TOMAS AGUON CAMACHO, Bishop's House, Chalan Kanoa, POB 500745, Saipan, MP 96950; tel. 234-3000; fax 235-3002; e-mail tcamacho@vzpacifica.net.

The Press

The weekly *Focus on the Commonwealth* is published in Guam, but distributed solely in the Northern Mariana Islands.

Marianas Observer: POB 502119, Saipan, MP 96950; tel. 233-3955; fax 233-7040; weekly; Publr JOHN VABLAN; Man. Editor ZALDY DANDAN; circ. 2,000.

Marianas Review: POB 501074, Saipan, MP 96950; tel. 234-7160; f. 1979 as *The Commonwealth Examiner*; weekly; English and Chamorro; independent; Publr LUIS BENAVENTE; Editor RUTH L. TIGHE; circ. 1,700.

Marianas Variety News and Views: POB 500231, Saipan, MP 96950; tel. 234-6341; fax 234-9271; Mon.–Fri.; English and Chamorro; independent; Mans ABED YOUNIS, PAZ YOUNIS; circ. 5,500.

North Star: Chalan Kanoa, POB 500745, Saipan, MP 96950; tel. 234-3000; fax 235-3002; e-mail north.star@saipan.com; internet www.cnmicatholic.org/north.htm; weekly: English and Chamorro; Roman Catholic; Publr BISHOP TOMAS A. CAMACHO; Editor RUY VALENTE M. POLISTICO.

Pacific Daily News (Saipan bureau): POB 500822, Saipan, MP 96950; tel. 234-6423; fax 234-5986; Publr LEE WEBBER; circ. 5,000.

Pacific Star: POB 505815 CHRB, Saipan, MP 96950; tel. 288-0746; fax 288-0747; weekly; Operational Man. NICK LEGASPI; circ. 3,000.

Pacifica: POB 502143, Saipan, MP 96950; monthly; Editor MIKE MALONE.

Saipan Tribune: POB 10001, PMB 34, Saipan, MP 96950-8901; tel. 235-8747; fax 235-3740; e-mail editor.tribune@saipan.com; internet www.tribune.co.mp; 2 a week; Editor-in-Chief MARK M. BROADHURST; Publr REX I. PALACIOS; circ. 3,500.

Broadcasting and Communications

TELECOMMUNICATIONS

Micronesian Telecommunications Corpn: Saipan, MP 96950.

BROADCASTING

Radio

Inter-Island Communications Inc: POB 500914, Saipan, MP 96950; tel. 234-7239; fax 234-0447; f. 1984; commercial; station KCNM-AM, or KZMI-FM in stereo; Gen. Man. HANS W. MICKELSON; Programme Dir KEN WARNICK; CEO ANGEL OCAMPO.

Far East Broadcasting Co: POB 500209, Saipan, MP 96950; tel. 322-9088; fax 322-3060; e-mail saipan@febc.org; internet www.febc.org; f. 1946; non-commercial religious broadcasts; Dir ROBERT SPRINGER; Pres. JIM R. BOWMAN.

KSAI-AM: tel. 234-6520; fax 234-3428; e-mail ksai@febc.org; f. 1978; local service; Station Man. HARRY BLALOCK.

KFBS-SW: tel. 322-9088; e-mail saipan@febc.org; international broadcasts in Chinese, Indonesian, Russian, Vietnamese, Burmese, Mongolian; Chief Engineer ROBERT SPRINGER.

Station KHBI-SW: POB 501837, Saipan, MP 96950; tel. 234-6515; fax 234-5452; fmrly KYOI; non-commercial station owned by the *Christian Science Monitor* (USA); Gen. Man. DOMINGO VILLAR.

Station KPXP: PMB 415, Box 10000, Saipan, MP 96950; tel. 235-7996; fax 235-7998; e-mail power99@saipan.com; internet www.radiopacific.com/p99/; f. 1981; acquired Station KRSI in 2000, which also broadcasts on Saipan; Gen. Man. CURTIS DANCOE.

Television

Marianas CableVision: Saipan, MP 96950; tel. 235-4628; fax 235-0965; e-mail mcv@saipan.com; internet www.kmcv.co.mp; 55-channel cable service provider, broadcasting US and Pacific Rim programmes.

Tropic Isles Cable TV Corpn: POB 501015, Saipan, MP 96950; tel. 234-7350; fax 234-9828; 33-channel commercial station, with 5 pay channels, broadcasting 24 hours a day; US programmes and local and international news; 5,000 subscribers; Gen. Man. FRED LORD.

KMCV-TV: POB 501298, Saipan, MP 96950; tel. 235-6365; fax 235-0965; f. 1992; 52-channel commercial station, with 8 pay channels, broadcasting 24 hours a day; US programmes and local and international news; 5,650 subscribers; Gen. Man. WAYNE GAMBLIN.

Finance

BANKING

Bank of Guam (USA): POB 678, Saipan, MP 96950; tel. 234-6467; fax 234-3527; Gen. Man. JAMES LYNN; brs on Tinian and Rota.

Bank of Hawaii: Bank of Hawaii Bldg, El Monte Ave, Garapan, POB 566, Saipan, MP 96950; tel. 234-6673; fax 234-3478; Vice-Pres. DAVID BUEHLER; 2 brs.

Bank of Saipan: POB 500690, Saipan, MP 96950; tel. 234-6260; fax 235-1802; e-mail bankofsaipan@gtepacifica.net.

City Trust Bank: Qualo Rai, POB 501867, Saipan, MP 96950; tel. 234-7773; fax 234-8664; Gen. Man. MARIA LOURDES JOHNSON.

First Savings and Loan Asscn of America (USA): Beach Rd, Susupe, POB 500324, Saipan, MP 96950; tel. 234-6617; Man. SUZIE WILLIAMS.

Guam Savings and Loan Bank: POB 503201, Saipan, MP 96950; tel. 233-2265; fax 233-2227; Gen. Man. GLEN PEREZ.

HSBC Ltd (Hong Kong): Middle Rd, Garapan, Saipan, MP 96950; tel. 234-2468; fax 234-8882.

Union Bank of California: Oleai Centre, Beach Rd, Chalan Laulau, POB 501053, Saipan, MP 96950; tel. 234-6559; fax 234-7438; Gen. Man. KEN KATO.

INSURANCE

Associated Insurance Underwriters of the Pacific Inc: POB 501369, Saipan, MP 96950; tel. 234-7222; fax 234-5367; Gen. Man. MAGGIE GEORGE.

General Accident Insurance Asia Ltd (Microl Insurance): POB 502177, Saipan, MP 96950; tel. 234-2811; fax 234-5462; Man. Dir ANDREW M. HOWLETT.

Marianas Insurance Co Ltd: POB 502505, Saipan, MP 96950-2505; tel. 234-5091; fax 234-5093; e-mail mic@itecnmi.com; Gen. Man. ROSALIA S. CABRERA.

Mitsui Marine and Fire Insurance Co Ltd: POB 502177, Saipan, MP 96950; tel. 234-2811; fax 234-5462; Man. Dir ANDREW M. HOWLETT.

Moylan's Insurance Underwriters (Int.) Inc: POB 500658, Saipan, MP 96950; tel. 234-6442; fax 234-8641; e-mail moylan70@ite.net.

Pacifica Insurance Underwriters Inc: POB 500168, Saipan, MP 96950; tel. 234-6267; fax 234-5880; e-mail norten@netpci.com; Pres. NORMAN T. TENORIO.

Primerica Financial Services: POB 500964, Saipan, MP 96950; tel. 235-2912; fax 235-7910; Gen. Man. JOHN SABLAN.

Staywell: POB 2050, Saipan, MP 96950; tel. 235-4260; fax 235-4263; Gen. Man. LARRY LAVEQUE.

Trade and Industry

GOVERNMENT AGENCIES

Commonwealth Development Authority: POB 502149, Wakins Bldg, Gualo Rai, Saipan, MP 96950; tel. 234-7145; e-mail cda@itecnmi.com; internet www.cda.gov.mp; govt lending institution; funds capital improvement projects and private enterprises; offers tax incentives to qualified investors; Chair. JUAN S. TENORIO.

Office of Public Lands, Board of Public Lands Management: POB 500380, Saipan, MP 96950; tel. 234-3751; fax 234-3755; e-mail opl@vzpacifica.net; manages public land, which constitutes 82% of total land area in the Commonwealth (14% on Saipan).

CHAMBER OF COMMERCE

Saipan Chamber of Commerce: Chalan Kanoa, POB 500806 CK, Saipan, MP 96950; tel. 233-7150; fax 233-7151; e-mail saipanchamber@saipan.com; internet www.saipanchamber.com; Pres. RICHARD A. PIERCE; Exec. Dir CARLENE REYES-TENORIO; Co-ordinator JADENE A. VILLAGOMEZ.

EMPLOYERS' ASSOCIATION

Association of Commonwealth Teachers (ACT): POB 5071, Saipan, MP 96950; tel. and fax 256 7567; e-mail cnmiteachers@netscape.net; internet http://silkleaf.tripod.com/cnmi-act; supports the teaching profession and aims to improve education in state schools.

Saipan Garment Manufacturers' Association (SGMA): Saipan, MP 96950; e-mail sgmacs@gtepacifica.net; internet www.sgma-saipan.org; Chair. RICHARD A. PIERCE (acting).

UTILITIES

Commonwealth Utilities Corpn: POB 501220, Saipan, MP 96950; tel. 235-7025; fax 235-6145; e-mail cucedp@gtepacifica.net.

TRADE UNION AND CO-OPERATIVES

International Brotherhood of Electrical Workers: c/o Micronesian Telecommunications Corpn, Saipan, MP 96950; Local 1357 of Hawaii branch of US trade union based in Washington, DC.

The Mariana Islands Co-operative Association, Rota Producers and Tinian Producers Associations operate in the islands.

Transport

RAILWAYS

There have been no railways operating in the islands since the Japanese sugar industry railway, on Saipan, ceased operations in the Second World War.

ROADS

In 1991 there were 494 km (307 miles) of roads on the islands, 320 km (199 miles) of which are on Saipan. First grade roads constitute 135 km (84 miles) of the total, 99 km (62 miles) being on Saipan. There is no public transport, apart from a school bus system.

SHIPPING

The main harbour of the Northern Mariana Islands is Port of Saipan, which underwent extensive renovation in the mid-1990s. There are also two major harbours on Rota and one on Tinian. Several shipping lines link Saipan, direct or via Guam, with ports in Japan, Asia, the Philippines, the USA and other territories in the Pacific.

Commonwealth Ports Authority: POB 501055, Saipan, MP 96950; tel. 664-3500; fax 234-5962; e-mail cpa.admin@saipan.com; internet www.cpa.gov.mp; Exec. Dir CARLOS H. SALAS; Chair. JOSE R. LIFOFOI.

Mariana Express Lines: POB 501937,CTS Building, Saipan, MP 96950; tel. 322-1690; fax 323-6355; e-mail ctsispn@aol.com; services between Saipan, Guam, Japan and Hong Kong.

Saipan Shipping Co Inc (Saiship): Saiship Bldg, Charlie Dock, POB 8, Saipan, MP 96950; tel. 322-9706; fax 322-3183; weekly barge service between Guam, Saipan and Tinian; monthly services to Japan and Micronesia.

Westpac Freight: POB 2048, Puerto Rico, Saipan, MP 96950; tel. 322-8798; fax 322-5536; e-mail westpac@gtepacifica.net; internet www.westpacfreight.com; services between Saipan, Guam and the USA; Man. MICHIE CAMACHO.

CIVIL AVIATION

Air services are centred on the main international airport, Isley Field, on Saipan. There are also airports on Rota and Tinian.

Continental Micronesia: POB 508778, A.B. Won Pat International Airport, Tamuning, MP 96911; tel. 647-6595; fax 649-6588; internet www.continental.com; f. 1968, as Air Micronesia, by Continental Airlines (USA); name changed 1992; wholly-owned subsidiary of Continental Airlines; hub operations in Saipan and Guam; services throughout the region and to destinations in the Far East and the mainland USA; Pres. BILL MEEHAN.

Freedom Air: POB 500239 CK, Saipan, MP 96950; tel. and fax 288-5663; scheduled internal flights.

Pacific Island Aviation: PPP 318, POB 10,000, Saipan, MP 96950; tel. 234-3600; fax 234-3604; e-mail piasaipan@saipan.com; internet www.pacificislandaviation.com; f. 1987; scheduled services to Rota and Guam; repair station; flight instruction; Pres. ROBERT F. CHRISTIAN; Gen. Man. FELICIDAD BODDY; Vice-Pres. PAZ PABALINAS.

Tourism

Tourism is the most important industry in the Northern Mariana Islands, earning US $430m. in 2001. In 1998 there were 3,942 hotel rooms. Most of the islands' hotels are Japanese-owned, and in 2001 75.5% of tourists came from Japan. The Republic of Korea and the

USA are also important sources of tourists. The islands received a total of 442,466 visitors in 2001 (a decrease of some 16.3% on the figure for the previous year). The islands of Asuncion, Guguan, Maug, Managaha, Sariguan and Uracas (Farallon de Pajaros) are maintained as uninhabited preserves. Visitors are mainly attracted by the white, sandy beaches and the excellent diving conditions. There is also interest in the *Latte* or *Taga* stones (mainly on Tinian), pillars carved from the rock by the ancient Chamorros, and relics from the Second World War.

Hotel Association of the Northern Mariana Islands: POB 501983, Saipan, MP 96950; tel. 234-3455; fax 234-3411; e-mail rds@itecnmi.com; internet www.marianashotels.org; f. 1985; Chair. RONALD D. SABLAN.

Marianas Visitors Authority: POB 500861 CK, Saipan, MP 96950; tel. 664-3200; fax 664-3237; e-mail mva@saipan.com; internet www.visit-marianas.com; f. 1976; responsible for the promotion and development of tourism in the Northern Mariana Islands; Man. Dir PERRY JOHN TENORIO.

Defence

The USA is responsible for the defence of the Northern Mariana Islands. The US Pacific Command is based in Hawaii (USA).

Education

School attendance is compulsory from six to 16 years of age. In 1999/2000 there were 11 state primary schools, with a total of 5,651 pupils enrolled, and there were six state secondary schools, with a total enrolment of 3,492 pupils. There was a total of 17 private schools, with a total enrolment of 2,842 pupils. There was one college of further education in 1993/94 with 3,051 students. Budgetary expenditure on education totalled US $49.6m. in 2000, equivalent to 22.0% of total government expenditure.

United States External Territories in the Pacific

Most of the external or unincorporated territories of the USA (except the US Virgin Islands and uninhabited Navassa Island, in the Caribbean Sea) are located in the Pacific Ocean. There are two territories with differing degrees of self-government. The Trust Territory of the Pacific Islands was terminated on 1 October 1994, when the Republic of Palau achieved independence from the USA under the Compact of Free Association. Most of the seven remaining island jurisdictions were annexed to the USA by the Guano Act of 1856, together with other, now-relinquished claims. In the federal government, the Secretary of the Navy is ultimately responsible for Kingman Reef and for Johnston Atoll, and the Secretary of the Air Force for Wake Island. Otherwise, the Secretary of the Interior is the responsible authority for the territories, although the administration may be exercised by another federal agency. Within the Department of the Interior, the Assistant Secretary for Policy, Management and Budget is responsible for the Office of Insular Affairs and acts on behalf of the Secretary in all matters relating to the insular governments and territories. The USA maintains membership, in its own right and in respect of its territories, of the Pacific Community (formerly the South Pacific Commission), the Colombo Plan and the UN's Economic and Social Commission for Asia and the Pacific (ESCAP).

Head of State: President GEORGE W. BUSH (took office 20 January 2001).

Department of the Interior, Office of Insular Affairs: C St between 18th and 19th Sts, NW, Washington, DC 20240, USA; tel. (202) 208-6816; fax (202) 208-3390.

Secretary of the Interior: GALE A. NORTON.

Director, Office of Insular Affairs: NIKALAO I. PULA.

Department of Defense: The Pentagon, Washington, DC 20301, USA; tel. (202) 697-5737; fax (202) 697-1656; internet www.defenselink.mil; for details of service depts, see under appropriate insular possessions.

AMERICAN SAMOA

Physical and Social Geography

American Samoa comprises the five islands of Tutuila, Ta'u, Olosega, Ofu and Aunu'u, and the atolls of Swain's Island (Olohenga) and uninhabited Rose Island. The islands lie in the South Central Pacific along latitude 14°S at about longitude 170°W, some 3,700 km south-west of Hawaii (USA). Swain's Island, administered as part of American Samoa since 1925, lies 340 km to the north-west of the main group. The territory's nearest neighbour is Samoa (formerly known as Western Samoa). The five principal islands are high and volcanic with rugged interiors and little flat land except along the coasts. The area of the islands is 201 sq km (77.6 sq miles).

At the 2000 census the population was 57,291, of whom the majority lived on Tutuila, where the main town, Pago Pago, is situated (the officially designated seat of government is the village of Fagatogo). Approximately 91,000 American Samoans are resident in the USA.

The islands are peopled by Polynesians and are thought to have been the origin of many of the people who now occupy islands further east. The Samoan language is believed to be the oldest extant form of Polynesian speech. Samoan society developed an intricate hierarchy of graded titles comprising titular chiefs and orator chiefs. The basis of Samoan society remains the aiga, or extended family unit, headed by a chiefly matai. One of the striking features of modern Samoa is the manner in which this system and the culture of the islands prior to European contact remains a dominant influence. It is referred to as *fa'a Samoa*, the Samoan Way. Most of the population are Christians.

History

The Samoan islands were first visited by Europeans in the 1700s, but it was not until 1830 that missionaries from the London Missionary Society settled there. In 1872 the Kingdom of Samoa, then an independent state, ceded Pago Pago harbour to the USA as a naval coaling station. The United Kingdom and Germany were also interested in the islands, but a treaty signed in 1889 by these powers and the USA guaranteed the neutrality of Samoa. The British withdrew in 1899, and in the same year, following internal conflicts between rival chiefs, the kingship was abolished and a further tripartite treaty left the Western islands for Germany to govern, while the Eastern islands passed under US influence. In 1900 the high chiefs, or Matai, of Tutuila formally ceded the islands of Tutuila and Aunu'u to the USA and, in 1904, the chiefs of the islands of Ta'u, Olosega, Ofu and Rose (Manu'a District) followed suit. These deeds of cession and American Samoa's annexation as a US territory, were enacted by Congress in the 1920s. The President of the USA was empowered to provide for the executive, legislative and judicial administration of the territory, this responsibility being vested in the Secretary of the Navy until 1951, and subsequently in the Secretary of the Interior. Since 1925 Swain's Island has also been administered by the USA as part of American Samoa. In December 1980 the USA and New Zealand signed a treaty (ratified in 1983) whereby New Zealand, on behalf of the territory of Tokelau, relinquished a claim to Swain's Island (Olohenga). At the same time, the USA relinquished its claim to Tokelau, which lies to the north of American Samoa.

From 1951 until 1978 American Samoa was administered by a Governor appointed by the US Department of the Interior, and a legislature comprising a Senate and a House of Representatives. In November 1977 the first popular vote to elect a Governor was held. In January 1978 the successful candidate, Peter Coleman, was inaugurated as Governor. He was re-elected to a second term in the election of November 1980, after three years in office instead of four (the normal term prescribed in the Constitution), to allow synchronization with US elections in that year. Coleman was ineligible to hold office for three consecutive terms and, at elections in November 1984, A. P. Lutali was elected Governor, and Eni Hunkin (who subsequently adopted the use of his chiefly name, Faleomavaega) was elected Lieutenant-Governor. In October 1986 a constitutional convention completed a comprehensive rewriting of the American Samoan Constitution. The draft revision, however, had yet to be submitted to the US Congress in mid-2002.

In July 1988 the territory's delegate to the US House of Representatives, Fofō Sunia, announced that he would not seek re-election, as he was then under federal investigation for alleged financial mismanagement. In October of the same year he was sentenced to a period of between five and 15 months in prison for fraud. Elections to choose a new delegate took place in November and were won by Faleomavaega, the Lieutenant-Governor. At the same time, Peter Coleman was elected Governor and Galea'i Poumele was elected Lieutenant-Governor.

In November 1990 a proposal that the Governor's powers of veto over legislative affairs should be restricted was defeated by a 75% majority in a referendum. Following the vote, Coleman announced that he favoured autonomy for American Samoa, and that he would seek negotiations on the matter. At gubernatorial elections in November 1992 Peter Coleman was defeated by A. P. Lutali. At elections to the House of Representatives in November 1994 about one-third of those members who sought re-election was defeated. Faleomavaega was re-elected as non-voting delegate.

In late 1994 and early 1995 American Samoa was among a number of Pacific islands to express concern at the proposed passage through their waters of regular shipments of plutonium, *en route* from Europe to Japan. Moreover, the decision by France to resume nuclear-testing in the South Pacific in September 1995 was fiercely criticized by Lutali, who described the action as an affront to the entire Pacific community.

A court action initiated by the Government of American Samoa against a US insurance company for its alleged failure to pay adequate compensation following a devastating hurricane in late 1991 was concluded in September 1995. The company (which had responded to a claim for US $50m. in 1991 with a payment of only US $6.1m.) was ordered by the court to pay a total of US $86.7m. to the islands in compensation.

Gubernatorial and legislative elections took place in November 1996. An estimated 87% of eligible voters participated in the election, at which only eight of the 18 members seeking re-election to the Fono were successful. At a second round of voting the incumbent

Lieutenant-Governor, the Democrat Tauese Sunia, was elected Governor with 51.3% of the votes, defeating Leala Peter Reid, Jr, who secured 48.7% of votes. Faleomavaega was re-elected as delegate to the US House of Representatives, with 56.5% of the votes, defeating Gus Hannemann, who won 43.5% of votes.

The decision in July 1997 by the Government of neighbouring Western Samoa to change the country's name to simply Samoa caused some controversy in the Territory. Legislation approved in March 1998 in the House of Representatives stated that American Samoa should not recognize the new name, which was viewed by many islanders as serving to undermine their own Samoan identity. Similarly, legislation prohibiting citizens of Samoa (formerly Western Samoa) from owning land in American Samoa was approved in response to the change.

In September 1998 a motion to impeach the Governor was introduced in the House of Representatives. Tauese Sunia was alleged to have used public funds to pay personal debts, to have sold government vehicles without following recognized procedure and to have used funds allocated for school building repairs to purchase and install a sauna at his home.

In November 1998 Faleomavaega was re-elected as delegate to the US House of Representatives. In the same month, following a dispute lasting several years, a legal settlement was reached between the five leading US tobacco companies and 46 US states and several of its territories, including American Samoa. It was agreed that between 1998 and 2025 American Samoa was to receive a total of some US $29m. in compensation for the harmful effects of cigarette smoking suffered by its inhabitants.

In March 1999 legislation was adopted introducing capital punishment (by lethal injection) for murder convictions. It was hoped that this would act as a deterrent to drugs-dealers and users. However, the decision was reversed when, in mid-2000, the territory's House of Representatives enacted legislation to abolish capital punishment; the legislation was to be presented to the Senate for approval. In April 2000 the House of Representatives rejected a bill proposing the legalization of gambling, on the grounds that this would foster social problems.

At elections held on 7 November 2000, Governor Tauese Sunia was narrowly re-elected, receiving 50.7% of votes cast, compared with 47.9% for opposition candidate, Senator Lealaifuaneva. However, it was later announced that a re-count of votes was to take place, although no date was set. At congressional elections, held concurrently, no candidate received the necessary 50% majority, Faleomavaega winning 45.7% of votes cast, compared with 30.3% for Hanneman. A second round of voting took place on 21 November, when Faleomavaega won a reported 61.1% of the votes and Hanneman received 38.9%. Faeomavaega thus returned to the US House of Representatives for a seventh two-year term.

The issue of US jurisdiction in the Territory was raised once more in September 2001, when the Senate approved a resolution urging discussion with the US Government regarding the conferral of limited federal jurisdiction to the High Court of American Samoa, the only US territory without a sitting federal judge. A congressional public survey, conducted in the same month, registered wide popular support for a Federal Court and Public Prosecutor. At a meeting of the UN General Assembly in January 2002, the UN accepted American Samoa's proposal of May 2001 that it be removed from the list of colonized territories. The Governor had sent a resolution to the UN Committee on Decolonization affirming American Samoa's wish to remain a US territory.

In mid-September 2002 the Territory's immigration procedures were amended to give the Attorney-General, rather than the Immigration Board, the ultimate authority to grant permanent resident status to aliens. The House of Representatives also approved a resolution to repeal legislation automatically conferring US citizenship in the Territory to foreign parents. In the same month the Territory's intelligence agencies claimed that the Speaker of the House of Representatives, Tuanaitau Tuia, had used public funds to purchase a car and to finance private travel for his wife. Meanwhile, in early June a former president of the Amerika Samoa Bank (now ANZ Amerika Samoa Bank), Will Cravens, was convicted of fraud in a scheme that had misappropriated US $75m. of investors' money; he was due to be sentenced in October.

The authorities were forced to introduce fuel rationing in October 2002 after a shipment was turned away from Pago Pago when it was discovered that its contents did not meet the specifications of the Environmental Protection Agency.

The federal government of the USA remains responsible for defence and foreign affairs.

Economy

In 1985, according to estimates by the World Bank, American Samoa's gross national product (GNP), measured at average 1983–85 prices, was about US $190m., equivalent to US $5,410 per head. GNP per head was estimated at some US $8,000 in 1992. Between 1973 and 1985, it was estimated, GNP increased, in real terms, at an average rate of 1.7% per year, with real GNP per head rising by only 0.1% per year. In 1990–98 the population increased by an average of 4.2% per year. An estimated 91,000 American Samoans live on the US mainland or Hawaii.

Agriculture, hunting, forestry and fishing engaged only 3.1% of the employed labour force in 2000. Agricultural production provides little surplus for export. Major crops are coconuts, bananas, taro, pineapples, yams and breadfruit. A state of disaster was declared in mid-1993, following the outbreak of taro-leaf blight in the islands, and in mid-1996 imports of root crops from Fiji were banned in an attempt to prevent the spread of a highly destructive beetle. Moreover, in 1998 the banana crop was severely reduced by aphid activity.

Tuna-canning plants at Pago Pago, process fish from US, Taiwanese and South Korean vessels. The Starkist Samoa and Samoa Packing plants are among the largest in the world. Canned tuna constituted almost 97% of total export revenue in 1998/99, when earnings reached US $334.2m. Fish-canning is the dominant industrial activity, engaging more than 42% of the employed work-force in the early 1990s; in 2001 70% of employees were guest workers from Samoa (formerly Western Samoa). In early July 2002 a shipment of tuna worth US $20m. was temporarily confiscated by the US Food and Drug Administration at the Port of Los Angeles, following concerns that it had been contaminated by 'bio-terrorist' groups. The delegate of American Samoa to the US Congress, Eni Faleomavaega, subsequently urged the Territory's canneries to buy more fish from US fishing boats rather than foreign fleets.

Other activities include meat-canning, handicrafts, dairy farming, orchid farming and the manufacture of soap, perfume, paper products and alcoholic beverages. A garment factory began operations at Tafuna in 1995, and in the following year employed more than 700 people (although almost one-half of these employees were foreign workers). However, the islands' garment manufacturing industry was adversely affected following a riot between local workers and Vietnamese employees at a clothing factory, during which a number of people were injured. The incident was widely condemned, and Governor Tauese Sunia stated that the future of the garment industry in American Samoa would require consideration. Exports of finished garments declined from US $15.4m. in 1997/98 to US $4.6m. in 1998/99. The construction sector engaged 6.4% of the employed labour force in 2000.

Service industries engage a majority of the employed labour force in American Samoa (55.2% in 2000). The Government alone employs almost one-third of workers, although in the mid-1990s a series of reductions in the number of public-sector employees were introduced. The tourist industry is developing slowly, and earned some US $10m. in 1998. Tourist arrivals rose from 41,050 in 1998 to 49,060 in 1999.

In late 1989 American Samoa experienced a severe financial crisis, in response to which, in early 1990, the Governor imposed pay cuts on 3,800 government workers and introduced the emergency 'freezing' of local prices. At the end of the year the budgetary deficit was estimated to have reached US $17.7m. (compared with US $7.5m. in the previous year). The Territory's total debt had reached some US $60m. by September 1992. Assistance from the USA totalled more than US $40m. in 1994. In 1996/97 the budget deficit was estimated at US $7.5m. In 2001 a fiscal surplus of US $200,000 was recorded, the Territory's first budgetary surplus in more than 20 years. Government revenues in 2001 surpassed budgeted expectations by more than US $4.2m.

The visible trade deficit rose from US $83.4m. in the year ending September 1998 to US $107m in 1999, when total imports reached US $452.6m. and exports totalled US $345.1m. Most of American Samoa's trade is conducted with the USA. Other trading partners in 1998/99 included New Zealand, which supplied 9.2% of total imports, Australia (8.6%) and Fiji (5.6%). The UN estimated that, during 1990–2000, the Territory's exports increased at an average annual rate of 2.4%, compared with the previous year, while imports increased at a rate of 3.2% a year. Annual inflation averaged 2.8% in 1990–96. Consumer prices rose by 1.7% in 1998 and by 0.9% in 1999. An inflation rate of 2.5% was recorded in the second quarter of 2002. An estimated 13% of the total labour force were unemployed in 2000.

The issue of American Samoa's minimum wage structure has caused considerable controversy. The situation (in which American Samoa has a lower minimum wage than the rest of the USA) has been largely attributed to the presence of the two tuna-canning plants on the islands, which provide much of the manufacturing employment on the islands and consequently exert substantial influence over the setting of wage levels; in 2001 approximately 80% of the employees at the canneries came from Samoa (formerly Western Samoa), an additional factor in wages being lower. In 1991, while the minimum wage on the US mainland increased by some 12%, the rate in American Samoa remained unchanged (leaving the Territory's minimum wage level some 50% below that of the mainland). A US recommendation for modest increases in wage levels, implemented in mid-1996, was strongly opposed by the American Samoan Government, which argued that, with higher costs, the Territory's tuna-canning industry would be unable to compete with other parts of the world. In May 2001 the American Samoan Government waived the provision requiring foreign workers to perform domestic duties for a year before being allowed to work. This move was welcomed by the tuna canneries, which were having difficulties recruiting new workers. In May 2002, however, a lawsuit seeking eviction from its premises for rent arrears was filed in the High Court against the tuna producer Starkist Samoa, the Territory's largest private employer (with some 2,500 workers).

American Samoa's continued financial problems have been compounded by the high demand for government services from an increasing population, the limited economic and tax base and natural disasters. Attempts to reduce the persistent budget deficit and achieve a greater measure of financial security for the islands have included severe reductions in the number of public-sector employees, increased fees for government services and plans to diversify the economy by encouraging tourism and expanding manufacturing activity. Economic development, however, is hindered by the islands' remote location, their vulnerability to adverse climatic conditions, the limited infrastructure and lack of skilled workers.

In February 1998 the American Samoa Economic Advisory Commission was established; it was hoped that the Commission would help the Territory attain self-sufficiency and reduce its budget deficit. Its task was facilitated in November of that year, when the so-called 'tobacco settlement' (see History) was reached. In late 1999 the Government opted to negotiate a loan of US $18.6m. from the US Department of the Interior, which was to be repaid from the proceeds of the 'tobacco settlement'. The money allowed the Government to pay outstanding debts—settlement of health care and utility bills were a condition stipulated by the USA—and to launch a programme of fiscal reforms. This was bolstered by an insurance settlement for damages sustained during Hurricane Val, in 1991, worth US $47.9m. In April 2002 the American Samoa Economic Advisory Commission published a report, further amended in July 2002, which outlined proposals for the development of a more diverse market economy in the Territory. The Commission identified four sectors—fisheries and agriculture, telecommunications and information technology, manufacturing and tourism—as growth industries with the most potential for development. The plan aimed to implement initiatives over a period of five to 10 years, leading ultimately to the creation of new enterprises and more small and medium-sized businesses.

American Samoa is a member of the Pacific Community (formerly the South Pacific Commission) and is an associate member of the UN's Economic and Social Commission for Asia and the Pacific (ESCAP). In mid-1986 the Governments of Western Samoa (now Samoa) and American Samoa signed a memorandum of understanding, in accordance with which a permanent committee was established to ensure mutual economic development.

Statistical Survey

Source (unless otherwise indicated): Statistics Division, Department of Commerce, Pago Pago, AS 96799; tel. 633-5155; fax 633-4195; internet www.amsamoa.com.

AREA AND POPULATION

Area: 201 sq km (77.6 sq miles); *by island* (sq km): Tutuila 137; Ta'u 46; Ofu 7; Olosega 5; Swain's Island (Olohenga) 3; Aunu'u 2; Rose 1.

Population: 46,773 at census of 1 April 1990; 57,291 (males 29,264; females 28,027) at census of 1 April 2000. *By island* (2000): Tutuila 55,400; Manu'a District (Ta'u, Olosega and Ofu islands) 1,378; Aunu'u 476; Swain's Island (Olohenga) 37.

Density (2000): 285.0 per sq km.

Ethnic Groups (2000 census): Samoan 50,545; part-Samoan 1,991; Asian 1,631; Tongan 1,598; Total (incl. others) 57,291.

Principal Towns (population at 2000 census): Pago Pago (capital) 4,278, Tafuna 8,409, Nu'uuli 5,154, Leone 3,568.

Births, Marriages and Deaths (1999): Registered live births 1,736; Registered marriages 272; Registered deaths 249.

Expectation of Life (years at birth, 1990): Males 68.5; Females 76.2.

Economically Active Population (persons aged 16 years and over, 2000 census): Agriculture, hunting, forestry, fishing and mining 517; Manufacturing 5,900; Construction 1,066; Trade, restaurants and hotels 2,414; Transport, storage, communications and utilities 1,036; Financing, insurance, real estate and business services 311; Community, social and personal services 5,474; Total employed 16,718 (males 9,804, females 6,914); Unemployed 909 (males 494, females 415); Total labour force 17,627 (males 10,298, females 7,329). Source: US Department of Commerce, *2000 Census of Population and Housing*.

AGRICULTURE, ETC.

Principal Crops (FAO estimates, '000 metric tons, 2000): Coconuts 5,000; Taro 2; Bananas 1. Source: FAO.

Livestock (FAO estimates, 2000): Pigs 10,700; Cattle 103; Chickens 37,000. Source: FAO.

Fishing (metric tons, live weight, 1999): Total catch 474 (Albacore 301). Source: FAO, *Yearbook of Fishery Statistics*.

INDUSTRY

Production (1994): Tinned fish 211,600 metric tons; Electric energy 158.60 million kWh (year ending September 1999). Source partly Bank of Hawaii.

FINANCE

Currency and Exchange Rates: United States currency is used. For details, see section on the Northern Mariana Islands.

Budget (US $ '000, year ending September 1997): *Revenue:* Local revenue 47,151 (Taxes 34,105, Charges for services 7,099); Grants from US Department of Interior 97,287 (Operating grant 23,056, Capital projects 4,015, Special revenue 70,216); Total 144,438. *Expenditure:* General government 21,615; Public safety 10,558; Public works 19,580; Health and recreation 41,706; Education and culture 43,533; Economic development 9,344; Capital projects 5,221; Debt-servicing 1,356; Total 152,912.

Cost of Living (Consumer Price Index; annual averages; base: July-Sept. 1997 = 100): 99.6 in 1997; 101.3 in 1998; 102.2 in 1999.

EXTERNAL TRADE

Principal Commodities (US $ million, year ending September 1999): *Imports:* Food 47.7 (Fish 13.1); Fuel and oil 49.0 (Diesel fuel 37.7); Textiles and clothing 7.1; Machinery and transport equipment 19.3 (Road motor vehicles and parts 12.5); Miscellaneous manufactured articles 44.9 (Tin plates 13.3); Construction materials 15.3; Total (incl. others) 187.8. *Exports:* Canned tuna 334.2; Total (incl. others) 345.1. Note: Figures for imports exclude the value of goods imported by the American Samoa Government ($5.0 million) and by the fish-canning sector ($259.9 million).

Principal Trading Partners (US $ million, year ending September 1999): *Imports:* Australia 16.1; Fiji 10.4; Japan 3.6; Korea, Republic 2.7; New Zealand 17.2; Samoa 5.2; Taiwan 2.0; USA 124.8; Total (incl. others) 187.7. *Exports:* Total 345.1 (almost entirely to the USA). Note: Figures for imports exclude the value of goods imported by the American Samoa Government and by the fish-canning sector. The total value of imports was $452.6 million in 1998/99.

TRANSPORT

Road Traffic ('000 motor vehicles in use, 1999): (Passenger cars 6.2; Commercial vehicles 0.7. Source: UN, *Statistical Yearbook*.

International Sea-borne Shipping (estimated freight traffic, '000 metric tons, 1990): Goods loaded 380; Goods unloaded 733. Source: UN, *Monthly Bulletin of Statistics*.

Civil Aviation (Pago Pago Int. Airport, year ending September 1999): Flights 7,748; Passengers 189,107 (Boarding 96,739, Disembarking 89,209, Transit 3,159); Freight and mail ('000 lb) 5,118 (Loaded 2,160, Unloaded 2,958).

TOURISM

Tourist Arrivals: (29,997 in 1997; 41,050 in 1998; 49,060 in 1999.

Tourist Arrivals by Country (1996): Australia 1,469; China 669; Germany 785; India 466; New Zealand 4,032; Philippines 671; Tonga 790; United Kingdom 1,514; USA 8,778; Total (incl. others) 21,366 Figures exclude arrivals from Samoa (formerly Western Samoa). Source: World Tourism Organization, *Yearbook of Tourism Statistics*.

Tourism Receipts (US $ million) 9 in 1996; 10 in 1997; 10 in 1998. Source: World Tourism Organization.

COMMUNICATIONS MEDIA

Daily Newspapers (1996): 2; estimated circulation 5,000*

Non-Daily Newspapers (1996): 1; estimated circulation 3,000*.

Radio Receivers (1997): 57,000* in use.

Television Receivers (1997): 14,000* in use.

Telephones (2000): 14,300† main lines in use.

Facsimile Machines (1999): 563 subscribers.

Mobile Cellular Telephones (1999): 2,377† subscribers.

* Source: UNESCO, *Statistical Yearbook*.

† Source: International Telecommunication Union.

EDUCATION

Pre-primary: 60 schools (1998); 123 teachers (1991/92); 3,293 pupils (2000).

Primary: 32 schools (1998); 524 teachers (1991/92); 11,418 pupils (2000).

Secondary: 10 high schools (1998); 266 teachers (1991/92); 4,645 pupils (2000).

Higher (2000): American Samoa Community College 1,474 students.

Source: mainly UN, *Statistical Yearbook for Asia and the Pacific* and US Department of Commerce, *2000 Census of Population and Housing*.

Directory

The Constitution

American Samoa is an Unincorporated Territory of the USA. Therefore not all the provisions of the US Constitution apply. As an unorganized territory it has not been provided with an organic act by Congress. Instead the US Secretary of the Interior, on behalf of the President, has plenary authority over the Territory and enabled the people of American Samoa to draft their own Constitution.

According to the 1967 Constitution, executive power is vested in the Governor, whose authority extends to all operations within the Territory of American Samoa. The Governor has veto power with respect to legislation passed by the Fono (Legislature). The Fono consists of the Senate and the House of Representatives, with a President and a Speaker presiding over their respective divisions. The Senate is composed of 18 members, elected, according to Samoan custom, from local chiefs, or Matai, for a term of four years. The House of Representatives consists of 20 members who are elected by popular vote for a term of two years, and a non-voting delegate from Swain's Island. The Fono meets twice a year, in January and July, for not more than 45 days and at such special sessions as the Governor may call. The Governor has the authority to appoint heads of government departments with the approval of the Fono. Local government is carried out by indigenous officials. In August 1976 a referendum on the popular election of a Governor and a Lieutenant-Governor resulted in an affirmative vote. The first gubernatorial elections took place on 8 November 1977 and the second occurred in November 1980; subsequent elections were to take place every four years.

American Samoa sends one non-voting delegate to the US House of Representatives, who is popularly elected every two years.

The Government

(September 2002)

Governor: TAUESE SUNIA (elected November 1996, re-elected November 2000).

Lieutenant-Governor: TOGIOLA TULAFONO.

GOVERNMENT OFFICES

Governor's Office: Pago Pago, AS 96799; tel. 633-4116; fax 633-2269; e-mail governorsoffice@asg-gov.com.

Department of the Interior, Office of Insular Affairs (OIA): Field Office of the OIA, Dept of the Interior, POB 1725, Pago Pago, AS 96799; tel. 633-2800; fax 633-2415; e-mail faleafine-nomura@samoatelco.com; Field Representative LYDIA FALEAFINE NOMURA.

Office of the Representative to the Government of American Samoa: Amerika Samoa Office, 1427 Dillingham Blvd, Suite 210, Honolulu HI 96817, USA; tel. (808) 847-1998; fax (808) 847-3420; Representative SOLOALI'I FAALEPO, Jr.

Department of Administrative Services: American Samoa Government, Pago Pago, AS 96799; tel. 633-4156; fax 633-1814.

Department of Agriculture: American Samoa Government, Executive Office Building, Utulei, Pago Pago, AS 96799; tel. 699-9272; fax 699-2567.

Department of Commerce: American Samoa Government, Pago Pago, AS 96799; tel. 633-1092, fax 633-2092.

Department of Education: American Samoa Government, Pago Pago, AS 96799; tel. 633-5237; fax 633-4240.

Department of Legal Affairs: American Samoa Government, Pago Pago, AS 96799; tel. 633-4163; fax 633-1838.

Department of Local Government: American Samoa Government, Pago Pago, AS 96799; tel. 633-5201; fax 633 5590.

Department of Health: American Samoa Government, Pago Pago; tel. 633-4606; fax 633-5379.

Department of Parks and Recreation: American Samoa Government, Pago Pago, AS 96799; tel. 699-9614; fax 699-4427.

Department of Port Administration: American Samoa Government, Pago Pago, AS 96799; tel. 633-4251; fax 633-5281.

Department of Public Safety: American Samoa Government, Pago Pago, AS 96799; tel. 633-1111; fax 633-7296.

Department of Public Works: American Samoa Government, Pago Pago, AS 96799; tel. 633-4141; fax 633-5958.

Department of Treasury: American Samoa Government, Pago Pago, AS 96799; tel. 633-4155; fax 633-4100.

Legislature

FONO

Senate

The Senate has 18 members, elected, according to Samoan custom, from local chiefs, or Matai, for a term of four years.

President: LETULI TOLOA.

House of Representatives

The House has 20 members who are elected by popular vote for a term of two years, and a non-voting delegate from Swain's Island.

Speaker: TUANAITAU F. TUIA.

CONGRESS

Since 1980 American Samoa has been able to elect, for a two-year term, a delegate to the Federal Congress, who may vote in committee but not on the floor of the House of Representatives. Elections to the post took place in November 2000.

Delegate of American Samoa: ENI F. H. FALEOMAVAEGA (October 2000), US House of Representatives, 2422 Rayburn House Office Bldg, Washington, DC 20515, USA; tel. (202) 225-8577; fax (202) 225-8757; e-mail eni@faleomavaega.house.gov.

Judicial System

The judicial system of American Samoa consists of the High Court, presided over by the Chief Justice and assisted by Associate Justices (all appointed by the Secretary of the Interior), and a local judiciary in the District and Village Courts. The judges for these local courts are appointed by the Governor, subject to confirmation by the Senate of the Fono. The High Court consists of three Divisions: Appellate, Trial, and Land and Titles. The Appellate Division has limited original jurisdiction and hears appeals from the Trial Division, the Land and Titles Division and from the District Court when it has operated as a court of record. The Trial Division has general jurisdiction over all cases. The Land and Titles Division hears cases involving land or Matai titles.

The District Court hears preliminary felony proceedings, misdemeanours, infractions (traffic and health), civil claims less than US $3,000, small claims, Uniform Reciprocal Enforcement of Support cases, and *de novo* trials from Village Courts. The Village Courts hear matters arising under village regulations and local customs.

Chief Justice: MICHAEL KRUSE.

Associate Justice: LYLE L. RICHMOND.

Attorney-General: MALAETASI M. TOGAFAU.

High Court: Office of the Chief Justice, High Court, Pago Pago, AS 96799; tel. 633-1261; e-mail Hcourt@samoatelco.com.

Judge of the District Court: JOHN L. WARD, II, POB 427, Pago Pago, AS 96799; tel. 633-1101.

Judge of the Village Court: FAISIOTA TAUANU'U, Pago Pago, AS 96799; tel. 633-1102.

Religion

The population is largely Christian, more than 50% being members of the Congregational Christian Church and about 20% being Roman Catholics.

CHRISTIANITY

American Samoa Council of Christian Churches: c/o CCCAS Offices, POB 1637, Pago Pago, AS 96799; f. 1985; six mem. churches; Pres. Cardinal PIO TAOFINU'U (Roman Catholic Archbishop of Samoa-Apia and Tokelau); Gen. Sec. Rev. ENOKA L. ALESANA (Congregational Christian Church in American Samoa).

The Roman Catholic Church

American Samoa comprises the single diocese of Samoa-Pago Pago, suffragan to the archdiocese of Samoa-Apia and Tokelau. At 31 December 2000 there were 12,000 adherents in the islands. The Bishop participates in the Catholic Bishops' Conference of the Pacific, based in Fiji.

Bishop of Samoa-Pago Pago: Rev. JOHN QUINN WEITZEL, Diocesan Pastoral Center, POB 596, Fatuoaiga, Pago Pago, AS 96799; tel. 699-1402; fax 699-1459; e-mail QUINN@samoatelco.com.

The Anglican Communion

American Samoa is within the diocese of Polynesia, part of the Church of the Province of New Zealand. The Bishop of Polynesia is resident in Fiji.

Protestant Churches

Congregational Christian Church in American Samoa (CCCAS): POB 1637, Pago Pago, AS 96799; 34,000 mems (22,000 in American Samoa) in 1985.

Other active Protestant groups include the Baptist Church, the Christian Church of Jesus Christ, the Methodist Church, Assemblies of God, Church of the Nazarene and Seventh-day Adventists. The Church of Jesus Christ of Latter-day Saints (Mormon) is also represented.

The Press

News Bulletin: Office of Public Information, American Samoa Government, Utulei; tel. 633-5490; daily (Mon.–Fri.); English; non-commercial; Editor PHILIP SWETT; circ. 1,800.

Samoa Journal and Advertiser: POB 3986, Pago Pago, AS 96799; tel. 633-2399; weekly; English and Samoan; Editor MICHAEL STARK; circ. 3,000.

Samoa News: POB 909, Pago Pago, AS 96799; tel. 633-5599; fax 633-4864; e-mail samoanews@samoatelco.com; 5 a week; English and Samoan; Publr LEWIS WOLMAN; circ. 4,500.

Broadcasting and Communications

TELECOMMUNICATIONS

American Samoa Telecommunications Authority: Pago Pago, AS 96799; internet www.samoatelco.com.

BROADCASTING

Radio

KSBS-FM: POB 793, Pago Pago, AS 96799; tel. 633-7000; fax 622-7839; internet www.samoanet.com/ksbsfm; commercial.

WVUV: POB 4894, Pago Pago, AS 96799; tel. 688-7397; fax 688-1545; fmr govt-administered station leased to Radio Samoa Ltd in 1975; commercial; English and Samoan; 24 hours a day; Man. VINCENT IULI.

Television

KVZK-TV: Office of Public Information, POB 3511, Pago Pago, AS 96799; tel. 633-4191; fax 633-1044; f. 1964; govt-owned; non-commercial; English and Samoan; broadcasts 18 hours daily on two channels; Gen. Man. VAOITA SAVALI; Technical Dir CARL SEVERA.

Finance

(cap. = capital; dep. = deposits; m. = million; amounts in US dollars)

BANKING

Commercial Banks

ANZ Amerika Samoa Bank: POB 3790, Pago Pago, AS 96799; tel. 633-5053; fax 633-5057; e-mail decourtb@samoatelco.com; internet www.anz.com.au/americansamoa; f. 1979; fmrly Amerika Samoa Bank; joined ANZ group in April 2001; cap. 6.6m., dep. 45.3m. (June 1995); Pres. and CEO HAROLD P. FIELDING; 4 brs.

Bank of Hawaii (USA): POB 69, Pago Pago, AS 96799; tel. 633-4226; fax 633-7197; f. 1897; total assets 12,674.6m. (Mar. 1993); Man. BRENT A. SCHWENKE.

Development Bank

Development Bank of American Samoa: POB 9, Pago Pago, AS 96799; tel. 633-4031; fax 633-1163; f. 1969; govt-owned and non-profit-making; cap. 6.4m. (1989); Chair. EUGENE G. C. H. REID; Pres. MANUTAFEA E. MEREDITH.

INSURANCE

American International Underwriters (South Pacific) Ltd: Pago Pago, AS 96799; tel. 633-4845.

National Pacific Insurance Ltd: Lumana'i Bldg, POB 1386, Pago Pago, AS 96799; tel. 633-4266; fax 633-2964; e-mail npi@samoatelco.com; f. 1977; Man. PETER MILLER.

Oxford Pacific Insurance Management: POB 1420, Pago Pago, AS 96799; tel. 633-4990; fax 633-2721; e-mail progressive_oxford@yahoo.com; f. 1977; represents major international property and life insurance cos; Pres. JULIAN E. ASHBY.

Trade and Industry

DEVELOPMENT ORGANIZATIONS

American Samoa Development Corporation: Pago Pago, AS 96799; tel. 633-4241; f. 1962; financed by private Samoan interests.

American Samoa Economic Advisory Commission: Pago Pago; Chair. JOHN WAIHEE.

Department of Commerce: Government of American Samoa, Pago Pago, AS 96799; tel. 633-5155; fax 633-4195; Dir ALIIMAU H. SCANLAN, Jr.

UTILITIES

American Samoa Power Authority: Pago Pago, AS 96799; tel. 644-2772; fax 644-5005; e-mail abe@aspower.com; supplies water and electricity throughout the islands; also manages sewer and solid waste collection.

MAJOR COMPANIES

COS Samoa Packing: POB 957, Pago Pago, AS 96799; tel. 644-5272; fax 644-2290; e-mail cos@samoatelco.com; US-owned; tuna-canning; Human Resources Man. ALFONSO PETE GALEA'I.

StarKist Samoa: Pago Pago, AS 96799; tuna-canning.

Transport

ROADS

There are about 150 km (93 miles) of paved and 200 km (124 miles) of secondary roads. Non-scheduled commercial buses operate a service over 350 km (217 miles) of main and secondary roads. There were an estimated 5,900 registered motor vehicles in the islands in 1996.

SHIPPING

There are various passenger and cargo services from the US Pacific coast, Japan, Australia (mainly Sydney) and New Zealand, that call at Pago Pago, which is one of the deepest and most sheltered harbours in the Pacific. Inter-island boats provide frequent services between Samoa and American Samoa.

Polynesia Shipping: POB 1478, Pago Pago AS 96799; tel. 633-1211; fax 633-1265; e-mail polyship@samoatelco.com.

CIVIL AVIATION

There is an international airport at Tafuna, 11 km (7 miles) from Pago Pago, and smaller airstrips on the islands of Ta'u and Ofu.

Samoa Aviation: POB 280, Pago Pago Int. Airport, Pago Pago, AS 96799; tel. 699-9106; fax 699-9751; e-mail samoaair@aol.com; f. 1986; operates service between Pago Pago and Samoa, Tonga and Niue; Pres. and Chair. JAMES PORTER.

Tourism

The tourist industry is encouraged by the Government, but suffers from the cost and paucity of air services linking American Samoa with its main sources of custom, particularly the USA. Pago Pago is an important mid-Pacific stop-over for large passenger aircraft. An estimated 21,366 tourists visited the islands in 1996. In that year 41.1% of tourists came from the USA, 18.9% from New Zealand, 7.1% from the United Kingdom, 6.9% from Australia, 3.7% from both Germany and Tonga, 3.1% from both China and the Philippines and 2.2% from India. In 1992 there were some 542 hotel beds available in the islands. The industry earned an estimated US $10m. in 1998. Tourist arrivals totalled 49,060 in 1999.

Office of Tourism: Convention Center, POB 1147, Pago Pago, AS 96799; tel. 633-1091; fax 633-2092; e-mail amsamoa@amsamoa.com; internet www.amsamoa.com/tourism; Dir SINIRA T. LUTU FUIMAONO.

Defence

The USA is responsible for the defence of American Samoa. The US Pacific Command is based in Hawaii, but the territory receives regular naval visits and assistance in surveillance of its waters.

Education

Education is compulsory for children between six and 18 years of age. The education system is based on the US pattern of eight years' attendance at an elementary school and four years' enrolment at a high school. In 1996 there were 32 consolidated elementary or primary schools, nine high schools and a community college. The Government's early childhood education division provides facilities for all children between three and five years of age. In 1996 pre-school facilities were available in 59 village centres. In the same year total enrolment in primary and secondary schools was 13,595 pupils, and the community college had 1,049 students. In 2000 there were 4,645 pupils attending secondary schools, and 1,474 were enrolled at the American Samoa Community College. Budgetary expenditure on education (and culture) in 1988/89 was US $30.4m., equivalent to 25.3% of total expenditure.

GUAM

Physical and Social Geography

Guam, the largest and southernmost of the Mariana Islands, covers an area of 549 sq km (212 sq miles). The island comprises a northern, coralline, limestone plateau and a mountainous area in the south, of volcanic origin, rising to some 395 m. It is situated about 2,400 km east of the Philippines, and its nearest neighbour is the Northern Mariana Islands, to the north. Guam has a tropical climate, with a mean annual temperature of 30°C (85°F), the hottest months being May and June. Most rain falls from July to October, and the island is sometimes subject to tropical storms and typhoons. The population is multiracial: some 45% are the indigenous Chamorro, 25% Filipino and 15% US immigrants. Most inhabitants profess the Christian religion, the largest denomination being Roman Catholic. Chamorro and, particularly, English are widely spoken and are both official languages. The population was recorded by the US Census Bureau 2000, as 154,805 excluding members of the US armed forces stationed on the island. The capital is Hagåtña (formerly Agaña).

History

The ancestors of the Micronesians first settled in Guam and the other Mariana Islands some 4,000 years ago. A society of matrilineal clans evolved. Members of a Spanish expedition, under the Portuguese navigator Fernão Magalhães (Ferdinand Magellan), were the first Europeans to discover Guam, visiting the island in 1521, during a voyage that accomplished the first circumnavigation of the globe. The island was claimed by Spain in 1565 and the first Jesuit missionaries arrived in 1668. The native Micronesian population is estimated to have fallen from 100,000 in 1521 to fewer than 5,000 in 1741, owing largely to a combination of massacres by the Spaniards and exposure to imported diseases. The present-day Chamorro population are the descendants of the Micronesians, mingled with Spaniards and immigrant Filipinos. Following the Spanish–American War of 1898, Spain ceded Guam to the USA, and then sold the other Mariana Islands to Germany. Japan obtained a League of Nations mandate over the German islands, including the Caroline and Marshall Islands, in 1919. Japanese forces seized Guam in 1941, but the island was recaptured by US troops in 1944.

Guam is an Unincorporated Territory of the USA: the population are US citizens, but do not take part in US presidential elections, and not all the provisions of the US Constitution apply. The territory has been organized, however, under a constitutional or organic act. The island, previously the responsibility of the US Navy, was transferred to the Department of the Interior in 1950, when the territory was granted its Constitution, and formally placed under the Secretary of the Interior's full jurisdiction in 1951. In 1970 the island elected its first Governor, and in 1972 a new law gave Guam one Delegate to the US House of Representatives. The Delegate may vote only in committee. In November 1986 a Democratic majority was elected in the Legislature, but the Republican candidates were elected as Delegate and Governor. The latter, Joseph Ada, was re-elected as Governor in November 1990.

In 1987 the previous Governor of Guam, Ricardo Bordallo, was found guilty on charges of bribery, extortion and conspiracy to obstruct justice. He claimed that the prosecution had been politically motivated, and, in October 1988, Bordallo won an appeal and his sentence of imprisonment was overturned. Bordallo was, however, convicted on two subsidiary charges. He and his family remained popular: in November 1987 his wife, Madeleine, was elected to the Guam Legislature, and was a strong, though unsuccessful, contender as the Democratic candidate at gubernatorial elections in November 1990, following Bordallo's suicide in January of that year.

At elections held in November 1988 and November 1990 the Democrats retained their majority in the unicameral Legislature. Ben Blaz, a Republican, was re-elected as Guam's non-voting Delegate to the US Congress on both occasions.

In September 1976, meanwhile, an island-wide referendum decided that Guam should maintain close ties with the USA, but that negotiations should be held to improve the island's status. In a further referendum in 1982, in which only 38% of eligible voters participated, the status of commonwealth was the most favoured of six options, attracting 48% of the votes cast. In August 1987, in a referendum held on the provisions of a draft law aimed at conferring the status of Commonwealth on the Territory, voters approved the central proposal, while rejecting articles empowering the Guam Government to restrict immigration and granting the indigenous Chamorro people the sole right to determine the island's future political status. In a further referendum, later that year, both outstanding provisions were approved. Negotiations between the Guam Commission for Self Determination and the USA continued throughout the late 1980s and early 1990s.

At legislative elections in November 1992 the Democrats increased their representation to 14 seats, while the Republicans secured only seven. Robert Underwood was elected as the new Democrat Delegate to the US House of Representatives, replacing the Republican Ben Blaz.

The issue of immigration re-emerged in early 1993, when a pressure group campaigning for the rights of indigenous people, 'Chamoru Nation', appealed for stricter control to be introduced. Members of the group expressed concern that the increased numbers of immigrants entering Guam would threaten the Chamorro culture as well as the political and social stability of the island.

In January 1994 the US Congress approved legislation providing for the transfer of 3,200 acres of land on Guam from federal to local control. This was a significant achievement for the Government of Guam, which had campaigned consistently for the return of 27,000 acres (some 20% of Guam's total area), appropriated by US military forces after the Second World War. Chamorro rights activists, however, opposed the move, claiming that land should not be transferred to the Government of Guam, but rather to the original landowners.

At gubernatorial elections in November 1994 the Democrat Carl Gutierrez defeated his Republican opponent, Tommy Tanaka, winning 54.6% of total votes cast, while Madeleine Bordallo (also a Democrat) was elected to the position of Lieutenant-Governor. Legislative elections held concurrently also resulted in a Democratic majority, with candidates of the party securing 13 seats, while the Republicans won eight. Robert Underwood was re-elected unopposed as Delegate to the US House of Representatives.

Reports that Chamorro rights activists had initiated a campaign for independence from the USA were denied by the Governor in July 1995. In September, however, at the Fourth World Conference on Women in Beijing, People's Republic of China, the Lieutenant-Governor, Madeleine Bordallo, expressed her support for the achievement of full autonomy for Guam and for the Chamorro people's desire for decolonization.

It was reported in 1995 that the US President, Bill Clinton, had appointed a team of Commonwealth negotiators to review the draft Guam Commonwealth Act. In late 1999 the proposals were still awaiting a full hearing in the US Congress, despite considerable pressure from the Democrat Governor, Carl Gutierrez, for a serious debate on Guam's political status. However, evidence of the US Government's renewed interest in the Act was reported in early 1997, although officials denied suggestions that this apparent increase in co-operation was as a result of the Territory's substantial financial contribution to Clinton's re-election campaign in 1996. Reports in mid-1996 that the US Government was seeking to have Guam removed from the UN's list of Non Self-Governing Territories prompted representatives of the Guam Landowners' Association to warn that consideration of the Commonwealth Act should not be viewed as a full debate on self-determination, and to reiterate their belief in the Chamorro people's right to autonomy. Guam's self-styled Commission on Decolonization was established in 1997, headed by the Governor. A plebiscite on Guam's political status was scheduled for September 2002.

At elections in November 1996 Republican members regained a majority in the Legislature, winning 11 seats, while Democrat candidates secured 10 seats. In a referendum held concurrently voters approved a proposed reduction in the number of Senators from 21 to 15 (effective from November 1998), and plans to impose an upper limit (2.5% of total budgetary expenditure) on legislative expenses. However, a proposal to restrict the number of terms that Senators can seek to serve in the Legislature was rejected by voters. Guam's Delegate to the US House of Representatives, Robert Underwood, was re-elected unopposed.

In March 1998 delegates from several Pacific island nations and territories met in Hawaii to discuss possible methods of controlling the increasing population of brown tree snakes in Guam. The reptile, which was accidentally introduced to the island from New Guinea after the Second World War, has been responsible for severe power cuts, as a result of climbing electricity lines, as well as major environmental problems (including the decimation of native bird populations); it was feared that, if left unchecked, the snakes could spread to other islands in the region. In 2002 government researchers from the US Department of Agriculture announced plans to poison the snakes using dead mice filled with a proprietary painkiller.

In June 1998 US authorities approved changing the name of the capital from Agaña to Hagåtña. The change was effected in order to reflect more accurately the original Chamorro language name for the town.

Robert Underwood was re-elected, with 70.2% of total votes, as Guam's Delegate to the US House of Representatives on 3 November 1998, defeating Manuel Cruz, who secured 20.1% of the votes. Concurrent gubernatorial and legislative elections resulted in the return to office, as Governor, of Carl Gutierrez, and, as Lieutenant-Governor, of Madeleine Bordallo. (In December former Governor Joseph Ada alleged that Gutierrez's victory had been achieved by fraudulent means, and later in the month a Guam court invalidated the election result and ordered a new poll to be held. In February 1999, however, the Superior Court of Guam found that no electoral malpractice had taken place and confirmed the appointments of Gutierrez and Bordallo.) In elections to the legislature, where the number of seats had been reduced from 21 to 15, 12 candidates of the Republican Party and three candidates of the Democratic Party were returned as Senators.

US President Bill Clinton visited Guam in November 1998. During his visit President Clinton approved the transfer of some 1,300 ha of federal land to the local administration and undertook to accelerate the transfer of a further 2,020 ha of former US air force and navy land. In August 2001 the US Army announced plans to move some combat weaponry and equipment stored in Europe to bases in Guam, as well as in Taiwan and Hawaii.

In mid-1999 it was announced that Guam was no longer able to support the growing numbers of illegal immigrants from the People's Republic of China, some 500 having arrived between April and June alone, seeking refugee status. The immigrants were to be diverted to and detained in the nearby Northern Mariana Islands, the immigration laws of which differ from those of Guam.

At elections held on 7 November 2000, Underwood was re-elected as Guam's delegate to the US House of Representatives, winning 78.1% of votes cast. At legislative elections, held concurrently, eight candidates of the Republican Party and seven candidates of the Democratic Party were returned as senators. The next elections were scheduled for November 2002.

In July 2002 Marilyn Manibusan, a former Senator, and another former government official were indicted by a federal grand jury. They were charged with conspiring to extort real estate developers.

Economy

In 2000, according to estimates by the Bank of Hawaii, Guam's gross national product (GNP), at current prices, was US $2,772.8m., equivalent to US $16,575 per head. Between 1988 and 1993, it was estimated, GNP increased, in real terms, at an average rate of some 10% per year. Real GNP rose by 3.9% in 1994. In 1990–2000, according to World Bank figures, the population increased at an average annual rate of 1.5%.

Guam's economy is based on tourism and the export of fish and handicrafts. The fishing industry expanded greatly during the late 1980s, and in 1997 there were 1,098 vessels operating from Guam (mainly Japanese, Korean and Taiwanese, fishing in the waters of the Federated States of Micronesia). The fishing catch totalled 37,486 metric tons in 1997. Fruit and vegetables, including watermelons, maize, cucumbers, bananas, runner beans, aubergines, squash, tomatoes and papaya are grown mainly for local consumption. Pigs are an important source of meat. Agriculture (including forestry, fishing and mining) engaged only 0.5% of the employed labour force in 2000.

Industrial enterprises, including a petroleum refinery (no longer operational) and textile and garment firms, were established in the early 1970s, in addition to existing smaller-scale manufacturing of soft drinks, confectionery and watches. Boat-building is also a commercial activity on Guam. The industrial sector accounted for some 15% of GDP in 1993. Construction engaged 9.7% and manufacturing (including textile and garment production and boat-building) 2.0% of the employed labour force in 2000. The Government has attempted to diversify Guam's economy by attracting increased foreign investment, principally from Asian manufacturers. Guam is a duty-free port and an important distribution point for goods destined for Micronesia. Re-exports constitute a high proportion of Guam's exports, major commodities being petroleum and petroleum products, iron and steel scrap, and eggs.

In 2001 some 1,159,426 tourists (of whom almost 78% were Japanese) visited the island, a decline of 10% compared with the previous year. Tourism earned some US $1,908m. in 1999. It accounted for more than 10% of government revenue and 18% of GDP in 1994. The services sector as a whole engaged some 87.8% of the employed labour force in 2000. The federal and territorial Governments alone employed 27.0% of workers in that year.

The Territory consistently records a visible trade deficit. Total exports were valued at US $75.7m. in 1999, compared with US $47.9m. in 1994, in which year imports of petroleum and petroleum products alone cost US $163.7m. In 1999 total imports (excluding petroleum and petroleum products) were valued at US $38.7m. In 1999 some 53.9% of Guam's exports were purchased by Japan, 24.5% by the Federated States of Micronesia, 6.2% by Palau and 2.0% by Taiwan. In 1991 the majority of imports were provided by the USA (44.6%) and Japan (31.6%).

In 1998 total budgetary expenditure stood at US $206.1m. and revenue at US $503.7m. In 2000 federal expenditure on the territory totalled US $888m., comprising military spending of US $451m., non-defence expenditure of US $388m. and other federal assistance of US $49m. The Government's total stood at US $440m. in early 2002. Unemployment declined to 1.9% of the labour force in mid-1989, the lowest rate in the USA and its territories, but stood at some 13.0% by 2001. The average annual rate of inflation was 10.1% in 1990–95, and stood at 5.3% in 1995. Consumer prices decreased by 0.5% in 1998 and by 0.3% in 1999.

In the 1990s Guam's economy benefited from increased foreign investment, notably from Japan and the Republic of Korea. Much of this investment resulted in the rapid expansion of the tourist industry from the 1980s. Guam continues to receive considerable financial support from the USA (direct federal grants totalled US $143m. in 1997) in addition to revenue from US military installations on the islands (which accounts for some US $400m. annually). In July 1999 it was announced that Guam was to receive a further US $5m. in funding from the USA. Considerable interest in establishing an 'offshore' financial centre on Guam was expressed in 1992. The development of such a centre, however, was dependent upon Guam's achievement of commonwealth status, which would allow the introduction of new tax laws. Guam's economy, particularly its important tourist industry, was seriously affected by the Asian financial crisis in the late 1990s. The announcement by the National Space Development Agency of Japan in mid-2001 that it was to build a rocket-tracking station on Guam was expected to enhance the territory's attraction to international investors. The project was scheduled for completion in November 2002. The tourism sector was badly affected by the repercussions of the terrorist attacks on the USA in September 2001, compounded by the continued economic difficulties in Japan (the principal source of visitors), but the number of tourist arrivals was expected to recover in 2002.

Guam is a member of the Pacific Community (formerly the South Pacific Commission) and an associate member of the UN's Economic and Social Commission for Asia and the Pacific (ESCAP). In early 1996 Guam joined representatives of the other countries and territories of Micronesia at a meeting in Hawaii, at which a new regional organization, the Council of Micronesian Government Executives, was established. The new body aimed to facilitate discussion of economic developments in the region and to examine possibilities for reducing the considerable cost of shipping essential goods between the islands.

Statistical Survey

Sources (unless otherwise stated): Department of Commerce, Government of Guam, 102 M St, Tiyan, GU 96913; tel. 475-0321; fax 477-9031; e-mail commerce@ns.gov.gu; internet www.admin.gov.gu/commerce/economy.

AREA AND POPULATION

Area: 549 sq km (212 sq miles).

Population: 133,152 at census of 1 April 1990; 154,805 (males 79,181; females 75,624) at census of 1 April 2000.

Density (2000): 282.0 per sq km.

Ethnic Groups (2000 census): Chamorro 57,297; Filipino 40,729; White 10,509; Other Asian 9,600; part-Chamorro 7,946; Chuukese 6,229; Total (incl. others) 154,805.

Principal Towns (population at 2000 census): Hagåtña (capital), 1,122; Tamuning 10,833; Mangilao 7,794; Yigo 6,391; Astumbo 5,207; Barrigada 4,417.

Births, Marriages and Deaths (2000, unless otherwise indicated): Registered live births 3,766 (birth rate 24.4 per 1,000); Registered marriages (1998) 1,514; Registered deaths 648 (death rate 4.2 per 1,000). Sources: National Center for Health Statistics, US Department of Health and Human Services; Office of Vital Statistics, Department of Public Health and Social Services, Government of Guam.

Expectation of Life (UN estimates, years at birth, 1997): 75.0 (males 73.0, females 77.0). Source: UN, *Statistical Yearbook for Asia and the Pacific*.

Economically Active Population (persons aged 16 and over, excl. armed forces, 2000 census): Agriculture, forestry, fishing and mining 296; Manufacturing 1,155; Construction 5,532; Transport, storage and utilities 4,319; Wholesale and retail trade 9,506; Arts, entertainment, recreation, accommodation and food services 10,278; Finance, insurance and real estate 3,053; Public administration 6,527; Education, health and social services 8,412; Professional, scientific, management and administrative services 4,277; Other services 3,698; Total employed 57,053 (males 31,609, females 25,444); Unemployed 7,399 (males 4,097, females 3,302); Total labour force 64,452 (males 35,706, females 28,746). Source: US Department of Commerce, *2000 Census of Population and Housing*.

AGRICULTURE, ETC.

Principal Crops: ('000 lb, 1998): Aubergines 111; Tomatoes 53; Cucumbers 332; Runner beans 224; Watermelons 265; Bittermelon 45; Bananas 49; Pepino 62; Papaya 54; Squash 91.

Livestock (head, 1998): Chickens 12,791; Pigs 3,025; Cattle 206; Goats 359; Horses 64; Water buffalo 43.
Source: Department of Agriculture, Government of Guam.

Livestock Products ('000 lb, 1997): Poultry meat 2,683; Hen eggs 40,057.

2000 ('000 metric tons, estimates): Hen eggs 1*.

* Source: FAO.

Fishing (metric tons, live weight, 1999): Capture 223 (Common dolphinfish 40, Wahoo 19, Skipjack tuna 19, Yellowfin tuna 15); Aquaculture 230* (Mozambique tilapia 150, Philippine catfish 20, Milkfish 28, Banana Prawn 25); Total catch 453.

* FAO estimate.
Source: FAO, *Yearbook of Fishery Statistics*.

INDUSTRY

Electric Energy (million kWh, estimates): 825 in 1996; 825 in 1997; 830 in 1998. Source: UN, *Industrial Commodity Statistics Yearbook*.

FINANCE

Currency and Exchange Rates: US currency is used. For details, see section on the Northern Mariana Islands.

Budget (estimates, US $ million, 1998): *Expenditure*: General Government 55.3; Defence 71.8; Community services 19.8; Recreation 5.9; Public health 3.3; Transportation 10.1; Environmental Protection 5.2; Economic development 5.8; Transfers to persons 17.7; Total (incl. others) 206.1. *Revenue*: Taxes 451.1; Federal contributions 2.9; Interest received 46.1; Total (incl. others) 503.7.

Cost of Living (Consumer Price Index; base: July–September 1996 = 100): 101.3 in 1997; 100.8 in 1998; 100.5 in 1999. Source: Cost of Living Office, Economic Research Center, Department of Commerce, Government of Guam.

Gross Domestic Product (US $ million at current prices): 3,020.5 in 1998; 2,718.5 in 1999; 2,772.8 in 2000. Source: Office of Insular Affairs, US Department of the Interior.

EXTERNAL TRADE

Principal Commodities (US $ '000, 1999): *Imports**: Travel goods, handbags, etc. 7,607; Meat, prepared or preserved 1,043; Bakery products 804; Watches 1,558. Jewellery articles 1,392; Meat and edible offals (beef, pork and poultry) 2,475; Fruits (incl. nuts) and vegetables 1,335; Passenger motor cars 2,767; Non-alcoholic beverages 1,304; Beer 1,516; Cigars and cigarettes 830; Total (incl. others) 38,709. *Exports*: Fish (chilled, fresh, frozen, dried and salted) 40,720; Tobacco, cigars, etc. 5,123; Petroleum oils and gases 15,183; Perfumes and toilet waters 2,726; Passenger motor cars 2,367; Total (incl. others) 75,748.

* Does not include figures for imports of petroleum and petroleum products (totalling US $163,685,000 in 1994).

Principal Trading Partners (US $ '000): *Imports (1991)*: Hong Kong 7,977.3; Japan 42,357.4; Korea, Republic 5,357.5; Philippines 3,281.3; Singapore 1,622.0; USA 59,837.8; Total (incl. others) 134,231.0. *Exports (1999)*: Hong Kong 1.5; Japan 40.8; Federated States of Micronesia 18.6; Palau 4.7; Papua New Guinea 0.9; Singapore 0.8; Taiwan 1.5; Thailand 1.4; USA 1.4. Total (incl. others) 75.7. Source: UN, *Statistical Yearbook for Asia and the Pacific*, and Economic Research Center, Department of Commerce, Government of Guam.

TRANSPORT

Road Traffic (registered motor vehicles, 1999): Private cars 65,887, Taxis 537, Buses 627, Goods vehicles 26,220, Motorcycles 633, Total (incl. others) 99,618. Source: Department of Revenue and Taxation, Government of Guam.

International Sea-borne Shipping (estimated freight traffic, '000 metric tons, 1991): Goods loaded 195.1; Goods unloaded 1,524.1; Goods transhipped 314.7. *Merchant Fleet* (total displacement, '000 grt at 31 December 1992): 1. Source: Lloyd's Register of Shipping.

Air Cargo ('000 lb): 36,691 in 1998.

TOURISM

Foreign Tourist Arrivals: 1,137,026 in 1998; 1,161,803 in 1999; 1,288,002 in 2000.

Tourist Arrivals by Country of Residence (2000): Japan 1,048,813; Korea, Republic 87,070; Taiwan 39,451; USA 41,664; Total (incl. others) 1,279,243. Note: Figures refer to air arrivals only. Arrivals by sea totalled 8,759. Source: Guam Visitors Bureau.

Tourism Receipts (US $ million): 2,361 in 1998; 1,908 in 1999. Source: World Tourism Organization.

COMMUNICATIONS MEDIA

Radio Receivers (1997): 221,000 in use*.

Television Receivers (1997): 106,000 in use*.

Telephones (2000): 80,300 main lines in use†.

Mobile Cellular Telephones (2000): 27,200 subscribers†.

Internet Users (estimate, 1999): 5,000†.

Daily Newspapers (1997): 1 (circulation 24,457).

Non-daily Newspapers (1988): 4 (estimated circulation 26,000)*.

* Source: UNESCO, *Statistical Yearbook*.
† Source: International Telecommunication Union.

EDUCATION

Institutions (public schools only, 1997/98): Elementary 24; Middle school 6; Senior high 5; Business colleges (private) 1; Guam Community College; University of Guam.

Teachers (public schools only, 1998/99): Elementary 1,063; Secondary 1,010.

Enrolment (public schools only, 1998/99): Elementary 16,102; Middle school 7,205; Senior high 8,364; Guam Community College 189; University of Guam 3,748;

Source: Department of Education, Government of Guam, and University of Guam.

Directory

The Constitution

Guam is governed under the Organic Act of Guam of 1950, which gave the island statutory local power of self-government and made its inhabitants citizens of the United States, although they cannot vote in presidential elections. Their Delegate to the US House of Representatives is elected every two years. Executive power is vested in the civilian Governor and the Lieutenant-Governor, first elected, by popular vote, in 1970. Elections for the governorship occur every four years. The Government has 48 executive departments, whose heads are appointed by the Governor with the consent of the Guam Legislature. The Legislature consists of 15 members elected by popular vote every two years (members are known as Senators). It is empowered to pass laws on local matters, including taxation and fiscal appropriations.

The Government

(September 2002)

Governor: Carl T. C. GUTIERREZ (Democrat—took office 1 March 1995; re-elected 3 November 1998 and 7 November 2000).

Lieutenant-Governor: MADELEINE Z. BORDALLO.

GOVERNMENT OFFICES

Government offices are located throughout the island.

Office of the Governor: POB 2950, Adelup, Hagåtña, GU 96932; tel. 475-8931; fax 477-4826; e-mail governor@mail.gov.gu; internet ns.gov.gu.

Department of the Interior, Office of Insular Affairs (OIA): Hagåtña, GU 96910; tel. 472-7279; fax 472-7309; Field Representative KEITH A. PARSKY.

Department of Administration: POB 884, Hagåtña, GU 96932; tel. 475-1101; fax 475-6788; e-mail doa@ns.gov.gu.

Department of Agriculture: 192 Dairy Rd, Mangilao, GU 96923; tel. 734-3942; fax 734-6569; e-mail agr@ns.gov.gu.

Department of Commerce: 102 M St, Tiyan, GU 96913; tel. 475-0321; fax 477-9031; e-mail commerce@mail.gov.gu; internet www.admin.gov.gu/commerce.

Department of Corrections: POB 3236, Hagåtña, GU 96932; tel. 734-4668; fax 734-4990; e-mail doc@mail.gov.gu.

Department of Customs and Quarantine: 1503 Central Ave Tiyan, Barrigada, GU 96921; tel. 475-6202; fax 475-62207; e-mail iperedo@ns.gov.gu.

Department of Education: POB DE, Hagåtña, GU 96932; tel. 475-0457; fax 472-5003; e-mail rtainato@doe.edu.gu; internet www.doe.edu.gu;

Department of Labor: POB 9970, Tamuning, GU 96931; tel. 475-0101; fax 477-2988; e-mail labor@ns.gov.gu; internet www.labor.gov.gu.

Department of Land Management: POB 2950, Hagåtña, GU 96932; tel. 475-5252. fax 477-0883; e-mail dlm@mail.gov.gu; internet www.gov.gu/dlm.

Department of Law: Suite 2-200E, Judicial Ctr. building, 120 West O'Brien Drive, Hagåtña, GU 96910; tel. 475-3324; fax 475-2493; e-mail law@ns.gov.gu; internet www.justice.gov.gu/dol.

Department of Parks and Recreation: POB 2950, 13-8 Seagull Ave, Tiyan, Hagåtña, GU 96932; tel. 475-6296; fax 472-9626; e-mail dpr@gov.gu; internet www.gov.gu/dpr.

Department of Public Health and Social Services: POB 2816, Hagåtña, GU 96932; tel. 735-7102; fax 734-5910; e-mail dennisr@mail.gov.gu; internet www.admin.gov.gu/pubhealth.

Department of Public Works: 542 North Marine Drive, Tamuning, GU 96911; tel. 646-4388; fax 649-6178; e-mail dpwdir@ns.gov.gu.

Department of Revenue and Taxation: POB 23607, Guam Main Facility, 13-1 Mariner Drive, Tiyan, Hagåtña, GU 96921; tel. 475-1817; fax 472-2643; e-mail revtax@ns.gov.gu; internet www.gov.gu/revtax.

Department of the Treasury: PDN Bldg, Suite 404, 238 Archbishop Flores St, Hagåtña, GU 96910.

Department of Youth Affairs: POB 23672, Guam Main Facility, GU 96921; tel. 734-2597; fax 734-7536; e-mail ddell@ns.gov.gu.

Legislature

GUAM LEGISLATURE

The Guam Legislature has 15 members, directly elected by popular vote for a two-year term. Elections took place in November 2000, when the Republican Party won eight seats and the Democratic Party seven.

Speaker: TONY UNPINGCO.

CONGRESS

Guam elects a Delegate to the US House of Representatives. An election was held in November 1998, when the Democrat candidate, Robert Underwood, was re-elected as Delegate.

Delegate: ROBERT UNDERWOOD, US House of Representatives, 2428 Rayburn HOB, Washington, DC 20515, USA; tel. (202) 225-1188; fax (202) 226-0341.

Judicial System

Attorney-General: JOHN F. TARANTINO.

Supreme Court of Guam: Suite 300, Guam Judicial Center, 120 West O'Brien Drive, Hagåtña, GU 96910; tel. 475-3162; fax 475-3140; e-mail justice@guamsupremecourt.com; internet www.guamsupremecourt.com.

District Court of Guam: 4th floor, US Courthouse, 520 West Soledad Ave, Hagåtña, GU 96910; Judge appointed by the President of the USA. The court has the jurisdiction of a Federal district court and of a bankruptcy court of the United States in all cases arising under the laws of the United States. Appeals may be made to the Court of Appeals for the Ninth Circuit and to the Supreme Court of the United States.

Presiding Judge: JOHN S. UNPINGCO.

Superior Court of Guam: 120 West O'Brien Drive, Hagåtña, GU 96910; tel. 475-3544; internet www.justice.gov.gu/superior; Judges are appointed by the Governor of Guam for an initial eight-year term and are thereafter retained by popular vote. The Superior Court has jurisdiction over cases arising in Guam other than those heard in the District Court.

Presiding Judge: ALBERTO C. LAMORENA III.

There are also Probate, Traffic, Domestic, Juvenile and Small Claims Courts.

Religion

About 90% of the population are Roman Catholic, but there are also members of the Episcopal (Anglican) Church, the Baptist churches and the Seventh-day Adventist Church. There are small communities of Muslims, Buddhists and Jews.

CHRISTIANITY

The Roman Catholic Church

Guam comprises the single archdiocese of Agaña. The Archbishop participates in the Catholic Bishops' Conference of the Pacific, based in Fiji, and the Federation of Catholic Bishops' Conferences of Oceania, based in New Zealand.

At 31 December 2000 there were 150,563 adherents in Guam.

Archbishop of Agaña: Most Rev. ANTHONY SABLAN APURON, Chancery Office, Cuesta San Ramón 196B, Hagåtña, GU 96910; tel. 472-6116; fax 477-3519; e-mail arch@ite.net.

BAHÁ'Í FAITH

National Spiritual Assembly: POB 20280, Guam Main Facility, Hagåtña, GU 96921; tel. 828-8639; fax 828-8112; mems resident in 19 localities in Guam and 10 localities in the Northern Mariana Islands.

The Press

NEWSPAPERS AND PERIODICALS

Bonita: POB 11468, Tumon, GU 96931; tel. 632-4543; fax 637-6720; f. 1998; monthly; Publr IMELDA SANTOS; circ. 3,000.

Directions: POB 27290, Barrigada, GU 96921; tel. 635-7501; fax 635-7520; f. 1996; monthly; Publr JERRY ROBERTS; circ. 3,800.

Drive Guam: POB 3191, Hagåtña, GU 96932; tel. 649-0883; fax 649-8883; e-mail glimpses@kuentos.guam.net; internet www.glimpsesofguam.com; f. 1991; quarterly; Publr STEPHEN V. NYGARD; circ. 20,000.

Guam Business News: POB 3191, Hagåtña, GU 96932; tel. 649-0883; fax 649-8883; e-mail glimpses@kuentos.guam.net; internet www.glimpsesofguam.com; f. 1983; monthly; Publr STEPHEN V. NYGARD; Editor MAUREEN MARATITA; circ. 2,600.

Guam Tribune: POB EG, Hagåtña, GU 96910; tel. 646-5871; fax 646-6702; Tue. and Fri.; Publr MARK PANGILINAN; Man. Editor ROBERT TEODOSIO.

Hospitality Guahan: POB 8565, Tamuning, GU 96931; tel. 649-1447; fax 649-8565; e-mail ghra@ghra.org; internet www.ghra.org; f. 1996; quarterly; circ. 3,000.

Latte Magazine: Tamuning, GU 96911; tel. 649-7736; fax 649-7737; e-mail editor@lattemag.com; internet www.lattemagazine.com; f. 1995; quarterly; Publr Manny Crisostomo Publications, Inc; circ. 40,000.

Pacific Daily News and **Sunday News:** POB DN, Hagåtña, GU 96932; tel. 471-9711; fax 472-1512; e-mail news@pdnguam.com; internet www.pdnguam.com; f. 1944; Publr LEE P. WEBBER; Man. Editor RINDRATY LIMTIACO; circ. 26,999 (weekdays), 25,115 (Sunday).

The Pacific Voice: POB 2553, Hagåtña, GU 96932; tel. 472-6427; fax 477-5224; f. 1950; Sunday; Roman Catholic; Gen. Man. TEREZO MORTERA; Editor Rev. Fr HERMES LOSBANES; circ. 6,500.

TV Guam Magazine: 237 Mamis St, Tamuning, GU 96911; tel. 646-4030; fax 646-7445; f. 1973; weekly; Publr DINA GRANT; Man. Editor EMILY UNTALAN; circ. 15,000.

NEWS AGENCY

United Press International (UPI) (USA): POB 1617, Hagåtña, GU 96910; tel. 632-1138; Correspondent DICK WILLIAMS.

Broadcasting and Communications

TELECOMMUNICATIONS

Guam Educational Telecommunication Corporation—KGTF: POB 21449, Guam Main Facility, Barrigada, GU 96921; tel. 734-2207; fax 734-5483; e-mail kgtfl2@ite.net.

Guam Telephone Authority: POB 9008, Tamuning, GU 96931; tel. 646-1427; fax 649-4821; e-mail gtagm@ite.net; internet www.gta.guam.net; Chair. PEDRO R. MARTINEZ; Gen. Man. RALPH TAITANO.

BROADCASTING

Radio

K-Stereo: POB 20249, Guam Main Facility, Barrigada, GU 96921; tel. 477-9448; fax 477-6411; operates on FM 24 hours a day; Pres. EDWARD H. POPPE; Gen. Man. FRANCES W. POPPE.

KGUM/KZGZ: 111 Chalan Santo, Hagåtña, GU 96910; tel. 477-5700; fax 477-3982; e-mail rex@spbguam.com; internet www.radiopacific.com; Chair. and CEO REX SORENSEN; Pres. JON ANDERSON.

KOKU-FM: 508 West O'Brien Drive, Hagåtña, GU 96910; tel. 477-5658; fax 472-7663; operates on FM 24 hours a day; Pres. LEE M. HOLMES; Gen. Man. ERNIE A. GALITO.

Radio Guam (KUAM): POB 368, Hagåtña, GU 96910; tel. 637-5826; fax 637-9865; e-mail kellykel@94jam2.com; internet www.kuam.com; f. 1954; operates on AM and FM 24 hours a day; Pres. PAUL M. CALVO; Gen. Man. JOEY CALVO.

Trans World Radio Pacific (TWR): POB CC, Hagåtña, GU 96932; tel. 477-9701; fax 477-2838; e-mail ktwr@twr.org; internet www.guam.net/pub/twr; f. 1975; broadcasts Christian programmes on KTWR and one medium-wave station, KTWG, covering Guam and nearby islands, and operates five short-wave transmitters reaching most of Asia, Africa and the Pacific; Pres. THOMAS LOWELL; Station Dir MICHAEL DAVIS.

Television

Guam Cable TV: 530 West O'Brien Drive, Hagåtña, GU 96910; tel. 477-7815; fax 477-7847; f. 1987; Pres. LEE M. HOLMES; Gen. Man. HARRISON O. FLORA.

KGTF—TV: POB 21449 Guam Main Facility, Barrigada, GU 96921; tel. 734-3476; fax 734-5483; e-mail kgtf12@ite.net; f. 1970; cultural, public service and educational programmes; Gen. Man. GERALDINE 'GINGER' S. UNDERWOOD; Operations Man. BENNY T. FLORES.

KTGM—TV: 692 Marine Dr, Tamuning 96911; tel. 649-8814; fax 649-0371.

KUAM—TV: POB 368, Hagåtña, GU 96932; tel. 687-5826; fax 637-9865; internet www.kuam.com; f. 1956; operates colour service; Gen. Man. JOEY CALVO.

Finance

(cap. = capital; res = reserves; = dep. = deposits; m. = million; brs = branches; amounts in US dollars)

BANKING

Commercial Banks

Allied Banking Corpn (Philippines): POB CT, Hagåtña, GU 96932; tel. 646-9143; fax 649-5002; e-mail abcguam@kuentos.guam.net; Man. NOEL L. CRUZ; 1 br.

Bank of Guam: POB BW, 134 W. Soledad Ave, Hagåtña, GU 96932; tel. 472-5300; fax 477-8687; e-mail customerservice@bankofguam.com; internet www.bankofguam.com; f. 1972; cap. 89m., res 11.3m., dep. 592m. (1998); Chair. ANTHONY A. LEON GUERRERO; Chair. JESUS S. LEON GUERRERO; 23 brs.

Bank of Hawaii (USA): POB BH, Hagåtña, GU 96932; tel. 479-3603; fax 479-3777; Exec. Vice-Pres. RON LEACH; Vice-Pres. THOMAS MICHELS; 3 brs.

BankPacific, Ltd.: 151 Aspinall Ave, POB 2888, Hagåtña, GU 96932; tel. 477-2671; fax 477-1483; e-mail philipf@bankpacific.com; internet www.bankpacific.com; f.1954; Pres. and CEO PHILIP J. FLORES; Exec. Vice-Pres. MARK O. FISH; 4 brs in Guam, 1 br. in Palau; 1 br. in Northern Mariana Islands.

Citibank NA (USA): 402 East Marine Drive, POB FF, Hagåtña, GU 96932; tel. 477-2484; fax 477-9441; Vice-Pres. RASHID HABIB; 2 brs.

Citizens Security Bank (Guam) Inc: POB EQ, Hagåtña, GU 96932; tel. 479-9000; fax 479-9090; Pres. and CEO DANIEL L. WEBB; 4 brs.

First Commercial Bank (Taiwan): POB 2461, Hagåtña, GU 96932; tel. 472-6864; fax 477-8921; Gen. Man. YAO DER CHEN; 1 br.

First Hawaiian Bank (USA): POB AD, 194 Hernan Cortes Ave, Hagåtña, GU 96910; tel. 477-8811; fax 472-3284; Vice-Pres. and Man. (Hagåtña) JOHN K. LEE; 2 brs.

First Savings and Loan Association (FSLA): 140 Aspinal Street, Hagåtña, GU 96910; affiliated to Bank of Hawaii; 6 brs.

HSBC Ltd (Hong Kong): POB 27C, Hagåtña, GU 96932; tel. 647-8588; fax 646-3767; CEO GUY N. DE B. PRIESTLEY; 2 brs.

Metropolitan Bank and Trust Co (Philippines): GCIC Bldg, 414 W Soledad Ave, Hagåtña, Guam 96913; tel. 477-9554; fax 477-8834; e-mail mbguam@metrobank.com.ph; f. 1975; Sen. Man. BENNETH A. REYES.

Union Bank of California (USA): 194 Hernan Cortes Ave, POB 7809, Hagåtña, GU 96910; tel. 477-8811; fax 472-3284; Man. KINJI SUZUKI; 2 brs.

CHAMBER OF COMMERCE

Guam Chamber of Commerce: Ada Plaza Center, Suite 102, 173 Aspinall Ave, POB 283, Hagåtña, GU 96932; tel. 472-6311; fax 472-6202; e-mail gchamber@guamchamber.com.gu; Pres. ELOISE R. BAZA; Chair. CARL PETERSON.

Trade and Industry

DEVELOPMENT ORGANIZATION

Guam Economic Development Authority (GEDA): Guam International Trade Center Bldg, Suite 511, 590 South Marine Drive, Tamuning, GU 96911; tel. 647-4332; fax 649-4146; f. 1965; e-mail gedamp@iftech.net; internet www.investguam; Administrator EDWARD G. UNTALAN.

EMPLOYERS' ORGANIZATION

Guam Employers' Council: 718 North Marine Drive, Suite 201, East-West Business Center, Upper Tumon, GU 96913; tel. 649-6616; fax 649-3030; e-mail tecinc@netpci.com; internet www.ecouncil.org; f. 1966; private, non-profit asscn providing management development training and advice on personnel law and labour relations; Exec. Dir JOSEPH BORJA.

UTILITIES

Electricity

Guam Energy Office: 1504 East Sunset Boulevard, Tiyan, GU 96913; tel. 477-0538; fax 477-0589; e-mail guamenergy@kuentos.guam.net.

Guam Power Authority: POB 2977, Hagåtña, GU 96932; tel. 649-6818; fax 649-6942; e-mail gpa@ns.gov.gu; autonomous government agency; supplies electricity throughout the island.

Water

Guam Waterworks Authority: POB 3010, Hagåtña, GU 96932; tel. 479-7823; fax 649-0158.

Public Utility Agency of Guam: Hagåtña, GU 96910; supplies the majority of water on the island.

TRADE UNIONS

Many workers belong to trade unions based in the USA such as the American Federation of Government Employees and the American Postal Workers' Union. About 4,000 of the island's working population of 65,380 (in 1991) belong to unions.

Guam Federation of Teachers (GFT): Local 1581, POB 2301, Hagåtña, GU 96932; tel. 735-4390; fax 734-8085; e-mail gft@netpci.com; f. 1965; affiliate of American Federation of Teachers; Pres. JOHN T. BURCH; Vice-Pres. BARBARA M. BLAS; 2,000 mems.

Guam Landowners' Association: Hagåtña; Sec. RONALD TEEHAN.

Transport

ROADS

There are 885 km (550 miles) of public roads, of which some 675 km (420 miles) are paved. A further 685 km (425 miles) of roads are classified as non-public, and include roads located on federal government installations.

SHIPPING

Apra, on the central western side of the island, is one of the largest protected deep-water harbours in the Pacific.

Port Authority of Guam: 1026 Cabras Highway, Suite 201, Piti, GU 96925; tel. 477-5931; fax 477-2689; e-mail pag4@netpci.com; internet www.netpci.com/~pag4; Gen. Man. FRANCISCO P. CAMACHO.

Ambyth, Shipping and Trading Inc: PAG Bldg, Suite 205, 1026 Cabras Highway, Piti, GU 96925; tel. 477-8000; fax 472-1264; agents for all types of vessels and charter brokers; Vice-Pres. GREGORY R. DAVID.

Atkins, Kroll Inc: 443 South Marine Drive, Tamuning, GU 96911; tel. 646-1866; f. 1914; Pres. ALBERT P. WERNER.

COAM Trading Co Ltd: PAG Bldg, Suite 110, 1026 Cabas Highway, Piti, GU 96925; tel. 477-1737; fax 472-3386.

Interbulk Shipping (Guam) Inc: Bank of Guam Bldg, Suite 502, 111 Chalan Santo Papa, Hagåtña, GU 96910.

Maritime Agencies of the Pacific Ltd: Piti, GU 96925; tel. 477-8500; fax 477-5726; e-mail rehmapship@kuentos.guam.net; f. 1976; agents for fishing vessels, cargo, dry products and construction materials; Pres. ROBERT E. HAHN.

Pacific Navigation System: POB 7, Hagåtña, GU 96910; f. 1946; Pres. KENNETH T. JONES, Jr.

Tucor Services: Tamuning, GU 96931; tel. 646-6947; fax 646-6945; e-mail tucor@tucor.com; general agents for numerous dry cargo, passenger and steamship cos; Pres. MICHELLE BOLL.

CIVIL AVIATION

Guam is served by the A. B. Won Pat International Airport. Work to triple the size of the airport terminal, at a cost of US $253m., was completed in late 1996.

Guam International Airport Authority: POB 8770, Tamuning, GU 96931; tel. 646-0300; fax 646-8823; e-mail rolendal@guamcell.net; internet www.airport.guam.net.

Continental Airlines: POB 8778, Tamuning, GU 96931; tel. 649-6594; fax 649-6588; internet www.continental.com; f. 1968, as Air Micronesia, by Continental Airlines (USA); name changed 1992; hub operations in Guam and Saipan (Northern Mariana Islands); services throughout the region and to destinations in the Far East and the mainland USA; Pres. BILL MEEHAN; Chair. D. BREEDING.

Freedom Air: POB 1578, Hagåtña, GU 96932; tel. 472-8009; fax 4728080; e-mail freedom@ite.net; f. 1974; Man. Dir JOAQUIN L. FLORES Jr.

Tourism

Tourism is the most important industry on Guam. In 2000 there were 1,288,002 visitor arrivals (including 8,759 arrivals by sea), compared with 769,876 in 1990. In 2000 some 82.0% of arrivals by air were visitors from Japan, 6.8% from the Republic of Korea, 3.3% from the USA and 3.1% from Taiwan. Most of Guam's hotels are situated in, or near to, Tumon, where amenities for entertainment are well-developed. Numerous sunken wrecks of aircraft and ships from Second World War battles provide interesting sites for divers. There were 10,110 hotel rooms on Guam at March 2001. A total of US $20.6m. was collected in hotel occupancy taxes in 2000. The industry as a whole earned some US $1,908m. in 1999.

Guam Visitors Bureau: 401 Pale San Vitores Rd, Tumon, GU 96911; tel. 646-5278; fax 646-8861; e-mail guaminfo@visitguam.org; internet www.visitguam.org; Gen. Man. JAMES E. NELSON III.

Defence

Guam is an important strategic military base for the USA, with about 1,600 members of the Air Force, 1,850 naval personnel and 40 army personnel stationed there in August 2001. In April 1992 it had been reported that the USA was to expand its military installations on the island considerably to compensate for the closure of a major naval base in the Philippines, despite continued requests by the Governor that the bases be returned to civilian use. However, the US Naval Air Station, Brewer Field, was returned to the Government of Guam for civilian use in 1995.

Education

School attendance is compulsory from six to 16 years of age. There were 24 public elementary schools, six junior high and five senior high schools, as well as a number of private schools operating on the island in 1997/98. Total secondary enrolment in public schools in 1998/99 was 15,758 students. Some 3,748 students were enrolled in tertiary education in that year. In 1990 the rate of adult illiteracy was 1.0%. Government expenditure on education was US $8.7m. in 1998 (equivalent to 4.2% of total expenditure).

OTHER TERRITORIES

Baker and Howland Islands: The uninhabited Baker and Howland Islands lie about 60 km apart in the Central Pacific Ocean, just north of the Equator and some 2,575 km south-west of Honolulu, Hawaii (USA). Both are low-lying coral atolls without lagoons, some 2.5 km long, surrounded by narrow, fringing reefs. The islands were sighted by American vessels in the early 19th century, although there is evidence of previous Polynesian settlement on Howland. Baker Island (also then known as New Nantucket and Phoebe Island) was named by an American, Michael Baker, who visited the island in 1832 and 1839. Baker is sparsely vegetated. It was mined for guano in the late 19th century and a settlement, known as Meyerton, was established by the USA in 1935. Howland Island, to the north and a little west of Baker, has an area of some 162 ha and is more thickly vegetated, with several trees; it was reputedly named by the American whaler, Capt. George Netcher, after the look-out who first sighted the atoll. Howland was also mined for guano in the late 19th century and an American settlement, known as Itascatown, was established in 1935. An airfield (which is now unusable) was completed in 1937. In that year the aviatrix Amelia Earhart and her navigator were attempting to reach this airfield when their aircraft mysteriously disappeared. The lighthouse on the island is known as the Amelia Earhart Light. Both islands were evacuated in 1942, owing to Japanese air attacks. Baker and Howland Islands were claimed by the USA in 1857 and were made the responsibility of the Secretary of the Interior in 1936. Actual administrative authority was transferred to the US Fish and Wildlife Service as from 27 June 1974; both islands are national wildlife refuges. In 1990 legislation before Congress proposed that the islands be included within the boundaries of the State of Hawaii. Permission to land is required from the US Department of the Interior, Department of Fish and Wildlife and Parks, 1849 C St, NW, Washington, DC 20240; tel. (202) 208-3171; fax (202) 208-6965; internet www.doi.gov.

Jarvis Island: The uninhabited Jarvis Island lies just south of the Equator, about 2,090 km south of Hawaii (USA) and 160 km east of Baker and Howland Islands. The nearest inhabited territory is Christmas Island or Kiritimati, some 320 km to the north-east in Kiribati. Jarvis is a low, basin-shaped coral island, with a diameter of about 2 km. There is a narrow fringing reef, but sparse vegetation, owing to the limited rainfall. Although known previously, under a variety of names, the island was officially discovered by a British sailor, Capt. Brown. Like Baker and Howland, Jarvis Island was claimed for the USA in 1857 (pursuant upon the Guano Act of 1856), mined for guano and then abandoned in 1879. The United Kingdom annexed the island in 1889 and some further guano mining took place. The island was reclaimed for the USA when a group of US settlers landed in 1935 and founded the village of Millersville and a weather station for the benefit of trans-Pacific aviation. This settlement was evacuated in 1942. Legislation before Congress in 1990 proposed that the island be included within the State of Hawaii. Jarvis Island was placed under the jurisdiction of the US Department of the Interior in 1936 but, as a national wildlife refuge, has been administered by the Department of Fish and Wildlife and Parks since 1974 (address as above, under Baker and Howland Islands).

Johnston Atoll: Johnston Atoll lies in the Pacific Ocean, about 1,319 km west-south-west of Honolulu, Hawaii (USA), and comprises Johnston Island (population 327 in 1980), Sand Island (uninhabited) and two man-made islands, North (Akua) and East (Hikina). It has an area of 2.6 sq km (1.0 sq mile). The group was discovered by a passing British vessel in 1807. In 1858 conflicting claims to sovereignty were lodged by the USA and the Kingdom of Hawaii, and these remained unresolved until Hawaii became a US territory in 1898. Following a period of unsuccessful attempts to establish guano mining operations, Johnston Atoll was placed, in 1926, under the supervision of the US Department of Agriculture as a refuge and breeding ground for native birds. For strategic reasons, however, administrative control was transferred in 1934 to the US Department of the Navy, with the proviso that the islands' use as a bird sanctuary should continue. Operational control was transferred to the Department of the Air Force in 1948 but subsequently, in 1973, the Defense Nuclear Agency (DNA) assumed responsibility. In 1985 construction of a chemical weapons disposal facility began on the atoll and by 1990 it was fully operational. The building of the facility cost US 0.5m. In 1989 the US Government agreed to remove artillery shells containing more than 400 metric tons of nerve gas from the Federal Republic of Germany to the facility on Johnston Atoll. The shells were moved in late 1990, after an accelerated environmental review, and were due for destruction. This plan was a cause for considerable concern in the region, and prompted a variety of unsuccessful legal and diplomatic attempts to prevent the transfer of the weapons from Europe. In January 1995, following a series of fires and accidental chemical releases during the previous year, the US army announced that it was to seek an extension to the 30 August 1995 deadline, the date by which the 400,000 weapons stored on the island were due to be destroyed. A facility capable of performing atmospheric nuclear-weapons tests remains operational on the atoll. A hurricane that struck Johnston Island in August 1994 forced the evacuation of 1,105 civilian and military personnel and resulted in damage estimated at some US $15m. In early 1996 the destruction programme was accelerated, and by May of that year it was reported that all nerve gases stored on the atoll had been destroyed. However, 1,000 tons of chemical agents remained contained in land mines, bombs and missiles at the site. In December 2000 it was announced that the destruction of the remaining stock of chemical weapons had been completed, and that the facility was to close. Johnston Atoll has been designated a Naval Defense Sea Area and Airspace Reservation, and is closed to public access. The atoll had an estimated population of 173 in 1990. The atoll is administered, on behalf of the DNA, by The Commander, Johnston Atoll (FCDNA), APO San Francisco, CA 96035.

Kingman Reef: Kingman Reef, located about 1,500 km south-west of Honolulu, Hawaii (USA), comprises a triangular, atoll-like reef and shoal, measuring about 8 km long and 15 km wide. Although the reef was first discovered in 1798, its precise location remained uncharted until 1853. In 1856 it was claimed for the USA. Kingman Reef posed a considerable hazard to the increasing volume of Pacific shipping during the second half of the 19th century, and was the site of notable shipwrecks in 1874, 1888 and 1893. The US Government formally took possession of the Reef in 1922, and in 1934 it was placed under the jurisdiction of the US Department of the Navy. Declared a National Defense Area in 1941, Kingman Reef now forms a Naval Defense Sea Area and Airspace Reservation, and public access to within a 5-km limit is forbidden. Legislation before the US Congress in 1990 proposed the inclusion of Kingman Reef within the boundaries of the State of Hawaii. The area is administered by the US Department of Defense, Department of the Navy, The Pentagon, Washington, DC 20530; tel. (202) 695-9020; internet www.navy.mil.

Midway Island: Midway Island is a coral atoll formed on a volcanic sea-mount at one end of the Hawaiian chain of islands. Midway was discovered in 1859 and was formally declared a US possession in 1867. Previously known as Brooks Island, the US Navy renamed it in recognition of its geographical location on the route between the USA and Japan. The group consists of Sand Island, Eastern Island and several small islets within the reef, and lies 1,850 km north-west of Hawaii. Midway has an area of about 5 sq km (2 sq miles) and in 1983 had a population of 2,200, although by 1990 the total had declined to 13. Since the transfer of the islands' administration from the US Department of Defense to the Department of the Interior in October 1996, limited tourism is permitted. A national wildlife refuge was established on the atoll of Midway Island, under an agreement with the Department of Fish and Wildlife and Parks. The territory is home to many species of birds, notably the frigate or gooney bird. Legislation before Congress in 1990 proposed the inclusion of the territory within the State of Hawaii. The atoll is administered by the US Department of the Interior, Department of Fish and Wildlife and Parks, 1849 C St, NW, Washington, DC 20240; tel. (202) 208-3171; fax (202) 208-6965; internet www.doi.gov.

Palmyra: Palmyra is a privately-owned atoll of islands, usually uninhabited, located some 1,600 km south of Honolulu, Hawaii (USA), and about midway between there and American Samoa. The territory consists of about 50 islets and a total area of 100 ha, thick with vegetation, but never more than 2 m above sea level. The Kingdom of Hawaii annexed the atoll in 1862 and it was formally annexed by the USA, with Hawaii, in 1898. The United Kingdom had annexed the atoll in 1889, and renewed British interest resulted in the USA dispatching a naval vessel to claim formal possession in 1912. Palmyra was, however, excluded from the boundaries of the State of Hawaii in 1959, and remains an unorganized and unincorporated territory of the USA, under the civil administration of the Department of the Interior since 1961. A Judge Cooper of Honolulu purchased the atoll in 1911 and 1912, and his heirs remain in possession of two islets, known as the Home Islets, following the sale of the bulk of the atoll to the Fullard-Leo family. During the Second World War the US Navy used and adapted the atoll and, until 1961, the US Air Force maintained the now unserviceable airstrip. The islands remain uninhabited. In 1990 legislation before Congress proposed the inclusion of Palmyra within the boundaries of the State of Hawaii. In mid-1996 it was announced that the owners (the Fullard-Leo family in Hawaii) were to sell the atoll to a US company, which, it was believed, planned to establish a nuclear waste storage facility in the Territory. The Government of Kiribati expressed alarm at the proposal, owing to Palmyra's proximity to the islands, and reiterated its intention to seek the reinclusion of the atoll within its own national boundaries. However, in June one of the Hawaiian Representatives to the US Congress proposed legislation in the US House of Representatives to prevent the establishment of such a facility, and a US government official subsequently announced that the atoll would almost certainly not be used for that purpose. In May 2000 it was announced that the island was to be purchased by The Nature Conservancy (internet www.tnc.org); the sale, for some US $30m., was confirmed in November 2000. The lagoons and surrounding waters within the 12 nautical mile zone of US territorial seas were transferred to the US Fish and Wildlife service in January 2001, and designated a National Wildlife Refuge.

Wake Island: Wake Island is a coral atoll consisting of three islets, Wake, Wilkes and Peale. The atoll, situated on a submerged volcano, lies in the Pacific on the direct route from Hawaii to Hong Kong, about 3,200 km west of Hawaii and 2,060 km east of Guam. The group is 7.2 km long and 2.4 km wide, and covers less than 8 sq km (3 sq miles). Wake Island may have been sighted by a Spanish expedition in 1568, but, following its formal discovery by a British vessel (commanded by Capt. William Wake, for whom the island is named) in 1796, its exact location was lost and not re-established until 1841 by a US naval expedition. The US Government took formal possession in 1899. In 1935 Wake Island was placed under the control of the US Department of the Navy, and in the same year a commercial seaplane base was established to service trans-Pacific passenger flights. The island was occupied by Japanese forces during the Second World War. Administrative responsibility passed to the US Department of the Interior in 1962, but the territory is actually administered by the US Air Force. In 1972 the responsibility for civil administration was delegated to the General Counsel of the Air Force, the agent being the Military Commander of Wake Island. In 1983 the population was 1,600, and in 1988 was estimated to be almost 2,000. These numbers have declined in recent years. In 1990 legislation before the US Congress proposed the inclusion of Wake Island within the boundaries of the territory of Guam. However, the Republic of the Marshall Islands, some 500 km to the south of Wake, then decided to exert its claim to the atoll, known as Enenkio to the Micronesians. President Amata Kabua of the Marshall Islands declared that Wake Island was a site of great importance to the traditional chiefly rituals of his islands and that the Marshall Islands, having achieved a measure of independence from the USA, could now claim the territory. Plans by a US company, announced in 1998, to establish a large-scale nuclear waste-storage facility on the atoll were condemned by environmentalists and politicians in the region. The group is administered by the US Department of Defense, Department of the Air Force (Pacific/East Asia Division), The Pentagon, Washington, DC 20330; tel. (202) 694-6061; fax (703) 696-7273; internet www.af.mil.

Vanuatu

Physical and Social Geography

The Republic of Vanuatu (formerly the New Hebrides) comprises an archipelago of some 80 islands covering a land area of 12,190 sq km (4,707 sq miles), including the Banks and Torres Islands, stretching from south of Solomon Islands to Hunter and Matthew Islands, east of New Caledonia, 900 km in all. The islands range in size from 12 ha to 3,600 sq km. The islands have rugged mountainous interiors, with narrow coastal strips where most of the inhabitants dwell. Three islands have active volcanoes on them. The climate is tropical. Temperatures in Port Vila, the capital, range from 16°C (61°F) to 33°C (92°F). There is a rainy season between November and April, and the islands are vulnerable to cyclones during this period; south-east trade winds blow between May and October. The population was estimated to be 192,910 at mid-2001. Most of the inhabitants (approximately 95%) are Melanesians, and there are small numbers of Europeans, Micronesians and Polynesians. The national language is Bislama (a Pidgin English), and English and French are also official languages. Most of the population profess Christianity, the largest denomination being Presbyterian. The capital is Port Vila, which is located on the island of Efate. The capital's population increased dramatically during the late 1980s and early 1990s, and was estimated to total some 31,000 by mid-2001.

History

The New Hebrides were governed until 1980 by an Anglo-French condominium, which was established in 1906. Under this arrangement there were three elements in the structure of administration: the British national service, the French national service and the condominium (joint) departments. Each power was responsible for its own citizens and other non-New Hebrideans who chose to be *ressortissant* of either power. Indigenous New Hebrideans were not permitted to claim either British or French citizenship. The result of this was two official languages, two police forces, three public services, three courts of law, three currencies, three national budgets, two resident commissioners in Port Vila (the capital) and two district commissioners in each of the four districts.

After the Second World War New Hebridean concern regarding the alienation of native land (more than 36% of the New Hebrides was owned by foreigners) prompted local political initiatives. Na-Griamel, one of the first political groups to emerge, had its source in cult-like activities. In 1971 Na-Griamel leaders petitioned the UN to prevent more land sales at a time when territory was being sold to US interests for development as tropical tourist resorts. In 1972 the New Hebrides National Party (NHNP) was formed with support from Protestant missions and covert support from British interests. French interests established the Union des communautés néo-hébridaises in 1974. In the same year discussions in the United Kingdom culminated in the replacement of the Advisory Council, established in 1957, by a Representative Assembly. Of the Assembly's 42 members, 29 were directly elected; this did not, however, fulfil nationalist aspirations.

The Representative Assembly was dissolved in early 1977 following a boycott by the NHNP, which had changed its name to the Vanuaaku Pati (VP) in 1976. However, the VP succeeded in reaching an agreement with the condominium powers for new elections for the Representative Assembly to be held, based on universal suffrage for all seats.

In July 1977 it was announced, at a conference of New Hebridean, British and French delegates, that the New Hebrides would become independent in 1980, following a referendum and elections. The VP, demanding immediate independence, boycotted this conference, refused to participate in the November 1977 elections and declared a 'people's provisional government'. A smaller (39-member) Assembly was, none the less, elected, and a degree of self-government was introduced in early 1978 with the creation of a Council of Ministers and of the office of Chief Minister, together with the inauguration of a single New Hebrides public service to replace the French, British and condominium services. In December 1978 a Government of National Unity was formed, with Fr Gérard Leymang, a Roman Catholic priest, as Chief Minister.

In November 1979 new elections resulted in victory for the VP, which secured 26 of the Assembly's 39 seats. The outcome provoked rioting on Espiritu Santo by Na-Griamel supporters, who threatened non-Santo 'foreigners'. In late November Fr Walter Lini, the President of the VP, was elected Chief Minister.

In June 1980 Jimmy Stevens, the leader of Na-Griamel, declared Espiritu Santo independent of the rest of the New Hebrides, renaming the island the 'Independent State of Vemarana'. Members of his movement, armed with bows and arrows (and allegedly assisted by French *colons* and supported by private US business interests), imprisoned government officers and police, who were later released and allowed to leave the island, together with other European and indigenous public servants. Later in the same month a peace-keeping force comprising about 200 British troops was dispatched to Espiritu Santo; this was strongly criticized by the French, who would not permit Britain's unilateral use of force on Espiritu Santo.

In mid-July 1980, however, agreement was reached between the two condominium powers and Lini, and the New Hebrides became independent within the Commonwealth, under the name of Vanuatu, on 30 July 1980. The former Deputy Chief Minister, George Kalkoa, who adopted the surname Sokomanu ('leader of thousands'), assumed the largely ceremonial post of President. Lini became Prime Minister. Shortly after independence, the Republic of Vanuatu signed a defence pact with Papua New Guinea, and in August units of the Papua New Guinea defence force replaced the British and French troops on Espiritu Santo and arrested the Na-Griamel rebels.

In February 1981 the French ambassador to Vanuatu was expelled, following the deportation from New Caledonia of the VP Secretary-General, who had been due to attend an assembly of the New Caledonian Independence Front. France immediately withdrew aid to Vanuatu but it was subsequently restored, and a new French ambassador was appointed. In June 1982 Vanuatu laid claim to the small, uninhabited islands of Matthew and Hunter, lying about 200 km south-east of Vanuatu's southern island of Aneityum, thus greatly increasing the size of the country's exclusive economic zone. France disputed the claim.

At a general election in November 1983 the VP retained a majority in Parliament. George Sokomanu resigned as President in February 1984, after pleading guilty in court to the late payment of road taxes, but was re-elected in the following month.

In mid-1986 the Government announced that it was to establish diplomatic relations with the USSR and Libya, both of which had hitherto been without diplomatic representation in the South Pacific region. This development, together with the Government's continued support for the Kanak National Liberation Front in its efforts to secure independence for New Caledonia, alarmed many of Vanuatu's Western trading partners (notably Australia, New Zealand and the USA), and attracted criticism of Lini's non-aligned foreign policy.

In October 1986 Vanuatu was one of a group of South Pacific island states to sign a five-year fishing agreement with the USA, whereby the US tuna fleet was granted a licence to operate vessels within Vanuatu's exclusive fishing zone. In January 1987, after protracted negotiations (and despite vigorous opposition from the leaders of other political parties), Lini concluded a one-year fishing agreement with the USSR. This agreement caused considerable disquiet among Australian and US officials, who expressed concern over the growing Soviet presence in the South Pacific. Furthermore, the proposed opening of a Libyan diplomatic mission in Vanuatu provoked censure from the Governments of Australia and New Zealand, and in May of that year it was announced that the establishment of diplomatic relations with Libya was to be postponed indefinitely.

In October 1987 the Government expelled the French ambassador, who, it was alleged, had provided 'substantial financial assistance' to the opposition Union of Moderate Parties (UMP). Elections to an enlarged legislature were held in December, at which the VP secured 26 seats and the UMP took the remaining 20 seats. Following the election, the Secretary-General of the VP, Barak Sope, unsuccessfully challenged Lini for the party presidency, but later accepted a portfolio in the Council of Ministers.

Rioting broke out in Port Vila in May 1988, at the time of a demonstration to protest against a government decision to abolish a local land corporation. Lini accused Sope of provoking the riots, and dismissed his rival from the Council of Ministers. Australia, New Zealand and Papua New Guinea guaranteed military support to Lini's Government in the case of a deterioration in the political situation. In July Sope and four colleagues resigned from the VP and were subsequently dismissed from Parliament at Lini's behest. Accusing Lini and the parliamentary Speaker of acting unconstitutionally, 18 members of the UMP boycotted successive parliamentary sessions and were in turn dismissed. (The Supreme Court subsequently upheld Lini's action.) In September Sope and his colleagues announced the formation of a new political party, the

Melanesian Progressive Pati (MPP), and in the following month the VP expelled 128 of its members for allegedly supporting the new organization.

In October 1988 the Court of Appeal ruled as unconstitutional the dismissal from Parliament of Sope and his colleagues but upheld the expulsion of the 18 members of the UMP. In the following month Sope resigned from Parliament. By-elections for the vacated parliamentary seats were held in December, at which the VP increased its majority, but there was a low level of electoral participation; Sokomanu dissolved Parliament and announced that Sope would act as an interim Prime Minister, pending a general election to be held in February 1989. Lini immediately denounced Sokomanu's actions, and the Governments of Australia, New Zealand and Papua New Guinea refused to recognize the interim Government. The islands' police force remained loyal to Lini, and later in December Sokomanu, Sope and other members of the interim Government were arrested and charged with treason. Fred Timakata, the former Minister of Health, assumed the presidency in January 1989. In an attempt to ensure impartiality, a judge from Solomon Islands presided over trials, which were held in March: Sokomanu was sentenced to six years' imprisonment, while Sope and the leader of the parliamentary opposition, Maxime Carlot Korman, received five-year prison sentences, after having been convicted of seditious conspiracy and incitement to mutiny. However, representatives of the International Commission of Jurists, who had been present at the trials, criticized the court's rulings, and in April the Court of Appeal reversed the sentences, citing insufficient evidence for the convictions.

Major changes were effected within the Government in 1990, with Lini assuming the functions of several ministries. There was diminishing support for his premiership within the Council of Ministers, and in August 1991 a motion of 'no confidence' in Lini's leadership was approved at the VP's congress. Donald Kalpokas, the Secretary-General of the VP, was unanimously elected to replace Lini as President of the party. In September a motion of 'no confidence' in Lini was narrowly approved in Parliament, and Kalpokas was elected Prime Minister. Lini stated that he would challenge his opponents at the general election scheduled for December 1991, and formed the National United Party (NUP).

Following the election of Kalpokas as Prime Minister, further defections to Lini's newly-formed NUP resulted in a narrowing of the VP's majority to two seats. At the election in December 1991 the UMP obtained 19 seats, while the VP and NUP each won 10 seats, the MPP four and the Tan Union, Fren Melanesia and Na-Griamel one each. The leader of the UMP, Maxime Carlot Korman, was appointed Prime Minister, and, in an unexpected move, a coalition Government was formed between his party and Lini's NUP.

The election of Carlot, Vanuatu's first francophone Prime Minister, helped to improve the country's uneasy relationship with France. However, the new Government reaffirmed its support for the Kanak independence movement in the French territory of New Caledonia, at a meeting with Kanak leaders in July 1992. The statement followed threats by Lini to withdraw from the Government unless Carlot moderated his pro-French policies.

The NUP-UMP coalition was beset by internal problems during 1993. A disagreement over the composition of the Council of Ministers led Lini to declare the coalition invalid, causing several NUP members to resign from government office, while several others expressed support for Carlot. During the following 30 days (the period required formally to dissolve the coalition) and while Carlot was overseas, the UMP President, Serge Vohor, negotiated an agreement with Lini to re-establish the two parties in government. Upon his return, however, Carlot rejected the agreement, deciding instead to form an alliance with the 'breakaway' members of the NUP, who had remained in their ministerial posts.

At a presidential election on 14 February 1994 neither the UMP's candidate, Fr Luc Dini, nor Fr John Bani, who was supported by the opposition, attained the requisite two-thirds of total votes cast. The election was rescheduled for March, and in the intervening period an atmosphere of political uncertainty prevailed, as parties sought to form alliances and several politicians changed party allegiances. The VP subsequently agreed to vote with the ruling UMP, in return for a guaranteed role in a future coalition government. As a result of this agreement, the UMP's candidate, Jean-Marie Leye, was elected to the presidency with 41 votes (Bani won only five.) The VP subsequently withdrew its support for the UMP when the Prime Minister refused to offer the party more than one ministerial post; the VP had requested three.

In May 1994 the 'breakaway' members of the NUP who had remained in their ministerial posts, Sethy Regenvanu, Edward Tabisari and Cecil Sinker, were expelled from the party. They subsequently formed the People's Democratic Party (PDP), and later that month signed an agreement with the UMP to form a new coalition Government, the third since the election of December 1991. The UMP-PDP coalition held a total of 26 legislative seats.

In August 1994 Parliament approved legislation providing for the introduction of a new system of local government, and in mid-September 11 local councils were dissolved and replaced by six provincial governments. Elections to the newly-formed provincial authorities took place in the following month, at which the Unity Front (an opposition coalition comprising the VP, the MPP, Tan Union and Na-Griamel), the NUP and the UMP each won control of two councils. In October 1995 the election results in two councils were declared invalid, following evidence of irregularities in the voting, and a third authority was suspended.

Widespread controversy concerning a series of decisions taken by Leye led, in October 1994, to the granting of a restraining order to the Government by the Supreme Court against further actions by the President. Members of the Government and the judiciary had become increasingly alarmed by Leye's exercise of his presidential powers, which had included orders to free 26 criminals (many of whom had been convicted of extremely serious offences) and to appoint a convicted criminal to the position of Police Commissioner (on the recommendation of the Prime Minister). The Government was granted the restraining order pending the hearing of its application to the Supreme Court to overrule several of the President's recent decisions. In May Leye's decision to release the 26 criminals was ruled to have been unconstitutional and therefore invalid.

The issue of press freedom was prominent in late 1994 and early 1995, following allegations concerning the censorship of news reports at the government-controlled Vanuatu Broadcasting and Television Corporation. In April 1995 Carlot attracted severe criticism from the Vanuatu-based regional news agency, Pacnews, when he dismissed two senior government officials for making comments critical of the Government; journalists who reported the comments were threatened with dismissal. The Prime Minister's increasing reputation for intolerance of criticism was compounded by allegations that, as part of his Government's policy of reducing the number of employees in the public service, civil servants believed to be opposition sympathizers were among the first to lose their jobs.

In mid-1995 the Carlot administration was virtually alone in the region in not condemning France's decision to resume nuclear-weapons testing in French Polynesia. Within Vanuatu, the Government's stance was criticized by the opposition, who claimed that it did not reflect the views of the vast majority of ni-Vanuatu. Moreover, the country's reputation for media censorship was further damaged by a government ban on all reports of the tests that had not been approved by the Government for broadcast or publication.

A general election took place in November 1995. The Unity Front coalition (now comprising the VP, the MPP and Tan Union) won 20 of the 50 seats in the enlarged Parliament, the UMP secured 17 seats, the NUP won nine, Fren Melanesia and Na-Griamel each obtained one, and independent candidates won two seats. A period of intense political manoeuvring ensued, as the Unity Front and UMP each sought to form coalitions with other parties in an attempt to secure a parliamentary majority. The situation was compounded by the emergence of two factions within the UMP, one comprising the supporters of Carlot and another led by Serge Vohor (the party's President). The Carlot faction of the UMP and the Unity Front both sought the political allegiance of the NUP. The latter's decision to accept the offer of a coalition with the UMP effectively excluded the Unity Front (the grouping with the largest number of seats) from government, and, in protest, its members boycotted the opening of Parliament in December, thus preventing the holding of a vote on the formation of a new government. At a subsequent parliamentary session Vohor was elected as Prime Minister. In January 1996, however, the Unity Front filed petitions in the Supreme Court against 12 members of the Government (among them Vohor and Carlot), alleging irregularities in their election—including the transfer of substantial funds from France to UMP activists for use in local projects aimed at securing support for the party shortly before the election.

In February 1996 seven dissident UMP members of Parliament proposed a motion of 'no confidence' in Vohor, supported by 22 other opposition members. However, Vohor announced his resignation as Prime Minister, thus preventing the vote taking place. A parliamentary session to elect a new premier was abandoned as a result of a boycott by supporters of Vohor, who was reported to have retracted his resignation. However, in a further sitting, Carlot was elected as Prime Minister with 30 parliamentary votes. A climate of instability persisted, and 25 elected members boycotted the opening of Parliament in March, following a declaration by the Chief Justice that rejected Vohor's application for reinstatement as Prime Minister and upheld the election of Carlot to the position. At the opening session President Jean-Marie Leye recommended an urgent review of the islands' Constitution, which he believed to contain inadequate provision for the avoidance of prolonged political turmoil such as that which had followed the inconclusive general election.

In July 1996 a report published by the national ombudsman revealed a serious financial scandal involving the issuing of 10 bank guarantees with a total value of US $100m. The Minister of Finance, Barak Sope, who had issued the guarantees in April (allegedly against the advice of the Attorney-General), had been persuaded by an Australian financial adviser, Peter Swanson, that the scheme could earn the country significant revenue. Swanson, who left Vanuatu after securing the guarantees, was subsequently traced and charged with criminal offences relating to his dealings with Sope. (In February 1998 the Supreme Court found Swanson guilty on seven charges arising from the scandal, sentencing him to 18 months' imprisonment.) Carlot, meanwhile, rejected demands for his resignation for his compliance with the scheme and resisted considerable pressure to dismiss Sope and the Governor of the Reserve Bank of Vanuatu. In the following month, however, Sope was dismissed, following his defection to the opposition after Carlot had transferred him to the Ministry of Commerce, Trade and Industry.

In September 1996 a motion of 'no confidence' in the Government was approved by 28 of the 50 members of Parliament. Vohor was again elected Prime Minister and appointed Sope as his deputy. His coalition Government comprised the pro-Vohor faction of the UMP, the NUP, the MPP, Tan Union and Fren Melanesia.

A dispute by members of the 300-strong paramilitary Vanuatu Mobile Force (VMF) over unpaid allowances, dating from 1993, led to the cancellation of the annual Constitution Day celebrations in October 1996. When the Government failed to resolve the dispute, members of the VMF briefly abducted the President and Deputy Prime Minister to demand a settlement. Both Leye and Sope expressed sympathy for the VMF members. In the same month the Chief Justice, Charles Vaudin d'Imecourt, who had been the subject of numerous allegations of misconduct and partiality since 1995, was dismissed (and deported as an 'undesirable alien'), following his decision to issue arrest warrants against several members of the VMF. Similarly, Sope was replaced as Deputy Prime Minister by Donald Kalpokas, and Fr Walter Lini was appointed Minister of Justice. Following a further incident in November in connection with their pay dispute, in which an official from the Department of Finance was abducted and allegedly assaulted, Lini ordered the arrest of more than half of the members of the VMF (although most were later released). Vohor claimed that his Government's decision to arrest the VMF personnel had averted a military coup, and revealed that documentary evidence detailing the force's plans to seize power and to install a military administration had been discovered. In June 1999 18 VMF members were charged with the alleged kidnapping of a number of government officers in 1996. One was found guilty and was referred to a court martial for sentencing.

In March 1997 a memorandum of agreement was signed between the VP, the NUP and the UMP, the three parties of the newly-formed governing coalition. The defection in May, however, of five NUP members of Parliament, including two cabinet ministers, to the VP (thus increasing the VP's representation to 20 seats) led to the party's expulsion from the Government. As a result, a new coalition, comprising the UMP, the MPP, Tan Union and Fren Melanesia, was formed. The subsequent designation of a new Cabinet was controversial for the appointment of Barak Sope to the position of Deputy Prime Minister and Minister of Commerce, Trade and Industry. Sope had been described in January by the national ombudsman, Marie-Noëlle Ferrieux-Patterson, in a further report on the financial scandal of the previous year, as unfit for public office. Ferrieux-Patterson also recommended the resignation or dismissal of the newly-appointed Minister of Finance, Willie Jimmy, who, together with ex-Prime Minister Carlot, had in 1993 made illegal 'compensation' payments to the 23 members dismissed from Parliament following their boycott of the legislature in 1988. In July 1997 legal action was initiated to recover the estimated US $300,000 of public funds paid to the members of Parliament. In the same month it was reported that the Government was preparing to amend legislation governing the powers of the ombudsman, in an attempt to contain increasingly vociferous criticism of certain public figures. In August the Tonga-based Pacific Islands News Association awarded its annual Freedom of Information prize to Ferrieux-Patterson. The decision was criticized by the Government as an interference in the country's affairs.

In November 1997 Parliament approved a private member's bill seeking the repeal of the Ombudsman Act. (Although the office of the ombudsman is guaranteed under the Constitution, the repeal of the Act, promulgated in 1995, would effectively curb the influence of Ferrieux-Patterson at a time when she was about to release a number of reports apparently damaging to several prominent public figures.) However, President Leye refused to sign the legislation, referring the bill to the Supreme Court for adjudication on its constitutionality.

The instability that had characterized political life in Vanuatu since the inconclusive general election of 1995 culminated in a constitutional crisis in late November 1997, when Carlot filed a parliamentary motion of 'no confidence' in Vohor's administration. In order to prevent debate of the motion, the Government withdrew all legislation from Parliament, whereupon the Speaker, Edward Natapei, declared the legislative session closed. In response, Leye announced the dissolution of Parliament, citing the need to restore institutional stability, and set new elections for January 1998. The sponsors of the 'no confidence' motion, protesting that their constitutional rights had been infringed, appealed to the Supreme Court, which overturned the President's dissolution order and also counter-manded the dismissal, during the crisis, of Barak Sope and the Minister of Lands, Energy and Natural Resources, Sato Kilman. The issue of the dissolution was further referred to the Court of Appeal, which in early January ruled that Leye's order to dissolve Parliament had been within his constitutional competence. Parliament was thus dissolved, and an election set for 6 March.

Despite the vote to repeal the Ombudsman Act, Ferrieux-Patterson continued to publish reports condemning the activities of numerous prominent political figures, and, as the election approached, the Government increasingly criticized the ombudsman for interfering in politics. In addition to a series of reports issued in late 1997 and early 1998 that sought the prosecution of Vohor and several of his ministers for their alleged involvement with a South Korean business executive in a scheme to sell 80,000 passports to Asian nationals, at a cost of 40,000m. vatu, Ferrieux-Patterson accused the Government of appointing foreign nationals as honorary consuls and trade representatives in return for financial contributions. Furthermore, the revelation, in late December 1997, that Jimmy, as Minister of Finance, had appointed a number of his associates to the board of the Vanuatu National Provident Fund (VNPF), to which all workers are obliged to make pension contributions, and that public figures had obtained housing loans at preferential rates from the fund, prompted public outcry as workers demanded the return of their savings. In mid-January 1998 there was rioting and looting in the capital as police used tear gas to disperse protesters who had gathered outside the offices of the VNPF. The violence in Port Vila and also in Luganville prompted the Government to impose a state of emergency (which remained in force in some areas until mid-February). Almost 500 arrests were made during this time: among those detained were reportedly members of Parliament, government officials and civil servants who had joined the rioting. Meanwhile, a new board of directors of the VNPF was appointed, and it was announced that contributors would be permitted to withdraw their savings from the fund. (The subsequent increase in liquidity arising from such withdrawals by some 28,000 members resulted in considerable monetary instability in the weeks preceding the election.)

Following a campaign dominated by allegations of corruption, the general election, on 6 March 1998, resulted in a loss of power for the UMP. According to the official results, the VP won 18 seats, the UMP 12, the NUP 11, the MPP six and the Tanna-based John Frum Movement two. Carlot was the only member of the Vanuatu Republikan Pati, formed by the former Prime Minister in January, to be elected, the other two seats being won by independents. In mid-March the VP and NUP reached agreement on the formation of a coalition, and at the end of the month Parliament formally approved the appointment of Kalpokas as Prime Minister (also Minister of Foreign Affairs, the Comprehensive Reform Programme (CRP) and the Public Service), with Lini as Deputy Prime Minister and Minister of Justice and Internal Affairs.

In June 1998, despite strong opposition notably by the UMP, Parliament approved a new 'leadership code'. Regarded as a key element in ensuring greater accountability and transparency in public life in accordance with the CRP, the code defined clear guidelines for the conduct of state officials (including a requirement that all public figures submit an annual declaration of assets to Parliament), and laid down strict penalties for those convicted of corruption. Shortly beforehand, the Supreme Court upheld the repeal of the Ombudsman Act, as approved by Parliament in November 1997.

In February 1998 the Supreme Court found Peter Swanson guilty on seven charges arising from the bank guarantees scandal revealed in 1996, sentencing him to 18 months' imprisonment. Convictions on five of these charges, together with the custodial sentence, were upheld by the Court of Appeal in July 1998. In late September the Court of Appeal ruled that the dismissal of Charles Vaudin d'Imecourt as Chief Justice in 1996 had been inadmissible; a further ruling on compensation was expected.

In October 1998 Kalpokas expelled the NUP from the governing coalition, following reports that Fr Walter Lini, the party's leader, had organized a series of meetings with prominent members of the opposition, with the aim of forming a new coalition government which would exclude the VP. Fr Walter Lini died in February 1999. At elections in March 1999 Fr John Bani was chosen by the electoral college to succeed Jean-Marie Leye as President of Vanuatu.

The governing coalition was threatened in August 1999 by a decision by the National Council of the UMP to oppose participation in the Government. The Council issued a directive to the 17 members of Jimmy's faction to resign from the Kalpokas administration. Following their refusal to comply with the directive, the National Council acted to suspend the members in October. However, later that month the suspensions were overruled by the Supreme Court. The two factions of the UMP had previously attempted reunification, but negotiations had stalled over the demands of Vohor's faction for two of the four ministerial positions held by Jimmy's faction. The UMP achieved reunification in November 2000.

At the end of August 1999 four by-elections took place, three of which were won by opposition parties, thus eliminating the Government's majority in Parliament. In November the Government staged a boycott of Parliament to avoid a proposed vote of 'no confidence' by opposition parties against the Kalpokas administration (at which time both the Government and the opposition controlled 26 seats in Parliament). However, the subsequent defection of two members to the opposition forced the resignation of Kalpokas prior to a 'no confidence' motion on 25 November. The Speaker, Edward Natapei, announced his resignation shortly afterwards, and Paul Rentari of the NUP was elected as his replacement. The leader of the MPP, Sope, was elected to lead a new Government, defeating Natapei (the newly-appointed President of the VP) with 28 votes to 24. Sope formed a five-party coalition Government, comprising the MPP, the NUP, the Vohor faction of the UMP, the VRP and the John Frum Movement. The composition of the new Council of Ministers was swiftly announced; it included Vohor as Minister of Foreign Affairs and Carlot as Minister of Lands and Mineral Resources, both of whom, with Sope, had been the subject to critical reports by the ombudsman. The new Government pledged to reduce the country's dependence on foreign advisers, review the recently-introduced value-added tax and ensures that adequate services were delivered to rural communities.

In May 2000 Parliament approved controversial legislation (the Public Services Amendment Bill and the Government Amendment Bill) giving the Government direct power to appoint and dismiss public servants. The opposition criticized the changes, claiming that they contravened the principles of the CRP (a programme of economic measures supported by the Asian Development Bank—ADB). President John Bani subsequently referred both pieces of legislation to the Supreme Court, which, in August, ordered that he approve them. The ADB reacted angrily to the development, arguing that it allowed for political bias in the public sector, and threatened to withhold further funds from Vanuatu. The bank's stance served to perpetuate an ongoing dispute between the organization and the Vanuatu Government, which had often expressed the view that the bank imposed harsh conditions in return for its finance.

An incident in August 2000 in which the Deputy Prime Minister, Reginald Stanley, was allegedly involved in the serious assult of two people and in causing criminal damage to property while drunk in a bar in Port Vila led to Stanley's dismissal from the post. He was replaced by Minister of Trade Development, James Bule. In October, however, the ombudsman recommended his complete dismissal from the Cabinet (he had retained the portfolios of infrastructure and public utilities).

In September 2000 opposition leader, Edward Natapei, invited the Vohor faction of the UMP to join the opposition and form a new government. Vohor declined the offer, saying that his priority was the stability of the current Government. The resignation of a VP member in the following month prevented the success of a 'no confidence' motion proposed in the Prime Minister. A further planned motion of 'no confidence' in the Prime Minister was withdrawn in December. In October the Government was forced to defend a controversial plan, which allowed a Thai company, Apex, to pay off a portion of government debt, allegedly in return for tax-haven privileges. The President of Apex, Amarendra Nath Ghosh, was also Vanuatu's recently-appointed honorary consul to Thailand. In January 2001 the Government deported Mark Neil-Jones, the publisher of the independent newspaper, *Trading Post*, on the grounds of instigating instability in the country. (The *Trading Post* had recently published several critical articles about the Government, including reports on the Government's financial dealings with Nath Ghosh.) However, the Supreme Court reversed the decision, declaring that the deportation order was illegal, and Neil-Jones was allowed to return to the country. An investigation was subsequently launched into the circumstances of the deportation.

In late January 2001 three members of the UMP resigned from the party, further reducing the Government's majority. The Government's problems intensified in March after the withdrawal of the UMP from the ruling coalition. Opposition attempts to vote on a motion of 'no confidence' were delayed as Sope initiated legal action against the motion, and the Speaker, Paul Ren Tari, refused to allow the vote while legal action was pending. The Chief Justice, however, ordered the vote to proceed, and after further postponements by the Speaker, the Sope Government was voted out of office on 13 April. A new Government, led by Edward Natapei of the VP, was elected. The incoming administration, a coalition of the VP and UMP, was sworn in on 17 April and pledged to continue the reform programme and to restore investor confidence. One of the Government's first acts was to remove Nath Ghosh from his diplomatic position. Vohor was appointed Deputy Prime Minister. In early May Parliament held an extraordinary session to debate a motion to remove Ren Tari as Speaker because of his conduct during the political crisis. Ren Tari responded by suspending Natapei, along with five other Members of Parliament who held cabinet posts, for breaching parliamentary procedure. Despite an order by the Chief Justice that they be allowed to return to Parliament to continue the extraordinary session, Ren Tari refused to open the legislature while he appealed to the Supreme Court against the order. In response, Ren Tari and his two deputies were arrested and charged with sedition. In May a new Speaker, Donald Kalpokas, President of the UMP, was elected, thus reducing Natapei's majority in Parliament to one. In September 2001 opposition leader Sope tabled a motion of 'no confidence' against the ruling coalition but was defeated.

In November 2001 Sope was ordered to appear in court to answer charges that he had forged two government-supported Letters of Guarantee, worth US $23m., while he was Prime Minister. It was reported that police were also investigating the activities of the former Minister of Finance, Morkin Steven, whose signature appeared on the documents. Meanwhile, Sope was under investigation for possible involvement in the illegal issuing of diplomatic passports and in connection with allegations of bribery. He was, however, able to contest the general election due to take place later in that year as the preliminary hearings into the forgery charges, originally scheduled to take place in February 2002, were postponed.

In March 2002 Parliament was dissolved after the Supreme Court ruled that its four-year term had expired. Prime Minister Natapei remained in charge of a 'caretaker' Government until the general election, scheduled for May 2002. Also in March it was announced that the newly established People's Progressive Party (PPP) and Fren Melanesia were to form a coalition with the ruling NUP to contest the forthcoming election. The announcement contradicted a statement issued earlier in the same month by the NUP, in which the party had declared that it would stand independently. Meanwhile, the Government dismissed the board of the Vanuatu Broadcasting and Television Corporation (VBTC), claiming that the organization had failed to consult with it over a number of important decisions and that it had incurred unnecessary costs. Later in March a total of 27 VBTC employees returned to work, having been dismissed in October 2001 for participating in a strike. They claimed to have been reinstated by the newly appointed government board—a claim denied by the board—and refused to leave. The individuals alleged to be responsible for the reinstatement subsequently resigned. Negotiations to settle the ongoing disputes began in April, amid allegations of political interference into the affairs of the company by government appointees. It was reported that the general election was to be monitored by an independent group of observers. The future of the Comprehensive Reform Programme was widely perceived to be the main issue at stake in the electoral campaign.

The general election was held on 2 May 2002. A total of 327 candidates contested the 52 seats available in Parliament. A record 136 candidates stood as independents, prompting Natapei to comment prior to the election that if Vanuatu were to attain political stability the electoral constituency should vote only for party candidates. Bad weather and problems with ballot papers delayed voting in some constituencies. After some initial uncertainty, it was announced that the UMP had won 15 seats in the new Parliament and that the VP had secured 14. The NUP won eight seats and the MPP, the Green Party and the VRP secured three apiece. The remaining seats went to independent candidates. In accordance with the terms of the coalition agreement, however, the VP was permitted to nominate the next Prime Minister. The new Government was formed on 3 June 2002, with Natapei duly re-elected Prime Minister and Henry Taga appointed as Speaker of Parliament.

In July 2002 former Prime Minister Barak Sope was convicted of fraud by the Supreme Court and sentenced to three years in prison. It was alleged soon afterwards that New Zealand had interfered in Vanuatu's internal affairs by funding the investigation that had led to Sope's conviction. In early August, following the controversial appointment of Mael Apisai as Vanuatu's new Police Commissioner, disaffected police officers staged a raid during which they arrested Apisai, Attorney-General Hamilton Bulu and 14 other senior civil servants on charges of seditious conspiracy. Following an investigation, the charges were abandoned owing to a lack of evidence. Prime Minister Natapei subsequently assumed the police and VMF portfolios from the Minister of Internal Affairs, Joe Natuman, in what was thought to be an attempt to distance Natuman from some members of the police force, with whom he had reportedly become too closely involved. Later in the month members of the VMF surrounded the police headquarters in Port Vila to serve arrest warrants on 27 of those who had been involved in the raid, including the acting police commissioner, Holis Simon, and the commander of the VMF, Api Jack Marikembo. Shortly afterwards, in an attempt to bring an end to the hostilities, the Government signed an agreement with representatives from the police department and the VMF during a traditional Melanesian reconciliation ceremony. The police officers involved, who had been suspended from their posts, were reinstated, the police and the VMF pledged to make no further arrests and it was agreed that Apisai's appointment would be reviewed by a newly appointed police services commission. At the same time it was decided that the allegations of conspiracy that had been brought against the 15 officials initially arrested would be considered by the judicial authorities. A new acting police commissioner, Lt-Gen. Arthur Coulton, was then appointed. In early

October 2002 it was announced that the charges against 18 of those arrested in connection with the August raid would be abandoned, leaving eight senior officers to face trial on charges of mutiny and incitement to mutiny; the trial was scheduled for early 2003. Meanwhile, the UMP urged the removal of the Australian High Commissioner, Steve Waters, while reportedly accusing Australia of interference into Vanuatu's internal affairs and of destabilizing the coalition Government by communicating solely with the VP at the expense of the UMP. Deputy Prime Minister Serge Vohor alleged that the Australian Federal Police (AFP) had been engaged in the surveillance of government ministers and other officials in Vanuatu. The AFP denied the charges.

In March 1988 Vanuatu signed an agreement with Papua New Guinea and Solomon Islands to form the 'Spearhead Group', which aimed to preserve Melanesian cultural traditions and to lobby for independence for New Caledonia. In 1994 the group concluded an agreement regarded as the first step towards the establishment of a free-trade area between the three countries. Fiji joined the group in early 1996.

Economy

In 2000, according to estimates by the World Bank, Vanuatu's gross national product (GNP), measured at average 1998–2000 prices, was US $228m., equivalent to US $1,140 per head, or US $2,940 per head on an international purchasing-power parity basis. During 1990–99, it was estimated, GNP per head decreased, in real terms, at an average annual rate of 3.4%. The population increased at an average annual rate of 3.1% in 1990–2000. According to the Asian Development Bank (ADB), Vanuatu's gross domestic product (GDP) decreased by 2.5% in 1999, grew by 3.7% in 2000, but contracted again, by 0.5%, in 2001.

Agriculture (including forestry and fishing) contributed an estimated 13.4% of GDP in 2001, compared with some 40% in the early 1980s. According to the ADB, the GDP of the agricultural sector was estimated to have decreased by an average annual rate of 0.7% in 1990–2001. Compared with the previous year, the sector's GDP was estimated to have decreased by 9.3% in 1999, increased by 2.5% in 2000, but declined by 14.9% in 2001. The performance of the agricultural sector in 2001 was severely affected by the devastation caused by two cyclones that struck Vanuatu early in the year. The principal cash crop is coconut. Fluctuations in levels of production of copra (the dried coconut meat that is the source of coconut oil) exemplify the vulnerability of Vanuatu's agricultural economy to adverse climatic conditions. Moreover, international prices for copra have tended to fluctuate widely. Revenue from copra accounted for 10.1% of total domestic export earnings in 2001, compared with 30.3% in 2000. Efforts have been made to diversify the agricultural sector, and the cultivation of cocoa is also significant. Exports of the crop accounted for 2.0% of total domestic earnings in 2001. Coffee is cultivated for export. More than 20,000 households are involved in the cultivation of kava, from which a narcotic drink is produced; the country's first commercial extraction plant was inaugurated in early 1998. However, it was feared that a European ban on kava imports, imposed from 2001 owing to concerns that its consumption might damage health, could affect the country's kava industry. In the early 1990s it was estimated that some 75% of the population were involved in subsistence cultivation, the principal staple crops being yams, taro, manioc, sweet potatoes, breadfruit and coconuts. In 2001 exports of beef contributed 7.5% of domestic exports. A project to breed goats for meat and cheese production was initiated in mid-2000. The Government derives substantial amounts of revenue from the sale of fishing rights to foreign fleets: sales of licences to Taiwanese and South Korean vessels contributed more than $A136,000 in 1997.

In mid-1993 it was announced that the Government had granted a Malaysian group of companies a licence to log 70,000 cu m of timber annually on the islands of Erromango, Malekula and Espiritu Santo (compared with previous licences for all operators of 5,000 cu m). The agreement caused extreme controversy, both for its lack of environmental provision and for the apparently unscrupulous terms under which it was negotiated. Following the publication of a report on the industry, financed by Australia, it was announced that from mid-1994 the export of round logs would be banned completely and logged wood would be restricted to an annual total of 25,000 cu m. These regulations were modified in late 1994, although the ban on round log exports was to be maintained. Timber exports contributed 10.5% of total export earnings in 2001.

The industrial sector contributed about 11.5% of GDP in 2001. Only 3.5% of the employed labour force were engaged in industrial activities in 1989. Compared with the previous year, according to the ADB, industrial GDP increased by 5.2% in 1999 and by 8.4% in 2000, before declining by 1.1% in 2001. Growth in the industrial sector during the late 1980s was largely attributable to an increase in construction activity, which contributed 4.2% of GDP in 2001. In 1990–2001 the GDP of the manufacturing sector increased by an average annual rate of only 1.7%. Manufacturing contributed about 5.0% of GDP in 2001. Most activities are agro-industrial: the processing of coconuts (to produce copra), fish and beef, for example. Governments have sought to promote the development of export-orientated industries, rather than of import-substitution.

Commercial extraction of manganese on Efate ceased in 1976. However, following investigations in the early 1990s, it was found that some 2m. metric tons of high-grade ore remained in the area, and in 1992 an Australian company announced plans to mine 60,000 tons of manganese per year for export to Japan and the People's Republic of China. In addition, an aerial geophysical survey of the islands, conducted in late 1994 (with Australian aid), identified several possibilities for gold- and copper-mining, as well as large deposits of petroleum around the islands of Malekula and Espiritu Santo. Electricity generation is thermal; in 1994 consumption of electricity totalled 29m. kWh. Imports of mineral fuels accounted for 13.7% of the value of total domestic imports in 2001. Funding to construct hydroelectric power stations on Espiritu Santo and Malekula was secured in the mid-1990s. In August 2000 Shofa province signed an agreement with an Australian company to establish an oil refinery on Efate.

The services sector contributed 75.0% of GDP in 2001. According to the ADB, the GDP of the services sector declined by 1.7% in 1999, before rising by 3.3% in 2000 and again by 3.3% in 2001. Tourism has become an important source of revenue, and it was estimated that as many as 5,000 ni-Vanuatu were engaged in tourism-related activities (the tourist industry is the largest generator of private-sector employment). Some 57,360 foreign visitors arrived in Vanuatu in 2000, while 30,530 cruise-ship passengers visited the islands in 1997. Revenue from tourism was US $58m. in 2000. The number of visitor arrivals declined by 2.6% in 1999, but increased by 13.0% in 2001. Social unrest in Port Vila and Luganville, followed by Cyclones Yali and Zuman led to a decline in visitor numbers in early 1998, and in the following year disruption to Air Vanuatu's services, together with negative publicity resulting from a domestic air crash, resulted in a further decrease in tourist arrivals.

Personal income taxes and taxes on company profits are not currently levied by the Government of Vanuatu (domestic tax revenue being derived principally from import duties). The country has thus become attractive as an 'offshore' financial centre and 'tax haven', earnings from which provided about 12% of annual GDP in the late 1980s. However, a restructuring of the tax base (effective from August 1998), as part of the Comprehensive Reform Programme (CRP—see below), included the introduction of a 12.5% value-added tax, offset by reductions in import duties and the abolition or adjustment of certain other levies. The Government has vehemently denied suggestions that Vanuatu's strict banking secrecy laws might conceal irregular transactions. The country's status as an offshore financial centre has, however, aroused international controversy, and in June 2000 the Paris-based Organisation for Economic Co-operation and Development (OECD) listed Vanuatu as one of a number of countries and territories operating as unfair tax havens. It was claimed that the country was being used to 'launder' the proceeds of illegal activities of the Russian mafia and drug cartels. Sanctions were threatened if Vanuatu failed to take action to prevent both 'money-laundering' and international tax evasion. This contributed to the introduction of anti 'money-laundering' legislation in August 2000. In September 2001 the Minister of Finance rejected demands to provide information on the country's revenue from its international tax haven facility. Furthermore, in February 2002 the Government stated that it would not co-operate with an international initiative intended to eliminate tax evasion by encouraging transparency in world-wide tax policies. Vanuatu thus remained on the OECD's list of unco-operative tax havens. The country also operates an 'offshore' shipping register: 316 ships were registered in 2001.

Vanuatu consistently records a visible trade deficit. However, such deficits are usually counterbalanced by receipts from tourism and the financial services sector and by official transfers from abroad. In 2001 there was a visible trade deficit of US $58.07m. and a deficit of US $14.53m. on the current account of the balance of payments. The principal exports are copra, cocoa, beef and timber, and the most significant markets for Vanuatu's export commodities were Indonesia (which took 34.8% of exports in 2001), Greece (15.5%) and Japan (14.2%). The principal imports in 2001 were machinery and transport equipment (which accounted for 23.8% of the value of total imports), food and live animals (16.6%), mineral fuels (13.7%) and basic manufactures (12.6%). Significant suppliers of goods to Vanuatu are Japan (which supplied 26.1% of Vanuatu's imports in 2001) and Australia (16.9%).

Budget estimates for 1999 projected an overall deficit of 375m. vatu, compared with a deficit of 3,057m. vatu in 1998. (However, almost 90% of the projected 1998 budget deficit was an exceptional payment to the Vanuatu National Provident Fund—VNPF, and to the Comprehensive Reform Programme—CRP.) The overall budget deficit decreased significantly, from 11.2% of GDP in 1998 to 1.4% in 1999. Australia, New Zealand, France, the United Kingdom,

Canada and Japan are significant suppliers of development assistance. In 2001/02 Australia provided aid of some $A19.5m. and development assistance from New Zealand totalled $NZ5.25m. in the same period. In February 2002 the European Union (EU) allocated Vanuatu 2,000m. vatu of aid to be disbursed over the next five years from the ninth European Development Fund; the funding was to be used principally for the development of education and human resources training. In 2000 Vanuatu's external debt totalled US $68.6m., of which US $67.2m. was long-term public debt. In that year the cost of debt-servicing was equivalent to 1.4% of the value of exports of goods and services. The annual rate of inflation averaged 2.9% in 1991–2001. Consumer prices increased by an average of 2.1% in 1999, by 2.5% in 2000 and by 3.2% in 2001. Vanuatu's unit of currency, the vatu, replaced the New Hebrides franc in March 1982.

Vanuatu's economic development has been impeded by its dependence on the agricultural sector, particularly the production and export of copra, which is vulnerable to adverse weather conditions and fluctuations in international commodity prices. Successive administrations, therefore, have attempted to encourage the diversification of the country's economy, and in the early 1990s various measures were undertaken with the aim of enhancing the performance of the tourism sector, such as the construction of new hotels and improvements in air transport facilities. It was hoped that a campaign, initiated in mid-1995, to establish Vanuatu as an important petroleum producer would significantly enhance the country's economic prospects. Economic development, however, remained inhibited by a shortage of skilled indigenous labour, a weak infrastructure and frequent foreign exploitation. In addition, political instability and a series of financial scandals (see History) prompted fears that foreign interests would be deterred from investing in the country.

Implementation of the CRP, sponsored by the ADB and with additional support from the country's bilateral and multilateral creditors, was regarded as crucial to Vanuatu's future economic prosperity. The programme's key aims included what was termed a 'right-sizing' of the public sector, involving a reduction of 10%–15% in civil service personnel, together with measures aimed at ensuring greater accountability and transparency in all areas of public administration. However, the political instability of late 1997, followed by rioting in early 1998 (see History), had a severe negative impact on the economy. Futhermore, the increase in liquidity arising from the release of funds by the VNPF precipitated considerable currency instability. In mid-1999 the ADB reported that despite a number of difficulties, mainly the impact of the Asian economic crisis on certain sectors of the economy, as well as a decline in output from the agricultural sector, which had been adversely affected by weather conditions throughout 1999, the Government had shown a strong level of commitment to the CRP: the number of ministries had been reduced from 34 to nine, and the number of civil service personnel had been decreased by 7%, creating a more efficient and autonomous public sector. Other improvements included the introduction of value-added tax (VAT) and the restructuring of the National Bank and the Development Bank. Development plans announced in early 2000 aimed to encourage growth in the rural sector with the establishment of an Agricultural Development Bank and in tourism with the construction of a major new airport. Moreover, legislation, approved in August 2000, facilitated the establishment of internet gambling services—an important additional source of revenue. In May 2001 there was a crisis in government finance owing to very low levels of revenue, which resulted in many government employees not being paid. In November 2001, after five years of negotiations, the World Trade Organization (WTO) offered Vanuatu membership. However, the Government rejected the offer on the grounds that it wished to delay its entry while it negotiated a more favourable tariff agreement. Prime Minister Natapei also voiced his concern that the opening of free trade between members of the Melanesian 'Spearhead Group' had proved harmful to businesses in Vanuatu. The economy experienced a deceleration in 2001; The renewed contraction of GDP was mainly attributable to the detrimental effect of adverse weather conditions upon the performance of the agricultural sector (and particularly upon exports of copra, which decreased by nearly 50%) and to the effects of the European ban on kava imports. However, the repercussions of the 11 September 2001 terrorist attacks on the USA also contributed to a decline in tourism, an important source of foreign revenue, in the final months of the year. GDP was forecast to increase by only 0.7% in 2002 as the Government's fiscal position continued to deteriorate.

Vanuatu is a member of numerous regional and international organizations, including the UN's Economic and Social Commission for Asia and the Pacific (ESCAP), the Pacific Community (formerly the South Pacific Commission), the Pacific Islands Forum (formerly the South Pacific Forum), the ADB and the Asian and Pacific Coconut Community. Vanuatu is a signatory to the South Pacific Regional Trade and Economic Agreement (SPARTECA) and to the Lomé Conventions and successor Cotonou Agreement with the EU.

Statistical Survey

Source (unless otherwise indicated): Vanuatu Statistics Office, PMB 19, Port Vila; tel. 22110; fax 24583; e-mail stats@vanuatu.com.vu; internet www.spc.int/stats/vanuatu.

AREA AND POPULATION

Area: 12,190 sq km (4,707 sq miles); *By island*: (sq km) Espiritu Santo 4,010; Malekula 2,024; Efate 887; Erromango 887; Ambrym 666; Tanna 561; Pentecost 499; Epi 444; Ambae 399; Vanua Lava 343; Gaua 315; Maewo 300.

Population: 142,419 at census of 16 May 1989; 186,678 (males 95,682, females 90,996) at census of 16–30 November 1999; 192,910 (estimate) at mid-2001. *By island* (mid-1999, official estimates): Espiritu Santo 31,811; Malekula 19,766; Efate 43,295; Erromango 1,554; Ambrym 7,613; Tanna 26,306; Pentecost 14,837; Epi 4,706; Ambae 10,692; Vanua Lava 2,074; Gaua 1,924; Maewo 3,385.

Density (mid-2001): 15.8 per sq km.

Capital: Port Vila, population 19,311 at census of 1989; mid-2001 (UN estimate, incl. suburbs) 31,000 (Source: UN, *World Urbanization Prospects: The 2001 Revision*).

Other Town: Luganville (population 6,983 at census of 1989; estimated at 11,360 in mid-1999).

Births and Deaths (estimates, 1995–2000): Birth rate 33.7 per 1,000; Death rate 6.1 per 1,000. Source: UN, *World Population Prospects: The 2000 Revision*.

Expectation of Life (WHO estimates, years at birth, 2000): Males 64.2; Females 68.1. Source: WHO, *World Health Report*.

Economically Active Population (census of May 1989): Agriculture, forestry, hunting and fishing 40,889; Mining and quarrying 1; Manufacturing 891; Electricity, gas and water 109; Construction 1,302; Trade, restaurants and hotels 2,712; Transport, storage and communications 1,030; Financing, insurance, real estate and business services 646; Community, social and personal services 7,891; Activities not adequately defined 11,126; Total labour force 66,597 (males 35,692; females 30,905).

HEALTH AND WELFARE

Key Indicators

Fertility (births per woman, 2000): 4.4.

Under-5 Mortality Rate (per 1,000 live births, 2000): 44.

Physicians (per 1,000 head, 1996): 0.12.

Health Expenditure (1998): US $ per head (PPP): 95.
% of GDP: 3.3.
public (% of total): 63.6.

Access to Water (% of persons, 2000): 88.

Access to Sanitation (% of persons, 2000): 100.

Human Development Index (2000): ranking: 131.
value: 0.542.

For sources and definitions, see explanatory note on p. vi.

AGRICULTURE, ETC.

Principal Crops (FAO estimates, '000 metric tons, 2001): Coconuts 248; Roots and tubers 63; Vegetables and melons 10; Bananas 13; Other fruit 7; Groundnuts (in shell) 2; Maize 1; Cocoa beans 2. Source: FAO.

Livestock (FAO estimates, 2001): Cattle 151,000; Pigs 62,000; Goats 12,000; Horses 3,100; Chickens 340,000. Source: FAO.

Livestock Products (FAO estimates, metric tons, 2001): Beef and veal 5,800; Pig meat 2,805; Cows' milk 3,100; Hen eggs 320; Cattle and buffalo hides 821; Goatskins 6. Source: FAO.

Forestry ('000 cu m, 2000): *Roundwood removals* (excl. bark): Sawlogs and veneer logs 40; Fuel wood 91; Total 131. *Sawnwood production* (all broadleaved, incl. railway sleepers): Total 18. Source: FAO.

Fishing ('000 metric tons, 1999): Skipjack tuna 35.8; Yellowfin tuna 9.7; Total catch 94.6. Source: FAO, *Yearbook of Fishery Statistics*.

FINANCE

Currency and Exchange Rates: Currency is the vatu. *Sterling, Dollar and Euro Equivalents* (31 May 2002): £1 sterling = 200.5 vatu; US $1 = 136.7 vatu; €1 = 128.3 vatu; 1,000 vatu = £4.986 = $7.314 = €7.791. *Average Exchange Rate* (vatu per US $): 129.08 in 1999; 137.64 in 2000; 145.31 in 2001.

Budget (estimates, million vatu, 1999): *Revenue:* Tax revenue 5,925 (Taxes on goods and services 3,370, Import duties 2,434); Non-tax revenue 828; Total 6,753, excluding grants from abroad (525). *Expenditure:* Wages and salaries 3,741. Purchases of goods and services 1,909; Interest payments 247; Transfers 612; Total 6,796 (excluding development expenditure 856). Source: IMF, *Vanuatu: Recent Economic Developments* (October 2000).

2001 (million vatu): Total revenue and grants 7,069; Total expenditure (incl. development) 9,350.

International Reserves (US $ million at 31 December 2001): IMF special drawing rights 0.99; Reserve position in IMF 3.14; Foreign exchange 33.53; Total 37.66. Source: IMF, *International Financial Statistics*.

Money Supply (million vatu at 31 December 2001): Currency outside banks 1,941; Demand deposits at banks 5,974; Total money (incl. others) 8,041. Source: IMF, *International Financial Statistics*.

Cost of Living (Consumer Price Index for low-income households in urban areas; base: 1995 = 100): All items 109.3 in 1999; 112.0 in 2000; 116.1 in 2001. Source: IMF, *International Financial Statistics*.

Expenditure on the Gross Domestic Product (million vatu at current prices, 1999): Government final consumption expenditure 8,470; Private final consumption expenditure 17,904; Increase in stocks −55; Gross fixed capital formation 6,537; Statistical discrepancy 528; *Total domestic expenditure* 33,384; Exports of goods and services 14,130; *Less* Imports of goods and services 18,308; *GDP in purchasers' values* 29,206. Source: Asian Development Bank, *Key Indicators of Developing Asian and Pacific Countries*.

Gross Domestic Product by Economic Activity (million vatu at current prices, 2001, estimates): Agriculture, forestry and fishing 4,270; Manufacturing 1,576; Electricity, gas and water 763; Construction 1,334; Wholesale and retail trade, restaurants and hotels 10,867; Transport, storage and communications 3,861; Finance 2,779; Public administration 3,839; Other services (net of imputed bank service charge) 2,542; GDP in purchasers' values 31,831. Source: Asian Development Bank, *Key Indicators of Developing Asian and Pacific Countries*.

Balance of Payments (US $ million, 2001): Exports of goods f.o.b. 19.89; Imports of goods f.o.b. −77.96; *Trade balance* −58.07; Exports of services 119.26; Imports of services −72.99; *Balance on goods and services* −11.80; Other income received 17.23; Other income paid −21.23; *Balance on goods, services and income* −15.80; Current transfers received 39.53; Current transfers paid −38.26; *Current balance* −14.53; Capital account (net) −16.03; Direct investment from abroad 18.00; Portfolio investment assets −4.33; Other investment assets −11.41; Other investment liabilities 10.48; Net errors and omissions 7.55; *Overall balance* −10.27. Source: IMF, *International Financial Statistics*.

EXTERNAL TRADE*

Principal Commodities (million vatu, 2001): *Imports*: Food and live animals 2,240; Mineral fuels, lubricants, etc. 1,859; Chemicals 1,449; Basic manufactures 1,704; Machinery and transport equipment 3,219; Miscellaneous manufactured articles 1,112; Total (incl. others) 13,532. *Exports:* Copra 323; Beef 239; Timber 334; Total (incl. others) 3,192. Source: Asian Development Bank, *Key Indicators of Developing Asian and Pacific Countries*.

Principal Trading Partners (US $ million, 2001): *Imports:* Australia 28.4; Fiji 8.1; France 7.9; Germany 18.4; Hong Kong 1.7; Japan 43.7; New Caledonia 3.1; New Zealand 11.3; Singapore 24.4; USA 0.9; Total (incl. others) 167.7. *Exports:* Bangladesh 1.3; Germany 1.6; Greece 8.3; Indonesia 18.7; Japan 7.6; Korea, Republic 0.6; USA 0.5; Total (incl. others) 53.7. Source: Asian Development Bank, *Key Indicators of Developing Asian and Pacific Countries*.

* Figures refer to domestic imports and exports only.

TRANSPORT

Road Traffic (estimates, '000 motor vehicles in use): 9.2 (Passenger cars 7.4) in 1995; 5.9 (Passenger cars 2.7) in 1996; 6.2 (Passenger cars 2.7) in 1997. Source: UN, *Statistical Yearbook*.

Shipping: *Merchant Fleet* (registered at 31 December 2001): Vessels 316; Total displacement ('000 grt) 1,496. Source: Lloyd's Register-Fairplay, *World Fleet Statistics*. *International Sea-borne Freight Traffic* (estimates, '000 metric tons, 1990): Goods loaded 80; Goods unloaded 55. Source: UN, *Monthly Bulletin of Statistics*.

Civil Aviation (traffic on scheduled services, 1998): Kilometres flown (million) 3; Passengers carried ('000) 89; Passenger-km (million) 179; Total ton-km (million) 19. Source: UN, *Statistical Yearbook*.

TOURISM

Foreign Tourist Arrivals: 52,085 in 1998; 50,746 in 1999; 57,364 in 2000.

Tourist Arrivals by Country of Residence (2000): Australia 36,751; New Caledonia 4,114; New Zealand 7,985; Total (incl. others) 57,364.

Tourism Receipts (US $ million): 52 in 1998; 56 in 1999; 58 in 2000 (Source: World Tourism Organization).

COMMUNICATIONS MEDIA

Radio Receivers (1997): 62,000 in use*.

Television Receivers (1997): 2,000 in use*.

Telephones (2001): 6,800 main lines in use‡.

Facsimile Machines (1996): 600 in use†.

Mobile Cellular Telephones (2001): 300 subscribers‡.

Internet Users (2001): 5,500‡.

Non-daily Newspapers (1996): 2 (estimated circulation 4,000)*.

* Source: UNESCO, *Statistical Yearbook*.
† Source: UN, *Statistical Yearbook*.
‡ Source: International Telecommunication Union.

EDUCATION

Pre-primary (1992): 252 schools; 49 teachers (1980); 5,178 pupils.

Primary (1995): 374 schools; 852 teachers (1992); 32,352 pupils.

Secondary:

General (1992): 27 schools (1995); 220 teachers; 4,269 students.

Vocational: 50 teachers (1981); 444 students (1992).

Teacher-training: 1 college (1989); 13 teachers (1983); 124 students (1991).

Source: mainly UNESCO, *Statistical Yearbook*.

Directory

The Constitution

A new Constitution came into effect at independence on 30 July 1980. The main provisions are as follows:

The Republic of Vanuatu is a sovereign democratic state, of which the Constitution is the supreme law. Bislama is the national language and the official languages are Bislama, English and French. The Constitution guarantees protection of all fundamental rights and freedoms and provides for the determination of citizenship.

The President, as head of the Republic, symbolizes the unity of the Republic and is elected for a five-year term of office by secret ballot by an electoral college consisting of Parliament and the Presidents of the Regional Councils.

Legislative power resides in the single-chamber Parliament, consisting of 39 members (amended to 46 members in 1987, to 50 in 1995 and further to 52 in 1998) elected for four years on the basis of universal franchise through an electoral system that includes an element of proportional representation to ensure fair representation of different political groups and opinions. Parliament is presided over by the Speaker elected by the members. Executive power is vested in the Council of Ministers which consists of the Prime Minister (elected by Parliament from among its members) and other ministers (appointed by the Prime Minister from among the members of Parliament). The number of ministers, including the Prime Minister, may not exceed a quarter of the number of members of Parliament.

Special attention is paid to custom law and to decentralization. The Constitution states that all land in the Republic belongs to the indigenous custom owners and their descendants. There is a National Council of Chiefs, composed of custom chiefs elected by their peers sitting in District Councils of Chiefs. It may discuss all matters relating to custom and tradition and may make recommendations to Parliament for the preservation and promotion of the culture and languages of Vanuatu. The Council may be consulted on any question in connection with any bill before Parliament. Each region may elect a regional council and the Constitution lays particular emphasis on the representation of custom chiefs within each one. (A reorganization of local government was initiated in May 1994, and resulted in September of that year in the replacement of 11 local councils with six provincial governments.)

The Constitution also makes provision for public finance, the Public Service, the Ombudsman, a leadership code and the judiciary (see Judicial System).

The Government

HEAD OF STATE

President: Fr John Bani (took office March 1999).

COUNCIL OF MINISTERS
(September 2002)

A coalition of the Vanuaaku Pati (VP) and the Union of Moderate Parties (UMP).

Prime Minister: Edward Nipake Natapei (VP).

Deputy Prime Minister and Minister of Foreign Affairs, External Trade and Telecommunications: SERGE VOHOR (UMP).

Minister of Agriculture, Livestock, Forestry and Fisheries: STEVEN KALSAKAU (UMP).

Minister of Internal Affairs: JOE NATUMAN (VP).

Minister of Education: JACQUES SESE (UMP).

Minister of Finance: SELA MOLISA (VP).

Minister of Health: DONALD KALPOKAS (VP).

Minister of Infrastructure and Public Utilities: WILLIE POSEN (UMP)

Minister of Lands and Mineral Resources: JACKLYN RUEBEN TITEK (VP).

Minister for ni-Vanuatu Business Development: NICHOLAS BROWN (Independent).

Minister of the Comprehensive Reform Programme: PHILIP BOETORO (VP).

Minister of Industry and Commerce: JEAN ALLAN MAHÉ (UMP).

Minister of Youth and Sports: RAPHAEL WORWOR (VP).

MINISTRIES AND DEPARTMENTS

Prime Minister's Office: PMB 053, Port Vila; tel. 22413; fax 22863; internet www.vanuatu.gov.vu.

Deputy Prime Minister's Office: PMB 057, Port Vila; tel. 22750; fax 27714.

Ministry of Agriculture, Livestock, Forestry and Fisheries: POB 39, Port Vila; tel. 23406; fax 26498.

Ministry of Civil Aviation, Meteorology, Postal Services, Public Works and Transport: PMB 057, Port Vila; tel. 22790; fax 27214.

Ministry of the Comprehensive Reform Programme: POB 110, Port Vila.

Ministry of Culture, Home Affairs and Justice: PMB 036, Port Vila; tel. 22252; fax 27064.

Ministry of Education, Youth and Sports: PMB 028, Port Vila; tel. 22309; fax 24569; e-mail andrews@vanuatu.com.vu.

Ministry of Energy, Lands, Mines and Rural Water Supply: PMB 007, Port Vila; tel. 27833; fax 25165.

Ministry of Finance: PMB 058, Port Vila; tel. 23032; fax 27937.

Ministry of Foreign Affairs, External Trade and Telecommunications: PMB 074, Port Vila; tel. 27045; e-mail depfa@vanuatu.com.vu.

Ministry of Health: PMB 042, Port Vila; tel. 22545; fax 26113.

Ministry of Trade, Industry, Co-operatives and Commerce: PMB 056, Port Vila; tel. 25674; fax 25677.

Ministry of Women's Affairs: PMB 028, Port Vila; tel. 25099; fax 26353.

Legislature

PARLIAMENT

Speaker: HENRI TAGA.

General Election, 2 May 2002 (provisional results)

	Seats
Union of Moderate Parties	15
Vanuaaku Pati	14
National United Party	8
Melanesian Progressive Pati	3
Green Party	3
Vanuatu Republikan Pati	3
Independents and others	6
Total	52

Political Organizations

Efate Laketu Party: Port Vila; f. 1982; regional party, based on the island of Efate.

Green Party: Port Vila; f. 2001, by breakaway group of the UMP; Leader GERARD LEYMANG.

Independence Front: Port Vila; f. 1995, by breakaway group of the UMP; Chair. PATRICK CROWBY.

Melanesian Progressive Pati (MPP): POB 39, Port Vila; tel. 23485; fax 23315; f. 1988, by breakaway group from the VP; Chair. BARAK SOPE; Sec.-Gen. GEORGES CALO.

National Democratic Party (NDP): Port Vila; f. 1986; advocates strengthening of links with France and the UK; Leader JOHN NAUPA.

National United Party (NUP): Port Vila; f. 1991 by supporters of Walter Lini, following his removal as leader of the VP; Pres. DIN VAN THAN; Sec.-Gen. WILLIE TITONGOA.

New People's Party (NPP): Port Vila; f. 1986; Leader FRASER SINE.

People's Democratic Party (PDP): Port Vila; f. 1994 by breakaway faction of the NUP.

People's Progressive Party (PPP): Port Vila; f. 2001; formed coalition with National United Party (NUP) and Fren Melanesia to contest 2002 elections; Pres. SATO KILMAN.

Tu Vanuatu Kominiti: Port Vila; f. 1996; espouses traditional Melanesian and Christian values; Leader HILDA LINI.

Union of Moderate Parties (UMP): POB 698, Port Vila; f. 1980; Pres. SERGE VOHOR; the UMP is divided into two factions, one led by SERGE VOHOR and the other by WILLIE JIMMY.

Vanuaaku Pati (VP) (Our Land Party): POB 472, Port Vila; tel. 22584; f. 1971 as the New Hebrides National Party; advocates 'Melanesian socialism'; Pres. EDWARD NATAPEI; First Vice-Pres. IOLU ABBIL; Sec.-Gen. SELA MOLISA.

Vanuatu Independent Alliance Party (VIAP): Port Vila; f. 1982; supports free enterprise; Leaders THOMAS SERU, GEORGE WOREK, KALMER VOCOR.

Vanuatu Independent Movement: Port Vila; f. 2002; Pres. WILLIE TASSO.

Vanuatu Labour Party: Port Vila; f. 1986; trade-union based; Leader KENNETH SATUNGIA.

Vanuatu Republikan Pati (VRP): Port Vila; f. 1998 by breakaway faction of the UMP; Leader MAXIME CARLOT KORMAN.

The **Na-Griamel** (Leader FRANKEY STEVENS), **Namaki Aute, Tan Union** (Leader VINCENT BULEKONE) and **Fren Melanesia** (Leader ALBERT RAVUTIA) represent rural interests on the islands of Espiritu Santo and Malekula. The **John Frum Movement** represents interests on the island of Tanna.

Diplomatic Representation

EMBASSIES AND HIGH COMMISSIONS IN VANUATU

Australia: KPMG House, POB 111, Port Vila; tel. 22777; fax 23948; e-mail australia_vanuatu@dfat.gov.au; internet www.vanuatu.embassy.gov.au; High Commissioner: STEPHEN WATERS.

China, People's Republic: PMB 071, Rue d'Auvergne, Nambatu, Port Vila; tel. 23598; fax 24877; e-mail trade@chinese-embassy.com.vu; Ambassador: WU ZURONG.

France: Kumul Highway, POB 60, Port Vila; tel. 22353; fax 22695; Ambassador: JEAN GARBE.

New Zealand: BDO House, Lini Highway, POB 161, Port Vila; tel. 22933; fax 22518; e-mail kiwi@vanuatu.com.vu; High Commissioner: BRIAN SMYTHE.

United Kingdom: KPMG House, rue Pasteur, POB 567, Port Vila; tel. 23100; fax 23651; e-mail bhcvila@vanuatu.com.vu; High Commissioner: MICHAEL HILL.

Judicial System

The Supreme Court has unlimited jurisdiction to hear and determine any civil or criminal proceedings. It consists of the Chief Justice, appointed by the President of the Republic after consultation with the Prime Minister and the leader of the opposition, and three other judges, who are appointed by the President of the Republic on the advice of the Judicial Service Commission.

The Court of Appeal is constituted by two or more judges of the Supreme Court sitting together. The Supreme Court is the court of first instance in constitutional matters and is composed of a single judge.

Magistrates' Courts have limited jurisdiction to hear and determine any civil or criminal proceedings. Island Courts have been established in several Local Government Regions, and are constituted when three justices are sitting together to exercise civil or criminal jurisdiction, as defined in the warrant establishing the court. A magistrate nominated by the Chief Justice acts as Chairman. The Island Courts are competent to rule on land disputes.

In late 2001 legislation was introduced to establish a new Land Tribunal which was intended to expedite the hearing of land disputes. The tribunal was to have three levels, and no cases were to go beyond the tribunal and enter either the Supreme Court or the Island Courts. The tribunal was to be funded by the disputing parties.

In 1986 Papua New Guinea and Vanuatu signed a memorandum of understanding, under which Papua New Guinea Supreme Court judges were to conduct court hearings in Vanuatu, chiefly in the Court of Appeal.

Supreme Court of Vanuatu: PMB 041, rue de Querios, Port Vila; tel. 22420; fax 22692.

Attorney-General: HAMILTON BULU (acting).

Chief Justice: VINCENT LUNABECK (acting).

Chief Prosecutor: HEATHER LINI LEO.

Religion

Most of Vanuatu's inhabitants profess Christianity. Presbyterians form the largest Christian group (with about one-half of the population being adherents), followed by Anglicans and Roman Catholics.

CHRISTIANITY

Vanuatu Christian Council: POB 13, Luganville, Santo; tel. 03232; f. 1967 as New Hebrides Christian Council; five mem. churches, two observers; Chair. Rt Rev MICHEL VISI; Sec. Rev. JOHN LIU.

The Roman Catholic Church

Vanuatu forms the single diocese of Port Vila, suffragan to the archdiocese of Nouméa (New Caledonia). At 31 December 2000 there were an estimated 28,600 adherents in the country. The Bishop participates in the Catholic Bishops' Conference of the Pacific, based in Fiji.

Bishop of Port Vila: Rt Rev. MICHEL VISI, Evêché, POB 59, Port Vila; tel. 22640; fax 25342; e-mail catholik@vanuatu.com.vu.

The Anglican Communion

Anglicans in Vanuatu are adherents of the Church of the Province of Melanesia, comprising eight dioceses: Vanuatu (which also includes New Caledonia), Banks and Torres and six dioceses in Solomon Islands. The Archbishop of the Province is the Bishop of Central Melanesia, resident in Honiara, Solomon Islands. In 1985 the Church had an estimated 16,000 adherents in Vanuatu.

Bishop of Vanuatu: Rt Rev. HUGH BLESSING BOE, Bishop's House, POB 238, Luganville, Santo; tel. 37065; fax 36026.

Bishop of Banks and Torres: Rt Rev. NATHAN TOME, Bishop's House, POB 19, Toutamwat, Torba Province.

Protestant Churches

Presbyterian Church of Vanuatu (Presbitirin Jyos long Vanuatu): POB 150, Port Vila; tel. 23008; fax 26480; f. 1948; 56,000 mems (1995); Moderator Pastor BANI KALSINGER; Assembly Clerk Pastor FAMA RAKAU.

Other denominations active in the country include the Apostolic Church, the Assemblies of God, the Churches of Christ in Vanuatu and the Seventh-day Adventist Church.

BAHÁ'Í FAITH

National Spiritual Assembly of the Bahá'ís of Vanuatu: POB 1017, Port Vila; tel. 22419; e-mail cbpierce@vanuatu.com.vu; f. 1953; Sec. CHARLES PIERCE; mems resident in 182 localities.

The Press

Hapi Tumas Long Vanuatu: POB 1292, Port Vila; tel. 23642; fax 23343; quarterly tourist information; in English; Publr MARC NEIL-JONES; circ. 12,000.

Logging News: Port Vila; environment and logging industry.

Pacific Island Profile: Port Vila; f. 1990; monthly; general interest; English and French; Editor HILDA LINI.

Port Vila Presse: 1st Floor, Raffea House, POB 637, Port Vila; tel. 22200; fax 27999; e-mail marke@presse.com.vu; internet www.presse.com.vu; f. 2000; daily; English and French; Publr MARKE LOWEN; Editor RICKY BINIHI.

The Trading Post: POB 1292, Port Vila; tel. 23111; fax 24111; e-mail tpost@vanuatu.com.vu; 2 a week; English; Publr MARC NEIL-JONES; circ. 2,000.

Vanuatu Weekly: PMB 049, Port Vila; tel. 22999; fax 22026; e-mail vbtcnews@vanuatu.com.vu; f. 1980; weekly; govt-owned; Bislama, English and French; circ. 1,700.

Viewpoints: Port Vila; weekly; newsletter of Vanuaaku Pati; Editor PETER TAURAKOTO.

Wantok Niuspepa: POB 1292, Port Vila; tel. 23642; fax 23343.

Broadcasting and Communications

TELECOMMUNICATIONS

Freedom Telecommunications Company (USA): Santo; f. 2000; provides services on Santo and islands in the north of Vanuatu.

Telecom Vanuatu Ltd (TVL): POB 146, Port Vila; tel. 22185; fax 22628; e-mail telecom@tvl.net.vu; internet www.vanuatu.com.vu; f. 1989 as a joint venture between the Government of Vanuatu, Cable & Wireless Ltd and France Câbles et Radio; operates all national and international telecommunications services in Vanuatu; Man. Dir RICHARD HALL.

BROADCASTING

Radio

Vanuatu Broadcasting and Television Corporation (VBTC): PMB 049, Port Vila; tel. 22999; fax 22026; e-mail vbtcnews@vanuatu.com.vu; internet www.vbtc.com.vu; fmrly Government Media Services, name changed in 1992; Gen. Man. JOE BOMAL CARLO; Chair. PHIL RICHARD; Dir of Programmes A. THOMPSON.

Radio Vanuatu: PMB 049, Port Vila; tel. 22999; fax 22026; f. 1966; govt-owned; broadcasts in English, French and Bislama; Dir JOE BOMAL CARLO.

Television

Vanuatu Broadcasting and Television Corporation (VBTC): (see Radio).

Television Blong Vanuatu: PMB 049, Port Vila; f. 1993; govt-owned; French-funded; broadcasts for four hours daily in French and English; Gen. Man. CLAUDE CASTELLY; Programme Man. GAEL LE DANTEC.

Finance

(cap. = capital; res = reserves; dep. = deposits; amounts in vatu unless otherwise indicated)

Vanuatu has no personal income tax nor tax on company profits and is therefore attractive as a financial centre and 'tax haven'.

BANKING

Central Bank

Reserve Bank of Vanuatu: POB 62, Port Vila; tel. 23333; fax 24231; e-mail resrvbnk@vanuatu.com.vu; f. 1981 as Central Bank of Vanuatu; name changed as above in 1989; cap. 100m., res 640.9m., total resources 5,598.1m. (Dec. 1996); Gov. ANDREW KAUSIAMA.

Development Banks

Development Bank of Vanuatu: rue de Paris, POB 241, Port Vila; tel. 22181; fax 24591; f. 1979; govt-owned; cap. 315m. (Nov. 1988); Man. Dir AUGUSTINE GARAE.

Agence Française de Développement: Kumul Highway, La Casa d'Andrea Bldg, BP 296, Port Vila; tel. 22171; fax 24021; e-mail afd.arep@vanuatu.com.vu; fmrly Caisse Française de Développement; provides finance for various development projects; Man. BERNARD SIRVAIN.

National Bank

National Bank of Vanuatu: POB 249, Air Vanuatu House, rue de Paris, Port Vila; tel. 22201; fax 27227; f. 1991, when it assumed control of Vanuatu Co-operative Savings Bank; govt-owned; cap. 600m., dep. 2,357m. (Dec. 2000); Chair. HAM BULE; Gen. Man. KEN MCARTHUR: 19 brs.

Foreign Banks

ANZ Bank (Vanuatu) Ltd: Lini Highway, POB 123, Port Vila; tel. 22536; fax 23950; e-mail vanuatu@anz.com; internet www.anz.com/vanuatu; f. 1971; cap. 3.7m., res 112.4m., dep. 14,271.2m. (Sept. 1998); Man. Dir MALCOLM TILBROOK; brs in Port Vila and Santo.

European Bank Ltd (USA): International Bldg, Lini Highway, POB 65, Port Vila; tel. 27700; fax 22884; e-mail info@europeanbank.net; internet www.europeanbank.net; cap. US $0.8m., res US $1.3m., dep. US $25.0m. (Dec. 2000); 'offshore' and private banking; Chair. THOMAS MONTGOMERY BAYER; Pres. ROBERT MURRAY BOHN.

Westpac Banking Corporation (Australia): Kumul Highway, POB 32, Port Vila; tel. 22084; fax 24773; e-mail westpacv@vanuatu.com.vu; Man. R. B. WRIGHT; 2 brs.

Financial Institution

The Financial Centre Association: POB 1128, Port Vila; tel. 27272; fax 27272; e-mail fincen@vanuatu.com.vu; f. 1980; group of banking, legal, accounting and trust companies administering 'offshore' banking and investment; Chair. MARK STAFFORD; Sec. ALISTAIR RODGERS.

INSURANCE

Pacific Insurance Brokers: POB 229, Port Vila; tel. 23863; fax 23089.

QBE Insurance (Vanuatu) Ltd: La Casa D'Andrea Bldg, POB 186, Port Vila; tel. 22299; fax 23298; e-mail info.van@qbe.com; Gen. Man. GEOFFREY R. CUTTING.

Trade and Industry

CHAMBER OF COMMERCE

Vanuatu Chamber of Commerce and Industry: POB 189, Port Vila; tel. 27543; fax 27542; e-mail vancci@vanuatu.com.vu; Pres. JOSEPH JACOBE.

MARKETING BOARD

Vanuatu Commodities Marketing Board: POB 268, Luganville, Santo; e-mail vcmb@vanuatu.com.vu; f. 1982; sole exporter of major commodities, including copra, kava and cocoa; Gen. Man. IAN G. BALTOR (acting).

UTILITIES

Electricity

Union Electrique du Vanuatu (Unelco Vanuatu Ltd): POB 26, rue Winston Churchill, Port Vila; tel. 22211; fax 25011; e-mail unelco@unelco.com.vu; private organization contracted for the generation and supply of electricity in Port Vila, Luganville, Tanna and Malekula, and for the supply of water in Port Vila; Dir-Gen. JEAN FRANÇOIS BARBEAU.

Village generators provide electricity in rural areas. The Department of Infrastructure, Utilities and Public Works provides recirculated water supplies to about 85% of urban and 30% of rural households.

CO-OPERATIVES

During the early 1980s there were some 180 co-operative primary societies in Vanuatu and at least 85% of goods in the islands were distributed by co-operative organizations. Almost all rural ni-Vanuatu were members of a co-operative society, as were many urban dwellers. By the end of that decade, however, membership of co-operatives had declined, and the organizations' supervisory body, the Vanuatu Co-operative Federation, had been dissolved, after having accumulated debts totalling some $A1m.

MAJOR COMPANIES

South Pacific Fishing Co: POB 237, Santo; tel. 36319; state-controlled exporters of fish.

Vanuatu Brewing Ltd: POB 169, Port Vila; tel. 22435; fax 22152; e-mail tusker@vanuatu.com.vu; f. 1990; 50% owned by Pripps Bryggerier (Sweden), 25% state-owned, 25% owned by Provident Fund of Vanuatu; production of Pripps Lager and Vanuatu Tusker Beer; Gen. Man. MURRAY PARSONS.

Vanuatu Maritime Services Ltd: POB 102, Port Vila; tel. 22454; fax 22884; e-mail security@vila.net; provides registry and administration of maritime services.

Vanuatu Registries Ltd: Port Vila; marketing and promotion of Vanuatu as a jurisdiction for company registration and ship registration; br. in Singapore.

TRADE UNIONS

Vanuatu Council of Trade Unions (VCTU): PMB 89, Port Vila; tel. 24517; fax 23679; e-mail synt@vanuatu.com.vu; Pres. OBED MASINGIOW; Sec.-Gen. EPHRAIM KALSAKAU.

National Union of Labour: Port Vila.

The principal trade unions include:

Oil and Gas Workers' Union: Port Vila; f. 1984.

Vanuatu Airline Workers' Union: Port Vila; f. 1984.

Vanuatu Public Service Association: Port Vila.

Vanuatu Teachers' Union: Port Vila; Gen. Sec. CHARLES KALO; Pres. OBED MASSING.

Vanuatu Waterside, Maritime and Allied Workers' Union: Port Vila.

Transport

ROADS

There are about 1,130 km of roads, of which 54 km, mostly on Efate Island, are sealed. In early 1998 Japan granted more than 400m. vatu to finance the sealing of the main road around Efate. In January 2002 an earthquake caused significant damage to the transport infrastructure around Efate. Several foreign donors, including New Zealand, contributed to funding urgent repairs to roads and bridges in the area.

SHIPPING

The principal ports are Port Vila and Luganville.

Vanuatu Maritime Authority: POB 320, Marine Quay, Port Vila; tel. 23128; fax 22949; e-mail vma@vanuatu.com.vu; domestic and international ship registry, maritime safety regulator; Commissioner of Maritime Affairs JOHN T. ROOSEN.

Ports and Marine Department: PMB 046, Port Vila; tel. 22339; fax 22475; Harbour Master Capt. PAUL PETER.

Burns Philp (Vanuatu) Ltd: POB 27, Port Vila.

Ifira Shipping Agencies Ltd: POB 68, Port Vila; tel. 22929; fax 22052; f. 1986; Man. Dir CLAUDE BOUDIER.

Sami Ltd: Kumul Highway, POB 301, Port Vila; tel. 24106; fax 23405.

South Sea Shipping: POB 84, Port Vila; tel. 22205; fax 23304; e-mail southsea@vanuatu.com.vu.

Vanua Navigation Ltd: POB 44, Port Vila; tel. 22027; f. 1977 by the Co-operative Federation and Sofrana Unilines; Chief Exec. GEOFFREY J. CLARKE.

The following services call regularly at Vanuatu: Compagnie Générale Maritime, Kyowa Shipping Co, Pacific Forum Line, Papua New Guinea Shipping Corpn, Sofrana-Unilines, Bank Line, Columbus Line and Bali Hai Shipping. Royal Viking Line, Sitmar and P & O cruises also call at Vanuatu.

CIVIL AVIATION

The principal airports are Bauerfield (Efate, for Port Vila) and Pekoa (Espiritu Santo, for Luganville). There are airstrips on all Vanuatu's principal islands and an international airport at White Grass on Tanna was completed in 1998. The Civil Aviation Corporation Act, approved by Parliament in August 1998, provided for the transfer of ownership of Vanuatu's airports to a commercially-run corporation, in which the Government is to have a majority shareholding. In early 2000 it was announced that a further three airports were to be built on the islands of Pentecost, Malekula and Tanna. Major improvements providing for the accommodation of larger aircraft at both Bauerfield and Pekoa airports began in mid-2000. Moreover, in September 2000 plans for a new international airport at Teouma (Efate) were announced, with finance from a private Thai investor. In late 2001 plans were also announced for the improvement of the international terminal at Bauerfield airport.

Air Vanuatu (Operations) Ltd: POB 148, Du Vanuatu House, rue de Paris, Port Vila; tel. 23838; fax 23250; e-mail service@airvanuatu.com.vu; internet www.pacificislands.com/airlines/vanuatu.html; f. 1981; govt-owned national carrier since 1987; regular services between Port Vila and Sydney, Brisbane and Melbourne (Australia), Nadi (Fiji), Nouméa (New Caledonia), Auckland (New Zealand), and Honiara (Solomon Islands); Man. Dir and CEO JEAN-PAUL VIRELALA.

Vanair: rue Pasteur, PMB 9069, Port Vila; tel. 22643; fax 23910; e-mail vias@vanuatu.com.vu; internet www.islandsvanuatu.com/vanair.htm; operates scheduled services to 29 destinations within the archipelago; CEO Capt YVES CHEVALIER.

Dovair: Port Vila; privately-owned; operates domestic services.

Tourism

Tourism is an important source of revenue for the Government of Vanuatu. Visitors are attracted by the islands' unspoilt landscape and rich local customs. The establishment of regular air services from Australia and New Zealand in the late 1980s precipitated a significant increase in the number of visitors to Vanuatu. In 2000 there were an estimated 57,364 foreign visitor arrivals in Vanuatu, an increase of 13.0% compared with the previous year. In 1997 passengers on cruise ships visiting the islands numbered 30,530. In 2000 some 64% of visitors were from Australia and 14% were from New Zealand. There was a total of 1,641 hotel beds at the end of 1996. Receipts from tourism totalled some US $58m. in 2000. The development of the tourist industry has hitherto been concentrated on the islands of Efate, Espiritu Santo and Tanna; however, the promotion of other islands as tourist centres is beginning to occur.

National Tourism Office of Vanuatu: Lini Highway, POB 209, Port Vila; tel. 22685; fax 23889; e-mail tourism@vanuatu.com.vu; internet www.vanuatutourism.com; Gen. Man. LINDA KALPOI.

Vanuatu Hotel and Resorts Association: POB 215, Port Vila; tel. 22040; fax 27579; Pres. JOHN GROCOCK.

Defence

Upon Vanuatu's achievement of independence in 1980, a defence pact with Papua New Guinea was signed. A 300-strong paramilitary force, the Vanuatu Mobile Force, exists. A security review was in progress in mid-1998. In 1997 the Government allocated 502m. vatu for public order and safety, equivalent to 7.9% of total recurrent budgetary expenditure.

Education

The abolition of nominal fees for primary education following independence resulted in a significant increase in enrolment at that level. Thus, at the beginning of the 1990s it was estimated that about 85% of children between the ages of six and 11 were enrolled at state-controlled primary institutions (which numbered 267 in 1995). Secondary education begins at 12 years of age, and comprises a preliminary cycle of four years and a second cycle of three years. In 1992 4,269 pupils attended the country's secondary schools (which numbered 27 in 1995). Vocational education and teacher-training are also available. The relatively low level of secondary enrolment is a cause of some concern to the Government, and a major programme for the expansion of the education system, costing US $17.8m., was inaugurated in 1989. The programme aimed to double secondary enrolment by 1996. Literacy rates are another cause of concern; it was estimated in 1997 that 64% of the population was illiterate.

An extension centre of the University of the South Pacific was opened in Port Vila in May 1989. Students from Vanuatu can also receive higher education at the principal faculties of that university (in Suva, Fiji), in Papua New Guinea or in France.

The 1997 budget allocated an estimated 1,396m. vatu to education (21.9% of total recurrent expenditure by the central Government).

Bibliography of the Pacific Islands

Akram-Lodhi, A.Haroon (Ed.). *Confronting Fiji Futures*. Canberra, Australian National University, 2000.

Aldrich, Robert, and Connell, John. *France's Overseas Frontier*. Cambridge, Cambridge University Press, 1992.

Aldrich, Robert. *The French Presence in the South Pacific, 1842–1940*. London, Macmillan, 1990.

France and the South Pacific since 1940. London, Macmillan, 1993.

Alkire, William H. *An Introduction to the Peoples and Cultures of Micronesia*. Menlo Park, CA, Cummings Publishing Co, 1977.

American Samoa Economic Advisory Commission. *Transforming the Economy of American Samoa: A Report to the President of the United States of America through the U. S. Department of the Interior*. Pago Pago, April 2002 (revised July 2002).

Australian National University. *Pacific History Bibliography and Comment, 1979–1987, Journal of Pacific History Bibliography -97, Journal of Pacific History*. Canberra, Australian National University.

Angleviel, Frédéric, Coppell, William and Charleux, Michel (Eds). *Bibliographie des Thèses sur le Pacifique*. Bordeaux, CRET, CEGET, Université de Bordeaux, 1991.

Angleviel, Frédéric, Atoloto, Malau amd Atonio, Takasi (Eds). *101 Mots Pour Comprendre Wallis et Futuna*. Nouméa, Iles de Lumiére, 1999.

Angleviel, Frédéric (Ed.). *La Nouvelle-Calédonie, Terre des Recherches—Bibliographie Analytique des Thèses et Memoires*. Nouméa, Association Thèse-Pac, 1995.

101 Mots Pour Comprendre l'Histoire de la Nouvelle-Calédonie. Nouméa, Ile de Lumière, 1997.

Antheaume, Benoît, and Bonnemaison, Joël. *Atlas des Iles et Etats du Pacifique Sud*. Montpellier-Paris, GIP Reclus/Publisud, 1988.

Australian Joint Parliamentary Committee on Foreign Affairs, Defence and Trade. *Australia's Relations with Papua New Guinea*. Canberra, 1991.

Bachimon, Philippe. *Tahiti Entre Mythes et Réalités: Essai d'Histoire Geographique*. Paris, Comité des Travaux Historiques et Scientifiques, 1989.

Ballard, J. A. (Ed.). *Policy-Making in a New State: Papua New Guinea 1972–77*. Melbourne, Oxford University Press, 1981.

Banks, Glenn, Bonnell, Susanne, and Filer, Colin (Eds). *Dilemmas of Development: the social and economic impact of the Porgera gold mine 1989–1994*. Canberra, Asia Pacific Press, Australian National University, 2000.

Bates, S. *The South Pacific Island Countries and France: A Study in International Relations*. Canberra, Australian National University, 1990.

Bayliss-Smith, T., Bedford, R., Brookfield, H., Latham, M., with Brookfield, M. *Islands, Islanders and the World: The Colonial and Post-Colonial Experience of Eastern Fiji*. Cambridge, Cambridge University Press, 1988.

Bellwood, Peter S. *The Polynesians: Prehistory of an island People*. London, Thames and Hudson, 1987.

Bellwood, Peter S. (Ed.). *The Austronesians: Historical and Comparative Perspectives*. Canberra, Australian University Press, 1995.

Bennett, Judith A. *Wealth of the Solomons*. Honolulu, HI, University of Hawaii Press, 1986.

Bensa, Alban and Leblic, Isabelle. *En Pays Kanak*. Paris, Edition de la Maison des Sciences de L'Homme, Mission du Patrimoine Ethnologique, Collection Ethnologie de la France, Cahier 14, 2000.

Bensa, Alban. *Nouvelle-Calédonie, un paradis dans la tourmente*. Paris, Gallimard, 1990.

Bird, I. *The Hawaiian Archipelago*. London, Picador, 1998.

Birkett, Dea. *Serpent in Paradise*. New York, NY, Doubleday, 1997.

Bonnemaison, J., Huffman, K., Kauffmann, C., and Tryon, D. *Arts of Vanuatu*. Bathurst, NSW, Crawford House Press, 1997.

Borofsky, Robert (Ed.). *Remembrance of Pacific Pasts: an invitation to remake history*. Honolulu, HI, University of Hawaii, 2000.

Brookfield, H. C. *Melanesia, a Geographical Interpretation of an Island World*. London, Methuen, 1971.

Colonialism, Development and Independence; the Case of the Melanesian Islands in the South Pacific. London, Methuen, 1972.

The Pacific in Transition: a Geographical Perspective on Adaptation and Change. Canberra, Australian National University, 1973.

Browne, C., and Scott, D. A. *Economic Development in Seven Pacific Island Countries*. Washington, DC, International Monetary Fund, 1989.

Bullard, Alice. *Exile to Paradise: Savagery and Civilization in Paris and the South Pacific, 1790–1900*. Stanford, CA, Stanford University Press, 2000.

Burt, Ben, and Clerk, Christian (Eds). *Environment and Development in the Pacific Islands*. Canberra, Australian National University, 1994.

Cameron, I. *Lost Paradise: the Exploration of the Pacific*. Massachusetts, Salem House, 1987.

Campbell, I. *A History of the Pacific Islands*. Christchurch, University of Canterbury, 1989.

Island Kingdom: Tonga Ancient and Modern. Christchurch, Canterbury University Press, 1992.

Campbell, Ian C., and Latouche, Jean-Pierre. *Les insulaires du Pacifique—histoire et situation politique*. Paris, Puf, 2001.

Carano, P., and Sanchez, P. C. *A Complete History of Guam*. Rutland, VT, Charles E. Tuttle.

Carrier, James. *History and Tradition in Melanesian Anthropology*. Berkeley, CA, University of California, 1992.

Chappell, David. *Double Ghost: Oceanian Voyagers on Euro-American Ships*. London, Armonk, 1997.

Chesneaux, Jean, and Maclellan, Nic. *La France dans le Pacifique, De Bougainville à Moruroa*. Paris, La Découverte, 1992.

After Mururoa—France in the South Pacific. Melbourne, Ocean Press, 1998.

Clark, R. S., and Sann, M. (Eds). *The Case against the Bomb: Marshall Islands, Samoa and Solomon Islands before the International Court of Justice*. Mansfield, OH, Book Masters, 1996.

Clifford, James. *Person and Myth: Maurice Leenhardt in the Melanesian World*. Los Angeles, University of California Press, 1982.

Cochrane, S. *Contemporary Art in Papua New Guinea*. Sydney, Craftsman House, 1997.

Cole, Rodney V., and Cuthbertson, S. *Population Growth in the South Pacific Island States—Implications for Australia*. Canberra, Bureau of Immigration, 1995.

Cole, Rodney V. (Ed.). *Pacific 2010—Challenging the Future*. Canberra, Development Studies Centre, Australian National University, 1993.

Cole, Rodney V., and Parny, T. G. (Eds). *Selected Issues in Pacific Island Development*. Canberra, Development Studies Centre, Australian National University, 1986.

Connell, John. *New Caledonia or Kanaky? The Political History of a French Colony*. Canberra, Development Studies Centre, Australian National University, 1987.

Connell, John. *Papua New Guinea: The Struggle for Development*. London, Routledge, 1997.

Connell, John et al. *Encyclopedia of the Pacific Islands*. Canberra, Australian National University, 1999.

Connell, John, and Lea, John (Eds). *Planning the Future: Melanesian Cities in 2010*. Canberra, Development Studies Centre, Australian National University, 1993.

Urbanisation in Polynesia. Canberra, Development Studies Centre, Australian National University, 1996.

Urbanization in the Island Pacific. London, Routledge, 2002.

Connell, John, and McCall, G. (Eds). *A World Perspective on Pacific Islander Migration: Australia, New Zealand and the USA*. Centre for Pacific Studies, University of New South Wales, 1992.

Coutau-Bégarie, H. *Géostratégie du Pacifique*. Paris, Economica, 1987.

Craig, Robert D. *Historical Dictionary of Polynesia*. Metuchen, NJ, Scarecrow Press, 1994.

Craig, Robert and King, Frank (Eds). *Historical Dictionary of Oceania*. London, Greenwood Press, 1981.

Crocombe, Ron. *The South Pacific*. Suva, Institute of Pacific Studies, University of the South Pacific, 1989 (revised 2001).

The Pacific Islands and the USA. Suva, Institute of Pacific Studies, 1995.

Crocombe, Ron, and Ali, A. *Politics in Melanesia*. Suva, Institute of Pacific Studies, University of the South Pacific, 1982.

Daniel, P., and Sims, R. *Foreign Investment in Papua New Guinea: Policies and Practices*. Canberra, Development Studies Centre, Australian National University, 1986.

Davidson, J. W. *Samoa Mo Samoa: the Emergence of the Independent State of Western Samoa*. Melbourne, Oxford University Press, 1967.

Davis, T. *Island Boy, an Autobiography*. Suva, Institute of Pacific Studies, University of the South Pacific, 1992.

Daws, G. *Shoal of Time. A History of the Hawaiian Islands*. Honolulu, HI, University of Hawaii Press, 1968.

A Dream of Islands. Queensland, Jacaranda Press, 1980.

Debsky, R. *The Organization of Development in the South Pacific*. Honolulu, Pacific Islands Studies Program, Center for Asian and Pacific Studies, 1986.

Decentralisation in the South Pacific: Local, Provincial and State Government in Twenty Countries. Suva, University of the South Pacific, 1986.

De Deckker, Paul and Kuntz, Laurence. *La Bataille de la Coutume*. Paris, L'Harmattan, 1997.

De Deckker, Paul, and Tryon, Darell (Eds). *Identités en Mutation dans le Pacifique à l'Aube du Troisième Millénaire, Iles et Archipels No. 26*. Cret, Coll., Université de Bordeaux III, 1998.

De Deckker, Paul. *Le Peuplement du Pacifique et de la Nouvelle-Calédonie au X1Xè siècle*. Paris, L'Harmattan & U.F.P., 1994.

De Deckker, Paul , and Faberon, Jean-Yves (Eds). *Custom and the Law*. Canberra, Asia Pacific Press 2001.

Delgado, James P. *Ghost fleet: The Sunken Ships of Bikini Atoll*. Honolulu, HI, University of Hawaii Press, 1996.

Denoon, Donald, Firth, S., Linnekin, J., Meleisea, M. and Nero, K. *The Cambridge History of the Pacific Islanders*. Cambridge, Cambridge University Press, 1998.

Denoon, Donald, and Mein-Smith, Philippa. *A History of Australia, New Zealand and the Pacific*. Malden, Blackwell, 2000.

Diamond, J. *Guns, Germs and Steel—The Fate of Human Societies*. New York, W. W. Norton, 1997.

Diaz, Vincente M. *Native Pacific Cultural Studies on the Edge*. Honolulu, HI, University of Hawaii Press, 2001.

Dibblin, Jane. *Day of Two Suns: US Nuclear Testing and the Pacific Islanders*. New York, NY, New Amsterdam Books, 1990.

Dinnen, Sinclair, and Ley, Alison (Eds). *Reflections on Violence in Melanesia*. Canberra, Asia Pacific Press, Australian National University, 2000.

Dinnen, Sinclair, May, Ron, and Regan, Anthony J. (Eds). *Challenging the State: The Sandline Affair in Papua New Guinea*. Canberra, Australian National University, 1998.

Dinnen, Sinclair. *Law and Order in a Weak State—Crime and Politics in Papua New Guinea, Pacific Islands Monograph Series, No.17*. Honolulu, HI, The University of Hawaii Press, 2001.

Diolé, P. *The Forgotten People of the Pacific*. London, Cassell, 1976.

Docherty, James. *Historical Dictionary of Australia, No.1*. Metchuen, NJ, Scarecrow Press, 1992.

Dorney, Sean. *The Sandline Affair: Politics and Mercenaries and the Bougainville Crisis*. ABC Books, 1998.

Dorrance, John C. *The United States and the Pacific Islands*. Westport, CT, Praeger, 1992.

Douglas, Bronwen. *Across the Great Divide—Journeys in History and Anthropology*. Amsterdam, Harwood Academic Publishers, 1998.

Douglas, Ngaire, and Norman, Douglas (Eds). *Pacific Islands Yearbook*. Suva, Fiji Times Ltd.

Doumenge, F. *L'Homme dans le Pacifique Sud; Etude Géographique*. Paris, Société des Océanistes, 1966.

Doumenge, J.P. *Du Terroir à la Ville, les Mélanésiens et leurs espaces en Nouvelle-Calédonie*. Bordeaux, CRET, CEGET, Université de Bordeaux 1982.

Dubois, Marie-Joseph. *Les Chefferies de Maré*. Paris, Librarie, H. Champion, 1977.

Dunmore, John. *Who's Who in Pacific Navigation*. Honolulu, HI, University of Hawaii Press, 1991.

Visions and Realities—France in the Pacific, 1695–1995. Auckland, Heritage Press, 1997.

Duroy, L. Hienghène, le désespoir calédonien. Barrault, 1988.

Dye, Bob (Ed). *World War Two in Hawaii from the pages of 'Paradise of the Pacific'*. Honolulu, HI, University of Hawaii Press, 2001.

Emberson-Bain, A. *Labour and Gold in Fiji*. Cambridge, Cambridge University Press, 1994.

Emberson-Bain, A. (Ed.). *Sustainable Development of Malignant Growth? Perspectives of Pacific Island Women*. Suva, Marama Publications, 1995.

Ernst, Manfred. *Winds of Change*. Suva, Pacific Conference of Churches, 1994.

Fairbairn, T. I. J. *Island Economies: Studies From the South Pacific*. Suva, Institute of Pacific Studies, University of the South Pacific, 1985.

Fairbairn, T. I. J., Morrison, C., Baker, R., and Groves, S. *The Pacific Islands*. Honolulu, HI, University of Hawaii Press, 1991.

Figiel, S. *Where We Once Belonged*. Auckland, Pasifika Press, 1997.

Finnegan Ruth and Orbell, Margaret. *South Pacific Oral Traditions*. Bloomington, IN, Indiana University Press, 1995.

Fischer, Steven Roger. *A History of the Pacific Islands*. Basingstoke, Palgrave Global Publishing, 2002.

Fleming, Euan, and Hardaker, Brian. *Pacific 2010: Strategies for Melanesian Agriculture for 2010: Tough Choices*. Canberra, National Centre for Development Studies, Australian National University, 1994.

Foerstel, L., and Gilliam, A. (Eds). *Confronting the Margaret Mead Legacy: Scholarship, Empire and the South Pacific*. Philadelphia, Temple University Press, 1992.

Forbes, David W. (Ed.). *Hawaiian National Bibliography, 1780–1900, Vol. 2: 1831–1850*. Honolulu, HI, University of Hawaii Press, 2001.

Foster, Robert (Ed.). *Nation-making Emergent Identities in Post-colonial Melanesia*. Ann Arbor, University of Michigan Press, 1995.

Franceschi, M. *La Démocratie Massacrée: Consensus ou Mystification à Nouméa?* Paris, Pygmalion, 1998.

Freeman, D. *Margaret Mead and Samoa: The Making and Unmaking of an Anthropological Myth*. Harmondsworth, Penguin, 1983.

Fry, Gerald and Rufino, Mauricio (Eds). *Pacific Basin and Oceania, World Bibliographical Series, Vol. 70*. Oxford. Clio Press, 1987.

Galipaud, Jean-Christophe and Lilley, Ian (Eds). *Le Pacifique de 5000 à 2000 avant le present—Supplements a L'Histoire d'une Colonisation*. Paris, Edition de l'Institut de Recherche pour le Development, 1999.

Gannicott, Ken. *Pacific 2010—Women's Education and Economic Development in Melanesia*. Canberra, National University Centre for Development Studies, 1994.

Garrett, John. *Island Exiles*. Melbourne, ABC Books, 1996.

To live among the stars—Christian origins in Oceania. Suva, University of the South Pacific, 1982.

Footsteps in the Sea—Christianity in Oceania Since World War II. Suva, University of the South Pacific, 1992.

Where Nets Were Cast—Christianity in Oceania Since World War II. Suva, University of the South Pacific, 1997.

Geddes, W. H., et al. *Atoll Economy: Social Change in Kiribati and Tuvalu, Islands on the Line Team Report No. 1*. Canberra, Australian National University Press, 1982.

Ghai, Y. *Law, Politics and Government in Pacific Island States*. Suva, University of the South Pacific, 1988.

Gill, W. W. *Cook Islands Customs*. Cook Islands, University of the South Pacific and the Ministry of Education, 1979.

Gille, Bernard et Toullelan, Pierre Yves. *De la Conquête à l'Exode—Histoire des Océaniens et de leurs Migrations dans le Pacifique. Tome 1. Les Migrations Contraintes en Océénia, Terres de Colonisation et D'immigration*. Papeete, Tahiti, Au Vent des Îles, 1999.

Goetzfridt, Nicholas. *Indigenous Literature of Oceania—A Survey of Criticism and Interpretation*. Westport, CT, Greenwood Press, 1995.

Goodman, R., Lepani, C., and Morawetz, D. *The Economy of Papua New Guinea: An Independent Review*. Canberra, Development Studies Centre, Australian National University, 1985.

Gorman, G.E. and Mills, J.J. (Eds). *Fiji,. World Bibliography, Volume 173*. Oxford, Clio Press, 1992.

Gostin, O. *Cash Cropping, Catholicism and Change: Resettlement among the Kuni of Papua*. Canberra, Development Studies Centre, Australian National University, 1986.

Grynberg, Roman. *Rules of Origin Issues in Pacific Island Development*. Canberra, Asia Pacific Press, Australian National University, 1998.

Gunson, W. N. (Ed.). *The Changing Pacific: Essays in Honour of H. E. Maude*. Melbourne, Oxford University Press, 1978.

Hanlon, David and White, Geoffrey. *Voyaging through the Contemporary Pacific*. New York, NY, Rowman, Littlefield and Publishers, 2000.

Harding, Thomas, Lockwood, Victoria, and Wallace, Ben (Eds). *Contemporary Pacific Societies: Studies in Development and Change*. Englewood Cliffs, Prentice Hall, 1993.

Hau'ofa, E., Naidu, V., and Waddell, E. (Eds). *A New Oceania: Rediscovering Our Sea of Islands*. Suva, University of the South Pacific, 1993.

Hayes, P., Zarskey, L., and Bello, W. *American Lake: Nuclear Peril in the Pacific*. Harmondsworth, Penguin, 1986.

Henningham, Stephen. *France and the South Pacific: A Contemporary History*. Sydney, Allen and Unwin, 1992.

Henningham, Stephen, and May, R.J. *Resources, Development and Politics in the Pacific Islands*. Bathurst, Crawford House Press, 1992.

Heyerdahl, Thor. *Green was the Earth on the Seventh Day*. London, Little Brown, 1997.

Hezel, F. X. *Strangers in Their Own Land: A Century of Colonial Rule in the Caroline and Marshall Islands*. Honolulu, HI, University of Hawaii Press, 1995.

The New Shape of Old Island Cultures—A Half Century of Social Change in Micronesia. Honolulu, HI, University of Hawaii Press, 2001.

Hintjens, Helen M., and Newitt, M. D. (Eds). *The Political Economy of Small Tropical Islands: The Importance of Being Small*. Exeter, University of Exeter Press, 1992.

History of Micronesia. Québec, Levesque Publications.

Hongo, G. *Volcano: A Memoir of Hawai'i*. Washington, Knopf, 1995.

Hooper, Antony (Ed.). *Culture and Sustainable Development in the Pacific*. Canberra, Australian National University, 2000.

Howard, Michael. *Mining, Politics and Development in the South Pacific*. Boulder, Westview Press, 1991.

Howe, Kerry, Kiste, Robert, and Lal, Brij (Eds). *Tides of History: The Pacific Islands in the Twentieth Century*. Sydney, Allen and Unwin, 1994.

Howe, Kerry. *The Loyalty Islands—A History of Culture Contacts 1840–1900*. Honolulu, HI, University of Hawaii Press, 1977.

Where the waves fall: A new South Seas islands history from first settlement to colonial rule. Honolulu, HI, University of Hawaii Press, 1984.

Nature, Culture and History—The 'Knowing' of Oceania. Honolulu, HI, University of Hawaii Press, 2000.

Huffer, Elise, and So'o, Asofou (Eds). *Governance in Samoa*. Canberra, Asia Pacific Press, Australian National University, 2000.

Huntsman, Judith, and Hooper, Antony. *Tokelau, A Historical Ethnography*. Honolulu, HI, University of Hawaii Press, 1997.

Institute of Pacific Studies, University of the South Pacific. *Micronesian Politics*. Suva, 1988.

Institute of Pacific Studies, University of the South Pacific, and Ministry of Education, Training and Culture, Kiribati. *Kiribati: Aspects of History*. 1979.

Jackson, Keith, and McRobie, Alan. *Historical Dictionary of New Zealand, No.5*. Metchuen, NJ, Scarecrow Press, 1996.

Jones, Peter D. *From Bikini to Belau: The Nuclear Colonization of the Pacific*. London, War Resisters International, 1988.

Kaeppler, Adrienne, and Nimmo, Arlo H. Eds). *Directions in Pacific Traditional Literature*. Honolulu, HI, Bishop Museum Press, 1976.

Kamisese, Ratu. *The Pacific Way: a Memoir*. Honolulu, HI, University of Hawaii Press, 1997.

Kaul, M. M. *Pearls in the Ocean: Security Perspectives in the South-West Pacific*. New Delhi, UBSPD, 1993.

Keating, Elizabeth. *Power Sharing—Language, Rank, Gender and Social Space in Pohnpei, Micronesia*. Oxford University Press, 1999.

Kernahan, M. *White Savages in the South Seas*. London, Verso, 1996.

King, D., and Ranck, S. *Papua New Guinea Atlas*. Robert Brown and University of Papua New Guinea, 1982.

Kirch, Vinton. P. (Ed.). *Island Societies—Archeological Approaches to Evolution and Transformation*. Cambridge, Cambridge University Press, 1986.

Kirch, Vinton P. *On the Road of the Wind—An Archeological History of the Pacific Islands before the European Contact*. Berkeley, CA, University of California Press, 2000.

Kirch, Vinton P. and Hunt, Terry L. (Eds). *Historical Ecology in the Pacific Islands: Prehistoric Environmental and Landscape Change*. Yale University Press, 1997.

Kluge, P. F. *The Edge of Paradise: America in Micronesia*. New York, NY, Random House, 1991.

Koburger, Charles W. *Pacific Turning Point: The Solomon Islands Campaign, 1942–1943*. London, Greenwood Publishing, 1995.

Kramer, Dr Anthony. *The Samoa Islands*. Auckland, Pasifika Press, 1994.

Kramer, Augustin. *The Samoa Islands: Volume 1: Constitution, Pedigrees and Traditions*. Honolulu, HI, University of Hawaii, 2000.

Krieger, M. *Conversations with Cannibals: the End of the Old Pacific*. Ecco Press, 1994.

Lal, Brij V. *Girmitiyas: the Origin of Fiji Indians*. Canberra, Journal of Pacific History, 1983.

Politics in Fiji: Studies in Contemporary History. Hawaii, Brigham Young University, Institute for Polynesian Studies, 1986.

Power and Prejudice: The Making of the Fiji Crisis. Wellington, New Zealand Institute of International Affairs, 1989.

Another way: the politics of constitutional reform in post-coup Fiji. Canberra, Australian National University, 1998.

Lacey, Rod. *'Whose voices are heard? Oral history and the Decolonisation of History' in Emerging from Empire?—Decolonisation in the Pacific*. Canberra, Australian National University, 1997, pp. 180–186.

Lal, Brij V. and Fortune, K. (Eds). *The Pacific Islands: An Encyclopedia*. Honolulu, HI, University of Hawaii Press, 2000.

Larmour, Peter (Ed.). *Governance and Reform in the South Pacific*. Canberra, Development Studies Centre, Australian National University, 1997.

Latukefu, S. *Church and State in Tonga*. Canberra, Australian National University, 1974.

Laux, Claire. *Les Théocraties Missionnaires en Polynésie (Tahiti, Hawaii, Cook, Tonga, Gambier, Wallis et Futuna) au XIVè siècle. Des Cités de Dieu dans les Mers du Sud?* Paris, L'Harmattan, 2000.

101 mots pour comprendre l'Océanie. Nouméa, Ile de Lumière 2002

Lawson, Stephanie. *Tradition versus Democracy in the South Pacific: Fiji, Tonga and Western Samoa*. Cambridge, Cambridge University Press, 1996.

Leckie, Jacqueline. *To Labour with the State: The Fiji Public Service Association*. Dunedin, University of Otago Press, 1997.

Leibowitz, A. *Defining Status: A Comprehensive Analysis of the United States' Territorial Relations*. Hingham, MA, Kluwer Academic Publishers, 1989.

Levantis, Theodore. *Papua New Guinea: employment, wages and economic development*. Canberra, Australian National University, 2000.

Levy, Neil M. *Micronesia Handbook*. Emeryville, CA, Moon Publications, 1999.

Lewis, D. *The Voyaging Stars—Secrets of the Pacific Island Navigators*. Sydney and London, Collins, 1978.

Lieber, M. D. (Ed.). *Exiles and Migrants in Oceania*. Honolulu, HI, University of Hawaii Press, 1977.

Lindstrom, Lamont. *Knowledge and Power in a South Pacific Society*. Washington, DC, Smithsonian Institute Press, 1990.

Lobban, Christopher, and Schefter, Maria. *Tropical Pacific Island Environments*. Hagåtña, University of Guam Press, 1998.

Löffler, E. *Geomorphology of Papua New Guinea*. Canberra, Australian National University, 1977.

Lummis, Trevor. *Life and Death in Eden: Pitcairn Island and the Bounty Mutineers*. London, Phoenix, 2000.

Lynch, John, and Mugler, France. *Pacific Languages in Education*. Suva, University of the South Pacific, 1996.

Mageo, Jeanette, M. *Cultural Memory—Reconfiguring History and Identity in the Postcolonial Pacific*. Honolulu, HI, University of Hawaii Press, 2001.

Marchal, H (Ed.). *De Jade et de Nacre—Patrimonie Artistique Kanak*. Paris, Réunion des Musées Nationaux, 1990.

McConnel, Frasier (Ed.). *Papua New Guinea. World Bibliography, Volume 90*. Oxford, Clio Press, 1990.

McInnes, D. (Ed.). *Encyclopaedia of Papua New Guinea*. Mount Waverley, Dellasta Pacific, 1996.

McKnight, Tom Lee. *Oceania—The Geography of Australia, New Zealand and the Pacific Islands*. Englewood, Prentice Hall, 1995.

Meleisea, M. *Lalaga: A Short History of Western Samoa*. Suva, University of the South Pacific, 1987.

Meller, Norman. *Constitutionalism in Micronesia*. Honolulu, HI, University of Hawaii Press, 1986.

Miles, J., and Shaw, E. *The French Presence in the South Pacific 1838–1990*. Auckland, Greenpeace, 1990.

Miles, John. *Infectious Diseases—Colonising the Pacific?* Dunedin, University of Otago Press, 1997.

Mills, Peter R. *Hawaii's Russian Adventure: A New Look at Old History*. Honolulu, HI, University of Hawaii Press, 2002.

Moorehead, A. *The Fatal Impact: The Invasion of the South Pacific 1767–1840*. London, Hamish Hamilton, 1966.

Murray, Spencer. *Pitcairn Island: The First 200 Years*. La Canada, CA, Bounty Sagas.

Naepels, Michel. *Histoires de Terrres Kanakes—Conflits Fonciers et Rapports Sociaux dans la Région de Houaïlou (Nouvelle Calédonie)*. Paris, Belin, 1998.

Narakobi Bernard Mullu. *The Melanesian Way*. Suva, Institute of Pacific Studies University, 1980.

Neemia, U. *Cooperation and Conflict: Costs, Benefits and National Interests in Pacific Regional Cooperation*. Suva, University of the South Pacific, Institute of Pacific Studies, 1986.

Newbury, C. *Tahiti Nui*. Honolulu, HI, University of Hawaii Press, 1980.

New Politics in the South Pacific. Suva, Institute of Pacific Studies, 1994.

Nicolson, Robert. *The Pitcairners*. Honolulu, HI, University of Hawaii Press, 1997.

Nordyke, E. C. *The Peopling of Hawaii*. Honolulu, HI, University of Hawaii Press, 1977.

Nunn, Patrick and Waddell Eric (Eds). *The Margin Fades—Geographical Itineraries on a World of Islands*. Suva, University of the South Pacific, 1994.

O'Callaghan, Mary-Louise. *Enemies Within: Papua New Guinea, Australia and the Sandline Crisis*. Doubleday Australia, 1998.

Oliver, Douglas L. *Native Cultures of the Pacific Islands*. Honolulu, HI, University of Hawaii Press, 1989.

The Pacific Islands. Honolulu, HI, University of Hawaii Press, 1989.

Black Islanders—A Personal Perspective of Bougainville 1937–1991. Melbourne, Hyland House Publishing, 1991.

Otto, Ton, and Borsboom, Ad. *Cultural Dynamics of Religious Change in Oceania*. Leiden, Netherlands, Kitlv Press, 1997.

Overton, John, and Scheyrens (Eds). *Strategies for Sustainable Development—Experiences from the Pacific*. Sydney, University of New South Wales Press, 1999.

Parmentier, R.J. *The Sacred Remains: Myth, History and Polity in Belau*. Chicago, University of Chicago Press, 1987.

Peterson, G. *Ethnicity and Interest at the 1990 Federated States of Micronesia Constitutional Convention*. Canberra, Australian National University, 1994.

Poirine, Bernard. *Les Petites Economies Insulaires: Théories et Stratégies de Développement*. Paris, L'Harmattan, 1995.

Pollock, Nancy J. *These Roots Remain: Food Habits in Islands of the Central and Eastern Pacific since Western Contact*. Honolulu, HI, University of Hawaii Press, 1992.

Poyer, Lin, Falgout, Suzanne, and Carucci, Laurence, M. (Eds). *The Typhoon of War, Micronesian Experiences of the Pacific War*. Honolulu, HI, University of Hawaii Press, 2001.

Quadling, P. *Bougainville—The Mine and the People*. Sydney, Centre for Independent Studies, 1991.

Quanchi, M., and Adams, R. (Eds). *Culture Contact in the Pacific: Essays on Contact Encounter and Response*. New York, Cambridge University Press, 1992.

Rainier, Chris, and Taylor, Meg. *Where Masks Still Dance: New Guinea*. London, Little Brown, 1997.

Rannels, J. *PNG—A Modern Fact Book on Papua New Guinea*. Melbourne, Oxford University Press, 1995.

Rapaport, Moshe (Ed.). *The Pacific Islands—Environment and Society*. Hawaii, HI, University of Hawaii Press, 1999.

Ravuvu, A. D. *Development or Dependence: The Pattern of Change in a Fijian Village*. Suva, Institute of Pacific Studies, University of the South Pacific, 1988.

Revue Tiers-Monde. *Le Pacifique Insulaire—Nations, Aides, Espaces, Numéro Special de la Revue Tiers-Monde, Tome XXXVIII, No.*149. Paris, Université de Paris, 1997.

Ridgell, Reilly. *Pacific Nations and Territories*. Honolulu, HI, University of Hawaii Press, 1998.

Robert, Craig, and King, Frank. *Historical Dictionary of Oceania*. London, Greenwood Press, 1981.

Robie, D. *Eyes of Fire: The Last Voyage of the Rainbow Warrior*. Auckland, Lindon Publishing, 1986.

Robie, D. (Ed.). *Tu Galala—Social Change in the Pacific*. Wellington, Bridget Williams Books, 1992.

Robillard, A. B. (Ed.). *Social Change in the Pacific Islands*. London, Kegan Paul International, 1992.

Rodman, Margaret C. *Houses Far From Home—British Colonial Space in the New Hebrides*. Honolulu, HI, University of Hawaii Press, 2001.

Rogers, R. F. *Destiny's Landfall: A History of Guam*. Honolulu, HI, University of Hawaii Press, 1996.

Rose, R. G. *Hawaii: The Royal Isles*. Honolulu, HI, Bishop Museum, 1980.

Ross, K. *Regional Security in the South Pacific: the Quarter-Century 1970–95*. Canberra, Strategic and Defence Studies Centre, Australian National University, 1993.

Rubinstein, H. J., and Zimmet, P. *Phosphate, Wealth and Health in Nauru: a study of lifestyle change*. Caulfield, Brolga Press, 1993.

Rumsey, Alan, and Weiner, James. *Emplaced Myth—Space, Narrative and Knowledge in Aboriginal Australia and Papua New Guinea*. Honolulu, HI, The University of Hawaii Press, 2001.

Sacks, O. *The Island of the Colorblind*. London, Picador, 1997.

Saffu, Y. (Ed.). *The 1992 Papua New Guinea Election—Change and Continuity in Electoral Politics*. Canberra, Australian National University, 1996.

Sahlins, M. *How 'Natives' Think: About Captain Cook, For Example*. Chicago, University of Chicago, 1996.

Sand, Christophe. *Le Temps d'Avant—La Préhistoire de la Nouvelle Calédonie*. Paris, L'Harmattan, 1995.

Scarr, Deryck. *A History of the Pacific Islands: Passages through Tropical Time*. London, Curzon Press, 2000.

Schoeffel, Penelope. *Sociocultural Issues and Economic Development in the Pacific Islands*. Manila, Asian Development Bank, Pacific Studies Series, 1996.

Segal, G. *Rethinking the Pacific*. London, Oxford University Press, 1990.

Seward, Robert. *Radio Happy Isles: Media and Politics at Play in the Pacific*. Honolulu, HI, University of Hawaii Press, 1998.

Sharphan, J. *Rabuka of Fiji: the Authorised Biography of Major-General Sitiveni Rabuka*. Queensland, Central Queensland University Press, 2000.

Shineberg, Dorothy. They came for Santalwood—A Study of the Santalwood Trade in the South-West Pacific, 1830–1865. Melbourne, Melbourne University Press, 1967.

The People Trade—Pacific Island Laborers and New Caledonia, 1865–1930, Pacific Island Monograph series No.16. Honolulu, HI, University of Hawaii Press, 1999.

Short, F. G. *Sinners and Sandalwood*. North Leura, NSW, Jomaru Press, 1997.

Sissons, J. *Nation and Destination: Creating a Cook Islands Identity*. Suva, Institute of Pacific Studies, University of South Pacific, 1999.

Skully, M. T. (Ed.). *Financial Institutions and Markets in the Southwest Pacific*. London, Macmillan, 1985.

Skully, M. T., and Fairbairn, T. I. J. *Private Sector Development in the South Pacific: Options for Donor Assistance*. Centre for South Pacific Studies, University of New South Wales, 1992.

Smith, Bernard. *European Vision and the South Pacific*. New Haven, CT, Yale University Press, 1989.

Smith, Gary. *Micronesia: Decolonization and US Military Interests in the Trust Territories of the Pacific Islands*. Canberra, Australian National University, 1991.

Somare, M. T. *Sana, an Autobiography*. Port Moresby, Niugini Press, 1975.

So'o, Asofou. *Universal Suffrage in Western Samoa: the 1991 General Elections*. Canberra, Australian National University, 1994.

Spate, O. H. K. *The Pacific Since Magellan*. Canberra, Australian National University. Vol. 1: The Spanish Lake, 1981; Vol. 2: Monopolists and Freebooters, 1983.

Speiser, F. *Ethnology of Vanuatu*. Bathurst, NSW, Crawford House Press, 1991.

Stanley, D. *South Pacific Handbook*. Emeryville, CA, Moon Publications, 1989.

Tahiti—Polynesia Handbook. Emeryville, CA, Moon Publications, 1999.

Fiji Islands Handbook. Emeryville, CA, Moon Publications, 2001.

Subramani. *South Pacific Literature—From Myth to Fabulation*. Suva, University of the South Pacific, 1992.

Swain, Tony, and Trompf, Gary. *The Religions of Oceania*. London, Routledge, 1995.

Syed, Saifullah, and Mataio, Ngatokorua. *Agriculture in the Cook Islands—New Directions*. Institute of Pacific Studies, and University of the South Pacific, 1993.

Tait, M. (Ed.). *The Papua New Guinea Handbook*. Canberra, Australian National University, irregular.

Taylor, M. (Ed.). *Fiji: Future Imperfect?* Sydney, Allen and Unwin, 1987.

Temu, Ila (Ed.). *Papua New Guinea: a 20/20 vision*. Canberra, Australian National University, 1997.

Thakur, R. (Ed.). *The South Pacific: Problems, issues and prospects*. Macmillan and the University of Otago, 1991.

Thawley, John (Ed.). *Australasia and South Pacific Islands Bibliography, Area Bibliograhpies No.12*. London, Scarecrow & Lanham, 1997.

Thomas, Nicholas. *In Oceania: Visions, Artifacts, Histories*. Durham, NC/London, Duke University Press, 1997.

Marquesan Societies - Inequality an Political Transformation in Eastern Polynesia. Oxford, Clarendon Press, 1990.

Tjibaou, Jean Marie, and Missotte, P. *Kanake, Melanesien de Nouvelle Caledonie*. Papeete, Tahiti, Les Editions du Pacifique, 1976.

Kanaké—the Melanesian Way. Papeete, Les Editions du Pacifique, with Suva, University of the South Pacific, 1982.

Tjibaou, Jean-Marie. *La Presence Kanak*. Paris, O. Jacob, 1996.

Tolron, Francine. *La Nouvelle- Zélande—Histoire et Représentations*. Avignon, Université d'Avignon, 2000.

Toohey, John. *Captain Bligh's Portable Nightmare*. Fourth Estate, 1998.

Treadgold, M. L. *Bounteous Bestowal: The Economic History of Norfolk Island*. Canberra, Development Studies Centre, Australian National University, 1988.

Tudor, J. (Ed.). *Pacific Islands Year Book and Who's Who*. Sydney, Pacific Publications, Ltd.

Turner, Ann (Ed.). *Historical Dictionary of Papua New Guinea No.4*. Metuchen, NJ, Scarecrow Press, 1994.

University of the South Pacific. *South Pacific Bibliography 1981, 1982, 1983, 1984, 1985, 1988, 1989-90, 1991, 1992-3, 1994-5*. Suva, Pacific Information Centre, University of the South Pacific.

University of the South Pacific. *South Pacific Bibliography 1996–97*. Suva, Pacific Information Centre, University of the South Pacific, 1998.

Uriam, K. K. *In Their Own Words—History and Society in Gilbertese Oral Tradition*. Canberra, Journal of Pacific History, 1996.

Usher, L. *Letters from Fiji 1987–1990*. Suva, Fiji Times Ltd, 1992.

Viviani, N. *Nauru*. Canberra, Australian National University, 1970.

Waiko, John Dademo. *A Short History of Papua New Guinea*. Oxford, Oxford University Press, 1995.

Ward, R. G. (Ed.). *Man in the Pacific Islands: Essays on Geographical Change in the Pacific Islands*. Oxford, Clarendon Press, 1972.

Ward, R. G., and Proctor, A. W. *South Pacific Agriculture: Choices and Constraints. South Pacific Agricultural Survey 1979*. Canberra, Australian National University, and Asian Development Bank, 1980.

Weeramantry, C. *Nauru—Environmental Damage Under International Trusteeship*. Melbourne, Oxford University Press, 1992.

Weightman, B. *Agriculture in Vanuatu: A Historical Review*. Cheam, British Friends of Vanuatu, 1989.

Wenkam, R., and Baker, B. *Micronesia*. Honolulu, HI, University of Hawaii Press, 1971.

White, Geoffrey M., and Lindstrom, Lamont (Eds). *Chiefs Today—Traditional Pacific Leadership and the Postcolonial State*. Cambridge, Cambridge University Press, 1998.

Wilson, Lynn. *Speaking to Power: Gender and Politics in the Western Pacific*. New York, Routledge, 1995.

Winchester, S. *The Pacific*. London, Hutchinson, 1991.

Wittersheim, Eric. *Melanesian Elites and Modern Politics in New Caledonia and Vanuatu, National Centre for Development Studies, Discussion and Policy Papers, No.3*. Canberra, Australian University Press, 1998.

Wurm, S. A., and Hattori, S. *Language Atlas of the Pacific Area. Part 1: New Guinea Area, Oceania, Australia*. Canberra, Australian Academy of the Humanities, and Tokyo, Japan Academy, Pacific Linguistics Series C, No. 66, 1981.

PAKISTAN

Physical and Social Geography

B. H. FARMER

The Islamic Republic of Pakistan covers an area of 796,095 sq km (307,374 sq miles), excluding Jammu and Kashmir (the sovereignty of which is disputed with India). The territory of Pakistan extends from 23° 45′ to 36° 50′ N and between 60° 55′ and 75° 30′ E, and is bounded to the west, north-west and north by Iran and Afghanistan (a narrow panhandle in the high Pamirs separates it from direct contact with Tajikistan), to the north-east by the People's Republic of China, to the east and south-east by India and by Jammu and Kashmir, and to the south by the Arabian Sea. Pakistan, like the Republic of India, became independent on 15 August 1947, and inherited, generally speaking, those contiguous districts of the former Indian empire that had a Muslim majority. Its former eastern wing became the independent People's Republic of Bangladesh after the Indo-Pakistan war of December 1971.

PHYSICAL FEATURES

Much of Pakistan is mountainous or, at any rate, highland. Its northernmost territories consist of the tangled mountains among which the western Himalayas run into the high Karakoram and Pamir ranges. From these the mighty River Indus breaks out through wild gorges to the plains. West of the Indus lies Chitral, a territory of hill ranges, deep gorges and high plateaux. South of this, on the Afghan border, structures are simpler, consisting essentially of a series of mountain arcs such as the Safed Koh, Sulaiman and Kirthar ranges, less complex in geological structure and lower in height than the Himalayas, Pamirs or Karakoram, breached by famous passes such as the Khaibar and Bolan, and enclosing belts of plateau country. Balochistan, the westernmost part of Pakistan's territory, is essentially a region of plateaux and ranges which run over the border into Iran.

Contrasting strongly with all this high and often mountainous terrain is the plain country to the south-east. Part of the great Indo-Gangetic plain, this consists for the most part of the alluvium brought down by the Indus and its tributaries, of which by far the most important are the five rivers of the Punjab, the Jhelum, Chenab, Ravi, Beas and Sutlej (part of whose course lies, however, in Indian or Kashmiri territory). The southern part of the border with India runs through the waterless wastes of the Thar Desert.

CLIMATE

The Pakistan plains, like those of northern India, have an annual cycle of three seasons. The 'cool season' (December to February) has relatively low average temperatures (Lahore, 12°C January) but warm days. Karachi, farther south and on the coast, is rather warmer (18°C January average). This season is dry, apart from rain brought by north-westerly disturbances. The 'hot season' (March to May) builds up to very high temperatures (Lahore, 31.5°C May average, but up to 48.5°C by day, and even hotter in that notorious hot-spot, Jacobabad; but rather less hot, 29.5°C May average, in Karachi); this season is dry. From June to September the south-west monsoon brings more wind, lower temperatures, and rains that are everywhere relatively light (3,430 mm in four months at Lahore) and that fall off to little or nothing westward into Balochistan and southward into Sindh and the Thar Desert. Much of Pakistan would, in fact, be agriculturally unproductive in the absence of irrigation. The mountains of Pakistan have a climatic regime modified by altitude and with a winter maximum of rainfall (such as it is) in the north-west, but, again, widely characterized by aridity.

VEGETATION AND NATURAL RESOURCES

There is very little 'natural' vegetation left, except for poor, semi-desert scrub in uncultivated portions of the plains of Pakistan (such as part of the Thal, between the Indus and Jhelum) and in Balochistan, and montane forests in parts of the western and northern hills (notably the Sulaimans). Even this surviving vegetation has been degraded by man: for instance, by the practice of pastoralism in Balochistan and elsewhere in the western hills and plateaux. Not surprisingly, Pakistan is desperately short of timber, and has actually planted irrigated forests, especially of shisham (*Dalbergia sissoo*), in the Thal and elsewhere.

The soils of the plains of Pakistan, like those in similar physiographic circumstances in India, exhibit considerable variety. Those of the Thar Desert tend to be poor and sandy, and there is a good deal of natural salinity in the more arid tracts, especially in Sindh. More fertile alluvium follows the main rivers and also spreads more widely in the Punjab, but there is, again as in India, the danger of man-induced salinity and alkalinity with the spread of irrigation, and consequent rise in the water-table and capillary ascent of salts to the surface. Indeed, large areas of land have gone out of cultivation for just this reason. The hill areas of Pakistan tend to have poor, skeletal mountain soils, though better conditions prevail in some innermost valleys.

Most of the mineral wealth is concentrated in the mountainous regions of Pakistan. Twenty types of mineral had been identified at the time of partition, but only coal (sub-bituminous and non-coking), rock salt, chromite, gypsum and limestone were mined. Fireclay, silica sand, celestite, ochres and iron ore are now also commercially exploited, and there may be commercial deposits of copper, manganese, bauxite and phosphates. Pakistan's most important energy resource is undoubtedly natural gas, found at Sui and other locations in the Indus plain and piped thence to Lahore, Karachi and other towns. Exploration has also revealed a number of oilfields, and there are hopes of self-sufficiency in petroleum.

POPULATION

According to the latest census, the population on 2 March 1998 was 130,579,571. The average annual rate of increase between 1990 and 1998 was 2.8%. The estimated population at 30 June 2001 was 140,470,000, giving an average density of 176 inhabitants per sq km. Pakistan has densities of more than 300 per sq km in well-watered districts such as Lyallpur. Pakistan also has sizeable conurbations in Karachi (population 9,269,000 at the 1998 census) and Lahore (population 5,063,000 in 1998).

There is considerable ethnic diversity within Pakistan. Tall, relatively fair and blue-eyed Pathans of the western hills contrast with darker, brown-eyed (though also often tall) 'plainsmen'—itself a heterogeneous category.

Although the population of Pakistan is overwhelmingly Muslim (about 95% at the 1981 census), it is divided, not only by race but also by linguistic and by tribal differences. Punjabi, Balochi and Pashtu (the language of the Pathans) are spoken; the official languages are Urdu and English. The Punjabi are the principal ethnic group, comprising about two-thirds of the total population. Other major groups are the Sindhi (13%), Pashtun (Iranian—8.5%), Urdu (7.6%) and Balochi (2.5%). Tribal divisions are most noticeable in the western hills, but also affect the plains where there are Janglis (once lawless nomads, now largely cultivators), Thiringiuzars (camel-herders) and other groups.

History*

SHARIF AL MUJAHID

Revised by IAN TALBOT and JOHN McGUIRE

Pakistan as a separate political entity came into being on 15 August 1947, under the leadership of Muhammad Ali Jinnah, popularly known as Quaid-i-Azam ('Great Leader'). The state of Pakistan was set up under the 3 June Partition Plan, often referred to as the Mountbatten Plan, which was accepted by the three main Indian parties—the Indian National Congress, the Muslim League and the Akali Dal, representing the Sikhs. The Indian Independence Act of July 1947, which was based on the Partition Plan, endowed the new state with its constitutional and legal sanction.

THE PROBLEMS OF PARTITION

From its very inception, Pakistan was faced with almost insurmountable problems. Some of these were inherent in the nature and logistics of its creation while others were engendered by forces hostile to its very existence.

Firstly, Pakistan was divided into two disparate sections. East Pakistan (the province of East Bengal), comprising only about one-seventh of the area, contained four-sevenths of the population, while West Pakistan (the provinces of Punjab, Sindh, the North-West Frontier Province (NWFP) and Balochistan), comprising six-sevenths of the area, had only three-sevenths of the population. This difference was to create anomalies in the application of the federal principle in subsequent years. Secondly, the two wings of Pakistan were about 1,600 km apart, separated by India. This led to an inter-wing communication problem, especially in view of India's traditional hostility. Thirdly, the most populous provinces, Bengal and the Punjab, were themselves partitioned, thus creating several problems for the newly created provinces. East Bengal lost both the capital and the chief port (Calcutta/Kolkata), and Punjab lost the water headworks to Eastern Punjab (India), turning vast tracts of its agricultural land into desert. East Bengal had to establish a makeshift capital at Dhaka, and trade through the undeveloped port at Chittagong. Fourthly, Pakistan did not inherit a central government, a capital, an administrative core, or an organized defence force. Karachi, with its extremely limited facilities, was the only city available to house the new nation's capital, and an improvised central government was established. The number of Muslims in the higher civil service was disappointingly low. Even the armed forces had to be built up out of those who had opted for Pakistan, many of whom were either in India or abroad at the time of partition.

The social and administrative resources of the country were meagre. The Punjab communal holocaust had caused extensive disruption. This, together with the mass migration of the Hindu and Sikh entrepreneurial and managerial classes, had badly damaged the economy. Furthermore, the nation was called upon to feed some 8m. refugees who had fled from the insecurities of the north Indian plains. Although it comprised about one-fifth of the subcontinent's area and population, Pakistan had less than one-tenth of the subcontinent's factories and industries. Its principal cash crops were jute in the East and cotton in the West; but all the jute and cotton mills were located in India. Pakistan lacked both capital and the technical expertise for industrial development.

Politically, however, the initial situation did not appear unfavourable. In Jinnah, Pakistan had a trusted and experienced leader, who fulfilled the nation's desperate need for imaginative, constructive and charismatic leadership, but he died within 13 months of independence. His chief lieutenant, Liaquat Ali Khan, the Prime Minister, was assassinated in 1951. The Muslim League failed to provide imaginative leadership capable of giving political coherence and direction in the formative stage. The political vacuum following Liaquat's assassination led to the rise of too many claimants for leadership, to frequent squabbles and conspiracies, and, in the end, to political instability.

Indo-Pakistani Disputes

Other problems were the result of the Radcliffe Boundary Commission's award and the peculiar nature of Indo-Pakistani relations. The state of Jammu and Kashmir had a large Muslim majority and was contiguous to Pakistan, with which all its economic interests and communications were linked. Without the award of the Muslim majority district of Gurdaspur to India, India would not have had physical access to it at all. India succeeded in annexing the state when the Hindu ruler's position was threatened by internal unrest and invasion by Pakistan tribesmen. The Kashmir issue has since marred relations between India and Pakistan. The award also broke up the irrigation system of the Punjab by awarding the headworks of the Punjab canals at Madhopur and Ferozepur to India. As early as April 1948 the water supply was cut off, and Pakistan had to conclude an agreement under duress, by which it surrendered essential riparian rights and agreed to make a payment to India for the use of water. The matter was taken up at an international level, culminating in an agreement reached through the good offices of, and a substantial loan from, the World Bank. India also withheld payment of Pakistan's share of the assets of the Reserve Bank of India, leading to a serious financial crisis within months of independence, pushing the new state to the verge of bankruptcy.

POLITICAL AND CONSTITUTIONAL DEVELOPMENTS, 1947–73

Pakistan, which had become an independent dominion under the Indian Independence Act 1947, was administered initially under the Government of India Act 1935, as adapted in Pakistan. The Indian Independence Act had abolished the special powers of the Governor-General. Moreover, a sovereign Constituent Assembly replaced the Indian Legislative Assembly. Yet, because of the unusual situation, the Governor-General was still vested with special powers to adapt the Government of India Act. However, they were to be exercised by the Governor-General on the advice of the Cabinet.

The Constituent Assembly, to which power was formally transferred on 14 August 1947, was a small chamber elected indirectly by the provincial legislatures on the basis of one member for a population of 1m. Initially comprising only 69 members, the number was later raised to 79, of whom 44 represented East Bengal.

Jinnah was the first Governor-General, although he derived his power chiefly from being the founder of the nation. He was also President of the Constituent Assembly and presided over cabinet meetings. Although he was only a titular head, he wielded immense power. After his death in September 1948, Liaquat Ali Khan became the chief executive and Khwaja Nazimuddin was appointed Governor-General.

The Drafting of a Constitution

The drafting of a constitution incorporating the principles of Islam was not easy. The only notable steps towards this during Liaquat Ali Khan's regime were the passing of the Objectives Resolution in 1949 and the presentation of the *Interim Report of the Basic Principles Committee* in 1950. On Liaquat Ali Khan's assassination in October 1951, the Governor-General, Khwaja Nazimuddin, became Prime Minister, but the focus of power now shifted to the new Governor-General, Ghulam Muhammad. Exploiting public discontent over food shortages,

* Since 1947 (for the pre-1947 history, see the chapter on India).

he dismissed Khwaja Nazimuddin in April 1953, even though the latter enjoyed the fullest confidence of the Assembly, and replaced him with Muhammad Ali Bogra, hitherto Pakistan's ambassador to the USA. This dismissal represented the first authoritarian thrust into Pakistan's body politic.

A Constitution was prepared on the basis of a formula set out by Muhammad Ali Bogra, under which the majority of the lower house was to come from East Pakistan on the basis of population and the majority of the upper house from the four units of West Pakistan, but the number was so fixed that in a joint session of the two houses the members from each wing numbered 175 (East Pakistan 165+10, and West Pakistan 135+40). When the Constitution was about to be passed as law, the Constituent Assembly was dissolved by the Governor-General in October 1954, presumably because the Constitution had sought to curtail his powers. As a result of the federal court ruling, however, a new Constituent Assembly was elected by the various provincial legislatures in mid-1955. Compared to its predecessor, which had only two parties, the new Assembly had six parties. The Muslim League, though still the largest party, was no longer dominant.

The Constitutions of 1956 and 1962

The new Constituent Assembly first amalgamated the four provinces of West Pakistan into one single province. Then, in March 1956, the Constitution was finally drawn up, passed by the Assembly and authenticated by the Governor-General. It established a federal republic of two provinces only, namely East and West Pakistan, with much decentralization, and established a parliamentary form of government. It recognized the principle of parity of representation for the two provinces and provided for only one house. It also incorporated several Islamic provisions among the directive principles. The head of state was to be a Muslim and, although Islam was not declared the state religion, no law was to be promulgated that conflicted with Islamic teachings. In addition, the existing laws were to be brought into conformity with Islam. The rights and personal laws of non-Muslims were, however, respected. The question of joint versus separate electorates was put aside to be settled by the legislatures. Urdu and Bengali were both recognized as state languages, although English was retained pro tem for official purposes.

However, the political parties were weak and disorganized, and the Governor-General, Iskandar Mirza, did not believe in parliamentary democracy. When the parliamentary system had become discredited—a situation to which he himself had substantially contributed—Iskandar Mirza abrogated the Constitution (on 7 October 1958), dismissed the Cabinet, abolished the legislatures, banned political parties and promulgated martial law under Gen. Ayub Khan, the Commander-in-Chief. Mirza may well have been motivated by the fact that he had no chance of being elected President under the 1956 Constitution.

On 27 October 1958 Ayub Khan removed Mirza, and himself became President. Martial law continued until a new Constitution was promulgated in June 1962. Its most important feature was the institution of 'basic democracies', which, as local governmental institutions, had been in existence since 1959. The Constitution provided for a presidential system of government. All executive power and much legislative power was concentrated in the hands of the President, who was practically irremovable during his five-year term. Unlike the 1956 Constitution, the 1962 Constitution tended towards centralization of power in the hands of the chief executive. The powers of the legislatures were limited, even in regard to finance. The system of election was indirect. Direct elections were, however, provided at the lowest level, the Basic Democrats (40,000 in East Pakistan and 40,000 in West Pakistan, later raised to 60,000 each) being elected by the vote of all registered voters. All the councils at the *tehsil*, district and division levels were indirectly elected, one after the other. For the election of the provincial and central assemblies and the President, the entire body of Basic Democrats formed an electoral college.

The Overthrow of Ayub Khan

In 1968 the regime made the grave mistake of celebrating the 10th anniversary of President Ayub's seizure of power as the 'decade of reforms'. Instead of popularizing the regime, the celebrations created precisely the opposite effect and brought to the surface all the hitherto submerged opposition to corruption, nepotism and autocratic controls. Religious elements and students took the lead in anti-Ayub agitation. Disturbances took place on a large scale and urban workers and peasants became involved, with the result that the regime was profoundly shaken. Ayub made a series of concessions to the political parties and held a conference with political leaders in February 1969, but all to no avail. Thus, in March when it became impossible to maintain law and order, he handed over power to his Commander-in-Chief, Gen. (later Field Marshal) Agha Muhammad Yahya Khan. Martial law was once more proclaimed. The new President and Chief Martial Law Administrator, however, lost no time in announcing that general elections would be held in October 1970, later postponed to December 1970.

Thus, the whole question of the Constitution of Pakistan was once more reopened. The President decided to dissolve the one unit and revive the old provinces, to replace the presidential by a parliamentary system, to hold direct elections and to apportion seats to the various provinces on population basis. The quantum of provincial autonomy and of the Islamic content was, however, left to be determined by the new National Assembly.

However, following postponement of the formation of a constituent assembly in March 1971, events took a serious turn in East Pakistan. Internal turmoil, followed by India's invasion, resulted in the secession of East Pakistan as Bangladesh in December 1971. Military defeat thoroughly exposed and discredited the military dictatorship. Yahya Khan fell, and Zulfikar Ali Bhutto, the founder and Chairman of the Pakistan People's Party (PPP), took over as President.

The National Assembly was convened, and in October 1972 a consensus was reached by the leaders of all the parties represented in the Assembly. A federal parliamentary system of government was agreed upon, with four units and two houses of legislature. The Prime Minister, answerable to the lower house, was to be the chief executive, while the President, elected by both houses voting together, was visualized as a constitutional head. The quantum of provincial autonomy was finally agreed upon by all the parties. The constitution committee of the National Assembly prepared a draft for the consideration of the Assembly. In April 1973 Pakistan at long last acquired a democratic Constitution, framed by a directly elected Assembly, which came into force on 14 August 1973. At the inauguration of the Constitution, President Bhutto became the Prime Minister of Pakistan.

POLITICAL PARTIES

A few years before the partition of India, the Muslim League, which had been founded in 1906, had become for all practical purposes the only party of the Muslims much in the same way as the Indian National Congress represented almost all Hindus. However, in the final phase of the freedom struggle, the League had transformed itself into a nationalist coalition representing diverse interests among Muslims. That diverse elements should come together under the banner of the League was a source of strength while the struggle for independence lasted. Yet, once the goal was achieved, the presence of heterogeneous elements in the League became a cause of weakness. Even so, the achievement of Pakistan had endowed the League with tremendous prestige and was responsible for discrediting other parties which had opposed the country's creation. Only the Congress survived among the Hindus of East Bengal. Thus, in the first Constituent Assembly (1947–54), there were initially only two parties: the Muslim League Assembly Party (MLAP) and a small opposition of 12 Hindus belonging to the Congress. Gradually new parties were founded by former members of the MLAP. Mamdot founded the Jinnah Muslim League in West Pakistan, and Suhrawardy the Awami League in East Bengal. Their programmes were, however, no different from those of the MLAP. A secession within the Constituent Assembly brought into being the Azad Pakistan Party in the Punjab in 1950/51.

In the provincial assembly elections in East Bengal in 1954, four parties opposed to the MLAP constituted a United Front under Fazlul Haq. It fought the elections on a 21-point programme, which emphasized provincial autonomy. The Front obtained 222 seats out of 309 while the MLAP won only nine seats. Soon, however, a rift developed between the component elements of the United Front, particularly between Fazlul Haq and the Awami League, headed by Suhrawardy. When, upon becoming Prime Minister in September 1956, Suhrawardy advocated a pronounced pro-Western policy, Bhashani first challenged Suhrawardy within the party and then, failing to carry the party with him, left it and formed his own National Awami Party (NAP) in 1957. In West Pakistan, though the Muslim League had won the provincial elections of 1951 in the Punjab, and subsequent elections in the NWFP and Sindh, a number of small parties, inspired by the MLAP's débâcle in East Bengal in 1954, continued to exist. Of particular importance was Maulana Maududi's Jamaat-e-Islami Pakistan (JIP), which advocated an Islamic constitution and the revival of Islamic values. The Muslim League split in 1956 over the nomination of Dr Khan Sahib, who was the NWFP Chief Minister at the time of partition, a Congressite and opposed to the creation of Pakistan, to the chief ministership of the newly constituted West Pakistan Province. Dr Khan's supporters launched the Republican Party under his leadership and with the backing of the Governor-General in April 1956.

Political parties, banned in the wake of the army take-over in October 1958, were allowed to function again only after the promulgation of a new Constitution in 1962. In the process of the revival of parties, the Muslim League was split. The original League party, dominated by the old guard, who were opposed to President Ayub and the 1962 Constitution, came to be known as Council Muslim League, whereas a faction comprising Leaguers in the lower echelons formed the Convention Muslim League and chose Ayub Khan as President. In East Pakistan, nine prominent political leaders formed the National Democratic Front (NDF) to fight for the democratization of the Constitution; and in 1964 several parties (including the Awami League, the NAP and Nizam-i-Islam) were revived.

For the presidential election, due in 1965, five opposition parties formed a Combined Opposition Party (COP): the Council Muslim League, the Awami League, the NAP, the Nizam-i-Islam and the JIP. The NDF also gave its general support to the COP. Fatima Jinnah, the elderly sister of Muhammed Ali Jinnah, was chosen as the COP's candidate. Initially, she made a favourable impression, but was unable to defeat the powerfully entrenched Field Marshal Ayub Khan. None the less, she demonstrated for the first time that the authority of Ayub Khan could be challenged.

In December 1967 Zulfikar Ali Bhutto, hitherto an enthusiastic supporter and minister of Ayub, formed the socialist-leaning PPP. In 1968 the NAP split, with one section, led by Wali Khan, in West Pakistan, and the other, by Bhashani, in the East. In late 1968 certain non-political figures like Air Marshal Asghar Khan, who later founded the Tehrik-i-Istiqlal (TI), also entered the political arena. Besides the JIP, two other organizations of Muslim religious scholars became active in 1970: Jamiat-e-Ulema-e-Islam (JUI) and Jamiat-e-Ulema-e-Pakistan (JUP). East Pakistan claimed several parties, the more important being the Awami League, headed by Mujibur Rahman, NAP (Bhashani) and the Pakistan Democratic Party (PDP), led by Nurul Amin, a former Chief Minister of East Bengal. The parties had no democratic base and regular membership did not exist. The working committees, organizing committees, co-ordination committees and conveners were seldom elected by the party membership at large. Leaders were mainly self-appointed. Most parties except the Muslim League were, in effect, regional or provincial parties, but for a long time the Muslim League had been divided.

LEGISLATIVE GOVERNMENT, 1970–77

The 1970 Elections and War with India

The first ever general elections were held in December 1970. Only two parties achieved overwhelming success, the Awami League in East Pakistan and the PPP in the two most populous provinces of West Pakistan—the Punjab and Sindh. The Awami League had fought the elections on the basis of 'Six Points', which were aimed at an extreme form of provincial autonomy and decentralization of authority. The Awami League, having secured nearly all the seats in East Pakistan, obtained an absolute majority in the central legislature. In the normal course, the largest party had the right to form the central Government, but in this case it was not a workable proposition because of the federal character of Pakistan as a state and the exclusively provincial character of the party concerned. The Awami League seemed inclined to coalesce with some of the smaller parties of West Pakistan, but the PPP chief vehemently opposed the idea. He sought assurances on certain constitutional issues before the calling of the session of the National Assembly. As the PPP was the second largest party in the Assembly, the President postponed the session to give the two largest parties an opportunity for arriving at a consensus on some of the remaining constitutional issues. Negotiations among the political parties themselves and between the President and the Awami League leader, Mujibur Rahman, followed. However, the situation in East Pakistan took an ugly turn when the Awami League sought independence for East Pakistan. In March 1971 the Pakistani Government imposed martial law and sent troops into East Pakistan, where in the wake of a brutal suppression, thousands of East Bengalis were slaughtered, with many others seeking refuge in West Bengal, India. The Pakistani Government claimed that India was the base for Bengali insurgents' training and incursions into East Pakistan. There followed border clashes between Indian and Pakistani troops and finally, in November, an invasion of East Pakistan by the Indian armed forces. However, the war did not remain confined to the East but spread to West Pakistan as well. The conflict was short but decisive. India achieved quick success, bringing about the surrender of Pakistani troops in the East, and a cease-fire in the West. It was followed by the declaration of Bangladesh as a new nation. East Pakistan ceased to exist.

In the aftermath of the war, Bhutto's Government embarked upon the task of drafting a new Constitution. The Constitution proposed in 1972 seemed to have the support of all parties. In early 1973, however, opposition parties of the right and left formed a United Democratic Front (UDF) to demand further amendments which would create 'a truly Islamic, democratic and federal Constitution'. Their fears that the Constitution would give too much power to the Prime Minister and the central Government were strengthened by events in Balochistan where tribal fighting was followed, in February 1973, by the imposition of direct presidential rule and the invocation of emergency powers.

The NAP was banned in February 1975 and many of its leading members were arrested, following the murder of the NWFP's most senior minister, Hayat Mohammed Sherpao. In the same month, although boycotted by the opposition parties, the National Assembly adopted a Constitution Bill empowering the Government to extend the state of emergency beyond six months without parliamentary approval. Meanwhile, a new party, the National Democratic Party (NDP), was launched in November 1975, with Sherbaz Khan Mazari, leader of the Independent Group in the National Assembly, as leader. It claimed the adherence of most of the former NAP leaders.

The 1977 Elections and the Fall of Zulfikar Ali Bhutto

In preparation for the national elections to be held on 7 March 1977, nine opposition parties formed a broadly-based opposition front, called the Pakistan National Alliance (PNA). The parties forming the Alliance were Air Marshal (retd) Asghar Khan's TI, Mian Tufail Muhammad's JIP, Maulana Mufti Mahmud's JUI, Maulana Shah Ahmed Noorani's JUP, the Pir of Pagara's Pakistan Muslim League (PML), Sherbaz Khan Mazari's NDP, Nawabzada Nasrullah Khan's PDP, Khan Muhammad Ashraf Khan's Khaksar Tehrik (KT), and Sardar Abdul Qayyum's Azad Kashmir Muslim Conference (AKMC). Although some other minor parties like the Qayyam Muslim League and Pakhtoon Khwa, chiefly in the NWFP and Balochistan respectively, and a considerable number of independents participated in the elections, the main contest was between the PNA and the ruling PPP, led by Bhutto. While Bhutto based his appeal on 'socio-economic reforms' introduced by him, the 'political stability' and 'economic prosperity' achieved during his previous term and his achievements in foreign affairs and other fields, the PNA concentrated on what they termed the gradual erosion of fundamental rights and of the authority and dignity of the courts, the concentration of power in the hands of the executive, and the 'undemocratic' and 'authoritarian' nature of the PPP regime.

The elections gave the PPP an overwhelming majority in the National Assembly: it won 155 seats, conceding only 36 seats to the PNA and one to the Qayyum Muslim League. However, the opposition front accused the Government of electoral malpractice. It called for a boycott of the provincial assembly polls scheduled for 9 March and for a country-wide strike on the following day. It demanded fresh elections under the supervision of the judiciary and the armed forces, the resignation of the Chief Election Commissioner and the establishment of a new impartial Election Commission. It also decided to launch a movement of country-wide civil disobedience from 14 March.

Although the malpractice charge was later confirmed by the Chief Election Commissioner and the Election Commission's findings, Bhutto denied the charges, but tried to appease opposition resentment by offering to hold the provincial polls again and by giving more power to the Election Commission. However, these concessions were to no avail, and the PNA launched the civil disobedience movement as scheduled. Within a week most of its leaders were in gaol, but the movement, though mostly confined to urban centres, continued to gain momentum, causing a breakdown of law and order in several places and of economic life in the principal industrial centres. The armed forces had to be called in at several places, a curfew had to be imposed for various periods in at least seven places and martial law was imposed in Karachi, Lahore and Hyderabad, continuing until 7 June. Official sources put the death toll at 275 and the injured at 2,000, but the unofficial figures were more than 1,000 dead and several thousand injured. Some 40,000 people were arrested.

Meanwhile, the new National Assembly met on 26 March 1977 and re-elected Bhutto as the leader of the house. He formed a new Cabinet. Subsequently, the newly elected provincial assemblies in all the four provinces were called to session, and new provincial governments were constituted. Weekly strike calls, processions and attempts to break the curfew and violate martial law regulations continued. The deepening crisis induced some Islamic countries, particularly Saudi Arabia, to mediate and finally bring the two sides to the negotiating table in early June. Four weeks of protracted negotiations resulted in an accord whereby the PNA withdrew its demand for Bhutto's resignation and Bhutto, for his part, accepted the PNA's original demands for fresh elections, the lifting of the emergency, and the restoration of fundamental rights and of the power of the judiciary. Elections were scheduled for 7 October. However, before the accord was formally signed, serious differences developed over the machinery being established to ensure free and fair elections, and this resulted in a further deadlock. Meanwhile, armed clashes had occurred between PPP and PNA supporters, and the country seemed on the verge of civil war.

MILITARY RULE

General Zia takes Power

On 5 July 1977 the armed forces intervened in the crisis, taking into 'temporary protective custody' the top echelons of both the PPP and the PNA leadership (including Bhutto). Martial law was imposed, the national and provincial assemblies and the Senate were disbanded, the federal and provincial cabinets were dismissed, and the armed forces took over the administration of the country. The Constitution was not abrogated, but some of its clauses were put in abeyance. The incumbent President was allowed to remain as Head of State, but provincial governors were replaced. Gen. Mohammad Zia ul-Haq, Chief of Army Staff, became martial law administrator, and a four-member military council (comprising the chiefs of the three services and Chairman of Joint Chiefs of Staff) was constituted. Political activity was banned for a month, but elections were promised for October as originally stipulated in the PPP-PNA accord.

However, on 1 October 1977 Gen. Zia postponed elections indefinitely, since it was felt that elections would be meaningless unless those holding public offices during the previous seven years were first made accountable, particularly for their misdemeanours on two counts—amassing of wealth through official position, and misuse of public office. Several charges were brought against Bhutto and a number of his ministers. In particular, Bhutto was accused of having instigated the murders of a PPP dissident and a member of his family in 1974. The Lahore High Court convicted Bhutto and four others and sentenced them to death in March 1978. The Supreme Court, which heard the appeal over a period of some nine months, confirmed the conviction by a majority decision in February 1979. After the dismissal of a review petition by the same court, Bhutto was hanged on 4 April 1979. The Government ordered the release of about 11,000 political detainees who had been imprisoned during the Bhutto regime, including the NAP leaders (in detention since 1975), and a general amnesty was declared in Balochistan in an attempt to conciliate the 'aggrieved' province. Although the official ban on political activity continued, limited activity was allowed.

The Zia Regime, 1978–88

In January 1978 Gen. Zia appointed a council of 16 advisers, and in August he formed a 22-member civilian Cabinet which included 15 PNA members. The PNA members left the Cabinet in April 1979, and a new Cabinet, comprising five army generals and 10 civilians, was installed. Meanwhile, President Fazal Elahi Chaudhri resigned in September 1978, for 'health reasons', and Gen. Zia became President.

Gen. Zia pursued the policy of bringing the country's laws into conformity with Islamic law (*Shari'a*) more zealously than any previous ruler. In February 1979 he announced the enforcement of Islamic penal laws with immediate effect, and the introduction of *zakat* (poor-tax) from July 1979, and of *ushr* (tax on agricultural produce), together with other measures concordant with Islamic economic practice. Interest-free banking was introduced in 1981. A federal Shari'a court, replacing the Shari'a benches of the high courts, was set up in May 1980. The Council of Islamic Ideology was broadened and reconstituted, and assigned the task of drafting an Islamic system of government in Pakistan.

The political situation continued to be fluid, however. Neither the PNA nor the PPP presented a united front. The TI left the PNA in November 1977, as did the JUP and the NDP, two other PNA components, in July and August 1978. When the NDP left the Alliance, the Balochi leaders joined the NDP, only to leave it in April 1979 and form a splinter group called the Pakistan National Party (PNP), headed by Ghaus Bakhsh Bizenjo, a former leader of the defunct NAP and a former Governor of Balochistan. Most of the PPP leadership, which had been in gaol or under house arrest since March 1978 for repeated attempts to organize demonstrations for Bhutto's release, were released after Bhutto's execution, and the PPP was reorganized under the leadership of Benazir Bhutto, the daughter of the executed leader.

The clamour of all the political parties for elections had earlier forced Gen. Zia to announce national elections for 17 November 1979. Subsequently, Gen. Zia announced a series of amendments to the Political Parties Act of 1962, which made it mandatory for all parties (i) to hold annual elections at every level within a specified period; (ii) to submit their accounts for audit to the Election Commission; and (iii) to register themselves with the Election Commission. Failure to fulfil any of these obligations was to render the parties ineligible for participation in the elections. All the major parties protested against the amendments, and vehemently opposed the registration clause.

By 30 September 1979, the deadline for the registration of political parties, only three major parties—the TI, the JUP and the JIP—had successfully registered, while four other major parties—the PPP, the PNA (except the JIP), the NDP and the PNP—had refused to register. Prolonged manoeuvres to induce the latter three parties to participate in the elections having failed, Gen. Zia finally announced on 16 October the indefinite postponement of elections, the dissolution of all political parties, and the reinforcement of martial law.

In March 1981 the Government promulgated a Provisional Constitution Order (PCO), which retained 119 articles, either wholly or in part, of the 1973 Constitution. The PCO provided for one or two Vice-Presidents, a *majlis-i-shura* (federal advisory council), and a framework for the functioning of political parties. The Lahore High Court subsequently ruled that the PCO was not a new legal order. The various political parties established the Movement for the Restoration of Democracy (MRD). However, the hijacking of a Pakistani civil aircraft to Kabul by PPP activists caused widespread public resentment against opposition activities, leading to the disbandment of the MRD by seven of its nine components. A new 23-member federal Cabinet was sworn in, composed chiefly of civilians and technocrats. This was closely followed by the setting up of provincial cabinets in the NWFP, the Punjab and Sindh. A 300-member *majlis-i-shura* was finally appointed in December 1981, and, subsequently, held several sessions. President Zia hoped that the *majlis-i-shura* would serve as a substitute for the legislature.

By July 1983 the Zia regime had survived six years without any major challenge to its authority. In August Gen. Zia announced a new political framework, promising provincial and national elections by March 1985. This, however, did not restrain the MRD from launching a non-violent civil disobedience movement, which it termed a 'Save Pakistan Movement'. The ban on public meetings was violated, and opposition leaders courted arrest in major cities. The movement was particularly intense in some rural areas of Sindh, where, with the active collaboration of some local landlords and *pirs* (religious leaders), it took the extreme form of a mass uprising. The consequent headlong confrontation between demonstrators and the law-enforcing agencies resulted in some 50 deaths and many more injured. Within six weeks, however, the 'Save Pakistan Movement' had collapsed, chiefly because the explosive events in rural Sindh had alienated and alarmed the other provinces.

In late 1984, in an unexpected development, Gen. Zia announced the holding of a national referendum on 19 December, to seek popular approval for his policies and to ensure the process of Islamization, as well as a five-year term for himself as President. An affirmative vote, he said, would ensure a peaceful transfer of power to the people's representatives in accordance with the 1983 plan, strengthening the country's ideological foundations and national solidarity. While the opposition alliance urged the electorate to boycott the poll, branding the referendum a 'farce', two political parties, the PML (Pagara Group) and the JIP supported it. Since Gen. Zia campaigned in the name of Islam, he was able to muster widespread support, especially in the rural areas. Official results claimed a 64% turn-out of voters, and a 97.7% 'yes' vote. The referendum result gave a new confidence to the regime, and elections to national and provincial assemblies were held respectively on 25 and 28 February 1985. The elections were held on a non-party basis, and public meetings and processions were forbidden. The MRD, once again, called for a boycott, but the call went largely unheeded. A 53% turn-out for the national poll and an even higher figure for the provincial one, plus the defeat of six ministers and several others who were identified with the regime, helped to give international credibility to the elections, as being reasonably free and fair within a given framework. The election of women's representatives to the national and provincial assemblies, and elections to the Senate, were completed by 21 March. The PML (Pagara Group) claimed a majority in the National Assembly and the Sindh assembly, and emerged as the largest single group in Punjab.

Meanwhile, Gen. Zia had announced the revival of the 1973 Constitution Order, which incorporated several far-reaching amendments to the Constitution, as part of his post-election plan gradually to lift martial law and to restore the Constitution. The amendments gave the President the power to appoint the Prime Minister and cabinet ministers, to dissolve the legislature, to order a national referendum on any national issue, and to appoint provincial Governors, the Chairman of the Joint Chiefs of Staff Committee, and the three armed forces chiefs. The amendments also codified the results of the December 1984 referendum, and envisaged the establishment of a National Security Council. The new National Assembly was, however, empowered to rescind these amendments by a two-thirds majority. Not surprisingly, the amendments attracted considerable criticism from various quarters.

On 23 March 1985, at a joint session of the National Assembly and the Senate, Gen. Zia was sworn in as President of Pakistan for a five-year term, and, under the March constitutional amendments, he nominated Muhammad Khan Junejo, a Sindhi politician of the PML (Pagara Group), as Prime Minister. A 20-member federal Cabinet, sworn in on 10 April, was expanded a month later. While pledging to work for an Islamic state, the new Prime Minister declared that a civilian government and martial law could not co-exist for very long, and promised that self-exiled politicians could safely return to Pakistan, and that the Government was ready to enter into negotiations with the opposition. Simultaneously, the opposition activists were released.

Within weeks of their convening, the assemblies generally displayed independence, and tried to assume an independent status. The NWFP and Punjab assemblies approved motions demanding the ending of martial law, while the National Assembly admitted a privilege motion proposing the termination of martial law. Similar motions were introduced in the Balochistan and Sindh assemblies. The MRD opposition intensified its campaign for the lifting of martial law. Consequently, Prime Minister Junejo's dramatic announcement in August 1985 that martial law would be lifted by the end of the year was widely welcomed.

In order to regulate political life after the lifting of martial law, the National Assembly adopted two important pieces of legislation. A last-minute compromise between the 190-member Official Parliamentary Group (OPG) and the 40-member Independent Parliamentary Group (IPG) facilitated the passage of the 22-clause Constitution (Eighth Amendment) Bill in October 1985, and it was approved unanimously. The main feature of the new legislation was the validation clause, indemnifying all acts and orders of the martial law regime, including the proclamation of 5 July 1977, the December 1984 referendum, and the PCO. The Government accepted the IPG's nine amendments, which deleted or delimited the discretionary powers of the President to dissolve the National Assembly without consulting the Prime Minister; limited the President's power to appoint or dismiss the Prime Minister, and to appoint provincial Governors; empowered the National Assembly to elect the Prime Minister and to amend any law, regulation or order of the martial law authorities; and withdrew protection of the Political Parties Act from judicial review. The comprehensive Political Parties (Amendment) Bill 1985 was approved in December, after more than 40 amendments, proposed by the IPG, were rejected, and despite the boycott by IPG members. The new law stipulated registration of all political parties by fulfilling specified requirements concerning each party's manifesto, funds and membership, and prohibited changes of political allegiance by members of parties and groups in the National Assembly and provincial assemblies.

By the beginning of 1986, there was a measure of political freedom in Pakistan. Not only martial law, but also the state of emergency (which had been imposed in March 1969 by President Yahya Khan and which continued throughout the Bhutto era) was lifted on 30 December 1985, thus restoring fundamental rights after more than 16 years. Junejo, who had earlier named the OPG as the PML parliamentary party, was unanimously elected President of the PML (Pagara Group) on 18 January 1986. The Chief Ministers in the four provinces and most members of provincial assemblies subsequently joined the official PML.

A turning-point in opposition activities came in April 1986, when Benazir Bhutto, the acting PPP Chairwoman, returned to Pakistan, where she received an unprecedented tumultuous welcome. Her four-week tour programme was a tremendous success. The mammoth processions that followed Benazir Bhutto helped to legitimize her claim to her father's former role, to silence dissidents, and to develop a personality cult similar to that of her father; she subsequently became Co-Chairwoman of the PPP. She demanded the ousting of Zia, and the holding of national elections in the latter half of 1986. Despite her preparations, Benazir's unilateral appeal for the observance of a 'Black Day' on 5 July (the anniversary of the day when Zia overthrew her father and seized power in 1977) proved to be largely unsuccessful, as was the movement that she launched in mid-August, in conjunction with the MRD, demanding mid-term elections. During 1986 four left-wing parties (the NDP, Sindh Awami Tehrik, the Mazdoor Kisan Party and a PNP breakaway faction) merged to form a new Awami National Party (ANP), with Abdul Wali Khan as its leader. In August Ghulam Mustafa Jatoi, who had been removed from the provincial presidency of the PPP in Sindh by Benazir Bhutto, summoned a convention in Lahore, where a left-of-centre National People's Party (NPP) was launched.

The Government surmounted a number of crises during 1986 and 1987. Terrorist bombings in several locations in the NWFP, and in Rawalpindi, Lahore and Karachi, were officially blamed on agents operating on behalf of Afghanistan and India. From October 1986 there were frequent violent clashes in Karachi, Quetta and Hyderabad, prompted, in part, by disputes between rival ethnic groups (Pathans, originally from the NWFP and Afghanistan, Punjabi settlers, native Sindhis, and the Urdu-speaking Mohajirs, who migrated to Pakistan from India at partition in 1947). Fighting also broke out in July 1987 in the Kurram tribal area between Sunni and Shi'a Muslim factions. The overall success of government economic measures, however, was, at this time, a factor in the opposition's loss of political momentum.

Local elections, which took place throughout the country in November 1987, were officially held on a non-party basis, but all the major parties, including the PPP (which thus ended an eight-year boycott of elections), presented and campaigned for candidates. The government-supported PML won the majority of seats, while the PPP obtained less than 20% of the total. The growth of ethnic communalism in Pakistan was reflected in the performance of the Mohajir party, the Mohajir Qaumi Movement (MQM), which won the majority of seats in Karachi and Hyderabad, and was also successful in other urban areas of Sindh.

By early 1988 the rift between President Zia and Prime Minister Junejo, on both personal and policy levels, had reached a crisis. The original understanding between them had been that Junejo would exercise full authority in internal matters, while Zia would hold authority regarding military and foreign relations. The Prime Minister, however, increasingly encroached on the President's territory. In May President Zia unexpectedly invoked his constitutional powers to dissolve the National Assembly and the four provincial assemblies. Zia also dissolved the Cabinet, accusing it of being corrupt, weak and inept, and of failing to suppress the rising tide of banditry, murders and kidnappings, as well as the growth of the separatist movement in Sindh. Zia stressed, however, that the Senate and the Constitution were to remain intact; that there was to be no ban on political parties or political rallies; that there were to be no restrictions imposed on the press; and that neither martial law nor a state of emergency were to be declared. A caretaker Government was formed in the following month, comprising nine ministers from the former civilian Cabinet and seven ministers from the earlier martial law administration. No Prime Minister was appointed, however, despite the constitutional requirement, as Zia was to act as Head of Government. Caretaker governments were also established in the provinces, apart from Sindh, where governor's rule was imposed after a virtual collapse of administration in the wake of increased ethnic violence. Most of the political parties, including the PPP, welcomed the dissolution of the assemblies and the Cabinet. In July President Zia announced that elections to the National Assembly and the provincial assemblies would be held, on a non-party basis, in November.

The political situation was, however, abruptly thrown into turmoil on 17 August 1988, when President Zia was killed in an air crash at Bahawalpur in eastern Pakistan. The US ambassador to Pakistan and several senior military figures were also killed. There was much speculation that sabotage was behind the incident. The Chairman of the Senate, Ghulam Ishaq Khan, was appointed acting President. An emergency National Council, composed of military chiefs, the four provincial Governors and four federal Chief Ministers, was appointed to take charge of government. A state of emergency was declared, but the acting President announced that the elections would still go ahead as scheduled.

Later in August 1988 the PML (Pagara Group) split into two factions, when Zia loyalists, with the support of the army, objected to Junejo's refusal to step down as President of the party. The breakaway faction, called the Fida Group, which was described by Junejo as illegal, included the three provincial acting Chief Ministers. The former Governor of the NWFP, Fida Mohammad Khan, was elected as President of the dissident faction, and the powerful acting Chief Minister of Punjab, Mohammad Nawaz Sharif, was elected as Secretary-General. The Junejo Group and the Fida Group agreed to co-operate with each other, however, during the campaign for the general election in November.

In late September 1988 the high court in Lahore ruled that the grounds given for the dissolution of Pakistan's legislative assemblies in May by President Zia were illegal and unconstitutional. However, the court rejected a request for the reinstatement of the dissolved assemblies and said that the scheduled elections should proceed in November. A few days later, the Supreme Court, by removing the last major restriction (the political party registration clause had been removed by the court in June), upheld Benazir Bhutto's constitutional petition and ruled that all political parties were eligible to contest the elections.

In October 1988 the PPP left the MRD, claiming that the latter was never intended to be an electoral alliance. The MRD was subsequently disbanded. In the same month, nine right-wing and Islamic parties, including the PML and the JIP, formed the Islamic Democratic Alliance (IDA), under the leadership of Ghulam Mustafa Jatoi and Mohammad Nawaz Sharif, to oppose the PPP in the elections.

PAKISTAN AFTER ZIA

The Government of Benazir Bhutto, 1988–90

The general election for a new National Assembly was held on 16 November 1988. It was, despite some alleged polling irregularities, described by foreign observers as having been fairly conducted. The PPP, with the acquisition of 93 of the 207 directly-elective seats, did not win an absolute majority, but it was the only party to secure seats in each of the four provinces. The IDA, under the leadership of Jatoi, won 54 seats, with the remaining 58 seats (polling in two constituencies was deferred, following the deaths of candidates) distributed among independents and candidates representing seven smaller parties. Several prominent political figures from the Zia period, including former Prime Minister Junejo, failed to secure election to the new Assembly.

The PPP's success in the general election was slightly undermined by its less decisive performance in the elections to the provincial assemblies, which were held on 19 November 1988. The PPP established coalition governments with the MQM and the ANP in Sindh and the NWFP respectively, while the IDA gained a majority in Punjab, the most populous province. Mohammad Nawaz Sharif, who was widely viewed as Benazir Bhutto's main rival, was re-elected as Punjab's Chief Minister. Following the signing of an agreement of co-operation between the MQM and the PPP, which together had a working majority in the National Assembly, Benazir Bhutto was appointed Prime Minister by the acting President on 1 December, thus becoming the first female leader of a Muslim country. On the same day, the state of emergency was repealed and the emergency National Council was dissolved. On 12 December, with the support of both the PPP and the IDA, Ghulam Ishaq Khan was elected President by an electoral college (comprising the National Assembly, the Senate and the four provincial assemblies), with 78% of the total valid votes cast.

In early 1989 the Prime Minister intensified her campaign for the repeal of the Eighth Amendment to the Constitution (which had been adopted in 1985 and which gave unprecedented powers to the President), describing it as an illegal document. However, the Government did not command the necessary two-thirds majority in the National Assembly necessary for amending the Constitution. The Government's determined attempt to unseat Mohammad Nawaz Sharif, by introducing a motion of 'no confidence' against him in the Punjab assembly in March, was unsuccessful, with 152 of the 258 members voting in favour of their Chief Minister.

In late April 1989 the coalition government between the ANP and the PPP in the NWFP broke down when, after months of tension, the ANP pulled out of the coalition following the resignation of five provincial ANP ministers. In the following month, the coalition government between the MQM and the PPP in Sindh also collapsed, following the resignation of the three MQM ministers from the provincial cabinet in the wake of increased ethnic violence in the province. The Government was faced with a further provincial upset in early June when the ANP entered into a formal alliance with the IDA in the

NWFP, thus posing a serious threat to the PPP-dominated provincial assembly. In the same month the opposition was strengthened by the establishment of an informal parliamentary grouping called the Combined Opposition Party (COP), which was composed of the ANP, the Jamiatul-Ulema-e-Islam, the Pakistan Awami Ittehad and the IDA.

In August 1989 a disagreement arose between the Prime Minister and the President over the retirement of the Chairman of the Joint Chiefs of Staff Committee, Adm. Iftikhar Ahmad Sirohey. The President insisted that it was his right, according to the Eighth Amendment to the Constitution, to appoint all senior officers and that, in any case, Sirohey's appointment had two more years to run. Benazir Bhutto argued, however, that although she did not have the right to appoint the army chiefs, she did have the right, as the head of the Ministry of Defence, to retire them. The crisis was resolved only when the Prime Minister finally climbed down. In October another dispute arose between Benazir Bhutto and Ghulam Ishaq Khan over the question as to which one of them had the constitutional right to appoint new judges. The dispute was amicably settled, however, when Benazir Bhutto again backed down, and a new Chief Justice of the Supreme Court was appointed by consensus in December.

In October 1989 the PPP-MQM alliance collapsed. The MQM alleged that the PPP Government had failed to honour any of its pledges and to fulfil any of the promises made in the Karachi Declaration. The MQM then transferred its parliamentary support to the opposition. This set-back for the PPP was followed by the introduction of a motion of 'no confidence' against the Bhutto Government in the National Assembly on 1 November. The opposition, however, could muster only 112 votes, seven short of the number required to unseat the Government. Before the voting took place, the Government managed to 'persuade' several opposition members to join its ranks, two of whom were sworn in as ministers immediately afterwards. The opposition, in turn, accused the Government of hard bargaining and political corruption.

The political strife between the PPP and the MQM in Sindh took a serious turn in January 1990, when the MQM organized a huge COP rally. The PPP accused the MQM of being involved in terrorism, while the MQM accused the PPP of using terrorist tactics and state agencies in an attempt to suppress it. Recurring violence and the kidnapping of political activists resulted in the holding of a general strike in Karachi by the MQM in February and a well-publicized hunger strike by the leader of the MQM, Altaf Hussain, in mid-April. Subsequent talks between the PPP and the MQM, which began in early May and which hoped to find a *modus vivendi* acceptable to both parties, failed to yield any positive results, chiefly because of the Sindh government's one-sided 'Operation Clean-up' to find and confiscate unauthorized arms and to arrest suspected terrorists. In May the law-enforcing agencies raided the Pucca Qila district in Hyderabad, a Mohajir locality, after cutting off the water, electric and gas supplies for three days. The police met with stiff resistance and about 100 people were killed. A crowd of women and children protesting against the stoppage of water and other facilities was also fired upon, 17 women and seven children being killed. These incidents prompted a strong and outraged reaction in Karachi and ethnic violence between Sindhis and non-Sindhis erupted throughout the Sindh Province. The army was called in, a curfew was imposed in the disturbed areas, and Sindh gradually returned to an uneasy calm.

In the mean time both the PPP and the IDA dissipated their energies in attempting to destabilize one another and to win over the loyalties of assembly members. The euphoria of December 1988 had evaporated; the law and order situation had, in general, worsened (particularly in Sindh); no significant legislation had been undertaken, and the burden of taxation and the rate of inflation had both greatly increased. The adverse situation was compounded by widespread charges of corruption against high-ranking officials.

In a dramatic move on 6 August 1990, President Ghulam Ishaq Khan, in accordance with powers conferred on him by the Constitution, dissolved the National Assembly, dismissed Prime Minister Benazir Bhutto and her Cabinet, declared a state of emergency and announced that a fresh general election was to be held on 24 October. The presidential order listed five specific alleged violations of the Constitution by the ousted Government, and charged it with corruption, nepotism, horse-trading, ineptitude and failure to maintain law and order. Ghulam Mustafa Jatoi, the leader of the COP in the erstwhile National Assembly, was given the post of caretaker Prime Minister of a deliberately broad-based Cabinet for the interim period. The four provincial assemblies were also dissolved and caretaker Chief Ministers appointed. Benazir Bhutto termed the dissolution of her administration as 'totally illegal' and a 'constitutional coup' and denied charges of corruption and nepotism. The caretaker Prime Minister, in turn, promised to initiate the accountability process, through the establishment of special tribunals, simultaneously with the preparation for the holding of the general election. At the end of August the former Prime Minister's husband, Asif Ali Zardari, was charged with possessing illegal arms, the former Minister of State for Labour was arrested (rapidly followed by the arrest of a number of other former ministers), and in early September Benazir Bhutto herself was charged with more than 10 counts of corruption and misuse of power. In early October Zardari was arrested in Karachi on charges of kidnapping a Pakistan-born British citizen, extorting US $800,000 from him, and misusing his wife's official position to obtain illegal bank loans (he was later acquitted on all counts). The caretaker Government's position was bolstered when, in mid-October, the Lahore High Court rejected the PPP's five petitions, and upheld the President's actions as legal and constitutional.

Both the PPP and the IDA felt obliged to forge alliances with other parties. Thus, the PPP, for the first time, entered into an electoral alliance with three small parties (the TI, Tehrik Nifaz Firqah Jafariya and the PML—Chatta Group). The alliance was named the People's Democratic Alliance (PDA). The IDA entered into an informal alliance with three regional parties, the MQM, the ANP and the Jamhuri Watan Party (JWP), which commanded substantial regional support in Sindh, the NWFP and Balochistan respectively, and which had all been components of the erstwhile COP.

The First Government of Mohammad Nawaz Sharif

The general election, which was held, as scheduled, on 24 October 1990, gave a verdict firmly in the IDA's favour. The IDA obtained 106 seats, while the PPP-dominated PDA won only 45 seats. The urban-based MQM, which again emerged as the third most popular party, obtained 15 seats, the ANP six, the JUI six, other minor parties eight, and independents 21 seats. Hence, the IDA (together with its allies) commanded a two-thirds majority, thus enabling it to amend the Constitution should it wish to do so. The provincial elections, held on 27 October, produced a similar pattern of results. The IDA and its allies obtained 325 of the 473 contested seats in the four legislatures, compared with the 65 won by the PDA. More surprisingly, the PDA failed to win even a bare majority in Benazir Bhutto's home province of Sindh. With a massive 208 out of a total 234 seats, the IDA formed the provincial government in the Punjab. It also held power in Sindh and Balochistan, and formed a coalition Government with the ANP in the NWFP. In the elections to the Senate, which were held in February 1991, the IDA won 24, and its electoral allies six, of the 46 contested seats. The 16 non-IDA coalition senators who took office, formed a nucleus opposition.

On 6 November 1990 Mohammad Nawaz Sharif, the former Chief Minister of the Punjab, was sworn in as Prime Minister, having received 153 votes, compared with the 39 for the PDA's candidate. Nawaz Sharif's first act as Prime Minister was to lift the state of emergency, which had been imposed on 6 August. From its inception, the Nawaz Sharif Government, though arguably politically more stable than any since the mid-1960s, was faced with a host of problems and several controversial issues, both political and economic. Despite the Prime Minister's call for reconciliation, Benazir Bhutto continuously adopted a confrontational posture, the PDA threatened *en masse* resignations and frequently boycotted the federal and Sindh assemblies.

Nawaz Sharif's Government faced a crisis of confidence during the Gulf War, which broke out in January 1991 as a result of Iraq's invasion and annexation of Kuwait in August 1990. Earlier, the caretaker Government had adopted a firm stand against Iraq, and had committed 11,000 troops to the UN-authorized,

US-led multinational force; but when hostilities actually commenced, this decision proved to be a divisive issue, polarizing the Government and popular opinion. The wave of anti-US feeling, fuelled by the recent suspension of US aid to Pakistan (see below), was exploited by several parties (including the PPP) to organize pro-Iraqi protests and rallies. The Government, however, succeeded in surviving the popular outcry.

One of the administrative failures of Benazir Bhutto's regime that had featured in the President's list of charges was the non-convocation of the Council of Common Interests and the National Finance Commission (NFC). Nawaz Sharif convened both, and, through them, reached settlements with provincial governments regarding the distribution of the Indus River waters, and regarding the division of financial resources (derived mainly from federal taxes) between the central Government and the provinces. Both these accords were considered to be important diplomatic achievements.

The Nawaz Sharif Government also successfully addressed the highly controversial issue of providing legal status to *Shari'a*. A bill officially to adopt the Islamic legal code, which had been a long and persistent demand in Pakistan and an election pledge by the IDA, was presented in the National Assembly in mid-April 1991; it was referred to a Select Committee for review and incorporation of amendments. The amended Shari'a Bill was adopted by the Assembly in mid-May and approved by the Senate two weeks later. At the committee stage, efforts had been made to meet various objections and incorporate amendments, so as to achieve maximum consensus. In order to make the Shari'a Bill effective, a series of legislative and administrative measures, termed as Islamic reforms, were adopted. These included the Constitution Amendment Bill, declaring *Shari'a* as the law of the land; legislation providing for the Islamization of the educational, judicial and economic systems, the promotion of Islamic values through the mass media, and the eradication of corruption, obscenity and other social evils. The various bills, however, provided protection for the existing political structure and institutions, including the parliamentary system, and to all contracts, whether individual, corporate or international, pending the development of an alternative economic system. Since it had been drawn up as a compromise, however, the Shari'a Bill could not satisfy fully the two extremes. Benazir Bhutto criticized it as a 'fundamentalist' bill, while the JUI claimed that the new law's provisions were not stringent enough. None the less, the Shari'a Bill was destined to be the most important piece of legislation in Pakistan since the National Assembly adopted the Constitutional Bill in 1973.

The chronic law and order problem defied all attempts to resolve it, thus undermining confidence in the Government. A spate of violence throughout Pakistan in 1991 led the National Assembly to give the Prime Minister the authority to establish impromptu trial courts to decide cases involving terrorism, kidnappings and armed robbery. Despite the establishment of these special courts, the law and order situation did not improve in Sindh in 1992. The kidnapping and/or murder of 14 businessmen by unidentified armed men in Karachi and its environs during April and May prompted the Government to launch another 'Operation Clean-up', whereby the army was to apprehend criminals and terrorists, and seize unauthorized weapons. Initially, it was generally assumed that the operations would be largely concentrated in rural Sindh, from where the majority of the kidnappers and dacoits (armed robbers) operated; a violent clash, however, between two factions of the MQM (the majority Altaf faction and the small breakaway Haqiqi faction) in Karachi in June gave the armed forces an opportunity to clamp down on the extremist elements within the MQM. More than 500 people were arrested; caches of arms were located and seized; and 'torture cells', allegedly operated by the MQM, were discovered. In response, the leader of the MQM (A), Altaf Hussain, accused the Inter-Services Intelligence Directorate of masterminding the whole incident with the co-operation of the MQM (H); he also accused the Government of attempting to crush the MQM through 'Operation Clean-up'. In protest, 12 of the 15 MQM members in the National Assembly and 24 of the 27 members in the Sindh Assembly resigned their seats. The Government, however, repeatedly gave assurances that the operations were against criminals, and not specifically against the MQM, and the Prime Minister cautioned against condemning the MQM outright for the misdeeds of only a relatively small number of its leaders and activists. Benazir Bhutto, on the other hand, who still held the MQM partly to blame for its part in her ousting in 1990, insisted upon calling the MQM a terrorist organization, and exploited the informal alliance of the IDA with the MQM to condemn the Nawaz Sharif Government and demand its resignation.

At the national level, Nawaz Sharif's Government faced several crises during 1991–92. An All Parties Conference (APC) was launched by the President of the PDP, Nawabzada Nasrullah Khan, in September 1991, and demanded the dismissal of the Nawaz Sharif Government and its replacement by a national government, and fresh elections under neutral auspices. Although the APC organized mass rallies throughout Pakistan in 1991/92, it did not prove successful chiefly because of the ambivalent attitude of Benazir Bhutto and her PDA. Although she concurred with the APC's objectives, she was averse to joining it formally or forging an electoral alliance with any of its components. Instead, she continued her own campaign, calling for the resignation of both the President and the Prime Minister, for the installation of a government of 'national unity' and for the holding of fresh elections.

In addition to the continuing troubles caused by the opposition, the Prime Minister was faced with a host of problems posed by member parties of the IDA. In March 1992, when a new Chief Minister was required to succeed the deceased Jam Sadiq Ali in Sindh, the NPP, led by Ghulam Mustafa Jatoi, switched alliances and joined the PDA, in an attempt to install an NPP nominee as Chief Minister. Following the victory of the IDA-supported nominee, Nawaz Sharif dismissed Jatoi's son from his post as Minister of Communications in the federal Cabinet, and expelled the NPP from the IDA. In May, the JIP, one of the founder members of the IDA, left the alliance, alleging that Nawaz Sharif's Government had failed to implement the IDA's manifesto. It was particularly aggrieved by the fact that, in its opinion, the Government had failed to fulfil its election pledge of establishing an Islamic order. With the departure of the JIP and the NPP from the alliance, and the resignations of most of the MQM members, the two-thirds majority commanded by the IDA in the National Assembly was somewhat reduced.

In mid-November 1992 the PDA intensified its campaign of political agitation and was now supported by the majority of the components of the newly-formed opposition National Democratic Alliance (NDA, including the NPP). The large-scale demonstrations and marches organized by Benazir Bhutto were, however, ruthlessly suppressed by the Government through mass arrests, road-blocks and the imposition of a two-month ban on the holding of public meetings in Islamabad and Rawalpindi and of travel restrictions on the former Prime Minister. By mid-December tension between the Government and opposition had eased considerably, and in January 1993, in an apparently conciliatory move on the part of Nawaz Sharif's administration, Benazir Bhutto was elected as Chairperson of the National Assembly's Standing Committee on Foreign Affairs. Shortly after Benazir Bhutto had accepted the nomination, her husband was released on bail.

In January 1993 Nawaz Sharif's short list of candidates for the post of Chief of Army Staff was overlooked by President Ghulam Ishaq Khan in favour of a relatively junior officer and fellow Pathan. In March the growing rift between the Prime Minister and the President became more evident when the Government initiated discussions regarding proposed modifications to the Eighth Constitutional Amendment, which afforded the President the power to dismiss the Government and dissolve assemblies, and to appoint judicial and military chiefs. Nawaz Sharif wished to abolish the clauses that had allowed for the dismissal of two governments over the past five years and that held his own government hostage. He was eager to complete his five-year term in office, and the recent consolidation of the alliance between the presidency and the army seemed to pose an imminent threat to the continuance of his administration. At stake in the ensuing controversy regarding the Amendment was who should have the overriding authority with respect to affairs of state—the indirectly elected President or the directly elected National Assembly through the Prime Minister. Nawaz Sharif believed that in order to strengthen the democratic process, the ultimate authority of the legislature should be established, and that this could be done only through a change in the Eighth Amendment. He maintained, therefore, that the presidential mandate should be curtailed and that all executive powers should be accredited to the Prime Minister's office. To which President Ishaq Khan countered, stating that it was his duty as President to defend the Constitution of which the Eighth Amendment was an integral part. Despite the President's open opposition, Nawaz Sharif appointed a committee to review the Amendment in detail, and to negotiate with other parties, especially the PPP, in the National Assembly, since any alteration to the Eighth Amendment required a two-thirds majority to become law. Nawaz Sharif also announced his intention to make peace with Benazir Bhutto (a process that had already been initiated—see above) and join forces with her in an attempt to repeal, or at least to modify, the Amendment.

In late March 1993 three cabinet ministers resigned in protest at Nawaz Sharif's nomination as President of the PML (Junejo Group), to succeed Muhammad Khan Junejo (who had died earlier that month), and voiced their support for Ghulam Ishaq Khan in his political struggle with the Prime Minister. While initial contacts between Nawaz Sharif and the PPP seemed favourable, Benazir Bhutto herself remained non-committal as regards extending support to the Prime Minister in his ongoing confrontation with the President. In a seemingly final attempt at reconciliation, the Cabinet unanimously decided, in early April, to nominate Ghulam Ishaq Khan as the PML's candidate for the forthcoming presidential election later that year. By mid-April, however, a total of eight ministers had resigned from the Cabinet in protest at Nawaz Sharif's continued tenure of the premiership.

On 18 April 1993 the President dissolved the National Assembly and dismissed the Prime Minister and his Cabinet, accusing Nawaz Sharif of 'maladministration, nepotism and corruption'. The provincial assemblies and governments, however, remained in power, despite demands by the PDA and the NDA for their dissolution. A member of the dissolved National Assembly, Mir Balakh Sher Mazari, was sworn in as acting Prime Minister. At the same time it was announced that elections to the National Assembly would be held on 14 July. In late April a large broadly-based interim Cabinet, including Benazir Bhutto's husband, was sworn in. In early May the PML (Junejo Group) split into two factions: one led by Nawaz Sharif, the other by Hamid Nasir Chattha, who was supported by the President. Following his dismissal, Nawaz Sharif adopted a confrontational stance—he travelled around the country, amassing considerable support among the general public (particularly from entrepreneurs and businessmen, who had welcomed the former Prime Minister's ambitious programme of economic reform), and vowing confidently to dislodge the President and to stage a return to office.

On 26 May 1993, in an historic and unexpected judgment, the Supreme Court ordered that the National Assembly, the Prime Minister and the Cabinet dismissed by the President in April be restored to power immediately, stating that President Khan's order had been unconstitutional. The President agreed to honour the Court's ruling, and the National Assembly and Nawaz Sharif's Government were reinstated with immediate effect. On the following day Nawaz Sharif's return to power was consolidated when he won a vote of confidence in the National Assembly. A few days later, however, the political scene was thrown into turmoil following the dissolution, through the machinations of supporters of the President, of the provincial assemblies in Punjab and the NWFP. Finding himself without any real authority in each of the four provinces, Nawaz Sharif resorted to the drastic measure of imposing federal government's rule on Punjab through a resolution passed by the National Assembly in late June. For its part, the Punjab provincial government refused to obey the federal Government's orders, claiming that they subverted provincial autonomy. The Government asked the Rangers, a federal paramilitary force, to arrange the take-over of the Punjab administration. The army's general headquarters intervened, however, at this point, to pull the Rangers out, claiming that the take-over was unconstitutional since the President had not signed the proclamation imposing direct rule. Meanwhile, an All Parties Conference (APC), including, amongst others, Benazir Bhutto and the Chief Ministers of Punjab and the NWFP, convened in Lahore to pass a resolution urging the President to dissolve the legislature, dismiss Nawaz Sharif's Government and hold fresh elections. In early July the Chief of Army Staff, following an emergency meeting of senior army officers, acted as an intermediary in talks between the President and Prime Minister in an attempt to resolve the political crisis. Benazir Bhutto, supported by her APC collaborators, announced a 'long march' on 16 July, with the intention of laying siege to the federal capital and forcing Nawaz Sharif to resign. Fearing the outbreak of serious violence, the army persuaded Benazir Bhutto to postpone the march, reportedly assuring her that both the President and the Prime Minister would resign and that a general election would be held under a neutral administration. On 18 July, in accordance with an agreement reached under the auspices of the army, both Ghulam Ishaq Khan and Nawaz Sharif resigned from their posts, the federal legislature and the provincial assemblies were dissolved, the holding of a general election in October was announced, and neutral administrations were established, at both federal and provincial level. As specified in the Constitution, Ghulam Ishaq Khan was succeeded by the Chairman of the Senate, Wasim Sajjad Jan, who was to hold the presidency for the remaining tenure of the deposed President—i.e. until November. A small interim apolitical Cabinet was sworn in, headed by Moeenuddin Ahmad Qureshi, a former Executive Vice-President of the World Bank, as interim Prime Minister.

While in office, Prime Minister Qureshi carried out a number of important political and economic measures: he introduced, for the first time, a tax on agricultural income, in an effort to replenish the greatly depleted foreign-exchange reserves, and he attempted to reduce political corruption involving financial misdeeds and illegal drugs-trafficking (politicians linked with either of these two crimes were disqualified from participating in the forthcoming general election).

The Return to Power and Second Dismissal of Benazir Bhutto

The general election, held on 6 and 9 October 1993 under military supervision, was widely considered to have been fair, although the turn-out, which some officials estimated to be less than 50%, was disappointing. The polling was closely contested between the PML faction led by Nawaz Sharif and the PPP (the MQM boycotted the elections to the National Assembly, claiming systematic intimidation by the army, but took part in the provincial assembly elections a few days later). Neither of the two leading parties, however, won an outright majority in the federal elections and, in the provincial elections, an outright majority was only procured, by the PPP, in Sindh. Following intensive negotiations with smaller parties and independents in the National Assembly, Benazir Bhutto was elected to head a coalition Government on 19 October. On the following day, a PPP-led coalition assumed control of the provincial administration in Punjab (traditionally a PML stronghold). The provincial governments in the NWFP and in Balochistan were, however, headed by alliances led by the PML (Nawaz).

On 13 November 1993 the PPP's candidate, the newly appointed Minister of Foreign Affairs, Sardar Farooq Ahmad Khan Leghari, was elected the country's President, having secured 274 votes (62% of the total) in the electoral college. The incumbent acting President, Wasim Sajjad Jan, who stood as the candidate of the PML (Nawaz), obtained 168 votes (38%). On assuming office, Leghari stated that he intended to end his political ties with the PPP and that he hoped for the repeal or modification of the controversial Eighth Constitutional Amendment in the near future.

In early December 1993 a feud within Benazir Bhutto's immediate family threatened to result in the emergence of a breakaway faction from the ruling party. The Prime Minister's mother, Nusrat Bhutto, challenged her own overthrow as Co-Chairwoman of the PPP, claiming that her nomination by her husband in 1977 had been for life. Relations between Benazir Bhutto (who was now sole Chairwoman of the PPP) and her mother had become increasingly strained in the latter half of 1993 regarding the future of the Prime Minister's brother, Mir Murtaza Bhutto, who returned to Pakistan from exile in November and who was immediately arrested and imprisoned on charges of insurgency (he was released on bail in June

1994). Nusrat Bhutto allegedly viewed her son, rather than her daughter, as the rightful heir to Zulfikar Ali Bhutto's political legacy.

In late January 1994 the Prime Minister announced the appointment of 11 new cabinet members. In late February the President dismissed the Chief Minister and Government in the NWFP, suspended the provincial legislature and imposed governor's rule, following the thwarted introduction of a vote of 'no confidence' against the PML (Nawaz)-led coalition by the PPP. The PPP consolidated its hold on federal power in early March by winning the majority of the contested seats in the elections to the Senate; however, the ruling party's candidate for the Senate's chairmanship lost to the opposition's nominee. In late April a PPP member was elected as Chief Minister of the newly revived provincial Government in the NWFP; the opposition alliance boycotted the proceedings.

It was reported that at least 20 people were killed in ethnic violence, allegedly instigated by members of the MQM (A), in Karachi in early May 1994. The army was deployed in an attempt to restore order: incidents were also reported in Hyderabad and Sukkur. In June 19 high-ranking members of the MQM (A), including its leader, Altaf Hussain, were each sentenced *in absentia* to 27 years of imprisonment on charges of terrorism.

The second half of 1994 witnessed a further intensification in the confrontation between Benazir Bhutto's Government and the main opposition party, the PML (Nawaz). Various strikes, marches and demonstrations were organized by the opposition group, yet, despite support from industrial and business bodies, which had their own grievances following the introduction of a new general sales tax, the 'Oust Bhutto' campaign rapidly lost momentum. The political conflict subsequently shifted literally to the floor of the National Assembly. On 14 November, the occasion of the presidential address to the joint parliamentary session, verbal insults and the unfurling of opposition banners degenerated into physical assaults and intimidation. The heated atmosphere was partly fuelled by the earlier arrest of Nawaz Sharif's elderly father, Mian Mohammad Sharif, the founder of the Ittefaq group of industries, on charges of fraud and tax evasion (he was later released on health grounds). The Prime Minister condemned the incident as undemocratic and an ugly attempt by the opposition to damage the political process.

The disturbances in the National Assembly followed an unexpected challenge to the Government's authority in the Malakand Division of the NWFP mounted by members of the Tehreek-i-Nifaz-i-Shariat-i-Mohammadi (TNSM), who were followers of Maulana Sufi Mohammad. This Islamist fundamentalist movement had been founded in mid-1989, but had only come to prominence in May 1994 when heavily armed tribesmen blocked the Malakand Pass as part of the TNSM's campaign for the replacement of civil law by *Shari'a*. However, the legal vacuum, which had been created by the Supreme Court's declaration that the Provincially Administered Tribal Area regulation for the Malakand Division was null and void, persisted. In early November the TNSM intensified its efforts to enforce Islamic law. Roads were blocked for five days, and TNSM activists took government officials hostage and occupied the Saidu Sharif airport. Amidst evidence that the movement had been infiltrated by Afghan militants sponsored by the drug 'barons' from the tribal belt, the Government took firm repressive action, deploying the Frontier Corps, whilst at the same time announcing the enforcement of *Shari'a* in the tribal area of Malakand. However, the deep divisions caused by the agitation (during which several hundred people had been killed) remained, and following a dispute over the refusal of an activist in Matta to pay 'unIslamic' land revenue tax, the TNSM resumed its campaign in mid-June 1995. The Government's response, with its combination of forbearance and harshness, including the arrest of Maulana Sufi Mohammad, defused the tension somewhat, although the poverty and underdevelopment of the tribal region, which had greatly aggravated the unrest, remained.

The Government was less successful in its attempts to bring under control the deteriorating law and order situation in Karachi. An increasingly unchecked outbreak of violence had begun following an incident at the Teen Hatti Bridge, which divides central and eastern Karachi, in late April 1994, when government troops fired on MQM protesters. The death toll rose dramatically in the wake of the army's hasty retreat from a futile two-year operation in the city in early December. In the first two weeks of December alone more than 100 people were killed in Karachi, including Muhammad Salahuddin, the editor of the influential Urdu weekly *Takbeer*. Rumours abounded in the absence of clear evidence regarding precise responsibility for the violence. The Indian consulate in Karachi was closed amidst claims that Indian secret service agents were attempting to destabilize the country in retaliation for alleged Pakistani involvement with Kashmiri separatists. Rivalries between Pakistani intelligence agencies were also purported to be exacerbating the violence, as also, it was claimed, were the drug mafias. Much of the unrest arose from clashes between the rival factions of the MQM. It was widely acknowledged that the MQM (H) had been patronized by the army after the launch of its June 1992 'Operation Clean-up', in order to fight a 'dirty war' against the mainstream MQM (A). Sectarian violence between Sunni and Shi'a Muslims also contributed to the death toll in Karachi. Each side attacked the other's mosques, as for example in the assault by Shi'a gunmen on the Masjid-e-Akbar in early December 1994, which left eight dead, including the city chief of the militant Sunni organization, Sipah-i-Sahaba Pakistan (SSP).

There was little respite for Karachi during the early months of 1995. In February a fresh wave of sectarian violence included a series of retaliatory attacks on mosques and other religious buildings. Twenty-five people were killed by unknown assailants in two incidents on 25 February alone. In the next month world attention was directed to Karachi following the murder in broad daylight of two US consular officials when their van was ambushed by unidentified armed gunmen on one of the city's busiest roads. The ensuing security crackdown reduced the number of violent deaths in April, but the respite proved very short-lived. Violence erupted again on 18 May with a day-long pitched battle between the security forces and the MQM (A) militants in North Nazimabad. During the following week there were repeated clashes in which more than 70 people were killed. Government control collapsed in large areas of central, eastern and western Karachi. The MQM held the advantage in what amounted to an insurgency until the end of June. Thereafter concerted action by the security forces, involving extra-judicial means, made inroads into the militant strongholds of the city.

The MQM campaign against government officials and the security forces in mid-1995 and the latter's sense of operating in 'foreign' territory was dangerously reminiscent of events in East Bengal in 1970–71. The almost total alienation of the Mohajir population from both the provincial government of Chief Minister Syed Abdullah Shah and the federal authorities was rooted in the excesses of law and order enforcement carried out during 'Operation Clean-up'. It was compounded by the Mohajirs' lack of a political voice in the administration of the city following the Sindh Government's refusal to call elections for local bodies. In fact, an almost irreparable division existed between the political interests of rural and urban Sindh. This situation was one of the crucial reasons for the failure to achieve a dialogue between the PPP and the MQM (A), despite the fact that such discussions would be vital in the restoration of peace to Karachi and in the removal of the wider threat that the violence posed both to the country's economic life and to national unity. Initially, the PPP national leadership refused to countenance dialogue with a 'terrorist' organization and insisted that Karachi's problems were to be solved by the implementation of 'law and order' rather than by political methods. Following the assassination of the two US consulate staff in March 1995, however, the army covertly and the President more openly began to support the idea of a negotiated settlement. In early July the MQM (A) adjusted its own hardline attitude. The weekly two-day strike call was cancelled, and talks between government officials and members of the MQM (A) were begun in the National Assembly. This directional change by the MQM (A) stemmed partly from the growing success of government 'counter-terrorist' activities, which were personally directed by the Minister of the Interior, Maj.-Gen. (retd) Naseerullah Khan Babar. It was also prompted by the way in which the PML (Nawaz) and other opposition parties had distanced themselves from the MQM (A) following the relaunch of its insurgency movement in May. Little progress was made in the talks, however, with both sides raising their conflicting 'charge sheets' against each other. The dialogue did not advance beyond the abortive 10-point agreement that had been drawn up between the MQM (A) and the Sindh Government in October 1994. It was apparent by August 1995 that although the Government had achieved some success in infiltrating and breaking up the networks of MQM militants, the rank and file public support for the Mohajir group remained intact.

The deteriorating law and order situation in Karachi throughout most of 1995 jeopardized the Government's efforts to encourage large-scale foreign investment in Pakistan. Nevertheless, progress was made in this respect in the energy sector and indeed much diplomatic activity was directed towards commercial areas. Benazir Bhutto's frequent overseas visits, although criticized by domestic opponents, were primarily aimed at stimulating foreign interest and at dispelling the negative image of the country as a 'terrorist' and 'fundamentalist' state. Instead, the Prime Minister portrayed Pakistan as a moderate Islamic state, open to outside business interests and willing to assist the West in its international struggle against drugs and terrorism. However, this reassuring image of a modern, peace-loving country was not only undermined by events in Karachi but also by the growing tide of sectarianism in the Punjab and by the highly publicized 'blasphemy' cases. In October 1994 the Sipah-e-Muhammad Pakistan (SMP), led by Allama Raza Naqvi, held a heavily armed rally in Lahore. In the following month members of the SMP attacked the offices of the Islamabad newspaper the *Pakistan Observer* because of its alleged links with the hated rival Sunni organization, the SSP. Much controversy, both within Pakistan itself and in the international community, was aroused in February 1995 by the death sentences imposed, under Pakistan's Islamic penal code, on a Christian youth and his uncle, who had been convicted of blasphemy. The sentences were later overruled by the High Court in Lahore, but the whole incident served to highlight the increasing persecution of religious minorities in Pakistan. Benazir Bhutto angered the country's Islamist fundamentalists when she said that she was 'shocked and saddened' by the court's initial imposition of the death sentence; in May, however, she assured Muslims that blasphemy would remain a capital offence.

There were a number of threats to Benazir Bhutto's Government during the latter half of 1995: a political crisis arose in the Punjab, Pakistan's most politically sensitive province; the violence in Karachi continued unabated; a small group of junior army officers attempted a coup; and, finally, increasing economic problems necessitated a tough mini-budget. The Government not only surmounted all these difficulties, however, but emerged from them much better than expected.

Punjab had proved the source of various troubles for Benazir Bhutto's first administration. In order to avoid a repetition, in October 1993 the PPP had formed a coalition provincial government in Punjab with the PML (Junejo Group) under the leadership of Mian Manzoor Ahmed Wattoo. By late 1995, however, the Chief Minister was resented not only by the dominant PPP partners in the coalition but also by his own party members, as he attempted to convert the provincial administrative services into his own personal preserve. The political manoeuvring in Lahore, which followed the Governor's dismissal of Wattoo in early September, could have either alienated the PPP's own supporters, or opened the way for a reunification of the PML under Nawaz Sharif's leadership. In the event, Benazir Bhutto's personal intervention ensured the installation in mid-September of a PPP-PML (Junejo Group) coalition under the much more compliant figure of Sardar Arif Nakai, with the PPP now dictating the administration of the province.

The violence in Karachi showed no sign of abatement during the second half of 1995. The number of people killed between late August and early November alone totalled about 500. In December Nasir Hussain, the elder brother of MQM (A) leader Altaf Hussain, was kidnapped and murdered by unknown assailants. Two weeks later Syed Ahsan Shah, the brother of the Chief Minister of Sindh, was killed in Karachi. These prominent deaths, however, marked the beginning of a return to relative normality rather than a renewed outbreak of violence. The improved atmosphere was most evident in early 1996, at the time of Ramadan and the Sixth Cricket World Cup fixtures, which were held in Karachi shortly afterwards.

As in previous years in the Indian state of Punjab, counter-insurgency measures adopted in Pakistan helped to reduce the threat of terrorism. Eleven police 'encounters' took place in January 1996 alone, resulting in the deaths of 23 MQM activists or sympathizers. A number of alleged leading terrorists died in what appeared to be staged confrontations with the police, who, together with the Rangers, seemed to have been given a free hand in dealing with the militants. In the absence of a meaningful political dialogue, however, the root of the disorder remained unchecked. Moreover, extra-judicial killings not only claimed their innocent victims, but further encouraged the brutalization of Pakistani society in general.

The coup attempt of Maj.-Gen. Zaheerul Islam Abbassi, Brig. Mustansar Billah, Col. Muhammad Azad Minhas and Col. Innayatullah Khan was thwarted in September 1995. The conspirators, together with a number of other junior officers, had secured weapons from the tribal areas and planned to storm a meeting of high-ranking army personnel on 30 September. They hoped that the liquidation of the military and political élite would pave the way for the establishment of an Islamic dictatorship in Pakistan. When the news of the plotters' arrests was finally made public, Benazir Bhutto attempted to secure Western sympathy and to use the episode to buttress further her regime's image as a bastion against fundamentalist forces. The conspiracy did not appear to have wide support within the army; significantly, it was uncovered shortly before the retirement of the Chief of Army Staff, Gen. Abdul Waheed Khan Khakar, who had established a reputation for non-intervention and professionalism. In keeping with this, he refused the Government's entreaties to extend his tenure on completing his term and was replaced by Gen. Jehangir Karamat in January 1996.

A less dramatic but equally dangerous threat to the Government was provided by the deteriorating economic situation at the end of 1995, which was illustrated most dramatically in the depletion of foreign-exchange reserves. The Government responded by introducing in October what was in effect a mini-budget. This sought to boost exports and raise revenues by devaluing the rupee by 7%, by increasing domestic fuel prices and by imposing a 10% regulatory duty on imports. In December the IMF provided Pakistan with a US $600m. stand-by loan in an effort to stabilize the foundering economy. These measures averted an economic collapse, although they were politically unpopular owing to the concomitant rise in the rate of inflation, which at this stage, according to government figures, stood at around 11%.

The danger that the political battles being waged by Islamist groups in the Middle East might extend to Pakistan was made evident by the suicide bomb attack on the Egyptian embassy in Islamabad in November 1995, as a result of which 18 people were killed and 16 injured. Early investigations led to the Islamic Jihad, an Egyptian militant group, being suspected of having carried out the attack. During 1994 the Pakistani Government had been co-operating with Egypt by attempting to apprehend and extradite members of illegal Islamist militant organizations operating in the NWFP or across the border in Afghanistan. (In 1993–95 the Pakistani authorities, concerned at being viewed as a centre for Islamist extremists, expelled more than 2,000 Arabs, the majority of whom were reported to have been or were still involved in the civil war in Afghanistan.) By early December 1995 16 Arab nationals had been arrested in Pakistan in connection with the bomb attack on the Egyptian embassy.

Despite all the threats (both internal and external) to Pakistan's stability, by the beginning of 1996 the Government of Benazir Bhutto appeared to have survived the worst of the crisis. Opposition was decidedly muted, and the PML (Nawaz) displayed a marked reluctance to organize public anti-Government demonstrations. The greatest interest provoked in the field of politics surrounded the political intentions of the popular former international cricketer, Imran Khan, who had attracted attention through his fund-raising campaign for the Shaukat Khanum Memorial Hospital. Khan's growing populist support and 'born-again' Islamist image created increasing tensions with Benazir Bhutto's administration. In retaliation to Khan's charges of corruption, the Government refused to broadcast his appeal for donations for the hospital on the state-owned television network and blocked the money he received from *zakat* funds. Imran Khan reciprocated by securing international media coverage for the Princess of Wales' visit to his hospital and a fund-raising dinner in late February 1996. It was only after the unexplained bomb explosion that wrecked the out-patient wing of the cancer hospital, that Khan established, in late April, a political reform movement, known as the Tehrik-e-Insaf (Movement for Justice). The new organization was promoted as an embryonic 'third force' in Pakistani politics, appealing directly to the middle classes.

The launching of the Tehrik-e-Insaaf in April 1996 coincided with a sharp downturn in the Government's fortunes. Even at the beginning of the previous month, the prospect of mid-term polls or a wider crisis had appeared remote. At this time the opposition was largely quiescent, and the ruthless tactics of the Minister of the Interior had curbed the violent campaign waged by the MQM militants in Karachi. Even concern about the worrying economic situation had been relegated to the background. The turning-point was provided by the Supreme Court's decision on 20 March to uphold the challenge mounted by the Rawalpindi lawyer Habib Wahabul Khairi to the PPP's legal appointments. This action, which meant that the Government no longer had the exclusive power to appoint judges to the higher courts, culminated in a trial of strength between the Government and the judiciary. The Supreme Court had agreed to hear Khairi's petition challenging the appointments and transfers of judges carried out on an *ad hoc* basis by Benazir Bhutto's Government in early November 1995. The ensuing attempts by the Government to pressurize the Supreme Court Chief Justice Sajjad Ali Shah through the intimidation of his son-in-law, Pervaiz Shah, inflicted immense damage on the Bhutto administration's image. This had earlier also been tarnished by the alleged human rights abuses in Karachi involving a reported series of extra-judicial killings as part of the clamp-down on the MQM. The 20 March judgment also abrogated the constitutional amendment imposed by Gen. Zia that allowed the transfer of High Court judges to the Federal Shari'a Court without their consent. In a move that further politicized the issue, lawyers in both Karachi and Lahore boycotted the PPP-appointed *ad hoc* judges. The impasse damaged the previously harmonious relations between the Prime Minister and President Leghari and the question was raised, for the first time during Benazir Bhutto's second premiership, of whether he would use his constitutional powers to move against the Government.

The Government's popularity was further undermined by the necessary introduction of an austere budget in mid-June 1996, in an attempt to reduce the large budget deficit, caused by ever-increasing defence expenditure and the burden of debt-servicing. Ensuing political protests focused on both the extent of the new taxes and on the fact that, in the absence of effective agricultural taxation, the onus would be inequitably shared. Anti-budget demonstrations were held in Islamabad and Rawalpindi in late June, during which three JIP protesters were shot dead by the police. Despite this, the JIP did not join the 16-party opposition alliance that was established in the following month. The party did, however, work with the MQM and other groups in organizing a strike in Sindh in late July. This formed part of a wave of mounting protests in which the broad opposition alliance, handicapped by its lack of ideological coherence, appeared to be responding to, rather than leading, events. The volatile political situation was intensified by a large bomb explosion at Lahore airport in late July. This attack occurred at the end of a seven-month period during which more than 80 people had been killed in mysterious bombings in Punjab. The danger of a recrudescence of violence in Karachi was also highlighted by the death of 12 SSP activists when unidentified gunmen opened fire on an Independence Day rally. Benazir Bhutto responded to the mounting political crisis by addressing large rallies in Karachi and in a number of Punjabi towns. In anticipation of a crisis occasioned by the Supreme Court ordering a hearing for Mian Manzoor Ahmed Wattoo's appeal against his dismissal as Chief Minister of Punjab, the Prime Minister spent a week in Lahore in mid-July. In the event, the hearing was postponed until early November, and the damage limitation exercise appeared to have been successful. The Prime Minister sought to consolidate further her position by expanding the federal Cabinet in late July. The inclusion of her husband, Asif Ali Zardari, generated yet more controversy, however, as did the appointment of Haji Nawaz Khokhar as Minister of Science and Technology. The latter politician possessed a reputation for unscrupulous behaviour and had been arrested in 1995 on charges of loan default. It appeared that his inclusion in the enlarged Cabinet was designed to signal the rewards that would await politicians like himself who defected from the opposition PML camp.

Pakistan's political outlook in mid-1996 was thus decidedly uncertain. Domestically, Benazir Bhutto's administration remained beleaguered. While the Government had withstood popular opposition to the budget, the economic prospects remained gloomy and pointed to the need for a continuation of harsh fiscal measures. The declining law and order situation in the strategic Punjab province (notably the increasing sectarian violence between Sunni and Shi'a Muslims), together with the formation of a broad opposition coalition, was disturbingly reminiscent of the situation that had preceded the 1977 military coup.

Pakistan was locked in mounting political and economic crisis from August 1996 onwards. Critics of the Bhutto Government accused it of gross corruption and financial mismanagement. Asif Ali Zardari was again at the centre of a controversy, which involved claims of misuse of government facilities to ship effects to a residence in the UK in what became known as the 'Surrey-gate' affair. Mir Murtaza Bhutto was especially bitter in his criticism of Zardari's influence over his sister and the PPP. This hostility formed the background to subsequent claims that Zardari was behind Murtaza's death during a police encounter in Karachi on 20 September. Three days earlier, one of Murtaza's long-time associates, Ali Mohammed Sonara, had been arrested on terrorist charges. Rumours circulated that he and other members of Murtaza's entourage were Indian intelligence agents. Murtaza, with typical boldness, clashed violently with the local police in attempting to secure Sonara's release. Sial was a witness to the later shoot-out and died, apparently having committed suicide (although his family claimed he was murdered), just a week later. Ghinwa Bhutto, Murtaza's wife, filed a petition in the Sindh High Court accusing senior police and intelligence officials of murdering her husband. An emotional Benazir Bhutto claimed that her brother had been murdered in a conspiracy aimed at eliminating the Bhutto family. This outburst fatally widened the breach between herself and President Leghari whom she had apparently implicated. Slogans appeared on buildings in Lahore accusing the President of Murtaza's murder. Simultaneously, the President filed a reference in the Supreme Court designed to expedite the 20 March judgment concerning the power to appoint judges to the superior courts. Less than a week later he met with Nawaz Sharif for the first time since he had assumed the presidency. Their five hours of discussions concluded with a statement in which Leghari significantly mentioned Article 58 (2b) under the Eighth Amendment of the Constitution, which allowed the President to dismiss the Government.

Benazir Bhutto also faced a political crisis in Punjab. The case which the former Chief Minister Wattoo had brought against his dismissal in September 1995 was a constant potential threat to the security of the replacement PPP-PML (Junejo Group) government of Sardar Arif Nakai. On 3 November 1996 the Lahore Court reinstated Wattoo as Chief Minister of Punjab. Asif Ali Zardari went to Lahore allegedly to buy support in a 'no confidence' vote against Wattoo. A number of observers have linked President Leghari's final decision to dismiss the Bhutto Government with this situation.

Benazir Bhutto's fall from power had also been precipitated, however, by the worsening economic crisis. The Prime Minister's meeting with IMF officials in early October 1996 during a visit to New York to address the UN General Assembly failed to soften significantly the Fund's stance at a time of dwindling foreign-exchange reserves. There thus seemed little option but to implement IMF conditionalities designed to reduce the budget deficit in order to receive the third tranche of the stand-by loan (US $80m.) which had been refused.

Despite this bleak political and economic scenario, Benazir Bhutto was taken totally by surprise when she was notified of her dismissal on 5 November 1996. While President Leghari's action appeared to have been taken hastily, it was undoubtedly made with the full support of the army high command. The caretaker administration headed by the octogenarian former PPP stalwart, Malik Meraj Khalid, suffered a lack of credibility and neutrality with the inclusion of such persons as Leghari's brother-in-law, Dr Zubair Khan, as Minister of Commerce and the bitter PPP critic, Mumtaz Bhutto, as Chief Minister of Sindh. The caretaker administration sought to introduce both major economic and financial reforms and to oversee an *Ehtesab* (accountability) exercise. The latter process became mired in controversy when the acting Minister of Law, Fakhruddin G. Ebrahim, resigned in protest at the amendment of the Accountability Ordinance, which was apparently designed to save Nawaz Sharif from disqualification in the forthcoming elections. The interim Government was also unable to bring any charges against Benazir Bhutto that would have disqualified her from standing for election. Economic and financial reforms were entrusted to Shahid Javed Burki, a Vice-President of the World Bank, who became Meraj Khalid's economic adviser. Burki sought to stabilize the rupee's exchange rate and to lower the fiscal deficit to the 4% of GDP demanded by the IMF. He attempted to broaden the tax base to include agricultural incomes, which, it was hoped, would realize US $2,000m. Burki also made changes in the management of the state-owned banks, and established a Resolution Trust Corporation to deal with the bad debts (these amounted to more than 100,000m. rupees) that had been accumulated by state-run banks and financial institutions. The caretaker Prime Minister highlighted the campaign to reduce public expenditure by closing VIP lounges at airports and setting an example of air travel by economy class. Despite Burki's public confidence in transforming the economy in a short time and securing IMF funds without difficulty, these aims appeared increasingly unattainable. In addition, the public was opposed to the price rises resulting from Burki's reforms.

Under the terms of the Constitution, elections were scheduled for 3 February 1997 following the dissolution of the National Assembly. There were serious doubts, however, whether these would be held. The doubts arose both from statements by cabinet members who mentioned the possibility of postponement, and from the uncertainty pending the outcome of Benazir Bhutto's appeal to the Supreme Court against her dismissal. The atmosphere was, however, very different from that of 1993 when Nawaz Sharif had been restored by the Court. The Bhutto Government's dismissal had been greeted with something akin to popular relief, most notably in commercial circles and in Karachi. Even in the PPP heartland of the interior of Sindh, the tide of opinion seemed to be turning from Benazir Bhutto to her estranged sister-in-law, Ghinwa Bhutto. The continuing court case into the circumstances of Mir Murtaza Bhutto's death led to vilification of Zardari. In November 1996 Ghinwa Bhutto had been appointed Chairwoman of the PPP (Shaheed Bhutto), a rival faction established by her deceased husband in 1995.

While the caretaker Government's inability to introduce an even-handed accountability process evoked considerable cynicism, two major institutional reforms were introduced during Meraj Khalid's tenure of power. The first, the introduction of adult franchise in Pakistan's Federally Administered Tribal Areas (FATA), was long overdue. The subsequent peaceful conduct of the elections in the FATA fully justified the decision. However, tribal custom resulted in women being unable to exercise their right to vote in many places. The acting Government's second institutional reform involved the formation of a 10-member Council of Defence and National Security (CDNS). The President was to chair the new body, which was to comprise the Prime Minister, four senior cabinet ministers, the Chairman of the Joint Chiefs of Staff and the three armed services chiefs. Its constitutionality and timing aroused considerable criticism. Qazi Hussain Ahmad, the leader of the JIP, even claimed that the establishment of the CDNS strengthened the 'Washington Plan' of imposing the hegemony of the World Bank and the IMF and diminishing the influence of the Islamist movements in Pakistan. The idea that the army should formally share decision-making with elected representatives dated to Zia's post-martial law proposals for a National Security Council. Despite its depiction as an advisory body, which could be disbanded by an incoming elected government, the CDNS inevitably appeared as a formalization of the power that the President and army had wielded together with the Prime Minister in what had been termed the 'troika' since the restoration of democracy in 1988. The notification order referred to the fixing of priorities in the co-ordination of defence policy with external and domestic policies and of advising the Government on economic and fiscal policies affecting defence and national security, all of which certainly indicated a more than advisory nature. Arguments that the CDNS's existence would prevent a military coup and ensure continuity in economic and foreign policy appeared unconvincing.

Nawaz Sharif's Return to Power

Uncertainty as to whether the polls should go ahead, bad weather and their coincidence with Ramadan all contributed to a low-key electioneering campaign for the 217 National Assembly seats and 460 provincial assembly constituencies. The JIP's boycott of the elections had a more marginal impact. The Supreme Court verdict upholding the dismissal of the Bhutto Government was announced just four days before the polling booths opened on 3 February 1997 and undoubtedly damaged the PPP's prospects. The party's impending débâcle was also hinted at by the defection of senior PPP members to the PML (Nawaz) and PPP (Shaheed Bhutto), or their decision to stand as independents. No commentators, however, anticipated the scale of the PML (Nawaz) victory. Indeed, much media attention had been devoted to the newcomers, Ghinwa Bhutto and Imran Khan. In the end, the PPP (Shaheed Bhutto) won just one National Assembly seat and two provincial assembly constituencies in Sindh. Begum Bhutto defeated her daughter-in-law in the Larkana NA-164 constituency. Imran Khan, the much touted 'third force' in Pakistani politics, fared even more dismally. His Tehrik-e-Insaaf party failed to win even a single seat. Imran Khan joined Benazir Bhutto in claiming that the polls had been rigged.

The European Union (EU) election observers, who had closely monitored the voting, reported that 'in general the poll was conducted in accordance with the rules' and in an 'equitable manner'. Their report also noted, however, that there were 'serious deficiencies' in the electoral register and identification of voters which 'excluded a significant proportion of those who had the right to vote'. The other losers in the general election besides the PPP were the religious parties. With the JIP and the JUP boycotting the polls, attention had focused on Fazlur Rehman's JUI. The JUI won just two National Assembly seats and eight provincial assembly seats (seven of which came from Balochistan, where the JUI joined the coalition Government of the Balochistan National Party and the Jamhuri Watan Party). The 134 seats that the PML (Nawaz) won in the National Assembly made this the first occasion since 1985 that a party possessed an absolute majority. The PPP's representation was reduced to just 18 seats in the National Assembly and to a small number of seats outside Sindh in the provincial assemblies. The Punjab once again proved to be the PML (Nawaz)'s key area of support, but it also made striking inroads into Sindh. The PPP, which had been decimated in Punjab where it won a paltry three of the 240 provincial assembly seats, was now no longer secure even in its traditional heartland of Sindh where it suffered a series of set-backs (at national and provincial level) in a number of districts. The 'Zardari factor' appeared to be at work here, although neither Asif Ali nor his father, Hakim Ali, contested the polls. In urban Sindh, the MQM (A) fended off an unexpectedly vigorous challenge from the PML (Nawaz), and won 12 National Assembly and 28 provincial assembly seats. The poor performance of the MQM (H) seemed further to confirm the exiled Altaf Hussain's claims that the smaller faction was merely a tool of the security forces without any electoral base. After some uncertainty, the MQM (A) formed an uneasy coalition government in Sindh with the PML (Nawaz) headed by Liaquat Jatoi. Little progress was made with the MQM (A)'s demands that cases against activists be lifted or that local-body elections be held. The MQM (A) also demanded that the Rangers paramilitary force be removed from its law-and-order duties in Karachi because of its 'patronizing' of the Haqiqi faction. The PML (Nawaz) had hoped that an MQM (A) nominee would be appointed as Governor of Sindh, but President Leghari had overridden this and insisted that the post be assigned to an establishment figure, Lt-Gen. (retd) Moinuddin Haider. The

President also secured his choice of the new Governor of Punjab when Shahid Hamid was sworn in on 11 March. The new Prime Minister's power in Pakistan's key province was demonstrated, however, by the fact that his brother, Mohammad Shahbaz Sharif, was appointed Chief Minister of Punjab.

Prime Minister Nawaz Sharif embarked on a series of populist measures designed to tackle such problems as corruption, the foreign-exchange crisis and environmental degradation. The most striking populist measure was the *qarz utaro, mulk sanvaro* ('retire debt, develop the country') scheme in which overseas Pakistanis were asked to boost foreign-exchange funds by depositing a minimum of US $1,000 as an interest-free loan in Pakistani banks for two to five years. Less eye-catching but more significant was the decision announced by the Minister of Finance, Sartaj Aziz, in the economic reform measures of 28 March to concentrate on supply-side economics through tax reductions and higher support prices to boost agricultural and textile production rather than attempt to continue the austerity measures demanded by the IMF stand-by arrangement. The suspension of this arrangement on 21 March indeed prompted what might be seen as a 'growing out of problems policy', although the IMF gave a guarded approval to the radical initiative. This departure was matched by an attempt to normalize relations with India in order to increase bilateral trade (see below).

The Nawaz Sharif Government used its huge majority in the National Assembly in May 1997 drastically to modify the Accountability Ordinance introduced by the caretaker regime in November 1996. This controversially gave the *Ehtesab* Cell, which was headed by the Prime Minister's personal friend, Senator Saifur Rehman, the power to investigate cases, thereby reducing the authority of the original *Ehtesab* Commission. Further questions concerning the impartiality of the accountability process were raised by the exemption of the period 1985–90 from review. Critics argued that this deliberately exempted Nawaz Sharif's Chief Ministership of the Punjab from scrutiny, despite the fact that there were alleged misuses of power during these years. Shortly afterwards, the controversial Fourteenth Amendment to the Constitution was passed, which was designed to curb the ability of legislators to defect from their party.

The most dramatic development of the early days of the Nawaz Sharif Government was the passage on 1 April 1997 of the Thirteenth Amendment Bill, which stripped the President of the power to dismiss the Prime Minister and dissolve the National Assembly. Benazir Bhutto unstintingly praised her rival for removing this potential threat, which had hung over every elected Government since 1988. She had been dismissed twice under Article 58 (2b) of the Constitution, and the incumbent Prime Minister once. Commentators had not expected such an early strike against the President, who was forced to accept what was in effect a *fait accompli*. The large and unanticipated PML (Nawaz) parliamentary majority had put the Prime Minister and a President eager to wield his influence on a collision course. The disagreement between the President and the Prime Minister over the appointment of the Governor of Sindh has already been mentioned (see above). Bitterness had also arisen when, against the wishes of many of his party, Nawaz Sharif had been forced by the President to award a seat in the Senate to the latter's cousin Maqsood Leghari. At a policy level, Farooq Leghari was uneasy with the Prime Minister's new supply-side economics. The curtailment of the President's authority should be understood, however, more in terms of a clash with the current holder of the office than as a permanent ending of the power of the unelected institutions of the State. The army had earlier distanced itself from the President because of reservations over such actions as the establishment of the CDNS. Despite Nawaz Sharif's bold and populist approach to government, there were still clouds on the horizon as Pakistan approached its Golden Jubilee (celebrating 50 years of independence). The economic crisis, fuelled by a trade deficit of US $3,000m. for 1995/96, was far from over. Kashmir still stood in the way of a much-needed normalization of relations with India.

Domestically, the attacks against the Christian community in Khanewal in early February 1997 were worrying, as were the violent sectarian clashes which showed no sign of abating. During June 1997 alone, 22 people were killed in sectarian violence in Punjab. Indeed, some observers believed that Saudi Arabia and Iran were almost fighting a proxy war in Pakistan. Tensions between Pakistan and Iran had certainly increased because of the rivalries between the two countries in Afghanistan and beyond it in Central Asia. In early July Asif Ali Zardari was formally charged with ordering the killing of Mir Murtaza Bhutto; 21 other former officials were simultaneously charged with murder and conspiracy in the death.

Four major issues dominated the second half of 1997: the serious allegations concerning the financial affairs of the former Prime Minister, Benazir Bhutto; the clash between the Chief Justice, Sajjad Ali Shah, and Prime Minister Nawaz Sharif which culminated on 2 December in the resignation of President Farooq Leghari and the dismissal of the Sindhi head of the Supreme Court; the increasing sectarian and ethnic violence in the Punjab and Karachi; and the increasing alienation of the minority provinces arising from the 'Punjabization' of the country.

The accountability process, which was orchestrated from the Prime Minister's Secretariat by his close associate Senator Saifur Rehman, displayed a single-minded, but far from even-handed, interest in the financial affairs of Benazir Bhutto and her controversial spouse. The Accountability Cell claimed a major breakthrough in September 1997, when it was disclosed that the Swiss Government had unprecedently 'frozen' four bank accounts held in the names of Zardari and Benazir Bhutto's mother, Nusrat Bhutto. Pakistani investigators were initially given a three-month deadline to ascertain whether the millions of dollars in the accounts had been acquired through illegal activities. Zardari's name was linked with drugs-dealing and with illegal commissions on such contracts as the purchase of submarines from France. Benazir Bhutto's accounts in London came under similar scrutiny, and much of her energy was to be subsequently expended in attempts to clear the family's name. Although the Accountability Cell found it difficult to bring hard evidence to court, the immense publicity surrounding its investigations discredited Benazir Bhutto in the view of the public.

A demoralized opposition and supine legislature provided Nawaz Sharif with the opportunity to fulfil his promise of bringing stability to Pakistan. This was cast aside, however, by the protracted struggle between him and the Chief Justice, which ended in triumph for the Prime Minister, but at the cost of politicizing the judiciary and weakening another important state institution. The struggle was variously viewed as symptomatic of Nawaz Sharif's increasingly dictatorial style; as an attempt to establish parliamentary sovereignty; and as another step towards the 'Punjabization' of Pakistan. The conflict was rooted in the encouragement to judicial activism given by the March 1996 verdict in the case regarding legal appointments. Chief Justice Sajjad Ali Shah's taking *suo motu* notice of cases involving the Government's handling of a wheat shipping contract from the USA and his opening cases, which had been pending, concerning the alleged illegal distribution of residential plots by the Prime Minister led to a heightening of the conflict. This intensified following the Supreme Court's disapproval of the parallel justice system of summary trial courts introduced in August 1997 under the controversial Anti-Terrorist Law. Shortly after this the Supreme Court Chief Justice sent a list of names of five judges to be added to the bench to deal with a backlog of cases. The Government, however, delayed in notifying their appointment, thereby precipitating the first stage of the crisis. This 'round' was won by Chief Justice Shah. Following a challenge from the Supreme Court Bar Association, Nawaz Sharif was forced to withdraw an ordinance that had reduced the strength of the Supreme Court from 17 to 12. On 30 October the Supreme Court invoked Clause 190 of the Constitution to order President Leghari to intervene and notify the appointment of the five judges. Tension mounted in Islamabad as the President refused to accept Nawaz Sharif's advice to dismiss the Chief Justice, despite the censure of the latter by an emergency session of the National Assembly. Nevertheless, following a clear sign of the army's disapproval of his action, the Prime Minister conceded defeat and on the evening of 31 October accepted the Chief Justice's recommendation concerning the elevation of the judges. This retreat from the brink was seen at the time as a major set-back for the Government; but Nawaz Sharif was soon to exact his revenge, although at the cost of dividing the supposedly independent judiciary on clear party political lines. The Balochistan circuit bench of the Supreme Court suspended Justice Shah and demanded a full bench petition hearing challenging his appointment shortly after the Prime Minister's brother, Shahbaz Sharif, had met Justice Irshad in Quetta. The Peshawar bench followed suit, paving the way for the existence of what amounted to two parallel Supreme Courts. A fight to the finish was signalled by the Chief Justice's decision to continue with a contempt of court trial against the Prime Minister. This occasioned extraordinary scenes in late November when PML (Nawaz) supporters, led by prominent figures, stormed the Supreme Court building forcing the trial to be abandoned. President Leghari's condemnation of this attack brought him into direct conflict with the Prime Minister. Fears that Leghari might still act to dissolve the National Assembly, despite the earlier passage of the Thirteenth Amendment Bill stripping the President of this power, led to rumours that the Government was considering impeachment charges. The final stages of the crisis saw the rival Supreme Court benches led by Justice Shah and Justice Saeeduzaman Siddiqi, respectively, repealing and almost immediately reinstating the Thirteenth Amendment. The attitude of the Chief of Army Staff, Gen. Jehangir Karamat, appeared to be decisive in the outcome of the conflict. The military's lack of intervention ensured that, in contrast to the situation in 1993, Nawaz Sharif emerged triumphant from his clash with the presidency. Leghari, following Justice Shah's removal from office, announced his resignation to a press conference at the presidential office on 2 December 1997. The Chairman of the Senate, Wasim Sajjad Jan, temporarily took his place. The presidency was filled on the last day of 1997 by the surprise nominee of the PML (Nawaz), Mohammad Rafiq Tarar. Tarar, a former Supreme Court Judge, was widely regarded as a pliant figure who owed his elevation to a close friendship with ('Abbaji') Mian Mohammad Sharif, the patriarch of the Sharif family. It was also feared that the appointment of the elderly new President, who was a strict Muslim, presaged a 'creeping fundamentalism' in the country. Finally, the triumphant Nawaz Sharif was portrayed in some quarters as a 'democratic dictator' who had gathered power to himself at the expense of all the other state institutions. Such an understanding, however, ignored both the role of the army in aiding the survival of the Prime Minister and the inherent weaknesses in the political system arising from poor institutionalization. This latter factor was to be brought home forcibly early in the following year when the army was deployed to undertake a number of tasks that in other polities would have been carried out by civilian administrators.

Another telling sign of a weak state was the inability to curb growing sectarian violence in the Punjab and ethnic strife in Karachi. The massacre that occurred in a Mominpura cemetery in January 1998 was especially embarrassing for Nawaz Sharif and his brother as it was perpetrated in broad daylight in the centre of their Lahore powerbase. The death of 24 Shi'a Muslims in the same month at the hands of masked gunmen from a breakaway group of the SSP, known as Lashkar-e-Jhangvi, led to extensive rioting in Lahore. The area also witnessed two bomb attacks on trains in early March. Indeed, during the first three months of 1998 there were 29 deaths and 12 bomb blasts in the Punjab. The culprits of these acts of terrorism were not apprehended. Sectarian motives could not be ruled out, although Nawaz Sharif claimed that the atrocities were the work of the Indian intelligence service. It was, in any case, clear that the controversial Anti-Terrorist Law, which had been introduced in August 1997 largely at the behest of Shahbaz Sharif, was ineffectual. In fact, the summary courts had decided on a mere 13 out of a total of 130 sectarian cases in the Punjab by April 1998 and one-third of the judges had resigned, largely due to death threats.

The link between influxes of weapons from Afghanistan and the influence of the Afghan Taliban movement was even clearer in the sectarian violence in the NWFP than in Punjab. The traditional Nauroz or New Year celebrations at Hangu provided an opportunity for a well-planned attack by a heavily armed war party (*lashkar*) on Shi'ite revellers. Thirty people were killed and hundreds were forced to flee their homes in the ensuing mayhem.

Religious extremism was also witnessed in the continuing persecution of minorities. According to a report by the Human Rights Commission of Pakistan, 35 members of the Ahmadi community were charged under the blasphemy laws in 1997. In many instances the accused were the victims of malicious and unsubstantiated claims. A similar case under Section 295-C of the Pakistan Penal Code, involving a Christian defendant, Ayub Masih, from Arifwala, achieved international notoriety in early May 1998 when John Joseph, the Roman Catholic Bishop of Faisalabad and Chairman of the National Commission for Peace and Justice, committed suicide in protest against the imposition of the death sentence on Masih by the Sahiwal Sessions Court. Local sources claimed that the case of blasphemy was instituted on the basis of a verbal complaint without circumstantial evidence and was motivated by a land dispute between the Christian minority and the dominant Muslim land-owning group in the area. Violence spread from Faisalabad to Lahore when Christians publicly observed 15 May as a day of mourning for Bishop Joseph.

Ethnic violence in Karachi arose from the factional fighting between the MQM(H) and the Muttahida Qaumi Movement — MQM(A)—(formerly known as the Mohajir Qaumi Movement) of Altaf Hussain. The assassination of a leading figure, Imtiaz Ahmad Koti, in the former group led to heavy fighting in late March 1998. The MQM(A)–MQM(H) conflict must be viewed in the context of the Karachi local bodies elections, which were scheduled to be held in April. The MQM(A) was concerned about its rivals on two accounts: first, that they would claim the mantle of a true mohajir movement following the various attempts by Altaf Hussain's group to broaden its appeal (e.g. its change in name), and, second, that they would use their 'street power' in parts of Karachi to ensure the return of their candidates. The demand that the authorities should move against the 'no-go' MQM(A) areas in such localities as Landi, Nazimabad, Shah Faisal and Liaquatabad threatened to break the fragile PML (Nawaz)–MQM(A) coalition government in Sindh. The security services and the army were, however, reluctant to move against the MQM(H) because it formed a useful counterbalance against the MQM(A), which the authorities continued to distrust. The decision to abandon the April polls in addition to the MQM(A)'s fear that if it left the provincial coalition it would be the victim of another army crackdown, ensured that the coalition held. By June, however, the fighting had intensified to almost the same levels experienced in 1995. To compound the infighting between the traditional MQM(A) and MQM(H) rivals, a third force had entered the fray; this was the Basic Association for the Citizens of Karachi, led by Altaf Hussain's former chief security guard, Umer Mehmood Khan (alias Goga). The inevitable claims soon emerged that this organization had been created by the security agencies as another ploy in their 'divide and rule' strategy in the dangerous port city.

Developments in the NWFP appeared calm in comparison with the turmoil in Karachi, although the long-standing informal alliance of convenience between the PML (Nawaz) and the ANP ended acrimoniously in late February 1998 amidst claims that the Prime Minister had reneged on his support for the renaming of the province as Pakhtoonkhwa (to reflect the Pakhtoon (Pashtun) ethnicity of the NWFP). In a replay of old animosities, Nawaz Sharif raised the issue of the opposition of the octogenarian ANP leader, Khan Abdul Wali Khan, to the Pakistan movement, along with that of his father, the celebrated Abdul Ghaffar Khan, the 'Frontier Gandhi'. In turn, Wali Khan claimed that the Punjabi leader was attempting to dominate the minority provinces in a ploy akin to the One Unit scheme of the 1950s.

Relations between the Punjab and the other provinces further deteriorated when Nawaz Sharif sought to take advantage of his heightened popularity following the May 1998 nuclear tests (see below) by announcing in the following month that the Kalabagh dam would be built. This project had been mooted for many years, but had been put on hold because of opposition to the scheme in Sindh and the NWFP. The dam, which would be designed to produce irrigation and hydroelectric power for the Punjab, was condemned on both environmental and political grounds in the neighbouring provinces. The reduced flow of the

Indus in Sindh was deemed likely to damage the mangrove forests in the Indus delta and increase the risk of salinity and desertification. While in the NWFP, which would be upstream from the proposed dam, there was the risk of the flooding of the Nowshera district. The mistrust arising from the Punjab's past 'theft' of Sindhi irrigation water from the Chasma–Jhelum Link Canal led some Sindhi nationalists to claim that the siting of the Kalabagh dam would give the Punjab a firm economic hold on its neighbour.

The elevation of the Punjabi Mohammad Rafiq Tarar to the presidency instead of a minority province candidate had also reopened the charge of Punjabi domination. It was noted by certain people that the President, the Prime Minister, the Chairman of the Senate and the Chief of Army Staff all originated from the Punjab. The dismissal of Chief Justice Shah in December 1997 was regarded by some Sindhis as a further affront to their province. The allocation of huge amounts of resources to Nawaz Sharif's favoured Islamabad–Peshawar motorway project when funds for development were being frozen elsewhere in the country raised claims of 'Punjabization' in Balochistan and Sindh. Further disquiet was engendered by the decision to freeze, at current levels, the Punjab's share of federal funds and level of political representation regardless of the outcome of the census. The first census since 1981 had finally been undertaken in March 1998, following its postponement in October 1997. Delays had occurred partly as a result of anxieties in the Punjab establishment regarding the changing population balance between the provinces. The census was also expected to reveal a rapid shift in population towards the urban areas, which would have important political repercussions. Equally contentious was the balance it was likely to reveal between Sindhi and Balochi 'sons of the soil' (i.e. families who had lived in these provinces for generations) and recent settlers. Resistance to the census was greatest, however, amongst the Pakhtoon population of Balochistan, who had long claimed that the Balochis over-enumerated their inhabitants. The Pakhtoonkhwa Milli Awami Party not only boycotted the census, but organized attacks on those conducting the census and stole documents from government offices. In such circumstances, the decision to deploy the army during the enumeration was understandable, although this was the first occasion in Pakistan's history that this course of action had to be taken.

More worrying was the increasing resort to the army to carry out routine administrative tasks, which now seemed beyond the competence of civilian agencies demoralized by endemic corruption and politicization. The most striking instance was the use of 1,400 army teams to eradicate 'ghost schools' amongst the 56,000 government-funded primary schools in the Punjab. The survey uncovered 4,000 such schools, which were costing the Government an estimated Rs 1,400m. per year. Shahbaz Sharif's decision to send in the military revealed the sure populist touch that the Chief Minister shared with his elder brother. The public had long been concerned at a situation in which many teachers emerged only monthly to draw their salary, or in which local notables appeared on the payroll of 'ghost schools'. Nevertheless, the quick solution of military inspection did nothing to address the root of the problem, which required careful institution building to address the collapse of the school inspectorate system. Less well known, but equally indicative of Pakistan's institutional crisis, was the resort to 'people friendly' army contractors, rather than their 'corrupt' civilian counterparts in a number of development projects in Punjab, including road-building projects. Army personnel were also to be deployed in the province to investigate 'ghost' health centres, deliver educational services and even tackle the Lahore Metropolitan Corporation's stray dog problem.

Institutional collapse, corruption and economic recession all appeared as great a compound weakness to Nawaz Sharif's Government as during his first tenure of office (1990–93). One-sided accountability and its pursuit, as in the independent power projects established by Benazir Bhutto, endangered the already fragile prospects of overseas investments. Equally misguided was the commitment to Punjabi-based large-scale development projects. The Government's supply-side economics failed to lift the economy out of recession. The foreign-exchange deficit was temporarily contained as falling imports coincided with a rise in overseas' remittances. The large domestic budget deficit, however, continued to expand beyond the IMF target of 5% of GDP. The long-standing issue of the bad debt of Pakistan's financial institutions remained unsolved. Budgetary reductions and down-sizing of the banking sector, at the IMF's behest, threatened stability. Farmers in Balochistan blocked highways and roads, bringing the province to a standstill, in protest at the imposition of a water-metering system by the state-owned Water and Power Development Authority in order to meet IMF demands to eliminate subsidies. A greater test for the Government was the ability to retain its support amongst the trading community following the introduction of a general sales tax. Mounting factional divisions within the Punjab PML (Nawaz) were brought to the surface during the infighting and violence that accompanied the local bodies elections, which were finally held in May 1998 after having been postponed five times. The sole consolation in all this was the absence of strong, united opposition forces to channel the unrest arising from increasing inflation and unemployment.

Despite the temporary public euphoria arising from the conduct of the nuclear tests in May 1998, the repercussions were to leave Pakistan in dire financial crisis. By July the country was facing the prospect of defaulting on its foreign debts, as the exchange reserves plummeted to less than US $1,000m., while debt repayments on the foreign debt of more than US $30,000m. amounted to more than US $350m. per month. The impending crisis drew little more response from the Government than the Prime Minister's symbolic gesture of sharing in the austerity drive by moving out of his official house and secretariat in Islamabad. A cabinet reshuffle in early August was largely driven by the Prime Minister's anxieties over the country's worsening economic outlook.

In late August 1998 Nawaz Sharif introduced the 15th Constitutional Amendment Bill to the National Assembly to replace the country's legal code with *Shari'a*. The Prime Minister attempted to allay fears of a move towards Islamist extremism by promising to ensure women's rights and to protect minorities. Some observers believed that the Prime Minister's decision to introduce full *Shari'a* arose from his desperation to hold the nation together at a time of great crisis, as well as from his wish to placate Pakistan's Islamist fundamentalists, who were angered by the recent US air-strikes against alleged bases of the Taliban-supported Saudi-born militant, Osama bin Laden, in Afghanistan. Some Islamist groups claimed that the Pakistani Government had been given prior warning of these attacks and had allowed the USA to use Pakistani airspace; these allegations were denied by the Government.

In early October 1998 the Chief of Army Staff, General Jehangir Karamat, resigned from his post after publicly criticizing the Government's economic and political policies and demanding that the armed forces be given a direct role in government decisions (rather than a purely advisory role, as with the CDNS). On the following day the 15th Constitutional Amendment Bill was passed in the National Assembly, by 151 votes to 16; the controversial law remained to be ratified by the Senate (within 90 days). The Prime Minister's critics claimed that the bill would give Pakistan a bad international image and would only serve to fuel the violence and anarchy that had beset the country. The Human Rights Commission of Pakistan called the bill 'regressive', claiming that it would allow Islamic courts to challenge every law in the Constitution and would over-expand the powers of the Prime Minister.

Pakistani politics at the end of the 20th century were dominated by the familiar themes of charges of corruption and the disputed fairness of accountability processes, and by relations with India, in which the question of Kashmir remained a central issue. Opposition claims that Pakistan was being ruled by Punjabis for the Punjabis also gathered pace, and were linked with the continuing centralization of power under the control of Nawaz Sharif. This process was revealed most clearly to international observers by the Government's attempts to curb the independent press. The earlier conflict between the Government and the *Jang* group of newspapers was overshadowed in the first half of 1999 by the arrest of the editor of the *Frontier Post*, Rehmat Shah Afridi, and the infamous Najam Sethi case involving the aforenamed respected editor of *The Friday Times*.

The long-running investigation into the alleged financial irregularities carried out by Benazir Bhutto and her spouse, Asif

Ali Zardari, culminated in the *Ehtesab* bench of the Lahore High Court in mid-April 1999, when they were each sentenced to five years' imprisonment, their property was confiscated, they were jointly fined US $8.6m. and they were automatically disqualified as members of the federal legislature. The Court found the couple guilty of corruption in a case involving the Swiss company, Société Générale de Surveillance. Benazir Bhutto, who was in London in self-imposed exile at the time of the judgment, claimed that the verdict represented a gross miscarriage of justice. She did not return to Pakistan, but mounted an increasingly vociferous campaign against the alleged corruption and human rights abuses being perpetrated by Nawaz Sharif's Government. Zardari had already been in custody for two-and-a-half years and was subsequently to be implicated in sensational torture allegations (see below).

The corruption issue showed no signs of abating, but accusations were now aimed at the ruling party and the Prime Minister's family. In late April 1999 the *Ehtesab* Cell finalized corruption cases against 30 incumbent and former PML legislators. In mid-May the Chief *Ehtesab* Commissioner, Justice Ghulam Mujaddid Mirza, rejected allegations against the Prime Minister that the latter had evaded millions of rupees in taxes and duties on the import of German cars. The finances of Nawaz Sharif's family had, however, appeared in a less favourable light in March when the London High Court had ordered members of the family, including the Punjab Chief Minister, Shahbaz Sharif, to return a loan of US $32.5m. to the Al-Towfeek Company, which had been given in respect of funds for Hudabiya Paper Mills. The media reporting of the Sharif family's questionable financial affairs proved a major factor in the subsequent action against independent journalists in May. Events came to a head on 8 May, when the editor of *The Friday Times*, Najam Sethi, was taken into custody. He was detained and interrogated by intelligence officials amidst charges that he had links with the Indian Research and Analysis Intelligence wing. The Pakistani High Commissioner in New Delhi aggravated the situation by claiming that Sethi's remarks during a seminar in the Indian capital represented 'contemptible treachery'. Sethi had, in fact, given the same paper at the Pakistan National Defence College where it had been favourably received. Sethi's detention was condemned by both the US and the EU as 'illegal'. Nawaz Sharif's opponents within Pakistan claimed that the real reason for Sethi's arrest was the journalist's co-operation with a documentary made by the British Broadcasting Corporation. When this was broadcast in early June it levelled serious charges of money 'laundering' against the Prime Minister and his family, as well as revealing the existence of four luxury flats in central London which were allegedly owned by Nawaz Sharif. Ultimately, to the Government's embarrassment, the charges against Sethi were withdrawn owing to lack of evidence.

The Sethi case coincided with two further developments which lowered the Pakistani Government's standing on the international stage. The first involved what was widely perceived as a concerted clampdown on non-governmental organizations (NGOs). There had been disquiet in government circles for some time concerning the alleged 'foreign links' of a number of NGOs and their involvement in opposition to such developments as the 15th Constitutional Amendment and in the peace and human rights lobbies. Political cover for curbing troublesome opponents was provided by the professed need to move against 'fraudulent' NGOs. The Punjab state administration, headed by the Prime Minister's brother, took the lead in the crackdown in early May 1999, when it dissolved almost 2,000 of the NGOs registered with its Social Welfare Department, in response to their alleged involvement in 'corrupt practices' and 'undesirable activity'. International concern was heightened when the Departmental Minister, Pir Bin Yamin, personally attacked such well-established women's organizations as Shirkat Gah for spreading 'vulgarity and obscenity'. These remarks seemed to provide evidence for claims of a furtive 'Talibanization' of Pakistan. Yamin also wrongly maintained that Shirkat Gah had misused Rs 80m. from the World Bank, when it had, in fact, never been in receipt of World Bank funds.

The second cause of international concern resulted from Pakistan's human rights record being placed under global scrutiny by the next development in the Asif Ali Zardari saga. In mid-May 1999 Benazir Bhutto's husband had been transferred from the Central Prison in Karachi for interrogation as prime suspect in the Justice Nizam Ahmed murder case. (The shooting of the Justice and his son had taken place in June 1996.) Zardari had been implicated in the incident at the beginning of 1999 following a confession extracted from, but later retracted by, a notorious criminal who had been apprehended for questioning regarding the murders. Zardari's interrogation resulted in his hospitalization. The police version of events was that the detainee had injured himself, and a case was registered against him of attempted suicide. Zardari's supporters maintained that he had been tortured by the police. Benazir Bhutto appealed directly to the US President, Bill Clinton, to protect her husband, and linked his case with the widespread human rights abuses reportedly perpetrated by the Nawaz Sharif Government.

The Pakistani Prime Minister attempted to counterbalance the problems with the US Government, which, in terms of regional relations, could not have come at a worse time, with a round of intensive diplomatic activity with China. Earlier, in April 1999, Nawaz Sharif had conducted a successful four-day visit to Moscow, the outcome of which had been the drawing up of a Russo-Pakistani agreement granting 'most favoured nation' economic status to each other. India, as always however, remained the fulcrum around which Pakistan's foreign policy turned. The first half of 1999 constituted one of the most dramatic periods in the tortured history of Indo-Pakistani relations. Euphoric hopes of a breakthrough in early 1999 were dramatically crushed once more by developments in Kashmir, which threatened to escalate into a full-scale war between two nuclear-armed powers.

Temporal proximity to the events inevitably hinders a measured judgement. Future historians, however, may well discern both the celebrated 'bus diplomacy' and the Lahore Declaration of February 1999 and the intensification of fighting in the Kargil area of Kashmir in May 1999 as outcomes of the nuclear tests of May 1998. The need for confidence-building measures to avert the unnecessary purchase of further costly weapons and an accidental nuclear exchange, together with international diplomatic and economic pressures were important factors in the background to the signing of the Lahore accord. The populist leanings of both Nawaz Sharif and the head of the Indian coalition Government, Atal Bihari Vajpayee, also contributed to what was termed in the premature elation of the February 1999 summit meeting in Lahore as 'a defining moment in South Asian history'. Preparations for the Lahore meeting had been made at talks held between the two Prime Ministers in New York in early September 1998 and during the resumption of discussions at foreign secretary level in mid-October in Islamabad. Despite intense international media speculation regarding a breakthrough on the Kashmir issue, the talks were primarily designed to restate positions and perceptions with the aim of building mutual trust and confidence. 'Bus diplomacy' was set in motion, however, in February 1999, when the Indian Prime Minister arrived at the Lahore summit meeting on the inaugural New Delhi–Lahore bus service. His Delhi Transport Corporation bus was greeted with much pomp and ceremony at the Wagah border on 20 February, and his arrival was covered by a joint Indian and Pakistani television broadcast (the first of its kind). The discussions ended with a joint statement, subsequently termed the Lahore Declaration, in which both Governments agreed to intensify their efforts for an early resolution of all issues, including the Kashmir situation, through bilateral talks. The foreign secretaries, K. Raghunath and Shamshul Ahmed Syed, also signed a memorandum of understanding concerned with confidence-building measures relating to security issues. These included commitments by the two countries to notify each other of nuclear accidents and ballistic missile tests and to abide by their respective unilateral moratoriums on conducting further nuclear test explosions. Amidst the immediate euphoria following the signing of the Lahore Declaration, it was even suggested that the two Prime Ministers be jointly nominated for the receipt of a Nobel peace prize. Even more cautious commentators maintained that, although the talks had not actually resolved any outstanding issues, a sound basis had been provided for the holding of future meaningful negotiations to resolve the subcontinent's disputes. Concern over the escalating arms race in South Asia was again deepened in April, following a series of ballistic missile tests carried out first by India and then by Pakistan (both countries, however, appeared to have adhered to the procedures incorporated in the Lahore Declaration, by informing each other of their test plans well in advance). By mid-1999, following dangerous developments in the Kashmir crisis, India and Pakistan stood on the brink of a full-scale war.

Part of the explanation for the abrupt thwarting of the hopes raised by the Lahore summit meeting may lie in the domestic difficulties the two countries were experiencing at the time of the military flare-up in Kargil in May 1999, following the reported infiltration of 600–900 well-armed Islamist militants across the Line of Control (LoC) into the Indian-held sector of Kashmir. Nawaz Sharif's problems arising from charges of corruption and of a creeping dictatorship have already been alluded to. Less obviously, it could be argued that this authoritarianism was based on deep insecurities involving the civilian Government's relationship with the army and the security service. Evidence of the tensions were apparent in Nawaz Sharif's attempts to ensure that if any blame attached to the Kargil episode, it would rest with the army. Yet the Prime Minister cannot have been ignorant of the army's ongoing logistical support for the militant 'intruders' in the Indian sector of Kashmir. It appeared that Nawaz Sharif had struck a major blow for civilian control of the military in October 1998, when he forced the retirement of Gen. Jehangir Karamat as Chief of Army Staff and installed his own choice, the relatively junior Lt-Gen. Pervez Musharraf, in the coveted post. On the Indian side, a number of commentators accused the Government of overreaction to events in Kargil and maintained that this was a direct consequence of the instability following the fall of the Vajpayee Government in mid-April 1999. On this reading of events, neither the caretaker BJP Government, nor the Congress-led opposition could afford to appear weak with regard to the Kashmir issue in the run-up to the mid-term elections later that year.

It appears that the militants' seizure of control of the strategic ridges of the Drass range overlooking the Srinagar to Leah route was perceived as a major set-back by the Indian army, which suffered heavy losses in its subsequent attempts to recapture them. The Indian troops launched a series of air-strikes against the militants at the end of May 1999, a move that seriously provoked Pakistan since it constituted the first peacetime use of air power in Kashmir. Within a few days the tension was heightened when a militant Kashmiri group claimed responsibility for shooting down an Indian helicopter gunship and Pakistani troops destroyed two Indian fighter aircraft which had reportedly strayed into Pakistani airspace. Artillery exchanges increased along the LoC and there was worrying talk of the massing of troops and evacuation of villages along the international border. If the Lahore Declaration had been held up as evidence of the supposed increased maturity in Indo-Pakistani relations since the nuclear test explosions of the previous year, the fighting in Kargil raised the possibility that a nuclear 'umbrella' could also encourage adventurism at even the risk of full-scale conventional conflict.

In one sense Nawaz Sharif was correct when he maintained, following his concession in the Washington Declaration of 4 July 1999 (see below), that the activities of the Islamist 'intruders' had achieved their 'basic purpose' of drawing the world's attention to the Kashmir dispute. However, Pakistan had been almost universally condemned for supporting the intrusion. Significantly, even China refused to provide any support. It seems that it was this diplomatic isolation, together with the fear of the withdrawal of IMF financial assistance and the realization that India might widen the conflict with potentially disastrous consequences, which prompted Nawaz Sharif's unexpected visit to Washington for talks with President Clinton in early July. Also crucial in preparing the ground for an end to the Kargil crisis through the withdrawal of all 'intruders' from Indian-controlled Kashmir, had been the visit to Pakistan of the Commander-in-Chief of the US Central Command, Gen. Anthony Zinni, some 10 days earlier.

Despite attempts to salvage something from the Washington Declaration in terms of President Clinton's expression of personal interest in the Kashmir situation and his intention to visit South Asia, in reality it represented a defeat, which government opponents in Pakistan declared a national 'betrayal'. Earlier denials by Pakistan of involvement in the infiltration of the militants were blatantly contradicted by its agreement to the withdrawal of its forces. The stated need for bilateral negotiations to resolve the Kashmir problem, also belied Pakistani attempts to 'internationalize' it.

Nawaz Sharif's subsequent efforts to pursue a non-belligerent policy in keeping with the Lahore Declaration threatened to isolate his Government on the domestic front, as it was already on the diplomatic front. Fellow politicians, much less the general public, had been ill-prepared for the Prime Minister's dramatic and precipitate trip to Washington. The abiding trait of the Nawaz Sharif Government—its lack of consultation—now became a major liability. Public opposition to the Washington Declaration was limited, however, to the protests organized by the JIP, including a 'Black Day' of protest on 6 July 1999 in Lahore, which provided the occasion for a number of vociferous rallies. Nevertheless, for many it seemed that the Kargil episode and its denouement represented a major turning point in the fortunes of the Nawaz Sharif Government.

Institutional decline arising from corruption and politicization had earlier forced Nawaz Sharif to induct the army into large areas of public life, while simultaneously attempting to grasp as much power for himself as possible. The army thus followed up its involvement in the 1998 census operations, with responsibility for tracking down defaulters and thieves of electric power. The management of the state-owned Water and Power Development Authority was put in 'safe' military keeping in order to prepare it for privatization. Mounting sectarian violence, together with a recrudescence of ethnic conflict in Karachi, had encouraged Nawaz Sharif to devolve further power to the military in November 1998 with the establishment of military courts in Sindh to try 'terrorist' cases. In mid-February 1999, however, the Supreme Court moved against the establishment of a parallel judicial system, ruling that the setting up of military courts for the trial of civilians was unconstitutional and without lawful authority. This resolution effectively barred the establishment of military courts throughout the country (as the Government had proposed the previous month). The Supreme Court ordered the transfer of the outstanding cases to civilian anti-terrorist courts.

The establishment of military courts in Karachi had followed on the imposition of governor's rule in Sindh in late October 1998. This decision was implemented after the murder of the province's former Governor, Hakim Mohammed Said, and marked a final parting of the ways between the PML (Nawaz) and its erstwhile MQM (A) ally in the Sindh coalition government. Despite the bitter legacy of Benazir Bhutto's second Government, in the following months the MQM (A) slowly moved closer to an agreement with the PPP. The two parties found common ground on the issues of resistance to the Prime Minister's authoritarianism and to Punjabi domination. A further stage in their developing relations was marked by the talks held in London between Altaf Hussain and the PPP Senior Vice-Chairman, Amin Fahim, in mid-June 1999.

Meanwhile, in December 1998 the PPP had edged closer to one of its erstwhile foes, the ANP, when Benazir Bhutto met Khan Abdul Wali Khan at Charsadda to discuss joint support for the demand for decentralization of power. The ANP had broken ties with the PML (Nawaz) earlier that year over the 'broken promise' of renaming the NWFP, Pakhtoonkhwa. The ANP had also been alienated by Nawaz Sharif's decision, in the wake of the nuclear test explosions, to announce approval for the construction of the controversial Kalabagh dam. The federal Government's decision to proceed with the project, despite the fact that the Sindh, NWFP and Balochistan assemblies had voted unanimously against it, was seen as further evidence of the Punjabization of Pakistan. In Balochistan, politicians already disaffected by the lack of consultation regarding the nuclear tests, were further affronted by the federal Government's decision to lease out the Gwadar Fish Harbour to a multinational company, thereby endangering the livelihoods of local fishermen. In response to the threat of centralization, including the Government's curtailment of the powers of the Senate owing to the latter's delay in implementing the 15th Constitutional Amendment, opposition groups in the smaller provinces formed the Pakistan Oppressed Nations Movement

(PONM) in late 1998. This new body was convened by Ajmal Khattak of the ANP and controlled by a 16-member council. In June 1999 even Benazir Bhutto, whose mainstream PPP was not a member of the PONM, took up the themes of Punjabization and the need for greater provincial autonomy in the wake of the dismissal of the non-partisan Governor of Sindh, Lt-Gen. (retd) Moinuddin Haider. While the former Prime Minister likened her bitter rival to the much-maligned Serb dictator, Slobodan Milošević, commentators on the Pakistan political scene saw worrying parallels in the dangers to the federation with the period 1970–71. In mid-September 1999 Nawaz Sharif's position looked increasingly precarious following the formation of a Grand Democratic Alliance by 19 conservative and centrist opposition parties, including the PPP, the MQM (A) and the ANP, which demanded the Prime Minister's immediate resignation. The various Islamist parties, including the JIP, also stepped up their anti-Government protests and rallies throughout the country. The opposition was weakened to some extent, however, by the fact that Benazir Bhutto was unwilling to return to Pakistan for fear of being arrested on charges of corruption.

The Coup of October 1999 and Beyond

Events took a dramatic turn on 12 October 1999, when, a few hours after Nawaz Sharif's announcement of his decision to dismiss the Chief of Army Staff and Chairman of the Joint Chiefs of Staff Committee, Gen. Pervez Musharraf, the army chief masterminded a bloodless military coup in Islamabad. Nawaz Sharif and his Government were overthrown, and the deposed Prime Minister was placed under house arrest. Gen. Musharraf was flying back from an engagement in Sri Lanka when he learned of his dismissal. His commercial flight was initially denied permission to land by the control tower at Karachi Airport and ordered to divert to a location outside the country. Troops loyal to the Chief of the Army took control of the airport and, running precariously low on fuel, the aircraft was eventually allowed to land at Nawabshah.

The fourth military coup since 1947 thus ended 11 years of competitive party politics. On 15 October 1999 Gen. Musharraf assumed the position of Chief Executive. He declared a state of emergency, and suspended the Constitution, National Assembly, Senate, the four provincial legislatures and all political officials. The President and judiciary were, however, left in place. A comparatively free press was allowed to operate. Political party activity was limited. Gen. Musharraf ensured, by means of a Provisional Constitution Order, that his actions could not be challenged by any court of law, thus imposing a virtual martial law. The lack of resistance to the coup within Pakistan, including his home province of Punjab, was indicative of the extent of Nawaz Sharif's perceived failure as Prime Minister. There were no large-scale popular demonstrations in favour of the deposed Prime Minister. At the same time, there was no sense of a new beginning for Pakistan. There was, rather, a mood of resignation. Neither the élites nor the public seemed to be sufficiently concerned to fight for a democratic regime. As well as the legacy inherited from Benazir Bhutto, ruthless political rivalry, incompetence and corruption had almost destroyed support for a Government that had gained power with a large majority only two-and-a-half years previously.

Nawaz Sharif's attempt to dismiss Gen. Musharraf as Chief of Army Staff and the retaliatory coup were the culmination of tense relations between the Prime Minister and the army during the former's entire second period of office. Firstly, as a result of advanced institutional decay in Pakistan, the Government had been forced to resort to the army to conduct routine administrative tasks (see above). This was likely to have reinforced the army's awareness that it remained the sole intact institution in Pakistan. Secondly, owing to growing mistrust and a concern to establish his own supremacy, Nawaz Sharif had intervened to change the leadership of the army. The most significant intervention occurred in October 1998, when Gen Jehangir Karamat was forced to resign from his position as the Chief of Army Staff and Chairman of the Joint Chiefs of Staff Committee, and was replaced by Gen. Musharraf. The latter, however, was not appointed Chairman of the Joint Chiefs of Staff Committee until March 1999, some five months after Gen. Karamat's dismissal. It was evident that, although the Prime Minister had replaced Gen. Karamat with Gen. Musharraf, he had less than full confidence in the new incumbent. Tense relations with the army were exacerbated by the Kargil episode. Nawaz Sharif's attempt to attribute responsibility for the crisis to the army greatly irritated the latter. The precise reason for Nawaz Sharif's attempt to replace Gen. Musharraf in October 1999 was unclear, but the events of previous years had indicated that the retaliatory coup of an already politicized army was highly likely.

It seemed that the military forces were aware of the severity of the task of governing Pakistan and not too inclined towards wielding power, as was previously often the case with the army. The army seized power to disable a Government that had failed to address the basic tasks of curbing corruption, reviving institutions and promoting development, while it had mismanaged civil-military relations. There was no indication of any long-term plot to resume overall military power in Pakistan. On his accession to power, Gen. Musharraf stated that the armed forces had no intention of remaining in charge any longer than was absolutely necessary 'to pave the way for true democracy to flourish in Pakistan'. However, it was not yet clear how and when he intended to achieve this.

The international reaction to the coup was relatively subdued. Japan, the USA, member nations of the British Commonwealth and Western Europe, as predicted, condemned the coup. However, the condemnation was not very forceful and was largely pronounced on principle. Nearly a week after the coup the Commonwealth effectively suspended Pakistan and banned it from attending meetings, including the conference to be held in South Africa in November 1999. A clear distinction was made between suspension and expulsion, which was not a considered alternative. The suspension from the Council of the Commonwealth (though not strictly from the Commonwealth itself) was duly confirmed at the conference. After earlier relaxation of some of the sanctions imposed on both India and Pakistan following their nuclear test explosions in 1998, the USA removed sanctions against India at the end of October 1999, but retained most of those placed on Pakistan. The two bans lifted on Pakistan were those on US commercial lending and on agricultural credit guarantees, already in use in relation to wheat exports: both measures were strongly in the interests of the USA, which was otherwise limited by the Foreign Assistance Act, prohibiting aid to countries whose Governments have been deposed by military coups. During a visit to Islamabad in late October, the Japanese State Secretary for Foreign Affairs insisted that Japan could provide no further foreign aid to Pakistan until it signed the CTBT and announced a schedule for the restoration of democracy. The EU also sent a mission to Pakistan and similarly advised the Chief Executive in early November that it could not continue aid until there was a timetable for the return to democratic governance.

From the beginning Gen. Musharraf was concerned to establish a self-consciously 'non-political', technocratic Government that would be able to command support both domestically and internationally and also pave the way for the reconstruction of Pakistani institutions. On 22 October 1999 he appointed four new provincial governors. Some four days later he announced a two-tier structure to head his administration: a National Security Council (NSC) and a civilian Cabinet. The precise division of powers between these two bodies was not clear, though there was evidently a strong military character to the NSC, which initially comprised, as well as the Chief Executive, the two other chiefs of armed forces and four civilian experts. Three of the four provincial governors were military figures, the other one a judge; they obtained the powers of the suspended Chief Ministers. In the Cabinet, the key position of Minister of Foreign Affairs was given to Abdul Sattar, a retired career Foreign Service officer and caretaker Minister of Foreign Affairs in 1993; the Minister of Finance was Shaukat Aziz, a banker of international repute. Provincial Cabinets were also appointed. In mid-August 2000 the NSC was reconstituted and redefined as the supreme executive body: it henceforth comprised the three chiefs of armed forces and the Ministers of Foreign Affairs, Interior, Finance and Commerce. The NSC thus more closely represented the military and technocratic character that Musharraf sought to promote for his Government. At the beginning of November 1999, meanwhile, as evidence of the military

Government's serious determination to confront official corruption, a National Accountability Bureau was established. An elaborate monitoring system was installed to provide continuous assessment of the administration and its impact. By January 2000 207 monitoring teams 'of impeccable integrity' were said to be functional.

By October 2000 it remained difficult to give any definitive judgement on the character and success of the regime, particularly its declared ambition to eliminate corruption and establish a 'real' democracy. Party mobilization was effectively banned, and the relatively free press was too limited to provide any balanced assessment of the Government. Furthermore, given the bans on political organization, there were not many events to report. The major political parties were occupied with internal problems. A year after the coup much of the activity was conducted in a discreet manner and was likely to take some time to emerge. The Government was not, however, entirely stable: during its first year in power, 12 ministers had resigned. In one important respect, the Government was similar to its recent antecedents: it was obsessed with destroying any remaining reputation of the previous head of state and ensuring that that person would never again enjoy freedom.

In mid-January 2000 Nawaz Sharif and six other senior officials (including Mohammad Shahbaz Sharif, the brother of the ousted Prime Minister and the former Chief Minister of Punjab) were formally charged with criminal conspiracy, hijacking (a charge that carries the maximum penalty of the death sentence), kidnapping and attempted murder in relation to the alleged refusal of landing rights to the commercial aircraft carrying Gen. Musharraf from Sri Lanka to Karachi on 12 October. The military authorities also charged Nawaz Sharif and his brother in November with corruption and non-repayment of bank loans. Nawaz Sharif was convicted on 6 April 2000 for hijacking and terrorism, but acquitted of kidnapping and attempted murder. He was sentenced to two terms of life imprisonment, fined Rs 1m., ordered to pay Rs 2m. in compensation to those on the flight, and his entire property was confiscated. The remaining six defendants were acquitted of all charges. In July Nawaz Sharif was convicted of a corruption charge by a 'National Accountability Court' for failing to declare the use of government funds to purchase a Russian helicopter. He was sentenced to a further 14 years' rigorous imprisonment and disqualified from holding office for 21 years. Nawaz Sharif continued to appeal against his convictions, arguing that he was engaged in a power struggle with Gen. Musharraf before the coup because of the army's rash conduct of the Kargil affair. At the end of August his counsel was warned by the Sindh High Court not to politicize the case. The international community doubted the fairness of the trials and criticized the harshness of the sentences. Following his conviction, Nawaz Sharif's position as head of the PML was subjected to scrutiny within the party, causing divisions among members. The Chief Executive's decree, announced in August, disqualifying those convicted by a court from holding office, however, meant that Nawaz Sharif was effectively barred from the post of President. In October 2000 the Sindh High Court overruled the life sentence for terrorism, but upheld that for hijacking. Ultimately, Musharraf resolved the problem by unexpectedly releasing Nawaz Sharif from prison in December and sending him into exile in Saudi Arabia. In return, Nawaz Sharif reportedly relinquished his personal and business assets, promised not to return to Pakistan for 10 years, and agreed not to take part in Pakistani politics for 21 years.

In November/December 2000 former leaders Nawaz Sharif and Benazir Bhutto, with 16 other smaller political parties, agreed to form the Alliance for the Restoration of Democracy, in an effort to end military rule and accelerate a return to democracy. The new alliance superseded the PPP-led Grand Democratic Alliance.

In the mean time, in August 2000 the National Accountability Bureau filed an application with the Lahore High Court to have the cases against Benazir Bhutto and her mother transferred to the Attock Fort Accountability Court. In early April 2001 the Supreme Court ordered that Benazir Bhutto's conviction for corruption be set aside and a retrial held, following the disclosure of tapes which allegedly proved that Nawaz Sharif's Government had forced the judge to convict Bhutto and her husband. Later that month the court concluded that the verdict had been politically motivated. Meanwhile, Bhutto and her husband faced further charges of corruption. In May a warrant was issued for Benazir Bhutto's arrest on her return to Pakistan. However, in the face of her continued absence in Dubai, she was sentenced *in absentia* in June 2001 to three years' imprisonment for not appearing in court to answer charges of corruption. Gen. Musharraf, therefore, managed to remove his two major opponents from the political arena by threatening imprisonment if they returned to Pakistan. The Government had reinforced this situation by declaring that any person convicted of a criminal charge was to be disqualified from holding public office.

In his first public broadcast to the nation, Gen. Musharraf promised an eventual return to civilian rule and announced wide-ranging measures to tackle corruption, loan defaulters, tax evasion, regional instability and religious extremism. He also stressed that he wished to maintain and promote amicable relations with the USA and the People's Republic of China. From around April 2000, however, there was a discernible rise in domestic criticism of the military regime. Frustration among political parties and journalists was mounting owing to the consistent refusal of Musharraf to announce a date for the restoration of competitive party democracy. In March he announced a plan to restore democracy at a local level, beginning with local elections. Candidates were to be elected to local councils, and the councils would in turn elect members of two higher councils in each district. One-third of seats were to be reserved for women, and 5% for religious minorities. The franchise was also to be lowered from 21 to 18. Elections were to be held between December 2000 and August 2001. In June the Minister of the Interior stated that the Chief Executive would begin a series of meetings with non-corrupt politicians in order to develop consensus on various issues. In August, however, it was announced that the new structure of local government was to be on a non-party basis. This provoked one of the clearest party interventions since the coup: most of the almost 40 parties attending a meeting condemned the plan. Although the Government avoided the subject of the restoration of democracy, it remained highly sensitive to the issue of its own legitimacy. Shortly after the coup, at the beginning of November 1999, Gen. Musharraf stated that the NSC was considering the idea of a 'referendum' to demonstrate popular approval of his assumption of power. This proposition was not pursued. However, in May 2000 the pro-Government Supreme Court unanimously endorsed the legitimacy of the military coup citing 'necessity' in the supreme interest of the public. The Court, however, ordered the Government to complete its declared objectives and restore civil rule by democratic elections to the National Assembly, Senate and provincial authorities within three years of the October 1999 coup. In response, Gen. Musharraf stated that he would comply with the Supreme Court ruling regarding the restoration of democracy. Furthermore, the Supreme Court gave the Chief Executive the powers to perform all legislative measures and even amend the Constitution under the same doctrine of 'state necessity'. This 'creative jurisprudence' was criticized by the British Government.

In terms of policy objectives, the campaign against corruption, the task of institution-building, and achievement of greater equity and integration among the Provinces were persistent themes in the rhetoric of the Government. The greatest economic problem facing Pakistan was pronounced to be that of debt, both domestic and, in particular, foreign, the Minister of Finance estimating the latter in June 2000 to be 56% of total debt. The long-standing deep social problems of Pakistan, including drug addiction and disabilities suffered by women have been marginally addressed. In August 2000 a National Commission for the Status of Women was established, although its objectives had yet to be formulated. In May a poverty-alleviation strategy was devised, to be implemented by the end of 2000. This was, however, a minimal improvement of Pakistan's underdeveloped social policy.

In terms of curbing religious extremism, the Government's actions were contradictory. In April 2000 the Minister of the Interior declared the Government's intention to deal with sectarianism firmly and, if necessary, ban sectarian parties and groups. In June the Government outlined an ambitious plan to curb networks of militant groups in Pakistan and Afghanistan.

In July, however, the Chief Executive issued a decree to revive the Islamic provisions of the suspended Constitution and to incorporate them in the provisional constitutional order, thereby supporting a ban on the passing of any law that conflicted with Islamic principles. Conversely, at the end of August Gen. Musharraf dismissed the Chief of General Staff, Lt-Gen. Mohammad Aziz, who was well known for his extreme Islamist views, and replaced him with the more liberal Lt-Gen. Mohammad Yusuf. In November human rights organizations accused the Pakistani authorities of ignoring attacks on the minority Ahmadi community, and urged them to condemn the violence and to take action. In January 2001 the English-language newspaper, *Frontier Post*, was closed down and several of its staff were arrested, on charges of printing blasphemous material. The newspaper was re-opened in June after it published an apology in a rival newspaper, claiming that it was the target of a conspiracy. In the same month its editor, Rehmat Shah Afridi, was sentenced to death by an anti-narcotics court for the possession of drugs. He was arrested in 1999 (see above) and detained without trial. He appealed against his conviction. At the same time a medical professor was sentenced to death under the blasphemy law. Meanwhile, separatist violence continued during 2001. Although the military Government appeared to be suppressing militant Islamism, attacks by extremist groups continued. In June the Cabinet approved an anti-terrorism law to curb ethnic violence and terrorism. This followed Gen. Musharraf's warning to Islamic clerics that Pakistan's international reputation for religious violence and Islamist extremist behaviour was damaging the country's standing and economic prospects.

When the first phase of local elections were held at the end of 2000, it was clear that Gen. Musharraf had been unable to remove party politics from the voting process: a significant number of elected members were associated with either the PML (Sharif) or the PPP. This continued to be the case in the next three phases of local elections. His problems were accentuated further by the growing influence of militant Islamist movements, particularly Jamaat-e-Islami Pakistan, which had won support from important elements within the military. Nevertheless, by mid-2001 Gen. Musharraf seemed more intent on strengthening his own position than on returning the country to civilian rule. His appointment of Lt-Gen. Muzaffar Hussain as Deputy Chief of Army Staff in May was largely seen as a move to enable himself to concentrate more on governing the country. In June 2001, following the trend set by two previous military leaders, Gen. Musharraf dismissed President Tarar and assumed the presidency himself. He was immediately sworn in by Chief Justice Irshan Khan. Gen. Musharraf also dissolved the National Assembly, the Senate and the provincial assemblies, which had been suspended since the coup. He instituted these changes on the grounds that they would strengthen his negotiating power at the forthcoming meeting with the Indian Prime Minister, and enable him to restore a democratic form of government within three years of the coup, as determined by the Supreme Court.

In the face of growing pressure from both within and outside Pakistan, President Musharraf declared on 14 August 2001 that federal and provincial elections would be held between 1 and 11 October 2002 in order to return the country to civilian rule just before the deadline imposed by the Supreme Court. He also voiced his intention to relax the ban on political activity by announcing that political parties would be given time to prepare for the elections.

Although President Musharraf's pronouncement was regarded as a conciliatory gesture to both the Pakistani public and the international community, there appeared to be little doubt that the military would be very reluctant to release its hold on power in return for what might be seen as democracy. Certainly, in agreeing, under pressure from the USA, that political parties would be able to contest the elections in 2002, Musharraf also emphasized that any politicians who had been previously convicted of a criminal charge would not be eligible to participate in the elections. In doing so, he attempted to exclude Nawaz Sharif and Benazir Bhutto, at least in a direct sense, from the electoral process. More significantly, he sought to weaken the positions of their political parties: the PML (Sharif) and PPP, respectively.

The shifts that occurred in both domestic and international politics after the massive suicide attacks on US citizens in New York and Washington, DC, in September 2001, gave President Musharraf the opportunity further to strengthen his position and weaken that of the main opposition parties. Whereas in the past the USA had been a strong critic of Pakistan's shift towards military rule, in the aftermath of the suicide attacks it recognized Pakistan's strategic importance in its efforts to carry out a campaign against the Afghanistan-based Islamist militant al-Qa'ida (Base) organization, held principally responsible for the attacks, and its Taliban hosts. At the same time Musharraf was quick to realize the extent to which he had been empowered by this change in foreign policy. As a result of ongoing dialogue between the USA and Pakistan, the former agreed to provide support to the South Asian country, both in terms of political recognition and aid, and in return Pakistan offered a base for the US-led military campaign. The Pakistani President utilized this situation to justify attacks on Pakistan-based Islamist militants, who had extended their violent campaign from across the LoC in Kashmir to within Pakistan. One instance of this violent campaign was the bombing in mid-March 2002 of a church close to the US embassy in Islamabad, which killed five people, including US citizens, and which led to the evacuation of US families as an emergency measure. Further attacks against Westerners and Christian communities, as well as sectarian attacks, appeared to undermine the success of Musharraf's counter-terrorism initiative.

Since senior elements within the army were sympathetic to a number of these Islamist groups, President Musharraf was careful to differentiate between militant and moderate religious organizations. He also exploited Pakistan's new relationship with the USA to strengthen his own position as President. In early April 2002 the Government approved a plan to hold a national referendum seeking endorsement for Musharraf's term of office as President to be extended by five years, and approval of the Government's political and economic programme. Despite widespread opposition from human rights organizations, the media and political parties, the referendum was held at the end of April. According to official figures, about 98% of those participating supported the proposal. The recent lowering of the voting age from 21 to 18 and the suspension of the electoral register made it impossible to check the eligibility of voters; estimates for the turn-out ranged between 5% and 70% (opposition parties and independent monitors reckoned the former was more realistic, whereas government estimates featured at the higher end of the spectrum). The referendum was viewed by some as an indication of Musharraf's success as a political leader, and regarded by others as a poll marred by gross irregularities.

The legitimacy of the process aside, it was clear that President Musharraf had considerably strengthened his position within Pakistani politics by isolating the militants, marginalizing his most dangerous opponents, and assuming the presidency for a period of five years, which ensured that he would later be in a position to strengthen constitutionally the role of the army in Pakistan's political system. Indeed, in July 2002 he introduced a set of reforms, including a range of proposed amendments to the Constitution. Musharraf's proposed reforms, which would transform Pakistan's prime-ministerial system into a presidential one, were heavily criticized. In opposition circles, his statements were seen as proof of his ambition to limit the rights of the National and Provincial Assemblies after the general elections of the National Assembly and the Provincial Assemblies, scheduled to be held on 10 October. Opposition parties immediately challenged his proposed constitutional reforms. His suggestion of a National Security Council, in which the armed forces would have ultimate power on matters relating to national security, was condemned. There was also concern that his perceived attempt to extend the powers of the head of state would undermine the authority of any government that might be elected, particularly as the President would have the authority to dissolve a government. Musharraf also suggested an amendment to the much maligned ordinance that candidates for the election should be educated to university degree level, and strengthened the presidency by noting that the Election Commission would realize this amendment with the approval of the President, rather than with the approval of the legislature. In the mean time, a campaign was under way to have the ban on political activities removed, so that opposition parties could engage in a fair election campaign. This movement was, initially, given further momentum by Benazir Bhutto's re-election as leader of the PPP at the end of July. Faced with the decree banning parties from contesting an election if any of its office-holders had been convicted of an offence, the PPP formed a new faction, the Pakistan People's Party Parliamentarians (PPPP), under a new leader, to challenge the forthcoming elections. Bhutto was barred from contesting the election, owing to her criminal conviction (see above).

Instead of presenting the constitutional changes proposed in July before the next legislature, President Musharraf unilaterally endorsed 29 amendments to the Constitution on 21 August 2002. His new powers allowed him to dissolve the elected National Assembly, extend his term in office and appoint Supreme Court judges. Significantly, the military was given a formal role in governing the country. In the mean time, the brother of Nawaz Sharif, Mian Shahbaz Sharif, the former Chief Minister of the Punjab, was named leader of the PML (Nawaz). Nawaz Sharif officially withdrew his candidacy in September, reportedly in solidarity with Bhutto. The PPPP and PML (Nawaz), both under new leadership, were permitted to take part in the elections. In response to criticisms, the President promised to restore democracy and transfer power to an elected government. Nevertheless, it was clear that, in the face of strong opposition from most of the political parties, the elections would bring to the fore all the underlying tensions.

During 2000/01 the IMF continued to review Pakistan's performance regarding economic reforms. Pakistan had not received any financial assistance from the IMF since 1999 and, in great need of sources to replenish its dwindling foreign-exchange reserves, sought to negotiate a loan that would enable it to service its foreign debts. By late 2000 the Government claimed to have met the criteria laid down by the IMF in relation to its economic performance. It soon transpired, however, that the IMF was concerned not only with implementing 'necessary economic reforms' but also with persuading Pakistan to sign the CTBT (see above). Although the Government was reluctant to sign the CTBT, it did reduce defence expenditure in the 2001/02 budget in order to meet the IMF demand that the budget deficit be lowered, an action that caused some concern within military circles. Having also endeavoured to meet the conditions laid down by the IMF with regard to structural adjustments through the removal of subsidies, the lowering of debt and other financial reforms, the IMF agreed to support a US $700m. World Bank loan in June 2001 to help facilitate further reforms. The loan, although not as large as was hoped, was an indication that the policies of the military regime had managed to satisfy the IMF. However, the Government was again faced with a decline in foreign investment, owing to uncertainties over possible political outcomes in Pakistan. At the same time the economic policies were viewed less favourably by the majority of Pakistanis, who felt the impact of consequent rising unemployment and prices; a situation that was compounded by a sustained drought, which caused a decline in agricultural production.

Pakistan's economy suffered as a result of the impact of the terrorist attacks on the USA on 11 September 2001. A fall in demand for Pakistan's major commodities led to a decline in exports. Trade was also adversely affected by the US-led military strikes, which disturbed safety and lines of communication, and caused the cost of insurance and other associated charges to increase. At the same time a reduction in international prices and an increase in domestic production of food products, caused imports to decline at an even greater rate than exports, resulting in a smaller trade deficit than the previous year. Owing to this movement in trade, the balance of payments in 2001/02 improved considerably. On a more general level, in response to the shift in geo-political terms from late 2001, Pakistan sought and gained more favourable economic conditions from international agencies. Sanctions that had been imposed after the coup in 1999 were lifted, debt payments were rescheduled and foreign loans and access to aid were more readily made available. As a result of these and other developments, foreign-exchange reserves nearly doubled in 2001/02 and the Pakistan rupee appreciated significantly. Indeed, while the IMF continued to pursue fiscal reforms, its review of Pakistan's economy for 2001/02 was quite favourable, with economic assistance for 2002/03 predicted to increase by nearly 14% to US $2,600m. In June 2002 the Supreme Court reversed its ruling that Pakistani banks should outlaw charging interest in the name of *Shari'a*.

FOREIGN POLICY

Relations with India

The foreign policy of Pakistan has been conditioned very largely by Indo-Pakistani relations. When the concept of Pakistan was mooted, it evoked great hostility among the Hindus, irrespective of the party to which they belonged; and even when the Congress, which became the successor authority in India, accepted the 3 June Partition Plan, it did so with extreme reservations. Pakistan was thus confronted from its inception with the problem of survival. India's territory and population were over four times those of Pakistan; its industrial potential was at least 10 times as great and its armed forces were three times those of Pakistan until 1962, and the ratio became adversely disturbed in the wake of massive Western military aid after the Sino-Indian clashes in that year. Moreover, Pakistan being divided into two wings, the ratio worked further to Pakistan's disadvantage. This explains why, since its creation, Pakistan has made many attempts to come to some arrangement whereby the two countries, instead of dissipating their energies against each other, would reach some clear and friendly understanding and settle the disputes by peaceful means.

Among the causes of early estrangement between Pakistan and India were the position of minorities and the question of evacuee property. The Canal Waters dispute and the dispute over some of the boundaries also proved difficult, but certain adjustments were made with regard to them. India's construction of the Farakka barrage in West Bengal was a later move which created dissatisfaction in Pakistan. Then there was the vital Kashmir question, to which a solution has not yet been found. Last but not least was the Bangladesh issue. The result has been that there have been occasions when the two countries have fought local wars, as in Kashmir (1947–48) and the Rann of Kutch (1965), and two full-scale wars in 1965 and 1971.

Following the war of December 1971, feeling grew in favour of an understanding with India on the principle of 'live and let live'. Partial success in this policy resulted in the Shimla Agreement of July 1972, which provided for the withdrawal of Indian and Pakistani troops from occupied territories. The return of prisoners, however, was delayed for more than a year until the signing of another Indo-Pakistani agreement in August 1973. The return of prisoners of war was completed in May 1974.

Linked with the problem of relations with India was the question of the recognition of Bangladesh. Pakistan's recognition of Bangladesh finally came in February 1974, but relations between the two countries improved only after the collapse of the Mujib regime in August 1975. Pakistan was the first country to recognize the new regime, and an exchange of envoys took place in January 1976; it also persuaded the West Asian Muslim countries to extend aid to Bangladesh. The visit by the Bangladesh President, Gen. Ziaur Rahman, to Islamabad in December 1977 and Gen. Zia's brief visit to the cyclone-devastated areas of Bangladesh in June 1985, along with the continuing identity of views of the two countries on most international issues, strengthened relations between the two states.

Relations with India, however, deteriorated again after the latter's nuclear test in May 1974. Further tension between the two countries was created in July as a result of alleged troop movements by India and Afghanistan on Pakistan's borders. The exchange of ambassadors was thus delayed a further two years. A goodwill visit by the Indian Minister of External Affairs to Pakistan in February 1978 resulted in further normalization. It also paved the way for an accord on the Salal Dam, after eight years of negotiations. The agreement, signed in New Delhi in April 1978, sought to safeguard Pakistan's vital interests in the flow of the Chenab waters, while ensuring benefits to India. The accord was hailed in both New Delhi and Islamabad as a step forward in increasing mutual understanding.

New Delhi's posture following Indira Gandhi's return to power in January 1980 caused a set-back. She not only refused to condemn Soviet intervention in Afghanistan (see below) but also did not consider it a threat to Pakistan's security. Secondly, New Delhi reacted adversely to the US offer of military aid to Pakistan, designed to bolster the country's defences in view of the Soviet threat. Thirdly, while protesting vehemently against Pakistan's nuclear programme for peaceful purposes, India officially affirmed its right to produce nuclear weapons, and successfully launched a four-stage rocket, of its own design, to place a satellite into orbit. India's nuclear and aerospace programme was viewed in Pakistan in the context of India's prepossession with military power, which included large arms purchases from the USSR and vast expansion of its armament industry. India also protested to the USA when it became known that the new Reagan administration had offered to help Pakistan in meeting its normal defence requirements. Indira Gandhi termed Pakistan's efforts to acquire modern equipment as a threat to India. On the other hand, Pakistan stoutly defended its sovereign right to acquire arms to meet its defence requirements. However, as a concession to India, Pakistan suggested that the parameters of the two countries' defence requirements be fixed and that the ratio of arms levels be maintained by both sides. These two principles were finally agreed upon by both countries during the visit of India's Minister of External Affairs in June 1981.

Zia's meeting with Indira Gandhi in New Delhi in 1982 led to the creation of the Indo-Pakistan Joint Commission. The first meeting of the commission in Islamabad in June 1983 postponed discussion of a proposed treaty of peace, friendship and co-operation but some general progress was made.

From 1984 a new irritant entered Indo-Pakistani relations—the Sikh problem. India accused Pakistan of abetting and assisting Sikh activists, and of giving widespread media coverage to the Punjab disturbances. The Pakistani Government, in turn, consistently denied the charges.

In December 1988, however, relations between Pakistan and India improved when Rajiv Gandhi visited Islamabad for discussions with the new Prime Minister, Benazir Bhutto. At this meeting, which constituted the first official visit of an Indian Prime Minister to Pakistan for nearly 25 years, the two leaders signed three agreements, including a formal pledge not to attack each other's nuclear installations. In June 1989 Pakistan and India moved one step closer to defusing tension created by the confrontation over the Siachen Glacier in the sensitive Kashmir border area, when high-level talks were held in Islamabad, at which the two countries agreed to attempt to find a formula to effect the eventual complete withdrawal of their troops from the area.

Relations between Pakistan and India reached a crisis in late 1989, when the outlawed Jammu and Kashmir Liberation Front (JKLF) and several other militant Muslim groups intensified their campaigns of terrorism, strikes and civil unrest, demanding an independent Kashmir or unification with Pakistan. These groups were verbally supported by the President of the Pakistani-controlled Azad (Free) Kashmir, Abdul Qayyum Khan. In response, the Indian Government sent troops into Jammu and Kashmir in December and placed the Srinagar valley under an indefinite curfew. India claimed that the violent uprising had been largely organized by militants trained and armed in Pakistan. The Pakistani Government, however, vehemently denied that it was officially involved in the insurgency, stressed that the Muslim Kashmiris were fighting independently for self-determination, and continued to state that it would prefer a settlement of the Kashmir problem in accordance with earlier UN resolutions (i.e. proposals to hold a plebiscite under the auspices of the UN in the two parts of the state). India, on the other hand, argued that the problem should be settled in accordance with the Shimla Agreement of 1972, which requires that all Indo-Pakistani disputes be resolved through bilateral negotiations. Pakistan also accused India of committing acts of brutality and suppressing human rights. Tension was heightened in early February 1990 after it was reported that three Pakistani civilians had been shot dead by Indian troops when they attempted to cross the cease-fire line into Indian-controlled Kashmir. Intense diplomatic efforts were begun at once in order to defuse what was viewed as a potentially major confrontation. The opposition parties in Pakistan organized nationwide strikes, to express their sympathy for the Muslims in Jammu and Kashmir, and urged the Government to take action.

In the mean time, there was a continuous exchange of bellicose statements between Pakistan and India, further heightening the tension between them. The Indian troops were reportedly massed on Pakistan's borders and Pakistani troops were put on alert. Despite the fact that neither side showed any desire to precipitate a war, there was, however, a considerable risk that a third war in Kashmir might start almost accidentally. The US President's special emissary to Islamabad and New Delhi helped to defuse the tension somewhat in April 1990, but the threat of war continued to hang over the subcontinent. In January 1991, however, Pakistan and India agreed to exchange instruments of ratification as regards the December 1988 agreement not to attack each other's nuclear facilities. In April 1991, following three rounds of talks, the two countries' Ministers of Foreign Affairs signed agreements providing that both sides would intimate troop movements and military exercises to each other in advance, and that each other's aircraft would be allowed to fly over and land in their territories through specified air corridors. A timetable was drawn up for further talks on certain controversial issues, including the delimitation of borders in the Siachen area and the decision by India, which caused great concern in Pakistan, to construct a barrage on the River Jhelum, in violation of the 1960 Indus Water Treaty. In the mean time, skirmishes along the border in Kashmir became more frequent, and the Nawaz Sharif Government adopted a firm stance in favour of finding a political solution to the Kashmir problem. In February and March 1992 the Pakistani Government deployed thousands of police and paramilitary forces in Azad Kashmir, to prevent planned protest marches (organized by Pakistani members of the JKLF) across the cease-fire line into Indian-controlled Kashmir, thus averting the danger of large-scale confrontation between Indian and Pakistani troops. A number of JKLF supporters were killed in the subsequent clashes between marchers and the Pakistani security troops.

In March 1993 relations between Pakistan and India reached an extremely low ebb when the Indian Government accused Pakistan of having been involved in bomb explosions in Mumbai (Bombay), which killed more than 300 people. The Pakistani Government closed its consulate in Mumbai in March 1994 as a result of deteriorating relations between the two countries. In June the Pakistani Prime Minister, Benazir Bhutto, described India's test firing of its surface-to-surface missile, Prithvi, as 'provocative' and warned of a missile race in the region. Indo-Pakistani relations were further strained in August when former Prime Minister Nawaz Sharif stated publicly that Pakistan possessed an atomic bomb and that it was prepared to use the weapon against India. In response, Pakistani officials reiterated the government position that it had acquired the capability to make nuclear weapons but had decided not to do so, and restricted the use of nuclear technology to peaceful purposes.

India gained a notable diplomatic victory over Pakistan in February 1994 when it was able to force the withdrawal, at the UN Commission on Human Rights, of a hostile resolution put forward by Pakistan condemning alleged human rights abuses by Indian security forces in Kashmir. However, in December Pakistan was successful in securing the passage of a resolution condemning reported violations by Indian troops in Kashmir at the summit meeting of the Organization of the Islamic Conference (OIC) held in Casablanca, Morocco. The OIC also agreed to establish a contact group on Kashmir. In February 1995 (and, again, in February 1996) Benazir Bhutto's Government organized a nation-wide general strike to express solidarity with the independence movement in Jammu and Kashmir and to protest against alleged atrocities carried out by the Indian forces. The entrenched Indo-Pakistani differences over Kashmir thus continued to be a major obstacle to the normalization of economic and political relations. Clashes persisted along the LoC during the usually quiet winter period in 1995/96. In January 1996 relations between the two countries deteriorated when the Pakistani Government accused the Indian forces of having launched a rocket attack on a mosque in Azad Kashmir, which killed 20 people. In response, the Indian authorities claimed that the deaths had been caused by Pakistani rockets which had been misfired. Tensions between Pakistan and India were also exacerbated in early 1996 by allegations that each side was on the verge of conducting nuclear tests. The depth to which relations had plunged was clearly indicated by the fact that in late January the Pakistani President felt it necessary to reassure the public that there was no possibility of war between the two countries. Later that year, India's decision to hold state assembly elections in Jammu and Kashmir (described as 'farcical' by Benazir Bhutto) and its refusal to sign the Comprehensive Test Ban Treaty did nothing to encourage an improvement in relations between Islamabad and New Delhi.

Hopes for improved relations with India were raised when Nawaz Sharif declared, just two days after the PML (Nawaz) party's election triumph in early February 1997, that 'we have to learn how to be as good neighbours, now is the time for serious dialogue'. During 28–31 March foreign-secretary level talks were resumed between Pakistan and India. The Ministers of Foreign Affairs themselves met in Delhi on 9 April at the end of the Non-aligned Foreign Ministers' Conference. Deve Gowda's replacement in that month by Inder Kumar Gujral, the former Minister of Foreign Affairs, as Indian Prime Minister did nothing to lessen speculation that a new departure in relations was now possible, although the Kashmir issue remained, as ever, an impasse to be overcome. Tensions were raised when it was reported by the US press in early June that Indian medium-range Prithvi missiles had been moved to a site near the city of Jullundur in the border state of Punjab. Conciliatory talks between Pakistan and India made little progress in 1997; Prime Minister Nawaz Sharif accused India of aggravating the situation by refusing to establish a joint working group on Kashmir. There was an upsurge in violence on the Kashmir border in September/October, with both sides shelling each other's positions and resulting in about 40 civilian deaths.

In 1998 Pakistan's foreign relations were dominated by the deteriorating relations with India following the installation of a right-wing BJP-led coalition Government in New Delhi in March. Tensions first mounted in Kashmir. Claims of a return to 'normalcy' under the state government of Dr Farooq Abdullah came under serious question following the fierce battle between militants and Indian forces at Aagam. In April Pakistan test-fired a long-range missile capable of hitting any target in India. The missile was named Ghauri after the 12th-century Turkish Muslim invader of India. None of these events, however, prepared the world for the five nuclear weapons tests that India conducted beneath the Rajasthan desert in mid-May. President Clinton of the USA immediately imposed sanctions, under the 1994 non-proliferation law, which were projected to cost India as much as US $20,000m. in lost aid. Japan followed suit, but other members of the G-8 group, who were meeting in Birmingham, in the United Kingdom, at the time, counselled caution. The US Deputy Secretary of State, Strobe Talbott, was sent to Islamabad to advise Pakistani restraint, but had nothing concrete to offer in exchange. Nawaz Sharif rejected such dictation, while Abdul Qadeer Khan, a leading figure in Pakistan's nuclear research programme, reiterated that he was only awaiting orders to carry out a successful test.

Fifty years of nation building based on animosity to the neighbouring 'other' state, which, in turn, had been preceded by the politicization of religious community and its 'essentialization' around the hostility of the religious 'other', culminated on 28 May 1998 with Pakistan's 'settling the account' and conducting its own five nuclear explosions at a test site in the rugged mountainous terrain of Chagai in Balochistan. Two decades of nuclear ambiguity were brought to an end as, henceforth, Pakistan and India were to face each other across the Wagah border armed with the 'Islamic' and 'Hindu' bombs. The impact of sanctions on a Pakistan economy teetering on the brink of collapse, led President Tarar to declare a state of emergency shortly after the news of the detonations had received international condemnation. Foreign-exchange accounts were 'frozen', a decision that dealt a further blow to the confidence of foreign investors already shaken by the disputes over power purchase tariffs between the Government and the independent power producers. When the Karachi Stock Exchange opened after a three-day closure on 1 June, the index fell to a record low, losing 12% of its value in a single session. Nawaz Sharif, in an echo of Zulfikar Ali Bhutto's famous phrase that Pakistanis would, if necessary, 'eat grass' to match India's nuclear capability, declared that 'if the nation will only take one meal a day, my children will only take one meal a day'. On 30 May Pakistan risked further international condemnation with the detonation of a further device. Pakistan's testing ceased when it had exploded six devices, one more than India. A special meeting of the G-8 nations was held in London on 12 June to discuss the escalating tensions in the subcontinent and to attempt to prevent a nuclear arms race in the region. In the event, the escalating tensions in Kosovo, Yugoslavia, between the Serbs and ethnic Albanians pushed Indo-Pakistani relations down the agenda. A slight easing of the situation in the subcontinent was, in any case, promised, as the preceding day Pakistan announced a unilateral moratorium on nuclear tests. In September, however, the Pakistani Minister of Foreign Affairs categorically stated that Pakistan would not sign the Comprehensive Test Ban Treaty until all of the sanctions were lifted and other legitimate concerns addressed. In the following month the USA lifted some of the sanctions imposed on Pakistan and India.

Despite a temporary and misleading improvement in Indo-Pakistani relations in early 1999, by the middle of the year the Kashmir crisis had escalated to a 'near-war' situation and the two countries appeared more hostile towards each other than ever (see above). Tension eased somewhat in July, following Pakistan's decision to support the withdrawal of all Muslim infiltrators from Indian-controlled Kashmir. Relations were greatly strained again in August as a result of the shooting-down of a Pakistani naval reconnaissance aircraft by the Indian armed forces at the Gujarat border; all 16 personnel on board were killed. The following day, in retaliation, Pakistani troops were reported to have opened fire on Indian military aircraft in the same area.

In October/November 1999 there was a notable increase in terrorist incidents in Kashmir, and Indian and Pakistani forces were reported to have resumed skirmishes across the LoC. Relations between the two countries worsened in early November after the success of the Indian Prime Minister in promoting the official condemnation of the new Pakistani military regime by the Commonwealth heads of government, following the military coup in Pakistan in mid-October. In December the Indian Government stated that it would not resume dialogue with Pakistan until the latter halted 'cross-border terrorism'.

In late December 1999 the Kashmir conflict came to international attention when five Islamist fundamentalists hijacked an Indian Airlines aircraft and held its passengers captive at Qandahar airport in southern Afghanistan for one week. Among the hijackers' demands was the release of 36 Islamist militants being held in Indian prisons who supported the Kashmiri separatist movement. Under increasing domestic pressure to prioritize the safety of the hostages, the Indian Government agreed to release three of the prisoners in exchange for the safe return of the captive passengers and crew. Despite Indian accusations of complicity, the Pakistani Government denied any links with the hijackers. In early January 2000 Prime Minister Vajpayee stated that India would 'work towards getting Pakistan declared a terrorist state'.

From March 2000 Gen. Musharraf repeatedly offered to take part in peace negotiations. However, India maintained that, while Pakistan appeared to be militarily and financially supporting Kashmiri insurgents, it was not prepared to resume dialogue. The US President's visit to the region in late March failed to bring Pakistan and India any closer together. India remained deeply suspicious of the Pakistani Chief Executive, associated with leading the Kargil affair. India continued to demand that Pakistan cease 'cross-border terrorism' as a precondition for talks, and Pakistan repeatedly denied arming and funding militants as well as giving them political support. Gen. Musharraf proclaimed that the Government gave only moral and diplomatic support for the Kashmiri people's 'struggle for self-determination'. In early June tension along the LoC increased, reducing the possibility of discussions between the two nations. On 24 July, however, the Kashmiri militant group, Hizbul Mujahideen, declared a three-month cease-fire on condition that India ended human rights violations and military operations against militants. Other militant groups denounced the cease-fire as a betrayal to the jihad (holy war). The Pakistani army denied a unilateral cease-fire, but continued to follow the policy of not firing first. The Government supported the cessation of hostilities, considering it a good opportunity to find a solution, but was allegedly being placed under pressure from separatist groups not to become involved in peace talks. The Hizbul Mujahideen later demanded tripartite discussions, incorporating Pakistan, on the future of Kashmir. India refused to involve Pakistan in the negotiations, renouncing the state again as 'terrorist'. The cease-fire ended in the second week of August. India accused Pakistan of orchestrating the entire episode. In mid-August Pakistan renewed its offer to resume negotiations, despite claims of increased violence by the Indian army towards Kashmiri militants. Violence in the region continued in August and September, and relations between the neighbouring nations remained unchanged.

As a result of the ongoing violence, militant Hindu groups within India called for more direct military action in dealing with Pakistan. Although the Indian BJP-led coalition Government did not heed these demands, in late August 2000 it voiced its objection to what it considered the long-standing Pakistan-sponsored violence in Kashmir, by instructing the Indian cricket team not to participate in a tournament against Pakistan in Toronto, Canada (much to the displeasure of the Indian Board of Control of Cricket). In the mean time, at the UN Millennium Summit meeting in early September, Gen. Musharraf identified Kashmir as the sole major problem between the two nations since 1947 and declared that he would welcome further discussions with India and any other form of help from the UN in resolving this problem. The Indian Prime Minister responded by demanding that cross-border violence cease as a condition for such a meeting, and in November he announced the suspension of combat operations against Kashmiri militants during the holy month of Ramadan. The cease-fire was extended periodically, despite the continuation of violent attacks by militant Kashmiri groups.

In January 2001, following the devastating earthquake centred in Gujarat, India, Gen. Musharraf immediately offered the neighbouring country humanitarian relief and established contact with his Indian counterpart. This development signified the improvement of Indo-Pakistani relations. Progress regarding the Kashmir question hitherto had been thwarted by India's delay in facilitating dialogue between the All-Party Hurriyat Conference (an organization that, to an extent, acted as the political voice for some of the militant groups) and the Pakistani Government, and by continuous violence perpetrated by separatist groups. However, as a result of the earthquake and the subsequent amelioration of relations, and also under pressure from the USA to arrive at a solution with regard to Kashmir, in May the Indian Government ended its cease-fire with an invitation to Pakistan to enter negotiations, which Gen. Musharraf (who later became President) duly accepted. It was agreed that a summit meeting would be held in mid-July, in Agra, where the Mughal emperor, Shah Jahan, had built the Taj Mahal in the 17th century. As India's most famous monument and built by a Muslim, it seemed, symbolically at least, an appropriate meeting place.

However, the seventh Indo-Pakistani summit in 50 years was, like its predecessors, constrained by the inability of the respective heads of state to engage in open and free discussion. Neither leader could afford to appear to be retreating from the entrenched principles that mould his country's foreign policy. Indeed, differences soon emerged over the agenda of the summit. The Pakistani Government insisted that Kashmir should be the focus of the talks, whereas the Indian Government was resolute that Kashmir should be considered in the context of cross-border terrorism and be one of a number of issues to form the basis of the negotiations. Ultimately, little was conceded by either side, the Kashmiris were excluded from the talks and rhetoric prevailed. The negotiations broke down after both leaders failed to agree on a joint communiqué. Nevertheless, President Musharraf managed to exploit the summit, through the media, to justify his assumption of the position of President, a move, it was argued, that enabled him to adopt a strong position in the negotiations.

Recriminations followed the summit meeting in mid-2001, with both sides voicing claims and counter claims. Prime Minister Vajpayee condemned President Musharraf for referring to the terrorists as 'freedom fighters', whereas Musharraf stated that the two sides had come close to signing a joint declaration. Furthermore, the Indian Prime Minister considered Musharraf's support of a mandate for the people of Jammu and Kashmir as hypocritical, given that the latter had denied Pakistani citizens such a right. Nevertheless, some progress appeared to have been achieved. For example, in the week prior to the summit, Vajpayee had instructed India's Director-General of Military Operations to visit his counterpart in Pakistan. In addition, the Indian Prime Minister accepted an invitation to visit Pakistan. In the weeks that followed these talks, both countries appeared to give some consideration to the idea of an Iran–India gas pipeline built across Pakistan, and to the possibility of wider trade links. However, in spite of all this, what could not be ignored was the extent to which Musharraf was constrained by the Islamist militant movements, in their various forms, and the fact that Vajpayee was primarily concerned with the BJP and *Hindutva* (Hinduness). The situation in Kashmir in 2001/02 did not improve, despite attempts by Musharraf and Vajpayee to seek some way out of the impasse. In actual fact , in response to the US-led military campaign against terrorism in Afghanistan, there was a significant increase in cross-border movement in Kashmir by militant Islamist groups from Pakistan, Afghanistan and elsewhere seeking to undermine the presence of the Indian army. Just over one week after the USA began military strikes against al-Qa'ida and its Taliban hosts in Afghanistan in October, India accused Pakistan of allowing militants to cross the LoC in Kashmir; Pakistan, however, claimed that the Indian army had opened fire on what appeared to be civilian targets. The policy of restraint that had been observed on both sides for more than a year had begun to break down. While India claimed that Pakistan was operating in collusion with the Taliban and other militants, Pakistan pointed out that India's actions could be considered as an attempt to undermine the new diplomatic relationship between Pakistan and the USA.

However, it was an attack on the Indian union parliament on 13 December 2001 by militant Islamists that caused tension between India and Pakistan to rise sharply. Although Musharraf strongly condemned the attack and ordered the arrest of the perpetrators, the Indian Government sought to use the situation to isolate Pakistan. In particular, the Indian Government ordered a large deployment of troops along the shared border, withdrew the Indian High Commissioner to Pakistan and closed public transport between the two countries.

The USA and its allies, however, pressed India to adopt a slightly less aggressive stance. In turn, President Musharraf used his national address in mid-January 2002, delivered in Urdu and English, skilfully to appease his domestic constituency and at the same time to assure the international community that he was intent on curbing the activities of militant groups, such as the Jaish-e-Mohammed. He also moved forces from the Afghan-Pakistani border to the border with India, in an attempt to match India's recent reinforcement of troops. Musharraf's attempts to dismantle these groups were, however, constrained by a number of factors, in particular the problematic nature of his own position within Pakistan's domestic political system, and the rise in militant attacks within Pakistan itself.

In the mean time, the more right-wing elements within the Indian Government were demanding stronger action, such as the aerial bombardment of Pakistan. Although the USA was quick to diminish such suggestions, attacks by militants on a bus and an army camp in Jammu and Kashmir, killing more than 30 people, mainly women and children, in mid-May 2002 caused tensions to rise very quickly again. The Indian Government claimed that the Pakistan Government had failed in its attempt to cease cross-border infiltration by terrorist groups and immediately expelled the Pakistani High Commissioner to India. In an address in late May, Musharraf emphasized the complexity of the situation that confronted Pakistan, but did little to appease India. Indeed, it appeared that, in his efforts to meet the demands of the USA, Musharraf had become alienated both from major religious groups and Pakistani political parties, and as a result his capacity to take action was becoming increasingly limited.

By the end of May 2002, the war-like rhetoric on both sides of the border had turned to the question of nuclear strikes. Both countries claimed to have deployed such missiles along the border. Certainly, when Pakistan ordered several 'routine' tests of three missiles in late May, it did little to calm the situation.

While some commentators saw the exercise as having limited significance, it led to sustained discussion about a range of nuclear possibilities. The political assessment of this development fluctuated on a daily basis; by mid-June, however, as a result of immense pressure from the USA and its allies, the threats of nuclear strikes had declined. The USA's warning to US citizens not to travel to India until further notice, and other more subtle forms of diplomatic pressure, encouraged India to adopt a less aggressive stance, a position that was enhanced by the USA's agreement to support India's efforts to install electronic sensors along the LoC, as a means of controlling terrorist movements.

However, the continued deployment of well over 1m. Indian and Pakistani troops in Kashmir, along with a rise in terrorist attacks within Pakistan, and the reorganization of the Indian Council of Ministers, which promoted militants such as L. K. Advani and demoted moderates like Jaswant Singh, made it unlikely that the issue would be brought under control in the immediate future. This was despite frequent attempts by visiting senior US and British officials to persuade the neighbouring countries to reduce the number of troops on their shared border and to contain rhetoric on nuclear weapons. The elections in Jammu and Kashmir, commencing in mid-September 2002 and ending three weeks later might prove to be a catalyst for future developments in one direction or another.

Relations beyond the Subcontinent

Relations with India have largely influenced Pakistan's relations with other nations. Pakistan felt in its early years that the Commonwealth was not a particularly useful instrument for the resolution of its disputes with India. In respect of the two major power blocs, Pakistan was inclined towards the West for some years and tried to come closer to the USA, particularly from 1954 onwards when a mutual defence assistance agreement was concluded. In the same year Pakistan became a member of SEATO. In 1955 it joined the Baghdad Pact (later known as CENTO) with the United Kingdom, Turkey, Iraq and Iran. To reinforce CENTO, a further bilateral agreement was concluded with the USA in 1959.

India's annexation of Goa in 1961 was a turning-point in the foreign policy of Pakistan, which then established closer relations with the People's Republic of China. The massive military aid to India by Western powers in 1962 forced Pakistan to strengthen its relations with China further and normalize those with the USSR. This led to a deterioration in relations with the USA and affected its economic and military aid to Pakistan. Closer relations with Turkey and Iran had been developed since 1964, and the policy paid dividends. During the Indo-Pakistan wars of 1965 and 1971, China, along with certain Islamic powers, proved to be the only supporters of Pakistan.

Pakistan withdrew from the Commonwealth in January 1972, in retaliation for the UK's role in the East Pakistan crisis. Attempts to rejoin it in the late 1970s were thwarted by India. In January 1989, however, India announced that it would no longer oppose Pakistan's application to rejoin the Commonwealth, following the restoration of democracy in Pakistan. During Benazir Bhutto's eight-day official visit to the UK in July, Pakistan was formally invited to rejoin the Commonwealth, which it did on 1 October 1989.

Relations with the USA improved when the US ban on arms sales to Pakistan was lifted after official visits by Zulfikar Ali Bhutto in 1973 and 1975. Pakistan withdrew from SEATO in 1972, but continued to attend CENTO ministerial council meetings. However, from 1976 relations with the USA deteriorated as a result of US opposition to the sale of a nuclear-reprocessing plant by France to Pakistan and the Carter administration's refusal to sell A-7 bombers. Bhutto also accused the USA of fostering a conspiracy to depose him, and threatened to leave CENTO. Relations with the USA improved under the Zia regime, but in August 1978 the Carter administration announced that it would suspend all economic aid to Pakistan for 1978–79 in response to Islamabad's intended purchase of the reprocessing plant. The threatened suspension of economic aid was actually carried out in April 1979 in the wake of Bhutto's execution, on the suspicion that Pakistan was secretly working towards producing an atomic bomb. Pakistan refused to participate in any military pact with the USA and joined the Non-aligned Movement (NAM) in September 1979.

Following the Islamic revolution in Iran in early 1979 and in consultation with the new regime, Pakistan left CENTO in March. Iran and Turkey also withdrew, and CENTO was disbanded. Further deterioration in US-Pakistani relations came in the wake of reports in the US press in late 1979 of alleged US government plans to destroy Pakistani nuclear installations through commando action. Relations were worsened by the burning down of the US embassy in Islamabad and information centre in Lahore in November by a mob protesting against the sacrilege of the Holy Ka'ba in Mecca. However, the USSR's intervention in Afghanistan in late December, which posed a common threat to the national interests of both Pakistan and the USA, helped to overcome mutual acrimony and bitterness, and the two countries, along with others, tried to evolve a common policy to curb Soviet adventurism in the region.

The USA showed a growing concern for Pakistan's security, and talks during 1981 resulted in a Pakistani-US accord on a US $3,000m., five-year programme of economic supporting funds, development assistance, and loans for foreign military sales. Under the new agreement, the USA agreed to sell 40 F-16 aircraft, to assist Pakistan in improving its air defence capabilities, and to the early delivery of selected defence equipment, urgently needed by Pakistan. This agreement caused relations with India to deteriorate, as the Indian Government felt that the provision of such equipment would upset the balance of power in the subcontinent and precipitate an arms race. Pakistan, which had earlier ruled out military ties with the USA, insisted, however, that the deal did not compromise the principles and purposes of the NAM and the OIC.

In April 1986, in spite of opposition by India, representatives of Pakistan and the USA concluded a new accord which stipulated that the USA would provide a six-year credit (1987–93), valued at US $4,020m., for economic assistance and purchases of military equipment, to support Pakistan's development priorities and its defence modernization programme. The release of the first instalment of this aid was postponed from October 1987 until January 1988, owing to the US Government's suspicion that Pakistan's nuclear development programme was being used for military purposes. Pakistan continued to resist US pressure to sign the Nuclear Weapons Non-Proliferation Treaty, declaring that it would accede to the treaty only after India had done so.

Benazir Bhutto's week-long official visit to the USA in June 1989 proved highly successful. Following the Pakistani Prime Minister's assurances to President George Bush and to the CIA that Pakistan had no intention of constructing a nuclear missile, the two leaders finalized a major arms deal under which Pakistan was to purchase a further 60 US-constructed F-16 aircraft at a cost of US $1,400m. In October 1990 the US Government announced that it was withholding US $564m. in economic and military aid (under the Pressler Amendment), following President Bush's failure to sign a certificate assuring Congress that Pakistan did not possess nuclear weapons. Pakistan, in turn, denied reports that it had secretly attempted three times in 1990 to buy special furnaces that could be used for constructing a nuclear bomb. The relations between Pakistan and the USA remained tense throughout 1991. Pakistan's bold stance on the Gulf crisis did not win any concessions from Washington on the nuclear waiver certification issue. Following the Soviet withdrawal from Afghanistan in the late 1980s and the amelioration in US-Soviet relations, Pakistan ceased to be considered as a front-line state, and relations between the USA and Pakistan were consequently downgraded. A Pakistani delegation to Washington in June 1991 made no progress in securing the resumption of aid. Pakistan's need to develop a nuclear programme to meet its growing energy requirements is rather acute. Hence, it is believed by some in Pakistan that the US objection to the Pakistani nuclear programme is based more on the industrialized countries' reluctance to share advanced industrial technology with the Third World countries than on its professed desire to prevent the proliferation of nuclear weapons. During 1992 both Pakistan and the USA made small but significant policy adjustments designed to ease the tension that had afflicted their relations owing to the former's suspected nuclear-weapons programme. In February, the Pakistani Government admitted for the first time that Pakistan had nuclear-weapons capability, but added that, presumably in view of the US demand, it had 'frozen' its nuclear programme at the level of October 1989, when it was still some way off from producing a nuclear device.

An issue that particularly troubled the Pakistani Government in the first half of 1993 was the fact that the USA had included Pakistan on its 'watch-list' of countries whose governments were suspected of directly sponsoring terrorism. India had long accused Pakistan of abetting the Sikh and Kashmiri separatists (see above), and had assiduously lobbied against Pakistan in the USA. During the conflict between the Soviet-backed Afghan Government and the *mujahidin* in the 1980s, Islamist militants from around the world, with the support of the USA and Saudi Arabia, had established representative offices in and around Peshawar in the NWFP, which served as conduits for volunteers and weapons to fight the Soviet and government forces in Afghanistan. Following the withdrawal of the Soviet troops from Afghanistan in 1988–89, however, these trained fundamentalist fighters increasingly became an embarrassment to the Pakistani authorities. Fearing US reprisals, the Government ordered foreigners without regular visas to leave Pakistan by mid-January 1993. Those who remained were arrested and imprisoned, or deported. The Nawaz Sharif Government also offered for inspection those areas that were suspected of accommodating terrorist training camps. In late April Brig. Imtiaz, the army intelligence chief, who allegedly had links with some suspected terrorist groups, was dismissed from his post. Consequently, Pakistan was finally removed from the US 'watch-list' in July and, thus, narrowly escaped being blacklisted as a terrorist country.

Relations between Pakistan and the USA were slightly improved following the revival in January 1995 of a bilateral consultative committee (abandoned in 1990), comprising senior defence officials. In March, however, the situation appeared less congenial, when two US consulate employees were shot dead by unidentified gunmen in Karachi. Prior to Prime Minister Benazir Bhutto's much-publicized 10-day official visit to the USA in April, a favourable image of Pakistan had been fostered through Pakistani participation in UN peace-keeping operations in Somalia, Haiti and Bosnia and Herzegovina and through the extradition of terrorists and drugs-traffickers. Whilst the nuclear issue and the continued sanctions under the terms of the 1990 Pressler Amendment remained high on the agenda during the Prime Minister's visit, considerable attention was also devoted to investment opportunities. This shift in emphasis from strategic to commercial issues in Pakistani-US relations had first been signalled during the visit to Pakistan of the US Secretary of Energy in October 1994. In September 1995 the US Senate voted in favour of the Brown Amendment, which allowed a limited resumption of defence supplies to Pakistan. The vote permitted the release of US $368m. worth of equipment but did not permit Pakistan to take delivery of the F-16 aircraft. The Brown Amendment (which was ratified by President Clinton in January 1996) also deleted the Pressler Amendment requirements for economic sanctions, thus paving the way for the resumption of US economic aid to Pakistan. In February 1996, however, the US Government was considering delaying the delivery of the military equipment to Pakistan because of the latter's suspected purchase of sensitive nuclear weapons-related equipment from China in 1995. These allegations were denied by both Pakistan and China. In August 1996 the first consignment of US military equipment released by the US Government after a six-year delay arrived in Pakistan. US-Pakistani relations suffered a set-back in November 1997 following the killing of four US oil executives in Karachi by unidentified gunmen, No group claimed responsibility for the attack, although it was speculated that the murders may have been perpetrated in retaliation for the conviction in the USA on the previous day of a Pakistani immigrant for the killing of two US government employees in 1993. Following the US air-strikes against the Saudi-born Islamist extremist, Osama bin Laden, in Afghanistan in August 1998 (which entailed the use of Pakistani airspace), the USA evacuated its non-essential embassy staff from Pakistan as part of a precautionary security alert. In December Prime Minister Nawaz Sharif held talks with President Clinton in the US capital in an attempt to gain support for Pakistan's ailing economy and to persuade the US leader further to ease the sanctions imposed on Pakistan following the nuclear tests carried out by the latter in May. The US Government agreed to return the entire payment made by Pakistan for 28 F-16 fighter aircraft, the delivery of which had been suspended since 1990 under the Pressler Amendment.

The USA's shift in allegiances was made apparent in late March 2000, when Clinton paid a cordial five-day visit to India, while spending only six hours in Pakistan. During his brief stopover, the US President warned Pakistan in a televised address that it faced international ostracism if it continued to adopt a belligerent stance towards Kashmir. In the course of his short meeting with Gen. Musharraf, Clinton urged the Chief Executive to reopen dialogue with India, to take action against terrorist groups operating in and from Pakistan, to sign the CTBT and to reintroduce democratic rule as soon as possible. Many considered President Clinton's visit as an endorsement of the military regime. However, it was clear that Pakistan was no longer of strategic use to the USA, the need to counter-balance the erstwhile close relationship between India and Russia having been superseded. The President's decision not to become involved in negotiations regarding Kashmir was a disappointment to Gen. Musharraf. The leaders of both Pakistan and India visited the USA in September. The cursory treatment of Gen. Musharraf, compared with the grand reception the Indian Prime Minister received, further emphasized the shift in allegiance. Indeed, somewhat worrying for Pakistan in the first half of 2001 was the manner in which the new US President, George W. Bush, became even more favourably disposed towards India as he redefined the USA's relationship with Asia. However, it would appear that the USA sought to stabilize Indo-Pakistani relations as a means of isolating China, although this was undermined somewhat by the growing trade ties between India and China.

Pakistan has had difficulties with Afghanistan since the outset of independence, the point at issue being the alleged desire of Pathans in the NWFP for an independent homeland, 'Pakhtoonistan' or 'Pashtunistan', which has been championed by Afghanistan but viewed by Pakistan as a gross interference in its internal affairs. Lt-Gen. Daud, who overthrew King Zahir Shah in 1973, revived the dormant Afghan claims to the Pakhtoon areas in Pakistan. During 1975–77 relations between the two countries were briefly improved by meetings and talks between Bhutto, and later Zia, and President Daud. However, after the April 1978 coup in Afghanistan, the Taraki regime in Kabul revived the 'Pakhtoonistan' question. The internal revolt in Afghanistan led thousands of Afghans to take refuge in the NWFP and Balochistan province of Pakistan.

The Soviet intervention in Afghanistan in late December 1979 caused an unprecedented deterioration in Pakistani-Afghan relations. Pakistan was obviously gravely concerned at this new development along its north-western frontier, and felt that the USSR had violated the UN charter and the Bandung principles. Along with other non-aligned countries, it sponsored a resolution in the UN Security Council demanding an 'immediate and unconditional withdrawal from Afghanistan'. In January 1980 an emergency session of the Islamic Foreign Ministers' Conference, held at Islamabad, suspended the membership of Afghanistan until such time as the Soviet intervention ended and declared complete solidarity with the Afghan *mujahidin*. Moscow and Kabul repeatedly accused Pakistan of providing military training to Afghan *mujahidin* and refugees. However, Pakistan consistently denied this charge and justified the assistance provided to the refugees on humanitarian grounds. By 1985 Pakistan was accommodating more than 3m. Afghan refugees.

Indirect negotiations regarding the Afghan crisis began in 1981, under UN auspices, and were continued in Geneva, Switzerland, between 1982 and 1988. Throughout this period there were many violations of the Afghanistan/Pakistan border, involving shelling, bombing and incursions into neighbouring airspace and resulting in casualties in border villages and encampments. An agreement on a complete Soviet withdrawal was eventually signed in April 1988. The Geneva accords comprised five documents: detailed undertakings by Pakistan and Afghanistan, relating to non-intervention and non-interference in each other's affairs; international guarantees of Afghan independence; arrangements for the voluntary return of more than 5m. Afghan refugees from Pakistan and Iran; a document linking the preceding documents with a timetable for a Soviet withdrawal; and the establishment of a 50-man UN monitoring force, which was to maintain surveillance of the Soviet troop departures and to monitor the return of the refugees. The withdrawal of Soviet troops commenced on 15 May and, as scheduled, was completed by 15 February 1989. Neither the *mujahidin* nor Iran played any part in the formulation of the Geneva accords, and, despite initial protests by Pakistan, there was no agreement incorporated in the accords regarding the composition of an interim coalition government in Afghanistan, or the 'symmetrical' cessation of Soviet aid to the Government in Kabul and US aid to the *mujahidin*. Accordingly, despite the departure of Soviet forces, the supply of arms to both sides was not halted and the violent conflict continued.

Pakistan repeatedly denied accusations, made by the Afghan Government, that it had violated the Geneva accords by continuing to harbour Afghan guerrillas and to act as a conduit for arms supplies to the latter from various sympathizers (notably the USA). Pakistan maintained its support for the guerrillas' cause in 1989–91, while vehemently denying accusations by the Afghan Government that it was taking an active military part in the Afghan conflict. The Pakistani Government welcomed the overthrow of the Afghan regime by the *mujahidin* in April 1992, and supported the interim coalition Government, which was to administer Afghanistan pending the holding of free elections. Relations between Pakistan and Afghanistan deteriorated, however, in 1994. The turbulence and increasingly anti-Pakistan feeling in Afghanistan threatened not only to result in an extension of the violence into the Pakhtoon areas of the NWFP, but also obstructed the trade route from the Central Asian republics of the former USSR to the Arabian Sea at Karachi. The situation worsened in September 1995 when the Pakistani embassy in Kabul was ransacked and burned down by a mob of about 5,000 Afghans protesting at Pakistan's alleged support for the Islamist Taliban militia. In the following month the Afghan ambassador to Pakistan was expelled from the country. Following the capture of Kabul by Taliban troops in late September 1996 and their assumption of power, the Pakistani Government issued a statement in which it recognized the Taliban regime as the new Afghan Government; the statement also said that Pakistan would send a delegation immediately to Kabul to establish contact with the new administration. At the same time, the Pakistani President stated that his country's stance as regards its neighbour's crisis was the need for an immediate cease-fire and multilateral dialogue regarding demilitarization. The success of the Taliban was seen as a mixed blessing by some Pakistani commentators, despite the increased trade prospects it brought. This was both because of the fear that armed Islamist militants within Pakistan would draw encouragement from the Taliban, and because of the possibility that Afghanistan might be divided on ethnic lines. In December 1999 there were signs of distinct changes in Pakistan's policy towards Afghanistan. Following the imposition of UN-mandated sanctions on Afghanistan the previous month for refusing to hand over the terrorist suspect bin Laden, Pakistan appeared to be exerting pressure on the Taliban to accede to Western demands by closing down a number of Afghan banking operations in Pakistan. In May 2000 the Afghan Minister of the Interior held talks with his Pakistani counterpart in Islamabad concerning transit trade, narcotics control and the repatriations of Afghan refugees. The Afghan delegation agreed to the repatriation of 100,000 refugees that year of the reported 1.7m. Afghan refugees still residing in Pakistan.

In January 2001 an estimated 1.2m. Afghan refugees remained in Pakistan. The Pakistani Government continued to offer financial and diplomatic support to the Taliban. Although Gen. Musharraf repeatedly and strongly denied giving military assistance to the Taliban, allegations regarding the involvement of Pakistan's special forces grew, following the latter's successful offensive in August–September 2000. The Government agreed to implement the UN sanctions imposed on Afghanistan in January 2001, but announced that it would attempt to mitigate the effect of the restrictions, warning of a steep increase in refugee numbers and a worsening of the civil war. In mid-April the military Government strongly denied allegations by the Afghan opposition that it was disregarding sanctions. Meanwhile, Afghanistan and Pakistan continued to conduct bilateral negotiations. In February Gen. Musharraf urged the international community to accept and integrate the Taliban, and to assist Afghanistan with its humanitarian crisis. More than 170,000 refugees had so far entered Pakistan as a result of the drought. The Government, however, rejected the request of the UN High Commissioner of Refugees for another camp to shelter the influx of Afghans and ordered 100,000 refugees to return to Afghanistan by mid-July. In mid-June the Minister of Foreign Affairs announced that Pakistan was unable to continue providing shelter for Afghan 'economic' refugees, but would still offer refuge to those seeking political asylum. In early August the Government and the UN agreed to screen 190,000 of the approximately 2m. refugees in Pakistan. It was agreed that those found to be genuine would be able to stay; the rest would be deported.

During 1982 the Khunjerab Pass on the Karakoram highway, linking China and Pakistan, was formally opened, and a joint Sino-Pakistani economic commission was established after Gen. Zia's visit to Beijing in October. In September 1986 China and Pakistan signed an agreement in Beijing for co-operation in the peaceful use of nuclear energy. In November 1989 the Chinese Prime Minister, Li Peng, made an official visit to Pakistan, during which he announced that China was to provide Pakistan with a 300,000-kW nuclear plant (see Economy). Relations with China remained strong, despite Pakistan's nuclear test explosions in 1998. Pakistan maintained support for China's policies, including the 'One China' policy (of not recognizing the Government of Taiwan), and in return received support from China on various issues at the international level. In July 2000 China was accused of aiding the development of Pakistan's long-range missile programme. China denied giving Pakistan any such assistance to develop missiles to carry nuclear weapons. In August the Pakistan Minister of Foreign Affairs declared that any co-operation between the two countries in missile technology was consistent with China's obligations under the Missile Technology Control Regime. Economic co-operation remained important. In August China decided to invest funds into Pakistan's telecommunications facilities and was also considering co-operation in terms of information technology, agriculture and infrastructure. China remained concerned about Pakistan's ties with the Taliban and therefore was keen to maintain good relations with the country. At the same time the USA's effort to isolate China and forge ties with India, as was displayed in July 2001 when the USA accused China of exporting missiles to Pakistan, provided a greater impetus for China to develop Sino-Pakistani relations. After the suicide attacks on the USA in September 2001, however, and as the USA shifted its focus to Afghanistan, Pakistan's relationship with the USA underwent a significant transformation. President Musharraf convinced the USA not to request the use of Pakistani soldiers in Afghanistan, but permitted US soldiers to utilize Pakistani military bases and the employment of US personnel in Pakistan.

In early 1992 the Economic Co-operation Organization (ECO), comprising Pakistan, Iran and Turkey, was reactivated, and by the end of the year had been expanded to include Afghanistan and the six Central Asian, mainly Muslim, republics of the former USSR; the 'Turkish Republic of Northern Cyprus' joined the ECO in April 1993. Trade delegations from Turkey and the new republics visited Pakistan, and an agreement for the restoration and construction of highways in Afghanistan to link Pakistan with these republics was signed. In order to meet the maritime trade requirements of the Muslim republics, the cargo facilities at Karachi Port are being modernized and expanded. In March 1995 Pakistan, China, Kazakhstan and Kyrgyzstan signed a transit trade agreement, restoring Pakistan's overland trade route with Central Asia, through China.

In 2000 the improvement of Pakistan's standing in the international community was largely affected by the global fear of terrorism. The coup did not cause a great deal of concern; however, Pakistan's acknowledgement of the Taliban regime in Afghanistan, the alleged presence of Taliban training camps in Pakistan and the general support for militant groups adversely affected Gen. Musharraf's efforts to improve Pakistan's foreign relations. Despite Gen. Musharraf's repeated requests for international mediation in Kashmir at the UN Millennium Summit in September, and his offers to enter dialogue with Indian leaders and make an agreement not to use military force, he failed to gain international support. The Pakistani

Government reiterated that the international community should deal with Afghanistan directly and that Pakistan's main concern was to maintain good relations with its neighbours.

As well as strongly denying that it provided the Taliban with military assistance, Pakistan stated that it was not in a position to control the movement of the Taliban along the borders of Pakistan and Afghanistan. However, as one of only three states to recognize the Taliban regime, it was pressed by the USA to help it locate groups associated with bin Laden. Pakistan rejected this request on the grounds that Afghanistan was its neighbour and that such activities were beyond its capabilities. The dilemma faced by Pakistan regarding the Taliban and Afghanistan became much more serious in the second week of September 2001, following the terrorist attacks against New York and Washington, DC, USA. The USA was quick to conclude that bin Laden, reportedly hiding in Afghanistan, was its prime suspect and informed Pakistan that it expected the country's full support in its efforts to identify and punish the perpetrators. Although the Taliban expressed regret for the events, they at first refused to surrender bin Laden, without detailed proof of his alleged role. Pakistan was placed in an extremely difficult situation. The Government was fully aware that if it did not agree to help the USA, it would be identified as an enemy and sympathetic to terrorism, and would risk severe economic penalties and possible invasion. It was also clear that if it supported the USA, the Government would face great resistance from within and outside Pakistan. It was feared that the Pakistani state would fragment, creating a highly unstable geopolitical situation on the sub-continent, if tensions that underpin Pakistan's society were released. Indeed, it was difficult to see how divisions within the army, ethno-nationalistic and regional differences, as well as other factors, and a massive flow of Afghan refugees into Pakistan would not dissipate whatever unity prevails. The Government sent a secret delegation to Afghanistan days after the attack in an attempt to work out a compromise; however, this failed, and President Musharraf declared Pakistan's support for the US-led anti-terrorism coalition. Despite increasing tension in the country, the Government agreed to grant the USA access to Pakistan's Inter-Services Intelligence (ISI) files on bin Laden and the Taliban. It also agreed to close the border with Afghanistan and halt the supply of fuel to the Taliban, and to grant permission to use Pakistani airspace in the event of military strikes. The two main political parties voiced their support for the President's position. On 17 September a Pakistani delegation, led by the head of the ISI, visited the spiritual leader of the Taliban, Mola Mohammad Omar, to warn the Taliban that they faced attack if they refused to expel bin Laden; however, the delegation failed to secure the surrender of the suspected terrorist. Consequently, Taliban fighters, armed with Scud missiles, began massing along the Afghan-Pakistani border. Pakistan faced a humanitarian catastrophe as hundreds of thousands of Afghan refugees also gathered on the frontier, in the hope of entering Pakistan, despite the latter's attempt to close the border. In the mean time, anti-US protests took place throughout Pakistan; religious party leaders and spiritual leaders warned of chaos and anarchy should Pakistan assist US retaliation. Islamist militants calling for jihad claimed that Pakistan's co-operation with the USA was a betrayal to Islam. Moderate Pakistanis demanded that the USA present evidence of bin Laden's culpability. It was later reported that Pakistan had agreed to allow US troops to be based at airfields near the Afghan border. In return the USA announced the lifting of economic sanctions on Pakistan, which had been imposed following the latter's nuclear tests in 1998. The USA also agreed to reschedule the debt owed by Pakistan. At the same time Pakistan temporarily withdrew its diplomatic staff from Kabul for 'security reasons'. Pakistan severed all diplomatic relations with the Taliban in November.

On 7 October 2001 the US-led coalition launched military strikes against Afghanistan. Pakistan decided to allow US forces to use at least two of its airports during the military strikes for emergency recovery operations. In the same month President Musharraf's tenure as Chief of Army Staff, which was due to end after a three-year term, was extended indefinitely. The President replaced the Chief of the ISI, Lt-Gen. Mahmood Ahmad, who was closely linked with the Taliban, with the more moderate Lt-Gen. Ehansul Haq. A reshuffle of the top ranks of the army command structure also took place, strengthening President Musharraf's power base and granting him greater flexibility to control the political crisis in Pakistan. The President and Indian Prime Minister were reported to have had a telephone conversation regarding attempts to curb terrorism, underlining what the expectations of the USA were in relation to Afghanistan.

Indeed, once Osama bin Laden and his al-Qa'ida network were held principally responsible for the attacks on the USA, President Musharraf was forced to support the USA and its 'coalition against terror'. Furthermore, during British Prime Minister Tony Blair's visit to Islamabad Musharraf was given little alternative but to reverse the policy on the Taliban, in other words to cease its political support and substantial economic aid. In doing so, Musharraf was also compelled to accept the United Islamic Front for the Salvation of Afghanistan (commonly known as the United Front or Northern Alliance) as a possible US replacement for the Taliban as the next government of Afghanistan. Protests against these actions spread throughout Pakistan, especially in the towns bordering Afghanistan. Popular protests against co-operation with the US-led coalition were fuelled by reports of civilian casualties of US bombing raids in Afghanistan. Reinforcing this picture of mass destruction was the growing influx of refugees fleeing the military operations. It was against this background that different elements of Pakistani society voiced their support for the Taliban and opposed the Government's official position.

None the less, President Musharraf was strongly supported by the US-led coalition, with both the US Secretary of State, Colin Powell, and US Secretary of Defense, Donald Rumsfeld, visiting Pakistan in October and November 2001, respectively. However, these visits were as much to remind Musharraf of his obligations to the USA, as they were to endorse his position within Pakistan. Gen. Powell, for example, informed him that Pakistan would have no influence in the formation of an Afghan interim administration and that his request for a suspension of bombing during the Muslim holy month of Ramadan had been denied. In the third week of October, US ground troops entered Afghanistan. The United Front made substantial territorial advances against the Taliban, taking Kabul in mid-November, and Qandahar in December. By the end of the year the Taliban had been effectively overthrown and an interim government, that appeared to be controlled by the Tajik United Front, had been installed. Although the return of 80,000 refugees from Pakistan to Afghanistan provided some relief, particularly in the overcrowded refugee camps, hundreds of thousands of displaced Afghans remained, creating a situation that placed great strains on the infrastructure of Pakistan. At the same time, as tension increased between Pakistan and India in the aftermath of the militant attack on the Indian parliament in December 2001, Pakistan began to move troops from the Afghan border to the eastern border in Kashmir.

By the beginning of 2002 President Musharraf appeared to have adopted a stronger stance against the activities of militant Islamists; in a speech in mid-January he condemned the extremist organizations based in Pakistan and announced the introduction of measures to combat terrorist activity and religious zealotry. In the months that followed he continued to struggle with a very complicated political situation. He was obliged to control the infiltration of terrorist activities across the border from Afghanistan. This became progressively more difficult as extremist attacks within Pakistan increased; the 'suicide bombing' in May that killed 14 people, mostly French engineers travelling on a bus in Karachi was the most notable. At the same time he was compelled to resist what he considered Indian attempts to undermine his position. Therefore, India's amassing of troops on the India–Pakistan border necessitated a similar response from President Musharraf. Moreover, instability in Afghanistan persisted, as was demonstrated by the assassination of Haji Abdul Qadir, the Vice-President of the newly established Transitional Administration, in early July. Indeed, as long as bin Laden (reportedly based somewhere between Afghanistan and Pakistan in mid-2002) remained free, the problem of terrorist attacks in Pakistan was likely to continue. In the mean time, Musharraf also had to deal with the public outrage after US forces bombed a wedding party in Afghanistan by mistake, killing at least 30 guests and injuring many others.

Economy

ASAD SAYEED

Revised by QAZI MASOOD AHMED

INTRODUCTION

'Pakistan is a puzzle, a miracle of levitation. With one of the lowest domestic savings rates in Asia, its economy has performed quite creditably. Since we do not believe in miracles, we have to wonder whether the capital inflows that have sustained the growth rate will last.' This statement by Professor Richard Eckaus aptly encapsulates the state of the Pakistani economy since the inception of the country in 1947. Initially a quintessentially agrarian economy, it has succeeded in diversifying the structure of production and employment a great deal. The worst extremes of poverty found elsewhere in South Asia are not to be seen in Pakistan. Yet, little, if anything, has been done to ensure a more equitable distribution of wealth. Although the country has witnessed periods of economic stagnation in the past, a deceleration in the rate of growth together with chronic macro-economic imbalances seem to have acquired greater permanence at the beginning of the 21st century. The consequences of the country's nuclear test explosions in May 1998, the overthrow of a democratically elected Government by the military and regional instability, especially with regard to militancy and religious fundamentalism, appear to have turned the 'miracle of levitation' into a more predictable slump.

The territories that in 1947 made up the new state of Pakistan were, before independence, essentially the hinterlands of the major economic centres of British India. In West Pakistan (which became, after 1971, the present Pakistan) there were some prosperous agricultural regions where irrigation had been developed in the late 19th century, but the surplus production of these areas, wheat and cotton, was exported to other industrially developed parts of British India. Although some small-scale industry existed in the Punjab, exports of wheat and cotton from the region meant that necessary linkages for industrialization were never forged. In East Pakistan or East Bengal, now Bangladesh, a densely-packed population cultivated rice for subsistence and jute for the factories of Calcutta (now known as Kolkata) or further abroad.

The task of achieving rapid economic growth was complicated by the effects of the partition of India which had brought Pakistan into existence. In the first place, the ties that had existed between, for example, the Punjab and Bombay (now known as Mumbai) were broken, and new economic links had to be forged. There was little co-operation from India, and in 1949, what there was ceased when the two currencies were separated. Secondly, although the country inherited a competent bureaucratic cadre at the top levels, the administrative infrastructure had to be built up more or less from nothing. Thirdly, the new state had to cope with a massive influx of refugees from India, most of whom had lost all their possessions and had to start from scratch. There was, it is true, no shortage of land vacated by refugees going in the opposite direction, but the resettlement was, nevertheless, a major administrative operation. Fourthly, the hostile relationship with India, as well as the greater institutional strength of the army, meant that a large quantum of resources was devoted to defence. This phenomenon has continued right up to the present, and Pakistan currently spends between 5% and 6% of its total annual GDP on defence. Finally, as new projects were embarked upon, especially in the irrigation sector, complex negotiations had to be conducted with its hostile neighbour, India. It was only in 1960, with help from the World Bank, that the Indus Waters Treaty reached a solution regarding the division of irrigation and hydroelectric resources.

Pakistan's economic legacy was therefore a mixed one. It had substantial agricultural potential, both for food grains and for cash crops. Although there was very little large-scale industry, sufficient technical and entrepreneurial skill was available in small-scale industry, especially in the Punjab. Moreover, many of the migrants from India brought relevant and applicable commercial and professional skills.

GENERAL STRATEGIES AND PATTERN OF DEVELOPMENT

While the new Government of Pakistan was establishing itself, it adopted a private-sector-led model of development, albeit with strict controls. The commodity boom that accompanied the Korean War (1950–53) benefited Pakistan's agricultural exports, especially of jute and cotton. The foreign exchange thus accumulated allowed the first stage of industrial development to be carried out through a partnership between the Government and the private sector. During the 1950s this process was greatly assisted by the creation of government institutions such as the Pakistan Industrial Development Corporation (PIDC). Pakistan's alliance with the West in the Cold War meant that its requests for foreign aid and assistance were sympathetically considered by many Western countries.

These processes were accelerated during Ayub Khan's regime (1958–69). Assured of power and with the co-operation of both the army and the civil bureaucracy, Ayub Khan adopted an approach to economic development that aimed to increase agricultural productivity through mechanization. In the industrial sphere, the first, albeit limited, spurt of industrialization was consolidated through patronizing a small coterie of traders turned industrialists to invest in and diversify the structure of industry. This strategy was incorporated in the Second Five-Year Plan (1960–65). With substantial technical and financial help from the USA, the economy, as a whole, grew at an average rate of 7% a year during this period. In the agricultural sector, the commercially viable farms in the irrigated areas prospered, and by the end of the 1960s the 'Green Revolution' (see Agriculture) was beginning to make an impact (wheat production more than doubled). In the industrial sector, the early concentration on textiles and other consumer goods was supplemented by fertilizer, cement and chemical factories. Large-scale manufacturing grew at double-digit rates. The Government ensured the supply of foreign exchange at cheap rates through a complex system of multiple exchange rates. By the late 1960s, however, in a deteriorating political climate, attention came to be focused on the degree to which the benefits of development had been monopolized by a small élite in West Pakistan. In industry particularly, the small group of traders turned industrialists was hence singled out for criticism. Economic discontent was a major factor in Ayub Khan's downfall in 1969.

The successor regime of Zulfikar Ali Bhutto, which assumed power following the secession of Bangladesh, had won the 1970 elections in West Pakistan on a platform of radical social and economic change. Soon after he came to power in December 1971, a number of large-scale industries and the banking and insurance sectors were nationalized. The new Government also instituted land reforms, but because Bhutto himself represented the landlords' lobby, their implementation was lax. Such tumultuous change obviously had a negative impact on economic growth. Private-sector investment fell to virtually zero, and since the gestation lag of investment in public-sector industries was long, economic growth in industry deteriorated considerably. Compared with average annual GDP growth of about 7% in the 1960s, during the tenure of power of Zulfikar Ali Bhutto (1971–77), GDP growth decelerated to an average of less than 5% per year. However, the period saw a marked improvement in the distribution of income, as a result of the Government's increased expenditure on welfare-related activities.

While Ayub Khan's regime had fallen partly because of popular discontent with the way the benefits of economic growth had been appropriated by the few, Zulfikar Ali Bhutto's regime fell in 1977 owing to unstable economic conditions and his assault on powerful economic interests. His successor, Gen. Zia ul-Haq, attempted to revert to the economic style of the Ayub Khan years. In this, he was only partially successful. Although nationalization was abandoned as government policy and fresh investment was encouraged in the private sector, the large public sector inherited by the regime was kept intact. In fact, in the early years of Zia ul-Haq's tenure of office, the regime depended heavily on investment in the public sector to develop and increase growth rates. The concept of planning within a five-year framework, which had been abandoned during the Zulfikar Ali Bhutto period, was restored, and the Fifth Five-Year Plan was launched in 1978. Over the following decade some aspects of the economy were stabilized: inflation was brought under control, essential commodities were available without difficulty or rationing, and average annual growth reached around 6%. During 1977–88 industrial output increased at an average annual rate of 9.6%. Agricultural output also improved, although not to the extent that the country became totally self-sufficient in food production. The economy proved incapable, however, of generating sufficient resources to finance its own further development. Levels of national savings, both private and public, were very low, and rates of borrowing, both domestic and foreign, were correspondingly high. The fiscal deficit rose to alarming heights, and deficit financing became a regular feature of public finance. External inflows were crucial in compensating for large fiscal and current-account deficits at that time. Among these the most important were remittances from overseas Pakistanis, mostly in the Gulf States. Remittances peaked at US $3,200m. in 1982/83 and annually exceeded US $2,500m. throughout the rest of the 1980s. Another external factor that helped to sustain the Zia Government was the concessional aid that it received from the USA and multilateral institutions on account of Pakistan's front-line status in containing Soviet occupation of Afghanistan.

By the time that Zia ul-Haq died in an aeroplane crash in 1988, external imbalances in the economy had started to undermine the high rates of growth achieved during his regime. Consequently, the interim Government that held power after the death of President Zia opted to enter Pakistan into a structural adjustment programme under the aegis of the IMF. The democratically elected Government of Benazir Bhutto (1988–90) inherited very few degrees of freedom in altering the broad contours of the economy. The Seventh Five-Year Plan (1988–93) had been drawn up under Zia's Government, but initially remained unaltered. Benazir Bhutto's Government was able to maintain the growth momentum of the early 1980s and also succeeded in reducing the budget deficit.

A major shift in economic policy was ushered in by the first Government of Mohammad Nawaz Sharif, which came into power following the 1990 elections. The Government, which enjoyed the benefits of a firm majority and the goodwill of the Pakistan establishment, decided that it would not simply pursue the policies of caution and stabilization that were required to correct the economic imbalances, but would embark on a radical programme of restructuring aimed at removing all the bureaucratic restraints on economic activity that had accumulated over the years. Restrictions on free movement of capital were lifted and restrictions on profit repatriation were removed from all foreign investment. Private commercial and investment banks were allowed to be established, and new avenues for private investment created, for example, in communications and power generation. In addition, most public-sector industries were scheduled for privatization. During Nawaz Sharif's first tenure of office (1990–93) 67 out of a total of 109 public-sector industrial units were privatized. Two of the six public-sector commercial banks were also transferred to private ownership. The initial response to these policies was positive as output and investment increased sharply in 1991/92. Soon after, however, following floods in mid-1992 and profligate spending by the Government, the budget deficit shot up to 8.7% of GDP and the balance-of-payments position deteriorated precipitously. The interim Government (led by an ex-World Bank functionary, Moeenuddin Ahmad Qureshi) which held power for several months in the latter half of 1993, signed another structural adjustment agreement with the IMF. The conditionalities of the agreement entailed a reduction of the budget deficit and further consolidation of liberalization measures, most important of which were a lowering of import tariffs and the removal of subsidies on electricity and gas.

The second Benazir Bhutto Government, which was in power during 1993–96, was initially successful in reducing the budget deficit, but in the latter part of her tenure, the deficit began to increase again, despite the fact that the Government imposed new taxes worth more than Rs 100,000m. over the three years. While Benazir Bhutto's Government did not substantially reduce import tariffs, it did succeed in significantly curtailing subsidies on electricity and gas tariffs. It also laid great emphasis on removing infrastructural obstacles in the energy sector. For this purpose, it initiated a private power policy, which elicited massive foreign investment (see Energy and Infrastructure). Benazir Bhutto's Government, however, could not contain a deterioration in the external account as foreign-currency reserves plummeted and the current-account deficit assumed mammoth proportions of around 7% of GDP.

The successor regime of Nawaz Sharif, which came to power in February 1997, launched a supply-side policy to combat the structural weaknesses in the economy. The salient features of this package were reductions in income and corporate tax rates, in import tariffs and in the rates of the General Sales Tax (GST). In October 1997 the Government also signed a US $1,600m. Extended Structural Adjustment Facility (ESAF) and Extended Fund Facility (EFF) loan with the IMF, which, together, helped the Government partially to tide over its balance-of-payments problems. This agreement was, however, annulled by the IMF after Pakistan's nuclear test explosions in May 1998, precipitating another balance-of-payments crisis. In January 1999 the Government signed a new agreement with the IMF, which was similar to the previous accord, although some of the conditionalities were stiffer and performance criteria more stringent. A more significant development was that, under the aegis of the IMF, a rescheduling arrangement regarding US $3,300m. of external debt was arranged on multilateral and bilateral debt through the 'Paris Club' of Pakistan's creditors in February.

The Nawaz Sharif Government was overthrown in a bloodless military coup in October 1999. The reasons given by the incoming military junta, led by Gen. Pervez Musharraf, were mismanagement and the dismal performance of the economy, as well as a number of political issues. The new economic team, led by Shaukat Aziz (a banker of international repute), announced an economic recovery plan. The salient features of the plan were to enhance the growth rate of the economy through revival of investor confidence, place greater emphasis on revenue generation through documentation of the economy and allocate Rs 15,000m. for poverty alleviation.

In November 2000 the IMF approved a 10-month US $596m. Standby Credit Arrangement for Pakistan. As dictated by this agreement, the policy focus was shifted towards macro-economic stabilization. Consequently, the aim of all policies was the reduction of fiscal deficit.

Although Pakistan has seen a number of different governments since the beginning of the 1990s, the essential thrust of economic policies has remained unchanged. Liberalization of the economy and reduction in the fiscal deficit have remained the most important policy areas. Concentration on these two areas has, however, not yet yielded good results for the economy.

An overview of the real sector performance reveals a decelerating growth momentum. In the 1980s GDP grew at an average annual rate of 6%, but declined to an average 5% per annum in the first half of the 1990s, before declining further to an average annual 3.2% in the latter half. In 2000/01 GDP declined to a record low of 2.6% and improved slightly in 2001/02 to reach 3.6%. The lower growth in these two years was mainly due to a poor performance of the agriculture sector. According to the Asian Development Bank (ADB), as a result of severe drought, the agricultural sector contracted by 2.6% in 2000/01; output improved in 2001/02 to reach growth of an estimated 1.4%. The drought also adversely affected hydroelectric power (HEP) generation, thereby creating a negative impact on the power and gas distribution sector. The large-scale manufacturing sector achieved high growth of 8.6% in 2000/01. In 2001/02, however, growth in this sector was only 4.0%, owing to the negative impact of the suicide attacks on New York and Washington, DC, USA on 11 September 2001. The services sector performed well, growing by 4.8% and 5.1% in 2000/01 and 2001/02, respectively.

Economic growth depends on capital accumulation, which is made possible only through investment. The rate of investment, therefore, is one of the most important determinants of the rate of growth of an economy. Hence, the economic slowdown in Pakistan might be attributed to a decline in the investment-GDP ratio. Total investment, which reached 18.7% of GDP in the 1980s, increased to 19.5% of GDP in the first half of the 1990s before decreasing to 17.1% of GDP in the latter half of the 1990s. Investment continued to decrease in 2000/01 and 2001/02, declining to 15.9% and 13.9% of GDP, respectively. The lower level of investment-GDP ratio, as well as Pakistan's sluggish economic growth, was due to a decline in sectoral (agriculture, industry etc.) as well as functional (private, public) categories of investment expenditure during the 1990s. Lack of investor confidence, owing to economic and non-economic factors, resulted in a decline in private investment. Reduction in public investment, meanwhile, was a result of a fiscal consolidation policy to control escalating budget deficits. Deteriorating infrastructure also led to lower productivity of private investment. This resulted in a decline in efficiency of capital utilization, which adversely affected overall growth of the economy. Inflow of foreign direct investment (FDI) also declined: in 1999/2000 FDI decreased by 0.5% and reduced further by 39% in 2000/01. The decline in FDI was particularly evident in the fertilizer, construction and financial businesses. However, the inflow of FDI in 2001/02 increased for the first time in five years, especially in the oil and gas sector. Growth would have been higher had it not been for the negative impact caused by the suicide attacks on the USA in September 2001.

Although the performance of the real sector of the economy was poor, the Government fared better in reducing fiscal and current-account deficits, as well as controlling the rate of inflation. The budget deficit was around 7.1% of GDP in the 1980s and remained at a similar level in the 1990s. Overall fiscal deficit decreased to 5.2% of GDP in 2000/01 and was projected to be 5.7% of GDP in 2001/02. Similarly, the current-account deficit declined from 4.5% in the 1990s to a marginal surplus in 2000/01. From July 2001 to March 2002 a current-account surplus of US $2,095m., or 3.4% of GDP had been recorded. The high rate of inflation—an average 9.2% per annum in 1990–2000, against an average of around 7% in the 1980s—was the main reason for the increase in poverty. However, an inflation rate of 2.6% was registered in 2001/02, largely owing to sufficient food supplies and lower economic growth. The slight reduction in budget deficit, an impressive improvement in the current-account balance and a lower inflation rate demonstrate the success of the stabilization programme.

The decline in economic growth can also be attributed to the policy of macro-stabilization. The main objectives of the stabilization programme were to reduce the escalating budget deficit and to control external deficit. The reduction in fiscal deficit was maintained by decreasing development expenditure. However, in order to increase expenditure without increasing fiscal and current-account deficit, additional revenue mobilization is required. The failure in the past to mobilize resources is evident in the decline of total revenue to GDP ratio (from 17.2% in the 1990s to 16% and 16.9% in 2000/01 and 2001/02, respectively). The reduction in external deficit was due to a decline in imports, especially capital equipment, rather than an increase in exports.

Unexpected events adversely affected the already unstable macro-economic situation. The first was Pakistan's nuclear test explosions in mid-1998. As a result of these tests, bilateral sanctions were imposed, and multilateral assistance was initially curbed. Skilful management of the crisis, as well as the debt-rescheduling arrangements with the 'Paris Club' (see above) in 1999 and 2001, succeeded in curtailing the crisis temporarily. The long-term damage to investor confidence as a result of the 'freezing' of foreign currency accounts (FCAs) would, however, continue to affect the Pakistani economy for a long time to come. The second event to have a negative impact on the economy was the severe drought that adversely affected the agriculture sector, distorted growth and caused more rural poverty. Thirdly, the 'freezing' of FCAs eroded private-investor confidence. The terrorist attacks that took place in the USA have again placed Pakistan in a precarious position. As a result of Pakistan's decision to support the USA against terrorism in the light of the attacks in September 2001, economic sanctions imposed after the country's 1998 nuclear tests have been lifted. However, one consequence of Pakistan's support for the US-led coalition has been an increase in militant activities within Pakistan, which has worsened the already deteriorating law and order situation. Increased tensions between India and Pakistan and the deployment of more than 1m. Indian and Pakistani troops on the two countries' shared border also disrupted Pakistan's fragile economy.

AGRICULTURE

As mentioned above, at independence Pakistan was largely an agricultural country, with more than one-half of national income derived from farming and with the great majority of the population employed directly or indirectly on the land. This situation has changed a great deal, with only one-quarter of national income now being provided by the agricultural sector. A commensurate reduction in agricultural employment has not, however, taken place, and about one-half of the labour force is still employed in agriculture. This indicates low labour productivity in the sector. In spite of three land reforms (in 1959, 1972 and 1977), the concentration of land in a few hands remains high. The last agricultural census, which was held in 1990, revealed that 7.4% of the landowners possessed around one-half of the cultivable land area.

In the early years following independence food-grain production actually fell, so that Pakistan became a net importer, but the implementation of new irrigation schemes, mechanization and expansion in credit for agriculture reversed this trend in the 1960s. In the late 1960s and 1970s the impact of the 'Green Revolution' made a major contribution, especially in wheat production. The 'Green Revolution' strategy comprises the introduction of high-yielding varieties of seeds for wheat and other crops, together with the availability of assured irrigation and fertilizer supplies. In the 1980s total agricultural production continued to grow at an average rate of 5.4% per year. Particularly pronounced was growth in the production of cotton, which increased from 4.2m. bales in 1980/81 to 8.6m. bales by the end of the decade. This also signalled a shift from food-grain production to the production of cash crops.

As a result of severe drought, the agriculture sector contracted by 2.6% in 2000/01. In 2001/02 the sector performed fairly well, despite continued drought, with growth in agriculture reaching 1.4%. The production of major crops in 2001/02 improved, owing to high growth in cotton and sugar cane cultivation and moderate growth in the production of wheat and gram. Nevertheless, the overall production of major crops declined by 0.5%, owing to a fall in the cultivation of the highly water-intensive crop, rice. Meanwhile, minor crops achieved growth of 1%. The reduction in the availability of water was the main factor behind lower growth in the agriculture sector, despite higher than average monsoon rains. Farmers relied heavily on ground water for irrigation purposes. This mode of irrigation proved more expensive, owing to higher energy costs, which in turn caused farmers to make optimal usage of this water.

Generally, the impact of water shortages would be reflected by a shift from water-intensive crops to crops requiring less water. However, the trend in crop substitution has been mixed. The area under cotton cultivation, which is a less water-intensive crop, increased by 6.5%, while the size of area for rice cultivation declined by 11.1%. However, the area cultivated under wheat (a less water-intensive crop) reduced by 2.4%, and the area for sugar cane (a crop requiring more water) increased by 4.1%. The reason for this mix in shifting is the distortion in market prices. The price of sugar cane and cotton were higher in 2000/01, encouraging farmers to allocate resources to these two crops the following year. The decline in the price of wheat, conversely, discouraged farmers from increasing wheat production. Thus, the cotton crop, by being less water-intensive and reasonably priced, was the most profitable. In the case of sugar cane, the price of the crop outweighed the water costs.

Real private investment in the agriculture sector declined by 6% in 2000/01 and by 15% in 2001/02. US $10,000m. was allocated to drought relief in 2001/02; US $6,000m. was allocated for 2002/03. A decline in credit disbursement and investment has brought about a decline in the capital stock in the agriculture sector, which in the past was considered the backbone bone of the economy.

The agricultural sector in Pakistan faces a number of major problems. Further expansion will have to be based almost entirely on improvements in productivity rather than on the expansion of the area under cultivation. One key element is irrigation, with approximately 80% of crops currently dependent on it. In many parts of the country, however, irrigation schemes have led to waterlogging and salinity, and more than one-half of the land area is affected to some extent. Due to severe drought in the early 21st century and disagreements among provinces on the formula of water sharing, the problem of water storage and distribution requires urgent attention. The Government has recently formed the Pakistan Irrigation Development Authority with the assistance of the World Bank. This authority was to privatize water channels in addition to increasing user charges on water; however, some three years after its establishment, the new authority has not managed to privatize water channels or improve the distribution infrastructure in the country. As mentioned above, large land holdings have been a contentious political issue in Pakistan. As well as ruling out land reforms, soon after coming to power the new military Government also mentioned distribution of state land to landless farmers. However, in similar fashion to previous governments on this issue, by late 2001 no significant progress had been made. The current emphasis in the agricultural sector is more on productivity enhancement, market reforms and infrastructure development. In the area of market reforms, Benazir Bhutto's second Government moved towards raising the procurement price for crops to bring them in line with international prices. The reform of land tenure does not feature in the agendas of the main political parties. Equity concerns have tended to focus more on the need to introduce direct taxes on agricultural incomes, thereby eliminating the current tax exemption. However, successive budgets in recent years have failed to introduce direct taxation on agricultural income, having left the decision to the provincial governments. While all four provinces have now imposed the agricultural tax, rates of taxation are extremely low and collection even lower. Thus, the introduction of the tax has yet to translate into the realization of its actual revenue potential.

In summary, prospects for future growth in the agriculture sector depend on water availability, the extent of price distortions and the impact of the agricultural tax. Where there are shortages of canal water, farmers will rely on irrigation via tube wells, a method that is more expensive, owing to higher energy prices. Taxation in such severe conditions will also increase input costs, particularly of fertilizers and pesticides. As well as the higher cost of production, distorted output prices will adversely affect profitability in this subsistent sector.

INDUSTRY

The share of industry in total GDP increased from a mere 2.2% in 1949/50 (when the first estimates were obtained) to reach a peak of 19.7% in 1984/85. It stabilized at about 18% before reaching about 25% in the early 21st century. The degree of backwardness of the industrial sector at the time of partition can be gleaned from the following statement made in 1948 by the Government of Pakistan—'A country producing nearly 75% of the world's production of jute does not possess a single jute mill. There is an annual production of 1.5m. bales of good quality cotton but very few textile mills to utilize it'. That the share of industry increased to roughly one-fifth of GDP in about 40 years can thus be termed as a genuine achievement.

For the most part of its history, the development of manufacturing in Pakistan has been dominated by the private sector, although up until the end of the 1980s it took place within the general framework of five-year plans and government controls. Only in the 1970s did investment in manufacturing take place in the public sector. Since the 1990s most government controls have been dismantled under the aegis of economic liberalization and whatever subsidies that the manufacturing sector hitherto enjoyed are also being withdrawn.

Industrial expansion in the 1950s was rapid. Starting from a virtually non-existent base, manufacturing growth averaged 15.4% per year during that decade. By the end of the 1950s the manufacturing sector had removed the 'structural disequilibrium' that the country inherited at the time of partition. 'Structural disequilibrium', a term coined by Professor Stephen Lewis, essentially meant that for a country with Pakistan's per caput income the share of manufacturing in GDP was abnormally low. The Government created specific incentives for traders who had migrated from India to Pakistan to invest in industry. The most important in this regard was an over-valued exchange rate, which meant that industrial machinery could be imported cheaply. This was accompanied by high tariffs as well as quotas and licences for imported goods. These incentives increased the profitability of these industries considerably. The Korean War (1950–53) helped Pakistan a great deal as traders accumulated capital by selling raw jute and cotton and then invested it in industry. The Government established the Pakistan Industrial Development Corporation (PIDC) in 1962, which helped to develop industries with more complex technologies and then sold them off to those traders turned industrialists to operate. Much of the industry established in the 1950s concentrated on processing raw cotton and jute into yarn, fabric and other products.

The policy thrust of the 1950s was further refined in the 1960s and the industrial base diversified to produce cement, chemicals and fertilizer. Not only was growth in manufacturing high throughout the decade, averaging 13.3% per year, but productivity also increased at a more rapid rate than most other developing countries at the time. Industrial development took place within the framework of the Second and Third Five-Year Plans, and the most important feature was the operation of multiple exchange rates, whereby imports of machinery and raw material could be brought in at an over-valued exchange rate while exporters received the market exchange rate. This also provided a fillip to manufactured exports. The negative aspect of industrial expansion in the 1960s was two-fold: firstly, industry was concentrated in the hands of a few families (the famous '22 families'), and secondly real wages for industrial workers were stagnant, in fact falling. The political backlash arising from these two factors was strong enough to delegitimize the entire development strategy of the 1960s.

When the Pakistan People's Party of Zulfikar Ali Bhutto came to power in 1971, it moved swiftly to nationalize a number of industries as well as the entire banking and insurance sectors. This created panic among the industrialists, who resorted to capital flight and investment in real estate and trading. The result was that industrial investment declined precipitously. The Government decided to counter this phenomenon by increasing public-sector investment in manufacturing. Most of this investment was in cement, fertilizers, chemicals and machine tools. Growth in manufacturing during the tenure of Zulfikar Ali Bhutto (1971–77) declined to an average rate of 2.0% per year. Inefficiency in the nationalized industries, the long gestation period of public-sector investment undertaken during the period, as well as the high inflation rate (mainly due to the petroleum crisis in 1973), all contributed to this downturn.

When Gen. Zia ul-Haq came to power in 1977, he attempted to restore private-sector confidence by announcing a moratorium on further nationalization of industry, although most of the industries nationalized during the Bhutto period were not restored to their original owners. By the late 1970s public-sector investments made earlier in the decade came to fruition and contributed to a revival in the manufacturing sector. The 1980s witnessed strong rates of growth in the manufacturing sector similar to those achieved in the 1960s. Average annual growth in manufacturing in the 1980s was 9.3%. Much of this growth was private-sector led and under the aegis of five-year plans, but the public sector also contributed to the recovery. There were marked differences in the 1980s compared with the 1960s: industrial ownership was much more diversified and productivity of manufacturing investment was low. Other factors that contributed to growth were high liquidity with banks, especially that of foreign exchange, because of the amount of remittances from overseas Pakistanis, and the revival of concessional aid to Pakistan in the wake of the Afghan civil war. Low productivity and high growth meant that much of the growth was coming through new investments and not necessarily through better utilization of resources. The 1980s also saw the initiation of the process of debt default by industrial units. By the end of the decade bad debt worth Rs 55,000m. had been accumulated by the banking sector, with a large portion of it owed by newly established manufacturing concerns.

Pakistan has performed well in the manufacturing sector since it gained independence in 1947. The sector grew by an annual average rate of 10% in the 1960s and 6% in the 1970s. Under the import-substitution policies, carried out in the 1960s and 1970s, high tariffs were established in order to protect the domestic industry. This protection undoubtedly helped the industry to expand; indeed, the large-scale manufacturing sector grew by an annual average 9% until the 1980s. However, this expansion was to the detriment of consumers. Manufacturers were guaranteed to earn a fair amount of profit and, therefore, never attempted to reduce their costs and improve the quality of their products. It would not be an exaggeration to say that national resources were for the most part utilized in an inefficient manner by businesses carrying higher protection, instead of being invested in areas of comparative advantage. However, incentives provided under this policy resulted in higher levels of output in the import-substitute industries in the 1960s and 1970s. The large-scale manufacturing sector diversified in the 1980s: import substitution declined, while the existence of protection encouraged export-orientated industry to grow. As a result, large-scale manufacturing grew by 8.2% in the 1980s. The growth rate of large-scale manufacturing decelerated in the 1990s to an average 4.8% per annum. This sharp decline was attributed to various reasons: the restructuring of the industrial sector, following a reduction in protection; contraction of the economy; lack of industrial diversity; increasing costs of production (precipitated by both external as well as internal factors); lower levels of investment, owing to the poor law and order situation in the country; reduction in public-sector development expenditure; political instability; the lack of quality and standardized products and the absence of a comprehensive industrial policy. The restructuring of tariffs, which began in the 1990s in compliance with a World Trade Organization agreement, affected the profitability of the industry sector. The reduction in protection was a result of the demands of globalization. An increase in the GST also helped to dismantle the 'walls' protecting Pakistani industry. The decline in the custom tariff reduced the prices of imported items and the increase in GST increased the prices of domestically manufactured products. As a result of cheaper imported goods, domestic prices had to fall. Consequently, the sector experienced lower profitability and new investment was discouraged. The decline in development expenditure and public investment in the 1990s contributed to a reduction in manufacturing growth.

The import of machinery and raw materials, an important indicator for manufacturing growth, has shown a decelerating trend since 1995. The principal reason for the deceleration in manufacturing growth in the 1990s was that the sector had yet to adjust to the liberalization of the economy. Import tariffs were reduced from a maximum rate of 90% in 1990/91 to 30% by June 2001, thus reducing protection to industry. At the same time as protection was reduced, the cost of production and of capital increased. Increase in cost of production was due to exchange-rate liberalization, which saw the value of the rupee depreciate by 75% between June 1991 and September 2001. This resulted in an escalation in the cost of raw material imports as well as of machinery. The cost of electricity and gas increased at an average rate of 20.9% and 16.5% per year, respectively, between 1991 and 1998. Similarly, interest-rate liberalization has meant that the cost of long-term capital is now in the range of 22%–24% per year, while working capital costs are even higher, in the range of 28%–35%. Although in 1999/2000 and 2000/01 interest rates declined somewhat, as a result of weak investor confidence on account of the 'freezing' of FCAs (see above), an unstable political situation from October 1999 and the military's campaign of action against loan defaulters, investors had yet to benefit from this reduction. All these factors not only resulted in decelerating rates of growth in manufacturing output and investment, but have also led to a large number of bank defaults and industrial closures. More than 3,500 industrial units have been shut down and bad debt from the manufacturing sector has reached the alarming level of about Rs 240,000m. The military Government confronted wilful bank defaulters and by mid-2001 had recovered an estimated Rs 22,000m. However, a number of structural impediments, which had led to defaults in the first place, had yet to be addressed. As mentioned above, a decline in public investment has meant that the necessary infrastructure for industrial development is not being created. Devaluation was intended to aid the export of manufactured goods, but the increasing cost of production has meant that the real exchange rate has commensurately increased.

The impressive growth performance of the large-scale manufacturing sector in 2000/01 contributed much in compensating for the adverse affect of the drought and enabled the economy to achieve growth of 2.6%. The only time the manufacturing sector had achieved such high growth in the 1990s was in 1990/91 and 1997/98. Taking into account broad-based growth, all sections of the large-scale manufacturing sector performed well in 2000/01, whereas the success of 1997/98 could only be attributed to the sugar industry. The annual average growth rate of the large-scale manufacturing sector declined to about 4% in the 1990s, before increasing significantly to 8.6% in 2000/01. Interestingly, this sharp increase cannot be attributed to the production of sugar or the performance of textiles, but to an improvement in the performance of non-traditional components, such as petroleum products, fertilizer, paper and board and automobiles. The manufacturing sector registered growth of 4.0% in 2001/02. This was attributed to improved production of textiles, food and beverages and tobacco, petroleum products, pharmaceuticals, electronics and tyres and tubes. The production of fertilizers, metal industries, automobiles, non-metallic minerals and engineering industries, however, declined.

The performance of the textile sector improved as a result of modernization in the industry as well as an increase in quota by European nations, in the aftermath of the suicide attacks on the USA on 11 September 2001. The dramatic increase in the production of phosphetic fertilizer (by 126%), owing to the installation of the new plant, Fauji Jordan, resulted in a growth of 8.6% in the chemical, rubber and plastic sector in 2000/01. However, a decline in demand for fertilizers, owing to the severe drought, caused excess carry-over stock for 2001/02. Food, beverages and tobacco also performed well in 2000/01: the sector achieved 8.8% growth, compared with a decline of 19.7% in the previous year. In 2001/02 the output of sugar and cooking oil increased, while the production of vegetable ghee, cigarettes and beverages registered negative growth.

Cement production experienced a slight improvement of 1.8% in 2001/02. A low number of public-sector development projects and a declining construction sector are the main reasons for the low demand for cement. The Government planned to introduce a range of incentives, such as the reduction of taxes on the import of coal plant and equipment, in order to revive the cement industry. Thus, it was hoped that an increase in development expenditure would result in higher demand for cement. The fact remains, however, that growth in this industry is heavily dependant on the policy of exemptions. The automobile industry grew by a high 23.2% in 2000/01, owing to the Government's protection policies, robust demand and the recent leasing of facilities to individuals. Consumers expected the prices of automobiles to decrease, owing to excess inventories and the appreciation of the rupee against the US dollar, but prevailing high prices in 2001/02 resulted in lower demand, causing a lower growth of 2.8%.

Perhaps for the first time in Pakistan's history, broad-based growth of the manufacturing sector was witnessed in 2000/01. This was due to the installation of a new fertilizer plant and oil refinery, and strong demand for automobiles. 2001/02, however, was adversely affected by factors such as the slowdown in international markets, particularly in the USA. Declining protection, as a result of the policy of liberalization and lower demand, owing to the national and global economic slowdown, are the main factors that will hinder growth in the future.

To provide a stimulus to the manufacturing sector, both the sequencing and modalities of liberalization need to be reformulated. It is imperative that the Government implements a strategic industrial policy whereby selective incentives and subsidies are given to those industries that exhibit high productivity growth and have the potential for fostering further technological developments. A coherent exit policy is also required which phases out, liquidates or merges ailing industrial units. Most important of all, however, is that public investment towards the provision of infrastructure is revived.

ENERGY AND INFRASTRUCTURE

Pakistan's total consumption of energy (including processing and transformation losses) in 2000/01 was estimated at about 45.1m. metric tons of petroleum equivalent. Approximately three-quarters of final consumption was met by commercial energy resources and the remainder by non-commercial, such as fuel wood, charcoal and cattle dung. Shortage of energy in all forms is a major constraint on the country's economic development.

In 1999/2000 46.6% of Pakistan's commercial energy originated from petroleum, 36.7% from natural gas, 12.1% from hydroelectricity, and 4.3% from coal. At present, around 37.6% of Pakistan's petroleum is produced domestically. Levels of production have stagnated in recent years. Compared with production of 58,797 barrels per day (b/d) in 1996/97, production declined to 57,064 b/d in 2000/01. The consumption of petroleum products declined by 0.7% in that year, and declined by a further 1.8% in the first nine months of 2001/02. Recoverable reserves are calculated to stand at 225m. barrels. The Government has been anxious to explore the country's reserves as quickly as possible and has invited foreign participation. There has also been limited offshore exploration in the Arabian Sea, which has yet proved fruitless. Pakistan's major suppliers of imported petroleum are Saudi Arabia and Kuwait, although the contribution by other Gulf states has recently increased.

In contrast to its, as yet, limited petroleum discoveries, Pakistan has been able to exploit extensive natural gas reserves, which are located principally in Balochistan. Total production in 2000/01 was estimated at 853,560m. cu ft, and reserves are reckoned to amount to 19,500,000m. cu ft. Production from the largest field has now peaked, and further discoveries are required to maintain the momentum. The consumption of gas increased by 8.3% in 2000/01 and by 15% in the first nine months of 2001/02. Coal reserves are estimated at 580m. metric tons, but the quality is mostly poor and production is limited. Plans to develop the deposits at Lakhra in Sindh province and to utilize them for power generation have been recently revived after being inactive for several years.

The energy shortage is at its most acute in the generation of electricity. Although the installation of new electrical capacity was a top governmental priority during the 1980s, little was actually done to mitigate the situation. Unscheduled power cuts are regular events and cause great difficulties for industry and domestic consumers. It is predicted that as electrification is extended to all rural areas, and as personal incomes increase, demand for electrical power will increase. In 2001 total installed capacity was 17,772 MW, of which about 28.8% was provided by hydroelectricity, mostly from large dams in the mountainous northern parts of the country. Almost all of the remainder was generated by conventional thermal stations powered by petroleum or natural gas. A small quantity was generated by Pakistan's one operating nuclear power station near Karachi, which has an installed capacity of 137 MW. The total installed capacity of electricity increased by 1.6% in 2001/02 and was largely provided by privately-owned power plants. The capacity of these power plants increased from 5,417 MW in 2000/01 to 5,652 MW in 2001/02. Rapid urbanization and the electrification of villages led to an increase in electricity consumption.

Future plans to increase power generation include substantial expansion of hydroelectricity capacity, which does not involve the utilization of scarce fossil resources. Existing schemes at Tarbela and Mangla have been expanded, but plans to construct a large, multi-purpose dam at Kalabagh in the Punjab, which would ultimately produce as much as 3,600 MW, have been delayed for many years, owing to objections from neighbouring provinces, whose land would be flooded and a large number of people displaced. The Government is now planning to build a greater number of smaller dams in place of the extravagant large projects.

As mentioned above, the Benazir Bhutto Government prioritized the development of the energy sector. The most important and subsequently the most controversial policy in this regard was to invite foreign private investment in thermal energy generation. The Government guaranteed a return of 6.5 US cents per unit to investors at a time when electricity costs in Pakistan averaged around 1.3 US cents. As a result, projects worth US $3,400m. and with a capacity to generate 3,000 MW of energy reached financial closure. This policy allegedly created a liquidity crisis for the state-operated Water and Power Development Authority (WAPDA) to meet the high per unit cost that was negotiated with the Independent Power Producers (IPPs). Nawaz Sharif's Government criticized the IPPs, accusing a number of them of having given bribes to Benazir Bhutto's Government for approval of their projects. A number of such projects have reduced the tariffs to 5.4 US cents per unit. The IPPs claim that the problem of WAPDA's liquidity is not a result of the high cost charged by them, but is a direct consequence of the extreme inefficiency and corruption within the organization itself. To illustrate this, they point to the distribution losses of 34%–37% incurred by WAPDA (a large portion of which is due to theft) compared with average losses in other developing countries in the range of 10%–12%. This controversy with the private-sector power producers, Hub Power Company (HUBCO), which began in March 1998, was finally resolved in December 2000. A settlement was reached in March 2001.

The Government identified oil and gas as one of the four major contributors to growth (agriculture, small and medium enterprises and information technology are the other three). It was acknowledged that the development of energy resources plays an important role in encouraging growth and well-being. Adequate availability of energy supplies was deemed necessary to support the policies of enhancing investment as well as economic growth.

Major achievements during 2000/01 were the commissioning of the Pak-Arab refinery (PARCO), which has an annual refining capacity of 4.5m. metric tons, and the Chashma Nuclear Power Plant (CHASHNUP), which has an installed capacity of 325 MW. Imports of petroleum products declined in 2001/02, while the import of crude oil increased, owing to the commissioning of PARCO. Production at this new oil refinery enabled Pakistan to export motor gasoline and naphtha. As part of the Government's plan to achieve optimal utilization of Pakistan's hydroelectric potential, Hydel plants with total installed capacity of 525 MW were scheduled for completion in 2006.

Apart from energy, other infrastructural areas require pressing attention. During the tenure of the first Nawaz Sharif Government, an ambitious road-building programme was initiated. This included the Lahore–Islamabad highway, which was alleged to cost 2% of GDP and was completed in December 1997. Other ambitious projects that the present Government intends to undertake are the Islamabad–Peshawar motorway and the construction of a new international airport at Lahore. The Government recently announced the initiation of a number of large-scale infrastructure projects. These include a new seaport at Gawadar, a highway linking Karachi with Gawadar and the construction of a northern bypass in Karachi. It is doubtful, however, that the Government will manage to raise enough resources to complete these projects in the short to medium term. With regard to the air network, the government monopoly was ended in August 1992. By mid-2000 two companies had gone bankrupt, and four private competitors to the state airline remained. Infrastructure has since been deteriorating, owing to insufficient public-sector investments. Indeed, sectoral analysis shows that capital stock in infrastructure has been declining.

TRADE, DEBT AND BALANCE OF PAYMENTS

Pakistan's economy is extremely vulnerable to external factors. In June 2001 roughly 40% of the country's gross national product (GNP) was exposed to international transactions through trade, loans and grants, debt-servicing and foreign investments and service payments made abroad. Owing to debt-rescheduling, the actual repayments in 1998/99 to 2000/01 were indeterminate. Foreign-exchange reserves, however, have remained stable in spite of the absence of multilateral assistance. In 2000/01 the Government succeeded in maintaining reserves of about US $1,677m. It was able to do so essentially through purchasing foreign exchange from the kerb (unofficial) market. It was estimated that such purchases reached US $1,300m. between mid-1999 and mid-2001. Purchases declined in 2001/02; at the end of June 2002 foreign-exchange reserves stood at US $4,333m.

In 2000/01 the trade deficit decreased slightly to US $1,269m., compared with US $1,412m. in the previous year. The trade deficit declined again in the first 11 months of 2001/02 to an estimated US $262m., compared with US $1,238m. in the corresponding period of 2000/01. The decline in the import bill was predominantly due to a fall in international oil prices as well as a decrease in the imports of petroleum and petroleum products: in 2000/01 the import bill for petroleum products was US $3,361m.; in 2001/02 it had declined to US $2,807m. The decline in imports despite a 6% appreciation of the Pakistani rupee is indicative of the continuing contraction experienced by the real economy. Exports in 2001/02 increased marginally, compared with the previous year.

Pakistan's trade suffers from a number of rigidities. On the export front, about 65% of exports were based on cotton in 2000/01. However, exports of cotton declined by about 82% in 2001/02, owing to lower international prices and an increase in consumption by the domestic market. As regards imports, petroleum and petroleum products account for about 27% of imports. Apart from these commodity imports, Pakistan's industry depends heavily on imports of components, machinery and raw materials. A substantial part of Pakistan's trade deficit has been covered, since the mid-1970s, by remittances from Pakistanis working abroad. In 1984 it was estimated that there were nearly 2m. Pakistanis working abroad, two-thirds of whom were in the Middle East. In 1982/83 remittances through official channels reached a peak of nearly US $3,000m., while nearly as much again may have come in through unofficial channels. The economies of most Middle East countries have been slowing down recently, however, and there is now a net return of migrants, especially since Pakistanis are facing increasing competition from workers from other developing countries. As a result, until 2000/01 the flow of remittances declined substantially, levelling off to about US $1,087m. In 2001/02, however, workers' remittances rose significantly, owing to the reverse capital flow from the expatriate Pakistani community after 11 September 2001 and the increased flow of remittances through official channels, precipitated by the narrowing of differences between exchange rates prevailing in the inter-bank and kerb markets.

The decline in trade deficit and increase in remittances in 2001/02 largely contributed to an improvement in the current-account balance: in the first 11 months of 2001/02 an estimated current-account surplus of US $2,664m. was registered. Closer inspection of all the factors of the current-account balance is necessary to determine the extent to which the improvements are reflective of gains in the real economy or are products of the shifting political situation in the aftermath of the terrorist attacks on the USA in September 2001. The trade balance, for example, improved as a result of a decline in imports. An improvement of the real economy would probably have led to a rise in imports and, therefore, an increase in the current-account deficit (unless the value of exports was higher than that of imports, which, considering the present economic circumstance, would have been impossible). The increase in remittances is expected to continue; however, if an improvement in the real economy does push the current-account balance into deficit, the difference between exchange rates prevailing in the inter-bank and kerb markets is likely to widen and shift the flow of remittances into unofficial channels; consequently, the current-account balance will worsen further. Increased levels of other incomes and official transfers were in response to the September 2001 terrorist attacks on the USA and are likely not to be repeated. It is widely considered that the current-account surplus is not sustainable and will turn into a deficit again, and that foreign-exchange purchases might re-emerge as the principal source of financing of the capital account.

Developing countries generally experience balance-of-payments deficits and, usually, current-account deficits are financed from capital-account surpluses. Pakistan followed this trend until mid-2000. From 2000/01 the situation reversed: the country experienced a current-account surplus, which was being used to support the capital account and to develop reserves.

Up until the beginning of the 1990s, Pakistan's external borrowing was in the form of long-term concessional bilateral and multilateral lending. In the 1990s, however, short-term commercial lending was resorted to. In a matter of nine years, commercial debt has risen from less than US $100m. to US $6,250m. (or 18.4% of the total debt stock of US $34,000m. in June 1999). Most of the foreign aid comes from the Pakistan Development Forum, previously known as the Aid to Pakistan Consortium, which is composed of a number of Western countries and multilateral agencies such as the World Bank and its affiliates and the ADB. Other substantial donors are Saudi Arabia and the other Gulf states. The USA has been in the past, for political reasons, the largest single donor to Pakistan, but the relationship between the two countries in recent years has been overshadowed by disputes over Pakistan's nuclear programme and the overthrow of a democratically elected Government. In October 1990 the USA suspended all new commitments of aid to Pakistan for this reason, but in January 1996 the embargo was lifted as a result of Pakistan's persistent lobbying in the US Congress. In the 1990s Japan emerged as the largest bilateral donor to Pakistan, but this situation was also expected to change as Japan was one of the first countries to impose sanctions on Pakistan after the nuclear detonations.

According to the State Bank of Pakistan, Pakistan's total sovereign external debt and liabilities had reached US $38,000m. in December 2001 (of which US $33,000m. was external debt and US $5,000m. was foreign-exchange liabilities). External debt comprised of public and publicly guaranteed debt (US $28,900m.), private loans and credit (US $2,300m.) and IMF loans (US $1,900m.). In the same month the 'Paris Club' agreed to restructure Pakistan's entire bilateral debt stock of more than US $12,500m. A repayment period of 38 years was granted, with a grace period of 15 years for official development assistance (ODA) loans and five years for non-ODA loans. The agreement was expected to save the country US $2,700m.–$2,900m. in 2001–04. In November 2001 the ADB announced a $350m. loan in support of Pakistan's judicial reform programme. Moreover, in December the IMF agreed to extend a US $1,320m. Poverty Reduction and Growth Facility (PRGF) to Pakistan, in support of a three-year social and economic reform programme to be implemented during October 2001–September 2004. The core of the reform programme was outlined in an Interim Poverty Reduction Strategy Paper (I-PRSP) and Memorandum of Economic and Financial Policies (MEFP), published by the Pakistani authorities in November 2001 as a draft document (to provoke debate and amendment) to be consolidated by the new government arising from parliamentary elections scheduled for October 2002. The crucial objectives identified by the I-PRSP were increased potential for economic growth, improved social provisions and reduced vulnerability to external factors. While the broad fiscal strategy was based on development of the successes achieved under the November 2000 stand-by agreement (with tax revenues projected to increase annually by 1.5% of GDP, over three years, to reach 14.3% of GDP in 2003/04), structural reform was concentrated in further improvements in governance through devolution of public service delivery, civil service reform, judicial reform and greater fiscal transparency. Privatization of the banking, energy and telecommunications sectors was to be reactivated. Poverty was also to be addressed directly through reorientation of public expenditure, increased support for rural development, job creation and social contingency programmes; development expenditure under the Public Sector Development Programme (PSDP) was projected to increase from 2.7% to 3.9% of GDP during 2001–2004. Medium-term projections arising from the I-PRSP include a gradual increase in GDP growth (fuelled by gains in productivity and increased private investment) to 5.2% in 2003/04, a stable annual rate of inflation of 5.0% and a reduction in the fiscal deficit to 3.2% of GDP by the end of the programme. The total annual saving as a result of the debt-rescheduling agreements was expected to increase, owing to the appreciation of the rupee in 2001/02, to Rs 65,000m.

Direct foreign investment has been low, despite recent government efforts to encourage it. The UK is the single largest foreign investor in Pakistan. While Japan has emerged as the most important source of technology and supplier of components and consumer goods, Japanese firms have been reluctant to make more than token equity investments. The first Government of Nawaz Sharif made major changes in the rules covering foreign investment in 1991. The obstacles to an increase in foreign investment derive as much, however, from world-wide perceptions of the general weakness of the economy and the political system in Pakistan, and there is unlikely to be a dramatic increase in the immediate future, whatever the policies are regarding investment.

PROSPECTS FOR THE FUTURE

Pakistan's key economic problems at the turn of the century can be located in four broad areas: the fiscal crisis of the State, declining productivity of investments, lack of human capital development, and the confidence crisis created in the wake of Pakistan's persistent political instability. The fiscal crisis of the State, in turn, has four different dimensions to it. The first is the inability of the State to collect revenues and expand the tax net. In spite of the implementation of a massive amount of new indirect taxation over several years, the Government has been unable to improve the tax–GDP ratio, which remains frozen at 11.5%–12.0% of GDP. One important reason for this is that the direct tax base is extremely narrow. As a result, much of the new taxation has been imposed on the same groups whose ability to pay has been stretched to the limit. This has also increased tax evasion. Two groups of potential tax payers remain outside the taxation net—the agriculturists and traders. Estimates show that the potential revenue impact of an agricultural tax is somewhere in the range of Rs 4,000m.–5,000m. Unless and until this source is tapped, not only will the fiscal crisis continue, but the perception of economic injustice inherent in this act of omission on the part of the State will remain a political issue in urban constituencies. The military Government embarked on an ambitious plan to document the economy, primarily with the purpose to bring traders and smugglers into the general sales tax (GST) and income tax net. The Government had to withdraw from the campaign against smugglers and agreed that, until their existing inventories were sold, they would not be held liable for payment of any form of tax. Documentation of wholesale and retail traders also resulted in country-wide strikes which disrupted economic activity in May and June 2000. It was eventually decided that the traders would not declare their inventory and, instead of a sales tax, those traders with an annual turnover of less than Rs 1m. would pay a turnover tax at 1% of their sales. The GST was extended to the retail sector in mid-2001. However, tax revenue collected in 2000/01 was roughly 15% lower than the projected figures. The trend of the previous five years continued in 2001/02. This shows that there have not been substantial recoveries as a result of the documentation campaign.

The second component of the fiscal crisis is the inability to reduce current expenditure. The dilemma, however, is that the expenditure profile of the federal Government is such that about 80% of its current expenditure is fixed, with 27% devoted to defence and another 50% going to debt-servicing. Most of the reduction in the budget deficit has, therefore, been as a result of reductions in public investment. This, in turn, has had a severe impact on economic growth. The major problem on the expenditure side is the rapid growth in debt-servicing payments. Whereas growth in other areas of expenditure (including defence) has remained virtually stagnant (in real terms) in the recent past, debt servicing has increased at a rate of 9.5% per year. The reprieve afforded successive debt rescheduling provides a temporary respite. However, an agreement with the IMF and the resultant debt reschedule with the 'Paris Club' will benefit the economy for more than 30 years. The 2002/03 budget was the first budget prepared in accordance with the macro-economic framework agreed under the PRGF. Expenditure was projected to decrease for the first time in Pakistan's history, owing to the ongoing decentralization of fiscal responsibilities and resources to lower levels of government, a decline in defence expenditure and the absence of one-time expenditures incurred during 2001/02. The underlying structural problems of investor confidence, restructuring of the manufacturing sector and the country's export profile, however, are not being addressed successfully by existing government policies.

Another fiscal problem still facing the State is the growing inability of different public-sector corporations to finance each other's debt. Total inter-governmental debt has increased by Rs 100,000m. in the last few years. The only solution to this problem is that governance within the public sector is improved. The Government has proved singularly incapable of achieving this over the last decade and appears unlikely to do so in the near future.

Yet another important symptom of the fiscal crisis in Pakistan is the private-sector default to nationalized commercial banks (NCBs). Although this phenomenon first appeared in the 1980s when the martial law regime used NCBs as clearing houses for political patronage, it continued unabated through the 1990s. This is best illustrated by the fact that whereas total bad debt in 1985 was Rs 23,440m., it had increased to an astronomical Rs 240,000m. by the end of December 1999. The military Government's campaign to increase accountability had resulted in the recovery of an estimated Rs 11,000m. of this debt by mid-2000. However, recent government and independent reports show that, despite efforts by the military Government, the amount of defaulted debt had increased by July 2002. The task of recovering bad debt was onerous, as it was exceedingly difficult to differentiate wilful default from that which occurred as a result of genuine business failures. On occasions, where wilful default was established, the value of domestic assets of those defaulters proved to be much less than the amount on which they had defaulted. The negative impact of the accountability drive was that banks became even more cautious in their lending policies, while borrowers feared being criminally charged even if projects failed as a result of genuine business-related conditions.

The second facet of Pakistan's economic tribulations is slackening productivity of capital. With the same investment-GDP ratio over the last two decades, the 1990s have seen the growth rate of GDP decelerate considerably. In the 1990s, however, the profile of investment has changed considerably. In the 1980s gross investment was dominated by the public sector, whereas in the 1990s private-sector investment has been increasing at the expense of public investment. As public investment is mainly in infrastructure, it appears that the problem is located in inadequate provision of infrastructure, which, in turn, 'crowds-in' productive private-sector investment. Because of this lack of complementary investment and because of high interest rates, private-sector funds available for investment are being increasingly channelled into short-term, high return investments and capital flight. This imbalance in the allocation of investment resources will have to be righted if productivity of scarce capital in the country is to be improved.

Another area that requires pressing attention is that of human capital formation. By all the usual criteria of literacy and availability of health services, Pakistan is substantially inferior to other countries with similar income levels. For example, according to the UN Development Programme's *Human Development Report 2002,* its adult literacy rate was only about 43.2% in 2000. The relative position of women in society is similarly much less favourable; literacy among rural women was estimated at only 18% in 2000. Some recent policy developments in this area, which initially appeared promising, have proved disappointing. The first phase of a major Social Action Programme (SAP) was launched in 1993, which was to concentrate on population control, primary education, rural health care and rural water and sanitation. A second phase was introduced in 1997. The marginal improvements in related social indicators do not appear to justify the more than Rs 150,000m. that has been spent on the SAP since 1993. Spending on poverty alleviation and social improvement projects under the PSDP (see above) was to increase from 3.4% to 4% of GDP during 2001–04.

The recent economic crisis has exposed the structural weaknesses of the Pakistani economy. The liquidity crisis has been resolved through the collective assistance of the IMF and the 'Paris Club', but the loss of confidence among both resident and non-resident Pakistanis as well as foreign investors, engendered as a result of the 'freeze' on FCAs, will take a long time to be redressed. So long as confidence in the guarantees of the Pakistani sovereign is not restored, not only is investment expected to decline sharply and thereby growth also, but macro-economic imbalances will remain or deepen, despite attempts by the 2002/03 budget to consolidate macro-economic stabilization.

To address the above problems, which are indeed formidable, requires innovative political and economic strategies. There is no doubt that whatever measures are undertaken to redress the situation, they will be accompanied by some difficult restructuring. In a country with a poor distributional profile and rising poverty, care has to be taken to minimize the burden of adjustment on the poor and disadvantaged. If this is not done, the social dislocations it will create may lead to a major political upheaval. Much will also depend on conditions in the global economy, which itself is going through a crisis; but if the internal problems are resolved, the Pakistani economy will be in a more resilient position to withstand exogenous disruptions. Pakistan's attempt to break from its isolationist and militant foreign policy by supporting the USA following terrorist attacks in September 2001 have led to the USA's removal of economic sanctions imposed on Pakistan after its nuclear tests. In addition, debt owed to the USA has been rescheduled. However, the long-term effects of the US-led retaliatory attacks against the Taliban in neighbouring Afghanistan could be devastating. Foreign investment has already decreased; export targets were not achieved. Optimistic export and growth targets for 2002/03 depend on internal and external factors, particularly the outcome of general election, scheduled for 10 October 2002. The relationship between the military and the newly elected government will be of immense importance and will determine the economic, political and social structure of Pakistan.

Statistical Survey

Source (unless otherwise stated): Development Advisory Centre, Karachi; tel. (21) 2631587; e-mail arsidiqi@fascom.com.

Area and Population

AREA, POPULATION AND DENSITY*

Area (sq km)	796,095†
Population (census results)	
1 March 1981	84,253,644
2 March 1998	
Males	67,840,137
Females	62,739,434
Total	130,579,571
Population (official estimates at mid-year)	
1999	134,510,000
2000	137,510,000
2001	140,470,000
Density (per sq km) at mid-2001	176.4

* Excluding data for the disputed territory of Jammu and Kashmir. The Pakistani-held parts of this region are known as Azad ('Free') Kashmir, with an area of 11,639 sq km (4,494 sq miles) and a population of 1,980,000 in 1981, and Northern Areas (including Gilgit and Baltistan), with an area of 72,520 sq km (28,000 sq miles) and a population of 562,000 in 1981. Also excluded are Junagardh and Manavadar. The population figures exclude refugees from Afghanistan (estimated to number more than 2m. in early 2002).

† 307,374 sq miles.

ADMINISTRATIVE DIVISIONS (population at 1998 census)

	Area (sq km)	Population (provisional)	Density (per sq km)
Provinces:			
Balochistan	347,190	6,510,000	18.8
North-West Frontier Province	74,521	17,555,000	235.6
Punjab	205,344	72,585,000	353.5
Sindh	140,914	29,991,000	212.8
Federally Administered Tribal Area	27,220	3,138,000	115.3
Federal Capital Territory: Islamabad	906	799,000	881.9
Total	796,095	130,578,000	164.0

Source: Ministry of Finance and Economic Affairs.

PRINCIPAL CITIES (population at 1998 census)

Karachi	9,269,265	Quetta	560,307
Lahore	5,063,499	Islamabad (capital)	524,500
Faisalabad (Lyallpur)	1,977,246	Sargodha	455,360
Rawalpindi	1,406,214	Sialkot	417,597
Multan	1,182,441	Bahawalpur	403,408
Hyderabad	1,151,274	Sukkur	329,176
Gujranwala	1,124,749	Jhang	292,214
Peshawar	988,005		

Source: UN, *Demographic Yearbook*.

BIRTHS AND DEATHS (UN estimates, annual averages)

	1985–90	1990–95	1995–2000
Birth rate (per 1,000)	41.5	39.9	37.9
Death rate (per 1,000)	13.3	12.0	10.8

Source: UN, *World Population Prospects: The 2000 Revision*.

Expectation of life (WHO estimates, years at birth, 2000): Males 60.1; Females 60.7 (Source: WHO, *World Health Report*).

Health and Welfare

KEY INDICATORS

Fertility (births per woman, 2000)	5.3
Under-5 mortality rate (per 1,000 live births, 2000)	110
HIV/AIDS (% of persons aged 15–49, 2001)	0.11
Physicians (per 1,000 head, 1997)	0.57
Hospital beds (per 1,000 head, 1993)	0.65
Health expenditure (1998): US $ per head (PPP)	67
% of GDP	4.0
public (% of total)	23.6
Access to water (% of persons, 1999)	88
Access to sanitation (% of persons, 1999)	61
Human Development Index (2000): ranking	138
value	0.499

For sources and definitions, see explanatory note on p. vi.

ECONOMICALLY ACTIVE POPULATION
(ISIC Major Divisions, '000 persons aged 10 years and over, excl. armed forces)*

	1999	2000	2001
Agriculture	17,570	17,780	18,160
Mining and manufacturing	3,780	4,240	4,330
Construction	2,330	2,120	2,170
Electricity and gas distribution	260	260	260
Transport	2,040	1,850	1,890
Trade	5,160	4,960	5,060
Total employed (incl. others)	37,190	36,720	37,500
Unemployed	2,330	3,120	3,190
Total labour force	39,520	39,840	40,690

* Excluding data for Jammu and Kashmir, Gilgit and Baltistan, Junagardh and Manavadar.

Source: *Economic Survey, 2001/02*, Government of Pakistan.

Agriculture

PRINCIPAL CROPS ('000 metric tons)

	1998	1999	2000
Wheat	18,694	17,856	21,079
Rice (paddy)	7,011	7,733	7,205
Barley	174	137	118
Maize	1,665	1,652	1,643
Millet	213	156	199
Sorghum	228	220	229
Potatoes	1,426	1,810	1,868
Other roots and tubers*	419	429	429
Sugar cane	53,104	55,191	46,333
Dry beans	116	91	95
Dry peas	82	93	78
Chick-peas	767	698	565
Other pulses	198	179	162
Nuts*	73	74	74
Groundnuts (in shell)	104	99	94
Sunflower seed	130	149	150
Rapeseed	292	279	290
Cottonseed	2,990	3,824	3,659†
Other oil-bearing crops*	75	77	90
Cabbages	60	62	62
Spinach	81	80	74
Tomatoes	325	332	283
Cauliflower	194	198	197
Pumpkins, squash and gourds*	240	245	245
Aubergines (Eggplants)*	76	76	76
Dry onions	1,077	1,138	1,648
Garlic	80	83	76
Green peas	72	72	71
Carrots	199	195	186
Okra*	109	109	109
Other vegetables*	1,134	1,135	1,131
Watermelons*	420	420	420
Cantaloupes and other melons*	400	400	400
Bananas	95	125	138
Oranges†	1,303	1,360	1,109
Tangerines, mandarins, clementines and satsumas†	484	505	412
Lemons and limes†	75	78	63
Apples	589	577	577*
Apricots	191	192	192*
Peaches and nectarines	48	53	53*
Plums	81	81*	81*
Grapes	76	76	76*
Mangoes	917	927	938
Dates	722	580	580*
Other fruits*	911	938	960
Pimento and allspice	137	115	115*
Other spices*	43	45	45
Cotton (lint)	1,496	1,912	1,829
Tobacco (leaves)	99	109	108

* FAO estimate(s). † Unofficial figure(s).

Source: FAO.

LIVESTOCK ('000 head, year ending September)

	1998	1999	2000
Cattle	21,192	21,600	22,000
Buffaloes	21,422	22,000	22,700
Sheep	23,800	23,900	24,100
Goats	44,183	45,800	47,400
Horses	327	300	300
Asses	3,200	3,800	3,800
Mules	151	150	200
Camels	800	800	800
Chickens*	145,000	148,000	150,000
Ducks*	3,500	3,500	3,500

* FAO estimates.

Source: FAO.

LIVESTOCK PRODUCTS ('000 metric tons)

	1998	1999	2000
Beef and veal*	340	350	357
Buffalo meat*	513	525	540
Mutton and lamb*	181	185	190
Goat meat*	308	315	323
Poultry meat	289	315	327
Other meat†	16	16	16
Cows' milk	9,682	8,039	8,192
Buffaloes' milk	16,456	16,910	17,454
Sheep's milk	30	31	31†
Goats' milk	546	586	607
Ghee	438.6	450.7	465.1
Hen eggs*	269.6	323.5	331.5
Other poultry eggs†	6.9	7.1	7.2
Wool: greasy	38.5	38.7	38.9
scoured*	23.0	23.1	23.4
Cattle hides	50.4	51.6	52.8
Buffalo hides	77.4	78.8	81.0
Sheepskins	39.9	40.7	41.8
Goatskins	93.7	97.2	100.6

* Unofficial figures. † FAO estimate(s).

Source: FAO.

Forestry

ROUNDWOOD REMOVALS ('000 cubic metres, excl. bark)

	1997	1998	1999
Sawlogs, veneer logs and logs for sleepers	1,685	1,729	1,785
Other industrial wood	585	600	620
Fuel wood	29,870	29,515	30,670
Total	32,140	31,844	33,075

2000: Production as in 1999 (FAO estimates).

Source: FAO.

SAWNWOOD PRODUCTION ('000 cubic metres, incl. railway sleepers)

	1997	1998	1999
Coniferous (softwood)	400	400	410
Broadleaved (hardwood)	624	651	665
Total	1,024	1,051	1,075

2000: Production as in 1999 (FAO estimates).

Source: FAO.

Fishing

('000 metric tons, live weight)

	1997	1998	1999
Capture	589.7	597.0	654.5
Freshwater fishes	167.5	163.5	179.9
Sea catfishes	54.4	55.9	51.7
Croakers and drums	20.4	19.6	24.7
Mullets	18.9	17.6	12.3
Indian oil sardine	51.9	44.1	30.6
Requiem sharks	31.2	35.4	32.5
Penaeus shrimps	28.8	25.4	24.5
Aquaculture	15.5	17.4	20.1*
Cyprinids	15.4	17.3	20.0*
Total catch	605.2	614.5	674.6

* FAO estimate.

Source: FAO, *Yearbook of Fishery Statistics*.

Mining

(metric tons, unless otherwise indicated, year ending 30 June)

	1998/99	1999/2000*	2000/01*
Barytes	18,000	26,000	28,000
Chromite	18,000	26,000	16,000
Limestone	9,466,000	9,589,000	10,868,000
Gypsum	242,000	355,000	364,000
Fireclay	153,000	139,000	164,000
Silica sand	158,000	167,000	155,000
Rock salt	1,190,000	1,358,000	1,394,000
Coal and lignite	3,378,000	3,164,000	3,269,000
Crude petroleum ('000 barrels)	19,950	20,400	21,080
Natural gas (million cu m)	21,090	23,170	24,780

* Revised figures.

Sources: *Economic Survey, 2001/02*, Government of Pakistan.

Industry

SELECTED PRODUCTS

('000 metric tons, unless otherwise indicated, year ending 30 June)

	1998/99	1999/2000	2000/01
Cotton cloth (million sq m)	384.6	437.2	490.2
Cotton yarn	1,540.3	1,669.9	1,721.0
Jute textiles	85.5	85.5	89.4
Refined sugar	3,542	2,429.3	2,789.1
Vegetable ghee	842	698.1	834.8
Cement	9,635	9,314	9,674
Urea	3,521.7	3,785.0	4,005.1
Superphosphate	21.6	145.8	159.6
Sulphuric acid	27.0	57.7	57.1
Soda ash	239.4	245.7	217.9
Caustic soda	120.4	141.3	145.5
Chlorine gas	11.3	14.2	14.5
Cigarettes (million)	51,578	46,976	58,259
Petroleum products	10,926	11,878	7,333*
Beverages (million bottles)	2,220.2	2,332.3	2,541.6
Ammonium nitrate	338.8	386.5	374.4
Nitrophosphate	285.0	261.3	282.5
Pig-iron	989.3	1,106.6	1,071.2
Billets	276.1	345.2	414.7
Paperboard	173.6	228.1	306.9
Tractors ('000)	25.6	35.0	32.4
Bicycles ('000)	504.0	534.1	569.6
Motor tyres ('000)	845	856	884
Bicycle tyres ('000)	3,665	3,766	4,051
Sewing machines ('000)	29.7	27.6	26.9
Electric energy (million kWh)	65,404	65,751	68,117

* Provisional figure.

Sources: *Economic Survey, 2001/02*, Government of Pakistan; State Bank of Pakistan; Asian Development Bank, *Key Indicators of Developing Asian and Pacific Countries*.

Finance

CURRENCY AND EXCHANGE RATES

Monetary Units

100 paisa = 1 Pakistani rupee.

Sterling, Dollar and Euro Equivalents (31 May 2002)

£1 sterling = 88.25 rupees;
US $1 = 60.17 rupees;
€1 = 56.48 rupees;
1,000 Pakistani rupees = £11.33 = $16.62 = €17.71.

Average Exchange Rate (Pakistani rupees per US $)

1999 49.118
2000 53.648
2001 61.927

Note: Data relating to exchange rates prior to May 1999 refer to the rate set by the State Bank of Pakistan (the buying rate until July 1998). Since May 1999 the figures refer to the rate determined in the interbank foreign exchange market.

CENTRAL GOVERNMENT BUDGET

(million rupees, year ending 30 June)

Revenue	2000/01*	2001/02*	2002/03†
Tax revenue	406,500	414,200	460,600
Income and corporate taxes‡	125,751	142,000	143,200
Taxes on property	1,812	400	—
Other direct taxes	6,337	4,100	5,200
Excise duty	52,200	47,100	50,000
Sales tax‡	155,800	170,100	205,700
Taxes on international trade	64,600	50,500	56,500
Non-tax revenue	118,450	164,697	153,793
Surcharges‡	33,000	53,902	60,500
Total	557,950	632,799	674,893

Expenditure	2000/01*	2001/02*	2002/03†
Current expenditure	579,682	648,589	607,958
Defence‡	131,637	151,669	146,022
Debt-servicing	308,103	320,114	289,695
Current subsidies	22,706	25,580	607,958
General administration	49,743	51,186	54,928
Social services	10,390	12,289	13,869
Development expenditure	102,432	124,700	134,000
Total	682,114	773,289	741,958

* Revised estimates.
† Projected estimates.
‡ Exclusively federal.

Source: Ministry of Finance, Economic Affairs and Statistics, Islamabad.

PLANNED DEVELOPMENT EXPENDITURE

(million rupees, year ending 30 June)

	1999/2000*	2000/01†	2001/02†
Sectoral programme:			
Agriculture (incl. subsidy for fertilizers)	329.1	329.2	665.2
Water	11,298.9	10,077.9	8,957.7
Power	2,963.0	2,682.5	
Industry	260.1	692.3	364.0
Fuels	1,170.0	2,238.7	—
Minerals	38.0	8.1	—
Transport and communication	3,188.2	4,057.1	754.3
Physical planning and housing	13,274.7	1,748.5	221.4
Science and technology and education and training	7,129.2	4,064.6	4,343.3
Social welfare, culture, tourism, sport and manpower and employment	457.8	263.6	381.5
Health	2,566.4	2,841.4	2,547.5
Population planning	2,200.0	2,200.0	1,800.0
Rural development	117.2	2,419.8	—
Mass media	126.0	126.9	207.3
Special programmes	3,500.0	—	20,170.0
Corporation	—	—	26,678.3
Provincial Development Programme	—	—	30,000.0
Provincial Social Action Programme Tied Allocation	—	—	11,000.0
Total planned development expenditure (incl. others)	116,296.6	120,432.5	130,000.0

* Revised estimates. † Provisional figures.

Source: Ministry of Finance, Economic Affairs and Statistics, Islamabad.

INTERNATIONAL RESERVES (US $ million, last Thursday of the year)

	1999	2000	2001
Gold*	543	543	595
IMF special drawing rights	n.a.	14	4
Foreign exchange	1,511	1,499	3,636
Total	2,054	2,056	4,235

* Revalued annually, in June, on the basis of London market prices.

Source: IMF, *International Financial Statistics*.

MONEY SUPPLY (million rupees, last Thursday of the year)

	1999	2000	2001
Currency outside banks	341,024	410,469	429,360
Demand deposits at scheduled banks	447,919	457,773	524,429
Total money*	795,370	876,014	964,921

* Including also private-sector deposits at the State Bank.

Source: IMF, *International Financial Statistics*.

COST OF LIVING (Consumer Price Index; base: 1990/91 = 100; year ending 30 June)

	1998/99	1999/2000	2000/01*
Food, beverages and tobacco	225.6	230.2	239.5
Clothing and footwear	200.4	211.3	216.7
Rent	217.1	216.5	223.0
Fuel and lighting	226.9	225.5	252.7
All items (incl. others)	215.7	223.4	233.0

* Provisional figures.

Source: *Economic Survey, 2000/01*, Government of Pakistan.

NATIONAL ACCOUNTS

(million rupees at current prices, year ending 30 June)

National Income and Product

	1995/96	1996/97	1997/98
Domestic factor incomes*	1,813,222	2,045,127	2,354,018
Consumption of fixed capital	138,338	156,801	179,262
Gross domestic product at factor cost	1,951,560	2,201,928	2,533,280
Indirect taxes	227,858	215,636	239,519
Less Subsidies	13,820	12,931	13,274
GDP in purchasers' values	2,165,598	2,404,633	2,759,525
Net factor income from abroad	-7,136	-19,127	-15,081
Gross national product (GNP)	2,158,462	2,385,506	2,744,444
Less Consumption of fixed capital	138,338	156,801	179,262
National income in market prices	2,020,124	2,228,705	2,565,182

* Compensation of employees and the operating surplus of enterprises. The amount is obtained as a residual.

Source: UN, *National Accounts Statistics*.

Expenditure on the Gross Domestic Product

	1999/2000	2000/01*	2001/02†
Government final consumption expenditure	351,624	350,376	425,902
Private final consumption expenditure	2,342,417	2,567,321	2,793,408
Increase in stocks	51,700	56,200	58,000
Gross fixed capital formation	452,280	488,180	459,457
Total domestic expenditure	3,198,021	3,462,077	3,736,767
Exports of goods and services	514,389	615,371	661,024
Less Imports of goods and services	565,243	661,196	671,180
GDP in purchasers' values	3,147,167	3,416,252	3,726,611
Net factor income from abroad	-44,906	-50,830	25,901
GNP in purchasers' values	3,102,261	3,365,422	3,752,512

* Revised figures. † Provisional figures.

Source: *Economic Survey, 2001/02*, Government of Pakistan.

Gross Domestic Product by Economic Activity

	1999/2000	2000/01*	2001/02†
Agriculture and livestock	755,348	761,979	800,563
Forestry and fishing	24,344	27,042	28,835
Mining and quarrying	17,393	20,856	22,803
Manufacturing	447,395	499,085	537,035
Electricity and gas distribution	114,064	105,244	106,614
Construction	97,517	100,164	103,157
Commerce	443,934	488,586	511,819
Transport, storage and communications	311,630	357,644	393,799
Banking and insurance	60,255	96,467	102,814
Ownership of dwellings	135,518	146,861	162,946
Public administration and defence	249,832	263,505	321,090
Other services	264,758	294,490	336,843
GDP at factor cost	2,921,988	3,161,923	3,428,318
Indirect taxes, *less* subsidies	225,179	254,329	298,293
GDP in purchasers' values	3,147,167	3,416,252	3,726,611

* Revised figures. † Provisional figures.

Source: *Economic Survey, 2001/02*, Government of Pakistan.

BALANCE OF PAYMENTS (US $ million)

	1998	1999	2000
Exports of goods f.o.b.	7,850	7,673	8,739
Imports of goods f.o.b.	-9,834	-9,520	-9,898
Trade balance	-1,984	-1,847	-1,159
Exports of services	1,404	1,373	1,380
Imports of services	-2,261	-2,146	-2,252
Balance on goods and services	-2,841	-2,620	-2,031
Other income received	83	119	118
Other income paid	-2,263	-1,959	-2,333
Balance on goods, services and income	-5,021	-4,460	-4,246
Current transfers received	2,801	3,582	4,188
Current transfers paid	-28	-42	-38
Current balance	-2,248	-920	-96
Direct investment abroad	-50	-21	-11
Direct investment from abroad	506	532	308
Portfolio investment liabilities	-57	46	-451
Other investment assets	44	-523	-437
Other investment liabilities	-2,316	-2,398	-2,514
Net errors and omissions	1,011	768	577
Overall balance	-3,110	-2,516	-2,624

Source: IMF, *International Financial Statistics*.

OFFICIAL DEVELOPMENT ASSISTANCE (US $ million)

	1996	1997	1998
Bilateral donors	274.3	66.2	528.0
Multilateral donors	609.4	527.7	521.8
Total	883.7	593.9	1,049.8
Grants	355.9	301.6	293.4
Loans	527.8	292.3	756.4
Per caput assistance (US $)	7.0	4.6	8.0

Source: UN, *Statistical Yearbook for Asia and the Pacific*.

External Trade

Note: Data exclude trade in military goods.

PRINCIPAL COMMODITIES (US $ million, year ending 30 June)

Imports c.i.f. (excl. re-imports)	1997/98	1998/99	1999/2000
Food and live animals	1,226.6	897.7	804.4
Wheat and meslin (unmilled)	709.0	407.0	283.5
Tea and maté	226.7	222.9	210.4
Crude materials (inedible) except fuels	555.5	655.7	719.0
Cotton	76.3	230.9	182.3
Mineral fuels, lubricants, etc.	1,775.2	1,500.8	2,873.1
Petroleum, petroleum products, etc.	1,572.1	1,463.5	2,804.4
Animal and vegetable oils, fats and waxes	844.1	912.9	503.2
Fixed vegetable fats and oils	779.3	837.4	436.1
Chemicals and related products	1,791.5	1,812.0	1,997.2
Organic chemicals	540.8	468.5	593.9
Medicinal and pharmaceutical products	248.9	263.8	259.4
Manufactured fertilizers	208.0	265.1	197.6
Basic manufactures	914.6	844.0	855.7
Iron and steel	320.6	292.8	304.5
Machinery and transport equipment	2,401.8	2,198.0	1,997.7
Power-generating machinery and equipment	462.4	235.1	141.7
Machinery specialized for particular industries	627.3	651.2	595.3
General industrial machinery, equipment and parts	229.7	346.8	224.7
Electrical machinery, apparatus, etc.	439.5	301.4	296.5
Road vehicles and parts (excl. tyres, engines and electrical parts)	350.6	312.4	345.5
Other transport equipment	132.5	232.3	218.6
Miscellaneous manufactured articles	245.9	238.8	263.1
Total (incl. others)	10,116.4	9,431.7	10,309.4

Exports f.o.b. (excl. re-exports)	1997/98	1998/99	1999/2000
Food and live animals	990.4	1,076.0	919.8
Rice	562.4	533.6	539.7
Sugar and honey	128.4	276.1	61.0
Crude materials (inedible) except fuels	275.0	126.6	210.9
Basic manufactures	4,779.4	4,172.2	4,628.5
Leather, leather manufactures and dressed furskins	217.3	181.9	183.8
Textile yarn, fabrics, etc.	4,502.6	3,944.7	4,383.7
Miscellaneous manufactured articles	2,438.1	2,230.8	2,550.7
Clothing and accessories (excl. footwear)	1,776.8	1,723.1	1,988.4
Total (incl. others)	8,626.7	7,779.3	8,568.6

2000/01 (US $ million, year ending 30 June): *Imports c.i.f. (excl. re-imports):* Wheat and meslin (unmilled) 15.4; Tea and maté 206.4; Sugar (incl. raw sugar) 393.3; Petroleum and petroleum products 3,360.8; Edible oils 327.6; Chemicals and related products 1,901.7 (Manufactured fertilizers 170.5; Medicinal and pharmaceutical products 238.7); Iron and steel 277.9; Machinery and transport equipment 2,066.2 (Power-generating machinery and equipment 197.9); Total (incl. others) 10,728.9. *Exports f.o.b. (excl. re-exports):* Rice 525.5; Cotton 139.3; Petroleum and petroleum products 183.9; Chemicals and related products 164.3; Leather and leather manufactures 658.4; Textile manufactures 5,755.6 (Cotton yarn 1,073.5; Woven cotton fabrics 1,032.5); Total (incl. others) 9,201.6.

2001/02 (US $ million, year ending 30 June): *Imports c.i.f. (excl. re-imports):* Wheat and meslin (unmilled) 50.0; Tea and mate 156.6; Sugar 23.5; Petroleum and petroleum products 2,807.0; Edible oils 393.0; Chemicals and related products 1,869.4 (Manufactured fertilizers 176.2; Medicinal and pharmaceutical products 228.1); Iron and steel 336.1; Machinery and transport equipment 2,207.5 (Power-generating machinery and equipment 203.8); Total (incl. others) 10,339.5. *Exports f.o.b. (excl. re-exports):* Rice 448.2; Cotton 24.7; Petroleum and petroleum products 190.7; Chemicals and related products 152.8; Leather and leather manufactures 623.1; Textile manufactures 5,778.1 (Cotton yarn 929.7; Woven cotton fabrics 1,130.8); Total (incl. others) 9,134.5.

Source: State Bank of Pakistan, *Annual Report*.

PRINCIPAL TRADING PARTNERS
(US $ million, year ending 30 June)

Imports c.i.f. (excl. re-imports)	1997/98	1998/99	1999/2000
Australia	413.3	285.8	366.7
Bahrain	111.5	78.4	114.6
Belgium	111.5	136.9	121.4
Canada	127.0	66.2	77.8
China, People's Republic	515.6	395.3	471.6
France	188.0	179.7	224.8
Germany	523.3	391.8	423.3
India	153.4	145.6	127.4
Indonesia	195.0	213.8	175.6
Iran	158.7	77.8	130.2
Italy	237.4	260.1	171.2
Japan	793.3	782.7	650.5
Korea, Republic	361.7	342.6	354.2
Kuwait	554.1	558.3	1,236.8
Malaysia	705.8	634.5	439.3
Netherlands	135.7	150.0	152.9
Saudi Arabia	681.3	643.0	923.0
Singapore	216.6	325.5	267.1
Switzerland	313.7	362.8	350.6
Thailand	136.2	155.5	159.4
Turkey	42.1	131.9	106.6
United Arab Emirates*	670.6	634.6	907.6
United Kingdom	410.2	410.8	355.7
USA	1,136.7	726.8	646.5
Total (incl. others)	10,118.0	9,431.7	10,309.4

* Abu Dhabi and Dubai only.

Exports f.o.b. (excl. re-exports)	1997/98	1998/99	1999/2000
Afghanistan	30.9	48.2	115.2
Australia	122.9	106.5	111.9
Bangladesh	97.9	119.4	120.4
Belgium	235.8	186.9	202.2
Canada	165.8	158.5	183.7
China, People's Republic	160.3	148.9	180.3
France	248.5	248.0	282.7
Germany	539.3	513.6	512.6
Hong Kong	611.6	549.6	524.9
Indonesia	143.9	174.8	52.9
Italy	232.3	206.5	209.3
Japan	363.1	271.3	267.5
Korea, Republic	171.5	192.3	245.4
Netherlands	272.0	243.0	229.1
Saudi Arabia	216.1	184.7	214.8
Spain	184.0	146.6	150.3
Sri Lanka	100.5	91.9	96.6
United Arab Emirates*	438.8	422.8	492.7
United Kingdom	591.9	516.0	579.5
USA	1,772.0	1,696.8	2,123.1
Total (incl. others)	8,626.7	7,779.3	8,568.6

2000/01 (US $ million, year ending 30 June): *Exports f.o.b. (excl. re-exports):* China, People's Republic 303.2; France 265.8; Germany 495.0; Hong Kong 504.5; Italy 230.3; Japan 193.6; Korea, Republic 278.4; Netherlands 233.2; Saudi Arabia 273.0; United Arab Emirates* 626.1; United Kingdom 576.0; USA 2,245.6; Total (incl. others) 9,201.6.

* Abu Dhabi and Dubai only.

Source: State Bank of Pakistan, *Annual Report*.

Transport

RAILWAYS (year ending 30 June)

	1998/99	1999/2000	2000/01
Passenger journeys ('000)	64,990	68,000	68,800
Freight ('000 metric tons)	5,450	4,770	5,900
Net freight ton-km (million)	4,330	3,612	4,520

Source: *Economic Survey, 2001/02*, Government of Pakistan.

ROAD TRAFFIC ('000 vehicles in use)

	1999	2000	2001
Motorcycles and scooters	1,976.9	2,113.0	2,140.5
Passenger cars	700.6	748.9	758.6
Jeeps	69.5	66.8	67.6
Station wagons	79.1	84.5	85.6
Road tractors	538.7	575.8	583.2
Buses	85.9	91.9	93.0
Taxicabs	67.9	72.6	73.5
Rickshaws	87.2	93.3	94.5
Delivery vans	172.1	184.0	186.4
Trucks	148.4	158.6	160.1
Total (incl. others)	4,016.6	4,277.8	4,332.5

Source: *Economic Survey, 2001/02*, Government of Pakistan.

SHIPPING

Merchant Fleet (displacement at 31 December)

	1999	2000	2001
Number of vessels	55	52	49
Total displacement ('000 grt)	308.0	260.3	247.4

Source: Lloyd's Register-Fairplay, *World Fleet Statistics*.

International Sea-borne Shipping
(port of Karachi, year ending 30 June)

	1998/99	1999/2000	2000/01
Goods ('000 long tons)			
Loaded	5,735	5,612	5,918
Unloaded	18,318	18,149	20,063

Source: State Bank of Pakistan, *Annual Report*.

CIVIL AVIATION
(PIA only, domestic and international flights, '000, year ending 30 June)

	1998/99	1999/2000	2000/01
Kilometres flown	70,697	76,155	54,830
Passengers carried	5,086	5,242	4,178
Passenger-km	10,722,000	11,650,000	9,739,000

Source: *Economic Survey, 2000/01*, Government of Pakistan.

Tourism

FOREIGN TOURIST ARRIVALS

Country of Nationality	1998	1999	2000
Afghanistan	20,275	25,586	27,913
Canada	10,931	11,429	12,956
China, People's Republic	10,747	7,957	6,191
Germany	12,988	12,778	14,121
India	67,050	63,225	66,061
Japan	17,479	16,589	12,794
United Kingdom	109,772	126,532	179,758
USA	49,795	48,488	71,518
Total (incl. others)	428,781	432,217	556,805

Receipts from tourism (US $ million): 98 in 1998; 76 in 1999; 86 (estimate) in 2000.

Source: World Tourism Organization, *Yearbook of Tourism Statistics*.

Communications Media

	1998	1999	2000
Television receivers ('000 in use)	12,500	16,000	18,500
Telephones ('000 main lines in use)	2,756.1	2,986.1	3,200.0
Mobile cellular telephones ('000 subscribers)	206.9	278.8	349.5
Facsimile machines ('000 in use)	268	n.a.	n.a.
Personal computers ('000 in use)	561	580	590
Internet users ('000)	61.9	80.0	133.9

Radio receivers ('000 in use): 13,500 in 1997 (Source: UNESCO, *Statistical Yearbook*).

Daily newspapers: 264 in 1996 (Source: UNESCO, *Statistical Yearbook*).

2001: Telephones ('000 main lines in use) 3,400; Mobile cellular telephones ('000 subscribers) 800; Personal computers ('000 in use) 600; Internet users ('000) 500.

Sources: *Economic Survey, 2000/01*, Government of Pakistan; International Telecommunication Union.

Education

(estimates, 2000/01)

	Institutions	Teachers	Students
Pre-primary and primary*	165,700	373,900	20,999,000
Middle	18,800	96,100	4,644,000
Secondary	12,800	224,000	1,932,000
Higher:			
Secondary vocational institutes	580	7,062	75,000
Arts and science colleges	853	26,942	791,000
Professional†	308	8,817	162,989
Universities	26	5,914	114,010

* Including mosque schools.

† Including educational colleges.

Source: *Economic Survey, 2000/01*, Government of Pakistan.

Adult literacy rate (UNESCO estimates): 43.2% (males 57.5%; females 27.9%) in 2000 (Source: UN Development Programme, *Human Development Report*).

Directory

The Constitution

The Constitution was promulgated on 10 April 1973, and amended on a number of subsequent occasions (see Amendments, below). Several provisions were suspended following the imposition of martial law in 1977. The (amended) Constitution was restored on 30 December 1985.

GENERAL PROVISIONS

The Preamble upholds the principles of democracy, freedom, equality, tolerance and social justice as enunciated by Islam. The rights of religious and other minorities are guaranteed.

The Islamic Republic of Pakistan consists of four provinces—Balochistan, North-West Frontier Province, Punjab and Sindh—and the tribal areas under federal administration. The provinces are autonomous units.

Fundamental rights are guaranteed and include equality of status (women have equal rights with men), freedom of thought, speech, worship and the press and freedom of assembly and association. No law providing for preventive detention shall be made except to deal with persons acting against the integrity, security or defence of Pakistan. No such law shall authorize the detention of a person for more than one month.

PRESIDENT

The President is Head of State and acts on the advice of the Prime Minister. He is elected by an electoral college, comprising the two chambers of the Federal Legislature and the four Provincial Assemblies, to serve for a term of five years. He must be a Muslim. The President may be impeached for violating the Constitution or gross misconduct.

FEDERAL LEGISLATURE

The Federal Legislature consists of the President, a lower and an upper house. The lower house, called the National Assembly, has 207 members elected directly for a term of five years, on the basis of universal suffrage (for adults over the age of 21 years), plus 10 members representing minorities. The upper house, called the Senate, has 87 members who serve for six years, with one-third retiring every two years. Each Provincial Assembly is to elect 19 Senators. The tribal areas are to return eight members and the remaining three are to be elected from the Federal Capital Territory by members of the Provincial Assemblies.

There shall be two sessions of the National Assembly and Senate each year, with not more than 120 days between the last sitting of a session and the first sitting of the next session.

The role of the Senate in an overwhelming majority of the subjects shall be merely advisory. Disagreeing with any legislation of the National Assembly, it shall have the right to send it back only once for reconsideration. In case of disagreement in other subjects, the Senate and National Assembly shall sit in a joint session to decide the matter by a simple majority.

GOVERNMENT

The Constitution provides that bills may originate in either house, except money bills. The latter must originate in the National Assembly and cannot go to the Senate. A bill must be passed by both houses and then approved by the President, who may return the bill and suggest amendments. In this case, after the bill has been reconsidered and passed, with or without amendment, the President must give his assent to it.

PROVINCIAL GOVERNMENT

In the matter of relations between Federation and Provinces, the Federal Legislature shall have the power to make laws, including laws bearing on extra-territorial affairs, for the whole or any part of Pakistan, while a Provincial Assembly shall be empowered to make laws for that Province or any part of it. Matters in the Federal Legislative List shall be subject to the exclusive authority of the Federal Legislature, while the Federal Legislature and a Provincial Assembly shall have power to legislate with regard to matters referred to in the Concurrent Legislative List. Any matter not referred to in either list may be subject to laws made by a Provincial Assembly alone, and not by the Federal Legislature, although the latter shall have exclusive power to legislate with regard to matters not referred to in either list for those areas in the Federation not included in any Province.

Four provisions seek to ensure the stability of the parliamentary system. First, the Prime Minister shall be elected by the National Assembly and he and the other Ministers shall be responsible to it. Secondly, any resolution calling for the removal of a Prime Minister shall have to name his successor in the same resolution which shall be adopted by not less than two-thirds of the total number of members of the lower house. The requirement of two-thirds majority is to remain in force for 15 years or three electoral terms, whichever is more. Thirdly, the Prime Minister shall have the right to seek dissolution of the legislature at any time even during the pendency of a no-confidence motion. Fourthly, if a no-confidence motion is defeated, such a motion shall not come up before the house for the next six months.

All these provisions for stability shall apply *mutatis mutandis* to the Provincial Assemblies also.

A National Economic Council, to include the Prime Minister and a representative from each province, shall advise the Provincial and Federal Governments.

There shall be a Governor for each Province, appointed by the President, and a Council of Ministers to aid and advise him, with a Chief Minister appointed by the Governor. Each Province has a provincial legislature consisting of the Governor and Provincial Assembly.

The executive authorities of every Province shall be required to ensure that their actions are in compliance with the Federal laws which apply in that Province. The Federation shall be required to consider the interests of each Province in the exercise of its authority in that Province. The Federation shall further be required to afford every Province protection from external aggression and internal disturbance, and to ensure that every Province is governed in accordance with the provisions of the Constitution.

To further safeguard the rights of the smaller provinces, a Council of Common Interests has been created. Comprising the Chief Ministers of the four provinces and four Central Ministers to decide upon specified matters of common interest, the Council is responsible to the Federal Legislature. The constitutional formula gives the net proceeds of excise duty and royalty on gas to the province concerned. The profits on hydroelectric power generated in each province shall go to that province.

OTHER PROVISIONS

Other provisions include the procedure for elections, the setting up of an Advisory Council of Islamic Ideology and an Islamic Research Institute, and the administration of tribal areas.

AMENDMENTS

Amendments to the Constitution shall require a two-thirds majority in the National Assembly and endorsement by a simple majority in the Senate.

In 1975 the Constitution (Third Amendment) Bill abolished the provision that a State of Emergency may not be extended beyond six months without the approval of the National Assembly and empowered the Government to detain a person for three months instead of one month.

In July 1977, following the imposition of martial law, several provisions, including all fundamental rights provided for in the Constitution, were suspended.

An amendment of September 1978 provided for separate electoral registers to be drawn up for Muslims and non-Muslims.

In October 1979 a martial law order inserted a clause in the Constitution establishing the supremacy of military courts in trying all offences, criminal and otherwise.

On 26 May 1980, the President issued a Constitution Amendment Order, which amended Article 199, debarring High Courts from making any order relating to the validity of effect of any judgment or sentence passed by a military court or tribunal granting an injunction; from making an order or entering any proceedings in respect of matters under the jurisdiction or cognizance of a military court or tribunal, and from initiating proceedings against the Chief Martial Law Administrator or a Martial Law Administrator.

By another amendment of the Constitution, the Federal Shari‘a Court was to replace the Shari‘a Benches of the High Courts. The Shari‘a Court, on the petition of a citizen or the Government, may decide whether any law or provision of law is contrary to the injunction of Islam as laid down in the Holy Koran and the Sunnah of the Holy Prophet.

In March 1981 the Government promulgated Provisional Constitution Order 1981, whereby provision is made for the appointment of one or more Vice-Presidents, to be appointed by the Chief Martial Law Administrator, and a Federal Advisory Council (*Majlis-i-Shura*) consisting of persons nominated by the President. All political parties not registered with the Election Commission on 13 September 1979 were to be dissolved and their properties made forfeit to the Federal Council. Any party working against the ideology, sovereignty or security of Pakistan may be dissolved by the President.

The proclamation of July 1977, imposing martial law, and subsequent orders amending the Constitution and further martial law regulations shall not be questioned by any court on any grounds.

All Chief Justices and Judges shall take a new oath of office. New High Court benches for the interior of the provinces shall be set up and retired judges are debarred from holding office in Pakistan for two years. The powers of the High Courts shall be limited for suspending the operation of an order for the detention of any person under any law provided for preventative detention, or release any person on bail, arrested under the same law.

The Advisory Council of Islamic Ideology, which was asked by the Government to suggest procedures for the election and further Islamization of the Constitution, recommended non-party elections, separate electorates, Islamic qualifications for candidates and a federal structure with greater devolution of power by changing the present divisions into provinces.

Under the Wafaqi Mohtasib Order 1982, the President appointed a Wafaqi Mohtasib (Federal Ombudsman) to redress injustice committed by any government agency.

In March 1985 the President, Gen. Zia ul-Haq, promulgated the Revival of the 1973 Constitution Order, which increased the power of the President by amendments such as those establishing a National Security Council, powers to dismiss the Prime Minister, the Cabinet and provincial Chief Ministers, to appoint judicial and military chiefs, and to call elections, and indemnity clauses to ensure the power of the President. The Constitution was then revived with the exception of 28 key provisions relating to treason, subversion, fundamental rights and jurisdiction of the Supreme Court. In October 1985 the Constitution (Eighth Amendment) Bill became law, incorporating most of the provisions of the Revival of the 1973 Constitution Order and indemnifying all actions of the military regime. In December the enactment of the Political Parties (Amendment) Bill allowed political parties to function under stringent conditions (these conditions were eased in 1988). In December Gen. Zia lifted martial law and restored the remainder of the Constitution.

In March 1987 the Constitution (Tenth Amendment) Bill reduced the minimum number of working days of the National Assembly from 160 days to 130 days.

In April 1997 the Constitution (Thirteenth Amendment) Bill repealed the main components of the Eighth Constitutional Amendment, thus divesting the President of the power to appoint and dismiss the Prime Minister and Cabinet, to dissolve the legislature, to order a national referendum, and to appoint provincial Governors, the Chairman of the Joint Chiefs of Staff and the three armed forces chiefs (these functions and appointments were, in future, to be carried out subject to a mandatory advice from the Prime Minister).

In October 1998 the Constitution (Fifteenth Amendment) Bill replaced the country's existing legal code with full Shari'a; the bill remained to be ratified by the Senate.

Note: Following the overthrow of the Government in a military coup on 12 October 1999, the Constitution was placed in abeyance on 15 October. On the same day a Provisional Constitution Order was promulgated, according to which executive power was transferred to a National Security Council, under the leadership of a Chief Executive. A federal Cabinet, which was to aid and advise the Chief Executive in the exercise of his functions, was to be appointed by the President on the advice of the Chief Executive. The President was to act on, and in accordance with, the advice of the Chief Executive. The National Assembly, Senate and the Provincial Assemblies were suspended and the Chairman and Deputy Chairman of the Senate ceased to hold office. Local elections were to be held nation-wide from December 2000. Under the reformed local government system, one-third of the seats would be reserved for women and 5% for religious minorities. The voting age would be lowered from 21 to 18. The publicly elected local councils would then select members of two higher councils in each district. The local elections were held between December 2000 and August 2001, on a non-party basis. In May 2000 the Chief Executive stated that he would comply with the Supreme Court's ruling that he should name a date, no later than 90 days before the expiry of the three-year period from 12 October 1999, for the holding of elections to the National Assembly, the Senate and provincial assemblies. In July 2000 the Chief Executive issued a decree to revive the Islamic principles of the suspended Constitution and to incorporate them in the Provisional Constitution Order. On 20 June 2001 the Proclamation of Emergency (Amendment) Order 2001 was promulgated, according to which the Chief Executive assumed the office of President of Pakistan. The National Assembly, Senate and Provincial Assemblies were dissolved with immediate effect. The Speaker and Deputy Speaker of the National Assembly and Provincial Assemblies ceased to hold office with immediate effect. The President later announced that elections to federal and provincial legislatures would be held on 10 October 2002 (see Recent History).

On 21 August 2002 the Legal Framework Order 2002 was promulgated, which sanctioned the President's 29 amendments to the Constitution, including the restoration of Article 58 (2-B), which authorized the President to dissolve the National Assembly (the article was also amended to allow the President to appoint provincial governors in consultation with the Prime Minister), the restoration of Article 243, which gave the President power to appoint the Chairman of the Joint Chiefs of Staff Committee and the three armed forces chiefs and the power to establish the National Security Council to provide consultation to the elected government on strategic matters. The President's term in office and role as Chief of Army Staff were to be extended for five years from the date of the election. Other amendments included the provision of constitutional protection to the offices of the National Accountability Bureau and the Governor of the State Bank of Pakistan, by placing them in 'Schedule Six'. Other provisions granted constitutional protection included the lowering of the voting age from 21 to 18, the Political Parties' Order and the autonomy of the Election Commission. The amendments would take effect from 12 October.

The Government

HEAD OF STATE

President: Gen. Pervez Musharraf (sworn in 20 June 2001).

NATIONAL SECURITY COUNCIL
(September 2002)

Chief Executive: Gen. Pervez Musharraf.

Ex-Officio Members:

Gen. Mohammad Aziz Khan
Gen. Mohammad Yusuf
Air Chief Marshal Mushaf Ali Mir
Adm. Abdul Aziz Mirza
Lt-Gen. (retd) Khalid Maqbool
Mian Mohammed Soomro
Lt-Gen. (retd) Iftikhar Hussain Shah
Justice (retd) Amir-ul-Mulk Mengal

CABINET
(September 2002)

Minister of Finance, Revenue, Economic Affairs and Statistics and of Planning and Development: Shaukat Aziz.

Minister of the Interior, Narcotics Division, Control and Capital Administration and Development Divisions: Lt-Gen. (retd) Moinuddin Haider.

Minister of Environment, Local Government and Rural Development: Shahida Jamil.

Minister of Labour, Manpower and Overseas Pakistanis: Owais Ghani.

Minister of Commerce, Industries and Production: Abdul Razzaq Daud.

Minister of Health, and of Women's Development, Social Welfare, Special Education and Population Welfare: Dr Abdul Malik Kasi.

Minister of Food, Agriculture, Co-operatives and Livestock: Khair Muhammad Junejo.

Minister of Petroleum and National Resources: Usman Aminuddin.

Minister of Culture, Sports, Minority Affairs and Youth: Col. (retd) S. K. Tressler.

Minister of Science and Technology, and of Education: Prof. Atta-ur-Rahman.

Minister of Communications and Railways, and of Housing and Works: Lt-Gen. (retd) Javed Ashraf.

Minister of Law, Justice, Human Rights and Parliamentary Affairs: Khalid Ranjhah.

Minister of Information and Media Development, and of Kashmir Affairs, Northern Areas and States and Frontier Region (SAFRON): Nisar A. Memon.

Minister of Religious Affairs, Zakat and Ushr: Owais Ahmed Ghani.

Minister of Privatization: Altaf M. Saleem.

Minister of State for Foreign Affairs: Inamul Haque.

Minister of State and Chairman of the National Kashmir Committee: Sardar MUHAMMAD ABDUL QAYYUM KHAN.

Minister of State and Chairman of the National Commission on Human Development: Dr NASIM ASHRAF.

Honorary Adviser to the Chief Executive for Foreign Affairs, Law, Justice and Human Rights: SYED SHARIFFUDIN PIRZADA.

Adviser to the Chief Executive for Food, Livestock and Agriculture: M. SHAFI NIAZ.

Chairman of the Federal Land Commission: IMTIAZ AHMAD SAHIBZADA.

Minister of State and Deputy Chairman of the Planning Commission: Dr SHAHID AMJAD CHAUDHRY.

MINISTRIES

Office of the President: Aiwan-e-Sadr, Islamabad; tel. (51) 9206060; fax (51) 9211018.

Office of the Chief Executive: Nishan-i-Imtiaz (Military), Tamgha-i-Basalat, Islamabad; tel. (51) 9202884; e-mail ce@pak.gov.pk.

Ministry of Commerce: Block A, Pakistan Secretariat, Islamabad; tel. (51) 9204548; fax (51) 9205241; e-mail mincom@meganet.com.pk.

Ministry of Communications: Block D, Pakistan Secretariat, Islamabad; tel. (51) 9210344; fax (51) 9217540; internet www.moc.gov.pk/moc.

Ministry of Culture, Sports, Tourism and Youth Affairs: Block D, Pakistan Secretariat, Islamabad; tel. (51) 9204556; fax (51) 9202347; internet www.heritage.gov.pk.

Ministry of Defence: Pakistan Secretariat, No. II, Rawalpindi 46000; tel. (51) 582980; fax (51) 580464.

Ministry of Education: Block D, Pakistan Secretariat, Islamabad; tel. (51) 9212020; fax (51) 9202851; e-mail pak@yahoo.com.

Ministry of Environment, Local Government and Rural Development: 8th Floor, UBL Bldg, Jinnah Avenue, Islamabad; tel. (51) 9224291; fax (51) 9202211; e-mail envir@isb.compol.com; internet www.environment.gov.pk.

Ministry of Finance, Economic Affairs and Statistics: Block Q, Pakistan Secretariat, Islamabad; tel. (51) 9203687; fax (51) 9213780; e-mail finance@isb.paknet.com.pk; internet www.finance.gov.pk.

Ministry of Food, Agriculture, Co-operatives and Livestock: Block B, Pakistan Secretariat, Islamabad; tel. (51) 9210088; fax (51) 9221246.

Ministry of Foreign Affairs: Constitution Ave, Islamabad; tel. (51) 9211942; fax (51) 9207217; e-mail pak.fm@usa.net; internet www.forisb.org.

Ministry of Health: Block C, Pakistan Secretariat, Islamabad; tel. (51) 9208139; fax (51) 9213933.

Ministry of Housing and Works: Constitution Ave, Islamabad; tel. (51) 9202952; internet www.pha.gov.pk.

Ministry of Human Rights: Pakistan Secretariat, Islamabad.

Ministry of Industries and Production: Block A, Pakistan Secretariat, Islamabad; tel. (51) 9210192; fax (51) 9206350; internet www.sec.gov.pk.

Ministry of the Interior and Narcotics Control: Block R, Pakistan Secretariat, Islamabad; tel. (51) 9212026; fax (51) 9202642.

Ministry of Kashmir Affairs and Northern Areas, States and Frontier Region (SAFRON), Housing and Works: Block R, Pakistan Secretariat, Islamabad; tel. (51) 9203022; fax (51) 9202494; e-mail safron@isb.perd.net.pk.

Ministry of Labour, Manpower and Overseas Pakistanis: Block B, Pakistan Secretariat, Islamabad; tel. (51) 9210077; fax (51) 9203462; internet www.labour.gov.pk.

Ministry of Law, Justice and Parliamentary Affairs: Block S&R, Pakistan Secretariat, Islamabad; tel. (51) 9212710; fax (51) 9215852; e-mail molaw1@comsats.net.pk.

Ministry of Petroleum and Natural Resources: 3rd Floor, Block A, Pakistan Secretariat, Islamabad; tel. (51) 9208233; fax (51) 9205437; e-mail info@mpnr.gov.pk; internet www.mpnr.gov.pk.

Ministry of Planning and Development: Block P, Pakistan Secretariat, Islamabad; tel. (51) 9202704; fax (51) 9202783.

Ministry of Railways: Block D, Pakistan Secretariat, Islamabad; tel. (51) 9208846; fax (51) 828846.

Ministry of Religious Affairs: Plot No. 20, Markaz Ramna-6, nr GPO, Islamabad; tel. (51) 9214856; fax (51) 821646; internet www.mra.gov.pk.

Ministry of Science and Technology: Block D, Pakistan Secretariat, Islamabad; tel. (51) 9208026; fax (51) 9202603; e-mail minister@most.gov.pk; internet www.most.gov.pk.

Ministry of Water and Power: Block A, 15th Floor, Shaheed-e-Millat, Pakistan Secretariat, Islamabad; tel. (51) 9212442; fax (51) 9203187.

Ministry of Women's Development, Social Welfare, Special Education and Population Welfare: State Building 5, Blue Area, China Chowk, Islamabad; tel. (51) 9224167; fax (51) 9203132; e-mail mowdswse@ibscomsate.net.pk.

Federal Legislature

SENATE

Normally, the Senate comprises 87 members, who are elected by the four provincial legislatures. Its term of office is six years, with one-third of the members relinquishing their seats every two years. Elections were scheduled for 12 November 2002.

NATIONAL ASSEMBLY

Normally, the 217-member National Assembly is elected for five years. It comprises 207 directly-elected Muslim members and an additional 10 seats reserved for Christians, Hindus and other minorities. In August 2002 the President announced that the size of the National Assembly would be increased to 342 seats, with 60 seats reserved for women and 10 for non-Muslims.

General Election, 10 October 2002

	Seats
Pakistan Muslim League (Quaid-e-Azam Group)	74
Pakistan People's Party Parliamentarians	63
Muttahida Majlis-e-Amal*	45
Pakistan Muslim League (Nawaz Group)	14
Muttahida Qaumi Movement	12
National Alliance†	13
Pakistan Muslim League (Functional Pir Pagara Group)	3
Pakistan Muslim League (Junejo Group)	2
Pakistan People's Party (Sherpao Group)	2
Balochistan National Party	1
Pakistan Tehrik-e-Insaf	1
Pakistan Muslim League (Ziaul Haq)	1
Jamhuri Watan Party	1
Pakistan Shia Political Party	1
Pakistan Awami Tehreek	1
Independents	28
Others and undeclared	10
Total‡	342

* Coalition comprising Jamaat-e-Islami Pakistan, Jamiat-e-Ulema-e-Pakistan, Jamiat-e-Ulema-Islam (S), Jamiat-e-Ulema-Islam (F), Islam Tehreek Pakistan and Jamiat-Ahl-e-Hadith.

† Coalition comprising the National People's Party, the Millat Party, the Sindh National Front, the Sindh Democratic Alliance and the National Awami Party.

‡ An election for 70 seats reserved for women and minorities, to be filled by proportional representation, according to party lists, was scheduled to take place by the end of October 2002.

Provinces

Pakistan comprises the four provinces of Sindh, Balochistan, Punjab and the North-West Frontier Province, plus the federal capital and 'tribal areas' under federal administration. Four new provincial governors were appointed by the new military administration on 22 October 1999. The new governors were to enjoy the functions and powers of a chief minister.

GOVERNORS

Balochistan: Justice (retd) AMIR-UL-MULK MENGAL.*

North-West Frontier Province: Lt-Gen. (retd) IFTIKHAR HUSSAIN SHAH.*

Punjab: Lt-Gen. (retd) KHALID MAQBOOL.*

Sindh: Mian MOHAMMED SOOMRO.*

* Member of the National Security Council.

CHIEF MINISTERS

Following the overthrow of the Government in a military coup on 12 October 1999, the four provincial legislatures were suspended on 15 October, and dissolved on 20 June 2001. Elections for the provincial legislatures were held on 10 October 2002.

Political Organizations

Some 62 parties, issued with election symbols by the Election Commission, were expected to contest the general election on 10 October 2002. Three alliances planned to contest the elections: the Alliance for the Restoration of Democracy (Leader NAWABZADA NASRULLAH KHAN; includes the Pakistan Muslim League (Nawaz) and the Pakistan People's Party Parliamentarians); the National Alliance (Chair. GHULAM MUSTAFA JATOI; includes the National People's Party, the Millat Party, the Sindh National Front; the Sindh Democratic Alliance and the National Awami Party); Muttahida Majlis-e-Amal (Chair. Maulana SHAH AHMED NOORANI; comprises Jamaat-e-Islami, Jamiat-e-Ulema-e-Pakistan, Jamiat-e-Ulema-e-Islam (S), Jamiat-e-Ulema-e-Islam (F), Islami Tehreek Pakistan and Jamiat Ahl-e-Hadith).

All Pakistan Jammu and Kashmir Conference: f. 1948; advocates the holding of a free plebiscite in the whole of Kashmir; Pres. Sardar SIKANDAR HAYAT KHAN.

Awami National Party (ANP) (People's National Party): Karachi; tel. (21) 534513; f. 1986 by the merger of the National Democratic Party, the Awami Tehrik (People's Movement) and the Mazdoor Kissan (Labourers' and Peasants' Party); federalist and socialist; Leader KHAN ABDUL WALI KHAN; Pres. ASFANDAR WALI KHAN.

Awami Qiyadat Party (People's Leadership Party): Lahore; f. 1995; Chair. Gen. (retd) ASLAM BEG.

Balochistan National Party: Quetta; Central leader Dr JAHANGIR JAMALUDDIN.

Balochistan National Movement: Quetta; Leader AYUB JATTAK.

Jamaat-e-Islami Pakistan (JIP): Mansoorah, Multan Rd, Lahore 54570; tel. (42) 5419520; fax (42) 5419505; e-mail amir@ji.org.pk; internet www.jamaat.org; f. 1941; seeks the establishment of Islamic order through adherence to teaching of Maulana Maududi, founder of the party; right-wing; Chair. Amir Qazi HUSSAIN AHMAD; Sec.-Gen. SYED MUNAWAR HASAN; c. 15,700 full mems (2002).

Jamhuri Watan Party (Bugti) Balochistan: Pres. Nawab AKBAR BUGTI.

Jamiat-e-Ulema-e-Islam (JUI): f. 1950; advocates adoption of a constitution in accordance with (Sunni) Islamic teachings; Leader Maulana FAZLUR REHMAN.

Jamiat-e-Ulema-e-Pakistan (JUP): Burns Rd, Karachi; f. 1948; advocates progressive (Sunni) Islamic principles and enforcement of Islamic laws in Pakistan; Pres. Maulana SHAH AHMED NOORANI SIDDIQUI; Gen. Sec. Gen. (retd) K. M. AZHAR KHAN.

Millat Party: 21-E/3, Gulberg III, Lahore; tel. (42) 5757805; fax (42) 5756718; e-mail millat@lhr.comsats.net.pk; advocates 'true federalism'; Chair. FAROOQ AHMAD KHAN LEGHARI.

Muttahida Qaumi Movement (MQM): 494/8 Azizabad, Karachi; tel. (21) 6313690; fax (21) 6329955; e-mail mqm@mqm.org; internet www.mqm.org; f. 1978 as All Pakistan Mohajir Students Organisation; name changed to Mohajir Qaumi Movement in 1984 and to Muttahida Qaumi Movement in 1997; represents the interests of Muslim, Urdu-speaking immigrants (from India) in Pakistan; seeks the designation of Mohajir as fifth nationality (after Sindhi, Punjabi, Pathan and Balochi); aims to abolish the prevailing feudal political system and to establish democracy; Pres. AFTAB SHEIKH.

National Awami Party: Peshawar; Pres. AJMAL KHATAK; Gen. Sec. ARBAB AYUB JAN.

National People's Party (NPP): 18 Kh-e-Shamsheer, Defence Housing Authority, Phase II, Karachi; tel. (21) 5854522; fax (21) 5873753; f. 1986; advocates a 10-point programme for the restoration of democracy; breakaway faction from PPP; right-wing; Chair. GHULAM MUSTAFA JATOI; Chief Organizer A. B. LEGHARI.

Pakhtoonkhwa Milli Awami Party (Quetta): Leader SAMAND ACHAKZAI.

Pakistan Awami Tehreek (PAT): 365-M Model Town, Lahore; tel. (42) 5169111; fax (42) 5169114; e-mail info@pat.com.pk; internet www.pat.com.pk; Chair. Dr MUHAMMAD TAHRIR-UL-QADRI.

Pakistan Democratic Party (PDP): f. 1969; advocates democratic and Islamic values; Pres. NAWABZADA NASRULLAH KHAN.

Pakistan Muslim League (PML): Muslim League House, Rawalpindi (Junejo Group); Muslim League House, 33 Agha Khan Rd, Lahore (Fida Group); f. 1906; in 1979 the party split into two factions, the pro-Zia Pagara Group and the Chatta Group (later renamed the Qasim Group, see below); the Pagara Group itself split into two factions when a group of army-supported Zia loyalists, known as the Fida Group, separated from the Junejo Group in August 1988; at the November 1988 general election, however, the Junejo Group and the Fida Group did not present rival candidates; by 2002 the PML had split into two main factions, one led by Mian MOHAMMAD NAWAZ SHARIF, known as the Nawaz Group (Pres. RAJA ZAFAR-UL-HAQ; Sec.-Gen. ANJAAM KHAN), and the other by Mian MOHAMMAD AZHAR, known as the PML Quaid-e-Azam Group (Sec.-Gen, Zafarullah Khan Jamali); other factions of the PML were led by HAMID NASIR CHATTA, known as the Chatta League, and Functional PML, led by PIR PAGARA.

Pakistan National Conference: Islamabad; Pres. Air Marshal (retd) MOHAMMAD ASGHAR KHAN; Sec.-Gen. Dr GHULAM HUSSAIN.

Pakistan People's Party (PPP): Zardari Hse, 8, St 19, F-8/2, Islamabad; tel. (51) 255264; e-mail ppp@comsats.net.pk; internet www.ppp.org.pk; f. 1967; advocates Islamic socialism, democracy and a non-aligned foreign policy; Chair. BENAZIR BHUTTO; Sr Vice-Pres. MAKHDOOM MOHAMMED ZAMAN TALIB-UL-MAULA; in 2002 the faction the Pakistan People's Party Parliamentarians was formed to contest the October general election; Leader MAKHDOOM AMIN FAHIM.

Pakistan People's Party (Shaheed Bhutto Group): 71 Clifton, Karachi; f. 1995 as a breakaway faction of the PPP; Chair. GHINWA BHUTTO; Sec.-Gen. Dr MUBASHIR HASAN.

Pakistan People's Party (Sherpao Group): Peshawar; breakaway faction of the PPP; Pres. ALTAB SHERPAO.

Punjabi Pakhtoon Ittehad (PPI): f. 1987 to represent the interests of Punjabis and Pakhtoons in Karachi; Pres. MALIK MIR HAZAR KHAN.

Qaumi Jamhori Party: Abbottabad; Pres. Air Marshal (retd) ASGHAR KHAN.

Sindh National Front: Pres. MUMTAZ BHUTTO.

Sindh Taraqi Passand Party (STPP): Leader Dr QADIR MAGSI.

Sipah-e-Sahaba Pakistan (SSP): Karachi; f. as a breakaway faction of Jamiat-e-Ulema-e-Islam; Sunni extremist; activities proscribed in January 2002; Leader Maulana TARIQ AZAM; Sec.-Gen. HAFIZ AHMED BUKHSH.

Tehrik-e-Insaf (Movement for Justice): Lahore; internet www.insaf.org.pk; f. 1996; Leader IMRAN KHAN; Sec.-Gen. MIRAJ MOHAMMAD KHAN.

Tehrik-i-Jafria-i-Pakistan (TJP): f. 1987 as a political party; Shi'a extremist; activities proscribed in January 2002; Leader Allama SAJID ALI NAQVI.

Diplomatic Representation

EMBASSIES AND HIGH COMMISSIONS IN PAKISTAN

Afghanistan: 8, St 90, G-6/3, Islamabad; tel. (51) 2824505; fax 2824504; Ambassador: RAHMATULLAH MUSA GHAZI.

Algeria: 107, St 9, E-7, POB 1038, Islamabad; tel. (51) 2206632; fax (51) 2820912; Ambassador: AISSA SEFERDJELI.

Argentina: 20 Hill Rd, Shalimar, F-6/3, POB 10151, Islamabad; tel. (51) 2825561; fax (51) 2825564; e-mail epaki@worldtelmeca.com; Ambassador: HORACIO R. BASSO.

Australia: Diplomatic Enclave 1, G-5/4, POB 1046, Islamabad; tel. (51) 2824345; fax (51) 2820189; High Commissioner: HOWARD BROWN.

Austria: 13, St 1, F-6/3, POB 1018, Islamabad 44000; tel. (51) 2279237; fax (51) 2828366; e-mail Islamabad-ob@bmaa.gv.at; Ambassador: Dr GUENTHER GALLOWITSCH.

Azerbaijan: 1, Nazimuddin Rd, F-10/4, Islamabad; tel. (51) 2291141; fax (51) 2211826; Ambassador: Dr EYNULLAH Y. MADATLI.

Bangladesh: 1, St 5, F-6/3, Islamabad; tel. (51) 2279267; fax (51) 2279266; High Commissioner: ALIMUL HAQUE.

Belgium: 14, St 17, F-7/2, POB 1016, Islamabad; tel. (51) 2827091; fax (51) 2822358; e-mail ambel-pk@isb.comsats.net.pk; Ambassador: IGOR HAUSTRATE.

Bosnia and Herzegovina: House No. 1, Kaghan Rd, F-8/3, Islamabad; tel. (51) 2261041; fax (51) 2261004; e-mail ambassador@bosnianembassypakistan.org; internet www.bosnianembassypakistan.org; Ambassador: AVDO HODZIĆ.

Brazil: 50 Atatürk Ave, G-6/3, POB 1053, Islamabad; tel. (51) 2279690; fax (51) 2823034; Ambassador: ABELARDO ARANTES JÚNIOR.

Brunei: 16, St 21, F-6/2, Islamabad; tel. (51) 2823038; fax (51) 2823138; High Commissioner: Brig. Gen. (retd) Dato' Paduka Haji IBRAHIM BIN MOHAMMAD.

Bulgaria: Plot No. 6-11, Diplomatic Enclave, Ramna-5, POB 1483, Islamabad; tel. (51) 2279196; fax (51) 2279195; Ambassador: IVAN DANTCHEV PETKOV.

Canada: Diplomatic Enclave, Sector G-5, POB 1042, Islamabad; tel. (51) 2279100; fax (51) 2279110; e-mail ferry.de-kerchkove@dfait.maeci.gc.ca; High Commissioner: FERRY DE KERCKHOVE.

China, People's Republic: Ramna 4, Diplomatic Enclave, Islamabad; tel. (51) 2826667; fax (51) 2279602; Ambassador: ZHANG CHUNXIANG.

Czech Republic: 49, St 27, Shalimar F-6/2, POB 1335, Islamabad; tel. (51) 2274304; fax (51) 2825327; e-mail islamabd@embassy.mzv.cz; internet www.mzv.cz/islamabad; Ambassador: PETR PŘIBÍK.

Denmark: 9, St 90, Ramna 6/3, POB 1118, Islamabad; tel. (51) 2824722; fax (51) 2823483; e-mail ambadane@comsats.net.pk; Chargé d'affaires a.i.: SVEN BILLE BJERREGAARD.

Egypt: 38–51, UN Blvd Diplomatic Enclave, Ramna 5/4, POB 2088, Islamabad; tel. (51) 2209072; fax (51) 2279552; Ambassador: HISHAM EL ZIAMAITY.

Finland: 11, St 88, G-6/3, Islamabad; tel. (51) 2828426; fax (51) 2828427; Ambassador: ANTTI KOISTINEN.

France: Constitution Ave, G-5, Diplomatic Enclave 1, POB 1068, Islamabad; tel. (51) 2278730; fax (51) 2822583; e-mail ambafra@isb.comsats.net.pk; Ambassador: YANNICK GÉRARD.

Germany: Ramna 5, Diplomatic Enclave, POB 1027, Islamabad 44000; tel. (51) 2279430; fax (51) 2279436; Ambassador: Dr CHRISTOPH BRÜMMER.

Greece: 22 Margalla Rd, F-6/3, Islamabad; tel. (51) 2822558; fax (51) 2825161; e-mail greece@isb.paknet.com.pk; internet www.greekembassy.netfirms.com; Ambassador: DIMITRIOUS MICHAIL LOUNDRAS.

Holy See: Apostolic Nunciature, St 5, Diplomatic Enclave 1, G-5, POB 1106, Islamabad 44000; tel. (51) 2278217; fax (51) 2820847; e-mail vatipak@isb.paknet.com.pk; Apostolic Nuncio: Most Rev. ALESSANDRO D'ERRICO, Titular Archbishop of Carini.

Hungary: House No. 12, Margalla Rd, F-6/3, POB 1103, Islamabad; tel. (51) 2823352; fax (51) 2825256; Ambassador: JÓZSEF KOVÁCS.

India: G-5, Diplomatic Enclave, Islamabad; tel. (51) 2206950; fax (51) 2823386; High Commissioner: HARSH KUMAR BHASIN.

Indonesia: Diplomatic Enclave 1, St 5, G-5/4, POB 1019, Islamabad; tel. (51) 2278736; fax (51) 2829145; e-mail unitkom@best.net.pk; Ambassador: JACK SAID GAFFAR.

Iran: 222–238, St. 2, G-5/1, Diplomatic Enclave, Islamabad; tel. (51) 2276270; fax (51) 2824839; Ambassador: Dr K. A. RAWI.

Iraq: 44, St 27, F-10, Islamabad; tel. (51) 2214570; fax (51) 2214572; e-mail iraqiya@sat.net.pk; Ambassador: ABDUL KAREEM MOHAMMAD ASWAD.

Italy: 54, Margalla Rd, F-6/3, POB 1008, Islamabad; tel. (51) 2829106; fax (51) 2829026; e-mail segreter@embassy.italy.org.pk; internet www.embassy.italy.org.pk; Ambassador: Dr ANGELO GABRIELE DE CEGLIE.

Japan: Plot No. 53-70, Ramna 5/4, Diplomatic Enclave 1, Islamabad 44000; tel. (51) 2279320; fax (51) 2279340; e-mail info@japanemb.org.pk; internet japanemb.org.pk; Ambassador: SADAAKI NUMATA.

Jordan: 131, St 14, E-7, POB 1189, Islamabad; tel. (51) 2823459; fax (51) 2823207; e-mail jordanemb@comsats.net.pk; Ambassador: Dr FAWAZ ABU TAYEH.

Kazakhstan: 2, St 4, F-8/2, Islamabad; tel. (51) 2262926; fax (51) 2262806; e-mail embkaz@comsats.net.pk; Ambassador: BEKZHASAR NARBAYEV.

Kenya: 10, St 9, F-7/3, Islamabad; tel. (51) 2279540; fax (51) 2279541; High Commissioner: JOHN W. K. MUKURIAH.

Korea, Democratic People's Republic: 9, St 18, F-8/2, Islamabad; tel. and fax (51) 2252754; Ambassador: RIM HOE SONG.

Korea, Republic: Block 13, St 29, G-5/4, Diplomatic Enclave 2, POB 1087, Islamabad; tel. (51) 2279380; fax (51) 2279391; e-mail koremi@isb.comsats.net.pk; Ambassador: YOON JEE-JOON.

Kuwait: Plot No.s 1, 2 and 24, University Rd, G-5, Diplomatic Enclave, POB 1030, Islamabad; tel. (51) 2279413; fax (51) 2279411; Ambassador: MOHAMAD AHMAD AL-MIJRIN AR-ROOMI.

Lebanon: 17, School Rd, F-6/1, Islamabad; tel. (51) 2278338; fax (51) 2826410; e-mail lebemb@comsats.net.pk; Ambassador: AL-AMEERA LEILA CHEHAB.

Libya: 12, Margalla Rd, F-8/3, Islamabad; tel. (51) 2254219; fax (51) 2261459; Chargé d'affaires a.i.: HADI M. AWSAJI.

Malaysia: 78, Margalla Rd, F-6/2, POB 1034, Islamabad; tel. (51) 2279570; fax (51) 2824761; e-mail mwislam@isb.comsats.net.pk; High Commissioner: Dato' SOPLAN BIN AHMAD.

Mauritius: 27, St 26, F-6/2, Islamabad; tel. (51) 2824657; fax (51) 2824656; High Commissioner: RAVINDRANATH DWARKA.

Morocco: 6, Gomal Rd, E-7, POB 1179, Islamabad; tel. (51) 2829656; fax (51) 2822745; e-mail sifmapk@comsats.net.pk; Ambassador: YOUSSEF FASSI FIHRI.

Myanmar: 12/1, St 13, F-7/2, Islamabad; tel. (51) 822460; fax (51) 828819; Ambassador: U SOE WIN.

Nepal: House No. 11, St 84, G-6/4, Islamabad; tel. (51) 2828838; fax (51) 2828839; e-mail nepemb@isb.comsats.net.pk; Ambassador: KUMAR P. GYAWALI.

Netherlands: PIA Bldg, 2nd Floor, Blue Area, POB 1065, Islamabad; tel. (51) 2279510; fax (51) 2279512; Ambassador: JAAP A. WALKATE.

Nigeria: 6, St 22, F-6/2, POB 1075, Islamabad; tel. (51) 823542; fax (51) 824104; High Commissioner: ABBAS ABDUL KADIR.

Norway: 25, St 19, F-6/2, POB 1336, Islamabad; tel. (51) 2279720; fax (51) 2279726; e-mail emb.islamabad@mfa.no; internet www.norway.org.pk; Ambassador: TORE TORENG.

Oman: 53, St 48, F-8/4, POB 1194, Islamabad; tel. (51) 2254869; fax (51) 2255074; Ambassador: SALIM MOHAMMAD SALIM AL-WAHAIBI.

Philippines: 8, St 60, F-8/4, Islamabad; tel. (51) 2824933; fax (51) 2277389; e-mail isdpe@isb.comsats.net.pk; Ambassador: JORGE V. ARIZABAL.

Poland: St 24, G-5/4, Diplomatic Enclave 2, POB 1032, Islamabad; tel. (51) 2279491; fax (51) 2279498; e-mail polemb@isb.comsats.net.pk; Ambassador: TOMASZ KOZLOWSKI.

Portugal: 66 Main Margalla Rd, F-7/2, POB 1067, Islamabad 44000; tel. (51) 2279531; fax (51) 2279532; e-mail portugal@isb.paknet.com.pk; Ambassador: Dr ALEXANDRE VASSALO.

Qatar: 20, University Rd, Diplomatic Enclave, G-6/4, Islamabad; tel. (51) 2270768; fax (51) 2270207; Ambassador: ABDULLAH FALAH ABDULLAH AD-DOSSARI.

Romania: 13, St 88, G-6/3, Islamabad; tel. (51) 2826514; fax (51) 2826515; e-mail romania@isb.comsats.net.pk; Ambassador: EMIL GHITULESCU.

Russia: Khayaban-e-Suhrawardy, Diplomatic Enclave, Ramna 4, Islamabad; tel. (51) 2278670; fax (51) 2826552; e-mail russia2@comsats.net.pk; Ambassador: EDWARD SHEVCHENKO.

Saudi Arabia: 14, Hill Rd, F-6/3, Islamabad; tel. (51) 2820156; fax (51) 2278816; Ambassador: ALI AWADH ASSERI.

Somalia: 21, St 56, F-6/4, Islamabad; tel. (51) 2279789; fax (51) 2826117; Ambassador: ABDI SALAM HAJI AHMAD LIBAN.

South Africa: House No. 48, Margalla Rd, Khayban-e-Iqbal, Sector F-8/2, Islamabad; tel. (51) 262354; fax (51) 250114; e-mail xhosa@isb.comsats.net.pk; High Commissioner: MOOSA MOHAMED MOOLLA.

Spain: St 6, G-5, Diplomatic Enclave 1, POB 1144, Islamabad; tel. (51) 2279480; fax (51) 2279489; Ambassador: ANTONIO SEGURA MORÍS.

Sri Lanka: St 55, F-6/4, Islamabad; tel. (51) 2828723; fax (51) 2828751; e-mail srilanka@isb.comsats.net.pk; High Commissioner: Gen. C. S. WEERASOORIYA.

Sudan: 7, St 1, G-6/3, Islamabad; tel. (51) 2827068; fax (51) 2827073; Ambassador: AWAD MOHAMED HUSSAN SAID.

Switzerland: St 6, G-5/4, Diplomatic Enclave, POB 1073, Islamabad; tel. (51) 279291; fax (51) 279286; e-mail swiemisl@isb.comsats.net.pk; Ambassador: CHRISTIAN DUNANT.

Syria: 30, Hill Rd, Shalimar 6/3, Islamabad; tel. (51) 2279470; fax (51) 2279472; Ambassador: SAIFI HAMWI.

Thailand: 10, St 33, Shalimar 8/1, Islamabad; tel. (51) 2280909; fax (51) 2256730; e-mail thailand@isb.comsats.net.pk; Ambassador: SAKSIT SRISORN.

Tunisia: 221, St 21, E-7, Islamabad; tel. (51) 827869; fax (51) 827871; Ambassador: LAMINE BENZARTI.

Turkey: 58 Atatürk Ave, G-6/3, Islamabad; tel. (51) 2278748; fax (51) 2278752; e-mail turkemb@isb.comsats.net.pk; Ambassador: KEMAL GUL.

Turkmenistan: H 22A, Nazim-Ud-Din Rd, Sector F-7/1, Islamabad; tel. (51) 2274913; fax (51) 2278799; e-mail turkmen@comsats.net.pk; Ambassador: SAPAR BERDINIYAZOV.

Ukraine: 20, St 18, F 6/2, Islamabad; tel. (51) 2274732; fax (51) 2274643; e-mail ukremb@isb.compol.com; internet www.ukremb.org.pk; Ambassador: VOLODYMYR S. PONOMARENKO.

United Arab Emirates: Plot No. 1-22, Diplomatic Enclave, Quaid-e-Azam University Rd, Islamabad; tel. (51) 2279052; fax (51) 2279063; Ambassador: ALI MOHAMMED AL-SHAMSI.

United Kingdom: Diplomatic Enclave, Ramna 5, POB 1122, Islamabad; tel. (51) 2822131; fax (51) 2823439; e-mail bhcmedia@isb.comsats.net.pk; internet www.britainonline.org.pk; High Commissioner: HILARY SYNNOTT.

USA: Diplomatic Enclave, Ramna 5, POB 1048, Islamabad; tel. (51) 826161; fax (51) 821193; e-mail isl@state.gov; Chargé d'affaires: NANCY POWELL.

Uzbekistan: 2, St 2, F-8/3, Kohistan Rd, Islamabad; tel. (51) 2264746; fax (51) 2261739; Ambassador: SHUHRAT KABILOV.

Yemen: 16, St 17, F-7/2, POB 1523, Islamabad 44000; tel. (51) 821146; fax (51) 826159; Ambassador: ABDUL MALIK MOHAMMAD WASEA AT-TAYYEB.

Yugoslavia: 14, St 87, Ramna 6/3, Islamabad; tel. (51) 829556; fax (51) 820965; e-mail fryemy@isb.comsats.net.pk; Chargé d'affaires: ZARKO MILOŠEVIĆ.

Judicial System

A constitutional amendment bill was passed in the National Assembly in October 1998 replacing the country's existing legal code with full Shari'a. The bill remained to be approved, however, by the Senate.

SUPREME COURT

Chief Justice: IRSHAD HUSSAN KHAN.

Attorney-General: AZIZ A. MUNSHI.

Deputy Attorney-General: KHWAJA SAEEDUZ ZAFAR.

Federal Shari'a Court

Chief Justice: FAZAL ELAHI KHAN.

Federal Ombudsman: Justice USMAN ALI SHAH.

Religion

ISLAM

Islam is the state religion. The majority of the population are Sunni Muslims, while about 5% are of the Shi'a sect and only about 0.001% are of the Ahmadi sect.

CHRISTIANITY

About 3% of the population are Christians.

National Council of Churches in Pakistan: 32-B, Shahrah-e-Fatima Jinnah, POB 357, Lahore 54000; tel. (42) 7592167; fax (42) 7569782; e-mail nccp@lhr.comsats.net.pk; f. 1949; four mem. bodies, nine associate mems; Gen. Sec. VICTOR AZARIAH.

The Roman Catholic Church

For ecclesiastical purposes, Pakistan comprises two archdioceses, four dioceses and one apostolic prefecture. At 31 December 2000 there were an estimated 1,263,934 adherents in the country.

Bishops' Conference: Pakistan Episcopal Conference, Sacred Heart Cathedral, 1 Mian Mohammad Shafi Rd, POB 909, Lahore 54000; tel. (42) 6366137; fax (42) 6368336; e-mail abishop@lhr.comsats.net.pk; f. 1976; Pres. Most Rev. SIMEON ANTHONY PEREIRA, Archbishop of Karachi; Sec.-Gen. Rt Rev. ANTHONY LOBO, Bishop of Islamabad-Rawalpindi.

Archbishop of Karachi: Most Rev. SIMEON ANTHONY PEREIRA, St Patrick's Cathedral, Shahrah-e-Iraq, Karachi 74400; tel. (21) 7781533; fax (21) 7781532.

Archbishop of Lahore: Most Rev. LAWRENCE J. SALDANHA, Sacred Heart Cathedral, 1 Mian Mohammad Shafi Rd, POB 909, Lahore 54000; tel. (42) 6366137; fax (42) 6368336; e-mail abishop@lhr.comsats.net.pk; internet www.rcarchdioceselahore.org.pk.

Protestant Churches

Church of Pakistan: Moderator Rt Rev. SAMUEL AZARIAH (Bishop of Raiwind), 17 Warris Rd, POB 2319, Lahore 3; fax (42) 7577255; f. 1970 by union of the fmr Anglican Church in Pakistan, the United Methodist Church in Pakistan, the United Church in Pakistan (Scots Presbyterians) and the Pakistani Lutheran Church; eight dioceses; c. 700,000 mems (1993); Gen. Sec. (vacant).

United Presbyterian Church of Pakistan: POB 395, Rawalpindi; tel. (51) 72503; f. 1961; c. 340,000 mems (1989); Moderator Sardar FEROZE KHAN; Sec. Rev. PIYARA LALL.

Other denominations active in the country include the Associated Reformed Presbyterian Church and the Pakistan Salvation Army.

HINDUISM

Hindus comprise about 1.8% of the population.

BAHÁ'Í FAITH

National Spiritual Assembly: POB 7420, Karachi 74400; tel. (21) 7216429; fax (21) 7215467; e-mail nsapk@cyber.net.pk.

The Press

The Urdu press comprises almost 800 newspapers, with *Daily Jang, Daily Khabrain, Nawa-i-Waqt, Jasarat* and *Mashriq* among the most influential. The daily newspaper with the largest circulation is *Daily Jang*. Although the English-language press reaches only a small percentage of the population, it is influential in political, academic and professional circles. The four main press groups in Pakistan are Jang Publications (the *Daily Jang, The News,* the *Daily News* and the weekly *Akhbar-e-Jehan*), the Dawn or Herald Group (the *Dawn,* the *Star,* the *Watan* and the monthly *Herald* and *Spider*), the Nawa-i-Waqt Group (the *Nawa-i-Waqt* and *The Nation*), and the National Press Trust (the *Mashriq*). The establishment of an independent press council was under consideration in 2002.

PRINCIPAL DAILIES

Islamabad

Al-Akhbar: Al-Akhbar House, Markaz, G-8, Islamabad; tel. (51) 852023; fax (51) 256522; Urdu; also publ. in Muzaffarabad; Editor GHULAM AKBAR.

The Nation: Nawa-i-Waqt House, Zero Point, Islamabad; tel. (51) 277631; fax (51) 278353; e-mail editor@nation.com.pk; internet www.nation.com.pk; English; Editor ARIF NIZAMI; circ. 15,000.

Pakistan Observer: Ali Akbar House, Markaz G-8, Islamabad 44870; tel. (51) 2852027; fax (51) 2262258; e-mail observer@best.net.pk; internet www.pakobserver.com; f. 1988; English; independent; Editor-in-Chief ZAHID MALIK.

Karachi

Aghaz: 11 Japan Mansion, Preedy St, Sadar, Karachi 74400; tel. (21) 7721688; fax (21) 7722125; internet www.aghaz.com; f. 1963; evening; Urdu; Editor MOHAMMAD ANWAR FAROOQI; Man. Editor BILAL FAROOQI; circ. 62,377.

Amn: Akhbar Manzil, Elender Rd; off I. I. Chundrigar Rd, Karachi 74200; tel. (21) 2634451; fax (21) 2634454; e-mail amn@aol.net.pk; Urdu; Editor AJMAL DEHLVI.

Business Recorder: Recorder House, Business Recorder Rd, Karachi 74550; tel. (21) 7210072; fax (21) 7228644; e-mail editor@brecorder.com; internet www.brecorder.com; f. 1965; English; Editor M. A. ZUBERI.

Daily Awam: HQ Printing House, I. I. Chundrigar Rd, POB 52, Karachi; tel. (21) 2637111; fax (21) 2636066; f. 1994; evening; Urdu; Editor-in-Chief Mir SHAKIL-UR-REHMAN.

Daily Beopar: 118 Bombay Hotel, I. I. Chundrigar Rd, Karachi; tel. (21) 214055; Urdu; Man. Editor TARIQ SAEED.

Daily Intekhab: Liaison Office, 3rd Floor, Mashhoor Mahal, Kucha Haji Usman, off I. I. Chundrigar Rd, Karachi; tel. (21) 2634518; fax (21) 2631092; Urdu; also publ. from Hub (Balochistan) and Quetta; Man. Editor SARKAR AHMAD; Publr and Editor ANWAR SAJIDI.

Daily Jang: HQ Printing House, I. I. Chundrigar Rd, POB 52, Karachi; tel. (21) 2637111; fax (21) 2634395; e-mail jang@jang-group.com.pk; internet www.jang-group.com.pk; f. 1940; morning; Urdu; also publ. in Quetta, Rawalpindi, Lahore and London; Editor-in-Chief SHAKIL-UR-RAHMAN; combined circ. 750,000.

Daily Khabar: A-8 Sheraton Centre, F. B. Area, Karachi; tel. (21) 210059; Urdu; Exec. Editor FAROOQ PARACHA; Editor and Publr SAEED ALI HAMEED.

Daily Khabrain: Sitara Market, Markaz G-7/2, Islamabad; tel. (51) 2204751; fax (51) 2204756.

Daily Mohasaba: Imperial Hotel, M.T. Khan Rd, Karachi; tel. (21) 519448; Urdu; Editor TALIB TURABI.

Daily News: Al-Rahman Bldg, I. I. Chundrigar Rd, Karachi; tel. (21) 2637111; fax (21) 2634395; f. 1962; evening; English; Editor S. M. FAZIL; circ. 50,000.

Daily Public: Falak Printing Press, 191 Altaf Hussain Rd, New Chhali, Karachi; tel. (21) 5687522; Man. Editor INQUILAB MATRI; Editor ANWAR SANROY.

Daily Sindh Sujag: 15/4, Namco Centre, Campbell St, New Challi, Karachi; tel. (21) 2625282; fax (21) 2623918; Sindhi; political; Editor NASIR DAD BALOCH.

Daily Special: Ahbab Printers, Beauty House, nr Regal Chowk, Abdullah Haroon Rd, Sadar, Karachi; tel. (21) 7771655; fax (21) 7722776; Urdu; Editor MOHAMMAD AT-TAYYAB.

Daily Standard: C-59, Mezzanine Floor, Main Korangi Rd, Defence Housing Authority, Phase II Extension, Karachi; tel. (21) 5804976; fax (21) 5384490; e-mail standard_pk@hotmail.com; English; Publr BILAL FAROOQI; circ. 30,000.

Dawn: Haroon House, Dr Ziauddin Ahmed Rd, POB 3740, Karachi 74200; tel. (21) 5670001; fax (21) 5683801; e-mail editor@dawn.com; internet www.dawn.com; f. 1947; English, Gujarati; also published from Islamabad and Lahore; Chief Exec. HAMEED HAROON; Editor SALIM ANSMI; circ. 110,000 (weekdays), 125,000 (Sundays).

Deyanet: Karachi; tel. (21) 2631556; fax (21) 2631888; Urdu; also publ. in Sukkur and Islamabad; Editor NAJMUDDIN SHAIKH.

The Finance: 903–905 Uni Towers, I. I. Chundrigar Rd, Karachi; tel. (21) 2411665; fax (21) 2422560; e-mail tfinance@super.net.pk; English; Chief Editor S. H. SHAH.

Financial Post: Bldg No. 106/C, 11 Commercial St, Phase II, Extension, Defence Housing Authority, POB 300, Karachi; tel. (21) 5381628; fax (21) 5802760; e-mail fpost@webnet.com.pk; f. 1994; English; Chief Editor and CEO QUDSIA K. KHAN; Publr M. AHSAN JAWAD.

Hilal-e-Pakistan: Court View Bldg, 2nd Floor, M. A. Jinnah Rd, POB 3737, Karachi 74200; tel. (21) 2624997; fax (21) 2624996; Sindhi; Editor MOHAMMAD IQBAL DAL.

Jago: Karachi; tel. (21) 2635544; fax (21) 2628137; f. 1990; Sindhi; political; Editor AGHA SALEEM.

Jasarat: Eveready Chambers, Muhammad Bin Qasim Rd, Karachi 74200; tel. (21) 2630391; fax (21) 2632102; e-mail jasarat@cyber.net.pk; f. 1970; Urdu; Editor MAHMOOD AHMAD MADANI; circ. 50,000.

Leader: Block 5, 609, Clifton Centre, Clifton, Karachi 75600; tel. (21) 5863801; fax (21) 5872206; e-mail dailyleader@hotmail.com; f. 1958; English; independent; Editor MANZAR-UL-HASSAN; Man. Editor MUNIR M. LADHA; circ. 3,000.

Mazdur: Spencer Bldg, I. I. Chundrigar Rd, Karachi 2; f. 1984; Urdu; Editor MOHAMMAD ANWAR BIN ABBAS.

Millat: 191 Altaf Hussain Rd, Karachi 2; tel. (21) 2411514; internet www.millat.com; f. 1946; Gujarati; independent; Editor INQUILAB MATRI; circ. 22,550.

Mohasib: Karachi; fax (21) 2632763; Urdu; also publ. from Abbotabad; Chief Editor ZAFAR MAJAZI; Editor NAEEM AHMAD.

The News International: Al-Rahman Bldg, I. I. Chundrigar Rd, POB 52, Karachi; tel. (21) 2630611; fax (21) 2418343; f. 1990; English; also publ. from Lahore and Rawalpindi/Islamabad; Editor-in-Chief Mir SHAKIL-UR-RAHMAN; Sr Editor SHAHEEN SEHBAI.

Parliament: 1013 Qasimabad, Karachi; tel. (21) 422030; f. 1988; English; Chief Editor FARRUGH AHMAD SIDDIQ.

Qaum (Nation): Karachi; Urdu; Editor and Publr MUSHTAQUE SOHAIL; Man. Editor MAMNOONUR REHMAN.

Qaumi Akhbar: 14 Ramzan Mansion, Dr Bilmoria St, off I. I. Chundrigar Rd, Karachi; tel. (21) 2633381; fax (21) 2635774; f. 1988; Urdu; Editor ILYAS SHAKIR.

Roznama Special: Falak Printing Press, 191 Altaf Hussain Rd, Karachi; tel. (21) 5687522; fax (21) 5687579; Publr and Man. Editor INQUILAB MATRI: Editor ANWAR SEN ROY.

Savera: 108 Adam Arcade, Shaheed-e-Millat Rd, Karachi; tel. (21) 419616; Urdu; Editor RUKHSANA SAHAM MIRZA.

Sindh Tribune: No. 246-D/6, PECHS, Karachi; tel. (21) 4535227; fax (21) 4332680; English; political; Editor YOUSUF SHAHEEN.

Star: Haroon House, Dr Ziauddin Ahmed Rd, Karachi 74200; evening; English; Editor KAMAL MAJEEDULLAH.

The Times of Karachi: Al-Falah Chambers, 9th Floor, Abdullah Haroon Rd, Karachi; tel. (21) 7727740; evening; English; independent; city news; Editor MOHAMMAD JAMI.

Lahore

Daily Pakistan: 41 Jail Rd, Lahore; tel. (42) 7576301; fax (42) 7586251; internet www.daily-pakistan.com; f. 1990; Urdu; Chief Editor MUJIBUR RAHMAN SHAMI.

Daily Times: 41-N, Industrial Area, Gulberg II, Lahore; tel. (42) 5878614; fax (42) 5878620; e-mail editorial@dailytimes.com.pk.

Mahgribi Pakistan: Lahore; tel. (42) 53490; Urdu; also publ. in Bahawalpur and Sukkur; Editor M. SHAFAAT.

The Nation: NIPCO House, 4 Sharah-e-Fatima Jinnah, POB 1815, Lahore 54000; tel. (42) 6367580; fax (42) 6367005; e-mail editor@nation.com; internet www.nation.com.pk; f. 1986; English; Chair. MAJEED NIZAMI; Editor ARIF NIZAMI; circ. 52,000.

Nawa-i-Waqt (Voice of the Time): 4 Sharah-e-Fatima Jinnah, Lahore 54000; tel. (42) 6302050; fax (42) 6367583; internet www.nawaiwaqt.com.pk; f. 1940; English, Urdu; also publ. edns in Karachi, Islamabad and Multan; Editor MAJID NIZAMI; combined circ. 560,000.

The Sun International: 15-L, Gulberg III, Ferozepur Rd, Lahore; tel. (42) 5883540; fax (42) 5839951; Editor MAHMOOD SADIQ.

Tijarat: 14 Abbot Rd, opp. Nishat Cinema, Lahore; Urdu; Editor JAMIL ATHAR.

Wifaq: 6A Waris Rd, Lahore; tel. (42) 302862; Urdu; also publ. in Rawalpindi, Sargodha and Rahimyar Khan; Editor MOSTAFA SADIQ.

Rawalpindi

Daily Jang: Murree Rd, Rawalpindi; internet www.jang.com.pk; f. 1940; also publ. in Quetta, Karachi and Lahore; Urdu; independent; Editor Mir JAVED REHMAN; circ. (Rawalpindi) 65,000.

Daily Wifaq: 7A C/A, Satellite Town, Rawalpindi; f. 1959; also publ. in Lahore, Sargodha and Rahimyar Khan; Urdu; Editor MUSTAFA SADIQ.

The News: Murree Rd, Rawalpindi; e-mail thenews@isb.comsats.net.pk; internet www.jang-group.com; f. 1991; also publ. in Lahore and Karachi; English; independent; Chief Editor Mir SHAKIL-UR-RAHMAN.

Other Towns

Aftab: Hyderabad; Sindhi; also publ. in Multan; Editor SHEIKH ALI MOHAMMAD.

Al Falah: Al Falah Bldg, Saddar Rd, Peshawar; f. 1939; Urdu and Pashtu; Editor S. ABDULLAH SHAH.

Al-Jamiat-e-Sarhad: Kocha Gilania Chakagali, Karimpura Bazar, Peshawar; tel. (91) 2567757; e-mail sagha@brain.net.pk; f. 1941; Urdu and Pashtu; Propr and Chief Editor S. M. HASSAN GILANI.

Balochistan Times: Jinnah Rd, Quetta; Editor SYED FASIH IQBAL.

Basharat: Peshawar; Urdu; general; also publ. in Islamabad; Chief Editor ANWAR-UL-HAQ; Editor KHALID ATHER.

Daily Awaz: Peshawar; political; Man. Editor ALI RAZA MALIK.

Daily Business Report: Railway Rd, Faisalabad; tel. (41) 642131; fax (41) 621207; f. 1948; Editor ABDUL RASHID GHAZI; circ. 26,000.

Daily Hewad: 32 Stadium Rd, Peshawar; tel. (521) 270501; Pashtu; Editor-in-Chief REHMAN SHAH AFRIDI.

Daily Ibrat Hyderabad: Ibrat Building, Gadi Khata, Hyderabad; tel. (221) 28571; fax (221) 784300; e-mail ibrat@hyd.compol.com; internet www.ibratgroup.com; Sindhi; Man. Editor QAZI ASAD ABID.

Daily Khadim-e-Waten: B-2, Civil Lines, Hyderabad; Editor MUSHATAQ AHMAD.

Daily Rehbar: Jamil Market, Circular Rd, Bahawalpur; tel. (621) 884664; e-mail dailyrehber@yahoo.co.uk; f. 1954; Urdu; Chief Editor AKHTER HUSSAIN ANJUM; circ. 250,000.

Daily Sarwan: 11-EGOR Colony, Hyderabad; tel. (221) 781382; Sindhi; Chief Editor GHULAM HUSSAIN.

Daily Shabaz: Peshawar; tel. (521) 220188; fax (521) 216483; Urdu; organ of the Awami National Party; Chief Editor Begum NASEEM WALI KHAN.

Frontier Post: 32 Stadium Rd, Peshawar; tel. (521) 79174; fax (521) 76575; e-mail editor@frontierpost.com.pk; internet www.frontierpost.com.pk; f. 1985; English; left-wing; also publ. in Lahore; closed down temporarily in January 2001, reopened in June; Editor-in-Chief REHMAT SHAH AFRIDI; Editor MUZAFFAR SHAH AFRIDI.

Jihad: 15A Islamia Club Bldg, Khyber Bazar, Peshawar; tel. (521) 210522; e-mail jehad@pes.comsats.net.pk; also publ. in Karachi, Rawalpindi, Islamabad and Lahore; Editor SHARIF FAROOQ.

Kaleem: Shahi Bazar Thalla, POB 88, Sukkur; tel. (71) 22086; fax (71) 22087; e-mail kaleem1@hyd.paknet.com.pk; Urdu; Editor SHAHID MEHR SHAMSI.

Kavish: Sindh Printing and Publishing House, Civil Lines, POB 43, Hyderabad; Chief Editor MUHAMMAD AYUB QAZI; Publr/Editor ASLAM A. QAZI.

Mashriq: Quetta; Chief Editor AZIZ MAZHAR.

Nawai Asma'n: Mubarak Ali Shah Rd, Hyderabad; tel. and fax (221) 21925; Urdu, Sindhi and Pashtu; Chief Editor DOST MUHAMMAD.

The News: Qaumi Printing Press, Peshawar; English; Editor KHURSHID AHMAD.

Punjab News: Kutchery Bazar, POB 419, Faisalabad; tel. (41) 30151; f. 1968; Chief Editor PERVAIZ PASHA; Man. Editor JAVAID HIMYARITE; circ. 20,000.

Sarhad: New Gate, Peshawar.

Sindh Guardian: Tulsi Das Rd, POB 300, Hyderabad; tel. and fax (221) 21926; English; Chief Editor DOST MUHAMMAD.

Sindh News: Garikhata, Hyderabad; tel. (221) 20793; fax (221) 781867; Editor Kazi SAEED AKBER.

Sindh Observer: POB 43, Garikhata, Hyderabad; tel. (221) 27302; English; Editor ASLAM AKBER KAZI.

Sindhu: Popular Printers, Ibrat Bldg, Garhhi Khata, Hyderabad; tel. (221) 783571; fax (221) 783570; Sindhi; political.

Watan: 10 Nazar Bagh Flat, Peshawar.

Zamana: Jinnah Rd, Quetta; tel. (81) 71217; Urdu; Editor Syed FASIH IQBAL; circ. 5,000.

SELECTED WEEKLIES

Akhbar-e-Jehan: Printing House, off I. I. Chundrigar Rd, Karachi; tel. (21) 2634368; fax (21) 2635693; f. 1967; Urdu; independent; illustrated family magazine; Editor-in-Chief Mir JAVED RAHMAN; circ. 278,000.

Amal: Shah Qabool Colony, POB 185, Peshawar; tel. 275605; e-mail pakbase@brain.com.pk; f. 1958; Urdu, Pashtu and English; Chief Editor F. M. ZAFAR KAIFI; Publr MUNAZIMA MAAB KAIFI.

Asianews: 4 Amil St, off Robson Rd, Karachi 1; multilingual news for and about Asians overseas; Man. Editor AMEEN TAREEN.

Badban: Nai Zindagi Publications, Rana Chambers, Old Anarkali, Lahore; Editor MUJIBUR REHMAN SHAMI.

Chatan: Chatan Bldg, 88 McLeod Rd, Lahore; tel. (42) 6311336; fax (42) 6374690; f. 1948; Urdu; Editor MASUD SHORISH.

Family Magazine: 4 Shara-i-Fatima Jinnah, Lahore 54000; tel. (42) 6367551; fax (42) 6367583; circ. 100,000.

The Friday Times: 45 The Mall, Lahore; tel. (42) 7355079; fax (42) 7355197; e-mail tft@lhr.comsats.net.pk; internet www.thefridaytimes.com; independent; Editor/Owner NAJAM SETHI.

Hilal: Hilal Rd, Rawalpindi 46000; tel. (51) 56134605; fax (51) 565017; f. 1951; Friday; Urdu; illustrated armed forces; Editor MUMTAZ IQBAL MALIK; circ. 90,000.

Insaf: P/929, Banni, Rawalpindi; tel. and fax (51) 5550903; fax (51) 4411038; e-mail insafrwp@isb.paknet.com.pk; f. 1955; Editor Mir WAQAR AZIZ.

Lahore: Galaxy Law Chambers, 1st Floor, Room 1, Turner Rd, Lahore 5; f. 1952; Editor SAQIB ZEERVI; circ. 8,500.

Mahwar: D23, Block H, North Nazimabad, Karachi; Editor SHAHIDA NAFIS SIDDIQI.

Memaar-i-Nao: 39 KMC Bldg, Leamarket, Karachi; Urdu; labour magazine; Editor M. M. MUBASIR.

The Muslim World: 49-B, Block-8, Gulshan-e-Iqbal, Karachi 75300; POB 5030, Karachi 74000; tel. (21) 4960738; fax (21) 466878; English; current affairs; Editor KHALID IKRAMULLAH KHAN.

Nairang Khayal: 8 Mohammadi Market, Rawalpindi; f. 1924; Urdu; Chief Editor SULTAN RASHK.

Nida-i-Millat: 4 Sharah-e-Fatima Jinnah, Lahore 54000.

Noor Jehan Weekly: 32A National Auto Plaza, POB 8833, Karachi 74400; tel. and fax (21) 7723946; f. 1948; Urdu; film journal; Editor KHALID CHAWLA.

Pakistan and Gulf Economist: 3A Falcon Arcade, BC-3, Block-7, Clifton, POB 4447, Karachi; tel. (21) 5869534; fax (21) 5876071; e-mail information@pak-economist.com; f. 1960; English; Editor SUHAIL ABBAS; circ. 30,000.

Pak Kashmir: Pak Kashmir Office, Soikarno Chowk, Liaquat Rd, Rawalpindi; tel. (51) 74845; f. 1951; Urdu; Editor MUHAMMED FAYYAZ ABBAZI.

Parsi Sansar and Loke Sevak: 8 Mehrabad, 5 McNeil Rd, Karachi 75530; tel. and fax (21) 5673717; e-mail ogra@cyber.net.pk; f. 1909; English and Gujarati; Editor MEHERJI P. DASTUR.

Parwaz: Madina Office, Bahawalpur; Urdu; Editor MUSTAQ AHMED.

Qallandar: Peshawar; f. 1950; Urdu; Editor M. A. K. SHERWANI.

Quetta Times: Albert Press, Jinnah Rd, Quetta; f. 1924; English; Editor S. RUSTOMJI; circ. 4,000.

Shahab-e-Saqib: Shahab Saqib Rd, Maulana St, Peshawar; f. 1950; Urdu; Editor S. M. RIZVI.

The Statesman: 260C, Central C/A, PECHS, Karachi 75400; tel. (21) 4525627; f. 1955; English; Editor MOHAMMAD OWAIS.

Takbeer: A-1, 3rd Floor, 'Namco Centre', Campbell St, Karachi 74200; tel. (21) 2626613; fax (21) 2627742; e-mail irfanfaruqi@usa.com; f. 1984; Urdu; Sr. Exec. IRFAN KALIM FAROOQ; circ. 70,000.

Tarjaman-i-Sarhad: Peshawar; Urdu and Pashtu; Editor MOHAMMAD SHAFI SABIR.

Times of Kashmir: P/929, Banni, Rawalpindi; tel. (51) 5550903; fax (51) 4411038; e-mail iqbalmir@yahoo.com; English; Editor Mir IQBAL AZIZ.

Ufaq: 44H, Block No. 2, PECHS, Karachi; tel. (21) 437992; f. 1978; Editor WAHAJUDDIN CHISHTI; circ. 2,000.

SELECTED PERIODICALS

Aadab Arz: 190 N. Ghazali Rd, Saman Abad, Lahore 54500; tel. (42) 7582449; monthly; Editor KHALID BIN HAMID.

Aalami Digest: B-1, Momin Sq., Rashid Minhas Rd, Gulshan-e-Iqbal, Karachi; monthly; Urdu; Editor ZAHEDA HINA.

Afsan Digest: B-436, Sector 11-A, North Kaveli, Karachi 36; tel. (21) 657074; Urdu; Editor SYED ASIM MAHMOOD.

Akhbar-e-Watan: 68-C, 13th Commercial St, Phase-II, Extension Defence, Karachi; tel. (21) 5886071; fax (21) 5890179; e-mail akhbarewatan@hotmail.com; f. 1977; monthly; Urdu; cricket; Man. Editor MUNIR HUSSAIN; circ. 57,000.

Albalagh: Darul Uloom, Karachi 14; monthly; Editor MOHAMMED TAQI USMANI.

Al-Ma'arif: Institute of Islamic Culture, Club Rd, Lahore 54000; tel. (42) 6363127; f. 1950; quarterly; Urdu; Dir and Editor-in-Chief Dr RASHID AHMAD JALLANDHRI.

Anchal: 24 Saeed Mansion, I. I. Chundrigar Rd, Karachi; monthly.

Architecture and Interiors: 99, Ghafoor Chambers, Abdullah Haroon Rd, Karachi; tel. (21) 7772397; fax (21) 7772417; e-mail aplusi@cyberaccess.com.pk; f. 2001; quarterly; English; Editor MUTJUBA HUSSAIN; Man. Editor MURTUZA SHIKOH.

Archi Times: Ghafoor Chambers, 7th Floor, Abdullah Haroon Rd, Karachi; tel. (21) 7772397; fax (21) 7772417; e-mail archtime@cyberaccess.com.pk; f. 1986; monthly; English; architecture; Editor MUJTABA HUSSAIN.

Asia Travel News: 101 Muhammadi House, I. I. Chundrigar Rd, Karachi 74000; tel. (21) 2424837; fax (21) 2420797; fortnightly; travel trade, tourism and hospitality industry; Editor JAVED MUSHTAQ.

Auto Times: 5 S. J. Kayani Shaheed Rd, off Garden Rd, Karachi; tel. (21) 713595; fortnightly; English; Editor MUHAMMAD SHAHZAD.

Bachoon Ka Risala: 108–110 Adam Arcade, Shaheed-e-Millat Rd, Karachi; tel. (21) 419616; monthly; Urdu; Editor RUKHSANA SEHAM MIRZA.

Bagh: 777/18 Federal B Area, POB 485, Karachi; tel. (21) 449662; monthly; Urdu; Editor RAHIL IQBAL.

Bayyenat: Jamia Uloom-e-Islamia, Binnori Town, Karachi 74800; tel. (21) 4927233; f. 1962; monthly; Urdu; religious and social issues; Editor Maulana MUHAMMAD YOUSUF LUDHIANVI.

Beauty: Plot No. 4-C, 14th Commercial St, Defence Housing Authority, Phase II Extension, Karachi; tel. (21) 5805391; fax (21) 5896269; e-mail mansuri@fascom.com; f. 2000; bi-monthly; English; Chief Editor RIAZ AHMED MANSURI.

Beemakar (Insurer): 85 Press Chambers, I. I. Chundrigar Rd, Karachi; monthly; Urdu; Man. Editor SHAMSHAD AHMAD; Editor A. M. HASHMI.

Chand: 190 N. Ghazali Rd, Saman Abad, Lahore 54500; tel. (42) 7582449; monthly; Editor MASOOD HAMID.

The Cricketer: Plot No. 4-C, 14th Commercial St, Defence Housing Authority, Phase II Extension, Karachi; tel. (21) 5805391; fax (21) 5896269; e-mail mansuri@fascom.com; f. 1972; monthly; English/Urdu; Chief Editor RIAZ AHMED MANSURI.

Dastarkhuan: Plot No. 4-C, 14th Commercial St, Defence Housing Authority, Phase II Extension, Karachi; tel. (21) 5805391; fax (21) 5896269; e-mail mansuri@fascom.com; f. 1998; bi-monthly; Urdu; Chief Editor RIAZ AHMED MANSURI.

Defence Journal: 16B, 7th Central St, Defence Housing Authority, POB 12234, Karachi 75500; tel. (21) 5894074; fax (21) 571710; f. 1975; monthly; English; Editor-in-Chief Brig. (retd) ABDUL RAHMAN SIDDIQI; circ. 10,000.

Dentist: 70/7, Nazimabad No. 3, Karachi 18; f. 1984; monthly; English and Urdu; Editor NAEEMULLAH HUSAIN.

Dosheeza: 108–110 Adam Arcade, Shaheed-e-Millat Rd, Karachi; tel. (21) 4930470; fax (21) 4934369; monthly; Urdu; Editor RUKHSANA SEHAM MIRZA.

Duniya-e-Tibb: Eveready Chambers, 2nd Floor, Mohd Bin Qasim Rd, off I. I. Chundrigar Rd, POB 1385, Karachi 1; tel. (21) 2630985; fax (21) 2637624; e-mail mcm@digicom.net.pk; f. 1986; monthly; Urdu; modern and Asian medicine; International Co-ordinator 'Parekh'; circ. 12,000.

Economic Review: Al-Masiha, 3rd Floor, 47 Abdullah Haroon Rd, POB 7843, Karachi 74400; tel. (21) 7728963; fax (21) 7728957; f. 1969; monthly; economic, industrial and investment research; Editor AHMAD MUHAMMAD KHAN.

Engineering Horizons: 3/II Shadman Plaza, Shadman Market, Lahore 54000; tel. (42) 7581743; fax (42) 7587422; e-mail mahmood@imtiaz-faiz.com; f. 1988; monthly; English.

Engineering Review: 305 Spotlit Chambers, Dr Billimoria St, off Chundrigar Rd, POB 807, Karachi 74200; tel. (21) 2632567; fax (21) 2639378; e-mail engineeringreview@yahoo.com; internet www.engineeringreview.com.pk; f. 1975; fortnightly; English; circ. 5,000.

Film Asia: 68-C, 13th Commercial St, Phase-II, Extension Defence, Karachi; tel. (21) 5886071; fax (21) 5890179; e-mail akhbarewatan@hotmail.com; f. 1973; monthly; film, television, fashion, art and culture; Man. Editor MUNIR HUSSAIN; circ. 38,000.

Good Food: Plot No. 4-C, 14th Commercial St, Defence Housing Authority, Phase II Extension, Karachi; tel. (21) 5805391; fax (21)

5896269; e-mail mansuri@fascom.com; f. 1997; bi-monthly; English; Chief Editor RIAZ AHMED MANSURI.

Hamdard-i-Sehat: Institute of Health and Tibbi Research, Hamdard Foundation Pakistan, Nazimabad, Karachi 74600; tel. (21) 6616001; fax (21) 6611755; e-mail hamdard@khi.paknet.com.pk; f. 1933; monthly; Urdu; Editor-in-Chief SADIA RASHID; circ. 12,000.

Hamdard Islamicus: Hamdard Foundation Pakistan, Nazimabad, Karachi 74600; tel. (21) 6616001; fax (21) 6611755; e-mail hamdard@khi.paknet.com.pk; f. 1978; quarterly; English; Editor-in-Chief SADIA RASHID; circ. 750.

Hamdard Medicus: Hamdard Foundation Pakistan, Nazimabad, Karachi 74600; tel. (21) 6616001; fax (21) 6611755; e-mail hamdard@khi.paknet.com.pk; f. 1957; quarterly; English; Editor-in-Chief SADIA RASHID; circ. 1,000.

Hamdard Naunehal: Hamdard Foundation Pakistan, Nazimabad, Karachi 74600; tel. (21) 6616001; fax (21) 6611755; e-mail hamdard@khi.paknet.com.pk; f. 1952; monthly; Urdu; Editor MASOOD AHMAD BARAKATI; circ. 30,000.

The Herald: Haroon House, Dr Ziauddin Ahmed Road, Karachi 74200; tel. (21) 5670001; fax (21) 5687221; e-mail subscribe.Herald@Dawn.com; f. 1970; monthly; English; Editor AAMER AHMED KHAN; circ. 38,000.

Hikayat: 26 Patiala Ground, Link McLeod Rd, Lahore; monthly; Editor INAYATULLAH.

Honhar-e-Pakistan: 56 Aurangzeb Market, Karachi; monthly; Editor MAZHAR YUSAFZAI.

Hoor: Hoor St, Lahore; monthly; Editor KHULA RABIA.

Islami Jumhuria: Laj Rd, Old Anarkali, Lahore; monthly; Editor NAZIR TARIQ.

Islamic Studies: Islamic Research Institute, Faisal Masjid Campus, POB 1035, Islamabad 44000; tel. (51) 850751; fax (51) 250821; e-mail amzia555@apollo.net.pk; f. 1962; quarterly; English, Urdu (Fikro-Nazar) and Arabic (Al Dirasat al-Islamiyyah) edns; Islamic literature, religion, history, geography, language and the arts; Editor Dr ZAFAR ISHAQ ANSARI (acting); circ. 3,000.

Jamal: Institute of Islamic Culture, 2 Club Rd, Lahore 3; tel. (42) 363127; f. 1950; annual; English; Dir and Editor-in-Chief MUHAMMAD SUHEYL UMAR.

Journal of the Pakistan Historical Society: c/o Hamdard Foundation, Nazimabad, Karachi 74600; tel. (21) 6616001; fax (21) 6611755; e-mail hamdard@khi.paknet.com.pk; f. 1953; quarterly; English; Editor Dr ANSAR ZAHID KHAN.

Khel-Ke-Duniya: 6/13 Alyusaf Chamber, POB 340, Karachi; tel. (21) 216888.

Khwateen Digest: Urdu Bazar, M. A. Jinnah Rd, Karachi; monthly; Urdu; Editor MAHMUD RIAZ.

Kiran: 37 Urdu Bazar, M. A. Jinnah Rd, Karachi; tel. (21) 216606; Editor MAHMUD BABAR FAISAL.

Leather News: Iftikhar Chambers, opp. UNI Plaza, Altaf Hussain Rd, POB 4323, Karachi 74000; fax (21) 2631545; f. 1989; Editor ABDUL RAFAY SIDDIQI.

Medical Variety: 108–110 Adam Arcade, Shaheed-e-Millat Rd, Karachi; tel. (21) 419616; monthly; English; Editor RUKHSANA SEHAM MIRZA.

Muslim World Business: 20 Sasi Arcade, 4th Floor, Main Clifton Rd, POB 10417, Karachi 6; tel. (21) 534870; f. 1989; monthly; English; political and business; Editor-in-Chief MUZAFFAR HASSAN.

Naey-Ufaq: 24 Saeed Mansion, I. I. Chundrigar Rd, Karachi; fortnightly.

NGM Communication: Gulberg Colony, POB 3041, Lahore 54660; tel. (42) 5713849; e-mail ngm@shoa.net; internet www.ngm.web-page.net; English; lists newly-released Pakistani publications on the internet; updated weekly; Editor NIZAM NIZAMI.

Pakistan Journal of Applied Economics: Applied Economics Research Centre, University of Karachi, POB 8403, Karachi 75270; tel. (21) 9243168; fax (21) 4829730; e-mail pjae@cyber.net.pk; twice a year; Editor Prof. Dr NUZHAT AHMAD.

Pakistan Journal of Scientific and Industrial Research: Pakistan Council of Scientific and Industrial Research, Scientific Information Centre, 39 Garden Rd, Saddar, Karachi 74400; tel. (21) 9215100; fax (21) 9215107; e-mail pcsirsys@super.net.pk; f. 1958; bi-monthly; English; Exec. Editor Dr A. RASHEED KHAN; circ. 1,000.

Pakistan Management Review: Pakistan Institute of Management, Management House, Shahrah Iran, Clifton, Karachi 75600; tel. (21) 9251711; e-mail pimkhi@pim.com.pk; internet www.pim.com.pk; f. 1960; quarterly; English; Editor IQBAL A. QAZI.

Pasban: Faiz Modh Rd, Quetta; fortnightly; Urdu; Editor MOLVI MOHD ABDULLAH.

Phool: 4 Sharah-e-Fatima Jinnah, Lahore 54000; e-mail phool@nawaiwaqt.com.pk; internet www.phool.com.pk; monthly; children's; circ. 40,000.

Progress: 4th Floor, PIDC House, Dr Ziauddin Ahmed Rd, POB 3942, Karachi 75530; tel. (21) 5681391; fax (21) 5680005; e-mail n_nusrat@ppl.com.pk; f. 1956; monthly; publ. by Pakistan Petroleum Ltd; Editor and Publr NUSRAT NASARULLAH; Chief Exec./Man. Dir S. MUNSIF RAZA.

Qaumi Digest: 50 Lower Mall, Lahore; tel. (42) 7225143; fax (42) 7233261; monthly; Editor MUJIBUR REHMAN SHAMI.

Sabrang Digest: 47–48 Press Chambers, I. I. Chundrigar Rd, Karachi 1; tel. (21) 211961; f. 1970; monthly; Urdu; Editor SHAKEEL ADIL ZADAH; circ. 150,000.

Sach-Chee Kahaniyan: 108–110 Adam Arcade, Shaheed-e-Millat Rd, Karachi; tel. (21) 4930470; fax (21) 4934369; monthly; Urdu; Editor RUKHSANA SEHAM MIRZA.

Sayyarah: Aiwan-e-Adab, Urdu Bazar, Lahore 54000; tel. (42) 7321842; f. 1962; monthly; Urdu; literary; Chief Editor NAEEM SIDDIQI; Man. Editor HAFEEZ-UR-RAHMAN AHSAN.

Sayyarah Digest: 16B Sanda Rd, Lahore; tel. (42) 7245412; e-mail sayyaradigest@brain.com.pk; f. 1963; monthly; Urdu; Chief Editor AMJAD RAUF KHAN.

Science Magazine: Science Book Foundation, Haji Bldg, Hassan Ali Efendi Rd, Karachi; tel. (21) 2625647; monthly; Urdu; Editor QASIM MAHMOOD.

Seep: Alam Market, Block No. 16, Federal B Area, Karachi; quarterly; Editor NASIM DURRANI.

Show Business: 108–110 Adam Arcade, Shaheed-e-Millat Rd, POB 12540, Karachi; tel. (21) 419616; monthly; Urdu; Editor RUKHSANA SEHAM MIRZA.

Sindh Quarterly: 36D Karachi Administrative Co-operative Housing Society, off Shaheed-e-Millat Rd, Karachi 75350; tel. (21) 4531988; f. 1973; Editor SAYID GHULAM MUSTAFA SHAH.

Smash: Plot No. 4-C, 14th Commercial St, Defence Housing Authority, Phase II Extension, Karachi; tel. (21) 5805391; fax (21) 5896269; e-mail mansuri@fascom.com; f. 2000; monthly; English; Chief Editor RIAZ AHMED MANSURI.

Spider: Haroon House, Dr Ziauddin Ahmed Rd, Karachi 74200; tel. (21) 5670001; fax (21) 5687221; e-mail info@spider.tm; internet spider.tm; f. 1998; internet monthly.

Sports International: Arshi Market, Firdaus Colony, Nazimabad, Karachi 74600; tel. (21) 622171; fax (21) 6683768; e-mail ibp-khi@cyber.net.pk; f. 1972; fortnightly; Urdu and English; Chief Editor KANWAR ABDUL MAJEED; Editor RAHEEL MAJEED.

Taj: Jamia Tajia, St 13, Sector 14/B, Buffer Zone, Karachi 75850; monthly; Editor BABA M. ATIF SHAH ANWARI ZAHEENI TAJI.

Talimo Tarbiat: Ferozsons (Pvt) Ltd, 60 Shahrah-e-Quaid-e-Azam, Lahore 54000; tel. (42) 6301196; fax (42) 6369204; f. 1941; children's monthly; Urdu; Chief Editor A. SALAM; circ. 50,000.

Textile Times: Arshi Market, Firdaus Colony, Nazimabad, Karachi 74600; tel. (21) 6683768; e-mail ibp-khi@cyber.net.pk; f. 1993; monthly; English; Chief Editor KANWAR ABDUL MAJEED; Exec. Editor RAHEEL MAJEED KHAN.

Trade Chronicle: Iftikhar Chambers, Altaf Hussain Rd, POB 5257, Karachi 74000; tel. (21) 2631587; fax (21) 2635007; e-mail arsidiqi@fascom.com; f. 1953; monthly; English; trade, politics, finance and economics; Editor ABDUL RAB SIDDIQI; circ. 6,000.

Trade Link International: Zahoor Mansion, Tariq Rd, Karachi; monthly; English; Man. Editor M. IMRAN BAIG; Editor IKRAMULLAH QUREISHI.

TV Times: Plot No. 4-C, 14th Commercial St, Defence Housing Authority, Phase II Extension, Karachi; tel. (21) 5805391; fax (21) 5896269; e-mail mansuri@fascom.com; f. 1987; monthly; English; Chief Editor RIAZ AHMED MANSURI.

UNESCO Payami: 30 UNESCO House, Sector H-8/1, Islamabad; tel. (51) 434196; fax (51) 431815; monthly; Urdu; publ. by Pakistan National Commission for UNESCO; Editor Dr MUNIR A. ABRO.

The Universal Message: D-35, Block-5, Federal 'B' Area, Karachi 75950; tel. (21) 6349840; fax (21) 6361040; f. 1979; journal of the Islamic Research Acad.; monthly; English; literature, politics, economics, religion; Editor ASADULLAH KHAN.

Urdu Digest: 21-Acre Scheme, Samanabad, Lahore 54500; tel. (42) 7589957; fax (42) 7563646; e-mail digest@lhr.paknet.com.pk; monthly; Urdu; Editor ALTAF HASAN QURESHEE.

Voice of Islam: Jamiatul Falah Bldg, Akbar Rd, Saddar, POB 7141, Karachi 74400; tel. (21) 7721394; f. 1952; monthly; Islamic Cultural Centre magazine; English; Editor Prof. ABDUL QADEER SALEEM; Man. Editor Prof. WAQAR ZUBAIRI.

Wings: 101 Muhammadi House, I. I. Chundrigar Rd, Karachi 74000; tel. (21) 2412591; fax (21) 2420797; monthly; aviation and defence; English; Editor and Publr JAVED MUSHTAQ.

Women's Own: Plot No. 4-C, 14th Commercial St, Defence Housing Authority, Phase II Extension, Karachi; tel. (21) 5805391; fax (21) 5896269; e-mail mansuri@fascom.com; f. 1987; monthly; English; Chief Editor RIAZ AHMED MANSURI.

Yaqeen International: Darut Tasnif (Pvt) Ltd, Main Hub River Rd, Mujahidabad, Karachi 75760; tel. (21) 2814432; fax (21) 2811304; f. 1952; English and Arabic; Islamic organ; Editor Dr HAFIZ MUHAMMAD ADIL.

Yaran-e-Watan: Overseas Pakistanis Foundation, Shahrah-E-Jamhuriate, G-5/2, POB 1470, Islamabad 44000; tel. (51) 9210175; fax (51) 9224518; e-mail opf@comsats.net.pk; f. 1982; monthly; Urdu; publ. by the Overseas Pakistanis Foundation; Editor HAROON RASHID.

Youth World International: 104/C Central C/A, Tariq Rd, Karachi; tel. (21) 442211; f. 1987; monthly; English; Editor Syed ADIL EBRAHIM.

NEWS AGENCIES

Associated Press of Pakistan (APP): 18 Mauve Area, Zero Point, G-7/1, POB 1258, Islamabad; tel. (51) 2826158; fax (51) 2821292; e-mail appnews@isb.comsats.net.pk; f. 1948; Dir-Gen. ASHFAQ AHMAD GONDAL.

National News Agency (NNA): 131 Posh Arcade Plaza, Markaz G-9, POB 455, Islamabad 44000; tel. (51) 2260082; fax (51) 2255967; e-mail nna@islamabad.net; internet www.nij.8m.net; Chief Editor SUHAIL ILYAS CHAUDHRY.

News Network International: 410 Khyber Plaza, Blue Area, Islamabad; tel. (51) 827442; fax (51) 218549; internet nni-news.com; Editor-in-Chief HAFIZ ABDUL KHALIQ.

Pakistan International Press Agency (PIPA): 6 Ground Floor, State Life Bldg, Karachi; tel. (21) 5683618; Bureau Chief S. M. SHAKEEL.

Pakistan Press Agency (PPA): 6, St 39, G-6/2, Islamabad; tel. (51) 272405; fax (51) 272403; Chief Exec. KHALID ATHAR.

Pakistan Press International (PPI): Press Centre, Shahrah Kamal Atatürk, POB 541, Karachi; tel. (21) 2631123; fax (21) 2637754; e-mail owais.ali@attglobal.net; f. 1956; Chair. OWAIS ASLAM ALI.

United Press of Pakistan (Pvt) Ltd (UPP): 1 Victoria Chambers, Haji Abdullah Haroon Rd, Karachi 74400; tel. 5683235; fax (21) 5682694; f. 1949; Man. Editor MAHMUDUL AZIZ; 6 brs.

Foreign Bureaux

Agence France-Presse (AFP): 90 Attaturk Ave, G-6/3, Islamabad; tel. (51) 111237475; fax (51) 2822203; e-mail islamabad@afp.com; Chief Rep. FRANÇOIS XAVIER HARISPE.

Agenzia Nazionale Stampa Associata (ANSA) (Italy): Islamabad; Bureau Chief ABSAR HUSAIN RIZVI.

Associated Press (AP) (USA): 6A, St 25, F-8/2, Islamabad; tel. (51) 260957; fax (51) 256176; Bureau Chief KATHY GANON.

Deutsche Presse-Agentur (dpa) (Germany): Islamabad; tel. (51) 821925; Correspondent ANWAR MANSURI.

Inter Press Service (IPS) (Italy): House 10, St 13, F-8/3, Islamabad; tel. (51) 853356; fax (42) 856430; Correspondent MUSHAHID HUSSAIN.

Reuters (UK): POB 1069, Islamabad, Pakistan; tel. (51) 2274757; e-mail simon.denyer@reuters.com; Bureau Chief: SIMON DENYER.

United Press International (UPI) (USA): Islamabad; tel. (51) 821472; Bureau Chief DENHOLM BARNETSON.

Xinhua (New China) News Agency (People's Republic of China): Islamabad; tel. (51) 856614; Chief Correspondent LI JIASHENG.

PRESS ASSOCIATIONS

All Pakistan Newspaper Employees Confederation: Karachi Press Club, M. R. Kayani Rd, Karachi; f. 1976; confed. of all press industry trade unions; Pres. ABDUL HAMEED CHAPRA; Sec.-Gen. PERVAIZ SHAUKAT.

All Pakistan Newspapers Society: 32 Farid Chambers, 3rd Floor, Abdullah Haroon Rd, Karachi 3; tel. (21) 5671256; fax (21) 5671310; e-mail apns44@hotmail.com; f. 1949; Pres. HAMEED HAROON; Sec.-Gen. KAZI ASAD ABID.

Council of Pakistan Newspaper Editors: c/o United Press of Pakistan, 1 Victoria Chambers, Haji Abdullah Haroon Rd, Karachi 74400; tel. (21) 5682694; fax (21) 5682694; Pres. AHMAD ALI KHAN; Gen. Sec. MUJIBUR RAHMAN SHAMI.

Publishers

Anjuman Taraqq-e-Urdu Pakistan: D-159, Block 7, Gulshan-e-Iqbal, Karachi 75300; tel. (21) 461406; f. 1903; literature, religion, textbooks, Urdu dictionaries, literary and critical texts; Pres. AFTAB AHMED KHAN; Hon. Sec. JAMIL UDDIN AALI.

Camran Publishers: Jalaluddin Hospital Bldg, Circular Rd, Lahore; f. 1964; general, technical, textbooks; Propr ABDUL HAMID.

Chronicle Publications: Iftikhar Chambers, Altaf Hussain Rd, POB 5257, Karachi 74000; tel. (21) 2631587; fax (21) 2635007; e-mail arsidiqi@fascom.com; f. 1953; reference, directories, religious books; Dir ABDUL RAUF SIDDIQI.

Economic and Industrial Publications: Al-Masiha, 3rd Floor, 47 Abdullah Haroon Rd, POB 7843, Karachi 74400; tel. (21) 7728963; fax (21) 7728434; f. 1965; industrial, economic and investment research.

Elite Publishers Ltd: D-118, SITE, Karachi 75700; tel. (21) 297035; fax (21) 295220; f. 1951; Chair. AHMED MIRZA JAMIL; Man. Dir KHALID JAMIL.

Ferozsons (Pvt) Ltd: 60 Shahrah-e-Quaid-e-Azam, Lahore; tel. (42) 626262; fax (42) 6369204; e-mail support@ferozsons.com.pk; f. 1894; books, periodicals, maps, atlases; Man. Dir A. SALAM; Dir ZAHEER SALAM.

Frontier Publishing Co: 22 Urdu Bazar, Lahore; tel. (42) 7355262; fax (42) 7247323; e-mail masim@brain.net.pk; internet www.brain.net.pk/~masim; academic and general; Execs MUHAMMAD ARIF, MUHAMMAD AMIR, MUHAMMAD ASIM.

Sh. Ghulam Ali and Sons (Pvt) Ltd: 199 Circular Rd, Lahore 54000; tel. (42) 7352908; fax (42) 6315478; e-mail niazasad@hotmail.com; internet www.ghulamali.com; f. 1887; general, religion, technical, textbooks; Dirs NIAZ AHMAD, ASAD NIAZ.

Harf Academy: G/307, Amena Plaza, Peshawar Rd, Rawalpindi.

Idara Taraqqi-i-Urdu: S-1/363 Saudabad, Karachi 27; f. 1949; general literature, technical and professional books and magazines; Propr IKRAM AHMED.

Ilmi Kitab Khana: Kabeer St, Urdu Bazar, Lahore; tel. (42) 62833; f. 1948; technical, professional, historical and law; Propr Haji SARDAR MOHAMMAD.

Indus Publications: 25 Fared Chambers, Abdullah Haroon Rd, Karachi; tel. (21) 5660242; fax (21) 2635276.

Islamic Book Centre: 25B Masson Rd, POB 1625, Lahore 54000; tel. (42) 6361803; fax (42) 6360955; e-mail lsaeed@paknetl.ptc.pk; religion in Arabic, Urdu and English; Islamic history, text books, dictionaries and reprints; Propr and Man. Dir SUMBLEYNA SAJID SAEED.

Islamic Publications (Pvt) Ltd: 3 Court St, Lower Mall, Lahore 54000; tel. and fax (42) 7248676; e-mail info@islamicpak.com.pk; internet www.islamicpak.com.pk; f. 1959; Islamic literature in Urdu and English; Man. Dir Prof. MUHAMMAD AMIN JAVED; Gen. Man. AMANAT ALI.

Jamiatul Falah Publications: Jamiatul Falah Bldg, Akbar Rd, Saddar, POB 7141, Karachi 74400; tel. (21) 7721394; f. 1952; Islamic history and culture; Pres. MUZAFFAR AHMED HASHMI; Sec. Prof. SHAHZADUL HASAN CHISHTI.

Kazi Publications: 121 Zulqarnain Chambers, Ganpat Rd, POB 1845, Lahore; tel. (42) 7311359; fax (42) 7117606; e-mail kazip@brain.net.pk; internet www.brain.net.pk/~kazip/; f. 1978; Islamic literature, religion, law, biographies; Propr/Man. MUHAMMAD IKRAM SIDDIQI; Chief Editor MUHAMMAD IQBAL SIDDIQI.

Lark Publishers: Urdu Bazar, Karachi 1; f. 1955; general literature, magazines; Propr MAHMOOD RIAZ.

Lion Art Press (Pvt) Ltd: 112 Shahrah-e-Quaid-e-Azam, Lahore 54000; tel. (42) 6363641; fax (42) 6304444; e-mail alij@brain.net.pk; f. 1919; general publs in English and Urdu; Man. Dir S. A. WAHEED; Dirs KHALID A. SHEIKH, S. A. JAMIL.

Maktaba Darut Tasnif: Main Hub River Rd, Mujahidabad, Karachi 75760; tel. (21) 2814432; fax (21) 2811307; f. 1951; Koran, Majeed and Islamic literature; Dir ABDUL BAQI FAROOQI.

Malik Sirajuddin & Sons: Kashmiri Bazar, POB 2250, Lahore 54000; tel. (42) 7657527; fax (42) 7657490; e-mail sirajco@brain.net.pk; f. 1905; general, religion, law, textbooks; Man. MALIK ABDUL ROUF.

Malik Sons: Karkhana Bazar, Faisalabad.

Medina Publishing Co: M. A. Jinnah Rd, Karachi 1; f. 1960; general literature, textbooks; Propr HAKIM MOHAMMAD TAQI.

Mehtab Co: Ghazni St, Urdu Bazar, Lahore; tel. (42) 7120071; fax (42) 7353489; e-mail shashraf@brain.net.pk; f. 1978; Islamic literature; Propr SHAHZAD RIAZ SHEIKH.

Mohammad Hussain and Sons: 17 Urdu Bazar, Lahore 2; tel. (42) 7244114; f. 1941; religion, textbooks; Partners MOHAMMAD HUSSAIN, AZHAR ALI SHEIKH, PERVEZ ALI SHEIKH.

Sh. Muhammad Ashraf: 7 Aibak Rd, New Anarkali, Lahore 7; tel. (42) 7353171; fax (42) 7353489; e-mail shashraf@brain.net.pk; f. 1923; books in English on all aspects of Islam; Man. Dir SHAHZAD RIAZ SHEIKH.

National Book Service: 22 Urdu Bazar, Lahore; tel. (42) 7247310; fax (42) 7247323; e-mail masim@brain.net.pk; internet www.brain.net.pk/~masim; academic and primary school books; Execs MUHAMMAD ARIF, MUHAMMAD AMIR, MUHAMMAD ASIM.

Oxford University Press: 5 Bangalore Town, Block 7–8, Sharah-e-Faisal, POB 13033, Karachi 75350; tel. (21) 4529025; fax (21) 4547640; e-mail ouppak@theoffice.net; internet www.oup.com.pk; academic, educational and general; Man. Dir AMEENA SAIYID.

Pakistan Law House: Pakistan Chowk, POB 90, Karachi 1; tel. (21) 2212455; fax (21) 2627549; e-mail plh_law_house@hotmail.com; f. 1950; importers and exporters of legal books and reference books; Man. K. NOORANI.

Pakistan Publishing House: Victoria Chambers 2, A. Haroon Rd, Karachi 75400; tel. (21) 5681457; f. 1959; Propr H. NOORANI; Gen. Man. AAMIR HUSSEIN.

Paramount Books: 152/0, Block 2, PECHS, Karachi 75400; tel. (21) 4310030; e-mail parabks@cyber.net.pk.

Pioneer Book House: 1 Avan Lodge, Bunder Rd, POB 37, Karachi; periodicals, gazettes, maps and reference works in English, Urdu and other regional languages.

Premier Bookhouse: Shahin Market, Room 2, Anarkali, POB 1888, Lahore; tel. (42) 7321174; Islamic and law.

Publishers International: Bandukwala Bldg, 4 I. I. Chundrigar Rd, Karachi; f. 1948; reference; Man. Dir KAMALUDDIN AHMAD.

Publishers United (Pvt) Ltd: 176 Anarkali, POB 1689, Lahore 54000; tel. (42) 7352238; textbooks, technical, reference, oriental literature in English, military and general; Man. Dir Maj. (retd) JAVED AMIN.

Punjab Religious Books Society: Anarkali, Lahore 2; tel. (42) 54416; educational, religious, law and general; Gen. Man. A. R. IRSHAD; Sec. NAEEM SHAKIR.

Reprints Ltd: 16 Bahadur Shah Market, M. A. Jinnah Rd, Karachi; f. 1983; Pakistani edns of foreign works; Chair. A. D. KHALID; Man. Dir AZIZ KHALID.

Sang-e-Meel Publications: 20 Shahrah-e-Pakistan, Lahore; tel. (42) 7220100; e-mail smp@sang-e-meel.com.

Sindhi Adabi Board (Sindhi Literary and Publishing Organization): Hyderabad; tel. (221) 771276; f. 1951; history, literature, culture of Sindh; in Sindhi, Urdu, English, Persian and Arabic; translations into Sindhi, especially of literature and history; Chair. MOHAMMAD IBRAHIM JOYO; Sec. GHULAM RABBANI A. AGRO.

Taj Co Ltd: Manghopir Rd, POB 530, Karachi; tel. (21) 294221; f. 1929; religious books; Man. Dir A. H. KHOKHAR.

The Times Press (Pvt) Ltd: C-18, Al-Hilal Society, off University Rd, Karachi 74800; tel. (21) 4932931; fax (21) 4935602; e-mail timekhi@cyber.net.pk; internet www.timespress.8m.com; f. 1948; printers, publishers and stationery manufacturers, including security printing (postal stationery and stamps); registered publishers of Koran, school textbooks, etc.; Dir S. M. MINHAJUDDIN.

Tooba Publishers: 85 Sikandar Block, Allama Iqbal Town, Lahore.

Urdu Academy Sind: 16 Bahadur Shah Market, M. A. Jinnah Rd, Karachi 2; tel. (21) 2634185; f. 1947; brs in Hyderabad and Lahore; reference, general and textbooks; Editor and Man. Dir A. D. KHALID.

West-Pak Publishing Co (Pvt) Ltd: 56N, Gulberg-II, Lahore; tel. (42) 7230555; fax (42) 7120077; f. 1932; textbooks and religious books; Chief Exec. SYED AHSAN MAHMUD.

Government Publishing House

Government Publications: Office of the Deputy Controller, Stationery and Forms, nr Old Sabzi Mandi, University Rd, Karachi 74800; tel. (21) 9231989; Dep. Controller MUHAMMAD AMIN BUTT.

PUBLISHERS' ASSOCIATION

Pakistan Publishers' and Booksellers' Association: YMCA Bldg, Shahrah-e-Quaid-e-Azam, Lahore; Chair. SYED AHSAN MAHMUD; Sec. ZUBAIR SAEED.

Broadcasting and Communications

TELECOMMUNICATIONS

Pakistan Telecommunications Authority (PTA): Mauve Area, G-10, Islamabad; tel. (51) 99257246; fax (51) 456375; e-mail ddpr_pta@yahoo.com; internet www.pta.gov.pk; f. 1995; regulatory authority; Chair. Mian AKHTAR BAJWA; Dir-Gen. CH. MOHAMMAD DIN.

Carrier Telephone Industries (Pvt) Ltd: 1-9/2 Industrial Area, POB 1098, Islamabad; tel. (51) 414856; fax (51) 414859; f. 1969; Man. Dir MALIK MOHAMMAD AMIN.

Instaphone: Pakcom Ltd, World Trade Centre, 10 Khayaban-e-Roomi, Clifton, Karachi; tel. (21) 5871171; fax (21) 5869051; private mobile telephone co.

Mobilink: Pakistan Mobile Communications (Pvt) Ltd, 205-B, E. I. Lines, Dr Daud Pota Rd, Karachi; tel. (21) 5670261; fax (21) 5670268; private mobile telephone co.

Pakistan Telecommunication Co Ltd (PTCL): G-8/4 Islamabad 44000; tel. (51) 4844463; fax (51) 4843991; e-mail gmpr@ptcl.com.pk; internet www.ptcl.com.pk; f. 1990; 88% state-owned; scheduled for transfer to the public sector; Chair. AKHTAR AHMED BAJWA.

Paktel Ltd: 1st Floor, State Life Bldg No. 3, Dr Ziauddin Ahmed Rd, Karachi; tel. (21) 5689231; fax (21) 5682537; private mobile telephone co.

Other telecommunications companies operating in Pakistan include Telephone Industries of Pakistan and Alcatel Pakistan Ltd.

RADIO

Pakistan Broadcasting Corporation: National Broadcasting House, Constitution Ave, Islamabad 4400; tel. (51) 9214278; fax (51) 9223827; e-mail cnoradio@isb.comsats.net.pk; internet www.radio.gov.pk; f. 1947 as Radio Pakistan; national broadcasting network of 23 stations; home service 408 hrs daily in 17 languages and dialects; external services 10 hrs daily in 11 languages; world service 11 hrs daily in two languages; 80 news bulletins daily; Dir-Gen. TARIQ IMMAM; Chair. SYED ANWAR MAHMOOD.

Azad Kashmir Radio: Muzaffarabad; state-owned; Station Dir MASUD KASHFI; Dep. Controller (Eng.) SYED AHMED.

Capital FM: Islamabad; f. 1995; privately-owned; broadcasts music and audience participation shows 24 hrs daily.

TELEVISION

Pakistan Television Corpn Ltd: Federal TV Complex, Constitution Ave, POB 1221, Islamabad; tel. (51) 9208651; fax (51) 9202202; e-mail md@ptv.com.pk; internet www.ptv.com.pk; f. 1964; transmits 240 hrs daily; four channels; Chair. SYED ANWAR MAHMOOD; Man. Dir YOUSAF BAIG MIRZA.

Shalimar Television Network: 36, H-9, POB 1246, Islamabad; tel. (51) 9257396; fax (51) 4434830; e-mail srbc@comsats.net.pk; f. 1989 as People's Television Network; 57% state-owned, 43% privately-owned; 12 terrestrial stations throughout Pakistan; Chief Exec. ANWAR JAHANGIR.

Finance

(cap. = capital; auth. = authorized; p.u. = paid up; res = reserves; dep. = deposits; m. = million; brs = branches; amounts in rupees unless otherwise stated)

BANKING

In January 1974 all domestic banks were nationalized. In December 1990 the Government announced that it intended to transfer the five state-owned commercial banks to private ownership. By late 1991 the majority of shares in the Muslim Commercial Bank Ltd and the Allied Bank of Pakistan Ltd had been transferred to private ownership. In 1991 the Government granted 10 new private commercial bank licences, the first since banks were nationalized in 1974. According to legislation introduced in early 2001, by the end of June 2002 all financial transactions were to be conducted in strict accordance with Shari'a law.

Central Bank

State Bank of Pakistan: Central Directorate, I. I. Chundrigar Rd, POB 4456, Karachi 2; tel. (21) 9212400; fax (21) 9212433; e-mail sbp-isd@cyber.net.pk; internet www.sbp.org.pk; f. 1948; bank of issue; controls and regulates currency and foreign exchange; cap. 100m., res 9,000m., dep. 312,625m. (June 1999); Gov. Dr ISHRAT HUSSAIN; Dep. Govs MUKHTAR NABI QURESHI, RASHID AKHTAR CHUGHTAI; 18 brs.

Commercial Banks

Allied Bank of Pakistan Ltd: Central Office, Karachi 75600; tel. (21) 5868770; fax (21) 5835525; e-mail int_div@abl.com.pk; f. 1942 as Australasia Bank Ltd; name changed as above 1974; cap. 1,063.2m., res 480.8m., dep. 93,107.3m. (Dec. 1999); 49% state-owned; Pres., Chair. and Chief Exec. KHALID A. SHERWANI; Sr Vice-Pres. KHALID MEHBOOB; 929 brs in Pakistan and four brs abroad.

Askari Commercial Bank Ltd: AWT Plaza, The Mall, POB 1084, Rawalpindi; tel. (51) 9272150; fax (51) 9272455; e-mail askari@comsats.net.pk; internet www.askaribank.com.pk/; f. 1992; cap. US $ 17.3m., res US $25.4m., dep. US $686.7m. (Dec. 2001); Chair. Lt-Gen. JAMSHAID GULZAR; Pres. and Chief Exec. KALIM UR-RAHMAN; 38 brs.

Bank Al Habib Ltd: M.M. Bldg, I.I. Chundrigar Rd, Karachi; tel. (21) 2412986; e-mail alhabib@cyber.net.pk; f. 1991; cap. 601.1m., res 565.0m., dep. 14,112.9m. (Dec. 1999); Chair. HAMID D. HABIB; Chief Exec. and Man. Dir ABBAS D. HABIB; 27 brs.

Bank Alfalah Ltd: BA Bldg, I.I. Chundrigar Rd, POB 6773, Karachi; tel. (21) 2414030; fax (21) 2417006; e-mail karachi@bankalfalah.com; internet www.bankalfalah.com; f. 1992 as Habib Credit and Exchange Ltd; name changed as above 1998; cap. 600.0m., res 286.0m., dep. 15,820.5m. (Dec. 1999); 70% owned by Abu Dhabi Consortium, 30% by Habib Bank; Chief Exec. MUHAMMAD SALEEM AKHTAR; 13 brs.

The Bank of Khyber: 24 The Mall, Peshawar; tel. (521) 279977; fax (521) 278146; e-mail mdbok1@pes.comsats.net.pk; internet www.bankofkhyber.com.pk; cap. 416.0m., res 253.0m., dep. 9,630.5m. (Dec. 1998); 100% state-owned; Exec. Dir SAJID ALI ABBASI; Man. Dir SAJID ALI ABBASI; 29 brs.

The Bank of Punjab: 7 Egerton Rd, POB 2254, Lahore 54000; tel. (42) 9200421; fax (42) 9200297; e-mail bop@lhr.comsats.net.pk; internet www.punjabbank.com; f. 1989; share cap. 1,004m., res 1,251m., dep. 22,433m. (June 2002); 51.6% owned by provincial govt; Chair. TARIQ SULTAN; Man. Dir SALIM JAN; 242 brs.

Bolan Bank Ltd: 92-514/A Madresa Rd, Quetta; tel. (81) 66562; fax (81) 67595; f. 1991; auth. cap. 600m.; Pres. and Chief Exec. SYED IJAZ HUSSAIN SHAH; 10 brs.

Habib Bank Ltd: 21 Habib Bank Plaza, I. I. Chundrigar Rd, Karachi 75650; tel. (21) 2418000; fax (21) 2414191; e-mail hfilsn@netvigator.com; f. 1941; cap. 12,178.5m., res 9,935.7m., dep. 258,097.1m. (Dec. 1998); 100% state-owned; scheduled for transfer to private sector; Pres. ZAKIR MAHMOOD; 1,859 brs in Pakistan.

Indus Bank Ltd: F.C. Trust Bldg, Suneri Masjid Rd, Peshawar; tel. (521) 271639; fax (521) 271072; f. 1991; cap. 300.0m., res 16.4m., dep. 2,197.5m. (Dec. 1998); Chair. and Pres. S. KHURSHID SOHAIL; Dep. Man. Dir ARIF ALI SIDDIQUI; 13 brs.

Khushhali Bank: 94 West, 4th Floor, Jinnah Ave, Blue Area, POB 3111, Islamabad; fax (51) 9206080; Chair. and Man. Dir GHALIB NISHTAR.

Metropolitan Bank Ltd: Spencer's Bldg, I. I. Chundrigar Rd, POB 1289, Karachi; tel. (21) 2636740; fax (21) 2630404; e-mail metro@paknet3.ptc.pk; f. 1992; cap. 500.0m., res 727.0m., dep. 15,839.4m. (Dec. 1999); Chair. and Chief Exec. KASSIM PAREKH; Sr Exec. Vice-Pres. and Gen. Man. A. SUBHAN SIDDIQUI; 19 brs.

Muslim Commercial Bank Ltd: Adamjee House, I. I. Chundrigar Rd, POB 4976, Karachi 74000; tel. (21) 2414091; fax (21) 2438441; e-mail mcbintl@cyber.net.pk; internet www.mcb.com.pk; f. 1947; cap. 2,423m., res 2,147m., dep. 154,439m. (June 2001); Chair. Mian MUHAMMAD MANSHA; Pres. and CEO MUHAMMAD AFTAB MANZOOR; 1,210 brs in Pakistan, 6 brs abroad.

National Bank of Pakistan (NBP): NBP Building, I. I. Chundrigar Rd, POB 4937, Karachi 2; tel. (21) 9212208; fax (21) 9212774; e-mail info@nbp.com.pk; internet www.nbp.com.pk; f. 1949; cap. 1,463.9m., res 6,376.4m., dep. 208,283.0m. (Dec. 1995); 100% state-owned; Pres. ALI RAZA; Sr Vice-Pres. MUHAMMAD YOUSUF; 1,491 brs in Pakistan and 23 brs abroad.

PICIC Commercial Bank Ltd: I. I. Chundrigar Rd, POB 572, Karachi 74200; tel. (21) 2637161; fax (21) 2636909; e-mail gcbl-fi@cyber.net.pk; f. 1994 as Schön Bank Ltd; name changed to Gulf Commercial Bank Ltd in 1998; 60% shares and full management of bank acquired by PICIC in February 2001, name changed to above in June 2001; cap. and res 690.9m., dep. 7,552.5m. (June 2001); Chair. MOHAMMAD ALI KHOJA; Pres. and CEO MOHAMMAD BILAL SHEIKH; 20 brs.

Platinum Commercial Bank Ltd: 76B, E-1, Main Blvd (next to Hafeez Centre), Gulberg III, Lahore 54000; tel. (42) 5764288; fax (42) 5755358; e-mail pcblglh@brain.net.pk; f. 1995; cap. 500m., res 154.8m., dep. 4,821.6m. (Dec. 1999); Chair. MOHAMMED ABID; Pres. and Chief Exec. S. M. WASEEM; 16 brs.

Prime Commercial Bank Ltd: 61 Main Blvd, Gulberg, Lahore; tel. (42) 5757788; fax (42) 5762323; e-mail info@primebank.com.pk; internet www.primebankpk.com; f. 1991; cap. 674.5m., res 305.9m., dep. 9,191.3m. (Dec. 1999); Pres. SAEED I. CHAUDHRY; Chair. ABDUL-RAZZAK M. EL-KHARAIJY; 17 brs.

Saudi Pak Commercial Bank Ltd: Hassan Ali St, off I. I. Chundrigar Rd, Karachi; tel. (21) 111001987; f. 1994 as Prudential Commercial Bank, acquired by Saudi Pak Industrial and Agricultural Investment Co (Pvt) Ltd and name changed to above in 2001; cap. 1,500m., res 74.3m., dep. 7,000m. (Dec. 2001); Chair./CEO MUHAMMAD RASHID ZAHIR; Vice-Chair. JAWED ANWAR; 24 brs.

Soneri Bank Ltd: 87 Shahrah-e-Quaid-e-Azam, POB 49, Lahore; tel. (42) 6368142; fax (42) 6368138; e-mail mainlhr@soneri.com; f. 1991; cap. 782.7m., res 760.3m., dep. 16,053.9m. (Dec. 2001); Chair. BADRUDDIN J. FEERASTA; Pres. and CEO SAFAR ALI K. LAKHANI; 24 brs.

Union Bank Ltd: New Jubilee Insurance House, I. I. Chandrigar Rd, Karachi 74200; tel. (21) 2416428; fax (21) 2400842; e-mail ubrokhi@digicom.net.pk; internet www.unionbankpk.com; f. 1991; cap. 655.0m., res 248.0m., dep. 22,900.5m. (Dec. 2000); Chair. SHAUKAT TARIN; Pres. and CEO MUNEER KAMAL; 27 brs.

United Bank Ltd: State Life Bldg, No. 1, I. I. Chundrigar Rd, POB 4306, Karachi 74000; tel. (21) 2417021; fax (21) 2413492; e-mail international@ubl.com.pk; internet www.ubl.com.pk; f. 1959; cap. 22,481.7m., res 4,087.9m., dep. 133,539.0m. (Dec. 2000); 100% state-owned; scheduled for transfer to private sector; Pres. AMAR ZAFAR KHAN; 1,349 brs in Pakistan and 19 brs abroad.

Principal Foreign Banks

ABN AMRO Bank NV (Netherlands): Avari Plaza, 242–243 Fatima Jinnah Rd, POB 4096, Karachi 74000; tel. (21) 5683097; fax (21) 5683432; f. 1948; Country Man. NAVEED A. KHAN; 3 brs.

American Express Bank Ltd (USA): Shaheen Commercial Complex, Dr Ziauddin Ahmed Rd, POB 4847, Karachi; tel. (21) 2634153; fax (21) 2631803; f. 1950; Sen. Dir and Country Man. NADEEM KARAMAT; 4 brs.

ANZ Grindlays Bank Ltd (Australia): I. I. Chundrigar Rd, POB 5556, Karachi 74000; tel. (21) 2412671; fax (21) 2414914; Gen. Man. (Pakistan) AZHAR HAMID; 15 brs.

Bank of America, NT & SA (USA): New Jubilee Insurance House, 5th Floor, I. I. Chundrigar Rd, POB 3715, Karachi; tel. (21) 2412520; fax (21) 2415371; f. 1961; Sr Vice-Pres. and Country Man. S. ALI RAZA; Vice-Pres. and Head of Financial Institutions, Trade, Finance and Global Payment Services HUSSAIN TEJANY; 4 brs.

Bank of Ceylon (Sri Lanka): Ground Floor, 252A Sarwar Shaheed Rd, Saddar, Karachi; tel. (21) 5684664; fax (21) 5686817; e-mail cm@ceybank.com.pk; Country Man. M. T. PERERA.

Bank of Tokyo-Mitsubishi Ltd (Japan): Shaheen Complex, 1st Floor, M. R. Kayani Rd, POB 4232, Karachi; tel. (21) 2630171; fax (21) 2631368; e-mail btmkarwr@cyber.net.pk; f. 1953; Gen. Man. K. ENDO; 1 br.

Chase Manhattan Bank, NA (USA): 13th Floor, Commercial Tower, Sidco Ave Centre, 264 R. A. Lines, Karachi; tel. (21) 5683568; fax (21) 5681467; f. 1982; Vice-Pres. RUDOLF VON WATZDORF; 2 brs.

Citibank, NA (USA): No. 1 State Life Bldg, 1.1. Chundrigar Rd, Karachi; tel. (21) 2638222; fax (21) 2638211; internet www.citibank.com/pakistan; f. 1961; Gen. Man. ZUBYR SOOMRO; 3 brs.

Crédit Agricole Indosuez (France): Muhammadi House, I. I. Chundrigar Rd, POB 6942, Karachi 74000; tel. (21) 2413720; fax (21) 2417503; f. 1973; Gen. Man. JEAN PIERRE RAYNAUD; 2 brs.

Deutsche Bank AG (Germany): Uni Tower Bldg, I. I. Chundrigar Rd, POB 4925, Karachi; tel. (21) 2416824; fax (21) 2411130; f. 1962; Gen. Man. (Pakistan) ARIF M. ALI; 2 brs.

Doha Bank Ltd (Qatar): 36/6-2 Lalazar Drive, off M. T. Khan Rd, Karachi; tel. (21) 5611313; fax (21) 5610764; Gen. Man. (Pakistan) MASOOD H. KHAN.

Emirates Bank International PJSC (United Arab Emirates): Emirates Bank Bldg, I. I. Chundrigar Rd, POB 831, Karachi; tel. (21) 2416648; fax (21) 2416599; e-mail timgibbs@emiratesbank.com; internet www.emiratesbank.com.pk; f. 1978; Gen. Man. (Pakistan) TIMOTHY P. GIBBS; 10 brs.

Faysal Islamic Bank Ltd (Bahrain): 11/13 Trade Centre, I. I. Chundrigar Rd, POB 472, Karachi; tel. (21) 2638011; fax (21) 2637975; e-mail fblpak@cyber.net.pk; internet www.faysalbank.com.pk; f. 1995; Chief Operating Officer and Country Gen. Man. FAROOQ BENGALI; 9 brs.

Habib Bank AG Zurich (Switzerland): Hirani Centre, I. I. Chundrigar Rd, POB 1424, Karachi; tel. (21) 2630526; fax (21) 2631418; Chief Exec. (Pakistan) MUHAMMAD HAROON AHMED.

The Hongkong and Shanghai Banking Corpn Ltd (Hong Kong): Shaheen Commercial Complex, M. R. Kayani Rd, POB 121, Karachi; tel. (21) 2632143; fax (21) 2631526; f. 1982; CEO PETER WATERHOUSE; Dep. CEO NICK D. GILMOUR; 2 brs.

Mashreq Bank PSC (United Arab Emirates): Ground and 1st Floor, Bahria Complex, 24 M.T. Khan Rd, POB 930, Karachi 74000; tel. (21) 5611271; fax (21) 5610661; f. 1978; Country Man. AZMAT ASHRAF; 3 brs.

Middle East Bank PJSC (United Arab Emirates): Mac Volk Bldg, I. I. Chundrigar Rd, POB 6712, Karachi; tel. (21) 2412986; f. 1978; Gen. Man. KALIM-UR-RAHMAN; 4 brs.

Rupali Bank Ltd (Bangladesh): Unitowers, I. I. Chundrigar Rd, POB 6440, Karachi 74000; tel. (21) 2410424; fax (21) 2414322; f. 1976; Country Man. (Pakistan) MD SELIM KHAN; 1 br.

Saudi Bahrain Investment Co: Karachi; Man. Dir RASHID ZAHID.

Société Générale (France): 3rd Floor, PNSC Bldg, Maulvi Tamizuddin Khan Rd, POB 6766, Karachi 74000; tel. (21) 111331331; fax (21) 5611672; Gen. Man. PAUL HENRI RUSCH; Dep. Gen. Man. FERNAND CLOP; 2 brs.

Standard Chartered Bank (UK): I. I. Chundrigar Rd, POB 4896, Karachi 74000; tel. (21) 2419075; fax (21) 2418788; Chief Exec. (Pakistan) ZAHID RAHIM; 6 brs.

Trust Bank Ltd (Kenya): Al-Falah Court, I. I. Chundrigar Rd, Karachi; tel. (21) 2633519; fax (21) 2636534; CEO (Pakistan) HUMAYUN ZIA.

Leasing Banks (Modarabas)

The number of leasing banks (modarabas), which conform to the strictures placed upon the banking system by Shari'a (the Islamic legal code), rose from four in 1988 to about 60 in 1992. The following are among the most important modarabas in Pakistan.

Asian Leasing Corporation Ltd: 85-B Jail Rd, Gulberg, POB 3176, Lahore; tel. (42) 484417; fax (42) 484418.

Atlas Lease Ltd: Ground Floor, Federation House, Shahrah-e-Firdousi, Main Clifton, Karachi 75600; tel. (21) 5866817; fax (21) 5870543; e-mail all@atlasgrouppk.com; Chair. YUSUF H. SHIRAZI.

B.R.R. Capital Modaraba: Dean Arcade, Block 8, Kehkeshan, Clifton, Karachi 75600; tel. (21) 572013; fax (21) 5870324.

Dadabhoy Leasing Co Ltd: 5th Floor, Maqbool Commercial Complex, JCHS Block, Main Sharhah-e-Faisal, Karachi; tel. (21) 4548171; fax (21) 4547301; Man. (Finance) MOHAMMAD AYUB.

English Leasing Ltd: M. K. Arcade, Ground Floor, 32 Davis Rd, Lahore; tel. (42) 6303855; fax (41) 6304251; e-mail englease@hotmail.com; Chair. JAVAID MAHMOOD; CEO MANZOOR ELAHI.

First Grindlays Modaraba: Grindlays Services of Pakistan (Pvt) Ltd, ANZ Grindlays Bank Bldg, I. I. Chundrigar Rd, POB 5556, Karachi 74000; tel. (21) 223917; fax (21) 2417197.

First Habib Bank Modaraba: 18 Habib Bank Plaza, I. I. Chundrigar Rd, Karachi 75650; tel. (21) 2412294; fax (21) 2411860; f. 1991; wholly-owned subsidiary of Habib Bank Ltd; auth. cap. 500.0m., cap. p.u. 397.1m. (1996); CEO MUHAMMAD NAWAZ CHEEMA; Co Sec. NAJEEB MAHMUD.

National Development Leasing Corpn Ltd: NIC Bldg, 10th Floor, Abbasi Shaheed Rd, off Shahrah-e-Faisal, POB 67, Karachi 74400; tel. (21) 5660671; fax (21) 5680454; e-mail ndlckar@cyberaccess.com.pk; 3 brs.

Pakistan Industrial and Commercial Leasing Ltd: 504 Park Ave, 24-A, Block 6, PECHS, Shahrah-e-Faisal, Karachi 75210; tel. (21) 4551045; fax (21) 4520655; e-mail picl@super.net.pk; f. 1987; Chief Exec. MINHAJ-UL-HAQ SIDDIQI.

Co-operative Banks

In 1976 all existing co-operative banks were dissolved and given the option of becoming a branch of the appropriate Provincial Co-operative Bank, or of reverting to the status of a credit society.

Federal Bank for Co-operatives: State Bank Bldg, G-5, POB 1218, Islamabad; tel. (51) 9205667; fax (51) 9205681; f. 1976; owned jtly by the fed. Govt, the prov. govts and the State Bank of Pakistan; provides credit facilities to each of six prov. co-operative banks and regulates their operations; they in turn provide credit facilities through co-operative socs; supervises policy of prov. co-operative banks and of multi-unit co-operative socs; assists fed. and prov. govts in formulating schemes for development and revitalization of co-operative movement; carries out research on rural credit, etc.; paid-up share cap. 200m., res 398m. (1998); Man. Dir M. AFZAL HUSSAIN; 4 regional offices.

Investment Banks

Al-Faysal Investment Bank Ltd: 15 West Jinnah Ave, Blue Area, Islamabad; tel. (51) 272579; fax (51) 272569; e-mail afibl@afibl.isb.sdnpk.org; f. 1991; cap. 978.7m., res 226.7m. (Dec. 1999); Pres. MOHAMMAD KHAN HOTI.

Al-Towfeek Investment Bank Ltd: 63 Shahrah-e-Quaid-e-Azam, Lahore; tel. (42) 7122395; fax (42) 2628610; e-mail atibl@lhr.comsats.pk.net; f. 1990; Chair. KHALID MAHMOOD BHAIMIA; Chief Exec. KHALID MAJID.

Asset Investment Bank Ltd: Room 1-B, 1st Floor, Ali Plaza, Khayaban-e-Quaid-e-Azam, Blue Area, Islamabad; tel. (51) 2270625; fax (51) 2272506; Chief Exec. SYED NAVEED ZAIDI.

Atlas Investment Bank Ltd: Ground Floor, Federation House, Shaheen-e-Firdoosi, Main Clifton, Karachi; tel. (21) 5832292; fax (21) 5863984; 15% owned by The Bank of Tokyo-Mitsubishi Ltd; Chief Exec. NAEEM KHAN.

Citicorp Investment Bank (Pak) Ltd: AWT Plaza, I. I. Chundrigar Rd, Karachi; tel. (21) 111777777; fax (21) 2638288; f. 1992; 60% owned by Citibank Overseas Investment Corpn; Chair. SHEHZAD NAQVI; CEO MUHAMMAD AZIMUDDIN.

Franklin Investment Bank Ltd: Bandukwala Bldg, I. I. Chundrigar Rd, Karachi; tel. (21) 2429721; fax (21) 2428642; Chief Executive MUHAMMAD ANWAR SULTAN.

Development Finance Organizations

Agricultural Development Bank of Pakistan: 1 Faisal Ave, POB 1400, Islamabad; tel. (51) 202089; fax (51) 812907; e-mail adbp@isb.paknet.com.pk; internet www.paknet.com.pk/users/adbp; f. 1961; provides credit facilities to agriculturists (particularly small-scale farmers) and cottage industrialists in the rural areas and for allied projects; auth. cap. 4,000m., res 1,739m. (June 1999); 100% state-owned; Chair. ISTIQBAL MEHDI; 49 regional offices and 349 brs.

Bankers Equity Ltd: Finance and Trade Centre, Shahrah-e-Faisal, Karachi 74400; tel. (21) 5670186; fax (21) 5660267; e-mail bel1@cyber.net.pk; f. 1979 to provide rupee and foreign currency financing and equity for the establishment of large- and medium-scale industrial projects in the private sector; auth. cap. 5,000m., cap. p.u. 656m. res 918m. (June 1997); State Bank of Pakistan seized control of Bankers Equity Ltd in August 1999; Pres. INAMUL HAQ; Chair. RAUF B. KADRI; 14 brs.

First Women Bank Ltd: A-115, 7th Floor, Mehdi Towers, Sindhi Muslim Co-operative Housing Society, Sharah-e-Faisal, POB 15549, Karachi; tel. (21) 4556093; fax (21) 4556983; e-mail fwblps@cyber.net.pk; f. 1989; cap. 200m., dep. 2,421m. (Dec. 1995); Pres. ZAREEN AZIZ; 38 brs.

House Building Finance Corpn: Finance and Trade Centre, Shahrah-e-Faisal, Karachi 74400; tel. (21) 9202314; fax (21) 9202360; provides loans for the construction and purchase of housing units; Man. Dir SOHAIL USMAN ALI.

Industrial Development Bank of Pakistan: State Life Bldg No. 2, Wallace Rd, off I. I. Chundrigar Rd, POB 5082, Karachi 74000; tel. (21) 2419160; fax (21) 2411990; e-mail idbp@idbp.com.pk; internet www.idbp.com.pk; f. 1961; provides credit facilities for small and medium-sized industrial enterprises in the private sector; cap. 157.0m., res 342.3m., dep. 20,119.9m. (June 1997); 100% state-owned; Chair. and Man. Dir JAVED SADIQ; 19 brs.

Investment Corpn of Pakistan: NBP Bldg, 5th Floor, I. I. Chundrigar Rd, POB 5410, Karachi 74400; tel. (21) 9212360; fax (21) 9212388; e-mail icp@paknet3.ptc.pk; f. 1966 by the Govt to encourage and broaden the base of investments and to develop the capital market; total assets 4,633.1m., cap. 200.0m., res 413.5m. (June 1997); Man. Dir ISTIQBAL MEHDI; Dep. Man. Dir BEHRAHM HASAN; 10 brs.

Khushhali Bank: POB 3111, Islamabad; f. 2000 by the Govt under the Asian Development Bank's micro-finance sector development programme; provides micro-loans to the poor and finances reforms in the micro-finance sector; cap. 1,705m. (Aug. 2000), Pres. GHALIB NISHTAR.

National Investment (Unit Trust) Ltd: NBP Bldg, 6th Floor, I. I. Chundrigar Rd, POB 5671, Karachi; tel. (21) 2419061; fax (21) 2430623; e-mail info@nit.com.pk; internet www.nit.com.pk; f. 1962; an open-ended Mutual Fund, mobilizes domestic savings to meet the requirements of growing economic development and enables investors to share in the industrial and economic prosperity of the country; 67,000 Unit holders (1999/2000); Man. Dir ISTIQBAL MEHDI.

Pakistan Industrial Credit and Investment Corpn Ltd (PICIC): State Life Bldg No. 1, I. I. Chundrigar Rd, POB 5080, Karachi 74000; tel. (21) 2414220; fax (21) 2417851; e-mail contact@picic.com; internet www.picic.com; f. 1957 as an industrial development bank to provide financial assistance in both local and foreign currencies, for the establishment of new industries in the private sector and balancing modernization, replacement and expansion of existing industries; merchant banking and foreign exchange activities; total assets 15,398m., cap. 736.8m., res 984.7m. (June 2001); held 91.4% and 8.7% by local and foreign investors respectively; Man. Dir MOHAMMAD ALI KHOJA; Chair. KURSHID K. MARKER; 19 brs.

Pakistan Investment Board (PIB): Government of Pakistan, Pakistan Secretariat, Block A, Rooms 108 and 109, 1st Floor, Islamabad; tel. (51) 211870; fax (51) 215554; Vice-Chair. SAFDAR ABBAS ZAIDI.

Pakistan Kuwait Investment Co (Pvt) Ltd: Tower 'C', 4th Floor, Finance and Trade Centre, Shahrah-e-Faisal, POB 901, Karachi 74200; tel. (21) 5660750; fax (21) 5683669; jt venture between the Govt and Kuwait to promote investment in industrial and agro-based enterprises; Man. Dir ZAIGHAM H. RIZVI.

Pak-Libya Holding Co (Pvt) Ltd: Finance and Trade Centre, 5th Floor, Tower 'C', Shahrah-e-Faisal, POB 10425, Karachi 74400; tel.

(21) 111111115; fax (21) 5682389; e-mail paklibya@paklibya.com.pk; jt venture between the Govts of Pakistan and Libya to promote industrial investment in Pakistan; Man. Dir KHALID SHARWANI.

Regional Development Finance Corpn: Ghausia Plaza, 20 Blue Area, POB 1893, Islamabad; tel. (51) 2825131; fax (51) 2201179; promotes industrial investment in the less developed areas of Pakistan; CEO MIRZA GHAGANFAR BAIG; 13 brs.

Saudi Pak Industrial and Agricultural Investment Co (Pvt) Ltd: Saudi Pak Tower, 61-A Jinnah Ave, Islamabad; tel. (51) 2273514; fax (51) 2273508; e-mail saudipak@saudipak.com; internet www.saudipak.com; f. 1981, jtly by Saudi Arabia and Pakistan to finance industrial and agro-based projects and undertake investmentrelated activities in Pakistan; cap. 2,000m., res. 732m., dep. 5,900m. (March 2001); CEO MUHAMMAD RASHID ZAHIR; Exec. Vice-Pres. ABDUL JALEEL SHAIKH; 1 br.

Small Business Finance Corpn: NBP Bldg, Ground Floor, Civic Centre, Islamabad 44000; tel. (51) 9214296; fax (51) 2826007; provides loans for small businesses; Man. Dir KAISER HANEEF NASEEM.

Youth Investment and Promotion Society: PIA Bldg, 3rd Floor, Blue Area, Islamabad; tel. (51) 815581; Man. Dir ASHRAF M. KHAN.

Banking Associations

Investment Banks Association of Pakistan: 7th Floor, Shaheen Commercial Complex, Dr Ziauddin Ahmed Rd, POB 1345, Karachi; tel. (21) 2631396; fax (21) 2630678.

Pakistan Banks' Association: National Bank of Pakistan, Head Office Bldg, 2nd Floor, I. I. Chundrigar Rd, POB 4937, Karachi 2; tel. and fax (21) 2416686; e-mail pba@cyber.net.pk; Chair. M. YOUNAS KHAN; Sec. A. GHAFFAR K. HAFIZ.

Banking Organizations

Pakistan Banking Council: Habib Bank Plaza, I. I. Chundrigar Rd, Karachi; tel. (21) 227121; fax (21) 222232; f. 1973; acts as a co-ordinating body between the nationalized banks and the Ministry of Finance, Economic Affairs and Statistics; Chair. MUHAMMAD ZAKI; Sec. Mir WASIF ALI.

Pakistan Development Banking Institute: 4th Floor, Sidco Ave Centre, Stratchen Rd, Karachi; tel. (21) 5688049; fax (21) 5688460.

STOCK EXCHANGES

Securities and Exchange Commission of Pakistan: NIC Bldg, 63 Jinnah Ave, Blue Area, Islamabad; tel. (51) 9205713; fax (51) 9204915; e-mail hilal-bult@seep.gov.pk; oversees and co-ordinates operations of exchanges and registration of companies; registration offices in Faisalabad (356-A, 1st Floor, Al-Jamil Plaza, People's Colony, Small D Ground, Faisalabad; tel. (41) 713841), Karachi (No. 2, 4th Floor, State Life Building, North Wing, Karachi; tel. (21) 2415855), Lahore (3rd and 4th Floors, Associated House, 7 Egerton Rd, Lahore; tel. (42) 9202044), Multan (61 Abdali Rd, Multan; tel. (61) 542609), Peshawar (Hussain Commercial Bldg, 3 Arbab Rd, Peshawar), Quetta (382/3, IDBP House, Shahrah-e-Hall, Quetta; tel. (81) 844138) and Sukkur (B-30, Sindhi Muslim Housing Society, Airport Rd, Sukkur; tel. (71) 30517); Chair. KHALID MIRZA.

Islamabad Stock Exchange: 4th Floor, Stock Exchange Bldg, 101E Faz-ul-haq Rd, Blue Area, Islamabad; tel. (51) 2829001; fax (51) 2272393; e-mail ise@ise.com.pk; internet www.ise.com.pk; f. 1991; 103 mems; Chair. OMAR IQBAL PASHA; Sec. YOUSUF H. MAKHDOOMI.

Karachi Stock Exchange (Guarantee) Ltd: Stock Exchange Bldg, Stock Exchange Rd, Karachi 74000; tel. (21) 2425502; fax (21) 2410825; e-mail gm@kse.com.pk; internet www.kse.com.pk; f. 1947; 200 mems, 762 listed cos; Chair. SALEEM CHANDNA; Man. Dir MUHAMMAD YAQOOB MEMON (acting).

Lahore Stock Exchange (Guarantee) Ltd: Lahore Stock Exchange Bldg, 19 Khayaban-e-Aiwan-e-Iqbal, Lahore 54000; tel. (42) 6300070; fax (42) 6368484; e-mail lstock@paknet4.ptc.pk; internet www.lahorestock.com; f. 1970; 576 listed cos, 151 mems; Pres. Group Capt. (retd) NASEEM A. KHAN; Man. Dir SAMEER AHMED.

INSURANCE

In 1995 legislation came into effect allowing foreign insurance companies to operate in Pakistan.

Insurance Division: Securities and Exchange Commission, 4th Floor, NIC Bldg, Jinnah Ave, Islamabad; tel. (51), 9208887; fax (51) 9208955; internet www.secp.gov.pk; under the Ministry of Finance and Economic Affairs; Commissioner of Insurance N. K. SHAHANI; Exec. Dir SHAFAAT AHMED.

Life Insurance

American Life Insurance Co (Pakistan) Ltd: Laksan Sq Bldg, Karachi 75400.

Metropolitan Life Assurance Co of Pakistan Ltd: 310-313 Qamar House, M. A. Jinnah Rd, Karachi 74000; tel. (21) 2311662; fax (21) 2311667; e-mail myunus@cyber.net.pk; Chief Exec. MAHEEN YUNUS.

Postal Life Insurance Organization: Tibet Centre, M. A. Jinnah Rd, Karachi; tel. (21) 723804; f. 1884; life and group insurance; Gen. Man and CEO Dr SALAHUDDIN AHMAD.

State Life Insurance Corpn of Pakistan: State Life Bldg No. 9, Dr Ziauddin Ahmed Rd, POB 5725, Karachi 75530; tel. (21) 5683233; fax (21) 5683266; e-mail dhasp@super.net.pk; internet www.statelife.com.pk; f. 1972; life and group insurance and pension schemes; Chair. SAMEE UL-HASAN.

General Insurance

ACE Insurance Ltd: 6th Floor, NIC Bldg, Abbasi Shaheed Rd, off Shahrah-e-Faisal, Karachi; tel. (21) 5681320; fax (21) 5683935; Country Gen. Man. SYED UMER ALI SHAH.

Adamjee Insurance Co Ltd: Adamjee House, 6th Floor, I. I. Chundrigar Rd, POB 4850, Karachi 74000; tel. (21) 2414607; fax (21) 2412627; e-mail info@adamjeeinsurance.com; internet www.adamjeeinsurance.com; f. 1960; Man. Dir and CEO MOHAMMED CHOUDHURY.

Agro General Insurance Co Ltd: 612, Qamar House, M. A. Jinnah Rd, POB 5920, Karachi 74000; tel. (21) 2313182; fax (21) 2310624; f. 1987; Man. Dir M. I. ANSARI.

Alpha Insurance Co Ltd: State Life Bldg No. 1B–1C, 2nd Floor, off I.I. Chungrigar Rd, POB 4359, Karachi 74000; tel. (21) 2412609; fax (21) 2419968; f. 1952; Chair. IQBAL M. QURESHI; Man. Dir V. C. GONSALVES; 9 brs.

Amicus Insurance Co Ltd: F-50, Block 7, Feroze Nana Rd, Bath Island, POB 3971, Karachi; tel. (21) 5831082; fax (21) 5870220; f. 1991; Chair. M. IRSHAD UDDIN.

Asia Insurance Co Ltd: Asia Insurance House, 7 Egerton Rd, POB 2289, Lahore; tel. (42) 6363692; fax (42) 6368966; f. 1980; Man. Dir ZAFAR IQBAL SHAIKH.

Askari General Insurance Co Ltd: 4th Floor, AWT Plaza, The Mall, POB 843, Rawalpindi; tel. (51) 9272425; fax (51) 9272424; f. 1995; Pres. and Chief Exec. M. JAMALUDDIN.

Business and Industrial Insurance Co Ltd: 65 East Pak Pavilions, 1st Floor, Fazal-e-Haq Rd, Blue Area, Islamabad; tel. (51) 2278957; fax (51) 2271914; f. 1995; Chair. and Chief Exec. Mian MUMTAZ ABDULLAH.

Capital Insurance Co Ltd: opp. ABL Paris Rd, Sialkot; tel. (432) 587643; fax (432) 583080; e-mail cicl@skt.comsats.net.pk; f. 1998; Chief Exec. Khawaja ZAKAUDDIN; Sec. M. I. BUTT.

Central Insurance Co Ltd: Dawood Centre, 5th Floor, M. T. Khan Rd, POB 3988, Karachi 75530; tel. (21) 5683194; fax (21) 5680218; f. 1960; Man. Dir M. HUSSAIN DAWOOD.

Century Insurance Co Ltd: Lakson Square Bldg No. 1, 2nd Floor, Block 'D', Sarwar Sheheed Rd, Karachi 74200; tel. (21) 5653519; fax (21) 5671665; e-mail cic@cyber.net.pk; f. 1988; Chair. and Chief Exec. IQBALALI LAKHANI; Dir MIR NADIR ALI.

CGU Inter Insurance PLC: 74/1-A, Lalazar, M. T. Khan Rd, POB 4895, Karachi 74000; tel. (21) 5611802; fax (21) 5611456; f. 1861; general and life insurance; Gen. Man. ABDUR RAHIM; 3 brs.

Commerce Insurance Co Ltd: 11 Shahrah-e-Quaid-e-Azam, POB 1132, Lahore 54000; tel. (42) 7325330; fax (42) 7230828; f. 1992; Chief Exec. SYED MOIN-UD-DIN.

Co-operative Insurance Society of Pakistan Ltd: Co-operative Insurance Bldg, Shahrah-e-Quaid-e-Azam, POB 147, Lahore; tel. (42) 7352306; fax (42) 7352794; f. 1949; Chief Exec. and Gen. Man. FAROOQ HAIDER JUNG.

Credit Insurance Co Ltd: Asmat Chambers, 68 Mazang Rd, Lahore; tel. (42) 6316774; fax (42) 6368868; f. 1995; Chief Exec. MUHAMMAD IKHLAQ BUTT.

Crescent Star Insurance Co Ltd: Nadir House, I. I. Chundrigar Rd, POB 4616, Karachi 74000; tel. (21) 2421207; fax (21) 2415474; f. 1957; Man. Dir MUNIR I. MILLWALA.

Dadabhoy Insurance Co Ltd: 5th Floor Maqbool Commercial Complex, JCHS Block, Main Shahrah-e-Faisal, Karachi; tel. (21) 4545704; fax (21) 4548625; f. 1983; Chief Exec. USMAN DADABHOY.

Delta Insurance Co Ltd: 101 Baghpatee Bldg, Altaf Hussain Rd, New Challi, Karachi; tel. (21) 2632297; fax (21) 2422942; f. 1991; Man. Dir SYED ASIF ALI.

East West Insurance Co Ltd: 410 Qamar House, M. A. Jinnah Rd, POB 6693, Karachi 74000; tel. (21) 2313304; fax (21) 2311904; f. 1983; Chief Exec. NAVEED YUNUS.

EFU General Insurance Ltd: Qamar House, M. A. Jinnah Rd, POB 5055, Karachi 74000; tel. (21) 2312379; fax (21) 2310450;

e-mail info@efuinsurance.com; internet www.efuinsurance.com; f. 1932; Man. Dir and Chief Exec. SAIFUDDIN N. ZOOMKAWALA.

Excel Insurance Co Ltd: S-07, 5th Floor, KDLB Bldg, 58 West Wharf Rd, Karachi 74000; tel. (21) 7738611; fax (21) 2310314; f. 1995; Chief Exec. BASHIR H. ALIMOHAMMAD.

Gulf Insurance Co Ltd: Gulf House, 1-A Link McLeod Rd, Patiala Grounds, Lahore; tel. (42) 7312028; fax (42) 7234987; f. 1988; Chief Exec. SH. ARIF SALAM.

Habib Insurance Co Ltd: Insurance House, 6 Habib Sq., M. A. Jinnah Rd, POB 5217, Karachi 74000; tel. (21) 2424038; fax (21) 2421600; f. 1942; Chair. HAMID D. HABIB; Man. Dir and Chief Exec. ALI RAZA D. HABIB.

Indus International Co Ltd: Indus House, 18-E-III, Model Town, POB 2002, Lahore 54700; tel. (42) 5865579; fax (42) 5866293; e-mail nation@paknet4.ptc.pk; f. 1993; Pres. and Man. Dir KHALID RASHID.

International General Insurance Co of Pakistan Ltd: Finlay House, 1st Floor, I. I. Chundrigar Rd, POB 4576, Karachi 74000; tel. (21) 2424976; fax (21) 2416710; e-mail igikhi@cubexs.net.pk; internet www.igi.com.pk; f. 1953; Gen. Man. BASIT HASSAN SYED.

Ittefaq General Insurance Co Ltd: H-16 Murree Rd, Rawalpindi; tel. (51) 71333; f. 1982; Man. Dir SYED ALI ASGHAR SHAH.

Jupiter Insurance Co Ltd: 4th Floor, Finlay House, I. I. Chundrigar Rd, POB 4655, Karachi 74000; tel. (21) 2427659; fax (21) 2427660; e-mail jicl20@hotmail.com; f. 1994; Chief Exec. MAHMUD HASAN.

Muslim Insurance Co Ltd: 3 Bank Sq., Shahrah-e-Quaid-e-Azam, POB 1219, Lahore; tel. (42) 7310658; fax (42) 7234742; f. 1935; Chief Exec. S. C. SUBJALLY.

National General Insurance Co Ltd: 401-B, Satellite Town, nr Commercial Market, Rawalpindi; tel. (51) 411792; fax (51) 427361; f. 1969; Gen. Man. F. A. JAFFERY.

National Insurance Corpn: NIC Bldg, Abbasi Shaheed Rd, Karachi 74400; tel. (21) 9202741; fax (21) 9202779; e-mail nicl@cyber.net.pk; internet www.niclpk.com; govt-owned; Chair. JAHAN ZEB KHAN.

New Hampshire Insurance Co: State Life Bldg No. 2, 8th Floor, Wallace Rd, POB 4693, Karachi 74000; tel. (21) 2434470; fax (21) 2419413; Country Man. for Pakistan MUJIB KHAN.

New Jubilee Insurance Co Ltd: 2nd Floor, Jubilee Insurance House, I. I. Chundrigar Rd, POB 4795, Karachi 74000; tel. (21) 2416022; fax (21) 2416728; e-mail nji@cyber.net.pk; internet www.nji.com.pk; f. 1953; Pres., Chief Exec. and Man. Dir MASOOD NOORANI.

North Star Insurance Co Ltd: 37–38 Basement, Sadiq Plaza, 69 The Mall, Lahore 54000; tel. (42) 6314308; fax (42) 6375366; e-mail northstarins@hotmail.com; f. 1995; Chief Exec./Man. Dir M. RAFIQ CHAUDHRY.

Orient Insurance Co Ltd: 2nd Floor, Dean Arcade, Block No. 8, Kahkeshan, Clifton, Karachi; tel. (21) 5865327; fax (21) 5865724; f. 1987; Man. Dir FAZAL REHMAN.

Pak Equity Insurance Co Ltd: M. K. Arcade, 32 Davis Rd, Lahore; tel. (42) 6361536; fax (42) 6365959; f. 1984; Chief Exec. CH. ATHAR ZAHOOR.

Pakistan General Insurance Co Ltd: 43 Al-Noor Bldg, Bank Square, POB 1028, Lahore; tel. (42) 7325281; fax (42) 7323051; f. 1948; Chair. CH. AZFAR MANZOOR; Pres. and Chief Exec. CH. ZAHOOR AHMAD.

Pakistan Guarantee Insurance Co Ltd: Al-Falah Court, 3rd and 5th Floors, I. I. Chundrigar Rd, POB 5436, Karachi 74000; tel. (21) 2636111; fax (21) 2638740; f. 1965; Chief Exec. SHAKIL RAZA SYED.

Premier Insurance Co of Pakistan Ltd: 2-A State Life Bldg, 5th Floor, Wallace Rd, off I. I. Chundrigar Rd, POB 4140, Karachi 74000; tel. (21) 2416331; fax (21) 2416572; f. 1952; Chair. ZAHID BASHIR; Adviser A. U. SIDDIQUI.

Prime Insurance Co Ltd: 505–507, Japan Plaza, M. A. Jinnah Rd, POB 1390, Karachi; tel. (21) 7770801; fax (21) 7725427; f. 1989; Chief Exec. ABDUL MAJEED.

Raja Insurance Co Ltd: Panorama Centre, 5th Floor, 256 Fatimah Jinnah Rd, POB 10422, Karachi 4; tel. (21) 5670619; fax (21) 5681501; f. 1981; Chair. RAJA ABDUL RAHMAN; Man. Dir SHEIKH HUMAYUN SAYEED.

Reliance Insurance Co Ltd: Reliance Insurance House, 181-A, Sindhi Muslim Co-operative Housing Society, POB 13356, Karachi 74400; tel. (21) 4539413; fax (21) 4539412; e-mail reli-ins@cyber.net.pk; Chief Exec. and Man. Dir ABDUL RAZAK AHMED.

Royal Exchange Assurance: P&O Plaza, I. I. Chundrigar Rd, POB 315, Karachi 74000; tel. (21) 2635141; fax (21) 2631369; Man. for Pakistan Dr MUMTAZ A. HASHMI.

Seafield Insurance Co Ltd: 86-Q, Block-2, Allama Iqbal Rd, PECHS, Karachi; tel. (21) 4556895; fax (21) 4527593; f. 1989; Man. Dir ADNAN HAFEEZ.

Security General Insurance Co Ltd: Nishat House, 53A Lawrence Rd, Lahore; tel. (42) 6279192; fax (42) 6303466; f. 1996; Man. Dir SYED JAWAD GILLANI.

Shaheen Insurance Co Ltd: D-27, Block 5, Kahkashan, Clifton, POB 707, Karachi; tel. (21) 5879705; fax (21) 5879072; f. 1996; CEO NASREEN RASHID.

Silver Star Insurance Co Ltd: Silver Star House, 2nd Floor, 5 Bank Square, POB 2533, Lahore; tel. (42) 7324488; fax (42) 7229966; e-mail silvrstr@nexlinx.net.pk; f. 1984; Man. Dir ZAHIR MUHAMMAD SADIQ.

Union Insurance Co of Pakistan Ltd: Adamjee House, 9th Floor, I. I. Chundrigar Rd, Karachi; tel. (21) 2427524; fax (21) 2420174; Chair. Mian MOHAMMED HANIF; Pres. NISHAT RAFFIQ.

United Insurance Co of Pakistan Ltd: Nizam Chambers, 5th Floor, Shahrah-e-Fatima Jinnah, POB 532, Lahore; tel. (42) 6361471; fax (42) 6375036; f. 1959; Man. Dir and CEO M. A. SHAHID.

Universal Insurance Co Ltd: Universal Insurance House, 63 Shahrah-e-Quaid-e-Azam, POB 539, Lahore; tel. (42) 7322972; fax (42) 7230326; e-mail mobin@am.lcci.org.pk; f. 1958; Chief Exec. OMAR AYUB KHAN; Man. Dir SARDAR KHAN.

Insurance Associations

Insurance Association of Pakistan: Jamshed Katrak Chambers, G. Allana Rd, POB 4932, Karachi 74000; tel. (21) 2311784; fax (21) 2310798; e-mail iapho@cyber.net.pk; f. 1948; mems comprise 46 cos (Pakistani and foreign) transacting general insurance business; issues tariffs and establishes rules for insurance in the country; regional office in Lahore; Chair. M. I. ANSARI; Sec. K. A. SIDDIQI.

Pakistan Insurance Institute: Shafi Court, 2nd Floor, Mereweather Rd, Karachi 4; f. 1951 to encourage insurance education; Chair. MOHAMMAD CHOUDHRY.

Trade and Industry

GOVERNMENT AGENCIES

Agricultural Marketing and Storage Ltd: Islamabad; tel. (51) 827407; fax (51) 824607.

Board of Investment (BOI): Govt of Pakistan, Attaturk Ave, Sector G-5/1, Islamabad; tel. (51) 9206161; fax (51) 9215554; e-mail boipr@isb.comsats.net.pk; internet www.pakboi.gov.pk; Chair. WASIM HAQUEE; Sec. SHUJA SHAH.

Commission for the Islamization of the Economy: Government of Pakistan, Finance Division, 2nd Floor, SNC Centre, 12-D, Fazl-ul-Haq Rd, Blue Area, Islamabad 44000; tel. (51) 9223679; fax (51) 9223684; f. 1991; Chair. RAJA MUHAMMAD ZAFARUL HAQ; Mem./Sec. ZULFIQAR KHAN.

Corporate and Industrial Restructuring Corpn: 13-C-II, M. M. Alam Rd, Gulberg III, Lahore; tel. (42) 5871532; fax (42) 5761650; e-mail info@cir-gov.cort; internet www.circ.gov.com.

Environmental Protection Agency: Govt of Sindh, EPA Complex, ST-2/1, Sector 23, Korangi Industrial Area, Karachi; tel. (21) 5065950; fax (21) 5065940.

Export Processing Zones Authority (EPZA): Landhi Industrial Area Extension, Mehran Highway, POB 17011, Karachi 75150; tel. (21) 5082001; fax (21) 5082005; e-mail epza@super.net.pk; internet www.epza.com.pk.

Export Promotion Bureau: 5th Floor, Block A, Finance and Trade Centre, Shahrah-e-Faisal, POB 1293, Karachi; tel. (21) 9202718; fax (21) 9202713; e-mail epb@epb.kar.erum.com.pk; internet www.epb.gov.pk; Chair. TARIQ IKRAM; Vice-Chair. EJAZ AHMED QURESHI.

Family Planning Association of Pakistan: 24, St 30, F-6/1, Islamabad.

Geological Survey of Pakistan: Sariab Rd, POB 15, Quetta; tel. (81) 9211032; fax (81) 9211018; e-mail geophy@gsp.qta.khi.sdnpk.undp.org; Dir-Gen. S. HASAN GAUHAR; Asst Dir MOHSIN ANWAR KAZIM.

Gwadar Port Authority: 2nd Floor, PNSC Bldg, M. T. Khan Rd, Karachi; tel. (21) 9204061; fax (21) 9204196; e-mail gwadarport@hotmail.com.

Information Technology Commission: IT and Telecom Division, Govt of Pakistan, 14, St 61, F-7/4, Islamabad; tel. (51) 9205889; fax (51) 9205992; e-mail secyitc@isb.comsats.net.pk; internet www.itcommission.gov.pk.

Investment Promotion Bureau: Kandawala Bldg, M. A. Jinnah Rd, Karachi.

Karachi Export Processing Zone (KEPZ): Landhi Industrial Area Extension, Mehran Highway, POB 17011, Karachi 75150; tel. (21) 7738995; fax (21) 7738188.

Karachi Metropolitan Corpn: M. A. Jinnah Rd, Karachi.

National Accountability Bureau: Government of Pakistan, Islamabad; e-mail info@nab.gov.pk; internet www.nab.gov.pk; Chair. Lt-Gen. KHALIF MAQBOOL.

National Database and Registration Authority (NADRA): Ministry of Interior, Awami Markaz, 5-A, Constitution Ave, F-5/1, Islamabad; tel. (51) 9204624; internet www.nadrapk.com.

National Economic Board: f. 1979 by the Govt as an advisory body to review and evaluate the state of the economy and to make proposals, especially to further the adoption of the socio-economic principles of Islam.

National Economic Council: supreme economic body; the governors and chief ministers of the four provinces and fed. ministers in charge of economic ministries are its mems; sr fed. and prov. officials in the economic field are also associated.

National Energy Conservation Centre (ENERCON): ENERCON Bldg, G-5/2, Islamabad; tel. (51) 9206001; fax (51) 9206004; Man. Dir ARIF ALAUDDIN.

National Highway Authority: 27, Mauve Area, G-9/1, Islamabad; tel. (51) 9260563; fax (51) 9261327; e-mail nhal2@comsats.net.pk.

National Housing Authority: Prime Minister's Office, Islamabad; tel. (51) 92008539; fax (51) 92008324.

National Technical Resources Pool: 414-C, National Reconstruction Bureau, Chief Executive's Secretariat II, Islamabad; tel. (51) 9207912.

Pakistan Electronic Media Regulatory Authority: Islambad; tel. (51) 2441600; f. 2002; Chair. Mian MUHAMMAD JAVED.

Pakistan Revenue Service: national tax authority; Chair. IQBAL FAREED.

Pakistan Software Export Board (Guarantee) Ltd: 2nd Floor, Evacuee Trust Complex, F-5/1, Aga Khan Rd, Islamabad; tel. (51) 9204074; fax (51) 9204075; e-mail info@pseb.org.pk; internet www.pseb.org.pk; Man. Dir SUHAIL SHAHID.

Pakistan Telecommunication Authority: F-5/1, Islamabad; internet www.pta.gov.pk; f. to regulate telecommunications services; to arrange deregulation of telecommunications; Chair. Gen. (retd) SHAHZADA ALAM MALIK.

Privatisation Commission: Experts Advisory Cell Bldg, 5A Constitution Ave, Islamabad 44000; tel. (51) 9216514; fax (51) 9203076; e-mail info@privatisation.gov.pk; internet www.privatisation.gov.pk; supervised by Ministry of Finance, Economic Affairs and Statistics; Chair. ALTAF M. SALEEM.

Sindh Katchi Abadi Authority: Karachi; tel. (21) 9211275; fax (21) 9211272; e-mail skaa@khi.compol.com; internet www.skaa.cutecity.com; govt agency established to regulate and improve slums in Pakistan's southern province; Dir-Gen. TASNEEM AHMAD SIDDIQUI.

Sindh Privatisation Commission: Sindh Secretariat, 4-A, Block 15, Court Rd, Karachi; tel. (21) 9202077; fax (21) 9202071; e-mail spcsecretary@yahoo.com; internet www.spc.gov.pk.

Sustainable Development Policy Institute: St 3, UN Boulevard Diplomatic Enclave 1; Islamabad; tel. (51) 2277146; fax (51) 2278135; e-mail yasin@sdpi.org.

DEVELOPMENT ORGANIZATIONS

Balochistan Development Authority: Civil Secretariat, Block 7, Quetta; tel. (81) 9202491; created for economic development of Balochistan; exploration and exploitation of mineral resources; development of infrastructure, water resources, etc.

Capital Development Authority: Islamabad; tel. (51) 823454; Chair. MOHAMMAD ZAFAR IQBAL.

Karachi Development Authority (KDA): Civic Centre, Gulshan-e-Iqbal, University Rd, Karachi; tel. (21) 9230653; fax (21) 9230670; responsible for planning and development of Karachi city; Dir-Gen. Brig. (retd) SYED ZAHEER KADRI.

Lahore Development Authority (LDA): LDA Plaza, Egerton Rd, Lahore.

Pakistan Industrial Technical Assistance Centre (PITAC): Maulana Jalaluddin Roomi Rd (Old Ferozepur Rd), Lahore 54600; tel. (42) 5864171; fax (42) 5862381; e-mail pitac@paknet4.ptc.pk; f. 1962 by the Govt to provide advanced training to industrial personnel in the fields of metal trades and tool engineering design and related fields; under Ministry of Industries and Production; provides human resource development programmes; design and production of tools, moulds, jigs, dies, gauges, fixtures, etc.; also operates as secretariat of National Productivity Council; Chair. SAJJAD HAIDER GILANI; Gen. Man. MOHAMMAD ABDUL JABBAR KHAN.

Pakistan Poverty Alleviation Fund: 6-A, Park Rd, F-8/2, Islamabad; tel. (51) 2253178; fax (51) 2251726; e-mail kamran@ppaf.org.pk; internet www.ppaf.org.pk; f. 1997 by the Government; funded by the World Bank; works with non-governmental organizations and private-sector institutions to alleviate poverty; Chief Exec. KAMAL HAYAT.

Peshawar Development Authority (PDA): PDA House, Phase V, Hayatabad, Peshawar; tel. (521) 9217035; fax (521) 9217030.

Sarhad Development Authority (SDA): PIA Bldg, Arbab Rd, POB 172, Peshawar; tel. (521) 73076; f. 1972; promotes industrial (particularly mining), commercial development in the North-West Frontier Province; Chair. KHALID AZIZ.

Small and Medium Enterprises Development Authority (SMEDA): 43-T, Gulberg II, Lahore 59660; fax (42) 5753545; f. 1998; 3 brs.

CHAMBERS OF COMMERCE

The Federation of Pakistan Chambers of Commerce and Industry: Federation House, Main Clifton, POB 13875, Karachi 75600; tel. (21) 5873691; fax (21) 5874332; e-mail fpcci@digicom.net.pk; internet www.fpcci.com; f. 1950; 163 mem. bodies; Pres. IFTIKHAR ALI MALIK; Sec.-Gen. Dr ANWAR-UL-HAQUE.

The Islamic Chamber of Commerce and Industry: ST-2/A, Block 9, KDA Scheme No. 5, Clifton, POB 3831, Karachi 75600; tel. (21) 5874756; fax (21) 5870765; e-mail icci@paknet3.ptc.pk; internet www.icci-oic.org; f. 1979; Pres. SHEIKH ISMAIL ABU DAWOOD; Sec.-Gen. AQEEL AHMAD AL-JASSEM.

Overseas Investors' Chamber of Commerce and Industry: Chamber of Commerce Bldg, Talpur Rd, POB 4833, Karachi; tel. (21) 2410814; fax (21) 2427315; e-mail info@oicci.org; internet www.oicci.org; f. 1860 as the Karachi Chamber of Commerce, name changed to above in 1968; 184 mem. bodies; Pres. KAMRAN HIVZA; Sec.-Gen. ZAHID ZAHEER.

Principal Affiliated Chambers

Bahawalpur Chamber of Commerce and Industry: 317-C, Satellite Town, Bahawalpur; tel. and fax (621) 80283; e-mail chamber@bcci.bwp.brain.net.pk; Pres. Khawaja MOHAMMAD ILYAS.

Balochistan Chamber of Commerce and Industry: Zarghoon Rd, POB 117, Quetta; tel. (81) 821943; fax (81) 821948; e-mail qcci@hotmail.com; f. 1984; Pres. Haji FAZAL KADIR SHERANI; Sec. SYED ZAHEER ALI.

Dadu Chamber of Commerce and Industry: Nooriabad, Dadu; tel. 4400114; fax 4547301.

Dera Ghazi Khan Chamber of Commerce and Industry: Block '34', Khakwani House, Dera Ghazi Khan, Punjab; tel. (641) 462338; fax (641) 464938; Pres. SHEIKH IFTIKHAR AHMED; Sec. MUHAMMAD MUJAHID.

Dera Ismail Khan Chamber of Commerce and Industry: Circular Rd, POB 5, D. I. Khan; tel. (961) 711334; fax (961) 811334; e-mail sjbdn@epistemics.net.

Faisalabad Chamber of Commerce and Industry: 2nd Floor, National Bank Bldg, Jail Rd, Faisalabad; tel. (41) 616045; fax (41) 615085; e-mail fcci@fsd.paknet.com.pk; Pres. Mian NAEEM-UR-REHMAN; Sec. Maj. (retd) MOHAMMAD WASIM.

Gujranwala Chamber of Commerce and Industry: Aiwan-e-Tijarat Rd, Gujranwala; tel. (431) 256701; fax (431) 254440; e-mail gcci@gjr.paknet.com.pk; internet www.gcci.org.pk; f. 1978; Pres. RANA NASIR MAHMOOD; Sec. SHAHID IMRAN RANA.

Hyderabad Chamber of Commerce and Industry: Aiwan-e-Tijarat Rd, Saddar, POB 99, Hyderabad; tel. (221) 784973; fax (221) 784972; e-mail hcci@paknet3.ptc.pk; Pres. Haji MOHAMMAD YAQOOB; Sec. A. U. MALIK.

Islamabad Chamber of Commerce and Industry: Aiwan-e-Sana't-o-Tijarat Rd, Mauve Area, Sector G-8/1, Islamabad; tel. (51) 2250526; fax (51) 2252950; e-mail icci@brain.net.pk; internet www.icci.com.pk; f. 1984; Pres. MUNAWAR MUGHAL; Sec. MAJID SHABBIR.

Jhelum Chamber of Commerce and Industry: Rani Nagar, GT Rd, Jhelum; tel. (541) 646532; fax (541) 646533; Pres. RAJA HABIB UR REHMAN; Sec. Capt. (retd) MUHAMMAD ZAMAN.

Karachi Chamber of Commerce and Industry: Aiwan-e-Tijarat Rd, off Shahrah-e-Liaquat, POB 4158, Karachi 74000; tel. (21) 2416091; fax (21) 2416095; e-mail ccikar@cyber.net.pk; internet www.karachichamber.com; f. 1960; 11,705 mems; Pres. A. Q. KHALIL; Sec. M. NAZIR ALI.

Khairpur Chamber of Commerce and Industry: Shop 8, Sachal Shopping Centre, Khairpur; tel. (792) 5105.

Lahore Chamber of Commerce and Industry: 11 Shahrah-e-Aiwan-e-Tijarat, POB 597, Lahore; tel. (42) 6305538; fax (42)

6368854; e-mail sect@lcci.org.pk; internet www.lcci.org.pk; f. 1923; 8,000 mems; Pres. SHEIKH ASIF; Sec. M. LATIF CHAUDHRY.

Larkana Chamber of Commerce and Industry: 21–23 Kenedy Market, POB 78, Larkana, Sindh; tel. (741) 40709; fax (741) 44633; Pres. KHAIR MUHAMMAD SHEIKH.

Mirpur, Azad Jammu and Kashmir Chamber of Commerce and Industry: 52, F/1 Kotli Rd, POB 12, Mirpur; tel. (582) 4890; fax (582) 2365; e-mail ajkcci@isb.paknet.com.pk; Pres. ZULFIQAR ABBASI.

Mirpur Khas Chamber of Commerce and Industry: POB 162, New Town, Mirpur Khas, Sindh; tel. (231) 6189; fax (231) 2221; Pres. ABDUL KHALIQUE KHAN; Sec. M. BASITULLAH BAIG.

Multan Chamber of Commerce and Industry: Sharah-e-Aiwan-e-Tijarat-o-Sanat, Multan; tel. (61) 517087; fax (61) 570463; e-mail mccimul@mul.paknet.com.pk; Pres. MUHAMMAD KHAN SADDOZAI; Sec. G. A. BHATTI.

Rawalpindi Chamber of Commerce and Industry: Chamber House, 108 Adamjee Rd, POB 323, Rawalpindi; tel. (51) 5566238; fax (51) 5586849; e-mail rcci@best.net.pk; f. 1952; Pres. SOHAIL A. SETHI; Sec. MUHAMMAD IFTIKHAR-UD-DIN.

SAARC Chamber of Commerce and Industry: H No. 5, St No. 59, F-8/4, Islamabad; tel. (51) 2281396; fax (51) 2281390; e-mail saarc@comsats.net.pk; internet www.saarc.sec.org; f. 1993; Pres. PADMA JYOTI.

Sarhad Chamber of Commerce and Industry: Sarhad Chamber House, Chacha Younis Park, G.T. Rd, Peshawar; tel. (91) 9213314; fax (91) 9213316; e-mail sccip@brain.net.pk; internet www.scci.org.pk; f. 1958; 1,758 mems; Pres. Col (retd) MALIK ZAHID HUSSAIN; Sec. FAQIR MUHAMMAD.

Sialkot Chamber of Commerce and Industry: Shahrah-e-Aiwan-e-Sanat-o-Tijarat, POB 1870, Sialkot 51310; tel. (432) 261881; fax (432) 268835; e-mail info@scci.com.pk; internet www.scci.com.pk; f. 1982; 4,500 mems; Pres. DAUD AHMAD CHATTHA; Sec. NAWAZ AHMED TOOR.

Sukkur Chamber of Commerce and Industry: Sukkur Chamber House, 1st Floor, Opposite Mehran View Plaza, Bunder Rd, Sukkur; tel. (71) 23938; fax (71) 23059; Pres. S. NAQEEB-UL-HUSSAIN MUSAVI; Sec. MIRZA IQBAL BEG.

Thatta Chamber of Commerce and Industry: Room D, Al-Haroon, 4th Floor, Garden Rd, Karachi; tel. (21) 7726243; fax (21) 7725628; e-mail malodhi@lodhico.khi2.erum.com.pk.

INDUSTRIAL AND TRADE ASSOCIATIONS

All Pakistan Cloth Exporters' Association: 30/7, Civil Lines, Faisalabad; tel. (41) 644750; fax (41) 617985; e-mail apcea@fsd.paknet.com.pk; Chair. CH. MOHAMMAD SIDDIQUE; Sec. AFTAB AHMAD.

All Pakistan Cloth Merchants' Association: 64, 4th Floor, Hussain Cloth Market, Dada Chambers, Mereweather Tower, M. A. Jinnah Rd, Karachi; tel. (21) 2444274; fax (21) 2419751; Chair. JAVED CHINOY.

All Pakistan Cotton Powerlooms' Association: P-79/3, Montgomery Bazaar, Faisalabad; tel. (411) 612929; fax (411) 28171; Chair. CHAUDRY JAVAID SADIQ.

All Pakistan Textile Mills' Association: APTMA House, 44A Lalazar, off Moulvi Tamizuddin Khan Rd, POB 5446, Karachi 74000; tel. (21) 5610191; fax (21) 5611305; e-mail aptma@cyber.net.pk; internet www.paktextile.com; Chair. NADEEM MAQBOOL; Sec.-Gen. Mian IFTIKHAR AFZAL.

Cigarette Manufacturers' Association of Pakistan: Mezzanine 1, Avanti Park View, 141-A, Block 2, PECHS, Allama Iqbal Rd, Karachi 75400; tel. and fax (21) 4526825; Sec. TARIQ FAROOQ.

Cotton Board: Dr Abbasi Clinic Bldg, 76 Strachan Rd, Karachi 74200; tel. (21) 215669; fax (21) 5680422; f. 1950; Chair. Mian HABIBULLAH; Dep. Sec. Dr MUHAMMAD USMAN.

Cotton Export Corpn of Pakistan (Pvt) Ltd: Finance and Trade Centre, Shahrah-e-Faisal, POB 3738, Karachi 74400; tel. (21) 5670162; fax (21) 5683968; f. 1973; raw cotton exports and imports in both the public sector and private sector; Chair. INAAMUL HAQUE.

Federal 'B' Area Industrial Association: F. B. Area, Karachi; Chair. (vacant).

Karachi Cotton Association: The Cotton Exchange, I. I. Chundrigar Rd, Karachi; tel. (21) 2410336; fax (21) 2413035; e-mail kca33@cyber.net.pk; internet www.kcapak.org; Chair. ZAHID BASHIR; Sec. FASIHUDDIN.

Korangi Association of Trade and Industry: ST-4/2,1st Floor, Aiwan-e-Sanat, Sector 23, Korangi Industrial Area, Karachi 74900; tel. (21) 5061211; fax (21) 5061215; e-mail korangi1@email.com; Chair. SHAIKH MANZAR ALAM.

Management Association of Pakistan: 36-A/4, Lalazar, opposite Beach Luxury Hotel, Karachi 74000; tel. (21) 5611683; fax (21) 5611683; e-mail info@mappk.org; Pres. SYED MASOOD ALI NAQVI; Exec. Dir FAROOQ HASSAN.

Pakistan Agricultural Machinery and Implements Manufacturers' Association: Samundari Rd, Faisalabad; tel. (41) 714517; fax (41) 722721; e-mail iqra@fsd.comsats.net.pk.

Pakistan Agricultural Pesticides Association: Karachi; Chair. ASIF MUHAMMAD KHAN.

Pakistan Art Silk Fabrics and Garments Exporters' Association: 405 Amber Estate, Shahrah-e-Faisal, Karachi; tel. (21) 4538814; fax (21) 4536164; Chair. MAHMOOD AHMED; Sec.-Gen. IFTIKHAR AHMED KHAN.

Pakistan Bedwear Exporters' Association: 245-1-V, Block 6, PECHS, Karachi; tel. (21) 4541149; fax (21) 2851429; e-mail nash2@attglobal.net; Chair. SHABIR AHMED; Sec. S. IFTIKHAR HUSSAIN.

Pakistan Beverage Manufacturers' Association: C, 1st Floor, Kiran Centre, M-28, Model Town Extension, Lahore; tel. (42) 5167306; fax (42) 5167316.

Pakistan Canvas and Tents Manufacturers' and Exporters' Association: 15/63, Shadman Commercial Market, Afridi Mansion, Lahore 3; tel. (42) 7578836; fax (42) 7577572; e-mail pctmea@wol.net.pk; Chair. ABDUL RAZAK CHHAPRA; Sec. IJAZ HUSSAIN.

Pakistan Carpet Manufacturers' and Exporters' Association: 401-A, 4th Floor, Panorama Center, Fatima Jinnah Rd, Saddar, Karachi 75530; tel. (21) 5212189; fax (21) 5679649; e-mail pcmeaho@gerrys.net; internet www.pakistanrug.com.pk; Chair. ABDUL LATIF MALIK; Sec. A. S. HASHMI.

Pakistan Chemicals and Dyes Merchants' Association: Chemical and Dye House, Jodia Bazar, Rambharti St, Karachi 74000; tel. (21) 2432752; fax (21) 2430117.

Pakistan Commercial Towel Exporters' Association: 207, 2nd Floor, Uni Plaza, I. I. Chundrigar Rd, Karachi; tel. (21) 2411389; fax (21) 2410135; Chair. JAMIL MAHBOOB MAGOON.

Pakistan Cotton Fashion Apparel Manufacturers' and Exporters' Association: Room 5, Amber Court, 2nd Floor, Shahrah-e-Faisal, Shaheed-e-Millat Rd, Karachi 75350; tel. (21) 4533936; fax (21) 4546711; e-mail faf@pcfa.khi.brain.net.pk; f. 1982; 650 mems; Chair. QASEEM FAZIL.

Pakistan Cotton Ginners' Association: 1119–1120, 11th Floor, Uni-Plaza, I. I. Chundrigar Rd, Karachi; tel. (21) 2411406; fax (21) 2423181; e-mail pcga@gem.net.pk; Chair. MUHAMMAD SAEED; Sec. AIJAZUDDIN GHAURI.

Pakistan Film Producers' Association: Regal Cinema Bldg, Shahrah-e-Quaid-e-Azam, Lahore; tel. (42) 7322904; fax (42) 7241264; Chair. SYED YAAR MUHAMMAD SHAH; Sec. SAMI DEHLVI.

Pakistan Footwear Manufacturers' Association: 6-F, Rehman Business Centre, 32-B-III, Gulberg III, Lahore 54660; tel. (42) 5750051; fax (42) 5750052; e-mail pfma@pfma.lcci.org.pk; internet www.pakfootwear.org; Chair. ZAHID HUSSAIN; Sec. Col (retd) ARSHAD AYYAZ.

Pakistan Gloves Manufacturers' and Exporters' Association: 349 Khadim Ali Rd, G. H. Jones Bldg, Tajpura, POB 1330, Sialkot; tel. (432) 551847; fax (432) 550182; Chair. Khawaja ABDUL QAVI; Sec. GULZAR AHMED SHAD.

Pakistan Hardware Merchants' Association: Mandviwala Bldg, Serai Rd, Karachi 74000; tel. (21) 2420610; fax (21) 2415743; f. 1961; more than 1,500 mems; Central Chair. WAJID RAFIQ; Central Sec. SYED ZAFRUN NABI.

Pakistan Hosiery Manufacturers' Association: Karachi; tel. (21) 4522769; fax (21) 4543774; Chair. SHAHZAD AZAM KHAN; Sec. YUNUS BIN AIYOOB.

Pakistan Iron and Steel Merchants' Association: Corner House, 2nd Floor, Preedy St, Saddar, Karachi; tel. (21) 519994; fax (21) 4550699; Pres. MALIK AHMAD HUSSAIN; Gen. Sec. S. S. REHMAN.

Pakistan Jute Mills Association: 8 Sasi Town House, Abdullah Haroon Rd, Civil Lines, Karachi 75530; tel. (21) 5676986; fax (21) 5676463; Chair. AHSAN SALEEM; Exec. Consultant M. Z. CHUGHTAI.

Pakistan Knitwear and Sweaters Exporters' Association: Rooms Nos 1014–1016, 10th Floor, Park Ave, Block 6, PECHS, Shahrah-e-Faisal, Karachi 95350; tel. (21) 4522604; fax (21) 4525747; Chair. NASIR HUSSAIN.

Pakistan Leather Garments Manufacturers' and Exporters' Association: 92-C, 1st Floor, Khayaban-e-Ittehad, DHA Phase II (Extension), Karachi; tel. (21) 5387356; fax (21) 5388799; e-mail info@plgmea.org; Chair. FAWAD EJAZ KHAN.

Pakistan Paint Manufacturers' Association: ST/6A, Block 14, Federal 'B' Area, Karachi 38; tel. (21) 6321103; fax (21) 2560468; f. 1953; Chair. WASSIM A. KHAN; Sec. SYED AZHAR ALI.

Pakistan Plastic Manufacturers' Association: 410 Mashrique Shopping Centre, St 6/A, Block No. 14, Gulshan-e-Iqbal, Karachi;

tel. (21) 4942336; fax (21) 4944222; e-mail ppmatpc@hotmail.com; Pres. ZAKARIA USMAN; Sec. FAYYAZ A. CHAUDHRY.

Pakistan Polypropylene Woven Sacks Manufacturers' Association: Karachi; Chair. SHOUKAT AHMED.

Pakistan Pulp, Paper and Board Mills Association: 402 Burhani Chambers, Abdullah Haroon Rd, Karachi 74400; tel. (21) 7726150; Chair. KAMRAN KHAN.

Pakistan Readymade Garments Manufacturers' and Exporters' Association: Shaheen View Bldg, Mezzanine Floor, Plot No. 18A, Block IV, PECHS, Shahrah-e-Faisal, Karachi; tel. (21) 4547912; fax (21) 4539669; e-mail info@prgmea.org; Chair. MASOOD NAQI.

Pakistan Ship Breakers' Association: 608, S.S. Chamber, Siemens Chowrangi, S.I.T.E., Karachi; tel. (21) 293958; fax (21) 256533.

Pakistan Silk and Rayon Mills' Association: Room Nos 44–48, Textile Plaza, 5th Floor, M. A. Jinnah Rd, Karachi 2; tel. (21) 2410288; fax (21) 2415261; f. 1974; Chair. M. ASHRAF SHEIKH; Sec. M. H. K. BURNEY.

Pakistan Small Units Powerlooms' Association: 2nd Floor, Waqas Plaza, Aminpura Bazar, POB 8647, Faisalabad; tel. (411) 627992; fax (411) 633567.

Pakistan Soap Manufacturers' Association: 148 Sunny Plaza, Hasrat Mohani Rd, Karachi 74200; tel. (21) 2634648; fax (21) 2563828; e-mail pakistansma@yahoo.com; Chair. YAQOOB KARIM.

Pakistan Software House Association (PASHA): Block 5, F-58, Park Lane, Clifton, Karachi 75600; tel. (21) 5870321; fax (21) 5870988; e-mail info@pasha.org.pk; internet www.pasha.org.pk; f. 1992; Pres. SYED HAMZA.

Pakistan Sports Goods Manufacturers' and Exporters' Association: Paris Rd, Sialkot 51310; tel. (432) 267962; fax (432) 261774; e-mail psga@brain.net.pk; Chair. ARIF MEHMOOD SHEIKH.

Pakistan Steel Melters Association: Lahore; Chair. AZIZ AHMED CHAUDHRY.

Pakistan Steel Re-rolling Mills' Association: Rashid Chambers, 6-Link McLeod Rd, Lahore 54000; tel. (42) 7227136; fax (42) 7231154; Chair. Mian TARIQ WAHEED; Sec. Lt-Col (retd) S. H. A. BUKHARI.

Pakistan Sugar Mills' Association: Mezzanine Floor, 24D Rashid Plaza, Jinnah Ave, Islamabad; tel. (51) 270525; fax (51) 274153; Chair. ASHRAF W. TABBANI; Sec.-Gen. K. ALI QAZILBASH.

Pakistan Tanners' Association: Plot No. 46-C, 21st Commercial St, Phase II Extension, Defence Housing Authority, Karachi 75500; tel. (21) 5880180; fax (21) 5880093; e-mail info@pakistantanners.org; Chair. MASOOD AHMED SHAIKH (acting).

Pakistan Tea Association: Suite 307, Business Plaza, Mumtaz Hassan Rd, off I. I. Chundrigar Rd, Karachi; tel. (21) 2422161; fax (21) 2422209; e-mail pta@cyber.net.pk; Chair. HANIF JANOO.

Pakistan Vanaspati Manufacturers' Association: No. 5-B, College Rd, F-7/3, Islamabad; tel. (51) 2274358; fax (51) 2272529; Chair. Mian MOHAMMAD IBRAHIM.

Pakistan Wool and Hair Merchants' Association: 27 Idris Chambers, Talpur Rd, Karachi; Pres. Mian MOHAMMAD SIDDIQ KHAN; Sec. KHALID LATEEF.

Pakistan Woollen Mills' Association: Republic Motors Bldg, 2nd Floor, Room No. 12, 87 Shahrah-e-Quaid-e-Azam, Lahore 54000; tel. (42) 6308398; fax (42) 6306879; e-mail pwma@lcci.org.pk; internet www.lcci.org.pk; Chair. Mian MUZAFFAR ALI; Sec. MUHAMMAD YASIN.

Pakistan Yarn Merchants' Association: Room Nos 802–3, Business Centre, 8th Floor, Dunolly Rd, Karachi 74000; tel. (21) 2410320; fax (21) 2424896; Central Chair. YAQOOB NAGARIA.

Towel Manufacturers' Association of Pakistan: 77-A, Block A, Sindhi Muslim Co-operative Housing Society, Karachi 74400; tel. (21) 4551628; fax (21) 4551628; Chair. TAHIR JAHANGIR.

EMPLOYERS' ORGANIZATION

Employers' Federation of Pakistan: 2nd Floor, State Life Bldg No. 2, Wallace Rd, off I. I. Chundrigar Rd, POB 4338, Karachi 74000; tel. (21) 2411049; fax (21) 2439347; e-mail efpak@cyber.net.pk; internet www.efpak.com; f. 1950; Pres. ASHRAF WALI MOHAMMAD TABANI; Sec.-Gen. MOHAMMED MUSTAFA SHARIF.

UTILITIES

Water and Power Development Authority (WAPDA): WAPDA House, Shahrah-e-Quaid-e-Azam, Lahore; tel. (42) 6366911; f. 1958 for development of irrigation, water supply and drainage, building of replacement works under the World Bank-sponsored Indo-Pakistan Indus Basin Treaty; flood-control and watershed management; reclamation of waterlogged and saline lands; inland navigation; generation, transmission and distribution of hydroelectric and thermal power; partial transfer to private ownership carried out in 1996; Chair. Lt-Gen. ZULFIKAR ALI KHAN.

Electricity

National Electric Power Regulatory Authority (NEPRA): 2nd Floor, OPF Bldg, G-5/2, Islamabad; tel. (51) 9207200; fax (51) 9210215; e-mail info@napra.org.pk; f. 1997; fixes the power tariff.

Hub Power Co Ltd (Hubco): Islamic Chamber Bldg, Block No. 9, Clifton, POB 13841, Karachi 75600; tel. (21) 5874677; fax (21) 5870397; f. 1991; supplies electricity; Chair. MOHAMMAD ALI RAZA; Chief Exec. VINCE HARRIS.

Karachi Electric Supply Corpn Ltd (KESC): Aimai House, Abdullah Haroon Rd, POB 7197, Karachi; tel. (21) 5685492; fax (21) 5682408; f. 1913; Chair. and Man. Dir KAMAL AZFAR.

Kot Addu Power Co (KAPCO): G.T.P, Kot Addu, District Muzaffargarh; tel. (697) 41336.

National Power Construction Corpn (Pvt) Ltd: 9 Shadman II, Lahore 54000; tel. (42) 7566019; fax (42) 7566022; e-mail npcc@wol.net.pk; internet www.npcc.com.pk; f. 1974; execution of power projects on turnkey basis, e.g. extra high voltage transmission lines, distribution networks, substations, power generation plants, industrial electrification, external lighting of housing complexes, etc.; Man. Dir MUHAMMAD AJAZ MALIK; Gen. Man. TAUQIR AHMED SHARIFI; project office in Jeddah (Saudi Arabia).

National Power International: D-15, Block-2, Khayaban-e-Ghalib, Clifton, Karachi 75600; tel. (21) 5860328; fax (21) 5860343; e-mail npower@www.fascom.com.

Pakistan Atomic Energy Commission (PAEC): POB 1114, Islamabad; tel. (51) 9209032; fax (51) 9204908; responsible for harnessing nuclear energy for development of nuclear technology as part of the nuclear power programme; operates Karachi Atomic Nuclear Power Plant—KANUPP (POB 3183, nr Paradise Point, Hawksbay Rd, Karachi 75400; tel. (21) 9202222; fax (21) 7737488; e-mail knpc@khi.comsats.net.pk) and Chasma Nuclear Power Plant (CHASNUP) at Chasma District Mianwali; building another nuclear power station at Kundian; establishing research centres, incl. Pakistan Institute of Nuclear Science and Technology (PINSTECH); promoting peaceful use of atomic energy in agriculture, medicine, industry and hydrology; searching for indigenous nuclear mineral deposits; training project personnel; Chair. PERVEZ BUTT; Gen. Man. (KANUPP) QAMRUL HODA.

Pakistan Electric Power Co: Lahore; f. 1998; Chair. JAVED BURKI.

Quetta Electric Supply Co Ltd: Zarghoon Rd, Quetta Cantt, Balochistan; tel. (81) 9202211; fax (81) 836554; e-mail qesco@qta.infolink.net.pk; f. 1998; CEO Brig. AGHA GUL.

Gas

Mari Gas Co Ltd (MGCL): 21 Mauve Area, 3rd Rd, Sector G10/4, Islamabad; tel. (51) 297679; fax (51) 297686; e-mail marigd@cyber.net.pk; 20% govt-owned; Chair. Lt-Gen. (retd) KHALID LATIF MOGHAL.

Oil and Gas Development Corpn Ltd (OGDCL): C-6, Masood Mansion, F-8, Markaz, Islamabad; tel. (51) 9260405; fax (51) 9260467; f. 1961; plans, promotes, organizes and implements programmes for the exploration and development of petroleum and gas resources, and the production, refining and sale of petroleum and gas; transfer to private ownership pending; Chair. Maj.-Gen. (retd) PERVEZ AKMAL; Man. Dir ZAKAUDDIN MALIK.

Pakistan Petroleum Ltd (PPL): PIDC House, 4th Floor, Dr Ziauddin Ahmed Rd, Karachi 75530; tel. (21) 5681391; fax (21) 5680005; e-mail info@ppl.com.pk; 93.7% govt-owned, 6.1% owned by International Finance Corpn; Pakistan's largest producer of natural gas; Chief Exec./Man. Dir S. MUNSIF RAZA.

Sui Northern Gas Pipelines Ltd: Gas House, 21 Kashmir Rd, POB 56, Lahore; tel. (42) 9201277; fax (42) 9201302; f. 1964; 36% state-owned; transmission and distribution of natural gas in northern Pakistan; sales 321,956m. (June 2002); Chair. Lt-Gen. (retd) GHULAM SAFDAR BUTT; Man. Dir ABDUL RASHID LONE.

Sui Southern Gas Co Ltd: 4B Sir Shah Suleman Rd, Block 14, Gulshan-e-Iqbal, Karachi 75000; tel. (21) 9231602; fax (21) 9231604; e-mail info@ssgc.com.pk; f. 1988; 70% state-owned; Man. Dir INAM-US-SAMAD (acting).

Water

Faisalabad Development Authority (Water and Sanitation Agency): POB 229, Faisalabad; tel. (411) 767606; fax (411) 782113; e-mail fwasa@fsd.paknet.com.pk; f. 1978; Man. Dir Lt-Col (retd) SYED GHIAS-UD-DIN.

Karachi Water and Sewerage Board: Block D, (Behind Subzazar Lawns), 9th Mile Office, Shahrae Faisal, Karachi; tel. (21) 9231882; fax (21) 9231814; e-mail water@cyber.net.pk; f. 1983; Man. Dir Brig. (retd) MUHAMMAD BAHRAM KHAN.

Lahore Development Authority (Water and Sanitation Agency): 4-A Gulberg V, Lahore; tel. (42) 5756739; fax (42) 5752960; f. 1967; Man. Dir IMRAN RAZA ZAIDI.

MAJOR COMPANIES

The following is a selection of the major companies in Pakistan:

Automobiles, Motorcycles and Tractors

Agriauto Industries Ltd: 5th Floor, House of Habib, 3JCHS, Shahrah-e-Faisal, Karachi 75350; tel. (21) 4541540; fax (21) 4549284; sales Rs 234m. (1994/95); manufactures spare parts and two-wheel vehicles; Chair. R. D. MINWALLA; Man. Dir SYED IKRAM HAIDER.

Al Ghazi Tractors Ltd: NIC Bldg, Abbasi Shaheed Rd, Karachi 74400; tel. (21) 5660881; fax (21) 5689387; e-mail agtl@khi.com pol.com; internet www.alghazitractors.com; sales Rs 6,163m. (1999/2000); CEO and Man. Dir PARVEZ ALI.

Atlas Group of Companies: 8th Floor, Adamjee House, I. I. Chundrigar Rd, Karachi; tel. (21) 2417744; fax (21) 2416851; e-mail yhs@atlasgrouppk.com; internet www.atlasgrouppk.com; sales Rs 15,000m. (2001); Chair. YUSUF H. SHIRAZI.

Awami Autos: West Wharf Rd, Karachi.

Dawood Yamaha Ltd: 40-C, Block 6, PECHS, Karachi 75400; tel. (21) 4541960; fax (21) 454677; e-mail dyl@cyber.net.pk.

Dewan Farooq Motors Ltd: Karachi; tel. (21) 5610552; fax (21) 5610326.

Gandhara Nissan Ltd: Gandhara House, 109/2 Clifton, POB 3812, Karachi 6; tel. (21) 576051; fax (21) 5830258; sales Rs 361m. (1994/95); mfr of automobiles and taxis; Chair. Gen. (retd) HABIBULLAH KHAN KHATTAK.

Hino Pak Motors Ltd: D-2, S.I.T.E., Manghopir Rd, Karachi; tel. (21) 298791; fax (21) 2426728; cap. and res Rs 419.9m., sales Rs 2,359.8m. (1996/97); Chair. KEITH STACK.

Indus Motor Co Ltd: 14 Bangalore Town Housing Society, Main Shahrah-e-Faisal, Karachi; tel. (21) 4545025; fax (21) 4549662; f. 1993; cap. and res Rs 1,372.7m., sales Rs 4,534.4m. (1996/97); mfrs Toyota passenger cars and diesel pick-ups; annual production capacity of 20,000 vehicles; Chair. ALI S. HABIB; 590 employees.

Mehran Motor Car Co: 150N, Block 2, Khalid Bin Waleed Rd, PECHS, Karachi; tel. (21) 4552886; fax (21) 4558037; agents for Daewoo Cars.

Millat Tractors Ltd: 9 Sheikhupura Rd, Lahore; tel. (42) 7925836; fax (42) 7925835; sales Rs 2,970m. (1994/95); Chair. SIKANDER M. KHAN.

National Motors Ltd: Hub Chouki Rd, S.I.T.E., POB 2706, Karachi 75730; tel. (21) 2560083; fax (21) 2564458; sales Rs 224m. (1994/95); manufactures and assembles trucks, buses and light commercial vehicles; Chair. RAZA KULI KHAN KHATTAK.

Novelty Enterprises Ltd: 192A Raja Sq., S.M.H. Society, Shahrah-e-Faisal, Karachi; tel. (21) 436424; fax (21) 4553027; assembles two-wheel Vespas and three-wheel rickshaws, distributes motor scooters.

Pak Suzuki Motor Co Ltd: 16 West Wharf Rd, Karachi; tel. (21) 750102; fax (21) 7737994; cap. and res Rs 1,300m., sales Rs 7,700m. (1997); Chair. and Man. Dir HIROFUMI NAGAO.

Pakistan Automobile Corpn Ltd (PACO): 2nd Floor, Finance and Trade Centre, Tower 'B', Shahrah-e-Faisal, POB 4271, Karachi; tel. (21) 525391; fax (21) 525320; f. 1972; Chair. KAMAL ASFAR.

Raja Autocars Ltd: 192-A Raja Sq., SMCHS Society, Karachi; tel. (21) 4550035; fax (21) 4553027; assembles/mfrs Vespa scooters and three-wheel auto rickshaws; Sec. HAKIMMUDIN SHEIKH.

Saif Nadeem Co: Corporate Office, 7/B, Malani Mahal, Frere Rd, Karachi; tel. (21) 7725762; operates plant in Lahore; assembles Kawasaki vehicles.

Shahnawaz Ltd: 19 West Wharf Rd, Karachi; tel. (21) 2313934; fax (21) 2310623; e-mail khi-vehdiv@shahnawazltd.com; agents for Mercedes Benz vehicles.

Sindh Engineering (Pvt) Ltd: West Wharf Rd, Karachi; assembles Mazda vehicles.

Suzuki Motorcycles Pakistan Ltd: F-14, S.I.T.E., Mauripur Link Rd, POB 2708, Karachi; tel. (21) 2573309; fax (21) 2563895; e-mail suzukimc@paknet3.ptc.pk; cap. and res Rs 439.0m., sales Rs 309m. (June 2002); Chair. MIDHAT A. KIDWAI.

Worldwide Motors (Pvt) Ltd: Worldwide House, C-17, Main Korangi Rd, Defence Housing Authority, Phase II (Extension), Karachi 75500; tel. (21) 5389901; fax (21) 5887467; e-mail worldwide_motors@yahoo.com; authorized distributors for Mitsubishi Motors; Dir (Marketing) S. KARIMUDDIN.

Cement

Attock Cement Pakistan Ltd: 5th Floor, PNSC Bldg, M. T. Khan Rd, Karachi 74000; tel. (21) 5611019; fax (21) 5610820; e-mail acpl@sat.net.pk; Chief Exec. BABAR BASHIR NAWAZ; 481 employees.

Chakwal Cement: 7/1, E-3, Main Boulevard, Gulberg III, Lahore; tel. (42) 5757108; fax (42) 5755760; cap. and res Rs 5,624.6m. (1997/98); Chair. and CEO KHAWAJA MOHAMMED JAWED.

Cherat Cement Co Ltd: Modern Motors House, Beaumont Rd, Karachi 75530; tel. (21) 5683566; fax (21) 5683425; cap. and res Rs 925.8m., sales Rs 1,302.1m. (1998); Chair. MOHAMMAD FAROOQUE.

Dadabhoy Cement Industries Ltd: 5th Floor, Maqbool Commercial Complex, Blocks 7 and 8, Jinnah Co-operative Housing Society, Main Shahrah-e-Faisal, Karachi 8; tel. (21) 4545704; fax (21) 4548625; sales Rs 750.0m. (1997); Chair. MOHAMMAD HUSSAIN DADABHOY.

Fecto Cement Ltd: 35 Darul-Aman-Housin Society, Blocks 7–8, Shahrah-e-Faisal, Karachi 75350; tel. (21) 4530120; fax (21) 4530123; cap. and res Rs 605.6m., sales Rs 1,098.9m. (1998); Chair. MOHAMMAD YASIN FECTO.

Gharibwal Cement Ltd: 26 Empress Rd, POB 1285, Lahore; tel. (42) 6365249; fax (42) 6278900: f. 1960; sales Rs 1,649m. (1994/95); Chair. MOHAMMAD TOUSIF PERACHA.

Javedan Cement Ltd: 2nd Floor, Al-Haroon, 10 Agha Khan III Rd, Karachi 74400; tel. (21) 9215281; fax (21) 7767302; 89% state-owned; sales Rs 682.9m. (1998/99); Chair. NAWAZ DIWANA; Man. Dir M. P. GANGWANI.

Kohat Cement Co Ltd: 1, 43 FCC, Gulberg IV, Lahore; tel. (42) 5754357; fax (42) 5754084; e-mail kccl@wol.net.pk; cap. and res Rs 408.3m., sales Rs 501.2m. (1997); Chair. ATTA MOHAMMAD SHEIKH.

Maple Leaf Cement Factory Ltd: 42 Lawrence Rd, Lahore; tel. (42) 6278904; fax (42) 6363184; e-mail cement@maple.lcci.org.pk; f. 1956; cap. and res Rs 3,130.1m., sales Rs 925.6m. (1998); Chair. TARIQ SAYEED SAIGOL.

Mustehkam Cement Ltd: 345 Bazar Rd, Westbridge, POB 174, Rawalpindi.

Pakland Cement Ltd: Trade Centre, A-14, Block 7–8, KCHS, Shahrah-e-Faisal, Karachi 75350; tel. (21) 4559171; fax (21) 4546992; f. 1985; cap. and res Rs 1,183m., sales Rs 922.2m. (1998); Chair. TARIQ MOHSIN SIDDIQUI; Gen. Man. N. H. MISTRY.

State Cement Corpn of Pakistan (Pvt) Ltd: PEC Bldg, 97-A/B-D Gulberg III, Lahore; tel. (42) 870341; f. 1973; operates public-sector cement plants; distributes cement; Chair. MALIK AMJAD ALI.

Thatta Cement Co Ltd: Al Farid Centre, Maulvi Tamizuddin Khan Rd, Karachi; tel. (21) 512772; Man. Dir Mr AKRAM.

Chemicals and Pharmaceuticals

Antibiotics (Pvt) Ltd: Iskanderabad (Daudkhel), Dist. Mianwali; tel. (459) 630.

Bayer Pakistan (Pvt) Ltd: B-28, KDA Scheme No. 1, Shahrah-e-Faisal, POB 4641, Karachi; tel. (21) 4547534; fax (21) 4549114; sales Rs 350m. (1997); Man. Dir B. HANS VENINGA.

Ciba-Geigy (Pakistan) Ltd: 15 West Wharf Rd, Karachi; tel. (21) 200112; fax (21) 2311009; sales Rs 2,685m. (1995); mfr of pharmaceuticals; Man. Dir A. E. DAPP.

Engro Asahi Polymer and Chemicals Ltd: Head Office, 1st Floor, Bahria Complex I, 24 M. T. Khan Rd, Karachi; tel. (21) 111411411; fax (21) 5611690; e-mail abnasim@engro.com; PVC resin plant at Port Qasim.

Federal Chemical and Ceramics Corpn Ltd: Ministry of Industries and Production, Government of Pakistan, 12 Ahmad Block, New Garden Town, Lahore; tel. (42) 5834956; fax (42) 5834837.

Hoechst Marion Roussel Pakistan Ltd: Hoechst House, Plot No. 23, Sector 22, Korangi Industrial Estate, Karachi; tel. (21) 5060221; fax (21) 5060358; e-mail hmritd@cyber.net.pk; cap. and res Rs 307.4m., sales Rs 1,420.7m. (1998); mfr of pharmaceuticals; Chair. SYED BABAR ALI.

ICI (Pakistan) Ltd: ICI House, 5 West Wharf, POB 4731, Karachi 74000; tel. (21) 2313717; fax (21) 2311739; e-mail iciccpa@fascom.com; internet www.ici.com.pk; sales Rs 11,062m. (1998); mfrs of soda ash, polyester staple fibre, pharmaceuticals, paints, pesticides and agricultural chemicals; 1,800 employees (1998).

Ittehad Chemicals Ltd: Kala Shah Kaku, Sheikhupura, POB 1414, Lahore; tel. (42) 290122; fax (42) 7990543; f. 1962; mfrs of hydrochloric and sulphuric acid, caustic soda and liquid chlorine.

Ittehad Pesticides: Kala Shah Kaku, Sheikhupura, POB 886, Lahore; tel. (42) 700128; fax (42) 700134; mfrs of BHC Technical and DDT Technical; Man. Dir CHAUDHRY G. S. MUSHTAQ.

National Fibres Ltd Pakistan: Schon Centre, I. I. Chundrigar Rd, Karachi 74200; tel. (21) 219551; fax (21) 2636325.

Nowshera PVC Co Ltd: Amangarh, POB 31, Nowshera 24100; tel. (21) 438044; fax (21) 438596; mfrs of PVC Cordrain pipes, alum and of liquid and powder insecticides; Man. Dir A. QADEEM JAN.

Pak Chemicals Ltd: Hakimsons Bldg, West Wharf Rd, POB 4739, Karachi 74000; tel. (21) 2313508; fax (21) 2314260; f. 1950; mfrs of sulphuric acid, hydrochloric acid, aluminium sulphate, magnesium sulphate, alum and sodium sulphate; Man. Dir S. M. KHALID; Man. (Marketing) S. H. ANSARI.

Pakdyes and Chemicals Ltd: Iskanderabad (Daudkhel) Distt. Mianwali; tel. (459) 2434; a project of Federal Chemicals and Ceramics Corpn (Pvt) Ltd; mfrs of all types of direct and acid dyestuffs for cotton, wool and leather.

Pakistan Agro Chemicals (Pvt) Ltd: 38-C/IV, Block 6, PECHS, Karachi 75400; tel. (21) 4534870; fax (21) 4548232.

Pakistan PVC Ltd: Al-Haroon, 4th Floor, Garden Rd, Karachi.

Pharmacia & Upjohn (Pvt) Ltd: Industrial Triangle, Kahuta Rd, POB 40, Rawalpindi; tel. (51) 8471237; fax (51) 422439; f. 1951; mfrs of pharmaceuticals; Pres. RAUL O. MONTEFUSCO.

Rhône-Poulenc Rorer Pakistan (Pvt) Ltd: G. T. Rd, Wah Cantt; tel. (51) 519359; fax (596) 3164; f. 1977; cap. Rs 30m.; mfrs of human pharmaceuticals; Chair. SAADAT HUSSAIN KHAN; Pakistan Rep. TARIQ MOHAMED AMIN.

Sandoz (Pakistan) Ltd: 5th and 6th Floors, Bahria Complex, 24 M. T. Khan Rd, Karachi; tel. (21) 5611405; fax (21) 5611062; sales Rs 2,288m. (1995); Chair. Dr MARTIN SYZ.

Silchem International (Pvt) Ltd: Office 107, 1st Floor, Fortune Centre, 45-A, Block 6, PECHS Shahrae Faisal, Karachi; e-mail silchem@khi.compol.com.

Sitara Chemical Industries Ltd: POB 442, Faisalabad; tel. (41) 689141; fax (41) 689147; e-mail ijaz@sitara.com.pk; Chief Exec. MUHAMMAD ADREES.

Sindh Alkalis Ltd: 1A, State Life Bldg, 3rd Floor, I. I. Chundrigar Rd, POB 4200, Karachi 74000; tel. (21) 2426783; fax (21) 2425710; sales Rs 526m. (1996/97); Chair. SAIF-UR-RAHMAN.

Electrical

Philips Electrical Industries of Pakistan: Islamic Chamber of Commerce, St.-2A, Block 9, KDA Scheme 5, Clifton, Karachi; tel. (21) 5874641; fax (21) 5874546; sales Rs 2,666m. (1995); mfr of domestic electrical appliances; Chair. S. NASEEM AHMED; 1,048 employees (1995).

Engineering

Heavy Mechanical Complex: Taxila 47050; tel. (51) 584165; fax (51) 584168; e-mail hmc@paknet2.ptc.pk; f. 1971; mfr and supplier of sugar, cement, chemical and petrochemical, fertilizer and oil and gas processing plants, boilers, road-rollers, steel structures, steel and iron castings, pressure vessels, machinery and equipment for thermal and hydel power plants, heavy and sophisticated steel structures, and steel and iron heavy castings and forgings; Man. Dir M. A. JANJUA.

Ittefaq Foundries (Pvt) Ltd: 32 Empress Rd, Lahore; tel. (42) 306961; fax (42) 305681; f. 1940; Chair. Mian MOHAMMAD SHARIF; Dir (Technical) Mian ILYAS MIRAJ.

National Engineering Services Pakistan (Pvt) Ltd (NESPAK): NESPAK House, 1-C, Block-N, Model Town Extension Scheme, POB 1351, Lahore 54700; tel. (42) 5160500; fax (42) 5160509; e-mail nespak@wol.net.pk; internet www.nespak.com.pk; f. 1973; multidisciplinary consulting company for engineering projects, including irrigation, dams, bridges, transmission lines, heating, ventilation and air-conditioning, power stations, roads, town planning, etc.; operates both in Pakistan and abroad; Pres. and Man. Dir SABIR P. CHOHAN; Gen. Man. (Business Development) KHALID NAWAZ.

Nowshera Engineering Co Ltd: P. O. Ferozsons Laboratory, Amangarh, Nowshera, Peshawar; f. 1959; Prin. Officer SYED PHOOL BADSHAH.

Pakistan Engineering Co Ltd: 6/7 Ganga Ram Trust Bldg, Shahrah-e-Quaid-e-Azam, Lahore 54000; tel. (42) 7320225; fax (42) 323108; e-mail peco@paknet4.ptc.pk; f. 1950; fmrly Batala Engineering Co Ltd; name changed following nationalization; cap. and res Rs 10m., sales Rs 241.7m. (1999); mfrs pumps, motors, turbines, power looms, concrete mixers, machine tools, bicycles, etc.; Chair. HUSSAIN A. SIDDIQUI.

Siemens Pakistan Engineering Co Ltd: B-72 Estate Ave, SITE, POB 7158, Karachi 75700; tel. (21) 2574910; fax (21) 2563563; internet www.siemens.com.pk; sales Rs 3,582m. (2000); CEO SOHAIL; 1,221 employees (2000).

Sindh Engineering Corpn Ltd: West Wharf, Karachi; Man. Dir JAMIL AHMAD SHAH.

State Engineering Corpn (Pvt) Ltd: 2nd Floor, Saeed Plaza, Jinnah Ave, Blue Area, Islamabad; tel. (51) 9204391; fax (51) 9220467; e-mail statc@isb.paknet.com.pk; internet www.sec.gov.pk; f. 1979; Chair. Mian SUHAIL ASLAM.

Fertilizers

Dawood Hercules Chemicals Ltd: 35A Shahrah-e-Abdul Hameed Bin Baadees, POB 1294, Lahore 54000; tel. (42) 6301601; fax (42) 6360343; e-mail dhcl@dawoodhercules.com.pk; internet www.dawoodhercules.com.pk; Chair. HUSSAIN DAWOOD; Exec. Dir A. G. GOHAR.

Engro Chemical Pakistan Ltd: 8th Floor, PNSC Bldg, Maulvi Tamizuddin Khan Rd, POB 5736, Karachi 74000; tel. (21) 5611060; fax (21) 5610688; e-mail info@engro.com; internet www.engro.com; cap. and res Rs 5,219m., sales Rs 8,394m. (2000); mfr of urea fertilizer; Chair. NISAR A. MEMON; Pres. and CEO ZAFFAR A. KHAN.

Fauji Fertilizer Co: 93 Harley St, POB 253, Rawalpindi; tel. (51) 5566593; fax (51) 5585442; e-mail ffcrwp@ffc.com.pk; internet www.ffc.com.pk; cap. and res Rs 7,527m., sales Rs 13,562m. (1997/98); Pakistan's largest private-sector producer of urea fertilizer; Chair. Lt Gen. (retd) MUHAMMAD MAWBOOL.

FFC-Jordan Fertilizer Co Ltd: 73 Harley St, Rawalpindi; tel. (51) 565401; fax (51) 582851; plant at Port Qasim, nr Karachi; Chair. L. G. M. ARIF BANGASH; Man. Dir Lt-Gen. (retd) IMTIAZ WARAICH.

Hazara Phosphate Fertilizers (Pvt) Ltd: Haripur Hazara, Hattar Rd, Haripur District, North-West Frontier Province; subsidiary of National Fertilizer Corporation of Pakistan (Pvt) Ltd (NFC).

Lyallpur Chemicals and Fertilizers Ltd: Jaranwala Rd, POB 13, Faisalabad; tel. (411) 42371; fax (468) 2628; f. 1953; also in Jaranwala; produces superphosphate fertilizer; subsidiary of NFC; Man. Dir A. MANNAN; Gen. Mans MUHAMMAD YOUNAS (Faisalabad), MUNIR AHMED (Jaranwala).

National Fertilizer Corpn of Pakistan (Pvt) Ltd: Al-Falah Bldg, 1st Floor, Shahrah-e-Quaid-e-Azam, POB 1730, Lahore; tel. (42) 6302904; fax (42) 6302918; 6 fertilizer plants; Chair. MOHAMMAD MOHSIN; Man. Dir WASEEM M. SANA.

Pak-American Fertilizer Ltd: Iskandarabad, Mianwali Dist.; tel. (459) 31538; fax (459) 31536; f. 1956; subsidiary of NFC; Chair. AGHA NEK MOHAMMAD.

Pak-Arab Fertilizers Ltd: P.O. Fertilizer Project, Khanewal Rd, Multan; tel. (61) 552123; fax (61) 553204; subsidiary of NFC; privately-owned; Man. Dir K. SAEED.

PakChina Fertilizers Ltd: House No. 56, St 88, G-6/3, Embassy Rd, Islamabad; tel. (51) 820667; fax (51) 272882; Man. Dir KHALID MUMTAZ.

Pak-Saudi Fertilizer (Pvt) Ltd: Mirpur Mathelo, Ghotki District 65050; tel. (71) 613001; fax (71) 612634; f. 1975; subsidiary of NFC; Man. Dir MUHAMMAD YOUNUS; Gen. Man. MEHMOOD AKHTAR; 900 employees.

Food and Food Products

Nestlé Milkpak Ltd: 308 Upper Mall, Lahore; tel. (42) 5757082; fax (42) 5711820; e-mail shahid.siddiqi@pk.nestle.com; sales Rs 7,900m. (2001); mfr and distributor of food, beverages and milk products; Man. Dir FRIEDRICH G. MAHLER.

Punjab Seed Corpn: 4 Lytton Rd, Lahore; tel. (42) 212512; seed trade, crop seed production and marketing.

Rafhan Maize Products Co Ltd: Rakh Canal East Rd, POB 62, Faisalabad; tel. (41) 540121; fax (41) 711016; e-mail rafhanmp@fsd.paknet.com.pk; f. 1953; sales Rs 3,126m. (2001); agri-based industry processing corn; Chair. JEFFREY B. HEBBLE; Chief Exec./Man. Dir RASHID ALI; 686 employees (2002).

Rice Export Corpn of Pakistan: 4th Floor, Block A, Finance and Trade Centre, Shahrah-e-Faisal, POB 457, Karachi; tel. (21) 517021; fax (21) 9202996; f. 1974; procures, mills, cleans, stores, packs and markets standard quality rice for export on monopoly basis; Chair. M. YOUNUS KHAN.

Sindh Sugar Corpn Ltd: Shaikh Sultan Trust Bldg, 6th Floor, Beaumont Rd, Karachi 3; Chair. ZAHEER SAJJAD.

Leather

Bata Pakistan Ltd: Batapur, G. T. Rd, Lahore; tel. (42) 331312; fax (42) 335086; sales Rs 1,828m. (1995); mfr of footwear, rubber and plastic products; Chair. M. OLDROYD.

Din Leather Ltd: Din House, 35-A/1, Lalazar Area, opp. Beach Luxury Hotel, POB 4696, Karachi 74000; tel. (21) 5610001; fax (21) 5610009; e-mail dingroup@cyber.net.pk.

East Pakistan Chrome Tannery: 45-50 Industrial Area, Gulberg III, Lahore; tel. (42) 5756192; fax (42) 5656194; e-mail epct@brain.net.pk.

Eastern Leather Co Pvt Ltd: Office Ferozpur Rd, Gulberg II, Lahore 54660; tel. (42) 5881138; fax (42) 5861346; e-mail eastern@brain.net.pk.

Elegant Footwear (Pvt) Ltd: 17-J, Gulberg III, Lahore 54660; tel. (42) 5858720; fax (42) 5758088; e-mail elegant@

lhr.paknet.com.pk; mfr and exporter of footwear for men; CEO NASIR ANWER SHEIKH.

HUB Leather Products Ltd: Cavish Court, A-35, Blocks 7 & 8, KCHSU, Shahrah-e-Faisal, POB 5218, Karachi 75350; tel. (21) 6310375; fax (21) 6313251; e-mail email@hubleather.com; internet www.hubleather.com; f. 1983; sales US $10m. (1999); mfr and exporter of leather garments and accessories; Gen. Man HAIDER M. TAMBAWALA; Man. (Sales) FARUKH TANVEER; 800 employees (1999).

Khawaja Tanneries (Pvt) Ltd: Mehr Manzil, Lahari Gate, POB 28, Multan; tel. (61) 511158; fax (61) 511262; e-mail ktm@brain.net.pk.

Leather Co-ordinators: Tufail Shaheed Rd, Sahiwal; tel. (441) 75847; fax (441) 61263; e-mail ytc@brain.net.pk.

Leather Master Private Ltd: Sublime Chowk, Wazirabad Rd, POB 16, Sialkot; tel. and fax (432) 553592; e-mail info@leathermaster.com.pk; internet www.leather.com.pk.

Mir Yousuf Leatherwear (Pvt) Ltd: POB 461, Sialkot; tel. (432) 552835; e-mail miryousuf@brain.net.pk.

Mohamed Ismail Mohamed Aslam (MIMA): Plot Nos 4-5, Sector 17, Korangi Industrial Area, Karachi 74900; tel. (21) 5060771; fax (21) 5060572; e-mail mima@fascom.com; Sr Asst Man. (Marketing and Sales) MANZOOR HASSAN MODAK.

Muhammad Shafi Tanneries (Pvt) Ltd: Shafi House, 35-A/3, M. T. Khan Rd, opp. Beach Luxury Hotel, Karachi 74000; tel. (21) 5610696; fax (21) 5610701; e-mail leather@fascom.com; internet www.shafi.com.

Royal Leather Industries Ltd: 26-B Sundar Das Rd, Zaman Park, Lahore; tel. (42) 636140; fax (42) 6361714; e-mail royal@brain.net.pk.

Service Industries Ltd: Service House, 38 Empress Rd, 2 Main Gulberg, Lahore; tel. (42) 571190; fax (42) 5711827; cap. and res Rs 438.4m., sales Rs 1,937m. (1998); mfr of leather products, footwear, clothes and textiles, rubber products and cars; Chair. CH. NAZAR MOHAMMAD; 500 employees.

Siddiq Leather Works (Pvt) Ltd: 51 G. T. Rd, Hide Market, POB 1676, Lahore 54900; tel. (42) 7970576; fax (42) 7970539; e-mail slwpvt@brain.net.pk; internet www.siddiqleather.com; subsidiary of Shafi Group of Pakistan since 1974; produces various types of finished leather for shoes and garments, mfrs leather goods and upholstery.

Universal Leather and Footwear Industries Ltd: Cavish Court, A-35, KCHSU, Blocks 7 & 8, Shahrah-e-Faisal, POB 5218, Karachi; tel. (21) 4531525; fax (21) 4535208; e-mail ulf@mimagrp.com; sales Rs 927m. (1994/95); Chair. S. M. SALEEM.

Zahur Sancho (Pvt) Ltd: Plot No. 46, Sector 7-A, Korangi Industrial Area, Karachi 74900; tel. (21) 5061786; fax (21) 5060343.

Metals

Pakistan Steel Fabricating Co (Pvt) Ltd: PSF Administrative Bldg No. 1, POB 9006, Bin Qasim, Karachi 50; tel. (21) 7732214; fax (21) 7732214.

Pakistan Steel Mills Corpn (Pvt) Ltd: Bin Qasim, POB 5429, Karachi 75000; tel. (21) 77694260; fax (21) 7733696; f. 1973; iron and steel mfrs; mfrs of coke, coal tar, ammonium sulphate, granulated slag; operates steel mill at Bin Qasim near Karachi, which started production in 1985; annual capacity 1.1m. metric tons; Chair. Lt-Col MUHAMMAD AFZAL KHAN; Sec. SAJID HUSSAIN; 15,000 employees.

Saindak Metals (Pvt) Ltd: Ramswamy Rd, off M. A. Jinnah Rd, Quetta; tel. (81) 65403; fax (81) 65387; state-owned; under Ministry of Petroleum and Natural Resources; technical and financial assistance from Chinese Metallurgical Corporation; Pakistan's largest copper and gold project; production commenced in 1996; ore to be sent to People's Republic of China for refinement; Man. Dir Maj.-Gen. (retd) MASOOD BURKI.

Oil and Petroleum

Attock Refinery Ltd: PO Refinery, Morgah, Rawalpindi 46000; tel. (51) 5487041; fax (51) 5487254; e-mail info@arl.com.pk; sales US $354m. (2000/01); refining of indigenous crude petroleum; production capacity of 37,500 b/d; produces LPG, gasoline, kerosene, diesel, jet fuel, furnace oil and asphalt; Chair. BASHIR AHMED; CEO M. RAZIUDDIN.

Bosicor Pakistan Ltd: 2nd Floor, Business Plaza, Mumtaz Husan Rd, Karachi; tel. (21) 2410099; fax (21) 2410722; refinery to be constructed at Mousa Kund, near Hub, Balochistan; Chief Exec. PERVEZ ABBASI.

Caltex Oil (Pakistan) Ltd: State Life Bldg No. 11, Abdullah Haroon Rd, Karachi; tel. (21) 5681371; fax (21) 5685014.

National Refinery Ltd: 7-B, Korangi Industrial Zone, Karachi 74900; tel. (21) 5064135; fax (21) 5054663; internet www.nrlpak.com; Sec. ASAD A. SIDDIQUI.

Pak-Arab Refinery Ltd: Corporate HQ, Pumping Station No. 1, Korangi Creek Rd, POB 12243, Karachi 75190; tel. (21) 5090100; fax (21) 5090929; e-mail parco@digicom.net.pk; Man. Dir SHAHID HAQ.

Pak Hy Oil Ltd: Korangi Industrial Area, Karachi; tel. (21) 310104; Gen. Man. A. A. KARIMI.

Pakistan Oilfields Ltd (POL): POL House, PO Refinery, Morgah, Rawalpindi; tel. (51) 487589; fax (51) 487598; e-mail polcms@paknet2.ptc.pk; f. 1950; cap. and res Rs 2,816.3m., sales Rs 1,846m. (1997/98); exploration, drilling and production; Attock Oil Co owns 53.8%, the Govt 34.7%, investment cos 6.1% and the public 5.4%; Chief Exec. ARIF KEMAL.

Pakistan Petroleum Ltd (PPL): PIDC House, 4th Floor, Dr Ziauddin Ahmed Rd, Karachi 75530; tel. (21) 5681391; fax (21) 5680005; e-mail info@ppl.com.pk; 93.7% govt-owned, 6.1% owned by International Finance Corpn; cap. and res Rs 6,536.7m., sales Rs 4,100m. (2000/01); oil and gas exploration and production; 175 wells drilled, nine gasfields and three oilfields discovered; four fields in production: Sui gasfield produced, on average, 722m. cu ft per day (2000/01), and Kandhkot gasfield produced 100m. cu ft per day; in 2000/01 Adhi gas-condensate field produced, on average, 2,477 barrels per day of NGL, 65 metric tons per day of LPG and 18m. cu ft per day of gas; in 2000/01 Block-22 (Shikarpur) produced, on average, 8m. cu ft per day of gas; Chief Exec./Man. Dir SYED MUNSIF RAZA; Gen. Man. (Production) RAO ALTAF HUSSAIN; 1,818 employees.

Pakistan Refinery Ltd: Korangi Creek Rd, POB 4812, Karachi; tel. (21) 5091771; fax (21) 5060145; e-mail prl@digicom.com.net.pk; cap. and res Rs 263.7m., sales Rs 15,295m. (1997/98); Chair. SALAHUDDIN QURESHI.

Pakistan State Oil Co Ltd: PSO House, Khayaban-e-Iqbal, Clifton, POB 3983, Karachi 75600; tel. (21) 9203866; fax (21) 9203717; e-mail psomd@cyber.net.pk; internet www.psocl.com; f. 1976; 25.5% state-owned; sales Rs 158,300m. (2001/02); import, export, storage, distribution, marketing and blending of all kinds of petroleum products, lubricants, LPG/CNG and petrochemicals; Man. Dir TARIQ KIRMANI; Co Sec. JALIL TARIN.

Petroman: 1st Floor, Musarrat Bldg, Sultan Ahmad Shah Rd, off Shaheed-e-Millat Rd, Karachi; tel. (21) 446131.

Shell Pakistan Ltd: Shell House, 6 Chaudhry Khaliq-us-Zaman Rd, Karachi 75530; tel. (21) 5689525; fax (21) 5660021; f. 1949; sales Rs 49,890m. (1999); Chair. and Man. Dir DAVID M. WESTON.

State Petroleum, Refining and Petrochemical Corpn (Pvt) Ltd (PERAC): 2nd Floor, PIDC House, Dr Ziauddin Ahmed Rd, Karachi 75530; tel. (21) 5685071; fax (21) 5680615; e-mail perac@digicom.net.pk; f. 1974; Chair. AINUDDIN SIDDIQI.

Total Atlas Lubricants Pakistan (Pvt) Ltd: 1 McLeod Rd, Lahore 54000; tel. (42) 7359053; fax (42) 7359081.

Computer Software Companies

2B Technologies (Pvt) Ltd: Continental Trade Centre, Block 8, Clifton, Karachi; tel. (21) 5861736; fax (21) 5867992; e-mail info@2bt.com.pk; internet www.2bt.com.pk.

CC Technologies (Pvt) Ltd: 6th Floor, Park Ave Bldg, Sharah-e-Faisal, Karachi 75400; tel. (21) 4539010; fax (21) 4539015; e-mail info@cctpak.com; internet www.cctpak.com.

Crescent Solutions: Suite No 408, Block 6, Business Ave, 96-A, Main Shahrah-e-Faisal, Karachi; tel. (21) 4532909; fax (21) 2416942; internet www.cresol.com.

CyberSoft Technologies (Pvt) Ltd: 123-A, Baber Block, New Garden Town, Lahore; e-mail info@cybersoft-tech.com; internet www.cybersoft-tech.com.

Diyatech Pakistan (Pvt) Ltd: Block 14, F-6, Islamabad; tel. (51) 2877803; fax (51) 2825155; e-mail info@diyatech.com; internet www.diyatech.com.

Fauji Software Company (Pvt) Ltd: Software Technology Park, 5-A, 1st Floor, Awami Markaz, Constitution Ave, Islamabad; (51) 2822848; fax (51) 2824831; e-mail info@faujisoft.com; internet www.faujisoft.com.

Fascom Systems: 39-A, Block 6, PECHS, Karachi; tel. (21) 4551001; fax (21) 4556701; e-mail sales@fascom.com.

Gem Net Internet Services (Pvt) Ltd: 310-311, Anum State, Main Shahrah-e-Faisal, Karachi; e-mail info@gem.net.pk; internet www.gem.net.pk.

Innovative Computers (Pvt) Ltd: 4-A, Old FCC, Ferozepur Rd, Lahore 54660; tel. (42) 111000911; fax (42) 5710376; e-mail jkhattak@innovative-pk.com; internet www.innovative-pk.com.

Kalsoft (Pvt) Ltd: Mezzanine Floor, 15-C, Rahat Commercial Lane 3, Khayaban-e-Rahat, DHA Phase VI, Karachi; tel. (21) 111403020;

fax (21) 5849780; e-mail info@kalsoft.com.pk; internet www.kalsoft.com.pk.

Techlogix: 50/A, FCC, Zahoor Elahi Rd, Gulberg IV, Lahore; tel. (42) 5763205; fax (42) 5876016; e-mail lahore@techlogix.com.

Textiles, Yarns and Fibres

Abbasi Textile Mills Ltd: 17 Abdullah Haroon Rd, Karachi 75530; tel. (21) 5681576; fax (21) 5681575; 47,480 spindles and 205 looms; Chief Exec. SYED WAJID ALI.

Al Ameen Denim Mills: A/4 S.I.T.E., Karachi 75700; tel. (21) 2578871; fax (21) 2562450; e-mail alameen@fascom.com; internet www.al-ameenmills.com.

Al-Karam Textile Mills (Pvt) Ltd: 3rd Floor, Karachi Dock Labour Board Bldg, 58 West Wharf Rd, Karachi; tel. (21) 2313031; fax (21) 2310625; e-mail headoffice@alkaram.com; internet www.alkaram.com; 80,616 spindles, 280 conventional looms and 324 shuttle-less looms; Chief Exec. ANWAR HAJI KARIM.

Burewala Textile Mills Ltd: 35A Shahrah-e-Abdul Hameed Bin Badees (Empress Rd), Lahore 54000; tel. (42) 6301601; fax (42) 6360343; e-mail btm@dawoodhercules.com.pk; internet www.burewala.com; f. 1954; sales US $8m. (2000); 42,912 spindles and 312 looms; Man. Dir SHAHZADA DAWOOD; *c.* 1,400 employees (2000).

Central Cotton Mills Ltd: 5th Floor, State Life Bldg, 2, Wallace Rd, Karachi; tel. (21) 5838612; fax (21) 5683051; 53,832 spindles; Chief Exec. MUNIR AHMED.

Chenab Ltd: Nishatabad, Faisalabad; tel. (41) 754472; fax (41) 752400; e-mail chenab@chenabgroup.com; sales Rs 3,210m. (2000); 7,000 employees (2000).

Crescent Textile Mills Ltd: 83 Babar Block, New Garden Town, Lahore; tel. (42) 5839631; fax (42) 5881976; e-mail crtxc@fsd.comsats.net.pk; internet www.ctm.com.pk; cap. and res Rs 1,253m., sales Rs 3,611m. (1997/98); 113,500 spindles and 1,000 rotors; 187 looms; complete processing unit; Chief Exec. MOHAMMAD ANWAR.

Dawood Cotton Mills Ltd: Dawood Centre, Moulvi Tamizuddin Khan Rd, POB 3952, Karachi 75530; tel. (21) 5686001; fax (21) 5684108; f. 1951; 53,724 spindles and 197 looms; mills at Landhi; Chief Exec. M. HUSSAIN DAWOOD; Sec. YOUSUF A. DESHI.

Dewan Salman Fibre Ltd: Dewan Centre, 3-A, Lalazar, Beach Luxury Hotel Rd, Karachi 74000; tel. (21) 5611098; fax (21) 5622341; cap. and res Rs 2,788m., sales Rs 5,337m. (1997/98); plant located at Hattar Industrial Estate, NWFP; produces fabrics, yarns and synthetic fibres; Chair. AKIRA YAMAMURA.

Dewan Textile Mills Ltd: Dewan Centre, 3A Lalazar, Beach Hotel Rd, Karachi 7400; tel. (21) 5611098; fax (21) 5610765; sales Rs 1,430m. (1994/95); 50,616 spindles; Chief Exec. DEWAN M. ZIA-UR-REHMAN FAROOQUI.

Fateh Textile Mills Ltd: 9th Floor, Adamjee House, I. I. Chundrigar Rd, Karachi; tel. (21) 2415910; fax (21) 2416748; sales Rs 2,555m. (1994/95); Chair. JAN ALAM.

Fazal Cloth Mills Ltd: 630, 6th Floor, Stock Exchange, I. I. Chundrigar Rd, Karachi; tel. (21) 226098; sales Rs 1,174m. (1994/95); 30,600 spindles; Chief Exec. SH. MUBARAK AHMAD.

Gatron (Industries) Ltd: 8th Floor, Textile Plaza, M. A. Jinnah Rd, POB 5801, Karachi 74000; tel. (21) 2417172; fax (21) 2416532; e-mail headoffice@gatron.com; internet www.gatronova.com; f. 1980; cap. and res Rs 1,514m., sales Rs 2,671m. (1997/98); mfr and exporter of polyester filament yarn and polyester chips (textile and bottle grade); Chair. PEER MOHAMMAD DIWAN; Dir A. RAZAK DIWAN.

Gul Ahmed Textile Mills Ltd: HT 4/B Landhi Industrial Area, Landhi, Karachi 75120; tel. (21) 5082626; fax (21) 5082625; e-mail gulahmed@gulahmed.com; internet www.gulahmed.com; sales Rs 4,996m. (2001); 97,000 spindles; full spinning, weaving, bleaching, dyeing and printing plant; Chief Exec. IQBAL ALIMOHAMMED; Dir (Marketing) BASHIR H. ALIMOHAMMED.

Hafiz Textile Mills Ltd: 97 Alliance Bldg, Moolji St, opp. Mereweather Tower, Karachi 2; tel. (21) 228815; 32,016 spindles and 136 looms; Chief Exec. FAKHRUDDIN USMANI.

Husein Industries Ltd: 6th Floor, Jubilee Insurance House, I. I. Chundrigar Rd, Karachi 7400; tel. (21) 2417601; fax (21) 2416549; 72,040 spindles, 210 shuttleless looms and 350 automatic looms; dyeing, bleaching, printing and finishing unit; garment, bedlinen and curtains division (with 1,500 sewing machines); Chief Exec. LATIF E. JAMAL.

Indus Dyeing and Manufacturing Co Ltd: Karachi Dock Labour Board Bldg, 58 West Wharf Rd, Karachi; tel. (21) 2310751; fax (21) 2313814; sales Rs 1,514m. (1994/95); 37,368 spindles; Chair. Mian MOHAMMED AHMED.

Khyber Textile Mills Ltd: 8th Floor, State Life Bldg No. 2, Wallace Rd, Karachi; tel. (21) 225885; fax (21) 2417138; 38,676 spindles and 160 looms; Chief Exec. FARID M. JADOON.

Kohinoor Industries Ltd: 6 Egerton Rd, Lahore; tel. (21) 6369840; fax (42) 630594; e-mail azamtex@paknet4.ptc.pk; sales Rs 2,387m. (1999/2000); 91,320 spindles, 654 looms and 15 shuttle-less looms; exporter and mfr of fine quality 100% cotton yarn; Chief Exec. Mian M. NASEEM SAIGOL; Man. Dir AZAM SAIGOL; 3,500 employees.

Kohinoor Textiles Mills Ltd: Peshawar Rd, Rawalpindi; tel. (51) 5477264; fax (51) 5473083; e-mail taufiquesaigol@hotmail.com; f. 1948; sales Rs 2,500m. (1999/2000); 75,000 spindles; producer of bed linen and home textiles; Chair. TARIQ S. SAIGOL; Chief Exec. TAUFIQUE S. SAIGOL.

Lyallpur Cotton Mills: Factory Area, POB 17, Faisalabad 30870; tel. (411) 610012; fax (411) 619684, a project of Bin Bak Industries (Pvt) Ltd; complete cloth-processing unit; 53,000 spindles; Chair. Haji ABDUL AZIZ AL-RAEE; Chief Exec. Haji ABDUL REHMAN AL-RAEE.

Mahmood Textile Mills Ltd: Mehr Manzil, Lohari Gate, Multan; tel. (61) 511158; fax (61) 511262; e-mail mtmltd@brain.net.pk; sales Rs 1,799m. (1994/95); Chair. Khawaja MUHAMMAD MASOOD; 3,000 employees (1999).

Masood Textile Mills Ltd: General Bus Stand, Faisalabad; tel. (411) 34494; 43,200 spindles; Chief Exec. Ch. MUHAMMAD NAZIR AHMAD.

Mohammed Farooq Textile Mills: Finlay House, 1.1. Chundrigar Rd, Karachi; tel. (21) 5011571; fax (21) 5011607; e-mail mftml@cyber.net.pk; internet www.mohammadfarooq.com.pk; mfr and export of textiles; CEO FAROOQ SUMAR.

Mohib Textile Mills Ltd: 6 FB Awani Complex, Usman Block, New Garden Town, Lahore; tel. (42) 5869800; fax (42) 5830756; sales Rs 1,808m. (1994/95); 36,312 spindles; Chief Exec. M. ASIF SAIGOL.

Nagina Cotton Mills Ltd: 2nd Floor, Shaikh Sultan Trust Bldg No. 2, 26 Civil Lines, Beaumont Rd, Karachi 75530; tel. (21) 5686263; fax (21) 5683215; 47,040 spindles; Chief Exec. SHAUKAT ELLAHI SHAIKH.

Nishat Mills Ltd: P.O. Nishatabad, Faisalabad; tel. (41) 754809; fax (41) 753105; e-mail nishat@fsd.comsats.net.pk; f. 1951; cap. and res Rs 3,968m., sales Rs 8,920m. (1997/98); 175,000 spindles and 460 looms; Chief Exec. Mian MUHAMMED MANSHA YAHYA; Exec. Sec. RIZWAN NIAZ: 7,200 employees.

Quetta Textile Mills Ltd: Ground Floor, Nadir House, I. I. Chundrigar Rd, Karachi 74000; tel. (21) 2414334; fax (21) 2419593; e-mail sales@quettagroup.com; internet www.quettagroup.com; sales Rs 1,443m. (1994/95); 67,000 spindles; Chief Exec. SHAIKH KHALID IQBAL.

Ravi Rayon Ltd: 130 Allama Iqbal Rd, Lahore; tel. (42) 6306754; fax (42) 6306753; mills at Kala Shah Kaku, Dist. Sheikhupura; Man. Dir Dr FAYYAZ A. MIAN.

Rupali Polyester Ltd: 4th Floor, IEP Bldg, 97-B/D-1, Gulberg III, Lahore; tel. (42) 5713101; fax (42) 5713095; e-mail rupali@nexlinx.net.pk; cap. and res Rs 1,374m., sales Rs 2,175m. (1999/2000); mfrs of polyester filament yarn and staple fibre; Chair. JAFFERALI M. FEERASTA; 1,356 employees.

Sapphire Textile Mills Ltd: 149 Cotton Exchange Bldg, I. I. Chundrigar Rd, Karachi 2; tel. (21) 2410930; fax (21) 2416705; e-mail sapphire@khi.compol.com; cap. and res Rs 670m., sales Rs 3,421m. (1996/97); 55,412 spindles and 1,152 rotors; CEO MUHAMMAD ABDULLAH.

Sargodha Textile Mills Ltd: Sultanabad, Faisalabad Rd, Sargodha Cantt.; tel. 720084; fax 710767; 42,240 spindles and 336 looms; dyeing and finishing; Chief Exec. Mian SAJJAD ASLAM; 2,000 employees.

Schon Textile Mills Ltd: Schon Centre, I. I. Chundrigar Rd, Karachi 74200; tel. (21) 2636000; fax (21) 2636325.

Shaffa International: 160 Y-C/A, Defence Society, Lahore 54792; tel. (42) 5892232; fax (42) 5731073; e-mail sales@shaffa.com; internet www.shaffa.com; mfrs and exporters of cotton and leather working gloves.

Sunshine Cotton Mills Ltd: 71-B/C-2, Gulberg-III, Lahore II; tel. (42) 870297; 58,088 spindles; Chief Exec. Mian AFTAB A. SHEIKH.

Tobacco

Lakson Tobacco Co Ltd: Lakson Sq., Bldg No. 2, Sarwar Shaheed Rd, Karachi 74200; tel. (21) 5689080; fax (21) 5683410; e-mail tabatlay@cyber.net.pk; cap. and res Rs 500m., sales Rs 6,698m. (1996/97); Chair. IQBALALI LAKHANI; Dir of Group Corporate Affairs TASLEEMUDDIN AHMED BATLAY.

Pakistan Tobacco Co Ltd: National Insurance Corpn Bldg, Abbasi Shaheed Rd, POB 4690, Karachi; tel. (21) 519051; fax (21) 5681537; e-mail paktobac@best.net.pk; cap. and res Rs 1,003m., sales Rs 14,245m. (1997/98); Chair. MICHAEL PAUL FENN.

Miscellaneous

Associated Industries Ltd: Amangarh Industrial Area, Nowshera; tel. (923) 610863; fax (923) 610830; e-mail ailpaknet.ptc.pk;

sales Rs 2,003m. (1999/2000); mfr and sale of edible oils and household chemicals; Chair. SH. AMJAD RASHID.

Gemstone Corpn of Pakistan Ltd: 15/C Railway Rd, University Town, Peshawar; tel. (521) 42062; fax (521) 841990; f. 1979; gem exploration, mining, cutting and polishing, jewellery manufacturing and marketing; Man. Dir Dr NASIR ALI BHATTI; Sec. PERVEZ ELAHI MALIK.

National Logistic Cell: Marketing Cell South Zone, POB 7020, Karachi; tel. (21) 2850398; fax (21) 2851316; transportation of bulk dry and liquid cargo (e.g. wheat, rice, machinery, oils, fertilizer, cement, etc.).

OCS Pakistan (Pvt) Ltd: Worldwide House, C-17, Korangi Rd, Defence House Authority, Phase II (Extension), Karachi 75500; tel. (21) 5803201; fax (21) 5880606; e-mail ocspak@cyber.net.pk; internet www.shipocs.com; domestic and international couriers.

Packages Ltd: Shahrah-e-Roomi, P.O. Amer Sidhu, Lahore; tel. (42) 5811541; fax (42) 5810879; sales Rs 3,926m. (1999); mfr and convertor of paper, board and plastic films; Chair. SAYED WAJI ALI.

Pakistan Industrial Development Corpn (PIDC): PIDC House, Dr Ziauddin Ahmad Rd, Karachi; tel. (21) 5688511; fax (21) 5685506; f. 1962; parastatal body; mfrs of woollen and cotton textiles, carpets, sugar; gas distributors; Chair. (vacant).

Trading Corpn of Pakistan (Pvt) Ltd: 4th and 5th Floor, Finance and Trade Centre, Shahrah-e-Faisal, Karachi 74400; tel. (21) 9202947; fax (21) 9202722; e-mail tcp@digicom.net.pk; f. 1967; premier public-sector trading house handling bulk import requirements, such as edible oil and other essential food items; deals in exports of Pakistani products, such as textiles, wheat, leather, rice, etc.; Chair. SYED MASOOD ALAM RIZVI.

Unilever Pakistan Ltd: POB 220, Karachi 74200; tel. (21) 519349; fax (21) 5680914; f. 1996 by merger; mfr of consumer goods.

Utility Store Corporation of Pakistan: Plot No. 2039, Jinnah Ave, Blue Area, Islamabad; tel. (51) 275650; supplies household articles at concessional rates.

TRADE UNIONS

National Trade Union Federation Pakistan: Bharocha Bldg, 2-B/6, Commercial Area, Nazimabad No. 2, Karachi 74600; tel. (21) 628339; fax (21) 6622529; e-mail ntuf@super.net.pk; f. 1999; 50 affiliated unions; covers following fields: steel, agriculture, textiles, garments, leather, automobiles, pharmaceuticals, chemicals, transport, printing, food, shipbuilding, engineering and power; Pres. MUHAMMAD RAFIQUE; Gen. Sec. SALEEM RAZA.

Pakistan National Federation of Trade Unions (PNFTU): Aiwan-E-Ittehad St, 37/4, Qasba Township, Manghopir Rd, Karachi 75890; tel. (21) 6693372; fax (21) 2313077; e-mail pnftu@cyber .net.pk; f. 1962; 177 affiliated feds; 218,468 mems; Pres. MUHAMMAD SHARIF; Sec.-Gen. ABDUL GHAFOOR BALOCH.

The principal affiliated federations are:

All Pakistan Federation of Labour (Durrani Group): Durrani Labour Hall, Khyber Bazar, Peshawar; tel. (91) 216411; fax (91) 274038; f. 1951; 300 affiliated unions, with 445,000 mems; affiliated to the World Federation of Trade Unions (WFTU); Pres. AURANGZEB DURRANI; Sec.-Gen. M. ZAFER IQBAL SAIF.

All Pakistan Federation of Trade Unions (APFTU): Bakhtiar Labour Hall, 28 Nisbet Rd, Lahore; tel. (42) 7229419; fax (42) 7239529; e-mail apftu@brain.net.pk; 520,100 mems; Pres. Haji MUHAMMAD AMIN RATHORE; Gen. Sec. KHURSHID AHMED.

Muttahida Labour Federation: Labour Welfare Society, Block D, Shershah Colony, Karachi 75730; tel. (21) 291576; c. 120,000 mems; Pres. KHAMASH GUL KHATTAK; Sec.-Gen. NABI AHMED.

Pakistan Central Federation of Trade Unions: 220 Al-Noor Chambers, M. A. Jinnah Rd, Karachi; tel. (21) 728891.

Pakistan Railway Employees' Union (PREM): City Railway Station, Karachi; tel. (21) 2415721; Divisional Sec. BASHIRUDDIN SIDDIQUI.

Pakistan Trade Union Federation: Khamosh Colony, Karachi; Pres. KANIZ FATIMA; Gen. Sec. SALEEM RAZA.

Pakistan Transport Workers' Federation: 110 McLeod Rd, Lahore; 17 unions; 92,512 mems; Pres. MEHBOOB-UL-HAQ; Gen. Sec. CH. UMAR DIN.

Other affiliated federations include: Pakistan Bank Employees' Federation, Pakistan Insurance Employees' Federation, Automobile, Engineering and Metal Workers' Federation, Pakistan Teachers Organizations' Council, Sarhad WAPDA Employees' Federation, and Balochistan Ittehad Trade Union Federation.

Transport

RAILWAYS

In 1994 the Government approved a US $700m., 850-km railway project, which was to link Pakistan with Turkmenistan via Afghanistan. In 1996 work was begun on the US $590m. Karachi mass transit system (KMTS), Pakistan's first urban train network; in mid-1998, however, work on the KMTS was suspended owing to the serious economic crisis.

Pakistan Railways: 31 Sheikh Abdul Hamid Bin Badees Rd, Lahore; tel. (42) 9201771; fax (42) 9201760; e-mail gmopr@pak rail.com; internet www.pakrail.com; state-owned; 11,515 km of track and 7,791 route km; seven divisions (Karachi, Lahore, Multan, Quetta, Rawalpindi, Peshawar and Sukkur); Chair. Lt-Gen. (retd) SAEED-UZ-ZAFAR; Gen. Man. IQBAL SAMAD KHAN.

ROADS

The total length of roads was 254,410 km (motorways 339 km, main 6,587 km, secondary 211,846 km, other roads 35,638 km) in 1999. In 1978 the 800-km Karakoram highway was opened, linking Xinjiang Province in the People's Republic of China with Havelian, north of Islamabad. In November 1997 a 340-km motorway between Islamabad and Lahore was opened. The road was Pakistan's first inter-city motorway and constituted the first section of a planned 2,000-km transnational motorway (the Indus Highway) from Peshawar to Karachi. In April 1997 the National Highways Authority announced a major road-building programme, the estimated cost of which was US $4,017m. Some 11 highway-building projects were under way in mid-2002.

Government assistance comes from the Road Fund, financed from a share of the excise and customs duty on sales of petrol and from development loans.

National Highways Authority: 27 Mauve Area, G/9–1, POB 1205, Islamabad; tel. (51) 859835; fax (51) 859903; f. 1991; jt venture between Govt and private sector; Chair. Maj.-Gen. (retd) WAQAR-UL-HAQ KHAN; Dir-Gen. Maj.-Gen. (retd) HIDAYATULLAH KHAN NIAZI.

Punjab Road Transport Board: Transport House, 11A Egerton Rd, Lahore.

SHIPPING

In 1974 maritime shipping companies were placed under government control. The chief port is Karachi. A second port, Port Qasim, started partial operation in 1980. A third port, Port Gwadar, is being developed as a deep-water seaport; the first phase of construction had been completed by mid-2002. Another port, Port Pasni, which is situated on the Balochistan coast, was completed in 1988. In 1991 the Government amended the 1974 Pakistan Maritime Shipping Act to allow private companies to operate. By mid-1992 31 private companies had been granted licences.

Mercantile Marine Dept: Government of Pakistan, 70/4, Timber Pond, N. M. Reclamation, Keamari, Karachi.

Al-Hamd International Container Terminal (Pvt) Ltd: Plot K&L, K-28, Trans Lyari Quarters, Hawkesbay Rd, New Truck Stand, Karachi; tel. (21) 2352651; fax (21) 2351556; e-mail info@aictpk.com; internet www.aicpakistan.com.

Engro Vopak Terminal Ltd: 1st Floor, Bahria Complex, 1 M. T. Khan Rd, POB 5736, Karachi 74000; tel. (21) 5610965; fax (21) 5611394; internet www.engro.com.

Karachi Port Trust (KPT): Eduljee Dinshaw Rd, Karachi 74000; tel. (21) 9214312; fax (21) 9214329; e-mail gmpd@kpt.gov.pk; internet www.kpt.gov.pk; Chair. Rear-Adm. AHMED HAYAT; Sec. Mr FAROZUDDIN.

Karachi International Container Terminal: Administrative Bldg, Berths 28–30, Dockyard Rd, West Wharf, Karachi; tel. (21) 2316410; fax (21) 2313816; internet www.kictl.com; f. 1996; Chief Exec. KHURRAM S. ABBAS.

Karachi Shipyard and Engineering Works Ltd: West Wharf, Dockyard Rd, POB 4419, Karachi 2; tel. (21) 9214045; fax (21) 9214020; e-mail ksew@fascom.com; f. 1956; building and repairing ships; general engineering; Man. Dir Rear-Adm. ARSHAD MUNIR AHMAD; Gen. Man. (Sales and Marketing) Capt. S. A. BOKHARI.

Korangi Fisheries Harbour Authority: Ghashma Goth, Landhi, POB 15804, Karachi 75160; tel. (21) 5013315; fax (21) 5015096; e-mail kfha@sat.net.pk.

National Tanker Co (Pvt) Ltd (Pak): 15th Floor, PNSC Bldg, M. T. Khan Rd, Karachi 74000; tel. (21) 5611843; fax (21) 5610780; f. 1981 by the Pakistan National Shipping Corpn and the State Petroleum Refining and Petrochemical Corpn Ltd; aims to make Pakistan self-reliant in the transport of crude petroleum and petroleum products; Chief Exec. Vice-Adm. A. U. KHAN; Dep. Chief Exec. TURAB ALI KHAN.

Pakistan National Shipping Corpn: PNSC Bldg, M. T. Khan Rd, POB 5350, Karachi 74000; tel. (21) 9203980; fax (21) 9203974; e-mail pnsckar@paknet3.ptc.pk; f. 1979 by merger; state-owned; Chair. Vice-Adm. S. T. H. NAQVI; Sec. ARIF SAEED.

Port Qasim Authority (PQA): Bin Qasim, Karachi 75020; tel. (21) 730101; fax (21) 730108; f. 1973; Chair. NAZAR MOHAMMAD SHAIKH; Sec. SYED MUMTAZ HUSSAIN SHAH.

Terminals Association of Pakistan: Molasses Exports Wing, Keamari, Karachi; tel. (21) 2410427; fax (21) 2416791; Chair. RASHID JAN MUHAMMAD.

Qasim International Container Terminal: Berths 5–7, Marginal Wharfs, POB 6425, Port Mohammad Bin Qasim, Karachi 75020; tel. (21) 730002; fax (21) 730021; e-mail info@qict.net; internet www.qict.net; f. 1994; CEO ALI HYDER STANHOPE; Gen. Man. DARAYUS DIVECHA.

Associations

All Pakistan Shipping Association: 01-E, 1st Floor, Sattar Chambers, West Wharf Rd, Karachi; tel. (21) 2200742; fax (21) 2200743; e-mail mfqshaheen@cyber.net.pk; Chair. MUHAMMAD F. QAISER.

Pakistan Ship Agents' Association: GSA House, 19 Timber Pound, Keamari, Karachi 75620; tel. (21) 2850837; fax (21) 2851528; e-mail psaa@cyber.net.pk; internet www.shipezee.com/psaa; Chair. FAROOQ H. RAHIM TOOLA.

Terminal Association of Pakistan: 8th Floor, Adamjee House, I. I. Chundrigar Rd, Karachi 74000; tel. (21) 2417131; fax (21) 2416477; Sec. AKHTAR SULTAN.

CIVIL AVIATION

Karachi, Lahore, Rawalpindi, Peshawar and Quetta have international airports.

In 1992 the Government ended the air monopoly held by the Pakistan International Airlines Corpn, and opened all domestic air routes to any Pakistan-based company.

Civil Aviation Authority: Jinnah Terminal, Karachi Airport, Karachi; tel. (21) 9248778; fax (21) 9248770; internet www.caapakistan.com; controls all the civil airports; Dep. Dir Gen. Air Vice-Marshal ALIDDIN.

Aero Asia International: 47-E/1, Block 6, PECHS, Karachi 75400; tel. (21) 4544951; fax (21) 4544940; e-mail aeroasia@cyber.net.pk; internet www.aeroasia.com; f. 1993; operates scheduled passenger and cargo services to domestic destinations and to the neighbouring Gulf states; Chair. MOHAMMED YAQUB TABANI; Man. Dir KHURSHID ANWAR.

Bhoja Air: Bhoja Air City Office, Court View Building, Court Road, Karachi 74200; tel. (21) 5683475; fax (21) 2625995; e-mail bhoja@mail.digicom.net.pk; internet www.bhojaair.com.pk; f. 1993; scheduled passenger services to domestic and international destinations; Chair. M. FAROUQ BHOJA; Man. Dir Capt. AIJAZ ALI FAIZI.

Pakistan International Airlines Corpn (PIA): PIA Bldg, Quaid-e-Azam International Airport, Karachi 75200; tel. (21) 4572011; fax (21) 4570419; e-mail info@fly-pia.com; internet www.piac.com.pk; f. 1954; merged with Orient Airways in 1955; 57.7% govt-owned; operates domestic services to 35 destinations and international services to 40 destinations in 31 countries; Chair. Lt-Gen. HAMID NAWAZ KHAN; Man. Dir AHMAD SAEED.

Shaheen Air International: 157B Clifton Rd, Clifton, Karachi 75600; tel. (21) 5872191; fax (21) 5873337; f. 1993; operates scheduled domestic services and international services to the Gulf region; Man. Dir ATAUR REHMAN.

Tourism

The Himalayan hill stations of Pakistan provide magnificent scenery, a fine climate and excellent opportunities for field sports, mountaineering, trekking and winter sports. The archaeological remains and historical buildings are also impressive.

In 2000 Pakistan received 556,805 foreign visitors, and in 2000 receipts from tourism amounted to around US $86m.

Pakistan Tourism Development Corpn: House No. 170, St 36, F-10/1, Islamabad 44000; tel. (51) 294189; fax (51) 294540; e-mail tourism@isb.comsats.net.pk; internet www.tourism.gov.pk; f. 1970; Chair. MUSHAHID HUSSAIN SAYED; Man. Dir IMTIAZ A. SYED.

Defence

In August 2001 the total strength of the armed forces was 62,0000 (including 513,000 reserves): army 550,000, navy 25,000, air force 45,000. There was also a paramilitary force of 288,000 men (including a National Guard of 185,000 men). Military service is voluntary.

Defence Expenditure: Budgeted at Rs 146,022m. for 2002/03.

Chairman of Joint Chiefs of Staff Cttee: Gen. MOHAMMAD AZIZ KHAN.

Chief of Army Staff: Gen. PERVEZ MUSHARRAF.

Chief of Air Staff: Air Chief Marshal MUSHAF ALI MIR.

Chief of Naval Staff: Adm. ABDUL AZIZ MIRZA.

Chief of General Staff and Vice Chief of Army Staff: Gen. MOHAMMAD YUSUF.

Education

At independence in 1947 Pakistan retained the education system that had been designed by the colonial British administration in India. Efforts to introduce educational reforms and to expand educational facilities were hampered by lack of finances. However, in 1972 the Pakistan Government formulated a new Education Policy which envisaged the enforcement of elementary education and an adult literacy programme, and emphasized the study of Islamiat—the ideological basis for the existence of Pakistan—and the introduction of an agro-technical bias in school education. All institutions, except missions, were nationalized and most colleges and universities became co-educational, although there are still colleges that admit only females.

The Education Policy provided a 10-year course in Islamiat, which includes study of the Koran, the life of Muhammad and the general code for a Muslim. Children of the Sunni and the Shi'a sects follow the same course for the first eight years, then dividing to study separately the rituals of the two sects. Agro-technical subjects are introduced in the seventh and eighth years of schooling.

Development expenditure on science and technology and education and training in 2001/02 was projected at Rs 4,343.3m. (only 3.3% of total development spending).

PRIMARY AND SECONDARY EDUCATION

Universal and free primary education is a constitutional right, but education is not compulsory. Primary education begins at five years of age and lasts for five years. Secondary education, beginning at the age of 10, is divided into two stages, of three and four years respectively. In 2000/01 there were an estimated 165,700 pre-primary and primary schools (including mosque schools), and total enrolment amounted to approximately 20,999,000. With the assistance of the World Bank, a Primary Education Project has been launched to increase educational facilities and improve the quality of instruction.

There were an estimated 18,800 middle schools and 12,800 secondary schools in 2000/01. Enrolment in that year was estimated at 4.64m. in middle schools and 1.93m. in secondary schools.

In 1991 the total enrolment at primary and secondary schools was equivalent to 44% of all school-age children (58% of boys; 29% of girls). Primary enrolment in 1993 was equivalent to 74% of children in the relevant age-group (101% of boys; 45% of girls), while the comparable ratio for secondary enrolment in 1991 was 26% (33% of boys; 17% of girls).

HIGHER EDUCATION

In 2000/01 there were 580 secondary vocational institutes, 853 arts and science colleges and 308 professional colleges (including educational colleges); enrolment totalled 75,000, 791,000 and 162,989 respectively. There were 26 universities and 114,010 enrolments in 2000/01. The Open University has been set up with the technical support of the British Open University.

With the assistance of the Asian Development Bank, 11 polytechnic institutes and a national teacher-training college are being established by the federal Government. Training is to be provided for teachers at polytechnic, commercial and vocational institutes.

Bibliography

GENERAL

Ahmad, Aziz. *Studies in Islamic Culture in the Indian Environment.* Karachi, Oxford University Press, 1970.

Ahmad, Kazi S. A. *Geography of Pakistan.* London, Oxford University Press, 1972.

Ahmed, Akbar S. *Jinnah, Pakistan and Islamic Identity—The Search for Saladin.* London, Routledge, 1997.

Allan, N (Ed.). *Karakorum Conquered.* Hampshire, Palgrave Publishers, 2002.

Aziz, K. K. *The Making of Pakistan.* Karachi, National Book Foundation, 1976.

Bolitho, Hector. *Jinnah: Creator of Pakistan.* London, John Murray, 1954.

Gustafson, Eric (Ed.). *Pakistan and Bangladesh: Bibliographic Essays in Social Science.* Islamabad, University of Islamabad Press, 1976.

Jain, Naresh Kumar. *Muslims in India: A Biographical Dictionary.* 2 Vols. New Delhi, Manohar.

Jalal, Hamid, et al (Eds). *Pakistan Past and Present.* London, Stacey International, 1977.

Jinnah, Fatima (Ed. Mujahid, Sharif Al). *My Brother.* Karachi, Quaid-i-Azam Academy, 1987.

Kapur, Ashok. *Pakistan's Nuclear Development.* London, Croom Helm Publishers, 1987.

Khan, Imran. *Indus Journey.* London, Chatto and Windus, 1990.

Khurshid, Anis. *Quaid-i-Azam Mohammad Ali Jinnah: An Annotated Bibliography; Vol. I, Western Languages; Vol. II, Eastern Languages.* Karachi, Quaid-i-Azam Academy, 1978–79.

Klein, Heinz Günther, and Nestvogel, Remote. *Women in Pakistan.* Lahore, Vanguard Books, 1992.

Malik, Hafeez (Ed.). *Iqbal: Poet-Philosopher of Pakistan.* New York, Columbia University Press, 1975.

Muslim Nationalism in India and Pakistan. Washington DC, Public Affairs Press, 1964.

Mohammad Ali, Chaudhri. *The Emergence of Pakistan.* New York, Columbia University Press, 1967.

Mujahid, Sharif Al (Ed.). *Ideological Orientation of Pakistan.* Karachi, National Book Foundation, 1976.

Quaid-i-Azam Jinnah: Studies in Interpretation. Karachi, Quaid-i-Azam Academy, 1981.

Mumtaz, Kamil Khan. *Architecture in Pakistan.* Singapore, Mirmar Books, 1986.

Mumtaz, Khawar, and Shaheed, Farida. *Women of Pakistan.* London, Zed Books Ltd, 1988.

Naim, C. M. (Ed.). *Iqbal, Jinnah and Pakistan: The Vision and the Reality.* Syracuse, NY, Maxwell Graduate School of Citizenship and Public Affairs, 1979.

Noman, Omar, and Weiner, M. *The Child and the State in India and Pakistan.* Oxford University Press, 1994.

Patel, Rashida. *Islamisation of Laws in Pakistan.* Karachi, Faiza Publishers, 1986.

Qureshi, Ishtiaq Husain. *The Muslim Community of the Indo-Pakistan Subcontinent.* Karachi, Ma'aref, 2nd Edn, 1977.

Sadullah, Mujahid, et al. (Eds). *Partition of the Punjab: A Compilation of Documents.* Lahore, National Documentation Centre, 1984.

Sayeed, Khalid bin. *Pakistan, the Formative Phase.* Karachi, Pakistan Publishing House, 1960.

Shah, Justice Nasim Hasan. *Judgements on the Constitution, Rule of Law and Martial Law in Pakistan.* Karachi, Oxford University Press, 1993.

Weiss, Anita M. (Ed.). *Islamic Reassertion in Pakistan: The Application of Islamic Laws in a Modern State.* Lahore, Vanguard Books Ltd, 1985.

Culture, Class and Development in Pakistan. Lahore, Vanguard Books, 1991.

Wolpert, Stanley. *Jinnah of Pakistan: A Life.* New York, Oxford University Press, 1984.

Yusuf, Kaniz F., *et al.* (Eds). *Pakistan Resolution Revisited.* Islamabad, National Institute of Historical and Cultural Research, 1990.

Zingel, Wolfgang Peter, and Lallemant, Stephanie (Eds). *Pakistan in the 80s: Ideology, Regionalism, Economy and Foreign Policy.* Lahore, Vanguard Books Ltd, 1985.

HISTORY AND POLITICS

Afzal, M. Rafique. *Pakistan: History and Politics, 1947–71.* Oxford, Oxford University Press, 2002.

Afzal, R. *Political Parties in Pakistan Vol. I, 1947–58; Vol. II, 1958–69.* Islamabad, National Commission on Historical and Cultural Research, 1976 and 1986.

Ahmad, Aziz. *Islamic Modernism in India and Pakistan (1857–1964).* London, Oxford University Press for Chatham House, 1967.

Ahsan Aitzaz. *The Indus Saga and the Making of Pakistan.* Karachi, Oxford University Press, 1996.

Aijazuddin, F. S. *Historical Images of Pakistan.* Lahore, Ferozensons, 1992.

Ayub Khan, Mohammad. *Friends not Masters: A Political Autobiography.* London, Oxford University Press, 1967.

Banerjee, Mukulika. *The Pathan Unarmed: Opposition and Memory in the North West Frontier.* 2000.

Baxter, Craig (Ed.). *Zia's Pakistan: Politics and Stability in a Frontline State.* Lahore, Vanguard Books Ltd, 1985.

Baxter, Craig, and Wasti, Syed Razi. *Pakistan: Authoritarianism in the 1980s.* Lahore, Vanguard Books, 1991.

Bennett Jones, O. *Pakistan: The Eye of the Storm.* New Haven, CT, Yale University Press, 2002.

Bhutto, Benazir. *Daughter of the East.* London, Hamish Hamilton, 1988.

Binder, Leonard. *Religion and Politics in Pakistan.* Berkeley, CA, University of California Press, 1961.

Braibanti, Ralph. *Research on the Bureaucracy of Pakistan.* Durham, NC, Duke University Press, 1966.

Burki, Shahed Javed. *Pakistan Under Bhutto.* London, Macmillan, 1980.

Pakistan: The Continuing Search for Nationhood. Lahore, Pak Book Corporation, 1992.

Burki, Shahed Javed, and Baxter, Craig (Eds). *Pakistan under the Military: Eleven Years of Zia ul-Haq.* Boulder, CO, Westview Press, 1991.

Callard, Keith. *Pakistan, A Political Study.* London, Allen and Unwin, 1957; Mystic, CT, Lawrence Verry, 1965.

Choudhury, G. W. *Constitutional Development in Pakistan.* Lahore and London, Longmans, 1959; New York, Institute of Pacific Relations, 1959.

The Last Days of United Pakistan. Bloomington, IN, Indiana University Press, 1974.

Pakistan: Transition from Military to Civilian Rule. London, Scorpian Publishing Ltd, 1988.

Feldman, Herbert A. *Revolution in Pakistan: A Study of the Martial Law Administration.* London and New York, Oxford University Press, 1967.

From Crisis to Crisis: Pakistan 1962–1969. London and Karachi, Oxford University Press, 1972.

The End and the Beginning: Pakistan 1969–1971. London and Karachi, Oxford University Press, 1976.

Goodson, Larry. *The Talibanization of Pakistan.* New York, NY, and Basingstoke, Palgrave Macmillan, 2002.

Halliday, Fred, and Alavi, Hamza. *State and Ideology in the Middle East and Pakistan.* London, Macmillan Education, 1988.

Hussain, Asif. *Elite Politics in an Ideological State: The Case of Pakistan.* Folkestone, Dawson, 1979.

Hyman, Anthony, Ghayur, Muhammad and Kaushik, Naresh. *Pakistan: Zia and After.* London, Asia Publishing House, 1988.

Jaffrelot, Christophe (Ed.). *Pakistan, Nationalism Without a Nation.* London, Zed Books, 2nd edn, 2002.

Jalal, Ayesha. *The State of Martial Rule: The Origins of Pakistan's Political Economy of Defence.* Cambridge, Cambridge University Press, 1990.

Democracy and Authoritarianism in South Asia. Cambridge, Cambridge University Press, 1995.

Jan, Tarik. *Issues in Pakistani Politics.* Islamabad, Institute of Policy Studies, 1992.

Jawed, Nasim Ahmad. *Islam's Political Culture: Religion and Politics in Predivided Pakistan.* Austin, TX, University of Texas Press, 1999.

Kennedy, Charles H. *Bureaucracy in Pakistan*. Karachi, Oxford University Press, 1987.

Khan, Asghar (Ed.). *Islam, Politics and the State: The Pakistan Experience*. London, Zed Books, 1985.

Khan, Lt-Gen. Gul Hassan. *Memoirs of Lt-Gen. Gul Hassan Khan*. Karachi, Oxford University Press, 1993.

Kothari, Smitu, and Mian, Zia (Eds). *Out of the Nuclear Shadow*. London, Zed Books, 2001.

Kukreja, V. *Contemporary Pakistan: Political Processes, Conflicts and Crises*. London, Sage Publications, 2002.

Lamb, A. *Kashmir—Origins of the Dispute*. Hertford, Roxford Books, 1994.

Lamb, Christina. *Waiting for Allah: Pakistan's Struggle for Democracy*. London, Hamish Hamilton, 1991.

Laporte, R., Jr. *Power and Privilege: Influence and Decision Making in Pakistan*. Los Angeles, CA, University of California Press, 1976.

Lari, S. Z. *A History of Sind*. Karachi, Oxford University Press, 1994.

Low, D. A. (Ed.). *The Political Inheritance of Pakistan*. Basingstoke, Macmillan, 1991.

Mahmood, Safdar. *Pakistan: Political Roots and Development 1947–99*. Oxford University Press, 2000.

Malik, I. H. State and Civil Society in Pakistan. Politics of Authority, Ideology and Ethnicity. Basingstoke, Macmillan Press Ltd, 1997.

Islam, Nationalism and the West: Issues of Identity in Pakistan. Basingstoke, Macmillan Press Ltd, 1999.

Malik, Muhammad Aslam. *The Making of the Pakistan Resolution*. Oxford University Press, 2001.

Manzooruddin, Ahmed (Ed.). *Contemporary Pakistan: Politics, Economy and Society*. Karachi, Royal Book Co, 1982

Mazari, Sherbaz Khan. *A Journey to Disillusionment*. Karachi, Oxford University Press, 2000.

Al-Mujahid, Sharif (Ed.). *Muslim League Documents 1900–1947, Vol. I, 1900–1908*. Karachi, Quaid-i-Azam Academy, 1990.

Nanda, Lt-Gen. K. K. *Conquering Kashmir—A Pakistani Obsession*. New Delhi, Lancer Books, 1994.

Nasr, Seyyed Vali Reza. *The Vanguard of the Islamic Revolution: The Jama'at-i Islami of Pakistan*. Berkeley, CA, University of California Press, 1996.

The Islam Leviathan: Islam and the Making of State Power (Religion and Global Politics). 2001.

Nayak, Dr Pandav. *Pakistan: Political Economy of a Developing State*. New Delhi, Patriot Publishers, 1988.

Noman, Omar. *Pakistan: Political and Economic History since 1947*. London, Kegan Paul International Ltd, 1991.

Rahman, Maitur. *Second Thoughts on Bangladesh*. London, News and Media, 1979.

Rizvi, Hasan Askari. *Internal Strife and External Intervention: India's Role in the Civil War in East Pakistan*. Lahore, Progressive Publishers, 1981.

The Military and Politics in Pakistan. Lahore, Progressive Publishers, 1987.

Pakistan and the Geostrategic Environment: A Study of Foreign Policy. London, St Martin's Press, 1993.

Samad, Yunas. *A Nation in Turmoil. Nationalism and Ethnicity in Pakistan, 1937–1958*. New Delhi, Sage Publications, 1995.

Sayeed, Khalid Bin. *The Political System of Pakistan*. London, Allen and Unwin, 1967.

Schofield, Victoria. *Kashmir in Conflict: India, Pakistan and the Unfinished War*. I. B. Tauris, 2000.

Shah, Syed Waqar Ali. *Ethnicity, Islam and Nationalism, Muslim Politics in the North-West Frontier Province 1937–47*. Karachi, Oxford University Press, 2000.

Sharma, R. (Ed.). *The Pakistan Trap*. London, Sangam Books, 2001.

Sherwani, L. A. (Ed.). *Pakistan Resolution to Pakistan*. Karachi, National Publishing House Ltd, 1969.

Sisson, Richard, and Rose, Leo E. *War and Secession: Pakistan, India and the Creation of Bangladesh*. Berkeley, University of California Press, 1990.

Talbot, Ian. *Provincial Politics and the Pakistan Movement. The Growth of the Muslim League in North-West and North-East India 1937–47*. Karachi, Oxford University Press, 1988.

Freedom's Cry: The Popular Dimension in the Pakistan Movement and the Partition Experience in North-West India. Karachi, Oxford University Press, 1996.

Pakistan: A Modern History. London, Hurst, 1999.

Talbot, Ian, and Singh, G. (Eds). *Region and Partition: Bengal, Punjab and the Partition of the Subcontinent*. Karachi, Oxford University Press, 1999.

Taylor, David. *Pakistan (World Bibliographical Series, No. 10)*. Oxford, Clio Press, 1990.

Von Vorys, K. *Political Development in Pakistan*. New Jersey, Princeton University Press, 1965.

Wilcox, W. A. *Pakistan: Consolidation of a State*. New York, NY, Columbia University Press, 1964.

Wolpert, Stanley. *Zulfi Bhutto of Pakistan: His Life and Times*. New York, NY, Oxford University Press, 1993.

Wriggins, H. (Ed.). *Pakistan in Transition*. Islamabad, University of Islamabad, 1975.

Zaidi, S. Akbar. *Regional Imbalances and National Questions in Pakistan*. Lahore, Vanguard Books, 1991.

Ziring, Lawrence. *The Ayub Khan Era: Politics in Pakistan 1958–69*. Syracuse University Press, New York, 1971.

Pakistan: The Enigma of Political Development. 1980.

Pakistan in the Twentieth Century: A Political History. Karachi, Oxford University Press, 1997.

Ziring, Lawrence, Braibanti, Ralph, and Wriggins, H. (Eds). *Pakistan: The Long View*. Durham, NC, Duke University Center for Commonwealth and Comparative Studies, 1977.

FOREIGN RELATIONS

Barnds, W. J. *India, Pakistan and the Great Powers*. New York, Praeger, for the Council on Foreign Relations, 1972.

Brines, R. *The Indo-Pakistan Conflicts*. New York, Pall Mall Press, 1968.

Burke, S. M. *Pakistan's Foreign Policy: An Historical Analysis*. London, Oxford University Press, 1973.

Main Springs of Indian and Pakistani Foreign Policies. Oxford University Press, 1975.

Cheema, Pervaiz Iqbal. *Pakistan's Defence Policy, 1947–58*. London, Macmillan Press, 1990.

Choudhury, G. W. *Pakistan's Relations With India*. New York, Praeger, 1968.

India, Pakistan, Bangladesh and the Major Powers. New York, The Free Press, and London, Collier Macmillan, 1975.

Dixit, J. N. *India-Pakistan in War and Peace*. London, Routledge, 2002.

Khan, M. Asghar. *Indo-Pakistan War: The First Round*. London, Islamic Information Service, 1979.

Khan, Rais Ahmad. *Forty Years of Pakistan–United States Relations*. Karachi, Royal Book Co, 1992.

Khan, Air Chief Marshal Zulfikar Ali. *Pakistan's Security: The Challenge and the Response*. Lahore, Progressive Publishers, 1987.

Kux, Dennis. *Pakistan: Flawed not Failed State*. Washington, DC, Foreign Policy Association, 2001.

The United States and Pakistan, 1947–2000: Dis enchanted Allies (The Adst-Dacor Diplomats and Diplomacy Series). Woodrow Wilson Centre Press, 2001.Lamb, A. *Asian Frontiers: Studies in a Continuing Problem*. London, Pall Mall Press, 1968.

Malik, Hafeez (Ed.) *Soviet-American Relations with Pakistan, Iran and Afghanistan*. New York, St Martin's Press, 1987.

Razvi, M. *The Frontiers of Pakistan: A Study of Frontier Problems in Pakistan's Foreign Policy*. Karachi, National Publishing House, 1971.

Rizvi, Hasan Askari. *Pakistan and the Geostrategic Environment: A Study of Foreign Policy*. London, St Martin's Press, 1993.

Rose, Leo E., and Husain, Noor A. (Eds). *United States—Pakistan Forum: Relations with the Major Powers*. Lahore, Vanguard Books Ltd, 1985.

Syed, Anwar Husain. *China and Pakistan: Diplomacy of Entente Cordiale*. London, University of Massachusetts Press, 1975.

Ziring, Lawrence (Ed.). *The Subcontinent in World Politics*. New York, Praeger Publishers, 1982.

ECONOMY

Addleton, Jonathan. *Undermining the Centre: The Gulf Migration and Pakistan*. Karachi, Oxford University Press, 1992.

Ahmad, V., and Amjad, R. *The Management of Pakistan's Economy: 1947–82*. Karachi, Oxford University Press, 1984.

Amjad, Rashid. *Private Industrial Investment in Pakistan, 1960–1980*. Cambridge, 1982.

Bhatia, B. M. *Pakistan's Economic Development*. Lahore, Vanguard Books, 1990.

Byerlee, Derek, and Husain, Tariq. *Farming Systems in Pakistan*. Lahore, Vanguard Books, 1992.

Central Statistical Office. *25 Years of Pakistan In Statistics: 1947–1972.* Karachi, Economic Affairs Division, Government of Pakistan, 1972.

Haq, Mahbubul, et al. *Employment Distribution and Basic Needs in Pakistan.* Lahore, Progressive Publishers, 1991.

Human Development in South Asia. Karachi, Oxford University Press, 1997.

Hasan, Parvez. *Pakistan's Economy at the Crossroads.* Karachi, Oxford University Press, 1998.

Husain, Ishrat. *Pakistan: The Economy of an Elitist State.* Karachi, Oxford University Press, 1999.

James, W. E., and Roy, S. (Eds). *Foundations of Pakistan's Political Economy.* Oxford University Press, 1993.

Kardar, Shahid. *Political Economy of Pakistan.* Lahore, Progressive Publishers, 1991.

Khan, Abdul Jabbar. *Non-Interest Banking in Pakistan: Concept, Practice and Evaluation.* Karachi, Royal Book Co, 1991.

Khan, Shahrukh Rafi. *Fifty Years of Pakistan's Economy: Traditional Topics and Contemporary Concerns.* Karachi, Oxford University Press, 1999.

Kibria, Ghulam. *A Shattered Dream: Understanding Pakistan's Underdevelopment.* Karachi, Oxford University Press, 1999.

Lefèvre, Alain. *Kinship, Honour and Money in Rural Pakistan.* Richmond, Curzon, 1999.

Michel, A. A. *The Indus Rivers: A study of the effect of Partition.* New Haven, CT, Yale University Press, 1967.

Nabi, Ijaz (Ed.). *The Quality of Life in Pakistan: Studies in Social Sector Economics.* Lahore, Vanguard Books, 1986.

Nasim, Anjum (Ed.). *Financing Pakistan's Development in the 1990s.* Karachi, Oxford University Press, 1992.

Noman, Omar. *Economic and Social Progress in Asia: Why Pakistan Did Not Become a Tiger.* Karachi, Oxford University Press, 1997.

Papanek, Gustav F. *Pakistan's Development: Social Goals and Private Incentives.* Cambridge, MA, Harvard University Press, and London, Oxford University Press, 1967.

Qureshi, Ejaz Aslam (Ed.). *Development Planning in Pakistan.* Lahore, Ferozsons, 1991.

Rajeev, P. V. *Resource Mobilization in India and Pakistan.* New Delhi, Deep and Deep Publications, 1991.

Siddiqi, Akhtar Husain. *Pakistan: Its Resources and Development.* Hong Kong, Asian Research Service, 1984.

Social Policy and Development Centre. *Social Development in Pakistan: Annual Review.* Karachi, Oxford University Press, 1999.

State Bank of Pakistan. *Development of the State Bank of Pakistan.* Karachi, 1994.

Zaidi, Syed Akbar. *Regional Imbalances and the National Question in Pakistan.* Lahore, Vanguard Books, 1992.

Issues in Pakistan's Economy. Oxford, Oxford University Press, 1999.

Related Territories

The status of Jammu and Kashmir has remained unresolved since the 1949 cease-fire agreement, whereby the area was divided into sectors administered by India and Pakistan separately. Pakistan administers Azad (Free) Kashmir and the Northern Areas as *de facto* dependencies, being responsible for foreign affairs, defence, coinage, currency and the implementation of UN resolutions concerning Kashmir.

AZAD KASHMIR

Area: 11,639 sq km (4,494 sq miles).

Population: 1,980,000 (1981 census).

Administration: Government is based on the Azad Jammu and Kashmir Interim Constitution Act of 1974. There are four administrative districts: Kotli, Mirpur, Muzaffarabad and Poonch.

Legislative Assembly: consists of 42 members: 40 directly elected and two women nominated by the other members.

Azad Jammu and Kashmir Council: consists of the President of Pakistan as Chairman, the President of Azad Kashmir as Vice-Chairman, five members nominated by the President of Pakistan, six members by the Legislative Assembly, and the Pakistan Minister of States, Northern Areas, Frontier Regions and Kashmir Affairs (ex officio).

President of Azad Kashmir: Maj.-Gen. (retd) MOHAMMAD ANWAR KHAN.

Prime Minister: Sardar SIKANDAR HAYAT.

NORTHERN AREAS

Area: 72,520 sq km (28,000 sq miles).

Population: 562,000 (1981 census).

Administration: There are three administrative districts: Baltistan, Diamir and Gilgit. The Northern Areas Council consists of 26 members (24 members are elected in a party-based election and two seats are reserved for women), headed by the federal Minister of Kashmir Affairs and Northern Areas, States and Frontier Regions (SAFRON).

THE PHILIPPINES

Physical and Social Geography

HARVEY DEMAINE

The combined land area of the 7,100 islands that constitute the Republic of the Philippines amounts to 300,000 sq km (115,831 sq miles). With the intervening seas, most of which rank as Philippines territorial waters, the country extends over a considerably larger area, from above 18°N to below 6°N, lying between the South China Sea and the Pacific Ocean.

Of its multitudinous islands, some 880 are inhabited and 462 have an area of 2.6 sq km (1 sq mile) or more. The two largest, namely Luzon in the north, covering 104,688 sq km, and Mindanao in the south, with an area of 94,630 sq km, account for 66.4% of its territory, and this figure is raised to 92.3% if the next nine largest (Samar, Negros, Palawan, Panay, Mindoro, Leyte, Cebu, Bohol and Masbate) are also included.

PHYSICAL FEATURES

Structurally, the Philippines forms part of the vast series of island arcs that fringe the East Asian mainland and also include Japan, the Ryukyus and Taiwan to the north, and extend into Sulawesi, Papua (formerly Irian Jaya) and other Indonesian territories to the south. Two main and nearly parallel lines of Tertiary folding run roughly north–south through Luzon, swing approximately north-west–south-east through the smaller islands surrounding the Sabayan, Visayan and Mindoro seas, and resume a north–south trend in Mindanao. In addition to these two, a less pronounced north-east–south-west pair extend from the central Philippines through Panay and the smaller islands of the Sulu archipelago, ultimately linking up with the similar Tertiary structures of the north-eastern tip of Borneo.

These major lines of folding largely determine the broad pattern of relief throughout the country. Over most of the islands Tertiary sediments and Tertiary-Quaternary eruptives predominate, and more than a dozen major volcanoes are still active. Nearly all the larger islands have interior mountain ranges, typically attaining heights of 1,200 m–2,400 m above sea-level, but, apart from narrow strips of coastal plain, few have any extensive lowlands. This is the country's greatest natural liability. The central plain of Luzon, which represents the only significant exception, has therefore assumed a dominant role.

CLIMATE

Because of its mountainous character and its alignment across the south-west monsoon and the north-east trade winds, the Philippines shows considerable regional variation in both the total amount and the seasonal incidence of rainfall. Thus, in general, the western side of the country receives most of its rain during the period of the south-west monsoon (late June–late September) whereas on most of the eastern side the wettest period of the year is from November to March when the influence of the north-east trades is at its greatest, though here, in contrast to the west, there is no true dry season. These differences can be seen by comparing Manila (on the west side of Luzon), which, out of an annual total of 2,100 mm, receives 1,100 mm in July–September and only 150 mm in December–April, with Surigao (in the north-east of Mindanao), which receives an annual total of 3,560 mm, 2,230 mm between the months of November and March inclusive, but with no monthly total falling below the August figure of 120 mm. In some sheltered valleys, however, totals may be as low as 1,020 mm, which, in association with mean annual sea-level temperatures that are rarely much below 26.7°C (80°F) anywhere in the country, makes farming distinctly precarious. On the other hand, a different kind of climatic hazard affects many of the more exposed parts of the country as a result of their exposure to typhoons, which are most common in the later months of the year and tend to be most severe in eastern Luzon and Samar.

NATURAL RESOURCES

The central lowlands of Luzon provide by far the best major food-producing region within the country, and although many of the smaller lowlands are also intensively cultivated, their soils are, in most cases, of only average fertility. Since the 1940s the only substantial areas of lowland offering scope for any important extension of cultivation have been in the southern island of Mindanao. Once described as the frontier of the Philippines, this island has become more densely populated in recent years, and the once extensive resources of tropical hardwoods have been disappearing.

While, as elsewhere in South-East Asia, rice forms the most important single item in the country's agricultural system, its predominance is less marked than in other parts of the region, and indeed in several of the islands, partly because of their relatively low rainfall, and partly because of the close cultural link with Latin America, maize is the leading food crop. So far as export crops are concerned, the emphasis has hitherto been mainly on coconuts, bananas, pineapples and sugar.

The Philippines has a fairly wide range of metallic mineral deposits, the most important of which are copper (with reserves mainly found on Cebu and at Marinduque), chromite and nickel. The country has been, on the other hand, sadly deficient in energy minerals. In the late 1990s more than one-half of energy requirements (mostly petroleum) were imported. The increasing costs of petroleum imports resulted in a frantic search for domestic energy supplies. Petroleum was discovered off the island of Palawan in 1977 and new reserves were located in 1990, but domestic production remained relatively insignificant. However, proven reserves of coal and lignite were estimated at 369m. tons, with potential reserves of 1,700m. tons. Hydroelectric power, which contributes about 8% of domestic energy requirements, and geothermal energy, which provides about 5%, are both the product of the youthful landscape and unstable geological structure of the archipelago.

POPULATION AND CULTURE

With an average annual growth rate of about 2.4% in 1995–2000, the population of the Philippines was enumerated at 76,498,735 at the May 2000 census, compared with the 68,616,536 recorded at the September 1995 census. At September 1995 the country had an average population density of 228.7 per sq km, which was nearly double the South-East Asian average and, in the region, exceeded only by that of Singapore. By May 2000 population density had increased to 255.0 per sq km. According to official estimates, the total population at mid-2001 had increased further to 77,925,894, with an average density of 259.8 per sq km. The shortage of lowland means that much the greater part of the population is concentrated in a relatively small area, and, particularly in the lowlands of central Luzon, the resultant pressure is now a serious problem and likely to become increasingly severe, owing to the exceptionally high rate of population growth.

Despite the existence of several regional languages spoken by the lowland Filipinos, the latter, who form the great majority of the population, share a basically common culture, which is much influenced by Roman Catholicism. In recent decades considerable progress has been made in developing Tagalog, the language of central Luzon, as a national language (Filipino), although, particularly among the largely *mestizo* élite elements, English is widely used.

Other than the Christian Filipinos, the only large indigenous group comprises the Muslim Moros inhabiting the southern and south-western peripheries of the country, who form approximately 5% of the total population. There are also a number of much smaller communities of animist hill peoples, principally in the remoter parts of Luzon and Mindanao, who together form perhaps 6% of the total. The Chinese population in the Philippines is very small, accounting for only about 1% of the total.

Largely because of its long history of colonial rule and its archipelagic nature, the Philippines now has numerous and widespread small administrative and market towns. Manila is the nation's capital, with a population of 1,581,082 at the 2000 census. However, this figure is misleading, since the boundaries of the administrative unit of Metropolitan Manila encompass a large number of former towns and districts, including Quezon City (2000 population of 2,173,831), and contain a total population of almost 7m. Other macro-regions of the country also have their urban focuses, however, with Davao City (1,147,116) in south-east Mindanao, Cebu City (718,821) in the Visayas and Zamboanga City (601,794) in south-west Mindanao being the largest.

History

IAN BROWN

Revised by MICHAEL PINCHES

HISTORICAL BACKGROUND

In March 1521 a Spanish expedition, led by the Portuguese navigator Fernão Magalhães (Ferdinand Magellan), which had sailed west from Spain in September 1519, in search of the Spice Islands, landed at Samar in the central Philippine archipelago. In April 1565 the first Spanish settlement was established in Cebu by Miguel López de Legaspi. By the early 1570s Spanish control extended over Cebu, Leyte, Panay, Mindoro and central Luzon; the capital of the new Spanish dominion was Manila, captured in May 1571. The extremely fragmented nature of indigenous political organization at that time made large-scale co-ordinated resistance impossible. Political authority was focused on the *barangay*, commonly a kinship community which contained between 30 and 100 families. These restricted communities were frequently at war with each other, but no nation-wide state organization emerged from these conflicts. Thus, the pre-colonial archipelago did not sustain the great indigenous empire, or powerful traditional kingdom, that provided a foundation for the modern nation-state in the rest of South-East Asia.

The principal aim of Spanish rule in the Philippines was religious conversion. In this, Spain exerted a profound influence over the indigenous population, although the animists of northern Luzon and, more particularly, the Muslims of Mindanao and Sulu effectively resisted Roman Catholicism; even in regions of widespread conversion, animist beliefs were by no means expelled. Spanish rule was financed primarily by the galleon trade; silver dollars and bullion were brought to Manila from Acapulco (Mexico) to be exchanged for Chinese silks, porcelain, bronzes and jade. The Spanish made little attempt to exploit the economic resources of the archipelago, and, by restriction and monopoly, prevented any other Europeans from doing so—at least until the beginning of the 19th century.

In 1834 the port of Manila was opened to unrestricted commerce, irrespective of nationality. Between 1855 and 1873 six provincial ports, including Iloilo and Cebu, were also opened, for the Spanish were now permitting other Westerners to engage in agriculture and manufacturing on the islands. From these initiatives there emerged the production and export of the crops—sugar, coconuts, Manila hemp (abaca) and tobacco—that were to become the foundation of the economy for the remaining decades of colonial rule and into the post-independence period. These economic changes had important repercussions, both socially and politically. An increase in agricultural production, from the middle of the 19th century onwards, encouraged the settlement of a vigorous Chinese entrepreneurial class in the regions. As time passed, a *mestizo*, or half-caste, élite emerged (sons of Chinese fathers and native mothers, brought up as natives and Roman Catholics). The *mestizo* derived their wealth and influence from land ownership, and frequently sent their children, known as *ilustrados* (enlightened ones), to universities in Manila and Europe. The *ilustrados* became the channels for Spanish culture and liberal thought in the Philippines. By the close of the 19th century they were also to challenge the repressive orthodoxy and exclusiveness of Spanish rule in the islands, as exposed in the writings of Dr José Rizal (1861–96). The *ilustrados* sought reform through a so-called 'Propaganda Movement', but the mass of rural and urban Filipinos, impoverished by loss of land, exploitative labouring wages and unemployment, were moving towards armed revolt against the colonial power.

The Philippine revolution erupted in late August 1896, launched by a secret society, the Katipunan (Association of Sons of the People), under the leadership of Andres Bonifacio, who had been born in the Tondo slum district of Manila. Although Rizal played no part in the revolt, he was subsequently seized by the Spanish, and tried on charges of rebellion, sedition and illicit association. On 30 December 1896 he was executed by a firing squad. Rizal's death provoked a major upsurge in revolutionary fervour. The most important initial military successes against the Spanish were achieved in the province of Cavite, south of Manila, under the leadership of Emilio Aguinaldo, the mayor of the town of Kawit. That success ensured a shift in the leadership of the revolution, away from Bonifacio and his dispossessed followers, to Aguinaldo and the provincial landed élite, the *principalia*; divisions also emerged in the revolutionary movement at this time. On 10 May 1897 Bonifacio was executed, having been sentenced to death by a military court that Aguinaldo had appointed. The struggle then turned against the Filipinos; and in December 1897 Aguinaldo and the *principalia* ceased hostilities, in return for exile in Hong Kong and a financial settlement. In the Philippines itself, the struggle was maintained.

In late April 1898 the USA declared war on Spain, following the sinking of the *USS Maine* in the harbour at Havana, Cuba. On 1 May the US Asiatic Squadron sailed into Manila Bay and destroyed the Spanish fleet. Aguinaldo, with US encouragement and assistance, returned to the Philippines, and on 12 June 1898 proclaimed Philippine independence. However, from this time onwards, a rift developed between the USA and its Filipino 'allies'. The US armed forces colluded with the Spanish colonial administration to stage a mock battle for Manila, so that the capital would be surrendered solely to US forces. On 14 August 1898 the Spanish capitulated; in the following December Spain ceded the Philippines to the USA for the payment of US $20m., under the terms of the Treaty of Paris.

On 23 January 1899 the Philippine Republic was inaugurated at Malolos, and Aguinaldo was sworn in as President. Early in the following month skirmishes occurred between the republican army and US occupying forces, leading rapidly to open conflict. For a year the new Republic fiercely resisted the US forces, but by early 1900 Aguinaldo's troops had been forced into retreat, in the mountains of northern Luzon. When Aguinaldo was captured in March 1901, major resistance was at an end. In April Aguinaldo took his oath of allegiance to the USA, and urged his fellow Filipinos to do the same. However, sporadic fighting by guerrillas, still motivated by the vision of *kalayaan* (freedom) which had inspired the initial outbreak of revolution in late 1896, continued to occur during the following decade.

US RULE

Under US dominance, the Philippines became even more heavily dependent on agricultural exports, and the rural masses found no relief from rigorously exploitative conditions of tenancy. Superficially, the US political administration did appear to constitute a decisive break with the past. While the Spanish had denied Filipinos even the prospect of political advancement, the new US administration moved rapidly to make political and bureaucratic positions accessible to them. Municipal elections were instituted in 1901; provincial government elections in 1902; an elective Lower-House Legislature in 1907; and an Upper House in 1916. By 1903 Filipinos occupied 49% of bureaucratic positions, although mainly at the lower levels; by 1913 they accounted for 71% of such positions; and by 1928 virtually the whole colonial Government (from clerks to cabinet ministers) was controlled by Filipinos. Crucially, however, these appointees were drawn almost exclusively from the ranks of the *ilustrados*, who, as soon as the leadership of the revolution had been wrested from the dispossessed in early 1897, had begun to collaborate closely with the new colonial power. The USA had strongly reinforced the dominant position of the *ilustrados* within Filipino society, in the interests of effective colonial administration. It was primarily for this reason that no significant attempt was made to reduce the extremely high levels of tenancy in the major regions of export production, for land reform would have threatened to destroy the foundation of *ilustrado* wealth and influence. Even colonial education policy, which was characterized by a major expansion of educational opportunity in the islands, reinforced the position of the *ilustrados* and their US promoters: the use of English as the medium of instruction in schools, and the introduction of a US-style school curriculum, brought an influx of US cultural values into the Philippines, which, in time, dissipated the intense indigenous identity that had animated the Filipino masses during the revolution and the resistance to US occupation.

Filipino politics were dominated in the period of US administration by the Nacionalista Party, led firstly by Sergio Osmeña, and then by Manuel L. Quezon; on numerous occasions the Nacionalista ranks were divided by the fierce personal ambitions of its leadership. In public, Nacionalista leaders fiercely demanded 'immediate, complete and absolute independence', but they were fully aware that they largely owed their power and privileged position to their relationship with the USA. As the prosperity of the islands increasingly came to depend on the free entry of its agricultural exports to the US market, dependence on the colonial power was reinforced. By the 1930s, whatever their public stance, the élite regarded the prospect of independence with increasing unease.

In the event, Philippine independence was secured less by Filipino agitation than by the USA's domestic rejection of its colonial role. Important elements in US society found it difficult to reconcile the proud heritage of independence in the USA with the acquisition of empire. As the USA plunged deeply into depression at the end of the 1920s, these elements were joined by the farming and labour lobbies in demanding protection against the free import of Philippine agricultural commodities—or, in effect, Philippine independence.

Under the Tydings-McDuffie Act, signed by President Franklin Roosevelt on 24 March 1934 and subsequently accepted by the Philippine legislature, the Philippines was to achieve full independence on 4 July 1946. This was to be preceded by a 10-year transitional period of internal self-government, during which the Philippine Commonwealth would remain under US control as far as foreign relations and national defence were concerned; the President of the USA would also be empowered to veto any constitutional amendment or any legislation affecting currency, coinage, imports or exports during this period. In July 1934 a commission was elected to draft a Philippine Constitution. The Constitution was approved by the US President and ratified by the Filipino electorate in May 1935. The Philippine Commonwealth was formally inaugurated on 15 November 1935, with Manuel L. Quezon as President and Sergio Osmeña as Vice-President.

During the 1920s and 1930s abuses on the part of landowners provoked an upsurge in peasant unrest. This period saw the emergence of large peasant unions, principally in central Luzon; the founding of the Partido Komunista ng Pilipinas (PKP—the Communist Party of the Philippines) in 1930; and the establishment of the *Sakdal* (Accusation) movement, which campaigned against the inequitable distribution of property, excessive taxes, and the large landholdings of the Roman Catholic Church, and demanded complete and immediate independence. In early May 1935 the *Sakdalistas*, drawn from the discontented peasantry in the provinces around Manila, began an uprising, but it was rapidly crushed. President Quezon responded to growing agrarian unrest by introducing a programme of 'Social Justice'. This involved much constructive legislation, establishing, for example, minimum wages for industrial and agricultural labourers, and written contracts between landowners and tenants. Quezon's legislative programme, however, proved virtually impossible to enforce against landed interests (including members of the President's own circle) who dominated both local administration and national politics.

In December 1941 Japanese forces landed in the Philippines. Manila was occupied in early January 1942. The political and bureaucratic élite remained largely intact during the occupation, except for Quezon, who escaped to Australia. On 14 October 1943 the Japanese declared the Philippines an independent Republic within the 'Greater East Asia Co-Prosperity Sphere'; the new President of the Republic was José P. Laurel. Japan's occupation did not go unchallenged. Particularly important here was the *Hukbalahap*, or *Huks* (People's Army Against Japan), formed in March 1942, and drawing its forces, in particular, from the militant peasant movement that had been approaching revolt in the late 1930s. Operating in central and southern Luzon, the *Huks* continuously harried Japanese forces; but they also strongly opposed the indigenous landlord class, and those Filipinos whom they saw as collaborating with the Japanese. In October 1944 US forces, under Gen. Douglas MacArthur, landed on Leyte island; US troops entered Manila in early February 1945 and operations continued for several months thereafter. In many areas, the US military advance was prepared by guerrilla groups, under the leadership of former officers of the US Armed Forces in the Far East and the *Huks*.

THE PHILIPPINE REPUBLIC

With a major part of the country's physical capital destroyed by the occupation and liberation, with the export economy in urgent need of rehabilitation, and with Filipino political life riven with charges and denials of wartime collaboration with the Japanese, the Philippines moved towards the attainment of full political independence on 4 July 1946. In the mean time, interim Commonwealth rule was re-established on 27 February 1945, under President Sergio Osmeña, who had succeeded Quezon as Head of the Government-in-exile on the latter's death in the USA in August 1944. In the presidential election of April 1946, Osmeña was narrowly defeated by Manuel Roxas (from the liberal wing of the Nacionalista Party), who had been a cabinet minister during the occupation, and a director of the wartime rice procurement agency which supplied the Japanese army, but who was now strongly supported by Gen. MacArthur. On his assumption of the presidency, Roxas's principal concern was to secure the Philippines' economic relationship with the USA. In March 1947 the USA and the new Republic concluded an agreement on military bases, whereby the USA received a 99-year lease on 23 bases in the islands. The lease was shortened to 25 years in subsequent negotiations. The principal military bases were Subic Bay Naval Base and Clark Air Base, both situated on the main island of Luzon. This agreement gave the US authorities extensive legal jurisdiction over Filipinos living within the bases, and, for this reason, it soon gave rise to major controversy.

Despite their resistance to the Japanese, the *Huks* were regarded with suspicion: the politicians who had collaborated with the Japanese during the war were aware that the *Huks'* open resistance could further expose them; landowners knew that, during the occupation, the *Huks* had been as ruthless with their class as with the Japanese; and the US administration, as well as the Philippine government élite, recognized the strong communist inspiration of the *Huks*. As the war came to a close, these forces combined in a strenuous attempt to suppress the movement. *Huk* units were disarmed, usually by force. In mid-1945 a group of *Huks*, on their way to Pampanga, were seized and executed by government forces, with the knowledge of the US military police in the area; a major part of the leadership was arrested, but subsequently released. In the immediate post-war months the *Huks*, working principally through the opposition Democratic Alliance (DA), sought entry into formal politics. In the April 1946 presidential and congressional elections, the *Huks* supported President Osmeña, while seven DA candidates (including the *Huk* leader, Luis Taruc) were elected to the legislature by the central Luzon peasantry. In mid-1946 Taruc offered to negotiate a cease-fire agreement with the Government of President Roxas, but the negotiations broke down over the demand that *Huks* surrender their weapons. Roxas then engineered the exclusion of successful DA candidates from the legislature, while Philippine army and police units launched a fierce and brutal campaign against the *Huks*. On 6 March 1948 Roxas declared the *Hukbalahap* to be an illegal organization.

Roxas died suddenly in April 1948. He was succeeded by his Vice-President, Elpidio Quirino. The new President immediately sought a truce with the *Huks*: indeed, agreement for an amnesty and surrender of arms was reached, and Luis Taruc, the leader of the *Hukbalahap*, was finally able to take his seat in the Philippine Congress. In mid-August 1948, however, Taruc suddenly left Manila, accusing the authorities of duplicity, primarily over the surrender of arms. The *Huks* were now in open revolt. Taruc announced that he had become a member of the PKP and in April 1949 he publicly declared, for the first time, that the *Hukbalahap* sought the overthrow of the Government.

Quirino sought re-election in 1949 as the Liberal candidate for the presidency, against the nominee of the Nacionalista Party, José Laurel, the wartime collaboration leader. After an election marred by fraud, violence and intimidation, Quirino was returned to office. He faced a deepening economic crisis and an intensified campaign of insurgency by the *Huks*. Many incompetent and corrupt army officers were dismissed, and a new Secretary of National Defense, Ramon Magsaysay, was appointed. Magsaysay pursued a dual policy. The excesses of the armed forces (which had done much to secure support for the *Huks* in rural districts) were sharply curtailed, and a programme for the rehabilitation of rebels who surrendered was instituted. In October 1950 the central committee of the *Hukbalahap* was seized in a number of army and police raids across Manila. The removal of a major part of the leadership, coupled with the Government's more calculated military strategy and more constructive response to rural grievances, which had been at the core of the revolt, including the first stage of a tenancy reform programme in Luzon, resulted in the elimination of the *Huks* as a political entity. On 17 May 1954 Luis Taruc, the *Huks'* leader, surrendered to the authorities. The urgency of demands for genuine agrarian reform waned and little further progress was made.

The disintegration of the *Hukbalahap* secured Magsaysay's prominence in Quirino's Cabinet. When it became clear that Quirino would seek re-election in 1953, Magsaysay left the Liberal Party and became the presidential candidate of the Nacionalistas. After a comparatively free and non-violent election campaign, Magsaysay won a convincing majority. During his presidency, Magsaysay reinforced the Philippines' relationship with the USA; in 1954 the Philippines became a founder-member of the US-inspired South East Asia Treaty Organization (SEATO), and in 1956 US parity with Filipinos in the exploitation of the Philippines' natural resources was extended to all economic activities until 1974, under the Laurel-Langley Agreement. In domestic policy, Magsaysay strongly emphasized his desire to improve the lot of the *tao* (common man), by amending land-tenure arrangements, providing agricultural credit and technical assistance, instituting community development projects and distributing some public lands to the landless. When Magsaysay died in an air accident in March 1957 he was succeeded by his Vice-President, Carlos P. Garcia, who won the presidential election held later that year. Garcia's presidency was initially characterized by austerity measures, and by a policy of economic nationalism (the 'Filipino First' policy) that was intended to lessen the Philippines' economic dependence on the USA, in particular. As Garcia's term of office came to a close, however, his Government foundered on rampant corruption, graft and financial scandal. In the 1961 presidential election Garcia was defeated by the Liberal Party nominee, Diosdado Macapagal. The new President instituted far-reaching economic reforms, encouraged by the USA and the International Monetary Fund (IMF). Macapagal's Government established a Philippine claim to Sabah, on the eve of its inclusion in the new Federation of Malaysia in August 1963. This act caused the Philippine Government to sever diplomatic relations with Malaysia in September; relations were not resumed until June 1966.

THE MARCOS YEARS

In the presidential election of November 1965, Macapagal was defeated by Ferdinand E. Marcos, the Senate President, who had earlier left the Liberal Party to become the Nacionalista candidate. During his first term there was an increase in government expenditure on infrastructure, financed by foreign loans. By the end of the 1960s the principal and interest payments fell due and the country faced a balance-of-payments crisis, which was aggravated by massive election spending in 1969. Marcos was re-elected by a large majority. The late 1960s and early 1970s saw the emergence of student activism, demanding social justice and national sovereignty, and an increasing challenge to central authority from the Moro National Liberation Front (MNLF), a Muslim secessionist movement based on the southern islands of Mindanao and Sulu. Dissension within the communists' ranks led in 1968 to a split in the PKP. A Maoist breakaway group, led by Jose Maria Sison, formed the Communist Party of the Philippines (CPP), whose military wing, the New People's Army (NPA), frequently clashed with government military forces. An umbrella organization, the National Democratic Front (NDF), which included the CPP, was formed in the early 1970s. The PKP, meanwhile, condemned the use of violence and continued to operate within the parliamentary framework.

Acts of political intimidation and violence, frequently perpetrated by private armies under the control of political figures, increased alarmingly after 1969. The number and size of student demonstrations escalated and they were violently dispersed, leaving scores of students dead. As the political and social fabric of the Republic disintegrated, a constitutional convention began the task of preparing a new constitution. Reports of corruption by Marcos and his wife, Imelda, were widespread and included allegations of bribery of members of the convention to extend Marcos's term of office, which, by the terms of the Constitution, had to end in 1973. In August 1971 an opposition rally was bombed; many died and a number of senatorial candidates were seriously injured. Marcos suspended the writ of *habeas corpus*. In September 1972, claiming a conspiracy between right-wing oligarchs and Maoist revolutionaries, Marcos declared martial law. Leading left- and right-wing opponents to Marcos, including both politicians and journalists, were arrested and detained, among them a former senator, Benigno S. Aquino, Jr. The new Constitution, which was drafted as martial law was declared, received ratification in January 1973 from Citizens' Assemblies throughout the Philippines. The new Constitution conferred the offices of both President and Prime Minister on Marcos, who was also empowered to determine when the interim National Assembly would be convened. Martial law continued under the new Constitution. The first elections to the interim Assembly were held in April 1978; local elections followed, in January 1980. On both occasions, the ruling Kilusan Bagong Lipunan (KBL—New Society Movement—formed in 1978 by Marcos and other former members of the Nacionalista Party) was successful, although there were claims by the opposition of widespread electoral malpractice. Marcos followed his electoral success with a period of slight political relaxation; Benigno Aquino was released in May 1980, enabling him to undergo medical treatment in the USA. Martial law was lifted in January 1981, although Marcos's powers remained largely intact. In the following April a national plebiscite approved constitutional amendments which, in effect, replaced the parliamentary form of regime with a mixed presidential-parliamentary Government, and César Virata was appointed Prime Minister.

In the mid-1970s the Muslim secessionist movement in the southern Philippines provoked a military confrontation between government troops and the MNLF. Although the secessionists were initially successful, the movement was neutralized in the late 1970s by the Tripoli Agreement, sponsored by Col Muammar al-Qaddafi of Libya. Marcos defeated the MNLF by ostensibly granting regional autonomy to the Muslim areas and by allegedly paying huge sums of money to some Moro leaders.

In August 1983 Benigno Aquino returned to the Philippines from exile in the USA. As he came down the steps of his aircraft, he was assassinated; the alleged assassin, Rolando Galman, was immediately shot by military guards. Benigno Aquino's death precipitated a major political crisis. Large-scale street demonstrations and labour strikes followed, demanding the resignation of Marcos. This pressure led to the appointment of an independent commission of inquiry into the assassination. In its report, published in October 1984, the commission concluded that Galman was not the assassin, and that Benigno Aquino had been the victim of a military conspiracy. It indicted 25 military officers (including the Chief of Staff of the Philippine Armed Forces, Gen. Fabian Ver), and a trial followed in February 1985.

It was widely believed that the President's immediate circle of associates, if not the President himself and his wife, Imelda, were implicated in Benigno Aquino's death. Rumours of the vast personal wealth that the Marcos family and their associates had accrued through questionable practices, and of the gross extravagance of Imelda Marcos, now began to circulate more openly. Human rights violations, including torture and killings, were documented by both the human rights organization, Amnesty International, and the US Congress. The communists and the legal opposition co-operated in daily demonstrations against the beleaguered regime. At the same time, the massively-indebted national economy was on the verge of collapse. Domestic political instability caused foreign creditors to suspend the short-term loans which had sustained the economy from the late 1970s onwards. New investment was curtailed, and capital fled the country. The Government of the USA brought pressure to bear on Marcos, urging him to submit his regime to electoral test.

On 3 November 1985 Marcos announced that the next presidential election, scheduled for May 1987, would take place in early 1986. At first Salvador Laurel, the President of the United Nationalist Democratic Organization (UNIDO—an alliance of opposition groups formed in 1982), was the only other declared contender. He was soon challenged by Eva Kalaw, one of the leaders of the Liberal Party, and also by Jovito Salonga, a former senator. Corazon Aquino (the widow of Benigno Aquino, Jr) was chosen by some cause-orientated groups and also by Lakas ng Bayan (the People's Power Movement, founded by Benigno Aquino in 1978) and the Pilipino Democratic Party (PDP), which had formed an alliance (PDP-Laban) in 1983, and which formed part of UNIDO. The fragmentation of the opposition groups continued until the end of November 1985, when efforts by the Roman Catholic primate, Cardinal Jaime Sin (the Archbishop of Manila), and the US Embassy in Manila, to encourage unity among opposition groups, resulted in a compromise; Laurel agreed to become the vice-presidential candidate, while Corazon Aquino consented to become the presidential candidate of UNIDO.

During the election campaign Gen. Ver and other military escorts of Benigno Aquino were acquitted of murder, in a trial that appeared to have been manipulated by Marcos. Confusion followed the election, which was held on 7 February 1986, when the two monitoring bodies, the National Movement for Free Elections (Namfrel), financed by the US-based National Endowment for Democracy, and the Government's Commission on Elections (Comelec), each alleged that the other had manipulated the enumeration of votes. Namfrel, basing its result on 70% of total votes, declared that Corazon Aquino had won a majority, while Comelec recorded Marcos in the lead from the outset, and completed the count, whereupon it declared Marcos's victory. A few days later, Marcos was recognized by the *Batasang Pambansa* (National Assembly) as the winner of the elections.

On 14 February 1986 a pastoral statement, issued by the Roman Catholic Church, declared that the election had been 'a fraud unparalleled in history'. US Senator Richard Lugar, a member of a congressional delegation that had observed the election, expressed similar conclusions. Two days later Aquino announced a campaign of non-violent civil disobedience in protest at the outcome of the election. On the evening of 21 February Juan Ponce Enrile, the Minister of National Defense, retreated to his office at Camp Aguinaldo, where he decided to resist his arrest by Marcos, following news that a coup plot by members of the Rebolusyonaryong Alyansang Makabayan (RAM—Nationalist Revolutionary Alliance—also known as the Reform the Armed Forces Movement), a group of right-wing reformist military officers, had been discovered. He was joined at Camp Aguinaldo by Lt-Gen. (later Gen.) Fidel Ramos, the Deputy Chief of Staff of the armed forces, and on 22 February both men announced that they had withdrawn their support from Marcos. Following an appeal by Cardinal Sin, over the church-owned radio station Veritas, for the populace to come to the aid of the two men, thousands of Filipinos flocked into the streets, effectively blocking the way of Marcos's troops. On 24 February the Government of the USA declared that it supported Enrile and Ramos. What had begun as a military revolt against Marcos had developed into a 'snap revolution', in which the strength of civilian support rendered Marcos's troops helpless. Enrile later declared that it was only because of the strength of civilian support for Corazon Aquino, manifested in 'people power', that he and Ramos had relinquished their own intention to form a government, including some civilians, and decided to ally with her. In spite of these events, Marcos insisted on a formal inauguration on 25 February, before being flown to safety in Hawaii, together with his family and associates, in two aircraft supplied by the US air force.

THE AQUINO GOVERNMENT

Corazon Aquino was inaugurated as President of the Philippines in a separate ceremony, also on 25 February 1986. Among those appointed to her Cabinet were Enrile, who retained the position of Minister of National Defense, and Ramos, who became the new Chief of Staff of the armed forces, replacing Ver. Continuity in economic policy between the Marcos administration and the new Aquino Government was established through José Fernandez, who was reappointed Governor of the Central Bank, and through Jaime Ongpin, who became the new Minister of Finance. Two new commissions were created: the Presidential Commission on Good Government, which was given the onerous task of recovering Marcos's ill-gotten wealth, and the Presidential Commission on Human Rights, which was formed to investigate allegations of violations of human rights under the Marcos regime, and to seek redress for the victims.

More than 500 political detainees were released within days of Aquino's inauguration (the armed forces and the US Government were alarmed that communist leaders, including Jose Maria Sison, were released with other political prisoners); the right of *habeas corpus* was restored in early March 1986; censorship of the media was abolished; and elderly pro-Marcos military officers were retired. However, there was some concern that President Aquino's powers were virtually dictatorial: in March she abolished the legislature, under an interim Constitution, and, at the same time, she demanded the resignation of several Supreme Court judges, and dismissed local officials. She also abolished the position of Prime Minister, within a few days of conferring it on Laurel. Disagreement emerged between supporters of UNIDO and PDP-Laban, especially over those appointed to local government positions. At the end of May a 50-member constitutional commission was convened. A new Constitution was presented to the Government in early September and approved by Aquino's Cabinet on 12 October.

By mid-1986 the new Government still awaited the results of its negotiations with creditor institutions, and no major economic initiative had been implemented. There was also growing doubt concerning the President's ability to produce a cohesive policy from the widely-varying opinions represented within her administration. Civil unrest was a serious problem and street rioting by pro-Marcos supporters frequently required armed intervention by the authorities. Marcos himself maintained daily contact with his Manila supporters, by telephone from his base in Hawaii, where he directed anti-Aquino operations. There were continuous rumours of impending political and military coups.

In June 1986 Aquino announced the beginning of formal negotiations with the outlawed NDF, which would aim to establish agreement for a cease-fire in the 17-year campaign by the NPA. However, the insurgents' apparent reluctance to observe a temporary cease-fire caused Enrile and Ramos to resume the government forces' anti-communist offensive while Aquino was out of the country. On her return, she came under strong pressure from members of the Cabinet and the armed forces, notably Enrile and Ramos, to adopt a tougher stance. In November a 60-day cease-fire was agreed, to be effective from 10 December. The pessimistic attitude of both the armed forces and the NDF, however, doomed the peace initiatives to failure and the cease-fire was broken.

In addition, the new Government sought to end the 16-year secessionist war being conducted by the MNLF in the southern Philippines. In August 1986 Agapito Aquino, the President's brother-in-law, and Nur Misuari, the Chairman of the MNLF, met in Saudi Arabia and, as a result, the Aquino Government agreed to grant autonomy to four mainly Muslim-populated provinces in Mindanao. A month later, Misuari returned to the Philippines and agreed to a truce, although there was doubt whether this would be observed by some factions within the MNLF. The initiatives were attacked by another Muslim secessionist grouping, the Moro Islamic Liberation Front (MILF), which was not included in the negotiations but claimed a wider membership than the MNLF. No agreement was achieved.

In July 1986, while Aquino was on a visit to Mindanao, Arturo Tolentino, Marcos's vice-presidential candidate in the February election, proclaimed himself acting president from the Manila Hotel, which had been seized by 300 rebel troops. He claimed to be acting on the instructions of Marcos and appointed a cabinet which included Enrile, the Minister of National Defense in Aquino's Government. Enrile immediately dissociated himself from the rebels, and ordered troops loyal to Aquino to surround the hotel; Tolentino and his supporters surrendered. Over the next two months, however, disagreement within the new Government intensified. By mid-October 1986 Enrile and Laurel, with some support from Ramos, were insisting upon the holding of a new presidential election and the adoption of a more forceful policy against the insurgents. In early November, following his appearance at an anti-Aquino rally, there were rumours of an impending coup by Enrile and his army supporters. Tensions increased with the assassination of Rolando Olalia, a trade union leader and prominent opponent of Enrile. Subsequent investigations implicated officers close to Enrile. On the night of 22–23 November there was an ill-co-ordinated uprising by officers at several military camps. Aquino reacted swiftly, dismissing Enrile as Minister of National Defense and demanding the resignation of the rest of the Cabinet.

The new Constitution, approved by Aquino's Cabinet in October 1986, was subject to a national plebiscite on 2 February 1987. In essence, it returned the Philippines to the constitutional form that had operated (except for the war years) from 1935 to 1973, with a US-style bicameral legislature and an executive presidency. The House of Representatives was to have 200 directly-elected members and up to 50 presidential 'appointees' chosen from party lists, interest groups (including labour and women's organizations) and tribal minorities. The members of the 24-seat Senate were to be directly elected in national elections. The Constitution provided for an extension of the term of the Presidential Commission on Good Government, which aimed to recover large quantities of Marcos's hidden wealth, and formally recognized 'People Power' organizations. Under the new Constitution, Aquino and her Vice-President, Salvador Laurel, were given a mandate to govern until 30 June 1992. Subsequent presidents would serve terms of six years, and would not be eligible for re-election. The Constitution did, however, empower the President to declare martial law in times of national emergency. The Constitution also stipulated that there should be no installation of nuclear weapons in the Philippines, thus directly threatening the maintenance and future of the US military bases.

The weeks immediately prior to the holding of the constitutional referendum were unusually tense. On 22 January 1987 some 10,000–15,000 demonstrators, gathered at the Mendiola Bridge in Manila in support of demands for accelerated land reforms, were attacked by government security forces, and at least 20 people were killed. The 'Mendiola Massacre' seriously damaged the international reputation of the Aquino Government and also reduced domestic support for the President. The NDF immediately withdrew from peace talks with the Government. Civil unrest intensified during the following days, and on 27 January troops belonging to secret organizations within the armed forces attacked military and civilian targets in Manila. Troops loyal to Aquino quashed the insurrection within hours, although a complete surrender by the rebels did not take place until four days had elapsed. On 28 January US officials thwarted an attempt by Marcos to return to Manila, from Hawaii, in order to take advantage of the disorder resulting from the attempted coup. Thirteen officers and 359 troops were subsequently detained by Ramos, pending their trial by court martial.

On 2 February 1987 Aquino's position was considerably strengthened, both in her negotiations with the communists and in her relationship with the armed forces, when the new Constitution was approved in a national referendum by 76% of voters. In the same month all members of the armed forces swore an oath of allegiance to the new Constitution; this was followed by an order disbanding military fraternities, such as the RAM, because they 'encouraged divisiveness'. Congressional elections were announced for 11 May. A Grand Alliance for Democracy (GAD) was formed by some anti-Government and anti-communist opposition groups, including the Nacionalista Party and the KBL, to contest the elections; its candidates for the 24-seat Senate included Enrile and Tolentino. Left-of-centre groups also formed a coalition, the Alliance for New Politics; its programme included the removal of US bases from the Philippines, as well as more radical land reform. The election resulted in a victory for President Aquino's Lagas ng Bayan alliance, which secured 180 of the 200 elective seats in the House of Representatives and 22 of the 24 senatorial seats.

In early 1987 it had become evident that the Government's armed forces lacked the ability to fight both the MNLF and the NPA at the same time. Talks between the Government and MNLF leaders in late 1986, under the auspices of the Organization of the Islamic Conference (OIC), resulted in an undertaking by MNLF leaders, in January 1987, to relinquish demands for complete independence in Mindanao and to accept autonomy. In western Mindanao, however, fierce fighting ensued, instigated by members of the MILF. Although the new Constitution provided for the eventual granting of autonomy to Muslim provinces in Mindanao, MNLF leaders claimed that this would not be sufficient to meet their demands, and in March the MILF reiterated that it would not recognize any agreement between the Government and the MNLF concerning the future of Mindanao. Talks continued, if sporadically, throughout April and May, when the Government announced that MNLF leaders were willing to form a joint commission to draft an autonomy settlement for Mindanao; following a deadlock in talks regarding autonomy provisions, however, the Government announced, in August, that it would no longer consult MNLF leaders.

In April 1987 government forces overcame an abortive coup by rebel soldiers. In July Marcos was forbidden to leave Hawaii by US officials, following the discovery of a pro-Marcos coup plot in Manila; and in the same month the Philippine Government initiated legal proceedings against Marcos, his family and associates (including Enrile and Jose Fernandez, the Governor of the Central Bank) in a Manila court, claiming damages of US $22,500m. for the sufferings of the Filipino people as a result of the Marcos Government's alleged corruption. Following the assassination of Jaime Ferrer, the Secretary of Local Government, by the NPA in August, there was an outbreak of strikes and violence in Manila. On 28 August Ramos and troops loyal to President Aquino averted a fifth attempted coup, when rebel officers, led by Col Gregorio Honasan (a former leader of the RAM and closely associated with Enrile), occupied the army headquarters. In subsequent fighting 53 people were killed. On the next day Honasan and his supporters fled, successfully evading capture until December.

In September 1987 Salvador Laurel resigned as the Secretary (formerly Minister) of Foreign Affairs, owing to differences of opinion regarding government policy in combating insurgency: he was replaced by Senator Raul Manglapus; however, he retained the post of Vice-President. In October Laurel announced that he and Enrile had agreed to form a new anti-Aquino alliance. During late 1987 the Government was accused of both 'leftism' and 'rightism' by its various opponents, and its reputation was damaged by allegations of abuses of human rights, owing to mass detentions and the creation (with government approval) of armed vigilante groups to combat insurgency in urban areas.

In January 1988 Ramos was appointed Secretary of National Defense. The government campaign against communist insurgents was immediately intensified, although the President continued to resist demands from the armed forces that a state of emergency be declared. Among numerous CPP officials captured by the army were its General Secretary, Rafael Baylosis, and the Commander-in-Chief of the NPA, Romulo Kintanar (who escaped from custody in November 1988). Although there were almost 2,000 deaths in insurgency-related violence during the first six months of 1988, Aquino was criticized by the military for not dealing sufficiently harshly with rebel elements.

The politically sensitive issue of US military bases in the Philippines came to the fore in 1988. Under an agreement signed in 1983 by the US and Philippine Governments, the continued use of six military bases, including Clark Air Base and Subic Bay Naval Base (both on Luzon island), had been permitted until 1989. In March 1986 Aquino had confirmed that the agreement would be respected, although the 1987 Constitution stated that foreign military bases would not be allowed in the country after 1991, unless under the provisions of a treaty approved by the Senate and ratified by voters in a referendum. Despite the strong nationalist feelings aroused by this issue, the bases had proved a useful source of employment and government revenue. Negotiations for a further two-year extension to 1991 were opened in April 1988 and were eventually concluded in October. Under the new agreement, the Philippine Government was to receive annual economic and military aid totalling US $481m., representing almost 2.5 times the previous level of receipts. The USA also secured the right for its military aircraft and warships to use the Philippines' facilities without a contingent obligation to declare the presence of nuclear weaponry.

In June 1988 the Government introduced a Comprehensive Agrarian Reform Programme (CARP), providing for an extensive redistribution of agricultural lands, over a 10-year period, to untenured farmers and farm workers. However, the extended timetable, together with numerous exemptions and complicated provisions for legal appeals, seriously impeded its implementation. These provisions were included in the programme as a result of the numerical domination of Congress, particularly the House of Representatives, by landowners. Also in June the PDP and Lakas ng Bansa formed a new pro-Aquino alliance, the Laban ng Demokratikong Pilipino (LDP).

Vice-President Laurel reasserted his opposition to Aquino's coalition in August 1988 by demanding the President's resignation and announcing his leadership of a broadly-based opposition front, the Union for National Action (UNA). Laurel also initiated a campaign against alleged corruption in the Aquino Government and among members of the President's family. In July 1988 the Presidential Commission on Good Government, which had been established to recover funds illegally acquired by Marcos, came under suspicion itself. The Head of the Commission was obliged to resign and a large-scale reorganization was ordered. In May 1989 Marcos's Nacionalista Party was revived, with Laurel elected as President and Enrile appointed Secretary-General.

In February 1989 the NDF offered to begin peace talks with the Government, if Aquino agreed not to renew the lease on US bases after 1991. After the Government's refusal of this offer, attacks were made by the NPA on US personnel and facilities. During the year the Government responded to accusations of human rights abuses by exposing atrocities allegedly committed by the NPA. In June revelations of irregularities in the administration of the CARP gave further embarrassment to the Government. Aquino's ensuing attempts to appoint as Secretary for Agrarian Reform Miriam Defensor Santiago (who had previously been in charge of the Commission on Immigration and Deportation and who had a reputation for combating corruption) were repeatedly rejected by members of the Commission on Appointments, influenced by landowning interests.

In September 1989 the Philippine Government began the first of 35 planned civil suits against the former President Marcos, in his absence, with the aim of regaining embezzled funds. At the end of the month, however, Marcos died in Hawaii. The Supreme Court prohibited (in the interests of national security) the return of Marcos's body for burial in the Philippines, as demanded by his supporters. (The trial of Imelda Marcos, on charges of fraud and of illegal transfer of stolen funds into the USA, began in New York in April 1990: she was acquitted of all charges in July.)

In November 1989 a plebiscite was held in 13 provinces and nine cities in Mindanao, on proposed legislation that envisaged the autonomy of these provinces and cities, with direct elections to a unicameral legislature in each province; this contrasted with the MNLF's demand for autonomy in 23 provinces, to be granted without a referendum. The MNLF appealed, with considerable success, to the Muslim population (about 28% of the inhabitants of the region) to abstain from participating in the referendum. The Christian inhabitants (about 66% of the regional population) were largely opposed to autonomy. Four provinces (Lanao del Sur, Maguindanao, Tawi-Tawi and Sulu) voted in favour of the government proposal and formed the Autonomous Region of Muslim Mindanao (ARMM).

In December 1989 an abortive coup was staged by members of two élite military units, the Marines and the Scout Rangers, in collusion with the illicit RAM and officers loyal to Marcos. Rebel soldiers captured an armed forces base and the air-force headquarters, which enabled them to launch air attacks on government strongholds and on the presidential palace. The progress of the coup prompted Aquino to request US air support to deter further aerial attacks by the rebels. This aim was achieved by the mere presence in the air of units of the US Air Force, which did not fire on rebel troops. Most of the rebel strongholds were captured within 24 hours. The coup was thought to involve many officers who had graduated with Honasan. Aquino subsequently accused Laurel and Enrile (who were both included in an eight-member provisional junta named by the rebels) of involvement in the coup attempt. Suspicion also fell on her estranged cousin, Eduardo Cojuangco, who had fled to the USA with Marcos in 1986 and returned secretly from exile shortly before the coup.

In February 1990 Enrile was arrested, on charges of 'rebellion complexed with murder'. He was also charged with harbouring Honasan, prior to the coup attempt. In March Rodolfo Aguinaldo, who had been suspended as Governor of Cagayan in January for supporting the attempted coup, launched an unsuccessful rebellion, following an attempt to arrest him. Arrests of those implicated in the attempted coup continued. In April Lt-Commdr Bilbastro Bibit, a suspected leader of the coup, was freed from prison by masked rebel soldiers. The soldiers claimed to be members of a military movement called the Young Officers' Union (YOU), which was alleged to have played an important role in the December 1989 coup attempt. In June the Supreme Court ordered the charge of 'rebellion complexed with murder' against Enrile and 22 other alleged rebels to be amended to 'simple rebellion' or 'illegal possession of firearms'. The court ruled that the original charge had been removed by Aquino from the statute book in 1986 by a presidential decree. As a result of the Supreme Court decision, Aguinaldo surrendered and was formally charged.

In May 1990 negotiations were resumed with the US Government on the future of US military bases in the Philippines after the expiry of the current agreement in 1991. There were violent confrontations between demonstrators, opposed to the retention of the bases, and police. In November 1990 it was announced that all US fighter aircraft and more than 1,800 military personnel would be withdrawn from the Philippines by the end of 1991. It was also announced that the two sides were to negotiate a new agreement to replace the existing security treaty, drafted in 1947.

In September 1990, following a trial lasting more than three years, a special court convicted 16 members of the armed forces of the murder of Benigno Aquino and Rolando Galman, the alleged assassin, and acquitted 20 defendants. It was recognized, however, that those responsible for planning the assassination had not been brought to justice.

In early October 1990 Col Alexander Noble, a former officer in Aquino's personal security corps, and allegedly an associate of Honasan, led a revolt on the island of Mindanao. The insurrection, which was launched in Cagayan de Oro and Butuan with 400 men, was ostensibly aimed at achieving independence for Mindanao. The Government swiftly destroyed the rebels' headquarters and communication building in an air strike, and Noble subsequently surrendered. However, the rebellion was widely assumed to be a further attempt to destabilize Aquino's Government, by forcing the transfer of troops from Manila to Mindanao.

The NPA killed 563 members of the armed forces between January and April 1991 and maintained an active presence in 55 of the 73 provinces. The fighting was most intense in the far north of the country, although clashes had occurred on the southern island of Mindanao. Following the eruption in June of the 1,780-m volcano Mt Pinatubo, situated on the boundary of the provinces of Tarlac, Zambales and Pampanga, the NDF offered to hold discussions with the Government, proposing a cease-fire in areas damaged by the volcano. Aquino rejected the offer, claiming that the NDF could not control the actions of certain members of the NPA. In July the armed forces captured the NPA's most important base, Camp Venus in Sagada, Mountain Province, representing a major success in the struggle against the communist insurgency. In early August Romulo Kintanar, the Commander-in-Chief of the NPA, became the 10th communist leader to be captured in two weeks.

In late August 1991, following negotiations extending over 14 months, the Philippines and the USA provisionally agreed a military bases treaty providing for a new 10-year lease on Subic Bay Naval Base, with generous US compensation for the Philippines. Following the agreement, Aquino, the armed forces and many business groups campaigned to gain the constitutionally-necessary support of a two-thirds' majority in the Senate. In September the NDF pledged an immediate cease-fire, pending a commitment by the Senate to reject the treaty. This commitment was subsequently given and the unilateral cease-fire duly implemented. Despite widespread popular support for the US installations, the Senate rejected the treaty by 12 votes to 11. The Government, however, rescinded the formal notice on termination of the previous lease, which had been served in May 1990, effectively extending the lease for another year.

In September 1991 Lt-Gen. Lisandro Abadio, the Chief of Staff of the armed forces since April, suspended all operations against Honasan and other military rebels in a concerted attempt to achieve national reconciliation. Abadio met Honasan twice in August and released 68 rebel soldiers as a gesture of goodwill. The Government was also attempting to negotiate an end to the communist insurgency.

At the end of July 1991 Aquino announced that Imelda Marcos and her family would be permitted to return to the Philippines to stand trial on charges of fraud and tax evasion. The decision to lift the travel ban on Imelda Marcos was prompted by a ruling of the Swiss Supreme Court in December 1990, which stated that the transfer of funds held in Swiss bank accounts to the Philippines was conditional on Imelda Marcos being brought to trial for fraud in a Philippine court before December 1991. In October Aquino relaxed the ban on the return of Marcos's remains, but stipulated that the burial should take place in his home province of Ilocos Norte, rather than in Manila. In November Imelda Marcos returned to the Philippines, and in December she pleaded 'not guilty' to charges of tax evasion. During the ensuing months she faced more than 80 civil and criminal charges.

During 1991 there was much political manoeuvring with a view to the presidential election, to be held in May 1992. In April 1991 Ramos officially joined the ruling LDP to compete with the Speaker of the House of Representatives, Ramon Mitra, for the party nomination. Although Ramos's candidacy elicited much support from the commercial sector, it was Mitra who was selected as the LDP's presidential candidate in November. Ramos then resigned from the LDP and formed a new party, the Partido Lakas Tao (People Power Party).

In January 1992 President Aquino endorsed the presidential candidacy of Ramos, thus ending speculation that (despite repeated denials) she might seek re-election. In the same month Ramos discarded the PPP and registered a new party called EDSA-LDP, with the support of 25 former LDP members of Congress. (EDSA was the popular acronym for Epifanio de los Santos Avenue, the main site of the uprising of February 1986.) The party subsequently altered its title to Lakas ng EDSA (Power of EDSA), and formed an electoral alliance with Raul Manglapus's National Union of Christian Democrats (NUCD) and the Partido Democratiko Sosyalista ng Pilipinas (Philippine Democratic Socialist Party). The grouping was subsequently known as Lakas-NUCD.

In February 1992 Comelec authorized the presidential candidacies of eight of a total of 78 nominees. They were: Eduardo Cojuangco; Joseph Estrada (a senator and former film actor); Salvador Laurel; Imelda Marcos (whose candidacy was supported by what remained of the KBL); Ramon Mitra (who received the endorsement of the Roman Catholic Archbishop of Manila, Cardinal Sin); Fidel Ramos; Jovito Salonga; and Miriam Defensor Santiago (who was supported by the newly-formed People's Reform Party). Enrile had withdrawn his candidacy earlier in the month, giving the support of his faction of the Nacionalista Party to Mitra. In March Estrada withdrew his presidential candidacy in order to compete for the vice-presidency, supporting Cojuangco.

On 11 May 1992 elections took place to select the President, Vice-President, 24 senators, 200 members of the House of Representatives and 17,014 local government councillors. Although more than 100 people were killed in election-related violence, the contest was regarded as relatively orderly, in comparison with previous occasions. Accusations of widespread electoral malpractice (voiced, in particular, by Santiago and Cojuangco) appeared to be largely unsubstantiated. Because of the protracted vote-counting procedure, the result of the presidential election was not proclaimed by Congress until 22 June. The victor was Ramos, with Estrada as the successful vice-presidential candidate. As a result of the country's 'first past the post' electoral system, Ramos had won with only 23.6% of the votes. His closest rivals were Santiago (with 19.7%) and Cojuangco (18.2%). The success of Ramos and the high degree of support for Santiago (whose electoral campaign had emphasized the need for eradicating corruption) were regarded as a rejection of traditional party politics, since neither candidate was supported by a large-scale party organization. In the legislative elections, however, the LDP (the only party that had local bases in every province) won 16 of the 24 seats in the Senate, and 89 of the 200 elective seats in the House of Representatives.

THE RAMOS GOVERNMENT

Ramos's ascent to the presidency was supported by three important political groups: retired yet still powerful military officers; business executives and technocrats, who were identified as economic and political reformers, some of whom had served under the Aquino Government; and traditional politicians from Lakas-NUCD. The principal appointees to Ramos's Cabinet, established after his inauguration on 30 June 1992, consequently came from these groups. Ramos declared that his administration's priorities were to restore political and civil stability through national reconciliation and an amnesty programme; to deregulate the economy and encourage foreign investment by dismantling monopolies; and to curb criminality and corruption.

In July 1992 Lakas-NUCD gained leadership in Congress by expanding its membership through defections from the LDP and other parties and by forging a 'Rainbow Coalition' with the Liberal Party, Cojuango's Nationalist People's Coalition (NPC) and the KBL to form a new majority. The Secretary-General of Lakas-NUCD, Jose de Venecia, a close ally of Ramos, assumed the post of Speaker of the House of Representatives. The LDP, however, retained control of the Senate, with Neptali Gonzales remaining as Senate President. In the same month Ramos submitted to Congress four initiatives to support his reconciliation programme: the repeal of the Anti-Subversion Law, which would in effect legalize the CPP and similar organizations; the granting of an amnesty to 4,485 former rebels; the creation of a National Unification Commission (NUC) to help frame the Government's peace and amnesty strategy; and the review of all cases of rebels under detention or serving a sentence. (Congress formally approved these initiatives seven months later in February 1993.) Ramos announced that his administration would pursue peace talks on three fronts: with the communist insurgents; the Muslim secessionists; and the military rebels. In July 1992 Ramos appointed a member of the House of Representatives, Jose Yap, as an official emissary to the NDF, thus giving government sanction to informal talks which were already taking place between Yap and rebel representatives. Also in July Ramos formed the Presidential Anti-Crime Commission (PACC) and named the popular Vice-President, Estrada, as its Head in an effort to curb the rising incidence of crime, especially kidnapping for ransom, which together with the acute energy crisis threatened the Government's plan to attract more foreign investment.

In mid-August 1992 Ramos authorized Yap to start exploratory talks with the expatriate leaders of the NDF, Luis Jalandoni and Jose Maria Sison, in the Netherlands. Ramos ordered the temporary release from prison of five communist leaders, including NDF negotiator, Saturnino Ocampo, and Romulo Kintanar, as well as 16 military rebels. Government and NDF emissaries held open but preliminary discussions in the Netherlands on 31 August and 1 September (the first since the failure of the peace talks in 1987). They agreed to recommend to their respective principals the resumption of formal talks, including the discussion of socio-political issues, in an attempt to secure a negotiated settlement of the insurgency. The Chairman of the NDF, Manuel Romero, immediately accepted the proposal, while Ramos promised to submit it to the NUC, which was created later in September. Ramos appointed Haydee Yorac, an elections commissioner and human rights lawyer, as Head of the NUC, and selected members from the legislature (including Yap), the Cabinet and the Catholic and Protestant churches. The NUC began its series of public consultations in early October. Meanwhile a breakthrough was made in the negotiations with the MNLF: a member of the NUC, Eduardo Ermita, met Nur Misuari in Tripoli, Libya, where the latter indicated his willingness to return home from self-exile to hold peace talks with the Government. Two weeks later Ramos agreed to negotiate with the MNLF, with the OIC acting as an observer. At the end of October, following a series of discrete talks with rebel leaders Honasan and Jose Maria Zumel, Yorac announced that the military rebels had submitted a framework for negotiations.

On 30 September 1992 the USA started to vacate Subic Bay Naval Base. In November Ramos called for a review of the 1951 Mutual Defense Treaty between the Philippines and the USA, declaring that it was not clear about the terms on which the USA would come to the aid of the Philippines in the event of an external attack. In the same month the USA completed its withdrawal from Subic Bay Naval Base and formally transferred command and control of the 56,000-ha facility to the Philippine Government. The Subic Bay Metropolitan Authority was established to oversee the conversion of the area to commercial use.

In January 1993 Edgardo Angara of the LDP was elected as Senate President, replacing Neptali Gonzales (also of the LDP) after realignments in the chamber brought together LDP and Lakas-NUCD senators in a new pro-Ramos majority. In another show of political dominance, the gubernatorial candidate supported by Ramos, Liningding Pangandaman, won 72% of the votes cast at elections in the ARMM on 25 March 1993.

The rift within the CPP, which had started in 1992 as a result of a Maoist purge initiated by the Chairman, Sison, worsened in 1993. In July the CPP's Metro Manila-Rizal organization declared their secession from the central leadership. Five months earlier, in November 1992, the party's Executive Committee had ordered the dissolution of the region's leading committee and its armed unit, the Alex Boncayao Brigade, purportedly for factionalism and military excesses. In October 1993 four communist leaders, including Romulo Kintanar and Arturo Tabara, the Secretary-General of the Central Philippine Command of the NPA, were expelled from the CPP and the NPA for refusing to recognize the authority of Sison.

In April 1993, following an extensive review of the Philippine National Police (PNP), in which corruption was found to be widespread, Ramos ordered the dismissal of hundreds of personnel, including 63 of the 194 senior officers. In July Ramos established a 60-day period during which the security forces were to disarm the 560 private armies in the Philippines, which were controlled mostly by provincial politicians and wealthy landowners. The September deadline for the dissolution of the private militias was, however, subsequently extended until the end of November, but even by this date little progress had been made.

In July 1993 Ramos gave permission for the remains of Ferdinand Marcos to be brought to the Philippines from Hawaii for a private burial in his native province of Ilocos Norte, with no state or military honours. The funeral, which took place in September, was attended by only a few thousand supporters. Later that month Imelda Marcos was convicted of corruption and sentenced to 18 years' imprisonment (although she remained at liberty pending an appeal).

Despite progress in early 1993, which had facilitated the reintegration of mutinous soldiers into active service, in February 1994 the military rebels announced that peace negotiations between the Government, the RAM and the YOU would continue to be suspended, pending the release of six military detainees. In the following month Ramos proclaimed a general amnesty for all rebels and for members of the security forces charged with offences committed during counter-insurgency operations, as recommended by the NUC. Crimes of torture, arson, massacre, rape and robbery were, however, exempted from the pardon. The RAM rejected the amnesty, on the grounds that it failed to address the causes of the rebellion, and reiterated its commitment to electoral, military, social and economic reform. Saturnino Ocampo also dismissed the proclamation, claiming that it was biased against communist rebels, since 80% of them had been charged with common crimes not covered by the amnesty.

In January 1994 an increase in petroleum prices took effect following the imposition of a levy by Ramos in September 1993, which had initially been charged to the Oil Price Stabilization Fund. A group of autonomous socialist organizations led by elements of the CPP, called the Philippine Left, organized a popular campaign in protest at price increases, creating the first crisis of Ramos's term of office. The Trade Union Congress of the Philippines threatened a general strike, and the still-active Alex Boncayao Brigade initiated bomb attacks on the country's three leading petroleum companies. At the end of February Ramos rescinded the levy, and established a committee to study alternative methods of raising government revenue.

The first formal negotiations between the Government and the MNLF took place in October 1993 in Jakarta, Indonesia, following two phases of exploratory talks earlier in the year. The MNLF demanded the creation of an autonomous Islamic state in the south, as provided for under the 1976 Tripoli Agreement. In November the two sides signed a memorandum of understanding and an interim cease-fire was agreed. In response to the progress of the negotiations, further violence occurred in the south, including an assault on a Roman Catholic cathedral in Davao City, followed by retaliatory attacks on three mosques by Christian extremists. In January 1994 the terms of the cease-fire were agreed, stipulating that both government and rebel forces should remain in place and refrain from provocative action. Nur Misuari subsequently gave an assurance that MNLF demands for a transitional government in Mindanao would not affect the terms of office of the officials of the existing ARMM, due to expire in 1996. The second round of formal peace negotiations between the Government and the MNLF took place in Jakarta in April 1994.

In February 1994 a federal court in Hawaii awarded US $1,200m. in punitive damages to 10,000 Filipinos who had been tortured under President Marcos's administration. This followed a court ruling in October 1992 that victims of human rights violations under the Marcos regime could sue his estate for compensation. Imelda Marcos announced that she would appeal against the decision. Lawyers acting for the Philippine Government also filed counter-claims to the money, citing an Aquino decree that stipulated that all properties recovered from the Marcoses should be used only to finance the Government's agrarian reform programme. In January 1995 the Hawaiian court ordered the estate of Marcos to pay a further US $774m. in compensatory damages to the 10,000 victims. At the end of that month the Philippine Supreme Court restored a 'freeze' on the assets of more than 500 companies controlled by former associates of Marcos, which had been revoked on technical grounds in 1991. In August 1995 the Swiss authorities approved the transfer of about US $475m. from Swiss bank accounts held by Marcos to an account in the Philippines.

In June 1994 the Government launched an offensive against Abu Sayyaf, a Muslim secessionist group, which was responsible for terrorist activities, including kidnapping, on the southern islands of Jolo and Basilan. In retaliation for the military assault, Abu Sayyaf planted a bomb in Zamboanga City, injuring 28 civilians. On the following day the armed forces captured the group's headquarters on Jolo Island, prompting Abu Sayyaf's seizure of 74 Christian hostages on Basilan. Many hostages were swiftly released, but 15 were killed in retaliation for government 'summary executions'. In mid-June 20 of the remaining 21 hostages were released following the alleged payment of a ransom by the local authority and the intercession of the MNLF. Abu Sayyaf, however, retained one hostage, a Roman Catholic priest, in order to protect themselves from government attacks. Government troops subsequently captured the group's main headquarters in Basilan; the priest was later released unharmed.

In May 1994 Ramos succeeded in enacting a law amending the system of value-added tax (VAT) in order to offset the losses in revenue arising from the rescission of the levy on petroleum prices. Popular opposition to the extended VAT system, however, gathered momentum during June, and Ramos's attempts to diminish dissent by granting exemptions for newspapers and school textbooks by executive order served only to confirm the public perception that the legislation was flawed. The VAT legislation provided a rallying point for opposition parties, which organized broad-based coalitions to oppose the law. Senators who initially supported the bill began to advocate its abrogation. At the end of June the Supreme Court issued an injunction on the legislation, preventing it from being implemented at the beginning of July, pending rulings on seven suits claiming that the legislation and its enactment violated the Constitution. In August the Supreme Court ruled that the VAT legislation was constitutional, but it still could not be implemented pending an appeal against the ruling by opposition groupings.

In July 1994 the majority leader of the House of Representatives, Ronaldo Zamora, defected from Lakas-NUCD to the NPC. A few days later he and 19 other members of the NPC resigned from the ruling coalition. However, in August Lakas-NUCD and the LDP formed an alliance, known as Lakas-Laban; the ruling coalition, which also comprised the Nacionalista Party, the Liberal Party and PDP-Laban, thus controlled 158 of the 215 seats in the House of Representatives and 19 of the 23 occupied seats in the Senate. The priority of Lakas-Laban was to present a common list for the 12 seats in the Senate that were to be contested in 1995. Ramos would, however, also benefit from support in the Senate to expedite the passage of vital legislation.

In August 1994 the RAM agreed to support government programmes that would benefit the population. Later that month it signed an agreement with the ruling administration on electoral reform. In July 1995 negotiations between the Government, the RAM and the YOU resumed, following a three-month hiatus owing to the elections. The military groupings pledged that they would refrain from organizing any further coup attempts.

In October 1994 negotiations resumed between the Government and the NDF in the Netherlands, but collapsed owing to disagreements over the NDF's insistence on granting immunity to government negotiators for future talks to be held in areas of the Philippines claimed by the NDF to be under its control. In May 1995 discussions scheduled for June were threatened by the arrest of a leading NDF member, Sotero Llamas. The peace talks did take place in Belgium in June, but were suspended by the Government following NDF demands for Llamas's release to enable him to join the negotiations. The Government subsequently announced that it would guarantee safe passage to all members of the NDF panel for future negotiations in the Philippines, but that it was no longer prepared to attend meetings overseas, as the discussions frequently collapsed owing to the unreasonable demands made by the insurgents. The NDF rejected the new conditions, and Sison announced that peace negotiations would be postponed until the expiry of Ramos's term of office in 1998.

In December 1994 clashes took place in North Cotabato between government forces and the MILF. The MILF, which was covered by the government cease-fire but was not a party to the peace talks, was widely suspected of having taken advantage of the continuing negotiations between the MNLF and the Government to strengthen its position, both by an accumulation of arms and the recruitment of young militants disaffected with the compliance of the MNLF. Negotiations between the Government and the MNLF proceeded in Mindanao in January 1995, at the end of which it was announced that the Government had agreed to the establishment of an MNLF provisional government in Mindanao, subject to congressional approval and the holding of a referendum. In April an attack by about 200 guerrillas on the largely Christian town of Ipil in Mindanao, in which more than 50 civilians were massacred, was attributed to Abu Sayyaf. Members of an MNLF splinter group, the Islamic Command Council, were alleged to have taken part in the attack on Ipil, which was denounced by Misuari as an attempt to sabotage the peace talks. Ramos, however, pledged to continue negotiations with the MNLF.

On 8 May 1995 elections were held to contest 12 of the 24 seats in the Senate and the 204 elective seats in the House of Representatives; 76 provincial governorships and more than 17,000 local government positions were also contested. Prior to the elections, in which an estimated 80% of all eligible voters participated, more than 80 people were killed in campaign violence. In Mindanao widespread violence caused voting to be postponed until 27 May, when 30,000 troops were dispatched to the island to ensure security. During the campaign Ramos declared that the elections should be regarded as a referendum on his three years in office and emphasized his administration's progress towards economic liberalization. Lakas-NUCD formed an electoral alliance with a small Mindanao-based moderate Islamic party for the election to the House of Representatives, in order to attract broad national support. The opposition parties, dominated by the NPC, focused on the Government's failure to prevent both the execution in Singapore of a Filipino domestic servant, Flor Contemplacion, who had been convicted of two murders, and the Muslim separatist attack on Ipil, emphasizing the Government's apparent inability to protect its nationals' interests at home and abroad.

In the event the ruling coalition won the vast majority (about 70%) of seats in the House of Representatives and Lakas-Laban won nine of the 12 seats in the Senate. One of the three opposition seats was secured by Honasan, despite a campaign by Aquino against his candidacy. In his opening address to Congress in July 1995 Ramos urged the adoption of radical legislation to reduce public bureaucracy and eliminate corruption in the police force and in the judicial system.

In October 1995 Ramos decided to assume personal responsibility for the campaign against organized crime, reducing the role of the PACC to that of a co-ordinating agency. Estrada was widely regarded as having failed in his position as head of the agency, despite his alleged sanctioning of extra-judicial executions to combat violent crime. The continuing increase in serious offences, often with the alleged involvement of members of PNP, adversely affected public perceptions of the Ramos administration, particularly in view of Ramos's past affiliation to the PNP. (In April 1996, however, the PACC's powers, and one-third of its former strength, were restored.)

In January 1996 the LDP withdrew from its alliance with Lakas-NUCD, leaving Ramos with a minority in the Senate, which threatened to undermine his reform programme, but still with a substantial majority in the House of Representatives. Ramos's administration had become increasingly unpopular as a result of rising crime, a national rice shortage (owing largely to mismanagement) and increasing inflation. Furthermore, the extended VAT legislation finally took effect in January, and in February an increase in the price of petrol was announced. Angara, the President of the LDP, claimed that the party had received no concessions in return for helping the administration to pass unpopular legislation, and that, contrary to agreement, Lakas-NUCD had contested LDP seats in the local government elections in May 1995. The LDP finally withdrew from the alliance, however, in protest against proposed anti-terrorist legislation, which it described as the effective introduction of martial law, designed to facilitate Ramos's extension of his term of office.

In 1995 formal peace negotiations continued between the Government and the MNLF in Jakarta regarding the proposed establishment of an expanded autonomous region in Mindanao. In August Misuari agreed for the first time to a referendum (as stipulated under the Constitution) prior to the establishment of an autonomous zone, but demanded the immediate establishment of a provisional MNLF government to ensure that the referendum was conducted fairly. (The MNLF had previously objected to a plebiscite, since a number of predominantly Christian regions were likely to vote against autonomy.) In April

1996 two bomb explosions in Zamboanga City were widely attributed to Abu Sayyaf or to other groups opposed to the peace negotiations. In June it was announced that the MNLF and the Government had finally reached agreement on a proposal by Ramos for the establishment of a transitional administrative council, to be known as the Southern Philippines Council for Peace and Development (SPCPD), which was to derive powers from the Office of the President. The five-member SPCPD, which was to be headed by Misuari, was to co-ordinate peace-keeping and development efforts in 14 provinces and 10 cities in Mindanao, with the assistance of an 81-member Consultative Assembly and a religious advisory council. After a period of three years a referendum was to be conducted in each province and city to determine whether it would join the existing ARMM. (The MNLF had abandoned its demands for autonomy in 23 provinces in Mindanao.) Also in June it was announced that negotiations between the Government and the NDF had resumed in the Netherlands, after a Manila court ordered the release 'in the interests of peace' of Sotero Llamas, the NDF member, who had been charged with a number of serious offences.

The announcement of the peace agreement between the Government and the MNLF prompted criticism from a number of Christian politicians and a series of protests by Christians in Mindanao, which culminated during an official visit by Ramos to the region, in July 1996, in an attempt to secure public support for the planned establishment of the SPCPD. The Government subsequently warned that opponents of the peace agreement could be charged with sedition, after a number of demonstrators displayed inverted Philippine flags (symbolizing a state of war). In the same month government officials announced that, under the peace agreement, Muslims were to be allocated one cabinet post, and were to be granted representation in state-owned companies and constitutional commissions. In addition, Ramos offered to support the candidacy of Misuari in the forthcoming gubernatorial election in the ARMM.

In early September 1996 the Government and the MNLF signed a final draft of the peace agreement in Jakarta; discussions continued regarding the integration of some 7,500 members of the MNLF's military wing into the national army and security forces (this commenced in March 1997), the establishment of a regional security force in Mindanao and the administrative structure of the SPCPD. The MILF refused to endorse the settlement, continuing to demand separatism for 23 provinces in Mindanao. On 9 September 1996 elections took place peacefully in Muslim Mindanao for the region's Governor and Assembly; Misuari, who, as agreed, contested the gubernatorial election with the support of Lakas-NUCD, was elected unopposed. (Critics of Misuari subsequently maintained that he was not permitted under law concurrently to chair the SPCPD and hold office as Governor of Muslim Mindanao.) Following his election as Governor, Misuari demanded reforms in the Senate whereby the number of seats would be increased from 24 to 72 (with 24 senators elected from Mindanao). In October he was officially appointed Chairman of the SPCPD.

MILF and government officials had met for preliminary peace discussions for the first time in August 1996, following the MILF's rejection of the peace agreement concluded by the MNLF. Clashes between government and MILF forces, which resulted in several deaths, were reported in October in North Cotabato and Maguindanao. Nevertheless, peace talks reconvened in January 1997, resulting in the announcement of a temporary cease-fire, but the high incidence of kidnappings by separatist rebels in Mindanao in early 1997 threatened to hinder the progress of the negotiations. In February members of Abu Sayyaf, who remained opposed to any peace agreement between the Government and the Muslim separatists, were responsible for the assassination of a Catholic bishop in Jolo. The abduction, allegedly by MILF rebels, of some 40 workers from the Philippine National Oil Co in mid-June resulted in the collapse of the peace talks and a renewed outburst of fierce fighting between government and MILF forces in Mindanao, with many thousands of civilians forced to evacuate the area. In an attempt to encourage the resumption of peace negotiations and to allow the citizens to return to their homes, President Ramos ordered a suspension of military offensives by the armed forces in early July. Prospects for peace appeared brighter following a meeting between MILF leaders and Misuari, at which the MILF reiterated its demands for the withdrawal of government forces from the region, and a new cease-fire agreement was subsequently signed by the Government and the MILF. Talks resumed later in July, with the negotiators aiming to reach a substantive agreement by the end of 1997.

During 1996–97 Ramos continued publicly to dissociate himself from efforts by his supporters to amend the constitutional stipulation that restricted the President to a single term in office. The business community criticized his prevarication, claiming that it was profoundly affecting investors' confidence in the Philippine economy. Ramos's attempt to transform Congress into a constituent assembly to revise the 1987 Constitution in early September prompted Cardinal Sin and Aquino to organize a protest demonstration on 21 September, the 25th anniversary of Marcos's declaration of martial law. Recognizing the support that the protest movement was already commanding (in the event, some 500,000 people took to the streets of Manila), Ramos issued a statement several hours before the demonstration was due to commence, declaring that he still believed that the Constitution should be amended, but that it should be changed after the 1998 presidential election, and that he was categorically not intending to offer his candidature.

The unsuccessful moves to introduce constitutional changes that would have enabled President Ramos to stand for a second term, greatly weakened the capacity of the ruling Lakas-NUCD to contest the presidential election. There was widespread apprehension within Lakas-NUCD, and more widely within the élite and business community, that Ramos was the only candidate able to defeat the populist Vice-President, Estrada, who had been nominated as the candidate of his own small party, the Partido ng Masang Pilipino (Party of the Filipino Masses). Moreover, Lakas-NUCD was divided over whom to support as party candidate: none of the contenders had wide popular appeal and any choice threatened to split the party. Contrary to early expectations, in December 1997 Ramos finally endorsed the Speaker of the House of Representatives and the most influential figure in the party, Jose de Venecia, in preference to the former Secretary of National Defense, Gen. Renato de Villa, a close associate of Ramos. De Villa promptly left the ruling party and declared his candidature for the Partido para sa Demokratikong Reporma—Lapiang Manggagawa Coalition (Party for Democratic Reform). In early 1998 a former senator, Gloria Macapagal Arroyo, the only candidate seriously to rival Estrada in opinion polls, withdrew from the presidential race, and from her own party, to become Lakas-NUCD's vice-presidential candidate. In June 1997 Estrada's party formed a coalition with two leading opposition parties, the LDP and the NPC. The resultant party, Laban ng Makabayang Masang Pilipino (LaMMP—the Struggle of Nationalist Filipino Masses), endorsed Estrada as its presidential candidate in December.

As the election approached, the only presidential candidates with significant popular followings were Estrada, de Venecia, Senator Raul Roco, the mayor of Manila, Alfredo Lim, and the former Governor of Cebu, Emilio Osmeña. Imelda Marcos, who did not command wide popular support, withdrew her candidature in support of Estrada. Only de Venecia and Estrada benefited from significant party organizations, while Lim had the endorsement of Cardinal Sin, the head of the Catholic Church, and the former President, Aquino.

The election on 11 May 1998 was one of the country's most peaceful (there were 53 deaths) and fair. As the opinion polls had predicted, the presidency was won by the former film actor, Estrada, with 39.9% of the votes cast; his nearest rival was de Venecia, who secured 15.9%. Estrada incorporated his family name into his professional name, becoming President Joseph Ejercito Estrada, and the LaMMP, which gained 66 seats in the House of Representatives (compared with 106 for Lakas-NUCD), was renamed Laban ng Masang Pilipino (LMP, Struggle of Filipino Masses). Exit polls showed that Estrada's strongest vote came from among lower socio-economic groups. Unlike all the other candidates, Estrada had built his public reputation and his campaign around his identity with the *masa* (masses). Despite a comfortable educated middle-class background, he prided himself on his failure to complete his education. Estrada had decades of political experience as a former mayor, senator and Vice-President, but, unlike many other politicians in the post-Marcos era, had not been stigmatized as a 'traditional politician'. Indeed, the 1998 elections continued a post-Marcos trend, the rise of populist politicians and a decline in what had always been a weak party system. Along with Estrada, several other film actors and celebrities were elected to positions of national and local authority. While Lakas-NUCD candidates won a majority of congressional seats, over one-half defected to Estrada's LMP soon after the election results were announced, as had occurred with the LDP after Ramos's election in 1992. Although a high proportion of those in Congress were younger and reputedly more idealistic than was the case in the past, Estrada was likely to encounter significant problems in trying to fulfil his plans to abolish 'pork barrel funds', which had hitherto supplied politicians with the means to reward their particular constituencies.

THE ESTRADA GOVERNMENT

President Estrada's Cabinet and coterie of advisers were reminiscent of the 'rainbow coalition' that marked the early period of Aquino's presidency. Among them were wealthy, mainly ethnic Chinese business executives, former Marcos cronies and political allies, friends from Estrada's mayoral days in San Juan, and activists formerly linked with the communist movement and left-wing non-governmental organizations. In a post-election climate of reconciliation, Ramos accepted a position as Senior Adviser, modelled on that of Singapore's former Prime Minister, Lee Kuan Yew. One of the most powerful figures to re-emerge alongside Estrada was a former close ally of Marcos, Eduardo Cojuangco, to whom Estrada was 'running mate' in 1992. In July 1998 Cojuangco became Chairman and CEO of the San Miguel corporation, the position he held during the Marcos years, and it appeared that the Government was to abandon its legal cases against him and another Marcos crony, Lucio Tan. Estrada announced his intention to disband the Presidential Commission on Good Government, established under Aquino to bring Marcos cronies to justice. Estrada also wanted to reach a compromise with the Marcos family over government claims to Marcos's Swiss bank accounts. However, Estrada prompted a public outcry when he agreed to allow the body of former President Marcos to be buried in the Cemetery of National Heroes and was forced to back down. While Estrada adopted a more conciliatory stance towards the leaders of the Marcos era than his two predecessors, he was also attempting to reassure the business community that he would continue the economically successful policies of liberalization, deregulation and privatization put in place under Ramos. Led by the Secretary of Education, Eduardo Angara (a former corporate lawyer), Estrada's coterie of advisers and cabinet secretaries on economic matters were people widely identified with these policies. Partly in response to the interests of the business community, Estrada also promised to address the problem of crime, and to create a more streamlined and transparent state bureaucracy.

What remained unclear, particularly in a climate of regional economic crisis, was how the Estrada administration would reconcile its free-market economic programme with its widely publicized promises of poverty alleviation, food security and agricultural development. With an impending budget deficit and substantial potential problems in reforming the tax system, the new regime would be struggling to fund the infrastructural and land reform programme it had promised. Attempting to implement some of the pro-poor policies would be the new Secretary for Agrarian Reform and the former head of the proscribed NDF, Horacio Morales. Morales claimed that he would complete the CARP land reform programme, started more than a decade earlier, within the next four years. While some former communists were participating in the Estrada Government, the leadership of what remained of the CPP-NDF condemned the new regime, much as it did that of Aquino and Ramos. Not long after taking office, on 30 July President Estrada approved a human rights agreement which had been negotiated with the NDF under Ramos, and invited the exiled NDF leadership to the Philippines for a resumption of peace negotiations. With the NDF demanding a reversal of the Government's liberalization policies, the next round of negotiations on social and economic reforms was likely to be difficult.

With continued Muslim secessionist pressures in western Mindanao, one of the foremost bills in Estrada's legislative agenda was an amendment to the Organic Act of the ARMM. A plebiscite was scheduled for the southern Philippines in 1999, with the intention of widening the ARMM beyond the four provinces it presently covers. However, with continuing disquiet over the implementation of the Organic Act and Nur Misuari's governorship of the ARMM, there were even threats from two provincial Governors that they would withdraw from the regional body. Alternating hostilities and short-term cease-fire agreements continued to characterize relations between the national Government and the secessionist MILF over the latter half of 1997 and 1998. Despite the 1996 settlement with the MNLF, this period witnessed the largest deployment of military personnel to western Mindanao since the mid-1970s. Nevertheless, both sides seemed committed to ongoing peace talks.

Over the course of his first year in office, President Estrada proved himself a much more adept leader than many of his critics had given him credit for. Not only did he maintain his mass popularity, but he also won the grudging acceptance of many opponents, notably from within the business community. Estrada's coalition party, the LMP (relaunched as the Lapian ng Masang Pilipino—LaMP, Party of the Filipino Masses—in August 1999), continued to hold the great majority of seats in both houses of Congress. While hardly spectacular, the Philippine economy continued its recovery under Estrada, and political stability was maintained. Where Ramos was noted for his work ethic and attention to detail, Estrada proved his skill in cultivating and drawing upon a range of experienced, generally well-respected advisers, who assumed key positions in the government and state bureaucracy. While factional tensions developed between some of the most powerful of these figures—notably the Executive Secretary, Ronaldo Zamora, and the Chief of the Presidential Management Staff, Leonora Vasquez-de Jesus—Estrada was able to negotiate a balance.

Some claimed that this system of particularistic authority had allowed Estrada to reduce bureaucratic inefficiency, but it also exposed him to accusations of cronyism. Rather than pursuing his predecessor's policies of liberalization, some critics argued that Estrada had overseen the creation of new monopolies, for instance in the petrochemical industry and port services, as well as a reconcentration of power in the area of telecommunications. Remaining at the centre of these accusations were former Marcos cronies, Eduardo Cojuangco and Lucio Tan, the majority owner of the heavily-indebted Philippine Airlines. Estrada was also censured for his relative inaction in seeking the recovery of the Marcos family's ill-gained wealth, although the cases against the Marcoses continued to be dealt with through the courts. In March 1999 the Supreme Court upheld a 1990 decision by the Bureau of Internal Revenue against the Marcos heirs for US $600m. in unpaid inheritance taxes. Later in the year an anti-graft court blocked an earlier US $150m. damages agreement between the Marcos family and about 10,000 victims of human rights abuses during the Marcos incumbency. The victims had agreed to abandon further claims in exchange for this settlement, but the court ruled against the release of funds from the US $590m. sequestered by the Government from Swiss bank accounts.

Just as Estrada's record on economic liberalization was uneven and even contradictory, so too was the stance of the mainstream political opposition. Under the leadership of the former President, Aquino, and the head of the Catholic Church, Cardinal Sin, this opposition continued to define itself as the defender of the democratic gains made in the wake of the overthrow of the Marcos regime. Amidst mounting concerns that Estrada's presidency was beginning to undermine these gains, a 'Rally for Democracy' was held on 20 August 1999, demanding an end to cronyism, presidential interference in the print media and government moves to amend the 1987 Constitution. As was the case at the end of the Ramos presidency, the campaign against constitutional change was largely aimed at retaining those provisions limiting an incumbent in political office to a maximum period of six years. Yet the campaign was also directed against Estrada's stated plans to extend economic deregulation by removing those provisions limiting foreign ownership of land and public utilities. Although further rallies were promised, Estrada had the support of most major business associations to continue with these constitutional reforms.

For many, the biggest expectations of the Estrada Government centred on its 'pro-poor' platform. Much was made of this in government rhetoric and in the creation of various state instrumentalities, like the National Anti-Poverty Commission, but the results were disappointing, an outcome that could only partly be attributed to the economic crisis. The principal aim was 'food security', which was to be achieved through agricultural modernization. To this end, the Agricultural and Fisheries Modernisation Act was passed with an increased budget allocation to fund such projects as rural credit and the improvement of irrigation, roads and other infrastructure. To complement this, the enclave development of Subic Bay was reorientated better to provide for its depressed Luzon hinterland. The dramatic increase in agricultural output in the early part of 1999 was, however, largely a result of the natural disasters that marred the previous year, rather than a measure of successful rural reform. There also appeared to have been little progress in the Government's plans to redistribute the remaining 1.3m. ha of land set aside under CARP. One of the few achievements under the pro-poor programme by mid-1999 was the rehousing of some 25,000 urban poor in Manila under a new state-sponsored mortgage scheme.

While Estrada still enjoyed wide popular support, his Government's continued failure to put its pro-poor rhetoric into practice threatened to bring significant political consequences. The communist movement remained small and fragmented, and, although its influence did not compare with that of a decade previously, it was recruiting growing numbers of people disillusioned with the mainstream political process and the social inequalities that continued to affect Philippine society. The NDF withdrew from peace negotiations with the Government in May 1999, following the Senate's ratification of a defence treaty with the USA (see below); Estrada, who had previously expressed dissatisfaction with the progress of the negotiations, and had imposed a deadline of December for a settlement, then assumed a position of outright hostility towards the movement. Nor did the Estrada Government succeed in placating the rural poor who were the major constituency of the MILF in the southern Philippines. Indeed, Estrada's stance towards the MILF vacillated between peace negotiations and promises of agricultural development and declarations of war. In early 1999, for example, the armed forces launched a major offensive on the MILF's main training camp in Maguindanao, with many killed or wounded, and thousands displaced. Peace negotiations resumed, but the national Government's standing among Muslim Filipinos remained tenuous. The national Government continued to delay the ARMM plebiscite it hoped would extend its authority over the region. Though the Estrada Government made little progress in dealing with the communist and Muslim secessionist movements, it achieved success in reducing crime. Most notably, it presided over a sharp reduction in the number of kidnappings, in large part a consequence of measures jointly formulated by Estrada and the Chinese business community.

In the latter months of 1999 and during most of 2000 the Estrada Government came under mounting pressure and criticism. Opponents of planned constitutional change, led by Cardinal Sin and Corazon Aquino, organized a rally involving some 80,000 protesters in Manila on 21 September 1999 to coincide with the anniversary of the declaration of martial law in 1972. This was followed, in October, by a march on the presidential palace by farmers protesting against proposed constitutional reforms that would open up land ownership to foreigners. Eventually, in January 2000, Estrada announced that constitutional change had been put on hold. While Estrada thus placated some opponents, others emerged within the trade union movement, whose wage claims Estrada rejected, and among teachers, whose promised bonuses were withdrawn. Opposition was also mounting among powerful sectors of the business community, represented by the Makati Business Club, which were critical of Estrada's tardiness in pushing further liberalization and privatization reforms through Congress, despite the ruling party occupying 80% of seats in the legislature, many more than those commanded by former President Ramos. To a degree this criticism was addressed in March 2000, when legislation was passed that allowed foreigners to enter the retail industry, and in May, when similar legislation gave foreigners the right to buy into domestic banks. In April the regime even oversaw a significant improvement in what had long been an abysmal record of tax collection.

Yet criticism and disappointment did not abate. Allegations of indecisiveness and inaction also surfaced increasingly in relation to Estrada's 'pro-poor' programme. World Bank funds intended for development projects, ostensibly aimed at benefiting the poor, were withdrawn in December 1999 because they had not been used, and almost a year later, in September 2000, similar funds from the Asian Development Bank and the Japan Bank for International Development were similarly unused, apparently because of government inaction. Earlier, in October 1999, the head of Estrada's mass housing programme, Karina Constantino-David, resigned over the slow pace of implementing housing reform and, in particular, over the growing influence of developers lobbying against it. In a tragedy that underlined ongoing inequalities and state neglect, hundreds of squatters were killed when a rubbish dump collapsed in Quezon City. It was claimed that the mayor's son was implicated in the accident through his interests in the trucking company that controlled the dumpsite. Despite Estrada's continued populist rhetoric, dissatisfaction was growing among the rural and urban poor, his main constituency. In March 2000, for example, oil price rises, which were affecting the whole region, resulted in widespread protests among Manila jeepney drivers, and the Government's continued failure to implement significant agricultural land reform also resulted in growing rural discontent. From a low of 6,000 armed guerrillas in 1994, the communist NPA had, by mid-2000, expanded its numbers to an estimated 9,500, mainly drawn from disaffected rural and urban youth.

Persistent accusations of corruption and favouritism also contributed to Estrada's growing unpopularity, particularly among the middle classes and the élite. Especially damaging, both to Estrada's claims to even-handedness and good economic management, was the accusation that he had intervened to protect one of his business associates from the charge of insider trading in March 2000, the result of which had been the near collapse of the Philippine Stock Exchange. The Estrada Government's suspension of flights to Taiwan in October 1999, in order to protect Philippine Airlines from what it regarded as unfair competition from two Taipei airlines, was also interpreted by some as a favour to its owner, reputed crony, Lucio Tan. With the resultant loss in exports, overseas contract work and Taiwanese investment, other critics simply interpreted the move as economic mismanagement and a retreat from the promised liberalization agenda. While Estrada reshuffled his Cabinet and dismissed several of his closest advisers in January 2000, partly in an effort to address accusations of favouritism and indecision, these allegations continued to plague his Government.

By April 2000 opinion polls showed that Estrada's net approval rating had fallen to 5%, compared with 65% less than one year earlier, and rumours were circulating that he would not complete his term of office and that plans of a coup or an assassination plot were afoot. Yet the principal formal opposition party, Lakas, lacked unity, occupying only a small minority of seats in Congress, and its leader, Vice-President Gloria Macapagal Arroyo, remained in Estrada's Cabinet and declared her continued support for the President. To some degree Lakas's opposition to the Government seemed to coalesce around former President Fidel Ramos, once a senior adviser to Estrada and subsequently one of his most outspoken critics.

Of all the crises faced hitherto by the Philippines under the Estrada regime, the most serious and costly, but also the one that regained some popularity for Estrada, involved the sharp escalation of hostilities in the Muslim south beginning in the early months of 2000. Despite promises of ongoing dialogue and the provision of greater development assistance, the Government's attitude towards the MILF increasingly assumed the profile of a military offensive. In February government aircraft bombed the MILF's Camp Omar and a secondary camp was seized, the military claiming that this was in retaliation for an earlier ambush. In May, after weeks of fierce fighting, government troops took control of an MILF-controlled section of highway near its headquarters in Camp Abubakar, Maguindanao, and continued their attack on MILF positions despite the offer of a cease-fire. By now hundreds had been killed, mostly on the MILF side, and well over 300,000 civilians, mainly

Muslim peasants, had been forced to flee to evacuation centres. In May bombs exploded in two Manila shopping malls, killing one person and wounding others. Though widely attributed to Muslim terrorists, they were just as likely to have been the work of military elements seeking further public support for their war in the south.

In July 2000, after further offensives into MILF-controlled territory, government soldiers finally captured and destroyed much of Camp Abubakar. In what had become characteristic of his political style in this conflict, President Estrada celebrated victory with his officers at Camp Abubakar with roast pork and alcohol. Now in retreat, and with no major camps left intact, the MILF leadership issued a call for a jihad (holy war) against the Philippine state. While government officials and the Catholic Church had long been anxious not to represent the war in the south in religious terms, a dangerous shift seemed to be taking place as more self-proclaimed Christian vigilantes had begun killing and terrorizing ordinary Muslims. Estrada announced plans to turn Camp Abubakar into a special economic zone for the mainly Muslim population of the region and, after initially putting a price on their heads, offered an amnesty to the MILF leadership. Rejecting these moves, but with most of its approximately 15,000-strong fighting force now fragmented, the MILF turned, once again, to guerrilla warfare, its leadership unbowed in its quest for an independent Islamic state.

In the Sulu archipelago to the west of Mindanao, the separate and much smaller secessionist group, Abu Sayyaf, resumed its campaign of terrorism with the kidnapping, in March 2000, of some 30 students and teachers, threatening to kill them unless various demands were met. A few weeks later, in April, as government troops were closing in, one Abu Sayyaf unit took the more dramatic step of kidnapping 21 tourists and staff, many of them European, from the island resort of Sipadan in eastern Malaysia, not far from Abu Sayyaf strongholds in Basilan and Jolo. In further bizarre developments, foreign journalists and a group of Filipino Christian evangelists who travelled to Jolo, with the aim of ending the crisis through prayer, were also taken hostage. In May 15 of the original Filipino hostages were freed by the military, but four others were found dead. By the end of September, after months of periodic military assaults, numerous civilian casualties and intermittent negotiation, involving the Governments of the Philippines, Malaysia, Libya, France, Germany, Finland and South Africa, nearly all of the hostages had been released. Most were freed in exchange for millions of dollars in ransom, much of it paid by the Libyan Government as 'development aid'. While Abu Sayyaf made massive gains in wealth, international publicity and new recruitment, it emerged from the drama less as a group of dedicated revolutionaries than a loose collection of brigands squabbling among themselves over spoils.

In October 2000 the Philippines was engulfed by a political crisis that arose as a result of allegations, made to an investigative committee of the Senate by the Governor of Ilocos Sur, Luis Singson, that President Estrada had accepted large sums of money as bribes from illegal gambling businesses and from provincial tobacco taxes. Despite the President's denial of these allegations in a televised statement to the nation, opposition parties announced their intention to begin, in late October, the process of impeaching the President. Earlier in the month Vice-President Gloria Macapagal Arroyo had announced her resignation from the Cabinet, in which she served as Secretary for Social Welfare and Development. The fact that she did not relinquish the vice-presidency at the same time led to speculation that she was preparing to succeed President Estrada in the event of his forced removal from office. On 13 November Estrada was impeached on charges of bribery, corruption, betrayal of public trust and culpable violation of the Constitution. The Speaker of the House of Representatives, Manuel Villar, ordered the transmittal of the articles of impeachment to the Senate without a vote, on the grounds that more than the required one-third of members had signed a petition endorsing impeachment. Villar and the President of the Senate, Franklin Drilon, were both replaced in their positions as they had resigned from the ruling coalition and urged Estrada's removal. A majority of two-thirds of the Senate, 15 of the 22 members, would be required to remove Estrada (who refused to resign) from office.

While the impeachment trial promised a balanced set of formal procedures to resolve the political uncertainties surrounding the corruption charges levelled against the President, a more volatile, extra-parliamentary process unfolded. The anti-Estrada street protests, which had begun with Singson's accusations, continued as growing numbers of Estrada allies withdrew their support, and public figures, like former President Fidel Ramos, repeated their calls for Estrada's resignation. On 30 December 2000, two weeks after the trial had started, Manila was rocked by five separate bomb explosions, resulting in 22 deaths and many more injured. While government sources blamed Estrada's political opponents or Muslim separatists, others attributed blame to Estrada's supporters, arguing that such violence was intended either to intimidate witnesses or to create an opportunity for the Government to declare martial law. However, the trial continued and damning testimony against Estrada emerged, notably that of Equitable PCI Bank's Senior Vice-President, Clarissa Ocampo, who alleged that she had been instructed to prevent the discovery of a bank account containing millions of dollars controlled by the President. Despite such testimony, the pro-Estrada majority in the Senate blocked a move by the prosecutors to open an envelope said to contain evidence of Estrada's corrupt banking practices.

With prosecutors resigning in protest, the trial came to an abrupt halt, more of Estrada's allies abandoned him, and the centre of political gravity moved to the street protests taking place at Manila's People Power monument, the scene of Marcos's overthrow in 1986. Covert lobbying by political, church and business leaders led the military and the police force to withdraw their support from Estrada in favour of Vice-President Gloria Macapagal Arroyo. Finally, on 20 January 2001, Estrada departed from the presidential palace and Macapagal Arroyo was sworn in as his successor.

THE MACAPAGAL ARROYO GOVERNMENT

Named People Power II by its supporters, the transition was welcomed by many, but it also aroused significant criticism because Estrada still appeared to have majority support, principally among his main constituency of urban and rural poor, and the transition created another political precedent, weakening the institutions of electoral democracy and the stability of the new regime. Although Estrada maintained his claim to the presidency and, hence, to immunity from prosecution, in March 2001 the Supreme Court ruled against both claims, reaffirmed Macapagal Arroyo as President and opened the way for charges of corruption, bribery and economic plunder to be brought against Estrada. In late April Estrada was imprisoned, awaiting trial.

Shortly afterwards, on 1 May 2001, mass protests were again staged in Manila, this time by Estrada's supporters. These disturbances were violent, resulting in several deaths and many injuries. President Macapagal Arroyo responded by declaring a week-long 'state of rebellion', and arrest orders, in response to an alleged aborted coup, were issued for Senators Juan Ponce Enrile and Gregorio Honasan, and for Estrada's former national police chief, Panfilo Lacson. Although Macapagal Arroyo withstood this challenge, doubt remained over her authority: it appeared likely that the President's coalition party, Lakas, would fare badly in elections for 13 of the 24 seats in the Senate, to the House of Representatives and to local administrations, scheduled for 14 May. In the event, however, Macapagal Arroyo emerged from the elections with a majority in both houses of Congress. While the veteran senator, Juan Ponce Enrile, lost his seat, both Honasan and Lacson, who remained in hiding, were returned to the Senate.

While Estrada's removal had much to do with the distaste he aroused among the élite and middle class, these represented President Macapagal Arroyo's principal, but not her only, basis of support: as the winning vice-presidential candidate in 1998 she had demonstrated a broad appeal, gaining the single largest number of votes of any candidate and thereby repeating an earlier performance in 1995, when she had received the most votes in elections to the Senate. In part she was able to take advantage of the fact that her father, Diosdado Macapagal, had been President before Marcos. However, she was also an experienced politician in her own right, having served two senatorial terms before becoming Vice-President; and as Under-

Secretary of Trade and Industry in the Aquino administration. In addition to her élite social and political credentials, Macapagal Arroyo (who had a doctorate in economics) was admired by many in the business community, having drafted many bills aimed at liberalizing the economy during the era of President Ramos. Indeed, figures such as Ramos and organizations such as the powerful Makati Business Club, which favoured ongoing liberalization of the economy, were among Macapagal Arroyo's staunchest supporters. Like former President Aquino, but in contrast to Estrada, Macapagal Arroyo also had a reputation as a devout and conservative Catholic, which gained her strong support from the upper echelons of the Catholic Church.

Following her inauguration in January 2001, President Macapagal Arroyo pledged to return the Philippines to the course that had been planned under the presidencies of Aquino and Ramos: more stable democratic institutions, a campaign against official corruption, a war on poverty and steady economic growth based on policies of increased liberalization. In fulfilling these promises, however, Macapagal Arroyo was confronted by major problems. One was the difficult task of accommodating within her administration the disparate interests and personalities who had supported her in the overthrow of Estrada: the Catholic Church, the business élite, the military, militant trade unions, a range of left-orientated non-governmental organizations and a number of former Estrada cronies. Policies ranging from economic liberalization to family planning aroused opposing views within this broad coalition, with potential impediments to the implementation of the reform agenda that many regarded as necessary in the Philippines. Many of those appointed to Macapagal Arroyo's Cabinet were associates of Aquino and Ramos, such as the former Secretary of the Budget under Aquino and new Secretary of Finance, Alberto Romulo, and the former Secretary of National Defense under Ramos and incoming Chief Security Adviser and Executive Secretary, Gen. (retd) Renato de Villa. However, Macapagal Arroyo was also obliged to rely on many former supporters of Estrada who had changed their allegiance in the final days of his presidency. Notably, Luis Singson, whose exposure of Estrada's bribe-taking prompted the impeachment trial, was appointed as the new Government's gambling consultant. Similarly, Macapagal Arroyo's first National Security Adviser was a retired general, who had been instrumental in gaining the support of the military for Macapagal Arroyo in the final days of Estrada's presidency, but who had also faced allegations of corrupt use of the military's pension fund. Although he was replaced, his appointment prompted the resignation of Secretary of National Defense, Orlando Mercado, himself a former member of the Government under Estrada. Such appointments raised doubts about the new President's capacity to eradicate corruption, a problem compounded by accusations that her husband, Mike Arroyo, had misused public lottery funds. However, the Macapagal Arroyo administration persisted in bringing several corruption charges against Estrada, the most serious being the embezzlement of US $80m. in state funds, a charge punishable by death. The trial began in October 2001.

The politicized class divide that seemed evident during the transition from Estrada to Macapagal Arroyo appeared to fade in the aftermath of the May 2001 elections, but the new President was still faced with the seemingly impossible task of implementing the liberal economic reforms of the Ramos era while, at the same time, addressing the deteriorating circumstances of the rural and urban poor. The Government's commitment to further liberalization appeared to be confirmed by the enactment, on 4 June 2001, of legislation, pending for five years, privatizing electric power supply. With regard to measures to combat poverty, President Macapagal Arroyo made a number of promises, undertaking fully to implement the CARP (see above), in particular its land reform provisions. The President also pledged to implement a housing and livelihood programme for the urban poor, and stated that the Government would grant loans and scholarships to the needy. However, Macapagal Arroyo's administration continued to be impeded by the high budget deficit inherited from the Estrada regime, by a corrupt and inadequate taxation system, by the high cost of servicing the country's foreign debt, and by a national economy severely weakened, both by domestic political turmoil and by the impact of the global economic downturn on major trading partners, such as the USA and Japan.

While investor confidence was stimulated by the change of government in early 2001, crime and rebellion continued to pose problems for the Macapagal Arroyo administration. The incidence of kidnapping for ransom increased sharply. The abductions were usually carried out by Manila-based and other urban syndicates, which mainly preyed on the wealthy Filipino-Chinese community; and by Abu Sayyaf, which targeted both wealthy Western tourists and Christian Filipinos, notably students and workers. The response of the Government was to intensify military intervention, in the case of Abu Sayyaf, and to establish a National Anti-Crime Commission. Despite these measures and a formal policy of non-negotiation, lucrative ransoms continued to be collected, while hostages were frequently killed, particularly by Abu Sayyaf. President Macapagal Arroyo continued to deploy the armed forces in attempts to free hostages held by Abu Sayyaf, but with only limited success.

While the Government continued efforts to combat Abu Sayyaf activities, it virtually abandoned the pursuit of a military solution to the conflicts with the MILF and the NPA. Between 1995 and 2000, in a context of widening wealth differences, the NPA was able almost to double its strength to more than 11,000 armed personnel. In March 2001 President Macapagal Arroyo declared a month-long cease-fire with the NPA and in April, in Norway, commenced formal peace talks with its leadership. Although the armed strength of the MILF had declined as a result of military action by the Estrada regime, it remained a potent force, with a strong recruitment base among ordinary Muslim Filipinos struggling with poverty and prejudice. In July, in Tripoli, Libya, a cease-fire between the Government and the MILF was concluded, and in August, after subsequent negotiations in Malaysia and a state visit to that country by President Macapagal Arroyo, a peace accord was reached. However, sporadic fighting between government and MILF forces continued. Moreover, the plebiscite held on 14 August in Mindanao, which the Government had hoped would increase the authority of the ARMM, was marked by a low turn-out and an emphatic 'no' vote, except in Basilan and Marawi City.

By mid-2002 President Macapagal Arroyo had fulfilled, or made substantial progress in implementing, many of the numerous pledges presented in her first State of the Nation address. Most surprisingly, in view of her own and her predecessor's respective bases of support, she had delivered more material benefits to the poor than had President Estrada. Notably, her Government was reported to have distributed more than 200,000 ha of land under the agrarian reform programme, to have provided security of tenure to over 180,000 urban poor families, and to have constructed some 150,000 houses for workers and others amongst the rural and urban poor. In addition, it had initiated a number of stores selling basic commodities at subsidized prices, and had established a national health insurance system (in which some 2.2m. had enrolled), which was largely designed to benefit the urban poor. The Macapagal Arroyo administration had also maintained its success, under new legislation, in promoting private sector involvement in infrastructural development, most notably in rural electrification, although excessive increases in power prices prompted widespread protests. The encouragement of a more liberalized, privatized economy continued in a number of sectors, and attracted broad support from the local business community.

Despite these successes, government efforts continued to be impeded by a large budgetary deficit, inadequate tax collection and a series of social and political problems. One of these was the continued widespread support enjoyed by detained former President Joseph Estrada, whose trials on charges of corruption and economic sabotage proceeded extremely slowly, protracted by appeals to the Supreme Court and the dismissal of trial judges and defence lawyers, amidst claims by Estrada that he remained the legitimate President. In the mean time, from his military hospital prison, Estrada campaigned for the holding of an immediate presidential election, delivered an alternative State of the Nation speech to that of Macapagal Arroyo, and applied to leave the country for medical treatment. Although the charges against him appeared to be overwhelming, they were not expected to be resolved for some considerable time. While there was no serious prospect of Estrada returning to the presidency, Macapagal Arroyo's authority was, nevertheless, hampered by the manner in which she came to office and this was likely to continue until the next presidential election, scheduled for 2004, an event for which several prospective candidates, including Macapagal Arroyo, appeared to be preparing. Popular opinion polls had generally been unfavourable to her, although in August 2002 her national approval rating in one survey had increased to 55%.

President Macapagal Arroyo's Lakas-NUCD party continued to command a majority in the lower house, but its control of the Senate remained tenuous. Indeed, as a consequence of the defection of one senator in June 2002, and the absence abroad of another, proceedings in the Senate, and consequently the Government's legislative agenda, were suspended for nearly two months. Macapagal Arroyo's presidency also suffered through the resignation at about the same time of two of her leading cabinet members, the Secretary of Foreign Affairs, Teofisto Guingona, and the Secretary of Education, Culture and Sports, Raul Roco, over the government decision to allow the deployment of US troops in the Philippines, and corruption charges, respectively. Both politicians claimed that Macapagal Arroyo's management of these issues were also as much the cause of their resignations, reflecting a criticism that had been levelled more widely at the President's technocratic style of leadership. Some observers, however, argued that these resignations were to be viewed in terms of the political manoeuvring, prior to the 2004 elections. Local government elections, which took place in July 2002, appeared to have little immediate bearing on national politics. Although a number of candidates, officials and others were killed, the authorities announced that the elections had been conducted in a relatively peaceful manner.

The main areas in which President Macapagal Arroyo had little success were in curbing official corruption and escalating crime, particularly on the part of kidnap-for-ransom syndicates. Both posed a growing threat to local and foreign business confidence in the country. In her second State of the Nation address in mid-2002, Macapagal Arroyo identified these problems for special attention. Among other measures, she established a new taskforce (replacing two earlier bodies for combating corruption and crime), transferred the police force to the authority of local government, and authorized the establishment of citizen self-defence units, but with little apparent impact. Corruption was curtailed in the highest political echelons, but continued to prove extremely difficult to eradicate within the state bureaucracy, while law enforcement agencies made little progress against organized crime.

RECENT FOREIGN RELATIONS

Just as the Estrada Government sought to reassure local business that it would continue with Ramos's economic reforms, so it seemed intent on winning international support by promising continuity of policy. Estrada retained Domingo Siazon, Jr, as his Secretary of Foreign Affairs, and announced that he would encourage the Senate to ratify the Visiting Forces Agreement (VFA) with the USA, concluded under Ramos's administration. While Siazon sided with Thailand at the ASEAN meeting in July 1998, in trying to reverse the regional association's policy of non-interference in member countries' internal affairs, Estrada was understood to oppose such a change.

Negotiations over the disputed sovereignty of the Spratly Islands, in the South China Sea, took place in January 1990, July 1991 and mid-1992; all parties agreed to reach a settlement by peaceful means and to develop jointly the area's natural resources. In December 1993 the Philippines and Malaysia agreed to co-operate on fishing rights for the disputed Spratly Islands in the area not claimed by the other four countries. Following a visit to Viet Nam (the first official visit by a Philippine Head of State to that country), Ramos appealed for the six countries with claims to the Spratly Islands (the Philippines, the People's Republic of China, Taiwan, Viet Nam, Brunei and Malaysia) to remove all armed forces from the area. In May 1994 the Philippine Government granted a permit to a US company to explore for petroleum off the coast of the south-western island of Palawan, which covered part of the disputed area of the Spratly Islands. The People's Republic of China reaffirmed sovereignty over the region and lodged an official complaint. In June 1994 de Venecia defused the issue by successfully inviting China to be a partner in the project.

In February 1995 it was revealed that Chinese forces had occupied an area of the Spratly Islands claimed by the Philippines (the first time that China had seized territory in the South China Sea from a country other than Viet Nam). The Philippine Government lodged a formal diplomatic protest with the Chinese Government, which had established several permanent structures on a reef (Mischief Reef) about 200 km from the Philippine island of Palawan. Although the Philippines ruled out the use of force to regain the territory, air and sea patrols in the region were increased, 62 Chinese fishermen and five Chinese vessels were detained in the area and Chinese territorial markers were destroyed. Bilateral discussions in March in Beijing failed to resolve the dispute. Following two days of consultations in August, however, the Chinese Government agreed for the first time to settle disputes in the South China Sea according to international law, rather than insisting that historical claims should take precedence. The Chinese and Philippine Governments issued a joint statement agreeing on a code of conduct to reduce the possibility of a military confrontation in the area. A similar agreement was signed with Viet Nam in November 1995. In March 1996 the Philippines and China agreed to co-operate in combating piracy, which was also a source of tension between the two countries since pirate vessels in the area often sailed under Chinese flags. In May, however, the Philippines, together with other nations in the region, expressed concern, after the Chinese Government announced new territorial claims.

Relations between the Philippines and China improved slightly in late 1996 when the Chinese President, Jiang Zemin, visited the Philippines in November and the two countries agreed to exchange military attachés. However, the construction of an airstrip by the Philippines on one of the Spratly Islands was criticized by China. The entry of Chinese warships into the waters around the Spratly Islands in April 1997 prompted a formal protest from the Philippine Government. Tension was heightened in May, when the Chinese flag, which had been raised on one of the islands, was replaced by the Philippine flag. Several Chinese fishermen, who had entered Philippine waters, were arrested by the Philippine authorities, and in late May negotiations were held between the two countries to resolve the situation. In August it was reported that the Philippine and Chinese Governments had agreed to put aside their territorial dispute and to concentrate on strengthening economic co-operation.

In March 1994 the East ASEAN Growth Area (EAGA), encompassing the southern Philippines, the eastern Malaysian states of Sabah and Sarawak, Brunei, and the Indonesian islands of Sulawesi and the Moluccas (Maluku), was formally conceived.

The escalating conflict over the Spratly Islands constituted the most urgent international issue confronting the Philippines during Estrada's first year of office. In November 1998 the Philippines protested to China over its construction of fort-like buildings on Mischief Reef, which the Philippines claims lies within its exclusive economic zone. The Philippine navy responded by arresting Chinese fishermen for illegal fishing in nearby waters, and impounded their boats. China, however, refused to dismantle the structures. Following unproductive talks between the two Governments in April 1999, relations deteriorated further in May when China claimed one of its fishing vessels had sunk after being deliberately rammed by a Philippine navy boat. A further Chinese fishing vessel sank in a collision with a Philippine navy vessel in July. In the mean time, Philippine relations with fellow ASEAN claimants of the Spratly Islands varied. Joint troop operations in the islands were agreed with Viet Nam, while in mid-1999 Malaysia stepped up its dispute with the Philippines with the construction of a two-storey building on Investigator Shoal, a reef claimed by both countries. The Philippines and Viet Nam drafted a new code of conduct for claimants of the Spratlys, which was approved by ASEAN.

As a result of China's expansionist policy in the South China Sea, relations between the Philippines and the USA improved considerably. Despite protests by the Catholic Church and the nationalist left, the May 1999 session of the Philippine Senate ratified the VFA between the Philippines and the USA, thereby allowing joint military operations to take place in the Philippines. Estrada campaigned strenuously for the ratification, despite his earlier support for the dismantling of the US military bases in 1992. Rationalized as an integral element to the modernization of the Philippine armed forces, the VFA also appeared to be part of the Government's strategy for dealing with its problems in the Spratly Islands and internal conflicts with the MILF and the communist movement.

Notwithstanding the ratification of the VFA, most of President Estrada's activities in foreign affairs focused on the region. All eight of his international visits, undertaken by mid-1999, were to neighbouring countries. While these generally worked at consolidating and building on existing alliances and economic agreements, Estrada also departed from ASEAN convention, raising the ire of the Malaysian Prime Minister, Mahathir Mohamad, by criticizing Malaysia over the arrest and beating of the former Deputy Prime Minister, Anwar Ibrahim.

The Estrada Government's largely inept handling, from March 2000, of the hostage crisis (see above), together with its fruitless suspension of flights to Taiwan (resumed in October), left it with a somewhat tarnished international reputation. On a more positive note, the Philippines did participate successfully in the UN peace-keeping force in East Timor, after the latter had opted for independence from Indonesia. Another achievement was a reduction in tensions with China over the Spratly Islands in the South China Sea. In Manila, in November 1999, China had rejected a code, prepared by ASEAN, for international conduct in the South China Sea, but it subsequently softened its hardline stance by circulating its own modified code. During a state visit to China in May 2000 President Estrada concluded a number of agreements and issued a joint statement with China's President Jiang in which they undertook to seek the peaceful resolution of regional disputes. President Estrada subsequently visited the USA, but was forced to abandon his visit owing to the hostage crisis in the Philippines. Earlier, in January 2000, the first joint military exercises between the USA and the Philippines for five years took place, amid local protests, under the new VFA. Although it was not publicly acknowledged, US military personnel were reported to have been directly involved in attempts to resolve the Abu Sayyaf hostage crisis.

During the remainder of the Estrada period and beyond, under the presidency of Gloria Macapagal Arroyo, Moro separatist activities continued to be at the forefront of international relations. During the latter part of the Estrada period, the MILF was reported to have been training radical Muslim fighters from Indonesia, while the bombing, in August 2000, of the Philippine ambassador's residence in Jakarta was believed by some to have been carried out by Indonesian supporters of the MILF. Conversely, under Macapagal Arroyo who assumed the presidency in early 2001, cease-fire agreements with the MILF were brokered through Libya and Malaysia. During this period President Macapagal Arroyo made her first state visit to Malaysia. Abu Sayyaf had continued to move in and out of Sabah with impunity, and in September 2000 had kidnapped three Malaysians from the resort of Pandanan, adding to the others it still held captive. The military freed a US hostage in April 2001, but in May Abu Sayyaf members took three more US citizens hostage, along with 17 Filipinos, from a luxury resort in Palawan. Abu Sayyaf later claimed to have beheaded one of the US captives. What most drew international attention to the activities of Abu Sayyaf was the hunt for members of the al-Qa'ida (Base) terrorist network of Osama bin Laden, following attacks, allegedly by that organization, on New York and Washington, DC, in September 2001. It was well known that Abu Sayyaf had been assisted by this group, some of whose members from the Middle East had spent time in the Philippines. Declaring her support for the US-led alliance against the al-Qa'ida network, President Macapagal Arroyo agreed to grant the USA access to Philippine military bases and air space, while the Congress adopted legislation aimed at combating 'money laundering'.

A major factor affecting Philippine internal politics and international relations from late 2001 was undoubtedly the US-led 'war on terror'. Not only was there continuing concern over Abu Sayyaf links to the al-Qa'ida terrorist network, but poor law enforcement in the Philippines appeared to make the country a potential haven for international terrorists. However, anti-Islamic sentiment among the majority Christian population and President Macapagal Arroyo's strident support for the US Government's position also made the Philippines the initial focus of the new US military presence in South-East Asia. In December the USA pledged US $100m. in military aid. In February 2002 660 US troops were deployed to the south as part of the six-month Balikatan campaign with the Philippine military to suppress Abu Sayyaf operations, although their role was to be limited to training, advice, surveillance and infrastructure development. While their presence attracted sharp criticism from the left, and from some nationalist politicians, including Vice-President Guingona, surveys indicated widespread popular support, at least among the Christian population. Despite concern that the US military presence would turn local secessionist sentiments in the Muslim south into popular support for the cause of al-Qa'ida, this did not appear to have transpired, in large part since US troops did not engage in direct combat and were concentrated in Basilan, Abu Sayyaf's stronghold, rather than in areas under the influence of the wider secessionist movement, led by the MILF. At the end of the six months the Balikatan campaign was declared a success, with the total of active Abu Sayyaf members reported to have declined from 4,000 to about 100. A number of Filipino military officers were expected to be court-martialled for collusion with Abu Sayyaf, but overall the government forces stationed in the south were believed to have improved in fighting power and discipline. While some hostages held by Abu Sayyaf were released during the campaign, at least two were killed, one US national and one Filipino, and other hostages were seized just before and soon after the campaign's completion. Indeed, two Filipinos were beheaded shortly after the departure of US forces. At the height of the campaign, US troops in the south were reinforced to number about 1,000, while a further 17,000 were engaged in military manoeuvres in the north. In October eight people were killed and some 150 injured in two bomb attacks in Zamboanga City, which were widely attributed to Abu Sayyaf. A further three people were subsequently killed when a bomb exploded on a bus in Manila. Five suspected members of Aby Sayyaf were arrested later that month.

The Macapagal Arroyo Government's co-operation with the US anti-terrorist effort also extended to the closer scrutiny of possible 'front' organizations involved in covert al-Qa'ida operations in the Philippines. In May 2002 the Government signed an agreement with Indonesia and Malaysia, which was aimed at preventing cross-border terrorist activity, with particular focus on members of Jemaah Islamiah, an organization reported to be furthering al-Qa'ida objectives in South-East Asia. In January, and again in March, the Philippine authorities arrested several Indonesian nationals suspected of producing or transporting bombs, while at the same time arrests of foreign nationals were made elsewhere in the region. In November 2001 the Malaysian Government arrested, and then transferred to the Philippine authorities, the former MNLF leader, Nur Misuari, who earlier had led a violent, but unsuccessful, attack on a military outpost in Jolo, after being forced to relinquish his position as Governor of the ARRM. Malaysia also continued to take a significant role in the peace negotiations between the Philippine Government and the MILF.

A further series of peace talks began between the Government and the MILF in October 2001, and in May 2002 an agreement was reached, whereby the Government would provide reparations for damaged MILF property and establish a state-funded aid body, to be administered by the MILF, in order to assist the many thousands of Muslims who had been displaced by fighting in Mindanao. This agreement even included plans to relinquish control of the MILF stronghold at Abubakar for non-military purposes, but these plans were abandoned owing to strong opposition from within the military and Congress. Moreover, despite the cease-fire agreement negotiated in 2001, sporadic military encounters continued, and by late 2002 the pace of peace discussions had slowed. Indeed, the future of relations between the Government and the MILF, and the Macapagal Arroyo doctrine of a non-military solution came under increasing pressure, following repeated claims that the MILF, rather than Abu Sayyaf, had the strongest links to international terrorist groups.

While regional inter-government co-operation was prompted by the need to address the increasing threat of transnational terrorist activity, the latter also intensified some long-standing disputes. In an attempt to exercise tighter control over its population and borders, the Malaysian Government introduced stringent new immigration laws in August 2002, aimed at the estimated 80,000 illegal Filipino workers and residents, most of them Muslims, who had long been settled in Sabah. As thousands of Filipinos were assembled in detention centres and deported to the Philippines, reports emerged of their abuse and mistreatment by the Malaysian authorities. Also confronted with the difficult prospect of accommodating these large numbers, mainly in Mindanao, the Philippine authorities protested to Malaysia, while some Filipino politicians urged a revival of the Philippines' long-standing claims on Sabah. Following the intervention of President Macapagal Arroyo and the protests of employers and human rights' activists in Malaysia, Prime Minister Mahathir suspended the mass deportations in early September.

Also affected by the US-led 'war on terror' were the CPP and NPA, which had become more active under the Macapagal Arroyo presidency. Apart from conventional guerrilla warfare, the NPA was believed to have supported some 400 candidates in the July 2002 local elections. It was also reported that NPA militia had been instructed to open fire on US troops at the start of the Balikatan campaign, although this did not, in effect, transpire. The exiled leader of the NPA, Joma Sison, as rumoured to have urged Filipino Muslims to join his movement. In August, following the renewed campaign against Abu Sayyaf, most of the Filipino troops stationed in the south were redeployed for a further campaign in areas known to contain NPA strongholds. At the same time the US authorities declared the NPA to be an international terrorist organization, thereby subjecting their supporters in the USA to the same legal sanctions as those associated with al-Qa'ida. Soon afterwards, the Dutch, British and Canadian authorities followed the US Government's example in freezing the assets of NPA groups and of their leaders, including Sison and many others who were exiled in the Netherlands. Although there had been ongoing efforts on both sides to reactivate peace talks between the Philippine Government and the CPP, Sison maintained that discussions would not resume while Macapagal Arroyo remained President. At the same time as these developments, various left-wing groups that had broken away from the CPP in the years following the overthrow of Marcos, announced that they were to unite as the Partido ng Manggagawang Pilipino (PMP—Filipino Workers' Party).

Economy

EDITH HODGKINSON

Since independence in 1946 the economic performance of the Philippines has almost constantly fallen below expectations. The Philippines shared many characteristics with the countries of the Far East that graduated to newly-industrialized status in the decades after the Second World War (Taiwan, the Republic of Korea and Singapore), with the added advantage of a plentiful natural resource base and a potentially enormous domestic market. Yet it only intermittently matched the rapid economic expansion recorded by the 'tiger' economies of the region, both the initial group and the second group of the 1980s and 1990s (comprising Thailand, Malaysia and Indonesia). The less rapid progress of the Philippines' economy was a result of major and basic structural deficiencies. Among these were: a dependence on imported intermediate and capital goods, following a period of protectionism; a grossly inequitable distribution of wealth; and a tendency for wealth to be acquired through ownership of monopoly privileges, derived from connections with influential persons, rather than through the development of productivity and efficiency. The Government that came to power after the overthrow of Ferdinand Marcos in 1986 espoused policies that would mitigate these features, and they were pursued with greater vigour and success by the administration of Gen. Fidel Ramos, who succeeded President Aquino in mid-1992. The economy was developed through the dismantling of domestic monopolies and the liberalization of the terms of entry of foreign goods and capital (notably in the banking sector). With investment rising, boosted by inflows of funds from the Philippine community overseas, and strong external markets for the country's manufactures, growth in gross national product (GNP) increased steadily in the mid-1990s, reaching 7.2% in 1996, and the Philippines seemed set at last to match the very rapid growth of other economies in the region, and to achieve newly-industrialized status by the end of the decade.

That movement was interrupted by the regional financial and currency crisis in 1997. The Philippines was forced to abandon the *de facto* pegging of the peso to the US dollar (which had made investment in Philippine bonds attractive and helped reduce inflation). The consequent depreciation of the currency could be restrained only by a steep increase in domestic interest rates. The much higher cost of credit, accompanied by reduced supply, as banks sought to reduce their exposure to bad debts, had a severe adverse effect on investment. While economic growth was sustained through late 1997 (the rise in GNP was reduced to 5.3% over the full year) and into early 1998 by continued dynamic foreign demand for Philippine manufactures, the drought associated with El Niño (a warm current, which periodically appears along the Pacific coast of South America, disrupting the usual weather patterns over a large area) caused a sharp fall in agricultural output in 1998. Finally the growing economic difficulties in Japan, a major export market and leading source of capital, meant that GNP growth reached only 0.4% in 1998. An improvement in agriculture raised GNP growth to 3.7% in 1999, and the pace of economic recovery quickened in 2000, when growth of 4.5% was registered. In line with its record of rather less dramatic rates of change than the region as a whole, GNP responded less markedly to the deceleration in the growth of US and, hence, world demand in 2001, increasing by 3.4% in that year and by 4.9% in the first three months of 2002. This resilience, despite the sharp fall in export earnings throughout the period, owed much to the strength of agricultural growth and rising remittances from Philippine workers overseas. With export earnings increasing throughout the second quarter of 2002, and some slowing in the agricultural sector notwithstanding, the expectation was that economic growth over the whole year would slightly exceed the 2001 rate.

GROWTH WITHOUT REFORM, 1946–85

On independence in 1946 the Philippines maintained the broad character of its economic policies as a US colony: freedom of trade with the USA, preferential entry for Philippine commodities into the US market and preferential treatment for US investment in the Philippines. However, with the vast increase in demand after the ravages of war, and despite reconstruction aid from the USA, import spending rose to levels far beyond the country's financing capacity. Consequently, import controls were imposed in 1949, and the country adopted the industrialization by import-substitution policy, which was to become the pattern among newly-independent developing countries. Very high tariffs on manufactured goods and quantitative controls were combined with a preferential exchange rate for the import of intermediate and capital goods, and interest 'ceilings', which underpriced capital. This set of measures served as a strong stimulus to manufacturing production, which grew by 12% a year in the 1950s, making the Philippines both the most industrialized country in South-East Asia by the end of the decade and the fastest-growing economy. The misuse of resources engendered by the policy of import-substitution, notably the recourse to capital-intensive processes in a country where labour was skilled and low-cost, was not immediately perceived. This was due to strong international prices for the country's agricultural exports, while the low population-to-land ratio allowed an expansion in the area under cultivation and, therefore, an increase in production. The Philippines was thus able to earn the foreign exchange needed to fund its dependence on imports.

However, at the beginning of the 1960s the prospects for a sustained growth in export earnings faded as a land constraint emerged. With rising imports threatening to create a balance-of-payments crisis, the Philippine Government took two significant steps towards stimulating export-manufacturing based on the country's factor endowment. The peso was devalued by around 100% and exchange controls were eliminated. However, other protectionist features were retained: high tariff rates, quantitative controls, and regulated and low interest rates. Thus, there was little incentive to switch from capital-intensive, domestic-orientated activities to labour-intensive export manufacture.

It was only after the introduction of martial law in 1972 that the Government implemented an effective policy, mainly through tax and tariff incentives, of encouraging export manufacture and attracting foreign investment. Coinciding with a period of buoyant world demand, the policy proved highly successful, increasing earnings from non-traditional manufactures by 25%–30% a year in 1973–78. With commodity prices booming in the 1970s, the rate of economic growth accelerated to an average 6.9% a year in 1973–79.

This record of success, and the ready availability of foreign funds as commercial banks sought to recycle 'petrodollars', prompted the Government to embark on a programme to widen the country's industrial base. The initiation of large-scale, mainly heavy industrial, projects was essentially aimed at enhancing self-sufficiency (only one was directed at export markets), but required massive inputs of foreign capital and technology. As a result, the foreign debt rose eightfold between 1975 and 1982. The debt-service payments required proved unsustainable when the international recession of the early 1980s brought a slowing in the growth in demand for Philippine manufactures. As a result, two-fifths of the country's foreign-exchange earnings were needed to cover the debt repayment and interest bill in 1982.

The deterioration in external economic conditions brought into sharp relief one of the characteristics of economic management under President Marcos: the concentration of ownership and control among members of the President's family and a group of close associates, in a system that came to be dubbed 'crony capitalism'. Government-mandated marketing monopolies were set up for the coconut and sugar industries, while subsidies and special privileges (including preferential access to bank credit and government guarantees for foreign borrowing) were awarded to companies owned by 'crony' interests. The failings of this pattern of economic management were masked when the economy was expanding rapidly, but as growth slowed sharply in the early 1980s, to an average 2.4% a year in 1981–83, many of the 'crony' companies, including commercial banks, found themselves in severe financial difficulties. As the economy moved into deep recession in 1984 and 1985, with GNP contracting by 8.9% and 7.0% respectively in those years, a number of companies collapsed. This in turn undermined the viability of the big government banks, whose portfolios included a high and growing proportion of non-performing assets, and which consequently recorded massive losses in these two years.

The rapid decline in the economy in 1983–85 was, however, precipitated by a political event: the assassination of President Marcos's leading opponent, Benigno Aquino, Jr, on his return from exile in August 1983. This immediately produced a collapse of confidence both domestically, prompting a flight of capital, and among the country's foreign creditors, who refused to renew short-term financing. The already fragile balance-of-payments situation thus tipped into crisis.

The first set of measures introduced to address the crisis were emergency ones, designed to halt the collapse of foreign-exchange reserves. A moratorium was declared on the repayment of external debts, rigorous exchange controls were imposed and the peso was devalued by almost one-quarter. This devaluation, which had long been urged by the International Monetary Fund (IMF) and the World Bank, allowed negotiations to begin on a rescheduling of foreign debt and the provision of new funds by the IMF and the commercial banks. The Philippines was required to implement a severe austerity programme, with harsh reductions in government spending, restrictions on the liquidity of banks and a steep rise in interest rates.

In addition to its short-term stabilization objective, the programme agreed with the IMF had a long-term aim: the development of a more efficient economy, based on the exploitation of the country's factor endowment, in labour and in agricultural resources. The distortions represented by an overvalued currency, high import tariffs and quantitative controls, and interest subsidies were to be removed, and the role of market forces enhanced through the reduction of government intervention in the economy, specifically through the ending of the agricultural monopolies and the restructuring of government financial institutions.

A PERIOD OF INCOMPLETE RESTRUCTURING

Economic reform was only intermittently implemented by President Marcos, since it weakened the power system he operated. It was adopted with greater commitment after his overthrow in February 1986. Within months the coconut and sugar marketing monopolies were dismantled and a wide range of tax exemptions eliminated. Non-performing assets were removed from the portfolios of the government banks, their operations rationalized and their special privileges removed to place them on an equal footing with private banks. Government corporate holdings were put up for sale.

Supported by the country's international creditors (see Foreign Debt, below), the new Government was able to embark on a rapid restimulation of the economy, mainly through an increase in spending on infrastructure and on an emergency rural employment programme. The boost from the fiscal side was reinforced by the sharp improvement in world coconut prices in both 1986 and 1987. With demand for Philippine export manufactures strong, and the Government committed to stimulating the private sector, in the late 1980s investment began to improve. The economy entered into another period of strong expansion, with GNP growth averaging 6% a year in 1987–89.

This process was abruptly halted at the end of 1989. The economy encountered the familiar problem of a burgeoning deficit on the current account of the balance of payments, as import growth continued to exceed export expansion. From a modest US $390m. in 1988, the deficit had risen to US $2,695m. in 1990. While debt restructuring by the country's commercial creditors, and new funds from official sources in 1989–90 (see below), reduced both total debt and the cost of servicing it, the balance of payments was adversely affected by the massive rise in the price of petroleum imports, following the Iraqi invasion of Kuwait in August 1990. The most serious reverse, however, was the severe shortfall of power in Luzon, the country's industrial centre (see below). The situation was compounded by the austere budgetary stance, which was the condition of IMF support, and GNP growth declined to about 1%–2% in 1991–93. It was only after electricity-generating capacity was rapidly expanded to meet the supply deficit that economic growth improved, increasing to just over 5% in both 1994 and 1995, and rising to 7.2% in 1996.

This surge in growth owed much to the major structural reforms that were implemented by the Ramos administration. These included the removal of nearly all foreign-exchange controls, the termination of monopolies in telephones, aviation and inter-island shipping and the ending of the 45-year ban on the entry of foreign banks. Privatization, which had been a major feature of the Aquino administration (30% of the country's largest bank, the government-owned Philippine National Bank—PNB, was transferred to the private sector, and the national airline was privatized), was pursued with increased vigour. The programme was extended to encompass strategic activities, including petroleum-refining and -marketing, and steel manufacture, with the aim of attracting the technology and access to markets of major foreign companies in addition to their capital. Moreover, the private sector was brought in to relieve one of the most serious constraints on economic growth, the inadequacy of the physical infrastructure, which could not be corrected by the public sector while budget finances were still precarious. The 'fast track' programme of capacity expansion that resolved the electricity supply crisis in 1993 employed a system of build-operate-transfer (BOT) schemes, under which private firms finance the installation of new facilities and contract to operate them for a fixed period, at the end of which they are transferred to government ownership. The same mechanism (or its development, the build-operate-own contract) was extended to other sectors, such as roads and commuter railways. Not all the liberalization targets had been achieved by the end of the Ramos administration in mid-1998, but the economy had been transformed from its state in 1986 when President Marcos left office. Although the new President, Joseph Estrada, pledged to continue economic liberalization, progress was slow during his period in office. While the ban on foreign participation in retail trade was lifted in early 2000, the long-mooted privatization of the state-owned electricity utility, the National Power Corporation, remained mired in congressional debate. One significant privatization—the disposal of the Government's residual equity in the PNB—was conducted in a way that confirmed growing unease about a recrudescence of 'crony capitalism'. Major supporters of the President's election campaign were repeatedly accorded favourable treatment. One former Marcos crony had voting control over sequestered equity returned to him, allowing him to take over the country's leading food conglomerate, while another had a massive tax evasion case abandoned and his investment in the former state airline underpinned by the Government's suspension of the country's aviation agreement with Taiwan. A new feature was the incoherence and inconsistency of policy implementation, as the President's detached style of government allowed personal rivalries to develop unchecked within the administration. Disquiet about the Estrada presidency grew markedly during early 2000, after he was alleged to have intervened to protect a close friend charged with share manipulation on the Philippine Stock Exchange (PSE). Finally persistent rumours of corruption at the highest level culminated in October of the same year when the President was accused of accepting profits from illegal gambling and diverting tobacco support funds. His replacement in January 2001 by Gloria Macapagal Arroyo prompted hopes of more effective government, and in June Congress finally approved the Electricity Power Industry Reform Act, which provided for the privatization of the state electricity utility. More significantly, the Government achieved its principal policy target, with the restoration of budgetary control, after a sharp increase in the fiscal deficit under President Estrada. (In 2001 the fiscal balance was 1.5% higher than the targeted level.)

POPULATION AND EMPLOYMENT

The rate of population growth has slowed in recent decades, from an annual average of 3% in the 1960s to a rate of 2.4% per year in the 1980s and 2.2% in 1990–2000. This reflected a decline in the birth rate, owing in part to birth-control programmes first implemented under the Marcos Government.

The rise in population numbers was not equalled by an increase in employment opportunities, and the constraint of land caused a significant migration to the urban areas, which failed to provide enough new jobs to absorb the addition to the labour force. Unemployment fluctuated between 7% and 10% in the 1990s, while underemployment was estimated to affect about one-fifth of the population. The rate of unemployment declined from 10.1% in 2000 to 9.8% in 2001. Unemployment would be greater were it not for the high level of emigration. Some 60,000–65,000 people a year emigrated officially in the first half of the 1990s, with the total declining to an annual average of 43,500 in 1998–2000. Much higher numbers (not classified as emigrants) undertake contract work abroad; in the 1990s overseas placements of Filipino workers averaged about 700,000 a year, equivalent to around 2% of the labour force. A total of some 6m. Filipinos were estimated by the Government to be living abroad in 1995.

AGRICULTURE, FORESTRY AND FISHING

In 2001 the agriculture, forestry and fishing sector contributed about 15.1% of gross domestic product (GDP) and engaged 37.4% of the employed labour force. Its share of GDP has been exceeded by that of manufacturing since the 1980s, and as early as the mid-1970s the agricultural sector had lost its primacy as export earner. The farming system is extremely diverse and includes a large number of rice, maize and coconut holdings that are farmed by agricultural tenants or workers, as well as sugar *haciendas* and large plantations, devoted mainly to non-traditional export crops such as bananas and pineapples.

During the 1970s agricultural production expanded by an annual average of 5%, stimulated by measures to achieve self-sufficiency in food grains as well as by the rise in the area under crops, particularly through the clearing of virgin forest in Mindanao. Growth slowed to an average of 2% a year in the following decade, as a land constraint emerged, producer prices fell under the marketing monopolies operated by associates of President Marcos, and government investment in infrastructure favoured urban areas. While limited improvement in rural incomes did result from measures introduced by the Aquino Government, including the removal of export taxes on agricultural commodities and the dismantling of monopolies, the sector overall has remained one of low growth, averaging just more than 2% per year in the 1990s.

Rice and maize are the principal food crops, the former accounting for around one-quarter of the cultivated area. The introduction of higher-yielding strains of rice, together with an expansion in supplies of fertilizer and pesticides, has made the country self-sufficient in rice (except in years of unfavourable weather conditions) since the late 1970s. An expansion in the area under cultivation, as well as an improvement in yields, brought the country self-sufficiency in maize for human consumption by the mid-1980s.

Coconuts are the most important cash crop, and the Philippines is the world's leading exporter of coconut products. Between 1975 and 1982 there was a rapid rise in annual output, from 1.9m. metric tons (copra equivalent) to 3.4m. tons. After 1983 output declined, largely owing to the ageing of trees, which reduced overall yields. A major replanting and rehabilitation programme was initiated in 1988, supported by World Bank funds, and began to have an impact in the mid-1990s, with output returning to 2m.–3m. tons a year.

Sugar, which was once a leading export crop, is now of minor importance. For many years a guaranteed share of the US market, at a fixed price, shielded the Philippine sugar industry from the effects of a long-term decline in productivity, but a lengthy period of world price weakness prompted a switch to higher-value crops and fish farming (in particular shrimps for export to Japan) in the early and mid-1980s. With rising domestic demand, imports of sugar have become necessary to supply the premium US market. Sugar has been exceeded as a dollar earner by bananas and pineapples, mainly grown on plantations developed in Mindanao by multinational companies. The production of mangoes and rubber has also grown in significance.

Agrarian Reform

One of the major requirements for sustained and broadly-based economic growth in the Philippines is land reform. Since independence, pressure for such a redistribution of resources has been continually resisted by the landed élite, who also constitute the political élite. In 1972 President Marcos launched a limited programme of agrarian reform covering land under rice and maize in holdings of 7 ha or more. By 1986 more than one-half of the 600,000-ha area covered by the programme still remained to be distributed. The Comprehensive Agrarian Reform Programme (CARP), introduced by the Aquino Government in 1988, provided for the redistribution of 4.5m. ha, or about 55% of all agricultural land, in three stages over a period of 10 years. The first phase involved unredistributed land covered by the Marcos programme and land held by the state—a total of some 1.09m. ha. The second phase, begun in 1989, involved private landholdings exceeding 50 ha, and the third phase, covering the vast majority of land to be redistributed, began in 1992. Landowners were allowed to retain 5 ha and their direct heirs 3 ha, but large estates could remain intact if they were made into corporate holdings with stock transfers substituting for land. Owing to obstruction by vested interests and reductions in government funding for landholder compensation, redistribution has remained well below target, and the completion date has been extended to 2008.

Fishing

The Philippines has extensive fishing resources, both marine and inland. Production increased rapidly to account for about 5% of GDP by the late 1980s. The fishing sector became a major source of foreign-exchange earnings, principally through the export of shrimps and prawns to Japan. While both freshwater ponds and most of the marine waters have not been fully developed, productivity in some areas has deteriorated because of pollution of coastal waters as the result of population growth, mining activities and destructive methods of exploitation. The infrastructure remains highly inadequate. Nevertheless, the total catch increased gradually in the 1990s, reaching 2.2m. in 1999.

Forestry

Forests were in the past one of the country's major resources, but suffered very severe depletion as the result of population pressure, shifting cultivation, illegal logging and inadequate reafforestation. In 1945 there was 15m. ha of virgin forest, but by 1999 the area was estimated at only 700,000 ha. A ban on logging in virgin forest, introduced in 1991, has proved largely ineffectual, and there is a prospect of its total elimination by 2010.

Government policy in the 1980s was to phase out exports of hardwood logs in order to stimulate the development of the local processing industry. An export ban has been in place since 1986, but substantial quantities of logs were believed to be illegally exported, with earnings put at about US $800m. a year in the late 1980s, more than three times the level of officially recorded lumber export earnings. The latter have fallen sharply, to US $20m. in 1999 and US $44m. in 2000. This also reflects the overall decline in output as the resource base has narrowed.

MINING

The Philippines has extensive deposits of gold, silver, copper, nickel, lead and chromium. Lesser, but still important, minerals include zinc, cobalt and manganese. However, around one-quarter of the land area remains to be surveyed and some of the richest deposits are unexploited. During the 1970s the Government gave high priority to the development of minerals, which resulted in a rapid growth of the sector. Since the mid-1980s, however, mining has been in overall decline, owing to weak prices and an unstable system of taxes and incentives. Output of copper, the country's leading mineral product, had declined to about one-eighth of its 1980 level by 2001, at 30,600 metric tons. The Philippines is also a significant producer of gold. Largely a by-product of copper mining, its output tends to reflect trends in the copper sector as well as in world prices.The non-metallic sector performed better in the 1980s, with the output of coal stimulated by energy conversion in the cement and mining industries. In 1993 production reached a peak of 1,531,000 metric tons, about six times the level of 1979, but has since averaged some 1.2m. tons per year.

While prospects for the sector's development have improved as the result of a mining law introduced in 1995, which permits 100% foreign ownership under special terms, investment remains low because of bureaucratic delay and legal challenges. In 2001 mining and quarrying accounted for 0.6% of GDP and engaged 0.3% of the employed labour force.

ENERGY

In 1973, at the time of the first major increase in international petroleum prices, the Philippines was dependent on imported oil for 95% of its energy supply. This level had fallen to 50%–55% by the late 1990s and early 2000s, reflecting the development of various domestic sources of energy, notably coal, hydroelectric power, geothermal steam, and non-conventional sources (mainly bagasse, agricultural waste and dendrothermal). Dependence was expected gradually to decline from 2002, with the beginning of production, in late 2001, at offshore gasfields.

The contribution of domestic petroleum production has been very limited. Petroleum deposits in commercial quantities were discovered off the island of Palawan in 1977. Production reached a peak in its first year, in 1979, of 42,000 barrels per day (b/d), but this level was not maintained, owing to operational difficulties. Despite the entry into production of other commercial oilfields in the 1980s and early 1990s, production had declined to about 1,000 b/d in 2000–01. A recovery was expected from the development of the offshore gasfields at Malampaya, where experimental operations in December 2001 yielded 8,000 b/d. Natural gas reserves at this field are estimated at more than 3,000,000m. cu ft, and production commenced in September 2001, with full commercial operations starting in 2002, serving three power plants with a total capacity of 2,700 MW.

The exploitation of geothermal resources has been actively pursued: in 2001 the Philippines had an installed capacity of 1,931 MW (a total exceeded only by the USA). Considerable resources remain to be exploited: some estimates suggest that the total potential exceeds 35,000 MW.

To reduce the country's dependence on imported petroleum, a nuclear power station, with a generating capacity of 620 MW, was constructed in Bataan, Luzon. Due to enter operation in 1986–87, this highly controversial project (it was located near a seismic fault) was abandoned by the incoming Aquino Government. The failure of the Aquino Government to replace the Bataan scheme with other additions to power capacity exacerbated the emerging power shortage on Luzon island (the three island grids are not connected) as accelerating economic growth increased consumption. Interruptions in electricity supply in the Manila region in 1990–91 were estimated to have reduced GNP by close to 1%. The incoming Ramos administration embarked on a 'fast track' programme to expand electricity-generating capacity, which had achieved its aim of ending daily blackouts in Luzon by late 1993. This investment in capacity proved excessive, as demand growth diminished from 1996, and installed capacity was 2,000 MW higher than the required level in 2002.

MANUFACTURING

Philippine manufacturing developed relatively early, reaching 22%–25% of GDP by the 1960s, a share it has since broadly maintained. (Manufacturing contributed 22.8% of GDP and engaged 9.6% of the employed labour force in 2001.) The sector was supported initially by exchange controls and, from the early 1960s, by tariffs and import quotas, which tended to promote production of consumer goods for the domestic market. Manufacturing for the export market was stimulated from the 1970s by the introduction of tax and duty exemptions for export producers and the establishment of four export-processing zones where 100% foreign ownership was permitted and companies were allowed to pay below the minimum wage. As a consequence there was a rapid growth of labour-intensive manufacturing, mainly textile products and electronic components, produced in many cases by Filipino enterprises working for multinationals on a subcontracting basis (these industries remained heavily dependent on imported inputs).

In the early 1980s the Government implemented a programme to develop the country's intermediate and heavy industrial base through 11 capital-intensive projects. Four of the 11 projects originally envisaged had become operational: a copper smelter, a coco-chemical manufacturing project, a phosphate fertilizer project and the manufacture of diesel-engine components. Nevertheless, despite these developments and the elimination of import quotas in the late 1980s and extensive reductions in tariffs since, Philippine manufacturing remains orientated towards the provision of consumer goods for the domestic market. Its performance has thus been very responsive to movements in domestic demand. The external market for Philippine manufacturers is, nevertheless, significant, with the export-processing zone pattern replicated in other zones and industrial estates established by the private sector since the early 1990s. In 2000 the zones registered exports of just less than US $20,000m., representing almost one-half of the country's export receipts. The four, longer-established government-run zones accounted for only one-third of these exports, since the privately-operated zones and estates had for some time been attracting most of the new investment. A major contribution to manufacturing, as well as to services such as tourism, transhipment and ship-repairing, is due to be made by the economic zone and free port at the former US naval base at Subic Bay. Another former US base, at Clark, is being developed similarly, and is centred on its airport facilities. However, the 1997 regional financial crisis, the cyclical downturn in the market for electronics (the major activity in this sector) and competition from other, lower-cost countries depressed the level of new investment. In 2001 approved investments in the export-processing zones (excluding Subic Bay and Clark) were valued at US $1,732m., less than one-third of the US $5,423m. recorded in 1997.

INFRASTRUCTURE

The country's physical infrastructure is characterized by marked regional disparity, which both reflects and reinforces the concentration of modern economic activity in Metropolitan Manila and regions immediately adjacent. Its efficiency was in decline from the mid-1980s as the result of reductions in budget expenditure under the austerity programme of that period. While considerable improvements were made in the 1990s as BOT contracts were used to mobilize private funds (both domestic and foreign) for investment in the transport infrastructure, overall the poor state of physical infrastructure remained a major constraint on economic growth.

The road network in the Philippines accommodates about 60% of freight and 80% of passenger traffic. In 2000 there were 201,994 km of roads, of which 30,013 km were highways and 49,992 km were secondary roads; an estimated 42,419 km of the network were paved. Feeder roads are in poor condition. However, new urban highways are being built in Metropolitan Manila and an extension to Subic.

The rail system is limited, with 740 km of single-line track in Luzon, and also in a poor state of repair. The network carried only an estimated 321,000 passengers in 1999. A mass transit system began operation in Manila in 1984, and has been undergoing extensive expansion since the late 1990s; an average 100m.–130m. passenger journeys per year were estimated in 2001.

The seaport network services about 40% of freight and carries 10% of passenger traffic. The most important ports are Manila (which handled 58.7m. metric tons of cargo in 1996) and Cebu (which handled 11.1m. tons in 1995); both have container facilities. The inter-island fleet is old, safety regulations are poor and maritime navigational aids inadequate.

There are about 90 national airports; international airports include Manila, Cebu and General Santos. The former US military facility at Clark Air Base has been developed as a joint principal airport, with the Ninoy Aquino International Airport at Manila, which is being modernized and upgraded.

FINANCE AND BANKING

During the 1970s there was a steady rise in government expenditure, associated with ambitious programmes of public investment, often in urban-based capital-intensive projects, in an effort to sustain growth. This trend became even more marked during the early 1980s, as government financial institutions intervened to rescue private corporations from bankruptcy (many of them connected with associates of Marcos). Tax revenues failed to keep pace with the expanded expenditure, largely because of the proliferation of exemptions, poor compliance, inefficiency in tax administration and widespread evasion, generating persistent and rising fiscal deficits. Although expenditure was curtailed in the final years of the Marcos regime, as a condition of IMF support during the crisis years, the contraction in the economy in that period depressed revenue, so that by 1986 the budget deficit was still slightly above the 1982 result, at 4.2% of GNP. The new Government undertook to reduce the deficit, both absolutely and as a percentage of GNP. With occasional backsliding because of unforeseeable pressures on the spending side—such as the oil price subsidy to counter the surge in world prices in 1990 and the Mt Pinatubo volcanic eruption in 1992—this objective was attained. Income was temporarily boosted by asset sales, such as the highly successful privatization of the country's national airline in 1992.

Under the administration of President Ramos,who took office in mid-1992, the budgetary balance moved for the first time into surplus, reaching 0.9% of GNP in 1994; this surplus was sustained, if at declining levels, in the following three years. This was due to a combination of higher than expected receipts from privatization and lower than projected interest, (owing to falling interest rates and some reduction in government debt). The slowing in economic growth and the rise in interest payments in the wake of the currency and financial crisis in 1997 again resulted in a budget deficit in 1998, of 49,981m. pesos (equivalent to 1.8% of GNP). The need to stimulate weak domestic demand meant that budget spending in 1999 was forecast to rise faster than revenue, but the deficit was even higher than projected, reaching 111,658m. pesos (3.6% of GNP), because internal tax receipts fell far below expectation, as the economic recovery proved slower and more fitful than predicted and was concentrated in sectors that are more lightly taxed (agriculture and exports). The budget balance deteriorated further in 2000, with the deficit, at 134,212m. pesos, more than double the target. This was in part the result of worsening investor sentiment because of the deepening political crisis, which meant that privatization proceeds were minimal (only 3,000m. pesos compared with the 23,000m. peso target), while interest outgoings were pushed up by the steep fall in the peso's value in October and the sharp rise in domestic interest rates to contain that fall. However, the most serious problem was the shortfall in internal tax revenue, which was about 43,000m. pesos below forecast.

In view of its legacy of about 70,000m. pesos in unpaid liabilities, the incoming Government of Macapagal Arroyo did not expect to reduce the budget deficit in 2001; consequently, its near-attainment of the relatively ambitious target of 145,000m. pesos (the outturn was a deficit of 147,023m. pesos) was viewed as a major achievement. Revenue receipts were increased by a reinforced tax collection effort, including a tax amnesty scheme, while expenditure activities were aided by lower than expected interest rates. The deficit as a proportion of GNP was unchanged from the level of 3.8% in 2000. For 2002 the Government hoped to reduce the deficit in both nominal terms and as a percentage of GNP, with a target of 130,000m. pesos. This was to be achieved by faster growth in revenue (10.8%) than in expenditure (6.1%). In the first half of the year, however, the deficit was equivalent to 41,460m pesos higher than the target of 78,260m. pesos, largely owing to the shortfall in tax revenue. With Congress still not having approved two proposed tax increases, in the levy on cigarettes, beer and liquor and a shift in the basis of income tax collection, observers were predicting a year-end deficit of some 20,000m. pesos above target. The Government was, however, maintaining the 2002 target and the medium-term objective of a zero budget balance by 2006, despite increasing the 2003 target deficit from 98,400m. pesos to 142,100m. pesos. The principal objective remained an increase in the tax ratio (tax revenue as a proportion of GNP) from the extremely high level of 12.6% registered in 2001 to a rate sufficient to fund adequate levels of government investment and services provision.

The banking and financial sector is still relatively undeveloped for an economy the size of the Philippines. Of the 45 commercial banks in operation at the end of 2001, 23 were small, with assets of less than 20,000m. pesos, and a number were still family-owned. The sector has, however, been developing rapidly since the mid-1990s, stimulated by the liberalization which has included the privatization of the largest commercial bank, the PNB, the removal in May 1994 of the ban on the establishment of foreign banks, and legislation raising the maximum foreign-ownership level of local banks. By the end of 2001 13 foreign banks had joined the four already in place since the 1950s. The banking system in the Philippines came under severe pressure as the result of the regional financial and currency crisis in 1997. However, it had relatively low exposure to the collapsing property sector, and the ratio of 'bad' loans in commercial banks' portfolios, while it had risen, was still relatively low, at 17.3%, at the end of 2001. This problem was expected to be eased by legislation (at a late stage of congressional consideration in August 2002), which would provide incentives for the sale of commercial banks' non-performing assets to asset management companies. The central bank was also quick to raise the requirements for capitalization and for loan-loss provisioning.

In the mid-1990s the local securities market was still small and speculative, but was developing fast. The market capitalization of the PSE was US $80,645m. at the end of 1996, six times the level at the end of 1992. This reflected new listings, enhanced by the privatization programme, and growing foreign confidence in the Philippines. This process was reversed in 1997, as the regional crisis affected both foreign fund inflows and domestic corporate results, causing a decline of 61% (in dollar values) in the PSE's capitalization, to US $31,270m. at the end of the year. Market capitalization had recovered to US $48,099m. at the end of 1999, and after a renewed decline in early 2000 owing to the deterioration in investors' perceptions of political risk in the Philippines and the narrowing interest differential with dollar assets, its value recovered to US $51,562m. by the end of 2000. After registering a slow decline in 2001, in line with international trends, the PSE was adversely affected by the aftermath of the terrorist attacks in the USA on 11 September, and capitalization had fallen to US $41,689m. by the end of the year.

TRADE AND THE BALANCE OF PAYMENTS

Until the final years of the 1990s merchandise trade was constantly in deficit, with the shortfall extremely sensitive to variations in GDP. Sudden surges in economic growth led to unsustainable increases in imports, and domestic demand was such that the trade deficit was never entirely eliminated. Thus, as economic growth gained momentum in the mid-1990s as a result of improved power supplies, the trade deficit rose nearly every year, reaching a record of US $11,342m. in 1996 (equivalent to 13% of GNP in that year). The deficit declined slightly in 1997 as a sharp fall in the value of the peso in the second half of the year and a steep rise in the cost of credit began to suppress import demand. However, it was the downturn in the economy in mid-1998 that reduced the deficit to the negligible level of US $28m. in that year. Contrary to the traditional pattern, the recovery in the economy in 1999 did not give rise to a surge in the trade deficit. Rather, a surplus, of US $4,958m., was registered. This was the result of unexpectedly rapid growth in exports, as an earthquake in Taiwan boosted demand for the Philippines' leading export, electronic goods, and a continuing fall in expenditure on imports. Although the trade surplus rose once again in 2000, to a new high of US $6,918m., there were indications of a reversal in the trend. Export growth was relatively robust, at 9% over the full year, but electronics, which accounted for around 60% of the total, rose by only 4.8%. With the depression in the electronics market combining with a rapid slackening in US demand growth, Philippine export earnings declined by 16.2% in 2001. The impact on the trade balance in 2001 was mitigated by the 6.2% fall in the cost of imports, but at US $2,746m., the surplus had declined by two-thirds, compared with 2000. However, there were signs of a resumption in export growth in early 2002. The surge in the US economy and a cyclical recovery in the electronics market produced double-digit export growth in April and May, increasing the five-month total to 2.7% above the year-on-year figure of 2001. While imports were showing some recovery, with a 3.3% rise in January–May, the expectation was that the overall trade surplus for 2002 would reach some US $2,000m. The USA and Japan continue to dominate Philippine international trade, with the level of transactions sustained by aid and private investment inflows at very important volumes. Changes in market shares have occurred among second-rank partners, as trade with other members of the Association of South East Asian Nations (ASEAN) has grown in importance as it has been liberalized. Their share of both imports and exports increased from only 2% in 1973 to 16% in 2000 and 2001.

Exports and Imports

The commodity composition of the Philippines' export trade has been transformed since the 1970s, when four primary commodities—coconut products, sugar, timber and copper—accounted for about one-half of the total. The general decline in world prices of these commodities and/or the fall in the volume of production coincided with the development of the export manufacturing sector and the diversification of agricultural production, with the result that by the end of the 1990s the four traditional exports accounted for under 5% of the total, while manufactures accounted for close to 90%. One category alone, electrical and electronic equipment and components, accounted for 62% of all export earnings in 1999. The sharp downturn in the information technology market had reduced the ratio to 53% by 2001.

Changes in imports have been less marked, although the fall in world prices and some changes in energy use reduced the proportion represented by crude petroleum to only 6% in 1996–98 from the 23% recorded in 1983. The subsequent surge in world petroleum prices still left the share at 9% in 2000–01. Imports of capital equipment and intermediates increased in significance in response to the post-1986 economic recovery, and played a major part in the sharp rise in the value of imports. Likewise, the economy's recession in 1998 had an adverse effect on demand for investment and production inputs, with the 21% fall in spending on raw materials and intermediates and the 12% fall in capital goods responsible for the steep decline in the value of imports in that year. Demand for both import commodities was registering a mild recovery by mid-2002.

Invisible Transactions

Invisible transactions (services, investment income and unrequited transfers) have always registered a significant surplus, owing primarily to inflows of remittances from Filipinos working abroad. These have tended to rise, reflecting the dependence of Philippine households on foreign wages and the strength of foreign demand for Filipino labour. In 2000–01 remittances from abroad averaged US $6,140m. per year, equivalent to almost one-fifth of merchandise export earnings. Tourism makes a useful, if much smaller, contribution, yielding a gross US $1,723m. in 2001. Tourist numbers have fluctuated moderately. During much of the 1980s this was in response to political instability in the Philippines. For most of the 1990s the overall trend was steadily upward, rising from 951,365 tourist arrivals in 1991 to the highest level of 2.22m. in 1997. Numbers subsequently declined gradually, with arrivals from Asian countries adversely affected by the regional economic crisis of the late 1990s, and the aftermath of the September 2001 terrorist attacks significantly reducing visits by overseas Filipinos (who normally accounted for one-twelfth of arrivals). Total arrivals declined to about 1.8m. in 2001.

The major outflow on the invisible account has been interest payments, reflecting the size of the foreign debt. However, as a consequence of the stabilizing of the debt (in dollar terms) in the 1990s and the reduction in interest rates, owing in large part to measures of debt relief, outflows declined from their peak of US $2,164m. in 1989 to US $1,518m. in 1993, before rising again, to average US $2,651m. a year in 1997–2000.

With the balance on merchandise trade turning positive, the surplus on invisible transactions, which previously had served to offset some of the trade deficit, has become incremental, moving the current account into very substantial surplus in both 1999 and 2000, at US $7,910m. and US $8,459m., respectively, equivalent to 10%–12% of GNP. Even in the more difficult external environment of 2001, the current account registered a surplus equivalent to 6% of GNP, at US $4,503m.

Capital Transactions

Traditionally, the capital account has been in surplus, more than offsetting the deficit on current payments in most years. This was largely the result of foreign borrowing. Although long-term loans remained the most significant inflow, the contribution of foreign investment, both direct and indirect, increased in the mid-1990s in response to the liberalization of the investment environment, political stability and sustained economic growth. Portfolio investment was by far the most important component, attracted by the strength of the peso and high domestic interest rates, but direct investment also rose rapidly, stimulated by the opportunities represented by strong external demand for Philippine manufactures. Like other long-term trends this was interrupted in 1997, when the sharp fall in portfolio investment inflows nearly halved the surplus on the capital account, to US $6,593m., which produced a deficit on the overall balance of payments of US $3,363m., compared with the surplus of US $4,107m. in 1996. While net capital inflows contracted sharply in 1998, in large part owing to the fall in foreign borrowing and in short-term inflows, and then became negative in 1999, as a result of the surplus on the current account, overall payments were back in surplus in both years, reaching US $3,659m. in 1999. Political uncertainties caused the sharp contraction on the portfolio account in 2000, which increased the negativity on capital transactions to a massive US $6,469m., and moved the overall balance of payments back into deficit by US $481m. The stabilization of the political environment in 2001 and a surge in bond issues by the Central Bank and the

Government in the final months of the year, reduced the deficit on the capital account, while that on the overall balance of payments remained low (at US $680m.).

CURRENCY

Ever since it was floated in February 1970, the peso has been in long-term decline, reflecting the economy's underlying external deficit. This has tended to enhance the competitiveness of Philippine export manufactures, while serving to sustain the level of inflation. From 1991 to mid-1997, however, the currency's value against the US dollar fluctuated within a narrow band, with the average in 1996 5% greater than the value five years earlier. This strength, during a period of persistently large trade imbalances, reflected rising remittances from the Filipino community overseas and inflows of portfolio investment. Then, in the turmoil on the currency markets during the regional financial crisis in Thailand in 1997, the Philippine peso fell sharply (if less than the currencies of some of the country's neighbours). Between July 1997 and January 1998 its value fell to US $1 = 44 pesos, representing a depreciation of more than one-third. Consistently good export performance, continued high inflows of remittances and reduced demand for dollars as imports fell resulted in the value of the peso increasing throughout the remainder of 1998 and the first half of 1999, to an average of US $1 = 39 pesos in the 18-month period. The peso then entered a period of weakness, initially owing to the rise in US federal fund rates, which lessened demand for peso-denominated assets, and subsequently to a marked deterioration in investor sentiment, after the stock-exchange scandal of January 2000 prompted a year of political uncertainty, culminating in the removal of President Estrada on 20 January 2001, prior to which the currency had reached a new low of US $1 = 55 pesos. It then stabilized, as the new administration became more entrenched and basic economic indicators remained sound. From December 2001 the value of the peso generally appreciated against the US dollar, in line with other currencies, and while inflation continued at a low rate, and both the trade and the current-payments accounts remained in surplus. Over the first half of 2002 the currency averaged US $1 = 51 pesos.

FOREIGN DEBT

Following the removal of Ferdinand Marcos, the Philippines was left with massive foreign indebtedness (equivalent to 96.4% of GNP at the end of 1986, with a high short-term component) and an unsustainable debt-service burden (34.6% of earnings from exports of goods and services in the same year). Thus, both the Aquino and the Ramos administrations were obliged to seek regular rounds of debt relief, the price of which was compliance with IMF requirements on structural change and fiscal austerity. These took the form of rescheduling, of both official and commercial credits, with grace periods when only interest payments were due. A new feature in 1990 was the 'buy-back' of debt, under which commercial banks sold US $1,340m. in Philippine debt to the Government at the secondary market rate, with the IMF, the World Bank and the USA providing funding. At the same time, the commercial banks agreed to provide new money, by buying 15-year government bonds at a reduced interest margin. A similar arrangement was agreed in 1992, when the consortium of the country's commercial bank creditors agreed to another 'buy-back' of US $1,260m. and the conversion of US $3,300m. to long-term, reduced-interest bonds. Against this background, the Government was able to return to the international capital market in February 1993, with its first sovereign bond issue since before the 1983 payments crisis, a US $150m. three-year Eurodollar flotation. The issue was a success despite the failure to agree on new IMF funding. Agreement was finally reached in May 1994, providing for a credit of SDR 475m. under the extended fund facility over a period of three years. The agreement was regarded by Manila as an 'exit facility' (i.e. the last such agreement it would need to reach with the IMF) in view of the progress it had achieved on structural reform (above all, improvement in the budgetary balance) and its ability to attract foreign investment capital. Thus, foreign debt, while still substantial at US $40,145m. at the end of 1996, represented much less of a burden. It was then equivalent to 47% of GNP; long-term debt to private creditors was predominantly in bonds rather than loans.

The reduced level of debt (in terms of the size of the economy), the stabilization of the current-account deficit, the increase in inflows of direct investment and the substantial growth in foreign-currency reserves (to over 10 times their end-1990 level by the end of 1996, at US $9,902m.) were all indicative of the improvement in the Philippines' payments position. However, the onset of the regional financial crisis in 1997 and its persistence throughout 1998 meant that the Philippines maintained a funding relationship with the IMF after the extended fund facility expired in March 1998. A 'precautionary stand-by arrangement' afforded access to US $1,370m. over a two-year period. This pledge of IMF support, the policy implications of a continuing relationship with the Fund, and the promise of policy continuation under the new Estrada administration helped to maintain foreign confidence in the Philippines during an uncertain period for the whole regional economy. The Philippines was therefore able to return to the international bond market in 1999, initially with a US $1,000m. global issue, which was oversubscribed, and then with Eurobond and further global issues through into the first half of 2000, to a total of US $1,130m. This foreign borrowing meant that the Government could fund a budget deficit that was essential to stimulate the economy, without putting pressure on domestic interest rates and thus threatening the recovery. However, as foreign sentiment against the Philippines hardened during the second half of 2000, owing to increasingly serious doubts about both the quality of the Estrada administration and the feasibility of its budgetary targets, the Government had to curb its foreign borrowing. With investment confidence stimulated by the inauguration of President Macapagal Arroyo, and the spread on Philippine debt consequently narrowing, the Government could once more embark on a programme of international borrowing. The Central Bank, meanwhile, was active throughout 2001 and into 2002 in raising funds on the international capital market to prepay higher-cost debt and also to offset the weakness in external markets for Philippine goods. Thus, by the end of 2001 foreign indebtedness, which had fallen by 6% in 2000 to US $50,063m., had again increased, to US $52,335m. equivalent to 69% of GNP.

Statistical Survey

Source (unless otherwise stated): National Statistics Office, Solicarel 1, Magsaysay Blvd, cnr Ampil St, POB 779, Metro Manila; tel. (2) 7160807; fax (2) 610794; internet www.census.gov.ph.

Area and Population

AREA, POPULATION AND DENSITY

Area (sq km)	300,000*
Population (census results)	
1 September 1995	
Males	34,584,170
Females	34,032,366
Total	68,616,536
1 May 2000	76,498,735
Population (official estimates at mid-year)†	
2000	76,348,114
2001	77,925,894
Density (per sq km) at mid-2001	259.8

* 115,831 sq miles.
† Figures not adjusted to take account of the May 2000 census results.

REGIONS (population at 2000 census)

	Area (sq km)	Population	Density (per sq km)
National Capital Region	636.0	9,932,560	15,617
Ilocos	12,840.2	4,200,478	327
Cagayan Valley	26,837.7	2,813,159	105
Central Luzon	18,230.8	8,030,945	441
Southern Tagalog	46,924.0	11,793,655	251
Bicol	17,632.5	4,674,855	265
Western Visayas	20,223.2	6,208,733	307
Central Visayas	14,951.5	5,701,064	381
Eastern Visayas	21,431.7	3,610,355	173
Western Mindanao	15,997.3	3,091,208	193
Northern Mindanao	14,033.0	2,747,585	196
Southern Mindanao	27,140.7	5,189,335	263
Central Mindanao	14,372.7	2,598,210	179
Cordillera Administrative Region	18,293.7	1,365,220	95
Autonomous Region of Muslim Mindanao	11,608.3	2,412,159	211
Caraga	18,847.0	2,095,367	111
Total†	300,000.3	76,498,735*	255

* Including Filipinos in Philippine embassies, consulates and missions abroad (2,851 persons).
† Total includes a statistical adjustment.

PRINCIPAL TOWNS (population at 2000 census)

Manila (capital)*	1,581,082	Gen. Santos City	411,822
Quezon City*	2,173,831	Marikina City	391,170
Caloocan City*	1,177,604	Muntinlupa City*	379,310
Davao City	1,147,116	Iloilo City	365,820
Cebu City	718,821	Pasay City*	354,908
Zamboanga City	601,794	Iligan City	285,061
Pasig City*	505,058	Mandaluyong City*	278,474
Valenzuela City	485,433	Butuan City	267,279
Las Piñas City	472,780	Angeles City	263,971
Cagayan de Oro City	461,877	Mandaue City	259,728
Parañaque City	449,811	Baguio City	252,386
Makati City*	444,867	Olongapo City	194,260
Bacolod City	429,076	Cotabato City	163,849

* Part of Metropolitan Manila.

BIRTHS, MARRIAGES AND DEATHS*

	Registered live births		Registered marriages		Registered deaths	
	Number	Rate (per 1,000)	Number	Rate (per 1,000)	Number	Rate (per 1,000)
1991	1,643,296	25.8	445,526	7.0	298,063	4.7
1992	1,684,395	25.8	454,155	7.0	319,579	4.9
1993	1,680,896	25.1	474,407	7.1	318,546	4.8
1994	1,645,011	24.0	490,164	7.2	321,440	4.7
1995	n.a.	n.a.	n.a.	7.4	324,737	4.7
1996	1,608,468	22.9	525,555	7.5	344,363	4.9
1997	1,653,236	23.1	562,808	7.9	339,400	4.7
1998	1,632,859	22.3	549,265	7.5	352,992	4.8

2000 (estimates, adjusted for under-registration): Birth rate 25.7; Death rate 5.77.

2001 (estimates, adjusted for under-registration): Birth rate 26.2; Death rate 5.83.

* Registration is incomplete. According to UN estimates, the average annual rates were: births 31.6 per 1,000 in 1990–95, 28.4 in 1995–2000; deaths 6.3 per 1,000 in 1990–95, 5.5 in 1995–2000 (Source: UN, *World Population Prospects: The 2000 Revision*).

Expectation of life (WHO estimates, years at birth, 2000): Males 64.6; Females 71.1 (Source: WHO, *World Health Report*).

ECONOMICALLY ACTIVE POPULATION*
('000 persons aged 15 years and over, January)

	1998	1999	2000
Agriculture, hunting, forestry and fishing	11,020	11,306	11,415
Mining and quarrying	116	104	110
Manufacturing	2,705	2,681	2,700
Electricity, gas and water	134	138	121
Construction	1,614	1,524	1,485
Wholesale and retail trade	4,237	4,383	4,590
Transport, storage and communications	1,821	1,927	1,991
Financing, insurance, real estate and business services	665	723	729
Community, social and personal services (incl. restaurants and hotels)	5,374	5,579	5,751
Activities not adequately defined	4	5	2
Total employed	27,689	28,368	28,895
Unemployed	2,551	2,800	2,953
Total labour force	30,240	31,168	31,848

* Figures refer to civilians only and are based on annual household surveys (excluding institutional households).

2001 (estimates, '000 persons): Agriculture, etc. 11,252; Mining and quarrying 104; Manufacturing 2,891; Total employed (incl. others) 30,090; Unemployed 3,271; Total labour force 33,361 (Source: Asian Development Bank, *Key Indicators of Developing Asian and Pacific Countries*).

Health and Welfare

KEY INDICATORS

Fertility (births per woman, 2000)	3.4
Under-5 mortality rate (per 1,000 live births, 2000)	40
HIV/AIDS (% of persons aged 15–49, 2001)	0.10
Physicians (per 1,000 head, 1996)	1.23
Hospital beds (per 1,000 head, 1993)	1.07
Health expenditure (1998): US $ per head (PPP)	144
% of GDP	3.6
public (% of total)	42.4
Access to water (% of persons, 1999)	87
Access to sanitation (% of persons, 1999)	83
Human Development Index (2000): ranking	77
value	0.754

For sources and definitions, see explanatory note on p. vi.

Agriculture

PRINCIPAL CROPS ('000 metric tons)

	1998	1999	2000
Rice (paddy)	8,554	11,787	12,389
Maize	3,823	4,585	4,511
Potatoes	65	64	64
Sweet potatoes	555	557	554
Cassava (Manioc)	1,734	1,890	1,771
Yams	30	25	26
Taro	114	97	96
Sugar cane	26,287*	23,780	21,546
Pulses	58	61	58
Groundnuts (in shell)	25	26	26
Coconuts	11,598	12,279	12,563
Vegetables (incl. melons)	4,605	4,723	4,726
Mangoes	945	866	855
Pineapples	1,489	1,530	1,524
Bananas and plantains	3,493	3,869	4,156
Soybeans	1	1	1
Garlic	13	9	14
Coffee (green)	122	117	117
Cocoa beans	7	8	7
Tobacco (leaves)	62	52	49
Natural rubber†	74	71	62

* FAO estimate. † Unofficial figure(s).

Source: FAO.

LIVESTOCK ('000 head, year ending 30 June)

	1998	1999	2000
Cattle	2,395	2,426	2,479
Pigs	10,210	10,397	10,711
Buffaloes	3,013	3,006	3,024
Horses†	230	230	230
Goats†	6,780	6,800	6,830
Sheep†	30	30	30
Chickens	138,000	114,000	115,000
Ducks	11,000*	11,000†	12,000†

* Unofficial figure. † FAO estimate(s).

Source: FAO.

LIVESTOCK PRODUCTS ('000 metric tons)

	1998	1999	2000
Beef and veal	156	190	190
Buffalo meat	56	57	58*
Pig meat	933	973	1,008
Poultry meat	511	517	550
Cows' milk	9	10	10
Buffalo milk†	18	18	n.a.
Hen eggs†	528	500	517
Other poultry eggs†	66	68	69
Cattle and buffalo hides	22	23	23

* Unofficial figure. † FAO estimate(s).

Source: FAO.

Forestry

ROUNDWOOD REMOVALS ('000 cu metres, excluding bark)

	1998	1999	2000
Sawlogs, veneer logs and logs for sleepers	478	568	375
Pulpwood	81	160	400
Other industrial wood	2,925	2,985	2,985
Fuel wood	13,832	13,720	13,615
Total	17,316	17,433	17,375

Source: FAO, *Yearbook of Forest Products*.

SAWNWOOD PRODUCTION
('000 cu metres, including railway sleepers)

	1998	1999	2000
Total	216	288	128

Source: FAO, *Yearbook of Forest Products*.

Fishing

('000 metric tons, live weight)

	1997	1998	1999
Capture	1,805.8	1,833.5	1,870.5
Scads (Decapterus)	234.8	250.8	254.2
Sardinellas	302.3	302.6	279.9
'Stolephorus' anchovies	78.7	77.0	78.1
Frigate and bullet tunas	108.5	106.4	111.3
Skipjack tuna	110.1	116.7	108.8
Yellowfin tuna	67.3	80.0	91.3
Freshwater molluscs	101.8	90.2	87.3
Aquaculture	330.4	312.1	328.4
Nile tilapia	78.5	60.7	62.9
Milkfish	161.4	162.4	170.7
Total catch	2,136.2	2,145.6	2,198.8

Note: Figures exclude aquatic plants ('000 metric tons): 627.6 (capture 0.5, aquaculture 627.1) in 1997; 643.1 (capture 0.5, aquaculture 642.6) in 1998; 621.1 (capture 0.4, aquaculture 620.6) in 1999.

Source: FAO, *Yearbook of Fishery Statistics*.

Mining

('000 metric tons, unless otherwise indicated)

	1998	1999	2000
Coal	900	1,300	1,300
Crude petroleum ('000 barrels)	300†	400	400
Chromium ore (gross weight)	53.9	19.6	20.9
Copper ore*	45.4	37.6	26.3
Salt (unrefined)	727.8	704.3	589.3
Nickel ore*	12.8	8.5	23.0
Gold (metric tons)*	34.8	31.1	36.5
Silver (metric tons)*	18.2	18.2	23.5
Limestone	5,997	1,679	9,000

* Figures refer to the metal content of ores and concentrates.
† Estimate.

Source: US Geological Survey.

Industry

SELECTED PRODUCTS

('000 metric tons, unless otherwise indicated)

	1997	1998	1999
Raw sugar*†	1,775	1,866	1,682
Plywood ('000 cubic metres)*‡	484	244	243
Mechanical wood pulp*‡	28	28	28
Chemical wood pulp*	94‡	94†	145†
Paper and paperboard*	613‡	780†	894†
Nitrogenous fertilizers(a)§	213	184	184
Phosphate fertilizers(b)§	273	217	193
Jet fuels ('000 barrels)‖	6,570	6,500	6,500
Motor spirit—petrol	292	300‡	1,460
Naphthas	648	585‡	n.a.
Kerosene ('000 barrels)‖	4,380	4,500	4,500‡
Distillate fuel oils ('000 barrels)‖	40,150	40,000	40,000‡
Residual fuel oils ('000 barrels)‖	47,450	47,000	47,000‡
Liquefied petroleum gas	454	427‡	n.a.
Cement	14,652	12,888	12,556
Smelter (unrefined) copper‖	206	198	192‡
Electric energy (million kWh)‡	39,816	41,207	41,337
Manufactured gas (terajoules)	205	205‡	n.a.

2000 ('000 metric tons, unless otherwise indicated): Raw sugar 1,676*; Plywood ('000 cubic metres) 282*; Mechanical wood pulp 28*‡; Chemical wood pulp 147*†; Paper and paperboard 870*.

* Source: FAO.

† Unofficial figure(s).

‡ Estimate(s).

§ Production of fertilizers is in terms of (a) nitrogen or (b) phosphoric acid.

‖ Source: US Geological Survey.

Sources: mainly UN, *Industrial Commodity Statistics Yearbook*; UN, *Statistical Yearbook for Asia and the Pacific*.

Finance

CURRENCY AND EXCHANGE RATES

Monetary Units

100 centavos = 1 Philippine peso.

Sterling, Dollar and Euro Equivalents (31 May 2002)

£1 sterling = 73.10 pesos;
US $1 = 49.84 pesos;
€1 = 46.78 pesos;
1,000 Philippine pesos = £13.68 = $20.07 = €21.38.

Average Exchange Rate (pesos per US $)

1999 39.089
2000 44.192
2001 50.993

GENERAL BUDGET (million pesos)

Revenue	1998	1999	2000
Tax revenue	416,585	431,686	460,034
Taxes on net income and profits	183,914	184,024	203,849
Excise tax	60,850	61,764	61,678
Sales taxes and licences	67,866	77,193	77,707
Import duties and taxes	76,005	86,497	93,742
Non-tax revenue	45,930	46,816	54,728
Bureau of the Treasury income	22,535	26,180	30,764
Fees and other charges	21,046	16,021	17,936
Total	462,515	478,502	514,762

Expenditure	1999	2000	2001
Current expenditure	522,240	585,396	647,744
Personal services	166,975	182,723	201,787
Maintenance and operating subsidy	141,591	149,313	143,579
Allotment to local government units	96,401	99,816	118,179
Interest payments	106,290	140,891	174,834
Capital outlay	61,195	60,408	58,583
Infrastructure	13,916	17,295	16,749
Equity investment	1,532	536	484
Net lending	3,193	2,634	3,944
Total	590,160	648,974	710,755

Total Revenue (million pesos): 563,732 (Tax 489,859; Non-tax 73,873) in 2001.

Source: Bureau of the Treasury.

INTERNATIONAL RESERVES (US $ million at 31 December)

	1999	2000	2001
Gold*	1,782	1,973	2,216
IMF special drawing rights	7	2	14
Reserve position in IMF	120	113	110
Foreign exchange	13,103	12,936	13,319
Total	15,012	15,024	15,659

* Valued at market-related prices.

Source: IMF, *International Financial Statistics.*

MONEY SUPPLY (million pesos at 31 December)

	1999	2000	2001
Currency outside banks	218,474	192,300	208,909
Demand deposits at commercial banks	172,874	192,982	191,940
Total money (incl. others)	395,557	390,548	406,483

Source: IMF, *International Financial Statistics.*

COST OF LIVING (Consumer Price Index; base: 1994 = 100)

	1998*	1999	2000
Food (incl. beverages and tobacco)	190.8	142.6	145.4
Fuel and light	190.2	132.9	146.4
Clothing (incl. footwear)	186.1	136.7	140.2
Rent	270.1	165.5	174.3
All items	204.0	145.9	152.3

* Base: 1990 = 100 (Source: ILO, *Yearbook of Labour Statistics*).

2001 (base: 1994 = 100): All items 161.6.

NATIONAL ACCOUNTS

National Income and Product (million pesos at current prices)

	1997	1998	1999
Compensation of employees	660,133	735,660	813,185
Operating surplus	1,305,132	1,452,747	1,642,335
Domestic factor incomes	1,965,265	2,188,407	2,455,520
Consumption of fixed capital	208,151	236,845	272,372
Gross domestic product (GDP) at factor cost	2,173,416	2,425,252	2,727,892
Indirect taxes	264,225	263,027	273,548
Less Subsidies	10,898	10,092	5,069
GDP in purchasers' values	2,426,743	2,678,187	2,996,371
Factor income from abroad *Less* Factor income paid abroad	101,578	137,072	272,989 113,725
Gross national product (GNP)	2,528,321	2,815,259	3,155,635
Less Consumption of fixed capital	208,151	236,845	272,372
National income in market prices	2,320,170	2,578,414	2,883,263
Other current transfers from abroad	86,537	46,911	67,088
Less Other current transfers paid abroad	17,435	13,169	6,457
National disposable income	2,389,272	2,612,156	2,943,894

Expenditure on the Gross Domestic Product
('000 million pesos at current prices)

	1999	2000	2001
Government final consumption expenditure	389.2	422.4	444.5
Private final consumption expenditure	2,161.6	2,335.5	2,561.2
Increase in stocks	−10.0	−7.3	15.5
Gross fixed capital formation	568.2	596.6	624.2
Statistical discrepancy	−136.9	−247.1	69.6
Total domestic expenditure	2,972.1	3,100.1	3,575.8
Exports of goods and services	1,532.2	1,859.4	1,794.9
Less Imports of goods and services	1,527.4	1,656.9	1,727.9
GDP in purchasers' values	2,976.9	3,302.6	3,642.8
GDP at constant 1985 prices	918.2	955.0	987.4

Source: IMF, *International Financial Statistics*.

Gross Domestic Product by Economic Activity
('000 million pesos at current prices)

	1999	2000	2001
Agriculture, hunting, forestry and fishing	510.5	525.9	549.4
Mining and quarrying	18.0	21.2	21.2
Manufacturing	644.0	745.9	831.6
Electricity, gas and water	86.1	97.5	116.3
Construction	162.9	174.4	182.4
Wholesale and retail trade, restaurants and hotels	419.3	473.0	517.5
Transport, storage and communications	159.3	199.0	247.6
Finance, insurance, real estate and business services	141.6	149.1	160.1
Public administration and defence	290.8	319.8	343.6
Other services	544.3	602.6	670.3
GDP in purchasers' values	2,976.9	3,308.3	3,640.0

Source: Asian Development Bank, *Key Indicators of Developing Asian and Pacific Countries*.

BALANCE OF PAYMENTS (US $ million)

	1999	2000	2001
Exports of goods f.o.b.	34,210	37,295	31,242
Imports of goods f.o.b.	−29,252	−30,377	−28,496
Trade balance	4,958	6,918	2,746
Exports of services	4,802	3,972	3,151
Imports of services	−7,515	−6,084	−5,090
Balance on goods and services	2,245	4,806	807
Other income received	8,081	7,804	7,348
Other income paid	−2,910	−4,588	−4,096
Balance on goods, services and income	7,416	8,022	4,059
Current transfers received	610	552	515
Current transfers paid	−116	−115	−71
Current balance	7,910	8,459	4,503
Capital account (net)	−9	38	−12
Direct investment abroad	59	107	161
Direct investment from abroad	573	1,241	1,792
Portfolio investment assets	−278	−806	234
Portfolio investment liabilities	5,094	693	178
Other investment assets	−5,669	−15,311	−13,893
Other investment liabilities	−714	7,579	7,211
Net errors and omissions	−3,307	−2,481	−854
Overall balance	3,659	−481	−680

Source: IMF, *International Financial Statistics*.

External Trade

PRINCIPAL COMMODITIES (distribution by SITC, US $ million)

Imports c.i.f.	1997	1998	1999
Food and live animals	2,564.6	2,473.6	2,253.2
Cereals and cereal preparations	955.4	1,148.1	822.7
Crude materials (inedible) except fuels	1,371.0	973.1	1,142.3
Mineral fuels, lubricants, etc.	3,305.6	2,237.1	2,573.0
Petroleum, petroleum products, etc.	2,932.1	1,924.7	2,267.8
Crude petroleum oils, etc.	2,565.4	1,524.5	2,066.8
Chemicals and related products	3,128.0	2,429.8	2,609.0
Basic manufactures	4,957.4	3,537.2	3,502.2
Textile yarn, fabrics, etc.	1,315.5	1,195.0	891.4
Iron and steel	1,423.1	849.7	1,052.0
Machinery and transport equipment	21,181.7	18,118.7	12,421.5
Machinery specialized for particular industries	1,690.1	1,183.0	1,020.4
General industrial machinery, equipment and parts	1,390.3	944.9	846.1
Office machines and automatic data-processing equipment	2,576.5	2,950.1	1,570.9
Parts and accessories for office machines, etc.	2,291.3	2,751.9	1,336.2
Telecommunications and sound equipment	2,305.2	1,269.5	1,054.4
Other electrical machinery, apparatus, etc.	9,588.1	10,051.3	6,196.5
Switchgear, resistors, printed circuits, switchboards, etc.	834.5	1,031.2	582.2
Thermionic valves, tubes, etc.	7,436.1	7,912.4	4,659.6
Electronic microcircuits	1,575.5	1,841.5	1,152.2
Road vehicles and parts (excl. tyres, engines and electrical parts)	1,555.2	630.6	874.8

Imports c.i.f. — *continued*	1997	1998	1999
Miscellaneous manufactured articles	1,710.8	1,462.9	1,228.9
Special transactions and commodities not classified according to kind	30.5	38.5	6,519.0
Total (incl. others)	38,580.9	31,529.9	32,568.2

Source: UN, *International Trade Statistics Yearbook*.

2000 (US $ million): Food and live animals 2,253; Crude materials (inedible) except fuels 948; Mineral fuels, lubricants, etc. 4,078; Chemicals and related products 2,883; Basic manufactures 3,530; Machinery and transport equipment 13,052; Miscellaneous manufactured articles 1,141; Total (incl. others) 33,807.

2001 (US $ million): Food and live animals 2,105; Crude materials (inedible) except fuels 853; Mineral fuels, lubricants, etc. 3,372; Chemicals and related products 2,515; Basic manufactures 3,072; Machinery and transport equipment 11,517; Miscellaneous manufactured articles 924; Total (incl. others) 31,358.

Source: Asian Development Bank, *Key Indicators of Developing Asian and Pacific Countries*.

Exports f.o.b.	1997	1998	1999
Food and live animals	1,330.7	1,262.6	1,175.0
Basic manufactures	1,297.3	1,102.7	1,054.9
Machinery and transport equipment	16,278.2	21,266.1	11,092.6
Office machines and automatic data-processing equipment	4,166.7	4,533.9	4,214.9
Automatic data-processing machines and units	2,169.9	2,411.1	3,158.2
Peripheral units	2,157.6	2,396.7	2,692.0
Parts and accessories for office machines, etc.	1,974.5	2,082.3	1,025.8
Telecommunications and sound equipment	1,279.3	1,165.4	747.7
Other electrical machinery, apparatus, etc.	10,012.5	14,707.8	5,374.4
Switchgear, resistors, printed circuits, switchboards, etc.	502.1	1,105.2	658.8
Thermionic valves, tubes, etc.	8,755.2	12,925.3	4,000.0
Diodes, transistors, etc.	1,015.2	880.9	662.8
Electronic microcircuits	7,507.4	11,750.3	3,003.0
Miscellaneous manufactured articles	4,018.3	3,972.1	2,331.1
Clothing and accessories (excl. footwear)	2,344.8	2,351.1	1,206.8
Special transactions and commodities not classified according to kind	6.8	6.5	17,928.6
Total (incl. others)	25,227.7	29,496.4	35,036.9

Source: UN, *International Trade Statistics Yearbook*.

2000 (US $ million): Food and live animals 1,283; Animal and vegetable oils, fats and waxes 477; Basic manufactures 1,222; Machinery and transport equipment 14,049; Miscellaneous manufactured articles 2,656; Total (incl. others) 38,078.

2001 (US $ million): Food and live animals 1,297; Animal and vegetable oils, fats and waxes 432; Basic manufactures 1,055; Machinery and transport equipment 12,378; Miscellaneous manufactured articles 2,431; Total (incl. others) 32,150.

Source: Asian Development Bank, *Key Indicators of Developing Asian and Pacific Countries*.

PRINCIPAL TRADING PARTNERS (US $ million)

Imports f.o.b.	1998	1999	2000
Australia	682.9	756.8	815.6
China, People's Republic	1,198.9	1,039.8	767.9
France (incl. Monaco)	492.1	305.8	347.7
Germany	822.0	800.6	734.2
Hong Kong	1,299.7	1,226.2	1,217.0
Indonesia	592.0	704.9	692.7
Iran	526.0	666.2	795.6
Japan	6,030.0	6,136.0	6,027.4
Korea, Republic	2,188.8	2,723.4	2,350.8
Malaysia	924.1	978.7	1,141.7
Netherlands	219.2	246.5	323.9
Saudi Arabia	606.7	810.5	1,048.1
Singapore	1,740.4	1,742.0	2,115.0
Taiwan	1,415.2	1,614.4	1,948.0
Thailand	793.8	821.7	846.0
United Kingdom	327.3	340.2	355.3
USA	6,560.2	6,365.1	5,323.3
Viet Nam	375.8	209.3	156.8
Total (incl. others)	29,659.9	30,742.5	31,387.4

Source: National Statistics Coordination Board.

2001 (US $ million): China, People's Republic 918; Germany 860; Hong Kong 1,642; Japan 7,258; Korea, Republic 2,250; Malaysia 1,166; Saudi Arabia 1,197; Singapore 2,365; Thailand 1,092; USA 6,602; Total (incl. others) 35,772.

Source: Asian Development Bank, *Key Indicators of Developing Asian and Pacific Countries*.

Exports f.o.b.	1998	1999	2000
China, People's Republic	343.7	574.8	663.3
Germany	1,035.1	1,229.0	1,328.6
Hong Kong	1,325.9	1,947.1	1,907.3
Japan	4,233.9	4,664.2	5,608.7
Korea, Republic	508.8	1,031.5	1,172.5
Malaysia	1,141.6	1,479.3	1,372.4
Netherlands	2,319.2	2,864.6	2,982.5
Singapore	1,832.3	2,466.7	3,124.2
Taiwan	1,757.1	2,993.4	2,861.3
Thailand	634.4	841.7	1,206.5
United Kingdom	1,756.9	1,766.4	1,506.3
USA	10,097.9	10,445.5	11,365.3
Total (incl. others)	29,496.4	35,036.9	38,078.3

Source: National Statistical Coordination Board.

2001 (US $ million): Germany 1,444; Hong Kong 1,732; Japan 5,725; Korea, Republic 1,223; Malaysia 1,331; Netherlands 2,146; Singapore 2,305; Thailand 1,327; United Kingdom 1,211; USA 9,762; Total (incl. others) 34,425.

Source: Asian Development Bank, *Key Indicators of Developing Asian and Pacific Countries*.

Transport

RAILWAYS (traffic)

	1994	1995	1996
Passengers ('000)	427	598	291
Passenger-km (million)	106	164	70
Freight ('000 metric tons)	13	14	6
Freight ton-km ('000)	3,080	4,000	1,476

Source: Philippine National Railways.

Passenger-km (million): 172 in 1997; 181 in 1998; 171 in 1999 (Source: UN, *Statistical Yearbook*).

ROAD TRAFFIC (registered motor vehicles)

	1998	1999	2000
Passenger cars	749,204	773,835	767,948
Utility vehicles	1,244,019	1,310,865	1,422,033
Buses	31,806	33,193	
Lorries and vans	231,342	243,443	248,369
Motorcycles and mopeds*	1,032,594	1,144,666	1,236,241
Trailers	27,852	27,730	26,612

* Includes tricycles.

Sources: Land Transportation Office, Manila, and International Road Federation, *World Road Statistics*.

SHIPPING

Merchant Fleet (registered at 31 December)

	1999	2000	2001
Number of vessels	1,897	1,865	1,697
Total displacement (grt)	7,650,058	7,002,097	6,029,876

Source: Lloyd's Register-Fairplay, *World Fleet Statistics*.

International Sea-borne Shipping (freight traffic)

	1994	1995	1996
Vessels ('000 net registered tons)			
Entered	53,453	61,298	n.a.
Cleared	53,841	61,313	n.a.
Goods ('000 metric tons)			
Loaded	14,581	16,658	15,687
Unloaded	38,222	42,418	51,830

CIVIL AVIATION (traffic on scheduled services)

	1996	1997	1998
Kilometres flown (million)	81	96	40
Passengers carried ('000)	7,263	7,475	3,944
Passenger-km (million)	15,132	16,392	7,503
Total ton-km (million)	1,893	2,086	925

Source: UN, *Statistical Yearbook*.

Tourism

FOREIGN TOURIST ARRIVALS

Country of Residence	1999	2000	2001
Australia	77,732	75,706	68,541
Canada	64,986	61,004	54,942
Germany	62,044	51,131	40,605
Hong Kong	160,152	146,858	134,408
Japan	387,513	390,517	343,840
Korea, Republic	133,068	174,966	207,957
Malaysia	49,667	42,067	30,498
Singapore	51,244	50,276	44,155
Taiwan	143,810	75,722	85,231
United Kingdom	88,920	74,507	60,147
USA	463,600	445,043	392,099
Total (incl. others)*	2,170,514	1,992,169	1,796,893

* Including Philippine nationals resident abroad (199,290 in 1999; 150,386 in 2000), not distributed by country.

Tourism receipts (US $ million): 2,831.2 in 1997; 2,412.9 in 1998; 2,534 in 1999.

Source: mainly Department of Tourism, Manila.

Communications Media

	1999	2000	2001
Television receivers ('000 in use)	8,200	11,000	n.a.
Telephones ('000 main lines in use)	2,892.4	3,061.4	3,100.0
Mobile cellular telephones ('000 subscribers)	2,850.0	6,454.4	10,568.0
Personal computers ('000 in use)	1,260	1,480	1,700
Internet users ('000)	1,320	2,000	2,000

Source: International Telecommunication Union.

Radio receivers ('000 in use): 11,500 in 1997.

Facsimile machines (estimated number in use): 50,000 in 1995.

Book production (titles, excluding pamphlets): 1,507 in 1996.

Daily newspapers: 47 (with average circulation of 5,700,000 copies) in 1996.

Non-daily newspapers: 243 (with average circulation of 153,000 copies) in 1995.

Sources: UN, *Statistical Yearbook*; UNESCO, *Statistical Yearbook*.

Periodicals (1990): 1,570 (estimated circulation 9,468,000).

Education

(1998/99)

	Institutions	Teachers	Pupils
Pre-primary	8,647	9,644*	n.a.
Primary schools	39,011	328,517	12,474,886
Secondary schools	7,021	108,981	5,066,190
University level	1,316	66,876†	2,481,809
Other tertiary level institutions	1,033	n.a.	4,134‡

* 1990/91 figure.

† 1993/94 figure.

‡ 1995/96 figure.

Sources: Department of Education, Culture and Sports; UNESCO, *Statistical Yearbook*.

Adult literacy rate (UNESCO estimates): 95.3% (males 95.1%; females 95.5%) in 2000 (Source: UN Development Programme, *Human Development Report*).

Directory

The Constitution

A new Constitution for the Republic of the Philippines was ratified by national referendum on 2 February 1987. Its principal provisions are summarized below:

BASIC PRINCIPLES

Sovereignty resides in the people, and all government authority emanates from them; war is renounced as an instrument of national policy; civilian authority is supreme over military authority.

The State undertakes to pursue an independent foreign policy, governed by considerations of the national interest; the Republic of the Philippines adopts and pursues a policy of freedom from nuclear weapons in its territory.

Other provisions guarantee social justice and full respect for human rights; honesty and integrity in the public service; the autonomy of local governments; and the protection of the family unit. Education, the arts, sport, private enterprise, and agrarian and urban reforms are also promoted. The rights of workers, women, youth, the urban poor and minority indigenous communities are emphasized.

BILL OF RIGHTS

The individual is guaranteed the right to life, liberty and property, under the law; freedom of abode and travel, freedom of worship, freedom of speech, of the press and of petition to the Government are guaranteed, as well as the right of access to official information on matters of public concern, the right to form trade unions, the right to assemble in public gatherings, and free access to the courts.

The Constitution upholds the right of habeas corpus and prohibits the intimidation, detention, torture or secret confinement of apprehended persons.

SUFFRAGE

Suffrage is granted to all citizens over 18 years of age, who have resided for at least one year previously in the Republic of the Philippines, and for at least six months in their voting district. Voting is by secret ballot.

LEGISLATURE

Legislative power is vested in the bicameral Congress of the Philippines, consisting of the Senate and the House of Representatives, with a maximum of 274 members. All members shall make a disclosure of their financial and business interests upon assumption of office, and no member may hold any other office. Provision is made for voters to propose laws, or reject any act or law passed by Congress, through referenda.

The Senate shall be composed of 24 members; Senators are directly elected for six years by national vote, and must be natural-born citizens, at least 35 years of age, literate and registered voters in their district. They must be resident in the Philippines for at least two years prior to election, and no Senator shall serve for more than two consecutive terms. One-half of the membership of the Senate shall be elected every three years. No treaty or international agreement may be considered valid without the approval, by voting, of at least two-thirds of members.

A maximum of 250 Representatives may sit in the House of Representatives. Its members may serve no more than three consecutive three-year terms. Representatives must be natural-born citizens, literate, and at least 25 years of age. Each legislative district may elect one representative; the number of legislative districts shall be determined according to population and shall be reapportioned following each census. Representatives must be registered voters in their district, and resident there for at least one year prior to election. In addition, one-fifth of the total number of representatives shall be elected under a party list system from lists of nominees proposed by indigenous, but non-religious, minority groups (such as the urban poor, peasantry, women and youth).

The Senate and the House of Representatives shall each have an Electoral Tribunal which shall be the sole judge of contests relating to the election of members of Congress. Each Tribunal shall have nine members, three of whom must be Justices of the Supreme Court, appointed by the Chief Justice. The remaining six members shall be members of the Senate or of the House of Representatives, as appropriate, and shall be selected from the political parties represented therein, on a proportional basis.

THE COMMISSION ON APPOINTMENTS

The President must submit nominations of heads of executive departments, ambassadors and senior officers in the armed forces to the Commission on Appointments, which shall decide on the appointment by majority vote of its members. The President of the Senate shall act as ex-officio Chairman; the Commission shall consist of 12 Senators and 12 members of the House of Representatives, elected from the political parties represented therein, on the basis of proportional representation.

THE EXECUTIVE

Executive power is vested in the President of the Philippines. Presidents are limited to one six-year term of office, and Vice-Presidents to two successive six-year terms. Candidates for both posts are elected by direct universal suffrage. They must be natural-born citizens, literate, at least 40 years of age, registered voters and resident in the Philippines for at least 10 years prior to election.

The President is Head of State and Chief Executive of the Republic. Bills (legislative proposals) that have been approved by Congress shall be signed by the President; if the President vetoes the bill, it may become law when two-thirds of members in Congress approve it.

The President shall nominate and, with the consent of the Commission on Appointments, appoint ambassadors, officers of the armed forces and heads of executive departments.

The President is Commander-in-Chief of the armed forces and may suspend the writ of habeas corpus or place the Republic under martial law for a period not exceeding 60 days when, in the President's opinion, public safety demands it. Congress may revoke either action by a majority vote.

The Vice-President may be a member of the Cabinet; in the event of the death or resignation of the President, the Vice-President shall become President and serve the unexpired term of the previous President.

THE JUDICIARY

The Supreme Court is composed of a Chief Justice and 14 Associate Justices, and may sit *en banc* or in divisions comprising three, five or seven members. Justices of the Supreme Court are appointed by the President, with the consent of the Commission on Appointments, for a term of four years. They must be citizens of the Republic, at least 40 years of age, of proven integrity, and must have been judges of the lower courts, or engaged in the practice of law in the Philippines, for at least 15 years.

The Supreme Court, sitting *en banc*, is the sole judge of disputes relating to presidential and vice-presidential elections.

THE CONSTITUTIONAL COMMISSIONS

These are the Civil Service Commission and the Commission on Audit, each of which has a Chairman and two other Commissioners, appointed by the President (with the approval of the Commission on Appointments) to a seven-year term; and the Commission on Elections, which enforces and administers all laws pertaining to elections and political parties. The Commission on Elections has seven members, appointed by the President (and approved by the Commission on Appointments) for a seven-year term. The Commission on Elections may sit *en banc* or in two divisions.

LOCAL GOVERNMENT

The Republic of the Philippines shall be divided into provinces, cities, municipalities and barangays. The Congress of the Philippines shall enact a local government code providing for decentralization. A region may become autonomous, subject to approval by a majority vote of the electorate of that region, in a referendum. Defence and security in such areas will remain the responsibility of the national Government.

ACCOUNTABILITY OF PUBLIC OFFICERS

All public officers, including the President, Vice-President and members of Congress and the Constitutional Commissions, may be removed from office if impeached for, or convicted of, violation of the Constitution, corruption, treason, bribery or betrayal of public trust.

Cases of impeachment must be initiated solely by the House of Representatives, and tried solely by the Senate. A person shall be convicted by a vote of at least two-thirds of the Senate, and will then be dismissed from office and dealt with according to the law.

SOCIAL JUSTICE AND HUMAN RIGHTS

The Congress of the Philippines shall give priority to considerations of human dignity, the equality of the people and an equitable distribution of wealth. The Commission on Human Rights shall investigate allegations of violations of human rights, shall protect human rights through legal measures, and shall monitor the Government's compliance with international treaty obligations. It may advise Congress on measures to promote human rights.

AMENDMENTS OR REVISIONS

Proposals for amendment or revision of the Constitution may be made by:

i) Congress (upon a vote of three-quarters of members);

ii) A Constitutional Convention (convened by a vote of two-thirds of members of Congress);

iii) The people, through petitions (signed by at least 12% of the total number of registered voters).

The proposed amendments or revisions shall then be submitted to a national plebiscite, and shall be valid when ratified by a majority of the votes cast.

MILITARY BASES

Foreign military bases, troops or facilities shall not be allowed in the Republic of the Philippines following the expiry, in 1991, of the Agreement between the Republic and the USA; except under the provisions of a treaty approved by the Senate, and, when required by Congress, ratified by the voters in a national referendum.

The Government

HEAD OF STATE

President: Gloria Macapagal Arroyo (inaugurated 20 January 2001).

Vice-President: Teofisto T. Guingona, Jr.

THE CABINET
(September 2002)

Executive Secretary: Alberto G. Romulo.

Secretary of Agrarian Reform: Hernani A. Braganza.

Secretary of Agriculture: Leonardo Q. Montemayor.

Secretary of the Budget and Management: Emilia T. Boncodin.

Secretary of Education, Culture and Sports: Edilberto C. de Jesus.

Secretary of Energy: Vicente S. Perez, Jr.

Secretary of Finance: Jose Isidro N. Camacho.

Secretary of Foreign Affairs: Blas F. Ople.

Secretary of Health: Manuel M. Dayrit.

Secretary of the Interior and Local Government: Jose D. Lina, Jr.

Secretary of Justice: Hernando B. Perez.

Secretary of Labor and Employment: Patricia A. Santo Thomas.

Secretary of National Defense: Gen. (retd) Angelo T. Reyes.

Secretary of Public Works and Highways: Simeon A. Datumanong.

Secretary of Science and Technology: Estrella F. Alabastro.

Secretary of Social Welfare and Development: Corazon Juliano N. Soliman.

Secretary of Tourism: Richard J. Gordon.

Secretary of Trade and Industry: Manuel A. Roxas II.

Secretary of Transportation and Communications: Leandro Mendoza.

Secretary of the Environment and Natural Resources: Heherson T. Alvarez.

Director-General of the National Economic and Development Authority: Dante B. Canlas.

Press Secretary: Ignacio R. Bunye.

MINISTRIES

Office of the President: New Executive Bldg, Malacañang Palace Compound, J. P. Laurel St, San Miguel, Metro Manila; tel. (2) 7356047; fax (2) 7358006; e-mail opnet@ops.gov.ph; internet www.opnet.ops.gov.ph.

Office of the Vice-President: PICC, 2nd Floor, CCP Complex, Roxas Blvd, Pasay City, Metro Manila; tel. (2) 8312658; fax (2) 8312614; e-mail gma@easy.net.ph.

Department of Agrarian Reform: DAR Bldg, Elliptical Rd, Diliman, Quezon City, Metro Manila; tel. (2) 9287031; fax (2) 9292527; e-mail nani@dar.gov.ph; internet www.dar.gov.ph.

Department of Agriculture: DA Bldg, 4th Floor, Elliptical Rd, Diliman, Quezon City, Metro Manila; tel. (2) 9288741; fax (2) 9285140; e-mail dnotes@da.gov.ph; internet www.da.gov.ph.

Department of the Budget and Management: DBM Bldg, Gen. Solano St, San Miguel, Metro Manila; tel. (2) 7354807; fax (2) 7354927; e-mail dbmbiss@dbm.gov.ph; internet www.dbm.gov.ph.

Department of Education, Culture and Sports: Ultra Complex, Meralco Ave, Pasig City, 1600 Metro Manila; tel. (2) 6321361; fax (2) 6320805; internet www.deped.gov.ph.

Department of Energy: Energy Center, Merritt Rd, Fort Bonifacio, Taguig, Metro Manila; tel. (2) 8441021; fax (2) 8442495; e-mail v_perez@doe.gov.ph; internet www.doe.gov.ph.

Department of the Environment and Natural Resources: DENR Bldg, Visayas Ave, Diliman, Quezon City, 1100 Metro Manila; tel. (2) 9296626; fax (2) 9204352; e-mail sechta@denr.gov.ph; internet www.denr.gov.ph.

Department of Finance: DOF Bldg, Roxas Blvd, cnr Pablo Ocampo St, Metro Manila; tel. (2) 5234955; fax (2) 5212950; e-mail camacho@dof.gov.ph; internet www.dof.gov.ph.

Department of Foreign Affairs: DFA Bldg, 2330 Roxas Blvd, Pasay City, Metro Manila; tel. (2) 8344000; fax (2) 8321597; e-mail webmaster@dfa.gov.ph; internet www.dfa.gov.ph.

Department of Health: San Lazaro Compound, Rizal Ave, Santa Cruz, 1003 Metro Manila; tel. (2) 7438301; fax (2) 7431829; e-mail mmdayrit@doh.gov.ph; internet www.doh.gov.ph.

Department of the Interior and Local Government: A. Francisco Gold Condominium II, Epifanio de los Santos Ave, cnr Mapagmahal St, Diliman, Quezon City, 1100 Metro Manila; tel. (2) 9250349; fax (2) 9250386; e-mail dilgmail@dilg.gov.ph; internet www.dilg.gov.ph.

Department of Justice: Padre Faura St, Ermita, Metro Manila; tel. (2) 5213721; fax (2) 5211614; e-mail sechbp@info.com.ph; internet www.asti.dost.gov.ph/doj.

Department of Labor and Employment: DOLE Executive Bldg, 7th Floor, Muralla Wing, Muralla St, Intramuros, 1002 Metro Manila; tel. (2) 5272131; fax (2) 5273494; e-mail osec@dole.gov.ph; internet www.dole.gov.ph.

Department of National Defense: DND Bldg, 3rd Floor, Camp Aguinaldo, Quezon City, Metro Manila; tel. (2) 9113300; fax (2) 9116213; e-mail osnd@philonline.com; internet www.dnd.gov.ph.

Department of Public Works and Highways: DPWH Bldg, Bonifacio Drive, Port Area, Metro Manila; tel. (2) 5274111; fax (2) 5275635; e-mail pilorin.beth.p@dpwh.gov.ph; internet www.dpwh.gov.ph.

Department of Science and Technology: DOST Compound, Gen. Santos Ave, Bicutan, Taguig, Metro Manila; tel. (2) 8372071; fax (2) 8372937; e-mail wgp@sunl.dost.gov.ph; internet www.dost.gov.ph.

Department of Social Welfare and Development: Batasang Pambansa, Constitution Hills, Quezon City, Metro Manila; tel. (2) 9317916; fax (2) 9318191; e-mail dinky@mis.dswd.gov.ph; internet www.dswd.gov.ph.

Department of Tourism: DOT Bldg, Teodoro F. Valencia Circle, Rizal Park, Metro Manila; tel. (2) 5251805; fax (2) 5256538; e-mail dotmprd@info.com.ph; internet www.tourism.gov.ph.

Department of Trade and Industry: Industry and Investments Bldg, 385 Sen. Gil J. Puyat Ave, Buendia, Makati City, 3117 Metro Manila; tel. (2) 8953611; fax (2) 8956487; e-mail mis@dti.dti.gov.ph; internet www.dti.gov.ph.

Department of Transportation and Communications: Columbia Tower, Ortigas Ave, Pasig City, 1555 Metro Manila; tel. (2) 7267106; fax (2) 7267104; e-mail dotc@i-next.net; internet www.dotcmain.gov.ph.

National Economic and Development Authority (NEDA—Department of Socio-Economic Planning): NEDA-sa-Pasig Bldg, 12 Blessed Josemaria Escriva St, Pasig City, 1605 Metro Manila; tel. (2) 6313747; fax (2) 6313282; e-mail info@neda.gov.ph; internet www.neda.gov.ph.

Philippine Information Agency (Office of the Press Secretary): PIA Bldg, Visayas Ave, Diliman, Quezon City, Metro Manila; tel. (2) 9247703; fax (2) 9204347; e-mail pia@ops.gov.ph; internet www.pia.ops.gov.ph.

President and Legislature

PRESIDENT

Election, 11 May 1998*

Candidate	Votes	% of votes
Joseph Ejercito Estrada (LaMMP)	10,722,295	39.86
Jose C. de Venecia, Jr (Lakas-NUCD)	4,268,483	15.87
Paul S. Roco (Aksyon Demokratiko)	3,720,212	13.83
Emilio R. Osmeña (PROMDI)	3,347,631	12.44
Alfredo S. Lim (LP)	2,344,362	8.71
Renato S. de Villa (Reporma)	1,308,352	4.86
Miriam Defensor Santiago (PRP)	797,206	2.96
Juan Ponce Enrile (Independent)	343,139	1.28
Santiago F. Dumlao, Jr (Bago)	32,212	0.12
Manuel L. Morato (PBM)	18,644	0.07
Total	26,902,536	100.00

* In January 2001, after the impeachment trial of President Estrada had been adjourned indefinitely, the Supreme Court declared the presidency vacant. Vice-President Gloria Macapagal Arroyo was sworn in as Estrada's successor.

THE CONGRESS OF THE PHILIPPINES

Senate

President of the Senate: Franklin M. Drilon.

Elections for 12 of the 24 seats in the Senate took place on 11 May 1998. The Laban ng Makabayang Masang Pilipino (LaMMP) won seven seats, while Lakas ng EDSA-National Union of Christian Democrats (Lakas-NUCD) won five seats. Elections for 13 of the 24 seats were held on 14 May 2001. The People Power Coalition (PPC) won eight seats and the Laban ng Demokratikong Pilipino-Puwersa ng Masa (LDP-PnM) won four. The remaining seat was taken by an independent candidate. The result thus gave President Macapagal Arroyo a narrow majority in the upper house, with 13 of the 24 seats being occupied by her supporters.

House of Representatives

Speaker of the House: Jose de Venecia.

General Election, 14 May 2001

	Seats
Lakas ng EDSA-National Union of Christian Democrats (Lakas-NUCD)	77
Nationalist People's Coalition (NPC)	51
Liberal Party (LP)	20
Laban ng Demokratikong Pilipino (LDP)	17
Independents	11
Alayon	4
PDP-Laban	3
Partido para sa Demokratikong Reporma-Lapiang Manggagawa Coalition (Reporma)	3
Probinsya Muna Development Initiatives (PROMDI)	3
United Negros Alliance (UNA)	3
Aksyon Demokratiko	2
Kabalikat ng Malayang Pilipino (KAMPI)	2
Partido ng Masang Pilipino (PMP)	2
Others	11
Total*	209

* Under the party list elections, which also took place on 14 May 2001, an additional five members of minority and cause-orientated groups were allocated seats in the House of Representatives.

Note: Results were provisional.

Autonomous Region

MUSLIM MINDANAO

The Autonomous Region of Muslim Mindanao (ARMM) originally comprised the provinces of Lanao del Sur, Maguindanao, Tawi-Tawi and Sulu. The Region was granted autonomy in November 1989. Elections took place in February 1990, and the formal transfer of limited executive powers took place in October. In August 2001 a plebiscite was conducted in 11 provinces and 14 cities in Mindanao to determine whether or not they would become members of the ARMM. The city of Marawi and the province of Basilan subsequently joined the Region. The regional Assembly, for which elections were held in November 2001, comprises 21 legislative seats.

Governor: Farouk Hussein (elected 26 November 2001).

Vice-Governor: Mahid Mutilan.

In October 1996 a transitional administrative council was established, which derived powers from the office of the President, to co-ordinate peace-keeping and development activities.

Southern Philippines Council for Peace and Development Chairman: Muslimin Sema.

Vice-Chairman: Edward S. Hagedorn.

Political Organizations

Akbayan (Citizens' Action Party): 14 Mapagkumbaba St, Sikatuna Village, Quezon City, Metro Manila; tel. (2) 4336933; fax (2) 9252936; e-mail secretariat@surfshop.net; internet www.akbayan.org; f. 1998; left-wing; Pres. Joel Rocamora; Sec.-Gen. Marie Victa Labajo.

Aksyon Demokratiko (Democratic Action Party): 16th Floor, Strata 2000 Bldg, Emerald Ave, Ortigas Centre, Pasig City, 1600 Metro Manila; tel. (2) 6385381; fax (2) 6343073; e-mail kabataan@raulroco.com; f. 1997 to support presidential candidacy of Raul Roco; Chair. Jaime Galvez Tan; Pres. Raul Roco.

Alayon: c/o House of Representatives, Metro Manila.

Bayan Muna: c/o House of Representatives, Metro Manila; e-mail bayanmuna@bayanmuna.net; internet www.bayanmuna.net; f. 1999; Pres. Satur Ocampo; Chair. Dr Reynaldo Lesaca, Jr.

Gabay ng Bayan (Nation's Guide): Metro Manila; fmrly Grand Alliance for Democracy; Leader Francisco Tadad.

Kabalikat ng Malayang Pilipino (KAMPI): c/o House of Representatives, Metro Manila; f. 1997.

Kilusang Bagong Lipunan (KBL) (New Society Movement): Metro Manila; f. 1978 by Pres. Marcos and fmr mems of the Nacionalista Party; Sec.-Gen. Vicente Mellora.

Kilusan para sa Pambansang Pagpapanibago (BAGO): Metro Manila; f. 1997 to support presidential candidacy of Santiago F. Dumlao, Jr.

Laban ng Demokratikong Pilipino (LDP) (Fight of Democratic Filipinos): Metro Manila; f. 1987, reorg. 1988 as an alliance of Lakas ng Bansa and a conservative faction of the PDP-Laban Party; mem. of Lapian ng Masang Pilipino (LAMP) until Jan. 2001; formed alliance with Puwersa ng Masa (PnM) to contest the 2001 elections to the Senate; Pres. Edgardo Angara; Sec.-Gen. Jose Cojuangco.

Lakas ng EDSA (Power of EDSA)**-National Union of Christian Democrats (Lakas-NUCD):** Metro Manila; e-mail mail@LAKAS-NUCD.com; internet www.lakas-nucd.com; f. 1992 as alliance to support the presidential candidacy of Gen. Fidel V. Ramos; formed alliance with UMDP to contest 1998 and 2001 elections, joined People Power Coalition (PPC) in Feb. 2001; Pres. Teofisto T. Guingona, Jr; Sec.-Gen. Gloria Macapagal Arroyo.

Lapian ng Masang Pilipino (LAMP) (Party of the Filipino Masses): Metro Manila; f. 1997 as Laban ng Makabayang Masang Pilipino (LaMMP, Struggle of Nationalist Filipino Masses), renamed Laban ng Masang Pilipino (LMP, Struggle of Filipino Masses) in 1998, present name adopted in 1999; originally coalition of Laban ng Demokratikong Pilipino (LDP), Nationalist People's Coalition (NPC) and Partido ng Masang Pilipino (PMP) until split in January 2001.

Liberal Party (LP): Metro Manila; f. 1946; represents centre-liberal opinion of the fmr Nacionalista Party, which split in 1946; endorsed Alfredo Lim as presidential candidate in 1998 election; joined People Power Coalition (PPC) in February 2001; Leader Florencio Abad.

Nacionalista Party (NP): Metro Manila; tel. (2) 854418; fax (2) 865602; Pres. Arturo Tolentino; Sec.-Gen. Rene Espina.

Nationalist People's Coalition (NPC): Metro Manila; f. 1991; breakaway faction of the Nacionalista Party led by Eduardo Cojuangco; mem. of Lapian ng Masang Pilipino (LAMP) from 1997 until Jan. 2001.

New National Alliance: Metro Manila; f. 1998; left-wing; Dep. Sec.-Gen. Teddy Casino.

Partido Bansang Marangal (PBM): Metro Manila; f. 1997 to support the presidential candidacy of Manuel L. Morato.

Partido Demokratiko Sosyalista ng Pilipinas (PDSP) (Philippine Democratic Socialist Party): Metro Manila; f. 1981 by mems of the Batasang Pambansa allied to the Nacionalista (Roy faction), Pusyon Visaya and Mindanao Alliance parties; joined People Power Coalition (PPC) in Feb. 2001; Leader Norberto Gonzales.

Partido Komunista ng Pilipinas (PKP) (Communist Party of the Philippines): f. 1930; Pres. Felicisimo Macapagal.

Partido Nacionalista ng Pilipinas (PNP) (Philippine Nationalist Party): Metro Manila; f. 1986 by fmr mems of KBL; Leader Blas F. Ople.

Partido ng Bayan (New People's Alliance): f. May 1986 by JOSE MARIA SISON (imprisoned in 1977–86), the head of the Communist Party of the Philippines (CPP); militant left-wing nationalist group.

Partido ng Manggagawang Pilipino (PMP) (Filipino Workers' Party): f. 2002 by fmr supporters of the CPP (see below).

Partido ng Masang Pilipino (PMP): Metro Manila; mem. of Lapian ng Masan Pilipino (LAMP) from 1997 until Jan. 2001; Leader JOSEPH EJERCITO ESTRADA.

Partido para sa Demokratikong Reporma-Lapiang Manggagawa Coalition (Reporma): c/o House of Representatives, Metro Manila; joined People Power Coalition (PPC) in Feb. 2001; Leader RENATO DE VILLA.

PDP-Laban Party: c/o House of Representatives, Metro Manila; f. February 1983 following merger of Pilipino Democratic Party (f. 1982 by fmr mems of the Mindanao Alliance) and Laban (Lakas ng Bayan—People's Power Movement, f. 1978 and led by Benigno S. Aquino, Jr. until his assassination in August 1983); centrist; formally dissolved in Sept. 1988, following the formation of the LDP, but a faction continued to function as a political movement; Pres. JUANITO FERRER; Sec.-Gen. AUGUSTO SANCHEZ.

People Power Coalition (PPC): c/o House of Representatives, Metro Manila; internet www.ppc.ph; formed to contest 2001 elections to the Senate; coalition of Aksyon Demokratiko, Lakas-NUCD, Liberal Party, PDSP, PROMDI and Reporma.

People's Reform Party (PRP): f. 1991 by MIRIAM DEFENSOR SANTIAGO to support her candidacy in the 1992 presidential election.

Probinsya Muna Development Initiatives (PROMDI): 7 Pasteur St, Lahug, Cebu City; tel (32) 2326692; fax (32) 2313609; e-mail emro@cebu.pw.net.ph; internet www.col.net.ph/emro; f. 1997; joined People Power Coalition (PPC) to contest 2001 elections; Leader EMILIO ('LITO') OSMEÑA.

Puwersa ng Masa (PnM): c/o House of Representatives, Metro Manila; f. 2001 by ex-President JOSEPH EJERCITO ESTRADA; formed an alliance with Laban ng Demokratikong Pilipino (LDP) to contest the 2001 elections to the Senate.

United Muslim Democratic Party (UMDP): Mindanao; moderate Islamic party; formed an electoral alliance with Lakas-NUCD for the election to the House of Representatives in May 2001.

United Negros Alliance (UNA): Negros Occidental.

The following organizations are, or have been, in conflict with the Government:

Abu Sayyaf (Bearer of the Sword): Mindanao; radical Islamic group seeking the establishment of an Islamic state in Mindanao; breakaway grouping of the MILF; est. strength 1,500 (2000); Leader KHADAFI JANJALANI.

Alex Boncayao Brigade (ABB): communist urban guerrilla group, fmrly linked to CPP, formed alliance with Revolutionary Proletarian Party in 1997; est. strength 500 (April 2001); Leader NILO DE LA CRUZ.

Islamic Command Council (ICC): Mindanao; splinter group of MNLF; Leader MELHAM ALAM.

Maranao Islamic Statehood Movement: Mindanao; f. 1998; armed grouping seeking the establishment of an Islamic state in Mindanao.

Mindanao Independence Movement (MIM): Mindanao; claims a membership of 1m.; Leader REUBEN CANOY.

Moro Islamic Liberation Front (MILF): Camp Abubakar, Lanao del Sur, Mindanao; aims to establish an Islamic state in Mindanao; comprises a faction that broke away from the MNLF in 1978; its armed wing, the Bangsa Moro Islamic Armed Forces, est. 10,000 armed regulars; Chair. HASHIM SALAMAT; Vice-Chair. and Chief of Armed Forces Haji MURAD.

Moro Islamic Reform Group: Mindanao; breakaway faction from MNLF; est. strength of 200 in 2000.

Moro National Liberation Front (MNLF): internet www.mnlf.org; seeks autonomy for Muslim communities in Mindanao; signed a peace agreement with the Govt in Sept. 1996; its armed wing, the Bangsa Moro Army, comprised an est. 10,000 mems in 2000; Chair. and Pres. of Cen. Cttee (vacant); Sec.-Gen. USTADZ MURSHI D. IBRAHIM.

Moro National Liberation Front—Islamic Command Council (MNLF—ICC): Basak, Lanao del Sur; f. 2000; Islamist separatist movement committed to urban guerrilla warfare; breakaway faction from MNLF; Cmmdrs DATU FIJRODIN, MUDS BAIRODIN, CALEB BEN MUHAMAD, ZAIDA BULLH, OMEN.

National Democratic Front (NDF): a left-wing alliance of 14 mem. groups; Chair. MARIANA OROSA; Spokesman GREGORIO ROSAL. The NDF includes:

Communist Party of the Philippines (CPP): f. 1968; a breakaway faction of the PKP; legalized Sept. 1992; in July 1993 the Metro Manila-Rizal and Visayas regional committees, controlling 40% of total CPP membership (est. 15,000 in 1994), split from the Central Committee; Chair. JOSE MARIA SISON; Gen. Sec. BENITO TIAMZON.

New People's Army (NPA): f. 1969 as the military wing of the CPP; based in central Luzon, but operates throughout the Philippines; est. strength 9,500; Leader JOVENCIO BALWEG; Spokesman GREGORIO ROSAL.

Revolutionary Proletarian Party: Metro Manila; f. 1996; comprises mems of the Metro Manila-Rizal and Visayas regional committees, which broke away from the CPP in 1993; has a front organization called the Bukluran ng Manggagawang Pilipino (Association of Filipino Workers); Leader ARTURO TABARA.

Diplomatic Representation

EMBASSIES IN THE PHILIPPINES

Argentina: ACT Tower, 6th Floor, 135 Sen. Gil J. Puyat Ave, Salcedo Village, Makati City, Metro Manila; tel. (2) 8108301; fax (2) 8936091; Ambassador: (vacant).

Australia: Doña Salustiana Dee Ty Bldg, 1st–5th Floors, 104 Paseo de Roxas, cnr Perea St, Makati City, 1200 Metro Manila; tel. (2) 7502850; fax (2) 7546268; e-mail public_affairs@mydestiny.net; internet www.australia.com.ph; Ambassador: RUTH PEARCE.

Austria: Prince Bldg, 4th Floor, 117 Rada St, Legaspi Village, Makati City, 1200 Metro Manila; tel. (2) 8179191; fax (2) 8134238; Ambassador: Dr CHRISTIAN KREPELA.

Bangladesh: Universal-Re Bldg, 2nd Floor, 106 Paseo de Roxas, Legaspi Village, Makati City, Metro Manila; tel. (2) 8175001; fax (2) 8164941; Ambassador: MOHAMMED FAROOQ.

Belgium: Multibancorporation Centre, 9th Floor, 6805 Ayala Ave, Makati City, Metro Manila; tel. (2) 8451869; fax (2) 8452076; e-mail manila@diplobel.org; Ambassador: RONALD VAN REMOORTELE.

Brazil: RCI Bldg, 6th Floor, 105 Rada St, Legaspi Village, Makati City, 1229 Metro Manila; tel. (2) 8928181; fax (2) 8182622; e-mail brascom@info.com.ph; Ambassador: CLAUDIO MARIA HENRIQUE DO COUTO LYRA.

Brunei: Bank of the Philippine Islands Bldg, 11th Floor, Ayala Ave, cnr Paseo de Roxas, Makati City, 1226 Metro Manila; tel. (2) 8162836; fax (2) 8916646; Ambassador: MAIMUNAH Dato' Paduka Haji ELIAS.

Cambodia: Unit 7A, 7th Floor, Country Space One Bldg, Sen. Gil J. Puyat Ave, Makati City, Metro Manila; tel. (2) 8189981; fax (2) 8189983; e-mail cam.emb.ma@netasia.net; Ambassador: EK SEREYWATH.

Canada: Allied Bank Center, 9th & 11th Floors, 6754 Ayala Ave, Makati City, 1200 Metro Manila; tel. (2) 8670001; fax (2) 8403547; e-mail manil.immigration@dfait-maeci.gc.ca; internet www.dfait-maeci.gc.ca/manila; Ambassador: ROBERT COLLETTE.

Chile: Doña Salustiana Dee Ty Bldg, 6th Floor, 104 Paseo de Roxas, Legaspi Village, Makati City, Metro Manila; tel. (2) 8103149; fax (2) 8150795; e-mail echileph@compass.com.ph; Ambassador: CARMEN LYNAM.

China, People's Republic: 4896 Pasay Rd, Dasmariñas Village, Makati City, Metro Manila; tel. (2) 8443148; fax (2) 8452465; e-mail emb-chn@pacific.net.ph; Ambassador: WANG CHUNGUI.

Colombia: Aurora Tower, 18th Floor, Araneta Center, Quezon City, Metro Manila; tel. (2) 9113101; fax (2) 9112846; Ambassador: (vacant).

Cuba: 101 Aguirre St, cnr Trasierra St, Cacho-Gonzales Bldg Penthouse, Legaspi Village, Makati City, Metro Manila; tel. (2) 8171192; fax (2) 8164094; Ambassador: RAMÓN DOMINGO ALONSO MEDINA.

Czech Republic: 30th Floor, Rufino Pacific Tower, Ayala Ave, cnr Herrera St, Makati City, Metro Manila; tel. (2) 8111155; fax (2) 8111020; e-mail manila@embassy.msv.cz; internet www.mzv.cz/manila; Ambassador: STANISLAV SLAVICKY.

Denmark: Doña Salustiana Dee Ty Bldg, 6th Floor, 104 Paseo de Roxas, Legaspi Village, Makati City, 1229 Metro Manila; POB 7707, Domestic Airport Post Office, 1301 Metro Manila; tel. (2) 8940086; fax (2) 8938075; e-mail mnlamb@um.dk; internet www.danish-embassies.dk/philippines; Ambassador: PETER ROSTING.

Egypt: 2229 Paraiso cnr Banyan St, Dasmariñas Village, Makati City, Metro Manila; tel. (2) 8439232; fax (2) 8439239; Ambassador: SABER ABDEL KADER MANSOUR.

Finland: 21st Floor, Far East Bank and Trust Center, Sen. Gil J. Puyat Ave, Makati City, Metro Manila; tel. (2) 8915011; fax (2) 8914107; Ambassador: RAIMO ANTTOLA.

France: Pacific Star Bldg, 16th Floor, Makati Ave, cnr Sen. Gil J. Puyat Ave, Makati City, Metro Manila; tel. (2) 8101981; fax (2)

8175047; e-mail consulat@france.com.ph; internet www.france.com.ph; Ambassador: RENÉE VEYRET.

Germany: Globalbank Centre, 6th Floor, 777 Paseo de Roxas, Makati City, 1226 Metro Manila; tel. (2) 8924906; fax (2) 8104703; e-mail germanembassymanila@surfshop.net.ph; internet www.germanembassy-philippines.com; Ambassador: HERBERT D. JESS.

Holy See: 2140 Taft Ave, POB 3364, 1099 Metro Manila (Apostolic Nunciature); tel. (2) 5210306; fax (2) 5211235; e-mail nuntiusp@info.com.ph; Apostolic Nuncio: Most Rev. ANTONIO FRANCO.

India: 2190 Paraiso St, Dasmariñas Village, POB 2123, Makati City, Metro Manila; tel. (2) 8430101; fax (2) 8158151; e-mail eimani@vasia.com; Ambassador: NAVREKHA SHARMA.

Indonesia: 185 Salcedo St, Legaspi Village, Makati City, Metro Manila; tel. (2) 8925061; fax (2) 8925878; Ambassador: SOERATMIN.

Iran: 2224 Paraiso St, cnr Pasay Rd, Dasmariñas Village, Makati City, Metro Manila; tel. (2) 8884757; fax (2) 8884777; Ambassador: GHOLAMREZA YOUSEFI.

Iraq: 2261 Avocado St, Dasmariñas Village, Makati City, Metro Manila; tel. (2) 8439838; fax (2) 8439839; Ambassador: (vacant).

Israel: Trafalgar Plaza, 23rd Floor, H. V. de la Costa St, Salcedo Village, Makati City, 1200 Metro Manila; POB 1697, Makati Central Post Office, 1256 Metro Manila; tel. (2) 8940441; fax (2) 8941027; e-mail israinfor@pacific.net.ph; Ambassador: IRIT BEN-ABBA.

Italy: Zeta Bldg, 6th Floor, 191 Salcedo St, Legaspi Village, Makati City, Metro Manila; tel. (2) 8924531; fax (2) 8171436; e-mail ambitaly@iname.com; Ambassador: UMBERTO COLESANTI.

Japan: 2627 Roxas Blvd, Pasay City, 1300 Metro Manila; tel. (2) 5515710; fax (2) 5515780; e-mail info@embjapan.ph; internet www.embjapan.ph; Ambassador: YOSHIHISA ARA.

Jordan: Golden Rock Bldg, 3rd Floor, Suite 502, 168 Salcedo St, Legaspi Village, Makati City, Metro Manila; tel. (2) 8177494; Ambassador: HASAN ZIYADEH.

Korea, Democratic People's Republic: Makati City, Metro Manila.

Korea, Republic: Pacific Star Bldg, 10th Floor, Sen. Gil J. Puyat Ave cnr Makati Ave, Makati City, 1226 Metro Manila; tel. (2) 8116139; fax (2) 8116148; Ambassador: SON SANG-HA.

Kuwait: 1230 Acacia Rd, Dasmariñas Village, Makati City, Metro Manila; tel. (2) 8876880; fax (2) 8876666; Ambassador: IBRAHIM MUHANNA AL-MUHANNA.

Laos: 34 Lapu-Lapu St, Magallanes Village, Makati City, Metro Manila; tel. and fax (2) 8525759; Ambassador: PHIANE PHILAKONE.

Libya: 1644 Dasmarinas St, cnr Mabolo St, Dasmariñas Village, Makati City, Metro Manila; tel. (2) 8177331; fax (2) 8177337; Ambassador: SALEM M. ADAM.

Malaysia: 107 Tordesillas St, Salcedo Village, Makati City, 1200 Metro Manila; POB 1967, Makati City, 1299 Metro Manila; tel. (2) 8174581; fax (2) 8163158; e-mail mwmanila@asiagate.net; Ambassador: MOHAMED TAUFIK BIN MOHAMED NOOR.

Malta: 6th Floor, Cattleya Condominium, 235 Salcedo St, Legaspi Village, Makati City, Metro Manila; tel. (2) 8171095; fax (2) 8171089; e-mail syquia@intlaw.com.ph; Ambassador: ENRIQUE P. SYQUIA.

Mexico: 18th Floor, Ramon Magsaysay Center, 1680 Roxas Blvd, Metro Manila; tel. (2) 5267461; fax (2) 5267425; e-mail ebmexfil@info.com.ph; Ambassador: ENRIQUE HUBBARD.

Myanmar: Zanland Center, 8th Floor, 152 Amorsolo St, Legaspi Village, Makati City, Metro Manila; tel. (2) 8172373; fax (2) 8175895; Ambassador: U TIN TUN.

Netherlands: King's Court Bldg, 9th Floor, 2129 Chino Roces Ave, POB 2448, Makati City, 1264 Metro Manila; tel. (2) 8125981; fax (2) 8154579; e-mail man@minbuza.nl; internet www.dutchembassy.ph; Ambassador: THEO ARNOLD.

New Zealand: Far East Bank Centre, 23rd Floor, Sen. Gil J. Puyat Ave, POB 3228, MCPO, Makati City, Metro Manila; tel. (2) 8915358; fax (2) 8915353; e-mail newzealand@embassy.com.ph; Ambassador: TERRY BAKER.

Nigeria: 2211 Paraiso St, Dasmariñas Village, Makati City, 1221 Metro Manila; POB 3174, MCPO, Makati City, 1271 Metro Manila; tel. (2) 8439866; fax (2) 8439867; e-mail embnigmanila@pacific.net.ph; Ambassador: Chief RAY O. INIJE.

Norway: Petron Mega Plaza, 21st Floor, 358 Sen. Gil J. Puyat Ave, Makati City, 1209 Metro Manila; tel. (2) 8863245; fax (2) 8863244; e-mail emb.manila@info.com.ph; internet www.noremb-manila.org; Ambassador: PAUL MOE.

Pakistan: Alexander House, 6th Floor, 132 Amorsolo St, Legaspi Village, Makati City, Metro Manila; tel. (2) 8172772; fax (2) 8400229; e-mail parepmnl@info.co.ph; Ambassador: IFTIKHAR HUSSAIN KAZMI.

Panama: Victoria Bldg, 5th Floor, 429 United Nations Ave, Ermita, Metro Manila; tel. (2) 5212790; fax (2) 5215755; e-mail panaembassy@i-manila.com.ph; Ambassador: JUAN CARLOS ESCALONA AVILA.

Papua New Guinea: 3rd Floor, Corinthian Plaza Condominium Bldg, cnr Paseo de Roxas and Gamboa St, Makati City, Metro Manila; tel. (2) 8113465; fax (2) 8113466; Ambassador: GRAHAM AINUI.

Peru: Unit 1604, Antel Corporate Centre, 139 Valero St, Salcedo Village, Makati City, Metro Manila; tel. (2) 8138731; fax (2) 8188191; e-mail eperfil@compass.com.ph; Ambassador: JORGE CHAVEZ.

Portugal: 14th Floor, Unit D, Trafalgar Plaza, 105 H.V. de la Costa St, Salcedo Village, Makati City, Metro Manila; tel. (2) 8483789; fax (2) 8483791; Ambassador: JOÃO CAETANO DA SILVA.

Qatar: 1601 Cypress St, Dasmariñas Village, Makati City, Metro Manila; tel. (2) 8874944; fax (2) 8876406; Ambassador: SALEH IBRAHIM AL-KUWARI.

Romania: 1216 Acacia Rd, Dasmariñas Village, Makati City, Metro Manila; tel. (2) 8439014; fax (2) 8439063; Ambassador: (vacant).

Russia: 1245 Acacia Rd, Dasmariñas Village, Makati City, Metro Manila; tel. (2) 8930190; fax (2) 8109614; e-mail RusEmb@i-manila.com.ph; Ambassador: ANATOLI I. KHMELNITSKI.

Saudi Arabia: Saudi Embassy Bldg, 389 Sen. Gil J. Puyat Ave Ext., Makati City, Metro Manila; tel. (2) 8909735; fax (2) 8953493; Ambassador: SALEH MUHAMMAD AL-GHAMDI.

Singapore: The Enterprise Centre, Tower I, 35th Floor, 6766 Ayala Ave, cnr Paseo de Roxas, Makati City, Metro Manila; tel. (2) 7512345; Ambassador: JACKY FOO.

Spain: ACT Tower, 5th Floor, 135 Sen. Gil J. Puyat Ave, Makati City, 1200 Metro Manila; tel. (2) 8183561; fax (2) 8102885; e-mail embspain@surfshop.net.ph; Ambassador: TOMÁS RODRÍGUEZ-PANTOJA.

Sri Lanka: 2260 Avocado Ave, Dasmariñas Village, Makati City, Metro Manila; tel. (2) 8439813; Ambassador: PITIDUWA GAMAGE KARUNASIRI.

Sweden: Equitable PCI Bank Tower II, 16th Floor, Makati Ave, Makati City, Metro Manila; POB 2322, MCPO 1263, Makati City, Metro Manila; tel. (2) 8191951; fax (2) 8153002; e-mail ambassaden.manila@foreign.ministry.se; internet www.swedemb-manila.com; Ambassador: ULF HÅKANSSON.

Switzerland: Equitable Bank Tower, 24th Floor, 8751 Paseo de Roxas, Makati City, 1226 Metro Manila; tel. (2) 7579000; fax (2) 7573718; e-mail vertretung@man.rep.admin.ch; Ambassador: Dr WERNER BAUMANN.

Thailand: 107 Rada St, Legaspi Village, Makati City, 1229 Metro Manila; tel. (2) 8154220; fax (2) 8154221; internet www.worldtelphil.com/~thaicomm; Ambassador: BUSBA BUNNAG.

Turkey: 2268 Paraiso St, Dasmariñas Village, Makati City, Metro Manila; tel. (2) 8439705; fax (2) 8439702; Ambassador: VEKA INAL.

United Arab Emirates: Renaissance Bldg, 2nd Floor, 215 Sakedo St, Legaspi Village, Makati City, Metro Manila; tel. (2) 8173906; fax (2) 8183577; Ambassador: MOHAMMED EBRAHIM ABDULLAH AL-JOWAID.

United Kingdom: Locsin Bldg, 15th–17th Floors, 6752 Ayala Ave, cnr Makati Ave, Makati City, 1226 Metro Manila; POB 1970 MCC, Metro Manila; tel. (2) 8167116; fax (2) 8197206; e-mail uk@info.com.ph; internet www.britishembassy.org.ph; Ambassador: ALAN COLLINS.

USA: 1201 Roxas Blvd, Metro Manila; tel. (2) 5231001; fax (2) 5224361; e-mail manila1@pd.state.gov; internet www.usembassy.state.gov/manila; Ambassador: FRANCIS RICCIARDONE.

Venezuela: Unit 17A, Multinational Bancorporation Center, 6805 Ayala Ave, Makati City, Metro Manila 1200; tel. (2) 8452841; fax (2) 8452866; e-mail embavefi@compass.com.ph; Ambassador: MILENA SANTANA-RAMÍREZ.

Viet Nam: 670 Pablo Ocampo St, Malate, Metro Manila; tel. (2) 5252837; fax (2) 5260472; e-mail sqvnplp@qinet.net; Ambassador: NGUYEN THAC DINH.

Judicial System

The February 1987 Constitution provides for the establishment of a Supreme Court comprising a Chief Justice and 14 Associate Justices; the Court may sit *en banc,* or in divisions of three, five or seven members. Justices of the Supreme Court are appointed by the President from a list of a minimum of three nominees prepared by a Judicial and Bar Council. Other courts comprise the Court of Appeals, Regional Trial Courts, Metropolitan Trial Courts, Municipal Courts in Cities, Municipal Courts and Municipal Circuit Trial Courts. There is also a special court for trying cases of corruption (the Sandiganbayan). The Office of the Ombudsman (Tanodbayan) investigates complaints concerning the actions of public officials.

Supreme Court

Taft Ave, cnr Padre Faura St, Ermita, 1000 Metro Manila; tel. (2) 5268123; e-mail infos@supremecourt.gov.ph; internet www.supremecourt.gov.ph.

Chief Justice: HILARIO G. DAVIDE, Jr.

Court of Appeals

Consists of a Presiding Justice and 50 Associate Justices.

Presiding Justice: JESUS M. ELBINIAS.

Islamic Shari'a courts were established in the southern Philippines in July 1985 under a presidential decree of February 1977. They are presided over by three district magistrates and six circuit judges.

Religion

In 1991 94.2% of the population were Christians: 84.1% were Roman Catholics, 6.2% belonged to the Philippine Independent Church (Aglipayan) and 3.9% were Protestants. There is an Islamic community, and an estimated 43,000 Buddhists. Animists and persons professing no religion number approximately 400,000.

CHRISTIANITY

Sangguniang Pambansa ng mga Simbahan sa Pilipinas (National Council of Churches in the Philippines): 879 Epifanio de los Santos Ave, Diliman, Quezon City, Metro Manila; tel. (2) 9288636; fax (2) 9267076; e-mail nccp-ga@philonline.com; f. 1963; 11 mem. churches, 10 assoc. mems; publishes NCCP news magazine quarterly and TUGON periodically; Gen. Sec. SHARON ROSE JOY RUIZ-DUREMDES.

The Roman Catholic Church

For ecclesiastical purposes, the Philippines comprises 16 archdioceses, 50 dioceses, six territorial prelatures and seven apostolic vicariates. In December 2000 there were an estimated 66,548,331 adherents in the country, representing 82.1% of the total population.

Catholic Bishops' Conference of the Philippines (CBCP): 470 General Luna St, Intramuros, 1002 Metro Manila; POB 3601, 1076 Metro Manila; tel. (2) 5274138; fax (2) 5274063; e-mail cbcp@cbcpnet.net; internet www.cbcp.com; f. 1945 (statutes approved 1952); Pres. Most Rev. ORLANDO B. QUEVEDO (Archbishop of Cotabato).

Archbishop of Caceres: Most Rev. LEONARDO Z. LEGASPI, Archbishop's House, Elias Angeles St, POB 6085, 4400 Naga City; tel. (54) 4738483; fax (54) 4732800.

Archbishop of Cagayan de Oro: Most Rev. JESUS B. TUQUIB, Archbishop's Residence, POB 113, 9000 Misamis Oriental, Cagayan de Oro City; tel. (88) 8571357; fax (88) 726304; e-mail orochan@cdo.weblinq.com.

Archbishop of Capiz: Most Rev. ONESIMO C. GORDONCILLO, Chancery Office, POB 44, 5800 Roxas City; tel. (36) 6215595; fax (36) 6211053.

Archbishop of Cebu: Cardinal RICARDO J. VIDAL, Archbishop's Residence, cnr P. Gomez St and P. Burgos St, POB 52, 6000 Cebu City; tel. (32) 2530123; fax (32) 2530616; e-mail adelito@skynet.net.

Archbishop of Cotabato: Most Rev. ORLANDO B. QUEVEDO, Archbishop's Residence, Sinsuat Ave, POB 186, 9600 Cotabato City; tel. (64) 4212918; fax (64) 4211446.

Archbishop of Davao: Most Rev. FERNANDO R. CAPALLA, Archbishop's Residence, 247 Florentino Torres St, POB 80418, 8000 Davao City; tel. (82) 2271163; fax (82) 2279771; e-mail bishop-davao@skyinet.net.

Archbishop of Jaro: Most Rev. ANGEL N. LAGDAMEO, D. D., Archbishop's Residence, Jaro, 5000 Iloilo City; tel. (33) 3294442; fax (33) 3293197; e-mail abpjaro@skyinet.net.

Archbishop of Lingayen-Dagupan: Most Rev. OSCAR V. CRUZ, Archbishop's House, 2400 Dagupan City; tel. (75) 52353576; fax (75) 5221878; e-mail oscar@rezcom.com.

Archbishop of Lipa: Most Rev. GAUDENCIO B. ROSALES, Archbishop's House, St Lorenzo Ruiz St, Lipa City, 4217 Batangas; tel. (43) 7562572; fax (43) 7560005; e-mail lipachancery@ala-eh.net.

Archbishop of Manila: Cardinal JAIME L. SIN, Arzobispado, 121 Arzobispo St, Intramuros, POB 132, 1099 Metro Manila; tel. (2) 5277631; fax (2) 5273955; e-mail aord@mailstation.net; internet www.geocities.com/aocmanila.

Archbishop of Nueva Segovia: Most. Rev. EDMUNDO M. ABAYA, Archbishop's House, Vigan, 2700 Ilocos Sur; tel. (77) 7222018; fax (77) 7221591.

Archbishop of Ozamis: Most Rev. JESUS A. DOSADO, Archbishop's House, POB 2760, 7200 Ozamis City; tel. (65) 5212820; fax (65) 5211574.

Archbishop of Palo: Most Rev. PEDRO R. DEAN, Archdiocesan Chancery, Bukid Tabor, Palo, 6501 Leyte; POB 173, Tacloban City, 6500 Leyte; (53) 3232213; fax (53) 3235607; e-mail rcap@mozcom.com.

Archbishop of San Fernando (Pampanga): Most Rev. PACIANO B. ANICETO, Chancery House, San José, San Fernando, 2000 Pampanga; tel. (45) 9612819; fax (45) 9616772; e-mail rca@pamp.pworld.net.ph.

Archbishop of Tuguegarao: Most Rev. DIOSDADO A. TALAMAYAN, Archbishop's House, Tuguegarao, 3500 Cagayan; tel. (78) 8441663; fax (78) 8462822; e-mail rcat@cag.pworld.net.ph.

Archbishop of Zamboanga: Most Rev. CARMELO DOMINADOR F. MORELOS, Sacred Heart Center, POB 1, Justice R. T. Lim Blvd, 7000 Zamboanga City; tel. (62) 9911329; fax (62) 9932608; e-mail aofzam@jetlink.com.ph.

Other Christian Churches

Convention of Philippine Baptist Churches: POB 263, 5000 Iloilo City; tel. (33) 3290621; fax (33) 3290618; e-mail gensec@iloilo.net; f. 1935; Gen. Sec. Rev. Dr NATHANIEL M. FABULA; Pres. DONATO ENABE.

Episcopal Church in the Philippines: 275 E. Rodriguez Sr Ave, Quezon City, 1102 Metro Manila; POB 10321, Broadway Centrum, Quezon City, 1112 Metro Manila; tel. (2) 7228478; fax (2) 7211923; e-mail ecpi@info.com.ph; internet www.episcopalphilippines.net; f. 1901; six dioceses; Prime Bishop Most Rev. IGNACIO C. SOLIBA.

Iglesia Evangélica Metodista en las Islas Filipinas (Evangelical Methodist Church in the Philippines): Beulah Land, Iemelif Center, Greenfields 1, Subdivision, Marytown Circle, Novaliches, Quezon City, Metro Manila; tel. (2) 9356519; fax (2) 4185017; e-mail iemelifph@yahoo.com; internet www.iemelif.com.ph; f. 1909; 40,000 mems (2000); Gen. Supt Bishop NATHANAEL P. LAZARO.

Iglesia Filipina Independiente (Philippine Independent Church): 1500 Taft Ave, Ermita, 1000 Metro Manila; tel. (2) 5237242; fax (2) 5213932; e-mail ifiphil@hotmail.com; internet www.ifi.dpinoyweb.com; f. 1902; 39 dioceses; 6.0m. mems; Obispo Maximo (Supreme Bishop) Most Rev. TOMAS MILLAMENA.

Iglesia ni Cristo: 1 Central Ave, New Era, Quezon City, 1107 Metro Manila; tel. (2) 9814311; fax (2) 9811111; f. 1914; 2m. mems; Exec. Minister Brother ERAÑO G. MANALO.

Lutheran Church in the Philippines: 4461 Old Santa Mesa, 1008 Metro Manila; POB 507, 1099 Metro Manila; tel. (2) 7157084; fax (2) 7142395; f. 1946; Pres. Rev. EDUARDO LADLAD.

Union Church of Manila: cnr Legaspi St and Rada St, Legaspi Village, Makati City, Metro Manila; tel. (2) 8126062; fax (2) 8172386; e-mail ucm@amdg.com.ph; internet www.unionchurch.ph; Interim Pastor Dr DOUGLAS BEYER.

United Church of Christ in the Philippines: 877 Epifanio de los Santos Ave, West Triangle, Quezon City, Metro Manila; POB 718, MCPO, Ermita, 1099 Metro Manila; tel. (2) 9240215; fax (2) 9240207; e-mail uccpnaof@manila-online.net; f. 1948; 900,000 mems (1996); Gen. Sec. Rev. ELMER M. BOLOCON (Bishop).

Among other denominations active in the Philippines are the Iglesia Evangélica Unida de Cristo and the United Methodist Church.

ISLAM

Some 14 different ethnic groups profess the Islamic faith in the Philippines, and Muslims comprised 4.6% of the total population at the census of 1990. Mindanao and the Sulu and Tawi-Tawi archipelago, in the southern Philippines, are predominantly Muslim provinces, but there are 10 other such provinces, each with its own Imam, or Muslim religious leader. More than 500,000 Muslims live in the north of the country (mostly in, or near to, Manila).

Confederation of Muslim Organizations of the Philippines (CMOP): Metro Manila; Nat. Chair. JAMIL DIANALAN.

BAHÁ'Í FAITH

National Spiritual Assembly: 1070 A. Roxas St, cnr Bautista St, Singalong Subd., Malate, 1004 Metro Manila; POB 4323, 1099 Metro Manila; tel. (2) 5240404; fax (2) 5245918; e-mail nsaphil@skyinet.net; mems resident in 129,949 localities; Chair. GIL MARVEL TABUCANON; Sec.-Gen. VIRGINIA S. TOLEDO.

The Press

The Office of the President implements government policies on information and the media. Freedom of the press and freedom of speech are guaranteed under the 1987 Constitution.

METRO MANILA

Dailies

Abante: Monica Publishing Corpn, Rooms 301-305, BF Condominium Bldg, 3rd Floor, Solana St, cnr. A. Soriano St, Intramuros, Metro Manila; tel. (2) 5273385; fax (2) 5274470; e-mail abante@

abante-tonite.com; internet www.abante.com.ph; morning; Filipino and English; Editor NICOLAS QUIJANO, Jr; circ. 417,000.

Abante Tonite: Monica Publishing Corpn, Rooms 301-305, BF Condominium Bldg, 3rd Floor, Solana St, cnr. A. Soriano St, Intramuros, Metro Manila; tel. (2) 5273385; fax (2) 5274470; e-mail tonite@abante-tonite.com; internet www.abante-tonite.com; afternoon; Filipino and English; Man. Editor NICOLAS QUIJANO, Jr; circ. 277,000.

Ang Pilipino Ngayon: 202 Railroad St, cnr 13th St, Port Area, Metro Manila; tel. (2) 401871; fax (2) 5224998; Filipino; Publr and Editor JOSE M. BUHAIN; circ. 286,452.

Balita: Liwayway Publishing Inc, 2249 China Roces Ave, Makati City, Metro Manila; tel. (2) 8193101; fax (2) 8175167; internet www.balita.org; f. 1972; morning; Filipino; Editor MARCELO S. LAGMAY; circ. 151,000.

Daily Tribune: Penthouse Suites, Plywood Industries Bldg, T. M. Kalaw St, cnr A. Mabini St, Ermita, Metro Manila; tel. (2) 5215511; fax (2) 5215522; e-mail nco@tribune.net.ph; internet www .tribune.net.ph; f. 2000; English; Publr and Editor-in-Chief NINEZ CACHO-OLIVARES.

Malaya: People's Independent Media Inc, 575 Atlanta St, Port Area, Metro Manila; tel. (2) 5277651; fax (2) 5271839; e-mail opinion@ malaya.com.ph; internet www.malaya.com.ph; f. 1983; English; Editor JOEY C. DE LOS REYES; circ. 175,000.

Manila Bulletin: Bulletin Publishing Corpn, cnr Muralla and Recoletos Sts, Intramuros, POB 769, Metro Manila; tel. (2) 5271519; fax (2) 5277534; e-mail bulletin@mb.com.ph; internet www.mb.com.ph; f. 1900; English; Publr EMILIO YAP; Editor BEN RODRIGUEZ; circ. 265,000.

Manila Standard: Leyland Bldg, 21st St, cnr Railroad St, Port Area, Metro Manila; tel. (2) 5278351; e-mail infoms@philonline.com; internet www.manilastandard.net; morning; English; Editor-in-Chief JULLIE YAP DAZA; circ. 96,000.

Manila Times: Liberty Bldg, 13th St, Port Area, Metro Manila; tel. (2) 5245664; fax (2) 5216887; e-mail newsboy1@manilatimes.net; internet www.manilatimes.net; f. 1945; morning; English; Publr, Chair and Pres. DANTE. A. ANG; Editor-in-Chief CIPRIANO S. ROXAS.

People Tonight: Philippine Journalist Inc, Railroad St, cnr 19th and 20th Sts, Port Area, Metro Manila; tel. (2) 5278421; fax (2) 5274627; f. 1978; English and Filipino; Editor FERDIE RAMOS; circ. 500,000.

People's Bagong Taliba: Philippine Journalist Inc, Railroad St, cnr 19th and 20th Sts, Port Area, Metro Manila; tel. (2) 5278121; fax (2) 5274627; Filipino; Editor MATEO VICENCIO; circ. 229,000.

People's Journal: Philippine Journalist Inc, Railroad St, cnr 19th and 20th Sts, Port Area, Metro Manila; tel. (2) 5278421; fax (2) 5274627; English and Filipino; Editor ROSAURO ACOSTA; circ. 219,000.

Philippine Daily Globe: Nova Communications Inc, 2nd Floor, Rudgen Bldg, 17 Shaw Blvd, Metro Manila; tel. (2) 6730496; Editor-in-Chief YEN MAKABENTA; circ. 40,000.

Philippine Daily Inquirer: Philippine Daily Inquirer Bldg, cnr Mascardo St and Yague St, Pasong Tamo, Makati City, 1220 Metro Manila; tel. (2) 8978808; fax (2) 8914793; e-mail feedback@inquirer .com.ph; internet www.inquirer.net; f. 1985; English; Chair. MARIXI R. PRIETO; Editor-in-Chief RIGOBERTO TIGLAO; circ. 250,000.

Philippine Herald-Tribune: V. Esguerra II Bldg, 140 Amorsolo St, Legaspi Village, Makati City, Metro Manila; tel. (2) 853711; f. 1987; Christian-orientated; Pres. AMADA VALINO.

Philippine Star: 13th and Railroad Sts, Port Area, Metro Manila; tel. (2) 5277901; fax (2) 5276851; e-mail philippinestar@hotmail.com; internet www.philstar.com; f. 1986; Editor BOBBY DE LA CRUZ; circ. 275,000.

Tempo: Bulletin Publishing Corpn, Recoletos St, cnr Muralla St, Intramuros, Metro Manila; tel. (2) 5278121; fax (2) 5277534; internet www.tempo.com.ph; f. 1982; English and Filipino; Editor BEN RODRIGUEZ; circ. 230,000.

Today: Independent Daily News, JAKA Macrima Bldg, 1666 Epifanio de los Santos Ave, cnr Escuela St, Makati City, Metro Manila; tel. (2) 8186133; fax (2) 8193982; f. 1993; Editor-in-Chief TEODORO L. LOCSIN, Jr; Man. Editor LOURDES MOLINA-FERNANDEZ; circ. 106,000.

United Daily News: 812 and 818 Benavides St, Binondo, Metro Manila; tel. (2) 2447171; f. 1973; Chinese; Editor-in-Chief CHUA KEE; circ. 85,000.

Selected Periodicals

Weeklies

Banawag: Liwayway Bldg, 2249 Pasong Tamo, Makati City, Metro Manila; tel. (2) 8193101; fax (2) 8175167; f. 1934; Ilocano; Editor DIONISIO S. BULONG; circ. 42,900.

Bisaya: Liwayway Bldg, 2249 Pasong Tamo, Makati City, Metro Manila; tel. (2) 8193101; fax (2) 8175167; f. 1934; Cebu-Visayan; Editor SANTIAGO PEPITO; circ. 90,000.

Liwayway: Liwayway Bldg, 2249 Pasong Tamo, Makati City, Metro Manila; tel. (2) 8193101; fax (2) 8175167; f. 1922; Filipino; Editor RODOLFO SALANDANAN; circ. 102,400.

Panorama: Manila Bulletin Publishing Corpn, POB 769, cnr Muralla and Recoletos Sts, Intramuros, Metro Manila; tel. and fax (2) 5277509; f. 1968; English; Editor RANDY V. URLANDA; circ. 239,600.

Philippine Starweek: 13th St, cnr Railroad St, Port Area, Metro Manila; tel. (2) 5277901; fax (2) 5275819; e-mail starweek@pacific .net.ph; internet www.philstar.com; English; Publr MAXIMO V. SOLIVEN; circ. 268,000.

SELECTED REGIONAL PUBLICATIONS

The Aklan Reporter: 1227 Rizal St, Kalibo, Panay, Aklan; tel. (33) 3181; f. 1971; weekly; English and Aklanon; Editor ROMAN A. DE LA CRUZ; circ. 3,500.

Baguio Midland Courier: 16 Kisad Rd, POB 50, Baguio City; English and Ilocano; Editor SINAI C. HAMADA; circ. 6,000.

Bayanihan Weekly News: Bayanihan Publishing Co, P. Guevarra Ave, Santa Cruz, Laguna; tel. (645) 1001; f. 1966; Mon.; Filipino and English; Editor ARTHUR A. VALENOVA; circ. 1,000.

Bohol Chronicle: 56 B. Inting St, Tagbilaran City, Bohol; tel. (32) 3100; internet www.boholchronicle.com; f. 1954; 2 a week; English and Cebuano; Editor and Publr ZOILO DEJARESCO; circ. 5,500.

The Bohol Times: 100 Gallares St, Tagbilaran City, Bohol; tel. (38) 4112961; fax (38) 4112656; e-mail times@bit.fapenet.org; internet www.calamay.bit.fapenet.org/btimes; Pblr Dr LILIA A. BALITE; Editor-in-Chief ATTY SALVADOR D. DIPUTADO.

The Kapawa News: 10 Jose Abad Santos St, POB 365, 6100 Bacolod City; tel. and fax (34) 4441941; e-mail ethel-lyn2001@ yahoo.com; f. 1966; weekly; Sat.; Hiligaynon and English; Editor ETHELYN MOLES; circ. 15,000.

Mindanao Star: 44 Kolambagohan-Capistrano St, Cagayan de Oro City; internet www.mindanaostar.com; weekly; Editor ROMULFO SABAMAL; circ. 3,500.

Mindanao Times: UMBN Bldg, Ponciano Reyes St, Davao City, Mindanao; tel. 2273252; e-mail timesmen@mozcom.com; internet www.mindanaotimes.com.ph; daily; Pblr JOSEFINA SAN PEDRO (acting); Editor-in-Chief VIC SUMALINOG; circ. 5,000.

Pagadian Times: Pagadian City, 7824 Zamboanga del Sur; tel. 586; e-mail pagtimes@mozcom.com; internet www.pagadian.moz com.com/pagtimes; f. 1969; weekly; English; Publr PEDE G. LU; Editor JACINTO LUMBAY; circ. 5,000.

Palihan: Diversion Rd, cnr Sanciangco St, Cabanatuan City, Luzon; f. 1966; weekly; Filipino; Editor and Publr NONOY M. JARLEGO; circ. 5,000.

Sorsogon Today: 2886 Burgos St, POB 20, East District, 4700 Sorsogon; tel. and fax (56) 2111340; e-mail sorsogontoday@mail city.com; f. 1977; weekly; Publr and CEO MARCOS E. PARAS, Jr; circ. 2,400.

The Tribune: Maharlika Highway, 2301 Cabanatuan City, Luzon; f. 1960; weekly; English and Filipino; Editor and Publr ORLANDO M. JARLEGO; circ. 8,000.

The Valley Times: Daang Maharlika, San Felipe, Ilagan, Isabela; f. 1962; weekly; English; Editor AUREA A. DE LA CRUZ; circ. 4,500.

The Visayan Tribune: 826 Iznart St, Iloilo City; tel. (33) 75760; f. 1959; weekly; Tue.; English; Editor HERBERT L. VEGO; circ. 5,000.

The Voice of Islam: Davao City; tel. (82) 81368; f. 1973; monthly; English and Arabic; official Islamic news journal; Editor and Publr NASHIR MUHAMMAD AL'RASHID AL HAJJ.

The Weekly Negros Gazette: Broce St, San Carlos City, 6033 Negros Occidental; f. 1956; weekly; Editor NESTORIO L. LAYUMAS, Sr; circ. 5,000.

NEWS AGENCIES

Philippines News Agency: PIA Bldg, 2nd Floor, Visayas Ave, Diliman, Quezon City, Metro Manila; tel. (2) 9206551; fax (2) 9206566; e-mail philna@ops.gov.ph; internet www.pna.ops.gov.ph; f. 1973; Gen. Man. GEORGE REYES; Exec. Editor SEVERINO SAMONTE.

Foreign Bureaux

Agence France-Presse (AFP): Kings Court Bldg 2, 5th Floor, Pasong Tamo, cnr de la Rosa St, Makati City, Metro Manila; tel. (2) 8112028; fax (2) 8112664; Bureau Chief MONICA EGOY.

Agencia EFE (Spain): 5th Floor, Singapore Airlines Bldg, 138 de la Costa St, Salcedo Village, Makati City, 1227 Metro Manila; tel.

(2) 8173663; fax (2) 8153395; e-mail efe@i-next.net; Bureau Chief MARÍA LUISA RUBIO.

Associated Press (AP) (USA): S&L Bldg, 3rd Floor, 1500 Roxas Blvd, Ermita, 1000 Metro Manila; tel. (2) 5259217; fax (2) 5212430; Bureau Chief DAVID THURBER.

Deutsche Presse Agentur (dpa) (Germany): Physicians Tower Bldg, 533 United Nations Ave, Ermita 1000, Metro Manila; tel. (2) 5221919; fax (2) 5221447; Representative GIRLIE LINAO.

Inter Press Service (IPS) (Italy): Amberland Plaza, Room 510, J. Vargas Ave, Ortigas Complex Pasig City, 1600 Metro Manila; tel. (2) 6353421; fax (2) 6353660; Correspondent JOHANNA SON.

Jiji Tsushin (Jiji Press) (Japan): Legaspi Tower, Suite 21, 3rd Floor, 2600 Roxas Blvd, Metro Manila; tel. (2) 5211472; fax (2) 5211474; Correspondent IPPEI MIYASAKA.

Kyodo News Service (Japan): Pacific Star Bldg, 4th Floor, Makati Ave, cnr Sen. Gil J. Puyat Ave, Makati City, Metro Manila; tel. (2) 8133072; fax (2) 8133914; Correspondent KIMIO OKI.

Reuters (UK): L.V. Locsin Bldg, 10th Floor, Ayala Ave, cnr Makati Ave, Makati City, 1226 Metro Manila; tel. (2) 8418900; fax (2) 8176267; Country Man. RAJU GOPALAKRISHNAN.

United Press International (UPI) (USA): Manila Pavilion Hotel, Room 526C, United Nations Ave, Ermita, 1000 Metro Manila; tel. (2) 5212051; fax (2) 5212074; Bureau Chief MICHAEL DI CICCO.

Xinhua (New China) News Agency (People's Republic of China): 705B Gotesco Twin Towers, 1129 Concepcion St, Ermita, Metro Manila; tel. (2) 5271404; fax (2) 5271410; Chief Correspondent CHEN HEGAO.

PRESS ASSOCIATION

National Press Club of the Philippines: National Press Club Bldg, Magallanes Drive, 1002 Intramuros, Metro Manila; tel. (2) 494242; f. 1952; Pres. MARCELO LAGMAY; Vice-Pres. RECAH TRINIDAD; 942 mems.

Publishers

Abiva Publishing House Inc: Abiva Bldg, 851 Gregorio Araneta Ave, Quezon City, 1113 Metro Manila; tel. (2) 7120245; fax (2) 7320308; e-mail mmrabiva@i-manila.com.ph; internet www.abiva.com.ph; f. 1937; reference and textbooks; Pres. LUIS Q. ABIVA, Jr.

Ateneo de Manila University Press: Bellarmine Bldg, Ateneo de Manila University, Katipunan Rd, Loyola Heights, Quezon City, Metro Manila; tel. (2) 4265984; fax (2) 4265909; e-mail unipress@admu.edu.ph; internet www.ateneouniversitypress.com; f. 1972; literary, textbooks, humanities, social sciences, reference books on the Philippines; Dir CORAZON E. BAYTION.

Bookman, Inc: 373 Quezon Ave, Quezon City, 1114 Metro Manila; tel. (2) 7124813; fax (2) 7124843; e-mail bookman@info.com.ph; f. 1945; textbooks, reference, educational; Pres. MARIETTA PICACHE MARTINEZ; Vice-Pres. LINA PICACHE ENRIQUEZ.

Capitol Publishing House, Inc: 13 Team Pacific Bldg, Jose C. Cruz St, cnr F. Legaspi St, Barrio Ugong, Pasig City, Metro Manila; f. 1947; tel. (2) 6712662; fax (2) 6712664; e-mail cacho@mozcom.com; Gen. Man. MANUEL L. ATIENZA.

Heritage Publishing House: 33 4th Ave, cnr Main Ave, Cubao, Quezon City, POB 3667, Metro Manila; tel. (2) 7248114; fax (2) 6471393; e-mail heritage@iconn.com.ph; internet www.iconn.com.ph/heritage; art, anthropology, history, political science; Pres. MARIO R. ALCANTARA; Man. Dir RICARDO S. SANCHEZ.

The Lawyers' Co-operative Publishing Co. Inc: 1071 Del Pan St, Makati City, 1206 Metro Manila; tel. (2) 5634073; fax (2) 5642021; e-mail lawbooks@info.com.ph; f. 1908; law, educational; Pres. ELSA K. ELMA.

Liwayway Publishing Inc: 2249 Chino Roces Ave, Makati City, Metro Manila; tel. (2) 8193101; fax (2) 8175167; magazines and newspapers; Pres. RENE G. ESPINA; Chair. DIONISIO S. BULONG.

Mutual Books Inc: 429 Shaw Blvd, Mandaluyong City, Metro Manila; tel. (2) 7257538; fax (2) 7213056; f. 1959; textbooks on accounting, management and economics, computers and mathematics; Pres. ALFREDO S. NICDAO, Jr.

Phoenix—SIBS Publishing House Inc: 927 Quezon Ave, Quezon City, 1104 Metro Manila; tel. (2) 3724733; fax (2) 3724732; e-mail sibsbook@info.com.ph; internet www.sibs.com.ph; f. 1958; sciences, languages, religion, literature, history; Pres. JESUS ERNESTO SIBAL; Gen. Man. JUAN CARLOS SIBAL.

Reyes Publishing Inc: Mariwasa Bldg, 4th Floor, 717 Aurora Blvd, Quezon City, 1112 Metro Manila; tel. (2) 7221827; fax (2) 7218782; e-mail reyespub@skyinet.net; f. 1964; art, history and culture; Pres. LOUIE REYES.

Sinag-Tala Publishers Inc: GMA Lou-Bel Plaza, 6th Floor, Chino Roces Ave, cnr Bagtikan St, San Antonio Village, Makati City, 0712 Metro Manila; tel. (2) 8971162; fax (2) 8969626; e-mail info@sinagtala.com; internet www.sinagtala.com; f. 1972; educational textbooks; business, professional and religious books; Man. Dir LUIS A. USON.

University of the Philippines Press: Epifanio de los Santos Ave, U. P. Campus, Diliman, Quezon City, 1101 Metro Manila; tel. (2) 9252930; fax (2) 9282558; e-mail press@up.edu.ph; internet www.upd.edu.ph/~uppress; f. 1965; literature, history, political science, sociology, cultural studies, economics, anthropology, mathematics; Officer in Charge RUTH JORDANA L. PISON.

Vibal Publishing House Inc: G. Araneta Ave, cnr Maria Clara St, Talayan, Quezon City, Metro Manila; tel. (2) 7122722; fax (2) 7118852; internet www.vibalpublishing.com; f. 1955; linguistics, social sciences, mathematics, religion; CEO ESTHER A. VIBAL.

PUBLISHERS' ASSOCIATIONS

Philippine Educational Publishers' Asscn: 84 P. Florentino St, Quezon City, 1104 Metro Manila; tel. (2) 7402698; fax (2) 7115702; e-mail dbuhain@cnl.net; Pres. DOMINADOR D. BUHAIN.

Publishers' Association of the Philippines Inc: Gammon Center, Alfaro St, Salcedo Village, Makati City, Metro Manila; f. 1974; mems comprise all newspaper, magazine and book publrs in the Philippines; Pres. KERIMA P. TUVERA; Exec. Dir ROBERTO M. MENDOZA.

Broadcasting and Communications

National Telecommunications Commission (NTC): NTC Bldg, BIR Rd, East Triangle, Diliman, Quezon City, Metro Manila; tel. (2) 9244042; fax (2) 9217128; e-mail ntc@ntc.gov.ph; internet www.ntc.gov.ph; f. 1979; supervises and controls all private and public telecommunications services; Dir Commr ELISEO M. RIO, jr.

TELECOMMUNICATIONS

BayanTel: Benpres Bldg, 5th Floor, Meralco Ave, cnr Exchange Rd, Pasig City, Metro Manila; tel. (2) 4493000; fax (2) 4492511; e-mail bayanserve@bayantel.com.ph; internet www.bayantel.com.ph; 359,000 fixed lines (1999); Pres. RODOLFO SALAZAR.

Bell Telecommunications Philippines (BellTel): Pacific Star Bldg, 3rd and 4th Floors, Sen. Gil J. Puyat Ave, cnr Makati Ave, Makati City, Metro Manila; tel. (2) 8400808; fax (2) 8915618; e-mail info@belltel.ph; internet www.belltel.ph; f. 1997; Pres. EDRAGDO REYES.

Capitol Wireless Inc: Dolmar Gold Tower, 6th Floor, 107 Carlos Palanca, Jr, St, Legaspi Village, Makati City, Metro Manila; tel. (2) 8159961; fax (2) 8941141; Pres. EPITACIO R. MARQUEZ.

Digital Telecommunications Philippines Inc: 110 Eulogio Rodriguez, Jr Ave, Bagumbayan, Quezon City, 1110 Metro Manila; tel. (2) 6330000; fax (2) 6339387; provision of fixed line telecommunications services; 564,304 fixed lines (1998); cap. and res 10,928m. pesos, sales 3,060m. pesos (1998); Chief Exec. RICARDO J. ROMULO; Pres. JOHN GOKONGWEI.

Domestic Satellite Philippines Inc (DOMSAT): Solid House Bldg, 4th Floor, 2285 Pasong Tamo Ext., Makati City, 1231 Metro Manila; tel. (2) 8105917; fax (2) 8671677; Pres. SIEGFRED MISON.

Globe Telecom (GMCR, Inc): Globe Telecom Plaza, 57th Floor, Pioneer St, cnr Madison St, 1552 Mandaluyong City, Metro Manila; tel. (2) 7302701; fax (2) 7302586; e-mail custhelp@globetel.com.ph; internet www.globe.com.ph; 700,000 fixed and mobile telephone subscribers (1999); Pres. and CEO GERARDO C. ABLAZA, Jr.

Philippine Communications Satellite Corpn (PhilcomSat): 12th Floor, Telecoms Plaza, 316 Sen. Gil J. Puyat Ave, Makati City, Metro Manila; tel. (2) 8158406; fax (2) 8159287; Pres. MANUEL H. NIETO.

Philippine Global Communications, Inc (PhilCom): 8755 Paseo de Roxas, Makati City, Metro Manila; tel. (2) 8162851; fax (2) 8162872; e-mail aong@philcom.com; internet www.philcom.com; Pres. EVELYN SINGSON.

Philippine Long Distance Telephone Co: Ramon Cojuangco Bldg, Makati Ave, POB 2148, Makati City, Metro Manila; tel. (2) 8168883; fax (2) 8186800; e-mail media@pldt.com.ph; internet www.pldt.com.ph; f. 1928; monopoly on overseas telephone service until 1989; retains 94% of Philippine telephone traffic; 2,516,748 fixed lines (1998); Chair. ANTONIO COJUANGCO; Pres. and CEO MANUEL PANGILINAN.

Pilipino Telephone Corpn (Piltel): Bankers Center, 9th Floor, 6764 Ayala Ave, Makati City, Metro Manila; tel. (2) 8913888; fax (2) 8171121; major cellular telephone provider; 400,000 subscribers (1999); Chair. ROBERTO V. ONGPIN; Pres. and CEO NAPOLEON L. NAZARENO.

Smart Communications, Inc (SCI): Rufino Pacific Tower, 12th Floor, Ayala Ave, cnr Herrera St, Makati City, Metro Manila; tel. (2) 8110213; fax (2) 5113400; 900,000 mobile telephone subscribers (1999); Pres. ORLANDO B. VEA.

BROADCASTING

Radio

Banahaw Broadcasting Corpn: Broadcast City, Capitol Hills, Diliman, Quezon City, 3005 Metro Manila; tel. (2) 9329949; fax (2) 9318751; 14 stations; Station Man. BETTY LIVIOCO.

Cebu Broadcasting Co: FJE Bldg, 105 Esteban St, Legaspi Village, Makati City, Metro Manila; tel. (2) 8159131; fax (2) 8125592; Chair. HADRIAN ARROYO.

Far East Broadcasting Co Inc: POB 1, Valenzuela, 0560 Metro Manila; 62 Karuhatan Rd, Karuhatan, Valenzuela City, 1441 Metro Manila; tel. (2) 2921152; fax (2) 2925790; e-mail febcomphil@febc.org.ph: internet www.febc.org.ph; f. 1948; 18 stations; operates a classical music station, eight domestic stations and an overseas service in 64 languages throughout Asia; Pres. CARLOS L. PEÑA.

Filipinas Broadcasting Network: Legaspi Towers 200, Room 306, Paseo de Roxas, Makati City, Metro Manila; tel. (2) 8176133; fax (2) 8177135; Gen. Man. DIANA C. GOZUM.

GMA Network Inc: GMA Network Centre, EDSA cnr Timog Ave, Diliman, Quezon City, 1103 Metro Manila; tel. (2) 9287021; fax (2) 4263925; e-mail yourgmafamily@gmanetwork.com; internet www.igma.tv; f. 1950; fmrly Republic Broadcasting System Inc; transmits nationwide through 44 television stations; Chair., Pres. and CEO FELIPE L. GOZON; Exec. Vice-Pres. GILBERTO R. DUAVIT Jr.

Manila Broadcasting Co: FJE Bldg, 4th Floor, 105 Esteban St, Legaspi Village, Makati City, Metro Manila; tel. (2) 8177043; fax (2) 8400763; f. 1946; 10 stations; Pres. RUPERTO NICDAO, Jr; Gen. Man. EDUARDO L. MONTILLA.

Nation Broadcasting Corpn: NBC Broadcast Center, Jacinta II Bldg, Epifanio de los Santos Ave, Guadelupe, Makati City, 1200 Metro Manila; tel. (2) 8821622; fax (2) 8821360; e-mail joey@nbc.ph; internet www.nbc.com.ph; f. 1963; 31 stations; Pres. FRANCIS LUMEN.

Newsounds Broadcasting Network Inc: Florete Bldg, Ground Floor, 2406 Nobel, cnr Edison St, Makati City, 3117 Metro Manila; tel. (2) 8430116; fax (2) 8173631; 10 stations; Gen. Man. E. BILLONES; Office Man. HERMAN BASBANO.

Pacific Broadcasting System: c/o Manila Broadcasting Co, FJE Bldg, 105 Esteban St, Legaspi Village, Makati City, Metro Manila; tel. (2) 8921660; fax (2) 8400763; Pres. RUPERTO NICDAO, Jr; Vice-Pres. RODOLFO ARCE.

PBN Broadcasting Network: Ersan Bldg, 3rd Floor, 32 Quezon Ave, Queen City, Metro Manila; tel. (2) 7325424; fax (2) 7438162; e-mail pbn@philonline.com.ph; Pres. JORGE BAYONA.

Philippines Broadcasting Service (PBS): Bureau of Broadcast Services, Office of the Press Sec., Philippine Information Agency Bldg, 4th Floor, Visayas Ave, Quezon City, Metro Manila; tel. (2) 9242607; fax (2) 9242745; Philippine overseas service (Radyo Pilipinas), Bureau of Broadcasts, Office of Media Affairs; Dir FERNANDO G. GAGELONIA.

Philippine Broadcasting System: FJE Bldg, 105 Esteban St, Legaspi Village, Makati City, Metro Manila; tel. (2) 8177043; fax (2) 8400763; Pres. RUPERTO NICDAO, Jr.

Philippine Federation of Catholic Broadcasters: 2307 Pedro Gil, Santa Ana, POB 3169, Metro Manila; tel. (2) 5644518; fax (2) 5637318; 48 radio stations and four TV channels; Pres. Fr FRANCIS LUCAS.

Radio Philippines Network, Inc: Broadcast City, Capitol Hills, Diliman, Quezon City, Metro Manila; tel. (2) 9318627; fax (2) 984322; f. 1969; seven TV stations, 14 radio stations; Pres. EDGAR SAN LUIS; Gen. Man. FELIPE G. MEDINA.

Radio Veritas Asia: Buick St, Fairview Park, POB 2642, Quezon City, Metro Manila; tel. (2) 9394692; fax (2) 9381940; e-mail rveritas-asia@rveritas-asia.org; internet www.rveritas-asia.org; f. 1969; Catholic short-wave station, broadcasts in 17 languages; Pres. and Chair. Cardinal JAIME L. SIN; Gen. Man. Fr CARLOS S. LARIOSA, SVD.

UM Broadcasting Network: Xanland Corporate Center, Room 7B, 152 Amorsolo St, Legaspi Village, Makati City, Metro Manila; tel. (2) 8158754; fax (2) 8173505; e-mail umbmmkt@mozcom.com; Exec. Vice-Pres. WILLY TORRES.

Vanguard Radio Network: J & T Bldg, Room 208, Santa Mesa, Metro Manila; tel. (2) 7161233; fax (2) 7160899; Pres. MANUEL GALVEZ.

Television

In July 1991 there were seven originating television stations and 105 replay and relay stations. The seven originating stations were ABS-CBN (Channel 2), PTV4 (Channel 4), ABC (Channel 5), GMA (Channel 7), RPN (Channel 9), IBC (Channel 13) and SBN (Channel 21). The following are the principal operating television networks:

ABC Development Corpn: APMC Bldg, 136 Amorsolo St, cnr Gamboa St, Legaspi Village, Makati City, Metro Manila; tel. (2) 8923801; fax (2) 8128840; CEO EDWARD U. TAN.

ABS-CBN Broadcasting Corpn: ABS-CBN Broadcasting Center, Sgt E. Esguerra Ave, cnr Mother Ignacia Ave, Quezon City, 1103 Metro Manila; tel. 9244101; fax (2) 9215888; Chair. EUGENIO LOPEZ III; Gen. Man. FEDERICO M. GARCIA.

AMCARA Broadcasting Network: Mother Ignacia St, cnr Sgt Esguerra Ave, Quezon City, Metro Manila; tel. (2) 4152272; fax (2) 4119646; Man. Dir MANUEL QUIOGUE.

Banahaw Broadcasting Corpn: Broadcast City, Capitol Hills, Quezon City, 3005 Metro Manila; tel. (2) 9329949; fax (2) 9318751; Station Man. BETTY LIVIOCO.

Channel V Philippines: Sagittarius Bldg, 6th Floor, H. V. de la Costa St, Salcedo Village, Makati City, Metro Manila; tel. (2) 8173747; fax (2) 8184192; e-mail channelv@i-next.net; Pres. JOEL JIMENEZ; Gen. Man. MON ALCARAZ.

GMA Network, Inc: RBS Bldg, Epifanio de los Santos Ave, Diliman, Quezon City, 1103 Metro Manila; tel. (2) 9287021; fax (2) 9243055; internet www.gmanetwork.com; f. 1950; transmits nation-wide through 44 TV stations and in South-East Asia through Aguila 2 satellite; Chair. FELIPE L. GOZON; Pres. and CEO MENARDO R. JIMENEZ.

Intercontinental Broadcasting Corpn: Broadcast City Complex, Capitol Hills, Diliman, Quezon City, Metro Manila; tel. (2) 9318781; fax (2) 9318743; 19 stations; Pres. and Chair. BOOTS ANSON-ROA.

Maharlika Broadcasting System: Metro Manila; tel. (2) 9220880; jtly operated by the Bureau of Broadcasts and the National Media Production Center; Dir ANTONIO BARRIERO.

People's Television Network Inc (PTV4): Broadcast Complex, Visayas Ave, Quezon City, Metro Manila; tel. (2) 9206514; fax (2) 9204342; f. 1992; public television network; Chair. LOURDES I. ILUSTRE.

Radio Mindanao Network: State Condominium, 4th Floor, Salcedo St, Legaspi Village, Makati City, Metro Manila; tel. (2) 8191073; fax (2) 8163680; Chair. HENRY CANOY; Pres. ERIC S. CANOY.

Radio Philippines Network, Inc: Broadcast City, Capitol Hills, Diliman, Quezon City, Metro Manila; tel. (2) 9315080; fax (2) 9318627; 7 primary TV stations, 14 relay stations; Pres. EDGAR SAN LUIS; Gen. Man. FELIPE G. MEDINA.

RJ TV 29: Save a Lot Bldg, Pasong Tamo Ext., Makati City, Metro Manila; tel. (2) 8942320; fax (2) 8942360; Gen. Man. BEA J. COLAMONICI.

Southern Broadcasting Network, Inc: Strata 200 Bldg, 22nd Floor, Ortigas Center, Emerald Ave, Pasig City, Metro Manila; tel. (2) 6365496; fax (2) 6365495; Pres. LUIS B. PACQUING.

United Broadcasting Network: FEMS Tower 1, 11th Floor, 1289 Zobel Roxas, cnr South Superhighway, Malate; tel. (2) 5216138; fax (2) 5221226; Gen. Man. JOSEPH HODREAL.

Association

Kapisanan ng mga Brodkaster sa Pilipinas (KBP) (Association of Broadcasters in the Philippines): LTA Bldg, 6th Floor, 118 Perea St, Legaspi Village, Makati City, Metro Manila; tel. (2) 8151990; fax (2) 8151989; e-mail kbp@pw.net; Chair. CERG REMONDE; Pres. JOSELITO YABUT.

Finance

(cap. = capital; res = reserves; dep. = deposits; m. = million; brs = branches; amounts in pesos, unless otherwise stated)

BANKING

Legislation enacted in June 1993 provided for the establishment of a new monetary authority, the Bangko Sentral ng Pilipinas, to replace the Central Bank of the Philippines. The Government was thus able to restructure the Central Bank's debt (308,000m. pesos).

In May 1994 legislation was promulgated providing for the establishment in the Philippines of up to 10 new foreign bank branches over the following five years (although at least 70% of the banking system's total resources were to be owned by Philippine entities). Prior to this legislation only four foreign banks (which had been in operation when the law restricting the industry to locally-owned banks was enacted in 1948) were permitted to operate. Two other foreign banks were subsequently licensed to organize locally-incorporated banks with minority Filipino partners. By the end of 2001 the number of foreign banks had increased to 17; at that time some 45 principal commercial banks were operating in the Philippines.

Central Bank

Bangko Sentral ng Pilipinas (Central Bank of the Philippines): A. Mabini St, cnr Vito Cruz St, Malate, 1004 Metro Manila; tel. (2) 5234832; fax (2) 5231252; e-mail bspmail@bsp.gov.ph; internet www.bsp.gov.ph; f. 1993; cap. 10,000m., res 97,851m., dep. 396,093m. (1998); Gov. RAFAEL B. BUENAVENTURA; 20 brs.

Principal Commercial Banks

Allied Banking Corpn: Allied Bank Centre, 6754 Ayala Ave, cnr Legaspi St, Makati City, 1200 Metro Manila; tel. (2) 8187961; fax (2) 8160921; internet www.alliedbank.com; f. 1977; cap. 495m., res 13,190m., dep. 83,079m. (Dec. 2000); Chair. PANFILO O. DOMINGO; Pres. REYNALDO A. MACLANG; 249 brs.

AsianBank Corporation: AsianBank Center, 328 Sen. Gil J. Puyat Ave, Salcedo Village, Makati City, 1200 Metro Manila; tel. (2) 8190611; fax (2) 8103867; e-mail francisv@mnl.sequel.net; f. 1978; cap. 3,877m., res 32,613m., dep. 22,424m. (Dec. 1998); merged with the Philippine Bank of Communications in early 1999 and into Globalbank in 2000; Chair. RAMON R. DEL ROSARIO; Pres. EDWARD S. GO; 98 brs.

Banco de Oro Universal Bank: 12 ADB Ave, Mandaluyong City, 1550 Metro Manila; tel. (2) 6366060; fax (2) 6317810; e-mail banc oro@bdo.com.ph; f. 1996; cap. 4,723m., dep. 41,515m. (March 1998); Chair. TERESITA T. SY; Pres. NESTOR V. TAN; 110 brs.

Bank of Commerce: Bankers' Center, 6764 Ayala Ave, Makati City, 1226 Metro Manila; tel. (2) 8174906; fax (2) 8172426; e-mail bk_commerce@mp.bkcomp.bridge.com; internet www.bank com.com.ph; f. 1983; fmrly Boston Bank of the Philippines; cap. 2,812m., dep. 8,621m. (Jan. 1999); Chair. ANTONIO COJUANGCO; Pres. RAUL B. DE MESA; 38 brs.

Bank of the Philippine Islands: BPI Bldg, Ayala Ave, cnr Paseo de Roxas, POB 1827, MCC, Makati City, 0720 Metro Manila; tel. (2) 8185541; fax (2) 8910170; f. 1851; merged with Far East Bank and Trust Co in Apr. 2000; cap. 15,323m., res 30,707m., dep. 296,254m. (Dec. 2000); Pres. XAVIER P. LOINAZ; Chair. JAIME ZOBEL DE AYALA; 340 brs.

China Banking Corpn: CBC Bldg, 8745 Paseo de Roxas, cnr Villar St, Makati City, 1226 Metro Manila; tel. (2) 8855555; fax (2) 8920220; e-mail postmaster@chinabank.com.ph; internet www.chinabank .com.ph; f. 1920; cap. 2,979m., res 2,082m., dep. 47,021m. (Dec. 2000); Chair. GILBERT U. DEE; Pres. and CEO PETER S. DEE; 138 brs.

DBS Bank Philippines, Inc: The Enterprise Center, 6766 Ayala Ave, cnr Paseo de Roxas, Makati City, Metro Manila; tel. (2) 8865888; internet www.dbs.com.ph; cap. 2,220m., dep. 6,099m. (Dec. 2000); Chair. CHONG KIE CHEONG; Pres. PASCUAL M. GARCIA III; 20 brs.

Development Bank of the Philippines: DBP Bldg, Makati Ave, cnr Sen. Gil J. Puyat Ave, Makati City, 1200 Metro Manila; POB 1996, Makati Central PO, Makati City, 1200 Metro Manila; tel. (2) 8189511; fax (2) 8128089; e-mail info@devbankphil.com.ph; internet www.devbankphil.com.ph; f. 1947 as the Rehabilitation Finance Corpn; govt-owned; provides medium- and long-term loans for agricultural and industrial developments; cap. 18,558m., dep. 36,740m. (June 2002); Chair. VITALIANO N. NAÑAGAS II; Pres. and CEO SIMON R.PATERNO; 77 brs; 16 area management offices.

East West Banking Corpn: 349 Sen. Gil J. Puyat Ave, Makati City, 1200 Metro Manila; f. 1994; tel. (2) 8905371; fax (2) 8928682; cap. 1,341m., dep. 2,857m. (March 1997); Chair. ANDREW L. GOTIANUM; Pres. ELREY T. RAMOS; 20 brs.

Equitable PCI Bank: Equitable PCI Bank Towers, 262 Makati Ave, cnr H. V. de la Costa St, Makati City, 1200 Metro Manila; tel. (2) 8407000; fax (2) 8941893; internet www.equitablepcib.com; f. 1950; formed by a merger between Equitable Banking Corpn and Philippine Commercial International (PCI) Bank in 1999; cap. 7,270m., res 37,396m., dep. 141,078m. (Dec. 2001); Chair. ANTONIO L. GO; Pres. RENE J. BUENAVENTURA; 420 brs.

Export and Industry Bank: 30 Paseo de Roxas, Makati City, 1226 Metro Manila; tel. (2) 8963311; fax (2) 8963310; cap. 1,638m., dep. 2,767m. (Dec. 1997); Chair. SERGIO R. ORTIZ-LUIS, Jr; Pres. BENJAMIN P. CASTILLO.

Global Business Bank (Globalbank): 777 Paseo de Roxas, cnr Sedeño St, Makati City, Metro Manila; tel. (2) 8948888; joint venture between Metrobank and Tokai Bank Ltd (Japan); merged with Philbank and Asianbank in 2000; Pres. ROBIN KING; 143 brs.

Land Bank of the Philippines: LBP Bldg, 319 Sen. Gil J. Puyat Ave, Makati City, 1200 Metro Manila; tel. (2) 8189411; fax (2) 8172536; e-mail corplan@mail.landbank.com; internet www.land bank.com; f. 1963; specialized govt bank with universal banking licence; cap. 14,220m., dep. 142,400m. (Dec. 1999); Chair. JOSE T. PARDO; Pres. FLORIDO P. CASUELA; 343 brs.

Maybank Philippines Inc: Legaspi Towers 300, Vito Cruz St, cnr Roxas Blvd, Malate, 1004 Metro Manila; POB 124, 1099 Metro Manila; tel. (2) 5216169; fax (2) 5218513; f. 1961; cap. 1,671m., dep. 2,701m. (Dec. 1997); Pres. and CEO YONG YUR WONG; 60 brs.

Metropolitan Bank and Trust Co (Metrobank): Metrobank Plaza, Sen. Gil J. Puyat Ave, Makati City, 1200 Metro Manila; tel. (2) 8988000; fax (2) 8176248; e-mail metrobank@metrobank.com.ph; internet www.metrobank.com.ph; f. 1962; cap. 32,673m., res 8,123m., dep. 350,486m. (Dec. 2000); Chair. GEORGE S. K. TY; Pres. ANTONIO S. ABACAN, Jr; 344 local brs; 6 overseas brs.

Philippine Bank of Communications: PBCOM Tower, 6795 Ayala Ave, cnr Herrera St, 1226 Makati City; tel. (2) 8307000; fax (2) 8182598; e-mail info@pbcom.com.ph; internet www.pbcom.com.ph; f. 1939; cap. 4,174m., dep. 23,904m. (Dec. 1998); merged with Asian-Bank Corporation in early 1999; Chair. LUY KIM GUAN; Pres. ISIDRO C. ALCANTARA, Jr; 45 brs.

Philippine Banking Corpn (Philbank): Philbank Bldg, 6797 Ayala Ave, Makati City, 1226 Metro Manila; tel. (2) 8170872; fax (2) 8170892; internet www.philbank.com.ph; f. 1935 as Square Deal Inc; present name adopted 1957; cap. 1,435m., dep. 12,104m. (Dec. 1999); Chair. SIY YAP CHUA; Pres. and CEO NORBERTO C. NAZARENO; 63 brs.

Philippine National Bank (PNB): PNB Financial Center, Roxas Blvd, Pasay City, POB 1844, 1300 Metro Manila; tel. 5263131; fax (2) 8331245; e-mail mainbranch@pnb.com.ph; internet www.pnb.com.ph; f. 1916; partially transferred to the private sector in 1996 and 2000, 17% govt-owned; cap. and res 20,471m., dep. 119,812m. (Dec. 2000); Chair. ROBERTO C. NAZARENO; Pres. and CEO FELICIANO L. MIRANDA, Jr; 324 local brs, 5 overseas brs.

Philippine Veterans Bank: 101 Herrera St, cnr de la Rosa St, Legaspi Village, Makati City, Metro Manila; tel. (2) 8943919; fax (2) 8940625; cap. 3.600m., dep. 10,400m. (June 1998); Chair. EMMANUEL DE OCAMPO; Pres. SUNDAY LAVIN; 38 brs.

Philtrust Bank (Philippine Trust Co): Philtrust Bank Bldg, United Nations Ave, cnr San Marcelino St, Ermita, 1045 Metro Manila; tel. (2) 5249061; fax (2) 5217309; e-mail ptc@bancnet.net; f. 1916; cap. 1,500m., dep. 20,540m. (Dec. 1999); Pres. ANTONIO H. OZAETA; Chair. EMILIO T. YAP; 32 brs.

Prudential Bank: Prudential Bank Bldg, 6787 Ayala Ave, Makati City, 1200 Metro Manila; f. 1952; tel. (2) 8178981; fax (2) 8175146; e-mail feedback@prudentialbank.com; f. 1951; merged with Pilipinas Bank in May 2000; cap. 829m., res 6,890m., dep. 39,456m. (Dec. 2000); Chair. and Pres. JOSE L. SANTOS; 117 brs.

Rizal Commercial Banking Corpn: Yuchengco Tower, RCBC Plaza, 6819 Alaya Ave, Makati City, POB 2202, 1200 Metro Manila; tel. (2) 8949000; fax (2) 8949958; f. 1960; cap. 8,281m., dep. 53,287m. (March 1997); Chair. ALFONSO T. YUCHENGCO; Pres. VALENTIN A. ARANETA; 166 brs.

Security Bank Corpn: 6776 Ayala Ave, Makati City, 0719 Metro Manila; tel. (2) 8676788; fax (2) 8132069; e-mail inquiry@ securitybank.com.ph; internet www.securitybank.com.ph; f. 1951; fmrly Security Bank and Trust Co; cap. 3,293m. (Dec. 2001), res 4,951m., dep. 47,020m. (Dec. 2000); Pres. RAFAEL F. SIMPAO, Jr; Chair. FREDERICK Y. DY; 118 brs.

TA Bank of the Philippines: Octagon Bldg, 4th Floor, San Miguel Ave, Ortigas Complex, Pasig City, Metro Manila; tel. (2) 6376162; fax (2) 6376279; cap. 1,378m., dep. 579m. (June 1998); Chair. Datuk TIAH THEE KIAN; Pres. EXEQUIEL VILLACORTA, Jr.

Traders Royal Bank: TRB Tower, Roxas Blvd, Pasay City, 1300 Metro Manila; tel. (2) 8312821; fax (2) 8312494; e-mail trbm@mnl .sequel.net; internet www.sequel.net; f. 1963; cap. 1,323.2m., dep. 6,553m. (Dec. 1999); Chair. JULITA C. BENEDICTO; Pres. RENATO H. PERONILLA; 55 brs.

Union Bank of the Philippines: SSS Makati Bldg, Ayala Ave, cnr Herrera St, Makati City, 1200 Metro Manila; tel. (2) 8920011; fax (2) 8186058; e-mail online@unionbankph.com; internet www.unionbankph.com; f. 1954; cap. 6,970m., dep. 19,694m. (Dec. 1998); Chair. JUSTO A. ORTIZ; Pres. and CEO ARMAND F. BRAUN, Jr; 120 brs.

United Coconut Planters' Bank: UCPB Bldg, Makati Ave, Makati City, 0728 Metro Manila; tel. (2) 8119000; fax (2) 8119706; e-mail crc@ucpb.com.ph; internet www.ucpb.com; f. 1963; cap. 10,727m., dep. 87,425m. (Dec. 2000); Chair. JERONIMO U. KILAYKO; Pres. LORENZO V. TAN; 178 brs.

United Overseas Bank Philippines: 17th Floor, Pacific Star Bldg, Sen. Gil J. Puyat Ave, cnr Makati Ave, Makati City, Metro Manila; tel. (2) 8788686; fax (2) 8115917; e-mail crd@uob.com.ph; internet www.uob.com.ph; f. 1999; cap. 2,731m., dep. 15,021m. (Dec. 1999); Chair. WEE CHO YAW; Pres. CHUA TENG HUI; 97 brs.

Urban Bank, Inc: Urban Bank Plaza, Urban Ave, Makati City, 1200 Metro Manila; tel. (2) 8164666; fax (2) 8879900; f. 1995; cap. 7,706m., dep. 4,103m. (March 1997); Chair. ARESENIO M. BARTOLOME; Pres. TEODORO C. BORLONGAN; 36 brs.

Rural Banks

Small private banks have been established with the encouragement and assistance (both financial and technical) of the Government in order to promote and expand the rural economy. Conceived mainly to stimulate the productive capacities of small farmers, merchants and industrialists in rural areas, and to combat usury, their principal objectives are to place within easy reach and access of the people credit facilities on reasonable terms and, in co-operation with other agencies of the Government, to provide advice on business and farm management and the proper use of credit for production and marketing purposes. The rural banks numbered 1,942 in 1998; their registered resources totalled 59,970m. pesos at 31 December 1998.

Thrift Banks

Thrift banks mobilize small savings and provide loans to lower income groups. The thrift banking system comprises savings and mortgage banks, stock savings and loan associations and private development banks. In 1998 there were 1,474 thrift banks; their registered resources totalled 216,440m. pesos.

Development Bank

1st e-Bank: 1st e-Bank Tower, 8737 Paseo de Roxas, Makati City, 1226 Metro Manila; tel. (2) 8158536; fax (2) 8195376; e-mail 1stecare@1stebank.com.ph; internet www.1stebank.com.ph; f. 1963, with World Bank assistance, as Private Development Corporation of the Philippines; 1992 converted into a development bank; name changed as above in May 2000; banking and lending services; financial advisory, trust and investment services; training and consultancy; insurance brokerage; cap. and res 2,079.7m., dep. 7,244.6m. (1996); Pres. and CEO CARLOS A. PEDROSA; 60 brs.

Foreign Banks

ANZ Banking Group Ltd (Australia and New Zealand): Ayala Triangle, Tower One, 3rd Floor, Ayala Ave, cnr Paseo de Roxas, Makati City, 1226 Metro Manila; tel. (2) 8485091; fax (2) 8485086; e-mail labrooyM2@anz.com; f. 1995; cap. 250m., dep. 2,000m. (Dec. 1999); Pres. MICHAEL LA BROOY.

Banco Santander Philippines, Inc: Tower One, 27th Floor, Ayala Triangle, Ayala Ave, cnr Paseo de Roxas, Makati City, 1200 Metro Manila; tel. (2) 7594144; fax (2) 7594190; cap. 1,351m., dep. 3,943m. (March 1997); Chair. ANA PATRICIA BOTIN; Dir and Pres. VICENTE B. CASTILLO.

Bangkok Bank Public Company Ltd (Thailand): Far East Bank Bldg, 25th Floor, Sen. Gil J. Puyat Ave, Makati City, 1200 Metro Manila; tel. (2) 8914011; fax (2) 8914037; f. 1995; cap. 266m. (Dec. 1996), dep. 647m. (March 1997); Pres. PREYAMIT HETRAKUL.

Bank of America NA (USA): BA–Lepanto Bldg, 2nd Floor, 8747 Paseo de Roxas, POB 1767, Makati City, 1257 Metro Manila; tel. (2) 8155000; fax (2) 8155895; f. 1947; cap. 210m. (Dec. 1996), dep. 5,015m. (June 1999); Sr Vice-Pres. and Country Man. JOSE L. QUERUBIN.

Bank of Tokyo-Mitsubishi Ltd (Japan): 6750 Ayala Ave, 5th Floor, Makati City, Metro Manila; tel. (2) 8921976; fax (2) 8160413; f. 1977; cap. 200m. (Dec. 1996), dep. 2,940m. (March 1997); Gen. Man. HISAO SAKASHITA.

Citibank NA (USA): Citibank Plaza, 8741 Paseo de Roxas, Makati City, 1226 Metro Manila; tel. (2) 8947700; fax (2) 8157703; f. 1948; cap. 2,536m., dep. 30,167m. (March 1997); CEO SURESH MAHARAJ; 3 brs.

Dao Heng Bank Inc: Pearl Bank Bldg, 11th Floor, 146 Salero St, Salcedo Village, Makati City, 1227 Metro Manila; tel. (2) 8403003; fax (2) 8178794; cap. 1,416m., dep. 2,797m. (March 1997); Chair. Tan Sri QUEK LENG CHAN; Pres. RENATO H. PERONILLA; 5 brs.

Deutsche Bank AG (Germany): Ayala Triangle, Tower One, 26th Floor, Ayala Ave, cnr Paseo de Roxas, Makati City, 1226 Metro Manila; tel. (2) 8946900; fax (2) 8946901; f. 1995; cap. 625m. (Dec. 1996), dep. 2,595m. (March 1997); Chief Country Officer PETER VERHOEVEN.

Development Bank of Singapore: Citibank Tower, 32nd Floor, Valero St, cnr Villar St, Legaspi Village, Makati City, 1229 Metro Manila; tel. (2) 8480461; fax (2) 8480478; f. 1995; cap. 202m. (Dec. 1996), dep. 13m. (March 1997); Gen. Man. SADASIVAN VIJAYAKUMAR.

Fuji Bank Ltd (Japan): Citibank Tower, 26th Floor, Valero St, cnr Villar St, Legaspi Village, Makati City, 1229 Metro Manila; tel. (2) 8480001; fax (2) 8153770; f. 1995; cap. 202m. (Dec. 1996), dep. 858m. (March 1997); Gen. Man. TAKUJI IWASAKI.

Hongkong and Shanghai Banking Corpn (Hong Kong): Enterprise Center, Tower I, 6766 Ayala Ave, cnr Paseo de Roxas, Makati City 1200; tel. (2) 8305300; fax (2) 8865343; internet www.asiapacific.hsbc.com; cap. HK $113,520m., res HK $42,280m., dep. HK $1,419,076m. (June 2002); CEO PAUL LAWRENCE; 5 brs.

ING Bank NV (The Netherlands): Ayala Triangle, Tower One, 21st Floor, Ayala Ave, cnr Paseo de Roxas, Makati City, 1200 Metro Manila; tel. (2) 8408888; fax (2) 8151116; f. 1995; cap. 643m., dep. 2,594m. (March 1997); Country Man. MANUEL SALAK.

International Commercial Bank of China (Taiwan): Pacific Star Bldg, Ground and 3rd Floors, Sen. Gil J. Puyat Ave, cnr Makati Ave, Makati City, 1200 Metro Manila; tel. (2) 8115807; fax (2) 8115774; cap. 188m., dep. 458m. (March 1997); Gen. Man. HERMAN C. CHEN.

Korea Exchange Bank: Citibank Tower, 33rd Floor, 8741 Paseo de Roxas, Makati City, 1229 Metro Manila; tel. (2) 8481988; fax (2) 8195377; cap. 257m., dep. 271m. (March 1997); Gen. Man. TAE-HONG JIN.

Standard Chartered Bank (Hong Kong): 6788 Ayala Ave, Makati City, 1226 Metro Manila; tel. (2) 8867888; fax (2) 8866866; f. 1873; cap. 1,500m. (Dec. 1996), dep. 3,770m. (March 1997); CEO EIRVIN B. KNOX.

Islamic Bank

Al-Amanah Islamic Investment Bank of the Philippines: 2nd Floor, Classica Tower I, H. V. de la Costa St, Salcedo Village, Makati City, Metro Manila; tel. (2) 8164258; fax (2) 8195249; internet www.islambnk@amanet.net/; f. 1989; Chair. and CEO FAROUK A. CARPIZO; Pres. ABDUL GAFFOOR ASHROOF.

Major 'Offshore' Banks

ABN AMRO Bank, NV (Netherlands): LKG Tower, 18th Floor, 6801 Ayala Ave, Makati City, 1200 Metro Manila; tel. (2) 8842000; fax (2) 8843954; Gen. Man. CARMELO MARIA L. BAUTISTA.

American Express Bank Ltd (USA): Ayala Bldg, 11th Floor, 6750 Ayala Ave, Makati City, Metro Manila; tel. (2) 8186731; fax (2) 8172589; f. 1977; Senior Dir and Country Man. VICENTE L. CHUA.

BankBoston NA (USA): 6750 Ayala Ave, 23rd Floor, Makati City, Metro Manila; tel. (2) 8170456; fax (2) 8191251; Country Man. BENJAMIN C. SEVILLA.

Bank Dagang Nasional Indonesia: Ayala Tower and Exchange Plaza, 19th Floor, Unit B, Ayala Ave, Makati City, Metro Manila; tel. (2) 8486189; fax (2) 8486176; Man. CONSUELO N. PADILLA.

Bank of Nova Scotia (Canada): Solidbank Bldg, 9th Floor, 777 Paseo de Roxas, Makati City, 1200 Metro Manila; tel. (2) 8179751; fax (2) 8178796; f. 1977; Man. M. S. (CORITO) SEVILLA.

Bankers Trust Co (USA): Pacific Star Bldg, 12th Floor, Makati Ave, Makati City, Metro Manila; tel. (2) 8190231; fax (2) 8187349; Man. Dir JOSE ISIDRO N. CAMACHO.

BNP Paribas (France): PCIB Tower Two, Makati Ave, cnr H. V. de la Costa St, Makati City, 1227 Metro Manila; tel. (2) 8158821; fax (2) 8179237; f. 1977; Country Man. PIERRE IMHOF.

Chase Manhattan International Finance Ltd: Corinthian Plaza, 4th Floor, 121 Paseo de Roxas, Makati City, Metro Manila; tel. (2) 8113348; fax (2) 8781290; Man. HELEN S. CIFRA.

Crédit Agricole Indosuez (France): Citibank Tower, 17th Floor, 8741 Paseo de Roxas, Makati City, 1200 Metro Manila; tel. (2) 8481344; fax (2) 8481380; f. 1977; Gen. Man. MARC MEULEAU.

Crédit Lyonnais (France): Pacific Star Bldg, 14th Floor, Makati Ave, cnr Sen. Gil J. Puyat Ave, Makati City, Metro Manila; POB 1859 MCC, 3117 Makati City, Metro Manila; tel. (2) 8171616; fax (2) 8177145; f. 1981; Gen. Man. PIERRE EYMERY.

KBC Bank, NV (Belgium): Far East Bank Center, 22nd Floor, Sen. Gil J. Puyat Ave, Makati City, 1200 Metro Manila; tel. (2) 8915331; fax (2) 8915352; Gen. Man. EDWIN YAPTANGCO.

PT Lippo Bank (Indonesia): Rufino Pacific Tower, 31st Floor, 6784 Ayala Ave, Makati City, Metro Manila; tel. (2) 8110515; fax (2) 8110516; Vice-Pres. and Gen. Man. EDNA D. REYES.

Overseas Union Bank Ltd: Corinthian Plaza, 7th Floor, Paseo de Roxas, Makati City, Metro Manila; tel. (2) 8179951; fax (2) 8113168; f. 1977; Man. TAN LYE OON.

Société Générale (France): Antel Corporate Center, 21st Floor, 139 Valero St, Salcedo Village, Makati City, Metro Manila; tel. (2) 8492000; fax (2) 8492940; f. 1980; CEO CLAUDE I. TOUITOU.

Standard Chartered Bank Ltd: 9th Floor, 6788 Ayala Ave, Makati City, Metro Manila; tel. (2) 8867888; fax (2) 8866866; Vice-Pres. and Gen. Man. IMELDA B. CAPISTRANO.

Union Bank of California (USA): ACE Bldg, 8th Floor, cnr Rada and de la Rosa Sts, Legaspi Village, Makati City, Metro Manila; tel. (2) 8923056; fax (2) 8170102; f. 1977; Branch Man. TERESITA MALABANAN.

Banking Associations

Bankers Association of the Philippines: Sagittarius Cond. Bldg, 11th Floor, H. V. de la Costa St, Salcedo Village, Makati City, Metro

Manila; tel. (2) 8103858; fax (2) 8103860; Pres. Dr PLACIDO L. MAPA, Jr; Exec. Dir LEONILO CORONEL.

Chamber of Thrift Banks: Cityland 10 Condominium Tower 1, Unit 614, H. V. de la Costa St, Salcedo Village, Makati City, Metro Manila; tel. (2) 8126974; fax (2) 8127203; Pres. DIONISIO C. ONG.

Offshore Bankers' Association of the Philippines, Inc: MCPO 3088, Makati City, 1229 Metro Manila; tel. (2) 8103554; Chair. ANTONIO DELOS ANGELES.

Rural Bankers' Association of the Philippines: RBAP Bldg, A. Soriano Ave, cnr Arzobispo St, Intramuros, Manila; tel. (2) 5272968; fax (2) 5272980; Pres. CARLITO B. FUENTES.

STOCK EXCHANGES

Securities and Exchange Commission: SEC Bldg, Epifanio de los Santos Ave, Greenhills, Mandaluyong City, Metro Manila; tel. (2) 7274543; fax (2) 7254399; e-mail mis@sec.gov.ph; internet www.sec.gov.ph; f. 1936; Chair. LILIA R. BAUTISTA.

Philippine Stock Exchange: Philippine Stock Exchange Center, Exchange Rd, Ortigas Centre, Pasig City, 1605 Metro Manila; tel. (2) 6360122; fax (2) 6345113; e-mail piac@pse.org.ph; internet www.pse.com.ph; f. 1994, following the merger of the Manila and Makati Stock Exchanges; Chair. VIVIAN YUCHENGCO; Pres. ERNEST C. LEUNG.

INSURANCE

At the end of 2000 a total of 156 insurance companies were authorized by the Insurance Commission to transact in the Philippines. Foreign companies were permitted to operate in the country.

Principal Domestic Companies

BPI/MS Insurance Corpn: BPI Bldg, 16th–18th Floors, Ayala Ave, Makati City, 1226 Metro Manila; tel. (2) 8409000; (2) 8910147; e-mail fguinsce@globe.com.ph; internet www.fguonline.com; f. 2002 as result of merger of FGU Insurance Corpn and FEB Mitsui Marine Insurance Corpn; joint venture of Bank of the Philippine Islands and Sumitomo Insurance Co (Japan); cap. 150m. (1997); Chair. JAIME AUGUSTO ZOBEL DE AYALA; Pres. ALFONSO L. SALCEDO, Jr.

Central Surety & Insurance Co: UniversalRe Bldg, 2nd Floor, 106 Paseo de Roxas, Legaspi Village, Makati City, 1200 Metro Manila; tel. (2) 8174931; fax (2) 8170006; f. 1945; bonds, fire, marine, casualty, motor car; Pres. CONSTANCIO T. CASTAÑEDA, Jr.

Commonwealth Insurance Co: Manila Bank Bldg, 4th Floor, Ayala Ave, Makati City, Metro Manila; tel. (2) 8187626; fax (2) 8138575; f. 1935; Chair. MARIO NOCHE.

Co-operative Insurance System of the Philippines: 80 Malakas St, Diliman, Quezon City, Metro Manila; tel. (2) 9240333; fax (2) 9240471; Chair. BIENVENIDO P. FAUSTINO; Gen. Man. ARTURO J. JIMENEZ.

Domestic Insurance Co of the Philippines: Domestic Insurance Bldg, Bonifacio Drive, Port Area, Manila; tel. (2) 472161; fax (2) 8162938; f. 1946; cap. 10m.; Pres. JULIAN J. CRUZ; Man. Dir MAR S. LOPEZ.

Dominion Insurance Corpn: Zeta II Annex Bldg, 6th Floor, 191 Salcedo St, Legaspi Village, Makati City, Metro Manila; tel. (2) 8925787; fax (2) 8183630; f. 1960; fire, marine, motor car, accident, engineering, bonds; Pres. JUAN DOMINO.

Empire Insurance Co: Prudential Life Bldg, 2nd Floor, 843 Arnaiz Ave, Legaspi Village, Makati City, 1229 Metro Manila; tel. (2) 8159561; fax (2) 8152599; f. 1949; fire, bonds, marine, accident, motor car, extraneous perils; Chair. SERGIO CORPUS; Pres. and CEO JOSE MA G. SANTOS.

Equitable Insurance Corpn: Equitable Bank Bldg, 4th Floor, 262 Juan Luna St, Binondo, POB 1103, Metro Manila; tel. (2) 2430291; fax (2) 2415768; e-mail info@equitableinsurance.com.ph; internet www.equitableinsurance.com.ph; f. 1950; fire, marine, casualty, motor car, bonds; Exec. Vice-Pres. ANTONIO C. OCAMPO; Vice-Pres. ERLINDA D. SANTIAGO.

Insular Life Assurance Co Ltd: Insular Life Corporate Centre, Insular Life Drive, Filinvest Corporate City, Alabang, 1781 Muntinlupa City; POB 8097, Parañaque Central Post Office, 1700 Parañaque City; tel. (2) 7711818; fax (2) 7711717; e-mail headofc@insular.com.ph; internet www.insularlife.com.ph; f. 1910; members' equity 8,300m. (Dec. 2000); Chair., Pres. and CEO VICENTE R. AYLLÓN.

Makati Insurance Co Inc: Far East Bank Center, 19th Floor, Sen. Gil J. Puyat Ave, Makati City, 1200 Metro Manila; tel. (2) 8459576; fax (2) 8915229; f. 1965; non-life; Pres. and Gen. Man. JAIME L. DARANTINAO; Chair. OCTAVIO V. ESPIRITU.

Malayan Insurance Co Inc: Yuchengco Tower, 4th Floor, 500 Quintin Paredes St, POB 3389, 1099 Metro Manila; tel. (2) 2428888; fax (2) 2412449; e-mail malayan@malayan.com; internet www.malayan.com; f. 1949; cap. 100m. (1998); insurance and bonds; Pres. YVONNE S. YUCHENGCO.

Manila Surety & Fidelity Co Inc: 66 P. Florentino, Quezon City, Metro Manila; tel. (2) 7122251; fax (2) 7124129; f. 1945; Pres. MA LOURDES V. PEÑA; Vice-Pres. EDITHA LIM.

Metropolitan Insurance Co: Ateneum Bldg, 3rd Floor, Leviste St, Salcedo Village, Makati City, Metro Manila; tel. (2) 8108151; fax (2) 8162294; f. 1933; non-life; Pres. JOSÉ M. PERIQUET, Jr; Exec. Vice-Pres. ROBERTO ABAD.

National Life Insurance Co of the Philippines: National Life Insurance Bldg, 6762 Ayala Ave, Makati City, Metro Manila; tel. (2) 8100251; fax (2) 8178718; f. 1933; Pres. BENJAMIN L. DE LEON; Sr Vice-Pres. JOSE L. BURGOS.

National Reinsurance Corpn of the Philippines: PS Bank Tower, 18th Floor, Sen. Gil J. Puyat Ave, cnr Tindalo St, Makati City, Metro Manila; tel. (2) 7595801; fax (2) 7595886; e-mail nrcp@nrcp.com.ph; internet www.nrcp.com.ph; f. 1978; Chair. WINSTON F. GARCIA; Pres. and CEO WILFRIDO C. BANTAYAN.

Paramount General Insurance Corpn: Sage House, 15th Floor, 110 Herrera St, Makati City, Metro Manila; tel. (2) 8127956; fax (2) 8133043; e-mail insure@paramount.com.ph; internet www.paramount.com.ph; f. 1950; fire, marine, casualty, motor car; Chair. PATRICK L. GO; Pres. GEORGE T. TIU.

Philippine American Life and General Insurance Co (Philamlife): Philamlife Bldg, United Nations Ave, Metro Manila; POB 2167, 0990 Metro Manila; tel. (2) 5216300; fax (2) 5217057; internet www.philamlife.com.ph; Pres. JOSE CUISIA.

Pioneer Insurance and Surety Corpn: Pioneer House-Makati, 108 Paseo de Roxas, Makati City, Metro Manila; tel. (2) 8179071; fax (2) 8171461; e-mail info@pioneer.com.ph; f. 1954; cap. 172.5m. (1997); Pres. and CEO DAVID C. COYUKIAT.

Rizal Surety and Insurance Co: Prudential Life Bldg, 3rd Floor, 843 Arnaiz Ave, Legaspi Village, Makati City, Metro Manila; tel. (2) 8403610; fax (2) 8173550; e-mail rizalsic@mkt.weblinq.com; f. 1939; fire, bond, marine, motor car, accident, extraneous perils; Chair. TOMAS I. ALCANTARA; Pres. REYNALDO DE DIOS.

Standard Insurance Co Inc: Standard Insurance Tower, 999 Pedro Gil St, cnr F. Agoncillo St, Metro Manila; tel. (2) 5223230; fax (2) 5261479; f. 1958; Chair. LOURDES T. ECHAUZ; Pres. ERNESTO ECHAUZ.

Tico Insurance Co Inc: Trafalgar Plaza, 7th Floor, 105 H. V. de la Costa St, Salcedo Village, Makati City, 1227 Metro Manila; tel. (2) 8140143; fax (2) 8140150; f. 1937; frmly Tabacalera Insurance Co Inc; Chair. and Pres. CARLOS CATHOLICO.

UCPB General Insurance Co Inc: 24th and 25th Floors, LKG Tower, 6801 Ayala Ave, Makati City, Metro Manila; tel. (2) 8841234; fax (2) 8841264; e-mail ucpbgen@ucpbgen.com; internet www.ucpbgen.com; f. 1989; non-life; Pres. ISABELO P. AFRICA; Chair. JERONIMO U. KILAYKO.

Universal Reinsurance Corpn: Ayala Life Bldg, 9th Floor, 6786 Ayala Ave, Makati City, Metro Manila; tel. (2) 7514977; fax (2) 8173745; f. 1949; life and non-life; Chair. JAIME AUGUSTO ZOBEL DE AYALA II; Pres. HERMINIA S. JACINTO.

Regulatory Body

Insurance Commission: 1071 United Nations Ave, Metro Manila; tel. (2) 5252015; fax (2) 5221434; e-mail oic@i-manila.com.ph; internet www.ic.gov.ph; regulates the private insurance industry by, among other things, issuing certificates of authority to insurance companies and intermediaries and monitoring their financial solvency; Commr EDUARDO T. MALINIS.

Trade and Industry

GOVERNMENT AGENCIES

Asset Privatization Trust: North Davao Mining Bldg, 104 Gamboa St, Legaspi Village, Makati City, 1229 Metro Manila; tel. (2) 8932383; fax (2) 8933453; f. 1986 to handle the privatization of govt assets; Chief Exec. RENATO V. VALDECANTOS.

Board of Investments: 385 Sen. Gil J. Puyat Ave, Makati City, Metro Manila; tel. (2) 8976682; fax (2) 8953521; e-mail OSAC@_boi.gov.ph; internet www.boi.gov.ph; Chair. MANUEL A. ROXAS II; Gov. JOSE ANTONIO C. LEVISTE.

Cagayan Economic Zone Authority: Westar Bldg, 7th Floor, 611 Shaw Blvd, Pasig City, 1603 Metro Manila; tel. (2) 6365781; fax (2) 6313997; e-mail cagayanecozone@pacific.net.ph; Administrator RODOLFO REYES.

Clark Development Corpn: Bldg 2127, C. P. Garcia St, cnr E. Quirino St, Clark Field, Pampanga; JMT Corporate Condominium,

15th Floor, ADB Ave, Ortigas Center, Pasig City, Metro Manila; tel. (2) 6338671; fax (2) 6338672; Pres. and CEO RUFO B. COLAYCO.

Industrial Technology Development Institute: DOST Complex, Gen. Santos Ave, Bicutan, Taguig, Metro Manila; tel. (2) 8372071; fax (2) 8373167; Man. Dr ROGELIO PANLASIGUI.

Maritime Industry Authority (MARINA): PPL Bldg, 1000 United Nations Ave, cnr San Marcelino St, Ermita, Metro Manila; tel. (2) 5238651; fax (2) 5242746; e-mail feedback@marina.gov.ph; internet www.marina.gov.ph; f. 1974; development of inter-island shipping, overseas shipping, shipbuilding and repair, and maritime power; Administrator OSCAR M. SEVILLA.

National Tobacco Administration: NTA Bldg, Scout Reyes St, cnr Panay Ave, Quezon City, Metro Manila; tel. (2) 3743987; fax (2) 3742505; e-mail nta_miscsd@pacific.net.ph; f. 1987; Administrator CARLITOS S. ENCARNACION.

Philippine Coconut Authority (PCA): Elliptical Rd, Diliman, Quezon City, 1104 Metro Manila; POB 3386, Metro Manila; tel. (2) 9278116; fax (2) 9216173; f. 1972; Administrator DANILO M. CORONACION.

Philippine Council for Advanced Science and Technology Research and Development (PCASTRD): DOST Main Bldg, Gen. Santos Ave, Bicutan, Taguig, 1631 Metro Manila; tel. (2) 8377522; fax (2) 8373168; e-mail aal@dost.gov.ph; internet www.dostweb.dost.gov.ph/pcastrd; f. 1987; Exec. Dir Dr IDA F. DALMACIO.

Philippine Economic Zone Authority: Roxas Blvd, cnr San Luis St, Pasay City, Metro Manila; tel. (2) 5513454; fax (2) 8916380; e-mail info@peza.gov.ph; internet www.peza.gov.ph; Dir-Gen. LILIA B. DE LIMA.

Subic Bay Metropolitan Authority: SBMA Center, Bldg 229, Waterfront Rd, Subic Bay Freeport Zone, 2222 Zambales; tel. (47) 2524895; fax (47) 2523014; e-mail fcpayumo@sbma.com; internet www.sbma.com; Chair. FELICITO PAYUMO.

DEVELOPMENT ORGANIZATIONS

Bases Conversion Development Authority: Metro Manila; internet www.bcda.gov.ph; f. 1992 to facilitate the conversion, privatization and development of fmr military bases; Chair. ROGELIO SINGSON.

Bureau of Land Development: DAR Bldg, Elliptical Rd, Diliman, Quezon City, Metro Manila; tel. (2) 9287031; fax (2) 9260971; Dir EUGENIO B. BERNARDO.

Capital Market Development Council: Metro Manila; Chair. ROMAN AZANZA.

Co-operatives Development Authority: Benlor Bldg, 1184 Quezon Ave, Quezon City, Metro Manila; tel. (2) 3723801; fax (2) 3712077; Chair. JOSE C. MEDINA, Jr; Exec. Dir CANDELARIO L. VERZONA, Jr.

National Development Co (NDC): NDC Bldg, 8th Floor, 116 Tordesillas St, Salcedo Village, Makati City, Metro Manila; tel. (2) 8404898; fax (2) 8404862; e-mail corplan@info.com; internet www.dti.gov.ph/ndc; f. 1919; govt-owned corpn engaged in the organization, financing and management of subsidiaries and corpns incl. commercial, industrial, mining, agricultural and other enterprises assisting national economic development, incl. jt industrial ventures with other ASEAN countries; Chair. MANUEL A. ROXAS; Gen. Man. OFELIA V. BULAONG.

Philippine National Oil Co: Energy Complex, Bldg 6, 6th Floor, Merritt Rd, Fort Bonifacio, Makati City, Metro Manila; tel. (2) 5550254; fax (2) 8442983; internet www.pnoc.com.ph; f. 1973; state-owned energy development agency mandated to ensure stable and sufficient supply of oil products and to develop domestic energy resources; sales 3,482m. pesos (1995); Chair. VINCENT S. PEREZ, Jr; Pres. and CEO THELMO Y. CUNANAN.

Southern Philippines Development Authority: Basic Petroleum Bldg, 104 Carlos Palanca, Jr St, Legaspi Village, Makati City, Metro Manila; tel. (2) 8183893; fax (2) 8188907; Chair. ROBERTO AVENTAJADO; Manila Rep. GERUDIO 'KHALIQ' MADUENO.

CHAMBERS OF COMMERCE AND INDUSTRY

American Chamber of Commerce of the Philippines: Corinthian Plaza, 2nd Floor, Paseo de Roxas, Makati City, 1229 Metro Manila; tel. (2) 8187911; fax (2) 8113081; e-mail info@amchamphilippines.com; internet www.amchamphilippines.com; Pres. TERRY J. EMRICK.

Cebu Chamber of Commerce and Industry: CCCI Center, cnr 11th and 13th Ave, North Reclamation Area, Cebu City 6000; tel. (32) 2321421; fax (32) 2321422; e-mail ccci@esprint.com; internet www.esprint.com/~ccci; f. 1921; Pres. SABINO R. DAPAT.

European Chamber of Commerce of the Philippines: PS Bank Tower, 19th Floor, Sen. Gil J. Puyat Ave, cnr Tindalo St, Makati City, 1200 Metro Manila; tel. (2) 8451324; fax (2) 8451395; e-mail info@eccp.com; internet www.eccp.com; f. 2000; 900 mems; Pres. WILLIAM BAILEY; Exec. Vice-Pres. HENRY J. SCHUMACHER.

Federation of Filipino-Chinese Chambers of Commerce and Industry Inc: Federation Center, 6th Floor, Muelle de Binondo St, POB 23, Metro Manila; tel. (2) 2419201; fax (2) 2422361; e-mail secretariat@ffcccii.com.ph; internet www.ffcccii.com.ph; Pres. BENJAMIN G. CHUA; Sec.-Gen. JOAQUIN SY.

Japanese Chamber of Commerce of the Philippines: Jaycem Bldg, 6th Floor, 104 Rada St, Legaspi Village, Makati City, Metro Manila; tel. (2) 8923233; fax (2) 8150317; e-mail jccipi@jccipi.com.ph; internet www.jccipi.com.ph; Pres. MASAHARU TAMAKI.

Philippine Chamber of Coal Mines (Philcoal): Rm 1007, Princeville Condominium, S. Laurel St, cnr Shaw Blvd, 1552 Mandaluyong City; tel. (2) 5330518; fax (2) 5315513; f. 1980; Exec. Dir BERTRAND GONZALES.

Philippine Chamber of Commerce and Industry: 14th Floor, Multinational Bancorporation Centre, 6805 Ayala Ave, Makati City, Metro Manila; tel. (2) 8445713; fax (2) 8434102; e-mail pcciintr@moz com.com; internet www.philcham.com; f. 1977; Pres. SERGIO R. ORTIZ-LUIS, Jr.

Philippine Chamber of Mines: Rm 204, Ortigas Bldg, Ortigas Ave, Pasig City, Metro Manila; tel. (2) 6354123; fax (2) 6354160; e-mail comp@vasia.com; f. 1975; Chair. GERARD H. BRIMO; Pres. ARTEMIO DISINI.

FOREIGN TRADE ORGANIZATIONS

Bureau of Export Trade Promotion: New Solid Bldg, 5th–8th Floors, 357 Sen. Gil J. Puyat Ave, Makati City, 1200 Metro Manila; tel. (2) 8990133; fax (2) 8904707; e-mail betpod@dti.gov.ph; internet www.dti.gov.ph/betp; Dir SERAFIN N. JULIANO.

Bureau of Import Services: Oppen Bldg, 3rd Floor, 349 Sen. Gil J. Puyat Ave, Makati City, Metro Manila; tel. (2) 8905418; fax (2) 8957466; e-mail bis@dti.gov.ph; internet www.dti.gov.ph/bis; Exec. Dir ALEXANDER B. ARCILLA.

Philippine International Trading Corpn (PITC): Philippines International Center, 46 Sen. Gil J. Puyat Ave, 1200 Makati City; POB 2253 MCPO; tel. (2) 8454376; fax (2) 8454476; e-mail pitc@info.com.ph; internet www.dti.gov.ph/pitc/; f. 1973; state trading company to conduct international marketing of general merchandise, industrial and construction goods, raw materials, semi-finished and finished goods, and bulk trade of agri-based products; also provides financing, bonded warehousing, shipping, cargo and customs services; Pres. ARTHUR C. YAP.

INDUSTRIAL AND TRADE ASSOCIATIONS

Chamber of Automobile Manufacturers of the Philippines: Metro Manila; Sec.-Gen. MARIO DE GRANO.

Cotton Development Administration: Rudgen Bldg 1, 2nd Floor, 17 Shaw Blvd, Pasig City, Metro Manila; tel. (2) 6312104; fax (2) 6312113; e-mail cotton@pworld.net.ph; Administrator Dr EUGENIO D. ORPIA, Jr.

Fiber Industry Development Authority: 1424 Asia Trust Annex Bldg, Quezon Ave, Quezon City, Metro Manila; tel. (2) 3739236; fax (2) 3739238; e-mail jjmt@i-manila.com.ph; Administrator JOAQUIN M. TEOTICO.

Philippine Fisheries Development Authority: Union Square 1 Bldg, 7th Floor, 145 15th Ave, Cubao, Quezon City, Metro Manila; tel. (2) 9113829; fax (2) 9113018; f. 1976; Gen. Man. PABLO B. CASIMINA.

Semiconductor and Electronic Industries in the Philippines (SEIPI): Unit 1102, Alabang Business Tower 1, Acacia Ave, Madrigal Business Park, Ayala Alabang, Muntinlupa City, 1780 Metro Manila; tel. (2) 8078458; fax (2) 8078459; e-mail philelectronics@seipi.org; internet www.seipi.org; Exec. Dir ERNIE SANTIAGO.

EMPLOYERS' ORGANIZATIONS

Employers' Confederation of the Philippines (ECOP): ECC Bldg, 4th Floor, 355 Sen. Gil J. Puyat Ave, Makati City, Metro Manila; tel. (2) 8904845; fax (2) 8958576; e-mail ecop@webquest.com; internet www.ecop.org.ph; f. 1975; Pres. MIGUEL B. VARELA; Dir-Gen. VICENTE LEOGARDO, Jr.

Filipino Shipowners' Association: Victoria Bldg, Room 503, United Nations Ave, Ermita, 1000 Metro Manila; tel. (2) 5227318; fax (2) 5243164; e-mail filiship@info.com.ph; f. 1950; 34 mems; Chair. and Pres. CARLOS C. SALINAS; Exec. Dir AUGUSTO Y. ARREZA, Jr.

Philippine Cigar and Cigarette Manufacturers' Association: Unit 508, 1851 Dr Antonio Vasquez St, Malate, Metro Manila; tel. (2) 5249285; fax (2) 5249514; Pres. ANTONIO B. YAO.

Philippine Coconut Producers' Federation, Inc: Wardley Bldg, 2nd Floor, 1991 Taft Ave, cnr San Juan St, Pasay City, 1300 Metro

Manila; tel. (2) 5230918; fax (2) 5211333; e-mail cocofed@pworld.net.ph; Pres. MARIA CLARA L. LOBREGAT.

Philippine Sugar Millers' Association Inc: 1402 Security Bank Centre, 6776 Ayala Ave, Makati City, 1226 Metro Manila; tel. (2) 8911138; fax (2) 8911144; e-mail psma@netasia-mnl.net; internet www.psma.com.ph; f. 1922; Pres. V. FRANCISCO VARUA; Exec. Dir JOSE MA T. ZABALETA.

Philippine Retailers' Association: Unit 2610, Jollibee Plaza, Emerald Ave, Ortigas Centre, Pasig City; tel. (2) 6874180; fax (2) 6360825; e-mail pra@nwave.net; internet www.philretailers.com; Pres. BIENVENIDO V. TANTOCO III.

Textile Mills Association of the Philippines, Inc (TMAP): Ground Floor, Alexander House, 132 Amorsolo St, Legaspi Village, Makati City, 1229 Metro Manila; tel. (2) 8186601; fax (2) 8183107; e-mail tmap@pacific.net.ph; f. 1956; 11 mems; Pres. HERMENEGILDO C. ZAYCO; Chair. JAMES L. GO.

Textile Producers' Association of the Philippines, Inc: Downtown Center Bldg, Room 513, 516 Quintin Paredes St, Binondo, Metro Manila; tel. (2) 2411144; fax (2) 2411162; Pres. GO CUN UY; Exec. Sec. ROBERT L. TAN.

UTILITIES

Energy Regulatory Commission: Pacific Center Bldg, 12th–18th Floors, San Miguel Ave, Ortigas Center, Pasig City, Metro Manila; tel. (2) 6334556; fax (2) 6315871; e-mail info@erb.gov.ph; Chair. FE B. BARIN; Exec. Dir ARNIDO O. INUMERABLE.

Electricity

Davao Light and Power Co: 163 C. Bangoy Sr St, Davao City 8000; tel. (82) 2212191; fax (82) 2212105; e-mail davaolight@davao-online.com; internet www.davaolight.com; the country's third largest electric utility with a peak demand of 175MW in 2000.

Manila Electric Co (Meralco): Lopez Bldg, Meralco Center, Ortigas Ave, Pasig City, 0300 Metro Manila; tel. (2) 6312222; fax (2) 6328501; e-mail wmtirona@meralco.com.ph; internet www.meralco.com.ph; f. 1903; supplies electric power to Manila and seven provinces in Luzon; largest electricity distributor, supplying 54% of total consumption in 2000; privatized in 1991, 34% govt-owned; cap. and res 54,382m., sales 85,946m. (1998); Chair. and CEO MANUEL M. LOPEZ; Pres. JESUS P. FRANCISCO.

National Power Corpn (NAPOCOR): Quezon Ave, cnr BIR Rd, Quezon City, Metro Manila; tel. (2) 9213541; fax (2) 9212468; e-mail pad@napocor.com.ph; internet www.napocor.com.ph; f. 1936; state-owned corpn supplying electric and hydroelectric power throughout the country; scheduled for privatization; installed capacity in 1998, 11,810 MW; sales 86,611m. pesos (Dec. 1998); 12,043 employees; Pres. JESUS ALCORDO; Chair. MARIO V. TIAOQUI.

Gas

First Gas Holdings Corpn: Benpres Bldg, 4th Floor, Exchange Rd, cnr Meralco Ave, Pasig City, Metro Manila; tel. (2) 6343428; fax (2) 6352737; internet www.firstgas.com.ph; major interests in power generation and distribution; Pres. PETER GARRUCHO.

Water

Regulatory Authority

Metropolitan Waterworks and Sewerage System: Katipunan Rd, Balaran, Quezon City, 1105 Metro Manila; tel. (2) 9223757; fax (2) 9212887; e-mail mwssoch@epic.net; govt regulator for water supply, treatment and distribution within Metro Manila; Administrator ORLANDO C. HONDRADE.

Distribution Companies

Davao City Water District: Km 5, J. P. Laurel Ave, Bajada, Davao City; tel. (82) 2219400; fax (82) 2264885; e-mail dcwd@interasia.com.ph; f. 1973; public utility responsible for the water supply of Davao City; Gen. Man. WILFRED G. YAMSON.

Manila Water: MWSS Compound, 2nd Floor, 489 Katipunan Rd, Balaran, Quezon City, Metro Manila; tel. (2) 9267999; fax (2) 9281223; e-mail info@manilawateronline.com; internet www.manilawateronline.com; f. 1998 following the privatization of Metro Manila's water services; responsible for water supply to Manila East until 2023; Pres. ANTONINO T. AQUINO.

Maynilad Water: MWSS Compound, Katipunan Rd, Balaran, Quezon City, Metro Manila; tel. (2) 4353583; fax (2) 9223759; e-mail dal@mayniladwater.com.ph; f. 1998 following the privatization of Metro Manila's water services; responsible for water supply, sewage and sanitation services for Manila West until 2021; Pres. RAFAEL M. ALUNAN III.

Metropolitan Cebu Water District: M. C. Briones St, cnr P. Burgos St, Cebu City 6000; tel. (32) 2560413; fax (32) 2545391; e-mail mcwd@cvis.net.ph; f. 1974; public utility responsible for water supply and sewerage of Cebu City and surrounding towns and cities; Chair. RUBEN D. ALMENDRAS; Gen. Man. DULCE M. ABANILLA.

MAJOR COMPANIES

(Amounts in pesos, unless otherwise stated)

Automobiles

Honda Cars Philippines, Inc: Laguna Technopark, Sta Rosa, Laguna; tel. (92) 8243390; fax (92) 8243396; f. 1990; sales 4,690m. (1994/95); 800 employees; Pres. and Gen. Man. KOJI MIYAJIMA.

Mitsubishi Motors Philippines Corpn: Ortigas Ave Ext., Cainta, Rizal; tel. (2) 6580911; fax (2) 6580671; internet www.mitsubishi-motors.com.ph; f. 1987; car assembly; sales 13,273m. (1995); 1,300 employees; Pres. MAKOTO MAEDA.

Toyota Motor Philippines Corpn: Km 15, South Superhighway, Parañaque, 1700 Metro Manila; tel. (2) 8244701; fax (2) 8244741; e-mail fbj@toyota.com.ph; internet www.toyota.com.ph; f. 1988; sales 7,648m. (1998); 1,518 employees (1998); Chair. Dr GEORGE S. K. TY; Pres. TAKESHI FUKUDA.

Cement

Alsons Cement Corpn: Alsons Bldg, 2285 Pasong Tamo Ext., Makati City, Metro Manila; tel. (2) 8175506; e-mail alcemir@pworld.net.ph; internet www.alsonscement.com; mfrs of cement and construction-related products; cap. and res 4,568m. (1998), sales 2,846m. (2000); Chair. and Pres. TOMAS I. ALCANTARA; Sec. A. A. PICAZO.

Bacnotan Consolidated Industries Inc: Phinma Bldg, 4th Floor, 166 Salcedo St, Legaspi Village, Makati City, Metro Manila; tel. (2) 8109526; fax (2) 8109252; e-mail phinma@bworldonline.com; internet www.phinma.com; f. 1957; holding co with subsidiaries in manufacture of cement and steel, incl. Bacnotan Cement Corpn; cap. and res 5,502m., sales 7,957m. (2000); 1,564 employees; Chair. RAMON V. DEL ROSARIO, Sr; Pres. OSCAR J. HILADO.

Davao Union Cement Corpn: Phinma Bldg, 2nd Floor, 166 Salcedo St, Legaspi Village, Makati City, Metro Manila; tel. (2) 8109526; fax (2) 8183384; mfrs of cement; scheduled for merger with Hi Cement Corpn and Bacnotan Cement in 2000; cap. and res 3,136m. (June 1998), sales 2,018m. (June 1999); Chair. RAMON V. DEL ROSARIO, Sr; Pres. MAGDALENO B. ALBARRACIN, Jr.

Fortune Cement Corpn: BPI Condominium, 2nd Floor, 8753 Paseo de Roxas, Salcedo Village, Makati City, Metro Manila; tel. (2) 8159121; f. 1967; cap.and res 3,191m. (1998), sales 1,606m. (2000); 440 employees; Chair. GILBERT GARCIA; Pres. HENRY SY, Sr.

Hi Cement Corpn: Kalayaan Bldg, 5th Floor, 164 Salcedo St, Legaspi Village, Makati City, 1200 Metro Manila; tel. (2) 8101831; fax (2) 8120813; scheduled for merger with Bacnotan Cement and Davao Union Cement Corpn in 2000; cap. and res 4,163m. (June 1998), sales 2,366m. (June 1999); Chair. RAMON V. DEL ROSARIO, Sr; Pres. MAGDALENO B. ALBARRACIN.

Southeast Asia Cement Holdings Inc: Chatham House Bldg, 17th Floor, 116 Valero St, cnr Herrera St, Salcedo Village, Makati City, 1229 Metro Manila; tel. (2) 8454201; fax (2) 8403559; cap. and res 4,699m. (1998), sales 2,443m. (2000); Chair. JEAN DESAZARS DE MONTGAILHARD; Pres. and CEO P. A. ROSEBERG.

Coconut Products

International Copra Export Corpn: LKG Tower, 38th Floor, 6801 Ayala Ave, Makati City; tel. (2) 8841271; fax (2) 8841389; f. 1961; wholesaler of coconut and coconut products; sales 3,771m. (1997); 350 employees; Chair. K. G. LUY; Pres. ENRIQUE LUY.

Legaspi Oil Co, Inc: UCPB Bldg, 16th Floor, Makati Ave, Makati City, 1200 Metro Manila; tel. (2) 8921961; fax (2) 8153370; f. 1929; processors of coconut oil; six subsidiaries; sales 2,892m. (1997); 150 employees; Chair. TIRSO ANTIPORDA; Pres. JEREMIAS B. BENICO.

Lu Do and Lu Ym Oleochemical Corpn: 101–103 Tupaz St, POB 18, Cebu City; tel. (32) 2531930; fax (32) 54102; f. 1948; mfrs of crude coconut oil, refined edible oil, copra meal products, corn starch, corn oil and gluten meal; net sales 260.3m. (1997); 538 employees; Pres. DOUGLAS LU YM; Exec. Vice-Pres. and Gen. Man. V. D. VELASCO; Chair. PATERNO LU YM.

Philippine Refining Co, Inc: 1351 United Nations Ave, Metro Manila; tel. (2) 504011; f. 1927; detergents, personal products, and food mfrs; processors of coconut oil; 1,550 employees; Pres. and Chair. CESAR B. BAUTISTA.

Procter and Gamble Philippine Manufacturing Corpn: Ayala Center, 14th–21st Floors, 6750 Ayala Ave, Makati City, Metro Manila; tel. (2) 8430621; fax (2) 8148551; internet www.pg.com; f. 1935; processors of coconut oil; toilet preparations and detergents;

food mfrs; sales US $367.2m. (1999); 2,000 employees; Pres. JOHNIP G. CUA.

Construction

Cityland Development Corpn: 2/F Cityland Condominium 10, Tower One, POB 5000, 6815 HV Dela Costa St, Ayala Ave, Makati City, 1226 Metro Manila; tel. (2) 8936060; fax (2) 8928656; e-mail investment@cityland.net; internet www.cityland.net; cap. and res 945,624m., sales 759,473m. (2000); Chairs VICENTE T. PATERNO, ANDREW I. LIUSON.

Construction Consultants Corpn: Zeta II Bldg, 5th Floor, Salcedo St, Makati City, 1200 Metro Manila; tel. (2) 877118; fax (2) 8185646; f. 1976; consulting, management, engineering; Pres. TEODORO GENER.

DMCI Holdings Inc: Dacon Bldg, 3rd Floor, 2281 Pasong Tamo Ext., Makati City, 1231 Metro Manila; tel. (2) 8920984; fax (2) 8167362; e-mail dmcihi@mozcom.com; internet www.dmchi.com; sales 4,592m. (2000); Pres. ISIDRO A. CONSUNJI.

Philippine National Construction Corpn (PNCC): PNCC Bldg, Epifanio de los Santos Ave, cnr Reliance St, Mandaluyong, Metro Manila; tel. (2) 6318431; fax (2) 6315362; 80% govt-owned; construction; design engineering; steel and concrete products, heavy machinery; sales 2,733m. (1998); Chair. VICTORINO A. BASCO; Pres. and CEO ROLANDO JOSE L. MACASAET.

Electrical and Electronics

Matsushita Communication Industrial Corpn of the Philippines: Laguna Technopark, Don Jose, Sta Rosa, Laguna; tel. (92) 8181263; fax (92) 8190313; e-mail mat_com@mozcom.com; f. 1987; mfr and sale of industrial communications products; sales 7,640m. (1998); 1,893 employees; Chair. and Pres. MORIMASA WADA.

Matsushita Electric Philippines Corpn: B. Mapandan, Ortigas Ave Ext., Taytay, Rizal, 1901 Metro Manila; tel. (2) 6352260; fax (2) 8189478; mfr of electrical appliances; cap. and res 2,627m. (March 1998), sales 7,679m. (March 2001); 1,800 employees; Pres. YUKIHARU KUBOTA.

Solid Group Inc: 2285 Pasong Tamo Ext., Makati City, 1200 Metro Manila; tel. (2) 8431511; fax (2) 8128273; mfr of consumer electronic products carrying the Sony and Aiwa brand names: cap. and res 7,459m., sales 4,149m. (2000); 1,550 employees; Chairs SUSAN L. TAN, DAVID S. LIM.

Temic Telefunken Microelectronics Philippines, Inc: FTI Complex, Bagsakan Rd, Taguig, Makati City, Metro Manila; tel. (2) 8158635; fax (2) 8158640; f. 1974; mfr of electronics components; sales 5,907m. (1996); 3,500 employees; Gen. Man. JOSE M. FACUNDO.

Texas Instruments (Philippines), Inc: Baguio Export Processing Zone, Laokan Rd, Baguio City, Benguet; tel. (74) 8450927; fax (2) 8931960; e-mail n-veria@ti.com; internet www.ti.com; f. 1979; mfr of semiconductors; sales US $1,391.1m. (1999); Pres. DONALD F. MIKA.

Food and Food Products

Coca-Cola Bottlers Philippines, Inc: Feliza Bldg, 6th Floor, Herrera St, Legaspi Village, Makati City, 1229 Metro Manila; tel. (2) 8188741; fax (2) 8188750; f. 1981; beverages; sales US $708.4m. (1999); 9,431 employees; Chair. ANDRES SORIANO.

Cosmos Bottling Corpn: RFM Bldg, 5th Floor, cnr Sheridan and Pioneer Sts, Mandaluyong City, Metro Manila; tel. (2) 6318101; fax (2) 6320839; e-mail cosmosmail@cosmos.com.ph; manufactures, markets and distributes soft drinks; cap. and res 6,531m., sales 4,077m. (1999); 4,811 employees; Chair. JOSE MARIE A. CONCEPCION, III.

Dole Philippines, Inc: BA-Lepanto Bldg, 4th Floor, 8747 Paseo de Roxas, Makati City, Metro Manila; tel. (2) 8102601; fax (2) 8166483; f. 1963; mfr or canned food; sales 5,259.3m. (1997); 4,550 employees; Chair. PAUL CUYEGKENG.

Jollibee Foods Corpn: Jollibee Plaza, 10th Floor, Emerald and Ruby Rd, Ortigas Center, Pasig City, Metro Manila; tel. (2) 6341111; fax (2) 6358888; e-mail president@jollibee.com.ph; internet www.jollibee.com.ph; operation of fast food chain; cap. 5,900m., sales 20,300m. (2000); Chair., Pres. and CEO TONY TAN CAKTIONG.

Nestlé Philippines, Inc: Jade Bldg, 335 Sen. Gil J. Pugat Ave, Makati City, 1200 Metro Manila; tel. (2) 8980001; fax (2) 8980089; f. 1961; mfr of food products; sales US $856.4m. (1999); 4,500 employees; Pres. JUAN B. SANTOS.

Pure Foods Corpn: JMT Corporate Condominium, ADB Ave, Ortigas Centre, Pasig City, POB 2695, Metro Manila; tel. (2) 6341010; fax (2) 6338747; e-mail dimayuga.teodoro@purefoods.com.ph; internet www.purefoods.co.ph; f. 1956; cap. and res 3,571m., sales 12,650,375m. (2000); 3,700 employees; Chair. EDUARDO M. COJUANGCO, Jr; Pres. ENRIQUE A. GOMEZ, Jr.

RFM Corpn: RFM Bldg, Pioneer St, cnr Sheridan St, Mandaluyong City, Metro Manila; tel. (2) 6318101; fax (2) 6315039; e-mail rfmmail@rfm.com.ph; internet www.rfm.com.ph; mfrs of flour, feeds, meat, snacks, fats and oil, etc.; cap. and res 5,929m., sales US $431.3m. (1999); Chair. JOSE A. CONCEPCION, Jr; Pres. and CEO JOSE A. CONCEPCION III.

San Miguel Corpn: 40 San Miguel Ave, Mandaluyong City, Makati City, Metro Manila; tel. (2) 6323000; fax (2) 6323099; internet www.sanmiguel.com.ph; f. 1890; breweries, food processing, packaging; cap. and res 65,612m., sales US $1,912.9m. (1999); 15,923 employees; Chair. EDUARDO COJUANGCO.

Swift Foods, Inc: RFM Corporate Centre, Pioneer Cnr, Sheridan, Mandaluyong City, 1603 Metro Manila; tel. (2) 6318101; fax (20 6315064; e-mail swiftmail@swiftfoods.com.ph; internet www.rfm.com.ph; mfr of processed meat products, poultry products and commercial feeds; cap. and res 3,302m., sales 9,171m. (2000); Chair. JOSE A. CONCEPCION III.

La Tondeña Distillers, Inc: Don Carlos Palanca Bldg, 453 Carlos Palanca, Sr St, Quiapo, 1001 Metro Manila; tel. (2) 7349701; fax (2) 7349584; e-mail csmapa@sanmiguel.com.ph; internet www.latondena.sanmiguel.com.ph; f. 1987; mfr of liquors and mineral water; cap. and res 4,312m. (1998), sales 14,188m. (2000); 1,200 employees; Chair. E. M. CONJUANGCO, Jr; Pres. P. A. MEDIARITO.

Universal Robina Corpn: URC Bldg, 110 E. Rodriguez Ave, Libis, Quezon City, Metro Manila; tel. (2) 6718246; fax (2) 6345276; f. 1954; mfr of snacks, chocolates, candies, biscuits, pasta and ice cream; cap. and res 14,288m. (Sept. 1998), sales 15,706m. (Sept. 2000); 6,300 employees; Chair. JOHN L. GOKONGWEI, Jr; Pres. JAMES L. GO.

Vitarich Corpn: 2316 Sarmiento Bldg, Pasong Tamo Ext., Makati City, Metro Manila; tel. (2) 8430236; fax (2) 8167236; internet www.vitarich.com; f. 1962; mfr of animal feeds; cap. and res 1,542m. (1997), sales 5,862m. (2000); 1,800 employees; Chair. ROGELIO M. SARMIENTO; Pres. RENATO P. SARMIENTO.

Metal Mining

Atlas Consolidated Mining and Development Corpn: Phelps Dodge Annex Bldg, 2nd Floor, Pioneer St, Mandaluyong City, 1554 Metro Manila; tel. (2) 6342311; fax (2) 6333759; f. 1953; mining of copper ore and recovery of by-products of gold, silver and pyrite at Cebu mines; mining of gold ore (with silver) at Masbate Gold Operations; cap. and res 4,488m., sales 306m. (1997); 400 employees; Chair. JOSE C. IBAZETA; Vice-Chair. ANDRES SORIANO, III.

Benguet Corpn: Corporate Plaza, 3rd Floor, 845 Arnaiz Ave., cnr Pasay Rd, Legaspi Village, Makati City, 1223 Metro Manila; tel. (2) 8121380; fax (2) 8136611; e-mail spp@benguetcorp.com.ph; internet www.benguetcorp.com; f. 1903; principal primary gold producer; cap. and res 1,275m., sales 406m. (1998); 480 employees; Chair., Pres. and CEO BENJAMIN PHILIP G. ROMUALDEZ.

Lepanto Consolidated Mining Co: BA-Lepanto Bldg, 21st Floor, 8747 Paseo de Roxas, Makati City, Metro Manila; tel. (2) 8159447; fax (2) 8105583; e-mail lepanto@i-next.net; f. 1936; copper, gold, silver and calcines; cap. and res 4,555m., sales 2,999m. (2000); 2,244 employees; Chair. and CEO FELIPE U. YAP; Pres. ARTEMIO F. DISINI.

Marinduque Mining and Industrial Corpn: 2283 Pasong Tamo Ext., Makati City, Metro Manila; tel. (2) 864011; f. 1949; nickel, copper and cement production; Pres. ALFREDO VELAYO; Exec. Vice-Pres. DAVID MYTTON.

Philex Mining Corpn: Philex Bldg, 27 Brixton St, Pasig City, 1660 Metro Manila; tel. (2) 6311381; fax (2) 6333242; e-mail philex@skyinet.net; internet www.philexmining.com.ph; mining; f. 1955; cap. and res 3,990m., sales 4,457m. (2000); 3,963 employees; Chair. GERARD H. BRIMO; Snr Vice-Pres. and CEO LEONARDO P. JOSEF.

Petroleum

Alsons Consolidated Resources Inc: Alsons Bldg, 2nd Floor, 2286 Pasong Tamo Ext., Makati City, 1231 Metro Manila; tel. (2) 8175506; fax (2) 8940655; e-mail acrinrel@pworld.net.ph; internet www.acr-alsons.com; exploration and development of petroleum and petroleum products and gas; cap. and res 6,919m., sales 7,415m. (1998); Chair. and Pres. NICASIO I. ALCANTARA; Sec. ROBERTO V. SAN JOSE.

Caltex (Philippines) Inc: 540 Padre Faura, Ermita, Metro Manila; tel. (2) 8136001; fax (2) 8944116; f. 1921; petroleum refining; sales US $939.5m. (1999); 878 employees; Chair. and Pres. WILLIAM S. TIFFANY.

Mobil Philippines Inc: The Orient Square, 17th Floor, Emerald Ave, Ortigas, Pasig City; tel. (2) 6382333; fax (2) 8151844; sales 2,194m. (1998); Pres. C. B. RICCI.

Petron Corpn: Petron Bldg, 7901 Makati Ave, Makati City, Metro Manila; tel. (2) 8929061; fax (2) 8152721; e-mail fmc@pet.com; internet www.petron.com; petroleum refining; 40% govt-owned, 40% owned by Saudi Arabian Oil Co; subsidiary of the state-owned

Philippine National Oil Co; cap. and res 17,950m., sales US $1,442.5m. (1999); Chair. NICASIO I. ALCANTARA

Pilipinas Shell Petroleum Corpn: Shell House, 156 Valero St, Salcedo Village, Makati City, 1227 Metro Manila; tel. (2) 8166501; fax (2) 8166565; internet www.shell.com.ph; f. 1959; petroleum refining and marketing; sales US $1,357.4m. (1999); 1,100 employees; Pres. OSCAR REYES.

Shell Gas Eastern, Inc: Shell House, 156 Valero St, Salcedo Village, Makati City, 1299 Metro Manila; tel. (2) 8166501; fax (2) 8166399; f. 1980; sales 6,803m. (1998); Pres. O. S. REYES.

Pharmaceuticals

Colgate-Palmolive Philippines: 1049 J. P. Rizal St, Makati City, 2800 Metro Manila; tel. (2) 8959444; fax (2) 8959457; f. 1947; mfr of cosmetics and toiletries; sales 4,600m. (1996); 480 employees; Pres. ROBERT GALAN.

Euro Med Laboratories Philippines, Inc: PPL Bldg, United Nations Ave, cnr San Marcelino, Metro Manila; tel. (2) 5240091; cap. and res 614,153m., sales 780,037m. (2000); Chairs Dr TOMAS P. MARAMBA, Jr, GEORGIANA S. EVIDENTE.

Metro Drug Distribution, Inc: Sta Maria Industrial Estate, Manalac Ave, Bicutan Tagig, Metro Manila; tel. (2) 8372121; fax (2) 8372912; e-mail zuellig@mni.sequel.net; f. 1932; mfr of pharmaceuticals; sales 6,723m. (1995); 1,340 employees; Pres. PAUL KLEINER.

Unilever Philippines (PRC), Inc: 1351 United Nations Ave, Paco, Metro Manila; tel. (2) 5623951; fax (2) 5647259; e-mail franklin.gomez@unilever.com; internet www.unilever.com; f. 1927; mfr of pharmaceutical products, detergents, toiletries and foods; sales 8,808m. (1998); 1,100 employees; CEO VENKATESH KASTURURANGAN.

United Laboratories, Inc: 66 United St, Mandaluyong City, Metro Manila; tel. (2) 6318501; fax (2) 6316774; f. 1953; sales 9,475m. (1998); 2,375 employees; Chair. JOSE Y. CAMPOS; Pres. DELFIN B. SAMSON, Jr.

Zuellig Pharma Corpn: Zuellig Bldg, Sen. Gil J. Puyat Ave, Makati City, 1265 Metro Manila; tel. (2) 8191561; fax (2) 8431495; e-mail zpc@zuelligpharma.com.ph; internet www.zuelligpharma.com; f. 1953; sales US $413.4m. (1999); 2,030 employees; Chair. and Pres. REINER W. GLOOR.

Sugar

Central Azucarera de Tarlac: Cojuangco Bldg, 119 de la Rosa St, Makati City, Metro Manila; tel. (2) 8183911; fax (2) 8179309; f. 1927; cap. and res 494m., sales 871m. (1998); Pres. and Chair. PEDRO COJUANGCO.

Central Azucarera Don Pedro: Cacho Gonzalez Bldg, 6th Floor, 101 Aquirre St, Legaspi Village, Makati City, Metro Manila; tel. (2) 8108901; fax (2) 8171875; f. 1930; sales 2,337m. (1997); 1,104 employees; Chair. PEDRO E. ROXAS; Vice-Chair. ANTONIO J. ROXAS.

Victorias Milling Co, Inc: VMC Bldg, 6th Floor, 165 Legaspi St, Legaspi Village, Makati City, 1200 Metro Manila; tel. (2) 8158101; fax (2) 8153204; f. 1919; sugar mfrs and refiners, agribusiness, property; sales 5,526m. (1994/95); 6,000 employees; Chair. CLAUDIO R. DE LUZURIAGA; Pres. GERARDO B. JAVELLANA.

Textiles

Litton Textile Mills: Amang Rodriguez Ave, Rosario, Pasig City, Metro Manila; tel. (2) 6413289; fax (2) 6417174; sales 1,634m. (1994/95); Pres. JAMES L. GO.

Ramie Textiles Inc: Boston Bank Center, 5th Floor, 6764 Ayala Ave, Makati City, Metro Manila; tel. (2) 8163301; fax (2) 8108616; f. 1956; 2,022 employees; Pres. RAMON H. DAVILA; Chair. ERNEST KAHN.

Solid Mills Inc: POB 1803, Makati City, Metro Manila; tel. (2) 8926416; fax (2) 8421631; f. 1971; 2,400 employees; sales 1,040m. (1995); Pres. PHILIP T. ANG; Chair. ANG BENG UH.

Tobacco

La Perla Industries Inc: Cheng Tsai Jun Bldg, 0165 Quirino Ave, Parañaque, Metro Manila; tel. (2) 8333211; fax (2) 8337452.

Wood and Wood Products

L. S. Sarmiento & Co, Inc and Sarmiento Industries, Inc: Sarmiento Bldg, 2 Pasong Tamo Ext., Makati City, Metro Manila; mfrs and exporters of plywood and panels; Pres. PABLO M. SARMIENTO, Jr (L. S. Sarmiento & Co Inc), DANILO P. SARMIENTO (Sarmiento Industries, Inc).

PICOP Resources Corpn: Moredel Bldg, 2nd Floor, 2280 Pasong Tamo Ext., Makati City, Metro Manila; tel. (2) 8135308; fax (2) 8410459; f. 1952; mfr of paper; cap. and res 3,352m. (1997), sales 2,417m. (2000); 3,648 employees; CEO LEONARDO T. SIGUION REYNA.

Steniel Manufacturing Corpn: Tektite Tower West, Unit 2902-B, Tektite Rd, Ortigas Center, Pasig City, Metro Manila; tel. (2) 6386286; fax (2) 6386289; e-mail info@firstpac.com.hk; internet www.steniel.com.ph; mfr of packaging products; cap. and res 1,391m. (1998), sales 1,698m. (2000); 703 employees; Chair. NAPOLEON L. NAZARENO; Pres. AUGIE PALISOC, Jr.

Zamboanga Wood Products Inc: GPL Bldg, Room 55, 5th Floor, 219 Sen. Gil J. Puyat Ave, Makati City, Metro Manila; tel. (2) 8159636; f. 1961; 1,090 employees; Pres. CLARITO ILLUSTRE.

Miscellaneous

Aboitiz Equity Ventures Inc: Aboitiz Corporate Center, Archbishop Reyes Ave, Banilad, Cebu City; tel. (32) 2312580; fax (32) 2314031; e-mail aev@aboitiz.com.ph; internet www.aev.aboitiz.com.ph; f. 1920; construction and fabrication; banking, power distribution; interests in shipping, shipyards, production of gases, operator of container terminal; cap. and res 10,916m. (1998), sales 11,343m. (2000); Chair. LUIS M. ABOITIZ, Jr; Pres. JON RAMON M. ABOITIZ.

Asian Terminals, Inc: Muelle de San Francisco St, South Harbor, Port Area, 1018 Metro Manila; tel. (2) 5278051; fax (2) 5272467; e-mail ati.sh@asianterminals.com.ph; internet www.asianterminals.com.ph; cap. and res 1,974m. (1998), sales 2,932m. (2000); Chair. Capt. RICHARD SETCHELL; Pres. EUSEBIO H. TANCO.

Atlantic, Gulf and Pacific Co of Manila, Inc: AG&P House, 351 Sen. Gil J. Puyat Ave, Makati City, Metro Manila; tel. (2) 878071; fax (2) 8172684; f. 1900; engineering, heavy industrial construction, fabrication and castings, marine repairs, offshore oil platform and marine structures, industrial manufacturing and machinery sales; sales 2,185m. (1997); Chair. ROBERTO G. VILLANUEVA; Pres. ROBERTO T. VILLANUEVA, Jr.

Ayala Corpn: Tower One, Ayala Triangle, Ayala Ave, Makati City, Metro Manila; tel. (2) 7594567; fax (2) 8485768; e-mail acquery@ayala.com.ph; internet www.ayala.com.ph; f. 1834; conglomerate with interests in food, real estate, hotels etc.; cap. and res 43,053m., sales US $883.5m. (1999); Chair. JAIME ZOBEL DE AYALA.

Ayala Land Inc: Tower One, Ayala Triangle, Ayala Ave, Makati City, Metro Manila; tel. (2) 8485643; fax (2) 8485336; e-mail iru@ayalaland.com.ph; internet www.ayalaland.com.ph; real estate and hotel operations; cap. and res 25,253m. (1998), sales 10,306m. (2000); Chair. JAIME ZOBEL DE AYALA.

EEI Corpn: Topy Industries Bldg, 2nd Floor, 3 Calle Economia, Bagumbayan, Quezon City, 1110 Metro Manila; tel. (2) 6350851; fax (2) 6350861; e-mail scl@eei.com.ph; internet www.eei.com.ph; f. 1931; industrial construction; general trading; overseas construction services; cap. and res 2,151m., sales 4,532m. (2000); 11,594 employees; Pres. SAMSON C. LAZO; Chair. and CEO RIZALINO S. NAVARRO.

Guoco Holdings (Philippines) Inc: BA-Lepanto Bldg, 17th Floor, 8747 Paseo de Roxas, Makati City, Metro Manila; tel. (2) 8927912; fax (2) 8132895; principal activities of group include investment holding, real estate, manufacturing and distribution of Pepsi Cola products; cap. and res 2,607m. (1998), sales 1,091m. (June 2000); Pres. KWEK LENG HAI.

J.G. Summit Holdings Inc: CFC Bldg, E. Rodriguez Ave, Bagong Ilog, Pasig City, 1600 Metro Manila; tel. (2) 6337641; internet www.jgsummit.com.ph; retailers of food and agro-industrial products; property, power generation, electronics manufacturing, etc; cap. and res 32,136m., sales US $658.4m. (1999); CEO JOHN GOKONGWEI, Jr.

Metro Pacific Corpn: Rufino Pacific Tower, 41st Floor, Ayala Ave, cnr Herrera St, Makati City, Metro Manila; tel. (2) 8110338; fax (2) 8110026; e-mail metro@metropacific.com; internet www.metropacific.com; principal activities include consumer products, packaging, telecommunications; cap. and res 13,277m. (1997), sales 9,826m. (2000); Chair. MANUEL V. PANGILINAN.

Pryce Corpn: Pryce Center, 17th Floor, 1179 Chino Roces Ave, cnr Bagtikan St, Makati City, 1203 Metro Manila; tel. (2) 8994401; fax (2) 8996865; principal activities include trade in gases, and land development projects; cap. and res 813,462m., sales 704,628m. (2000); Chair. SALVADOR P. ESCANO.

Rustan Commercial Corpn: Rustan Bldg, Epifanio de los Santos Ave, Mandaluyong City, 1501 Metro Manila; tel. (2) 7270226; fax (2) 7212432; f. 1951; retailer; sales 9,232m. (2000); 3,940 employees; Chair. BIENVENIDO TANTOCO, Jr.

TRADE UNION FEDERATIONS

In 1986 the Government established the Labor Advisory Consultation Committee (LACC) to facilitate communication between the Government and the powerful labour movement in the Philippines. The LACC granted unions direct recognition and access to the Government, which, under the Marcos regime, had been available only to the Trade Union Congress of the Philippines (KMP-TUCP). The KMP-TUCP refused to join the Committee.

In May 1994 a new trade union alliance, the Caucus for Labor Unity, was established; its members included the KMP-TUCP and three groups that had dissociated themselves from the former Kilusang Mayo Uno.

Katipunang Manggagawang Pilipino (KMP-TUCP) (Trade Union Congress of the Philippines): TUCP Training Center Bldg, TUCP-PGEA Compound, Masaya St, cnr Maharlika St, Diliman, Quezon City, 1101 Metro Manila; tel. (2) 9222185; fax (2) 9219758; e-mail tucp@easy.net.ph; internet www.tucp.org.ph; f. 1975; 1.5m. mems; Pres. DEMOCRITO T. MENDOZA; Gen. Sec. ERNESTO F. HERRERA; 39 affiliates:

Associated Labor Unions—Visayas Mindanao Confederation of Trade Unions (ALU—VIMCONTU): ALU Bldg, Quezon Blvd, Port Area, Elliptical Rd, cnr Maharlika St, Diliman, Quezon City, 1101 Metro Manila; tel. (2) 9222185; fax (2) 9223199; f. 1954; 350,000 mems; Pres. DEMOCRITO T. MENDOZA.

Associated Labor Union for Metalworkers (ALU—METAL): TUCP-PGEA Compound, Diliman, Quezon City, 1101 Metro Manila; tel. (2) 9222575; fax (2) 9223199; 29,700 mems; Pres. CECILIO T. SENO.

Associated Labor Union for Textile Workers (ALU—TEXTILE): TUCP-PGEA Compound, Elliptical Rd, Diliman, Quezon City, 1101 Metro Manila; tel. (2) 9222575; fax (2) 9223199; 41,400 mems; Pres. RICARDO I. PATALINJUG.

Associated Labor Unions (ALU—TRANSPORT): 1763 Tomas Claudio St, Baclaran, Paranaque, Metro Manila; tel. (2) 8320634; fax (2) 8322392; 49,500 mems; Pres. ALEXANDER O. BARRIENTOS.

Associated Professional, Supervisory, Office and Technical Employees Union (APSOTEU): TUCP-PGEA Compound, Elliptical Rd, Diliman, Quezon City, 1101 Metro Manila; tel. (2) 9222575; fax (2) 9223199; Pres. CECILIO T. SENO.

Association of Independent Unions of the Philippines: Vila Bldg, Mezzanine Floor, Epifanio de los Santos Ave, Cubao, Quezon City, Metro Manila; tel. (2) 9224652; Pres. EMMANUEL S. DURANTE.

Association of Trade Unions (ATU): Antwel Bldg, Room 1, 2nd Floor, Santa Ana, Port Area, Davao City; tel. (82) 2272394; 2,997 mems; Pres. JORGE ALEGARBES.

Confederation of Labor and Allied Social Services (CLASS): Doña Santiago Bldg, TUCP Suite 404, 1344 Taft Ave, Ermita, Metro Manila; tel. (2) 5240415; fax (2) 5266011; f. 1979; 4,579 mems; Pres. LEONARDO F. AGTING.

Federation of Agrarian and Industrial Toiling Hands (FAITH): Kalayaan Ave, cnr Masigla St, Diliman, Quezon City, Metro Manila; tel. (2) 9225244; 220,000 mems; Pres. RAYMUNDO YUMUL.

Federation of Consumers' Co-operatives in Negros Oriental (FEDCON): Bandera Bldg, Cervantes St, Dumaguete City; tel. (32) 2048; Chair. MEDARDO VILLALON.

Federation of Filipino Civilian Employees Association (FFCEA): 14 Murphy St, Pagasa, Olongapo City; tel. (2) 8114267; fax (2) 8114266; 21,560 mems; Pres. ROBERTO A. FLORES.

Federation of Unions of Rizal (FUR): Perpetual Savings Bank Bldg, 3rd Floor, Quirino Ave, Parañaque, Metro Manila; tel. and fax (2) 8320110; 10,853 mems; Officer-in-Charge EDUARDO ASUNCION.

Lakas sa Industriya ng Kapatirang Haligi ng Alyansa (LIKHA): 32 Kabayanihan Rd Phase IIA, Karangalan Village, Pasig City, Metro Manila; tel. (2) 6463234; fax (2) 6463234; e-mail jbvlikha@yahoo.com; Pres. JESUS B. VILLAMOR.

National Association of Free Trade Unions (NAFTU): CVC Bldg, Room 3, AD Curato St, Butuan City; tel. (8822) 3620941; 7,385 mems; Pres. JAIME RINCAL.

National Congress of Unions in the Sugar Industry of the Philippines (NACUSIP): 7431-A Yakal St, Barangay San Antonio, Makati City, Metro Manila; tel. (2) 8942758; fax (2) 8437284; e-mail nacusip@compass.com.ph; 32 affiliated unions and 57,424 mems; Nat. Pres. ZOILO V. DELA CRUZ, Jr.

National Mines and Allied Workers' Union (NAMAWU): Unit 201, A. Dunville Condominium, 1 Castilla St, cnr Valencio St, Quezon City, Metro Manila; tel. (2) 7265070; fax (2) 4155582; 13,233 mems; Pres. ROBERTO A. PADILLA.

Pambansang Kilusan ng Paggawa (KILUSAN): TUCP-PGEA Compound, Elliptical Rd, Diliman, Quezon City, 1101 Metro Manila; tel. (2) 9284651; 13,093 mems; Pres. AVELINO V. VALERIO; Sec.-Gen. IGMIDIO T. GANAGANA.

Philippine Agricultural, Commercial and Industrial Workers' Union (PACIWU): 5 7th St, Lacson, Bacolod City; fax (2) 7097967; Pres. ZOILO V. DELA CRUZ, Jr.

Philippine Federation of Labor (PFL): FEMII Bldg, Suite 528, Aduana St, Intramuros, Metro Manila; tel. (2) 5271686; fax (2) 5272838; 8,869 mems; Pres. ALEJANDRO C. VILLAVIZA.

Philippine Federation of Teachers' Organizations (PFTO): BSP Bldg, Room 112, Concepcion St, Ermita, Metro Manila; tel. (2) 5275106; Pres. FEDERICO D. RICAFORT.

Philippine Government Employees' Association (PGEA): TUCP-PGEA Compound, Elliptical Rd, Diliman, Quezon City, Metro Manila; tel. (2) 6383541; fax (2) 6375764; e-mail eso_pgea@hotmail.com; f. 1945; 65,000 mems; Pres. ESPERANZA S. OCAMPO.

Philippine Integrated Industries Labor Union (PIILU): Mendoza Bldg, Room 319, 3rd Floor, Pilar St, Zamboanga City; tel. (992) 2299; f. 1973; Pres. JOSE J. SUAN.

Philippine Labor Federation (PLF): ALU Bldg, Quezon Blvd, Port Area, Cebu City; tel. (32) 71219; fax (32) 97544; 15,462 mems; Pres. CRISPIN B. GASTARDO.

Philippine Seafarers' Union (PSU): TUCP-PGEA Compound, Elliptical Rd, Diliman, Quezon City, 1101 Metro Manila; tel. (2) 9222575; fax (2) 9247553; e-mail psumla@info.com.ph; 10,000 mems; Pres. DEMOCRITO T. MENDOZA; Gen. Sec. ERNESTO F. HERRERA.

Philippine Transport and General Workers' Organization (PTGWO—D): Cecilleville Bldg, 3rd Floor, Quezon Ave, Quezon City, Metro Manila; tel. (2) 4115811; fax (2) 4115812; f. 1953; 33,400 mems; Pres. VICTORINO F. BALAIS.

Port and General Workers' Federation (PGWF): Capilitan Engineering Corpn Bldg, 206 Zaragoza St, Tondo, Manila; tel. 208959; Pres. FRANKLIN D. BUTCON.

Public Sector Labor Integrative Center (PSLINK): 9723 C. Kamagong St, San Antonio Village, Makati City, Metro Manila; tel. (2) 8961573; fax (2) 9243525; 35,108 mems; Pres. ERNESTO F. HERRERA; Gen. Sec. ANNIE GERON.

United Sugar Farmers' Organization (USFO): SPCMA Annex Bldg, 3rd Floor, 1 Luzuriaga St, Bacolod City; Pres. BERNARDO M. REMO.

Workers' Alliance Trade Unions (WATU): Delta Bldg, Room 300, Quezon Ave, cnr West Ave, Quezon City, Metro Manila; tel. (2) 9225093; fax (2) 975918; f. 1978; 25,000 mems; Pres. TEMISTOCLES S. DEJON, Sr.

INDEPENDENT LABOUR FEDERATIONS

The following organizations are not affiliated to the KMP-TUCP:

Associated Marine Officers and Seamen's Union of the Philippines (AMOSUP): Seaman's Centre, cnr Cabildo and Sta Potenciana Sts, Intramuros, Metro Manila; tel. (2) 495415; internet www.amosup.org/; f. 1960; 23 affiliated unions with 55,000 mems; Pres. GREGORIO S. OCA.

Federation of Free Workers (FFW): FFW Bldg, 1943 Taft Ave, Malate, Metro Manila; tel. (2) 5219435; fax (2) 4006656; f. 1950; affiliated to the Brotherhood of Asian Trade Unionists and the World Confed. of Labour; 300 affiliated local unions and 400,000 mems; Pres. RAMON J. JABAR.

Lakas ng Manggagawa Labor Center: Rm 401, Femii Bldg Annex, A. Soriano St, Intramuros, Metro Manila; tel. and fax (2) 5280482; a grouping of 'independent' local unions; Chair. OSCAR M. ACERSON.

Manggagawa ng Komunikasyon sa Pilipinas (MKP): 22 Libertad St, Mandaluyong City, Metro Manila; tel. (2) 5313701; fax (2) 5312109; f. 1951; Pres. PETE PINLAC.

National Confederation of Labor: Suite 402, Carmen Bldg, Ronquillo St, cnr Evangelista St, Quiapo, Metro Manila; tel. and fax (2) 7334474; f. 1994 by fmr mems of Kilusang Mayo Uno; Pres. ANTONIO DIAZ.

Philippine Social Security Labor Union (PSSLU): Carmen Bldg, Suite 309, Ronquillo St, Quiapo, Metro Manila; f. 1954; Nat. Pres. ANTONIO B. DIAZ; Nat. Sec. OFELIA C. ALAVERA.

Samahang Manggagawang Pilipino (SMP) (National Alliance of Teachers and Office Workers): Fersal Condominium II, Room 33, 130 Kalayaan Ave, Quezon City, 1104 Metro Manila; tel. and fax (2) 9242299; Pres. ADELISA RAYMUNDO.

Solidarity Trade Conference for Progress: Rizal Ave, Dipolog City; tel. and fax (65) 2124303; Pres. NICOLAS E. SABANDAL.

Trade Unions of the Philippines and Allied Services (TUPAS): Med-dis Bldg, Suites 203–204, Solana St, cnr Real St, Intramuros, Metro Manila; tel. (2) 493449; affiliated to the World Fed. of Trade Unions; 280 affiliated unions and 75,000 mems; Nat. Pres. DIOSCORO O. NUÑEZ; Sec.-Gen. VLADIMIR R. TUPAZ.

Transport

RAILWAYS

The railway network is confined mainly to the island of Luzon.

Light Rail Transit Authority (Metrorail): Adm. Bldg, LRTA Compound, Aurora Blvd, Pasay City, Metro Manila; tel. (2) 8320423; fax (2) 8316449; e-mail railnet@pacific.net.ph; internet www.lrta.gov.ph; managed and operated by Light Rail Transit Authority (LRTA); electrically-driven mass transit system; Line 1 (14.8 km, Baclaran to Monumento) began commercial operations in Dec. 1984; Line 1 South Extension (12 km, Baclaran to Bacoot) and Line 2 (14 km, Santolan to Recto) were scheduled to be operational in 2004; Administrator TEODORO B. CRUZ, Jr.

Philippine National Railways: PNR Management Center, Torres Bugallon St, Kalookan City, Metro Manila; tel. (2) 3654716; fax (2) 3620824; internet www.pnr.gov.ph; f. 1887; govt-owned; northern line services run from Manila to Caloocan, 6 km (although the track extends to San Fernando, La Union) and southern line services run from Manila to Legaspi, Albay, 479 km); Chair. and Gen. Man. JOSE M. SARASOLA II.

ROADS

In 2000 there were 201,994 km of roads in the Philippines, of which 30,013 km were highways and 49,992 km were secondary roads; an estimated 42,419 km of the network were paved. Bus services provided the most widely-used form of inland transport.

Department of Public Works and Highways: Bonifacio Drive, Port Area, Metro Manila; tel. (2) 5274111; fax (2) 5275635; e-mail pilorin.beth.p@dpwh.gov.ph; internet www.dpwh.gov.ph; responsible for the construction and maintenance of roads and bridges; Sec. GREGORIO R. VIGILAR.

Land Transportation Franchising and Regulatory Board: East Ave, Quezon City, Metro Manila; tel. (2) 4262505; fax (2) 4262515; internet www.ltfrb.gov.ph; f. 1987; Chair. DANTE LANTIN.

Land Transportation Office (LTO): East Ave, Quezon City, Metro Manila; tel. (2) 9219072; fax (2) 9219071; internet www.lto.gov.ph; f. 1987; plans, formulates and implements land transport rules and regulations, safety measures; registration of motor vehicles; issues licences; Assistant Sec. ROBERTO LASTIMOSO.

SHIPPING

In 2000 there were 102 national and municipal ports, 20 baseports, 58 terminal ports and 270 private ports. The eight major ports are Manila, Cebu, Iloilo, Cagayan de Oro, Zamboanga, General Santos, Polloc and Davao.

Pangasiwaan ng Daungan ng Pilipinas (Philippine Ports Authority): Marsman Bldg, 22 Muelle de San Francisco St, South Harbour, Port Area, 1018 Metro Manila; tel. (2) 5274856; fax (2) 5274853; e-mail alcusi@ppa.com.ph; internet www.ppa.com.ph; f. 1977; supervises all ports within the Philippine Ports Authority port system; Gen. Man. ALFONSO G. CUSI.

Domestic Lines

Albar Shipping and Trading Corpn: 2649 Molave St, United Parañaque 1, Parañaque, Metro Manila; tel. (2) 8232391; fax (2) 8233046; e-mail admin@albargroup.com.ph; internet www.albargroup.com.ph; f. 1974; manning agency (maritime), trading, ship husbanding; Chair. AKIRA S. KATO; Pres. JOSE ALBAR G. KATO.

Candano Shipping Lines, Inc: Victoria Bldg, 6th Floor, 429 United Nations Ave, Ermita, 2802 Metro Manila; tel. (2) 5238051; fax (2) 5211309; f. 1953; inter-island chartering and Far East, cargo shipping; Pres. and Gen. Man. JOSE CANDANO.

Carlos A. Gothong Lines, Inc: Quezon Blvd, Reclamation Area, POB 152, Cebu City; tel. (32) 211181; fax (32) 212265; Exec. Vice-Pres. BOB D. GOTHONG.

Delsan Transport Lines Inc: Magsaysay Center Bldg, 520 T. M. Kalaw St, Ermita, Metro Manila; tel. (2) 5219172; fax (2) 2889331; Pres. VICENTE A. SANDOVAL; Gen. Man. CARLOS A. BUENAFE.

Eastern Shipping Lines, Inc: ESL Bldg, 54 Anda Circle, Port Area, POB 4253, 2803 Metro Manila; tel. (2) 5277841; fax (2) 5273006; e-mail eastship@skyinet.net; f. 1957; services to Japan; Pres. ERWIN L. CHIONGBIAN; Exec. Vice-Pres. ROY L. CHIONGBIAN.

Loadstar Shipping Co Inc: Loadstar Bldg, 1294 Romualdez St, Paco, 1007 Metro Manila; tel. (2) 5238381; fax (2) 5218061; Pres. and Gen. Man. TEODORO G. BERNARDINO.

Lorenzo Shipping Corpn: Birch Tree Plaza Bldg, 6th Floor, 825 Muelle dela Industria St, Binondo, Metro Manila; tel. (2) 2457481; fax (2) 2446849; Pres. Capt. ROMEO L. MALIG.

Luzteveco (Luzon Stevedoring Corpn): Magsaysay Bldg, 520 T.M. Kalaw St, Ermita, Metro Manila; f. 1909; two brs; freight-forwarding, air cargo, world-wide shipping, broking, stevedoring, salvage, chartering and oil drilling support services; Pres. JOVINO G. LORENZO; Vice-Pres. RODOLFO B. SANTIAGO.

National Shipping Corpn of the Philippines: Knights of Rizal Bldg, Bonifacio Drive, Port Area, Metro Manila; tel. (2) 473631; fax (2) 5300169; services to Hong Kong, Taiwan, Korea, USA; Pres. TONY CHOW.

Negros Navigation Co Inc: Rufino Pacific Tower, 33rd Floor, 6784 Ayala Ave, cnr Herrera St, Makati City, Metro Manila; tel. (2) 8110115; fax (2) 8183707; Chair. DANIEL L. LACSON; Man. Dir MANUEL GARCIA.

Philippine Pacific Ocean Lines Inc: Delgado Bldg, Bonifacio Drive, Port Area, POB 184, Metro Manila; tel. (2) 478541; Vice-Pres. C. P. CARANDANG.

Philippine President Lines, Inc: PPL Bldg, 1000–1046 United Nations Ave, POB 4248, Metro Manila; tel. (2) 5249011; fax (2) 5251308; trading world-wide; Chair. EMILIO T. YAP, Jr; Pres. ENRIQUE C. YAP.

Sulpicio Lines, Inc: 1st St, Reclamation Area, POB 137, Cebu City; tel. (32) 73839; Chair. ENRIQUE S. GO; Man. Dir CARLOS S. GO.

Sweet Lines Inc: Pier 6, North Harbour, Metro Manila; tel. (2) 201791; fax (2) 205534; f. 1937; Pres. EDUARDO R. LOPINGCO; Exec. Vice-Pres. SONNY R. LOPINGCO.

Transocean Transport Corpn: Magsaysay Bldg, 8th Floor, 520 T. M. Kalaw St, Ermita, POB 21, Metro Manila; tel. (2) 506611; Pres. and Gen. Man. MIGUEL A. MAGSAYSAY; Vice-Pres. EDUARDO U. MANESE.

United Philippine Lines, Inc: UPL Bldg, Santa Clara St, Intramuros, POB 127, Metro Manila; tel. (2) 5277491; fax (2) 5271603; e-mail uplines@skyinet.net; services world-wide; Pres. FERNANDO V. LISING.

WG & A Philippines, Inc: South Harbour Center 2, cnr Railroad St, South Harbour, Metro Manila; tel. (2) 5274605; fax (2) 5360945; internet www.wgasuperferry.com; f. 1996 following the merger of William Lines, Aboitiz Shipping and Carlos A. Gothong Lines; passenger and cargo inter-island services; Pres. ENDICA ABOITIZ; Chair. W. L. CHIONGBIAN.

CIVIL AVIATION

In March 1999 there were 92 national and 103 private airports in the Philippines. In addition to the international airports in Metro Manila (the Ninoy Aquino International Airport), Cebu (the Mactan International Airport), Angeles City (the Clark International Airport), and Olongapo City (the Subic Bay International Airport), there are five alternative international airports: Laoag City, Ilocos Norte; Davao City; Zamboanga City; Gen. Santos (Tambler) City; and Puerto Princesa City, Palawan. A further international airport was being developed in Laguindingan, Mindanao. The upgrading of the airport at the former US military installation, Clark Air Base (which was to be the country's principal airport), commenced in mid-1996, when a new international terminal (with an initial capacity of 300 passengers on charter flights) was opened.

Air Transportation Office: MIA Rd, Pasay City, Metro Manila; tel. (2) 8323308; fax (2) 8340143; internet www.ato.gov.ph; implements govt policies for the development and operation of a safe and efficient aviation network; Dir Gen. Capt. JACINTO F. ORTEGA, Jr; Gen. Man. Gen. (retd) ADELBERTO F. YAP.

Civil Aeronautics Board: Airport Rd, Pasay City, Metro Manila; tel. (2) 8317266; fax (2) 8336911; internet www.cab.gov.ph; exercises general supervision and regulation of, and jurisdiction and control over, air carriers, their equipment facilities and franchise; Dir MANUEL C. SAN JOSE.

Air Philippines: Multinational Bancorporation Center, 15th Floor, Ayala Ave, Makati City, 6805 Metro Manila; tel. (2) 8437001; fax (2) 8451983; internet www.airphilippines.com; f. 1994; operates flights between Manila, Cebu City and Davao City; was expected to commence regional services in 1996; Chair. and Pres. WILLIAM GATCHALIAN.

Asian Spirit: G & A Bldg, 3rd Floor, 2303 Don Chino Roces Ave, Makati City, Metro Manila; tel. (2) 8403811; fax (2) 8130183; e-mail info@asianspirit.com; internet www.asianspirit.com; Man. ANTONIO BUENDIA.

Cebu Pacific Air: 30 Pioneer St, cnr Epifanio de los Santos Ave, Mandaluyong City, Metro Manila; tel. (2) 6371810; fax (2) 6379170; e-mail feedback@cebupacificair.com; internet www.cebupacificair.com; f. 1995; domestic and international services; Pres. LANCE GOKONGWEI; Vice-Pres. (Corporate Planning and External Affairs) PEGGY P. VERA.

Grand Air: Philippines Village Airport Hotel, 8th Floor, Pasay City, Metro Manila; tel. (2) 8312911; fax (2) 8917682; f. 1994; Pres. REBECCA PANLILI.

Manila International Airport Authority (MIAA): NAIA Complex, Pasay City, Metro Manila; tel. (2) 8322938; fax (2) 8331180;

e-mail gm@miaa.gov.ph; internet www.miaa.gov.ph; Gen. Man. EDGARDO C. MANDA.

Philippine Airlines Inc (PAL): PAL Corporate Communications Dept, PAL Center, Ground Floor, Legaspi St, Legaspi Village, Makati City, Metro Manila; tel. (2) 8316541; fax (2) 8136715; e-mail rgeccd@pal.com.ph; internet www.philippineairlines.com; f. 1941; in Jan. 1992 67% of PAL was transferred to the private sector; operates domestic, regional and international services to destinations in the Far East, Australasia, the Middle East, the USA and Canada; Chair. LUCIO TAN; Pres. AVELINO ZAPANTA.

Tourism

Tourism, although adversely affected from time to time by political unrest, remains an important sector of the economy. In 2001 arrivals totalled 1,796,893, compared with 1,992,169 in the previous year. Visitor expenditure totalled US $2,534m. in 1999 (compared with $2,412.9m. in 1998).

Philippine Convention and Visitors' Corpn: Legaspi Towers, 4th Floor, 300 Roxas Blvd, Metro Manila; tel. (2) 5259318; fax (2) 5216165; e-mail pcvcnet@info.com.ph; internet www.dotpcvc.gov.ph; Chair. Secretary of Tourism; Exec. Dir DANIEL G. CORPUZ.

Philippine Tourism Authority: Department of Tourism Bldg, T. M. Kalaw St, Ermita, 1000 Metro Manila; tel. (2) 5241032; fax (2) 5232865; e-mail info@philtourism.com; internet www .philtourism.com; Gen. Man. NIXON T. KUA.

Defence

In August 2001 the total strength of the armed forces was estimated at 107,000: army 67,000, navy an estimated 24,000 (including 8,000 Marines and a 2000-strong Coast Guard), air force an estimated 16,000. The Citizen Armed Forces Geographical Units (CAFGU), which replaced the civil home defence force, numbered about 40,000. Military service is voluntary. In early 2002 the US Government dispatched troops to support the Philippine armed forces in a six-month counter-terrorist operation. Most of the US forces were withdrawn in July, but it was announced that some 400 were to remain in the Philippines to assist in training the military.

Defence Expenditure: 34,939m. pesos in 2001.

Chief of Staff of the Armed Forces: Lt-Gen. BENJAMIN P. DEFENSOR.

Chief of Staff (Army): Lt-Gen. DIONISIO R. SANTIAGO.

Chief of Staff (Navy): Rear-Adm. VICTORINO S. HINGCO.

Chief of Staff (Air Force): Lt-Gen. NESTOR R. SANTILLAN.

Education

The 1987 Constitution commits the Government to provide free elementary and high school education; elementary education is compulsory. The organization of education is the responsibility of the Department of Education, Culture and Sports.

There are both public and private schools. The private schools are either sectarian or non-sectarian. Education in the Philippines is divided into four stages: pre-school (from the age of three); elementary school, which begins at seven years of age and lasts for six years; secondary or high school, which begins at 13 and lasts for five years (extended in 1994 from four years); and higher education, normally lasting four years. The public schools offer a general secondary curriculum and there are private schools which offer more specialized training courses. There is a common general curriculum for all students in the first and second years and more varied curricula in the third and fourth years leading to either college or technical vocational courses.

Total enrolment at pre-primary level in 1998/99 was equivalent to 30.7% (males 31.5%; females 30.0%) of children in the relevant age-group. . In 1998/99 enrolment in primary education was equivalent to 113.2% (males 113.0%; females 113.3%) of children in the relevant age group, while enrolment at secondary level included 50.9% of the appropriate age-group (males 48.7%; females 53.1%). In that year total enrolment at tertiary level was equivalent to 29.5% of the relevant age-group (males 26.1%; females 32.9%). Instruction is in both English and Filipino at elementary level and English is the usual medium at the secondary and tertiary levels. In 1998/99 there were 2,349 tertiary level institutions in the country. The 2002 budget allocated 105,300m. pesos (13.5% of total national expenditure) to education.

Bibliography

GENERAL

Adib Majul, Cesar. *The Political & Constitutional Ideas of the Philippine Revolution*. Metro Manila, University of the Philippines Press, 1999.

Muslims in the Philippines. Metro Manila, University of the Philippines Press, 1999.

Abueva, Jose V. (Ed.). *The Making of the Filipino Nation and Republic*. Metro Manila, University of the Philippines Press, 1999.

Barreveld, Dirk J. *Terrorism in the Philippines: the Bloody Trail of Abu Sayyaf, Bin Laden's East Asian Connection*. San Jose, CA, Writers Club Press, 2002.

Broad, Robin, and Cavanagh, John. *Plundering Paradise: The Struggle for the Environment in the Philippines*. Berkeley, CA, University of California Press, 1993.

Burley, T. M. *The Philippines. An Economic and Social Geography*. London, G. Bell and Sons, 1973.

Gowing, P. G., and Scott, W. H. (Eds). *Acculturation in the Philippines: Essays in Changing Societies*. Quezon City, New Day Publishers, 1971.

Guthrie, G. M. (Ed.). *Six Perspectives on the Philippines*. Manila, Bookmark Inc, 1971.

Hedman, Eva-Lotta, and Sidel, John T. (Eds). *Philippine Politics and Society in the Twentieth Century: Colonial Legacies, Post-Colonial Trajectories*. London, Routledge, 2000.

McCoy, Alfred W., and de Jesus, Ed C. (Eds). *Philippine Social History*. Quezon City, Metro Manila, Ateneo de Manila University Press, 1982.

Putzel, James. *A Captive Land*. London, Catholic Institute for International Relations, 1992.

San Juan, Jr, E. *From Exile to Diaspora*. Boulder, CO, Westview Press, 1998.

Wernstedt, F. L., and Spencer, J. E. *The Philippine Island World: A Physical, Cultural and Regional Geography*. Berkeley and Los Angeles, University of California, 1967.

HISTORY

Alfonso, Oscar M. *Theodore Roosevelt and the Philippines, 1897–1908*. Quezon City, University of the Philippines, 1970.

Bain, David Haward. *Sitting in Darkness: Americans in the Philippines*. Boston, MA, Houghton Mifflin, 1985.

Bankoff, Greg, and Weekley, Kathleen. *Post-Colonial National Identity in the Philippines: Celebrating the Centennial of Independence*. London, Ashgate Publishing Company, 2002.

Bresnan, John (Ed.). *Crisis in the Philippines: The Marcos Era and Beyond*. Princeton, NJ, Princeton University Press, 1987.

The Burden of Proof. Quezon City, University of the Philippines Press, 1984.

Carlson, Keith Thor. *The Twisted Road to Freedom*. Metro Manila, University of the Philippines Press, 1996.

Connaughton, R., Pimlott, J., and Anderson, D. *The Battle for Manila*. London, Bloomsbury, 1995.

Constantino, L. R. *The Snap Revolution*. Quezon City, Karrel Inc, 1986.

Constantino, R. *History of the Philippines: From the Spanish Colonization to the Second World War*. New York and London, MR Press, 1976.

Constantino, R., and Constantino, L. R. *The Philippines: The Continuing Past*. Quezon City, Foundation for Nationalist Studies, 1979.

George, T. J. S. *Revolt in Mindanao: The Rise of Islam in Philippine Politics*. Oxford University Press, 1980.

Hamilton-Paterson, James. *America's Boy: The Rise and Fall of Ferdinand Marcos and Other Misadventures of US Colonialism in the Philippines*. New York, Henry Holt, 1999.

Jones, Gregg R. *Red Revolution, Inside the Philippine Guerilla Movement*. Boulder, CO, Westview Press, 1989.

Kessler, Richard. *Rebellion and Repression in the Philippines*. New Haven, CT, Yale University Press, 1990.

Magno, A., Quiros, C., and Ofreneo, R. *The February Revolution*. Quezon City, Karrel Inc, 1986.

May, Anthony. *Battle for Batangas: A Philippine Province at War.* New Haven, CT, Yale University Press, 1991.

McFerson, Hazel M. (Ed.). *Mixed Blessing: the Impact of the American Colonial Experiences on Politics and Society in the Philippines (Contributions in Comparative Colonial Studies).* Westport, CT, Greenwood Publishing Group, 2002.

Mojares, Resil B. *The War Against the Americans: Resistance and Collaboration in Cebu, 1899–1906.* Metro Manila, University of the Philippines Press, 1999.

Muslim, M. *The Moro Armed Struggle in the Philippines.* Marawi City, Mindanao State University, 1994.

Paredus, R. R. (Ed.). *Philippine Colonial Democracy.* New Haven, CT, Yale University Press, 1988.

Reid, Robert H., and Guerrero, Eileen. *Corazon Aquino and the Brushfire Revolution.* Baton Rouge, Louisiana State University Press, 1996.

Rosenberg, David A. (Ed.). *Marcos and Martial Law in the Philippines.* Ithaca, NY and London, Cornell University Press, 1979.

Salman, Michael. *The Embarrassment of Slavery: Controversies over Bondage and Nationalism in the American Colonial Philippines.* Berkeley, CA, University of California Press, 2001.

Schirmer, D. B. *Republic or Empire: American Resistance to the Philippine War.* Mass, Schenkman Publishing Co, 1972.

Shaw, Angel V. and Francia, Luis, H. (Eds). *Vestiges of War: the Philippine-American War and the Aftermath of an Imperial Dream 1899–1999.* New York, NY, New York University Press, 2002.

Stanley, Peter W. (Ed.). *Reappraising an Empire: New Perspectives on Philippine-American History.* Cambridge, MA, Harvard University Press, 1985.

Timberman, David G. *A Changeless Land: Continuity and Change in Philippine Politics.* Singapore, Institute of Southeast Asian Studies, 1992.

ECONOMY

Aguilar, Jr, Filomeno V. *Clash of Spirits: The History of Power and Sugar Planter Hegemony on a Visayan Island.* Metro Manila, University of the Philippines Press, 1998.

Baldwin, R. E. *Foreign Trade Regimes and Economic Development: The Philippines.* Vol. V. New York, National Bureau of Economic Research, 1975.

Balisacan, Arsenio M., and Hill, Hal (Eds). *Philippine Economy: Development, Policies and Challenges.* Oxford, Oxford University Press, 2002.

Bautista, Germelino M. *Natural Resources, Economic Development and the State: The Philippine Experience.* Singapore, Institute of Southeast Asian Studies, 1994.

Boyce, James K. *The Philippines: The Political Economy of Growth and Impoverishment in the Marcos Era.* Metro Manila, University of the Philippines Press, 1993.

Center for Research and Communications. *The Philippines at the Crossroads: Some Visions for the Nation.* Manila, Center for Research and Communications, 1986.

Constantino, R. *The Nationalist Alternative.* Quezon City, Foundation for Nationalist Studies, 1979.

Corpuz, O. D. *An Economic History of the Philippines.* Quezon City, University of the Philippines Press, 1999.

de Dios, Emanuel (Ed.). *An Analysis of the Philippine Economic Crisis: A Workshop Report.* Quezon City, University of the Philippines, 1984.

Dolan, Ronald E. (Ed.). *The Philippines: A Country Study.* Washington DC, Federal Reserve Division, Library of Congress, 1993.

Eaton, Kent. *Politicians and Economic Reform in New Democracies: Argentina and the Philippines in the 1990s.* Philadelphia, PA, University Of Pennsylvania Press, 2002.

Eder, James F. *A Generation Later: Household Strategies and Economic Change in the Rural Philippines.* Metro Manila, University of the Philippines Press, 1999.

Estanislao, Jesus P. *The Philippine Economy: An Emerging Asian Tiger.* Singapore, Institute of Southeast Asian Studies, 1997.

Fast, Jonathan, and Richardson, Jim. *Roots of Dependency.* Quezon City, Foundation for Nationalist Studies, 1980.

Feder, Ernest. *Perverse Development.* Quezon City, Foundation for Nationalist Studies, 1983.

Gonzalez, III, Joaquin, L. *Philippine Labour Migration: Critical Dimensions of Public Policy.* Singapore, Institute of Southeast Asian Studies, 1998.

Hodgkinson, Edith. *The Philippines to 1993: Making Up Lost Ground.* London, Economist Intelligence Unit, 1988.

Hutchcroft, Paul D. *Booty Capitalism: The Politics of Banking in the Philippines.* Ithaca, NY, Cornell University Press, 1999.

Jorgensen, Erika, et al. *A Strategy to Fight Poverty: The Philippines.* Washington, DC, World Bank, 1996.

José, V. R. (Ed.). *Mortgaging the Future: The World Bank and IMF in the Philippines.* Quezon City, Foundation for Nationalist Studies, 1982.

Krinks, P. *The Economy of the Philippines.* London, Routledge Curzon, 2002.

Mearl, L., et al. *Rice Economy of the Philippines.* Quezon City, University of the Philippines, 1974.

Ofreneo, Rene. *Capitalism in Philippine Agriculture.* Quezon City, Foundation for Nationalist Studies, 1980.

Philippine Center for Investigative Journalism. *Saving the Earth: The Philippine Experience.* Manila, 1992.

Power, J. H., and Sicat, G. P. *The Philippines: Industrialization and Trade Policies.* London, Oxford University Press, 1971.

Van Den Top, Gerhard. *The Social Dynamics of Deforestation in the Philippines: Actions, Options and Motivations.* Copenhagen, Nordic Institute of Asian Studies, 2002.

Villegas, Edberto M. *Studies in Philippine Economy.* Manila, Silangan Publishers, 1983.

World Bank. *The Philippines: A Framework for Economic Recovery.* Washington, DC, 1987.

POLITICS AND GOVERNMENT

Abinales, P. (Ed.). *The Revolution Falters: The Left in Philippine Politics after 1986.* Ithaca, NY, Cornell University Press, 1996.

Making Mindanao: Cotabato and Davao in the Formation of the Philippine Nation-State. Quezon City, Ateneo de Manila University Press, 2001.

ABS-CBN Broadcasting Corpn. *People Power 2: Lessons and Hopes.*

Alejo, Albert E. *Generating Energies in Mount Apo: Cultural Politics in a Contested Environment.* Honolulu, HI, University of Hawaii Press, 2001.

Bonner, Raymond. *Waltzing with a Dictator: The Marcoses and the Making of American Policy.* New York, Times Books, 1987.

Canoy, Reuben R. *The Counterfeit Revolution: Martial Law in the Philippines.* Manila, 1980.

Catholic Institute for International Relations. *The Philippines: Politics and Military Power.* London, 1992.

Coronel, Sheila S. (Ed.). *Pork and Other Perks.* Manila, Philippine Center for Investigative Journalism, 1998.

EDSA 2: A Nation in Revolt. Manila, AsiaPix/Anvil, 2001.

Investigating Estrada: Millions, Mansions and Mysteries. Manila, Philippine Centre for Investigative Journalism, 2001.

Franco, Jennifer C., and Kerkvliet, B. J. T. *Elections and Democratization in the Philippines (Comparative Studies of Democratization).* New York, NY, Garland Publishing, 2001.

Goodno, James B. *Land of Broken Promises.* London, Zed Press, 1991.

Gutierrez, Eric. *The Ties that Bind: A Guide to Business, Family and Other Interests in the House of Representatives.* Manila, Philippine Center for Investigative Journalism and Institute for Popular Democracy, 1993.

Gutierrez E., Torrente I., and Narca N. *All in the Family: A Study of Elites and Power Relations in the Philippines.* Quezon City, Institute for Popular Democracy, 1992.

Hedman, Eva-Lotta, and Sidel, John T. (Eds). *Philippine Politics and Society in the Twentieth Century: Colonial Legacies, Post-Colonial Trajectories.* London, Routledge, 2000.

Hodder, Rupert. *Between Two Worlds – Society, Politics and Business in the Philippines.* London, Curzon Press Ltd, 2002.

Kerkvliet, B. J. T. *Political Change in the Philippines: Studies of Local Politics Preceding Martial Law.* Honolulu, HI, University of Hawaii Press, 1974.

Everyday Politics in the Philippines: Class and Status Relations in a Central Village. Berkeley, CA, University of California Press, 1991.

Kudeta: The Challenge to Philippine Democracy. Philippine Center for Investigative Journalism and the Photojournalist Guild of the Philippines, 1991.

The Huk Rebellion: a Study of Peasant Revolt in the Philippines. Lanham, MD, Rowman & Littlefield, 2002.

Kerkvliet, B. J. T., and Mojares, R. (Eds). *From Marcos to Aquino: Local Perspectives on Political Transition in the Philippines.* Honolulu, HI, University of Hawaii Press, 1992.

Landé, Carl H. *Leaders, Factions and Parties: The Structure of Philippine Politics.* Yale University Press, Southeast Asia Studies, Monograph Series No. 6.

Post-Marcos Politics: A Geographical and Statistical Analysis of the 1992 Presidential Election. Singapore, Institute of Southeast Asian Studies, 1996.

May, R. J., and Nemenzo, Francisco (Eds). *The Philippines After Marcos.* Beckenham, Kent, Croom Helm, 1985.

Nadeau, Kathleen M. *Liberation Theology in the Philippines: Faith in a Revolution.* Westport, CT, Praeger Publications, 2001.

Pesigan, Guillermo, and MacDonald, Charles J. (Eds). *Old Ties and New Solidarities: Studies on Philippine Communities.* Honolulu, HI, University of Hawaii Press, 2001.

Philippine Center for Investigative Journalism. *People Power Uli! A Scrapbook About EDSA 2.* Manila, 2001.

Philippine Center for Investigative Journalism and Ateneo Center for Social Policy and Public Affairs. *1992 and Beyond: Forces and Issues in the Philippine Elections.* Manila, 1992.

Silliman, G., and Noble, L. *Organizing for Democracy: NGOs, Civil Society and the Philippine State.* Quezon City, Ateneo de Manila University Press, 1998.

Timberman, David G. *The Philippines: New Directions in Domestic Policy and Foreign Relations.* Singapore, Institute of Southeast Asian Studies, 1998.

Tordesillas, Ellen, and Hutchinson, Greg. *Hot Money, Warm Bodies: The Downfall of Philippine President Joseph Estrada.* Manila, Anvil, 2001.

Vitug, Marites Danguilan, and Gloria, Glenda. *Under the Crescent Moon: Rebellion in Mindanao.* Manila, Ateneo Center for Social Policy and Public Affairs/Institute for Popular Democracy, 2000.

Wurfel, D. *Filipino Politics: Development and Decay.* Quezon City, Ateneo de Manila University Press, 1988.

SINGAPORE

Physical and Social Geography

HARVEY DEMAINE

The Republic of Singapore is an insular territory, with an area of 659.9 sq km (254.8 sq miles), lying to the south of the Malay peninsula, to which it is joined by a causeway, 1.2 km long, carrying a road, a railway and a water pipeline across the intervening Straits of Johor. Singapore Island, which is situated less than 1.5° north of the Equator, occupies a focal position at the turning-point on the shortest sea-route from the Indian Ocean to the South China Sea.

PHYSICAL FEATURES

The mainly granitic core of the island, which rises in a few places to summits of over 100 m, is surrounded by lower land, much of it marshy, though large areas are now intensively cultivated. Singapore City has grown up on the firmer ground adjacent to the Mt Faber ridge, the foreshore of which provides deep water anchorage in the lee of two small offshore islands, Pulau Sentosa and Pulau Brani. In recent years suburban growth has been rapid towards the north and along the eastern foreshore, and since 1961 a large expanse of mangrove swamp to the west of the dock area has been reclaimed to provide industrial estates for the Jurong Town Corporation.

The climate, like that of the Malay peninsula, is hot and humid, with no clearly defined seasons, although February is usually the sunniest month and December often the least sunny. Rainfall averages 2,367 mm annually, and the average daytime temperature is 26.6°C, falling to an average minimum of 23.7°C at night.

POPULATION AND CULTURE

According to the census of 30 June 2000, the population (including non-residents) was 4,017,733. At mid-2001 the population was officially estimated at 4,131,200, giving a population density of 6,260.3 per sq km, one of the highest in the world. Of the total population (excluding non-residents) at the 2000 census, 76.8% were Chinese, 13.9% Malay and 7.9% Indian. In 2000 the birth rate was estimated at 11.6 per 1,000 (compared with 18.4 in 1990) and the death rate at 3.9 per 1,000.

There are four official languages: Chinese (in 1990 as a first language Mandarin was spoken by 26% of the population, Chinese dialects by 36.7%), English (used by nearly 20% in 1990), Malay and Tamil. Chinese dialects were spoken as a first language by 24% of the population in 2000.

History

C. M. TURNBULL

ORIGINS AND EARLY DEVELOPMENT

The island of Singapore has a record of human habitation going back possibly some 2,000 years, but its early history is obscure, and the very name of Singapura (Sanskrit for 'Lion City') is unexplained, since the lion is not native to the region. The original seaport, Temasek, may have been part of the great Sumatran maritime empire of Srivijaya, which disintegrated in the 13th century. The earliest historical chronicle, the *Malay Annals*, described 14th-century Temasek as a prosperous trading centre. At about this time it became known as Singapura. However, the island's prosperity brought it into the sphere of rival expanding empires: Thai Ayudhya and Javanese Majapahit. Attacked by both and torn further by internal strife, the city was destroyed in the final years of the 14th century. The ruler and his followers fled to found a more auspicious settlement at Melaka (Malacca), which became the centre of a renowned Empire.

Following this violent episode, Singapore remained almost deserted for more than 400 years, home of a few tribes of *orang laut* (boat people), who lived by fishing, piracy and petty trading and owed allegiance to the Malay Riau-Johor Empire, centred nearby in the Riau archipelago. Soon all that remained of the old city were a few crumbling ramparts and the neglected graves of its former rulers on the hill above the Singapore river. Riau itself was a prosperous emporium for regional commerce, but Singapore merely battened on the piratical fringe of that trade.

In the early 19th century the Straits of Melaka and the southern part of the Malay peninsula assumed a new commercial and strategic importance when Britain's East India Co sought bases to protect its China trade and to challenge the Dutch commercial monopoly in the Malay peninsula and archipelago. In 1819 Sir Stamford Raffles, an official of the East India Co, obtained permission, from the Sultan of Johor and the local chief, to establish a trading post at the mouth of the Singapore river, and five years later the two Malay chiefs ceded the island in perpetuity to the East India Co and its successors, in return for money payments and pensions.

The Straits Settlements

In 1826 the East India Co united Singapore with its two other dependencies on the west coast of the Malay peninsula: Pinang (Penang), acquired in 1786, and Melaka, ceded by the Dutch in 1824. These scattered territories remained one political entity, known as the Straits Settlements, for the next 120 years. Under the protection of the East India Co, the new port, conveniently situated and free from customs duties or restrictions, attracted traders and settlers from all over the region. They came first from the nearby ports of Riau, Melaka and Pinang, but soon others began to arrive from further afield in the Indonesian archipelago, and from Thailand, Indo-China, Burma (now Myanmar), Borneo, the Philippines, India, China and Europe.

In 1833 the East India Co lost its monopoly of the China trade, after which it had no further use for the Straits Settlements. It continued to administer them but on a severely constrained budget. The very laxness of government and freedom from taxation attracted further steady immigration and trade, but the European merchants of Singapore became increasingly dissatisfied with administrative inefficiency and the lack of representative institutions. In 1857 Singapore's merchants petitioned that the Straits Settlements be separated from India and brought under direct British rule, and in 1867 the Straits Settlements became a crown colony, with a constitution that remained basically unchanged until the Second World War. A Governor, appointed by the British Government, ruled with the assistance of an Executive and a Legislative Council, the latter comprising a majority of officials with unofficial members nominated by the Governor. Over the years the number of 'unofficials' and of Asian councillors increased, so that by the 1920s there were equal numbers of officials and 'unofficials' on the Legislative Council, with the Governor having the casting vote. By that time some 'unofficials' were nominated by the chambers of commerce but there were no elected members as such.

The transfer of the Straits Settlements to direct colonial rule was soon followed by two events which gave a new impetus to Singapore's development: the opening of the Suez Canal in 1869, and the first treaties of protection made between the British and rulers of the Malay states in 1874. With the opening of the Suez Canal, the India–Melaka Straits route, on which Singapore was situated in a dominating position, became the main highway from Europe to the Far East. The 1874 treaties with the west coast Malay states of Perak, Selangor and Sungei Ujong marked the first step in bringing all the Malay states under British protection. Singapore provided a political focal point as the base of the Governor of the Straits Settlements Colony, who was also High Commissioner of the Malay States and the chief authority for the three British-protected Borneo states of Sarawak, North Borneo and Brunei.

In the late 19th and early 20th century Singapore became the commercial and financial centre for the whole region. Growing Western interests in South-East Asia, the increasing use of steamships (which from the 1880s replaced sailing ships as the main carriers) and the development of telegraphs all put Singapore, with its fine natural sheltered harbour, at the hub of international trade in South-East Asia. It became a vital link in the chain of British ports which stretched from Gibraltar, through the Mediterranean Sea and the Indian Ocean, to the Far East.

The 60 years from the opening of the Suez Canal to the onset of the Great Depression in 1929 were a time of almost unbroken peace, steady economic expansion and population growth in Singapore. A more sophisticated administration gradually brought the population into the pale of the Government and the law courts. In the early years the different immigrant groups lived in specified districts of the town, largely supervised by their own community leaders or *kapitans*. As early as 1827 the Chinese were the biggest single community in Singapore and by the beginning of the 20th century constituted three-quarters of the population, a proportion which has remained fairly constant since that time. Most Chinese came from the troubled Guangdong and Fujian Provinces of southern China, representing a variety of dialect groups, chiefly Fukien, Cantonese, Teochew, Hakka and, in the later years of the century, Hainanese. Most were young adult men who aimed to make money abroad and return to their native China, so that, well into the 20th century, the population was transitory and shifting, with very few women, children or old people. As the years passed more women came to Singapore, and a large number of immigrants settled permanently and raised families. By the early 20th century there was a sizeable Straits-born Asian community, who were British subjects and sometimes English-educated. Some Straits-born Asians collaborated with the colonial establishment as Legislative and Municipal Councillors or Justices of the Peace, while many others worked as clerks and assistants. In the 1930s the colonial regime created a Straits civil service, Straits legal service and Straits medical service which offered the first openings to Asian British subjects in professional government work, but only at subordinate levels. All senior administrative and technical posts in Singapore were held by British European officials.

There was little interest in local politics. From the mid-1920s, a Legislative Councillor, Tan Cheng Lock, began to call for elected representation on the Legislative Council for those who had made the Straits Settlements their home, but he found little backing even among his fellow Straits Chinese. There was no indigenous nationalist movement or desire for independence and any political interest was directed more to China or India.

Immigration reached a peak in the boom year of 1927, when an all-time record of 360,000 Chinese landed in Singapore. However, the Great Depression of 1929–33 hit Singapore hard, leading to the first restrictions. In 1930 an Immigration Restriction Ordinance imposed a quota on Chinese men, but it did not affect women for some years, which encouraged the trend towards permanent family settlement.

THE SECOND WORLD WAR AND JAPANESE OCCUPATION

After the First World War, Singapore acquired a new strategic significance as a naval and military base. However, this did not deter Japan from attacking Malaya in December 1941 as part of a campaign to seize the raw materials it needed from South-East Asia. After a lightning campaign down the Malay peninsula, culminating in a week of fighting on the island itself, Singapore capitulated to the Japanese in February 1942.

Renamed Syonan, or 'Light of the South', it remained under Japanese occupation for more than three years. Japan intended to retain Singapore as a permanent colony and military base, a focal point in its proposed 'Greater East Asia Co-Prosperity Sphere', but wartime priorities and difficulties precluded the Japanese from developing this concept. They destroyed the colonial economy without replacing it by an Asian alternative, and tried to suppress the English language and colonial education without building up Japanese in its place. Japan did nothing to promote indigenous politics in Singapore, although the island for a time became the regional base for the collaborationist Indian National Army and the Indian Independence League. The occupation was a time of misery, hunger and fear, which came to an abrupt end in August 1945, when Japan surrendered after atom bombs were dropped on two of its own cities, thus sparing Singapore the ordeal of an Allied invasion.

THE POST-WAR PERIOD

In September 1945 the British set up a temporary military administration in preparation for a return to colonial government under a new structure. They aimed to unite the peninsula by creating a Malayan Union comprising all the Malay states, together with Pinang and Melaka, but separating Singapore as a crown colony. In April 1946 civil rule was restored and the Malayan Union and Singapore Crown Colony came into being. These decisions were taken because of Singapore's special position as a free port, its importance as a military base and the complications of trying to absorb it into a Malaya embarking on the road to self-government and independence. However, Singapore's separation was not intended to be permanent.

The proposals provoked protest in Singapore, leading in 1945 to the creation of its first political party, the Malayan Democratic Union (MDU), which campaigned for the island's incorporation in the Malayan Union. The party joined other opposition groups in the peninsula to form the All-Malaya Council of Joint Action, which put forward proposals calling for the inclusion of Singapore in a Malayan federation. However, these were swept aside by the intensity of peninsular Malay nationalism, reacting against the Malayan Union, the loss of state identity, and the proposed liberal granting of citizenship to immigrants. As a result, in 1948 a Federation of Malaya replaced the Malayan Union. Singapore remained separated, but this time on racial grounds, since the Malay leaders did not want to upset the ethnic balance of the federation by including a predominantly Chinese Singapore.

Constitutional Development, 1948–65

Meanwhile, Singapore was being prepared for eventual self-government, and in 1948 the first elections were held for six members of the Legislative Council. The MDU, now heavily communist-infiltrated, boycotted the election, and most of the elected seats went to the Singapore Progressive Party. This upper-middle-class English-educated group supported British plans for gradual constitutional reform while maintaining the economic status quo. There was little popular enthusiasm for this experiment. Voting was confined to British subjects, registration was voluntary, and the activities of the English-speaking Legislative Council were remote from the majority of the population, with their problems of poverty, unemployment, bad housing and inadequate vernacular education. The outbreak of a communist 'Emergency' in the Federation of Malaya in 1948 led to a period of severe repression of all radical politics in Singapore. While the colony was not directly involved in the revolt, the same emergency regulations were enforced. The Malayan Communist Party was proscribed in 1948 and the MDU disbanded itself.

As the Malayan 'Emergency' was brought under control, the authorities permitted a greater level of political activity in

Singapore. In 1955 a new Constitution was granted in an effort to speed up constitutional reform and encourage a sense of real participation and responsibility. The new Legislative Assembly had an elected majority (25 out of 32 members), voters were registered automatically, and the leader of the largest party in the Assembly, as Chief Minister, would form a Council of Ministers responsible to the Assembly.

Two new rival left-wing parties were created to fight the election, both headed by lawyers: the Labour Front under David Marshall and the People's Action Party (PAP), led by Lee Kuan Yew. Unexpectedly, the two radical parties routed the Progressives and other conservatives, and Marshall's Labour Front formed a minority Government. However, in 1955–56 the communist left wing of the PAP made a determined bid for power through the trade union movement and Chinese middle schools. For a time they even wrested control of the PAP Central Executive Committee away from Lee Kuan Yew. The Labour Front Government curbed them by using emergency regulations to imprison their leaders and by taking steps to remove genuine grievances. A 1957 Education Ordinance gave parity to the four main language streams; in the same year citizenship was offered on generous terms to nearly all residents, and a new public services commission was set up to achieve rapid localization of the civil service. In 1958 terms were agreed for full internal self-government, and at elections held in 1959 to implement this, the PAP won an outright majority (43 out of 51 seats). Lee Kuan Yew took office as Prime Minister, and the party remained in power in the early 21st century.

The new Government committed itself to a programme of rapid industrialization and social reform, with ambitious schemes for education, housing and a far-reaching Women's Charter. It also aspired within its four-year term to achieve full independence through a merger with the Federation of Malaya, which had itself secured independence in 1957. Such a union was seen as vital to provide the military security and free access to a Malayan market, which were considered essential for Singapore's survival. However, the implementation of this policy quickly led to dissension in the party, and to challenges from the extreme left wing, which threatened to tear the party apart and plunge Singapore into chaos.

The Federation of Malaya, which was originally reluctant to draw closer to Singapore because of its large Chinese population and left-wing tendencies, now realized the need to exercise direct control on the near-communist state emerging on its doorstep. To do this, in May 1961 the Malayan Prime Minister, Tunku Abdul Rahman, proposed a closer association between the federation and Singapore, by bringing in the three Borneo territories to achieve racial equilibrium. The PAP leadership eagerly took up this idea, but the prospect of merging Singapore in a conservative, anti-communist Malayan federation so alarmed members of the party's radical left wing that in July 1961 they made a bid to topple Lee Kuan Yew's Government. Having failed by a narrow margin at a dramatic all-night session of the Assembly, the rebels then broke away to form an opposition socialist front, the Barisan Sosialis (BS).

Despite vigorous protests by the BS, a public referendum in 1962 endorsed Singapore's entry, and in July 1963 the Malaysia Agreement was finally signed, under which Singapore was to join Malaya, Sarawak and Sabah (North Borneo) in forming the Federation of Malaysia on 31 August 1963. The implementation was deferred until mid-September to enable United Nations (UN) representatives to ascertain the wishes of the people of the Borneo states. Singapore took advantage of this delay to declare its own unilateral independence from colonial rule and to call an election. Having survived the 1961 crisis, the moderate element of the PAP had reorganized and strengthened the party, and profited from the success of the Malaysia merger to secure a comfortable victory.

However, the association was strained. 'Confrontation' by Indonesia, which objected to the formation of the Malaysian federation, severely damaged Singapore's trade and led to acts of violence by Indonesian saboteurs. Simultaneously, the central Government and Singapore clashed over what each perceived as undue interference in the other's internal affairs. In July and September 1964 communal riots in Singapore further strained relations with Kuala Lumpur, while the ruling Alliance Party in Malaysia objected to the PAP's contesting the 1964 general elections. Finally, Lee Kuan Yew's attempts to unite all Malaysian opposition parties brought the crisis to a head, and on 9 August 1965, the central Government forced Singapore to agree to a separation.

REPUBLIC OF SINGAPORE

In this way Singapore became independent against the wishes of its own leaders. It joined the UN in September 1965 and was admitted as a member of the Commonwealth the following month. The new Republic was committed to multiracial, non-communist, democratic socialist policies, and to co-operation with Malaysia, particularly in economic and defence matters.

Politically, the transition to full independence was smooth. The machinery of government remained almost intact, with small constitutional amendments, notably the appointment of a non-executive President as Head of State. Effective power lay in the hands of the Prime Minister and his Cabinet, responsible to the single-chamber Parliament (formerly the Legislative Assembly), which was elected for a five-year term by all adult Singapore citizens. Other adjustments were more painful. Few, if any, had visualized a separate independent Singapore on the grounds that such a tiny state, with a large population and no natural resources, could neither sustain its economy nor defend itself. Initially, the British defence 'umbrella' continued to shelter Malaysia and Singapore, but in 1966 the United Kingdom decided to withdraw its bases from 'east of Suez' during the mid-1970s. Singapore introduced compulsory national service and was working to build up a credible defence force when, less than two years later, the British Government advanced the withdrawal date to 1971. The accelerated timetable threatened Singapore's economy, since the bases accounted for 20% of the country's gross national product (GNP), but the Government took advantage of the situation to call an election in 1968, when it won a mandate to pass far-reaching labour legislation curbing trade union activity, to provide the right climate for foreign investment. As hopes for access to the Malaysian market evaporated, Singapore stepped up its efforts to achieve rapid export-orientated industrialization. To attract foreign and local capital and expertise, the Government rejected doctrinaire socialism in favour of a mixed economy, largely privately owned and managed, but with a sizeable public ownership stake used by the Government to give impetus and direction to industrialization.

With independence suddenly thrust upon it, Singapore needed to create a sense of nationhood. In the early years this was done by stressing the unique qualities and differences that distinguished Singapore from its neighbours, resulting in an abrasive foreign policy. While the Republic was a founder member of the Association of South East Asian Nations (ASEAN), formed in 1967 along with Malaysia, Thailand, Indonesia and the Philippines (and joined in 1984 by Brunei, in 1995 by Viet Nam, in 1997 by Myanmar and Laos, and in 1999 by Cambodia), at first it made little practical contribution to regional co-operation. However, the British withdrawal, the sharp increase in oil prices in 1974 (petroleum refining is Singapore's largest industry), followed by the fall of South Viet Nam to the communists in 1975, induced Singapore to draw closer to its neighbours. It led the way in supporting regional solidarity, particularly after the first ASEAN summit meeting in Bali in 1976.

The Singapore Government was anxious to maintain cordial relations and to forge economic links with all countries: the West, communist states, developing countries, the Middle East, Japan, Taiwan and the People's Republic of China. Despite developing substantial economic relations with China, however, the Singapore Government waited until 1990 before establishing formal links at ambassadorial level, in order to minimize its image as an ethnic Chinese nation.

Any desire to be readmitted to the Federation of Malaysia disappeared with growing confidence in the country's viability as an independent state and the maturing sense of nationhood. After an initially troubled period, in the early 1970s the relationship between the two countries became friendlier and they maintained close co-operation in matters of mutual concern: combating subversion and illicit trading in narcotic drugs, and protecting the Straits of Melaka.

Independence was followed by eight years of international boom, when Singapore achieved an 'economic miracle' in industrialization. Official policy aimed to improve living standards without creating a welfare state: it encouraged full employment and subsidized education, housing and public health. Social reform was initially accompanied by a strict policy of family limitation and population control, together with stringent immigration curbs. In the 1960s and 1970s a vigorous education programme concentrated on promoting bilingualism in primary and secondary schooling, while developing technical skills appropriate to the Republic's economy. English became increasingly accepted as the language of development and modernization. An energetic programme of urban renewal and the construction of new townships meant that by the end of the century about 90% of households owned their homes, the highest rate of home-ownership in the world.

After the 1961 crisis, the Government pursued a consistently anti-communist policy, using the emergency regulations—a legacy of colonial times—to imprison 'hard-core' subversives. The BS refused to acknowledge Singapore's independence in 1965, and boycotted the Parliament, opting to oppose the Government by extra-constitutional means. After the communist victories in Indo-China in 1975, the extreme left wing re-grouped to attempt a resurgence in Singapore and Malaysia, but the Government arrested leading cadres of the Malayan National Liberation Front, the militant satellite of the Communist Party of Malaya.

From 1968 until October 1981 the PAP held every seat in Parliament, and the party leadership maintained a remarkable cohesion, which contributed to the country's stability but tended to stifle criticism. Radio and television services are state-owned. Newspapers, all concentrated under the ownership of one public company, Singapore Press Holdings Ltd, require annual licences and incline towards self-censorship. This concentration of power and patronage, and the acknowledgement of the considerable achievements and success of PAP policies, emphasized the lack of credible alternatives. Seven opposition parties contested the 1980 parliamentary elections, but the ruling party achieved its widest margin of victory, winning all seats for the fourth successive election and capturing nearly 78% of the votes. In two decades of remarkable economic progress, Singapore had achieved the third highest per caput income in Asia (excluding the Middle East), after Brunei and Japan. The Republic was also acquiring a sense of nationhood, and the 1980 census showed that more than 78% of the population were Singapore-born. In the more relaxed climate, numbers of political prisoners were released, leaving only a small band of committed left-wingers in detention.

However, a nation that had begun to take its relatively high standard of living for granted became less tolerant of the more arbitrary aspects of PAP policies. The victory of J. B. Jeyaretnam, the Secretary-General of the opposition Workers' Party, at a parliamentary by-election in 1981 was an unsettling event for the ruling PAP, which had enjoyed a virtual monopoly of power since 1968. At the 1984 general election the PAP's share of the total vote declined to below 63% and the party lost a second seat, this time to Chiam See Tong, founder and Secretary-General of the Singapore Democratic Party (SDP). This reverse caused consternation among the PAP's leadership. While two opposition members in Parliament posed no serious threat to the Government (Jeyaretnam subsequently lost his seat in 1986 and was disbarred from Parliament for five years, following his conviction for perjury), and there was still no viable alternative to the PAP, the period of the party's unchallenged dominance was over. After the 1984 election Lee Kuan Yew remained as Prime Minister but delegated daily government administration to younger men, led by Goh Chok Tong, the First Deputy Prime Minister. Lee Kuan Yew's elder son, Brig.-Gen. Lee Hsien Loong, was appointed a junior minister in 1985 and Minister for Trade and Industry in the following year.

An economic recession in 1985–86 prompted the Government to review some of its policies and to adopt new strategies for economic development and social policy. In 1987 a New Population Policy was introduced, since strict population control had resulted in a decline in fertility to below replacement levels. Early marriage was encouraged, as was a return to three-child families, particularly among the more prosperous and better-educated groups. The 1990 census recorded a resident population of 2.7m., and in 1991 an official Concept Plan set a target of 4m. by 2010. The Government aimed to achieve this by raising fertility, encouraging the immigration of talented Asians, and discouraging emigration by making life in Singapore more attractive.

The Government placed even greater emphasis on the need for political stability, in order to attract investors. In 1986 press laws were extended to reduce the circulation of those foreign publications that were considered to be unduly critical of Singapore. These were invoked against several journals, and in 1990, following a dispute between the Government and three foreign publications, which had allegedly interfered in Singapore's politics, the Newspaper and Printing Presses Act was amended: all publications of which the 'contents and editorial policy were determined outside Singapore' and which dealt with politics and current events in South-East Asia would be required to obtain a ministerial licence, renewable annually and limiting the number of copies sold. Punitive damages were awarded against *The International Herald Tribune* and the author of articles that were published in 1994 implying nepotism and the Government's use of a compliant judiciary to suppress opposition by bankrupting rival opposition politicians. This increased caution in reporting on Singapore by journals that circulated locally, although Singapore continued to attract opposition from the US liberal media.

In 1987 the Government alleged that it had discovered a 'Marxist network' which had infiltrated student and church groups and the Workers' Party and arrested a group of alleged activists under the Internal Security Act, which permitted indefinite detention, without trial, of persons suspected by the authorities of subversion. The detainees were mainly young, English-speaking university-educated professionals, and, as such, differed from political dissidents of former years. In 1988 the Internal Security Act was tightened to put detention beyond the review of the law courts. Despite the most vigorous campaigning for 20 years, Chiam See Tong of the SDP was again the only successful non-PAP candidate in the 1988 general election. The electorate once more responded to the Government's slogan of 'More Good Years', and economic growth resumed its upward movement. With the expansion of population and migration to new towns, constituencies were redelineated and the number of elective parliamentary seats was increased from 58 in 1967 to 83 in 1997. In 1988 MPs were allocated a role as town councillors in managing new towns, and 39 constituencies were reorganized into 13 group representation constituencies. These were contested by teams of three from the same party, including at least one candidate from a minority community. (This was changed in 1991 to a minimum of three and a maximum of four candidates, and in 1996 the maximum was raised to six, in a measure that the Government claimed would facilitate town council operations, but that also made it more difficult for opposition parties to present electoral teams.) In 1990 Parliament approved legislation enabling the Government to appoint up to six unelected MPs for a two-year term. Independent, well-educated people, successful in their own field, these Nominated Members of Parliament (NMPs)were expected to provide constructive non-partisan criticism and to improve the quality of parliamentary debate. They had the right to vote on all legislative proposals except those concerning financial and constitutional affairs.

In 1990 the Republic celebrated its 25th anniversary of independence with the slogan 'one people, one nation, one Singapore'. However, government leaders expressed concern that the population was too cosmopolitan and individualistic, and in danger of being overwhelmed by foreign cultures. Instead the authorities supported the concept of an ethnic and racial mosaic, respecting individual cultural roots. To the minority communities, however, the formulation of a new national ideology, which stressed core values of Confucian morality, family loyalty and placing society before self, was suggestive of Chinese cultural chauvinism. It threatened to detract from the PAP's own considerable success over the past quarter of a century in creating a modern, secular, multiracial society. The Malays, in particular, feared relegation to the status of an underclass, and responded with the formation of an Association of Muslim Professionals. In 1990 the Government ended the automatic waiver of tertiary education fees for Malays, although it awarded a S $10m. grant to help impoverished Malay students.

Over the years a 'Speak Mandarin' campaign, which had originally been adopted in 1979, had successfully diverted the Chinese-educated from using regional dialects. By the early 1990s, however, Mandarin itself was threatened by the rapidly-increasing use of English, which was promoted as the essential language for modernization, particularly after 1987 (when English became the medium of instruction for all schools). From 1992, therefore, the 'Speak Mandarin' campaign concentrated on encouraging the English-educated to maintain their Mandarin.

Goh Chok Tong's Premiership

In November 1990 Lee Kuan Yew stepped down as Prime Minister in favour of Goh Chok Tong, but remained in the Cabinet as Senior Minister, kept his influential post as PAP Secretary-General, and continued to travel extensively abroad promoting Singapore's interests. Lee Hsien Loong and Ong Teng Cheong, formerly the Second Deputy Prime Minister (and also the Secretary-General of the National Trades Union Congress—NTUC), were appointed Deputy Prime Ministers of supposedly equal rank, but Lee Hsien Loong was to act in the Prime Minister's absence.

Goh offered a more open political system and, at his inauguration, invited 'fellow citizens to join me, to run the next lap together'. An official programme, entitled *The Next Lap*, which was published in 1991, promised to make Singapore 'more prosperous, gracious and interesting over the next 20 to 30 years', befitting an affluent, well-educated society. Censorship of films, television and magazines was relaxed, the new Prime Minister embarked on an extensive programme of community visits and exhorted the public to participate and express its views. This gained him considerable support among the Malay and Indian minorities, who were traditionally wary of the PAP. The changes, however, represented a difference of style rather than of substance. Goh still stressed the virtues of hard work, meritocracy, sound education, economic growth, the need to avoid the pitfalls of a welfare state and a defence policy based on national resilience. The public was invited to offer constructive criticism, but not to advocate radical change. Restrictions on the foreign press remained in force. Although all political detainees were released from prison by June 1990, Goh refused to repeal the Internal Security Act, and it was only in November 1998 that the final residential restrictions were lifted on the movements of Chia Thye Poh, Singapore's last political prisoner, who had been arrested in 1966. Even then he was prohibited from engaging in politics.

Seeking popular endorsement for his style of government, the Prime Minister called a 'snap' election in August 1991, two years ahead of schedule, arguing that consensus and national unity precluded the need for a formal opposition. The opposition parties, in a plan conceived by Chiam See Tong, decided to contest only 40 out of the 81 seats, conceding victory to the ruling PAP by default, but inviting voters to create a strong opposition. In the event, the PAP's share of the vote dropped to 61.0% (from 63.2% in 1988), and the party won 77 seats, compared with 80 in 1988. Jeyaretnam was unable to contest the election as his disqualification still remained in force, but the Workers' Party won in one constituency while Chiam's SDP secured three seats. During the election campaign the Prime Minister warned there would be a return to a more authoritarian and paternalistic form of government if he failed to receive a popular mandate. However, Goh subsequently announced that he would continue his style of government but would implement reforms more slowly.

In November 1992 the Government announced that both Deputy Prime Ministers were suffering from cancer, although Ong Teng Cheong's case was low grade and Lee Hsien Loong gained complete remission by April 1993. In the mean time Lee Hsien Loong relinquished his office, and the illness of both men gave urgency to holding a by-election, which the Prime Minister had pledged to stage to counter Jeyaretnam's claim to have been deliberately excluded by the early timing of the 1991 general election. In an astute move, Goh held the contest in his own four-member group representation constituency in December 1992; Jeyaratnam was unable to enter the contest, since the Workers' Party did not have the required minimum of four candidates. The PAP secured 72.9% of the vote; this result, Lee Hsien Loong's indisposition and Goh's unanimous election earlier in the month as Secretary-General of the PAP (replacing Lee Kuan Yew who proposed his candidacy), put the Prime Minister in a stronger personal position than at any time since he assumed office.

Following many years of public discussion, in 1991 Parliament approved a constitutional change in the presidency. Instead of a ceremonial figurehead appointed by Parliament, the new-style President was chosen directly by the electorate, and was empowered to safeguard the large financial reserves that had been accumulated over the previous 30 years and to veto senior civil service and judicial appointments. Only those who had served as cabinet ministers, chief justice, senior civil servants or the head of a large company would be eligible as presidential candidates.

In 1993 Ong Teng Cheong was elected President for a six-year term, securing 58.7% of the votes cast. The election of Ong, who had been nominated by the NTUC and who enjoyed strong PAP support, was almost a foregone conclusion; however, the only other candidate, a former accountant-general, Chua Kim Yeow, who adopted an apolitical platform, attracted a significant 41.3% of the vote.

In January 1994 Goh reorganized the Cabinet, appointing Lee Hsien Loong to supervise both the trade and industry and the defence portfolios. By mid-1994 senior ministers were once more expressing concern about the difficulty of recruiting able people into public service and, most particularly, into the Cabinet. The consequent decision to increase ministerial salaries to a level comparable with private-sector leaders provoked some protest, especially from the SDP. The ruling party also encouraged junior MPs simultaneously to hold posts as professionals and top business executives, provided there were no conflicts of interest. The PAP subsequently sought to recruit younger parliamentary candidates of a high calibre and with the potential for ministerial office.

When the term of office of the six NMPs expired in 1994, the system was made permanent on the basis of two-year appointments, with the possibility of reappointment. A Maintenance of Parents Bill, introduced by NMP Dr Walter Woon in 1995, offered destitute parents the right to claim maintenance from their children. As a Private Member's Bill, this was open to free discussion and provoked spirited debate both in Parliament and the press. The legislation, which gained widespread support and set up a tribunal in 1996, was designed to address one of Singapore's most serious problems: the ageing of the population and the consequent concern to reduce pressure on health care and other social services by enforcing family responsibility for the older generation. The birth rate continued to decline, despite government measures to encourage marriage and child-bearing, and in 1998 the retirement age was raised from 60 to 62.

Profiting from the booming regional economy, Singapore consolidated its reputation as a leading financial centre. Largely as a result of the swift and professional actions of Singapore officials to contain the crisis, the Republic emerged unscathed from the collapse of the British banking group, Barings PLC, in London in 1995, following massive losses incurred by a British trader based in Singapore. In 1996 the Organisation for Economic Co-operation and Development (OECD) promoted Singapore from the list of developing countries eligible for aid to the rank of 'more advanced developing country'. Goh Chok Tong and Lee Kuan Yew, however, continued to stress the Republic's vulnerability and the need for good government and a disciplined people to sustain the momentum of a dynamic economy.

Many of the benefits of economic success were passed on to the general population in the form of generous tax rebates, ongoing programmes to upgrade Housing and Development Board flats, Edusave Merit bursaries for bright students from low-income families, and contributions to citizens' Medisave accounts. An amended Women's Charter was passed, after much discussion, in 1996, which widened the provisions protecting families in case of violence and divorce. Over the years, however, rising living standards and expectations led to more open debate and dissatisfaction with the 'nanny state'. The Prime Minister and Senior Minister reacted sharply to mildly critical articles that appeared in the local press in late 1994, countering that critics should enter the political arena themselves if they wanted to set a political agenda. Leaders insisted that the elected Government must establish the limits on consultation, which should not extend to challenging those in authority as equals or to damaging respect for the Prime Minister.

Under the slogan 'Singapore 21: make it our best home', the Prime Minister contested the general election of January 1997 on three key issues: his own impressive track record; a solid programme offering political stability, economic growth, high-quality education and rising living standards; and a capable leadership being prepared for the 21st century. Goh's programme specified five goals: to create wealth for the nation, to share the fruits of success among citizens, to invest in the young, care for the old, and bond the people together.On the eve of the election seven opposition parties came to an agreement to avoid splitting the anti-PAP vote in most constituencies, but, despite their promising performance in the 1991 general election, the opposition was in an unstable state. The SDP was divided by personal feuds and became more confrontational under the leadership of Chee Soon Juan, a former university lecturer, who was elected Secretary-General in 1995. Chee's book, *Dare to Change*, which he had published in 1994 as a counterbalance to the PAP's *The Next Lap,* argued for greater democracy and was adopted as the SDP's policy. Articulate and vocal, the new SDP leaders received substantial coverage in the local press, but their strident anti-Government censure was frequently criticized by journalists and many of the public as unpatriotic. Meanwhile, Chiam was expelled from the party and in July 1995 formed the Singapore People's Party, which aimed to revive the original moderate policy of the early SDP. The new party sought to liberalize publishing and the internal security laws and to create a 'caring and civic society in which people could enter politics without fear'.

Unopposed in 47 of the 83 seats, the PAP was assured of being returned to power. Nevertheless, Goh conducted an energetic campaign, emphasizing the successes of his six years in office. He insisted that the principal role of government was to improve the quality of life by providing a stable and secure environment in which citizens could better themselves. At the same time he proposed to give Singaporeans more say in municipal affairs and in determining their living environment by creating geographic communities with mayors and Community Development Councils. He likened the Cabinet to a board of trustees of which he was chairman, accountable for the people's welfare and steering the economy forward, to enable the general population to share the benefits of success.

The opposition parties had no specific programmes to match those of the PAP, but Goh's declaration that priority in upgrading housing and community services would be given to wards that showed commitment by voting in favour of the PAP was attacked by the opposition candidates, and attracted criticism from the US State Department. The Workers' Party, and the SDP in particular, accused the Government of using the upgrading issue as a bribe and of denying people the right to an alternative voice in Parliament. The last bitter days of the election campaign were dominated by the racial issue. Alarmed by the emotional response of Chinese-educated voters at rallies of a Workers' Party candidate, Tang Liang Hong, a lawyer and newcomer to politics, Goh and Lee Kuan Yew campaigned vigorously in the constituency that Tang was contesting. They denounced Tang as an anti-Christian Chinese chauvinist, while he in turn accused PAP leaders of lying. The PAP secured the constituency, but the Workers' Party team won a creditable 45% of the vote.

Overall the PAP achieved its best result since the 1984 general election, winning all but two seats, increasing its share of the contested votes to 65% (up from 61% in 1991), and regaining two opposition seats. Low Thia Kiang of the Workers' Party retained his seat with a slightly increased vote, Chiam was returned for a fourth term but as leader of the Singapore People's Party with a reduced majority, while Chee and the SDP were completely routed. Jeyaretnam was declared a Non-Constituency MP, under a constitutional amendment that provided for the highest-scoring losers to be admitted to Parliament if there were fewer than three opposition members; Non-Constituency MPs are prohibited from voting on constitutional and financial matters.

The new Cabinet incorporated no important changes in the senior posts but introduced several younger ministers. The Prime Minister appealed for unity following the election, but acrimonious court disputes ensued. The Prime Minister, Senior Minister and other PAP leaders sued Tang for defamation and he subsequently fled to Johor, declaring that he had received threats against his life. In his absence, the court ordered Tang to pay a record S $8m. in damages and costs. The Court of Appeal later substantially reduced the damages but Tang, by this time settled in Australia, refused to pay and was declared bankrupt. The PAP leadership also sued Jeyaretnam, following remarks made at an election rally concerning two police reports submitted by Tang that accused the PAP leadership of criminal conspiracy and of lying. Jeyaretnam insisted that the legal suits were an attempt to bankrupt him and thus disqualify him from Parliament. The High Court found against Jeyaretnam, but ordered the payment of only modest damages of S $20,000 (one-tenth of the amount claimed by Prime Minister Goh) and 60% of the costs. Observers from Amnesty International and the Geneva-based International Commission of Jurists monitored the trial, and the report subsequently made to the Commission accused the court of being compliant in its procedures. In July 1998, however, the Court of Appeal dismissed Jeyaretnam's appeal, increased the damages fivefold to S $100,000 and awarded full costs against him.

The number of NMPs was increased to nine in 1997, by which time Parliament comprised 93 representatives, of whom six were women and 17 were selected from the minority communities. The Prime Minister urged a change of attitude: instead of expecting activity to emanate from just a few leaders, all Singaporeans should feel responsible for solving local issues and shaping their own communities. Nine Community Development Councils were created to encompass all constituencies, including the two opposition wards; however, opposition MPs could not be chairmen of the councils or have power to disburse funds. Goh also called for adaptability to tackle new challenges. Despite impressive progress in education over the past 30 years, the Republic still suffered from a shortage of graduates. The Government planned to upgrade tertiary institutions, increase local student numbers and attract more foreign students, while Singaporeans working abroad were urged to return home. The Government attempted to encourage talented foreigners to settle in Singapore by relaxing immigration rules and allocating affordable housing to immigrants. Under an 'Intelligent Island' programme, Singapore aimed to lead the world in connecting all households as well as businesses to a multimedia computer network. The Republic aspired to become 'the Boston of the East'. By October 2000 six leading tertiary institutions in the United States and Europe had linked up with the National University of Singapore to run joint degree courses and exchange programmes. Existing universities (the National University of Singapore—NUS— and the Nanyang Technological University) were upgraded, a Singapore Management University, which was devoted to business studies, opened in July 2000, while consideration was given to creating a fourth university. In May 2002 the NUS announced that it was to establish two new campuses by 2010, of which one would take 3,000 undergraduates for practice-based engineering programmes each year, and the second provide post-graduate medical education. A fifth polytechnic was due to open in 2003, bringing the total polytechnic student intake to 22,000.

In February 1998 the Government banned political parties from making videos and from promoting their views on television, with the reported aim of maintaining the propriety of political debate. At that time 22 opposition parties were registered, of which 13 were dormant and the remainder rarely met. Even Chiam's Singapore People's Party had no fixed address or listed telephone number. The SDP was devastated by its general election defeat. In the period immediately after the election, the party held no meetings and issued no publications. In early 1999 Chee was convicted twice under the Public Entertainment Act after deliberately refusing to apply for licences to make two public speeches, in which he criticized government policy; he served two brief spells in prison for refusing to pay the fines. In May Jeyaretnam and Chee jointly declared an 'Open Singapore

Centre', with the aim of pressing public and private bodies to release information and promote democratic accountability.

The Workers' Party was active immediately after the 1997 election, with Jeyaretnam meeting the public at regular weekly sessions, but he ended these when he became involved in legal proceedings. In addition to the damages and costs owed to the PAP leaders, in November 1998 10 members of a Tamil Language Committee won defamatory damages from Jeyaretnam and the Workers' Party for an article published in the party's journal, *The Hammer*. An appeal against the order was rejected, and in May 2000 Jeyaretnam was briefly declared bankrupt for failing to pay the instalment of damages due. He managed to meet the instalment, but could not raise sufficient funds to pay off the rest of the debt and was finally declared bankrupt in January 2001, consequently losing his non-constituency seat and becoming barred from contesting the next general election. In May 2001, at the age of 76, Jeyaretnam relinquished the post of Secretary-General of the Workers' Party, which he had held for the past 30 years, and was succeeded by the former Assistant Secretary-General, Low Thia Khiang, MP. Finally, students from the Ngee Ann Polytechnic were forced to withdraw a film about Jeyaretnam, entitled *A Vision of Persistence*, which they had entered for the 2001 Singapore International Film Festival, on the grounds that it contravened legislation banning political films. Meanwhile, associations began to form outside of the formal political arena. The Association of Women for Action and Research aimed to achieve full equality for women in public and private life and was influential in gaining significant amendments to the Women's Charter concerning domestic violence. The Association of Malay/Muslim Professionals sought to raise the educational, economic and social status of the Malay/Muslim community. 'Roundtable', a discussion group of young professionals, urged a review of the Societies, Internal Security, and Public Entertainments Acts.

Political stability, a sound economic infrastructure and massive foreign-exchange reserves placed Singapore in a better position than its neighbours to withstand the economic crisis that beset the region from mid-1997. Nevertheless, since the economy was driven primarily by external demand, the crisis posed the most serious challenge faced by Goh's Government since it first took office. Growth decelerated markedly in 1998, tax revenue declined for the first time in a decade and key manufacturing and commercial sectors showed negative growth. The Housing and Development Board upgrading programme, which was financed out of budget surpluses, was scaled down. Both the Prime Minister and the leader of the NTUC stressed the importance of full employment with wage adjustments to curb costs and to save jobs. Ministerial and senior civil service salaries were 'frozen', civil service annual bonuses were cut, but by November Singapore was formally in recession. and the Government introduced far-reaching measures to reduce business costs, which included wage cuts and the halving of employers' Central Provident Fund (CPF) contributions from 20% to 10%. Ministers and senior civil servants suffered substantial pay cuts. At the same time, the Government reduced corporate and property taxes, stamp duty, vehicle taxes, utility charges, Housing and Development Board rents and mortgage interest rates in order to lower costs and to ease the burden on individuals. However, it resisted pleas from the business community for more positive intervention, insisting that its priority was to continue heavily to invest in education, training programmes, defence and the economic infrastructure, in order to strengthen Singapore's future prospects of profiting from the eventual upturn in the regional economy.

In June 1999 President Ong Teng Cheong, whose six-year mandate was due to expire in September, announced that he did not intend to seek a second term in office, citing the difficulties he had experienced as Singapore's first elected President: notably, restrictions placed on the presidential right of veto, official obstruction of his efforts to establish the details of the Republic's financial reserves, and disappointment at not being approached to release the funds needed to help Singapore through the recession. In response, the Government insisted that net investment income lay outside of the President's jurisdiction and that the surplus accumulated during the current Parliament would be sufficient to finance measures to be implemented up to the year 2000 without the need to use reserves. In July 1999 Parliament endorsed a set of rules agreed between Ong and the Prime Minister to ensure a smooth future working relationship: it was decreed that a President could block the sale of land holdings and prohibit unreasonable disposals but could not fetter the day-to-day operations of government; furthermore, the President would be obliged to give warning before blocking any transaction, while the Government in turn undertook regularly to furnish the President with information. Public speculation about the potential impact of the appointment of a new President was quickly dispelled by Senior Minister Lee Kuan Yew, who emphasized that there could be only one centre of executive power and that the powers of the President were confined to preventing the squandering of reserves or the making of unsuitable appointments by an irresponsible administration; otherwise, the role of President remained largely ceremonial. S. R. Nathan, a former Singaporean ambassador to the USA whose presidential candidature was supported by the Cabinet and welcomed by the NTUC, was chosen as the new President without an election being held, since the two other potential contestants failed to meet the criteria for nomination. Reviewing the position in 1999, the Prime Minister concluded that although the Republic had prospered since independence, it was still a fragile society with racial divisions. The 'Singapore 21' concept, which was the result of two years' wide-ranging consultation, was embodied in a book, entitled *Singapore 21: Together We Make The Difference*, and debated in a marathon parliamentary session in May 1999. It aspired to be a 'total vision', for the country's future in the next millennium. This went beyond mere material achievement to developing a partnership between the public and private sectors and the citizens of the Republic, with the aim of building—over one or two generations—a multi-racial nation, in which each community would have its own distinctive identity but overlap with other communities, and in which English would be the common language and equal opportunities would be enjoyed by all. The population target of 4m. envisaged in the 1991 Concept Plan was achieved in 1999, 11 years ahead of schedule, principally as the result of an influx of foreign immigrants, and the target was raised to 5m. by the middle of the 21st century. While the Government retained a strict immigration policy, skilled professionals were welcomed. In 1999 the period for which permanent residents had to wait to attain citizenship was reduced from 10 to six years, and Singaporean women were permitted to sponsor their husbands for citizenship after two years' permanent residency.

By May 1999 Singapore was technically no longer in recession, and the economy experienced greater growth than expected for the rest of the year and throughout 2000. This prompted the National Wages Council to recommend wage increases, bonus payments and the restoration, at a more rapid rate then the proposed five-year period, of the 10% CPF reduction. Some 2% of the CPF decrease was restored in April 2000, and a further 4% by January 2001. In August 2000 Goh Chok Tong announced plans to revive the programme to upgrade Housing Development Board (HDB) flats.

In contrast to the previous two years, Singapore celebrated National Day in August 2000 in ebullient mood, but the Prime Minister warned of 'grave problems', notably falling fertility, emigration, and a widening gap between rich and poor. The optimum population of about 5m. could only be achieved through extensive immigration. Despite tax incentives introduced in the mid-1980s to encourage the educated classes to have more children, the fertility rate had declined sharply to less than 1.5 and was still falling, and already one-quarter of the population were non-Singaporeans. In August 2000 incentives were announced in the form of bonus payments and improved maternity leave for those parents producing a second and third child. To compound the fertility problem, competition from other countries to recruit talent in a global economy was encouraging many Singaporeans to emigrate, thus raising salaries among the most highly-paid echelons. This was a particular threat to the public service, which had not kept pace with the private sector during the recession and, in July 2000, in order to curb rising resignations, the Government announced a radical overhaul of civil service rewards. All ministers and senior officials were given substantial salary increases and enhanced bonuses, linked partly to personal performance and partly to the national economy. Life-long tenure was to be replaced by fixed 10-year appointments, and outstanding young officials could expect accelerated promotion. Opposition MPs objected to the large increases, urging that public service demanded some sacrifice, but the press gave cautious approval.

While the upsurge in the economy created many new jobs for professionals and technicians, unemployment continued to increase among the unskilled, who had suffered most during the 1997–98 crisis. The gap between those earning 'First World' salaries and 'Third World' wages was widening, and in the midst of affluence, 4% of Singaporeans were living below the poverty line. The Government acknowledged that it was impossible to resist the economic transformation created by globalization, and that high achievers must be paid their international worth, but also that the State should help the poor and the old, while simultaneously creating jobs for the younger generation. While rejecting the Workers' Party demand for widespread welfare measures, which it believed would encourage dependency, in August 2000 the Government announced a grants programme, providing for, in particular, help for the elderly, the poor and families with young children, and including CPF and medical insurance 'top-up' sums and HDB mortgage discounts. Furthermore, there was to be continued emphasis on areas such as education, retraining and upgrading skills.

While a very high proportion of Singaporeans were educated to upper secondary and tertiary level, the Government remained concerned at the low academic standards and high drop-out rates at some private schools, notably in *madrasahs* (Islamic religious schools). A minimum level of schooling had never hitherto been enforced, for fear of offending the sensitivities of the Malay/Muslim community, and a proposal made in October 1999 to introduce six years' minimum compulsory education by 2003 and require all schools to achieve specified standards, provoked heated exchanges between the Association of Muslim Professionals (AMP) and the Singapore authorities. The AMP was particularly incensed at remarks passed by Lee Kuan Yew about Malays in the Singapore Armed Forces, which implied doubts about their loyalty. The Association called for an end to discrimination, particularly in promotions to top military posts, and proposed a system of 'collective leadership' of 'independent-non-political' Malay leaders, as a counterweight to the 11 PAP Malay MPs. The Prime Minister insisted that there was no intention of abolishing *madrasahs*, provided they achieved an acceptable standard, and, addressing a large gathering of Muslims at the second National Convention organised by the AMP in November 2000, he objected vigorously to their parallel leadership suggestion, warning this would lead to race-based politics. In the following month the AMP abandoned its controversial proposal, a meeting with Lee Kuan Yew in March 2001 eased the tension, and Malay MPs drew up a blueprint to ensure the progress of the Malay community.

In celebrating National Day in August 1999 Goh Chok Tong had outlined a vision of Singapore as a 'world-class renaissance city', with excellence in education, arts and sport to match a world-class economy, which would attract foreign talent and encourage Singaporeans to remain in the country. President Nathan developed this theme in his inaugural address to Parliament in October and also appealed for constructive disagreement. In 1997 Goh Chok Tong had told Parliament that Singapore needed a civil society 'to harness the talents and energies of its people and to build a cohesive and vibrant nation'. In October 1999 he declared consultation and participation to be among the Government's main objectives, encouraging citizens to turn the republic into 'a nation of ideas'. In September 2000 a 'Speakers' Corner' was designated, which would be open seven days a week for any Singapore citizen to register and speak freely, provided they did not endanger law and order, respected racial and religious sensitivities, and avoided libel. Opposition politicians were wary, however, and 'Speakers' Corner' generated little public interest. The PAP leaders maintained their stance that politics was the domain of elected politicians, since they alone had a popular mandate and were accountable to the electorate. In 1999 Goh Chok Tong had insisted that 'meaningful politics must mean joining a political party', and Lee Kuan Yew repeated a warning about would-be critics crossing 'out of bounds markers'. The Prime Minister insisted that the press should inform and educate but that it was not entitled to set the national agenda. In May 2000 a Political Donations Bill was passed, which aimed to keep Singapore politics free of foreign interference. Political parties were required to keep lists of donors, accept donations only from Singaporean and local companies, and to declare any single donation exceeding S $10,000. Associations promoting purely social causes would not be affected, but any organization would be gazetted as political if its activities related wholly or mainly to politics in Singapore or if it pressed for changes in the political or legal structure. While agreeing that foreigners should be kept out of Singapore politics, all three opposition MPs registered spirited resistance to the Bill, arguing that it would place a heavy burden on small parties to keep detailed records and would deter donors, who were often reluctant to make their support for opposition parties known.

Confidence in the recovery of the economy was shaken in March 2001 when the manufacturing sector contracted for the first time in two years, and the situation worsened with the deceleration in the US economy. By July 20,000 workers faced retrenchment, and in August exports fell to a record low. The terrorist attacks on New York and Washington, DC, on 11 September 2001 destroyed immediate prospects of global recovery. Since the Republic was heavily dependent on the US economy, and already facing considerable problems, the crisis threatened to prolong the downturn in its fortunes, and by the last few months in 2001 Singapore was suffering from the deepest recession since independence.

Appalled by the 11 September 2001 attacks, the Singapore Government immediately pledged its support for the US effort to create a worldwide alliance to counter terrorism, urging in particular that Muslim and developing countries should be included in the coalition. The Republic undertook to co-operate on intelligence, eliminate terrorist networks and monitor financial transactions, but both the Government and the press insisted that the military front was not the most important, and that the 'war on terrorism' could only be won by fighting both the causes and symptoms, and, in particular, by resolving the Israeli–Palestinian conflict.

In order to gain a strong mandate and convince foreign and local investors that the PAP had the electorate's confidence to address the economic crisis and terrorist threat, the Government decided to bring forward the date of the general election (which was required to be held no later than August 2002). The election was scheduled for 3 November 2001, allowing only the minimum legal nine-day notice period, prompting protests from the opposition. The PAP had prepared a new electoral team, recruited after lengthy search and comprising prospective cabinet ministers from the senior ranks of the private sector, together with well-qualified younger candidates, including a number of women and representatives of ethnic minorities. As an alternative to the PAP, in July 2001 three opposition parties, the Singapore People's Party, the National Solidarity Party and the Singapore Malay National Organization, formed a Singapore Democratic Alliance (SDA), under the leadership of Chiam See Tong, but both Low Thia Khiang's Workers' Party and Chee Soon Juan's SDP refused to join the new coalition. A Workers' Party team, which planned to contest a Group Representation Constituency, was disqualified by failing to submit the correct nomination papers, and at the elections the PAP was unopposed in 55 of the 84 elective seats and consequently returned to power with the largest number of outright victories since the 1968 election. Nevertheless, the party contested the election with customary vigour, campaigning on its good record, promising to overcome recession and to have a strong new leadership in place by the next election in five years' time. Unlike previous parliamentary contests, the campaign was not marred by racial or religious discord, although inaccurate allegations about a proposed loan to Indonesia, directed at Goh Chok Tong and Lee Kuan Yew by Chee Soon Juan, briefly caused controversy. (Threatened with legal action, Chee made a public apology.)

Despite Goh's warning that the recession might continue for up to two years, with unemployment rising further and retrenchment being inevitable to safeguard jobs and ensure competitiveness, the PAP won an overwhelming 73.3% of votes cast in the poll, the biggest margin since the 1980 election. This represented a 10% transfer of the vote since the 1997 election, and the party emerged with 82 of the elective 84 seats. Low

Thia Khiang and Chiam See Tong retained their seats, but with smaller majorities. Chiam, who had represented his constituency for 17 years, was now the longest ever serving opposition member, but his majority fell to 52.4%. Low won for the third time, but his proportion of the vote had declined from 58% to 55%. As the losing candidate with the highest number of votes, Steve Chia of the SDA became a non-constituency MP. Although the SDP was overwhelmingly defeated, Chee Soon Juan declared that he would not relinquish the leadership of the party. Owing to the large numbers of uncontested seats, the 'Roundtable' discussion group demanded changes in the electoral system, but Lee insisted that Group Representation Constituencies were essential to ensure minority candidates entered Parliament.

Goh announced that he would remain in office throughout the period of recession, but would resign prior to the next general election in favour of a younger team. Immediately after the election, the Prime Minister appointed his new Cabinet. The Deputy Prime Minister, Lee Hsien Loong, assumed control of the Ministry of Finance from Dr Richard Hu, who had resigned during the election, and Tony Tan Keng Kam continued as Second Deputy Prime Minister and Minister of Defence. Five first-term MPs were appointed Ministers of State; all of them were young and from the private sector, rather than government officials or military officers as in the past, but no women were appointed to senior office.

The Government embarked immediately on addressing economic problems, giving highest priority to saving jobs and helping the unemployed. New Singapore shares were issued to all citizens, with greater allocations to the poor. In December 2001 unemployment reached its highest level for 15 years, while figures indicated that the overall economy had contracted in that year. By mid-2002 optimism about signs of recovery and hopes that the economy would return to its pre-recession level by the end of that year were restrained by concern over the state of the US economy following various accountaning scandals there. In his National Day address in August 2002, Goh tried to dispel the gloom by expressing confidence that Singapore was recovering from recession and would attract investment if it confronted challenges over the necessity for new skills and flexibility.

Meanwhile, in December 2001 an Economic Review Committee was appointed, under the chairmanship of Lee Hsien Loong, with seven sub-committees chaired by prominent politicians and businessmen. The Committee's remit was to recommend long-term economic restructuring to meet the changes in the global economy, notably China's increasing influence and the transfer in emphasis to North-East Asia, which threatened to marginalize the South-East Asian markets. In April 2002 the committee recommended a major revision of taxation and employment benefits, in order to liberalize the labour market and create jobs. It proposed the reduction of direct corporate and personal taxes, including income tax, in favour of increasing indirect general sales taxes. These recommendations were implemented in the budget in May 2002, but with the stipulation that, in order to lessen the impact on the poor of transfer to indirect taxation, at least five years' financial aid would be required, such as in rebates on public housing service charges. Addressing the issue of company structure, the Economic Review Committee recommended that, in principle, the Government should remain involved only in strategic areas, such as the Port of Singapore, and withdraw from enterprises that the private sector could manage (but that this should be undertaken gradually and methodically). Regarding the CPF, in July 2002 the Committee proposed the imposition of a permanent 'freeze' on employers' contributions at the level of 16% for the age group of over 50 years, in order to keep jobs competitive for older workers, a measure that was accepted with reservations by the trade unions.

A parallel 'Remaking Singapore Committee' was established in February 2002, comprising younger citizens under the chairmanship of the Minister of State for National Development. Continuing the research of the Singapore 21 Committee, this body was to make a comprehensive review of political, social and cultural affairs, including the arts and censorship. In March 2002 the PAP invited its MPs to speak and vote according to their personal views, except on matters of critical national importance, such as the budget, the Constitution or security. For the first time the 2002 NMPs included candidates from the areas of community activities, the media and sports, and academia, including the President of the 'Roundtable' political discussion group, and five women. The greater relaxation in party control resulted in some unusually vigorous criticism in Parliament in July 2002 over the Government's decision to increase public transport fares, but official reaction, while conciliatory in tone, was not influenced into modifying the policy.

In November 2001, implementing a concept first proposed by Goh five years earlier, Singapore was divided into five districts, each with a mayor (who would become an MP with the same rank as a Minister of State), and managed by their own Community Development Councils. The aim was to improve community spirit and to allow local government to administer social services, such as welfare, health and sports.

The atmosphere in Singapore following the 11 September 2001 attacks remained calm. Muslim leaders condemned terrorism, and there was no harassment of Muslims by other communities. Nevertheless, the authorities feared that the peace was fragile, that Singapore itself was vulnerable to attack and that al-Qaida had links with neighbouring Indonesia, Malaysia and the Philippines. A new national security secretariat was created, and in December 15 alleged terrorists were arrested, of whom 13 received two-year sentences of imprisonment under the Internal Security Act. Of these, all but one were Singapore citizens, while none of them had been educated at *madrasahs,* or involved in mosque activities or Muslim community organizations, and six had served as full-time national servicemen. They were members of *Jemaah Islamiyah,* a secret network of at least three active groups, part of a larger network in Malaysia and Indonesia, which had been established in 1995 with the aim of creating a Java-based Islamic state, incorporating Indonesia, Malaysia, Singapore and the southern Philippines. Trained in Afghanistan and led by Indonesian militants, *Jemaah Islamiyah* had long planned action against targets in Singapore, including the hijacking of an aeroplane to crash into Changi Airport, attacks against US service personnel and US naval vessels, and a simultaneous offensive against US embassies in Singapore, Kuala Lumpur and Jakarta.

Singapore Muslim leaders expressed strong support for the government action against terrorist suspects, and there were no signs of an adverse reaction against the Muslim community. Goh, in his Chinese New Year message in February 2002, emphasized that security was a greater problem than the economic crisis, which was likely to be severe but brief, whereas security and racial harmony were crucial. The Government sought even greater national cohesion, such as compliance with legislation banning Malay girls in primary schools from wearing the head covering (*tudung*), which provoked protests from some parents. In January 2002 new 'grassroots' community groups, known as 'Inter-racial Confidence Circles' were established in each constituency, and Goh, together with Lee Hsien Loong and other senior ministers, organized a secret meeting of some 1,700 community leaders to discuss the impact of the arrests of *Jemaah Islamiyah* suspects.

In January 2002 an Indonesian man, code-named Mike, who was implicated in the terrorist conspiracy to attack Singapore targets, was arrested in the Philippines. In July a Canadian of Kuwaiti origin, code-named Sammy, who had planned the offensive, was seized in Oman.

FOREIGN RELATIONS

The terrorist threat from 2001 gave even greater impetus to Singapore's aim to establish cordial relations with neighbouring countries. The Republic had consistently supported the promotion of the proposed ASEAN Free Trade Area (AFTA), which had been agreed at the summit held in Singapore in 1992, and the fostering of regional security. The Republic welcomed the entry of Viet Nam, Myanmar, Laos and Cambodia as members of ASEAN in the 1990s. Singapore supported ASEAN's policy of 'constructive engagement' and gentle persuasion to reform Myanmar's autocratic military regime, rather than the European Union's recommendations for economic sanctions. Singapore was anxious to restore the influence of ASEAN, which had failed collectively to address the 1997 regional economic crisis, while relations between its member states had suffered as a result of increased pressure, dissipating the confidence of overseas investors as a consequence. At ASEAN summit meeting in December 1998 and November 2000, and at meetings of ASEAN Ministers of Foreign Affairs, Singapore was foremost in securing substantial measures to increase regional trade and attract capital back to South-East Asia. At the ASEAN summit held in Singapore in November 2000, some resentment was expressed, particularly on the part of Malaysia, at Singapore's moves to conclude bilateral free trade pacts with New Zealand, the USA, Australia and other countries, ahead of the ASEAN arrangement scheduled for 2003. Despite this, the Republic pressed for further economic integration and persuaded ASEAN to undertake a feasibility study on proposals to link the regional economies to those of China, Japan and South Korea. In July 2002 Singapore welcomed the significant decision of ASEAN to expedite progress towards the 2010 deadline for complete free trade, by allowing more advanced countries to open up sectors of their markets before the other member nations. Prime Minister Goh took the initiative in promoting the development of the Singapore-Johor-Riau 'Growth Triangle'. While this would benefit both Malaysia and Indonesia, it was particularly crucial to Singapore, offering the Republic's economy the opportunity to compensate for the geographical constraints of land and labour shortages. The Asian economic crisis strained relations between Singapore and the Republic's immediate neighbours but, at the National Day rally in August 1998, Goh emphasized Singapore's dependence upon Indonesia and Malaysia. The Republic continued to hold reserves in Indonesian and Malaysian currencies, provided humanitarian aid to Indonesia and proposed a loan to support the Indonesian currency (although this was not accepted). Goh visited Jakarta three times between October 1997 and February 1998, and in January 1999 Singapore signed a long-term trade agreement with Indonesia for the supply of natural gas from West Natuna to Singapore. The Singapore authorities co-operated closely with the Government of President Suharto on economic enterprises, but relations with President B. J. Habibie, who took office following the resignation of Suharto in May 1998, were fraught with difficulties. Habibie and several of his senior advisers accused the Republic of having done too little to help Indonesia in the country's time of need and of discriminating against its own Malay minority community (an allegation that was quickly denied by Malay organizations in Singapore). Relations improved for a time, following the appointment of his successor, President Abdurrahman Wahid, who was warmly received in Singapore on a brief tour of ASEAN countries in November 1999. Senior Minister Lee Kuan Yew accepted Indonesia's invitation to join an international advisory council to help accelerate the country's recovery, and Singapore took the initiative in encouraging investment in Indonesia. The Indonesian President caused a disturbance in December 2000, when, in a speech at the Indonesian embassy in Singapore, he accused the Republic of profiteering and threatened to stop its water supply. Senior Indonesian politicians and officials were quick to disown these remarks, and President Wahid and Goh launched the West Natuna gas pipeline in January 2001. However, the Singapore Government welcomed the end of Wahid's 'wayward presidency' in July 2001, followed by the swift and peaceful transition to power of the new Indonesian President, Megawati Sukarnoputri, and her call for unity. In February 2002 Singapore proposed the extension of the free trade agreement being negotiated with the USA to Indonesia, to support its manufacturing base and attract investment. However, relations were strained for a time, after Lee Kuan Yew publicly reprimanded the Indonesian Government for allegedly allowing terrorists to remain at large, provoking Indonesian protests of interference and unsubstantiated charges. In March President Megawati urged a relaxation of tension and it was agreed to settle the issue peacefully through normal diplomatic means.

Full diplomatic relations were restored between Singapore and the Philippines in January 1996, following an acrimonious dispute in the previous year, which caused the deepest rift between ASEAN partners for more than a quarter of a century when Singapore insisted in March 1995 on hanging a Filipino woman found guilty of murder, despite pleas from President Fidel Ramos for a stay of execution. When President Joseph Estrada of the Philippines visited Singapore in October 1998 a few months after his election, the Republic welcomed his pledge to retain an open economy and pro-market policies. At the ASEAN summit meeting (held in Hanoi) in December, the two countries signed a Philippine-Singapore Action Plan to develop closer bilateral co-operation in trade. Goh Chok Tong welcomed the efforts of the Thai Prime Minister, Thaksin Shinawatra, to revive the Thai economy, and in February 2002 proposed an extension of their existing co-operation in the form of the Singapore-Thailand Enhanced Economic Relationship (Steer).

Singapore and Malaysia grew closer in the mid-1990s, agreeing to settle all their differences amicably, including the long-standing dispute over the ownership of the island of Pedra Branca (Batu Putih) and to work together to promote investment in emerging Asian economies. In 1995 the two countries launched a bilateral defence forum, signed a Defence Co-operation Pact, and agreed on the permanent boundary of their territorial waters after 15 years of negotiations. By mid-1996 Singapore was well on the way to becoming the top investor in Malaysia, but underlying tensions between the two countries were demonstrated in that year, when indiscreet remarks by Lee Kuan Yew provoked a ferocious response from the Malaysian press and the United Malays National Organization (UMNO), the dominant element in the Malaysian ruling coalition. Goh met the Malaysian Prime Minister, Dr Mahathir Mohamad, three times between October 1997 and January 1998 and, after a cordial two-day working session in Kuala Lumpur in February, it appeared that Singapore and Malaysia had put aside their differences. The two Prime Ministers discussed ways to help restore economic confidence in the region, and agreed to co-operate in the areas of banking and finance and to encourage private investment in each other's economies. Mahathir announced that bilateral problems could be solved, given flexibility. However, friction escalated over conflicting interpretations of the Points of Agreement which had been signed between the two countries in 1990 covering the status and development of Malayan Railway land in Singapore, under which land at Tanjong Pagar, Kranji and Woodlands would be developed jointly by the two countries. In accordance with a long-standing arrangement, Singapore prepared to transfer railway customs, immigration and quarantine facilities from Tanjong Pagar to the frontier at Woodlands in August 1998; however, Malaysia refused to do likewise and ended talks with Singapore abruptly at the end of July. In September Malaysia imposed restrictions on the use of its airspace by Singaporean military aircraft, complained that Malaysian ports were losing trade to Singapore, and withdrew from a Five Power Defence Arrangement exercise, citing tensions with Singapore as well as economic difficulties. The publication of the first volume of Lee Kuan Yew's memoirs in September 1998 revived old contentions and provoked protests from the Malaysian Prime Minister and other Malay leaders in Kuala Lumpur. However, Singapore politicians continued to emphasize the need for good relations with Malaysia and the importance of maintaining racial harmony in Singapore. In November 1998 Goh visited Malaysia at the invitation of Mahathir, and at the ASEAN summit meeting in Hanoi in the following month the two Prime Ministers agreed upon an arrangement to settle all outstanding issues. Officials met several times over the next few months, but discussions were abandoned in May 1999. Contact was resumed unexpectedly by Senior Minister Lee Kuan Yew, who paid a four-day informal visit to Malaysia in August 2000 for the first time in 10 years. After receiving a very cordial welcome, including meetings with Mahathir and other ministers, Lee declared that, given compromise on both sides, all disputes could be settled within a few months. Lee's second volume of memoirs, published in September 2000, was warmly received in Malaysia, and the two Prime Ministers had discussions at the time of the ASEAN summit meeting in Singapore in November 2000. A joint naval exercise was held that month, and in February 2001 the Malaysian Deputy Prime Minister brought a large delegation for informal discussions, at which a compromise over the railway station was agreed in principle, and ideas were mooted for a new bridge to replace the causeway and an undersea rail tunnel. Meeting in Kuala Lumpur in August 2001, the Malaysian Prime Minister and Senior Minister Lee Kuan Yew agreed a compromise in principle on all outstanding issues, leaving the detailed arrangements to be worked out by officials.

In March 2002 a delegation of 60 members of Malaysia's Barisan Nasional Youth met their PAP counterparts in an amicable visit to Singapore and agreed to establish a joint secretariat, but the negotiations between the government officials of the two countries remained fraught with difficulties. The main issue of contention was the price of water supplied by Malaysia under two agreements, made in 1961 and 1962, which could not be changed unilaterally and were due to remain in force until 2011 and 2061, respectively. Malaysia had undertaken to supply water at a cost of 3 sen (Malaysian cents) per 1,000 gallons, but in early 2001 the Malaysian Government complained about the price. In September of that year Singapore offered to pay 45 sen for the period between 2011 and 2061, (although not legally required to do so), and Malaysia pledged to continue the supply after 2061, probably raising the charge to 60 sen per 1,000 gallons, with a price review every five years.

In spite of Lee Hsien Loong visiting Kuala Lumpur to ease differences, the Malaysian national press and politicians continued what Singapore's Minister of Foreign Affairs described as 'pyschological warfare'. Complaints about Singapore profiting from cheap water were followed for several months from February 2002 by vociferous objections to Singapore's reclamation projects at Tuas and Pulau Tekong, on the grounds that they encroached on Johor territory, would cause environmental damage and would restrict access to Malaysia's new ports in the Johor Strait. Singapore insisted that the reclamation would cause no damage and was entirely within the Republic's territorial waters. In April unfounded allegations that members of the Singapore armed forces had landed on the Johor island of Pulau Pisang, where Singapore maintained a lighthouse, caused a minor dispute, and the two Governments were at conflict over the possible replacement for the causeway.

Apart from the issue of sovereignty over Pedra Branca, which was to be submitted to the International Court of Justice in The Hague, Singapore aimed to resolve all outstanding issues in one settlement, which would include water, the location of Customs, Immigration and Quarantine facilities in Singapore, the redevelopment of Malaysian railway land in Singapore, the early release of CPF money to West Malaysian contributors, the use of Malaysian airspace and the construction of a bridge to replace the causeway. However, Malaysia insisted, at a meeting of ministers responsible for foreign affairs in Kuala Lumpur in July 2002, on settling the issue of water separately. Singapore aimed to fix the future water price to the cost of producing recycled 'new water' to avoid future disputes, whereas Malaysia sought a higher rate, comparable to that agreed between Hong Kong and China.

The Malaysian Minister of Foreign Affairs offered to supply Singapore with water for another hundred years after 2061, if a fair price could be agreed. For its part, Singapore sought to reduce its dependence on Malaysia, aiming to make the Republic self-sufficient after 2061, if necessary. In December 2001 approval was given for the first desalination plant, which would produce the equivalent of 10% of the Republic's current consumption by 2005. Two new fresh water reservoirs were to be constructed and all reservoirs linked by 2009. 'New water', which could be produced at one-half of the cost of treating sea water, would begin to supply industrial plants early in 2003, when two plants would commence operations, with a further two by 2011. Indeed, the recycled 'new water' was being promoted as safe drinking water, not just for industrial use, and thousands of bottles were distributed on National Day in August 2002. In the mean time, in May 2002 Taiwan's prominent shipping line, Evergreen, decided to transfer headquarters from Singapore to Malaysia's new port of Tanjung Pelepas on the Johor Strait later in the year, following the example of a major Danish shipping line. Singapore continued to maintain friendly relations with the People's Republic of China. By 2001 earlier problems over the progress of the Sino-Singaporean Suzhou joint venture, from which Singapore had contemplated withdrawing, had been overcome, and Singapore continued to encourage investment and commercial links. Lee Kuan Yew travelled frequently to China, always receiving a warm welcome. In April 2000 Goh Chok Tong paid an official visit, reaffirming co-operation with the People's Republic, and in 2001 Singapore established institutions for closer business links, following China's admission to the World Trade Organization. In April 2002 the Chinese Vice-President, Hu Jintao, who was expected to assume the leadership of the Chinese Communist Party from President Jiang Zemin later in the year and to become President himself in 2003, made an official visit to Singapore. He and Goh agreed to establish a high-level joint council to investigate potential areas of practical co-operation, such as an early start of talks to form a China–ASEAN Free Trade Agreement, and Beijing also offered Singapore military training facilities on Hainan Island as an alternative to Taiwan.

Anxious to avoid conflict in the region, Singapore hoped that Taiwan would reach an agreement with China, with a view to reunification. Singapore had hosted the first Taiwan-China talks in 1993, but a second round of discussions, proposed for 1999, was abandoned, when the then Taiwanese President, Lee Teng-hui, declared that relations with China were 'state-to-state'. The election of President Chen Shui-bian, who represented a pro-independence party, prompted escalating tension between China and Taiwan in mid-2000. In October 2001 Lee Kuan Yew made a four-day visit to Taiwan (his first in six years) on his own initiative, and not at the invitation of the Taiwan Government. He was received with respect, although his views differed from those of President Chen. Lee Kuan Yew argued that Taiwan should accept the 'one China' reunification principle on the terms proposed by the Chinese Government, rather than after losing its economic prosperity to mainland China. Consequently, Singapore was critical of President Chen's proposal in August 2002 for a referendum on declaring independence.

The maintenance of good relations with the USA continued to be of crucial importance to Singapore. Singapore had distanced itself from the US Government's hostile stance towards China during the Clinton administration in 1994–2000, and during 1993–96 the Clinton Government relegated the Republic to *persona non grata* status, following the sentence of caning imposed on a young US national, who had been convicted for vandalism. However, the measures taken by the Singaporean Government to mitigate the Republic's domestic financial problems following the onset of the regional economic crisis in 1997 won praise in the US press. Goh Chok Tong met with US President Bill Clinton in Washington in September 1998, and he was the first South-East Asian leader to meet President George W. Bush in Washington in June 2001, when he urged a permanent US interest in South-East Asia. In recognition of Singapore's strong support after the 11 September attacks, the US Government designated Singapore 'a friendly foreign country', with privileged access to technology and eligible to take part in co-operative programmes in research development and defence. The Republic warmly welcomed the Joint Declaration for Co-operation to Combat International Terrorism agreed between ASEAN and the USA and signed by the US Secretary of State, Colin Powell, in Brunei in July 2002. The agreement, reached at meetings of ASEAN ministers responsible for foreign affairs and their 13 dialogue partners, provided for sharing intelligence, blocking terrorist funds, and tightening border security, without increasing US troops in the region or creating new military bases.

Economy

GAVIN PEEBLES

Revised for this edition by CHRISTOPHER TORRENS

INTRODUCTION

Despite its small size, with a population of about 4m. people, the city-state of Singapore plays an important part in the world economy. Illustrating the nature of international fragmentation in production, amongst other aspects of globalization, Singapore presents some of the most extreme examples of economic features, has been one of the fastest growing economies in the world over the last four decades and provides evidence for different sides of the various arguments about the correct foundations for economic development. To some Singapore is an epitome of economic freedom, usually being ranked the second most economically free economy in the world after Hong Kong; able to transform itself from colonial neglect and the status of a fishing village to first world status in four decades through discipline, not democracy. To others it is an Orwellian nightmare of social and economic control by a single, all-intrusive political party that has been in power for more than 40 years, placed restrictions on many aspects of life and repressed wages in order to benefit foreign capital; its high growth rates the result of massive levels of investment and not technological progress. Even institutions that rank it as economically free can say that the ruling political party controls all aspects of social and economic life.

Another distinguishing feature of this small, seemingly very vulnerable economy, is that during the Asian financial crisis of the late 1990s it suffered less than its larger neighbours. Growth stopped in 1998, but growth rates of 5.9% and 9.9% were achieved in 1999 and 2000 respectively, and unemployment did not rise significantly. In 1998 there was mild deflation, with the consumer price index (CPI) falling by 0.3%, and in the following two years the inflation rates were zero and 1.3%. In 2000 gross domestic product (GDP) at current prices reached S $159,042m. and gross national product (GNP) was S $169,597m. However, in 2001, when GDP at current prices declined to S $153,455m., Singapore experienced its worst recession since independence in 1965. Nevertheless, prospects for recovery in 2002 remained good, with a strong performance in the second quarter of the year. An increase in GDP of 3.2% (following a 2.6% fall in the first quarter) raised hopes of continuing economic growth, supported by a second-quarter expansion of 7.5% in the manufacturing sector, which accounted for 30% of GDP. Low interest rates and renewed government spending were expected to fuel domestic demand, although it was possible that rising unemployment would limit this effect. The Economist Intelligence Unit projected 3.8% growth for 2002, with further recovery to 5.7% in 2003. In the July–September quarter of 2002, however, GDP was estimated to have expanded by 3.7%, well below expectations.

Singapore has had positive net factor income flows since the mid-1980s. GNP per caput was S $24,740 in 2000. In terms of purchasing power parity, Singapore's GNP per caput puts it in the leading 10 countries in the world. Singapore has what is probably the highest gross national saving rate (equivalent to 52% of GNP), one of the lowest levels of personal consumption, a high investment rate and a very large current account surplus. The typical recent profile of expenditures on GDP is: private consumption 40%; government consumption 10%; investment 31%; and net exports of goods and services 19%. This is a very different profile from economies of the same level of per caput GNP, where private consumption is usually a larger proportion, as is government consumption, and there is less investment, slower growth and a smaller export surplus.

The dependence on exports, especially electronics, and having the USA as its most important export market and investor, has always been seen as one of the vulnerabilities of the economy. This was highlighted in 2001 when reductions in investment in the USA decreased the demand for electronic products from many Asian economies, and as feared, Singapore sank into recession, with a contraction of 2.0% in GDP. In an attempt to pre-empt this, the Government in 2000 had announced a 10-year plan to create a 'New Singapore', intended to form a new social contract whereby the lower paid would receive more help than usual.

Singapore both receives large inflows of direct foreign investment and is increasingly investing abroad, but has a policy of aiming for balance-of-payments surpluses and a stable trade-weighted exchange rate. Recent years have witnessed continuing balance-of-payments surpluses but at a much lower rate than previously. This contributes to the increasing official foreign reserves held by Singapore, which, on a per caput basis, are among the highest in the world. Singapore has had a low rate of inflation, and emphasis has been placed on trade. In the 1970s the average annual real GDP growth rate was 9.4%, in the 1980s 7.4%, and 7.6% in the 1990s. Despite rapid growth and rising standards of living, some in the Government do not yet feel that Singapore is a developed country due to its reliance on exports, especially of electronic products to the USA, and its dependence on foreign capital and labour. Furthermore, they have realised that formerly successful policies of government ownership, control and protection of certain sectors are no longer viable and there has been a paradigm shift in the Government's approach to managing the economy, especially in the financial sector and in trade agreements.

DEVELOPMENT STRATEGY AND INSTITUTIONS

Interpretations of this remarkable record of growth tend to elicit comparisons between Singapore and Hong Kong. The similarities between the two city-sized economies in terms of their dimension, entrepôt role and free trade policies, maintenance of certain British institutions and majority Chinese populations have led some commentators to assume that there must be resemblances in the nature of their economic policies. Both are sometimes hailed as examples of dynamic Asian capitalism, achieving rapid growth through free-market policies and free trade. Although both of these economies are characterized by a very high level of economic freedom, they are not at all similar in the nature of their development strategies.

Singapore is a 'planned' economy in the sense that the mobilization, co-ordination, improvement and allocation of resources is subject to strong guidance from the public sector, which also decides which sectors should be subsidized. Furthermore, a significant part of Singapore's output has been produced by public-sector bodies such as the statutory boards and hundreds of government-linked companies (GLCs). GLCs have benefited from access to cheaper bank loans, as bankers believed that they would always be supported by the Government.

The principal planning body in Singapore is the Economic Development Board (EDB), a statutory board under the Ministry of Trade and Industry (MTI), established in August 1961. The EDB's main aims became, and remain, the attraction of foreign investment into Singapore, the fostering of the development of local enterprises and, from the mid-1990s, the promotion of outflows of investment from Singapore. Singapore's industrialization drive and growth have been based on attracting world-class, foreign multinational corporations (MNCs). To address the problem of unemployment in the late 1960s, labour-intensive investments were initially encouraged. The first significant foreign investors were in the electronics industry, which has become the core of Singapore's manufacturing sector. These investors were Texas Instruments (now Micron Semiconductor Asia) and National Semiconductors, which in 1968 located their labour-intensive assembly operations in Singapore. Singapore adopted a welcoming policy towards MNCs, granting favourable tax status, allowing complete foreign operation and imposing no restrictions on the employment of foreign workers. The EDB became a 'one stop' agency at which foreign investors could receive all necessary help and co-ordination with other agencies, enabling them to start production within a very short period of time.

The EDB's plan, Manufacturing 2000 (M2000), was to ensure that manufacturing continued to account for a minimum of 25% of GDP and more than 20% of employment. Industry 21 (I21), launched in January 1999, focused more on knowledge-intensive activities and reflected the Government's intention to build a knowledge-based economy (KBE). The strategic plan known as Manpower 21 was to co-ordinate the development of the labour force in order to meet the output target set by the EDB. The continued emphasis on manufacturing contained in I21, probably reflected the view that a large part of the labour force was not yet suitable for employment in the service sector and that a manufacturing sector that exported to a diverse range of countries was more stable than a service sector that served the regional economies only. This plan also included the aim of increasing the share of manufacturing services (such as research and development, product design and testing and marketing) from 3% to 6% of GDP by 2010. Although companies were encouraged to relocate some of their activities in neighbouring countries, the Government seemed unwilling to allow basic manufacturing activity to contract to the extent seen in Hong Kong, for example.

The EDB managed to maintain a high level of investment commitment by foreign firms despite the uncertainties caused by the Asian financial crisis of the late 1990s. In 2000 48% of investment commitments were in the electronics sector and 30% in chemicals and chemical products, a sector the Government has been developing. Historically, as much as 80% of investment in manufacturing each year came from outside Singapore. In 2000 the USA provided 40% of fixed investment in manufacturing, Japan 16%, the European Union (EU) 18% and Singapore 21%. The USA's investment in 1999 rose 56% above the 1998 level, as a result of investment in some major chemical projects, and it then increased its investment commitments slightly in 2000. In 2000 Japan also increased its commitments by 27%, having reduced them by 35% in 1999 following a 10% reduction in 1998. The EU has become a more significant investor in Singapore's manufacturing sector. Singaporean investment declined by 32% in 1999 compared with 1998 but increased by 10% in 2000. Total investment commitments in manufacturing reached S $9,151.5m. in 2001. The areas that the EDB has stressed are wafer-fabrication plants and the petrochemicals sector and a desire to create knowledge-based jobs. Another initiative that the EDB has co-ordinated is the building of a fourth pillar of the economy through the development of the life sciences sector, which draws on the pharmaceuticals sector, medicine, medical equipment design and manufacture, health promotion and research in such areas as molecular biology and biotechnology. The EDB has co-ordinated the work of a ministerial committee and an international advisory board on how to develop this sector. It has funds to co-invest with suitable foreign investors and for education programmes totalling about S $1,000m. The EDB co-invests with MNCs and local firms to develop targeted sectors in Singapore and to encourage outward investment. In 1995 the EDB established the Promising Local Enterprises (PLEs) programme, which initially identified 100 local companies for support in order to increase their annual sales to S $100m. each by the year 2005. By 1999 45 PLEs had achieved revenue of more than S $100m., compared with 31 companies in the previous year, and by 2000 this had increased to 52. Tax incentives, financial assistance, innovation grants, the arrangement of strategic partnerships and the development of business contacts for the PLEs are the methods used by the EDB. In 2000 there were about 300 PLEs in both the manufacturing and service sectors that had benefited from the programme. Many are being helped to set up operations abroad. In 1999 15 PLEs were listed on the stock exchange and, in 2000, 13.

Another government initiative, the Technopreneurship 21 (T21) programme, was announced in April 1999. The four aspects of this programme were: to develop a pro-enterprise environment; to develop suitable physical infrastructure; to develop a venture investment infrastructure and to develop the education system to encourage entrepreneurship, initiative and risk taking. These policies can be seen as moves away from a development strategy based on public enterprises managed by civil servants to a more entrepreneurial one aimed at responding to the needs of the knowledge-based economy. However, much of the funding for such programmes will come from the public sector such as the Technopreneurship fund (which will also have a private-sector contribution) and the use of government funds managed by the Government of Singapore Investment Corporation Special Investments, a branch of the Government's wholly-owned company, the Government of Singapore Investment Corporation Pte Ltd (GIC), which manages its reserves.

The budget announced in February 2001 was hailed as one of the best ever, as it attempted to address the grievances of the small domestic production sector, which has long complained of being crowded out by government companies. Corporate tax reductions applied to all companies but small ones were given generous tax exemptions, with the expectation that two-thirds of taxable companies would pay half as much tax as before. In 2001 the Government announced it would allow the establishment of limited partnerships and limited liability partnerships to encourage company formation.

A very important aspect of Singapore's planning system has been the Government's policy towards land ownership and allocation. Various pieces of legislation, especially the Land Acquisition Act of 1966, have allowed the Government to acquire land from the private sector. Together with the transfer of land to the Government from the British forces and land reclamation, this active procurement policy increased the State's ownership of land from 44% of total land area in 1960 to 76% in 1985 and to about 85% by 2000. This has had a huge impact on the nature of Singapore's development. Sales of leases on state land have produced large revenues for the state budget, and the Government has been able quickly to acquire and allocate land to its chosen projects. The Urban Redevelopment Authority (URA) is the statutory board that plans and co-ordinates the development and sale of land. In June 2001 a new statutory board, the Singapore Land Authority (SLA), was established by merging four land associated departments.

Many important sectors have been dominated by public enterprises. Electricity, water and piped gas were provided by the Public Utility Board (PUB), a statutory board which was corporatized in October 1995. The PUB remains the water authority and is the regulator of the divested suppliers of electricity and gas. The crucial port facilities have been administered by the Port of Singapore Authority (PSA), another statutory board, corporatized in October 1997. Apart from some 50 statutory boards, the public sector consists of hundreds of government-linked companies. There are four major government-owned holding companies under the Ministry of Finance: Temasek Holdings Pte Ltd, the most important, Singapore Technologies Holdings Pte Ltd, MND Holdings Pte Ltd and Health Corporation of Singapore Pte Ltd. They own various stakes in hundreds of GLCs. Other crucial and distinctive institutions in Singapore's development include the following. The National Wages Council (NWC), established in 1972, brings together the Government, employers and trade union in negotiations and advises the government on wages policies. It makes annual recommendations on wage increases and bonus payments that, while not binding, are (when accepted by the Government) used as guidelines for negotiations over pay increases. Since the late 1980s Singapore has had a flexible wage system that pays variable components and bonuses depending on the performance of the economy (based on the growth rate of GDP) or the individual company. In the late 1990s about 16% of the typical annual salary in the private sector consisted of a variable component, and for civil servants it was at least 20%; this had risen from the overall average of 11% in 1987. The NWC was instrumental in introducing the 'high wage policy' of the late 1970s and early 1980s which attempted to encourage companies to move to higher value-added and capital- and skill-intensive activities, and which also led to the move to cut wages in the recessionary environment of the late 1990s. In May 2001, after a brief period of optimism in 2000, the NWC told workers to expect lower wage rises in 2001. In November 2001 the NWC began to advise companies under economic pressure to 'freeze' salaries.

Another important institution is the National Trades Union Congress (NTUC), virtually a branch of the Government, which has a government minister as its Secretary-General. Affiliated to it are 67 trade unions, giving it a total of 314,478 members in 2000, 99% of all trade union membership. This organization relays government policy to the unions and provides training and recreation facilities for its members. It operates the largest taxi company, a major insurance company, a chain of supermarkets (on co-operative principles) and also a radio station. This relationship ensures smooth industrial relations and an almost complete absence of industrial disputes. It is said that since 1978 there have been no strikes except for a two-day action in 1986. For five consecutive years Business Environment Risk Intelligence (Beri) ranked the Singaporean labour force as the best in the world based on four criteria: legal framework, relative productivity, worker attitude and technical skills. Singapore was judged the second best destination after Switzerland for foreign investment. Foreign investors consistently state that the nature of labour relations is the most important factor in their investment decision, ahead of tax and other incentives. In 2000 231 industrial disputes were recorded, compared with 246 in 1999. The vast majority of disputes, most of them involving wages or conditions of service, were duly resolved, with only five referred for arbitration.

The Central Provident Fund (CPF) plays a crucial role in financing Singapore's development and in public housing policy. Established under the colonial administration in July 1955, this statutory board was intended to provide retirement benefits for civil servants, financed from contributions from both employees and employers. The system was subsequently extended to all employees, and the self-employed can opt in. Contributions are paid into three accounts, which are owned by the member, accumulate and are available for withdrawal, subject to maintaining a minimum sum, at the age of 55 or at death or on permanent disability or on leaving Singapore. Over the years, the Government has used this institution in areas of social policy by allowing members to use their funds for various approved purposes. Members have been allowed to use their funds to buy and upgrade flats built by public housing authorities, to buy private residential properties and land, for investment in approved shares and unit trusts and gold. CPF funds can be used to finance the education of members' children at local tertiary institutions.

Furthermore, the rates of contribution to CPF funds were increased steadily, thus improving Singapore's very high saving rate. By 1994 the long-term goal of having equal contribution rates of 20% from both employer and employee had been achieved. The measures introduced by the Government in 1998 to reduce costs included an amendment of these rates, however, and the Government subsequently implied that the rates might not be restored to their previous levels. It has been estimated that by the mid-1980s about 64% of gross national saving was done by the public sector, 30% was through the CPF scheme and the remainder was voluntary saving. Discussion of the adequacy of individual private saving for retirement is a sensitive issue, and debate is not facilitated by the lack of good data on households' saving patterns and resources. Ministers have frequently stated that current savings rates are insufficient for people to finance their retirements and that the CPF scheme is inadequate and should be reformed to include private-sector participation. The returns the CPF pays on CPF funds are based on short-term interest rates and have been essentially zero in real terms over the last decade or so. Since 1965, with the exception of 1993 when withdrawals of CPF funds exceeded contributions owing to the demand for SingTel shares, net contributions have been positive. In 1965 net contributions were only S $38m. In 1998 they reached S $2,390m. (only 54% of the amount recorded in 1997), and in 1999 net contributions declined to only S $38m., a remarkably low figure that resulted from a 20% decrease in the amount of contributions, owing to the reduction in employers' contributions announced in 1998. In 2000 the amount due to members was S $90,288m. To reduce wage costs, employers' CPF rates were halved from 1 January 1999 to 10% of salary, increased by two percentage points from 1 April 2000 and by a further four percentage points from 1 January 2001.

In July 2002 the Deputy Prime Minister and Minister of Finance, Lee Hsien Loong, announced CPF reforms, including a reduction to the aggregate contribution rate for workers aged 50–55 years, from 36% to 32%, as part of efforts to encourage employers to retain older workers. The Government also limited CPF withdrawals for home loans at 150% of the property value, to be reduced to 120% over five years. Finally, the Government was to grant financial institutions priority over the pension board in mortgage default claims.

Regionalization

During the early 1990s there was increased emphasis by the Government on encouraging companies to invest in the region. The implementation of more market- and trade-orientated policies by such former centrally-planned economies as the People's Republic of China, Viet Nam, Laos and Cambodia have created opportunities for such investment. Both the private sector and GLCs, with support from such agencies as the EDB, are encouraged to take advantage of these opportunities. The EDB is keen to enter joint ventures with companies, including GLCs and MNCs, for this purpose. This sector of the Singapore economy is called the 'external wing'. The EDB also arranges training schemes for managers under its Initiatives in New Technology (Rationalization) programme. In 2000 there were 7,526 Singaporean companies outside the country with a stock of direct equity investment of S $59,4000m.

Emphasis is being placed upon assistance to local firms to encourage them to venture outside Asia to such places as Mexico and Central and Eastern Europe because of their proximity to the USA and the EU respectively. The main sectors were financial services and manufacturing, but Singapore is also developing tourist sites in the region. Despite the regional recession and the related uncertainty, in 1999 and 2000 Singapore was the largest investor in Viet Nam, the third largest in Indonesia, the fourth largest in Malaysia and Thailand, the eighth largest in the Philippines and the ninth largest in India. These investment links will boost trade, just as Japan's investment in Singapore contributed to commercial growth between those two countries. In terms of earnings from these investments, it is estimated that Singapore's factor income from abroad (FIFA) reached 14% of GDP plus FIFA in 2000. Some of these investments abroad have followed the Singaporean development pattern of establishing industrial parks by public-sector agencies in joint ventures and making them available for Singaporean and foreign firms. The JTC has been involved in ventures to develop a number of industrial townships in such places as China, Viet Nam, Thailand, India and Indonesia. However, there were reports that Singapore's major 7,000-ha China-Singapore Suzhou Industrial Park, not far from Shanghai, was not developing in a satisfactory manner. In a speech in China the Senior Minister, Lee Kuan Yew, publicly criticized the Chinese authorities for their constantly changing policies and seeming lack of support for the development. The central Government in Beijing replied that it fully supported the scheme. In 2001 the Singapore Government reduced its stake from 65% to 35%, thereby transferring ownership of the project to China. The measure followed difficulties arising from differences in business practices and expectations, as well as the existence of competition in the form of an earlier established park.

LABOUR FORCE

Singapore's labour market suffered in 2001. In contrast to strong gains of 108,500 new workers in 2000, employment growth remained negligible for the whole year as many companies halted their recruitment programmes. A survey of Singapore firms in late 2001 indicated that about 18% of firms had 'frozen wages', 26% expected to do so, while 4% had introduced pay cuts. Some 40% of companies had reduced working hours, while an overwhelming 68% had suspended recruitment.

Job vacancies fell to a record low, prompted by the international economic slowdown, and the 11 September terrorist attacks. According to the Ministry of Manpower, by June 2001 the labour force had reached 2.12m., of a total population of 4.1m. in that year. In 2000 women comprised 39.6% of the labour force. Manufacturing employment increased by 28,000 in 2000, whereas employment in the service industries rose by 82,700, mostly in business services (23,200), wholesale and retail trade (15,900), transport and communications (10,800) and 'other services' (20,200). These increases were associated with the revival of tourism. By contrast, in 2001 the only sector to register positive growth was business services (36,900), with job losses in other sectors such as manufacturing (14,300) and construction (20,500). The seasonally-adjusted unemployment rate for December 2001 was 4.7% (the highest rate since 1987). A total of 25,800 workers were made redundant in 2001, a sharp increase on the 11,600 retrenchments in 2000. Overall unemployment in 2001 averaged 3.3%, compared with an average of 3.1% in 2000, 3.6% in 1999 and 2.4% in 1998. In June 2002 the NTUC announced that Singapore had lost more than 42,000 jobs over the past five years as companies moved facilities to lower-cost sites, many in China. The Government envisaged an increase in the unemployment rate from 4.4% in 2001 to more than 5.5% in 2002.

The average age of Singapore's workforce rose gradually, from 36.9 years to 37.8 years, between 1997 and 2001. While the 15–29 age-group represented 41% of the workforce in 1989, by 2001 this had dropped to 27.4%. The Government responded by raising the retirement age from 60 to 62 years from 1 January 1999, with an eventual plan to raise it to 67 years.

Of the 2001 population of 4,131,200, 3,319,100 were resident in Singapore as citizens or permanent residents. The 812,100 non-nationals, who had resided in the country for more than one year, thus comprised 19.7% of the total. Singapore's resident population growth rate is rather low and has been decreasing. The average annual growth rate of the resident population during 1990–2000 was 1.8%, whereas that of non-residents was 9.3%, giving a growth rate for the total population of 2.8% per year. The Government was planning for a population of 5.5m. by the year 2040. As in other developed countries, the Government in Singapore was very concerned about the falling birth rate, and in August 2000 announced a new incentive to encourage procreation. On the birth of a married couple's second and third child, the Government would open a Children Development Account ('baby bonus'), into which it would pay up to S $1,500 or S $3,000 for every second or third child, respectively, until the child reached six years of age. In addition, for every dollar placed in the account by the parents, the Government would make a matching dollar-for-dollar contribution of up to S $1,000 a year for the second and up to S $2,000 for the third child. The parents are free to decide how the funds should be used.

Recent policy changes have allowed a higher ratio of foreigners to be employed in key sectors such as construction and ship-repairing. There have been some key appointments of foreigners in local banks and even at the Monetary Authority of Singapore (MAS). Foreign workers are employed in jobs that Singaporeans dislike, and if there is a downturn in a sector, such as construction, the foreign worker will lose his job. The official view is that if two workers are equally productive and it is necessary to dismiss one worker, then the foreigner should be made redundant. In 2001 redundancies increased in the manufacturing sector, and banking and finance sectors, as mergers took place. It is possible that many of the older workers displaced from manufacturing might enter low-level service sectors, such as retailing and tourism, and displace foreign workers employed there.

STRUCTURAL CHANGE

Singapore's strategy of industrializing a basically service-based, entrepôt economy has had profound effects on its production structure. In 1965 manufacturing accounted for only 15.2% of GDP. The contributions of other sectors were: commerce 27.2%; transport and communications 11.5%; financial and business services 16.6%; utilities 2.2%; construction 6.5%; and other services 17.6%. By 1995 manufacturing had reached 24.9% of GDP with the contributions of other sectors being: commerce 18.6%; transport and communications 11.1%; financial and business services 26.9%; utilities 1.5%; construction 6.7%; and other services 10.0%. This illustrated the increased importance of the manufacturing and financial services sectors (52% of GDP in 1995, compared with 32% in 1965) and the decline in commerce. In 1999 manufacturing was still producing 25.0% of GDP and financial and business services 23.3%.

Singapore's strategy of attracting export-orientated MNCs and high infrastructure investment and fixed capital formation has had profound implications for the structure of expenditures in the economy. In 1965 private consumption expenditure made up 79.2% of GDP, and government consumption expenditures represented 10.4%. With gross fixed capital formation at 21.1% of GDP and stock accumulation at 0.8%, net exports had to be equivalent to 12% of GDP (imports exceeded exports), showing that Singapore was borrowing from abroad in order to finance domestic expenditures, which were 112% of domestic production. Use of the CPF scheme to increase forced saving, persistent fiscal surpluses and surpluses of statutory boards have restrained consumption expenditures and have boosted national saving. By 1995 personal consumption expenditure had been reduced to 40.7% of GDP and, with government consumption expenditure at only 8.5% of GDP, Singapore's gross fixed capital formation reached 33% of GDP and net exports were equivalent to 18.1% of GDP. Net exports only became positive in the mid-1980s, and this had implications for Singapore's balance-of-payments accounts (see below). The reduction of private consumption expenditure as a proportion of GDP means that private consumption expenditures continue to grow in real terms each year but at a slower rate than that of overall output.

The distribution of income is likely to have altered in view of such structural changes. Only in 1998 did Singapore produce provisional data of the income-based estimates of GDP. Official estimates show the distribution of GDP into indirect taxes, gross operating surplus and remuneration (wages and salaries). In 1997 indirect taxes took 10% of GDP, remuneration 43% and profits 47%. This relatively low remuneration share is similar to that of Hong Kong (45.9%), but lower than that of developed economies such as the USA (58.2%) and Japan (55.3%). The remuneration rate rose significantly over the period 1980–85 when the NWC's high wage policy was implemented. The profit-to-remuneration ratio in Singapore in the late 1990s (1.11 in 1997) was the highest amongst the Asian newly-industrializing economies (compared with 1.05 for Hong Kong and 0.70 for Taiwan) and the developed economies (0.59 for the USA, 0.66 for Japan and 0.65 for Canada). This was interpreted as showing that the economy remained competitive and provided adequate returns for companies in Singapore. The recessionary environment of the late 1990s and the recovery had a strong impact on the structure of the economy. In 1998 33.9% of GDP was received by resident foreign companies and resident foreigners, but by 2000 this share had increased to 34.8%.

MANUFACTURING

Singapore's export-orientated policy, together with the constant pressure to move to higher levels of technology, has created a significant manufacturing sector based on a few important industries. Factories, as they are often built for high-technology, exporting MNCs, tend to be large, much bigger than those of Hong Kong. In terms of output, the average foreign company produces 12 times the amount of an average local firm. Foreign firms tend to be more profitable than local ones, with those in manufacturing in 1998—a year of declining demand—for example, making a rate of return on assets of 11.9% compared with the 3.6% rate achieved by local firms. Foreign firms produce about 76% of total manufacturing output. During 1965–84 manufacturing output increased at an average annual rate of 21%. After the global recession of 1985–86, growth resumed at a rate of 12% per annum until 1995. By 2000 manufacturing accounted for 25% of GDP and employed some 434,901 people. In 2000 electronics comprised 47.8% of manufacturing value added, chemicals and chemical products 15.8% and transport equipment and machinery 10.7%. Fabricated metal products account for 4.5% of manufacturing value added, petroleum products 4.8% and printing and publishing 3.6%. By far the most important electronic products are computer disk drives, followed by communications equipment and televisions. Direct exports constituted 64% of total manufacturing output in 1999. The export performance of the manufacturing sector is strongly influenced by world electronics demand, especially from the USA.

In the three years from 1998 to 2000 the growth rates of the manufacturing sector were 0.6%, 13.6% and 15.2%, and these were associated with GDP growth rates of 0.1%, 5.9% and 9.9%. Manufacturing was the most significant contributor to growth in these years and brought the economy out of recession. In these three years the growth rates of external demand, which is the largest component of demand, were 4.4%, 6.9% and 15.2%.

Those parts of the manufacturing sector that experienced rapid growth in 2000 were: electronics (25.2% growth); machinery and equipment (25.3%); rubber and plastic products (24.1%); and printing and publishing (13.7%). Chemicals and chemical products increased output only by 6.8% in 2000, having produced growth rates of 25.8%, 25.3% and 27.1% in the three years between 1997 and 1999. In 2001, however, there were some heavy falls in manufacturing, including electronics (11.5%), machinery and equipment (16.3%), chemicals and chemical products (21.3%) and rubber and plastic products (25.0%). Only transport equipment saw significant growth, with 23.0%. In 2001, according to the Asian Development Bank, the overall contribution of manufacturing to GDP declined slightly, to 22.1%.

Singapore is often criticized for over-reliance on electronics exports, but it must be remembered that 'electronics' is just a statistical categorization and that there has been restructuring within this sector with less reliance on items associated with older technologies, such as personal desk-top computers, and more investments from abroad in components for new technologies such as hand phones, portable computers and so on. The EDB has recently secured large commitments from Japanese companies to invest in these areas in Singapore. There are still large investment commitments for the manufacturing sector, generally in the currently favoured sectors of electronics and chemicals, and mostly from sources outside Singapore. Investment commitments in biomedical sciences comprised 9% of total manufacturing investment commitments in 2000. These inflows will continue to increase the supply-side capacity of the manufacturing sector significantly.

MONETARY SYSTEM AND POLICY

The Singapore dollar was first issued only in June 1967, nearly two years after nationhood. Singapore had previously been part of a currency union with Malaysia and Brunei, which had been operating for 29 years. In that month the three countries issued their own currencies and the Singapore dollar was interchangeable at par with the Malaysian ringgit and the Brunei dollar. The old Malaysian currency was withdrawn from circulation in Singapore by January 1969. After 1967 the three currencies could still be used in the other two countries at par. In June 1973, when the Singapore dollar was floated, it was delinked from the Malaysian ringgit but remained exchangeable at par against the Brunei dollar which was also delinked from the Malaysian ringgit. The Singapore and Brunei currencies (unlike the Malaysian ringgit) remain 'customary currencies', are exchangeable at par and can be used for transactions in either country.

The Singapore dollar is issued by the Board of Commissioners of Currency, Singapore (BCCS), established in April 1967, and not by the MAS, established in 1971, which is Singapore's de facto central bank and the regulator of the banking and financial sectors. For this reason it is sometimes said that Singapore still operates a currency board system. It is true that the BCCS maintains foreign reserves equal to more than the entire note and coin issue, so this aspect of a currency board system exists. (In fact, these reserves are not even managed by the BCCS, but by the government-owned company, Government of Singapore Investment Corporation Pte. Ltd, reflecting its importance in the saving-investment nexus in Singapore). It is generally agreed, however, that Singapore does not operate a currency board system as the authorities do not fix any exchange rate for the Singapore dollar against any currency or commodity, or against any clearly defined basket of currencies, and there is no mechanism to enable people to convert local currency at this rate. This view is sometimes challenged by the authorities in Singapore. The official statement of exchange rate policy is that the Singapore dollar is managed against an undefined basket of major relevant currencies, with the aim of achieving both price stability and international competitiveness. Singapore thus has a managed floating system. Official policy since the early 1980s has been to ensure a 'strong' dollar to offset any effects of imported inflation. Trade-weighted indexes of the value of the Singapore dollar show a long-term nominal and real appreciation. In mid-1998, a year after the onset of the Asian financial crisis, senior officials of the MAS placed on record their exchange-rate policy. They stressed that the value of the Singapore dollar was essentially set by market forces, but that the MAS would intervene to counter unwarranted speculation. The managed aspect of their policy is that it is managed within a band against a trade-weighted basket. Not only is the band quite wide, but it can be adjusted. Furthermore, even when the value of the dollar moves outside the band, this does not automatically mean that the MAS will intervene. Sharp movements might be counteracted, but generally there is no predetermined policy. Singapore has maintained persistent balance-of-payments surpluses since the early 1970s, implying excess demand for the currency at prevailing exchange rates. The MAS policy has been to intervene by selling Singapore dollars to prevent too rapid an appreciation of the local currency. This explains the steady increase in Singapore's official foreign-exchange reserves, which at the end of 2000 totalled S $139,260m. (US $80,362m.), 4% more than at the end of 1999, in US dollar terms. At the end of 2001 official foreign reserves increased slightly, to S $139,942m. (US $75,800m.).

INFLATION

In terms of its CPI and GDP deflator, Singapore has achieved a remarkable record of low and relatively stable inflation. Since the 1960s the average annual rate of inflation has been about 4%. Consequently, the 1999 consumer price level was only 2.9 more than its 1965 level. (In comparison, the USA's 1996 price level was 4.4 more than its 1965 level). There have been significant departures from this average, however. In 1973 the CPI increased by 19.6%, and in 1974 by 22%. These sharp increases were due to external factors such as commodity price increases (especially of food) and, subsequently, petroleum price increases. The second 'oil shock' raised the inflation rates for 1980 and 1981, to 8.5% and 8.2%, respectively. In the years 1995, 1996 and 1997 inflation rates were only 1.7%, 1.4% and 2.0%, respectively. The rate of inflation declined by 0.3% in 1998, and neither increased nor declined (using the new index) in 1999. The overall GDP deflator declined by 1.8% and 1.3% in 1998 and 1999, respectively. In 2000 the CPI rose by 1.3%, compared with 1999, with the rate subsiding slightly in 2001, to 1.0%. In 2002–03 deflationary effects were expected to force CPI downwards, with further redundancies expected and a continuing decline in the rate of growth of housing costs. The Economist Intelligence Unit projected a constant CPI rate in 2002, with an increase of 1.3% in 2003, when unemployment was expected to subside.

The main source of inflation in the 1990s was domestic, as monetary policy (that is exchange-rate policy) was aimed at offsetting any external inflationary pressures. Of the 2.0% increase recorded in 1997, it was estimated that 1.8% was due to domestic factors. Historically, many prices have been set by public-sector suppliers, and their changes were subject to government influence. The best statistical explanation of domestic inflation is the movement in Unit Labour Costs and these were reduced substantially after 1998 as an anti-recessionary policy.

When aspects of asset inflation are examined, the trends in the 1990s have been very different. There were significant increases in the prices of residential properties, with prices of both private and public housing approximately quadrupling over the period 1991–96. This led some economists to warn of the possibility of Singapore suffering from the problems of a 'bubble' economy, as was the case in Japan. In May 1996 the Government introduced measures aimed at halting the price rises. These included taxing gains on properties sold within three years of purchase, higher stamp dues on such sales, extending stamp duties to other sales and limiting the extent of housing loans to 80% of a property's value. These measures made owning a house less attractive, and thus reduced the price that potential buyers would be willing to pay. By 1998 private residential property prices were about 33% lower than their 1996 peak, but by 1999 had increased by 2.5% over the 1998 level. Office rentals in 1999 were as much as 25% lower than their 1996 level.

EXTERNAL TRADE AND BALANCE OF PAYMENTS

Singapore's export-orientated development strategy has resulted in a remarkable increase in its external trade volume (goods and services) from a total of S $7,698m. in 1965 (2.6 times that year's GDP) to S $485,986m., (63 times as much in nominal terms and 3.4 times GDP) in 1997. Total exports of goods and services in 1997 were 67 times their 1965 level and imports were 59 times their 1965 level, in nominal terms. Trade decelerated in 1998 to total S $405,689m., or 2.9 times GDP. Total trade in goods declined by 7.5% in that year, but increased by 8.1% in 1999 and then by 23% in 2000. In 2001, according to International Enterprise Singapore, external trade fell by 9.4% from 2000, to S $425,718m. The drop stemmed largely from a sharp downturn in global demand for electronics and the overall slowdown in the US economy. Trade in volume terms declined even further, by 10%, compared with 16% expansion in 2000. Similarly, export volume shrank by 8.6%, with domestic exports and re-exports contracting by 11% and 5.4%, respectively. Import volume also declined by 12%.

The composition of trade has changed. In 1965 food, crude materials and petroleum were the main export categories, contributing 51% of exports. In 1995 machinery and transport equipment comprised 66% of exports, and oil only 8.3%. Of the machinery and transport equipment exports, electronic components and parts accounted for 25%. In 1965 primary commodities comprised 55% of imports, but by 1995 machinery and transport equipment contributed 58% of imports and oil only 8.1%. Electronic components and parts accounted for 32% of machinery and transport equipment imports. Despite Singapore's establishment of a substantial manufacturing sector and the perceived decline in its entrepôt role, some economists still designate Singapore as a 're-export economy'. Strictly speaking, re-exports are those goods that are imported and then simply repackaged and exported elsewhere. In 2000 re-exports constituted of 43% of total exports, compared with 61% in 1970. However, many domestic exports, such as electronics, require the import of parts. Thus, machinery and transport equipment constitute the bulk of both imports and exports. Oil has declined from being 15.3% of total trade in 1980 to 9.3% in 2000. In 2000 electronic valves made up 25% of exports, data-processing machines 14.1%, petroleum products 9.3%, parts for office and data-processing machines 8.2%, telecommunication equipment 4.4%, electrical machinery and electrical circuits 4.9% and musical instruments and parts 1.8%. According to the IMF, a trade surplus of US $11,400m. was recorded in 2001 on a balance of payments basis. Exports totalled US $138,931m. and imports US $127,531m. Of the total major sectoral exports in 2001, according to the Ministry of Trade and Industry, machinery and equipment accounted for 64.5%, followed by chemicals (8.1%), manufactured goods (4.4%) and food (2.1%). Major imports commodities in 2001 were machinery and equipment (59.7%), manufactured goods (7.3%), chemicals (5.9%) and food (3.4%).

Singapore's exports are destined for geographically diverse countries in Asia, Europe and the Americas. This diversification has been an important factor in protecting the country to some extent from recession in one of these regions, although it did not help in 2001. Singapore's main export markets in 2000 were Malaysia (18.2%), USA (17.3%), the EU (13.2%), Hong Kong (7.9%) Japan (7.5%), Taiwan (6.0%), Thailand (4.3%), China (3.9%), the Republic of Korea (3.6%) and the Philippines (2.5%). Trade with Malaysia is highly correlated with global sales of computer chips and consists of cross-border shippings by MNCs who have plants in both Singapore and Malaysia.

Exports to the USA and Europe increased by 10.7% and 9.8% respectively in 2000, whereas those to China increased by 39.8%, Japan by 24.5%, the Republic of Korea by 40.7%, Taiwan by 49.8% and Viet Nam by 42.6%. Despite this shift, the deceleration in the USA in 2001 was the main factor in Singapore's own slowdown. In that year Malaysia accounted for 17.4% of exports, the USA 15.4% and Hong Kong 8.9%.

The sources of imports are slightly different, with Japan, Kuwait, China and Saudi Arabia being more important as sources of products than as export markets. Relevant shares of imports for 2000 were: Japan 17.2%; Malaysia 17.0%; the USA 15.1%; EU 11.3%; China 5.3%; Thailand 4.3%; Taiwan 4.4%; the Republic of Korea 3.6%; Saudi Arabia 3.2%; and Hong Kong 2.6%. There are no official statistics of trade between Singapore and Indonesia available from Singapore sources. The Government declined a request from a Nominated Member of Parliament in June 1998 to make public the trade statistics for Singapore and Indonesia. In 2001 Malaysia became the principal supplier of imports (comprising 17.3% of the total), followed by the USA (16.5%) and Japan (13.9%).

There are no taxes on international trade except for duties on vehicles, petrol, alcohol and tobacco. Singapore has adopted a policy to sign bilateral free-trade agreements with such countries as New Zealand, Australia, Japan and the USA, in an effort to encourage the membership of the Association of South East Asian Nations (ASEAN) to expand its trading and investment beyond the limits of the Association and the rules of the ASEAN Free Trade Area (AFTA). Pressure from the USA during current negotiations for a bilateral free-trade agreement are likely to lead to further liberalization of the financial and banking sectors.

Singapore has always had a positive services balance, and the export orientation of foreign MNCs in the manufacturing sector reduced the merchandise trade deficit significantly, so that by the mid 1980s the current account became positive. The goods balance itself became positive in the mid-1990s and the current account became extremely large, reaching 24% of GNP in 1999 and 22% in 2000.

The 1970s and 1980s witnessed large capital account surpluses because of the inflow of foreign direct investment. These inflows continue, but recently outward direct investment from Singapore has increased. The net capital account has been negative recently, but (as it is smaller than the current-account surplus) there have been substantial balance-of-payments surpluses. The current-account surplus increased from US $20,334m. in 1998 to US $21,750m. in 1999, rising slightly to US $21,797m. The overall balance-of-payments surplus declined from US $7,940m. in 1997, to US $2,965m. in 1998, but increased to US $4,194m. in 1999 and US $6,806m. In 2001 the balance of payments moved into deficit, which was estimated at US $894m.

EXCHANGE RATES

Owing to persistent balance-of-payments surpluses, there has been excess demand for the Singapore dollar, which has therefore appreciated against most currencies. Some of the appreciations have been very large. For example, since 1975, following the general floating of world currencies in 1973, the exchange rate against the US dollar has fallen from S $2.4895 to S $1.6755 at the end of 1997 (compared with S $1.3998 at the end of 1996). The pound sterling has decreased from S $5.0381 in 1975 to S $2.7771 at the end of 1997 and the Malaysian ringgit from S $0.9618 in 1975 (having been at par before 1973) to S $0.4307 at the end of 1997. The price of 100 Japanese yen rose from S $0.8161 in 1975 to S $1.2893 at the end of 1997.

Between the onset of the Asian financial crisis in July 1997 and mid-1998, the Singapore dollar appreciated markedly against the Thai baht (a 37% increase over 1997), Malaysian ringgit (38%), Korean won (30%) and Indonesian rupiah (410%). Given the MAS's statements that it manages the value of the Singapore dollar against a basket of currencies, it was clear that the depreciation against non-Asian countries was expected. The official position was that in 1997 the trade-weighted exchange rate remained 'relatively stable'. In 1999 the Singapore dollar continued to depreciate against the US dollar and the Japanese yen but, compared with significant depreciation against the pound sterling and the Deutsche Mark in 1998, the Singapore dollar appreciated slightly against them in 1999 while remaining at a lower value than in 1997. The Asian economic recovery of 1999 led to an appreciation of regional currencies against the Singapore dollar, which nevertheless, remained stronger against them in relation to 1997 when they had fallen significantly. As the Malaysian ringgit is effectively pegged to the US dollar and the Hong Kong dollar is linked to the US dollar, the Singapore dollar depreciated against these two regional currencies in 1999. The marked slowdown in the economy in 2001 resulted in a depreciation of the Singapore dollar against the US dollar. In March the MAS eased a number of currency controls on the Singapore dollar, as the exchange rate rose to an average of US $1 = S $1.7917 for the year. The exchange rate was expected to settle at about US $1 = S $1.75 in 2003.

FISCAL POLICY

The Government is committed to a policy of ensuring significant budget surpluses, defended by the view that the country's reserves are the mainstay of Singapore and overall budget surpluses were significant in the 1990s. The Government's economic policy is pro-business, but does not necessarily favour economic freedom. The Government has consistently used tax breaks and incentives in an attempt to attract MNCs and more specialized foreign enterprises into Singapore. In the 1990s income tax rates were reduced from a range of 2.5%–30% in 1994 to between 2% and 28% in 1997. The corporate tax rate was reduced to 27% in 1994 and from 1997 was further reduced to 26%. Income tax rebates were increased after the introduction of the goods and services tax at 3% in 1994. From 1 July 1996 the property tax rate was reduced from 13% to 12%. There is no capital gains tax, apart from a few exceptions such as when house selling is considered to be trading.

In May 2002 the Government announced broad tax reforms for business and individuals, in a budget intended to counteract the economic downturn of 2001, which had resulted from a sharp drop in external demand, particularly from the USA. The changes were designed to make Singapore more competitive by reducing business operating costs. The corporate tax rate has been reduced from 24.5% to 22%, making it much lower than China's 33%, Malaysia's 28% and Taiwan's 25%, though still above Hong Kong's 16% rate. Meanwhile, the tax rate for individuals has fallen from 26% to 22% (and will be reduced further to 20% within three years). The Government has also improved its incentive schemes. These include: lowering the minimum tax rate to 5% under the development and expansion initiative; and providing a double tax deduction for approved research and development expenses for all service companies. The Government was confident that these measures would be effective. There is no widespread public social security or unemployment benefit scheme. Publicly-funded pensions are available only to senior civil servants, members of the judiciary and parliament and military officers. The CPF scheme and private savings are supposed to provide for the retirement needs of the rest of the population, but this is privately, not publicly, funded (although the Government has occasionally 'topped up' certain accounts of citizens by small amounts in the manner of a company paying extra dividends), and government ministers admit that CPF savings are not sufficient for these needs and more reforms to the system are necessary. The Public Assistance Scheme provides very small benefits for the aged poor, the totally disabled and chronically ill, after a means test. The unemployed are supposed to finance themselves through savings or through the support of their family.

In the 1999 fiscal year most of the tax changes were to provide incentives for the financial sector to promote the bond market and 'boutique' funds' managers and for the organizers of international conferences in Singapore. As many people do not pay any income tax in Singapore, they were helped through rebates on the rentals of public housing and reductions in local authority service and conservancy charges on households. In the budget for the fiscal year 2000 the corporate tax rate was permanently lowered to 25.5%, to be effective from the following tax year. The prevailing rate in 1999 was 26%, but with the one-off rebates the effective rate payable by companies was 23.4%. The tax rebate of that year would be withdrawn. A 10% personal tax rebate was given in 1999, but this was reduced to 5% in the budget of 2000. In that budget the Government also announced a S $250 'top-up' to be paid into citizens' CPF accounts. An innovation to the CPF scheme announced in the budget was to allow voluntary additional contributions by employees into their CPF accounts, under a Supplementary Retirement Scheme that would be tax deductible and taxable on withdrawals. Whether this would prove to be attractive was debatable as returns paid on CPF funds have been virtually zero in real terms. Furthermore, a voluntary Special Retirement Scheme was established by 2001, enabling foreigners to make tax-deductible contributions, which would be taxed on withdrawal. In August 2000 the Government announced that it would use S $2,000m. to enhance the CPF accounts of all adult Singaporean citizens who had paid at least S $100 into their CPF accounts between 1 January 1998 and 31 December 2000. Instead of the usual method of an equal payment for all (as the 2000 budget had given), this time those earning more than S $2,000 a month would receive S $500, those earning between S $1,200 and S $2,000 would receive S $1,000 and those earning less than S $1,200 would receive S $1,500. The self-employed and those whose incomes could be ascertained from CPF records would receive the enhancement according to the type of house they lived in. The payments were to be made in two instalments, with the first being in January 2001.

In July 2002 the CPF proposed changes to its S $64,000m. (US $36,000m.) national pension system, which might boost the stock market but at the cost of weakening property prices. The economic review committee has proposed shifting pension savings from property to financial investments in an effort gain better returns. The Government has no plans to scale back contributions to the CPF, which amounted to some 40% of a worker's annual salary in 2002.

In 2000 government operating revenue and tax revenue both increased by 17%. The budget announced in February 2001 took advantage of this and was welcomed as pro-local business and the best ever. The corporate tax rate was reduced from 25.5% to 24.5%, against all expectations, since a rate below 25% is considered by some countries to be unfair and to denote the country as a tax haven. The top marginal income tax rate was reduced from 28% to 26% and the property tax rate was reduced from 12% to 10%.

FINANCIAL AND BUSINESS SERVICES

The financial part of this sector consists of banking, insurance, stockbroking, fund management and currency and futures trading and so on and the business part of such activities as real estate, legal services, advertising, consultancies, information technology services and so on. These two sectors' combined contribution to GDP increased from 16.6% in 1965 to about 25% of GDP in 1997, after rapid growth in 1996 and 1997. Employment in this sector prior to the Asian financial crisis totalled 273,500 people and was equivalent to some 15% of total employment. In 1998 output in the financial services sector contracted by 8.1% while business services grew by 5.1%; in 1999 financial services experienced no growth and business services expanded by just 0.1%. In 2000 financial services grew by 4.1% and business services by 6.6%. In the same year financial services employment increased by 8,100 and business services employed 23,200 more people. In 2001 financial and business services together contributed 26.1% of total GDP.

The financial sector's development was aided by government policy and tax concessions. In 1968, responding to suggestions by a US bank, the Government allowed the establishment within banks and merchant banks of departments known as Asian Currency Units (ACUs). These are separate legal and accounting departments of the banks in which they are located and were given special tax treatment, and this has continued over the years thus contributing to their rapid growth. They operate in the Asian dollar market. At the end of 1997 their total assets/ liabilities, at US $557,194m., were 1,429 times their 1970 level. In 1998 the assets of the Asian dollar market contracted by 9.6% and in 1999 by 4.6% as non-bank customers wished to borrow much less.

Other important parts of the financial sector have been the Stock Exchange of Singapore (SES), the foreign-exchange market and the financial futures market, formerly known as the Singapore International Monetary Exchange (SIMEX). SIMEX started operations in September 1984 and has established links with the Chicago Mercantile Exchange through its system of mutual offsets. It is said to be the first financial futures exchange in Asia, as it assumed the functions of the Gold Exchange of Singapore, which had earlier commenced financial futures trading. On 1 December 1999, following the demutualization of both stock and futures exchanges, SIMEX and the SES were merged to form a new company known as Singapore Exchange Limited (SGX), which presents itself as the first demutualized, integrated securities and derivatives exchange in the Asia-Pacific region. There were plans to make a public offer of its shares after a private placement, so that up to 65% of its shares could be placed with foreign investors. Its majority shareholders were former members of the SES and SIMEX, who were expected to retain about 35% of the shares.

The first stages of the Asian financial crisis brought business to the financial markets in 1997, which witnessed high turnover on the foreign-exchange market and stock exchange, increased earnings and rapid growth of the financial sector. In 1998 the turnover of the stock exchange was 14% lower than in 1997. The domestic market recovered in 1999 when the value of turnover on the Singapore Exchange Securities Trading (SGX-ST, formerly the SES) more than doubled to reach S $197,000m. In 1999 the trading volume of derivative contracts on the Singapore Exchange Derivatives Trading (SGX-DT, formerly SIMEX) declined by 7.2% from the record level of 1998. In June 2000 the SGX-DT launched a futures contract based on the Straits Times Index, the second product to be based on that index in Singapore. The SGX-DT offers the widest range of Asian stock index futures in the world, and three new contracts were introduced in 1999, with plans to increase the number of products considerably in the future. About 86% of its trade was derived from outside Singapore. The foreign-exchange market in 2000 recorded an average daily turnover of just below US $100,000m., which was 19% below the 1999 level, which itself was 19% below that of the previous year. The volume of foreign-exchange transactions in Singapore ranks it as the fourth busiest in the world. Trade is mainly of US dollars against the Japanese yen and the US dollar against the euro. These two trades account for 48% of total turnover. These changes in business were responsible for the overall zero growth of the financial services sector in 1999.

Responding to long-held beliefs that the financial sector has been over-regulated by the MAS and other authorities, stifling development and innovation, the Government established the Financial Sector Review Group in 1997, and the recommendations of its subcommittees were publicized during 1998. The Corporate Finance Committee recommended a move towards a US system of fuller disclosure by companies, with investors taking more responsibility for their own decisions. Overall, securities regulation should be removed from the Stock Exchange of Singapore, the Securities Industry Council and other bodies and responsibility centralized in the MAS in a 'super regulator'. It was felt that the Singapore Exchange had been taking into account too many restrictive criteria when deciding whether a listing should be allowed. Other recommendations included consolidating securities market laws and updating them, promoting listings by foreign and smaller local companies, encouraging the use of technology and encouraging internet trading.

In recent years the Government's policies to increase the presence of fund managers in Singapore, through favourable tax treatment and making funds available for them to manage, have begun to yield noticeable results. The Government also accepted the recommendation to issue a 10-year government bond to establish a benchmark for the yield curve. This would facilitate the corporate issue of bonds. In 2000 further issues of government bonds were to be made for this purpose. Following the recommendations of a Committee on Banking Disclosure Standards, most of which were accepted by the Government, local banks will be required to stop the practice of keeping hidden reserves. Furthermore, the limit of S $200m. put on loans to residents by foreign banks was increased to S $300m. for each bank in any year and was subsequently further raised to S $1,000m. In 1998 further liberalization of the banking system took place and by the end of 2001 the Government had issued six new licences for a new category of banks, known as as Qualifying Full Banks. As the foreign banks cannot share the automated teller machines (ATM) network of the local banks their ability to compete is restricted.

The limit of 40% on foreign ownership of Singapore bank shares was removed in 1999, and also in that year all banks were allowed to offer interest on current accounts and the restrictions on the size and duration of fixed deposits they could accept was removed. The view within the industry is that the pace of liberalization is rather slow and that the degree of competition has not significantly increased, while the main four foreign banks that received licences had not co-operated in setting up their own ATM network.

The Government declared its commitment to a five-year plan of consolidating the banking sector and allowing more competition. In July 1998 the Post Office Savings Bank system (a statutory board) was merged with the Development Bank of Singapore (DBS) for S $1,600m. The Chairman of the MAS, one of the two Deputy Prime Ministers, Brig.-Gen. Lee Hsien Loong, received praise from the foreign financial community for this liberalization of the banking sector and for the realization that competition is better than protection at this stage of development. In June 2000 the Government announced that it would introduce legislation to require local banks to divest themselves of all non-core assets within three years, signalling that, as voluntary compliance with government suggestions had not been adopted, legislation would be used. These assets are mainly in the property development and manufacturing sectors. The government view is that there is only room for two domestic banks in Singapore, and in mid-2001 there was an unprecedented frenzy of hostile takeover activities, resulting in two large, private, local banks merging to become larger than the DBS.

Liberalization has been extended to the insurance industry, which had been protected by the Government. Only one company had been allowed to enter the industry since 1986, a policy that the Government now recognizes 'stifled new products and efficiency'. In 1999 there was strong growth in the insurance sector, and rapid growth continued in 2000, with most of the new business coming from outside Singapore. The domestic market continued to experience declines in rates owing to increased competition. In September 1998 Malaysia linked its currency to the US dollar and imposed capital controls. One consequence was that the holdings of some 170,000 people with shares in Malaysian companies that were traded on Singapore's Central Limit Order Book International Market (CLOB) were 'frozen'. An arrangement was reached (accepted by 94% of the owners who owned 98% of the shares), providing for the gradual release of their shares from June 2000 in weekly batches over 13 weeks. This issue and its solution elicited strong expressions of discontent from the Singapore shareholders, who were highly critical of the Stock Exchange, the Government and the Malaysian authorities.

On 1 July 2002 the second stage of the Securities and Futures Act 2001 (SFA) went into effect. Under the new measures, intended to improve disclosure and streamline the listing process, companies must submit prospectuses to the MAS rather than the Singapore Exchange. There were 32 initial public offers in the first nine months of 2001. This represented a decline from the 47 new listings that had come to market in the same period in 2000. A total of 85 public offers took place in 2000, compared with 53 in 1999 and 24 in 1998. Six foreign firms were listed on the Singapore Exchange in the year to August 2001, increasing the total number of locally listed foreign firms to 90.

TOURISM

Although Singapore has few areas of natural beauty, it has always been an important tourist destination, mainly for those going in transit or who include a visit to Singapore as part of a trip to some combination of Indonesia, Malaysia and Thailand. By 2000 the average length of stay by a tourist was 3.2 days, having declined steadily since the early 1990s, and was much shorter than the length of visits to such places as Indonesia and the Philippines at 10 days each and Thailand at 7.4 days. Average per caput daily expenditure has also fallen since the early 1990s. Combining a modern, efficient city with diverse examples of Asian culture, it has been called 'Asia for beginners'. For many years Singapore was promoted as a 'shoppers' paradise' but, despite the continuing annual 'Great Singapore Sale' in May and June or July, this aspect has faded, mainly owing to the appreciation of the Singapore dollar. Visitors can obtain a rebate of the goods and services tax on purchases of more than S $300 in any participating retail outlet. During the economic crisis tourism, and hence the retail and hotel sectors, suffered from the strength of the Singapore dollar, the decline in incomes in neighbouring countries and the return of smoke pollution from forest fires in Indonesia, which was particularly bad in September and October of that year. The impact on the economy continued into 1998. The total of 7,197,871 visitors in 1997 was 1.3% lower than in 1996, but in 1998 this number decreased to 6,242,152, 13.3% less than in 1997. In 1999 the number of visitors rose to 6,958,201, an increase of 11.5%, and in 2000 by 10.5%, to reach 7,691,399. In 2001 the number of visitor arrivals contracted by 2.2%, to an estimated 7,518,584. At more than 83% in 2000, the hotel occupancy rate in the second quarter of 2002 averaged 75%, a year-on-year decline of 2.9% compared with 2001, but still above its its lowest rate of 71.3% in 1998. Total revenue from the sector increased from US $5,162m. in 1998 to US $5,974m. in 1999, and to an estimated US $6,370m. in 2000.

The Tourism 21 plan, adopted by the Singapore Tourist Promotion Board (STPB), featured more promotions with neighbouring Asian countries and Western Australia. One aspect of its marketing is to link tourism with Singapore's plans to become an arts hub ('Global city for the arts' being the slogan), and tourist promotions have been linked to Singapore's hosting of popular musical and theatrical events. Another important aspect of tourism development is the promotion of Singapore as the location for major international conferences, conventions and exhibitions. The successful hosting of the inaugural World Trade Organization's Ministerial Conference in December 1996 provided much publicity and experience. A new exhibition centre near Changi International Airport began operations in 1999, adding to the substantial convention facilities near the Central Business District that were completed in the mid-1990s. Singapore has ranked as Asia's foremost convention centre since the mid-1980s and is regarded as one of the best in the world.

INFRASTRUCTURE

With such a huge volume of trade and people passing through such a small place, and with the need to provide international communications together with the building of factories, infrastructural development has been crucial to Singapore's overall progress. In the 1990s construction output accounted for an average of about 6.5% of GDP, having reached as much as 10% of GDP in 1985 as a result of a boom in public-sector housing and a decline in overall GDP in that year. Although construction output rose by 15.3% in 1997, it increased by only 4.4% in 1998, declined by about 9% in 1999 and continued to contract by 4.6% in 2000. This contraction in 1999 was mainly due to a significant reduction in public-sector contracts. In 2001 the construction sector contributed 5.8% of GDP, compared with 5.9% in 2000. The Government has launched Construction 21, a strategic plan to restructure Singapore's construction industry which, it has admitted, has suffered from negative productivity growth and heavy reliance on unskilled foreign workers.

There are some significant projects under way that will add considerably to supply-side capacity. To the south of Singapore extensive reclamation by the JTC continues between a group of seven islands. This will produce a 3,000 ha petrochemical complex, Jurong Island, to be completed by 2015. The area is already used for refining, petrochemical and chemical production and will become the main site for this important part of Singapore's industrial sector as envisioned in the EDB's plans. Singapore's first petroleum refinery had been established by Shell in 1961 on the small island of Pulau Bukum.

Singapore obtains about one-half of its water supply from Malaysia. Whenever political tensions arise between Malaysia and Singapore, fears are expressed that Malaysia might discontinue water supplies and not renew the two supply agreements, which expire in the years 2011 and 2061, although Malaysia has stated that it will renew the contracts, whatever the circumstances. Singapore is building a water desalination plant in Tuas and has plans for two more before the year 2011. New technology has recently been introduced to recycle waste water into potable supplies. It is possible that a scheme to build a 200-km pipeline from Indonesia to deliver water to Singapore will be undertaken and is scheduled to be completed by 2005. Furthermore, treated sewage is to be processed into 'new water', which is pure enough to be used by the very high technological level wafer fabrication plants that Singapore is still attracting.

Transport

In February 1996 six new stations and 16 kms of track were added to the railway system, the Mass Rapid Transit (MRT) system operated by the MRTC, which was a statutory board before September 1995, when it was reconstituted as part of the Land Transport Authority. In December 1996 work commenced on the 20-km North–East line, which was to add 16 underground stations and connect with the existing system at two central stations, with some stations also being developed into offices and retail developments. Originally due to open in 2004, the North–East line was likely to be completed in 2006. A new 6.4-km. line, linking the East–West line with Changi International Airport, was completed in 2001. Another central line was scheduled for completion in 2004. Light Rapid Transit (LRT) systems were under construction to link new towns to the wider MRT network. By 2005 the MRT/LRT system was expected to cover an area 50% greater than in 2000.

Designs for the planned third terminal for Changi International Airport at Changi were made public in 1998, and construction commenced in October 2000. The new terminal was due to open in 2006, with the two existing terminals being upgraded in the meantime. However, with air passenger traffic declining 3.4% in the first quarter of 2002, this deadline could be extended, or even abandoned. Airport development depends in part on the fortunes of Singapore Airlines (SIA), the national carrier. SIA has expanded its business interests significantly through a 49% share in the British carrier Virgin Atlantic. Nevertheless, in September 2002 Mitsubishi Heavy Industries and Mitsubishi Corporation of Japan gained a US $76.87m. order from the Civil Aviation Authority of Singapore for a new automated people mover (APM) for Changi International Airport. The order involved 6.4 km of elevated track for an APM that connected the three terminals of Changi Airport, shuttling airport users via unmanned rubber-wheeled trains. Installation was due for completion by June 2006.

Work on a major extension of the container port at Pasir Panjang has been undertaken. Singapore was developing the port's facilities to cope with large cruise ships, as the country sought to become a regional hub for this expanding leisure industry. Singapore remains the busiest port in the world in terms of shipping tonnage and is the world's largest supplier of bunkers (fuel used by ships). However, the decision by Taiwan's Evergreen Marine Corporation in April 2002 to move its transhipment business to Tanjung Pelepas in Malaysia, following Denmark's Maersk Sealand International, which moved in 2000, has slowed down the process to privatize the Port of Singapore Authority and could affect future port development.

In January 1998 a new toll road bridge, financed equally by Singapore and Malaysia and linking the west of Singapore to Malaysia, was opened. This was intended to reduce congestion on the existing causeway that provides road, rail and water pipeline links to Malaysia. The new link is, so far at least, surprisingly underutilized, with Malaysian commercial drivers citing the cost of the toll and the longer travelling distances as the main reasons for not using it. Malaysia was therefore considering legislation to require lorries to use the new link.

Singapore's high volume of trade requires a good, uncongested road system. This has been planned since 1990 by strictly controlling the growth in the number of vehicles through a government-determined quota for vehicles sales. In order to buy a vehicle, buyers must purchase at a monthly auction a Certificate of Entitlement (COE). In early 2000 a COE for a luxury car cost between S $43,000 and S $51,000 and for a small car about S $42,000. This non-proportionality to the price of the car has made large cars relatively cheaper in Singapore. There are, however, plans to change the nature of the auction system used to allocate COEs. In addition, substantial import duties contribute to high car prices.

In addition to the quota system, the Government tries to influence road usage by charging drivers for access to such areas as the Central Business District (CBD). This has been done by requiring drivers to buy and display a licence either for daily or monthly use. In April 1998 road pricing took a technological leap with the introduction of what is said to be the world's first use of Electronic Road Pricing (ERP), although this claim has been disputed. Access to the roads currently subject to charges requires vehicles to be fitted with an in-vehicle unit (IU) on the dashboard that can be read by cameras placed at points on the restricted roads. Units were supplied and fitted free for a limited period. Drivers of cars visiting Singapore can hire the units. Charges for usage are deducted from a cash card placed in the unit. Charges for access vary according to the time of day. Overall, the Government aims for 3% growth in the vehicle population each year, adjusting the number of COEs accordingly. However, the Government has stated that if this system of road pricing keeps the roads free of congestion, it might increase the number of COEs in the future.

Communications

Efficient telecommunications are vital for a financial and trading centre such as Singapore. Plans for a more competitive telecommunications system became clearer in April 1998. After a competitive bidding process, a licence for fixed-line telecommunications, along with one for mobile phone operations, was awarded to StarHub, which is owned by Singapore Technologies Communications (34.5%), Singapore Power (22.5%), British Telecom (20%) and Nippon Telegraph & Telephone (20%). Originally it was planned that StarHub would be the sole competitor for the former monopoly supplier, SingTel, from 1 April 2000 for two years. The Government compensated SingTel for the earlier than agreed loss of its monopoly by granting it S $1,500m. However, in January 2000, in an unexpected move, the Government announced that it would no longer stand by its original commitment and announced that from 1 April it would open up the telecommunications market. The Government also announced that it would appoint advisers to suggest the extent of compensation appropriate for the two companies that would be affected and in September awarded compensation of S $859m. to SingTel and S $1,082m. to StarHub. Furthermore, it insisted that StarHub install the nation-wide infrastructure to serve the fixed-line residential customers. Despite the fear that this change of policy might discourage further foreign investment in Singapore, the Government stated that it thought this liberalization would bring in S $3,000m. in further investment and 2,500 new jobs over three years. Within a few months of the change in policy 58 new licences had been issued, and competition had reduced phone rates and increased the variety of products.

One of SingTel's major current investments is through its subsidiary City-to-City, which has awarded contracts for the construction of a 17,000-km cable network, at a cost of US $2,000m., to link Hong Kong, Japan, the Republic of Korea, Taiwan, the Philippines, Singapore and, it is hoped, the People's Republic of China. This is necessary to deal with the expected rapid growth in internet usage. Mobile phones and pagers are widely used, and Singapore in 2000 probably still had the highest penetration rate for pagers in the world. The rate reached 76.7% in September 2001, according to Singapore's new statutory board, the Infocommunications Development Authority of Singapore (IDA). However, this had fallen to 68.9% by November 2001 after SingTel started to close more than 650,000 inactive accounts. Singapore's IT2000 plan includes the development of Singapore ONE (One Network for Everyone), which will link the entire population through developing a multimedia broadband infrastructure. Officially launched in June 1998, and initiated by the Government, private-sector participation is being encouraged. Singapore ONE now has more than 250,000 users; and according to a local internet research firm, NetValue, from October 2001 to March 2002 the number of broadband users rose 35% to 172,000, with 71,000 households connected. Overall, there are over 35 internet service providers (ISPs) and 20 International Simple Resellers (ISRs) selling overseas calls. At the end of 2000 the number of internet users, at 2.2m., was nearly three times the number in 1999. Research by NetValue conducted in September 2001 also indicated that one-third of those 'wired' Singaporeans now use online banking services.

The Government is promoting the growth of electronic commerce, and some international companies have located their Asian headquarters for electronic commerce in Singapore. These developments are being encouraged by the IDA, which had been created by the merger of the National Computer Board and the Telecommunications Authority of Singapore in December 1999. The IDA promotes greater use of information technology in Singapore, and even has a strategic planning branch that is responsible for anticipating new developments in 'hot' areas such as broadband and mobile commerce. In a bid to boost Singapore's competitiveness in international electronic commerce, the IDA has encouraged businesses to invest more heavily in the information technology sector. In 2000 total business spending in information communications and the media industry increased by 29% year-on-year to reach S $730m. The IDA itself introduced a S $30m. incentive programme in October 2000 to encourage businesses to increase their electronic commerce levels. The same month, the IDA also launched 'Wired with Wireless', a S $200m. programme to give Singapore a fully integrated wired and wireless infrastructure.

Training and Research

Education and training have always been an important part of Singapore's supply-side policies. The public sector dominates although there are private schools, mainly in commercial, computing and fine arts education. At the tertiary level many students can study through correspondence and internet courses with foreign universities, and the Singapore Institute of Management (SIM) offers Open University courses. At the post-secondary level the four polytechnics, two universities and the Institute of Technical Education are all Statutory Boards under the Ministry of Education. From 2000 students will be able to enter the privately-run Singapore Management University (SMU). In mid-2000 the number of students at Singapore's three universities totalled 49,856, and there were 58,374 students at the four polytechnics. There were plans of establishing a fourth university and a fifth polytechnic was to open in 2003. Foreign business schools from the USA and Europe are also establishing campuses in Singapore. Recently, schools have been encouraging creative thinking, while at higher levels emphasis has been placed on research. More junior colleges will be built and the aim is that by 2010 25% of Primary One students will eventually reach a local university, rather than the current 20%.

It has long been observed that the amount spent on research and development has been rather low compared with other countries. In the past much of the research expenditure from which Singapore benefited was probably being made in other locations, but many MNCs and local companies have started conducting research and development in Singapore. Total research and development expenditure reached 1.9% of GDP in 1999, a higher rate than in 1998. Most of the research and development is being carried out by the private sector (63% of the total in 1999) and mainly in the areas of electronics, chemicals, engineering, information technology and telecommunications. The electricity market was to be liberalized and it was expected that foreign firms were to establish power generation companies.

THE CURRENT SITUATION AND SINGAPORE'S PROSPECTS

The economy of Singapore is small, open and heavily dependent upon foreign capital, expertise and workers, as well as upon overseas markets. It is often argued that the Republic's manufacturing sector is too dependent upon the electronics sub-sector; this is a cause for concern, as the demand for electronic products is cyclical. Other sectors such as petroleum and tourism are similarly vulnerable: tourism, which is very important to both the retail and transport sectors, is susceptible to regional and international instability, as demonstrated by the impact of the terrorist attacks on the USA in September 2001. The tourism sector has also suffered from the effects of smoke pollution in the region since the late 1990s, particularly in late 1997. This pollution has recurred on several occasions since then, but to a milder extent in Singapore than in neighbouring countries, most notably in July 2000. This has prompted the Government to review the National Green Plan (launched in 1991), in which it aimed to: limit carbon dioxide emissions to their 1991 level by 2000; phase out controlled chlorofluorocarbons (CFCs) by 2000; and tighten safety procedures on the storage, handling and transport of hazardous products. The authorities have made some progress in these areas, including the ban on CFCs in 1996, the phasing out of leaded petrol in 1998 and the implementation of new anti-pollution regulations in January 2001. However, environmental degradation remained a priority, particularly with continuing problems from smog caused by forest fires. The Government has therefore presented new National Green Plan targets for 2012. Four key areas, agreed following public consultations in 2001, have been identified: 'quality living environment' (limiting air pollution, increasing the use of natural gas, reducing landfill levels through increased recycling); 'working in partnership with the community' (building greater community responsibility and gathering public feedback); reducing noise levels; and 'doing our part for the global environment' (helping to enforce international environmental commitments).

The region has shown greater political instability and violence in the last few years. Foreign demand can be rather unstable and consists of about 80% of the demand for Singapore's output. The domestic market is small, and personal consumption (at about 40% of expenditure on GDP) is much lower than in other developed economies. Domestic demand is also vulnerable to changes in the stock market and in property prices. The Singaporean economy has been affected by the industrialization and liberalization of the economies of neighbouring countries, and by their competition for foreign direct investment, some of which has come from Singapore, but some of which has been committed by sources that might otherwise have chosen to invest in Singapore. The Government is particularly concerned by the threat posed by China as a potentially more desirable destination for foreign investments. In view of the above, it might be construed that the economy of Singapore is by nature very vulnerable and might therefore have been likely to suffer rather badly as a result of the Asian economic crisis that began in 1997. However, Singapore was the Asian country least affected by the crisis in terms of growth rates, inflation and unemployment; the deceleration in the economy could be attributed to the external factors that had repercussions through trade and tourism and not to any inherent problems in the economy. Foreign direct investment commitments did not decline significantly during the crisis years. The supply capacity of the economy continues to expand significantly.

In 2000, according to the Asian Development Bank, the economy increased by 10.3%, its highest rate since 1994, with manufacturing expanding by 15.2% and the services sector by 8.8%. Many of the vulnerabilities of the economy that have long been discussed came to prominence in 2001. Capital investment in the USA fell in late 2000 and Singapore's exports and manufacturing output were affected very quickly. In 2001 GDP contracted by 2.0%.

On the economic side, the Government introduced an off-budget set of policies in July 2001 similar to earlier policies aimed at reducing business costs and maintaining the profitability of firms. This package included reductions in charges by government agencies, rental rebates and grants to companies of up to S $600 a month for hiring retrenched workers. Plans to fully restore the employers' CPF rate were postponed. In addition, some public sector projects were brought forward. At a value of S $2,200m., this package was about 1.4% of GDP, much less than that required at the time of the Asian financial crisis. The co-operative trade union movement, through its chain of supermarkets, decided to reduce the prices of a range of staple commodities to help the lower-paid population. The CPF and HDB have said they will reschedule mortgage payments for families that experience financial difficulties. The Government is preparing the population for a possible long period of slow growth, increased retrenchments and higher unemployment. Mergers in the banking sector are likely to lead to retrenchments there. The global electronics slowdown has led many foreign MNCs to retrench workers in their foreign operations, including in Singapore. In the first half of 2001 there were about 9,000 retrenchments, of which 40% were in the electronics sector, and total retrenchments for that year reached 26,500. In the past, MNCs that closed down production operations in Singapore would often relocate them to Malaysia. The Government fears that the future destination of these jobs will be China, but the nature of globalization is illustrated by the fact that, when one US telecommunications equipment company recently closed down its manufacturing operations in Singapore, it relocated them to Ireland. The Government retains its strong commitment to helping retrenched workers learn new skills, but if the electronics sector contracts much more, they may be forced into lower-level service jobs. The Government has told older workers not to be too selective when searching for new employment.

In the wake of the feared slowdown of 2001, the Prime Minister has reiterated his aim to create a 'New Singapore' within 10 years. This 'New Singapore' will be a global city ('globapolis') with people from all over the world well connected to all parts of the globe. There will be abundant opportunities for Singaporeans and talented foreigners to work, do well and enjoy excellent recreational and artistic facilities. Singapore's economic activity will expand beyond its limited space and this restricted size will not restrain its growth but will encourage it to become one of the world's most habitable cities. Foreign advisers had long supported a move towards a more service-based economy and more entertainment and artistic venues that would attract foreign professionals.

The main policies required for this were to increase the productivity and standards of service of the domestic sector, which is behind that of the MNCs and other foreign firms in Singapore. Diversification away from electronics was required. The Prime Minister also argued that the country needed to alter its entire mindset. Singaporeans needed to be more innovative, rather than merely copying the ideas of others, and should be more willing to take risks and to expand further into the region. Towards this end he argued that Singaporeans should accept non-conformist thinking, be more tolerant of people who make mistakes in their business affairs and not be resentful of private entrepreneurs who 'make it big.' (Income distribution has become more unequal during the 1990s and the Government expects the income gap to widen further.) To encourage innovation, and here, the Prime Minister acknowledged the irony of using a 'top-down' approach, the Government would establish the National Innovation Council (NIC). Another irony was that Parliament was simultaneously passing legislation that would restrict the ability of internet web sites not registered as political organizations to discuss and endorse politicians.

The Prime Minister promised that this 'New Singapore', in which competition would become increasingly fierce, would also be accompanied by a 'new social compact' with the people. The Government would continue to subsidize housing, education and healthcare. In addition, it would introduce 'New Singapore' shares' that would be distributed to all citizens and would provide a guaranteed dividend for a fixed number of years and a bonus when the economy did well. On 1 March 2002 the CPF credited a total of 12,340,000 New Singapore Shares (NSS) to the accounts of 2,080,000 NSS shareholders. Each shareholder earned a dividend ranging from 1 to 17 bonus NSS, according to the number of shares held as of mid-February.

In December 2001 the Government launched the Economic Review Committee (ERC), which was to give an open assessment of economic strategy by September 2002. The ERC and its affiliated bodies made a number of recommendations throughout the first nine months of 2002, including advice included in the 2002/03 budget, which was presented to Parliament in May 2002. The ERC's main goal is to boost economic recovery and make Singapore more competitive in the region. There will be further liberalization in the banking and power generation sectors and the Government will have to learn how to regulate these sectors rather than being the producer itself. Furthermore, the Government might have to deal with a protracted slowdown and rising unemployment, possibly accompanied by a significant and permanent loss of manufacturing jobs, without an immediate increase in suitable service sector jobs. The Government has continually expressed the need to attract foreign talent into those sectors it hopes will expand, such as life sciences, which require skilled personnel and researchers. There is likely to be a greater foreign presence in the financial and service sectors. The local banking takeovers showed a definite culture clash with the US advisers to the DBS, who discussed in a way considered too blunt the nature of local bank management. The Government has envisaged a more competitive, free market environment in which there is likely to be a greater foreign presence in areas that were reserved for local firms. In the period before a general election, the Government has more than usual to manage. Many of the latest features of the proposed 'New Singapore' are in stark contrast to those believed by some observers to have brought about its economic success thus far.

Statistical Survey

Source (unless otherwise stated): Department of Statistics, 100 High St, 05-01 The Treasury, Singapore 179434; tel. 63327686; fax 63327689; e-mail info@singstat.gov.sg; internet www.singstat.gov.sg.

Area and Population

AREA, POPULATION AND DENSITY

Area (sq km)	659.9*
Population (census results)†	
30 June 1990	3,047,132‡
30 June 2000	
Males	2,061,800§
Females	1,955,900§
Total	4,017,733
Population (official estimates at mid-year)	
1998	3,865,600
1999	3,893,600
2001	4,131,200
Density (per sq km) at mid-2001	6,260.3

* 254.8 sq miles.

† Includes non-residents, totalling 311,264 in 1990 and 754,524 in 2000.

‡ Includes resident population temporarily residing overseas.

§ Provisional.

ETHNIC GROUPS (at census of 30 June 2000)*

	Males	Females	Total
Chinese	1,245,782	1,259,597	2,505,379
Malays	228,174	225,459	453,633
Indians	134,544	123,247	257,791
Others	21,793	24,613	46,406
Total	1,630,293	1,632,916	3,263,209

* Figures refer to the resident population of Singapore.

BIRTHS, MARRIAGES AND DEATHS*

	Registered live births		Registered Marriages		Registered deaths	
	Number	Rate (per 1,000)	Number	Rate (per 1,000)†	Number	Rate (per 1,000)
1993	50,225	15.4	25,298	7.8	14,461	4.4
1994	49,554	14.7	24,662	7.3	14,946	4.4
1995	48,635	14.0	24,974	7.2	15,569	4.5
1996	48,577	13.4	24,111	6.7	15,590	4.3
1997	47,333	12.7	25,667	6.9	15,307	4.1
1998	43,838	11.3	23,106	6.0	15,656	4.1
1999	43,193	11.1	25,648	6.6	15,516	4.0
2000	46,631	11.6	22,561	5.6	15,692	3.9

* Data are tabulated by year of registration, rather than by year of occurrence.

† Provisional.

Source: mainly UN, *Demographic Yearbook*.

Expectation of life (WHO estimates, years at birth, 2000): Males 75.4; Females 80.2 (Source: WHO, *World Health Report*).

ECONOMICALLY ACTIVE POPULATION
('000 persons aged 15 years and over, at June of each year)

	1998	1999	2000
Agriculture, hunting, forestry and fishing	4.3	5.5	5.1
Mining and quarrying	1.5	1.4	0.7
Manufacturing	404.4	395.6	434.9
Electricity, gas and water supply	8.2	8.9	7.1
Construction	131.3	130.7	274.0
Wholesale and retail trade; repair of motor vehicles, motorcycles and personal and household goods	281.2	278.9	286.8
Hotels and restaurants	118.9	121.2	114.5
Transport, storage and communications	206.4	203.7	196.5
Financial intermediation	108.5	104.6	96.3
Real estate, renting and business activities	184.3	196.8	226.2
Public administration and defence; compulsory social security	118.5	121.9	105.9
Education, health and social work	137.5	142.0	127.4
Other community, social and personal service activities; private households with employed persons	161.9	172.4	217.3
Extra-territorial organizations and bodies	2.7	2.3	2.1
Total employed	1,869.7	1,885.9	2,094.8
Unemployed	62.1	90.1	97.5
Total labour force	1,931.8	1,976.0	2,192.3
Males	1,125.1	1,138.6	1,324.3
Females	806.7	837.3	868.0

Source: ILO, *Yearbook of Labour Statistics*.

Mid-2001 (estimates in '000): Agriculture, etc. 5; Mining and quarrying 1; Manufacturing 385; Total employed 2,047; Unemployed 73; Total labour force 2,120 (Source: Asian Development Bank, *Key Indicators of Developing Asian and Pacific Countries*).

Health and Welfare

KEY INDICATORS

Fertility (births per woman, 2000)	1.5
Under-5 mortality rate (per 1,000 live births, 2000)	4
HIV/AIDS (% of persons aged 15–49, 2001)	0.20
Physicians (per 1,000 head, 1998)	1.63
Hospital beds (per 1,000 head, 1994)	3.05
Health expenditure (1998): US $ per head (PPP)	744
% of GDP	3.6
public (% of total)	35.4
Access to water (% of persons, 2000)	100
Access to sanitation (% of persons, 2000)	100
Human Development Index (2000): ranking	25
value	0.885

For sources and definitions, see explanatory note on p. vi.

Agriculture

PRINCIPAL CROPS (FAO estimates, '000 metric tons)

	1998	1999	2000
Vegetables	4.8	4.8	4.8

Source: FAO.

LIVESTOCK (FAO estimates, '000 head, year ending September)

	1998	1999	2000
Pigs	190	190	190
Chickens	2,000	2,000	2,000
Ducks	600	600	600

Source: FAO.

LIVESTOCK PRODUCTS ('000 metric tons)

	1998	1999	2000
Pig meat	84.1	50.0	50.0*
Poultry meat	69.6	69.6	69.6
Hen eggs	15.9	16.0	16.0*

* FAO estimate.

Source: FAO.

SELECTED OTHER PRODUCTS

	1988	1989	1990
Paints ('000 litres)	48,103.6	52,746.9	58,245.9
Broken granite ('000 metric tons)	6,914.0	7,007.5	6,371.7
Bricks ('000 units)	103,136	116,906	128,386
Soft drinks ('000 litres)	269,689.4	252,977.6	243,175.1
Plywood, plain and printed ('000 sq m)	31,307.0	28,871.3	26,106.9
Vegetable cooking oil (metric tons)	75,022	103,003	102,854
Animal fodder (metric tons)	110,106	115,341	104,541
Electricity (million kWh)	13,017.5	14,039.0	15,617.6
Gas (million kWh)	681.1	722.4	807.1
Cassette tape recorders ('000 sets)	15,450	14,006	18,059

Source: UN, *Industrial Commodity Statistics Yearbook*.

Plywood ('000 cu m, estimates): 280 per year in 1991–2000 (Source: FAO).

Electricity (million kWh): 29,520 in 1999; 31,665 in 2000; 33,089 in 2001 (Source: Asian Development Bank, *Key Indicators of Developing Asian and Pacific Countries*).

Forestry

SAWNWOOD PRODUCTION
(FAO estimates, '000 cubic metres, incl. railway sleepers)

	1990	1991	1992
Coniferous (softwood)	5	10	5
Broadleaved (hardwood)	50	20	20
Total	55	30	25

1993–2000: Annual production as in 1992 (FAO estimates).

Source: FAO.

Fishing

(metric tons, live weight)

	1997	1998	1999
Capture	9,250	8,155	5,052
Sea catfishes	385	358	240
Clupeoids	430	406	257
Shrimps and prawns	706	621	522
Common squids	470	462	376
Aquaculture	4,088	3,706	4,029
Indonesian snakehead	100	200	380
Milkfish	370	148	378
Green mussel	2,836	2,640	2,358
Total catch	13,338	11,861	9,081

Note: Figures exclude crocodiles, recorded by number rather than by weight. The number of estuarine crocodiles caught was: 296 in 1997; 416 in 1998; 350 in 1999.

Source: FAO, *Yearbook of Fishery Statistics*.

Industry

PETROLEUM PRODUCTS ('000 metric tons)

	1996	1997	1998*
Liquefied petroleum gas	875	965	965
Naphtha	5,850*	5,100*	5,200
Motor spirit (petrol)	5,231	5,032	4,920
Kerosene	3,025*	3,100*	3,250
Jet fuel	9,029	7,995	8,463
Gas-diesel (distillate fuel) oils	19,200*	19,500*	19,650
Residual fuel oil	16,200*	17,000*	17,800
Lubricating oils	648*	849*	849
Petroleum bitumen (asphalt)	1,132*	1,480*	1,480

* Estimate(s).

Source: UN, *Industrial Commodity Statistics Yearbook*.

Finance

CURRENCY AND EXCHANGE RATES

Monetary Units

100 cents = 1 Singapore dollar (S $).

Sterling, US Dollar and Euro Equivalents (31 May 2002)

£1 sterling = S $2.6188;
US $1 = S $1.7855;
€1 = S $1.6760;
S $100 = £38.19 = US $56.01 = €59.66.

Average Exchange Rate (Singapore dollars per US $)

1999	1.6950
2000	1.7240
2001	1.7917

BUDGET (S $ million)

Revenue*	1998	1999	2000
Tax revenue	22,154.1	21,578.1	25,277.4
Income tax	10,966.0	11,623.5	13,422.9
Assets taxes	1,849.5	1,181.1	1,484.7
Taxes on motor vehicles	1,547.5	1,337.2	2,179.7
Customs and excise duties	1,611.9	1,536.5	1,766.2
Betting taxes	1,266.6	1,309.3	1,452.2
Stamp duty	1,080.8	1,280.1	1,380.0
Goods and services tax	1,688.7	1,776.7	2,244.0
Others	2,143.1	1,533.7	1,347.7
Fees and charges	3,354.9	3,732.8	5,572.3
Total (incl. others)	28,212.5	28,619.2	33,526.6

* Figures refer to operating revenue only. The data exclude investment income and capital revenue.

Expenditure	1998	1999	2000
Operating expenditure	14,236.4	13,907.4	18,896.9
Security	7,189.8	7,063.0	8,882.9
Social and community services	5,254.4	4,859.6	6,047.4
Education	3,327.4	2,967.2	3,901.9
Health	934.2	874.7	990.2
Environment	319.1	321.9	357.2
Public Housing	166.5	169.1	185.6
Others	507.2	526.8	612.4
Economic services	976.0	1,143.3	3,053.0
National development	236.0	222.7	132.7
Communications	317.7	458.0	2,427.8
Trade and Industry	334.7	340.8	391.3
Labour	87.6	121.9	101.2
General services	816.2	841.4	913.7
Development expenditure	10,557.1	11,039.3	9,117.6
Total	24,793.5	24,946.7	28,014.5

INTERNATIONAL RESERVES (US $ million at 31 December)

	1999	2000	2001
Gold and foreign exchange	76,304	79,685	74,851
IMF special drawing rights	122	137	150
Reserve position in the IMF	416	310	374
Total	76,843	80,132	75,376

Source: IMF, *International Financial Statistics*.

MONEY SUPPLY (S $ million at 31 December)

	1999	2000	2001
Currency outside banks	11,315	11,289	11,863
Demand deposits at commercial banks	19,794	21,973	24,251
Total money	31,109	33,262	36,114

Source: IMF, *International Financial Statistics*.

COST OF LIVING (National Consumer Price Index; base: year ending October 1998 = 100)

	1999*	2000	2001
Food	112.0	101.4	101.9
Transport and communication	106.3	100.7	99.4
Clothing	104.4	97.1	97.5
Housing	106.5	100.6	101.8
Education	121.3	102.9	105.1
Health	118.4	102.3	105.7
All items (incl. others)	109.2	101.1	102.1

* Base: year ending September 1993 = 100.

NATIONAL ACCOUNTS (S $ million at current prices)

Composition of the Gross National Product

	1994	1995	1996
Gross domestic product (GDP) at factor cost	96,773.6	108,393.7	119,220.2
Indirect taxes, *less* subsidies	11,731.6	12,687.1	13,409.1
GDP in purchasers' values	108,505.2	121,080.8	132,629.3
Net factor income from abroad	1,186.4	300.4	1,143.1
Gross national product (GNP)	109,691.6	121,381.2	133,772.4

Expenditure on the Gross Domestic Product

	1999	2000	2001
Government final consumption expenditure	14,091.0	16,834.3	18,319.5
Private final consumption expenditure	57,555.2	64,158.9	64,796.7
Increase in stocks	-2,521.8	3,428.1	-7,581.1
Gross fixed capital formation	47,181.5	47,086.5	44,829.6
Statistical discrepancy	-2,815.9	-304.9	-231.6
Total domestic expenditure	113,490.0	131,202.9	120,133.1
Trade in goods and services (net)	26,580.4	28,685.3	33,322.1
GDP in purchasers' values	140,070.4	159,888.2	153,455.2

Source: Asian Development Bank, *Key Indicators of Developing Asian and Pacific Countries*.

Gross Domestic Product by Economic Activity

	1999	2000	2001
Agriculture, fishing and quarrying	211.3	204.2	189.3
Manufacturing	34,432.8	42,921.1	35,974.9
Electricity, gas and water	2,376.6	2,538.8	3,033.6
Construction	11,186.8	9,950.0	9,413.0
Wholesale and retail trade	21,921.6	26,663.2	25,407.1
Transport and communications	16,554.6	17,757.4	17,289.5
Finance and business services	37,408.7	40,909.7	42,582.0
Other services	25,028.1	27,345.1	29,177.3
Sub-total	149,120.5	168,289.5	163,066.7
Import duties	822.5	1,048.2	1,105.3
Less Imputed bank service charge	9,872.3	9,449.5	10,716.3
GDP in purchasers' values	140,070.4	159,888.2	153,455.2

Source: Asian Development Bank, *Key Indicators of Developing Asian and Pacific Countries*.

BALANCE OF PAYMENTS (US $ million)

	1998	1999	2000
Exports of goods f.o.b.	110,561	115,518	138,931
Imports of goods f.o.b.	-95,782	-104,361	-127,531
Trade balance	14,779	11,157	11,400
Exports of services	19,149	23,985	27,040
Imports of services	-17,623	-18,929	-21,408
Balance on goods and services	16,305	16,213	17,033
Other income received	12,969	14,975	15,253
Other income paid	-7,843	-8,274	-9,130
Balance on goods, services and income	21,432	22,914	23,155
Current transfers received	136	134	132
Current transfers paid	-1,234	-1,297	-1,490
Current balance	20,334	21,750	21,797
Capital account (net)	-226	-191	-163
Direct investment abroad	-555	-4,011	-4,276
Direct investment from abroad	6,316	7,197	6,390
Portfolio investment assets	-7,677	-9,228	-11,775
Portfolio investment liabilities	669	2,143	-2,082
Other investment assets	-3,555	-21,074	-5,291
Other investment liabilities	-17,012	6,693	5,635
Net errors and omissions	4,670	915	-3,429
Overall balance	2,965	4,194	6,806

Source: IMF, *International Financial Statistics*.

External Trade

PRINCIPAL COMMODITIES (distribution by SITC, US $ million)

Imports c.i.f.	1997	1998	1999
Mineral fuels, lubricants, etc.	12,588.3	8,198.7	10,117.1
Chemicals and related products	7,384.7	6,007.6	6,418.5
Basic manufactures	13,314.9	9,196.5	8,927.1
Iron and steel	2,930.4	1,996.9	1,679.5
Machinery and transport equipment	76,128.1	61,300.0	66,764.7
Power-generating machinery and equipment	2,782.3	2,367.1	2,326.5
Machinery specialized for particular industries	4,497.0	3,453.8	3,545.0
General industrial machinery, equipment and parts	5,849.7	4,184.9	4,252.1
Office machines and automatic data-processing equipment	16,662.0	13,419.0	14,387.1
Telecommunications and sound equipment	7,858.2	5,337.5	5,780.0
Other electrical machinery, apparatus, etc.	29,857.3	26,094.7	30,440.0
Transport equipment (excl. road vehicles) and parts*	5,455.2	4,450.4	3,734.3
Miscellaneous manufactured articles	14,064.7	10,239.0	4,068.1
Professional, scientific and controlling instruments, etc.	3,099.3	2,337.4	2,893.2
Total (incl. others)	132,441.7	101,731.6	111,060.9

* Data on parts exclude tyres, engines and electrical parts.

Exports f.o.b.	1997	1998	1999
Mineral fuels, lubricants, etc.	8,810.3	8,232.4	9,123.5
Chemicals and related products	7,357.2	6,961.9	8,923.0
Organic chemicals	2,594.8	2,397.3	3,353.6
Basic manufactures	7,053.6	5,052.1	5,037.4
Machinery and transport equipment	82,425.3	72,955.3	75,973.1
General industrial machinery, equipment and parts	3,642.2	2,809.0	2,806.3
Office machines and automatic data-processing equipment	34,121.9	30,677.4	30,287.4
Telecommunications and sound equipment	9,974.8	7,420.5	7,276.1
Other electrical machinery, apparatus, etc.	27,794.8	25,872.0	30,075.4
Miscellaneous manufactured articles	9,689.3	9,064.2	9,768.2
Total (incl. others)	124,988.1	109,905.0	114,681.8

Source: UN, *International Trade Statistics Yearbook.*

2000 (S $ million): Total imports 232,175.1; Total exports 237,826.3.

2001 (S $ million): Total imports 207,692; Total exports 218,026 (Source: Asian Development Bank, *Key Indicators of Developing Asian and Pacific Countries*).

PRINCIPAL TRADING PARTNERS (US $ million)

Imports c.i.f.	1999	2000	2001
China, People's Republic	5,697	7,116	7,195
Hong Kong	3,188	3,516	2,785
Japan	18,505	23,189	16,091
Germany	3,608	4,236	3,835
Korea, Republic	4,171	4,822	3,823
Malaysia	17,292	22,848	20,094
Saudi Arabia	3,248	4,338	4,229
Thailand	5,246	5,801	5,160
United Kingdom	2,727	2,741	2,440
USA	19,022	20,270	19,159
Total (incl. others)	111,071	134,630	116,018

Exports f.o.b.	1999	2000	2001
China, People's Republic	3,920	5,377	5,329
Hong Kong	8,810	10,842	10,820
Germany	3,259	4,277	4,297
Japan	8,513	10,404	9,341
Korea, Republic	3,557	4,916	4,688
Malaysia	18,994	25,042	21,122
Netherlands	3,858	4,089	4,035
Thailand	5,041	5,872	5,304
United Kingdom	4,277	3,550	2,851
USA	22,055	23,891	18,755
Total (incl. others)	114,730	137,932	121,717

Source: Asian Development Bank, *Key Indicators of Developing Asian and Pacific Countries.*

Transport

ROAD TRAFFIC (registered vehicles)

	1998	1999	2000
Private cars*	370,804	378,024	386,780
Motor cycles and scooters	133,375	134,346	131,937
Motor buses	11,429	11,827	12,569
Goods vehicles (incl. private)	141,051	139,473	134,756
Others	24,422	25,141	26,765
Total	681,081	688,811	692,807

* Including private and company cars.

SHIPPING

Merchant Fleet (at 31 December)

	1999	2000	2001
Number of vessels	1,736	1,728	1,729
Displacement (grt)	21,780,112	21,491,085	21,022,604

Source: Lloyd's Register-Fairplay, *World Fleet Statistics.*

International Sea-borne Shipping
(vessels of over 75 net registered tons)

	Ships Entered	Ships Cleared	Cargo Discharged ('000 freight tons)	Cargo Loaded ('000 freight tons)
1995	104,014	104,123	175,259.7	130,224.3
1996	117,723	117,662	179,572	134,592
1997	130,333	130,237	188,234	159,272

1998 Ships entered 140,922; Ships cleared 140,838.

Source: mainly UN, *Statistical Yearbook.*

Note: One freight ton equals 40 cubic feet (1.133 cubic metres) of cargo.

CIVIL AVIATION

	1995	1996	1997
Passengers			
Arrived	10,919,739	11,587,394	11,915,969
Departed	10,823,457	11,542,408	11,883,259
In Transit	1,453,046	1,384,446	1,375,116
Mail (metric tons)			
Landed	9,521	10,572	10,813
Dispatched	9,543	10,380	10,978
Freight (metric tons)			
Landed	577,749	622,019	696,710
Dispatched	528,024	568,438	639,544

Source: Civil Aviation Authority of Singapore.

1998: Kilometres flown (million) 293; Passengers carried ('000) 13,316; Passenger-km (million) 58,174; Total ton-km (million) 10,381 (Source: UN, *Statistical Yearbook*).

Tourism

FOREIGN VISITOR ARRIVALS ('000, incl. excursionists)

Country of Nationality	1998	1999	2000
Australia	410.5	441.5	484.6
China, People's Republic	293.4	372.7	440.0
Germany	172.9	181.6	184.6
Hong Kong	173.8	158.4	160.5
India	298.0	344.7	410.0
Indonesia	874.9	1,179.2	1,293.2
Japan	892.0	905.4	978.8
Korea, Republic	109.7	256.0	365.0
Malaysia*	415.0	411.7	459.6
Philippines	150.7	164.6	185.2
Taiwan	364.8	317.7	292.8
Thailand	160.9	205.5	222.7
United Kingdom	458.8	498.6	559.9
USA	372.7	374.2	406.1
Total (incl. others)*	6,242.2	6,958.2	7,691.4

* Figures exclude arrivals of Malaysians by land.

Source: World Tourism Organization, *Yearbook of Tourism Statistics.*

2001: Total visitor arrivals 7,518,584 (Source: Singapore Tourism Board).

Tourism receipts (US $ million): 5,402 in 1998; 5,974 in 1999; 6,370 in 2000 (Source: World Tourism Organization).

Communications Media

(at 31 December)

	1999	2000	2001
Television receivers ('000 in use)	1,200	1,200	n.a.
Telephones ('000 main lines in use)	1,876.6	1,946.5	1,948.5
Mobile cellular telephones ('000 subscribers)	1,630.8	2,747.4	2,858.8
Personal computers ('000 in use)	1,700	1,941	2,100
Internet users ('000)	950	1,200	1,500

Sources: International Telecommunication Union; UN, *Statistical Yearbook*.

Radio receivers ('000 in use): 2,550 in 1997.

Facsimile machines ('000 in use, estimate): 100 in 1998.

Daily newspapers: 8 (with average circulation of 1,095,000 copies) in 1996.

Non-daily newspapers: 2 in 1996.

Sources: mainly UNESCO, *Statistical Yearbook*; UN, *Statistical Yearbook.*

Education

(June 2000)

	Institutions	Students	Teachers
Primary	201	305,992	12,287
Secondary	163	176,132	9,462
Centralized Institutes / Junior Colleges	17	24,975	1,878
Institute of Technical Education	10	15,974	1,257
Polytechnics	4	58,374	3,931
National Institute of Education	1	3,308	561
Universities	3	49,856	2,826
Total	399	634,611	32,202

Adult literacy rate (UNESCO estimates): 92.3% (males 96.3%; females 88.4%) in 2000 (Source: UN Development Programme, *Human Development Report*).

Directory

The Constitution

A new Constitution came into force on 3 June 1959, with the establishment of the self-governing State of Singapore. This was subsequently amended as a consequence of Singapore's affiliation to Malaysia (September 1963 to August 1965) and as a result of its adoption of republican status on 22 December 1965. The Constitution was also amended in January 1991 to provide for the election of a President by universal adult suffrage, and to extend the responsibilities of the presidency, which had previously been a largely ceremonial office. A constitutional amendment in October 1996 placed restrictions on the presidential right of veto. The main provisions of the Constitution are summarized below:

HEAD OF STATE

The Head of State is the President, elected by universal adult suffrage for a six-year term. He normally acts on the advice of the Cabinet, but is vested with certain functions and powers for the purpose of safeguarding the financial reserves of Singapore and the integrity of the Public Services.

THE CABINET

The Cabinet, headed by the Prime Minister, is appointed by the President and is responsible to Parliament.

THE LEGISLATURE

The Legislature consists of a Parliament of 84 elected members, presided over by a Speaker who may be elected from the members of Parliament themselves or appointed by Parliament although he may not be a member of Parliament. Members of Parliament are elected by universal adult suffrage for five years (subject to dissolution) in single-member and multi-member constituencies.* Additionally, up to three 'non-constituency' seats may be offered to opposition parties, in accordance with a constitutional amendment approved in 1984, while legislation approved in 1990, and amended in 1997, enables the Government to nominate up to nine additional, politically-neutral members for a term of two years; these members have restricted voting rights.

A 21-member Presidential Council, chaired by the Chief Justice, examines material of racial or religious significance, including legislation, to see whether it differentiates between racial or religious communities or contains provisions inconsistent with the fundamental liberties of Singapore citizens.

CITIZENSHIP

Under the Constitution, Singapore citizenship may be acquired either by birth, descent or registration. Persons born when Singapore was a constituent State of Malaysia could also acquire Singapore citizenship by enrolment or naturalization under the Constitution of Malaysia.

*A constitutional amendment was introduced in May 1988, whereby 39 constituencies were merged to form 13 'group representation constituencies' which would return 'teams' of three Members of Parliament. At least one member of each team was to be of minority (non-Chinese) racial origin. In January 1991 the Constitution was further amended, stipulating that the number of candidates contesting 'group representation constituencies' should be a minimum of three and a maximum of four. The maximum was increased to six by constitutional amendment in October 1996.

The Government

HEAD OF STATE

President: SELLAPAN RAMANATHAN (S. R.) NATHAN (took office 1 September 1999).

THE CABINET
(September 2002)

Prime Minister: GOH CHOK TONG.

Senior Minister in the Prime Minister's Office: LEE KUAN YEW.

Deputy Prime Minister and Minister of Finance: Brig.-Gen. (retd) LEE HSIEN LOONG.

Deputy Prime Minister and Minister of Defence: Dr TONY TAN KENG YAM.

Minister of Law and of Foreign Affairs: Prof. SHANMUGAM JAYAKUMAR.

Minister of Trade and Industry: Brig.-Gen. (retd) GEORGE YONG BOON YEO.

Minister of Home Affairs: WONG KAN SENG.

Minister of Health and Second Minister of State for Finance: LIM HNG KIANG.

Acting Minister of Information, Communications and the Arts and Senior Minister of State for Defence: DAVID LIM TIK EN.

Minister of Manpower: Dr LEE BOON YANG.

Minister of Transport: YEO CHEOW TONG.

Minister in the Prime Minister's Office and Second Minister of Foreign Affairs: LEE YOCK SUAN.

Minister in the Prime Minister's Office: LIM BOON HENG.

Minister of National Development: MAH BOW TAN.

Acting Minister of Community Development and Sports and Minister in charge of Muslim Affairs: Dr YAACOB IBRAHIM.

Minister of Education and Second Minister of Defence: Rear-Adm. (retd) TEO CHEE HEAN.

Minister of the Environment: LIM SWEE SAY.

MINISTRIES

Office of the President: The Istana, Orchard Rd, Singapore 238823; internet www.istana.gov.sg.

Office of the Prime Minister: Orchard Rd, Istana Annexe, Istana, Singapore 238823; tel. 62358577; fax 67324627; e-mail goh_chok_tong@pmo.gov.sg; internet www.pmo.gov.sg.

Ministry of Community Development and Sports: 512 Thomson Rd, MCD Bldg, Singapore 298136; tel. 62589595; fax 63548324; e-mail mcds_home@mcds.gov.sg; internet www.mcds.gov.sg.

Ministry of Defence: Gombak Drive, off Upper Bukit Timah Rd, Mindef Bldg, Singapore 669645; tel. 67608844; fax 67646119; e-mail mfu@starnet.gov.sg; internet www.mindef.gov.sg.

Ministry of Education: 1 North Buona Vista Drive, MOE Bldg, Singapore 138675; tel. 68721110; fax 67755826; e-mail contact@moe.edu.sg; internet www.moe.gov.sg.

Ministry of the Environment: 40 Scotts Rd, Environment Bldg, 22nd Floor, Singapore 228231; tel. 67327733; fax 67319456; e-mail contact_env@env.gov.sg; internet www.env.gov.sg.

Ministry of Finance: 100 High St, 06-03 The Treasury, Singapore 179434; tel. 62259911; fax 63327435; e-mail mof_qsm@mof.gov.sg; internet www.mof.gov.sg.

Ministry of Foreign Affairs: Tanglin, Singapore 248163; tel. 63798000; fax 64747885; e-mail mfa@mfa.gov.sg; internet www.mfa.gov.sg.

Ministry of Health: 16 College Rd, College of Medicine Bldg, Singapore 169854; tel. 63259220; fax 62241677; e-mail moh_info@moh.gov.sg; internet www.moh.gov.sg

Ministry of Home Affairs: New Phoenix Park, 28 Irrawaddy Rd, Singapore 329560; tel. 62359111; fax 62546250; e-mail mha_feedback@mha.gov.sg; internet www.mha.gov.sg.

Ministry of Information, Communications and the Arts: MITA Bldg, 02-02 140 Hill St, Singapore 179369; tel. 62707988; fax 68379840; e-mailmita_pa@mita.gov.sg; internet www.mita.gov.sg.

Ministry of Law: 100 High St, 08-02 The Treasury, Singapore 179434; tel. 63328840; fax 63328842; e-mail mlaw_enquiry@minlaw.gov.sg; internet www.minlaw.gov.sg.

Ministry of Manpower: 18 Havelock Rd, 07-01, Singapore 059764; tel. 65341511; fax 65344840; e-mail mom_hq@mom.gov.sg; internet www.mom.gov.sg.

Ministry of National Development: 5 Maxwell Rd, 21/22-00, Tower Block, MND Complex, Singapore 069110; tel. 62221211; fax 63257254; e-mail mnd_hq@mnd.gov.sg; internet www.mnd.gov.sg.

Ministry of Trade and Industry: 100 High St, 09-01 The Treasury, Singapore 179434; tel. 62259911; fax 63327260; e-mail mti_email@mti.gov.sg; internet www.mti.gov.sg.

Ministry of Transport: 460 Alexandra Rd, 39-00 PSA Bldg, Singapore 119963; tel. 62707988; fax 63757734; e-mail mot@mot.gov.sg; internet www.mot.gov.sg.

President and Legislature

PRESIDENT

On 18 August 1999 SELLAPAN RAMANATHAN (S. R.) NATHAN was nominated as President by a state-appointed committee. S. R. Nathan was the sole candidate for the Presidency, following the rejection by the committee of the only two other potential candidates, and was officially appointed to the post on 1 September.

PARLIAMENT

Parliament House: 1 Parliament Place, Singapore 178880; tel. 63326666; fax 63325526; e-mail parl@parl.gov.sg; internet www.gov.sg/parliament/.

Speaker: ABDULLAH TARMUGI.

General Election, 3 November 2001

	Seats
People's Action Party	82*
Workers' Party	1
Singapore Democratic Alliance	1
Total	84

* 55 seats were unopposed.

Political Organizations

Angkatan Islam (Singapore Muslim Movement): Singapore; f. 1958; Pres. MOHAMED BIN OMAR; Sec.-Gen. IBRAHIM BIN ABDUL GHANI.

National Solidarity Party: Blk 531, Upper Cross St, Hong Lim Complex, 03-30, Singapore 050531; fax 65366388; e-mail nsp@nsp-singapore.org; internet www.nsp.org.sg; f. 1987; joined Singapore Democratic Alliance (SDA) in July 2001; Pres. YIP YEW WENG; Sec.-Gen. STEVE CHIA.

People's Action Party (PAP): Blk 57B, PCF Bldg, 01-1402 New Upper Changi Rd, Singapore 463057; tel. 62444600; fax 62430114; e-mail paphq@pap.org.sg; internet www.pap.org.sg; f. 1954; governing party since 1959; 12-member Cen. Exec. Cttee; Chair. Dr TONY TAN KENG YAM; Sec.-Gen. GOH CHOK TONG.

Pertubuhan Kebangsaan Melayu Singapura (PKMS) (Singapore Malay National Organization): 218F Changi Rd, 4th Floor, PKM Bldg, Singapore 1441; tel. 64470468; fax 63458724; f. in 1950 as the United Malay National Organization (UMNO) of Malaysia; renamed as UMNO Singapore in 1954 and as PKMS in 1967; seeks to advance the implementation of the special rights of Malays in Singapore, as stated in the Constitution, to safeguard and promote the advancement of Islam and to encourage racial harmony and goodwill in Singapore; joined Singapore Democratic Alliance (SDA) in July 2001; Pres. Haji BORHAN ARIFFIN; Sec.-Gen. MOHD RAHIZAN YAACOB.

Singapore Democratic Alliance (SDA): Singapore; f. 2001 to contest 2001 general election; coalition of Pertubuhan Kebangsaan Melayu Singapura (PKMS), Singapore People's Party (SPP),

National Solidarity Party and the Singapore Justice Party; Chair. CHIAM SEE TONG.

Singapore Democratic Party (SDP): 1357A Serangoon Rd, Singapore 328240; tel. and fax 63981675; e-mail speakup@singaporedemocrats.org; internet www.singaporedemocrats.org; f. 1980; 12-mem. Cen. Cttee; Chair. LING HOW DOONG; Sec.-Gen. CHEE SOON JUAN.

Singapore Justice Party: Singapore; f. 1972; joined Singapore Democratic Alliance (SDA) in July 2001; Pres. A. R. SUIB; Sec.-Gen. MUTHUSAMY RAMASAMY.

Singapore People's Party (SPP): Singapore; f. 1993; a breakaway faction of the SDP, espousing more moderate policies; joined Singapore Democratic Alliance (SDA) in July 2001; 12-mem. Cen. Executive Cttee; Chair. SIN KEK TONG; Sec.-Gen. CHIAM SEE TONG.

Workers' Party: 411B Jalan Besar, Singapore 209014; tel. 62984765; fax 64544404; e-mail wp@wp.org.sg; internet www.wp.org.sg; f. 1961; active as opposition party in Singapore since 1957, merged with Barisan Sosialis (Socialist Front) in 1988; seeks to establish a democratic socialist govt with a constitution guaranteeing fundamental citizens' rights; Chair. Dr TAN BIN SENG; Sec.-Gen. LOW THIA KHIANG.

Other parties are the Alliance Party Singapura, Barisan Sosialis (Socialist Front), The Democratic People's Party, the Democratic Progressive Party, the National Party of Singapore, the Partai Rakyat, the People's Front, the Parti Kesatuan Ra'ayat (United Democratic Party), the People's Republican Party, the Persatuan Melayu Singapura, the Singapore Chinese Party, the Singapore Indian Congress, the Singapore National Front, the United National Front, the United People's Front and the United People's Party.

Diplomatic Representation

EMBASSIES AND HIGH COMMISSIONS IN SINGAPORE

Argentina: 9 Temasek Blvd, 44-03 Suntec Tower 2, Singapore 038989; tel. 68830415; fax 68830410; e-mail eargsing@pacific.net.sq; internet www.ar.c-d.org/sg/; Ambassador: ALFREDO RAÚL MORELLI.

Australia: 25 Napier Rd, Singapore 258507; tel. 68364100; fax 67337134; e-mail public-affairs-sing@dfat.gov.au; internet www.singapore.embassy.gov.au; High Commissioner: GARY QUINLAN.

Austria: 1 Scotts Rd, 24-05/06 Shaw Centre, Singapore 228208; tel. 62354087; fax 67371202; e-mail embassy@austria.org.sg; internet www.austria.org.sg; Chargé d'affaires a.i.: WOLFGANG MAYERHOFER.

Bangladesh: 100 Thomson Rd, 05-04 United Sq., Singapore 307591; tel. 62550075; fax 62551824; e-mail bdoot@singnet.com.sg; internet www.bangladesh.org.sg; High Commissioner: SYED MAUDUD ALI.

Belgium: 8 Shenton Way, 14-01 Temasek Tower, Singapore 068811; tel. 62207677; fax 62226976; e-mail singapore@diplobel.org; internet www.embelsing.org.sg; Ambassador: ERIC DUCHENE.

Brazil: 101 Thomson Rd, 10-05 United Sq., Singapore 307591; tel. 62566001; fax 62566619; e-mail cinbrem@singnet.com.sg; internet web.singnet.com.sg/~cinbrem; Ambassador: PAULO DYRCEU PINHEIRO.

Brunei: 325 Tanglin Rd, Singapore 247955; tel. 67339055; fax 67375275; High Commissioner: Haji ADNAN Haji ZAINAL.

Cambodia: 152 Beach Rd, 11-05 Gateway East, Singapore 189721; tel. 62993028; fax 62993622; e-mail cambodiaembasy@pacific.net.sg.

Canada: 80 Anson Rd, 14-00 and 15-01/02 IBM Towers, Singapore 079907; tel. 63253200; fax 63253297; e-mail echiesg@pacific.net.sg; internet www.dfait-maeci.gc.ca/singapore; High Commissioner: DOREEN STEIDLE.

Chile: 105 Cecil St, 25-00 The Octagon, Singapore 069534; tel. 62238577; fax 62250677; e-mail echilesg@pacific.net.sg; internet www.conchile.org.sg; Ambassador: JUAN SCAFF MARTABIT.

China, People's Republic: 70-76 Dalvey Rd, Singapore 259470; tel. 67343200; fax 67344737; e-mail emprc@singnet.com.sg; Ambassador: ZHANG JIUHUAN.

Czech Republic: 7 Temasek Blvd, 18-02 Suntec Tower 1, Singapore 038987; tel. 63322378; fax 63322372; e-mail singapore@embassy.mzv.cz; internet www.mfa.cz/singapore; Chargé d'affaires: RUDOLF HYKL.

Denmark: 101 Thomson Rd, 13-01/02 United Sq., Singapore 307591; tel. 63555010; fax 62533764; e-mail embassy@denmark.com.sg; internet www.denmark.com.sg; Ambassador: JØRGEN ØRSTRØM MØLLER.

Egypt: 75 Grange Rd, Singapore 1024; tel. 67371811; fax 67323422; Ambassador: NADIA KAFAFI.

Finland: 101 Thomson Rd, 21-03 United Sq., Singapore 307591; tel. 62544042; fax 62534101; e-mail sanomat.sin@formin.fi; Ambassador: YRJÖ KIM DAVID LUOTONEN.

France: 101–103 Cluny Park Rd, Singapore 259595; tel. 68807800; fax 68807801; e-mail ambassadeur@france.org.sg; internet www.france.org.sg; Ambassador: MICHEL FILHOL.

Germany: 545 Orchard Rd, 14-00 Far East Shopping Centre, Singapore 238882; tel. 67371355; fax 67372653; e-mail germany@singnet.com.sg; internet www.germanembassy-singapore.org.sg; Ambassador: ANDREAS MICHAELIS.

Greece: 61B Duxton Rd, Singapore 089525; tel. and fax 62212364.

Holy See: 55 Waterloo St 6, Singapore 187954 (Apostolic Nunciature); tel. 63372466; fax 63372466; Apostolic Nuncio: Most Rev. ADRIANO BERNARDINI, Titular Archbishop of Faleri.

Hungary: 250 North Bridge Rd, 29-01 Raffles City Tower, Singapore 179101; tel. 68830882; fax 68830177; e-mail humemsin@singnet.com.sg; Ambassador: Dr GYÖRGY NANOVFSZKY.

India: 31 Grange Rd, India House, Singapore 239702; tel. 67376777; fax 67326909; e-mail indiahc@pacific.net.sg; internet www.embassyofindia.com; High Commissioner: P. P. SHUKLA.

Indonesia: 7 Chatsworth Rd, Singapore 249761; tel. 67377422; fax 67375037; Ambassador: Dr DJOHAN SYAHPERI SALEH.

Ireland: Ireland House, 541 Orchard Rd, 8th Floor, Liat Towers, Singapore 238881; tel. 62387616; fax 62387615; e-mail ireland@magix.com.sg; Ambassador: HUGH SWIFT.

Israel: 58 Dalvey Rd, Singapore 259463; tel. 68349200; fax 67337008; e-mail singapor@israel.org; internet www.israelbiz.org.sg; Ambassador: ITZHAK SHOHAM.

Italy: 101 Thomson Rd, 27-02 United Sq., Singapore 307591; tel. 62506022; fax 62533301; e-mail ambitaly@italyemb.org.sg; internet www.italyemb.org.sg; Ambassador: GUIDO SCALICI.

Japan: 16 Nassim Rd, Singapore 258390; tel. 62358855; fax 67331039; e-mail eojs04@singnet.com.sg; internet www.japanemb.org.sg; Ambassador: KUNIHIKO MAKITA.

Korea, Democratic People's Republic: 7500A Beach Rd, 09-320 The Plaza, Singapore 199591; tel. 64403498; fax 63482026; Ambassador: YU JAE HAN.

Korea, Republic: 47 Scotts Rd, 08-00 Goldbell Towers, Singapore 228233; tel. 62561188; fax 62543191; e-mail info@koreaembassy.org.sg; Ambassador: HAHM MYUNG-CHUL.

Laos: 101 Thomson Rd, 05-03A United Sq., Singapore 307591; tel. 62506044; fax 62506014; e-mail laoembsg@singnet.com.sg; Ambassador: LEUANE SOMBOUNKHAN.

Malaysia: 301 Jervois Rd, Singapore 249077; tel. 62350111; fax 67336135; e-mail mwspore@mbox3.singnet.com.sg; High Commissioner: HAMIDON ALI.

Mexico: 152 Beach Rd, 06-07/08 Gateway East, Singapore 189721; tel. 62982678; fax 62933484; e-mail singmx@singnet.com.sg; Ambassador: ANDRÉS CARRAL CUEVAS.

Myanmar: 15 St Martin's Drive, Singapore 257996; tel. 67350209; fax 67356236; e-mail ambassador@mesingapore.org.sg; Ambassador: U HLA THAN.

Netherlands: 541 Orchard Rd, 13-01 Liat Towers, Singapore 238881; tel. 67371155; fax 67371940; e-mail nlgovsin@singnet.com.sg; internet www.nethemb.org.sg; Ambassador: H. J. VAN PESCH.

New Zealand: 391A Orchard Rd, 15-06/10 Ngee Ann City, Singapore 238873; tel. 62359966; fax 67339924; e-mail enquiries@nz-high-com.org.sg; internet www.nz-high-com.org.sg; High Commissioner: NIGEL MOORE.

Nigeria: 350 Orchard Rd, 16-09/10 Shaw House, Singapore 238868; tel. 67321741; fax 67321742; High Commissioner: ALEX CHIKE ANIEGBO.

Norway: 16 Raffles Quay, 44-01 Hong Leong Bldg, Singapore 048581; tel. 62207122; fax 62202191; e-mail emb.singapore@mfa.no; Ambassador: ENOK NYGAARD.

Pakistan: 1 Scotts Rd, 24-02/04 Shaw Centre, Singapore 228208; tel. 67376988; fax 67374096; e-mail parep@singnet.com.sg; internet www.parep.org.sg; High Commissioner: ABDUL MOIZ BOKHARI.

Panama: 16 Raffles Quay, 41-06 Hong Leong Bldg, Singapore 048581; tel. 62218677; fax 62240892; e-mail pacosin@pacific.net.sg; Ambassador: JORGE LUIS ALEMÁN.

Peru: 390 Orchard Rd, 12-03 Palais Renaissance, Singapore 238871; tel. 67388595; fax 67388601; e-mail embperu@pacific.net.sg; Ambassador: JUAN CARLOS CAPUNAY.

Philippines: 20 Nassim Rd, Singapore 258395; tel. 67373977; fax 67339544; e-mail php@pacific.net.sg; internet www.rpsing.org; Ambassador: JESUS I. YABES.

Poland: 100 Beach Rd, 33-11/12 Shaw Towers, Singapore 189702; tel. 62942513; fax 62950016; e-mail polish_embassy@pacific.net.sg; Chargé d'affaires a.i.: WŁODZIMIERZ PACZEŚNY (acting).

Portugal: 55 Waterloo St, 09-03A, Singapore 187954; tel. 63341231; fax 65334943.

Romania: 48 Jalan Harom Setangkai, Singapore 258827; tel. 64683424; fax 64683425; e-mail comofrom@cyberway.com.sg; Chargé d'affaires: Marian Sjate.

Russia: 51 Nassim Rd, Singapore 258439; tel. 62351834; fax 67334780; e-mail rosposol@pacific.net.sg; internet www.singapore.mid.ru; Ambassador: Sergei B. Kiselev.

Saudi Arabia: 40 Nassim Rd, Singapore 258449; tel. 67345878; fax 67385291; Chargé d'affaires: Mohammad A. al-Hamdan.

South Africa: 331 North Bridge Rd, 15/01-06 Odeon Towers, Singapore 188720; tel. 63393319; fax 63396658; e-mail sahcp@singnet.com.sg; internet www.singnet.com.sg/~satrade2; High Commissioner: S. J. Schoeman.

Sri Lanka: 13-06/12 Goldhill Plaza, 51 Newton Rd, Singapore 308900; tel. 62544595; fax 62507201; e-mail slhcs@lanka.com.sg; internet www.lanka.com.sg; High Commissioner: Chitranganee Wagiswara.

Sweden: 111 Somerset Rd, 05-01, Power Bldg, Singapore 238164; tel. 64159720; fax 64159747; e-mail swedemb@singnet.com.sg; internet www.swedemb.org.sg; Ambassador: Teppo Tauriainen.

Switzerland: 1 Swiss Club Link, Singapore 288162; tel. 64685788; fax 64668245; e-mail vertretung@sin.rep.admin.ch; internet www.eda.admin.ch/singapore_emb/e/home.html; Ambassador: Raymond Loretan.

Thailand: 370 Orchard Rd, Singapore 238870; tel. 67372158; fax 67320778; e-mail thaisgp@singnet.com.sg; Ambassador: Somkiati Ariyapruchya.

Turkey: 20B Nassim Rd, Singapore 258397; tel. 67329211; fax 67381786; e-mail turksin@starhub.net.sg; Ambassador: Hayri Erol.

Ukraine: 20-03 Shenton House, 3 Shenton Way, Singapore 068805; tel. 62279400; fax 62247374; e-mail ukraine@singnet.com.sg; Ambassador: Oleksandr O. Horin.

United Kingdom: 100 Tanglin Rd, Singapore 247919; tel. 64244200; fax 64244218; e-mail brit–1>hc@pacific.net.sg; internet www.britain.org.sg; High Commissioner: Sir Stephen Brown.

USA: 27 Napier Rd, Singapore 258508; tel. 64769100; fax 64769340; internet www.usembassysingapore.org.sg; Ambassador: Franklin L. Lavin.

Viet Nam: 10 Leedon Park, Singapore 267887; tel. 64625938; fax 64625936; e-mail vnemb@singnet.com.sg; Ambassador: Do Cong Minh.

Judicial System

Supreme Court: St Andrew's Rd, Singapore 178957; tel. 63381034; fax 63379450; e-mail supcourt–1>qsm@supcourt.gov.sg; internet www.supcourt.gov.sg.

The judicial power of Singapore is vested in the Supreme Court and in the Subordinate Courts. The Judiciary administers the law with complete independence from the executive and legislative branches of the Government; this independence is safeguarded by the Constitution. The Supreme Court consists of the High Court and the Court of Appeal. The Chief Justice is appointed by the President if the latter, acting at his discretion, concurs with the advice of the Prime Minister. The other judges of the Supreme Court are appointed in the same way, in consultation with the Chief Justice. At 1 March 2002 there were three judges of appeal, including the Chief Justice, seven judges and four judicial commissioners, in the Supreme Court. Under a 1979 constitutional amendment, the position of judicial commissioner of the Supreme Court was created 'to facilitate the disposal of business in the Supreme Court'. A judicial commissioner has the powers and functions of a judge, and is appointed for such period as the President thinks fit.

The Subordinate Courts consist of District Courts and Magistrates' Courts. In addition, there are also specialized courts such as the Coroner's Court, Family Court, Juvenile Court, Mentions Court, Night Court, Sentencing Courts and Filter Courts. The Primary Dispute Resolution Centre and the Small Claims Tribunals are also managed by the Subordinate Courts. The Subordinate Courts have also established the Multi-Door Courthouse, which serves as a one-stop centre for the screening and channelling of any cases to the most appropriate forum for dispute resolution.

District Courts and Magistrates' Courts have original criminal and civil jurisdiction. District Courts try offences for which the maximum penalty does not exceed 10 years of imprisonment and in civil cases where the amount claimed does not exceed S $250,000. Magistrates' Courts try offences for which the maximum term of imprisonment does not exceed three years. The jurisdiction of Magistrates' Courts in civil cases is limited to claims not exceeding S $60,000. The Coroners' Court conducts inquests. The Small Claims Tribunal has jurisdiction over claims relating to a dispute arising from any contract for the sale of goods or the provision of services and any claim in tort in respect of damage caused to any property involving an amount that does not exceed S $10,000. The Juvenile Court deals with offences committed by young persons aged under 16 years.

The High Court has unlimited original jurisdiction in criminal and civil cases. In its appellate jurisdiction it hears criminal and civil appeals from the District Courts and Magistrates' Courts. The Court of Appeal hears appeals against the decisions of the High Court in both criminal and civil matters. In criminal matters, the Court of Appeal hears appeals against decisions made by the High Court in the exercise of its original criminal jurisdiction. In civil matters, the Court of Appeal hears appeals against decisions made by the High Court in the exercise of both its original and appellate jurisdiction.

With the enactment of the Judicial Committee (Repeal) Act 1994 in April of that year, the right of appeal from the Court of Appeal to the Judicial Committee of the Privy Council in the United Kingdom was abolished. The Court of Appeal is now the final appellate court in the Singapore legal system.

Attorney-General: Chan Sek Keong.

Chief Justice: Yong Pung How.

Judges of Appeal: L. P. Thean, Chao Hick Tin.

Judges of the High Court: Lai Kew Chai, S. Rajendran, M. P. H. Rubin, Kan Ting Chiu, Lai Siu Chiu, Judith Prakash, Tan Lee Meng.

Judicial Commissioners: Choo Han Teck, Lee Seiu Kin, Tay Yong Kwang, Woo Bih Li.

Religion

According to the 2000 census, 64.4% of ethnic Chinese, who constituted 76.8% of the population, professed either Buddhism or Daoism (including followers of Confucius, Mencius and Lao Zi) and 16.5% of Chinese adhered to Christianity. Malays, who made up 13.9% of the population, were 99.6% Muslim. Among Indians, who constituted 7.9% of the population, 55.4% were Hindus, 25.6% Muslims, 12.1% Christians and 6.3% Sikhs, Jains or adherents of other faiths. There are small communities of Zoroastrians and Jews. Freedom of worship is guaranteed by the Constitution.

BAHÁ'Í FAITH

National Spiritual Assembly: 110D Wishart Rd, Singapore 098733; tel. 62733023; fax 62732497.

BUDDHISM

Buddhist Union: 28 Jalan Senyum, Singapore 418152; tel. 64435959; fax 64443280.

Singapore Buddhist Federation: 12 Ubi Ave 1, Singapore 408932; tel. 67444635; fax 67473618; f. 1948.

Singapore Buddhist Sangha Organization: 88 Bright Hill Drive, Singapore 579644.

Evangelical Fellowship of Singapore (EFOS): Singapore; f. 1980.

CHRISTIANITY

National Council of Churches: 6 Mount Sophia, Singapore 228457; tel. 63372150; fax 63360368; e-mail nccs@cyberway.com.sg; f. 1948; six mem. churches, six assoc. mems; Pres. Bishop John Tan; Gen. Sec. Rev. Canon Dr James Wong.

Singapore Council of Christian Churches (SCCC): Singapore; f. 1956.

The Anglican Communion

The Anglican diocese of Singapore (also including Indonesia, Laos, Thailand, Viet Nam and Cambodia) is part of the Province of the Anglican Church in South-East Asia.

Bishop of Singapore: The Rt Rev. Dr John Hiang Chea Chew, 4 Bishopsgate, Singapore 249970; tel. 64741661; fax 64791054; e-mail bpoffice@anglican.org.sg.

Orthodox Churches

The Orthodox Syrian Church and the Mar Thoma Syrian Church are both active in Singapore.

The Roman Catholic Church

Singapore comprises a single archdiocese, directly responsible to the Holy See. In December 2000 there were an estimated 151,655 adherents in the country, representing 3.8% of the total population.

Archbishop of Singapore: Most Rev. NICHOLAS CHIA, Archbishop's House, 31 Victoria St, Singapore 187997; tel. 63378818; fax 63334725; e-mail nc@veritas.org.sg.

Other Christian Churches

Brethren Assemblies: Bethesda Hall (Ang Mo Kio), 601 Ang Mo Kio Ave 4, Singapore 569898; tel. 64587474; fax 64566771; e-mail bethesda@pacific.net.sg; f. 1864; Hon. Sec. WONG TUCK KEONG.

Methodist Church in Singapore: 2 Cluny Rd, 02–00, Singapore 259570; tel. 64715665; fax 64736754; e-mail mcsbp@cyberway.com.sg; internet www.methodist.org.sg; f. 1885; 30,393 mems (July 2000); Bishop Dr ROBERT SOLOMON.

Presbyterian Church: 3 Orchard Rd, cnr Penang Rd, Singapore 238825; tel. 63376681; fax 63391979; e-mail orpcenglish@orpc.org.sg; f. 1856; services in English, Chinese (Mandarin), Indonesian and German; 2,000 mems; Chair. Rev. DAVID BURKE.

Singapore Baptist Convention: 01 Goldhill Plaza, 03–19 Podium Block, Singapore 308899; tel. 62538004; fax 62538214; e-mail sbcnet@singnet.com.sg; internet www.baptistconvention.org.sg; Chair. Rev. M. S. SONG; Sec. RUSSELL MORRIS.

Other denominations active in Singapore include the Lutheran Church and the Evangelical Lutheran Church.

HINDUISM

Hindu Advisory Board: c/o 397 Serangoon Rd, Singapore 218123; tel. 62963469; fax 62929766; e-mail heb@pacific.net.sg; Chair. AJAIB HARI DASS; Sec. E. SANMUGAM.

Hindu Endowments Board: 397 Serangoon Rd, Singapore 218123; tel. 62963469; fax 62929766; e-mail heb@pacific.net.sg; internet www.gov.sg/heb; Chair. V. R. NATHAN; Sec. SATISH APPOO.

ISLAM

Majlis Ugama Islam Singapura (MUIS) (Islamic Religious Council of Singapore): Islamic Centre of Singapore, 273 Braddell Road, Singapore 579702; tel. 62568188; fax 62537572; e-mail maarof@muis.gov.sg; internet www.muis.gov.sg; f. 1968; Pres. Haji MAAROF Haji SALLEH.

Muslim Missionary Society Singapore (JAMIYAH): 31 Lorong, 12 Geylang Rd, Singapore 399006; tel. 67431211; fax 67450610; e-mail info@jamiyah.org.sg; internet www.jamiyah.org.sg; Pres. Haji ABU BAKAR MAIDIN; Sec.-Gen. ISMAIL ROZIZ.

SIKHISM

Sikh Ad: c/o 2 Towner Rd, 03-01, Singapore 327804; tel. and fax 62996440; Chair. BHAJAN SINGH.

The Press

Compulsory government scrutiny of newspaper management has been in operation since 1974. All newspaper enterprises must be public companies. In August 1986 there were more than 3,700 foreign publications circulating in Singapore. The Newspaper and Printing Presses (Amendment) Act 1986 empowers the Government to restrict the circulation of foreign periodicals that are deemed to exert influence over readers on domestic political issues. An amendment to the Newspaper and Printing Presses Act was promulgated in October 1990. Under this amendment, all publications of which the 'contents and editorial policy were determined outside Singapore' and which dealt with politics and current events in South-East Asia would be required to obtain a ministerial licence, renewable annually. The permit would limit the number of copies sold and require a deposit in case of legal proceedings involving the publication. Permits could be refused or revoked without any reason being given. In November, however, a statement was issued exempting 14 of the 17 foreign publications affected by the amendment, which came into effect in December.

DAILIES

English Language

Business Times: 1000 Toa Payoh North, Singapore 318994; tel. 63196319; fax 63198277; e-mail btnews@sph.com.sg; internet www.business-times.asia1.com.sg; f. 1976; morning; Editor PATRICK DANIEL; circ. 36,000 (Singapore only).

The New Paper: 1000 Toa Payoh North, Annexe Blk, Level 6, Singapore 318994; tel. 63196319; fax 63198266; e-mail tnp@sph.com.sg; internet www.newpaper.asia1.com.sg; f. 1988; afternoon tabloid; Editor IVAN FERNANDEZ; circ. 121,000 (Singapore only).

Streats: 1000 Toa Payoh North, Podium Blk, Level 1, Singapore 318994; tel. 63192421; fax 63198191; e-mail streats@sph.com.sg; Editor KEN JALLEH, Jr.

The Straits Times: 1000 Toa Payoh North, Singapore 318994; tel. 63196319; fax 67320131; e-mail stlocal@sph.com.sg; internet www.straitstimes.asia1.com.sg; f. 1845; morning; Editor LESLIE FONG; circ. 392,611 (Singapore only).

Chinese Language

Lianhe Wanbao: 1000 Toa Payoh North, Podium Blk, Level 4, Singapore 318994; tel. 63196319; fax 63198133; e-mail wanbao@sph.com.sg; f. 1983; evening; Editor KOH LIN HOE; circ. 127,656 (week), 123,283 (weekend) in Feb. 2001.

Lianhe Zaobao: 1000 Toa Payoh North, Podium Blk, Level 4, Singapore 318994; tel. 63196319; fax 63198199; e-mail zaobao@zaobao.com.sg; internet www.zaobao.com.sg; f. 1923; Editor LIM JIM KOON; circ. 200,761.

Shin Min Daily News (S) Ltd: 1000 Toa Payoh North, Podium Blk, Level 4, Singapore 318994; tel. 63196319; fax 63198166; e-mail shinmin@sph.com.sg; f. 1967; evening; Editor TOH LAM HHAT; circ. 128,383.

Malay Language

Berita Harian: 1000 Toa Payoh North, Singapore 318994; tel. 63196319; fax 63198255; e-mail bharian@cyberway.com.sg; internet www.cyberita.asia1.com.sg; f. 1957; morning; Editor MOHD GUNTOR SADALI; circ. 68,000 (Singapore only).

Tamil Language

Tamil Murasu: 151 Chin Swee Rd, 01-52 Manhattan House, Singapore 169876; tel. 67366077; fax 67366033; e-mail murasu4@cyberway.co.sg; internet www.tamilmurasu.asia1.com.sg; f. 1935; Editor CHITRA RAJARAM; circ. 14,000 (daily), 23,000 (Sunday).

WEEKLIES

English Language

Sunday Times: 1000 Toa Payoh North, Singapore 318994; tel. 63195397; fax 67320131; e-mail stlocal@sph.com.sg; internet www.straitstimes.asia1.com.sg; f. 1845; Editor-in-Chief CHEONG YIP SENG; circ. 387,000 (Singapore only).

Malay Language

Berita Minggu: 1000 Toa Payoh North, Singapore 318994; tel. 63196319; fax 63198255; e-mail bharian@cyberway.com.sg; internet www.cyberita.asia1.com.sg; f. 1957; Sunday; Editor MOHD GUNTOR SADALI; circ. 73,500 (Singapore only).

SELECTED PERIODICALS

English Language

Accent: Accent Communications, 215 Intrepid Warehouse Complex, 4 Ubi Ave, Singapore 1440; tel. 67478088; fax 67472811; f. 1983; monthly; lifestyle; Senior Editor DORA TAY; circ. 65,000.

Cherie Magazine: 12 Everton Rd, Singapore 0208; tel. 62229733; fax 62843859; f. 1983; bimonthly; women's; Editor JOSEPHINE NG; circ. 20,000.

8 Days: 298 Tiong Bahru Rd, 19-01/06 Tiong Bahru Plaza, Singapore 168730; tel. 62789822; fax 62724800; e-mail feedback@8daysonline.com; internet www.8days.mediacorppublishing.com; f. 1990; weekly; Editor-in-Chief TAN LEE SUN; circ. 113,258.

Go Flirt: Times Periodicals Pte Ltd, 422 Thomson Rd, Singapore 298131; tel. 62550011; fax 62568016; e-mail tpgo@cyberway.com.sg; f. 1980; monthly; women's; Editor LYNN LEE; circ. 29,632.

Her World: Times Periodicals Pte Ltd, 422 Thomson Rd, Singapore 298131; tel. 62550011; fax 62568016; e-mail herworld@cyberway.com.sg; internet www.herworld.asiaone.com.sg; f. 1960; monthly; women's; Editor CAROLINE NGUI; circ. 64,042.

Home and Decor: Times Periodicals Pte Ltd, 422 Thomson Rd, Singapore 298131; tel. 62550011; fax 62568016; e-mail hdecor@cyberway.com.sg; f.1981; 6 a year; home-owners; Editor SOPHIE KHO; circ. 25,385.

LIME: 65 Io Ang Mo Kio St, 01-06/08 Techpoint, Singapore 569059; tel. 64837118; fax 64837286; f. 1996; Editor PAMELA QUEK; circ. 34,947.

Man—Life & Style: 55 Cuppage Rd, 08-06 Cuppage Centre, Singapore 0922; tel. 67386166; fax 67386122; f. 1986; monthly; men's; Editor SU MANN ONG; circ. 130,000.

Mondial Collections: Singapore; f. 1990; bimonthly; arts; Chair. CHRIS CHENEY; circ. 100,000.

NSman: Times Periodicals Pte Ltd, 422 Thomson Rd, Singapore 298131; tel. 62550011; fax 62568016; e-mail timesp@cyberway.com.sg; f. 1973; bimonthly; publication of the SAF National Service; Editor KOH BOON PIN; circ. 130,705.

Republic of Singapore Government Gazette: Singapore National Printers Ltd, 1 Kim Seng Promenade, 18-01 Great World City East Tower, Singapore 237994; tel. 68338680; fax 67321866; e-mail egazinfo@snp.com.sg; internet www.egazette.com.sg; weekly; Friday.

Reservist: 5200 Jalan Bukit Merah, Singapore 0315; tel. 62786011; fax 6273441; f. 1973; bimonthly; men's; Editor SAMUEL EE; circ. 130,000.

Singapore Medical Journal: Singapore Medical Association, Level 2, Alumni Medical Centre, 2 College Rd, Singapore 169850; tel. 62231264; fax 62247827; e-mail smj@sma.org.sg; internet www.sma.org.sg/smj; monthly; Editor Dr C. RAJASOORYA.

Times Guide to Computers: 1 New Industrial Rd, Times Centre, Singapore 536196; tel. 62848844; fax 62850161; e-mail ttd@corp.tpl.com.sg; internet www.tpl.com.sg; f. 1986; annually; computing and communications; Vice-Pres. LESLIE LIM; circ. 30,000.

Visage: Ubi Ave 1, 02-169 Block 305, Singapore 1440; tel. 67478088; fax 67472811; f. 1984; monthly; Editor-in-Chief TENG JUAT LENG; circ. 63,000.

WEEKENDeast: 82 Genting Lane, News Centre, Singapore 349567; tel. 67401200; fax 67451022; e-mail focuspub@cyberway.com.sg; f. 1986; Editor VICTOR SOH; circ. 75,000.

Woman's Affair: 140 Paya Lebar Rd, 04-10 A-Z Bldg, Singapore 1440; tel. 67478088; fax 67479119; f. 1988; 2 a month; Editor DORA TAY; circ. 38,000.

Young Parents: Times Periodicals Pte Ltd, 422 Thomson Rd, Singapore 298131; tel. 62550011; fax 62568016; e-mail yparents@cyberway.com.sg; f. 1986; monthly; family; Editor GLORIA CHAN (acting); circ. 10,725.

Chinese Language

Characters: 1 Kallang Sector, 04-04/04-05 Kolam Ayer Industrial Park, Singapore 349276; tel. 67458733; fax 67458213; f. 1987; monthly; television and entertainment; Editor SAM NG; circ. 45,000.

The Citizen: People's Association, 9 Stadium Link, Singapore 397750; tel. 63405138; fax 63468657; monthly; English, Chinese, Tamil and Malay; Man. Editor OOI HUI MEI.

i-weekly: 298 Tiong Bahru Rd, 19-01/06 Tiong Bahru Plaza, Singapore 168730; tel. 62789822; fax 62724811; f. 1981; weekly; radio and television; Editor-in-Chief LOKE TAI TAY; circ. 113,000.

Punters' Way: 4 Ubi View (off Ubi Rd 3), Pioneers and Leaders Centre, Singapore 408557; tel. 67458733; fax 67458213; e-mail pnlhldg@pcl.com.sg; f. 1977; biweekly; English and Chinese; sport; Editor T. S. PHAN; circ. 90,000.

Racing Guide: 1 New Industrial Rd, Times Centre, Singapore 1953; tel. 62848844; fax 62881186; f. 1987; 2 a week; English and Chinese; sport; Editorial Consultant BENNY ORTEGA; Chinese Editor KUEK CHIEW TEONG; circ. 20,000.

Singapore Literature: Singapore Literature Society, 122B Sims Ave, Singapore 1438; quarterly; Pres. YAP KOON CHAN; Editor LUO-MING.

Tune Monthly Magazine: Henderson Rd 06-04, Block 203A, Henderson Industrial Park, Singapore 0315; tel. 62733000; fax 62749538; f. 1988; monthly; women's and fashion; Editor CHAN ENG; circ. 25,000.

Young Generation: SNP Media Asia Pte Ltd, 97 Ubi Avenue 4, SNP Building, Singapore 408754; tel. 67412500; fax 68463890; e-mail yg@snp.com.sg; internet www.snp.com.sg; monthly; children's; Editor EVELYN TANG; circ. 80,000.

NEWS AGENCIES

Foreign Bureaux

Agence France-Presse (AFP): 10 Hoe Chiang Rd, 07-03 Keppel Towers, Singapore 089315; tel. 62228581; fax 62247465; e-mail afpsin@afp.com; Bureau Chief ROBERTO Z. COLOMA.

Agenzia Nazionale Stampa Associata (ANSA) (Italy): Blk 628, 8 Hougang Ave, 04-94, Singapore 530628; tel. 63855514; fax 63855279; e-mail kuttynng@pacific.net.sg; Correspondent N. G. KUTTY.

Associated Press (AP) (USA): 10 Anson Rd, 32-11 International Plaza, Singapore 079903; tel. 62201849; fax 62212753; e-mail sgutkin@ap.org; Chief of South-East Asian Services STEVEN GUTKIN.

Central News Agency Inc (CNA) (Taiwan): 78A Lorong N, Telok Kurau, Ocean Apartments, Singapore 425223; tel. 63445746; fax 63467645; e-mail cnanews@singnet.com.sg; South-East Asia Correspondent SHERMAN SHEAN-SHEN WU.

Inter Press Service (IPS) (Italy): Marine Parade Rd, 10-42 Lagoon View, Singapore 1544; tel. 64490432; Correspondent SURYA GANGADHARAN.

Jiji Tsushin (Jiji Press) (Japan): 10 Anson Rd, 24-16A International Plaza, Singapore 079903; tel. 62244212; fax 62240711; e-mail jijisp@jiji.com.sg; internet www.jiji.com; Bureau Chief AMANO KAZUTOSHI.

Kyodo News (Japan): 138 Cecil St, Cecil Court, Singapore; tel. 62233371; fax 62249208; e-mail goinrk@kyodonews.or.jp; Chief NORIKO GOI.

Reuters Singapore Pte Ltd: 18 Science Park Drive, Singapore 118229; tel. 68703080; fax 67768112; e-mail singapore.newsroom@reuters.com; Bureau Chief RICHARD HUBBARD.

Rossiiskoye Informatsionnoye Agentstvo—Vesti (RIA—Vesti) (Russia): 8 Namly Grove, Singapore 1026; tel. 64667998; fax 64690784; Correspondent MIKHAIL I. IDAMKIN.

United Press International (UPI) (USA): Singapore; tel. 63373715; fax 63389867; Man. DEAN VISSER.

Bernama (Malaysia), United News (India) and Xinhua (People's Republic of China) are also represented.

Publishers

ENGLISH LANGUAGE

Addison-Wesley (S) Pte Ltd: 25 First Lok Yang Rd, Jurong City, Singapore 629734; tel. 62682666; fax 62641740; e-mail enquiry@awl.com.sg; educational, computing and professional books; Gen. Man. CHWEE LEONG LOW.

Butterworths Asia: 1 Temasek Ave, 17-01 Millenia Tower, Singapore 039192; tel. 63369661; fax 63369662; e-mail sales@butterworths.com.sg; internet www.lexisnexis.com.sg/butterworths-online; f. 1932; law texts and journals; Man. Dir GRAHAM J. MARSHALL.

Caldecott Publishing Pte Ltd: 10 Ang Mo Kio St 65, 01-06/08 Techpoint, Singapore 569059; tel. 64837118; fax 64837286; f. 1990; CEO MICHAEL CHIANG; Editor-in-Chief TAN LEE SUN.

Chopmen Publishers Pte Ltd: 865 Mountbatten Rd, 05–28, Singapore 1543; tel. 63543936; fax 63440180; e-mail mighty@singnet.com.sg; f. 1963; scholarly, academic, children's and general; Man. Dir T. SINGH.

EPB Publishers Pte Ltd: Block 162, 04-3545 Bukit Merah Central, Singapore 150162; tel. 62780881; fax 62782456; e-mail epb@sbg.com.sg; fmrly Educational Publications Bureau Pte Ltd; textbooks and supplementary materials, general, reference and magazines; English and Chinese; Gen. Man. ROGER PHUA.

FEP International Pte Ltd: 11 Arnsal Chetty Rd 03-02, Singapore 239949; tel. 67331178; fax 67375561; f. 1960; textbooks, reference, children's and dictionaries; Gen. Man. RICHARD TOH.

Flame of the Forest Publishing Pte Ltd: Block 5, Ang Mo Kio Industrial Park 2A, 07-22/23, AMK Tech II, Singapore 567760; tel. 64848887; fax 64842208; e-mail editor@flameoftheforest.com; internet www.flameoftheforest.com; Man. Dir ALEX CHACKO.

Graham Brash Pte Ltd: 45 Kian Teck Drive, Blk 1, Level 2, Singapore 628859; tel. 62624843; fax 62621519; e-mail graham_brash@giro.com.sg; internet www.grahambrash.com.sg; f. 1947; general, academic, educational; English, Chinese and Malay; CEO CHUAN I. CAMPBELL; Dir HELENE CAMPBELL.

HarperCollins, Asia Pte Ltd: 970 Toa Payoh North, 04-24/26, Singapore 1231; tel. 62501985; fax 62501360; f. 1983; educational, trade, reference and general; Man. Dir FRANK FOLEY.

Institute of Southeast Asian Studies: 30 Heng Mui Keng Terrace, Pasir Panjang Rd, Singapore 119614; tel. 67780955; fax 67781735; e-mail publish@iseas.edu.sg; internet www.iseas.edu.sg; f. 1968; scholarly works on contemporary South-East Asia and the Asia-Pacific; Dir Prof. CHIA SIOW YUE.

Intellectual Publishing Co: 113 Eunos Ave 3, 04-08 Gordon Industrial Bldg, Singapore 1440; tel. 67466025; fax 67489108; f. 1971; Man. POH BE LECK.

Pearson Education Asia Pte Ltd: 23/25 First Lok Yang Rd, Jurong Town, Singapore 629733; tel. 63199388; fax 62641740; educational; Pres. WONG WEE WOON.

Simon & Schuster Asia Pte Ltd: 317 Alexandra Rd, 04-01 Ikea Bldg, Singapore 159965; tel. 64764688; fax 63780370; e-mail prenhall@signet.com.sg; f. 1975; educational; Man. Dir GUNAWAN HADI.

Singapore University Press Pte Ltd: National University of Singapore, 31 Lower Kent Ridge Rd, Singapore 119078; tel. 67761148; fax 67740652; e-mail supbooks@nus.edu.sg; internet www.nus.edu.sg/SUP; f. 1971; scholarly; Editor and Man. PATRICIA TAY.

Stamford College Publishers: Colombo Court 05-11A, Singapore 0617; tel. 63343378; fax 63343080; f. 1970; general, educational and journals; Man. LAWRENCE THOMAS.

Times Editions Pte Ltd: Times Centre, 1 New Industrial Rd, Singapore 536196; tel. 62139288; fax 62844733; e-mail tpl@tpl.com.sg; internet www.tpl.com.sg; f. 1978; political, social and cultural books, general works on Asia; Chair. LIM KIM SAN; Pres. and CEO LAI SECK KHUI.

Times Media Pte Ltd (Education Division): Times Centre, 1 New Industrial Rd, Singapore 536196; tel. 62139463; fax 62889254; e-mail tmesales@tpl.com.sg; internet www.timesone.com.sg/fpl; f. 1957; educational, children's, general and reference books; Vice-Pres. and Gen. Man. JUNE OEI.

World Scientific Publishing Co Pte Ltd: 5 Toh Tuck Link, Singapore 596224; tel. 64665775; fax 64677667; e-mail wspc@wspc.com.sg; internet www.worldscientific.com; f. 1981; academic texts and science journals; Man. Dir DOREEN LIU.

MALAY LANGUAGE

Malaysia Press Sdn Bhd (Pustaka Melayu): Singapore; tel. 62933454; fax 62911858; f. 1962; textbooks and educational; Man. Dir ABU TALIB BIN ALLY.

Pustaka Nasional Pte Ltd: 2 Joo Chiat Rd, 05-1125 Joo Chiat Complex, Singapore 420002; tel. 67454321; fax 67452417; e-mail webmaster@pustaka.com.sg; internet www.pustaka.com.sg; f. 1965; Malay and Islamic religious books and CD-Roms; Man. Dir SYED AHMAD BIN MUHAMMED.

CHINESE LANGUAGE

Shanghai Book Co (Pte) Ltd: 231 Bain St, 02-73 Bras Basah Complex, Singapore 180231; tel. 63360144; fax 63360490; e-mail shanghaibook@pacific.net.sg; f. 1925; educational and general; Man. Dir MA JI LIN.

Shing Lee Publishers Pte Ltd: 120 Hillview Ave, 05-06/07 Kewalram Hillview, Singapore 2366; tel. 67601388; fax 67625684; e-mail shingleebook@sbg.com.sg; f. 1935; educational and general; Man. PEH CHIN HUA.

Union Book Co (Pte) Ltd: 231 Bain St 03-01, Bras Basah Complex, Singapore 0718; tel. 63380696; fax 63386306; general and reference; Gen. Man. CHOW LI-LIANG.

TAMIL LANGUAGE

EVS Enterprises: Singapore; tel. 62830002; f. 1967; children's books, religion and general; Man. E. V. SINGHAN.

Government Publishing House

SNP Corpn Ltd: 1 Kim Seng Promenade, 18–01 Great World City East Tower, Singapore 237994; tel. 68269600; fax 68203341; e-mail btsypang@snpcorp.com; internet www.snpcorp.com; f. 1973; printers and publishers; Pres. and CEO YEO CHEE TONG.

PUBLISHERS' ORGANIZATIONS

National Book Development Council of Singapore (NBDCS): Singapore; promotes reading and jointly organizes the annual Singapore Book Fair with the Singapore Book Publishers' Association.

Singapore Book Publishers' Association: c/o Chopmen Publrs, 865 Mountbatten Rd, 05-28 Katong Shopping Centre, Singapore 1543; tel. 63441495; fax 63440180; Pres. N. T. S. CHOPRA.

Broadcasting and Communications

TELECOMMUNICATIONS

Infocomm Development Authority of Singapore: 8 Temasek Blvd, 14-00 Suntec Tower Three, Singapore 038988; tel. 62110888; fax 62112222; e-mail info@ida.gov.sg; internet www.ida.gov.sg; f. 1999 as result of merger of National Computer Board and Telecommunication Authority of Singapore; the national policy maker, regulator and promoter of telecommunications in Singapore; CEO LEONG KENG THAI (acting).

Netrust: 10 Collyer Quay, 09-05/06 Ocean Bldg, Singapore 049315; tel. 62121388; fax 62121366; e-mail infoline@netrust.net; internet www.netrust.net; f. 1997; the first Internet Certification Authority (CA), jointly formed by the National Computer Board and the Network for Electronic Transfers; the authority verifies the identity of parties doing business or communicating in cyberspace through the issuing of electronic identification certificates.

Singapore Telecommunications Ltd (SingTel): Comcentre, 31 Exeter Rd, Singapore 239732; tel. 68383388; fax 67383769; e-mail contact@singtel.com; internet www.singtel.com; f. 1992; a postal and telecommunications service operator and a holding company for a number of subsidiaries; 68%-owned by Temasek Holdings (Private) Ltd (a government holding company), 32% transferred to the private sector; Chair. ANG KONG HUA; Pres. and CEO LEE HSIEN YANG.

StarHub Pte Ltd: Head Office, 51 Cuppage Rd, 07–00, StarHub Centre, Singapore 229469; tel. 68255000; fax 67215000; e-mail customercare@starhub.com.sg; internet www.starhub.com.sg; f. 2000; telecommunications service provider; consortium includes Singapore Technologies Telemedia Pte Ltd, Singapore Power Ltd, Nippon Telegraph and Telephone Corpn (NTT) and British Telecom (BT); CEO and Pres. TERRY CLONTZ.

Singapore Technologies Telemedia: 51 Cuppage Rd, 10-11/17, Starhub Centre, Singapore 229469; tel. 67238777; fax 67207277; e-mail contactus@stt.st.com.sg; internet www.stt.st.com.sg; Pres. LEE THENG KIAT.

BROADCASTING

Regulatory Authority

Singapore Broadcasting Authority: MITA Bldg 04–01, 140 Hill St, Singapore 179369; tel. 68379973; fax 63368023; internet www.sba.gov.sg; f. 1994; regulates the broadcasting industry in Singapore; licenses and regulates broadcasting services, regulates the use of broadcasting apparatus, ensures public service broadcasting obligations, collects licence fees, establishes guidelines on programme quality and balance in subject matter and censorship, liaises with foreign broadcasters and film producers to promote and market Singapore as a regional hub, acts as representative of Singapore on matters relating to international broadcasting, encourages the development of broadcasting and related services, also manages the Internet by emphasizing industry self-regulation and public education and by establishing a regulatory framework; Chair. NIAM CHIANG MENG; CEO LIM HOCK CHUAN.

Radio

Far East Broadcasting Associates: 30 Lorong Ampas, 07-01 Skywaves Industrial Bldg, Singapore 328783; tel. 62508577; fax 62508422; e-mail febadmin@febasgp.com; f. 1960; Chair. GOH EWE KHENG; Exec. Dir Rev. JOHN CHANG.

Media Corporation of Singapore: Caldecott Broadcast Centre, Andrew Rd, Singapore 299939; tel. 63333888; fax 62515628; e-mail cherfern@mediacorpradio.com; internet www.mediacorpsingapore .com; f. 1994 as Singapore International Media (SIM), following the corporatization of the Singapore Broadcasting Corpn; holding co for seven operating cos—Television Corpn of Singapore (TCS), Singapore Television Twelve (STV12), Radio Corpn of Singapore (RCS), MediaCorp Studios, MediaCorp News, MediaCorp Interactive and MediaCorp Publishing; Chair. CHENG WAI KEUNG.

Radio Corpn of Singapore Pte Ltd (RCS): Caldecott Broadcast Centre, Radio Bldg, Andrew Rd, Singapore 299939; tel. 62518622; fax 62569533; e-mail feedback@rcs.com.sg; internet www.media corpradio.com; f. 1936; operates 12 domestic services—in English (five), Chinese (Mandarin) (three), Malay (two), Tamil (one) and foreign language (one)—and three international radio stations (manages Radio Singapore International (RSI)—services in English, Mandarin and Malay for three hours daily and service in Bahasa Indonesia for one hour daily); Chief Operating Officer CHUA FOO YONG.

Radio Heart: Singapore; internet www.heart913.org.sg; f. 1991; first private radio station; broadcasts in English, Chinese (Mandarin), Malay and Tamil; 2 channels broadcasting a total of 280 hours.

Rediffusion (Singapore) Pte Ltd: 6 Harper Rd, 04-01/08 Leong Huat Bldg, Singapore 369674; tel. 63832633; fax 63832622; e-mail md@rediffusion.com.sg; internet www.rediffusion.com.sg; f. 1949; commercial audio wired broadcasting service and wireless digital audio broadcasting service; broadcasts two programmes in Mandarin (18 hours daily) and English (24 hours daily); Man. Dir WONG BAN KUAN.

SAFRA Radio: Defence Technology Towers, Tower B, 5Depot Rd, 12–04, Singapore; tel. 63731924; fax 62783039; e-mail power98@ pacific.net.sg; internet www.power98.com.sg/; f. 1994; broadcasts in Chinese (Mandarin) and English.

Television

CNBC Asia Business News (S) Pte Ltd: 10 Anson Rd, 06-01 International Plaza, Singapore 079903; tel. 63230488; fax 63230788; e-mail talk2us@cnbcasia.com; internet www.cnbcasia.com.sg; f. 1998; cable and satellite broadcaster of global business and financial news; US controlled; broadcasts in English (24 hours daily) and Mandarin; Pres. PAUL FRANCE.

Media Corporation of Singapore: (see Radio).

Singapore CableVision: Singapore; internet www.scv.com.sg; f. 1992; broadcasting and communications co, subscription television service; three channels; launched cable service with 33 channels in June 1995; offers broadband access services.

Singapore Television Twelve Pte Ltd (STV12): 12 Prince Edward Rd, 05-00 Bestway Bldg, Singapore 079212; tel. 62258133; fax 62203881; internet www.stv12.com.sg; f. 1994; terrestrial television station; 2 channels—Suria (Malay, 58 hours weekly) and Central (110.5 hours weekly); Chief Operating Officer WOON TAI HO.

Television Corpn of Singapore (TCS): Caldecott Broadcast Centre, Andrew Rd, Singapore 299939; tel. 62560401; fax 62538119; e-mail webmaster@mediacorptv.com; internet www.mediacorptv.com; f. 1994 following the corporatization of Singapore Broadcasting Corporation; four channels—TCS 5 (English), TCS 8 (Mandarin), Suria (Malay) and Central; teletext service on two channels; also owns TVMobile, Singapore's first digital television channel, and Digital TV; Chair. CHENG WAI KEUNG; CEO LIM HUP SENG.

Finance

(cap. = capital; res = reserves; dep. = deposits; m. = million; brs = branches; amounts in Singapore dollars)

BANKING

The Singapore monetary system is regulated by the Monetary Authority of Singapore (MAS) and the Ministry of Finance. The MAS performs all the functions of a central bank, except the issuing of currency, a function which is carried out by the Board of Commissioners of Currency. In March 2002 there were 122 commercial banks (6 local, 116 foreign) and 57 representative offices in Singapore. Of the foreign banks, 22 had full licences, 19 had restricted licences and 75 foreign banks had 'offshore' banking licences.

Government Financial Institutions

Board of Commissioners of Currency, Singapore: 109 Pasir Panjang Rd, Singapore 118536; tel. 63776868; fax 63776800; e-mail currency@bccs.gov.sg; internet www.singaporecurrency.gov.sg; Chair. Brig.-Gen. (retd) LEE HSIEN LOONG; Dep. Chair. LIM SIONG GUAN.

Monetary Authority of Singapore (MAS): 10 Shenton Way, MAS Bldg, Singapore 079117; tel. 62255577; fax 62299229; e-mail webmaster@mas.gov.sg; internet www.mas.gov.sg; cap. 100m., res 13,857m., dep. 78,004m. (Dec. 2001); Chair. Brig.-Gen. (retd) LEE HSIEN LOONG; Man. Dir KOH YONG GUAN.

Domestic Full Commercial Banks

Bank of Singapore Ltd: 01-01 Tong Eng Bldg, 101 Cecil St, 01-01 Tong Eng Bldg, Singapore 069533; tel. 63893000; fax 63893016; internet www.bankofsingapore.com; f. 1954; subsidiary of Oversea-Chinese Banking Corpn Ltd; cap. 50m., res 207m., dep. 2,984.5m. (Dec. 1997); Chair. and CEO ALEXANDER AU SIU KEE; 1 local br.

DBS Bank (Development Bank of Singapore Ltd): 6 Shenton Way, DBS Bldg, Tower One, Singapore 068809; tel. 68788888; fax 64451267; e-mail dbs@dbs.com; internet www.dbs.com; f. 1968; 29% govt-owned; merged with Post Office Savings Bank in 1998; cap. 1,307m., res 9,187.5m., dep. 93,422.7m. (Dec. 2000); Chair. S. DHANABALAN; Pres. JACKSON TAI; 100 local brs, 14 overseas brs.

Far Eastern Bank Ltd: 156 Cecil St, 01-00 FEB Bldg, Singapore 069544; tel. 62219055; fax 62242263; internet www.uobgroup.com; f. 1959; subsidiary of United Overseas Bank Ltd; cap. 24.4m., res 53m., dep. 577.0m. (Dec. 2000); Chair. and CEO WEE CHO YAW; Pres. WEE EE CHEONG; 4 brs.

Industrial and Commercial Bank Ltd: Unity Tower One, 2 Shenton Way 01-01, Singapore 068804; tel. 62211711; fax 62259777; internet www.uobgroup.com; f. 1954; subsidiary of United Overseas Bank Ltd; cap. 168.3m., res 406.0m., dep. 3,097.5m. (Dec. 2000); Chair. and CEO WEE CHO YAW; Pres. WEE EE CHONG; 10 brs.

Oversea-Chinese Banking Corpn (OCBC) Ltd: 65 Chulia St, 08-00 OCBC Centre, Singapore 049513; tel. 65357222; fax 65337955; e-mail info@obc.com.sg; internet www.ocbc.com; f. 1932; merged with Keppel TatLee Bank Ltd in August 2001; cap. 1,286m., res 4,348.8m., dep. 41,715.2m. (Dec. 2000); Chair. LEE SENG WEE; Vice-Chair. and CEO ALEXANDER AU SIU KEE; 37 local brs, 44 overseas brs.

United Overseas Bank Ltd: 80 Raffles Place, UOB Plaza, Singapore 048624; tel. 65339898; fax 65342334; internet www.uobgroup.com; f. 1935; merged with Overseas Union Bank Ltd in Jan. 2002; cap. 1,052.5m., res 4,004.8m., dep. 46,718.0m. (Dec. 2000); Chair. and CEO WEE CHO YAW; Pres. WEE EE CHEONG; 49 local brs, 15 overseas brs.

Foreign Banks

Full Commercial Banks

ABN AMRO Asia Pacific Pte Ltd (Netherlands): 63 Chulia St, Singapore 049514; tel. 62318888; fax 65323108; Country Rep. DAVID WONG SEE HONG; Country Admin. Officer ROBERT DAVIS.

Bangkok Bank Public Co Ltd (Thailand): 180 Cecil St, Bangkok Bank Bldg, Singapore 069546; tel. 62219400; fax 62255852; Sr Vice-Pres. and Gen. Man. TORPHONG CHARUNGCHAREONVEJI.

Bank of America NA (USA): 9 Raffles Place, 18-00 Republic Plaza Tower 1, Singapore 048619; tel. 62393888; fax 62393188; CEO ALAN KOH; Man. Dir GOETZ EGGELHOEFER.

Bank of China (People's Republic of China): 4 Battery Rd, Bank of China Bldg, Singapore 049908; tel. 65352411; fax 65343401; Gen. Man. ZHU HUA.

Bank of East Asia Ltd (Hong Kong): 137 Market St, Bank of East Asia Bldg, Singapore 048943; tel. 62241334; fax 62251805; Gen. Man. KHOO KEE CHEOK.

Bank of India (India): 01-01, 02-01, 03-01, Hong Leong Centre, 138 Robinson Rd, Singapore 068906; tel. 62220011; fax 62254407; Chief Exec. B. R. PARTHASARATHI; Gen. Man. RAJIV KUMAR BAKSHI.

PT Bank Negara Indonesia (Persero) Tbk (Indonesia): 158 Cecil St, 01-00 to 04-00 Dapenso Bldg, Singapore 069545; tel. 62257755; fax 62254757; e-mail ptbni@starhub.net.sg; Gen. Man. SUWOKO SINGOASTRO.

Bank of Tokyo-Mitsubishi Ltd (Japan): 9 Raffles Place, 01-01 Republic Plaza, Singapore 048619; tel. 65383388; fax 65388083; Gen. Man. HISAO SAKASHITA; Dep. Gen. Man. KAZUAKI IWAMOTO.

BNP Private Paribas (France): 20 Collyer Quay, 01-01 Tung Centre, Singapore 049319; tel. 62103888; fax 62103671; internet www.bnpparibas.com.sg; CEO SERGE FORTI.

Citibank NA (USA): 3 Temasek Ave, 12-00 Centennial Tower, Singapore 039190; tel. 62242611; fax 6325880; internet www.citibank.com.sg; Country Corporate Officer SUNIL SREENIVASAN.

Crédit Agricole Indosuez (France): 6 Raffles Quay, 17-00 John Hancock Tower, Singapore 048580; tel. 65354988; fax 65322422; e-mail cai.singapore@sg.ca-indosuez.com; internet www.ca-indosuez.com; f. 1905; Senior Country Man. JEAN-FRANCOIS CAHET.

HL Bank (Malaysia): 20 Collyer Quay, 01-02 and 02-02 Tung Centre, Singapore 049319; tel. 65352466; fax 65339340; Country Head GAN HUI TIN.

Hongkong and Shanghai Banking Corpn Ltd (Hong Kong): 14-01 HSBC Bldg, 21 Collyer Quay, Singapore 049320; tel. 65305000; fax 62250663; e-mail HSBC@hsbc.com.sg; internet www.hsbc.com.sg; CEO (Singapore) ERIC W. GILL.

Indian Bank (India): 3 Raffles Place, Bharat Bldg, Singapore 048617; tel. 65343511; fax 65331651; e-mail ceibsing@mbox3.singnet.com.sg; Chief Exec. V. SRINIVASAN.

Indian Overseas Bank (India): POB 792, 64 Cecil St, IOB Bldg, Singapore 049711; tel. 62251100; fax 62244490; Chief Exec. A. C. KHER.

JP Morgan Chase Bank (USA): 168 Robinson Rd, 17th Floor, 14-01 Capital Tower, Singapore 068912; tel. 68822888; fax 68821756; Senior Country Officer JEANETTE WONG KAI YUAN.

Maybank (Malaysia): Maybank Chambers, 2 Battery Rd 01-00, Singapore 049907; tel. 65352266; fax 65327909; internet www.maybank2u.com.sg; Sr Gen. Man. SPENCER LEE TIEN CHYE.

RHB Bank Bhd (Malaysia): 90 Cecil St 01-00, Singapore 069531; tel. 62253111; fax 62273805; Asst Gen. Man. (Head of Singapore Operations) ANTHONY YEO.

Southern Bank Bhd (Malaysia): 39 Robinson Rd, 01-02 Robinson Point, Singapore 068911; tel. 65321318; fax 65355366; Dir YEAP LAM YANG.

Standard Chartered Bank (UK): 6 Battery Rd, Singapore 049909; tel. 62258888; fax 64230965; internet www.standardchartered.com.sg; Group Exec. Dirs MIKE DENOMA, KAI NARGOLWALA; Chief Exec. (Singapore) EULEEN GOH.

Sumitomo Mitsui Banking Corpn (Japan): 3 Temasek Ave, 06-01 Centennial Tower, Singapore 039190; tel. 68820001; fax 68870330; Gen. Man. HITOSHI YOSHIMATSU.

UCO Bank (India): 3 Raffles Place, 01-01 Bharat Bldg, Singapore 048617; tel. 65325944; fax 65325044; e-mail general@ucobank.com.sg; Chief Exec. R. K. MUKHERJEE.

Restricted Banks

American Express Bank Ltd (USA): 16 Collyer Quay, Hitachi Tower, Singapore 049318; tel. 65384833; fax 65343022; Sr Country Exec. S. LACHLAN HOUGH.

Barclays Bank plc (UK): 23 Church St, 13-08 Capital Sq., Singapore 049481; tel. 63953000; fax 63953139; Regional Head JAMES LOH; Country Man. QUEK SUAN KIAT.

Bayerische Landesbank Girozentrale (Germany): 300 Beach Rd, 37-01 The Concourse, Singapore 199555; tel. 62933822; fax 62932151; e-mail sgblb@blb.de; Gen. Man. and Sr Vice-Pres. MANFRED WOLF; Exec. Vice-Pres. HEINZ HOFFMANN.

Chiao Tung Bank Co Ltd (Taiwan): 80 Raffles Place, 23-20 UOB Plaza II, Singapore 048624; tel. 65366311; fax 65360680; Sr Vice-Pres. and Gen. Man. FRANK WEI KUANG HUA.

Commerzbank AG (Germany): 8 Shenton Way, 41-01 Temasek Tower, Singapore 068811; tel. 63110000; fax 62253943; Gen. Man. MICHAEL OLIVER.

Crédit Suisse First Boston (Switzerland): 1 Raffles Link, 03/04-01 South Lobby, Singapore 039393; tel. 62122000; fax 62123100; Br. Man. ERIC M. VARVEL.

Deutsche Bank AG (Germany): 6 Shenton Way, 15-08 DBS Bldg, Tower Two, Singapore 068809; tel. 64238001; fax 62259442; Gen. Man. RONNY TAN CHONG TEE.

Dresdner Bank AG (Germany): 20 Collyer Quay, 22-00 Tung Centre, Singapore 049319; tel. 62228080; fax 62244008; Man. Dirs PHILIP DEFORD, RAYMOND B. T. KOH, LEE SIEW CHIANG; CEO BAUDOUIN GROONENBERGHS.

First Commercial Bank (Taiwan): 76 Shenton Way, 01-02 ONG Bldg, Singapore 079119; tel. 62215755; fax 62251905; e-mail fcbsin@singnet.com.sg; Vice-Pres. and Gen. Man. YANG TAY-PYNG.

Fuji Bank Ltd (Japan): 1 Raffles Place, 20-00 OUB Centre, Singapore 048616; tel. 65343500; fax 65327310; Gen. Man. FUSATO SUZUKI.

Habib Bank Ltd (Pakistan): 3 Phillip St, 01-03 Commerce Point, Singapore 048693; tel. 64380055; fax 64380644; e-mail gmhbl@singnet.com.sg; Regional Gen. Man. ASHRAF MAHMOOD WATHRA.

IntesaBci SpA (Italy): 9 Raffles Place, 49-02 Republic Plaza, Singapore 048619; tel. 62201333; fax 62271619; Gen. Man. GIORGIO MARIA ROSICA.

Korea Exchange Bank (Republic of Korea): 30 Cecil St, 24-03/08 Prudential Tower, Singapore 049712; tel. 65361633; fax 65382522; e-mail kebspore@singnet.com.sg; Gen. Man. KIM SEONG JUNG.

Moscow Narodny Bank Ltd (UK): 50 Robinson Rd, MNB Bldg, Singapore 068882; tel. 62209422; fax 62250140; Man. Dir EVGENY MIKHAILOVICH GREVTSEV.

Rabobank International (Netherlands): 77 Robinson Rd, 09-00 SIA Bldg, Singapore 068896; tel. 65363363; fax 65363236; Exec. Vice-Pres. CHRISTIAN H. A. M. MOL.

Societé Generale (France): 80 Robinson Rd, 25-00, Singapore 068898; tel. 62227122; fax 62252609; CEO and Country Man. DANIEL MOLLE.

UBS AG (Switzerland): 5 Temasek Blvd, 18-00 Suntec City Tower, Singapore 038985; tel. 64318000; fax 64318188; e-mail rolf-w.gerber@wdr.com; Man. Dir and Head of Br. (Singapore) ROLF GERBER.

UFJ Bank Ltd (Japan): 6 Raffles Quay, 24-01 John Hancock Tower, Singapore 048580; tel. 65384838; fax 65384636; Gen. Man. GEN TOMII.

'Offshore' Banks

ABSA Bank Ltd (South Africa): 7 Temasek Blvd, 16-01 Suntec Tower One, Singapore 038987; tel. 63331033; fax 63331066; Gen. Man. DAVID MEADOWS.

Agricultural Bank of China (People's Republic of China): 80 Raffles Place, 27-20 UOB Plaza 2, Singapore 048624; tel. 65355255; fax 65387960; Gen. Man. WANG GANG.

Arab Bank PLC (Jordan): 80 Raffles Place, 32-20 UOB Plaza 2, Singapore 048624; tel. 65330055; fax 65322150; e-mail abplc@pacific.net.com.sg; Exec. Vice-Pres. and Area Exec. Asia Pacific KIM EUN-YOUNG.

Arab Banking Corpn (BSC) (Bahrain): 9 Raffles Place, 35-01 Republic Plaza, Singapore 048619; tel. 65359339; fax 65326288; Gen. Man. JOHN MEADS.

Australia and New Zealand Banking Group Ltd (Australia): 10 Collyer Quay, 17-01/07 Ocean Bldg, Singapore 049315; tel. 65358355; fax 65396111; Regional Gen. Man. JOHN WINDERS.

Banca Monte dei Paschi di Siena SpA (Italy): 10 Collyer Quay, 13-01 Ocean Bldg, Singapore 0104; tel. 65352533; fax 65327996; Gen. Man. GIUSEPPE DE GIOSA.

Banca Nazionale del Lavoro SpA (Italy): 9 Raffles Place, 50-01 Republic Plaza, Singapore 048619; tel. 65366063; fax 65365213; e-mail bnlsing@pacific.net.sg; Sen. Vice-Pres. and Gen. Man. FRANCO UNGARO.

Banca di Roma (Italy): 9 Raffles Place, 20-20 Republic Plaza II, Singapore 048619; tel. 64387509; fax 65352267; e-mail bdrsi@singnet.com.sg; Gen. Man. MARIO FATTORUSSO.

Bank Brussels Lambert (Belgium): 1 Raffles Place, 42-00 OUB Centre, Singapore 048616; tel. 65324088; fax 65305750; Gen. Man. ALAIN CORDENIER.

Bank of Communications (People's Republic of China): 50 Raffles Place, 26-04 Singapore Land Tower, Singapore 048623; tel. 65320335; fax 65320339; Gen. Man. DU PING.

PT Bank Mandiri (Persero) (Indonesia): 16 Collyer Quay, 28-00 Hitachi Tower, Singapore 049318; tel. 65320200; fax 65320206; Gen. Man. ERWIN ALIMUDIN.

Bank of New York (USA): 1 Temasek Ave, 02-01 Millenia Tower, Singapore 039192; tel. 64320222; fax 63374302; Sr Vice-Pres. and Man. Dir JAI ARYA.

Bank of New Zealand (New Zealand): 5 Temasek Blvd, 15-01 Suntec City Tower, Singapore 038985; tel. 63322990; fax 63322991; Gen. Man. VICTOR CHUA BENG KHOON.

Bank of Nova Scotia (Canada): 10 Collyer Quay, 15-01/09 Ocean Bldg, Singapore 049315; tel. 65358688; fax 65363325; Country Head, Vice-Pres. and Man. SEONG KOON WAH SUN.

Bank of Scotland (UK): 50 Raffles Place, 16-06 Singapore Land Tower, Singapore 048623; tel. 64382721; fax 64382706; Regional Dir and CEO ADAM R. ION.

Bank One NA (USA): 9 Raffles Place, 29-02 Republic Plaza, Singapore 048619; tel. 64382488; fax 64382070; e-mail Yew_Chong_Tan@bankone.com; Regional Head and Gen. Man. DENNIS PORTELLI.

Bank of Taiwan (Taiwan): 80 Raffles Place, 28-20 UOB Plaza 2, Singapore 048624; tel. 65365536; fax 65368203; Vice-Pres. and Gen. Man. CHANG SHOU-HSING.

Bayerische Hypo- und Vereinsbank AG (Germany): 30 Cecil St, 26-01 Prudential Tower, Singapore 049712; tel. 64133688; fax 65368591; Gen. Man. PETER NG POH LIAN.

Bumiputra Commerce Bank Berhad (Malaysia): 7 Temasek Blvd, 37-01/02/03 Suntec Tower One, Singapore 038987; tel. 63375115; fax 63371335; e-mail bpsp3700@pacific.net.sg; Gen. Man. Raja SULONG AHMAD BIN Raja ABDUL RAZAK.

Canadian Imperial Bank of Commerce (Canada): 16 Collyer Quay, 04-02 Hitachi Tower, Singapore 049318; tel. 65352323; fax 65357565; Br. Man. NORMAN SIM CHEE BENG.

Chang Hwa Commercial Bank Ltd (China): 1 Finlayson Green, 08-00, Singapore 049246; tel. 65320820; fax 65320374; Gen. Man. YANG JIH-CHENG.

China Construction Bank (China): 9 Raffles Place, 33-01/02 Republic Plaza, Singapore 048619; tel. 65358133; fax 65386616; Gen. Man. KONG YONG XIN.

Chohung Bank (Republic of Korea): 50 Raffles Place, 04-02/03 Singapore Land Tower, Singapore 048623; tel. 65361144; fax 65331244; Gen. Man. HA-WOOK PARK.

Commonwealth Bank of Australia (Australia): 50 Raffles Place, 22-02 Singapore Land Tower, Singapore 048623; tel. 62243877; fax 62245812; Gen. Man. ROBERT LEWIS BUCHAN.

Crédit Industriel et Commercial (France): 9 Raffles Place, 23-01/02 Republic Plaza, Singapore 048619; tel. 65366008; fax 65367008; internet www.cic.com.sg; Gen. Man. JEAN-LUC ANGLADA.

Crédit Lyonnais (France): 3 Temasek Ave, 11-01 Centennial Tower, Singapore 039190; tel. 63336331; fax 63336332; Gen. Man. PIERRE EYMERY.

Crédit Suisse (Switzerland): 1 Raffles Link, 05-02, Singapore 039393; tel. 62126000; fax 62126200; internet www.cspb.com.sg; Br. Man. PIERRE-FRANCOIS BAER.

Dai-Ichi Kangyo Bank Ltd (Japan): 168 Robinson Rd, 13-00 Capital Tower, Singapore 068912; tel. 64230330; fax 64230012; Gen. Man. NOBORU TAKAGI.

Dexia Banque Internationale à Luxembourg (Luxembourg): 9 Raffles Place, 42-01 Republic Plaza, Singapore 048619; tel. 62227622; fax 65360201; Gen. Man. ALEXANDRE JOSSET.

DZ Bank AG Deutsche Zentral (Germany): 50 Raffles Place, 40-01 Singapore Land Tower, Singapore 048623; tel. 64380082; fax 62230082; Gen. Man. KLAUS GERHARD BORIG.

Fleet National Bank (USA): 150 Beach Rd, 07-00 Gateway West, Singapore 189720; tel. 62962366; fax 62960998; Regional Man. ANTHONY LOH.

Fortis Bank SA/NV (Belgium/Netherlands): 30 Raffles Place, 18-00 Caltex House, Singapore 048622; tel. 65394988; fax 65394933; Gen. Man. GIJSBERT SCHOT.

Hamburgische Landesbank Girozentrale (Germany): 3 Temasek Ave, 32-02 Centennial Tower, Singapore 039190; tel. 65509000; fax 65509003; e-mail info@hamburglb.com.sg; Gen. Man. and Exec. Dir DETLEV REHMKE.

Hana Bank (Republic of Korea): 8 Cross St, 23-06 PWC Bldg, Singapore 048424; tel. 64384100; fax 64384200; Gen. Man. SHIN JOON-SANG.

Hang Seng Bank Ltd (Hong Kong): 21 Collyer Quay, 14-01 HSBC Bldg, Singapore 049320; tel. 65363118; fax 65363148; e-mail sgp@hangseng.com; Country Man. ALEX CHEN CHARNG-TERK (acting).

Hanvit Bank (Republic of Korea): 5 Shenton Way, 17-03 UIC Bldg, Singapore 068808; tel. 62235855; fax 62259530; e-mail combksp@singnet.com.sg; Gen. Man. PARK DONG YOUNG.

HSBC Bank USA: 21-00 HSBC Bldg, 21 Collyer Quay, Singapore 049320; tel. 62240077; fax 62255769; Man. Dir and Country Chief JOHN C. HANSON.

Hua Nan Commercial Bank Ltd (Taiwan): 80 Robinson Rd, 14-03, Singapore 068898; tel. 63242566; fax 63242155; Gen. Man. GEENG JENG FANG.

Industrial and Commercial Bank of China (People's Republic of China): 6 Raffles Quay, 12-01 John Hancock Tower, Singapore 048580; tel. 65381066; fax 65381370; e-mail icbcsg@singnet.com.sg; Gen. Man. SHI QILU.

Industrial Bank of Japan Ltd (Japan): 16 Collyer Quay, 14-00 Hitachi Tower, Singapore 049318; tel. 65387366; fax 65387779; Gen. Man. NAOKI IZAWA.

ING Bank NV (Netherlands): 9 Raffles Place, 19-02 Republic Plaza, Singapore 048619; tel. 65353688; fax 65338329; Country Head J. KESTEMONT.

International Commercial Bank of China (Taiwan): 6 Battery Rd, 39-03, Singapore 049909; tel. 62277667; fax 62271858; Vice-Pres. and Gen. Man. YEN-PING HSIANG.

KBC Bank NV (Belgium): 30 Cecil St, 12-01/08 Prudential Tower, Singapore 049712; tel. 63952828; fax 65342929; Gen. Man. YIN MIN YONG.

Korea Development Bank (Republic of Korea): 8 Shenton Way, 07-01 Temasek Tower, Singapore 068811; tel. 62248188; fax 62256540; Gen. Man. KIM KI CHEOL.

Krung Thai Bank Public Co Ltd (Thailand): 65 Chulia St, 32-05/08 OCBC Centre, Singapore 049513; tel. 65336691; fax 65330930; e-mail ktbs@pacific.net.sg; Gen. Man. PERMPOM SITTIPIYASAKUL.

Landesbank Baden-Württemberg (Germany): 25 International Business Park, 01-72 German Centre, Singapore 609916; tel. 65627722; fax 65627729; Man. Dr WOLFHART AUER VAN HERRENKIRCHEN.

Lloyds TSB Bank PLC (UK): 3 Temasek Ave 19-01, Centennial Tower, Singapore 039190; tel. 65341191; fax 65322493; e-mail mktg@lloydstsb.com.sg; Country Head BARRY LEA.

Mitsubishi Trust and Banking Corpn (Japan): 50 Raffles Place, 42-01/06 Singapore Land Tower, Singapore 048623; tel. 62259155; fax 62241857; Gen. Man. MIKIO KOBAYASHI.

Natexis Banques Populaires (France): 50 Raffles Place, 41-01, Singapore Land Tower, Singapore 048623; tel. 62241455; fax 62248651; Gen. Man. PHILIPPE PETITGAS.

National Australia Bank Ltd (Australia): 5 Temasek Blvd, 15-01 Suntec City Tower Five, Singapore 038985; tel. 63380038; fax 63380039; Gen. Man. VICTOR CHUA BENG KHOON.

National Bank of Kuwait SAK (Kuwait): 20 Collyer Quay, 20-00 Tung Centre, Singapore 049319; tel. 62225348; fax 62245438; Gen. Man. R. J. MCKEGNEY.

Nedcor Bank Ltd (South Africa): 30 Cecil St, 10-05 Prudential Tower, Singapore 049712; tel. 64169438; fax 64388350; e-mail ned sing@nedcor.com; Gen. Man. BRIAN SHEGAR.

Norddeutsche Landesbank Girozentrale (Germany): 6 Shenton Way, 16-08 DBS Bldg Tower Two, Singapore 068809; tel. 63231223; fax 63230223; e-mail nordlb.singapore@nordlb.com; Gen. Man. and Regional Head Asia/Pacific HEINZ WERNER FRINGS.

Nordea Bank Finland Plc (Finland): 50 Raffles Place, 15-01 Singapore Land Tower, Singapore 048623; tel. 62258211; fax 62255469; e-mail singapore@nordea.com; Gen. Man. PETRI SANDELL.

Norinchukin Bank (Japan): 80 Raffles Place, 53-01 UOB Plaza 1, Singapore 048624; tel. 65351011; fax 65352883; Gen. Man. JUNICHI KOBAYASHI.

Den norske Bank ASA (Norway): 8 Shenton Way, 48-02 Temasek Tower, Singapore 068811; tel. 62206144; fax 62249743; e-mail dnb.singapore@dnb.no; Gen. Man. PÅL SKOE.

Northern Trust Company (USA): 80 Raffles Place, 46th Floor, UOB Plaza 1, Singapore 048624; tel. 64376666; fax 64376609; e-mail hynl@ntrs.com; Sr Vice-Pres. LAWRENCE AU.

Philippine National Bank (Philippines): 96 Somerset Rd, 04-01/04 UOL Bldg, Singapore 238183; tel. 67374646; fax 67374224; e-mail singapore@pnb.com.ph; Vice-Pres. and Gen. Man. RODELO G. FRANCO.

Raiffeisen Zentralbank Oesterreich Aktiengesellschaft (Austria): 50 Raffles Place, 45-01 Singapore Land Tower, Singapore 048623; tel. 62259578; fax 62253973; Gen. Man. RAINER SILHAVY.

Royal Bank of Canada (Canada): 20 Raffles Place, 27-03/08 Ocean Towers, Singapore 048620; tel. 65369206; fax 65322804; Gen. Man. LARRY YAN KING NAM.

Royal Bank of Scotland PLC (UK): 50 Raffles Place, 08-00 Singapore Land Tower, Singapore 048623; tel. 64168600; fax 62259827; Regional Man. ROBERT. I. GARDEN.

San Paolo IMI SpA (Italy): 6 Temasek Blvd, 42/04-05 Suntec Tower Four, Singapore 038986; tel. 63338270; fax 63338252; e-mail singapore.sg@sanpaoloimi.com; Gen. Man. GUIDO IMBIMBO.

Skandinaviska Enskilda Banken AB Publ (Sweden): 50 Raffles Place, 36-01 Singapore Land Tower, Singapore 048623; tel. 62235644; fax 62253047; Gen. Man. PER ENGSTRÖM.

Siam Commercial Bank Public Company Ltd (Thailand): 16 Collyer Quay, 25-01 Hitachi Tower, Singapore 049318; tel. 65364338; fax 65364728; Vice-Pres. and Gen. Man. NATTAPONG SAMIT AMPAIPISARN.

State Bank of India (India): 6 Shenton Way, 22-08 DBS Bldg Tower Two, Singapore 068809; tel. 62222033; fax 62253348; e-mail sbinsgsg@pacific.net.sg; CEO PADMA RAMASUBBAN.

State Street Bank and Trust Co (USA): 8 Shenton Way, 33-03 Temasek Tower, Singapore 068811; tel. 63299600; fax 62259377; Br. Man. LEE YOW FEE.

Sumitomo Trust & Banking Co Ltd (Japan): 8 Shenton Way, 45-01 Temasek Tower, Singapore 068811; tel. 62249055; fax 62242873; Gen. Man. HIDEHIKO ASAI.

Svenska Handelsbanken AB (publ) (Sweden): 65 Chulia St, 21-01/04 OCBC Centre, Singapore 049513; tel. 65323800; fax 65344909; Gen. Man. MAJ-LISS OLSSON.

Toronto-Dominion (South East Asia) Ltd (Canada): 15-02 Millenia Tower, 1 Temasek Ave, Singapore 039192; tel. 64346000; fax 63369500; Man. Dir HENRY SCHINDELE.

UniCredito Italiano SpA (Italy): 80 Raffles Place, 51-01 UOB Plaza 1, Singapore 048624; tel. 62325728; fax 65344300; e-mail singaporebranch@gruppocredit.it; Gen. Man. GIANNI FRANCO PAPA.

Union de Banques Arabes et Françaises (UBAF) (France): 6 Temasek Blvd, 25-04-05 Suntec Tower Four, Singapore 038986; tel. 63336188; fax 63336789; e-mail ubafsg@singnet.com.sg; Gen. Man. BENOIT GUEROULT.

Westdeutsche Landesbank Girozentrale (Germany): Centennial Tower, 3 Temasek Ave 33-00, Singapore 039190; tel. 63332388; fax 63332399; Gen. Man. KLAUS R. GERRITZEN.

Westpac Banking Corpn (Australia): 77 Robinson Rd, 19-00 SIA Bldg, Singapore 068896; tel. 65309898; fax 65326781; e-mail yhlee@westpac.wm.au; Gen. Man. LEE YEW HUAT.

Association

Association of Banks in Singapore: 10 Shenton Way, 12-08 MAS Bldg, Singapore 079117; tel. 62244300; fax 62241785; e-mail banks@abs.org.sg; internet www.abs.org.sg; Dir ONG-ANG AI BOON.

STOCK EXCHANGE

Singapore Exchange Limited (SGX): 2 Shenton Way, 19-00 SGX Centre One, Singapore 068804; tel. 62368888; fax 65356994; e-mail webmaster@sgx.com; internet www.sgx.com; f. 1999, as a result of the merger of the Stock Exchange of Singapore (SES, f. 1930) and the Singapore International Monetary Exchange Ltd (SIMEX, f. 1984); Chair. J. Y. PILLAY; CEO TOM KLOET; Pres. ANG SWEE TIAN.

INSURANCE

The insurance industry is supervised by the Monetary Authority of Singapore (see Banking). In March 2002 there were 145 insurance companies, comprising 54 direct insurers (eight life insurance, 40 general insurance, six composite insurers), 43 professional reinsurers (one life reinsurer, 34 general reinsurers, eight composite reinsurers) and 48 captive insurers.

Domestic Companies

Life Insurance

Asia Life Assurance Society Ltd: 2 Finlayson Green, 05-00 Asia Insurance Bldg, Singapore 049247; tel. 62243181; fax 62239120; e-mail asialife@asialife.com.sg; internet www.asialife.com.sg; f. 1948; Chair. TAN ENG HENG.

John Hancock Life Assurance Co Ltd: 6 Raffles Quay, 21-00 John Hancock Tower, Singapore 048580; tel. 65383333; fax 65383233; internet www.jhancock.com.sg; f. 1954; Pres. MALCOLM J. J. ARNEY.

OUB Manulife Pte Ltd: 491B River Valley Rd, 07-00 Valley Point, Singapore 248373; tel. 67371221; fax 67378488; e-mail custrve@oubmanulife.com.sg; internet www.oubmanulife.com.sg; Pres. KEITH WEAVER.

Prudential Assurance Co Singapore (Pte) Ltd: 30 Cecil St, 30-01 Prudential Tower, Singapore 049712; tel. 65358988; fax 65354043; e-mail customer.service@prudential.com.sg; internet www.prudential.com.sg; CEO TAN SUEE CHIEH.

UOB Life Assurance Ltd: 156 Cecil St, 10-01 Far Eastern Bank Bldg, Singapore 069544; tel. 62278477; fax 62243012; internet www.uob.com.sg; Man. Dir RAYMOND KWOK CHONG SEE.

General Insurance

Allianz Insurance Company of Singapore Pte Ltd: 3 Temasek Ave, 03-01 Centennial Tower, Singapore 039190; tel. 62972529; fax 62971956; e-mail askme@allianz.com.sg; internet www.allianz.com.sg; formed by merger between Allianz Insurance (Singapore) Pte Ltd and AGF Insurance (Singapore) Pte Ltd; Man. Dir NEIL BASSETT EMERY.

Asia Insurance Co Ltd: 2 Finlayson Green, 03-00 Asia Insurance Bldg, Singapore 049247; tel. 62243181; fax 62214355; e-mail asiains@asiainsurance.com.sg; internet www.asiainsurance.com.sg; f. 1923; cap. p.u. S $75m.; Chair. TAN ENG HENG; Man. Dir LOO SUN MUN.

Asian Securitization and Infrastructure Assurance (Pte) Ltd: 9 Temasek Blvd, 38-01 Suntec Tower 2, Singapore 038989; tel. 63342555; fax 63342777; e-mail general@asialtd.com; Dir ELEANOR L. LIPSEY.

Axa Insurance Singapore Pte Ltd: 143 Cecil St, 01-01 GB Bldg, Singapore 069542; tel. 63387288; fax 63382522; e-mail customer.service@axa-insurance.com.sg; internet www.axainsurance.com.sg; fmrly East West-USI Insurance Pte Ltd; Pres. and CEO CLAUDE MARX.

Cigna Insurance Singapore Ltd: 152 Beach Rd, 25-05 Gateway East, Singapore 189721; tel. 63910501; fax 62981323; Prin. Officer PAUL HARTLEY.

Cosmic Insurance Corpn Ltd: 410 North Bridge Rd, 04-01 Cosmic Insurance Bldg, Singapore 188726; tel. 63387633; fax 63397805; internet www.cosmic.com.sg; f. 1971; Gen. Man. TEO LIP MOH.

ECICS-COFACE Guarantee Co (Singapore) Ltd: 7 Temasek Blvd, 11-01 Suntec City Tower 1, Singapore 038987; tel. 63374779; fax 63389267; e-mail ecics@ecics.com.sg; internet www.ecics.com.sg; Chair. KWAH THIAM HOCK; Asst Vice-Pres. JONATHAN TANG.

First Capital Insurance Ltd: 80 Robinson Rd, 09-02/03, Singapore 068898; tel. 62222311; fax 62223547; e-mail enquiry@fcc.com.sg; internet www.first-insurance.com.sg; Gen. Man. TAN THIAM SENG.

India International Insurance Pte Ltd: 64 Cecil St, 04-00/05-00 IOB Bldg, Singapore 049711; tel. 62238122; fax 62244174; e-mail insure@iii.com.sg; internet www.iii.com.sg; f. 1987; all non-life insurance; CEO R. ATHAPPAN.

Kemper International Insurance Co (Pte) Ltd: 3 Shenton Way, 22-09 Shenton House, Singapore 068805; tel. 68369120; fax 68369121; e-mail vchia@kemper.com.sg; internet www.kemper.com.sg; Gen. Man. VIOLET CHIA.

Liberty Citystate Insurance Pte Ltd: 51 Club St, 03-00 Singapore 069428; tel. 62218611; fax 62263360; e-mail koh.peter@libertycitystate.com.sg; internet www.libertycitystate.com.sg; fmrly Citystate Insurance Pte Ltd; Man. Dir PETER KOH TIEN HOE.

Mitsui Sumitomo Insurance (Singapore) Pte Ltd: 16 Raffles Quay, 24-01 Hong Leong Bldg, Singapore 048581; tel. 62209644; fax 62256371; internet www.ms-ins.com.sg; fmrly Mitsui Marine and Fire Insurance (Asia) Private Ltd; merged with The Sumitomo Marine and Fire Insurance Co Ltd and name changed as above; Man. Dir YOSHIO IIJIMA; Dep. Gen. Man. NOBORI OMORI.

The Nanyang Insurance Co Ltd: 302 Orchard Rd, 09-01 Tong Bldg, Singapore 238862; tel. 67388211; fax 67388133; e-mail tnicl@nanyanginsurance.com.sg; f. 1956; Dir and Principal Officer FREDDIE YEO.

Overseas Union Insurance Ltd: 50 Collyer Quay, 02-02 Overseas Union House, Singapore 049321; tel. 62251133; fax 62246307; internet www.oub.com.sg; f. 1956; Gen. Man. PETER YAP KIM KEE; Asst Gen. Man. YEO TIAN CHU.

Royal & Sun Alliance Insurance (Singapore) Ltd: 77 Robinson Rd, 18-00 SIA Bldg, Singapore 068896; tel. 62201188; fax 65350855; CEO EDMUND LIM.

Singapore Aviation and General Insurance Co (Pte) Ltd: 25 Airline Rd, 06-A Airline House, Singapore 819829; tel. 65423333; fax 65450221; f. 1976; Man. AMARJIT KAUR SIDHU.

Standard Steamship Owners' Protection and Indemnity Association (Asia) Ltd: 140 Cecil St, 10-02 PIL Bldg, Singapore 069540; tel. 62211060; fax 62211082; e-mail central@ctg-ap.com; internet www.standard-club.com; Prin. Officer DAVID ALWYN.

Tenet Insurance Co Ltd: 10 Collyer Quay, 04-01 Ocean Bldg, Singapore 049315; tel. 65326022; fax 65333871; Chair. ONG CHOO ENG.

The Tokio Marine & Fire Insurance Co (Singapore) Pte Ltd: 6 Shenton Way, 23-08 DBS Bldg Tower Two, Singapore 068809; tel. 62216111; fax 62240895; Man. Dir KYOZO HANAJIMA.

United Overseas Insurance Ltd: 156 Cecil St, 09-01 Far Eastern Bank Bldg, Singapore 069544; tel. 62227733; fax 62242718; internet www.uoi.com.sg; Man. Dir DAVID CHAN MUN WAI.

Winterthur Insurance (Far East) Pte Ltd: 5 Shenton Way, 06-01 UIC Bldg, Singapore 068808; tel. 65368669; fax 65368870; Man. Dir ANG YEW LEE.

Yasuda Fire and Marine Insurance Co (Asia) Pte Ltd: 50 Raffles Place, 03-03 Singapore Land Tower, Singapore 048623; tel. 62235293; fax 62257947; e-mail yasudaqa@yasudaasia.com; internet www.yasudaasia.com; f. 1989; Man. Dir and Gen. Man. KOJI OTSUKA

Zürich Insurance (Singapore) Pte Ltd: 78 Shenton Way, 06-01, Singapore 079120; tel. 62202466; fax 62255749; Prin. Officer and Man. Dir RONALD CHENG JUE SENG.

Composite Insurance

Great Eastern Life Assurance Co Ltd: 1 Pickering St, 13-01 Great Eastern Centre, Singapore 048659; tel. 62482000; fax 65322214; e-mail wecare@lifeisgreat.com.sg; internet www.lifeisgreat.com.sg; f. 1908; Dir and CEO TAN BENG LEE.

Insurance Corpn of Singapore Ltd: 4 Shenton Way, 23-01 SGX Centre Two, Singapore 068807; tel. 68277988; fax 68277900; e-mail prd_div@cguasia.com; internet www.icsinsurance.com.sg; f. 1969; Prin. Officer KEITH PERKINS.

Keppel Insurance Pte Ltd: 10 Hoe Chiang Rd, 13-00 Keppel Towers, Singapore 089315; tel. 62256111; fax 62212188; internet www.keppelinsurance.com.sg; Prin. Officer ALBERT KOH.

NTUC Income Insurance Co-operative Ltd: 75 Bras Basah Rd, NTUC Income Centre, Singapore 189557; tel. 63363322; fax 63381500; e-mail inbox@income.wm.sg; internet www.income.com.sg; CEO TAN KIN LIAN; Gen. Man. ALOYSIUS TEO SENG LEE.

Overseas Assurance Corpn Ltd: 1 Pickering St, 13-01 Great Eastern Centre, Singapore 048659; tel. 62482000; fax 65322214; e-mail general@oac.com.sg; internet www.oac.com.sg; f. 1920; Chair. MICHAEL WONG PAKSHONG.

Associations

General Insurance Association of Singapore: 103 Amoy St, Singapore 069923; tel. 62218788; fax 62272051; internet www.gia.org.sg; f. 1965; Pres. LAW SONG KENG; Vice-Pres. DAVID CHAN.

Life Insurance Association: 30 Cecil St, 23-04A Prudential Tower, Singapore 049712; tel. 64388900; fax 64386989; e-mail lifeinsassn@pacific.net.sg; internet www.lia.org.sg; f. 1967; Pres. TAN BENG LEE.

Reinsurance Brokers' Association: c/o Ins Communications Pte, 55-58 Amoy St, Singapore 069881; tel. 62245583; fax 62241091; e-mail rbas@asiainsurancereview.com; internet www.rbas.org.sg; Chair. RICHARD AUSTEN.

Singapore Insurance Brokers' Association: 138 Cecil St, 15-00 Cecil Court, Singapore 069538; tel. 62227777; fax 62220022; Pres. ANTHONY LIM; Vice-Pres. DAVID LUM.

Singapore Reinsurers' Association: 85 Amoy St, Singapore 069904; tel. 63247388; fax 62248910; e-mail secretariat@sraweb.org.sg; internet www.sraweb.org.sg; f. 1979; Chair. PHUA KIA TING.

Trade and Industry

GOVERNMENT AGENCIES

Housing and Development Board: 3541 Bukit Merah Rd, HDB Centre, Singapore 159459; tel. 62739090; fax 62780144; e-mail hdbmailbox@hdb.gov.sg; internet www.hdb.gov.sg; f. 1960; public housing authority; Chair. NGIAM TONG DOW.

Urban Redevelopment Authority (URA): 45 Maxwell Rd, URA Centre, Singapore 069118; tel. 62216666; fax 62263549; e-mail ura_main_registry@ura.gov.sg; internet www.ura.gov.sg; statutory board; responsible for national planning.

DEVELOPMENT ORGANIZATIONS

Applied Research Corpn (ARC): independent non-profit-making research and consultancy org. aiming to facilitate and enhance the use of technology and expertise from the tertiary institutions to benefit industry, businesses and joint institutions.

Asian Infrastructure Fund (AIF): Singapore; f. 1994; promotes and directs investment into regional projects; Chair. MOEEN QURESHI.

Economic Development Board (EDB): 250 North Bridge Rd, 24-00 Raffles City Tower, Singapore 179101; tel. 63362288; fax 63396077; e-mail webmaster@edb.gov.sg; internet www.sedb.com.sg; f. 1961; statutory body for industrial planning, development and promotion of investments in manufacturing, services and local business; Chair. Philip Yeo; Man. Dir Liew Heng San.

Government of Singapore Investment Corp Pte Ltd (GSIC): 250 North Bridge Rd, 38-00 Raffles City Tower, Singapore 179101; tel. 63363366; fax 63308722; internet www.gic.com.sg; f. 1981; Chair. Lee Kuan Yew; Man. Dir Lee Ek Tieng.

Jurong Town Corpn: 8 Jurong Town Hall Rd, Singapore 609434; tel. 65600056; fax 65655301; e-mail askjtc@jtc.gov.sg; internet www.jtc.gov.sg; f. 1968; statutory body responsible for developing and maintaining industrial estates; Chair. Lim Neo Chian; CEO Chong Lit Cheong.

Infocomm Development Authority of Singapore (IDA): see under Telecommunications.

Agency for Science, Technology and Research (A*STAR): 10 Science Park Rd, 01/01-03 The Alpha, Singapore Science Park II, Singapore 117684; tel. 67797066; fax 67771711; e-mail astar_contact@a-star.gov.sg; internet www.a-star.gov.sg; f. 1990; fmrly National Science and Technology Board; statutory board; responsible for the development of science and technology; Chair. Philip Yeo; Man. Dir Boon Swan Foo.

Singapore Productivity and Standards Board (PSB): PSB Bldg, 2 Bukit Merah Central, Singapore 159835; tel. 62786666; fax 62786667; e-mail queries@psb.gov.sg; internet www.psb.gov.sg; f. 1996; merger of Singapore Institute of Standards and Industrial Research and the National Productivity Board; carries out activities in areas including workforce development, training, productivity and innovation promotion, standards development, ISO certification, quality programmes and consultancy, technology application, product and process development, system and process automation services, testing services, patent information, development assistance for small and medium-sized enterprises; Chief Exec. Lee Suan Hiang.

Trade Development Board: 230 Victoria St, 07-00 Bugis Junction Office Tower, Singapore 188024; tel. 63376628; fax 63376898; e-mail enquiry@tdb.gov.sg; internet www.tdb.gov.sg; f. 1983 to develop and expand international trade; due to be renamed International Enterprise Singapore in 2002; statutory body; Chair. Stephen Lee; CEO Lee Yi Shyan.

CHAMBERS OF COMMERCE

Singapore Federation of Chambers of Commerce and Industry: 47 Hill St, 03-01 Chinese Chamber of Commerce Bldg, Singapore 179365; tel. 63389761; fax 63395630; e-mail sfcci@singnet.com.sg; f. 1978; Pres. Kwek Leng Joo; Hon. Sec.-Gen. Lim Sah Soon; mems comprise the following:

Singapore Chinese Chamber of Commerce and Industry: 47 Hill St, 09-00 Singapore 179365; tel. 63378381; fax 63390605; e-mail corporate@sccci.org.sg; internet www.sccci.org.sg; f. 1906; promotes trade and industry and economic development of Singapore.

Singapore Confederation of Industries: The Enterprise 02-02, 1 Science Centre Rd, Singapore 609077; tel. 68263000; fax 68228828; e-mail scihq@sci.org.sg; internet www.sci.org.sg; f. 1932; Pres. Robin Lau Chung Keong; Sec.-Gen. Tham Hock Chee.

Singapore Indian Chamber of Commerce and Industry: 101 Cecil St, 23-01/04 Tong Eng Bldg, Singapore 069533; tel. 62222855; fax 62231707; e-mail sicci@singnet.com.sg; internet www.sicci.com.

Singapore International Chamber of Commerce: 6 Raffles Quay, 10-01 John Hancock Tower, Singapore 048580; tel. 62241255; fax 62242785; e-mail general@sicc.com; internet www.sicc.com.sg; f. 1837.

Singapore Malay Chamber of Commerce: 72A Bussorah St, Singapore 199485; tel. 62979296; fax 63924527; e-mail smcci@singnet.com.sg.

INDUSTRIAL AND TRADE ASSOCIATIONS

Association of Singapore Marine Industries (ASMI): 1 Maritime Sq., 10–32 World Trade Centre, Singapore 099253; tel. 62704730; fax 62731867; e-mail asmi@pacific.net.sg; internet www.asmi.com; f. 1968; 12 hon. mems, 67 assoc. mems, 51 ord. mems (2001); Pres. Heng Chiang Gnee; Exec. Dir Winnie Low.

Singapore Commodity Exchange (SICOM): 111 North Bridge Rd, 23-04/05 Peninsula Plaza, Singapore 179098; tel. 63385600; fax 63389116; e-mail marketing@sicom.com.sg; internet www.sicom.com.sg; f. 1968 as Rubber Association of Singapore, adopted present name 1994; to regulate, promote, develop and supervise commodity futures trading in Singapore, including the establishment and dissemination of official prices for various grades and types of rubber; provides clearing facilities; endorses certificates of origin and licences for packers, shippers and mfrs; Chair. Victor Liew Cheng San; Gen. Man. Lim Toh Eng.

EMPLOYERS' ORGANIZATION

Singapore National Employers' Federation: 19 Tanglin Rd, 10-01/07 Tanglin Shopping Centre, Singapore 247909; tel. 68276827; fax 68276800; e-mail webmaster@snef.org.sg; internet www.sgemployers.com; f. 1948; Pres. Stephen Lee; Vice-Pres Alex Chan, Bob Tan Beng Hai.

UTILITIES

Electricity and Gas

Singapore Power Ltd: 111 Somerset Rd 16-01, Singapore Power Bldg, Singapore 238164; tel. 68238888; fax 68238188; e-mail prdiv@spower.com.sg; internet www.spower.com.sg; incorporated in 1995 to take over the piped gas and electricity utility operations of the Public Utilities Board (see Water) which now acts as a regulatory authority for the privately-owned cos; 100% owned by government holding company, Temasek Holdings Pte Ltd; subsidiaries include PowerGrid, PowerGas, Power Supply, Singapore Power International, Development Resources, Power Automation, SP E-Services, SP Systems, Singapore District Cooling and SP Telecommunications; Chair. Ng Kee Choe; Pres. and CEO Kwek Siew Jin.

Water

Public Utilities Board: 111 Somerset Rd 15-01, Singapore 238164; tel. 62358888; fax 67313020; e-mail pub_pr@pub.gov.sg; internet www.pub.gov.sg; authority responsible for water supply; regulatory body for privatized electricity and piped gas industries; Chair. Tan Gee Paw.

MAJOR COMPANIES

(cap. = capital; res = reserves; m. = million;

amounts shown are in Singapore dollars unless otherwise stated)

Building and Building Materials

AsiaMedic Ltd: 350 Orchard Rd, 08-00 Shaw House, Singapore 238868; tel. 67898888; fax 67384136; cap. and res 15m., sales 10m. (1998/99); precision plastic moulding, mould manufacture and medical services; Chair. Djeng Shih Kien.

Econ International Ltd: 2 Ang Mo Kio St 64, Ang Mo Kio Industrial Park 3, Singapore 569084; tel. 64842222; fax 64842221; e-mail corp@econ.com.sg; internet www.econ.com.sg; investment holding co with subsidiaries engaged in manufacture and trading of building materials and construction; cap. and res 143m., sales 351m. (1999/2000); Chair. Chew Tiong Kheng; Exec Dir Joseph Sin Kam Choi.

Hong Leong Corpn: 16 Raffles Quay, 26-00 Hong Leong Bldg, Singapore 048581; tel. 62208411; fax 62200087; sales 2,100m. (1995, est.); mfr and retailer of concrete, metal packaging, plastic packaging and containers; Pres. Peter H. Ren; 1,500 employees.

Jurong Cement Ltd: 15 Pioneer Crescent, Jurong Town, Singapore 628551; tel. 62618816; fax 62659178; e-mail jcibd@singnet.com.sg; f. 1973; cap. and res 127m., sales 77m. (1999/2000); mfrs of cement; Chair. Tay Joo Soon; Man. Dir Tan Eng Sim.

Lee Kim Tah Holdings Ltd: 20 Jalan Afifi, 07-01 CISCO Centre, Singapore 409179; tel. 67453318; fax 67451218; e-mail info@leekimtah.com; internet www.leekimtah.com; cap. and res 148m., sales 79m. (1999); investment holding co with subsidiaries engaged in manufacture of precast concrete building products and other building materials, building and civil engineering construction and property develolpment; Chair. Lee Soon Teck.

Low Keng Huat (S) Ltd: 80 Marine Parade Rd, 18-05/09 Parkway Parade, Singapore 449269; tel. 63442333; fax 63457841; cap. and res 119m., sales 193m. (1999/2000); property management, construction and building materials; Chair. Tan Sri Dato' Low Keng Huat; Man. Dir Low Keng Boon.

Sembawang Resources Ltd: 391A Orchard Rd, 18-00 Ngee Ann City Tower A, Singapore 238873; tel. 67352222; fax 67352006; cap. and res 83m., sales 295m. (1998); quarrying of granite, manufacture of ready-mixed concrete, asphalt premix, premix paving and waste disposal; Chair. Cheong Quee Wah; Pres. Goh Song How.

Ssangyong Cement (Singapore) Ltd: 17 Pioneer Crescent, Jurong Town, Singapore 628552; tel. 62654588; fax 62640371; cap. and res 209m., sales 97m. (1998/99); mfrs and retailers of cement, concrete, vermiculite and building materials; Chair. Park Young Il; Man. Dir and CEO Tan Cheng Gay.

Tuan Sing Holdings Ltd: 30 Robinson Rd, 12-01 Robinson Towers, Singapore 048546; tel. 62237211; fax 62241085; e-mail tuansing@pacific.net.sg; internet www.tuansing.com; cap. and res 408m., sales 365m. (2000); investment holding co with interests in property, manufacturing, construction and trading; Chair. Patrick Yeoh Khwai Hoh; Man. Dir John P. Garrity.

Wearnes International (1994) Ltd: 45 Leng Kee Rd, Singapore 159103; tel. 64716288; fax 62733839; cap. and res 178m., sales 237m.

(1998/99); mfrs of food equipment, retailers of building materials, suppliers of industrial, laundry, kitchen and food-processing equipment; Chair. TANG I-FANG; Man. Dir SOH YEW HOCK.

Chemicals and Petroleum

BHP Petroleum Trading and Marketing Pte Ltd: 5 Tamesek Bvd 04-003, Singapore 049315; tel. 63333370; fax 63333340; f. 1892; sales 1,400m. (1994); retailer of petroleum products; CEO ROGER WHITBY.

BP Singapore Pte Ltd: 396 Alexandra Rd, 18-00 BP Tower, Singapore 119954; tel. 63718888; fax 63718855; internet www.bp.com; sales 3,328m. (1995); retailer of petroleum products; Pres. KOH KIM WAH.

Caltex Trading Pte Ltd: 30 Raffles Place, 25-00 Caltex House, Singapore 048622; tel. 65333000; fax 64391790; f. 1989; sales 20,062m. (1998); retailing and refining of petroleum products; Chair. Pres. LEO LONERGAN.

Chemical Industries (Far East) Ltd: 3 Jalan Sumulun, Singapore 629127; tel. 62650411; fax 62656690; cap. and res 97m., sales 34m. (1999/2000); mfrs and retailers of chemicals; Chair. and Man. Dir LIM SOO PENG.

Cosmo Oil International Pte Ltd: 6 Shenton Way, 24-08 DBS Bldg Tower 2, Singapore 068809; tel. 63243722; fax 63241022; f. 1985; sales 3,005m. (1994); retailer of petroleum and associated products; Man. Dir SUMIO TANAKA.

Fuji Offset Plates Manufacturing Ltd: 54 Tanjong Penjuru, Singapore 609035; tel. 62659111; fax 62710811; internet www.fuji-group.com.sg/fop/index.html; cap. and res 26m., sales 24m. (1999); mfrs of aluminium offset plates and related industrial chemicals for printing industry; Chair. DAVID TEO KEE BOCK; Man. Dir STEVEN TEO KEE CHONG.

Idemitsu International (Asia) Pte: 16 Raffles Quay, 31-01 Hong Leong Bldg, Singapore 048581; tel. 62226477; fax 62240508; sales 1,500m. (1994, est.); retailer of petroleum products; Man. Dir Z. SUDA.

Itochu Petroleum Co (Singapore) Pte Ltd: 9 Raffles Place, 48-01, Singapore; tel. 65323542; fax 65323809; f. 1984; sales 1,039m. (1995); retailer of petroleum products; Chair. J. TANIUCHI.

Marubeni International Petroleum (Singapore) Pte Ltd: 16 Raffles Quay, 40-01 Hong Leong Bldg, Singapore 048581; tel. 62240446; fax 62215458; sales 1,979m. (1994/95); retailer of petroleum and related products; CEO FUMIYA KOKUBU.

Mobil Oil Singapore Pte Ltd: 18 Pioneer Rd, Singapore 628498; tel. 62650000; fax 62656570; f. 1963; sales 3,286m. (1995); petroleum refining; retailing of petroleum products; Gen. Man. G. H. KOHLENBURGER; 640 employees.

Nippon Oil (Asia) Pte Ltd: 6 Battery Rd, 29-02/03, Singapore 049909; tel. 62236732; fax 62248921; f. 1980; sales 1,243m. (1995); retailer of petroleum products; Man. Dir K. YONEMITSU.

Nissho Iwai Petroleum Pte Ltd: 77 Robinson Rd, 33-00 SIA Bldg, Singapore 065896; tel. 64382566; fax 64382577; f. 1991; sales 4,573m. (1994/95); petroleum and petroleum products; Man. Dir AKISHIGE KATO.

Shell Eastern Petroleum (Pte) Ltd, Shell Eastern Trading (Pte) Ltd, Seraya Chemicals Singapore Pte Ltd, Shell Research Eastern (Pte) Ltd, Shell Singapore Trustees Pte Ltd: Shell House, 83 Clemenceau Ave, Singapore 239920; tel. 63848000; internet www.shell.com.sg; Chair. LEE TZU YANG; 1,500 employees.

Singapore Petroleum Co Ltd: 1 Maritime Sq. 1010 World Trade Centre, Singapore 099253; tel. 62766006; fax 62756006; internet www.spc.com.sg; cap. and res 523m., sales 1,963m. (1998/99); petroleum refining, tanker transport, trading, distribution and marketing; Chair. CHOO CHIAU BENG.

Yukong International Pte Ltd: 5 Shenton Way, 34-04 UIC Bldg, Singapore 068808; tel. 62201266; fax 62211225; sales 3,891m. (1994/95); petroleum products; Man. Dir C. K. LEE.

Electrical and Electronics

Acma Ltd: 17 Jurong Port Rd, Singapore 619092; tel. 62687733; fax 62663998; f. 1965; cap. and res 136m., sales 425m. (1999/2000); mfrs, retailers and servicers of electrical and electronic equipment; Chair. QUEK SIM PIN; Man. Dir RAJ RAJEN.

Amcol Holdings Ltd: 9 Temasek Blvd, 42-00 Suntec Tower 2, Singapore 038989; tel. 63371722; fax 63321800; cap. and res 555m., sales 981m. (1995/96); mfrs and retailers of electronic and electrical products; Chair. SUDWIKATMONO; Man. Dir HENRY PRIBADI.

Avimo Group Ltd: 34 Bukit Pasoh Rd, Singapore 089848; tel. 63252620; fax 63233002; e-mail info@avimo.com.sg; internet www.avimogroup.com; cap. and res 48m., sales 218m. (1998/99); designers, developers, mfrs, marketers and servicers of advanced precision optics, electro-optics instruments, laser equipment; custom plating processing of component products; Chair. BERNARD JEAN-NOEL ROCQUEMONT; Man. Dir IAN CLARK BOOTH.

Aztech Systems Ltd: 31 Ubi Rd 1, Aztech Bldg, Singapore 408694; tel. 67417211; fax 67418678; internet www.aztech.com.sg; cap. and res 88m., sales 171m. (1998/99); designers, mfrs and distributors of multimedia products; Pres. MICHAEL MUN HONG YEW; Sec. PAVANI NAGARAJAH.

Clipsal Industries (Holdings) Ltd: 5 Fourth Chin Bee Rd, Singapore 619699; tel. 62665936; fax 62662989; e-mail clipsal@singnet.com.sg; internet www.clipsal.com.sg; cap. and res 213m., sales 203m. (1998/99); investment holding co with subsidiaries engaged in manufacture and marketing of electrical installation products; Chair. VICTOR LO CHUNG WING; Man. Dir CHAU KWOK WAI; 2,600 employees.

Conner Peripherals Pte Ltd: 151 Lorong Chuan, 06-01 New Tech Park, Singapore 556741; tel. 62845366; fax 62845060; sales 1,400m. (1994, est.); mfr of computer components.

Creative Technology Ltd: 31 International Business Park, Creative Resource, Singapore 609921; tel. 68954000; fax 68954999; internet www.creative.com; cap. and res US $779m., sales US $1,344m. (1999/2000); multimedia products peripherals; Chair. and CEO SIM WONG HOO.

Eltech Electronics Ltd: 20 Raffles Place, 17-00 Ocean Towers, Singapore 048620; tel. 65350733; fax 62211306; cap. and res 62m., sales 174m. (1999); electronics equipment; Chair. TAN CHEOW KOON; Man. Dir TAN GEH.

General Magnetics Ltd: 625 Lorong 4, Toa Payoh, Singapore 319519; tel. 62595511; fax 62593723; e-mail genmag@singnet.com.sg; cap. and res 52m., sales 36m. (1998/99); mfrs and retailers of magnetic media and related products and telecommunication equipment; Chair. and Man. Dir OH LOON LIAN; Sec. LOH WENG YEW.

Giken Sakata (S) Ltd: 40 Jalan Pemimpin 04-05, Tat Ann Bldg, Singapore 577185; tel. 62599133; fax 62599822; cap. and res 16m., sales 150m. (1999/2000); parts for electronics equipment; Chair. SAKAE YOKOTA; Chair. SHIGEO NAKAGAWA.

GP Batteries International Ltd: 50 Gul Crescent, Singapore 629543; tel. 68622088; fax 68623313; e-mail gpbi@gpbatteries.com.sg; internet www.gpbatteries.com.sg; cap. and res 221m., sales 531m. (1999/2000); batteries and related products; Chair. and CEO ANDREW NG SUNG ON.

Hewlett-Packard Singapore (Pte) Ltd: 450 Alexandra Rd, Singapore 119960; tel. 62733888; fax 62756839; internet www.hp.com.sg; f. 1970; sales 5,547m. (1995); mfrs of opto-electronic components, inkjet printers and peripherals, PCs, imaging products, hand held devices and integrated circuits; Man. Dir CHEAH KEAN HUAT; 6,515 employees.

Hitachi Consumer Products (S) Pte Ltd: 206 Bedok South Ave 1, Singapore 469334; tel. 62419444; fax 64444572; f. 1972; sales 200m. (1995); mfrs of TV and radio receivers, tape-recorders, vacuum cleaners, air purifiers; Man. Dir H. NAKAJIXA; 1000 employees.

IPC Corpn Ltd: 23 Tai Seng Drive, IPC Bldg, Singapore 535224; tel. 67442688; fax 67430691; internet www.ipc.com.sg; cap. and res -49m., sales 25m. (1999); mfrs and retailers of computers and electronic products; Pres. BERNARD NGIAM MIA HAI; Chair. and CEO PATRICK NGIAM MIA JE.

Matsushita Electronics (S) Pte Ltd: 202 Bedok South Ave 1, Singapore 469332; tel. 64437744; fax 64453168; f. 1977; sales 680m. (1995); mfrs of radio receivers, tape-recorders and stereophonic equipment; Man. Dir A. KUNI; 2,800 employees.

Maxtor Peripherals (Singapore) Pte Ltd: 2 Ang Mo Kio St 63, Ang Mo Kio Ind. Park 3, Singapore 569448; tel. 64821100; fax 64815513; f. 1990; sales 1,900m. (1994, est.); mfr of hard disk drives and other computer peripherals; Vice-Pres. NGO PATRICK.

Micron Semiconductor Asia Ltd: 990 Bendemeer Rd, Singapore 339942; tel. 62903191; fax 62903690; internet www.micron.com; sales 4,621m. (1995); provider of semiconductor memory solutions.

Motorola Electronics Pte Ltd: 12 Ang Mo Kio Ind. Park 3, St 64, Singapore 569088; tel. 64812000; fax 64823879; mfr of mobile telephones, pagers, cable modems; Man. Dir E. L. TAY.

Pentex-Schweizer Circuits Ltd: 55 Penjuru Rd, Singapore 609140; tel. 62664311; fax 62665872; cap. and res 56m., sales 124m. (1999/2000); mfrs and retailers of double-sided printed circuit boards; Chair. CHRISTOPH OSKAR SCHWEIZER.

Philips Singapore Pte Ltd: 620A Lorong 1, Toa Payoh, Singapore 319762; POB 340, Toa Payoh Central Post Office, Singapore 9131; tel. 63502000; fax 62533395; f. 1951; sales 1,700m. (1994); mfrs of consumer electronic products, domestic appliances and telecommunications equipment; Chair. and Pres. VICTOR K. H. LOH; 7,500 employees.

Powermatic Data Systems Ltd: 135 Joo Seng Rd, 08-01 PM Industrial Bldg, Singapore 368363; tel. 62888220; fax 62809947;

mfrs and distributors of computer hardware and software; cap. and res 50m., sales 44m. (1999/2000); Chair. and Man. Dir Dr CHEN MUN; 203 employees.

Samsung Asia Pte Ltd: 80 Robinson Rd, 20-00, Singapore 068898; tel. 65353075; fax 62215510; sales 2,265m. (1995); retailers of semiconductors and telecommunications equipment; 70 employees.

Sanyo Industries (S) Pte Ltd: 117–119 Neythal Rd, Singapore 628604; tel. 62650077; fax. 62653015; f. 1966; cap. p.u. 2m.; mfrs of electrical household appliances; Chair. K. IUE; Man. Dir NG GHIT CHEONG; 500 employees.

Seagate Technology International (Singapore) Pte Ltd: 06-01 New Tech Park, 151 Lorung Chuan, Singapore 556741; tel. 62870700; fax 64887525; f. 1987; sales 4,900m. (1994); mfr of personal computers and computer components; Vice-Pres. DON KENNEDY.

Siemens Components Pte Ltd: Blk 28 Ayer Rajah Crescent, 06-08, Singapore 139959; tel. 63709666; fax 67738070; internet www.siemens.com.sg/hearing; f. 1970; sales 1,900m. (1997); mfr of electronic components; Pres. and Man. Dir LOH KIN WAH.

Singapore Technologies Industrial Corpn Ltd: 9 Bishan Place, 10-00 Junction 8, Singapore 579837; tel. 63542227; fax 63541711; internet www.stic.com.sg; cap. and res 545m., sales 1,415m. (1997); intermediate holding co with subsidiaries involved in electronics, telecommunications and engineering; Chair. WONG KOK SIEW; Pres. TAY SIEW CHOON.

Singatronics Ltd: 506 Chai Chee Lane, Singatronics Bldg, Singapore 469026; tel. 64486211; fax 64452506; e-mail corp_hq@singatronics.com.sg; cap. and res 500m., sales 62m. (2001); engaged in manufacture and retailing of computer-related, telecommunication and other electronic products, property development and leasing, hotel ownership; Chair. EDDIE FOO CHIK KIN.

ST Microelectronics Asia Pacific (Pte) Ltd: 28 Ang Mo Kio Industrial Park 2, Singapore 569508; tel. 64821411; fax 64820240; internet www.st.com; f. 1969; sales 1,700m. (1995); manufacturing, marketing and sales, design of integrated circuits; Pres. J.C. MARQUET; 3,800 employees.

Thakral Corpn Ltd: 20 Upper Circular Rd, The Riverwalk 03-06A, Singapore 058416; tel. 63368966; fax 63367225; e-mail tcloct96@thakralcorp.com.sg; internet www.thakral.com; cap. and res 157m., sales 584m. (2001); distributor of consumer electronic and domestic electrical products with operations in Hong Kong and China; Chair. KARTAR SINGH THAKRAL; Man. Dir INDERBETHAL SINGH THAKRAL.

Toshiba Electronics Asia (S) Pte Ltd: 460 Alexandra Rd, 21-00 PSA Bldg, Singapore 119963; tel. 62785252; fax 62715155; sales 2,314m. (1994/95); electronic components retailers; CEO K. HIROSE; 80 employees.

Venture Manufacturing (Singapore) Ltd: 138 Cecil St, 15-00 Cecil Court, Singapore 069538; tel. 62227777; fax 64820122; internet www.venture-mfg.com.sg; mfrs and traders for companies in electronic and computer-related industries; cap. and res 513m., sales 1,455m. (2000); Chair. GOPALA ACHUTA MENON; Man. Dir WONG NGIT LIONG.

Vikay Industrial Ltd: 1100 Lower Delta Rd, Vikay Industrial Bldg, Singapore 169206; tel. 62700300; fax 62706989; mfrs of electronic products; cap. and res 50m., sales 97m. (1996); Chair. HERMAN TANIHAHA.

Western Digital (S) Pte Ltd: 750B Chai Chee Road Block E, Chai Chee Ind. Park, Singapore 496002; tel. 64433443; fax 64456107; sales 2,187m. (1994/95); mfr of personal computer components; Man. Dir VINCE MASTROPIETRO.

Food and Beverages

Asia Pacific Breweries (S) Pte Ltd: 21-00 Alexandra Point, 438 Alexandra Rd, Singapore 119958; tel. 62729488; fax 62710811; internet www.tigerbeer.com; f. 1990; cap. and res 654m., sales 1,326m. (1998/99); brewers of beer and stout; Chair. Dr MICHAEL FAM; 400 employees.

Auric Pacific Group Ltd: 24 Raffles Place, 19-01 Clifford Centre, Singapore 048621; tel. 65351221; fax 65351771; sales 136m. (1997/98); food manufacturing; Chair. JAMES T. RIADY.

Cerebos Pacific Ltd: 1 Kim Seng Promenade 11-01/06, Great World City East Office Tower, Singapore 237994; tel. 67324111; fax 67329971; e-mail cerebos.com.sg; internet www.cerebos.com; cap. and res 362m., sales 543m. (1999/2000); subsidiaries engaged in manufacture and marketing of food products; Chair. LEE KIM YEW; Man. Dir EIJI KOIKE.

Cold Storage Singapore Ltd: 1 Sophia Rd, 06-38 Peace Centre, Singapore 228149; tel. 63332766; fax 63372766; f. 1960; sales 300m. (1994); retailers and distributors of food, mfrs of food and beverages; Chair. MICHAEL P. K. KOK.

Fraser and Neave Ltd: 21-00 Alexandra Point, 438 Alexandra Rd, Singapore 119958; tel. 62729488; fax 62710811; internet www.fraserandneave.com; f. 1964; cap. and res 3,027m., sales 2,606m. (1999/2000); investment holding company with subsidiaries involved in the production of soft drinks, beer, stout and dairy products, and in packaging; Pres. Tan Sri TAN CHIN TUAN; Chair. MICHAEL Y. O. FAM.

Khong Guan Flour Milling Ltd: 2 MacTaggart Rd, Singapore 368078; tel. 62822511; fax 62855868; cap. and res 34.7m., sales 31.2m. (2000/01); producers of wheat flour and corn meals; Chair. LEE SEOW GEK; Man. Dir CHEW CHOO HAN.

Kuok Oils and Grains Pte Ltd: 1 Kim Seng Promenade, Great World City, 05-01 Singapore 237994; tel. 67388622; fax 67356366; e-mail trading@kuokoil.com; f. 1989; sales 2,516m. (2000); mfr of edible oils and fats; Man. Dir KWOK KIAN HAI; 160 employees.

Network Foods International Ltd: 5 Shenton Way, 29-00 UIC Bldg, Singapore 068808; tel. 6757704; fax 67570300; internet www.networkfoods.com; cap. and res 0.6m., sales 56m. (1998); mfrs and marketers of chocolate and other cocoa-based products, biscuits and confectioneries; Chair. KOK QUAN TAN; Exec. Dir SUSHIA PREMCHAND.

Prima Ltd: 201 Keppel Rd, Singapore 099419; tel. 62728811; fax 62732933; e-mail enquiry@prima.com.sg; internet www.prima.com.sg; f. 1961; cap. 38m., sales 66m. (2001); producers of wheat flour, wheat bran and pollard; fish and meat; Chair. CHENG CHIH KWONG PRIMUS.

QAF Ltd: 224 Pandan Loop, Singapore 128411; tel. 67751338; fax 67779536; f. 1958; cap. and res 160m., sales 460m. (1998/99); wholesalers and retailers of food and beverages; Chair. DIDI DAWIS; Man. Dir TAN KONG KING.

Yeo Hiap Seng Ltd: 3 Senoko Way, Singapore 758057; tel. 67522122; fax 67523122; cap. and res 377m., sales 404m. (2000); mfrs and distributors of food and beverages; Chair. ROBERT CHEE SIONG NG; Man. Dir and CEO LEONG HORN KEE.

Metals and Engineering

Amtek Engineering Ltd: 1 Kian Teck Drive, Singapore 628818; tel. 62640033; fax 62652510; e-mail sales@ammail.amtek.com.sg; internet www.amtek.com.sg; cap. and res 149m., sales 552m. (1999/2000); mfrs and stampers of precision metal parts; precision rubber components and moulds; mechanical assemblies; computer enclosures; Chair. LEE AH BEE; Man. Dir LAI FOOK KUEN.

Carnaudmetalbox Asia Ltd: 750-D Chai Chee Ind. Park, 08-02/03 Chai Chee Rd, Singapore 469004; tel. 62421788; fax 62423722; internet www.sciencepark.com.sg/data/IO5.html; cap. and res 275m., sales 241m. (1999); investment holding co and mfrs of metal packaging; Chair. and CEO WILLIAM HENRY VOSS.

GB Holdings Ltd: 29 Loyang Crescent, Singapore 509015; tel. 65452929; fax 65430029; internet www.grandbanks.com; cap. and res 43m., sales 66m. (1999/2000); investment holding co with subsidiaries engaged in manufacture and retailing of diesel-powered cruisers, sailing boats; yacht repairers; Chair. ROBERT W. LIVINGSTON; 870 employees.

Hitachi Zosen Singapore Ltd: 15 Benoi Rd, Singapore 629888; tel. 68616622; fax 68614393; f. 1970; cap. and res 170m., sales 228m. (1998); ship-building and repair, steel structures, industrial engineering; Chair. TAKESHI TENJIN; Man. Dir FOO MENG KEE.

Jurong Engineering Ltd: 25 Tanjong Kling Rd, Singapore 628050; tel. 62653222; fax 62684211; e-mail webmaster@jel.com.sg; internet www.jel.com.sg; cap. and res 159m., sales 297m. (1998/99); construction and engineering services; Chair. CHEE KENG SOON; Man. Dir MASAO UEDA.

Jurong Shipyard Ltd: 5 Jalan Samulun, Jurong Industrial Estate, Singapore 629122; tel. 62651766; fax 62610738; cap. and res 689m., sales 472m. (1998); ship-builders and repairers; Chair. WONG KOK SIEW; Man. Dir TAN KWI KIN; 1,800 employees.

Keppel Corpn Ltd: 23 Church St, 15-01 Capital Square, Singapore 049481; tel. 68857390; fax 68857391; internet www.keppelcorporation.com; f. 1859; cap. and res 3,475m., sales 6,325m. (2000); Chair. LIM CHEE OMN; Man. Dir LOH WING SIEW; 15,947 employees.

Keppel FELS Ltd: 31 Shipyard Rd, Singapore 628130; tel. 68637200; fax 62617719; e-mail marketing@keppelfels.com.sg; internet www.keppelfels.com.sg; f. 1967; cap. and res 894m., sales 656.5m. (2001); builders and repairers of offshore production facilities; Chair. and Man. Dir CHOO CHIAU BENG; Man. Dir TONG CHONG HEONG; 1,970 employees.

Liang Huat Aluminium Ltd: 51 Benoi Rd, Blk 8, 07-05 Liang Huat Industrial Complex, Singapore 629908; tel. 68622228; fax 68624962; e-mail lhg_corpadm1@pacific.net.sg; cap. and res 79m., sales 67m. (2001); aluminium products; Man. Dir PETER TAN YONG KEE.

Lion Asiapac Ltd: 10 Arumugam Rd, 10-00 Lion Industrial Bldg, Singapore 409957; tel. 67459677; fax 67479493; f. 1974; cap. and res 88m., sales 31m. (1999/2000); mfrs and retailers of containers, and investment holding; Chair. OTHMAN WOK; Man. Dir SAM CHONG KEEN.

NatSteel Ltd: 22 Tanjong Kling Rd, Jurong Town, Singapore 628048; tel. 62651233; fax 62658317; internet www.natsteel.com.sg; fmrly National Iron and Steel Mills; cap. and res 1,622m., sales 1,441m. (2000); manufacturing and marketing of iron and steel products, building materials, electronics and lime products; Chair. Dr CHAM TAO SOON; Pres. ANG KONG HUA; 17,363 employees.

Pacific Can Investment Holdings Ltd: 1 Sixth Lok Yang Rd, Singapore 628099; tel. 62656877; fax 62683280; cap. and res 9m., sales 58m. (1997/98); investment holding co with subsidiaries engaged in production of cans and components, packaging, printing; Chair. LOW HUA KIN; Man. Dir and CEO KO CHING-SHUEI.

Sembcorp Marine: 29 Tanjong Kling Rd, Singapore 628054; tel. 62651766; fax 62650201; internet www.sembcorpmarine.com.sg; f. 1968; cap. and res 849m., sales 763m. (2000); maritime services, shipping, civil construction, construction of oil rigs and specialized marine equipment; also active in industrial and venture sectors; Chairs WONG KOK SIEW, TAN KWI KIN.

Singapore Technologies Aerospace Ltd: 540 Airport Rd, Paya Lebar, Singapore 539938; tel. 62871111; fax 62809713; e-mail mktg.aero@stengg.com; internet www.stengg.com/aero/; cap. 362m. (1995), sales 1,031.2m. (2001); maintenance, modification and refurbishment of military and civilian aircraft, engines and components; Pres. TAY KHOK KHIANG; 4,695 employees.

Singapore Technologies Marine Ltd: 7 Benoi Rd, Singapore 629882; tel. 68612244; fax 68613028; internet www.stengg.com; cap. and res 169m., sales 220m. (1995); naval and commercial shipbuilding and repair, engineering equipment; Chair. JAMES LEO CHIN LIAN.

Singmarine Industries Ltd: 55 Gul Road, Singapore 629353; tel. 68613007; fax 68623645; cap. and res 388m., sales 176m. (1995); holding co with subsidiaries engaged in shipbuilding and repair, marina management and processing of copper slag; Chair. LOH WING SIEW; 1,092 employees.

Straits Trading Co Ltd (THE): 9 Battery Rd, 21-00 Straits Trading Bldg, Singapore 049910; tel. 65354722; fax 65327939; e-mail straits@stc.com.sg; f. 1887; cap. and res 1,040m. (1997), sales 105m. (2001); tin smelting; Pres. NORMAN IP KA CHEUNG; Chair. and CEO HOWE YOON CHONG.

Superior Metal Printing Ltd: 7 Benoi Sector, Singapore 629842; tel. 62683933; fax 62657151; cap. and res 61m., sales 73m. (1998); mfrs of metal containers and packaging; Chair. STEVEN CHAN CHENG.

United Engineers Ltd: 257 Jalan Ahmad Ibrahim, Singapore 629147; tel. 62662388; fax 62686993; cap. and res 660m., sales 397m. (2000); civil, mechanical, electrical and environmental engineering; fabrication of industrial, construction and agricultural machinery; Chair. TANG I-FANG; Man. Dir JACKSON CHEVALIER YAP KIT SIONG.

Van der Horst Ltd: 11 Pandan Crescent, Singapore 128467; tel. 67750333; fax 67792363; cap. and res -52m., sales 25m. (1998/99); engaged, with subsidiary, in remanufacture and electroplating of marine, oilfield and general industrial precision equipment, manufacture of wedge-wire screens, pressure vessels; Chair. JOHANNES B. KOTJO; Man. Dir MICHAEL A. OXBOROW.

Wepco Ltd: 5 Kwong Min Rd, Singapore 628708; tel. 62614933; fax 62618340; cap. and res 8m., sales 24m. (1995); electroplating and industrial engineering services; Chair. NG KAH TIE; Man. Dir FONG LOON HING.

Wood and Paper Products

Hiap Moh Corpn Ltd: Block 162, Bukit Merah Central, 08-3545, Singapore 150162; tel. 62735333; fax 62789707; internet www.collection.com.hk/sta/hiapmoh/eindex.htm; cap. and res 33m., sales 50m. (1998/99); mfrs and traders of paper products; Chair. JOSHUA NG HOCK HWA; Man. Dir NG KAH LIN.

United Pulp and Paper Co Ltd: 20 Liu Fang Rd, Jurong Town, Singapore 628675; tel. 62652622; fax 62643973; e-mail uppgroup@singnet.com.sg; cap. and res 62m., sales 52m. (1999); investment holding co with subsidiaries engaged in manufacture and retail of paper products; Chair. HO POH CHOON.

Miscellaneous

Ace Dynamics Ltd: 1 Shipyard Rd, Singapore 628128; tel. 62664868; fax 62662026; e-mail acepower@pacific.net.sg; cap. and res 35m., sales 17.4m. (1999/2000); investment holding co, with subsidiaries engaged in distribution of industrial welding and safety equipment and the manufacture and supply of industrial gases; Man. Dir JOHN LEE SOK KHIAN.

Alliance Technology and Development Ltd; 139 Joo Seng Rd, 06-01, ATD Centre, Singapore 368362; tel. 67491090; fax 62825377; cap. and res 36m., sales 34m. (1998/99); investment holding co with subsidiary engaged in manufacture of contact lenses and related eye-care products, property investment and development, leisure and entertainment, hospitality and Underwater World; Chair. CHANG CHING CHUAN; Exec. Vice-Chair. and CEO CHANG WHE HAN.

Bonvests Holdings Ltd: 541 Orchard Rd, 16-00 Liat Towers, Singapore 238881; tel. 67325533; fax 67379166; cap. and res 328m., sales 321m. (1998/99); investment holding co with subsidiary engaged in property development, waste collection and cleaning services, buying and selling luxury goods; Chair. and Man. Dir HENRY NGO.

British-American Tobacco Co (Singapore) Ltd: 57 Senoko Drive, Singapore 758236; tel. 67588555; fax 67557798; cap. and res 56m., sales 230m. (1998); investment holding co with subsidiaries engaged in manufacturing, importing and retailing tobacco products; Chair. RICHARD SAMUEL WOODING; 500 employees.

Bukit Sembawang Estates Ltd: 65 Chulia St, 49-05 OCBC Centre, Singapore 049513; tel. 65361836; fax 65361858; cap. and res 160m., sales 46m. (2000/01); property development; Chair. CECIL VIVIAN RICHARD WONG.

Centrepoint Properties Ltd: 438 Alexandra Rd, 21-00 Alexandra Point, Singapore 119958; tel. 62729488; fax 62710811; cap. and res 1,629m., sales 377m. (1999/2000); property ownership and development; Chair. Dr MICHAEL FAM.

City Developments Ltd: 36 Robinson Rd, 20-01 City House, Singapore 068877; tel. 62212266; fax 62232746; internet www.cdl.com.sg; cap. and res 3,846m., sales 2,626m. (2000); property ownership and development; Chair. KWEK LENG BENG; Man. Dir KWEK LENG JOO.

Comfort Group Ltd: 383 Sin Ming Drive, Singapore 575717; tel. 64576255; internet www.comfortgroup.com.sg; cap. and res 410m., sales 414m. (2000/01); management and investment holding co, with subsidiaries involved in the provision of transport-related services; Chair. LIM JIT POH; Man. Dir GOH CHEE WEE.

Cycle and Carriage Ltd: 239 Alexandra Rd, Singapore 159930; tel. 64733122; fax 64757088; internet www.cyclecarriage.com.sg; f. 1899; cap. 234m., sales 2,990m. (2000); retailer of motor vehicles; property investment; Chair. Tan Sri Dato' Seri MOHD SALEH SULONG; Man. Dir PHILIP ENG HENG NEE.

Datacraft Asia Ltd: 6 Shenton Way 24-11, DBS Bldg Tower Two, Singapore 068809; tel. 63237988; fax 63237933; internet www.datacraft-asia.com; cap. and res 319m. (2000), sales 567.3m. (2001); management and investment holding, data communication systems; Chair. PATRICK QUARNBY; CEO RON CATTELL.

DBS Land Ltd: 39 Robinson Rd 18-01, Robinson Point, Singapore 068911; tel. 65361188; fax 65363788; internet www.dbsland.com; cap. and res 3,791m., sales 1,383m. (1998/99); property investment and development; Chair. LAU CHAN SIN; CEO HAN CHENG FONG; 1,818 employees.

First Capital Corpn Ltd: 20 Collyer Quay, 02-02 Tung Centre, Singapore 049319; tel. 65356455; fax 65326196; f. 1976; cap. and res 1,059m. (1999/2000); investment holding co with principal activities consisting of investment holding and property development; Chair. SAT PAL KHATTAR; CEO QUEK CHEE HOON.

Gold Coin Services (S) Pte Ltd: 99 Bukit Timah Rd, Alfa Centre 05-03/06 Singapore 229835; tel. 63374300; fax 63376911; f. 1983; cap. 40m., sales 347m. (1990); investment holding co with subsidiaries engaged in manufacturing animal feeds and marketing and distribution of industrial, agricultural and consumer products; Man. Dir LOUIS SCHENBERG.

Goldtron Ltd: 53 Ubi Rd 1, Singapore 408698; tel. 67471616; fax 67413525; cap. and res -80m., sales 266m. (1999/2000); investment holding co with subsidiaries engaged in manufacture and retail of telecommunication products; Chair. MOKHZANI BIN MAHATHIR.

Haw Par Corpn Ltd: 178 Clemenceau Ave 08-00, Haw Par Glass Tower, Singapore 239922; tel. 63379102; fax 63369232; f. 1969; cap. and res 544m., sales 158m. (2000); investment holding co with subsidiaries engaged in property, investments and manufacture of industrial products, sports products and pharmaceutical products; Chair. WEE CHO YAW; Pres. and CEO Dr HONG HAI; 691 employees.

Hotel Properties Ltd: 50 Cuscaden Rd, 08-01 HPL House, Singapore 249724; tel. 67345250; fax 62350729; cap. and res 851m., sales 408m. (2000); hotels; leisure; food retailing; Chair. PETER FU YUN SIAK; Man. Dir ONG BENG SENG.

Htl International Holdings Ltd: 11 Gul Circle, Singapore 629567; tel. 67475050; fax 67478497; cap. and res 77.2m., sales 223m. (2001); furniture, fabrics; Chair. PHUA YONG PIN; Man. Dir PHUA YONG TAT.

Hwa Hong Corpn Ltd: 60 Martin Rd, 07-38, Singapore 239065; tel. 62355088; fax 67377625; e-mail hwahong@pacific.net.sg; cap. and res 409m., sales 172m. (1999); investment holding co with subsidiaries engaged in general insurance and related activities, packaging of edible oil products, construction and engineering; Chair. and Man. Dir ONG CHOO ENG.

Inchcape Motors Ltd: 31/33 Leng Kee Rd, Singapore 159101; tel. 64755383; fax 64741970; cap. and res 251m., sales 1,021m. (2000); marketing of consumer goods, business machines, pharmaceuticals and industrial parts and equipment; Chair. THAI CHEE KEN; Man. Dir EDDIE NG YUK CHEUNG; 2,000 employees.

Jack Chia-MPH Ltd: 47 Scotts Rd, 18-02 Goldeell Towers, Singapore 228233; tel. 67341515; fax 67322241; f. 1927; cap. and res 193m., sales 727m. (1997/98); investment holding co; activities of subsidiaries: publication, distribution and retail of books and magazines, manufacture and distribution of confectionary products, residential home building; Chair. DANAI CHIARAPURK; Sec. KOK HWEE LENG; 2,552 employees.

Keppel Land Ltd: 230 Victoria St, 15-05 Bugis Junction Towers, Singapore 188024; tel. 63388111; fax 63377168; e-mail marketg@kepland.com.sg; internet www.keppelland.com.sg; cap. and res 2,240m., sales 500m. (2000); property investment, development and management; hotel and resort operations; retail management; Chair. LIM CHEE ONN; 3,591 employees (1999).

Kim Eng Holdings Ltd: 9 Temasek Blvd, 39-00 Suntec Tower 2, Singapore 038989; tel. 63369090; fax 63396003; cap. and res 506m., sales 214m. (1999/2000); sharebrokers, stockbrokers and investment holding co; Chair. GLORIA LEE KIM YEW; Man. Dir RONALD ANTHONY OOI THEAN YAT.

Marco Polo Developments Ltd: 501 Orchard Rd, 04-01/03 Lane Crawford Place, Singapore 238880; tel. 67388660; fax 67359833; internet www.mpdl.com; cap. and res 750m., sales 511m. (1999/2000); property development; Chair. GONZAGA W. J. LI; Man. Dir DAVID J. LAWRENCE.

MCL Land Ltd: 78 Shenton Way, 23-01, Singapore 079120; tel. 62218111; fax 62253383; cap. and res 876m., sales 174m. (2000); investment holding, property investment and management; Chair. KEI MEI RIN; Man. Dir EE SENG LIM.

Orchard Parade Holdings Ltd: 14 Scotts Rd, 06-01 Far East Plaza, Singapore 228213; tel. 62352411; cap. and res 465m., sales 131m. (2001); management and investment holding, property investment and development; Chair. PHILIP NG CHEE TAT; Man. Dir CHAU TIAN CHU.

Overseas Union Enterprise Ltd: 333 Orchard Rd, Overseas Union Bank Bldg, Singapore 238867; tel. 67374411; fax 67372620; cap. and res 823m., sales 168m. (2000); advertising; hotels and leisure; property; Chair. and Man. Dir Dr LIEN YING CHOW.

Parkway Holdings Ltd: 80 Marine Parade Rd, 22-01/09 Parkway Parade, Singapore 449269; tel. 63458822; fax 63440356; internet www.pgh.parkway.com.sg; cap. and res 793m., sales 390m. (1999); hospital ownership and management; wholesale of medicines and medical products; Man. Dir TONY TAN CHOON KEAT.

Rothmans Industries Ltd: 15 Senoko Loop, Singapore 758168; tel. 63388998; fax 63388181; cap. and res 113m., sales 318m. (1996/97); investment holding co with subsidiaries engaged in manufacture, import and retail of cigarettes, pipe tobaccos, cigars and other tobacco-related products; Chair. ALAN YEO CHEE YEOW.

San Teh Ltd: 701 Sims Drive, 06-01 LHK Bldg, Singapore 387383; tel. 67476666; cap. and res 261m., sales 144m. (1998/99); mfrs of specialized silicone rubber products; Chair. KAO SHIN PING; Man. Dir CHUANG WEN-FU.

Singapore Press Holdings Ltd: News Centre, 82 Genting Lane, Singapore 349567; tel. 67438800; fax 67484919; internet www.sph.com.sg; cap. and res 2,055m., sales 1,053m. (1999/2000); publishing, printing and distribution of newspapers and magazines; Chair. LIM KIM SAN.

SM Summit Holdings Ltd: 45 Ubi Rd 1, Summit Bldg, Singapore 408696; tel. 67453288; fax 67489612; e-mail co@smsummit.com.sg; internet www.smsummit.com.sg; cap. and res 66m., sales 44m. (1999); mfrs and retailers of compact discs, audio tapes and related products; Chair. and Man. Dir LEE KERK CHONG.

Sumitomo Corporation (Singapore) Pte Ltd: 20 Cecil St, 23/24-01/08, Singapore 049705; tel. 65337722; fax 65339693; sales 4,502m. (1995); retailing and project management; CEO TOYOHARA SAWADA; 135 employees.

Toepfer International Asia Pte: 100 Beach Rd, 31-01 Shaw Towers, Singapore 189702; tel. 62932366; fax 62927556; sales 1,400m. (1994, est.); sale of commodities.

United Overseas Land Ltd: 101 Thomson Rd, 33-00 United Sq., Singapore 307591; tel. 62550233; fax 62529822; e-mail uol@pacific.net.sg; internet www.uol.com.sg; cap. and res 1,879m., sales 297m. (2000); property development; hotels; Chair. WEE CHO YAW; Pres. and CEO GWEE LIAN KHENG.

United Industrial Corpn Ltd: 5 Shenton Way, 02-16 UIC Bldg, Singapore 068808; tel. 62201352; fax 62240278; cap. and res 1,897m., sales 401m. (1998/99); investment holding co with subsidiaries engaged in manufacture of detergent products, toiletries and electronic systems; Chair. WEE CHO YAW; Pres. and CEO LIM HOCK SAN.

WBL Corpn Ltd: 65 Chulia St, 41-08 OCBC Centre, Singapore 049513; tel. 65333444; fax 63838940; cap. and res 478m., sales 908m. (1999/2000); investment holding co with subsidiaries engaged in manufacture of vehicles, industrial machinery, electronic components and products, building materials and precision engineering products, property development and investment, provision of management services; Pres. TAN CHIN TUAN; Chair. TANG I-FANG.

Wing Tai Holdings Ltd: 107 Tampines Rd, Wing Tai Industrial Centre, Singapore 535129; tel. 62809111; fax 63838940; internet www.wingtaiasia.com.sg; cap. and res 1,568m., sales 199m. (1999/2000); investment holding co with subsidiaries engaged in property development and hospitality, trading in fabrics, garments and architectural products and the provision of internet-related services; Chair. and Man. Dir CHENG WAI KEUNG.

TRADE UNIONS

In 1998 there were 86 registered trade unions and associations with 287,062 members, and three employer unions.

In December 1998 the largest private-sector union, the United Workers of Electronics and Electrical Industries, had 40,433 members, while the largest public-sector union, the Amalgamated Union of Public Employees, had 20,872 members.

National Trades Union Congress (NTUC): NTUC Trade Union House, 73 Bras Basah Rd, Singapore 189556; tel. 62226555; fax 63343373; internet www.ntuc.org.sg; f. 1961; 66 affiliated unions and 6 affiliated associates, 337,712 mems (Oct. 2001); Pres. JOHN DE PAYVA; Sec.-Gen. LIM BOON HENG.

Transport

RAILWAYS

In 1993 there was 26 km of 1-m gauge railway, linked with the Malaysian railway system and owned by the Malayan Railway Pentadbiran Keretapi Tanah Melayu—KTM. The main line crosses the Johore causeway (1.2 km) and terminates near Keppel Harbour. Branch lines link it with the industrial estate at Jurong.

Construction began in 1983 on the Mass Rapid Transit (MRT) system. The first section was completed in 1987, and the remaining sections by 1990. The system extends for 83 km and consists of two lines with 48 stations (32 elevated, 15 under ground and one at ground level). The construction of a further 20-km line, the North–East Line, began in 1997; the line has 16 stations and one depot, and was completed in 2002. In 2002 the extension of the East–West line to Changi Airport was completed; the Changi Airport Line (CAL) has one underground and one elevated station. In 2001 construction was under way on the Circle Line, a 34-km orbital line running entirely under ground which was to link all the radial lines into the city. The line was to start at Dhoby Ghaut and terminate at Harbour Front and was to be implemented in five stages, the last of which was scheduled for completion in 2010.

Singapore's first Light Rapid Transit (LRT) system, the Bukit Panjang LRT (a 7.8-km line with 14 stations), was completed in April 1998. Work on two further LRT lines, in Sengkang and Punggol, was also under way, and these lines were expected to be completed in 2002 and 2004 respectively.

Land Transport Authority: 460 Alexandra Rd, 28-00 PSA Bldg, Singapore 119963; tel. 63757100; fax 63757200; internet www.lta.gov.sg; Chair. FOCK SIEW WAH; Chief Exec. Maj.-Gen. HAN ENG JUAN.

ROADS

In 1999 Singapore had a total of 3,066 km of roads, of which 150 km were motorway; in that year 100% of the road network was paved. In 1990 the Government introduced a quota system to control the number of vehicles using the roads. A manual road-pricing system was introduced on one expressway in June 1996 and extended to two further expressways in May 1997. It was replaced by a system of Electronic Road Pricing (ERP) in 1998, whereby each vehicle was charged according to road use in congested areas. The ERP was first introduced on one expressway in April 1998, and was subsequently extended to include two other expressways and the Area Licensing Scheme gantry areas by early September of that year. In 2001 construction of the12-km Kallang–Paya Lebar expressway was progressing. It was scheduled for completion in 2006.

SHIPPING

The Port of Singapore is the world's busiest in tonnage terms; Singapore handled an estimated 146,265 vessels with a total displacement of 960.1m. grt in 2001.

The Port of Singapore Authority operates six cargo terminals: Tanjong Pagar Terminal, Keppel Terminal, Brani Terminal, Pasir Panjang Terminal, Sembawang Terminal and Jurong Port.

Tanjong Pagar Terminal and Keppel Terminal have the capacity to handle 10.7m. 20-foot equivalent units (TEUs).

The third container terminal, Brani, built on an offshore island connected to the mainland by a causeway, has a capacity of 5.5m. TEUs.

Pasir Panjang Terminal, Singapore's main gateway for conventional cargo (particularly timber and rubber), has five deep-water berths and eight coastal berths and 17 lighter berths.

Sembawang Terminal has three deep-water berths and one coastal berth. This terminal is the main gateway for car carriers as well as handling steel and timber products.

Jurong Port (which handles general and dry-bulk cargo, is situated in south-western Singapore, and serves the Jurong Industrial Estate) has 20 deep-water berths and one coastal berth.

A new container terminal at Pasir Panjang was under construction in the late 1990s. Upon completion, the terminal, which was to be built in four phases, was to have 49 berths and a handling capacity of 36m. TEUs.

Maritime and Port Authority of Singapore: 460 Alexandra Rd, 18-00 PSA Bldg, Singapore 119963; tel. 63751600; fax 62759247; internet www.mpa.gov.sg; f. 1996; regulatory body responsible for promotion and development of the port, overseeing all port and maritime matters in Singapore.

Port of Singapore Authority: 460 Alexandra Rd, PSA Bldg, Singapore 119963; tel. 63751600; fax 62759247; internet www.psa.gov.sg; f. 1964 as a statutory board under the Ministry of Communications; made a corporate entity in 1997 in preparation for privatization; responsible for the provision and maintenance of port facilities and services; Chair. Dr Yeo Ning Hong; Pres. Khoo Teng Chye.

Major Shipping Companies

American President Lines Ltd (APL): 456 Alexandra Rd, 08-00 NOL Bldg, Singapore 119962; tel. 62789000; fax 62742113; e-mail hung-song-goh@apl.com; internet www.apl.com; container services to North and South Asia, the USA, the Middle East, India and Pakistan; Chief Operating Officer Ed Aldridge.

Glory Ship Management Private Ltd: 24 Raffles Place 17-01/02, Clifford Centre, Singapore 048621; tel. 65361986; fax 65361987; e-mail gene@gloryship.com.sg.

Guan Guan Shipping Pte Ltd: 2 Finlayson Green, 13-05 Asia Insurance Bldg, Singapore 049247; tel. 65343988; fax 62276776; e-mail golden@golden.com.sg; f. 1955; shipowners and agents; cargo services to East and West Malaysia, Indonesia, Pakistan, Sri Lanka, Bengal Bay ports, Persian (Arabian) Gulf ports, Hong Kong and China; Man. Dir Richard Thio.

IMC Shipping Co Pte Ltd: 5 Temasek Blvd, 12-01 Suntec City Tower, Singapore 038985; tel. 63362233; fax 63379715; e-mail commercial@imcshipping.com.sg; internet www.imcshipping.com; Man. Dir Peter Chew.

Nedlloyd Lines Singapore Pte Ltd: 138 Robinson Rd, 01-00 Hong Leong Centre, Singapore 068906; tel. 62218989; fax 62255267; f. 1963; Gen. Man. F. C. Schuchard.

Neptune Orient Lines Ltd: 456 Alexandra Rd, 05-00 NOL Bldg, Singapore 119962; tel. 63715300; fax 63716489; e-mail shirley_ting@ccgate.apl.com; internet www.nol.com.sg; f. 1968; liner containerized services on the Far East/Europe, Far East/North America, Straits/Australia, South Asia/Europe and South-East Asia, Far East/Mediterranean routes; tankers, bulk carriers and dry cargo vessels on charter; 36% govt-owned; Chair. Lua Cheng Eng; Man. Dir Flemming Jacobs.

New Straits Shipping Co Pte Ltd: 51 Anson Rd, 09-53 Anson Centre, Singapore 0207; tel. 62201007; fax 62240785.

Ocean Tankers (Pte) Ltd: 41 Tuas Rd, Singapore 638497; tel. 68632202; fax 68639480; e-mail admin@oceantankers.com.sg; Marine Supt V. Lim.

Osprey Maritime Ltd: 8 Cross St, 24-02/03 PWC Bldg, Singapore 048424; tel. 62129722; fax 65570450; internet www.ospreymaritime.com; CEO Peter George Costalas.

Pacific International Lines (Pte) Ltd: 140 Cecil St, 03-00 PIL Bldg, POB 3206, Singapore 069540; tel. 62218133; fax 62273933; e-mail sherry.chua@sgp.pilship.com; shipowners, agents and managers; liner services to South-East Asia, the Far East, India, the Red Sea, the Persian (Arabian) Gulf, West and East Africa; container services to South-East Asia; world-wide chartering, freight forwarding, container manufacturing, depot operators, container freight station operator; Exec. Chair. Y. C. Chang; Man. Dir S. S. Teo.

Petroships Private Ltd: 460 Alexandra Rd, 25-04 PSA Bldg, Singapore 119963; tel. 62731122; fax 62732200; e-mail gen@petroships.com.sg; Man. Dir Kenneth Kee.

Singa Ship Management Private Ltd: 78 Shenton Way 16-02, Singapore 079120; tel. 62244308; fax 62235848; e-mail agency@singaship.com.sg; Chair. Ole Hegland; Man. Dir Eileen Leong.

Syabas Tankers Pte Ltd: 10 Anson Rd, 34-10 International Plaza, Singapore 0207; tel. 62259522.

Tanker Pacific Management (Singapore) Private Ltd: 1 Temasek Ave, 38-01 Millenia Tower, Singapore; tel. 63365211; fax 63375570; Man. Dir Hugh Hung.

CIVIL AVIATION

Singapore's international airport at Changi was opened in 1981. Construction on a third terminal at Changi began in October 2000, and was scheduled to be completed in 2006, increasing the airport's total capacity to 64m. passengers a year. A second airport at Seletar operates as a base for charter and training flights.

Civil Aviation Authority of Singapore: Singapore Changi Airport, POB 1, Singapore 918141; tel. 65412222; fax 65421231; e-mail thennarasee_R@caas.gov.sg; internet www.caas.gov.sg; responsible for regulatory and advisory services, air services development, airport management and development and airspace management and organization; Chair. Tjong Yik Min; Dir-Gen. Wong Woon Liong.

SilkAir: Singapore Airlines Superhub, Airfreight Terminal 5, Core L, 5th Storey, 30 Airline Rd, Singapore 819830; tel. 65428111; fax 65426286; internet www.silkair.net; f. 1975; fmrly Tradewinds Private; wholly-owned subsidiary of Singapore Airlines Ltd; began scheduled services in 1989; Chair. Chew Choon Seng; Gen. Man. Paul Tan.

Singapore Airlines Ltd (SIA): Airline House, 25 Airline Rd, Singapore 819829; tel. 65415880; fax 65456083; e-mail publicaffairs@singaporeair.com.sg; internet www.singaporeair.com; f. 1972; passenger services to 88 destinations in 42 countries; Chair. Michael Fam; Dep. Chair. and CEO Cheong Choong Kong.

Tourism

Singapore's tourist attractions include a blend of cultures and excellent shopping facilities. Tourist arrivals totalled 7,518,584 in 2001. Receipts from tourism totalled an estimated US $6,370m. in 2000.

Singapore Tourism Board: Tourism Court, 1 Orchard Spring Lane, Singapore 247729; tel. 67366622; fax 67369423; e-mail feedback@stb.com.sg; internet www.stb.com.sg; f. 1964; Chair. Wee Ee-chao; Chief Exec. Yeo Khee Leng.

Defence

In August 2001 the total strength of the armed forces was 60,500 (39,800 conscripts): army 50,000 (35,000 conscripts), navy an estimated 4,500 (1,800 conscripts), air force 6,000 (3,000 conscripts). Military service lasts 24-30 months. Army reserves numbered an estimated 312,500. Paramilitary forces of an estimated 94,000 comprised the Singapore police force. marine and Gurkha guard battalions, and a civil defence force. Singapore is a participant in the Five-Power Defence Arrangements with Malaysia, Australia, New Zealand and the United Kingdom.

Defence Expenditure: Budgeted at S $7,800m. in 2001.

Chief of the Defence Forces: Lt-Gen. Bey Soo Khiang.

Chief of the Army: Maj.-Gen. Ng Yat Chung.

Chief of the Air Force: Brig.-Gen. Raymund Ng Teck Heng.

Chief of the Navy: Rear-Adm. Richard Lim Cherng Yih.

Education

Education in Singapore is not compulsory. All children are entitled to at least six years' free primary education, which may be completed in eight years by less able pupils, under the New Primary Education System implemented in 1979.

In 1996 the number of children attending primary schools was equivalent to 94% of children in the relevant age-group (males 95%; females 93%) and secondary school enrolment was equivalent to 74% of children in the relevant age-group. Expenditure on education by the central Government in the 2001/01 finanical year was S $3,901.9m. to education (13.9% of total expenditure).

The policy of bilingualism ensures that children are taught two languages, English and one of the other official languages, Chinese, Malay or Tamil. The option to study French, German or Japanese is offered in secondary schools to interested pupils with linguistic ability as a third language, and as a second language to pupils not of Chinese, Malay or Tamil ethnic origin.

Primary education focuses on the core subjects of English, Mathematics and the mother tongue (Chinese, Malay or Tamil). After four years pupils are streamed according to their abilities into the normal bilingual course (six years' primary education), extended bilingual course (eight years) or the monolingual course (eight years). Pupils of the bilingual courses take the Primary School Leaving Examination (PSLE) on completion of their primary education and are streamed, depending on their performance in the PSLE, into the Special course (four years), the Express course (four years) or the Normal course (five years). Pupils of Special and Express courses will take the Singapore-Cambridge General Certificate of Education (GCE) 'Ordinary' Level Examination. Normal course pupils will sit the GCE 'Normal' Level Examination after four years, and those who do well may take the GCE 'O' Level after the fifth year. Based on 'O' Level results, pupils may follow a two-year or three-year pre-university course leading to the GCE 'Advanced' Level Examination. Pupils of the monolingual course may continue their education in the technical or commercial institutes under the Institute of Technical Education.

HIGHER EDUCATION

There were seven tertiary institutions in 2000, including the National University of Singapore, the Nanyang Technological University, the Ngee Ann Polytechnic, the Singapore Polytechnic, the Nanyang Polytechnic and the Temasek Polytechnic. In June of that year the total enrolment in the universities and colleges was 108,230.

VOCATIONAL AND INDUSTRIAL TRAINING

The Institute of Technical Education provides and regulates vocational training. It conducts institutional training for school-leavers, offers part-time continuing education and training programmes and registers apprentices. It is also responsible for setting national skills standards, the conduct of public trade testing and certification of skills.

Bibliography

GENERAL

Barr, Michael D. *Lee Kuan Yew: The Beliefs Behind the Man.* Washington, DC, Georgetown University Press, 2000.

Bedlington, Stanley S. *Malaysia and Singapore: The Building of New States.* Ithaca, NY, Cornell University Press, 1978.

Bloodworth, Dennis. *The Tiger and the Trojan Horse.* Singapore, Times Books International, 1986.

Buchanan, Iain. *Singapore in Southeast Asia; An Economic and Political Appraisal.* London, G. Bell, 1972.

Chan Heng Chee. *Singapore: Politics of Survival 1965–1967.* Singapore, Oxford University Press, 1971.

A Sensation of Independence: Singapore's David Marshall. Singapore, Oxford University Press, 1984.

Chee Soon Juan. *Dare to Change.* Singapore, 1994.

Singapore: My Home Too. Singapore, Melodies Press Co, 1995.

Cherian, George. *Singapore: The Air-Conditioned Nation—Essays on the Politics of Comfort and Control, 1990–2000.* Singapore, Landmark Books, 2001.

Chew, Ernest C. T., and Lee, Edwin (Eds). *A History of Singapore.* Singapore, Oxford University Press, 1991.

Chew, Melanie. *Leaders of Singapore.* Singapore, Resource Press, 1996.

Chua Beng-Huat. *Communitarian Ideology and Democracy in Singapore.* London, Routledge, 1997.

Political Legitimacy and Housing—Singapore's Stakeholder Society. London, Routledge, 1997.

Clammer, John. *Singapore: Ideology, Society, Culture.* Singapore, Chapman, 1985.

Clutterbuck, Richard. *Conflict and Violence in Singapore and Malaysia 1945–1983.* Singapore, Graham Brash, 1984.

da Cunha, Derek. *Debating Singapore (Reflective Essays).* Singapore, Institute of Southeast Asian Studies, 1994.

The Price of Victory: The 1997 Singapore General Election and Beyond. Singapore, Institute of Southeast Asian Studies, 1997.

Singapore in the New Millennium: Challenges Facing the City-State. Singapore, Institute of Southeast Asian Studies, 2001.

Darusman, Suryono. *Singapore and the Indonesian Revolution 1945–50: Recollections of Suryono Darusman.* Singapore, Institute of Southeast Asian Studies, 1992.

Drysdale, John. *Singapore: Struggle for Success.* Singapore, Times Books International, 1984.

Gomez, James. *Self-Censorship: Singapore's Shame.* Singapore, Think Center, 2000.

Han Fook Kwang, Fernandez, Warren, and Tan, Sumiko. *Lee Kuan Yew: The Man and his Ideas.* Singapore, 1997.

Harper, R. W. E., and Miller, Harry. *Singapore Mutiny: The Story of a Little 'Local Disturbance'.* Singapore, Oxford University Press, 1984.

Hassan, Riaz (Ed.). *Singapore: Society in Transition.* Kuala Lumpur, Oxford University Press, 1976.

Josey, Alex. *Lee Kuan Yew: The Struggle for Singapore.* Sydney, Angus & Robertson, 1980.

Lam Peng Er, and Tan, Kevin (Eds). *Managing Politics in Singapore: the Elected Presidency.* London and New York, Routledge, 1997.

Lee's Lieutenants. Singapore, Allen and Unwin, 1999.

Lau, Albert. *A Moment of Anguish.* Singapore, 1998.

Lee Kuan Yew. *The Battle for Merger.* Singapore, Ministry of Culture, 1961.

The Singapore Story: Memoirs of Lee Kuan Yew. Prentice Hall/ Simon & Schuster Asia, Singapore, 1998.

From Third World to First: The Singapore Story: 1965–2000. Singapore, Times Media Private and Straits Times Press, 2000.

Leifer, Michael. *Singapore's Foreign Policy—Coping with Vulnerability.* London, Routledge, 2000.

Lim Pui Huen P., and Wong, Diana (Eds). *War and Memory in Malaysia and Singapore.* Singapore, Institute of Southeast Asian Studies, 1999.

Lim, R. *Got Singapore.* Singapore, Angsana Books, 2002.

Liu, Gretchen. *Singapore—A Pictorial History 1819–2000.* London, Curzon Press, 2001.

Mahizhnan, Arun, and Lee Tsao Yuan (Eds). *Singapore: Re-Engineered Success.* Oxford, Oxford University Press, 2002.

Makepeace, Walter, Brooke, Gilbert E., and Braddell, Roland St J. (Eds). *One Hundred Years of Singapore.* 2 vols, 1921, 1991.

Milne, R. S., and Mauzy, Diane K. *Singapore: The Legacy of Lee Kuan Yew.* Boulder, CO, Westview Press, 1990.

Singapore Politics: Under the People's Action Party. London, Routledge, 2002.

Minchin, James. *No Man is an Island.* London, Unwin Hyman, 1987.

Mulliner, K. *Historical Dictionary of Singapore.* Lanham, MD, Scarecrow Press, 2002.

Nair, C. V. Devan. *Socialism That Works: The Singapore Way.* Singapore, Federal Publications, 1977.

Pang Cheng Lian. *Singapore's People's Action Party.* Singapore, Oxford University Press, 1971.

Quah, Jon S. T., Chan Heng Chee and Seah Chee Meow (Eds). *Government and Politics of Singapore.* Singapore, Oxford University Press, 1985.

Rappa, Antonio, L. *Modernity and Consumption: Theory, Politics and the Public in Singapore and Malaysia.* Singapore, World Scientific Publishing Co, 2002.

Régnier, Philippe. *Singapore, City-State in South East Asia.* London/ Honolulu, Hurst Publishers/Hawaii University Press, 1991.

Saw Swee Hock. *Asian Metropolis: Singapore in Transition.* University of Pennsylvania and Oxford University Press, 1970.

The Population of Singapore. Singapore, Institute of Southeast Asian Studies, 1999.

Selvan, T. S. *Singapore the Ultimate Island (Lee Kuan Yew's Untold Story).* Victoria, Freeway Books, 1990.

Seow, Francis. *To Catch a Tartar.* New Haven, CT, Yale University Press, 1994.

The Media Enthralled: Singapore Revisited. Boulder, CO, and London, Lynne Rienner, 1998.

Singapore Government. *The Next Lap.* Singapore, 1991.

Singh, Bilveer. *Whither PAP's Dominance? An Analysis of Singapore's 1991 General Elections.* Petaling Jaya, Pelanduk Publications, 1992.

Song Ong Siang. *One Hundred Years' History of the Chinese in Singapore.* Oxford University Press, 1923, 1967, 1984.

Suryadinata, L. *Ethnic Chinese in Singapore and Malaysia.* Singapore, Times Academic Press, 2002.

Tamney, Joseph B. *The Struggle over Singapore's Soul: Western Modernization and Asian Culture.* Berlin and New York, Walter de Gruyter, 1996.

Thio, Eunice (Ed.). *Singapore 1819–1969.* University of Singapore, Journal of South-East Asian History, March 1969.

Times Editions. *Singapore: Island. City. State.* Singapore, 1990.

Turnbull, C. M. *A History of Singapore 1819–1988.* Oxford University Press, 1989.

A History of Malaysia, Singapore, and Brunei. Sydney, Allen and Unwin, 1989.

The Straits Settlements, 1826–67. London, Athlone Press, and Kuala Lumpur, Oxford University Press, 1972.

Dateline Singapore: 150 Years History of the Straits Times. Singapore, Singapore Press Holdings, 1995.

Vasil, Raj. *Governing Singapore: A History of National Development and Democracy.* Singapore, Institute of Southeast Asian Studies, 2000.

Warren, J. F. *Rickshaw Coolie.* Singapore, Oxford University Press, 1986.

Ah Ku and Karayuki-san: Prostitution in Singapore 1870–1940. Singapore, Oxford University Press, 1993.

Wei-Bin Zhang. *Singapores Modernization: Westernization and Modernizing Confucian Manifestations.* New York, NY, Nova Science Publishers, 2002.

Wilson, H. E. *Social Engineering in Singapore: Educational Policies and Social Change, 1819–1972.* Singapore, Singapore University Press, 1978.

Worthington, Ross. *Governance in Singapore.* London, RoutledgeCurzon, 2002.

Wurtzburg, C. E. *Raffles of the Eastern Isles.* London, Hodder and Stoughton, 1954, 1984.

Yeo Kim Wah. *Political Development in Singapore, 1945–1955.* Singapore, Singapore University Press, 1973.

Yong Chin Fatt. *Tan Kah-Kee: The Making of a Legend.* Singapore, Oxford University Press, 1987.

Zahari, Said. *Dark Clouds at Dawn: A Political Memoir.* Kuala Lumpur, INSAN, 2001.

ECONOMY

Board of Commissioners of Currency. *Currency Board System: A Stop-gap Measure or a Necessity: Currency Board System Symposium '97.* Singapore, 1997.

Dent, Christopher. *The Foreign Economic Policies of Singapore, South Korea and Taiwan.* Cheltenham, Edward Elgar Publishing, 2002.

Deutsch, Antal, and Zowall, Hanna. *Compulsory Savings and Taxes in Singapore.* Singapore, Institute of Southeast Asian Studies, 1988.

Doshi, Tilak. *The Singapore Petroleum Industry.* Singapore, Institute of Southeast Asian Studies, 1989.

Freeman, Nick, Chia Siow Yue, Venkatesan, R., and Malvea, S. V. (Eds). *Growth and Development of the IT Industry in Bangalore and Singapore: A Comparative Study.* Singapore, Institute of Southeast Asian Studies, 2001.

Goh Keng Swee. *The Economics of Modernization and Other Essays.* Singapore, Asia Pacific Press, 1972.

The Practice of Economic Growth. Singapore, Federal Publications, 1977.

Wealth of East Asian Nations: Speeches and Writings by Goh Keng Swee. Singapore, Kuala Lumpur and Hong Kong, Federal Publications, 1995.

Gwartney, James, Lawson, Robert, and Block, Walter. *Economic Freedom of the World 1975–1995.* Vancouver, The Fraser Institute, 1996.

Hiroshi, Shimizu and Hitoshi, Hirakawa. *Japan and Singapore in the World Economy: Japan's Economic Advance into Singapore 1870–1965.* London, Routledge, 1999.

Huff, Gregg. *The Economic Growth of Singapore: Trade and Development in the Twentieth Century.* Cambridge, Cambridge University Press, 1994.

Krause, Lawrence B., Koh Ai Tee, and Lee Yuan. *Singapore Economy Reconsidered.* Singapore, Institute of Southeast Asian Studies, 1987.

Lee Sheng-Yi. *Public Finance and Public Investment in Singapore.* Singapore, Institute of Banking and Finance, 1978.

The Monetary and Banking Development of Singapore and Malaysia (3rd Edn). Singapore, Singapore University Press, 1990.

Lee Tsao Yuan. *Growth Triangle: The Johor-Singapore-Riau Experience.* Singapore, Institute of Southeast Asian Studies, 1991.

Lee Tsao Yuan and Low, Linda. *Local Entrepreneurship in Singapore: Private and State.* Singapore, Times Academic Press, 1990.

Lim, Chong Yah, et al. *Policy Options for the Singapore Economy.* Singapore, McGraw-Hill Book Co, 1988.

Lim Chong Yah (Ed.). *Economic Policy Management in Singapore.* Singapore, Addison-Wesley, 1996.

Lim, L., and Eng Fong, P. *Trade, Employment and Industrialization in Singapore.* Geneva, International Labour Office, 1985.

Lingle, Christopher. *Singapore: Authoritarian Capitalism: Asian Values, Free Market Illusions and Political Dependency.* Barcelona, Edicions Sirocco, 1996.

Low, Linda. *The Political Economy of a City-State: Government-Made Singapore.* Singapore, Oxford University Press, 1998.

Low, Linda, Toh Mun Heng, Soon Teck Wong, Tan Kong Yam and Hughes, Helen. *Challenge and Response: Thirty Years of the Economic Development Board.* Singapore, Times Academic Press, 1993.

Low, Linda and Aw, T. C. *Housing a Healthy, Educated and Wealthy Nation Through the CPF.* Singapore, Times Academic Press for The Institute of Policy Studies, 1997.

Luckett, Dudley G., Schulze, David L., and Wong, Raymond W. Y. *Banking, Finance and Monetary Policy in Singapore.* Singapore, McGraw-Hill, 1994.

Mirza, Hafiz. *Multinationals and the Growth of the Singapore Economy.* London, Croom Helm, 1986.

Murray, Geoffrey, and Perera, Audrey (Eds). *Singapore: The Global City State.* Richmond, Surrey, Curzon Press, 1996.

Peebles, Gavin, and Wilson, Peter. *The Singapore Economy.* Cheltenham, and Brookfield, USA, Edward Elgar Publishing, 1996.

Economic Growth and Development in Singapore. Singapore, Singapore University Press, 2002.

Quak Ser Khoon. *Marketing Abroad: Competitive Strategies and Market Niches for the Singapore Construction Industry.* Singapore, Institute of Southeast Asian Studies, 1991.

Rajan, Ramkishen S., Sen, Rahul, and Siregar, Reza. *Singapore and Free Trade Agreements: Economic Relations with Japan and the United States.* Singapore, Institute of Southeast Asian Studies, 2001.

Rodan, Garry. *The Political Economy of Singapore's Industrialisation: National State and International Capital.* London, Macmillan, 1989.

Sharma, Shankar. *The Role of the Petroleum Industry in Singapore's Economy.* Singapore, Institute of Southeast Asian Studies, 1989.

Siddique, Sharon, and Puru Shotam, Nirmala. *Singapore's Little India: Past, Present and Future* (Second Edn with Epilogue). Singapore, Institute of Southeast Asian Studies, 1982.

Singh Sandhu, Kernial, and Wheatley, Paul (Eds). *Management of Success: The Moulding of Modern Singapore.* Singapore, Institute of Southeast Asian Studies, 1990.

Tan Chwee Huat, *Singapore Financial and Business Sourcebook.* Singapore, Singapore University Press, 2002.

Tan Ern Ser, Yeoh, Brenda S. A., and Wang, Jennifer (Eds). *Tourism Management and Policy: Perspectives from Singapore.* Singapore, World Scientific Publishing Co, 2002.

Tan Sook Yee. *Private Ownership of Public Housing in Singapore.* Singapore, Times Academic Press, 1998.

Toh Mun Heng, and Low, Linda. *Economic Impact of the Withdrawal of the GSP on Singapore.* Singapore, Institute of Southeast Asian Studies, 1991.

Toh Mun Heng, and Tan Kong Yam (Eds). *Competitiveness of the Singapore Economy: A Strategic Perspective.* Singapore, Singapore University Press and World Scientific, 1998.

Tremewan, Peter. *The Political Economy of Social Control in Singapore.* London, St. Martin's Press, 1994.

Vasil, Raj. *Asianising Singapore: The PAP's Management of Ethnicity.* Singapore, Institute of Southeast Asian Studies, 1995.

Walter, Ingo. *High-Performance Financial Systems: Blueprint for Development.* Singapore, Institute of Southeast Asian Studies, 1993.

You Poh Seng, and Lim Chong Yah. *The Singapore Economy.* Singapore, Eastern Universities Press, 1971.

SRI LANKA

Physical and Social Geography

B. H. FARMER

Revised by G. H. PEIRIS

The Democratic Socialist Republic of Sri Lanka (formerly known as Ceylon) comprises one large island and several islets, lying east of the southern tip of the Indian subcontinent. The maximum north–south length of the island, which (including adjacent small islands) covers an area of 65,525 sq km (25,299 sq miles), is 435 km, and its greatest width is 225 km. The Bay of Bengal lies to its north and east, and the Arabian Sea to its west. Sri Lanka is separated from India by the Gulf of Mannar and the Palk Strait, between which there lies, in very shallow water, a chain of small islands linking Sri Lanka and India. Sri Lanka extends from 5° 55′ to 9° 50′ N and from 79° 42′ to 81° 53′ E.

PHYSICAL FEATURES

Sri Lanka consists almost entirely of hard ancient crystalline rocks (although recent work has cast doubt on the age of some of them). Unaltered sedimentary rocks are largely confined to the Jaffna peninsula in the north and a strip down the north-west coast.

The highest land in Sri Lanka occupies the south-centre, the 'up-country', and rises to more than 1,500 m above sea-level. The highest point is Piduruthalagala (2,524 m). From the up-country, the land falls by steps to a rolling coastal plain, narrow in the west and south-west, broadest in the north (though even there, isolated hills rise above the general level). The rivers, apart from the longest, the Mahaweli Ganga (which has a complicated course), are generally short and run radially outwards from the up-country.

CLIMATE

Sri Lanka has temperatures appropriate to its near-equatorial position, modified by altitude up-country. In Colombo, at sea-level, mean monthly temperatures fluctuate only between 25°C in January and 28°C in May. At Nuwara Eliya, at 1,889 m, temperatures range between 14°C in January and 16°C in May.

A fundamental division in Sri Lanka, so far as rainfall and therefore agriculture are concerned, is that between the wet and dry zones. The former occupies the south-western quadrant of the island, and normally receives rain from both the south-west and north-east monsoons. Colombo, for example, has a mean annual rainfall of 2,365 mm: it receives 69 mm in February, the driest month, and 371 mm in May, the wettest. The dry zone, covering the lowlands of the north and east and extending in modified form into the eastern up-country, has a period of severe drought in the south-west monsoon and most of its rain from the north-east. Trincomalee, for example, with a mean annual rainfall of 1,648 mm, receives on average only 69 mm, 28 mm and 51 mm in May, June and July respectively (and mean *expectation* is less than the mean rainfall); but it receives over 356 mm in both November and December. Commercial crops such as tea and rubber are almost entirely confined to the wet zone.

SOILS AND NATURAL RESOURCES

The contrast between the wet zone and the dry zone extends into other environmental diversities such as those of soil and vegetation. For example, the 'red-yellow podzolic soils', which are confined to the wet zone, comprise a leached lateritic soil susceptible to rapid degradation when exposed through removal of vegetation to processes of weathering and erosion. The 'reddish-brown earths', are found extensively in those parts of the dry zone with a sub-surface of crystalline rocks; this non-lateritic loamy soil has a potential for sustained high productivity under conditions of sound management. Among the other more important edaphic formations found in Sri Lanka are the 'latosolic soils', which cover the limestone rock strata of the northern and north-western littoral, the 'alluvials' found in association with riverine terrain, and the 'regosols' (sandy soils), which extend over much of the coastal fringe.

The zonal differences in vegetation are reflected in the remnants of natural forests—'wet evergreen forest' (modified by elevation in the highlands to 'sub-montane' and 'montane' types) of the wet zone, and 'dry mixed evergreen forests' (modified in areas of lowest rainfall into shrub and thorn forest) of the dry zone. Rapid deforestation has reduced the aggregate extent of natural forest cover to no more than about 15% of the country. The fertility of the soil, and the biotic characteristics of the forests, now reflect in abundance the impact of ecological disruptions caused by many centuries of intensive use of the land for agriculture and human settlements. Accordingly, both conservation of the soil as well as the preservation of the fauna and flora have become matters of major concern to Sri Lanka.

Gemstones (including high-value varieties such as sapphire, ruby, chrysoberyl, spinel, beryl and topaz), graphite, ilmenite, quartz, mica, industrial clays, limestone and salt are the more important economically useful minerals found in Sri Lanka. The resource base in metallurgical minerals is considered poor, the only commercially exploitable metals known hitherto being titanium, monazite and zircon contained in the beach sands over certain stretches of the sea coast. Of fossil fuels, the only known resource is the low-grade peat found along the swamps adjacent to the west coast. In the absence of both coal and petroleum, biomass (extracted from forests, and by-products of agriculture) and river water harnessed for hydropower are significant as locally available sources of commercial energy.

POPULATION AND ETHNIC GROUPS

According to the provisional results of the census of July 2001, Sri Lanka had a population of 16,864,544 in 18 out of 25 districts where enumeration was carried out completely. Enumeration was only partially conducted in Mannar, Vavuniya, Batticaloa and Trincomalee districts, owing to security concerns; data from these districts brought the total enumerated population to approximately 17,560,000. The census was not conducted in the districts of Jaffna, Mullaitivu and Kilinochchi, also owing to security concerns. The total estimated population for the entire country at July 2001 was 18,732, 255. The crude birth rate fell from 37 per 1,000 in 1960 to 22.4 per 1,000 in 1986, and to an estimated 17.3 per 1,000 in 1999. The average population density at mid-2001 was 286 per sq km, although the population is very unevenly distributed. The wet zone and most of the up-country have a dense rural population and also contain the principal conurbation, Colombo (estimated population 642,163 at mid-2001), and a number of other towns, e.g. Kandy (110,049 at mid-1997). Some of the dry zone remains sparsely peopled, despite considerable colonization since the 1930s.

Sri Lanka has a plural society. The majority group, the Sinhalese, speak a distinctive language (Sinhala) related to the Indo-Aryan tongues of north India, and are mainly Buddhist. There are two groups of Tamils: 'Sri Lankan Tamils', the descendants of Tamil-speaking groups who migrated from South India many years ago, and 'Indian Tamils', comparatively recent immigrants (who came to Sri Lanka to work on plantations) and their descendants: both are predominantly Hindu. There are also groups of Muslims (comprising 'Moors' and 'Malays') and Christians (drawn from the Sinhalese, Tamil and other communities).

History

KINGSLEY M. de SILVA

HISTORICAL BACKGROUND

Sri Lanka has had a long and troubled history that goes back over 2,500 years. The Sinhalese and Tamils, the main component elements of its society, have a common Indian origin, Indo-Aryan and Dravidian respectively. Indo-Aryan settlement and colonization in the island began around the fifth century BC, a few centuries earlier than the arrival of Dravidian Tamil settlers in any large numbers. These latter were always a small minority, although a distinctive one.

The early settlements were located in the dry zone, with rice as the main crop. The Sinhalese developed a highly sophisticated irrigation system, which became the basis of a thriving economy; indeed, Sri Lanka became, in time, one of the great irrigation civilizations of the ancient world. The Buddhist religion was the bedrock of its culture and civilization, while a linkage between Buddhism and national identity fostered the self-image of the Sinhalese as a 'chosen' people destined to protect and preserve Buddhism in Sri Lanka. Hinduism established itself as the religion of the Tamils; trade links with the Indian Ocean states brought Islam to the island through small groups of Moorish traders who settled in the island from around the eighth century AD.

The Sinhalese kingdom of Sri Lanka's northern plain became, in time, an integral part of the power politics of southern India. It was highly vulnerable to invasion from that quarter, and such incursions were frequent. While the Sinhalese demonstrated a remarkable resilience in the face of invasions, and recovery from their ill-effects never proved too difficult, yet, over the centuries, foreign onslaughts, in combination with succession disputes in the Sinhalese kingdoms and other features of political instability, sapped the vitality, and contributed powerfully to the eventual collapse of the Sinhalese kingdom in the 13th century. Thereafter the Sinhalese abandoned the north-central plains and moved to the wetter, hilly and more densely forested south-west quarter. A Tamil kingdom, which survived for over two centuries, was established in the north of the island at this time.

Western influence began with the Portuguese intrusion into the affairs of the littoral. By 1600 the Portuguese were well established there despite prolonged resistance from the Sinhalese; within 60 years they were displaced by the Dutch, with the active support of the Sinhalese, and the Dutch, in their turn, by the British in 1795–96. Throughout this period much of the interior of the island remained independent under the Kandyan kings. The Kandyan kingdom maintained its independence until 1815–18, when it was absorbed into the British colony of Ceylon, and, for the first time in several centuries, one power controlled all of Sri Lanka. One notable feature of European rule was the introduction of Christianity in all its sectarian variety. None of the Protestant groups, however, developed any strong roots in the island, unlike Roman Catholicism. Under British rule, the economy was transformed through the development of plantation agriculture, with coffee the dominant crop in the earlier stages, to be replaced later on by tea, rubber and coconut. Immigrant Indian workers on the plantations settled in the island in large numbers in the last quarter of the 19th century.

The first phase in the emergence of nationalism in Sri Lanka occurred in the last quarter of the 19th century; this incipient nationalism was primarily religious—Buddhist—in outlook and content. It developed a more positive political content and ideology in the early 20th century. In the first two decades of the 20th century the British successfully withstood pressure from sections of the Sri Lanka élite for a share in the administration in the country. The keynotes of the Sri Lankan reform movement were restraint and moderation. The formation of the Ceylon National Congress in 1919 was evidence of the strength of these attitudes rather than any radical departure from them.

The 1920s brought bolder political initiatives, and also a significant heightening of working-class activity and trade union agitation. Foreseeing the eventual transfer of a substantial portion of power to the Sri Lankan political leadership, minority groups, led by the Tamils, were engaged in a determined effort to secure protection of their interests as the price of their support for this process. Constitutional reforms, introduced in 1931, amounted to the first really significant step towards self-government. Equally important was the introduction in that year of universal suffrage. Sri Lanka was the first of the United Kingdom's Asian colonies to secure this right, and few events in Sri Lanka's recent history have had so profound an impact on its politics and society as this.

The final phase in the transfer of power began under the leadership of Stephen Senanayake, the country's first Prime Minister, who was guided by a strong belief in ordered constitutional evolution to dominion status on the analogy of constitutional development in the white dominions. In response to the agitation in Sri Lanka, the British Government appointed the Soulbury Commission in 1944 to examine the island's constitutional problem. The Constitution that emerged from their deliberations was based substantially on one drafted for Senanayake in 1944 by his advisers. It gave the island internal self-government while retaining some imperial safeguards in defence and external affairs, but Sri Lanka's leaders pressed, successfully, for the removal of these restrictions, and the island was granted independence, with dominion status, on 4 February 1948. The transfer of power was smooth and peaceful, a reflection of the moderate tone of the dominant strand of the country's nationalist movement. In general, the situation in the country seemed to provide an impressive basis for a solid start in nation-building and national regeneration.

INDEPENDENCE AND AFTER, 1948–70

Stephen Senanayake's policies for the transfer of power in the early years of independence were based on his acceptance of the reality of a plural society. He sought the reconciliation of the legitimate interests of the majority and minority ethnic and religious groups within the context of an all-island polity. This held out the prospect of peace and stability in the vital first phase of independence. It was expected that the new Government would be threatened from the left, but the Marxist parties were too divided to pose an effective challenge. Within a year of the granting of independence, Stephen Senanayake's United National Party (UNP) had entrenched its position in the country and strengthened its hold on Parliament.

The first major challenge to the UNP-dominated Government emerged with Solomon Bandaranaike's formation of the Sri Lanka Freedom Party (SLFP) in September 1951, two months after he had crossed over to the opposition. The SLFP's populist programme sought to attract the large protest vote that went to the Marxist parties for want of a democratic alternative to the UNP, and looked for support in the rural areas which formed the basis of the UNP's hold on political power in the country.

Stephen Senanayake's death in March 1952, far from upsetting the political equilibrium that he had established, actually helped to stabilize it. When, two months later, his son and successor as Prime Minister, Dudley Senanayake, won a massive electoral victory, the verdict of the electorate was in many ways an endorsement of his father's life's work. Nevertheless, by the mid-1950s the UNP's position in the country was being undermined, even though its hold on Parliament appeared to be as strong as ever. The economy was faltering, after a period of prosperity, and an attempt to reduce the budgetary allocation for food subsidies provoked violent opposition, organized by the left-wing parties, in August 1953. Moreover, religious, cultural and linguistic issues were gathering momentum and developing into a force too powerful for the existing social and political establishment to accommodate or absorb. Neither the Government nor its left-wing critics showed much understanding of the sense of outrage and indignation of the Buddhists at what they regarded as the historic injustices suffered by their religion under European rule.

Solomon Bandaranaike successfully channelled this discontent into a massive campaign which swept the UNP out of office in 1956. His decisive victory was a significant point in Sri Lanka's history, for it represented the rejection of the concept of a Sri Lanka nationalism, based on plurality, which Stephen Senanayake had striven to nurture, and the substitution of a more democratic and populist nationalism which was at the same time fundamentally divisive in its impact on the country because it was unabashedly Sinhalese and Buddhist in content. Against the background of the world-wide celebration in 1956 of the 2,500th anniversary of the death of the Buddha, an intense religious fervour became the catalyst of a populist nationalism the explosive effect of which was derived from its interconnection with language. Language became the basis of nationalism and Sinhala nationalism was consciously or unconsciously treated as being identical with Sri Lanka nationalism, and this the minorities, especially the Tamils, rejected. As a result, in 1956 there began almost a decade of ethnic and linguistic tensions erupting occasionally into race riots and religious confrontation.

With the emergence of this linguistic nationalism there was increased pressure for the close association of the State with Buddhism, and a corresponding decline of Christian influence. On the whole Bandaranaike's Government was much more cautious in handling matters relating to the Christian minority than it was on the language issue. The language struggle took precedence over all else, and there was no desire to add to the problems of the Government by taking on an issue which was just as combustible.

At the time of his assassination in September 1959, the culmination of a bitter struggle for power within his own party, Bandaranaike's hold on the electorate was not as strong as it had been in 1956–57. However, his assassination dramatically changed the political situation and, after a few months of drift and regrouping, the SLFP emerged, under the leadership of his widow, Sirimavo Bandaranaike, more powerful than ever before. Unlike her husband, Sirimavo Bandaranaike was not reluctant to address two inflammable issues simultaneously. As well as pursuing her husband's policy on language, she made a determined bid to bring schools under state control and to secularize education, thus antagonizing the Roman Catholics as decisively as her language policy alienated the Tamils.

A wide variety of economic enterprises, foreign and local, were nationalized. Socialism was viewed as a means of redressing the balance in favour of the Sinhalese Buddhists and Sri Lankan nationals in a situation in which the island's trade was largely dominated by foreign capitalists and the minorities were disproportionately influential within the indigenous capitalist class. This extension of state control over trade and industry was justified on the grounds that it helped to curtail the influence of foreign interests and the minorities.

Two significant events in 1964 were the Bandaranaike-Shastri pact, which laid the basis for an equitable settlement of Sri Lanka's Indian problem, and the establishment of a coalition Government between the SLFP and the Trotskyist Lanka Sama Samaja Party (LSSP). This shift to the left by the SLFP was designed to stabilize the Government after the political turmoil of the early years of Sirimavo Bandaranaike's regime, which saw extended periods of rule under emergency powers in the wake of ethnic and religious confrontations, and an abortive plot by high-ranking police, military and naval officers to overthrow the Government. While the dominance of the SLFP in national politics had resulted in a corresponding decline in the electoral fortunes of the Marxist groups, the *apertura a sinistra* was regarded as a necessity for keeping the UNP out of power. In joining the SLFP in a coalition, the LSSP came to accept the SLFP's stand on religion and did so in order to protect its mass base. However, far from stabilizing the Government, the SLFP's shift to the left had the immediate effect of causing a rift which precipitated its fall in December 1964, and contributed to its subsequent defeat in the general election of March 1965.

Dudley Senanayake's UNP-dominated coalition enjoyed a five-year term of office (1965–70). A resolute endeavour was made to maximize agricultural productivity, with self-sufficiency in food as the prime objective. The very considerable success achieved in this field gave the whole economy a boost. Yet, while its agricultural policies achieved substantial success, the Government's popularity was eroded by inflation and its conspicuous failure to solve the problem of educated unemployment. The rising expectations of an increasingly educated population had created an almost unmanageable problem for the Government. Sri Lanka, by now, was very much a prime example of population explosion undermining a country's political stability.

Dudley Senanayake made ethnic and religious reconciliation the keynote of his policy. Yet his Government was placed on the defensive from the moment the Federal Party opted to join it in coalition. By a virulent campaign of ethnic hostility directed against Senanayake's policy of ethnic and religious reconciliation, the opposition prevented the Prime Minister from implementing some of the key legislative and administrative measures that would have made his policy effective. The limits of that policy were thus clearly demonstrated.

It was evident that the two Bandaranaikes between them had established a new equilibrium of forces within the country, and that their supporters and associates, such as the Marxist groups, as well as their opponents, such as the UNP, had to accommodate themselves to this. The primary feature of the new balance of forces was the acceptance of the predominance of the Sinhalese Buddhists within the Sri Lanka polity, and a sharp decline in status of the ethnic and religious minorities.

THE UNITED FRONT, 1970–77

In their election campaign and their manifesto of 1970, the parties of Sirimavo Bandaranaike's United Front (UF)—the SLFP, the LSSP and the Communist Party of Sri Lanka—held out the distinct assurance of purposeful, systematic and fundamental changes in every sphere of life. However, within a few weeks of their victory, they were confronted by precisely the combination of factors that had brought down their predecessor—unemployment, rising prices and scarcities of food items—and the UF Government floundered just as badly as Dudley Senanayake's administration. More significantly, there was growing opposition from a section of its erstwhile supporters. By mid-March 1971 the Government was faced with a very serious threat from the Janatha Vimukthi Peramuna (JVP, or People's Liberation Front), a radical left-wing organization dominated by educated youths, unemployed or disadvantageously employed. The JVP insurrection that broke out in April, although suppressed with considerable ruthlessness, had a marked influence on future developments. It undoubtedly hastened the proceedings begun under the UF in 1970 for an autochthonous constitution for Sri Lanka; and it gave a tremendous impetus to the adoption of a series of radical economic and social changes, the most far-reaching of which were the Land Reform Law of 1972 and the nationalization of the plantations in 1975. Over the period 1970–75, state control in trade and industry was accelerated and expanded to the point where the State had established a dominance of the commanding heights of the economy.

However, the economic situation deteriorated rapidly. The serious balance-of-payments problem, inherited by the UF Government, was aggravated to a grave crisis partly through the operation of external forces beyond its control. The crux of the problem was that the prices of the country's principal imports, particularly its food, rose to unprecedented levels, especially in 1973–74, while there was no corresponding rise in the price of its exports. The Government was compelled to reduce food subsidies, which were absorbing too much foreign exchange, and cuts in welfare expenditure, begun in 1971, continued through 1973. With inflationary pressures never greater and the problem of unemployment as serious as ever, the Government lost public support, as was evident from its dismal record in by-elections to Parliament. By the middle of 1972 the UNP had recovered from its débâcle at the 1970 polls and re-emerged as a viable democratic alternative to the UF regime.

To save itself from further embarrassment, the Government became increasingly authoritarian. A new republican and indigenous Constitution was adopted in May 1972, under which the state power of the Republic was vested in the National State Assembly (a unicameral legislature). Thus, one of its distinctive features was the absence of meaningful institutional or constitutional checks on executive power. While the new Constitution was a notable landmark in the island's recent history, opposition parties were antagonized by two issues stemming from its adoption. First, the ruling coalition gave itself an extended term of two years (to May 1977) beyond the five years for which it was elected in May 1970. Second, the adoption of the Constitution gave rise to a new phase of communal antagonism in the island especially as regards relations between the Sinhalese and the indigenous Tamils and prompted the gradual conversion of a large section of the Tamils of the north to the idea of a separate Tamil state.

In 1974 Sirimavo Bandaranaike negotiated the settlement of the vexed question of the status of the Indians in Sri Lanka. Nearly half a million of them would eventually be integrated into the Sri Lankan polity, and Sri Lankan citizenship would confer on them the political legitimacy which, as an ethnic group, they had not had since 1948. However, the Government's relations with the leadership of the Ceylon Workers' Congress (CWC), the most powerful trade union-dominated political party of the Indians in Sri Lanka, were as unfriendly as those with the leadership of the indigenous Tamils.

By 1975 sharp differences of opinion over the mechanics of the nationalization of foreign-owned plantations on the island led to acrimonious bickering between the SLFP and the LSSP, the two major components of the UF, which culminated in October 1975 in the expulsion of the LSSP from the Government. The political consequences were not immediately evident. On the contrary, the Government sought to stabilize its position by exploiting any political advantages to be gained from staging the non-aligned nations' conference in Colombo in August 1976. The coalition was disintegrating rapidly, however. By the end of February 1977 the UF coalition had been dissolved and what remained was a dispirited and demoralized SLFP Government confronting Sri Lanka's worst wave of strikes for 20 years, which had been engineered by its erstwhile coalition partners. For the first time since March 1960 there was no electoral pact against the UNP.

RETURN OF THE UNP

In the general election of July 1977 the UNP, under the leadership of Junius Richard Jayewardene, won 140 out of 168 seats in the National State Assembly. Jayewardene had twice rebuilt the UNP—once, following defeat in 1956, and again after he took control of it in 1973. The SLFP won only nine seats (compared with 90 in 1970), while every candidate of the Marxist left was defeated, many of them quite decisively. As a result of the peculiar demographic profile of the island, with a concentration of the Tamils in the north and, to a lesser extent, in the east of the island, the Tamil United Liberation Front (TULF), with the equivalent of only about one-fifth of the popular vote secured by the SLFP, had more than double the number of seats won by the SLFP and emerged as the main parliamentary opposition party. For the first time since independence a Tamil, Appapillai Amirthalingam, became leader of the opposition.

High on the Government's list of priorities was a reassessment of Sri Lanka's constitutional framework. In late September 1977 the National State Assembly adopted a constitutional amendment establishing a presidential form of government, and the Prime Minister, J. R. Jayewardene, became the first executive President of Sri Lanka on 4 February 1978. The new Constitution, promulgated in September 1978, was a blend of some of the functional aspects of Sri Lanka's previous Constitutions and features of the US, French and British systems of government. One important innovation incorporated in the new Constitution was the introduction of proportional representation on the list system in place of the 'first-past-the-post' principle of representation which had been based on the British model. Article 19 of the Constitution declared that Sinhala and Tamil were to be the national languages of Sri Lanka (with Sinhala remaining the sole official language), a major departure from the language policy established since the mid-1950s. Equally important was the abolition of the distinction between citizens by descent and citizens by registration, such as the Indian Tamils, thus removing the stigma of second-class citizenship attached to the latter. Combined with the lifting, in December 1977, of the bar on plantation workers resident on estates voting in local government elections, which had been in force since the 1930s, this ensured that citizens of Indian origin, in the main plantation workers, were treated on a par with Sri Lankan citizens by descent. The position of the Indians resident in Sri Lanka was further improved by affording to stateless persons the same civil rights guaranteed by the Constitution to citizens of the country. No previous Constitution, not even that of 1946–48, had offered the minorities a more secure position within the Sri Lankan polity.

The Indian Tamils responded more positively to these conciliatory gestures than the TULF. When S. Thondaman, leader of the CWC, the main political party-cum-trade union of the Indian plantation workers, entered the Cabinet following the introduction of the new Constitution in September 1978, it marked a major breakthrough in Sri Lanka's politics for it brought the Indian Tamils within Sri Lanka's 'political nation' for the first time since the 1930s.

The Jayewardene Government inherited a stagnant economy, in which, with the nationalization of the plantations, the state sector was in a position of overwhelming dominance. Unemployment was high and inflation a serious problem. The Government's budgetary policy was far removed from that of its predecessors, and aimed at creating a free-market economy after almost 20 years of controls and restrictions. The rate of economic growth improved quite dramatically from 1977 and was sustained at a uniformly high level, explaining, to a large extent, the Government's success in the management of the 'political market', in retaining the initiative in politics, and in keeping its rivals at bay.

From the beginning of its term of office in 1977, the Jayewardene Government benefited greatly from the disarray in the ranks of its opponents. The SLFP, the main opposition party, was unable to implement an effective political challenge to the Government; the party was torn apart by a leadership crisis, aggravated by Sirimavo Bandaranaike's expulsion from Parliament (the National State Assembly having been renamed thus in August 1978) in October 1980 after a presidential commission of inquiry found her guilty on charges of abuse of power. The decline of the 'old' left, particularly the LSSP, was a notable factor in Sri Lanka's politics at this time. The 'new' left, with the factionalized JVP in the vanguard, was as hostile to the 'traditional' left and the SLFP as it was to the Government.

The TULF, now very much a party of the indigenous Tamils, adopted a somewhat ambiguous attitude to the UNP Government. It began, in August 1977, as an opposition party, and an advocate of a separate state for the Tamils. The commitment to separatism was later put aside, however, after negotiations with the Government. Yet the leaders of the TULF were conscious of the challenge from their youth wing, and especially extreme terrorist groups who combined an adherence to various forms of Marxism with a passionate commitment to separatism. While the TULF leadership sought to maintain a discreet distance from these terrorist groups, ties between them were never completely abandoned.

Despite a creditable record of innovative and imaginative attempts to accommodate the minorities, the Jayewardene Government's term of office was punctuated by ethnic conflict between the Sinhalese majority and the Tamil minority, in particular the Sri Lankan Tamils. One of the major points of controversy between successive Sri Lankan Governments and the Tamils has been the question of the devolution of authority to regional units of administration. Jayewardene's Government took the initiative in providing for a scheme of decentralized administration through district development councils. In August 1980 Parliament approved legislation establishing 24 of these councils, for which elections were held in the following year. The establishment of the councils failed, however, to result in any lasting peace. The country was faced with the problem of a Tamil separatist movement (including a number of guerrilla groups) operating in the north and east of the island. The threat that this movement posed to the Sri Lankan polity was compounded by the existence of a great deal of Tamil separatist sympathy and a strong sense of Tamil ethnic identity in the southern Indian state of Tamil Nadu.

If the results of the 1977 general election appeared to herald a major change of direction in Sri Lankan politics, the presidential election in October 1982 provided confirmation of this. By winning that election, Junius Jayewardene became the first Sri Lankan Head of Government to win two consecutive terms of office. Jayewardene followed this with a deft legal and constitutional, but nevertheless controversial, move—the holding of a referendum on 22 December to ask for a mandate to extend the life of the Parliament, elected in 1977, by a period of six years from August 1983. Although the electorate endorsed this by a large majority, thus effectively guaranteeing the UNP its huge majority in Parliament until 1989, the referendum was widely viewed as a retrograde and undemocratic measure. The opposition had hardly recovered from the referendum when, early in 1983, it was announced that by-elections would be held for 18 seats in which the Government had fared badly at the presidential election and the referendum. These by-elections were held on 18 May, and the UNP won 14 of them. This was accompanied by the ruling party's notable success in the local government elections held on the same date and on 20 May. The UNP won all but five of the local bodies in the Sinhalese areas, with the SLFP winning one and independents four. Neither the JVP nor the 'traditional' left made any significant impact at these elections. As in 1979, only the TULF, which won control of the local bodies in the Tamil areas, stood between the UNP and a clean sweep. However, violence organized by terrorist groups, marred the local government elections in the Jaffna peninsula. The TULF won these elections in a very low poll, but in other parts of the northern and eastern regions it won comfortably in a normal poll.

A TIME OF TROUBLES: 1983–88

The unusually prolonged period of electioneering raised political tension to dangerous levels, and, in recognition of this, a state of emergency was declared in May 1983. This proved to be wholly ineffective in confronting the pressures that were released by an eruption of ethnic violence, directed against the Tamils, in July, the worst such outbreak since 1958. These riots were very widespread, but the most severely affected area was the city of Colombo and its suburbs. The Government needed nearly a week to re-establish its authority and quell the violence.

In early August 1983 a ban on the advocacy of separatism was imposed through the sixth amendment to the Constitution. One immediate result of this was that all TULF members opted to resign from their seats in Parliament. Anura Bandaranaike, the son of Sirimavo Bandaranaike, took over as leader of the parliamentary opposition from Appapillai Amirthalingam. In 1986, when Sirimavo Bandaranaike's civic and political rights were restored as a result of a presidential pardon, she surprised many political observers by her decision to remain outside Parliament as the head of the SLFP while her son continued as leader of the opposition in Parliament.

Another immediate consequence of the political tension of May–July 1983 was pressure from India on behalf of the Tamils, with Indira Gandhi's Government assuming the role of mediator in the conflict between the Sri Lankan Government and Tamil groups. A conference, in which most Sri Lankan political groups (with the exception of the SLFP) and also representatives of religious organizations participated, began in January 1984 and continued throughout the year. As a result of these deliberations, a consensus appeared to have been reached on the crucially important issue of the devolution of power to regional bodies, and much progress had been achieved in regard to other matters, including language policy. By the end of the year, however, this consensus had evaporated amid political controversy. The TULF eventually rejected the proposals as inadequate, while representatives of Buddhist opinion opposed them because they were perceived to be conceding too much to the Tamils. The Government withdrew its own support for the proposals in December 1984. Within a few months, the collapse of the conference led to more formal diplomatic negotiations between the Governments of Sri Lanka and India, and eventually to a meeting between Jayewardene and the Indian Prime Minister, Rajiv Gandhi, in June 1985. A three-month cease-fire was established, and talks were held, under Indian auspices, in Bhutan in July and August 1985 between representatives of the Sri Lankan Government and representatives of the various Tamil separatist groups, including the TULF. Although these talks failed, negotiations continued in New Delhi and eventually yielded a set of proposals for devolution of power in Sri Lanka on the basis of provincial councils. This was the essence of the Delhi Accord of August 1985. The Accord was initialled by the Sri Lankan and Indian Governments, but the Tamil groups that had been consulted during the negotiations refused to sign it. Nevertheless, the principal features of the 1985 Delhi Accord became the basis of future negotiations between the two Governments and Sri Lanka's Tamil groups.

The TULF and some of the Tamil separatist groups continued to press for a single regional unit, encompassing the northern and eastern provinces, as a Tamil ethno-region. Both the Government and the SLFP were strongly opposed to a merger of these two provinces, as were the Muslims resident there. (The Tamils constitute only 40% of the population of the eastern province.) The main Tamil separatist group, the Liberation Tigers of Tamil Eelam (LTTE), however, would accept nothing short of a separate Tamil state. In a sustained effort to break this deadlock, Indian negotiators made various proposals throughout the second half of 1986, some of which formed part of the 19 December 1986 formula, which the Indian Government proposed as the basis for further negotiations between the Sri Lankan Government and the Tamils. The LTTE, however, rejected this formula as totally unacceptable.

These negotiations took place against the background of regular outbursts of ethnic violence, especially in the north and east of the island, and conflicts between the security forces and Tamil guerrillas and terrorist groups. In addition, there was fierce internecine fighting among these Tamil separatist groups, in the course of which the LTTE prevailed over its main rivals. The Tamil guerrillas and terrorist groups had the advantage of training facilities and bases in Tamil Nadu and in other parts of India. The existence of the terrorist bases in Tamil Nadu, as well as the refusal of the Indian Government officially to acknowledge their existence (much less to close them down), remained a constant irritant in Indo-Sri Lankan relations. The guerrillas were also helped by a decision of the Sri Lankan Government, taken in mid-1985, to keep its forces in the north of the island within their barracks or camps, as part of an understanding that was reached with the Government of India on the mediatory process. The result of this decision was to give the armed separatist groups effective control over the Jaffna peninsula, which they used to consolidate their position there. From mid-1984, attacks by guerrillas and terrorists increased, but those directed against the security forces were generally repulsed. When, however, the terrorist attacks were directed against unarmed Sinhalese civilians in the eastern and northern central parts of the island, the death toll was heavy. The most serious of such attacks occurred on 14 May 1985, when a heavily-armed group of terrorists made a surprise raid on Anuradhapura, killing nearly 150 civilians. The killings continued during 1986–87, two of the worst such incidents being the bus massacre of more than 120 people near Habarana, in the eastern province, and the bomb explosion (killing more than 100 people) in the main bus station in Colombo, both of which took place in April 1987.

In early 1987 attempts by the LTTE to make a unilateral declaration of independence in the north of the island were treated by the Sri Lankan authorities as gravely provocative. In February government security forces moved into the eastern and northern provinces and cleared them (with the exception of the crowded Jaffna peninsula) of the LTTE and other separatist groups.

Faced with the prospect of a serious erosion of political support as a result of the terrorist outrages in April 1987 (see above), the Government decided to make an attempt to regain control of the Jaffna peninsula. The most important aspect of the subsequent 'Operation Liberation' was to take control of the strategically important Vadamarachchi division of the north-eastern part of the peninsula, to prevent the hitherto easy movement of men and materials from Tamil Nadu. By the end of May the Sri Lankan forces had gained control of this area by means of a remarkably effective military operation. Tamil Nadu responded with a well-publicized monetary grant of US $3.2m. to the LTTE and its allies. The Indian central Government, far from condemning this act of interference in Sri Lankan affairs, also gave its support by making an offer of food aid and petroleum supplies to Jaffna, to be shipped there in Indian vessels. When the first shipment was turned back by the Sri Lankan navy on 3 June, the Indian air force blatantly violated Sri Lankan airspace to drop food parcels and medical supplies in Jaffna on the following day. This constituted an unmistakable demonstration of Indian support for the Tamil separatist movement in Sri Lanka. The Indian supply of food to Jaffna continued over the next few weeks by sea. While this second phase of Indian aid had the formal, but clearly reluctant, approval of the Sri Lankan Government, it was, none the less, as unwelcome as the earlier air-drop of food. The result was that, by the end of June, Indo-Sri Lankan relations were dominated by mutual recrimination and deep suspicion.

By mid-July 1987, however, there were signs of an unforeseen change in attitude and the emergence of a breakthrough in negotiations on a settlement of Sri Lanka's ethnic conflict. By the end of July, the Indian and Sri Lankan Governments had reached agreement on the basis of an accord, and, on 29 July, the Indian Prime Minister, Rajiv Gandhi, arrived in Colombo to sign the accord with Jayewardene. The main points of the accord were: the provision of Indian military assistance to help with its implementation (more than 7,000 Indian troops were drafted into Sri Lanka in August); a complete cessation of hostilities, and the surrender of all weapons held by the Tamil militants within 72 hours of the implementation of the accord; the establishment of a system of provincial councils in the island, based on the island's nine provincial units; the linking of the northern and eastern provinces into one administrative unit with an elected provincial council (to be elected within three months); the holding of a referendum in the eastern province, at a date set by the Sri Lankan President, to determine whether the mixed population of Tamils, Sinhalese and Muslims supported this official merger with the northern province into a single Tamil-dominated province; a general amnesty for all Tamil militants after they had surrendered their arms; the repatriation of about 100,000 Tamil refugees in India to Sri Lanka; the resumption of the repatriation of Indian citizens from Sri Lanka, under the terms of agreements reached between the Governments of Sri Lanka and India in 1964 and 1974; the prevention of the use of Indian territory by Tamil militants for military or propaganda purposes; the prevention of the military use of Sri Lankan ports, Trincomalee in particular, by any country in a manner prejudicial to Indian interests; and the provision that Tamil has equal status with Sinhala as an official language. The signing of the accord led to violent protests and widespread civil unrest among the Sinhalese majority in and around Colombo and in the south-west of the country. These demonstrations had the support of the SLFP, of sections of the *sangha* (the Buddhist order), and of a revived JVP.

The early indications of a successful implementation of the accord were encouraging. Sri Lankan security forces in the northern and eastern provinces returned to their barracks and the paramilitary forces were disarmed, as part of the Sri Lankan Government's obligations under the terms of the accord. Tamil separatist groups, including the LTTE and the Eelam Revolutionary Organization of Students (EROS), began to surrender their weapons. In September 1987, however, the surrender of arms by the Tamil militant groups became more sporadic, and the implementation of the peace accord was impeded by further bitter factional fighting among the Tamil militias (involving the LTTE in particular), which, in mid-September, necessitated direct intervention by the Indian peace-keeping troops. By early October the surrender of arms had virtually ceased and Tamil guerrillas had launched a series of terrorist attacks on Sinhalese citizens in the eastern province. The destabilization of the eastern province, a region which had, hitherto, been relatively secure under the protection of the Sri Lankan forces, soon reached a point that compelled the Sri Lankan Government to insist on firm action by the Indian Peace-Keeping Force (IPKF) to prevent any further deterioration of the situation. Accordingly, troops of the IPKF were now dispatched to disarm the LTTE and, when faced with resistance, launched a major attack on the guerrilla strongholds in the Jaffna peninsula in the second week of October. Despite obstinate opposition from the LTTE (necessitating the deployment of thousands of reinforcements), the militants' control over the peninsula was eventually ended. The LTTE then withdrew to the forests of the northern province, whence, from the beginning of 1988, it continued the struggle. In the mean time, the size of the IPKF increased from 7,000 in the early months of its presence on the island, to between 75,000 and 100,000 by mid-1988. These numbers were gradually reduced, but in early 1989 the IPKF still had at least 45,000 men in the north and east of the island.

Legislation to give effect to some of the major provisions of the peace accord was approved by the Sri Lankan Parliament in the latter half of 1987. Of these, the most important and controversial was the 13th amendment to the Constitution, establishing a system of provincial councils. The SLFP opposed this legislation, as did the JVP. The latter, which had been officially banned in August 1983 and which was based mainly in the south of the island, initiated a campaign of sporadic violence directed at person and property. The JVP was widely believed to have been involved in an assassination attempt on President Jayewardene in Parliament on 18 August 1987, in which one district minister was killed and several cabinet ministers and members of Parliament were seriously wounded. Another district minister was assassinated in May 1988. It was estimated that, altogether, more than 1,000 members of the UNP, including the party's Chairman and General Secretary, had been killed by the JVP by July 1988. The JVP was also believed to have instigated the murder of the leader of the left-wing Sri Lanka Mahajana Party (SLMP), Vijaya Kumaratunga, who supported the accord. As soon as the Government had definitely decided to hold provincial council elections, the SLFP joined the JVP in organizing a boycott of the elections. The JVP's violence increased in a campaign of intimidation, which was directed at all parties supporting the accord and at candidates for election to the provincial councils.

In February 1988 a new opposition force emerged, when an alliance, named the United Socialist Alliance (USA), was formed by the SLMP, the LSSP, the Communist Party of Sri Lanka, the Nava Sama Samaja Party and, most notably, the Tamil rights group entitled the Eelam People's Revolutionary Liberation Front (EPRLF). Although the USA group, led by Chandrika Bandaranaike Kumaratunga (a daughter of Sirimavo Bandaranaike and the widow of the SLMP's assassinated leader), comprised opposition parties, it expressed full support for the peace accord.

At the elections to seven of the new provincial councils (elections in the northern and eastern provinces were postponed indefinitely), which were held in April and June 1988 (in defiance of the JVP's threats and violence), the UNP won a majority and effective control in all of them, while the USA emerged as the main opposition group. A 'surprise' peace agreement, which was purportedly signed by government officials and alleged representatives of the JVP in May, proved to be a hoax; Rohana Wijeweera, the leader of the JVP, denied that anyone had been authorized to negotiate on behalf of his party. The Government, however, decided to proceed with its decision to rescind the ban on the JVP.

In September 1988, following President Jayewardene's decision not to seek a third term of office, the Prime Minister, Ranasinghe Premadasa, was nominated as the candidate of the ruling UNP for the presidential election, which was due to be held on 19 December. Sirimavo Bandaranaike emerged as the main opposition candidate, with support from an alliance of eight opposition parties, collectively called the Democratic People's Alliance, including the SLFP, the JVP and other minor political groups. In September the President officially authorized the merger of the northern and eastern provinces into a single north-eastern province, prior to the provincial council elections. The JVP reacted violently, and was widely believed to have been responsible for the murder of the Minister of Rehabilitation and Reconstruction, Lionel Jayatilleke, at the end of the month. On 9 October President Jayewardene vested the leadership of the UNP in the Prime Minister. In protest against the proposed election in the new north-eastern province, the JVP organized a series of disruptive strikes, systematic acts of sabotage, prison riots and violent demonstrations in the central, western and southern provinces of the island in October. In an attempt to arrest the escalating violence, the Government invoked emergency regulations, imposed strict curfews in the troubled areas, and deployed armed riot police. In November, however, the JVP intensified its campaign of violence and protest; it demanded a boycott of the presidential election by the SLFP, the dissolution of Parliament, the establishment of a caretaker Government, and the holding of a fresh general election. In mid-November the moderate and pro-accord Tamil groups, the EPRLF and the Eelam National Democratic Liberation Front (ENDLF), together with the Sri Lanka Muslim Congress (SLMC), emerged strongly from the elections to the new provincial council of the north-eastern province, while the UNP won only one seat. The poll was boycotted, however, by the LTTE, the TULF and the Sinhalese population in the eastern province. In late November the EPRLF nominated a regional cabinet to administer the new province. In early December Parliament unanimously approved a Constitution Amendment Bill to make Tamil one of the country's two official languages (with Sinhala), thus fulfilling one of the major commitments envisaged in the peace accord.

THE PRESIDENCY OF RANASINGHE PREMADASA

On 19 December 1988 the presidential election took place, in an environment of unprecedented disruption, and was boycotted by the LTTE and the JVP. None the less, it was estimated that about 55% of the total electorate voted. The UNP's candidate, Prime Minister Ranasinghe Premadasa, won by a narrow margin, with 50.4% of the total votes, while Sirimavo Bandaranaike, the President of the SLFP, received 44.9%. On the following day Parliament was dissolved in preparation for the general election, which was to be held in February 1989 (six months before schedule). In early January Premadasa was sworn in as Sri Lanka's new President, and an interim Cabinet was appointed. In the same month, in a conciliatory gesture to the JVP and the LTTE alike, the Government decided to repeal the state of emergency, which had been in force since May 1983, and to abolish the Ministry of National Security. Shortly after his inauguration, Premadasa offered to negotiate with the extremists and invited all groups to take part in the electoral process. The JVP and the LTTE, however, intensified their campaigns of violence, in protest at the forthcoming general election. In early February the moderate, pro-accord Tamil groups, the EPRLF, the ENDLF and the Tamil Eelam Liberation Organization (TELO), formed a loose alliance, under the leadership of the TULF, to contest the general election. In the election, which was held on 15 February and which was, like the presidential poll, characterized by widespread violence, the UNP won 125 of the 225 contested seats. The new system of proportional representation, which was introduced at this election, was especially advantageous to the SLFP, which became the major opposition force in Parliament, with 67 seats. The comparatively low level of participation (64% of the electorate) confirmed, again, that intimidatory tactics, employed by the LTTE and the JVP, had had an effect on the voters. A few days later, President Premadasa appointed a new Cabinet and in early March he named the Minister of Finance, Dingiri Banda Wijetunga, as the country's new Prime Minister. Although both the LTTE and the JVP rejected a conciliatory offer made by the President in April, in a surprising development, representatives of the LTTE began discussions with government officials in Colombo in the following month.

Negotiations also commenced between Sri Lankan and Indian officials, regarding the withdrawal of the IPKF. Between January and April 1989, five battalions of the IPKF left Sri Lanka, and in early June the Sri Lankan Government announced, in an apparent effort to appease the LTTE and the JVP, that it wanted all Indian troops to have left by the end of July (two years after the arrival of the first troops). With the exception of the EPRLF, which administered the north-eastern province, all other Sri Lankan political groups welcomed this call for a speedy Indian withdrawal. India itself responded cautiously to Premadasa's demand, which had been made without warning or consultation, saying only that it would withdraw at an 'early date'. Rajiv Gandhi stressed that the timetable for a complete withdrawal of troops would have to be decided mutually, and that, before the Indian forces left, he wanted to ensure the security of the Tamils and the devolution of genuine power to the elected local government in the north-eastern province, so that it would resist any post-withdrawal destabilization.

The resultant deadlock in Indo-Sri Lankan relations provoked a wave of anti-Indian feeling in Sri Lanka, and demonstrations and strikes were organized by the JVP to protest against the continued presence of the IPKF in Sri Lanka. The JVP's renewed campaign of violence reached a peak in June/July 1989, and compelled the Government to reimpose a state of emergency on 20 June, granting the army virtually unlimited powers of arrest and detention.

In the mean time, the LTTE decided to transform its temporary cease-fire agreement with the Sri Lankan army into a general cessation of hostilities against the Government. In response, the Government announced that it would henceforth collaborate with the LTTE to secure the withdrawal of the IPKF from Sri Lanka. This agreement was reached despite the Government's suspicions about the LTTE's involvement in the murder of several prominent Tamil leaders, including the Secretary-General of the TULF, Appapillai Amirthalingam, and the leader of the People's Liberation Organization of Tamil Eelam (PLOTE), Kadirkamam Uma Maheswaran. Although it initially denied any connection with the killings, the LTTE subsequently assumed responsibility for them.

On 13 September 1989 Premadasa convened an All-Party Conference (APC) to discuss the country's ethnic crisis. Some 70 delegates from 21 parties, including the LTTE and the moderate Tamil groups (but excluding the JVP), attended the conference. On 18 September the Governments of Sri Lanka and India signed an agreement in Colombo, whereby India promised to make 'all efforts' to withdraw its remaining 45,000 troops from Sri Lanka by the end of the year and the IPKF was to declare an immediate unilateral cease-fire. In return, the Sri Lankan Government pledged immediately to establish a peace committee for the north-eastern province in an effort to reconcile the various Tamil groups and to incorporate members of the LTTE into the peaceful administration of the province. A co-ordination committee for the withdrawal of the IPKF was established in mid-October.

The JVP suffered a very serious set-back when its leader, Rohana Wijeweera, and his principal deputy, Upatissa Garmanayake, were shot dead by the security forces in November 1989. In the following month the leader of the military wing of the JVP, Saman Piyasiri Fernando, was killed in an exchange of gunfire in Colombo. Between September 1989 and the end of January 1990 the Sri Lankan security forces effectively destroyed the JVP as a political force, thus substantially transforming the country's political scene. All but one member of the JVP's political bureau and most leaders at district level had been killed. It was estimated, however, that the number of people killed in the lengthy struggle between the JVP and the Government might have been as high as 25,000–50,000.

As the Indian troops increased the speed of their withdrawal from Sri Lanka in the latter half of 1989, the LTTE initiated a campaign of violence against its arch-rivals, the more moderate Indian-supported EPRLF, which was mustering a so-called Tamil National Army, with Indian help, in the north-eastern province, to resist the LTTE. The LTTE accused the EPRLF and its allies of forcibly conscripting thousands of Tamil youths into the Tamil army. Following months of peace talks with the Government, however, the political wing of the LTTE was recognized as a political party by the commissioner of elections in December. The LTTE leaders then proclaimed that the newly recognized party would take part in the democratic process (it demanded immediate fresh elections in the north-eastern province) under the new name of the People's Front of the Liberation Tigers (PFLT). By the end of 1989 the inexperienced and undisciplined Tamil National Army had been virtually destroyed by the LTTE, which now appeared to have the tacit support of the central Government and had taken control of much of the territory in the north-eastern province being progressively evacuated by the IPKF.

Following further talks between the Governments of Sri Lanka and India, the completion date for the withdrawal of the IPKF was postponed until the end of March 1990. In early February President Premadasa reconvened the APC in a fresh attempt to end the continuing violence. In early March the EPRLF-dominated north-eastern provincial council, under the leadership of Annamalai Varadharajah Perumal, renamed itself the 'National Assembly of the Free and Sovereign Democratic

Republic of Eelam' and gave the central Government a one-year ultimatum to fulfil a 19-point charter of demands. Two weeks later, however, Perumal was reported to have fled to Madras (now known as Chennai) in southern India. The last remaining IPKF troops left Sri Lanka on 24 March, a week ahead of schedule. Their departure was welcomed by both the Government and the LTTE. In the next month the Government eased emergency regulations (including the ban on political rallies) in an effort to restore a degree of normality to the country after years of violence. At the same time, Sri Lanka's security forces, encouraged by the relative lull in violence, halted all military operations against the now much-weakened JVP and the Tamil militant groups.

Thus, a fragile peace was maintained while talks (mainly concerning the proposed dissolution of the north-eastern provincial council and the holding of fresh elections there) continued between the Government and the LTTE until early June 1990, when quite unexpectedly the LTTE attacked and captured about 20 police stations in the Batticaloa and Trincomalee districts, abducting more than 600 Sinhalese and Muslim policemen and subsequently massacring a large number of them. Later in the month an LTTE execution squad, operating in Tamil Nadu in India, raided a block of apartments in Madras in which Annamalai Varadharajah Perumal and other leaders of the EPRLF were living as refugees (see above), killing 13 of them (including the party's General Secretary, Kandaswamy Padmanabha). In mid-June the Government dissolved the north-eastern provincial council (despite protests by the EPRLF), and the holding of fresh elections in the province was postponed indefinitely pending the LTTE's agreement to participate in them (as earlier promised). By the end of June up to 1,000 people had been killed in the renewed fighting, and many thousands had been made homeless. Attempts to establish a cease-fire foundered, and the Sri Lankan security forces launched a counter-attack. By the end of July, after fierce fighting, the security forces had established control over most parts of the north-eastern province (including Batticaloa, Trincomalee and Amparai), outside the densely-populated Jaffna peninsula. Several fortified LTTE camps in the jungles in the north-east were targeted for attack, and, by the end of the year, many of them had fallen to the security forces. The LTTE, however, continued to control a number of fortified jungle hide-outs, from which they launched occasional raids.

In August 1990 the LTTE intensified its campaign of violence in the eastern province against the Muslim population; the renewed strife between the country's two largest minority groups resulted in more than 400 deaths. At the end of August the Government launched an all-out offensive against the Tamil strongholds in the Jaffna peninsula, and, by mid-September, had succeeded in relieving the three-month siege by the LTTE of the old army fort (the fort was later abandoned by the security forces). In October the LTTE launched an attack on the Muslim settlements in the Mannar district of the northern province, and succeeded in expelling the Muslim population from there. The Muslims fled to various parts of the north-central and north-western provinces where they took up residence as refugees. Although the army later re-established control in the Mannar region and repulsed the LTTE, most of the Muslims were reluctant to return to their homes. In January 1991 the LTTE suffered an apparent set-back when the Indian central Government dismissed the state government in Tamil Nadu, on account of the latter's alleged support for the Tamil militants in Sri Lanka. In early March it was widely suspected that the LTTE was responsible for the assassination of a senior Sri Lankan cabinet member, the Minister of Plantation Industries and Minister of State for Defence, Ranjan Wijeratne. Wijeratne had been in charge of both the government forces' successful offensive against the JVP, several years earlier, and the ongoing offensive against the LTTE. The LTTE presence in the jungles of the north and east continued, while the army strengthened its hold on the towns and main roads there. In July the LTTE made a concerted effort to capture the army camp at Elephant Pass, which guards the entrance to the Jaffna peninsula. They suffered heavy losses when the security forces successfully repulsed the attack. Thereafter, the LTTE strongholds in the Jaffna peninsula came under regular attack by the Sri Lankan forces, which maintained a limited but conspicuous presence there—at the port of Kankesanthurai, the airport at Palaly, and at the naval base of Karainagar.

Throughout 1991 a considerably weakened, but by no means defeated, LTTE made occasional offers of further talks with the Government, but the latter responded by laying down conditions, which were unacceptable to the militant group. Suspected LTTE bomb squads carried out a number of successful missions in Colombo: the assassination of Ranjan Wijeratne (see above) and the bomb attack on an armed-forces building in a residential part of Colombo in late June. More significantly for its regional implications, the LTTE was widely believed to have been responsible for the assassination of the former Indian Prime Minister Rajiv Gandhi (whose party, Congress (I), had reportedly pressurized the Indian Government into dismissing the administration in Tamil Nadu earlier that year), on 21 May near Madras. In early 1992 the Indian Government proscribed the LTTE in India and banned its activities on Indian soil. The LTTE's access to bases and other resources in Tamil Nadu was sharply curtailed, while rigorous patrolling of the seas by the Indian navy cut off the LTTE's traditional sources of arms supplies.

President Premadasa, for his part, consolidated his position within the country, by treating the local government elections in May 1991 as a national 'referendum' on his period in office. Premadasa took a calculated risk in doing so, but the decisive victory of the UNP provided him with the clear mandate that had eluded him in the presidential election of 1988 and the parliamentary election of 1989, owing to the relatively low turnout on those occasions and the pervasive violence. In early September 1992 the Supreme Court, following a lengthy hearing spanning two-and-a-half years, rejected Sirimavo Bandaranaike's election petition against Premadasa, thus confirming the validity of his election.

In August–September 1991 opposition groups, supported by a dissident section of the UNP, began proceedings for the impeachment of President Premadasa. The impeachment motion listed 24 items of alleged abuses of power, including illegal land deals and failing to consult the Cabinet (thus violating the Constitution). The UNP group that supported the motion included two cabinet members, the Minister of Education, Lalith Athulathmudali, and the Minister of Labour and Vocational Training, G. M. Premachandra, and one former cabinet member, Gamini Dissanayake, all of whom protested against the President's alleged autocratic behaviour. These initiatives heralded the beginning of a significant challenge to the authority of President Premadasa. Although the impeachment motion was rejected by the Speaker of Parliament in early October, and the rebel group was expelled from the party, these events provided evidence of a major split in the UNP. The subsequent establishment of the Democratic United National Front (DUNF) by the dissident UNP group in December appeared to signify a very important change in Sri Lanka's political system: the emergence of a third party with wide political support. This was especially so because the SLFP continued to suffer the debilitating effects of a prolonged and bitter leadership struggle, and remained in a state of unresolved crisis over the succession to Sirimavo Bandaranaike, who had been the head of the party since 1960.

The campaign against the LTTE suffered a serious set-back in early August 1992, when 10 senior officers, including the northern military commander, Brig.-Gen. Denzil Kobbekaduwa, and the Jaffna peninsula commander, Brig. Wijaya Wimalaratne, were killed in a mine explosion near Jaffna. The new leadership of the security services, however, recommenced the stalled efforts to re-establish government control over the areas hitherto dominated by the LTTE—i.e. parts of the northern province and the Jaffna peninsula. Tension between the Muslim and Tamil populations in the north-eastern district of Polonnaruwa drastically increased following the massacre of more than 170 Muslim villagers by suspected LTTE guerrillas in October. In the next month the LTTE were also widely believed to have been responsible for the murder of the naval commander, Vice-Admiral Clancy Fernando, in Colombo. The LTTE themselves lost one of their most senior leaders when Commander Sathasivam Krishnakumar, Velupillai Prabhakaran's chief deputy, was killed at sea in January 1993.

Once the elections for the provincial councils were announced for 17 May 1993 there was a sharp increase in political activity, since the outcome of the poll was expected to affect the results of the presidential election scheduled to be held in October/ November 1994. The campaign itself was relatively peaceful until 23 April 1993, when the leader of the DUNF, Lalith Athulathmudali, was assassinated. This precipitated a dangerous political crisis, since, at first, it was widely believed that persons close to the Government were involved in the murder, if indeed they had not planned it. In fact, it subsequently appeared that the assassination was the work of the LTTE. The Athulathmudali killing overshadowed all other issues in the run-up to the provincial council elections, until the assassination, in a 'suicide bomber' attack, of President Premadasa on 1 May, which also killed 23 others. The assassination raised fears about a long period of instability in the country. President Premadasa was the most prominent victim of the LTTE so far, and the manner of the killing had many parallels with the assassination of the former Indian Prime Minister Rajiv Gandhi. However, in a remarkably smooth transition, the incumbent Prime Minister, Dingiri Banda Wijetunga, was first sworn in as acting President, and subsequently unanimously elected President by Parliament in accordance with the terms of the Constitution. President Wijetunga appointed Ranil Wickremasinghe, who had been Leader of the House since 1989, to replace him in the premiership. The incoming President quickly established a hold on the political system, and introduced a new style of government which was more open and more democratic than that of his predecessor.

The results of the provincial council elections held in May 1993 proved a set-back for the UNP. While the ruling party won control of four of the seven councils (no polling was carried out in the area covered by the now defunct north-eastern province), the three others went to a combination of the SLFP, the 'traditional' left and the DUNF. Although the UNP received 47% of the votes, as against 36% for the SLFP and the 'traditional' left, it was the first time since 1977 that its percentage of total votes had fallen below 50%, evidence of an erosion of its support base which became more pronounced in the early part of 1994.

The Sri Lankan forces achieved considerable success in their fight against ethnic violence in the eastern province in 1993, but were forced to abandon a massive military offensive in the Jaffna peninsula in October owing to the ferocity of the LTTE resistance. In the following month both sides suffered heavy casualties in the course of the battle over the military base at Pooneryn on the Jaffna lagoon. As a result of this military débâcle, in which, according to official figures, more than 600 army and naval personnel were either killed or captured, the Government established a new combined security forces command for the Jaffna and Kilinochchi districts to counter the LTTE threat.

THE PEOPLE'S ALLIANCE IN POWER

In late 1993 and in the first two months of 1994 the SLFP seemed hopelessly divided; Anura Bandaranaike's decision to defect to the UNP appeared to provide further evidence of this. Despite the continuing violence, local government elections were held in the eastern province and in the northern town of Vavuniya in early March 1994; the UNP secured the greatest number of seats, while independent Tamil groups also performed well. The LTTE and the TULF boycotted the poll. The ruling party suffered its first major electoral reverse in 17 years at the end of the month, however, when an opposition grouping known as the People's Alliance (PA), of which the main constituents were the SLFP and the traditional Marxist left and which was headed by the former leader of the USA group, Chandrika Kumaratunga, won a clear majority in elections to the southern provincial council. In early May, however, Wijetunga's Government defeated a parliamentary motion of 'no confidence' by 111 votes to 71. On 24 June, in an apparent attempt to catch the opposition by surprise and to enhance his prospects in the forthcoming presidential election, the President dissolved Parliament and announced that early legislative elections were to be held on 16 August, ahead of the presidential election. Wijetunga's ploy failed, however: the PA obtained 48.9% of the votes, thus securing a narrow victory over the UNP, which received 44% of the poll. Under the prevailing system of proportional representation, this translated to 105 seats for the PA and 94 for the UNP in the 225-seat Parliament. The 17-year rule of the UNP had thus come to an end. On 18 August President Wijetunga abandoned hope of forming a UNP minority Government and appointed Kumaratunga as Prime Minister, the PA having secured the support of the SLMC, the TULF, the Democratic People's Liberation Front and a small, regional independent group. A new Cabinet was appointed on the following day, all members of which belonged to the SLFP, with the exception of four ministers and the President. In line with her electoral pledge to abolish the executive presidency and to establish a parliamentary system in its place, the Prime Minister removed the finance portfolio from the President and assumed responsibility for it herself. Although Wijetunga retained the title of Minister of Defence, actual control of the ministry was expected to be exercised by the Deputy Minister of Defence. The Prime Minister's mother, Sirimavo Bandaranaike, was appointed as Minister without Portfolio. With regard to the Tamil question, overtures were made between the new Government and the LTTE concerning unconditional peace talks (these commenced in mid-October) and at the end of August, as a gesture of goodwill, the Government partially lifted the economic blockade on LTTE-occupied territory. In addition, the Prime Minister created a new Ministry of Ethnic Affairs and National Integration and assumed the portfolio herself, thus revealing her determination to seek an early solution to the civil strife.

In early September 1994 Chandrika Kumaratunga was unanimously elected by the PA as its candidate for the forthcoming presidential polls, while Gamini Dissanayake, the leader of the opposition (who had left the DUNF and returned to the UNP in 1993), was chosen as the UNP's candidate. The election campaign was thrown into turmoil, however, on 24 October 1994, when Dissanayake was assassinated by a suspected LTTE 'suicide bomber' in a suburb of Colombo; more than 50 other people, including the General Secretary of the UNP, Gamini Wijesekara, and the leader of the SLMP, Ossie Abeyagoonasekera, were killed in the blast. The Government declared a state of emergency and suspended the ongoing peace talks with the LTTE. Dissanayake had been an outspoken critic of these talks and had been one of the architects of the 1987 Indo-Sri Lankan accord. In a surprising move, his widow, Srima Dissanayake, was chosen by the UNP to replace him as the party's presidential candidate. The state of emergency was revoked on 7 November (with the exception of the troubled areas in the north and east) to facilitate the fair and proper conduct of the presidential election, which was held on 9 November. Kumaratunga won the election, with 62.3% of the votes, while Srima Dissanayake obtained 35.9%. The Government viewed the victory as a clear mandate for the peace process initiated earlier that year. Sirimavo Bandaranaike was subsequently appointed Prime Minister, for the third time. The new President pledged to abolish the executive presidency before mid-July 1995, on the grounds that she believed that the post vested too much power in one individual, and promised to initiate a programme of social, economic and constitutional change.

The Government and the LTTE resumed peace talks in early January 1995, which resulted in the drawing up of a preliminary agreement on the cessation of hostilities as a prelude to political negotiations. This important development constituted the first formal truce since fighting was renewed in the north-east in June 1990. As an inducement to ending the violence, the Government offered to implement a US $816m.-rehabilitation and development programme in the war-torn northern region. A further incentive was the Government's decision to employ foreign observers to monitor the cease-fire. Towards the end of the month, the LTTE modified its central demand and indicated that it would be willing to accept some form of devolution under a federal system, rather than full independence. In April 1995, however, following several rounds of deadlocked negotiations, with both sides accusing each other of making unreasonable demands and proposals, the LTTE unilaterally ended the truce, withdrew from the peace talks and resumed hostilities against the government forces. (As feared, the LTTE had apparently used the 14-week truce period to fortify and consolidate its strategic positions, notably in the eastern province.) In response, the Government cancelled all the concessions made to the guerrillas during the peace negotiations and placed the security forces on alert. A disturbing escalation in the violence was demonstrated at the end of the month by the LTTE's deployment, for the first time, of surface-to-air missiles.

With so much of its political energies invested in the peace process, the resurgence of violence in April 1995 constituted a major set-back for the Government. At this point, Kumaratunga's administration adopted a different, 'hearts and minds' approach, namely the preparation of a range of constitutional proposals, including a more comprehensive devolution of power to the provinces than the system prevailing. Details of these proposals were announced at various stages, and in early August an official statement was issued explaining that the proposed new structure was, in essence, a federal system in which the units were named regions rather than provinces. Meanwhile, in July 1995 the Government candidly admitted that one of its principal election proposals, the abolition of the executive presidency, could not be effected by 15 July as earlier promised. In the same month the Government launched another major offensive in the Jaffna peninsula. 'Operation Leap Forward', as it was named, made some initial gains but appeared to have stalled by the end of the month, in part owing to a deliberate decision by the Government to do so, and in part owing to LTTE counter-attacks. Outside the Jaffna peninsula, LTTE 'suicide attacks' on army positions at Weli-Oya in the eastern province resulted in the most significant reversal that the LTTE had suffered at the hands of the Sri Lankan army since 1992; more than 300 LTTE militants were killed for the loss of just two defenders. Although 'Operation Leap Forward' was initially an anti-climax both for the Government and the armed forces alike, the victory at Weli-Oya was very much a morale booster.

As the Government's offensive against the Jaffna peninsula was intensified in mid-October 1995, under the code name 'Operation Riviresa' ('Operation Sunshine'), tens of thousands of civilians were compelled by the LTTE to flee the area. In retaliation against the army's attack, rather than actively confronting the troops, the LTTE activated explosives on the country's two largest petroleum storage facilities near Colombo, which received virtually all of Sri Lanka's imported petroleum. As a result, about 20% of the island's petroleum supply was destroyed. In mid-November two LTTE 'suicide bombers' caused 18 deaths and more than 50 injuries in Colombo. In early December, however, the Sri Lankan army achieved a major victory in capturing the city of Jaffna and subsequently much of the Jaffna peninsula. Although the LTTE's military strength and morale were undermined, the rebels, as expected, reverted to guerrilla warfare and further terrorist activity.

The Government's two-pronged approach to the Tamil problem (i.e. military and political), which was adopted in 1995, was continued throughout the second half of the 1990s. Thus, in 1996 the Government's devolution proposals went through the normal political and constitutional processes. The political processes included discussions within a parliamentary select committee, in which the Government needed to convince the opposition UNP that the proposals merited the support of all parties. In the event of their approval by the select committee, the proposals would need to secure a two-thirds parliamentary majority if they were to become law. Once that stage had been reached, the proposals would then have to be approved by a simple majority in a national referendum. In mid-January a draft legal document of devolution proposals was introduced to facilitate discussion on this controversial subject, while the army launched a fresh offensive in the Jaffna peninsula, codenamed 'Operation Rivikirana' to consolidate the gains made in that area. The LTTE retaliated by exploding a truck-bomb at the Central Bank building in Colombo, which resulted in more than 100 deaths and more than 1,400 injuries. The army resumed its offensive in the Jaffna peninsula in April through 'Operation Riviresa II', and once more met with very little resistance. With 'Operation Riviresa III', which was launched in mid-May, the army completed a successful campaign to bring the whole of the Jaffna peninsula under its control for the first time since 1984–85. When the army offensive in the Jaffna peninsula was at its peak at the end of 1995, the LTTE had forced the population of the areas potentially under attack by the army to move out of the peninsula to the Kilinochchi and Mullaitivu districts. Thousands of people had followed these instructions. After the completion of 'Operation Riviresa III', however, these people moved back to their homes, which constituted a considerable embarrassment for the LTTE.

Although the army had secured control over the whole of the Jaffna peninsula by mid-1996, the LTTE maintained a presence there, and engaged in occasional guerrilla attacks on the troops. In one such attack on 4 July, a female 'suicide bomber' killed 23 soldiers in a motorcade accompanying the Minister of Housing, Construction and Public Utilities, Nimal Siripala de Silva, who was on a visit to Jaffna. While the Minister escaped with minor injuries, the Jaffna town commander was among those killed in the incident. On 18 July the LTTE demonstrated its capacity for surprise attacks on army positions, when the isolated military base at Mullaitivu on the north-eastern coast of Sri Lanka was overrun by the LTTE, inflicting very heavy casualties on the army (according to the LTTE, at least 1,200 government soldiers were killed; according to official figures, the army death toll was about 300) and a defeat on the scale of the Pooneryn incident of November 1993. The LTTE also again demonstrated its capacity to launch bomb attacks in the city of Colombo; a bomb in a crowded suburban train left more than 70 people dead on 24 July 1996. In late September the army seized control of the northern town of Kilinochchi, which had served as the LTTE's new headquarters since April. In October Velupillai Prabhakaran and nine other militants were charged with more than 700 criminal acts of terrorism, including the bombing of the Central Bank in January. This constituted the first occasion that the Government had initiated legal action against the LTTE leader. Fierce fighting between the Tamil militants and government troops continued into 1997, both in the north and east of the country; in early March it was estimated that more than 50,000 people had died as a result of the 14-year civil war.

By the beginning of 1997 the Government's political initiative on devolution had clearly stalled. While discussions in the parliamentary select committee continued, there were few signs of any consensus being reached between the Government and the UNP on these reforms. The election promise to abolish the executive presidency, which had originally been scheduled for mid-July 1995, was once again shelved. The long-postponed local government elections were, however, held on 21 March 1997 (voting did not take place in the troubled northern and eastern provinces). Although the Government secured control over a majority of the local bodies, its share of the total popular vote fell to 48%, compared with the 62% it achieved in the presidential election of November 1994. The UNP obtained nearly 42% of the poll. The Government's victory was tarnished, however, by allegations of widespread electoral malpractice. In April 1997 UK officials brokered an agreement between the PA Government and the opposition UNP, aimed at creating a bipartisan approach to ending the civil conflict. In an exchange of letters, Kumaratunga agreed to brief Wickremasinghe on any significant developments in the war, while the opposition pledged not to undermine the Government's attempts to negotiate peace with the LTTE.

In May 1997 the Government resumed its offensive against the LTTE; 'Operation Jayasikuru' ('Operation Certain Victory') was launched with the objective of gaining control of 75 km of the main road (the A9) between Vavuniya and Elephant Pass, which is the point of entry to the Jaffna peninsula. The northern highway, if opened, would provide the military with a vital land route to the Jaffna peninsula (hitherto during the civil war, all government troops and supplies had had to be transported by sea or air). This campaign, which was the largest military operation undertaken by the PA Government since the capture of the Jaffna peninsula, had some early successes. The section of the road between Vavuniya and Mankulam was brought under military control, but, owing to the stiff resistance mounted by the LTTE, the campaign made rather slow progress thereafter. In June 1998 the Government imposed an indefinite 'total ban' on news coverage (both local and foreign) of the ongoing civil war. By recapturing Kilinochchi in September, which it had lost to the army nearly two years earlier, the LTTE compelled the government forces to reconsider the rationale behind their campaign. By October 'Operation Jayasikuru', which was estimated to have cost the lives of more than 3,000 government troops, had been abandoned, despite the army's seizure the previous month of Mankulam, the last major town held by the guerrillas on the vital northern highway. (The operation was officially cancelled by the Government in December.) In November Sri Lankan intelligence reports indicated that the LTTE was in the process of acquiring helicopters and military aircraft. By late 1998 there were also signs that the army had a serious manpower problem (it needed to recruit 20,000 fresh troops), caused partly by desertions and growing numbers of casualties.

Meanwhile, in late August 1997 the Government announced that it would submit its devolution proposals for parliamentary debate in October. In mid-October, however, 18 people were killed and more than 100 injured (including about 35 foreigners) when a truck-bomb exploded in the car park of a Colombo hotel, leading to several hours of shooting between troops and suspected LTTE terrorists in the city's business district. It was widely believed that the LTTE deliberately targeted foreigners in this attack following the US Government's decision a few days earlier to place the organization on its official list of proscribed international terrorist groups. At the end of the month, despite protests from the UNP, the draft of the proposed constitutional amendments was presented to Parliament. The prospect of peace, however, appeared increasingly remote in late January 1998 when 16 people were killed in a suspected LTTE 'suicide bombing' in Kandy at Sri Lanka's most sacred Buddhist temple, the Dalada Maligawa ('Temple of the Tooth'). This attack was particularly provocative because, aside from the loss of life, the temple itself, one of the most important religious sites in the Buddhist world, suffered severe damage. The following day the Government retaliated by formally outlawing the LTTE, thus apparently ruling out the prospect of further peace negotiations in the near future and focusing instead on a military solution. In addition, the main ceremonies of the 50th anniversary of Sri Lanka's independence, which had been scheduled to be held in Kandy on 4 February, were hastily shifted to Colombo. The Government suffered another set-back in late January when the UNP effectively rejected the proposed devolution package. The UNP disagreed with the Government's proposal to devolve wide-ranging powers to regional councils—including a Tamil-administered area—and favoured the concept of power-sharing at the centre. Also at the end of January, polls were conducted in Jaffna for the first time in 15 years. The local authority elections, which were monitored by tens of thousands of troops, were contested by a number of moderate Tamil political parties but were, not surprisingly, boycotted by the LTTE. The largest number of seats was won by the Eelam People's Democratic Party, but the turn-out was a mere 28%, owing to LTTE threats to disrupt the voting.

In late January 1998 a special court in Chennai (as Madras had recently been renamed), India, sentenced 10 Indians and 16 Sri Lankans to death for their involvement in the assassination of the former Indian Prime Minister Rajiv Gandhi in 1991. (In May 1999, however, the Supreme Court in New Delhi acquitted 19 defendants and commuted the sentences of three others.)

In February and March 1998 47 people were killed and hundreds injured in Colombo as a result of two 'suicide bombings'. In mid-May the recently elected mayor of Jaffna (the first person to hold that position in 14 years), Sarojini Yogeswaran, who was a member of the moderate TULF, was assassinated by two suspected LTTE gunmen after refusing demands by Tamil militants to resign. In September Yogeswaran's replacement, Ponnuthurai Sivapalan, who was also a leading member of TULF, was killed, along with 19 others, in a suspected LTTE bomb explosion in Jaffna city hall.

The Government's political calculations, in the wake of the attack on the 'Temple of the Tooth' in Kandy, were determined by the need to deal with elections to five provincial councils, which were scheduled to be held in August 1998. Claiming that the security situation would make it virtually impossible to ensure a peaceful election campaign, the Government sought the support of the UNP to introduce a constitutional amendment to postpone the elections. Following the UNP's refusal to support such a move, except on its own terms, the Government was faced with the difficult choice of either proceeding with the holding of the elections or postponing them through a resort to the declaration of a state of emergency. In the mean time the electoral process was initiated, nominations of candidates were received and processed, and the Commissioner of Elections declared 28 August as the date for the elections. On 4 August, however, the Government declared a nation-wide state of emergency. A presidential regulation under the emergency was issued on the following day, formally postponing indefinitely the holding of the provincial elections. The opposition claimed that the Government had deliberately engineered the postponement of the important polls since it was concerned about performing badly in them. At the beginning of 1999 an election was called for the north-western provincial council, which was not among the five where elections had been postponed. The campaign culminated on 25 January in the most violent and corrupt election in the island's history. The systematic 'ballot-stuffing' and booth-capturing organized by the ruling PA was on an unprecedented scale. Civil rights groups and religious leaders joined the opposition UNP in forthright condemnation of the Government for these blatant infringements of electoral laws. The Commissioner of Elections rejected as many as 50,000 votes as clearly fraudulent. Although the PA wrested control of the council from the UNP, the legality of the whole election was challenged before the courts.

The Government's reputation, already badly tarnished by the manner in which the election to the north-western provincial council was conducted, suffered another severe blow, when, on the day after the polling, the Supreme Court in Colombo overruled President Kumaratunga's order, made in August 1998, postponing elections to five other provincial councils. The Court stated that the presidency had no constitutional right to postpone the elections through the declaration of a state of emergency and asked the election commission to hold the polls within the next three months and to hold all five of them on a single day. The provincial elections, which were eventually held on 6 April 1999, gave the Government no cause for satisfaction. The difference in the percentage of votes gained by the PA and the UNP was reduced to a mere 1%. The Government secured a majority in three councils, but in the two principal councils, the western and central, the PA was forced to head a minority administration. An election to the southern province, which was held in May, also resulted in a PA-led minority administration. One notable feature of this series of provincial elections was the recovery of the JVP as a credible political force (it won around 8% of the vote in total in all of the contested provincial councils, and, specifically, as much as 20% in the Hambantota district of the southern province).

Meanwhile, the LTTE leader presented a carefully worded peace offer in December 1998, which included a demand for third-party mediation. The Government responded by insisting that certain conditions be met before peace talks could commence. Once the north-east monsoon rains had subsided, the army launched another offensive in early March 1999 in the areas controlled by the LTTE in the Mullaitivu district of the northern province. This offensive, which was code-named 'Operation Ranagosa' ('Operation The Sound of War') and the objective of which was to reduce the area under the effective control of the LTTE, was waged intermittently during 1999, along with other minor operations in parts of the northern province. In mid-June, in an unprecedented order, the President temporarily dissolved the powerful National Security Council and stripped the Chief of Defence Staff of sweeping powers. Prospects of achieving a peace settlement in Sri Lanka appeared even more remote in late July, following the assassination by a suspected LTTE 'suicide bomber' in Colombo of the TULF Vice-President, Neelan Tiruchelvam, who was a leading peace campaigner and human rights activist. In the same month Kumaratunga promoted 15 PA members to the position of deputy minister, in a move that was widely viewed as an attempt to ensure that politicians remained loyal to the alliance prior to and during the forthcoming general election. The move was heavily criticized by opposition members as financially profligate.

Sri Lanka's fourth presidential election, which was called in October 1999, was held on 21 December, about 11 months ahead of schedule. For the second time in succession the results of a Sri Lankan presidential election were affected by actions of the LTTE. On this occasion, this phenomenon happened initially with the LTTE inflicting a series of defeats on the Sri Lankan army in the north of the country in October and November 1999 during a brief and very successful campaign, as a result of which the government forces lost control of large areas of territory that they had secured between 1995 and 1997. These demoralizing defeats (amidst reports of large-scale desertions and mutiny in the army ranks) embarrassed the Government of President Kumaratunga and gave the prospects of her principal opponent, Ranil Wickremasinghe of the UNP, an unexpected boost. As a result, the latter's electoral campaign gained in credibility, and by the end of November he seemed a potential victor in the contest. Wickremasinghe sustained this favourable position until a failed assassination attempt by a LTTE 'suicide bomber' on 18 December, the last day of campaigning, left the terrorists' target, Chandrika Kumaratunga, slightly injured and helped to reverse the emerging pro-UNP trend in the election process. The shock of the failed assassination attempt (which killed more than 20 people) was cleverly exploited by the Government through the use of the state-controlled electronic media, particularly television broadcasts, and through hastily organized, small public meetings virtually throughout the country, in direct violation of the ban imposed by electoral laws on any form of electioneering for two days immediately prior to the holding of the election. The principal theme of the Government's last-minute campaign was that the LTTE had planned the assassination to help Wickremasinghe's cause. The margin of Kumaratunga's victory, by 51% of the total votes to 43% for her and Wickremasinghe respectively, was substantially below that of 1994. The JVP candidate's relatively poor performance in the election (which was contested by 13 candidates and attracted a 73% turn-out of the electorate) benefited the incumbent President. Had the JVP garnered more support, Kumaratunga's margin of victory would have been even lower. With allegations made by neutral observers, as well as by the defeated UNP candidate, of widespread electoral violence, blatant malpractices and vote-rigging, the flawed presidential election cost the Government heavily in terms of integrity. In addition, the Government was faced with a serious legal challenge to the validity of the election. In early January 2000, despite tightened security in the capital, another suspected LTTE 'suicide bomber' killed herself and 12 other people outside the office of Prime Minister Bandaranaike in Colombo in what police described as a failed assassination attempt. In June a 'suicide bomber' killed at least 20 people, including the Minister of Industrial Development, Clement V. Gunaratna, at a parade in the capital marking the country's first 'War Heroes' Day'.

Once the President had recovered sufficiently from the trauma of the pre-election attempt on her life (in which she had sustained wounds in her right eye) Kumaratunga applied herself once more to the process of constitutional reform, and by mid-February 2000 she had succeeded in persuading Wickremasinghe and the UNP to send a delegation to participate in the preparation of a new constitution (based on the proposals regarding devolution presented by the Government in 1997). The first of such meetings took place on 9 March. Meanwhile, in mid-February the Norwegian Minister of Foreign Affairs, Knut Vollebæk, during a visit to Colombo announced that the Norwegian Government had accepted a request from the Sri Lankan President and the LTTE to serve as a mediator to bring the two parties together for discussions—for a year or so Norway had been posited as a potential facilitator. The Norwegian initiative had little effect in checking the LTTE's military operations, which had continued throughout November and December 1999. It was clear that the successes achieved by the LTTE in the last weeks of 1999 were a prelude to a determined bid to capture the large army base at Elephant Pass, on the strategically important isthmus that links the Jaffna peninsula to the rest of the island. The garrison (which had been under government control since the IPKF's withdrawal in 1990) was seized by the LTTE in late April 2000, the LTTE's most spectacular military victory in recent times. In response, a panic-stricken Sri Lankan Government appealed for assistance to deal with the rapidly advancing LTTE, both from regional powers and from elsewhere. Adopting a more circumspect policy than its predecessor had done in the 1980s, the Indian central Government decided that it would not interfere directly in the Sri Lankan conflict. All requests for military assistance in the form of weaponry from the Sri Lankan Government were turned down. All that was on offer from India was humanitarian assistance, a pronouncement interpreted in Colombo as including the transfer of Sri Lankan troops out of the Jaffna peninsula presumably by Indian ships, should the need for such an evacuation arise. India also announced, however, that it was extending its ban on the outlawed LTTE for a further two years. A more fruitful initiative by the Sri Lankan authorities was the restoration of diplomatic ties with Israel and successful negotiations with that country for the supply of sophisticated weaponry and military aircraft. Other countries too responded with the supply of arms: namely, Pakistan, China and Russia. On 3 May President Kumaratunga put Sri Lanka on a war footing by invoking the Public Security Ordinance; this constituted the first use of the measure, which gave the police extensive powers of arrest and confiscation, since the country became independent in 1949. At the same time, the President imposed a ban on strikes and political rallies, and stricter censorship on all forms of media reporting.

The resurgence of the LTTE in 1999–2000 had a noticeable effect on Tamil Nadu politicians in the form of a revival in pro-LTTE sentiment, which had largely been dormant since the assassination of Rajiv Gandhi in 1991. In early June 2000 the Chief Minister of Tamil Nadu, Muthuvel Karunanidhi, called for a partition of Sri Lanka, on the model of the former Czechoslovakia, into two states, one of which would be a Tamil state. There was immediate opposition to this proposal, both within Tamil Nadu and in other parts of India. Karunanidhi's proposition and the outpouring of pro-LTTE sentiment among other Indian politicians belonging to parties of the current governing coalition in New Delhi were acutely embarrassing to the Indian Government. The administration of Atal Bihari Vajpayee indicated clearly enough, and repeatedly, that it would not countenance the establishment of a separate Tamil state in Sri Lanka, and indicated, rather, a preference for the allocation of greater autonomy to the Tamil areas of the island.

Meanwhile, in response to the escalating military crisis, the Sri Lankan Government imposed draconian security measures, banning all activities perceived as a threat to national security and giving sweeping powers to the armed forces and police, and renewed press censorship on the foreign media. By early May 2000 LTTE forces, buoyed up by their recent military gains, were close enough to Jaffna town to suggest that they were poised to drive the Sri Lankan army away from Jaffna and the Jaffna peninsula and to compel the government forces to abandon the airport at Palali and the naval base of Karainagar, which the LTTE had never been able to control previously. Within a month, however, the LTTE advance had lost its early momentum. Whether this was because of a change of leadership in the Sri Lankan army in the Jaffna peninsula, with two experienced generals with exemplary records as field commanders being posted there, whether it was the recent provision of high-tech weaponry, which the army had lacked at the time of the fall of Elephant Pass, that enabled the Sri Lankan security forces to regain the initiative, or whether it was a combination of the two was difficult to assess. The fact remains, however, that by mid-June the threat poised by the LTTE to the Government's control over Jaffna town and the Jaffna peninsula had clearly receded. By early September the army was making efforts to compel the LTTE to move out of some of the towns in the vicinity of Jaffna. Despite early set-backs, these attempts began to prove successful by mid-September. In mid-2000 it was estimated that since the instigation of the civil conflict in 1983 65,000 people had been killed in Sri Lanka as a result of the violence, 1m. had been internally displaced and 600,000 had fled overseas.

In any event, the successful holding operation by the army in Jaffna gave the Government the opportunity to return to its preparation of a new constitution through discussions with the UNP. The Government's avowed objective was to have a new constitution presented to and approved by Parliament in July or August 2000, always bearing in mind the fact that the national legislature's term of office expired on 24 August (unless it was dissolved earlier). The discussions with the UNP leadership on the draft of the new constitution proceeded smoothly enough until early July, when complications arose in the form of sharp disagreements over the role of the current President in a new parliamentary system. While the Government insisted that Kumaratunga should have a dual role, as the new Prime Minister after parliamentary elections, should the elections be won by the PA, and as executive President until the expiry of her current six-year term, the UNP argued that her tenure of the presidency should come to end within a short time of the promulgation of any new constitution. Approval of the new constitution required a two-thirds parliamentary majority, which was not possible, however, once the UNP leadership had declared its opposition to the draft constitution; the Tamil parliamentary parties—the EPDP, the Democratic People's Liberation Front and the TULF—also rejected the proposals as giving inadequate autonomy to the Tamil regions of the country. The Government sought to overcome this by attempting to persuade UNP deputies to support the new constitution in Parliament; in the event, a number of UNP MPs did cross over to the opposition during the debate on the constitution in early August. However, the members who did so fell far short of the Government's targeted number. When this situation became clear, the draft constitution was not presented for a vote (voting on the controversial bill was postponed indefinitely). Instead, after an inconclusive and acrimonious debate, amidst large and vociferous crowds expressing their opposition to the draft constitution, Parliament was dissolved on 18 August, and new parliamentary elections were scheduled for October.

Meanwhile, on 10 August 2000 Sirimavo Bandaranaike resigned as Prime Minister and retired from political life at the age of 84; the veteran politician was replaced in the premiership by the erstwhile Minister of Public Administration, Home Affairs and Plantation Industries, Ratnasiri Wickramanayake, who was regarded as a Sinhalese hardliner close to the Buddhist clergy. In mid-September the Minister of Shipping and Shipping Development and President of the SLMC, Mohamed H. M. Ashraff, was killed in a helicopter crash in Kegalle district; a high-level investigation into the incident was immediately ordered amidst speculation that the aircraft had been shot down by LTTE guerrillas.

The results of the parliamentary election of 10 October 2000 were a disappointment to both the PA and the UNP. The election, which according to official figures attracted a turn-out of 75%, was marred by widespread electoral malpractice and systematic violence and intimidation (particularly on the part of the incumbent PA). The PA secured only 45% of the votes cast, and the UNP received 40%. The JVP gained 10 seats (6% of the vote), and from the beginning considered itself a possible balancing force in a Parliament in which the PA nor the UNP had won an absolute majority (with 107 and 89 of the 225 seats, respectively). After much bargaining by the two main parties, the PA, having gained the support of the EPDP, National Unity Alliance (NUA) and SLMC, was able to form a coalition with a very narrow majority. It was evident that the Government would be vulnerable to shifts of opinion within Parliament, and throughout the country.

The death of Sirimavo Bandaranaike, on the day of the election, deprived the SLFP of its leader for 40 years, as well as a respected stabilizing influence. The election of Anura Bandaranaike, a member of the UNP and the President's estranged brother, as parliamentary Speaker by a unanimous vote of Parliament was seen, in the early stages at least, as heralding the beginning of a period of greater co-operation between the PA and the UNP. However, in fact, the establishment of a 44-member cabinet, with 38 Deputy Ministers, underlined the inherent instability of the Government, and its potential vulnerability in the face of a challenge by the UNP. Every group in the coalition was represented in the Cabinet, including the SLMC and its affiliate, the NUA. It was evident very soon that President Kumaratunga's principal concern was to ensure the survival of the Government in a situation where, under the terms of the Constitution, Parliament could not be dissolved for at least one year after the previous election, in this instance until 10 October 2001.

The priority for the new Government was established by the LTTE, which declared a unilateral cease-fire to begin on 24 December 2000 as a prelude to talks with the Government, which, it proposed, would be facilitated in the early stages by a Norwegian representative. Although the Government readily accepted the principle of a Norwegian facilitator, it refused to accept the LTTE's offer. The Government also refused to lift the proscription on the Tamil group. Instead, it insisted on a set of conditions as a prelude to accepting a unilateral cessation of hostilities. The LTTE, nevertheless, implemented a cease-fire, and regularly renewed it until the end of April 2001, ignoring the conditions set by the Government. The Government evidently suspected the LTTE of seeking a period of time during which it could rebuild its forces and its equipment. The low-intensity conflict continued in the north and east.

By June 2001, however, the Government's priorities had shifted more emphatically to its political survival, as a result of a serious miscalculation on the part of the President. Kamaratunga dismissed the leader of the SLMC, Rauf Hakeem, from his position as Minister of Internal and International Trade, Commerce, Muslim Religious Affairs and Shipping Development, in the belief that his party would not stand by him. However, as a result, six other members of the SLMC withdrew their support from the PA, thereby reducing the coalition Government to a minority in Parliament. The UNP was able to claim, subsequently, that the anti-PA coalition had a parliamentary majority, with 115 of the 225 seats, and challenged the Government with a parliamentary motion of 'no confidence'. A debate in Parliament was proposed to take place in mid-July. As the census was scheduled to take place at this time, the Government suggested mid-August as an appropriate time.

However, in early July 2001 the President unexpectedly prorogued Parliament for two months to forestall an attempt to overthrow the Government and ordered a referendum on 21 August to seek a mandate for a new constitution. The former decision breached a settled principle of democratic government that Parliament must not be prorogued when the government faces a vote of 'no confidence', especially when it has lost its majority. The second ruling was unconstitutional: the special provisions in the constitution that dictate the procedures for constitutional reform had been deliberately ignored.

President Kumaratunga's decisions, which had been taken without prior consultation with the Cabinet, plunged the country into a constitutional crisis. The UNP-led opposition embarked on a campaign of peaceful popular resistance demanding a revocation of the prorogation of parliament. The protests became violent at times. There was also opposition within the Cabinet, especially to the referendum. As a result, in early August the President considered it expedient to postpone the referendum to mid-October. The announcement was made two weeks after the LTTE's attack on Colombo's international airport, and adjacent air base at the end of July. This raid demonstrated serious flaws in the air force and airport's security system. It also resulted in severe damage to the country's economy and tourist industry. Violence between the Tamil guerrillas and Government escalated, following the attack. Earlier that month the President had circumvented Parliament and reimposed state of emergency legislation under anti-terrorism laws. The President also passed an order to reimpose the ban on the LTTE. Unsurprisingly, recent events led to the further erosion of the Government's political credibility.

In an attempt to resolve the crisis, the Prime Minister and some senior Cabinet members conducted negotiations with the UNP on a possible coalition Government. Although the UNP showed some interest in this, it eventually decided to join opposition parties to form a UNP-led coalition. The President objected to a UNP government or a UNP-led opposition coalition, and began negotiations with the radical, left-wing JVP. The JVP agreed to support the Government and in early September, a Memorandum of Understanding was signed binding the two parties for one year to a PA-led minority Government, sustained by JVP votes. The left-wing party set 28 conditions in the memorandum, one of which was a reduction of the Cabinet to 20 members. A 22-member cabinet was subsequently sworn in, but three senior Cabinet members had refused to join, an indication of the instability of the Government. According to the JVP's demands, the President also cancelled the referendum on constitutional reform and ordered Parliament to reconvene a day earlier. The JVP also insisted that there should be no negotiations with the LTTE during the one-year period.

In October 2001 the SLFP removed its General Secretary, S. B. Dissanayake, as the Government faced a vote of 'no confidence', which was to be held on 11 October. It had become clear that the Government would face defeat in the parliamentary vote after 13 members of the coalition, including several ministers, defected to the opposition. President Kumaratunga, therefore, dissolved Parliament one day before the scheduled vote and announced that a general election would be held in early

December. The dissolution was condemned by the opposition, which was prevented from proving its majority. However, the decision was constitutional, as the President had waited until one year after the previous election had passed before she dissolved the legislature. Meanwhile, violence between the LTTE and Government continued and showed no signs of abating.

THE UNITED NATIONAL FRONT IN OFFICE

The general election of 5 December 2001, like that of October 2000, was marred by electoral malpractice, the blatant exploitation of state resources and vote-rigging (often crude and some times adroit) on the part of the outgoing PA. In addition, during both elections the state's print and electronic media were fully and almost exclusively reserved for the election campaign of government candidates. All these occurrences were in defiant and open disregard of election laws. Furthermore, both elections were marred by systematic violence directed against opposition members under the alleged instruction of senior government officials. The December 2001 parliamentary elections were reported to be the more violent of the two; however, on this occasion the electorate turned against the outgoing Government and the vote-rigging failed decisively.

The UNP-led coalition won a comprehensive victory, securing most of the polling divisions and all but one of the polling districts outside of the northern province. The UNP won 109 of the 225 seats (45.6% of the vote) and the PA obtained 77 seats (37.2%). The JVP secured 16 seats (9.1%) and the TNA won 15 seats (3.9%). Political analysts considered that the margin of victory for the UNP and its allies would have been much wider had the election been free and fair. In order to ensure a majority in Parliament and in recognition of the support received from and through coalition partners, the UNP leader, Ranil Wickremesinghe, formed a United National Front (UNF) Government with the SLMC, Tamil National Alliance and several members of the former PA administration who had defected to the UNP after the election.

The new Government consolidated its position at the local government elections in March 2002. Apart from a few incidents of election violence—well below the levels witnessed in 1999, 2000 and 2001 in terms of intensity or geographical range—the elections were free and fair, in a deliberate and permanent return to the practices of the early 1990s. The PA was overwhelmingly defeated, managing to secure only four out of 247 councils, compared with the UNP's victory in 240 municipal legislatures. The UNP won almost 57% of the total vote, while the PA secured 31% and the JVP nearly 6%.

The political cohabitation between the PA President, and the UNF Government proved to be uncomfortable. Sri Lanka was not accustomed to the Prime Minister and President representing two opposing parties (the last time this occurred was in 1984) and the conventions and practices that would reduce friction between the two parties had not yet developed. One essential factor was the right of the President to dissolve Parliament after one year from the date of the last election. Confronted with the prospect of an election called at the President's convenience after 5 December 2002, the UNF Government proposed that future elections be called on the basis of a parliamentary resolution; however, the President refused to support this suggestion. The other proposal was a constitutional amendment, known as the 19th amendment, which would restrict the right of the President to dissolve Parliament when the governing party has a majority in the legislature. The proposed statute was introduced in Parliament in mid-September; a debate was scheduled for early October.

One of the principal political developments that followed the UNF's accession to power was a strengthening of the peace process. An informal cease-fire took effect in December 2001. On 22 February 2002 the Prime Minister and the LTTE leader, Velupillai Prabhakaran, signed a Memorandum of Understanding (MOU), agreeing to an internationally monitored indefinite cease-fire, with the Norwegian Government serving as facilitators. The MOU committed the two sides to specified courses of action and stipulated the conditions for implementation prior to the commencement of peace talks. A Sri Lanka Monitoring Mission, operated by several Scandinavian countries and led by Norwegians, conducted the supervision of the implementation of the MOU.

The assumption was that the two parties would maintain the cease-fire and commence peace talks on or before 2 August 2002. This latter deadline was missed but the cessation of hostilities was upheld. On 4 September the Government removed the official ban on the LTTE, a condition that the LTTE insisted upon as a prelude to negotiations. The three-day peace talks began nearly two weeks later, on 16 September in Bangkok, Thailand. During the negotiations the LTTE unexpectedly abandoned its long-standing demand for independence and instead agreed to regional autonomy and self-government. The successful talks ended with both sides agreeing to establish a committee to deal with the return of more than 800,000 internally displaced people to high-security zones operated by the Sri Lankan military; to form a joint task force for humanitarian and reconstruction activities; and to appeal to international donors to support the humanitarian efforts. They also agreed to hold three more rounds of negotiations in October, December and January 2003, at which it was expected that the two sides would discuss the formation of an interim administration in the Tamil-controlled areas.

Economy

S. W. R. de A. SAMARASINGHE

With a population of 18.9m. at mid-2002, Sri Lanka has many of the features that characterize a 'small' developing economy in its early stages of industrialization. In 2000 income per head was a modest US $837. At least one-quarter of the population live below the poverty line. About 40% of those who were gainfully employed were in agriculture. Earnings from the export of the three leading primary products (tea, rubber and coconut) accounted for about 17% of total visible export earnings. The relative importance of these three products has sharply declined over the last two decades. In 2001 the three products together accounted for only 4.7% of the gross domestic product (GDP). Neither do they dominate exports as in the past. Garments, textiles and other manufactured exports accounted for 77% of total visible export earnings during 2000/01. The country's manufacturing industry contributed 16% to the GDP in 2001. The inability of the economy to raise the share of manufactures above this level for a period of over 20 years has been one of the more disappointing features of economic performance. Against a backdrop of an increase in the population from 7.5m. to over 18.9m. between independence in 1948 and 2002, maintaining a high economic growth rate to create productive job opportunities with adequate pay for a rapidly increasing labour force together with the alleviation of poverty have become two of the most pressing socio-economic problems. The civil war of two decades has drained the country's resources for military activity and has discouraged investment, thereby acting as a major constraint on economic progress. A cease-fire was under way in 2002 and peace negotiations between the Government and the Liberation Tigers of Tamil Eelam (LTTE) commenced in September. If long-term peace is achieved, the economy will be given a huge boost.

The atypical features of Sri Lanka's economy have attracted a great deal of international attention. Using gross national product (GNP) per head as the criterion, in 2000 the World Bank classified Sri Lanka as 140th from the top among 206 countries in the world; this means that it is among the poorest one-third of nations. If Sri Lanka's national output is measured in US dollars in terms of internationally comparable purchasing power parity (PPP), GNP per caput in 2000 was about US $3,460. The rank is slightly higher at 133. This may not, however, be an adequate measure of the country's development. The Human Development Index (HDI) for 2000, computed by the United Nations Development Programme (UNDP), using life expectancy at birth, adult literacy and school gross enrollment at primary, secondary and tertiary levels, and real PPP GDP per caput as indices, ranks Sri Lanka 89th from the top on a list of 173 countries (which is 19 positions higher than real PPP GDP per caput ranking). This comparatively high HDI ranking can be attributed to the relatively high adult literacy rate (92%), high school enrolment ratio (70%), and high life expectancy at birth (72 years).

In 1977 Sri Lanka was one of the first developing countries to adopt a programme of economic liberalization cum structural adjustment, abandoning a two-decade-old *dirigisme* economic policy. The international donor community, led by the World Bank and the IMF, supported the new policy with substantial aid. The reform package adopted then included the liberalization of imports, reductions in exchange controls, price controls and rationing, the abolition of the State's monopoly in the import of certain key goods, the establishment of a unified (and pegged floating) exchange rate, the transfer to private-sector ownership of selected state enterprises, and lowering of corporate and personal taxes. Despite political difficulties such as the ethnic war, these reforms have been sustained over two decades and further strengthened in the last few years with an accelerated programme of privatization, reform of the public service and further liberalization of current and capital account transactions in the balance of payment. What is even more remarkable is that now there is bipartisan support for a market economy. Thus, the People's Alliance (PA), which was in office from 1994 to 2001, and which consisted of parties that in the past adhered to 'socialism', was also committed to pursuing pro-market policies.

GROSS DOMESTIC PRODUCT

GDP for 2001, at current market prices, has been estimated at Rs 1,400,117m. (US $15,700m.). The composition of real GDP has undergone a considerable change following the introduction of economic liberalization in 1977, with the share of value added by agriculture (including the processing of export crops) declining from 39.6% of GDP in 1975–77 to 19.7% in 1999–2001. The contribution of mining and quarrying has remained virtually unchanged, at about 2.0% of the GDP, throughout this period. The contribution of construction increased from 3.7% to 7.5%, that of banking, insurance and real estate from 1.4% to 8.3%, that of transport, storage and communication from 8.0% to 11.9%, that of electricity, gas, water and sanitary services from 0.7% to 1.3%, and that of trade from 18.9% to 21.9%. However, during the 1980s there was no significant structural change in the economy in favour of manufacturing. The share of manufacturing in GDP, which was about 12% when the liberalization program was initiated had moved up to about 16% by the late 1980s. In 2001 this figure was still 15.8%. The share of public administration and defence increased significantly between 1975–77 and 1999–2001, from 3.3% to 5.3%. This was partly due to the expansion of the military during that period. The annual real GDP growth rate averaged 2.9% over 1970–77, and 6.1% between 1978 and 1984. In the second half of the 1980s the economic growth rate dropped to about 3.0% due to a decline in investment caused largely by political instability. In the first half of the 1990s economic growth was fairly robust, with the rate averaging about 5.5% per year. The average rate of growth of GDP decelerated in the second half of the decade to around 4.0%–4.5% per year. The economy grew by 6.0% in 2000. However, in 2001, for the first time since Sri Lanka's independence in 1948, the country registered a negative GDP growth rate of -1.4%.

AGRICULTURE

The Sri Lankan economy is dominated by agriculture, especially as an avenue of employment. In 2001 of a 6.7m.-strong labour force, about 2.2m. (33%) living outside the northern and eastern provinces were employed in that sector. Sri Lanka's agriculture consists of export-orientated commercial crops and part-subsistence and part-market food crops. The agricultural labour force divides itself roughly equally between the two sectors. The commercial crops are cultivated both in large plantations with hired labour as well as in owner-operated smallholdings. About 1.7m. ha (26%) of the nation's total land area is under cultivation. Of this amount, about 770,000 ha (46% of cultivated land) are under tea, rubber, and coconut, the three principal export crops, and the remainder under food crops (chiefly rice). Smallholders produce the bulk of the coconut crop, 60% of the tea output and a significant proportion of the rubber. Over the past three decades the small-scale farming sector growing food crops have got increasingly commercialized.

Export Crops

All three principal export crops are grown largely in the south-west quadrant (wet zone) of the island, which receives a well-distributed and reliable rainfall of over 1,900 mm per year. Tea is grown in elevations ranging from a few hundred meters above sea-level to above 2,000 m, although teas with the best flavours are usually found at elevations above 1,200 m. Rubber is grown mostly on slopes below 600 m. from sea-level, and coconut is concentrated on the western and southern lowlands. In addition to these three staples, Sri Lanka also cultivates a number of minor export crops such as cocoa, pepper, cloves, nutmeg, cardamom, cinnamon and citronella. In 2001 about 180,000 ha were cultivated with tea and 157,000 ha with rubber. Around 430,000 ha were under coconut in 2001. The minor export crops together accounted for a further 75,000 ha.

In 1972 and 1975, under the land reform, a large proportion of the estates owned by foreign and local private individuals and all estates owned by public companies were nationalized with compensation. The Government became the owner of about 60% of the tea land, 30% of the rubber, and 10% of the coconut. However, the state-owned companies that managed the plantations faced chronic losses in their operations. Thus, in 1992 the Government handed over the management of state-owned plantations to private companies for a five-year period. In 1995 a program was initiated to extend these leases for a further 50 years with the companies purchasing 51% of the shares. This, in effect, reversed the 1972 Land Reform Act and moved the plantations back into private ownership. By the end of 2001 all but three of the 20 plantation companies were in private hands.

There is also continuing fragmentation of some of the larger estates into smaller units, caused partly by the pressure of population on land, partly by the division of large estates into smaller units when selling, and partly by a government policy of land redistribution. As a result, more than 60% of the tea crop is now produced by 'smallholders' who cultivate units smaller than 8 ha. In the case of rubber, smallholders account for about one-third of the total output.

State-aided schemes have been in operation since the 1950s to replant tea and rubber land with high-yielding varieties. This effort has been more successful in rubber, where, by the end of 1989, the total area had been replanted. In 1990 the programme completed its first 20-year cycle and entered the second. In tea the proportion was only 37% at the end of 2001. Under a state-sponsored crop diversification programme, an effort is also being made to put uneconomical tea and rubber lands to more profitable agricultural uses. In the case of coconut, some of the land in the more urban areas (especially in the western province) is being lost to urban construction.

Food Crops

According to the 2001 census, only an estimated 15% of Sri Lanka's population lived in urban areas and about 8% lived in rural areas (including estates). The former figure is probably a substantial underestimate, considering that the urban population at the 1981 census was an estimated 21.5%. The decline in the intervening period was caused by a change in classification of a large number of 'town council' areas, from urban in 1981 to rural in 2001. If this adjustment and urban growth between 1981 and 2001 were taken into account, a well-informed estimate of the urban population would be about 30%. That would still render Sri Lanka a predominantly rural country, where agriculture plays an important role in the economy.

Paddy rice, which is the staple food in Sri Lanka, is the pre-eminent crop in peasant agriculture, having about 878,000 ha—a little more than 50% of all cultivated land—under asweddumized conditions, spread throughout the island. However, when adequate irrigation is available, the dry zone (i.e. the drier parts of the country outside the south-west quadrant) is considered to be better suited to paddy.

Only about 25% of Sri Lanka's paddy land consists of units of two ha or more. About one-third consists of units of one ha or under. Thus, the 1972 Land Reform Act, which fixed a 'ceiling' of 10.1 ha on paddy holdings per family, left paddy ownership practically untouched. However, the small size of the typical paddy unit reflects the severe pressure on existing land, especially in the densely populated wet zone in the south-west of the country. The settlement of farming families on undeveloped state-owned land in the dry zone (land colonization) has been the Government's answer to this problem. This programme, which began in the late 1920s, received a major boost under the massive Accelerated Mahaweli Diversion Programme (AMDP). By the end of 2001 about 90,000 ha of new land had been brought under cultivation with the help of new irrigation facilities under this programme. In addition, a further 84,000 ha of land already under cultivation were provided with additional water from the AMDP. The programme has been the single largest development project ever undertaken in Sri Lanka. In addition to the agricultural sector, two other main benefits of the AMDP have been hydroelectric power (HEP) generation and flood control. The total investment made in the project between 1969 and 2001 exceeded US $1,500m.

Since the early 1950s, paddy cultivation has shown one of the most impressive growth records in the Sri Lankan economy. The annual output of paddy rice increased more than six-fold from about 450,000 metric tons in the early 1950s to a record 2.9m. tons in 2000. This was the result of both an expansion in area under cultivation and a rise in land productivity under the impact of the 'Green Revolution'. This brought Sri Lanka to the verge of self-sufficiency in the country's staple food. Helped by two bumper crops in 1999 and 2000, rice imports were reduced to an inconsequential level in the latter year. In 2001 rice production declined by 6%, mainly owing to drought. Consequently, there was a small increase in rice imports.

MINERAL AND POWER RESOURCES

No comprehensive assessment has been made of Sri Lanka's mineral resources. However, the country has a variety of economically useful minerals such as gem stones, graphite, ilmenite, limestone, quartz, mica, industrial clays, salt, titanium, monazite and zircon. There are no known deposits of coal or petroleum.

A few local industries, such as ceramics, cement, glass, salt and bricks, are based on extraction of minerals. Graphite, gemstones and ilmenite are the only three minerals that are extracted in commercially significant quantities for export. In 2001 Sri Lanka exported graphite valued at Rs 225m. (less than 0.5% of the total value of visible exports). Sri Lanka is one of the world's leading suppliers of gemstone. The rapid expansion of the international market for precious and semi-precious stones from the early 1970s has boosted Sri Lankan gem exports. However, during the 1970s, when foreign exchange was strictly controlled, it was suspected that that a significant proportion of the gemstones were smuggled out of the country. The liberalization of foreign exchange after 1977 reduced the incentive to smuggle gemstones. The Government has also attempted to tighten the law and to provide tax incentives to channel the trade to more legitimate avenues. Although no production figures are available, State Gem Corporation data indicate that the value of exports of precious and semi-precious stones rose from only US $1.5m. in 1972 to US $82m. in 2001. Jewellery exports earned an additional US $18m. in 2001. The USA, Europe, Japan and Thailand provide the principal markets for Sri Lankan gems. Sri Lanka is also developing a diamond cutting and polishing industry. The diamond market was adversely affected by the Asian economic crisis. However, exports recovered after 1998 to reach US $166m. in 2001.

In 1999 Sri Lanka's total commercial energy consumption per head in terms of kg of oil equivalent, was 406 kg. This was equivalent to only about 11% of average consumption in high-income countries. An estimated 47% of energy requirements in the country are met by 'non-commercial' biomass sources such as fuel wood and agricultural residues. Petroleum, which is the principal source of commercial energy, accounts for about 30% of total energy consumption and hydroelectricity accounts for about 23%. At the end of 2001 Sri Lanka's installed capacity for electricity generation was 1,901 MW (1,161 MW HEP, 737 MW thermal power and 3 MW wind power). The AMDP has made a major contribution to the country's HEP capacity; about one-half of total electricity generated comes from AMDP sources. Private investors in the electricity generation industry accounted for about 10% of installed capacity; their share was set to grow.

MANUFACTURING INDUSTRY

In 1958 Sri Lanka's manufacturing sector (including cottage industries) accounted for barely 6% of GDP. In the 1960s, with the help of a protected market, it grew by some 6% per year and by the end of the decade contributed about 10% of GDP. By the late 1980s the proportion had risen to about 16%, and it has remained around that level through the 1990s.

The output of producer goods is less important than the production of consumer goods in Sri Lanka's manufacturing industry. Until the end of the 1980s almost all the large-scale manufacturing units were run by state industrial corporations, of which there were 26 at the end of 1989. In 1990 the situation began to change following the launching of an ambitious privatization programme. Between 1990 and 2001 35 state-owned industrial enterprises and two state-owned graphite mines were privatized. Since then the Government has renationalized four companies that were not successful under private ownership. The Government has found it difficult to find buyers at the prices it expects for the remaining 10 industrial ventures that it wants to privatize. Some are not very profitable ventures; moreover, there have been fewer prospective buyers from East Asia since the economic crisis of 1997–98.

The 1960s and 1970s can be characterized as the first phase of Sri Lanka's industrialization, which was driven by an import substitution strategy dominated by the state sector. In the 1980s and 1990s the country entered a second phase, with the private sector playing an increasingly dominant role, aided by the liberal economic policies of the Government and the programme of privatization. Traditionally, the private sector covered a wide range of light consumer goods industries and a small number of producer goods industries such as machine tools and building materials. Now, having taken over state-owned factories, it is also in industries such as steel, fertilizers, tyres, gas, hardware and cement.

The Board of Investment of Sri Lanka (BOISL), which was established in 1978 under the name of the Greater Colombo Economic Commission, acts as a 'one stop' centre for approval of industries throughout the country. Its task is to promote investment, especially foreign private investment, in export-orientated industry in Investment Promotion Zones (IPZs) and elsewhere. The BOISL has statutory powers to grant a wide range of concessions to investors, including tax 'holidays' of seven to 10 years. Foreign investors are encouraged to invest under 'Build, Operate and Own' (BOO) or 'Build, Operate and Transfer' (BOT) arrangements. By the end of 2001, 1,561 firms, with 386,034 employees, were in commercial production under BOISL sponsorship. The Government is also providing special incentives to private investors to start industries outside the Colombo metropolitan area where most of the country's manufacturing activity currently takes place.

FOREIGN TRADE AND BALANCE OF PAYMENTS

In 2001 the USA was the largest purchaser of Sri Lanka's exports, accounting for about 38.9% of the total value, followed by the United Kingdom (10.8%), Germany (4.4%), Japan (4.0%), and France (2.8%). Traditionally, exports to India and other South Asian countries have been limited. However, in recent years, partly aided by a free trade agreement, the volume and value of exports to this region have risen. In 2001 Sri Lankan exports to South Asia accounted for 3.4% of the total, with India as the largest purchaser, followed by the Maldives. During the 1990s imports from India to Sri Lanka rose steadily. In 2001 India contributed 9.9% of Sri Lanka's total imports. The market share of some of Sri Lanka's traditional suppliers, such as Japan (4.8%) and the United Kingdom (3.5%) has declined in recent years. In contrast, the newly industrializing South-East and

East Asian countries, notably Taiwan, the Republic of Korea, Singapore, Hong Kong, Malaysia and the People's Republic of China, have become important suppliers of goods to Sri Lanka (collectively accounting for more than 43% of the imports). The USA supplied only 3.2% of Sri Lanka's imports in 2001, thus creating a substantial trade balance in favour of the latter.

Balance of Payments

Sri Lanka has suffered from a chronic deficit in the balance of trade and of payments since the late 1950s. The combined impact of import liberalization coupled with increased economic activity, periodic adverse movements in the terms of trade, and either stagnant or fluctuating output in the three major commodity exports worsened this situation after 1977.

Textiles and clothing exports account for about one-half of gross merchandise export earnings. According to the Asian Development Bank (ADB), in 2001 the gross value of industrial exports decreased by 13%, compared with an increase of 20% in the previous year. In 2001 Sri Lanka's total merchandise export earnings also contracted by US $705m., or 13%. In 2001 the merchandise import bill decreased by US $1,345m., compared with the previous year. The trade deficit decreased from US $1,798m. in 2000 to US $1,158m. in 2001 (7.4% of GDP). In 2001 the services account recorded a surplus of US $108m. Receipts from services amounted to US $1,267m., with tourism contributing US $213m. (a decline of 15%, compared with tourism receipts in the preceding year). Interest payments on the foreign debt, which has been growing in recent years, totalled US $109m. in 2001. The goods and services account produced a deficit of US $1,330m. which was US $734m. less than the deficit in 2000. Substantial net private transfers (totalling US $938m.) with about two-thirds of this figure coming from remittances of more than 300,000 Sri Lankan workers in West Asia, helped to meet part of this deficit. The overall deficit in the current-account balance decreased to US $370m. in 2001 from US $1,066m. in the preceding year.

Since 1977 Sri Lanka has been receiving substantial sums in foreign aid, mainly from Western sources. In 2001 US $62m. was received as grants. The Government also borrowed, on concessional terms, a further US $217m. from donors, which was primarily used to repay debt. The ethnic disturbances after 1983 and political disturbances in the south in the late 1980s adversely affected private foreign direct investment (FDI), which increased substantially following the introduction of economic liberalization policies in 1977. Between 1991 and 1993, however, FDI recovered steadily. Foreign portfolio investment also increased substantially during this period, encouraged by the opening of the Colombo stock market to foreign investors. In 1995, following the change of government, FDI declined sharply to US $16m., compared with US $187m. in 1993 and US $158m. in 1994. The trend was reversed in 1996, but annual growth since then has been nominal. In 2001 total FDI was US $82m.; an additional US $90m. was earned through privatization. Foreign portfolio investment, which reached a peak of US $67m. in 1993, has been negative in recent years. In 2001 it registered a negative US $11m., which partly reflected the uncertainty in the Asian investment climate owing to the East Asian economic crisis, but, more importantly, highlighted the lack of investor confidence in the Colombo market. After three years of decline, the country's external reserves increased in 2001 from US $2,131m. to US $2,238m. By the end of 2001 they were equal to about 3.8 months of visible imports for that year. Between January and December 2001 the rupee depreciated against the US dollar (11.3%), pound sterling (8.8%), French franc (by 6.7%), German Mark (by 6.7%), and the Indian rupee (2.4%). The Sri Lankan rupee appreciated marginally against the Japanese yen (by 1.5%) . The Central Bank of Sri Lanka's decision at the beginning of 2001 to allow the Sri Lankan rupee to 'float' independently in the currency market was the main reason for the depreciation of its value.

FINANCE

Banking and Investment Finance

The Central Bank of Sri Lanka, the sole bank of issue, also acts as a financial adviser to the Government and administers monetary policy. Over the last five decades it has played an increasingly important role in helping to develop credit facilities for special groups such as peasant farmers, small businesses and the self-employed, who normally do not enjoy access to established lending institutions. It has also created special credit schemes for industrialists and exporters.

In 2001 one new domestic commercial bank opened in Sri Lanka, making a total of 11 domestic banks. In the same year the total number of foreign banks operating branch offices in the country decreased from 16 to 14. At the end of 2001 the foreign banks had a total of 46 bank offices, with few, if any, outside Colombo. In contrast, the domestic banks had a branch network of 1,082 offices. The system is dominated by the two state-owned banks, the Bank of Ceylon and the People's Bank, which together accounted for the vast majority of the branch offices and for more than 60% of total bank deposits. By the end of 2001 there was a commercial bank office for every 16,700 of Sri Lanka's inhabitants. Until 1984 the trend was for the bank branch network to increase rapidly. In the second half of the 1980s banks, and the two state banks in particular, slowed down the expansion of the branch office network partly in order to rationalize and consolidate existing operations. In the 1990s expansion resumed but at a more measured pace; between 1999 and 2001 the number of branch offices rose by 73 (6.9%).

Over the past two decades Sri Lanka's financial system has undergone considerable change. The private banks and allied institutions play a larger role than ever in the provision of credit and collection of private savings. For example, private finance companies that play a key role in the financing of consumer durables and transportation equipment are a significant presence in the market. The Government and the central bank have encouraged several innovative steps including the establishment of an offshore banking facility, merchant banking, leasing companies, and venture capital suppliers. The state-owned provident funds have been permitted to invest in the share market. The Central Bank has also made a bid to develop a secondary market for government bills and bonds. In addition, the Colombo stock market has been liberalized, permitting foreign investors to invest. At the same time, the regulatory framework governing market activity has been strengthened.

Public Finance

In 2001 total central government expenditure (including net lending) amounted to an estimated Rs 383,686m. and total revenue to Rs 231,463m. (27.4% and 16.5% of GDP, respectively). About 13% of the budget deficit of Rs 152,223m. was financed with foreign grants and loans and 82% with local loans. The remaining 5% (Rs 8,589m.) was derived from privatization proceeds, which amounted to only about one-third of the total anticipated by the Government at the beginning of the fiscal year.

The principal sources of government tax revenue in Sri Lanka in 2001 were sales and excise taxes, national security levy, import duties, corporate taxes, personal income taxes and stamp duties (in that order). Export duties, which in the past were a major source of revenue, were totally abolished in 1998. Although national income rose faster after 1977 than at anytime before, the growth of tax revenue has not been buoyant; the ratio of tax revenue to GDP in the late 1990s stood at 15% of GDP, and in 2001 was only 14.6%.

ECONOMIC DEVELOPMENT

Performance

In broad terms, the period between 1948 and 1977 was one of missed economic opportunities compounded by generally poor economic policy. The country failed to diversify its economy by utilizing the substantial foreign exchange reserves that it had accumulated during the Second World War (1939–45). It also neglected to exploit the steady and rapid-post war growth of world markets and world trade. Instead, Sri Lanka continued to rely heavily on its three traditional export crops and attempted to build an industrial sector that largely catered to a small domestic market protected by high tariffs and quantitative import restrictions. The 'socialist' economic ideology that guided this programme demanded extensive nationalization and state control. It stifled entrepreneurship, discouraged foreign investment, and created a set of mainly inefficient and loss-making state enterprises. Economic growth at best was sluggish and the rate of unemployment had reached a crisis level of 25% by 1977. The economy itself reached a crisis point by the mid-1970s. It could no longer fiscally support the social welfare system that had produced commendable results in human development.

The post-1977 export-orientated and liberal economic strategy has led to a higher level of economic activity and a more diversified and dynamic economy. Between the late 1970s and the mid-1980s total investment expenditure more than doubled in real terms. Rough estimates suggest that, during the same period, about 1.7m. new jobs were created, making a substantial impact on the level of unemployment, which fell from 25% of the labour force to 15%. The agricultural sector registered an annual overall real growth rate of 3% during the period 1978–86, and output of paddy rice alone increased by 55% between 1977 and 1986.

Economic growth decelerated in the second half of the 1980s, partly owing to the uncertain economic climate created by the widespread political unrest and the ethnic civil war. Economic growth accelerated after 1990 when political stability was restored in the southern part of the country. For example, manufacturing output doubled in real terms from Rs 69,000m. in 1990 to Rs 149,000m. in 2000. During the same period industrial exports increased from US $1,031m. to US $4,302m. The economic structure had undergone two important structural transformations during the last two decades. Firstly, the share of the labour force in agriculture decreased from about 45% in the early 1980s to about 33% in 2000. Secondly, in exports, in 1980, the three primary exports—tea, rubber and coconut products—accounted for about 60% of exports and about 33% of industrial products. In 2000 the shares were 17% and 78%, respectively.

The balance of payments registered an overall surplus every year from 1990 to 1998 with the exception of 1996. However, deficits of US $263m. and US $522m. were recorded in 1999 and 2000, respectively, according to the ADB. These deficits that were mainly owing to high import bills, were caused partly by the higher oil prices, and partly by a substantial rise in imports of military supplies. A decline in earnings from tourism in 2000 also contributed to the widening of the deficit. The rising deficit caused a significant reduction in the nation's external reserves, which caused the Central Bank to review its policy on the exchange rate. From 1977 Sri Lanka has had a managed floating rate with a crawling peg that required the Central Bank to quote a price for the US dollar, the principal currency to which the rupee was pegged. In January 2001 this system was replaced with an independent floating system that allowed the market to determine the rate. This led to a sharp depreciation of the rupee by about 29%, from Rs 75 to one US dollar in January 2001 to Rs 97 in September 2002. The new rate reflected market conditions and also improved the competitiveness of Sri Lankan exports. It also released the Central Bank from having to maintain relatively high interest rates to defend the rupee. Consequently, since January 2001 there has been a decline in market interest rates, which has made credit somewhat cheaper. In comparative terms, in the past two decades Sri Lanka has generally maintained a relatively low level of inflation with annual increases in consumer prices varying between 10% and 15% and rarely exceeding 20%. In 1997–2000 the annual inflation rate was no higher than 9%. It is likely that the consumer price index understates the true rate of inflation; however, the index is acceptable as an indicator of general direction of change and its rough order of magnitude. This reasonable degree of price stability has been a bright spot in an otherwise discouraging economic picture. However, even this achievement was threatened by the downturn of the economy in 2001.

In poverty alleviation and equity, Sri Lanka's record is mixed. The percentage living below the poverty line is estimated to be between 25% and 40% of the population, numbers believed to be no worse than figures for other South Asian countries. The lower income groups in Sri Lanka receive some state assistance by way of food stamps and poverty-alleviation grants. However, the distribution of income in the country is only marginally more equitable than that of its South Asian neighbours. In 1996/97 the Gini Index was estimated to be 0.43, the lowest quintile received 5.5% of the income and the highest 50.2%. It is estimated that at least one-third, if not more, of children under five suffer from malnutrition. Sri Lanka's total fertility rate has declined from 3.5 live births per 1,000 women of child-bearing age in 1980 to 2.1 per 1,000 in 2000, one of the lowest rates in the developing world. In terms of gender equity, Sri Lanka performs quite well in international comparative terms. For example, according to the UNDP, in 2000 Sri Lanka ranked 70th in its Gender-related Development Index whereas it occupies a position four places below that in the overall Human Development Index ranking for 173 countries. The unemployment estimates reveal that the female unemployment rate, which stood at around 20% in the early 1990s, decreased to about 11% in 2000. During the same period the male unemployment rate declined from about 10% to 6.5%.

The environmental sustainability of Sri Lanka's development effort is becoming an increasingly important theme in public discourse. Between 1980 and 1990 about 300 sq km of land was annually deforested. Encouragingly, this average annual rate of deforestation fell to about 200 sq km during 1990–95. The total forest cover is estimated have fallen from over 40% in the late 1940s to about 20% in 2000. Industrial pollution, urban solid waste disposal, and damage to the sea coast caused by construction are some of the other key environmental problems confronting the country.

Problems, Challenges and Prospects

The year 2001 was a decisive turning point in Sri Lanka's post-independence economy. Real GDP declined by 1.4% for the first time since 1948. The two most important sectors of the economy, agriculture and manufacturing, deteriorated by almost equal measures, contracting by 3.7% and 4.0%, respectively. The value of exports in US dollars decreased by 12.8%, while the value of imports diminished by 18.4%. Furthermore, investment as a proportion of GDP declined from 28% in 2000 to 22% in 2001, affecting privately-owned as well as state enterprises. Domestic savings also decreased, from 17.4% to 15.3%. The country was experiencing an economic recession of significant magnitude, worsened by the high inflation rate of about 11%.

The reasons for the recession were both external and internal. The global economic slowdown was a major external factor. According to the IMF, the growth rate of the industrial economies declined from 3.9% in 2000 to 1.2% in 2001. As a result, the demand for exports by this group of countries that usually provide the main markets for Sri Lanka's products, contracted by 1.5% in 2001, compared with an 11.6% increase in 2000. These events had severe repercussions on the Sri Lankan economy as reflected, for example, in the negative growth of the country's exports.

Internal factors, several of which were created by the Government, added to the economic difficulties. Whether the LTTE attack on Colombo airport in July 2001 was preventable was open to debate; nevertheless, its occurrence had devastating consequences on the economy. The effect on the tourist industry was damaging and was later compounded by the fear of travelling, precipitated by the terrorist attacks on New York and Washington, DC, USA on 11 September 2001. In the first half of 2001 tourist arrivals increased by 10.5%, compared with the corresponding period of the preceding year. In the second half of 2001, however, visitor arrivals declined sharply; by the end of the year the total number of tourist arrivals (336,794) had decreased by 19%, compared with the previous year.

The extended period of drought, caused by the failure of three successive monsoons beginning in mid-2000, had a major impact on agriculture and HEP generation. In 2001 production of all four major agricultural products—tea, rubber, coconut, and rice—declined by amounts ranging from 1.8% (rubber) to 9.7% (coconut), compared with the previous year. HEP generation decreased by 3%, and overall power generation declined by a similar percentage. The Government was forced to ration power supplies by one hour per day from July 2001; this period was gradually increased to eight hours in September. The rationing was suspended during the December 2001 general election, and reimposed after the polls until mid-2002. The reduction in power supply had a serious negative impact on industry.

Political uncertainty that prevailed throughout 2001, culminating in a general election in December (the second within 15 months), served to weaken further investor confidence. Political instability, LTTE attacks, power-rationing and a war that the Government appeared unable to win, led to a decline in investment. FDI in Board of Investment (BOI) projects declined from US $1,906m. in 2000 to US $106m. in 2001. BOI local private investment also decreased, from US $51m. to US $43m. Thus, a decline of as much as 21% in the rate of investment was to be expected.

In principle, the recession should have had an impact on employment, consumption level, and welfare. Data on unemployment and real wages are incomplete and must be interpreted with caution. The total number of unemployed in the fourth quarter of 2000 was estimated to be 497,000. This increased by 2% in the first three quarters of 2001 to reach 528,000. The rate of unemployment grew from 7.4% to 7.8% in that period. Real wages were compressed during the year. The rate of real wages of workers whose pay rates are fixed by official wages boards declined by an average of 8.2%. However, the Government increased its spending on social welfare from Rs 83,000m. in 2000 to Rs 103,000m. in 2001. Adjusted for inflation this represents a rise of 11%. The general election of December 2001 was one factor that motivated the PA Government to maintain welfare spending while it was in power.

Aside from the recession, evidence was emerging that Sri Lanka's recent development has produced sharp regional differences within the country. The western province, and in particular Colombo and Gampaha Districts, is the most urbanized of the country's nine provinces and houses almost one-third of the nation's population; however, it has a significantly higher annual average personal income level and a significantly lower consumption poverty level than the rest of the country. It is possible that the north, which suffers the most from the war, is the least urbanized and hinders the development of the country as a whole. One of the challenges of development would be to address this structural imbalance. The Government, which appeared to be aware of this issue, had established five regional ministries of development to provide a stronger regional orientation to its development programme. It also wished to create regional boards of investment. However, these institutional structures will be effective only once financial and other resources, that were in short supply in mid-2002, are made available.

The economic crisis was not entirely caused by external factors and short-term difficulties, such as drought. The economic situation had been deteriorating for some time. There were several policy failures and acts of political inexpediency, inefficiency and mismanagement together with structural factors that significantly contributed to the crisis. Often these worked in combination with one another. The power crisis was one example. The country's demand for power had grown at an annual rate of about 10%, but the actual capacity growth since 1993 had reached about 3%, despite warnings from power engineers to the decision-makers about the impending crisis. The situation was exacerbated by mismanagement of the state power company, which accumulated a massive debt, financed largely by the state banks, and was accused of corruption.

The single most important factor that contributed to the 2001 economic crisis was probably the civil war of the previous two decades. There are various estimates on the total economic cost of the war over that period. The specific numbers are debatable, but it is accepted by all that the loss amounted to thousands of millions of US dollars. The economy in the north contracted during the war. Between 1990 and 1995 the annual output of the northern province declined from US $350m. to US $250m., resulting in a negative growth rate of 6.2% per annum. The decline might have decelerated or ceased after the Government captured the Jaffna peninsula from the LTTE in 1995; however, there was almost certainly no appreciable economic growth in that region until the end of 2001.

The war diverted a growing amount of funds in the government budget from development and social welfare to the military. In 1982, just before the conflict intensified, the Government spent US $54m. (3.1% of the budget) on the security forces. In 1990 the amount was US $364m. (12.5%), in 2000 it had risen to US $1,018m. (17%). This increase in expenditure on the military was the single main reason for the Government's fiscal difficulties.

In the five-year period 1997–2001 the overall budget deficit as a percentage of GDP never declined below 7.5%. This trend was considered unsustainable and a serious constraint on investment in the private sector, owing to the drain on budgetary resources and its 'crowding out' effect. In 2001 the original budget projected a deficit of 8.5% but the actual figure was 10.9%. In the latter months of 2001 the Government, entirely motivated by narrow partisan political considerations in the months preceding the general election, aggravated the fiscal problem by instituting some hasty spending measures, such as substantial salary increases for public-sector employees.

Donor assistance has been an important source of funding required to cover the budget deficit. In 1980–2001 annual average donor assistance to Sri Lanka amounted to slightly less than US $400m.; the record US $700m. was received in 1991 and the lowest, US $201m., was donated in 2000. In the 1980s donors generally did not question the use of their assistance and helped finance about one-half of the budget deficit. However, from the late 1980s some donors appeared less keen to fund a Government that seemed to be engaged in a war it could not win. From 1998 assistance to Sri Lanka decreased dramatically. The reduction was such that from 1996 the net inflow of assistance to the country was negative. However, the war was not the only reason for this change. The reduction in global donor resources, the diversion of more assistance to sub-Saharan Africa and the former USSR, as well as Sri Lanka's progress from a low-income country to a lower-middle-income country, contributed to this change in donor attitude towards the country.

Sri Lanka also failed to utilize fully the assistance that it received. Between 1996 and 1999, for example, only about 30% of the grants were used. In 2000 only 20% were utilized. Equally, an average 15% of loans in 1996–2000 were used. A variety of reasons, including the lack of counterpart local funds, limited capacity for implementation of projects, and the Government being distracted by the war and local political power struggles, contributed to this situation.

Given the economic crisis that paralysed Sri Lanka, it was hoped in mid- to late 2002 that the peace negotiations between government and LTTE representatives in Thailand would generate a permanent solution to the civil strife. Indeed, the two sides agreed to hold three more rounds of negotiations, following the success of the first set of talks in September. Peace alone would ensure that Sri Lanka would be able to rebuild its economy and realize its full potential. However, even if a permanent truce is achieved, the economic challenges that confront the country are formidable. About 800,000 internally displaced persons require resettling, for example, the cost of which is estimated to be at least US $100m. The resettling of another approximately 70,000 Sri Lankan refugees residing in India would require more funds. An unknown number of refugees from western countries might also return.

The physical infrastructure in the north was almost derelict after two decades of conflict. Some towns were completely destroyed by the war and exist only in name. The south was also drained of resources that would otherwise have been invested in infrastructure. The road network that connects the main towns and the state-owned railway system were in serious need of capital. The Government estimated that it required a minimum of US $500m. to fund some of these immediate needs.

The international community declared its willingness to assist Sri Lanka to rebuild its economy. In early September 2002 the IMF released US $65m. under a stand-by agreement. The United Kingdom pledged new funds for rehabilitation, and the Dutch and Japanese Governments as well as the World Bank also promised to help. However, there were two prerequisites to this assistance: a serious commitment from the Government to a comprehensive restructuring programme for the economy and a permanent peace arrangement between the Government and the LTTE.

With regard to the first condition, the Government is committed to restructuring some principal state-owned enterprises, including the two banks, Sri Lanka Insurance, Ceylon Petroleum Corporation, and the state power company. However, the opposition voiced some objections to these proposals, and most of the employees of these enterprises opposed privatization. In regard to the second issue, there was no guarantee that the rounds of negotiations would result in a permanent peace. Similar efforts in the past that commenced with the considerable goodwill and hope witnessed in Thailand, failed. However, there was some evidence at the negotiations in September 2002 to suggest that both local and international conditions were more favourable on this occasion than in the past to generate a successful outcome. In particular, the US-led campaign against terrorism has made it more difficult for the LTTE to resume violence.

The political structure that would be established in the north-east would have a crucial bearing on the economic progress of that region. The Government, it appeared, had agreed to allow the LTTE to establish an interim administration. The latter was already engaged in establishing a so-called basic institutional structure for its regime. This included banks and a taxation authority that levies a variety of taxes from businesses and residents in LTTE-controlled areas. These would have to be regularized under an interim administration.

The provision of foreign aid to the north-east is one of the more sensitive issues that will need to be resolved. The direct transfer of financial assistance to the north-east would be construed as a violation of the sovereignty of Sri Lanka, and a significant step towards the *de facto* establishment of a separate Tamil state ('Eelam'). However, the LTTE insists on playing a major role in deciding how aid for the north-east should be allocated. A likely solution would be the establishment of a mechanism in Colombo to which the LTTE would contribute and through which the funds would be distributed.

In its country report on Sri Lanka released in September 2002, the IMF forecast a GDP growth rate of 3.5% to 4.0% for 2002. In the first quarter of the year growth was only 0.1%. Although that did not augur well, the revival of the economy in the north, the end to reductions in power supply and the momentum that the economy had shown since April, might precipitate improved growth rates. There were indications that business confidence was slowly returning. The all-share price index of the Colombo stock exchange that registered 621 at the end of 2001 had risen to over 800 (a gain of 29%) by mid-September 2002. Nevertheless, these incipient gains will be consolidated only if peace returns to this troubled island.

Statistical Survey

Source (unless otherwise stated): Department of Census and Statistics, 15/12 Maitland Crescent, POB 563, Colombo 7; tel. (1) 682176; fax (1) 697594; e-mail dcensus@lanka.ccom.lk; internet www.statistics.gov.lk

Area and Population

AREA, POPULATION AND DENSITY

Area (sq km)	65,525*
Population (census results)	
17 March 1981	14,846,750
17 July 2001 (provisional)†	
Males	8,343,964
Females	8,520,580
Total	16,864,544
Population (official estimates at mid-year)‡	
1998	18,774,000
1999	19,043,000
2000	19,359,000
Density (per sq km) at July 2001	286§

* 25,299 sq miles. This figure includes inland water (3,189 sq km).

† Figures refer to 18 out of 25 districts where enumeration was carried out completely. Enumeration was only partially conducted in Mannar, Vavuniya, Batticaloa and Trincomalee districts, owing to security concerns; data from these districts brought the total enumerated population to approximately 17,560,000. The census was not conducted in the districts of Jaffna, Mullaitivu and Kilinochchi, also owing to security concerns. The total estimated population for the entire country at July 2001 was 18,732,255.

‡ Not adjusted to take account of the July 2001 census results.

§ Including adjustment for underenumeration.

ETHNIC GROUPS (census results)

	1981	2001*†
Sinhalese	10,979,561	13,810,664
Sri Lankan Tamil	1,886,872	736,484
Indian Tamil	818,656	855,888
Sri Lankan Moors	1,046,926	1,349,845
Others	114,735	111,663
Total	14,846,750	16,864,544

* Provisional.

† Figures refer to 18 out of 25 districts.

DISTRICTS (population at 2001 census)

	Area (sq km, excl. inland water)*	Population (provisional)	Density (persons per sq km)
Colombo	676	2,234,289	3,305
Gampaha	1,341	2,066,096	1,541
Kalutara	1,576	1,060,800	673
Kandy	1,917	1,272,463	664
Matale	1,952	442,427	227
Nuwara Eliya	1,706	700,083	410
Galle	1,617	990,539	613
Matara	1,270	761,236	599
Hambantota	2,496	525,370	210
Jaffna†	929	490,621	528
Mannar†	1,880	115,577	81
Vavuniya†	1,861	149,835	80
Mullaitivu†	2,415	121,667	49
Kilinochchi†	1,205	127,263	106
Batticaloa†	2,610	486,447	186
Ampara	4,222	589,344	140
Trincomalee†	2,529	340,158	351
Kurunegala	4,624	1,452,369	314
Puttalam	2,882	705,342	245
Anuradhapura	6,664	746,466	112
Polonnaruwa	3,077	359,197	117
Badulla	2,827	774,555	274
Monaragala	5,508	396,173	72
Ratnapura	3,236	1,008,164	312
Kegalle	1,685	779,774	463
Total	62,705	18,732,255	299

* Revised total land area is 62,336 sq km.

† Official estimates where census was not conducted or only partially conducted.

PRINCIPAL TOWNS
(provisional, population at 2001 census)

Colombo (capital)	642,163	Jaffna	145,600*
Dehiwala-Mount Lavinia	209,787	Kotte	115,826
Moratuwa	177,190	Kandy	110,049
		Galle	90,934

* Estimated population at mid-1997 (Source: Provincial Councils, Department of Elections).

BIRTHS, MARRIAGES AND DEATHS*

	Registered live births		Registered marriages		Registered deaths	
	Number	Rate (per 1,000)	Number	Rate (per 1,000)	Number	Rate (per 1,000)
1992	356,842	20.5	155,345	8.9	98,380	5.6
1993	350,707	19.9	152,423	8.6	96,179	5.5
1994	356,071	19.9	162,489	9.1	100,394	5.6
1995	343,224	18.9	169,220	9.3	104,707	5.8
1996	340,649	18.6	170,444	9.3	122,161	6.7
1997	332,626	17.9	n.a.	n.a.	113,078	6.1
1998†	329,148	17.5	169,209	9.0	112,657	6.0
1999†	329,121	17.3	n.a.	n.a.	114,392	6.0

* Data are tabulated by year of registration, rather than by year of occurrence.

† Provisional.

Source: partly UN, *Demographic Yearbook* and *Population and Vital Statistics Report*.

Expectation of life (WHO estimates, years at birth, 2000): Males 67.6; Females 77.8 (Source: WHO, *World Health Report*).

ECONOMICALLY ACTIVE POPULATION*

('000 persons aged 10 years and over, January–March of each year)

	1998	1999	2000
Agriculture, hunting, forestry and fishing	2,472.2	2,536.3	2,290.0
Mining and quarrying	78.2	68.7	77.8
Manufacturing	914.7	843.3	1,013.2
Electricity, gas and water	35.3	31.7	25.0
Construction	309.3	279.1	320.6
Trade, restaurants and hotels	593.7	577.8	767.7
Transport, storage and communications	268.0	333.2	278.1
Financing, insurance, real estate and business services	117.1	87.8	122.6
Community, social and personal services	1,006.7	1,110.6	1,153.7
Activities not adequately defined	150.4	290.0	258.5
Total employed	5,946.1	6,159.0	6,307.7
Unemployed	701.0	580.0	546.1
Total labour force	6,647.2	6,739.1	6,853.8

2001 ('000 persons aged 10 years and over, January–March): Total employed 6,212.4; Unemployed 518.3; Total labour force 6,730.7.

2002 ('000 persons aged 10 years and over, January–March): Total employed 6,662.8; Unemployed 632.8; Total labour force 7,295.6.

* Excluding northern and eastern provinces.

Health and Welfare

KEY INDICATORS

Fertility (births per woman, 2000)	2.1
Under-5 mortality rate (per 1,000 live births, 2000)	19
HIV/AIDS (% of persons aged 15–49, 2001)	<0.10
Physicians (per 1,000 head, 1999)	0.37
Hospital beds (per 1,000 head, 1990)	2.74
Health expenditure (1998): US $ per head (PPP)	99
% of GDP	3.4
public (% of total)	51.3
Access to water (% of persons, 2000)	83
Access to sanitation (% of persons, 2000)	83
Human Development Index (2000): ranking	89
value	0.741

For sources and definitions, see explanatory note on p. vi.

Agriculture

PRINCIPAL CROPS ('000 metric tons)

	1998	1999	2000
Rice (paddy)	2,692	2,868	2,859
Maize	34	31	31
Potatoes	26	27	48
Sweet potatoes	52	52	52
Cassava (Manioc)	257	252	249
Sugar cane	946	1,021	1,066
Dry beans	16	14	14*
Dry cow-peas	13	12	12*
Cashew nuts*	15	15	15
Coconuts	1,916	2,149	2,353
Copra	70	64	64*
Cabbages	47	52	53
Tomatoes	36	40	44
Pumpkin, squash and gourds*	170	170	170
Cucumbers and gherkins*	28	28	28
Aubergines (Eggplants)	69	74	69
Chillies and green peppers	62	60	56
Dry onions	55	105	79
Green beans	29	32	35
Carrots	25	27	26
Other vegetables*	68	69	69
Plantains*	725	750	780
Lemons and limes*	20	20	21
Mangoes	95	86	86
Pineapples*	62	62	62
Other fresh fruit*	68	68	68
Coffee (green)	10	11	10
Tea (made)	280	284	306
Pepper	18	17	17
Cinnamon	12	12	12
Other spices*	27	28	28
Natural rubber	96	97	88

* FAO estimate(s).

LIVESTOCK ('000 head, year ending September)

	1998	1999	2000
Buffaloes	721	728	694
Cattle	1,599	1,617	1,557
Sheep	12	12	11
Goats	519	514	495
Pigs	76	74	71
Chickens	9,566	9,923	10,622

LIVESTOCK PRODUCTS ('000 metric tons)

	1998	1999	2000
Beef and veal	25.0	23.6	24.6
Goat meat	1.6	1.7	1.7
Pig meat	1.9	1.7	1.9
Poultry meat	59.0	57.0	63.3
Cows' milk	216.5	219.9	221.2
Buffaloes' milk	68.5	69.7	68.1
Goats' milk	5.5	5.4	5.2
Hen eggs	49.7	50.9	52.3
Cattle and buffalo hides	4.9	4.8	4.8

Sources: FAO; Department of Census and Statistics, Colombo.

Forestry

ROUNDWOOD REMOVALS
('000 cubic metres, excl. bark)

	1998	1999	2000
Sawlogs, veneer logs and logs for sleepers*	59	59	59
Other industrial wood*	572	577	577
Fuel wood*	6,005	5,955	5,907
Total	6,636	6,591	6,543

* FAO estimates.

Source: FAO.

SAWNWOOD PRODUCTION
(FAO estimates, '000 cubic metres, incl. railway sleepers)

	1998	1999	2000
Total	5	5	5

Source: FAO.

Fishing*

('000 metric tons)

	1997	1998	1999†
Inland waters:			
Freshwater fishes	27.3	29.9	31.5
Indian Ocean:			
Marine fishes	208.4	233.5	241.9
Other marine animals	6.4	6.5	6.5
Total catch	242.1	269.9	279.9

* Excluding (a) quantities landed by Sri Lanka craft in foreign ports, and (b) quantities landed by foreign craft in Sri Lanka ports.

† Provisional estimates.

Source: Ministry of Fisheries and Aquatic Resources Development, Colombo.

Mining

('000 metric tons, unless otherwise indicated)

	1998	1999	2000
Ilmenite concentrates	34.1	n.a.	n.a.
Zirconium concentrates (metric tons)	8,814*	13,000	n.a.
Natural graphite (metric tons)	5,910	4,592	5,902
Salt—unrefined	67*	79	n.a.
Kaolin	11	13	12
Natural phosphates	38	32	36

* Estimate.

Sources: US Geological Survey; UN, *Industrial Commodity Statistics Yearbook*.

Industry

SELECTED PRODUCTS ('000 barrels, unless otherwise indicated)

	1998	1999	2000
Raw sugar ('000 metric tons)	62	66	64
Plywood ('000 cu m)	7	7	n.a.
Jet fuel	450	500	550
Motor gasoline—petrol	1,900	1,950	2,000
Kerosene	1,550	1,500	1,550
Distillate fuel oil	4,500	4,600	4,700
Residual fuel oil	5,400	5,300	5,300
Cement ('000 metric tons)	874	976	1,008
Electric energy (million kWh)	5,683	6,184	6,844

1997: Naphtha ('000 metric tons) 99.

2001: Raw sugar ('000 metric tons) 48; Electric energy (million kWh) 6,602.

Sources: US Geological Survey; Asian Development Bank, *Key Indicators of Developing Asian and Pacific Countries*; UN, *Industrial Commodity Statistics Yearbook*.

Finance

CURRENCY AND EXCHANGE RATES

Monetary Units

100 cents = 1 Sri Lanka rupee.

Sterling, Dollar and Euro Equivalents (31 May 2002)

£1 sterling = 141.10 rupees;
US $1 = 96.20 rupees;
€1 = 90.30 rupees;
1,000 Sri Lanka rupees = £7.087 = $10.395 = €11.074.

Average Exchange Rate (rupees per US $)

1999 70.635
2000 77.005
2001 89.383

BUDGET (million rupees)

Revenue	2000	2001*	2002†
Taxation	181,657	204,723	237,149
Taxes on income	27,224	34,618	38,992
Taxes on goods and services	44,473	45,603	87,835
National Security levy	34,136	42,939	17,211
Excise levy	41,682	44,911	52,321
Stamp duty	8,564	8,442	3,407
Taxes on international trade	23,444	26,096	29,775
Non-tax revenue	29,464	26,740	41,053
Interest	8,742	6,074	11,203
Sales and charges	6,177	5,938	7,629
Total	211,121	231,463	278,202

Expenditure	2000	2001*	2002†
Current expenditure	254,117	300,440	332,564
General public services	36,610	46,185	46,392
National security and defence	70,773	68,290	64,050
Interest payments	71,200	94,307	117,184
Transfers to other institutions	33,719	39,104	49,467
Provincial councils	23,220	26,405	31,684
Social safety	41,513	51,318	54,700
Pension	21,602	26,325	31,863
Samurdhi	9,661	12,574	9,950
Capital expenditure and net lending	81,545	83,246	81,062
Public investment	80,956	82,743	84,909
Acquisition of fixed assets	32,934	33,414	43,716
Capital transfers	26,617	26,585	21,385
Provincial transfers	8,218	7,844	5,531
On-lending	13,187	14,900	14,277
Other expenditure	589	503	–3,847
Total	335,662	383,686	413,626

* Provisional figures.

† Forecasts.

Source: Central Bank of Sri Lanka, Colombo.

INTERNATIONAL RESERVES (US $ million at 31 December)

	1999	2000	2001
IMF special drawing rights	1	—	1
Reserve position in IMF	65	62	60
Foreign exchange	1,569	976	1,226
Total (excl. gold)	1,636	1,039	1,287

Source: IMF, *International Financial Statistics.*

MONEY SUPPLY (million rupees at 31 December)

	1999	2000	2001
Currency outside banks	58,481	62,647	65,536
Demand deposits at commercial banks	50,059	55,788	56,665
Total money (incl. others)	108,554	118,478	122,211

Source: IMF, *International Financial Statistics.*

COST OF LIVING
(Consumer Price Index for Colombo; base: 1990 = 100)

	1997	1998	1999
Food (incl. beverages)	214.2	237.6	247.1
Fuel and light	193.4	200.2	203.2
Clothing (excl. footwear)	138.3	139.7	141.5
Rent	100.0	100.0	100.0
All items (incl. others)	207.1	226.5	237.2

2000: Food 258.1; All items 251.8.

Source: ILO, *Yearbook of Labour Statistics.*

2001: Food 297.4; All items 287.5 (Source: UN, *Monthly Bulletin of Statistics*).

NATIONAL ACCOUNTS (million rupees at current prices)

Expenditure on the Gross Domestic Product

	1998	1999	2000
Government final consumption expenditure	99,745	99,851	131,583
Private final consumption expenditure	723,506	790,379	906,186
Increase in stocks	175	95	40
Gross fixed capital formation	255,714	301,728	352,632
Total domestic expenditure	1,079,140	1,192,053	1,390,441
Exports of goods and services	368,957	392,437	490,676
Less Imports of goods and services	430,111	478,526	624,048
Sub-total	—	—	1,257,069
Statistical discrepancy*	—	—	565
GDP in purchasers' values	1,017,986	1,105,964	1,257,634

* Referring to the difference between the sum of the expenditure components and official estimates of GDP, compiled from the production approach.

Source: IMF, *International Financial Statistics.*

Gross Domestic Product by Economic Activity

	1999	2000	2001
Agriculture, hunting, forestry and fishing	205,599	218,408	242,532
Mining and quarrying	18,322	21,547	23,869
Manufacturing	163,103	189,331	198,073
Construction	75,538	82,684	94,547
Electricity, gas and water	14,425	13,415	16,127
Transport, storage and communications	113,814	131,669	154,595
Wholesale and retail trade, restaurants and hotels	211,376	254,100	274,796
Finance	80,696	91,186	105,496
Public administration	52,412	58,020	69,409
Other services	59,445	64,899	73,301
GDP at factor cost	994,730	1,125,259	1,252,744
Indirect taxes, *less* subsidies	111,234	132,375	147,373
GDP in purchasers' values	1,105,964	1,257,634	1,400,117

Source: Asian Development Bank, *Key Indicators of Developing Asian and Pacific Countries.*

BALANCE OF PAYMENTS (US $ million)

	1998	1999	2000
Exports of goods f.o.b.	4,808.0	4,596.2	5,439.6
Imports of goods f.o.b.	5,313.4	–5,365.5	–6,483.6
Trade balance	505.4	–769.3	–1,004.0
Exports of services	916.6	964.3	938.7
Imports of services	1,361.6	–1,413.7	–1,621.4
Balance on goods and services	950.5	–1,218.6	–1,726.7
Other income received	214.2	166.7	149.0
Other income paid	394.5	–419.3	–448.4
Balance on goods, services and income	1,130.8	–1,471.2	–2,026.2
Current transfers received	1,054.5	1,078.1	1,166.5
Current transfers paid	151.3	–168.2	–182.7
Current balance	227.7	–561.3	–1,042.4
Capital account (net)	79.9	80.0	50.7
Direct investment from abroad	193.4	176.4	172.9
Portfolio investment assets	88.9	71.8	19.1
Portfolio investment liabilities	112.9	–84.6	–63.4
Other investment assets	75.9	23.2	–238.0
Other investment liabilities	99.7	226.6	683.9
Net errors and omissions	26.3	–27.3	56.4
Overall balance	223.6	–95.2	–360.8

Source: IMF, *International Financial Statistics.*

OFFICIAL DEVELOPMENT ASSISTANCE (US $ million)

	1996	1997	1998
Bilateral donors	276.0	225.8	280.0
Multilateral donors	209.0	103.4	209.9
Total	485.0	329.2	489.9
Grants	236.9	204.3	194.5
Loans	248.1	124.9	295.4
Per caput assistance (US $)	26.5	17.7	26.1

Source: UN, *Statistical Yearbook for Asia and the Pacific.*

External Trade

PRINCIPAL COMMODITIES
(distribution by SITC, million rupees)

Imports c.i.f.	1998	1999	2000
Food and live animals	43,751	43,928	49,127
Beverages and tobacco	7,217	7,149	8,076
Crude materials (inedible) excluding fuels	6,192	5,974	7,359
Mineral fuels, lubricants, etc.	22,698	21,601	44,118
Animal, vegetable oil and fats	4,492	5,033	3,247
Chemicals	17,175	18,276	21,974
Basic manufactures	134,314	140,887	173,888
Machinery and transport equipment	87,688	87,616	106,554
Miscellaneous manufactured articles	44,993	47,543	61,940
Total (incl. others)	369,014	378,509	477,487

Exports f.o.b.	1998	1999	2000
Food and live animals	68,788	63,549	78,240
Tea	50,280	43,728	53,133
Desiccated coconut	2,975	5,095	4,951
Beverages and tobacco	2,904	2,816	3,108
Crude materials (inedible) excluding fuels	549	311	399
Rubber	2,808	2,305	2,179
Copra	458	631	587
Mineral fuels, lubricants, etc.	783	1,364	2,016
Animal, vegetable oil and fats	355	450	525
Coconut oil	199	247	249
Chemicals	2,021	1,869	2,299
Basic manufactures	52,205	51,489	60,736
Machinery and transport equipment	11,147	13,436	17,342
Miscellaneous manufactured articles	160,413	175,211	231,147
Total (incl. others)	305,850	318,810	412,733

Source: Asian Development Bank, *Key Indicators of Developing Asian and Pacific Countries.*

PRINCIPAL TRADING PARTNERS (US $ million)

Imports c.i.f.	1999	2000	2001
China, People's Republic	161.5	251.1	404.0
Germany	136.0	157.0	174.1
Hong Kong	459.1	515.9	420.1
India	511.6	600.1	660.2
Japan	560.8	646.1	318.5
Korea, Republic	386.8	396.4	368.1
Malaysia	168.4	217.3	207.8
Singapore	451.8	496.0	435.1
United Kingdom	251.1	311.4	233.7
USA	216.2	254.9	215.4
Total (incl. others)	6,255.2	6,688.0	6,672.9

Exports f.o.b.	1999	2000	2001
France	101.7	114.2	140.9
Germany	215.7	230.2	221.5
Italy	64.7	69.1	63.0
Japan	159.1	229.7	203.6
Netherlands	107.5	104.3	75.3
Russia	87.9	109.8	70.1
Turkey	59.8	53.9	59.5
United Arab Emirates	122.2	135.1	134.5
United Kingdom	604.1	736.7	541.6
USA	1,791.8	2,192.6	1,956.6
Total (incl. others)	4,621.8	5,458.8	5,036.2

Source: Asian Development Bank, *Key Indicators of Developing Asian and Pacific Countries.*

Transport

RAILWAYS

	1998	1999	2000*
Passengers (million)	82.0	82.8	84.2
Freight carried ('000 metric tons)	1,051	1,160	1,194

* Provisional.

Source: Sri Lanka Railways.

ROAD TRAFFIC (motor vehicles in use at 31 December)

	1997	1998	1999
Passenger cars	202,456	208,593	219,125
Buses and coaches	56,751	60,097	62,672
Lorries and vans	273,561	292,391	323,809
Road tractors	93,912	116,901	123,661
Motor cycles and mopeds	909,922	752,009	794,506
Total	1,536,602	1,429,991	1,523,773

Source: International Road Federation, *World Road Statistics.*

SHIPPING

Merchant Fleet (registered at 31 December)

	1999	2000	2001
Number of vessels	64	65	69
Displacement ('000 grt)	194.6	150.0	153.7

Source: Lloyd's Register-Fairplay, *World Fleet Statistics.*

International Sea-borne Shipping
(freight traffic, '000 metric tons)

	1996	1997	1998
Goods loaded	7,678	9,507	9,290
Goods unloaded	11,885	13,884	16,633

Source: UN, *Statistical Yearbook for Asia and the Pacific.*

CIVIL AVIATION (traffic on scheduled services)

	1997	1998	1999
Kilometres flown (million)	25.2	26.0	31.7
Passengers carried ('000)	1,231.9	1,212.5	1,421.8
Passenger-km (million)	4,249.1	4,136.1	5,156.0
Total ton-km (million)	588.5	553.2	669.7

Tourism

FOREIGN TOURIST ARRIVALS*

Country of Residence	1998	1999	2000
Australia	10,329	13,218	16,443
Belgium	4,992	5,643	10,224
France	26,874	34,458	25,992
Germany	74,058	77,259	70,584
India	37,356	42,315	31,860
Italy	15,867	19,815	16,883
Japan	13,785	16,332	10,266
Netherlands	22,977	29,670	22,618
Pakistan	10,782	11,421	10,005
Switzerland	9,048	8,310	8,490
United Kingdom	66,432	80,919	84,693
USA	9,987	10,572	9,816
Total (incl. others)	381,063	436,440	400,414

* Excluding Sri Lanka nationals residing abroad.

Tourist arrivals: 336,794 in 2001.

Tourism receipts (US $ million): 230 in 1998; 275 in 1999; 253 (estimate) in 2000.

Sources: Ceylon Tourist Board; World Tourism Organization.

Communications Media

	1998	1999	2000
Television receivers ('000 in use)	1,800	1,900	2,100
Telephones ('000 main lines in use)	523.5	669.1	767.4
Mobile cellular telephones ('000 subscribers)	174.2	256.7	430.2
Personal computers ('000 in use)	90	105	135
Internet users ('000)	55	65	121.5
Daily newspapers	181	174	180
Books published			
Number of titles	5,839	4,655	1,818
Number of copies ('000)	58,157.5	n.a.	25,459.3

Facsimile machines (in use)*: 11,000 in 1994.
Radio receivers ('000 in use): 3,850 in 1997.

2001 ('000): Telephones (main lines in use) 828.0; Mobile cellular telephones (subscribers) 720.0; Personal computers (in use) 150; Internet users 150.0.

* Estimate.

Sources: UN, *Statistical Yearbook*, UNESCO, *Statistical Yearbook*, Telecommunications Regulatory Commission of Sri Lanka and International Telecommunication Union.

Education

(1995)

	Institutions	Teachers	Students
Primary	9,657	70,537	1,962,498
Secondary	5,771*	103,572	2,314,054
Universities and equivalent	n.a.	2,344	40,035
Distance learning	n.a.	206	20,601

* 1992 figure.

1996: Primary: 9,554 institutions, 66,339 teachers, 1,843,848 students.
1997: Primary: 60,832 teachers, 1,807,751 students; Secondary: 2,313,511 students.
1998: Primary: 1,798,162 students.

Sources: UNESCO, *Statistical Yearbook*; Ministry of Education, Colombo.

Adult literacy rate (UNESCO estimates): 91.6% (males 94.4%; females 89.0%) in 2000 (Source: UN Development Programme, *Human Development Report*).

Directory

The Constitution

The Constitution of the Democratic Socialist Republic of Sri Lanka was approved by the National State Assembly (renamed Parliament) on 17 August 1978, and promulgated on 7 September 1978. The following is a summary of its main provisions.

FUNDAMENTAL RIGHTS

The Constitution guarantees the fundamental rights and freedoms of all citizens, including freedom of thought, conscience and worship and equal entitlement before the law.

THE PRESIDENT

The President is Head of State, and exercises all executive powers including defence of the Republic. The President is directly elected by the people for a term of six years, and is eligible for re-election. The President's powers include the right to:

(i) choose to hold any portfolio in the Cabinet;
(ii) appoint or dismiss the Prime Minister or any other minister;
(iii) preside at ceremonial sittings of Parliament;
(iv) dismiss Parliament at will; and
(v) submit to a national referendum any Bill or matter of national importance which has been rejected by Parliament.

LEGISLATURE

The Parliament is the legislative power of the people. It consists of such number of representatives of the people as a Delimitation Commission shall determine. The members of Parliament are directly elected by a system of modified proportional representation. By-elections are abolished, successors to members of Parliament being appointed by the head of the party which nominated the outgoing member at the previous election. Parliament exercises the judicial power of the people through courts, tribunals and institutions created and established or recognized by the Constitution or established by law. Parliament has control over public finance.

OTHER PROVISIONS

Religion

Buddhism has the foremost place among religions and it is the duty of the State to protect and foster Buddhism, while assuring every citizen the freedom to adopt the religion of their choice.

Language

The Constitution recognizes two official languages, Sinhala and Tamil. Either of the national languages may be used by all citizens in transactions with government institutions.

Amendments

Amendments to the Constitution require endorsement by a two-thirds majority in Parliament. In February 1979 the Constitution was amended by allowing members of Parliament who resigned or were expelled from their party to retain their seats, in certain circumstances. In January 1981 Parliament amended the Constitution to increase its membership from 168 to 169. An amendment enabling the President to seek re-election after four years was approved in August 1982. In February 1983 an amendment providing for by-elections to fill vacant seats in Parliament was approved. An amendment banning parties that advocate separatism was approved by Parliament in August 1983. In November 1987 Parliament adopted an amendment providing for the creation of eight provincial councils (the northern and eastern provinces were to be merged as one administrative unit). In December 1988 Parliament adopted an amendment allowing Tamil the same status as Sinhala, as one of the country's two official languages.

The Government

HEAD OF STATE

President: CHANDRIKA BANDARANAIKE KUMARATUNGA (sworn in 12 November 1994; re-elected 21 December 1999).

CABINET

(September 2002)

Prime Minister and Minister of Policy Development and Implementation: RANIL WICKREMASINGHE.

Minister of Foreign Affairs: TYRONNE FERNANDO.

Minister of Finance: K. N. CHOKSY.

Minister of Interior: JOHN AMARATUNGA.

Minister of Home Affairs, Provincial Councils and Local Government: ALICK ALUVIHARE.

Minister of Defence, and of Transport, Highways and Aviation: THILAK MARAPANE.

Minister of Agriculture and Livestock, and of Samurdhi: S. B. DISSANAYAKE.

Minister of Enterprise Development, Industrial Policy and Investment Promotion, and of Constitutional Affairs: Prof. G. L. PEIRIS.

Minister of Women's Affairs: AMARA PIYASEELI RATNAYAKE.

Minister of Justice, Law Reform and National Integration, and of Buddha Sasana: W. J. M. LOKUBANDARA.

Minister of Irrigation and Water Management: GAMINI JAYAWICKRAMA PERERA.

Minister of Environment and Natural Resources: Rukman Senanayake.

Minister of Health, Nutrition and Welfare: P. Dayaratne.

Minister of Power and Energy: Karu Jayusuriya.

Minister of Tourism: Gamini Lokuge.

Minister of Human Resources Development, Education and Cultural Affairs: Dr Karunasena Kodituwakku.

Minister of Mass Communication: Imithiyas Bakeer Makar.

Minister of Employment and Labour: Mahinda Samarasinghe.

Minister of Commerce and Consumer Affairs: Ravi Karunanayake.

Minister of Economic Reforms and of Science and Technology: Milinda Moragoda.

Minister of Public Administration, Management and Reforms: Vajira Abeywardena.

Minister of Housing and Plantation Infrastructure: Arumugan Thondaman.

Minister of Plantation Industries: Lakshman Kiriella.

Minister of Fisheries and Ocean Resources: Mahinda Wijesekera.

Minister of Lands: Rajitha Senaratne.

Minister of Community Development: P. Chandrasekaran.

Minister of Port Development and Shipping, and of Eastern Development and Muslim Religious Affairs: Rauf Hakeem.

Minister of Southern Region Development: Ananda Kularatne.

Minister of Western Region Development: M. H. Mohamed.

Minister of Central Region Development: Tissa Attanayake.

Minister of Rural Economy: Bandula Gunawardane.

Minister of Co-operatives: A. R. M. Abdul Cader.

MINISTRIES

President's Secretariat: Republic Sq., Colombo 1; tel. (1) 24801; internet www.priu.gov.lk/execpres/presecretariat.html.

Prime Minister's Office: Sir Ernest de Silva Mawatha, Colombo 7; tel. (1) 575317; fax (1) 575454.

Ministry of Agriculture and Livestock: 'Govijana Mandiraya', 82 Rajamalwatta Rd, Battaramulla, Colombo; tel. (1) 868922; fax (1) 863497; e-mail minagr@slt.lk.

Ministry of Buddha Sasana: 135 Anagarika Dharmapala Mawatha, Colombo 7; tel. (1) 326126; fax (1) 437997.

Ministry of Central Region Development: Colombo.

Ministry of Commerce and Consumer Affairs: Rakshana Mandiraya, 21 Vauxhall St, Colombo 2; tel. (1) 435601; fax (1) 447669.

Ministry of Community Development: 45 St Michael's Rd, Colombo 3; tel. (1) 441849; fax (1) 328117; e-mail secomdev@sltnet.lk.

Ministry of Constitutional Affairs: 73/1 Galle Rd, Colombo 3; tel. (1) 327553; fax (1) 449402; e-mail mnindder@slt.lk.

Ministry of Co-operative Development: 349 Galle Rd, Colombo 3; tel. (1) 421211; fax (1) 301476; e-mail coopacct@sltnet.lk.

Ministry of Defence: 15/5 Baladaksha Mawatha, POB 572, Colombo 3; tel. (1) 430860; fax (1) 541529.

Ministry of Eastern Development and Muslim Religious Affairs: 45 Leyden Bastian Rd, Colombo 1; tel. (1) 438344; fax (1) 435142; e-mail minpds@slpa.lk.

Ministry of Economic Reform, Science and Technology: 561/3 Etvigala Mawatha, Colombo 5; tel. (1) 554848; fax (1) 554845; e-mail milindamora@sltnet.lk; internet www.most.gov.lk.

Ministry of Employment and Labour: 2nd Floor, Labour Secretariat, Kirula Rd, Narahenpita, Colombo; tel. (1) 581991; fax (1) 582938; e-mail mlabour@slt.lk; internet www.labour.gov.lk.

Ministry of Enterprise Development, Industrial Policy and Investment Promotion: Colombo; www.industry.gov.lk.

Ministry of Environment and Natural Resources: 'Sampathpaya', 82 Rajamalwatte Rd, Battaramulla, Colombo.

Ministry of Finance and Planning: Galle Face Secretariat, Colombo 1; tel. (1) 433937; fax (1) 449823; e-mail dst@sltnet.lk; internet www.eureka.gov.lk/fpea.

Ministry of Fisheries and Ocean Resources: Maligawatte, Colombo 10; tel. (1) 446184; fax (1) 541184.

Ministry of Foreign Affairs: Republic Bldg, Colombo 1; tel. (1) 325371; internet www.lanka.net/fm.

Ministry of Health, Nutrition and Welfare: 'Suwasiripaya', 385 Wimalawansha Mawatha, Colombo 10; tel. (1) 698471; fax (1) 693869; internet www.lk/government.html.

Ministry of Home Affairs, Provincial Councils and Local Government: 330 Union Place, Colombo 2.

Ministry of Housing and Plantation Infrastructure: Colombo.

Ministry of Human Resource Development, Education and Cultural Affairs: Colombo; internet www.mca.gov.lk.

Ministry of Interior: Colombo.

Ministry of Irrigation and Water Management: 500 T. B. Jayah Mawatha, Colombo 10; tel. (1) 673013; fax (1) 677247.

Ministry of Justice, Law Reform and National Integration: Superior Courts Complex Bldg, Colombo 12; tel. (1) 323022; fax (1) 320785; e-mail justices@sri.lanka.net; internet www.justiceministry.gov.lk.

Ministry of Land: 'Govijana Mandiraya', 80/5 Rajamalwatte Rd, Battaramulla, Colombo.

Ministry of Mass Communication: Level 7&18, West Tower, World Trade Centre, Echelon Sq, Colombo 1.

Ministry of North-West Region Development: Colombo.

Ministry of Plantation Industries: Vauxhall Lane, Colombo 2; tel. (1) 320901; fax (1) 438031.

Ministry of Policy Development and Implementation: Colombo.

Ministry of Port Development and Shipping: 45 Leyden Bastian Rd, Colombo 1; tel. (1) 438344; fax (1) 435142; e-mail minpds@slpa.lk.

Ministry of Power and Energy: 80 Flower Rd, Colombo 7.

Ministry of Public Administration, Management and Reforms: Independence Sq., Colombo 7; tel. (1) 696211; fax (1) 695279; e-mail minister@pubad.gov.lk; internet www.gov.lk/public/index.htm.

Ministry of Rehabilitation, Resettlement and Refugees: Colombo.

Ministry of Rural Economy: Janakala Kendraya, Pelawatte, Battaramulla, Colombo.

Ministry of Samurdhi: 7A Ried Ave, Colombo 7; tel. (1) 689589; fax (1) 688945.

Ministry of Southern Region Development: Colombo.

Ministry of Tourism: 64 Galle Rd, Colombo 3; tel. (1) 385241; fax (1) 441505; internet www.slmts.slt.lk.

Ministry of Transport, Highways and Aviation: 1 D. R. Wijewardene Mawatha, POB 588, Colombo 10; tel. (1) 687212; fax (1) 687284; www.transport.gov.lk.

Ministry of Urban Public Utilities: 29 Galle Face Terrace, Colombo 3; tel. (1) 307831; fax (1) 307827; e-mail sec_upu@sltnet.lk.

Ministry of Western Region Development: Colombo.

Ministry of Women's Affairs: 177 Nawala Rd, Narahenpita, Colombo 5; tel. (1) 598371; internet www.womens-affairs.gov.lk.

Ministry of Youth Affairs and Sports: 7a Ried Ave, Colombo 7.

President and Legislature

PRESIDENT

Presidential Election, 21 December 1999

Candidate	Valid votes	Percentage of votes
Chandrika Bandaranaike Kumaratunga (PA)	4,312,157	51.12
Ranil Wickremasinghe (UNP)	3,602,748	42.71
M. D. Nandana Gunathilaka (JVP)	344,173	4.08
Total (incl. others)	8,435,754	100.00

PARLIAMENT

Speaker: Joseph Michael Perera (UNP).

Deputy Speaker: (vacant).

General Election, 5 December 2001

Party	Seats
United National Party (UNP)	109
People's Alliance (PA)	77
Janatha Vimukthi Peramuna (JVP)	16
Tamil National Alliance (TNA)	15
Sri Lanka Muslim Congress (SLMC)	5
Eelam People's Democratic Party (EPDP)	2
Democratic People's Liberation Front (DPLF)	1
Total	225

Notes: Direct elections were held for 196 of the 225 seats on the basis of a proportional representation system involving preferential voting; the remaining 29 were chosen from party lists according to each party's national share of the vote.

Political Organizations

Ceylon Workers' Congress (CWC): 'Savumia Bhavan', 72 Ananda Coomarasamy Mawatha, POB 1294, Colombo 7; tel. (1) 565082; fax (1) 301355; e-mail cwcctuc@slt.lk; f. 1939; represents the interests of workers in the mercantile and local government sectors and of workers (mainly of Indian Tamil origin) on tea plantations; 250,000 mems; Pres. and Gen. Sec. S. R. Arumugan Thondaman.

Democratic People's Liberation Front (DPLF): has operated as a national political party since Sept. 1988; political wing of the People's Liberation Organization of Tamil Eelam (PLOTE); Leader Dharmalingam Sithadthan.

Democratic Workers' Congress (DWC) (Political Wing): 70 Bankshall St, POB 1009, Colombo 11; tel. (1) 439199; fax (1) 435961; f. 1939 as trade union, f. 1978 as political party; aims to eliminate discrimination against the Tamil-speaking Sri Lankans of recent Indian origin; 201,382 mems (1994); Pres. and Gen. Sec. Mano Ganeshan.

Desha Vimukthi Janatha Party (National Liberation People's Party): has operated as a national political party since Sept. 1988.

Deshapriya Janatha Viyaparaya (DJV) (Patriotic People's Movement): militant, Sinhalese group; associated with the JVP.

Eelam National Democratic Liberation Front (ENDLF): Kilinochchi; Tamil; supports 1987 Indo-Sri Lankan peace accord; has operated as a national political party since Sept. 1988; Gen. Sec. G. Gnanasekaran; Dep. Gen. Sec. P. Rajaratnam.

Eelam People's Democratic Party (EPDP): Tamil; Sec.-Gen. Douglas Devananda.

Eelavar Democratic Front: fmrly known as Eelam Revolutionary Organization of Students (EROS); Tamil separatist group; Leader Velupillai Balakumar.

Eksath Lanka Jathika Peramuna: f. by fmr mems of the UNP.

Janatha Vimukthi Peramuna (JVP) (People's Liberation Front): 198/19 Panchikawattha Rd, Colombo 10; tel. (1) 822379; fax (1) 819775; e-mail contact@jvpsrilanka.com; internet www.jvpsrilanka.com; f. 1964, banned following a coup attempt in 1971, regained legal status in 1977, banned again in 1983, but regained legal status in 1988; Marxist; Sinhalese support; c. 2,000 mems; Leader Tilwin Silva.

Liberal Party: Colombo.

Mahajana Eksath Peramuna (MEP) (People's United Front): Gothami Rd, Borella, Colombo 8; tel. (1) 595450; f. 1956; Sinhalese and Buddhist support; left-wing; advocates economic self-reliance; Pres. Dinesh C. R. Gunawardena.

Muslim United Liberation Front: has operated as a national political party since Sept. 1988.

National Unity Alliance (NUA): affiliate party of the Sri Lanka Muslim Congress; has operated as a national political party since 1986; Leader Fariel Ashraff.

Nava Sama Samaja Party (NSSP) (New Equal Society Party): 17 Barracks Lane, Colombo 2; tel. (1) 324053; fax (1) 305963; e-mail nssp@visual.lk; internet www.nssp.info; f. 1977; Trotskyist; Gen. Sec. Dr Vickramabahu Bandara Karunarathne; Popular leaders Neil Wijetilake, Linus Jayatilake, V. Thirunnakarasu.

People's Alliance (PA): f. 1993 as a left-wing alliance, incl. communists and Trotskyists; Leader Chandrika Bandaranaike Kumaratunga; Gen. Sec. D. M. Jayaratne.

Communist Party of Sri Lanka (CPSL): 91 Dr N. M. Perera Mawatha, Colombo 8; tel. (1) 694945; fax (1) 691610; f. 1943; advocates establishment of socialist society; seeks broadening of democratic rights and processes, political solution to ethnic problem, defence of social welfare and presses for social justice; supports national sovereignty, territorial integrity and national unity of the country; Chair. Pieter Keuneman; Gen. Sec. Raja Collure.

Democratic United National Front (DUNF): f. 1991 by a dissident group of UNP politicians; 500,000 mems; Leader Srimani Athulathmudali; Gen. Sec. G. M. Premachandra.

Lanka Sama Samaja Party (LSSP) (Lanka Equal Society Party): 457 Dr Colvin R. de Silva Mawatha, Colombo 2; tel. (1) 679544; f. 1935; Trotskyist; Gen. Sec. Batty Weerakoon.

Sri Lanka Freedom Party (SLFP): 301 T. B. Jayah Mawatha, Colombo 10; tel. (1) 696289; internet www.slfp.lk; f. 1951; democratic socialist; advocates a non-aligned foreign policy, industrial development in both the state sector and the private sector, rapid modernization in education and in the economy, and safeguards for minorities; Pres. Pres. Chandrika Bandaranaike Kumaratunga; Gen. Sec. (vacant).

Sri Lanka Mahajana (People's) Party (SLMP): Colombo; tel. (1) 696038; f. 1984 by fmr mems of the SLFP; social democrats; Leader Sarath Kongahage; Gen. Sec. Premasiri Perera.

People's Front of the Liberation Tigers (PFLT): f. 1989; political wing of the LTTE (see below); Leader Gopalswamy Mahendrarajah ('Mahathya'); Gen. Sec. Yogaratnam Yogi.

Singhalaye Nithahas Peramuna (Sinhalese Freedom Front): Sri Panchananda Charity Bldg, Kelani Railway Station Rd, Colombo; f. 1994; nationalist, Buddhist; Pres. Arya Sena Tera; Sec. Prof. Nalin de Silva.

Sri Lanka Muslim Congress: Colombo; internet www.slmc.org; Leader Rauf Hakeem.

Sri Lanka Progressive Front: c/o Parliament, Colombo.

Tamil National Alliance (TNA): c/o Parliament, Colombo; f. 2001; alliance of Tamil parties.

All Ceylon Tamil Congress: Colombo; f. 1944; aims to secure Tamil self-determination.

Eelam People's Revolutionary Liberation Front (EPRLF): Tamil rights group; c. 1,000 mems; Leader Annamalai Varadharajah Perumal; Gen. Sec. Suresh K. Premachandran.

Tamil Eelam Liberation Organization (TELO): supports 1987 Indo-Sri Lankan peace accord; has operated as a national political party since Sept. 1988; Leader Sri Sabaratnam.

Tamil United Liberation Front (TULF): 30/1B Alwis Place, Colombo 3; tel. (1) 347721; fax (1) 384904; f. 1976, following merger of All Ceylon Tamil Congress (f. 1945) and Federal Party (f. 1949); Pres. Veerasingham Anandasangaree; Sec.-Gen. R. Sampanthan.

United National Party (UNP): Sirikotha, 400 Kotte Rd, Sri Jayawaredenepura; tel. (1) 865375; fax (1) 865347; e-mail unpweb@yahoo.com; internet www.unplanka.org; f. 1946; democratic socialist; aims at a non-aligned foreign policy, supports Sinhala and Tamil as the official languages and state aid to denominational schools; Leader Ranil Wickremasinghe; Chair. Karu Jayasuriya; Gen. Sec. Gamini Atukorale.

Up-Country People's Front: represents interests of workers (mainly of Indian Tamil origin) on tea plantations.

Tamil separatist groups also include the Liberation Tigers of Tamil Eelam (LTTE; Leader Velupillai Prabhakaran), the Tamil Eelam Liberation Front (TELF; Gen. Sec. M. K. Eelaventhan), the People's Liberation Organization of Tamil Eelam (PLOTE; Leader Dharmalingam Siddharthan; Vice-Pres. Karuvai A. Srikanthasami), the People's Revolutionary Action Group, the Ellalan Force and the Tamil People's Protection Party.

Diplomatic Representation

EMBASSIES AND HIGH COMMISSIONS IN SRI LANKA

Australia: 3 Cambridge Place, POB 742, Colombo 7; tel. (1) 698767; fax (1) 686939; High Commissioner: David Alexander Ritchie.

Bangladesh: 286 Bauddhaloka Mawatha, Colombo 7; tel. (1) 502198; fax (1) 681309; High Commissioner: Masum Ahmed Chowdhury.

Canada: 6 Gregory's Rd, Cinnamon Gdns, POB 1006, Colombo 7; tel. (1) 695841; fax (1) 687049; e-mail clmbo@dfait-maeci.gc.ca; High Commissioner: Valerie Raymond.

China, People's Republic: 381A Bauddhaloka Mawatha, Colombo 7; tel. (1) 694494; Ambassador: Jiang Qinzheng.

Egypt: 39 Dickman's Rd, Colombo 5; tel. (1) 583621; fax (1) 585292; Ambassador: Ramzy Y. Allam.

Finland: 81 Barnes Place, Colombo 7; tel. (1) 698819.

France: 89 Rosmead Place, POB 880, Colombo 7; tel. (1) 698815; fax (1) 699039; e-mail ambfrclb@sltnet.lk; internet www.ambafrance.lk; Ambassador: MARIE-FRANCE PAGNIER.

Germany: 40 Alfred House Ave, POB 658, Colombo 3; tel. (1) 580431; fax (1) 580440; e-mail germaemb@sltnet.lk; internet www.germanyembassy.lk; Ambassador: JÜRGEN ELIAS.

Holy See: 220 Bauddhaloka Mawatha, Colombo 7 (Apostolic Nunciature); tel. (1) 582554; fax (1) 580906; e-mail aponun@sri.lanka.net; Apostolic Nuncio: Most Rev. Dr THOMAS YEH SHENG-NAN, Titular Archbishop of Leptis Magna.

India: 36–38 Galle Rd, Colombo 3; tel. (1) 421605; fax (1) 446403; High Commissioner: GOPALKRISHNA GANDHI.

Indonesia: 400/50 Sarana Rd, off Bauddhaloka Mawatha, Colombo 7; tel. (1) 674337; Ambassador: MOHAMMAD SALEH.

Iran: 17 Bullers Lane, Colombo 7; tel. (1) 501137; Ambassador: ALIREZA MOTEVALI ALAMUTI.

Iraq: 19 Barnes Place, POB 79, Colombo 7; tel. (1) 698733; fax (1) 697676; e-mail iraqiya@sol.lk; Ambassador: AMER NAJI.

Italy: 55 Jawatta Rd, Colombo 5; tel. (1) 588388; fax (74) 712272; e-mail itembgen@lankacom.net; internet www.italianembassy.lk; Ambassador: MAURIZIO TEUCCI.

Japan: 20 Gregory's Rd, POB 822, Colombo 7; tel. (1) 393831; fax (1) 698629; Ambassador: YOJI SUGIYAMA.

Korea, Democratic People's Republic: Colombo; Ambassador: PAK MYONG GU.

Korea, Republic: 98 Dharmapala Mawatha, Colombo 7; tel. (1) 699036; fax (1) 672358; e-mail kesl@koreanembassy.net; Ambassador: LEE NAM-SOO.

Libya: 120 Horton Place, POB 155, Colombo 7; tel. (1) 693700; fax (1) 695671; e-mail libya@eureka.lk; Secretary of the People's Bureau: ABDUL KARIM ALI ABDUL KARIM.

Malaysia: 47/1 Jawatta Rd, Colombo 5; tel. (1) 508773; fax (1) 508972; High Commissioner: SHAMSUDDIN BIN ABDULLAH.

Maldives: 25 Melbourne Ave, Colombo 4; tel. (1) 586762; fax (1) 581200; High Commissioner: ABDUL AZEEZ YOOSUF.

Myanmar: 17 Skeleton Gdns, Colombo 5; tel. (1) 587607; fax (1) 681196; Ambassador: U AUNG GYI.

Nepal: 290 R. A. de Mel Mawatha, Colombo 4; tel. (1) 575510; Ambassador: NILAMBER ACHARYA.

Netherlands: 25 Torrington Ave, Colombo 7; tel. (1) 596914; fax (1) 502855; e-mail nethemb@sri.lanka.net; Ambassador: H. C. R. M. PRINCEN.

Norway: 34 Ward Place, Colombo 7; tel. (1) 469611; fax (1) 695009; e-mail noremb@panlanka.net; Ambassador: JON WESTBORG.

Pakistan: 211 De Saram Place, Colombo 10; tel. (1) 696301; fax (1) 695780; e-mail hcpakl@sltnet.lk; High Commissioner: ASHRAF QURESHI.

Philippines: 10 Gregory's Rd, Colombo 7.

Poland: 120 Park Rd, Colombo 5.

Romania: 6A Samudra Mawatha, Mount Lavinia, Greater Colombo; tel. (1) 203153; fax (1) 723256; e-mail romanial@embassy.org; Chargé d'affaires a.i.: CRISTIAN OVIDIU MATEESCU.

Russia: 62 Sir Ernest de Silva Mawatha, Colombo 7; tel. (1) 573555; Ambassador: VICTOR G. ZOTIN.

Sweden: 49 Buller's Lane, POB 1072, Colombo 7; tel. (1) 688452; fax (1) 688455; e-mail sweden@panlanka.net; Chargé d' affaires a.i.: ANN MARIE FALLENIUS.

Switzerland: 63 Gregory's Rd, POB 342, Colombo 7; tel. (1) 695117; fax (1) 695176; Ambassador: FRANCO BESOMI.

Thailand: 43 Dr C. W. W. Kannangara Mawatha, Colombo 7; tel. (1) 689037; Ambassador: SAMROENG LAKSANASUT.

United Kingdom: 190 Galle Rd, Kollupitiya, POB 1433, Colombo 3; tel. (1) 437336; fax (1) 430308; e-mail bhc@eureka.lk; High Commissioner: LINDA J. DUFFIELD.

USA: 210 Galle Rd, POB 106, Colombo 3; tel. (1) 448007; fax (1) 437345; e-mail ecpo@eureka.lk; internet www.usia.gov/posts/sri_lanka; Ambassador: E. ASHLEY WILLS.

Judicial System

The judicial system consists of the Supreme Court, the Court of Appeal, the High Court, District Courts, Magistrates' Courts and Primary Courts. The last four are Courts of the First Instance and appeals lie from them to the Court of Appeal and from there, on questions of law or by special leave, to the Supreme Court. The High Court deals with all criminal cases and the District Courts with civil cases. There are Labour Tribunals to decide labour disputes.

The Judicial Service Commission comprises the Chief Justice and two judges of the Supreme Court, nominated by the President. All judges of the Courts of First Instance (except High Court Judges) and the staff of all courts are appointed and controlled by the Judicial Service Commission. The Supreme Court consists of the Chief Justice and not fewer than six and not more than 10 other judges. The Court of Appeal consists of the President and not fewer than six and not more than 11 other judges.

Chief Justice of the Supreme Court: G. P. S. DE SILVA.

Attorney-General: TILAK MARAPANA.

Religion

According to the 2001 census, the distribution of the population by religion in 18 out of 25 districts was: Buddhist 76.7%, Muslim 8.5%, Hindu 7.9%, Roman Catholics 6.1%, Other Christians 0.8%. The census results did not cover the Tamil-dominated northern and eastern districts.

BUDDHISM

Theravada Buddhism is the predominant sect. There are an estimated 53,000 Buddhist Bhikkhus (monks), living in about 6,000 temples.

All Ceylon Buddhist Congress: 380 Bauddhaloka Mawatha, Colombo 7; tel. (1) 691695; f. 1919; Pres. Dr SUDATH DEVAPURA; Jt Secs PAJAPALA SRI GUNAWARDENA, SUNIL SARATH KURAGAMA.

Sri Lanka Regional Centre of the World Fellowship of Buddhists: 380 Bauddhaloka Mawatha, Colombo 7; tel. (1) 681886; e-mail palitha@panlanka.net; Pres. FRANCIS WANIGASEKERA; Sec. S. PALITHA KANNANGARA.

HINDUISM

The majority of the Tamil population are Hindus. In March 1981 the Hindu population was 2,252,000.

CHRISTIANITY

National Christian Council of Sri Lanka: 368/6 Bauddhaloka Mawatha, Colombo 7; tel. (1) 671723; fax (1) 671721; e-mail nccsl@eureka.lk; f. 1945; 13 mem. bodies; Gen. Sec. Rev. W. P. EBENEZER JOSEPH.

The Anglican Communion

The Church of Ceylon (Sri Lanka) comprises two Anglican dioceses. In 1985 there were about 78,000 adherents.

Bishop of Colombo: Rt Rev. DULEEP KAMIL DE CHICKERA, Bishop's House, 358/2 Bauddhaloka Mawatha, Colombo 7; tel. (1) 696208; fax (1) 684811; e-mail bishop@eureka.lk; diocese f. 1845.

Bishop of Kurunegala: Rt Rev. KUMARA BANDARA SAMUEL ILLANGASINGHE, Bishop's House, Kandy Rd, Kurunegala; tel. (37) 22191; fax (37) 26806; e-mail bishopkg@sltnet.lk; diocese f. 1950.

The Roman Catholic Church

For ecclesiastical purposes, Sri Lanka comprises one archdiocese and 10 dioceses. At 31 December 2000 there were an estimated 1,299,935 adherents in the country.

Catholic Bishops' Conference in Sri Lanka: 19 Balcombe Place, Cotta Rd, Borella, Colombo 8; tel. (1) 597110; fax (1) 699619; e-mail neildias@rocketmail.com; f. 1975; Pres. Rt Rev. Dr OSWALD THOMAS COLMAN GOMIS, Archbishop of Colombo; Sec.-Gen. Rt Rev. MARIUS PEIRIS.

Archbishop of Colombo: Most Rev. Dr OSWALD THOMAS COLMAN GOMIS, Archbishop's House, 976 Gnanarthapradeepaya Mawatha, Colombo 8; tel. (1) 695471; fax (1) 692009; e-mail cyrilsp@sltnet.lk; internet www.ceylon.net/catholicchurchcolombo.

The Church of South India

The Church comprises 21 dioceses, including one, Jaffna, in Sri Lanka. The diocese of Jaffna, with an estimated 18,500 adherents in 1997, was formerly part of the South India United Church (a union of churches of the Congregational and Presbyterian/Reformed traditions), which merged with the Methodist Church in South India and the four southern dioceses of the (Anglican) Church of India to form the Church of South India in 1947.

Bishop in Jaffna: Rt Rev. Dr S. JEBANESAN, 41 4th Cross St, Jaffna; tel. (21) 2029; fax (1) 584836; e-mail jdcsiacm@panlanka.net.

Other Christian Churches

Dutch Reformed Church: General Consistory Office, 363 Galle Rd, Colombo 6; tel. (1) 585861; fax (1) 582469; e-mail drc1642@sltnet.lk; f. 1642; Pres. of Gen. Consistory Rev. CHARLES N. JANSZ; Admin. Sec. GODFREY B. EVENEZER.

Methodist Church: Methodist Headquarters, 252 Galle Rd, Colombo 3; tel. (1) 575707; fax (1) 436090; e-mail methhq@sltnet.lk; internet www.gbgm-umc.org/methchsrilan; 30,139 mems (2000); Pres. of Conference Rev. A. NOEL P. FERNANDO; Sec. of Conference Rev. NIMAL L. S. MENDIS.

Other denominations active in the country include the Sri Lanka Baptist Sangamaya.

BAHÁ'Í FAITH

Spiritual Assembly: Bahá'í National Centre, 65 Havelock Rd, Colombo 5; tel. and fax (1) 587360.

The Press

NEWSPAPERS

Newspapers are published in Sinhala, Tamil and English. There are five main newspaper publishing groups:

Associated Newspapers of Ceylon Ltd: Lake House, D. R. Wijewardene Mawatha, POB 248, Colombo 10; tel. (1) 435641; fax (1) 449069; e-mail webmgr@sri.lanka.net; internet www.lanka.net/lakehouse; f. 1926; nationalized 1973; publr of *Daily News, Evening Observer, Thinakaran, Janatha* and *Dinamina* (dailies), three Sunday papers: *Sunday Observer, Silumina* and *Thinakaran Vaara Manjari,* and 11 periodicals; Chair. ALOY N. RATNAYAKE; Sec. B. A. JINADASA.

Express Newspapers (Ceylon) Ltd: 185 Grandpass Rd, POB 160, Colombo 14; tel. (1) 320881; fax (1) 439987; e-mail kesari10@virakesari.lk; internet www.virakesari.lk; publr of *Virakesari Daily, Mithran Varamalar, The Weekend Express* and *Virakesari Weekly* (Sunday); Man. Dir KUMAR NADESAN; Editor S. NADARAJAH.

Leader Publications (Pvt) Ltd: No. 101, 2nd Floor, Collettes Bldg, D. S. Senanayake Mawatha, Colombo 8; tel. (1) 686047; fax (1) 699968; e-mail leader@sri.lanka.net; internet www.thesundayleader.lk; publr of *The Sunday Leader* and *Irida Peramuna*.

Upali Newspapers Ltd: 223 Bloemendhal Rd, POB 133, Colombo 13; tel. (1) 324001; fax (1) 448103; f. 1981; publr of *The Island, Divaina* (dailies), two Sunday papers, *Sunday Island* and *Sunday Divaina*, four weeklies, *Vidusara, Navaliya, Bindu* and *The Island International* (for sale abroad only); and one bi-weekly, *Vathmana-News Magazine*; English and Sinhala; Editor-in-Chief (vacant); Man. Dir J. H. LANEROLLE.

Wijeya Newspapers Ltd: 8 Hunupitiya Cross Rd, Colombo 2; tel. (1) 441070; fax (1) 449504; f. 1979; publr of *Daily Mirror, The Sunday Times, Sri Lankadipa, Woman's Weekly, Men's Weekly, Children's Weekly*; Sinhala and English.

Dailies

Daily Mirror: 8 Hunupitiya Cross Rd, Colombo 2; tel. (1) 436998; fax (1) 753308; e-mail mirror@wijeya.lk; f. 1996; English and Sinhala; Editor LATITH ALAHAKOON; circ. 45,500.

Daily News: Lake House, D. R. Wijewardene Mawatha, POB 248, Colombo 10; tel. (1) 429429; fax (1) 429210; e-mail editor@dailynews.lk; internet www.dailynews.lk; f. 1918; morning; English; Editor GEOFF WIJEYESINGHE; circ. 65,000.

Dinakara: 95 Maligakanda Rd, Colombo 10; tel. (1) 595754; f. 1978; morning; Sinhala; publ. by Rekana Publrs; Editor MULEN PERERA; circ. 12,000.

Dinamina: Lake House, D. R. Wijewardene Mawatha, POB 248, Colombo 10; tel. (1) 21181; f. 1909; morning; Sinhala; Editor G. S. PERERA; circ. 140,000.

Divaina: 223 Bloemendhal Rd, POB 133, Colombo 13; tel. (1) 24001; fax (1) 448103; internet www.divaina.com; f. 1982; morning and Sunday; Chief Editor UPALI TENNAKOON.

Eelanadu: Jaffna; tel. (21) 22389; f. 1959; morning; Tamil; Chair. S. RAVEENTHIRANATHAN; Editor M. SIVANANTHAM; circ. 15,000.

The Island: 223 Bloemendhal Rd, Colombo 13; tel. (1) 324001; internet www.island.lk; f. 1981; English; Editor GAMINI WEERAKOON; circ. 80,000.

Janatha: Janata Lake House, D. R. Wijewardene Mawatha, Colombo 10; tel. (1) 421181; f. 1953; evening; Sinhala; Editor MOHAN LAL PIYADASA; circ. 15,000.

Evening Observer: Associated Newspapers of Ceylon Ltd, Lake House, D. R. Wijewardene Mawatha, POB 248, Colombo 10; tel. (1) 434544; fax (1) 449069; f. 1834; evening (weekdays) and Sunday morning; Editor AJITH SAMARANAYAKE; circ. 10,000 (evening), 95,000 (Sunday).

Peraliya: 2nd Floor, Borella Supermarket Complex, Colombo 8; Editor SUJEEWA GAMAGE.

Sri Lankadeepa: 8 Hunupitiya Cross Rd, Colombo 2; tel. (1) 448321; fax (1) 438039; e-mail siri@wijeya.lk; internet www.lankadeepa.com; f. 1986; Sinhala and English; Editor SIRI RANASINGHE; circ. 160,000.

Thinakaran: Lake House, D. R. Wijewardene Mawatha, POB 248, Colombo 10; tel. (1) 21181; f. 1932; morning; Tamil; Editor R. SIVAGURUNATHAN; circ. daily 14,000.

Uthayan: Jaffna; internet www.uthayan.com; Tamil; Associate Editor N. VITHIYADHARAN.

Virakesari Daily: 185 Grandpass Rd, POB 160, Colombo 14; tel. (1) 320881; fax (1) 439987; e-mail virakesari@lanka.ccom.lk; internet www.virakesari.lk; f. 1931; morning; Tamil; Man. Dir M. G. WENCESLAUS; Editor S. NADARAJAH; circ. 49,500.

Sunday Newspapers

Janasathiya: 47 Jayantha Weerasekara Mawatha, Colombo 10; f. 1965; Sinhala; publ. by Suriya Publishers Ltd; Editor SARATH NAWANA; circ. 50,000.

Mithran Varamalar: 185 Grandpass Rd, Colombo 14; tel. (1) 320881; fax (1) 448205; e-mail virakesari@lanka.ccom.lk; internet www.virakesari.lk; f. 1969; Tamil; Man. Dir M. G. WENCESLAUS; Editor P. SURIYAKUMARY; circ. 29,000.

Silumina: Lake House, 35 D. R. Wijewardene Mawatha, Colombo 10; tel. (1) 324772; fax (1) 449069; f. 1930; Sinhala; Editor NIWAL HORANA; circ. 264,000.

Sunday Island: 223 Bloemendhal Rd, POB 133, Colombo 13; tel. (1) 421599; fax (1) 609198; e-mail manik@unl.upali.lk; f. 1981; English; Editor MANIK DE SILVA; circ. 40,000.

The Sunday Leader: No. 101, 2nd Floor, Collettes Bldg, D. S. Senanayake Mawatha, Colombo 8; tel. (1) 686047; fax (1) 699968; internet www.lanka.net/sundayleader; English; Editor LASANTHA WICKRAMATUNGA.

Sunday Observer: D. R. Wijewardene Mawatha, POB 248, Colombo 10; tel. (1) 429239; fax (1) 429230; e-mail editor@sundayobserver.lk; internet www.sundayobserver.lk; f. 1923; English; Editor H. L. D. MAHINDAPALA.

The Sunday Times: 8 Hunupitiya Cross Rd, Colombo 2; tel. (1) 326247; fax (1) 449504; e-mail editor@suntimes.is.lk; internet www.is.lk/times/index.html; f. 1986; English and Sinhala; Editor SINGHA RATNATUNGA; circ. 116,000.

Thinakaran Vaara Manjari: Lake House, 35 D. R. Wijewardene Mawatha, Colombo 10; tel. (1) 21181; f. 1948; Tamil; Editor R. SRIKANTHAN; circ. 35,000.

Virakesari Weekly: 185 Grandpass Rd, Colombo 14; tel. (1) 320881; fax (1) 448205; e-mail virakesari@lanka.ccom.lk; internet www.virakesari.lk; f. 1931; Tamil; Man. Dir M. G. WENCESLAUS; Editor S. NADARAJAH; circ. 69,000.

The Weekend Express: 185 Grandpass Rd, Colombo 14; tel. (1) 320881; fax (1) 613982; e-mail express@sri.lanka.net; Chief Editor SUKUMAR ROCKWOOD; circ. 27,500.

PERIODICALS

(weekly unless otherwise stated)

Athavan: Colombo; Tamil.

Aththa: 91 Dr N. M. Perera Mawatha, Colombo 8; tel. (1) 691450; fax (1) 691610; f. 1964; Sinhala; publ. by the Communist Party of Sri Lanka; Editor GUNASENA VITHANA; circ. 28,000.

Business Lanka: Trade Information Service, Sri Lanka Export Development Board, Level 7, 42 Navam Mawatha, POB 1872, Colombo 2; tel. (1) 300677; fax (1) 300715; e-mail tisinfo@tradenetsl.lk; f. 1981; quarterly; information for visiting businessmen etc.; Editor Mrs S. D. ISAAC.

Ceylon Commerce: The National Chamber of Commerce of Sri Lanka, NCCSL Bldg, 450 D. R. Wijewardene Mawatha, POB 1375, Colombo 10; tel. (1) 689597; fax (1) 689596; e-mail nccsl@slt.lk; internet www.nationalchamberlk.org; monthly.

Ceylon Medical Journal: 6 Wijerama Mawatha, Colombo 7; tel. (1) 693324; fax (1) 698802; e-mail slma@eureka.lk; internet www.medinet.lk/cmj; f. 1887; quarterly; Editors Prof. COLVIN GOONARATNA, Prof. H. JANAKA DE SILVA.

The Economic Times: 51/1 Sri Dharmarama Rd, Colombo 9; tel. (1) 686337; fax (1) 670889; f. 1970; Editor THIMSY FAHIM.

The Financial Times: 323 Union Place, POB 330, Colombo 2; tel. (1) 26181; quarterly; commercial and economic affairs; Man. Editor CYRIL GARDINER.

Gnanarthapradeepaya: Colombo Catholic Press, 2 Gnanarthapradeepaya Mawatha, Borella, Colombo 8; tel. (1) 695984; f. 1866;

Sinhala; Roman Catholic; Chief Editor Rev. Fr W. Don Benedict Joseph; circ. 26,000.

Janakavi: 47 Jayantha Weerasekera Mawatha, Colombo 10; fortnightly; Sinhala; Assoc. Editor Karunaratne Amerasinghe.

Manasa: 150 Dutugemunu St, Dehiwala; tel. (1) 553994; f. 1978; Sinhala; monthly; science of the mind; Editor Sumanadasa Samarasinghe; circ. 6,000.

Mihira: Lake House, 35 D. R. Wijewardene Mawatha, Colombo 10; tel. (1) 21181; f. 1964; Sinhala children's magazine; Editor M. Newton Pinto; circ. 145,000.

Morning Star: 39 Fussels Lane, Colombo 6; tel. (1) 511233; fax (1) 584836; e-mail jdcsiacm@panlanka.net; f. 1841; English and Tamil; publ. by the Jaffna diocese of the Church of South India.

Nava Yugaya: Lake House, 35 D. R. Wijewardene Mawatha, Colombo 10; tel. (1) 21181; f. 1956; literary fortnightly; Sinhala; Editor S. N. Senanayake; circ. 57,000.

Navaliya: 223 Bloemendhal Rd, Colombo 13; tel. (1) 324001; fax (1) 448103; internet www.navaliya.com; Sinhala; women's interest; Editor Chandani Wijetunge; circ. 148,260.

Pathukavalan: POB 2, Jaffna; tel. (21) 22300; f. 1876; Tamil; publ. by St Joseph's Catholic Press; Editor Rev. Fr Ruban Mariampillai; circ. 7,000.

Puthiya Ulaham: 115, 4th Cross St, Jaffna; tel. (21) 22627; f. 1976; Tamil; six a year; publ. by Centre for Better Society; Editor Rev. Dr S. J. Emmanuel; circ. 1,500.

Ravaya: Colombo; Sinhala; Editor Victor Ivan.

Samajawadhaya: 91 Dr N. M. Perera Mawatha, Colombo 8; tel. (1) 595328; monthly; theoretical; publ. by the Communist Party of Sri Lanka.

Sarasaviya: Lake House, 35 D. R. Wijewardene Mawatha, Colombo 10; tel. (1) 21181; f. 1963; Sinhala; films; Editor Granville Silva; circ. 56,000.

Sinhala Bauddhaya: Maha Bodhi Mandira, 130 Rev. Hikkaduwe Sri Sumangala Nahimi Mawatha, Colombo 10; tel. (1) 698079; f. 1906; publ. by The Maha Bodi Society of Ceylon; Editor-in-Chief Kirthi Kalahe; circ. 25,000.

Sri Lanka Government Gazette: Government Press, POB 507, Colombo; tel. (1) 93611; f. 1802; official govt bulletin; circ. 54,000.

Sri Lanka News: Lake House, 35 D. R. Wijewardene Mawatha, Colombo 10; tel. (1) 429429; fax (1) 449069; f. 1938; digest of news and features; printing temporarily suspended from March 2002; Editor Ruwan Godage.

Sri Lanka Today: Government Dept of Information, 7 Sir Baron Jayatilaka Mawatha, Colombo 1; tel. (1) 28376; English; quarterly; Editor Manel Abhayaratne.

Subasetha: Lake House, 35 D. R. Wijewardene Mawatha, Colombo 10; tel. (1) 21181; f. 1967; Sinhala; astrology, the occult and indigenous medicine; Editor Capt. K. Chandra Sri Kularatne; circ. 100,000.

Tharunee: Lake House, 35 D. R. Wijewardene Mawatha, Colombo 10; tel. (1) 21181; f. 1969; Sinhala; women's journal; Editor Sumana Sapramadu; circ. 95,000.

Vidusara: 223 Bloemendhal Rd, Colombo 13; tel. (1) 324001; fax (1) 448103; internet www.vidusara.com; Sinhala; Editor Anura Siriwardena; circ. 103,992.

NEWS AGENCIES

Lankapuvath (National News Agency of Sri Lanka): Transworks House, Lower Chatham St, Colombo 1; tel. (1) 433173; fax (1) 433173; f. 1978; Chair. D. E. W. Gunasekara; Editor G. L. W. Wijesinha.

Press Trust of Ceylon: Negris Bldg, POB 131, Colombo 1; tel. (1) 31174; Chair. R. Bodinagoda; Sec. and Gen. Man. A. W. Amunugama.

Foreign Bureaux

Agence France-Presse (AFP): Colombo Bureau, 100 Barnes Place, Colombo 7; tel. (1) 694384; fax (1) 694385; Chief of Bureau Amal Jayasinghe.

Deutsche Presse-Agentur (dpa) (Germany): Independent Newspapers Ltd, 5 Gunasena Mawatha, Colombo 12; tel. (1) 545327; Correspondent Rex de Silva.

Iraqi News Agency: Dinakara, 301 Darley Rd, Colombo 10; tel. (1) 595323; Correspondent Sarath Cooray.

Press Trust of India (PTI): Colombo; Correspondent K. Dharmarajan.

Reuters (UK): Level 27, East Tower, World Trade Centre, Echelon Sq., Colombo 1; tel. (1) 431187; fax (1) 338302; Sr Co Rep. Dion Schoorman.

United Press International (UPI) (USA): 'Jasmin Court', 60/1 Wijerama Lane, Udahamulla, Nugegoda; tel. (1) 853923; fax (1) 856496; Correspondent Iqbal Athas.

Xinhua (New China) News Agency (People's Republic of China): 24 Pathiba Rd, Colombo 5; tel. (1) 589092; e-mail xhco@eureka.lk; Chief Correspondent Zhang Yadong.

Prensa Latina (Cuba) is also represented.

PRESS ASSOCIATIONS

Press Association of Ceylon: Negris Bldg, POB 131, Colombo 1; tel. (1) 31174; Pres. K. Sivapiragasam; Gen. Sec. U. L. D. Chandratillake.

Sri Lanka Foreign Correspondents' Association: 20 1/1 Regent Flats, Sir Chittampalan Gardiner Mawatha, Colombo; tel. (1) 31224.

Publishers

W. E. Bastian and Co (Pvt) Ltd: 23 Canal Row, Fort, Colombo 1; tel. (1) 432752; f. 1904; art, literature, technical; Dirs H. A. Munideva, K. Hewage, N. Munideva, G. C. Bastian.

Buddhist Publication Society Inc.: 54 Sangharaja Mawatha, POB 61, Kandy; tel. (8) 237283; fax (8) 223679; e-mail bps@ids.lk; internet www.lanka.com/dhamma; philosophy, religion and theology; Editor-in-Chief Bhikkhu Bodhi.

Colombo Catholic Press: 2 Gnanarthapradeepaya Mawatha, Borella, Colombo 8; tel. (1) 695984; f. 1865; religious; publrs of *The Messenger, Gnanartha Pradeepaya, The Weekly;* Exec. Dir Rev. Fr Bertram Dabrera.

M. D. Gunasena and Co Ltd: 217 Olcott Mawatha, POB 246, Colombo 11; tel. (4) 323981; fax (1) 323336; e-mail mdgunasena@mail.ewisl.net; f. 1913; educational and general; Chair M. D. Percy Gunasena; Man. Dir M. D. Ananda Gunasena.

Lake House Printers and Publishers Ltd: 41 W. A. D. Ramanayake Mawatha, POB 1458, Colombo 2; tel. (1) 433271; fax (1) 449504; e-mail rstimes@lanka.ccom.lk; f. 1965; Chair. R. S. Wijewardene; Sec. D. P. Anura Nishantha Kumara.

Pradeepa Publishers: 34/34 Lawyers' Office Complex, Colombo 12; tel. (1) 435074; fax (1) 863261; academic and fictional; Propr K. Jayatilake.

Saman Publishers Ltd: 49/16 Iceland Bldg, Colombo 3; tel. (1) 23058; fax (1) 447972.

Sarexpo International Ltd: Caves Bookshop, 81 Sir Baron Jayatilleke Mawatha, POB 25, Colombo 1; tel. (1) 422676; fax (1) 447854; f. 1876; history, arts, law, medicine, technical, educational; Man. Dir C. J. S. Fernando.

K. V. G. de Silva and Sons (Colombo) Ltd: 49 Abdulgaffor Mawatha, Colombo 3; tel. (1) 301490; fax (1) 588875; f. 1898; art, philosophy, scientific, technical, academic, 'Ceyloniana', fiction; Man. Frederick Jayaratnam.

PUBLISHERS' ASSOCIATION

Sri Lanka Association of Publishers: 112 S. Mahinda Mawatha, Maradana, Colombo 10; tel. (1) 695773; fax (1) 696653; e-mail dayawansajay@hotmail.com; Pres. Dayawansa Jayakody; Sec.-Gen. Gamini Wijesuriya.

Broadcasting and Communications

TELECOMMUNICATIONS

Lanka Communication Services (Pvt) Ltd: 6th Floor, City Bank Bldg, 65c Dharmapala Mawatha, Colombo 7; tel. (1) 437545; fax (1) 537547; Man. Dir D. Hanly.

Lanka Internet Services Ltd: World Trade Center, 24th Floor, Echelon Sq., Colombo 1; tel. (1) 346441; CEO Dr P. Samaratunga.

MTN Networks (Pvt) Ltd: 502 R. A. de Mel Mawatha, Colombo 3; tel. (1) 594329; fax (1) 594337; Chief Exec. H. Suria.

Sri Lanka Telecom Ltd: Telecom Headquarters, 7th Floor, Lotus Rd, POB 503, Colombo 1; tel. (1) 335010; fax (1) 424800; e-mail md@slt.lk; 35% owned by Nippon Telegraph and Telephone Corpn (Japan), 61.5% by Govt of Sri Lanka and 3.5% by employees; Chair. H. Fernando; CEO Hideaki Kamitsuma.

Regulatory Authority

Telecommunications Regulatory Commission of Sri Lanka: 276 Elvitigala Mawatha, Manning Town, Colombo 8; tel. (1) 689345; fax (1) 689341; e-mail dgtsl@slt.lk; internet www.trc.gov.lk; Chair. S. S. Ediriweera; Dir-Gen. R. D. Somasiri.

RADIO

Sri Lanka Broadcasting Corpn: Independence Sq., POB 574, Colombo 7; tel. (1) 697491; fax (1) 695488; e-mail slbcweb@srilankanet; f. 1967; under Ministry of Posts, Telecommunications and the Media; controls all broadcasting in Sri Lanka; regional stations at Anuradhapura, Kandy and Matara; transmitting stations at Ambewela, Amparai, Anuradhapura, Diyagama, Ekala, Galle, Kanthalai, Mahiyangana, Maho, Matara, Puttalam, Ratnapura, Seeduwa, Senkadagala, Weeraketiya; home service in Sinhala, Tamil and English; foreign service also in Tamil, English, Sinhala, Hindi, Kannada, Malayalam, Nepali and Telugu; 893 broadcasting hours per week: 686 on domestic services, 182 on external services and 126 on education; Chair. JANADASA PEIRIS; Dir-Gen. ERIC FERNANDO.

Colombo Communications (Pvt) Ltd: 2/9 2nd Floor, Liberty Plaza, 250 R. A. de Mel Mawatha, Colombo 3; tel. (1) 577924; fax (1) 577929; commercial station; three channels broadcast 24 hrs daily in English, Sinhala and Tamil.

Lite FM: No. 52 5th Lane, Colombo 3; tel. (1) 575000; fax (1) 301082; e-mail tnlradio@sri.lanka.net; internet www.lite892.com; commercial station; broadcasts 24 hrs daily in English; Exec. Dir NIRAJ WICKREMESINGHE.

MBC Networks (Pvt) Ltd: Colombo; tel. (1) 689234; commercial station; broadcasts 24 hrs daily in English and Sinhala.

TNL Radio: No. 52, 5th Lane, Colombo 3; tel. (1) 575000; fax (1) 301082; e-mail tnlradio@sri.lanka.net; internet www.tnlradio.com; commercial station; broadcasts 24 hrs daily in English; Exec. Dir NIRAJ WICKREMESINGHE.

Trans World Radio: 125/3, 3rd Lane, Subadrarama Rd, POB 123, Nugegoda; tel. (75) 559321; fax (1) 817749; e-mail rkoch@twr.org; f. 1978; religious station; broadcasts 3 hours every morning and 6.75 hours each evening to Indian subcontinent; Dir (Finance) ROGER KOCH; Eng. P. VELMURUGAN.

TELEVISION

Sri Lanka Rupavahini Corpn (SLRC): Independence Sq., POB 2204, Colombo 7; tel. (1) 580136; fax (1) 500373; e-mail ddge@rupavahini.lk; internet www.rupavahini.lk; f. 1982; studio at Colombo; transmitting stations at nine locations; broadcasts 18 hrs daily on 1st channel, 12 hrs daily on 2nd channel; Chair. Prof. DAMMIKA GANGANATH DISSANAYAKE; Dep. Dir-Gen. (Eng.) UPALI ARAMBEWALE.

Independent Television Network (ITN—Sri Lanka): Wickremasinghepura, Battaramulla; tel. (1) 865494; fax (1) 864591; e-mail itnch@slt.lk; internet www.itnsl.lk; broadcasts about 6 hrs daily; Chair. NEWTON GUNARATNE; Gen. Man. S. LOKUGAMAGE.

EAP Network (Pvt) Ltd: 676 Galle Rd, Colombo 3; tel. (1) 503819; fax (1) 503788; e-mail eapnet@slt.lk; Chair. SOMA EDIRISINGHE; Man. Dir JEEVAKA EDIRISINGHE.

MTV Channel (Pvt) Ltd: Araliya Uyana, Depanama, Pannipitiya.

Telshan Network (Pvt) Ltd (TNL): 9D, Tower Bldg, 25 Station Rd, Colombo 4; tel. (1) 501681; fax (1) 501683; Chair. and Man. Dir SHANTILAL NILKANT WICKREMESINGHE.

Finance

(cap. = capital; res = reserves; dep. = deposits; m. = million; brs = branches; amounts in Sri Lanka rupees, unless otherwise indicated)

BANKING

Central Bank

Central Bank of Sri Lanka: 30 Janadhipathi Mawatha, POB 590, Colombo 1; tel. (1) 477000; fax (1) 477677; e-mail cbslgen@sri.lanka.net; internet www.centralbanklanka.org; f. 1950; sole bank of issue; cap. 15m., res 985m., dep. 70,210m. (Dec. 1999); Gov. and Chair. of the Monetary Board A. S. JAYAWARDENA; Dep. Govs P. M. NAGAHAWATTA, W. A. WIJEWARDENA; 3 regional offices.

Commercial Banks

Bank of Ceylon: 4 Bank of Ceylon Mawatha, POB 241, Colombo 1; tel. (1) 446811; fax (1) 447171; e-mail agmint@boc.lanka.net; internet www.bankofceylon.net; f. 1939; 100% state-owned; cap. 2,600m., res 8,512.6m., dep. 131,126.7m. (Dec. 2000); Chair. DESAMANYA K. BALENDRA; Gen. Man. A. SARATH DE SILVA; 296 brs in Sri Lanka, 7 brs abroad.

Commercial Bank of Ceylon Ltd: Commercial House, 21 Bristol St, POB 856, Colombo 1; tel. (1) 430416; fax (1) 449889; e-mail e-mail@combank.net; internet www.combank.net; f. 1969; 29.77% owned by DFCC Bank, 29.91% by govt corpns and 40.32% by public; cap. 1,324.4m., res 5,420.4m., dep. 46,533.5m. (Dec. 2001); Chair. M. J. C. AMARASURIYA; Man. Dir A. L. GOONERATNE; 86 brs.

Hatton National Bank Ltd: 10 R. A. de Mel Mawatha, POB 837, Colombo 3; tel. (1) 421885; fax (1) 434057; e-mail moreinfo@hnb.net; internet www.hnb.net; f. 1970; 15.7% owned by Standard Finance Ltd, 29.9% by public and 54.5% by others; cap. 650m., res 4,897.9m., dep. 62,757.8m. (Dec. 2000); Chair. J. CHRISANTHA R. COORAY; Gen. Man. and CEO RIENZIE T. WIJETILLEKE; 96 brs.

Nations Trust Bank Ltd: 76 York St, Colombo 1; tel. (1) 447655; fax (1) 447659; e-mail bank@nationstrust.lk; internet www.nationstrust.com; f. 1999; privately-owned; cap. 500.0m., res 85.5m., dep. 2,196.2m. (Dec. 2000); Chair. VIVENDRA LINTOTAWELA; CEO MOKSEVI R. PRELIS.

Pan Asia Bank Ltd: 450 Galle Rd, Colombo 3; tel. (1) 565556; fax (1) 565562; e-mail panasia@itmin.com; internet www.pabnk.lk; f. 1995; 100% privately-owned; cap. 445.0m., res 92.8m., dep. 2,995.6m. (Dec. 2000); Chair. Dr W. M. TILAKARATNA; Gen. Man. and CEO DAYA MUTHUKUMARANA; 11 brs.

People's Bank: 75 Sir Chittampalam A. Gardiner Mawatha, POB 728, Colombo 2; tel. (1) 327841; fax (1) 446407; e-mail info@people.is.lk; internet www.peoplesbank.lk; f. 1961; 92% owned by Govt, 8% by co-operatives; cap. 1,202m., res –7,511.3m., dep. 115,864.7m. (Dec. 2000); Chair. MANO TITTAWELLA; CEO/Gen. Man. DERECK J, KELLY; 323 brs.

Sampath Bank Ltd: 110 Sir James Peiris Mawatha, POB 997, Colombo 2; tel. (1) 300153; fax (1) 300143; e-mail mgr@oper.sampath.lk; internet www.sampath.lk; f. 1987; cap. 442.8m., res 2,090.9m., dep. 29,668.8m. (Dec. 2001); Chair. EDGAR GUNATUNGA; Man. Dir/CEO ANIL AMARASURIYA; 40 brs.

Seylan Bank Ltd: Ceylinco Seylan Towers, 90 Galle Rd, POB 400, Colombo 3; tel. (1) 456789; fax (1) 456456; e-mail info@seylan.lk; internet www.eseylan.com; f. 1988; cap. 446.1m., res 1,791.9m., dep. 47,859.5m. (Dec. 2001); Chair. J. L. B. KOTELAWALA; Gen. Man./CEO/Dir Mrs ROHINI L. NANAYAKKARA; 90 brs.

Union Bank of Colombo Ltd: Level 28, East Tower, World Trade Centre, Echelon Sq., POB 348, Colombo 1; tel. (1) 346357; fax (74) 714452; e-mail shan@unionb.com; internet www.unionb.com; f. 1995; cap. 360.0m., res 20.9m., dep. 4,804.0m. (Dec. 1999); Chair. CHANAKA DE SILVA; CEO and Man. Dir SHAN SHANMUGANATHAN.

Development Banks

Agricultural and Industrial Credit Corpn of Ceylon: POB 20, Colombo 3; tel. (1) 23783; f. 1943; loan cap. 30m.; Chair. V. P. VITTACHI; Gen. Man. H. S. F. GOONEWARDENA.

DFCC Bank: 73/5 Galle Rd, POB 1397, Colombo 3; tel. (1) 440366; fax (1) 440376; e-mail dfcc@sri.lanka.net; internet www.dfcc.com; f. 1956 as Development Finance Corpn of Ceylon; name changed as above 1997; provides long- and medium-term credit, investment banking and consultancy services; cap. 352.5m., res 4,684.6m., dep. 2,666.8m. (March 2000); Chair. E. M. WIJENAIKE; Gen. Man. Dir and CEO N. FONSEKA; 3 brs.

National Development Bank of Sri Lanka: 40 Navam Mawatha, Colombo 2; tel. (1) 437701; fax (1) 440262; e-mail info@ndb.org; internet www.ndb.org; f. 1979; provides long-term finance for projects, equity financing and merchant banking services; cap. 537.5m., res 5,115.5m. (March 2000); Chair. SARATH KUSUM WICKREMESINGHE; Gen. Man. and Chief Exec./Dir RANJIT MICHAEL SAMUEL FERNANDO.

State Mortgage and Investment Bank: 269 Galle Road, POB 156, Colombo 3; tel. (1) 573563; fax (1) 573346; e-mail smibgm@itmin.com; internet www.lanka.net/smib; f. 1979; Chair. Dr GAMINI FERNANDO; Gen. Man. U. H. D. PATHMASIRI.

Merchant Banks

Merchant Bank of Sri Lanka Ltd: Bank of Ceylon Merchant Tower, 28 St. Michael's Rd, POB 1987, Colombo 3; tel. (74) 711711; fax (74) 711743; e-mail mbslbank@mbslbank.com; internet www.mbslbank.com; f. 1982; 53.8% owned by Bank of Ceylon; public ltd liability co; cap. p.u. 500m. (1999), total assets 3,398m. (1994); Chair. DESAMANYA K. BALENDRA; Man. Dir/CEO SUNIL G. WIJESINHA; 3 brs.

People's Merchant Bank Ltd: Level 4, Hemas House, 75 Braybrooke Place, Colombo 2; tel. (1) 300191; fax (1) 300190; e-mail pmbank@sltnet.lk; f. 1983; total assets 610m. (1999); Chair. Dr G. FERNANDO.

Foreign Banks

ABN AMRO Bank NV (Netherlands): 103A Dharmapala Mawatha, Colombo 7; tel. (1) 448448; fax (1) 446986; Gen. Man. MICHAEL MOORMANN.

American Express Bank Ltd (USA): 104 Dharmapala Mawatha, Colombo 7; tel. (1) 682787; fax (1) 682786; Dir of Operations K. BALACHANDRARAJAN.

ANZ Grindlays Bank Ltd (UK): 37 York St, POB 112, Colombo 1; tel. (1) 446150; fax (1) 446158; e-mail iossifij@anz.com; f. 1881; Gen. Man. JOHN IOSSIFIDIS.

Citibank NA (USA): 67 Dharmapala Mawatha, POB 888, Colombo 7; tel. (1) 447316; fax (1) 445487; Vice-Pres. KAPILA JAYAWARDENA.

Crédit Agricole Indosuez (France): 1st Floor, Ceylinco House, 69 Janadhipathi Mawatha, POB 303, Colombo 1; tel. (1) 436181; fax (1) 541537; f. 1979; Gen. Man. FRANCIS DUBUS.

Deutsche Bank AG (Germany): 86 Galle Rd, POB 314, Colombo 3; tel. (1) 447062; fax (1) 447067; Gen. Man. MATTHIAS KLUG.

Emirates Bank International Ltd (United Arab Emirates): 64 Lotus Rd, POB 358, Colombo 1; tel. (1) 23467; Gen. Man. N. C. VITARANA.

Habib Bank Ltd (Pakistan): 140–142 Second Cross St, POB 1088, Colombo 11; tel. (1) 326565; fax (1) 447827; e-mail habiblk@serendib.ccom.lk; f. 1941; Sr Vice-Pres. and Gen. Man. MUHAMMAD YOUNUS PINGAL.

Hongkong and Shanghai Banking Corpn Ltd (Hong Kong): 24 Sir Baron Jayatilaka Mawatha, POB 73, Colombo 1; tel. (1) 325435; fax (1) 448388; internet www.asiapacific.hsbc.com; CEO NIK CHERRILL.

Indian Bank (India): 22 & 24 Mudalige Mawatha, POB 624, Colombo 1; tel. (1) 323402; fax (1) 447562; e-mail ibcol@slnet.lk; Chief Exec. C. S. RAMANI.

Indian Overseas Bank (India): 139 Main St, POB 671, Colombo 11; tel. (1) 324422; fax (1) 447900; e-mail iobch@lgo.lk; Country Head K. LAKSHMI NARASIMHAN; 1 br.

Mashreq Bank PSC (United Arab Emirates): 245 Dharmapala Mawatha, Colombo 7; tel. (1) 679000; fax (75) 331849; e-mail mshqgen@sri.lanka.net; Country Man. KHURRAM HUSSAIN.

Overseas Trust Bank Ltd (Hong Kong): YMCA Bldg, 39 Bristol St, POB 835, Colombo 1; tel. (1) 547655.

Public Bank Berhad (Malaysia): Ground and First Floor, Jewelarts Bldg, 324 Galle Rd, Colombo 3; tel. (1) 576289; fax (1) 573958.

Standard Chartered Bank PLC (UK): 17 Janadhipathi Mawatha, POB 27, Colombo 1; tel. (1) 26671; fax (1) 432522; f. 1853; Man. J. M. MORRISON.

State Bank of India: 16 Sir Baron Jayatilleke Mawatha, POB 93, Colombo 1; tel. (1) 26133; fax (1) 547166; f. 1955; Chief Man. B. P. AGRAWAL.

Financial Association

The Finance Houses' Association of Sri Lanka: 84 Ward Place, Colombo 7; tel. (1) 699295; fax (1) 697205; f. 1958; represents the finance cos registered and licensed by the Central Bank of Sri Lanka; Chair. KITHSIRI B. WANIGASEKERA; Sec. M. M. N. DE SILVA.

STOCK EXCHANGE

Colombo Stock Exchange: 04–01, West Block, World Trade Centre, Echelon Sq., Colombo 1; tel. (1) 446581; fax (1) 445279; e-mail cse@cse.lk; internet www.cse.lk; f. 1896; stock market; 15 mem firms and 241 listed cos; Chair. AJIT D. GUNEWARDENE; Dir-Gen. HIRAN MENDIS.

INSURANCE

Ceylinco Insurance Co Ltd: Ceylinco House, 4th Floor, 69 Janadhipathi Mawatha, Colombo 1; tel. (1) 485706; fax (1) 485769; e-mail jagath@lanka.ccom.lk; f. 1987; Chair. and Man. Dir J. L. B. KOTELAWALA.

Eagle Insurance Co Ltd: 'Eagle House', 75 Kumaran Ratnam Rd, Colombo 2; tel. (1) 437090; fax (1) 447620; e-mail eaglehouse@eureka.lk; internet www.eagle.com.lk; f. 1988 as CTC Eagle Insurance Co Ltd; general and life insurance; mem. of the Zurich Group; Chair. Dr F. A. SCHNEWLIN; Man. Dir CHANDRA JAYARATNE.

Hayleys Ltd: Hayley Bldg, 400 Deans Rd, Colombo 10; internet www.hayleys.com; f. 1952; Chair. SUNIL MENDIS; Dep. Chair. R. YATAWARA.

National Insurance Corpn Ltd: 47 Muttiah Rd, POB 2202, Colombo 2; tel. (1) 445738; fax (1) 445733; general; Chair. T. M. S. NANAYAKKARA; Sec. A. C. J. DE ALWIS.

Sri Lanka Insurance Corporation Ltd: 'Rakshana Mandiraya', 21 Vauxhall St, POB 1337, Colombo 2; tel. (1) 325311; fax (1) 447742; e-mail jww@eureka.lk; internet www.lk.rakshana; f. 1961; all classes of insurance; Chair. Prof. J. W. WICKRAMASINGHE; Exec. Dir K. L. SAMARASINGHE.

Union Assurance Ltd: Union Assurance Centre, 20 St. Michael's Rd, Colombo 3; tel. (1) 344171; fax (1) 343065; e-mail info@union-assurance.com; internet www.union-assurance.com; f. 1987; general and life insurance; Chair. KEN BALENDRA; Dep. Chair. R. SIVARATNAM.

Trade and Industry

GOVERNMENT AGENCIES

Board of Investment of Sri Lanka: World Trade Centre, West Tower, 15th-17th Floor, Echelon Sq., Colombo 1; tel. (1) 434403; fax (1) 447995; e-mail info@boisrilanka.org; internet www.boisrilanka.org; f. 1978, as the Greater Colombo Economic Commission; promotes foreign direct investment and administers the five Export Processing Zones at Katunayake, Biyagama, Koggala, Mirigama and Malwatta; also administers industrial township at Watupitiwala and industrial parks at Seetawaka and Kandy; Chair. LALITH DE MEL.

National Gem and Jewellery Authority: 25 Galle Face Terrace, Colombo 3; tel. and fax (1) 329352; e-mail ngja@sri.lanka.net; f. 1971 as State Gem Corpn; Chair. Prof. P. G. R. DHARMARATNE; Dir-Gen. T. PIYADASA.

Sri Lanka Gem and Jewellery Exchange: 310 Galle Rd, Colombo 3; tel. (1) 574274; fax (1) 576171; e-mail ngja@sri.lanka.net; f. 1990; import and export facilities, testing and certification of gems, assaying and hallmarking, trading booths; Dir-Gen. T. PIYADASA; Man.(Export Promotion) G. H. A. P. PERERA.

Public Enterprises Reform Commission (PERC): 11–01 West Tower, World Trade Centre, Colombo 1; tel. (1) 338756; fax (1) 326116; e-mail dg@perc.gov.lk; internet www.perc.gov.lk; f. 1995 to advise Govt on privatization and restructuring of loss-making state-sector enterprises; Chair. Dr P. B. JAYASUNDERA; Dir-Gen. MANO TITTAWELLA.

Trade Information Service: Sri Lanka Export Development Board, Colombo Renaissance Hotel Complex, 115 Sir Chittampalam A. Gardiner Mawatha, POB 1872, Colombo 2; tel. (1) 438523; fax (1) 438404; f. 1981 to collect and disseminate commercial information and to provide advisory services to trade circles; Dir Mrs G. I. UNAMBOOWE.

DEVELOPMENT ORGANIZATIONS

Industrial Development Board of Ceylon (IDB): 615 Galle Rd, Katubedda, Moratuwa; tel. 605887; fax 607002; e-mail idbch@sltnet.lk; internet www.nsf.ac.lk/idb; f. 1969; under Ministry of Industrial Development; promotes industrial development through provincial network; Chair. C. T. S. B. PERERA; Gen. Man. CHANDRASIRI KALUPAHNAGE.

Centre for Entrepreneurship Development and Consultancy Services: 615 Galle Rd, Katubedda, Moratuwa; tel. (1) 632156; f. 1989; Dir T. M. KULARATHNE (acting).

Centre for Industrial and Technology Information Services (CITIS): 615 Galle Rd, Katubedda, Moratuwa; tel. (1) 605372; fax (1) 607002; e-mail citis@slt.lk; internet www.nsf.ac.lk/idb; f. 1989; Dir CHANDRASIRI KALUPAHANAGE (acting).

Sri Lanka Export Development Board: Level 7, Trade Information Service, 42 Navam Mawatha, Colombo 2; tel. (1) 300705; fax (1) 300715; e-mail tisinfo@edb.tradenetsl.lk; internet www.tradenetsl.lk; Chair. G. L. J. HEWAWASAM (acting).

Coconut Development Authority: 11 Duke St, POB 386, Colombo 1; tel. (1) 421027; fax (1) 447602; e-mail cocoauth@panlanka.net; internet www.cda.lk; f. 1972; state body; promotes the coconut industry through financial assistance for mfrs of coconut products, market information, consultancy services and quality assurance; Chair. H. A. THILAKARATNE.

Janatha Estates Development Board: 55/75 Vauxhall St, Colombo 2; tel. (1) 320901; fax (1) 446577; f. 1975; manages 18 tea and spice plantations; 10,164 employees; 1 regional office.

CHAMBERS OF COMMERCE

Federation of Chambers of Commerce and Industry of Sri Lanka: 29 Gregory's Rd, Colombo 7; tel. (1) 698225; fax (1) 699530; internet www.fccisl.org; f. 1973; Pres. LAL DE MEL.

All Ceylon Trade Chamber: Colombo; tel. (1) 432428; Pres. MUDLIYAR N. W. J. MUDALIGE; Gen. Sec. Y. P. MUTHUKUMARANA.

Ceylon Chamber of Commerce: 50 Navam Mawatha, POB 274, Colombo 2; tel. (1) 421745; fax (1) 449352; e-mail info@chamber.lk; internet www.chamber.lk; f. 1839; 517 mems; Chair. TILAK DE ZOYSA; Sec.-Gen. RENTON DE ALWIS.

Ceylon National Chamber of Industries: Galle Face Court 2, Room 20, 1st Floor, POB 1775, Colombo 3; tel. (1) 423734; fax (1) 423734; f. 1960; 300 mems; Chair. LAL DE MEL; Chief Exec. JOE SOTHINATHAN.

International Chamber of Commerce Sri Lanka: 1st Floor, CNAPT Centre, 51 Sir Marcus Fernando Mawatha, POB 1733, Colombo 7; tel. and fax (1) 691290; e-mail iccsl@itmin.com; f. 1955; Chair. M.J.C. AMARASURIYA; CEO P. A. PATHIRANA.

The National Chamber of Commerce of Sri Lanka: NCCSL Bldg, 450 D. R. Wijewardene Mawatha, POB 1375, Colombo 10; tel. (1) 689600; fax (1) 689596; e-mail nccsl@slt.lk; internet www.nationalchamberlk.org; f. 1948: Pres. ASOKA DE Z. GUNASEKERA; Sec.-Gen. NEIL C. SENEVIRATNE.

INDUSTRIAL AND TRADE ASSOCIATIONS

The Association of Computer Training Organizations: 5 Clifford Ave, Colombo 3; tel. (1) 565193; fax (1) 713821; e-mail info tel@sri.lanka.net; internet www.actoslanka.org; f. 1991; 29 mems; Pres. KITHSIRI MANCHANAYAKE.

Ceylon Coir Fibre Exporters' Association: c/o Volanka Ltd, 193 Minuwangoda Rd, Kotugoda; tel. (1) 232938; fax (1) 237365; e-mail volanka@sri.lanka.net; internet www.slcfa.lk; Chair. INDRAJITH PIYASENA.

Ceylon Hardware Merchants' Association: 20B Central Rd, Colombo 12; tel. and fax (1) 435920; Pres. S. THILLAINATHAN.

Ceylon Planters' Society: 40/1 Sri Dharmadara Mawatha, Ratmalana; tel. (1) 715656; fax (1) 716758; e-mail plansoty@sltnet.lk; f. 1936; 1,660 mems (plantation mans); 25 brs and nine regional organizations; Pres. J. W. Y. K. DE SILVA; Sec. D. S. P. HETTIARACHCHI.

Coconut Products Traders' Association: c/o Ceylon Chamber of Commerce, 50 Navam Mawatha, POB 274, Colombo 2; tel. (1) 421745; fax (1) 449352; f. 1925; Chair. N. PIERIS; Sec. C. G. JAYASURIYA.

Colombo Rubber Traders' Association: c/o Ceylon Chamber of Commerce, 50 Navam Mawatha, POB 274, Colombo 2; tel. (1) 380150; fax (1) 449352; e-mail kanchana@chamber.lk; internet www.chamber.lk; f. 1918; Chair. W. T. ELLAWALA; Sec. RENTON DE ALWIS.

Colombo Tea Traders' Association: c/o Ceylon Chamber of Commerce, 50 Navam Mawatha, POB 274, Colombo 2; tel. (1) 380150; fax (1) 449352; e-mail kanchana@chamber.lk; internet www.chamber.lk; f. 1894; 198 mems; Chair. MAHEN DAYANANDA; Sec. RENTON DE ALWIS.

Free Trade Zone Manufacturers' Association: Plaza Complex, Unit 6 (Upper Floor), IPZ, Katunayake; tel. (1) 252813; Administrative Sec. TUWAN SAMAHOON.

The Industrial Association of Sri Lanka: c/o Ceylon Chamber of Commerce, 50 Nawam Mawatha, POB 274, Colombo 2; tel. (1) 422084.

Sea Food Exporters' Association: c/o Andriesz & Co Ltd, 39 Nuge Rd, Peliyagoda; tel. 530021.

Software Exporters' Association: c/o Project Management Division, Sri Lanka Export Development Board, 42 Nawam Mawatha, Colombo 2; e-mail it@eureka.lk; internet www.islandsoftware.org.

Sri Lanka Apparel Exporters' Association: 45 Rosmead Place, Colombo 7; tel. (1) 670778; fax (1) 683118; e-mail srilanka-apparel@eureka.lk; internet www.srilanka-apparel.com; f. 1982; Chair. RANJAN CASIE CHETTY; Sec. HEMAMALI SIRISENA.

Sri Lanka Association of Manufacturers and Exporters of Rubber Products (SLAMERP): 341/12 Kotte Rd, Rajagirya; tel. (1) 863429; fax (74) 410557; e-mail slamerp@panlanka.net; internet www.tradenetsl.lk/slamerp; f. 1984; Chair. ANANDA CALDERA; Sec.-Gen. C. DIAS BANDARANAYAKE.

Sri Lanka Association of Printers: 593 Kularatne Mawatha, Colombo 10; tel. (1) 687557; fax (1) 572875; e-mail christo@itmin.com; f. 1993; Pres. CHRISTOPHER R. DIAS; Sec. KOSALA THILLEKARATNE.

Sri Lanka Chamber of the Pharmaceutical Industry: 15 Tichbourne Passage, Colombo 10; tel. (1) 694823; fax (1) 671877; e-mail nimjay@sltnet.lk; Pres. N. DIAS JAYASINHA; Sec. NAUSHAD ISMAIL.

Sri Lanka Fruit and Vegetables Producers, Processors and Exporters' Association: c/o Sri Lanka Export Development Board, 42 Navam Mawatha, Colombo 2; tel. (1) 300705; fax (1) 300715; e-mail ead@edb.tradenetsl.lk; internet www.tradenetsl.lk; Sec. M. A. JUNAID.

Sri Lanka Importers, Exporters and Manufacturers' Association (SLIEMA): 28 Rajamalwatte Rd, POB 12, Colombo 15; tel. (1) 696321; fax (1) 522524; e-mail sliema@isplanka.lk; f. 1955; Pres. WILLIAM JOHN TERRENCE PERERA.

Sri Lanka Jewellery Manufacturing Exporters' Association: Colombo; tel. (1) 445141; fax (1) 445105; Pres. IFTHIKHAR AZIZ; Sec. CHANAKA ELLAWELA.

Sri Lanka Shippers' Council: c/o Ceylon Chamber of Commerce, 50 Nawam Mawatha, POB 274, Colombo 2; tel. (1) 422156; internet www.slcs.ws.

Sri Lanka Tea Board: 574 Galle Rd, POB 1750, Colombo 3; tel. (1) 582236; fax (1) 589132; e-mail tboard@sri.lanka.net; internet www.pureceylontea.com; f. 1976 for development of tea industry through research and promotion in Sri Lanka and in world markets; Chair. RONNIE WEERAKOON; Dir-Gen. S. WIRITHAMULLA.

Sri Lanka Wooden Furniture and Wood Products Manufacturers' and Exporters' Association: c/o E. H. Cooray & Sons Ltd, 411 Galle Rd, Colombo 3; tel. (1) 509227; fax (1) 575198; Pres. PATRICK AMARASINGHE; Sec. PINSIRI FERNANDO.

Sugar Importers' Association of Sri Lanka: c/o C. W. Mackie & Co Ltd, 36 D. R. Wijewardena Mawatha, POB 89, Colombo 10; tel. (1) 423554; fax (1) 438069; Pres. M. THAVAYOGARAJAH; Sec. C. KAPUWATTA.

EMPLOYERS' ORGANIZATION

Employers' Federation of Ceylon: 385 J3 Old Kotte Rd, Rajagiriya, Colombo; tel. (1) 867966; fax (1) 867942; e-mail gkbd@eureka.lk; internet www.empfed.lk; f. 1928; mem. International Organization of Employers and Confederation of Asian Pacific Employers; 440 mems; Chair. R. SIVARATNAM; Dir-Gen. G. K. B. DASANAYAKA.

UTILITIES

Electricity

Ceylon Electricity Board: 50 Sir Chittampalam A. Gardiner Mawatha, POB 540, Colombo 2; tel. (1) 320953; fax (1) 323935; e-mail chairceb@sri.lanka.net; f. 1969; Chair. ARJUN DERANIYAGALA.

Water

National Water Supply and Drainage Board (NWSDB): Galle Rd, Ratmalana; tel. (1) 638999; fax (1) 636449; e-mail gmswe@sltnet.lk; f. 1975; govt corpn; Gen. Man. S. WEERARATNE.

CO-OPERATIVES

In 2000 there were an estimated 11,793 co-operative societies in Sri Lanka, with membership totalling 17,235,000.

MAJOR COMPANIES

ACL Cables Ltd: 21 Norris Canal Rd, Colombo 10; tel. (1) 697652; fax (1) 696058; f. 1962; sales Rs 1,410m. (1999/2000); manufacture and marketing of cables and conductors; Chair. and Man. Dir U. G. MADANAYAKE; Exec. Dir H. A. S. MADANAYAKE; 515 employees.

Aitken Spence and Co Ltd: Vauxhall Towers, 305 Vauxhall St, POB 5, Colombo 2; tel. (1) 308308; fax (1) 445406; e-mail info@aitkenspence.lk; internet www.aitkenspence.com; f. 1868; sales Rs 4,311m. (1999/2000); conglomerate with vested interests in hotels, inbound and outbound travel, cargo logistics services, printing and packaging, plantations, ship agency services, property and infrastructure development, and light engineering; agents for Lloyds of London since 1876 and for various airlines; Chair./Man. Dir R. SIVARATNAM; 4,000 employees (2000).

Allied Industries Ltd: 95 Hyde Park Corner, Colombo 2; tel. (1) 687395; fax (1) 687007; manufactures and exports razor blades, disposable razors and pens; Chair. M. P. S. WIJAYAWARDENA; Man. Dir VAJIRA KALINGA WIJAYAWARDENA.

Asbestos Cement Industries Ltd: 175 Sri Sumanatissa Mawatha, POB 1361, Colombo 12; tel. (1) 435115; fax (1) 449537; e-mail aciho@sltnet.lk; f. 1955; cap. Rs 257m., sales Rs 1,305m. (1999); factory at Ratmalana; asbestos cement roofing, ceiling and moulded products; Chair. SEPALA WIMALADHARMA MOLLIGODA; Man. Dir MAHESAN GANESAN; 774 employees (1999).

Asian Electrical and Mineral Industries Ltd: 411 Ferguson Rd, POB 1091, Colombo 15; tel. (1) 522431; fax (1) 522943; f. 1969; mfrs of Tungslite electric light bulbs; Chair. RAY DE COSTA; Gen. Man. L. S. SENEVIRATNE; 100 employees.

Associated Battery Manufacturers (Ceylon) Ltd: POB 42, Mount Lavinia; tel. (71) 3113; f. 1960; sales Rs 416m. (1994/95); mfrs of hard rubber and polypropylene automotive and motor-cycle batteries, battery components and antimonial lead; Gen. Man. Maj.-Gen. H. G. SILVA; 226 employees.

Associated Motorways Ltd: 185 Union Place, Colombo 2; tel. (1) 433371; fax (1) 449909; e-mail amw@eureka.lk; f. 1949; sales Rs 1,659.8m. (1997/98); tyre rebuilding, rubber goods and rubber compounds; Chair. AJITA DE ZOYSA; Dep. Chair. and Man. Dir TILAK DE ZOYSA; 1,500 employees.

BCC Lanka Ltd: Hulftsdorp Mills, Meeraniya St, POB 281, Colombo 12; tel. (1) 422111; fax (1) 447139; e-mail bccl@sltnet.lk; sales Rs 236.2m. (1996/97); mfrs and shippers of coconut oil, household and toilet soaps, detergents, etc.; Chair. ROHAN DE ALWIS; 259 employees.

Blue Diamonds Jewellery Worldwide Ltd: 55 1/1 Iceland Bldg, Galle Rd, Colombo 3; tel. (1) 684275; fax (1) 438417; f. 1990; sales

Rs 569.4m. (1996/97); mfr and exporter of jewellery (particularly gold and diamonds); Chair. J. L. B. KOTELAWA; Dep. Chair. D. R. SENANAYAKE; 180 employees.

Bogala Graphite Lanka Ltd: 63 Elvitigala Mawatha, POB 233, Colombo 8; tel. (1) 696145; fax (1) 698708; e-mail bogalag@slt.lk; f. 1991; sales Rs 165.4m. (1997/98); mining, processing and export of graphite; Chair. D. KALANSOORIYA; Dir and Gen. Man. W. A. D. N. GREGORY; 600 employees.

Browns Group Industries Ltd: 481 T. B. Jaya Mawatha, POB 200, Colombo 10; tel. (1) 697111; fax (1) 698489; e-mail damasin_browns@mail.ewisl.net; f. 1982; sales Rs 2,000m. (1999); air conditioners, ceiling fans, radiators, marine engines, 2-wheel tractors, agricultural trailers and implements, hardware, plastic goods etc.; Chair. J. C. R. COORAY; Man. Dir D. P. FERNANDO; 1,100 employees (1999).

Buildings Materials Corpn Ltd: 541 Sri Sangaraja Mawatha, Colombo 12; tel. (1) 326701; fax (1) 445614; e-mail bmc@panlanka.net; f. 1971; sales Rs 1,431m. (1999); import, supply, distribution and sale of building materials; Chair./Man. Dir WIJERATNE SIRIWARDENA; 1,054 employees (1999).

Care Products (Pvt) Ltd: 96 Parakrama Rd, Peliyagoda; tel. (1) 912879; fax (1) 912878; e-mail nirmal@sltnet.lk; mfrs and exporters of detergents, disinfectants and cleaning products; Chair. D. S. MADANAYAKE; CEO N. A. MADANAYAKE.

Carson Cumberbatch & Co Ltd: 83 George R. De Silva Mawatha, Colombo 13; tel. (1) 343361; fax (1) 436119; f. 1913; sales Rs 2,598.8m. (1998/99); plantations and export of tea, insurance, financial services, real estate, brewing, hotelier; Chair. WIJAYA UNAMBOOWE; Dep. Chair. HARI SELVANATHAN; 1,000 emploees.

H. Don Carolis & Sons Ltd: 64 Keyzer St, POB 48, Colombo 11; tel. (1) 325676; fax (1) 447862; e-mail dons@eureka.lk; internet www.eureka.lk/doncarolis; f. 1860; sales Rs 161.8m. (1996/97); manufacturers and exporters of wooden furniture; Chair. SINGHA WEERASEKERA; 350 employees.

Ceylon Agro-Industries Ltd: 346 Negombo Rd, Seeduwa; tel. (1) 253527; fax (1) 253537; e-mail gm.cai@prima.com.lk; f. 1992; sales US $18m. (1998); mfrs and exporters of instant noodles, bakery products and oil; poultry processing; Gen. Man. Dr LIM BENG JOO; 800 employees.

Ceylon Cold Stores Ltd: 1 Justice Akbar Mawatha, POB 220, Colombo 2; tel. (1) 328221; fax (1) 447422; e-mail coldstor@keells.com; internet www.keels.com; f. 1866; sales Rs 1,699.6m. (1997/98); mfrs, wholesalers, retailers of food and beverages; exports sea foods, spices, essential oils, fruit juices and processed meats; br. at Trincomalee; Chair. K. BALENDRA; Gen. Man. D. N. MARASINGHE; 1,990 employees.

Ceylon Fertilizer Co Ltd: 62 Chatham St, POB 841, Colombo 1; tel. (1) 422431; fax (1) 343991; Personnel Man. W. N. FERNANDO.

Ceylon Fisheries Corpn: Rock House Lane, Mutwal, Colombo 15; tel. (1) 523227; fax (1) 523385; f. 1964; fisheries harbour at Mutwal; cold storage, freezing and processing facilities, fish trading, ice production and trading, fish filleting, and export/import of fish and fish products; Chair. NIMAL PUNCHIHEWA; 550 employees.

Ceylon Galvanising Industries Ltd: Lady Catherine Drive, POB 35, Ratmalana; tel. (63) 636711; fax (63) 435649; f. 1967; cap. p.u. Rs 4.5m.; sales Rs 262m. (1999); mfrs of galvanized steel sheets; Man. Dir V. BALASUBRAMANIAM; 50 employees.

Ceylon Glass Co Ltd: 148 Maligawa Rd, Borupana, Ratmalana; tel. (1) 635481; fax (1) 635484; f. 1956; sales Rs 560.8m. (1997/98); production of glass containers; Chair. E. M. WIJENAIKE; Man. Dr Dr C. T. S. B. PERERA; 510 employees.

Ceylon Grain Elevators Ltd: 15 Rock House Lane, Colombo 15; tel. (1) 522556; fax (1) 524163; e-mail cgechin@sri.lanka.net; f. 1982; sales Rs 2,725.8m. (1997); mfr and exporter of animal feed; poultry and shrimp farming; manufacture and transport of agricultural equipment; Exec. Chair. CHENG TSANG MAN; Exec. Dir CHENG CHIH KWONG; 1,000 employees.

Ceylon Heavy Industries & Construction Co Ltd: Office and Works, Oruwela, Athurugiriya; tel. (1) 561213; fax (1) 561449; e-mail chicoltd@lk; f. 1961 as Ceylon Steel Corpn Ltd; steel rolling; mfrs of wire products, steel castings, machine tools; welding electrodes; soldering lead; metallographic work and testing, etc.; Chair. and Man. Dir J. M. KIM.

Ceylon Hotels Corpn: 411 Galle Rd, POB 259, Colombo 4; tel. (1) 503497; fax (1) 503504; f. 1966; state-owned; Chair. ASOKA FERNANDO.

Ceylon Leather Products Ltd: 141 Church Rd, Mattakkuliya, POB 1488, Colombo 15; tel. (1) 521776; fax (1) 521702; e-mail clpl@slt.lk; internet www.colombocityguide.com/clpl; f. 1990; sales Rs 385.7m. (2001/02); mfrs and exporters of leather, including footwear, sports and leather goods; Chair. NIMAL SAMARAKKODY; Gen. Man. SISIRA K. PERERA; 378 employees.

Ceylon Oxygen Ltd: 50 Sri Pannananda Mawatha, Colombo 15; tel. (1) 524381; fax (1) 523044; f. 1936; production and supply of industrial and medical gases, including liquid and gaseous oxygen, nitrogen and carbon dioxide; Chair. R. N. HAPUGALLE; Man. Dir L. WOLDERLING.

Ceylon Paint Industries Ltd: Lady Catherine's Drive, Ratmalana; tel. (1) 632831; fax (1) 698831; e-mail mbdj@eureka.lk; f. 1934; mfrs of 'Crown' paints of England, Glasso automotive refinishes from Glassurit GmbH (BASF) of Germany, PVA, textile binders, adhesives and alkyd resins; Chair. and Pres. MARSH B. DODANWELA; Man. Dir SRIYA DODANWELA; 64 employees.

Ceylon Pencil Co Ltd: 96 Parakrama Rd, Peliyagoda; tel. (1) 912879; fax (1) 912878; e-mail nirmal@sltnet.lk; produces ball-point pens, pencils and school stationery; Chair. D. S. MADANAYAKE; CEO N. A. MADANAYAKE.

Ceylon Petroleum Corpn: 113 Galle Rd, POB 634, Colombo 3; tel. (1) 325231; fax (1) 448143; f. 1961; state-owned; exploration, refining and distribution of petroleum and petrolum products; terminal at Kolonnawa, Colombo; refinery at Sapugaskanda; subsidiary: Lanka Lubricants Ltd; Chair. A. J. OBEYESEKERE; Gen. Man. R. PIYASENA.

Ceylon Synthetic Textile Mills Ltd: 752 Baseline Rd, Colombo 9; tel. (1) 92255; synthetic textiles.

Ceylon Tea Services Ltd: 111 Negombo Rd, POB 1938, Peliyagoda; tel. (1) 933070; fax (1) 933080; e-mail info@dilmahtea.com; internet www.dilmahtea.com; f. 1981; sales Rs 1,071.4m. (1997/98); production and export of tea bags, herbal infusions, packeted and bulk tea; Chair. and Man. Dir MERRILL J. FERNANDO; Sec. DESMOND FERNANDO; 600 employees.

Ceylon Tobacco Co Ltd: 178 Srimath Ramanathan Mawatha, Colombo 15; tel. (1) 434231; fax (1) 541255; e-mail dinesh_dharmadasa&bat.com; f. 1932; manufacture and marketing of cigarettes and smoking tobacco, export of cigarettes and leaf tobacco, and financial and consultancy services; Chair. and Man. Dir P. HILTERMANN; 389 employees.

Chemical Industries (Colombo) Ltd: 199 Kew Rd, Colombo 2; tel. (1) 328421; fax (1) 446922; f. 1964; sales Rs 3,287.8m. (1996/97); manufacture and sale of agro-chemicals, paints and industrial plastics; Chair. and Man. Dir B. R. L. FERNANDO; Sec. P. R. SALDIN; 225 employees.

Contracts and Supplies (Mfg) Ltd: POB 487, Colombo; tel. (1) 598436; f. 1974; sales Rs 36m. (1986/87); govt-approved manufacturing of CEYGMA water pumps; Man. Dir R. CUMARASAMY; Tech. Dir N. FERNANDO; 208 employees.

Dankotuwa Porcelain Ltd: Kurunegala Rd, Dankotuwa; tel. (31) 58181; fax (31) 58145; e-mail ceodpl@sri.lanka.net; internet www.dankotuwa.com; f. 1984; sales Rs 706.2m. (1998); manufacture of porcelainware; Chair. D. J. GUNARATNE; 976 employees.

Dipped Products Ltd: Hayley Bldg, 400 Deans Rd, Colombo 10; tel. (1) 683964; fax (1) 699018; e-mail postmast@dplgroup.com; f. 1976; sales Rs 2,179.8m. (1997/98); manufacture and export of household and industrial gloves from natural and synthetic latex; tea and rubber plantations and plantation management; Chair. S. MENDIS; Man. Dir N. G. WICKREMERATNE.

Distilleries Co of Sri Lanka Ltd: 110 Norris Canal Rd, Colombo 10; tel. (1) 695295; fax (1) 522913; f. 1989; sales Rs 3,626.9m. (1999/2000); producer of alcoholic beverages; incl. Arrack (exclusive to Sri Lanka); Chair. Dr V. P. VITTACHI; Man. Dir D. H. S. JAYAWARDHENA; 1,283 employees (2000).

Eastern Merchants Ltd: 341 Union Place, POB 611, Colombo 2; tel. (1) 325736; fax (1) 448474; e-mail chiraath@sltnet.lk; sales Rs 800m. (1999); exporters of rubber, cinnamon, dessicated coconut, tea and fibre.

James Finlay & Co (Colombo) Ltd: Finlay House, 186 Vauxhall St, Colombo 2; tel. (1) 421931; fax (1) 448216; e-mail jfcmb@sri.lanka.net; f. 1893; sales Rs 3,846m. (2001); corporate management services, insurance provision, environmental services, airline, tourism and travel services, marketing of industrial and agrochemicals; cultivates and exports tea; Chair. R. L. JURIANSZ; Exec. Dirs E. R. CROOS MORAES, C. L. K. P. JAYASURIYA, N. K. H. RATWATTE.

Formosa's Communication Co: 28B Rajamalwatte Rd, POB 12, Colombo 15; tel. (1) 696321; fax (1) 522524; f. 1945; manpower consultants; Propr WILLIAM JOHN TERRENCE PERERA.

Glaxo Wellcome Ceylon Ltd: POB 80, Mount Lavinia; tel. (1) 636341; fax (1) 635000; f. 1956; sales Rs 731.8m. (1997); manufacture and sale of pharmaceuticals; Chair. V. THYAGARAJAN; Man. Dir E. M. ANDREE.

Hayleys Ltd: 400 Deans Rd, POB 70, Colombo 10; tel. (1) 696331; fax (1) 699299; e-mail hayleys@sri.lanka.net; internet www.hayleys.com; f. 1878 as Chas. P. Hayley and Co; name changed as above 1952; issued share cap. Rs 330m., sales Rs 9,000m. (1999/2000); 60 subsidiary and 13 assoc. cos involved in processing and packing coir fibre, coir yarn and twine and coir brush mats for export; processing and export of essential oils and spices; manufacture of agricultural machinery and implements, activated carbon and textile dyestuff; formulation of crop protection and household chemicals; manufacture of pesticides and disinfectants, printing inks and graphic supplies, industrial and household brushes and rubber gloves; courier agents; marketing of industrial chemicals and machinery, photographic products, medicines and miscellaneous products on the local market; engineering contractors and suppliers; consultancy services; freight forwarding and warehousing; insurance; travel agency; hotels; and plantations; Chair. and Chief Exec. SUNIL MENDIS; Dep. Chair. M. J. C. AMARASURIYA; more than 30,000 employees (2000).

Hemas Pharmaceuticals (Pvt) Ltd: 36 Bristol St, POB 911, Colombo 1; tel. (1) 541095; fax (1) 437695; e-mail hmpharma@sri.lanka.net; internet www.hemas.com; f. 1949; sales Rs 750m. (1994); imports and markets pharmaceuticals, veterinary medicine, diagnostic products, surgical products and medical equipment.

Hirdaramani Industries Ltd: 69 Chatham St, Colombo 1; tel. (1) 335858; fax (1) 446135; mfrs of clothing.

Indo-Ceylon Leather Co Ltd: 148 Prince St, Colombo 11; tel. (1) 23503; fax (1) 437615; tanners.

Jinasena Group: 4 Hunupitiya Rd, POB 196, Colombo 2; tel. (1) 448848; fax (1) 448849; e-mail jinasena@sri.lanka.net; internet www.xasia.lk/jinasena.jinasena.htm; f. 1905; sales Rs 5,000m. (1996/97); comprises Jinasena Ltd and several other companies; mfrs of agricultural machinery, water pumps, electric motors, paddy threshers, foundry castings, carbon seals; exports lobsters, ladies' garments and tyres; Man. Dir T. N. JINASENA; Financial Dir R. T. JINASENA; 5,500 employees.

John Keells Holdings Ltd: 130 Glennie St, POB 76, Colombo 2; tel. (1) 421101; fax (1) 447087; e-mail jkh@keells.com; internet www.keells.com; f. 1979; sales Rs 11,777.3m. (2001/02); holding co with interests in food and beverages, retailing, restaurants, transport, shipping, freight-forwarding, plantation management, tea production, travel agencies and resort ownership, stockbroking, investment banking, computers and business systems, commercial banking, infrastructure, software development, insurance, printing and management and investment trusts; Chair. V. LINOTAWELA; 19,405 employees (2001/02).

Kelani Tyres Ltd: 203 Union Place, Colombo 2; tel. (1) 434183; fax (1) 911598; f. 1991; sales Rs 471m. (1999/2000); factory at Kelaniya; Chair. CHANAKA DE SILVA; Man. Dir ROHAN T. FERNANDO; 506 employees (2000).

Korea Ceylon Footwear Mfg Co Ltd: 36 D. R. Wijewardena Mawatha, Colombo 10; tel. (1) 452640; fax (1) 452548; f. 1980; sales Rs 594.1m. (1996/97); Chair. A. G. L. PERERA; Exec. Dir S. S. SENARATNE.

Kundanmals Group of Cos: 110-114 Main St, POB 16, Colombo 11; tel. (1) 323641; fax (1) 447618; e-mail kundan@slt.lk; f. 1930; sales US $50m. (1999); mfr and exporter of ready-made garments; Chair. M. KUNDANMAL; 3,000 employees.

Lakstar Garments (Pvt) Ltd: 63 Upananda Mawatha, Attidiya, Dehiwala; tel. (1) 724269; fax (1) 712802; Chair. R. GANEGODA; Man. Dir P. COORAY.

Lanka Canneries Ltd: Nawala Rd, Narahenpita, POB 341, Colombo 5; tel. (1) 586622; fax (1) 501183; f. 1981; sales Rs 250m. (1998); canned and bottled products; Chair. M. F. DOSSA; Man. Dir L. R. P. DOSSA; 334 employees.

Lanka Ceramic Ltd: 696 Galle Rd, Colombo 3; tel. (1) 587526; fax (1) 503359; e-mail ceramicsm@eureka.lk; f. 1991; sales Rs 3,102m. (2000); five mining and processing facilities; five manufacturing facilities; 13 retail outlets; makes entire range of ceramic tableware, sanitary ware; refines its own kaolin and supplies refined kaolin to other industries; mines ball clay, quartz and feldspar; exports tableware; subsidiaries: Lanka Wall Tiles Meepe (Pvt) Ltd, Meepe; Lanka Refractories Ltd, Meepe; Lanka Wall Tiles Ltd, Balangoda; LCL Distributors Ltd; Ceradec (Pvt) Ltd, Jalatara; Gen. Man. SARATH SILVA; 1,600 employees.

Lanka Milk Foods (CWE) Ltd: Welisara, Ragama; tel. (1) 956263; fax (1) 956266; f. 1981; sales Rs 1,968.2m. (1997/98); production, import, export and packaging of milk and related products; transferred to the private sector in 2001; Chair. Dr V. P. VITTACHI; Man. Dir D. H. S. JAYAWARDENA; 267 employees.

Lanka Mineral Sands Ltd: 167 Sri Vipulasena Mawatha, POB 1212, Colombo 10; tel. (1) 694631; fax (1) 699132; e-mail ilmenite@slt.lk; f. 1957; ilmenite, rutile, zircon and monazite plants at Pulmoddai; Chair. and Man. Dir D. JAYASEKERA; Dir and Gen. Man. S. A. NANDADEVA.

Lanka Plywood Products Ltd: 420 Bauddhaloka Mawatha, POB 1148, Colombo 7; tel. (1) 694879; state-owned; Chair. D. K. FERNANDO.

Lanka Tiles Ltd: 34/5 W. A. D. Ramanayake Mawatha, Colombo 2; sales Rs 380m. (1994); mfr of ceramic tiles and other flooring products.

Lanka Walltile Ltd: 215 Nawala Rd, Narahenpita, Colombo 5; tel. (1) 865454; f. 1975; sales Rs 2,140.4m. (1999/2000); mfr and exporter of floor and wall tiles; Chair. B. MAHADEVA; Man. Dir Prof. C. L. V. JAYATILLEKE.

Lankaloha Hardware Ltd: 196 Kandy Rd, Yakkala; tel. 3326010; fax 3326716; e-mail lankaloha@asianet.lk; f. 1963; hardware factory at Yakkala, cast iron foundry at Enderamulle; Chair. DAVE SIRIWARDENA; Man. Dir N. MUMTAZ SIRIWARDENA.

C. W. Mackie & Co Ltd: 36 D. R. Wijewardena Mawatha, Colombo 10; tel. (1) 423554; fax (1) 440228; f. 1923; sales Rs 3,402.5m. (1996/97); manufacture and export of rubber and rubber products, import of industrial products, welding equipment and accessories; Chair. B. M. AMARASEKARA; Man. Dir and Chief Exec. A. G. L. PERERA; 275 employees.

Maliban Biscuit Manufactories Ltd: 389 Galle Rd, Ratmalana; tel. (1) 738551; fax (1) 734556; e-mail malibist@slt.lk; internet malibanbiscuit.com; f. 1954; sales Rs 3,000m. (1997); Gen. Man. S. P. GAMAGE; 1,200 employees.

Mercantile Credit Ltd: POB 1166, Colombo; tel. (1) 438471; fax (1) 448900; merchant banking, financiers, brokers (stock, financial and produce), shipping, engineers, manufacturers, hoteliers, insurance agents, exporters, travel agents, dealers in motor vehicles; Chair. A. N. U. JAYAWARDENA; Pres N. U. JAYAWARDENA.

Mercantile Investments Ltd: 28 Sunethra Devi Rd, Kohuwela Nugegoda; tel. 852327; f. 1969; automotive and general engineers, used car dealers; Chair. G. ONDAATJIE; Man. (Workshop) N. C. ONDAATJIE; 75 employees.

The Modern Confectionery Works: 663 Prince of Wales Ave, Colombo; tel. (1) 431783; fax (1) 440325; f. 1945.

National Paper Co Ltd: 356 Union Place, POB 1367, Colombo 2; tel. (1) 324701; fax (1) 446381; state-owned; paper boards, printing, pulp; Chair. W. H. S. WIJERATNE; Gen. Man. M. A. JUSTIN; factories at Valaichchenai and Embilipitiya.

National Small Industries' Corpn: Colombo; tel. (1) 22781.

National Textile Corpn: 16 Gregory's Rd, Colombo 7; tel. (1) 595891; factories at Veyangoda, Thulhiriya, Mattegama and Pugoda.

Nestlé Lanka Ltd: 440 T. B. Jayah Mawatha, Colombo 10; tel. (1) 699991; fax (1) 699437; e-mail priyasath.saparamadu@lk.nestle.com; internet www.coconutmilk.nestle.lk; f. 1980; sales Rs 6,963.8m. (2001); Chair. and Man. Dir G. TARNERO; 660 employees.

Paranthan Chemicals Corpn: 292 Galle Rd, POB 1489, Colombo 3; tel. (1) 575321; factory at Paranthan.

Pelwatte Sugar Industries Ltd: 27 Melbourne Ave, POB 1992, Colombo 4; tel. (1) 501195; fax (1) 500674; f. 1983; sales Rs 1,306m. (1997/98); cultivation and manufacture of sugar and molasses; Chair. M. P. B. SENANAYAKE; Dep. Chair. E. H. W. JAYASEKERA.

Pure Beverages Co Ltd: 140A Vauxhall St, Colombo 2; tel. (1) 324211; fax (1) 421147; f. 1955; sales Rs 1,405.9m. (1997/98); mfr and bottler of soft drinks; Chair. W. D. M. FERNANDO; Man. Dir ANA PUCHIHEWA.

Reckitt and Colman of Ceylon Ltd: Borupana Ferry Rd, POB 16, Ratmalana; tel. (1) 636051; fax (1) 636059; e-mail reckitts@sri.lanka.net; f. 1962; sales Rs 1,366.5m. (1998); mfrs and distributors of pharmaceuticals, and food and household products; Chair. J. C. L. DE MEL; Man. Dir A. H. C. DE SILVA; 450 employees.

Richard Pieris and Co Ltd: 310 High Level Rd, Nawinna, Maharagama; tel. (1) 802522; fax (1) 804787; e-mail cpu@arpico.com; internet www.arpico.com; f. 1940; sales Rs 3,677m. (2001/02); mfrs and exporters of goods from rubber foam mattresses, rubber mats, polyurethane foam, tyre retreading and plastics; tea and rubber plantations; financial services and real estate developers; Chair. HENRY A. PIERIS; Dep. Chair. and Man. Dir P. IAN PIERIS.

Royal Ceramics Lanka Ltd: 51/1 Fife Rd, Colombo 5; tel. (1) 502042; fax (1) 508945; e-mail langres@sri.lanka.net; internet www.royal-ceramics.com; f. 1990; sales Rs 700m. (1999/2000); mfr of ceramic products; Chair. M. M. UDESHI; Dep. Chair. A. M. WEERASINGHE; 457 employees.

Salu Sala Ltd: 93 Jawatte Rd, Colombo 5; tel. (1) 581727; fax (1) 586752; state-owned; manufactures textiles and garments.

D. Samson Industries Ltd: 110 Kumaran Ratnam Rd, POB 778, Colombo 2; tel. (1) 320978; fax (1) 440890; e-mail dsicmb@slt.lk; internet www.dsi.lk; f. 1962; sales Rs 4,100m. (1998); mfrs and exporters of footwear and rubber goods; Chair. D. SAMSON RAJAPAKSA; Man. Dir D. K. RAJAPAKSA; 6,000 employees (1998).

Shell Co of Sri Lanka Ltd: 161 Sri Gnanendra Mawatha, Nawala, Rajagiriya, Colombo; fax (1) 698139; exploration and production of petroleum and gas and distribution of petroleum products.

Sigiri Garments Ltd: 216 2nd Cross St, Colombo 1; tel. (1) 329347; fax (1) 449331; manufacture of textiles and clothing.

Sri Lanka Cement Corpn: 130 W. A. D. Ramanayaka Mawatha, POB 1382, Colombo 2; tel. (1) 540201; state-owned; cement works at Puttalam, Kankesan and Ruhunu; combined capacity of cement works meets about 60% of the country's requirements and provides for export; Chair. C. H. D. TISSERA; Gen. Man. R. M. JAYATILLAKE.

Sri Lanka Distilleries Ltd: Wadduwa; tel. 32523; fax 32630; e-mail sldlgarc@sltnet.lk; f. 1945; distillers of coconut spirit and neutral alcohol; Chair. H. E. P. COORAY; Man. Dir G. A. R. COORAY; 65 employees.

Sri Lanka Sugar Corpn: 651 Alvitigala Mawatha, Colombo 5; tel. (1) 582231; factories at Kantalai and Hingurana.

State Engineering Corpn: 130 W. A. D. Ramanayake Mawatha, POB 194, Colombo 2; tel. (1) 430061; e-mail gmsec@itmin.com.

State Fertilizer Manufacturing Corpn: Sapugaskanda, Kelaniya; tel. (1) 911833; f. 1966; Chair. A. A. JUSTIN DIAS.

State Timber Corpn: 82 Rajamalwatte Rd, Battaramulla; tel. 866601; fax 866600; f. 1968; extraction of timber, saw milling, running of timber sales depots, timber seasoning, preservation, import of timber, manufacture of furniture, and special projects connected with timber industry; Chair. W. A. B. L. DE SILVA.

Tea Smallholder Factories Ltd: 320/1 Union Place, Colombo 2; tel. and fax (1) 335870; e-mail rpk@keells.com; internet www.keells.com; f. 1991; cap. Rs 150m., sales Rs 1,091.1m. (2000); tea processors; Chair. C. WIJENAIKE; Man. Dir J. S. RATWATTE; 1,220 employees.

Tri-Star Group of Cos: 182 Galle Rd, Bambalapitiya, Colombo 4; tel. (1) 503256; fax (1) 508758; manufactures garments; Chair. KUMAR DEWAPURA; Dep. Chair. UPALI GAJANAYAKE.

Unilever Ceylon Ltd: 258 M. Vincent Perera Mawatha, Colombo 14; tel. (1) 24281; f. 1938; soaps, cosmetics, toilet preparations, margarine, oils and fats; Chair. M. C. THOMPSON.

United Motors Lanka Ltd: 100 Hyde Park Corner, POB 697, Colombo 2; tel. (1) 448112; fax (1) 448113; e-mail umll@itmin.com; f. 1945; nationalized 1972 and incorporated 1989; sales Rs 1,000.4m. (1998/99); imports and markets Mitsubishi motor vehicles and spare parts; imports agricultural machinery, reconditioned vehicles and machinery, tyres and batteries; Chair. MAHENDRA AMARASURIYA; Man. Dir D. A. WIJESINGHE; 397 employees.

Usha Industries Ltd: 68 Attidiya Rd, Ratmalana; tel. (1) 637381; fax (1) 636921; e-mail haylect@sri.lanka.net; f. 1961; mfrs of sewing machines, electric fans, etc.; Chair. S. MENDIS; Dir G. S. DEWARAJA; 70 employees.

P.P.K. Vellaiappa Nadar (Pvt) Ltd: 148 Prince St, Pettah, Colombo 11; tel. (1) 341437; fax (1) 347970; f. 1919; sales US $500,000 (1998); tanners and dealers in shoe materials; Chair. and Man. Dir RAM KANAGARAJAN.

Veyangoda Textile Mills Ltd: 323 Galle Rd, Colombo 4; tel. (1) 500267; fax (1) 580086; f. 1982; sales Rs 728.6m. (1996/97); manufacture and sale of fabrics; Chair. S. MUKUNTHAN; Man. Dir S. LOGANATHAN.

TRADE UNIONS

At the end of 2000 there were 1,588 trade unions functioning in Sri Lanka.

All Ceylon Federation of Free Trade Unions (ACFFTU): 94-1/6 York Bldg, York St, Colombo 1; tel. (1) 431847; fax (1) 470874; e-mail nwccmb@itmin.com; nine affiliated unions; 80,000 mems; Pres. Mrs M. C. RAJAHMONEY; Sec.-Gen. ANTONY LODWICK.

Ceylon Federation of Labour (CFL): 457 Union Place, Colombo 2; tel. (1) 94273; f. 1957; 16 affiliated unions; 155,969 mems; Pres. Dr COLVIN R. DE SILVA; Gen. Sec. R. WEERAKOON.

Ceylon Mercantile, Industrial and General Workers' Union (CMU): Colombo; Sec. G. JAGANATHAN.

Ceylon Trade Union Federation (CTUF): Colombo; tel. (1) 20365; f. 1941; 24 affiliated unions; 35,271 mems; Sec.-Gen. L. W. PANDITHA.

Ceylon Workers' Congress (CWC): 'Savumia Bhavan', 72 Ananda Coomarasamy Mawatha, POB 1294, Colombo 7; tel. (1) 301359; fax (1) 301355; e-mail cwcctuc@slt.lk; f. 1939; represents mainly plantation workers of Indian Tamil origin; 50 district offices and 7 regional offices; 250,000 mems; Pres. and Gen. Sec. S. ARUMUGAN THONDAMAN.

Democratic Workers' Congress (DWC): 70 Bankshall St, POB 1009, Colombo 11; tel. (1) 423746; fax (1) 435961; f. 1939; 201,382 mems (1994); Pres. MANO GANESHAN; Gen. Sec. R. KITNAN.

Government Workers' Trade Union Federation (GWTUF): 457 Union Place, Colombo 2; tel. (1) 95066; 52 affiliated unions; 100,000 mems; Leader P. D. SARANAPALA.

Jathika Sevaka Sangamaya (JSS) (National Employees' Union): 416 Kotte Rd, Pitakotte, Colombo; tel. (1) 565432; f. 1959; 357,000 mems; represents over 70% of unionized manual and clerical workers of Sri Lanka; Pres. W. A. NEVILLE PERERA; Sec. SIRINAL DE MEL.

Lanka Jathika Estate Workers' Union (LJEWU): 60 Bandaranayakepura, Sri Jayawardenepura Mawatha, Welikada, POB 1918, Rajagiriya; tel. (1) 865138; fax (1) 862262; e-mail ctucljew@sri.lanka.net; f. 1958; 350,000 mems; Pres. RANIL WICKREMASINGHE; Gen. Sec. RAJAH SENEVIRATNE.

Public Service Workers' Trade Union Federation (PSWTUF): POB 500, Colombo; tel. (1) 31125; 100 affiliated unions; 100,000 mems.

Sri Lanka Nidahas Sewaka Sangamaya (Sri Lanka Free Workers' Union): 301 T. B. Jayah Mawatha, POB 1241, Colombo 10; tel. and fax (1) 694074; f. 1960; 478 br. unions; 193,011 mems; Gen. Sec. LESLIE DEVENDRA.

Union of Post and Telecommunication Officers: 11/4 Lotus Rd, POB 15, Colombo 1; tel. (1) 324100; fax (1) 341626; f. 1945; Pres. S. T. B. WICKRAMASINGHE; Sec. N. P. HETTIARACHCHI.

Transport

RAILWAYS

Sri Lanka Railways (SLR): Olcott Mawatha, POB 355, Colombo 10; tel. (1) 431177; fax (1) 446490; e-mail slrail@itmin-com; internet www.sciencelandlk-railway; f. 1864; under Ministry of Transport and Highways; operates 1,447 track-km; there are 9 railway lines across the country and 164 stations, with 134 sub-stations (1997); Gen. Man. W. K. B. WERAGAMA.

ROADS

In 1999 there were an estimated 96,695 km of roads in Sri Lanka, of which 11,462 km were main roads. In April 2002 a major highway linking the Jaffna peninsula with the rest of the country was opened for the first time in 12 years.

Office of the Minister of Transport and Highways: 1 D. R. Wijewardene Mawatha, POB 588, Colombo 10; tel. (1) 687311; fax (1) 694547; maintains 11,147 km of national highways and 4,441 bridges through the Road Development Authority.

Department of Motor Traffic: 581-341 Elvitigala Mawatha, POB 533, Colombo 5; tel. (1) 694331; fax (1) 694338; e-mail dmtsl@sltnet.lk.

Sri Lanka Central Transport Board: 200 Kirula Rd, POB 1435, Colombo 5; tel. (1) 581121; f. 1958; nationalized organization responsible for road passenger transport services consisting of a central transport board, 11 Cluster Bus Cos and one regional transport board; fleet of 8,900 buses (2001); Chair. THILAK IDDAMALGODA; Sec. R. ARIYAGAMA.

SHIPPING

Colombo is one of the most important ports in Asia and is situated at the junction of the main trade routes. The other main ports of Sri Lanka are Trincomalee, Galle and Jaffna. Trincomalee is the main port for handling tea exports.

Ceylon Association of Ships' Agents (CASA): 56 Ward Place, Colombo 7; tel. (1) 696227; fax (1) 698648; e-mail casa@itmin.com; f. 1966; primarily a consultative organization; represents mems in dealings with govt authorities; 116 mems; Chair. A. R. PERERA; Sec.-Gen. N. K. WARUSAVITHARANA.

Sri Lanka Ports Authority: 19 Church St, POB 595, Colombo 1; tel. (1) 421201; fax (1) 440651; e-mail ch@slpa.lk; internet www.slpa.lk; f. 1976; responsible for all cargo handling operations and harbour development and maintenance in the ports of Colombo, Galle, Kankasanthurai and Trincomalee; Chair. PARAKRAMA DISSANAYAKE; Man. Dir M. COLONNE.

Shipping Companies

Ceylon Ocean Lines Ltd: 'Sayuru Sevana', 46/12 Nawam Mawatha, Colombo 2; tel. (1) 434928; fax (1) 439245; e-mail oceanlines@col.lk; f. 1956; shipping agents, freight forwarders, charterers, container freight station operators and bunkers; Dirs Capt. L. P. WEINMAN, Capt. A. V. RAJENDRA.

Ceylon Shipping Corpn Ltd: 6 Sir Baron Jayatilleke Mawatha, POB 1718, Colombo 1; tel. (1) 328772; fax (1) 449486; e-mail cscemail@sri.lanka.netA21CE846(COMTEXT); f. 1971 as a govt corpn; became govt-owned limited liability co in 1992; operates fully-containerized service to Europe, the Far East, the Mediterranean, USA and Canada (East Coast); Chair. SUNDRA JAYAWARDHANA; Gen. Man. M. S. P. GUNAWARDENA.

Ceylon Shipping Lines Ltd: 450 D.R. Wijewardena Mawatha, POB 891, Colombo 10; tel. (1) 689500; fax (1) 689510; shipping agents, travel agents, off dock terminal operators; Chair. E. A. WIRASINHA; Man. Dir T. D. V. GUNARATNE.

Ceyoceanic Ltd: 80 Reclamation Rd, POB 795, Colombo 11; tel. (1) 36071; Dir M. T. G. ANAAM.

Colombo Dockyard Ltd: Port of Colombo, Graving Docks, POB 906, Colombo 15; tel. (1) 522461; fax (1) 446441; e-mail coldock@cdl.lk; internet www.cdl.lk; f. 1974; 51% owned by Onomichi Dockyard Co Ltd, Japan, and 49% by Sri Lankan public and government institutions; four dry-docks, seven repair berths (1,200 m), repair of ships up to 125,000 dwt, and builders of steel/aluminium vessels of up to 3,000 dwt; Chair. K. YAMANAKA; Gen. Man. M. P. B. YAPA.

Mercantile Shipping Co Ltd: 108 Aluthmawatha Rd, Colombo 15; tel. 331792; fax (1) 331799.

Sri Lanka Shipping Co Ltd: 46/5 Navam Mawatha, POB 1125, Colombo 2; tel. (1) 336853; fax (1) 437420; e-mail lankaship@slsc.lk; f. 1956.

INLAND WATERWAYS

There are more than 160 km of canals open for traffic.

CIVIL AVIATION

Civil aviation is controlled by the Government's Department of Civil Aviation. There are airports at Batticaloa, Colombo (Bandaranaike for external flights and Ratmalana for internal), Gal Oya, Palali, Jaffna and Trincomalee. In April 2002 the Government lifted a six-year ban on domestic flights and permitted commercial airlines to resume services to Jaffna.

SriLankan Airlines Ltd: 22-01 East Tower, World Trade Centre, Echelon Sq., Colombo 1; tel. (1) 735555; fax (1) 735122; e-mail admin@srilankan.lk; internet www.srilankan.lk; f. 1979 as Air Lanka Ltd, name changed as above in 1999; 60% state-owned, 44% owned by Emirates Airline (UAE) and 6% by employees; international services to Europe, the Middle East, Far East and Australasia; Chair. D. PELPOLA; CEO P. M. HILL.

Helitours: Air Headquarters, POB 594, Colombo 2; tel. (1) 508927; fax (1) 20541; e-mail slafgops@slklk.

Lionair (Pvt) Ltd: Asian Aviation Centre, Colombo Airport, Ratmalana, Colombo; tel. (1) 622622; fax (1) 611540; e-mail lionair@sri.lanka.net; f. 1994; scheduled and charter services to eight domestic destinations; Chair. CHANDRAN RUTNAM; Man. Dir ASOKA PERERA.

Sky Cabs: 294 1/1 Union Place, POB 683, Colombo 2; tel. (1) 333105; fax (1) 635575; e-mail skycabs@lanka.com.lk; internet www.skycab.com; f. 1991; commenced operations 1993; privately-owned; scheduled passenger and cargo services to Bahrain, India, Oman, the Maldives and Pakistan; Chair. ALI AKBER S. JEEVUNJEE; Man. Dir SURENDRA DE SILVA.

Tourism

As a stopping place for luxury cruises and by virtue of the spectacle of its Buddhist festivals, ancient monuments and natural scenery, Sri Lanka is one of Asia's most important tourist centres. Good motor roads connect Colombo to the main places of interest.

Owing to the continuing intercommunal violence, tourist arrivals decreased from 403,101 in 1995 to 302,265 in 1996 and tourism receipts fell from US $224m. to $168m. The tourism sector, however, recovered well in 1997; total arrivals rose by 21% to reach 366,165 and receipts increased by 26% to stand at US $212m. Tourism receipts in 1999 were estimated at US $275m., while arrivals rose by 14.5% compared with 1998 to reach 436,440. At the end of 2000 the industry appeared to be improving, although arrivals decreased to 400,414 in that year. However, the LTTE attack on Colombo's international airport in July 2001 caused severe damage to the tourist industry. One half of Sri Lankan Airlines' fleet was out of service as a result of the raid, and tourists were advised not to visit the country. The industry was also adversely affected by the increased insurance costs payable by airlines. The number of tourist arrivals in 2001 decreased to 336,794.

Ceylon Tourist Board: 80 Galle Rd, Colombo 3; tel. (1) 437059; fax (1) 437953; e-mail tourinfo@sri.lanka.net; internet www.lanka.net/ctb; f. 1966; Chair. H. M. S. SAMARANAYAKE; Dir-Gen. TISSA WARNASURIYA.

Defence

In August 2001 the total strength of the armed forces (including recalled reservists) was some 118,000–123,000: army an estimated 90,000–95,000, navy 18,000, air force 10,000; there were also paramilitary forces of around 88,600 (including an estimated 15,000 National Guard, 13,000 Home Guard and a 3,000-strong anti-guerrilla unit). Military service is voluntary.

Defence Budget: Estimated at Rs 64,050m. for 2002.

Chief of Combined Defence Staff: Lt-Gen. ROHAN DALUWATTE.

Chief of Staff of Army: Maj.-Gen. L. C. GOONEWARDENE.

Chief of Staff of Navy: Adm. DAYA SANDAGIRI.

Chief of Staff of Air Force: Air Marshal G. D. PERERA.

Education

The formulation of educational policy is the responsibility of the Ministry of Education and Higher Education. The administration and management of the school system is divided into 15 regions. Projected expenditure on education by the central Government in 2002 was Rs 32,123m. (7.8% of total government spending).

Since 1945 education has been available free of charge. In 1997 about 4.3m. pupils attended schools and teachers numbered an estimated 187,539. The total number of schools (including denominational schools and pirivenas, which are attended by Buddhist clergy and lay students) in 1997 was estimated at 10,983.

School attendance is officially compulsory for nine years between five and 14 years of age, and each year about 350,000 new pupils start school. Schools are streamed according to the language medium used, either Sinhala or Tamil. Improving the standard of English, which is a compulsory second language, is one of the policy priorities of the Government. In 1960 almost all denominational schools were brought under state control.

ELEMENTARY AND SECONDARY EDUCATION

Elementary education lasts five years from the ages of five to 10. Its first phase is organized as kindergarten classes. Secondary schooling, beginning at 10 years of age, lasts for up to eight years, comprising a first cycle of six years and a second of two years. A new system of public examinations, the National Certificate of General Education (NCGE), came into effect in 1975 to replace the British examination system. It places emphasis on practical subjects such as mathematics, science, health and physical education, social studies and pre-vocational studies. The Higher National Certificate of Education (HNCE) is more employment-orientated. The pre-university course is being revised to benefit not merely the 10% who enter university, but also those who seek employment on terminating the course. In 1995 the total enrolment at primary and secondary schools was equivalent to 89% of the school-age population (boys 87%; girls 90%). Primary enrolment in 1996 was equivalent to 109% of children in the relevant age-group (boys 110%; girls 108%); the comparable ratio for secondary enrolment was 75% (boys 72%; girls 78%) in 1995.

HIGHER EDUCATION

Two-year full-time courses in engineering, industry, commerce and agriculture are available at technical institutes and colleges, and may include a year of job experience. Vocational technical education to develop occupational skills begins after eight years of general education and includes two-year full-time craft or trade courses, some of which may also be part-time.

The University of Sri Lanka was founded in 1972 as a single institution with six campuses. These, however, developed a high degree of autonomy and in 1979 became six independent universities. There are 26 teacher-training colleges and 12 universities. There are also 13 polytechnic institutes, eight junior technical colleges and an open university. A university grants commission supervises and administers all aspects of higher education.

Bibliography

GENERAL

Arasaratnam, S. *Ceylon*. Englewood Cliffs, NJ, Prentice-Hall, 1964.

Champion, Stephen. *Lanka 1986–1992*. London, Garnet, 1993.

Cooray, L. J. M. *An Introduction to the Legal System of Ceylon*. Colombo, Lake House Investments Ltd, 1972.

de Silva, Daya, and de Silva, C. R. *Sri Lanka (Ceylon) Since Independence 1948–1976; A Bibliographical Survey of the Literature in the Field of Social Sciences in Sri Lanka*. Hamburg, Institute of Asian Affairs, 1978.

de Silva, K. M. (Ed.). *Sri Lanka, A Survey*. London, C. Hurst & Co, 1977.

Dharmadasa, K. N. O. *Language, Religion and Ethnic Assertiveness, The Growth of Sinhalese Nationalism in Sri Lanka*. Ann Arbor, The University of Michigan Press, 1992.

Farmer, B. H. *Ceylon*. in O. H. K. Spate and A. T. A. Learmonth, *India and Pakistan*, 3rd Edn, London, Methuen, 1967.

Goonatilake, Susantha. *Anthropologizing Sri Lanka: A Eurocentric Misadventure*. Indiana University Press, 2001.

Jayasuriya, J. E. *Education in Ceylon Before and After Independence 1939–1968*. Colombo, Associated Educational Publishers, 1969.

Johnson, B. L. C., and Scrivenor, M. le M. *Sri Lanka, Land, People and Economy*. London, Heinemann, 1981.

Ludowyk, E. F. C. *The Story of Ceylon*. London, Faber and Faber, 1962.

Malalgoda, K. *Buddhism in Sinhalese Society, 1750–1900*. Berkeley, University of California Press, 1976.

Mortimer, L. R. (Ed.). *Sri Lanka: A Country Study*. Area Handbook Series, Washington, DC, Library of Congress, 1995.

Paranavitana, S. *Art of the Ancient Sinhalese*. Colombo, Lake House Investments Ltd, 1972.

Peiris, G. H. *Development and Change in Sri Lanka*. New Delhi, Macmillan, 1996.

Pieris, Ralph. *Sinhalese Social Organisation*. Colombo, University of Ceylon Press, 1956.

Raghavan, M. D. *Tamil Culture in Ceylon*. Colombo, Kalai Nilayam Ltd, 1972.

Rahula, Bhikkhu. *History of Buddhism in Ceylon: The Anuradhapura Period*. Colombo, Gunasena, 1956.

Wickramasinghe, Nira. *Global Civil Society in Sri Lanka*. London, Sage Publications, 2002.

HISTORY AND POLITICS

Chandraprema, C. A. *Sri Lanka: The Years of Terror—The JVP Insurrection, 1987–89*. Colombo, 1992.

de Mel, Neloufer. *Women and the Nation's Narrative: Gender and Nationalism in Twentieth Century Sri Lanka*. Oxford, Rowman and Littlefield Publishers, 2002.

de Silva, Colvin R. *Ceylon Under the British Occupation*. Colombo, 2 vols, Colombo Apothecaries Press, 1950.

de Silva, K. M. *History of Sri Lanka*. London, Hurst, 1981.

Managing Ethnic Tensions in Multi-ethnic Societies: Sri Lanka 1880–1985. Lanham and New York, 1986.

de Silva, K. M. (Ed.). *The University of Ceylon, History of Ceylon, Vol. 3*. Colombo, University of Ceylon Press, 1973.

Sri Lanka: Problems of Governance. New Delhi, Konark Publishers, 1993.

de Silva, K. M., and Wriggins, Howard. *J. R. Jayewardene of Sri Lanka: A Political Biography, Volume One: The First Fifty Years, 1906–1956*. London, Anthony Blond/Quartet, 1988; Volume Two: 1956–1989. London, Leo Cooper, 1994.

Dixit, J. N. *Assignment Colombo*. Delhi, Konark Publishers, 1998.

Gunaratna, Rohan. *Sri Lanka's Ethnic Crisis and National Security*. Colombo, South Asian Network on Conflict Research, 2000.

Jayaweera, Swarna. *Women in Post-Independence Sri Lanka*. London, Sage Publications, 2001.

Jiggins, J. *Caste and Family in the Politics of the Sinhalese*. Cambridge University Press, 1979.

Jupp, J. *Sri Lanka, Third World Democracy*. London, Frank Cass, 1978.

Kearney, R. N. *Communalism and Language in the Politics of Ceylon*. Durham, NC, Duke University Press, 1967.

The Politics of Ceylon (Sri Lanka). Ithaca and London, Cornell University Press, 1973.

Kemper, S. *The Presence of the Past: Chronicles, Politics and Culture in Sinhala Nationalism*. Ithaca, NY, Cornell University Press, 1992.

Ludowyk, E. F. C. *The Modern History of Ceylon*. London, Weidenfeld and Nicolson, 1966.

McGowan, William. *Only Man is Vile: The Tragedy of Sri Lanka*. London, Picador and New York, Farrar, Straus and Giroux, 1994.

Mendis, G. C. *Early History of Ceylon*. Colombo, 4th Edn, 1946.

Mukarji, Apraim. *The War in Sri Lanka*. Har Anand Publications, 2001.

Narayan Swamy, M. R. *Tigers of Lanka: From Boys to Guerrillas*. Delhi, Konark Publishers, 1994.

Nicholas, C. W., and Paranavitana, S. A. *A Concise History of Ceylon*. Colombo, University of Ceylon Press, 1961.

Paranavitana, S. (Ed.). *The University of Ceylon, History of Ceylon, Vol. 1 (Parts 1 & 2)*. Colombo, University of Ceylon Press, 1959–60.

Sabaratnam, Lakshmanan. *Ethnic Attachments: The Deployment of Modern Sinhala and Tamil Ethnicity*. 2001.

Samarasinghe, S. W. R. de A., and Samarasinghe, Vidyamali. *Historical Dictionary of Sri Lanka*. London, The Scarecrow Press, 1998.

Sivarajah, Ambalavanar. *Politics of Tamil Nationalism in Sri Lanka*. International Academic Publishers, 2000.

Tambiah, S. J. *Sri Lanka: Ethnic Fratricide and the Dismantling of Democracy*. Chicago, 1986.

Buddhism Betrayed? Religion, Politics and Violence in Sri Lanka. Chicago, IL, University of Chicago Press, 1992.

Wilson, A. Jeyaratnam. *Politics in Sri Lanka, 1947–1973*. London, Macmillan, 1974.

Electoral Politics in an Emergent State: The Ceylon General Elections of May 1970. Cambridge University Press, 1975.

The Gaullist System in Asia, The Constitution of Sri Lanka, 1978. London, Macmillan, 1980.

S. J. V. Chelvanayakam and the Crisis of Tamil Nationalism, 1947–1977. Honolulu, HI, University of Hawaii Press, 1994.

Sri Lankan Tamil Nationalism: Its Origins and Development in the 19th and 20th Centuries. Seattle, WA, University of Washington Press, 2000.

Woodward, C. A. *The Growth of a Party System in Ceylon*. Providence, Rhode Island, Brown University Press, 1969.

Wriggins, W. Howard. *Ceylon: Dilemmas of a New Nation*. Princeton, NJ, Princeton University Press, 1960.

ECONOMY

Athukorala, Premachandra, and Rajapatirana, Sarath. *Liberalization and Industrial Transformation in Sri Lanka*. Oxford University Press, 2000.

Central Bank of Sri Lanka. *Review of the Economy*. Colombo, Central Bank of Sri Lanka, annual.

The Alleviation of Poverty in Sri Lanka. Colombo, Central Bank of Sri Lanka, 1987.

Economic Progress of Independent Sri Lanka. Colombo, Central Bank of Sri Lanka, 1998.

de Silva, W. Indralal. *Population Projections for Sri Lanka: 1921–2041*. Colombo, Institute of Policy Studies, Human Resource Development Series No. 2, 1997.

Department of Census and Statistics. *Statistical Profile of Sri Lanka: A Statistical Compendium to Commemorate the 50th Anniversary of Independence in Sri Lanka*. Colombo, Department of Census and Statistics, 1998.

Dunham, David, and Edwards, Chris. *Rural Poverty and Agrarian Crisis in Sri Lanka, 1985–95: Making Sense of the Picture*. Colombo, Institute of Policy Studies, 1997.

Government of Sri Lanka. *Connecting to Growth: Sri Lanka's Poverty Reduction Strategy*. Colombo, 2002.

National Framework for Relief, Rehabilitation and Reconciliation. Colombo, June 2002.

Hettiarachchi, Wimal. *Globalization—Liberalizing the Capital Account in Sri Lanka*. Colombo, Institute of Policy Studies, 1998.

Indraratna, A. D. V. de S. *Fifty Years of Sri Lanka's Independence, A Socio-Economic Review*. Colombo, Sri Lanka Institute of Social and Economic Studies (SLISES), 1998.

Institute of Policy Studies. *Sri Lanka: State of the Economy*. Colombo, annual.

Kember, Steven. *Buying and Believing*. Chicago, IL, University of Chicago Press, 2002.

Knight-John, Malathy. *Performance Contracting: A Strategy for Public Enterprise Reform in Sri Lanka?* Colombo, Institute of Policy Studies, 1997.

Lakshman, W. D. (Ed.). *Dilemmas of Development—Fifty Years of Economic Change in Sri Lanka*. Colombo, Sri Lanka Association of Economics, 1997.

Lakshman, W. D., and Tisdell, Clement A. *Sri Lanka's Development since Independence—Socio-Economic Perspectives and Analysis*. Nova Science Publishers, 2000.

Peebles, Patrick. *The Plantation Tamils of Ceylon*. Leicester, Continuum Publishing Group (Leicester University Press), 2001

Ranasinghe, Malik. *A Method to Analyze Viability of Private Sector Participation in New Infrastructure Projects in Sri Lanka*. Colombo, Institute of Policy Studies, 1998.

Snodgrass, D. *Ceylon: An Export Economy in Transition*. Homewood, IL, Richard D. Irwin, 1966.

THAILAND

Physical and Social Geography

HARVEY DEMAINE

The Kingdom of Thailand (formerly Siam) occupies the centre of the South-East Asian mainland, bordered by Myanmar (Burma) to the west, by Laos and Cambodia to the east, and by Peninsular Malaysia to the south. Its total area is 513,115 sq km (198,115 sq miles). Most of this territory lies to the north of the Bight of Bangkok, and hence well removed from the main shipping routes across the South China Sea between Singapore and Hong Kong, though peninsular Thailand, extending south to the Malaysian border approximately at latitude 6°N, has a coastline of some 960 km facing the Gulf of Thailand, and a somewhat shorter one facing the Andaman Sea. Between these two the peninsula narrows at the isthmus of Kra to a straight-line distance of only 56 km between salt water on both sides.

PHYSICAL AND CLIMATIC ENVIRONMENT

Apart from peninsular Thailand, which (except in the far south) consists of mainly narrow coastal lowlands backed by low and well-wooded mountain ranges, the country comprises four main upland tracts—in the west, north, north-east and south-east—surrounding a large central plain drained by the principal river, the Menam Chao Phraya. Because of its position, while experiencing tropical temperatures throughout its entire area, Thailand receives relatively less rainfall than either Myanmar to the west or most parts of Indo-China to the east. In general, rainfall is highest in the south and south-east, and in the uplands of the west and, to some extent, in the higher hills in the north, but most of the rest of the country, in effect, constitutes a rain-shadow area where the total annual fall is below 1,500 mm.

The western hills are formed by a series of north–south ridges, thickly covered by tropical monsoon forest with much bamboo, and drained by the Kwei Noi and Kwei Yai rivers. Although summit levels here are only of the order of 600 m–900 m, the ridge-and-furrow pattern makes this generally inhospitable country. In the northern uplands, which represent the southernmost portion of the great Yunnan-Shan-Laos plateau, altitudes are higher than in the west, reaching an upper limit of about 1,500 m, and the upland surface is fairly well forested, although the natural cover has clearly deteriorated in many areas as a result of shifting cultivation. However, in the four parallel valleys of the Ping, Wang, Yom and Nan rivers, which flow through these uplands and subsequently converge farther south to form the Chao Phraya, there are relatively broad lowlands with a more open vegetation, now largely cleared for rice cultivation.

The north-eastern plateau, also known as the Korat plateau, is mostly of much lower altitude than the two uplands just described. On its western and southern edges it presents a continuous rim usually exceeding 300 m, and in places much higher than that, but elsewhere it consists of a relatively low and undulating surface, draining eastwards, via the Nam Si and the Nam Mun, to the Mekong, which flows along its entire northern and eastern edge.

In contrast to most of the other uplands, the Korat plateau is an area of barely adequate rain, which during the dry season presents a barren and desiccated appearance. Since the main rivers flowing across it rise within this same area of low rainfall, Korat is less favourably placed in respect of irrigation water than the central plain, which, though likewise receiving an annual rainfall of less than 1,500 mm, is well watered by the Chao Phraya system.

Because of its focal position, its fertile alluvial soils, and the well developed system of natural waterways, the central plain forms by far the most important single region within the country; and within this region, the delta, which begins about 190 km from the coast, enjoys all these advantages to a more pronounced extent.

NATURAL RESOURCES

Thailand's main natural resources lie in its agricultural potential, and in particular in the capacity of the central plain (and to a lesser extent the Korat plateau) to produce a substantial surplus of rice. In addition, since the late 1950s substantial areas of upland have been opened up in these areas for the cultivation of maize, cassava (tapioca), kenaf (upland jute), beans and, more recently, cotton and pineapple. The more humid and more truly equatorial coastal plains of the southern peninsula of Thailand have similarly expanded their production of rubber. Unfortunately, this expansion has been very much at the expense of the country's timber resources, which are estimated to have contracted to less than 20% of the total area, with the once famous teak of the northern hills now in extremely short supply.

Thailand is not especially well endowed with minerals. Tin was traditionally the most important, but this was superseded as an export by gypsum in 1993. In 1995 large-scale extraction of potash began in Chaiyaphum. Various other minerals, including tungsten, lead, fluorite and lignite, are being worked, and the country's heavy dependence on energy imports has begun to lessen, following the initial exploitation of reserves of natural gas in the Gulf of Thailand. These reserves are estimated at 172,000m. cu m, and there is a prospect of a substantial increase in Thailand's total reserves, following onshore discoveries in the Nam Phong area of Khonkaen province, on the north-east plateau. Small quantities of petroleum have also been identified in the north-central plain province of Kampaengphet. In addition, massive rock-salt deposits are known to underlie the Korat plateau.

POPULATION AND ETHNIC GROUPS

According to the census of 1 April 2000, the population totalled 60,606,947, giving an average density of 118.1 per sq km. At mid-2001, according to official estimates, the population was 62,914,000, the average density being 122.6 per sq km. Although average densities fall to between one-quarter and one-half of this in the west and north, the total area of really sparsely populated upland is small. The proportion formed by indigenous minority peoples is low. Apart from some 700,000 Muslim Malays in the far south, a smaller number of Cambodians near the eastern borders, and a total of 300,000 scattered hill peoples—Meo, Lahu, Yao, Lisu, Lawa, Lolo and Karen—mainly in the far north and west, virtually the entire indigenous population belongs to the Thai ethnic group (which also includes the Shan and Lao) and subscribes to Buddhism, predominantly of the Hinayana (Theravada) form. However, it should be added that the inhabitants of the north-east tend to be closer in speech and custom to the Lao populations on the other side of the Mekong than to those of central Thailand. Excluding the Lao groups, the largest minority in Thailand may be said to be the ethnic Chinese. However, estimates as to their proportion of the total population vary and many Chinese have been assimilated into the Thai culture. Most have become Thai citizens.

Thailand shows only a relatively limited degree of urbanization. The urban scene is totally dominated by the single great complex of Bangkok Metropolis (including Thonburi), which had a population of 6,320,174 at 1 April 2000. According to UN estimates, the population of Bangkok Metropolis had risen to 7,527,000 by mid-2001.

History

RUTH McVEY

Revised by PATRICK JORY

PREHISTORY AND EARLY PERIOD

Recent archaeological findings show very ancient civilizations to have existed in what is now Thailand, but the earliest evidence that we have of the Thai people is as part of a population speaking related languages and inhabiting mountainous areas of what is now Yunnan Province in the People's Republic of China. These Thai-speaking groups gradually spread southward into the highland areas of present-day Laos, northern Viet Nam, north-eastern Myanmar (Burma) and northern Thailand, where many preserve their identity as 'hill tribes' which are only very partially integrated into modern nation-states. The mountainous terrain in which they lived ensured that their polities remained small and simply organized, but in some river valleys of northern Thailand the development of irrigated rice cultivation led to relatively dense population and complex states controlling water distribution systems. Southward migration of these people brought them to the edge of the great central plain of the Chao Phraya river system; there, in AD 1238, they established the first historical Thai (Siamese) Kingdom of Sukothai.

Sukothai was initially subject to the major mainland power, the Khmer (Cambodian) empire of Angkor, but the growth of its population enabled it to express an increasingly Thai character and finally to assert independence under King Ramkamheng (reigned 1283–c. 1317). He extended the Kingdom's influence against both the Khmers and the Mons to the south and west, establishing Thai power over the central plain and making it a major element in the South-East Asian state system. Ramkamheng is also credited with establishing the standard Thai writing system, which was derived, under Mon and Khmer influence, from Indian scripts, reflecting the great prestige which Indian culture and statecraft had for the ancient civilizations of South-East Asia. The religion of Sukothai was Hinayana (Theravada) Buddhism, which spread initially from Sri Lanka and became the dominant faith of the major population groups of mainland South-East Asia.

The continued southward movement of the Thais on to the central plain brought the establishment in the mid-14th century of a new centre of Siamese power, called Ayudhya, at a point on the Chao Phraya river attainable by seagoing vessels. In 1368 it conquered Angkor and established Siam as a power with interests in Cambodia. Ayudhya's great King Trailok (reigned 1448–88) pursued its extension against the Burmese to the west, Thai principalities in the north, and Malay sultanates in the southern peninsula. He greatly strengthened Siamese state organization, making the first efforts at a centralized bureaucratic structure and ranking system and codifying customary rules into law. None the less, Ayudhya's power was diffuse by modern standards resting, as in the earliest Thai states, on the ability of a population centre (*muang*), under its lord (*chao muang*), to enforce authority over, and extract tribute from, the rural areas around it. Those who commanded larger resources in population and wealth, usually by virtue of strategic location on a river system which enabled them to control trade, established themselves as overlords; the strongest of these might make himself king. However, the monarch's control remained uncertain, and the borders of the kingdoms shifted with the waxing and waning of the central *muang's* ability to exact loyalty from its more distant tributaries.

Ayudhya's position on the central river, near enough to the sea to become involved in the developing trade between Europe and the Far East, gave it a particular advantage in the accumulation of power. The Portuguese, then the dominant European power in South-East Asia, sent a mission to Siam soon after their conquest of Melaka (Malacca) in 1511; thereafter, Ayudhya became increasingly involved in European rivalries until, under King Narai (1657–88), it accepted a French military mission. Narai's death brought a reaction against the involvement with foreigners and inaugurated a long period of isolation. Ayudhya's reduced resources and unstable leadership enabled rising Burmese power to challenge it, and in 1767 the city was laid waste.

EMERGENCE OF A MODERN STATE

On Ayudhya's fall, a new Thai state centre was founded by the Chinese war-lord Taksin at Thonburi, near the mouth of the Chao Phraya. He was overthrown in 1782 by the house of Chakri, and the capital was moved across the river to Bangkok. The early Chakri kings were anxious to consolidate Thai power against Burmese and, increasingly, European threats. They pressed the extension of Siamese authority over Laos, western Cambodia and the northern Malay states, and sought to strengthen the central administrative structure and to substitute tax farming for the older tributary system. This concern for increased efficiency received a forceful impetus in 1855, when the Bowring Treaty, imposed by the British, deprived Thai rulers of important income from tolls and monopolies on foreign trade. Under Kings Mongkut (Rama IV, 1851–68) and Chulalongkorn (Rama V, 1868–1910), interest in Western technology and ideas grew rapidly among the royal and noble élite, and Chulalongkorn was able to implement a major reorganization of the State, which substituted a modern centralized bureaucracy and fiscal system for the old *chao muang* arrangement.

By its internal reforms and concessions to European interests, Siam was able to maintain formal independence, but it had to concede to France its claims to suzerainty over Laos and western Cambodia, and to the United Kingdom its claims over the Malay states of Kedah, Perlis, Kelantan, and Trengganu. In order to placate the Europeans, to improve its expertise, and to finance economic and administrative modernization, Siam sought foreign loans and accepted European and US advisers in key governmental posts. It attempted to prevent any one country from having predominance but, as the United Kingdom was by far the strongest power in the region, it fell effectively within the British sphere of influence.

However, at the same time that Siam suffered under unequal relationships, it prospered with the development of the international rice trade, which provided the major source of finance for the modern Thai state. The extension of rice lands led to a rapid expansion of settlement throughout the central Thai plain. Bangkok developed into a major trading centre, in which (as in colonized South-East Asia) European firms dominated large-scale international activity and immigrant Chinese took roles as shopkeepers, middlemen and labourers. Central control over Siam's remaining territories was strengthened, though not without alienating people in the north, north-east and south who were still loyal to their customary chiefs. Although unrest was rigorously suppressed in 1902, Bangkok's authority in these regions never penetrated as deeply as in the central plain.

The bureaucracy which was developed to administer the new Siam consisted, in part, of people drawn from the old nobility and partly of commoners recruited through a rapidly expanding modern educational system. Influenced by Western ideas of progress and efficiency, its members soon acquired an ethos which clashed with the principle of royal absolutism and patronage. In 1912 an attempt by young army officers to overthrow King Wachirawut (Rama VI, 1910–25) in favour of a republic had already revealed the potential for a rift between royal authority and the new bureaucratic élite. King Wachirawut responded by identifying royalty with the new ideological force of nationalism: 'Nation, Religion, King' became, and remains, the central patriotic slogan. This preserved the royal symbol but not, in the end, royal power, for tension between royal and bureaucratic authority came to a head over financial stringencies that were imposed by the collapse of the international rice market during the Great Depression. In 1932 a bloodless coup brought to an end the absolute rule of King Prajadhipok (Rama VII, 1925–35).

MILITARY-BUREAUCRATIC RULE, 1932–44

The 'Revolution' of 1932 was led by European-educated radicals of lesser noble rank, Pridi Phanomyang and Maj. (later Marshal) Phibun Songkhram, and by the highest-ranking military officer of commoner background, Col Phahon Phonphayuhasena. The leaders of this faction saw themselves as representing the Thai public interest, but they were very much divided as to what this entailed beyond substituting their own wisdom for that of royalty in managing national affairs. Pridi, influenced by French Utopian socialist ideas, presented an economic plan whose emphasis on land nationalization and abolition of private trade probably owed as much to Thai absolutist traditions as to European socialist concepts. However, his programme antagonized the conservative members of the new ruling élite, who had increased their private wealth and financial security with Siam's economic development and the decline in royal prerogatives, and who were no more willing to entrust their welfare to socialism than they were to subject it to the royal whim. They allied with still-strong monarchist forces against Pridi, who was branded a communist and went into exile.

After a period of instability, a conservative constitutionalist regime was established under Phahon. However, real power lay increasingly with the radical Phibun Songkhram, who brought back Pridi; but, at the same time, the illegality of communism was confirmed, parties were banned, and press censorship was instituted. With little possibility of organizing popular support, civilian politicians could only represent competing factions within the Bangkok élite, and power increasingly rested with the army.

Neither Pridi nor other civilian radicals had tried to mobilize mass support while they had the opportunity, for there seemed to them little possibility that people could be aroused to follow anything but the dictates of local officials and customary chiefs. Thailand's great economic development had taken place without much change in its social structure at the mass level: peasants could plant more rice than they had before with little alteration in organization or technology, and profits from the rice trade were such that the State could take its share and still allow the peasants enough to encourage them to produce a surplus. Moreover, the later Chakri kings had seen in peasant smallholders a source of social stability and so had limited landholdings and the possibility of seizing land in payment of debt; this prevented a drastic rural upheaval akin to that experienced by Burma (now Myanmar) during the Great Depression. A certain amount of rural indebtedness and absentee landholding had occurred in the area near Bangkok, largely as a result of real estate investment by members of the capital's élite, but this inspired migration to the city rather than peasant protest.

Nor did there seem to be a basis for urban political mobilization. The only sizeable town was the capital; until the 1970s it so dwarfed other urban centres in size and importance as to be the only place that counted politically. The working class was overwhelmingly Chinese; some of it was radical—indeed, a small communist party was established illegally in the early 1930s—but it was interested in Chinese affairs and had almost no involvement in Thai politics. A few journalists and writers formed a tiny intelligentsia, continuing a tradition of iconoclastic writing that had begun in the late 19th century and reached something of a height in the 1920s under Wachirawut, when the King himself took to journalism to set forth his ideas and reply to his critics. However, whatever potential they had for influencing public opinion disappeared with the introduction of the new press laws. The independent middle class was overwhelmingly Chinese, uninterested in Thai intellectual affairs and anxious to avoid the displeasure of the officials on whom depended their chance of trade and their permission to stay in the country. All power and virtually all political participation lay with an élite employed in government service, and most particularly the military part of it. Politics became, in effect, a struggle for office and patronage by 'strongmen' and their associates within the bureaucracy. Whether Thailand's outward form was constitutional or dictatorial, the basic locus of power and the means of exercising it changed little.

This 'bureaucratic polity' was inefficient as an administrative machine, since its members were more involved with internecine power struggles and the maintenance of patronage networks than they were in performing their duties. Conscious of this weakness, which they saw as evidence that Siam was insufficiently modernized, radical Thai leaders made more drastic efforts at renovation. Phibun, who became Prime Minister in 1938, took fascism as his model. He embarked on a militantly anti-Chinese and anti-Western campaign, encouraging a rise of Japanese influence, as a counter to the dominant British, and playing upon popular resentment at the Chinese minority's powerful economic position. Stressing his role as supreme leader and pioneer of a modern society, he changed the country's name from Siam to Thailand in 1939, decreed new words of greeting, and imposed modes of dress that he considered modern. He acted ruthlessly against his opponents, encouraged the beginnings of state-sponsored industrialism in order to achieve autarchy in basic military supplies, and took an expansionist course aimed at securing, with Japanese aid, the lands which had earlier been lost to the British and French.

In 1940 Thailand attacked Indo-China, then cut off from France by war, and, in a Japanese-sponsored settlement, acquired the Laotian lands west of the Mekong River and the north-western provinces of Cambodia. Japanese troops landed in peninsular Thailand on 8 December 1941, and from there spread south to Malaya. Phibun elected to become Japan's ally, declaring war on the United Kingdom and the USA in January 1942. In 1943 Japan awarded Thailand two of the Shan states which had been incorporated into British Burma and the four states that Siam had been compelled to cede to Malaya.

The fact that Thailand experienced the war as an ally of Japan rather than under its military occupation meant that it underwent far less economic, social and political upheaval than that experienced by the other South-East Asian states. None the less, the war caused considerable privation, and, as it became evident that the Japanese were going to lose, it grew increasingly unpopular. Fortunately, some prominent Thais had always opposed the Japanese alignment, among them the ambassador to the USA, Seni Pramoj. With US help, he established the Free Thai movement, which made contact with Pridi, then regent for King Ananda (Rama VIII, 1935–46, still a child and at school in Switzerland). Pridi set up an anti-Japanese resistance which enjoyed some immunity from the Thai authorities. In August 1944 Phibun was formally deposed by the National Assembly, and in September 1945 Seni Pramoj was named Prime Minister.

POST-WAR DEMOCRACY AND TURBULENCE, 1945–47

The initial post-war years brought considerable turmoil, particularly in the life of the capital, for times were hard and inflation rampant. The political system's principal element, the armed forces, had been removed by the failure of the Japanese alliance and by the need to maintain the good graces of the Allies. The civilian leaders were occupied with securing US support against extensive British demands for reparations (the lands that had been gained with Japanese aid were lost). Constitutional democracy was restored, and free play was given to the formation of political parties, but these groupings were little more than the personal followers of politicians in the capital. They included the conservative Democrat Party (DP), which counted among its adherents Seni Pramoj and his brother Kukrit. The parties were unable to discipline themselves, much less to agree on a common course of policy or to gain control over an increasingly corrupt and demoralized civil service.

In March 1946 Pridi became Prime Minister, but in spite of his long association with Phibun, he was still feared as a socialist by many conservatives. Phibun still had a strong following in the armed forces, which increased as he put himself forward as the spokesman for resentment at civilian corruption and mismanagement. In June the young King Ananda died in mysterious circumstances, and Phibun had a major role in assigning the blame to Pridi, who was forced to resign. In November 1947 the army seized power, in a coup led by Gen. (later Marshal) Phin Choonhavan. He acted on behalf of Phibun, who took power in his own name in April 1948.

One factor that emboldened Phibun was a shift in the international situation. Hitherto, he and the army had been the objects of Allied displeasure; but, with the 'Cold War' beginning, Burma apparently near collapse, and Indo-China embroiled in revolution, Thailand seemed a possible centre of stability. In February 1949 an attempted coup by Pridi's supporters sent that leader into exile in China. In November 1951 a bloodless coup by Phibun ended what remained of Thai democracy. The Constitution was abrogated, political parties were banned, radical leaders were imprisoned or executed, and dissent was stifled. Thailand embarked on a new international career as an anti-communist ally of the USA, receiving considerable US military and economic aid, and in 1954 becoming a founding member of the South-East Asian Treaty Organization (SEATO), which established its seat in Bangkok.

PHIBUN'S SECOND DICTATORSHIP, 1948–57

Political power in this period rested with a triumvirate composed of Phin, Phibun, and Phin's son-in-law, Gen. Phao Sriyanon, head of the police. Aside from the alliances consolidated by patronage and intermarriage among the country's leading military and bureaucratic families, there were informal (but increasingly close) ties between political power-holders and wealthy local Chinese. In the early days of his post-war rule Phibun had revived some of his economic nationalism and persecution of the Chinese minority, but in the boom that accompanied the Korean War the chance to profit from Chinese capital and economic expertise was too much to resist, and increasingly generals found themselves on the boards of directors of Chinese-run enterprises. The Chinese themselves were becoming more assimilated, by force of circumstances and by the fact that immigration from China had ceased. There was an increasing identity of interest between Thailand's political and economic leadership, but the Thai élite remained overwhelmingly in control of the bureaucracy, through which they extracted tribute and gifts from the politically weak entrepreneurs.

Increasingly, Phibun found it difficult to defend his position against the ambitions of his associates, particularly the new Bangkok army head, Gen. (later Marshal) Sarit Thanarat. He attempted to recoup his position by changing the sources of his support: in 1955, after a trip to Europe and the USA, he restored free speech, allowed the formation of political parties, and announced elections for 1957. These took place amid growing turbulence and accusations of corruption; the Government's victory resulted only in it being discredited, so blatantly was the vote rigged. Sarit, who prudently stayed clear of the campaign, used the opportunity to seize power, first installing the SEATO Secretary-General, Pote Sarasin, as Prime Minister and finally, in October 1958, assuming the leadership himself.

SARIT AND AUTHORITARIAN DEVELOPMENT, 1958–72

Sarit stamped out the brief democracy of the election campaign, and urged a restoration of traditional values, including (for the first time since the 1932 Revolution) an appeal for loyalty to the King. As it was no longer likely that royalty could challenge military rule, Sarit could restore it as a major element in a nationalist appeal for popular support. His cultural and political conservatism was accompanied, however, by a conviction that Thailand should open itself to rapid economic modernization. He removed the limits on land-holding and welcomed foreign investment. The time was propitious, for US involvement in the Viet Nam War was creating the conditions for both an economic boom and profitable foreign entanglement. Soon Thailand became a major provider of US military bases and supplies, Bangkok was a rest-and-recreation centre for US troops, and Thai troops were serving, at a price, in the Indo-China campaign.

In the countryside, US-funded road-building for security purposes rapidly increased communications and transport; peasants became deeply involved in the money economy, moved to towns to seek construction work, or sought to give their children an education that would raise them above peasant status. Both in the cities and the countryside, the old social structures were weakening. In the cities the clash of cultures, generations and interests was more obvious, but the contrast was perhaps more serious in the countryside, as hitherto lightly-ruled peasants and hill peoples in the distant provinces were confronted with officials who were determined to impose their will in the name of security and development. Rural resentment was encouraged by Chinese, Vietnamese and Pathet Lao aid to rebel groups in the north and north-east, but even in the southern peninsula unrest flared into rebellion. In 1965 a China-based Thai Patriotic Front proclaimed a 'war of national liberation', and by the end of the decade most of the provinces outside the central plain were, to some degree, insecure.

Sarit had died in 1963; he was discovered to have appropriated vast sums of public money, but the scandal was soon forgotten in a wave of nostalgia for his despotic but highly successful rule. His successors, the duumvirate Gen. Thanom Kittikachorn and Gen. Praphat Charusathien, were less dynamic leaders, though initially they prospered, not only because of the Indo-China War boom but also because of increasing Japanese investment in trade, manufacturing and agribusiness. In 1968 they sought to broaden their power base by a cautious revival of constitutional democracy. This brought more criticism than they had bargained for, and in November 1971 they again seized full power; but by now their authority was severely compromised.

The US Government's decision to withdraw from Viet Nam and to seek a *rapprochement* with China brought great uncertainty. The economic boom was ending, creating hardship in the capital, which had been swollen by rural immigrants. The great expansion of education and bureaucratic recruitment in the preceding decade had to be curtailed for lack of cash, at the cost of considerable popular resentment. In rural areas, peasants were turning from rice to better-paying cash crops, for the Government, anxious to husband its declining profit from the rice trade and to keep the domestic price low enough to satisfy the urban populace, was not offering a worthwhile price. In the more distant countryside, revolt was spreading. There was a general weariness of corrupt military rulers; within the army itself, those outside the Thanom-Praphat faction resented their long separation from profitable office, while within it annoyance grew at the slow rate of promotion and the inability of their leaders to address Thailand's problems.

THE 'DEMOCRATIC REVOLUTION', 1973–76

During 1972 student-led demonstrations began in protest at the regime. Army leaders outside the ruling faction came increasingly to feel that the military should withdraw from direct responsibility for rule, in order not to be identified with the unpopular economic measures any successor government would need to take. In October 1973, when Thanom and Praphat tried to halt the demonstrators by armed action, the army refused to support them. Additionally, King Bhumibol Adulyadej (Rama IX,1946–) withdrew his support, thus depriving the duumvirate of any legitimacy. The military regime collapsed, and its leaders went into exile.

The upheaval of October 1973 was no more a revolution, in the sense of mass armed action, than had been the Revolution of 1932 but, like its predecessor, it marked a watershed in the development of the Thai political system. It, too, was the culmination of gradual social, economic and ideological changes which finally overwhelmed the old bases of rule. The demonstrations that brought the downfall of military rule were only the beginning of a turbulent three years of political participation. Not only students in the capital, but also those in the new provincial universities, demonstrated for social reform; organized under the National Student Centre of Thailand (NSCT), they presented increasingly radical demands to the Government and worked to organize peasants and labourers against economic exploitation and ill-treatment by officials. The peasants and workers were, in contrast to earlier democratic periods, receptive to urgings for organized action to secure redress: particularly in the central plain, peasants began to form farmers' associations and to send delegations to the capital. Workers in Bangkok's now numerous textile mills began to strike against the low pay and hard working conditions that had attracted international investment to Thai industry. Even the Buddhist monkhood, hitherto apolitical except for a generalized support for established authority, was caught up in the fervour. Younger monks, concerned at social inequality and at the growing secularism and materialism of modern Thai culture, called for the religious to protect the poor from injustice, and aided peasants in pressing their claims.

Though the democratic institutions of 1973–76 allowed the expression of such sentiments, they did very little to satisfy demands. A caretaker regime under a university rector, Sanya Thammasak, was appointed by the King following the collapse of the Thanom-Praphat regime and presided over a period of frenetic party formation, with elections held in January 1975. With great difficulty—as none of the numerous parties had a working majority—a coalition Government was formed under Kukrit Pramoj, who had broken with the DP, under his brother Seni, and now headed the Social Action Party (SAP). His regime lasted for less than a year; new elections in April 1976 brought Seni and the DP to power in a centre-right coalition, but this, too, proved unable to formulate, let alone execute, a coherent policy.

The Governments of the period were markedly more conservative than the non-parliamentary expressions of public opinion; moreover, the general electoral trend was to the right, while the demands of the petitioners, strikers and demonstrators were increasingly radical. Most workers and peasants were still politically passive and either did not participate in elections or voted as directed by village headmen or district officials. The less likely it seemed to them that they could change things by voting, the less attempt they made at challenging the establishment electorally, and the more they did so by rejecting it altogether: hence an increasingly conservative trend in voting was accompanied by an alarming rise in rural insurgency. Thais who had benefited from the recent economic development, and who had hoped for further reform, became alarmed at the gathering disorder and the possibility that economic collapse might endanger their hard-won prosperity. Increasingly, there was not only renewed conservatism in the middle classes but sympathy for a radical-right response to leftist demands. Rightist mobilization was apparent even among the Buddhist monkhood, where Kittiwutto Bhikku, hitherto noted for his efforts at founding a socially-relevant monastic educational system, broke with the Buddhist precept against taking life to announce that the slaying of communists was not a sin.

The parties themselves were poorly organized and still bound largely by ties of personal loyalty and patronage. However, they were, for the first time, active in the provinces as well as in the capital, and the DP, in particular, had consolidated a national following as the representative of conservative reform. Further to the right were parties composed of leading military, bureaucratic and business figures; the most important of these was the Chart Thai (Thai Nation) party, which centred on the heirs of the old Phin-Phao-Phibun military clique. However, these parties were not merely military-bureaucratic factions, for the Thai élite was being drawn increasingly into business endeavours. A growing sector of big business—particularly the banks—was now Thai-owned and confident enough to take an open role in politics. This impelled the Thai right wing away from statist solutions; parties confronted economic dilemmas more seriously and policy differences, as well as personal loyalties, determined the élite coalitions that formed the basis of the right.

Far weaker were the parties of the left. Led by intellectuals and with little popular appeal, they were undermined by the communists, who were pursuing victory by armed action, and by students and other militants who saw extra-parliamentary pressure as the way to achieve reform. From the right they were victimized by a rising tide of counter-revolutionary violence.

As civilian governments showed themselves unable even to keep order, military officers and their civilian allies became increasingly restive. Gen. Krit Siwara, who had become Army Commander-in-Chief just before the fall of the Thanom-Praphat regime and had gained general acclaim for his refusal to fire upon the students, was unwilling to overthrow a constitutionalist system which he, as well as other moderate conservatives, saw as the best ultimate guarantee of stability. While he hesitated, military rightists gave funds and encouragement to groups advocating mass action: the Nawaphon movement, of which Kittiwutto was a prominent advocate; the strong-arm Red Gaur squads; and the rural vigilantes of the Village Scout organization. All of these took King Wachirawut's slogan of 'Nation, Religion, King' as their cry, and stressed loyalty to the monarch as the touchstone of Thai nationalism.

REPRESSION AND RESTORATION, 1976–88

Krit's death in April 1976 hastened the return to military rule, an increasingly popular solution as the urban middle classes came to see authoritarian government as preferable to paralysis and disorder. On 6 October 1976 Red Gaurs and police attacked a student sit-in at Thammasat University and bloodily dispersed it. A military-dominated National Administrative Reform Council took over, banning political parties, dissolving the National Assembly, and setting up a Government which was headed by a right-wing Supreme Court judge, Thanin Kraivixien. Left-wing activists were arrested; many student leaders fled to the jungle, where they joined the communist forces. Labour unions, left-wing parties and farmers' associations were firmly suppressed, and the already marked level of violence against worker and peasant organizers grew with officially-sanctioned killings. Legally-expressed dissent was silenced, but revolutionary protest grew apace, bolstered not only by new recruits but by confidence and material flowing from communism's 1975 victories in Indo-China.

The political harshness of Thanin's regime alienated a great many people who had earlier looked to a military solution, provided the communists with a good deal of talent and considerable legitimacy, and did nothing to restore the economy or Thailand's international reputation. Previous military clampdowns had brought killing and imprisonment, but these had involved only a small number of socially obscure or marginal dissidents. Now the repression affected a significant part of the population; moreover, the students who were the chief targets of the reaction were also the offspring of the ruling élite. In October 1977 the armed forces Commander-in-Chief, Gen. Kriangsak Chomanan, seized power, and restored some elements of democracy by reducing censorship, releasing detainees, and permitting the resumption of party activity under arrangements that ensured conservative control of the legislature and key government appointments.

In March 1980, having failed to find economic policies that were both realistic and acceptable to the élite, Kriangsak was replaced as Prime Minister by the Army Commander-in-Chief and Defence Minister, Gen. Prem Tinsulanonda. Prem's regime, like Kriangsak's, was based on a combination of the military and centre-right party politicians. Ultimate power lay with the armed forces, but the political parties played a major role in linking military, civilian, bureaucratic and business interests. The result was a ruling élite too powerful to dislodge but not sufficiently united to govern effectively.

None the less, in this period the evolution of foreign affairs and domestic society combined to reduce greatly the pressures on the Thai polity. Viet Nam's invasion of Cambodia had brought disunity among communist supporters, and a breach between Viet Nam and China, which greatly reduced support for the Thai communist insurgency. Refugees from Laos and Cambodia, and Viet Nam, burdened Thai facilities but also provided testimony against the rigours of communist rule. Thailand found common cause with China as well as the USA in supporting the deposed Pol Pot against the Viet Nam-sponsored Heng Samrin regime. Insurgents in the north and north-east, long accustomed to material support from and refuge in neighbouring Laos, Viet Nam and China, were demoralized by their patrons' quarrel. The students who had joined them were increasingly disillusioned by the Thai Communist Party leadership's rigid insistence on the outdated Maoist doctrine of protracted rural warfare. The relative liberalism of the post-1977 regimes began to attract them, and, following the announcement of an amnesty for dissidents, many of them returned. Later Prem extended the amnesty to the rank and file of the communist insurgency; this resulted in mass defections from the rebellion in late 1982 and early 1983.

These achievements were somewhat marred by lack of success in responding to the consolidation of power by communist regimes in Indo-China. A Thai military operation to dislodge the Laotians from a disputed border territory ended ingloriously with a truce in March 1988. On the Cambodian border the Thai army showed little ability to respond to Vietnamese incursions, but the Thai Government argued strongly against any compromise on the Cambodian issue by the Association of South East

Asian Nations (ASEAN), of which it had been an enthusiastic member since that group's founding in 1967.

While maintaining an unyielding stance towards its communist neighbours, the Thai Government quietly restored US military aid projects and training schemes, which had been rejected following the 1973 uprising and the defeat of the USA in Viet Nam. In late 1985 US forces began to participate in Thai military exercises on a substantial scale; in April 1986 plans were devised for the establishment of a stockpile of US weapons in Thailand, the first occasion for a US reserve of weapons in a country without US military bases.

Towards the end of the 1970s the discovery of petroleum and natural gas in the Gulf of Thailand helped revive local economic optimism. At the same time foreign investors, realizing that Thailand was not after all about to fall to communism, began to move funds into the country. In particular, Japan, seeking new sources of cheap manufacturing labour and outlets for its capital, contributed greatly to a new wave of economic development. The pattern of expansion begun in the 1960s was resumed, and the outlines of a major social transformation became more apparent. Industrial, agribusiness, and construction sectors expanded rapidly, with Thai as well as foreign business interests prominent in them. The middle and working classes grew in importance and self-confidence, pressing for such reforms as the establishment of a social security system. Secondary urban centres began to flourish, challenging the capital's monopoly on political power.

The growth of the 1980s differed from that of Sarit's time in that it lacked any clear leadership or ideology. The regimes of Kriangsak and Prem were reactive rather than dynamic, and they confined their innovative efforts to the search for a constitutional formula that would create strong yet controllable political parties. The Government attempted to remove the army from the political process while safeguarding its interests, an effort which found support in the early 1980s from the Democratic Officers Movement (DOM), whose leaders argued that this was necessary for the sake of national progress, military unity, and professionalism. Indeed, the basis of politics appeared to be changing from the old personalist ties of patron-client relations to alliances based on interest groups and political ideals. Banking, manufacturing, and agribusiness interests began to play a significant role in politics; partly because of their participation the parties seemed to acquire more substance, and young army officers began to form groups supporting particular political objectives rather than an individual patron or faction.

The effort to reform the system culminated in the constitutional changes endorsed by the general election to the House of Representatives in April 1983, which greatly reduced the power of the appointed Senate and banned the appointment of civil servants (including military officers) to positions in the Council of Ministers. Such attacks on entrenched interests did not go unchallenged, both by senior officers aspiring to national leadership and young ones who sought a more dynamic role for the army, and the State in general, in developing the country. Already in 1981 radical nationalist middle-rank officers had attempted a coup. In 1983 Gen. Arthit Kamlang-ek, Supreme Commander of the Armed Forces and Commander-in-Chief of the Army, formed an alliance with these 'Young Turks' in his attempt to consolidate military support against the constitutional reforms. This culminated in a coup attempt in September 1985, led by Col Manoon Roopkachorn and quietly supported by senior military officers. Its failure resulted in Arthit's replacement as Supreme Commander of the Armed Forces and Army Commander-in-Chief by Gen. Chavalit Yongchaiyudh, one of Prem's closest advisers and the acknowledged leader of the successful campaign against the communist insurgency.

Chavalit had once been prominent in the DOM, but soon after his elevation he began to voice opinions which seemed more in line with the ideas of the 'Young Turks'. He began to call for a state-led 'revolution' that would transform the country's political, economic, and social structure. Increasingly, he appeared as a dynamic alternative to Prem. The latter's administration had been re-endorsed by elections in July 1986, which gave the DP a strong plurality in the House of Representatives. However, the government coalition (comprising the DP, Chart Thai, the SAP and Rassadorn) was highly unstable, and the influence of political parties remained small compared with that of the armed forces. The notable growth of interest-group politics and the middle class meant increased participation but, often enough, political deadlock as well. During the 1970s and 1980s the King became a pivotal figure in political negotiations, his opinion being sought as a means of breaking the impasse resulting from conflicting interests. Prem, though excellent at the manoeuvring and compromise necessary for political survival, was not able to provide a sense of direction. As a result, what was in many ways a very successful regime was characterized by a high level of popular frustration. Out of this arose the opportunity for a revival of parliamentary government.

PARLIAMENTARY RULE, 1988–91

In July 1988 a general election for the House of Representatives was held: it was marred by vote-buying and campaign violence. The results endorsed the existing coalition Government but also revealed a severe decline in the power of the DP, which split, and the growth of the right-wing Chart Thai, which had established itself as the representative of powerful Thai business interests and had spent lavishly on the campaign. The King asked Prem to continue as Prime Minister, but he refused in favour of the leader of Chart Thai, Gen. Chatichai Choonhavan.

Chatichai was not only a retired general but also the son of Phin Choonhavan, founder of the Phin-Phao-Phibun military clique that led Thailand from 1948 to 1957. His accession was seen, however, as a major step towards democracy: for the first time since 1976, an elected leader was in charge of the Government. Chatichai was known as a politician rather than as a military man, and he was the architect of Chart Thai's business orientation. The size of the business community's financial support for Chart Thai's campaign reflected not only appreciation of the party's attitude but also a new respect for the importance of party politics and a departure from reliance on the protection of powerful individuals rather than political organizations. Chatichai's coalition Government comprised Chart Thai, the SAP, the DP, Rassadorn, the United Democratic Party and Muan Chon.

Chatichai initiated reforms that opened Thailand to a major expansion of the business sector. At the same time, he asserted a concern for developing the country's poorer regions, and secured the passage of Thailand's first social security law. In November 1988 all logging of Thailand's rain forest was banned, an act that aroused some astonishment given the very powerful interests that it affected. (In fact, however, Thailand's forested area had been almost exhausted, and the Government intended to compensate the politically well-connected logging interests with a major new field of exploitation, Myanmar—formerly Burma.)

Chatichai's innovations were particularly notable in foreign affairs. Overcoming considerable bureaucratic and military resistance, he abandoned the previously intransigent Thai stance on the Indo-China question, declaring his ambition to turn Indo-China 'from a battlefield into a market-place'. In particular, he hoped to transform the north-east of Thailand into a centre for trade and industry, linking Laos and eventually the rest of Indo-China to Thailand. In November 1988 he succeeded in settling the border dispute with Laos. The Vietnamese withdrawal from Cambodia in September 1989 presented him with an opportunity to stress, against army opposition, a willingness to improve relations with the rest of Indo-China.

In December 1988 Chavalit visited Myanmar, earning the gratitude of its internationally-isolated regime. A principal purpose of his trip was to arrange for Myanma timber, hitherto smuggled via Thailand to the world market, to be exported by firms recommended by the Thai Government to Myanmar's state Timber Corporation. There ensued a rush for logging concessions by politically well-connected Thai businesses. In addition, Thai interests obtained favourable agreements for fishing rights and the exploitation of minerals, and for the supply of urgently-needed goods. From having been the agrarian victim of unequal economic relationships with industrialized countries, Thailand was itself becoming the exploiter of a poorer and more backward economy.

In spite of these initiatives, Chatichai's regime began to falter in late 1989. Commerce expanded but was accompanied by a widespread feeling of unease at Thailand's precipitate capitalist development. The country was experiencing unprecedented prosperity but also growing inequality; the promises to aid the poorer regions had not been fulfilled. Public concern mounted over corruption, the high rate of inflation, traffic congestion in Bangkok, pollution and other environmental issues, drug addiction and AIDS. Once again, the demand rose for strong leadership to address the country's ills. In 1990 a series of no-confidence motions was brought against the Government in the House of Representatives, and Chatichai engaged in increasingly desperate government reshuffles. He attempted to allay military disaffection by giving Chavalit unrestricted responsibility for senior military appointments. Chavalit took advantage of this to allot key posts to the leaders of the powerful Class 5 Group, based on the 1958 graduates of Chulachomklao Military Academy.

Military Academy class membership had long been an important source of faction and patronage within the army. Previously, Prem and Kriangsak had been careful, as government leaders, to ensure that no one class dominated the military power structure. Class 5 was a particularly large and cohesive group, whose ties had been strengthened by marriages and business relationships among its principal figures. Chavalit relied for his influence over Class 5 on his generous patronage of it and especially on the presumed personal loyalty of its leader, Gen. Suchinda Kraprayoon, whom he named Deputy Commander-in-Chief of the Army in September 1989. Chavalit also acted to establish himself as an opposition figure within the parliamentary context, resigning from his official posts in 1990 and forming the New Aspiration Party (NAP) to contest the next elections. In establishing himself formally in political opposition, he had given up his official sources of military power. His place as Supreme Commander of the Armed Forces was taken by Gen. Sunthorn Kongsompong, who was regarded as favourable to Class 5. The position of Commander-in-Chief of the Army was assumed by Suchinda, whose brother-in-law, Gen. Issarapong Noonpakdi, became his deputy.

RETURN TO MILITARY RULE

The Prime Minister, alarmed at this entrenchment of Class 5, attempted to rally its opponents in the army, but only succeeded in bringing the situation to a climax. On 23 February 1991 Chatichai was seized in a bloodless military coup. A National Peace-keeping Council (NPC), headed by Sunthorn, took command of the country. Martial law was declared, the Constitution suspended and the National Assembly dissolved.

Although politically-active Thais had believed that an unquestioned military intervention was no longer possible, there was little reaction to the country's 17th coup. The public was too disenchanted with the corruption and unscrupulous capitalism of Chatichai's regime to be willing to defend it. The domestic and international business interests, which had been its chief source of support, were easily persuaded by the perpetrators of the coup that they intended merely to install a more honest and competent rule of experts. The President of the Federation of Thai Industries, Anand Panyarachun, was appointed Prime Minister. Anand appointed a predominantly civilian 35-member interim Cabinet comprising respected technocrats and former ministers and including only eight members of the armed forces. It was declared that an interim National Legislative Assembly would be created to draft a new constitution and prepare for a general election. The Assembly, however, consisted overwhelmingly of senior military officers (149 of its 292 members). The other members were business executives, bureaucrats and others known for their conservatism and military connections. The new rulers dissolved trade unions in the public sector, announced a new anti-communist campaign and an offensive against crime and corruption, and declared a revival of the 'hard-line' policy on Cambodia. They did not, however, ban political parties, as had occurred following every previous military take-over.

Although parties remained legal, they were in complete disarray. An Assets Examination Committee installed by the new regime identified leaders of the major parties, in particular the former Prime Minister, Chatichai, as possessing 'unusual wealth'. Politicians seeking new allegiance were attracted to the NAP of Chavalit, who had declared himself opposed to the overthrow of parliamentary rule. To offset this the Class 5 ally, Air Chief Marshal Kaset Rojananin (a member of the NPC), sponsored the Samakkhi Tham party as a vehicle for supporters of the new regime. In addition, Chart Thai, reportedly in exchange for the abandoning of corruption charges against its major leaders, aligned itself in support of the military regime under a new leader, Air Chief Marshal Somboon Rahong. During the next months Class 5 strengthened its hold on the government machinery, and in August 1991 Suchinda replaced Sunthorn as Supreme Commander of the Armed Forces and appointed Issarapong as Commander-in-Chief of the Army.

In December 1991 the new Constitution was proclaimed, which ensured the protection of conservative, military-bureaucratic interests. The new basic law was greeted with some popular dismay but little organized protest. Public opinion endorsed Anand's competent and honest governance, though Thais were increasingly disenchanted with the military's blatant profiting from its hold on politics.

On 22 March 1992 National Assembly elections were held under the new dispensation. They provided encouragement for neither the military nor its opponents. With a bare majority, they returned a weak coalition led by Samakkhi Tham, Chart Thai, and the SAP, and also including Prachakorn Thai and Rassadorn. None of these presented a credible candidate for Prime Minister, and finally, despite his previous assurances to the contrary, Suchinda assumed the premiership.

Rule by a non-elected military man was sanctioned by the new Constitution and was historically very familiar. Suchinda seemed to have an invincible military-political machine at his call. However, his assumption of the premiership crystallized civilian unease, and resulted in demonstrations demanding an elected Prime Minister. These culminated in a dramatic hunger strike by Maj.-Gen. (retd) Chamlong Srimuang, who had been the highly popular and effective Governor of Bangkok, and was the leader of the Palang Dharma (Righteous Force) party. On 17–20 May 1992, after unsuccessfully trying to wait out the protests, Suchinda and his chief supporters resorted to violence that led to the deaths of an estimated 100 Bangkok demonstrators. As increasingly in major Thai political crises, royal intervention was required to achieve a settlement. On 24 May (the day after the declaration of an amnesty for all 'offenders' in the recent demonstrations—including those responsible for the deaths of protesters) Suchinda submitted his resignation.

THE RE-ESTABLISHMENT OF DEMOCRATIC RULE

Following Suchinda's resignation, the five government coalition parties nominated Somboon Rahong, the leader of Chart Thai, as Prime Minister. The fact that Somboon was perceived, however, as having close links with the military leaders led to fears of new unrest, and his appointment was not confirmed. Instead, on 10 June 1992, the King again appointed Anand Panyarachun Prime Minister. Anand announced that he would organize new elections within four months. On the same day as his appointment, the National Assembly approved constitutional amendments, reducing the powers of the non-elected Senate and stipulating that the Prime Minister must be an elected member of the Assembly. Anand formed an administration that comprised many of the apolitical figures whom he had appointed during his previous term of office. At the end of June a 'National Democratic Front' was formed by four parties that had opposed the military Government: the DP, the NAP, Palang Dharma and Ekkaparb. In July Chatichai declined the leadership of Chart Thai (offered to him after the resignation of Somboon from that post) and formed a new party, Chart Pattana (National Development).

In August 1992 Anand demoted the military leaders regarded as being responsible for the violent repression of the May demonstrations, and appointed in their place officers who had a reputation as professional soldiers of integrity. The new Commander-in-Chief of the army, Gen. Wimol Wongwanit, promised that the army would not interfere in politics during his period of command. Anand also reduced military control of state enterprises, appointing civilians instead of military officers to head the national airline, the communications and telephone authorities, and other institutions hitherto regarded as the preserve of the armed forces.

In the general election of 13 September 1992 Thailand's oldest party, the DP, won the largest number of seats (79), while Chart Thai won 77 and Chart Pattana 60. With the other parties that belonged to the 'National Democratic Front', the DP was able to form a coalition Government, commanding 185 of the 360 seats in the House of Representatives: Chuan Leekpai, the leader of the DP, became Prime Minister. In order to increase the coalition's narrow majority, the SAP (which had won 22 seats) was also invited to join the coalition, despite its participation in the previous Government.

Major formal shifts in the way Thailand was ruled were not accompanied by clear and consistent changes in public opinion. The underlying reason for the popular rejection of both Chatichai's and Suchinda's regimes was not so much the institutional form of their rule as dismay at blatant corruption and abuse of office. Prime Minister Anand, although he served the military regime and was not himself elected, was perfectly acceptable to public opinion because he was seen as honest and competent. This public opinion was largely middle-class and located in Bangkok, characteristics which no longer reflected, as in the past, the failure of national politics to penetrate the provinces, but rather the urban middle class's growing strength. This could be seen in the importance of business opinion to the smooth acceptance of both the 1991 military coup and Suchinda's downfall. Such opinion was not yet committed to any particular set of political institutions, although it was beginning to express itself particularly through political parties, but was concerned to find competent and reasonably honest rule. At the same time, those powerful business executives who had access to political decision-makers were reluctant to forgo the advantages of the old patronage system, and they found a new source of strength in the rising power of provincial business and political leaders. These relied on relationships of patronage to make profits and to garner votes; money, not principle, was the basis for their loyalties. Since vote-buying and local 'pork-barrel' projects were the only benefits most rural people realized from government, they tended to support leaders who offered the most immediate financial return; and as 90% of the National Assembly seats went to provincial districts, this gave the politics of patronage great electoral strength.

On assuming office as Prime Minister, Chuan had declared his intention to eradicate corrupt practices, to decentralize government from Bangkok to the provinces and to pay increased attention to rural development. However, although he was regarded as an able and honest politician, he did not appear a forceful leader, and his tenure was devoted largely to holding together his unsteady coalition. There was little business-political support for his reforms, and the decentralization efforts aroused the anger of the still-powerful bureaucracy. Nevertheless, with Chuan's Government in office, the military appeared to move into the political background. Chavalit indeed served as Minister of the Interior, but this was as much due to the importance of his NAP to the ruling coalition as it was to his continuing influence in military circles. Business executives and technocrats, not military leaders, were increasingly seen as the source of dynamism and reform.

In June 1993 the position of Chuan's administration was consolidated by its decisive survival of a motion of 'no confidence' in the Cabinet introduced by Chart Pattana and Chart Thai. In early September the SAP announced that it was to merge with four opposition parties, including Chart Pattana, under the leadership of Chatichai, while remaining in the ruling coalition. This appeared to be an attempt to secure the premiership for Chatichai, as the new SAP would command more seats than any other member of the coalition. However, four days after the merger plans were announced the SAP was expelled from the Government. It was replaced by the Seritham Party, which controlled only eight seats, compared with 21 for the SAP, bringing the coalition's total representation to 193 seats.

On 31 March 1994 a joint session of the upper and lower houses of the National Assembly was held to consider government proposals to democratize the Constitution, principally by reducing the powers of the appointed Senate and broadening the method by which its members were chosen. The senators, most of whom had been appointed under the Suchinda regime, were understandably reluctant to diminish their powers; together with the opposition parties from the House of Representatives, they defeated the government plan and put forward instead proposals to strengthen the Constitution's authoritarian aspects. A crisis was avoided by the appointment of a joint committee to formulate a compromise reform programme; while it was debating, the Government was attacked not only by conservative critics but also by radicals who wanted more comprehensive constitutional reform.

In September 1994 Chamlong resumed the leadership of Palang Dharma in party elections. He subsequently persuaded the party executive committee to approve the replacement of all 11 of Palang Dharma's cabinet members. Chamlong's nominations for the cabinet posts, which included Thaksin Shinawatra, a prominent business executive, and Vichit Surapongchai, a former President of the Bangkok Bank, as Minister of Foreign Affairs and Minister of Transport and Communications respectively, provoked strong protests within the divided party, which were led by Prasong, who opposed the selection of non-elected candidates and objected to Chamlong's authoritarian style of leadership. The appointments were confirmed in a cabinet reorganization in late October, when Chamlong was named Deputy Prime Minister.

In December 1994 the NAP withdrew from the ruling coalition over a constitutional amendment providing for the future election of local government representatives, including village headmen. Chavalit voted against the Government in what was widely viewed as an attempt to ingratiate himself with powerful local interests who would control many votes at the next election. The NAP's defection to the opposition left the ruling coalition with a minority of seats in the House of Representatives. Chuan therefore found it necessary to invite Chatichai's Chart Pattana to join the coalition, although this severely compromised the Government's claims to represent honesty and reform.

In January 1995 Chuan finally managed to secure the approval of a joint session of the National Assembly for a series of amendments to the Constitution aimed at expanding the country's democratic base. The reforms included a lowering of the minimum voting age from 20 years to 18, a reduction in the size of the appointed military-dominated Senate to two-thirds that of the elective House of Representatives, equality for women and the prohibition of senators and members of the Government from holding monopolistic concessions with government or state bodies. This last amendment necessitated the resignation of Thaksin as Minister of Foreign Affairs, owing to his extensive business interests.

In December 1994 the Minister of Agriculture and Co-operatives, Niphon Phromphan, and his Deputy Minister, Suthep Thuaksuwan, had resigned prior to a planned motion of 'no confidence' in the Government, owing to allegations of corruption in connection with a land distribution scheme promoted by Chuan as the centre-piece of his administration's programme. Following a government investigation, in April 1995 land titles were removed from seven deed-holders, and a senior official was dismissed from the land reform department. However, opposition parties tabled a motion of 'no confidence' in the Government in May, and Chamlong announced that Palang Dharma would not support the coalition in the 'no confidence' vote. Chuan dissolved the House of Representatives on 19 May and announced that a general election would take place in early July.

The elections held on 2 July 1995 marked the triumph of provincially-based money politics. Chart Thai secured the largest number of seats (92), not one of them from the more sophisticated electorate in Bangkok. The party's leader, Banharn Silapa-Archa, became Prime Minister. A self-made businessman and politician from the central Thai province of Suphanburi, he had been one of those leaders accused of being 'unusually rich' by the military junta that seized power in 1991. Banharn headed a seven-party coalition comprising Chart Thai, the NAP, Palang Dharma (led by Thaksin since late May), the SAP, Prachakorn Thai, Nam Thai (a new, overtly technocratic, business-orientated party formed in 1994 by Amnuay Viravan, a former minister and former head of Bangkok Bank) and the Muan Chon party. His Cabinet, unlike Chuan's, eschewed technocrats in favour of patronage-based politicians. Banharn presented himself as a dynamic leader, willing to ignore legalities and sensitivities in order to achieve progress. He defined his Government's aims much as his predecessor had, for these were issues generally conceded to be urgent, even if their solutions were not agreed. However, Banharn's ability to outperform Chuan was sharply curtailed by the instability of his coalition and by his dependence on serving the interests of provincial patronage. Thus, although resolving Bangkok's infamous traffic congestion was a prime test of effective leadership, he allocated Palang Dharma's new leader, Thaksin, responsibility for the management of traffic in inner Bangkok, and gave the Prachakorn Thai leader, Samak Sundaravej, control of traffic in outer Bangkok. Such politicization of decision-making on a critical issue led to much public disillusionment, culminating in August 1995 in an unprecedented criticism of government incompetence by the King.

The interior portfolio caused even greater problems, as the leaders of powerful factions within Chart Thai, Narong Wongwan and Vatana Asavahame, both demanded control of the Ministry. The US Government, however, threatened a deterioration in bilateral relations if either representative (both of whom had been refused a visa to enter the USA owing to allegations of involvement in the narcotics trade) were appointed to the Cabinet. Finally, Banharn himself assumed the interior portfolio pending the findings of a commission established to investigate the US allegations. The commission was headed by an outspoken critic of the USA, Thanat Khoman, who later accused the US embassy of conspiring with Chuan to discredit Vatana.

In September 1995 the Minister of Defence, Chavalit, took the unprecedented step of rejecting recommendations for promotions by the outgoing Commander-in-Chief of the Army, Wimol, and appointed his own close associate, Gen. Pramon Phalasin, to replace him. This was a set-back to Banharn, who was close to Wimol, but he managed to strengthen his position by the appointment of Gen. Viroj Saengsanit as Supreme Commander of the Armed Forces. Viroj, a Class 5 member and supporter of the 1991 coup, was considered to be unsympathetic to Chavalit. Increasingly Chavalit, who was also Deputy Prime Minister, appeared as Banharn's unspoken rival and most likely successor. His NAP party, with 57 seats, was the third largest party in the legislature and the second largest in the governing coalition. He had a strong base in the military, which he consolidated both through controlling appointments and by increasing weapons purchases and the opportunities for military participation in business. As a result, Thai military appropriations rose in accordance with patronage, rather than technical demands. Chavalit also endeavoured to increase his support among business interests, by promoting privatization, and among the bureaucracy, by advocating strong central administration. Although he urged rule through parliamentary institutions rather than by military junta, he emphasized his view that the army had a legitimate and important role in politics.

By early 1996 it was evident that Thailand had replaced weak but relatively honest and competent rule with a weak and patently venal administration. The Banharn Government attempted to regain credibility by pursuing some of the political reform projects it had promised at its inception, and in March the Prime Minister appointed a new Senate that included only 39 military officers, a considerable step towards democratizing that institution. At the end of March the Government also announced a major programme of investment in education, which it hoped would both alleviate rural discontent and meet business demands for a better-trained work-force. It announced a plan for financial decentralization, which was intended to promote rural development. Most of the Government's efforts were blocked, however, by disagreements within the ruling coalition and by the requirements of the all-pervasive patronage system. Impatience over the failure to address long-standing questions of agricultural reform led to mass protests in March and April, when thousands of farmers camped outside Banharn's office, demanding action on such issues as land rights and indebtedness.

In May 1996 the Government faced a vote of 'no confidence' in which 10 cabinet ministers were accused by the opposition of incompetence and/or corruption. These included Banharn but not Chavalit, despite widespread criticism of the latter's role in military procurement. Evidently the opposition parties, led by the DP, were leaving a line open for future negotiations with the powerful Minister of Defence. The Government won without difficulty, as it held 233 of the 391 seats in the House of Representatives. None the less, public disillusionment eroded support for the coalition parties: this was shown in the Bangkok gubernatorial elections of 2 June, when Palang Dharma, hitherto the capital's most popular political party, lost to the independent candidate, Bhichit Rattakul. In August Palang Dharma withdrew from the Government, following a cabinet dispute over bribery in the awarding of bank licences. Speculation grew that Banharn would come to an agreement with Chatichai Choonhavan to bring Chart Pattana into the ruling coalition, a move that would both strengthen the latter's parliamentary position and support Banharn in his rivalry with the increasingly powerful Chavalit. In September Banharn was only able to secure the support of his coalition partners in a scheduled motion of 'no confidence' in his administration by undertaking to resign from the premiership to make way for another candidate. However, the inability of the coalition partners to agree on the appointment of a new Prime Minister led to the dissolution of the House of Representatives by the King on 27 September.

The general election, which was held on 17 November 1996, was characterized by extensive campaign violence and vote-buying on a massive scale. The NAP gained a plurality with 125 seats secured mostly through patronage politics in the impoverished rural north-east of the country. The DP, which secured 123 seats, appealed to the more sophisticated electorate, winning 29 of Bangkok's 37 seats, thus contributing to the reduction of Palang Dharma's representation to only one seat from 23 at the previous election.

The Chavalit Coalition

On 25 November the King formally appointed Chavalit as Prime Minister leading a coalition (comprising the NAP, Chart Pattana, the SAP, Prachakorn Thai, the Seritham Party and Muan Chon) that commanded a total of 221 seats in the House of Representatives. Initially, Chavalit's coalition appeared to offer the prospect of more stable government, after the months of incapacitating dissension between the parties of the Banharn coalition. Besides holding the Premiership, Chavalit also retained control of the powerful Ministry of Defence, a portfolio he had held in the previous Government. The key position of Minister of the Interior was awarded to Sanoh Thienthong, the former Secretary-General of Chart Thai, as a reward for Sanoh's support for Chavalit's bid for the premiership prior to the general election and his subsequent defection from the Chart Thai Party to Chavalit's NAP. Most other influential (and lucrative) ministries were awarded to NAP or Chart Pattana members. Gen. Mongkon Ampornpisit, the Supreme Commander of the Armed Forces, and Gen. Chettha Thanajaro, the Army Commander-in-Chief, were both Chavalit appointees; thus Chavalit was in a position of great control over the armed forces. This also gave Chavalit much influence in the sensitive and politicized process of annual promotions and appointments in the military.

As evidence of Chavalit's avowed intention to revive the economy, he allocated the finance portfolio and the deputy premiership with responsibility for economic affairs to Amnuay Viravan, a respected technocrat. However, Chavalit subsequently failed to give Amnuay the necessary support to overcome the obstacles imposed by other coalition members anxious to prevent the implementation of austere fiscal policies. The Government's indecisive handling of the economy contributed to a financial crisis in mid-1997, following a series of sustained attacks on the Thai baht by currency speculators. In June Amnuay resigned and was replaced by the little-known Thanong Bidaya, the President of the Thai Military Bank. At the end of July 1997 the Governor of the Central Bank, Rerngchai Marakanonda, also resigned, citing political interference. The deterioration in the state of the economy in 1997 was reflected in an increase in popular protests. The most significant of these was an encampment of more than 10,000 representatives of the Assembly of the Poor (a non-governmental organization campaigning for the improvement of conditions for impoverished farmers and landless agricultural labourers) outside the Prime Minister's office in January, demanding the implementation of agricultural reforms. In May, following the establishment of a fund to compensate villagers for relocation and destruction caused by government infrastructure projects, the protest ended. In response to expressions of popular discontent, the Government introduced measures in June to constrain media attacks on the authorities and to limit mass protests.

At the end of August 1997 Chavalit and Thanong had an audience with the King to discuss the economic crisis. Later that month Chavalit implemented a cabinet reorganization in an attempt to regain public confidence. On the advice of the former Prime Minister, Prem, the former Minister of Finance, Virabongsa Ramangkura, an outspoken critic of the Government's handling of the economic crisis, was appointed Deputy Prime Minister with responsibility for economic affairs. Thaksin, who had resigned as leader of Palang Dharma, following the party's disastrous performance in the general election, joined the Cabinet as Deputy Prime Minister with responsibility for regional development and trade. Despite these changes the opposition threatened to introduce a motion of 'no confidence' in the Government.

For much of Chavalit's first year in office the major issue on the political agenda was the drafting of a new Constitution by the Constitutional Drafting Assembly, presided over by long-time political activist, Uthai Pimchaichon. The draft Constitution was promoted by its supporters (including the former Prime Minister, Anand Panyarachun) as providing the basis for a truly democratic system of government in Thailand. Many of the provisions sought to address the endemic problems of political corruption and vote-buying that had plagued Thai politics for decades. Some of the major amendments contained in the new draft Constitution included the reduction of the number of senators to 200; the introduction of direct elections for the Senate (in place of the system whereby senators were appointed by the Prime Minister); a clause requiring members of the National Assembly who became ministers to resign from the legislature; a requirement that the minimum level of education for a member of the National Assembly be a degree; a provision that 50,000 eligible voters could initiate investigations into corruption by members of the National Assembly; and restrictions on media censorship by the State. By September 1997 the draft Constitution had gained the support of all opposition parties and most of the print media. However, considerable opposition to the new charter came from within the Chavalit coalition and sections of the Senate. Sanoh was the most outspoken in his opposition to the new draft, invoking the communist threat to dissuade potential supporters. Chavalit himself reneged on his pledge to support the overwhelmingly popular draft, but then finally gave it his endorsement following the application of pressure by both business representatives and the armed forces.

Chavalit ensured his survival of a 'no confidence' motion tabled by the opposition by scheduling the censure debate prior to the vote on the draft Constitution. If defeated Chavalit could thus dissolve the National Assembly rather than resign, delaying the vote on the draft Constitution and forcing fresh elections under the existing Constitution. In the event the Government won the 'no confidence' vote and the draft Constitution was passed on 27 September 1997 with 578 votes in favour, 16 opposed, 17 abstentions and 40 absences. Chavalit was then prohibited by law from dissolving the National Assembly and was allowed 240 days to complete enabling legislation for the new Constitution, prior to a general election (although the King subsequently urged the accelerated completion of the necessary reforms). The new Constitution was promulgated on 11 October.

In October 1997, following the resignation of the Minister of Finance, Thanong Bidaya, Chavalit effected a reorganization of the Cabinet. However, unprecedented criticism of the Chavalit administration in the Thai media, based on the perception that the Government was out of its depth in handling the worsening economic crisis, as well as on opposition to the new draft Constitution, led in early November to Chavalit's resignation as Prime Minister. In the political manoeuvring that followed, the DP succeeded in persuading 12 members of Prachakorn Thai (later dubbed the 'Cobra faction' by the media) to defect and join the Democrats. With the support of Chart Thai and other minor parties, the DP was able to form a new eight-party coalition commanding the support of 207 members of the 393-member House of Representatives, which gave it the right to form a government.

The Government of Chuan Leekpai

On 9 November 1997 the leader of the DP, Chuan Leekpai, was appointed Prime Minister. The majority of the key portfolios in the new Cabinet were awarded to DP members. Despite some opposition from within the armed forces, Chuan himself assumed the post of Minister of Defence concurrently with the Prime Ministership, thus becoming the first non-military figure to occupy the position in recent history. The DP Secretary-General, Sanan Kajornprasart, assumed responsibility for the influential post of Minister of the Interior. The key Ministries of Finance and of Commerce were headed by the two former bankers, Tarrin Nimmanhaeminda and Supachai Panichpakdi respectively, while Surin Pitsuwan, also of the DP, became Thailand's first Muslim Minister of Foreign Affairs.

Thailand's political agenda in 1998 was dominated by the economy which, despite the change of government, showed little sign of improvement. The value of the baht continued to fall, reaching a new all-time low of 55 to the US dollar in January 1998. However, the new Government enjoyed an extended 'honeymoon' period, assisted by a supportive media, which perceived in the Chuan administration a more credible team of economic managers. Regular meetings between the IMF and Thailand's economic ministers resulted in the Government's acceptance of most of the IMF's demands for macro-economic reform in exchange for a badly-needed rescue programme of US $17,200m. As a consequence of Thailand's co-operation with the IMF, the Chuan Government received considerable international support. In March Chuan visited the USA and received strong praise from President Bill Clinton, as well as from other US political and business leaders, for the Government's handling of the economic crisis. The visit did much to repair relations with the USA (a long-standing ally of Thailand), which had become strained at the height of the financial crisis, when strong criticism of the USA's perceived abandonment of Thailand in the country's hour of greatest need had been voiced in the Thai press and by certain parliamentarians. The visit also afforded Chuan the opportunity to differentiate Thailand's economic predicament from the worsening situation in Indonesia, where President Suharto's intransigence towards the IMF's demands had led to social and political turmoil and was to result in his eventual resignation in May. Largely as a result of Thailand's adherence to the conditions of the IMF rescue programme, by April the currency had recovered to a rate of around 40 baht to the US dollar.

Throughout 1998 the austerity measures imposed by the Government in accordance with IMF recommendations began to take effect. Extensive redundancies of factory workers became regular occurrences. Meanwhile, government forecasts estimated that the number of unemployed would rise to 2m. by the end of 1998. Fuelled by impatience at the apparent slow progress of the Government in rectifying Thailand's economy, a perception grew in the Thai media that the administration was interested only in solving the 'problems of the rich'. Protesters from farming groups, mostly from the impoverished north-east, regularly rallied outside the National Assembly to criticize the Government's failure to address their problems. Increasing resentment towards the IMF, particularly in relation to the way in which the IMF appeared to be dictating Thailand's economic policy, was expressed in the press and intellectual circles; the IMF's policy of maintaining high interest rates, along with the pressure it was placing on the Government to privatize state enterprises, were perceived by many as an attempt to force Thailand to sell off its assets to foreign interests. A 'Thai Help Thai' campaign was launched by the Government to solicit contributions and donations from the public in an attempt to alleviate Thailand's foreign debt. Television commercials urged Thais to practise moderation in their spending habits. A 'Buy Thai' campaign encouraged Thai consumers to avoid foreign products and to purchase local ones instead, in order to improve Thailand's balance-of-payments problem. Despite these pressures, however, the Chuan Government continued to enjoy a relatively high degree of stability. In early March the Government easily survived a censure debate led by Chuan's predecessor, Chavalit, which did more harm to the opposition's credibility than to that of the Government. Popular support for the Government was demonstrated at the elections to the Bangkok city council, which took place on 26 April, when the DP won 22 of the 60 seats, followed by the non-political supporters of the incumbent Governor, Bhichit Rattakul, who secured 20 seats. By August Thailand's economic situation appeared to have stabilized, although the future was to a great extent dependent on the moribund Japanese economy which, by mid-1998, was officially in recession.

New electoral legislation was passed in May 1998, enabling polls to be held six months subsequently. Despite pressure from the opposition, Chuan stated that elections would not be held until certain economic reforms had been put in place. Under the new legislation, however, it appeared likely that 12 of the members of the ruling coalition who had defected from Prachakorn Thai to help form the Government in November 1997 might lose their legal status as legislators, thus placing in jeopardy the Government's parliamentary majority. (The 12 were formally expelled from Prachakorn Thai in October 1998 but continued to form part of the coalition Government.) A new political party, Thai Rak Thai, was formed by the former Deputy Prime Minister, Thaksin Shinawatra, in July 1998.

In August 1998, following a change in the attitude of the Thai press towards Chuan from May, Queen Sirikit, in an unusual move, praised Prime Minister Chuan and urged support for the efforts of his Government to stabilize the economy. During the same period, however, the Government was afflicted by allegations of corruption, which resulted in the resignation in September of the Minister of Public Health, Rakkeit Sugthana, and subsequently, in October, of the Deputy Minister of Agriculture, Virat Rattanaset. On 5 October Prime Minister Chuan reorganized his Government, bringing the Chart Pattana party into the ruling coalition. The inclusion of Chart Pattana reinforced the Government's majority in the House of Representatives, increasing the number of seats held by the coalition to 257. Five new ministers were appointed to the Cabinet, including the Chart Pattana Secretary-General, Suwat Liptapallop, who was assigned the industry portfolio. Many of the most influential portfolios, however, were retained by the DP. Later the same month the Government announced its intention to remain in power until at least mid-1999.

The widespread support that the Chuan Government had enjoyed in its first year began to diminish in its second year as public frustration grew over the depressed state of the economy. The Government was constantly accused in the media and in the National Assembly of 'selling out the nation' as a result of its economic policies, and a perception persisted that the Government was failing to deal decisively with a series of scandals. In December 1998 and January 1999 there was intense debate in the National Assembly and in the media concerning 11 'Economic Recovery Bills' introduced by the Government. Ostensibly designed to restore confidence in the economy, the bills were also intended partly to meet IMF recommendations for its restructuring. Among the most controversial aspects of the bills were new bankruptcy laws that made it much easier for creditors to prosecute debtors defaulting on loans. Another controversial bill allowed foreigners to hold shares in state enterprises. The Government came under strongest criticism from leading members of the Senate, most notably the upper house's President, Meechai Rachupan, who protested that the bills would lead to foreign control of the Thai economy. Senate opposition to the bills was not, however, entirely based on nationalistic motives. It was revealed that the bills would also affect the business interests of a number of influential senators, including Prachai Leophairatana, chief executive of Thai Petrochemical Industry Public Co Ltd, which had outstanding debts to both Thai and foreign banks of more than US $4,000m. Despite such opposition, and under considerable pressure from the Government, the bills were eventually passed by the Senate in March 1999.

In December 1998 the opposition had filed a motion to remove Chuan and the Minister of Finance, Tarrin Nimmanhaeminda, from office, on the grounds that they had allegedly acted in breach of the Constitution by submitting four Letters of Intent to the IMF without first securing the approval of the House of Representatives; the motion was unsuccessful. In January 1999 a motion of censure was filed by the opposition against three DP ministers (Tarrin, the Deputy Prime Minister and Minister of the Interior, Maj.-Gen. Sanan Kajornprasart, and the Minister of Transport and Communications, Suthep Thaungsuban), who were accused by the opposition of corruption, nepotism, incompetence and dishonesty. As expected, all three ministers survived the vote on the motion; however, there was some concern that the censure debate could potentially undermine popular confidence in the Government.

A series of minor bombings of government buildings, which occurred in December 1998 and January 1999, and included an attack on the DP headquarters in mid-January, was believed by a number of observers to be politically motivated. The Government reportedly attributed the bombings to a group of unidentified opposition sympathizers, and some observers suggested that the campaign of violence had been timed deliberately to cause unrest and instability in the period leading up to the censure debate in late January. The opposition, however, denied any involvement in the bombings.

The Government's standing was further damaged in December 1998 when the media uncovered evidence implicating Sanan in a land scandal in Kanchanaburi province. Government agencies under the administration of the Ministry of the Interior were found to have illegally built resort houses and a road on land reserved for forest. A more damaging issue for the personal reputation of the Prime Minister, who also held the defence portfolio, was the revelation, in March, that he had countersigned an army recommendation awarding Field Marshal Thanom Kittikachorn an honorary appointment as a Royal Guards officer. A military dictator of the 1960s and 1970s, Thanom was notorious for his role in the attempt violently to suppress the 1973 pro-democracy demonstrations in Bangkok in which some 80 (mainly student) protesters were killed. Despite considerable pressure from the media for the appointment to be withdrawn, Chuan declined to interfere on the grounds that it was an internal matter for the Armed Forces and that his signature was simply a matter of procedure; however, Thanom subsequently resigned from the position. In April 1999 Chavalit resigned as leader of the NAP; he was expected to stand for re-election to the post, however, in an attempt to outmanoeuvre his political rivals and increase his influence within the party in advance of the next general election.

Meanwhile, public impatience mounted over the dilatory nature of the investigation into a controversial Buddhist sect, Dhammakaya, which had been accused of distorting Buddhist teachings, employing questionable fund-raising methods, and improperly amassing large areas of land throughout the country. In May 1999 the Government's popularity received a further set-back, owing to its apparent inability to prosecute the perpetrators of a blatant attempt to falsify the results of a municipal election held in Samut Prakan province that month. Television cameras covering the election captured on film two unidentified figures opening a ballot box and emptying a bag of ballot slips into the box in full view of electoral officials. An official recount revealed that over 20,000 illegal votes had been cast, most of which favoured the party led by Chonsawat Asawahem, son of Deputy Minister of the Interior and long-standing National Assembly member for Samut Prakan, Wathana Asawahem. Public suspicion of the Government's tardiness in resolving the issue was partly related to the fact that Wathana's support had been instrumental in the DP's formation of the new Government in 1997 (he led the defection of 12 members of Prachakorn Thai to join the Democrats). In July 1999 the Government was further damaged by allegations that a group of eight armed men, led by an aide to Deputy Prime Minister and senior Democrat Trairong Suwankhiri, had entered the office of the *Thai Post* newspaper and intimidated journalists for publishing an article critical of Trairong. Trairong and Chuan refused to apologize for the incident. In the same month intense infighting within the SAP concerning the allocation of cabinet positions forced the party to withdraw from the governing coalition. In the ensuing cabinet reshuffle Chart Pattana further strengthened its position, notably with the controversial decision to award the important post of Deputy Minister of Commerce to a party fund-raiser and influential business figure, Gonpote Aswinvijit.

In mid-1999, meanwhile, campaigning by Thaksin Shinawatra's party, Thai Rak Thai, intensified in anticipation of an early election. Speculation that Thai Rak Thai was using financial inducements to recruit members of other parties was confirmed by the senior Democrat ministers, Chamni Sakdiset and Khunying Supatra Massdit, who opened a public debate on the issue, partly as an attempt to prevent support flowing from the Democrats to Thai Rak Thai. Despite such criticism, the media reported a groundswell of support for the new party, especially in the northern provinces (Thaksin being a native of Chiang Mai) and in November Chavalit pledged his willingness to support Thai Rak Thai in the pending general election in the event of his own NAP performing poorly at the polls. By August 1999, with public approval of the Government declining, the Democrats found themselves trying to forestall growing demands from opposition parties and numerous public figures to dissolve the House of Representatives and call fresh elections. In late August, following a 10-month investigation into the landholdings and fund-raising methods of Dhammakaya, the Ministry of the Interior approved a warrant for the arrest of the leader of the Buddhist sect, Phra Dhammachayo, on fraud, embezzlement and corruption charges. However, Dhammachayo refused to surrender to the security forces without a guarantee that he would be released on bail. Following a two-day impasse between riot police and some 20,000 of Dhammachayo's supporters, who had barricaded him inside his headquarters on the outskirts of Bangkok, bail was granted and Dhammachayo allowed himself to be taken into custody. Also in August 1999 a report on the state-owned Krung Thai Bank, which exposed the bank's dubious loan policies and other irregularities, was leaked to the Senate and the press. The report led to criticism of the Government for its handling of the bank, and also resulted in direct allegations of corruption being made against Tarrin, whose brother, Sirin Nimmanhaeminda, had been the President of Krung Thai Bank until his resignation in January. Although the Government was reported in October to have exonerated a number of senior Krung Thai executives, including Sirin, of allegations of inefficiency and dishonesty relating to the findings of the report, the controversy surrounding the bank continued adversely to affect the Government throughout November and early December; it constituted the main focus of a joint no-confidence motion filed by three main opposition parties against the Government in December, in which the ruling coalition was accused of mismanagement of the economy and of condoning corruption. As expected, the Government survived the censure debate, winning 229 votes against the opposition's 125. However, the debate exposed divisions within the governing coalition (particularly between the DP and Chart Thai), and also proved particularly damaging to Tarrin and to Sanan.

Although polls of public opinion carried out in the early months of 2000 indicated that the DP-led Government continued to command a significant level of support, the DP suffered a loss of support in the provincial elections held in February, possibly reflecting discontent amongst the rural population with the Government's refusal to subsidize crop prices. In late January, however, the opposition NAP had also suffered a serious reverse when as many as 40 of its legislators, led by the former NAP Secretary-General, Sano Thianthong, boycotted a gathering intended to reaffirm their allegiance to the party in the approach to the anticipated elections. Sano, who had been forcibly removed from his position within the party leadership in March 1999, was subsequently reported to have claimed that the dissident legislators were engaged in negotiations with representatives of Thai Rak Thai on the subject of a possible merger between the two groups.

On 4 March 2000 elections to the new 200-member Senate were held as required under the 1997 Constitution. The elections were contested by more than 1,500 candidates, and a voter participation level of 71.89% was reported. The power of the new Election Commission (EC), which had been established under the reformist Constitution to oversee the elections, was demonstrated when it disqualified 78 of the 200 winning candidates on the grounds of either vote-buying or fraudulent conduct. The EC subsequently announced that a second round of polling would be held in the 78 affected constituencies on 29 April, in which all but two of the disqualified contestants would be permitted to stand again. A total of 66 senators were duly elected, including more than one-half of those disqualified after the first round of polling. The EC announced that a third round of polling would be held in June to elect senators to the 12 remaining seats, and rejected calls for the dismissal of the allegations of fraud in the interest of political continuity. (While the final results of the elections remained in dispute, none of the declared winners were able to assume their seats as they lacked the necessary quorum, resulting in a backlog of legislation and obliging the outgoing Senate to remain in office in an interim capacity.) The EC also announced that a number of prominent individuals were likely to be prosecuted for their involvement in electoral misconduct. While the insistence of the EC on the holding of a further round of polls led to fears that the recent constitutional reforms were perhaps overzealous and could result in the paralysis of the legislature, the disclosures of electoral fraud were welcomed by many as demonstrating the Government's commitment to the elimination of political corruption. However, it was also recognized that the disruption of the legislative process caused by the delay in the appointment of the new Senate could have implications for the timing of the pending general elections, as a number of bills scheduled to be passed before the Senate were thought likely by many observers to be critical to the electoral prospects of the ruling coalition. On 4 June the third round of polling was duly held, which resulted in the election of a further eight senators, although voter participation was officially registered at a mere 41.28%. Further allegations of electoral fraud necessitated fourth and fifth rounds of polling on 9 and 22 July respectively, both of which attracted voter turnouts of some 31%. On 27 July the last of the 200 members of the Senate were finally endorsed, and on 1 August the new Senate was officially sworn in. A significant feature of the composition of the new Senate was the greatly reduced proportion of senators coming from military and bureaucratic backgrounds, and increased numbers from academia, the media and NGOs.

Meanwhile, in March 2000 the DP was set back by the findings of the National Anti-Corruption Commission's (NACC) investigation into Deputy Prime Minister, Minister of the Interior and Secretary-General of the DP, Sanan Kajornprasart, which, in a watershed decision, indicted Sanan on charges of falsifying his assets statement. Sanan immediately resigned from his ministerial positions and was replaced by Banyat Bantadtan; Sanan's position as Secretary-General of the DP was eventually taken by Anant Anatakul, a former permanent secretary in the Ministry of the Interior, following the former's conviction, in August, of corruption charges by the Constitutional Court, which resulted in a five-year ban from holding political position. While the NACC's findings damaged the credibility of the DP, Sanan's resignation also spared the party the difficulty of facing a new election with Sanan, whose tarnished image was increasingly seen as a liability. The Government's difficulties were, however, ameliorated by the growing disarray in the ranks of the core party of the opposition, the NAP. In March the party was hit by a scandal in which Surasak Nananukkol, the NAP's chief economic adviser and a former Deputy Minister of Finance, was arrested in the USA on charges of involvement in an oil smuggling deal with Iraq, which violated UN sanctions on Iraqi oil exports as well as US law. Furthermore, rumours abounded that in the run-up to the next election large numbers of NAP deputies, including the influential Wang Nam Yen faction controlled by Sano, were preparing to desert Chavalit's NAP in order to join Thai Rak Thai. In June the NAP leadership took the step of urging NAP deputies to resign from their seats in the House of Representatives in a bid to force the Government into calling an early election. The controversial strategy revealed the deep divisions within the NAP, with at least 20 NAP deputies refusing to take part in the mass resignation (although almost 100 did resign), including former NAP Secretary-General Chaturon Chaisaeng. The NAP's mass defection had little effect on the DP-led coalition, however, which now faced a greatly-reduced opposition in the House of Representatives. In July a second opposition party, the SAP, also resigned from the House of Representatives.

The turmoil within the NAP was taken advantage of by Thai Rak Thai, which was emerging as the DP's likely major rival in the next election. However, Thai Rak Thai was also faced with its own difficulties. Its candidate in the Bangkok gubernatorial election, Sudarat Keyuraphan, was decisively defeated by the veteran leader of Prachakorn Thai, Samak Sundaravej. In the largest ever elector turn-out for a gubernatorial election (58.87% according to official figures) Samak became the first candidate in the history of the election to poll over 1m. votes. The result was interpreted by many observers as a set-back to Thai Rak Thai's hopes of winning seats in Bangkok in the forthcoming legislative elections. Thai Rak Thai's image continued to be damaged by ongoing criticism in the media that it was offering financial incentives in order to recruit deputies from other parties. Several high profile deputies, including SAP leader Suwit Khunkitti and Chart Pattana's Yingphan Manasikarn, confirmed that they would run under the Thai Rak Thai banner in the next legislative elections. Concern had also been raised over Thaksin's controversial acquisition in late May of a significant stake in a television station that had been established following the pro-democracy demonstrations in 1992 as a supposedly independent media organization. In September it was announced that Thaksin was to be investigated on possible charges of corruption.

In November 2000 Prime Minister Chuan Leekpai ended months of speculation by dissolving the legislature and setting 6 January 2001 as the date for an election to the House of Representatives, the first under the 1997 Constitution. The announcement came at a time when the Government was suffering from rapidly-declining public support as a result of the continued stagnation of the Thai economy, a perception in the media that the Government's policies were addressing only the problems of major businesses, and ongoing criticisms that the Government had capitulated to the demands of the IMF and the foreign investment community at the expense of national interests. However, Thai Rak Thai, which in the short time of its existence had emerged as the DP's major rival, was faced with an internal problem in the form of a major corruption scandal involving its leader, Thaksin Shinawatra. After a lengthy investigation, on 26 December Thaksin was indicted by the National Counter Corruption Commission (NCCC) on charges that he and his wife had violated assets disclosure regulations (laid out in the new Constitution) by deliberately concealing shares worth thousands of millions of baht. The NCCC alleged that Thaksin had transferred the shares to his household staff. Refusing to accept the verdict, Thaksin launched an immediate appeal to the 15-member Constitutional Court, another so-called 'independent body', like the NCCC, established under the new Constitution. If found guilty, Thaksin faced the prospect of being banned from politics for five years.

The Thai Rak Thai election campaign was characterized by its sophisticated use of the mass media, which portrayed Thai Rak Thai as the party of 'the new generation', summed up by its election slogan, 'New Ideas, New Actions'. Thaksin was represented as a successful business executive who would bring his skills from the corporate world to government, in contrast to Chuan, who was depicted as indecisive, ineffective, and mired in bureaucratic process. Thai Rak Thai also made a series of populist election promises, including: development fund grants of 1m. baht for each of Thailand's 77,000 villages in a bid to stimulate the rural economy; a public health programme that would see Thais pay just 30 baht for each hospital consultation; and a three-year debt moratorium for Thailand's indebted farmers. The Thai Rak Thai campaign received an unexpected boost after unprecedented public expressions of support from the heads of two of the country's biggest corporate groups: Dhanin Chiaravanont, head of the agribusiness company, Charoen Pokphand Group; and Chatri Sophonpanich, Chairman of the Bangkok Bank. The DP's campaign focused on highlighting the Government's record of guiding the Thai economy out of the economic crisis of the late 1990s and its implementation of vital economic reforms, while at the same time accusing Thaksin of trying to buy votes at the election in the same way that he had used his enormous financial resources to recruit politicians to Thai Rak Thai.

The election result was an overwhelming victory for Thai Rak Thai. The final outcome (following a second round of elections in a number of constituencies on 29 January 2001 as a result of voting irregularities in the earlier poll) gave Thai Rak Thai 248 seats, almost double that of the party with the next highest number of seats, the Democrat Party, which secured 128.

The Government of Thaksin Shinawatra

Following Thaksin's successful negotiation of a merger between the Seritham Party and Thai Rak Thai, the party became the first in Thai history to hold an absolute majority in the House of Representatives. To further consolidate its position, Thai Rak Thai elected to form a coalition with Chart Thai and the NAP to give the Government an ample majority of 339 seats. One of the most significant outcomes of the election was the eclipse of a number of long-standing provincial political dynasties, as a result of electoral rules set out in the new Constitution that were designed to decrease the influence of smaller parties in the interests of more stable government. Thaksin impressed his dominance on the coalition Government by filling 27 out of the 36 Cabinet positions with Thai Rak Thai appointees, including the key Ministries of the Interior, Finance, Commerce, Industry, Education, Foreign Affairs, Health, Agriculture and Cooperatives, and Justice. Given his substantial personal financial assets, his extensive media interests, his control of the Thai Rak Thai party, and Thai Rak Thai's dominance of the coalition Government, Thaksin was thus in a more powerful political position than any previous civilian Prime Minister.

From the start, the new Government emphasized its nationalist credentials and distanced itself from the previous administration, which had been widely portrayed in the media as being too accommodating with regard to 'the West'. The new Minister of Foreign Affairs, Surakiart Sathirathai, announced a redirection of Thailand's foreign policy to focus on strengthening economic relations with Thailand's Asian neighbours, dismissing his predecessor's perceived preoccupation with broader issues of human rights and democracy, which, while winning praise from Western nations, had aggravated numerous governments within ASEAN. In a speech in February 2001 Thaksin declared that Thailand must, 'cease being a slave to the world', and abandon policies that worked against 'Thai interests'. In another controversial and widely-reported address to the UN Economic and Social Commission for Asia and the Pacific (ESCAP) in April, Thaksin appeared to indicate that Thailand would be following a more inward-looking, self-sufficient economic policy, and would give more support to 'small and medium enterprise industries'. The Prime Minister also discussed the importance of promoting greater economic integration among Asian countries. Following adverse reports in the Western media, Thaksin was later at pains to assure the international business community that Thailand would maintain an open economy and continue to welcome foreign investment.

Early in Thai Rak Thai's tenure of office, concerns were raised about apparent attempts by the Government to limit the powers of a number of the so-called 'independent bodies' established under the 1997 Constitution. Following a decision by the Electoral Commission (one the most active of these bodies) to disqualify 10 Senators for alleged violations of electoral laws, the Government mounted a legal challenge to limit the Commission's extensive powers. The NCCC similarly came under pressure from the Government after its investigation into the Thaksin share concealment case. Three members of the NCCC were accused by the Government of violating constitutional regulations, which eventually resulted in the resignation of the leader of the investigation. Thaksin also expressed his intention of reviewing the powers of the Constitutional Court by making amendments to the Constitution. In May, after weeks of tension over interest rate policy, Thaksin dismissed the Governor of the central bank, Chatu Mongol Sonakul, and replaced him with Pridiyathorn Davakula. Despite the Prime Minister's insistence that the dismissal was primarily due to personality differences, concerns were raised about government interference in the independence of the Bank of Thailand. The Thai media were also targeted by the Government. Accusations were made that the Government was attempting systematically to cajole the media into presenting the Government in a favourable light. These accusations were strengthened considerably when one of Thai Rak Thai's own members of the House of Representatives, the maverick Piyanat Wacharaporn, publicly expressed concerns about government interference in the media, which prompted a sharp rebuke from the Prime Minister. In August the Public Relations Department's Channel 11 cancelled a popular current affairs talk show hosted by a Senator and former academic, Chirmsak Pinthong.

In early August 2001 months of uncertainty over Thaksin's political future finally ended when the Constitutional Court controversially acquitted him of corruption charges by an eight-to-seven ruling. The decision came after campaigns of public support for Thaksin had put pressure on the Court to return an acquittal verdict, while numerous Thai Rak Thai politicians had warned that a guilty verdict would have an adverse effect on the Thai economy, and could even lead to political violence.

While the Court's decision received considerable public support, concern was expressed in certain quarters that a number of the judges might have been placed under pressure, or even bribed, into returning a verdict of acquittal. The allegations were sufficiently serious to prompt the Senate to begin an inquiry into the Court's decision.

Thaksin's increasing control over the political process was strengthened in April 2002, when the long-expected merger of the NAP, which had been a major force in Thai politics during the 1990s, with Thai Rak Thai finally took place. NAP leader Chavalit, however, retained his post as Minister of Defence and Deputy Prime Minister. Thai Rak Thai's position in the House of Representatives was further consolidated with the defection of Chart Pattana from the opposition to the Government, giving Thai Rak Thai 368 seats, out of a total of 500, with the DP, the next largest party in the House of Representatives, commanding only 129. Not only did the merger of the NAP and the defection of Chart Pattana reinforce Thai Rak Thai's dominance over the opposition, but it also gave Thaksin increased authority over factions within his own party, especially the 'Wang Nam Yen' group of 50 legislators, controlled by veteran politician Sanoh Thienthong. The Government's increased majority enabled it to survive easily a three-day no-confidence debate in May 2002. The Prime Minister also extended his influence over the military with his appointment of Gen. Somdhat Attanand, known to have close links with the Thai Rak Thai party, to the key post of Commander-in-Chief of the Army during the annual military reshuffle, which took place in August 2002. In addition, the Government moved to strengthen its control over the bureaucracy, completing a major reform of the sector by October 2002. This included a reorganization of ministries and departments, as well as an increase in the existing number of ministries, from 14 to 20. The principal feature of the provincial administration reforms was the creation of what were dubbed 'CEO governors' through a strengthening of the powers of the provincial governor over the myriad of bureaucratic agencies at provincial and local government level. The policy was, however, criticized by the opposition and sections of the media as being an apparent reversal of the policy of decentralization favoured by the previous Democrat administration, a claim denied by the Government.

Thai Rak Thai's remarkable dominance of the House of Representatives, and Thaksin's often abrasive style of leadership (the Prime Minister being an open admirer of Malaysia's Prime Minister, Mahathir Mohamad), provoked accusations from the political opposition, sections of the print media, numerous academics and even members of his own party, that Thaksin was acting like a 'dictator'. In a rare public rebuke, the King singled the Prime Minister out for criticism in his birthday address on 4 December 2001, warning that Thailand was heading for 'catastrophe' and calling for increased unity amongst all politicians. The King's comments led to a sharp decline in the Prime Minister's popularity in the opinion polls and encouraged further criticism in the media. Thaksin also ran foul of the Western news media, owing partly to statements (which he had made regarding Thailand's economy soon after becoming Prime Minister) that were interpreted as being anti-Western in orientation. A report in the Hong Kong-based news weekly, the *Far Eastern Economic Review*, in March 2002, concerning the apparent tensions between the Government and the Palace, led to moves to have the two journalists involved in the publication of the article expelled from the country, a decision that was later reversed following negotiations between the Government and the *Review*. In the same month an issue of another leading current affairs weekly, *The Economist*, containing a special feature on Thailand, was banned from circulation in the country, ostensibly for portraying the Thai royal family in an unfavourable light. While both the domestic and international media protested against what they perceived to be direct attacks on the freedom of the press, Thaksin was able to gain some domestic support for the Government by representing his actions as constituting a defence of the monarchy against foreign criticism. The domestic media were also targeted by the Government. In March 2002 the Nation Multimedia Group, a publisher of newspapers in both Thai and English, as well as a broadcaster of television and radio programmes, which had been one of Thaksin's most prominent critics, was warned by the Ministry of Defence to delete political content from one radio programme after it aired an interview with an opposition MP critical of the Government. The Nation Multimedia Group was also at the centre of another controversy when senior members were placed under investigation by the Anti-Money Laundering Office. Following an outcry in the media, the investigation was eventually abandoned. To counter what it perceived to be inaccurate media reporting, the Government initiated the establishment of a new agency intended to implement guide-lines to be followed by the state controlled media. In October 2001 Shin Corporation, the telecommunications conglomerate which Thaksin had founded, and in which his family retained a controlling interest, increased its share in ITV, the only non-state-owned television station, from an initial 25% (which it had acquired in 2000), to 77%. There were even accusations, strongly denied by Thaksin, that the Government was using advertising accounts worth thousands of millions of baht to reward media sources that were sympathetic towards the Government. Thus, during its second year in office, the Government appeared to be complementing its dominance of the legislature with an increasingly effective control over the media.

Despite these criticisms, the Thai Rak Thai-led Government managed to maintain a relatively high level of popularity. A prominent 'social order' campaign, implemented by the Minister of the Interior, Purachai Piumsombun, one of the Prime Minister's close associates and, like Thaksin, a former police officer with a doctorate in criminology, was publicly well received. The campaign involved an uncharacteristically stringent nationwide campaign against illegal entertainment establishments. Entertainment venues violating zoning laws were closed down, opening and closing times were strictly enforced, and under-age youths were prohibited from attending such venues. Despite lobbying from the nighttime entertainment industry, from members of the House of Representatives who belonged to his own party—including the powerful Sanoh Thienthong—and from sections of the military with links to the industry, the policy remained in place.

The Government's fortunes were also improved by an apparent recovery in Thailand's economic prospects. In the first quarter of 2002 the economy expanded at a healthy rate of 3.9%, despite the depressed state of the US economy and the disruptions to the world economy that had occurred in the wake of the terrorist attacks on the USA on 11 September 2001. In June 2002 the Stock Exchange of Thailand was the best performing exchange in Asia. Consumer spending had also increased; the Government attributed this to its 'village development fund', established by Thai Rak Thai following its election. In August a leading international rating agency upgraded its assessment of the Thai economy, from 'stable' to 'positive'. In July the Government conducted negotiations with Malaysia and Indonesia over the establishment of a rubber cartel, which would control rubber prices on the world market. Not only did the cartel promise to improve incomes for Thailand's rubber producers, it also had the potential to enhance the Government's popularity in the Democrats' heartland of southern Thailand, where most of the country's rubber continued to be produced.

One of the opposition's major criticisms of the Thaksin Government (and one that had been raised in the no-confidence censure motion debated in May) was that the Prime Minister was allegedly using his public office to further his private business interests. In August 2001 the House of Representatives approved legislation reducing the limit on foreign ownership of telecommunications companies from 49% to 25%. While the decision was presented in nationalist rhetoric concerning the need to protect Thailand's national interests from foreign influence—a theme that Thai Rak Thai had successfully exploited during the election campaign—the decision directly benefited Shin Corporation, the major telecommunications organization controlled by the Shinawatra family, which continued to dominate the domestic telecommunications market. Several of the accusations of a conflict of interest involved Shin Corporation's satellite services branch, Shin Satellite, or 'Sattel'. In February 2002 the Prime Minister made a sudden visit to India, where it was alleged that he negotiated a deal between Sattel and India's Department of Space. Sattel already had a substantial stake in India's satellite cable television market. Sattel's wholly-owned subsidiary, Camshin, also maintained a significant presence in the Cambodian mobile telecommunications market. In May 2002 Sattel announced a US $13m. deal with the Myanma government agency, Bagan Cybertech (headed by the son of Gen. Khin Nyunt, Secretary of the ruling State Peace and Development Council (SPDC), the military junta of Myanmar) to provide technology and satellite services for a telephone network in rural Myanmar. Sattel was also preparing to launch a new-generation broadband satellite system, 'iPSTAR', which would provide most of the Asian continent with high-speed telecommunications, internet and multimedia services at a fraction of the current costs. Sattel had already been awarded a contract by the Thai Government to equip 40,000 state schools and educational institutions with iPSTAR technology. According to company projections, iPSTAR would provide US $300m. in annual earnings for Sattel. Given Shin Corporation's interests in Sattel, the success or otherwise of its iPSTAR venture, and, indeed, of the company's other regional business interests, was expected to have direct implications for Thaksin's political fortunes.

RECENT FOREIGN AFFAIRS

Thai regimes since the mid-1980s, whether military or civilian, had attempted to achieve a *modus vivendi* between established military-bureaucratic élites and the increasingly powerful interests of capitalism. Domestic and international business interests greatly circumscribed the ability of Thailand's rulers to change policy from the *laissez-faire*, export-promoting course on which the country had embarked. It was not possible, for example, for the military to restore the 'hard line' on Indo-China as Suchinda's regime had announced on seizing power in 1991. Thai business interests were already too deeply engaged in Laos and keen to penetrate Cambodia, while ASEAN and other countries were increasingly determined to reach an Indo-China settlement. Consequently, the military regime's leaders quietly acceded to Chatichai's vision of Thailand as the capitalist focus for the economically-feeble socialist states that surrounded it, and they adopted policies toward Cambodia, Laos, and Myanmar that favoured the penetration of Thai interests. Under the democratic regime of Chuan Leekpai, this line was pursued with vigour. In February 1993 Thailand, Viet Nam, Laos and Cambodia signed a joint communiqué that resulted in the establishment of a Bangkok-based commission for developing the Mekong river basin. In October 1993 Thailand was accepted as a full member of the Non-aligned Movement.

Thailand's efforts to establish itself as a patron to its economically weaker neighbours were complicated in Cambodia by the involvement of powerful Thai business and military interests with the communist dissident faction, the Khmers Rouges, a lucrative source of concessions for logging and gem-mining. At the beginning of 1993 Thailand formally closed its borders to trade with the Khmers Rouges, in accordance with UN sanctions. Unofficial dealings continued, however, straining Thai relations not only with the UN but with the USA, which Thailand was otherwise eager to accommodate. In December the Government was deeply embarrassed by the seizure of a large shipment of weapons from a Thai army stockpile, which was evidently on its way to the Khmers Rouges. In January 1994 Chuan became the first Thai Prime Minister to pay an official visit to Cambodia. Thereafter, his Government made increasing efforts to disentangle Thai military and business interests from the Khmers Rouges. In December 1994 Chuan issued an order to governors and military commanders of the border provinces to cease their co-operation with Cambodian guerrillas. This was largely successful, and co-operation between the Thai and Cambodian armies on the border increased notably during 1995, although there continued to be clashes between Thai and Cambodian troops as a result of incursions into Thai territory by the latter in pursuit of Khmer Rouge guerrillas. In mid-1996 Thai interests switched to support the breakaway Khmer Rouge faction of Ieng Sary, which controlled the border area on which the gem and timber trade was centred. In the subsequent negotiations between Ieng Sary and the Cambodian Government, Thailand played a major mediating role.

Thailand refused to join in the international boycott of the Myanma military regime, proclaiming instead a policy of 'constructive engagement'. The profitability of this remained considerable, in spite of Myanmar's cancellation of many Thai logging and fishing concessions at the end of 1992. The Myanma military's increasing domination of border areas led to a new influx of refugees into Thailand in 1992–93; Thai authorities accommodated them but took care to prevent their aiding insurgents. They also moved to reduce possible clashes with the Myanma regime by joint demarcation of the border, and by supporting mediated settlements of Myanmar's ethnic rebellions. At the same time Thai diplomacy within ASEAN successfully secured a more positive approach by the regional organization to Myanmar; Thailand invited the Myanma Minister of Foreign Affairs, Ohn Gyaw, to attend an ASEAN ministerial meeting in Bangkok in August 1994.

In January and February 1995 about 10,000 members of the Kayin (formerly Karen) National Union (KNU) fled to Thailand, following an assault by Myanma government forces on the rebels' headquarters on the Moei river. Attacks on the refugee camps where the disarmed Kayins were held prompted Thailand to move the refugees to a site 10 km inside Thailand and to warn Myanmar that it would retaliate against border incursions. Bilateral relations deteriorated further in March when Myanmar closed its only land border with Thailand, in retaliation for alleged Thai support for raids in the area by the Mong Tai Army controlled by the 'opium warlord', Khun Sa. In September Chavalit visited Yangon and assured the Myanma regime that Thailand did not intend to support Khun Sa and his Shan followers.

Thailand achieved mixed results in its efforts to 'open up' its socialist neighbours. Once the countries of what Thai leaders liked to call the 'Greater Mekong Sub-region' had established connections with a range of foreign capitalist interlocutors they tried to reduce their dependence on Thai patronage. In 1995 Cambodia gave preference to investment from Malaysia and Singapore. Myanmar became less pliable to Thai interests and likewise encouraged investment from Singapore. Relations with Viet Nam were marred by competition over fishing rights in the Gulf of Siam, leading in May 1995 to an armed clash between Thai and Vietnamese naval patrol boats. Even Laos, which normally preferred avoidance to assertion in its international relations, demanded that the headquarters of the Mekong River Commission be removed to Vientiane, and attempted to balance its Thai connections by renewed dealings with China and Viet Nam. None the less, Thailand's political and economic centrality to the mainland South-East Asian area led to increasing international acknowledgement of its regional importance.

Thailand's foreign business investments were not limited to raw material extraction from its poorer neighbours. Increasingly, major Thai banks and businesses looked abroad for profit, particularly to mainland China's booming economy. At the same time, trade with the rest of ASEAN grew rapidly, and Thailand's professed objective of making Bangkok an investment hub for mainland South-East Asia and inland southern China began to be taken seriously by foreign observers. This increasing Asian orientation had an effect on Thai-US relations, with growing tension over issues such as investment access, US import quotas, and intellectual property rights. Thailand, too, was distancing itself from its traditional patron, as its economic interests and diplomatic possibilities diversified. The USA was unsure of Thailand's commitment to the war on drugs, and in 1995 refused visas to three senior politicians it considered to be involved in drugs-trafficking. However, Thailand's growing attraction as a market-place and as a base for business in the ASEAN area brought increasing US investment, counterbalancing tensions aroused over other issues.

In July 1993 Thailand, Malaysia and Indonesia endorsed the concept of a 'growth triangle' that would enhance economic development in northern Sumatra, the five southernmost states of Thailand, and the north-western border states of Malaysia. For Thailand, this was an economic initiative with profound political implications: whereas once Thai authorities had been concerned to sever the cross-border connections of the largely Muslim and Malay-speaking south, they now seemed confident that economic advantage would outweigh the risk of encouraging sympathy for Muslim separatism.

Under Chavalit, Thailand's foreign policy included a number of new initiatives. The most important and controversial of these was increased defence links with the People's Republic of

China. In early April 1997 Chavalit led a high-level delegation, including senior ministers, military representatives, senior bureaucrats and the police chief, to Beijing for talks with the Chinese authorities. While agreements were reached on increasing trade relations between the two countries, media attention focused on China's pledge to strengthen defence ties. The Chinese Ministry of Defence offered to sell military equipment including battle tanks and an air defence system to the Thai military at 'friendly prices' with favourable conditions of payment. In May a follow-up visit to China was made by senior Thai military officials in which further talks were conducted regarding the procurement of Chinese military hardware.

Chavalit continued Thailand's policy of strengthening bilateral relations with its neighbours by making trips to Viet Nam, Myanmar and Cambodia. On most of these trips the agenda was dominated by security issues. There was continuing instability on Thailand's western border with Myanmar where tens of thousands of Kayin, Karenni and Mon refugees had crossed into Thailand as a result of campaigns by the Myanma military against ethnic insurgents. By mid-1997 it was estimated that as many as 100,000 refugees were housed in refugee camps inside the Thai border with Myanmar. Despite the unstable situation on Thailand's border with Myanmar, however, Thailand's support was a key factor in Myanmar's admission into ASEAN as a full member in July 1997. In Cambodia the fragile alliance between the Co-Prime Ministers, Hun Sen and Prince Ranariddh, broke down in July, with fighting erupting between forces loyal to the two rival leaders. Fierce battles between the two forces spilled over into Thailand's eastern border with Cambodia, with thousands of refugees fleeing the fighting and crossing into Thailand. Border issues preoccupied the Armed Forces' Survey Directorate throughout 1997. Talks continued with the Laotian and Myanma Governments on disputed border demarcations, while an agreement was reached with Viet Nam regarding its maritime boundaries with Thailand.

Under the Chuan administration, there was a substantial improvement in relations with Malaysia. By April 1998 Chuan and the Malaysian Prime Minister, Mahathir Mohamad, had met an unprecedented five times in as many months to discuss regional and economic issues affecting the two countries. The most important outcome of these discussions was the agreement by Malaysia to end all support for the Muslim separatist movement in the troubled border region of southern Thailand, and to take a more assertive stance in suppressing the activity of known Muslim separatists operating on Malaysian soil. In the months following the agreement, a number of key separatist leaders were apprehended or gave themselves up to the Thai authorities. Discussions were held regarding the use of common currencies in the conduct of bilateral trade instead of relying on US dollars. In April the two Prime Ministers also witnessed an agreement signed by the two respective state-owned oil companies of Thailand and Malaysia on the development of gas reserves in the Thai-Malaysian Joint Development Area, once a disputed region between the two countries. The gas development deal was part of the Indonesia-Malaysia-Thailand Economic Triangle co-operation agreement, which gained added significance as a result of the economic slump in the region in the late 1990s.

Work on the controversial Yadana gas pipeline running between Thailand and Myanmar was approaching completion in 1998. The purpose of the pipeline was to give Thailand access to gas reserves being developed by the Myanma Government in Myanmar's Andaman Sea; however, the project attracted strong criticism from Thai environmentalists and human-rights activists, causing tension in Thailand's relations with Myanmar. Relations with Myanmar were further strained by a series of other issues, the most serious of which were the continuing incursions across the Thai-Myanma border by Myanma troops and the ongoing refugee problem resulting from continued fighting between Myanma government forces and rebel ethnic groups on the border. The Myanma ruling junta's continued restrictions on the movements and political activities of opposition leader Aung San Suu Kyi also received considerable media attention in Thailand. In August a number of Thai activists, along with other foreign nationals, were detained in Yangon by the Myanma authorities; the activists were charged with distributing anti-Government material and sentenced to five-year prison terms before the sentences were overturned and the group was eventually deported. In early 1998, with Thailand's economic crisis resulting in increasing levels of unemployment, the large numbers of illegal migrant labourers who had been working in the country since the years of the economic boom were also becoming a major concern to the Thai Government. According to official statistics, almost 1m. illegal migrant labourers remained in Thailand, most of whom were Myanma nationals, with the remainder coming from Laos and Cambodia. In March the Government announced plans for the forced repatriation of several hundred thousand illegal Myanma migrant workers; however, the Government subsequently announced that it would reconsider its plans, as some industries were encountering difficulties in finding local replacements for the foreign workers.

In mid-1998 Thailand's new Minister of Foreign Affairs, Surin Pitsuwan, signalled a change in Thailand's approach to regional relations within ASEAN. Instead of 'constructive engagement', which effectively meant that ASEAN members were to refrain from commenting on the internal affairs of other member countries, Surin proposed a new policy of 'flexible engagement', in accordance with which ASEAN nations would have the right to discuss the domestic affairs of another member country if those affairs had an impact beyond that country's borders. The proposed change in policy had been prompted by a number of recent regional issues, including the violent events in Cambodia in July 1997, the devastating forest fires in Indonesia which had severely affected the air quality (and the tourist industries) of neighbouring countries, the continuing abuse of human rights by the military regime in Myanmar and the problem, experienced by several ASEAN nations, of large numbers of illegal foreign workers. While Surin's proposal was welcomed by US, European and Australian government officials as a sign of a new political openness in the region, it met with a generally negative response from most other ASEAN members. At the meeting of ASEAN Ministers of Foreign Affairs in Manila in July, the only regional support Thailand received for the 'flexible engagement' concept came from the Philippines, while Indonesia, Malaysia, Myanmar and Viet Nam strongly rejected any modification of ASEAN's long-standing principle of non-interference.

A major issue dominating Thailand's foreign agenda for much of 1998–99 was the impasse over the appointment of the next Director-General of the World Trade Organization (WTO). The Thai candidate, Deputy Prime Minister and Minister of Commerce, Supachai Panichpakdi, who was supported by the majority of Asian nations, was involved in a contest with former New Zealand Prime Minister, Michael Moore. Intense criticism in the Thai media regarding the apparent support of the USA for Moore turned the issue into one of national pride, and Chuan wrote to President Clinton to express his wish that the USA remain neutral with regard to the appointment. The perception that the USA was obstructing Supachai's bid for the position fuelled growing criticism of the USA by Thai politicians and the Thai media concerning the effects of the economic crisis and the perceived political influence of the IMF in Thailand. Anti-US sentiment was further provoked by 'Operation Desert Fox' and the punitive air-strikes conducted against Iraq in December 1998, which, although they were not condemned by the Thai Government, were widely criticized in the Thai media. The impasse concerning the WTO appointment was finally resolved in July 1999 after Supachai agreed to an Australian proposal for the post to be divided into two consecutive three-year terms, with Supachai taking the second term.

Undoubtedly, the major foreign affairs issue for the Thai Government in 1999 was its high-profile participation in the UN-organized International Force for East Timor (Interfet). In the frantic diplomatic activity that followed the outbreak of militia violence in East Timor in the wake of the referendum on independence, held on 30 August, the Thai Government agreed to commit 1,500 troops to the Interfet force. The Thai contingent was the largest of those sent by ASEAN nations (and the second largest after the Australian contribution), and a Thai general, Maj.-Gen. Songkitti Chakrapatr, was appointed Deputy Commander of Interfet. The situation was a very sensitive one for the Thai Government, given that it risked breaking the accepted convention of non-interference in the internal affairs of an ASEAN member state. Prime Minister Chuan and the Minister of Foreign Affairs, Surin Pitsuwan, repeatedly stated that they had agreed to take part in the mission only after being invited to do so by Indonesia's President Habibie, Gen. Wiranto (then Commander-in-Chief of the Indonesian National Defence Forces) and the UN. The Thai opposition expressed concern over the cost of such an operation at a time of severe economic hardship in the country. The prominent Thai participation in Interfet contrasted with the initially reluctant responses by other South-East Asian nations, most of which sent only token forces. Malaysia's Prime Minister, Mahathir Mohamad, was highly critical of the West's role in East Timor, claiming that it was a 'plot to split up Indonesia'. Singapore's former Prime Minister, Lee Kuan Yew, publicly questioned what he perceived as the West's preoccupation with the issue of East Timor. Within Thailand the Government was accused by the opposition and some sections of the media, especially a number of Thai Muslim news magazines, of pandering to the West and breaking ranks with ASEAN members.

In 1999 Thailand's relations with Myanmar were strained over the issue of drugs-trafficking into Thailand. By the late 1990s amphetamine addiction had come to be regarded not only as a serious social issue but also as a problem of national security. The Thai authorities publicly accused the United Wa State Army, based in north-east Myanmar, of being behind the production and trafficking of millions of amphetamine tablets across the border into Thailand. The Wa have signed a peace agreement with the Myanma Government and were co-operating with the Myanma military in the suppression of Kayin insurgents. In August, on the advice of the National Security Council, the Thai Government closed a major border trading point at San Ton Du in Chiang Mai province, which was regarded as one of the main entry points of amphetamines into Thailand. Thai border police and military units reported intermittent clashes with suspected Wa traffickers who had crossed into Thai territory. Meanwhile, in Thailand's southern provinces bordering Malaysia a series of violent incidents occurred in July and August, including the shooting of a policeman, and bombings and arson attacks directed against government property. The Thai authorities blamed the attacks, the first for some time, on a renewed campaign of violence carried out by Muslim separatists. Malaysia promised to co-operate in apprehending anyone suspected of involvement in the attacks who was using Malaysian territory to evade capture by the Thai authorities.

On 1 October 1999 Thai–Myanma relations were strained further when a group of heavily armed Myanma students stormed the Myanma embassy in Bangkok taking all 89 people in the compound hostage, including 13 diplomats. The gunmen demanded that all political prisoners in Myanmar be released, that a dialogue between the military junta and other political parties be opened, and that the elected legislature be convened. The situation was further complicated as the Thai Minister of the Interior, Sanan Kajornprasart, and the Deputy Minister of Foreign Affairs, Sukhumphand Paripatra, publicly appeared to express sympathy with the pro-democracy aspirations of the students. The situation was, however, resolved within 24 hours when the group agreed to release the hostages in exchange for the Thai Government's guarantee of a safe passage by helicopter to the Thai-Myanma border. Sukhumphand also agreed to act as a hostage for the duration of the flight. The ruling military junta in Myanmar was quick to express its displeasure at the way in which the hostage crisis had been handled by the Thai Government. In a series of retaliatory measures, it closed the border with Thailand, cancelled fishing concessions and refused to allow Thai fishing vessels into Myanma waters. Relations between the two countries deteriorated further when, in November, the Thai Government began forced repatriations of thousands of illegal Myanma migrant workers. The deterioration in relations between the two countries was eventually halted at the end of November when, following a visit by Thai Minister of Foreign Affairs, Surin Pitsuwan, Myanmar agreed to reopen both the common border and its territorial waters to Thai fishing vessels. The importance that the Thai Government now placed on cordial relations with the junta in Myanmar was evident with the handling of a second hostage crisis in January 2000: 10 armed Myanma rebels from God's Army, an ethnic Kayin faction fighting an armed insurgency against the Myanma Government, took control of a hospital in Ratchaburi Province, close to the Myanmar border, holding more than 500 patients, doctors and nurses hostage. They demanded that the shelling of Kayin positions by the Thai military should cease, that medical assistance should be given to injured Kayin fighters, and that the Thai military should cease its co-operation with the Myanma forces in suppressing Kayin military activity on the Thai-Myanma border. In contrast to its peaceful handling of the earlier siege at the Myanma embassy, the Thai Government acted decisively; a team of commandos stormed the hospital in a pre-dawn raid, killing all 10 hostage-takers (according to some hostage reports after they had already surrendered). The brutal resolution of the incident was praised by the military Government in Myanmar, and many observers viewed the Thai Government's handling of the incident as signalling a broader campaign by the Thai authorities on dissident activity by ethnic Myanma opposition groups operating in Thailand. In another sign of a change in the formerly-relaxed Thai policy towards the tens of thousands of Myanma and Kayin refugees housed in camps in Thailand, the Government appealed to the UN to organize the rapid resettlement of the refugees to third countries.

Despite the new Thai Rak Thai Government's announcement of a redirection in foreign policy that would focus on strengthening relations with Thailand's neighbours, relations between Thailand and Myanmar reached a new low point soon after the new administration took office. In February 2001 thousands of ethnic Shan villagers were forced to cross the border into Thailand, as a result of a renewed campaign by the Myanma Government against Shan insurgents. During the fighting, Myanma forces shelled Thai villages in the border region of Chiang Rai province, as well as crossing into Thai territory on a number of occasions in pursuit of the insurgents. The Myanma Government's actions were apparently linked to public accusations by Thai government officials that the Myanma Government was aiding the flow of amphetamines produced in the ethnic Wa-controlled regions into Thailand. Thaksin himself had highlighted in a number of speeches the importance of stemming the flow of narcotics from Myanmar to Thailand. The Myanma regime's official daily newspaper, *The New Light of Myanmar,* published an unprecedented series of articles highly critical of Thailand, even at one point obliquely criticizing the Thai royal family, which prompted an immediate protest from the Thai Ministry of Foreign Affairs. In March an explosion that destroyed a Thai Airways' airliner shortly before it was due to transport the Prime Minister to a conference on the issue of cross-border drug trafficking was initially linked to the Prime Minister's stance on the drugs issue. An investigation later revealed that the explosion was most likely to have been caused by faulty wiring. Meanwhile, Thai nationalist sentiments were being fuelled by a popular film *Bang Rachan*, which dramatized the famous story of the battle of Bang Rachan village in the 18th century when, according to Thai historical sources, marauding Burmese forces invaded the Thai Kingdom and destroyed the royal capital of Ayudhya. The rapid deterioration in relations was eventually halted when Thaksin made a long-delayed official visit to Yangon in June. Thaksin's visit was followed by a further visit by the Minister of Defence, Gen. Chavalit Yongchaiyudh, known to have long-standing personal relations with a number of the Myanma junta officials. In September a junta leader, Gen. Khin Nyunt, paid a reciprocal visit to Bangkok, during which he was warmly received by the Government.

Tensions between Thailand and Myanmar persisted, however, principally owing to Thai accusations that the Myanma Government was not doing enough to curb the flow of amphetamines across the border into Thailand, and to ongoing Myanma complaints that the Thai military was assisting the ethnic insurgent group, the Shan State Army (SSA), in the Myanma military's campaign against it. In June 2002 a series of articles appeared in *The New Light of Myanmar* on the subject of Thai and Myanma history, which the Thai Government deemed to be insulting. The publication of an article critical of the late 16th-century Thai King Naresuan (who was credited with having recovered the independence of the kingdom of Ayuthaya from the Burmese) led to a major diplomatic incident. The Supreme Command of the Thai military launched an official protest against the article, which it claimed was offensive to the Thai monarchy itself, whilst radio and television stations, under the control of the Thai military, aired anti-Myanmar programmes for several days. Yangon responded by closing its border entry points with Thailand. Opposition legislator Sukhumphand Paripatra, former Deputy Minister of Foreign Affairs, accused the Government of appeasing the Myanma regime by refusing to demand a formal apology from the junta. The incident was finally closed when the Vice-Chairman of the SPDC, Gen. Maung Aye, delivered a message to the Thai Government promising to prevent the state-controlled media from publishing articles deemed to be insulting to the Thai monarchy. However, relations continued to be strained when 15 Thai journalists were 'blacklisted' from Myanmar, ostensibly in response to the Thai Government's ban on the author of the allegedly anti-Thai articles that had appeared in the Myanma press. Thaksin's relations with the Thai military itself were also tested when he urged the army not to react to alleged border incursions by the Myanma military. Both opposition and press sources accused the Government of failing to respond more resolutely to the Myanma regime in order to protect the business interests of the Prime Minister and the Minister of Defence, Chavalit, in Myanmar.

In early July 2000 a group of some 60 Laotians and Thais, believed to have links to a rebel Lao political group, unsuccessfully attacked a customs and immigration check-point on the Thai-Laotian border. It was reported that six of the rebels had been killed during the fighting and that, after being repelled by Lao Government troops, 28 members of the group had fled into Ubon Ratchathani Province in Thailand, where they were arrested by Thai police. The Laotian authorities officially requested the extradition of the 28 'international terrorists'; however, the Thai Government insisted that the rebels would first face trial in Thailand on charges of illegally entering the country and possessing weapons of war. Representatives from the two countries subsequently met in Chong Mek, Thailand, to discuss measures to prevent similar occurrences in the future. In August around 30 Laotian soldiers moved onto the Mano I and Mano II islands in the Mekong River between the two countries, forcing numerous Thai farmers to leave. Under the Siam-Franco treaty of 1926, all islands on the Mekong River belong to Laos, and many observers believed that the occupation was an attempt on behalf of the Laotian administration to assert its territorial rights over the islands prior to the demarcation of the river boundary between the two countries.

In accordance with the Thai Rak Thai Government's declaration that it was to adopt a more regionally-focused foreign policy, the Prime Minister and the Minister of Foreign Affairs paid official visits to most of Thailand's Asian neighbours, including China, Japan, Indonesia and India. In December 2001 Thaksin led his Cabinet on a week-long official trip to the USA, amidst accusations by the opposition that government policies had led to a decline in Thai-US relations. The issues that were said to be contributing to US dissatisfaction with the new Thai Government included: Thaksin's criticism of Western media sources soon after his accession to office; accusations that the Government was limiting media freedoms in Thailand; and a perception that the Thai Government had given unenthusiastic support to the US 'war on terror' that had been declared in the wake of the 11 September attacks, a charge vehemently denied by the Prime Minister. Following the visit, the opposition claimed that the US Administration had effectively rebuffed Thaksin, comparing his reception unfavourably with that accorded to the leaders of Malaysia and Indonesia during their respective visits.

Economy

CHRIS DIXON

In 1997 the strong economic growth that Thailand had experienced since the mid-1980s came to an abrupt halt in the wake of major currency and financial crises. In 1997 and 1998, respectively, gross domestic product (GDP) contracted by 0.4% and 9.4%, industrial output declined by 5.9% and 13.5% and unemployment rose from 2.2% in February 1997 to 5.25% at the end of 1998. This unprecedented negative growth followed speculative action against the Thai currency, the baht, and the virtual collapse of the financial and property sectors. In August 1997 the depth of the crisis forced the Government to seek assistance from the IMF, and that month a 'rescue' programme valued at a total of some US $17,200m. was agreed. Conditions attached to this agreement included: the enforcement of tight monetary policy; an increase in value-added tax (VAT) from 7% to 10%; no subsidies to be given to public utilities to prevent price rises; substantial cuts in public expenditure; increased private-sector involvement in infrastructural projects; and the implementation of major liberalization and privatization programmes, particularly aimed at opening the economy to foreign activity and ownership. The implementation of this programme was accompanied by two years of recession and financial turmoil.

By the end of 1999 it was evident that the macroeconomic crisis was over; during that year GDP had expanded by 4.2%, the value of exports by 7.5%, industrial output by 7.6% and industrial capacity utilization had recovered from its 1998 record low of 52.2%, to reach 64.3%. In addition, interest rates, inflation and currency values and continued net inflows of direct investment had broadly stabilized. These positive indicators persisted into the first half of 2000, with GDP for that year projected to grow by 6.3% and the value of exports by 8.8%. In June 2000 Thailand departed from the IMF rescue programme, having received generally favourable comments regarding both the Government's handling of the crisis and the country's prospects for sustained economic recovery. However, in the event this proved to be a highly optimistic view; by the end of 2000 GDP had grown by a respectable, but disappointing, 4.3%. Although export levels had greatly exceeded expectations, the 19.7% rate of increase had to be placed in the context of a 31.7% rise in imports (see Foreign Trade). At the end of 2000 industrial capacity utilization had declined to 56.6%. This contraction continued into 2001, reaching a new low of 51.9% in June, before recovering slightly to 54% by the end of that year. In addition, from mid-2001 the currency began to depreciate, a process that continued into July (see Finance and Banking). Provisional figures for 2001 suggest that GDP only expanded by 1.8% in that year, industrial capacity utilization recovered slightly to 54%, and export earnings declined. A sustained recovery would depend heavily upon the export sector, which continued to be undermined by global and regional economic conditions, and by Thailand's maintenance of a weak competitive position (see Future Developments and Prospects).

The abrupt reversal in the progress of the Thai economy during 1997 could to a degree be attributed to the weaknesses of the financial sector and to its liberalization, to poor central regulation and to ineffective macro-economic management by the Bank of Thailand (see Finance and Banking). These problems were compounded by the failure of the Government and the central bank to take early and effective action. In 1996 there was negligible growth in export earnings, a widening balance-of-payments deficit, escalating private-sector debt, increasing short-term speculative capital movements and the 'over-heating' of the property and financial sectors. None of these was regarded as a cause for alarm, given the high rate of GDP growth and the continued influx of foreign funds. While no observers predicted the 1997 crisis and subsequent recession, from the early 1990s doubts had been raised concerning the sustainability of Thailand's high rates of growth and structural change. Particular attention focused on the inadequate infrastructure and shortages of skilled labour that were increasing the costs and difficulty of operating in Thailand at a time when the rapid re-engagement of the People's Republic of China and Viet Nam with international capital were providing cheaper alternative

Asian locations for investment in labour-intensive manufacturing.

The 1997 crisis must, however, be seen in the context of a remarkable period of growth and structural change lasting from 1986 to 1996. Between 1986 and 1991 Thailand became one of the fastest-growing economies in the world. During this period the value of exports grew at 30% per year and GDP at 9.2%. Subsequently, expansion decelerated slightly, but remained rapid and remarkably consistent, with GDP growth averaging 8.2% annually in 1992–96. The most striking feature of the whole period from 1986 was the expansion of manufacturing. This sector increased its share of GDP from 21% in 1985 to 30% in 1995, and its share of export earnings from 43% to 81%. Overall, from the mid-1980s Thailand experienced a period of accelerated integration into the Asian and global economies. Between 1986 and 1995 the openness ratio (the value of trade expressed as a percentage of gross national product—GNP) increased from 43.9% to 77.6%.

The rapid growth of the Thai economy attracted a great deal of attention. It was not only increasingly referred to as one of the next newly-industrializing countries (NICs), but was also presented as a new model of development—one that was more appropriate to the other less-developed Asian economies than that of the NICs. However, the rapid expansion and changing composition of GDP and export earnings had yet to be fully reflected in employment or residence patterns. In 2000 agriculture accounted for 50% of employment, and 57% of the population still lived in rural areas. When set alongside the heavy dependence of post-1985 growth on the influx of foreign investment and the continued heavy reliance on imported raw materials and components, the description of 'NIC' looked remarkably premature even before the 1997 crisis.

The accelerated growth that the Thai economy had experienced during the 1986–91 period was the result of a number of interrelated factors. During 1986 the export of manufactured goods began to expand significantly. The devaluation and re-alignment of the baht substantially improved the competitiveness of Thai exports. Thai exporters were remarkably successful in expanding sales in established markets and penetrating new ones. This expansion initially involved the redirecting of surplus manufacturing capacity towards the export market. From 1987 there was a surge of domestic and foreign investment in export-orientated, labour-intensive manufacturing industry. Thailand has become a major destination for East Asian investment. The loss of comparative advantage in labour-intensive assembly work resulted in a relocation of these activities away from the Republic of Korea, Hong Kong and Taiwan. Thailand was seen by investors as the Asian economy whose location, political and economic stability and low labour costs better suited their purposes.

As economic growth accelerated, the Government implemented a wide range of liberalization measures, some of which had been originally advocated during the early 1980s by the World Bank and the IMF. These included the removal of subsidies and marketing restrictions on a wide range of products, simplification of investment promotion procedures, the reduction of tariff levels and a considerable measure of financial liberalization, including the virtual elimination of foreign-exchange controls. The furtherance of such measures formed a key element in the Seventh (1992–96) and Eighth (1997–2001) National Plans. Under these Plans the Government aimed to reduce its role as the 'principal economic stimulator' by limiting public expenditure and encouraging private investment, and by becoming the 'co-ordinator, adviser and facilitator to the private sector'. To this end, a wide-ranging programme of privatization was announced. However, the programme was subject to considerable debate, opposition and delay. Overall, liberalization accompanied and furthered Thai economic growth, rather than preceding it and playing any significant role in its initiation.

Liberalization from the late 1980s has to be viewed in the context of the increased political influence of business interests that expected to gain through deregulation and the easing of access to international capital. There was also considerable pressure for liberalization from Thailand's principal trading partners and from international agencies. In addition, tariff reductions and the removal of restrictions on foreign market access and ownership became necessary conditions for membership of the Association of South East Asian Nations (ASEAN) Free Trade Area (AFTA) and the World Trade Organization (WTO). Between 1997 and 2000 liberalization was assigned a greater degree of urgency under the IMF programme. However, there was considerable debate over, and resistance to, many of the measures. In consequence, reform was slow, uneven and far from consistent in its implementation.

STRUCTURAL PROBLEMS

By the early 1990s the rapid growth that Thailand had experienced since 1985 had begun to expose serious long-term structural problems. The lack of infrastructure, particularly port and air freight facilities, roads, water supply and telephones, was creating serious congestion and raising production costs (see Communications and Infrastructure). Shortages, and, in some cases, the high prices of domestically-produced materials and components, constrained production and accelerated the growth of imports—a problem exacerbated by the limited development of many basic industries and the continuation of tariff protection and import restrictions. Similarly, the lack of adequate technical training schemes resulted in a serious shortage of skilled labour, which began to restrict the growth of the manufacturing sector. In 2000 only 22% of the labour force had more than primary level education, and Thailand has practically the lowest secondary and tertiary education participation rates in South-East Asia. In addition, the quality of secondary and tertiary education is often poor, with a curriculum that is ill-suited to the requirements of a modern economy. There is a particular shortage of science and technology graduates. Overall, the limited participation in, and deficiencies of, the education system remain a major barrier to the development of more technology- and skill-intensive production, while Thailand's comparative advantage in labour-intensive manufacturing has been eroded. This situation has only been partly and temporarily reversed by the post-July 1997 currency depreciations. Since the early 1990s there have been a variety of government schemes aimed at resolving the skills shortage. The 1997 Constitution guaranteed all children education until the age of 12, but this was not scheduled to be implemented before 2003. The 1999 National Education Act set out a three-year programme of education reform. In addition, during 2001 a Skill Development Act was formulated and a new Skill Development Fund established. The scope of the proposed training schemes is very broad. However, there are concerns over the scale of funding, how the scheme will operate in practice, and the nature of its relationship with other programmes. During 2002 the World Bank reported that there were some 17 separate organizations involved in a range of overlapping and largely unco-ordinated educational and skills enhancement programmes. While it is significant that the Government is addressing this critical issue, it has become clear that even if the reforms are fully implemented there can be no rapid solution to the skills problem.

The growth in the Thai economy has been heavily concentrated in the Bangkok Metropolitan Region (BMR) and its immediate environs. Particularly since 1986 there has been a sharp increase in the level of income disparity between the BMR and the rest of the Kingdom. In 2000 the official incidence of poverty was less than 1% in the BMR, 5% in the Central Region, 11% in the South, 12% in the North, and 28% in the North-East. Despite the establishment of various programmes aimed at promoting investment in provincial areas, there has been little success. Congestion and land shortages have begun to extend development into the fringes of the 10 provinces adjacent to the BMR. Similarly, despite the still variable infrastructural provision, there has been considerable expansion along the Eastern Seaboard. However, these developments represent the extension of the BMR rather than any dispersal of economic growth.

There has been serious, long-term neglect of the rural areas, and shortages of funds, vested interest and unwieldy administration have limited the impact of programmes directed at such areas as credit, water supply and land reform. In many rural areas there is an acute shortage of land, with much landlessness, illegal forest clearance and cultivation of unsuitable land (including some on watersheds, which are prone to soil erosion). There is increasing official recognition of the environmental consequences of unrestrained development, but the controls and planning mechanisms remain weak.

The long-term growth of the Thai economy has been associated with a significant decline in the incidence of poverty. The percentage of the population living below the official poverty line declined from 23.0% in 1980 to 18.0% in 1990 and to 11.4% in 1996. However, as a result of the 1997 crisis, the overall incidence of poverty rose to 15.9% in 1999, before falling to 14.2% in 2000. The rapid decline in levels of poverty before 1997 was particularly striking given the limited efforts directed at finding a solution to the problem. However, the success in reducing poverty has to be set against an increase in disparities of income. By 1996 the UN Development Programme (UNDP) had concluded that Thailand had one of the world's most uneven distributions of income. In addition, poverty has become heavily concentrated in rural areas. In 2000 the official incidence was 20% in rural areas, 9% in the semi-urbanized sanitary districts and 1% in urban areas. This situation was exacerbated by the 1997 crisis, which contributed to substantial remigration to rural areas in the wake of the collapse of much urban employment and the reduction of remittance flows. The returning population, as well as increasing levels of rural poverty, brought many 'urban problems' to villages, including drugs, organized crime and HIV/AIDS. The persistence of high levels of income disparity, the low income-generating capacity of agriculture, and the concentration of poverty in rural areas has precipitated large-scale protests, particularly since the 1997 crisis. These have played a significant role in increasing the concern of policymakers with the agricultural sector (see Agriculture), but, as with education and infrastructure, there can be no quick solutions.

Even before the 1997 crisis there were signs that structural problems and the apparent inability of the Government to deal with them were casting serious doubt over the sustainability of the Kingdom's pattern of rapid economic growth and structural change. From the early 1990s there were calls from a variety of areas, including business groups, for a more pro-active, interventionist and effective Government, prepared to address training and infrastructural deficiencies and the economic and social consequences of growth. Such views have been reinforced by the 1997 crisis and its aftermath. However, there were indications that the Government of Thaksin Shinawatra, elected in January 2001, was, at least in part, responding to these demands (see Future Prospects).

AGRICULTURE

The agricultural sector employs some 50% of the labour force and directly supports a similar proportion of the population. However, between 1980 and 2002 the sector's contribution to GDP declined from 40% to 10%, and its share of export earnings from 60% to 7.3%. However, Thailand is one of only two net food exporters in Asia (the other is Viet Nam). It is the world's largest exporter of rice (a position it attained in 1981), rubber and cassava, and the second largest exporter of sugar. As well as providing a continuing contribution to export earnings and supplying domestic foodstuffs and raw materials, the agricultural sector is the basis of the rapidly-expanding agro-business sector. However, Thailand is becoming a comparatively high-cost producer of agricultural goods and is losing markets to new low-cost producers.

The rapid economic growth that Thailand experienced between 1986 and 1996 posed a number of problems for the agricultural sector, particularly in the areas adjacent to the BMR. Good-quality agricultural land has been lost to housing, industry, infrastructure and leisure developments. Increasing pressure on water supplies restricted irrigation, particularly for rice, sugar cane, maize and intensive vegetable production; and increased employment opportunities resulted in rising labour costs.

Most of Thai agriculture remains unintensive in character, and until comparatively recently accommodated increases in production and population by expansion of the area cultivated. Between 1950 and 1975 the cultivated area increased at an average annual rate of 2.7%. The rate of expansion slowed to 1.2% between 1975 and 1988 and to 0.6% between 1989 and 1993. Subsequently, expansion has almost ceased, with clearance for upland and tree crops, often of land that is unsuited to permanent cultivation, being offset by land passing out of cultivation owing to salination, declining fertility and erosion. Controls over clearance have been generally ineffective, even within forestry reserves. As a result, forest cover declined rapidly, from 54.6% of the country in 1965 to an estimated 12% in 2000. By the late 1980s the expansion of agriculture, weak controls over logging and limited replanting schemes had effectively eliminated the Thai forestry industry.

The long-term expansion has for many crops been associated with stagnant or declining yields. This is largely accounted for by the progressive clearance of less reliable and less fertile land, reinforced by low and uncertain price levels, the high cost of fertilizer, and insecure land tenure. Since the early 1980s the deceleration in the rate of expansion of the cultivated area and the emergence of land shortage in many areas has resulted in some intensification of production and increasing yields. However, by 2000, yields and rates of fertilizer application for almost all the Kingdom's major crops remained among the lowest in Asia. This was particularly striking with respect to rice. Production remains remarkably extensive in character, with relatively low yields: the only significant South-East Asian rice-producing country with a lower yield than Thailand is Cambodia.

While rice continues to dominate Thai agriculture, since the early 1960s there has been significant diversification of production. The spread of such crops as maize and cassava brought much land unsuited to rice production into cultivation. Thus, the percentage of land planted with rice fell from 88% in 1950 to 68% in 1970 and 50% by 2000. These developments were reinforced from the late 1970s by a second wave of diversification, which contributed to the reduction of the rice sector's share of the cultivated area to 52% in 1990 and 50% in 2000. The later programme involved horticulture, aquaculture, tree crops and intensive livestock farming. Some of these developments involved substantial capital inputs and were associated with the emergence of a major agribusiness sector, either through direct control or various contractual arrangements. Particular growth areas for the export market have been frozen chickens, canned fruit (notably pineapples), frozen fruit and vegetables, fresh fruit and vegetables and cut flowers. In addition, for the domestic market, the growth of Western-style supermarkets and the rise of a comparatively wealthy middle class in the BMR have led to the development of packaging and grading of a wide range of produce.

In the wake of the post-1997 recession the Government has focused increased attention on the agricultural sector as a principal area for economic growth. Priority has been given to the expansion of exports and the creation of employment, and a series of agricultural development and promotion programmes has been announced. This increased official attention, at least in part, reflects the contraction of urban employment, particularly during 1997–8, the resultant large-scale return of migrants to rural areas, notably in the north-east, and evidence of subsequent, sharp increases in rural unemployment, poverty and public protest.

During early 1998 the Cabinet approved a Master Plan for Agriculture, aimed at stimulating the production and export of rice, rubber, cassava, canned seafood and fresh and frozen shrimps. In addition, the Master Plan for Industrial Restructuring, approved in April 1998, included provisions which aimed to stimulate industries that use agricultural products, notably the food, animal feed, rubber and rubber products industries. Also during 1998 the Agricultural Sector Programme Loan scheme was introduced, funded by the Asian Development Bank (ADB) and the Japanese Overseas Economic Co-operation Fund. This is a broad-based programme involving irrigation, land reform and extension work all aimed at upgrading agricultural production and raising yields. During 1999 the Government made efforts to develop new markets and facilitate agricultural trade, with little sign of immediate effect. In August 2000 the Board of Investment (BOI) implemented a new range of incentives aimed at the agricultural sector, and the Thaksin administration stressed its commitment to the development of the agricultural sector and wealth creation in rural areas. Policies announced during 2001 included: a moratorium on farmers' debt, a renewed attempt to raise agricultural productivity, and the establishment of the Village Development Fund.

Under the latter, each of Thailand's 75,000 villages was to receive US $23,000 to provide credit and working capital for small-scale enterprises. Against all these post-1997 programmes had to be considered the extent of the problems, doubts over the utility of the measures themselves, and the limited resources directed at them. The agricultural sector's share of public expenditure declined from 10.6% in 1996 to 7.6% in 1999, rising only marginally to 8% in 2001.

FISHING

Thailand has one of the largest marine fishing sectors in Asia, along with the People's Republic of China, Japan and Indonesia. However, in recent years over-fishing has depleted inshore fish stocks. The expansion of catches from 1.6m. tons in 1980 to 3.0m. tons in 1999 resulted from agreements with Oman, India and Bangladesh on the exploration of distant waters, and agreements with Indonesia and Myanmar over joint exploitation of their territorial waters. However, since 1992 there have been an increasing number of disputes with neighbouring countries relating to fishing by Thai vessels in their territorial waters. Since the late 1980s the most rapidly-growing fishing sub-sector has been coastal aquaculture. Output increased from 151,600 tons in 1987 to 602,800 tons in 1999, of which 225,000 tons were giant tiger prawns. Since the mid-1990s Thailand has been the world's largest producer and exporter of prawns and shrimps, accounting for more than 30% of global production. However, there is increasing concern over the environmental damage caused by farming, particularly where mangroves are removed to facilitate production. In addition, since 1998, in an attempt to protect rice fields from pollution, the Government has imposed a total ban on inland (freshwater) shrimp and prawn farming.

For the Thai market, much fish is dried, salted, fermented or turned into paste or sauce for preservation. Since 1975 the development of canning and freezing facilities has greatly expanded the export of seafood, particularly shrimps, prawn and squid. Since the mid-1980s the frozen seafood sector has also expanded rapidly. The main export markets are Japan, where there is increasing competition from cheaper Chinese produce, the USA and the European Union (EU), in both of which the markets are being threatened by increased levels of protectionism, particularly since 1999.

Since the early 1980s Thailand has emerged as the world's largest exporter of canned tuna, accounting for about 80% of world trade. The principal market, the USA, where Thai tuna accounts for 60% of sales, is jeopardized not only by increased tariffs but also by the US ban on tuna caught with drift-nets and by consumer reaction to fishing methods that are harmful to dolphins. However, Unicord, which is the largest exporter of canned tuna fish in Asia, established a firm hold on the US market in 1990 with the purchase of Bumble Bee Seafoods, the third largest US producer. Subsequently, Unicord has shipped increasing amounts of frozen tuna fish to the USA for canning, thus avoiding the higher tariffs on the imported canned product.

The freshwater sector is highly subsistent in character, and official production figures (228,898 tons in 1997) are almost certainly a considerable underestimate. It remains, however, of vital importance to rural protein supply, and small-scale aquaculture is being widely promoted as a means of raising and diversifying rural incomes. Some inland commercial development has taken place with the stocking of the larger irrigation reservoirs.

MINING

Despite the depressed state of the international market and declining production, tin remains Thailand's most important metallic mineral resource. In terms of mineral content, reserves are estimated at some 1m. tons, representing 10% of the world's total reserves. A wide range of other minerals are present in commercial quantities: notably, gold, lignite, gypsum, potash, antimony, iron, tungsten, lead, manganese, copper, zinc and a range of precious and semi-precious gem stones. Most established mineral production is small in scale, with large-scale operations confined to lead, zinc, gypsum, lignite, and, most recently, potash. The large-scale extraction of potash began in Chaiyaphum during 1995, and in 1996 there were further discoveries of deposits in north-east Thailand. It was believed that these deposits might become Thailand's most important mineral asset.

The Lampang lignite field is responsible for the majority of Thai production, almost all of which is used for electricity generation; since 1996 some 25% of national electricity output has been produced this way. Lignite production peaked at 23.4m. tons in 1996, subsequently contracting to 17.7m. tons in 2002, in the wake of rising costs, concern over pollution and increased oil and gas output (see Energy section). During 2001 these factors led to the cancellation of plans for two new lignite-fuelled power plants.

Thailand remains an important source of a wide range of stones, including sapphires, rubies, zircon, garnet, quartz and jadeite. Since the early 1980s the expansion of production has been closely related to the development of the Thai jewellery industry, but has become increasingly incapable of supplying its needs. While by the early 1990s Thailand had become the world's principal exporter of jewellery, the industry had become increasingly dependent on imported stones, particularly from Sri Lanka, Myanmar and Cambodia.

The Thai tin industry comprises a small number of large dredging concerns and numerous small-scale producers, using very simple hydraulic technology. Many of these enterprises are highly marginal, reworking old alluvial deposits, and move in and out of production depending on the prevailing price levels. Since the early 1980s low world prices, increasing operating costs and the expansion of production in lower-cost producers have resulted in the almost complete collapse of the industry. Large numbers of operations have closed, and production of tin concentrates, with a metal content of some 73%, declined from a peak of 46,547 metric tons in 1980 to 14,393 tons in 1991, to 3,926 tons in 1994 and to 800 tons in 1997. Subsequently, despite the contraction of industrial production, the high cost of imports resulted in an expansion of tin output to 2,000 tons in 1998,to 3,400 tons in 1999 and to 2,400 tons in 2000.

MANUFACTURING

Since the early 1980s there has been rapid expansion and diversification of the Thai manufacturing sector. Between 1980 and 2001 the sector increased its shares of: export earnings, from 28.8% to 82.0%; GDP, from 21.3% to 34.6%; and the labour force, from 2.0% to 15.0%. This rapid expansion was led by the textile and garment sector and from the mid-1980s by electronics and electrical goods.

The electrical goods sector initially emerged during the early 1970s, led by foreign and later by Thai companies producing for the highly-protected domestic market. Electronic assembly work for export began during the late 1970s, involving almost exclusively foreign capital. Expansion was rapid after 1986, with heavy investment and relocation of production by companies based particularly in Japan, the Republic of Korea, Taiwan and Singapore. Between 1989 and 1996 the number of foreign semiconductor factories increased from six to 13 to include such major transnationals as ATT, Hana and Sony. In 1980 the electronics and electrical sector contributed 15.2% of the earnings from manufactured exports; this figure rose to 24.5% in 1991 and to 39.0% in 2001—32% of total merchandise export earnings. This rise was accompanied by significant changes in the composition of exports. In 1980 91.0% of exports were integrated circuits; however, by 1999 these accounted for only 16.7% of the total value of exports, while computers and computer parts (particularly disk drives) accounted for 32.6% and electrical appliances and machinery 36.8%. Nevertheless, the extent of skill and technological upgrading remains limited, and the industry is basically a labour-intensive assembly activity. As a result, little value-added is generated: the Bangkok Bank has estimated that 85%–90% of the contents of computers is imported; 75%–90% of radios and televisions; 60%–70% of air-conditioners; and 60% of microwave ovens.

Despite the relaxation of regulations and tariffs since 1991, sufficient barriers remain for Thai-owned concerns to control most of the domestic market for electrical and electronic products. The situation may well change dramatically with the full implementation of AFTA and Thailand's obligations under membership of the WTO. While many Thai companies are involved in sub-contracting, the export market remains dominated by Japanese and NIC concerns.

Textiles have been a major sector since the 1960s, first for the internal market, and later for export. From 1986 textiles were the largest source of export earnings until overtaken by the electronics sector in 1994. Textiles' share of export earnings fell from 14.6% in 1988 to 6.7% in 2001. Expansion has been impeded by the existence of a surplus in the world textile market and by the imposition of quotas and tariff barriers by the EU and the USA in particular. Considerable efforts have been made to develop new, largely 'non-quota', markets in the Middle East, Eastern Europe, Australia and Japan. These developments presented the Thai textile industry with an increasingly diversified market, which made it less vulnerable to increase in protection or reduction in quotas on the part of the EU or USA.

The textile sector remains heavily dependent on imported raw materials and machinery. Domestic production of cotton is small and of low quality and 90% of requirements are imported. Similarly, despite the recent expansion of synthetic fibre production from 231,443 tons in 1990 to 728,400 tons in 2000, representing over 95% of the sector's needs, all the raw materials are imported. Despite the long-term success of textiles, increasing concern has been expressed regarding the large number of outdated plants, ineffective controls on standards, the poor development of dyeing and finishing sections and the shortage of skilled labour. In 2000 less than 25% of the 4m. workers employed in the sector were classed as 'skilled', while Thailand faced the loss of comparative advantage to such lower-cost locations as Bangladesh and the People's Republic of China. In 1996 it was reported that the hourly labour costs in the Thai textile industry were US $1.49, compared with US $0.48 in China; even after the depreciation in the value of the baht, these two countries still maintained a labour cost advantage over Thailand. During 2000 the Government began to consider the textile sector a 'problem' industry and, early in 2001, a World Bank project was implemented aimed at encouraging investment and moves into high value-added areas of production.

The heavy dependence of the textile sector on imports is typical of much of Thai industry. However, during the 1990s the expansion of domestic steel, cement and refined petroleum products began to reduce some of the serious deficiency in basic manufacturing industry. This expansion has combined with the continuing recession to create over-capacity in a number of areas. In consequence, the cement industry has begun to develop export markets, mainly in Malaysia, Myanmar, Singapore and Viet Nam. In 2000 some 30% of output was exported. Similarly, since 1996, the opening of two new refineries by Shell and Caltex, along with the expansion of capacity by Esso, has enabled a small export trade to develop.

As the manufacturing sector has expanded there has been a general increase in the size of manufacturing concerns: the proportion of workers employed in plants with more than 50 employees rose from 19.1% in 1980 to 45.2% in 1996. However, the manufacturing sector remains dominated by small-scale operations. In addition, much of the expansion in textiles, garments, and other labour-intensive production has taken place through casual employment, out-work and subcontracting to large numbers of very small workshops. These developments must be set against the emergence of a number of very large companies, notably Siam City Cement, which before the 1997 crisis had a controlling interest in over 40 companies and was probably the largest manufacturing group in ASEAN.

Following the 1997 crisis, some of the major concerns restructured their operations; Charoen Pokphand, for example, disposed of a number of domestic and overseas subsidiaries and reconcentrated on its core agro-business activities. However, there were few major corporate mergers. This reflected in part the continuing problematic nature of Thai regulations governing mergers, take-overs and bankruptcy, and the slow progress of debt restructuring (see Banking and Finance). In August 2002, after three years of negotiations, Siam City Cement agreed to merge its two steel concerns with the NTS Steel Group. The resultant Millennium Corporation would therefore control 25% of Thai steel-making capacity. This was by far the largest post-1997 industrial merger. However, whether this heralded the beginning of a major wave of mergers, as some observers suggested, remained highly debatable. A similar inhibition of foreign mergers and take-overs, despite the relaxation of controls over foreign ownership (see Investment), had continued to prevail. Between 1997 and the end of 2000 only 25 manufacturing firms were either taken over or merged with foreign firms.

Following the currency depreciation of 1997, Thai manufacturing regained some of its competitiveness. However, this gave only a temporary respite, and from the latter part of 2001 there were indications that competitiveness was declining. Unless the problems of low productivity, skill shortages and infrastructural deficiencies are rapidly addressed, Thailand will be unable effectively to gain an advantage in the face of competition elsewhere in the region. Concerns have also been expressed over the impact of the progressive implementation of AFTA and obligations to the WTO. These will, in many cases, give domestic manufacturers access to cheaper components, raw materials and machinery, but will also open the national market to foreign competition, which may undermine some domestically-orientated manufacturing and result in substantial business failures and loss of employment.

ENERGY

Thailand has substantial offshore natural gas resources with 13 proven fields in the Gulf of Thailand and rather more limited onshore oil reserves in three small fields, the most successful at Kamphaengphet. Gas began to be piped ashore in 1981, and from 1990 production expanded at some 20% per year; by 2000 it had risen to 323,700 b/d of natural gas, 54,300 b/d of condensate and 46,700 b/d of crude petroleum. This enabled 60% of national gas, crude oil and refined oil products demand to be supplied from domestic production and refining. The expansion of oil, gas and lignite production (see Mining, above) has reduced Thailand's dependence on imported energy from a peak of 90% in 1992 to 66% in 2000. However, the level of imports still makes the economy vulnerable to increases in international oil prices. In consequence, there are plans to reduce imports by 10% by 2003. This is to be achieved through energy-saving campaigns. More significant in the longer term will be increased access to energy resources in neighbouring countries.

Thailand has been importing electrical power from Laos since 1978; this involves almost the entire 150,000 kW output of the Nam Ngum plant. In May 2000 agreement was reached over the supply of electricity from Laos's largest hydropower plant, Nam Thuen 2, which is scheduled to commence in 2006. Further negotiations are in train to develop additional supplies from Laos and Cambodia. In addition, since 1998 the Petroleum Authority of Thailand (PTT) has contracted to import increasing amounts of gas from Myanmar's Yadana and Yetagun fields. However, the failure to construct a power plant dedicated to utilizing the Yadana gas, together with increased Thai production, led to negotiations that were aimed at reducing both the volume and the price of the Yadana supplies. These negotiations have proved increasingly problematic given the deteriorating relationship between the two countries (see History). In addition, work started early in 2001 on the exploitation, with Malaysia, of the offshore gas reserves of the Joint Development Area. It was expected that the completion of gas pipelines and an associated separation plant would, by 2007, give Thailand access to gas that would increase the Kingdom's reserves by 40%. However, protests by local people and environmental groups have resulted in substantial delays; it is now unlikely that the project will be completed before 2009. Even more problematic is the exploitation of the substantial offshore gas reserves believed to lie in a 2,600 sq km area, of which the ownership is disputed with Cambodia.

In the energy sector, as with Thai infrastructure as a whole (see Communications and Infrastructure, below), the Government has increasingly looked to the private sector to finance developments. During 1996 EGAT reached agreement with two private companies to construct power plants. In addition, the Ratchaburi Electricity Holding Company, the largest generating plant in the country, was sold in late 2000, following the withdrawal of opposition by the labour unions. However, while both EGAT and the PTT are scheduled for privatization, progress has been slow and the subject of considerable opposition and debate. In November 2001 30% of the PTT was sold, leaving Government firmly in control of policy and prices, a situation much criticized by foreign investors. The privatization of EGAT was planned for 2003.

INVESTMENT

During the late 1970s and early 1980s investment was equivalent to between 25% and 28% of GDP, rising very sharply from 26% in 1986 to 40% in 1990 and then fluctuating between 38% and 41% until the 1997 crisis. The increase in the level of investment from the mid-1980s was almost entirely financed by the inflow of foreign funds, initially in the form of direct investment, but later also increasingly as loans to the private sector. Despite the rapid growth of the 1986–96 period, Thailand has not been able to generate the high levels of domestic savings and investment that characterized the economies of Singapore and the Republic of Korea, and remains heavily dependent on foreign sources of funding.

Prior to 1986 direct foreign investment in Thailand was relatively small, compared with that of other ASEAN countries. In general, Thailand was unattractive to multinational corporations and foreign investors because of poor international communications, uncertainty over the country's long-term political stability, and the absence of any significant labour cost advantages. However, between 1986 and 1991 a combination of rising costs elsewhere in the region and the appearance of economic and political stability made Thailand one of the most attractive investment locations in Asia, particularly for investors from Japan and the Asian NICs. During the period 1987–96 33.3% of net foreign investment was from Japan, 36.6% from Hong Kong, Taiwan and Singapore, 16.5% from the USA and 9.3% from the EU. Since the late 1980s there has been a general decline in the share of Japanese investors and an increase in the share of those from the NICs.

The foreign investment boom began to falter during the early 1990s, with inflows contracting particularly sharply during 1994. This reflected the beginnings of problems associated with inadequate infrastructure, congestion, skilled labour shortages, and increased competition from Viet Nam and China. Until 1994 foreign investment had been increasingly in the manufacturing sector, which increased its share from 20% in 1983 to 48.7% in 1993. Within the manufacturing sector the most significant growth was in electronics and electrical equipment, the share of which increased from 14.3% in 1983 to 44.6% in 1992. Renewed growth of foreign investment from 1995 was associated with a decline in the share of manufacturing (to 32.0% in 1996) and greater flows into the property sector, which increased its share of net inflows from 5.5% in 1993 to 33.5% in 1996. Despite the 1997 financial crisis, net inflows continued to rise throughout 1998, but declined from US $4,300m. in 1998, to US $3,220m. in 1999 and US $2,900m. in 2000, before recovering to a provisional level of US $3,819m. in 2001. Since 1998, despite the problems suffered by the sector, industry's share of foreign investment has risen—from 34% in 1999 to 64% in 2000 and to a provisional 70% in 2001. The inflows since 1997 have tended to reflect the recapitalization of the corporate sector, including an increase in foreign ownership, rather than any new developments.

Since 1959 the BOI has co-ordinated a programme of investment promotion, under which both Thai and foreign firms were issued with 'promotional certificates', which exempted them from restrictions on repatriating profits and capital, and on foreign ownership of land, import duties and taxes on equipment. The certificates were also guarantees against nationalization or competition from state enterprises. From 1982 the promotional programme became more selective; privileges were proportional to the degree to which the firms complied with criteria on employment, the use of Thai raw materials, provincial location and the level of exports. In addition, priority was given to the promotion and financing of research into new technology and particular emphasis has been given to biotechnology, computer software, solar cells and microwave insulators. Since 1996 the Ministry of Industry has offered additional incentives to those provided by the BOI for firms producing electrical appliances and parts, precision instruments, medical equipment and vehicle parts, packaging, jewellery and processed food. In August 2000 the BOI revised the investment privileges, principally in order to reduce the indirect subsidy element in order to conform to WTO agreements. Tax exemptions were removed for companies that do not export and the length of corporate tax 'holidays' was reduced. However, in order fully to comply with WTO requirements, many of the regulations regarding levels of exports and the use of domestically produced components and raw materials will also have to be removed. During December 2001 a revised incentive programme was announced, which included tax concessions for companies establishing their regional headquarters in Thailand.

Since 1972 the BOI has also offered greater incentives to firms locating outside of the BMR. In the mid-1980s the Kingdom was divided into three zones for promotional purposes, generally reflecting levels of development. Both the levels of privileges and the zones themselves have been the subject of various minor revisions and in 1998 the BOI announced the abolition of the whole system owing to its lack of success in encouraging investment outside of the BMR. However, the zones were retained and were further revised in August 2000. Zone 1 comprises the BMR and has the lowest level of privileges. Zone 2 comprises the provinces of Ang Thong, Ayutthaya, Chatchoengsai, Chonburi, Kanchanaburi, Nakhon Nayok, Phuket, Ratchaburi, Rayong, Samut Songkhram, Saraburi and Suphanburi. These provinces have all received increased levels of investment and economic activity as a result of the spreading of development from the BMR. Zone 3 contains the remaining 53 provinces and has the highest level of privileges. During 2002 further modifications were implemented, particularly with respect to the promotion of industrial estates. However, there is little evidence to suggest that the BOI incentives have any significant impact on decisions regarding location.

Particularly since the mid-1980s, despite a number of streamlining measures and changes in regulations, the BOI has continued to be criticized for application procedures, bureaucratic delays, and the rejection of applications in order to protect established influential producers. Some critics have also seen the privileges as ineffective in attracting investment, particularly since 1986, as an increasing numbers of investors chose not to apply. In 1998 the Government approved a new foreign investment law that effectively replaced the restrictive 1972 Alien Business Law. This had required that every registered business in Thailand should have majority Thai ownership and prohibited even minority foreign ownership in certain industries. The only exception to this were those US-based corporations that were permitted to have 100% foreign ownership under the 1966 Thai-US Treaty of Amity and Co-operation. The 1998 act opened up all areas of the economy except land ownership to foreign investment. Further changes effective from October 1999 permitted up to 49% foreign ownership of real estate. This was increased to 100% in March 2000 as part of a further amendment allowing 100% foreign ownership within a range of service and manufacturing sectors. Restrictions remained in some 57 specified activities on the grounds of national security, cultural considerations and environmental issues. However, Thailand has given a commitment to the WTO to allow full access to all service areas by 2006.

The substantial relaxation of long-standing restrictions on foreign ownership was widely expected to lead to substantial numbers of take-overs and mergers by foreign firms. Indeed, between 1997 and the end of 2000 there were some 68 mergers or take-overs involving foreign firms. These were valued at US $15,500m., compared with less than US $2m. worth of cross-border mergers and acquisitions during 1995 and 1996. Despite this, there is little evidence of the large-scale 'fire sale' that many predicted in the wake of the 1997 crisis, and foreign ownership remains limited. This is a reflection of the continuing depressed and uncertain state of the Thai economy, the existence of more attractive investments elsewhere, the slow progress in the restructuring and reform of governance in the corporate structure and major shortcomings in national regulation. In particular, there are problems regarding take-overs, mergers and bankruptcy procedures, as well as continuing concerns over the effectiveness of the legal system as a whole. Furthermore, investors are concerned that, whatever changes are made to the regulations governing foreign ownership, the Government and administration may well not facilitate them. Until the end of 2001 the Thaksin Government appeared to take a more nationalist approach to investment than its immediate predecessors, a reflection of its election pledges. Privatization was represented as being 'privatization for Thais'; the Prime Minister, for example, stated that no foreign concern would be invited to purchase shares in Thai International Airways. While such claims might have been no more than political rhetoric, they did not send reassuring messages to foreign investors. However, in December 2001 a new programme to promote foreign investment was announced; this was accompanied by commitments to invite foreign participation in the sale of state enterprises and to match foreign funds invested in the Stock Exchange of Thailand (SET). When this is considered in conjunction with the reversal of restrictions on foreign ownership in the telecommunications sector imposed in November 2001 (see Communications and Infrastructure), and a general reduction in statements of economic nationalism, it does appear that there has been a major shift in policy.

FINANCE AND BANKING

The 1997 crisis arose from the rapid liberalization of the financial regime from 1990 onwards without significant development of any system of central regulation. From 1991 virtually all restrictions on foreign-exchange and capital movements were removed. Lending rates were liberalized, deposit interest rates (except those for savings) were freed, and a conduit for international capital, the Bangkok International Banking Facility (BIBF), was created in March 1993. The BIBF licensed 32 foreign banks to provide 'offshore' facilities for Thailand, including 12 of the 14 foreign banks already fully licensed to operate branches within the country. This facility in particular, combined with the financial liberalization, gave Thai companies easy access to cheap international funds. The freedom of financial movements, combined with the volatile and ineffectively regulated SET, the promotion of overseas corporate bond issues and a currency that was remarkably stable from the early 1980s until 1997, encouraged speculative movements of capital. These movements became increasingly large and erratic. With the benefit of hindsight, it was clear that from mid-1996 an extremely unstable financial situation was emerging. The Bank of Thailand, while expressing concern over speculative movements, took no action to regulate matters. Subsequently, much attention focused on the unsatisfactory nature of the central bank's monitoring and management procedures. During the latter part of 1996, however, speculative pressure on the baht, a reflection of its degree of linkage with the US dollar and the size of the current-account deficit, resulted in a massive intervention by the Bank of Thailand. The attempt to support the currency was doomed to failure, and in early 1997 the baht was placed on a 'managed float'. This resulted almost immediately in a 20% depreciation. Further depreciation meant that by 12 January 1998 the baht had reached an historic low against the US dollar of 55.5, a 45% depreciation since July 1997. This was an undervaluation, and the baht then began to appreciate against the dollar, reaching 40.8 by mid-1998 and 37.8 by January 1999. From mid-2000 the currency came under renewed pressure as a result of currency depreciation elsewhere in the region, rising oil prices and the level of foreign debt. In consequence, the baht depreciated from 38.54 against the dollar in July 2000, to 42.27 by December 2000 and 45.28 by June 2001. There was subsequently a gradual appreciation—the baht had reached 42.75 against the dollar by June 2002.

The 1997 financial crisis resulted in the suspension of the activities of 58 of the 91 major financial institutions (42 at the behest of the IMF), 56 of which were subsequently closed and 12 placed under state management. During 1998 six banks (Krung Thai Bank, Siam City Bank, Bangkok Bank of Commerce, Union Bank of Bangkok, Laem Thong Bank and Bangkok Metropolitan Bank) and five finance companies were nationalized, owing to their inability to recapitalize. In addition, several banks were closed or merged. In order to manage the assets of closed institutions and to fill the gap left by the closures, two new state-controlled banks were established: the Bankthai in 1999 and the Radanasin Bank Public Co Ltd in 1998. The latter was the result of the merger of Laem Thong Bank with Radanasin Bank. During 1999 three banks were sold to foreign interests (see below), and in 2002 the Siam City Bank and the Bangkok Metropolitan Bank were merged. By 2002 the 15 Thai-owned commercial banks that were in operation before the 1997 crisis had been reduced to nine.

Prior to the 1997 economic crisis, foreign banks had only been permitted to open three branches, one of which had to be in the provinces, and they were excluded from the purchase of majority ownership of Thai banks. The latter restriction was removed shortly after the economic crisis, permitting the sale of the Radanasin Bank to the Singapore-based United Overseas Bank in 1999, the acquisition of the Bank of Asia by the Dutch-based ABM AMRO and the sale of the Thai Danu Bank to the Development Bank of Singapore. While further foreign purchases had been expected, these did not materialize. During 2000 attempts to sell Siam City Bank to Newbridge Capital failed, and HSBC Holdings withdrew from negotiations to buy the Bangkok Metropolitan Bank. Potential purchasers were discouraged by the consistently high level of non-performing loans (NPLs) in the sector, continued operating difficulties, the failure of the existing foreign banks to expand their market shares and the large losses that they had recorded. This situation was reflected in the closure during 2001 of the Thai operations of the Sukbank (of Japan), the Dresdner Bank (of Germany), and the Ibducto Bank (of Japan). However, renewed foreign activity in the banking sector was believed to have played a significant part in its rapid modernization, increasing the accessibility of branches and encouraging the spreading of automatic teller machines (ATMs) and online banking.

The crisis and subsequent process of liberalization have also significantly transformed the insurance sector. Since 1997 the number of insurance companies has expanded rapidly owing to the relaxation of restrictions on the issue of licences. Foreign investment in the sector has been stimulated by the fact that companies with up to 25% foreign ownership and an equal proportion of foreign directors were permitted to operate within it. Majority ownership and a 50% foreign directorship will be permitted from 2004 in order to comply with WTO regulations. By the end of 2001 there were foreign stakes in 13 of the 25 life insurance concerns in Thailand. However, there is a long-standing exception to the controls over foreign ownership—the American International Assurance Co Ltd, which dominates the life insurance sector, commanding 50% of market share in 2001. This wholly-US-owned company has operated in Thailand since the 1960s under the terms of the 1966 Thai-US Treaty of Amity and Co-operation.

In response to the 1997–98 financial crisis a number of new institutions were set up to manage the sector's restructuring and improve regulation. The most notable of these were: the Bank of Thailand's Financial Institutions Development Fund (FIDF), which was established in order to guarantee the deposits and liabilities of the financial institutions; the Financial Restructuring Authority (FRA), which was formed to handle and sell the assets of the closed finance companies; and the Asset Management Corporation (AMC), established to purchase those assets that could not be disposed of by the FRA in any other way. Progress in the sale of assets and restructuring has been slow. This reflects the scale of the operations, the limited resources and expertise of the new financial bodies, a difficulty in finding buyers, a reluctance to raise new loans, and the cumbersome procedures in place to deal with asset sales and bankruptcy. These procedures have continued to be adhered to despite reforms and the establishment of a new Central Bankruptcy Court. Early in 2002 the World Bank reported that there were over 65,000 debt- and asset-related cases pending in the Civil Court system—a backlog that could take up to seven years to clear. Despite these issues, the Ministry of Finance estimated that the level of financial sector NPLs had fallen to 17.9% by the end of 2001, and to 10.1% by mid-2002, compared with 38.6% at the end of 1999 and a peak of 47.7% in May 1999. However, the rate of reduction of NPLs has declined, while the rate of reversion to NPL status has increased. More significantly, the World Bank has suggested that the official NPL statistics have become a poor indication of the extent of effective restructuring. The Bank concluded that, once allowances had been made for changes in the definition of NPLs adopted by the Thai system, reversions and write-offs, in mid-2002 the level of 'distressed' loans was still some 35%.

In July 2001 a centralized debt-restructuring institution was established—the Thai Asset Management Corporation (TAMC)—in order to purchase NPLs from the banking sector through the sale of up to 300,000m. baht (US $6,600m.) of

10-year bonds guaranteed by the FIDF. By December 2001 700,000m. baht (US $15,400m.) had been transferred to the TAMC, leaving some 250,000m. baht (US $5,500m.) of mostly small loans in the hands of the state banks and the AMC. The Government set the TAMC the ambitious task of restructuring 500,000m. baht (US $11,000m.) of NPLs in 2002. While the TAMC had succeeded in restructuring 200,000m. baht (US$4,400m.) by mid-year, doubts were expressed as to whether the target could be met, particularly in the light of the increasing number of restructured loans that had reverted to NPL status. By June 2002 the debt burden of the FIDF had reached US $33,000m. (1,343,000m. baht). In an attempt to remedy this situation the Government announced that bonds would be issued between mid-2002 and 2006. This has to be seen in the context of previous bond issues for the FIDF in 1998 (555,000m. baht) and 2000 (112,000m. baht). While such bond issues lessened the impact on public-sector borrowing, this has expanded dramatically as a direct result of the Government's assumption of responsibility for NPLs and for the debts of the banking and financial sector. According to the Ministry of Finance, public-sector debt increased from 37.0% of GDP in 1996 to 53% in 1999 and to 57.6% in 2001, and was projected to exceed 60% during 2002. Some two-thirds of the increase is directly related to the debt crisis; the remainder reflects increased budget deficits (see below).

Since 1999 the Government has initiated a series of programmes in an attempt to stimulate economic recovery. Initially, US $3,000m. was directed to the support of debt-laden companies unable to secure finance from banks, many of which are still also overburdened with NPLs. A further US $1,400m. programme was announced in March 2000. This included tax reductions aimed at boosting consumer demand and reducing business costs, measures to reduce energy costs and schemes aimed at generating 486,000 jobs, principally in rural areas, through small-scale infrastructure and public-works projects. The tax cuts included the reduction of value-added tax (VAT) from 10% to 7% until March 2001 (thus reversing the 1997 increase demanded by the IMF), elimination of the 1.5% VAT levied on small businesses, increased personal tax allowances and the reduction of fuel-oil tax from 17.5% to 5%. During 2001 corporation tax was reduced from 30% to 25% for a five-year period. Tariffs were decreased on some 500 categories during 2000 and on some 9,000 further items during 2001. These changes reflected attempts to reduce costs, as well as moves to implement AFTA. However, the tariff reductions increased government dependence on tax income at a time when the depressed state of the economy was exacerbating the problems of low collection rates, thus increasing the pressure on the budget deficit and public-sector borrowing. The budget deficit as a proportion of GDP increased from 2.2% in 2000 to 2.7% in 2001, and to a projected 4.1% in 2002. However, according to the World Bank, with the inclusion of all the quasi-fiscal measures, the public-sector deficit was 3% in 2001 and would rise to some 6% during 2002.

Prior to the 1997 economic crisis, Thailand was by no means a heavily-indebted country. Indeed, rapid growth of GDP and export earnings, combined with the emergence of government budget surpluses that enabled the repayment of some debts, reduced the debt-service ratio from 30.0% in 1986 to 13.0% in 1991 and to 10.5% in 1995. However, from 1996 a sharp contraction in export earnings and the depreciation of the currency increased the debt-service ratio to 15.5% in 1997, 22.0% in 1999 and to 20.8% by the end of 2001. There were also marked changes in the composition of debt. In 1996 38% of foreign debt was short-term, and 74% of medium- and long-term debt was owed by the private sector. By the end of 2000 short-term debt had fallen to 18.4%, and the private sector's share of medium- and long-term debt to 57.4%, levels that altered little during 2001 and the first half of 2002. These changes in debt structure largely reflected restructuring and the extent to which the Government had assumed responsibility for the debts of the financial sector. Overall, Thailand's external debt fell from a peak of US $109,000m. (72% of GDP) in 1997, to US $71,000m. (61% of GDP) by the end of 2001.

FOREIGN TRADE

Since the early 1980s the composition of Thailand's exports has changed dramatically. In 1980 68.4% of export earnings were derived from the agricultural sector and 28.8% from manufacturing. By 2001 the manufacturing sector's share of export earnings had grown to 82.0%, while that of agriculture had declined to 7.3%. This spectacular expansion of manufactured exports was associated with an increase in the share of import expenditure on machinery, components and raw materials (excluding fuels and lubricants) from 48.5% in 1980 to 72.9% in 2001. While between 1986 and 1995 the annual increase in export earnings averaged 18.5%, this failed to keep pace with the growth of imports. To some extent the resultant widening trade gap was offset by the growth of tourism and remittances from overseas workers. However, from the early 1990s these inflows were countered by the increasing number of Thais who travelled abroad.

The increasing trade deficit, reinforced by higher international interest rates and the level of profit repatriation from the substantial inflow of foreign business and investment that had taken place since the mid-1980s, resulted in a substantial rise in the balance-of-payments current-account deficit from US $6,364m. in 1993 (equivalent to 5.7% of GDP) to US $14,691m. in 1996 (the equivalent of 8.1% of GDP). The deficit fell sharply to US $3,024m. in 1997 (the equivalent of 0.9% of GDP). Subsequently, the balance of payments went into surpluses of US $16,200m. (the equivalent of 12.8% of GDP) in 1998, US $12,600m. (the equivalent of 9.1% of GDP) in 1999, US $9,196m. (the equivalent of 7.5% of GDP) in 2000 and a provisional US $6,200m. in 2001 (the equivalent of 5.4% of GDP). These high levels of surplus were not the result of any major recovery of the export sector. While there had been substantial trade surpluses in 1998 and 1999, these reflected declines in imports rather than any return to the high levels of export growth enjoyed during the 1986–95 period. During 1998 the surplus resulted from the contraction of imports by 33.7% and of exports by 6.9%, while in 1999 exports expanded by 7.5% and imports contracted by 17.9%. Only in 2000 was there a marked recovery of exports, which grew at 19.7%. However, the dependence of much of the Thai export sector on imports was reflected in a 31.7% increase in the cost of imports. The expansion was short-lived, however; provisional figures suggested that export earnings had contracted by 6.9% during 2001 and were projected to decline by a further 1.7% in 2002 (see Future Prospects).

From the early 1980s onwards Thailand became increasingly dependent on the USA as a destination for exports and on Japan and the NICs as sources of imports. In 2001 Japan accounted for 15.3% of exports and 22.4% of imports, while the USA took 20.3% of exports and contributed 11.6% of imports, and the EU supplied 9.8% of imports and purchased 13.6% of exports. The contraction of many Asian-Pacific markets and government and private-sector efforts reduced the share of Thailand's exports to the region from 44.7% in 1996 to 35.8% in 1999. However, counter to this trend there has been a significant increase in trade with the People's Republic of China. The slow establishment of AFTA has resulted in Thailand's investigation of a variety of bilateral free trade agreements, notably with Australia, New Zealand, South Africa, Mexico, the Republic of Korea, Chile and India. Similarly, there have been discussions with the EU over mutual tariff reductions.

TOURISM

Tourism has been Thailand's largest single source of foreign exchange since 1982. In 2001 it accounted for 11% of foreign-exchange earnings and reached the equivalent of 6% of GDP. The number of tourists increased from 4.2m. in 1988 to 10.1m. in 2001. However, prior to the 1997 financial crisis, despite continued growth the industry was experiencing a number of problems. Rising prices had made Bangkok, Pattaya and Phuket amongst the most expensive locations in South-East Asia. This was compounded by the adverse publicity attendant on the drugs trade and the sex industry and the associated treatment of women and children, and by increased competition from other Asian-Pacific tourist centres. In addition, many major tour companies were beginning to avoid Bangkok because of the levels of pollution and congestion. Bangkok, none the less, remains the gateway to the southern coastal locations, despite the increase in direct international flights to provincial centres. The increased pollution of the Gulf of Thailand was also having an adverse effect on the coastal resorts. As a result, growth in the number of tourist arrivals since 1993 has been principally in the low-spending sector, while the more expensive Bangkok hotels have become heavily dependent on business travellers.

The depreciation of the currency during 1997–98 substantially increased Thailand's attraction for tourists. In 1998 the number of arrivals increased by 7.6%, in 1999 by 10.5%, and in 2000 by 10.8%. Arrivals slowed in 2001, increasing by only 5.7%. The deceleration in the latter year reflected reduced levels of international travel from, in particular, North America and Europe, in the wake of the terrorist attacks on the USA on 11 September 2001. To some extent, however, this was offset by the arrival of increasing numbers of visitors from the Middle-East, India and China. As in the pre-crisis period, growth has been principally in such southern coastal resorts as Phuket and Koh Samui. Bangkok, which had a substantial surplus of rooms before the financial crisis and depends heavily on business travellers, remained extremely depressed.

COMMUNICATIONS AND INFRASTRUCTURE

The rapid growth that the Thai economy has experienced since 1986 has put very considerable pressure on the Kingdom's infrastructure. It is apparent that even before the present period of accelerated growth there were serious deficiencies in the provision of roads, railways, port facilities, power generation, water supply and telephones. These problems are at their most acute in the BMR and its immediate environs, where the majority of the recent growth has been concentrated.

In Bangkok the lack of an effective water supply system has resulted in increased levels of exploitation of underground sources. Some 40% of the population are dependent on deep wells for their water supply. The abstraction in conjunction with the weight of modern buildings is resulting in serious and widespread subsidence. In parts of eastern Bangkok the annual rate of subsidence exceeds 10 cm and in many central areas averages 5–10 cm. These movements are resulting in serious damage to buildings, bridges, roads, drainage and water supplies.

The capital's road system is inadequate in two ways. First, in terms of the area devoted to roads (12.5% of the city area, compared with 20%–25% in European cities); and second, by the low level of integration. The latter is a reflection of the largely uncontrolled manner in which the urban area has expanded. By the early 1990s the average speed of traffic was less than 7 km per hour, and the World Bank costed commuting time as the equivalent of 1.7% of GDP. There is little to suggest that there has been any substantial improvement in this situation in recent years.

A rail mass-transit system for Bangkok was proposed as long ago as 1971. In 1993 plans were finalized and contracts awarded for three projects that would together provide 100 km of elevated track. Subsequently operations were halted, and the plans were revised to put the central parts of the system underground. Construction finally began in mid-1996 but was disrupted by further changes of plan and disputes with contractors and landowners. In December 1999 the first project, run by the Bangkok Mass Transit System and comprising a 23-km elevated railway system, began operating, three years behind schedule. However, by mid-2002 it was still only recording an average of 200,000 daily passenger trips compared with the expected 600,000. This was attributed to some continuing operating problems and, more significantly, to the limited network and the high level of fares. The 20-km central subway project, the Blue Line, is not scheduled to begin operation until 2004, while the third line (the Hopewell project), which would have connected the other two lines to suburban areas, has been cancelled. However, during 2001 the Mass Rapid Transit Authority (MRTA) announced plans to extend the central subway project by 13 km. Serious doubts have been expressed over the viability of this extension. The protracted history of the development of the system is indicative of the difficulty that successive Thai Governments have encountered in developing major infrastructural projects.

The port facilities at Klongtoey have long been regarded as inadequate. The opening of the new port at Laem Chabang on the Eastern Seaboard in 1992 did not provide either as high or as rapid a level of relief as expected: firstly, because of the delay in completing links with Bangkok (the road link was completed during 2000 but plans for a high-speed rail link have been suspended) and secondly, owing to inadequate provision of container and handling facilities.

The increasing congestion at Don Muang airport has led to plans to produce a second facility at Nong Ngu Hao. However, this development was seriously disrupted by the severe floods of 1995, delays in relocating residents and disputes regarding the allocation of contracts. During 1997 the project was abandoned only to be reactivated later in the year following a change of government. It is not expected that the capital's second airport will be operational before 2004 and the rail link before 2005. Some decentralization of air traffic may result from the upgrading to international status of facilities at Chiang Mai, Hat Yai, Ngu Hao, Phuket and Utapoa.

There have been considerable improvements in telecommunications since the early 1990s. The number of telephone lines per 100 people increased from 4.7 in 1993 to 8.4 in 1999. A major factor in the expansion of provision has been the entry of private companies since 1992. However, the Thai telephone system still compares unfavourably with that of Malaysia, which had 19.8 lines per 100 people. Similar unfavourable comparisons can be made with regard to mobile cellular telephones; there were 32 per 1,000 people in Thailand compared to 99 per 1,000 people in Malaysia. The limitations of the Thai telecommunications sector are particularly apparent with respect to internet connections, with only 2% of the population having access to facilities in 2000 and only 15% of business making active use of them. The limited business use is a reflection of the weak development of higher technology activity in Thailand. However, the high level of charges for lines remains a major disincentive. The line infrastructure is controlled by two state corporations, the Telephone Organization of Thailand (TOT) and the Communications Authority of Thailand (CAT). While both are scheduled for privatization, there have been repeated postponements (see Future Prospects). Considerable vested interests exist within the ranks of the Thaksin Government and its supporters that are opposed to rapid liberalization of the telecommunications sector and increased foreign participation. This was reflected during 2001 by the reduction of the permitted level of foreign ownership in the sector from 49% to 25%. This caused problems for several companies, which already had foreign partners owning more than 25% stakes. In consequence, after much debate, the decision was reversed in July 2002. Such uncertainty and reversals of policy have typified much of the post-1997 liberalization and privatization programmes.

Since the late 1980s successive governments have increasingly looked to the private sector to finance the development of infrastructure. This view was reinforced by the IMF following the 1997 financial crisis and appears to remain the official position. In addition, under prevailing economic conditions and levels of public-sector debt, the prospects of substantial government expenditure on infrastructure appear remote. More disturbing is that while there has been some success with telecommunications, the progress of privatization has been slow, and the private sector has shown little interest in providing infrastructure under the prevailing economic and regulatory conditions.

FUTURE DEVELOPMENT AND PROSPECTS

In mid-2002 the outlook for the Thai economy was far from clear, and there was a considerable divergence of opinion among established commentators. The provisional figures for 2001 confirmed the pessimistic views that were emerging even before the impact of the events of 11 September 2001 on the international economy became apparent. However, it could be argued that the performance of the Thai economy during 2001 was far from disastrous given the general economic climate. To a considerable extent this can be attributed to the comparatively diverse nature of the Thai economy and to government policy. The Thaksin Government was significantly more interventionist and proactive in managing the economy than its immediate predecessors. It made various attempts to stimulate the economy through measures such as: tax concessions; incentive programmes; deregulation; direction of lending by the state banks; and public expenditure. It would be an exaggeration to assert (as some observers have) that Thailand has returned to sustained growth through spending, but there is no doubt that such areas as consumption, the property market and the SET have benefited from both policies and expenditure. On the basis of provisional figures for the first half of the year, GDP was projected to grow by 3.7% in 2002, a significant improvement on 2001. Mitigating against this was the fact that export earnings were projected to contract by 1.7%. However, this would still represent an improvement on their 2001 level.

In contrast to these positive aspects of government policy, the implications of the nationalist economic approach upon which the Thaksin Government came to power required consideration. While this approach seemed to have been largely abandoned by December 2001, it did little to encourage foreign investment and fuller participation in the Thai economy. In addition, some commentators considered that levels of expenditure and effort were still inadequate to solve the Kingdom's long-term structural and competitive problems. Meanwhile, other critics drew attention to the high levels of expenditure and the associated rapid expansion of public-sector debt, suggesting that government policies might lead to another major economic crisis. While some of the debt was expected to be recouped by the sale of financial sector assets, nationalized financial institutions and the privatization of state corporations, progress in these areas continued to be extremely slow.

The slow progress in privatization is a reflection of opposition within the legislature and from bureaucrats, the public-sector unions and some business groups, and continuing legal and procedural difficulties. The approval of the Corporatization Act early in 2000, which allowed state enterprises to be transformed into limited companies, appeared to be a significant move towards easing the process of privatization. Indeed, the listing of the PTT and Internet Thai and subsequent sale of 30% and 50% of shares, respectively, suggested that the new approach could be effective. However, a number of major privatization plans were repeatedly postponed: the listing of Thai Airways, Siam City Bank, Bangkok Metropolitan Bank, and the Port Authority of Thailand, all scheduled to take place during 2002, were postponed owing to their poor financial positions. However, in July 2002 the Government announced that it would sell 30% of its share in the Port Authority of Thailand, 23% of Thai Airways International, and facilitate the listing of the TOT and the CAT. The latter move reflects a reversal of the 2002 decision to merge the TOT and the CAT before they were listed.

There were a number of promising signs for the Thai economy in 2002, notably the prospect of some economic recovery in Japan and a related new series of relocations of manufacturing activity overseas. Thailand's much more positive approach to the attraction of foreign investment since the end of 2001 could combine with perceptions that the country enjoys both economic and political stability to make the Kingdom an attractive location for business. Mitigating against this, however, were the uncertainties that remained concerning the global economic situation (and in particular that of the USA), renewed decline in the electronics sector and competition from the People's Republic of China. The latter's membership of the WTO from late 2001 might substantially increase its competitiveness compared with such locations as Thailand. This prospect increased the urgency of addressing Thailand's weak, and perhaps declining, competitive position. In addition, the effective operation of many parts of the economy continued to be constrained by the heavy debt burden, the related protracted negotiations over restructuring, a shortage of operating capital and a reluctance to raise new loans. Setting aside questions of direct operating costs, the state of the country's legal system and cumbersome procedural considerations were increasingly giving Thailand poor ratings in terms of operating environment. These ratings were further impaired by increased internal complaints over the repression of the media, the concentration of power in the hands of the Prime Minister, disputes with foreign journalists and publications, conflicts with the bureaucracy and the divisive nature of the policies of the Thaksin Government. The King highlighted these divisions when he publicly criticized the Prime Minister in December 2001. However, the Government was attempting to address many of the Kingdom's long-term structural problems, major decisions were being made and the administration was showing considerable dynamism in its attempts to manage the economy successfully.

Statistical Survey

Source (unless otherwise stated): National Statistical Office, Thanon Larn Luang, Bangkok 10100; tel. (2) 281-8606; fax (2) 281-3815; internet www.nso.go.th.

Area and Population

AREA, POPULATION AND DENSITY

Area (sq km)	513,115*
Population (census results)†	
1 April 1990	54,548,530
1 April 2000	
Males	29,844,870
Females	30,762,077
Total	60,606,947
Population (official estimates at mid-year)	
1999	61,560,000
2000	62,320,000
2001	62,914,000
Density (per sq km) at mid-2001	122.6

* 198,115 sq miles.

† Excluding adjustment for underenumeration.

REGIONS (2000 census)

	Area (sq km)	Population	Density (per sq km)
Bangkok	1,565	6,320,174	4,038.4
Central Region (excl. Bangkok)	102,335	14,101,530	137.8
Northern Region	169,645	11,367,826	67.0
Northeastern Region	168,855	20,759,899	122.9
Southern Region	70,715	8,057,518	113.9
Total	513,115	60,606,947	118.1

PRINCIPAL TOWNS (population at 2000 census)

Bangkok Metropolis*	6,320,174	Pak Kret	141,788
Samut Prakan	378,694	Si Racha	141,334
Nanthaburi	291,307	Khon Kaen	141,034
Udon Thani	220,493	Nakhon Pathom	120,657
Nakhon Ratchasima	204,391	Nakhon Si Thammarat	118,764
Hat Yai	185,557	Thanya Buri	113,818
Chon Buri	182,641	Surat Thani	111,276
Chiang Mai	167,776	Rayong	106,585
Phra Padaeng	166,828	Ubon Ratchathani	106,552
Lampang	147,812	Khlong Luang	103,282

* Formerly Bangkok and Thonburi.

Mid-2001 (UN estimate, including suburbs): Bangkok 7,527,000 (Source: UN, *World Urbanization Prospects: The 2001 Revision*).

BIRTHS, MARRIAGES AND DEATHS*

	Registered live births		Registered marriages		Registered deaths	
	Number	Rate (per 1,000)	Number	Rate (per 1,000)	Number	Rate (per 1,000)
1993	957,832	16.5	484,569	8.4	285,731	4.9
1994	960,248	16.4	n.a.	n.a.	305,526	5.2
1995	963,678	16.2	470,751	7.9	324,842	5.5
1996	944,118	15.7	436,831	7.3	342,645	5.7
1997	897,604	14.8	396,928	6.5	303,918	5.0
1998	897,495	14.7	324,262	5.3	317,793	5.2
1999	754,685	12.3	348,803	5.7	362,607	5.9
2000	773,009	12.4	339,443	5.4	365,741	5.9

* Registration is incomplete. According to UN estimates, the average annual rates in 1990–95 were: Births 19.9 per 1,000; Deaths 5.7 per 1,000; and in 1995–2000: Births 19.6 per 1,000; Deaths 6.1 per 1,000 (Source: UN, *World Population Prospects: The 2000 Revision*).

Source: mainly Ministry of Public Health, Ministry of the Interior, Thailand.

Expectation of life (WHO estimates, years at birth, 2000): Males 66.0; Females 72.4 (Source: WHO, *World Health Report*).

ECONOMICALLY ACTIVE POPULATION*
(million persons aged 15 years and over)

	1999	2000	2001
Agriculture, hunting, forestry and fishing	13.88	13.89	13.59
Mining and quarrying	0.64	0.45	0.47
Manufacturing	4.60	4.99	5.68
Electricity, gas, water and sanitary services	0.16	0.17	0.17
Construction	1.40	1.50	1.58
Trade, financing, insurance and real estate	4.76	4.89	4.49
Transport, storage and communications	1.01	0.97	1.02
Other services (incl. restaurants and hotels)	4.79	4.83	5.60
Total employed	30.66	31.29	32.17
Unemployed	2.06	1.93	1.75
Total labour force	32.72	33.22	33.92

* Excluding the armed forces.

Source: IMF, *Thailand: Selected Issues and Statistical Appendix* (September 2002).

Health and Welfare

KEY INDICATORS

Fertility (births per woman, 2000)	2.1
Under-5 mortality rate (per 1,000 live births, 2000)	29
HIV/AIDS (% of persons aged 15–49, 2001)	1.79
Physicians (per 1,000 head, 1995)	0.24
Hospital beds (per 1,000 head, 1995)	1.99
Health expenditure (1998): US $ per head (PPP)	197
% of GDP	3.9
public (% of total)	61.4
Access to water (% of persons, 2000)	80
Access to sanitation (% of persons, 2000)	96
Human Development Index (2000): ranking	70
value	0.762

For sources and definitions, see explanatory note on p. vi.

Agriculture

PRINCIPAL CROPS ('000 metric tons)

	1998	1999	2000
Rice (paddy)	22,999	24,172	25,608
Maize	4,617	4,286	4,397
Sorghum	146	142	148
Sweet potatoes	90	100	91
Cassava (Manioc, Tapioca)	15,591	16,507	19,064
Dry beans	226	249	233
Soybeans (Soya beans)	321	319	324
Groundnuts (in shell)	135	137	135
Coconuts	1,372	1,381	1,400
Dry onions	279	316	270
Other vegetables†	2,180	2,182	2,201
Watermelons†	390	400	400
Sugar cane	50,332	53,494	51,210
Bananas†	1,720	1,720	1,720
Mangoes†	1,250	1,350	1,350
Pineapples	1,786	2,372	2,287
Other fruits†	2,562	2,588	2,588
Tobacco (leaves)	74	79	74
Natural rubber	2,162	2,199	2,236

* Unofficial figure.
† FAO estimate(s).

Source: FAO.

LIVESTOCK ('000 head, year ending September)

	1998	1999	2000*
Horses*	15	16	16
Cattle	6,328	5,677	6,100
Buffaloes	2,286	1,912	1,900
Pigs	7,082	6,370	6,500
Sheep	41*	42†	43
Goats	130†	130†	130
Chickens	229,083	230,000*	232,000
Ducks	19,748	21,000*	22,000
Geese*	400	420	420

* FAO estimate(s). † Unofficial figure.

Source: FAO.

LIVESTOCK PRODUCTS ('000 metric tons)

	1999	2000	2001
Beef and veal	188	170	180
Buffalo meat	57	54	54
Pig meat	426	450	475
Chicken meat*	1,087	1,117	1,260
Duck meat	102	103†	105*
Cows' milk	455	469	520*
Hen eggs	496	515	530†
Other poultry eggs†	280	280	280
Cattle hides (fresh)†	40	40	40
Buffalo hides (fresh)	7	6	6

* Unofficial figures.
† FAO estimate(s).

Source: FAO.

Forestry

ROUNDWOOD REMOVALS ('000 cubic metres, excl. bark)

	1998	1999	2000
Sawlogs, veneer logs and logs for sleepers	50	50	46
Other industrial wood*	2,822	2,848	2,848
Fuel wood*	20,549	20,548	20,553
Total	23,421	23,446	23,447

* FAO estimates.

Source: FAO.

SAWNWOOD PRODUCTION
('000 cubic metres, incl. railway sleepers)

	1998	1999	2000
Coniferous (softwood)	4	41	52
Broadleaved (hardwood)	99	137	242
Total	103	178	294

Source: FAO.

Fishing

('000 metric tons, live weight)

	1997	1998	1999
Capture	2,877.6	2,900.3	3,004.9
Sardinellas	202.8	204.8	211.0*
Anchovies, etc.	157.3	158.9	165.0*
Indian mackerels	181.5	183.1	192.0*
Aquaculture	539.9	607.7	602.8
Giant tiger prawn	223.6	247.5	225.1
Total catch	3,417.5	3,508.0	3,607.7

* FAO estimate.

Source: FAO, *Yearbook of Fishery Statistics.*

Mining

(production in metric tons, rounded, unless otherwise indicated)

	1998	1999	2000
Tin concentrates*	2,000	3,400	2,400
Tungsten concentrates*	100	—	—
Lead ore*	15,300	23,800	24,800
Zinc ore*	195,100	185,700	186,500
Antimony ore*	500	100	200
Iron ore*	90,700	122,600	100
Gypsum	4,333,800	5,005,200	5,842,600
Lignite	20,200,000	18,200,000	17,700,000
Fluorite†	3,700	23,000	24,200
Manganese ore	100	700	200
Crude petroleum (million barrels)	10.4	12.0	20.9
Natural gas ('000 million cu ft)	621.5	680.3	713.0

* Figures refer to the gross weight of ores and concentrates.
† Metallurgical grade.

Source: IMF, *Thailand: Statistical Appendix* (August 2001).

2001: Crude petroleum (million barrels) 22.2; Natural gas ('000 million cu ft) 693.5 (Source: Bank of Thailand, Bangkok).

Industry

SELECTED PRODUCTS
('000 metric tons, unless otherwise indicated)

	1999	2000	2001
Synthetic fibre*	696	735	727
Raw sugar	5,630	6,447	4,865
Cement	25,354	25,499	27,913
Galvanized iron sheets	299	369	434
Pulp	854	917	n.a.
Petroleum products (million litres)	41,414	41,060	n.a.
Beer (million litres)	1,042	1,165	1,238
Integrated circuits (million pieces)	5,182	7,070	n.a.
Tin metal	17	17	n.a.

* Source: Asian Development Bank, *Key Indicators of Developing Asian and Pacific Countries.*.

Sources: IMF, *Thailand: Statistical Appendix* (August 2001), and Bank of Thailand, Bangkok.

Finance

CURRENCY AND EXCHANGE RATES

Monetary Units

100 satangs = 1 baht.

Sterling, Dollar and Euro Equivalents (31 May 2002)

£1 sterling = 62.15 baht;
US $1 = 42.37 baht;
€1 = 39.78 baht;
1,000 baht = £16.09 = $23.60 = €25.14.

Average Exchange Rate (baht per US $)

1999 37.814
2000 40.112
2001 44.432

Note: Figures refer to the average mid-point rate of exchange available from commercial banks. In July 1997 the Bank of Thailand began operating a managed 'float' of the baht. In addition, a two-tier market was introduced, creating separate exchange rates for purchasers of baht in domestic markets and those who buy the currency overseas.

BUDGET (million baht, year ending 30 September)

Revenue	1998/99	1999/2000	2000/01
Tax revenue	641,000	691,000	741,100
Taxes on income and profits	213,700	235,400	253,600
Individual taxes	101,200	87,400	97,000
Corporate taxes	101,300	137,400	139,600
Taxes on consumption	319,400	322,000	341,500
Business tax/value-added tax	132,100	138,000	144,200
Excise taxes	166,500	167,400	184,600
Taxes on international trade	68,100	87,100	93,100
Import duties	66,400	84,900	91,000
Non-tax revenue	98,100	99,800	155,500
Profits	46,400	38,500	53,300
Other	51,700	61,300	102,300
Total	739,100	790,800	896,600

Expenditure	1998/99	1999/2000	2000/01
General public services	35,600	39,300	83,000
Defence	73,100	71,500	73,000
Public order and safety	44,400	47,700	51,800
Education	170,900	171,700	181,300
Health	63,400	61,500	65,800
Social security and welfare	37,000	56,400	60,200
Housing and community amenities	9,400	14,100	18,800
Recreational, cultural and religious affairs and services	5,900	5,300	5,300
Economic affairs and services	72,400	91,400	140,400
Fuel and energy	1,700	9,100	8,400
Agriculture, forestry, fishing and hunting	40,700	44,100	43,400
Mining and mineral resources, manufacturing and construction	4,600	4,600	11,500
Transportation and communication	10,400	13,300	14,100
Other purposes	84,400	96,500	109,500
Total	1,160,200	883,300	1,013,000
Current expenditure	596,500	655,500	789,100
Capital expenditure	563,700	227,800	223,900

Source: IMF, *Thailand: Selected Issues and Statistical Appendix* (September 2002).

INTERNATIONAL RESERVES (US $ million at 31 December)

	1999	2000	2001
Gold*	718	645	686
IMF special drawing rights	258	83	5
Foreign exchange	33,805	31,933	32,350
Total	34,781	32,661	33,041

* Revalued annually on the basis of the London market price.

Source: IMF, *International Financial Statistics.*

MONEY SUPPLY (million baht at 31 December)

	1999	2000	2001
Currency outside banks	472,407	406,841	440,884
Demand deposits at deposit money banks	94,868	113,988	134,371
Total money (incl. others)	739,660	684,256	639,955

Source: IMF, *International Financial Statistics.*

COST OF LIVING (Consumer Price Index; base: 1990 = 100)

	1998	1999	2000
Food (incl. beverages)	168.4	166.9	165.1
Fuel and light	152.4	152.7	164.6
Clothing (incl. footwear)	151.0	152.8	154.3
Rent	125.7	126.3	126.1
All items (incl. others)	152.7	153.2	155.6

Source: ILO, *Yearbook of Labour Statistics.*

2001 (base: 2000 = 100): All items 101.7 (Source: IMF, *International Financial Statistics*).

NATIONAL ACCOUNTS (million baht at current prices)

National Income and Product

	1998	1999	2000*
Compensation of employees	1,440,186	1,450,914	1,542,959
Operating surplus	2,030,906	2,005,769	2,149,228
Domestic factor incomes	3,471,092	3,456,683	3,692,187
Consumption of fixed capital	679,148	703,867	728,287
Gross domestic product (GDP) at factor cost	4,150,240	4,160,550	4,420,474
Indirect taxes, *less* subsidies	476,207	471,582	484,251
GDP in purchasers' values	4,626,447	4,632,132	4,904,725
Net factor income from abroad	-160,044	-126,436	-76,874
Gross national product	4,466,403	4,505,696	4,827,851
Less Consumption of fixed capital	679,148	703,867	728,287
National income in market prices	3,787,255	3,801,829	4,099,564

* Provisional figures.

Source: National Economic and Social Development Board.

Expenditure on the Gross Domestic Product

	1999	2000*	2001*
Government final consumption expenditure	533,507	560,767	593,202
Private final consumption expenditure	2,591,129	2,751,901	2,903,664
Increase in stocks	-16,693	31,853	35,175
Gross fixed capital formation	966,343	1,082,651	1,188,965
Statistical discrepancy	-25,114	50,148	69,657
Total domestic expenditure	4,049,172	4,477,320	4,788,663
Exports of goods and services	2,703,308	3,289,675	3,379,634
Less Imports of goods and services	2,120,348	2,862,270	3,070,655
GDP in purchasers' values	4,632,132	4,904,725	5,099,642

* Provisional figures.

Sources: National Economic and Social Development Board and Asian Development Bank, *Key Indicators of Developing Asian and Pacific Countries.*

Gross Domestic Product by Economic Activity

	1999	2000*	2001*
Agriculture, forestry and fishing	497,149	504,513	436,160
Mining and quarrying	87,352	116,798	125,869
Manufacturing	1,446,554	1,570,842	1,706,695
Construction	166,332	150,333	148,996
Electricity and water	130,378	146,155	167,850
Transport and communications	376,777	396,667	410,701
Wholesale and retail trade, restaurants and hotels	743,185	784,478	875,850
Banking, insurance and real estate services	164,109	157,306	319,623
Ownership of dwellings	123,101	125,008	
Public administration and defence	204,102	212,515	229,425
Other services	693,093	740,110	678,473
GDP in purchasers' values	4,632,132	4,904,725	5,099,642

* Provisional figures.

Sources: National Economic and Social Development Board and Asian Development Bank, *Key Indicators of Developing Asian and Pacific Countries.*

BALANCE OF PAYMENTS (US $ million)

	1999	2000	2001
Exports of goods f.o.b.	56,775	67,894	63,202
Imports of goods f.o.b.	-42,762	-56,193	-54,620
Trade balance	14,013	11,701	8,582
Exports of services	14,635	13,868	13,024
Imports of services	-13,583	-15,460	-14,619
Balance on goods and services	15,066	10,109	6,987
Other income received	3,092	4,235	3,839
Other income paid	-6,083	-5,616	-5,200
Balance on goods, services and income	12,075	8,727	5,626
Current transfers received	806	952	990
Current transfers paid	-452	-366	-389
Current balance	12,428	9,313	6,227
Direct investment abroad	-346	23	-162
Direct investment from abroad	6,213	3,366	3,820
Portfolio investment assets	-2	-160	-287
Portfolio investment liabilities	77	-546	-932
Other investment assets	-1,755	-2,203	250
Other investment liabilities	-15,261	-10,914	-6,597
Net errors and omissions	33	-685	155
Overall balance	1,388	-1,806	2,475

Source: IMF, *International Financial Statistics.*

External Trade

PRINCIPAL COMMODITIES (distribution by SITC, US $ million)

Imports c.i.f.	1997	1998	1999
Food and live animals	2,443.0	1,993.3	2,019.4
Crude materials (inedible) except fuels	2,674.7	1,812.2	2,047.3
Mineral fuels, lubricants, etc.	5,838.9	3,479.5	4,879.3
Petroleum and petroleum products	5,714.0	3,428.9	4,775.5
Crude petroleum	4,694.2	2,905.4	3,897.1
Refined petroleum products	915.2	468.2	802.6
Chemicals and related products	5,994.0	4,680.7	5,448.1
Organic chemicals	1,680.4	1,309.1	1,391.2
Artificial resins, plastic materials, etc.	1,261.7	1,053.1	1,237.6
Basic manufactures	10,684.4	7,932.1	9,816.9
Textile yarn, fabrics, etc.	1,248.9	1,158.4	1,345.1
Non-metallic mineral manufactures	1,154.7	889.6	1,125.5
Iron and steel	3,635.8	1,944.4	2,728.7
Ingots and other primary forms	1,242.7	630.8	1,157.6
Universals, plates and sheets	1,477.4	758.9	949.1
Non-ferrous metals	1,404.7	991.4	1,103.6
Other metal manufactures	2,045.8	2,098.6	2,509.4

Imports c.i.f. — *continued*	1997	1998	1999
Machinery and transport equipment	29,319.5	18,489.5	21,675.9
Power-generating machinery and equipment	1,410.1	1,389.7	1,035.3
Machinery specialized for particular industries	2,794.3	1,126.2	1,219.7
General industrial machinery, equipment and parts	1,388.0	702.5	710.3
Office machines and automatic data-processing equipment	3,307.8	2,165.8	2,567.7
Parts and accessories for office machines, etc.	2,649.2	1,846.5	2,138.1
Telecommunications and sound equipment	2,102.6	960.4	1,256.3
Other electrical machinery, apparatus, etc.	10,032.7	8,751.4	9,739.4
Switchgear, etc., and parts	1,786.4	1,623.0	1,522.9
Thermionic valves, tubes, etc.	5,451.7	4,910.4	5,928.1
Road vehicles and parts*	2,306.8	519.4	1,304.7
Parts and accessories for cars, buses, lorries, etc.*	1,412.7	290.6	724.4
Other transport equipment	2,067.1	749.5	2,108.6
Aircraft, associated equipment and parts	1,687.6	605.9	1,809.4
Miscellaneous manufactured articles	3,716.1	2,757.8	3,011.1
Total (incl. others)	62,461.7	42,370.1	50,309.1

* Excluding tyres, engines and electrical parts.

Exports f.o.b.	1997	1998	1999
Food and live animals	10,390.0	9,460.1	9,687.7
Fish, crustaceans and molluscs	4,211.0	4,023.9	4,095.7
Fresh, chilled, frozen, salted or dried crustaceans and molluscs	1,885.3	1,754.8	1,648.3
Prepared or preserved fish, crustaceans and molluscs	1,882.0	1,875.8	2,016.0
Cereals and cereal preparations	2,331.8	2,309.5	2,165.9
Milled rice	2,039.2	2,050.1	1,906.9
Vegetables and fruit	1,467.1	1,087.8	1,409.1
Sugar and honey	1,070.2	689.5	582.0
Crude materials (inedible) except fuels	2,612.1	2,117.7	2,104.5
Natural rubber	1,854.6	1,343.8	1,160.8
Chemicals and related products	2,441.7	2,391.2	2,942.4
Basic manufactures	6,919.0	6,396.9	6,917.5
Textile yarn, fabrics, etc.	2,059.9	1,786.2	1,833.1
Non-metallic mineral manufactures	1,576.3	1,160.0	1,421.4
Machinery and transport equipment	22,335.6	21,869.5	24,490.8
General industrial machinery, equipment and parts	1,710.2	1,504.3	1,747.5
Office machines and automatic data-processing equipment	7,443.5	8,042.2	8,211.8
Automatic data-processing machines and units	2,776.1	1,810.7	1,935.3
Parts and accessories for office machines, etc.	4,353.1	5,917.8	6,033.0
Telecommunications and sound equipment	3,327.3	3,091.3	2,997.1
Other electrical machinery, apparatus, etc.	6,906.7	6,694.3	8,153.5
Thermionic valves, tubes, etc.	3,380.6	3,169.2	4,031.1
Miscellaneous manufactured articles	9,818.2	8,947.8	9,075.9
Clothing and accessories (excl. footwear)	3,721.7	3,576.0	3,495.9
Total (incl. others)	58,282.6	53,583.5	58,423.1

Source: UN, *International Trade Statistics Yearbook*.

2000 (US $ million): Total imports 63,241; Total exports 69,871.

Source: IMF, *Thailand: Statistical Appendix* (August 2001).

PRINCIPAL TRADING PARTNERS (US $ million)

Imports c.i.f.	1999	2000	2001
Australia	977	1,160	1,380
China, People's Repub.	2,495	3,377	3,711
Germany	1,589	1,947	2,562
Japan	12,256	15,315	13,881
Korea, Repub.	1,770	2,165	2,121
Malaysia	2,512	3,344	3,078
Oman	1,060	958	1,264
Singapore	2,980	3,416	2,854
United Arab Emirates	872	1,766	1,529
USA	6,443	7,291	7,198
Total (incl. others)	50,350	61,923	62,057

Exports f.o.b.	1999	2000	2001
Australia	1,315	1,615	1,358
China, People's Repub.	1,861	2,806	2,863
Germany	1,459	1,640	1,568
Hong Kong	2,979	3,474	3,298
Japan	8,259	10,164	9,964
Malaysia	2,124	2,813	2,722
Netherlands	2,197	2,245	2,028
Singapore	5,073	5,997	5,287
United Kingdom	2,090	2,357	2,328
USA	12,667	14,706	13,246
Total (incl. others)	58,495	68,961	65,112

Source: Asian Development Bank, *Key Indicators of Developing Asian and Pacific Countries*.

Transport

RAILWAYS ('000)

	1991	1992	1993
Passenger journeys	86,906	87,769	87,183
Passenger-km	12,819,567	14,135,915	14,717,667
Freight (ton-km)	3,365,431	3,074,786	3,059,043
Freight carried (metric tons)	7,990	7,600	7,498

Source: The State Railway of Thailand.

1994: Passenger-km ('000) 14,496,000; Freight (ton-km, '000) 3,072,000.
1995: Passenger-km ('000) 12,975,000; Freight (ton-km, '000) 3,242,000.
1996: Passenger-km ('000) 12,205,000; Freight (ton-km, '000) 3,286,000.
1997: Passenger-km ('000) 11,804,000.
1998: Passenger-km ('000) 10,947,000.
1999: Passenger-km ('000) 9,894,000.

Source: UN, *Statistical Yearbook for Asia and the Pacific*.

ROAD TRAFFIC ('000 motor vehicles in use at 31 December)

	1999	2000	2001
Passenger cars	2,124	2,111	2,281
Buses and trucks	731	775	804
Vans and pick-ups	3,098	3,209	3,341
Motor cycles	13,245	13,817	15,236

Source: Ministry of Transport and Communications.

SHIPPING

Merchant Fleet (registered at 31 December)

	1999	2000	2001
Number of vessels	551	561	568
Total displacement ('000 grt)	1,956.1	1,944.5	1,771.4

Source: Lloyd's Register-Fairplay, *World Fleet Statistics*.

International Sea-borne Freight Traffic
(Ports of Bangkok and Laem Chabang)

	1998	1999	2000
Goods loaded ('000 metric tons)	10,009	10,743	12,152
Goods unloaded ('000 metric tons)	17,151	18,569	20,055
Vessels entered	5,325	5,475	6,145

Source: Port Authority of Thailand.

CIVIL AVIATION

	1988	1989	1990
Kilometres flown	85,003,000	93,871,689	101,589,000
Passengers carried			
Number	6,282,438	7,394,199	8,272,516
Passenger-km ('000)	16,742,348	18,876,972	19,869,143
Freight carried			
Tons	157,964	165,502	199,399
Ton-km ('000)	589,064	626,497	799,267
Mail carried			
Tons	7,636	8,893	9,287
Ton-km ('000)	33,576	39,104	39,070

Source: Airport Authority of Thailand and the Department of Aviation.

Kilometres flown ('000): 140,300 in 1996; 153,000 in 1997; 158,000 in 1998. Passengers carried ('000): 14,078 in 1996; 14,236 in 1997; 15,015 in 1998. Passenger-km (million): 29,801 in 1996; 30,827 in 1997; 34,340 in 1998. Total ton-km (million): 4,075 in 1996; 4,460 in 1997; 4,682 in 1998.

Sources: UN, *Statistical Yearbook*, and UN, *Statistical Yearbook for Asia and the Pacific*.

Tourism

FOREIGN TOURIST ARRIVALS

Country of origin	1999	2000	2001
Australia	306,583	326,003	366,468
China, People's Republic	776,059	704,463	695,372
France	228,183	240,568	238,550
Germany	384,086	387,904	407,353
Hong Kong	438,791	495,153	531,300
India	164,279	203,221	206,541
Indonesia	132,520	145,375	153,734
Italy	114,335	120,159	120,368
Japan	1,071,482	1,206,549	1,179,202
Korea, Republic	338,266	448,207	553,441
Malaysia	993,020	1,055,933	1,161,490
Singapore	608,384	659,539	669,166
Sweden	163,715	210,504	224,268
Switzerland	110,528	114,030	122,701
Taiwan	563,023	711,702	728,953
United Kingdom	429,302	480,303	522,117
USA	432,164	485,701	494,920
Total (incl. others)	8,651,260	9,578,826	10,132,509

Receipts from tourism (million baht): 220,754 in 1997; 242,177 in 1998; 269,882 in 1999.

Source: Tourism Authority of Thailand.

2000: Receipts from tourism (US $ million) 7,119 (Source: World Tourism Organization).

Communications Media

	1999	2000	2001
Television receivers ('000 in use)	16,700	17,200	n.a.
Telephones ('000 main lines in use)	5,215.6	5,591.1	5,973.5
Mobile cellular telephones ('000 subscribers)	2,339.4	3,056.0	7,550.0
Personal computers ('000 in use)	1,382	1,471	1,700
Internet users ('000)	950	2,300	3,536

Source: International Telecommunication Union.

Radio receivers ('000 in use): 13,959 in 1997.

Facsimile machines ('000 in use): 150 in 1997.

Daily newspapers: 35 (with average circulation of 2,766,000 copies) in 1994; 35 (with average circulation of 2,700,000* copies) in 1995; 30 (with average circulation of 3,808,000 copies) in 1996.

Non-daily newspapers: 280 in 1995; 320 in 1996.

* Provisional.

Sources: UNESCO, *Statistical Yearbook*; UN, *Statistical Yearbook*.

Education

(1999)

	Institutions	Teachers	Students
General education	37,828	583,779	11,531,383
Vocational education	1,105	46,482	1,148,272
Higher education*	58	8,618	407,967
Others	4,115†	89,869‡	3,719,736‡
Total (incl. others)	43,106	728,748	16,807,358

* Office of Rajhabat Institutes Council and Department of Physical Education only.

† Institutions in non-formal education under Department of Vocational Education and Office of the Private Education Commission only.

‡ For students and teachers under Department of Non-Formal Education, Department of Vocational Education and Office of the Private Education Commission.

Adult literacy rate (UNESCO estimates): 95.5% (males 97.1%; females 93.9%) in 2000 (Source: UN Development Programme, *Human Development Report*).

Directory

The Constitution

On 27 September 1997 the National Assembly approved a new Constitution, which was endorsed by the King and promulgated on 11 October. The main provisions are summarized below.

GENERAL PROVISIONS

Sovereignty resides in the people. The King as Head of State exercises power through the National Assembly, the Council of Ministers (Cabinet) and the Courts in accordance with the provisions of the Constitution. The human dignity, rights and liberty of the people shall be protected. The people, irrespective of their origin, sex or religion, shall enjoy equal protection under the Constitution. The Constitution is the supreme law of the State.

THE KING

The King is a Buddhist and upholder of religions. He holds the position of Head of the Thai Armed Forces. He selects and appoints qualified persons to be the President of the Privy Council and not more than 18 Privy Councillors to constitute the Privy Council. The Privy Council has a duty to render such advice to the King on all matters pertaining to His functions as He may consult. Whenever the King is absent from the Kingdom or unable to perform His functions, He will appoint a Regent. For the purposes of maintaining national or public safety or national economic security, or averting public calamity, the King may issue an Emergency Decree which shall have the force of an Act.

RIGHTS, LIBERTIES AND DUTIES OF THE THAI PEOPLE

All persons are equal before the law and shall enjoy equal protection under the law. Men and women shall enjoy equal rights. Unjust discrimination against a person on the grounds of origin, race, language, sex, age, physical or health condition, personal status, economic or social standing, religious belief, education or constitutionally political view, shall not be permitted. A person shall enjoy full liberty to profess a religion, a religious sect or creed, and observe religious precepts or exercise a form of worship in accordance with his or her belief, provided that it is not contrary to his or her civic duty, public order or good morals. A person shall enjoy the liberty to express his or her opinion, make speeches, write, print, publicize, and make expression by other means. A person shall enjoy an equal right to receive the fundamental education for the duration of not less than 12 years which shall be provided by the State without charge. A person shall enjoy the liberty to assemble peacefully and without arms, to unite and form an association, a union, league, co-operative, farmer group, private organization or any other group, and to unite and form a political party. A person shall enjoy an equal right to receive standard public health service, and the indigent shall have the right to receive free medical treatment from public health centres of the State. Every person shall have a duty to exercise his or her right to vote at an election. Failure to vote will result in the withdrawal of the right to vote as provided by law.

THE NATIONAL ASSEMBLY

The National Assembly consists of the House of Representatives and the Senate. The President of the House of Representatives is President of the National Assembly. The President of the Senate is Vice-President of the National Assembly. A bill approved by the National Assembly is presented by the Prime Minister to the King to be signed within 20 days from the date of receipt, and shall come into force upon its publication in the Government Gazette. If the King refuses his assent, the National Assembly must re-deliberate such bill. If the National Assembly resolves to reaffirm the bill with a two-thirds' majority, the Prime Minister shall present such bill to the King for signature once again. If the King does not sign and return the bill within 30 days, the Prime Minister shall cause the bill to be promulgated as an Act in the Government Gazette as if the King had signed it.

The House of Representatives consists of 500 members, 100 of whom are from the election on a party-list basis and 400 of whom are from the election on a constituency basis. Election is by direct suffrage and secret ballot. The list of any political party receiving votes of less than 5% of the total number of votes throughout the country shall be regarded as one for which no person listed therein is elected and such votes shall not be reckoned in the determination of the proportional number of the members of the House of Representatives. A person seeking election to the House of Representatives must be of Thai nationality by birth, be not less than 25 years of age, have graduated with not lower than a Bachelor's degree or its equivalent, except for the case of having been a member of the House of Representatives or a Senator before, and be a member of any and only one political party, for a consecutive period of not less than 90 days, up to the date of applying for candidacy in an election. The term of the House of Representatives is four years from the election day. The King has the prerogative power to dissolve the House of Representatives for a new election of members of the House. Members of the House may not renounce their party affiliation without resigning their seats.

The Senate consists of 200 members, elected by direct suffrage and secret ballot. A person seeking election to the Senate must be of Thai nationality by birth, of not less than 40 years of age, and have graduated with not lower than a Bachelor's degree or its equivalent. The term of the Senate is six years as from the election day.

When it is necessary for the interests of the State, the King may convoke an extraordinary session of the National Assembly.

The Election Commission consists of a Chairman and four other Commissioners appointed, by the King with the advice of the Senate, from persons of apparent political impartiality and integrity. Election Commissioners shall hold office for a term of seven years.

The National Human Rights Commission consists of a President and 10 other members appointed, by the King with the advice of the Senate, from persons having apparent knowledge and experiences in the protection of rights and liberties of the people. The term of office of members of the National Human Rights Commission is six years. The National Human Rights Commission has the duty to examine and report the commission or omission of acts which violate human rights or which do not comply with obligations under international treaties to which Thailand is a party.

THE COUNCIL OF MINISTERS

The King appoints the Prime Minister and not more than 35 other Ministers to constitute the Council of Ministers (Cabinet) having the duties to carry out the administration of state affairs. The Prime Minister must be appointed from members of the House of Representatives and must receive the approval of more than half the total number of members of the House. No Prime Minister or Ministers shall be members of the House of Representatives or Senators simultaneously. A Minister must be of Thai nationality by birth, of not less than 35 years of age and be a graduate with not lower than a Bachelor's degree or its equivalent.

The State shall establish the National Economic and Social Council to be charged with the duty to give advice and recommendations to the Council of Ministers on economic and social problems. A national economic and social development plan and other plans as provided by law shall obtain opinions of the National Economic and Social Council before they can be adopted and published.

LOCAL GOVERNMENT

Any locality which meets the conditions of self-government shall have the right to be formed as a local administrative organization as provided by law. A local administrative organization shall have a local assembly and a local administrative committee or local administrators. Members of a local assembly shall be elected by direct suffrage and secret ballot. A local administrative committee or local administrators shall be directly elected by the people or by the approval of a local assembly. Members of a local assembly, local administrative committee or local administrators shall hold office for a period of four years. A member of a local administrative committee or local administrator shall not be a government official holding a permanent position or receiving a salary, or an official or an employee of a state agency, state enterprise or local administration.

AMENDMENT OF THE CONSTITUTION

A motion for amendment must be proposed either by the Council of Ministers or by not less than one-fifth of the total number of members of the House of Representatives or the National Assembly as a whole. A motion for amendment must be proposed in the form of a draft Constitution Amendment and the National Assembly shall consider it in three readings. Promulgation must be approved by the votes of more than half of the total number of members of both Houses.

The Government

HEAD OF STATE

HM King BHUMIBOL ADULYADEJ (King RAMA IX); succeeded to the throne June 1946.

PRIVY COUNCIL

Gen. (retd) PREM TINSULANONDA (President).
Dr SANYA DHARMASAKTI.
M. L. CHIRAYU NAVAWONGS.
Dr CHAOVANA NASYLVANTA.
THANIN KRAIVIXIEN.
Rear-Adm. M. L. USNI PRAMOJ.
Air Vice-Marshal KAMTHON SINDHAVANANDA.
Air Chief Marshal SIDDHI SAVETSILA.
CHULANOPE SNIDVONGS.
M. R. ADULKIT KITIYAKARA.
Gen. PICHITR KULLAVANIJAYA.
AMPOL SENANARONG.
CHAMRAS KEMACHARU.
M. L. THAWISAN LADAWAN.
M. R. THEP DEVAKULA.
SAKDA MOKKAMAKKUL.
PALAKORN SUWANNARAT.
KASEM WATANACHAI.

CABINET
(October 2002)

A coalition of the Thai Rak Thai, Chart Thai and Chart Pattana.

Prime Minister: THAKSIN SHINAWATRA.

Deputy Prime Ministers: CHAVALIT YONGCHAIYUDH, KORN DABBARANSI, SUWIT KHUNKITTI, PROMMIN LERTSURIDEJ, CHATURON CHAISAENG, WISSANU KREA-NGAM.

Minister of Defence: THAMMARAK ISSARANGKUN NA AYUTTHAYA.

Minister of Labour and Social Welfare: SUWAT LIPTAPANLOP.

Minister of Finance: SOMKID JATUSRIPITAK.

Minister of Culture: URAIWAN TIENGTHONG.

Minister of Education: PONGPOL ADIREKSARN.

Minister of Foreign Affairs: SURAKIART SATHIRATHAI.

Minister of the Interior: WAN MUHAMAD NOR MATHA.

Minister of Justice: PURACHAI PIEMSOMBOON.

Minister of Natural Resources and Environment: PRAPAT PANYACHARTRAK.

Minister of Energy: PONGTHEP THEPKANJANA.

Minister of Agriculture and Co-operatives: SORA-AT KLINPRATUM.

Minister of Tourism and Sport: SONTHAYA KHUNPLUEM.

Minister of Transport: SURIYA JUNGRUNGRUANGKIT.

Minister of Commerce: ADISAI PHOTHARAMIK.

Minister of Public Health: SUDARAT KEYURAPHUN.

Minister of Industry: SOMSAK THEPSUTHIN.

Minister of Information and Communications Technology: SURAPONG SUEBWONGLEE.

Minister of Science and Technology: PINIT JARUSOMBAT.

Minister of Social Development and Human Security: ANURAK JUREEMAT.

MINISTRIES

Office of the Prime Minister: Government House, Thanon Nakhon Pathom, Bangkok 10300; tel. (2) 280-3526; fax (2) 282-8792; internet www.pmoffice.go.th.

Ministry of Agriculture and Co-operatives: Thanon Ratchadamnoen Nok, Bangkok 10200; tel. (2) 281-5955; fax (2) 282-1425; internet www.moac.go.th.

Ministry of Commerce: Thanon Sanamchai, Pranakorn, Bangkok 10200; tel. (2) 282-6171; fax (2) 280-0775; internet www.moc.go.th.

Ministry of Culture: Bangkok.

Ministry of Defence: Thanon Sanamchai, Bangkok 10200; tel. (2) 222-1121; fax (2) 226-3117; internet www.mod.go.th.

Ministry of Education: Wang Chankasem, Thanon Ratchadamnoen Nok, Bangkok 10300; tel. (2) 281-9809; fax (2) 281-8218; e-mail website@emisc.moe.go.th; internet www.moe.go.th.

Ministry of Energy: Bangkok.

Ministry of Finance: Thanon Rama VI, Samsennai, Phaya Thai, Rajatevi, Bangkok 10400; tel. (2) 273-9021; e-mail foc@vayu.mof.go.th; internet www.mof.go.th.

Ministry of Foreign Affairs: Thanon Sri Ayudhya, Bangkok 10400; tel. (2) 643-5000; fax (2) 225-6155; e-mail thaiinfo@mfa.go.th; internet www.mfa.go.th.

Ministry of Industry: 75/6 Thanon Rama VI, Ratchathewi, Bangkok 10400; tel. (2) 202-3000; fax (2) 202-3048; internet www.industry.go.th.

Ministry of Information and Communications Technology: Bangkok.

Ministry of the Interior: Thanon Atsadang, Bangkok 10200; tel. (2) 222-1141; fax (2) 223-8851; internet www.moi.go.th.

Ministry of Justice: Thanon Ratchadaphisek, Chatuchak, Bangkok 10900; tel. (2) 502-8051; fax (2) 502-8059; internet www.moj.go.th.

Ministry of Labour and Social Welfare: Thanon Mitmaitri, Dindaeng, Huay Kwang, Bangkok 10400; tel. (2) 245-4782; fax (2) 246-1520; internet www.molsw.go.th.

Ministry of Natural Resources and Environment: Bangkok.

Ministry of Public Health: Thanon Tiwanon, Amphoe Muang, Nonthaburi 11000; tel. (2) 591-8495; fax (2) 591-8492; internet www.moph.go.th.

Ministry of Science and Technology: Thanon Phra Ram VI, Ratchathewi, Bangkok 10400; tel. (2) 246-0064; fax (2) 247-1449; internet www.moste.go.th.

Ministry of Social Development and Human Security: Bangkok.

Ministry of Tourism and Sport: Bangkok.

Ministry of Transport: 38 Thanon Ratchadamnoen Nok, Khet Pom Prab Sattruphai, Bangkok 10100; tel. (2) 283-3044; fax (2) 280-1714; internet www.motc.go.th.

Ministry of University Affairs: 328 Thanon Sri Ayudhya, Bangkok 10400; tel. (2) 246-0025; fax (2) 245-8636; internet www.inter.mua.go.th.

Legislature

RATHA SAPHA
(National Assembly)

Woothi Sapha
(Senate)

A constitutional amendment was enacted in January 1995, limiting the membership of the Senate to two-thirds of that of the House of Representatives.

On 22 March 1996 the Prime Minister appointed a new Senate, comprising 260 members, only 39 of whom were active members of the armed forces. (Under the new Constitution promulgated in October 1997, the Senate was to comprise 200 directly-elected members.) Elections to the new 200-member Senate were held on 4 March 2000; however, owing to the repeated incidence of electoral fraud, a second round of voting took place in April and a third round was held in a number of constituencies in June, by which time only 197 members had been elected to the new Senate, which had yet to take office pending the election of its three remaining members. A fourth round of polling was held in June/July, which resulted in the election of a further two members to the Senate. At a fifth round of voting held later that month the final member was elected to the Senate. The 200-member Senate was subsequently sworn in on 1 August 2000.

President of the Senate: Maj.-Gen. MANOONKRIT ROOBKAJORN.

Sapha Poothaen Rassadorn
(House of Representatives)

Speaker of the House of Representatives and President of the National Assembly: UTHAI PHIMCHAICHON.

General Election, 6 January 2001*

Party	Seats
Thai Rak Thai	248
Democrat Party	128
Chart Thai	41
New Aspiration Party	36
Chart Pattana	29
Seritham Party	14
Social Action Party	1
Independents	3
Total	500

* The new Constitution of 1997 provided for an increase in the number of deputies in the House of Representatives from 393 to 500. Of those who gained seats in January 2001, 400 contested the election in single-member constituencies and 100 through a party-list system.

Political Organizations

Chart Pattana (National Development): c/o House of Representatives, Bangkok; f. 1992; Leader KORN DABBARANSI; Sec.-Gen. SUWAT LIPTAPALLOP.

Chart Thai (Thai Nation): 1 Thanon Pichai, Dusit, Bangkok; tel. (2) 243-8070; fax (2) 243-8074; internet www.chartthai.or.th; f. 1981; right-wing; founded political reform policy; includes mems of fmr United Thai People's Party and fmr Samakkhi Tham (f. 1991); Leader BANHARN SILAPA-ARCHA.

Democrat Party (DP) (Prachatipat): 67 Thanon Setsiri, Samsen Nai, Phyathai, 10400 Bangkok; tel. (2) 270-0036; fax (2) 279-6086; e-mail admin@democrat.or.th; internet www.democrat.or.th; f. 1946; liberal; Leader CHUAN LEEKPAI; Sec.-Gen. Maj.-Gen. SANAN KAJORNPRASART.

Ekkaparb (Solidarity): 670/104 Soi Thepnimit, Thanon Jaransanitwong, Bangpaid, Bangkok 10700; tel. (2) 424-0291; fax (2) 424-8630; f. 1989; opposition merger by the Community Action Party, the Prachachon Party, the Progressive Party and Ruam Thai; Leader CHAIYOS SASOMSAP; Sec.-Gen. NEWIN CHIDCHOB.

Muan Chon (Mass Party): 630/182 Thanon Prapinklao, Bangkok 10700; tel. and fax (2) 424-0851; f. 1985; dissolved after defection of leader Capt. Chalerm Yoobamrung to New Aspiration Party (NAP); re-formed in 2002 following merger of NAP with Thai Rak Thai; Leader Gen. VORAVIT PIBOONSILP; Sec.-Gen. KAROON RAKSASUK.

Nam Thai (Leadership of Thailand): c/o House of Representatives, Bangkok; f. 1994; business-orientated; Leader AMNUAY VIRAVAN.

Palang Dharma (PD) (Righteous Force): 445/15 Ramkhamhaeng, 39 Bangkapi, Bangkok 10310; tel. (2) 718-5626; fax (2) 718-5634; internet www.pdp.or.th; f. 1988; Leader CHAIWAT SINSUWONG; Sec.-Gen. RAVEE MASCHAMADOL.

Prachakorn Thai (Thai Citizens Party): 1213/323 Thanon Srivara, Bangkapi, Bangkok 10310; tel. (2) 559-0008; fax (2) 559-0016; f. 1981; right-wing; monarchist; Leader SAMAK SUNDARAVEJ; Sec.-Gen. YINGPAN MANSIKARN.

Seritham Party (Justice Freedom Party): c/o House of Representatives, Bangkok; f. 1992; merged with Thai Rak Thai in June 2001; Leader PRACHUAB CHAIYASARN.

Social Action Party (SAP) (Kij Sangkhom): 126 Soi Ongkarak Samsen, 28 Thanon Nakhon Chaisi, Dusit, Bangkok 10300; tel. (2) 243-0100; fax (2) 243-3224; f. 1981; conservative; Leader MONTREE PONGPANIT; Sec.-Gen. SUWIT KHUNKITTI.

Thai Party: 193 Thanon Amnauy Songkram, Dusit, Bangkok; tel. and fax (2) 669-4367; f. 1997; Leader THANABORDIN SANGSATHAPORN; Gen. Sec. Rear Adm. THAVEEP NAKSOOK.

Thai Freedom Party: c/o House of Representatives, Bangkok; f. Aug. 2002; Leader NIT SORASIT.

Thai Rak Thai (Thais Love Thais): c/o House of Representatives, Bangkok; f. 1998; tel. (2) 668-2000; fax (2) 668-6000; e-mail public@thairakthai.or.th; internet www.thairakthai.or.th; Leader THAKSIN SHINAWATRA.

Groupings in armed conflict with the Government include:

National Revolutionary Front: Yala; Muslim secessionists.

Pattani United Liberation Organization (PULO): e-mail p_u_l_@hotmail.com; internet www.pulo.org; advocates secession of the five southern provinces (Satun, Narathiwat, Yala, Pattani and Songkhla); Leader SIAMA-IL TAHNAM.

Diplomatic Representation

EMBASSIES IN THAILAND

Argentina: 16th Floor, Suite 1601, Glas Haus Bldg, 1 Soi Sukhumvit 25, Klongtoey, Bangkok 10110; tel. (2) 259-0401; fax (2) 259-0402; e-mail embtail@mozart.inet.co.th; Ambassador: CARLOS FAUSTINO GARCÍA.

Australia: 37 Thanon Sathorn Tai, Bangkok 10120; tel. (2) 287-2680; fax (2) 287-2029; e-mail austembassy.bangkok@dfat.gov.au; internet www.austembassy.or.th; Ambassador: MILES KUPA.

Austria: 14 Soi Nandha, off Thanon Sathorn Tai, Soi 1, Bangkok 10120; tel. (2) 287-3970; fax (2) 287-3925; e-mail austrian@loxinfo.co.th; Ambassador: GEORG ZNIDARIC.

Bangladesh: 727 Thanon Thonglor Sukhumvit, Soi 55, Bangkok 10110; tel. (2) 392-9437; fax (2) 391-8070; e-mail bdoot@samart.co.th; Ambassador: HEMAYETUDDIN.

Belgium: 17th Floor, Sathorn City Tower, 175 Thanon Sathorn Tai, Tungmahamek, Sathorn, Bangkok 10120; tel. (2) 679-5454; fax (2) 679-5467; e-mail bangkok@diplobel.org; Ambassador: PIERRE VAESEN.

Bhutan: 375/1 Soi Ratchadanivej, Thanon Pracha-Uthit, Huay Kwang, Bangkok 10320; tel. (2) 274-4740; fax (2) 274-4743; e-mail bht_emb_bkk@yahoo.com; Ambassador: CHENKYAB DORJI.

Brazil: 34F Lumpini Tower, 1168/101 Thanon Rama IV, Sathorn, Bangkok 10120; tel. (2) 679-8567; fax (2) 679-8569; e-mail EMBRASbkk@mozart.inet.co.th; Ambassador: MARCO ANTÔNIO DINIZ BRANDÃO.

Brunei: 132 Sukhumvit, Soi 23, Thanon Sukhumvit, Bangkok 10110; tel. (2) 204-1476; fax (2) 204-1486; Ambassador: Dato' Paduka Haji MOHD YUNOS BIN Haji MOHD HUSSEIN.

Bulgaria: 64/4 Soi Charoenmitr, Sukhumvit 63, Wattana, Bangkok 10110; tel. (2) 391-6180; fax (2) 391-6182; e-mail bulgemth@asianet.co.th; Ambassador: ROUMEN IVANOV SABEV.

Cambodia: 185 Thanon Ratchadamri, Lumpini, Bangkok 10330; tel. (2) 254-6630; fax (2) 253-9859; e-mail recanbot@loxinfo.co.tlt; Ambassador: UNG SEAN.

Canada: Abdulrahim Bldg, 15th Floor, 990 Thanon Rama IV, Bangrak, Bangkok 10500; tel. (2) 636-0540; fax (2) 636-0565; e-mail bngkk@dfait-maeci.gc.ca; internet www.bangkok.gc.ca; Ambassador: Dr ANDREW MCALISTER.

Chile: 10th Floor, Charan Tower, 19 Thanon Sukhumvit, Soi 43, Wattana, Bangkok 10110; tel. (2) 260-3870; fax (2) 260-4328; e-mail embajada@chile-thai.com; internet www.chile-thai.com; Ambassador: LUIS ALBERTO SEPÚLVEDA.

China, People's Republic: 57 Thanon Ratchadaphisek, Bangkok 10310; tel. (2) 245-7043; internet www.chinaembassy.or.th; Ambassador: YAN TINGAI.

Czech Republic: 71/6 Soi Ruamrudi 2, Thanon Ploenchit, Bangkok 10330; tel. (2) 255-3027; fax (2) 253-7637; e-mail bangkok@embassy.mzv.cz; internet www.mfa.cz/bangkok; Ambassador: Dr JIŘI SITLER.

Denmark: 10 Soi Attakarn Prasit, Thanon Sathorn Tai, Bangkok 10120; tel. (2) 213-2021; fax (2) 213-1752; e-mail bkkamb@bkkamb.um.dk; internet www.denmark-embassy.or.th; Ambassador: ULRIK HELWEG-LARSEN.

Egypt: 49 Soi Ruam Rudee, Thanon Ploenchit, Bangkok 10330; tel. (2) 253-0161; fax (2) 254-9489; e-mail egyptemb@loxinfo.co.th; Ambassador: ABDUL MOHSEN OMAR MAKHYOUN.

Finland: Amarin Tower, 16th Floor, 500 Thanon Ploenchit, Bangkok 10330; tel. (2) 256-9306; fax (2) 256-9310; e-mail Sanomat.BAN@formin.fi; Ambassador: HEIKKI TUUANEN.

France: 35 Soi Rong Phasi Kao, Thanon Charoenkrung, Bangkok 10500; tel. (2) 266-8250; fax (2) 236-7973; e-mail press@ambafrance-th.org; internet www.ambafrance-th.org/; Ambassador: CHRISTIAN PRETTRE.

Germany: 9 Thanon Sathorn Tai, Bangkok 10120; tel. (2) 287-9000; fax (2) 287-1776; e-mail rk@german-embassy.or.th; internet www.german-embassy.or.th; Ambassador: ANDREAS VON STECHOW.

Greece: Thai Wah Tower II, 30th Floor, 21/159 Thanon Sathorn Tai, Bangkok 10120; tel. (2) 679-1462; fax (2) 679-1463; e-mail bagremb@ksc.th.com; Ambassador: NICHOLAS ZAFIROPOLOUS.

Holy See: 217/1 Thanon Sathorn Tai, POB 12–178, Bangkok 10120 (Apostolic Nunciature); tel. (2) 212-5853; fax (2) 212-0932; e-mail vatemb@mozart.inet.co.th; Apostolic Nuncio: Most Rev. ADRIANO BERNARDINI (Titular Archbishop of Faleri).

Hungary: Oak Tower, 20th Floor, President Park Condominium, 95 Sukhumvit Soi 24, Prakhanong, Bangkok 10110; tel. (2) 661-1150; fax (2) 661-1153; e-mail huembbgk@mozart.inet.co.th; Ambassador: SANDOR JOLSVAI.

India: 46 Soi Prasarnmitr, 23 Thanon Sukhumvit, Bangkok 10110; tel. (2) 258-0300; fax (2) 258-4627; e-mail indiaemb@mozart.inet.co.th; internet www.indiaemb.or.th; Ambassador: L. K. PONAPPA.

Indonesia: 600–602 Thanon Phetchburi, Phyathai, Bangkok 10400; tel. (2) 252-3135; fax (2) 255-1267; Ambassador: Air Chief Marshall (retd) SUTRIA TUBAGUS.

Iran: 602 Thanon Sukhumvit, between Soi 22–24, Bangkok 10110; tel. (2) 259-0611; fax (2) 259-9111; e-mail emb@mozart.inet.co.th; Ambassador: RASOUL ESLAMI.

Iraq: 47 Thanon Pradipat, Samsen Nai, Phya Thai, Bangkok 10400; tel. (2) 278-5355; fax (2) 271-4218; e-mail iraqthi@email.com; Chargé d'affaires: THAMIR M. S. KADHIM.

Israel: Ocean Tower II, 25th Floor, 75 Sukhumvit, Soi 19, Thanon Asoke, Bangkok 10110; tel. (2) 204-9200; fax (2) 204-9255; e-mail bangkok@israel.org; Ambassador: DAVID MATNAI.

Italy: 399 Thanon Nang Linchee, Thungmahamek, Yannawa, Bangkok 10120; tel. (2) 285-4090; fax (2) 285-4793; e-mail ambitbkk@loxinfo.co.th; internet www.ambasciatabangkok.org; Ambassador: STEFANO STARACE JANFOLLA.

Japan: 1674 Thanon Phetchburi Tadmai, Bangkok 10320; tel. (2) 252-6151; fax (2) 253-4153; internet embjp-th.org; Ambassador: ATSUSHI TOKINOYA.

Kazakhstan: Suite 3E1–3E2, 3rd Floor, 139 Rimco House, Sukhumvit 63, Klongton Nua, Wattana, Bangkok 10110; tel. (2) 714-9890; fax (2) 714-7588; e-mail kzdipmis@asianet.co.th; Ambassador: RASHIT RAKHIMBEKOV.

Korea, Democratic People's Republic: 14 Mooban Suanlaemthong 2, Thanon Pattanakarn, Suan Luang, Bangkok 10250; tel. (2) 319-2686; fax (2) 318-6333; Ambassador: JO IN CHOL.

Korea, Republic: 23 Thanon Thiam-Ruammit, Huay Kwang, Bangkok 10320; tel. (2) 247-7537; fax (2) 247-7535; e-mail korembas@kormail.net; Ambassador: CHOI HYUCK.

Kuwait: 100/44 Sathorn Nakhon Tower, 24th Floor, Thanon Sathorn Nua, Bangrak, Bangkok 10500; tel. (2) 636-6600; fax (2) 636-7363; e-mail hamood@mozart.inet.co.th; Ambassador: HAMOOD Y. AL-ROUDHAN.

Laos: 520/502/1–3 Soi Sahakarnpramoon, Thanon Pracha Uthit, Wangthonglang, Bangkok 10310; tel. (2) 539-6667; fax (2) 539-3827; e-mail sabaidee@bkklaoembassy.com; internet www.bkklaoembassy.com; Ambassador: HIEM PHOMMACHANH.

Malaysia: 35 Thanon Sathorn, Tungmahamek, Sathorn, Bangkok 10120; tel. (2) 679-2190; fax (2) 679-2208; e-mail mwbngkok@samart.co.th; Ambassador: Dato' SYED NORULZAMAN SYED KAMARULZAMAN.

Mexico: 20/60–62 Thai Wah Tower I, 20th Floor, Thanon Sathorn Tai, Bangkok 10120; tel. (2) 285-0995; fax (2) 285-0667; e-mail mexthai@loxinfo.co.th; internet www.sre.gob.mx/tailandia; Ambassador: JAVIER RAMON BRITO MONCADA.

Mongolia: 90/3 Soi Areesamphan I, Thanon Phaholyothin, Phyathai, Bangkok 10400; tel. (2) 278-5792; fax (2) 278-4927; e-mail mongemb@loxinfo.co.th; Ambassador: LUVSANDORJ DAWAGIV.

Morocco: One Pacific Place, 19th Floor, 140 Thanon Sukhumvit, between Soi 4–6, Bangkok 10110; tel. (2) 653-2444; fax (2) 653-2449; e-mail sifambkk@samart.co.th; Ambassador: SAMIR ARROUR.

Myanmar: 132 Thanon Sathorn Nua, Bangkok 10500; tel. (2) 233-2237; fax (2) 236-6898; e-mail mebkk@asianet.co.th; Ambassador: U MYO MYINT.

Nepal: 189 Soi 71, Thanon Sukhumvit, Bangkok 10110; tel. (2) 390-2280; fax (2) 381-2406; e-mail nepembkk@asiaaccess.net.th; internet www.royalnepaleseembassy.org; Ambassador: JANAK BAHADUR SINGH.

Netherlands: 106 Thanon Witthayu, Bangkok 10330; tel. (2) 254-7701; fax (2) 254-5579; e-mail ban@minbuza.nl; Ambassador: G. J. H. C. KRAMER.

New Zealand: M Thai Tower, 14th Floor, All Season's Place, 87 Thanon Witthayu, Lumpini, Bangkok 10330; tel. (2) 254-2530; fax (2) 253-9045; e-mail nzembbkk@loxinfo.co.th; Ambassador: ALAN WILLIAMS.

Nigeria: 100 Sukhumvit, Soi 38, Prakhanong, Klongtoey, Bangkok 10110; tel. (2) 391-5197; fax (2) 391-8819; Ambassador: Prince ADEMOLA O. ADERELE.

Norway: UBC II Bldg, 18th Floor, 591 Thanon Sukhumvit, Soi 33, Bangkok 10110; tel. (2) 261-0230; fax (2) 262-0218; e-mail emb.bangkok@mfa.no; internet www.emb-norway.or.th/; Ambassador: RAGNE BIRTE LUND.

Oman: 82 Saeng Thong Thani Tower, 32nd Floor, Thanon Sathorn Nua, Bangkok 10500; tel. (2) 235-4222; fax (2) 639-9390; e-mail oman_embassy@pacific.net.th; Ambassador: MOHAMMED YOUSUF DAWOOD SHALWANI.

Pakistan: 31 Soi Nana Nua, Thanon Sukhumvit, Bangkok 10110; tel. (2) 253-0288; fax (2) 253-0290; e-mail parepbkk@ji-net.com; Ambassador: Maj.-Gen. (retd) MUHAMMAD HASAN AQAEL.

Panama: 14 Sarasin Bldg, 7th Floor, 14 Thanon Surasak, Bangrak, Bangkok 10500; tel. (2) 237-9008; fax (2) 237-9009; e-mail ptybkk@ksc.th.com; Chargé d'affaires a.i.: VICTORIA ENRIQUE.

Peru: Glas Haus Bldg, 16th Floor, 1 Soi Sukhumvit 25, Khet Wattana, Bangkok 10110; tel. (2) 260-6243; fax (2) 260-6244; e-mail peru@peruthai.or.th; internet www.peruthai.or.th; Ambassador: GABRIEL GARCIA.

Philippines: 760 Thanon Sukhumvit, Bangkok 10110; tel. (2) 259-0139; fax (2) 259-2809; e-mail bangkokpe@dfa.gov.ph; internet www.philembassy-bangkok.net; Ambassador: SONIA C. BRADY.

Poland: Sriyukon Bldg, 84 Sukhumvit, Soi 5, Bangkok 10110; tel. (2) 251-8891; fax (2) 251-8895; Ambassador: JERZY SURDYKOWSKI.

Portugal: 26 Bush Lane, Thanon Charoenkrung, Bangkok 10500; tel. (2) 234-2123; fax (2) 238-4275; e-mail jose@loxinfo.co.th; Ambassador: JOSÉ TADEU DA COSTA SOUSA SOARES.

Romania: 20/1 Soi Rajakhru, Phaholyothin Soi 5, Thanon Phaholyothin, Phayathai, Bangkok 10400; tel. (2) 617-1551; fax (2) 617-1113; e-mail romembkk@ksc.th.com; Ambassador: CRISTIAN TEODORESCU.

Russia: 78 Thanon Sap, Bangrak, Bangkok 10500; tel. (2) 234-9824; fax (2) 237-8488; e-mail rosposol@cscoms.com; internet www.thailand.mid.ru; Ambassador: YEVGENY OSTROVENKO.

Saudi Arabia: Sathorn Thani Bldg, 10th Floor, 82 Thanon Sathorn Nua, Bangkok 10500; tel. (2) 639-2999; fax (2) 639-2950; Chargé d'affaires: WAHEEB M. AL-SEHLI.

Singapore: Rajanakarn Bldg, 9th and 18th Floors, 183 Thanon Sathorn Tai, Bangkok 10120; tel. (2) 286-2111; fax (2) 287-2578; e-mail singemb@pacific.net.th; internet www.mfa.gov.sg/bangkok; Ambassador: CHAN HENG WING.

Slovakia: Thai Wah Tower II, 22nd Floor, 21/144 Thanon Sathorn Tai, Bangkok 10120; tel. (2) 677-3445; fax (2) 677-3447; e-mail slovakemb@actions.net; Ambassador: MARIAN TOMASIK.

South Africa: The Park Place, 6th Floor, 231 Soi Sarasin, Lumpini, Bangkok 10330; tel. (2) 253-8473; fax (2) 253-8477; e-mail saembbkk@loxinfo.co.th; Ambassador: BUYISIWE MAUREEN PHETO.

Spain: Diethelm Towers, 7th Floor, 93/1 Thanon Witthayu, Bangkok 10330; tel. (2) 252-6112; fax (2) 255-2388; e-mail embesp@bkk3.loxinfo.co.th; internet www.embesp.or.th; Ambassador: JOSÉ EUGENIO SALARICH FERNÁNDEZ DE VALDERRAMA.

Sri Lanka: Ocean Tower II, 13th Floor, 75/6–7 Sukhumvit, Soi 19, Bangkok 10110; tel. (2) 261-1934; fax (2) 261-1936; e-mail slemb@ksc.th.com; Ambassador: H. M. G. S. PALIHAKKARA.

Sweden: First Pacific Place, 20th Floor, 140 Thanon Sukhumvit, Bangkok 10110; tel. (2) 263-7200; fax (2) 263-7260; e-mail ambassaden.bangkok@foreign.ministry.se; internet www.embassy-sweden.or.th; Ambassador: JAN NORDLANDER.

Switzerland: 35 Thanon Witthayu, Bangkok 10330; tel. (2) 253-0156; fax (2) 255-4481; e-mail vertretung@ban.rep.admin.ch; internet www.eda.admin.ch/bangkok_emb/e/home.html; Ambassador: HANS-PETER ERISMANN.

Turkey: 61/1 Soi Chatsan, Thanon Suthisarn, Huaykwang, Bangkok 10310; tel. (2) 274-7262; fax (2) 274-7261; e-mail tcturkbe@mail.cscoms.com; Ambassador: MUMIN ALANAT.

United Arab Emirates: 82 Seng Thong Thani Bldg, 25th Floor, Thanon Sathorn Nua, Bangkok 10500; tel. (2) 639-9820; fax (2) 639-9818; Ambassador: SALIM ISSA ALI AL-KATTAM AL-ZAABI.

United Kingdom: 1031 Thanon Witthayu, Pathumwan, Bangkok 10330; tel. (2) 305-8333; fax (2) 255-8619; e-mail info.bangkok@fco.gov.uk; internet www.britishemb.or.th; Ambassador: LLOYD BARNABY SMITH.

USA: 120/22 Thanon Witthayu, Bangkok 10330; tel. (2) 205-4000; fax (2) 254-2990; internet www.usa.or.th/; Ambassador: DARRYL N. JOHNSON.

Viet Nam: 83/1 Thanon Witthayu, Lumpini, Pathumwan, Bangkok 10330; tel. (2) 251-7202; fax (2) 251-7201; e-mail vnembassy@bkk.a-net.net.th; Ambassador: DO NGOC SON.

Judicial System

SUPREME COURT

Sarn Dika: Thanon Ratchadamnoen Nai, Bangkok 10200. The final court of appeal in all civil, bankruptcy, labour, juvenile and criminal cases. Its quorum consists of three judges. However, the Court occasionally sits in plenary session to determine cases of exceptional importance or where there are reasons for reconsideration or overruling of its own precedents. The quorum, in such cases, is one-half of the total number of judges in the Supreme Court.

President (Chief Justice): PRAMAN TEEYAPAIBOONFIN.

Vice-President: UDOM FRUNGFOONG.

COURT OF APPEALS

Sarn Uthorn: Thanon Ratchadaphisek, Chatuchak, Bangkok 10900. Appellate jurisdiction in all civil, bankruptcy, juvenile and criminal matters; appeals from all the Courts of First Instance throughout the country, except the Central Labour Court, come to this Court. Two judges form a quorum.

Chief Justice: KAIT CHATANIBAND.

Deputy Chief Justices: PORNCHAI SMATTAVET, CHATISAK THAMMASAKDI, SOMPOB CHOTIKAVANICH, SOMPHOL SATTAYA-APHITARN.

COURTS OF FIRST INSTANCE

Civil Court (Sarn Pang): Thanon Ratchadaphisek, Chatuchak, Bangkok 10900. Court of first instance in civil and bankruptcy cases in Bangkok. Two judges form a quorum.

Chief Justice: PENG PENG-NITI.

Criminal Court (Sarn Aya): Thanon Ratchadaphisek, Bangkok 10900. Court of first instance in criminal cases in Bangkok. Two judges form a quorum.

Chief Justice: PRADIT EKMANEE.

Central Juvenile and Family Court (Sarn Yaowachon Lae Krobkrow Klang): Thanon Rachini, Bangkok 10200; fax (2) 224-1546. Original jurisdiction over juvenile delinquency and matters affecting children and young persons. Two judges and two associate judges (one of whom must be a woman) form a quorum.

Chief Justice: JIRA BOONPOJANASUNTHON.

Central Labour Court (Sarn Rang Ngan Klang): 404 Thanon Phra Ram IV, Bangkok 10500. Jurisdiction in labour cases throughout the country.

Chief Justice: CHAVALIT PRAY-POO.

Central Tax Court (Sarn Phasi-Arkorn Klang): Thanon Ratchadaphisek, Chatuchak, Bangkok 10900. Jurisdiction over tax cases throughout the country.

Chief Justice: SANTI TAKRAL.

Provincial Courts (Sarn Changwat): Exercise unlimited original jurisdiction in all civil and criminal matters, including bankruptcy, within their own district, which is generally the province itself. Two judges form a quorum. At each of the five Provincial Courts in the south of Thailand (i.e. Pattani, Yala, Betong, Satun and Narathiwat) where the majority of the population are Muslims, there are two Dato Yutithum or Kadis (Muslim judges). A Kadi sits with two trial judges in order to administer Shari'a (Islamic) laws and usages in civil cases involving family and inheritance where all parties concerned are Muslims. Questions on Islamic laws and usages which are interpreted by a Kadi are final.

Thon Buri Civil Court (Sarn Pang Thon Buri): Civil jurisdiction over nine districts of metropolitan Bangkok.

Thon Buri Criminal Court (Sarn Aya Thon Buri): Criminal jurisdiction over nine districts of metropolitan Bangkok.

South Bangkok Civil Court (Sarn Pang Krungthep Tai): Civil jurisdiction over southern districts of Bangkok.

South Bangkok Criminal Court (Sarn Aya Krungthep Tai): Criminal jurisdiction over southern districts of Bangkok.

Magistrates' Courts (Sarn Kwaeng): Adjudicate in minor cases with minimum formality and expense. Judges sit singly.

Religion

Buddhism is the predominant religion, professed by more than 95% of Thailand's total population. About 4% of the population are Muslims, being ethnic Malays, mainly in the south. Most of the immigrant Chinese are Confucians. The Christians number about 305,000, of whom about 75% are Roman Catholic, mainly in Bangkok and northern Thailand. Brahmins, Hindus and Sikhs number about 85,000.

BUDDHISM

Sangha Supreme Council: The Religious Affairs Dept, Thanon Ratchadamnoen Nok, Bangkok 10300; tel. (2) 281-6080; fax (2) 281-5415; governing body of Thailand's 350,000 monks, novices and nuns.

Supreme Patriarch of Thailand: SOMDEJ PHRA YANSANGWARA.

The Buddhist Association of Thailand: 41 Thanon Phra Aditya, Bangkok 10200; tel. (2) 281-9563; f. 1934 under royal patronage; 4,183 mems; Pres. PRAPASANA AUYCHAI.

CHRISTIANITY

The Roman Catholic Church

For ecclesiastical purposes, Thailand comprises two archdioceses and eight dioceses. At 31 December 2000 there were an estimated 273,147 adherents in the country, representing about 0.4% of the population.

Catholic Bishops' Conference of Thailand: 122/6–7 Soi Naaksuwan, Thanon Nonsi, Yannawa, Bangkok 10120; tel. (2) 681-5361; fax (2) 681-5370; e-mail cbct@ksc.th.com; f. 1969; Pres. Cardinal MICHAEL MICHAI KITBUNCHU, Archbishop of Bangkok.

Catholic Association of Thailand: 57 Soi Burapa, Bangrak, Bangkok 10500; tel. (2) 233-2976.

Archbishop of Bangkok: Cardinal MICHAEL MICHAI KITBUNCHU, Assumption Cathedral, 40 Thanon Charoenkrung, Bangrak, Bangkok 10500; tel. (2) 237-1031; fax (2) 237-1033; e-mail arcdibkk@loxinfo.co.th.

Archbishop of Tharé and Nonseng: Most Rev. LAWRENCE KHAI SAEN-PHON-ON, Archbishop's House, POB 6, Sakon Nakhon 47000; tel. (42) 711718; fax (42) 712023.

The Anglican Communion

Thailand is within the jurisdiction of the Anglican Bishop of Singapore (q.v.).

Other Christian Churches

Baptist Church Foundation (Foreign Mission Board): 90 Soi 2, Thanon Sukhumvit, Bangkok 10110; tel. (2) 252-7078; Mission Admin. TOM WILLIAMS, POB 832, Bangkok 10501.

Church of Christ in Thailand: CCT Bldg, 13th Floor, 109 Thanon Surawong, Bangkok 10500; tel. (2) 236-2900; fax (2) 238-3520; e-mail cctecume@loxinfo.co.th; f. 1934; 129,935 communicants; Moderator Rev. Dr BOONRATNA BOAYEN; Gen. Sec. Rev. Dr SINT KIMHACHANDRA.

ISLAM

Office of the Chularajmontri: 100 Soi Prom Pak, Thanon Sukhumvit, Bangkok 10110; Sheikh Al-Islam (Chularajmontri) Haji SAWASDI SUMALAYASAK.

BAHÁ'Í FAITH

National Spiritual Assembly: 77/1 Soi Lang Suan 4, Thanon Ploenchit, Lumpini Patumwan, Bangkok 10330; tel. (2) 252-5355; fax (2) 254-4199; mems resident in 76 provinces.

The Press

DAILIES

Thai Language

Baan Muang: 1 Soi Pluem-Manee, Thanon Vibhavadi Rangsit, Bangkok 10900; tel. (2) 513-3101; fax (2) 513-3106; Editor MANA PRAEBHAND; circ. 200,000.

Daily News: 1/4 Thanon Vibhavadi Rangsit, Laksi, Bangkok 10210; tel. (2) 561-1456; fax (2) 940-9875; internet www.dailynews.co.th; f. 1964; Editor PRACHA HETRAKUL; circ. 800,000.

Dao Siam: 60 Mansion 4, Thanon Rajdamnern, Bangkok 10200; tel. (2) 222-6001; fax (2) 222-6885; f. 1974; Editor SANTI UNTRAKARN; circ. 120,000.

Khao Panich (Daily Trade News): 22/27 Thanon Ratchadaphisek, Bangkok 10900; tel. (2) 511-5066; Editor SAMRUANE SUMPHANDHARAK; circ. 30,000.

Khao Sod (Fresh News): Bangkok; Editor-in-Chief KIATICHAI PONGPANICH; circ. 350,000.

Krungthep Turakij Daily: Nation Multimedia Group Public Co Ltd, 44 Moo 10, Thanon Bangna-Trad, Bangna, Prakanong, Bangkok 10260; tel. (2) 317-0042; fax (2) 317-1489; e-mail ktwebmaster@bangkokbiznews.com; internet www.bangkokbiznews.com; f. 1987; Publr and Group Editor SUTHICHAI YOON; Editor ADISAK LIMPRUNGPATANAKIT; circ. 75,882.

Matichon: 12 Thanon Thedsaban Naruban, Prachanivate 1, Chatuchak, Bangkok 10900; tel. (2) 589-0020; fax (2) 589-9112; e-mail matisale@matichon.co.th; internet www.matichon.co.th; f. 1977; Man. Editor PRASONG LERTRATANAVISUTH; circ. 180,000.

Naew Na (Frontline): 96 Moo 7, Thanon Vibhavadi Rangsit, Bangkok; tel. (2) 521-4647; fax (2) 552-3800; Editor WANCHAI WONGMEECHAI; circ. 200,000.

Siam Daily: 192/8–9 Soi Vorapong, Thanon Visuthikasat, Bangkok; tel. (2) 281-7422; Editor NARONG CHARUSOPHON.

Siam Post: Bangkok; internet www.siampost.co.th; Man. Dir PAISAL SRICHARATCHANYA.

Siam Rath (Siam Nation): 12 Mansion 6, Thanon Rajdamnern, Bangkok 10200; tel. (2) 224-1952; fax (2) 224-1982; f. 1950; Editor ASSIRI THAMMACHOT; circ. 120,000.

Sue Tuakij: Bangkok; f. 1995; evening; business news.

Thai: 423–425 Thanon Chao Khamrop, Bangkok; tel. (2) 223-3175; Editor VICHIEN MANA-NATHEETHORATHAM.

Thai Rath: 1 Thanon Vibhavadi Rangsit, Bangkok 10900; tel. (2) 272-1030; fax (2) 272-1324; internet www.thairath.co.th; f. 1948; Editor PITHOON SUNTHORN; circ. 800,000.

English Language

Asia Times: 102/1 Thanon Phra Arthit, 5th Floor, Pranakorn, Bangkok 10200; tel. (2) 288-4160; fax (2) 288-4161; internet www.atimes.com; f. 1995; regional; business news; Editor PANSAK VINYARATN; Deputy Editor UWE VON PARPART.

Bangkok Post: Bangkok Post Bldg, 136 Soi Na Ranong, Klongtoey, Bangkok 10110; tel. (2) 240-3700; fax (2) 240-3666; e-mail editor@bangkokpost.co.th; internet www.bangkokpost.net; f. 1946; morning; Editor PICHAI CHUENSUKSAWADI; circ. 49,378 (Dec. 1999).

Business Day: Olympia Thai Tower, 22nd Floor, 444 Thanon Ratchadaphisek, Huay Kwang, Bangkok 10310; tel. (2) 512-3579; fax (2) 512-3565; e-mail info@bday.net; internet www.bday.net; f. 1994; business news; Man. Editor CHATCHAI YENBAMROONG.

The Nation: 44 Moo 10, Thanon Bangna Trad, km 4.5 Bangna, Phra Khanong, Bangkok 10260; tel. (2) 317-0420; fax (2) 317-2071; e-mail info@nationgroup.com; internet www.nationmultimedia.com; f. 1971; morning; Publr and Group Editor SUTHICHAI YOON; Editor PANA JANVIROJ; circ. 55,000.

Thailand Times: 88 Thanon Boromrajachonnee, Taling Chan, Bangkok; tel. (2) 434-0330; Editor WUTHIPONG LAKKHAM.

Chinese Language

Kia Hua Tong Huan: 108 Thanon Suapa, Bangkok; tel. (2) 221-4182; f. 1959; Editor SURADECH KORNKITTICHAI; circ. 80,000.

New Chinese Daily News: 1022–1030 Thanon Charoenkrung, Talad-Noi, Bangkok; tel. (2) 234-0684; fax (2) 234-0684; Editor PUSADEE KEETAWORANART; circ. 72,000.

Sing Sian Yit Pao Daily News: 267 Thanon Charoenkrung, Bangkok 10100; tel. (2) 222-6601; fax (2) 225-4663; e-mail singpau@loxinfo.co.th; f. 1950; Man. Dir NETRA RUTHAIYANONT; Editor TAWEE YODPETCH; circ. 70,000.

Tong Hua Daily News: 877/879 Thanon Charoenkrung, Talad-Noi, Bangkok 10100; tel. (2) 236-9172; fax (2) 238-5286; Editor CHART PAYONITHIKARN; circ. 85,000.

WEEKLIES

Thai Language

Bangkok Weekly: 533–539 Thanon Sri Ayuthaya, Bangkok 10400; tel. (2) 245-2546; fax (2) 247-3410; Editor VICHIT ROJANAPRABHA.

Mathichon Weekly Review: 12 Thanon Thedsaban Naruban, Prachanivate 1, Chatuchak, Bangkok 10900; tel. (2) 589-0020; fax (2) 589-9112; Editor RUANGCHAI SABNIRAND; circ. 150,000.

Satri Sarn: 83/35 Arkarntrithosthep 2, Thanon Prachathipatai, Bangkok 10300; tel. (2) 281-9136; f. 1948; women's magazine; Editor NILAWAN PINTONG.

Siam Rath Weekly Review: 12 Mansion 6, Thanon Rajdamnern, Bangkok 10200; Editor PRACHUAB THONGURAI.

Skul Thai: 58 Soi 36, Thanon Sukhumvit, Bangkok 10110; tel. (2) 258-5861; fax (2) 258-9130; Editor SANTI SONGSEMSAWAS.

Wattachak: 88 Thanon Boromrajachonnee, Talingchan, Bangkok 10170; tel. (2) 434-0330; fax (2) 435-0900; e-mail rattanasingha@wattachak.com; internet www.wattachak.com; Editor PRAPHAN BOONYAKIAT; circ. 80,000.

English Language

Bangkok Post Weekly Review: U-Chuliang Bldg, 3rd Floor, 968 Thanon Phra Ram Si, Bangkok 10500; tel. (2) 233-8030; fax (2) 238-5430; f. 1989; Editor ANUSSORN THAVISIN; circ. 10,782.

Business Times: Thai Bldg, 1400 Thanon Phra Ram IV, Bangkok 10110.

FORTNIGHTLIES

Thai Language

Darathai: 9-9/1 Soi Sri Ak-Sorn, Thanon Chuapleung, Tungmahamek, Sathorn, Bangkok 10120; tel. (2) 249-1576; fax (2) 249-1575; f. 1954; television and entertainment; Editor USA BUKKAVESA; circ 80,000.

Dichan: 1400 Thai Bldg, Thanon Phra Ram Si, Bangkok; tel. (2) 249-0351; fax (2) 249-9455; Editor KHUNYING TIPYAVADI PRAMOJ NA AYUDHYA.

Lalana: 44 Moo 10, Thanon Bangna-Trad, Bangna, Bangkok 10260; tel. (2) 317-1400; fax (2) 317-1409; f. 1972; Editor NANTAWAN YOON; circ. 65,000.

Praew: 7/9–18 Thanon Arun-Amarin, Bangkoknoi, Bangkok 10700; tel. (2) 434-0286; fax (2) 433-8792; e-mail praew@amarin.co.th; internet www.amarin.com; f. 1979; women and fashion; Editorial Dir SUPAWADEE KOMARADAT; Editor NUANCHAN SUPANIMIT; circ. 150,000.

MONTHLIES

Bangkok 30: 98/5–6 Thanon Phra Arthit, Bangkok 10200; tel. (2) 282-5467; fax (2) 280-1302; f. 1986; Thai; business; Publr SONCHAI LIMTHONGKUL; Editor BOONSIRI NAMBOONSRI; circ. 65,000.

Chao Krung: 12 Mansion 6, Thanon Rajdamnern, Bangkok 10200; Thai; Editor NOPPHORN BUNYARIT.

The Dharmachaksu (Dharma-vision): Foundation of Mahamakut Rajavidyalai, 241 Thanon Phra Sumeru, Bangkok 10200; tel. (2) 629-1417; fax (2) 629-4015; e-mail books@mahamakuta.inet.co.th; internet www.mahamakuta.inet.co.th; f. 1894; Thai; Buddhism and related subjects; Editor WASIN INDASARA; circ. 5,000.

Grand Prix: 4/299 Moo 5, Soi Ladplakhao 66, Thanon Ladplakhao, Bangkhan, Bangkok 10220; tel. (2) 971-6450; fax (2) 971-6469; e-mail grandprix@grandprixgroup.com; internet www.grandprixgroup.com/gpi/maggrandprix/grandprix.asp; Editor VEERA JUNKAJIT; circ. 80,000.

The Investor: Pansak Bldg, 4th Floor, 138/1 Thanon Petchburi, Bangkok 10400; tel. (2) 282-8166; f. 1968; English language; business, industry, finance and economics; Editor TOS PATUMSEN; circ. 6,000.

Kasikorn: Dept of Agriculture, Catuchak, Bangkok 10900; tel. (2) 561-4677; fax (2) 579-5369; f. 1928; Thai; agriculture and agricultural research; Editor-in-Chief ORANAN LEKAGUL; Editor PANNEE WICHACHOO.

Look: 1/54 Thanon Sukhumvit 30, Pra Khanong, Bangkok 10110; tel. (2) 258-1265; Editor KANOKWAN MILINDAVANIJ.

Look East: 52/38 Soi Saladaeng 2, Silom Condominium, 12th Floor, Thanon Silom, Bangkok 10500; tel. (2) 235-6185; fax (2) 236-6764; f. 1969; English; Editor ASHA SEHGAL; circ. 30,000.

Motorcycle Magazine: 4/299 Moo 5, Soi Ladplakhao 66, Thanon Ladplakhao, Bangkhan, Bangkok 10220; tel. (2) 971-6450; fax (2) 971-6469; e-mail motorcycle@grandprixgroup.com; internet www.grandprixgroup.com/gpi/magmotor/motorcycle.asp; monthly; Publr PRACHIN EAMLAMNOW; circ. 70,000.

Saen Sanuk: 50 Soi Saeng Chan, Thanon Sukhumvit 42, Bangkok 10110; tel. (2) 392-0052; fax (2) 391-1486; English; travel and tourist attractions in Thailand; Editor SOMTAWIN KONGSAWATKIAT; circ. 85,000.

Satawa Liang: 689 Thanon Wang Burapa, Bangkok; Thai; Editor THAMRONGSAK SRICHAND.

Villa Wina Magazine: Chalerm Ketr Theatre Bldg, 3rd Floor, Bangkok; Thai; Editor BHONGSAKDI PIAMLAP.

NEWS AGENCIES

Foreign Bureaux

Agence France-Presse (AFP): 18th Floor, Alma Link Bldg, 25 Soi Chidlom, Thanon Ploenchit, Lumpini Patumwan, Bangkok 10330; tel. (2) 650-3230; fax (2) 650-3234; e-mail afpbgk@samart.co.th; Bureau Chief PHILIPPE AGRET.

Associated Press (AP) (USA): Charn Issara Tower, 14th Floor, 942/51 Thanon Phra Ram IV, POB 775, Bangkok; tel. (2) 234-5553; Bureau Chief DENIS D. GRAY.

Jiji Tsushin (Jiji Press) (Japan): Boonmitr Bldg, 8th Floor, 138 Thanon Silom, Bangkok; tel. (2) 236-8793; fax (2) 236-6800; Bureau Chief JUNICHI ISHIKAWA.

Kyodo News Service (Japan): U Chuliang Bldg, 2nd Floor, 968 Thanon Phra Ram IV, Bangkok 10500; tel. (2) 236-6822; Bureau Chief YOSHISUKE YASUO.

Reuters (UK): Maneeya Centre Bldg, 518/5 Thanon Ploenchit, 10330 Bangkok; tel. (2) 637-5500; Man. (Myanmar, Thailand and Indo-China) GRAHAM D. SPENCER.

United Press International (UPI) (USA): U Chuliang Bldg, 968 Thanon Phra Ram IV, Bangkok; tel. (2) 238-5244; Bureau Chief JOHN B. HAIL.

Viet Nam News Agency (VNA): 3/81 Soi Chokchai Ruamit, Bangkok; Bureau Chief NGUYEN VU QUANG.

Xinhua (New China) News Agency (People's Republic of China): Room 407, Capital Mansion, 1371 Thanon Phaholyothin, Saphan Kwai, Bangkok 10400; tel. and fax (2) 271-1413; Chief Correspondent YU ZUNCHENG.

PRESS ASSOCIATIONS

Confederation of Thai Journalists: 55 Mansion 8, Thanon Ratchadamnoen Klang, Bangkok 10200; tel. (2) 629-0022; fax (2) 280-

0337; internet www.ctj.in.th; Pres. SMARN SUDTO; Sec.-Gen. SUWAT THONGTHANAKUL.

Press Association of Thailand: 299 Thanon Ratchasima, Dusit, Bangkok 10300; tel. (2) 241-2064; e-mail webmaster@thaipressasso.com; internet www.thaipressasso.com; f. 1941; Pres. PREECHA SAMAKKIDHAM.

There are also regional press organizations and journalists' organizations.

Publishers

Advance Media: 1400 Rama IV Shopping Centre, Klongtoey, Bangkok 10110; tel. (2) 249-0358; Man. PRASERTSAK SIVASAHONG.

Bhannakij Trading: 34 Thanon Nakornsawan, Bangkok 10100; tel. (2) 282-5520; fax (2) 282-0076; Thai fiction, school textbooks; Man. SOMSAK TECHAKASHEM.

Chalermnit Press: 108 Thanon Sukhumvit, Soi 53, Bangkok 10110; tel. (2) 662-6264; fax (2) 662-6265; e-mail chalermnit@hotmail.com; internet www.chalermnit.com; f. 1937; dictionaries, history, literature, guides to Thai language, works on Thailand and South-East Asia; Man. Dir Dr PARICHART (JUMSAI) SUKSONGKROH.

Dhamabuja: 5/1–2 Thanon Asadang, Bangkok; religious; Man. VIROCHANA SIRI-ATH.

Graphic Art Publishing: 105/19–2 Thanon Naret, Bangkok 10500; tel. (2) 233-0302; f. 1972; textbooks, science fiction, photography; CEO Mrs ANGKANA SAJJARAKTRAKUL.

Prae Pittaya Ltd: POB 914, 716–718 Wangburabha, Bangkok; tel. (2) 221-4283; general Thai books; Man. CHIT PRAEPANICH.

Praphansarn: Siam Sq., Soi 2, Thanon Phra Ram I, Bangkok; tel. (2) 251-2342; e-mail editor@praphansarn.com; internet www.praphansarn.com; Thai pocket books; Man. Dir SUPHOL TAECHATADA.

Ruamsarn (1977): 864 Wangburabha, Thanon Panurangsri, Bangkok 10200; tel. (2) 221-6483; fax (2) 222-2036; f. 1951; fiction and history; Man. PITI TAWEWATANASARN.

Ruang Silpa: 663 Thanon Samsen Nai, Bangkok; Thai pocket books; Propr DHAMNOON RUANG SILPA.

Sermvitr Barnakarn: 222 Werng Nakorn Kasem, Bangkok 10100; general Thai books; Man. PRAVIT SAMMAVONG.

Silkworm Books: 104/5 Thanon Chiang Mai-Hot, M.7, T. Suthep, Muang, Chiang Mai 50200; tel. (53) 271-889; fax (53) 275-178; e-mail silkworm@loxinfo.co.th; internet www.silkwormbooks.info; f. 1991; South-East Asian studies.

Suksapan Panit (Business Organization of Teachers' Institute): 128/1 Thanon Ratchasima, Bangkok 10300; tel. (2) 811-845; e-mail ssp@suksapan.or.th; internet www.suksapan.or.th; f. 1950; general, textbooks, children's, pocket books; Pres. PANOM KAW KAMNERD.

Suriyabarn Publishers: 14 Thanon Pramuan, Bangkok 10500; tel. (2) 234-7991; f. 1953; religion, literature, Thai culture; Man. Dir PRASIT SAETANG.

Thai Watana Panit: 599 Thanon Maitrijit, Bangkok 10100; tel. (2) 221-0111; children's, school textbooks; Man. Dir VIRA T. SUWAN.

Watana Panit Printing and Publishing Co Ltd: 31/1–2 Soi Siripat, Thanon Mahachai, Samranrat, Pranakorn, Bangkok 10120; tel. (2) 222-1016; fax (2) 225-6556; school textbooks; Man. ROENGCHAI CHONGPIPATANASOOK.

White Lotus Co Ltd: 11/2 Soi 58, Thanon Sukhumvit, POB 1141, Bangkok 10250; tel. (2) 332-4915; fax (2) 311-4575; e-mail ande@loxinfo.co.th; internet www.thailine.com/lotus; f. 1992; regional interests; Chief Exec. D. ANDE.

PUBLISHERS' ASSOCIATION

Publishers' and Booksellers' Association of Thailand: 947/158–159 Moo 12, Thanon Bang Na-Trad, Bang Na, Bangkok 10260; tel. (2) 744-0863; fax (2) 744-0873; e-mail pubat@usa.net; internet www.pubat.or.th; Pres. M. L. MANICH JUMSAI; Gen. Sec. PLEARNPIT PRAEPANIT.

Broadcasting and Communications

TELECOMMUNICATIONS

Post and Telegraph Department: Thanon Phaholyothin, Payathai, Bangkok 10400; tel. (2) 271-0151; fax (2) 271-3511; e-mail webadmin@ptd.go.th; internet www.ptd.go.th; Dir-Gen. SETHAPORN CUSRIPITUCK.

Advanced Info Service Public Co Ltd: 414 Thanon Phaholyothin, Shinawatra Tower I, Phayathai, Bangkok 10400; tel. (2) 299-5000; fax (2) 299-5719; e-mail callcenter@ais900.com; internet www.ais900.com; mobile telephone network operator; Chair. PAIBOON LIMPAPHAYOM.

Communications Authority of Thailand (CAT): 99 Thanon Changwattana, Laksi, Bangkok 10002; tel. (2) 506-3299; fax (2) 573-6507; e-mail prcat@cat.or.th; internet www.cat.or.th; state-owned; telephone operator; *de facto* regulator; scheduled for partial transfer to the private sector; Chair. SRISOOK CHANDRANGSU; Pres. and CEO DHIRAPHONG SUDDHINOND.

Samart Corpn Public Co Ltd: Moo 4, Software Park Bldg, 38th Floor, 99 Thanon Chaengwattana, Klong Gluar, Pak-kred, Nonthaburi 11120; tel. (2) 502-6000; fax (2) 502-6043; e-mail nikhila@samartcorp.com; internet www.samartcorp.com; telecommunications installation and distribution; cap. and res 700m., sales 4,692m. (1996); Chair. PICHAI VASANASONG; Exec. Chair. CHAROENRATH VILAILUCK.

Telecomasia Corpn Public Co Ltd: Telecom Tower, 18 Thanon Ratchadaphisek, Huay Kwang, Bangkok 10320; tel. (2) 643-1111; fax (2) 643-9669; e-mail iroffice@asianet.co.th; internet www.telecomasia.co.th; telecommunications services; Chair. DHANIN CHEARAVANONT; Pres. and CEO SUPACHAI CHEARAVANONT.

Telephone Organization of Thailand (TOT): 89/2 Moo 3, Thanon Chaengwattana, Thungsonghong, Laksi, Bangkok 10210; tel. (2) 505-1000; internet www.tot.co.th; state-owned; telephone operator; *de facto* regulator; scheduled for partial transfer to the private sector; Pres. SUTHAM MALILA.

Thai Telephone and Telecommunication Public Co Ltd (TT&T): Muang Thai Phatra Complex Tower 1, 24th Floor, 252/30 Thanon Ratchadaphisek, Huay Kwang, Bangkok; tel. (2) 693-2100; fax (2) 693-2126; internet www.ttt.co.th; distributors of telecommunications equipment and services; Chair. DHONGCHAI LAMSAM; Pres. and CEO Dr PISIT LEEAHTAM.

Total Access Communications Public Co Ltd: Chai Bldg, 19th Floor, 333/3 Moo 4, Thanon Vibhavadi Rangsit, Ladyao Chatuchak, Bangkok 10900; tel. (2) 202-8000; fax (2) 202-8102; internet www.dtac.co.th; mobile telephone network operator; 71.6% owned by United Communication Industry Public Co Ltd; Chair. and Man. Dir BOONCHAI BENCHARONGKUL.

United Communication Industry Public Co Ltd: 499 Moo 3, Benchachinda Bldg, Thanon Vibhavadi Rangsit, Chatuchak, Bangkok 10900; tel. (2) 953-1111; fax (2) 953-0248; e-mail hr@ucom.co.th; internet www.ucom.co.th; telecommunications service provider; Chair. SRIBHUMI SUKHANETR; Pres. and Chief Exec. BOONCHAI BENCHARONGKUL.

BROADCASTING

Regulatory Authority

Radio and Television Executive Committee (RTEC): Programme, Administration and Law Section, Division of RTEC Works, Government Public Relations Department, Thanon Ratchadamnoen Klang, Phra Nakhon Region, Bangkok 10200; constituted under the Broadcasting and TV Rule 1975, the committee consists of 17 representatives from 14 government agencies and controls the administrative, legal, technical and programming aspects of broadcasting in Thailand.

Radio

Radio Thailand (RTH): National Broadcasting Services of Thailand, Government Public Relations Dept, Soi Aree Sampan, Thanon Phra Ram VI, Khet Phayathai, Bangkok 10400; tel. (2) 618-2323; fax (2) 618-2340; internet www.prd.go.th/mcic/radio.htm; f. 1930; govt-controlled; educational, entertainment, cultural and news programmes; operates 109 stations throughout Thailand; Dir of Radio Thailand SOMPHONG VISUTTIPAT.

Home Service: 12 stations in Bangkok and 97 affiliated stations in 50 provinces; operates three programmes; Dir CHAIVICHIT ATISAB.

External Services: f. 1928; in Thai, English, French, Vietnamese, Khmer, Japanese, Burmese, Lao, Malay, Chinese (Mandarin), German and Bahasa Indonesia; Dir AMPORN SAMOSORN.

Ministry of Education Broadcasting Service: Centre for Innovation and Technology, Ministry of Education, Bangkok; tel. (2) 246-0026; f. 1954; morning programmes for schools (Mon.–Fri.); afternoon and evening programmes for general public (daily); Dir of Centre PISAN SIWAYABRAHM.

Pituksuntirad Radio Stations: stations at Bangkok, Nakorn Rachasima, Chiangmai, Pitsanuloke and Songkla; programmes in Thai; Dir-Gen. PAITOON WAIJANYA.

Radio Saranrom: Thanon Ratchadamnoen, POB 2-131, Bangkok 10200; tel. (2) 224-4904; fax (2) 226-1825; f. 1968 as Voice of Free Asia; name changed as above in 1998; operated by the Ministry of Foreign Affairs; broadcasts in Thai; Dir of Broadcasting PAIBOON KUSKUL.

Television

Radio and Television Executive Committee (RTEC): (see Radio).

Bangkok Broadcasting & TV Co Ltd (Channel 7): 998/1 Soi Sirimitr, Phaholyothin, Talad Mawchid, POB 456, Bangkok 10900; tel. (2) 278-1255; fax (2) 270-1976; e-mail prdept@ch7.com; internet www.ch7.com; commercial.

Bangkok Entertainment Co Ltd (Channel 3): 1126/1 Thanon Petchburi Tadmai, Bangkok 10400; tel. (2) 204-3333; fax (2) 204-1384; internet www.tv3.co.th; Programme Dir PRAVIT MALEENONT.

Independent Television (ITV): 19 SCB Park Plaza, East Tower 3, Thanon Rachadapisek, Bangkok; tel. (2) 937-8080; e-mail webmaster@itv.co.th; internet www.itv.co.th; f. 1996; owned by a consortium including Nation Publishing Co, Siam Commercial Bank Public Co Ltd and Daily News media group.

The Mass Communication Organization of Thailand (Channel 9): 222 Thanon Asoke-Dindaeng, Bangkok 10300; tel. (2) 245-1844; fax (2) 245-1855; e-mail webmaster@mcot.or.th; internet www.mcot.or.th; f. 1952 as Thai Television Co Ltd; colour service; Dir-Gen. (vacant).

The Royal Thai Army Television HSA-TV (Channel 5): Thanon Phaholyothin, Sanam Pao, Bangkok 10400; tel. (2) 278-1470; fax (2) 279-0430; internet www.tv5.co.th; f. 1958; operates channels nationwide; Dir-Gen. Maj. Gen. VIJIT JUNAPART.

Television of Thailand (Channel 11): Public Relations Dept, Fortune Town Bldg, 26th Floor, Thanon Ratchadaphisek, Huay Kwang, Bangkok 10310; tel. and fax (2) 248-1601; internet www.prd.go.th/prdnew/thai/tv11; operates 16 colour stations; Dir-Gen. (vacant).

Thai Sky TV: 21 Vibhavadi Rangsit, Bangkok; tel. (2) 273-8977; pay-television; owned by Wattachak Co.

TV Pool of Thailand: c/o Royal Thai Army HSA-TV, Thanon Phaholyothin, Sanam Pao, Bangkok 10400; tel. (2) 271-0060; fax (2) 279-0430; established with the co-operation of all stations to present coverage of special events; Chair. Maj.-Gen. SOONTHORN SOPHONSIRI.

Finance

(cap. = capital; p.u. = paid up; res = reserves; dep. = deposits; m. = million; brs = branches; amounts in baht)

BANKING

Central Bank

Bank of Thailand: POB 154, 273 Thanon Samsen, Bangkhunprom, Bangkok 10200; tel. (2) 283-5353; fax (2) 280-0449; e-mail webmaster@bot.or.th; internet www.bot.or.th; f. 1942; bank of issue; cap. 20m., res 75,502m., dep. 748,072m. (Dec. 2000); Gov. PRIDIYATHORN DAVAKULA; Asst Gov. BANDID NIJATHAWORN; 4 brs.

Commercial Banks

Bangkok Bank Public Co Ltd: 333 Thanon Silom, Bangkok 10500; tel. (2) 231-4333; fax (2) 236-8281; internet www.bbl.co.th; f. 1944; cap. 14,668m., res 145,928m., dep. 1,083,352m. (Dec. 2000); 49% foreign-owned; Chair. CHATRI SOPHONPANICH; Pres. CHARTSIRI SOPHONPANICH; 548 brs.

Bank of Asia Public Co Ltd: 191 Thanon Sathorn Tai, Khet Sathorn, Bangkok 10120; tel. (2) 287-2211; fax (2) 287-2973; e-mail webmaster@boa.co.th; internet www.bankasia4u.com; f. 1939; cap. 50,954m., res 8,560m., dep. 142,462m. (June 2002); 78.85%-owned by ABN AMRO Bank N.V.; Pres. and CEO CHULAKORN SINGHAKOWIN; 129 brs.

Bank of Ayudhya Public Co Ltd: 1222 Thanon Rama III, Bangkok 10120; tel. (2) 296-2000; fax (2) 683-1304; e-mail prs007@bay.co.th; internet www.bay.co.th; f. 1945; cap. 18,503m., res 35,965m., dep. 365,390m. (Dec. 2000); Chair. KRIT RATANARAK; Pres. JAMLONG ATIKUL; 424 brs.

Bankthai Public Co Ltd: 44 Thanon Sathorn, Silom, Bangrak, Bangkok 10500; tel. (2) 638-8000; fax (2) 633-9026; e-mail bankthai_pr2@hotmail.com; internet www.bankthai.co.th; f. 1998; cap. 70,631m., dep. 186,606m. (Aug. 2002); Chair. PRAMON SUTIVONG; Pres. PHIRASILP SUBHAPHOLSIRI; 80 brs.

DBS Thai Danu Bank Public Co Ltd: 393 Thanon Silom, Bangkok 10500; tel. (2) 230-5000; fax (2) 236-7939; internet www.dbs.co.th; f. 1949; cap. 17,001m., res 20,116m., dep. 72,407m. (Dec. 2000); fmrly Thai Danu Bank Public Co Ltd, 51.8% share purchased by DBS Bank (Singapore) in 1999; Chair. PAKORN THAVISIN; Pres. and CEO PORNSANONG TUCHINDA; 96 brs.

Krung Thai Bank Public Co Ltd (State Commercial Bank of Thailand): 35 Thanon Sukhumvit, Klongtoey, Bangkok 10110, POB 44 BMC, Bangkok 10000; tel. (2) 255-2222; fax (2) 255-9391; e-mail ptsirana@ktb.co.th; internet www.ktb.co.th; f. 1966; cap. 219,850m., res 34,747m., dep. 854,011m. (Dec. 1999); taken under the control of the central bank in 1998, pending transfer to private sector; merged with First Bangkok City Bank Public Co Ltd in 1999; Chair. SUPHACHAI PHISITVANICH; Pres. VIROJ NUALKHAIR; 617 local brs, 8 overseas brs.

Siam City Bank Public Co Ltd: POB 488, 1101 Thanon Petchburi Tadmai, Bangkok 10400; tel. (2) 208-5000; fax (2) 253-1240; e-mail webmaster@siamcity.co.th; internet www.siamcity.co.th; f. 1941; cap. 31,421m., res –4,613m., dep. 248,035m. (Dec. 2000); taken under the control of the central bank in Feb. 1998; merged with Bangkok Metropolitan Bank Public Co Ltd in April 2002; Pres. SOMPOL KIATPHAIBOOL; 211 brs.

Siam Commercial Bank Public Co Ltd: 9 Thanon Ratchadaphisek, Lardyao, Chatuchak, Bangkok 10900; tel. (2) 544-1111; fax (2) 937-7754; e-mail ccs@telecom.scb.co.th; internet www.scb.co.th; f. 1906; cap. 60,175m., res 22,808m., dep. 593,107m. (Dec. 2000); Chair. Dr CHIRAYU ISARANGKUN NA AYUTHAYA; Pres. and CEO JADA WATTANSIRITHAM; 477 brs.

Standard Chartered Nakornthon Bank Public Co Ltd: 90 Thanon Sathorn Nua, POB 2731, Bangkok 10500; tel. (2) 233-2111; fax (2) 236-1968; e-mail suteel@samart.co.th; internet www.ntb.co.th; f. 1933 as Wang Lee Bank Ltd, renamed 1985; cap. 7,003m., res 114m., dep. 55,220m. (Dec. 1999); taken under the control of the central bank in July 1999, 75% share sold to Standard Chartered Bank (United Kingdom); name changed as above in September 1999; CEO and Pres. VISHNU MOHAN; 67 brs.

Thai Farmers Bank Public Co Ltd: 1 Thai Farmers Lane, Thanon Ratburana, Bangkok 10140; tel. (2) 470-1122; fax (2) 470-1144; internet www.tfb.co.th; f. 1945; cap. 27,072m., dep. 664,846m. (Dec. 2001); 48.98% foreign-owned; Chair. BANYONG LAMSAM; Pres. BANTHOON LAMSAM; 529 brs.

Thai Military Bank Public Co Ltd: 3000 Thanon Phahon Yothin, Bangkok 10900; tel. (2) 299-1111; fax (2) 273-7121; e-mail tmbir@tmb.co.th; internet www.tmb.co.th; f. 1957; cap. 36,102m., res 10,906m., dep. 268,588m. (Dec. 2000); Pres. and CEO SOMCHAI SAKULSURARAT; 367 brs.

UOB Radanasin Bank Public Co Ltd: 690 Thanon Sukhumvit, Bangkok 10110; tel. (2) 260-0090; fax (2) 260-5310; internet www.uob-radanasin.co.th; f. 1998 as the result of the merger of Laem Thong Bank Ltd with Radanasin Bank; name changed as above Nov. 1999; cap. 19,795m., res –7,618m., dep. 40,870m. (Dec. 1998); Chair. WEE CHO YAW; CEO SAMUEL POON HON THANG; 68 brs.

Foreign Banks

ABN AMRO Bank N.V. (Netherlands): Bangkok City Tower, 1st–4th Floors, 179/3 Thanon Sathorn Tai, Bangkok 10120; tel. (2) 679-5900; fax (2) 679-5901; cap. p.u. 2,003m., dep. 903m. (March 1996); Country Man. BURNO SCHRIEKE.

Bank of America, NA (USA): Bank of America Centre, 2/2 Thanon Witthayu, Bangkok 10330; tel. (2) 251-6333; fax (2) 253-1905; f. 1949; cap. p.u. 2,000m. (May 1998); Man. Dir and Country Man. FREDERICK CHIN.

Bank of China (People's Republic of China): Bangkok City Tower, 179 Thanon Sathorn Tai, Bangkok 10120; tel. (2) 268-1010; fax (2) 268-1020.

Bank of Tokyo-Mitsubishi Ltd (Japan): Harindhorn Tower, 54 Thanon Sathorn Nua, Bangrak, Bangkok 10500; tel. (2) 266-3011; fax (2) 266-3055; cap. p.u. 3,100m., dep. 17,213m. (March 1996); Dir and Gen. Man. HIROSHI MOTOMURA.

Bharat Overseas Bank Ltd (India): 221 Thanon Rajawongse, Sumpphanthawongse, Bangkok 10100; tel. (2) 224-5412; fax (2) 224-5405; f. 1974; cap. p.u. 225m., dep. 1,254m. (March 1996); Man. K. S. GANAPATHY.

Chase Manhattan Bank, NA (USA): Bubhajit Bldg, 2nd Floor, 20 Thanon Sathorn Nua, Silom Bangrak, Bangkok 10500; tel. (2) 234-5992; fax (2) 234-8386; cap. p.u. 615m., dep. 2,720m. (Aug. 1993); Man. Dir RAYMOND C. C. CHANG.

Citibank, NA (USA): 82 Thanon Sathorn Nua, Bangrak, Bangkok 10500; tel. (2) 232-2000; fax (2) 639-2564; cap. p.u. 3,849m., dep. 9,483m. (Feb. 1996); Man. DAVID L. HENDRIX.

Crédit Agricole Indosuez (France): CA Indosuez House, 152 Thanon Witthayu, POB 303, Bangkok 10330; tel. (2) 651-4590; fax (2) 651-4586; cap. p.u. 1,400m., dep. 2,241m. (April 1996); Man. Dr JEAN-FRANÇOIS CAHET.

Deutsche Bank AG (Germany): 208 Thanon Witthayu, Bangkok 10330; tel. (2) 651-5000; fax (2) 651-5151; cap. p.u. 1,200m., dep. 3,703m. (March 1996); Man. GERHARD HEIGL.

Hongkong and Shanghai Banking Corpn (HSBC) (Hong Kong): HSBC Bldg, 968 Thanon Rama IV, Silom, Bangkok 10500; tel. (2) 614-4000; fax (2) 632-4818; cap. p.u. 2,000m., dep. 8,328m. (March 1996); Man. R. J. O. CROMWELL.

International Commercial Bank of China (Taiwan): 36/12 P. S. Tower Asoke, 21 Thanon Sukhumvit, Phrakhanong, Bangkok 10110; tel. (2) 259-2000; fax (2) 259-1330; cap. p.u. 500m., dep. 1,334m. (Feb. 1996); Gen. Man. CHIA-NAN WANG.

Oversea-Chinese Banking Corpn Ltd: (Singapore): Charn Issara Tower, 2nd Floor, 942/80 Thanon Rama IV, Suriwongse, Bangkok 10500; tel. (2) 236-6730; fax (2) 237-7390; cap. p.u. 651m., dep. 455m. (Feb. 1996); Gen. Man. NEW JING YAN.

RHB Bank Bhd (Malaysia): Liberty Sq. Bldg, 10th Floor, 287 Thanon Silom, Bangrak, Bangkok 10500; tel. (2) 631-2010; fax (2) 631-2018; Man. LEH THIAM GUAN.

Standard Chartered Bank (UK): POB 320, 990 Thanon Rama IV, Bangkok 10500; tel. (2) 636-1000; fax (2) 636-1199; cap. p.u. 1,200m., dep. 5,585m. (March 1996); Man. BRUCE DARRINGTON.

Sumitomo Mitsui Banking Corpn (Japan): Boon-Mitr Bldg, 138 Thanon Silom, Bangkok 10500; tel. (2) 353-8000; fax (2) 353-8100; cap. p.u. 3,200m., dep. 8,343m. (Feb. 1996); Gen. Rep. YOSHIHIRO YOSHIMURA.

Development Banks

Bank for Agriculture and Agricultural Co-operatives (BAAC): 469 Thanon Nakorn Sawan, Dusit, Bangkok 10300; tel. (2) 280-0180; fax (2) 280-0442; e-mail train@baac.or.th; internet www.baac.or.th/eng_baac/home.htm; f. 1966 to provide credit for agriculture; cap. 22,761m., dep. 180,563m. (Dec. 2000); Exec. Chair. VARATHEP RATANAKORN; Pres. PITTAYAPOL NATTARADOL; 491 brs.

Export-Import Bank of Thailand (EXIM THAILAND): EXIM Bldg, 1193 Thanon Phaholyothin, Phayathai, Bangkok 10400; tel. (2) 271-3700; fax (2) 271-3204; e-mail info@exim.go.th; internet www.exim.go.th; f. 1993; provides financial services to Thai exporters and Thai investors investing abroad; cap. 6,500m. (Dec. 2001); Chair. Dr SOMCHAI RICHUPAN; Pres. (vacant); 7 brs.

Government Housing Bank: 212 Thanon Phra Ram IX, Huay Kwang, Bangkok 10310; tel. (2) 246-0303; fax (2) 246-1789; f. 1953 to provide housing finance; cap. 9,483m., assets 152,973m., dep. 80,251m. (Dec. 1995); Chair. Dr SOMCHAI RICHUPAN; Pres. SIDHIJAI TANPHIPHAT; 120 brs.

Savings Bank

Government Savings Bank: 470 Thanon Phaholyothin, Phayathai, Bangkok 10400; tel. (2) 299-8000; fax (2) 299-8490; e-mail vicheal@gsb.or.th; internet www.gsb.or.th; f. 1913; cap. 0.1m., res 4,647m., dep. 377,773m. (Dec. 1999); Chair. SUPHACHAI PHISITVANICH; Dir-Gen. PAIBOON WATTANASIRITHAM; 566 brs.

Bankers' Association

Thai Bankers' Association: Lake Rachada Office Complex, 4th Floor, 195/8–10 Thanon Ratchadaphisek, Klongtoey, Bangkok 10110; tel. (2) 264-0883; fax (2) 264-0888; e-mail atmpool@tba.or.th; internet www.tba.or.th; Chair. CHATRI SOPHONPANICH.

STOCK EXCHANGE

Stock Exchange of Thailand (SET): The Stock Exchange of Thailand Bldg, 62 Thanon Ratchadaphisek, Klongtoey, Bangkok 10110; tel. (2) 229-2000; fax (2) 654-5649; e-mail clientsupport@set.or.th; internet www.set.or.th; f. 1975; 27 mems; Pres. KITTIRAT NA RANONG; Chair. CHAVALIT THANACHANAN.

Securities and Exchange Commission: Diethelm Towers B, 10th/13th–16th Floors, 93/1 Thanon Witthayu, Lumpini, Patumwan, Bangkok 10330; tel. (2) 252-3223; fax (2) 256-7711; e-mail info@sec.or.th; internet www.sec.or.th; f. 1992; supervises new share issues and trading in existing shares; Chair. Minister of Finance; Sec.-Gen. PRASORN TRAIRVOSAKUL.

INSURANCE

In March 1997 the Government granted licences to 12 life assurance companies and 16 general insurance companies, bringing the total number of life insurance companies to 25 and non-life insurance companies to 83.

Selected Domestic Insurance Companies

American International Assurance Co Ltd: American International Tower, 181 Thanon Surawong, Bangkok 10500; tel. (2) 634-8888; fax (2) 236-6452; internet www.aia.co.th; f. 1983; ordinary and group life, group and personal accident, credit life; Snr Vice-Pres. and Gen. Man. DHADOL BUNNAG.

Ayudhya Insurance Public Co Ltd: Ploenchit Tower, 7th Floor, Thanon Ploenchit, Pathumwan, Bangkok 10330; tel. (2) 263-0335; fax (2) 263-0589; internet www.ayud.co.th; non-life; Chair. KRIT RATANARAK.

Bangkok Insurance Public Co Ltd: Bangkok Insurance Bldg, 25 Thanon Sathorn Tai, Bangkok 10120; tel. (2) 285-8888; fax (2) 677-3777; e-mail corp.comm@bki.co.th; internet www.bki.co.th; f. 1947; non-life; Chair. and Pres. CHAI SOPHONPANICH.

Bangkok Union Insurance Public Co Ltd: 175–177 Thanon Surawongse, Bangkok 10500; tel. (2) 233-6920; fax (2) 237-1856; f. 1929; non-life; Chair. MANU LIEWPAIROT.

China Insurance Co (Siam) Ltd: 36/68–69, 20th Floor, PS Tower, Thanon Asoke, Sukhumvit 21, Bangkok 10110; tel. (2) 259-3718; fax (2) 259-1402; f. 1948; non-life; Chair. JAMES C. CHENG; Man. Dir FANG RONG-CHENG.

Indara Insurance Public Co Ltd: 364/29 Thanon Si Ayutthaya, Ratchthewi, Bangkok 10400; tel. (2) 247-9261; fax (2) 247-9260; e-mail webmaster@indara.co.th; internet www.indara.co.th; f. 1949; non-life; Chair. PRATIP WONGNIRUND; Man. Dir SOPHON DEJTHEVAPORN.

International Assurance Co Ltd: 488/7–9 Thanon Henri Dunant, Patumwan, Bangkok 10330; tel. (2) 658-1919; fax (2) 285-8679; f. 1952; non-life, fire, marine, general; Chair. PICHAI KULAVANICH; Man. Dir SOMCHAI MAHASANTIPIYA.

Mittare Insurance Co Ltd: 295 Thanon Si Phraya, Bangrak, Bangkok 10500; tel. (2) 237-4646; fax (2) 236-1376; internet www.mittare.com; f. 1947; life, fire, marine, health, personal accident, automobile and general; fmrly Thai Prasit Insurance Co Ltd; Chair. SURACHAN CHANSRICHAWLA; Man. Dir SUKHATHEP CHANSRICHAWLA.

Ocean Life Insurance Co Ltd: 170/74–83 Ocean Tower I Bldg, Thanon Rachadapisek, Klongtoey, Bangkok 10110; tel. (2) 261-2300; fax (2) 261-3344; e-mail info@oiclife.com; internet www.oiclife.com; f. 1949; life; Chair. and Man. Dir KIRATI ASSAKUL.

Paiboon Insurance Co Ltd: Thai Life Insurance Bldg, 19th–20th Floors, 123 Thanon Ratchadapisek, Bangkok 10310; tel. (2) 246-9635; fax (2) 246-9660; f. 1927; non-life; Chair. ANUTHRA ASSAWANONDA; Pres. VANICH CHAIYAWAN.

Prudential TS Life Assurance Public Co Ltd: Sengthong Thani Tower, 30th–32nd Floors, 82 Thanon Sathorn Nua, Bangkok 10500; tel. (2) 639-9500; fax (2) 639-9699; e-mail customer.service.ptsl@ibm.net; internet www.prudential.co.th; f. 1983; Chair. Prof. BUNCHANA ATTHAKOR; Vice-Chair. DAN R. BARDIN.

Siam Commercial New York Life Insurance Public Co Ltd: 4th Floor, SCB Bldg 1, 1060 Thanon Petchburi, SCB Chidlom, Ratchathewi, Bangkok 10400; tel. (2) 655-3000; fax (2) 256-1517; e-mail don@scnyl.com; internet www.scnyl.com; f. 1976; life; Pres. and CEO C. DONALD CARDEN.

Southeast Insurance (2000) Co Ltd (Arkanay Prakan Pai Co Ltd): Southeast Insurance Bldg, 315G, 1–3 Thanon Silom, Bangrak, Bangkok 10500; tel. (2) 631-1331; f. 1946; life and non-life; Chair. CHAYUT CHIRALERSPONG; Gen. Man. NATDANAI INDRASUKHSRI.

Syn Mun Kong Insurance Public Co Ltd: 279 Thanon Srinakarin, Bangkapi, Bangkok 10240; tel. (2) 379-3140; fax (2) 731-6590; e-mail info@smk.co.th; internet www.smk.co.th; f. 1951; fire, marine, automobile and personal accident; Chair. THANAVIT DUSADEESURAPOJ; Man. Dir RUENGDEJ DUSADEESURAPOJ.

Thai Commercial Insurance Public Co Ltd: TISCO Tower Bldg, 12th Floor, 48/21 Thanon Sathorn Nua, Bangrak, Bangkok 10500; tel. (2) 236-5987; fax (2) 236-5990; f. 1940; automobile, fire, marine and casualty; Chair. SUKIT WANGLEE, SUCHIN WANGLEE; Man. Dir SURAJIT WANGLEE.

Thai Health Insurance Co Ltd: 123 Thanon Ratchadaphisek, Ding-Daeng, Bangkok 10320; tel. (2) 246-9680; fax (2) 246-9806; f. 1979; Chair. APIRAK THAIPATANAKUL; Man. Dir PRANEET VIRAKUL.

Thai Insurance Public Co Ltd: 34/3 Soi Lang Suan, Thanon Ploenchit, Lumpini, Pathumwan, Bangkok 10330; tel. (2) 652-2880; fax (2) 652-2870; e-mail tic@thaiins.com; internet www.thaiins.com; f. 1938; non-life; Chair. KAVI ANSVANANDA.

Thai Life Insurance Co Ltd: 123 Thanon Ratchadaphisek, Din-Daeng, Bangkok 10320; tel. (2) 247-0247; fax (2) 246-9945; e-mail prcenter@thailife.com; internet www.thailife.com; f. 1942; life; Chair. and CEO VANICH CHAIYAWAN; Pres. APIRAK THAIPATANAGUL.

Viriyah Insurance Co Ltd: Viriya Panich Bldg, 1242 Thanon Krung Kasem, Pomprapsattrupuy, Bangkok 10100; tel. (2) 223-0851; fax (2) 224-9876; e-mail info@viriyah.co.th; internet www.viriyah.co.th; Man. Dir SUVAPORN THONGTHEW.

Wilson Insurance Co Ltd: 18th Bangkok Insurance/YWCA Bldg, 25 Thanon Sathorn Tai, Thungmahamek, Sathorn, Bangkok 10120; tel. (2) 677-3999; fax (2) 677-3978; f. 1951; fire, marine, motor car, general; Chair. CHOTE SOPHONPANICH; Pres. NOPADOL SANTIPAKORN.

Associations

General Insurance Association: 223 Soi Ruamrudee, Thanon Witthayu, Bangkok 10330; tel. (2) 256-6032; fax (2) 256-6039; e-mail general@thaigia.com; internet www.thaigia.com; Exec. Dir CHALAW FUANGAROMYA.

Thai Life Assurance Association: 36/1 Soi Sapanku, Thanon Rama IV, Thungmahamek, Sathorn, Bangkok 10120; tel. (2) 287-4596; fax (2) 679-7100; e-mail tlaa@tlaa.org; internet www.tlaa.org; Pres. SUTTI RAJITRANGSON.

Trade and Industry

GOVERNMENT AGENCIES

Board of Investment (BOI): 555 Thanon Vipavadee Rangsit, Chatuchak, Bangkok 10900; tel. (2) 537-8111; fax (2) 537-8177; e-mail head@boi.go.th; internet www.boi.go.th; f. 1958 to publicize investment potential and encourage economically and socially beneficial investments and also to provide investment information; Chair. The Prime Minister; Sec.-Gen. SOMPHONG WANAPHA.

Board of Trade of Thailand: 150/2 Thanon Rajbopit, Bangkok 10200; tel. (2) 221-1827; fax (2) 225-3995; e-mail bot@tcc.or.th; internet www.tcc.or.th/bot/index2.htm; f. 1955; mems: chambers of commerce, trade asscns, state enterprises and co-operative societies (large and medium-sized companies have associate membership); Chair. AIVA TAULANANDA.

Central Sugar Marketing Centre: Bangkok; f. 1981; responsible for domestic marketing and price stabilization.

Financial Sector Restructuring Authority (FSRA): 130–132 Tower 3, Thanon Witthayu, Patumwan, Bangkok 10330; tel. (2) 263-2620; fax (2) 650-9872; e-mail webmaster@fra.or.th; internet www.fra.or.th; f. 1997 to oversee the restructuring of Thailand's financial system; Chair. KAMOL JUNTIMA, Sec. Gen. MONTRI CHENVIDAYAKAM.

Forest Industry Organization: 76 Thanon Ratchadamnoen Nok, Bangkok 10200; tel. (2) 282-3243; fax (2) 282-5197; e-mail info@fio.or.th; internet www.fio.or.th; f. 1947; oversees all aspects of forestry and wood industries; Man. Col M. R. ADULDEJ CHAKRABANDHU.

Office of the Cane and Sugar Board: Ministry of Industry, Thanon Phra Ram Hok, Bangkok 10400; tel. (2) 202-3291; fax (2) 202-3293; e-mail wimonlak@narai.oie.go.th.

Rubber Estate Organization: Nabon Station, Nakhon Si Thammarat Province 80220; tel. (75) 411554; internet www.reothai.com; Man. Dir SOMPHOL ISARATHANACHAI.

DEVELOPMENT ORGANIZATIONS

Industrial Finance Corpn of Thailand (IFCT): 1770 Thanon Petchburi Tadmai, Bangkok 10320; tel. (2) 253-7111; fax (2) 253-9677; e-mail info@ifct.co.th; internet www.ifct.co.th; f. 1959 to assist in the establishment, expansion or modernization of industrial enterprises in the private sector; organizes pooling of funds and capital market development; makes medium- and long-term loans, complementary working capital loans, investment advisory services, underwriting shares and securities and guaranteeing loans; Chair. Dr ARAN THAMMANO; Pres. ANOTHAI TECHAMONTRIKUL.

National Economic and Social Development Board: 962 Thanon Krung Kasem, Bangkok 10100; tel. (2) 282-8454; fax (2) 628-2871; e-mail mis@nesdb.go.th; internet www.nesdb.go.th; economic and social planning agency; Sec.-Gen. (vacant).

Royal Developments Projects Board: Office of the Prime Minister, Bangkok; internet www.rdpb.go.th; Sec.-Gen. Dr SUMET TANTIVEJKUL.

Small Industries Finance Office (SIFO): 24 Mansion 5, Thanon Ratchadamnoen, Bangkok 10200; tel. (2) 224-1919; f. 1964 to provide finance for small-scale industries; Chair. PISAL KONGSAMRAN; Man. VICHIEN OPASWATTANA.

CHAMBER OF COMMERCE

Thai Chamber of Commerce: 150 Thanon Rajbopit, Bangkok 10200; tel. (2) 622-1880; fax (2) 225-3372; e-mail tcc@tcc.or.th; internet www.tcc.or.th; f. 1946; 2,000 mems, 10 assoc. mems (1998); Chair Dr. AJVA TAULANANDA, Pres. VICHIEN TEJAPHAIBOON.

INDUSTRIAL AND TRADE ASSOCIATIONS

Bangkok Rice Millers' Association: 14/3 Thanon Sathorn Tai, Bangkok 10120; tel. (2) 286-8298.

The Federation of Thai Industries: Queen Sirikit National Convention Center, Zone C, 4th Floor, 60 Thanon Ratchadaphisek Tadmai, Klongtoey, Bangkok 10110; tel. (2) 229-4255; fax (2) 229-4941; e-mail fa-dept@off.fti.or.th; internet www.fti.or.th; f. 1987, fmrly The Association of Thai Industries; 4,800 mems; Chair. TAWEE BUTSUNTORN.

Mining Industry Council of Thailand: 222/2 Soi, Thai Chamber of Commerce University, Thanon Vibhavadi Rangsit, Dindaeng, Huay Kwang, Bangkok 10400; tel. (2) 275-7684; fax (2) 275-7686; f. 1983; intermediary between govt organizations and private mining enterprises; Pres. DARMP TEWTHONG; Sec.-Gen. PUNYA ADULYAPICHIT.

Rice Exporters' Association of Thailand: 37 Soi Ngamdupli, Thanon Phra Ram IV, Bangkok 10120; tel. (2) 287-2674; fax (2) 287-2678; e-mail reat@ksc.th.com; Chair. SMARN OPHASWONGSE.

Rice Mill Association of Thailand: 81–81/1 Trok Rongnamkheng, 24 Thanon Charoenkrung, Talat Noi, Sampanthawong, Bangkok 10100; tel. (2) 235-7863; fax (2) 234-7286; Pres. NIPHON WONGTRAGARN.

Sawmills Association: 101 Thanon Amnuaysongkhram, Dusit, Bangkok 10300; tel. (2) 243-4754; fax (2) 243-8629; e-mail smassoc@mail.cscoms.com; Pres. VITOON PONGPASIT.

Thai Diamond Manufacturers Association: Bangkok; tel. (2) 390-0341; 11-mem. board; Pres. CHIRAKITTI TANGKATHAC.

Thai Food Processors' Association: Tower 1, Ocean Bldg, 9th Floor, 170/21–22 Thanon Rajchadapisaktadmai, Klongtoey, Bangkok 10110; tel. (2) 261-2995; fax (2) 261-2996-7; e-mail thaifood@thaifood.org; internet www.thaifood.org.

Thai Jute Mill Association: Sivadol Bldg, 10th Floor, Rm 10, 1 Thanon Convent, Silom, Bangrak, Bangkok 10500; tel. (2) 234-1438; fax (2) 234-1439.

Thai Lac Association: 66 Soi Chalermkhetr 1, Thanon Yukul, Pomprab, Bangkok 10100; tel. (2) 233-8331.

Thai Maize and Produce Traders' Association: Sathorn Thani II Bldg, 11th Floor, 92/26–27 Thanon Sathorn Nua, Bangrak, Bangkok 10500; tel. (2) 234-4387; fax (2) 236-8413.

Thai Pharmaceutical Manufacturers Association: 188/107 Thanon Charansanitwongs, Banchanglaw, Bangkoknoi, Bangkok 10700; tel. (2) 863-5106; fax (2) 863-5108; e-mail tpma@asiaaccess.net.th; f. 1969; Pres. CHERNPORN TENGAMNUAY.

Thai Rubber Traders' Association: 57 Thanon Rongmuang 5, Pathumwan, Bangkok 10500; tel. (2) 214-3420; f. 1951; Pres. SANG UDOMJARUMANCE.

Thai Silk Association: Textile Industry Division, Soi Trimitr, Thanon Rama IV, Klongtoey, Bangkok 10110; tel. (2) 712-4328; fax (2) 391-2896; e-mail thsilkas@thaitextile.org; internet www.thaitextile.org/tsa; f. 1962; Pres. MONTIGAN LOVICHIT.

Thai Sugar Producers' Association: 8th Floor, Thai Ruam Toon Bldg, 794 Thanon Krung Kasem, Pomprap, Bangkok 10100; tel. (2) 282-0990; fax (2) 281-0342.

Thai Sugar Manufacturing Association: 20th Floor, Gypsum Metropolitan Tower, 539/2 Thanon Sri Ayudhya, Rajdhareé, Bangkok 10400; tel. (2) 642-5248; fax (2) 642-5251; e-mail tsma2000@cscoms.com.

Thai Tapioca Trade Association: Sathorn Thani II Bldg, 20th Floor, 92/58 Thanon Sathorn Nua, Silom, Bangkok 10500; tel. (2) 234-4724; fax (2) 236-6084; e-mail ttta@loxinfo.co.th; internet www.ttta-tapioca.org; Pres. SEREE DENWORALAK.

Thai Textile Manufacturing Association: 454–460 Thanon Sukhumvit, Klongton, Klongtoey, Bangkok 10110; tel. (2) 258-2023; fax (2) 260-1525; e-mail ttma@thaitextile.org; internet www.thaitextile.org/ttma.

Thai Timber Exporters' Association: Ratchada Trade Centre, 4th Floor, 410/73–76 Thanon Ratchadaphisek, Bangkok 10310; tel. (2) 278-3229; fax (2) 259-0481.

Timber Merchants' Association: 4 Thanon Yen-Arkad, Thung-Mahamek, Yannawa, Bangkok 10120; tel. (2) 249-5565.

Union Textile Merchants' Association: 562 ESPREME Bldg, 4th Floor, Soi Watgunmatuyalarm, Thanon Rajchawong, Samphanthawong, Bangkok 10100; tel. (2) 622-6711; fax (2) 622-6714; e-mail utma@thaitextile.org; internet www.thaitextile.org/utma; Chair. SURAPHOL TIYAVACHRAPONG.

UTILITIES

Electricity

Cogeneration Public Co Ltd: Grand Amarin Tower, 29th Floor, 1550 Thanon Petchburi Tadmai, Rachtavee, Bangkok 10320; tel. (2) 207-0970; fax (2) 207-0910; generation and supply of co-generation power; cap. and res 5,634m., sales 3,424m. (1996/97); Chair. PIERRE CHARLES E. SWARTENBROEK; Pres. CHANCHAI JIVACATE.

Electricity Generating Authority of Thailand (EGAT): 53 Thanon Charan Sanit Wong, Bang Kruai, Nothaburi, Bangkok 11130; tel. (2) 436-4800; fax (2) 436-4879; internet www.egat.or.th; f. 1969; scheduled for transfer to the private sector; Gov. VITAYA KOTCHARUG.

Electricity Generating Public Co Ltd (EGCO): EGCO Bldg, 222 Moo 5, Thanon Vibhavadi Rangsit, Tungsonghong, Laksi, Bangkok 10210; tel. (2) 955-0955; fax (2) 955-0956; e-mail electric@egco.com; internet www.egco.com; a subsidiary of the Electricity Generating

Authority of Thailand (EGAT); 59% transferred to the private sector in 1994–96; 14.9%-owned by China Light and Power Co (Hong Kong); Pres. SITTHIPORN RATANOPAS.

The Metropolitan Electricity Authority: 30 Soi Chidlom Ploenchit, Lumpini, Pathumwan, Bangkok 10330; tel. (2) 254-9550; fax (2) 253-1424; internet www.mea.or.th; one of the two main power distribution agencies in Thailand; Gov. YONGYUTH SRICHAROEN.

The Provincial Electricity Authority: 200 Thanon Ngam Wongwan, Chatuchak, Bangkok 10900; tel. (2) 589-0100; fax (2) 589-4850; e-mail vibulya@pca.or.th; f. 1960; one of the two main power distribution agencies in Thailand.

Water

Metropolitan Waterworks Authority: 18/137 Thanon Prachachuen, Don Muang, Bangkok 10210; tel. (2) 504-0123; fax (2) 503-9493; e-mail mwa1125@water.mwa.or.th; internet www.mwa.or.th; f. 1967; state-owned; provides water supply systems in Bangkok; Gov. CHUANPIT DHAMASIRI.

Provincial Waterworks Authority: 72 Thanon Chaengwattana, Don Muang, Bangkok 10210; tel. (2) 551-1020; fax (2) 552-1547; e-mail pwait2000@yahoo.com; internet www.pwa.thaigov.net; f. 1979; provides water supply systems except in Bangkok Metropolis; Gov. THANYA HARNPOL; Dep. Gov. WANCHAI GHOOPRASERT.

CO-OPERATIVES

In 1992 there were 4m. members of co-operatives, including 1.6m. in agriculture.

MAJOR COMPANIES

(cap. = capital; res = reserves; m. = million; amounts in baht, unless otherwise stated)

Advance Agro Public Co Ltd: 1 Moo 2, Tha Toom District, Amphur Sri Mata Phote, Prachinburi 25140; tel. (37) 208-800; fax (37) 208-850; e-mail shs@sshs.co.th; internet www.advanceagro.com; mfrs of paper; cap. and res 4,709m., sales 14,962m. (2000); Chair. CHANCHAI LEETAVORN.

AIG Finance (Thailand) Public Co Ltd: 102 Soi Aree, Sukhumvit 26, Bangkok 10110; tel. (2) 259-0063; fax (2) 259-7390; e-mail agift1@samart.co.th; internet www.aigfinance.th; finance and securities co; cap. and res 804m. (2000), sales 881m. (1998); Chair. TSE EDMUND SZE WING; Man. Dir SORNTHEP GOMUTPUTRA.

Alphatec Electronics Public Co Ltd: Times Square Bldg, 19th Floor, 246 Sukhumvit, Soi 12-14, Bangkok 10110; tel. (2) 229-4678; fax (2) 229-4677; internet www.alphatec.co.th; mfr of integrated circuits; cap. and res 3,857m., sales 12,241m. (1996); Chair. THAMNU WANGLEE; Chief Exec. ROBERT MOLLERSTEUN (acting).

American Standard Sanitary Ware (Thailand) Public Co Ltd: 1/6 Moo 1, Thanon Phaholyothin, Km 32, Tambol Klongnung, Amphur Klongluang, Pathumthani 12120; tel. (2) 901-4455; fax (2) 901-4422; internet www.americanstandard.com; f. 1969; mfrs of sanitary ware; cap. and res 1,056m., sales 1,414m. (2000); Chair. CHALERMBHAND SRIVIKORN; Man. Dir NORMAN D. LIVINGSTONE; 1,300 employees.

Asia Fiber Public Co Ltd: Wall Street Tower, 27th Floor, 33/133–136 Thanon Surawong, Bangkok 10500; tel. (2) 632-7071; fax (2) 236-1982; e-mail afcny6@ksc.th.com; internet www.asiafiber.com; f. 1970; mfrs of nylon filament yarn, nylon textured yarn, filament woven fabrics; cap. and res 769m., sales 1,643m. (1999/2000); Chair. PIPAT SIRIKIETSOONG; Pres. CHEN NAMCHAISIRI; 1,424 employees.

Bangchak Petroleum Public Co Ltd: 38 Thanon Srinakarin, Prawet, Bangkok 10260; tel. (2) 301-2700; fax (2) 301-2726; internet www.bangchak.co.th; f. 1984; refining and distribution of petroleum; cap. and res 4,463m., sales 52,118m. (2000); Chair. SOMMAI PHASEE.

Bangkok Agro-Industrial Products Public Co Ltd: C.P. Tower, 313 Thanon Silom, Bangrak, Bangkok 10500; tel. (2) 231-0231; fax (2) 238-1921; mfrs and distributors of animal feedstuffs, animal husbandry, poultry and swine breeding, fruit production; cap. and res 3,066m., sales 4,596m. (1998); Chair. JARAN CHIARAVANONT; Pres. ADIREK SRIPRATAK; 1,650 employees.

Bangkok Expressway Public Co Ltd: 238/7 Thanon Asoke-Dindaeng, Bangkapi, Huay Kwang, Bangkok 10320; tel. (2) 641-4611; fax (2) 641-4610; engaged in the construction and management of Thailand's second stage expressway project; cap. and res -35,087m., sales 5,531m. (2000); Chair. VIRABONGSA RAMANGKURA.

Bangkok Produce Merchandizing PCL: CP Tower Bldg, 18th Floor, 313 Thanon Silom, Bangkok 10500; tel. (2) 638-2000; fax (2) 631-0787; f. 1978; production of processed chicken; cap. and res 1,316m., sales 18,495m. (1995); Chair. DHANIN CHIRAVANONT; Pres. EAM NGAMDAMRONK; 4,000 employees.

Bangkok Rubber Public Co Ltd: 611/40 Soi Watchan Nai, Bangklo, Bangkloaem, Bangkok 10120; tel. (2) 689-9500; fax (2) 291-1353; f. 1974; mfrs of sports shoes and other footwear; cap. and res 2,946m., sales 5,800m. (2000); Chair. NARONG CHOKWATANA; Pres. BOONSONG TONDULYAKUL; 2,369 employees.

Bangkok Steel Industry Public Co Ltd: United Flour Mill Bldg, 5th and 7th Floors, 205 Thanon Rajawongse, Chakkawad, Sampantawongse, Bangkok 10100; tel. (2) 225-0200; fax (2) 222-7497; f. 1964; mfrs of steel products; cap. and res 4,681m., sales 4,071m. (1999); Chair. PRASERT TANGTRONGSAKDI; Pres. PICHIT NITHIVASAN; Man. Dir JARAY BHUMICHITRA; 1,200 employees.

Banpu Public Co Ltd: Grand Amarin Tower, 26th–28th Floors, 1550 Thanon Petchburi Tadmai, Bangkok 10310; tel. (2) 207-0688; fax (2) 207-0697; e-mail piyanuch_j@banpu.co.th; internet www.banpu.co.th; mineral mining and power generation; cap. and res 5,257m., sales 4,439m. (1999/2000); Chair. METHA AUAPINYAKUL, CHANIN VONGKUSOLIT; 884 employees.

Berli Jucker Public Co Ltd: Berli Jucker House, 99 Soi Rubia, 42 Thanon Sukhumvit, Klongtoey, Prakanong, Bangkok 10110; tel. (2) 367-1111; fax (2) 367-1000; e-mail bjc@berlijucker.co.th; internet www.berlijucker.co.th; f. 1882; engineering; mfr and distribution of consumer, imaging and technical products and packaging; cap. and res 5,991m., sales 11,497m. (2000); Chair. PITI SITHI-AMNUAI; Pres. DAVID NICOL; 5,700 employees.

Boon Rawd Brewery Co Ltd: 999 Thanon Samsen, Dusit, Bangkok 10300; tel. (2) 669-2050; fax (2) 669-2089; e-mail nanthawan@boonrawd.co.th; internet www.boonrawd.co.th; f. 1933; mfrs of beer and soft drinks; sales 24,010m. (1994); Chair. PIYA BHIROM BHAKDI; 2,300 employees.

Caltex Oil (Thailand) Ltd: 14–26 Sun Towers B, 123 Thanon Vibhavadi Rangsit, Jautchak, Bangkok 10900; tel. (2) 617-6888; fax (2) 617-6828; e-mail nanthapolc@caltex.co.th; internet www.caltex.co.th; f. 1946; distributors of petroleum products; sales 20,144m. (1994); Chief Exec. STEPHEN LONG; 350 employees.

Central Pattana Public Co Ltd: Central Plaza Lardprao, 12th–13th Floors, 1693 Thanon Phaholyothin, Lardyao, Chatuchak, Bangkok 10900; tel. (2) 937-1555; fax (2) 937-1578; e-mail cpnternt@ksc11.ksc.co.th; internet www.centralpattana.co.th; engaged in property investment, development, management and construction; cap. and res 3,642m. (2000), sales 550m. (1998); Chair. VANCHAI CHIRATHIVAT.

CH Karnchang Public Co Ltd: 587 Thanon Sutthisarn, Dindaeng Dindaeng, Bangkok 10400; tel. (2) 277-0460; fax (2) 275-7029; constructor and sub-contractor, engaged in general construction; cap. and res -618m., sales 5,633m. (2000); Chair. THAVORN TRIVISVAVET; Pres. PLEW TRIVISVAVET.

Charoen Pokphand Foods Public Co Ltd: CP Tower, 14th Floor, 313 Thanon Silom, Bangkok 10500; tel. (2) 638-2936; fax (2) 638-2942; e-mail iroffice@cp-foods.com; internet www.cp-foods.com; f. 1921; mfrs of feed for poultry, pigs and prawns; poultry and pig breeding; cap. and res 22,708m., sales 61,958m. (2000); Chair. and CEO DHANIN CHEARAVANONT; Pres. PHONG VISEDPAITOON; 3,953 employees.

Charoen Pokphand Northeastern Public Co Ltd: C.P. Tower, 14th Floor, 313 Thanon Silom, Bangkok 10500; tel. (2) 631-0671; fax (2) 631-0863; f. 1984; animal food mfr; cap. and res 1,043m., sales 5,308m. (1998); Chair. PRASERT POONGKUMARN; Man. Dir ADIREK SRIPRATAK.

Christiani and Nielsen (Thai) PCL: 50/670 Thanon Sukhumvit, 105 (Soi La Salle) Baangna, Bangkok 10260; tel. (2) 398-0158; fax (2) 398-9860; e-mail cnt@cn-thai.co.th; internet www.cn-thai.co.th; f. 1930; construction and property investment; cap. and res 209m., sales 8,846m. (1999); Chair. ANANT ASAVABHOKHIN: Chair. and Man. Dir SUTHEP PONSOMBOON; 16,200 employees.

Delta Electronics (Thailand) Public Co Ltd: 909 Moo 4, Tambon Prakasa, Amphur Muang, Samutprakarn 10280; tel. (2) 709-2800; fax (2) 709-3790; e-mail mae@delta.co.th; internet www.delta.co.th; design and manufacture of electronic and electrical equipment; cap and res 13,529m., sales 27,037m. (2000); Chair. JAMES NG KONG MENG.

Diethelm and Co Ltd: Diethelm Towers, 93/1 Thanon Witthayu, Lumpini Pathumwan, Bangkok 10330; tel. (2) 251-1700; fax (2) 256-0267; f. 1906; retailers of industrial equipment; sales 13,737m. (1994); Chair. MARK DIETHELM; 2,712 employees.

Esso (Thailand) Public Co Ltd: 3195/17–29 Thanon Phra Rama IV, Klongtoey, Bangkok 10110; tel. (2) 262-4000; fax (2) 262-4800; internet www.exxon.com; f. 1965; distributors of petroleum products; sales US $1,601m. (1998); Man. Dir WILLIAM M. COLTON.

GFPT Public Co Ltd: 69/6–13 Thanon Suksawatdi, Ratburana, Bangkok 10140; tel. (2) 463-0040; fax (2) 463-5751; f. 1981; producers of frozen chicken; cap. and res 1,677m., sales 5,835m. (1998); Chair. CHAROEN SIRIMONGKOLKASEM; Man. Dir VIRACH SIRIMONGKOLKASEM; 4,856 employees.

Grammy Entertainment Public Co Ltd: 209/1 CMIC Tower-B, Thanon Asoke, Klongtoey, Bangkok 10110; tel. (2) 664-4000; fax (2)

664-0248; internet www.grammy.co.th; operators of media businesses, including television and radio; cap. and res 3,198m., sales 2,232m. (2000); Chair. PAIBOON DAMRONGCHAITHAM.

GSS ARRAY Technology Public Co Ltd: 94 Moo 1, Hi-Tech Industrial Estate, Thanon Banlane, A. Bang Pa-In, Ayudhya 13160; tel. (3) 535-0890; fax (3) 535-0945; f. 1985; electronics contract manufacturing; cap. and res 633m., sales 9,766m. (1998); Chair. GARY M. STICKLES, ROBERT E. ZIMM; 3,112 employees.

Hemaraj Land and Development Public Co Ltd: UM Tower, 18th Floor, 9 Thanon Ramkhamhaeng, Suanluang, Bangkok 10250; tel. (2) 719-9555; fax (2) 719-9546; e-mail sales@hemaraj.com; internet www.hemaraj.com; engaged in property development; cap. and res 1,829m., sales 577m. (1999); Chair. SAWASDI HORRUNGRUANG; Man. Dir DAVID NARDONE.

Honda Automobile (Thailand) Co Ltd: 2754/1 Soi Sukhumvit 66/1, Thanon Sukhumvit, Khwang Bangna, Khet Bangna, Bangkok 10260; tel. (2) 744-7744; fax (2) 744-7755; internet www.honda.th.com; f. 1983; mfrs of motor vehicles; sales 24,895m. (1994); Chair. SAICHIRO FUJIE; Man. Dir NOBUNARI MATSUSHITA.

ICC International Public Co Ltd: 757/10 Soi Pradoo, 1 Thanon Sadhupradit, Yannawa, Bangkok 10120; tel. (2) 294-0281; fax (2) 294-3024; e-mail webmaster@icc.co.th; internet www.icc.co.th; distributors of consumer goods; cap. and res 7,191m., sales 8,034m. (2000); Chair. SOM CHATUSRIPITAK; Pres. BOONKIET CHOKWATANA; 4,126 employees.

Italian-Thai Development Corpn PCL: 2034/132-161 Italthai Tower, Thanon Petchburi Tadmai, Bangkapi, Bangkok 10320; tel. (2) 716-1600; fax (2) 716-1488; e-mail itdmail@italian-thai.co.th; internet www.italian-thai.co.th; f. 1958; construction; cap. and res 2,106m., sales 14,696m. (2000); Chair. Dr CHAIJUDH KARNASUTA; Pres. PREMCHAI KARNASUTA.

Jalaprathan Cement Public Co Ltd: 2974 Thanon Petchburi Tadmai, Bangkapi, Huay Kwang, Bangkok 10320; tel. (2) 318-7111; fax (2) 318-3469; f. 1956; mfrs of cement; cap. and res 2,109m., sales 1,418m. (2000); Chair. Gen. AYUPOON KARNASUTA; Man. Dirs XAVIER MARCEL HERVE BLUTEL and RAPEE SUKHAYANGA; 766 employees.

Jasmine International PCL: 29th–30th Floors, 200 Thanon Chaengwatana, Pakkred, Nonthaburi, Bangkok 11120; tel. (2) 502-3000; fax (2) 502-3150; e-mail webmaster@jasmine.th.com; internet www.jasmine.com; mfrs and distributors of telecommunications equipment; cap. and res -3,891m., sales 4,469m. (2000); Chair. THANPUYING NIRAMOL SURIYASAT; 1,075 employees.

KGI Securities (Thailand) Public Co: 323 United Center Bldg, 9th Floor (Trading Rm), Thanon Silom, Bangkok 10500; tel. (2) 231-1111; fax (2) 231-1524; e-mail ebusiness@securities-one.com; internet www.kgieworld.co.th; finance co engaged in securities broking, dealing and investment advice; cap. and res 5,459m. (2000), sales 1,219m. (1998); 51% owned by a Taiwan-based co; Chair. ANGELO KOO JOHN YNN.

Krungthai Thanakit Public Co Ltd: Sermitt Tower, 14–17th Floors, 159 Thanon Sukhumvit 21 (Asoke), Khweang Klongtoey Nua, Khet Klongtoey, Bangkok 10110; tel. (2) 261-7373; fax (2) 261-7447; state-owned finance and securities co; cap. and res -747m., sales 5,641m. (1998); Chair. SIRIN NIMMANAHAEMINDA; Pres. PHIRASILP SUBHAPHOLSIRI.

Lee Feed Mill Public Co Ltd: Wall Street Tower, 28th Floor, 33/137 Thanon Surawongse, Bangkok 10500; tel. (2) 632-7300; fax (2) 236-7751; f. 1984; mfrs of feed for livestock; cap. and res 1,293m., sales 2,385m. (2000); Chair. VISITH LEELASITHORN; Man. Dir NIPON LEELASITHORN.

Loxley Public Co Ltd: 102 Thanon Na Ranong, Klongtoey, Bangkok 10110; tel. (2) 240-3000; fax (2) 240-3101; e-mail editor@loxley.co.th; internet www.loxley.co.th; f. 1939; information technology, infrastructure, telecommunications, consumer electronics, consumer products, chemicals, construction materials, environment, media and entertainment; cap. and res 1,198m., sales 8,428m. (2001); Chair. PIROTE LAMSAM; Man. Dir DHONGCHAI LAMSAM.

Luckytex (Thailand) Public Co Ltd: Bubhajit Bldg, 5th Floor, 20 Thanon Sathorn Nua, Silom, Bangrak, Bangkok 10500; tel. (2) 266-6600; fax (2) 238-3957; e-mail luckeytex@loxinfo.co.th; internet www.toray.com; mfrs of spun fabrics and yarn; cap. and res 1,735m., sales 6,116m. (2000/01); Chair. MINORU KADOWAKI; 2,426 employees.

Millennium Steel Public Co Ltd: UM Tower, 19th Floor, 9 Thanon Ramkhamhaeng, Suanluang, Bangkok 10250; tel. (2) 719-9800; fax (2) 719-9820; e-mail karnchana@nts.co.th; f. 2002 following merger between steel-producing facilities of Siam Cement Public Co Ltd and NTS Steel Group Public Co Ltd; mfrs of steel rods and bars; Chair. SAWASDI HORRUNGRUANG.

Minebea (Thai) Ltd: Thanon Paholyothin 1, Chiangkraknoi, Ayudhya 13180; tel. (35) 361429; fax (35) 361177; internet www.minebea.co.th; f. 1984; mfrs of electrical goods and electronic components; sales 22,308m. (1994/95); Man. Dir RYUSUKE MIZUKAMI.

Natural Park Public Co Ltd: 88 Soi Klang (Sukhumvit 49), Klongton Nua Wattana, Bangkok 10110; tel. (2) 259-4800; fax (2) 260-5059; developers of real estate; cap. and res -13,143m., sales 779m. (1999); Chair. VIRAVUDH ASSAKUL; Man. Dir THOSAPONG JARUTHAVEE.

NEP Realty and Industry Public Co Ltd: 41 Thanon Phaholyothin, Soi 5, Phayathai, Bangkok 10400; tel. (2) 271-4213; fax (2) 271-4416; e-mail nepgroup@tcc.or.th; mfrs and distributors of jute products; cap. and res 361m., sales 750m. (1999); Chair. PHORNSAKE KARNCHANACHARI; Man. Dir NISAN PRATHANRASNIKORN; 1,200 employees.

Padaeng Industry Public Co Ltd: CTI Tower, 26th–27th Floors, 191/18–25 Thanon Ratchadaphisek, Klongtoey, Bangkok 10110; tel. (2) 661-9900; fax (2) 661-9490; e-mail padaeng@inet.co.th; internet www.padaeng.co.th; f. 1981; miners and refiners of zinc ingot and zinc alloy; cap. and res 2,346m. (2000), sales 5,222m. (2001); Chair. ARSA SARASIN; CEO PINIT VONGMASA; Man. Dir ANDRE R. VAN DER HEYDEN; 751 employees.

Pakfood Public Co Ltd: 103 Soi Ruammitr, Thanon Nonsee, Yannawa, Bangkok 10120; tel. (2) 295-1991; fax (2) 295-2002; f. 1984; processors and exporters of frozen seafood; cap. and res 300m. (2000), sales 6,745m. (2001); Pres. YONG AREECHAROENLERT; Man. Dir WIWAT KANOKWATANAWAN; 3,788 employees.

Petroleum Authority of Thailand (PTT): 555 Thanon Vibhavadi Rangsit, Bangkok 10900; tel. (2) 537-2000; fax (2) 537-3499; internet www.ptt.or.th; f. 1978; activities relate to the development, exploitation, production and distribution of petroleum and gas; regrouped its business into two subsidiaries in February 1996: PTT Oil, comprising all domestic operations and PTT International; 100% state-owned; scheduled for transfer to the private sector; Chair. SIVAVONG CHANGKASIRI; Gov. VISET CHOOPIBAN.

Phoenix Pulp and Paper Public Co Ltd: Ocean Tower II, 42nd Floor, 75/120–121 Sukhumvit Soi 19, North Klongtoey, Wattana, Bangkok 10110; tel. (2) 661-7755; fax (2) 665-7231-3; e-mail vashi@phoenixpulp.com; mfrs of pulp and paper; cap. and res 2,369m. (1998), sales 4,318m. (2001); Chair. CHUMPOL NALAMLIENG; Exec. Dir VASHI T. PURSWANI.

Pranda Jewelry PLC: 333 Soi Rungsang, Thanon Bangna-Trat, Bangna, Bangkok 10260; tel. (2) 361-3311; fax (2) 399-4877; e-mail prida@pranda.co.th; producers and exporters of jewellery; cap. and res 98m., sales 2,187m. (1999); Chair. PRIDA TIASUWAN; 2,631 employees.

PTT Exploration and Production PCL (PTTEP): PTTEP Bldg, 555 Thanon Rangsit Vibhavadi, Chatuchak, Bangkok 10900; tel. (2) 537-4000; fax (2) 537-4444; internet www.pttep.com; f. 1985; extraction and refining of petroleum; cap. and res 19,385m., sales 21,519m. (2000); Chair. MANU LEOPAIROTE; Pres. CHITRAPONGSE KWANGSUKSTITH.

Rubber Estate Organization: Nabon Station, Nakhon Si Thammarat Province 80220; tel. (75) 411554; 100% state-owned; Man. Dir SOMPHOL ISARATHANACHAI.

Saha-Union Public Co Ltd: 1828 Thanon Sukhumvit, Phrakanong, Bangkok 10250; tel. (2) 311-5111; fax (2) 332-5616; internet www.sahaunion.co.th; f. 1972; holding co whose subsidiaries produce textiles, plastic and rubber products, garment accessories and footwear; cap. and res 9,991m., sales 18,181m. (2000); Chair. ANAND PANYARACHUN; Pres. KAMOL KHOOSUWAN; 16,564 employees.

Sahaviriya Steel Industries Public Co Ltd: 2nd–3rd Floors, Prapawit Bldg, 28/1 Thanon Surasek, Silom Bangrak, Bangkok 10500; tel. (2) 238-3063-82; fax (2) 236-8890; internet www.ssi-steel.com; f. 1990; mfrs of hot-rolled coils; cap. and res 5,022m., sales 16,325m. (2000); Chair. MARUAY PHADOONSIDHI; Chair. WIT VIRIYAPRAPAIKIT; 719 employees.

Sanyo Universal Electric Public Co Ltd: 19 Soi Udomsuk (103), Moo 5, Thanon Sukhumvit, Pravej, Bangkok 10260; tel. (2) 398-0120; fax (2) 398-4708; f. 1958; mfrs and distributors of electronic equipment and electrical appliances; cap. and res -602m., sales 3,988m. (1999); Chair. Squadron Leader PRAMUDE BURANASIRI, SURADEJ BOOTYAWATANA; 3,918 employees.

Seagate Technology (Thailand) Ltd: Moo 7, 1627 Thanon Theparak, Theparak Muang, Samutprakan 10270; tel. (2) 383-5779; fax (2) 383-5736; internet www.seagate.com; f. 1983; mfrs of computer hardware; sales 32,429m. (1994); Man. Dir JIRAPANNEE SUPRATCHYA.

Serm Suk Public Co Ltd (The): Muang Thai Phatra Complex, 27th–28th Floors, 252/35–36 Thanon Ratchadaphisek, Huay Kwang, Bangkok 10310; tel. (2) 693-2255; fax (2) 693-2266; e-mail sermsuk@thai.com; f. 1952; mfrs and distributors of carbonated soft drinks; cap. and res 3,712m., sales 14,095m. (2000); Chair. and Chief Exec. NETR CHANTRASMI; Pres. SOMCHAI BULSOOK; 8,276 employees.

Sharp Appliances (Thailand) Ltd: Moo 5, 64 T. Bang Samak, Pakong, Cachoengsao 24130; tel. (38) 538663; fax (38) 538863;

f. 1987; mfrs of kitchen equipment and other electronic household appliances; sales 9,656m. (1994/95); Man. Dir YASUO SHIN.

Shell Company of Thailand Ltd, The: 10 Thanon Soonthornkosa, Klongtoey, Bangkok 10110; tel. (2) 249-0491; fax (2) 249-8393; internet www.shell.com; distributors of petroleum products; sales 44,677m. (1995, est.); Chair. J. WITHRINGTON.

Shin Corporation Public Co Ltd: Shinawatra Tower, 414 Thanon Paholyothin, Samsennai, Payathai, Bangkok 10400; tel. (2) 299-5000; fax (2) 299-5224; e-mail investor@shincorp.com; internet www.shincorps.com; f. 1983; mfrs and distributors of mobile telephones, pagers and other telecommunications equipment; cap. and res 12,484m., sales 6,868m. (2000); Chair. BHANAPOT DAMAPONG; 1,620 employees.

Shin Satellite Public Co Ltd: 41/103 Thanon Rattanathibet, Nonthaburi 11000; tel. (2) 591-0736; fax (2) 591-0705; e-mail richardw@thaicom.net; internet www.thaicom.net; operation and administration of satellite projects; cap. and res -2,878m., sales 4,017m. (2000); Chair. PARON ISRASENA NA AYUDHAYA.

Siam Cement Public Co Ltd: 1 Thanon Siam Cement, Bangsue, Bangkok 10800; tel. (2) 586-3333; fax (2) 587-2199; internet www.siamcement.com; f. 1913; parent company of Siam Cement Group, Thailand's largest industrial group, with subsidiaries manufacturing cement and construction materials, machinery, electrical goods, pulp and paper; cap. and res 66,085m., sales 122,643m. (2001); Chair. CHAOVANA NA SYLVANTA; Pres. CHUMPOL NA LAMLIENG; 25,000 employees.

Siam City Cement Public Co Ltd: 14th Floor, Ploenchit Tower, 898 Thanon Ploenchit, Bangkok 10330; tel. (2) 272-5555; fax (2) 263-0555; e-mail pr@sccc.co.th; internet www.siamcitycement.com; f. 1969; mfrs of cement and ready-mixed concrete; cap. and res 14,030m., sales 14,256m. (2000); Chair. KRIT RATANARAK; Man. Dir VINCENT BICHET; 6,288 employees.

Siam Nissan Automobile Co Ltd: 74 Moo 2 Soi, Thanon Bang-Na Trad Km 21, Yai Bang Phili, Samutprakarn 10540; tel. (2) 215-0830; fax (2) 215-9433; f. 1973; mfrs of motor vehicles; sales 20,576m. (1994); Man. Dir PHOMPONG PHORNPRAPHA.

Siam Pulp and Paper Public Co Ltd: 1 Thanon Siam Cement, Bangsue, Bangkok 10800; tel. (2) 586-3333; fax (2) 587-0738; e-mail chantimn@cementthai.co.th; internet www.cementthai.co.th; mfrs of paper pulp; cap. and res 8,742m., sales 27,350m. (2000); chair. CHUMPOL NA LAMLIENG; Man. Dir CHAISAK SAENG-XUTO; 4,074 employees.

Siam Tyre Public Co Ltd: 32 Thanon Poochaosmingprai, Samrongklang, Phrapradaeng, Samuthprakarn 10130; tel. (2) 615-0177; fax (2) 615-0180; f. 1962; mfrs and distributors of tyres and auto accessories; subsidiary of Siam Cement Public Co Ltd; sales 11,482m. (1998); Chair. OSOT KOSIN; Pres. CHALALUCK BUNNAG; 950 employees.

Siam Yamaha Co Ltd: 1 Thanon Dindang, Samseannai, Phyathai, Bangkok 10400; tel. (2) 245-7820; fax (2) 246-2779; f. 1964; mfrs of motor vehicles; sales 14,010m. (1995, est.); Pres. KASEM NARONGDEJ.

Siew National Sales and Service Co Ltd: 48/17–18 Moo 9, Thanon Ladprao, Wangthonghang, Bangkok 10310; tel. (2) 514-0500; fax (2) 538-3728; f. 1970; distributors of domestic electronic goods; sales 9,242m. (1994); Man. Dir K. WATANABE.

Srithai Superware Public Co Ltd: 355 Soi 36, Thanon Suksawat, Bangpakok, Rasburana, Bangkok 10140; tel. (2) 427-0088; fax (2) 871-1378; internet www.srithaisuperware.com; f. 1964; mfrs of plastic products and melamine tableware; cap. and res US $63m., sales US $73m. (2001); Chair. SUMIT LERTSUMITKUL; Pres. SANAN ANGUBOLKUL; 3,500 employees.

Thai Arrow Products Ltd: 460/1-9 Soi Siam Sq. Zone 4, Rama 1 Rd, Pathumwam, Bangkok 10330; tel. (2) 254-7860; fax (2) 255-4457; f. 1963; mfrs of electrical equipment for motor vehicles; sales 10,602m. (1995); Chair. YAZUMI OISHI.

Thai-Asahi Glass Public Co Ltd: Cathay Trust Bldg, 3rd Floor, 1016 Thanon Phra Ram IV, Bangkok 10500; tel. (2) 633-8800; fax (2) 633-8836; e-mail tag-mkt@ksc.th.com; internet www.thaiasahi.com; mfrs of plain glass; cap. and res 1,161m., sales 1,259m. (1999); Chair. AKIO TAKABE; Man. Dirs CHAIKIRI SRIFUENGFUNG, OSAMU YOSHIDA; 600 employees.

Thai Carbon Black Public Co Ltd: Mahatun Plaza Bldg, 16th Floor, 888/162-163, Thanon Ploenchit, Lumpini, Patumwan, Bangkok 10330; tel. (2) 253-6745; fax (2) 254-9031; e-mail pawantcb@loxinfo.co.th; internet www.thaicarbon.com; chemical products; cap. and res 2,929m., sales 3,015m. (2000); Chair. KUMAR MANGALAM BIRLA.

Thai Central Chemical Public Co Ltd: Metro Bldg, 180–184 Thanon Rajawongse, Bangkok 10100; tel. (2) 225-0135; fax (2) 226-1263; e-mail tccc@thaicentral.co.th; internet www.tcccthai.com; f. 1973; mfrs of chemical fertilizers; cap. and res 430m., sales 8,424m. (2000); Chair. Adm. NIRAN SIRINAVIN; Pres. TAKASHI HIRABAYASHI; 960 employees.

Thai-German Ceramic Industry Public Co Ltd: 1/2 Moo 1, Thanon Paholyothin, Klongnueng, Klongluang, Pathumthani, Bangkok 10120; tel. (2) 516-8611; fax (2) 516-8106; internet www.tgci.co.th; mfrs and distributors of glazed wall tiles, glazed and unglazed floor tiles; cap. and res 2,852m., sales 863m. (1999); Chair. VONGVUTHI VUTHINANTHA; Man. Dir PRABHOL BURANASIRI; 487 employees.

Thai Glass Industries Public Co Ltd: 15 Moo 1, Thanon Rajaburana, Bangkok 10140; tel. (2) 427-0060; fax (2) 427-6603; e-mail faxadmin@berlijucker.co.th; internet www.berlijucker.co.th; f. 1951; mfrs and distributors of glassware and glass containers; cap. and res 1,345m., sales 3,092m. (2000); Chair. DAVID NICOL; Man. Dir PRASERT MAEKWATTANA; 1,730 employees.

Thai Hino Motor Sales Ltd: 45/13 Thanon Wiphavadi Rangsit, Don Muang, Bangkok 10210; tel. (2) 552-0020; fax (2) 552-2936; f. 1962; distributors of industrial motor vehicles; sales 12,170m. (1994); Man. Dir KEIICHI SUGIYAMA.

Thailand Oil Co Ltd (Thaioil): POB 2387, Bangkok 10501; tel. (38) 351-555; fax (38) 351-554; e-mail rhino@thaioil.co.th; internet www.thaioil.com.th; petroleum-refining; 100% state-owned; sales US $1,594.2m. (1993); Chair. MANU LEOPAIROTE.

Thai Petrochemical Industry Public Co Ltd: 299 Moo 5, Thanon Sukhumvit, Cherng Noen, Meung, Rayong Province; tel. (38) 802-5509; fax (38) 612-8123; e-mail tpiadmin@tpigroup.co.th; internet www.tpigroup.co.th; f. 1978; mfrs of plastics; cap. and res 32,365m., sales 56,365m. (1999); declared insolvent in March 2000; Chair. SUNTHORN HONGLADAROM; Chief Exec. PRACHAI LEOPHAIRATANA.

Thai Plastic and Chemical Public Co Ltd: Rajanakarn Bldg, 14th–15th Floors, 183 Thanon Sathorn Tai, Yannawa, Sathorn, Bangkok 10120; tel. (2) 676-6000; fax (2) 676-6045; e-mail tpc@thaiplastic.co.th; internet www.thaiplastic.co.th; f. 1966; mfrs of PVC resins and compounds; cap. and res 5,473m., sales 13,670m. (2000); Chair. YOS EUARCHUKIATI; Man. Dir DHEP VONGVANICH; 1,060 employees.

Thai Rayon Public Co Ltd: Mahatun Plaza Bldg, 12th Floor, 888/127 Thanon Ploenchit, Lumpini, Pathumwan, Bangkok 10330; tel. (2) 627-3801; fax (2) 627-3804; e-mail rayon@thairayon.com; internet www.thairayon.com; mfrs and distributors of fibre and chemicals; cap. and res 4,498m. (1998/99), sales 4,196m. (2001); Chair. PRACHITR YOSSUNDARA; Pres. P. M. BAJAJ; 850 employees.

Thai Union Frozen Products Public Co Ltd: 979/12 M Floor, SM Tower, Thanon Paholyothin, Samsennai-Phayathai, Bangkok 10400; tel. (2) 298-0537; fax (2) 298-0548; e-mail chansiri@mail.thaiunion.co.th; internet www.thaiuniongroup.com; manufacture and export of frozen and canned foods; cap. 749.9m., sales 19,120m. (2000); Chair. KRAISON CHANSIRI; Pres. THIRAPHONG CHANSIRI.

Thai Wah Public Co Ltd: Thai Wah Tower, 21st–22nd Floors, 21/63–66 Thanon Sathorn Tai, Bangkok 10120; tel. (2) 285-0040; fax (2) 285-0269; e-mail starch@thaiwah.com; internet www.thaiwah.com; f. 1947; mfrs of tapioca products; cap. and res 339m., sales 2,399m. (1999); Chair. HO KWON PING; Man. Dir PINAI KIATTEPPAWAN.

Thailand Fishery Coldstorage Public Co Ltd: 592 Moo 2, Thanon Thayban, Amphur Muang, Samutprakarn 10280; tel. (2) 387-1171; fax (2) 387-2227; freezers and exporters of shrimps and squids; cap. and res 271m., sales 4,082m. (1998); Chair. and Chief Exec. THAVESAKDI LAOTRAKUL; Pres. and Man. Dir YUWAREE AUKARNJAN-AWILAI; 885 employees.

Thailand Tobacco Monopoly: Ministry of Finance, 443 Thanon Sri Ayudthya, Phaya Thai, Rajatevi, Bangkok 10400; fax (2) 255-4220; 100% state-owned.

Thonburi Automotive Assembly Plant Co Ltd: Soi 3, 72 Thanon Klang Ratchadamneon, Bowon Niwet, Phranakhon, Bangkok 10200; tel. (2) 226-0021; fax (2) 384-2246; f. 1960; mfrs of motor vehicles; sales 28,363m. (1994); Man. Dir PARKPIEN WIRIYAPANT.

Tipco Asphalt Public Co Ltd: 118/1 Thanon Ram VI, Samsen Nai, Phayathai, Bangkok 10400; tel. (2) 273-6000; fax (2) 273-6030; e-mail adm-tipc@mozart.inet.co.th; internet www.tipco.co.th; f. 1979; mfrs of construction materials; cap. and res 1,669m., sales 4,743m. (2000); Chair. PRASIT SUPSAKORN; Man. Dir SOMCHIT SERTTHIN.

Toyota Motor Thailand Co. Ltd: Moo 1, 186/1 Thanon Old Railway, Samrongtai, Phra Pradaeng, Samutprakarn 10130; tel. (2) 386-1000; fax (2) 384-1891; e-mail pr@toyota.co.th; internet www.toyota.co.th; f. 1962; mfrs and traders of motor vehicles; sales 48,980m. (1999); Pres. YOSHIAKI MURAMATSU.

TPI Polene Public Plc: 26/56 Thanon Chan Tad Mai, Thungmahamek, Sathorn, Bangkok 10120; tel. (2) 285-5090; fax (2) 213-1035; e-mail tpiadmin@tpigroup.co.th; internet www.tpigroup.co.th; f. 1978; mfrs and distributors of cement and LDPE; cap. and res 16,899m., sales 14,096m. (2000); Chair. SUNTHORN HONGLADAROM; Chief Exec. PRACHAI LEOPHAIRATANA; 3,392 employees.

Tuntex (Thailand) Public Co Ltd: 54 BB Bldg, 18th Floor, Room 1812, 54 Sukhumvit 21 (Soi Asoke), Thanon Sukhumvit, Klongtoey

Nua, Wattana, Bangkok 10110; tel. (2) 260-8020; fax (2) 260-8012; e-mail tuntex01@asiaaccess.th.com; manufacture and distribution of polyester products; cap. and res 6,702m., sales 6,640m. (1999); Chair. SHAN HUA SHEN.

Unicord Public Co Ltd: 404 Thanon Phayathai, Wangmai, Patumwan, Bangkok 10330; tel. (2) 216-0200; fax (2) 216-1468; f. 1977; mfrs of canned seafood; cap. and res 3,090m., sales 11,952m. (1995); Chair. KAMCHORN SATHIRAKUL; Pres. PORNPHUN KONUNTAKIET; 6,800 employees.

Union Mosaic Industry Public Co Ltd: Chamnan Phenjati Business Center Bldg, 29th Floor, 65 Thanon Phra Ram IX, Huay Kwang, Bangkok 10310; tel. (2) 248-7007; fax (2) 248-7005; e-mail export@umi-tiles.com; internet www.umi-tiles.com; f. 1973; mfrs of tiles; cap. and res 320m. (2000), sales 1,650m. (2001); CEO PAWEENA LAOWIWATWONG; 1,600 employees.

United Flour Mill Public Co Ltd: UFM Bldg, 9th Floor, 177–179 205 Thanon Rajawong, Sumpuntawong, Bangkok 10100; tel. (2) 226-0680; fax (2) 224-5670; f. 1961; wheat flour milling; cap. and res 315m., sales 2,219m. (2000); Chair. PRASERT TANGTRONGSAKDI, PRACHA RAKSINCHAROENSAK; 243 employees.

United Foods Public Co Ltd: 19/111 Moo 7, Thanon Thakam, Semae Daam, Bang Khun Thien, Bangkok 10150; tel. (2) 415-0035; fax (2) 415-1211; e-mail united@unitedfoods.com; internet www.unitedfoods.com; f. 1985; mfrs of biscuits and confectionery; cap. and res 223m., sales 1,072m. (1999); Chair. NARONG SUTHISAMPHAT; 1,100 employees.

Unocal Thailand Ltd: SCB Park Plaza, Tower III, 5th Floor, 19 Thanon Ratchadaphisek, Chatuchak, Bangkok 10900; tel. (2) 541-1970; fax (2) 541-1436; internet www.unocal.com; f. 1962; mining of petroleum and natural gas; sales 30,394m. (1997); Pres. BRIAN MARCOTTE.

Vanachai Group Public Co Ltd: 2/1 Thanon Pibulsongkram, Bangsue, Bangkok 10800; tel. (2) 585-4900; fax (2) 587-0516; e-mail woodtek@loxinfo.co.th; internet www.vanachai.com; manufacturer of wood-based panels; cap. and res 1,206m., sales 3,702m. (2000); Chair. SOMPON SAHAVAT.

Vinythai Public Co Ltd: Green Tower, 14th Floor, 3656/41 Thanon Rama IV, Khet Klongtoey, Bangkok 10110; tel. (2) 240-2425; fax (2) 240-1383; e-mail vinythai@solvay.com; production and distribution of chemicals; cap. and res 4,515m., sales 6,158m. (2000); Chair. PHISIT PAKKASEM.

TRADE UNIONS

Under the Labour Relations Act (1975), a minimum of 10 employees are required in order to form a union; by August 1997 there were an estimated 1,028 such unions.

Confederation of Thai Labour (CTL): 25/20 Thanon Sukhumvit, Viphavill Village, Tambol Paknam, Amphur Muang, Samutprakarn, Bangkok 10270; tel. (2) 756-5346; fax (2) 323-1074; represents 44 labour unions; Pres. AMPORN BANDASAK.

Labour Congress of Thailand (LCT): 420/393–394 Thippavan Village 1, Thanon Teparak, Samrong-Nua, Muang, Samutprakarn, Bangkok 10270; tel. and fax (2) 384-6789; e-mail lct_org@hotmail.com; f. 1978; represents 224 labour unions, four labour federations and approx. 140,000 mems; Pres. PRATNENG SAENGSANK; Gen. Sec. SAMAM THOMYA.

National Congress of Private Employees of Thailand (NPET): 142/6 Thanon Phrathoonam Phrakanong, Phrakanong, Klongtoey, Bangkok 10110; tel. and fax (2) 392-9955; represents 31 labour unions; Pres. BANJONG PORNPATTANANIKOM.

National Congress of Thai Labour (NCTL): 1614/876 Samutprakarn Community Housing Project, Sukhumvit Highway Km 30, Tai Baan, Muang, Samutprakarn, Bangkok 10280; tel. (2) 389-5134; fax (2) 385-8975; represents 171 unions; Pres. PANAS THAILUAN.

National Free Labour Union Congress (NFLUC): 277 Moo 3, Thanon Ratburana, Bangkok 10140; tel. (2) 427-6506; fax (2) 428-4543; represents 51 labour unions; Pres. ANUSSAKDI BOONYAPRANAI.

National Labour Congress (NLC): 586/248–250 Moo 2, Mooban City Village, Thanon Sukhumvit, Bang Phu Mai, Mueng, Samutprakarn, Bangkok 10280; tel. and fax (2) 709-9426; represents 41 labour unions; Pres. CHIN THAPPHLI.

Thai Trade Union Congress (TTUC): 420/393–394 Thippavan Village 1, Thanon Teparak, Tambol Samrong-nua, Amphur Muang, Samutprakarn, Bangkok 10270; tel. and fax (2) 384-0438; f. 1983; represents 172 unions; Pres. PANIT CHAROENPHAO.

Thailand Council of Industrial Labour (TCIL): 99 Moo 4, Thanon Sukhaphibarn 2, Khannayao, Bungkum, Bangkok; tel. (2) 517-0022; fax (2) 517-0628; represents 23 labour unions; Pres. TAVEE DEEYING.

Transport

RAILWAYS

Thailand has a railway network of 4,623 km, connecting Bangkok with Chiang Mai, Nong Khai, Ubon Ratchathani, Nam Tok and towns on the isthmus.

State Railway of Thailand: Thanon Rong Muang, Pathumwan, Bangkok 10330; tel. (2) 220-4567; fax (2) 225-3801; e-mail fad@srt moct.co.th; internet www.srt.or.th; f. 1897; 4,623 km of track in 1995; responsible for licensing a 4,044-km passenger and freight rail system, above ground; Chair. TERDSAK SEDTHAMANOP; Gov. CHITSANTI DHANASOBHON.

Bangkok Mass Transit System Corpn Ltd: Alma Link Bldg, 9th Floor, 25 Soi Chidlom, Thanon Ploenchit, Lumpini, Bangkok 10330; fax (2) 255-8651; responsible for the construction of the Skytrain, a two-line, 23.5-km elevated rail system, under the supervision of the Bangkok Metropolitan Area, the initial stage of which was opened in December 1999; the remaining sections were scheduled for completion in 2002 and 2003; Chair. KASAME CHATIKAVANIJ; Exec. Vice-Pres. DAVID RACE.

Mass Rapid Transit Authority of Thailand: 175 Thanon Rama IX, Huay Kwang, Bangkok 10320; tel. (2) 246-5733; fax (2) 246-3687; e-mail pr@mrta.or.th; internet www.mrta.or.th; in September 1995 it was announced that 21 km of the planned rail network for Bangkok would be underground; Gov. THEERAPONG ATTAIJARUSIT.

ROADS

The total length of the road network was an estimated 64,600 km in 1999, of which 97.5% was paved. A network of toll roads has been introduced in Bangkok in an attempt to alleviate the city's severe congestion problems.

Bangkok Mass Transit Authority (BMTA): 131 Thanon Thiam Ruammit, Huay Kwang, Bangkok 10310; tel. (2) 246-0973; fax (2) 247-2189; e-mail cnai.bmta@motc.go.th; internet www.bmta .motc.go.th; controls Bangkok's urban transport system; Chair. WANCHAI SARAIHUHIHAT; Dir and Sec. PHIRAPHONG ISARABHAKDI.

Department of Highways: Thanon Sri Ayudhaya, Ratchathevi, Bangkok 10400; tel. (2) 246-1122; e-mail prosdoh@motc.go.th; internet www.doh.motc.go.th; Dir-Gen. JARUK ANUPONG.

Department of Land Transport: 1032 Thanon Phaholyothin, Chatuchak, Bangkok 10900; tel. (2) 272-5671; fax (2) 272-5680; e-mail admin@dlt.motc.go.th; internet www.dlt.motc.go.th; Dir-Gen. PREECHA ORPRASIRTH.

Express Transportation Organization of Thailand (ETO): 485/1 Thanon Sri Ayudhaya, Ratchathevi, Bangkok 10400; tel. (2) 245-3231; internet www.eto.motc.go.th; f. 1947; Pres. KOVIT THANYARATTAKUL.

SHIPPING

There is an extensive network of canals, providing transport for bulk goods. The port of Bangkok is an important shipping junction for South-East Asia, and consists of 37 berths for conventional and container vessels.

Harbour Department: 1278 Thanon Yotha, Talardnoi, Samphanthawong, Bangkok 10100; tel. (2) 266-3972; fax (2) 233-7167; e-mail webmaster@hd.motc.go.th; internet www.hd.motc.go.th; Dir-Gen. WIT WORAKUPT.

Office of the Maritime Promotion Commission: 19 Thanon Phra Atit, Bangkok 10200; tel. (2) 281-9367; e-mail motc@motc.go.th; internet www.ompc.moto.go.th; f. 1979; Sec.-Gen. SOMSAK PIENSAKOOL.

Port Authority of Thailand: 444 Thanon Tarua, Klongtoey, Bangkok 10110; tel. (2) 269-3000; fax (2) 249-0885; e-mail patodga@ loxinfo.co.th; internet www.pat.or.th; 18 berths at Bangkok Port, 12 berths at Laem Chabang Port; Chair. Gen. Dr WICHAI SUNGPRAPAI; Dir-Gen. MANA PATRAM.

Principal Shipping Companies

Jutha Maritime Public Co Ltd: Mano Tower, 2nd Floor, 153 Soi 39, Thanon Sukhumvit, Bangkok 10110; tel. (2) 260-0050; fax (2) 259-9825; e-mail jutha@loxinfo.co.th; services between Thailand, Malaysia, Korea, Japan and Viet Nam; Chair. Rear-Adm. CHANO PHENJATI; Man. Dir CHANET PHENJATI.

Precious Shipping Public Co Ltd: Cathay House, 7th Floor, 8/30 Thanon Sathorn Nua, Khet Bangrak, Bangkok 10500; tel. (2) 237-8700; fax (2) 633-8460; e-mail psl@preciousshipping.com; internet www.preciousshipping.com; Chair. Adm. AMNARD CHANDANAMATTHA; Man. Dir HASHIM KHALID MOINUDDIN.

Regional Container Lines Public Co Ltd: Panjathani Tower, 30th Floor, 127/35 Thanon Ratchadaphisek, Chongnonsee Yannawa,

Bangkok 10120; tel. (2) 296-1088; fax (2) 296-1098; e-mail rclbkk@rclgroup.com; Chair. KUA PHEK LONG; Pres. SUMATE TANTHUWANIT.

Siam United Services Public Co Ltd: 30 Thanon Ratburana, Bangprakok, Ratburana, Bangkok 10140; tel. (2) 428-0029; fax (2) 427-6270; f. 1977; Chair. and Man. Dir MONGKHOL SIMAROJ.

Thai International Maritime Enterprises Ltd: Sarasin Bldg, 5th Floor, 14 Thanon Surasak, Bangkok 10500; tel. (2) 236-8835; services from Bangkok to Japan; Chair. and Man. Dir SUN SUNDISAMRIT.

Thai Maritime Navigation Co Ltd: Manorom Bldg, 15th Floor, 51 Thanon Phra Ram IV, Klongtoey, Bangkok 10110; tel. (2) 249-0100; fax (2) 249-0108; internet www.tmn.co.th; services from Bangkok to Japan, the USA, Europe and ASEAN countries; Chair. VORASUGDI VORAPAMORN; Vice-Chair. ORMSIN CHIVAPRUCK.

Thai Mercantile Marine Ltd: 599/1 Thanon Chua Phloeng, Klongtoey, Bangkok 10110; tel. (2) 240-2582; fax (2) 249-5656; e-mail tmmbkk@asiaaccess.net.th; f. 1967; services between Japan and Thailand; Chair. SUTHAM TANPHAIBUL; Man. Dir TANAN TANPHAIBUL.

Thai Petroleum Transports Co Ltd: 355 Thanon Sunthornkosa, POB 2172, Klongtoey, Bangkok 10110; tel. (2) 249-0255; Chair. C. CHOWKWANYUN; Man. Capt. B. HAM.

Thoresen Thai Agencies Public Co Ltd: 26/26–27 Orakarn Bldg, 8th Floor, 26–27 Soi Chidlom, Thanon Ploenchit, Kwang Lumpinee, Khet Pathumwan, Bangkok 10330; tel. (2) 254-8437; fax (2) 253-9497; e-mail tta@thoresen.th.com; transports bulk cargo around Asia and the Middle East; Chair. M. R. CHANDRAM S. CHANDRATAT; Man. Dir ARNE TEIGEN.

Unithai Group: 11th Floor, 25 Alma Link Bldg, Soi Chidlom, Thanon Ploenchit, Pathumwan, Bangkok 10330; tel. (2) 254-8400; fax (2) 253-3093; e-mail gerrit.d@unithai.com; internet www.unithai.com; regular containerized/break-bulk services to Europe, Africa and Far East; also bulk shipping/chartering; Chair. SIVAVONG CHANGKASIRI; CEO GERRIT J. DE NYS.

CIVIL AVIATION

Bangkok, Chiang Mai, Chiang Rai, Hat Yai, Phuket and Surat Thani airports are of international standard. U-Tapao is an alternative airport. In May 1991 plans were approved to build a new airport at Nong Ngu Hao, south-east of Bangkok, at an estimated cost of US $1,200m. Construction began in 1995, and the project was scheduled for completion in 2000. In January 1997, however, it was announced that, due to the Government's financial problems, the Nong Ngu Hao project was to be suspended; priority was, instead, to be given to the existing airport at Don Muang in Bangkok, which was to be expanded to handle 45m. passengers annually by 2007, compared with 25m. in 1997. In December 2001 construction of the passenger terminal complex of Bangkok's second airport, Suvarnabhumi International Airport, commenced. The project was scheduled for completion in 2004.

In May 1996 the Government approved the creation of a second national airline; a proposal for the project made by a private consortium was approved in 1997.

Airports Authority of Thailand: Bangkok International Airport, 171 Thanon Vibhavadi Rangsit, Don Muang, Bangkok 10210; tel. (2) 535-1111; fax (2) 535-5559; e-mail aatpr@airportthai.or.th; internet www.airportthai.or.th; f. 1998; Man. Dir Air Chief Marshal TERDSAK SUJJARUK.

Department of Aviation: 71 Soi Ngarmduplee, Thanon Phra Ram IV, Tung Mahamek, Sathorn District, Bangkok 10120; tel. (2) 287-0320; fax (2) 286-1295; e-mail tiva@aviation.go.th; internet www.aviation.go.th; f. 1963; Dir-Gen. SUPOTE KUMPEERA.

Air Andaman: 87 Nailert Bldg, 4th Floor, Unit 402A, Thanon Sukhumvit, Bangkok; tel. (2) 2514905; fax (2) 6552378; internet www.airandaman.com; f. 2000; regional, scheduled passenger and charter services; Pres. ATICHART ATHAKRAVISUNTHORN.

Bangkok Airways: 60 Queen Sirikit Nat. Convention Centre, Thanon Ratchadaphisek Tadmai, Klongtoey, Bangkok 10110; tel. (2) 229-3434; fax (2) 229-3450; e-mail reservation@bangkokair.co.th; internet www.bangkokair.com; f. 1968 as Sahakol Air, name changed as above in 1989; privately-owned; scheduled and charter passenger services to regional and domestic destinations; Pres. and CEO Dr PRASERT PRASARTTONG-OSOTH.

Kampuchea Airlines (OX): 138/70 Jewellery Centre, 17th Floor, Thanon Nares, Bangrak, Bangkok 10500; tel. (2) 267-3210; fax (2) 267-3216; e-mail bondmx@yahoo.com; f. 1997; owned by Cambodian govt (51%) and Orient Thai Airlines (49%); regional passenger flights from Phnom-Penh to Hong Kong and Bangkok; CEO UDOM TANTIPRASONGCHAI.

PB Air: 101 Thanon Samsen, Bangkok 10300; tel. (2) 669-2066; fax (2) 669-2092; internet www.pbair.com; f. 1990; scheduled domestic passenger services; Chair. PIYA BHIROM BHAKDI.

Phuket Airlines: 1168/71, 25th Floor, Lumpini Tower Bldg, Thungmahamek, Bangkok; tel. (67) 982-3840; internet www.phuketairlines.com; f. 1999; domestic passenger services linking Ranong to Bangkok, Had Yai and Phuket.

Thai Airways International Public Co Ltd (THAI): 89 Thanon Vibhavadi Rangsit, Bangkok 10900; tel. (2) 513-0121; fax (2) 513-0203; e-mail public.info@thaiairways.co.th; internet www.thaiair.com;f. 1960; 93% govt-owned; shares listed in July 1991, began trading in July 1992; merged with Thai Airways Co in 1988; scheduled for partial privatization in late 2000; domestic services from Bangkok to 20 cities; international services to over 50 destinations in Australasia, Europe, North America and Asia; Chair. THANONG BHIDAYA; Pres. KANOK ABHIRADEE.

Tourism

Thailand is a popular tourist destination, noted for its temples, palaces, beaches and islands. In 2001 tourist arrivals totalled 10.13m. Revenue from tourism totalled 269,882m. baht in 1999 and, according to the World Tourism Organization, was an estimated US $7,119m. in 2000.

Tourism Authority of Thailand (TAT): Head Office: Le Concorde Building, 202 Thanon Ratchadaphisek, Huay Kwang, Bangkok 10310; tel. (2) 694-1222; fax (2) 694-1220; e-mail center@tat.or.th; internet www.tat.or.th; f. 1960; Chair. ADISAI BODHACAMIK; Gov. PRADECH PHAYAKVICHIEN.

Tourist Association of Northern Thailand: 51/20 Thanon Mahidol (Northern Tour), Chiang Mai 50100; tel. (53) 276-848; fax (53) 272-394; Pres. AURAWAN NIMANANDA.

Defence

In August 2001 the total strength of the armed forces was 306,000: army 190,000 (70,000 conscripts), navy 68,000 (27,000 conscripts), air force 48,000. Paramilitary forces numbered approximately 104,000, including a National Security Volunteer Corps of 50,000. Military service lasts for two years between the ages of 21 and 30 and is compulsory.

Defence Expenditure: Budgeted at an estimated 77,200m. baht for 2001/02.

Supreme Commander of the Armed Forces: Gen. SURAYUD CHULANONT.

Commander-in-Chief of the Army: Gen. SOMDHAT ATTANAND.

Commander-in-Chief of the Air Force: Air Chief Marshal KHONGSAK WANTHANA.

Commander-in-Chief of the Navy: Adm. THAWEESAK SOMAPA.

Education

Education in Thailand is free and compulsory for six years between the ages of six and 11 years. From 1996 the Government planned to extend the period of compulsory education to nine years. There are four types of schools: (i) Government schools established and maintained by government funds; (ii) Local schools which are usually financed by the Government; however, if they are founded by the people of the district, funds collected from the public may be used in supporting such schools; (iii) Municipal schools, a type of primary school financed and supervised by the municipality; (iv) Private schools set up and owned by private individuals under the provisions of the 1954 Private Schools Act. The National Scheme of Education provides for education on four levels: (i) Pre-School Education (nursery and kindergarten), which is not compulsory; (ii) Primary Education; (iii) Secondary Education; (iv) Higher Education. Budgetary expenditure on education in was estimated to be 181,300m. baht, or 17.9% of total planned spending.

Pre-primary education begins at three years and enrolment was equivalent to 63% of the relevant age-group in 1996. Primary education starts at the age of six and lasts for six years. In 1996 enrolment at primary level was equivalent to 87% of the relevant age-group. Secondary education, which also lasts for six years, is divided into two three-year cycles. In 1996 enrolment at secondary schools was equivalent to 56% of the school-age population. In 1995 there were 20 state universities and 26 private universities and colleges in Thailand, offering both undergraduate and graduate courses in all fields. Other higher education establishments include the various Military and Police Academies providing a standard of training equivalent to that of civil establishments, and teacher-training establishments. Enrolment in higher education was equivalent to 22% of the relevant age-group in 1995.

Bibliography

GENERAL

Askew, Marc. *Bangkok: Place, Practice and Representation*. London, Routledge, 2002.

Brummelhuis, Hanten, and Kemp, J. (Eds). *Strategies and Structures in Thai Society*. Amsterdam, University of Amsterdam Antropologisch-Sociologisch Centrum, 1984.

Bunnag, Jane. *Buddhist Monk, Buddhist Layman*. Cambridge University Press, 1973.

Calavan, M. *Decisions against Nature: An Anthropological Study of Agriculture in Northern Thailand*. Northern Illinois Centre for Southeast Asian Studies, 1977.

Connors, Michael Kelly. *Democracy and National Identity in Thailand*. London, RoutledgeCurzon, 2002.

Donner, W. *Five Faces of Thailand*. London, C. Hurst, 1978.

Hanks, Lucien. *Rice and Man*. Ithaca, NY, Cornell University Press, 1972.

Ishii, Yoneo. *Sangha, State and Society: Thai Buddhism in History*. Honolulu, HI, University of Hawaii Press, 1986.

Ishii, Yoneo (Ed.). *Thailand, A Rice-Growing Society*. Honolulu, HI, University of Hawaii Press, 1978.

Kaufman, H. K. *Bangkhuad: A Community Study in Thailand*. Prentice Hall, 1978.

Klausner, William J. *Thai Culture in Transition: Collected Writings*. Bangkok, Siam Society, 1998.

McKinnon, J., and Vienne, B. (Eds). *Hill Tribes Today: Problems in Change*. Bangkok and Paris, White Lotus-ORSTOM, 1991.

McKinnon, John, and Wanat Bhruksari. *Highlanders of Thailand*. Kuala Lumpur, Oxford University Press, 1983.

Piprell, Collin, and Boyd, Ashley J. *Thailand's Coral Reefs: Nature Under Threat*. Bangkok, White Lotus, 1996.

Rajadhon, Phya Anuman. *Popular Buddhism in Siam and other Essays on Thai Studies*. Bangkok, Thai Inter-Religions Commission for Development, 1985.

Reynolds, Craig I. (Ed.). *National Identity and its Defenders: Thailand, 1939–1989*. Victoria, Monash University, 1993.

Sanitsuda, Ekachai. *Behind the Smile: Voices of Thailand*. Bangkok, Thai Development Support Committee and Post Publishing, 1990.

Sato, T. *Field Crops of Thailand*. Kyoto University, South-East Asia Centre, 1966.

Seidenfaden, E. *The Thai Peoples*. Bangkok, The Siam Society, 1963.

Sharp, L., and Hanks, L. *Bang Chan: Social History of a Rural Community in Thailand*. Ithaca, NY, Cornell University Press, 1978.

Skinner, G. W. *Chinese Society in Thailand*. Ithaca, NY, Cornell University Press, 1957.

Skinner, William G., and Kirsch, Thomas A. (Eds). *Change and Persistence in Thai Society*. Ithaca, NY, Cornell University Press, 1975.

Takaya, Yoshikazu. *Agricultural Development of a Tropical Delta: A Study of the Chao Phraya Delta*. Honolulu, HI, University of Hawaii Press, 1987.

Tambiah, S. J. *World Conqueror and World Renouncer: A Study of Buddhism and Polity in Thailand Against a Historical Background*. Cambridge University Press, 1975.

Tanabe, Shigeharu, and Keyes, Charles F. (Eds). *Cultural Crisis and Social Memory: Modernity and Identity in Thailand and Laos*. London, RoutledgeCurzon, 2002.

Tapp, Nicholas. *Sovereignty and Rebellion: The White Hmong of Northern Thailand*. Singapore, Oxford University Press, 1990.

Wijeyewardene, Gehan, and Chapman, E. C. (Eds). *Patterns and Illusions: Thai History and Thought*. Canberra, Australian National University and Singapore, Institute of Southeast Asian Studies, 1993.

HISTORY

Brailey, Nigel (Ed.). *Two Views of Siam on the Eve of the Chakri Reformation*. Arran, Kiscadale Publications, 1990.

Bunnag, Tej. *The Provincial Administration of Siam 1892–1915*. Oxford University Press, 1977.

Callahan, William A. *Imagining Democracy—Reading 'The Events of May' in Thailand*. Singapore, Institute of Southeast Asian Studies, 1999.

Chakrabongse, Prince Chula. *Lords of Life: the Paternal Monarchy of Bangkok, 1782–1932*. New York, Taplinger and London, Alvin Redman, 1960.

Chaloemtiarana, Thak (Ed.). *Thai Politics 1932–1957*. Bangkok, Social Sciences Association of Thailand, 1978.

Chaloemtiarana, Thak. *Thailand: The Politics of Despotic Paternalism*. Bangkok, Social Sciences Association of Thailand, 1979.

Fineman, Daniel Mark. *A Special Relationship—The United States and Military Government in Thailand, 1947–1958*. Honolulu, HI, University of Hawaii Press, 1997.

Haseman, J. B. *The Thai Resistance Movement During World War II*. Washington, DC, University of Washington Press, 2002.

Hong Lysa. *Thailand in the Nineteenth Century: Evolution of the Economy and Society*. Singapore, Institute of Southeast Asian Studies, 1984.

Peleggi, Maurizio. *Lords of Things: The Fashioning of the Siamese Monarchy's Modern Image*. Honolulu, HI, University of Hawaii Press, 2002.

Stowe, Judith A. *Siam Becomes Thailand: A Story of Intrigue*. London, Hurst, 1991.

Suksamran, Somboon. *Political Buddhism in Southeast Asia: The Role of the Sangha in the Modernisation of Thailand*. London, Hurst, 1977.

Terweil, B. J. *A History of Modern Thailand 1767–1942*. St Lucia, University of Queensland Press, 1983.

Wood, W. A. R. *A History of Siam*. Bangkok, Chalermnit, 1959.

Wright, Joseph J. *The Balancing Act: A History of Modern Thailand*. Oakland, Pacific Rim Press, 1991.

Wyatt, D. K. *Thailand: A Short History*. New Haven, CT, Yale University Press, 1984.

Young, Ernest. *The Kingdom of the Yellow Robe*. Oxford University Press, 1982.

ECONOMICS AND POLITICS

Arghiros, Daniel. *Democracy, Development and Decentralization in Provincial Thailand*. London, Curzon Press, 2001.

Bello, Walden, Cunningham, Shea, and Li, Kheng Poh. *A Siamese Tragedy—Development and Disintegration in Modern Thailand*. London, Zed Books, 1999.

Brown, I. *The Elite and the Economy in Siam c. 1890–1920*. Singapore, Oxford University Press, 1989.

The Creation of the Modern Ministry of Finance in Siam, 1985–1910. Basingstoke, Macmillan, 1992.

Dhiravegin, Likhit. *Demi Democracy*. Singapore, Times Academic Pres, 1993.

Dixon, Chris. *The Thai Economy: Uneven Development and Internationalisation*. London, Routledge, 1999.

Girling, J. L. S. *Thailand: Society and Politics*. Ithaca, NY, and London, Cornell University Press, 1981.

Hewison, K. *The Development of Capital and the Role of the State in Thailand*. New Haven, CT, Yale University Press, 1988.

Power and Politics in Thailand. Manila, Journal of Contemporary Asia Publishers, 1990.

Political Change in Thailand: Democracy and Participation. London and New York, Routledge, 1997.

Hirst, P. *Development Dilemmas in Rural Thailand*. Singapore, Oxford University Press, 1990.

Ingram, J. C. *Economic Change in Thailand 1850–1970*. 2nd Edn, Stanford, CA, Stanford University Press, 1971.

Kerdphol, Gen. Saiyud. *The Struggle for Thailand: Counter-Insurgency 1965–1985*. Bangkok, South Research Centre, 1986.

Keyes, Charles F. *Thailand: Buddhist Kingdom as Modern Nation-State*. Boulder, CO, Westview Press, 1987.

Kulick, Elliott, and Wilson, Dick. *Thailand's Turn: Profile of a New Dragon*. New York, St Martin's Press, 1993.

Laothamatus, Anek. *Business Associations and the New Political Economy of Thailand*. Singapore, Institute of Southeast Asian Studies, 1993.

McCargo, Duncan. *Politics and the Press in Thailand: Media Machinations*. London, Routledge, 2000.

McVey, Ruth T. (Ed.). *Money and Power in Provincial Thailand.* Singapore, Institute of Southeast Asian Studies, 2000.

Morell, D., and Chai-Anan Samudvanij. *Thailand: Reform, Reaction and Revolution.* Cambridge, MA, Oelgeschlager, Gunn and Hain, 1981.

Muscat, Robert J. *Thailand and the United States: Development, Security, and Foreign Aid.* New York, Columbia University Press, 1990.

na Pombhejra, Vichitvong. *Readings in Thailand's Political Economy.* Bangkok Printing Enterprise, 1978.

Neher, C. D. *Modern Thai Politics: From Village to Nation.* Cambridge, MA, Schenkman, 1979.

Parnwell, M. (Ed.). *Uneven Development in Thailand.* Aldershot, Avebury, 1995.

Phongpaichit, Pasuk, and Baker, Chris. *Thailand: Economy and Politics.* Kuala Lumpur, Oxford University Press, 1996.

Thailand's Boom and Bust. Chiang Mai, Silkworm Books, 1998.

Thailand's Crisis. Chiang Mai, Silkworm Books, 2000.

Phongpaichit, Pasuk, and Piriyarangsan, Sungsidh. *Corruption and Democracy in Thailand.* Chiang Mai, Silkworm Books, 1998.

Phongpaichit, Pasuk, Piriyarangsan, Sungsidh, and Treerat, Nualnoi. *Guns, Girls, Gambling, Ganja—Thailand's Illegal Economy and Public Policy*. Chiang Mai, Silkworm Books, 1999.

Pian, Kobkua Suwannathat. *Kings, Country and Constitutions: Thailand's Political Development 1932–2000.* London, Routledge Curzon, 2002.

Rigg, Jonathan (Ed.). *Counting the Costs: Economic Growth and Environmental Change in Thailand.* Singapore, Institute of Southeast Asian Studies, 1996.

Samudvanija, Chai-Anan. *The Thai Young Turks.* Singapore, Institute of Southeast Asian Studies, 1982.

Silcock, T. H. (Ed.). *The Economic Development of Thai Agriculture.* Ithaca, NY, Cornell University Press, 1970.

Suehiro, Akira. *Capital Accumulation in Thailand 1955–1985.* Tokyo, Centre for East Asian Cultural Studies, Toyo Bunko, 1989.

Suksamran, Somboon. *Buddhism and Politics in Thailand.* Singapore, Institute of Southeast Asian Studies, 1982.

Unger, Daniel. *Building Social Capital: Fibers, Finance, and Infrastructure*. Cambridge University Press, Cambridge, 1998.

Unphakorn, P., et al. *Finance, Trade and Economic Development in Thailand.* Bangkok, 1973.

Van Roy, E. *Economic Systems of Northern Thailand.* Ithaca, NY, Cornell University Press, 1971.

Warr, Peter. *Thailand Beyond the Crisis.* London, Routledge, 2002.

Wedel, Yuengrat. *The Thai Radicals and the Communist Party.* Singapore, Maruzen Asia, 1983.

Xuto, Somsakdi (Ed.). *Government and Politics of Thailand.* Hong Kong, Oxford University Press, 1987.

VIET NAM

Physical and Social Geography

HARVEY DEMAINE

The Socialist Republic of Viet Nam covers a total area of 331,114 sq km (127,844 sq miles) and lies along the western shore of the South China Sea, bordered by the People's Republic of China to the north, by Laos to the west and by Cambodia to the south-west. The capital is Hanoi.

PHYSICAL FEATURES AND CLIMATE

The fundamental geographical outlines of the country are determined by the deltas and immediate hinterlands of the Mekong and Songkoi (Red River) which are linked by the mountain backbone and adjacent coastal lowlands of Annam.

Of the two rivers which are thus of major significance in the geography of Viet Nam, the Songkoi, rising, like the Mekong, in south-western China, is much the shorter, and its delta, together with that of a series of lesser rivers, forms a total area of some 14,500 sq km, which is less than one-half that of the great Mekong delta in the south. The north of Viet Nam also includes a much more extensive area of rugged upland, mainly in the north and west, which represents a southward continuation of the Yunnan and adjacent plateaux of south-western China, and forms an inhospitable and sparsely populated divide, some 900–1,500 m above sea-level, between North Viet Nam and northern Laos.

Both the Songkoi and its main right-bank tributary, the Songbo (Black River), flow in parallel north-west/south-east gorges through this upland before their confluence some 100 km above the apex of the delta, while a third main river, the Songma, also follows a parallel course still further to the south, beyond which rises the similarly north-west/south-east trending Annamite chain or Cordillera. This, in relief if not in structure, constitutes a further prolongation of the massive upland system already described, and extends without a break to within about 150 km of the Mekong delta.

With an average breadth of 150 km, and an extremely rugged and heavily-forested surface, at many points exceeding 1,500 m in altitude, the Annamite chain, which lies mainly in southern Viet Nam, provides an effective divide between the Annam coast and the middle Mekong valley of southern Laos and eastern Cambodia. Moreover, from the Porte d'Annam (latitude 18°N) southwards, the chain not only reaches to within a few miles of the coast, but also sends off a series of spurs, which terminate in rocky headlands overlooking the sea. Thus, along the 1,000-km stretch of coast between latitudes 18° and 11°N, the continuity of the coastal plain is repeatedly interrupted and it dwindles to an average width of less than 16 km and often to less than half that figure; but thereafter it broadens out to merge with the vast deltaic plain of the Mekong and its associated natural waterways, the whole forming an almost dead flat surface covering some 37,800 sq km.

In forming the western hinterland of the South China Sea virtually from the tropic of Cancer to within 9°N of the Equator, Viet Nam might be assumed to be wholly within the zone of the tropical monsoon climate. The greater part of the country does merit such a designation, and the city of Hué, practically at the mid-point of the coastal zone, has a mean monthly temperature range from 20°C in January to 30°C in August, and a total rainfall of 2,600 mm, of which 1,650 mm falls between September and November. However, the Songkoi delta in the north is not strictly tropical in the climatological sense, as, owing to its exposure to cold northern air during the season of the north-east monsoon, it experiences a recognizable cool season from December to March, and in both January and February the mean monthly temperatures in Hanoi are only 17°C. This fact is of great importance since the cooler weather gives greater effectiveness to the 130–150 mm of rain that fall during these months, and so makes it possible to raise a 'winter' as well as a summer crop of rice in this part of the country.

NATURAL RESOURCES

In terms of agricultural potential, the two river deltas are of overriding importance. The uplands, until recently, have offered far less opportunity for supporting population, not only because of the extremely restricted prospects for rice cultivation but also because of their intensely malarial character. Owing to increasing pressure on land resources in the Tongking delta in particular, great efforts are being made to develop the uplands for cash cropping, although there are suggestions that this may be at the expense of environmental stability. In respect of mineral wealth, on the other hand, the uplands, particularly in the north, contain a wide variety of lesser metallic ores, and also some useful apatite (a source of phosphates), though economically the most important mineral is in the anthracite field of Quang-Yen immediately to the north-east of the Songkoi delta. Reserves here are put at some 20m. metric tons, and total coal reserves are estimated at 3,500m. metric tons. Petroleum has been discovered off shore in the north and south of the country, and the Bach Ho oilfield, 160 km to the east of Ho Chi Minh City, came into operation in 1986. There are also plans to exploit reserves of natural gas.

POPULATION AND ETHNIC GROUPS

The population of Viet Nam totalled 76,324,753 at the census of 1 April 1999, according to provisional figures, (compared with the April 1989 census total of 64,411,713). By mid-2001 the population had increased further to 79,175,000, according to UN estimates, and there was an average population density of 239.1 per sq km. This average, however, is highly misleading, firstly because the great majority of the population (and practically all of the Vietnamese proper) live within the lowlands, and secondly because these regions comprise rather more than one-third of the total area of southern Viet Nam, but barely one-sixth of that of northern Viet Nam. Thus, whereas most of the vast Mekong delta supports rural densities varying from 40 to 200 per sq km, the comparable figures for the Songkoi delta are between four and five times as great. The South, however, shows the higher degree of urbanization. At mid-1993 the largest town in Viet Nam was Ho Chi Minh City, in the South, with a population of 4,322,300, while the largest towns in the North, the capital Hanoi and its port, Haiphong, had populations of 2,154,900 and 1,583,900, respectively. The distribution of population in Viet Nam changed considerably following a vast resettlement programme: 3.5m. people were moved after 1975 and 2.1m. after 1981, mostly to Viet Nam's New Economic Zones or to the Central Highlands.

Vietnamese, who are ethnically related to the southern Chinese, form 80% of the population. There are also significant minority groups, notably the Tai in the North (numbering some 2m.), some 750,000 Hmong and related groups and a number of smaller groups of people in the Central Highlands, usually known as *montagnards* and numbering up to 1m. There are perhaps 600,000 Cambodians along Viet Nam's south-western border and a now uncertain number of Chinese, still primarily concentrated in the southern city of Cholon, but much reduced in numbers by migration.

History

RALPH SMITH

Revised for this edition by ZACHARY ABUZA

EARLY HISTORY

Recent archaeological work suggests that Viet Nam had a distinctive bronze age civilization, perhaps by 1000 BC. The present northern Viet Nam became incorporated into the Chinese Han empire in 112 BC and remained effectively a province of China for the ensuing millennium. During these centuries there occurred a gradual interaction of Vietnamese and Chinese ideas and institutions, and the Chinese language was introduced, although it did not supplant Vietnamese. The Chinese religions of Daoism, Confucianism and Mahayana Buddhism also became widespread.

With the dissolution of the Tang empire in the early part of the 10th century, Viet Nam came under the rule of an independent southern dynasty. However, this regime's army was defeated by the Vietnamese in 931 and 938, and it is from the latter year that the Vietnamese usually date their independence. During the next four centuries Viet Nam (or Dai Viet) gradually developed into a strong and fairly centralized state, with a capital in Hanoi and institutions modelled on those of China. Under the dynasties of the Ly (1009–1225) and Tran (1225–1400), Dai Viet was strong enough to resist further Chinese attempts at reconquest: by the Song in 1075–77, and by the Yuan (Mongols) in the years 1282–88. A new Chinese attack succeeded in 1407, but the Chinese were once more driven out by Le Loi, founder of the Le dynasty (1428–1789).

Meanwhile, the region now comprising central Viet Nam belonged to the kingdom of Champa, with a culture strongly influenced by Hindu-Buddhist culture, while the Mekong delta belonged to Angkor (cf. Cambodia). Dai Viet annexed areas of Cham territory in 1070, 1306 and 1470, reducing Champa to a small principality which was finally extinguished in 1695.

CONFLICTS, DIVISION AND UNIFICATION

The 15th century was the 'golden age' of Confucian culture in Viet Nam and a period of general stability. In the early 16th century, however, the kingdom began to break up under the stress of conflict between rival clans, one of which established the Mac dynasty (1527–92). After intermittent civil war in the 16th century, the next 100 years saw a more lasting division of Viet Nam between two powerful clans: the Trinh in the north and the Nguyen in central Viet Nam. It was the Nguyen who led the way in a further southward expansion, beginning about 1658, which established their control over the greater part of what is now southern Viet Nam. Also in this period, Christian missions were established in both parts of Viet Nam.

In the 1770s, however, the Tay Son rebellion cast the entire country into a state of civil war. Although the Tay Son established a new dynasty and defeated a Chinese invasion in 1789, they could not bring new stability. The last Nguyen survivor recaptured Saigon (now Ho Chi Minh City) and from there went on to conquer the centre and north by 1802. He proclaimed himself Emperor at Hué, with the title Gia Long, and for the first time in its history the present area of Viet Nam was brought under the control of a single ruler. For a brief period Minh Mang (1820–41) also extended his control to embrace much of Cambodia. During the reign of Tu Duc (1847–83), however, the Vietnamese were confronted by the challenge of French colonialism.

In 1858–59 a Franco-Spanish fleet attacked Tourane (Da Nang), and then Saigon. French annexation of three provinces of Cochin-China (the southernmost part of Viet Nam) was formally recognized by Tu Duc in 1862. In 1867 the French annexed another three provinces. A new Franco-Vietnamese treaty, signed in 1874, recognized French possession of all Cochin-China and permitted the French to trade in Tongking (Tonkin). In 1883 the French imposed a treaty of 'protection' on the Vietnamese empire. Two years later, after a border war with China, the French secured Chinese recognition of their protectorate.

FRENCH RULE AND VIETNAMESE OPPOSITION

By 1885 the whole of Viet Nam was under French colonial rule: Cochin-China, in the south, as a directly administered colony; Tongking and Annam (the north and centre) as protectorates. In 1887 they were united with Cambodia to form the Union Indochinoise, to which Laos was added in 1893. By 1901 the administration of the Union had become an effective central authority with financial control over the whole of Indo-China.

The French administration promoted the mining of coal and minerals in Tongking, the cultivation of rubber and other plantation crops in the hill areas, the export of rice from Cochin-China, and the construction of several railways. They also created several new towns, notably Saigon and Hanoi, which for a time were alternate capitals of the Union and which attracted the growth of a small urban, French-educated élite among the Vietnamese population. In the countryside, on the other hand, the peasantry enjoyed few benefits from French rule. Their taxes were increased several times from about 1897, but they were given little help in increasing productivity. During the 1930s, with the economic slump, followed by a new inflation, the economic condition of the peasantry declined seriously and many of the poor and landless villagers became permanently indebted to their richer neighbours. The political developments of the 1930s and 1940s must be seen against this background of social conflict. At the same time the development of French education tended to undermine traditional values and to accentuate economic inequalities.

Opposition to French rule was essentially 'traditional' before about 1900: a long sequence of local risings led by scholars or military men who had had some status in the old society, but who had no effective means of defeating the new regime. During the first decade of the 20th century a new opposition movement began, strongly influenced by the model of Japanese modernization and by Chinese revolutionary aspirations. However, an anti-taxation revolt and a nationalist education movement in 1907–08 were both suppressed by the French. The two most prominent opposition leaders of this period, Phan Chau Trinh and Phan Boi Chau, spent long periods in exile.

The growth of constitutionalist opposition to Western colonial rule throughout Asia, from about 1916, was reflected in Viet Nam by the Constitutionalist Party, founded in Cochin-China in 1917. The party participated in elections for the Colonial Council, but was not allowed to operate outside Cochin-China: the French did not permit a nation-wide constitutional opposition movement comparable to the Congress Party in India. Consequently, from about 1925 Vietnamese nationalism began to produce revolutionary organizations, some of which became communist. In 1930 it also found expression in a number of open revolts, quickly suppressed. A peasant movement that emerged in mid-1930 in parts of Cochin-China, and in Nghe An, Ha Tinh and Annam, reached more serious proportions. It was organized largely by the Communist Party of Indo-China (CPIC), which was formally established in 1930. The movement, generally known as the 'Nghe Tinh Soviets', continued until 1931, when it was suppressed with the use of French air power. As a result many communist leaders (including several future members of the North Vietnamese Politburo) spent the years 1930–36 in prison.

In 1936 the Popular Front Government in France allowed an amnesty of political prisoners and a measure of press freedom and open political activity. Among those who took advantage of it to organize meetings and to write articles were Pham Van Dong, Vo Nguyen Giap and Dang Xuan Khu (Truong Chinh). Meanwhile, the CPIC held its first National Congress at Macau in 1935, and a clandestine leadership was created by Le Hong Phong, who had trained in Moscow. During the same period Trotskyist and Stalinist movements emerged. Following the outbreak of war in Europe in 1939, the various left-wing groups were again banned, but in the North, at least, the communists managed to maintain a secret network of cells throughout the war period, under the leadership of Truong Chinh.

A different type of political movement, which developed in the South during the 1920s and 1930s, was associated with a number of religious sects, including the Caodaists, formally established in 1926, and the Hoa Hao Buddhists. These groups tended to draw political inspiration and support from Japan. Also during the 1930s there was a revival of more orthodox Mahayana Buddhism in all regions of Viet Nam, although it did not play an active role in politics until the 1960s. In addition, Roman Catholicism made considerable progress under the French, so that by 1954 there were probably over 2m. Vietnamese adherents.

REVOLUTION, WAR AND PARTITION

In July 1941 the Japanese advanced into southern Indo-China. Administrative control, however, was left in French hands, with a French admiral acting as Governor and accepting the authority of Vichy France. Among the Vietnamese, pro-Japanese groups gained support, notably the Cochin-Chinese sects and the new Dai Viet (Great Viet Nam) Party. The Japanese finally deposed the French administration and disarmed its forces in March 1945, in order to prevent its playing any role that would assist the allies in the closing stages of the war. At Japan's behest, the Emperor Bao Dai revoked the treaties of 1884–85 which had made Annam and Tongking into protectorates, and proclaimed their independence. It was not until August, however, that he was permitted to revoke the treaties concerning Cochin-China, signed in 1862 and 1874. In April 1945 Bao Dai appointed a new Government, led by the pro-Japanese Tran Trong Kim, which made some effort to institute reforms. However, in wartime conditions, with most communications destroyed by US bombing, this regime was unable to control the country or to relieve the famine which had afflicted northern Viet Nam since late 1944.

Meanwhile, in southern China, a number of Vietnamese political groups were active, of which the communists were by far the most effective. Their leader in China was Ho Chi Minh, who as Nguyen Ai Quoc had played a significant part in founding the CPIC and who now returned from Moscow as its Comintern-appointed leader. In June 1941 the Chinese-based leaders and the leaders of the party still active in Tongking decided to found the Viet Nam Doc Lap Dong Minh Hoi (Revolutionary League for the Independence of Viet Nam), usually known as the Viet Minh. During the next few years the communists survived a series of French punitive campaigns against them.

In early 1945, after a period of imprisonment at the hands of the Chinese Nationalists, Ho Chi Minh made contact with the US forces operating behind Japanese lines, and obtained their assistance in expanding his base areas inside Tongking. When the Japanese removed the French administration, the Viet Minh soon emerged as the most effective political force within the country. After the Japanese surrender, the Viet Minh quickly gained control of many provinces throughout the country. On 24 August Bao Dai abdicated in their favour, and on 2 September Ho Chi Minh, as President of the new provisional Government, read the declaration of independence which marked the foundation of the Democratic Republic of Viet Nam. In the next month, the Viet Minh leaders carried out the first stages of what amounted to a political and social revolution. They were stronger in the North, where they had been active throughout the war. In the South they had only a loosely arranged front organization, in which their allies and rivals included the formerly pro-Japanese sects and various other small groups. Their provisional committee took over in Saigon but was not very firmly established in power.

The Allied powers had agreed at the Potsdam Conference in August 1945 on the temporary occupation of Viet Nam by British and Chinese Nationalist forces, respectively south and north of the 16th parallel. In the South, Franco-British co-operation enabled the French to recover control in Saigon and to land reinforcements there in October. By the end of the year the British zone was virtually under French control, apart from a number of rural areas where guerrillas held out; the British themselves left in early 1946. In the North, the French were obliged to negotiate first with the Chinese, who agreed to withdraw in March 1946, and then with Ho Chi Minh's Government in Hanoi. Elections for a National Assembly were held in the North, and some parts of the South, in January 1946. The Viet Minh dominated the polls, although they reserved a number of seats for Nationalist members, and they had the upper hand in the coalition Government formed in February. The withdrawal of the Chinese troops in the next few months left the Nationalists with very little power.

Negotiations between the French and the Viet Minh permitted the return of a French army to Tongking in early 1946, but a semi-formal *modus vivendi* broke down, when Cochin-China was granted independence. In May 1946 Ho Chi Minh led a delegation to France for further discussions, which collapsed by the end of the year. An attempted Viet Minh rising in Hanoi on 19 December was defeated by the French, and the Viet Minh withdrew to the countryside to plan a more protracted guerrilla war. The French began a series of negotiations with Vietnamese anti-communists (including Bao Dai) which led to the establishment of the Associated State of Viet Nam in 1949. If the French could recover firm control over the country, it was to be united under the new regime, with France retaining control of defence and other important policy areas. The new state had a succession of Prime Ministers between then and 1954, and was internationally recognized by the Western powers in early 1950. At about the same time, China and the USSR recognized the Democratic Republic of Viet Nam.

In 1950–51 communist victories in neighbouring China resulted in closer links with Viet Nam, while the USA responded by offering aid to the French side. The CPIC re-emerged in 1951, renamed as the Viet Nam Workers' (Lao Dong) Party, and held its second National Congress that year. The conflict assumed a 'cold war' dimension. Despite defeats in early 1951, the Viet Minh armies gained in strength, with the steady supply of Chinese material: the military conflict culminated in the siege of Dien Bien Phu, a fortress-encampment near the Laos border, which fell to the Viet Minh in May 1954.

In May 1954 an international conference on Indo-China began in Geneva. On 21 July a cease-fire agreement was signed by representatives of the French and Viet Minh high commands, and an international declaration by 14 governments set forth conditions for an eventual political settlement, emphasizing that politically Viet Nam remained one country. In effect, however, two zones were created, to be administered by the two existing Vietnamese Governments: that of the Democratic Republic in Hanoi and that of the State of Viet Nam in Saigon, with latitude 17°N as the boundary between them. A period of 300 days was allowed for regrouping, during which almost 130,000 people moved north, while as many as 900,000 people (mainly Roman Catholics) moved to the South.

SOUTH VIET NAM AND THE WAR

The State of Viet Nam, originally within the French Union, concluded an independence agreement with France in June 1954. After the cease-fire agreements at Geneva in July, French forces withdrew, leaving the state's jurisdiction limited to the zone south of 17°N. Complete sovereignty was transferred by France in December. For a little over 20 years after the Geneva agreements, the area south of the 17th parallel remained a separate state with an anti-communist administration. A French community continued to look after its own interests there, notably the large rubber estates north of Saigon. However, economically, culturally and, above all, militarily, South Viet Nam moved out of the French ambit and into the US sphere of influence, developing much closer relations with other US-aligned states: the Philippines, Thailand and the Republic of Korea. It very soon became dependent for its survival on US aid.

From 1954 to 1963 Ngo Dinh Diem and his brother, Ngo Dinh Nhu, who headed the secret security forces, dominated the politics of South Viet Nam. Coming from a family of Roman Catholic mandarins (a combination characteristic of the colonial period), Diem had been a minister at Hué briefly in 1933 but had since become strongly anti-French, as well as being deeply anti-communist. He became Prime Minister at the behest of the USA in June 1954. His position was initially very insecure; by October 1955, however, he was strong enough to hold a referendum, the result of which enabled him to depose Bao Dai and to proclaim himself President of the Republic of Viet Nam. He also repudiated the Geneva declaration and rejected plans to hold elections which it had envisaged for July 1956. During the next few years, he attempted to destroy the Viet Minh (or, as he termed it, Viet Cong) network in the South. Many communists and their sympathizers who had remained in the South in 1954 were imprisoned. In May 1959 the communist leadership in Hanoi authorized a political, and limited military, campaign in the South. In December 1960 the communists created the National Front for the Liberation of South Viet Nam (NLF), to unite opposition to Diem.

In 1961–62, determined to prevent any communist advance in South-East Asia, President Kennedy provided US troops (numbering 8,000 by the end of 1962) to act as advisers to the South Vietnamese army. US confidence in Diem, whose increasingly brutal tactics included the systematic repression of Buddhist monks, was beginning to decline, and in November 1963 he was overthrown by a military coup with tacit US approval. Diem himself was killed during the coup. However, a change of government in Saigon did not provide protection against a growing rural guerrilla movement. During the latter half of 1963 the communists adopted a more offensive strategy and by the end of the year the situation of the Saigon Government was precarious. French proposals to neutralize Viet Nam were unacceptable to the USA; and, soon after the death of President Kennedy in November, his successor, Lyndon Johnson, committed the USA to a policy of defending South Viet Nam at all costs.

It did not prove easy to create a stable and legitimate regime to succeed Diem. Following a second military coup in January 1964 Gen. Nguyen Khanh assumed power. In February 1965 he was ousted by a group of younger officers led by the air force commander, Air Gen. Nguyen Cao Ky. A nominally civilian government under Phan Huy Quat was followed, in June 1965, by a new military regime, with Lt-Gen. Nguyen Van Thieu as Head of State and Nguyen Cao Ky as Prime Minister.

By that time the USA had decided to reinforce the Saigon Government by sending its own combat troops to fight in Viet Nam. An incident involving US ships in the Gulf of Tongking in August 1964 enabled President Johnson to obtain virtually unrestricted authority from the US Congress, and he used the power granted to him at that time to deal with the Vietnamese situation without any formal declaration of war. The number of US forces in Viet Nam increased from 23,000 at the beginning of 1965 to more than 500,000 by March 1968; in addition, contingents were sent from the Republic of Korea, Australia, the Philippines and Thailand. As a result, the conflict escalated into a war of major proportions, with the communists obliged to send regular North Vietnamese troops to the South, and to rely increasingly on aid from China and the USSR. The USA commenced aerial bombardment of the North in March 1965.

A measure of political stability gradually returned to Saigon, when Nguyen Cao Ky defeated a Buddhist revolt in early 1966. A new Constitution for South Viet Nam came into effect in 1967. As a result, Gen. Nguyen Van Thieu was elected President in September 1967, with Gen. Ky as his Vice-President; elections were also held for the upper and lower houses of a legislature based on the US model. Thieu remained President from October 1967 until April 1975.

Despite their successes in the countryside, communist leaders aimed to cause heavy damage in the urban areas. In January–February 1968 the communists launched an offensive to coincide with the lunar New Year (known as *Tet*). It was on a larger scale than any previous operation, and included attacks on Saigon, Hué and many other towns. There was also heavy fighting just south of the 17th parallel. The *Tet* offensive, although a military defeat, was a political victory that forced the USA to reconsider its policy. Faced with a major financial crisis, and increasing opposition to the fighting, President Johnson decided against a further expansion of the war. Discussions between US and North Vietnamese representatives began in Paris in May. In October Washington and Hanoi agreed to extend the negotiations and the USA thereupon ended its bombing raids against the North. Heavy bombing continued, however, to be an essential part of US strategy in the South, and the talks led to no further decrease in the fighting.

In January 1969, after the transfer of power in the USA from President Johnson to Richard Nixon, the informal talks in Paris were transformed into a formal conference between representatives of the USA, North Viet Nam, South Viet Nam and the NLF. In June 1969 the NLF was supplemented by the creation of a new Provisional Revolutionary Government of South Viet Nam. During 1969–70 the conflict continued: although the USA began to withdraw its own troops, fears that the North Vietnamese might take advantage of the withdrawal led to a sequence of moves by the USA which tended, in fact, to intensify the war. The most spectacular was the invasion of Cambodia (q.v.) in April 1970, following US-supported moves to overthrow the Government of Prince Sihanouk in Phnom-Penh. Equally important was the 'Lam Son' operation of February 1971 in Laos, which damaged North Vietnamese supply lines even though it ended in South Vietnamese retreat. By this time the communist war effort in the South was heavily dependent on the presence of North Vietnamese regular troops.

In March 1972, with US forces reduced to about 95,000, the North Vietnamese launched a new offensive, which led to some of the most intense fighting of the war. The US Government reacted by renewing its bombing of the North and by mining Haiphong and other harbours. By September it was clear that the situation had reached an impasse, while in the USA itself there was mounting pressure to bring the war to a speedy end. Secret meetings in Paris between President Nixon's foreign policy adviser, Dr Henry Kissinger, and Le Duc Tho of the Vietnamese Politburo, which had taken place several times since 1969, began to show progress, following Dr Kissinger's visit to Moscow in September 1972. In December, however, discussions collapsed, and, in order to pressurize the Vietnamese Politburo to resume negotiations, US planes conducted the heaviest bombing raids of the war against North Viet Nam. Only after that was the cease-fire agreement finally signed in Paris in January 1973.

The Paris Agreement provided for the complete withdrawal of all US troops from Viet Nam, together with the return of US prisoners of war, by the end of March 1973. That part of the agreement was largely fulfilled. However, the remaining terms of the agreement, including provisions for political freedom in the South and the creation of a National Council of Reconciliation and Concord were virtually ignored during the next two years. For the USA the war was over. Since 1961 they had suffered 45,941 combat deaths and over 10,000 deaths from other causes in Viet Nam, as well as 150,000 casualties. In the same period, it was estimated, nearly 2m. Vietnamese on both sides had been killed in the war.

For the Vietnamese the war was not yet over: the Paris Agreement provided for a cease-fire, without any requirement that North Vietnamese forces be withdrawn from the South. Nor was there any provision for action by the USA to enforce the agreement, or to end the fighting in neighbouring Cambodia, and in July 1973 the US Congress made any further US military action in Indo-China illegal. The international commission set up to supervise the cease-fire was not able to prevent frequent outbreaks of fighting between the two sides, while the North Vietnamese were now free to undertake a final offensive. Following the fall of the entire province of Phuoc Long in January 1975, the pace was accelerated. By the end of March the communists controlled Hué and Da Nang and were advancing southwards along the coast. In April they threatened Saigon. Thieu resigned, to be succeeded for a few days by his Vice-President and then by Gen. Duong Van Minh. On 30 April the last members of the US embassy and other personnel were evacuated and the communists entered Saigon, which they renamed Ho Chi Minh City.

NORTH VIET NAM

During the same 20-year period following the Geneva agreements, Viet Nam north of the 17th parallel underwent a political and social revolution under a communist-led regime. A land reform programme, carried out in 1953–56, proved controversial, with an estimated 15,000 people killed during its implementation. Its object was to eliminate as a class the landlords and rich peasants who—often through money-lending as much as through actual ownership of land—had dominated the economic life of the villages. Land was confiscated and redistributed, and in many cases the former owners were publicly disgraced, imprisoned or killed. This social revolution in the countryside was followed in 1959–60 by a movement for the widespread introduction of co-operatives. During the 10 years from 1956 a series of national economic plans made some progress towards developing agricultural and industrial production, using a limited amount of material and technical aid from the major communist countries. However, these programmes were impeded by the separation from the southern half of the country.

There was an inevitable conflict of priorities between the desire to implement a socialist revolution in the North, and the policy of 'completing the revolution' in the South and bringing about national reunification. It was probably not finally settled until 1960, when the Hanoi leaders decided on a combination of support for the NLF in the South, and the simultaneous implementation of a Five-Year Plan (1961–65) in the North. Meanwhile, important changes in leadership took place in 1956–57, with the removal of Truong Chinh as party Secretary-General and the emergence (by October 1957) of Le Duan as a major figure in Hanoi; previously he had led the party in the South.

At the beginning of 1960 a new Constitution came into effect, and in May elections were held for a new National Assembly to take the place of that elected in 1946. The third National Congress of the Lao Dong Party, in September 1960, established the broad framework of policy within which the country was to develop, despite the ravages of war, over the next 15 years. The policy adopted in 1960 assumed a substantial measure of economic and military aid from the USSR. However, North Viet Nam, which also aimed to continue good relations with China, faced a growing division between the two major communist powers after 1959. The escalation of the war in the South in 1965 made it imperative to secure more Soviet aid, but Hanoi sought to maintain good relations with both Moscow and Beijing for the next 10 years.

The North was involved in the war as the 'rear area' of the NLF, following a decision in 1960 that the South Vietnamese should, in principle, achieve their own revolution, with as much support from the North as they needed. By 1973 there were 150,000 regular North Vietnamese troops in the South, but their status there continued to be denied. The war seriously disrupted life in the North during the years of US bombing, from March 1965 until November 1968, and again in 1972. During 1965–66, to defend the economy against this aerial bombardment, the Hanoi Government devised a system of decentralized activity which may well have had long-term significance for economic development. However, by 1969, when Ho Chi Minh died, it became concerned about the possibility that in a more liberal system, capitalist agriculture might again become established. During 1969–70 Truong Chinh led a movement to expand the co-operative system and to limit the encroachments of individualism. Nevertheless, during the early 1970s it became clear that Le Duan was the dominant leader in the party; he placed more emphasis on economic modernization than on ideological purity. Even after the Paris Agreement of January 1973, there continued to be a strong emphasis on combining defence and production.

THE SOCIALIST REPUBLIC OF VIET NAM

The period from the fall of Saigon in April 1975 to mid-1976 was one of transition. At first it appeared that the northern and southern parts of the country might continue to have a separate existence for several years, although it was clear that the ultimate authority in both halves was a single united party, with its Political Bureau and Secretariat in Hanoi and a southern bureau in Ho Chi Minh City. In May 1975 revolutionary committees were created at all levels in the South. The South was recognized as having its own distinctive problems, arising from the fact that its 'national democratic' revolution had still to be completed, whereas the North was already in the stage of 'socialist' revolution. A first priority in the South was to bring the economy under control, and, following the closure of private banks in August, the traders who had dominated the Saigon economy under Nguyen Van Thieu were accused of hoarding commodities and their stores were confiscated; their savings (in piastres) were rendered valueless by the introduction of a new currency which could be regulated more easily. Although it was still permissible for small capitalist enterprises to continue operating, the state took steps to control, if not to own, capitalist enterprises left behind by foreign investment. Foreign banks and enterprises were no longer allowed. Former members of the South Vietnamese army and civil service were obliged to undergo 're-education' courses, sometimes in camps where study was combined with labour. More than 300,000 Saigonese officials were sentenced to long-term re-education.

In November 1975 a reunification conference was held in Ho Chi Minh City, presided over by Truong Chinh (representing the North) and Pham Hung (representing the South), which formally decided that reunification should take place through elections to be held throughout the country during 1976. Accordingly, a single National Assembly was elected in April, and when it met on 2 July it declared the inauguration of the Socialist Republic of Viet Nam, with its capital in Hanoi. The Assembly also established a committee to draft a new Constitution. The new Government included a few members of the former Provisional Revolutionary Government of South Viet Nam, but it was dominated for the most part by the leaders of the former Democratic Republic and, in effect, of the Political Bureau of the Viet Nam Workers' Party, which was restyled the Communist Party of Viet Nam (Dang Cong San Viet Nam) at the fourth Party Congress in December. The Congress decided that the immediate economic priorities were the development of agriculture and light industry, with heavy industry (the ultimate goal) temporarily assuming secondary importance.

In 1976 Viet Nam joined the IMF and the World Bank, and in 1977 it sought Western investment in Vietnamese industrial projects. During the same year there were moves towards the 'normalization' of relations between Viet Nam and the USA, which abandoned its opposition to Vietnamese membership of the UN, to which Viet Nam was subsequently admitted in September 1977. However, the US Congress had voted in May to forbid aid to Viet Nam, while the Vietnamese, until mid-1978, made the establishment of full diplomatic relations conditional on aid. A trend towards increased dependence on the USSR began in 1977, and in June 1978 Viet Nam became a full member of the (now-defunct) Soviet trading bloc, the Council for Mutual Economic Assistance (CMEA). During the same period, a new phase of economic transformation began, and led eventually to the abolition of private trading and street markets in the South and the unification of the currencies (March–April 1978). These changes were accompanied by a programme to convert agriculture to a system of co-operatives and to transform private industry in the South, and to step up the 'redeployment' of labour from cities to the New Economic Zones (NEZs).

The economic decisions of mid-1977 were part of a much more fundamental shift in Viet Nam's orientation towards the USSR and away from the People's Republic of China. When Pham Van Dong visited Beijing in June of that year, the Chinese Government presented a memorandum suggesting that Viet Nam had not honoured agreements made in the 1950s concerning Sino-Vietnamese borders (both on land and in the Gulf of Bac Bo), and the problem of citizenship of Chinese residents living in Viet Nam. A third issue was China's insistence on maintaining close relations with the Pol Pot regime in Cambodia, which by this time was positively hostile towards Viet Nam. The Vietnamese wanted to draw Phnom-Penh into close ties with Viet Nam and Laos, in an 'Indo-Chinese Federation', whereas China wished to maintain direct relations with Cambodia and Laos independently of Hanoi, thereby thwarting Soviet ambitions in the region.

From September 1977 there was a growing military confrontation between Viet Nam and Cambodia (or Kampuchea, as it was known between 1976 and 1989). It became clear in late 1978 that the Chinese were unable or unwilling to escalate their own military involvement, and it was impossible for the Cambodians to hold out indefinitely. In December the Vietnamese invaded, ostensibly in support of the Kampuchean National United Front for National Salvation, and gained control of Phnom-Penh and other major centres during the early part of 1979, enabling a pro-Vietnamese Government under Heng Samrin to take power (although Pol Pot forces continued to resist in more remote areas). In February 1979 this Government signed a treaty of friendship with Viet Nam, comparable to that already signed with Laos, and was willing to accept the continuing presence of Vietnamese forces which by mid-1984 were estimated at 160,000 to 180,000.

By that time relations with the People's Republic of China had deteriorated drastically. The socialist measures that were introduced in early 1978 had especially affected the Chinese community in southern Viet Nam, which dominated the commercial sector. This fact, combined with fears among Chinese in northern Viet Nam that sooner or later there might be a Sino-Vietnamese war, led to a major exodus of Chinese residents. Between April and July 1978 (when China closed its border), 160,000 of them had fled by land into China; others began to leave by sea, hoping to find refuge elsewhere in South-East Asia. Until this point China had continued to give economic aid to Viet Nam, but between May and July 1978 they abandoned all projects, leaving the Vietnamese more dependent than ever on the USSR and Eastern Europe. In November 1978 Le Duan and Pham Van Dong signed a formal treaty of friendship and co-operation with the USSR. In due course it became evident that the Soviet navy had been granted facilities at Cam Ranh Bay, once a major US base. Over the next few years, the USSR was able to convert it into a naval base for its own use. By 1984 there were said to be several thousand military and civilian advisers from the USSR in Viet Nam.

China was dissatisfied with Viet Nam's invasion of Cambodia, with its orientation towards Moscow, and with its treatment of Chinese residents; by early 1979 there were also serious frontier clashes. On 17 February China sent a punitive force into Viet Nam, and fierce fighting lasted for a month. After capturing the town of Lang Son, but also suffering heavy casualties, the Chinese withdrew in March. Negotiations held in April and May produced no formal agreement but it was decided in May to start the exchange of prisoners of war.

Meanwhile, Vietnamese policy towards the Chinese residents (also known as 'Hoa' people) had become so severe that vast numbers of them were taking to ships in the South China Sea, hoping to reach land or to be picked up by larger vessels. It was said that the Vietnamese authorities had now ceased to object to their leaving, but charged large sums in gold or Western currencies for exit papers. More Chinese also crossed into the People's Republic of China at this time. By mid-1979 it was estimated that there were 200,000 such refugees from Viet Nam in China, and perhaps another 200,000 had reached other countries of South-East Asia, Hong Kong, Taiwan or Australia. Many thousands more were thought to have drowned at sea. As a result of a UN conference in July, Viet Nam agreed to allow an Orderly Departure Programme, sponsored by the UN High Commissioner for Refugees (UNHCR): by June 1992 354,500 people had left the country in this way. Illegal departures continued, however.

Important political changes occurred during 1980–81, starting with a government reshuffle in January 1980. In December, after four years of debate, a new Constitution was finally adopted, under which a newly-elected National Assembly met in July 1981 and appointed both a State Council (which was to constitute a collective presidency) and a new Council of Ministers. Truong Chinh became President of the former, and therefore Head of State, while Pham Van Dong remained Chairman of the Council of Ministers (Prime Minister) with slightly reduced powers. Le Duan, still dominant in the Communist Party, was not included in either of the principal state organs. The party's fifth Congress, twice postponed, was eventually held at the end of March 1982. It became clear, from the reports of preparatory congresses at provincial level, that the party was deeply divided and that some elements in the leadership were being blamed for the country's severe economic failures. When the Congress finally met, a number of prominent figures were removed from the new Politburo (including Gen. Vo Nguyen Giap) and others from the Central Committee. A number of younger men were promoted, but the generation of the 1950s had still not finally relinquished control.

In the early 1980s tension between Viet Nam and Thailand led to greater involvement of the member states of the Association of South East Asian Nations (ASEAN) in the Cambodian question. ASEAN countries promoted an alliance between Pol Pot's Khmer Rouge forces and the non-communist groups, led by Prince Sihanouk and Son Sann, with the result that those three elements formed the coalition Government-in-exile of Democratic Kampuchea in June 1982. The Democratic Kampuchean resistance forces continued to oppose the presence of Vietnamese troops, and were able to establish base camps along the border between Cambodia and Thailand, with the support of the ASEAN states, China and the USA. In early 1985 the Vietnamese captured and destroyed the bases of all three resistance groups, but were unable to defeat the more mobile guerrilla forces. In 1984 Viet Nam announced that it anticipated the total withdrawal of its troops from Cambodia within five to 10 years, and in August 1985 the deadline was established as 1990. However, there appeared to be little reason to believe that either the Government in Hanoi or that in Phnom-Penh genuinely desired a compromise with the forces of Democratic Kampuchea. Meanwhile, the Chinese continued to exert pressure on Viet Nam's northern frontier, forcing Hanoi to keep a substantial part of its armed forces in that area.

REFORM INITIATIVES

By 1985 relations between Viet Nam and the USSR were so close that it was impossible for the changes that followed the emergence of Mikhail Gorbachev as Soviet leader not to have some impact in Hanoi. In mid-1985 the USSR promised to increase its aid to Viet Nam, notably in the fields of petroleum exploration and refining, petrochemicals and metallurgy, while emphasizing the need to apply in Viet Nam the same kind of economic restructuring as was taking place elsewhere in the socialist world: a reduction of the role of centralized planning and state subsidies and the introduction of 'socialist accounting'. The Eighth Plenum of the Central Committee, convened in Hanoi in June, decided to implement such reforms; but a poorly-managed change of currency in September led to rampant inflation, for which the reformers were blamed. The policy of reform was thus slowed throughout 1986.

Significant changes in the Vietnamese leadership occurred during 1986–87. In July 1986 Le Duan died, and was succeeded as General Secretary of the Communist Party by Truong Chinh, who had previously held the post from 1951 to 1956. Truong Chinh retained the position of President (the first occasion on which the top party and state posts had been combined in Viet Nam since the death of Ho Chi Minh). At the sixth Party Congress in December 1986, it was announced that the three most senior members of the Politburo would all retire, to become advisers to the Central Committee: Truong Chinh himself, Pham Van Dong and Le Duc Tho. Nguyen Van Linh was elected the new General Secretary of the party. Linh had played an important role in the South from 1945 to 1975 and had then become party leader in Ho Chi Minh City from 1975 to 1986. He had been responsible for a number of economic experiments in the South, but in 1982 had been removed from the Politburo, only to resume his place there in June 1985, when the need for reform was again accepted. In February 1987 the Minister of Defence, Van Tien Dung, was forced to retire and was succeeded by another veteran of the southern struggle, Le Duc Anh. At that time, several other appointments were made as part of a major restructuring of government ministries in the economic field. Truong Chinh and Pham Van Dong, however, continued to hold their state offices until their retirement in July 1987. At that time a new National Assembly, elected in April, appointed Vo Chi Cong as President of the State Council (and Head of State) and Pham Hung as Chairman of the Council of Ministers. They too were southern veterans, as was Vo Van Kiet, the reform-orientated head of the State Planning Commission and senior Deputy Chairman of the Council of Ministers. Thus, in the course of one year, the incumbents of all the highest positions had changed, and there was a significant shift of power in favour of southerners, who tended to be more supportive of the economic reform programme.

Viet Nam also had to adjust to the new Soviet policy towards Asia, first indicated in a comprehensive way by Gorbachev in July 1986 in a major speech delivered in Vladivostok (USSR). He advocated not only an improvement in Sino-Soviet relations, which by then was already in progress, but also an eventual restoration of relations between China and Viet Nam, which in turn required a concerted effort to resolve the conflict in Cambodia. Incidents on the Sino-Vietnamese border decreased in number in the second half of the year. More fighting occurred, however, in January 1987, when a major battle on the Yunnan sector of the border was alleged by the Vietnamese to have resulted in the deaths of more than 1,500 Chinese troops. The

Chinese leadership now regarded Cambodia as the principal obstacle to a normalization of Sino-Soviet relations. Beijing insisted that the USSR should at least put pressure on Viet Nam to withdraw its troops, instead of continuing to provide the support that enabled the Vietnamese occupation to continue. The Cambodian situation also remained an obstacle to any attempt by Viet Nam itself to open up its own economy to foreign investment. The USA, Japan, the ASEAN countries and the European Community (EC, now the European Union—EU) had all made it clear that the lifting of their embargo on economic relations with Viet Nam, imposed in 1979–80, was conditional upon the withdrawal of Vietnamese troops from Cambodia and upon the conclusion of a comprehensive political settlement. In March 1986 an eight-point peace proposal, submitted by the coalition Government of Democratic Kampuchea, was summarily rejected by the Vietnamese, although it was later regarded as the first step towards negotiations. It called for a supervised withdrawal of Vietnamese troops, followed by the establishment of a quadripartite coalition government including the Phnom-Penh administration and the three resistance groups. In January 1987 the Phnom-Penh regime announced its willingness to negotiate with the resistance groups, but this was immediately rejected by the Khmers Rouge. Viet Nam's urgent need of Western aid, and increasing pressure from the USSR, prompted an announcement in May 1988 that Viet Nam would repatriate 50,000 (of an estimated total of 100,000) troops from Cambodia by the end of 1989. The Vietnamese military high command left Cambodia in June, placing the remainder of the Vietnamese forces under Cambodian control. In July Viet Nam was represented at an informal meeting in Jakarta with the four Cambodian factions and the six members of ASEAN. In January 1989 a commitment to repatriate all Vietnamese troops by September was declared, provided that a political settlement had been achieved in Cambodia.

Meanwhile, the Vietnamese leadership appeared committed to the advancement of reform, although the continuing influence of 'hardliners' remained an obstacle to progress. Following the death of the Chairman of the Council of Ministers, Pham Hung, a meeting of the National Assembly in June took the unprecedented step of nominating Vo Van Kiet, an advocate of political reform, to oppose the Central Committee's more conservative candidate, Do Muoi (ranked third in the Politburo), in the election for the chairmanship of the Council of Ministers. Do Muoi was elected by a majority to the post, but Vo Van Kiet received unexpectedly strong support (36% of the votes). The 'retired' Le Duc Tho continued to exert considerable influence until his death in October 1990. Widespread dissatisfaction with the slow progress towards 'renovation' (*doi moi*) of the economy, often due to the refusal of officials to implement new policies, led to the removal of hundreds of cadres from government posts. In March 1989 a reshuffle of senior economic ministers took place, adjusting the balance further towards reform and strengthening the position of the party leader, Nguyen Van Linh. In the late 1980s he implemented a number of significant economic reforms: a foreign investment law in December 1987; the liberalization of private agricultural production in April 1988; the opening up of interprovincial trade; and measures to encourage private industrial activity, particularly in Ho Chi Minh City.

While economic reforms were undertaken, there were few concurrent measures to liberalize the political system. Municipal elections to provincial and district councils took place in November 1989. Under new legislation, adopted during a meeting of the National Assembly in June, candidates who were not members of the Communist Party were allowed to participate for the first time. (Large numbers of non-Communist Party candidates won posts in November 1994 at the subsequent local government elections.) In December 1989 the National Assembly approved legislation that imposed new restrictions on the press. Open dissension towards the policy of the Communist Party also became a criminal offence. In late 1989 progress towards political reform under *doi moi* was adversely affected by government concern over the demise of socialism in Eastern Europe. At a meeting of the Central Committee in March 1990, tension over the issue of political pluralism resulted in the dismissal of a member of the Politburo, Tran Xuan Bach, who had openly advocated political reform. In early April the Council of State announced an extensive ministerial reorganization.

Following the death in October 1990 of Le Duc Tho, division within the Government on issues of political and economic policy increased. In early 1991, after the publication of articles criticizing government policy and the socialist system, the Communist Party increased surveillance of dissidents and ordered the media to publish retaliatory articles condemning party critics. The seventh party Congress took place in June, following a series of delays which were attributed to increasing dissension within the party. The Congress approved two draft reports presented by the Central Committee, one of which comprised a 10-year programme of economic liberalization, while the other reaffirmed the party's commitment to a socialist political system. Seven members of the Politburo, including Nguyen Van Linh, were retired from their posts. Do Muoi was elected General Secretary of the Communist Party. There seemed to be a consensus within the party leadership, however, that a measure of political reform had become vital, both for the success of economic reform and in order to obviate any potential challenge to the party's monopoly of political power. There was also a notable attempt at the seventh Congress to emphasize the distinctiveness and national character of Vietnamese communism. While Viet Nam's leaders robustly and repeatedly rejected any idea of political pluralism following the collapse of the USSR in December 1991, they remained aware that the success of the country's economic reforms required a move away from archaic Leninist political structures.

The ninth session of the National Assembly (eighth legislature), which took place between late July and early August 1991, elected the reformist, Vo Van Kiet, to replace Do Muoi as Chairman of the Council of Ministers. The Minister of Foreign Affairs, Nguyen Co Thach, and the Minister of the Interior, Mai Chi Tho, who were former associates of Le Duc Tho (and opposed the restoration of links with China), were removed from their positions both in the Government and the Politburo. In addition, the National Assembly considered extensive amendments to the Constitution, whereby the power of the premier and individual ministers would be greatly increased. The postponement of decisions about these constitutional amendments, at a plenum of the party Central Committee in December, indicated that conservatives remained unhappy with the proposed democratic changes. The amendments, which required at least three drafts, were finally ratified by the National Assembly in April 1992. Like the previous (1980) Constitution, it emphasized the central role of the Communist Party; however, it stipulated that the party must be subject to the law. While affirming adherence to a state-regulated socialist economic system, the new Constitution guaranteed protection for foreign investment in Viet Nam, and permitted foreign travel and overseas investment for Vietnamese. Land was to remain the property of the State, although the right to long-term leases, which could be inherited or sold, was granted. The National Assembly was to be reduced in number, but was to have greater power. The Council of State was to be replaced by a single President as Head of State: he or she would be responsible for appointing (subject to approval of the National Assembly) a Prime Minister and senior members of the judiciary, and would command the armed forces (which were now obliged under the Constitution to defend the socialist regime). The new Constitution was to enter into effect after the forthcoming general election.

Under the provisions of the new Constitution, elections to the Ninth National Assembly took place on 19 July 1992. The delays in enacting the legislative amendments, however, confirmed the fears of many in the party leadership that political reform would inevitably undermine the Communist Party's monopoly of power. The elections and the manner in which they were conducted emphasized the continuing influence of party conservatives. While there was a choice of candidates in all constituencies (a total of 601 candidates contested 395 seats), about 90% were members of the ruling Communist Party. Even this figure was misleading. In the past, candidates had to be sponsored by the Viet Nam Fatherland Front, an official body encompassing mass organizations, such as the trade unions. Under the new Constitution, however, private individuals were permitted to stand for election without the endorsement of the Fatherland Front. In practice, only two independent candidates contested the elections, both of whom failed to win a seat, while 41 others who had applied subsequently withdrew their candidature or were disqualified. Only 105 deputies, however, were re-elected from the Eighth National Assembly.

At the first session of the new National Assembly (ninth legislature) in September 1992 the conservative Gen. Le Duc Anh, a former Minister of National Defence and a high-ranking member of the Politburo, was elected to the new post of President, and Nguyen Thi Binh, a member of the National Assembly, was elected as Vice-President (the first woman to hold such a senior position). Vo Van Kiet was re-elected as Prime Minister. At the beginning of October the National Assembly approved the membership of the new National Defence and Security Council and the new Cabinet. The anticipated streamlining of bureaucracy did not take place; indeed, several posts were upgraded to ministerial rank. Four Ministers, all of whom had been implicated in corruption scandals, were replaced.

During 1993 and subsequently there were indications that the National Assembly was beginning to play a greater role in the political life of Viet Nam. In July, after lengthy debate, the Assembly adopted legislation on agriculture that stopped short of recognizing private ownership of land, but liberalized land-holding rights for the country's 55m. peasants. Under the law, farmers were to be permitted to purchase, sell, transfer and rent as well as inherit the right to use land, even though it was to remain the property of the State. The new legislation marked a further step in the phasing-out of collective agriculture. Nevertheless, intense disputes over access to land and land usage continued. In February 1995 the Prime Minister amended the 1993 land law by decree in order to curtail land speculation. This was followed in March by the declaration that rice land could not be converted to other purposes, except under special circumstances. Both actions led to critical comments by deputies in the National Assembly.

Despite the country's economic liberalization, however, there was no toleration of political dissent. In August 1993 14 people were convicted of having conspired to overthrow the Government, and sentenced to terms of imprisonment, and in November several Buddhist monks were imprisoned for having, it was alleged, incited anti-Government demonstrations. In late 1994 two senior Buddhist dissidents, Thich Huyen Quang and Thich Quang Do, were taken into custody. In August of the same year political dissidents associated with the Tan Dai Viet Party (Movement for National Unification and Democracy Building) and officials of the opposition Unified Buddhist Church of Viet Nam were put on trial separately. In June 1995 two Communist Party dissenters, Do Trung Hieu and Hoang Minh Chinh, were arrested. Le Hong Ha, a retired senior police official, was expelled from the party for protesting at their arrests. Hieu and Chinh were sentenced in November to 15 and 12 months in prison, respectively. Chinh's appeal was turned down in the following year. In December 1995 the State took further steps to silence dissent. Le Hong Ha and biologist Ha Si Phu were arrested for political dissent, while Lu Phuong, a southern intellectual, was expelled from the Communist Party. In August 1996 Nguyen Thanh Huyen was given a 15-month suspended sentence for his role in passing classified state documents to Ha and Phu. Ha and Phu were each sentenced to gaol, receiving terms of two years and 12 months respectively.

In January 1994, at a mid-term conference of the Communist Party, Do Muoi praised the country's recent economic achievements and its expanding relations with foreign countries, but emphasized the continuing prevalence of poverty, the increase in corruption and crime, and the inadequacy of the educational system; he also strongly criticized the party for disunity and poor organization. Immediately before the conference four new members were appointed to the Politburo, including the Minister of Foreign Affairs, Nguyen Manh Cam, and during the conference 20 new members (all under the age of 55) were elected to the party's Central Committee. This reflected a recruitment drive during 1994, when some 60,000 new members joined the Communist Party (an increase of 20%, compared with the previous year).

In February 1994 a former Minister of Energy (who had been dismissed in 1992) was sentenced to three years' imprisonment for corruption. Further cases of abuse of office at senior levels continued to be exposed during 1994 as the Government pursued its campaign against corruption. In May 1995 Do Muoi urged the dismissal of 'corrupt elements . . . regardless of their ranks and positions'.

In June 1994 the National Assembly approved new legislation, including a labour law which guaranteed the right of workers to strike (providing the 'social life of the community' was not adversely affected). Strikes subsequently occurred in some southern provinces and, in August, the first incident of industrial action in Hanoi was reported. At a plenum of the Central Committee of the party, held in late July–early August, Do Muoi reasserted the need to strengthen Viet Nam's 'open-door' policy in order to attract wider foreign investment; attention was also drawn to the increasing income differential between the urban and rural economies.

In October 1994 the National Assembly held a 12-day session to consider its legislative programme for 1995; priority was assigned to further administrative and legislative reforms, including the draft civil code. This priority was reaffirmed at a plenum of the Central Committee of the Communist Party, held in January 1995. In March–April the National Assembly finally approved legislation on state enterprises, determining various categories of enterprise and the degree of government control over ownership. (In 1996 there were an estimated 6,000 state enterprises whose status was still to be determined.) The Assembly also approved laws on civil aviation and people's courts. At its end-of-year session in November, the legislature finally adopted the civil code whose 12 drafts had been under consideration since 1980. The Assembly also approved a major restructuring of ministerial portfolios: eight separate ministries (or state commissions) were merged into three new ministries (of agriculture and rural development, of industry, and of planning and investment). At its session in March 1996 the Assembly approved the organic budget law, the law on co-operatives and the law on mining.

The end-of-year Plenum (November 1995) of the Communist Party adopted the confidential draft documents to be presented to the eighth national Congress scheduled for the following year. Included was a controversial amendment to the party statutes, which abolished the Secretariat and replaced it with a more powerful Standing Board of the Politburo. This drew attention to the party leadership issue, and provoked heated disagreement among conservatives and reformers. In February 1996 the conservatives launched a campaign against 'social evils', including pornography, prostitution, gambling and drug abuse. The campaign adopted an anti-foreign stance when English-language advertising signs were painted over, and 'pubs' and karaoke bars frequented by visiting businessmen were closed down by the police. In September the authorities in Ho Chi Minh City renewed their campaign against 'social evils' by detaining prostitutes, drug addicts and homeless persons.

Conservative party leaders also made a concerted effort to bring about the retirement of key reformers and to capture the party's most senior leadership post. Signs of internal party division soon emerged in public. Prime Minister Vo Van Kiet was attacked by conservatives for a confidential memorandum he had written in August 1995, shortly after the normalization of relations with the USA. In this document, Kiet downgraded the importance of ideology, argued for the curtailment of party interference in day-to-day state affairs, and recommended thorough-going reform of state-owned enterprises. The conservatives countered in October in a document widely circulated within party ranks. They argued that the normalization of relations with the USA would result in greater interference in Viet Nam's internal affairs. Viet Nam, they asserted, was the target of a 'hostile campaign of peaceful evolution' aimed at overthrowing Communist Party rule. In April the party Central Committee's 10th Plenum released to the public draft policy documents to be presented to the eighth Congress and, in an unexpected decision, announced the expulsion from the party of leading conservative Nguyen Ha Phan for 'having committed serious mistakes in his past activities'. Phan was in charge of the party's economic commission and also of a special personnel commission charged with examining the suitability of delegates to the eighth Congress. Shortly after Phan's demise, his ideological and political mentor, senior Politburo member Dao Duy Tung, was reportedly placed under house arrest. The party leadership then moved to reselect delegates to the forthcoming national Congress.

At the Eighth Congress (28 June–1 July 1996) party delegates acted to restore internal party unity. The three senior leaders, Secretary-General Do Muoi, State President Le Duc Anh and Prime Minister Vo Van Kiet were retained in office, despite strong rumours that they would step down. Their retention underscored the party's desire to maintain political stability and policy continuity. The new Politburo was expanded to 19 members, the largest in the party's history. Included in this number were four representatives of the military and two from the Ministry of the Interior, a clear indication that firm control would be maintained over the party, State and society. Delegates also endorsed, with several notable modifications, the compromise policy documents drafted in late 1995 by the reformist and conservative camps. The new documents made clear that Viet Nam would not embark on any destabilizing political reforms. Political pluralism and multi-party democracy were condemned in fulsome terms. Priority was given to the state sector which was to continue to dominate the economy, but private-sector activities were also to be allowed. Viet Nam was to continue its 'open-door' policy. Priority was to be given to improving the legal and legislative base to support continued foreign direct investment. At the same time, however, the party emphasized the establishment of cells in private enterprises and joint ventures. A key theme emerging from the eighth Congress was the stress on economic modernization and industrialization in the years to come. In an unexpected move prompted by the intervention of a lone delegate in the final moments of the Congress, the delegates voted to delete the powers accorded to the Politburo Standing Board from the draft party statutes. The statutes were then approved.

In 1995 the party launched a major recruitment drive to mark the 65th anniversary of its founding. Figures released a year later indicated that although the party had increased its membership by 85,900 new members (the highest intake since 1986) to a total of 2.13m., recruitment had not kept pace with population growth. More women, ethnic minorities and better-educated individuals were recruited, but figures for the under-30 age group showed a decline. Party membership in the over-60 category increased slightly. The percentage of urban party members increased, while that of peasant farmers fell from one-third to just over one-quarter of total membership. Official figures released in 1996 and 1997 indicated that membership of the party increased in those years by 90,000 and 103,000 respectively. Of the members that joined in 1997—the highest number to join the party in any single year for a decade—24.3% were women, 12.8% were from ethnic minority groups and 19% were college graduates. In August 1998 it was reported that more than 47,600 new members had been admitted to the party in the first six months of that year.

In 1996 two high-profile corruption cases received extensive media attention. The first involved Tamexco, a trading firm with connections to the Ho Chi Minh City party apparatus. Several leading officers of the Viet Nam Commercial Bank were also implicated. In January 1997 the Ho Chi Minh City Court sentenced four of the 15 defendants to death by firing squad; this decision was upheld in March by the Appeals Court, and in January 1998 three of the four who had been sentenced to death were executed in front of thousands of onlookers. The second corruption case involved directors of the Minh Phung Export Garment Company and Epco, a trading firm: the head of the former engaged in real estate speculation using collateral provided by the latter for use in securing a loan from the Viet Nam Commercial Bank. The fraud was revealed when Minh Phung's director could not repay the bank loan and it was discovered that the collateral was missing. In early 1998, in an illustration of the Government's commitment to countering corruption, the Communist Party announced that in 1997 it had disciplined and expelled some 18,000 members, and sentenced 469 to terms of imprisonment. Further members of the party were reported to have been disciplined over corruption-related offences in July 1998. Also in 1998 it was reported that allegations of corruption made against one of the members of the Politburo Standing Board, Pham The Duyet, were under investigation by Communist Party leaders. Political analysts alternatively speculated that the emergence of the allegations suggested a power struggle within the Politburo or served as evidence of a rift between the current leadership of the Communist Party and the party 'old guard'.

In November 1996 the 10th session of the Ninth National Assembly brought about a major cabinet reorganization (three ministerial-level posts were abolished) and reshuffle that reflected personnel changes on the new party Central Committee selected by the eighth national Congress: for example, Le Minh Huong was appointed Minister of the Interior, replacing Bui Thien Ngo, who retired. In a surprising move, the National Assembly rejected the Prime Minister's nominee for the transport and telecommunications portfolio; this position remained vacant for a year. In all, 12 positions were vacated and eight new ministers appointed. The National Assembly also voted to remove Le Thanh Dao from his post as head of the Supreme People's Organ of Control because of corruption in his business dealings. On 16 November, a few days after the session, President Le Duc Anh suffered a serious stroke; he remained incapacitated until 31 January 1997, when he made a brief appearance on Vietnamese television. Anh later addressed the 11th session of the National Assembly in April. The National Assembly also decided to increase the number of provinces from 53 to 61 (since several were becoming too powerful), and raised the status of Da Nang (directly responsible to the central government).

The party convened the second plenary session of the Central Committee in December 1996. This meeting adopted two important resolutions dealing with 'the strategic orientations and tasks until the year 2000' in the fields of education and training, and science and technology. In late January 1997 the Politburo issued an anti-corruption resolution. The next meeting of the Central Committee was held against a background of widespread rural unrest in central Viet Nam, especially in the province of Thai Binh. These disturbances had been preceded by violent protests in May and December 1996 by peasants living near Hanoi airport, who were protesting against the repossession of their land in order to build a golf course. Details of the unrest in Thai Binh in 1997 were initally sketchy, as the foreign press was prohibited from visiting the area and the official media was kept silent. It was only in September 1997 that detailed reports appeared in the party and army newspapers. These sources indicated that, in May, an estimated 3,000 farmers from 128 villages had marched on a district office to protest against the imposition of numerous taxes and fees as well as corruption by local officials. In June 1997 rural protests escalated in intensity and spread to the provincial capital. According to official reports issued later, these incidents were serious in nature, and 'extremist actions', such as physical assault on local officials and their property, were alleged to have occurred. Special police units were dispatched to restore law and order; party leaders in Hanoi also responded by sending a member of the Politburo to make two inspection visits. In November, as unrest continued, the Government pledged to provide financial aid to Thai Binh province. In July 1998 more than 30 people were sentenced to terms of imprisonment for their involvement in the unrest. In order to combat continued unrest, the Politburo authorized local police and army units to establish temporary detainment camps, where individuals could be held for up to two years without trial.

The Third Plenum of the Central Committee, held in June 1997, considered these events and passed a major resolution on 'developing the people's right to be masters of the nation'; in other words, in order to regain peasant support the party decided to implement policies that would give farmers greater influence at the basic level. At the same time, more scope was to be given to representatives from 'people's organizations' at local level in the political process. These initiatives were designed to provide checks and balances on local authorities. The third plenum also made the decision to expand the party's Central Control Commission by including two new members, to enhance its effectiveness in dealing with abuse by party and state officials. More importantly, the third plenum adopted a second major resolution, which set out the guidelines for developing a personnel strategy for cadres employed by the State. Finally, the third plenum also decided on the procedures to be followed in the forthcoming elections for the 10th legislature (1997–2002) of the National Assembly. On the eve of the plenum it was announced that President Le Duc Anh, Prime Minister Vo Van Kiet and nine other cabinet-level officials, as well as Secretary-General Do Muoi, would not be standing for re-election. According to foreign press reports, the plenum endorsed Phan Van Khai, Deputy Prime Minister, to replace Vo Van Kiet; it also endorsed the retention of Nong Duc Manh as Chairman of the National Assembly Standing Committee. The plenum could not, however, reach consensus on Le Duc Anh's replacement as President.

Viet Nam's National Assembly elections proved to be a watershed. Under a revised electoral law, the National Assembly was expanded from 395 to 450 seats organized in multi-member constituencies, which were contested by a record 663 candidates. The party-controlled pre-selection process was modified to enable more independent (or self-nominated) candidates to stand than previously. On 20 July 1997 the elections resulted in the selection of a younger and better-educated legislature. The number of women and ethnic minority deputies rose markedly, while the number of non-party deputies nearly doubled from 8% to 15% of the total. Significantly, 11 independent candidates qualified to stand, and three of these—a northern businessman, a southern surgeon and former member of the South Vietnamese army, and a woman from the H'mong ethnic minority—were elected.

The convening of the first session of the 10th legislature was preceded by the holding of the party Central Committee's Fourth Plenum in September. This meeting once again considered nominees for the office of President, as well as other leadership posts. There were two main contenders for the Presidency, namely Nguyen Manh Cam, the Minister of Foreign Affairs, and Doan Khue, the Minister of National Defence. Once again, however, deadlock ensued, but a compromise was eventually reached: Deputy Prime Minister Tran Duc Luong, a technocrat, was selected as a candidate. The National Assembly convened in September and duly endorsed the party's nominees. Tran Duc Luong was elected President after Doan Khue stepped aside. President Luong then nominated Nguyen Thi Binh as Vice-President, Nong Duc Manh as Chairman of the Assembly's Standing Committee and Phan Van Khai as Prime Minister; all were elected.

Prime Minister Khai then successfully proposed that the number of Deputy Prime Ministers be expanded from three to five and that each be given responsibility for an enlarged portfolio. Nguyen Tan Dung, at 48 the youngest member of the Politburo, was elected as First Deputy Prime Minister with responsibility for internal and economic affairs; Nguyen Manh Cam, who retained his previous post as Minister for Foreign Affairs, was given responsibility for foreign political and economic relations; Nguyen Cong Tan, the former Minister for Agriculture and Rural Development, was made responsible for rural development and water resources; Phan Gia Khiem, the former Minister for Science, Technology and the Environment, was charged with overseeing culture, education and environmental matters; and Ngo Xuan Loc, the former Minister of Construction, was placed in charge of industry, construction and transport. Prime Minister Khai also proposed a Cabinet consisting of 31 persons (29 men and two women). Included in this number were seven new ministers (Agriculture and Rural Development; Construction; Defence; Education and Training; Population and Family Planning; Science, Technology and the Environment; and Trade). Unexpectedly, however, the National Assembly rejected by a vote of 250 to 195 Phan Van Khai's nominee for Governor of the State Bank of Viet Nam, Cao Sy Kiem. Kiem's rejection was due to his implication in several scandals and debt-management problems in the banking sector during the previous year. In May 1998 Deputy Prime Minister Nguyen Tan Dung was appointed Governor of the State Bank of Viet Nam.

At the enlarged Fourth Plenum of the Central Committee, which met in December 1997, Do Muoi resigned and was replaced as party General Secretary by Le Kha Phieu. (Phieu had served as a political officer in the army before being appointed to the party Secretariat in 1992 and subsequently being placed in charge of the party's Internal Political Protection Commission.) Following the resignation from the Politburo of Do Muoi, Le Duc Anh and Vo Van Kiet, four new members—Phan Dien, Nguyen Minh Triet, Nguyen Phu Trong and Gen. Pham Thanh Ngan—were appointed. These appointments strengthened the conservative influence within the party. Immediately after his election, Phieu reshuffled the Politburo Standing Board and effected a major reorganization of the military hierarchy. Tran Duc Luong, Phan Van Khai, Nong Duc Manh and Pham The Duyet were appointed to the Politburo Standing Board. The National Minister of Defence, Pham Van Tra, was promoted to the rank of Senior Lieutenant-General; Gen. Pham Thanh Ngan was appointed head of the army's General Political Department; new heads were also appointed to lead the Technical and Logistics General Departments. Gen. Dao Trong Lich was appointed Deputy Minister of National Defence and Chief of the General Staff (in May 1998, however, he was killed in an air crash in Laos, along with 13 other senior officers).

In addition to the leadership question, the party Central Committee's Fourth Plenum also considered economic issues. The Committee resolved to accord priority to the improvement of Viet Nam's economic efficiency and international competitiveness and to mobilize domestic capital; particular emphasis was to be placed on the labour-intensive, export-orientated processing industries. It was also decided to continue with the equitization of state-owned enterprises although at a cautious pace. The Government was ordered to reduce spending, balance the budget and practise thrift. The party Central Committee held its fifth plenary session in July 1998. Two principal issues were discussed: namely, the challenge posed to Vietnamese identity and culture by the forces of globalization and the impact on the country's economy of the Asian financial crisis. Regarding Viet Nam's response to the regional economic crisis, the plenum stressed the importance of the mobilization of domestic capital resources to offset the shortfall in foreign direct investment. At the same time, new capital markets in Europe and the USA would need to be found to offset the decline of those in North-East Asia. In the same month Prime Minister Phan Van Khai issued a decree authorizing the creation of a securities market as the first step towards the creation of a stock exchange.

In August 1998 the release of more than 5,000 prisoners under a general amnesty was announced by the Government. Among those released were prominent dissidents Doan Viet Hoat and Nguyen Doan Que; the release of both men was, however, reported to be conditional upon their immediate exile from Viet Nam. Following his release, Hoat sought exile in the USA while Que, who refused to emigrate, was placed under house arrest. On 4 March 1999 the scientist and dissident writer, Nguyen Thanh Giang, was rearrested on charges of possessing anti-socialist propaganda; he was released from custody in May. On 7 May Vietnamese security police raided an evangelical bible reading in Hanoi and detained 20 persons, including Pastor Tran Dinh (Paul) Ai, for participating in an 'illegal religious event'; Ai was released in early June. In October of the previous year the Special Rapporteur on religious intolerance of the UN Commission on Human Rights, Abdelfattah Amor, visited Viet Nam to investigate assertions made by the Vietnamese authorities that greater freedom of religious expression was being tolerated in the country. At the end of his visit, Amor stated that his investigation had been obstructed by government officials and that he had been prevented from meeting key religious dissidents.

In early September 1999 it was announced that the Government was to free 1,712 prisoners and to reduce the sentences of more than 4,000 others under an amnesty to mark the 54th anniversary of the country's declaration of independence.

Viet Nam's deteriorating economic circumstances were addressed by the Communist Party Central Committee's sixth plenum (first session) in October 1998. Although the final communiqué noted that Viet Nam's 'economic growth rate has slowed, and output and trade have become less effective', it declared, none the less, that Viet Nam had achieved considerable success in maintaining political stability and in the attainment of a GDP growth rate of 6% in 1998. The plenum accorded priority to agriculture and rural development, and noted that Viet Nam continued to possess plentiful untapped domestic resources that could be used to stimulate development. In particular, it highlighted the mobilization of domestic savings and funds from overseas Vietnamese as sources of investment. The plenum indicated that an effort would also be made to revitalize rural co-operatives in an attempt to reassert central control following a period of prolonged decentralization. During the sixth plenum Viet Nam's leaders once again demonstrated their unwillingness to adopt the comprehensive reform programme being urged upon them by international financial institutions and donor countries. Their central concern instead was to maintain internal stability and party unity, while preserving Vietnamese culture and values in the face of the intrusive forces of globalization. These concerns were heightened by a marked rise in citizens' complaints about corruption and continued rural unrest during 1998. In December the international donor community pledged US $2,700m. in aid to Viet Nam; an additional 'package' of US $500m. was made conditional upon Viet Nam's adoption of accelerated reforms.

After two postponements, the Communist Party Central Committee held the second session of the Sixth Plenum from 25 January to 2 February 1999. The session was held against a background of several important developments. First, the Communist Party announced that an exceptionally high number of new members—106,000—had been recruited in 1998, a level of intake that exceeded that achieved in all years since 1986, when 'doi moi' was adopted; more than half of the newly-recruited members were under 30 years of ago. Second, the party was faced with a new uprising of internal party dissent, spearheaded by very senior, retired party officials such as Gen. Tran Do, the former head of the party's Ideology and Culture Commission. Tran Do was aroused to protest by peasant unrest in his native province of Thai Binh in late 1997. As a consequence of his criticisms, he was expelled from the party in January 1999, provoking renewed protests. Third, the session was held amidst speculation, precipitated by the death of Politburo member and former Minister of Defence, Doan Khue, that forecast major changes in the party and state leadership. However, no consensus could be reached as to who would replace him on the ruling body. During its second session, the sixth plenum considered the best ways and means by which the efficiency and administrative performance of the Communist Party in the implementation of Viet Nam's reform programme might be improved, and focused in particular upon the need to counter degradation in the party's ranks caused by corruption, excessive bureaucracy, 'individualism', and internal disunity. The plenum resolved to launch a three-year 'criticism and self-criticism' campaign, designed to rid the party of its degenerate members and to restore unity. Party officials were charged with the task of establishing guidelines on the question of the extent to which a party member and his or her family members should be allowed to participate in private economic activities; a committee was also set up to formulate a plan to reduce party and state bureaucracies, and was to report back to the next Central Committee meeting. The discussion of any reorganization of the party leadership was, however, postponed by the plenum. In June the official Vietnamese media published the text of a Politburo decision prohibiting party members from speaking out publicly against party decisions or inciting others to do so; party members also continued to be banned from distributing documents at variance with official party policy. The Central Committee's Seventh Plenum met in Hanoi from 9 to 16 August. It focused on issues relating to the organization and apparatus of the political system, wages and social allowances funded by the state budget, and preparations for the forthcoming ninth national party congress, which was scheduled for the first quarter of 2001.

Two large-scale corruption trials were held in Viet Nam in 1999. The trial of 74 people accused of smuggling (more than one-half of whom were reported to be former government officials) opened in late March; two of the defendants were subsequently sentenced to death, and the remainder to terms of imprisonment, in April. In May 77 businessmen, bankers and government officials appeared in court charged with the fraudulent procurement of state loans; subsequently, in early August, six of the defendants were sentenced to death and six others to life imprisonment, while the remainder received various other terms of imprisonment.

In June 1999 it was reported that a nationwide census was to be held in order to assess the health of Vietnamese who had been exposed to the chemical defoliant, Agent Orange, during the Viet Nam War; the chemical, which had been sprayed in large quantities by the US armed forces, was believed to be responsible for widespread health problems, including genetic damage to unborn children. In 2000 Viet Nam authorized the US Government to dispatch a team of researchers to study the impact of Agent Orange; in July the US Ford Foundation for the first time granted aid to Vietnamese victims of Agent Orange.

The political situation in Viet Nam throughout 1999–2000 was affected by the continued debate between reformist and conservative party members over the pace and extent of the economic reform programme. The Vietnamese economy remained weak in 1998–2000, and grew only slightly in 1999, failing to provide sufficient employment for the rapidly-increasing labour force. Foreign investment fell dramatically in the late 1990s, as a result of the severe negative impact of the Asian economic crisis. Although Viet Nam received substantial international assistance in June 2000, the World Bank and IMF again withheld lending until the Government adopted a 'more comprehensive approach to reform'. However, the leadership continued to resist any attempts radically to reform the economy, preferring not to jeopardize political stability.

Fierce debates over changes in leadership and policies caused the seventh party Plenum, held in August 1999, to be delayed on five occasions. One of the most controversial issues was a proposal to rationalize the Government by eliminating 15% of posts. The First Deputy Prime Minister, Nguyen Tan Dung, resigned from the office of Governor of the State Bank of Vietnam; he was replaced by the Deputy Governor, Le Duc Thuy. However, the reform programme suffered several reverses. In September 1999 the authorities took a number of suppressive measures against dissent. Three Buddhist monks were arrested, some 24 people were sentenced to terms of imprisonment for allegedly attempting to overthrow the Government, while a leading political dissident, Gen. Tran Do, was denied permission to publish a newspaper. Then, at a meeting in October, the Politburo rejected the bilateral trade agreement with the USA that had been reached in principle in July (see below). Continued corruption scandals assumed particular significance in the later part of the year. In October the Customs Chief, Phan Van Dinh, was dismissed, and 22 department officials were charged with corruption in December. In November the Ministry of Finance conducted a government audit and discovered evidence of considerable misuse of public funds. In December Phan Van Khai's principal aide, Nguyen Thai Nguyen, was detained, while the Deputy Prime Minister, Tran Xuan Gia, was dismissed for his involvement in a development project in Hanoi, which had been associated with malpractice. The head of the illicit United Buddhist Church, Thich Huyen Quang, was detained in that month, after meeting with a US diplomat. In December 1999 the National Assembly adopted a new penal code; significantly, the number of capital crimes was reduced from 44 to 29.

At the Eighth Plenum in January 2000 there was an extensive government reorganization: Vu Khoan replaced Truong Dinh Tuyen as Minister of Trade, while the hitherto Deputy Foreign Minister, Nguyen Dy Nien, replaced Nguyen Manh Cam as Minister of Foreign Affairs (although Manh Cam remained in his post of Deputy Prime Minister.) There were also several changes in the party leadership. The Ho Chi Minh City party leader, Truong Tan Sang, was promoted to head the Central Committees Economic Commission, which was to supervise national-level economic policies; Sang was replaced by his deputy, Nguyen Minh Triet. The member replaced by Sang, Phan Dien, was appointed as the Da Nang party leader, a significant position with responsibility for supervising massive economic reconstruction of the Central Coast, where monsoons had killed more than 700 people in late 1999. A new party leader was also appointed for Haiphong. A further increase in membership was announced; the party remained divided, however. Frustrated at conservative opposition to the reform programme, Khai tendered his resignation in March 2000, although it was rejected. The Ninth Plenum, held in April 2000, began to make preparations for changes in leadership and the drafting of the political report for the Ninth Party Congress, provisionally scheduled for March 2001. At the Plenum the Minister of Planning and Investment, Tran Xuan Gia, was reprimanded for corruption, while disciplinary action was taken against two other Central Committee members. It was announced that there would be a revision of the nation's cultural sector as part of measures to combat social ills.

Nationwide celebrations were held for the 25th anniversary of the fall of Saigon and the unification of the country. For the first time since 1975, public recognition of the NLF's contribution was made, and a nationwide amnesty for 12,000 prisoners was granted. Following the celebrations, it was announced that Pham Van Dong, the wartime Prime Minister, and last of the political leaders of that era, had died. In May 2000 the authorities of Ho Chi Minh City, having become frustrated with bureaucratic delays in Hanoi, which, they believed, were acting as a disincentive to foreign investors, announced that they would unilaterally approve foreign investment if the approval process in Hanoi continued for more than two weeks. The National Assembly has also become more critical of the Government following the economic crisis, censuring several cabinet ministers and questioning many government policies in May. One government initiative that was highly scrutinized was the planned construction of a highway along the famous Ho Chi Minh Trail.

At the 10th Plenum in June 2000 the future of state ownership was debated, although none of the anticipated leadership reorganizations were discussed. Proposed changes to the party's Constitution, which would allow the party General Secretary to serve concurrently as the head of state, were raised, but were subsequently rejected. The refusal to address the economic difficulties for fear of increasing factional dissent prompted the country's most prominent war hero, Gen. Vo Nguyen Giap, to criticize the slow pace of economic reforms.

Massive peasant protests erupted in the politically-sensitive Central Highlands region in February 2001, prompting great concern on the part of the Government, which rapidly dispatched troops to quell the unrest. The demonstrators belonged to ethnic minority groups, and many of them had been allied with, and served as mercenaries for, the USA during the war. Although the Government claimed that it had defeated a local guerrilla group, known as the United Front for the Liberation of Oppressed Races, in the early 1990s, it contended that this movement, and indirectly the US Government, had organized the demonstrations. However, the unrest had, in fact, erupted for domestic reasons; Hanoi had forced migration to the sparsely-populated border regions since 1975, disturbing the ethnic balance there, while a further 3.6m. Vietnamese had migrated to the area in later years to establish coffee plantations. The Government was prepared for more unrest, since the Son La hydroelectric project was expected to force the relocation of some 100,000 additional people to the Central Highlands region.

The continuing campaign against corruption dominated political life throughout the year. In September 2000 the Government dispatched missions to 18 of the country's 61 provinces to investigate complaints of local-level corruption. There were several dismissals of prominent officials throughout the year. The head of the Communist Party's Committee for Ethnic Minorities and Mountainous Areas, who had held the office since 1982, was reprimanded for corruption and mismanagement in the agency, which had disbursed little of the allocated funds of some US $100m. to ethnic minority groups. Two provincial party leaders were replaced in early 2001. Some 160,000 party members were investigated, and the Government announced that 43% of the examined party organs had been involved in corrupt practices. (Viet Nam was rated as the most corrupt country in Asia).

The most significant political event in 2000 was the Ninth Party Congress, at which the General Secretary of the Communist Party, Le Kha Phieu, was replaced. Phieu had been criticized for his mismanagement of the economy, nepotism and misuse of the security services for clandestine surveillance of political rivals. In an attempt to establish a more youthful leadership, an age limit of 65 years for election to the post was established, on the proposal of the three senior members of the party and advisers to the Central Committee, Do Muoi, Le Duc Anh and Vo Van Kiet.Throughout the last quarter of 2000 and the first quarter of 2001 there was intense political debate, as Le Kha Phieu struggled to retain his position. At the end of the 11th Plenum's first session in January 2001, it was reported that Phieu was almost certain to be dismissed. After the rural unrest in the Central Highlands, however, Phieu was able to convince the Politburo that the country needed political stability in times of crisis. (Although he was over the 65-year age limit, an exception for principal party officials was made.) At the party Plenum in March the Minister of Defence and the Chief of the General Staff department, both Central Committee members, received the party's highest reprimand for 'management shortcomings'. It was later revealed that the two, who were close allies of Phieu, had been disciplined for allowing the military intelligence service to use clandestine surveillance against Phieu's rivals. At the 12th Plenum in early April the Politburo voted to re-elect Phieu, but the Central Committee, in an unprecedented action, subsequently rejected the Politburo's endorsement of Phieu. (The Central Committee, which had become dominated by provincial leaders, had been critical of the Government's management of the economy.) The Central Committee overwhelmingly elected the hitherto Chairman of the National Assembly and a prominent advocate of reforms, Nong Duc Manh, as the new General Secretary. The Ninth Congress elected a Central Committee (which had been reduced from 170 members to 150) and Politburo (reduced from 19 members to 15). The military lost several of its seats on the Politburo, although it maintained its level in the Central Committee. Both the incumbent party President, Tran Duc Luong, and Prime Minister, Phan Van Khai, were re-elected to their posts. In June a member of the Politburo, Nguyen Van An, was elected as the new Chairman of the National Assembly.

The Ninth Congress took place, amidst continued economic recession. Although foreign investment rates improved during 2000, and in the first quarter of 2001, almost all the capital was invested in projects in, or near, Ho Chi Minh City, while declining commodity prices in the international market placed considerable pressure on the economy. The Political Report issued at the Ninth Congress urged the Government to double GDP by 2010, although it provided few details on how this was to be achieved. In mid-2000 a proposal by the Ho Chi Minh City authorities for greater autonomy was rejected by the central Government, although they were granted greater powers over economic matters.

The Government ordered suppressive measures against dissidents prior to the Congress, which intensified in strength throughout the second half of 2001 and into 2002. Ha Si Phu, a dissident Catholic priest, Father Nguyen Van Ly, and the leader of the clandestine Unified Buddhist Church, Thich Quang Do, were all under house arrest, while Le Quang Liem, the 82-year old leader of the Hoa Hao Buddhist sect, was also detained. In October 2001 Father Ly was sentenced to 10 years' imprisonment; and was subsequently adopted by Amnesty International as a 'Prisoner of Conscience'. The Government continued to view organized religion as a threat to its monopoly of power, and, in particular, made efforts to suppress the activities of religious leaders, who avoided party control. Evangelical Protestantism, the fastest-growing religion in the country, was granted official status and legalized. Unrest continued in the Central Highlands region, following the trial, conducted in secret, of 14 members of ethnic minorities who had protested against the Government in February 2001, and received sentences of between six and 12 years in prison, after being denied legal council. In March 2001 a Buddhist nun committed self-immolation in protest at the lack of religious freedom. In late 2001 the three senior editors of the popular newspaper, *Thanh Nien,* were removed, on grounds of anti-Government propaganda, after publishing the results of a 2000 public opinion survey that demonstrated the then US President, Bill Clinton, to be the second most popular international politician (after Ho Chi Minh, but ahead of Phan Van Khai). The writer, Nguyen Vu Binh, was detained in July 2002, after he dispatched a testimony to a US Congressional caucuson Viet Nam. The dissident community suffered a further reverse, when, on 8 August 2002, the most prominent critic of the Government, Gen. Tran Do, died. Although a representative of the Communist Party Central Committee gave a eulogy at the funeral of the war hero (who was himself a former member of the Central Committee), this included the statement that Do 'had made mistakes at the end of his life'. Unusually, a protest erupted during the funeral, following Tran Do's son's speech, in which he rejected the official party eulogy and verdict.

Despite the Government's uncompromising stance on dissent, there were several signs that gradual political reform was under way. At the Fourth Plenum in November 2001, the Central Committee protested at the December 2000 border treaty with China, which had been negotiated by the ousted General Secretary, Le Kha Phieu, and there were calls for the National Assembly to reject the treaty. At the Fifth Plenum in March 2002, the Communist Party enshrined the role of the private sector in the economy and allowed party members themselves to engage in private entrepreneurial activities. At the same Plenum, General Secretary Nong Duc Manh urged the decentralization of political power and the empowerment of 'grassroots' political organizations. At the final session of the 10th National Assembly in March, the delegates prepared for the parliamentary elections, scheduled for 19 May. For the first time private businessmen were permitted to contest the elections. There was also greater transparency in the election process, the Viet Nam News Agency published details of all candidates. Although 85% of the candidates were party members, they were better educated and more professional. At the March 2002 session the National Assembly adopted legislation requiring that at least 25% of the deputies become full time members, thereby acknowledging the need for more professional and skilled lawmakers. The legislation also increased educational requirements for deputies. At the elections to the 11th National Assembly on 19 May, the 498 seats (increased from the previous 450-member Assembly) were contested by 759 candidates, only 13 of whom were independent. Of the candidates who were not members of the Communist Party, 51 secured seats, while independent candidates won two, the remainder being taken by party members. The first session of the 11th National Assembly, which took place from July to August 2002, approved a significant reorganization in the leadership. Although President Tran Duc Luong, Prime Minister Phan Van Khai and the Chairman of the National Assembly, Nguyen Van An, were all re-elected to their positions, Vu Khoan was promoted from the Ministry of Trade to one of the deputy premierships, while the hitherto Minister of Public Security, Le Minh Huong, was replaced by the Party's top disciplinarian and Politburo member, Le Hong Anh. The 'hardline' Politburo member, Truong Quang Duoc, also became the Vice-Chairman of the National Assembly, reinforcing the party's control over the increasingly independent and assertive legislature.

Corruption continued to provoke extreme controversy within the Communist Party. In July 2002 two members of the party's élite Central Committee were expelled, owing to their connections to the notorious criminal leader, Truong Van Cam, known as Nam Cam. In addition, a high-ranking public security official, two prosecutors, members of the security forces and a radio celebrity were also arrested. Deputy Prime Minister, Nguyen Minh Triet, who took a leading role in the arrest of Nam Cam and officials who abetted him, gained in prominence. Triet, along with Prime Minister Khai and other reformers, urged the adoption of further economic reforms, especially in the state-owned sector. In August the Government announced more generous cash payments for redundant workers and demanded that the private sector take the lead in employment generation. Overall, Vietnamese leaders believed that prospects for economic recovery were favourable.

RECENT FOREIGN POLICY

In the 1980s severe unemployment and poverty remained urgent problems. Refugees—'economic migrants' in addition to victims of political oppression—continued to leave Viet Nam for South-East Asia or for Hong Kong. The increasing reluctance of Western countries to provide resettlement opportunities led to a meeting in Malaysia, in March 1989, at which representatives of 30 nations drafted a programme of action. Members of ASEAN subsequently ceased to accept refugees for automatic resettlement and instituted a screening procedure to distinguish genuine refugees from economic migrants. A similar procedure had been in effect since June 1988 in Hong Kong, and an agreement had been signed in November, whereby Viet Nam agreed to accept voluntary repatriation of refugees from Hong Kong, funded by the UNHCR and the United Kingdom, with UN supervision to protect the returning refugees from punitive measures by the Vietnamese Government. Between March 1989 and March 1995 more than 73,000 Vietnamese were voluntarily repatriated. In June 1989, at a UN-sponsored conference, Western countries committed themselves to the resettlement of the 55,000 'boat people' who had arrived in reception countries before March 1989 (June 1988 in the case of Hong Kong). The USA and Viet Nam agreed to expand the Orderly Repatriation Programme. Despite pressure from the United Kingdom and Hong Kong (where Vietnamese refugees totalled 43,000 in June 1989), the conference rejected proposals of forced repatriation to Viet Nam. In December 1989 the United Kingdom initiated a programme of mandatory repatriation, which, however, was halted as a result of continued opposition from the USA and Viet Nam's refusal to accept deportations. In July 1990 the USA accepted in principle a UN plan, which involved the 'involuntary' repatriation of Vietnamese classed as economic migrants who did not actively oppose deportation. In September the United Kingdom, Viet Nam and UNHCR reached an agreement, whereby the Vietnamese Government would no longer refuse refugees who were repatriated 'involuntarily'.

In October 1991 the British and Vietnamese Governments concluded an agreement on the deportation of about 300 Vietnamese refugees who had been voluntarily repatriated but had returned to Hong Kong. Later in that month the agreement was extended to include all Vietnamese who were not considered to be political refugees. The policy appeared to have deterred all but a few Vietnamese from fleeing to Hong Kong during 1992. In that year more than 12,000 Vietnamese returned from Hong Kong under the voluntary repatriation programme. At the end of 1993 there remained about 31,000 Vietnamese in Hong Kong camps, and a further 20,000 in Indonesia, Malaysia and other parts of South-East Asia. In February 1994 representatives of 31 nations attended a conference in Geneva on the issue of Indo-Chinese refugees. It was agreed that political conditions in Viet Nam were now sufficiently favourable to permit the repatriation of the remaining 51,000 'boat people' by the end of 1995. In February 1995 Viet Nam and the Philippines reached an agreement on the orderly return of 'boat people' who had not qualified as refugees under international law. A further international conference on the issue of Vietnamese refugees was held in Geneva in March 1995. It was decided to end the UN programme for 'boat people' and to support the repatriation of those remaining in camps, either voluntarily or through the Orderly Repatriation Programme. However, the 1995 deadline was not met. Refugees in Hong Kong delayed the process of repatriation through a series of demonstrations in detention camps as well as court appeals. Approximately 6,000 boat people volunteered to return to Viet Nam under a US State Department programme that offered hope of resettlement in the USA only after an immigration interview had been conducted in Viet Nam.

In 1996 decisive steps were taken by the international community to resolve the long-standing problem of Vietnamese refugees in South-East Asia. In mid-January a UN-sponsored meeting in Bangkok agreed that all camps outside Hong Kong should be cleared of refugees by June 1996. The UNHCR terminated its financial assistance on 30 June. Throughout the year Indonesia, Malaysia, the Philippines, Singapore and Thailand took steps to empty their camps. Vietnamese 'boat people' were offered the choice of returning voluntarily or being forcibly repatriated. This new policy provoked rioting and violent resistance by camp inmates in the Philippines, Thailand and Malaysia. While Malaysia succeeded in emptying its camps of those who refused voluntary return, the Philippines abandoned forcible repatriation after violent protests. At 30 September 1996 refugee figures stood at approximately 1,000 in the Philippines and 1,700 in Thailand. China brought pressure to bear on Hong Kong to empty its camps before 30 June 1997 when the United Kingdom was to relinquish control of the territory. Funding for the Hong Kong refugee camps was terminated at the end of 1996; the European Union, however, agreed to provide a further US $20m. to assist in resettlement, in addition to a US $75m. ongoing programme to assist with the reintegration of returnees. In March 1997 6,000 refugees remained in Hong Kong, a number that was reduced to 1,800 by 1 July 1997. Of this number, roughly 500 were stateless ethnic Chinese whom Viet Nam refused to accept, while another 900 were persons who had been repeatedly rejected for resettlement in a third country. Viet Nam continued to co-operate with the Government in Hong Kong in meeting its obligations under the Orderly Departure Programme following the return of Hong Kong to

Chinese sovereignty in 1997. The number of boat people declined to fewer than 2,000 in 1999. In April 1999 it was reported that a total of 13,495 refugees had been repatriated from Hong Kong to Viet Nam since October 1991 under the Orderly Repatriation Programme. In July 1999 Hong Kong announced that the remaining Vietnamese refugees would be given permanent residency, while a group of 500 recent arrivals would be returned home as illegal immigrants. Also in July, the European Union announced that it was terminating its support for the Returnee Assistance Programme, which had provided credit and job-training schemes for returning 'boat people'. In December 1998 it was reported that the UNHCR had announced the closure of its office in Ho Chi Minh City; the agency was, however, to maintain a small office in Hanoi. Viet Nam and the USA were co-operating in a programme under which boat people in South-East Asian camps who agreed to return to Viet Nam would be interviewed for resettlement in the USA. Approximately 2,000 persons per month were interviewed during 1998. In February 2000 the remaining 1,400 refugees in Hong Kong were granted permanent residency.

The necessity of securing greater foreign investment, through the removal of the international embargo on economic relations with Viet Nam, placed the Vietnamese Government under increasing pressure to fulfil its commitment to withdraw all Vietnamese troops from Cambodia in 1989. In September Viet Nam unilaterally withdrew its 26,000 remaining forces from Cambodia, but without international verification. In July 1990, the USA finally acknowledged that all Vietnamese troops had departed. The Khmer Rouge, however, repeatedly charged that Vietnamese troops remained in the country. The Cambodian conflict was eventually settled by the intervention of the five permanent members of the UN Security Council in support of regional diplomatic efforts. Intense diplomatic efforts throughout 1990 and 1991 led to the convening of the Paris International Conference on Cambodia in October 1991. This conference adopted a comprehensive political agreement on Cambodia (see chapter on Cambodia).

Following the elections in Cambodia in May 1993, the status of Vietnamese residents became a political issue between Cambodia and Viet Nam. The Vietnamese Government was concerned by the Cambodian National Assembly's adoption in August 1994 of a new immigration law, which, it claimed, contravened international agreements on human rights and might lead to discrimination against the Vietnamese minority in Cambodia. In the following month such concerns appeared substantiated by two incidents involving the persecution and killing of Vietnamese villagers in Cambodia by Khmer Rouge guerrillas. In December Prince Norodom Ranariddh, the First Prime Minister of Cambodia, visited Viet Nam. The two countries agreed to resolve their outstanding problems on the basis of previous joint communiqués dated January 1992, August 1993 and April 1994. It was also agreed to establish two expert working groups, one on the status of Vietnamese residents in Cambodia and the other on border demarcation issues. Relations improved further in December 1995 when King Norodom Sihanouk paid an official visit to Viet Nam, his first in 20 years. In the following year, however, the question of relations with Viet Nam became a controversial issue in internal Cambodian politics. In January 1996 Norodom Ranariddh alleged that Viet Nam had encroached into Svay Rieng province and relocated border markers. Vietnamese local authorities subsequently claimed that Cambodian troops had opened fire on unarmed civilians without provocation. Two months later Ranariddh threatened military action to curb what he termed Viet Nam's 'border invasion'. This prompted a visit by Prime Minister Vo Van Kiet in mid-April to defuse the situation. Both parties agreed to follow a set of procedures under which negotiation of border incidents would be dealt with first by local and then by provincial officials before being raised at national level. High-level talks on the border issue were held in Ho Chi Minh City in May 1996, but in July Ranariddh once again charged that Viet Nam was encroaching on Cambodian territory. Viet Nam refrained from involving itself in internal Cambodian affairs in the aftermath of the July 1997 action by Second Prime Minister Hun Sen, which ousted First Prime Minister Ranariddh from power. Viet Nam initially supported Cambodia's entry into ASEAN, but soon accepted the ASEAN consensus to delay Cambodia's membership until 'free and fair' elections were held. Representatives of Viet Nam were included in a delegation sent by ASEAN to observe elections held in Cambodia in July 1998. (Subsequently, the Vietnamese Government expressed its approval of the results of the election.) Also in 1998, Viet Nam protested against the violent persecution of ethnic Vietnamese living in Cambodia and vandalism of monuments in Cambodia commemorating Vietnamese volunteers who had served in Cambodia. In June 1999 the General Secretary of the Central Committee of the Vietnamese Communist Party, Lt.-Gen. Le Kha Phieu, paid an official visit to Cambodia at the invitation of King Norodom Sihanouk; subsequently, in July, the Chairman of the Central Committee of the Cambodian People's Party, Chea Sim, made an official friendship visit to Viet Nam. Although there were several high-level exchanges of visits between 1999 and 2001, no agreement was reached on either the border demarcation or on the ethnic Vietnamese in Cambodia. Relations between the two countries became strained in February 2001, when, following the Vietnamese Government's suppression of unrest in the Central Highlands region, large numbers of protesters fled to Cambodia seeking sanctuary. Viet Nam demanded their return, but under US and UN pressure, the Cambodian authorities allowed 24 refugees to emigrate to the USA, following a review of their cases. At mid-2001 many protesters continued to remain in Cambodia, and the UNHCR had failed to receive guarantees from the Vietnamese Government that they would not be prosecuted for involvement in the unrest if they were returned. In 1989–90 the dramatic political changes in Eastern Europe prompted renewed efforts by Viet Nam to restore political and economic links with the People's Republic of China. A secret 'summit' meeting of senior party officials was held in Chengdu, in southern China, in September 1990. The October 1991 comprehensive political agreement on Cambodia, which *inter alia* called on all external parties to cease military support for the Cambodian protagonists, removed the last remaining major obstacle to the restoration of normal relations. In early November the resumption of political relations between the two countries was formally announced during a Sino-Vietnamese 'summit' meeting in Beijing. Territorial disputes between the two countries, however, remained unresolved. In May 1992 Viet Nam made a formal protest against China's unilateral decision to grant a US company petroleum exploration rights in an area in the Gulf of Tongking, which was claimed as territorial waters by Viet Nam. In June discussions took place in Yogyakarta, Indonesia, concerning the sovereignty of the Spratly Islands which have been the subject of a protracted dispute involving Viet Nam, China, the Philippines, Malaysia, Taiwan and Brunei, which claim all or part of the archipelago (believed to be rich in mineral resources). In July Viet Nam protested when Chinese troops landed on another islet in the Spratlys. (Viet Nam maintained a military presence on 21 of the islands, China on seven.)

In September 1992 China agreed to discuss land border disputes and the disagreement over the Gulf of Tongking, but ruled out negotiations on the Spratlys. The discussions, which took place in October, failed to achieve significant progress. However, in November–December the Chinese Premier, Li Peng, paid an official visit to Viet Nam (the first by a Chinese head of government since 1971); new accords on economic, scientific and cultural co-operation were concluded, and the two Governments agreed to accelerate the negotiations on disputed territory. The first round of border discussions was duly held in August 1993, and in October the two countries concluded an agreement to avoid the use of force in resolving territorial disputes. However, armed confrontation between Chinese and Vietnamese ships in the disputed waters was only narrowly avoided in April 1994, and in July two Chinese warships blocked access to Vietnamese oil-prospecting facilities on one of the Spratly Islands. In September Vice-Prime Minister Phan Van Khai visited Beijing to discuss the matter, and agreement was reached to continue seeking a negotiated settlement. In the following month China renewed diplomatic protests at Viet Nam's decision to invite foreign oil companies to develop areas of the Gulf of Tongking. These protests came on the eve of a visit to Hanoi in November by the Chinese President and Communist Party General Secretary, Jiang Zemin. This represented the highest-level visit by a Chinese official since the resumption of normal bilateral relations in late 1991. The joint communiqué issued at the end of the visit called for an early settlement of territorial disputes by peaceful means. Various economic agreements were also signed, including the establishment of a joint trade commission. In the following month, Viet Nam and China held the third round of talks on border and territorial issues, which concentrated on demarcating the Gulf of Tongking. Problems in Sino-Vietnamese relations were exacerbated in early 1995, when it was discovered that the Chinese had occupied Mischief Reef, located in an area of the Spratlys claimed by the Philippines. This was the first such incident involving China in a direct dispute with an ASEAN member, and it served as a welcome opportunity for Viet Nam to demonstrate its solidarity with ASEAN prior to its membership of the Association (see below).

Sino-Vietnamese relations have alternated between the exchange of high-level delegations (and progress on economic matters) and contention over contested territory. In November 1995 Do Muoi led a senior party delegation to China to accelerate the pace of economic relations. Although Viet Nam and China had signed some 20 economic and commercial agreements since the normalization of relations in 1991, the only tangible result of this visit was the decision to reopen rail links between Kunming in Yunnan Province with Hanoi and Haiphong in February 1996. Despite the fact that cross-border trade was valued officially at US $378m. in 1996, in 1998 freight trade along the reopened rail line from Kunming to Haiphong had yet to develop. Little progress was made on more contentious issues, such as outstanding territorial disputes. In November 1995 the first round of talks was held on maritime issues between expert groups of the two countries. In January and April 1996 the seventh and eighth round of bilateral talks on border issues were held, but no progress was recorded. In mid-April Prime Minister Vo Van Kiet and his Chinese counterpart, Li Peng, held bilateral discussions while attending the Asia-Europe Summit Meeting in Bangkok. In June 1996 Premier Li Peng visited Viet Nam to attend the eighth party Congress. Relations became strained once again, however, when Viet Nam announced the award of a petroleum exploration and production rights contract to Conoco, a US company, in an offshore block claimed by China. The seventh meeting of the joint Sino-Vietnamese working group on the delineation of the Gulf of Tongking took place in Hanoi in August 1996. At the end of the year, however, tensions flared again when an armed Chinese naval vessel came to the assistance of a boat in the Gulf of Tongking, which Vietnamese authorities had stopped on suspicion of smuggling; two Vietnamese patrol boats were seized by the Chinese. In early 1997 Viet Nam seized several Chinese fishing boats in waters off Da Nang and held 65 fishermen in detention.

In March 1997 two Chinese tugboats towed an oil rig into disputed waters off Viet Nam's central coast, resulting in a Vietnamese protest to China and intense lobbying by Viet Nam among ASEAN members. China then agreed to host discussions at the level of Deputy Minister. In April Beijing announced that the oil rig had completed its work and was being withdrawn. This announcement prepared the way for a visit to Beijing by Do Muoi in July and for a reaffirmation of the 'fraternal relations' between the two countries. In August 1997 Viet Nam and China held their fifth round of talks on the land border issue and agreed to reach a settlement by 2000. In January 1998 Viet Nam accused China of a 'serious violation' of border treaties when Chinese workers reclaimed land along a border river causing a diversion of water into Vietnamese territory; however, Vietnamese officials denied that border tensions increased in 1998. The sixth around of talks between the two countries on the land border issue was held in September 1998.

In mid-October 1998 it was announced that the Vietnamese Prime Minister, Phan Van Khai, would pay his first official visit to China later the same month. On the eve of Khai's departure, however, the official Chinese news agency, Xinhua, issued a critical review of the state of the Vietnamese economy. During Khai's visit to Beijing, the Vietnamese Prime Minister and his Chinese counterpart, Zhu Rongji, discussed the implementation of economic reforms in their respective countries, concluding jointly that the maintenance of 'socialist stability' was the most important consideration for both Viet Nam and China, thereby underscoring the main concern of the Communist Party that too rapid an introduction of economic reforms could lead to political instability. Following his visit to China, Khai stated that the Vietnamese Government would give careful consideration to the Chinese model of economic reform. The Chinese Vice-President, Hu Jintao, visited Viet Nam in December 1998 during the second informal summit meeting of South-East Asian heads of government, to attend the China-ASEAN leadership meeting. While in Hanoi, Hu held talks with his Vietnamese counterparts, emphasizing the need for the resolution of border issues and for closer bilateral co-operation between Viet Nam and China; an agreement on economic and technical co-operation was also signed, in which China pledged to provide 10m. yuan in non-refundable aid to Viet Nam. During the visit of the Vietnamese Communist Party General Secretary, Le Kha Phieu, to Beijing in February 1999, a further agreement on economic and technical co-operation, valued at 20m. yuan, was signed. In discussions held between Phieu and Chinese President Jiang Zemin, both parties reiterated their determination to conclude a border agreement by the end of the year and to agree on the demarcation of the Gulf of Tongking by 2000. According to the final communiqué, Phieu once again reaffirmed that 'Viet Nam will have only unofficial economic and trade ties, and not official relations, with Taiwan'. In 1999–2000 some 80 high-level visits were made by both sides. A significant land border agreement came into effect in January 2000. At an ASEAN summit meeting in September, chaired by Viet Nam, member countries and China reached consensus on some major principles of a regional code of conduct governing activities in the South China Sea.

Relations continued to progress in 2000, and in that year bilateral trade between the two states reached US $2,000m. Following success in efforts to resolve the bilateral territorial dispute, President Tran Duc Luong travelled to China in December 2000 to sign an 'agreement on the demarcation of the territorial waters, exclusive economic zone, and continental shelf in the Gulf of Tonkin'. A second agreement on fishing co-operation in the Gulf of Tonkin was signed at the same time. The agreement did not cover the Spratly Islands, which continued to be problematic to bilateral relations. In February Viet Nam announced that it was to establish a civilian administration for the Spratly Islands. The Chinese Government responded angrily, while Viet Nam claimed that China was acting more aggressively in the South China Sea. Relations between the two nations continued to progress, however, and the Chinese Minister of Defence, Chi Haotian, made a six-day working visit to Viet Nam in February and the Chinese Vice-President, Hu Jintao, led the Chinese delegation to the Communist Party's Ninth Congress in April 2001. In September 2001 the Chinese Politburo member, Li Peng, visited Hanoi. Although high-level exchanges continued throughout 2001 and 2002 (with more than 100 in 2001 alone), there was considerable mistrust of China and dissatisfaction over the border agreement. At the Central Committee's Fourth Plenum in November 2001, members urged the National Assembly to reject the treaty. In order to placate the Chinese Government, General Secretary Nong Duc Manh travelled to Beijing in that month and reaffirmed the land border treaty and the demarcation of the Gulf of Tonking. A general framework agreement on economic and technical co-operation was also signed during the visit, although no further issues were discussed. In February 2002 the Chinese President, Jiang Zemin, travelled to Viet Nam (his first visit since 1994) and offered some US $12.1m. in credit and grants to Viet Nam.

In the aftermath of the collapse of the USSR and the ending of the 'Cold War', and the settlement in Cambodia in 1991, the 'cornerstones' of Vietnamese foreign policy—alliances with the USSR, Eastern Europe, Laos and Cambodia—were broken. Viet Nam has readjusted its foreign policy so decisively that ideological factors now appear to play little or no role in the Government's considerations. Viet Nam has opened relations with former enemies and, after a short period of readjustment, placed relations with old allies on a new footing.

In the early 1990s Viet Nam sought to consolidate relations with the successor states of the USSR, as well as with the newly-democratic countries of Eastern Europe. In June 1994 Prime Minister Vo Van Kiet visited Ukraine, Kazakhstan and Russia at the head of a large delegation composed of his Minister of Foreign Affairs, 13 deputy ministers or deputy chiefs of state organizations, senior military officials and at least 20 business representatives. The visit focused on economic relations, and Viet Nam's outstanding debt, as well as the issue of Vietnamese workers residing in republics of the former USSR. Defence ties were also discussed, including continued Russian access to Cam Ranh Bay (finally agreed in mid-1995), the supply of spare parts for Viet Nam's military, and co-operation in a new security system for Asia. While in Moscow, Kiet renegotiated the 1978 Soviet-Vietnamese treaty of friendship and co-operation. The new document merely stipulated bilateral consultations in the event of a crisis. Viet Nam and Russia also reached agreement on the sale of six Sukhoi Su-27 fighter bombers (two of which were delivered to Viet Nam in 1995), anti-aircraft missiles and air defence radars, and two *Tarantul*-class missile patrol boats. The value of the sale was placed at US $180m. In February 1996 the commander of the Russian Pacific Fleet visited Viet Nam and announced Russia's intention 'to maintain and develop' Cam Ranh Bay after the current access agreement expires in 2004. In November 1997 the Russian Prime Minister, Viktor Chernomyrdin, paid an official visit to Viet Nam, where he witnessed the signing of four bilateral co-operation agreements on tourism, trade and science, oil and gas exploitation, and veterinary sciences. He also discussed with his counterparts the sale of military aircraft and the question of Viet Nam's outstanding debt. President Tran Duc Luong paid a reciprocal visit to Russia and to Belarus in August 1998. While in Moscow, President Luong signed agreements on oil, gas and energy, weapons sales and support services, narcotics control, and legal relations, but was unable to resolve the issue of Hanoi's outstanding debt to Moscow. In 1998 Russia ranked first among foreign investors in Viet Nam for that year; Russia's profile in Viet Nam was further enhanced by the announcement that the Russian economic federation, Zarubezhneft, and Petrovietnam had received a joint licence to build a US $1,100m. petroleum refinery at Dung Quat in central Viet Nam. In March 1999 the Russian First Deputy Prime Minister, Vadim Gustov, visited Viet Nam to attend the sixth meeting of the Intergovernmental Committee for Economic, Commercial and Scientific and Technological Co-operation. Following discussions, the two countries agreed jointly to establish a group of experts to investigate possible ways of resolving the issue of Viet Nam's debts to Russia. The Vietnamese Minister of Defence visited Ukraine to negotiate military assistance and the purchase of Ukrainian armaments.

Relations with Russia improved significantly in 2001. A visit by Phan Van Khai to Moscow in September 2000 contributed greatly to resolving the issue of Viet Nam's debt to Russia. In February 2001 the Russian President, Vladamir Putin, visited Viet Nam, prompting further rapid exchanges of bilateral visits. Putin, who was welcomed warmly in the country, resolved the long-standing bilateral dispute by drastically reducing the amount of Viet Nam's debt to the former USSR from US $11,000m. to about US $1,600m., and extended the terms of repayment to 23 years. Viet Nam was henceforth to pay Russia US $100m. per year. Both countries pledged to renew their historical friendship. Viet Nam favoured Putin's neo-Soviet leanings, strong image and his willingness to act forcefully in relations with the US Government. The two countries signed a 'Strategic Partnership Declaration'. Putin indicated his desire to extend the lease on the naval and signals intelligence facility in Cam Ranh Bay, which was due to expire in 2004, but the Vietnamese Government demanded a much higher rent. The Minister of Foreign Affairs, Nguyen Dy Nien, visited Moscow in June 2001, with an offer of US $2,000m. for a 10-year lease, which the Russians rejected. In mid-2001 Viet Nam indicated that it would not renew the lease and would develop the naval base into an export-processing zone. Russia formally transferred the facilities of the naval base in Cam Ranh Bay to Viet Nam in July 2002, prior to the expiry of the lease in 2004. Nevertheless, bilateral relations remained strong, owing to increased economic co-operation and military sales. Bilateral trade reached US $570m. in 2001, and the heads of state of both countries pledged to increase the total to US $1,000m. in 2002. The Russian Government provided US $100m. in credit for two hydroelectric installations, while Russian companies invested US $1,500m. in 38 projects, making Russia Viet Nam's ninth-largest foreign investor. Its most important investment, a joint-venture petroleum refinery at Dung Quat, valued at US $1,300m., has fallen greatly behind schedule. The 20-year old joint venture, Vietsovpetro, accounted for 80% of Viet Nam's crude petroleum output, and the Dung Quat refinery was expected to provide 50% of Viet Nam's demand for refined petroleum products. Russian military sales to Viet Nam have advanced significantly. In 2002 Viet Nam purchased 50 surface-to-air defence missiles, valued at US $64m., while it was reported that the Russian Government envisaged the establishment of a regional maintenance centre for its airplanes in Viet Nam.

Viet Nam's relations with ASEAN have been transformed from confrontation to accommodation to membership. Agreement was reached on the repatriation of refugees from ASEAN countries (see above). In October 1991, after the Cambodian peace agreement had been signed, Vo Van Kiet visited Indonesia, Singapore and Thailand, where he signed a number of economic agreements. In addition, Singapore announced the resumption of trade relations with Viet Nam (in 1993 Singapore was Viet Nam's largest trading partner). In January 1992 Vo Van Kiet visited Malaysia, and in late February he visited the remaining ASEAN members, Brunei and the Philippines.

Trade and investment from various ASEAN states has grown considerably. Between 1990 and 1997 bilateral trade between Viet Nam and ASEAN increased at an annual average rate of 26.9%. Bilateral trade between Viet Nam and ASEAN was valued at US $5,300m. (about 30% of Viet Nam's total foreign trade) for the first 10 months of 1999. ASEAN investment increased 10-fold between 1991 and 1994, thus comprising 16% of total direct foreign investment. By 1996 the three ASEAN states, Singapore, Malaysia and Thailand, were involved in 274 projects with a paid-up capital of US $4,300m. Singapore was the largest ASEAN investor, with 153 projects capitalized at nearly US $2,600m., and the third largest overall foreign investor. Thirty-seven co-operation agreements have been signed between business representatives of Viet Nam and ASEAN. In August 1996 the ASEAN Secretary-General, Ajit Singh, told Vietnamese leaders that they would be required to draw up a master plan to eliminate import quotas and other non-tariff barriers for approval by ASEAN economic ministers. Singh also urged greater transparency in Viet Nam's trading system. However, in the following month ASEAN's plans to adopt an agreement outlining a mechanism for the settlement of trade disputes were stymied when Vietnamese officials refused to sign, claiming that they had no authority to do so. Viet Nam has overlapping territorial claims with several ASEAN states. Viet Nam and Indonesia have held 17 rounds of talks regarding disputed territory near the Natuna Islands, but with no result. In September 1992 Viet Nam reached agreement with Malaysia and Thailand on co-operation in the use of waters in the Gulf of Thailand. As a result of continuing friction between Thai and Vietnamese fishing boats, the two countries' Ministers of Foreign Affairs met in Hanoi in April 1996 and agreed to establish a joint commission to resolve the matter. In early September Nong Duc Manh, Chairman of the National Assembly's Standing Committee, visited Bangkok to discuss this issue. However, in mid-October another incident took place between Thai fishing trawlers and a Vietnamese naval vessel, in which two Thais were killed. This incident prompted Thailand and Viet Nam to intensify their efforts to reach a *modus vivendi* for the maritime area in which their territorial claims conflicted. The Ministers of Foreign Affairs from the two countries met in March 1997 to discuss this issue, and also to consider ways in which bilateral economic co-operation might be increased. Finally, in October 1997, Viet Nam and Thailand reached an agreement to delimit their maritime boundary (continental shelf and exclusive economic zone) in the Gulf of Thailand. This agreement was expected to lead to joint naval patrols, fishery surveys and petroleum and gas exploration. In 1996 Thailand was Viet Nam's 13th largest foreign investor. Also in 1996 Viet Nam and Malaysia reached an agreement jointly to develop an area in the Gulf of Thailand where they had overlapping claims not involving a third country. In the same year Viet Nam and the Philippines began discussions on the joint development of their overlapping territorial claims in the South China Sea. In March 1998 President Tran Duc Luong visited Malaysia and Singapore, where he sought assistance in the drafting of Viet Nam's individual plan of action that was a prerequisite for the country's potential admission to the Asia-Pacific Economic Co-operation forum (APEC) (see below).

In July 1992 Viet Nam signed the 1976 ASEAN Treaty on Amity and Co-operation, and was granted observer status at its annual meeting of foreign ministers. In July 1994 Viet Nam became a founding member of the ASEAN Regional Forum, a security discussion group. On 28 July 1995, at ceremonies in Brunei, Viet Nam became ASEAN's seventh member. On the same occasion Viet Nam announced its intention to join the ASEAN Free Trade Area. ASEAN members granted Viet Nam a three-year grace period, until 2003, to lower its tariff barriers. As an ASEAN member, Viet Nam attended the first 'summit' meeting of all 10 heads of government in South-East Asia held in Bangkok in December 1995. At the 31st annual ASEAN ministerial meeting in July 1998, Viet Nam opposed a Thai initiative to modify ASEAN's long-standing policy of non-interference in the internal affairs of member countries in favour of a policy of 'flexible engagement'. Viet Nam hosted the sixth ASEAN summit in Hanoi in December of that year. Viet Nam joined other regional states in endorsing the South-East Asia Nuclear-Weapon Free Zone Treaty. In November 1996 ASEAN members successfully supported Viet Nam's application for membership of APEC; formal admission took place in November 1998. In 1996 and 1998 Viet Nam attended the first and second Asia-Europe Meetings, held in Kuala Lumpur and London respectively. Relations with ASEAN remained strained, owing to continued pressure from Thailand and the Philippines for greater intervention in the internal affairs of other member states. From July 2000 to July 2001 Viet Nam held the rotating chairmanship of ASEAN, but was criticized for its continued support of Myanmar and refusal to challenge ASEAN's non-interference principle. Relations with Thailand appeared stable, however, and, following the discovery of a bomb at the Vietnamese embassy in Bangkok, the Thai Government committed itself to preventing groups from using Thailand as a base of operations against the Vietnamese Government. At the ASEAN summit in July in Hanoi, the organization urged wealthier member nations to assist the development of the poorer ones. Viet Nam exhibited concern that its development was again behind that of the other states in the region. Earlier in March the Deputy Prime Minister, Nguyen Tan Dung, travelled to Singapore to promote foreign investment and to demonstrate a pledge to the Singaporean business community of Viet Nam's commitment to reform. The newly-elected Indonesian President, Megawati Sukarnoputri, visited Viet Nam in August 2001. President Tran Duc Luong visited Brunei, the Philippines and Indonesia, in November 1991, prior to the ASEAN summit. In May 2002 President Luong visited Myanmar, where he met with the leader of the State Peace and Development Council, Than Shwe. ASEAN states continued to be economically important for Viet Nam, which received some US $330m. in total ASEAN investment in 2001.

Viet Nam's relations with other Asian countries also improved markedly after 1991. Diplomatic relations with the Republic of Korea (already an important trading partner and investor in Viet Nam) were restored in December 1992; they had remained severed since the fall of Saigon in 1975. Defence attachés were exchanged in 1996, and in November of that year the President of the Republic of Korea, Kim Young-Sam, visited Hanoi accompanied by a delegation that included nearly 70 business executives. The Prime Minister of the Republic of Korea, Lee Han-Dong, visited Hanoi in April 2002, demonstrating the continuing importance of the bilateral economic relationship between the two states: the Republic of Korea is the fourth largest investor in Viet Nam, with some US $3,000m. allocated to 322 projects, while bilateral trade in 2001 totalled more than US $2,000m. However, Viet Nam has been careful not to antagonize its former ally, the Democratic People's Republic of Korea, and in mid-2002 President Tran Duc Luong travelled to its capital to meet with Kim Jong Il.

In September 1993 full diplomatic relations were re-established between Viet Nam and Japan. In the mid-1990s Japan became Viet Nam's largest aid donor and principal trading partner. Between 1991 and 1998 Japan pledged US $3,200m. of development assistance, most of which was in the form of 'soft' loans related to infrastructure projects. In late March 1999 the Vietnamese Prime Minister, Phan Van Khai, made an official visit to Japan; each country extended 'most favoured nation' status to the other. In April, in response to a written request from Prime Minister Khai, Japan informed South-East Asian Ministers of Finance that it would include Viet Nam in the US $30,000m. Miyazawa Plan; Viet Nam was allocated US $160m. in concessional loans under this plan. In mid-2000 six Vietnamese students were accepted by the Japanese National Defence Academy, providing for increased bilateral military activity. The Japan Bank for International Cooperation provided Viet Nam with a US $54m. loan for the Bai Chay Bridge near Hai Phong, the destination of much Japanese foreign investment. In 2001 Japan provided US $540m. in aid for five additional infrastructure projects. By this time Viet Nam had received more than US $7,000m. in aid from Japan since 1992, 40% of all bilateral aid committed to Viet Nam. Japan was Viet Nam's third-largest investor, with more than US $4,000m. allocated to 335 projects. Bilateral trade in 2001 totalled more than US $5,000m.

In July 1998 the Prime Minister of Laos, Gen. Sisavat Keobounphan, made an official visit to Viet Nam, and in June 1999 the President of Viet Nam, Tran Duc Luong, visited Laos. In mid-2000, following ethnic and political violence in Laos, the Lao army commander visited Viet Nam to appeal for military assistance. The Vietnamese Government agreed to increase aid to Laos, but publicly refused to send troops to assist in the suppression of dissident activity (despite reports of the transport of Vietnamese forces to Laos). Viet Nam and Laos continued their close relations and exchanged many high-level visits throughout 2000–2001, culminating in sending reciprocal delegations to their respective party congresses. The Ministers of Defence of the two countries signed a protocol for co-operation and mutual assistance in February 2001. The Vietnamese Government remained extremely concerned over the spread of ethnic minority unrest from Laos into Viet Nam and intensified military aid. The new party General Secretary, Nong Duc Manh, made a prominent visit to Laos in July 2001, and Laos continued to be Viet Nam's most important ally. In May 2002 the Lao Head of State, Khamtay Siphandone, made a visit to Hanoi to celebrate 40 years of diplomatic relations, and the 25th anniversary of the Treaty of Friendship and Cooperation, demonstrating that the 'special relationship' between the two states remained very strong, despite the fact that bilateral trade was in 2000 valued at only US $177m. Viet Nam was at that time the 14th-largest foreign investor in Laos and an agreement to reduce the taxation on Vietnamese investments was reached in late 2001. Viet Nam remained the most important source of education and technical training for Lao officials.

In January 1999 the Vietnamese Deputy Prime Minister and Minister of Foreign Affairs, Nguyen Manh Cam, paid an official visit to India to attend the ninth session of the Intergovernmental Committee for Economic, Cultural, Scientific and Technical Co-operation. On the eve of his visit it was announced that Viet Nam and India had reached agreement on co-operation over nuclear energy. Close military relations between the two countries were consolidated in 2000, with the visit to Viet Nam of the Indian Minister of Defence. Agreement was reached on joint naval exercises, while Viet Nam pledged to assist the Indian army in guerrilla warfare training. The Indian Prime Minister, Atal Bihari Vajpayee, visited Viet Nam in March 2001, although plans for an agreement on naval construction co-operation were not realized.

Relations between Viet Nam and the USA remained in part an exception to the general improvement in Hanoi's relations with the outside world during 1991–94, owing to the lingering problem of the more than 2,600 US servicemen listed as 'missing in action' (MIA) during the Viet Nam War. In 1986 and 1987 agreements were reached for Vietnamese co-operation in the search for missing servicemen, in return for a promise of humanitarian aid from the USA. The Vietnamese Government also agreed in principle to permit the emigration to the USA of former re-education camp detainees and their families, subject to assurances that they would not engage in 'anti-Vietnamese' activities. Between November 1988 and January 1989 the remains of 86 soldiers were returned to the US Government. In October 1990 the Vietnamese Minister of Foreign Affairs, Nguyen Co Thach, met leading US officials in Washington (the first visit by a Vietnamese delegate in 15 years) to discuss the UN peace plan for Cambodia, and the possible release of information concerning the MIA. The meeting represented a significant move towards the establishment of diplomatic relations between the two countries. In early 1991 a US representative was stationed in Hanoi to supervise inquiries into MIA, the first official US presence in Viet Nam since 1975. In April the USA proposed a four-stage programme for the establishment of normal diplomatic relations with Viet Nam, conditional on Vietnamese co-operation in reaching a diplomatic settlement in Cambodia, and in accounting for the remaining MIA. In December 1991 the USA ended restrictions on US citizens travelling to Viet Nam. In March 1992 relations improved further when the US Assistant Secretary of State, Richard Solomon, visited Hanoi, the most senior US official to do so since 1986. In exchange for enhanced co-operation on the MIA issue, Solomon announced that the USA would grant Viet Nam US $3m. in humanitarian aid. He reiterated, however, that there would be no deviation from the four-stage programme for normalization. Despite the public urging of allies such as Thailand, Australia and the United Kingdom, in September 1992 the USA extended the trade embargo against Viet Nam for a further year. In October, following the discovery of more than 4,000 photographs of the remains of MIA, discussions took place between the Vietnamese Minister of Foreign Affairs and the US Secretary of Defense, Richard Cheney.

However, expectations that the coming to power in the USA of a Democratic administration under President Bill Clinton (who took office in January 1993) would lead to the early normalization of relations between Viet Nam and the USA were not realized. Nevertheless, in July the USA did withdraw its long-standing opposition to loans to Viet Nam from the IMF, the World Bank and the ADB. As a result, in October (having paid its arrears to the IMF with the help of donor countries) Viet Nam was granted US $223m. in credits by the IMF, and large loans from the ADB (for irrigation) and the World Bank (for education and road repairs) followed. In December a conference of international aid organizations and governments agreed to provide US $1,860m. in aid to Viet Nam over the ensuing year, and in the same month creditor nations agreed to reschedule part of Viet Nam's external debt. The resumption of large-scale external aid was expected to give impetus to the improvement of the country's infrastructure, regarded as essential for its economic development. However, despite increased Vietnamese endeavours to assist in the search for MIA and despite the stationing of US diplomats in Hanoi from August 1993, President Clinton announced in September a renewal of the embargo against Viet Nam (although US businesses were to be permitted greater access to the country).

Viet Nam was not kept isolated from the international community during the period when the US embargo was in effect. Australia was the first Western country to restore direct development assistance, a decision that was made in October 1991 in anticipation of a comprehensive political settlement in Cambodia. Australia has consistently maintained its position among foreign investors in Viet Nam since then. In May 1993 Vo Van Kiet visited Australia, and reportedly agreed to receive a delegation of parliamentarians. In the following year the Australian Prime Minister paid a return visit. The question of a parliamentary consultative delegation 'on human rights' proved to be a contentious matter, and it was not until 1995 that such a mission was permitted to make a brief visit. Later in the year Australia's Governor-General visited Hanoi, while Do Muoi visited Australia (and also New Zealand). Bilateral relations with Viet Nam were briefly strained when the new Australian Government, elected in March 1996, sought to withdraw the financial support for the My Thuan bridge in the Mekong Delta, which the previous Government had pledged. This policy was reversed during a visit to Hanoi by the new Australian Minister for Foreign Affairs.In1997Australia quietly opened a regional security dialogue with defence officials in Hanoi; the first formal dialogue took place in May 1998.

In February 1999 Australia and Viet Nam held the fifth meeting of their Joint Trade and Economic Co-operation Committee. In 1998 bilateral trade between the two countries increased by 39%, reaching a record US $1,000m. The Vietnamese Prime Minister, Phan Van Khai, paid an official visit to Australia in March 1999; at the same time, Australia announced it was to increase its official development aid to Viet Nam to US $236m. for the 1998–2001 period; a separate agreement on co-operation in the areas of education and training was also signed. The completion of the My Thuan bridge in mid-2000 was a significant point in bilateral relations between Australia and Viet Nam. Australia signed a Defence Co-operation Agreement with Viet Nam in 2000, and from 1999 commenced training Vietnamese security forces, with the aim of improving co-operation in law enforcement and establishing a narcotics intelligence database. Australia also funded a 10-year US $15m. rural development programme in Quang Ngai province to alleviate rural poverty.

In February 1993 President Mitterrand of France became the first Western Head of State to visit Viet Nam since its reunification. (He was followed in early 1995 by the French Minister of Foreign Affairs, and in early 1997 by the Chief of Staff of the French army.) In November 1997 President Jacques Chirac of France made an official visit to Viet Nam, which was hosting a summit meeting of French-speaking countries. In July 1993 Vo Van Kiet visited several West European countries, including the UK, France and Germany. In 1995 Viet Nam and the EU signed a co-operation agreement which included a provision for the protection of human rights. In July 1996 an agreement between Viet Nam and the EU on the export of garments and textiles was completed. Germany's relations with Viet Nam have been strained by the issue of Vietnamese illegal residents in Germany who refuse to return home. Some Vietnamese gangs were implicated in the smuggling of cigarettes, while others attracted publicity as a result of violent gang warfare; Viet Nam has been reluctant to accept them back. In January 1995 Germany pledged DM 100m. in development assistance (suspended since 1990) and an equivalent amount in export credits in return for which Viet Nam agreed to accept, by the year 2000, 40,000 of an estimated 95,000 Vietnamese living in Germany. The remaining 55,000 would be given official residence permits. In January 1999 Germany agreed to waive the debt of US $21.6m. owed to the country by Viet Nam as a contribution towards the financing of environmental protection measures in Viet Nam. In April 1999 the Vietnamese Minister of Foreign Affairs, Nguyen Manh Cam, paid a nine-day working visit to Germany. In June Germany pledged continued support for a programme to assist Vietnamese nationals returning to Viet Nam from Germany. In February 1999 the Danish Minister of Foreign Affairs, Niels Helveg Petersen, visited Viet Nam and announced Denmark's contribution of US $111m. towards the funding of land-mine clearance; a 'soft' loan agreement of US $40m. for 1999–2000 was also signed. In March 1999 Prince Andrew of the United Kingdom paid a five-day friendship visit to Viet Nam to promote bilateral trade between Viet Nam and the United Kingdom. In September Prime Minister Phan Van Khai paid official visits to Sweden, Finland, Norway and Denmark, where he signed a number of aid agreements. The party General Secretary visited France and Italy in May 2000 (one of his first overseas visits to non-communist states). In April of that year Canada suspended diplomatic relations with Viet Nam, after the Vietnamese authorities executed a Canadian citizen for drug-trafficking (despite evidence, provided by the Canadian Government, indicating the victim's innocence). EU officials were angered at Viet Nam's support for Myanmar during its chairmanship of ASEAN. In early 2001 a Belgian national, who was a member of the European Parliament, was expelled from Viet Nam for protesting at the lack of religious freedom. The EU has steadily increased its economic co-operation with Viet Nam, in 2002 providing US $150m. in financial assistance over the following five years for poverty reduction and sustainable development in the countryside. By 2002 the EU had provided over US $2,400m. in aid to Viet Nam (75% in grants, 25% in loans), making it the third-largest donor, after Japan and the World Bank.

In February 1994 President Clinton announced the lifting of the US economic embargo. He expressed the hope that this would encourage the Vietnamese to give further assistance in the investigations of MIAs (the number of whom was now believed to be about 1,600). In May Viet Nam and the USA agreed to open liaison offices in their respective capitals; the USA opened its office in Hanoi in February 1995. The restoration of full diplomatic relations was finally announced by President

Clinton on 11 July. In the following month the US Secretary of State, Warren Christopher, visited Hanoi to inaugurate the new US embassy there. The posting of a US ambassador was delayed, however, until April 1997 on account of the refusal of Senator Jesse Helms, chairman of the Senate Foreign Relations Committee, to approve President Clinton's nominee for the position, Douglas Peterson. In April 1996 a US commercial office was opened in Hanoi. In July President Clinton's national security adviser, Anthony Lake, visited Hanoi on the first anniversary of the normalization of relations, to discuss three sets of issues: economic co-operation, refugee resettlement and regional co-operation. However, Lake made clear that the full accounting of MIAs remained the USA's 'highest priority.'

By 1995 the USA had become the sixth largest foreign investor in Viet Nam, and maintained that ranking in 1996, with US $1,300m. invested in 64 projects. In April 1997 US Secretary of the Treasury, Robert Rubin, visited Viet Nam and signed an agreement settling a US $150m. debt issue outstanding since the end of the Viet Nam War. During the course of his visit, Rubin stated that Viet Nam would be required to undertake a series of measures, such as protecting intellectual property and agreeing to a trade accord, before the USA would grant Most Favoured Nation (MFN) trading status (now Normal Trade Relations—NTR). Although an agreement on intellectual property rights was signed, negotiations on a trade agreement made little progress in the face of US demands that Viet Nam open its markets, remove various trade barriers, abandon investment licensing and grant 'national treatment' to US banks, law firms and advertising agencies. In late June 1997 the US Secretary of State, Madeleine Albright, made a brief visit to Hanoi, where she signed an agreement on copyright protection and urged Viet Nam to initiate *doi moi 2* (renewed reforms). In March 1998, however, Viet Nam's co-operation with the USA on a resettlement programme for Vietnamese boat people in camps in South-East Asia (see above) resulted in President Clinton's decision to waive the Jackson-Vanik Amendment to the 1974 Trade Act; this amendment prohibits the USA from trading with or providing investment funds to countries that do not permit free emigration. As a result of the waiver, the Overseas Private Investment Corporation (OPIC) and the Export-Import Bank were permitted to commence operations in Viet Nam. (OPIC provides special insurance cover for US firms doing business in Viet Nam, while the Export-Import Bank provides loans to US companies to assist their exports to Viet Nam.) During 1998 Viet Nam and the USA intensified negotiations on trade and aviation agreements. In late September 1998 Deputy Prime Minister and Minister of Foreign Affairs, Nguyen Manh Cam, made an official visit to the USA at the invitation of the US Secretary of State.

In February 1999 President Clinton affirmed that Viet Nam was 'fully co-operating in good faith' in all areas of bilateral relations in which the USA itself sought progress (particularly in the area of joint searches for the remains of MIAs). Viet Nam also intensified its co-operation with the USA on immigration issues in 1999: following some initial difficulties, the Vietnamese Government gave permission for refugees in overseas camps to return to Viet Nam for processing, in preparation for emigration to the USA under the Resettlement of Vietnamese Returnees Programme, and also expedited the processing of former re-education camp detainees. Improved Vietnamese co-operation in these areas led to President Clinton's agreement to the second waiver of the Jackson-Vanik Amendment, as a consequence of which US export promotion and investment support programmes offered by the Export-Import Bank, OPIC, the US Department of Agriculture and the United States Trade and Development Agency were permitted to recommence. In 1999 Viet Nam and the USA made substantial progress in their negotiations of a Bilateral Trade Agreement, and considerable progress was achieved in particular during the eighth round of negotiations held in mid-June. On several occasions when an impasse was reached, the USA sought the intervention of the Vietnamese Deputy Prime Minister and Politburo member, Nguyen Tan Dung. During negotiations, Viet Nam was extremely reluctant to grant the USA access to certain protected sectors, such as telecommunications. The most contentious issues during the final round of negotiations were those of non-tariff barriers and tariff reduction schedules; also, Viet Nam sought an eight-year time frame for the full implementation of the agreement, whereas the USA insisted on a time frame of four years. Once enacted, the Agreement would allow Vietnamese exports access to the US market on a 'normal trade relations' basis. The World Bank estimated that Vietnamese exports to the USA would double in the first year following the enactment of the Agreement, from US $470m. to nearly US $1,000m. On 25 July the USA and Viet Nam announced that they had finally reached agreement in principle upon the terms of the Bilateral Trade Agreement. It was expected that, once all the outstanding technical details had been completed, the Agreement would finally be signed in September and then submitted to the US Congress for approval. However, a visit to Viet Nam by the US Secretary of State, Madeleine Albright, in September to inaugurate a new US consulate in Ho Chi Minh City (and especially Albright's meeting with the General Secretary of the Communist Party, Le Kha Phieu) was reported not to have proceeded well, and hopes that the trade agreement would be signed at the APEC summit held in the same month in Auckland, New Zealand, were dispelled. In October the Politburo rejected the trade accord. The Vietnamese Government attempted to renegotiate certain provisions of the agreement, although the USA steadfastly refused, offering only to clarify certain aspects. The USA made efforts to continue discussions on the issue, with a series of high-level visits in the first half of 2000.

The US Secretary of Defense, William Cohen, finally travelled to Viet Nam in April 2000, after his visit had been twice postponed by the Vietnamese authorities. Although the visit represented progress in improving bilateral military links, the Vietnamese Government appeared reluctant to support Cohen's suggestion that Viet Nam and the USA were potential allies against 'growing hegemony' in the region and to allow port visits of US naval vessels. The USA praised Viet Nam for its co-operation regarding the search for MIAs, although Hanoi made little progress in appealing to the US Government for aid to locate the remains of some 300,000 servicemen. Cohen's visit coincided with the 25th anniversary of the fall of Saigon, which the Vietnamese celebrated throughout April. The anniversary gave rise to some tension, with the assertion of the US Senator, John McCain, that he and other captured US servicemen had been tortured, antagonizing the Vietnamese Government. A resolution by the US Congress condemning the communist regime in April also prompted hostility. The continuing effects of the huge amounts of Agent Orange used in South Viet Nam during the war remained a contentious political issue; the US Government agreed to conduct joint research, but refused to pay reparations. In mid-2000 the Vietnamese authorities, which had sentenced 86 drug-traffickers to death in 1999, pledged to co-operate with the USA in measures to prevent the passage of illicit drugs through the country. Nevertheless, bilateral relations suffered certain reverses. In May Hanoi charged a dissident, Ha Si Phu, with treason, prompting five other dissidents to submit a joint appeal to the National Assembly. His case was supported by several US legislators, infuriating the Vietnamese Government, which rejected their intervention as interference in its internal affairs. The nomination of a dissident Buddhist monk, Thich Quang Do, for the Nobel Peace Prize also antagonized the Politburo, which increasingly urged continued vigilance against foreign conspiracies to undermine the regime through 'peaceful evolution'. Viet Nam attempted to gain credibility for its claim of being committed to the improvement of human rights with its election in May to the UN Economic and Social Council's Human Rights and Social Development Committee; however, allegations of continued violations of human and religious rights persisted.

In July 2000 the newly-appointed Trade Minister, Vu Khoan, travelled to Washington at the invitation of the US Trade Representative, Charlene Barshefsky. As expected, the bilateral trade agreement was finally signed. Viet Nam was accorded Normal Trade Relations, effectively lowering tariff rates on exports from 40% to 3%. The US Government ceded to Vietnamese demands that foreign companies would only be allowed to become minority partners in the telecommunications sector, but in return accepted a three-year period of introduction for other components of the accord, as opposed to the four years that had been previously negotiated. The agreement laid the foundations for Vietnamese membership of the World Trade Organisation, which Viet Nam hoped to join by 2003. Both the US Congress and the Vietnamese National Assembly for domestic political reasons delayed ratification of the bilateral trade agreement. The US Congress finally ratified the agreement in August 2001, while the National Assembly endorsed it in November.

President Bill Clinton visited Viet Nam in November 2000, the first visit by a US President to a unified Viet Nam. Clinton had a cold official reception and there was little ceremony surrounding the visit, although he was welcomed by the public. Despite the visit, little goodwill between the two states was generated. In January 2001 the official visit by the Commander in Chief of US forces in the Pacific, Adm. Denis Blair, was cancelled shortly beforehand by the Vietnamese, who provided no reason for the decision. Military co-operation suffered a further reverse in April, when a helicopter carrying a mission of US and Vietnamese military personnel to search for MIA remains crashed in the Quang Binh province, killing all passengers. The crash prompted renewed controversy over the efficacy of continuing the searches. As of mid-2001 65 joint missions had been carried out and the remains of more than 600 US military personnel had been repatriated.

Viet Nam continued to react with hostility to what it considered unwarranted interference in its internal affairs. In February 2001 a congressional commission, the US Commission on International Religious Freedom, conducted hearings on Viet Nam and, concluding that the Vietnamese Government practised systemic repression, recommended that the World Bank suspend financing. At the same time the US Government granted asylum to 24 members of ethnic minority groups, who had fled to Cambodia after leading the protests in the Central Highlands. In September the US Congress adopted the Viet Nam Human Rights Act, thereby angering the Vietnamese Government. In February 2002, however, Viet Nam approved a mission from the US Commission on International Religious Freedom. In March US and Vietnamese government scientists held their first meeting to discuss the effects of the chemical defoliant Agent Orange, which had been sprayed in large quantities over 10% of South Viet Nam's land area during the war. The US scientists denied that the chemical had caused severe long-term health problems, including birth defects, and the US Government refused to accept any financial liability. The USA and Viet Nam undertook to co-operate on further research.

Viet Nam responded cautiously to the US Government's announcement of a 'war on terror', following the attacks against New York and Washington, DC, on 11 September 2001. While condemning the terrorist acts against the USA and supporting UN and ASEAN resolutions, Viet Nam was highly critical of the US use of military force in Afghanistan. Nevertheless, Viet Nam granted US military planes overflight rights to Vietnamese territory. The alleged conspiracy by terrorists linked to the al-Qa'ida organization (the network of fundamentalist Islamic militants believed to be responsible for the September acts) to attack US naval vessels in Singapore prompted the US Commander-in-Chief of Pacific Forces, Adm. Dennis Blair, to make the issue of port access to Cam Ranh Bay a priority. The Vietnamese Government had rejected initial requests from both the USA and China for access to the former Russian base, but had not refused to permit port visits.

Economy

ADAM McCARTY

INTRODUCTION

Viet Nam was a country ruled by colonists, divided, or at war for most of the 20th century. Unification of the country in 1976 was followed by the invasion of Cambodia in 1978, and a subsequent brief but violent war with the People's Republic of China. This legacy had profound consequences for economic development in general, and for attempts to impose central planning in particular. Central planning was introduced in North Viet Nam in the 1950s, and in South Viet Nam after 1976, but less extensively. The implementation of central planning was therefore both brief and incomplete.

Viet Nam's economic transition, which is typically identified as having been initiated in 1986, was a relatively smooth period of structural adjustment and stabilization—at least for the first decade. The state sector was never large in Viet Nam, where 80% of the population lived in rural areas and were mostly engaged in the cultivation of rice. Furthermore, by 1986 the planned part of the economy was thoroughly undermined. The collapse of trading relations with the Council for Mutual Economic Assistance (CMEA—which Viet Nam joined as a full member in 1978) forced a restructuring of the modest state-owned enterprise sector, which disposed of almost one-quarter of its labour force during 1988–92. Institutional reforms also generated growth in the urban household services economy, which offset the increase in the numbers of unemployed. The shift to markets was relatively easy without the burden of a large military-industrial complex, and goods hitherto exported to the CMEA found new Western markets without difficulty.

During the 1990s the economy of Viet Nam underwent a transformation. Structural changes occurred during 1987–91, but changes in institutions were slower to occur, and the legacy of administrative control continued. Furthermore, important services, such as accounting, banking and the legal system, remained highly rudimentary. In some regards, therefore, 'transition' involved a generational process.

Before Reunification

In 1954 Viet Nam was divided into two zones at the 17th parallel. In the North under the rule of the Viet Nam Workers' Party (now the Communist Party of Viet Nam), a central economic plan following the Stalinist model was adopted and implemented much as it had been in China, commencing with a campaign to collectivize agricultural production. The purging of rich peasants and landlords in the late 1950s suppressed opposition to collectivization and extended Communist Party economic control to the village level. The absence of a campaign of enforced collectivization in the South after reunification, similar to that which had taken place in the North, was a major factor in the failure to collectivize agriculture in the Mekong delta area. The inefficiency of collectivization also became evident. Yields of paddy rice per ha in the North had fallen from 2,290 kg in 1959 to 1,840 kg in 1960, accounting for most of the decline in total rice production from 5.19m. tons in 1959 to 4.18m. tons in 1960. Average annual rice production during 1960–69 remained low (4.2m. tons). Collectivization had placed the entire Northern economy under pressure.

Agricultural production in North Viet Nam fluctuated during the war years, but rice output exceeded the 1959 level only in 1974. The weaknesses of the centrally-planned model were disguised by the war, and by annual inflows of about US $1,000m. of economic aid, mainly from the USSR, but also from other Eastern European countries and China. Official statistics showed a three-fold increase in the value of industrial production from 1960 to 1975, but this was at uncompetitive, inflated prices, compared with international prices, and was not reflected in data for per caput production.

Until 1976 the economy of South Viet Nam was dominated by the inflow of US military and civilian funding. Aid funds provided infrastructure. Industrial development was pursued through import substitution. Farmers benefited by selling their agricultural surplus. The non-traded goods sector, particularly services, grew rapidly as consumer demand increased. The effects of war, import substitution and the growth of services, resulted in rapid urbanization. The market economy was vigorous but overdeveloped. When US forces withdrew, therefore, the consumer demand that had supported the economy collapsed.

After Reunification

After reunification in 1976 Viet Nam was a poor country attempting to recover from a prolonged period of war. As a result of the war, 52% of the population of 49m. were women, and only 21% of the population lived in urban areas. The North could barely feed its population of 25m., owing to the stagnation of agricultural production that had resulted from two decades of war and central planning. Between 1958 and 1975 the Northern population had grown by 64%, while the production of staples had increased by only 11%. There was little industrial and almost no infrastructural and service development. Markets were clandestine and hence ill developed. Although market transactions persisted to a considerable degree in the South, reunification resulted in an immediate decline in living standards.

The national economic strategy for recovery was to integrate the two economies by imposing Northern central planning upon the South. A five-year Plan, which aimed to 'achieve basic socialist transition in the South', was initiated in 1976. All financial activity was brought under the control of the central bank, and a campaign to collectivize the villages of the Mekong delta commenced. The aim was also to merge the South's predominantly light industry, its system of import substitution and privately-owned enterprises with the North's centrally-planned 'heavy' industries. The 1976–80 Plan failed as a result of the inherent inefficiencies of planning and the unwillingness to take measures that would collectivize and extract an economic surplus from Southern agriculture. Amid resistance to collectivization in the South, Viet Nam's output of staple foods declined by 9%, and the paddy rice yield per ha by 18% in 1976–78. Farmers refused to harvest crops, or refused to sell them at low official prices, slaughtered their livestock, and abandoned land. It was estimated that over 1m. tons of rice were fed to pigs each year. By the end of the decade, the Mekong delta remained largely uncollectivized. Most of the production collectives and co-operatives that did exist had limited functions. The planned industrial growth from enhanced North-South economic integration also failed to materialize. Weak infrastructure, together with barriers to internal trade (tolls and travel permits), increased transport and transaction costs. Output figures recorded a decline: in 1980 total quantities produced of coal, cement, steel, fertilizer, cloth, and paper were all below 1976 levels. State enterprises were reportedly operating at only 30%–50% of their productive capacity.

Failure of the 1976–80 Plan was already apparent in early 1978, but the military demands of Viet Nam's invasion of Cambodia, and the subsequent decline in foreign aid and the war with China, precipitated a crisis. The central planning system, already greatly compromised by unplanned production and market activities, albeit illegal, broke down. Reductions in aid, particularly Chinese assistance, decreased supplies of cheap inputs for state enterprises. Viet Nam was still attempting to maintain an army of more than 1m. until the late 1980s, but state procurement of staple products declined in 1978 and 1979. Unplanned economic activity proliferated. State enterprises had to work outside the plan in order to provide minimal living wages for employees, and workers found additional jobs to supplement those incomes. Central state management weakened when cheap inputs disappeared. The central authorities did not have an economic surplus to support the state sector, which itself did not produce a surplus.

Liberalization after 1978 was a spontaneous process, which placed great pressure on authorities to sanction economic realities and to permit further compromises to central planning. The first official steps towards liberalization were taken at the Communist Party's Sixth Plenum in September 1979, which adopted plans to stimulate agricultural production. Procurement quotas for paddy rice, and the agricultural tax, were fixed for five years, and state procurement prices were increased. Above-quota production could be sold on the free market. Markets were officially sanctioned, so that extensive legal market activity began to co-exist with central planning (unlike most other centrally-planned economies).

During the period of the five-year Plan, instead of imposing an already diminished Northern development model on the South, Southern practices were extended throughout Viet Nam. The economy that emerged in the 1980s was as much a product of 'southernizing' the North, as it was of 'northernizing' the South. Strict central planning no longer dominated resource allocations. From 1979 Viet Nam became more a 'command' economy than a centrally-planned economy. After the economic crisis of 1978–79 the State periodically tried to re-establish the dominance of central planning, but was too weak to do so. Owing to the inherent inefficiencies of planning, economic resources were under-utilized, and hence even modest liberalization was able to generate strong supply responses. Short periods of growth after liberalization measures were viewed by the authorities as opportunities to reimpose central control, which only precipitated further crises. The liberalization initiated in 1979 continued into the early 1980s. In 1981 an 'end-product system' replaced the system of work points in agricultural co-operatives. Co-operatives were allocated production quotas above which output could continue to be sold on markets or at 'negotiated' state prices that were close to market prices and included some bartering, such as the provision of cheap fertilizer to farmers. Central-planning controls over state enterprises were also officially relaxed. In January 1981 a 'Three-Plan System', which legalized the already extensive market activities of state enterprises, was introduced.

During the early 1980s a confusing policy of pragmatic liberalization and attempts to recentralize economic authority were implemented. Without a domestic economic surplus, the State could expand only through aid or by reducing the real incomes paid to workers. Both strategies were pursued. In response, state enterprises expanded 'unplanned' activities to supplement official salaries, and employees increasingly found additional work. It was reported that the supplementary incomes earned by state workers increased after 1979, reaching almost 60% of total income in 1986, but declined slowly thereafter.

In 1976 some 45% of total budgetary revenue was derived from external sources. This share declined as relations with China and industrial countries worsened, but rose again to 41% in 1980, after the USSR increased its support. The trade deficit with the CMEA countries increased from 380m. roubles in 1980 to 721m. roubles in 1985 (when Viet Nam's CMEA exports covered only about one-third of imports). Soviet aid also financed 40 large construction projects and supported more than 200 state enterprises during 1981–85. In 1985 it was reported that Soviet projects accounted for 35% of electricity generation, 95% of coal production and 51% of cement output. Foreign assistance was never large in relation to the whole economy, but because it was entirely directed to the state sector, its supporting role was vital. Without foreign assistance, the State could not have maintained its position during the 1980s. By 1985 the state sector was again under strain. Agricultural production had stagnated, real incomes had declined, and 'unplanned' economic activity continued to increase. The recentralizing policies pursued after 1982 again undermined the economy. Increases in the money supply induced inflation in the free market, which state prices had to follow. This resulted in a so-called 'leading effect' of the parallel, or open, market that made the transition process in Viet Nam differ from that of the USSR or other socialist countries in Eastern Europe.

In September 1985, in an unsuccessful attempt to solve the problem of high free-market prices, the authorities increased state prices and introduced a currency reform. The price rises were accompanied by increases in loans to state enterprises and in wages. The monetary reform introduced a new dông, equivalent to 10 old dông, with limits per person (as also happened in 1978). Since personal savings had been predominantly in gold and US dollars, the main impact of this reform was to eliminate the cash holdings of state enterprises. Without commodity convertibility, the bank deposits of state enterprises had little direct influence on the price level, but a significant increase in budgetary deficits and a sharp rise in inflation were inevitable. In 1984 budgetary revenue had covered 81% of expenditure; in 1985 receipts covered only 55% of expenditure. In 1986 the general price index rose by 487%.

Official planners were unable to disregard the markets. The State maintained constant prices until the breakdown of planning in 1978–79. In the late 1970s, market inflation was running at about 30% annually, eroding the real value of state procurement prices. Official price increases, above the prevailing market inflation rate, were consequently required in 1981–82 to raise the real state price being paid for agricultural produce. Thereafter, state prices followed free market trends closely. In 1979 state procurement of staples in the Mekong delta had totalled 380,000 tons; after the price reforms, procurement rose to 1.9m. tons in 1984. The failure to maintain strong central planning made it possible to undertake drastic price reform in 1989. Repressed inflation associated with a monetary 'overhang' had been eliminated by free market exchanges (commodity convertibility) and annual inflation of more than 300% during the preceding three years. Free market prices had come to dominate economic activity, with the notable exception of key industrial sector inputs, where low prices were maintained through the subsidized trading and aid relationship with CMEA countries. Thus, the issue of prices was already significant when the Vietnamese authorities began dismantling the old planning system.

The 'reforms' of 1985 were the last attempt to maintain the system of central planning. The failure of the 1985 policies strengthened the position of reformers who advocated a more market-orientated economy. The pro-market forces included a rising commercial interest group within the state sector and Southern liberals within the Communist Party. The death of the General Secretary of the Communist Party, Le Duan, in July 1986, created the opportunity for fundamental change within the existing political structure. The Sixth Party Congress of December 1986 was an ideological turning-point, which initiated the transition to a market economy in Viet Nam.

The Transition to a Market Economy

In fact, the Sixth Party Congress in December 1986 introduced a period of policy disarray. Liberalization continued to be selective, and the planned economy remained protected. When interprovincial trade barriers were abolished in 1987, rice prices declined. Central Committee policy decrees issued during 1987–88 relaxed control over foreign investment, land, foreign trade, banking, state industrial management, the private and household sectors, and agriculture. Reforms accelerated in 1988, when the co-operative method of agricultural production was abandoned in favour of household production, and small private enterprises were officially encouraged. However, the fundamental contradictions of maintaining a two-price system remained. The budget deficit grew to 7.1% of gross domestic product (GDP) in 1988, and the trade deficit increased as the State tried to compensate for the rapid decline in aid. Most of the deficit was financed by central bank borrowings. Inflation remained high, at an annual rate of about 300%. In early 1989 any residual planning still in place had to be abandoned.

In March 1989 the Vietnamese Government introduced several stabilization measures. Although direct subsidies and price controls on electricity, coal and some other products remained, most were removed. Government expenditure for the first half of the year was tightened, declining from 14.1% of GDP in 1988 to 12.3% in 1989. Bank interest rates were raised to high positive levels. They were accompanied by credit restrictions on lending to state enterprises. The foreign-exchange rate was brought close to the black market equilibrium rate. Gold trading was liberalized, while a relaxation of trade regulations facilitated a rapid increase in rice exports. The effect was impressive. Inflation, which increased at a monthly rate of 13.6% during 1988, nevertheless rose by 9.2% in February 1989, but then progressively declined, with prices falling between May and July of that year. Central bank financing of the budget deficit in the second half of 1989 brought monthly inflation down to around 2.5%, and this level was maintained into mid-1990.

The 1989 reforms addressed the difficulties of money flow, rather than any perceived money stock problem (the 'monetary overhang'), which had been the focus of the 1978 and 1985 monetary reforms. Money supply (M1) rose from 9.2% to 15.2% of GDP. Budget and credit policies were tightened as indicated, and strong monetary growth was absorbed by a one-off 'monetization' of the economy and 'sterilization' of increased household deposits in the banking system. Credit limits restricted lending to state enterprises, while the underdeveloped legal and banking systems further constrained non-state lending options.

After years of near hyperinflation, the 'monetization' of the economy and of household saving portfolios in early 1989 prompted a revival of confidence in the domestic currency. In a significant change in savings behaviour, households shifted into monetary assets. The real purchasing power of gold and US dollars fell by about 25% in the three months prior to May 1989, as households shifted into dông and bank deposits. During the 10 months after March 1989, household deposits in the commercial banks increased from 0.8% to 3.8% of GDP. Universal poverty and the distortions of the period up to 1986 resulted in the high supply responses to later reforms, particularly to the ending of active discrimination against private enterprise, but also in a continuing distrust of the banking system. Other forms of saving than the dông were still preferred. In 1993 a national survey reported that only 6% of the Vietnamese population used banks.

The 'monetization' of the economy in 1989 helped to limit the inflationary impact of radical price reforms and monetary expansion. The estimated GDP growth of 8% in 1989 resulted from supply responses in the agricultural sector and also in services, as well as from reaction to changes introduced in 1988, which more than offset the 2.8% decline in industrial production. The fiscal expansion of late 1989 continued into 1990. Inflation returned, and real interest rates again became negative in August of that year. Despite increases in budget revenues, notably from petroleum exports in 1990, inflation stood at 68%. The fundamental causes (money-financed budget deficits and state enterprise subsidies) continued. The Government reacted by reducing current and capital expenditures, with the consequence that the budget deficit decreased from 6% of GDP in 1990 to 2.5% of GDP in 1991.

At a meeting of the Central Committee of the Communist Party in December 1991, macroeconomic stability and control of inflation were declared the priority policy objectives to 1995. An anti-inflationary campaign followed, characterized by large-scale selling of dollar and gold reserves to remove dông from circulation. This, and the delayed response to tighter fiscal policies in 1991, reduced the annual inflation rate to 18% for 1992. Indirect subsidies to state enterprises were also lowered significantly in 1992. The momentum was maintained, with the effect that inflation declined to 5% in 1993, although it rose to 14% in 1994. Relative stability of the exchange rate, and in gold buying and selling, was also maintained from 1991. The interest rate (the monthly rate for three-month deposits) was lowered progressively by the central bank from 2.0% to 1.4%.

Control of inflation continued to improve. Diversified financing of the deficit, including experimental bond floats, reduced the growth of money supply. The growth of M2 (M1 and sight deposits) was estimated at 28% for 1994, compared with 19% in 1993 and 34% in 1992. With non-inflationary financing of the budget deficit from 1992 to 1994, the annual inflation rate did not return to pre-1992 levels. In 1993 current budget revenues increased by 13%, owing, in part, to the rise in prices of petroleum, postal services, and electricity, although these areas continued to be lightly taxed by international standards. Steady increases in revenue from external trade taxes from 1991 were also beneficial.

Macroeconomic stability in the mid-1990s became more threatened by trade and exchange rate policies than by fiscal management. In 1995 the trade deficit grew to 11.5% of GDP. This rose to about 19% of GDP in 1996, with imports exceeding exports by US $3,200m. These deficits were only partly covered by aid and foreign investment inflows. A regulated contraction of imports was the policy response that achieved a reduction in the trade deficit in the late 1990s, at the cost of lowering imports.

The Economy in the 1990s

The economic performance of Viet Nam in the 1990s would be classified as 'miraculous' if such achievements were not so common in the latter half of the 20th century. Annual GDP growth rates ranged between 8.1% and 9.5% during 1992–97, led by industry and services, but with average growth in the agricultural sector still an impressive 4.8% per year. Viet Nam's performance was exceptional prior to the Asian financial crisis, even compared with the most successful regional economies.

From a low base, both economic growth and exports were increasing dramatically. The period from 1986, however, was not without problems. Many of these difficulties, such as rural–urban income inequality and migration, were more typical of a fast-growing developing economy than a transitional one. In 2000 Viet Nam remained a very poor country, where concerns about food production and ownership of agricultural land continued to prevail.

Growth and Development after the Asian Crisis

The Asian financial crisis, which had severe effects on the economies of most of the countries in the region in late 1997, had relatively little immediate impact on those countries without open capital accounts and foreign-currency rationing. Viet Nam, like Myanmar, was therefore able to maintain reasonable rates of growth. Longer-term prospects were more favourable. Foreign direct investment in Viet Nam decelerated dramatically. Despite strong growth in trade volumes in the late 1990s, it was expected to be several more years before Viet Nam returned to GDP growth rates in excess of 6%. Thus, despite the Asian financial crisis and apparent hesitation in Viet Nam to adopt further structural change, the economy continued to grow quite rapidly. Major economic indicators showed a general recovery from 1998, with real GDP increasing by about 6.1% in 2000 and by 5.8% in 2001, according to the Asian Development Bank (ADB). Since December 1998 there has been little inflationary pressure in the economy. The rate of inflation was 4.1% in 1999; however, consumer prices declined by 1.7% in 2000 and by 0.4% in 2001. This reflected a decline in food and rice prices in the international market. Total export earnings grew by 25% in 2000 (owing, in part, to an increase in the international prices for some agricultural products and crude petroleum), and non-petroleum exports increased substantially, by 16% in 1999 and again in 2000. Sustained high rates of development would, however, require a return of foreign investment, an increased rate of gross savings as a percentage of GDP, and development of a private corporate sector in Viet Nam.

EMPLOYMENT

During the early years of economic transition, from 1986 to 1991, substantial structural change took place in Viet Nam's labour force. Total state sector employment decreased by about 250,000 persons each year during 1989–91. About 500,000 soldiers were demobilized. Returning worker migrants added to the labour force. Furthermore, the number of persons of working age increased by 3.7% per year (39% of the Vietnamese population was under 15 years of age in 1990). During this 'first phase', the expanding household sector absorbed the growing supply of workers. Unemployment and underemployment, while severe, were never at socially dangerous levels. Unemployment during this period was estimated at between 1.9m. and 6m. persons. In the 'second phase', beginning around 1992–93, change in the structure of employment was less dramatic. In 2000 the threat of large-scale unemployment and under-employment remained a serious problem for Viet Nam, both in terms of political stability and efficient resource use. The sustained growth of the private household sector absorbed some of this labour force growth, but the ability of the economy to generate jobs with higher value-added was essential.

Employment: the First Phase

The 1989–91 shedding of workers was mainly a result of the collapse of CMEA trade, and of a tightening of state enterprise budget constraints during the 1989 stabilization period. At about the same time, however, the removal of internal trade barriers and official decrees supporting the development of the private sector created incentives and opportunities for Viet Nam's household businesses. This process of co-ordinated reform allowed state enterprise employment to decline from 8.7% of total employment in 1989 to 6.2% in 1991, but without causing a huge rise in unemployment, since the private sector created jobs for 4,369,000 workers. The capacity for the private sector to absorb more employment was, however, very limited without further institutional change. Value-added and profit margins in private household activities were very low. Since household economic activities were also very competitive, the scope for one-off household-based employment creation through institutional reforms is limited. The only prospect for creating employment was the promotion of private small and medium enterprises (the private corporate sector).

Employment: the Second Phase

The labour supply is in surplus, as a result of the sharp increase in the population in the 1990s. The excess of supply over demand has become more evident as Viet Nam has developed a more market-orientated economy, and the underemployment of central planning has been revealed. Before 1986 the labour force was concentrated in the state and collective sectors as the two main components of the national economy. With the development of a multi-sector economy during the economic reforms, that share has fallen at a steady rate. The Vietnamese labour market has become fragmented, with the majority of employed workers working in the non-state sector. During 1996–2000 total employment increased by 2.3m., of whom the state sector absorbed nearly 700,000, or 33% of total employment generation, while the non-state sector recruited about 1.2m., accounting for more than 50% of total job creation over that period.

During 1990–98 the number of state businesses was reduced by 6,600, but the total employment in the state sector still slightly increased, owing to lack of finance to pay labourers loss of employment allowances. The private sector was crucial in generating employment. For example, in 1998 the private industrial sector accounted for only 22% of output, but employed 64% of the total labour force in the industrial sector. The private sector provided about 40% of the total new jobs for the country in 2000.

The labour force continued to increase at a rate of about 3% annually, so that a further 1.4m. entered the labour market every year. Unemployment and underemployment were very high, owing to the slow rate of transformation of the rural economic structure. The Government's target was to transform the economy from an agricultural to an industrial one; however, during 1990–2000, the employment in the industry and services sectors increased by 14.2%, while agricultural employment declined by only 4%. Viet Nam is an agricultural country, with 68% of the total employment in the agricultural sector. At present 25%–35% of labourers in the agricultural sector are underemployed. Unemployment of up to 25–30% in rural areas is also a serious problem.

The 'open door' policy has resulted in the creation of a foreign-invested sector in Viet Nam. Total employment in firms with foreign investment increased from 146,000 in 1996 to 218,350 in 2000. In 1996 foreign invested firms therefore accounted for about one-quarter of industrial output, while employing about 5% of the industrial labour force. However, employment in the foreign direct investment sector remained modest, accounting for less than 1% of the labour force in 1999. This was partly from greater productivity in foreign-invested firms, but also because much of the foreign investment has been channelled into heavy and capital intensive industries, with little job-creation capacities. Generally, policies, either directly or indirectly, remained biased towards the development of capital-intensive industries, thereby severely hindering a growth process that generated employment.

AGRICULTURE

Agricultural Reform

The productive economy in Viet Nam remained reliant on the agricultural sector, which employed 62.6% of the labour force in 2000, and contributed 24.3% of GDP in 2000 and an estimated 22% of GDP in 2001 (compared with 34% in 1992). The performance of the agricultural sector has therefore largely determined the direction of political and policy reforms since 1976. The contribution of the agricultural sector to a country's GDP typically declines in relation to the process of development, although agricultural output rises in absolute terms. However, this was not the case in Viet Nam under its system of central planning. In the late 1980s the agricultural share of GDP rose as a result of official price increases rather than output gains, and despite falling productivity indicators. It was not until the 1990s that a clear trend of increasing aggregate output and productivity, and a declining share of GDP, became evident. Real growth in agricultural GDP was somewhat lower in 2001, with an expansion of only 2.3% (compared with 4.0% in 2000). The most significant growth was in the fisheries sector, which accounted for only 12% of the sector's GDP, however. Farming, which accounted for 80% of agricultural GDP, demonstrated almost no growth in 2001.

The basis for a quick supply response to the sharp rise in official prices in early 1989 was the removal of internal trade barriers in 1987 and the return to household production in 1988. In 1993 the National Assembly approved a new Land Law, granting annual crop farmers 20-year renewable tenure rights to their land for up to a maximum of 3 ha. The new code allowed citizens to transfer, exchange, lease and inherit rights to farmland, and to use land as collateral for farm loans. With more secure property rights, the Agriculture Bank acted as a lending agency in rural areas. Total rice output grew annually by 3%–6% during 1993–97, and by 5.9% in 1998, to 31.9m. tons. Rice production totalled 31.4m. tons in 1999, 32.5m. tons in 2000, but declined by 31.9m. in 2001 (the first time in a decade that output had not increased). The decrease in rice production was attributable to a 2.4% reduction in land area under rice cultivation, as lower yield areas were increasingly shifted into aquaculture and production of other crops. However, rice production still accounted for 65% of total crop farming in Viet Nam. Higher output in cash crops, such as coffee (5.5% volume growth), tea (18% volume growth) and cashew (4% volume growth), was not sufficient to offset the decline in rice production. Rice exports increased steadily, reaching 3,477m. tons in 2000, which accounted for 4.6% of total export value in that year, and 3,729.5m. tons in 2001. Wholesale trading of rice used to be highly regulated. Producer prices were held below world prices, and the rationing of export quotas provided a lucrative rent-seeking opportunity. In 1996 the UN estimated that the rice quota system had an effect equivalent to a tax received by trading monopolies on 30% of the value of the paddy crop. In the late 1990s, however, rice exporting was liberalized through policies to abolish the quota allocation system. The exporting sector of the rice industry became more competitive through these measures. The primary beneficiaries of this policy were rice-producing farmers, despite the continuation of provincial cartels.

Food

The rise in gross food output has been a notable feature of Viet Nam's successful economic performance. Total food production increased by 50% during 1988–97 (and by 30% on a per caput basis), while livestock numbers and industrial crop production increased even faster. This extraordinary performance enabled Viet Nam to become a major rice exporter, and led to a steady decline in the incidence of poverty. Liberalization of markets and a strengthening of property rights have generated strong supply responses in the agriculture sector during transition. Long-term investments in annual and perennial crops by households have had a dramatic impact on living standards. The benefits, however, have not been evenly distributed. More farmers have lost their land, while those who were growing only enough crops to survive have not been incorporated in the reforms. Improving the situation of the poorest households was viewed as a more complex task than that involving those who were capable of producing a surplus for markets.

Cash Crops

The expansion of cash crop production has been an important element of Viet Nam's economic reforms. Since 1993 Viet Nam has been a leading exporter of groundnuts and cashew nuts, with cashew nuts providing US $125m. in export earnings in 1997 and US $130m. in 2000. Other successful cash crops include rubber, coffee, and tea. Rubber output more than doubled between 1990 and 1995, and increased from 225,700 tons in 1998, to 291,000 tons in 2000 and to 305,000 in 2001. The Government aimed to further increase production. Notably, in 1991 Viet Nam became Asia's second largest producer of robusta coffee: in 1998 exports rose to 382,000 tons, and to 482,000 tons in 1999 and 694,000 tons in 2000. In 2001 coffee remained Viet Nam's second largest agricultural export after rice, with the country having rapidly become one of the world's major exporters of the commodity. According to the ADB, in 1999 coffee exports were valued at US $585m., compared with revenue of US $1,025m. from exports of rice. By 2001, however, revenue from coffee exports had declined to US $385m., compared with US $588m. from rice exports.

Nevertheless, Viet Nam has suffered as a result of its own success. Despite a steady increase in export volume, from 122,000 tons in 1996 to 212,000 tons in 1999 and 280,000 tons in 2000 and 300,000 tons in 2001, revenue from rubber has decreased similarly to coffee exports, as a result of a decline in the international price for the commodity. The value of rubber exports, according to the ADB, declined from US $255m. in 1996, to US $191m. in 1997, and to US 127m. in 1998. Revenue from rubber exports recovered to US $147m. in 1999 and to US $170m. in 2000, declining again in 2001, to US $161m. Viet Nam's Institute of Agriculture Planning and Design favoured doubling rubber output by 2010, and proposed expanding the area planted from 400,000 ha to 700,000 ha and increasing yields. It was hoped that the smallholdings would raise their share of rubber area from 29% to as much as 50% of the total. This method of increasing production was also applicable for pepper and cashew. From being a minor pepper exporter in the early 1990s, by 2001 Viet Nam had become the second largest exporter of this product. However, the expansion in output has lowered prices from US $4,000–6,000 per ton in 1997–99 to about US $1,330 by December 2001 (an increase in output of 56%, but a decline in revenue of 39%). Similarly, Viet Nam exported 20% more cashews in 2001 than in 2000, a total of 41,000 tons. However, the export value actually fell by 14% in that year, as the international price weakened.

Aquatic exports, a leading sub-sector, is based on a diverse and sophisticated industry, increasingly reliant on fish and shrimp farming. The main markets are the USA (which contributed 27% of the value of shipments), Japan (26%) and China (20%). Private suppliers produce almost all the fish and shrimp and handle 30% of seafood exports. Viet Nam's agricultural exporters are likely to continue to be affected by the low international prices for commodities. For example, coffee prices were projected to decline by 18.5% in 2002 and by 3.3% in 2003. Such continuously falling prices discouraged farmers from investing in future crops, thereby restraining growth. However, the Government lowered taxes on imports of fertilizer and insecticides for several months until June 2002.

Land

In 2000 it appeared that land scarcity was continuing to increase in most regions of the country. An average farming family of five cultivated about 0.5 ha of land, with farmers in the Mekong and Central Highlands averaging 1 ha. The People's Committees had less scope to reallocate land, or to find unused land for newly-formed families. Families with three or more children (often the poorer families) could no longer expect to receive more land on this account. There were reports of land consolidation (purchase of user rights) by larger commercial farmers (especially in the South), or by developers converting land to industrial, residential or recreational use). A new class of landless families was thus being created, who worked for wages on other people's land, who might find off-farm activities, or who joined the increasing flow of people seeking work in urban areas. In 1996 at least 2m. rural residents were officially estimated to have migrated to cities in search of employment (equal to 7% of the nation's working-age population). The authorities of Ho Chi Minh City reported a rural influx of 700,000 persons in 1996 (of whom an estimated 85% were without permanent registration documents.

Forestry

According to estimates by the United Nations Development Programme (UNDP), the area of forest declined from 44% of total land area in 1943 to 23% in 1995. Forestland coverage recovered to 33.2% in 2000, however, due to active afforestation and reforestation efforts, especially in the north-east and north-west regions of the country. The 1979 land use survey of the country put the total area of forest at 13.4m. ha. By 1994 it was estimated that Viet Nam's forested area had decreased to 9.4m. ha. In 2001 the total area of forest in Viet Nam increased to 11.4m. ha. In 1997 Viet Nam had 19.6m. ha of forestry land, accounting for two-thirds of the total natural land area. The forest area was only 10.1m. ha, of which 8.78m. ha was natural and 1.37m. ha was planting area. Wasteland and barren hill areas totalled 10m. ha in the same year. Deforestation remained a major problem, with about 200,000 ha being lost annually in the mid-1990s. In 1998 there were 17,408 ha of 'fired forest' and 20,475 ha of 'destroyed forest'. It was estimated that if this rate were to be maintained, the country would be without forests before the middle of the 21st century. However, deforestation was dramatically reduced in 1999 and 2000. Over the first nine months of 2000, the forest area destroyed totalled 4,000 ha.

Since the Viet Nam war, when an estimated 5% of the country's forests were destroyed and a further 50% damaged, forests have continued to be lost through a combination of uncontrolled logging, population pressure, and 'slash and burn' agriculture. Deforestation also threatened to have a detrimental effect on agriculture in the delta provinces, where forests were an important aspect of flood control. Furthermore, most household energy was derived from fuel wood. In view of the seriousness of the problem, the Government has repeatedly taken measures to curb the rate of deforestation, including since 1992 a ban on the export of logs and low value-added timber products. A number of areas have also been designated national parks. As indicated by the rate of deforestation, enforcement has proved to be difficult. Accordingly, Viet Nam has enlisted the services of the FAO to undertake several forest farming projects, with the aim of increasing the planting rate. Between 1990 and 2000 it was expected that a total of 18 forest projects, at an estimated cost of US $272.7m would be undertaken to plant 785,000 ha of forest. In fact, Viet Nam planted more than 1.9m. ha of forest over this 10-year period.

MINING AND ENERGY

Mining

Interest in mineral resources was one of the factors that attracted the French to Tongking in the late 1880s. Their exploitation was an important feature of the colonial economy, and was further developed by the Japanese during their brief control of the region during 1940–45. The Vietnamese themselves continued this development from the 1950s with the assistance of Soviet geologists. Viet Nam has commercially viable reserves of coal, iron ore, bauxite, chromite, copper, tin, titanium, zinc, gold, apatite and gemstones, although many of these remained underexploited. Coal reserves are located in the north-eastern province of Quang Ninh and in Bac Thai province in the Thai Nguyen Basin. Proven reserves of coal were estimated to be approximately 3,500m. tons, although the actual figure for reserves of all types of coal (bituminous coal, anthracite, lignite and peat) was possibly as high as 30,000m. tons. Iron ore deposits of around 500m. tons have been located in a mine at Thac Khe. Proven bauxite reserves were estimated to be 4,000m. tons, mainly in the southern province of Lam Dong. Deposits of zinc and lead have been located in the North, although the size of the reserves remained unknown in 2000. Son La province was active in mining slate for both domestic use and export.

The most important mining activity arises from the coal deposits. Output expanded considerably in the early 1970s, but stagnated for some years after 1977, following the widespread withdrawal of Chinese labourers after the deterioration of Sino-Vietnamese relations. Production reached 6.9m. tons in 1988, but averaged only 4.4m. tons per year in 1989–91. Production subsequently recovered, with annual coal output averaging 6.8m. tons in 1993–96, increasing to 10.7m. tons in 1998, and slightly declining to 9.6m. tons in 1999. The Viet Nam Coal Corporation, Vinacoal (which assumed sole responsibility for production and distribution in 1994), adopted the target of increasing Viet Nam's annual coal production to 12m. tons. However, external market conditions permitted the production of only 10.8m. tons in 2000. In 1999 mines under the control of Vinacoal were being closed. Exports of coal declined for three years in succession from 1977 to only 600,000 tons in 1980, and in 1987 the level of exports was estimated at only 233,000 tons. By 1990, however, coal exports had recovered to 788,500 tons. Further rapid increases were subsequently achieved, and in 1996 coal exports were 3.6m. tons, valued at US $115m., before a decline to 3.2m. tons (US $102m.) in 1998 and 3m. tons in 2000. Since the 1980s the Government has sought to promote foreign investment in the mining sector. However, this has remained at a relatively low level despite the 1996 mining law.

Petroleum and Natural Gas

In June 1986 Viet Nam finally became an oil-producing nation when petroleum began to flow from the Bach Ho oilfield, which was developed jointly with the USSR by Vietsovpetro. By mid-1987 this field, located 160 km east of Ho Chi Minh City in the South China Sea, was producing some 5,000 barrels per day (b d) and, in the absence of a domestic refinery, Viet Nam was exporting petroleum to Japan. In 1996 output of crude petroleum was approximately 8.8m. tons. In 1994 two new fields (Dai Hung and Rong) entered into production. However, only a fraction of the petroleum produced was refined locally, at a small plant in Ho Chi Minh City, which was built with French assistance. As a result of increases in the international price, the value of Viet Nam's petroleum exports rose from US $1,200m. in 1998 to US $2,100m. in 1999.

The project to build a new refinery at Dung Quat in the central province of Quang Ngai, with a capacity of 130,000 b/d, was well advanced in 2000. Although the installation was originally due to be operational by 2000, with a second refinery of similar capacity scheduled for construction several years later, the project proved highly controversial. The initial group of foreign investors withdrew after the location in central Viet Nam was announced. Furthermore, another group later withdrew and claimed that the project was not economically viable; the Government finally proceeded without external financing. In early 1998 Zarubezhneft, a Russian foreign economic association, agreed to assist in financing the proposed US $1,300m. refinery, enabling the project to progress. In October, however, it was reported that construction of the refinery had been postponed indefinitely, owing to a dispute between the US contractor and the other companies involved.

In the mid-1990s Viet Nam's production level of crude petroleum was approximately equivalent to that of a minor producer such as Romania, but still well below that of neighbouring Malaysia and Indonesia. (In 2000 Viet Nam's petroleum reserves were estimated to be about one-third of those of Indonesia.) During 1995–98 petroleum production increased by 22% annually, reaching 12.5m. tons in 1998, but increased by only 7% in 1999–2000, to 16.3m tons. Between 1988 and 1999 the Government allocated 35 production-sharing contracts to foreign oil companies, with a total of about US $3,100m. invested. However, in terms of commercially viable finds, the results have been disappointing. In 1995 less than 25% of the country's petroleum blocks had been allocated, and it was believed that some of the most promising areas had yet to be explored. Nearly all the major international oil companies were represented in Viet Nam, including those from the USA, following the removal of the US trade embargo in early 1994.

Viet Nam also aimed to exploit its natural gas resources, with proven reserves of 300,000m. cu m., and prospective reserves of 1,700,000m. cu m. Since production at the offshore gas field of Tien Hai reached its highest point in 1987, Viet Nam produced only associated gas from Bach Ho (nearly all of which was burnt off). However, in 1995 a gas pipeline from Bach Ho to Ba Ria (near the oil centre of Vung Tau) was completed, thereby allowing the utilization of gas for power generation, and gas production increased by 154% during 1995–98. A three-stage programme for the industry has been drafted, with 14,000m. cu m of gas expected to be produced in the final phase (2005–10).

By 2002 prospects for the petroleum industry appeared to be less favourable, with the increase in production believed to have nearly slowed to a standstill. The large Bach Ho oilfield was projected to maintain output levels for a further five years before they fell sharply, with the Su Tu Den and Su Tu Vang oilfields then compensating for the deficit. However, prospects for the natural gas industry were more promising. Total proven gas reserves were estimated at slightly more than the proven reserves of oil (of 500 tons). Much of the gas was to be brought ashore in the Nam Con Son pipeline in the south by Petrovietnam, Viet Nam's state-owned petroleum and gas corporation. Petrovietnam also planned to construct a pipeline to transmit gas from off the south coast to Ca Mau province. The amount of oil and gas produced annually was, in practice, closer to 18m. tons, than the 20m. tons estimated in the late 1990s.

Power Generation

By 1975 the total power generation of both zones of the country was only 3,000m. kWh. Production in 1980 was put at approximately 3,720m. kWh. Although the situation has improved since the mid-1980s, there were frequent power shortages, particularly in the South during the 1990s. With energy demand rising at a rate of about 20% per year, electricity output has failed to keep pace. Electricity demand was projected to reach 25,000m.–27,000m. kWh in 2000. Power generation in the South increased by an estimated 16.5% in 1993. The additional output was largely due to the newly inaugurated gas turbine generators at the Ba Ria-Vung Tau power plant, as well as to increased generation at the Da Nhim and Tri An hydroelectric power stations. Further important developments were the construction of a new generator at the hydroelectric power station at Hoa Binh, the completion of the 1,500-km North–South power line in May 1994 and two hydroelectric power stations in the centre and the South, YALY and Thacmo. Total electricity output rose from 19,253m. kWh in 1997 to 21,847m. kWh in 1998. It was projected that generating capacity would reach 33,000m. kWh by 2002. Nevertheless, an overhaul of the distribution system and the establishment of a regulatory framework to attract foreign investment remained an urgent requirement. Some 19% of the electricity generated by power stations was lost in transmission in 1997. The Government aimed to supply electricity to 80% of rural households by 2005 (compared with 63% in 1995). During 1998–99 the Government also announced its intention to reduce the country's dependence on hydroelectric power, anticipating greater reliance on gas and coal.

Electricity production increased by 13% in 2000 and by 15% in 2001. Debate continued about the form of the proposed Son La power installation in North Viet Nam, which was to have the design capacity of 2,400 MW. Some members of the legislature have doubted the wisdom of these plans, which would necessitate the reallocation of 700,000 people.

INDUSTRY

To avoid competition with French imports, only a limited range of industrial activity was allowed to develop during the colonial period. Apart from mining, the only significant industries in Indo-China before 1940 were those of cement at Haiphong and textiles at Nam Dinh and Hanoi. After 1954 the Vietnamese aimed to develop both existing and new industries. In the South there was some development of light industry in the late 1950s and early 1970s, mainly related to the production or assembly of consumer goods, and a cement works was established at Ha Tien, near the Cambodian border.

'Socialist construction' entailed the creation of a heavy industrial base for the new economy. However, US bombing destroyed the development of industry before 1965. After 1968 a gradual decline in the emphasis on heavy industry was perceived. One of the principal aims of the second National Plan was to expand light and consumer goods industries, in an effort to relieve the shortages of basic commodities, which were causing further discontent among the long-suffering population. In practice, however, these policies made little progress until the advent of economic reforms in the 1980s. Although emphasis continued to be placed on heavy industry, the expansion of light industry, which began in the early 1980s, was furthered in the 1990s. Between 1990 and 2000, according to the ADB, the average annual growth rate in industry was 11.3%, despite the slow down in 1997–98. Following recovery from the Asian economic crisis, industrial growth increased to 7.7% in 1999, to 10.1% in 2000, and to an estimated 9.7% in 2001. Some of the large-scale state-owned industries performed well during the early 1990s (although many did not), following the input of foreign capital and technology in the form of joint-venture agreements. According to official figures, state industry and the non-state sector grew at about the same rate in 1998 but differed in 2000 with an estimated 12.2% for the state sector and 18.5% for both the non-state and foreign invested sector. Light industrial growth was also strong. In 1998 industry (including mining, manufacturing, construction and power) constituted 32.7% of GDP and employed 16% of the working population. The contribution of industry to GDP rose to 35.4% in 2000 (when the sector engaged 13.1% of the labour force), and to 36.6% in 2001, reflecting the strong effect of the Government's development programme and a rise in consumer confidence. Industry (including construction) remained a principal contributor of total economic growth. In 2001 the increase in non-state domestic industrial production was greatest, at 20%. The state and foreign investment sector experienced more modest, but still vigorous, growth rates of about 12%.

Four areas of manufacturing showed particular promise in the 1990s: textiles, footwear and garments; agro-processing; electrical industries; and automobile and motorcycle assembly. In 1999 textiles and garments represented a significant source of export earnings (US $1,747m.) and were also among the strongest performing commodities in the industrial sector in 2000 (US $1,815m.), with 17.5% and 13.1% growth, respectively, after a stagnant year in 1998. In 2001 textile production increased by 5.7%, to US $2000m. Footwear exports were US $1,350m. in 1999, US $1,402m. in 2000, and US $1,600m. in 2001. In April 2000 the Government negotiated a 27% increase in the size of its European Union (EU) quota, which, combined with access to the US market, should result in a continuation of strong growth in the sector. Viet Nam remained price competitive in garments, but less so following the currency devaluations of regional producers in 1997.

In the early 1990s electronics and automobile production were still at an early stage of development. Both were import-substitution industries protected by tariffs and non-tariff barriers, and had fulfilled the demand of the domestic market by 2000. In 1993 foreign companies assembling electronics goods in Viet Nam included Daewoo, Hitachi, and Philips. From 1995 the sector expanded considerably, with output of assembled television sets almost trebling in the period 1995–98, to reach 364,000 pieces in 1998. The 30%–40% growth rates in the electronics industry of the early 1990s declined to about 10% annually by 2000, but recovered to 52% in 2001.

By 1997 14 foreign joint ventures in the automobile industry had been licensed. Investment totalled US $940m., with assembly capacity estimated at 144,660 cars annually, and with 45 different models. Of the 14 joint ventures, seven companies (Mekong Corporation, Vina Star Motor Corporation, Viet Nam Motor Corporation, Mercedes-Benz Viet Nam, Ford Viet Nam, Toyota Viet Nam, Isuzu Viet Nam, Suzuki Corporation and the Daihatsu Motor Company of Japan) were in production. Only 6,882 cars were assembled in 1999 (compared with 6,404 in 1998), which was less than 10% of projected domestic demand for the period 2000–05. In 2000 and early 2001 there was a surge in second-hand car imports (about 10,000 units over the first half of 2001). Only 11 vehicle assembly joint ventures were still in operation, with an estimated total output of 12,500 units in 2000. Domestic sales recorded 8,700 units over six months in 2000; most joint ventures were therefore operating at as little as 10% of total capacity. In 1998 212,000 motorcycles were assembled in Viet Nam, increasing to 509,000 in 1999 and to an estimated 1.6m in 2000, meeting domestic market potential, which was estimated at 1m. annually for 1997–2005. The automobile industry has become the fastest expanding sub-sector, with a 41% increase in sales for 2001.

The cement and steel sectors continued to receive special priority. Annual growth of cement demand was 22% during 1991–96, while production increased by 15% in 1999, and 27.3% in 2000. Cement output increased from 2.5m. tons in 1990 to 5.8m. tons in 1995, 9.3m. tons in 1998, 13.3m tons in 2000, and 15.4 m. tons in 2001. Crude steel production was 408,000 tons in 1996 and 853,000 tons in 1998. Import of cement increased almost three-fold during 1994–96, but sharply declined to only 10,000 tons in 1999 (compared with 1.3m tons in 1996) owing to increased domestic production. Imports of steel in the same period (1994–96) more than doubled. In 1998, however, prompted by declining demand and rising domestic production, the Government banned steel imports. Nevertheless, an increasing import trend continued with 2.2m tons in 1999 and 2.6m. tons in 2000 accounting for 5.2m.% of total principal import of 2000.

Another emerging industrial sector is plastics, with output reaching 200,000 tons in 1994. In view of the rapidly expanding requirements of the packaging industry, it was planned to increase plastics production eightfold by 2000. However, a joint venture to produce PVC (with accompanying import protection) resulted in an increase in local costs, forcing the industry into a position of import substitution. The import of plastic raw materials reached US $477m. in 2000.

TRANSPORT AND COMMUNICATIONS

In 2000 a significant factor that continued to constrain development was the inadequacy of the country's infrastructure. During the French colonial period Viet Nam was provided with a railway system, the main lines of which linked Hanoi to Ho Chi Minh City (then Saigon) and Haiphong to Yunnan Province in the People's Republic of China. After 1954 the Chinese assisted in the construction of a third major route between Hanoi and the Chinese province of Guangxi via Lang Son. The system was badly damaged during the war, in both North and South Viet Nam, and its reconstruction was a priority from 1975. The lines to China, however, were closed towards the end of 1978, and further stretches were damaged, as a result of the war with China during February–March 1979. Improved Sino-Vietnamese relations led to the reopening of the cross-border rail link in February 1996. Other lines remained in extreme need of modernization. In 1999 the journey of 1,730 km between Hanoi and Ho Chi Minh City by express train took 32 hours. In that year some 25% of Viet Nam's estimated 400 engines remained coal-powered. In 1995 the Government estimated that investment of more than US $3,670m. was required for the modernization and expansion of the railway system. In 2002, as a direct result of frequent visits of some leaders of Viet Nam and China, the two countries were to investigate the feasibility of upgrading the railway between Haiphong and Kunming.

Road transport became increasingly important in the 1960s, although roads and bridges suffered heavy damage during the war. In the South, the USA constructed a new highway between Ho Chi Minh City and Bien Hoa, as well as a large number of lesser roads. However, the road transport sector continued to be perceived as a 'weak link' in the economy. A large proportion of the US $13,040m. pledged by foreign aid donors during 1993–98 was allocated to improving the road network. This assistance was most apparent in the upgraded North–South nationwide Road No 1 and the newly constructed Hanoi –Haiphong highway. However, most road bridges in Viet Nam had a maximum weight capacity of only 10 tons and, of the country's 105,500 km of highways, only 25% were paved. A six-lane highway, linking Hanoi with Noi Bai airport, was opened in 1994, but a new airport terminal was to be brought into full use only in September 2001, substantially behind schedule.

The principal port facilities before 1975 were at Haiphong, Da Nang and Ho Chi Minh City. By 1978 projects had been initiated to construct a new port at Cua Lo, as well as to modernize Haiphong in order to increase its capacity to 2.7m. tons per year. Upgrading work was ongoing in the mid-1990s and, pending its completion, severe congestion in Haiphong was expected to continue. In the southern-central provinces, it was decided to modernize the ports of Quy Nhon and Nha Trang, to enable them to cope with timber exports. In the region of the Mekong delta the development of a new container facility at Ho Chi Minh City and the upgrading of several of the river ports to take ocean-going vessels were planned. Haiphong and Can Tho ports required dredging to reduce chronic silting, while new container terminals were also planned at Haiphong, and Tan Thuan. Vung Tau port was due for extensive upgrading. Although large amounts of foreign financial aid and investment have been pledged, their disbursement and implementation were delayed by problems associated with bureaucracy and the low level of domestic capital mobilization. Aid disbursements reportedly totalled US $5,300m. during 1993–98 (equivalent to 39% of commitments).

As a result of rapid economic and political developments in recent years, by 1997 more than 17 foreign airlines served Viet Nam. In the early 1990s a major programme of airport development was under way, with Noi Bai (Hanoi), Tan Son Nhat (Ho Chi Minh City) and Da Nang airports as principal objectives. The airport at Tan Son Nhat was scheduled to be able to accommodate 10m. passengers and 1m. tons of freight annually by 2010. The number of passengers carried by Vietnamese airlines increased from 500,000 in 1990 to more than 2.7m. in 1996 and some 2.8m in 2000, while the volume of freight increased from 4,000 in 1990 to 50,100 in 1997. Viet Nam Airlines expanded its operation to 20 domestic and 20 international routes in 2001.

With the implementation of reform, Viet Nam's telecommunications network also received attention. In 1991 there were only two telephones per 1,000 people; by 1997 there were 130 per 1,000. By the end of 2000 the number of telephone subscribers was 3.3m, nearly 26 times more than that in 1991, ranking Viet Nam among 30 countries with subscribers of more than 2m. In the late 1990s Viet Nam has achieved high growth in telecommunication. In 2001 there were four new foreign direct investment projects on transport and communication, with the total value of commitment reaching US $231 m. The international telecommunication charge levied by the Viet Nam Posts and Telecommunication Corporation was reduced by 15% by December 2001, in response to the emergence of a competing telephone service provided by the army. The introduction of competition made further price reductions certain.

FINANCE

In contrast to the negligible role that the financial sector played in centrally planned economies, financial intermediation is a crucial factor in the functioning of markets. Reform of the financial sector was consequently a test of the transition to a market economy. The Vietnamese financial sector remained dominated by a few large banks. In the late 1990s, the banking sector constituted only 2% of GDP, reflecting its undeveloped nature.

Interest Rate Policy

Prior to 1989 government policy kept interest rates strongly negative with obligatory enterprise and household deposits. In early 1989 rates were set at levels that were strongly positive in real terms, and it was announced that explicit account of inflation would determine future changes. The correlation between interest rates and inflation during 1989 was very weak; however, it was not until after 1991 that interest rate movements became discernibly related to inflation trends. Even so, a deposit of a three-month rolling term would have accrued a real interest return of 132% over the 30 months between July 1992 and December 1994. In 2000 interest rates remained controlled, and hence consequent problems of miscalculation, rationing, resource wastage, corruption, and patronage continued. In 2000 the central bank, the State Bank of Vietnam (SBV), introduced a more flexible interest rate policy, allowing more freedom for commercial banks to determine the price of their loans. In the first half of 2000 the SBV announced an interest rate band, with a base rate of 0.7% per month. From August 2000 credit institutions were allowed to offer any rate up to the new ceiling rate; consequently, banks can price their loan differently to prime and non-prime customers, subject to the ceiling. Lending in foreign currency is anchored to the Singapore inter-bank market. On 1 June 2001 the SBV removed the interest rate ceiling on both US dollar loans and dông loans. Deregulating the limit on these rates is a key step in decentralizing the financial system. It was announced in August that locally based companies could borrow foreign exchange from overseas lenders at a rate negotiated by the two sides. In November the SBV reduced reserve requirement for foreign deposit from 15% to 10%, with a view to help commercial banks equipped to supply the high demand for dollars. Nominal interests favoured the dông to the US dollar, but the real rate reversed from the gradual devaluation of the dông, 4.3% in 2001 and 2.9% in the first three months of 2002.

Government Banks

A move towards financial sector reform was made in 1988 when the Agriculture Bank of Viet Nam (VBA, now Bank for Agriculture and Rural Development—VBARD) and the Industrial and Commercial Bank of Viet Nam were created as commercial banks from departments of the SBV. They subsequently dominated commercial deposits and lending. Two existing small specialized banks, the Bank for Foreign Trade of Viet Nam (Vietcombank) and the Bank for Investment and Development of Viet Nam, constituted the formal financial sector. Establishing the two-tier banking system in 1988 had little effect until monetization in 1989, when the World Bank considered that deposit growth caused a 'transformation of the degree of penetration of the banking system in the economy'. Deposits increased to 3.8% of GDP, but by international standards this was still low. In 1991 the ADB considered the financial sector to be a major constraint to economic growth. Although the first round of banking reforms of 1988–91 were conducted and the structure of the banking system has diversified and fiscal control has improved, the current banking system remained considerably behind that of the region. Total bank credits totalled about 22% and bank deposits about 8% of GDP in 2000. Four state-owned commercial banks have continued to dominate total lending and policy lending.

The proportion of non-state enterprise lending began to increase after 1991. The non-state sector's share of net domestic credit rose from 10% in December 1990 to 38% in March 1995. Increased bank autonomy and experience supported the trend for non-state lending, as did tighter budget constraints on state enterprises, and the improved institutional environment, which was reducing the risks associated with non-state enterprise lending. The VBA adapted promptly to changing circumstances. Within six months of the authorization of lending to farm households in July 1991, the Bank had lent 405,000m. dông (about US $36m.) to 558,680 households (about US $65 per household). By 1995 the VBA had reportedly lent to 7m. households, with an average of about US $110 per household. The monthly lending rate was uniformly 1.25%, which was below market rates, thus requiring government subsidization and rationing mechanisms.

The SBV continued to subsidize state commercial banks, owing to the interest rate regime and the asset portfolio with which the banks were established. The two large state commercial banks (VBA and Incombank) were probably insolvent when they were formed in 1988. These four banks' share of non-performing loans (NPLs) in outstanding credit was estimated at US $1,000m. by the Vietnamese Government and US $4,500m. by the World Bank. Notably, in 2000 the four SOCBs accounted for 88% of new credit, and for the first half of 2001 accounted for nearly one-half. However, the NPLs' total asset ratio continued to increase in the past 18 months, suggesting a significant and ongoing deterioration of the banks' credit portfolio. Based on Viet Nam's Accounting Standards (VAS), the rate was 10% at the end of August 2001, and it was at least 30% for the 1996–1998 period, if International Accounting Standards (IAS) were used. Also based on VAS, the capital-asset ratios have fallen to an average of below 5% at the end of July 2001.

A detailed restructuring plan for the four large state commercial banks was created, with the development of a phased recapitalization fund from the Government. The master plan began with financial audits of the large state commercial banks by international auditors using the IAS. The auditing of the VBARD and the Bank for Investment and Development of Vietnam have been completed, and the other two were scheduled for completion by the end of 2002.

The 80% recapitalization capital comes partially from the Government, with the rest funded by bond issues. The World Bank estimated the recapitalization requirements of the commercial banks at 6% of GDP in 1991. A Debt Resolution Committee subsequently identified the extent of existing bad debts, and facilitated the payment of some outstanding debts, in some cases through liquidation proceedings. The Government also authorized the cancellation of some bank debts. However, Vietnamese officials announced that the 2006 deadline might not be met, owing to the exceptionally high NPLs (mentioned above). Restructuring of joint-stock banks (JSBs) has been conducted by their closure, merger, or rehabilitation. By February 2002 13 JSBs had been closed or merged, reducing the total number from 52 to 38. Several JSBs have been rehabilitated through stakeholders providing additional capital. This process was expected to be finalized in 2002.

The legal and property rights framework has been strengthened gradually. The devolution of economic and legal autonomy from the Communist Party and the State to rights for individuals has not been easy to accept. The task of developing a commercial rights-based legal system was formidable, both technically and politically, and required much greater progress. Several commercial laws have been adopted since 1986. Legislation introduced in 1987 provided for the private use of allotted land in agriculture. A series of ordinances on economic contracts in 1989, on economic arbitration in 1990, and on civil contracts in 1991 began to codify contractual procedures. Legislation on private enterprises and on companies was introduced in 1990. Changes to the Constitution in 1992 allowed individuals to exercise property rights over income-producing assets and personal property. Legislation relating to bankruptcy was introduced in 1993, as was a new land law that clarified property rights and allowed mortgages on land. 'Codification' and clear documentation of rights were important initial developments in the formulation of an effective legal and property rights framework, but the effective, transparent, and fair enforcement of these new laws remained to be implemented. The legacy of the domination of the legal system by the Communist Party was that courts had yet to 'develop a high level of commercial expertise or a robust form of independence'.

Regulatory Framework

Efficient financial intermediation is severely constrained by the lack of appropriate monitoring capacity at the SBV. In 1991 it was reported that no department at the SBV was responsible for the collection and processing of reports of joint-venture banks and that the SBV did not even have complete lists of joint-stock and housing banks in Viet Nam. By 2000 comprehensive supervision of all financial sector organizations was the responsibility of the SBV, although it lacked powers of direct intervention. Implementation of the SBV's limited authority continued to be constrained by skill shortages and poor administrative procedures. Its supervisory capacity was also dependent on the perceived credibility of its role as an autonomous agent of monetary policy. In 2000 this role was compromised by the necessity to act as a 'frequent lender' to the state commercial banks that were unable to make profits from financial intermediation. In 2000 new regulations were also issued for the operations of banks with respect to calculating provisions against their non-performing loans on a quarterly basis. A legal framework for creditor rights and resolution of assets was to be established, with the aim of securing transparency and accountability for all banks, allowing them to become more competitive. The Government has established the National Financial and Monetary Policy Consultancy Council, chaired by the First Deputy Prime Minister. The SBV Governor, Le Duc Thuy, was to be the standing member. The precise purpose of the Council was unclear, but it might introduce an element of political supervision over the activities of the SBV.

FOREIGN TRADE

Buoyant trade growth has been a remarkable feature of Viet Nam's transition. The value of total trade increased steadily from 1988, with only a slight levelling-out in 1990 when CMEA-area trade collapsed. Using the exchange rates of the Bretton Woods institutions, the total volume of CMEA trade was not large prior to 1987 and fell subsequently. Relations with the CMEA permitted Viet Nam to run a large trade deficit for only a short period to 1988. After 1988 trade with the convertible area was always larger. The collapse of the CMEA in 1990–91, therefore, had no significant adverse effects on the economy as a whole. The impact was mainly in the loss of subsidies to state industrial enterprises.

Viet Nam's total trade as a percentage of GDP increased from 32% to 88% in the eight years to 1999. Exports rose to US $14,448m. (46% of GDP) in 2000, and reached US $15,027m. in 2001, with a growth rate of about 4.0% (a slowdown from 2000, owing to weak external demand and low commodity prices). Exports to Japan, along with imports from Hong Kong, grew consistently. Of the growth in total export earnings in 2000, 60% was attributable to exports to Asian markets outside ASEAN, mainly Japan and China. The US and Canada market also expanded significantly from a low level, accounting for almost 40% of export earnings. The US export market ranked fifth in 2000. The switch to hard currency exporting was achieved largely because Viet Nam's main exports were primary products that found an international market without difficulty. Labour-intensive manufactures and assembly operation exports ('light industry') increased in the 1990s, as a result of investments by Asian economies utilizing Viet Nam as a low-wage export base. Owing to the dramatic return of Viet Nam as a net exporter of rice in 1989 and the steady growth in petroleum exports, the collapse of CMEA trade in 1990 appeared only as a brief interruption in a strong upward trend. Petroleum exports increased almost fourfold between 1989 and 1992, and doubled between 1995 and 1999 in both volume and value. This was an important contribution to both exports and economic growth. The strong export performance, together with rising capital inflows, facilitated a rapid rise in imports of machinery and spare parts.

The sharp decline in exports and foreign direct investment that followed the Asian financial crisis of 1997 prompted the Vietnamese authorities to remove restrictions on exports, including the abolition of the requirement for private companies to obtain export licences. Strong export performance during 1999–2000 was, in part, a result of these institutional reforms (although about one-half of growth in receipts at that time was due to the higher international price for petroleum). The eventual signing of the Normal Trade Relations (NTR) treaty with the USA in 2000 was welcomed as a significant step in the political and economic reform process in Viet Nam. The NTR was to reduce tariffs for the US market and was expected to increase future export activity. Export revenue for 2002 and 2003 was projected to increase by 7.7% and 17.8%, respectively.

The value of imports, according to the ADB, increased from US $10,568m. in 1999, to US $14,073m. in 2000 and to US 14,546m. in 2001. Imports grew slower than exports, at a rate of 3.4% in 2001, mainly in the sectors of construction materials, such as steel and glass, and motor vehicles. Export growth rates were expected to reach 10% in 2002 and 21.1% in 2003, owing to a stronger domestic demand and an increase in the import of key production inputs. According to the ADB, the trade surplus had declined from US $972m. in 1999 to US $375m. in 2000, but increased to US $481m. in 2001.

Trade Policies

Viet Nam's trade and investment policies can be characterized as 'export-led protectionism', whereby import substitution is encouraged with trade protection, and export industries are promoted by providing subsidies to counterbalance the high relative costs of intermediary products. This should not be interpreted simply as a model similar to that of the Republic of Korea, but rather as protectionism based on central planning, combined with a crude interpretation of export-led development.

The legacy of central planning is, most importantly, a strong belief in self-sufficiency through import substitution. Another important aspect is the continuing belief in the role of the Government to manage and to make frequent adjustments to the whole economy, and a consequent disregard for the costs of price distortions and uncertainty created by this approach in a market economy.

A new tariff code was introduced in 1993. It had over 20 different rates ranging from zero to 200%, making it too complex to be effectively administered. The new rates were generally higher than those set in 1991, but for many goods they were still in an acceptable range, according to the World Bank. The average (unweighted) rate was 12%. Almost 80% of tariff lines were set at 20% or lower. In 1994 the requirement for import permits for all but 15 products (refined petroleum, fertilizer, cement, and some consumer items) were eliminated. An import duty exemption scheme was improved in 1994, with the result that a company was not required to pay duties on those imports used to produce exports. A process of imposing international standards of free trade on Viet Nam began in 1996, following the country's admission to the Association of South East Asian Nations (ASEAN) Free Trade Area (AFTA). This transition was expected to take many years to be effective, particularly in view of the allowances made for poor developing countries like Viet Nam. Quantitative import restrictions on eight out of 19 groups of products were removed in 2000. In addition, the plan for AFTA tariff reductions for 2001–06 was approved: most tariff lines were to be reduced to 20% by early 2003 and to 5% by early 2006. In February 2002 the Government detailed a list of goods and tax rates for implementing the Agreement on Common Effect Preferential Tariffs Scheme for Asian countries for the year 2002. Based on the schedule, 481 items were transferred to the inclusion list, with tariffs lower than 20%.

A further measure was the removal of qualification requirements multilaterally on all tariff lines of the following groups of products: liquor, clinker, paper, floor tiles, construction glass, several types of steel, and vegetable oils. Moreover, the Government for the first time established import and export plans for a five-year period, rather than the year-on-year review. This was expected to significantly reduce the risk for long-term planning among traders. With a view to support the agricultural producer in tough times, the Government has reduced import tariff on fertilizer, as well as established an export support credit sourced from the State Development Assistance Fund to promote exports for enterprises, economic organizations and individuals. There has been much discussion of stricter controls over imports of parts for cars and motorcycles. The Ministry of Finance has resisted lobbying from foreign-invested enterprises for greater protection of the domestic electronic goods sector. The Ministry argued that under 'common effective preferential tariff' obligations, Viet Nam would have to reduce its duty on audio and video products from ASEAN countries to 0%–5%.

Customs duties comprised 25% of government revenue by the late 1990s. This, however, was only one of the objectives assigned to this policy instrument. Consequently, the tariff schedule was complex and constantly changing. The number of tariff rates decreased from 36 in 1995 to 31 in 1996, then increased to 35 in 1997, but was subsequently reduced to 26 rates, ranging from 0% to 60%, in 1998. The schedule in February 1998 identified 3,163 separate items, and within one item there may be many relevant minimum import prices applied. Despite the ASEAN agreement to remove all surcharges by 1996, Viet Nam maintained surcharges (export taxes) on a small number of important products. Customs surcharges were subsequently applied for various periods of time to imported petroleum, some types of iron and steel, and fertilizer. Surcharges were also applied on exports of coffee, unprocessed cashew nuts, and rubber in the late 1990s, purportedly as part of a price stabilization fund process. These surcharge rates have been changed frequently. Between mid-1994 and 2000, the rates on petroleum products were changed 14 times. Rates on petroleum products differed between North and South Viet Nam until 1996. Rates between 2% and 10% were applied to eight different types of iron and steel products.

In 1998 foreign-exchange management controls became a more prominent instrument of economic policy in Viet Nam, and these were used to meet macroeconomic and specific trade and industry policy objectives. The increased emphasis on financial controls preceded the removal of import licensing, and was most probably a response to the Asian financial crisis and dwindling capital inflows. That is, an emerging shortage of foreign capital promoted a strengthening of foreign-exchange controls that, as usual, were then also employed to pursue other development strategy objectives. In 1999 foreign exchange controls were slightly relaxed by reducing the foreign exchange surrender requirement of foreign exchange earnings from 80% to 50%, and subsequently to 40%. Vietnamese trade policy reforms of the late 1990s might be interpreted as generally protectionist, although in some instances they were merely codifying existing policies. The most obvious trend of the trade reform process has been one of contradictory liberalization: both protectionist and liberalizing measures were being introduced every year. Publication of the tariff reduction schedule and the abolition of import licences in 1998 appeared to indicate one course, while foreign-exchange controls, combined with the gradual increase in the use of quotas, bans and surcharges, pointed to the other direction.

Therefore, it is difficult to suggest that Viet Nam is firmly moving towards the fulfilment of its trade liberalization commitments to AFTA and Asia-Pacific Economic Co-operation (APEC). If anything, trade policies became more restrictive during 1996–2000. Most non-tariff barriers have been strengthened, with only licensing and rice-exporting notably weaker. Viet Nam's trade regime in 2000 remained restrictive by international standards. The policy framework continued to be very much a legacy of central planning. The planning vision of development and role of the State impeded the pace of liberalization. Entrenched interest groups, particularly state enterprises and corporations, slowed the liberalization process even further. Such a combination of conflicting ideologies, interests and economic perspectives could not be expected to produce a 'liberal' trading regime in the short term.

FOREIGN INVESTMENT

The promotion of foreign investment was an early and relatively straightforward stage in Viet Nam's reform process. Viet Nam enacted its first foreign investment law in December 1987, with amendments in June 1990 and in December 1992. Although the law was intended to reassure foreign investors with regard to their rights and provided the usual incentives in the form of tax concessions and other privileges, it was ineffective until a realistic exchange rate was established in 1989. Even then, the weak legal framework, the continuing US trade and investment embargo, and the lengthy process of approving foreign investment projects prevented a significant rise in commitments until the mid-1990s. As in China, foreign investment was begun informally by Asian developing countries investing in labour-intensive export production outside the approval procedure and statistical structure.

'Total capital' foreign direct investment commitments to Viet Nam exceeded US $3,400m. in 1998 and US $3,718m. in the first seven months of 2001. This included the Vietnamese partner's contribution, typically land, to joint venture projects. About three-quarters of projects with foreign investment were joint ventures, with the Vietnamese contribution averaging 25%–30% of the official value. After deflating total capital by 22% (30% of three-quarters), the 262 licensed projects amounted to an investment of US $3,700m. in 1994, equivalent to about 19% of Viet Nam's GDP in that year. Foreign direct investment commitments reached US $8,500m. in 1996, but subsequently declined steadily. In 1999 commitments totalled US $1,300m., and they reached US $2,400m. in 2001 (a 23% increase, compared with 2000). Japan was the largest investor, in terms of disbursement, but was expected to be overtaken by Taiwan and Singapore.

Remarkably, in 1999 the Paris Club rescheduled Viet Nam's debt to Russia, lowering Viet Nam's debt burden and debt ratio. Other positive developments included progress on the economic reform process, political stability, and the signing in 2001 of bilateral trade agreements with the USA. Several additional changes in policy have caused a positive change in investors' assessment of Viet Nam. There was a reduction in the number of items that foreign invested enterprises have to export, from 24 to 14, which included tiles, ceramic, footwear, electric fans, plastic products, and common paints. Foreign invested enterprises are also permitted to export coffee, certain wood products, and certain textiles. Export-orientated foreign direct investment is now automatically registered. Recent amendments to the Law on Petroleum have made the regulatory environment for foreign investment in the oil and gas sector more attractive. Overseas Vietnamese are allowed to hold land-use rights, allowing them to buy homes and raise the volume of inward remittances. Joint venture and foreign banks are allowed to take land-use rights and land certificates as collateral. The State now formally publishes detailed guidelines listing all necessary documentation for foreign-invested enterprises to mortgage land-use rights.

Disbursements have typically failed to keep pace with commitments. In 1993 the net inflow of foreign investment totalled only US $300m., less than one-sixth of net inflows for Thailand and Indonesia during the 1991–93 period. In 1996–97 annual disbursements totalled about US $2,300m., but this average fell to US $700m. during 1998–2000. Three large foreign direct investment projects in energy were signed in late 2000 and early 2001 and were expected to generate inflows of nearly US $2,500m. for 2001–03.

Serious obstacles remain in provisions that allowed minority partners, often state enterprises or government entities, the veto powers in a joint venture. Foreign investment projects required the approval of several investment agencies. Although the central Government processed all large projects directly, the approval process remained lengthy, arbitrary, and tedious by regional standards. The absence of legislation governing the implementation of contractual agreements continued. In this situation, the lack of an adequate dispute resolution mechanism was a serious problem. Local authorities had considerable power and their approval was as necessary as that of central agencies. Disputes over problems such as site clearance for hotels caused prolonged delays. Property rights remained unclear. These weaknesses increased the evident risks of investing in a country that continued to subscribe to 'market socialism'. In June 2000 the Law on Foreign Investments was amended to include covered land issues and transfer rights, but was not particularly broad or encouraging.

In 2000 an initial focus on petroleum and gas projects was replaced by manufacturing and infrastructure projects. Seven projects in the construction sector, with investment capital of US $9.1m., were licensed in the first seven months of 2001. Investments in hotels and tourism remained strong throughout the 1990s, with the total capital in this sector increasing to US $3,506m. by July 2001. More than two-thirds of investments came from Asian countries in the 1990s. Taiwan was the largest investor, followed by Hong Kong and the Republic of Korea. Total Japanese commitments involved 110 projects, with total capital pledges of US $1,700m. by July 1995. This was 10% of total commitments, less than commitments from Western Europe (14%), but greater than that from the USA (6%). By July 2001 total Japanese commitments were US $3,995m., allocated to 311 projects, with more than 67% of these commitments implemented. The USA ranked 13th, with US $986m., and more than 45% implemented. The US Bilateral Trade Agreement showed its effect of increasing foreign direct investment in labour intensive industries (services, light industry, food, and construction). By mid-2001 Singapore was the largest investor, with US $6,809m., followed by Taiwan and Japan, with US $4,862m. and US $3,981m., respectively.

SOCIAL WELFARE

Poverty Alleviation

Following near famine conditions in 1988, and with one-quarter of Vietnamese people in a situation of food poverty in the early 1990s, the number of Vietnamese in poverty has since declined sharply. Nevertheless, in the late 1990s almost one-half of the rural population remained in general poverty. Alleviating poverty requires access to markets and facilities, and education. In Viet Nam 37% of rural households lacked access to electricity in 1995, and only 38% had safe drinking water. The Central Highlands and the Mekong delta suffered the most from weak facilities. There were few all-weather roads penetrating rural areas. Integrated efforts were required to link rural people to markets (roads, bridges), to improve access to facilities and resources (land rights) and to strengthen personal capacities and information flows (education).

It would appear, however, that rapid economic growth in Viet Nam has not been accompanied by a markedly worsening income distribution. According to Viet Nam Living Standards Survey data, greater inequality in urban areas, particularly in northern Viet Nam, resulted in a marginal national increase. Vietnamese survey data demonstrated erratic and marginal changes in income distribution throughout Viet Nam during 1994–97, with an apparent reversal of the inequality trend in 1997. Therefore, both the absolute level of inequality and the trend did not appear to be matters for concern, and by international standards Viet Nam remained a relatively equitable society.

Per caput GDP in Viet Nam was only about one-third the average level recorded in the countries of the East Asia and Pacific region. According to reports by IMF country staff, poverty has declined in all regions of Viet Nam, but cross-regional inequalities have increased. Poverty is particularly high in the mountainous areas and those in large ethnic minorities. Inequality has risen, but is still modest by international standards.

From the late 1990s rural income came under pressure, as a result of the decline in commodity prices on the international market. The rural economy has suffered from a reduced inflow of resources. The actual loss to the rural areas is greater than that of the urban areas as urban consumers still pay lower prices. The gap between the North and the South has decreased, but remains large. The Government planned to use US $590m. over five years in the Northern mountains to subsidize new rice cultivation, provide better seeds, build schools, health centres and phone lines, subsidize migration to border and lowland areas, with the aim of halving the poverty rate by 2005. Meanwhile, the Ministry of Education planned to build boarding schools in every district of these provinces and to expand local universities. A separate plan was formulated for the central Highlands. More than US $2,300m. was to be spent over a five-year period. This amount included projected government spending of US $800m., with private investment envisaging substantial investments in farm and forest product processing, mining, and hydroelectricity. It was unlikely, however, that this would help to address the ethnic tension in the area or the problem of people being displaced from their land. The Land Management Services of Dak Lak planned to transfer 17,000 ha of unused land managed by some state-owned enterprises to minority households. Around 77% of the province's total area was under the control of 106 state-owned farms in 2001.

Health and Education

One underlying cause of Viet Nam's success was the relatively strong system of primary health care and basic education prior to the reform period. Achievements in areas such as literacy and life expectancy were both a cause and a consequence of Viet Nam's rapid development during the 1990s. By 1998 Vietnam's literacy rate was above that of China and Indonesia, despite the much higher GDP per caput of those two countries.

During the period of transition, the collapse of subsidies and payments in kind from the planning system was not immediately followed by the introduction of monetary equivalents, which were constantly eroded by a high level of inflation until about 1992. Teachers left schools, and rising costs resulted in an increase in the rate of student drop-outs. Health services declined, particularly in rural areas. Recovery since 1992 has been evident but incomplete. Education services have improved markedly. Teacher shortages have continued, but drop-out rates have fallen, and government funding of the sector has risen. School enrolment rates have increased significantly both for male and female. State funding of health services, however, has been less generous. De facto privatization of education and health services has allowed services to increase in line with rising household incomes. It was possible, however, that access to health and education services for those in poverty was worse than in 1985.

Informal and formal social security systems have also come under pressure to adapt to a more market-based economy. Increased factor mobility, of land use and workers, has undermined traditional systems of welfare support. Extended family ties have been important through this transitional phase, as welfare systems became monetized and community organizations developed. The formal social security system has experienced less change. The 1995 Labour Code was essentially an attempt to expand the existing system to cover the non-state sector. It failed to address the fundamental design and delivery problems that made it financially unsustainable and an obstacle to labour mobility. Health insurance remained in crisis during 2000.

Both the health and education sectors were in decline until about 1992–93, when increased government spending, development assistance, and selective policy liberalization reversed the trend. The number of grade school teachers had been declining since 1988–89, but so did the numbers of students. The number of grade school students decreased by 8% to 11.7m. during 1987–90. Numbers of both students and teachers again recovered in the 1990s (the number of secondary school students did not rise until 1992–93). The teacher to student ratio had therefore been somewhat steady at 1:27, but subsequently rose to 1:31 in 1997–98. During 1999–2000, the number of both teachers and students strongly increased, giving a teacher to student ratio of 1:28. Additionally, education facilities experienced an increase of 31.3%. The number of kindergarten teachers had stagnated until the 1990s, when liberalization (leading to the establishment of private kindergartens) prompted a dramatic increase in teacher numbers and schools.

Health data presented a less clear picture of decline and recovery. Although the number of doctors has increased each year, the number of nurses has fallen sharply. The number of hospital beds has increased since 1994 (after falling steadily from 224,000 beds in 1987), but these figures fail to reflect other trends. For example, although the number of hospital beds totalled 198,000 in both 1992 and 1997, availability in rural areas decreased from 69,600 to 63,800. Although it was possible that the deterioration in health services, particularly in rural areas, was continuing, this was not reflected as a priority concern in the central government budget.

Central budget education expenditures increased steadily as a percentage of GDP, from about 1% in 1991 to 2.4% in 1997, then dropped slightly to 2.3% in 1998. Health sector expenditure trends have been less consistent: rising from 0.8% of GDP in 1991 to 1.3% in 1994, but subsequently declining to about 1% of GDP in 1998 and 0.7% in 1999. These education and health sector shares remained low by international standards. The increases have not compensated for substantial reductions in local government funding during the transition period. Furthermore, expenditure is inequitably directed at urban areas.

PROSPECTS FOR THE 21ST CENTURY

Viet Nam's transition is undoubtedly one of success. Incomes have risen, poverty has declined, and farmers have benefited. This success, however, is largely due to the failure to implement extensive central planning after 1976. Furthermore, as a poor developing country, with largely unprocessed agricultural exports, and a labour force willing and able to work at wages slightly above subsistence level, Viet Nam differs significantly from most transitional economies. Structural transformation of Viet Nam's 'residual element' of central planning was therefore achieved during the first decade of transition without dramatic adverse effects, with the exception of a short-term decrease in industrial production. It was reported, however, that social services and support systems also experienced a decline, followed by gradual recovery.

Viet Nam's reform process, it has been suggested, decelerated in the late 1990s. Nevertheless, transition is a long process, and overall progress in that decade was impressive. Structural reform in Viet Nam between 1988 and 1992 was considerable: macroeconomic stabilization, state enterprise reform (the sector shedding 22% of its work-force during 1989–91), a reorientation of international trade, and an increase in private rural and urban household economic activity, owing largely to fundamental institutional reforms. Reforms in the latter part of the 1990s invariably appeared comparatively less impressive. Following the election of a new Government in May 2002, administrative reform became a priority, with the implementation of a 2001–10 plan that was aimed at raising the effectiveness of the state apparatus and the party leadership. It was obvious that the Government's determination to keep the country's poorer regions and ethnic minority involved in the economic and political mainstream is an effort to reduce political instability. The campaign against corruption was expected to be vigorous.

The future prospects, however, remained favourable, provided that incomes continued to rise and jobs were created. Concern regarding a steady increase in the number of unemployed continued. Rural–urban migration was also increasing. This 'employment imperative' was not being addressed through policies promoting capital-intensive import substitutes, or by ongoing protection of the state enterprise sector. The development of a private corporate sector was particularly slow, yet remained the prerequisite for sustained long-term development, and hence the ability to generate increasing levels of income transfer in order to achieve welfare aims. In 2001 the private sector accounted for around 40% of GDP in Viet Nam, compared with 50% in China, but mainly in agriculture and for only one-third of industrial output. World Bank studies indicated that small to medium-sized enterprises were required to contribute a much larger share of economic activity for Viet Nam to sustain GDP growth at 6–8%.

External forces, notably the international recession, were expected to result in slower than anticipated rates of export and GDP growth during 2001–05. The recession has impeded Viet Nam's export growth and real GDP growth in 2001 and in the first quarter of 2002. Exports would, however, remain relatively robust, as the main negative impact was on Asian electronics exporters, which did not include Viet Nam. A modest recovery was expected for the last three quarters of 2002, mainly from greater domestic private consumption and investment. Assuming a reasonable rate of ongoing domestic liberalization, such as state enterprise and state bank restructuring, Viet Nam's economy was likely to grow at about 5% annually, thereby enabling political stability.

Statistical Survey

Sources (unless otherwise stated): General Statistical Office of the Socialist Republic of Viet Nam, 2 Hoang Van Thu, Hanoi; tel. (4) 8464385; fax (4) 264345; Communist Party of Viet Nam.

Area and Population

AREA, POPULATION AND DENSITY

Area (sq km)	331,114*
Population (census results)	
1 April 1989	64,411,713
1 April 1999†	
Males	37,519,754
Females	38,804,999
Total	76,324,753
Population (official estimates at mid-year)	
2000	77,686,000
Density (per sq km) at mid-2000	234.6

* 127,844 sq miles.
† Provisional.

ADMINISTRATIVE DIVISIONS (mid-1993)

Provinces and Cities	Area (sq km)	Population ('000)*	Density (per sq km)
North Mountains and Midlands	102,964.6	12,109.3	118
Ha Giang	7,831.1	520.4	66
Tuyen Quang	5,800.9	628.5	108
Cao Bang	8,444.7	624.7	74
Lang Son	8,187.2	671.9	82
Lai Chau	17,130.6	501.2	29
Lao Cai	8,049.5	535.4	66
Yen Bai	6,808.1	638.2	94
Bac Thai†	6,502.9	1,144.5	176
Son La	14,210.0	776.0	55
Hoa Binh	4,611.8	712.9	155
Vinh Phu	4,834.8	2,203.2	456
Ha Bac‡	4,614.4	2,262.8	490
Quang Ninh	5,938.6	889.6	150
Red River Delta	12,510.7	13,808.8	1,104
Hanoi	920.6	2,154.9	2,341
Haiphong	1,503.5	1,583.9	1,053
Hai Hung	2,551.4	2,658.0	1,042
Ha Tay	2,147.0	2,217.8	1,033
Thai Binh	1,508.7	1,768.4	1,172
Nam Ha	2,492.0	2,585.9	1,038
Ninh Binh	1,387.5	839.9	605
North Central Coast	15,187.6	9,516.9	186
Thanh Hoa	11,168.3	3,311.9	296
Nghe An	16,380.6	2,680.6	164
Ha Tinh	6,054.0	1,293.6	214
Quang Binh	7,983.5	736.7	92
Quang Tri	4,592.0	520.9	113
Thua Thien-Hué	5,009.2	973.2	194
South Central Coast	45,876.0	7,374.7	161
Quang Nam-Da Nang	11,985.4	1,911.7	159
Quang Ngai	5,856.3	1,149.5	196
Binh Dinh	6,075.9	1,373.1	226
Phu Yen	5,278.0	708.9	134
Khanh Hoa	5,258.0	923.7	176
Ninh Thuan	3,430.4	449.1	131
Binh Thuan	7,992.0	858.7	107
Central Highlands	55,568.9	2,903.5	52
Gia Lai	15,661.9	737.7	47
Kon Tum	9,934.4	249.6	25
Dac Lac	19,800.0	1,173.3	59
Lam Dong	10,172.6	742.9	73
North-East South	23,450.7	8,692.9	371
Ho Chi Minh City	2,090.3	4,322.3	2,068
Song Be	9,519.4	1,081.7	114
Tay Ninh	4,020.0	868.9	216
Dong Nai	5,864.4	1,762.9	301
Ba Ria-Vung Tau	1,956.6	657.1	336
Mekong River Delta	39,555.1	15,531.6	393
Long An	4,338.3	1,224.8	282
Dong Thap	3,276.3	1,462.9	446
An Giang	3,423.5	1,933.8	565
Tien Giang	2,339.2	1,622.0	693
Ben Tre	2,247.0	1,309.4	583
Vinh Long	1,487.3	1,041.3	700
Tra Vinh	2,369.4	938.5	396
Can Tho	2,950.6	1,780.6	603
Soc Trang	3,191.0	1,172.6	367
Kien Giang	6,243.1	1,326.6	212
Minh Hai	7,689.4	1,719.1	224
Total	331,113.6	70,982.5	214

* Figures are provisional. The revised total is 71,025,600.
† On 1 January 1997 Bac Thai province was split into Thai Nguyen province (estimated data: area 3,541 sq km; population 1,019,300; density 287.9 persons per sq km) and Bac Can province (estimated data: area 4,795 sq km; population 268,000; density 55.9 persons per sq km).
‡ On 1 January 1997 Ha Bac province was split into Bac Giang province (estimated data: area 3,816 sq km; population 1,400,000; density 366.9 persons per sq km) and Bac Ninh province (estimated data: area 798 sq km; population 920,000; density 1,152.9 persons per sq km).

PRINCIPAL TOWNS
(estimated population, excluding suburbs, at mid-1992)

Ho Chi Minh City (formerly Saigon)	3,015,743*	Cam Pha	209,086
Hanoi (capital)	1,073,760	Nam Dinh	171,699
Haiphong	783,133	Qui Nhon	163,385
Da Nang	382,674	Vung Tau	145,145
Buon Ma Thuot	282,095	Rach Gia	141,132
Nha Trang	221,331	Long Xuyen	132,681
Hué	219,149	Thai Nguyen	127,643
Can Tho	215,587	Hong Gai	127,484
		Vinh	112,455

* Including Cholon.

Source: UN, *Demographic Yearbook*.

Mid-2000 (UN estimates, including suburbs): Ho Chi Minh City 4,619,000; Hanoi 3,751,000; Haiphong 1,676,000 (Source: UN, *World Urbanization Prospects: The 2001 Revision*).

BIRTHS AND DEATHS (UN estimates, annual averages)

	1985–90	1990–95	1995–2000
Birth rate (per 1,000)	32.5	28.3	21.5
Death rate (per 1,000)	9.3	8.1	7.0

Source: UN, *World Population Prospects: The 2000 Revision*.

Expectation of life (WHO estimates, years at birth, 2000): Males 66.7; Females 71.0 (Source: WHO, *World Health Report*).

EMPLOYMENT ('000 persons)

	1995	1996	1997
Agriculture	24,537	24,543	24,814
Forestry	228	232	
Industry*	3,379	3,442	3,656
Construction	996	975	977
Trade and catering	2,290	2,677	2,672
Transport	512	799	856
Communications	56	57	
Science	38	39	41
Education	973	994	999
Culture, arts and sport	94	96	96
Public health	358	359	296
Other activities	1,128	1,579	2,587
Total employed	34,590	35,792	36,994

* Comprising manufacturing, mining and quarrying, electricity, gas and water.

Source: IMF, *Vietnam: Statistical Appendix* (July 1999).

1998 ('000): Total employment 37,877, of which 26,070 in agriculture, fisheries, and forestry; 3,656 in industry; and 980 in construction.
1999 ('000): Total employment 38,546, of which 26,591 in agriculture, fisheries, and forestry; 3,674 in industry; and 982 in construction.

Source: IMF, *Vietnam: Statistical Appendix* (August 2000).

2000 ('000): Total employment 36,206, of which 22,670 in agriculture, fisheries, and forestry and 4,744 in industry and construction.

Source: IMF, *Vietnam: Selected Issues and Statistical Appendix* (January 2002).

Health and Welfare

KEY INDICATORS

Fertility (births per woman, 2000)	2.4
Under-5 mortality rate (per 1,000 live births, 2000)	39
HIV/AIDS (% of persons aged 15–49, 2001)	0.30
Physicians (per 1,000 head, 1998)	0.48
Hospital beds (per 1,000 head, 1997)	1.67
Health expenditure (1998): US $ per head (PPP)	49
% of GDP	3.9
public (% of total)	39.1
Access to water (% of persons, 2000)	56
Access to sanitation (% of persons, 2000)	73
Human Development Index (2000): ranking	109
value	0.688

For sources and definitions, see explanatory note on p. vi.

Agriculture

PRINCIPAL CROPS ('000 metric tons)

	1999	2000	2001
Rice (paddy)	31,394	32,530	31,925
Maize	1,753	2,006	2,118
Potatoes	330*	316	316*
Sweet potatoes	1,745	1,611	1,610
Cassava (Manioc)	1,801	1,986	2,050
Dry beans	144	145	147
Other pulses*	101	100	100
Soybeans (Soya beans)	147	149	156
Groundnuts (in shell)	318	355	375
Coconuts	1,104	885	887
Vegetables (including melons)*	4,841	4,905	4,905
Fruit (excluding melons)*	4,046	4,043	4,087
Sugar cane	17,760	15,044	15,089
Coffee (green)	510	803	800
Tea (made)	70	77	77*
Tobacco (leaves)	36	27	29
Natural rubber	249	291	305

* FAO estimate(s).

Source: FAO.

LIVESTOCK ('000 head, year ending September)

	1999	2000	2001
Horses	150	127	190*
Cattle	4,064	4,128	4,200
Buffaloes	2,956	2,897	2,950
Pigs	18,886	20,194	20,200
Goats	471	544	600*
Chickens	125,500†	137,300*	150,000*
Ducks	53,800†	54,500*	57,000*

* FAO estimate(s).
† Unofficial figure.

Source: FAO.

LIVESTOCK PRODUCTS ('000 metric tons)

	1999	2000	2001
Beef and veal	85.5	92.3	97.0*
Buffalo meat	90.3	92.5	96.8
Pig meat	1,318.2	1,409.0	1,415.5
Chicken meat	261.8	286.5	302.0†
Duck meat	63.6	64.5	69.6
Cows' milk	39.6	52.1	60.0
Buffaloes' milk	30.0	30.0	30.0
Poultry eggs	164.6†	166.0*	168.0*
Cattle hides (fresh)	15.1	15.7	15.7*
Buffalo hides (fresh)	16.8	17.2	18.0

* FAO estimate.
† Unofficial figure.

Source: FAO.

Forestry

ROUNDWOOD REMOVALS
('000 cubic metres, excluding bark)

	1998	1999	2000
Sawlogs, etc.:			
Coniferous*	173	173	173
Broadleaved*	2,243	2,243	2,243
Other industrial wood*	2,109	2,140	2,140
Fuel wood (all broadleaved)	26,695	26,695	26,686
Total	31,220	31,251	31,242

* FAO estimates.

Source: FAO.

SAWNWOOD PRODUCTION
('000 cubic metres, including railway sleepers)

	1998	1999	2000
Coniferous (softwood)*	96	96	96
Broadleaved (hardwood)*	625	625	625
Total	721	721	721

* FAO estimates.

Source: FAO.

Fishing

(FAO, estimates, '000 metric tons, live weight)

	1997	1998	1999
Capture	1,078.7	1,130.7	1,200.0
Freshwater fishes	66.5	68.0	73.0
Marine fishes	677.7	700.4	770.0
Marine crabs	190.0	195.0	185.0
Natantian decapods	70.0	80.0	80.0
Aquaculture	494.0	521.9	594.9
Freshwater fishes	342.6	359.0	407.8
Crustaceans	131.8	141.6	157.0
Total catch	1,572.7	1,652.5	1,794.0

Source: FAO, *Yearbook of Fishery Statistics.*

Mining

('000 metric tons)

	1998	1999*	2000*
Coal	10,708	10,460†	11,300†
Chromium ore	54	55	53
Phosphate rock	576	580	600
Salt (unrefined)	717	720	730
Crude petroleum ('000 barrels)	89,696	109,991†	114,877†

* Estimates.
† Reported figure.

Source: US Geological Survey.

Industry

SELECTED PRODUCTS
('000 metric tons, unless otherwise indicated)

	1993	1994	1995
Raw sugar*	369	364	517
Beer ('000 hectolitres)	2,300	3,666	5,120
Cigarettes (million packets)	1,713	1,941	2,146
Cotton yarn (pure and mixed)	38	44	51
Woven cotton fabrics (million metres)	215	228	222
Garments (million)	81	121	145
Leather footwear ('000 pairs)	12,004	22,383	35,663
Chemical fertilizers	714	841	931
Insecticides	14	14	16
Washing preparations	88	97	106
Bricks (million)	5,000	5,797	6,890
Cement	4,849	5,371	5,828
Crude steel	252	288	408
Machine tools (number)	1,517	1,538	1,358
Television receivers ('000)	650	792	635
Clocks ('000)	28	39	45
Bicycles ('000)	324	286	236
Tractors (number)	2,316	2,808	2,709
Threshing machines (number)	30,882	43,942	36,398
Electric energy (million kWh)	10,851	12,476	14,665

1996 ('000 metric tons): Raw sugar 637*; Chemical fertilizers 965†; Cement 6,585†; Crude steel (including crude steel for casting): 310‡; Electric energy (million kWh) 16,962†.
1997 (estimates, '000 metric tons): Raw sugar 649*; Chemical fertilizers 982†; Cement 8,019†; Electric energy (million kWh) 19,253†.
1998 (estimates, '000 metric tons): Raw sugar 736*; Chemical fertilizers 978†; Cement 9,738†; Electric energy (million kWh) 21,694†.
1999 (estimates, '000 metric tons): Raw sugar 947*; Cement 10,489†; Electric energy (million kWh) 23,599†.
2000 (estimates, '000 metric tons): Raw sugar 1,165*; Cement 13,347†; Electric energy (million kWh) 26,682†.
2001: Electric energy (million kWh) 30,801†.

* Source: FAO.
† Source: Asian Development Bank, *Key Indicators of Developing Asian and Pacific Countries.*
‡ Source: US Geological Survey.

Finance

CURRENCY AND EXCHANGE RATES

Monetary Units
100 xu = 1 new đông.

Sterling, Dollar and Euro Equivalents (31 May 2002)
£1 sterling = 22,383.3 đông;
US $1 = 15,261.0 đông;
€1 = 14,325.5 đông;
100,000 new đông = £4.468 = $6.553 = €6.981.

Average Exchange Rate (new đông per US $)
1999 13,943.2
2000 14,167.7
2001 14,725.2

Note: The new đông, equivalent to 10 former đông, was introduced in September 1985.

BUDGET ('000 million đông)

Revenue	1998	1999	2000
Tax revenue	55,700	60,300	64,100
Corporate income tax	13,100	14,500	19,800
Individual income tax	1,800	1,900	1,800
Capital user charge	1,700	1,500	1,400
Land and housing tax	300	300	400
Licence tax	300	400	400
Tax on properties transfer	1,000	1,000	900
Tax on land use right	400	300	200
Value added tax (VAT)	11,800	17,200	17,100
Excises	5,600	4,500	5,300
Agricultural tax	2,000	2,000	1,800
Taxes on trade	14,900	14,400	13,500
Other taxes on trade	1,500	1,000	100
Other taxes	1,400	1,200	1,400
Non-tax revenue	15,200	15,800	24,700
Fees and charges	4,100	3,600	5,100
Rental of land	500	600	500
Income from natural resources	3,300	4,600	6,700
Net profit after tax	2,100	2,900	8,700
Capital revenues	800	800	800
Other	4,300	3,400	2,800
Grants	2,100	2,400	1,900
Total	73,000	78,500	90,700

Expenditure	1998	1999	2000
Current expenditure	52,900	55,100	65,700
General administrative services	6,700	6,800	6,300
Economic services	4,800	4,800	5,400
Social services	24,400	25,600	32,200
Education	7,700	8,000	10,700
Health	3,100	3,100	3,700
Pensions and social relief	8,700	9,000	11,300
Other services (incl. defence)	14,800	15,700	18,700
Interest on public debt	900	n.a.	n.a.
Capital expenditure	20,500	26,700	33,600
Lending	5,400	7,100	10,400
Total	78,800	88,900	109,700

Source: IMF, *Vietnam: Selected Issues and Statistical Appendix* (January 2002).

INTERNATIONAL RESERVES
(US $ million at 31 December)

	1999	2000	2001
Gold*	97.3	93.1	90.6
IMF special drawing rights	1.5	0.3	14.6
Foreign exchange	3,324.7	3,416.2	3,660.0
Total	3,423.5	3,509.6	3,765.2

* National valuation.

Source: IMF, *International Financial Statistics.*

MONEY SUPPLY ('000 million dông at 31 December)

	1999	2000	2001
Currency outside banks	41,254	52,208	66,320
Demand deposits at banks	27,106	38,781	46,089
Total money	68,360	90,989	112,409

Source: IMF, *International Financial Statistics.*

COST OF LIVING
(Consumer price index; base: previous year = 100)

	1998	1999	2000
Staples (mainly rice)	119.1	101.3	89.9
Other food	106.2	105.0	97.6
All non-food	104.9	103.9	101.7
All items	107.3	104.1	98.3

Source: IMF, *Vietnam: Selected Issues and Statistical Appendix* (January 2002).

2001 (base: previous year = 100): All items 99.6 (Source: IMF, *International Financial Statistics*).

NATIONAL ACCOUNTS ('000 million dông at current prices)

Expenditure on the Gross Domestic Product

	1999	2000	2001
Government final consumption expenditure	27,137	28,346	30,145
Private final consumption expenditure	274,553	293,507	314,695
Increase in stocks	7,704	8,970	9,726
Gross fixed capital formation	102,799	121,857	139,895
Total domestic expenditure	412,193	452,680	494,461
Exports of goods and services	199,836	243,049	267,927
Less Imports of goods and services	211,254	252,927	277,772
Sub-total	400,775	442,802	484,616
Statistical discrepancy*	−833	−1,156	−124
GDP in purchasers' values	399,942	441,646	484,492
GDP at constant 1994 prices	256,272	273,666	292,376

* Referring to the difference between the sum of the expenditure components and official estimates of GDP, compiled from the production approach.

Source: IMF, *International Financial Statistics.*

Gross Domestic Product by Economic Activity*

	1998	1999	2000*
Agriculture, hunting, forestry and fishing	93,072	101,723	107,913
Mining and quarrying	24,196	33,703	42,219
Manufacturing	61,906	70,767	82,992
Electricity, gas and water	10,339	11,725	12,993
Construction	20,858	21,764	24,461
Trade, restaurants and hotels	55,783	59,384	64,460
Transport, storage and communications	14,076	15,546	17,601
Finance, insurance, real estate and business services	6,274	7,488	8,457
Public administration, defence and social security	34,124	35,368	38,159
Other community, social and personal services	40,388	42,474	44,884
Total	361,016	399,942	444,139

* Estimates.

Source: Asian Development Bank, *Key Indicators of Developing Asian Countries.*

BALANCE OF PAYMENTS (US $ million)

	1998	1999	2000
Exports of goods f.o.b.	9,361	11,540	14,448
Imports of goods f.o.b.	−10,350	−10,568	−14,073
Trade balance	−989	972	375
Exports of services	2,616	2,493	2,702
Imports of services	−3,146	−3,040	−3,252
Balance on goods and services	−1,519	425	−175
Other income received	127	142	185
Other income paid	−804	−571	−782
Balance on goods, services and income	−2,196	−4	−772
Current transfers received	1,122	1,181	1,732
Current balance	−1,074	1,177	960
Direct investment from abroad	1,671	1,412	1,298
Other investment assets	−537	−786	−2,089
Other investment liabilities	512	432	475
Net errors and omissions	−535	−925	−534
Overall balance	37	1,310	110

Source: IMF, *International Financial Statistics.*

External Trade

SELECTED COMMODITIES (US $ million)

Imports c.i.f.	1998	1999	2000
Petroleum products	832	1,047	2,058
Fertilizers	474	458	509
Iron and steel	535	626	812
Machinery and equipment	2,187	2,005	2,482
Leather and garment material	821	1,096	1,334
Motorcycles	351	386	787
Total (incl. others)	11,527	11,742	15,200

Exports f.o.b.	1998	1999	2000
Petroleum	1,232	2,092	3,503
Rice	1,020	1,025	667
Coffee	594	585	501
Marine products	818	974	1,479
Clothing	1,450	1,746	1,892
Footwear	1,031	1,387	1,465
Electronic goods and components	497	585	783
Total (incl. others)	9,365	11,540	14,449

Source: IMF, *Vietnam: Selected Issues and Statistical Appendix* (January 2002).

PRINCIPAL TRADING PARTNERS (US $ million)

Imports c.i.f.	1999	2000	2001
China, People's Republic	673.1	1,691.0	2,032.9
France	309.3	291.9	442.4
Hong Kong	504.7	599.3	602.6
Indonesia	286.8	396.7	428.1
Japan	1,618.3	2,172.2	1,986.2
Korea, Republic	1,485.8	1,854.6	1,904.8
Malaysia	305.0	522.9	523.5
Singapore	1,878.5	2,344.4	2,315.7
Thailand	561.8	921.3	872.2
USA	323.1	381.8	499.6
Total (incl. others)	11,740.9	15,552.3	16,652.7

Exports f.o.b.	1999	2000	2001
Australia	814.6	1,254.8	1,258.8
China, People's Republic	746.4	844.7	1,078.3
France	354.9	463.9	579.7
Germany	654.3	990.5	999.6
Japan	1,786.2	2,397.3	2,447.7
Korea, Republic	319.9	293.7	350.7
Netherlands	342.9	343.5	320.2
Singapore	876.4	745.1	772.5
United Kingdom	421.2	470.9	555.9
USA	504.1	782.0	1,021.3
Total (incl. others)	11,541.3	12,881.3	13,981.4

Source: Asian Development Bank, *Key Indicators of Developing Asian and Pacific Countries*.

Transport

RAILWAYS (traffic)

	1995	1996*	1997*
Passengers carried (million)	8.8	8.4	9.3
Passenger-km (million)	2,133.3	2,259.0	2,444.0
Freight carried (million metric tons)	4.5	4.4	4.7
Freight ton-km (million)	1,750.6	1,678.0	1,525.0

* Source: Reed Business Information, *Railway Directory*.

1998: Passenger-km ('000) 2,542; Freight ton-km ('000) 1,369.
1999: Passenger-km ('000) 2,723; Freight ton-km ('000) 1,387.

Source: UN, *Statistical Yearbook*.

ROAD TRAFFIC

	1993	1994	1995
Passengers carried (million)	419.2	440.6	472.2
Passenger-km (million)	10,601.3	11,150.0	16,757.0
Freight carried (million metric tons)	46.0	49.4	55.9
Freight ton-km (million)	2,437.0	2,645.6	2,967.8

INLAND WATERWAYS

	1993	1994	1995
Passengers carried (million)	86.4	104.1	109.8
Passenger-km (million)	1,310.6	1,412.0	1,427.9
Freight carried (million metric tons)	16.8	17.5	20.1
Freight ton-km (million)	2,335.0	1,971.3	2,248.2

SHIPPING

Merchant Fleet (registered at 31 December)

	1999	2000	2001
Number of vessels	640	691	700
Total displacement ('000 grt)	864.7	1,001.5	1,073.6

Source: Lloyd's Register-Fairplay, *World Fleet Statistics*.

International Sea-Borne Shipping
(estimated freight traffic, '000 metric tons)

	1988	1989	1990
Goods loaded	305	310	303
Goods unloaded	1,486	1,510	1,510

Source: UN, *Monthly Bulletin of Statistics*.

CIVIL AVIATION (traffic on scheduled services)

	1996	1997	1998
Kilometres flown (million)	29	35	33
Passengers carried ('000)	2,108	2,527	2,373
Passenger-km (million)	2,954	3,785	3,644
Total ton-km (million)	352	448	426

Source: UN, *Statistical Yearbook*.

Tourism

TOURIST ARRIVALS BY NATIONALITY ('000)

Country	1999	2000	2001
Australia	63,056	68,162	84,085
Cambodia	74,366	124,557	76,620
China, People's Republic	484,102	626,476	672,846
France	86,026	86,492	99,700
Japan	113,514	152,755	204,860
Korea, Republic	43,333	53,452	75,167
Taiwan	173,920	212,370	200,061
United Kingdom	43,869	56,355	64,673
USA	210,377	208,642	230,470
Total (incl. others)*	1,781,754	2,140,100	2,330,050

Source: Vietnam National Administration of Tourism.

Tourism receipts (US $ million): 88 in 1997; 86 in 1998 (Source: World Bank).

Communications Media

	1999	2000	2001
Television receivers ('000 in use)	14,500	14,750	n.a.
Telephones ('000 main lines in use)	2,105.9	2,542.7	3,049.9
Facsimile machines ('000 in use)	31	n.a.	n.a.
Mobile cellular telephones ('000 subscribers)	328.7	788.6	1,251.2
Personal computers ('000 in use)	600	700	800
Internet users ('000)	100	200	400

Source: International Telecommunication Union.

Radio receivers ('000 in use): 8,200 in 1997.
Book production: 8,186 titles (169,800,000 copies) in 1995.
Daily newspapers: 10 (with estimated circulation of 300,000 copies) in 1996.

Sources: mainly UN, *Statistical Yearbook*, and UNESCO, *Statistical Yearbook*.

Education

(1999/2000, '000)

	Teachers	Students
Pre-primary	96.3	2,214.1
Primary	340.9	10,063.0
Secondary	273.9	7,743.6
Higher*	26.1	682.3

* 1998/99.

Source: UN, *Statistical Yearbook for Asia and the Pacific*.

Adult literacy rate (UNESCO estimates): 93.4% (males 95.5%; females 91.4%) in 2000 (Source: UN Development Programme, *Human Development Report*).

Directory

The Constitution

On 15 April 1992 the National Assembly adopted a new Constitution, a revised version of that adopted in December 1980 (which in turn replaced the 1959 Constitution of the Democratic Republic of Viet Nam). The National Assembly approved amendments to 24 articles of the Constitution on 12 December 2001. The main provisions of the Constitution (which originally entered into force after elections in July 1992) are summarized as follows:

POLITICAL SYSTEM

All state power belongs to the people. The Communist Party of Viet Nam is a leading force of the state and society. All party organizations operate within the framework of the Constitution and the law. The people exercise power through the National Assembly and the People's Councils.

ECONOMIC SYSTEM

The State develops a multi-sectoral economy, in accordance with a market mechanism based on state management and socialist orientations. All lands are under state management. The State allots land to organizations and individuals for use on a stabilized and long-term basis: they may transfer the right to the use of land allotted to them. Individuals may establish businesses with no restrictions on size or means of production, and the State shall encourage foreign investment. Legal property of individuals and organizations, and business enterprises with foreign invested capital, shall not be subjected to nationalization.

THE NATIONAL ASSEMBLY

The National Assembly is the people's highest representative agency, and the highest organ of state power, exercising its supreme right of supervision over all operations of the State. It elects the President and Vice-President, the Prime Minister and senior judicial officers, and ratifies the Prime Minister's proposals for appointing members of the Government. It decides the country's socio-economic development plans, national financial and monetary policies, and foreign policy. The term of each legislature is five years. The National Assembly Standing Committee supervises the enforcement of laws and the activities of the Government. Amendments to the Constitution may only be made by a majority vote of at least two-thirds of the Assembly's members.

THE PRESIDENT OF THE STATE

The President, as Head of State, represents Viet Nam in domestic and foreign affairs. The President is elected by the National Assembly from among its deputies, and is responsible to the National Assembly. The President's term of office is the same as that of the National Assembly. He or she is Commander-in-Chief of the people's armed forces, and chairs the National Defence and Security Council. The President asks the National Assembly to appoint or dismiss the Vice-President, the Prime Minister, the Chief Justice of the Supreme People's Court and the Chief Procurator of the Supreme People's Organ of Control. According to resolutions of the National Assembly or of its Standing Committee, the President appoints or dismisses members of the Government, and declares war or a state of emergency.

THE GOVERNMENT

The Government comprises the Prime Minister, the Vice-Prime Ministers, ministers and other members. Apart from the Prime Minister, ministers do not have to be members of the National Assembly. The Prime Minister is responsible to the National Assembly, and the term of office of any Government is the same as that of the National Assembly, which ratifies the appointment or dismissal of members of the Government.

LOCAL GOVERNMENT

The country is divided into provinces and municipalities, which are subordinate to the central Government; municipalities are divided into districts, precincts and cities, and districts are divided into villages and townships. People's Councils are elected by the local people.

JUDICIAL SYSTEM

The judicial system comprises the Supreme People's Court, local People's Courts, military tribunals and other courts. The term of office of the presiding judge of the Supreme People's Court corresponds to the term of the National Assembly, and he or she is responsible to the National Assembly. The Supreme People's Organ of Control ensures the observance of the law and exercises the right of public prosecution. Its Chief Procurator is responsible to the National Assembly. There are local People's Organs of Control and Military Organs of Control.

The Government

HEAD OF STATE

President: TRAN DUC LUONG (elected by the 10th National Assembly on 24 September 1997).

Vice-President: NGUYEN THI BINH.

CABINET

(October 2002)

Prime Minister: PHAN VAN KHAI.

First Deputy Prime Minister: NGUYEN TAN DUNG.

Deputy Prime Ministers: VU KHOAN, PHAM GIA KHIEM.

Minister of National Defence: Lt-Gen. PHAM VAN TRA.

Minister of Public Security: LE HONG ANH.

Minister of Foreign Affairs: NGUYEN DY NIEN.

Minister of Justice: UONG CHU LUU.

Minister of Finance: NGUYEN SINH HUNG.

Minister of Labour, War Invalids and Social Welfare: NGUYEN THI HANG.

Minister of Education and Training: Prof. NGUYEN MINH HIEN.

Minister of Public Health: TRAN THI TRUNG CHIEN.

Minister of Culture and Information: PHAM QUANG NGHI.

Minister of Construction: NGUYEN HONG QUAN.

Minister of Transport and Communications: DAO DINH BINH.

Minister of Agriculture and Rural Development: LE HUY NGO.

Minister of Aquatic Resources: Dr TA QUANG NGOC.

Minister of Industry: HOANG TRUNG HAI.

Minister of Trade: TRUONG DINH TUYEN.

Minister of Planning and Investment: VO HONG PHUC.

Minister of Internal Affairs: DO QUANG TRUNG.

Minister of Science and Technology: HOANG VAN PHONG.

Minister of Natural Resources and the Environment: MAI AI TRUC.

Minister of Posts and Telecommunications: DO TRUNG TA.

State Inspector-General: QUACH LE THANH.

Minister, Chairman of the Ethnic Minorities and Mountain Region Commission: KSOR PHUOC.

Minister, Head of the Government's Personnel and Organization Commission: DO QUANG TRUNG.

Minister, Head of the Government Office: DOAN MANH GIAO.

Minister, Chairman of the Committee for Physical Training and Sports: NGUYEN DANH THAI.

Minister, Chairman of the Committee for Population, Family and Children: LE THI THU.

MINISTRIES AND COMMISSIONS

All ministries are base in Hanoi.

Ministry of Agriculture and Rural Development: 2 Ngoc Ha, Ba Dinh District, Hanoi; tel. (4) 8468160; fax (4) 8454319.

Ministry of Aquatic Resources: 57 Ngoc Khanh, Ba Dinh District, Hanoi; tel. (4) 8346269; fax (4) 8326702.

Ministry of Construction: 37 Le Dai Hanh, Hai Ba Trung District, Hanoi; tel. (4) 8268271; fax (4) 8215591.

Ministry of Culture and Information: 51–53 Ngo Quyen, Hoan Kiem District, Hanoi; tel. (4) 8255349; fax (4) 8267101; internet www.cinet.vnn.vn.

Ministry of Education and Training: 54 Dai Co Viet, Hai Ba Trung District, Hanoi; tel. (4) 8694795; fax (4) 8694085; e-mail intlaff@iupui.edu; internet www.iupui.edu.

Ministry of Finance: 8 Phan Huy Chu, Hoan Kiem District, Hanoi; tel. (4) 8264872; fax (4) 8262266.

Ministry of Foreign Affairs: 1 Ton That Dam, Ba Dinh District, Hanoi; tel. (4) 8453973; fax (4) 8445905; e-mail bc.mfa@mofa.gov.vn; internet www.mofa.gov.vn.

Ministry of Industry: 54 Hai Ba Trung, Hoan Kiem District, Hanoi; tel. (4) 8267870; fax (4) 8269033.

Ministry of Justice: 25A Cat Linh, Ba Dinh District, Hanoi; tel. (4) 8231138; fax (4) 8431431.

Ministry of Labour, War Invalids and Social Welfare: 12 Ngo Quyen, Hoan Kiem District, Hanoi; tel. (4) 8246137; fax (4) 8248036.

Ministry of National Defence: 1A Hoang Dieu, Ba Dinh District, Hanoi; tel. (4) 8468101; fax (4) 8265540.

Ministry of Planning and Investment: 2 Hoang Van Thu, Ba Dinh District, Hanoi; tel. (4) 8458261; fax (4) 8232494; internet www.khoahoc.vnn.vn/mpi_website.

Ministry of Public Health: 138A Giang Vo, Ba Dinh District, Hanoi; tel. (4) 8464051; fax (4) 8460701.

Ministry of Public Security: 15 Tran Binh Trong, Hoan Kiem District, Hanoi; tel. (4) 8268231; fax (4) 8260774.

Ministry of Science, Technology and Environment: 39 Tran Hung Dao, Hoan Kiem District, Hanoi; tel. (4) 8252731; fax (4) 8252733.

Ministry of Trade: 31 Trang Tien, Hoan Kiem District, Hanoi; tel. (4) 8253881; fax (4) 8264696.

Ministry of Transport and Communications: 80 Tran Hung Dao, Hoan Kiem District, Hanoi; tel. (4) 8254012; fax (4) 8267291; e-mail tic_mot@hn.vnn.vn; internet www.mt.gov.vn.

National Committee for Population and Family Planning: 12 Ngo Tat To, Hanoi; tel. (4) 8260020; fax (4) 8258993; e-mail htqt@vietnam.org.vn.

State Inspectorate: 28 Tang Bat Ho, Hanoi; tel. (4) 8254497.

NATIONAL DEFENCE AND SECURITY COUNCIL

President: TRAN DUC LUONG.

Vice-President: PHAN VAN KHAI.

Members: NONG DUC MANH, NGUYEN MANH CAM, Lt-Gen. PHAM VAN TRA, LE MINH HUONG.

Legislature

QUOC HOI

(National Assembly)

Elections to the 11th National Assembly were held on 19 May 2002. The new Assembly comprised 498 members (compared with 450 in the previous Assembly), elected from among 759 candidates; 51 non-party candidates were elected.

Standing Committee

Chairman: NGUYEN VAN AN.

Vice-Chairmen: NGUYEN VAN YEU, NGUYEN PHUC THANH, TRUONG QUANG DUOC.

Political Organizations

Dang Cong San Viet Nam (Communist Party of Viet Nam): 1 Hoang Van Thu, Hanoi; e-mail cpv@hn.vnn.vn; internet www.cpv.org.vn; f. 1976; ruling party; fmrly the Viet Nam Workers' Party, f. 1951 as the successor to the Communist Party of Indo-China, f. 1930; c. 2.2m. mems (1996); Gen. Sec. of Cen. Cttee NONG DUC MANH.

POLITBURO

NONG DUC MANH, TRAN DUC LUONG, PHAN VAN KHAI, NGUYEN MINH TRIET, NGUYEN TAN DUNG, LE MINH HUONG, NGUYEN PHU TRONG, PHAN DIEN, LE HONG ANH, TRUONG TAN SANG, Lt-Gen. PHAM VAN TRA, NGUYEN VAN AN, TRUONG QUANG DUOC, TRAN DINH HOAN, NGUYEN KHOA DIEM.

SECRETARIAT

NONG DUC MANH, LE HONG ANH, NGUYEN VAN AN, TRAN DINH HOAN, NGUYEN KHOA DIEM, LE VAN DUNG, TONG THI PHONG, TRUONG VINH TRONG, VU KHOAN.

Ho Chi Minh Communist Youth Union: 60 Ba Trieu, Hanoi; tel. (4) 9435709; fax (4) 9348439; e-mail cydeco@hn.vnn.vn; f. 1931; 4m. mems; First Sec. HOANG BINH QUAN.

People's Action Party (PAP): Hanoi; Leader LE VAN TINH.

Viet Nam Fatherland Front: 46 Trang Thi, Hanoi; f. 1930; replaced the Lien Viet (Viet Nam National League), the successor to Viet Nam Doc Lap Dong Minh Hoi (Revolutionary League for the Independence of Viet Nam) or Viet Minh; in 1977 the original organization merged with the National Front for the Liberation of South Viet Nam and the Alliance of National, Democratic and Peace Forces in South Viet Nam to form a single front; 200-member Cen. Cttee; Pres. Presidium of Cen. Cttee PHAM THE DUYET; Gen. Sec. TRAN VAN DANG.

Vietnam Women's Union: 39 Hang Chuoi, Hanoi; tel. (4) 9717225; fax (4) 9713143; e-mail VWUnion@netnam.org.vn; f. 1930; 11.4m. mems; Pres. HA THI KHIET.

Diplomatic Representation

EMBASSIES IN VIET NAM

Algeria: 13 Phan Chu Trinh, Hanoi; tel. (4) 8253865; fax (4) 8260830; Ambassador: TEWFIK ABADA.

Argentina: Daeha Business Centre, 360 Kim Ma, Ba Dinh District, Hanoi; tel. (4) 8315262; fax (4) 8315577; e-mail embarg@hn.vnn.vn; internet www.embargentina.org.vn; Ambassador: TOMÁS FERRARI.

Australia: 8 Dao Tan St, Ba Dinh District, Hanoi; tel. (4) 8317755; fax (4) 8317710; internet www.ausinvn.com; Ambassador: MICHAEL MANN.

Belgium: Daeha Business, 5th Floor, 360 Kim Ma, Ba Dinh District, Kimma, Hanoi; tel. (4) 8315240; fax (4) 8315242; e-mail walbru.hanoi@fpt.vn; internet www.wbri.be/hanoi; Ambassador: ZÉNON KOWAL.

Brazil: 14 Thuy Khue, T72 Hanoi; tel. (4) 8430817; fax (4) 8432542; e-mail ambviet@netnam.org.vn; Ambassador: CHRISTIANO WHITAKER.

Bulgaria: Van Phuc, Nui Truc, Hanoi; tel. (4) 8452908; fax (4) 8460856; Chargé d'affaires a.i.: STANILAV BAEV.

Cambodia: 71 Tran Hung Dao, Hanoi; tel. (4) 9424788; fax (4) 9423225; e-mail arch@fpt.vn; Ambassador: VAR SIM SAMRETH.

Canada: 31 Hung Vuong, Hanoi; tel. (4) 8235500; fax (4) 8235333; e-mail hanoi@dfait.maeci.gc.ca; Ambassador: RICHARD LECOQ.

China, People's Republic: 46 Hoang Dieu, Hanoi; tel. (4) 8453736; fax (4) 8232826; Ambassador: QI JIANGUO.

Cuba: 65 Ly Thuong Kiet, Hanoi; tel. (4) 9424775; fax (4) 9422426; Ambassador: FREDESMAN TURRÁ GONZÁLEZ.

Czech Republic: 13 Chu Van An, Hanoi; tel. (4) 8454131; fax (4) 8233996; e-mail hanoi@embassy.mzv.cz; internet www.mfa.cz/hanoi; Ambassador: LUBOS NOVÝ.

Denmark: 19 Dien Bien Phu, Hanoi; tel. (4) 8231888; fax (4) 8231999; e-mail hanamb@vn.dk; internet www.dk.vn.dk; Ambassador: BJARNE H. SORENSEN.

Egypt: 336 Nghi Tam, Quang An, Tay Ho, Hanoi; tel. (4) 8294999; fax (4) 8294997; Ambassador: MUHAMMAD EL SAYED TAHA.

Finland: 6th Floor, Central Bldg, 31 Hai Ba Trung, Hanoi; tel. (4) 8266788; fax (4) 8266766; e-mail finnemb@fpt.vn; Ambassador: KARI ALANKO.

France: 57 Tran Hung Dao, Hanoi; tel. (4) 8252719; fax (4) 8264236; e-mail ambafrance@hn.vnn.vn; internet www.ambafrance-vn.org; Ambassador: ANTOINE POUILLIEUTE.

Germany: 29 Tran Phu St, Hanoi; tel. (4) 8453836; fax (4) 8453838; e-mail germanemb.hanoi@fpt.vn; internet www.germanembhanoi.org.vn; Ambassador: Dr WOLFGANG MASSING.

Hungary: 360 Kim Ma St, Hanoi; tel. (4) 7715714; fax (4) 7715716; e-mail hungemb@hn.vnn.vn; Ambassador: ERNŐ BOHÁR.

India: 58–60 Tran Hung Dao, Hanoi; tel. (4) 8244990; fax (4) 8244998; e-mail india@netnam.org.vn; Ambassador: SAURABH KUMAR.

Indonesia: 50 Ngo Quyen, Hanoi; tel. (4) 8253353; fax (4) 8259274; Ambassador: AIYUB MOSHIN.

Iran: 54 Tran Phu, Ba Dinh District, Hanoi; tel. (4) 8232068; fax (4) 8232120; Ambassador: HOSSEIN EBRAHIM KHANI.

Iraq: 66 Tran Hung Dao, Hanoi; tel. (4) 9424141; fax (4) 9424055; Ambassador: SHA'ALAN H. HAMOD.

Israel: 68 Nguyen Thai Hoc, Hanoi; tel. (4) 8433141; fax (4) 8435760; e-mail hanoi@israel.org; Ambassador: WALID MANSOUR.

Italy: 9 Le Phung Hieu, Hanoi; tel. (4) 8256256; fax (4) 8267602; e-mail embitaly@embitaly.org.vn; internet www.embitalyvietnam.org; Ambassador: LUIGI SOLARI.

Japan: 27 Lieu Giai, Ba Dinh District, Hanoi; tel. (4) 8463000; fax (4) 8463043; Ambassador: RYUICHIRO YAMAZAKI.

Korea, Democratic People's Republic: 25 Cao Ba Quat, Hanoi; tel. (4) 8453008; fax (4) 8231221; Ambassador: RI HONG.

Korea, Republic: 4th Floor, Daeha Business Centre, 360 Kim Ma, Ba Dinh District, Hanoi; tel. (4) 8315111; fax (4) 8315117; Ambassador: PAIK NAK WHAN.

Laos: 22 Tran Binh Trong, Hanoi; tel. (4) 9424576; fax (4) 8228414; Ambassador: VILAYVANH PHOMKEHE.

Libya: A3 Van Phuc Residential Quarter, Hanoi; tel. (4) 8453379; fax (4) 8454977; e-mail libpbha@yahoo.com; Secretary: SALEM ALI SALEM DANNAH.

Malaysia: 16th Floor, Fortuna Tower, 6B Lang Ha, Hanoi; tel. (4) 8313400; fax (4) 8313402; e-mail mwhanoi@hn.vnn.vn; Ambassador: Dato' MOHAMED RADZI BIN ABDUL RAHMAN.

Mongolia: 5 Van Phuc Quarter, Hanoi; tel. (4) 8453009; fax (4) 8454954; e-mail mongembhanoi@hn.vnn.vn; Ambassador: AGVAANDORJIIN TSOLMAN.

Myanmar: A3 Van Phuc Diplomatic Quarter, Hanoi; tel. (4) 8453369; fax (4) 8452404; e-mail myan.emb@fpt.vn; Ambassador: U KHIN AUNG.

Netherlands: Daeha Office Tower, 6th Floor, 360 Kim Ma, Ba Dinh, Hanoi; tel. (4) 8315650; fax (4) 8315655; e-mail han@minbuza.nl; internet www.netherlands-embassy.org.vn; Ambassador: GERBEN S. DE JONG.

New Zealand: 32 Hang Bai, Hanoi; tel. (4) 8241481; fax (4) 8241480; e-mail nzembhan@fpt.vn; Ambassador: MALCOLM MCGOUN.

Pakistan: 8th Floor, Daeha Business Centre, 360 Kim Ma, Ba Dinh District, Hanoi; tel. (4) 7716420; fax (4) 7716418; e-mail parephanoi@hn.vnn.vn; Ambassador: MOHAMMAD YOUNIS KHAN.

Philippines: 27B Tran Hung Dao, Hanoi; tel. (4) 9437873; fax (4) 9435760; e-mail phvn@hn.vnn.vn; Ambassador: GUILLERMO G. WONG.

Poland: 3 Chua Mot Cot, Hanoi; tel. (4) 8452027; fax (4) 8236914; Ambassador: WIESLAW SCHOLZ.

Romania: 5 Le Hong Phong, Hanoi; tel. (4) 8452014; fax (4) 8430922; e-mail romambhan@fpt.vn; Ambassador: CONSTANTIN LUPEANU.

Russia: 191 La Thanh, Hanoi; tel. (4) 8336991; fax (4) 8336995; e-mail moscow.vietnam@hn.vnn.vn; Ambassador: ANDREI ALEXEEVICH TATARINOV.

Singapore: 41–43 Tran Phu, Hanoi; tel. (4) 8233965; fax (4) 7337627; e-mail singemb@hn.vnn.vn; Ambassador: TAN SENG CHYE.

Slovakia: 6 Le Hong Phong, Hanoi; tel. (4) 8454334; fax (4) 8454145; Ambassador: ANTON HAJDUK.

Sweden: 2, Nui Truc St, Van Phuc, Khu Ba Dinh, Hanoi; tel. (4) 8454824; fax (4) 8232195; e-mail embassy.hanoi@sida.se; internet www.hanoi.embassy.ud.se; Ambassador: MARIE SJÖLANDER.

Switzerland: 44B Ly Thuong Kiet St, 15th Floor, Hanoi; tel. (4) 9346589; fax (4) 9346591; Ambassador: THOMAS FELLER.

Thailand: 63–65 Hoang Dieu, Hanoi; tel. (4) 8235092; fax (4) 8235088; e-mail thaiemhn@netnam.org.vn; Ambassador: KRIENGSAK DEESRISUK.

United Kingdom: Central Bldg, 31 Hai Ba Trung, Hanoi; tel. (4) 9360500; fax (4) 9360561; e-mail behanoi@fpt.vn; internet www.uk-vietnam.org; Ambassador: WARWICK MORRIS.

USA: 7 Lang Ha, Ba Dinh District, Hanoi; tel. (4) 7721500; fax (4) 7721510; e-mail irchano@pd.state.gov; internet www.usembassy.state.gov/vietnam; Ambassador: RAYMOND BURGHARDT.

Yugoslavia: 47 Tran Phu, Hanoi; tel. (4) 8452343; fax (4) 8456173; Chargé d'affaires a.i.: MILOMIR MIHALJEVIĆ.

Judicial System

Supreme People's Court: 48 Ly Thuong Kiet, Hanoi.

The Supreme People's Court in Hanoi is the highest court and exercises civil and criminal jurisdiction over all lower courts. The Supreme Court may also conduct trials of the first instance in certain cases. There are People's Courts in each province and city which exercise jurisdiction in the first and second instance. Military courts hear cases involving members of the People's Army and cases involving national security. In 1993 legislation was adopted on the establishment of economic courts to consider business disputes. The observance of the law by ministries, government offices and all citizens is the concern of the People's Organs of Control, under a Supreme People's Organ of Control. The Chief Justice of the Supreme People's Court and the Chief Procurator of the Supreme People's Organ of Control are elected by the National Assembly, on the recommendation of the President.

Chief Justice of the Supreme People's Court: TRINH HONG DUONG.

Chief Procurator of the Supreme People's Organ of Control: HA MANH TRI.

Religion

Traditional Vietnamese religion included elements of Indian and all three Chinese religions: Mahayana Buddhism, Daoism and Confucianism. Its most widespread feature was the cult of ancestors, practised in individual households and clan temples. In addition, there were (and remain) a wide variety of Buddhist sects, the sects belonging to the 'new' religions of Caodaism and Hoa Hao, and the Protestant and Roman Catholic Churches. The Government has guaranteed complete freedom of religious belief.

BUDDHISM

In the North a Buddhist organization, grouping Buddhists loyal to the Democratic Republic of Viet Nam, was formed in 1954. In the South the United Buddhist Church was formed in 1964, incorporating several disparate groups, including the 'militant' An-Quang group (mainly natives of central Viet Nam), the group of Thich Tam Chau (mainly northern emigrés in Saigon) and the southern Buddhists of the Xa Loi temple. In 1982 most of the Buddhist sects were amalgamated into the state-approved Viet Nam Buddhist Church (which comes under the authority of the Viet Nam Fatherland Front; number of adherents estimated at 7% of total population in 1991). The Unified Buddhist Church of Viet Nam is an anti-Government organization.

Viet Nam Buddhist Church: Pres. Exec. Council Most Ven. THICH TRI TINH; Gen. Sec. THICH MING CHAU.

Unified Buddhist Church of Viet Nam: Patriarch THICH HUYEN QUANG.

CAODAISM

Formally inaugurated in 1926, this is a syncretic religion based on spiritualist seances with a predominantly ethical content, but sometimes with political overtones. A number of different sects exist, of which the most politically involved (1940–75) was that of Tay Ninh. Another sect, the Tien Thien, was represented in the National Liberation Front from its inception. There are an estimated 2m. adherents, resident mainly in the South.

Leader: Cardinal THAI HUU THANH.

CHRISTIANITY

In 1991 the number of Christian adherents represented an estimated 7% of the total population.

The Roman Catholic Church

The Roman Catholic Church has been active in Viet Nam since the 17th century, and since 1933 has been led mainly by Vietnamese priests. Many Roman Catholics moved from North to South Viet Nam in 1954–55, but some remained in the North. The total number of adherents was estimated at 5,301,329 in 2000, representing 6.6% of the population. For ecclesiastical purposes, Viet Nam comprises three archdioceses and 22 dioceses.

Committee for Solidarity of Patriotic Vietnamese Catholics: 59 Trang Thi, Hanoi; Pres. Rev. VUONG DINH AI.

Bishops' Conference: Conférence Episcopal du Viet Nam, 40 Pho Nha Chung, Hanoi; tel. (4) 8254424; fax (4) 8285920; e-mail ttgmhn@hn.vnn.vn; f. 1980; Pres. Cardinal PAUL JOSEPH PHAM DINH TUNG, Archbishop of Hanoi.

Archbishop of Hanoi: Cardinal PAUL JOSEPH PHAM DINH TUNG, Archevêché, 40 Pho Nha Chung, Hanoi; tel. (4) 8254424; fax (4) 8285920; e-mail ttgm@fpt.vn.

Archbishop of Ho Chi Minh City: Most Rev. JEAN-BAPTISTE PHAM MINH MÂN, Archevêché, 180 Nguyen Dinh Chieu, Ho Chi Minh City 3; tel. (8) 9303828; fax (8) 9300598.

Archbishop of Hué: Most Rev. ETIENNE NGUYEN NHU THE, Archevêché, 37 Phan Dinh Phung, Hué; tel. (54) 823100; fax (54) 833656; e-mail tgmhue@dng.vnn.vn.

The Protestant Church

Introduced in 1920 with 500 adherents; the total number is estimated at 180,000.

HOA HAO

A new manifestation of an older religion called Buu Son Ky Huong, the Hoa Hao sect was founded by Nguyen Phu So in 1939, and at one time claimed 1.5m. adherents in southern Viet Nam.

ISLAM

The number of Muslims was estimated at 50,000 in 1993.

The Press

The Ministry of Culture and Information supervises the activities of newspapers, news agencies and periodicals.

DAILIES

Hanoi

Le Courrier du Viet Nam: 33 Le Thanh Tong, Hanoi; tel. (4) 9334587; fax (4) 8258368; French; publ. by the Viet Nam News Agency; Editor-in-Chief NGUYEN TUONG.

Hanoi Moi (New Hanoi): 44 Le Thai To, Hanoi; tel. (4) 8253067; fax (4) 8248054; f. 1976; organ of Hanoi Cttee of the Communist Party of Viet Nam; Editor HO XUAN SON; circ. 35,000.

Lao Dong (Labour): 51 Hang Bo, Hanoi; tel. (4) 8252441; fax (4) 8254441; e-mail baolaodong@hn.vnn.vn; internet www.laodong.com.vn; f. 1929; organ of the Viet Nam General Confederation of Labour; Editor-in-Chief PHAM HUY HOAN; circ. 80,000.

Nhan Dan (The People): 71 Hang Trong, Hoan Kiem District, Hanoi; tel. (4) 8254231; fax (4) 8255593; e-mail toasoan@nhandan.org.vn; internet www.nhandan.org.vn; f. 1946; official organ of the Communist Party of Viet Nam; Editor-in-Chief DINH THE HUYNH; circ. 180,000.

Quan Doi Nhan Dan (People's Army): 7 Phan Dinh Phung, Hanoi; tel. (4) 8254118; f. 1950; organ of the armed forces; Editor NGUYEN PHONG HAI; circ. 60,000.

Viet Nam News: 79 Ly Thuong Kiet, Hanoi; tel. (4) 8222884; fax 9424908; e-mail vnnews@vnagency.com.vn; internet www.vietnamnews.vnagency.com.vn; f. 1991; English; publ. by the Viet Nam News Agency; Editor-in-Chief TRAN MAI HUONG; circ. 25,000 (Mon.-Sat.), 20,000 Sun. edn (Viet Nam News Sunday); circ. 60,000.

Ho Chi Minh City

Sai Gon Giai Phong (Saigon Liberation): 432 Nguyen Thi Minh Khai, Ho Chi Minh City; tel. (8) 8395942; fax (8) 8334183; internet www.sggp.org.vn; f. 1975; organ of Ho Chi Minh City Cttee of the Communist Party of Viet Nam; Editor-in-Chief VU TUAT VIET; circ. 100,000.

Saigon Times: 35–37 Nam Ky Khoi Nghia St, District 1, Ho Chi Minh City; tel. (8) 8295936; fax (8) 8294294; e-mail sgt@hcm.vnn.vn; internet www.saigon-news.com; f. 1991; Vietnamese, English and French; business issues; Editor-in-Chief VO NHU LANH.

PERIODICALS

Dai Doan Ket (Great Unity): 66 Ba Trieu, Hanoi; and 176 Vo Thi Sau St, Ho Chi Minh City; tel. (4) 8262420; f. 1977; weekly; organ of the Viet Nam Fatherland Front; Editor NGUYEN QUANG CANH.

Dau Tu: 175 Nguyen Thai Hoc, Hanoi; tel. (4) 8450537; fax (4) 8457937; e-mail vir@hn.vnn.vn; internet www.vir.com.vn; 3 a week business newspaper publ. in Vietnamese; Man. Dir ROSS DUNKLEY; Editor-in-Chief NGUYEN TRI DUNG; circ. 40,000.

Dau Tu Chung Khoan: 175 Nguyen Thai Hoc, Hanoi; tel. (4) 8450537; fax (4) 8457937; e-mail vir@hn.vnn.vn; internet www.vir.com.vn; weekly; stock market news publ. in Vietnamese; Editor-in-Chief NGUYEN TRI DUNG; circ. 40,000.

Giao Thong-Van Tai (Communications and Transport): 1 Nha Tho, Hanoi; tel. (4) 8255387; f. 1962; weekly; Thursday; organ of the Ministry of Transport and Communications; Editor NGO DUC NGUYEN; circ. 10,000.

Giao Duc Thoi Dai (People's Teacher): Le Truc, Hanoi; tel. (4) 8252849; f. 1959; weekly; organ of the Ministry of Education and Training; Editor NGUYEN NGOC CHU.

Hoa Hoc Tro (Pupils' Flowers): 5 Hoa Ma, Hanoi; tel. (4) 8211065; weekly; Editor NGUYEN PHONG DOANH; circ. 150,000.

Khoa Hoc Ky Thuat Kinh Te The Gioi (World Science, Technology and Economy): 5 Ly Thuong Kiet, Hanoi; tel. (4) 8252931; f. 1982; weekly.

Khoa Hoc va Doi Song (Science and Life): 70 Tran Hung Dao, Hanoi; tel. (4) 8253427; f. 1959; weekly; Editor-in-Chief TRAN CU; circ. 30,000.

Nghe Thuat Dien Anh (Cinematography): 65 Tran Hung Dao, Hanoi; tel. (4) 8262473; f. 1984; fortnightly; Editor DANG NHAT MINH.

Nguoi Cong Giao Viet Nam (Vietnamese Catholic): 59 Trang Thi, Hanoi; f. 1984; tel. (4) 8256242; internet www.vietcatholic.org; weekly; organ of the Cttee for Solidarity of Patriotic Vietnamese Catholics; Editor-in-Chief SO CHI.

Nguoi Dai Bieu Nhan Dan (People's Deputy): 35 Ngo Quyen, Hanoi; tel. (4) 8252861; f. 1988; bi-monthly; disseminates resolutions of the National Assembly and Council of State; Editor NGUYEN NGOC THO.

Nguoi Hanoi (The Hanoian): 19 Hang Buom, Hanoi; tel. (4) 8255662; f. 1984; Editor VU QUAN PHUONG.

Nha Bao Va Cong Luan (The Journalist and Public Opinion): 59 Ly Thai To, Hanoi; tel. (4) 8253609; fax (4) 8250797; f. 1985; monthly review; organ of the Viet Nam Journalists' Asscn; Editor-in-Chief PHAN DUOC TOAN; circ. 40,000.

Nong Nghiep Viet Nam (Viet Nam Agriculture): 14 Ngo Quyen, Hanoi; tel. (4) 8256492; fax (4) 8252923; f. 1987; weekly; Editor LE NAM SON.

Phu Nu (Woman): Vietnam Women's Union, International Relations Dept, 39 Hang Chuoi St, Hanoi; e-mail VWunion@netnam.org.vn; f. 1997; fortnightly; women's magazine; circ. 100,000.

Phu Nu Thu Do (Capital Women): 72 Quan Su, Hanoi; tel. (4) 8247228; fax (4) 8223989; f. 1987; weekly; magazine of the Hanoi Women's Union; Editor-in-Chief MAI THUC.

Phu Nu Viet Nam (Vietnamese Women): 39 Hang Chuoi, Hanoi; tel. (4) 8253500; weekly; magazine of the Vietnamese Women's Union; Editor-in-Chief PHUONG MINH.

San Khau (Theatre): 51 Tran Hung Dao, Hanoi; tel. (4) 8264423; f. 1976; monthly; Editor (vacant).

Suc Khoe Va Doi Song (Health and Life): 138 A Giang Vo, Hanoi; tel. (4) 8443144; weekly; published by the Ministry of Public Health; Editor LETHAU; circ. 20,000.

Tap Chi Cong San (Communist Review): 1 Nguyen Thuong Hien, Hanoi; tel. (4) 9422061; fax (4) 8222846; e-mail bbttccs@hn.vnn.vn; internet www.tapchicongsan.org.vn; f. 1955 as *Hoc Tap*; fortnightly; political and theoretical organ of the Communist Party of Viet Nam; Editor-in-Chief HA DANG; circ. 50,000.

Tap Chi Tac Pham Van Hoc: 65 Nguyen Du, Hanoi; tel. (4) 8252442; f. 1987; monthly; organ of the Viet Nam Writers' Asscn; Editor-in-Chief NGUYEN DINH THI; circ. 15,000.

Tap Chi Tu Tuong Van Hoa (Ideology and Culture Review): Hanoi; f. 1990; organ of the Central Committee Department of Ideology and Culture; Editor PHAM HUY VAN.

Tap Chi Van Hoc (Literature Magazine): 20 Ly Thai To, Hanoi; tel. (4) 8252895; monthly; published by the Institute of Literature; Editor HA MINH DUC.

The Thao Van Hoa (Sports and Culture): 5 Ly Thuong Kiet, Hanoi; tel. (4) 8267043; fax (4) 8264901; f. 1982; weekly; Editor-in-Chief NGUYEN HUU VINH; circ. 100,000.

The Thao Viet Nam (Viet Nam Sports): 5 Trinh Hoai Duc, Hanoi; f. 1968; weekly; Editor NGUYEN HUNG.

Thieu Nhi Dan Toc (The Ethnic Young): 5 Hoa Ma, Hanoi; tel. (4) 9317133; bi-monthly; Editor PHAM THANH LONG; circ. 60,000.

Thieu Nien Tien Phong (Young Pioneers): 5 Hoa Ma, Hanoi; tel. (4) 9317133; three a week; Editor PHAM THANH LONG; circ. 210,000.

Thoi Bao Kinh Te Viet Nam: 175 Nguyen Thai Hoc, Hanoi; tel. (4) 8452411; fax (4) 8432755; f. 1993; 2 a week; Editor-in-Chief PAVEF DAONGUYENCAT; circ. 37,000.

Thoi Trang Tre (New Fashion): 12 Ho Xuan Huong, Hanoi; tel. (4) 8254032; fax (4) 8226002; f. 1993; monthly; Editor VU QUANG VINH; circ. 80,000.

Thuong Mai (Commerce): 100 Lo Duc, Hanoi; tel. (4) 8263150; f. 1990; weekly; organ of the Ministry of Commerce; Editor TRAN NAM VINH.

Tien Phong (Vanguard): 15 Ho Xuan Huong, Hanoi; tel. (4) 8264031; fax (4) 8225032; f. 1953; four a week; organ of the Ho Chi Minh Communist Youth Union and of the Forum of Vietnamese Youth; Editor DUONG XUAN NAM; circ. 165,000.

Tuan Tin Tuc (News Weekly): 5 Ly Thuong Kiet, Hanoi; tel. (4) 8252931; f. 1982; Vietnamese.

Van Hoa (Culture and Arts): 26 Dien Bien Phu, Hanoi; tel. (4) 8257781; f. 1957; fortnightly; Editor PHI VAN TUONG.

Van Nghe (Arts and Letters): 17 Tran Quoc Toan, Hanoi; tel. (4) 8264430; f. 1949; weekly; organ of the Vietnamese Writers' Union; Editor HUU THINH; circ. 40,000.

Van Nghe Quan Doi (Army Literature and Arts): 4 Ly Nam De, Hanoi; tel. (4) 8254370; f. 1957; monthly; Editor NGUYEN TRI HUAN; circ. 50,000.

Vietnam Business Forum: 9 Dao Duy Anh, Dong Da District, Hanoi; tel. (4) 5743063; fax (4) 5742052; e-mail vbfhn@vnn.vn; fortnightly magazine in English; publ. by the Chamber of Commerce and Industry of Vietnam; Editor-in-Chief VU TIEN LOC.

Viet Nam Courier: 5 Ly Thuong Kiet, Hanoi; tel. (4) 8261847; fax (4) 8242317; weekly; English; publ. by the Viet Nam News Agency; Editor-in-Chief NGUYEN DUC GIAP.

Viet Nam Cultural Window: 46 Tran Hung Dao, Hanoi; tel. (4) 8253841; fax (4) 8269578; e-mail vncw@hn.vnn.vn; internet www.vnn.vn/english/vncw/; f. 1998; monthly; English; Dir MAI LY QU'ANG.

Viet Nam Economic Times: 175 Nguyen Thai Hoc, Hanoi; tel. (4) 8452411; fax (8) 8356716; e-mail dist@vethan.com.vn; internet www.vneconomy.com.vn; f. 1994; twice weekly; in Vietnamese (with bi-monthly circ. 38,900; edn in English); Editor-in-Chief Prof. DAO NGUYEN CAT.

Viet Nam Investment Review: 175 Nguyen Thai Hoc, Hanoi; tel. (4) 8450537; fax (4) 8457937; e-mail vir@hn.vnn.vn; internet www.vir.com.vn; f. 1990; weekly; publ. in English and Vietnamese; economic and political news; Editor-in-Chief NGUYEN TRI DUNG; circ 30,000.

Viet Nam Renovation: Hanoi; f. 1994; quarterly magazine on reform of the agricultural sector; in Vietnamese, Chinese and English.

Vietnam Review: 79 Ly Thuong Kiet, Hanoi; tel. (4) 9422297; fax (4) 8221152; e-mail vnreview@vnagency.com.vn; internet www.vietnam.vnagency.com.vn; f. 1954; monthly online, in Vietnamese, English, French, Chinese, Spanish and Russian; Editor-in-Chief VU KHANH; circ. 138,000.

Viet Nam Social Science: 27 Tran Xuan Soan, Hanoi; tel. (4) 8261578; f. 1984; quarterly; publ. in English, French and Russian; organ of National Centre for Social and Human Sciences; Editor PHAM XUAN NAM.

Vietnamese Studies: 46 Tran Hung Dao, Hanoi; tel. (4) 8253841; fax (4) 8269578; e-mail thegioi@hn.vnn.vn; f. 1964; quarterly; English and French edns; Dir MAI LY QUANG.

NEWS AGENCIES

Viet Nam News Agency (VNA): 5 Ly Thuong Kiet, Hanoi; tel. (4) 8255443; fax (4) 8252984; e-mail btk@vnagency.com.vn; internet www.vnagency.com.vn; mem. of Organization of Asian and Pacific News Agencies; Dir-Gen. LE QUOC TRUNG.

Foreign Bureaux

Agence France-Presse (AFP): 76 Ngo Quyen, BP 40, Hanoi; tel. (4) 8252045; fax (4) 8266032; e-mail afphanoi@fpt.vn; Bureau Chief PHILLIPPE PERDRIAU.

Informatsionnoye Telegrafnoye Agentstvo Rossii—Telegrafnoye Agentstvo Suverennykh Stran (ITAR—TASS) (Russia): Trung Tam Da Nganh, Thanh Xuan Bac, Dong Da, Hanoi; tel. and fax (4) 8541381; Correspondent SERGEI A. BLAGOV.

Kyodo News Service (Japan): Room 304, 8 Tran Hung Dao, Hanoi; tel. (4) 8259622; fax (4) 8255848; Bureau Chief KAZUHISA MIYAKE.

Polska Agencja Prasowa (PAP) (Poland): B5 Van Phuc Residential Quarter, Hanoi; tel. (4) 8252601; Chief TOMASZ TRZCINSKI.

Prensa Latina (Cuba): 66 Ngo Thi Nham, Hanoi; tel. (4) 9434366; fax (4) 9434866; e-mail plvietnam@hn.vnn.vn; Correspondent FELIX ALBISU CRUZ.

Reuters (UK): Room 402, 8 Tran Hung Dao, Hanoi; tel. (4) 8259623; fax (4) 8268606; e-mail hanoi.newsroom@reuters.com.

Rossiiskoye Informatsionnoye Agentstvo—Novosti (RIA—Novosti) (Russia): 55A Tran Phu, Hanoi; tel. (4) 8431607; fax (4) 8230001; e-mail riahanoi@hn.vnn.vn; internet www.rian.ru; f. 1955; Bureau Chief ANDREI P. SHAMSHIN.

Xinhua (New China) News Agency (People's Republic of China): 6 Khuc Hao, Hanoi; tel. (4) 8232521; fax (4) 8452913; Chief Correspondent ZHANG JIAXIANG.

PRESS ASSOCIATION

Viet Nam Journalists' Association: 59 Ly Thai To, Hanoi; tel. (4) 8269747; fax (4) 8250797; e-mail vja@hn.vnn.vn; f. 1950; asscn of editors, reporters and photographers working in the press, radio, television and news agencies; 11,000 mems (2000); Pres. HONG VINH; Vice-Pres. TRAN MAI HANH.

Publishers

All publishing enterprises are controlled by the Ministry of Culture and Information.

Am Nhac Dia Hat (Music) **Publishing House:** 61 Ly Thai To, Hoan Kiem District, Hanoi; tel. (4) 8256208; f. 1986; produces cassettes, videocassettes, books and printed music; Dir PHAM DUC LOC.

Cong An Nhan Dan (People's Public Security) **Publishing House:** 167 Mai Hac De, Hai Ba Trung District, Hanoi; tel. (4) 8260910; f. 1981; managed by the Ministry of the Interior; cultural and artistic information, public order and security; Dir PHAM VAN THAM.

Giao Thong Van Tai (Communications and Transport) **Publishing House:** 80B Tran Hung Dao, Hanoi; tel. (4) 8255620; f. 1983; managed by the Ministry of Transport and Communications; Dir TO KHANH THO.

Khoa Hoc Va Ky Thuat (Science and Technology) **Publishing House:** 70 Tran Hung Dao, Hanoi; tel. (4) 9424786; fax (4) 8220658; e-mail todanghai@hn.vnn.vn; internet www.nxbkhkt.com.vn; f. 1960; scientific and technical works, guide books, dictionaries, popular and management books; Dir Prof. Dr TO DANG HAI.

Khoa Hoc Xa Hoi (Social Sciences) **Publishing House:** 61 Phan Chu Trinh, Hanoi; tel. (4) 8255428; f. 1967; managed by the Institute of Social Science; Dir Dr NGUYEN DUC ZIEU.

Kim Dong Publishing House: 62 Ba Trieu, Hanoi; tel. (4) 9434730; fax (4) 8229085; e-mail kimdong@hn.vnn.vn; internet www.nxbkimdong.com.vn; f. 1957; children's; managed by the Ho Chi Minh Communist Youth Union; Dir and Editor NGUYEN THANG VU.

Lao Dong (Labour) **Publishing House:** 54 Giang Vo, Hanoi; tel. (4) 8515380; f. 1945; translations and political works; managed by the Viet Nam General Confederation of Labour; Dir LE THANH TONG.

My Thuat (Fine Arts) **Publishing House:** 44B Hamlong, Hanoi; tel. (4) 8253036; f. 1987; managed by the Plastic Arts Workers' Association; Dir TRUONG HANH.

Nha Xuat Ban Giao Duc (Education) **Publishing House:** 81 Tran Hung Dao, Hanoi; tel. (4) 8220554; fax (4) 8262010; f. 1957; managed by the Ministry of Education and Training; Dir PHAM VAN AN; Editor-in-Chief Prof. NGUYEN NHU Y.

Nha Xuat Ban Hoi Nha Van (Writers' Association) **Publishing House:** 65 Nguyen Du, Hoan Kiem District, Hanoi; tel. and fax (4) 8222135; f. 1957; managed by the Vietnamese Writers' Association; Editor-in-Chief and Dir (acting) NGO VAN PHU.

Nong Nghiep (Agriculture) **Publishing House:** DH 14, Phoung Mai Ward, Dong Da District, Hanoi; tel. (4) 8523887; f. 1976; managed by the Ministry of Agriculture and Rural Development; Dir DUONG QUANG DIEU.

Phu Nu (Women) **Publishing House:** 16 Alexandre De Rhodes, Hanoi; tel. (4) 8294459; f. 1957; managed by the Vietnamese Women's Union; Dir TRAN THU HUONG.

Quan Doi Nhan Dan (People's Army) **Publishing House:** 25 Ly Nam De, Hanoi; tel. (4) 8255766; managed by the Ministry of National Defence; Dir DOAN CHUONG.

San Khau (Theatre) **Publishing House:** 51 Tran Hung Dao, Hanoi; tel. (4) 8264423; f. 1986; managed by the Stage Artists' Association.

Su That (Truth) **Publishing House:** 24 Quang Trung, Hanoi; tel. (4) 8252008; fax (4) 8251881; f. 1945; managed by the Communist Party of Viet Nam; Marxist-Leninist classics, politics and philosophy; Dir TRAN NHAM.

Thanh Nien (Youth) **Publishing House:** 270 Nguyen Dinh Chieu, District 3, Hanoi; tel. and fax (4) 8222612; f. 1954; managed by the Ho Chi Minh Communist Youth Union; Dir BUI VAN NGOI.

The Duc The Thao (Physical Education and Sports) **Publishing House:** 7 Trinh Hoai Duc, Hanoi; tel. (4) 8256155; f. 1974; managed by the Ministry of Culture and Information; Dir NGUYEN HIEU.

The Gioi Publishers: 46 Tran Hung Dao, Hanoi; tel. (4) 8253841; fax (4) 8269578; e-mail thegioi@hn.vnn.vn; f. 1957; foreign language publications; managed by the Ministry of Culture and Information; Dir MAI LY QUANG.

Thong Ke (Statistics) **Publishing House:** 96 Thuy Khe, Hanoi; tel. (4) 8257814; f. 1980; managed by the Gen. Statistical Office; Dir NGUYEN DAO.

Van Hoa (Culture) **Publishing House:** 43 Lo Duc, Hanoi; tel. (4) 8253517; f. 1971; managed by the Ministry of Culture and Information; Dir QUANG HUY.

Van Hoc (Literature) **Publishing House:** 49 Tran Hung Dao, Hanoi; tel. (4) 8252100; f. 1948; managed by the Ministry of Culture and Information; Dir LU HUY NGUYEN.

Xay Dung (Building) **Publishing House:** 37 Le Dai Hanh, Hanoi; tel. (4) 8268271; fax (4) 8215369; f. 1976; managed by the Ministry of Construction; Dir NGUYEN LUONG BICH.

Y Hoc (Medicine) **Publishing House:** 4 Le Thanh Ton, Phan Chu Trinh, Hoan Kiem District, Hanoi; tel. (4) 8255281; e-mail xuatbanyhoc@netnam.vn; managed by the Ministry of Public Health; Dir HOANG TRONG QUANG.

Broadcasting and Communications

TELECOMMUNICATIONS

Directorate General for Posts and Telecommunications (DGPT): Department of Science-Technology and International

Cooperations, 18 Nguyen Du St, Hanoi; tel. (4) 8226580; fax (4) 8226590; industry regulator; Sec.-Gen. Dr MAI LIEM TRUC.

Board of the Technical and Economic Programme on Information Technology: 39 Tran Hung Dao St, Hanoi; e-mail nyenet@itnet.gov.vn; Gen. Dir Dr DO VAN LOC.

Army Electronics and Communications Corporation: military-owned communications company; awarded a licence in 1998 to provide national telephone services, including a fixed network and mobile and paging systems.

Saigon Post and Telecommunications Service Corpn: 45 Le Duan, District 1, Ho Chi Minh City; tel. (8) 8220121; fax (8) 8220120; e-mail saigonpostel@saigonpostel.com.vn; internet www.saigonpostel.com.vn; partially owned by the state; granted a licence in 1997 to operate services in southern Viet Nam; Chair. TRAN NGOC BINH; Gen. Dir NGUYEN THANH VAN.

Viet Nam Posts and Telecommunications Corporation (VNPT): 18 Nguyen Du, Hai Ba Trung District, Hanoi; tel. (4) 8265104; fax (4) 8255851; e-mail infocen2@hn.vnn.vn; internet www.vnpt.com.vn; f. 1995; state-owned communications company; Chair. DO TRUNG TA; Pres. and CEO DANG DINH LAM.

RADIO

In 1998 there were 390 FM stations, 567 district radio stations and 6,505 commune radio stations in Viet Nam. The Ministry of Culture and Information is responsible for the management of radio services.

Voice of Viet Nam (VOV): 58 Quan Su St, Hanoi; tel. (4) 8255669; fax (4) 8261122; e-mail qhqt.vov@hn.vnn.vn; internet www.vov.org.vn; f. 1945; five domestic channels in Vietnamese; foreign service in English, Japanese, French, Khmer, Laotian, Spanish, Thai, Cantonese, Mandarin, Indonesian, Vietnamese and Russian; Dir-Gen. VU HIEN.

TELEVISION

At the end of 1994 there were 53 provincial television stations and 232 relay stations in Viet Nam. The Ministry of Culture and Information is responsible for the management of television services.

Viet Nam Television (VTV): 43 Nguyen Chi Thanh, Hanoi; tel. (4) 8318123; fax (4) 8318124; e-mail webmaster@vtv.org.vn; internet www.vtv.org.vn; television was introduced in South Viet Nam in 1966 and in North Viet Nam in 1970; broadcasts from Hanoi (via satellite) to the whole country and Asia region; Vietnamese, French, English; Dir-Gen. VU VAN HIEN.

Finance

(cap. = capital; res = reserves; dep. = deposits; m. = million; brs = branches)

BANKING

In early 1990 the Government established four independent commercial banks, several joint-venture banks, and introduced legislation to permit the operation of foreign banks in Viet Nam. At the end of 1998 the Vietnamese banking system comprised six state-owned banks, four joint-venture banks, 24 foreign bank branches, 51 joint-stock commercial banks, 977 People's Credit Funds, two joint-stock finance companies, three corporation-subordinated finance companies and eight leasing companies. At the beginning of 2002 there were 27 foreign bank branches and 42 representative offices of foreign financial institutions in Viet Nam.

Central Bank

State Bank of Viet Nam: 47–49 Ly Thai To, Hanoi; tel. (4) 9342524; fax (4) 8268765; e-mail sf-sbv@hn.hnn.vn; f. 1951; central bank of issue; provides a national network of banking services and supervises the operation of the state banking system; Gov. LE DUC THUY; 61 brs and sub-brs.

State Banks

Bank for Agriculture and Rural Development: 2 Lang Ha St, Hanoi; tel. (4) 8313710; fax (4) 8313717; e-mail qhqt@fpt.vn; f. 1988; Chair. NGUYEN QUOC TOAN; Gen. Dir TRINH HUU DAN; 1,291 brs.

Bank for Foreign Trade of Viet Nam (Vietcombank): 198 Tran Quang Khai, Hanoi; tel. (4) 8265503; fax (4) 8269067; f. 1963; authorized to deal in foreign currencies and all other international banking business; cap. 1,099,258m. dông, res 780,469m. dông, dep. 58,591,190m. dông (Dec. 2000), total assets 65,633,108m. dông (Dec. 2000); Chair. LE DAC CU; Dir-Gen. VU VIET NGOAN; 22 brs.

Bank for Investment and Development of Vietnam (Vietinde Bank): 194 Tran Quang Khai St, Hanoi; tel. (4) 8266966; fax (4) 8266959; e-mail bidv@hn.vnn.vn; internet www.bidv.com.vn; Chair. PHUNG THI VAN ANH; Gen. Dir TRINH NGOC HO.

Industrial and Commercial Bank of Viet Nam (VIETINCOMBANK): 108 Tran Hung Dao, Hanoi; tel. (4) 9421066; fax (4) 9421143; e-mail sonbk@fpt.vn; internet www.icb.com.vn; f. 1987; state-owned; authorized to receive personal savings, extend loans, issue stocks and invest in export-orientated cos and jt ventures with foreigners; cap. and res 1,624,210m. dông, dep. 40,745,050m. dông (Dec. 2000); Chair. NGUYEN VAN BINH; Gen. Dir PHUNG KHAO KE; 101 brs and 29 sub-brs.

Saigon Bank for Industry and Trade: 18–20 Ton Duc Thang, District 1, Ho Chi Minh City; tel. (8) 8257994; fax (8) 8235668; e-mail saigonbank@hcm.vnn.vn; cap. 145,000m. dông, res 17,492m. dông, dep. 1,152,609m. dông (Dec. 2001); specializes in trade and industry activities; Dir DUONG XUAN MINH.

Vietnam Export-Import Commercial Joint-Stock Bank (Vietnam Eximbank): 7 Le Thi Hong Gam, Ho Chi Minh City; tel. (8) 8210055; fax (8) 8216913; e-mail icbr.eximbank@hcm.vnn.vn; f. 1989; authorized to undertake banking transactions for the production and processing of export products and export-import operations; cap. 300,000m. dông (Apr. 2001); res 30,913m. dông, dep. 2,567,279m. dông (Dec. 2000); Chair. NGUYEN THANH LONG; Dir-Gen. TRUONG VAN PHUOC; 3 brs.

Viet Nam Technological and Commercial Bank: 24 Ly Thuong Kiet, Hoan Kiem, Hanoi; tel. (4) 8250305; Dir DANG TRONG CUONG.

Joint-Stock and Other Banks

CBD (Codo Rural Share Commercial Bank): Co Do, Thoi Dong, O Mon, Can Tho Province; tel. (71) 61642; Dir TRAN NGOC HA.

Chohung Vina Bank: 3-5 Ho Tung Mau, District 1, Ho Chi Minh City; tel. (8) 8291581; fax (8) 8291583; e-mail hcmc.fvb.@hcm.vnn.vn; f. 1993; joint venture between the Bank for Foreign Trade of Viet Nam and Korea First Bank; cap. US $20m.; Chair. VIET NGOAN VU.

DS Bank (Dongthap Commercial Joint-Stock Bank): 48 Rad 30/4, Cao Lanh Town, Dong Thap Province; tel. (67) 51441; fax (67) 51878; Dir HOANG VAN TU.

Ficombank (Denhat Joint-Stock Commercial Bank): 67A Le Quang Sung, District 6, Ho Chi Minh City; tel. (8) 5857089; fax (8) 8557093; Dir VAN DUONG.

Indovina Bank Ltd: 36 Ton That Dam, District 1, Ho Chi Minh City; tel. (8) 8224995; fax (8) 8230131; e-mail ivbhcm@hcm.vnn.vn; f. 1990; joint venture of the United World Chinese Commercial Bank and the Industrial and Commercial Bank of Viet Nam; also has brs in Hanoi, Hai-phong and Can Tho; cap. US $20m., res US $2.3m., dep. US $61.7m. (2001); Chair. PHUNG KHAC KE; Gen. Dir PENG YUO LUNG.

Maritime Bank: 5A Nguyen Tri Phuong Hai Phong, Ho Chi Minh City; tel. (8) 31823076; fax (8) 31823063; e-mail maritimebank@fpt.vn; Gen. Dir TRAN VAN NGHI.

Phuongnam Bank—Phuongnam Commercial Joint-Stock Bank: 258 Minh Phung, District 11, Ho Chi Minh City; tel. (8) 8556050; fax (8) 8556047; commercial bank; Dir HOANG VAN TOAN.

Quedo Joint-Stock Bank: 1-3-5 Can Giuoc, District 8, Ho Chi Minh City; tel. (8) 8562418; fax (8) 8553596; Dir BAO LAN.

VID Public Bank: Ground Floor, Hanoi Tungshing Square, 2 Ngo Quyen, Hanoi; tel. (4) 8268307; fax (4) 8268228; e-mail vpb.han@hn.vnn.vn; f. 1992; joint venture between the Bank for Investment and Development (Viet Nam) and the Public Bank Berhad (Malaysia); commercial bank; cap. US $20m. (2001); Chair. TRINH NGOC HO; Gen. Man. LEE WING CHEW; 4 brs.

Viet Hoa Bank (Viet Hoa Joint-Stock Commercial Bank): 203 Phung Hung, District 5, Ho Chi Minh City; tel. (8) 8554231; fax (8) 8554244; f. 1992; cap. 70,000m. dông; Chair. of Bd of Administration TRAN TUAN TAI; Gen. Man. VU NGOC NHUNG; 7 brs.

VinaSiam Bank: 2 Pho Duc Chinh, District 1, Ho Chi Minh City; tel. (8) 8210557; fax (8) 8210585; e-mail vsb@hcm.vnn.vn; internet www.vinasiambank.com; f. 1995; joint venture between Bank for Agriculture and Rural Development, Siam Commercial Bank (Thailand) and Charoen Pokphand Group (Thailand).

VP Bank (Viet Nam Commercial Joint-Stock Bank for Private Enterprises): 18B Le Thanh Tong, Hanoi; tel. (4) 8245246; fax (4) 8260182; Dir BUI HUY HUNG.

Foreign Banks

Australia and New Zealand Banking Group Ltd (Australia): 14 Le Thai To, Hanoi; tel. (4) 8258190; fax (4) 8258188; Gen. Man. ADIL AHMED.

Bangkok Bank Public Co Ltd (Thailand): Harbour View Tower, 35 Nguyen Hue St, District 1, Ho Chi Minh City; tel. (8) 8214396; fax (8) 8213772; e-mail bblhcm@hcm.vnn.vn; Man. WITTAYA SUPATANAKUL.

Bank of Tokyo-Mitsubishi Ltd (Japan): The Landmark, 8th Floor, 5B Ton Duc Thang, District 1, Ho Chi Minh City; tel. (8) 8231560; fax (8) 8231559.

BNP Paribas (France): 8 Tran Hung Dao, Hanoi; tel. (4) 8253175; fax (4) 8266982.

Crédit Agricole Indosuez (France): Somerset Chancellor Court, 4th Floor, 21–23 Nguyen Thi Minh Khai St, District 1, Ho Chi Minh City; tel. (8) 8295048; fax (8) 8296065; e-mail cai.vietnam@hcm.vnn.vn; Gen. Man. Olivier Prechac.

Crédit Lyonnais SA (France): Han Nam Officetel, 4th Floor, 65 Nguyen Du, District 1, Ho Chi Minh City; tel. (8) 8299226; fax (8) 8296465; e-mail contact_vnhcmc@creditlyonnais.fr; f. 1993; also has br. in Hanoi.

Natexis Banques Populaires (France): Rm 16-02, Prime Ctr, 53 Quang Trung, Hanoi; tel. (4) 9433667; fax (4) 9433665; e-mail natexis-vn@hcm.vnn.vn; Rep. Mme Ut.

Shinhan Bank (Republic of Korea): Yoco Bldg, 7th Floor, 41 Nguyen Thi Minh Khai St, District 1, Ho Chi Minh City; tel. (8) 8230012; fax (8) 8230009; Gen. Man. Hae-Soo Kim.

Thai Military Bank Public Co Ltd (Thailand): Unit 113, First Floor, Saigon Trade Center, 37 Ton Due Thang, Ben Nghe Ward, District 1, Ho Chi Minh City; tel. (8) 9100606; fax (8) 9100505; Man. Tossatis Rodprasert.

STOCK EXCHANGE

Securities Trading Centre: 45–47 Chuong Duong, Ho Chi Minh City; f. July 2000 by the State Securities Commission (see Development Organization).

INSURANCE

In January 1994 it was announced that foreign insurance companies were to be permitted to operate in Viet Nam. In 1995 it was announced that Baoviet's monopoly of the insurance industry was to be ended. A number of new insurance companies were subsequently established, including Bao Minh, Nha Long Co, Pijico, PetroViet Nam Insurance Co and Vinare. In August 1996 Viet Nam's first joint-venture insurance company, Viet Nam International Assurance, was founded. By late 1996 some 30 foreign insurance companies had opened representative offices in Viet Nam.

Baoviet (Viet Nam Insurance Co): Head Office, 35 Hai Ba Trung St, Hoan Kiem District, Hanoi; tel. (4) 8262632; fax (4) 8257188; e-mail service@baoviet.com.vn; internet www.baoviet.com.vn; f. 1965; property and casualty, personal accident, liability and life insurance; total assets 3,257,000m. dông (2000); Chair. and CEO Prof. Truong Moc Lam.

Viet Nam International Assurance (VIA): 8th Floor, The Landmark, 5B Ton Duc Thang, District 1, Ho Chi Minh City; tel. and fax (8) 8221340; e-mail hcm@via.com.vn; internet www.via.com.vn; f. 1996; joint-venture co, 51% owned by Baoviet, 24.5% owned by Commercial Union (UK), 24.5% owned by Tokyo Marine and Fire Insurance Co (Japan); non-life insurance and reinsurance for foreign cos.

Bao Long (Nharong Joint-Stock Insurance Co): 185 Dien Bien Phu, District 1, Ho Chi Minh City; tel. (8) 8239219; fax (8) 8239223; internet www.nharong.com; cap. 22,000m. dông (1994); Dir Tran Van Binh.

Inchibrok Insurance: 27 Ly Thai To, Hanoi; tel. (4) 8262686; fax (4) 8243983; f. 1993; 50% joint venture between Baoviet and Inchcape Group.

Thanhhoa Insurance: 666 Ba Trieu, Thanh Hoa City, Thanh Hoa Province; tel. (37) 52347; fax (37) 53007; Dir Nguyen Minh Khan.

Trade and Industry

GOVERNMENT AGENCIES

State Financial and Monetary Council (SFMC): f. 1998; established to supervise, review and resolve matters relating to national financial and monetary policy.

Vinacontrol (Viet Nam Superintendence and Inspection Co): 54 Tran Nhan Tong, Hanoi; tel. (4) 9433840; fax (4) 9433844; e-mail vinacontrolvn@hn.vnn.vn; internet www.vinacontrol.com.vn; f. 1957; brs in all main Vietnamese ports; controls quality and volume of exports and imports and transit of goods, and conducts inspections of deliveries and production processes; price verification, marine survey, damage survey, claim settling and adjustment; Gen. Dir Le Viet Su.

DEVELOPMENT ORGANIZATION

State Securities Commission: Hanoi; internet www.ssc.gov.vn; f. 1997; responsible for developing the capital markets, incl. the establishment of a stock exchange; 14 mems; Chair. Nguyen Duc Quang.

CHAMBER OF COMMERCE

VCCI (Viet Nam Chamber of Commerce and Industry): 9 Dao Duy Anh St, Hanoi; tel. (4) 5742022; fax (4) 5742030; e-mail vcci@hn.vnn.vn; internet www.vcci.com.vn; f. 1963; offices in Ho Chi Minh City, Da Nang, Haiphong, Can Tho, Vung Tau, Nha Trang, Thanh Hoa and Vinh; promotes business and investment between foreign and Vietnamese cos; protects interests of businesses; organizes training activities, exhbns and fairs in Viet Nam and abroad; provides information about and consultancy in Viet Nam's trade and industry; represents foreign applicants for patents and trade mark registration; issues certificates of origin and other documentation; helps domestic and foreign businesses to settle disputes by negotiation or arbitration; in 1993 foreign businesses operating in Viet Nam and Vietnamese businesses operating abroad were permitted to become assoc. mems; Pres. and Chair. Doan Duy Thanh; Vice-Pres Doan Ngoc Bong, Pham Chi Lan, Dao Duy Chu, Vu Tien Loc; Sec.-Gen. Hoang Van Dung; associated organizations: Viet Nam International Arbitration Centre, Viet Nam General Average Adjustment Committee, Advisory Board.

Viet Nam International Arbitration Centre: 9 Dao Duy Anh, Hanoi; tel. (4) 5742022; fax (4) 5742020; e-mail viac-vcci@hn.vnn.vn; adjudicates in disputes concerning both domestic and international economic relations.

INDUSTRIAL AND TRADE ORGANIZATIONS

Agrexport (Viet Nam National Agricultural Produce Export-Import Corpn): 6 Trang Tien, Hanoi; tel. (4) 8254234; fax (4) 8265550; f. 1958; imports and exports agricultural produce and coffee, natural silk, insecticides and agrochemicals; Gen. Dir Nguyen Viet Van.

Agrimex (Viet Nam National Agricultural Products Corpn): 173 Hai Ba Trung, District 3, Ho Chi Minh City; tel. (8) 8241049; fax (8) 8291349; e-mail agrimex@hcm.fpt.vn; f. 1956; imports and exports agricultural products; Gen. Dir Nguyen Bach Tuyet.

Airimex (General Civil Aviation Import-Export and Forwarding Co): Le Van Kim, Gia Lam District, Hanoi; tel. (4) 8271939; fax (4) 8271925; e-mail airimex@fpt.vn; f. 1989; imports and exports aircraft, spare parts and accessories for aircraft and air communications; Dir Nguyen Chi Can.

An Giang Afiex Co (An Giang Agriculture and Foods Import and Export Co): 34–36 Hai Ba Trung St, Long Xuyen Town, An Giang Province; tel. (76) 841021; fax (76) 843199; e-mail xnknstpagg@hcm.vnn.net; f. 1992; mfr and sale of agricultural products, also beverages; Dir Pham Van Bay.

Artexport–Hanoi (Viet Nam Handicrafts and Art Articles Export-Import Corpn): 31–33 Ngo Quyen, Hanoi; tel. (4) 8252760; fax (4) 8259275; e-mail artexport.hn@fpt.vn; internet www.artexport.com.vn; f. 1964; deals in craft products and art articles; Gen. Dir Mai Van Nghiem.

Barotex (Viet Nam National Bamboo and Rattan Export-Import Co): 15 Ben Chuong Duong, District 1, Ho Chi Minh City; tel. (8) 8295544; fax (8) 8295352; e-mail barotex@saigonnet.vn; f. 1971; specializes in art and handicrafts, sports shoes, ceramics, fibres, agricultural and forest products; Gen. Dir Ta Quoc Toan.

Bimson Cement Co: Lam Son Hamlet, Bim Con Town, Thanh Hoa Province; tel. (52) 824242; fax (37) 824046; mfr of cement; Dir Le Van Chung.

Binh Tay Import-Export Co (BITEX): 78–82 Hau Giang, District 6, Ho Chi Minh City; tel. (8) 8559669; fax (8) 8557846; e-mail bitex@hcm.vnn.vn; trade in miscellaneous goods; Dir Nguyen Van Thien.

B12 Petroleum Co: Cai Lan, Bay Chay Sub-District, Ha Long City, Quang Ninh Province; tel. (33) 846360; fax (33) 846349; distribution of petroleum products; Dir Vu Ngoc Hai.

Centrimex (Viet Nam National General Import-Export Corpn): 48 Tran Phu, Nha Trang City, Khanh Hoa; tel. (58) 821239; fax (58) 821914; e-mail centrimex@dng.vnn.vn; internet www.centrimexhn.com.vn; exports and imports goods for five provinces in the south-central region of Viet Nam; Gen. Dir Le Van Ngoc.

Coalimex (Viet Nam National Coal Export-Import and Material Supply Corpn): 47 Quang Trung, Hanoi; tel. (4) 9423166; fax (4) 9422350; e-mail coalimex@fpt.vn; internet www.coalimex.com.vn; f. 1982; exports coal, imports mining machinery and equipment; Gen. Dir Ninh Xuan Son.

Cocenex (Central Production Import-Export Corpn): 80 Hang Gai, Hanoi; tel. (4) 8254535; fax (4) 8294306; f. 1988; Gen. Dir Bui Thi Thu Huong.

Coffee Supply, Processing and Materials Co: 38B Nguyen Bieu, Nha Trang City, Khanh Hoa Province; tel. (58) 21176; coffee producer.

Cokyvina (Post and Telecommunication Equipment Import-Export Service Corpn): 178 Trieu Viet Vuong St, Hanoi; tel. (4) 9782362;

fax (4) 9782368; e-mail cokyvina@hn.vnn.vn; f. 1987; imports and exports telecom equipment, provides technical advice on related subjects, undertakes authorized imports, joint ventures, joint co-ordination and co-operation on investment with foreign and domestic economic organizations; Dir NGUYEN KIM KY.

Constrexim (Viet Nam National Construction Materials and Technique Export-Import Corpn): 39 Nguyen Dinh Chieu, Hanoi; tel. (4) 8263448; fax (4) 8262701; e-mail constrexim@fpt.vn; internet www.constrexim.com.vn; f. 1982; exports and imports building materials, equipment and machinery; undertakes construction projects in Viet Nam and abroad, and production of building materials with foreign partners; assists Vietnamese enterprises in forming joint-venture projects with foreign partners; also involved in investment promotion and projects management, real estate development, and human resources development and training; Gen. Dir NGUYEN QUOC HIEP.

Culturimex (State Enterprise for the Export and Import of Works of Art and other Cultural Commodities): 22B Hai Ba Trung, Hanoi; tel. (4) 8252226; fax (4) 8259224; f. 1988; exports cultural items and imports materials for the cultural industry; Dir NGUYEN QUOC HIEP.

Epco Ltd (Export Import and Tourism Co Ltd): 1 Nyuyen Thuong Hien, District 3, Ho Chi Minh City; tel. (8) 8324392; fax (8) 8324744; f. 1986; processes seafood; tourism and hotel business.

Foocosa (Food Co Ho Chi Min City): 57 Nguyen Thi Minh Khai, District 1, Ho Chi Minh City; tel. (8) 9309070; fax (8) 9304552; e-mail foocosa@hcm.vnn.vn; internet www.foocosa.com.vn; mfr and distributor of food products (rice, instant noodles, porridge, sauces, biscuits); Dir NGO VAN TAN.

Genecofov (General Co of Foods and Services): 64 Ba Huyen Thanh Quan, District 3, Ho Chi Minh City; tel. (8) 9325366; fax (8) 9325428; f. 1956; import and export of food products; under the Ministry of Commerce; Dir TO VAN PHAT.

Generalexim (Viet Nam National General Export-Import Corpn): 46 Ngo Quyen, Hoan Kiem, Hanoi; tel. (4) 8264009; fax (4) 8259894; e-mail generalexim@bdvn.vnd.net; f. 1981; export and import on behalf of production and trading organizations, also garment processing for export and manufacture of toys; Gen. Dir YUONG VAN TU.

Generalimex (Viet Nam National General Import-Export Corpn): 66 Pho Duc Chinh, Ho Chi Minh City; tel (8) 8292990; fax (8) 8292968; e-mail generalimex@hcm.fpt.vn; exports of agricultural products and spices, imports of machinery, vehicles, chemicals and fertilizers; Gen. Dir NGUYEN VAN HOANG.

Geruco (Viet Nam General Rubber Corpn): 236 Nam Ky Khoi Nghia, District 3, Ho Chi Minh City; tel. (8) 9325235; fax (8) 9327341; e-mail grc-imexdept@hcm.vnn.vn; internet www.vngeruco.com; merged with Rubexim (rubber export-import corpn) in 1991; manages and controls the Vietnamese rubber industry, including the planting, processing and trading of natural rubber; also imports chemicals, machinery and spare parts for the industry; Dir-Gen. LE QUANG THUNG.

Haprosimex (Hanoi General Production and Import-Export Company): 22 Hang Luoc St, Hanoi; tel. (4) 8266601; fax (4) 8264014; e-mail hapro@fpt.vn; internet www.hapro.com.vn; specializes in handicrafts, textiles, clothing and agricultural and forestry products; Gen. Dir NGUYEN CU TAM.

Hatien Cement Co No 1: Km 8 Highway Hanoi, Thu Duc, Ho Chi Minh City; tel. (8) 8966608; fax (8) 8967635; mfr of cement; Dir NGUYEN NGOC ANH.

Hatien Cement Co No 2: Kien Luong Town, Ha Tien, Kien Giang Province; tel. (77) 53004; fax (77) 53005; mfr of cement; Dir NGUYEN MANH.

Haugiang Petrolimex (Haugiang Petrol and Oil Co): 21 Cach Mang Thang 8, Can Tho City, Can Tho Province; tel. (71) 21657; fax (71) 12746; distributor of fuel; Dir TRINH MANG THANG.

Hoang Thach Cement Co: Minh Tan Hamlet, Kim Mon, Hai Hung Province; tel. (32) 821092; fax (32) 821098; sale of construction materials; Dir NGUYEN DUC HOAN.

Machinoimport (Viet Nam National Machinery Export-Import Corpn): 8 Trang Thi, Hoan Kiem, Hanoi; tel. (4) 8253703; fax (4) 8254050; e-mail machino@hn.vnn.vn; internet www.machinoimport.com.vn; f. 1956; imports and exports machinery, spare parts and tools; consultancy, investment, joint-venture, and mfring services; comprises 12 cos; Chair. NGUYEN TRAN DAT; Gen. Dir HO QUANG HIEU.

Marine Supply (Marine Technical Materials Import-Export and Supplies): 276A Da Nang Rd, Ngo Quyen, Haiphong; tel. (31) 847308; fax (31) 845159; f. 1985; imports and exports technical materials for marine transportation industry; Dir PHAN TRANG CHAN.

Mecanimex (Viet Nam National Mechanical Products Export-Import Co): 37 Trang Thi, Hoan Kiem District, Hanoi; tel. (4) 8257459; fax (4) 9349904; e-mail mecahn@fpt.vn; exports and imports mechanical products and hand tools; Gen. Dir TRAN BAO GIOC.

Minexport (Viet Nam National Minerals Export-Import Corpn): 35 Hai Ba Trung, Hanoi; tel. (4) 8253674; fax (4) 8253326; e-mail minexport@fpt.vn; internet www.minexport.com; f. 1956; exports minerals and metals, quarry products, chemical products; imports metals, chemical products, industrial materials, fuels and oils, fertilizers; Gen. Dir VO TRONG CUONG.

Nafobird (Viet Nam Forest and Native Birds, Animals and Ornamental Plants Export-Import Enterprises): 64 Truong Dinh, District 3, Ho Chi Minh City; tel. (8) 8290211; fax (8) 8293735; f. 1987; exports native birds, animals and plants, and imports materials for forestry; Dir VO HA AN.

Naforimex (Hanoi Forest Products Export-Import and Production Corpn): 19 Ba Trieu, Hoan Kiem District, Hanoi; tel. (4) 8261254; fax (4) 8259264; e-mail naforimexhanoi@fpt.vn; f. 1960; imports chemicals, machinery and spare parts for the forestry industry, linseed oil and essences; exports oils, forest products, gum benzoin and resin; Dir PHAM CAO CHINH.

Packexport (Viet Nam National Packaging Technology and Import-Export Co): 31 Hang Thung, Hanoi; tel. (4) 8262792; fax (4) 8269227; e-mail packexport-vn@vnn.vn; f. 1976; manufactures packaging for domestic and export demand, and imports materials for the packaging industry; Gen. Dir TRINH LE KIEU.

Petec-Trading and Investment Corpn: 70 Ba Huyen Thanh Quan, District 3, Ho Chi Minh City; tel. (8) 8299299; fax (8) 8299686; f. 1981; imports equipment and technology for oil drilling, exploration and oil production, exports crude petroleum, rice, coffee and agricultural products; invests in silk, coffee, financial and transport sectors; Gen. Dir TRAN HUU LAC.

Petrol and Oil Co (Zone 1): Duc Gliang Town, Gia Lam, Hanoi; tel. (4) 8271400; fax (4) 8272432; sales of oil and gas; Dir PHAN VAN DU.

Petrolimex (Viet Nam National Petroleum Corpn): 1 Kham Thien, Dong Da, Hanoi; tel. (4) 8512603; fax (4) 8519203; e-mail xttm@petrolimex.com.vn; internet www.petrolimex.com.vn; f. 1956; import, export and distribution of petroleum products and liquefied petroleum gas; Chair. NGUYEN MANH TIEN.

Petrolimex Saigon Petroleum Co (Zone 2): 15 Le Duan, District 1, Ho Chi Minh City; tel. (8) 8292081; fax (8) 8222082; sales of petroleum products; Dir CAI XUAN HUNG.

Petrovietnam (Viet Nam National Petroleum Corpn): 22 Ngo Quyen St, Hoan Kiem District, Hanoi; tel. (4) 8252526; fax (4) 8265942; e-mail webmaster@hn.pv.com.vn; internet www.petrovietnam.com.vn; f. 1975; exploration and production of petroleum and gas; Chair. HO SI THOANG; Pres. and CEO NGO THUONG SAN.

Saigon Brewery Co: 187 Nguyen Chi Thanh, District 5, Ho Chi Minh City; tel. (8) 8396342; fax (8) 8296856; producer of beer; Dir HOANG CHI QUY.

Seaco (Sundries Electric Appliances Co): 64 Pho Duc Chinh, District 1, Ho Chi Minh City; tel. (8) 8210961; fax (8) 8210974; deals in miscellaneous electrical goods; Dir MAI MINH CUONG.

Seaprodex Saigon (Ho Chi Minh City Sea Products Import-Export Corpn): 87 Ham Nghi, District 1, Ho Chi Minh City; tel. (8) 8293669; fax (8) 8224951; e-mail seaprodex.saigon@bdvn.vnd.net; internet www.seaprodexsg.com; f. 1978; exports frozen and processed sea products; imports machinery and materials for fishing and processing; Gen. Dir PHUNG QUOC MAN.

Seaprodex Hanoi (Hanoi Sea Products Export-Import Co): 20 Lang Ha, Hanoi; tel. (4) 8344437; fax (4) 8354125; e-mail seaprodexhn@hn.vnn.vn; Dir DANG DINH BAO.

SJC (Saigon Jewellery Co): 2D Nguye Trung Truc, District 1, Ho Chi Minh City; tel. (8) 8222827; fax (8) 8294420; e-mail sjc@hcm.vnn.vn; internet www.sjcvn.com; distributor of jewellery; Dir NGUYEN THANH LONG.

Technimex (Viet Nam Technology Export-Import Corpn): 70 Tran Hung Dao, Hanoi; tel. (4) 8256751; fax (4) 8220377; e-mail hanoi.technimex@bdvn.vnmail.vnd.net; f. 1982; exports and imports machines, equipment, instruments, etc.; Dir NGUYEN HUY BINH.

Technoimport (Viet Nam National Complete Equipment and Technics Import-Export Corpn): 16–18 Trang Thi, Hanoi; tel. (4) 8254974; fax (4) 8254059; e-mail technohn@netnam.org.vn; internet www.technoimport.com.vn; f. 1959; imports and exports equipment, machinery, transport equipment, spare parts, materials and various consumer commodities; exports products by co-investment and joint-venture enterprises; provides consulting services for trade and investment, transport and forwarding services; acts as import-export brokering and trading agents; Gen. Dir PHAN MAI PHUONG.

Terraprodex (Corpn for Processing and Export-Import of Rare Earth and Other Specialities): 35 Dien Bien Phu, Hanoi; tel. (4) 8232010; fax (4) 8256446; f. 1989; processing and export of rare earth products and other minerals; Dir TRAN DUC HIEP.

Tocontap Saigon (Viet Nam National Sundries Import-Export Corpn): 18 Nguyen Hue, District 1, Ho Chi Minh City; tel. (8) 9325687; fax (8) 9325963; e-mail tocontapsaigon@hcm.vnn.vn; internet www.tocontapsaigon.com; f. 1956; imports and exports miscellaneous consumer goods; Gen. Dir LE THI THANH HUONG.

Vegetexco (Viet Nam National Vegetables and Fruit Export-Import Corpn): 2 Trung Tu, Dong Da, Hanoi; tel. (4) 5740779; fax (4) 8523926; e-mail vegetexcovn@fpt.vn; internet www.vegetexcovn.tripod.com; f. 1971; exports fresh and processed vegetables and fruit, spices and flowers, and other agricultural products; imports vegetable seeds and processing materials; Gen. Dir DINH VAN PHUOC.

Vienametal (Viet Nam National Steel Corpn): D2 Ton That Tung, Dong Da, Hanoi; tel. (4) 8525537; fax (4) 8262657; distributor of metal products; Dir NGO HUY PHAN.

Vietgoldgem (Viet Nam National Gold, Silver and Gemstone Corpn): 23B Quang Trung, Hoan Kiem, Hanoi; tel. (4) 8260453; fax (4) 8260405; sales of precious metals and gems; Dir NGUYEN DUY HUNG (acting).

Vietrans (Viet Nam National Foreign Trade Forwarding and Warehousing Corpn): 13 Ly Nam De, Hoan Kiem, Hanoi; tel. (4) 8457801; fax (4) 8455829; e-mail vietrans@hn.vnn.vn; internet www.vietrans.com.vn; f. 1970; agent for forwarding and transport of exports and imports, diplomatic cargoes and other goods, warehousing, shipping and insurance; Gen. Dir THAI DUY LONG.

Vietranscimex (Viet Nam Transportation and Communication Import-Export Co): 22 Nguyen Van Troi, Phu Nhuan District, Ho Chi Minh City; tel. (8) 8442993; fax (8) 8445240; exports and imports specialized equipment and materials for transportation and communication; Gen. Dir PHAM QUANG VINH.

Viettronimex (Viet Nam Electronics Import-Export Corpn): 74–76 Nguyen Hue, Ho Chi Minh City; tel. (8) 8228249; fax (8) 8292964; e-mail viettronimex@hcm.vnn.vn; f. 1981; imports and exports electronic goods; Dir NGUYEN CANH THANH.

Vigecam (Viet Nam General Corpn of Agricultural Materials): 16 Ngo Tat To, Dong Da District, Hanoi; tel. (4) 8231972; fax (4) 7474647; exports and imports agricultural products; Dir HUYNH KY.

Vimedimex (Viet Nam Medical Products Export-Import Corpn): 246 Cong Quynh, 1st District, Ho Chi Minh City; tel. (8) 8398441; fax (8) 8325953; e-mail vietpharma@hcm.vnn.vn; internet www.vietpharma.com.vn; f. 1984; exports and imports medicinal and pharmaceutical materials and products, medical instruments; Gen. Dir NGUYEN TIEN HUNG.

Vinacafe (Viet Nam National Coffee Import-Export Corpn): 5 Ong Ich Khiem, Ba Dinh District, Hanoi; tel. (4) 8235449; fax (4) 8456422; e-mail vinacafe@hn.vnn.vn; internet www.vinacafe.com.vn; f. 1995; exports coffee, and imports equipment and chemicals for coffee production; Chair. TRAN KHAI; Pres. and CEO THAI DOAN LAI.

Vinacement (Viet Nam National Cement Corpn): 228 Le Duan, Dong Da, Hanoi; tel. (4) 8510593; fax (4) 8512778; f. 1980; manufactures and exports cement and clinker; Gen. Dir NGUYEN MAN.

Vinachimex (Viet Nam National Chemicals Import-Export Corpn): 4 Pham Ngu Lao, Hanoi; tel. (4) 8256377; fax (4) 8257727; f. 1969; exports and imports chemical products, minerals, rubber, fertilizers, machinery and spare parts; Dir NGUYEN VAN SON.

Vinafim (Viet Nam Film Import, Export and Film Service Corpn): 73 Nguyen Trai, Dong Da, Hanoi; tel. (4) 8244566; f. 1987; export and import of films and video tapes; film distribution; organization of film shows and participation of Vietnamese films in international film festivals; Gen. Man. NGO MANH LAN.

Vinafimex (Viet Nam National Agricultural Produce and Foodstuffs Import and Export Corpn): 58 Ly Thai To, Hanoi; tel. (4) 8255768; fax (4) 8255476; e-mail fime@hn.vnn.vn; f. 1984; exports cashews, peanuts, coffee, rubber and other agricultural products, and garments; imports malt, fertilizer, insecticide, seeds, machinery and equipment, etc.; Pres. NGUYEN TOAN THANG; Gen. Dir NGUYEN VAN THANG.

Vinafood Hanoi (Hanoi Food Import-Export Co): 4 Ngo Quyen, Hanoi; tel. (4) 8256771; fax (4) 8258528; f. 1988; exports rice, maize, tapioca; imports fertilizers, insecticides, wheat and wheat flour; Dir NGUYEN DUC HY.

Vinalivesco (Vietnam National Livestock Corporation): 519 Minh Khai, Hanoi; tel. (4) 8626763; fax (4) 8623645; f. 1996; imports and exports animal and poultry products, animal feeds and other agro-products, and foodstuffs; Gen. Dir NGUYEN VAN KHAC.

Vinamilk (Viet Nam Milk Co): 36–38 Ngo Duc Ke, District 1, Ho Chi Minh City; tel. (8) 8298054; fax (8) 8238117; internet www.hcm.fpt.vn/adv/vinamilk/vn; producer of dairy products; Dir MAI TRIUE LIEN.

Vinataba (Viet Nam National Tobacco Corpn): 25A Ly Thuong Kiet St, Hoan Kiem District, Hanoi; tel. (4) 8265778; fax (4) 8265777; mfr of tobacco products; Dir NGUYEN HANH TUYEN.

Vinatea (Viet Nam National Tea Development Investment and Export-Import Co): 46 Tang Bat Ho St, Hanoi; tel. (4) 8212005; fax (4) 8212663; e-mail thitruong@vinatea.com.vn; exports tea, imports tea-processing materials; Gen. Dir NGUYEN KIM PHONG.

Vinatex (Viet Nam National Textile and Garment Corpn): 25 Ba Trieu St, Hoan Kiem District, Hanoi; tel. (4) 8257700; fax (4) 8262269; e-mail vinatexhn@hn.vnn.vn; internet www.vinatex.com; f. 1995; imports textile machinery and materials, spare parts accessories, dyestuffs; exports textiles, garments, handicrafts, carpets, jute, silk; Gen. Dir BUI XUAN KHU.

Vocarimex (National Co. for Vegetable Oils, Aromas, and Cosmetics of Viet Nam): 58 Nguyen Binh Khiem, District 1, Ho Chi Minh City; tel. (8) 8294513; fax (8) 8290586; e-mail vocar@hcm.vnn.vn; f. 1976; producing and trading vegetable oils, oil-based products and special industry machinery; packaging; operating port facilities; Gen. Dir DUONG THI NGOC TRINH.

Xunhasaba (Viet Nam State Corpn for Export and Import of Books, Periodicals and other Cultural Commodities): 32 Hai Ba Trung, Hanoi; tel. (4) 8262989; fax (4) 8252860; e-mail xunhasaba@hn.vnn.vn; internet www.xunhasaba.com.vn; f. 1957; exports and imports books, periodicals, postage stamps, greetings cards, calendars and paintings; Dir TRAN PHU SON.

UTILITIES

Electricity

Power Co No 1 (PC1): 20 Tran Nguyen Han, Hoan Kiem, Hanoi; tel. (4) 8255074; fax (4) 8244033; e-mail anhdn@pc1.com.vn; manages the generation, transmission and distribution of electrical power in northern Viet Nam; Dir DO VAN LOC.

Power Co No 2 (PC2): 72 Hai Ba Trung, District 1, Ho Chi Minh City; tel. (8) 8297151; fax (8) 8299680; manages the distribution of electrical power in southern Viet Nam; Dir NGUYEN VAN GIAU.

Power Co No 3 (PC3): 16 Rue Le Thanh Ton, Da Nang; manages the generation, transmission and distribution of electrical power in central Viet Nam.

Viet Nam National Electrical Power Corporation (VNEPC): produces electrical power; Vice-Dir TRAN VIETN NGAI.

Water

Hanoi Water Business Co: 44 Yen Phu Road, Hanoi; tel. (4) 8292478; fax (4) 8294069; f. 1954; responsible for the supply of water to Hanoi and its five urban and two suburban districts; Dir Gen. BUI VAN MAT.

Ho Chi Minh City Water Supply Co: 1 Cong Truong Quoc Te, District 3, Ho Chi Minh City; tel. (8) 8291974; fax (8) 8241644; e-mail hcmcwater@hcm.vnn.vn; f. 1966; manages the water supply system of Ho Chi Minh City; Dir VO QUANG CHAU.

CO-OPERATIVES

Viet Nam Co-operatives Alliance: Hanoi; f. 1993 (fmrly Viet Nam Co-operatives Council); Chair. (vacant).

TRADE UNIONS

Tong Lien doan Lao dong Viet Nam (Viet Nam General Confederation of Labour): 82 Tran Hung Dao St, POB 627, Hanoi; tel. and fax (4) 8253781; e-mail doingoaitld@hnn.vnn.vn; f. 1929; merged in 1976 with the South Viet Nam Trade Union Fed. for Liberation; 4,000,000 mems; Pres. CU THI HAU; Vice-Pres NGUYEN AN LUONG, DANG NGOC CHIEN, DO DUC NGO, NGUYEN DINH THANG.

Cong Doan Nong Nghiep Cong Nghiep Thu Pham Viet Nam (Viet Nam Agriculture and Food Industry Trade Union): Hanoi; f. 1987; 550,000 mems.

National Union of Building Workers: 12 Cua Dong, Hoan Kiem, Hanoi; tel. (4) 8253781; fax (4) 8281407; f. 1957; Pres. NGUYEN VIET HAI.

Vietnam National Union of Industrial Workers: 54 Hai Ba Trung, Hanoi; tel. (4) 9344426; fax (4) 8245306; f. 1997; Pres. VU TIEN SAU.

Transport

RAILWAYS

Duong Sat Viet Nam (DSVN) (Viet Nam Railways): 118 Le Duan, Hanoi; tel. (4) 8220537; fax (4) 9424998; e-mail vr.hn.irstd@fpt.vn; 2,600 km of main lines (1996); lines in operation are: Hanoi–Ho Chi Minh City (1,726 km), Hanoi–Haiphong (102 km), Hanoi–Dong Dang (167 km), Hanoi–Lao Cai (296 km), Hanoi–Thai Nguyen (75 km), Thai Nguyen–Kep–Bai Chay (106 km); Gen. Dir Dr NGUYEN HUU BANG.

ROADS

In 1999 there were an estimated 93,300 km of roads, of which 25.1% were paved. In 1995 the Government announced plans to upgrade 430 km of the national highway which runs from Hanoi in the north to Ho Chi Minh City in the south. In 1997 the Government announced plans to build a new 1,880-km north–south highway in the east of the country. In 2001 the Government also announced plans to upgrade the section of the national highway that runs between the northern provinces of Hoa Binh and Son La.

SHIPPING

The principal port facilities are at Haiphong, Da Nang and Ho Chi Minh City. In 2001 the Vietnamese merchant fleet (700 vessels) had a combined displacement totalling 1,073,618 grt. In 1994 there were 150 shipping companies with a combined capacity of 800,000 dwt.

Cong Ty Van Tai Duong Bien Viet Nam (VOSCO) (Viet Nam Ocean Shipping Co): 215 Tran Quoc Toan, Ngo Quyen District, Haiphong; tel. (31) 846951; fax (31) 845107; controlled by the Viet Nam Gen. Dept of Marine Transport; Dir TRAN VAN LAM; Dir-Gen. TRAN XUAN NHON.

Dai Ly Hang Hai Viet Nam (VOSA) (VOSA group of companies): Unit 1003, 10/F Harbour View Tower, 35 Nguyen Hue, District 1, Ho Chi Minh City; tel. (8) 9140422; fax (8) 8211290; e-mail vosagroup@rcen.vnn.vn; internet www.vosagroup.com; f. 1957; formerly the Viet Nam Ocean Shipping Agency; controlled by the Viet Nam National Shipping Lines (VINALINES); in charge of merchant shipping; arranges ship repairs, salvage, passenger services, air and sea freight forwarding services; main br. office in Haiphong; brs in Hanoi, Da Nang, Hong Gai, Cam Pha, Ben Thuy, Qui Nhon, Nha Trang, Vung Tau and Can Tho; Dir-Gen. HA CAM KHAI (acting).

Transport and Chartering Corpn (Vietfracht): 74 Nguyen Du, Hanoi; tel. (4) 9422355; fax (4) 9423679; e-mail vfhan@hn.vnn.vn; internet www.vietfracht.com.vn; f. 1963; ship broking, chartering, ship management, shipping agency, international freight forwarding; consultancy services, import-export services; Gen. Dir DO XUAN QUYNH.

Viet Nam Sea Transport and Chartering Co (Vitranschart): 428–432 Nguyen Tat Thanh, District 4, Ho Chi Minh City; tel. (8) 9404027; fax (8) 9404711; e-mail vitrans@fmail.vnn.vn; Dir VO PHUNG LONG.

CIVIL AVIATION

Viet Nam's principal airports are Tan Son Nhat International Airport (Ho Chi Minh City) and Thu Do (Capital) International Airport at Noi Bai (Hanoi). They cater for domestic and foreign traffic. Airports at Da Nang, Hué, Nha Trang, Da Lat, Can Tho, Haiphong, Muong Thanh (near Dien Bien Phu), Buon Ma Thuot and Lien Khuong handle domestic traffic. In 1990 a programme to expand Tan Son Nhat, Noi Bai and Da Nang airports was initiated. In 1997 it was announced that numerous abandoned wartime airstrips were to be repaired and returned into service under a programme scheduled for completion in 2010, by which time the Government also aims to expand the annual capacity of Tan Son Nhat to 30m. passengers and 1m. tons of freight.

Viet Nam Airlines: Gialem Airport, Hanoi; tel. (4) 8732732; fax (4) 8272291; internet www.vietnamair.com.vn; fmrly the Gen. Civil Aviation Admin. of Viet Nam, then Hang Khong Viet Nam; wholly state-owned; operates domestic passenger services from Hanoi and from Ho Chi Minh City to the principal Vietnamese cities, and international services to 18 countries; Pres. and CEO NGUYEN XUAN HIEN.

Pacific Airlines: 112 Hong Ha, Tan Binh District, Ho Chi Minh City; tel. (8) 8450090; fax (8) 8450085; f. 1991; operates charter cargo flights, also scheduled passenger and cargo services to Taiwan; Man. Dir DUONG CAO THAI NGUYEN.

Tourism

In the 1990s the Vietnamese Government encouraged tourism as a source of much-needed foreign exchange, with the objective of attracting some 4m. tourists annually by the year 2005. About 2.3m. foreign tourists visited Viet Nam in 2001. In 1998 revenue from tourism totalled US $86m.

Viet Nam National Administration of Tourism (VNAT): 80 Quan Su, Hanoi; tel. (4) 9421061; fax (4) 9424115; e-mail icdvnat@vietnamtourism.com; internet www.vietnamtourism.com; f. 1960; Gen. Dir NGO HUY PHUONG.

Hanoi Tourism Service Company (HANOI TOSERCO): 8 To Hien Thanh, Hanoi; tel. (4) 9780004; fax (4) 8226055; e-mail hanoitoserco@hn.vnn.vn; internet www.fpt.vn/adv/toserco; f. 1988; manages the development of tourism, hotels and restaurants in the capital and other services including staff training; Dir TRAN TIEN HUNG.

Saigon Tourist: 23 Le Loi St, District 1, Ho Chi Minh City; tel. (8) 8225887; fax (8) 8291026; e-mail saigontourist@sgtourist.com.vn; internet www.saigon-tourist.com; f. 1975; tour operator; Gen. Dir DO VAN HOANG.

Unitour (Union of Haiphong Tourist Co): 40 Tran Quang Khai, Haiphong; tel. (31) 8247295.

Viet Nam Tourism in Haiphong: 60A Dien Bien Phu St, Haiphong; tel. and fax (31) 823651; f. 1960; hotel services, travel arrangements, visa service; Dir NGUYEN HUU BONG.

Defence

In August 2001 the total strength of the armed forces was an estimated 484,000: army 412,000; navy 42,000; air force 30,000. Men are subject to a two-year minimum term of compulsory military service between 18 and 35 years of age. Paramilitary forces number 4–5m. and include the urban People's Self Defence Force and the rural People's Militia. Border defence troops number an estimated 40,000. The defence budget for 2001 was estimated at US $1,800m.

Commander-in-Chief of the Armed Forces: TRAN DUC LUONG.

Chief of General Staff (Army): PHUNG QUANG THANH.

Commander of the Navy: Adm. DO XUAN CONG.

Education

Primary education, which is compulsory, begins at six years of age and lasts for five years. Secondary education, beginning at the age of 11, lasts for up to seven years, comprising a first cycle of four years and a second cycle of three years. In 1999/2000 some 96.3% of children in the relevant age-group were enrolled in primary schools, while total secondary enrolment included 61.4% of children in the appropriate age-group (boys 64.4%; girls 58.3%). In 1999/2000 an estimated total of 10,063,000 pupils attended 22,199 primary schools. In that school year there were 7,743,600 students in secondary education; a further 177,600 students were enrolled in technical secondary education in 1998/99. In 1999/2000 total enrolment at tertiary level was equivalent to 9.7% of students in the relevant age-group (males 11.2%; females 8.1%). In 1998/99 there were 123 universities and colleges of higher education, with a total enrolment of 682,300 students and 26,100 teachers. In 1989 Viet Nam's first private college since 1954, Thang Long College, was opened in Hanoi to cater for university students. In the budget for 2000 the Government allocated 10,700,000m. dông (9.8% of total expenditure) to education.

Bibliography

See also Cambodia and Laos

Amer, Ramses. *The Ethnic Chinese in Vietnam and Sino-Vietnamese Relations*. Petaling Jaya, Forum, 1992.

Anderson, Kym. *Vietnam's Transforming Economy and WTO Accession*. Singapore, Institute of Southeast Asian Studies, 1999.

Ang Cheng Guan. *The Vietnam War from the Other Side*. London, RoutledgeCurzon, 2002.

Archer, Robert. *Vietnam: The Habit of War*. London, Catholic Institute for International Relations, 1984.

Bao Ninh. *The Sorrow of War*. London, Secker and Warburg, 1994.

Beresford, Melanie. *Vietnam: Politics, Economics and Society*. London, Pinter, 1988.

National Unification and Economic Development in Vietnam. Basingstoke, Macmillan, 1989.

Beresford, Melanie, and Dang Phong. *Economic Transition in Vietnam—Trade and Aid in the Demise of a Centrally Planned Economy*. Cheltenham, Edward Elgar, 2000.

Bertram, Trent, and McCarty, Adam. *Enterprise Reform Project: Labour Market and Employment Issues*. Hanoi, Ministry of Planning and Investment /Asian Development Bank, 1997.

Bilton, Michael, and Sim, Kevin. *Four Hours in My Lai*. London, Viking, 1992.

Boettcher, T. D. *Vietnam: The Valour and the Sorrow*. Boston, MA, Little, Brown and Co, 1986.

Boothroyd, Peter, and Pham Xuan Nam (Eds). *Socio-Economic Renovation in Vietnam—The Origin, Evolution and Impact of Doi Moi*. Singapore, Institute of Southeast Asian Studies, 2000.

Braestrup, P. (Ed.). *Vietnam as History: Ten Years after the Paris Peace Accords*. Washington, DC, University Press of America, for the Wilson Center, 1984.

Brazier, Chris. Vietnam: *The Price of Peace*. Oxford, Oxfam, 1992.

Brownmiller, Susan. *Seeing Vietnam: Encounters of the Road and Heart*. New York, HarperCollins, 1994.

Bruton, Christopher, and Genovese, Mathilde. *Vietnam: An Investor's Appraisal*. Hong Kong, Business International, 1990.

Bui Tin. *Following Ho Chi Minh: Memoirs of a North Vietnamese Colonel*. New South Wales, Crawford House, 1996.

Butler, D. *The Fall of Saigon*. New York City, Simon and Schuster, 1986.

Buttinger, J. *Vietnam, a Political History*. London, André Deutsch, 1969.

Vietnam: a Dragon Embattled. London, Pall Mall Press, 1967.

Cable, James. *The Geneva Conference of 1954 on Indochina*. London, Macmillan, 1986.

Cameron, A. W. *Vietnam Crisis, a Documentary History (1940–56)*. Ithaca, NY, Cornell University Press, 1971.

Chaliand, G. *The Peasants of North Vietnam*. Harmondsworth, Penguin Books, 1969.

Chanda, Nayan. *Brother Enemy: The War After the War*. A History of Indochina since the Fall of Saigon. San Diego, New York and London, Harcourt Brace Jovanovich, 1986.

Chen, K. *Vietnam and China, 1938–54*. Princeton, NJ, Princeton University Press, 1969.

Chesneaux, J., Boudarel, G., Hemery, D., et al. *Tradition et Révolution au Vietnam*. Paris, Editions Anthropos, 1971.

Cohen, J. A. *Investment Law and Practice in Vietnam*. Hong Kong, Longman Professional Intelligence Reports, 1991.

Dahm, Henrich. *French and Japanese Economic Relations with Vietnam since 1975*. Richmond, Curzon Press, 1999.

Dalloz, J. *La Guerre d'Indochine 1945–1954*. Paris, Le Seuil, 1987.

Decaro, Peter A. *Rhetoric of Revolt: Ho Chi Minh's Discourse for Revolution*. Westport, CT, Praeger Publishers, 2002.

Devillers, P. *Histoire du Viet Nam de 1940 à 1952*. Paris, Le Seuil, 1952.

Devillers, P., and Lacouture, J. *End of a War, Indochina 1954*. London, Pall Mall Press, 1969.

Duiker, William J. *The Rise of Nationalism in Vietnam, 1900–1941*. Ithaca, NY, Cornell University Press, 1976.

Historical Dictionary of Vietnam. Metuchen, NJ, Scarecrow Press, 1989.

Victory in Vietnam: the Official History of the People's Army of Vietnam. Lawrence, KS, University Press of Kansas, 2002.

Eisen, Arlene. *Women and Revolution in Vietnam*. London, Zed Books, 1985.

Engelman, Larry. *Tears before the Rain: An Oral History of the Fall of South Vietnam*. New York, Oxford University Press, 1991.

Evans, Grant, and Rowley, Kelvin. *Red Brotherhood at War: Indochina Since the Fall of Saigon*. London, Verso Editions, 1985 (revised edn 1990).

Fall, B. *The Two Viet Nams, a Political and Military Analysis*. 2nd Edn, London, Pall Mall Press, 1967.

Street Without Joy: Insurgency in Indochina, 1946–63. London, Pall Mall Press, 1963.

Hell in a very Small Place: the Siege of Dien Bien Phu. London, Pall Mall Press, 1967.

Fforde, Adam. *The Limits of National Liberation: Economic Management and the Re-Unification of the Democratic Republic of Vietnam*. London, Croom Helm, 1984.

The Agrarian Question in North Viet Nam 1974–1979: A Study of Cooperator Resistance to State Policy. New York, M. E. Sharpe, 1990.

Doi Moi: Ten Years after the 1986 Party Congress. Political and Social Change Monograph 24. Canberra, Australian National University, 1997.

Fforde, Adam, and de Vylder, Stefan. *From Plan to Market: The Economic Transition in Viet Nam*. Boulder, CO, Westview Press, 1996.

Forbes, Dean K., Hull, Terrence H., Marr, David G. and Brogan, Brian (Eds). *Doi Moi: Vietnam's Renovation—Policy and Performance. Political and Social Change Monograph 14*. Canberra, Australian National University, 1991.

Franklin, H. Bruce. *M.I.A. or Mythmaking in America*. New York, Lawrence Hill Books, 1992.

Gainsborough, Martin. *Changing Political Economy of Vietnam*. London, RoutledgeCurzon, 2002.

Gelb, L. H., and Betts, R. K. *The Irony of Vietnam*. Washington, DC, Brookings Institution, 1979.

Gibbons, William C. *The US Government and the Vietnam War* (2 vols). Princeton University Press, 1986.

Gough, K. *Political Economy in Vietnam*. Berkeley, CA, Folklore Institute, 1990.

Grant, Zalin. *Over the Beach*. New York, W. W. Norton, 1987.

Halberstam, D. *The Best and the Brightest*. London, Barrie and Jenkins, 1973.

Hammer, E. J. *The Struggle for Indochina*. 2nd Edn, Stanford, CA, Stanford University Press, 1966.

Hannah, Norman B. *The Key to Failure: Laos and the Vietnam War*. New York, Madison Books, 1989.

Hardy, Andrew. *Red Hills: Migrants and the State in the Highlands of Vietnam*. Honolulu, HI, University of Hawaii Press, 2002.

Haughton, Dominique, Haughton, Jonathan, Bales, Sarah, Truong Thi Kim Chuyen, and Nguyen Nguyet Nga (Eds). *Health and Wealth in Vietnam (An Analysis of Household Living Standards)*. Singapore, Institute of Southeast Asian Studies, 1999.

Herring, G. C. *America's Longest War: The United States and Vietnam 1950–1975*. New York, Wiley, 1979.

Hickey, G. C. *Village in Vietnam*. New Haven, CT, Yale University Press, 1964.

Hiebert, Murray *Vietnam Notebook*. Hong Kong, Review Publishing Co Ltd, 1993 (revised edn 1998).

Chasing the Tigers—A Portrait of the New Vietnam. London, Kodansha Europe, 1997.

Hodgkin, T. *Vietnam, the Revolutionary Path*. London, Macmillan, 1981.

Houtart, François, and Lemercinier, Genevieve. *Hai Van: Life in a Vietnamese Commune*. London, Zed Press, 1984.

Hue-Tam Ho Tai. *Millenarianism and Peasant Politics in Vietnam*. Cambridge, MA, Harvard University Press.

Hurst, Steven. *The Carter Administration and Vietnam*. London, Macmillan, 1996.

Huynh Kim Khanh. *Vietnamese Communism 1925–1945.* Ithaca, NY, Cornell University Press, 1982.

International Monetary Fund. *Vietnam Economic Development.* Hanoi, International Monetary Fund, 1998.

Isaacs, A. R. *Without Honour: Defeat in Vietnam and Cambodia.* Baltimore, Johns Hopkins University Press, 1983.

Kahin, G. McT. *Intervention. How America became involved in Vietnam.* New York, Alfred Knopf, 1986.

Karnow, Stanley. *Vietnam, A History.* Harmondsworth, Penguin Books, 1984.

Kerkvliet, Benedict, and Porter, Doug (Eds). *Vietnam's Rural Transformation.* Boulder, CO, Westview Press, 1995.

Kimura, Tetsusaburo. *The Vietnamese Economy 1975–86.* Tokyo, Institute of Developing Economies, 1989.

Kleinen, John. *Facing The Future, Reviving The Past. A Study of Social Change in a Northern Vietnamese Village.* Singapore, Institute of Southeast Asian Studies, 1999.

Kolko, Gabriel. *Vietnam: Anatomy of a Peace.* London, Routledge, 1997.

Lacouture, J. *Ho Chi Minh.* London, Penguin Books, 1968.

Lancaster, D. *The Emancipation of French Indochina.* London, Oxford University Press, 1961.

Lansdale, E. G. *In the Midst of Wars: an American Mission to South-East Asia.* New York, Harper and Row, 1972.

Le Thanh Khoi. *Le Viet Nam, Histoire et Civilisation.* Paris, Editions de Minuit, 1955.

Leung, Suiwah (Ed.). *Vietnam Assessment: Creating a Sound Investment Climate.* Singapore, Institute of Southeast Asian Studies, 1996.

Lewy, G. *America in Vietnam.* New York, Oxford University Press, 1978.

Ljunggren, Börje (Ed.). *The Challenge of Reform in Indochina.* Cambridge, MA, Harvard Institute for International Development, 1993.

Lockhart, Greg. *Nation in Arms: The Origins of the People's Army of Vietnam.* Sydney, Allen and Unwin, 1989.

Logevall, Frederik. *Choosing War: the Lost Chance for Peace and the Escalation of War in Vietnam.* Berkeley, CA, University of California Press, 2001.

Luong, Hy Van. *Revolution in the Village: Tradition and Transformation in North Vietnam, 1925–1988.* Honolulu, University of Hawaii Press, 1992.

McAleavy, H. *Black Flags in Vietnam.* London, Allen and Unwin, 1968.

McAlister, J. T. *Viet Nam, the Origins of Revolution.* London, Allen Lane, 1970.

McCoy, A. W. *The Politics of Heroin in South-East Asia.* New York, Harper and Row, 1972.

Macdonald, Peter. *Giap: The Victor in Vietnam.* London, 4th Estate, 1994.

McKelvey, Robert S. *A Gift of Barbed Wire: America's Allies Abandoned in South Vietnam.* Seattle, WA, University of Washington Press, 2002.

McNamara, Robert S. *In Retrospect: The Tragedy and Lessons of Vietnam.* New York, NY, Times Books, 1995.

Malarney, Shaun. *Culture, Ritual and Revolution in Vietnam.* London, RoutledgeCurzon, 2002.

Mangold, Tom, and Penycate, John. *The Tunnels of Cu Chi.* Sevenoaks, Kent, Hodder and Stoughton, 1985.

Marr, D. G. *Vietnamese Anticolonialism, 1885–1925.* Berkeley, CA, University of California, 1971.

Vietnamese Tradition on Trial, 1920–45. Berkeley, CA, University of California, 1981.

Vietnam 1945: The Quest for Power. Berkeley, CA, University of California, 1996.

Marr, David G., and White, Christine (Eds). *Postwar Vietnam: Dilemmas in Socialist Development.* Southeast Asia Program, Ithaca, Cornell University, 1988.

Mio, Tadashi (Ed.). *Indochina in Transition: Confrontation or Co-prosperity.* Japan Institute of International Affairs, Tokyo, 1989.

Moise, Edwin. *Land Reform in China and North Vietnam: Consolidating the Revolution at the Village Level.* Chapel Hill, NC, University of North Carolina Press, 1983.

Tonkin Gulf and the Escalation of the Vietnam War. Chapel Hill, NC, University of North Carolina Press, 1996.

Morley, James W. and Masashi, Nishihara (Eds). *Vietnam Joins the World.* New York, M. E. Sharpe, 1997.

Morris, Stephen J. *Why Vietnam Invaded Cambodia (Political Culture and the Causes of War).* Cambridge, Cambridge University Press, 1998.

Neale, Jonathan. *The American War.* London, Bookmarks Publications, 2001.

Ng Chee Yuen, Freeman, Nick J., and Hiep Huynh, Frank. *State-Owned Enterprise Reform in Vietnam: Lessons from Asia.* Singapore, Institute of Southeast Asian Studies, 1996.

Ngo Vinh Long. *Before the Revolution: the Vietnamese Peasants under the French.* Cambridge, MA, MIT Press, 1973.

Nguyen Long, with Kendall, Harry H. *After Saigon Fell: Daily Life under the Vietnamese Communists.* Los Angeles, University of California Press, 1981.

Nguyen, Nicholas. *Vietnam: The Second Revolution.* Brighton, In Print Publishing, 1996.

Nguyen Tien Hung, G. *Economic Development of Socialist Vietnam, 1955–1980.* New York, Praeger Publishers, 1977.

Nguyen Tien Hung and Schecter, Jerrold L. *The Palace File.* New York, Harper & Row, 1987.

Nguyen Van Canh. *Vietnam under Communism, 1975–1982.* Stanford, CA, Hoover Institution Press, 1983.

Nixon, Richard. *No More Vietnams.* New York, NY, Arbor House, 1985.

Osborne, M. E. *The French Presence in Cochin-China and Cambodia: Rule and Response (1859–1905).* Ithaca, NY, Cornell University Press, 1969.

Palmer, General Bruce. *The 25-Year War.* New York, Harper and Row Publishers, 1985.

Palmujoki, Eero. *Vietnam and the World: Marxist-Leninist Doctrine and the Changes in International Relations, 1975–93.* London, Macmillan, 1997.

Patti, A. L. A. *Why Vietnam? Prelude to America's Albatross.* University of California, 1981.

The Pentagon Papers: the Defense Department History of US Decision-making on Vietnam. 'Senator Gravel Edition', 4 vols. Boston, MA, Beacon Press, 1971.

Pike, D. *Viet Cong, the Organization and Techniques of the National Liberation Front of South Vietnam.* Cambridge, MA, MIT Press, 1966.

PAVN: People's Army of Viet Nam. Oxford, Brassey's Defence Publishers, 1986.

Vietnam and the Soviet Union. Boulder, CO, and London, Westview Press, 1987.

Popkin, Samuel L. *The Rational Peasant: The Political Economy of Rural Society in Viet Nam.* Los Angeles, CA, University of California Press, 1979.

Porter, G. *Vietnam: The Politics of Bureaucratic Socialism.* Ithaca, NY, Cornell University Press, 1993.

Prados, John. *The Blood Road—The Ho Chi Minh Trail and the Vietnam War.* New York, NY, John Wiley & Sons, 1999.

Quinn-Judge, Sophie. *Ho Chi Minh: the Missing Years.* Berkeley, CA, University of California Press, 2002.

Race, J. *War comes to Long An: Revolutionary Conflict in a Vietnamese Province.* Berkeley, CA, University of California, 1972.

Ronnas, Per, and Ramamurthy, Bhargavi (Eds). *Entrepreneurship in Vietnam: Transformation and Dynamics.* Singapore, Institute of Southeast Asian Studies, 2001.

Ronnas, Per, and Sjöberg, O. *Socio-Economic Development in Vietnam: The Agenda for the 1990s.* Stockholm, Swedish International Development Authority, 1991.

Ronnas, Per and Sjöberg, O. (Eds). *Doi Moi—Economic Reforms and Development Policies in Vietnam.* Stockholm, Swedish International Development Authority, 1990.

Salemink, Oscar. *The Ethnography of Vietnam's Central Highlanders.* London, RoutledgeCurzon, 2002.

Salisbury, Harrison. *Vietnam Reconsidered.* New York, Harper and Row Publishers, 1985.

Sansom, R. L. *The Economics of Insurgency in the Mekong Delta of Vietnam.* Cambridge, MA, MIT Press, 1970.

Schoenl, William (Ed.). *New Perspectives on the Vietnam War: Our Allies Views.* Lanham, MD, University Press of America, 2002.

Shaplen, R. *The Lost Revolution in Vietnam, 1945–65.* London, 1965.

Smith, R. *Viet Nam and the West.* London, Heinemann Educational, 1968.

Smith, R. B. *An International History of the Vietnam War: Vol. 1—Revolution versus Containment, 1955–1961; Vol. 2—The Struggle for South-east Asia, 1961–65; Vol. 3—Making of a United War, 1965–66.* London, Macmillan, 1983, 1985, 1990.

Snepp, F. *Decent Interval, an Insider's Account of Saigon's Indecent End.* New York, Random House, 1978.

Sorley, Lewis. *A Better War: the Unexamined Victories and Final Tragedy of America's Last Years in Vietnam.* New York, NY, Harcourt Brace & Co., 1999.

Spector, Ronald H. *After Tet: The Bloodiest Year in Vietnam.* New York, Vintage Books, 1994.

Stern, Lewis M. *Renovating the Vietnamese Communist Party* Singapore, Institute of Southeast Asian Studies, 1993.

Tana, Li. *Peasants on the Move: Rural–Urban Migration in the Hanoi Region.* Singapore, Institute of Southeast Asian Studies, 1996.

Templer, Robert. *Shadows and Wind: A View of Modern Vietnam.* London, Little Brown, 1998.

Thakur, R., and Thayer, C. A. *Soviet Relations with India and Vietnam.* London, Macmillan, 1992.

Than, Mya, and Tan, Joseph L. H. (Eds). *Vietnam's Dilemmas and Options: The Challenge of Economic Transition in the 1990s.* Singapore, Institute of Southeast Asian Studies, 1993.

Thayer, Carlyle A. *War by Other Means: National Liberation and Revolution in Vietnam.* Sydney, Allen and Unwin, 1989.

The Vietnam People's Army Under Doi Moi. Pacific Strategic Paper No. 7, Singapore, Institute of Southeast Asian Studies, 1994.

Thayer, Carlyle A., and Amer, Ramses (Eds). *Vietnamese Foreign Policy in Transition.* Singapore, Institute of Southeast Asian Studies, 1999.

Thayer, Carlyle A., and Marr, David G. (Eds). *Vietnam and the Rule of Law. Political and Social Change Monograph No. 19.* Canberra, Australia National University, 1993.

Thierry d'Argenlieu, Admiral. *Chronique d'Indochine, 1945–1947.* Paris, Albin Michel, 1986.

Thrift, Nigel, and Forbes, Dean. *The Price of War: Urbanisation in Vietnam 1954–85.* Sydney, Allen and Unwin, 1986.

Tonnesson, Stein. *The Vietnamese Revolution of 1945: Roosevelt, Ho Chi Minh and de Gaulle in a World at War.* Oslo/London, International Peace Research Institute/Sage Publications, 1992.

Tran, Khanh. *The Ethnic Chinese and Economic Development in Vietnam.* Singapore, Institute of Southeast Asian Studies, 1993.

Tran Thi Que. *Vietnam's Agriculture: The Challenges and Achievements.* Singapore, Institute of Southeast Asian Studies, 1998.

Tran Tri Vu. *Lost Years. My 1,632 Days in Vietnamese Re-education Camps.* Berkeley, CA, Institute of East Asian Studies, University of California, 1989.

Truong Buu Lam. *Patterns of Vietnamese Response to Foreign Intervention 1858–1900.* New Haven, CT, Yale University Press, 1967.

Truong Chinh. *Primer for Revolt.* B. B. Fall (Ed.), New York, Praeger, 1963.

Truong Nhu Tong. *Journal of a Viet-Cong.* London, Cape, 1986.

Turley, William S. (Ed.). *Vietnamese Communism in Comparative Perspective.* Boulder, CO, Westview Press, 1980.

Turley, W. S. *The Second Indo-China War: A Short Political and Military History.* Boulder, CO, Westview Press, 1986.

Turley, W. S., and Selden, M. (Eds). *Reinventing Vietnamese Socialism.* Boulder, CO, Westview Press, 1993.

Turner, Robert, F. *Vietnamese Communism: Its Origins and Development.* Stanford, Hoover Institution Press, 1975.

Van Dyke, J. M. *North Vietnam's Strategy for Survival.* Palo Alto, CA, 1972.

Vickerman, A. *The Fate of the Peasantry: A Premature 'Transition to Socialism' in the Democratic Republic of Vietnam.* New Haven, CT, Yale University Press, 1987.

Vo Dai Luoc (Ed.). *Investment and Trade Policies and the Development of Major Industries in Vietnam.* Nha Xuat Ban Khoa hoc Xa hoi, Hanoi, 1998.

Vo Nguyen Giap. *People's War, People's Army.* New York, Praeger, 1962.

Vo Nhan Tri. *Croissance Economique de la République Démocratique du Viet Nam.* Hanoi, 1967.

Vietnam's Economic Policy Since 1975. Singapore, Institute of Southeast Asian Studies, 1990.

Vu Tuan Anh. *Development in Vietnam: Policy Reforms and Economic Growth.* Singapore, Institute of Southeast Asian Studies, 1994.

Weller, Keith. *The Birth of Vietnam.* Berkeley, CA, University of California Press, 1985.

Werner, Jayne and Huynh, Luu Doan (Eds). *The Vietnam War—Vietnamese and American Perspectives.* Armonk, NY, M. E. Sharpe, 1993.

Wiegersma, N. *Vietnam: Peasant Land, Peasant Revolution: Patriarchy and Collectivity in the Rural Economy.* New York, St. Martin's Press, 1988.

Willenson, K. *The Bad War: An Oral History of the Vietnam War.* New York, New American Library, 1987.

Williams, Michael C. *Vietnam at the Crossroads.* London, Royal Institute of International Affairs/Pinter Publishers, 1992.

Woodside, A. B. *Vietnam and the Chinese Model: a Comparative Study of Vietnamese and Chinese Government in the first half of the Nineteenth Century.* Cambridge, MA, Harvard University Press, 1971.

Community and Revolution in Modern Vietnam. Boston, MA, Houghton and Mifflin, 1976.

Zasloff, J., and Brown, McA. (Eds). *Communism in Indochina: New Perspectives.* Lexington, MA, Heath and Co, 1975.

PART THREE

Regional Information

REGIONAL ORGANIZATIONS

THE UNITED NATIONS IN THE FAR EAST AND AUSTRALASIA

Address: United Nations Plaza, New York, NY 10017, USA.

Telephone: (212) 963-1234; **fax:** (212) 963-4879; **internet:** www.un.org.

The United Nations (UN) was founded on 24 October 1945. The organization, which has 191 member states, aims to maintain international peace and security and to develop international co-operation in addressing economic, social, cultural and humanitarian problems. The principal organs of the UN are the General Assembly, the Security Council, the Economic and Social Council (ECOSOC), the International Court of Justice and the Secretariat. The General Assembly, which meets for three months each year, comprises representatives of all UN member states. The Security Council investigates disputes between member countries, and may recommend ways and means of peaceful settlement: it comprises five permanent members (the People's Republic of China, France, Russia, the United Kingdom and the USA) and 10 other members elected by the General Assembly for a two-year period. The Economic and Social Council comprises representatives of 54 member states, elected by the General Assembly for a three-year period: it promotes co-operation on economic, social, cultural and humanitarian matters, acting as a central policy-making body and co-ordinating the activities of the UN's specialized agencies. The International Court of Justice comprises 15 judges of different nationalities, elected for nine-year terms by the General Assembly and the Security Council: it adjudicates in legal disputes between UN member states.

Secretary-General of the United Nations: Kofi Annan (Ghana) (1997–2006).

MEMBER STATES IN THE FAR EAST AND AUSTRALASIA

(with assessments for percentage contributions to UN budget for 2003, and year of admission)

Afghanistan	0.00900	1946
Australia	1.62700	1945
Bangladesh	0.01000	1974
Bhutan	0.00100	1971
Brunei	0.03300	1984
Cambodia	0.00200	1955
China, People's Republic*	1.53200	1945
East Timor†	n.a.	2002
Fiji	0.00400	1970
India	0.34100	1945
Indonesia	0.20000	1950
Japan	19.51575	1956
Kiribati	0.00100	1999
Korea, Democratic People's Republic	0.00900	1991
Korea, Republic	1.85100	1991
Laos	0.00100	1955
Malaysia	0.23500	1957
Maldives	0.00100	1965
Marshall Islands	0.00100	1991
Micronesia, Federated States	0.00100	1991
Mongolia	0.00100	1961
Myanmar	0.01000	1948
Nauru	0.00100	1999
Nepal	0.00400	1955
New Zealand	0.24100	1945
Pakistan	0.06100	1947
Palau	0.00100	1994
Papua New Guinea	0.00600	1975
Philippines	0.10000	1945
Samoa	0.00100	1976
Singapore	0.39300	1965
Solomon Islands	0.00100	1978
Sri Lanka	0.01600	1955
Thailand	0.29400	1946
Tonga	0.00100	1999
Tuvalu	0.00100	2000
Vanuatu	0.00100	1981
Viet Nam	0.01600	1977

* From 1945 to 1971 the Chinese seat was occupied by the Republic of China (confined to Taiwan since 1949).

† East Timor was admitted, as the Democratic Republic of Timor-Leste, on 27 September 2002.

SOVEREIGN COUNTRY NOT IN THE UNITED NATIONS

China (Taiwan)

PERMANENT MISSIONS TO THE UNITED NATIONS

(with Permanent Representatives—October 2002)

Afghanistan: 360 Lexington Ave, 11th Floor, New York, NY 10017; tel. (212) 972-1212; fax (212) 972-1216; e-mail afgwatan@aol.com; Dr Ravan A. G. Farhâdi.

Australia: 150 East 42nd St, New York, NY 10017; tel. (212) 351-6600; fax (212) 351-6610; e-mail australia@un.int; internet www.un.int/australia; John Dauth.

Bangladesh: 821 United Nations Plaza, 8th Floor, New York, NY 10017; tel. (212) 867-3434; fax (212) 972-4038; e-mail bangladesh@un.int; internet www.un.int/bangladesh; Anwarul Karim Chowdhury.

Bhutan: 2 United Nations Plaza, 27th Floor, New York, NY 10017; tel. (212) 826-1919; fax (212) 826-2998; e-mail bhutan@un.int; Lyonpo Om Pradhan.

Brunei: 771 United Nations Plaza, New York, NY 10017; tel. (212) 697-3465; fax (212) 697-9889; e-mail brunei@un.int; Serbini Ali.

Cambodia: 866 United Nations Plaza, Suite 420, New York, NY 10017; tel. (212) 223-0676; fax (212) 223-0425; e-mail cambodia@un.int; internet www.un.int/cambodia; Ouch Borith.

China, People's Republic: 350 East 35th St, New York, NY 10016; tel. (212) 655-6100; fax (212) 634-7626; e-mail china@un.int; internet www.china-un.org/eng/index.html; Wang Ying-Fan.

East Timor: Dr José Luís Guterres.

Fiji: 630 Third Ave, 7th Floor, New York, NY 10017; tel. (212) 687-4130; fax (212) 687-3963; e-mail fji@un.int; Amraiya Naidu.

India: 235 East 43rd St, New York, NY 10017; tel. (212) 490-9660; fax (212) 490-9656; e-mail india@un.int; internet www.un.int/india; Vijay Kunhianandan Nambiar.

Indonesia: 325 East 38th St, New York, NY 10016; tel. (212) 972-8333; fax (212) 972-9780; e-mail indonesia2@un.int; internet www.indonesiamission-ny.org; Chargé d'affaires M. Slamet Hidayet.

Japan: 866 United Nations Plaza, 2nd Floor, New York, NY 10017; tel. (212) 223-4300; fax (212) 751-1966; e-mail mission@un-japan.org; internet www.un.int/japan; Koichi Haraguchi.

Korea, Democratic People's Republic: 820 Second Ave, 13th Floor, New York, NY 10017; tel. (212) 972-3105; fax (212) 972-3154; e-mail dprk@un.int; Pak Gil Yon.

Korea, Republic: 335 East 45th St, New York, NY 10017; tel. (212) 439-4000; fax (212) 916-1083; e-mail korea@un.int; internet www.un.int/korea; Sun Joun-Yung.

Laos: 317 East 51st St, New York, NY 10022; tel. (212) 832-2734; fax (212) 750-0039; e-mail laos@un.int; internet www.un.int/lao; Alounkèo Kittikhoun.

Malaysia: 313 East 43rd St, New York, NY 10017; tel. (212) 986-6310; fax (212) 490-8576; e-mail malaysia@un.int; internet www.un.int/malaysia; Agam Hasmy.

Maldives: 800 Second Ave, Suite 400E, New York, NY 10017; tel. (212) 599-6195; fax (212) 661-6405; e-mail maldives@un.int; internet www.un.int/maldives; Hussain Shihab.

Marshall Islands: 800 Second Ave, 18th Floor, New York, NY 10017; tel. (212) 983-3040; fax (212) 983-3202; e-mail marshallislands@un.int; Alfred Capelle.

Micronesia, Federated States: 820 Second Ave, Suite 17A, New York, NY 10017; tel. (212) 697-8370; fax (212) 697-8295; e-mail micronesia@un.int; Masao Nakayama.

Mongolia: 6 East 77th St, New York, NY 10021; tel. (212) 861-9460; fax (212) 861-9464; e-mail mongolia@un.int; internet www.un.int/mongolia; JARGALSAIKHANY ENKHSAIKHAN.

Myanmar: 10 East 77th St, New York, NY 10021; tel. (212) 535-1310; fax (212) 737-2421; e-mail myanmar@un.int; KYAW TINT SWE.

Nauru: 800 Second Ave, Suite 400D, New York, NY 10017; tel. (212) 937-0074; fax (212) 937-0079; VINCI NEIL CLODUMAR.

Nepal: 820 Second Ave, Suite 17B, New York, NY 10017; tel. (212) 370-3988; fax (212) 953-2038; e-mail nepal@un.int; internet www.un.int/nepal; MURARI RAJ SHARMA.

New Zealand: 1 United Nations Plaza, 25th Floor, New York, NY 10017; tel. (212) 826-1960; fax (212) 758-0827; e-mail nz@un.int; internet www.un.int/newzealand; DONALD JAMES MACKAY.

Pakistan: Pakistan House, 8 East 65th St, New York, NY 10021; tel. (212) 879-8600; fax (212) 744-7348; e-mail pakistan@un.int; internet www.un.int/pakistan; MUNIR AKRAM.

Papua New Guinea: 201 East 42nd St, Suite 405, New York, NY 10017; tel. (212) 557-5001; fax (212) 557-5009; e-mail png@un.int; ROBERT GUBA AISI.

Philippines: 556 Fifth Ave, 5th Floor, New York, NY 10036; tel. (212) 764-1300; fax (212) 840-8602; e-mail misunphil@aol.com; ALFONSO TIAOQUI YUCHENGCO.

Samoa: 800 Second Ave, Suite 400D, New York, NY 10017; tel. (212) 599-6196; fax (212) 599-0797; e-mail samoa@un.int; TUILOMA NERONI SLADE.

Singapore: 231 East 51st St, New York, NY 10022; tel. (212) 826-0840; fax (212) 826-2964; e-mail singapore@un.int; KISHORE MAHBUBANI.

Solomon Islands: 800 Second Ave, Suite 400L, New York, NY 10017; tel. (212) 599-6193; fax (212) 661-8925; e-mail solomonislands@un.int; Chargé d'Affaires a.i. JEREMIAH MANELE.

Sri Lanka: 630 Third Ave, 20th Floor, New York, NY 10017; tel. (212) 986-7040; fax (212) 986-1838; e-mail srilanka@un.int; CHITHAMBARANATHAN MAGENDRAN.

Thailand: 351 East 52nd St, New York, NY 10022; tel. (212) 754-2230; fax (212) 754-2535; e-mail thailand@un.int; CCHUCHAI KASEMSARN.

Tonga: 800 Second Ave, Suite 400B, New York, NY 10017; tel. (212) 599-6190; fax (212) 808-4975; e-mail tongaunmission@aol.com; S. TU'A TAUMOEPEAU-TUPOU.

Tuvalu: 800 Second Ave, Suite 400B, New York, NY 10017; tel. (212) 490-0534; fax (212) 808-4975; ENELE SOSENE SOPOAGA.

Vanuatu: 42 Broadway, Suite 1200–18, New York, NY 10004; tel. (212) 425-9600; fax (212) 425-9653; e-mail vanuatu@un.int; Chargé d'affaires a.i. SELWYN ARUTANEAI.

Viet Nam: 866 United Nations Plaza, Suite 435, New York, NY 10017; tel. (212) 644-0594; fax (212) 644-5732; e-mail vietnam@un.int; internet www.un.int/vietnam; NGUYEN THANH CHAU.

Observers

Asian-African Legal Consultative Organization: 404 East 66th St, Apt 12C, New York, NY 10021; tel. (212) 734-7608; e-mail aalco@un.int; K. BHAGWAT-SINGH.

Commonwealth Secretariat: 800 Second Ave, 4th Floor, New York, NY 10017; tel. (212) 599-6190; fax (212) 808-4975; e-mail comsec@thecommonwealth.org.

International Committee of the Red Cross: 801 Second Ave, 18th Floor, New York, NY 10017; tel. (212) 599-6021; fax (212) 599-6009; e-mail redcrosscommittee@un.int; SYLVIE JUNOD.

Organization of the Islamic Conference: 130 East 40th St, 5th Floor, New York, NY 10016; tel. (212) 883-0140; fax (212) 883-0143; e-mail oic@un.int; internet www.un.int/oic; MOKHTAR LAMANI.

World Conservation Union—IUCN: 406 West 66th St, New York, NY 10021; tel. and fax (212) 734-7608.

The African, Caribbean and Pacific Group of States, the Economic Co-operation Organization and the Pacific Islands Forum are among several intergovernmental organizations that have a standing invitation to participate as observers but do not maintain permanent offices at the UN.

United Nations Information Centres

Afghanistan: (temporarily inactive).

Australia: 46–48 York St, Level 5, Sydney, NSW 2000; GPO 4045, Sydney, NSW 2001; tel. (2) 9262-5111; fax (2) 9262-5886; e-mail unsyd@ozemail.com.au; office also covers Fiji, Kiribati, Nauru, New Zealand, Samoa, Tonga, Tuvalu and Vanuatu.

Bangladesh: GPO Box 3658, Dhaka 1000; tel. (2) 8118600; fax (2) 8112343; e-mail unic.dhaka@undp.org; internet www.unicdhaka.org.

India: 55 Lodi Estate, New Delhi 110003; tel. (11) 462-3439; fax (11) 462-0293; e-mail feodor@giasd101.vsnl.net.in; internet www.unic.org.in; office also covers Bhutan.

Indonesia: Gedung Dewan Pers, 5th Floor, 32–34 Jalan Kebon Sirih, Jakarta; tel. (21) 3900292; fax (21) 3900274; e-mail unicjak@cbn.net.id.

Japan: UNU Bldg, 8th Floor, 53–70 Jingumae S-chome, Shibuya-ku, Tokyo 150-0001; tel. (3) 5467-4451; fax (3) 5467-4455; e-mail unictok@untokyo.jp; internet www.unic.or.jp; office also covers Palau.

Myanmar: 6 Natmauk Rd, POB 230, Yangon; tel. (1) 292619; fax (1) 292911; e-mail unic.myanmar@undp.org.

Nepal: POB 107, UN House, Kathmandu; tel. (1) 524366; fax (1) 523991; e-mail registry.np@undp.org.

Pakistan: House No. 26, 88th St, G-6/3, POB 1107, Islamabad; tel. (51) 270610; fax (51) 271856; e-mail unic@isb.paknet.com.pak; internet www.un.org.pk/unic.

Philippines: POB 7285 (DAPO), Room 301, NEDA Bldg, 106 Amorsolo St, Legaspi Village, Makati City, Manila; tel. (2) 8920611; fax (2) 8163011; e-mail infocentre@unicmanila.org; office also covers Papua New Guinea and Solomon Islands.

Sri Lanka: 202–204 Bauddhaloka Mawatha, POB 1505, Colombo 7; tel. (1) 580691; fax (1) 581116; e-mail anusha.atukorale@undp.org.

Thailand: UN Bldg, Rajdamnern Ave, Bangkok 10200; tel. (2) 288-1866; fax (2) 288-1052; e-mail unisbkk.unescap@un.org; internet www.unescap.org/unis; office also covers Cambodia, Hong Kong, Laos, Malaysia, Singapore and Viet Nam.

Economic and Social Commission for Asia and the Pacific—ESCAP

Address: United Nations Bldg, Rajdamnern Ave, Bangkok 10200, Thailand.

Telephone: (2) 288-1234; **fax:** (2) 288-1000; **e-mail:** unisbkk.unescap@un.org; **internet:** www.unescap.org.

The Commission was founded in 1947 to encourage the economic and social development of Asia and the Far East; it was originally known as the Economic Commission for Asia and the Far East (ECAFE). The title ESCAP, which replaced ECAFE, was adopted after a reorganization in 1974.

MEMBERS

Afghanistan	Korea, Democratic People's Republic	Papua New Guinea
Armenia	Korea, Republic	Philippines
Australia	Kyrgyzstan	Russia
Azerbaijan	Laos	Samoa
Bangladesh	Malaysia	Singapore
Bhutan	Maldives	Solomon Islands
Brunei	Marshall Islands	Sri Lanka
Cambodia	Micronesia, Federated States	Tajikistan
China, People's Republic	Mongolia	Thailand
Fiji	Myanmar	Tonga
France	Nauru	Turkey
Georgia	Nepal	Turkmenistan
India	Netherlands	Tuvalu
Indonesia	New Zealand	United Kingdom
Iran	Pakistan	USA
Japan	Palau	Uzbekistan
Kazakhstan		Vanuatu
Kiribati		Viet Nam

ASSOCIATE MEMBERS

American Samoa	Hong Kong	Northern Mariana Islands
Cook Islands	Macao	
French Polynesia	New Caledonia	
Guam	Niue	

Organization

(October 2002)

COMMISSION

The Commission meets annually at ministerial level to examine the region's problems, to review progress, to establish priorities and to decide upon the recommendations of the Executive Secretary or the subsidiary bodies of the Commission.

Ministerial and intergovernmental conferences on specific issues may be held on an *ad hoc* basis with the approval of the Commission, although, from 1998, no more than one ministerial conference and five intergovernmental conferences may be held during one year.

COMMITTEES AND SPECIAL BODIES

The following advise the Commission and help to oversee the work of the Secretariat:

Committee on the Environment and Natural Resources Development: meets annually.

Committee on Regional Economic-Co-operation: meets every two years, with a high-level Steering Group, which meets annually to discuss and develop policy options.

Committee on Socio-economic Measures to Alleviate Poverty in Rural and Urban Areas: meets annually.

Committee on Statistics: meets every two years.

Committee on Transport, Communications, Tourism and Infrastructure Development: meets annually.

Special Body on Least-Developed and Land-locked Developing Countries: meets every two years.

Special Body on Pacific Island Developing Countries: meets every two years.

In addition, an Advisory Committee of permanent representatives and other representatives designated by members of the Commission functions as an advisory body.

SECRETARIAT

The Secretariat operates under the guidance of the Commission and its subsidiary bodies. It consists of two servicing divisions, covering administration and programme management, in addition to the following substantive divisions: Development research and policy analysis; International trade and industry; Environment and natural resources development; Social development; Population and rural and urban development; Transport, communications, tourism and infrastructure development; and Statistics.

The Secretariat also includes the ESCAP/UNCTAD Joint Unit on Transnational Corporations and the UN information services.

Executive Secretary: KIM HAK-SU (Republic of Korea).

SUB-REGIONAL OFFICE

ESCAP Pacific Operations Centre (EPOC): Private Bag 004, Port Vila, Vanuatu; tel. 23458; fax 23921; e-mail escappoc@escap.org.vu; f. 1984, to provide effective advisory and technical assistance at a sub-regional level and to identify the needs of island countries. Dir NIKENIKE VUROBARAVU.

Activities

ESCAP acts as a UN regional centre, providing the only intergovernmental forum for the whole of Asia and the Pacific, and executing a wide range of development programmes through technical assistance, advisory services to governments, research, training and information.

In 1992 ESCAP began to reorganize its programme activities and conference structures in order to reflect and serve the region's evolving development needs. The approach that was adopted focused on regional economic co-operation, poverty alleviation through economic growth and social development, and environmental and sustainable development.

Regional economic co-operation. Provides technical assistance and advisory services. Aims to enhance institutional capacity-building; gives special emphasis to the needs of least developed, land-locked and island developing countries, and to economies in transition in accelerating their industrial and technological advancement, promoting their exports, and furthering their integration into the region's economy; supports the development of electronic commerce and other information technologies in the region; and promotes the intra-regional and inter-subregional exchange of trade, investment and technology through the strengthening of institutional support services such as regional information networks.

Development research and policy analysis. Aims to increase the understanding of the economic and social development situation in the region, with particular attention given to sustainable economic growth, poverty alleviation, the integration of environmental concerns into macroeconomic decisions and policy-making processes, and enhancing the position of the region's disadvantaged economies. The sub-programme is responsible for the provision of technical assistance, and the production of relevant documents and publications.

Social development. The main objective of the sub-programme is to assess and respond to regional trends and challenges in social policy and human resources development, with particular attention to the planning and delivery of social services and training programmes for disadvantaged groups, including the poor, youths, women, the disabled, and the elderly. Implements global and regional mandates, such as the Programme of Action of the World Summit for Social Development and the Jakarta Plan of Action on Human Resources Development and Action for the Asian and Pacific Decade of Disabled Persons 1993–2002. In addition, the sub-programme aims to strengthen the capacity of public and non-government institutions to address the problems of marginalized social groups and to foster partnerships between governments, the private sector, community organizations and all other involved bodies. In 1998 ESCAP initiated a programme of assistance in establishing a regional network of Social Development Management Information Systems (SOMIS). Feasibility studies were conducted in three pilot countries in 1998–2000. In 2001 ESCAP undertook regional preparations for the World Summit on Sustainable Development, which was held in Johannesburg, South Africa, in September 2002, and collaborated with other agencies towards the adoption, in November 2001, of a Regional Platform on Sustainable Development for Asia and the Pacific.

Population and rural and urban development. Aims to assess and strengthen the capabilities of local institutions in rural and urban development, as well as increasing the capacity of governmental and non-governmental organizations to develop new approaches to poverty alleviation and to support food security for rural households. Promotes the correct use of agro-chemicals in order to increase food supply and to achieve sustainable agricultural development and administers the Fertilizer Advisory Development and Information Network for Asia and the Pacific (FADINAP). Rural employment opportunities and the access of the poor to land, credit and other productive assets are also considered by the sub-programme. Undertakes technical co-operation and research in the areas of ageing, female economic migration and reproductive health, and prepares specific publications relating to population. Implements global and regional mandates, such as the Programme of Action of the International Conference on Population and Development. The Secretariat co-ordinates the Asia-Pacific Population Information Network (POPIN). The fifth Asia and Pacific Population Conference was scheduled to be held in Bangkok, Thailand, in December 2002.

Environment and natural resources development. Concerned with strengthening national capabilities to achieve environmentally-sound and sustainable development by integrating economic concerns, such as the sustainable management of natural resources, into economic planning and policies. The sub-programme was responsible for implementation of the Regional Action Programme for Environmentally Sound and Sustainable Development for the period 1996–2000. Other activities have included the promotion of integrated water resources development and management, including water quality and a reduction in water-related natural disasters; strengthening the formulation of policies in the sustainable development of land and mineral resources; the consideration of energy resource options, such as rural energy supply, energy conservation and the planning of power networks; and promotion of the use of space technology applications for environmental management, natural disaster monitoring and sustainable development.

Transport, communications, tourism and infrastructure development. Aims to develop inter- and intra-regional transport links to enhance trade and tourism, mainly through implementation of an Asian Land Transport Infrastructure Development project. Other activities are aimed at improving the planning process in developing infrastructure facilities and services, in accordance with the regional action programme of the New Delhi Action Plan on Infrastructure Development in Asia and the Pacific, which was adopted at a ministerial conference held in October 1996, and at enhancing private sector involvement in national infrastructure development through financing, management, operations and risk-sharing. A Ministerial Conference on Infrastructure Development was organized by ESCAP in November 2001. The meeting concluded a memorandum of understanding, initially signed by ESCAP, Kazakhstan, the Republic of Korea, Mongolia and Russia, to facilitate the transport of container goods along the Trans-Asian Railway. The sub-programme aims to reduce the adverse environmental impact of the provision of infrastructure facilities and to promote more equitable and easier access to social amenities. Tourism concerns include the development of human resources, improved policy planning for tourism development, greater investment in the industry, and minimizing the environmental impact of tourism.

Statistics. Provides training and advice in priority areas, including national accounts statistics, gender statistics, population censuses and surveys, and the management of statistical systems. Supports co-ordination throughout the region of the development, implementation and revision of selected international statistical standards. Disseminates comparable socio-economic statistics, with increased use of the electronic media, promotes the use of modern information technology in the public sector and trains senior-level officials in the effective management of information technology.

Throughout all the sub-programmes, ESCAP aims to focus particular attention on the needs and concerns of least developed, land-locked and island developing nations, and economies in transition in the region.

CO-OPERATION WITH THE ASIAN DEVELOPMENT BANK

In July 1993 a memorandum of understanding was signed by ESCAP and the Asian Development Bank (ADB—q.v.), outlining priority areas of co-operation between the two organizations. These were: regional and sub-regional co-operation; issues concerning the least-developed, land-locked and island developing member countries; poverty alleviation; women in development; population; human resource development; the environment and natural resource management; statistics and data bases; economic analysis; transport and communications; and industrial restructuring and privatization. The two organizations were to co-operate in organizing workshops, seminars and conferences, in implementing joint projects, and in exchanging information and data on a regular basis.

ASSOCIATED BODIES

Asian and Pacific Centre for Transfer of Technology: Off New Qutab Institutional Area, POB 4575, New Delhi 110 016, India; tel. (11) 6966509; fax (11) 6856274; e-mail infocentre@apctt.org; internet www.apctt.org; f. 1977 to assist countries of the ESCAP region by strengthening their capacity to develop, transfer and adopt technologies relevant to the region, and to identify and to promote regional technology development and transfer. Dir Dr JÜRGEN H. BISCHOFF. Publs *Asia Pacific Tech Monitor, VATIS Updates on Biotechnology, Food Processing, Ozone Layer Protection, Non-Conventional Energy,* and *Waste Technology* (each every 2 months), *International Technology and Business Opportunities Update* (quarterly).

ESCAP/WMO Typhoon Committee: c/o UNDP, POB 7285, ADC, Pasay City, Metro Manila, Philippines; tel. (632) 3733443; fax (2) 3733419; e-mail tcs@philonline.com; f. 1968; an intergovernmental body sponsored by ESCAP and WMO for mitigation of typhoon damage. It aims at establishing efficient typhoon and flood warning systems through improved meteorological and telecommunication facilities. Other activities include promotion of disaster preparedness, training of personnel and co-ordination of research. The committee's programme is supported from national resources and also by UNDP and other international and bilateral assistance. Mems: Cambodia, People's Republic of China, Hong Kong, Japan, Democratic People's Republic of Korea, Republic of Korea, Laos, Macao, Malaysia, Philippines, Singapore, Thailand, USA, Viet Nam. Co-ordinator of Secretariat Dr ROMAN L. KINTANAR.

Regional Co-ordination Centre for Research and Development of Coarse Grains, Pulses, Roots and Tuber Crops in the Tropics of Asia and the Pacific (CGPRT Centre): Jalan Merdeka 145, Bogor 16111, Indonesia; tel. (251) 343277; fax (251) 336290; e-mail cgprt@cbn.net.id; internet www.cgprt.org.sg; f. 1981; initiates and promotes research, training and publications on the production, marketing and use of these crops. Dir Dr NOBUYOSHI MAENO. Publs *Palawija News* (quarterly), working paper series, monograph series and statistical profiles.

Statistical Institute for Asia and the Pacific: 2-2 Wakaba 3-chome, Mihama-ku, Chiba-shi, Chiba 261-8787, Japan; tel. (43) 2999782; fax (43) 2999780; e-mail staff@unsiap.or.jp; internet www.unsiap.or.jp; f. 1970; trains government statisticians; prepares teaching materials, provides facilities for special studies and research of a statistical nature, assists in the development of training on official statistics in national and sub-regional centres. Dir TOMAS P. AFRICA (Philippines).

WMO/ESCAP Panel on Tropical Cyclones: Technical Support Unit, c/o Pakistan Meteorological Dept, POB 1214, H-8, Islamabad, Pakistan; tel. (51) 9257314; fax (51) 432588; e-mail tsupmd@hotmail.com; f. 1973 to mitigate damage caused by tropical cyclones in the Bay of Bengal and the Arabian Sea. Mems: Bangladesh, India, Maldives, Myanmar, Pakistan, Sri Lanka, Thailand. Co-ordinator of Secretariat Dr QAMAR-UZ-ZAMAN CHAUDHRY.

Finance

For the two-year period 2000–01 ESCAP's regular budget, an appropriation from the UN budget, was US $57.0m. (compared with $67.5m. in 1998–99). The regular budget is supplemented annually by funds from various sources for technical assistance.

Publications

Annual Report.

Agro-chemicals News in Brief (quarterly).

Asia-Pacific Development Journal (2 a year).

Asia-Pacific in Figures (annually).

Asia-Pacific Population Journal (quarterly).

Asia-Pacific Remote Sensing and GIS Journal (2 a year).

Atlas of Mineral Resources of the ESCAP Region.

Confluence (water resources newsletter, 2 a year).

Economic and Social Survey of Asia and the Pacific (annually).

Environmental News Briefing (every 2 months).

ESCAP Energy News (2 a year).

ESCAP Human Resources Development Newsletter (2 a year).

ESCAP Population Data Sheet (annually).

ESCAP Tourism Newsletter (2 a year).

Fertilizer Trade Information Monthly Bulletin.

Foreign Trade Statistics of Asia and the Pacific (annually).

Government Computerization Newsletter (irregular).

Industry and Technology Development News for Asia and the Pacific (annually).

Poverty Alleviation Initiatives (quarterly).

Regional Network for Agricultural Machinery Newsletter (3 a year).

Small Industry Bulletin for Asia and the Pacific (annually).
Social Development Newsletter (2 a year).
Space Technology Applications Newsletter (quarterly).
Statistical Indicators for Asia and the Pacific (quarterly).
Statistical Newsletter (quarterly).
Statistical Yearbook for Asia and the Pacific.
Trade and Investment Information Bulletin (monthly).
Transport and Communications Bulletin for Asia and the Pacific (annually).
Water Resources Journal (quarterly).

Bibliographies; country and trade profiles; commodity prices; statistics.

United Nations Development Programme—UNDP

Address: One United Nations Plaza, New York, NY 10017, USA.

Telephone: (212) 906-5315; **fax:** (212) 906-5364; **e-mail:** hq@undp.org; **internet:** www.undp.org.

The Programme was established in 1965 by the UN General Assembly. Its central mission is to help countries eradicate poverty and achieve a sustainable level of human development.

Organization

(October 2002)

UNDP is responsible to the UN General Assembly, to which it reports through the UN Economic and Social Council (ECOSOC).

EXECUTIVE BOARD

The Executive Board is responsible for providing intergovernmental support to and supervision of the activities of UNDP and the UN Population Fund (UNFPA), of which UNDP is the governing body. It comprises 36 members: eight from Africa, seven from Asia, four from eastern Europe, five from Latin America and the Caribbean and 12 from western Europe and other countries.

SECRETARIAT

Offices and divisions at the Secretariat include: an Operations Support Group; the Emergency Response Division; Offices of the United Nations Development Group, the Human Development Report, Audit and Performance Review, and Communications; and Bureaux for Resources and Strategic Partnerships, Development Policy, and Management. Five regional bureaux, all at the Secretariat in New York, cover: Africa; Asia and the Pacific; the Arab states; Latin America and the Caribbean; and Europe and the Commonwealth of Independent States.

Administrator: MARK MALLOCH BROWN (United Kingdom).

Assistant Administrator and Director, Regional Bureau for Asia and the Pacific: HAFIZ PASHA.

COUNTRY OFFICES

In almost every country receiving UNDP assistance there is an office, headed by the UNDP Resident Representative, who usually also serves as the UN Resident Co-ordinator, responsible for the co-ordination of all UN technical assistance and operational development activities, advising the Government on formulating the country programme, ensuring that field activities are carried out, and acting as the leader of the UN team of experts working in the country. The offices function as the primary presence of the UN in most developing countries.

OFFICES OF UNDP REPRESENTATIVES IN THE FAR EAST AND AUSTRALASIA

Afghanistan: (currently operating from Pakistan office).

Bangladesh: POB 224, 8A, Begum Rokeya Sharani Sher-e-Bangla Nagar, Dhaka 1207; tel. (2) 8118600; fax (2) 8113196; e-mail registry.bd@undp; internet www.un-bd.org/undp.

Bhutan: UN House, GPO Box 162, Dremton Lam, Thimphu; tel. (2) 322424; fax (2) 322657; e-mail fo.btn@undp.org; internet www.undp.org.bt/Index2.htm.

Cambodia: 53 rue Pasteur, Boeung Keng Kang, POB 877, Phnom-Penh; tel. (23) 216167; fax (23) 216257; e-mail registry@undp.forum.org.kh; internet www.un.org.kh/undp.

China, People's Republic: 2 Liangmahe Nan Lu, 100600 Beijing; tel. (10) 65323730; fax (10) 65322567; e-mail registry.cn@undp.org; internet www.unchina.org/undp.

East Timor: Caicoli St 14, Dili; tel. (390) 312481; fax (390) 312408; e-mail registry.tp@undp.org; internet www.undp.east-timor.org.

Fiji: Private Mail Bag, Reserve Bank Bldg, Pratt St, Suva; tel. 331-2500; fax 330-1718; e-mail fo.fiji@undp.org.fj; internet www.undp.org.fj (also covers French Polynesia, Kiribati, Marshall Islands, Federated States of Micronesia, Nauru, New Caledonia, Palau, Solomon Islands, Tonga, Tuvalu, Vanuatu and Wallis and Futuna).

India: POB 3059, 55 Lodhi Estate, New Delhi 110003; tel. (11) 4628877; fax (11) 4627612; internet www.undp.org.in.

Indonesia: POB 2338, 14 Jalan M. H. Thamrin, Jakarta 10240; tel. (21) 314-1308; fax (21) 314-4251; e-mail media.id@undp.org; internet www.un.or.id/undp.

Japan: UNU Bldg, 8th Floor, 5-53-70, Jingumae, Shibuya-ku, Tokyo 150-0001; tel. (3) 5467-4751; fax (3) 5467-4753; e-mail fo.jpn@undp.org; internet www.undp.or.jp/indexe.htm.

Korea, Democratic People's Republic: POB 27, 21 Munsudong, Pyongyang; tel. (2) 3817566; fax (2) 3817603; e-mail fo.prk@undp.org; internet undp-dprk.apdip.net.

Korea, Republic: Central POB 143, 794-4 Hannam Dong, Yongsan-ku, Seoul 140-210; tel. (2) 790-9562; fax (2) 749-1417; internet www.undp.or.kr.

Laos: POB 345, Route Phon Kheng, Vientiane; tel. (21) 213390; fax (21) 214819; e-mail fo.lao@undp.org; internet www.undplao.org.

Malaysia: Block C, Damansara Offices Complex, Jalan Dungun, Damansara Heights, 50490 Kuala Lumpur; tel. (3) 2559122; fax (3) 2552870; e-mail info.my@undp.org.my; internet www.undp.org.my (also covers Brunei and Singapore).

Maldives: POB 2058, UN Bldg, Buruzu Magu, Radhdebai Higun, Malé; tel. 324501; fax 324504; e-mail registry.mv@undp.org; internet www.mv.undp.org.

Mongolia: POB 49/207, 7 Erkhuu St, Ulan Bator; tel. (1) 327585; fax (1) 326221; e-mail registry.mn@undp.org; internet www.un-mongolia.mn/undp.

Myanmar: POB 650, No. 6 Natmauk Rd, Yangon; tel. (1) 92637; fax (1) 92739; internet www.mm.undp.org.

Nepal: POB 107, UN Bldg, Pulchowk, Kathmandu; tel. (1) 523200; fax (1) 523986; e-mail registry.np@undp.org; internet www.undp.org.np.

Pakistan: POB 1051, Saudi Pak Towers, 9th Floor, Islamabad; tel. (51) 280-0133; fax (51) 280-0031; e-mail webmaster@undp.un.org.pk; internet www.un.org.pk/undp.

Papua New Guinea: POB 1041, ADF House, 3rd Level, Musgrave St, Port Moresby; tel. 3212877; fax 3211224; e-mail fo.png@undp.org; internet www.undp.org.pg.

Philippines: POB 2865, NEDA Sa Makati Bldg, 106 Amorsolo St, Legaspi Village, Makati City; tel. (2) 8920611; fax (2) 8164061; e-mail registry.ph@undp.org; internet www.undp.org.ph.

Samoa: Lauofo Meti's Bldg, Four Corners, Matautu-uta, Private Mail Bag, Apia; tel. 23670; fax 23555; e-mail registry.ws@undp.org; internet www.undp.org.ws (also covers Cook Islands, Niue and Tokelau).

Sri Lanka: POB 1505, 204 Bauddhaloka Mawatha, Colombo 7; tel. (1) 580691; fax (1) 581116; e-mail registry.lk@undp.org; internet www.undp.lk.

Thailand: GPO Box 618, UN Bldg, 12th Floor, Rajdamnern Ave, Bangkok 10200; tel. (2) 2882138; fax (2) 2800556; e-mail registry.th@undp.org; internet www.undp.or.th (also covers Hong Kong).

Viet Nam: 25–29 Phan Bôi Chan, Hanoi; tel. (4) 9421495; fax (4) 9422267; e-mail registry@undp.org.vn; internet www.undp.org.vn.

Activities

As the world's largest source of grant-funded technical assistance for developing countries, UNDP provides advisory and support services to governments and UN teams. Assistance is mostly non-monetary, comprising the provision of experts' services, consultancies, equipment and training for local workers, including fellowships for advanced study abroad. UNDP supports programme countries in attracting aid and utilizing it efficiently. The Programme is committed to allocating some 88% of its regular resources to low-income developing countries. Developing countries themselves contribute significantly to the total project costs in terms of personnel, facilities, equipment and supplies.

Since the mid-1990s UNDP has strengthened its focus on results, streamlining its management practices and promoting clearly defined objectives for the advancement of sustainable human development. Under 'UNDP 2001', an extensive internal process of reform initiated during the late 1990s, UNDP placed increased emphasis on its activities in the field and on performance and accountability, focusing on the following priority areas: democratic governance; poverty reduction; crisis prevention and recovery; energy and environment; promotion of information and communications technology; and combating HIV/AIDS. In 2001 UNDP established six Thematic Trust Funds, covering each of these areas, to enable increased support of its programme activities. Gender equality and the provision of country-level aid co-ordination services are also important focus areas. In accordance with the more results-oriented approach developed under the 'UNDP 2001' process the Programme has introduced a new Multi-Year Funding Framework (MYFF), the first phase of which covers the period 2000–03. The MYFF outlines the country-driven goals around which funding is to be mobilized, integrating programme objectives, resources, budget and outcomes. It provides the basis for the Administrator's Business Plans for the same duration and enables policy coherence in the implementation of programmes at country, regional and global levels. A Results-Oriented Annual Report (ROAR) was produced for the first time in 2000 from data compiled by country offices and regional programmes. It was hoped that UNDP's greater focus on performance would generate increased voluntary contributions from donors, thereby strengthening the Programme's core resource base. In September 2000 the first ever Ministerial Meeting of ministers of development co-operation and foreign affairs and other senior officials from donor and programme countries, convened in New York, USA, endorsed UNDP's new orientation.

From the mid-1990s UNDP also determined to assume a more active and integrative role within the UN system-wide development framework. UNDP Resident Representatives—usually also serving as UN Resident Co-ordinators, with responsibility for managing inter-agency co-operation on sustainable human development initiatives at country level—were to play a focal role in implementing this approach. In order to promote its co-ordinating function UNDP allocated increased resources to training and skill-sharing programmes. In late 1997 the UNDP Administrator was appointed to chair the UN Development Group (UNDG), which was established as part of a series of structural reform measures initiated by the UN Secretary-General, with the aim of strengthening collaboration between all UN funds, programmes and bodies concerned with development. The UNDG promotes coherent policy at country level through the system of UN Resident Co-ordinators (see above), the Common Country Assessment mechanism (CCA, a country-based process for evaluating national development situations), and the UN Development Assistance Framework (UNDAF, the foundation for planning and co-ordinating development operations at country level, based on the CCA). Within the framework of the Administrator's Business Plans for 2000–03 a new Bureau for Resources and Strategic Partnerships was established to build and strengthen working partnerships with other UN bodies, donor and programme countries, international financial institutions and development banks, civil society organizations and the private sector. The Bureau was also to serve UNDP's regional bureaux and country offices through the exchange of information and promotion of partnership strategies.

UNDP has a catalyst and co-ordinating function as the focus of UN system-wide efforts to achieve the so-called Millennium Goals, pledged by governments attending a summit meeting of the UN General Assembly in September 2000. The objectives included a reduction by 50% in the number of people with income of less than US $1 a day and those suffering from hunger and lack of safe drinking water by 2015. Other commitments made concerned equal access to education for girls and boys, the provision of universal primary education, the reduction of maternal mortality by 75%, and the reversal of the spread of HIV/AIDS and other diseases.

UNDP aims to help governments to reassess their development priorities and to design initiatives for sustainable human development. UNDP country offices support the formulation of national human development reports (NHDRs), which aim to facilitate activities such as policy-making, the allocation of resources and monitoring progress towards poverty eradication and sustainable development. In addition, the preparation of Advisory Notes and Country Co-operation Frameworks by UNDP officials help to highlight country-specific aspects of poverty eradiction and national strategic priorities. In January 1998 the Executive Board adopted eight guiding principles relating to sustainable human development that were to be implemented by all country offices, in order to ensure a focus to UNDP activities. A network of Sub-regional Resource Facilities (SURFs) has been established to strengthen and co-ordinate UNDP's technical assistance services. Since 1990 UNDP has published an annual global *Human Development Report*, incorporating a Human Development Index, which ranks countries in terms of human development, using three key indicators: life expectancy, adult literacy and basic income required for a decent standard of living. In 1997 a Human Poverty Index and a Gender-related Development Index, which assesses gender equality on the basis of life expectancy, education and income, were introduced into the Report for the first time.

UNDP's activities to facilitate poverty eradication include support for capacity-building programmes and initiatives to generate sustainable livelihoods, for example by improving access to credit, land and technologies, and the promotion of strategies to improve education and health provision for the poorest elements of populations (with a focus on women and girls). In March 1996 UNDP launched the Poverty Strategies Initiative (PSI) to strengthen national capacities to assess and monitor the extent of poverty and to combat the problem. All PSI projects were intended to involve representatives of governments, the private sector, social organizations and research institutions in policy debate and formulation. With the World Bank, UNDP helps governments of developing countries applying for international debt relief to draft Poverty Reduction Stategy Papers. In May 2001 UNDP signed a memorandum of understanding with the Asian Development Bank to provide for strengthened collaboration, in particular in joint activities relating to poverty measurement and assessment. In 1997 a UNDP scheme to support private-sector and community-based initiatives to generate employment opportunities, MicroStart, became operational.

Approximately one-quarter of all UNDP programme resources support national efforts to ensure efficient and accaountable governance and to build effective relations between the state, the private sector and civil society, which are essential to achieving sustainable development. UNDP undertakes assessment missions to help ensure free and fair elections and works to promote human rights, a transparent and competent public sector, a competent judicial system and decentralized government and decision-making. In September 1999 the Regional Bureau for Asia and the Pacific inaugurated a Regional Governance Programme, with the aim of supporting the implementation of reforms required at national level for the achievement of these goals. In May/June 1999 a World Conference on Governance was held in Manila, the Philippines, attended by some 1,000 government officials and representatives of the private sector and non-governmental organizations. UNDP sponsored a series of meetings held on the subject of Building Capacities for Governance. In July 2000 a sub-regional conference on urbanization and good governance was held at the SAARC secretariat, in Kathmandu, Nepal, jointly organized by the Nepalese Government and UNDP. The meeting adopted the Kathmandu Declaration, which incorporated a strategic vision on governance in South Asia. During 2001 UNDP undertook a large-scale civic education campaign to ensure a peaceful general election in East Timor, which was conducted in late August.

UNDP plays a role in developing the agenda for international co-operation on environmental and energy issues, focusing on the relationship between energy policies, environmental protection, poverty and development. UNDP supports the development of national programmes that emphasize the sustainable management of natural resources, for example through its Sustainable Energy Initiative, which promotes more efficient use of energy resources and the introduction of renewable alternatives to conventional fuels. UNDP is also concerned with forest management, the aquatic environment and sustainable agriculture and food security. Its 'Africa 2000' networks support small-scale agricultural projects, such as irrigation schemes, to help eradicate poverty and promote environmentally sustainable development. Within UNDP's framework of urban development activities the Local Initiative Facility for Urban Environment (LIFE) undertakes small-scale environmental projects in low-income communities, in collaboration with local authorities and community-based groups. Other initiatives include the Urban Management Programme and the Public-Private Partnerships Programme for the Urban Environment which aimed to generate funds, promote research and support new technologies to enhance sustainable environments in urban areas. In 1996 UNDP initiated a process of collaboration between city authorities world-wide to promote implementation of the commitments made at the 1995 Copenhagen summit for social development (see below) and to help to combat aspects of poverty and other urban problems, such as poor housing, transport, the management of waste disposal, water supply and sanitation. The first Forum of the so-called World Alliance of Cities Against Poverty was convened in October 1998, in Lyon, France. The second Forum took place in April 2000 in Geneva, Switzerland, and the third Forum was held in April 2002 in Huy, Belgium.

UNDP is a co-sponsor, jointly with WHO, the World Bank, UNDCP, UNICEF, UNESCO, ILO and UNFPA, of the Joint UN Programme on HIV/AIDS (UNAIDS), which became operational on 1 January 1996. UNDP has initiated a regional programme to help to counter the HIV/AIDS epidemic, which was to be implemented through four sub-regional components and one region-wide development project. Some US $5.6m. was committed to the programme over the three-year period 1999–2001.

UNDP has responsibility for co-ordinating activities following global UN conferences. In March 1995 government representatives attending the World Summit for Social Development, held in Copenhagen, Denmark, approved initiatives to promote the eradication of poverty, to increase and reallocate official development assistance to basic social programmes and to promote equal access to education. The Programme of Action adopted at the meeting advocated that UNDP support the implementation of social development programmes, co-ordinate these efforts through its field offices and organize efforts on the part of the UN system to stimulate capacity-building at local, national and regional levels. The PSI (see above) was introduced following the Summit. A special session of the UN General Assembly to review the implementation of the Summit's objectives was convened in June 2000. Following the UN Fourth World Conference on Women, held in Beijing, People's Republic of China, in September 1995, UNDP led inter-agency efforts to ensure the full participation of women in all economic, political and professional activities and assisted with further situation analysis and training activities. UNDP also created a Gender in Development Office to ensure that women participate more fully in UNDP-supported activities. In June 2000 a special session of the UN General Assembly was convened to review the conference, entitled Women 2000: Gender Equality, Development and Peace for the 21st Century (Beijing + 5). UNDP played an important role, at both national and international levels, in preparing for the second UN Conference on Human Settlements (Habitat II), which was held in Istanbul, Turkey, in June 1996. At the conference UNDP announced the establishment of a new facility, which was designed to promote private-sector investment in urban infrastructure. A special session of the UN General Assembly, entitled Istanbul + 5, was held in June 2001 to report on the implementation of the recommendations of the Habitat II conference.

UNDP collaborates with other UN agencies in countries in crisis and with special circumstances to promote relief and development efforts, in order to secure the foundations for sustainable human development, and thereby increase national capabilities to prevent or pre-empt future crises. In particular, UNDP is concerned to achieve reconciliation, reintegration and reconstruction in affected countries, as well as to support emergency interventions and manage the delivery of programme aid. UNDP has established a mine action unit within its Bureau for Crisis Prevention and Recovery in order to strengthen national de-mining capabilities. UNDP is the focal point within the UN system for strengthening national capacities for natural disaster reduction (prevention, preparedness and mitigation relating to natural, environmental and technological hazards). Its Disaster Management Programme oversees the system-wide Disaster Management Training Programme. In March 1998, in response to the financial crisis that emerged in South-East Asia in late 1997, UNDP initiated a programme of Special Assistance to Countries in Economic Crisis in Asia, which aimed to assist governments with planning policies to address the social consequences of the economic downturn. UNDP undertook rehabilitation activities in East Timor prior to its independence in May 2002. Following the devastating earthquake that occurred in Gujarat, India, in January 2001, UNDP undertook a major role in the co-ordination of aid, and facilitation of assistance and reconstruction efforts. It aimed to reduce the future vulnerability of rural communities through improved reconstruction standards and the establishment of disaster management mechanisms. In January 2002 UNDP, the World Bank and the Asian Development Bank announced the results of a jointly-prepared preliminary 'needs assessment' report for reconstruction efforts in Afghanistan: it was estimated that US $15,000m. in donor financing would be required over 10 years, of which US $5,000m. would need to be provided in the first 2.5 years. In mid-2002 UNDP was implementing a Recovery and Employment Afghanistan Programme (REAP), assisting the Afghan Interim Authority with the development of a database to track aid donations and supporting civil service reforms.

UNDP supports the Tumen River Area Development Programme, under which China, the Democratic People's Republic of Korea, the Republic of Korea, Mongolia and Russia collaborate to study the feasibility of joint development activity. In December 1995 the Governments agreed to pursue more formal arrangements for promoting economic and technical co-operation in the Tumen River Economic Development Area. A Secretariat, to administer an inter-governmental Consultation Commission and a Co-ordination Committee, was subsequently established in Beijing, China. In April 1995 the Governments of Cambodia, Laos, Thailand and Viet Nam signed an agreement for sustainable development in the Mekong River Basin, following two years of negotiations, during which UNDP provided technical support and encouragement. UNDP provided financing for the preparatory assistance phase of the implementation of the agreement, and supports the institutional capacity development of the Mekong River Commission as an independent intergovernmental organization to supervise the development, conservation and management of the river basin and its resources.

UNDP aims to ensure that, rather than creating an ever-widening 'digital divide', ongoing rapid advancements in information technology are harnessed by poorer countries to accelerate progress in achieving sustainable human development. UNDP advises governments on technology policy, promotes digital entrepreneurship in programme countries and works with private-sector partners to provide reliable and affordable communications networks. UNDP and the World Bank jointly host the secretariat of the Digital Opportunity Task Force, a partnership between industrialized nations, developing countries, business and non-governmental organizations that was established in 2000. The Bureau for Development Policy operates the Information Technology for Development Programme, which aims to promote sustainable human development through increased utilization of information and communications technologies globally. The Programme aims to establish technology access centres in developing countries. A Sustainable Development Networking Programme focuses on expanding internet connectivity in poorer countries through building national capacities and supporting local internet sites. UNDP has used mobile internet units to train people even in isolated rural areas.

In 1999 UNDP, in collaboration with an international communications company, Cisco Systems, and other partners, launched NetAid, an internet-based forum (accessible at www.netaid.org) for mobilizing and co-ordinating fundraising and other activities aimed at alleviating poverty and promoting sustainable development. With Cisco Systems and other partners, UNDP has worked to establish academies of information technology to support training and capacity-building in developing countries. By February 2002 70 academies had been established in 34 countries.

In 1996 UNDP implemented its first corporate communications and advocacy strategy, which aimed to generate public awareness of the activities of the UN system, to promote debate on development issues and to mobilize resources by increasing public and donor appreciation of UNDP. UNDP sponsors the International Day for the Eradication of Poverty, held annually on 17 October.

Finance

UNDP and its various funds and programmes are financed by the voluntary contributions of members of the United Nations and the Programme's participating agencies, as well as by cost-sharing by recipient governments. In 2000 total voluntary contributions amounted to US $2,400m., of which US $634m. was for regular (core) resources (compared with US $681m. in 1999). Donor co-finance, including trust funds and cost-sharing by third parties, amounted to US $571m. in 2000, while cost-sharing by programme country governments amounted to more than US $900m. It was hoped that the introduction of a new Multi-Year Funding Framework for the four-year period 2000–03 and of Results-Oriented Annual Reports from 2000 (see above) would increase UNDP's resource base by stimulating an increase in voluntary contributions. In 2000 field programme expenditure under UNDP's regular programme totalled US $1,458m.

Publications

Annual Report of the Administrator.

Choices (quarterly).

Global Public Goods: International Co-operation in the 21st Century.

Human Development Report (annually).

Poverty Report (annually).

Results-Oriented Annual Report.

Associated Funds and Programmes

UNDP is the central funding, planning and co-ordinating body for technical co-operation within the UN. Associated programmes, financed separately by means of voluntary contributions, provide specific services through the UNDP network.

UNITED NATIONS CAPITAL DEVELOPMENT FUND—UNCDF

The Fund was established in 1966 and became fully operational in 1974. It invests in poor communities in developing countries through local governance projects and microfinance operations, with the aim of increasing such communities' access to essential local infrastructure and services and thereby improving their productive capacities and self-reliance. UNCDF encourages participation by local people and local government in the planning, implementation and monitoring of projects. The Fund aims to promote the interests of women in community projects and to enhance their earning capacities. By 1999 56 countries had received UNCDF assistance, including 15 nations from the Asia and Pacific region. In 1998 UNCDF nominated 15 countries (including Bangladesh, Bhutan, Cambodia and Nepal) in which to focus subsequent programmes. A Special Unit for Microfinance (SUM) was established in 1997 as a joint UNDP/UNCDF operation, was fully integrated into UNCDF in 1999. UNCDF's annual programming budget amounts to some US $40m.

Executive Secretary: NORMAND LAUZON.

UNITED NATIONS DEVELOPMENT FUND FOR WOMEN—UNIFEM

UNIFEM provides direct financial and technical support to enable low-income women in developing countries to increase earnings, gain access to labour-saving technologies and otherwise improve the quality of their lives. It also funds activities that include women in decision-making related to mainstream development projects. UNIFEM collaborates with other UN organizations, governments and non-government organizations to promote women's issues in the planning and implementation of projects. In 2000 UNIFEM approved 77 new projects and continued to support some 159 ongoing programmes world-wide. UNIFEM has supported the preparation of national reports in 30 countries and used the priorities identified in these reports and in other regional initiatives to formulate a Women's Development Agenda for the 21st century. Through these efforts, UNIFEM played an active role in the preparation for the UN Fourth World Conference on Women, which was held in Beijing, China, in September 1995. UNIFEM participated in a special session of the UN General Assembly convened in June 2000 to review the conference, entitled Women 2000: Gender Equality, Development and Peace for the 21st Century (Beijing + 5). In March 2001 UNIFEM, in collaboration with International Alert, launched a Millennium Peace Prize for Women. In January 2002 UNIFEM appealed for US $12m. to support women's leadership in the ongoing peace-building and reconstruction process in Afghanistan. Programme expenditure in 2000 amounted to US $25.4m.

Director: NOELEEN HEYZER (Singapore).

UNITED NATIONS VOLUNTEERS—UNV

The United Nations Volunteers is an important source of middle-level skills for the UN development system, supplied at modest cost, particularly in the least-developed countries. Volunteers expand the scope of UNDP project activities by supplementing the work of international and host-country experts and by extending the influence of projects to local community levels. One of the most important parts of UNV's work is the support of technical co-operation within and among the developing countries by encouraging specialists and field workers from the countries themselves and by forming regional exchange teams made up of such volunteers. The UN Short-term Advisory (UNISTAR) Programme, which is the private-sector development branch of the UNV, has increasingly focused its attention upon countries in the process of economic transition. In addition to development activities, UNV has been increasingly involved in areas such as election and human-rights monitoring, peace-building and community-based programmmes concerned with environmental management and protection.

Since 1994 UNV has administered UNDP's Transfer of Knowledge Through Expatriate Nationals (TOKTEN) programme, which was initiated in 1977 to enable specialists and professionals from developing countries to contribute to development efforts in their countries of origin through short-term technical assignments.

By January 2002 2,946 UNVs were serving in 132 countries. At that time more than 30,000 people had served under the initiative amounted in some 140 countries.

Executive Co-ordinator: SHARON CAPELING-ALAKIJA.

GLOBAL ENVIRONMENT FACILITY—GEF

The GEF, which is managed jointly by UNDP, the World Bank and UNEP, began operations in 1991 for an initial pilot phase covering 1991–94. Its aim is to support projects for the prevention of climate change, conserving biological diversity, protecting international waters, and reducing ozone layer depletion. UNDP is responsible for capacity-building, targeted research, pre-investment activities and technical assistance. UNDP also administers the Small Grants Programme of the GEF, which supports community-based activities by local non-governmental organizations. During the pilot phase of the GEF total funding was US $1,500m. In 1994 representatives of 34 countries agreed to provide US $2,000m. to replenish GEF funds. In 1998 36 donor countries pledged US $2,750m. for the next replenishment of GEF funds (GEF-2) covering the period 1 July 1998–30 June 2002. At 30 June 2000 the GEF portfolio comprised 165 projects; 94 projects had been completed at that time. During 1991–99 some US $939m. in funding was approved for the GEF-UNDP project portfolio. The GEF administers a regional project on the prevention and management of marine pollution in East Asian seas and a South Pacific Biodiversity Programme.

United Nations Environment Programme—UNEP

Address: POB 30552, Nairobi, Kenya.

Telephone: (20) 621234; **fax:** (20) 624489; **e-mail:** cpiinfo@unep.org; **internet:** www.unep.org.

The United Nations Environment Programme was established in 1972 by the UN General Assembly, following recommendations of the 1972 UN Conference on the Human Environment, in Stockholm, Sweden, to encourage international co-operation in matters relating to the human environment.

Organization

(October 2002)

GOVERNING COUNCIL

The main functions of the Governing Council, which meets every two years, are to promote international co-operation in the field of the environment and provide general policy guide-lines for the direction and co-ordination of environmental programmes within the UN system. It comprises representatives of 58 states, elected by the UN General Assembly, for four-year terms, on a rotating basis. The Council is assisted in its work by a Committee of Permanent Representatives.

HIGH-LEVEL COMMITTEE OF MINISTERS AND OFFICIALS IN CHARGE OF THE ENVIRONMENT

The Committee was established by the Governing Council in 1997, with a mandate to consider the international environmental agenda and to make recommendations to the Council on reform and policy issues. In addition, the Committee, comprising 36 elected members, was to provide guidance and advice to the Executive Director, to enhance UNEP's collaboration and co-operation with other multilateral bodies and to help to mobilize financial resources for UNEP.

SECRETARIAT

Offices and divisions at UNEP headquarters include the the Office of the Executive Director; the Secretariat for Governing Bodies; Offices for Evaluation and Oversight, Programme Co-ordination and Management, and Resource Mobilization; and divisions of communications and public information, early warning and assessment, policy development and law, policy implementation, technology and industry and economics, regional co-operation and representation, environmental conventions, and GEF co-ordination.

Executive Director: Dr KLAUS TÖPFER (Germany).

REGIONAL OFFICES

Asia and the Pacific: UN Bldg, 10th Floor, Rajdamnern Ave, Bangkok 10200, Thailand; tel. (2) 288-1870; fax (2) 280-3829; e-mail unep.unescap@un.org; internet www.roap.unep.org.

West Asia: POB 10880, Manama, Bahrain; tel. 276072; fax 276075; e-mail www.uneprowa@unep.org.bh.

OTHER OFFICES

Convention on International Trade in Endangered Species of Wild Fauna and Flora (CITES): 15 chemin des Anémones, 1219 Châtelaine, Geneva, Switzerland; tel. (22) 9178139; fax (22) 7973417; e-mail cites@unep.ch; internet www.cites.org; Sec.-Gen. WILLEM WOUTER WIJNSTEKERS.

Global Programme of Action for the Protection of the Marine Environment from Land-based Activities: POB 16227, 2500 The Hague, The Netherlands; tel. (70) 411460; fax (70) 3456648; e-mail gpa@unep.nl; internet www.gpa.unep.org; Co-ordinator VEERLE VANDEWEERD.

Regional Co-ordinating Unit for East Asian Seas: UN Bldg, 10th Floor, Rajdamnern Ave, Bangkok 10200, Thailand; tel. (2) 228-

1860; fax (2) 281-2428; e-mail kirkman.unescap@un.org; internet www.roap.unep.org/easrcu/index.htm.

Secretariat of the Basel Convention: 15 chemin des Anémones, 1219 Châtelaine, Geneva, Switzerland; tel. (22) 9178128; fax (22) 7973454; e-mail sbc@unep.ch; internet www.basel.int; Exec. Sec. SACHIKO KUWABARA-YAMAMOTO.

Secretariat of the Convention on Biological Diversity: World Trade Centre, 393 St Jacques St, Suite 300, Montréal, QC H2Y 1N9, Canada; tel. (514) 288-2220; fax (514) 288-6588; e-mail secretariat@biodiv.org; internet www.biodiv.org; Exec. Sec. Dr HAMDALLAH ZEDAN.

Secretariat of the Multilateral Fund for the Implementation of the Montreal Protocol: 1800 McGill College Ave, 27th Floor, Montréal, QC H3A 3J6, Canada; tel. (514) 282-1122; fax (514) 282-0068; e-mail secretariat@unmfs.org; internet www.unmfs.org; Chief Dr OMAR EL-ARINI.

UNEP Chemicals: 11-13 chemin des Anémones, 1219 Châtelaine, Geneva, Switzerland; tel. (22) 9178111; fax (22) 7973460; e-mail opereira@unep.ch; internet www.chem.unep.ch; Dir JAMES B. WILLIS.

UNEP Division of Technology, Industry and Economics: Tour Mirabeau, 39–43 quai André Citroen, 75739 Paris Cédex 15, France; tel. 1-44-37-14-41; fax 1-44-37-14-74; e-mail unep.tie@unep.fr; internet www.uneptie.org; Dir JACQUELINE ALOISI DE LARDEREL.

UNEP International Environmental Technology Centre: 2-110 Ryokuchi koen, Tsurumi-ku, Osaka 538-0036, Japan; tel. (6) 6915-4581; fax (6) 6915-0304; e-mail ietc@unep.or.jp; internet www.unep.or.jp; Dir STEVE HALLS.

UNEP Ozone Secretariat: POB 30552, Nairobi, Kenya; tel. (20) 623885; fax (20) 623913; e-mail ozoneinfo@unep.org; internet www.unep.org/ozone/; Officer-in-Charge MICHAEL GRABER.

UNEP Secretariat for the UN Scientific Committee on the Effects of Atomic Radiation: Vienna International Centre, Wagramerstrasse 5, 1400 Vienna, Austria; tel. (1) 26060-4330; fax (1) 26060-5902; e-mail norman.gentner@unvienna.un.or.at; internet www.unscear.org; Sec. NORMAN GENTNER.

UNEP/CMS (Convention on the Conservation of Migratory Species of Wild Animals) **Secretariat:** Martin-Luther-King-Str 8, 53175 Bonn, Germany; tel. (228) 8152401; fax (228) 8152449; e-mail cms@unep.de; internet www.wcmc.org.uk/cms; Exec. Sec. ARNULF MÜLLER-HELMBRECHT.

Activities

UNEP serves as a focal point for environmental action within the UN system. It aims to maintain a constant watch on the changing state of the environment; to analyse the trends; to assess the problems using a wide range of data and techniques; and to promote projects leading to environmentally sound development. It plays a catalytic and co-ordinating role within and beyond the UN system. Many UNEP projects are implemented in co-operation with other UN agencies, particularly UNDP, the World Bank group, FAO, UNESCO and WHO. About 45 intergovernmental organizations outside the UN system and 60 international non-governmental organizations have official observer status on UNEP's Governing Council, and, through the Environment Liaison Centre in Nairobi, UNEP is linked to more than 6,000 non-governmental bodies concerned with the environment.

In February 1997 the Governing Council, at its 19th session, adopted a ministerial declaration (the Nairobi Declaration) on UNEP's future role and mandate, which recognized the organization as the principal UN body working in the field of the environment and as the leading global environmental authority, setting and overseeing the international environmental agenda. In June a special session of the UN General Assembly, referred to as 'Rio + 5', was convened to review the state of the environment and progress achieved in implementing the objectives of the UN Conference on Environment and Development (UNCED) in Rio de Janeiro, Brazil, in June 1992. The meeting adopted a Programme for Further Implementation of Agenda 21 (a programme of activities to promote sustainable development, adopted by UNCED) in order to intensify efforts in areas such as energy, freshwater resources and technology transfer. The meeting confirmed UNEP's essential role in advancing the Programme and as a global authority promoting a coherent legal and political approach to the environmental challenges of sustainable development. An extensive process of restructuring and realignment of functions was subsequently initiated by UNEP, and a new organizational structure reflecting the decisions of the Nairobi Declaration was implemented during 1999. UNEP played a leading role in preparing for the World Summit on Sustainable Development (WSSD), held in August/September 2002 in Johannesburg, South Africa, to assess strategies for strengthening the implementation of Agenda 21. Governments participating in the conference made commitments to attaining several objectives, including a reduction by one-half in the proportion of people world-wide lacking access to clean water or good sanitation by 2015, the restocking of depleted fisheries by 2015, a reduction in the ongoing loss in biodiversity by 2010, and the production and utilization of chemicals without causing harm to human beings and the environment by 2020. Participants also determined to increase usage of renewable energy sources. A large number of partnerships between governments, private sector interests and civil society groups were announced at the conference.

In May 2000 UNEP sponsored the first annual Global Ministerial Environment Forum (GMEF), held in Malmö, Sweden, and attended by environment ministers and other government delegates from more than 130 countries. Participants reviewed policy issues in the field of the environment and addressed issues such as the impact on the environment of population growth, the depletion of the earth's natural resources, climate change and the need for fresh water supplies. The Forum issued the Malmö Declaration which identified the effective implementation of international agreements on environmental matters at national level as the most pressing challenge for policy makers. The Declaration emphasized the importance of mobilizing domestic and international resources and urged increased co-operation from civil society and the private sector in achieving sustainable development. The second GMEF, held in Nairobi, Kenya in February 2001, addressed means of strengthening international environmental governance, and established an Open-Ended Intergovernmental Group of Ministers or Their Representatives to prepare a report on possible reforms. GMEF-3, held in Cartagena, Colombia, in February 2002, considered UNEP's participation in the forthcoming WSSD, with a focus on environmental guidance issues.

ENVIRONMENTAL ASSESSMENT AND EARLY WARNING

The Nairobi Declaration resolved that the strengthening of UNEP's information, monitoring and assessment capabilities was a crucial element of the organization's restructuring, in order to help establish priorities for international, national and regional action, and to ensure the efficient and accurate dissemination of emerging environmental trends and emergencies.

In 1995 UNEP launched the Global Environment Outlook (GEO) process of environmental assessment. UNEP is assisted in its analysis of the state of the global environment by an extensive network of collaborating centres. Reports on the process are issued every two–three years. (The first *Global Environment Outlook, GEO-1*, was published in January 1997, the second, *GEO 2000*, in September 1999, and *GEO-3* in May 2002.) UNEP is leading a major Global International Waters Assessment (GIWA) to consider all aspects of the world's water-related issues, in particular problems of shared transboundary waters, and of future sustainable management of water resources. UNEP is also a sponsoring agency of the Joint Group of Experts on the Scientific Aspects of Marine Environmental Pollution and contributes to the preparation of reports on the state of the marine environment and on the impact of land-based activities on that environment. In November 1995 UNEP published a Global Biodiversity Assessment, which was the first comprehensive study of biological resources throughout the world. The UNEP-World Conservation Monitoring Centre (UNEP-WCMC), established in June 2000, provides biodiversity-related assessment. UNEP is a partner in the International Coral Reef Action Network—ICRAN, which was established in 2000 to manage and protect coral reefs world-wide. In June 2001 UNEP launched the Millennium Ecosystems Assessment, which was expected to be completed in 2004. Other major assessments under way in 2002 included the Assessment of Impact and Adaptation to Climate Change; the Solar and Wind Energy Resource Assessment; the Regionally-Based Assessment of Persistent Toxic Substances; the Land Degradation Assessment in Drylands; and the Global Methodology for Mapping Human Impacts on the Biosphere (GLOBIO) project.

UNEP's environmental information network includes the Global Resource Information Database (GRID), which converts collected data into information usable by decision-makers. The INFOTERRA programme facilitates the exchange of environmental information through an extensive network of national 'focal points'. By early 2002 177 countries were participating in the network. Through INFOTERRA UNEP promotes public access to environmental information, as well as participation in environmental concerns. UNEP aims to establish in every developing region an Environment and Natural Resource Information Network (ENRIN) in order to make available technical advice and manage environmental information and data for improved decision-making and action-planning in countries most in need of assistance. UNEP aims to integrate all its information resources in order to improve access to information and to promote its international exchange. This has been pursued through UNEP.net, an internet-based interactive environmental information- and data-sharing facility, and Mercure, a telecommunications service using satellite technology to link a network of 16 earth stations throughout the world.

UNEP's information, monitoring and assessment structures also serve to enhance early-warning capabilities and to provide accurate information during an environmental emergency.

POLICY DEVELOPMENT AND LAW

UNEP aims to promote the development of policy tools and guidelines in order to achieve the sustainable management of the world environment. At a national level it assists governments to develop and implement appropriate environmental instruments and aims to co-ordinate policy initiatives. Training workshops in various aspects of environmental law and its applications are conducted. UNEP supports the development of new legal, economic and other policy instruments to improve the effectiveness of existing environmental agreements.

UNEP was instrumental in the drafting of a Convention on Biological Diversity (CBD) to preserve the immense variety of plant and animal species, in particular those threatened with extinction. The Convention entered into force at the end of 1993; by September 2002 185 countries and the European Community were parties to the CBD. The CBD's Cartagena Protocol on Biosafety (so-called as it had been addressed at an extraordinary session of parties to the CBD convened in Cartagena, Colombia, in February 1999) was adopted at a meeting of parties to the CBD held in Montreal, Canada, in January 2000. The Protocol regulates the transboundary movement and use of living modified organisms resulting from biotechnology (such as genetically modified—GM—seeds and crops), in order to reduce any potential adverse effects on biodiversity and human health. It provides for an Advanced Informed Agreement procedure to govern the import of such organisms. By September 2002 35 countries and the European Community were parties to the Protocol. In January 2002 UNEP launched a major project aimed at supporting developing countries with assessing the potential health and environmental risks and benefits of GM crops, in preparation for the Protocol's entry into force. In February the parties to the CBD and other partners convened a conference, in Montreal, to address ways in which the traditional knowledge and practices of local communities could be preserved and used to conserve highly-threatened species and ecosystems. In April the sixth conference of parties to the CBD adopted detailed global guidelines on the management of genetic resources. UNEP supports co-operation for biodiversity assessment and management in selected developing regions and for the development of strategies for the conservation and sustainable exploitation of individual threatened species (e.g. the Global Tiger Action Plan). It also provides assistance for the preparation of individual country studies and strategies to strengthen national biodiversity management and research. UNEP administers the Convention on International Trade in Endangered Species of Wild Flora and Fauna (CITES), which entered into force in 1975.

In October 1994 87 countries, meeting under UN auspices, signed a Convention to Combat Desertification, which aimed to provide a legal framework to counter the degradation of drylands. An estimated 75% of all drylands have suffered some land degradation, affecting approximately 1,000m. people in 110 countries. UNEP continues to support the implementation of the Convention, as part of its efforts to protect land resources. UNEP also aims to improve the assessment of dryland degradation and desertification in co-operation with governments and other international bodies, as well as identifying the causes of degradation and measures to overcome these.

UNEP is the lead UN agency for promoting environmentally sustainable water management. It regards the unsustainable use of water as the most urgent environmental and sustainable development issue, and estimates that two-thirds of the world's population will suffer chronic water shortages by 2025. This is attributed to rising demand for drinking water as a result of growing populations, decreasing quality of water because of pollution, and the increasing requirements of industries and agriculture. In 2000 UNEP adopted a new water policy and strategy, comprising assessment, management and co-ordination components. The Global International Waters Assessment (see above) is the primary framework for the assessment component. The management component includes the Global Programme of Action (GPA) for the Protection of the Marine Environment from Land-based Activities (adopted in November 1995), and UNEP's freshwater programme and regional seas programme. The GPA for the Protection of the Marine Environment for Land-based Activities focuses on the effects of activities such as pollution on marine biodiversity and the coastal ecosystems of small-island developing states. UNEP aims to develop a similar global instrument to ensure the integrated management of freshwater resources. It promotes international co-operation in the management of river basins and coastal areas and for the development of tools and guidelines to achieve the sustainable management of freshwater and coastal resources. UNEP provides scientific, technical and administrative support to facilitate the implementation and co-ordination of 14 regional seas conventions and 13 regional plans of action, and is developing a strategy to strengthen collaboration in their implementation. The new water policy and strategy emphasizes the need for improved co-ordination of existing activities. UNEP aims to play an enhanced role within relevant co-ordination mechanisms, such as the UN open-ended informal consultation process on oceans and the law of the sea .

In 1996 UNEP, in collaboration with FAO, began to work towards promoting and formulating a legally-binding international convention on prior informed consent (PIC) for hazardous chemicals and pesticides in international trade, extending a voluntary PIC procedure of information exchange undertaken by more than 100 governments since 1991. The Convention was adopted at a conference held in Rotterdam, Netherlands, in September 1998, and was to enter into force on being ratified by 50 signatory states. It aimed to reduce risks to human health and the environment by restricting the production, export and use of hazardous substances and enhancing information exchange procedures.

In conjunction with UN-Habitat, UNDP, the World Bank and other regional organizations and institutions, UNEP promotes environmental concerns in urban planning and management through the Sustainable Cities Programme, as well as regional workshops concerned with urban pollution and the impact of transportation systems. In 1994 UNEP inaugurated an International Environmental Technology Centre (IETC), with offices in Osaka and Shiga, Japan, in order to strengthen the capabilities of developing countries and countries with economies in transition to promote environmentally-sound management of cities and freshwater reservoirs through technology co-operation and partnerships.

UNEP has played a key role in global efforts to combat risks to the ozone layer, resultant climatic changes and atmospheric pollution. UNEP worked in collaboration with the World Meteorological Organization to formulate a Framework Convention on Climate Change (UNFCCC), with the aim of reducing the emission of gases that have a warming effect on the atmosphere, and has remained an active participant in the ongoing process to review and enforce its implementation. UNEP was the lead agency in formulating the 1987 Montreal Protocol to the Vienna Convention for the Protection of the Ozone Layer (1985), which provided for a 50% reduction in the production of chlorofluorocarbons (CFCs) by 2000. An amendment to the Protocol was adopted in 1990, which required complete cessation of the production of CFCs by 2000 in industrialized countries and by 2010 in developing countries; these deadlines were advanced to 1996 and 2006, respectively, in November 1992. In 1997 the ninth conference of the parties to the Vienna Convention adopted a further amendment which aimed to introduce a licensing system for all controlled substances. The eleventh conference of parties, meeting in Beijing, People's Republic of China in November/December 1999, adopted the Beijing Amendment, which imposed tighter controls on the import and export of hydrochlorofluorocarbons, and on the production and consumption of bromochloromethane (Halon-1011, an industrial solvent and fire extinguisher). The Beijing Amendment entered into force in December 2001. A Multilateral Fund for the Implementation of the Montreal Protocol was established in June 1990 to promote the use of suitable technologies and the transfer of technologies to developing countries. UNEP, UNDP, the World Bank and UNIDO are the sponsors of the Fund, which by July 2001 had approved financing for some 3,850 projects in 124 developing countries at a cost of US $1,200m. Commitments of US $440m. were made to the fourth replenishment of the Fund, covering the three-year period 2000–02.

POLICY IMPLEMENTATION

UNEP's Division of Environmental Policy Implementation incorporates two main functions: technical co-operation and response to environmental emergencies.

With the UN Office for the Co-ordination of Humanitarian Assistance, UNEP has established a Joint Environment Unit to mobilize and co-ordinate international assistance and expertise for countries facing environmental emergencies and natural disasters. In December 2001 UNEP established a new Post-conflict Assessment Unit. During 2002 the Unit undertook activities in Afghanistan.

UNEP, together with UNDP and the World Bank, is an implementing agency of the Global Environment Facility (GEF, q.v.), which was established in 1991 as a mechanism for international co-operation in projects concerned with biological diversity, climate change, international waters and depletion of the ozone layer. UNEP services the Scientific and Technical Advisory Panel, which was established to provide expert advice on GEF programmes and operational strategies.

TECHNOLOGY, INDUSTRY AND ECONOMICS

The use of inappropriate industrial technologies and the widespread adoption of unsustainable production and consumption patterns have been identified as being inefficient in the use of renewable resources and wasteful, in particular in the use of energy and water. UNEP aims to encourage governments and the private sector to develop and adopt policies and practices that are cleaner and safer, make efficient use of natural resources, incorporate environmental costs, ensure the environmentally sound management of chemicals, and reduce pollution and risks to human health and the environment. In collaboration with other organizations and agencies UNEP works to define and formulate international guide-lines and agreements to address these issues. UNEP also promotes the transfer of appropriate technologies and organizes conferences and training workshops to provide sustainable production practices. Relevant information is disseminated through the International Cleaner Production Information Clearing House. UNEP, together with UNIDO, has established eight National Cleaner Production Centres to promote a preventive approach to industrial pollution control. In October 1988 UNEP adopted an International Declaration on Cleaner Production, with a commitment to implement cleaner and more sustainable production methods and to monitor results; the Declaration had 317 signatories at April 2002, including representatives of 47 governments. In 1997 UNEP and the Coalition for Environmentally Responsible Economies launched the Global Reporting Initiative, which, with participation by corporations, business associations and other organizations and stakeholders, develops guide-lines for voluntary reporting by companies on their economic, environmental and social performance. In April 2002 UNEP launched the 'Life-Cycle Initiative', which aims to assist governments, businesses and other consumers with adopting environmentally-sound policies and practice, in view of the upward trend in global consumption patterns.

UNEP provides institutional servicing to the Basel Convention on the Control of Transboundary Movements of Hazardous Wastes and their Disposal, which was adopted in 1989 with the aim of preventing the disposal of wastes from industrialized countries in countries that have no processing facilities. In March 1994 the second meeting of parties to the Convention agreed to ban exportation of hazardous wastes between OECD and non-OECD countries by the end of 1997. The third meeting of parties to the Convention, held in September 1995, proposed that the ban should be incorporated into the Convention as an amendment. The resulting so-called Ban Amendment required ratification by three-quarters of the 62 signatory states present at the time of its adoption before it could enter into effect; by September 2002 the Ban Amendment had been ratified by 32 parties. The fourth full meeting of parties to the Convention, held in February 1998, attempted to clarify the classification and listing of hazardous wastes. At September 2002 the number of parties to the Convention totalled 152. In December 1999 132 states adopted a Protocol to the Convention to address issues relating to liability and compensation for damages from waste exports. The governments also agreed to establish a multilateral fund to finance immediate clean-up operations following any environmental accident.

The UNEP Chemicals office was established to promote the sound management of hazardous substances, central to which was the International Register of Potentially Toxic Chemicals (IRPTC). UNEP aims to facilitate access to data on chemicals and hazardous wastes, in order to assess and control health and environmental risks, by using the IRPTC as a clearing house facility of relevant information and by publishing information and technical reports on the impact of the use of chemicals.

UNEP's OzonAction Programme works to promote information exchange, training and technological awareness. Its objective is to strengthen the capacity of governments and industry in developing countries to undertake measures towards the cost-effective phasing-out of ozone-depleting substances. UNEP also encourages the development of alternative and renewable sources of energy. To achieve this, UNEP is supporting the establishment of a network of centres to research and exchange information on environmentally-sound energy technology resources.

REGIONAL CO-OPERATION AND REPRESENTATION

UNEP maintains six regional offices. These work to initiate and promote UNEP objectives and to ensure that all programme formulation and delivery meets the specific needs of countries and regions. They also provide a focal point for building national, sub-regional and regional partnership and enhancing local participation in UNEP initiatives. Following UNEP's reorganization a co-ordination office was established at headquarters to promote regional policy integration, to co-ordinate programme planning, and to provide necessary services to the regional offices.

UNEP provides administrative support to regional conventions, organizes conferences, workshops and seminars at national and regional levels, and may extend advisory services or technical assistance to individual governments.

A new CITES Tiger Enforcement Task Force met for the first time in New Delhi, India, in April 2001; all trade in tigers and tiger parts is prohibited under CITES. In May UNEP launched the Great Apes Survival Project (GRASP), which supports, in 23 countries in South-East Asia and Africa, the conservation of orang-utans, gorillas, chimpanzees and bonobos.

CONVENTIONS

UNEP aims to develop and promote international environmental legislation in order to pursue an integrated response to global environmental issues, to enhance collaboration among existing convention secetariats, and to co-ordinate support to implement the work programmes of international instruments.

UNEP has been an active participant in the formulation of several major conventions (see above). The Division of Environmental Conventions is mandated to assist the Division of Policy Development and Law in the formulation of new agreements or protocols to existing conventions. Following the successful adoption of the Rotterdam Convention in September 1998, UNEP played a leading role in formulating a multilateral agreement to reduce and ultimately eliminate the manufacture and use of Persistent Organic Pollutants (POPs), which are considered to be a major global environmental hazard. The agreement on POPs, concluded in December 2000 at a conference sponsored by UNEP in Johannesburg, South Africa, was adopted by 127 countries in May 2001.

UNEP has been designated to provide secretariat functions to a number of global and regional environmental conventions (see above for list of offices).

COMMUNICATIONS AND PUBLIC INFORMATION

UNEP's public education campaigns and outreach programmes promote community involvement in environmental issues. Further communication of environmental concerns is undertaken through the media, an information centre service and special promotional events, including World Environment Day, photograph competitions and the awarding of the Sasakawa Prize to recognize distinguished service to the environment by individuals and groups. In 1996 UNEP initiated a Global Environment Citizenship Programme to promote acknowledgment of the environmental responsibilities of all sectors of society.

Finance

UNEP derives its finances from the regular budget of the United Nations and from voluntary contributions to the Environment Fund. A budget of US $119.9m. was authorized for the two-year period 2002–03, of which US $100m. was for programme activities, US $14.9m. for management and administration, and US $5m. for fund programme reserves.

Publications

Annual Report.

APELL Newsletter (2 a year).

Cleaner Production Newsletter (2 a year).

Climate Change Bulletin (quarterly).

Connect (UNESCO-UNEP newsletter on environmental degradation, quarterly).

EarthViews (quarterly).

Environment Forum (quarterly).

Environmental Law Bulletin (2 a year).

Financial Services Initiative (2 a year).

GEF News (quarterly).

Global Environment Outlook (every 2–3 years).

Global Water Review.

GPA Newsletter.

IETC Insight (3 a year).

Industry and Environment Review (quarterly).

Leave it to Us (children's magazine, 2 a year).

Managing Hazardous Wastes (2 a year).

Our Planet (quarterly).

OzonAction Newsletter (quarterly).

Tourism Focus (2 a year).

UNEP Chemicals Newsletter (2 a year).

UNEP Update (monthly).

World Atlas of Coral Reefs.

World Atlas of Desertification.

Studies, reports, legal texts, technical guide-lines, etc.

United Nations High Commissioner for Refugees—UNHCR

Address: CP 2500, 1211 Geneva 2 dépôt, Switzerland.

Telephone: (22) 7398111; **fax:** (22) 7397312; **e-mail:** unhcr@unhcr.ch; **internet:** www.unhcr.ch.

The Office of the High Commissioner was established in 1951 to provide international protection for refugees and to seek durable solutions to their problems.

Organization

(October 2002)

HIGH COMMISSIONER

The High Commissioner is elected by the United Nations General Assembly on the nomination of the Secretary-General, and is responsible to the General Assembly and to the UN Economic and Social Council (ECOSOC).

High Commissioner: RUUD LUBBERS (Netherlands).

Deputy High Commissioner: MARY ANN WYRSCH (USA).

EXECUTIVE COMMITTEE

The Executive Committee of the High Commissioner's Programme (ExCom), established by ECOSOC, gives the High Commissioner policy directives in respect of material assistance programmes and advice in the field of international protection. In addition, it oversees UNHCR's general policies and use of funds. ExCom, which comprises representatives of 57 states, both members and non-members of the UN, meets once a year.

ADMINISTRATION

Headquarters include the Executive Office, comprising the offices of the High Commissioner, the Deputy High Commissioner and the Assistant High Commissioner. There are separate offices for the Inspector General, the Special Envoy in the former Yugoslavia, the Director of the UNHCR liaison office in New York, and the Director of the Emergency Response Service. The other principal administrative units are the Division of Communication and Information, the Department of International Protection, the Division of Resource Management, and the Department of Operations, which is responsible for the five regional bureaux covering Africa; Asia and the Pacific; Europe; the Americas and the Caribbean; and Central Asia, South-West Asia, North Africa and the Middle East. At July 2002 there were 268 UNHCR field offices in 114 countries. At that time UNHCR employed 5,523 people, including short-term staff, of whom 84% were working in the field.

OFFICES IN THE FAR EAST AND AUSTRALASIA

Regional Office for Australia, New Zealand, Papua New Guinea and the South Pacific: 9 Terrigal Crescent, O'Malley, ACT 2606, Australia; tel. (2) 6290-1355; fax (2) 6290-1315; e-mail aul@unhcr.ch.

People's Republic of China: Tayuan Diplomatic Office, Bldg 14, Liangmahe Nanlu, Beijing 100600, People's Republic of China; e-mail chibe@unhcr.ch; also covers Mongolia.

Indonesia: POB 4505, Jakarta, Indonesia; e-mail insja@unhcr.ch.

Japan: 4-14, Akasaka 8-chome, Minato-ku, Tokyo 107, Japan; tel. (3) 3475-1615; fax (3) 3475-1647; e-mail jpnto@unhcr.ch; also covers Republic of Korea.

UNHCR also maintains branch and liaison offices in several countries in the region.

Activities

The competence of the High Commissioner extends to any person who, owing to well-founded fear of being persecuted for reasons of race, religion, nationality or political opinion, is outside the country of his or her nationality and is unable or, owing to such fear or for reasons other than personal convenience, remains unwilling to accept the protection of that country; or who, not having a nationality and being outside the country of former habitual residence, is unable or, owing to such fear or for reasons other than personal convenience, is unwilling to return to it. This competence may be extended, by resolutions of the UN General Assembly and decisions of ExCom, to cover certain other 'persons of concern', in addition to refugees meeting these criteria. Refugees who are assisted by other UN agencies, or who have the same rights or obligations as nationals of their country of residence, are outside the mandate of UNHCR.

In recent years there has been a significant shift in UNHCR's focus of activities. Increasingly UNHCR is called upon to support people who have been displaced within their own country, i.e. with similar needs to those of refugees but who have not crossed an international border, or those threatened with displacement as a result of armed conflict. Operations involving internally displaced populations may be undertaken only at the request of the UN Secretary-General or the General Assembly and with the consent of the country concerned. In addition, UNHCR is providing greater support to refugees who have returned to their country of origin, to assist their reintegration, and is working to enable the local community to support the returnees, frequently through the implementation of Quick Impact Projects (QIPs). At December 2001, according to provisional figures, the refugee population world-wide totalled 12.1m. and UNHCR was concerned with an estimated further 940,800 asylum-seekers, 462,700 recently returned refugees and 6.3m. others (of whom an estimated 5.0m. were internally displaced persons—IDPs).

The first annual World Refugee Day, sponsored by UNHCR, was held on 20 June 2001.

INTERNATIONAL PROTECTION

As laid down in the Statute of the Office, UNHCR's primary function is to extend international protection to refugees, and its second function is to seek durable solutions to their problems. In the exercise of its mandate UNHCR seeks to ensure that refugees and asylum-seekers are protected against *refoulement* (forcible return), that they receive asylum, and that they are treated according to internationally recognized standards of treatment. UNHCR pursues these objectives by a variety of means that include promoting the conclusion and ratification by states of international conventions for the protection of refugees, particularly the 1951 UN Convention relating to the Status of Refugees, extended by a Protocol adopted in 1967. The Convention defines the rights and duties of refugees and contains provisions dealing with a variety of matters which affect their day-to-day lives. UNHCR has attempted to deal with the problem of military attacks on refugee camps by formulating and encouraging the acceptance of a set of principles to ensure the safety of refugees. UNHCR promotes the adoption of liberal practices in granting asylum, so that refugees and asylum-seekers are granted admission by states, at least on a temporary basis.

UNHCR has actively encouraged states to accede to the 1951 United Nations Refugee Convention and the 1967 Protocol: 144 states had acceded to either or both of these basic refugee instruments by mid-2002. An increasing number of states have also adopted domestic legislation and/or administrative measures to implement the international instruments, particularly in the field of procedures for the determination of refugee status. UNHCR has sought to address the specific needs of refugee women and children, and has also attempted to deal with the problem of military attacks on refugee camps, by adopting and encouraging the acceptance of a set of principles to ensure the safety of refugees. In recent years it has formulated a strategy designed to address the fundamental causes of refugee flows. In 2001, in response to widespread concern about perceived high numbers of asylum-seekers and large-scale international economic migration and human trafficking, UNHCR initiated a series of Global Consultations on International Protection with the signatories to the 1951 Convention and 1967 Protocol, and other interested parties, with a view to strengthening both the application and scope of international refugee legislation. In July 2001 the High Commissioner urged the fair treatment of asylum-seekers in industrialized countries pending the outcome of their applications. He condemned the practice of detaining them, supported the introduction of new clearly defined systems for dealing separately with asylum-seekers and economic migrants, and expressed concern at incidences of manipulation and misreporting of the issues involved by politicians and the media. Following the major terrorist attacks perpetrated in September against targets in the USA, UNHCR issued a list of concerns relating to possible negative consequences for asylum-seekers and refugees, including the threat of increased xenophobia and discrimination. In addition, with the subsequent threat of action by a US-led global coalition against countries suspected of harbouring and promoting terrorist organizations, UNHCR reassessed its contingency plans for possible large-scale population displacement in Central Asia, South-West Asia and the Middle East.

ASSISTANCE ACTIVITIES

The first phase of an assistance operation uses UNHCR's capacity of emergency preparedness and response. This enables UNHCR to address the immediate needs of refugees at short notice, for example, by employing specially-trained emergency teams and maintaining stockpiles of basic equipment, medical aid and materials. A significant proportion of UNHCR expenditure is allocated to the next phase of an operation, providing 'care and maintenance' in stable refugee circumstances. This assistance can take various forms, including the provision of food, shelter, medical care and essential supplies. Also covered in many instances are basic services, including education and counselling.

As far as possible, assistance is geared towards the identification and implementation of durable solutions to refugee problems—this being the second statutory responsibility of UNHCR. Such solutions generally take one of three forms: voluntary repatriation, local integration or resettlement in another country. Voluntary repatriation is increasingly the preferred solution, given the easing of political tension in many regions from which refugees have fled. Where voluntary repatriation is feasible, the Office assists refugees to overcome obstacles preventing their return to their country of origin. This may be done through negotiations with governments involved, or by providing funds either for the physical movement of refugees or for the rehabilitation of returnees once back in their own country.

When voluntary repatriation is not feasible, efforts are made to assist refugees to integrate locally and to become self-supporting in their countries of asylum. In cases where resettlement through emigration is the only viable solution to a refugee problem, UNHCR negotiates with governments in an endeavour to obtain suitable resettlement opportunities, to encourage liberalization of admission criteria and to draw up special immigration schemes.

In the early 1990s UNHCR aimed to consolidate efforts to integrate certain priorities into its programme planning and implementation, as a standard discipline in all phases of assistance. The considerations include awareness of specific problems confronting refugee women, the needs of refugee children, the environmental impact of refugee programmes and long-term development objectives. In an effort to improve the effectiveness of its programmes, UNHCR has initiated a process of delegating authority, as well as responsibility for operational budgets, to its regional and field representatives, increasing flexibility and accountability. An Evaluation and Policy Analysis Unit, established in 1999, reviews systematically UNHCR's operational effectiveness.

REGIONAL ASSISTANCE

In June 1989 an international conference was convened by UNHCR in Geneva to discuss the ongoing problem of refugees and displaced persons in and from the Indo-Chinese peninsula. The participants adopted the Comprehensive Plan of Action for Indo-Chinese Refugees (CPA), which provided for the 'screening' of all Vietnamese arrivals in the region to determine their refugee status, the resettlement of 'genuine' refugees and the repatriation (described as voluntary 'in the first instance') of those deemed to be economic migrants. A steering committee of the international conference met regularly to supervise the plan. In March 1996 UNHCR confirmed that it was to terminate funding for the refugee camps (except those in Hong Kong) at the end of June to coincide with the formal conclusion of the CPA; however, it pledged to support transitional arrangements regarding the completion of the repatriation process and maintenance of the remaining Vietnamese 'non-refugees' during the post-CPA phase-out period, as well as to continue its support for the reintegration and monitoring of returning nationals in Viet Nam and Laos. The prospect of forcible repatriation provoked rioting and violent protests in many camps throughout the region. By mid-1996 more than 88,000 Vietnamese and 22,000 Laotians had returned to their countries of origin under the framework of the CPA, with Malaysia and Singapore having completed the repatriation process. In late July the Philippines Government agreed to permit the remaining camp residents to settle permanently in that country. In September the remaining Vietnamese refugees detained on the island of Galang, in Indonesia, were repatriated, and in February 1997 the last camp for Vietnamese refugees in Thailand was formally closed. In mid-June of that year the main Vietnamese detention camp in Hong Kong was closed. However, the scheduled repatriation of all remaining Vietnamese before the transfer of sovereignty of the territory to the People's Republic of China (PRC) at the end of June was not achieved. In early 1998 the Hong Kong authorities formally terminated the policy of granting a port of first asylum to Vietnamese 'boat people'. In February 2000 UNHCR, which had proposed the integration of the remaining Vietnamese as a final durable solution to the situation, welcomed a decision by the Hong Kong authorities to offer permanent residency status to the occupants of the last remaining Vietnamese detention camp (totalling 973 refugees and 435 'non-refugees'). By the end of May, when the camp was closed, more than 200 Vietnamese had failed to apply for residency. At 31 December 2001 UNHCR was providing assistance to an estimated further 295,276 Vietnamese refugees in mainland PRC. In 1995, in accordance with an agreement concluded with the Chinese Government, UNHCR initiated a programme to redirect its local assistance to promote long-term self-sufficiency in the poorest settlements, including support for revolving-fund rural credit schemes. UNHCR favours the local integration of the majority of the Vietnamese refugee population in the PRC as a durable solution to the situation.

The conclusion of a political settlement of the conflict in Cambodia in October 1991 made possible the eventual repatriation of some 370,000 Cambodian refugees and displaced persons. A landmine survey was prepared in order to identify the risk to returnees posed by unexploded mines (mine clearance was subsequently undertaken under UN auspices). The actual repatriation operation began in March 1992 and was completed in April 1993. At the same time, however, thousands of ethnic Vietnamese (of whom there were estimated to be 200,000 in Cambodia) were fleeing to Viet Nam, as a result of violence perpetrated against them by Cambodian armed groups. In March 1994 25,000 supporters of the Khmers Rouges in Cambodia fled across the border into Thailand, following advances by government forces. The refugees were immediately repatriated by the Thai armed forces into Khmer Rouge territory, which was inaccessible to aid agencies. In July 1997 armed conflict between opposing political forces in northern Cambodia resulted in large-scale population movement. A voluntary repatriation programme was initiated in October, and in late March 1999 UNHCR announced that the last Cambodian refugees had left camps in Thailand, the majority having been repatriated to north-western Cambodia. A UNHCR programme was initiated to monitor the welfare of returnees and assist in their reintegration; this was terminated at the end of 2000. At 31 December 2001 there were still some 15,945 Cambodian refugees in Viet Nam. In January 2002 UNHCR signed an agreement with the Governments of Viet Nam and Cambodia for the safe repatriation of an estimated 1,000 Montagnards who had fled from the Central Highland provinces of Viet Nam during 2001. UNHCR was to be permitted unlimited access to the region to assist and monitor the return process. In March 2002, however, UNCHR withdrew from the agreement owing to alleged intimidation of refugees and UN staff.

From 1979, as a result of civil strife in Afghanistan, there was a massive movement of refugees from that country into Pakistan and Iran creating the world's largest refugee population, which reached a peak of almost 6.3m. people in 1990. In 1988 UNHCR agreed to provide assistance for the voluntary repatriation of refugees, both in ensuring the rights of the returning population and in providing material assistance such as transport, immunization, and supplies of food and other essentials. In April 1992, following the establishment of a new Government in Afghanistan, refugees began to repatriate in substantial numbers (hitherto only a small proportion had returned), although, meanwhile, large numbers of people continued to flee into Pakistan as a result of persisting insecurity. From October 1996 an escalation of hostilities in northern and western regions of Afghanistan resulted in further massive population displacement. During 1997 UNHCR operated a pilot scheme to organize group repatriations to specific areas in Afghanistan, under the protection of international observers; despite initial successes, however, the scheme was suspended in late 1998. In early 1998 UNHCR initiated a new returnee monitoring system to evaluate the situation of returnees in Afghanistan. By the end of the year the total number of returnees from Iran and Pakistan since 1988 amounted to more than 4.2m. In recent years UNHCR, with other UN agencies, attempted to meet the immediate needs of IDPs and recent returnees in Afghanistan through systematic monitoring (see above) and, for example, by initiating small-scale multi-sectoral QIPs to improve shelter, rural water supply and local infrastructure; organizing income-generating and capacity-building activities; and providing food and tools. However, the ongoing civil conflict, as well as successive severe droughts and harsh winter conditions, caused renewed population displacement, precluding a settlement of the refugee situation and entailing immense difficulties in undertaking comprehensive relief efforts. Activities were disrupted by periodic withdrawals of UN international personnel owing to security concerns. The humanitarian crisis worsened considerably during 2000. At the end of that year, an estimated total of 1.3m. Afghan refugees were sheltering in Iran (the same as at the end of 1999), 2m. in Pakistan (compared with 1.2m. at end-1999), 15,350 in Tajikistan, and some 12,760 in India. In mid-2001 UNHCR warned that the food insecurity in the country was continuing to deteriorate and that population movements were ongoing. In September, prompted by the threat of impending military action directed by a US-led global coalition against targets in the Taliban-administered areas of Afghanistan, UNHCR launched an appeal for US $252m. to finance an emergency relief operation to cope with a potentially large further movement of Afghan refugees and IDPs. Although all surrounding countries imposed 'closed border' policies (with Pakistan reportedly permitting limited entry to Afghans in possession of correct travel documentation), it was envisaged that, were the security situation to deteriorate significantly, large numbers of Afghans might attempt to cross into the surrounding countries (mainly Iran and Pakistan) at unsecured points of entry. UNHCR urged the adoption of more liberal border policies and began substantially to reinforce its presence in Iran and Pakistan. Activities being undertaken included the supply of basic relief items such as tents and health and hygiene kits and assistance with the provision of community services such as education for school-age children. The construction and maintenance of new camps near the Pakistan-Afghanistan border was initiated in co-operation with the Pakistan Government and other agencies, and it was also planned to construct new refugee shelters in Iran. Emergency contingency plans were also formulated for a relief initiative to assist a projected further 500,000 IDPs (in addition to the large numbers of people already displaced) inside Afghanistan. Large population movements out of cities were reported from the start of the international political crisis. An estimated 6m. Afghans (about one-quarter of the total population) were believed to be extremely vulnerable, requiring urgent food aid and other relief supplies. In mid-September all foreign UN field staff were withdrawn from Afghanistan for security reasons; meanwhile, in order to address the humanitarian situation, a Crisis Group was established by several UN agencies, including UNHCR, and a crisis management structure came into operation at UNHCR headquarters. In October (when air-strikes were initiated against Afghanistan) UNHCR opened a staging camp at a major crossing point on the Afghanistan-Pakistan border, and put in place a system for monitoring new refugee arrivals (implemented by local people rather than by UNHCR personnel). It was estimated that from October 2001–January 2002 about 50,000 Afghan refugees entered Pakistan officially, while about 150,000 crossed into the country at unofficial border points; many reportedly sought refuge with friends and relatives. Much smaller movements into Iran were reported. Spontaneous repatriations also occurred during that period (reportedly partly owing to the poor conditions at many camps in Pakistan), and UNHCR-assisted IDP returns were also undertaken. UNHCR resumed operations within Afghanistan in mid-November 2001, distributing supplies and implementing QIPs, for example the provision of warm winter clothing. From that month some 130,000 Afghan refugees in Pakistan were relocated from inadequate accommodation to new camps. At December 2001 there were an estimated 1.48m. Afghan refugees in Iran, 2.20m. in Pakistan and 15,300 in Tajikistan. On 1 March 2002 UNHCR initiated, jointly with the new interim Afghan administration, an assisted repatriation programme. Each returning family was to receive food and basic household items, as well as information about security and mine-awareness. UNHCR also concluded tripartite accords on repatriation with the Afghan authorities and with Iran and Pakistan. The pace of returns far exceeded expectations, and by early August more than 1.2m. Afghan refugees had registered to return under the programme, while some 200,000 had returned spontaneously. UNHCR had assisted a further 200,000 IDPs to return to their home areas.

In 1991–92 thousands of people of Nepalese ethnic origin living in Bhutan sought refuge from alleged persecution by fleeing to Nepal. In December 2000 Bhutan and Nepal reached agreement on a joint verification mechanism for the repatriation of the refugees, which had been hitherto the principal issue precluding a resolution of the situation. Progress towards settling a remaining disagreement concerning categorizing the refugees was achieved during 2001. The first verification of Bhutanese refugees was undertaken in March, and it was envisaged that voluntary repatriations would commence during 2002. At the end of 2001 there were an estimated 110,780 Bhutanese refugees in Nepal, the majority of whom were receiving UNHCR assistance in the form of food, shelter, medical care and water.

A temporary cessation of hostilities between the Sri Lankan Government and Tamil separatists in early 1995 greatly facilitated UNHCR's ongoing efforts to repatriate Sri Lankan Tamils who had fled to India. However, later in that year an offensive by Sri Lankan government troops against the northern Jaffna peninsula caused a massive displacement of the local Tamil population and effectively ended the repatriation process. Increasing insecurity from late 1999 prompted further population displacements. However, fewer movements were recorded in 2001. In July UNHCR suspended its activities in Mallavi, northern Sri Lanka, owing to security concerns. By 31 December there were 683,286 Sri Lankan internally displaced persons of concern to UNHCR, as well as an estimated 64,061 Sri Lankan refugees in 116 camps in southern India. At that time India's total refugee population of some 169,549 also included 11,972 refugees from Afghanistan and 92,344 from the PRC (mainly Tibetans).

From April 1991 increasing numbers of Rohingya Muslims in Myanmar fled into Bangladesh to escape brutality and killings perpetrated by the Myanma armed forces. UNHCR launched an international appeal for financial aid for the refugees, at the request of Bangladesh, and collaborated with other UN agencies in providing humanitarian assistance. UNHCR refused to participate in a programme of repatriation of the Myanma refugees agreed by Myanmar and Bangladesh, on the grounds that no safe environment existed for them to return to. In May 1993 a memorandum of understanding between UNHCR and Bangladesh was signed, whereby UNHCR would be able to monitor the repatriation process and ensure that people were returning of their own free will. In November a memorandum of understanding, signed with the Myanma Government, secured UNHCR access to the returnees. The first refugees returned to Myanmar with UNHCR assistance at the end of April 1994. They and all subsequent returnees were provided with a small amount of cash, housing grants and two months' food rations, and were supported by several small-scale reintegration projects. In January 1997 the Bangladesh and Myanma Governments agreed to conclude the mass repatriation programme by the end of March, later extended to August. In July, in advance of the revised deadline, Rohingya activists initiated a hunger-strike in protest at alleged efforts by the Bangladesh authorities to repatriate forcibly the remaining refugees. The repatriation process resumed in November 1998 although remained slow. During 2001 UNHCR renewed its efforts to negotiate with both governments a solution to the refugee problem. Attempts by UNHCR to find a local solution for those unwilling to return to Myanmar have been met with resistance by the Bangladeshi Government. By the end of December an estimated 22,106 Myanma refugees still remained in camps in Bangladesh and were receiving basic care from UNHCR.

In the early 1990s members of ethnic minorities in Myanmar attempted to flee attacks by government troops into Thailand; however, the Thai Government refused to recognize them as refugees or to offer them humanitarian assistance. Throughout 1997 the border camps were vulnerable to attacks by rival Karen (Kayin) factions and by Myanma Government forces. In December Thailand and Myanmar agreed to commence 'screening' the refugees to determine those who had fled persecution and those who were economic migrants. By the end of 2001 there were an estimated 110,313 people in camps along the Myanma–Thai border, the majority of whom were Karen refugees. UNHCR's priorities in 2002 were to ensure that any new arrivals were treated in accordance with international standards, as well as to continue to seek a durable solution to the problem and to ensure that, in the meantime, the fundamental rights of the refugees were respected.

In April 1999, following the announcement by the Indonesian Government, in January, that it would consider a form of autonomy or independence for East Timor, some 26,000 Indonesian settlers left their homes as a result of clashes between opposing groups and uncertainty regarding the future of the territory. The popular referendum on the issue, conducted at the end of August, and the resulting victory for the independence movement, provoked a violent reaction by pro-integration militia. UNHCR, along with other international personnel, was forced to evacuate the territory in early September. At that time there were reports of forced mass deportations of East Timorese to West Timor, while a large number of others fled their homes into remote mountainous areas of East Timor. In mid-September UNHCR staff visited West Timor to review the state of refugee camps, allegedly under the control of militia, and to persuade the authorities to permit access for humanitarian personnel. It was estimated that 250,000–260,000 East Timorese had fled to West Timor, of whom some 230,000 were registered in 28 camps at the end of September. At that time there were also an estimated 190,000–300,000 people displaced within East Timor, although the International Committee of the Red Cross estimated that a total of 800,000 people, or some 94% of the population, had been displaced, or deported, during the crisis. The arrival of multinational troops, from 20 September, helped to stabilize the region and enable the safe receipt and distribution of food supplies, prompting several thousands to return from hiding. Most homes, however, along with almost all other buildings in the capital, Dili, had been destroyed. In early October UNHCR, together with the International Organization for Migration, initiated a repatriation programme for the refugees in West Timor. However, despite an undertaking by the Indonesian Government in mid-October that it would ensure the safety of all refugees and international personnel, persistent intimidation by anti-independence militia impeded the registration and repatriation processes. The operation was also hindered by the Indonesian Government's decision to reduce the provision of food aid to the camps from the beginning of July 2000. UNHCR initially aimed to complete the repatriation programme by mid-2001, prior to the staging of elections to a Constituent Assembly by the UN Transitional Administration in East Timor (UNTAET, which assumed full authority over the territory in February 2000). However, in September 2000 UNHCR suspended its activities in West Timor, following the murder by militiamen of three of its personnel. A UN Security Council resolution, adopted soon afterwards, deplored this incident and strongly urged the Indonesian authorities to disable the militia and to guarantee the future security of all refugees and humanitarian personnel. In mid-September UNTAET and the Indonesian Government signed a Memorandum of Understanding on co-operation in resolving the refugee crisis. However, despite a subsequent operation by the Indonesian security forces to disarm the militia, intimidation of East Timorese refugees reportedly persisted, and UNHCR did not redeploy personnel to West Timor. The Office has, however, liaised with other humanitarian organizations to facilitate continuing voluntary repatriations, which have been encouraged by the Indonesian authorities. UNHCR's operation in East Timor has aimed to promote the safe voluntary repatriation of refugees, monitor returnees, support their reintegration through the implementation of QIPs, pursue efforts towards sustainable development and the rehabilitation of communities, and promote reconciliation and respect for human rights. At the beginning of January 2002 the Indonesian Government terminated the provision of food assistance to refugees remaining in camps in West Timor. In July, following a series of protests by refugees, the Government announced that it would resume the distribution of rice, although it reiterated that all repatriation assistance would terminate on 31 August. In mid-May East Timor achieved independence. At that time almost 205,000 East Timorese refugees were reported to have returned to East Timor since October 1999, while more than 50,000 were believed to remain in West Timorese camps. UNHCR and the newly-elected administration were co-operating to encourage further repatriation, as well as to assist with East Timor's accession to the international instruments of protection and with the development of new national refugee protection legislation.

In late August 2001 UNHCR expressed concern when the Australian authorities refused entry into that country to some 430 Afghan asylum-seekers who had been rescued at sea by a Norwegian vessel near the Australian external territory of Christmas Island. In September the Afghans were removed on an Australian naval ship to Nauru, Papua New Guinea and New Zealand. At the request of the Nauru authorities, UNHCR dispatched a team there to assist with ascertaining the refugee status and resettlement needs of members of the group. Further groups of asylum-seekers at sea were subsequently similarly redirected, mainly to Nauru and Papua New Guinea; in mid-September the Australian Government successfully appealed a ruling by the Federal Court of Australia demanding that it reverse its decision, and stricter legislation aimed at deterring future asylum-seekers was swiftly adopted, including removing the external territories from Australia's migration zone. At 31 December 2001 Australia was sheltering an estimated 13,670 asylum-seekers (compared with 4,920 at the end of 2000), in addition to some 55,146 refugees. In February 2002 the High Commissioner urged the Australian Government to reconsider its policy of holding asylum-seekers in detention centres pending the outcome of their applications, following widely-publicized protests by a number of such detainees against conditions and delays in processing their applications. UNHCR aimed to undertake public awareness activities in Australia during that year.

PERSONS OF CONCERN TO UNHCR IN THE FAR EAST AND AUSTRALASIA*

(31 December 2001, '000s, provisional figures)

Country	Refugees	Asylum seekers	Returned refugees	Others of concern†
Afghanistan	—	—	26.1	1,200.0
Australia	55.1	13.7	—	—
Bangladesh	22.2	—	—	—
China, People's Republic	295.3	—	—	—
East Timor	—	—	18.2	—
India	169.5	0.2	—	—
Indonesia	73.6	0.8	—	—
Malaysia	50.5	0.3	—	—
Nepal	130.9	—	—	—
Pakistan	2,198.8	0.6	—	—
Sri Lanka	—	—	—	683.3
Thailand	110.7	0.3	—	—
Viet Nam	15.9	—	—	—

* Figures are provided mostly by governments, based on their own records and methods of estimations. Countries with fewer than 10,000 persons of concern to UNHCR are not listed.

† Mainly internally displaced persons (IDPs) or recently-returned IDPs.

CO-OPERATION WITH OTHER ORGANIZATIONS

UNHCR works closely with other UN agencies, intergovernmental organizations and non-governmental organizations (NGOs) to increase the scope and effectiveness of its emergency operations. Within the UN system, UNHCR co-operates, principally, with the World Food Programme in the distribution of food aid, UNICEF and the World Health Organization in the provision of family welfare and child immunization programmes, OCHA in the delivery of emergency humanitarian relief, UNDP in development-related activities and in the preparation of guide-lines for the continuum of emergency assistance to development programmes, and the Office of the UN High Commissioner for Human Rights. UNHCR also has close working relationships with the International Committee of the Red Cross and the International Organization for Migration. In 2001 UNHCR worked with 537 NGOs as 'implementing partners', enabling UNHCR to broaden the use of its resources, as well as to benefit from local knowledge and skills, while maintaining a co-ordinating role in the provision of assistance.

TRAINING

UNHCR organizes training programmes and workshops to enhance the capabilities of field workers and non-UNHCR staff, in the following areas: the identification and registration of refugees; people-orientated planning; resettlement procedures and policies; emergency response and management; security awareness; stress management; and the dissemination of information through the electronic media.

Finance

The United Nations regular budget finances a proportion of UNHCR administrative expenditure. The majority of UNHCR's programme expenditure is funded by voluntary contributions, mainly from governments. The Private Sector and Public Affairs Service, established in 2001, aims to increase funding from non-governmental donor sources, for example by developing partnerships with foundations and corporations. UNHCR assistance activities are financed from the Unified Annual Budget. Following approval of the Budget any subsequently-identified requirements are managed by Supplementary Programmes, financed by separate appeals. Of the total US $828.6m. approved under the programme budget for 2001, South-West Asia was allocated US $59.8m., South Asia US $21.5m., and East Asia and the Pacific US $18.2m.At February 2002 Supplementary Programmes had been approved for South-West Asia, amounting to US $167.1m., and for East Asia and the Pacific (US $6.9m.).

Publications

Refugees (quarterly, in English, French, German, Italian, Japanese and Spanish).

Refugee Survey Quarterly.

State of the World's Refugees (every 2 years).

UNHCR Handbook for Emergencies.

United Nations Peace-keeping Operations

Address: Department of Peace-keeping Operations, Room S-3727-B, United Nations, New York, NY 10017, USA.

Telephone: (212) 963-8077; **fax:** (212) 963-9222; **internet:** www.un.org/Depts/dpko/.

United Nations peace-keeping operations have been conceived as instruments of conflict control. The UN has used these operations in various conflicts, with the consent of the parties involved, to maintain international peace and security, without prejudice to the positions or claims of parties, in order to facilitate the search for political settlements through peaceful means such as mediation and the good offices of the Secretary-General. Each operation has been established with a specific mandate, which requires periodic review by the Security Council. United Nations peace-keeping operations fall into two categories: peace-keeping forces and observer missions.

Peace-keeping forces are composed of contingents of military and civilian personnel made available by member states. These forces assist in preventing the recurrence of fighting, restoring and maintaining peace, and promoting a return to normal conditions. To this end, peace-keeping forces are authorized as necessary to undertake negotiations, persuasion, observation and fact-finding. They run patrols and interpose physically between the opposing parties. Peace-keeping forces are permitted to use their weapons only in self-defence.

Military observer missions are composed of officers (usually unarmed), who are made available, on the Secretary-General's request, by member states. A mission's function is to observe and report to the Secretary-General (who in turn informs the UN Security Council) on the maintenance of a cease-fire, to investigate violations and to do what it can to improve the situation.

Peace-keeping forces and observer missions must at all times maintain complete impartiality and avoid any action that might affect the claims or positions of the parties.

The UN's peace-keeping forces and observer missions are financed in most cases by assessed contributions from member states of the organization. In recent years a significant expansion in the UN's peace-keeping activities has been accompanied by a perpetual financial crisis within the organization, as a result of the increased financial burden and some member states' delaying payment. By 31 August 2002 outstanding assessed contributions to the peace-keeping budget amounted to some US $1,770m.

UNITED NATIONS MILITARY OBSERVER GROUP IN INDIA AND PAKISTAN—UNMOGIP

Headquarters: Rawalpindi, Pakistan (November–April), Srinagar, India (May–October).

Chief Military Observer: Maj.-Gen. PERTTI JUHANI PUONTI (Finland).

The Group was established in 1948 by UN Security Council resolutions aiming to restore peace in the region of Jammu and Kashmir, the status of which had become a matter of dispute between the Governments of India and Pakistan. Following a cease-fire which came into effect in January 1949, the military observers of UNMOGIP were deployed to assist in its observance. There is no periodic review of UNMOGIP's mandate. In 1971, following the signature of a new cease-fire agreement, India claimed that UNMOGIP's mandate had lapsed, since it was originally intended to monitor the agreement reached in 1949. Pakistan, however, regarded UNMOGIP's mission as unchanged, and the Group's activities have continued, although they have been somewhat restricted on the Indian side of the 'line of control', which was agreed by India and Pakistan in 1972.

At 31 July 2002 there were 44 military observers deployed on both sides of the 'line of control', supported by 63 international and local civilian personnel. The operation was allocated US $6.2m. from the regular budget of the UN for 2002.

UNITED NATIONS MISSION OF SUPPORT IN EAST TIMOR—UNMISET

Headquarters: Dili, East Timor.

Special Representative of the UN Secretary-General and Transitional Administrator: KAMALESH SHARMA (India).

Commander: Maj.-Gen. TAN HUCK GIM (Singapore).

Chief Military Observer: (acting) Col ABDUL LATIF HARUN.

Chief of Civilian Police: Chief Superintendent PETER MILLER (Canada).

UNMISET was established on 20 May 2002, initially with a mandate for one year, when East Timor attained its independence. It succeeded the UN Transitional Administration in East Timor (UNTAET), which had been established in October 1999 to govern the territory on an interim basis following the outcome of a popular referendum in support of independence from Indonesia. UNMISET was to provide assistance to core administrative structures, to extend interim law enforcement and public security services, to assist the development of a national police force, and to contribute to the maintenance of external and internal security. The civilian component of UNMISET was to include a Serious Crimes Unit and a Human Rights Unit, as well as focal points for gender and HIV/AIDS. The Mission was mandated to devolve all operational responsibilities to the East Timorese authorities within two years.

At 30 June 2002 UNMISET comprised 4,789 troops, 939 civilian police officers and 119 military observers, supported by 1,291 international and local civilian personnel. The cost of the operation for the period 1 July 2002–30 June 2003 was estimated at US $316m; this was to be financed by a Special Account.

Food and Agriculture Organization—FAO

Address: Viale delle Terme di Caracalla, 00100 Rome, Italy.

Telephone: (06) 57051; **fax:** (06) 5705-3152; **e-mail:** fao-hq@fao.org; **internet:** www.fao.org.

FAO, the first specialized agency of the UN to be founded, aims to alleviate malnutrition and hunger, and serves as a co-ordinating agency for development programmes in the whole range of food and agriculture, including forestry and fisheries. It helps developing countries to promote educational and training facilities and the creation of appropriate institutions.

Organization

(October 2002)

CONFERENCE

The governing body is the FAO Conference of member nations. It meets every two years, formulates policy, determines the Organization's programme and budget on a biennial basis, and elects new members. It also elects the Director-General of the Secretariat and the Independent Chairman of the Council. In alternate years, FAO also holds conferences in each of its five regions (the Near East, Asia and the Pacific, Africa, Latin America and the Caribbean, and Europe).

COUNCIL

The FAO Council is composed of representatives of 49 member nations, elected by the Conference for staggered three-year terms. It is the interim governing body of FAO between sessions of the Conference. The most important standing Committees of the Council are: the Finance and Programme Committees, the Committee on Commodity Problems, the Committee on Fisheries, the Committee on Agriculture and the Committee on Forestry.

SECRETARIAT

The total number of FAO staff in May 2002 was 3,700, of whom 1,500 were professional staff and 2,200 general service staff. About one-half of the Organization's staff were based at headquarters. Work is supervised by the following Departments: Administration and Finance; General Affairs and Information; Economic and Social Policy; Agriculture; Forestry; Fisheries; Sustainable Development; and Technical Co-operation.

Director-General: JACQUES DIOUF (Senegal).

REGIONAL AND SUB-REGIONAL OFFICES

Regional Office for Asia and the Pacific: Maliwan Mansion, 39 Phra Atit Rd, Bangkok 10200, Thailand; tel. (2) 281-7844; fax (2) 280-0445; e-mail fao-rap@fao.org; internet www.fao.or.th; Regional Rep. R. B. SINGH.

Sub-regional Office for the Pacific Islands: Private Mail Bag, Apia, Samoa; tel. 22127; fax 22126; e-mail fao-sapa@fao.org; Sub-regional Rep. V. A. FUAVAO.

Activities

FAO aims to raise levels of nutrition and standards of living, by improving the production and distribution of food and other commodities derived from farms, fisheries and forests. FAO's ultimate objective is the achievement of world food security, 'Food for All'. The organization provides technical information, advice and assistance by disseminating information; acting as a neutral forum for discussion of food and agricultural issues; advising governments on policy and planning; and developing capacity directly in the field.

In November 1996 FAO hosted the World Food Summit, which was held in Rome and was attended by heads of state and senior government representatives of 186 countries. Participants approved the Rome Declaration on World Food Security and the World Food Summit Plan of Action, with the aim of halving the number of people afflicted by undernutrition, at that time estimated to total 828m. world-wide, by no later than 2015. A review conference, World Food Summit: Five Years Later, held in Rome in June 2002, reaffirmed commitment to this objective.

In November 1999 the FAO Conference approved a long-term Strategic Framework for the period 2000–15, which emphasized national and international co-operation in pursuing the goals of the 1996 World Food Summit. The Framework promoted interdisciplinarity and partnership, and defined three main global objectives: constant access by all people to sufficient nutritionally adequate and safe food, ensuring that levels of undernourishment were reduced by 50% by 2015; the continued contribution of sustainable agriculture and rural development to economic and social progress and well-being; and the conservation, improvement and sustainable use of natural resources. It identified five corporate strategies (each supported by several strategic objectives), covering the following areas: reducing food insecurity and rural poverty; ensuring enabling policy and regulatory frameworks for food, agriculture, fisheries and forestry; creating sustainable increases in the supply and availability of agricultural, fisheries and forestry products; conserving and enhancing sustainable use of the natural resource base; and generating knowledge. The November 2001 the FAO Conference adopted a medium-term plan covering 2002–07 and a work programme for 2000–03, both on the basis of the Strategic Framework.

FAO organizes an annual series of fund-raising events, 'TeleFood', some of which are broadcast on television and the internet in order to raise public awareness of the problems of hunger and malnutrition. Since its inception in 1997 public donations to TeleFood have exceeded US $9m., financing more than 1,000 'grass-roots' projects in more than 100 countries. The projects have provided tools, seeds and other essential supplies directly to small-scale farmers, and have been especially aimed at helping women.

In 1999 FAO signed a memorandum of understanding with UNAIDS on strengthening co-operation. In December 2001 FAO, IFAD and WFP determined to strengthen inter-agency collaboration in developing strategies to combat the threat posed by the HIV/AIDS epidemic to food security, nutrition and rural livelihoods. During that month experts from those organizations and UNAIDS held a technical consultation on means of mitigating the impact of HIV/AIDS on agriculture and rural communities in affected areas.

The Technical Cooperation Department has responsibility for FAO's operational activities, including policy development assistance to member countries; investment support; and the management of activities associated with the development and implementation of country, sub-regional and regional programmes. The Department manages the technical co-operation programme (TCP, which funds 13% of FAO's field programme expenditures), and mobilizes resources.

AGRICULTURE

FAO's Field Programme provides training and technical assistance to enable small-scale farmers to increase crop production by a number of methods, including improved seeds and fertilizer use, soil conservation and reafforestation, better techniques for the management of water resources, upgrading storage facilities, and improvements in processing and marketing. Governments are advised on the conservation of genetic resources, on improving the supply of seeds and on crop protection. In the Far East and Australasia the production of 'miracle rice', a new hybrid, has been encouraged, in order to help satisfy the rapidly-growing demand for the region's most important food crop. In 1999 FAO and the International Rice Research Institute (IRRI, q.v.) agreed to strengthen their collaboration to promote the development and use of hybrid rice, which studies conducted in the People's Republic of China had shown to yield up to 20% more than conventional varieties. In May an FAO-organized intergovernmental meeting, convened in Bangkok, recommended the establishment of a Seed Network for Asia and the Pacific to strengthen local seed production and distribution, including the harmonization of seed regulations, support for technical developments, and improvements to seed supply and marketing.

Plant protection, weed control, and animal health programmes form an important part of FAO's work as farming methods become more intensive, and pests more resistant to control methods. In 1985 the FAO Conference approved an International Code of Conduct on the Distribution and Use of Pesticides, and in 1989 the Conference adopted an additional clause concerning 'Prior Informed Consent' (PIC), whereby international shipments of newly-banned or restricted pesticides should not proceed without the agreement of importing countries. Under the clause FAO aims to inform governments about the hazards of toxic chemicals and to encourage them to take proper measures to curb trade in highly toxic agrochemicals, while keeping the pesticides industry informed of control actions. In 1996 FAO publicized a new initiative which aimed to increase awareness of, and to promote international action on, obsolete and hazardous stocks of pesticides remaining throughout the world (estimated in 2001 to total some 500,000 metric tons). In September 1998 an international conference held in Rotterdam, the Netherlands, adopted the legally-binding Convention on the Prior Informed Consent Procedure for Certain Hazardous Chemicals and Pesticides in International Trade. The so-called Rotterdam Convention, which was to enter into force on being ratified by 50 countries, aimed to protect the health of farmers, workers and consumers in developing nations and to reduce threats to the environment by obliging countries to halt production of the most dangerous compounds, and by specifying that all hazardous chemicals and pesticides banned or severely restricted in at least two countries should not be exported unless explicitly agreed by the importing country. FAO was co-operating with UNEP to provide an interim secretariat for the Convention. In July 1999 a conference on the Rotterdam Convention, held in Rome, established an Interim Chemical Review Committee with responsibility for recommending the inclusion of chemicals or pesticide formulations in the PIC procedure. By March 2002 the treaty had been ratified by 20 states. In 1988 the Integrated Pest Management (IPM) programme was initiated in Asia and the Pacific in an attempt to reduce the environmental risks posed by over-reliance on pesticides. The IPM strategy includes biological control methods, such as the introduction of natural predators (including spiders and wasps) to reduce pest infestation, crop rotation and the use of pest-resistant crop varieties. IPM principles have since been introduced into other regions, based on the Asian experience and are a central concept of FAO's plant protection strategy. FAO's Joint Division with the International Atomic Energy Agency (IAEA), tests controlled-release formulas of pesticides and herbicides that can limit the amount of agrochemicals needed to protect crops, and is engaged in exploring biotechnologies and in developing non-toxic fertilizers (especially those that are locally available) and improved strains of food crops (especially from indigenous varieties). FAO's plant nutrition activities aim to promote nutrient management, such as the Integrated Plant Nutritions Systems (IPNS), which are based on the recycling of nutrients through crop production and the efficient use of mineral fertilizers. In February 2001 FAO warned that some 30% of pesticides sold in developing countries did not meet internationally accepted quality standards.

In June 1996 representatives of more than 150 governments attending a conference in Leipzig, Germany, organized by FAO, adopted a Global Plan of Action to conserve and improve the use of plant genetic resources, in order to enhance food security throughout the world. The Plan included measures to strengthen the development of plant varieties and to promote the use and availability of local varieties and locally-adapted crops to farmers, in particular following a natural disaster, war or civil conflict. The conservation and sustainable use of plant and animal genetic resources are promoted by FAO's Global System for Plant Genetic Resources, which includes five databases, and the Global Strategy on the Management of Farm Animal Genetic Resources. An FAO programme supports the establishment of gene banks, designed to maintain the world's biological diversity by preserving animal and plant species threatened with extinction. FAO, jointly with UNEP, has published a document listing the current state of global livestock genetic diversity. In November 2001 the FAO Conference adopted the International Treaty on Plant Genetic Resources for Food and Agriculture, which was to provide a framework to ensure access to plant genetic resources and to related knowledge, technologies and funding. The Treaty was to enter into force once it had been ratified by 40 signatory states.

FAO's work on soil conservation includes erosion control and the reclamation of degraded land, such as reafforestation after indiscriminate tree-cutting. The fertilizer programme demonstrates to farmers and government officials the benefits of fertilizers, including locally available organic wastes. In 1983 a network of research institutions was set up in 17 Asian countries to provide information on biological nitrogen fixation.

An Emergency Prevention System for Transboundary Animal and Plant Pests and Diseases (EMPRES) was established in 1994 to strengthen FAO's activities in the prevention, control and, where possible, eradication of pests and of highly contagious livestock diseases (which the system categorizes as epidemic diseases of strategic importance, such as rinderpest or foot-and-mouth; diseases requiring tactical attention at international or regional level, e.g. Rift Valley fever; and emerging diseases, e.g. bovine spongiform encephalopathy—BSE). During 1994 EMPRES published guidelines on all aspects of desert locust monitoring, commissioned an evaluation of recent control efforts and prepared a concept paper on desert locust management. FAO has assumed responsibility for technical leadership and co-ordination of the Global Rinderpest Eradication Campaign. The Campaign aims to eradicate the disease, which still affects parts of southern India, Pakistan and Afghanistan, by 2010.

FAO's organic agriculture programme provides technical assistance and policy advice on the production, certification and trading of organic produce. In July 2001 the FAO/WHO Codex Alimentarius Commission adopted guide-lines on organic livestock production, covering organic breeding methods, the elimination of growth hormones and certain chemicals in veterinary medicines, and the use of good quality organic feed with no meat or bone meal content.

FISHERIES

FAO's Fisheries Department consists of a multi-disciplinary body of experts who are involved in every aspect of fisheries development from coastal surveys, conservation management and use of aquatic genetic resources, improvement of production, processing and storage, to the compilation and analysis of statistics, development of computer databases, improvement of fishing gear, institution building and training. In November 1993 the FAO Conference established an Indian Ocean Tuna Commission to facilitate the management and conservation of those resources. In March 1995 a ministerial meeting of fisheries adopted the Rome Consensus on World Fisheries, which identified a need for immediate action to eliminate overfishing and to rebuild and enhance depleting fish stocks. In November the Conference adopted a Code of Conduct for Responsible Fishing, which incorporated many global fisheries and aquaculture issues (including fisheries resource conservation and development, fish catches, seafood and fish-processing, commercialization, trade and research) to promote the sustainable development of the sector. In February 1999 the FAO Committee on Fisheries adopted new international measures, within the framework of the Code of Conduct, in order to reduce over-exploitation of the world's fish resources, as well as plans of action for the conservation and management of sharks and the reduction in the incidental catch of seabirds in longline fisheries. The voluntary measures were endorsed at a ministerial meeting, held in March and attended by representatives of some 126 countries, which issued a declaration to promote the implementation of the Code of Conduct and to achieve sustainable management of fisheries and aquaculture. FAO promotes the use of aquaculture as a source of animal protein and as an income-generating activity for rural communities. A new Programme of Fisheries Assistance for Small Island Developing States, which had been formulated by FAO in consultation with South Pacific member states and with the Alliance of Small Island States, was approved at a session of the Committee on Fisheries in March 1997. The second phase of the South Pacific Aquaculture Development Project covered the period May 1994–May 1999. With funding from the Japanese Government, the project aimed to develop subsistence aquaculture, as well as commercial aquaculture for domestic and export markets, and to enhance aquaculture resources in 15 countries in the region. In February 2000 FAO and the Network of Aquaculture Centres in Asia and the Pacific (NACA, q.v.) jointly convened a Conference on Aquaculture in the Third Millennium, which was held in Bangkok, Thailand, and attended by participants representing more than 200 governmental and non-governmental organizations. The Conference debated global trends in aquaculture and future policy measures to ensure the sustainable development of the sector. It adopted the Bangkok Declaration and Strategy for Aquaculture Beyond 2000. In December 2001 FAO issued a report based on the technical proceedings of the conference. In March 2001 FAO adopted an international plan of action to address the problem of so-called illegal, unreported and unregulated fishing. In October FAO and the Icelandic Government jointly organized the Reykjavik Conference on Responsible Fisheries in the Marine Ecosystem, which adopted a declaration on pursuing responsible and sustainable fishing activities in the context of ecosystem-based fisheries management (EBFM). EBFM involves determining the boundaries of individual marine ecosystems, and maintaining or rebuilding the habitats and biodiversity of each of these so that all species will be supported at levels of maximum production.

FORESTRY

FAO focuses on the contribution of forestry to food security, on effective and responsible forest management and on maintaining a balance between the economic, ecological and social benefits of forest resources. The Organization has helped to develop national forestry programmes and to promote the sustainable development of all types of forest. FAO administers the global Forests, Trees and People Programme, which promotes the sustainable management of tree and forest resources, based on local knowledge and management practices, in order to improve the livelihoods of rural people in developing countries. In Asia and the Pacific the Programme is implemented in collaboration with organizations and institutions in Bangladesh, the People's Republic of China, India, Indonesia, Nepal, Philippines, Thailand and Viet Nam. FAO's Strategic Plan for Forestry was approved in March 1999; its main objectives were to maintain the environmental diversity of forests, to realize the economic potential of forests and trees within a sustainable framework, and to expand access to information on forestry.

PROCESSING AND MARKETING

An estimated 20% of all food harvested is lost before it can be consumed. FAO helps reduce immediate post-harvest losses, with the introduction of improved processing methods and storage systems. It also advises on the distribution and marketing of agricultural produce and on the selection and preparation of foods for optimum nutrition. FAO continues to favour the elimination of export subsidies and related discriminatory practices, in particular those which create unfavourable trading conditions for developing countries dependent on agricultural products as their main source of foreign income. FAO has organized regional workshops and national projects in order to help member states to implement new World Trade Organization regulations, in particular with regard to agricultural policy, intellectual property rights, sanitary and phytosanitary measures, technical barriers to trade and the international standards of the Codex Alimentarius. FAO evaluates new market trends and helps to develop improved plant and animal quarantine procedures. In November 1997 the FAO Conference adopted new guidelines on surveillance and on export certification systems in order to harmonize plant quarantine standards. In August 1999 FAO announced the establishment of a new forum, PhAction, to promote post-harvest research and the development of effective post-harvest services and infrastructure.

ENVIRONMENT

At the UN Conference on Environment and Development, held in Rio de Janeiro in June 1992, FAO participated in several working parties and supported the adoption of Agenda 21, a programme of activities to promote sustainable development. FAO was subsequently designated as the UN agency responsible for the chapters of Agenda 21 concerned with water resources, forests, fragile mountain ecosystems and sustainable agriculture and rural development. FAO was designated by the UN General Assembly as the lead agency for co-ordinating the International Year of Mountains (2002), which aimed to raise awareness of mountain ecosystems and to promote the conservation and sustainable development of mountainous regions.

NUTRITION

In December 1992 an International Conference on Nutrition was held in Rome, administered jointly by FAO and WHO. The Conference approved a World Declaration on Nutrition and a Plan of Action, with the aim of eliminating hunger and reducing levels of malnutrition by incorporating nutritional objectives into national development polices and governmental programmes. Since the conference, more than 100 countries have formulated national plans of action for nutrition, many of which were based on existing development plans such as comprehensive food security initiatives, national poverty alleviation programmes and action plans to attain the targets set by the World Summit for Children in September 1990. In January 2001 a joint team of FAO and WHO experts issued a report concerning the allergenicity of foods derived from biotechnology (i.e. genetically modified—GM foods). In July the Codex Alimentarius Commission agreed the first global principles for assessing the safety of GM foods, and approved a series of maximum levels of environmental contaminants in food. In April 2002 FAO and WHO announced a joint review of their food standards operations, including the activities of the Commission.

FOOD SECURITY

FAO's food security policy aims to encourage the production of adequate food supplies, to maximize stability in the flow of supplies, and to ensure access on the part of those who need them. FAO was actively involved in the formulation of a Plan of Action on food security, adopted at the World Food Summit in November 1996, and was to be responsible for monitoring and promoting its implementation. FAO's Special Programme for Food Security (SPFS), which was initiated in 1994, was designed to assist target countries, i.e. low-income countries with a food deficit, to increase food production and productivity as rapidly as possible. This was to be achieved primarily through the widespread adoption by farmers of available improved production technologies, with emphasis on areas of high potential. In March 1999 FAO signed agreements with IFAD and the WFP, in order to increase co-operation within the framework of the SPFS. At May 2002 82 countries were categorized as 'low-income food-deficit', of which 24 were in Asia. The SPFS was operational in 69 countries. The Programme promotes South-South co-operation to improve food security and the exchange of knowledge and experience. In 2002 26 bilateral co-operation agreements were in force, for example, between Pakistan and Swaziland and Viet Nam and Benin.

FAO's Global Information and Early Warning System (GIEWS), which became operational in 1975, maintains a database on and monitors the crop and food outlook at global, regional, national and sub-national levels in order to detect emerging food supply difficulties and disasters and to ensure rapid intervention in countries experiencing food supply shortages. From early 1997 the GIEWS intensified efforts to monitor weather developments resulting from the periodic warming of the tropical Pacific Ocean (the so-called 'El Niño' effect) and the consequent prospects for crops and food security. FAO provided technical advice to strengthen agricultural systems against the effects of El Niño, for example by introducing drought- and cyclone-resistant crop patterns, farming and fishing practices in South Asian countries. In October 1999 FAO published the first *State of Food Insecurity in the World,* based on data compiled by a new Food Insecurity and Vulnerability Information and Mapping Systems programme. In July 2002 the GIEWS issued a special report on the food production situation in the Democratic People's Republic of Korea. A report on the situation in Afghanistan was published in the following month.

FAO INVESTMENT CENTRE

The Investment Centre was established in 1964 to help countries prepare viable investment projects that would attract external financing. In 1993 the Centre focused its evaluation of projects on two fundamental concerns: promotion of sustainable activities for land management, forestry development and environmental protection, and the alleviation of rural poverty. In 2000–01 90 projects were approved, representing a total investment of US $3,700m.

EMERGENCY RELIEF

FAO works to rehabilitate agricultural production following natural and man-made disasters by providing emergency seed, tools and technical and other assistance. New projects approved by FAO's Special Relief Operations Service in 2001 included the emergency provision of essential inputs for drought- and conflict-affected farmers in Afghanistan, procurement of drought-resistant wheat, chickpea seed and fertilizer for drought-affected farmers, supply of vegetable kits to returnee families, and the distribution to farmers in the Afghan central highlands of seed, fertilizer and equipment for seed multiplication; emergency control of a PPR ('peste des petits ruminants') epidemic in Bangladesh; emergency provision of rice seed for flood-affected households in Cambodia; support for a double-cropping and crop diversification programme in the Democratic People's Republic of Korea (DPRK) and emergency provision of fertilizers to flood-affected areas of that country; support for urgent maize and rice seed multiplication in local communities in East Timor; emergency provision of seeds to flood-affected provinces of Indonesia (West Sumatra, Jambi and North Sumatra) and emergency food production support for returnee farmers in North Maluku; assistance for the Mongolian national programme for the protection of livestock from drought and harsh winter weather conditions in that country; and the emergency supply of seed and agricultural materials to communities affected by flooding in Viet Nam and assistance to flood-affected fish farmers in that country. Since the 1980s FAO has provided support for the agricultural sector in Afghanistan (devastated for many years by civil conflict and drought). Following the establishment of the Afghan Interim Administration in December 2001, FAO supported its newly-developed food security strategy, which aimed to move emphasis from relief to rehabilitation efforts. In January 2002, under the UN's Immediate and Transitional Assistance Programme for the Afghan People, FAO appealed for US $18m. for emergency activities and US $21m. for medium-term activities. Under the UN inter-agency appeal for the DPRK in 2002 FAO appealed for US $16m. for the procurement of agricultural inputs. FAO also appealed for US $2m. to fund the emergency agricultural relief component of the 2002 UN inter-agency appeal for Indonesia. Jointly with the United Nations, FAO is responsible for the WFP (see below), which provides emergency food supplies and food aid in support of development projects.

INFORMATION

FAO functions as an information centre, collecting, analysing, interpreting and disseminating information through various media. It issues regular statistical reports, commodity studies, and technical manuals in local languages (see list of publications below). Other materials produced by the FAO include information booklets, reference papers, reports of meetings, training manuals and audiovisual materials.

FAO 's internet-based interactive World Agricultural Information Centre (WAICENT) offers access to agricultural publications, technical documentation, codes of conduct, data, statistics and multimedia resources. FAO compiles and co-ordinates an extensive range of international databases on agriculture, fisheries, forestry, food and statistics, the most important of these being AGRIS (the International Information System for the Agricultural Sciences and Technology) and CARIS (the Current Agricultural Research Information System). Statistical databases include GLOBEFISH databank and electronic library, FISHDAB (the Fisheries Statistical Database), FORIS (Forest Resources Information System), and GIS (the Geographical Information System). In addition, FAOSTAT provides access to updated figures in six agricultural-related topics.

Regional Commissions

Asia and Pacific Commission on Agricultural Statistics: c/o FAO Regional Office, Bangkok; f. 1962 to review the state of food and agricultural statistics in the region and to advise on the development and standardization of agricultural statistics. Mems: 24 states.

Asia and Pacific Plant Protection Commission: c/o FAO Regional Office, Bangkok; f. 1956 (adopted present name 1983) to strengthen international co-operation in plant protection to prevent the introduction and spread of destructive plant diseases and pests; Exec. Sec. Prof. C. Y. SHEN. Mems: 25 states.

Asia-Pacific Fishery Commission: c/o FAO Regional Office, Bangkok; f. 1948 to develop fisheries, encourage and co-ordinate research, disseminate information, recommend management measures to governments, propose standards in technique and nomenclature. Mems: 20 states.

Asia-Pacific Forestry Commission: Viale delle Terme di Caracalla, 00100 Rome, Italy; f. 1949 to advise on the formulation of forestry policy and review and co-ordinate its implementation throughout the region; to exchange information and advise on technical problems. Mems: 29 states.

Commission for Controlling the Desert Locust in the Eastern Region of its distribution area in South West Asia: Viale delle Terme di Caracalla, 00100 Rome, Italy; f. 1964 to carry out all possible measures to control plagues of the desert locust in the region. Mems: Afghanistan, India, Iran, Pakistan.

Indian Ocean Fishery Commission: c/o FAO Fisheries Dept, Viale delle Terme di Caracalla, 00100 Rome, Italy; f. 1967 to promote national programmes, research and development activities, and to examine management problems; Sec. B. P. SATIA. Mems: 41 states.

International Rice Commission: Viale delle Terme di Caracalla, 00100 Rome, Italy; f. 1948 to promote national and international action on production, conservation, distribution and consumption of rice, except matters relating to international trade. Mems: 60 states.

Regional Animal Production and Health Commission for Asia and the Pacific: c/o FAO Regional Office, Bangkok; f. 1973 to promote livestock development in general, and national and international research and action with respect to animal health and husbandry problems in the region. Mems: 15 states.

Finance

FAO's Regular Programme, which is financed by contributions from member governments, covers the cost of the FAO Secretariat, its Technical Co-operation Programme (TCP) and part of the cost of several special action programmes. The budget for the two years 2002–03 totalled US $651.8m. Much of FAO's technical assistance programme is funded from extra-budgetary sources. The single largest contributor is the United Nations Development Programme (UNDP), which in 1999 accounted for US $26m., or 8.5% of total field project expenditures. More important are the trust funds that come mainly from donor countries and international financing institutions. In 1999 they totalled US $228m., or 76.5% of field project expenditures. FAO's contribution under the TCP (FAO's regular budgetary funds for the Field Programme) was some US $39m., or 13% of field project expenditures in that year, while the Organization's contribution under the Special Programme for Food Security was US $5m., or some 1.7% of the total of US $298m. In 2001 total field programme expenditure amounted to US $367m.

World Food Programme—WFP

Address: Via Cesare Giulio Viola 68, Parco dei Medici, 00148 Rome, Italy.

Telephone: (06) 651-31; **fax:** (06) 651-328-40; **e-mail:** wfpinfo@wfp.org; **internet:** www.wfp.org.

WFP Asia Bureau: f. Aug. 2001; covers Bangladesh, Bhutan, Cambodia, People's Republic of China, East Timor, India, Indonesia, Democratic Republic of Korea, Laos, Myanmar, Nepal and Sri Lanka; Chief JOHN POWELL.

WFP, which became operational in 1963, is the principal food aid agency of the UN. It aims to alleviate acute hunger by providing emergency relief following natural or man-made humanitarian disasters, to eradicate chronic undernourishment, and to support social development. Priority is given to vulnerable groups, such as children and pregnant women. Since the mid-1990s WFP has placed particular emphasis on the needs and interests of girls and women, believing that—through improving levels of income, health and nutrition—the education of girls contributes significantly both to individual empowerment and to national development and the eradication of poverty. During 2001 WFP benefited some 77m. people world-wide, of whom 20m. received aid through development projects, 43m. through emergency operations, and 14m. through rehabilitation programmes. Total food deliveries in that year amounted to 4.2m. metric tons in 82 countries.

Through its development activities WFP aims to alleviate poverty in developing countries by promoting self-reliant families and communities. Food is supplied, for example, as an incentive in labour-intensive projects that provide employment and strengthen self-help capacity. WFP supports activities to boost agricultural production, to rehabilitate and improve local infrastructure, particularly transport systems, and to encourage education, training and health programmes. Some WFP projects are intended to alleviate the effects of structural adjustment programmes (particularly programmes that involve reductions in public expenditure and in subsidies for basic foods). During 2001 operational expenditure on development projects undertaken in Asia amounted to an estimated US $79.2m., or 35.2% of WFP's total development expenditure world-wide. School feeding projects benefited 15m. children during that year. In 2001 WFP initiated a new Global School Feeding Campaign to strengthen international co-operation to expand educational opportunities for poor children and to improve the quality of the teaching environment.

In the early 1990s there was a substantial shift in the balance between emergency relief and development assistance provided by WFP, owing to the growing needs of victims of drought and other natural disasters, refugees and displaced persons. Following a comprehensive evaluation of its activities, WFP became increasingly focused on linking its relief and development activities to provide a continuum between short-term relief and longer-term rehabilitation and development. In order to achieve this objective, WFP has aimed to integrate elements that strengthen disaster mitigation into development projects, including soil conservation, reafforestation, irrigation infrastructure and transport construction and rehabilitation, and to promote capacity-building elements within relief operations, e.g. training, income-generating activities and environmental protection measures. A new programme of emergency response training was inaugurated in 2000, while security concerns for personnel was incorporated as a new element into all general planning and training activities. In 1999 WFP adopted a new Food Aid and Development policy, which aims to use food assistance both to cover immediate requirements and to create conditions conducive to enhancing the long-term food security of vulnerable populations. During that year Protracted Relief and Recovery Operations (PRROs) were introduced, where the emphasis is on fostering stability, rehabilitation and long-term development after an emergency. In these operations, which are undertaken in collaboration with UNHCR and other international agencies, WFP is responsible for mobilizing basic food commodities and for related transport, handling and storage costs. Countries in which PRROs were implemented in 2001 included Afghanistan, Bangladesh, Cambodia, India, Indonesia, Myanmar, Nepal and Sri Lanka. During that year WFP's operational expenditure on relief operations in Asia amounted to an estimated US $463.8m., equivalent to 33.2% of world-wide relief expenditure.

The key elements of WFP's emergency response capacity are its strategic stores of food and logistics equipment, stand-by arrangements to enable the rapid deployment of personnel, communications and other essential equipment, and the Augmented Logistics Intervention Team for Emergencies (ALITE), which undertakes capacity assessments and contingency-planning. In 2000 a new UN Humanitarian Response Depot was opened in Brindisi, Italy, under the direction of WFP experts, for the storage of essential rapid response equipment. In that year WFP also led efforts, undertaken with other UN humanitarian agencies, for the design and application of local UN Joint Logistics Centre facilities, which aimed to co-ordinate resources in an emergency situation. A Vulnerability Analysis and Mapping (VAM) Unit provides food security analysis, enabling WFP to identify populations affected by or at risk of hunger and malnutrition and to target its food aid as effectively as possible. VAM projects have been conducted in Afghanistan, Cambodia, the People's Republic of China, Laos and Pakistan.

In recent years WFP has been actively concerned wth the food situation in the Democratic People's Republic of Korea (DPRK), which has required substantial levels of emergency food supplies owing to natural disasters and consistently poor harvests. In September/October 1998 WFP, together with UNICEF and the EU, conducted the first random nation-wide nutritional survey in the DPRK, which identified some 16% of young children as suffering acute malnutrition and 60% suffering long-term malnutrition. By mid-1999 an estimated 1.5m.–3.5m. people had died of starvation in the DPRK since 1995. In 2002 WFP aimed to provide food assistance to some 4.5m. people in that country and support to 2m. others, particularly through 'food for work' activities. In September, however, WFP announced that it had suspended the delivery of cereals assistance to some 3m. people in the DPRK, owing to a shortfall in funding for its emergency activities there. WFP has also been active in Afghanistan, where civil conflict and severe drought have caused massive food insecurity and population displacement. In March 2001 WFP launched an appeal for US $76m. to fund a new one-year emergency operation to assist 3.8m. people. In August WFP reported a substantial cereal deficit in the country and identified widespread pre-famine conditions. Accordingly, the operation was expanded to provide assistance to 5.5m. people, with new funding requirements amounting to US $151m., in order to meet its objectives, which included delivering food to those threatened with starvation, providing subsidized bread to urban communities, and encouraging farmers to engage in productive activities. In mid-September, however, the delivery of food aid to Afghanistan was suspended and all international personnel were withdrawn owing to a deterioration in the security situation and expectation of imminent military action by a US-led coalition against the Taliban regime. Food shipments to northern areas of the country were resumed later in that month. Meanwhile, in readiness for a predicted mass influx of refugees from Afghanistan were international military action to be initiated, WFP staff were mobilized in neighbouring countries and emergency supplies stockpiled in border regions. The first delivery of humanitarian supplies by air was undertaken in late October. However, despite the swift withdrawal of the Taliban authorities, and the establishment of the Afghan Interim Administration in December, the distribution of aid was still seriously hampered by poor rural infrastructure, adverse weather conditions and ongoing security concerns. In April 2002 WFP launched a new nine-month US $285m. operation for Afghanistan with a focus on recovery and rehabiliation rather than relief. In addition to the provision of 1.2m. metric tons of emergency food aid, activities aimed at assisting 9m. Afghans included food for workers engaged in reconstructing the country's infrastructure and for farmers concerned with rehabilitating irrigation systems, an expansion of bakery projects staffed by women, and support for school feeding projects targeting 1m. children.

WFP Executive Director: JAMES T. MORRIS (USA).

FAO Publications

Animal Health Yearbook.
Commodity Review and Outlook (annually).
Environment and Energy Bulletin.
Fertilizer Yearbook.
Food Crops and Shortages.
Food Outlook (5 a year).
Plant Protection Bulletin.
Production Yearbook.
Quarterly Bulletin of Statistics.
The State of Food and Agriculture (annually).
The State of Food Insecurity in the World (annually).
The State of World Fisheries and Aquaculture (every 2 years).
The State of the World's Forests (every 2 years).
Technical Co-operation Among Developing Countries Newsletter.
Trade Yearbook.
Unasylva (quarterly).
Yearbook of Fishery Statistics.
Yearbook of Forest Products.
World Animal Review (quarterly).
World Watch List for Domestic Animal Diversity.

International Bank for Reconstruction and Development—IBRD, and International Development Association—IDA (World Bank)

Address: 1818 H St, NW, Washington, DC 20433, USA.

Telephone: (202) 477-1234; **fax:** (202) 477-6391; **e-mail:** pic@worldbank.org; **internet:** www.worldbank.org.

The IBRD was established in December 1945. Initially it was concerned with post-war reconstruction in Europe; since then its aim has been to assist the economic development of member nations by making loans where private capital is not available on reasonable terms to finance productive investments. Loans are made either directly to governments, or to private enterprises with the guarantee of their governments. The 'World Bank', as it is commonly known, comprises the IBRD and the International Development Association (IDA), which was founded in 1960. The affiliated group of institutions, comprising the IBRD, the IDA, the International Finance Corporation (IFC, q.v.) the Multilateral Investment Guarantee Agency (MIGA, q.v.) and the International Centre for Settlement of Investment Disputes (ICSID, see below), is referred to as the World Bank Group. Only members of the International Monetary Fund (IMF, q.v.) may be considered for membership in the Bank. Subscriptions to the capital stock of the Bank are based on each member's quota in the IMF, which is designed to reflect the country's relative economic strength. Voting rights are related to shareholdings.

Organization

(October 2002)

Officers and staff of the IBRD serve concurrently as officers and staff in the International Development Association (IDA). The World Bank has offices in Brussels, New York, Paris (for Europe), Frankfurt, Geneva, London and Tokyo, as well as in more than 100 countries of operation. Country Directors are located in some 28 country offices.

BOARD OF GOVERNORS

The Board of Governors consists of one Governor appointed by each member nation. Typically, a Governor is the country's finance minister, central bank governor, or a minister or an official of comparable rank. The Board normally meets once a year.

EXECUTIVE DIRECTORS

The general operations of the World Bank are conducted by a Board of 24 Executive Directors. Five Directors are appointed by the five members having the largest number of shares of capital stock, and the rest are elected by the Governors representing the other members. The President of the Bank is Chairman of the Board.

OFFICERS

President and Chairman of Executive Directors: JAMES D. WOLFENSOHN (USA).

Vice-President, South Asia Regional Office: MIEKO NISHIMIZU.

Vice-President, East Asia and the Pacific Regional Office: JEMAL-UD-DIN KASSUM.

Activities

FINANCIAL OPERATIONS

The IBRD's capital is derived from members' subscriptions to capital shares, the calculation of which is based on their quotas in the IMF. In April 1988 the Board of Governors approved an increase of about 80% in the IBRD's authorized capital, to US $171,000m. At 30 June 2001 the total subscribed capital of the IBRD was US $189,505m., of which the paid-in portion amounted to US $11,476m. (6.1%); the remainder is subject to call if required. Most of the IBRD's lendable funds come from its borrowing in world capital markets, and also from its retained earnings and the flow of repayments on its loans. Bank loans carry a variable interest rate, rather than a rate fixed at the time of borrowing.

IBRD loans are usually for a period of 20 years or less. Loans are made to governments, or must be guaranteed by the government concerned. IDA assistance is aimed at the poorer developing countries (i.e. those with an annual per caput GNP of less than US $885 during 1999/2000 qualified for assistance in 2000/01). Under IDA lending conditions, credits can be extended to countries whose balance of payments could not sustain the burden of repayment required for IBRD loans. Terms are more favourable than those provided by the IBRD; credits are for a period of 35–40 years, with a 'grace' period of 10 years, and no interest charges. In September 2001 the World Bank granted Indonesia temporary access to IDA resources as part of measures to resolve that country's financial difficulties.

IDA's development resources, consisting of members' subscriptions and supplementary resources (additional subscriptions and contributions) are replenished periodically by contributions from the more affluent member countries. In March 1996 representatives of more than 30 donor countries concluded negotiations for the 11th replenishment of IDA funds (and for a one-year interim fund), to finance the period July 1996–June 1999. New contributions over the three-year period were to amount to US $11,000m., while total funds available for lending, including past donor contributions, repayments of IDA credits and the World Bank's contributions, were to amount to US $22,000m. In November 1998 representatives of 39 donor countries agreed to provide US $11,600m. for the 12th replenishment of IDA funds, enabling total lending to amount to an estimated US $20,500m. in the period July 1999–June 2002. The new IDA-12 resources were to be directed towards the following objectives: investing in people; promoting good governance; promoting broad-based growth; and protecting the environment. Discussions on the 13th replenishment of IDA resources were undertaken in 2001/02, and for the first time involved representatives of borrowing countries, civil society and other public groups. A final commitment, providing for some US $23,000m. in resources in the period 1 July 2002–30 June 2005, was concluded in early July 2002.

The World Bank's primary objectives are the achievement of sustainable economic growth and the reduction of poverty in developing countries. In March 1997 the Board of Executive Directors endorsed a 'Strategic Compact', providing for a programme of reforms, to be implemented over a period of 30 months, to increase the effectiveness of the Bank in achieving its central objective of poverty reduction. The reforms included greater decentralization of decision-making, and investment in front-line operations, enhancing the administration of loans, and improving access to information and co-ordination of Bank activities through a knowledge management system comprising four thematic networks: the Human Development Network; the Environmentally and Socially Sustainable Development Network; the Finance, Private Sector and Infrastructure Development Network; and the Poverty Reduction and Economic Management Network. In 2000/01 the Bank adopted a new two-year Strategic Framework which emphasized two essential approaches for Bank support: strengthening the investment climate and prospects for sustainable development in a country, and supporting investment in the poor. In September 2001 the Bank announced that it was to join the UN as a full partner in implementing the so-called Millennium Development Goals, and was to make them central to its development agenda. The objectives, which were approved by governments attending a special session of the UN General Assembly in September 2000, included a reduction by 50% in the number of people with an income of less than US $1 a day and those suffering from hunger and lack of safe drinking water by 2015. The Bank was closely involved in preparations for the International Conference on Financing for Development, which was held in Monterrey, Mexico, in March 2002, and incorporated discussions on achieving the Millennium Goals.

The Bank compiles country-specific assessments and formulates country assistance strategies (CASs) to review and guide the Bank's country programmes. Since 1998 the Bank has published CASs, with the approval of the governments concerned. In 1989/90 systematic 'screening' of all new projects was introduced, in order to assess their environmental impact. In addition, the Bank supports individual countries to prepare and implement national environmental action plans (NEAPs) and to strengthen their institutional capacity for environmental planning and management. In 1998/99 the Bank's Executive Directors endorsed a Comprehensive Development Framework (CDF) to effect a new approach to development assistance based on partnerships and country responsibility. The Framework, which aimed to enhance the overall effectiveness of development assistance, was formulated after a series of consultative meetings, organized by the Bank and attended by representatives of governments, donor agencies, financial institutions, non-governmental organizations, the private sector and academics.

In December 1999 the Bank introduced a new approach to implement the principles of the CDF, as part of its strategy to enhance the debt relief scheme for heavily indebted poor countries (see below). Applicant countries were requested to formulate a national strategy to reduce poverty, to be presented in the form of a Poverty Reduction Strategy Papers (PRSP). In cases where there might be some delay in issuing a full PRSP, it was permissible for a country to submit a less detailed 'interim' PRSP (I-PRSP) in order to secure the preliminary qualification for debt relief. During 2000/01 32 countries issued full and interim PRSPs for consideration by the Bank and IMF, compared with 12 in the previous year. During that year the Bank introduced a new Poverty Reduction Support Credit to help low-income countries to implement the policy and institutional reforms outlined in their PRSP. The first credits were approved for Uganda and Viet Nam in May and June respectively. It was envisaged that in 2001/02 each CAS presented for an IDA country would be based on a PRSP. In January 2002 a PRSP public review conference, attended by more than 200 representatives of donor agencies, civil society groups, and developing country organizations was held as part of an ongoing review of the scheme by the Bank and the IMF.

In September 1996 the World Bank/IMF Development Committee endorsed a joint initiative to assist heavily indebted poor countries (HIPCs) to reduce their debt burden to a sustainable level, in order to make more resources available for poverty reduction and economic growth. A new Trust Fund was established by the World Bank in November to finance the initiative. The Fund, consisting of an initial allocation of US $500m. from the IBRD surplus and other contributions from multilateral creditors, was to be administered by IDA. Of the 41 HIPCs identified by the Bank, only three—Laos, Myanmar and Viet Nam—were in the Far East and Australasia region. Countries were required to have implemented extensive programmes of economic and social reform for at least three years before being considered eligible for assistance under the scheme, and for a total of at least six years before receiving any assistance. In September 1999 the Bank and IMF reached an agreement on an enhanced HIPC scheme to allow more countries to benefit from the initiative, to accelerate the process by which a country may qualify for assistance and to enhance the effectiveness of debt relief. Additional revenue was to be generated through the revaluation of a percentage of IMF gold reserves. Under the enhanced initiative it was agreed that, during the initial phase of the process to ensure suitability for debt relief, each applicant country should formulate a PRSP, and should demonstrate prudent financial management in the implementation of the strategy for at least one year, with support from the IDA and IMF. At the pivotal 'decision point' of the process, having thus developed and successfully applied the poverty reduction strategy, applicant countries still deemed to have an unsustainable level of debt were to qualify for interim debt relief from the IMF and IDA, as well as relief on highly concessional terms from other official bilateral creditors and multilateral institutions. In the majority of cases a sustainable level of debt was targeted at 150% of the net present value (NPV) of the debt in relation to total annual exports (compared with 200%–250% under the original HIPC scheme). Other countries with a lower debt-to-export ratio were to be eligible for assistance under the initiative, providing that their export earnings were at least 30% of GDP (lowered from 40%) and government revenue at least 15% of GDP (reduced from 20%). During the ensuing 'interim period' countries were required successfully to implement further economic and social development reforms, as a final demonstration of suitability for securing full debt relief at the 'completion point' of the scheme. At July 2002 debt relief valued at US $25,102m. in NPV terms had been approved under the initiative, of which the Bank's contribution was US $6,394m.

During 1997/98 the extreme financial difficulties confronting several Asian economies tested the Bank's capacity to respond effectively to major financial challenges and accelerated its process of internal reform. A Special Financial Operations Unit was established to help to alleviate the consequences of the crisis in all affected countries, while collaboration with external partners was enhanced. The Bank pledged some US $16,000m., in addition to its regular lending programme, to help to alleviate the social consequences of the crisis by protecting social services and strengthening social security and other public funding for the poor and disadvantaged, mainly in Thailand and Indonesia. The Bank also helped to formulate programmes to strengthen legal and institutional frameworks and to restructure the financial services sector and corporate governance. In April 1998 the Bank agreed to administer a new US $40m. Asian Financial Crisis Response Trust Fund, which had been established at the second Asia-Europe Meeting (ASEM, see p. 1532). By 30 June 2000 the Trust Fund had provided support for 69 activities in seven countries, mainly relating to corporate and banking sector reforms, at a total cost of some US $43m. In June a Japan Social Development Fund, with resources amounting to some US $93m., was established by the Japanese Government to fund social programmes to assist the poorest communities affected by the financial crisis and other grassroots capacity-building activities. The Bank is a trustee, with the Asian Development Bank, of the Trust Fund for East Timor, which was established in December 1999, with donations of some US $147m., to channel support during the transition towards independence. In May 2002 an Afghanistan Reconstruction Trust Fund was established to provide a co-ordinated financing mechanism to support the interim administration in that country. The Bank is the Administrator of the Trust, which is managed jointly by the Bank, Asian Development Bank, Islamic Development Bank and UNDP.

During the year ending 30 June 2001 31% of Bank assistance approved was for the Far East and Australasia: the total amount for the region was US $5,380.3m. (compared with US $5,091.5m. in the previous financial year), of which US $3,171.1m. was in the form of IBRD loans and US $2,209.2m. in IDA credits (see table).

TECHNICAL ASSISTANCE

The provision of technical assistance to member countries is a major component of Bank activities. The economic and sector work (ESW) undertaken by the Bank is the vehicle for considerable technical assistance. In addition, project loans and credits may include funds designated specifically for feasibility studies, resource surveys, management or planning advice, and training. The Economic Development Institute has become one of the most important of the Bank's activities in technical assistance. It provides training in national economic management and project analysis for government officials at the middle and upper levels of responsibility. It also runs overseas courses aiming to build up local training capability, and administers a graduate scholarship programme.

In 1992 the Bank established an Institutional Development Fund (IDF) to provide rapid, small-scale financial assistance, to a maximum value of US $500,000, for capacity-building proposals.

ECONOMIC RESEARCH AND STUDIES

In the 1990s the World Bank's research, carried out by its own research staff, was increasingly concerned with providing information to reinforce the Bank's expanding advisory role to developing countries. Consequently the principal areas of current research focus on issues such as maintaining sustainable growth while protecting the environment and the poorest sectors of society, encouraging the development of the private sector, and reducing and decentralizing government activities. The Bank, together with UNDP, UNEP and FAO, sponsors the Consultative Group on International Agricultural Research (CGIAR), which was formed in 1971 to raise financial support for research on improving crops and animal production in developing countries. The Group supports 16 research centres.

CO-OPERATION WITH OTHER ORGANIZATIONS

The World Bank co-operates closely with other UN bodies, through consultations, meetings and joint activities. It collaborates with the IMF in implementing economic adjustment programmes in developing countries. The Bank holds regular consultations with the European Community and OECD on development issues, and the Bank-NGO Committee provides an annual forum for discussion with non-governmental organizations (NGOs). The Bank chairs meetings of donor governments and organizations for the co-ordination of aid to particular countries. The Bank also conducts co-financing and aid co-ordination projects with official aid agencies, export credit agencies and commercial banks.

In 1997 a Partnerships Group was established to strengthen the Bank's work with development institutions, representatives of civil society and the private sector. The Group established a Development Grant Facility to support partnership initiatives in key areas of concern and to co-ordinate all of the Bank's grant-making activities. Also in 1997 the Bank, in partnership with the IMF, UNCTAD, UNDP, the World Trade Organization (WTO) and International Trade Commission, established an Integrated Framework for Trade-related Assistance to Least Developed Countries, at the request of the WTO, to assist those countries to integrate into the global trading system and improve basic trading capabilities. Strengthening co-operation with external partners was a fundamental element of the Comprehensive Development Framework, which was adopted in 1998/99 (see above). In March 1998 the Bank helped to organize the first Asia Development Forum, which convened some 300 representatives of government, the private sector and academia to discuss the region's prospects for economic recovery. A second Forum was held in June 2000, in Singapore, and the third, organized by the bank with the Asian Development Bank, the ADB Institute, and ESCAP to enhance further development capacity, was convened in June 2001, in Bangkok, Thailand. A fourth Forum was scheduled to be held in Seoul, Republic of Korea, in November 2002, on the theme of trade and poverty.

The Bank conducts co-financing and aid co-ordination projects with official aid agencies, export credit institutions and commercial banks. During the year ending 30 June 2001 co-financing contributions to Bank-funded projects amounted to US $5,470m., or some 29% of the total cost.

The World Bank administers the Global Environment Facility (GEF), which was established in 1990 in conjunction with UNDP and UNEP (see p. 1474). In June 1995 the World Bank joined other international donors (including regional development banks, other UN bodies, Canada, France, the Netherlands and the USA) in establishing a Consultative Group to Assist the Poorest (CGAP) with an initial credit of approximately US $200m. The Bank manages the CGAP Secretariat, which is responsible for the administration of external funding and for the evaluation and approval of project financing. In addition, the CGAP provides training and information services on microfinance for policy-makers and practitioners.

EVALUATION

The Bank's Operations Evaluation Department is an independent unit within the World Bank, which studies and publishes the results of projects after a loan has been fully disbursed, so as to identify problems and possible improvements in future activities. Internal auditing is also carried out, to monitor the effectiveness of the Bank's operations and management.

In September 1993 the Bank's Board of Executive Directors agreed to establish an independent Inspection Panel, consistent with the Bank's objective of improving project implementation and accountability. The Panel, which became operational in September 1994, was to conduct independent investigations and reports on complaints concerning the design, appraisal and implementation of development projects supported by the Bank. The first project considered by the Panel was that of the Arun III hydroelectric facilities in Nepal, which the panel ruled to be a violation of IDA social and environmental policies. In June 1995 the Panel reported the findings of its investigations into the main areas of concern regarding the project, namely environmental assessment, involuntary resettlement and treatment of indigenous peoples. In August the Bank decided not to finance the project. By the end of 2001 the panel had received 22 formal requests for inspection, and had undertaken 12 investigations.

IBRD INSTITUTIONS

World Bank Institute—WBI: founded in March 1999 by merger of the Bank's Learning and Leadership Centre, previously responsible for internal staff training, and the Economic Development Institute (EDI), which had been established in 1955 to train government officials concerned with development programmes and policies. The new Institute aimed to emphasize the Bank's priority areas through the provision of training courses and seminars relating to poverty, crisis response, good governance and anti-corruption strategies. The WBI also aimed to take the lead in co-ordinating a process of consultation and dialogue with researchers and other representatives of civil society to examine poverty for the 2000/01 *World Development Report.* During 1999/2000 the WBI expanded its programmes through distance learning, global knowledge networks, and use of new technologies. Under the EDI a World Links for Development programme was initiated to connect schools in developing countries with partner establishments in industrialized nations via the internet. A new initiative, Global Development Learning Network, aimed to expand access to information and learning opportunities through the internet, videoconferences and organized exchanges. Vice-Pres. FRANNIE LÉAUTIER (Tanzania/France).

International Centre for Settlement of Investment Disputes—ICSID: founded in 1966 under the Convention of the Settlement of Investment Disputes between States and Nationals of Other States. The Convention was designed to encourage the growth of private foreign investment for economic development, by creating the possibility, always subject to the consent of both parties, for a Contracting State and a foreign investor who is a national of another Contracting State to settle any legal dispute that might arise out of such an investment by conciliation and/or arbitration before an impartial, international forum. The governing body of the Centre is its Administrative Council, composed of one representative of each Contracting State, all of whom have equal voting power. The President of the World Bank is (*ex officio*) the non-voting Chairman of the Administrative Council.

At March 2002 134 states had ratified the Convention to become ICSID Contracting States. At the end of 2001 the number of cases registered with the Centre totalled 95. Sec.-Gen. KO-YUNG TUNG.

WORLD BANK OPERATIONS IN THE FAR EAST AND AUSTRALASIA

IBRD Loans Approved, 1 July 2000–30 June 2001

Country	Purpose	Amount (US $ million)
China, People's Republic	Inland waterways III project	100.0
	Liao river basin project	100.0
	Jiangxi highway II project	200.0
	Shijiazhuang urban transport project	100.0
	Huai river pollution control project	105.5
	Water conservation	74.0
	Urumqi urban transport improvement project	100.0
	Financial sector technical assistance (supplemental loan)	8.0
India	Karnataka economic restructuring*	75.0
	Grand trunk road improvement project	589.0
	Karnataka state highways improvement project	360.0
	Powergrid system development II project	450.0
	Rajasthan power sector restructuring project	180.0
	Gujarat State highway project	381.0
Indonesia	Provincial health II project*	63.2
	Kecamatan development II project*	208.9
	Western Java environmental management project*	11.7
Philippines	Metro Manila urban transport integration project	60.0
	Land administration and management project	4.8

IDA Credits Approved, 1 July 2000–30 June 2001

Country	Purpose	Amount (US $ million)
Bangladesh	Legal and judicial capacity building project	30.6
	Post-literacy and continuing education for human development project	53.3
	Poverty alleviation microfinance II project	151.0
	HIV/AIDS prevention project	40.0
	Air quality management project	4.7
Cambodia	Flood rehabilitation social fund II project (supplemental credit)	10.0
	Flood emergency rehabilitation project	35.0
India	Rajasthan second district primary education project	74.4
	Karnataka watershed development project	100.4
	Karnataka economic restructuring*	75.0
	National leprosy elimination II project	30.0
	Madhya Pradesh district poverty initiatives project	110.1
	Kerala rural water supply and environmental sanitation project	65.5
	Technician education III project	64.9
Indonesia	Provincial health II project*	40.0
	Kecamatan development II project	111.3
	Western Java environmental management project*	5.8
	Library development project	4.1
	Kecamatan development project (supplemental credit)	48.2
Laos	Agricultural development project	16.7
	Road maintenance	25.0
Mongolia	Energy project	30.0
	Transport development	34.0
Pakistan	Structural adjustment credit	350.0
	North West Frontier Province on-farm water management project	21.3
	Trade and transport facilitation project	3.0
Samoa	Health sector management	5.0
Sri Lanka	Central bank strengthening project	30.3
	Land titling and related services project	5.0
	Distance learning project	2.0
Vanuatu	Education II project	3.5
Viet Nam	Community-based rural infrastructure project	102.8
	Poverty reduction support credit	250.0
	Ho Chi Minh City environmental sanitation (Nhieu Loc-Thi Nghe basin) project	166.3
	Mekong transport and flood protection project	110.0

* Jointly funded projects.

Source: *World Bank Annual Report 2001.*

Publications

Abstracts of Current Studies: The World Bank Research Program (annually).

Annual Report on Operations Evaluation.

Annual Report on Portfolio Performance.

Global Development Finance (annually, also on CD-Rom and online).

Global Economic Prospects (annually).

ICSID Annual Report.

News from ICSID (2 a year).

Poverty Reduction Strategies Newsletter (quarterly).

Research News (quarterly).

Staff Working Papers.

Transition (6 a year)

World Bank Annual Report.

World Bank Atlas (annually).

World Bank Economic Review (3 a year).

The World Bank and the Environment (annually).

World Bank Research Observer (2 a year).

World Development Indicators (annually, also on CD-Rom and online).

World Development Report (annually, also on CD-Rom).

World Tables (annually).

International Finance Corporation—IFC

Address: 2121 Pennsylvania Ave, NW, Washington, DC 20433, USA.

Telephone: (202) 477-1234; **fax:** (202) 974-4384; **e-mail:** information@ifc.org; **internet:** www.ifc.org/.

IFC was founded in 1956 as a member of the World Bank Group to encourage the growth of productive private enterprise in its member countries, particularly in the less-developed areas.

Organization

(October 2002)

IFC is a separate legal entity in the World Bank Group. Executive Directors of the World Bank also serve as Directors of IFC. The President of the World Bank is, *ex officio*, Chairman of the IFC Board of Directors, which has appointed him President of IFC. Subject to his overall supervision, the day-to-day operations of IFC are conducted by its staff under the direction of the Executive Vice-President.

PRINCIPAL OFFICERS

President: JAMES D. WOLFENSOHN (USA).

Executive Vice-President: PETER L. WOICKE (Germany).

OFFICES IN THE REGION

Bangladesh: 3A Paribagh, Dhaka 1000; tel. (2) 861-1056; fax (2) 861-7521; Resident Rep. HAFEEZUDIN AHMAD.

Cambodia: 113 Norodom Blvd, Sangkat Chaktomuk, Phnom Penh; tel. (23) 210922; fax (23) 215157; Country Man. DEEPAK KHANNA.

China, People's Republic: 9/F Tower B, Fuhua Mansion, 8 Chaoyangmen Beidajie, Dongcheng District, Beijing 100027; tel. (10) 65544191; fax (10) 65544192; Resident Rep. KARIN FINKELSTON.

India: No. 1, Panchsheel Marg, Chanakyapuri, POB 416, New Delhi 110021; tel. (11) 6111306; fax (11) 6111281; Dir. MARY ELLEN ISKENDERIAN.

Indonesia: Stock Exchange Bldg, Tower II, 13th Floor, Jalan Jenderal Sudirman Kav. 52-53, 12190 Jakarta; tel. (21) 5299-3001; fax (21) 5299-3002; Regional Rep. AMITAVA BANERJEE.

Japan: Fukoku Seimei Bldg, 10th Floor, 2-2-2, Uchisaiwai-cho, Chiyoda-ku, Tokyo 100; tel. (3) 3597-6657; fax (3) 3597-6698; Special Rep. MORINOBU IRITANI.

Korea, Republic: Youngpoong Bldg, 11th Floor,Chongro-ku, Seoul 110-110; tel. (2) 399-0905; fax (2) 399-0915; Resident Rep. DEEPAK KHANNA.

Nepal: c/o World Bank, Yak and Yeti Hotel Complex, GPO Box 798, Kathmandu; tel. (1) 226793; fax (1) 225112; Resident Rep. SUDHIR MITTAL.

Pakistan: 20A Shahrah e Jamhuriat, Ramna 5 (G 5/1), POB 3033, Islamabad; tel. (51) 279631; fax (51) 824335; e-mail fbatta@ifc.org; Regional Rep. RAYMOND CHIU.

Philippines: Tower One, 11th Floor, Ayala Triangle, Ayala Ave, Makati 1226, Manila; tel. (2) 8487333; fax (2) 8487339; Country Man. VIPUL BHAGHAT.

Singapore: 10 ShentonWay, 15-08 MAS Bldg, Singapore 079 117; tel. 63244612; fax 63244615; Principal Investment Officer FRANCOIS GROSSAS.

Thailand: Diethelm Tower A, 17th Floor, 93/1 Wireless Rd, Bangkok 10330; tel. (2) 650-9253; fax (2) 650-9259; Country Man. TIMOTHY R. RYAN.

Viet Nam: 63 Ly Thai To, 7th Floor, Hoan Kiem, Hanoi; tel. (4) 9342282; fax (4) 9342289; Country Man. DEEPAK KHANNA.

Activities

IFC aims to promote economic development in developing member countries by assisting the growth of private enterprise and effective capital markets. It finances private sector projects, through loans, the purchase of equity, quasi-equity products, and risk management services, and assists governments to create conditions that stimulate the flow of domestic and foreign private savings and investment. IFC also mobilizes additional resources from other financial institutions, in particular through syndicated loans, thus providing access to international capital markets. IFC provides a range of advisory services to help to improve the investment climate in developing countries and offers technical assistance to private enterprises and governments.

IFC's authorized capital is US $2,450m. At 30 June 2001 IFC's paid-in capital was US $2,360m. The World Bank is the principal source of borrowed funds, but IFC also borrows from private capital markets. In the financial year ending 30 June 2001, project financing approved amounted to US $5,357m. for 240 projects, compared with US $5,846m. for 259 projects in the previous year. Of the total approved in 2000/01 US $3,742m. was for IFC's own account, while US $1,615m. was used in loan syndications and underwriting of securities issues and investment funds.

Since the economic crisis in east Asia in the late 1990s IFC focused its activities on restructuring and strengthening corporate and financial sectors in market economies and promoting the development of market institutions in transition economies. IFC's other priority areas in Asia and the Pacific have been to finance and advise small and medium-sized enterprises, to support private participation in infrastructure and social services, and to promote use of information technology, communications and software throughout the region. During 2000/01 IFC approved total financing of US $1,359m. for 65 projects in Asia and the Pacific (excluding Afghanistan), compared with US $1,064m. for 54 projects in the previous year. Examples of projects approved in the region in 2000/01 include investment in a rural microfinance institution in India, refurbishment of hotels in Laos, investment in a life insurance company in the People's Republic of China, construction and upgrading of hospital facilities in the Philippines and Sri Lanka, and investment in a trade enhancement facility in Bangladesh.

IFC provides advisory services, particularly in connection with privatization and corporate restructuring, private infrastructure, and the development of capital markets. Under the Technical Assistance Trust Funds programme (TATF), established in 1988, IFC manages resources contributed by various governments and agencies to provide finance for feasibility studies, project identification studies and other types of technical assistance relating to project preparation. IFC, together with the World Bank, administers the Foreign Investment Advisory Service (FIAS), which provides advice to governments on attracting foreign investment and strengthening the country's investment framework. During 1999/2000 IFC and the World Bank combined their advisory services creating the Private Sector Advisory Services. FIAS was to operate within the framework of the new unit, alongside a Corporate Finance Services facility, which supports private-sector involvement in state-owned and -operated sectors. IFC technical assistance activities undertaken during 2000/01 included assessements and strengthening of financial institutions in Cambodia, the People's Republic of China and Samoa; projects to strengthen the arrangements for foreign direct investment in Cambodia, East Timor, Indonesia, and Palau;

and preparation of initiatives to encourage small and medium-sized businesses in Bangladesh, China and Indonesia. Regional initiatives included preparation of a strategy for promoting sustainable private mining investments, study of foreign investment issues in the development of tuna management plans of Solomon Islands, Palau and Vanuatu, and a feasibility study for a regional telemedicine sector.

In February 1995 IFC established a Pacific Island Investment Facility to support the development of small and medium-sized enterprises, which was intended to complement the activities of the South Pacific Project Facility (see below).

MEKONG PROJECT DEVELOPMENT FACILITY

The Facility was established in November 1996 to support the development of small and medium-sized enterprises in Cambodia, Laos and Viet Nam, mainly through technical assistance, training and the mobilization of capital. The three core programmes of the Facility are investment evaluation and promotion; institution building; and support for the Mekong Financing Line, which was to provide additional credit for enterprises in the region. IFC contributes US $4m. for the administration of the Facility and provided US $5m. for the establishment of the Mekong Financing Line.

Headquarters: 21–23 N. T. Minh Khai, Ho Chi Minh City, Viet Nam; tel. (8) 8235266; fax (8) 8235271; internet www.mpdf.org; Gen. Man. MARIO FISCHEL.

SOUTH PACIFIC PROJECT FACILITY (SPPF)

The South Pacific Project Facility (SPPF) was established in 1991 and assists entrepreneurs in IFC's South Pacific island member countries (Fiji, Kiribati, Marshall Islands, the Federated States of Micronesia, Palau, Papua New Guinea, Samoa, Solomon Islands, Tonga and Vanuatu) to establish new businesses or to expand or diversify existing ones. While SPPF does not fund projects directly, it contributes finance towards market, technical and feasibility studies, and helps to raise resources from other sources. SPPF also helps in locating appropriate technology and provides technical assistance during the implementation of projects. An SPPF mission was opened in Port Moresby, Papua New Guinea, in 1997.

Headquarters: Level 18, CML Bldg, 14 Martin Pl., Sydney, NSW 2000, GPO Box 1612, Sydney, NSW 2000, Australia; tel. (2) 9223-7773; fax (2) 9223-2553; e-mail sppf-info@ifc.org; Gen. Man. DENISE ALDOUS.

IFC Publications

Annual Report.
Emerging Stock Markets Factbook (annually).
Emerging Stock Markets Review (monthly).
Impact (quarterly).
Lessons of Experience (series).
Results on the Ground (series).
Review of Small Businesses (annually).

Multilateral Investment Guarantee Agency—MIGA

Address: 1818 H Street, NW, Washington, DC 20433, USA.

Telephone: (202) 477-1234; **fax:** (202) 477-6391; **internet:** www.miga.org/.

MIGA was founded in 1988 as an affiliate of the World Bank, to encourage the flow of investments for productive purposes among its member countries, especially developing countries, through the provision of political risk insurance and investment marketing services to foreign investors and host governments, respectively.

Organization

(October 2002)

MIGA is legally and financially separate from the World Bank. It is supervised by a Council of Governors (comprising one Governor and one Alternate of each member country) and an elected Board of Directors (of no less than 12 members).

President: JAMES D. WOLFENSOHN (USA).

Executive Vice-President: MOTOMICHI IKAWA (Japan).

Activities

The convention establishing MIGA took effect in April 1988. Authorized capital was US $1,082m. In April 1998 MIGA's Board of Directors approved an increase in MIGA's capital base. A grant of US $150m. was transferred from the IBRD as part of the package, while the capital increase (totalling US $700m. callable capital and US $150m. paid-in capital) was approved by MIGA's Council of Governors in April 1999. At 30 June 2001 subscriptions to capital stock amounted to US $1,713m., of which US $328m. was paid-in.

MIGA guarantees eligible investments against losses resulting from non-commercial risks, under four main categories:

transfer risk resulting from host government restrictions on currency conversion and transfer;

risk of loss resulting from legislative or administrative actions of the host government;

repudiation by the host government of contracts with investors in cases in which the investor has no access to a competent forum;

the risk of armed conflict and civil unrest.

Before guaranteeing any investment, MIGA must ensure that it is commercially viable, contributes to the development process and is not harmful to the environment. During the fiscal year 1998/99 MIGA and IFC appointed the first Compliance Adviser and Ombudsman to consider the concerns of local communities directly affected by MIGA or IFC sponsored projects. In February 1999 the Board of Directors approved an increase in the amount of political risk insurance available for each project, from US $75m. to US $200m.

During the year ending 30 June 2002 MIGA issued 58 investment insurance contracts for 33 projects in 24 countries, with a value of US $1,357m. (compared with 66 guarantees issued amounting to US $2,000m. in the previous financial year). The amount of direct investment associated with the contracts in 2001/02 totalled approximately US $4,700m.

MIGA also provides policy and advisory services to promote foreign investment in developing countries and in transitional economies, and to disseminate information on investment opportunities. In October 1995 MIGA established a new network on investment opportunities, which connected investment promotion agencies (IPAs) throughout the world on an electronic information network. The so-called IPA*net* aimed to encourage further investments among developing countries, to provide access to comprehensive information on investment laws and conditions and to strengthen links between governmental, business and financial associations and investors. A new version of IPA*net* was launched in 1997 (accessible at www.ipanet.net). In June 1998 MIGA initiated a new internet-based facility, 'PrivatizationLink', to provide information on investment opportunities resulting from the privatization of industries in developing economies. In April 2002 MIGA launched a new service, 'FDIXchange', to provide potential investors, advisers and financial institutions with up-to-date market analysis and information on foreign direct investment opportunities in emerging economies (accessible at www.fdixchange.com).

In November 2000 MIGA organized a series of seminars and informal meetings in east Asia to promote its guarantee programme. In addition, during 2000/01 MIGA provided capacity-building and investment marketing services throughout the region in order boost private sector growth.

Publications

Annual Report.
Investment Promotion Quarterly (electronic news update).
MIGA News (quarterly).

International Fund for Agricultural Development—IFAD

Address: Via del Serafico 107, 00142 Rome, Italy.

Telephone: (06) 54591; **fax:** (06) 5043463; **e-mail:** ifad@ifad.org; **internet:** www.ifad.org.

IFAD was established in 1976, following a decision of the 1974 World Food Conference, with a mandate to combat hunger and eradicate poverty on a sustainable basis in the low-income, food-deficit regions of the world. Funding operations began in January 1978.

Organization

(October 2002)

GOVERNING COUNCIL

Each member state is represented in the Governing Council by a Governor and an Alternate. Sessions are held annually, with special sessions convened as required. The Governing Council elects the President of the Fund (who also chairs the Executive Board) by a two-thirds majority for a four-year term. The President is eligible for re-election.

EXECUTIVE BOARD

The Board consists of 18 members and 18 alternates, elected by the Governing Council, who serve for three years. The Executive Board is responsible for the conduct and general operation of IFAD and approves loans and grants for projects; it conducts three regular sessions each year.

Following agreement on the fourth replenishment of the Fund's resources in February 1997, the governance structure of the Fund was amended. Former Category I countries (i.e. industrialized donor countries) were reclassified as List A countries and were awarded a greater share of the 1,800 votes in the Governing Council and Executive Board, in order to reflect their financial contributions to the Fund. Former Category II countries (petroleum-exporting developing donor countries) were reclassified as List B countries, while recipient developing countries, formally Category III countries, were termed as List C countries, and divided into three regional Sub-Lists. Where previously each category was ensured equal representation on the Executive Board, the new allocation of seats was as follows: eight List A countries, four List B, and two of each Sub-List C group of countries.

President and Chairman of Executive Board: LENNART BÅGE (Sweden).

Vice-President: JOHN WESTLEY (USA).

Activities

The Fund's objective is to mobilize additional resources to be made available on concessionary terms for agricultural development in developing member states. IFAD provides financing primarily for projects and programmes specifically designed to introduce, expand or improve food production systems and to strengthen related policies and institutions within the framework of national priorities and strategies. In allocating resources IFAD is guided by: the need to increase food production in the poorest food-deficit countries; the potential for increasing food production in other developing nations; and the importance of improving the nutrition, health and education of the poorest people in developing countries i.e. small-scale farmers, artisanal fishermen, nomadic pastoralists, indigenous populations, rural women, and the rural landless. All projects emphasize the participation of beneficiaries in development initiatives, both at the local and national level. IFAD is committed to achieving the so-called Millennium Goal, pledged by governments attending a special session of the UN General Assembly in September 2000, of reducing by 50% the proportion of people living in extreme poverty by 2015. IFAD's Strategic Framework for 2002–06 reiterates its commitment to enabling the rural poor to overcome their poverty. Accordingly, the Fund's efforts were to focus on the following objectives: strengthening the capacity of the rural poor and their organizations; improving equitable access to productive natural resources and technology; and increasing access to financial services and markets. Within this Framework the Fund has also formulated regional strategies for rural poverty reduction. With respect to Asia and the Pacific IFAD identified the following aspects as fundamental to a regional approach to reducing poverty: improving the gender balance, including women's participation in community management; enhancing productivity of staple food in less favoured areas; reforming property and other rights of minorities and indigenous peoples; and expanding the capabilities of the poor and vulnerable through greater access to skills, training and new technology. IFAD intended with all its projects in the region to complement government poverty reduction initiatives and projects funded by multilateral donors concerning health, education and infrastructure.

PROJECTS IN ASIA AND THE PACIFIC APPROVED IN 2001

Country	Purpose	Loan amount (SDR m.*)
Bangladesh	Sunamganh community-based resource management project	17.6
India	Livelihood security project for earthquake-affected rural households in Gujarat	11.7
Nepal	Western uplands poverty-reduction project	15.6
Pakistan	Development project for Barani Area in North-West Frontier Province	11.2
Philippines	Northern Mindanao community initiatives and resource management project	11.6
Viet Nam	Rural income diversification project in Tuyen Quang Province	16.4

* The average value of the SDR—Special Drawing Rights—in 2001 was US $1.27304.

IFAD is empowered to make both grants and loans. Grants are limited to 75% of the resources committed in any one financial year. Loans are available on highly concessional, intermediate and ordinary terms. Highly concessional loans, which carry no interest but have an annual service charge of 0.75%, and are repayable over a 40-year period, form about two-thirds of IFAD's total annual loan commitments. In 2001 all six of the projects approved for Asia and the Pacific were on highly concessional terms. To avoid duplication of work, the administration of loans, for the purposes of disbursements and supervision of project implementation, is entrusted to competent international financial institutions, with the Fund retaining an active interest. In order to increase the impact of its lending resources on food production, the Fund seeks as much as possible to attract other external donors and beneficiary governments as co-financiers of its projects.

IFAD's development projects usually include a number of components, such as infrastructure (e.g. improvement of water supplies, small-scale irrigation and road construction); input supply (e.g. improved seeds, fertilizers and pesticides); institutional support (e.g. research, training and extension services); and producer incentives (e.g. pricing and marketing improvements). IFAD also attempts to enable the landless to acquire income-generating assets: by increasing the provision of credit for the rural poor, it seeks to free them from dependence on the capital market and to generate productive activities. The Fund supports projects that are concerned with environmental conservation, in an effort to alleviate poverty that results from the deterioration of natural resources. It also extends assessment grants to review the environmental consequences of projects under preparation.

IFAD is a leading repository of knowledge, resources and expertise in the field of rural hunger and poverty alleviation. During 1995 a team established to review IFAD's activities focused on IFAD's role as an innovator, emphasizing the importance of pioneering practices and strategies that can be replicated, and of making its knowledge available to relevant agencies and governments. Through its technical assistance grants, IFAD aims to promote research and capacity-building in the agricultural sector, as well as the development of technologies to increase agricultural production and help to alleviate rural poverty. In mid-1998 IFAD inaugurated the Electronic Networking for Rural Asia/Pacific Projects (ENRAP), initially as a pilot project in eight countries in the region to bring the benefits of the internet to rural development projects. A Poverty Alleviation Training Programme for Asia and the Pacific (PATAP) was initiated in 1995 with pilot projects in Bangladesh, Bhutan, India, the Maldives, Nepal, Pakistan and Sri Lanka. In 1998 IFAD undertook a series of case studies to assess the impact of the Asian economic crisis on the rural poor, and to formulate appropriate responses.

Also in 1998 IFAD's Executive Board endorsed a policy framework for the Fund's role in providing development assistance in post-conflict situations, with the aim of achieving a continuum from emerging relief to a secure basis from which to pursue sustainable development. At the end of that year IFAD was involved in a project to rehabilitate crops and livestock following extensive flooding in the Democratic People's Republic of Korea. In February 1998 IFAD inaugurated a new Trust Fund to complement the multilateral debt initiative for heavily indebted poor countries (HIPCs—see World Bank p. 1488). The Fund was intended to assist IFAD's poorest members deemed to be eligible under the initiative to channel resources from debt repayments to communities in need. In February 2000 the Governing Council resolved that IFAD should participate in the enhanced HIPC initiative, which aimed to accelerate the process of approving concessional lending to countries assessed as having an unsustainable level of debt. During 1999/2000 IFAD conducted a detailed study of rural poverty, the conclusions and recommendations of which were issued as the *Rural Poverty Report 2001*.

In 2001 six projects were approved for the Asia and the Pacific region under the Regular Programme, amounting to approximately US $107.1m., equivalent to 26.6% of total IFAD loans approved during that year. At the end of 2001 cumulative IFAD financing for the region, since 1978, amounted to some US $2,379.5m. for 153 projects in 21 countries.

Finance

The 2001 programme of work envisaged loans and grants to be allocated totalling some US $433.9m. IFAD's provisional administrative budget for 2001 was US $53.6m. The fifth replenishment of IFAD funds, covering the period 2000–02, amounting to US $460m., became effective in September 2001.

Publications

Annual Report.
IFAD Update (2 a year).
Rural Poverty Report (annually).
Staff Working Papers (series).

International Monetary Fund—IMF

Address: 700 19th St, NW, Washington, DC 20431, USA.

Telephone: (202) 623-7430; **fax:** (202) 623-6220; **e-mail:** publicaffairs@imf.org; **internet:** www.imf.org.

The IMF was established concurrently with the World Bank (IBRD) in 1945, to promote international monetary co-operation, to facilitate the expansion and balanced growth of international trade and to promote stability in foreign exchange.

Organization

(October 2002)

BOARD OF GOVERNORS

The highest authority of the Fund is exercised by the Board of Governors, on which each member country is represented by a Governor and an Alternate Governor. The Board normally meets annually. The International Monetary and Financial Committee (formerly the Interim Committee) advises and reports to the Board on matters relating to the management and adaptation of the international monetary and financial system, sudden disturbances that might threaten the system and proposals to amend the Articles of Agreement. The voting power of each country is related to its quota in the Fund.

BOARD OF EXECUTIVE DIRECTORS

The 24-member Board of Executive Directors is responsible for the day-to-day operations of the Fund. The USA, the United Kingdom, Germany, France and Japan each appoint one Executive Director. There is also one Executive Director each from Russia, Saudi Arabia and the People's Republic of China, while the remainder are appointed by groups of the remaining member countries.

OFFICERS

Managing Director: HORST KÖHLER (Germany).

First Deputy Managing Director: ANNE KRUEGER (USA).

Deputy Managing Directors: SHIGEMITSU SUGISAKI (Japan); EDUARDO ANINAT (Chile).

Director, Asia and Pacific Department: YUSUKE HORIGUCHI (Japan).

REGIONAL OFFICE

Regional Office for Asia and the Pacific: 21F Fukoku Seimei Bldg, 2-2-2, Uchisaiwai-cho, Chiyodu-ku, Tokyo 100, Japan; tel. (3) 3597-6700; fax (3) 3597-6705; e-mail oap@imf.org; f. 1997; Dir HIROYUKI HINO (Japan).

Activities

The purposes of the IMF, as set out in the Articles of Agreement, are:

(i) To promote international monetary co-operation through a permanent institution which provides the machinery for consultation and collaboration on monetary problems;

(ii) To facilitate the expansion and balanced growth of international trade, and to contribute thereby to the promotion and maintenance of high levels of employment and real income and to the development of members' productive resources;

(iii) To promote exchange stability, to maintain orderly exchange arrangements among members, and to avoid competitive exchange depreciation;

(iv) To assist in the establishment of a multilateral system of payments in respect of current transactions between members and in the elimination of foreign exchange restrictions which hamper the growth of trade;

(v) To give confidence to members by making the general resources of the Fund temporarily available to them, under adequate safeguards, thus providing them with the opportunity to correct maladjustments in their balance of payments, without resorting to measures destructive of national or international prosperity; and

(vi) In accordance with the above, to shorten the duration of and lessen the degree of disequilibrium in the international balances of payments of members.

In joining the Fund, each country agrees to co-operate with the above objectives. Under Article IV of the Articles of Agreement the Fund monitors members' compliance by holding an annual consultation with each country, in order to survey the country's exchange rate policies and determine its need for assistance.

In accordance with its objective of facilitating the expansion of international trade, the IMF encourages its members to accept the obligations of Article VIII, Sections two, three and four, of the IMF Articles of Agreement. Members that accept Article VIII undertake to refrain from imposing restrictions on the making of payments and transfers for current international transactions and from engaging in discriminatory currency arrangements or multiple currency practices without IMF approval. By mid-2002 152 members had accepted Article VIII status. In April 1997 the Interim Committee endorsed proposals to amend the Articles of Agreement in order to recognize the promotion of liberalizing capital accounts as a specific objective of the IMF and to extend the organization's jurisdiction over capital movements. The proposed amendment remained under consideration in 2001.

In mid-1997 the devaluation of the Thai baht, following intense speculation of the currency and market losses, initiated a period of severe financial and economic turmoil in several Asian countries. The widespread effect of the crisis dominated the work of the IMF in 1997/98 and placed a substantial strain on its financial resources: by August 1998 the Fund had disbursed approximately US $26,000m. to assist the countries most affected by the Asian crisis, i.e. Indonesia, the Republic of Korea and Thailand. The IMF led efforts to mobilize additional funding from international sources, and aimed to help restore confidence in those economies, to support structural reforms, including the reform of financial systems, and to address governance issues, such as links between commerce and government and the question of economic transparency. The IMF established new resident representative offices in the Republic of Korea and in Thailand, and expanded the existing office in Indonesia, in order to co-ordinate the assistance programmes.

MEMBERSHIP AND QUOTAS IN THE FAR EAST AND AUSTRALASIA (million SDR)*

Country	23 September 2002
Afghanistan†	(161.9) 120.4
Australia	3,236.4
Bangladesh	533.3
Bhutan	6.3
Brunei†	(215.2) 150.0
Cambodia	87.5
China, People's Republic‡	6,369.2
East Timor	8.2
Fiji	70.3
India	4,158.2
Indonesia	2,079.3
Japan	13,312.8
Kiribati	5.6
Korea, Republic	1,633.6
Laos	52.9
Malaysia	1,486.6
Maldives	8.2
Marshall Islands	(3.5) 2.5
Micronesia, Federated States	5.1
Mongolia	51.1
Myanmar	258.4
Nepal	71.3
New Zealand	894.6
Pakistan	1,033.7
Palau	3.1
Papua New Guinea	131.6
Philippines	879.9
Samoa	11.6
Singapore	862.5
Solomon Islands	10.4
Sri Lanka	413.4
Thailand	1,081.9
Tonga	6.9
Vanuatu	17.0
Viet Nam	329.1

* The Special Drawing Right (SDR) was introduced in 1970 as a substitute for gold in international payments, and was intended eventually to become the principal reserve asset in the international monetary system. Its value (which was US $1.32269 at 30 September 2002 and averaged US $1.27304 in 2001) is based on the currencies of the five largest exporting countries. Each member is assigned a quota related to its national income, monetary reserves, trade balance and other economic indicators; the quota approximately determines a member's voting power and the amount of foreign exchange it may purchase from the Fund. A member's subscription is equal to its quota. In December 1994 the Executive Board resolved that the Ninth General Review, which increased total quotas from SDR 90,035m. to SDR 135,200m., had provided substantial additional resources and concluded the Tenth General Review without any amendment of quotas. In February 1998 the Board of Governors adopted a resolution in support of an earlier decision of the Executive Board of an increase in total quotas of some 45%. The resolution completed the Eleventh General Review; however, the increase was subject to approval by member countries with at least 85% of total quotas (as at December 1997). Sufficient consent had been granted by January 1999 to enable the overall increase in quotas to enter into effect. At September 2002 total quotas in the Fund amounted to SDR 212,666.1m.

† Afghanistan had overdue obligations and was therefore ineligible to consent to any increase, while Brunei had not yet consented to the new quota by September 2002. The figures listed are those determined under the Eighth and Ninth General Reviews, respectively, while the figures in parentheses are the proposed Eleventh General Review quotas.

‡ In February 2001 the Board of Governors approved an increase in China's quota, from SDR 4,687.2m., to reflect its economic position following its resumption of sovereignty over Hong Kong.

The financial crises in the late 1990s contributed to widespread discussions concerning the strengthening of the international monetary system. In April 1998 the Executive Board identified the following fundamental aspects of the debate: reinforcing international and domestic financial systems; strengthening IMF surveillance; promoting greater availability and transparency of information regarding member countries' economic data and policies; emphasizing the central role of the IMF in crisis management; and establishing effective procedures to involve the private sector in forestalling or resolving financial crises. During 1999/2000 the Fund implemented several measures in connection with its ongoing efforts to appraise and reinforce the global financial architecture, including, in March 2000, the adoption by the Executive Board of a strengthened framework to safeguard the use of IMF resources. During 2000 the Fund established the IMF Center, in Washington, DC, which aimed to promote awareness and understanding of its activities. In September the Fund's new Managing Director announced his intention to focus and streamline the principles of conditionality (which links Fund financing with the implementation of specific economic policies by the recipient countries) as part of the wider reform of the international financial system. A comprehensive review was undertaken, during which the issue was considered by public forums and representatives of civil society. New guide-lines on conditionality, which *inter alia* aimed to promote national ownership of policy reforms and to introduce specific criteria for the implementation of conditions given different states' circumstances, were approved by the Executive Board in September 2002. In 2000/01 the Fund established an International Capital Markets Department to improve its understanding of financial markets, and a separate Consultative Group on capital markets to serve as a forum for regular dialogue between the Fund and representatives of the private sector. In early 2002 a position of Director for Special Operations was created to enhance the Fund's ability to respond to critical situations affecting member countries.

RESOURCES

Members' subscriptions form the basic resource of the IMF. They are supplemented by borrowing.

Under the General Arrangements to Borrow (GAB), established in 1962, the 'Group of Ten' industrialized nations (Belgium, Canada, France, Germany, Italy, Japan, the Netherlands, Sweden, the United Kingdom and the USA) and Switzerland (which became a member of the IMF only in May 1992, but which was a full participant in the GAB from April 1984) undertake to lend the Fund up to SDR 17,000m. (increased from SDR 6,400m. in December 1983) in their own currencies, so as to help meet the balance-of-payments requirements of any member of the group, or to meet requests to the Fund from countries with balance-of-payments problems that could threaten the stability of the international monetary system. In May 1996 GAB participants concluded an agreement in principle to expand the resources available for borrowing to SDR 34,000m., by securing the support of other countries with the financial capacity to support the international monetary system. The New Arrangements to Borrow was approved by the Executive Board in January 1997. It was to enter into force, for an initial five-year period, as soon as the five largest potential creditors (of the anticipated 25 member countries and institutions participating in the NAB) had approved the initiative and the total credit arrangement of participants endorsing the scheme had reached at least SDR 28,900m. While the GAB credit arrangement was to remain in effect, the NAB was expected to be the first facility to be activated in the event of the Fund requiring supplementary resources. In July 1998 the GAB was activated for the first time in more than 20 years in order to provide funds totalling US $6,300m. in support of an IMF emergency assistance package for Russia (the first time the GAB had been used for a non-participant). The NAB became effective in November, and was used for the first time as part of an extensive programme of support for Brazil, which was adopted by the IMF in early December.

DRAWING ARRANGEMENTS

Exchange transactions within the Fund take the form of members' purchases (i.e. drawings) from the Fund of the currencies of other members for the equivalent amounts of their own currencies. Fund resources are available to eligible members on an essentially short-term and revolving basis to provide members with temporary assistance to contribute to the solution of their payments problems. Before making a purchase, a member must show that its balance of payments or reserve position make the purchase necessary. Apart from this requirement, reserve tranche purchases (i.e. purchases that do not bring the Fund's holdings of the member's currency to a level above its quota) are permitted unconditionally.

With further purchases, however, the Fund's policy of 'conditionality' means that a member requesting assistance must agree to adjust its economic policies, as stipulated by the IMF. All requests other than for use of the reserve tranche are examined by the Executive Board to determine whether the proposed use would be consistent with the Fund's policies, and a member must discuss its proposed adjustment programme (including fiscal, monetary, exchange and trade policies) with IMF staff. Purchases outside the reserve tranche are made in four credit tranches, each equivalent to 25% of the member's quota; a member must reverse the transaction by repurchasing its own currency (with SDRs or currencies specified by the Fund) within a specified time. A credit tranche purchase is usually made under a 'Stand-by Arrangement' with the Fund, or under the Extended Fund Facility. A Stand-by Arrangement is normally of one or two years' duration, and the amount is made available in instalments, subject to the member's observance of 'performance criteria'; repurchases must be made within three-and-a-quarter to five years. An Extended Arrangement is normally of three years' duration, and the member must submit detailed economic programmes and progress reports for each year; repurchases must be made within four-and-a-half to 10 years. A member whose payments imbalance is large in relation to its quota may make use of temporary facilities established by the Fund using borrowed resources, namely the 'enlarged access policy' established in 1981, which helps to finance Stand-by and Extended Arrangements for such a member, up to a limit of between 90% and 110% of the member's quota annually. In October 1994 the Executive Board agreed to increase, for three years, the annual access limit under IMF regular tranche drawings, Stand-by Arrangements and Extended Fund Facility credits from 68% to 100% of a member's quota, with the cumulative access limit remaining at 300% of quota. The arrangements were extended, on a temporary basis, in November 1997. In July an Emergency Financing Mechanism, which had been established in 1995 to facilitate rapid approval of financial support in emergency situations, was activated for the first time, in response to a request by the Philippines Government to extend and increase its three-year Extended Facility in order to reinforce the country's international reserves, which had been depleted in support of the national currency. The Mechanism was again used in August 1997 in support of a Stand-by Arrangement of SDR 2,900m. approved for Thailand. The funding commitment activated a 'package' of financial assistance from other countries, international organizations and financial companies, totalling some US $17,200m. A three-year Stand-by Arrangement of SDR 7,228m. was approved for Indonesia in November, as part of an initial international credit 'package' amounting to some US $23,000m. The disbursement of funds to Indonesia was disrupted during 1998 owing to disagreements between the IMF and the Indonesian authorities regarding the management and reform of the economy; however, in July the Fund agreed to provide additional funds amounting to US $1,300m. (supplemented by US $5,000m. from multilateral and bilateral sources) in order to alleviate the social consequences of the financial collapse in that country.

During 2000/01 Stand-by Arrangements were approved for Pakistan (amounting to SDR 465.0m.), Papua New Guinea (SDR 85.5m.), and Sri Lanka (SDR 200.0m.). An Extended Arrangement of SDR 3,628.0m. was approved for Indonesia.

In December 1997 a new Supplemental Reserve Facility (SRF) was activated immediately to provide SDR 9,950m. to the Republic of Korea, as part of a Stand-by Arrangement amounting to SDR 15,500m., the largest amount ever committed by the Fund. With additional financing from governments and international institutions, the total assistance 'package' for the Republic of Korea reached an estimated US $57,000m.

The Compensatory Financing Facility (CFF, known as the Compensatory and Contingency Financing Facility—CCFF—until January 2000) provides compensation to members whose export earnings are reduced owing to circumstances beyond their control, or who are affected by excess costs of cereal imports. In December 1997 the Executive Board established the SRF (see above) to provide short-term assistance to members experiencing exceptional balance-of-payments difficulties resulting from a sudden loss of market confidence. Repayments were to be made within one to one-and-a-half years of the purchase, unless otherwise extended by the Board. In April 1999 an additional facility, the Contingent Credit Lines (CCL), was established to provide short-term financing on similar terms to the SRF in order to prevent more stable economies being affected by adverse international financial developments and to maintain investor confidence. Under the CCL member countries were to have access to up to 500% of their quota, subject to meeting various economic criteria stipulated by the Fund.

In November 1999 the Fund's existing facility to provide balance-of-payments assistance on concessionary terms to low-income member countries, the Enhanced Structural Adjustment Facility, was reformulated as the Poverty Reduction and Growth Facility (PRGF), with greater emphasis on poverty reduction as a key element of growth-orientated economic strategies. Assistance under the PRGF was to be matched to specific national requirements, and based upon a national poverty reduction strategy, to be formulated in collaboration with non-governmental organizations, representatives of civil society, and bilateral and multilateral institutions and presented in a Poverty Reduction Strategy Paper. PRGF loans carry an interest rate of 0.5% per year and are repayable over 10 years, with a five-and-a-half-year grace period; each country is permitted to borrow up to 140% of its quotas (in exceptional circumstances the maximum access can be raised to 185%). A PGRF Trust replaced the former ESAF Trust.

During 2000/01 the IMF approved new PRGF arrangements for Laos (amounting to SDR 31.7m.) and Viet Nam (SDR 290.0m.). A PRGF for Cambodia, amounting to SDR 58.5m., remained in effect at 30 April 2001.

The PRGF supports, through long-maturity loans and grants, IMF participation in a joint initiative, with the World Bank, to provide exceptional assistance to heavily indebted poor countries (HIPCs) in order to help them achieve a sustainable level of debt management. The initiative was formally approved at the September 1996 meeting of the Interim Committee, having received the support of the 'Paris Club' of international creditors which agreed to increase the relief on official debt relief from 67% to 80%. In early 1999 the IMF and World Bank initiated a comprehensive review of the HIPC scheme, in order to consider modifications of the initiative and to strengthen the link between debt relief and poverty reduction. A consensus emerged among the financial institutions and leading industralized nations to enhance the scheme, in order to make it available to more countries, and to accelerate the process of providing debt relief. In September the IMF Board of Governors expressed its commitment to undertaking an off-market transaction of a percentage of the Fund's gold reserves (i.e. a sale, at market prices, to central banks of member countries with repayment obligations to the Fund, which were then to be made in gold), as part of the funding arrangements of the enhanced HIPC scheme. The transactions were undertaken between December 1999 and April 2000. Of a total of 41 nations that have been identified as HIPCs, only three are in the Far East and Australasia region (Laos, Myanmar and Viet Nam). Total assistance under the HIPC initiative committed at July 2002 amounted to US $25,102m., of which the Fund had pledged US $2,043m.

SURVEILLANCE

Under its Articles of Agreement the Fund is mandated to oversee the effective functioning of the international monetary system and to review the policies of individual member countries to ensure the stability of the exchange rate system. The Fund's main tools of surveillance are regular consultations with member countries conducted in accordance with Article IV of the Articles of Agreement, which cover fiscal and monetary policies, balance of payments and external debt developments, as well as policies that affect the economic performance of a country, such as the labour market, social and environmental issues and good governance and aspects of the country's capital accounts, and finance and banking sectors. In April 1997, in an effort to improve the value of surveillance by means of increased transparency, the Executive Board agreed to the voluntary issue of Press Information Notices (PINs) (on the internet and in *IMF Economic Reviews*), following each member's Article IV consultation with the Board, to those member countries wishing to make public the Fund's views. Other background papers providing information on and analysis of economic developments in individual countries continued to be made available. In addition, World Economic Outlook discussions are held, normally twice a year, by the Executive Board to assess policy implications from a multilateral perspective and to monitor global developments.

In April 1996 the IMF established the Special Data Dissemination Standard (SDDS), which was to improve access to reliable economic statistical information for member countries that have, or are seeking access to, international capital markets. In March 1999 the IMF undertook to strengthen the Standard by the introduction of a new reserves template. By mid-2002 50 countries had subscribed to the Standard. The Fund maintains a Dissemination Standards Bulletin Board (accessible at dsbb.imf.org), which aims to ensure that information on SDDS subscribing countries is widely available. In December 1997 the Executive Board approved a new General Data Dissemination System (GDDS) to encourage all member countries to improve the production and dissemination of core economic data. The operational phase of the GDDS commenced in May 2000.

In April 1998 the then Interim Committee adopted a voluntary Code of Good Practices on Fiscal Transparency: Declaration on Principles, which aimed to increase the quality and promptness of reports on economic indicators, and in September 1999 adopted a Code of Good Practices on Transparency in Monetary and Financial Policies: Declaration of Principles. The IMF and World Bank jointly established a Financial Sector Assessment Programme (FSAP) in May 1999, initially as a pilot project, which aimed to promote greater global financial security through the preparation of confidential detailed evaluations of the financial sectors of countries. Assessments were undertaken of 12 industrialized countries, emerging market economies and developing countries. During 2000 the FSAP was extended to cover a further 24 countries. It remained under regular review by the Boards of Governors of the Fund and World Bank. As part of the FSAP, Fund staff may conclude a Financial System Stability Assessment (FSSA), addressing issues relating to macroeconomic stability and the strength of a country's financial system. A separate component of the FSAP are Reports on the Observance of Standards and Codes, which are compiled after an assessment of a country's implementation and observance of internationally recognized financial standards. In March 2000 the Executive Board adopted a strengthened framework to safeguard the use of IMF resources. All member countries making use of Fund resources were to be required to publish annual central bank statements audited in accordance with internationally accepted standards. It was also agreed that any instance of intentional misreporting of information by a member country should be publicized. In the following month the Executive Board approved the establishment of an Independent Evaluation Office to conduct objective evaluations of IMF policy and operations.

In April 2001 the Executive Board agreed on measures to enhance international efforts to counter money-laundering, in particular through the Fund's ongoing financial supervision activities and its programme of assessment of offshore financial centres. In November the IMFC, in response to the terrorist attacks against targets in the USA, which had occurred in September, resolved, *inter alia*, to strengthen the Fund's focus on surveillance, and, in particular, to extend measures to counter money-laundering to include the funds of terrorist organizations. It determined to accelerate efforts to assess offshore centres and to provide technical support to enable poorer countries to meet international financial standards.

TECHNICAL ASSISTANCE

Technical assistance is provided by special missions or resident representatives who advise members on every aspect of economic management; more specialized technical assistance is provided by the IMF's various departments. In 2000/01 the IMFC determined that technical assistance should be central to IMF's work in crisis prevention and management, in capacity-building for low-income countries, and in restoring macroeconomic stability in countries following a financial crisis. Technical assistance activities subsequently underwent a process of review and reorganization to align them more closely with IMF policy priorities and other initiatives, for example the Financial Stability Assessment Programme. The majority of technical assistance is provided by the Departments of Monetary and Exchange Affairs, of Fiscal Affairs and of Statistics, and by the IMF Institute.The Institute, founded in 1964, trains officials from member countries in financial analysis and policy, balance-of-payments methodology and public finance; it also gives assistance to national and regional training centres. The IMF-Singapore Regional Training Institute (an affiliate of the IMF Institute) was inaugurated in May 1998 and organizes seminars and courses for officials in Asia and the Pacific. During 2000 the IMF Institute established, with the People's Bank of China, a joint training programme for government officials in the People's Republic of China comprising six courses and a high-level seminar. From the early 1990s, owing to an increase in membership of the Fund and demand for technical assistance, greater emphasis was placed on co-operation with other agencies and co-financing of projects. The IMF is a co-sponsor, with the UNDP and the Japan Administered Account, of the Joint Vienna Institute, which provides training for public officials and business executives from countries with economies in transition.

Publications

Annual Report.

Balance of Payments Statistics Yearbook.

Direction of Trade Statistics (quarterly, with yearbook).

Global Financial Stability Report (quarterly).

Government Finance Statistics Yearbook.

International Financial Statistics (monthly, with yearbook).

Staff Papers (quarterly).

Finance and Development (quarterly, published jointly with the World Bank).

IMF Economic Review (3 a year).

IMF Survey (2 a month).

World Economic Outlook (2 a year).

Occasional papers, country reports, economic reviews, books and pamphlets.

United Nations Educational, Scientific and Cultural Organization—UNESCO

Address: 7 place de Fontenoy, 75352 Paris, France.

Telephone: 1-45-68-10-00; **fax:** 1-45-67-16-90; **e-mail:** scg@unesco .org; **internet:** www.unesco.org.

UNESCO was established in 1946 'for the purpose of advancing, through the educational, scientific and cultural relations of the peoples of the world, the objectives of international peace and the common welfare of mankind'.

Organization

(October 2002)

GENERAL CONFERENCE

The supreme governing body of the Organization, the Conference meets in ordinary session once in two years and is composed of representatives of the member states.

EXECUTIVE BOARD

The Board, comprising 58 members, prepares the programme to be submitted to the Conference and supervises its execution; it meets at least twice a year.

SECRETARIAT

Director-General: KOICHIRO MATSUURA (Japan).

REGIONAL OFFICES

Principal Regional Office for Asia and the Pacific: 920 Sukhumvit Rd, POB 967, Prakanong Post Office, Bangkok 10110, Thailand; tel. (2) 391-0577; fax (2) 391-0866; e-mail bangkok@unesco .org; internet www.unescobkk.org; f. 1961; the main function of the office is to provide programme delivery and advisory services to member states in Asia and the Pacific in the fields of education, social and human sciences and culture, at national, regional and sub-regional levels. Aims to enhance the capacity of member states to manage, access and use information and to promote inter-country co-operation in information exchange. The office serves as a permanent secretariat to periodic regional conferences of ministers of education or of economic planning. A documentation and clearing house service is available for Governments and institutions of member states in the region. Dir SHELDON SCHAEFFER. Publs *Statistical Indicators, ACEID Newsletter, Adolescence Education Newsletter,* reports, digests, instructional materials, etc.

Regional Bureau for Communication and Information: B-5/29, Safdarjung Enclave, New Delhi 110057, India; tel. (11) 671-3000; fax (11) 671-3001; e-mail newdelhi@unesco.org; internet unescodelhi.nic.in; f. 1948 as UNESCO New Delhi Office; aims to widen access to information and knowledge resources, with a special focus on reaching the poor or illiterate people and other marginalized groups; Dir Prof. MOSHEN TAWFIK. Publs *Annual Report, Library Accessions List* (monthly), *Quarterly Newsletter*.

Regional Office for Science and Technology for South-East Asia: UN Bldg, Jalan Thamrin 14, Tromolpos 1273/JKT, Jakarta 10002, Indonesia; tel. (21) 3141308; fax (21) 3150382; e-mail jakarta @unesco.org; internet www.unesco.or.id; f. 1951; major programmes undertaken by the office have included studies in science and technology policy, earth sciences, water resources, appropriate technology and energy development. It also organizes conferences, seminars, workshops, short-term training courses and other meeting and seminars in the region. Dir Prof. STEPHEN C. HILL. Publs *Annual Report*, research reports.

UNESCO Apia Office: POB 5766, Matautu, Apia, Samoa; tel. 24276; fax 22253; e-mail apia@unesco.org; f. 1984; represents Australia, New Zealand and the Pacific Island states; Dir EDNA TAIT. Publ. *UNESCO Pacific News* (2 or 3 a year).

Other field offices are located in Dhaka, Bangladesh; Phnom-Penh, Cambodia; Beijing, the People's Republic of China (also representing the Democratic People's Republic of Korea and Mongolia); Hanoi, Viet Nam; Islamabad, Pakistan; Kuala Lumpur, Malaysia; and Kathmandu, Nepal.

Activities

In November 2001 the General Conference approved a medium-term strategy to guide UNESCO during the period 2002–07. The Conference adopted a new unifying theme for the organization: 'UNESCO contributing to peace and human development in an era of globalization through education, the sciences, culture and communication'. UNESCO's central mission as defined under the strategy was to contribute to peace and human development in the globalized world through its four programme domains (Education, Natural and Social and Human Sciences, Culture, and Communication and Information), incorporating the following three principal dimensions: developing universal principles and norms to meet emerging challenges and protect the 'common public good'; promoting pluralism and diversity; and promoting empowerment and participation in the emerging knowledge society through equitable access, capacity-building and knowledge-sharing. Programme activities were to be focused particularly on supporting disadvantaged and excluded groups or geographic regions. The organization aimed to decentralize its operations in order to ensure more country-driven programming. UNESCO's overall work programme for 2002–03 comprised the following major programmes: education; natural sciences; social and human sciences; culture; and communication and information. Basic education; fresh water resources and ecosystems; the ethics of science and technology; diversity, intercultural pluralism and dialogue; and universal access to information, especially in the public domain, were designated as the priority themes. The work programme incorporated two transdisciplinary projects—eradication of poverty, especially extreme poverty; and the contribution of information and communication technologies to the development of education, science and culture and the construction of a knowledge society. UNESCO aims to promote a culture of peace. The UN General Assembly designated UNESCO as the lead agency for co-ordinating the International Decade for a Culture of Peace and Non-Violence for the Children of the World (2001–10), with a focus on education. In the implementation of all its activities UNESCO aims to contribute to achieving the UN Millennium Goal of halving levels of extreme poverty by 2015.

EDUCATION

Since its establishment UNESCO has devoted itself to promoting education in accordance with principles based on democracy and respect for human rights. UNESCO supports the Asia-Pacific Network for International Education and Values Education to secure this objective.

In March 1990 UNESCO, with other UN agencies, sponsored the World Conference on Education for All, which was held in Jontien, Thailand. 'Education for All' was subsequently adopted as a guiding principle of UNESCO's contribution to development. UNESCO advocates 'Literacy for All' as a key component of 'Education for All', regarding literacy as essential to basic education and to social and human development. In April 2000 several UN agencies, including UNESCO and UNICEF, and other partners sponsored the World Education Forum, held in Dakar, Senegal, to assess international progress in achieving the goal of 'Education for All' and to adopt a strategy for further action (the 'Dakar Framework'), with the aim of ensuring universal basic education by 2015. The Forum launched the Global Initiative for Education for All. The Dakar Framework emphasized the role of improved access to education in the reduction of poverty and in diminishing inequalities within and between societies. UNESCO was appointed as the lead agency in the implementation of the Framework. UNESCO's role in pursuing the goals of the Dakar Forum was to focus on co-ordination, advocacy, mobilization of resources, and information-sharing at international, regional and national levels. It was to oversee national policy reforms, with a particular focus on the integration of 'Education for All' objectives into national education plans, which were to be produced by all member countries by 2002. UNESCO's work programme on Education for 2002–03 aimed to promote an effective follow-up to the Forum and comprised the following two main components: Basic Education for All: Meeting the Commitments of the Dakar World Education Forum; and Building Knowledge Societies through Quality Education and a Renewal of Education Systems. 'Basic Education for All', signifying the promotion of access to learning opportunities throughout the lives of all individuals, including the most disadvantaged, was designated as the principal theme of the programme and was deemed to require urgent action. The second part of the strategy was to improve the quality of educational provision and renew and diversify education systems, with a view to ensuring that educational needs at all levels were met. This component included updating curricular programmes in secondary education, strengthening science and technology activities and ensuring equal access to education for girls and women. (UNESCO supports the UN Girls' Education Initiative, established following the Dakar Forum.) The work programme focused on the importance of knowledge, information and communication in the increasingly globalized world, and the significance of education as a means of empowerment for the poor and of enhancing basic quality of life.

Two co-operative programmes, the Asia-Pacific Programme of Education for All (APPEAL) and the Asia-Pacific Programme of Educational Innovation for Development (APEID), are responsible for undertaking UNESCO's educational strategies in the region. In 1991 an Asia-Pacific Co-operative Programme for Reading Promotion and Book Development was established, in order to support literacy initiatives, the development of primary reading materials, rural reading centres and mobile libraries, as well as support to national publishing industries. In December 1993 the heads of government of nine highly-populated countries, including Bangladesh, the People's Republic of China, India, Indonesia and Pakistan, meeting in Delhi, India, agreed to co-operate with the objective of achieving comprehensive primary education for all children and of expanding further learning opportunities for children and adults. By September 1999 all of the so-called 'E-9' countries had officially signed the so-called Delhi Declaration. An evaluation of the 'E-9' initiative was to be conducted during the period of UNESCO's 2002–03 work programme. In May 1997 an Asia Regional Literacy Forum, convened in Manila, Philippines, urged greater focus on literacy issues in the region. A second Forum was held in New Delhi, in February 1998, organized jointly by UNESCO, the National Literacy Mission of India and the International Literacy Institute (itself a co-operative venture of UNESCO and the University of Pennsylvania, USA), and attended by government representatives and officials from 22 Asian countries. A third forum was held in Beijing, People's Republic of China, in October 1999. In March/April 1998 UNESCO hosted a conference entitled 'Education in the 21st Century in the Asia and Pacific Region', held in Melbourne, Australia, at which it was agreed to establish working parties on a series of concerns, including access to technology and the role of higher education in preparing for the future.

Within the UN system, UNESCO is responsible for providing technical assistance and educational services in the context of emergency situations. This includes providing education to refugees and displaced persons, as well as assistance for the rehabilitation of national education systems.

UNESCO is concerned with improving the quality, relevance and efficiency of higher education. It assists member states in reforming their national systems, organizes high-level conferences for Ministers of Education and other decision-makers, and disseminates research papers. A World Conference on Higher Education was convened in October 1998 in Paris, France. The Conference adopted a World Declaration on Higher Education for the 21st Century, incorporating proposals to reform higher education, with emphasis on access to education, and educating for individual development and active participation in society.

The International Institute for Educational Planning and the International Bureau of Education undertake training, research and the exchange of information on aspects of education. A UNESCO Institute for Education, based in Hamburg, Germany, researches literacy activities and the evolution of adult learning systems. UNESCO aims to promote the use of new information and communication technologies in the expansion of learning opportunities. A joint UNESCO/ILO committee of experts has been established to consider strategies for enhancing the status of the teaching profession.

The April 2000 World Education Forum recognized the global HIV/AIDS pandemic to be a significant challenge to the attainment of 'Education for All'. UNESCO, as a co-sponsor of the Joint UN Programme on HIV/AIDS—UNAIDS, takes an active role in promoting formal and non-formal preventive health education.

NATURAL SCIENCES

In November 1999 the General Conference endorsed a Declaration on Science and the Use of Scientific Knowledge and an agenda for action, which had been adopted at the World Conference on Science, held in June/July 1999, in Budapest, Hungary. UNESCO was to co-ordinate the follow-up to the conference and, in conjunction with the International Council for Science (q.v.), to promote initiatives in international scientific partnership. The following were identified as priority areas of UNESCO's work programme on Natural Sciences for 2002–03: Science and Technology: Capacity-building and Management; and Sciences, Environment and Sustainable Development. Water Security in the 21st Century was designated as the principal theme, involving addressing threats to water resources and their associated ecosystems. UNESCO was to be the lead UN agency involved in the preparation of the first *World Water Development Report*, due to be issued in 2003. The Science and Technology component of the programme focused on the follow-up of the World Conference on Science, involving the elaboration of national policies on science and technology; strengthening science education; improving university teaching and enhancing national research capacities; and reinforcing international co-operation in mathematics, physics, chemistry, biology, biotechnology and the engineering sciences. UNESCO aims to contribute to bridging the divide between community-held traditional knowledge and scientific knowledge.

UNESCO aims to improve the level of university teaching of the basic sciences through training courses, establishing national and regional networks (for example, the Asian Physics Education Network) and centres of excellence, and fostering co-operative research. In carrying out its mission, UNESCO relies on partnerships with non-governmental organizations and the world scientific communities. In 1996 UNESCO initiated a 10-year World Solar Programme, which aimed to promote the application of solar energy and to increase research, development and public awareness of all forms of ecologically-sustainable energy use.

UNESCO has established various forms of intergovernmental co-operation concerned with the environmental sciences and research on natural resources, in order to support the recommendations of the June 1992 UN Conference on Environment and Development and, in particular, the implementation of 'Agenda 21' to promote sustainable development. The International Geological Correlation Programme, undertaken jointly with the International Union of Geological Sciences, aims to improve and facilitate global research of geological processes. In the context of the International Decade for Natural Disaster Reduction (declared in 1990), UNESCO has conducted scientific studies of natural hazards and means of mitigating their effects and has organized several disaster-related workshops. The International Hydrological Programme considers scientific aspects of water resources assessment and management; and the Intergovernmental Oceanographic Commission (IOC) focuses on issues relating to oceans, shorelines and marine resources, in particular the role of the ocean in climate and global systems. The IOC has been actively involved in the establishment of a Global Coral Reef Monitoring Network. It is developing a Global Ocean Observing System. An initiative on Environment and Development in Coastal Regions and in Small Islands is concerned with ensuring environmentally-sound and sustainable development by strengthening management of the following key areas: freshwater resources; the mitigation of coastline instability; biological diversity; and coastal ecosystem productivity. UNESCO hosts the secretariat of the World Water Assessment Programme on freshwater resources.

UNESCO's Man and the Biosphere Programme supports a world-wide network of biosphere reserves (comprising 408 sites in 94 countries at May 2002), which aim to promote environmental conservation and research, education and training in biodiversity and problems of land use. Following the signing of the Convention to Combat Desertification in October 1994, UNESCO initiated an International Programme for Arid Land Crops, based on a network of existing institutions (including the Institute for Desert Research at the Chinese Academy of Sciences in Lanzhou, People's Republic of China, the Faculty of Agriculture Sciences at the University of Queensland in Brisbane, Australia, and the Central Arid Zone Research Institute in Jodhpur, India) in order to assist the implementation of the Convention., to assist implementation of the Convention.

The Regional Office for Science and Technology (ROSTAS) organizes courses and studies on the teaching of basic science, computer science, hydrology, oceanography, geophysics, soil biology, geomorphology and seismology. It provides regional seminars, training courses and consultancy missions. As part of its programmes in arid zone research, UNESCO has helped to establish research institutes in Iraq and Saudi Arabia, and has given financial aid to Egypt's Desert Research Institute.

SOCIAL AND HUMAN SCIENCES

UNESCO is mandated to contribute to the world-wide development of the social and human sciences and philosophy, which it regards as of great importance in policy-making and maintaining ethical vigilance. The structure of UNESCO's Social and Human Sciences programme takes into account both an ethical and standard-setting dimension, and research, policy-making, action in the field and future-oriented activities. UNESCO's work programme for 2002–03 on Social and Human Sciences comprised three main components: The Ethics of Science and Technology; Promotion of Human Rights, Peace and Democratic Principles; and Improvement of Policies Relating to Social Transformations and Promotion of Anticipation and Prospective Studies. The priority Ethics of Science and Technology element aimed to reinforce UNESCO's role as an intellectual forum for ethical reflection on challenges related to the advance of science and technology; oversee the follow-up of the Universal Declaration on the Human Genome and Human Rights (see below); promote education in science and technology; ensure UNESCO's role in promoting good practices through encouraging the inclusion of ethical guiding principles in policy formulation and reinforcing international networks; and to promote international co-operation in human sciences and philosophy. The Social and Human Sciences programme had the main intellectual and conceptual responsibility for the transdisciplinary theme 'eradication of poverty, especially extreme poverty'.

UNESCO aims to promote and protect human rights and acts as an interdisciplinary, multicultural and pluralistic forum for reflection on issues relating to the ethical dimension of scientific advances, for example in biogenetics, new technology, and medicine. In May 1997 the International Bioethics Committee, a group of 36 specialists who meet under UNESCO auspices, approved a draft version of a Universal Declaration on the Human Genome and Human Rights, in an attempt to provide ethical guide-lines for developments in human genetics. The Declaration, which identified some 100,000 hereditary genes as 'common heritage', was adopted by the UNESCO General Conference in November and committed states to promoting the dissemination of relevant scientific knowledge and co-operating in genome research. The November Conference also resolved to establish an 18-member World Commission on the Ethics of Scientific Knowledge and Technology (COMEST) to serve as a forum for the exchange of information and ideas and to promote dialogue between scientific communities, decision-makers and the public. UNESCO hosts the secretariat of COMEST, which met for the first time in April 1999 in Oslo, Norway. Its second meeting, which took place in December 2001 in Berlin, Germany, focused on the ethics of energy, fresh water and outer space.

UNESCO aims to assist the building and consolidation of peaceful and democratic societies. An international network of institutions and centres involved in research on conflict resolution is being established to support the promotion of peace. Other training, workshop and research activities have been undertaken in countries which have suffered conflict. The Associated Schools Project (ASPnet—comprising more than 6,700 institutions in 166 countries in 2001) has, for nearly 50 years, promoted the principles of peace, human rights, democracy and international co-operation through education. An International Youth Clearing House and Information Service (INFOYOUTH) aims to increase and consolidate the information available on the situation of young people in society, and to heighten awareness of their needs, aspirations and potential among public and private decision-makers. UNESCO also focuses on the educational and cultural dimensions of physical education and sport and their capacity to preserve and improve health.

In 1994 UNESCO initiated an international social science research programme, the Management of Social Transformations (MOST), to promote capacity-building in social planning at all levels of decision-making. UNESCO sponsors several research fellowships in the social sciences. In other activities UNESCO promotes the rehabilitation of underprivileged urban areas, the research of socio-cultural factors affecting demographic change and the study of family issues.

Fundamental to UNESCO's mission is the rejection of all forms of discrimination. It disseminates scientific information aimed at combating racial prejudice, works to improve the status of women and their access to education, and promotes equality between men and women.

CULTURE

In undertaking efforts to preserve the world's cultural and natural heritage UNESCO has attempted to emphasize the link between culture and development. In November 2001 the General Conference adopted the UNESCO Universal Declaration on Cultural Diversity, which affirmed the importance of intercultural dialogue in establishing a climate of peace. The work programme on Culture for 2002–03 included the following interrelated components: Reinforcing Normative Action in the Field of Culture; Protecting Cultural Diversity and Promoting Cultural Pluralism and Intercultural Dialogue; and Strengthening Links between Culture and Development. The focus was to be on all aspects of cultural heritage, and on the encouragement of cultural diversity and dialogue between cultures and civilizations. Under the 2002–03 programme UNESCO aimed to launch the Global Alliance on Cultural Diversity, a six-year initiative to promote partnerships between governments, non-governmental bodies and the private sector, with a view to supporting cultural diversity through the strengthening of cultural industries and the prevention of cultural piracy. UNESCO was designated as the lead agency for co-ordinating the UN Year for Cultural Heritage, celebrated in 2002.

UNESCO's World Heritage Programme, inaugurated in 1978, aims to protect historic sites and natural landmarks of outstanding universal significance, in accordance with the 1972 UNESCO Convention Concerning the Protection of the World Cultural and Natural Heritage, by providing financial aid for restoration, technical assistance, training and management planning. By June 2002 the 'World Heritage List' comprised 730 sites in 125 countries, of which 563 had cultural significance, 144 were natural landmarks, and 23 were of 'mixed' importance. UNESCO participated in the successful safeguarding campaign of the Buddhist temple at Borobudur, Indonesia (1973–83), the conservation and management of the Angkor complex in Cambodia and in preliminary work on saving the ancient city of Moenjodaro in Pakistan. Asian and Pacific sites appearing on the 'World Heritage List' include the 12th century minaret and archaeological remains of Jam (Afghanistan), Great Barrier Reef (Australia), the Great Wall of China, the Taj Mahal (India), the Kathmandu Valley (Nepal), the sacred city of Anuradhapura (Sri Lanka), the Himeji Castle (Japan), Sukhothai (Thailand), Luang Prabang (Laos) and numerous other historic sites and nature reserves in the region. UNESCO also maintains a 'List of World Heritage in Danger'. At June 2002 this comprised 33 sites world-wide, including the minaret of Jam in Afghanistan and the Angkor complex in Cambodia. Through the World Heritage Information Network (WHIN), a world-wide network of more than 800 information providers, UNESCO promotes global awareness and information exchange. In May 1999 UNESCO sponsored an Asia-Pacific conference on the economics of heritage, held in Penang, Malaysia. UNESCO supports efforts for the collection and safeguarding of humanity's non-material heritage (oral traditions, music, dance, medicine, etc.). In May 2001 UNESCO awarded the title of 'Masterpieces of the Oral and Intangible Heritage of Humanity' to 19 cultural spaces (i.e. physical or temporal spaces hosting recurrent cultural events) and popular forms of expression deemed to be of outstanding value, such as the Japanese Nôgaku theatre and the Hudhud chants of the Ifuqao community in the Philippines. In co-operation with the International Council for Philosophy and Humanistic Studies, UNESCO is compiling a directory of endangered languages. In early 2001 UNESCO condemned an alleged edict by the then fundamentalist Islamist Taliban regime in Afghanistan ordering the destruction of all statues in that country which, owing to their representation of human likenesses, were regarded as non-Islamic. In March UNESCO protested strongly against the reported destruction by order of the Taliban of two ancient monuments of Buddha at Bamiyan. In January 2002, following the overthrow of the Taliban in late 2001, the newly-appointed Afghan Interim Administration requested UNESCO to co-ordinate all international and bilateral activities to protect Afghanistan's cultural heritage. In March a memorandum of understanding was concluded between UNESCO and the Interim Administration providing for UNESCO to manage international efforts towards rehabilitating the national museum in Kabul, where a number of artefacts had been destroyed under Taliban rule. During that year UNESCO initiated an Afghan cultural heritage campaign to assess preservation requirements.

In 1992 a World Heritage Centre was established to enable rapid mobilization of international technical assistance for the preservation of cultural sites. In addition, UNESCO supports efforts for the collection and safeguarding of humanity's non-material 'intangible' heritage, including oral traditions, music, dance and medicine. UNESCO produces an *Atlas of the World's Languages in Danger of Disappearing*. The most recent edition, issued in February 2002, reported that, of some 6,000 languages spoken world-wide, about one-half were endangered.

In November 2001 the General Conference adopted the Convention on the Protection of the Underwater Cultural Heritage, covering the protection from commercial exploitation of shipwrecks, submerged historical sites, etc. situated in the territorial waters of signatory states. UNESCO also administers the 1954 Hague Convention on the Protection of Cultural Property in the Event of Armed Conflict and the 1970 Convention on the Means of Prohibiting and Preventing the Illicit Import, Export and Transfer of Ownership of Cultural Property.

UNESCO encourages the translation and publication of literary works, publishes albums of art, and produces records, audiovisual programmes and travelling art exhibitions. It supports the development of book publishing and distribution, including the free flow of books and educational material across borders, and the training of editors and managers in publishing. UNESCO is active in preparing and encouraging the enforcement of international legislation on copyright.

In December 1992 UNESCO established the World Commission on Culture and Development, to strengthen links between culture and development and to prepare a report on the issue. UNESCO was the leading agency for promoting the UN's World Decade for Cultural Development (1988–97). In the framework of the World Decade UNESCO launched the Silk Roads Project, as a multidisciplinary study of the interactions among cultures and civilizations along the routes linking Asia and Europe. The Vaka Moana (Ocean Roads) Programme studied traditional and contemporary culture in the Pacific islands, means of reinforcing traditional links, the conservation of resources and the interaction between culture and development in the region.

COMMUNICATION AND INFORMATION

In 2001 UNESCO introduced a major programme, 'Information for All', as the principal policy-guiding framework for the Communication and Information sector. The organization works towards establishing an open, non-exclusive knowledge society based on information-sharing and incorporating the socio-cultural and ethical dimensions of sustainable development. It promotes the free flow of, and universal access to information, knowledge, data and best practices, through the development of communications infrastructures, the elimination of impediments to freedom of expression, and the promotion of the right to information; through encouraging international co-operation in maintaining libraries and archives; and through efforts to harness informatics for development purposes and strengthen member states' capacities in this field. Activities include assistance with the development of legislation and training programmes in countries where independent and pluralistic media are emerging; assistance in the monitoring of media independence, pluralism and diversity; promotion of exchange programmes and study tours; and improving access and opportunities for women in the media. UNESCO recognizes that the so-called global 'digital divide', in addition to other developmental differences between countries, generates exclusion and marginalization, and that increased participation in the democratic process can be attained through strengthening national communication and information capacities. UNESCO promotes the upholding of human rights in the use of cyberspace. The organization was to participate in the World Summit on the Information Society, scheduled to take place in Geneva, Switzerland, in December 2003. The work programme on Communication and Information for 2002–03 comprised the following components: Promoting Equitable Access to Information and Knowledge Especially in the Public Domain; and Promoting Freedom of Expression and Strengthening Communication Capacities. During 2002–03 UNESCO was to evaluate its interactive internet-based WebWorld Portal, which aims to provide global communication and information services at all levels of society. UNESCO's Memory of the World project aims to preserve in digital form, and thereby to promote wide access to, the world's documentary heritage.

In regions affected by conflict UNESCO supports efforts to establish and maintain an independent media service. This strategy is largely implemented through an International Programme for the Development of Communication (IPDC). IPDC provides support to communication and media development projects in the developing world, including the establishment of news agencies and newspapers and training editorial and technical staff. Since its establishment in 1982 IPDC has provided around US $85m. to finance some 900 projects. UNESCO has participated in the restructuring of the media in Cambodia in the context of the process of national reconciliation.

In March 1997 the first International Congress on Ethical, Legal and Societal Aspects of Digital Information ('InfoEthics') was held in Monte Carlo, Monaco. At the second 'InfoEthics' Congress, held in October 1998, experts discussed issues concerning privacy, confidentiality and security in the electronic transfer of information. UNESCO maintains an Observatory on the Information Society, which provides up-to-date information on the development of new information and communications technologies, analysis of major trends, and aims to raise awareness of related ethical, legal and societal issues. The UNESCO Institute for Information Technologies in Education was established in Moscow, Russia in 1998. In 2001 the UNESCO Institute for Statistics was established in Montréal, Canada.

Finance

UNESCO's activities are funded through a regular budget provided by member states and extrabudgetary funds from other sources, particularly UNDP, the World Bank, regional banks and other bilateral Funds-in-Trust arrangements. UNESCO co-operates with many other UN agencies and international non-governmental organizations.

UNESCO's proposed Regular Programme budget for the two years 2002–03 was US $544.4m., unchanged from the previous biennium. Extrabudgetary funds for 2002–03 were estimated at US $320m.

Publications

(mostly in English, French and Spanish editions; Arabic, Chinese and Russian versions are also available in many cases)

Atlas of the World's Languages in Danger of Disappearing.

Copyright Bulletin (quarterly).

Education for All: Status and Trends.

International Review of Education (quarterly).

International Social Science Journal (quarterly).

Museum International (quarterly).

Nature and Resources (quarterly).

Prospects (quarterly review on education).

UNESCO Sources (monthly).

UNESCO Statistical Yearbook.

World Communication Report.

World Culture Report.

World Education Report (every 2 years).

World Heritage Newsletter.

World Heritage Review (quarterly).

World Information Report.

World Science Report (every 2 years).

Books, databases, video and radio documentaries, statistics, scientific maps and atlases.

World Health Organization—WHO

Address: avenue Appia 20, 1211 Geneva 27, Switzerland.

Telephone: (22) 7912111; **fax:** (22) 7913111; **e-mail:** info@who.int; **internet:** www.who.int.

WHO was established in 1948 as the central agency directing international health work.

Organization

(October 2002)

WORLD HEALTH ASSEMBLY

The Assembly meets annually in Geneva; it is responsible for policy making, and the biennial programme and budget; it appoints the Director-General, admits new members and reviews budget contributions.

EXECUTIVE BOARD

The Board is composed of 32 health experts designated by, but not representing, their governments; they serve for three years, and the World Health Assembly elects 10–12 member states each year to the Board. It meets at least twice a year to review the Director-General's programme, which it forwards to the Assembly with any recommendations that seem necessary. It advises on questions referred to it by the Assembly and is responsible for putting into effect the decisions and policies of the Assembly. It is also empowered to take emergency measures in case of epidemics or disasters.

Chair.: MYRIAM ABEL (Vanuatu).

SECRETARIAT

Director-General: Dr GRO HARLEM BRUNDTLAND (Norway).

Executive Directors: Dr ANARFI ASAMOA-BAAH (Ghana) (Health Technology and Pharmaceuticals), MARYAN BAQUEROT (General Management), Dr DAVID L. HEYMANN (USA) (Communicable Diseases), CHRISTOPHER MURRAY (USA) (Evidence and Information for Policy), Dr DAVID NABARRO (United Kingdom) (Sustainable Development and Healthy Environments), Dr TOMRIS TÜRMEN (Turkey) (Family and Community Health), Dr DEREK YACH (South Africa) (Non-communicable Diseases and Mental Health); NADIA YOUNES (Egypt) (External Relations and Governing Bodies).

Chef de Cabinet (Office of the Director-General): DENIS AITKIN (United Kingdom).

.

REGIONAL OFFICES

South-East Asia: World Health House, Indraprastha Estate, Mahatma Gandhi Rd, New Delhi 110002, India; tel. (11) 3370804; fax (11) 3379507; e-mail pandeyh@whosea.org; internet w3.whosea.org/index.htm; Regional Dir Dr UTON MUCHTAR RAFEI (Indonesia).

Western Pacific: POB 2932, 1000 Manila, Philippines; tel. (2) 5288001; fax (2) 5211036; e-mail postmaster@who.org.ph; internet www.wpro.who.int; Regional Dir Dr SHIGERI OMI (Japan).

Activities

WHO's objective is stated in the constitution as 'the attainment by all peoples of the highest possible level of health'. In November 2001 WHO issued the International Classification of Functioning, Disability and Health (ICF) to act as an international standard and guide-line for determining health and disability.

It acts as the central authority directing international health work, and establishes relations with professional groups and government health authorities on that basis.

It provides, on request from member states, technical and policy assistance in support of programmes to control or eradicate disease, train health workers best suited to local needs and strengthen national health systems. Aid is provided in emergencies and natural disasters.

A global programme of collaborative research and exchange of scientific information is carried out in co-operation with about 1,200 leading national institutions. Particular stress is laid on the widespread communicable diseases of the tropics, and the countries directly concerned are assisted in developing their research capabilities.

It keeps communicable and non-communicable diseases and other health problems under constant surveillance, promotes the exchange of prompt and accurate information and of notification of outbreaks of diseases, and administers the International Health Regulations.

It sets standards for the quality control of drugs, vaccines and other substances affecting health.

It collects and disseminates health data and carries out statistical analyses and comparative studies in such diseases as cancer, heart disease and mental illness.

It receives reports on drugs observed to have shown adverse reactions in any country, and transmits the information to other member states. All available information on effects on human health of the pollutants in the environment is critically reviewed and published.

Co-operation among scientists and professional groups is encouraged. The organization negotiates and sustains national and global partnerships. It may propose international conventions and agreements, and develops and promotes international norms and standards. The organization promotes the development and testing of new technologies, tools and guide-lines. It assists in developing an informed public opinion on matters of health.

In 1980 the Asian Charter for Health Development was signed by a number of countries in the region. The Charter serves to declare health priorities, to enable the mobilization of funds and resources, to promote inter-country co-operation, and to provide a common basis for formulating health plans. It lists the following priority areas: primary health care; appropriate manpower development; provision of safe water and sanitation; promotion of maternal and child health; control of communicable diseases (especially malaria and the diseases against which effective immunization agents are available); and the improvement of nutrition.

HEALTH FOR ALL

WHO's first global strategy for pursuing 'Health for all' was adopted in May 1981 by the 34th World Health Assembly. The objective of 'Health for all' was identified as the attainment by all citizens of the world of a level of health that would permit them to lead a socially and economically productive life, requiring fair distribution of available resources, universal access to essential health care, and the promotion of preventive health care. In May 1998 the 51st World Health Assembly renewed the initiative, adopting a global strategy in support of 'Health for all in the 21st century', to be effected through regional and national health policies. The new approach was to build on the primary health care approach of the initial strategy, but was to strengthen the emphasis on quality of life, equity in health and access to health services. The following have been identified as minimum requirements of 'Health for All':

(i) Safe water in the home or within 15 minutes' walking distance, and adequate sanitary facilities in the home or immediate vicinity;

(ii) Immunization against diphtheria, pertussis, tetanus, poliomyelitis, measles and tuberculosis;

(iii) Local health care, including availability of essential drugs, within one hour's travel; and

(iv) Trained personnel to attend childbirth, and to care for pregnant mothers and children up to at least one year old.

In July 1998 Dr Gro Harlem Brundtland officially took office as the new Director-General of WHO. She immediately announced an extensive reform of the organization, including restructuring the WHO technical programmes into the following groups, each headed by an Executive Director (see above): Communicable Diseases; Non-communicable Diseases and Mental Health; Family and Community Health; Sustainable Development and Healthy Environments; Health Technology and Pharmaceuticals; Evidence and Information for Policy; External affairs and Governing Bodies; and General Management. The Office of the Director-General (including audit, oversight and legal activities) is headed by a Chef de Cabinet. In 2000 WHO adopted a new corporate strategy, entailing a stronger focus on performance and programme delivery through standardized plans of action, and increased consistency and efficiency throughout the organization.

The Tenth General Programme of Work, for the period 2002–05, defined a policy framework for pursuing the principal objectives of building healthy populations and combating ill health. The Programme took into account: increasing understanding of the social, economic, political and cultural factors involved in achieving better health and the role played by better health in poverty reduction; the increasing complexity of health systems; the importance of safeguarding health as a component of humanitarian action; and the need for greater co-ordination among development organizations. It incorporated four interrelated strategic directions: lessening excess mortality, morbidity and disability, especially in poor and marginalized populations; promoting healthy lifestyles and reducing risk factors to human health arising from environmental, economic, social and behavioural causes; developing equitable and financially fair health systems; and establishing an enabling policy and an institutional environment for the health sector and promoting an effective health dimension to social, economic, environmental and development policy.

In May 1997 WHO signed a Memorandum of Understanding with the Association of South East Asian Nations (ASEAN), in order to promote collaboration between the two organizations in key areas of disease prevention and control, and research into health-related issues. WHO also collaborates with the Asian Development Bank in promoting and reinforcing health development in Asia and the Pacific.

COMMUNICABLE DISEASES

WHO identifies infectious and parasitic communicable diseases as a major obstacle to social and economic progress, particularly in developing countries, where, in addition to disabilities and loss of productivity and household earnings, they cause nearly one-half of all deaths. Emerging and re-emerging diseases, those likely to cause epidemics, increasing incidence of zoonoses (diseases passed from animals to humans either directly or by insects) attributable to environmental changes, outbreaks of unknown etiology, and the undermining of some drug therapies by the spread of antimicrobial resistance are main areas of concern. In recent years WHO has noted the global spread of communicable diseases through international travel, voluntary human migration and involuntary population displacement.

WHO's Communicable Diseases group works to reduce the impact of infectious diseases world-wide through surveillance and response; prevention, control and eradication strategies; and research and product development. Combating malaria and tuberculosis (TB) are organization-wide priorities and, as such, are supported not only by their own areas of work but also by activities undertaken in other areas. The group seeks to identify new technologies and tools, and to foster national development through strengthening health services and the better use of existing tools. It aims to strengthen global monitoring of important communicable disease problems. The group advocates a functional approach to disease control. It aims to create consensus and consolidate partnerships around targeted diseases and collaborates with other groups at all stages to provide an integrated response. In April 2000 WHO and several partner institutions in epidemic surveillance established a Global Outbreak Alert and Response Network. Through the Network WHO aims to maintain constant vigilance regarding outbreaks of disease and to link world-wide expertise to provide an immediate response capability. A Global Fund to Fight AIDS, TB and Malaria was established, with WHO participation, in 2001 (see below).

A Ministerial Conference on Malaria, organized by WHO, was held in October 1992, attended by representatives from 102 member countries. The Conference adopted a plan of action for the 1990s for the control of the disease, which kills an estimated 1m. people every year and affects a further 300m.–500m. Some 90% of all cases are in sub-Saharan Africa; the remainder are concentrated in India, Brazil, Sri Lanka, Viet Nam, Colombia and Solomon Islands. WHO assists countries where malaria is endemic to prepare national plans of action for malaria control in accordance with WHO's Global Malaria Control Strategy, which emphasized strengthening local capabilities, for example through training, for effective health control. In July 1998 WHO declared the control of malaria a priority concern, and in October the organization formally launched the 'Roll Back Malaria' programme, in conjunction with UNICEF, the World Bank and UNDP, which aimed to halve the prevalence of malaria 2010. Emphasis was to be placed on strengthening local health systems and on the promotion of inexpensive preventative measures, including the use of bednets treated with insecticides. The global Roll Back Malaria partnership, linking governments, development agencies, and other partners, aims to mobilize resources and support for controlling the disease. WHO, with several private- and public-sector partners, supports the development of more effective anti-malaria drugs and vaccines through the 'Medicines for Malaria' venture. The global prevalence of dengue fever, another mosquito-carried infection, and dengue haemorrhagic fever (a severe complication) has increased in recent years, with an estimated 20m. cases occurring annually. Prevalence is highest in the South-East Asia and Western Pacific regions. WHO has produced guide-lines for dengue surveillance and mosquito control.

In 1995 WHO established a Global Tuberculosis Programme to address the challenges of the TB epidemic, which had been declared a global emergency by the Organization in 1993. According to WHO estimates, one-third of the world's population carries the TB bacillus, and 2m.–3m. people die from the disease each year. WHO provides technical support to all member countries, with special attention given to those with high TB prevalence, to establish effective national tuberculosis control programmes. WHO's strategy for TB control includes the use of DOTS (direct observation treatment, short-course), standardized treatment guide-lines, and result accountability through routine evaluation of treatment outcomes. Simultaneously, WHO is encouraging research with the aim of further disseminating DOTS, adapting DOTS for wider use, developing new tools for prevention, diagnosis and treatment, and containing new threats such as the HIV/TB co-epidemic. In March 1999 WHO announced the launch of a new initiative, 'Stop TB', in partnership with the World Bank, the US Government and a coalition of non-governmental organizations, which aimed to promote DOTS to ensure its use in 85% of cases by 2005 (compared with around one-quarter in 1999). In 2000 Bangladesh, the People's Republic of China and Viet Nam were reported to be successfully controlling TB through the use of DOTS. However, inadequate control of DOTS in some areas, leading to partial and inconsistent treatments, has resulted in the development of drug-resistant and, often, incurable strains of the disease. The incidence of so-called multidrug-resistant TB (MDR-TB) strains, that are unresponsive to the two main anti-TB drugs, has risen in recent years. During 2001 WHO was developing and testing DOTS-Plus, a strategy for controlling the spread of MDR-TB in areas of high prevalence. In 2001 WHO estimated that more than 8m. new cases of TB were occurring world-wide each year, of which the largest concentration was in South-East Asia. It envisaged a substantial increase in new cases by 2005, mainly owing to the severity of the HIV/TB co-epidemic. TB is the principal cause of death for people infected with the HIV virus. In March 2001 the Global TB Drug Facility was launched under the 'Stop TB' initiative; this aimed to increase access to high-quality anti-TB drugs for sufferers in developing countries. In October the 'Stop TB' partnership announced a Global Plan to Stop TB, which envisaged the expansion of access to DOTS; the advancement of MDR-TB prevention measures; the development of anti-TB drugs entailing a shorter treatment period; and the implementation of new strategies for treating people with HIV and TB.

One of WHO's major achievements was the eradication of smallpox. Following a massive international campaign of vaccination and surveillance, begun in 1958 and intensified in 1967, the last case was detected in 1977 and the eradication of the disease was declared in 1980. In May 1996 the World Health Assembly resolved that, pending a final endorsement, all remaining known stocks of the smallpox virus were to be destroyed on 30 June 1999, although 500,000 doses of smallpox vaccine were to remain, along with a supply of the smallpox vaccine seed virus, in order to ensure that a further supply of the vaccine could be made available if required. In May 1999, however, the Assembly authorized a temporary retention of stocks of the virus until 2002. In late 2001, in response to fears that illegally-held virus stocks could be used in acts of biological terrorism (see below), WHO reassembled a team of technical experts on smallpox. In January 2002 the Executive Board determined that stocks of the virus should continue to be retained, to enable research into more effective treatments and vaccines. In 1988 the World Health Assembly declared its commitment to the eradication of poliomyelitis and launched the Global Polio Eradication Initiative. At the end of 2001 10 countries were still known to be or suspected of being polio endemic, including Afghanistan, India and Pakistan (which were all regarded as areas with high-intensity transmission). By that time the number of reported polio cases world-wide had declined to 480, from 35,000 in 1988 (although the actual number of cases in 1988 was estimated at around 350,000). In 2001 WHO adopted a strategic plan for the eradication of polio covering the period 2001–05, which envisaged the effective use of national immunization days (NIDs) to secure global interruption of polio transmission by the end of 2002, with a view to achieving certification of the global eradication of polio by the end of 2005. Meanwhile, routine immunization services were to be strengthened. In 2001 575m. children in 94 countries world-wide were immunized through the use of NIDS.

WHO is committed to the elimination of leprosy (the reduction of the prevalence of leprosy to less than one case per 10,000 population). The use of a highly effective combination of three drugs (known as multi-drug therapy—MDT) resulted in a reduction in the number of leprosy cases world-wide from 10m.–12m. in 1988 to 597,000 in 2000. The Global Alliance for the Elimination of Leprosy, launched in November 1999 by WHO, in collaboration with governments of affected countries and several private partners, including a major pharmaceutical company, aims to bring about the eradication of the disease by the end of 2005, through the continued use of MDT treatment. The world-wide prevalence rate stood at 1.4 cases per 10,000 people in 2000, although the rate in the 11 most endemic countries was 4.5 cases per 10,000. India accounts for more than one-half of the global total of active leprosy cases.

The Special Programme for Research and Training in Tropical Diseases, established in 1975 and sponsored jointly by WHO, UNDP and the World Bank, as well as by contributions from donor countries, involves a world-wide network of some 5,000 scientists working on the development and application of vaccines, new drugs, diagnostic kits and preventive measures, and an applied field research on practical community issues affecting the target diseases.

The objective of providing immunization for all children by 1990 was adopted by the World Health Assembly in 1977. Six diseases (measles, whooping cough, tetanus, poliomyelitis, tuberculosis and diphtheria) became the target of the Expanded Programme on Immunization (EPI), in which WHO, UNICEF and many other organizations collaborated. As a result of massive international and national efforts, the global immunization coverage increased from 20% in the early 1980s to the targeted rate of 80% by the end of 1990. This coverage signified that more than 100m. children in the developing world under the age of one had been successfully vaccinated against the targeted diseases, the lives of about 3m. children had been saved every year, and 500,000 annual cases of paralysis as a result of polio had been prevented. In 1992 the Assembly resolved to reach a new target of 90% immunization coverage with the six EPI vaccines; to introduce hepatitis B as a seventh vaccine (with the aim of an 80% reduction in the incidence of the disease in children by 2001); and to introduce the yellow fever vaccine in areas where it occurs endemically.

In June 2000 WHO released a report entitled 'Overcoming Antimicrobial Resistance', in which it warned that the misuse of antibiotics could render some common infectious illnesses unresponsive to treatment. At that time WHO issued guide-lines which aimed to mitigate the risks associated with the use of antimicrobials in livestock reared for human consumption.

NON-COMMUNICABLE DISEASES AND MENTAL HEALTH

The Non-communicable Diseases and Mental Health group comprises departments responsible for the surveillance, prevention and management of uninfectious diseases (such as those arising from an unhealthy diet), and departments for health promotion, disability, injury prevention and rehabilitation, mental health and substance abuse. Surveillance, prevention and management of non-communicable diseases, tobacco, and mental health are all organization-wide priorities.

Unhealthy diet, physical inactivity and tobacco use are regarded as common, preventable risk factors for the four most prominent non-communicable diseases: cardiovascular diseases, cancer, chronic respiratory disease and diabetes. WHO aims to monitor the global epidemiological situation of non-communicable diseases, to co-ordinate multinational research activities concerned with prevention and care, and to analyse determining factors such as gender and poverty. In mid-1998 the Organization adopted a resolution on measures to be taken to combat non-communicable diseases, the prevalence of which was anticipated to increase, particularly in developing countries, owing to rising life expectancy and changes in lifestyles. For example, between 1995 and 2025 the number of adults affected by diabetes was projected to increase from 135m. to 300m. In February 1999 WHO initiated a new programme, 'Vision 2020: the Right to Sight', which aimed to eliminate avoidable blindness (estimated to be as much as 80% of all cases) by 2020. Blindness was otherwise predicted to increase by as much as twofold, owing to the increased longevity of the global population. WHO's programmes for diabetes mellitus, chronic rheumatic diseases and asthma assist with the development of national initiatives, based upon goals and targets for the improvement of early detection, care and reduction of long-term complications. In co-operation with the International Association for the Study of Obesity (IASO, q.v.) WHO has studied obesity-related issues affecting countries in Asia and the Pacific. In October 2001 the first Asia-Oceania Conference on Obesity was convened in Japan under the auspices of IASO; a second conference was to be held in Kuala Lumpur, Malaysia, in September 2003. The International Task Force on Obesity, affiliated to the IASO, aims to encourage the development of new policies for managing obesity in Asia and the Pacific.

WHO works to assess the impact of injuries, violence and sensory impairments on health. The health promotion division promotes decentralized and community-based health programmes and is concerned with developing new approaches to population ageing and encouraging healthy life-styles and self-care. It also seeks to relieve the negative impact of social changes such as urbanization, migration and changes in family structure upon health. WHO advocates a multi-sectoral approach—involving public health, legal and educational systems—to the prevention of injuries, which represent 16% of the global burden of disease. It aims to support governments in developing suitable strategies to prevent and mitigate the consequences of violence, unintentional injury and disability. Several health promotion projects have been undertaken, in collaboration between WHO regional and country offices and other relevant organizations, including: the Global School Health Initiative, to bridge the sectors of health and education and to promote the health of school-age children; the Global Strategy for Occupational Health, to promote the health of the working population and the control of occupational health risks; Community-based Rehabilitation, aimed at providing a more enabling environment for people with disabilities; and a communication strategy to provide training and support for health communications personnel and initiatives. In 2000 WHO, UNESCO, the World Bank and UNICEF adopted the joint Focusing Resources for Effective School Health (FRESH Start) approach to promoting life skills among adolescents.

Mental health problems, which include unipolar and bipolar affective disorders, psychosis, epilepsy, dementia, Parkinson's disease, multiple sclerosis, drug and alcohol dependency, and neuropsychiatric disorders such as post-traumatic stress disorder, obsessive compulsive disorder and panic disorder, have been identified by WHO as significant global health problems. Although, overall, physical health has improved, mental, behavioural and social health problems are increasing, owing to extended life expectancy and improved child mortality rates, and factors such as war and poverty. WHO aims to address mental problems by increasing awareness of mental health issues and promoting improved mental health services and primary care. The Organization formulates guide-lines and protocols for the prevention and management of mental problems.

The Substance Abuse department is concerned with problems of alcohol, drugs and other substance abuse. Within its Programme on Substance Abuse (PSA), which was established in 1990 in response to the global increase in substance abuse, WHO provides technical support to assist countries in formulating policies with regard to the prevention and reduction of the health and social effects of psychoactive substance abuse. The PSA's sphere of activity includes epidemiological surveillance and risk assessment, advocacy and the dissemination of information, strengthening national and regional prevention and health promotion techniques and strategies, the development of cost-effective treatment and rehabilitation approaches, and also encompasses regulatory activities as required under the international drugs-control treaties in force.

The Tobacco or Health Programme aims to reduce the use of tobacco, by educating tobacco-users and preventing young people from adopting the habit. In 1996 WHO published its first report on the tobacco situation world-wide. According to WHO, about one-third of the world's population aged over 15 years smoke tobacco, which causes approximately 3.5m. deaths each year (through lung cancer, heart disease, chronic bronchitis and other effects). In 1998 the 'Tobacco Free Initiative', a major global anti-smoking campaign, was established. In May 1999 the World Health Assembly endorsed the formulation of a Framework Convention on Tobacco Control (FCTC) to help to combat the increase in tobacco use (although a number of tobacco growers expressed concerns about the effect of the convention on their livelihoods). It was envisaged that the Framework Convention would be adopted in 2003; a draft of the treaty was released in July 2002. The greatest increase in tobacco use is forecast to occur in developing countries.

FAMILY AND COMMUNITY HEALTH

WHO's Family and Community Health group addresses the following areas of work: child and adolescent health, research and programme development in reproductive health, making pregnancy safer, women's health, and HIV/AIDS. Making pregnancy safer and HIV/AIDS are organization-wide priorities. The group's aim is to improve access to sustainable health care for all by strengthening health systems and fostering individual, family and community development. Activities include newborn care; child health, including promoting and protecting the health and development of the child through such approaches as promotion of breast-feeding and use of the mother-baby package, as well as care of the sick child, including diarrhoeal and acute respiratory disease control and support to women and children in difficult circumstances; the promotion of safe motherhood and maternal health; adolescent health, including the promotion and development of young people and the prevention of specific health problems; women, health and development, including addressing issues of gender, sexual violence, and harmful traditional practices; and human reproduction, including research related to contraceptive technologies and effective methods. In addition, WHO aimed to provide technical leadership and co-ordination on reproductive health and to support countries in their efforts to ensure that people: experience healthy sexual development and maturation; have the capacity for healthy, equitable and responsible relationships; can achieve their reproductive intentions safely and healthily; avoid illnesses, diseases and injury related to sexuality and reproduction; and receive appropriate counselling, care and rehabilitation for diseases and conditions related to sexuality and reproduction.

WHO's Division of Diarrhoeal and Acute Respiratory Disease Control encourages national programmes aimed at reducing the estimated 3.5m. yearly childhood deaths as a result of diarrhoea, particularly through the use of oral rehydration therapy and preventive measures. The Division is also seeking to reduce deaths from pneumonia in infants through the use of a simple case-management strategy involving the recognition of danger signs and treatment with an appropriate antibiotic. In September 1997 WHO, in collaboration with UNICEF, formally launched a programme advocating the Integrated Management of Childhood Illness (IMCI), following successful regional trials in more than 20 developing countries during 1996–97. IMCI recognizes that pneumonia, diarrhoea, measles, malaria and malnutrition cause some 70% of the approximately 11m. childhood deaths each year, and recommends screening sick children for all five conditions, in order to enable health workers to reach a more accurate diagnosis than may be achieved from the results of a single assessment.

The HIV/AIDS epidemic represents a major threat to human well-being and socio-economic progress. Some 95% of those known to be infected with HIV/AIDS live in developing countries. At December 2001 an estimated 40m. adults and children world-wide were living with HIV/AIDS, of whom 5m. were newly infected during that year. At that time 6.1m. people were reported to be living with HIV/AIDS in South and South-East Asia and 1m. in East Asia and the Pacific. The highest reported prevalence rates in the Asia and Pacific region were in Cambodia, Myanmar, Thailand, India and Papua New Guinea. The rate of HIV infection is also reported to have risen significantly in the People's Republic of China in recent years. WHO's Global Programme on AIDS, initiated in 1987, was concluded in December 1995. A Joint UN Programme on HIV/AIDS (UNAIDS) became operational on 1 January 1996. It is sponsored by WHO, the World Bank, UNICEF, UNDCP, UNDP, UNESCO, UNFPA and ILO. The UNAIDS secretariat is based at WHO headquarters. WHO established an Office of HIV/AIDS and Sexually-Transmitted Diseases in order to ensure continuity of its global response to the problem, which included support for national control and education plans, improving the safety of blood supplies and improving the care and support of AIDS patients. In addition, the Office was to liaise with UNAIDS and to make available WHO's research and technical expertise. Sufferers of HIV/AIDS in developing countries have often failed to receive advanced antiretroviral (ARV) treatments that are widely available in industrialized countries, owing to their high cost. In May 2000 the World Health Assembly adopted a resolution urging WHO member states to improve access to the prevention and treatment of HIV-related illnesses and to increase the availability and affordability of drugs. WHO, with UNAIDS, UNICEF, UNFPA, the World Bank, and major pharmaceutical companies, participates in the 'Accelerating Access' initiative, which aims to expand access to care, support and ARVs for people with HIV/AIDS. In March 2002, under its 'Access to Quality HIV/AIDS Drugs and Diagnostics' programme, WHO published a comprehensive list of HIV-related medicines deemed to meet standards recommended by the Organization. In April WHO issued the first treatment guide-lines for HIV/AIDS cases in poor communities, and endorsed the inclusion of HIV/AIDS drugs in its *Model List of Essential Drugs* in order to encourage their wider availability. A WHO-UNAIDS HIV Vaccine Initiative was launched in 2000. In July 2001 a meeting of the Group of Seven industrialized nations and Russia (G-8), convened in Genoa, Italy, announced the formation of a new Global Fund to Fight AIDS, TB and Malaria (as previously proposed by the UN Secretary-General and recommended by the World Health Assembly). The Fund, a partnership between governments, UN bodies (including WHO) and other agencies, and private-sector interests, aimed to disburse US $700m.–$800m. in grants during 2002, thereby increasing annual global expenditure on combating those diseases by about 50%. WHO supports governments in developing effective health-sector responses to the HIV/AIDS epidemic through enhancing the planning and managerial capabilities, implementation capacity, and resources of health systems.

SUSTAINABLE DEVELOPMENT AND HEALTHY ENVIRONMENTS

The Sustainable Development and Healthy Environments group focuses on the following areas of work: health in sustainable development; nutrition; health and environment; food safety; and emergency preparedness and response. Food safety is an organization-wide priority.

WHO promotes recognition of good health status as one of the most important assets of the poor. The Sustainable Development and Healthy Environment group seeks to monitor the advantages and disadvantages for health, nutrition, environment and development arising from the process of globalization; to integrate the issue of health into poverty reduction programmes; and to promote human rights and equality. Adequate and safe food and nutrition is a priority programme area. An estimated 780m. people world-wide cannot meet basic needs for energy and protein, more than 2,000m. people lack essential vitamins and minerals, and 170m. children are estimated to be malnourished.

WHO collaborates with FAO, WFP, UNICEF and other UN agencies in pursuing its objectives relating to nutrition and food safety. In December 1992 an International Conference on Nutrition, co-sponsored by FAO and WHO, adopted a World Declaration on Nutrition and a Plan of Action designed to make the fight against malnutrition a development priority. In pursuing the objectives of the Declaration WHO promotes the elaboration and implementation of national plans of action for nutrition and aims to identify and support countries with high levels of malnutrition, which includes protein energy deficiencies, and deficiencies of iron, vitamin A and iodine. A strategy of universal salt iodization was launched in 1993 (iodine deficiency causes mental handicap.) In collaboration with other international agencies, WHO is implementing a comprehensive strategy for promoting appropriate infant, young-child and maternal nutrition, and for dealing effectively with nutritional emergencies in large populations. Areas of emphasis include promoting health-care practices that enhance successful breast-feeding; appropriate complementary feeding; refining the use and interpretation of body measurements for assessing nutritional status; relevant information, education and training; and action to give effect to the International Code of Marketing of Breast-milk Substitutes. The Food Safety Programme aims to eliminate risks, such as biological or chemical contaminants in foods which are a major cause of diarrhoea and malnutrition in children. WHO, together with FAO, establishes food standards (through the work of the Codex Alimentarius Commission) and evaluates food additives, pesticide residues and other contaminants and their implications for health. The Programme provides expert advice on such issues as food-borne pathogens (e.g. listeria), production methods (e.g. aquaculture) and food biotechnology (e.g. genetic modification). In March 2002 an intergovernmental task force established by the Codex Alimentarius Commission finalized 'principles for the risk analysis of foods derived from biotechnology', which were to provide a framework for assessing the safety of genetically-modified—GM—foods and plants. In the following month WHO and FAO announced a joint review of their food standards operations.

WHO's programme area on environment and health undertakes a wide range of initiatives to tackle the increasing threats to health and well-being from a changing environment, especially in relation to air pollution, water quality, sanitation, protection against radiation, management of hazardous waste, chemical safety and housing hygiene. The major part of WHO's technical co-operation in environmental health in developing countries is concerned with community water supply and sanitation. In order to contribute to the solution of environmental health problems associated with the rapid urbanization of cities in the developing world, the Programme was promoting globally in the 1990s the Healthy City approach that had been initiated in Europe. WHO is also working with other agencies to consider the implications on human health of global climate change.

Following the major terrorist attacks perpetrated against targets in the USA in September 2001, WHO focused renewed attention on the potential deliberate use of infectious diseases, such as anthrax and smallpox, or of chemical agents, in acts of biological or chemical terrorism. In that month WHO issued draft guide-lines entitled 'Health Aspects of Biological and Chemical Weapons.'

Through its Division of Emergency and Humanitarian Action, WHO acts as the 'health arm' of disaster relief undertaken by the UN system. Its emergency preparedness activities include co-ordination, policy making and planning, awareness-building, technical advice, training, publication of standards and guide-lines, and research. Its emergency relief activities include organizational support, the provision of emergency drugs and supplies, and conducting technical emergency assessment missions. The Division's objective is to build the capacity of disaster-vulnerable member states to reduce the adverse health consequences of disasters. In responding to emergency situations, WHO always tries to develop projects and activities that will assist the national authorities concerned in rebuilding or strengthening their own capacity to handle the impact of such situations. Under the UN's Consolidated Appeals Process for 2002, launched in November 2001, WHO requested funding of US $8.4m. (to supplement US $5.7m. already pledged) for emergency health care provision and health sector reconstruction activities in Afghanistan, US $7.2m. for ensuring availability of essential drugs, supporting immunization activities, provision of basic health services, training, and control of communicable diseases in the Democratic Republic of Korea, and US $1.7m. for strengthening health services, disease surveillance and mental health care and psychosocial support in Indonesia.

HEALTH TECHNOLOGY AND PHARMACEUTICALS

WHO's Health Technology and Pharmaceuticals group, made up of the departments of essential drugs and other medicines, vaccines and other biologicals, and blood safety and clinical technology, covers the following areas of work: essential medicines—access, quality and rational use; immunization and vaccine development; and world-wide co-operation on blood safety and clinical technology. Blood safety and clinical technology are an organization-wide priority.

In January 1999 the Executive Board adopted a resolution on WHO's Revised Drug Strategy, which placed emphasis on the inequalities of access to pharmaceuticals, and also covered specific aspects of drugs policy, quality assurance, drug promotion, drug donation, independent drug information and rational drug use. Plans of action involving co-operation with member states and other international organizations were to be developed in order to monitor and analyse the pharmaceutical and public health implications of international agreements, including trade agreements. In April 2001 experts from WHO and the World Trade Organization participated in a workshop to address ways of lowering the cost of medicines in less developed countries. In the following month the World Health Assembly adopted a resolution urging member states to promote equitable access to essential drugs, noting that this was denied to about one-third of the world's population. WHO participates with other partners in the 'Accelerating Access' initiative, which aims to expand access to antiretroviral drugs for people with HIV/AIDS (see above).

WHO reports that 2m. children die each year of diseases for which common vaccines exist. In September 1991 the Children's Vaccine Initiative (CVI) was launched, jointly sponsored by the Rockefeller Foundation, UNDP, UNICEF, WHO and the World Bank, to facilitate the development and provision of children's vaccines. The CVI has as its ultimate goal the development of a single oral immunization shortly after birth that will protect against all major childhood diseases. In 1998 the CVI reported that 4m. children die each year of diseases for which there are existing, common vaccines. In 1999 WHO, UNICEF, the World Bank and a number of public- and private-sector partners formed the Global Alliance for Vaccines and Immunization (GAVI), which aimed to expand the provision of existing vaccines and to accelerate the development and introduction of new vaccines and technologies, with the goal of protecting children of all nationalities and from all socio-economic backgrounds against vaccine-preventable diseases.

WHO supports states in ensuring access to safe blood, blood products, transfusions, injections, and health-care technologies.

EVIDENCE AND INFORMATION FOR HEALTH POLICY

The Evidence and Information for Health Policy group addresses the following areas of work: evidence for the development of health policy; health information management and dissemination; and research policy and the promotion and organization of health systems. The group aims to assist policy-makers assess health needs, choose intervention strategies, design policy and monitor performance, and thereby improve the performance of national health systems. The group also supports international and national dialogue on health policy.

In July 2001 WHO and six leading medical publishers announced an initiative to enable relevant authorities in developing countries to access nearly 1,000 biomedical journals through the internet at no or greatly reduced cost, in order to improve the world-wide circulation of scientific information.

Finance

WHO's regular budget is provided by assessment of member states and associate members. An additional fund for specific projects is provided by voluntary contributions from members and other sources. Funds are received from the UNDP for particular projects and from UNFPA for population programmes. A regular budget of US $842.7m. was proposed for the 2002–03 biennium, of which US $93.0m. (11%) was for South-East Asia and US $73.3 (8.7%) for the Western Pacific.

Publications

Bulletin of WHO (monthly).

Environmental Health Criteria.

International Digest of Health Legislation (quarterly).

International Statistical Classification of Diseases and Related Health Problems, Tenth Revision, 1992–94.

Model List of Essential Drugs (biennially).

Weekly Epidemiological Record.

WHO Drug Information (quarterly).

World Health Report (annually).

World Health Statistics Annual.

Series of technical reports.

Other UN Organizations Active in the Far East and Australasia

OFFICE FOR THE CO-ORDINATION OF HUMANITARIAN AFFAIRS

Address: United Nations Plaza, New York, NY 10017, USA.

Telephone: (212) 963-1234; **fax:** (212) 963-9489; **e-mail:** ochany@un.org; **internet:** www.reliefweb.int/ocha_ol.

The Office was established in January 1998 as part of the UN Secretariat, with a mandate to co-ordinate international humanitarian assistance and to provide policy and other advice on humanitarian issues. It administers the Humanitarian Early Warning System, as well as Integrated Regional Information Networks to monitor the situation in different countries and a Disaster Response System.

Under Secretary-General for Humanitarian Affairs and Emergency Relief Co-ordinator: KENZO OSHIMA (Japan).

OFFICE FOR DRUG CONTROL AND CRIME PREVENTION—ODCCP

Address: Vienna International Centre, POB 500, 1400 Vienna, Austria.

Telephone: (1) 26060-0; **fax:** (1) 26060-5866; **e-mail:** odccp@odccp.org; **internet:** www.odccp.org.

The Office was established on 1 November 1997 to strengthen the UN's integrated approach to issues relating to drug control, crime prevention and international terrorism. It comprises two principal components: the United Nations International Drug Control Programme (UNDCP) and the Centre for International Crime Prevention (CICP), both headed by the ODCCP Executive Director.

Executive Director: ANTONIO MARIA COSTA (Italy).

OFFICE OF THE UNITED NATIONS HIGH COMMISSIONER FOR HUMAN RIGHTS

Address: Palais Wilson, 52 rue de Paquis,, 1201 Geneva, Switzerland.

Telephone: (22) 9179290; **fax:** (22) 9179022; **e-mail:** secrt.hchr@unog.ch; **internet:** www.unhchr.ch.

The Office is a body of the UN Secretariat and is the focal point for UN human rights activities. Since September 1997 it has incorporated the Centre for Human Rights. The High Commissioner is the UN official with principal responsibility for UN human rights activities.

High Commissioner: SERGIO VIEIRA DE MELLO (Brazil).

UNITED NATIONS HUMAN SETTLEMENTS PROGRAMME—UN-Habitat

Telephone: (20) 621234; **fax:** (20) 624266; **e-mail:** infohabitat@un-habitat.org; **internet:** www.unhabitat.org.

UN-Habitat was established, as the United Nations Centre for Human Settlements, in 1978 to service the inter-governmental Commission on Human Settlements. It became a full UN programme on 1 January 2002, serving as the focus for human settlements activities in the UN system.

Executive Director: ANNA KAJUMULO TIBAIJUKA (Tanzania).

UNITED NATIONS CHILDREN'S FUND—UNICEF

Address: 3 United Nations Plaza, New York, NY 10017, USA.

Telephone: (212) 326-7000; **fax:** (212) 888-7465; **e-mail:** netmaster@unicef.org; **internet:** www.unicef.org.

UNICEF was established in 1946 by the UN General Assembly as the UN International Children's Emergency Fund, to meet the emergency needs of children in post-war Europe and China. In 1950 its mandate was enlarged to emphasize programmes giving long-term benefits to children everywhere, particularly those in developing countries who are in the greatest need. UNICEF continues to provide relief and rehabilitation assistance in emergency situations and advocates for the rights of all children.

Executive Director: CAROL BELLAMY (USA).

Regional Office for East Asia and the Pacific: POB 2-154, Bangkok 10200, Thailand; tel. (2) 280-5931; fax (2) 280-3563; e-mail eapro@unicef.org.

Regional Office for South Asia: POB 5815, Leknath Marg, Kathmandu, Nepal; tel. 417082; fax 419479; e-mail unicefrosa@uncrosa.mos.com.np.

UNITED NATIONS CONFERENCE ON TRADE AND DEVELOPMENT—UNCTAD

Address: Palais des Nations, 1211 Geneva 10, Switzerland.

Telephone: (22) 9071234; **fax:** (22) 9070057; **e-mail:** ers@unctad .org; **internet:** www.unctad.org.

UNCTAD was established in 1964. It is the principal organ of the UN General Assembly concerned with trade and development, and is the focal point within the UN system for integrated activities relating to trade, finance, technology, investment and sustainable development. It aims to maximize the trade and development opportunities of developing countries, in particular least-developed countries, and to assist them to adapt to the increasing globalization and liberalization of the world economy. UNCTAD undertakes consensus-building activities, research and policy analysis and technical co-operation.

Secretary-General: RUBENS RICÚPERO (Brazil).

UNITED NATIONS POPULATION FUND—UNFPA

Address: 220 East 42nd St, New York, NY 10017, USA.

Telephone: (212) 297-5020; **fax:** (212) 297-4911; **internet:** www.unfpa.org.

UNFPA was initially established in 1967, as the Trust Fund for Population Activities, to increase awareness of population issues and to help member states to formulate and implement population policies. The Fund became a subsidiary organ of the UN General Assembly in 1979. It adopted its current name in 1987, retaining its original acronym.

Executive Director: THORAYA A. OBAID (Saudi Arabia).

UN Specialized Agencies

INTERNATIONAL ATOMIC ENERGY AGENCY—IAEA

Address: POB 100, Wagramerstrasse 5, 1400 Vienna, Austria.

Telephone: (1) 26000; **fax:** (1) 26007; **e-mail:** official.mail@iaea.org; **internet:** www.iaea.org/worldatom.

The Agency was founded in 1957 as an autonomous intergovernmental organization, although it is administratively part of the UN system and reports annually to the UN General Assembly. Its main objectives are to enlarge the contribution of atomic energy to peace, health and prosperity throughout the world, and to ensure that materials and services provided by the Agency are not used to further any military purpose.

Director-General: Dr MOHAMED EL-BARADEI (Egypt).

INTERNATIONAL CIVIL AVIATION ORGANIZATION—ICAO

Address: 999 University St, Montréal, QC H3C 5H7, Canada.

Telephone: (514) 954-8219; **fax:** (514) 954-6077; **e-mail:** icaohq@icao.int; **internet:** www.icao.int.

ICAO was founded in 1947, on the basis of the Convention on International Civil Aviation, signed in Chicago, in 1944, to promote and regulate the safe and orderly development of civil air transport throughout the world.

Secretary-General: RENATO CLAUDIO COSTA PEREIRA (Brazil).

Regional Office for Asia and the Pacific: POB 11, Samyaek Ladprao, Bangkok 10901, Thailand; tel. (2) 537 8189; fax (2) 537 8199.

INTERNATIONAL LABOUR ORGANIZATION—ILO

Address: 4 route des Morillons, 1211 Geneva 22, Switzerland.

Telephone: (22) 7996111; **fax:** (22) 7988685; **e-mail:** ilo@ilo.org; **internet:** www.ilo.org.

ILO was founded in 1919 to work for social justice as a basis for lasting peace. It carries out this mandate by promoting decent living standards, satisfactory conditions of work and pay and adequate employment opportunities. Methods of action include the creation of international labour standards; the provision of technical co-operation services; and research and publications on social and labour matters.

Director-General: JUAN O. SOMAVÍA (Chile).

Regional Office for Asia and the Pacific: POB 1759, Bangkok 2, Thailand.

INTERNATIONAL MARITIME ORGANIZATION—IMO

Address: 4 Albert Embankment, London, SE1 7SR, United Kingdom.

Telephone: (20) 7735-7611; **fax:** (20) 7587-3210; **e-mail:** info@imo.org; **internet:** www.imo.org.

The Inter-Governmental Maritime Consultative Organization (IMCO) began operations in 1959, as a specialized agency of the UN to facilitate co-operation among governments on technical matters affecting international shipping. Its main aims are to improve the safety of international shipping, and to prevent pollution caused by ships. IMCO became IMO in 1982.

Secretary-General: WILLIAM A. O'NEIL (Canada).

INTERNATIONAL TELECOMMUNICATION UNION—ITU

Address: place des Nations, 1211 Geneva 20, Switzerland.

Telephone: (22) 7305111; **fax:** (22) 7337256; **e-mail:** itumail@itu .int; **internet:** www.itu.int.

Founded in 1865, ITU became a specialized agency of the UN in 1947. It acts to encourage world co-operation for the improvement and use of telecommunications, to promote technical development, harmonize national policies in the field, and to promote the extension of telecommunications throughout the world.

Secretary-General: YOSHIO UTSUMI (Japan).

UNITED NATIONS INDUSTRIAL DEVELOPMENT ORGANIZATION—UNIDO

Address: Vienna International Centre, POB 300, 1400 Vienna, Austria.

Telephone: (1) 260260; **fax:** (1) 2692669; **e-mail:** unido@ unido.org; **internet:** www.unido.org.

UNIDO began operations in 1967 and became a specialized agency in 1985. Its objectives are to promote sustainable and socially equitable industrial development in developing countries and in countries with economies in transition. It aims to assist such countries to integrate fully into global economic system by mobilizing knowledge, skills, information and technology to promote productive employment, competitive economies and sound environment.

Director-General: CARLOS ALFREDO MAGARIÑOS (Argentina).

UNIVERSAL POSTAL UNION—UPU

Address: Weltpoststr., 3000 Berne 15, Switzerland.

Telephone: (31) 3503111; **fax:** (31) 3503110; **e-mail:** info@upu.int; **internet:** www.upu.int.

The General Postal Union was founded by the Treaty of Berne (1874), beginning operations in July 1875. Three years later its name was changed to the Universal Postal Union. In 1948 UPU became a specialized agency of the UN. It aims to develop and unify the international postal service, to study problems and to provide training.

Director-General: THOMAS E. LEAVEY (USA).

WORLD INTELLECTUAL PROPERTY ORGANIZATION—WIPO

Address: 34 chemin des Colombettes, 1211 Geneva 20, Switzerland.

Telephone: (22) 3389111; **fax:** (22) 7335428; **e-mail:** wipo.mail@ wipo.int; **internet:** www.wipo.int.

WIPO was established in 1970. It became a specialized agency of the UN in 1974 concerned with the protection of intellectual property (e.g. industrial and technical patents and literary copyrights). WIPO formulates and administers treaties embodying international norms and standards of intellectual property, establishes model laws, and facilitates applications for the protection of inventions, trademarks etc. WIPO provides legal and technical assistance to developing countries and countries with economies in transition and advises countries on obligations under the World Trade Organization's agreement on Trade-Related Aspects of Intellectual Property Rights (TRIPS).

Director-General: Dr KAMIL IDRIS (Sudan).

WORLD METEOROLOGICAL ORGANIZATION—WMO

Address: 7 bis ave de la Paix, CP 2300, 1211 Geneva 2, Switzerland.

Telephone: (22) 7308111; **fax:** (22) 7308181; e-mail: ipa@wmo.ch; **internet:** www.wmo.ch.

WMO was established in 1950 and was recognized as a Specialized Agency of the UN in 1951. It aims to improve the exchange of information in the fields of meteorology, climatology and operational hydrology, and its applications. WMO jointly implements the UN Framework Convention on Climate Change with UNEP.

Secretary-General: Prof. G.O.P. OBASI (Nigeria).

ASIA-PACIFIC ECONOMIC CO-OPERATION—APEC

Address: 438 Alexandra Rd, 14th Floor, Alexandra Point, Singapore 119958.

Telephone: 62761880; **fax:** 62761775; **e-mail:** info@mail.apecsec.org.sg; **internet:** www.apecsec.org.sg.

Asia-Pacific Economic Co-operation (APEC) was initiated in November 1989, in Canberra, Australia, as an informal consultative forum. Its aim is to promote multilateral economic co-operation on issues of trade and investment.

MEMBERS

Australia	Japan	Philippines
Brunei	Korea, Republic	Russia
Canada	Malaysia	Singapore
Chile	Mexico	Taiwan*
China, People's Republic	New Zealand	Thailand
Hong Kong	Papua New Guinea	USA
Indonesia	Peru	Viet Nam

* Admitted as Chinese Taipei.

Organization

(October 2002)

ECONOMIC LEADERS' MEETINGS

The first meeting of APEC heads of government was convened in November 1993, in Seattle, USA. Subsequently, each annual meeting of APEC ministers of foreign affairs and of economic affairs has been followed by an informal gathering of the leaders of the APEC economies, at which the policy objectives of the grouping are discussed and defined. The 10th Leaders' Meeting was held in Mexico, in late October 2002; the 2003 meeting was scheduled to be held in Bangkok, Thailand, in October.

MINISTERIAL MEETINGS

APEC ministers of foreign affairs and ministers of economic affairs meet annually. These meetings are hosted by the APEC Chair, which rotates each year, although it was agreed, in 1989, that alternate Ministerial Meetings were to be convened in an ASEAN member country. A Senior Officials' Meeting (SOM) convenes regularly between Ministerial Meetings to co-ordinate and administer the budgets and work programmes of APEC's committees and working groups. Other meetings of ministers are held on a regular basis to enhance co-operation in specific areas.

SECRETARIAT

In 1992 the Ministerial Meeting, held in Bangkok, Thailand, agreed to establish a permanent secretariat to support APEC activities, and approved an annual budget of US $2m. The Secretariat became operational in February 1993. The Executive Director is appointed from the member economy chairing the group and serves a one-year term. A Deputy Executive Director is appointed by the member economy designated to chair APEC in the following year.

Executive Director: ALEJANDRO DE LA PEÑA NAVARRETE (Mexico).

Deputy Executive Director: PIAMSAK MILINTACHINDA (Thailand).

COMMITTEES AND GROUPS

Budget and Management Committee—BMC: f. 1993 as Budget and Administrative Committee, present name adopted 1998; advises APEC senior officials on budgetary, administrative and managerial issues. The Committee reviews the operational budgets of APEC committees and groups, evaluates their effectiveness and conducts assessments of group projects.

Committee on Trade and Investment—CTI: f. 1993 on the basis of a Declaration signed by ministers meeting in Seattle, USA, in order to facilitate the expansion of trade and the development of a liberalized environment for investment among member countries. The CTI undertakes initiatives to improve the flow of goods, services and technology in the region. In May 1997 an APEC Tariff Database was inaugurated, with sponsorship from the private sector. A new Market Access Group was established in 1998 to administer CTI activities concerned with non-tariff measures. In 2001 the CTI finalized a set of non-binding Principles on Trade Facilitation. The development of the nine principles was intended to help eliminate procedural and administrative impediments to trade and to increase trading opportunities.

Economic Committee—EC: f. 1994 following an agreement, in November, to transform the existing *ad hoc* group on economic trends and issues into a formal committee. The Committee aims to enhance APEC's capacity to analyse economic trends and to research and report on issues affecting economic and technical co-operation in the region. In addition, the Committee is considering the environmental and development implications of expanding population and economic growth.

Sub-Committee on Economic and Technical Co-operation—ESC: f. 1998 to assist the SOM with the co-ordination of APEC's economic and technical co-operation programme (ECOTECH). The ESC monitors and evaluates project implementation and also supervises the work of the Group on Economic Infrastructure (GEI), which carries out projects designed to strengthen economic and technical co-operation in infrastructure. The ESC co-ordinated the development of APEC's Human-Capacity Building Strategy in 2001.

In addition, the following Working Groups promote and co-ordinate practical co-operation between member countries in different activities: Agricultural technical co-operation; Energy; Fisheries; Human resources development; Industrial science and technology; Marine resource conservation; Small and medium enterprises (SMEs); Telecommunications and Information; Tourism; Trade promotion; and Transportation. (See below for more detailed information.)

ADVISORY COUNCIL

APEC Business Advisory Council—ABAC: Equitable Card Center Bldg, 8th Floor, 203 Salcedo St, Legaspi Village, Makati City 1229, Philippines; tel. (2) 8436001; fax (2) 8454832; e-mail abacsec@pfgc.ph; internet www.abaconline.org; an agreement to establish ABAC, comprising up to three senior representatives of the private sector from each APEC member economy, was concluded at the Ministerial Meeting held in November 1995. ABAC was mandated to advise member states on the implementation of APEC's Action Agenda and on other business matters, and to provide business-related information to APEC fora. ABAC meets three or four times each year and holds a dialogue with APEC economic leaders prior to their annual informal meeting. ABAC's first meeting, convened in June 1996 in Manila, the Philippines, resolved to accelerate the liberalization of regional trade. In 1998 ABAC focused on measures to alleviate the effects of the financial crisis in Asia, in particular, by enhancing confidence in the private sector, as well as efforts to support SMEs, to develop electronic commerce in the region and to advise on APEC Individual Action Plans (IAPs, see below). In 2000 ABAC addressed the relevance of APEC to the challenges of globalization and, in its annual report to APEC leaders, issued several recommendations, including support for a new round of multilateral trade negotiations; enhancement of the IAP process, with increased implementation of electronic IAPs (e-IAPS); implementation of a proposed food system for member states; the establishment of an APEC Institute of Directors Forum; and the adoption of a regulatory framework conducive to the development of e-commerce. In 2001 ABAC concentrated on the challenges posed by globalization; the impact on APEC members of the global economic slowdown; and capacity-building in financial systems. ABAC's declared theme for 2002 was Sharing Development to Reinforce Global Security. At a meeting in February 2002 the Council considered the relationship between global security and its work to facilitate trade and investment flows. Chair. JAVIER PRIETO DE LA FUENTE (Mexico).

Activities

APEC was initiated in 1989 as a forum for informal discussion between the then six ASEAN members and their six dialogue partners in the Pacific, and, in particular, to promote trade liberalization in the Uruguay Round of negotiations, which were being conducted under the General Agreement on Tariffs and Trade (GATT). The Seoul Declaration, adopted by ministers meeting in the Republic of Korea in November 1991, defined the objectives of APEC.

ASEAN countries were initially reluctant to support any more formal structure of the forum, or to admit new members, owing to concerns that it would undermine ASEAN's standing as a regional grouping and be dominated by powerful non-ASEAN economies. In August 1991 it was agreed to extend membership to the People's Republic of China, Hong Kong and Taiwan (subject to conditions imposed by the People's Republic of China, including that a Taiwanese official of no higher than vice-ministerial level should attend the annual meeting of ministers of foreign affairs). Mexico and Papua New Guinea acceded to the organization in November 1993, and Chile joined in November 1994. The summit meeting held in

November 1997 agreed that Peru, Russia and Viet Nam should be admitted to APEC at the 1998 meeting, but imposed a 10-year moratorium on further expansion of the grouping.

In September 1992 APEC ministers agreed to establish a permanent secretariat. In addition, the meeting created an 11-member non-governmental Eminent Persons Group (EPG), which was to assess trade patterns within the region and propose measures to promote co-operation. At the Ministerial Meeting in Seattle, USA, in November 1993, members agreed on a framework for expanding trade and investment among member countries, and to establish a permanent committee (the CTI, see above) to pursue these objectives.

In August 1994 the EPG proposed the following timetable for the liberalization of all trade across the Asia-Pacific region: negotiations for the elimination of trade barriers were to commence in 2000 and be completed within 10 years in developed countries, 15 years in newly-industrialized economies and by 2020 in developing countries. Trade concessions could then be extended on a reciprocal basis to non-members in order to encourage world-wide trade liberalization, rather than isolate APEC as a unique trading bloc. In November 1994 the meeting of APEC heads of government adopted the Bogor Declaration of Common Resolve, which endorsed the EPG's timetable for free and open trade and investment in the region by the year 2020. Other issues incorporated into the Declaration included the implementation of GATT commitments in full and strengthening the multilateral trading system through the forthcoming establishment of the World Trade Organization (WTO), intensifying development co-operation in the Asia-Pacific region and expanding and accelerating trade and investment programmes.

During 1995 meetings of APEC officials and other efforts to substantiate the trade liberalization agreement revealed certain differences among members regarding the timetable and means of implementing the measures, which were to be agreed upon at the 1995 Economic Leaders' Meeting. The principal concern, expressed notably by the USA, focused on whether tariff reductions were to be achieved by individual trade liberalization plans or based on some reciprocal or common approach. In August the EPG issued a report, to be considered at the November Leaders' Meeting, which advocated acceleration of tariff reductions and other trade liberalization measures agreed under GATT; the establishment of a dispute mediation service to reduce and settle regional trade conflicts; and a review of new trade groupings within the APEC region. Further proposals for the implementation of the Bogor Declaration objectives were presented, in September, by the Pacific Business Forum, comprising APEC business representatives. The recommendations included harmonization of product quality, the establishment of one-stop investment agencies in each APEC country, training and technology transfers and the implementation of visa-free business travel by 1999. In November 1995 the Ministerial Meeting decided to dismantle the EPG, and to establish an APEC Business Advisory Council (ABAC), consisting of private-sector representatives.

In November 1995 APEC heads of government, meeting in Osaka, Japan, adopted an Action Agenda as a framework to achieve the commitments of the Bogor Declaration. Part One of the Agenda identified action areas for the liberalization of trade and investment and the facilitation of business, for example, customs procedures, rules of origin and non-tariff barriers. It incorporated agreements that the process was to be comprehensive, consistent with WTO commitments, comparable among all APEC economies and non-discriminatory. Each member economy was to ensure the transparency of its laws, regulations and procedures affecting the flow of goods, services and capital among APEC economies and to refrain from implementing any trade protection measures. A second part of the Agenda was to provide a framework for further economic and technical co-operation between APEC members in areas such as energy, transport, infrastructure, SMEs and agricultural technology. In order to resolve a disagreement concerning the inclusion of agricultural products in the trade liberalization process, a provision for flexibility was incorporated into the Agenda, taking into account diverse circumstances and different levels of development in APEC member economies. Liberalization measures were to be implemented from January 1997 (i.e. three years earlier than previously agreed) and were to be subject to annual reviews. A Trade and Investment Liberalization and Facilitation Special Account was established to finance projects in support of the implementation of the Osaka Action Agenda. In May 1996 APEC senior officials met in Cebu, the Philippines, to review Individual Action Plans—IAPs, annual reports submitted by each member state on progress in the implementation of trade liberalization measures—and to achieve some coherent approach to tariff liberalization prior to the Leaders' Meeting in November.

In November 1996 the Economic Leaders' Meeting, held in Subic Bay, the Philippines, approved the Manila Action Plan for APEC (MAPA), which had been formulated at the preceding Ministerial Meeting, held in Manila. MAPA incorporated the IAPs and other collective measures aimed at achieving the trade liberalization and co-operation objectives of the Bogor Declaration, as well as the joint activities specified in the second part of the Osaka Agenda. Heads of government also endorsed a US proposal to eliminate tariffs and other barriers to trade in information technology products by 2000 and determined to support efforts to conclude an agreement to this effect at the forthcoming WTO conference; however, they insisted on the provision of an element of flexibility in achieving trade liberalization in this sector.

The 1997 Economic Leaders' Meeting, held in Vancouver, Canada, in November, was dominated by concern at the financial instability that had affected several Asian economies during 1997. The final declaration of the summit meeting endorsed a framework of measures that had been agreed by APEC deputy ministers of finance and central bank governors at an emergency meeting convened in the previous week in Manila, the Philippines (the so-called Manila Framework for Enhanced Asian Regional Co-operation to Promote Financial Stability). The meeting, attended by representatives of the IMF, the World Bank and the Asian Development Bank, committed all member economies receiving IMF assistance to undertake specified economic and financial reforms, and supported the establishment of a separate Asian funding facility to supplement international financial assistance (although this was later rejected by the IMF). APEC ministers of finance and governors of central banks were urged to accelerate efforts for the development of the region's financial and capital markets and to liberalize capital flows in the region. Measures were to include strengthening financial market supervision and clearing and settlement infrastructure, the reform of pension systems, and promoting co-operation among export credit agencies and financing institutions. The principal item on the Vancouver summit agenda was an initiative to enhance trade liberalization, which, the grouping insisted, should not be undermined by the financial instability in Asia. The following 15 economic sectors were identified for 'early voluntary sectoral liberalization' ('EVSL'): environmental goods and services; fish and fish products; forest products; medical equipment and instruments; toys; energy; chemicals; gems and jewellery; telecommunications; oilseeds and oilseed products; food; natural and synthetic rubber; fertilizers; automobiles; and civil aircraft. The implementation of EVSL was to encompass market opening, trade facilitation, and economic and technical co-operation activities. The heads of government subsequently requested the authorities in each member state to formulate details of tariff reductions in these sectors by mid-1998, with a view to implementing the measures in 1999. (In June 1998, however, ministers of trade, meeting in Malaysia, failed to conclude an agreement on early tariff reductions, in part owing to Japan's reluctance to liberalize trade in fish and forest products.) In Vancouver APEC Economic Leaders also declared their support for an agreement to liberalize financial services (which was successfully negotiated under the auspices of the WTO in December 1997) and for the objective of reducing the emission of 'greenhouse gases', which was under consideration at a global conference, held in Kyoto, Japan, in December (resulting in the adoption of the Kyoto Protocol to the UN Framework Convention on Climate Change).

In May 1998 APEC finance ministers met in Canada to consider the ongoing financial and economic crisis in Asia and to review progress in implementing efforts to alleviate the difficulties experienced by several member economies. The ministers agreed to pursue activities in the following three priority areas: capital market development, capital account liberalization and strengthening financial systems (including corporate governance). The region's economic difficulties remained the principal topic of discussion at the Economic Leaders' Meeting held in Kuala Lumpur, Malaysia, in November. A final declaration reiterated their commitment to co-operation in pursuit of sustainable economic recovery and growth, in particular through the restructuring of financial and corporate sectors, promoting and facilitating private-sector capital flows, and efforts to strengthen the global financial system. The meeting endorsed a proposal of ABAC to establish a partnership for equitable growth, with the aim of enhancing business involvement in APEC's programme of economic and technical co-operation. Other initiatives approved included an Agenda of APEC Science and Technology Industry Co-operation into the 21st Century (for which the People's Republic of China announced it was to establish a special fund), and an Action Programme on Skills and Development in APEC. Japan's persisting opposition to a reduction of tariffs in the fish and forestry sectors again prevented the conclusion of tariff negotiations under the EVSL scheme, and it was therefore agreed that responsibility for managing the tariff reduction element of the initiative should be transferred to the WTO. The meeting was divided by political differences regarding human rights, and in particular, the treatment by the Malaysian authorities of the imprisoned former Deputy Prime Minister, Anwar Ibrahim. A declaration of support for the democratic reform movement in Malaysia by the US representative, Vice-President Gore, dominated discussions at the start of the summit meeting and provoked a formal complaint from the Malaysian Government.

In September 1999 political dialogue regarding the civil conflict in East Timor dominated the start of the annual meetings of the grouping, held in Auckland, New Zealand, although the issue remained separate from the official agenda. Ministers of foreign affairs, convened in emergency session, declared their support for the establishment of a multinational force, under UN auspices, to restore peace in the territory and determined to provide humanitarian and technical assistance to facilitate the process of reconstruction and rehabilitation. The Economic Leaders' Meeting considered measures to sustain the economic recovery in Asia and endorsed the APEC Principles to Enhance Competition and Regulatory Reform (for example, transparency, accountability, non-discrimination) as a framework to strengthen APEC markets and to enable further integration and implementation of the IAPs. The meeting endorsed a report prepared during the year by an *ad hoc* task force concerning an ABAC proposal for the development of an APEC food system. Also under discussion was the forthcoming round of multilateral trade negotiations, to be initiated by the WTO. The heads of government proposed the objective of completing a single package of trade agreements within three years and endorsed the abolition of export subsidies for agricultural products. The meeting determined to support the efforts of the People's Republic of China, Russia, Taiwan and Viet Nam to accede to WTO membership.

The Economic Leaders' Meeting for 2000, held in Brunei in November, noted the generally strong recovery from the Asian economic crisis of 1997–98 and reiterated support for APEC's goals. The heads of government urged that an agenda for the now-stalled round of multilateral trade negotiations should be formulated without further delay. The meeting endorsed a plan of action to promote the utilization of advances in information and communications technologies in member economies, for the benefit of all citizens. It adopted the aim of tripling the number of people in the region with access to the internet by 2005, and determined to co-operate with business and education sector interests to attract investment and expertise in the pursuit of this goal. A proposal that the Democratic People's Republic of Korea be permitted to participate in APEC working groups was approved at the meeting.

The 2001 Economic Leaders' Meeting, held in mid-October, in Shanghai, the People's Republic of China, condemned the terrorist attacks against targets in the USA of the previous month and resolved to take action to combat the threat of international terrorism. The heads of state declared terrorism to be a direct challenge to APEC's vision of free, open and prosperous economies, and concluded that the threat made the continuing move to free trade, with its aim of bolstering economies, increasing prosperity and encouraging integration, even more of a priority. The meeting stressed the importance of sharing the benefits of globalization. The leaders also expressed their determination to address the effects on APEC countries of the prevailing global economic downturn. They noted that the reforms carried out after the 1997–98 financial crisis had strengthened APEC economies, and advocated timely policy actions in the coming year to rebuild confidence and boost growth. Human capacity-building was a central theme. The heads of state committed support to the launch of the next round of WTO multilateral trade negotiations and applauded the recent successful conclusion of negotiations on WTO membership for the People's Republic of China. The meeting adopted the Shanghai Accord, which identified development goals for APEC during its second decade and clarified measures for achieving the Bogor goals within the agreed timetable. Among other initiatives, the Accord suggested broadening and updating the Osaka Action Agenda to reflect developments in the new economy. The meeting also outlined the e-APEC Strategy developed by the e-APEC Task Force established after the Brunei Economic Leaders' meeting. Considering issues of entrepreneurship, structural and regulatory reform, competition, intellectual property rights and information security, the strategy aimed to facilitate technological development in the region.

In September 2002 a meeting of APEC ministers of finance was held in Los Cabos, Mexico. Ministers discussed the importance of efforts to combat money-laundering and the financing of terrorism. The meeting also focused on ways to strengthen global and regional economic growth, to advance fiscal and financial reforms and to improve the allocation of domestic savings for economic development.

WORKING GROUPS

APEC's structure of working groups aims to promote practical and technical co-operation in specific areas, and to help implement individual and collective action plans in response to the directives of the Economic Leaders and meetings of relevant ministers. APEC recognizes sustainable development as a key issue cross-cutting all forum activities. In 1997 APEC leaders declared their commitment to the integration of women into the mainstream of APEC activities.

Agricultural Technical Co-operation: Formally established as an APEC Expert's Group in 1996, and incorporated into the system of working groups in 2000. The group aims to enhance the role of agriculture in the economic growth of the region and to promote co-operation in the following areas: conservation and utilization of plant and animal genetic resources; research, development and extension of agricultural biotechnology; processing, marketing, distribution and consumption of agricultural products; plant and animal quarantine and pest management; development of an agricultural finance system; sustainable agriculture; and agricultural technology transfer and training. The group has primary responsibility for undertaking recommendations connected with the implementation of the proposed APEC food system. In 2001 the group conducted projects on human resource development in post-harvest technology and on capacity-building, safety assessment and communication in biotechnology.

Energy: Responsible for the development of the energy component of the 1995 Action Agenda. APEC ministers responsible for energy convened for the first time in 1996 to discuss major energy challenges confronting the region and to provide guidance for the working group. The group's main objectives were determined as: the enhancement of regional energy security and improvement of the fuel supply market for the power sector; the development and implementation of programmes of work promoting the adoption of environmentally sound energy technologies and promoting private-sector investment in regional power infrastructure; the development of energy efficiency guide-lines; and the standardization of testing facilities and results. In March 1999 the group resolved to establish a business network to improve relations and communications with the private sector. The first meeting of the network took place in April. In October 1998 APEC energy ministers, meeting in Okinawa, Japan, emphasized the role of the energy sector in stimulating economic activity and stressed the need to develop infrastructure, improve energy efficiency and accelerate the development of natural gas reserves. In May 2000 ministers meeting in San Diego, USA, launched the APEC 21st Century Renewable Energy Initiative, which aims to encourage co-operation in and advance the utilization of renewable energy technologies, envisaging the establishment of a Private Sector Renewable Energy Forum.

Fisheries: Aims to maximize the economic benefits and sustainability of fisheries resources for all APEC members. Recent concerns include food safety, the quality of fish products and resource management. In 1996 the group initiated a four-year study on trade and investment liberalization in the sector, in the areas of tariffs, non-tariff barriers and investment measures and subsidies. In 1997 the group organized two technical workshops on seafood inspection systems, and conducted a workshop addressing destructive fishing techniques. The first APEC Aquaculture Forum, which considered the sustainable development of aquaculture in the region and the development of new markets for APEC fish products, was held in Taipei, Taiwan, in June 1998. In May 1999 new guide-lines were adopted to encourage the participation of the private sector in the activities of the working group. The group's first business forum was convened in July 2000.

Human Resources Development: Comprises three networks promoting co-operation in different areas of human resources, training and education: the Capacity Building Network, with a focus on human capacity building, including management and technical skills development and corporate governance; the Education Network, promoting effective learning systems and supporting the role of education in advancing individual, social and economic development; and the Labour and Social Protection Network, concerned with promoting social integration through the strengthening of labour markets, the development of labour market information and policy, and improvements in working conditions and social safety net frameworks. The working group undertakes activities through these networks to implement ministerial and leaders' directives, as well as the 'Medium Term Strategic Priorities', which were formulated in January 1997. A voluntary network of APEC Study Centers links higher education and research institutions in member economies. In January 1998 the working group established a Task Force on the Human Resource and Social Impacts of the Financial Crisis. Private-sector participation in the working group has been strengthened by the establishment of a network of APEC senior executives responsible for human resources management. Recent activities have included programmes on information technology in the learning society; the implementation of standards and accreditation in supply chain management; and child labour.

Industrial Science and Technology: Aims to contribute to sustainable development in the region, improve the availability of information, enhance human resources development in the sector, improve the business climate, promote policy dialogue and review and facilitate networks and partnerships. Accordingly, the group has helped to establish an APEC Virtual Centre for Environmental Technology Exchange in Japan; a Science and Technology Industrial Parks Network; an International Molecular Biology Network for the APEC Region; an APEC Centre for Technology Foresight, based in Thailand; and the APEC Science and Technology Web, an online database. In 2001 the group worked on developing a Strategy to Combat HIV/AIDS and Other Infectious Diseases, as requested by the Economic Leaders' meeting in 2000. A dialogue on the subject was initiated with the World Health Organization.

Marine Resource Conservation: Promotes initiatives within APEC to protect the marine environment and its resources. In 1996 a five-year project was initiated for the management of red tide and harmful algal blooms in the APEC region. An APEC Action Plan for Sustainability of the Marine Environment was adopted by ministers responsible for the environment, meeting in June 1997. The Plan aimed to promote regional co-operation, an integrated approach to coastal management, the prevention, reduction and control of marine pollution, and sustainable development. Efforts were also being undertaken to establish an Ocean Research Network of centres of excellence in the Pacific. In December 1997 the group organized a workshop, in Hong Kong, on the impact of destructive fishing practices on the marine environment. A workshop was held in Australia, in April 1998, on preventing maritime accidents and pollution in the Pacific region. In April 1999 the group organized a training course, held in Hong Kong, on the satellite remote sensing of algal blooms. Strategies to encourage private-sector participation in promoting the sustainable management of marine resources were endorsed by the group in June 2000. Four main themes were identified for the Action Plan in the 21st century: balancing coastal development and resource protection; ensuring sustainable fisheries and aquaculture; understanding and observing the oceans and seas; and promoting economic and technical co-operation in oceans management.

Small and Medium Enterprises: The group was established in 1995, as the Ad Hoc Policy Level Group on Small and Medium Enterprises, with a temporary mandate to oversee all APEC activities relating to SMEs. It supported the establishment of an APEC Centre for Technical Exchange and Training for Small and Medium Enterprises, which was inaugurated at Los Baños, near Manila, the Philippines, in September 1996. A five-year action plan for SMEs was endorsed in 1998. The group was resdesignated as a working group, with permanent status, in 2000. In 2000 and 2001 the group considered issues relating to globalization, innovation, human resource development, information technology and e-commerce, financing, and the forming of strategic alliances with other SMEs and larger firms.

Telecommunications and Information: Incorporates four steering groups concerned with different aspects of the development and liberalization of the sector—Liberalization; Business facilitation; Development co-operation; and Human resource development. Activities are guided by directives of ministers responsible for telecommunications, who first met in 1995, in the Republic of Korea, and adopted a Seoul Declaration on Asia Pacific Information Infrastructure (APII). The second ministerial meeting, held in Gold Coast, Australia, in September 1996, adopted more detailed proposals for liberalization of the sector in member economies. In June 1998 ministers, meeting in Singapore, agreed to remove technical barriers to trade in telecommunications equipment (although Chile and New Zealand declined to sign up to the arrangement). At their fourth meeting, convened in May 2000 in Cancún, Mexico, telecommunications ministers approved a programme of action that included measures to bridge the 'digital divide' between developed and developing member economies, and adopted the APEC Principles on International Charging Arrangements for Internet Services and the APEC Principles of Interconnection.

Tourism: Established in 1991, with the aim of promoting the long-term sustainability of the tourism industry, in both environmental and social terms. The group administers a Tourism Information Network and an APEC Centre for Sustainable Tourism. In 1998 the group initiated a project to assess the impact of the Asian financial crisis on regional tourism and to identify strategies to counter any negative effects. The first meeting of APEC ministers of tourism, held in the Republic of Korea in July 2000, adopted the Seoul Declaration on the APEC Tourism Charter. The group's work plan is based on four policy goals inherent in the Seoul Declaration, namely, the removal of impediments to tourism business and investment; increased mobility of visitors and increased demand for tourism goods and services; sustainable management of tourism; and enhanced recognition of tourism as a vehicle for economic and social development. At a meeting of the working group in April 2001, APEC and the Pacific Asia Travel Association (PATA) adopted a Code for Sustainable Tourism. The Code is designed for adoption and implementation by a variety of tourism companies and government agencies. It urges members to conserve the natural environment, ecosystems and biodiversity; respect local traditions and cultures; conserve energy; reduce pollution and waste; and ensure that regular environmental audits are carried out. In November 2001 the working group considered the impact on tourism of the September terrorist attacks on the USA. The group noted that while the short-term negative effects could be substantial, a return to long-term growth could be expected in the following year. The group advocated work to improve the quality and timeliness of tourism data, to enable accurate assessment of the situation. In July 2002 APEC ministers of tourism met for the second time, in Manzanillo, Mexico, and adopted a declaration that reiterated the importance of tourism to regional economies.

Trade Promotion: Aims to promote trade, as a key aspect of regional economic co-operation, through activities to enhance trade financing, skills and training, information and networking (for example, through the establishment of APEC Net, providing information to the business community via the internet, accessible at www.apecnet.org.sg), and co-operation with the private sector and public agencies, including trade promotion organizations. Organizes an APEC International Trade Fair, the fourth of which was held in Jakarta, Indonesia, in October 2000.

Transportation: Undertakes initiatives to enhance the efficiency and safety of the regional transportation system, in order to facilitate the development of trade. The working group focuses on three main areas: improving the competitiveness of the transportation industry; promoting a safe and environmentally-sound regional transportation system; and human resources development, including training, research and education. The group has published surveys, directories and manuals on all types of transportation systems, and has compiled an inventory on regional co-operation on oil spills preparedness and response arrangements. A Road Transportation Harmonization Project aims to provide the basis for common standards in the automotive industry in the Asia-Pacific region. The group has established an internet database on ports and the internet-based Virtual Centre for Transportation Research, Development and Education. It plans to develop a regional action plan on the implementation of Global Navigation Satellite Systems, in consultation with the relevant international bodies.

Publications

ABAC Report to APEC Leaders (annually).

APEC Economic Outlook (annually).

APEC Economies Beyond the Asian Crisis.

APEC Energy Handbook (annually).

APEC Energy Statistics (annually).

Foreign Direct Investment and APEC Economic Integration (irregular).

Guide to the Investment Regimes of the APEC Member Economies.

Key APEC Documents (annually).

The State of Economic and Technical Co-operation in APEC.

Towards Knowledge-based Economies in APEC.

Trade and Investment Liberalization in APEC.

Working group reports, regional directories, other irregular surveys.

ASIAN DEVELOPMENT BANK—ADB

Address: 6 ADB Ave, Mandaluyong City, 0401 Metro Manila, Philippines; POB 789, 0980 Manila, Philippines.

Telephone: (2) 6324444; **fax:** (2) 6362444; **e-mail:** information@adb.org; **internet:** www.adb.org.

The ADB commenced operations in December 1966. The Bank's principal functions are to provide loans and equity investments for the economic and social advancement of its developing member countries, to give technical assistance for the preparation and implementation of development projects and programmes and advisory services, to promote investment of public and private capital for development purposes, and to respond to requests from developing member countries for assistance in the co-ordination of their development policies and plans.

MEMBERS

There are 44 member countries and territories within the ESCAP region and 17 others (see list of subscriptions below).

Organization

(October 2002)

BOARD OF GOVERNORS

All powers of the Bank are vested in the Board, which may delegate its powers to the Board of Directors except in such matters as admission of new members, changes in the Bank's authorized capital stock, election of Directors and President, and amendment of the Charter. One Governor and one Alternate Governor are appointed by each member country. The Board meets at least once a year.

BOARD OF DIRECTORS

The Board of Directors is responsible for general direction of operations and exercises all powers delegated by the Board of Governors, which elects it. Of the 12 Directors, eight represent constituency groups of member countries within the ESCAP region (with about 65% of the voting power) and four represent the rest of the member countries. Each Director serves for two years and may be re-elected.

Three specialized committees (the Audit Committee, the Budget Review Committee and the Inspection Committee), each comprising six members, assist the Board of Directors in exercising its authority with regard to supervising the Bank's financial statements, approving the administrative budget, and reviewing and approving policy documents and assistance operations.

The President of the Bank, though not a Director, is Chairman of the Board.

Chairman of Board of Directors and President: TADAO CHINO (Japan).

Vice-Presidents: JOSEPH B. EICHENBERGER (USA); JOHN LINTJER (Netherlands); MYOUNG-HO SHIN (Republic of Korea).

ADMINISTRATION

The Bank had 2,163 staff at 31 December 2001.

On 1 January 2002 the Bank implemented a new organizational structure, which had been under review in 2001. The reorganization aimed to strengthen the Bank's country and sub-regional focus, as well as its capacity for poverty reduction and implementing its long-term strategic framework. Five regional departments cover East and Central Asia, the Mekong, the Pacific, South Asia, and South East Asia. Other departments and offices include Private Sector Operations, Central Operations Services, Regional and Sustainable Development, Strategy and Policy, Cofinancing Operations, and Economics and Research, as well as other administrative units.

There are Bank Resident Missions in Bangladesh, Cambodia, the People's Republic of China, India, Indonesia, Kazakhstan, Kyrgyzstan, Laos, Mongolia, Nepal, Pakistan, Sri Lanka, Uzbekistan and Viet Nam, all of which report to the head of the regional department. In addition, there is a country office in the Philippines, Extended Missions in Gujarat, India and in Papua New Guinea, Special Liaison Offices in East Timor and Afghanistan, and a South Pacific Regional Mission, based in Vanuatu. Representative Offices are located in Tokyo, Japan, Frankfurt am Main, Germany (for Europe), and Washington, DC, USA (for North America).

Secretary: BINDU N. LOHANI.

General Counsel: GERALD A. SUMIDA.

INSTITUTE

ADB Institute—ADBI: Kasumigaseki Bldg, 8th Floor, 2–5 Kasumigaseki 3-chome, Chiyoda-ku, Tokyo 100-6008, Japan; tel. (3) 3593-5500; fax (3) 3593-5571; e-mail info@adbi.org; internet www.adbi.org; f. 1997 as a subsidiary body of the ADB to research and analyse long-term development issues and to disseminate development practices through training and other capacity-building activities. Dean MASARU YOSHITOMI (Japan).

FINANCIAL STRUCTURE

The Bank's ordinary capital resources (which are used for loans to the more advanced developing member countries) are held and used entirely separately from its Special Funds resources (see below). A fourth General Capital Increase (GCI IV), amounting to US $26,318m. (or some 100%), was authorized in May 1994. At the final deadline for subscription to GCI IV, on 30 September 1996, 55 member countries had subscribed shares amounting to $24,675.4m.

At 31 December 2001 the position of subscriptions to the capital stock was as follows: authorized US $43,834m.; subscribed $43,628m.

The Bank also borrows funds from the world capital markets. Total borrowings during 2001 amounted to US $1,607m. (compared with $1,693m. in 2000). At 31 December 2001 total outstanding borrowings amounted to $24,880.8m.

In July 1986 the Bank abolished the system of fixed lending rates, under which ordinary operations loans had carried interest rates fixed at the time of loan commitment for the entire life of the loan. Under the new system the lending rate is adjusted every six months, to take into account changing conditions in international financial markets.

SPECIAL FUNDS

The Asian Development Fund (ADF) was established in 1974 in order to provide a systematic mechanism for mobilizing and administering resources for the Bank to lend on concessionary terms to the least-developed member countries. In 1998 the Bank revised the terms of ADF. Since 1 January 1999 all new project loans are repayable within 32 years, including an eight-year grace period, while quick-disbursing programme loans have a 24-year maturity, also including an eight-year grace period. The previous annual service charge was redesignated as an interest charge, including a portion to cover administrative expenses. The new interest charges on all loans are 1%–1.5% per annum. At 31 December 2001 total ADF loans approved amounted to US $25,714m. for 917 loans, while cumulative disbursements from ADF resources totalled $17,552m.

Successive replenishments of the Fund's resources amounted to US $809m. for the period 1976–78, $2,150m. for 1979–82, $3,214m. for 1983–86, $3,600m. for 1987–90, $4,200m. for 1992–95, and $6,300m. for 1997–2000. In September 2000 25 donor countries pledged $2,910m. towards the ADF's seventh replenishment (ADF VIII), which totalled $5,650m. to provide resources for the period 2001–04; repayments of earlier ADF loans were to provide the remaining $2,740m. ADF VIII became effective in June 2001.

The Bank provides technical assistance grants from its Technical Assistance Special Fund (TASF). By the end of 2001, the Fund's total resources amounted to US $911.0m., of which $829.7m. had been utilized or committed. The Japan Special Fund (JSF) was established in 1988 to provide finance for technical assistance by means of grants, in both the public and private sectors. The JSF aims to help developing member countries restructure their economies, enhance the opportunities for attracting new investment, and recycle funds. The Japanese Government had committed a total of 94,300m. yen (equivalent to some $813.5m.) to the JSF by the end of 2001 (of which $774.2m. had been utilized). In March 1999 an Asian Currency Crisis Support Facility (ACCSF) was established, for a three-year period, as an independent component of the JSF to provide additional technical assistance, interest payment assistance and guarantees to countries most affected by financial instability, i.e. Indonesia, Republic of Korea, Malaysia, Philippines and Thailand. At the end of 2001 the Japanese Government, as the sole financier of the fund, had contributed 27,500m. yen (some $241.0m.) to the new Facility. The Japanese Government also funds the Japan Scholarship Program, under which 1,334 scholarships had been awarded to recipients from 34 member countries between 1988 and 2001, and the ADB Institute Special Fund, which was established to finance the initial operations of the new Institute (see above). By 31 December 2001 cumulative commitments to the Special Fund amounted to 7,500m. yen (or $61.5m.). In May 2000 the Japan Fund for Poverty Reduction was established, with an initial contribution of 10,000m. yen (approximately $92.6m., supplemented in 2001 by an additional 7,900m. yen, of $65.0m.) from the Japanese Government, to support ADB-financed poverty reduction and social development activities. A Japan Fund for Information and Community Technology (ICT) was established in July 2001, for a three-year period, to promote the development and use of ICT in developing member countries. The Fund was established with an initial contribution of 1,273m. yen (or $10.7m.) from the Japanese Government.

The majority of grant funds in support of the Bank's technical assistance activities are provided by bilateral donors under channel financing arrangements (CFAs). Since 1980, when the first CFA was negotiated, 151 technical assistance grants had been financed under CFAs at the end of 2001, with a total value of $73.7m. CFAs may also be processed as a thematic financing tool, for example concerned with renewable energy, water or poverty reduction, enabling more than one donor to contribute.

Activities

Loans by the ADB are usually aimed at specific projects. In responding to requests from member governments for loans, the Bank's staff assesses the financial and economic viability of projects and the way in which they fit into the economic framework and priorities of development of the country concerned. In 1987 the Bank adopted a policy of lending in support of programmes of sectoral adjustment, not limited to specific projects; such loans were not to exceed 15% of total Bank public sector lending. In 1999 the Board of Directors increased the ceiling on programme lending to 20% of the annual total. In 1985 the Bank decided to expand its assistance to the private sector, hitherto comprising loans to development finance institutions, under government guarantee, for lending to small and medium-sized enterprises; a programme was formulated for direct financial assistance, in the form of equity and loans without government guarantee, to private enterprises. In 1992 a Social Dimensions Unit was established as part of the central administrative structure of the Bank, which contributed to the Bank's increasing awareness of the importance of social aspects of development as essential components of sustainable economic growth. During the early 1990s the Bank also aimed to expand its role as project financier by providing assistance for policy formulation and review and promoting regional co-operation, while placing greater emphasis on individual country requirements. In accordance with its medium-term strategy for 1995–98 the Bank resolved to promote sound development management, by integrating into its operations and projects the promotion of governance issues, such as capacity-building, legal frameworks and openness of information. During that period the Bank also introduced a commitment to assess development projects for their impact on the local population and to avoid all involuntary resettlement where possible and established a formal procedure for grievances, under which the Board may authorize an inspection of a project, by an independent panel of experts, at the request of the affected community or group. In 1998 the Bank approved a new anticorruption strategy.

The currency instability and ensuing financial crises affecting many Asian economies in the second half of 1997 and in 1998 prompted the Bank to reflect on its role in the region. The Bank resolved to strengthen its activities as a broad-based development institution, rather than solely as a project financier, through lending policies, dialogue, co-financing and technical assistance. A Task Force on Financial Sector Reform was established to review the causes and effects of the regional financial crisis. The Task Force identified the Bank's initial priorities as being to accelerate banking and capital market reforms in member countries, to promote market efficiency in the financial, trade and industrial sectors, to promote good governance and sound corporate management, and to alleviate the social impact of structural adjustments. In mid-1999 the Bank approved a technical assistance grant to establish an internet-based Asian Recovery Information Centre, within a new Regional Monitoring Unit, which aimed to facilitate access to information regarding the economic and social impact of the Asian financial crisis, analyses of economic needs of countries, reform programmes and monitoring of the economic recovery process. In November the Board of Directors approved a new overall strategy objective of poverty reduction, which was to be the principal consideration for all future Bank lending, project financing and technical assistance. The strategy incorporated key aims of supporting sustainable, grass-roots based economic growth, social development and good governance. The Board also approved a health sector policy, to concentrate resources on basic primary healthcare, and initiated reviews of the Bank's private sector strategy and the efficiency of resident missions. During 2000 the Bank began to refocus its country strategies, projects and lending targets to complement the poverty reduction strategy. In addition, it initiated a process of wide-ranging discussions to formulate a long-term strategic framework for the next 15 years, based on the target of reducing by 50% the incidence of extreme poverty by 2015. The framework, establishing the operational priorities and principles for reducing poverty, was approved in March 2001. At the same time a medium-term strategy, for the period 2001–05, was approved, which aimed to enhance the development impact of the Bank's assistance and to define the operational priorities within the context of the strategic agenda.

SUBSCRIPTIONS AND VOTING POWER*
(31 December 2001)

Country	Subscribed capital (% of total)	Voting power (% of total)
Regional:		
Afghanistan	0.034	0.366
Australia	5.892	5.053
Azerbaijan	0.453	0.701
Bangladesh	1.040	1.171
Bhutan	0.006	0.344
Cambodia	0.050	0.379
China, People's Republic	6.562	5.588
Cook Islands	0.003	0.341
Fiji	0.069	0.394
Hong Kong	0.555	0.783
India	6.447	5.497
Indonesia	5.546	4.776
Japan	15.893	13.053
Kazakhstan	0.821	0.996
Kiribati	0.004	0.342
Korea, Republic	5.130	4.443
Kyrgyzstan	0.305	0.583
Laos	0.014	0.350
Malaysia	2.773	2.557
Maldives	0.004	0.342
Marshall Islands	0.003	0.341
Micronesia, Federated States	0.004	0.342
Mongolia	0.015	0.351
Myanmar	0.555	0.783
Nauru	0.004	0.342
Nepal	0.150	0.459
New Zealand	1.564	1.590
Pakistan	2.218	2.114
Papua New Guinea	0.096	0.415
Philippines	2.426	2.280
Samoa	0.003	0.342
Singapore	0.347	0.616
Solomon Islands	0.007	0.344
Sri Lanka	0.591	0.811
Taiwan	1.109	1.226
Tajikistan	0.292	0.572
Thailand	1.386	1.448
Tonga	0.004	0.342
Turkmenistan	0.258	0.545
Tuvalu	0.001	0.340
Uzbekistan	0.686	0.888
Vanuatu	0.007	0.344
Viet Nam	0.348	0.617
Sub-total	63.674	65.515
Non-regional:		
Austria	0.347	0.616
Belgium	0.347	0.616
Canada	5.327	4.600
Denmark	0.347	0.616
Finland	0.347	0.616
France	2.370	2.235
Germany	4.405	3.863
Italy	1.840	1.811
Netherlands	1.045	1.175
Norway	0.347	0.616
Spain	0.347	0.616
Sweden	0.347	0.616
Switzerland	0.594	0.814
Turkey	0.347	0.616
United Kingdom	2.080	2.003
USA	15.893	13.053
Sub-total	36.326	34.485
Total	100.000	100.000

*Portugal was admitted as a non-regional member of the Bank in April 2002; East Timor became the Bank's 61st member in July.

In 2001 the Bank approved 76 loans in 60 projects amounting to US $5,339.0m. (compared with $5,653m. for 74 projects in 2000). Loans from ordinary capital resources in 2001 totalled $3,977.4m., while loans from the ADF amounted to $1,361.6m. Private-sector operations approved amounted to $67.9m., which included direct loans without government guarantee of $37.5m. and equity investments of $30.4m. The largest proportion of assistance, amounting to some 27% of total lending, was allocated to transport and communications projects. Disbursements of loans during 2001 amounted to $3,873.9m., bringing cumulative disbursements to $62,168.0m.

In 2001 grants approved for technical assistance (e.g. project preparation, consultant services and training) amounted to US $146.4m. for 257 projects, with $59.8m. deriving from the Bank's ordinary resources and the TASF, $53.8m. from the JSF, $16.1m. from the ACCSF, and $16.7m. from bilateral and multilateral sources. The Bank's Operations Evaluation Office prepares reports on completed projects, in order to assess achievements and problems. In April 2000 the Bank announced that, from 2001, some new loans would be denominated in local currencies, in order to ease the repayment burden on recipient economies.

The Bank co-operates with other international organizations active in the region, particularly the World Bank group, the IMF, UNDP and APEC, and participates in meetings of aid donors for developing member countries. In May 2001 the Bank and UNDP signed a memorandum of understanding (MOU) on strategic partnership, in order to strengthen co-operation in the reduction of poverty, for example the preparation of common country assessments and a common database on poverty and other social indicators. Also in 2001 the Bank signed an MOU with the World Bank on administrative arrangements for co-operation, providing a framework for closer co-operation and more efficient use of resources. In early 2002 the Bank worked with the World Bank and UNDP to assess the preliminary needs of the interim administration in Afghanistan, in preparation for an International Conference on Reconstruction Assistance to Afghanistan, held in late January, in Tokyo. The Bank pledged to work with its member governments to provide highly concessional grants and loans of some US $500m., with a particular focus on road reconstruction, basic education, and agricultural irrigation rehabilitation. A new policy concerning co-operation with non-governmental organizations (NGOs) was approved by the Bank in 1998. During 2001 57% of the public sector projects were prepared with NGO involvement.

Finance

Internal administrative expenses amounted to US $220.7m. in 2001, and were projected to total $240.0m. in 2002.

Publications

ADB Business Opportunities (monthly).
ADB Institute Newsletter.
ADB Review (6 a year).
Annual Report.
Asian Development Outlook (annually).
Asian Development Review (2 a year).
Basic Statistics (annually).
Key Indicators of Developing Asian and Pacific Countries (annually).
Law and Policy Reform Bulletin (annually).
Loan Disbursement Handbook.
Studies and technical assistance reports, information brochures, guide-lines, sample bidding documents, staff papers.

Statistics

BANK ACTIVITIES BY SECTOR

	Loan Approvals (US $ million)		
	2001		1968–2001
Sector	Amount	%	%
Agriculture and natural resources	603.48	11.30	18.34
Energy	662.90	12.42	20.87
Finance	565.02	10.58	14.53
Industry and non-fuel minerals	86.00	1.61	3.47
Social infrastructure	492.10	9.22	16.10
Transport and communications	1,425.50	26.70	20.17
Multi-sector and others	1,504.00	28.17	6.51
Total	5,339.00	100.00	100.00

LENDING ACTIVITIES BY COUNTRY (US $ million)

Country	Loans approved in 2001 Ordinary Capital	ADF	Total
Bangladesh	138.70	159.20	297.90
Bhutan	—	7.00	7.00
Cambodia	—	75.20	75.20
China, People's Republic	997.00	—	997.00
India	1,500.00	—	1,500.00
Indonesia	400.00	100.00	500.00
Kyrgyzstan	—	75.00	75.00
Laos	—	65.00	65.00
Maldives	—	17.50	17.50
Marshall Islands	4.00	8.00	12.00
Micronesia, Federated States	—	13.02	13.02
Mongolia	—	35.69	35.69
Nepal	—	95.60	95.60
Pakistan	593.20	363.60	956.80
Papua New Guinea	70.00	5.90	75.90
Philippines	105.00	—	105.00
Samoa	—	6.00	6.00
Sri Lanka	60.00	86.00	146.00
Tajikistan	—	3.60	3.60
Uzbekistan	72.00	—	72.00
Viet Nam	17.50	243.09	260.59
Regional	20.00	—	20.00
Total	3,977.40	1,361.60	5,339.00

LENDING ACTIVITIES (in %)

	1993–97		1998–2001	
Country	Ordinary Capital	ADF	Ordinary Capital	ADF
Bangladesh	0.2	21.2	1.8	15.9
Bhutan	—	0.3	—	0.8
Cambodia	—	2.5	—	5.4
China, People's Republic	23.4	—	25.5	—
Cook Islands	—	0.2	—	0.0
Fiji	0.2	—	—	—
India	13.0	—	20.8	—
Indonesia	22.2	3.7	22.9	5.3
Kazakhstan	1.6	0.8	0.3	—
Kiribati	—	—	—	0.2
Korea, Republic	18.4	—	—	—
Kyrgyzstan	—	3.5	—	5.5
Laos	—	5.8	—	3.4
Malaysia	0.9	—	—	—
Maldives	—	0.2	—	0.6
Marshall Islands	—	0.5	0.0	0.5
Micronesia, Federated States	—	0.5	—	0.4
Mongolia	—	4.8	—	2.6
Nauru	—	—	0.0	—
Nepal	0.2	5.2	—	8.5
Pakistan	4.1	20.5	8.0	14.3
Papua New Guinea	0.2	0.6	1.1	1.0
Philippines	6.7	3.1	9.2	0.2
Samoa	—	0.0	—	0.5
Solomon Islands	—	0.0	—	0.7
Sri Lanka	0.0	7.8	0.8	12.2
Tajikistan	—	—	—	2.1
Thailand	8.5	—	5.9	—
Tonga	—	0.2	—	—
Tuvalu	—	—	—	0.1
Uzbekistan	0.3	0.3	2.2	—
Vanuatu	—	0.1	—	0.4
Viet Nam	0.1	18.2	0.6	15.4
Regional	—	—	0.9	4.0
Total	100.0	100.0	100.0	100.0
Value (US $ million)	21,828.8	7,139.5	16,941.0	5,011.7

Source: *ADB Annual Report 2001.*

ASSOCIATION OF SOUTH EAST ASIAN NATIONS—ASEAN

Address: 70A Jalan Sisingamangaraja, POB 2072, Jakarta 12110, Indonesia.

Telephone: (21) 7262991; **fax:** (21) 7398234; **e-mail:** public@asean.or.id; **internet:** www.aseansec.org.

ASEAN was established in August 1967 in Bangkok, Thailand, to accelerate economic progress and to increase the stability of the South-East Asian region.

MEMBERS

Brunei	Malaysia	Singapore
Cambodia	Myanmar	Thailand
Indonesia	Philippines	Viet Nam
Laos		

Organization

(October 2002)

SUMMIT MEETING

The highest authority of ASEAN, bringing together the heads of government of member countries. The first meeting was held in Bali, Indonesia, in February 1976. The 30th anniversary of the founding of ASEAN was commemorated at an informal gathering of heads of government in Kuala Lumpur, Malaysia, in December 1997. The sixth summit meeting was convened in Hanoi, Viet Nam, in December 1998 and informal summit meetings were held in Manila, Philippines, in November 1999 and in Singapore, in November 2000. The seventh summit meeting took place in Bandar Seri Begawan, Brunei, in November 2001. The eighth meeting was scheduled to be held in Phnom-Penh, Cambodia, in November 2002.

MINISTERIAL MEETINGS

The ASEAN Ministerial Meeting (AMM), comprising ministers of foreign affairs of member states, meets annually, in each member country in turn, to formulate policy guide-lines and to co-ordinate ASEAN activities. These meetings are followed by 'post-ministerial conferences' (PMCs), where ASEAN ministers of foreign affairs meet with their counterparts from countries that are 'dialogue partners' as well as with ministers from other countries. Ministers of economic affairs also meet once a year, to direct ASEAN economic co-operation. Joint Ministerial Meetings, consisting of ministers of foreign affairs and of economic affairs are convened prior to a summit meeting, and may be held at the request of either group of ministers. Other ministers meet regularly to promote co-operation in different sectors.

STANDING COMMITTEE

The Standing Committee normally meets every two months. It consists of the minister of foreign affairs of the host country and ambassadors of the other members accredited to the host country.

SECRETARIATS

A permanent secretariat was established in Jakarta, Indonesia, in 1976 to form a central co-ordinating body. The Secretariat comprises four bureaux relating to: Programme Co-ordination and External Relations; Trade, Industry and Services; Investment, Finance and Surveillance; and Economic and Functional Co-operation. The Secretary-General holds office for a five-year term, and is assisted by two Deputy Secretaries-General. In each member country day-to-day work is co-ordinated by an ASEAN National Secretariat.

Secretary-General: (until Nov. 2002) RODOLFO CERTEZA SEVERINO (Philippines); (designate) ONG KENG YOUNG (Singapore).

Deputy Secretaries-General: TRAN DUC MINH (Viet Nam), AHMAD MOKHTAR SELAT (Malaysia).

COMMITTEES AND SENIOR OFFICIALS' MEETINGS

Ministerial meetings are serviced by 29 committees of senior officials, supported by 122 technical working groups. There is a network of subsidiary technical bodies comprising sub-committees, expert groups, *ad hoc* working groups and working parties.

To support the conduct of relations with other countries and international organizations, ASEAN committees (composed of heads of diplomatic missions) have been established in 14 foreign capitals: those of Australia, Belgium, Canada, the People's Republic of China, France, India, Japan, the Republic of Korea, New Zealand, Pakistan, Russia, Switzerland, the United Kingdom and the USA. There is also an ASEAN committee in New York (USA).

Activities

ASEAN was established in 1967 with the signing of the ASEAN Declaration, otherwise known as the Bangkok Declaration, by the ministers of foreign affairs of Indonesia, Malaysia, the Philippines, Singapore and Thailand. Brunei joined the organization in January 1984, shortly after attaining independence. Viet Nam was admitted as the seventh member of ASEAN in July 1995. Laos and Myanmar joined in July 1997 and Cambodia was formally admitted in April 1999, fulfilling the organization's ambition to incorporate all 10 countries in the sub-region.

TRADE AND ECONOMIC CO-OPERATION

A Basic Agreement on the Establishment of ASEAN Preferential Trade Arrangements was concluded in 1977, but by mid-1987 the system covered only about 5% of trade between member states, since individual countries were permitted to exclude any 'sensitive' products from preferential import tariffs. In December 1987 the meeting of ASEAN heads of government resolved to reduce such exclusions to a maximum of 10% of the number of items traded and to a maximum of 50% of the value of trade, over the next five years (seven years for Indonesia and the Philippines).

In January 1992 heads of government, meeting in Singapore, signed an agreement to create an 'ASEAN Free Trade Area' (AFTA) by 2008. In accordance with the agreement, a common effective preferential tariff (CEPT) scheme came into effect in January 1993. The CEPT covered all manufactured products, including capital goods, and processed agricultural products (which together accounted for two-thirds of intra-ASEAN trade), but was to exclude unprocessed agricultural products. Tariffs were to be reduced to a maximum of 20% within a period of five to eight years and to 0%–5% during the subsequent seven to 10 years. Fifteen categories were designated for accelerated tariff reduction, including vegetable oils, rubber products, textiles, cement and pharmaceuticals. Member states were, however, still to be permitted exclusion for certain 'sensitive' products. In October 1993 ASEAN trade ministers agreed to modify the CEPT, with only Malaysia and Singapore having adhered to the original tariff reduction schedule. The new AFTA programme, under which all member countries except Brunei were scheduled to begin tariff reductions from 1 January 1994, substantially enlarged the number of products to be included in the tariff-reduction process and reduced the list of products eligible for protection. In September 1994 ASEAN ministers of economic affairs agreed to accelerate the implementation of AFTA: tariffs were to be reduced to 0%–5% within seven to 10 years, or within five to eight years for products designated for accelerated tariff cuts. In July 1995 Viet Nam was admitted as a member of ASEAN and was granted until 2006 to implement the AFTA trade agreements (this deadline was subsequently advanced to 2003). In December 1995 heads of government, at a meeting convened in Bangkok, agreed to maintain the objective of achieving AFTA by 2003, while pursuing efforts to eliminate or reduce tariffs to less than 5% on the majority of products by 2000. Liberalization was to be extended to certain service industries, including banking, telecommunications and tourism. In July 1997 Laos and Myanmar became members of ASEAN and were granted a 10-year period, from 1 January 1998, to comply with the AFTA schedule. (This deadline was subsequently advanced to 2005.)

In December 1998, meeting in Hanoi, Viet Nam, heads of government approved a Statement on Bold Measures, detailing ASEAN's strategies to deal with the economic crisis that had prevailed in the region since late 1997. These included incentives to attract investors, for example a three-year exemption on corporate taxation, accelerated implementation of the ASEAN Investment Area (AIA, see below), and advancing the AFTA deadline, for the original six members, to 2002, with some 85% of products to be covered by the arrangements by 2000, and 90% by 2001. It was envisaged that the original six members and the new members would achieve the elimination of all tariffs by 2015 and 2018, respectively. The Hanoi Plan of Action, which was also adopted at the meeting as a framework for the development of the organization over the period 1999–2004, incorporated a series of measures aimed at strengthening macroeconomic and financial co-operation and enhancing economic integration. In April 1999 Cambodia, on being admitted as a full member of ASEAN, signed an agreement to implement the tariff reduction programme over a 10-year period, commencing 1 January 2000. Cambodia also signed a declaration endorsing the commitments of the 1998 Statement on Bold Measures. In May 2000 Malaysia was granted a special exemption to postpone implementing tariff reductions on motor vehicles for two years from 1 January 2003. In November 2000 a protocol was approved permitting further temporary exclusion of products from the CEPT scheme for countries experiencing economic difficulties. In September 2001 ASEAN ministers of economic affairs reviewed progress in the completion of the free trade area and the AIA, and reported that the grouping's six original members had achieved the objective of reducing to less than 5% (specifically, reaching a level of 3.2%) trade restrictions on 90% of products. Consequently, AFTA was formally realized, among the original six signatories, on 1 January 2002.

To complement AFTA in facilitating intra-ASEAN trade, member countries are committed to the removal of non-tariff barriers (such as quotas), the harmonization of standards and conformance measures, and the simplification and harmonization of customs procedures. In June 1996 the Working Group on Customs Procedures completed a draft legal framework for regional co-operation, designed to simplify and harmonize customs procedures, legislation and product classification. The agreement was signed in March 1997 at the inaugural meeting of ASEAN finance ministers. (Laos and Myanmar signed the customs agreement in July and Cambodia assented to it in April 1999.) In 2001 ASEAN finalized its system of harmonized tariff nomenclature. Implementation began in 2002, with training on the new system to be given to public- and private-sector officials over the course of the year.

At the seventh summit meeting, held in Brunei, in November 2001 heads of government noted the challenges posed by the severe global economic slowdown, at a time when ASEAN countries were beginning to emerge from the 1997–98 crisis. Members discussed moving beyond the group's existing free-trade and investment commitments by deepening market liberalization. Specifically, it was proposed that negotiations on the liberalization of intra-ASEAN trade in services be accelerated. The third round of negotiations on liberalizing trade in services began at the end of 2001; it was scheduled to be completed by 2004. Members also agreed to start negotiations on mutual recognition arrangements for professional services. The summit meeting stated that tariff preferences would be extended to ASEAN's newer members from January 2002, under the ASEAN Integration System of Preferences (AISP), thus allowing Cambodia, Laos, Myanmar and Viet Nam tariff-free access to the more developed ASEAN markets earlier than the previously agreed target date of 2010.

In November 2000 heads of government endorsed an Initiative for ASEAN Integration (IAI), which aimed to reduce economic disparities within the region through effective co-operation, in particular, in training and other educational opportunities. In July 2002 the AMM endorsed an IAI Work Plan, which focused on the following priority areas: human resources development; infrastructure; information communications technology; and regional economic integration. An IAI Development Co-operation Forum was held in August.

In 1991 ASEAN ministers discussed a proposal of the Malaysian Government for the formation of an economic grouping, to be composed of ASEAN members, the People's Republic of China, Hong Kong, Japan, the Republic of Korea and Taiwan. In July 1993 ASEAN ministers of foreign affairs agreed a compromise, whereby the grouping was to be a caucus within APEC, although it was to be co-ordinated by ASEAN's meeting of economy ministers. In July 1994 ministers of foreign affairs of nine prospective members of the group held their first informal collective meeting; however, no progress was made towards forming the proposed East Asia Economic Caucus. There was renewed speculation on the formation of an East Asian grouping following the onset of the Asian financial crisis of the late 1990s. At an informal meeting of leaders of ASEAN countries, China, Japan and the Republic of Korea, held in November 1999, all parties (designating themselves 'ASEAN + 3') issued a Joint Statement on East Asian Co-operation, in which they agreed to strengthen regional unity, and addressed the long-term possibility of establishing an East Asian common market and currency. Meeting in May 2000, in Chiang Mai, Thailand, ASEAN + 3 ministers of economic affairs proposed the establishment of an enhanced currency-swap mechanism, enabling countries to draw on liquidity support to defend their economies during balance-of-payments difficulties or speculative currency attacks and to prevent future financial crises. In July ASEAN + 3 ministers of foreign affairs convened an inaugural formal summit in Bangkok, Thailand, and in October ASEAN + 3 economic affairs ministers agreed to hold their hitherto twice-yearly informal meetings on an institutionalized basis. In November an informal meeting of ASEAN + 3 leaders approved further co-operation in various sectors and initiated a feasibility study into a proposal to establish a regional free trade area. In May 2001 ASEAN + 3 ministers of economic affairs endorsed a series of projects for co-operation in information technology, environment, small and medium-sized enterprises, Mekong Basin development, and harmonization of standards. In the same month the so-called Chiang Mai initiative on currency-swap arrangements was formally approved by ASEAN + 3 finance ministers. A meeting of the ASEAN + 3 leaders was held alongside the seventh ASEAN summit in November 2001. Malaysia offered to host an ASEAN + 3 secretariat; however the establishment of a formal secretariat for the grouping remained under discussion in 2002. In October 2001 ASEAN + 3 agriculture and forestry ministers met for the first time, and discussed issues of poverty alleviation, food security, agricultural research and human resource development. The first meeting of ASEAN + 3 tourism ministers was held in January 2002. In July ASEAN + 3 ministers of foreign affairs declared their support for other regional initiatives, namely an Asia Co-operation Dialogue, which was initiated by the Thai Government in June, and an Initiative for Development in East Asia (IDEA), which had been announced by the Japanese Government in January. An IDEA ministerial meeting was convened in Tokyo, in August.

INDUSTRY

The ASEAN-Chambers of Commerce and Industry (CCI) aims to enhance ASEAN economic and industrial co-operation and the participation in these activities of the private sector. In March 1996 a permanent ASEAN-CCI secretariat became operational at the ASEAN Secretariat. The first AIA Council-Business Sector Forum was convened in September 2001, with the aim of developing alliances between the public and private sectors. The seventh ASEAN summit in November resolved to encourage the private sector to convene a regular ASEAN Business Summit. It was also agreed to set up an ASEAN Business Advisory Council.

The ASEAN Industrial Co-operation (AICO) scheme, initiated in 1996, encourages companies in the ASEAN region to undertake joint manufacturing activities. Products derived from an AICO arrangement benefit immediately from a preferential tariff rate of 0%–5%. The AICO scheme superseded the ASEAN industrial joint venture scheme, established in 1983. The attractiveness of the scheme is expected slowly to diminish as ASEAN moves towards the full implementation of the CEPT scheme. ASEAN has initiated studies of new methods of industrial co-operation within the grouping, with the aim of achieving further integration.

The ASEAN Consultative Committee on Standards and Quality (ACCSQ) aims to promote the understanding and implementation of quality concepts, considered to be important in strengthening the economic development of a member state and in helping to eliminate trade barriers. ACCSQ comprises three working groups: standards and information; conformance and assessment; and testing and calibration. In September 1994 an *ad hoc* Working Group on Intellectual Property Co-operation was established, with a mandate to formulate a framework agreement on intellectual property co-operation and to strengthen ASEAN activities in intellectual property protection. ASEAN aims to establish, by 2004, a regional electronic database, to strengthen the administration of intellectual property. ASEAN is also developing a Regulatory Trademark Filing System, as a first step towards the creation of an ASEAN Trademark System.

In 1988 the ASEAN Fund was established, with capital of US $150m., to provide finance for portfolio investments in ASEAN countries, in particular for small and medium-sized enterprises (SMEs). The Hanoi Plan of Action, which was adopted by ASEAN heads of state in December 1998, incorporated a series of initiatives to enhance the development of SMEs, including training and technical assistance, co-operation activities and greater access to information.

FINANCE, BANKING AND INVESTMENT

In 1987 heads of government agreed to accelerate regional financial co-operation, to support intra-ASEAN trade and investment. They adopted measures to increase the role of ASEAN currencies in regional trade, to assist negotiations on the avoidance of double taxation, and to improve the efficiency of tax and customs administrators. An ASEAN Reinsurance Corporation was established in 1988, with initial authorized capital of US $10m. In December 1995 the summit meeting proposed the establishment of an ASEAN Investment Area (AIA). Other measures to attract greater financial resource flows in the region, including an ASEAN Plan of Action for the Promotion of Foreign Direct Investment and Intra-ASEAN Investment, were implemented during 1996.

In February 1997 ASEAN central bank governors agreed to strengthen efforts to combat currency speculation through the established network of foreign-exchange repurchase agreements. However, from mid-1997 several Asian currencies were undermined by speculative activities. Subsequent unsuccessful attempts to support the foreign-exchange rates contributed to a collapse in the value of financial markets in some countries and to a reversal of the region's economic growth, at least in the short term, while governments undertook macro-economic structural reforms. In early December ASEAN ministers of finance, meeting in Malaysia, agreed to liberalize markets for financial services and to strengthen surveillance of member country economies, to help prevent further deterioration of the regional economy. The ministers also endorsed a proposal for the establishment of an Asian funding facility to provide emergency assistance in support of international credit and structural reform programmes. At the informal summit meeting held later in December, ASEAN leaders issued a joint statement in which they expressed the need for mutual support to counter the region's financial crisis and urged greater international assistance to help overcome the situation and address the underlying problems. The heads of government also resolved to accelerate the implementation of the AIA.

In July 1998 the ASEAN Ministerial Meeting endorsed the decisions of finance ministers, taken in February, to promote greater use of regional currencies for trade payments and to establish an economic surveillance mechanism. In October ministers of economic affairs, meeting in Manila, the Philippines, signed a framework agreement on the AIA, which was expected to provide for equal treatment of domestic and other ASEAN direct investment proposals within the grouping by 2010, and of all foreign investors by 2020. The meeting also confirmed that the proposed ASEAN Surveillance Process (ASP), to monitor the economic stability and financial systems of member states, would be implemented with immediate effect, and would require the voluntary submission of economic information by all members to a monitoring committee, to be based in Jakarta, Indonesia. The ASP and the framework agreement on the AIA were incorporated into the Hanoi Plan of Action, adopted by heads of state in December 1998. The December summit meeting also resolved to accelerate reforms, particularly in the banking and financial sectors, in order to strengthen the region's economies, and to promote the liberalization of the financial services sector.

In March 1999 ASEAN ministers of trade and industry, meeting in Phuket, Thailand, as the AIA Council, agreed to open their manufacturing, agriculture, fisheries, forestry and mining industries to foreign investment. Investment restrictions affecting those industries were to be eliminated by 2003 in most cases, although Laos and Viet Nam were granted until 2010. In addition, ministers adopted a number of measures to encourage investment in the region, including access to three-year corporate income-tax exemptions, and tax allowances of 30% for investors. The AIA agreement formally entered into force in June 1999, having been ratified by all member countries. Under the agreement, member countries submitted individual action plans for 2000–04, noting specific action to be taken in the areas of investment promotion, facilitation and liberalization. In September 2001 ministers agreed to accelerate the full realization of the AIA for non-ASEAN investors in manufacturing, agriculture, forestry, fishing and mining sectors. The date for full implementation was advanced to 2010 for the original six ASEAN members and to 2015 for the newer members.

In November 2001 ASEAN heads of state considered the difficulties facing member countries as a result of the global economic and political uncertainties following the terrorist attacks on the USA in September. The summit meeting noted the recent decline in foreign direct investment and the erosion of the region's competitiveness. Short-term priorities were stated to be the stimulation of economies to lessen the impact of reduced external demand, and the adoption of appropriate fiscal and monetary policies, together with a renewed commitment to structural reform.

In April 2002 ASEAN economy ministers signed an agreement to facilitate intra-regional trade in electrical and electronic equipment by providing for the mutual recognition of standards (for example, testing and certification). The agreement was also intended to lower the costs of trade in those goods, thereby helping to maintain competitiveness.

SECURITY

In 1971 ASEAN members endorsed a declaration envisaging the establishment of a Zone of Peace, Freedom and Neutrality (ZOPFAN) in the South-East Asian region. This objective was incorporated in the Declaration of ASEAN Concord, which was adopted at the first summit meeting of the organization, held in Bali,

Indonesia, in February 1976. (The Declaration also issued guidelines for co-operation in economic development and the promotion of social justice and welfare.) Also in February 1976 a Treaty of Amity and Co-operation was signed by heads of state, establishing principles of mutual respect for the independence and sovereignty of all nations, non-interference in the internal affairs of one another and settlement of disputes by peaceful means. The Treaty was amended in December 1987 by a protocol providing for the accession of Papua New Guinea and other non-member countries in the region; it was reinforced by a second protocol, signed in July 1998.

In December 1995 ASEAN heads of government, meeting in Bangkok, signed a treaty establishing a South-East Asia Nuclear-Weapon Free Zone (SEANWFZ). The treaty was also signed by Cambodia, Myanmar and Laos. It was extended to cover the offshore economic exclusion zones of each country. On ratification by all parties, the Treaty was to prohibit the manufacture or storage of nuclear weapons within the region. Individual signatories were to decide whether to allow port visits or transportation of nuclear weapons by foreign powers through territorial waters. The Treaty entered into force on 27 March 1997. ASEAN senior officials were mandated to oversee implementation of the Treaty, pending the establishment of a permanent monitoring committee. In July 1999 the People's Republic of China and India agreed to observe the terms of the SEANWFZ.

In January 1992 ASEAN leaders agreed that there should be greater co-operation on security matters within the grouping, and that ASEAN's post-ministerial conferences (PMCs) should be used as a forum for discussion of questions relating to security with dialogue partners and other countries. In July 1992 the ASEAN Ministerial Meeting issued a statement calling for a peaceful resolution of the dispute concerning the strategically significant Spratly Islands in the South China Sea, which are claimed, wholly or partly, by the People's Republic of China, Viet Nam, Taiwan, Brunei, Malaysia and the Philippines. (In February China had introduced legislation that defined the Spratly Islands as belonging to its territorial waters.) Viet Nam's accession to ASEAN in July 1995, bringing all the Spratly Islands claimants except China and Taiwan into the grouping, was expected to strengthen ASEAN's position of negotiating a multilateral settlement on the islands. In mid-1999 ASEAN established a special committee to formulate a code of conduct for the South China Sea to be observed by all claimants to the Spratly Islands. Proposals under consideration were a ban on the building of all new structures, which had been the cause of escalating tensions in 1998, and a declaration rejecting the use of force to resolve disputes. A draft code of conduct was approved in November 1999. China, insisting that it would adopt the proposed code only as a set of guide-lines and not as a legally-binding document, resolved not to strengthen its presence on the islands. In 2000 and 2001 it participated in discussions with ASEAN officials concerning the document.

In July 1997 ASEAN ministers of foreign affairs reiterated their commitment to the principle of non-interference in the internal affairs of other countries. However, the group's efforts in Cambodia (see below) marked a significant shift in diplomatic policy towards one of 'constructive intervention', which had been proposed by Malaysia's Deputy Prime Minister in recognition of the increasing interdependence of the region. At the Ministerial Meeting in July 1998 Thailand's Minister of Foreign Affairs, supported by his Philippine counterpart, proposed that the grouping formally adopt a policy of 'flexible engagement'. The proposal, based partly on concerns that the continued restrictions imposed by the Myanma authorities on dissident political activists was damaging ASEAN relations with its dialogue partners, was to provide for the discussion of the affairs of other member states when they have an impact on neighbouring countries. While rejecting the proposal, other ASEAN ministers agreed to pursue a more limited version, referred to as 'enhanced interaction', and to maintain open dialogue within the grouping. In September 1999 the unrest prompted by the popular referendum on the future of East Timor and the resulting humanitarian crisis highlighted the unwillingness of some ASEAN member states to intervene in other member countries and undermined the political unity of the grouping. A compromise agreement, enabling countries to act on an individual basis rather than as representatives of ASEAN, was formulated prior to an emergency meeting of ministers of foreign affairs, held during the APEC meetings in Auckland, New Zealand. Malaysia, the Philippines, Singapore and Thailand declared their support for the establishment of a multinational force to restore peace in East Timor and committed troops to participate in the Australian-led operation. At their informal summit in November 1999 heads of state approved the establishment of an ASEAN Troika, which was to be constituted as an *ad hoc* body comprising the foreign ministers of the Association's current, previous and future chairmanship with a view to providing a rapid response mechanism in the event of a regional crisis.

On 12 September 2001 ASEAN issued a ministerial statement on international terrorism, condemning the attacks of the previous day in the USA and urging greater international co-operation to counter terrorism. The seventh summit meeting in November issued a Declaration on a Joint Action to Combat Terrorism. This condemned the September attacks, stated that terrorism was a direct challenge to ASEAN's aims, and affirmed the grouping's commitment to strong measures to counter terrorism. The summit encouraged member countries to sign (or ratify) the International Convention for the Suppression of Financing of Terrorism, to strengthen national mechanisms against terrorism, and to work to deepen co-operation, particularly in the area of intelligence exchange; international conventions to combat terrorism would be studied to see if they could be integrated into the ASEAN structure, while the possibility of developing a regional anti-terrorism convention was discussed. The summit noted the need to strengthen security co-operation to restore investor confidence. In its Declaration and other notes, the summit explicitly rejected any attempt to link terrorism with religion or race, and expressed concern for the sufferings of innocent Afghanis during the US military action against the Taliban authorities in Afghanistan. The summit's final Declaration was worded so as to avoid any mention of the US action, to which Muslim ASEAN states such as Malaysia and Indonesia were strongly opposed. Several ASEAN countries offered to assist in peace-keeping and reconstruction in Afghanistan, following the removal of the Taliban and establishment of an interim authority.

In June 1999 the first ministerial meeting to consider issues relating to transnational crime was convened. Regular meetings of senior officials and ministers were subsequently held. The third ministerial meeting, in October 2001, considered initiatives to combat transnational crime, which was defined as including terrorism, trafficking in drugs, arms and people, money-laundering, cyber-crime, piracy and economic crime. In May 2002 ministers responsible for transnational crime issues convened a Special Ministerial Meeting on Terrorism, held in Kuala Lumpur, Malaysia. The meeting approved a work programme to implement a plan of action to combat transitional crime, including information exchange, the development of legal arrangements for extradition, prosecution and seizure, the enhancement of co-operation in law enforcement, and the development of regional security training programmes. In a separate initiative Indonesia, Malaysia and the Philippines signed an agreement on information exchange and the establishment of communication procedures. Cambodia acceded to the agreement in July.

ASEAN Regional Forum—ARF: In July 1993 the meeting of ASEAN ministers of foreign affairs sanctioned the establishment of a forum to discuss and promote co-operation on security issues within the region, and, in particular, to ensure the involvement of the People's Republic of China in regional dialogue. The ARF was informally initiated during that year's PMC, comprising the ASEAN countries, its dialogue partners (at that time—Australia, Canada, the EC, Japan, the Republic of Korea, New Zealand and the USA), and the People's Republic of China, Laos, Papua New Guinea, Russia and Viet Nam. The first formal meeting of the ARF was conducted in July 1994, following the Ministerial Meeting held in Bangkok, Thailand, and it was agreed that the ARF would be convened on an annual basis. The 1995 meeting, held in Brunei, in August, attempted to define a framework for the future of the Forum. It was perceived as evolving through three stages: the promotion of confidence-building (including disaster relief and peace-keeping activities); the development of preventive diplomacy; and the elaboration of approaches to conflict. The 19 ministers of foreign affairs attending the meeting (Cambodia participated for the first time) recognized that the ARF was still in the initial stage of implementing confidence-building measures. The ministers, having conceded to a request by China not to discuss explicitly the Spratly Islands, expressed concern at overlapping sovereignty claims in the region. In a further statement, the ministers urged an 'immediate end' to the testing of nuclear weapons, then being undertaken by the French Government in the South Pacific region. The third ARF, convened in July 1996, which was attended for the first time by India and Myanmar, agreed a set of criteria and guiding principles for the future expansion of the grouping. In particular, it was decided that the ARF would only admit as participants countries that had a direct influence on the peace and security of the East Asia and Pacific region. The ARF held in July 1997 reviewed progress made in developing the first two 'tracks' of the ARF process, through the structure of inter-sessional working groups and meetings. The Forum's consideration of security issues in the region was dominated by concern at the political situation in Cambodia; support was expressed for ASEAN mediation to restore stability within that country. Myanmar and Laos attended the ARF for the first time. Mongolia was admitted into the ARF at its meeting in July 1998. India rejected a proposal that Pakistan attend the meeting to discuss issues relating to both countries' testing of nuclear weapons. The meeting ultimately condemned the testing of nuclear weapons in the region, but declined to criticize specifically India and Pakistan. In July 1999 the ARF warned the Democratic People's Republic of Korea (DPRK) not to conduct any further testing of missiles over the Pacific. At the seventh meeting of the ARF, convened in Bangkok, Thailand, in July 2000, the DPRK was admitted to the Forum. The meeting considered the positive effects and challenges of globalization, including the possibilities for greater economic interdependence and for a growth in transnational crime. The eighth ARF meeting in July 2001 in Hanoi, Viet Nam, pursued these themes, and also discussed the widening development gap between nations. The meeting agreed to enhance the role of the ARF Chairman, enabling him to issue statements on behalf of ARF participants and to organize events during the year. In March and April 2002 ARF workshops were held on financial measures against terrorism and on the prevention of terrorism, respectively. The ninth ARF meeting, held in Bandar Seri Begawan, Brunei, in July, assessed regional and international security developments, and issued a statement of individual and collective intent to prevent any financing of terrorism. The statement included commitments by participants to freeze the assets of suspected individuals or groups, to implement international financial standards and to enhance co-operation and the exchange of information. In October the Chairman, on behalf of all ARF participants, condemned the terrorist bomb attacks committed against tourist targets in Bali, Indonesia.

Since 2000 the ARF has published the *Annual Security Outlook*, to which participating countries submit assessments of the security prospects in the region.

EXTERNAL RELATIONS

ASEAN's external relations have been pursued through a dialogue system, initially with the objective of promoting co-operation in economic areas with key trading partners. The system has been expanded in recent years to encompass regional security concerns and co-operation in other areas, such as the environment. The ARF (see above) emerged from the dialogue system, and more recently the formalized discussions of ASEAN with Japan, China and the Republic of Korea (ASEAN + 3) has evolved as a separate process with its own strategic agenda.

European Union: In March 1980 a co-operation agreement was signed between ASEAN and the European Community (EC, as the EU was known prior to its restructuring on 1 November 1993), which provided for the strengthening of existing trade links and increased co-operation in the scientific and agricultural spheres. A Joint Co-operation Committee met in November (and annually thereafter). An ASEAN-EC Business Council was launched in December 1983, and three European Business Information Councils have since been established, in Malaysia, the Philippines and Thailand, to promote private-sector co-operation. The first meeting of ministers of economic affairs from ASEAN and EC member countries took place in October 1985. In December 1990 the Community adopted new guide-lines on development co-operation, with an increase in assistance to Asia, and a change in the type of aid given to ASEAN members, emphasizing training, science and technology and venture capital, rather than assistance for rural development. In October 1992 the EC and ASEAN agreed to promote further trade between the regions, as well as bilateral investment, and made a joint declaration in support of human rights. An EU-ASEAN Junior Managers Exchange Programme was initiated in November 1996, as part of efforts to promote co-operation and understanding between the industrial and business sectors in both regions. An ASEAN-EU Business Network was established in Brussels in 2001, to develop political and commercial contacts between the two sides.

In May 1995 ASEAN and EU senior officials endorsed an initiative to strengthen relations between the two economic regions within the framework of an Asia-Europe Meeting of heads of government (ASEM). The first ASEM was convened in Bangkok, Thailand, in March 1996, at which leaders approved a new Asia-Europe Partnership for Greater Growth (see EU, p. 1532). The second ASEM summit meeting, held in April 1998, focused heavily on economic concerns. In February 1997 ministers of foreign affairs of countries participating in ASEM met in Singapore. Despite ongoing differences regarding human rights issues, in particular concerning ASEAN's granting of full membership status to Myanmar and the situation in East Timor (which precluded the conclusion of a new co-operation agreement), the Ministerial Meeting issued a final joint declaration, committing both sides to strengthening co-operation and dialogue on economic, international and bilateral trade, security and social issues. A protocol to the 1980 co-operation agreement was signed, enabling the participation of Viet Nam in the dialogue process. In November 1997 a session of the Joint Co-operation Committee was postponed and later cancelled, owing to a dispute concerning objections by the EU to the participation of Myanmar. A compromise agreement, allowing Myanma officials to attend meetings as 'silent' observers, was concluded in November 1998. However, a meeting of the Joint Co-operation Committee, scheduled to take place in January 1999, was again cancelled, owing to controversy over perceived discrimination by the EU against Myanmar's status. The meeting was finally convened in Bangkok, Thailand, in late May. The third ASEM summit meeting was convened in Seoul, Korea in October 2000. In December an ASEAN-EU Ministerial Meeting was held in Vientiane, Laos. Both sides agreed to pursue dialogue and co-operation and issued a joint declaration that accorded support for the efforts of the UN Secretary-General's special envoy towards restoring political dialogue in Myanmar. Myanmar agreed to permit an EU delegation to visit the country, and opposition leaders, in early 2001. In September 2001 the Joint Co-operation Committee met for the first time since 1999 and resolved to strengthen policy dialogue, in particular in areas fostering regional integration. Four new EC delegations were to be established—in Cambodia, Laos, Myanmar and Singapore. The fourth ASEM summit meeting was held in September 2002, in Copenhagen, Denmark.

People's Republic of China: Efforts to develop consultative relations between ASEAN and China were initiated in 1993. Joint Committees on economic and trade co-operation and on scientific and technological co-operation were subsequently established. The first formal consultations between senior officials of the two sides were held in April 1995. In July 1996, in spite of ASEAN's continued concern at China's territorial claims to the Spratly Islands in the South China Sea, China was admitted to the PMC as a full dialogue partner. In February 1997 a Joint Co-operation Committee was established to co-ordinate the China-ASEAN dialogue and all aspects of relations between the two sides. Relations were further strengthened by the decision to form a joint business council to promote bilateral trade and investment. China participated in the informal summit meeting held in December, at the end of which both sides issued a joint statement affirming their commitment to resolving regional disputes through peaceful means. A second meeting of the Joint Co-operation Committee was held in March 1999. China was a participant in the first official ASEAN + 3 meeting of foreign ministers, which was convened in July 2000. An ASEAN-China Experts Group was established in November, to consider future economic co-operation and free trade opportunities. The Group held its first meeting in April 2001 and proposed a Framework on Economic Co-operation and the establishment of an ASEAN-China free-trade area within 10 years (with differential treatment and flexibility for newer ASEAN members). Both proposals were endorsed at the seventh ASEAN summit meeting in November 2001. China also agreed to grant preferential tariff treatment for some goods from Cambodia, Laos and Myanmar.

Japan: The ASEAN-Japan Forum was established in 1977 to discuss matters of mutual concern in trade, investment, technology transfer and development assistance. The first meeting between the two sides at ministerial level was held in October 1992. At this meeting, and subsequently, ASEAN requested Japan to increase its investment in member countries and to make Japanese markets more accessible to ASEAN products, in order to reduce the trade deficit with Japan. Since 1993 ASEAN-Japanese development and cultural co-operation has expanded under schemes including the Inter-ASEAN Technical Exchange Programme, the Japan-ASEAN Co-operation Promotion Programme and the ASEAN-Japan Friendship Programme. In December 1997 Japan, attending the informal summit meeting in Malaysia, agreed to improve market access for ASEAN products and to provide training opportunities for more than 20,000 young people in order to help develop local economies. In December 1998 ASEAN heads of government welcomed a Japanese initiative, announced in October, to allocate US $30,000m. to promote economic recovery in the region. At the same time the Japanese Prime Minister announced a further package of $5,000m. to be made available as concessionary loans for infrastructure projects. In mid-2000 a new Japan-ASEAN General Exchange Fund (JAGEF) was established to promote and facilitate the transfer of technology, investment and personnel. In November 1999 Japan, along with the People's Republic of China and the Republic of Korea, attending an informal summit meeting of ASEAN, agreed to strengthen economic and political co-operation with the ASEAN countries, to enhance political and security dialogue, and to implement joint infrastructure and social projects. Japan participated in the first official ASEAN + 3 meeting of foreign ministers, which was convened in July 2000. An ASEAN-Japan Experts Group, similar to that for China, was to be established to consider how economic relations between the two sides can be strengthened. In recent years Japan has provided information technology (IT) support to ASEAN countries, and has offered assistance in environmental and health matters and for educational training and human resource development (particularly in engineering).

Australia and New Zealand: In 1999 ASEAN and Australia undertook to development the ASEAN-Australia Development Co-operation Programme (AADCP), to replace an economic co-operation programme which had begun in 1974. In August 2002 the two sides signed a formal memorandum of understanding on the AADCP. It was to comprise three core elements, with assistance amounting to $A45m.: a Program Stream, to address medium-term issues of economic integration and competitiveness; a Regional Partnerships Scheme for smaller collaborative activities; and the establishment of a Regional Economic Policy Support Facility within the ASEAN Secretariat. All components were to be fully operational by 2003. Co-operation relations with New Zealand are based on the Inter-Institutional Linkages Programme and the Trade and Investment Promotion Programme, which mainly provide assistance in forestry development, dairy technology, veterinary management and legal aid training. An ASEAN-New Zealand Joint Management Committee was established in November 1993, to oversee the implementation of co-operation projects. New Zealand's English Language Training for Officials Programme is among the most important of these projects. In September 2001 ASEAN ministers of economic affairs signed a Framework for Closer Economic Partnership (CEP) with their counterparts from Australia and New Zealand (the Closer Economic Relations—CER—countries), and agreed to establish a Business Council to involve the business communities of all countries in the CEP. The CEP was perceived as a first step towards the creation of a free-trade area between ASEAN and CER countries. The establishment of such an area would strengthen the grouping's bargaining position regionally and multilaterally, and bring benefits such as increased foreign direct investment and the possible relocation of industry.

Other countries: The USA gives assistance for the development of small and medium-sized businesses and other projects, and supports a Center for Technology Exchange. In 1990 ASEAN and the USA established an ASEAN-US Joint Working Group, whose purpose is to review ASEAN's economic relations with the USA and to identify measures by which economic links could be strengthened. In recent years, dialogue has increasingly focused on political and security issues. In early August 2002 ASEAN ministers of foreign affairs met with their US counterpart, and signed a Joint Declaration for Co-operation to Combat International Terrorism. ASEAN-Canadian co-operation projects include fisheries technology, the telecommunications industry, use of solar energy, and a forest seed centre. A Working Group on the Revitalization of ASEAN-Canada relations met in February 1999. At a meeting in Bangkok in July 2000, the two sides agreed to explore less formal avenues for project implementation.

In July 1991 the Republic of Korea was accepted as a 'dialogue partner' in ASEAN, and in December a joint ASEAN-Korea Chamber of Commerce was established. In 1995 co-operation projects on human resources development, science and technology, agricultural development and trade and investment policies were implemented. The Republic of Korea participated in ASEAN's informal summit meetings in December 1997 and November 1999 (see above), and took part in the first official ASEAN + 3 meeting of foreign ministers, convened in July 2000. The Republic's assistance in the field of information technology (IT) has become particularly valuable in recent years. In March 2001, in a sign of developing co-operation, ASEAN and the Republic of Korea exchanged views on political and security issues in the region for the first time. The ASEAN-Korea Work Programme for 2001–03 covers, among other areas, the environment, transport, science and technology and cultural sectors.

In July 1993 both India and Pakistan were accepted as sectoral partners, providing for their participation in ASEAN meetings in sectors such as trade, transport and communications and tourism. An ASEAN-India Business Council was established, and met for the first time, in New Delhi, in February 1995. In December 1995 the ASEAN summit meeting agreed to enhance India's status to that of a full dialogue partner; India was formally admitted to the PMC in July 1996. At a meeting of the ASEAN-India Working Group in March 2001 the two sides agreed to pursue co-operation in new areas, such as health and pharmaceuticals, social security and rural development. The fourth meeting of the ASEAN-India Joint Co-operation Committee in January 2002 agreed to strengthen co-operation in these areas and others, including technology. The first ASEAN-India meeting at the level of heads of state was scheduled to be held in November. An ASEAN-Pakistan Joint Business Council met for the first time in February 2000. In early 2001 both sides agreed to co-operate in projects relating to new and renewable energy resources, IT, agricultural research and transport and communications.

In March 2000 the first ASEAN-Russia business forum opened in Kuala Lumpur, Malaysia.

Indo-China: In July 1992 Viet Nam and Laos signed ASEAN's Treaty on Amity and Co-operation and subsequently participated in ASEAN meetings and committees as observers. Viet Nam was admitted as a full member of ASEAN in July 1995. In that month Myanmar signed ASEAN's Treaty on Amity and Co-operation. In July 1996 ASEAN granted Myanmar observer status and admitted it to the ARF, despite the expression of strong reservations by (among others) the Governments of Australia, Canada and the USA owing to the human rights situation in Myanmar. In November ASEAN heads of government, attending an informal summit meeting in Jakarta, Indonesia, agreed to admit Myanmar as a full member of the grouping at the same time as Cambodia and Laos. While Cambodia's membership was postponed, Laos and Myanmar were admitted to ASEAN in July 1997.

Cambodia was accorded observer status in July 1995. In May 1997 ASEAN ministers of foreign affairs confirmed that Cambodia, together with Laos and Myanmar, was to be admitted to the grouping in July of that year. In mid-July, however, Cambodia's membership was postponed owing to the deposition of Prince Ranariddh, and the resulting civil unrest. Later in that month Cambodia's *de facto* leader, Second Prime Minister Hun Sen, agreed to ASEAN's pursuit of a mediation role in restoring stability in the country and in preparing for democratic elections. In early August the ministers of foreign affairs of Indonesia, the Philippines and Thailand, representing ASEAN, met Hun Sen to confirm these objectives. A team of ASEAN observers joined an international monitoring mission to supervise the election held in Cambodia in July 1998. International approval of the conduct of the election, and consequently of Hun Sen's victory, prompted ASEAN to agree to reconsider Cambodia's admission into the Association. In December, following the establishment of a coalition administration in Cambodia, the country was welcomed, by the Vietnamese Government, as the 10th member of ASEAN, despite an earlier meeting of ministers of foreign affairs failing to reach a consensus decision. Its formal admission took place on 30 April 1999.

In June 1996 ministers of ASEAN countries, and of the People's Republic of China, Cambodia, Laos and Myanmar adopted a framework for ASEAN-Mekong Basin Development Co-operation. The initiative aimed to strengthen the region's cohesiveness, with greater co-operation on issues such as drugs-trafficking, labour migration and terrorism, and to facilitate the process of future expansion of ASEAN. Groups of experts and senior officials were to be convened to consider funding issues and proposals to link the two regions, including a gas pipeline network, rail links and the establishment of a common time zone. In December 1996 the working group on rail links appointed a team of consultants to conduct a feasibility study of the proposals. The completed study was presented at the second ministerial conference on ASEAN-Mekong Basin Development Co-operation, convened in Hanoi, Viet Nam, in July 2000. At the November 2001 summit China pledged US $5m. to assist with navigation along the upper stretches of the Mekong River, while other means by which China could increase its investment in the Mekong Basin area were considered. At the meeting the Republic of Korea was invited to become a core member of the grouping. Other growth regions sponsored by ASEAN include the Brunei, Indonesia, Malaysia, Philippines, East ASEAN Growth Area (BIMP-EAGA), the Indonesia, Malaysia, Singapore Growth Triangle (IMS-GT), the Indonesia, Malaysia, Thailand Growth Triangle (IMT-GT), and the West-East Corridor within the Mekong Basin Development initiative.

AGRICULTURE, FISHERIES AND FORESTRY

In October 1983 a ministerial agreement on fisheries co-operation was concluded, providing for the joint management of fish resources, the sharing of technology, and co-operation in marketing. In July 1994 a Conference on Fisheries Management and Development Strategies in the ASEAN region resolved to enhance fish production through the introduction of new technologies, aquaculture development, improvements of product quality and greater involvement by the private sector.

Co-operation in forestry is focused on joint projects, funded by ASEAN's dialogue partners, which include a Forest Tree Seed Centre, an Institute of Forest Management and the ASEAN Timber Technology Centre. In April 1995 representatives of the ASEAN Secretariat and private-sector groups met to co-ordinate the implementation of a scheme to promote the export of ASEAN agricultural and forestry products. In recent years ASEAN has urged member countries to take action to prevent illegal logging in order to prevent the further degradation of forest resources.

ASEAN holds an emergency rice reserve, amounting to 87,000 metric tons, as part of its efforts to ensure food security in the region. There is an established ASEAN programme of training and study exchanges for farm workers, agricultural experts and members of agricultural co-operatives. During 1998 ASEAN was particularly concerned with the impact of the region's economic crisis on the agricultural sector, and the possible effects of climatic change. In September ministers of agriculture and forestry, meeting in Hanoi, Viet Nam, endorsed a Strategic Plan of Action on ASEAN Co-operation in Food, Agriculture and Forestry for 1999–2004. The Plan focused on programmes and activities aimed at enhancing food security, the international competitiveness of ASEAN food, agriculture and forestry products, promoting the sustainable use and conservation of natural resources, encouraging greater involvement by the private sector in the food and agricultural industry, and strengthening joint approaches on international and regional issues. An ASEAN Task Force has been formed to harmonize regulations on agricultural products derived from biotechnology. In December 1998 heads of state resolved to establish an ASEAN Food Security Information Service to enhance the capacity of member states to forecast and manage food supplies. In 1999 agriculture ministers endorsed guide-lines on assessing risk from genetically modified organisms (GMOs) in agriculture, to ensure a common approach. In 2001 work was undertaken to increase public and professional awareness of GMO issues, through workshops and studies.

MINERALS AND ENERGY

The ASEAN Centre for Energy (ACE), based in Jakarta, Indonesia, provides an energy information network, promotes the establishment of interconnecting energy structures among ASEAN member countries, supports the development of renewable energy resources and encourages co-operation in energy efficiency and conservation. An ASEAN energy business forum is held annually and attended by representatives of the energy industry in the private and public sectors. Efforts to establish an ASEAN electricity grid were initiated in 1990. An ASEAN Interconnection Masterplan Study Working Group was established in April 2000 to formulate a study on the power grid. In November 1999 a Trans-ASEAN Gas Pipeline Task Force was established. In July 2002 ASEAN ministers of energy signed a Memorandum of Understanding to implement the pipeline project, involving seven interconnections. The meeting also approved initial plans for the implementation of the regional power grid initiative. ASEAN has forged partnerships with the EU and Japan in the field of energy, under the ASEAN Plan of Action for Energy Co-operation, running from 1999–2004.

A Framework of Co-operation in Minerals was adopted by an ASEAN working group of experts in August 1993. The group has also developed a programme of action for ASEAN co-operation in the development and utilization of industrial minerals, to promote the exploration and development of mineral resources, the transfer of mining technology and expertise, and the participation of the private sector in industrial mineral production. The programme of action is implemented by an ASEAN Regional Development Centre for Mineral Resources, which also conducts workshops and training programmes relating to the sector.

TRANSPORT AND COMMUNICATIONS

ASEAN aims to promote greater co-operation in the transport and communications sector, and in particular, to develop multi-modal transport; to harmonize road transport laws and regulations; to improve air space management; to develop ASEAN legislation for the carriage of dangerous goods and waste by land and sea; and to achieve interoperability and interconnectivity in telecommunications. The summit meeting of December 1998 agreed to work to develop a trans-ASEAN transportation network by 2000, comprising principal routes for the movement of goods and people. (The deadline for the full implementation of the agreement was subsequently moved to the end of 2000.) In September 1999 ASEAN ministers of transport and communications resolved to establish working groups to strengthen co-operation within the sector and adopted a programme of action for development of the sector in 1999–2004. By September 2001, under the action programme, a harmonized road route numbering system had been completed, a road safety implementation work plan agreed, and two pilot courses, on port management and traffic engineering and safety, had been adopted. A Framework Agreement on Facilitation of Goods in Transport entered into force in October 2000.

ASEAN is seeking to develop a Competitive Air Services Policy, possibly as a first step towards the creation of an ASEAN Open Skies Policy. In September 2000 a meeting of transport ministers agreed to embark on a study to formulate maritime shipping policy, to cover, *inter alia*, issues of transshipment, the competitiveness of ports, liberalization, and the integration of maritime shipping into the overall transport system. In October 2001 ministers approved the third package of commitments for the air and transport sectors under the ASEAN framework agreement on services (according to which member countries were to liberalize the selling and marketing of air and maritime transport services. The summit meeting held in November reaffirmed the large-scale Singapore–Kunming rail link as a priority transport project. Emphasis was also put on smaller-scale (and cheaper) projects in 2001.

In October 1999 an e-ASEAN initiative was launched, aiming to promote and co-ordinate electronic commerce and internet utilization. In November 2000 the informal meeting of ASEAN heads of government approved an e-ASEAN Framework Agreement to further the aims of the initiative. The Agreement incorporated commitments to develop and strengthen ASEAN's information infrastructure, in order to provide for universal and affordable access to communications services. Tariff reduction on IT products was to be accelerated, with the aim of eliminating all tariffs in the sector by 2010. In July 2001 ministers of foreign affairs discussed measures for the economic liberalization of IT products and for developing IT capabilities in poorer member countries. In the same month the first meeting of ASEAN ministers responsible for telecommunications was held, in Kuala Lumpur, Malaysia, during which a Ministerial Understanding on ASEAN co-operation in telecommunications and IT was signed. In September ASEAN ministers of economic affairs approved a list of information and communications technology (ICT) products eligible for the elimination of duties under the e-ASEAN Framework Agreement. This was to take place in three annual tranches, commencing in 2003 for the six original members of ASEAN and in 2008 for the newer member countries. During 2001 ASEAN continued to develop a reference framework for e-commerce legislation; it aimed to have e-commerce legislation in place in all member states by 2003. The second ASEAN telecommunications ministerial meeting was held in Manila, Philippines, in August 2002. The meeting issued a declaration incorporating commitments to exploit ASEAN's competitive position in the field of ICT and to fulfill the obligations of the e-ASEAN Framework Agreement. The ministers also resolved to enhance co-operation with China, Japan and Korea with regard to ICT.

SCIENCE AND TECHNOLOGY

ASEAN's Committee on Science and Technology (COST) supports co-operation in food science and technology, meteorology and geophysics, microelectronics and IT, biotechnology, non-conventional energy research, materials science and technology, space technology applications, science and technology infrastructure and resources development, and marine science. There is an ASEAN Science Fund, used to finance policy studies in science and technology and to support information exchange and dissemination.

The Hanoi Plan of Action, adopted in December 1998, envisaged a series of measures aimed at promoting development in the fields of science and technology, including the establishment of networks of science and technology centres of excellence and academic institutions, the creation of a technology scan mechanism, the promotion of public- and private-sector co-operation in scientific and technological (particularly IT) activities, and an increase in research on strategic technologies. In September 2001 the ASEAN Ministerial Meeting on Science and Technology, convened for its first meeting since 1998, approved a new framework for implementation of ASEAN's Plan of Action on Science and Technology during the period 2001–04. The Plan aimed to help less developed member countries become competitive in the sector and integrate into regional co-operation activities.

ENVIRONMENT

A ministerial meeting on the environment in April 1994 approved long-term objectives on environmental quality and standards for the ASEAN region, aiming to enhance joint action in addressing environmental concerns. At the same time, ministers adopted standards for air quality and river water to be achieved by all ASEAN member countries by 2010. In June 1995 ministers agreed to co-operate to counter the problems of transboundary pollution.

In December 1997 ASEAN heads of state endorsed a Regional Haze Action Plan to address the environmental problems resulting from forest fires, which had afflicted several countries in the region throughout that year. A Haze Technical Task Force undertook to implement the plan in 1998, with assistance from the UN Environment Programme. In March ministers of the environment requested international financial assistance to help mitigate the dangers of forest fires in Indonesia, which had suffered an estimated US $1,000m. in damage in 1997. Sub-regional fire-fighting arrangement working groups for Sumatra and Borneo were established in April 1998 and in May the Task Force organized a regional workshop to strengthen ASEAN capacity to prevent and alleviate the haze caused by the extensive fires. A pilot project of aerial surveillance of the areas in the region most at risk of forest fires was initiated in July. In December heads of government resolved to establish an ASEAN Regional Research and Training Centre for Land and Forest Fire Management by 2004. In March 2002 members of the workings groups on sub-regional fire-fighting arrangements for Sumatra and Borneo agreed to intensify early warning efforts and surveillance activities in order to reduce the risks of forest fires. In June ASEAN ministers of the environment signed an Agreement on Transboundary Haze Pollution, which was intended to provide a legal basis for the Regional Haze Action Plan. The Agreement required member countries to co-operate in the prevention and mitigation of haze pollution, for example, by responding to requests for information by other states and facilitating the transit of personnel and equipment in case of disaster. The Agreement also provided for the establishment of an ASEAN Co-ordination Centre for Transboundary Haze Pollution Control. An ASEAN Specialized Meteorological Centre (ASMC) based in Singapore, plays a primary role in long-range climatological forecasting, early detection and monitoring of fires and haze.

In April 2000 ministers adopted a Strategic Plan of Action on the Environment for 1999–2004. Activities under the Plan focus on issues of coastal and marine erosion, nature conservation and biodiversity, the implementation of multilateral environmental agreements, and forest fires and haze. Other ASEAN environmental objectives include the implementation of a water conservation programme and the formation and adoption of an ASEAN protocol on access to genetic resources. An ASEAN Regional Centre for Biodiversity Conservation (ARCBC) was established in February 1999. It held several workshops in 2000 and 2001, on issues including genetically modified organisms, access to genetic resources and data sharing. In May 2001 environment ministers launched the ASEAN Environment Education Action Plan (AEEAP), with the aim of making citizens 'environmentally literate', and willing and able to participate in sustainable regional development.

SOCIAL DEVELOPMENT

ASEAN concerns in social development include youth development, the role of women, health and nutrition, education, labour affairs and disaster management. In December 1993 ASEAN ministers responsible for social affairs adopted a Plan of Action for Children, which provided a framework for regional co-operation for the survival, protection and development of children in member countries. ASEAN supports efforts to combat drug abuse and illegal drugs-trafficking. It aims to promote education and drug-awareness campaigns throughout the region, and administers a project to strengthen the training of personnel involved in combating drug abuse. In October 1994 a meeting of ASEAN Senior Officials on Drug Matters approved a three-year plan of action on drug abuse, providing a framework for co-operation in four priority areas: preventive drug education; treatment and rehabilitation; law enforcement; and research. In July 1998 ASEAN ministers of foreign affairs signed a Joint Declaration for a Drug-Free ASEAN, which envisaged greater co-operation among member states, in particular in information exchange, educational resources and legal procedures, in order to eliminate the illicit production, processing and trafficking of narcotic substances by 2020. (This deadline was subsequently advanced to 2015.)

The seventh ASEAN summit meeting, held in November 2001, declared work on combating HIV and AIDS to be a priority. The second phase of a work programme to combat AIDS and provide help for sufferers was endorsed at the meeting. Heads of government expressed their readiness to commit the necessary resources for prevention and care, and to attempt to obtain access to cheaper drugs. More than 1.5m. people in South-East Asia were known to be infected with the HIV virus. An ASEAN task force on AIDS has been operational since March 1993.

In December 1998 ASEAN leaders approved a series of measures aimed at mitigating the social impact of the financial and economic crises that had affected many countries in the region. Plans of Action were formulated on issues of rural development and poverty eradication, while Social Safety Nets, which aimed to protect the most vulnerable members of society, were approved. The summit meeting emphasized the need to promote job generation as a key element of strategies for economic recovery and growth. The fourth meeting of ministers of social welfare in August 2001 noted the need for a holistic approach to social problems, integrating social and economic development. The summit meeting in November considered the widening development gap between ASEAN members and concluded that bridging this gap was a priority, particularly with respect to developing human resources and infrastructure and providing access to IT.

In January 1992 the ASEAN summit meeting resolved to establish an ASEAN University Network (AUN) to hasten the development of a regional identity. A draft AUN Charter and Agreement were adopted in 1995. The Network aims to strengthen co-operation within the grouping, develop academic and professional human resources and transmit information and knowledge. The 17 universities linked in the network carry out collaborative studies and research programmes. At the seventh ASEAN summit in November 2001 heads of government agreed to establish the first ASEAN University, in Malaysia.

TOURISM

National Tourist Organizations from ASEAN countries meet regularly to assist in co-ordinating the region's tourist industry, and a Tourism Forum is held annually to promote the sector. The first formal meeting of ASEAN ministers of tourism was held in January 1998, in Cebu, the Philippines. The meeting adopted a Plan of Action on ASEAN Co-operation in Tourism, which aimed to promote intra-ASEAN travel, greater investment in the sector, joint marketing of the region as a single tourist destination and environmentally sustainable tourism. In January 1999 the second meeting of ASEAN ministers of tourism agreed to appoint country co-ordinators to implement various initiatives, including the designation of 2002 as 'Visit ASEAN Millennium Year'; research to promote the region as a tourist destination in the 21st century, and to develop a cruise-ship industry; and the establishment of a network of ASEAN Tourism Training Centres to develop new skills and technologies in the tourism industry by 2001. The third meeting of tourism ministers, held in Bangkok, Thailand, in January 2000, agreed to reformulate the Visit ASEAN Millennium Year initiative as a long-term Visit ASEAN programme. This was formally launched in January 2001 at the fourth ministerial meeting. The first phase of the programme, implemented in 2001, promoted brand awareness through an intense marketing effort; the second phase, initiated at the fifth meeting of tourism ministers, held in Yogyakarta, Indonesia, in January 2002, was to direct campaigns towards end-consumers. Ministers urged member states to abolish all fiscal and non-fiscal travel barriers, to encourage tourism, including intra-ASEAN travel. A seminar on sustainable tourism was held in Malaysia in October 2001.

CULTURE AND INFORMATION

Regular workshops and festivals are held in visual and performing arts, youth music, radio, television and films, and print and interpersonal media. In addition, ASEAN administers a News Exchange and provides support for the training of editors, journalists and information officers. In 2000 ASEAN adopted new cultural strategies, with the aims of raising awareness of the grouping's objectives and achievements, both regionally and internationally. The strategies included: producing ASEAN cultural and historical educational materials; promoting cultural exchanges (especially for young people); and achieving greater exposure of ASEAN cultural activities and issues in the mass media. It was agreed to work towards the creation of an ASEAN Cultural Heritage Network, for use by professionals and the public, by 2002.

In July 1997 ASEAN ministers of foreign affairs endorsed the establishment of an ASEAN Foundation to promote awareness of the organization and greater participation in its activities; this was inaugurated in July 1998 and is based at the ASEAN secretariat building (www.aseanfoundation.org). The Foundation's work programme for 2000–03 has four major goals: promotion of awareness of ASEAN activities; reinforcement of ASEAN solidarity; promotion of development co-operation in poverty alleviation and related issues; and organizational development.

Publications

Annual Report.

AFTA Brochure.

ASEAN Investment Report (annually).

ASEAN State of the Environment Report (1st report: 1997; 2nd report: 2000).

ASEAN Update (6 a year).

Business ASEAN (6 a year).

Public Information Series, Briefing Papers, Documents Series, educational materials.

THE COMMONWEALTH

Address: Marlborough House, Pall Mall, London, SW1Y 5HX, United Kingdom.

Telephone: (20) 7839-3411; **fax:** (20) 7930-0827; **e-mail:** info@commonwealth.int; **internet:** www.thecommonwealth.org.

The Commonwealth is a voluntary association of 54 independent states (at September 2002), comprising more than one-quarter of the world's population. It includes the United Kingdom and most of its former dependencies, and former dependencies of Australia and New Zealand (themselves Commonwealth countries). All Commonwealth countries accept Queen Elizabeth II as the symbol of the free association of the independent member nations and as such the Head of the Commonwealth.

MEMBERS IN THE FAR EAST AND AUSTRALASIA

Australia	Maldives	Singapore
Bangladesh	Nauru	Solomon Islands
Brunei	New Zealand	Sri Lanka
Fiji*	Pakistan†	Tonga
India	Papua New Guinea	Tuvalu
Kiribati	Samoa	Vanuatu
Malaysia		

* In October 1987, following a military coup, the Constitution of Fiji was revoked, and Fiji's membership of the Commonwealth was subsequently declared to have lapsed by the meeting of Commonwealth Heads of Government. It was readmitted on 1 October 1997, but was suspended from participation in meetings of the Commonwealth in June 2000.

† Pakistan withdrew from the Commonwealth in 1972, and rejoined in October 1989. It was suspended from participation in meetings of the Commonwealth in October 1999.

DEPENDENCIES

Australia	New Zealand	United Kingdom
Christmas Island	Cook Islands	Pitcairn Islands
Cocos (Keeling) Islands	Niue	
Coral Sea Islands Territory	Tokelau	
Norfolk Island		

Organization

(October 2002)

The Commonwealth is not a federation: there is no central government nor are there any rigid contractual obligations such as bind members of the United Nations.

The Commonwealth has no written constitution but its members subscribe to the ideals of the Declaration of Commonwealth Principles unanimously approved by a meeting of heads of government in Singapore in 1971. Members also approved the 1977 statement on apartheid in sport (the Gleneagles Agreement); the 1979 Lusaka Declaration on Racism and Racial Prejudice; the 1981 Melbourne Declaration on relations between developed and developing countries; the 1983 New Delhi Statement on Economic Action; the 1983 Goa Declaration on International Security; the 1985 Nassau Declaration on World Order; the Commonwealth Accord on Southern Africa (1985); the 1987 Vancouver Declaration on World Trade; the Okanagan Statement and Programme of Action on Southern Africa (1987); the Langkawi Declaration on the Environment (1989); the Kuala Lumpur Statement on Southern Africa (1989); the Harare Commonwealth Declaration (1991); the Ottawa Declaration on Women and Structural Adjustment (1991); the Limassol Statement on the Uruguay Round of multilateral trade negotiations (1993); the Millbrook Commonwealth Action Programme on the Harare Declaration (1995); the Edinburgh Commonwealth Economic Declaration (1997); the Fancourt Commonwealth Declaration on Globalization and People-centred Development (1999); and the Coolum Declaration on the Commonwealth in the 21st Century: Continuity and Renewal (2002).

MEETINGS OF HEADS OF GOVERNMENT

Meetings are private and informal and operate not by voting but by consensus. The emphasis is on consultation and exchange of views for co-operation. A communiqué is issued at the end of every meeting. Meetings are normally held every two years in different capitals in the Commonwealth. The last meeting was held in Brisbane, Australia, in March 2002.

OTHER CONSULTATIONS

Meetings at ministerial and official level are also held regularly. Since 1959 finance ministers have met in a Commonwealth country in the week prior to the annual meetings of the IMF and the World Bank. Meetings on education, legal, women's and youth affairs are held at ministerial level every three years. Ministers of health hold annual meetings, with major meetings every three years, and ministers of agriculture meet every two years. Ministers of trade, labour and employment, industry, science and the environment also hold periodic meetings.

Senior officials—cabinet secretaries, permanent secretaries to heads of government and others—meet regularly in the year between meetings of heads of government to provide continuity and to exchange views on various developments.

COMMONWEALTH SECRETARIAT

The Secretariat, established by Commonwealth heads of government in 1965, operates as an international organization at the service of all Commonwealth countries. It organizes consultations between governments and runs programmes of co-operation. Meetings of heads of government, ministers and senior officials decide these programmes and provide overall direction.

The Secretariat is headed by a secretary-general (elected by heads of government), assisted by three deputy secretaries-general. One deputy is responsible for political affairs, one for economic and social affairs, and one for development co-operation (including the Commonwealth Fund for Technical Co-operation—see below). The Secretariat comprises 12 Divisions in the fields of political affairs; legal and constitutional affairs; information and public affairs; administration; economic affairs; human resource development; gender and youth affairs; science and technology; economic and legal advisory services; export and industrial development; management and training services; and general technical assistance services. It also includes a non-governmental organizations desk, a unit for strategic planning and evaluation, and a human rights unit.

In 2000 the Secretariat adopted the following as its guiding mission: working for all people of the Commonwealth as a force for democracy and good governance, as a platform for global consensus-building, and as a source of practical assistance for sustainable development.

Secretary-General: DONALD (DON) C. MCKINNON (New Zealand).

Deputy Secretary-General (Political): FLORENCE MUGASHA (Uganda).

Deputy Secretary-General (Economic and Social): (vacant).

Deputy Secretary-General (Development Co-operation): WINSTON A. COX (Barbados).

Activities

INTERNATIONAL AFFAIRS

In October 1991 heads of government, meeting in Harare, Zimbabwe, issued the Harare Commonwealth Declaration, in which they reaffirmed their commitment to the Commonwealth Principles declared in 1971, and stressed the need to promote sustainable development and the alleviation of poverty. The Declaration placed emphasis on the promotion of democracy and respect for human rights and resolved to strengthen the Commonwealth's capacity to assist countries in entrenching democratic practices. The meeting also welcomed the political reforms introduced by the South African Government to end the system of apartheid and urged all South African political parties to commence negotiations on a new constitution as soon as possible. The meeting endorsed measures on the phased removal of punitive measures against South Africa. In December a group of six eminent Commonwealth citizens was dispatched to observe multi-party negotiations on the future of South Africa and to assist the process where possible. In October 1992, in a fresh attempt to assist the South African peace process, a Commonwealth team of 18 observers was sent to monitor political violence in the country. A second phase of the Commonwealth Mission to South Africa (COMSA) began in February 1993. COMSA issued a report in May in which it urged a concerted effort to build a culture of political tolerance in South Africa. In a report on its third phase, issued in December, COMSA appealed strongly to all political parties to participate in the transitional arrangements leading to democratic elections. In October the Commonwealth heads of government, meeting in Limassol, Cyprus, agreed that a democratic and non-racial South Africa would be invited to join the organization. They endorsed the removal of all economic sanctions against South Africa, but agreed to retain the arms embargo until a post-apartheid, democratic government had been established.

In November 1995 Commonwealth heads of government, convened in New Zealand, formulated and adopted the Millbrook Commonwealth Action Programme on the Harare Declaration, to promote adherence by member countries to the fundamental principles of democracy and human rights (as proclaimed in the 1991 Declaration). The Programme incorporated a framework of measures to be pursued in support of democratic processes and institutions, and actions to be taken in response to violations of the Harare Declaration principles, in particular the unlawful removal of a democratically-elected government. A Commonwealth Ministerial Action Group on the Harare Declaration (CMAG) was to be established to implement this process and to assist the member country involved to comply with the Harare principles. On the basis of this Programme, the leaders suspended Nigeria from the Commonwealth with immediate effect, following the execution by that country's military Government of nine environmental and human rights protesters and a series of other violations of human rights. The meeting determined to expel Nigeria from the Commonwealth if no 'demonstrable progress' had been made towards the establishment of a democratic authority by the time of the next summit meeting. In addition, the Programme formulated measures to promote sustainable development in member countries, which was considered to be an important element in sustaining democracy, and to facilitate consensus-building within the international community. Earlier in the meeting a statement was issued declaring the 'overwhelming majority' of Commonwealth governments to be opposed to nuclear-testing programmes being undertaken in the South Pacific region. However, in view of events in Nigeria, the issue of nuclear testing and disagreement among member countries did not assume the significance anticipated.

In December 1995 CMAG convened for its inaugural meeting in London. The Group, comprising the ministers of foreign affairs of Canada, Ghana, Jamaica, Malaysia, New Zealand, South Africa, the United Kingdom and Zimbabwe (with membership to be reconstituted periodically), commenced by considering efforts to restore democratic government in the three Commonwealth countries then under military regimes, i.e. The Gambia, Nigeria and Sierra Leone. At the second meeting of the Group, in April 1996, ministers commended the conduct of presidential and parliamentary elections in Sierra Leone and the announcement by The Gambia's military leaders to proceed with a transition to civilian rule. In June a three-member CMAG delegation visited The Gambia to reaffirm Commonwealth support of the transition process in that country and to identify possible areas of further Commonwealth assistance. In August the Gambian authorities issued a decree removing the ban on political activities and parties, although shortly afterwards they prohibited certain parties and candidates involved in political life prior to the military take-over from contesting the elections. CMAG recommended that in such circumstances no Commonwealth observers should be sent to either the presidential or parliamentary elections, which were held in September 1996 and January 1997 respectively. Following the restoration of a civilian Government in early 1997, CMAG requested the Commonwealth Secretary-General to extend technical assistance to The Gambia in order to consolidate the democratic transition process. In April 1996 it was noted that the human rights situation in Nigeria had continued to deteriorate. CMAG, having pursued unsuccessful efforts to initiate dialogue with the Nigerian authorities, outlined a series of punitive and restrictive measures (including visa restrictions on members of the administration, a cessation of sporting contacts and an embargo on the export of armaments) that it would recommend for collective Commonwealth action in order to exert further pressure for reform in Nigeria. Following a meeting of a high-level delegation of the Nigerian Government and CMAG in June, the Group agreed to postpone the implementation of the sanctions, pending progress on the dialogue. (Canada, however, determined, unilaterally, to impose the measures with immediate effect; the United Kingdom did so in accordance with a decision of the European Union to implement limited sanctions against Nigeria.) A proposed CMAG mission to Nigeria was postponed in August, owing to restrictions imposed by the military authorities on access to political detainees and other civilian activists in that country. In September the Group agreed to proceed with the visit and to delay further a decision on the implementation of sanction measures. CMAG, without the participation of the representative of the Canadian Government, undertook its ministerial mission in November. In July 1997 the Group reiterated the Commonwealth Secretary-General's condemnation of a military coup in Sierra Leone in May, and decided that the country's participation in meetings of the Commonwealth should be suspended pending the restoration of a democratic government.

In October 1997 Commonwealth heads of government, meeting in Edinburgh, the United Kingdom, endorsed CMAG's recommendation that the imposition of sanctions against Nigeria be held in abeyance pending the scheduled completion of a transition programme towards democracy by October 1998. It was also agreed that CMAG be formally constituted as a permanent organ to investigate abuses of human rights throughout the Commonwealth. Jamaica and South Africa were to be replaced as members of CMAG by Barbados and Botswana, respectively.

In March 1998 CMAG, at its ninth meeting, commended the efforts of ECOWAS in restoring the democratically-elected Government of President Ahmed Tejan Kabbah in Sierra Leone, and agreed to remove all restrictions on Sierra Leone's participation in Commonwealth activities. Later in that month, a representative mission of CMAG visited Sierra Leone to express its support for Kabbah's administration and to consider the country's needs in its process of reconstruction. At the CMAG meeting held in October members agreed that Sierra Leone should no longer be considered under the Group's mandate; however, they urged the Secretary-General to continue to assist that country in the process of national reconciliation and to facilitate negotiations with opposition forces to ensure a lasting cease-fire. A Special Envoy of the Secretary-General was appointed to co-operate with the UN, ECOWAS and the OAU (now African Union—AU) in monitoring the implementation of the Sierra Leone peace process, and the Commonwealth has supported the rebuilding of the Sierra Leone police force. In September 2001 CMAG recommended that Sierra Leone be removed from its remit, but that the Secretary-General should continue to monitor developments there.

In April 1998 the Nigerian military leader, Gen. Sani Abacha, confirmed his intention to conduct a presidential election in August, but indicated that, following an agreement with other political organizations, he was to be the sole candidate. In June, however, Abacha died suddenly. His successor, Gen. Abdulsalam Abubakar, immediately released several prominent political prisoners, and in early July agreed to meet with the Secretaries-General of the UN and the Commonwealth to discuss the release of the imprisoned opposition leader, Chief Moshood Abiola. Abubakar also confirmed his intention to abide by the programme for transition to civilian rule by October. In mid-July, however, shortly before he was to have been liberated, Abiola died. The Commonwealth Secretary-General subsequently endorsed a new transition programme, which provided for the election of a civilian leader in May 1999. In October 1998 CMAG, convened for its 10th formal meeting, acknowledged Abubakar's efforts towards restoring a democratic government and recommended that member states begin to remove sanctions against Nigeria and that it resume participation in certain Commonwealth activities. The Commonwealth Secretary-General subsequently announced a programme of technical assistance to support Nigeria in the planning and conduct of democratic elections. Staff teams from the Commonwealth Secretariat observed local government, and state and governorship elections, held in December and in January 1999, respectively. A Commonwealth Observer Group was also dispatched to Nigeria to monitor preparations and conduct of legislative and presidential elections, held in February. While the Group reported several irregularities in the conduct of the polling, it confirmed that, in general, the conditions had existed for free and fair elections and that the elections were a legitimate basis for the transition of power to a democratic, civilian government. In April CMAG voted to readmit Nigeria to full membership on 29 May, upon the installation of the new civilian administration.

In 1999 the Commonwealth Secretary-General appointed a Special Envoy to broker an agreement in order to end a civil dispute in Honiara, Solomon Islands. An accord was signed in late June, and it was envisaged that the Commonwealth would monitor its implementation. In October a Commonwealth Multinational Police Peace Monitoring Group was stationed in Solomon Islands; this was renamed the Commonwealth Multinational Police Assistance Group in February 2000. Following further internal unrest, however, the Group was disbanded. In June CMAG determined to send a new mission to Solomon Islands in order to facilitate negotiations between the opposing parties, to convey the Commonwealth's concern and to offer assistance. The Commonwealth welcomed the peace accord concluded in Solomon Islands in October, and extended its support to the International Peace Monitoring Team which was established to oversee implementation of the peace accords. CMAG welcomed the conduct of parliamentary elections held in Solomon Islands in December 2001.

In June 1999 an agreement was concluded between opposing political groups in Zanzibar, having been facilitated by the good offices of the Secretary-General; however, this was only partially implemented. In mid-October a special meeting of CMAG was convened to consider the overthrow of the democratically-elected Government in Pakistan in a military coup. The meeting condemned the action as a violation of Commonwealth principles and urged the new authorities to declare a timetable for the return to democratic rule. CMAG also resolved to send a four-member delegation, comprising the ministers of foreign affairs of Barbados, Canada, Ghana and Malaysia, to discuss this future course of action with the military regime. Pakistan was suspended from participation in meetings of the Commonwealth with immediate effect. The suspension, pending the restoration of a democratic government, was endorsed by heads of government, meeting in November, who requested that CMAG keep the situation in Pakistan under review. (A Commonwealth team of observers was to monitor provincial and legislative elections scheduled to be held in Pakistan in October 2002.) At the meeting, held in Durban, South Africa, CMAG was reconstituted to comprise the ministers of foreign affairs of Australia, Bangladesh, Barbados, Botswana, Canada, Malaysia, Nigeria and the United Kingdom. It was agreed that no country would serve for more than two consecutive two-year terms. CMAG was requested to remain actively involved in the post-conflict development and rehabilitation of Sierra Leone and the process of consolidating peace. In addition, it was urged to monitor persistent violations of the Harare Declaration principles in all countries. Heads of government also agreed to establish a new ministerial group on Guyana and to reconvene a ministerial committee on Belize, in order to facilitate dialogue in ongoing territorial disputes with neighbouring countries. The meeting established a 10-member Commonwealth High Level Review Group to evaluate the role and activities of the Commonwealth. In 2000 the Group initiated a programme of consultations to proceed with its mandate and established a working group of experts to consider the Commonwealth's role in supporting information technology capabilities in member countries.

In June 2000, following the overthrow in May of the Fijian Government by a group of armed civilians, and the subsequent illegal detention of members of the elected administration, CMAG suspended Fiji's participation in meetings of the Commonwealth pending the restoration of democratic rule. In September, upon the request of CMAG, the Secretary-General appointed a Special Envoy to support efforts towards political dialogue and a return to democratic rule in Fiji. The Special Envoy under took his first visit in December. In December 2001, following the staging of democratic legislative elections in August/September, Fiji was readmitted to Commonwealth meetings on the recommendation of CMAG.

In March 2001 CMAG resolved to send a ministerial mission to Zimbabwe, in order to relay to the government the Commonwealth's concerns at the ongoing violence and abuses of human rights in that country, as well as to discuss the conduct of parliamentary elections and extend technical assistance. The mission was rejected by the Zimbabwe Government, which queried the basis for CMAG's intervention in the affairs of an elected administration. In September, under the auspices of a group of Commonwealth foreign ministers partly derived from CMAG, the Zimbabwe Government signed the Abuja Agreement, which provided for the cessation of illegal occupations of white-owned farms and the resumption of the rule of law, in return for financial assistance to support the ongoing process of land reform in that country. In January 2002 CMAG expressed strong concern at the continuing violence and political intimidation in Zimbabwe. Commonwealth observers arrived in Zimbabwe from early February to monitor the presidential election scheduled to be held there during March. The summit of Commonwealth heads of government convened in early March (see below) also expressed concern at the situation in Zimbabwe, and, having decided on the principle that CMAG should be permitted to engage with any member Government deemed to be in breach of the organization's core values, mandated a Commonwealth Chairperson's Committee on Zimbabwe to determine appropriate action should the forthcoming presidential election be found not to have been conducted freely and fairly. Following the publication by the observer team of an unfavourable report on the conduct of the election, the Committee decided to suspend Zimbabwe from meetings of the Commonwealth for one year.

In September 2001 it was announced that the next meeting of Commonwealth heads of government, originally scheduled to be held in early October, in Brisbane, Australia, would be postponed in view of the international political crisis that followed major terrorist attacks perpetrated against targets in the USA in early September. The meeting was eventually convened in March 2002, in Brisbane. It adopted the Coolum Declaration on the Commonwealth in the 21st Century: Continuity and Renewal, which reiterated commitment to the organization's principles and values. Leaders at the meeting condemned all forms of terrorism; welcomed the Millennium Goals of the UN General Assembly; called on the Secretary-General to constitute a high-level expert group on implementing the objectives of the Fancourt Declaration; pledged continued support for small states; and urged renewed efforts to combat the spread of HIV/AIDS. The meeting adopted a report on the future of the Commonwealth drafted by the High Level Review Group. The document recommended strengthening the Commonwealth's role in conflict prevention and resolution and support of democratic practices; enhancing the good offices role of the Secretary-General; better promoting member states' economic and development needs; strengthening the organization's role in facilitating member states' access to international assistance; and promoting increased access to modern information and communications technologies. The meeting expanded CMAG's mandate to enable the Group to consider action against serious violations of the Commonwealth's core values perpetrated by elected administrations (such as that in Zimbabwe, see above) as well as by military regimes. A the summit CMAG was reconstituted to comprise the ministers of foreign affairs of Australia, the Bahamas, Bangladesh, Botswana, India, Malta, Nigeria and Samoa.

Political Affairs Division: assists consultation among member governments on international and Commonwealth matters of common interest. In association with host governments, it organizes the meetings of heads of government and senior officials. The Division services committees and special groups set up by heads of government dealing with political matters. The Secretariat has observer status at the United Nations, and the Division manages a joint office in New York to enable small states, which would otherwise be unable to afford facilities there, to maintain a presence at the United Nations. The Division monitors political developments in the Commonwealth and international progress in such matters as disarmament, the concerns of small states, dismantling of apartheid and the Law of the Sea. It also undertakes research on matters of common interest to member governments, and reports back to them. The Division is involved in diplomatic training and consular co-operation.

In 1990 Commonwealth heads of government mandated the Division to support the promotion of democracy by monitoring the preparations for and conduct of parliamentary, presidential or other elections in member countries at the request of national governments. By the end of 2000 the Commonwealth had dispatched more than 30 electoral missions in accordance with this mandate.

A new expert group on good governance and the elimination of corruption in economic management convened for its first meeting in May 1998. In November 1999 Commonwealth heads of government endorsed a Framework for Principles for Promoting Good Governance and Combating Corruption, which had been drafted by the group.

LAW

Legal and Constitutional Affairs Division: promotes and facilitates co-operation and the exchange of information among member governments on legal matters. It administers, jointly with the Commonwealth of Learning, a distance training programme for legislative draftsmen and assists governments to reform national laws to meet the obligations of international conventions. The Division organizes the triennial meeting of ministers, Attorneys General and senior ministry officials concerned with the legal systems in Commonwealth countries. It has also initiated four Commonwealth schemes for co-operation on extradition, the protection of material cultural heritage, mutual assistance in criminal matters and the transfer of convicted offenders within the Commonwealth. It liaises with the Commonwealth Magistrates' and Judges' Association, the Commonwealth Legal Education Association, the Commonwealth Lawyers' Association (with which it helps to prepare the triennial Commonwealth Law Conference for the practising profession), the Commonwealth Association of Legislative Counsel, and with other international non-governmental organizations. The Division provides in-house legal advice for the Secretariat. The quarterly *Commonwealth Law Bulletin* reports on legal developments in and beyond the Commonwealth.

The Division's Commercial Crime Unit assists member countries to combat financial and organized crime, in particular transborder criminal activities, and promotes the exchange of information regarding national and international efforts to combat serious commercial crime through a quarterly publication, *Commonwealth Legal Assistance News,* and the *Crimewatch* bulletin.

ECONOMIC CO-OPERATION

In October 1997 Commonwealth heads of government, meeting in Edinburgh, the United Kingdom, signed an Economic Declaration that focused on issues relating to global trade, investment and development and committed all member countries to free-market economic principles. The Declaration also incorporated a provision for the establishment of a Trade and Investment Access Facility within the Secretariat in order to assist developing member states in the process of international trade liberalization and promote intra-Commonwealth trade.

In May 1998 the Commonwealth Secretary-General appealed to the Group of Eight industrialized nations to accelerate and expand the initiative to ease the debt burden of the most heavily indebted poor countries (HIPCs) (see World Bank and IMF). In October Commonwealth finance ministers, convened in Ottawa, Canada, reiterated their appeal to international financial institutions to accelerate the HIPC initiative. The meeting also issued a Commonwealth Statement on the global economic crisis and endorsed several proposals to help to counter the difficulties experienced by several countries. These measures included a mechanism to enable countries to suspend payments on all short-term financial obligations at a time of emergency without defaulting, assistance to governments to attract private capital and to manage capital market volatility, and the development of international codes of conduct regarding financial and monetary policies and corporate governance. In March 1999 the Commonwealth Secretariat hosted a joint IMF-World Bank conference to review the HIPC scheme and initiate a process of reform. In November Commonwealth heads of government, meeting in South Africa, declared their support for measures undertaken by the World Bank and IMF to enhance the HIPC initiative. At the end of an informal retreat the leaders adopted the Fancourt Commonwealth Declaration on Globalization and People-Centred Development, which emphasized the need for a more equitable spread of wealth generated by the process of globalization, and expressed a renewed commitment to the elimination of all forms of discrimination, the promotion of people-centred development and capacity-building, and efforts to ensure developing countries benefit from future multilateral trade liberalization measures. In June 2002 the Commonwealth Secretary-General urged more generous funding of the HIPC initiative.

In February 1998 the Commonwealth Secretariat hosted the first Inter-Governmental Organizations Meeting to promote co-operation between small island states and the formulation of a unified policy approach to international fora. A second meeting was convened in March 2001, where discussions focused on the forthcoming WTO ministerial meeting and the OECD's harmful tax competition initiative. In September 2000 Commonwealth finance ministers, meeting in Malta, reviewed the OECD initiative and agreed that the measures, affecting many member countries with offshore financial centres, should not be imposed on governments. The ministers mandated the involvement of the Commonwealth Secretariat in efforts to resolve the dispute; a joint working group was subsequently established by the Secretariat with the OECD. In April 2002 a meeting on international co-operation in the financial services sector, attended by representatives of international and regional organizations, donors and senior officials from Commonwealth countries, was held under Commonwealth auspices in Saint Lucia.

The first meeting of governors of central banks from Commonwealth countries was held in June 2001 in London, United Kingdom.

Economic Affairs Division: organizes and services the annual meetings of Commonwealth ministers of finance and the ministerial group on small states and assists in servicing the biennial meetings of heads of government and periodic meetings of environment ministers. It engages in research and analysis on economic issues of interest to member governments and organizes seminars and conferences of government officials and experts. The Division undertook a major programme of technical assistance to enable developing Commonwealth countries to participate in the Uruguay Round of multilateral trade negotiations and has assisted the African, Caribbean and Pacific (ACP) group of countries in their trade negotiations with the European Union. It continues to help developing countries to strengthen their links with international capital markets and foreign investors. The Division also services groups of experts on economic affairs that have been commissioned by governments to report on, among other things, protectionism; obstacles to the North-South negotiating process; reform of the international financial and trading system; the debt crisis; management of technological change; the special needs of small states; the impact of change on the development process; environmental issues; women and structural adjustment; and youth unemployment. A Commonwealth Secretariat Debt Recording and Management System has been developed by the Economic and Legal Advisory Services Division, which operates the system for the benefit of member countries and concerned organizations. The Economic Affairs Division co-ordinates the Secretariat's environmental work and manages the Iwokrama International Centre for Rainforest Conservation and Development.

The Division played a catalytic role in the establishment of a Commonwealth Equity Fund, initiated in September 1990, to allow developing member countries to improve their access to private institutional investment, and promoted a Caribbean Investment Fund. The Division supported the establishment of a Commonwealth Private Investment Initiative (CPII) to mobilize capital, on a regional basis, for investment in newly-privatized companies and in small and medium-sized businesses in the private sector. The first regional fund under the CPII was launched in July 1996. The Commonwealth Africa Investment Fund (Comafin), was to be managed by the United Kingdom's official development institution, the Commonwealth Development Corporation, to assist businesses in 19 countries in sub-Saharan Africa, with initial resources of US $63.5m. In August 1997 a fund for the Pacific Islands was launched, with an initial capital of $15.0m. A $200m. South Asia Regional Fund was established at the Heads of Government Meeting in October. In October 1998 a fund for the Caribbean states was inaugurated, at a meeting of Commonwealth finance ministers. The 2001 summit of Commonwealth heads of government authorized the establishment of a new fund for Africa: this was inaugurated in March 2002, and was expected to attract capital in excess of $200m.

HUMAN RESOURCES

Human Resource Development Division: consists of two departments concerned with education and health. The Division co-operates with member countries in devising strategies for human resource development.

The **Education Department** arranges specialist seminars, workshops and co-operative projects, and commissions studies in areas identified by ministers of education, whose three-yearly meetings it also services. Its present areas of emphasis include improving the quality of and access to basic education; strengthening the culture of science, technology and mathematics education in formal and non-formal areas of education; improving the quality of management in institutions of higher learning and basic education; improving the performance of teachers; strengthening examination assessment systems; and promoting the movement of students between Commonwealth countries. The Department also promotes multi-sectoral strategies to be incorporated in the development of human resources. Emphasis is placed on ensuring a gender balance, the appropriate use of technology, promoting good governance, addressing the problems of scale particular to smaller member countries, and encouraging collaboration between governments, the private sector and other non-governmental organizations.

The **Health Department** organizes ministerial, technical and expert group meetings and workshops, to promote co-operation on health matters, and the exchange of health information and expertise. The Department commissions relevant studies and provides professional and technical advice to member countries and to the Secretariat. It also supports the work of regional health organizations and promotes health for all people in Commonwealth countries.

Gender and Youth Affairs Division: consists of the Gender Affairs Department and the Commonwealth Youth Affairs Department.

The **Gender Affairs Department** is responsible for the implementation of the 1995 Commonwealth Plan of Action on Gender and Development, which was endorsed by the Heads of Government in order to achieve gender equality in the Commonwealth. The main objective of the Plan is to ensure that gender is incorporated into all policies, programmes, structures and procedures of member states and of the Commonwealth Secretariat. A further gender equality plan, 'Advancing the Commonwealth Agenda in the New Millennium', covers the period 2000–05. The Department is also addressing specific concerns such as the integration of gender issues into national budgetary processes, increasing the participation of women in politics and conflict prevention and resolution (with the objective of raising the level of female participation to 30%), and the promotion of human rights, including the elimination of violence against women and girls.

The **Youth Affairs Department** administers the Commonwealth Youth Programme (CYP), funded through separate voluntary contributions from governments, which seeks to promote the involvement of young people in the economic and social development of their countries. The CYP was awarded a budget of £2.2m. for 2000/01. It provides policy advice for governments and operates regional training programmes for youth workers and policy-makers through its centres in Africa, Asia, the Caribbean and the Pacific. It conducts a Youth Study Fellowship scheme, a Youth Project Fund, a Youth Exchange Programme (in the Caribbean), and a Youth Service Awards Scheme, holds conferences and seminars, carries out research and disseminates information. In 1995 a Commonwealth Youth Credit Initiative was launched, in order to provide funds, training and advice to young entrepreneurs. In May 1998 a Commonwealth ministerial meeting, held in Kuala Lumpur, Malaysia, approved a new Plan of Action on Youth Empowerment to the Year 2005. In March 2002 Commonwealth heads of government approved the Youth for the Future initiative involving technology and skills development and promoting youth enterprise.

SCIENCE

Science and Technology Division: is partially funded and governed by the Commonwealth Science Council, consisting of 35 member governments, which aims to enhance the scientific and technological capabilities of member countries, through co-operative research, training and the exchange of information. Current priority areas of work are concerned with the promotion of sustainable development and cover biological diversity and genetic resources, water resources, and renewable energy.

TECHNICAL CO-OPERATION

Commonwealth Fund for Technical Co-operation (CFTC): f. 1971 to facilitate the exchange of skills between member countries and to promote economic and social development. It is administered by the Commonwealth Secretariat and financed by voluntary subscriptions from member governments. The CFTC responds to requests from member governments for technical assistance, such as the provision of experts for short- or medium-term projects, advice on economic or legal matters, in particular in the areas of natural resources management and public-sector reform, and training programmes. Since 1995 the CFTC has operated a volunteer scheme, the Commonwealth Service Abroad Programme, for senior professionals willing to undertake short-term assignments. The CFTC also administers the Langkawi awards for the study of environmental issues, which is funded by the Canadian Government. The CFTC budget for 2000–01 amounted to £20.5m.

CFTC activities are implemented by the following divisions:

Economic and Legal Advisory Services Division: serves as an in-house consultancy, offering advice to governments on macro-economic and financial management, capital market and private-sector development, debt management, the development of natural resources, and the negotiation of maritime boundaries and fisheries access agreements;

Export and Industrial Development Division: advises on all aspects of export marketing and the development of tourism, industry, small businesses and enterprises. Includes an Agricultural Development Unit, which provides technical assistance in agriculture and renewable resources;

General Technical Assistance Services Division: provides short- and long-term experts in all fields of development;

Management and Training Services Division: provides integrated packages of consultancy and training to enhance skills in areas such as public sector reform and the restructuring of enterprises, and arranges specific country and overseas training programmes.

The Secretariat also includes an Administration Division, a Strategic Planning and Evaluation Unit, and an Information and Public Affairs Division, which produces information publications, and radio and television programmes, about Commonwealth co-operation and consultation activities.

Finance

The Secretariat's budget for 2000/01 was £11.0m. Member governments meet the cost of the Secretariat through subscriptions on a scale related to income and population.

Publications

Commonwealth Currents (quarterly).

Commonwealth Law Bulletin (2 a year).

Commonwealth Organisations (directory).

In Common (quarterly newsletter of the Youth Programme).

International Development Policies (quarterly).

Link In to Gender and Development (annually).

Report of the Commonwealth Secretary-General (every 2 years).

The Commonwealth Yearbook.

Numerous reports, studies and papers (catalogue available).

Commonwealth Organizations

(In the United Kingdom, unless otherwise stated.)

PRINCIPAL BODIES

Commonwealth Foundation: Marlborough House, Pall Mall, London, SW1Y 5HY; tel. (20) 7930-3783; fax (20) 78398157; e-mail geninfo@commonwealth.int; internet www.commonwealthfoundation.com; f. 1966; intergovernmental body promoting people-to-people interaction, and collaboration within the non-governmental sector of the Commonwealth; supports non-governmental organizations, professional associations and Commonwealth arts and culture. Awards an annual Commonwealth Writers' Prize. Funds are provided by Commonwealth govts. Chair. GRACA MACHEL (Mozambique); Dir COLIN BELL (United Kingdom). Publ. *Common Path* (quarterly).

The Commonwealth of Learning (COL): 1285 West Broadway, Suite 600, Vancouver, BC V6H 3X8, Canada; tel. (604) 775-8200; fax (604) 775-8210; e-mail info@col.org; internet www.col.org; f. 1987 by Commonwealth Heads of Government to promote the devt and sharing of distance education and open learning resources, including materials, expertise and technologies, throughout the Commonwealth and in other countries; implements and assists with national and regional educational programmes; acts as consultant to international agencies and national governments; conducts seminars and studies on specific educational needs. COL is financed by Commonwealth governments on a voluntary basis; in 1999 heads of government endorsed an annual core budget for COL of US $9m. Pres. and CEO Dato' Prof. GAJARAJ DHANARAJAN (Malaysia). Publs *Connections, EdTech News*.

The following represents a selection of other Commonwealth organizations:

AGRICULTURE AND FORESTRY

Commonwealth Forestry Association: 6–8 South Parks Rd, Oxford, OX1 3UB; tel. (1865) 271037; fax (1865) 275074; e-mail cfa_ox@hotmail.com; f. 1921; produces, collects and circulates information relating to world forestry and promotes good management, use and conservation of forests and forest lands throughout the world. Mems: 1,000. Chair. Prof. JULIAN EVANS. Publs *International Forestry Review* (quarterly), *Commonwealth Forestry News* (quarterly), *Commonwealth Forestry Handbook* (irregular).

Standing Committee on Commonwealth Forestry: Forestry Commission, 231 Corstorphine Rd, Edinburgh, EH12 7AT; tel. (131) 314-6137; fax (131) 334-0442; e-mail libby.jones@forestry.gsi.gov.uk; f. 1923 to provide continuity between Confs, and to provide a forum for discussion on any forestry matters of common interest to mem. govts which may be brought to the Cttee's notice by any member country or organization; 54 mems. 1997 Conference: Victoria Falls, Zimbabwe; 2005 Conference: Sri Lanka. Sec. LIBBY JONES. Publ. *Newsletter* (quarterly).

COMMONWEALTH STUDIES

Institute of Commonwealth Studies: 28 Russell Sq., London, WC1B 5DS; tel. (20) 7862-8844; fax (20) 7862-8820; e-mail ics@sas.ac.uk; internet www.sas.ac.uk/commonwealthstudies/; f. 1949 to promote advanced study of the Commonwealth; provides a library and meeting place for postgraduate students and academic staff engaged in research in this field; offers postgraduate teaching. Dir Prof. PAT CAPLAN. Publs *Annual Report, Collected Seminar Papers, Newsletter, Theses in Progress in Commonwealth Studies.*

COMMUNICATIONS

Commonwealth Telecommunications Organization: Clareville House, 26–27 Oxendon St, London, SW1Y 4EL; tel. (20) 7930-5516; fax (20) 7930-4248; e-mail info@cto.int; internet www.cto.int; f. 1967; aims to enhance the development of telecommunications in Commonwealth countries and contribute to the communications infrastructure required for economic and social devt, through a devt and training programme. Exec. Dir Dr DAVID SOUTER. Publ. *CTO Briefing* (3 a year).

EDUCATION AND CULTURE

Association of Commonwealth Universities (ACU): John Foster House, 36 Gordon Sq., London, WC1H 0PF; tel. (20) 7380-6700; fax (20) 7387-2655; e-mail info@acu.ac.uk; internet www.acu.ac.uk; f. 1913; organizes major meetings of Commonwealth universities and their representatives; publishes factual information about Commonwealth universities and access to them; acts as a liaison office and general information centre and provides a recruitment advertising and publicity service; hosts a management consultancy service; supplies secretariats for the Commonwealth Scholarship Comm., the Marshall Aid Commemoration Comm. and the Commonwealth Universities Study Abroad Consortium; administers various other fellowship and scholarship programmes. Mems: 480 universities in 36 Commonwealth countries or regions. Sec.-Gen. Prof. MICHAEL GIBBONS. Publs include: *Commonwealth Universities Yearbook, ACU Bulletin* (5 a year), *Report of the Council of the ACU* (annually), *Awards for University Teachers and Research Workers, Awards for Postgraduate Study at Commonwealth Universities, Awards for First Degree Study at Commonwealth Universities, Awards for University Administrators and Librarians, Who's Who of Executive Heads: Vice-Chancellors, Presidents, Principals and Rectors,* Student Information Papers (study abroad series).

Commonwealth Association for Education in Journalism and Communication—CAEJC: c/o Faculty of Law, University of Western Ontario, London, ON N6A 3K7, Canada; tel. (519) 6613348; fax (519) 6613790; e-mail caejc@julian.uwo.ca; f. 1985; aims to foster high standards of journalism and communication education and research in Commonwealth countries and to promote co-operation among institutions and professions. c. 700 mems in 32 Commonwealth countries. Pres. Prof. SYED ARABI IDID (Malaysia); Sec. Prof. ROBERT MARTIN (Canada). Publ. *CAEJAC Journal* (annually).

Commonwealth Association of Science, Technology and Mathematics Educators—CASTME: c/o Education Dept, Human Resource Development Division, Commonwealth Secretariat, Marlborough House, Pall Mall, London, SW1Y 5HX; tel. (20) 7747-6282; fax (20) 7747-6287; e-mail v.goel@commonwealth.int; f. 1974; special emphasis is given to the social significance of education in these subjects. Organizes an Awards Scheme to promote effective teaching and learning in these subjects, and biennial regional seminars. Pres. Sir HERMANN BONDI; Hon. Sec. Dr VED GOEL. Publ. *CASTME Journal* (quarterly).

Commonwealth Council for Educational Administration and Management: c/o International Educational Leadership Centre, School of Management, Lincoln University Campus, Brayford Pool, Lincoln, LN6 7TS; tel. (1522) 886071; fax (1522) 886023; e-mail athody@lincoln.ac.uk; f. 1970; aims to foster quality in professional development and links among educational administrators; holds nat. and regional confs, as well as visits and seminars. Mems: 24 affiliated groups representing 3,000 persons. Pres. Prof. ANGELA THODY; Sec. GERALDINE BRISTOW. Publs *Managing Education Matters* (2 a year), *International Studies in Educational Administration* (2 a year).

Commonwealth Institute: 230 Kensington High St, London, W8 6NQ; tel. (20) 7603-4535; fax (20) 7602-7374; e-mail info@commonwealth.org.uk; internet www.commonwealth.org.uk; f. 1893 as the Imperial Institute; restructured as an independent pan-Commonwealth agency Jan. 2000; governed by a Bd of Trustees elected by the Bd of Governors; Commonwealth High Commissioners to the United Kingdom act as ex-officio Governors; the Inst. houses a Commonwealth Resource and Literature Library and a Conference and Events Centre; supplies educational resource materials and training throughout the United Kingdom; provides internet services to the Commonwealth; operates as an arts and conference centre, running a Commonwealth-based cultural programme; a new five-year strategic plan, entitled 'Commonwealth 21', was inaugurated in 1998. Chair. DAVID A. THOMPSON; Chief Exec. DAVID FRENCH. Publ. *Annual Review*.

League for the Exchange of Commonwealth Teachers: 7 Lion Yard, Tremadoc Rd, London, SW4 7NQ; tel. (20) 7498-1101; fax (20) 7720-5403; e-mail lectcom_exchange@compuserve.com; internet www.lect.org.uk; f. 1901; promotes educational exchanges between teachers in Australia, the Bahamas, Barbados, Bermuda, Canada, Guyana, India, Jamaica, Kenya, Malawi, New Zealand, Pakistan, South Africa and Trinidad and Tobago. Dir ANNA TOMLINSON. Publs *Annual Report, Exchange Teacher* (annually).

HEALTH

Commonwealth Medical Association: BMA House, Tavistock Sq., London, WC1H 9JP; tel. (20) 7272-8492; fax (20) 7272-1663; e-mail office@commat.org; internet www.commat.org; f. 1962 for the exchange of information; provision of tech. co-operation and advice; formulation and maintenance of a code of ethics; provision of continuing medical education; devt and promotion of health education programmes; and liaison with WHO and the UN on health issues; meetings of its Council are held every three years. Mems: medical asscns in Commonwealth countries. Sec. Dr JANE RICHARDS.

Commonwealth Pharmaceutical Association: 1 Lambeth High St, London, SE1 7JN; tel. (20) 7572-2364 ; fax (20) 7572-2508; e-mail bfalconbridge@rpsgb.org.uk; f. 1970 to promote the interests of pharmaceutical sciences and the profession of pharmacy in the Commonwealth; to maintain high professional standards, encourage links between members and the creation of nat. asscns; and to facilitate the dissemination of information. Holds confs (every four years) and regional meetings. Mems: 39 pharmaceutical asscns. Sec. TONY MOFFAT. Publ. *Quarterly Newsletter*.

Commonwealth Society for the Deaf: 34 Buckingham Palace Rd, London, SW1W 0RE; tel. (20) 7233-5700; fax (20) 7233-5800; e-mail sound.seekers@btinternet.com; internet www.sound-seekers.org.uk; promotes the health, education and general welfare of the deaf in developing Commonwealth countries; encourages and assists the development of educational facilities, the training of teachers of the deaf, and the provision of support for parents of deaf children; organizes visits by volunteer specialists to developing countries; provides audiological equipment and organizes the training of audiological maintenance technicians; conducts research into the causes and prevention of deafness. CEO Brig. J. A. DAVIS. Publ. *Annual Report*.

Sight Savers International (Royal Commonwealth Society for the Blind): Grosvenor Hall, Bolnore Rd, Haywards Heath, West Sussex, RH16 4BX; tel. (1444) 446600; fax (1444) 446688; e-mail generalinformation@sightsavers.org; internet www.sightsavers.org; f. 1950 to prevent blindness and restore sight in developing countries, and to provide education and community-based training for incurably blind people; operates in collaboration with local partners, with high priority given to training local staff; Chair. Sir JOHN COLES; Dir RICHARD PORTER. Publ. *Sight Savers News*.

INFORMATION AND THE MEDIA

Commonwealth Broadcasting Association: 17 Fleet St, London, EC4Y 1AA; tel. (20) 7583-5550; fax (20) 7583-5549; e-mail cba@cba.org.uk; internet www.cba.org.uk; f. 1945; gen. confs are held every two years (2002: Manchester, United Kingdom). Mems: 97 in 57 countries. Acting Pres. GEORGE VALARINO; Sec.-Gen. ELIZABETH SMITH. Publs *Commonwealth Broadcaster* (quarterly), *Commonwealth Broadcaster Directory* (annually).

Commonwealth Institute: see under Education.

Commonwealth Journalists Association: 17 Nottingham St, London, W1M 3RD; tel. (20) 7486-3844; fax (20) 7486-3822; e-mail ian.cjalon@virgin.net; internet www.ozemail.com.au/~pwessels/cja.html; f. 1978 to promote co-operation between journalists in Commonwealth countries, organize training facilities and confs, and foster understanding among Commonwealth peoples. Pres. MURRAY BURT; Exec. Dir IAN GILLHAM.

Commonwealth Press Union (Asscn of Commonwealth Newspapers, News Agencies and Periodicals): 17 Fleet St, London, EC4Y 1AA; tel. (20) 7583-7733; fax (20) 7583-6868; e-mail 106156.3331@compuserve.com; f. 1950; promotes the welfare of the Commonwealth press; provides training for journalists and organizes biennial confs. Mems: c. 1,000 newspapers, news agencies, periodicals in 42 Commonwealth countries. Dir ROBIN MACKICHAN. Publs *CPU News, Annual Report*.

LAW

Commonwealth Lawyers' Association: c/o The Law Society, 114 Chancery Lane, London, WC2A 1PL; tel. (20) 7320-5911; fax (20) 7831-0057; e-mail cla@lawsociety.org.uk; internet www.commonwealthlawyers.com; f. 1983 (fmrly the Commonwealth Legal Bureau); seeks to maintain and promote the rule of law throughout the Commonwealth, by ensuring that the people of the Commonwealth are served by an independent and efficient legal profession; upholds professional standards and promotes the availability of legal services; assists in organizing the triennial Commonwealth law confs. Pres. (1999–2003) CYRUS DAS; Exec. Sec. CHRISTINE AMOH. Publs *The Commonwealth Lawyer*, *Clarion*.

Commonwealth Legal Advisory Service: c/o British Institute of International and Comparative Law, Charles Clore House, 17 Russell Sq., London, WC1B 5JP; tel. (20) 7862-5151; fax (20) 7862-5152; e-mail info@biicl.org; financed by the British Institute and by contributions from Commonwealth govts; provides research facilities for Commonwealth govts and law reform commissions.

Commonwealth Legal Education Association: c/o Legal and Constitutional Affairs Division, Commonwealth Secretariat, Marlborough House, Pall Mall, London, SW1Y 5HX; tel. (20) 7747-6415; fax (20) 7747-6406; e-mail clea@commonwealth.int; internet www.clea.org.uk; f. 1971 to promote contacts and exchanges and to provide information regarding legal education. Gen. Sec. JOHN HATCHARD. Publs *Commonwealth Legal Education Association Newsletter* (3 a year), *Directory of Commonwealth Law Schools* (every 2 years).

Commonwealth Magistrates' and Judges' Association: Uganda House, 58/59 Trafalgar Sq., London, WC2N 5DX; tel. (20) 7976-1007; fax (20) 7976-2395; e-mail info@cmja.org; internet www.cmja.org; f. 1970 to advance the administration of the law by promoting the independence of the judiciary, to further education in law and crime prevention and to disseminate information; confs and study tours; corporate membership for asscns of the judiciary or courts of limited jurisdiction; assoc. membership for individuals. Pres. DAVID ARMATI; Sec.-Gen. Dr KAREN BREWER. Publ. *Commonwealth Judicial Journal* (2 a year).

PARLIAMENTARY AFFAIRS

Commonwealth Parliamentary Association: Westminster House, Suite 700, 7 Millbank, London, SW1P 3JA; tel. (20) 7799-1460; fax (20) 7222-6073; e-mail hq.sec@comparlhq.org.uk; internet www.comparlhq.org.uk; f. 1911 to promote understanding and co-operation between Commonwealth parliamentarians; organization: Exec. Cttee of 32 MPs responsible to annual Gen. Assembly; 148 brs throughout the Commonwealth; holds annual Commonwealth Parliamentary Confs and seminars; also regional confs and seminars; Sec.-Gen. ARTHUR DONAHOE. Publ. *The Parliamentarian* (quarterly).

PROFESSIONAL AND INDUSTRIAL RELATIONS

Commonwealth Association of Architects: 66 Portland Pl., London, W1N 4AD; tel. (20) 7490-3024; fax (20) 72532592; e-mail caa@gharchitects.demon.co.uk; internet www.archexchange.org; f. 1964; an asscn of 38 socs of architects in various Commonwealth countries. Objectives: to facilitate the reciprocal recognition of professional qualifications; to provide a clearing house for information on architectural practice, and to encourage collaboration. Plenary confs every three years; regional confs are also held. Exec. Dir TONY GODWIN. Publs *Handbook, Objectives and Procedures: CAA Schools Visiting Boards, Architectural Education in the Commonwealth* (annotated bibliography of research), *CAA Newsnet* (2 a year), a survey and list of schools of architecture.

Commonwealth Association for Public Administration and Management—CAPAM: 1075 Bay St, Suite 402, Toronto, ON

M5S 2B1, Canada; tel. (416) 920-3337; fax (416) 920-6574; e-mail capam@capam.ca; internet www.capam.comnet.mt/; f. 1994; aims to promote sound management of the public sector in Commonwealth countries and to assist those countries undergoing political or financial reforms. An international awards programme to reward innovation within the public sector was introduced in 1997, and is awarded every 2 years. Pres. Sir RICHARD MOTTRAM (United Kingdom); Exec. Dir ART STEVENSON (Canada).

Commonwealth Trade Union Council: Congress House, 23–28 Great Russell St, London, WC1B 3LS; tel. (20) 7467-1301; fax (20) 7436-0301; e-mail info@commonwealthtuc.org; internet www.commonwealthtuc.org; f. 1979; links trade union national centres (representing more than 30m. trade union mems) throughout the Commonwealth; promotes the application of democratic principles and core labour standards, works closely with other international trade union orgs. Dir ANNIE WATSON. Publ. *Annual Report*.

SCIENCE AND TECHNOLOGY

Commonwealth Engineers' Council: c/o Institution of Civil Engineers, One Great George St, London, SW1P 3AA; tel. (20) 7222-7722; fax (20) 7222-7500; e-mail international@ice.org.uk; f. 1946; the Council meets every two years to provide an opportunity for engineering institutions of Commonwealth countries to exchange views on collaboration; there is a standing cttee on engineering education and training; organizes seminars on related topics. Sec. J. A. WHITWELL.

Commonwealth Geological Surveys Forum: c/o Commonwealth Science Council, CSC Earth Sciences Programme, Marlborough House, Pall Mall, London, SW1Y 5HX; tel. (20) 7839-3411; fax (20) 7839-6174; e-mail comsci@gn.apc.org; f. 1948 to promote collaboration in geological, geochemical, geophysical and remote sensing techniques and the exchange of information. Geological Programme Officer Dr SIYAN MALOMO.

SPORT

Commonwealth Games Federation: Walkden House, 3–10 Melton St, London, NW1 2EB; tel. (20) 7383-5596; fax (20) 7383-5506; e-mail commonwealthgamesfederation@abtinternet.com; internet www.commonwealthgames-fed.org; the Games were first held in 1930 and are now held every four years; participation is limited to competitors representing the mem. countries of the Commonwealth; held in Manchester, United Kingdom, in 2002. Mems: 72 affiliated bodies. Pres. HRH The Earl of WESSEX; Chair. MICHAEL FENNELL.

YOUTH

Commonwealth Youth Exchange Council: 7 Lion Yard, Tremadoc Rd, London, SW4 7NQ; tel. (20) 7498-6151; fax (20) 7720-5403; e-mail mail@cyec.demon.co.uk; f. 1970; promotes contact between groups of young people of the United Kingdom and other Commonwealth countries by means of educational exchange visits, provides information for organizers and allocates grants; 224 mem. orgs. Dir V. S. G. CRAGGS. Publs *Contact* (handbook), *Exchange* (newsletter), *Safety and Welfare* (guide-lines for Commonwealth Youth Exchange groups).

Duke of Edinburgh's Award International Association: Award House, 7-11 St Matthew St, London, SW1P 2JT; tel. (20) 7222-4242; fax (20) 7222-4141; e-mail sect@intaward.org; internet www.intaward.org; f. 1956; offers a programme of leisure activities for young people, comprising Service, Expeditions, Physical Recreation, and Skills; operates in more than 60 countries (not confined to the Commonwealth). International Sec.-Gen. PAUL ARENGO-JONES. Publs *Award World* (2 a year), *Annual Report*, handbooks and guides.

MISCELLANEOUS

British Commonwealth Ex-Services League: 48 Pall Mall, London, SW1Y 5JG; tel. (20) 7973-7263; fax (20) 7973-7308; links the ex-service orgs in the Commonwealth, assists ex-servicemen of the Crown and their dependants who are resident abroad; holds triennial confs. Grand Pres. HRH The Duke of EDINBURGH; Sec.-Gen. Col BRIAN NICHOLSON. Publ. *Annual Report.*

Commonwealth Countries League: 14 Thistleworth Close, Isleworth, Middlesex, TW7 4QQ; tel. (20) 8737-3572; fax (20) 8568-2495; f. 1925 to secure equal opportunities and status between men and women in the Commonwealth, to act as a link between Commonwealth women's orgs, and to promote and finance secondary education of disadvantaged girls of high ability in their own countries, through the CCL Educational Fund; holds meetings with speakers and an annual Conf., organizes the annual Commonwealth Fair for fund-raising; individual mems and affiliated socs in the Commonwealth. Sec.-Gen. SHEILA O'REILLY. Publ. *CCL Newsletter* (3 a year).

Commonwealth War Graves Commission: 2 Marlow Rd, Maidenhead, Berks, SL6 7DX; tel. (1628) 634221; fax (1628) 771208; e-mail general.enq@cwgc.org; casualty and cemetery enquiries casualty.enq@cwgc.org; internet www.cwgc.org; f. 1917 (as Imperial War Graves Commission); responsible for the commemoration in perpetuity of the 1.7m. members of the Commonwealth Forces who died during the wars of 1914–18 and 1939–45; provides for the marking and maintenance of war graves and memorials at some 23,000 locations in 150 countries. Mems: Australia, Canada, India, New Zealand, South Africa, United Kingdom. Pres. HRH The Duke of KENT; Dir-Gen. R. KELLAWAY.

Joint Commonwealth Societies' Council: c/o Royal Commonwealth Society, 18 Northumberland Ave, London, WC2N 5BJ; tel. (20) 7930-6733; fax (20) 7930-9705; e-mail jcsc@rcsint.org; internet www.commonwealthday.com; f. 1947; provides a forum for the exchange of information regarding activities of mem. orgs which promote understanding among countries of the Commonwealth; co-ordinates the distribution of the Commonwealth Day message by Queen Elizabeth, organizes the observance of the Commonwealth Day and produces educational materials relating to the occasion; mems: 16 unofficial Commonwealth orgs and four official bodies. Chair. Sir PETER MARSHALL; Sec. N. J. HERCULES.

Royal Commonwealth Society: 18 Northumberland Ave, London, WC2N 5BJ; tel. (20) 7930-6733; fax (20) 7930-9705; e-mail info@rcsint.org; internet www.rcsint.org; f. 1868; to promote international understanding of the Commonwealth and its people; organizes meetings and seminars on topical issues, and cultural and social events; library housed by Cambridge University Library. Chair. Sir MICHAEL MCWILLIAM; Dir STUART MOLE. Publs *Annual Report, Newsletter* (3 a year), conference reports.

Royal Over-Seas League: Over-Seas House, Park Place, St James's St, London, SW1A 1LR; tel. (20) 7408-0214; fax (20) 7499-6738; internet www.rost.org.uk; f. 1910 to promote friendship and understanding in the Commonwealth; club houses in London and Edinburgh; membership is open to all British subjects and Commonwealth citizens. Chair. Sir GEOFFREY ELLERTON; Dir-Gen. ROBERT F. NEWELL. Publ. *Overseas* (quarterly).

The Victoria League for Commonwealth Friendship: 55 Leinster Sq., London, W2 4PW; tel. (20) 7243-2633; fax (20) 7229-2994; f. 1901; aims to further personal friendship among Commonwealth peoples and to provide hospitality for visitors; maintains Student House, providing accommodation for students from Commonwealth countries; has brs elsewhere in the UK and abroad. Chair. COLIN WEBBER; Gen. Sec. JOHN ALLAN. Publ. *Annual Report*.

ECONOMIC CO-OPERATION ORGANIZATION—ECO

Address: 1 Golbou Alley, Kamranieh St, POB 14155-6176, Tehran, Iran.

Telephone: (21) 2831733; **fax:** (21) 2831732; **e-mail:** registry@ecosecretariat.org; **internet:** www.ecosecretariat.org.

The Economic Co-operation Organization (ECO) was established in 1985 as the successor to the Regional Co-operation for Development, founded in 1964.

MEMBERS

Afghanistan	Kyrgyzstan	Turkey
Azerbaijan	Pakistan	Turkmenistan
Iran	Tajikistan	Uzbekistan
Kazakhstan		

The 'Turkish Republic of Northern Cyprus' has been granted special guest status.

Organization

(October 2002)

SUMMIT MEETING

The first summit meeting of heads of state and of government of member countries was held in Tehran in February 1992. Summit meetings are generally held at least once every two years. The sixth summit meeting was convened in Tehran in June 2000. The seventh summit meeting was scheduled to be held in Turkey in October 2002.

COUNCIL OF MINISTERS

The Council of Ministers, comprising ministers of foreign affairs of member states, is the principal policy- and decision-making body of ECO. It meets at least once a year.

REGIONAL PLANNING COUNCIL

The Council, comprising senior planning officials or other representatives of member states, meets at least once a year. It is responsible for reviewing programmes of activity and evaluating results achieved, and for proposing future plans of action to the Council of Ministers.

COUNCIL OF PERMANENT REPRESENTATIVES

Permanent representatives or Ambassadors of member countries accredited to Iran meet regularly to formulate policy for consideration by the Council of Ministers and to promote implementation of decisions reached at ministerial or summit level.

SECRETARIAT

The Secretariat is headed by a Secretary-General, who is supported by two Deputy Secretaries-General. The following Directorates administer and co-ordinate the main areas of ECO activities: Trade and investment; Transport and communications; Energy, minerals and environment; Industry and agriculture (to be renamed Human Development); Project research; Economic research and statistics; and Co-ordination and international relations.

Secretary-General: Sayed Mojtaba Arastou (Iran).

Activities

The Regional Co-operation for Development (RCD) was established in 1964 as a tripartite arrangement between Iran, Pakistan and Turkey, which aimed to promote economic co-operation between member states. ECO replaced the RCD in 1985, and seven additional members were admitted to the Organization in November 1992. The main areas of co-operation are transport (including the building of road and rail links, of particular importance as seven member states are landlocked), telecommunications and post, trade and investment, energy (including the interconnection of power grids in the region), minerals, environmental issues, industry, and agriculture. ECO priorities and objectives for each sector are defined in the Quetta Plan of Action and the İstanbul Declaration; an Almaty Outline Plan, which was adopted in 1993, is specifically concerned with the development of regional transport and communication infrastructure. The period 1998–2007 has been designated as the ECO Decade of Transport and Communications.

In 1990 an ECO College of Insurance was inaugurated. A joint Chamber of Commerce and Industry was established in 1993. The third ECO summit meeting, held in Islamabad, Pakistan, in March 1995, concluded formal agreements on the establishment of several other regional institutes and agencies: an ECO Trade and Development Bank, in İstanbul, Turkey (with main branches in Tehran, Iran, and Islamabad, Pakistan), a joint shipping company, airline, and an ECO Cultural Institute, all to be based in Iran, and an ECO Reinsurance Company and an ECO Science Foundation, with headquarters in Pakistan. In addition, heads of state and of government endorsed the creation of an ECO eminent persons group and signed the following two agreements in order to enhance and facilitate trade throughout the region: the Transit Trade Agreement (which entered into force in December 1997) and the Agreement on the Simplification of Visa Procedures for Businessmen of ECO Countries (which came into effect in March 1998). The sixth ECO summit meeting, held in June 2000 in Tehran, urged the completion of the necessary formalities for the creation of the planned ECO Trade and Development Bank and ECO Reinsurance Company. In May 2001 the Council of Ministers agreed to terminate the ECO airline project, owing to its unsustainable cost, and to replace it with a framework agreement on co-operation in the field of air transport.

In September 1996, at an extraordinary meeting of the ECO Council of Ministers, held in Izmir, Turkey, member countries signed a revised Treaty of Izmir, the Organization's fundamental charter. An extraordinary summit meeting, held in Ashgabat, Turkmenistan, in May 1997, adopted the Ashgabat Declaration, emphasizing the importance of the development of the transport and communications infrastructure and the network of transnational petroleum and gas pipelines through bilateral and regional arrangements in the ECO area. In May 1998, at the fifth summit meeting, held in Almaty, Kazakhstan, ECO heads of state and of government signed a Transit Transport Framework Agreement and a memorandum of understanding to help combat the cross-border trafficking of illegal goods. The meeting also agreed to establish an ECO Educational Institute in Ankara, Turkey. In June 2000 the sixth ECO summit encouraged member states to participate in the development of information and communication technologies through the establishment of a database of regional educational and training institutions specializing in that field. The ECO heads of state and government also reconfirmed their commitment to the Ashgabat Declaration. In December 2001 ECO organized its first workshop on energy conservation and efficiency in Ankara.

Convening in conference for the first time in early March 2000, ECO ministers of trade signed a Framework Agreement on ECO Trade Co-operation (ECOFAT), which established a basis for the expansion of intra-regional trade. The Framework Agreement envisaged the eventual adoption of an ECO Trade Agreement (ECOTA), providing for the gradual elimination of regional tariff and non-tariff barriers between member states. ECO and the International Trade Centre are jointly implementing a project on expanding intra-ECO trade. In November the first meeting of ECO ministers responsible for energy and petroleum, convened in Islamabad, adopted a plan of action for regional co-operation on energy and petroleum matters over the period 2001–05. The first meeting of ECO ministers of agriculture, convened in July 2002, in Islamabad, Pakistan, adopted a declaration on co-operation in the agricultural sector, which specified that member states would contribute to agricultural rehabilitation in Afghanistan, establishing a special fund for the purpose, and considered instigating a mechanism for the regional exchange of agricultural and cattle products.

ECO staged its third trade fair in Bandar Anzali, Iran, in July 1998. The fourth fair, scheduled to be held in Karachi, Pakistan, in May 2002, was postponed. The Organization maintains ECO TradeNet, an internet-based repository of regional trade information. ECO has co-operation agreements with several UN agencies and other international organizations in development-related activities. An ECO-UN International Drug Control Programme (UNDCP) Project on Drug Control and Co-ordination Unit commenced operations in Tehran in July 1999. ECO has been granted observer status at the UN, OIC and WTO.

In November 2001 the UN Secretary-General requested ECO to take an active role in efforts to restore stability in Afghanistan and to co-operate closely with his special representative in that country. In June 2002 the ECO Secretary-General participated in a tripartite ministerial conference on co-operation for development in Afghanistan that was convened under the auspices of the UN Development Programme and attended by representatives from Afghanistan, Iran and Pakistan.

Finance

Member states contribute to a centralized administrative budget.

Publications

ECO Annual Economic Report.
ECO Bulletin (quarterly).

EUROPEAN UNION*

MEMBERS

Austria	Germany	Netherlands
Belgium	Greece	Portugal
Denmark	Ireland	Spain
Finland	Italy	Sweden
France	Luxembourg	United Kingdom

The European Union (EU)'s relations with the developed countries of the Far East and Australasia have been dominated by problems of competition in trade. The traditional agricultural exports to the United Kingdom by Australia and New Zealand clash with EU preferences, although the EU has made some concessions on meat and butter. Regular consultations are held with Australia at ministerial level on co-operation in the areas of trade, industry, science and technology, energy, development assistance and the environment. In March 1994 an EU-Australia wine agreement entered into effect, entailing improved access for Australian wines to EU markets and the phasing out of the use of European geographical indicators by Australian producers. Negotiations to conclude a new partnership and co-operation agreement between the EU and Australia were suspended in late 1996, owing to a dispute regarding the inclusion of a human-rights clause. A joint declaration, committing both sides to greater political, cultural and economic co-operation, was signed in June 1997. During 1996 extensive negotiations between the New Zealand Government and EU officials failed to conclude an agreement on import duties for a substantial sector of its butter industry and related products. In March 1997 New Zealand took the dispute to the World Trade Organization (WTO), which later ruled against the EU's policy of subjecting the disputed sector to a different tariff regime, and in June 1999 the European Commission agreed to comply with the ruling. A joint declaration detailing areas of co-operation and establishing a consultative framework to facilitate the development of these was signed in May 1999. Mutual recognition agreements were also signed with Australia and New Zealand in 1999, with the aim of facilitating bilateral trade in industrial products. A National Europe Centre, based at the Australian National University in Canberra, was established in April 2001 jointly by the EU and the University to consolidate Australia-EU relations.

In 1987 an EC-Japan Centre for Industrial Co-operation was established in Tokyo. (An office in Brussels was opened in June 1996.) However, the EU's substantial trade deficit with Japan was a continuing source of friction between the two sides. In 1990 a joint committee was established, with the aim of reducing the deficit. In July 1991 the heads of government of Japan and the Community signed a joint declaration on closer co-operation, to be undertaken not only in economic matters, but also with regard to political questions and security; annual meetings of heads of government were to take place. Under an agreement concluded in the same month exports of Japanese cars to the EC/EU were limited until the end of 1999, withall restrictions abolished by the EU from 1 January 2000. The agreement exempted cars produced in Europe by Japanese companies. During 1993 Japan undertook to reduce significantly its volume of exports to the EC. In early 1994 the EU initiated a scheme to promote European exports to Japan by providing advice and financial support to companies undertaking trade missions to Japan, and organizing training programmes. During 1995 the EU's ongoing policy of enhancing political dialogue with Japan and of holding regular low-profile negotiations between EU and Japanese government and business representatives on trade and economic co-operation was considered to be an important factor contributing to its steadily improving trade balance with Japan. Nevertheless, that country's restrictive trading practices continued to be a source of concern. In October 1996 the WTO upheld a long-standing complaint brought by the EU that Japanese taxes on alcoholic spirits discriminated against certain European products. Other areas of dispute were the treatment of foreign shipping companies in Japanese ports, trade restrictions on access to the Japanese photographic film and paper markets and policies for trade in semiconductors. In April 1997 the EU reintroduced a reference price for semiconductors in order to protect the European electronic industry from alleged underpriced imports from Japan and the Republic of Korea. In January 1998 an EU–Japan summit meeting was held, followed by a meeting at ministerial level in October. Subsequent summits aimed to strengthen political dialogue and deepen negotiations, and the tenth summit, held in December 2001, adopted an action plan aimed at strengthening co-operation over the following ten years, in the areas of peace and security, economic and trade partnership, global and other challenges, and cultural dialogue. Progress in the implementation of the action plan was reviewed at the 11th summit, held in July 2002.

Textiles exports by Asian countries have caused concern in the EU, owing to the depressed state of its own textiles industry. During 1982 bilateral negotiations were held under the Multi-Fibre Arrangement (MFA) with Asian producers, notably Hong Kong, the Republic of Korea and Macao. Agreements were eventually reached involving reductions in clothing quotas, 'anti-surge' clauses to prevent flooding of European markets, and measures to be imposed in the event of fraud. In 1986 new bilateral negotiations were held under the MFA and agreements were reached with the principal Asian textile exporters; in most cases a slight increase in quotas was permitted by the EC. In 1993 the MFA, which was due to expire on 31 December, was extended by one year. In accordance with the WTO's transitional Agreement on Textiles and Clothing (ATC), which replaced the MFA on 1 January 1995, the EU was gradually to liberalize its textiles trade regime and the quotas determined under the MFA were to be phased out in four stages over a ten-year period. The ATC was to expire at the end of December 2004.

Bilateral non-preferential trading and co-operation agreements were signed with Bangladesh, India, Pakistan and Sri Lanka between 1973 and 1976. A further agreement with India, extended to include co-operation in trade, industry, energy, science and finance, came into force in December 1981. A third agreement, which entered into effect in August 1994, included commitments to develop co-operation between the two sides and improve market access, as well as for the observance of human rights and democratic principles. The first EU–India summit meeting was held in Lisbon in June 2000. Both parties agreed to examine obstacles to trade and investment in India, to work to improve co-operation within the framework of the WTO, and to hold regular summits and senior officials' and ministerial meetings. A new and extended agreement with Pakistan on commercial and economic co-operation entered into force in May 1986; in May 1992 an agreement was signed on measures to stimulate private investment in Pakistan. A new accord with Sri Lanka, designed to promote co-operation in areas such as trade, investment and protection of the environment, was signed in July 1994 and entered into force in April 1995. A similar agreement was signed with Nepal in November 1995 and entered into force in June 1996. These co-operation agreements, which incorporated provisions for respect for human rights and democratic principles, did not include a financial protocol. In July 1996 EU Governments authorized the European Commission to conclude similar agreements with Bangladesh and Pakistan. A draft co-operation agreement was initialled with Pakistan in April 1998; in December the Commission proposed that the agreement be concluded. However, following the October 1999 military coup in Pakistan, negotiations were suspended. Political dialogue with Pakistan recommenced in November 2000, and the new agreement was eventually signed in November 2001. In August 2002 the EU Presidency issued a statement strongly condemning ongoing political violence in Pakistan and Kashmir.

* The European Union (EU) was formally established on 1 November 1993 under the Treaty on European Union; prior to that date it was known as the European Community (EC).

The new co-operation accord with Bangladesh was signed in May 2000 and came into force in March 2001.

A trade agreement with the People's Republic of China (PRC), signed in 1978, was replaced in May 1985 by a new trade and economic co-operation agreement. In June 1989, following the violent repression of the Chinese pro-democracy movement, EC heads of government agreed to impose sanctions on the PRC, including the cancellation of official contacts and the suspension of loans by member states. In October 1990 the Community resolved that relations with the PRC should be 'progressively normalized'. Regular meetings continued to be held between Chinese and European representatives, focusing on issues relating to human rights, economic reforms in PRC and bilateral trade relations. The EU supported the PRC's involvement in the international community and, in particular, its application for membership of the WTO. By 1994 trade between the two sides amounted to US $40,000m., compared with US $12,000m. in 1985. In November 1994 a PRC-Europe International Business School was inaugurated in Shanghai. In 1995 the EU sought to focus on the PRC as a key area for export promotion, and five events were held in the PRC to assist European companies to gain access to new market opportunities. A joint declaration was signed with the PRC in October 1996 to strengthen co-operation in the energy sector. In October 1997 senior representatives of the EU and the Chinese authorities signed a memorandum on future co-operation. The first meeting of the two sides at the level of heads of government was convened in April 1998. In November the President of the Commission made an official visit to the PRC and urged that country to remove trade restrictions imposed on European products. In the same month the EU and Hong Kong signed a co-operation agreement to combat drugs-trafficking and copyright piracy. The agreement was the first international accord to be signed by the territory since its reversion to Chinese sovereignty in July 1997. An agreement of science and technology was signed by the EU and the PRC in January 1999. A second meeting of EU-PRC heads of state was convened in December. In May 2000 the PRC and the EU concluded a bilateral trade agreement, removing a major barrier to WTO accession (which was eventually achieved in December 2001). The EU announced that it would continue disbursing aid to the PRC after accession, to help smooth the country's transition to a market economy. A third EU–PRC summit meeting was held in Beijing in October 2000. At the fourth summit, in September 2001, the two sides agreed to strengthen and widen political dialogue and to continue their dialogue on human rights. Negotiations on an EU-PRC maritime transport agreement were also formally opened in September. EU-PRC trade amounted to €103,400m. in 2001; the EU had a trade deficit with the PRC of €45,000 in that year. The fifth EU-PRC summit meeting was held in September 2002. It was envisaged that the EU would commit €200m. to co-operation projects in the PRC during 2002–06.

In November 1992 the EC and the Republic of Korea signed an arrangement on scientific and technical co-operation; the EC also ended a suspension of tariff preferences for imports from the Republic of Korea, following that country's decision to end discrimination against the Community in the field of intellectual property. Further removal of trade barriers by the Republic of Korea prompted the EU, in October 1994, to announce that a new bilateral trade agreement was to be negotiated. During negotiations, initiated in May 1995, the EU expressed concern at restrictions on European car exports to the Republic of Korea, and advocated deregulation of that country's financial sector. A customs co-operation agreement was initialled with the Republic of Korea in July 1996. In October the two sides signed a framework trade and co-operation agreement, aiming to increase co-operation in trade and industry, scientific research, technology and environmental protection. In October 1997 the parties signed an agreement regarding a reciprocal opening of markets for telecommunications equipment, following a protracted dispute, which had led the EU to lodge a complaint with the WTO. In September 1997, however, the Commission submitted a further complaint to the WTO, accusing the Republic of Korea of tax discrimination against European spirits exporters. In May 2000 the EU noted that the extremely low prices offered by shipyards in the Republic of Korea were causing severe pressures in the global market. A dialogue was opened with the Republic of Korea on this issue; however, in September 2002 it was announced that the negotiations had failed and that the EU was to register the case with the WTO. The framework trade and co-operation agreement entered into force in April 2001.

In September 1997 the European Atomic Energy Community (Euratom—an integral part of the EU) formally acceded to the executive board of the Korean Peninsula Energy Development Organization (KEDO), which aims to enhance nuclear safety and reduce the threat of nuclear proliferation from the energy programme of the Democratic People's Republic of Korea (DPRK). Political dialogue between the EU and the DPRK was initiated in 1998. In March 2001 the EU determined to strengthen its efforts to establish peace and stability in the Korean peninsula. A high-level EU delegation visited the DPRK in May. Later in that month, the EU announced that it would establish diplomatic relations with the DPRK, with the aim of facilitating inter-Korean reconciliation and alleviating food insecurity in the DPRK.

In June 1992 the EC signed trade and co-operation agreements with Mongolia and Macao, with respect for democracy and human rights forming the basis for the envisaged co-operation. A co-operation accord was formally signed with Viet Nam in July 1995, under which the EU agreed to increase quotas for Vietnamese textile products by 15%, support the country's efforts to join the WTO and provide aid for environmental and public management projects. The agreement, which came into effect on 1 June 1996, incorporated a commitment by Viet Nam to guarantee human rights and allowed for the gradual repatriation of some 40,000 Vietnamese refugees from Germany, who lost their legal status (granted by the Government of East Germany) after reunification. In October 1997 the EU agreed to increase Viet Nam's textile quotas by some 30%, in exchange for improved market access for EU exports. The agreement was ratified by both sides in September 1998. A third textile and clothing agreement was signed in October 2000, allowing increased access for Viet Nam to EU markets. Non-preferential co-operation agreements (without financial protocols) were initialled with Laos and Cambodia in November 1996 and signed in April 1997. The agreement with Laos entered into force on 1 December; however, the agreement with Cambodia was postponed, owing to adverse political developments in that country. In 1998 the EU provided financial assistance to support preparations for a general election in Cambodia, and dispatched a 200-member team to monitor the poll, which was conducted in July. The co-operation agreement with Cambodia finally came into force in November 1999. The first meeting of the EU-Laos Joint Committee was held in June 1998 and the first meeting of the EU-Cambodia Joint Committee in May 2000, when an agreement on textiles was also signed.

Concern at the human-rights situation in Myanmar and the lack of progress towards establishing a democratic government in that country has been a source of friction between the EU and Asian governments. In October 1996 the EU imposed strict limits on entry visas for Myanma officials, owing to Myanmar's refusal to permit a Commission delegation to investigate allegations of forced labour in certain government industries. In March 1997 ministers of foreign affairs agreed to revoke Myanmar's special trade privileges under the Generalized System of Preferences. In November a meeting of EU and ASEAN senior officials was postponed, owing to Myanmar's insistence (then as a full member of the ASEAN grouping) that it attend with full observer status. After several further delays, the meeting was finally convened, with Myanmar as a 'silent' observer, in late May 1999. In April 2002 the EU extended until October 2002 its ban on arms exports to Myanmar and its prohibition on the issuing of visas. In September a fourth EU mission was sent to Myanmar to assess the human rights situation there and outline EU policy on Myanmar.

In February 2000, in support of a UN Security Council Resolution to that effect, the European Council adopted a regulation prohibiting flights in EU airspace by airlines controlled by the Afghan Taliban, and freezing funds and other financial resources of the regime. The EU also adopted resolutions expressing concern at the nature of the Taliban regime and at the situation prevailing in Afghanistan. In December 2001, following the overthrow of the Taliban regime, the EU agreed to support the UN-mediated Bonn Agreement (concluded during that month) on the future of Afghanistan, to provide technical support for rehabilitation and humanitarian assistance for vulnerable members of the population, to promote democracy and human rights in Afghanistan (with a special focus on the position of women), and to strengthen efforts to combat terrorism and trafficking in illegal drugs. The EU pledged support totalling €2,300m. for reconstruction efforts during 2002–06 at the International Conference on Reconstruction Assistance to Afghanistan, held in Tokyo in January 2002. An ECHO office opened in Afghanistan during that month, and an EU representative office in Kabul became operational in February. An EU Special Representative to Afghanistan, based in Kabul, liaises with local leaders with a view to promoting peace and stability.

In 2000 the EU contributed €19m. to a Trust Fund established by the World Bank to finance reconstruction activities in East Timor. In December the EU hosted the third multilateral conference of donors to East Timor. In July 2001 the EU agreed to fund an observer mission to monitor the elections (held in the following month) to a new Constituent Assembly in the territory. An EU observer team monitored the presidential election held in April 2002 prior to East Timor's accession to independence in the following month.

Relations between the EU and ASEAN (q.v.) are based on the Co-operation Agreement of 1980. Under this agreement, joint committee meetings are held approximately every 18 months. The 14th joint committee meeting took place in Brussels in September 2001. There are also regular ministerial meetings and post-ministerial conferences. In addition, the EU is a member of the ASEAN Regional Forum (ARF), a security grouping designed to promote peace and stability, established in 1994. In December 1994 the European Council endorsed a new strategy for Asia, which recognized the region's increasing economic and political importance and pledged to strengthen bilateral and regional dialogue. The strategy aimed to enhance the development of trade and investment, promote peace and security, and assist the less-developed countries in Asia. In May 1995 ASEAN and EU senior officials endorsed an initiative to convene an Asia-Europe Meeting of heads of government (ASEM). The first meeting, attended by heads of state and government of EU member states, ASEAN countries, Japan, the PRC and the Republic of Korea was held in March 1996 in Bangkok, Thailand. The meeting concluded a new Asia-Europe Partnership for Greater Growth, which aimed to strengthen links between the two economic regions in order to contribute to long-term prosperity and regional and global stability. In addition to measures to promote an expansion in trade and investment, the agreement incorporated provisions for co-operation in human resources development, technology and science and for educational and cultural exchanges. A controversial linkage of human rights criteria to trade, demanded by some non-governmental organizations prior to the meeting and discussed previously by European Governments, was avoided: the final statement of the meeting agreed on the promotion of 'fundamental rights', but incorporated a commitment for non-intervention in internal affairs. Among the initiatives agreed in order to pursue the objectives of the Partnership were the establishment of an Asia-Europe Business Forum, to promote private-sector trade and investment, an Asia-Europe Foundation, based in Singapore, for academic and cultural exchanges, and a Centre for Environmental Technology, based in Thailand. The meeting also proposed the initiation of a transport project linking the trans-Asian and trans-European railway networks. The first meeting of ministers of foreign affairs of countries participating in ASEM was held in Singapore, in February 1997. The meeting reviewed co-operation initiatives between the two regions and agreed to consolidate the process of economic and political dialogue. An agreement was signed to provide for the establishment of the Asia-Europe Foundation. The second ASEM summit, convened in April 1998, was dominated by concerns regarding the economic and financial situation in Asia, and both sides' declared intention to prevent a return to protectionist trading policies. A special statement, issued at the end of the meeting, identified the need for economic reform in individual countries and urged a reinforcement of international financial institutions. The meeting established an ASEM Asian Financial Crisis Response Trust Fund, under the auspices of the World Bank, to alleviate the social impact of the crisis. Other initiatives adopted by ASEM were an Asia–Europe Co-operation Framework, to guide, focus and co-ordinate political, economic and financial co-operation, a Trade Facilitation Action Plan, and an Investment Promotion Action Plan, incorporating a new Investment Experts Group. The meeting resolved to promote efforts to strengthen relations in all areas, and to set up a series of working bodies; however, it was decided not to establish a permanent secretariat for the ASEM arrangement. In September 2000 an ASEM senior officials' meeting agreed to permit the DPRK to participate in future ASEM co-operation initiatives. ASEM heads of government convened for the third time in Seoul, Republic of Korea, in October. ASEM III welcomed the ongoing *rapprochement* between the two Korean nations, declared a commitment to the promotion of human rights, and endorsed several initiatives related to globalization and information technology, including an Initiative to Address the Digital Divide and the creation of a Trans-Eurasia Information Network. Initiatives aimed at combating money-laundering, corruption and transnational crime were also adopted. The meeting established a new Asia-Europe Co-operation Framework (AECF), identifying ASEM's principles and priorities for the next 10 years. The fourth ASEM summit meeting, held in September 2002, in Copenhagen, Denmark, adopted a declaration and a co-operation programme on combating international terrorism, and determined to convene an ASEM seminar on the issue. Leaders participating in the summit also agreed to establish an *ad hoc* consultative mechanism that would enable senior officials of member countries to hold extraordinary meetings to address relevant international events. The summit endorsed a conference on cultures and civilizations, adopted a declaration on achieving peaceful reconciliation in the Korean peninsula, declared commitment for the new round of WTO multilateral trade negotiations agreed at Doha, Qatar in November 2001, and authorized the creation of an ASEM Task Force on Closer Economic Partnership to address interregional trade, investment and finance.

In September 2001 the EU adopted a new Communication on relations with Asia for the coming decade. Representing an updating of the 1994 strategy, this focused on strengthened partnership, particularly in the areas of politics, security, trade and investment. It aimed to reduce poverty and to promote democracy, good governance and the rule of law throughout the region. Partnerships and alliances on global issues were to be forged. A fundamental aim was to strengthen the EU's presence in Asia, promoting mutual awareness and knowledge on both sides. To this end, the EU established a scholarship scheme in the PRC and increased the number of EU delegation offices in the region.

In 2000 EU financial and technical co-operation with Asia amounted to €300m., while economic co-operation totalled €100m. During 2000 assistance granted through the European Community Humanitarian Office (ECHO) included €15m. for victims of drought in Afghanistan and €5.8m. for those affected by the drought in India; €5.5m. for victims of the earthquakes in Indonesia, as well as for refugees from East Timor and the population of Irian Jaya (now Papua); €4.5m. for development in Myanmar and aid in the camps housing Myanma refugees; €1.7m. for Pakistan; €1.5m. for Bangladesh; and €1.2m. for Sri Lanka. A €4m. action plan for South-East Asia was adopted under the EU's Natural Disaster Prevention and Preparedness Programme (Dipecho) in 2000. The plan aimed to improve local capabilities and set up early-warning systems.

EUROPEAN UNION-ACP PARTNERSHIP

From 1976 to February 2000 the principal means of co-operation between the Community and developing countries were the Lomé Conventions, concluded by the EU and African, Caribbean and Pacific (ACP) countries. The latter include 14 Pacific states: Cook Islands, Fiji, Kiribati, Marshall Islands, Federated States of Micronesia, Nauru, Niue, Palau, Papua New Guinea, Samoa, Solomon Islands, Tonga, Tuvalu and Vanuatu, as well as 48 African and 16 Caribbean nations.

The first Lomé Convention (Lomé I), which was concluded at Lomé, Togo, in February 1975 and came into force on 1 April 1976, replaced the Yaoundé Conventions and the Arusha Agreement and was designed to provide a new framework of co-operation, taking into account the varying needs of developing ACP countries. Under Lomé I, the Community committed ECU 3,052.4m. for aid and investment, through the European Development Fund (EDF) and the European Investment Bank (EIB). Provision was made for over 99% of ACP (mainly agricultural) exports to enter the EC market duty free, while certain products competing directly with Community agriculture, such as sugar, were given preferential treatment but not free access. The Stabex (Stabilization of Export Earnings) scheme was designed to help developing countries to withstand fluctuations in the price of their agricultural products, by paying compensation for reduced export earnings.

The second Lomé Convention (January 1981–28 February 1985) envisaged Community expenditure of ECU 5,530m.; it extended some of the provisions of Lomé I, and introduced new fields of co-operation, including a new scheme, Sysmin, to safeguard exports of mineral products. Lomé III provided a total of ECU 8,500m. (about US $6,000m. at 30 January 1985) in assistance to the ACP states over the five years from March 1985, representing little or no increase, in real terms, over the amount provided by Lomé II.

The fourth Lomé Convention entered partially into force (trade provisions) on 1 March 1990, and fully into force on 1 September 1991. It was to cover the 10-year period 1990–99 (but was subsequently extended until February 2000). The financial protocol for 1990–95 made commitments of ECU 12,000m., of which ECU 10,800m. was from the EDF (including ECU 1,500m. for Stabex and ECU 480m. for Sysmin) and ECU 1,200m. from the EIB. Under Lomé IV the obligation of most of the ACP states to contribute to the replenishment of Stabex resources, including the repayment of transfers made under the first three Conventions, was removed. In addition, special loans made to ACP member countries were to be cancelled, except in the case of profit-orientated businesses. Other innovations included the provision of assistance for structural adjustment programmes, measures to avoid increasing recipient countries' indebtedness (e.g. by providing Stabex and Sysmin assistance in the form of grants, rather than loans), and increased support for the private sector, environmental protection and control of population growth.

In September 1993 the EC announced plans to revise and strengthen its relations with the ACP countries under the Lomé Convention. A mid-term review of the Convention was initiated in May 1994. The EU reiterated its intention to maintain the Convention as an aid instrument. It emphasized, however, that stricter conditions relating to the awarding of aid would be imposed, based on standards of human rights, human resource development and environmental protection. In February 1995 a joint EU-ACP ministerial council, which was scheduled to conclude the negotiations, was adjourned, owing to significant disagreement among EU member states concerning reimbursement of the EDF for the period 1995–2000. In June EU heads of government reached an agreement, which was subsequently endorsed by an EU-ACP ministerial group. The accord was to provide ECU 14,625m. for the second phase of Lomé IV, with ECU 12,967m. allocated from the EDF and ECU 1,658m. in loans from the EIB. Agreement was also reached on revision of the country-of-origin rules for manufactured goods; expansion of the preferential system of trade for ACP products; a new protocol on the sustainable management of forest resources; and a joint declaration on support for the banana industry. The revised Convention was signed in November, in Mauritius. The new agreement included a reference to the observance of human rights, respect for democracy and the rule of law as essential elements of the preferential trading arrangement accorded under the Convention. Financial resources were to be made available to support institutional and administrative reforms to strengthen these principles in contracting states. In addition, the Convention provided for reforms in the administration of aid, including assistance to support structural economic adjustments. The revised Convention formally entered into force on 1 June 1998, having been ratified by all 15 EU member states.

In March 1997 the Commission proposed the provision of debt relief assistance worth ECU 25m. per year for the period 1997–2000 to the 11 heavily indebted poor countries (as identified by the World Bank and IMF) that formed part of the ACP group. The funding was intended to support international efforts to reduce outstanding debt and to encourage economic prospects. In May 2001 the EU announced that it would cancel all outstanding debts arising from its trade accords with former colonies of member states. It was believed that the loans made under the Lomé Conventions could be as high as US $200m. In November 1997 the first summit meeting of heads of state of ACP countries was held, in Libreville, Gabon. The principal issues under consideration at the meeting were the strategic challenges confronting the ACP group of countries and, in particular, relations with the EU beyond 2000, when Lomé IV was scheduled to expire. The summit mandated ACP ministers of finance and of trade and industry to organize a series of regular meetings in order to strengthen co-ordination within the grouping.

Formal negotiations on the conclusion of a successor agreement to the Lomé Convention were initiated on 30 September 1998. The negotiations were concluded in February 2000, and the new partnership accord was signed by ACP and EU heads of state and government in June 2000 in Cotonou, Benin. The so-called Cotonou Agreement was to enter into effect following ratification by the European Parliament and the ACP national legislatures, and was to cover the period 2000–20. (Cuba, admitted as an ACP state in December 2000, and South Africa, which has a special arrangement with the EU, are not signatories of the Cotonou Agreement.) The Agreement comprised the following main elements: increased political co-operation; the enhanced participation of civil society in ACP–EC partnership affairs; a strong focus on the reduction of poverty (addressing the economic and technical marginalization of developing nations was a primary concern); reform of the existing structures for financial co-operation; and a new framework for economic and trade co-operation. Under the provisions of the new accord, the EU was to negotiate free-trade arrangements (replacing the previous non-reciprocal trade preferences) with the most developed ACP countries during 2000–08; these would be structured around a system of regional free-trade zones, and would be designed to ensure full compatibility with WTO provisions. Once in force, the agreements would be subject to revision every five years. An assessment to be conducted in 2004 would identify those mid-ranking ACP nations also capable of entering into such free-trade deals. Meanwhile, the least-developed ACP nations were to benefit from an EU initiative to allow free access for most of their products by 2005. The preferential agreements currently in force would be retained initially (phase I), in view of a waiver granted by the WTO; thereafter ACP–EU trade was to be gradually liberalized over a period of 12–15 years (phase II). It was envisaged that Stabex and Sysmin would be eliminated gradually.

The first meeting of the ACP-EU Joint Parliamentary Assembly following the signing of the Cotonou Agreement was held in Brussels in October 2000. In total, the EU provided €3,612m. in financing for ACP countries in 2000. The EDF had funds of €13,500m. to cover the first five years of operation of the Cotonou Agreement. In February 2001, under its 'everything but arms' (EBA) policy, the EU agreed to phase out trade barriers on imports of everything but military weapons from the world's 48 least developed countries, 39 of which were in the ACP group. Duties on sugar, rice, bananas and some other products were to remain until 2009. In May the ACP Council of Ministers appealed to all parties to accelerate the process of ratification of the Cotonou Agreement, noting that the release of funds under the ninth EDF was contingent on the entry into force of the Agreement. By July 2002 10 European states and 61 ACP countries had ratified the accord.

ACP-EU INSTITUTIONS

Council of Ministers: one minister from each signatory state; one co-chairman from each of the two groups; meets annually.

Committee of Ambassadors: one ambassador from each signatory state; chairmanship alternates between the two groups; meets at least every six months.

Joint Assembly: EU and ACP are equally represented; attended by parliamentary delegates from each of the 77 ACP countries and an equal number of members of the European Parliament; one co-chairman from each of the two groups; meets twice a year.

Secretariat of the ACP-EU Council of Ministers: 175 rue de la Loi, 1048 Brussels, Belgium; tel. (2) 285-61-11; fax (2) 285-74-58.

Centre for the Development of Enterprise (CDE): 52 ave Hermann Debroux, 1160 Brussels, Belgium; tel. (2) 679-18-11; fax (2) 679-18-31; e-mail info@cde.int; internet www.cdi.be; f. 1977 (as the Centre for the Development of Industry: present name adopted 2001) to encourage investment in the ACP states by providing contacts and advice, holding promotion meetings and helping to finance feasibility studies; Dir FERNANDO MATOS ROSA.

Technical Centre for Agricultural and Rural Co-operation: Postbus 380, 6700 AJ Wageningen, Netherlands; tel. (317) 467100; fax (317) 460067; e-mail cta@cta.nl; internet www.agricta.org; f. 1983 to provide ACP states with better access to information, research, training and innovations in agricultural development and extension; Dir CARL B. GREENIDGE.

ACP INSTITUTIONS

ACP Council of Ministers.

ACP Committee of Ambassadors.

ACP Secretariat: ACP House, 451 ave Georges Henri, 1200 Brussels, Belgium; tel. (2) 743-06-00; fax (2) 735-55-73; e-mail info@acpsec.org; internet www.acpsec.org; Sec.-Gen. JEAN-ROBERT GOULONGANA (Gabon).

ORGANIZATION OF THE ISLAMIC CONFERENCE—OIC

Address: Kilo 6, Mecca Rd, POB 178, Jeddah 21411, Saudi Arabia.

Telephone: (2) 680-0800; **fax:** (2) 687-3568; **e-mail:** info@oic-oci.org; **internet:** www.oic-oci.org.

The Organization was formally established in May 1971, when its Secretariat became operational, following a summit meeting of Muslim heads of state at Rabat, Morocco, in September 1969, and the Islamic Foreign Ministers' Conference in Jeddah in March 1970, and in Karachi, Pakistan, in December 1970.

MEMBERS

Afghanistan*	Brunei	Egypt
Albania	Burkina Faso	Gabon
Algeria	Cameroon	The Gambia
Azerbaijan	Chad	Guinea
Bahrain	The Comoros	Guinea-Bissau
Bangladesh	Côte d'Ivoire	Guyana
Benin	Djibouti	Indonesia
Iran	Mozambique	Suriname
Iraq	Niger	Syria
Jordan	Nigeria†	Tajikistan
Kazakhstan	Oman	Togo
Kuwait	Pakistan	Tunisia
Kyrgyzstan	Palestine	Turkey
Lebanon	Qatar	Turkmenistan
Libya	Saudi Arabia	Uganda
Malaysia	Senegal	United Arab Emirates
Maldives	Sierra Leone	Uzbekistan
Mali	Somalia	Yemen
Mauritania	Sudan	
Morocco		

* Afghanistan's membership of the OIC was suspended in 1996; however, it was reported to have resumed full membership following the establishment of an interim authority in late 2001.

† Nigeria renounced its membership in May 1991; however, the OIC has not formally recognized this decision.

Note: Observer status has been granted to Bosnia and Herzegovina, the Central African Republic, Thailand, the Muslim community of the 'Turkish Republic of Northern Cyprus', the Moro National Liberation Front (MNLF) of the southern Philippines, the United Nations, the African Union, the Non-Aligned Movement, the League of Arab States, the Economic Co-operation Organization, the Union of the Arab Maghreb and the Co-operation Council for the Arab States of the Gulf.

Organization

(October 2002)

SUMMIT CONFERENCES

The supreme body of the Organization is the Conference of Heads of State, which met in 1969 at Rabat, Morocco, in 1974 at Lahore, Pakistan, and in January 1981 at Mecca, Saudi Arabia, when it was decided that summit conferences would be held every three years in future. Ninth Conference: Doha, Qatar, November 2000.

CONFERENCE OF MINISTERS OF FOREIGN AFFAIRS

Conferences take place annually, to consider the means for implementing the general policy of the Organization, although they may also be convened for extraordinary sessions.

SECRETARIAT

The executive organ of the Organization, headed by a Secretary-General (who is elected by the Conference of Ministers of Foreign Affairs for a four-year term, renewable only once) and four Assistant Secretaries-General (similarly appointed).

Secretary-General: Dr ABDELOUAHED BELKEZIZ (Morocco).

At the summit conference in January 1981 it was decided that an International Islamic Court of Justice should be established to adjudicate in disputes between Muslim countries. Experts met in January 1983 to draw up a constitution for the court; however, by 2002 it was not yet in operation.

STANDING COMMITTEES

Al-Quds Committee: f. 1975 to implement the resolutions of the Islamic Conference on the status of Jerusalem (Al-Quds); it meets at the level of foreign ministers; maintains the Al-Quds Fund; Chair. King MUHAMMAD VI of Morocco.

Standing Committee for Economic and Commercial Co-operation (COMCEC): f. 1981; Chair. AHMET NECDET SEZER (Pres. of Turkey).

Standing Committee for Information and Cultural Affairs (COMIAC): f. 1981. Chair. ABDOULAYE WADE (Pres. of Senegal).

Standing Committee for Scientific and Technological Co-operation (COMSTECH): f. 1981; Chair. Gen. PERVEZ MUSHARRAF (Pres. of Pakistan).

Other committees comprise the Islamic Peace Committee, the Permanent Finance Committee, the Committee of Islamic Solidarity with the Peoples of the Sahel, the Eight-Member Committee on the Situation of Muslims in the Philippines, the Six-Member Committee on Palestine, and the *ad hoc* Committee on Afghanistan. In addition, there is an Islamic Commission for Economic, Cultural and Social Affairs and OIC contact groups on Bosnia and Herzegovina, Kosovo, Jammu and Kashmir, and Sierra Leone.

Activities

The Organization's aims, as proclaimed in the Charter that was adopted in 1972, are:

(i) To promote Islamic solidarity among member states;

(ii) To consolidate co-operation among member states in the economic, social, cultural, scientific and other vital fields, and to arrange consultations among member states belonging to international organizations;

(iii) To endeavour to eliminate racial segregation and discrimination and to eradicate colonialism in all its forms;

(iv) To take necessary measures to support international peace and security founded on justice;

(v) To co-ordinate all efforts for the safeguard of the Holy Places and support of the struggle of the people of Palestine, and help them to regain their rights and liberate their land;

(vi) To strengthen the struggle of all Muslim people with a view to safeguarding their dignity, independence and national rights; and

(vii) To create a suitable atmosphere for the promotion of co-operation and understanding among member states and other countries.

The first summit conference of Islamic leaders (representing 24 states) took place in 1969 following the burning of the Al Aqsa Mosque in Jerusalem. At this conference it was decided that Islamic governments should 'consult together with a view to promoting close co-operation and mutual assistance in the economic, scientific, cultural and spiritual fields, inspired by the immortal teachings of Islam'. Thereafter the foreign ministers of the countries concerned met annually, and adopted the Charter of the Organization of the Islamic Conference in 1972.

At the second Islamic summit conference (Lahore, Pakistan, 1974), the Islamic Solidarity Fund was established, together with a committee of representatives which later evolved into the Islamic Commission for Economic, Cultural and Social Affairs. Subsequently, numerous other subsidiary bodies have been set up (see below).

ECONOMIC CO-OPERATION

A general agreement for economic, technical and commercial co-operation came into force in 1981, providing for the establishment of joint investment projects and trade co-ordination. This was followed by an agreement on promotion, protection and guarantee of investments among member states. A plan of action to strengthen economic co-operation was adopted at the third Islamic summit conference in 1981, aiming to promote collective self-reliance and the development of joint ventures in all sectors. In 1994 the 1981 plan of action was revised; the reformulated plan placed greater emphasis on private-sector participation in its implementation. Although several meetings of experts were subsequently held to discuss some of the 10 priority focus areas of the plan, little progress was achieved in implementing it during the 1990s.

The fifth summit conference, held in 1987, approved proposals for joint development of modern technology, and for improving scientific and technical skills in the less developed Islamic countries. The first international Islamic trade fair was held in Jeddah, Saudi Arabia, in March 2001.

In 1991 22 OIC member states signed a framework agreement concerning the introduction of a system of trade preferences among member states. It was envisaged that, if implemented, this would represent the first step towards the eventual establishment of an Islamic common market. In May 2001 the OIC Secretary-General urged increased progress in the ratification of the framework agreement. An OIC group of experts was considering the implications of the proposed creation of such a common market.

CULTURAL CO-OPERATION

The Organization supports education in Muslim communities throughout the world, and was instrumental in the establishment of Islamic universities in Niger and Uganda (see below). It organizes seminars on various aspects of Islam, and encourages dialogue with the other monotheistic religions. Support is given to publications on Islam both in Muslim and Western countries. The OIC organizes meetings at ministerial level to consider aspects of information policy and new technologies.

HUMANITARIAN ASSISTANCE

Assistance is given to Muslim communities affected by wars and natural disasters, in co-operation with UN organizations, particularly UNHCR. The countries of the Sahel region (Burkina Faso, Cape Verde, Chad, The Gambia, Guinea, Guinea-Bissau, Mali, Mauritania, Niger and Senegal) receive particular attention as victims of drought. In April 1999 the OIC resolved to send humanitarian aid to assist the displaced ethnic Albanian population of Kosovo and Metohija, in southern Serbia. Several member states have provided humanitarian assistance to the Muslim population affected by the conflict in Chechnya. During 2001 the OIC was providing emergency assistance to Afghanistan, and in October established an Afghan People Assistance Fund. The OIC also administers a Trust Fund for the urgent return of refugees and the displaced to Bosnia and Herzegovina.

POLITICAL CO-OPERATION

Since its inception the OIC has called for vacation of Arab territories by Israel, recognition of the rights of Palestinians and of the Palestine Liberation Organization (PLO) as their sole legitimate representative, and the restoration of Jerusalem to Arab rule. The 1981 summit conference called for a *jihad* (holy war—though not necessarily in a military sense) 'for the liberation of Jerusalem and the occupied territories'; this was to include an Islamic economic boycott of Israel. In 1982 Islamic ministers of foreign affairs decided to establish Islamic offices for boycotting Israel and for military co-operation with the PLO. The 1984 summit conference agreed to reinstate Egypt (suspended following the peace treaty signed with Israel in 1979) as a member of the OIC, although the resolution was opposed by seven states.

In August 1990 a majority of ministers of foreign affairs condemned Iraq's recent invasion of Kuwait, and demanded the withdrawal of Iraqi forces. In August 1991 the Conference of Ministers of Foreign Affairs obstructed Iraq's attempt to propose a resolution demanding the repeal of economic sanctions against the country. The sixth summit conference, held in Senegal in December, reflected the divisions in the Arab world that resulted from Iraq's invasion of Kuwait and the ensuing war. Twelve heads of state did not attend, reportedly to register protest at the presence of Jordan and the PLO at the conference, both of which had given support to Iraq. Disagreement also arose between the PLO and the majority of other OIC members when a proposal was adopted to cease the OIC's support for the PLO's *jihad* in the Arab territories occupied by Israel, in an attempt to further the Middle East peace negotiations.

In August 1992 the UN General Assembly approved a non-binding resolution, introduced by the OIC, that requested the UN Security Council to take increased action, including the use of force, in order to defend the non-Serbian population of Bosnia and Herzegovina (some 43% of Bosnians being Muslims) from Serbian aggression, and to restore its 'territorial integrity'. The OIC Conference of Ministers of Foreign Affairs, which was held in December, demanded anew that the UN Security Council take all necessary measures against Serbia and Montenegro, including military intervention, in order to protect the Bosnian Muslims.

A report by an OIC fact-finding mission, which in February 1993 visited Azad Kashmir while investigating allegations of repression of the largely Muslim population of the Indian state of Jammu and Kashmir by the Indian armed forces, was presented to the 1993 Conference. The meeting urged member states to take the necessary measures to persuade India to cease the 'massive human rights violations' in Jammu and Kashmir and to allow the Indian Kashmiris to 'exercise their inalienable right to self-determination'. In September 1994 ministers of foreign affairs, meeting in Islamabad, Pakistan, agreed to establish a contact group on Jammu and Kashmir, which was to provide a mechanism for promoting international awareness of the situation in that region and for seeking a peaceful solution to the dispute. In December OIC heads of state approved a resolution condemning reported human rights abuses by Indian security forces in Kashmir.

In July 1994 the OIC Secretary-General visited Afghanistan and proposed the establishment of a preparatory mechanism to promote national reconciliation in that country. In mid-1995 Saudi Arabia, acting as a representative of the OIC, pursued a peace initiative for Afghanistan and issued an invitation for leaders of the different factions to hold negotiations in Jeddah.

A special ministerial meeting on Bosnia and Herzegovina was held in July 1993, at which seven OIC countries committed themselves to making available up to 17,000 troops to serve in the UN Protection Force in the former Yugoslavia (UNPROFOR). The meeting also decided to dispatch immediately a ministerial mission to persuade influential governments to support the OIC's demands for the removal of the arms embargo on Bosnian Muslims and the convening of a restructured international conference to bring about a political solution to the conflict. In December 1994 OIC heads of state, convened in Morocco, proclaimed that the UN arms embargo on Bosnia and Herzegovina could not be applied to the Muslim authorities of that Republic. The Conference also resolved to review economic relations between OIC member states and any country that supported Serbian activities. An aid fund was established, to which member states were requested to contribute between US $500,000 and $5m., in order to provide further humanitarian and economic assistance to Bosnian Muslims. In relation to wider concerns the conference adopted a Code of Conduct for Combating International Terrorism, in an attempt to control Muslim extremist groups. The code commits states to ensuring that militant groups do not use their territory for planning or executing terrorist activity against other states, in addition to states refraining from direct support or participation in acts of terrorism. In a further resolution the OIC supported the decision by Iraq to recognize Kuwait, but advocated that Iraq comply with all UN Security Council decisions.

In July 1995 the OIC contact group on Bosnia and Herzegovina (at that time comprising Egypt, Iran, Malaysia, Morocco, Pakistan, Saudi Arabia, Senegal and Turkey), meeting in Geneva, declared the UN arms embargo against Bosnia and Herzegovina to be 'invalid'. Several Governments subsequently announced their willingness officially to supply weapons and other military assistance to the Bosnian Muslim forces. In September a meeting of all OIC ministers of defence and foreign affairs endorsed the establishment of an 'assistance mobilization group' which was to supply military, economic, legal and other assistance to Bosnia and Herzegovina. In a joint declaration the ministers also demanded the return of all territory seized by Bosnian Serb forces, the continued NATO bombing of Serb military targets, and that the city of Sarajevo be preserved under a Muslim-led Bosnian Government. In November the OIC Secretary-General endorsed the peace accord for the former Yugoslavia, which was concluded, in Dayton, USA, by leaders of all the conflicting factions, and reaffirmed the commitment of Islamic states to participate in efforts to implement the accord. In the following month the OIC Conference of Ministers of Foreign Affairs, convened in Conakry, Guinea, requested the full support of the international community to reconstruct Bosnia and Herzegovina through humanitarian aid as well as economic and technical co-operation. Ministers declared that Palestine and the establishment of fully-autonomous Palestinian control of Jerusalem were issues of central importance for the Muslim world. The Conference urged the removal of all aspects of occupation and the cessation of the construction of Israeli settlements in the occupied territories. In addition, the final statement of the meeting condemned Armenian aggression against Azerbaijan, registered concern at the persisting civil conflict in Afghanistan, demanded the elimination of all weapons of mass destruction and pledged support for Libya (affected by the US trade embargo). Ministers determined that an intergovernmental group of experts should be established in 1996 to address the situation of minority Muslim communities residing in non-OIC states.

In December 1996 OIC ministers of foreign affairs, meeting in Jakarta, Indonesia, urged the international community to apply pressure on Israel in order to ensure its implementation of the terms of the Middle East peace process. The ministers reaffirmed the importance of ensuring that the provisions of the Dayton Peace Agreement for the former Yugoslavia were fully implemented, called for a peaceful settlement of the Kashmir issue, demanded that Iraq fulfil its obligations for the establishment of security, peace and stability in the region and proposed that an international conference on peace and national reconciliation in Somalia be convened. The ministers elected a new Secretary-General who confirmed that the organization would continue to develop its role as an international mediator. In March 1997, at an extraordinary summit held in Pakistan, OIC heads of state and of government reiterated the organization's objective of increasing international pressure on Israel to ensure the full implementation of the terms of the Middle East peace process. An 'Islamabad Declaration' was also adopted, which pledged to increase co-operation between members of the OIC. In June the OIC condemned the decision by the US House of Representatives to recognize Jerusalem as the Israeli capital. The Secretary-General of the OIC issued a statement rejecting the US decision as counter to the role of the USA as sponsor of the Middle East peace plan.

In early 1998 the OIC appealed for an end to the threat of US-led military action against Iraq arising from a dispute regarding access granted to international weapons inspectors. The crisis was averted by an agreement concluded between the Iraqi authorities and the UN Secretary-General in February. In March OIC ministers of foreign affairs, meeting in Doha, Qatar, requested an end to the international sanctions against Iraq. Additionally, the ministers urged all states to end the process of restoring normal trading and diplomatic relations with Israel pending that country's withdrawal from the occupied territories and acceptance of an independent Palestinian state. In April the OIC, jointly with the UN, sponsored new peace negotiations between the main disputing factions in Afghanistan, which were conducted in Islamabad, Pakistan. In early May, however, the talks collapsed and were postponed indefinitely. In September the Secretaries-General of the OIC and UN agreed to establish a joint mission to counter the deteriorating security situation along the Afghan–Iranian border, following the large-scale deployment of Taliban troops in the region and consequent military manoeuvres by the Iranian authorities. They also reiterated the need to proceed with negotiations to conclude a peaceful settlement in Afghanistan. In December the OIC appealed for a diplomatic solution to the tensions arising from Iraq's withdrawal of co-operation with UN weapons inspectors, and criticized subsequent military air-strikes, led by the USA, as having been conducted without renewed UN authority. An OIC Convention on Combating International Terrorism was adopted in 1998. An OIC committee of experts responsible for formulating a plan of action for safeguarding the rights of Muslim communities and minorities met for the first time in 1998.

In early April 1999 ministers of foreign affairs of the countries comprising OIC's contact group met to consider the crisis in Kosovo. The meeting condemned Serbian atrocities being committed against the local Albanian population and urged the provision of international assistance for the thousands of people displaced by the conflict. The group resolved to establish a committee to co-ordinate relief aid provided by member states. The ministers also expressed their willingness to help to formulate a peaceful settlement and to participate in any subsequent implementation force. In June an OIC Parliamentary Union was inaugurated; its founding conference was convened in Tehran, Iran.

In early March 2000 the OIC mediated contacts between the parties to the conflict in Afghanistan, with a view to reviving peace negotiations. Talks, held under OIC auspices, ensued in May. In November OIC heads of state attended the ninth summit conference, held in Doha, Qatar. In view of the significant deterioration in relations between Israel and the Palestinian (National) Authority during late 2000, the summit issued a Declaration pledging solidarity with the Palestinian cause and accusing the Israeli authorities of implementing large-scale systematic violations of human rights against Palestinians. The summit also issued the Doha Declaration, which reaffirmed commitment to the OIC Charter and undertook to modernize the organization's organs and mechanisms. Both the elected Government of Afghanistan and the Taliban sent delegations to the Doha conference. The summit determined that Afghanistan's official participation in the OIC, suspended in 1996, should not yet be reinstated. In early 2001 a high-level delegation from the OIC visited Afghanistan in an attempt to prevent further destruction of ancient statues by Taliban supporters.

In May 2001 the OIC convened an emergency meeting, following an escalation of Israeli-Palestinian violence. The meeting resolved to halt all diplomatic and political contacts with the Israeli government, while restrictions remained in force against Palestinian-controlled territories. In June the OIC condemned attacks and ongoing discrimination against the Muslim Community in Myanmar. In the same month the OIC Secretary-General undertook a tour of six African countries—Burkina Faso, The Gambia, Guinea, Mali, Niger and Senegal, to promote co-operation and to consider further OIC support for those states. In August the Secretary-General condemned Israel's seizure of several Palestinian institutions in East Jerusalem and aerial attacks against Palestinian settlements. The OIC initiated high-level diplomatic efforts to convene a meeting of the UN Security Council in order to discuss the situation.

In September 2001 the OIC Secretary-General strongly condemned major terrorist attacks perpetrated against targets in the USA. Soon afterwards the US authorities rejected a proposal by the Taliban regime that an OIC observer mission be deployed to monitor the activities of the Saudi Arabian-born exiled militant Islamist fundamentalist leader Osama bin Laden, who was accused by the US Government of having co-ordinated the attacks from alleged terrorist bases in the Taliban-administered area of Afghanistan. An extraordinary meeting of OIC ministers of foreign affairs, convened in early October, in Doha, Qatar, to consider the implications of the terrorist atrocities, condemned the attacks and declared its support for combating all manifestations of terrorism within the framework of a proposed collective initiative co-ordinated under the auspices of the UN. The meeting, which did not pronounce directly on the recently-initiated US-led military retaliation against targets in Afghanistan, urged that no Arab or Muslim state should be targeted under the pretext of eliminating terrorism. It determined to establish a fund to assist Afghan civilians. In February 2002 the Secretary-General expressed concern at statements of the US administration describing Iran and Iraq (as well as the Democratic People's Republic of Korea) as belonging to an 'axis of evil' involved in international terrorism and the development of weapons of mass destruction. In early April OIC foreign ministers convened an extraordinary session on terrorism, in Kuala Lumpur, Malaysia. The meeting issued the 'Kuala Lumpur Declaration', which reiterated member states' collective resolve to combat terrorism, recalling the organization's 1994 code of conduct and 1998 convention to this effect; condemned attempts to associate terrorist activities with Islamists or any other particular creed, civilization or nationality, and rejected attempts to associate Islamic states or the Palestinian struggle with terrorism; rejected the implementation of international action against any Muslim state on the pretext of combating terrorism; urged the organization of a global conference on international terrorism; and urged an examination of the root causes of international terrorism. In addition, the meeting strongly condemned Israel's ongoing military intervention in areas controlled by the Palestinian (National) Authority. The meeting adopted a plan of action on addressing the issues raised in the declaration. Its implementation was to be co-ordinated by a 13-member committee on international terrorism. Member states were encouraged to sign and ratify the Convention on Combating International Terrorism in order to accelerate its implementation. In June ministers of foreign affairs, meeting in Khartoum, Sudan, issued a declaration reiterating the OIC call for an international conference to be convened, under UN auspices, in order clearly to define terrorism and to agree on the international procedures and mechanisms for combating terrorism through the UN. The conference also repeated demands for the international community to exert pressure on Israel to withdraw from all Palestinian-controlled territories and for the establishment of an independent Palestinian state. It endorsed the peace plan for the region that had been adopted by the summit meeting of the League of Arab States in March.

In June 2002 the OIC Secretary-General expressed his concern at the escalation of tensions between Pakistan and India regarding Kashmir. He urged both sides to withdraw their troops and to refrain from the use of force. In the following month the OIC pledged its support for Morocco in a territorial dispute with Spain over a small, uninhabited island, but called for a negotiated settlement to resolve the issue.

Finance

The OIC's activities are financed by mandatory contributions from member states. The budget for 2002/03 totalled US $11.4m.

SUBSIDIARY ORGANS

Islamic Centre for the Development of Trade: Complexe Commercial des Habous, ave des FAR, BP 13545, Casablanca, Morocco; tel. (2) 314974; fax (2) 310110; e-mail icdt@icdt.org; internet www.icdt.org; f. 1983 to encourage regular commercial contacts, harmonize policies and promote investments among OIC mems. Dir-Gen. ALLAL RACHDI. Publs *Tijaris: International and Inter-Islamic Trade Magazine* (bi-monthly), *Inter-Islamic Trade Report* (annually).

Islamic Jurisprudence (Fiqh) Academy: POB 13917, Jeddah, Saudi Arabia; tel. (2) 667-1664; fax (2) 667-0873; internet www.fiqhacademy.org.sa; f. 1982. Sec.-Gen. Sheikh MOHAMED HABIB IBN AL-KHODHA.

Islamic Solidarity Fund: c/o OIC Secretariat, POB 178, Jeddah 21411, Saudi Arabia; tel. (2) 680-0800; fax (2) 687-3568; f. 1974 to meet the needs of Islamic communities by providing emergency aid and the finance to build mosques, Islamic centres, hospitals, schools and universities. Chair. Sheikh NASIR ABDULLAH BIN HAMDAN; Exec. Dir ABDULLAH HERSI.

Islamic University in Uganda: POB 2555, Mbale, Uganda; tel. (45) 33502; fax (45) 34452; e-mail iuiu@info.com.co.ug; Kampala Liaison Office: POB 7689, Kampala; tel. (41) 236874; fax (41) 254576; f. 1988 to meet the educational needs of Muslim populations in English-speaking African countries; mainly financed by OIC. Principal Officer Prof. MAHDI ADAMU.

Islamic University of Niger: BP 11507, Niamey, Niger; tel. 723903; fax 733796; f. 1984; provides courses of study in *Shari'a* (Islamic law) and Arabic language and literature; also offers courses in pedagogy and teacher training; receives grants from Islamic Solidarity Fund and contributions from OIC member states. Rector Prof. ABDELALI OUDHRIRI.

Islamic University of Technology—IUT: GPO Box 3003, Board-Bazar, Gazipur 1704, Dhaka, Bangladesh; tel. (2) 980-0960; fax (2) 980-0970; e-mail dg@iit.dhaka.edu; internet www.iitoic-dhaka.edu; f. 1981 as the Islamic Centre for Technical and Vocational Training and Resources, named changed to Islamic Institute of Technology in 1994, current name adopted in June 2001; aims to develop human resources in OIC mem. states, with special reference to engineering, technology, tech. and vocational education and research; 224 staff and 1,000 students; library of 23,000 vols. Vice-Chancellor Prof. Dr M. ANWAR HOSSAIN. Publs *News Bulletin* (annually), annual calendar and announcement for admission, reports, human resources development series.

Research Centre for Islamic History, Art and Culture—IRCICA: POB 24, Beşiktaş 80692, İstanbul, Turkey; tel. (212) 2591742; fax (212) 2584365; e-mail ircica@superonline.com; internet www.ircica.org; f. 1980; library of 50,000 vols. Dir-Gen. Prof. Dr EKMELEDDİN İHSANOĞLU. Publs *Newsletter* (3 a year), monographical studies.

Statistical, Economic and Social Research and Training Centre for the Islamic Countries: Attar Sok 4, GOP 06700, Ankara, Turkey; tel. (312) 4686172; fax (312) 4673458; e-mail oicankara@sesrtcic.org; internet www.sesrtcic.org; f. 1978. Dir-Gen. ERDINÇ ERDÜN. Publs *Journal of Economic Co-operation among Islamic Countries* (quarterly), *InfoReport* (quarterly), *Statistical Yearbook* (annually).

SPECIALIZED INSTITUTIONS

International Islamic News Agency—IINA: King Khalid Palace, Madinah Rd, POB 5054, Jeddah, Saudi Arabia; tel. (2) 665-8561; fax (2) 665-9358; e-mail iina@ogertel.com; internet www.islamicnews.org; f. 1972; distributes news and reports daily on events in the Islamic world, in Arabic, English and French. Dir-Gen. ABDULWAHAB KASHIF.

Islamic Development Bank: POB 5925, Jeddah 21432, Saudi Arabia; tel. (2) 636-1400; fax (1) 636-6871; e-mail archives@isdb.org.sa; internet www.isdb.org; f. 1975; promotes the economic and social development of OIC member countries and Muslim communities in non-member countries; provides assistance in the form of loans and grants for technical aid, in accordance with the principles of the Islamic *Shari'a* (sacred law). Pres. and Chair. Dr AHMED MOHAMED ALI; Sec.-Gen. Dr ABDERRAHIM OMRANA.

Islamic Educational, Scientific and Cultural Organization—ISESCO: BP 755, Rabat 10104, Morocco; tel. (7) 772433; fax (7) 772058; e-mail cid@isesco.org.ma; internet www.isesco.org.ma; f. 1982. Dir-Gen. Dr ABDULAZIZ BIN OTHMAN AL-TWAIJRI. Publs *ISESCO Newsletter* (quarterly), *Islam Today* (2 a year), *ISESCO Triennial*.

Islamic States Broadcasting Organization—ISBO: POB 6351, Jeddah 21442, Saudi Arabia; tel. (2) 672-1121; fax (2) 672-2600; e-mail isbo@isbo.org; internet www.isbo.org; f. 1975. Sec.-Gen. HUSSEIN AL-ASKARY.

AFFILIATED INSTITUTIONS

International Association of Islamic Banks—IAIB: King Abdulaziz St, Queen's Bldg, 23rd Floor, Al-Balad Dist, POB 9707, Jeddah 21423, Saudi Arabia; tel. (2) 651-6900; fax (2) 651-6552; f. 1977 to link financial institutions operating on Islamic banking principles; activities include training and research; mems: 192 banks and other financial institutions in 34 countries. Sec.-Gen. SAMIR A. SHAIKH.

Islamic Chamber of Commerce and Industry: POB 3831, Clifton, Karachi 75600, Pakistan; tel. (21) 5874756; fax (21) 5870765; e-mail icci@icci-oic.org; internet icci-oic.org; f. 1979 to promote trade and industry among member states; comprises nat. chambers or feds of chambers of commerce and industry. Sec.-Gen. AQEEL AHMAD AL-JASSEM.

Islamic Committee for the International Crescent: POB 17434, Benghazi, Libya; tel. (61) 95823; fax (61) 95829; f. 1979 to attempt to alleviate the suffering caused by natural disasters and war. Sec.-Gen. Dr AHMAD ABDALLAH CHERIF.

Islamic Solidarity Sports Federation: POB 5844, Riyadh 11442, Saudi Arabia; tel. and fax (1) 482-2145; f. 1981. Sec.-Gen. Dr MOHAMMAD SALEH GAZDAR.

Organization of Islamic Capitals and Cities—OICC: POB 13621, Jeddah 21414, Saudi Arabia; tel. (2) 698-2141; fax (2) 698-1053; e-mail secrtriat@oicc.org; internet www.oicc.org; f. 1980 to promote and develop co-operation among OICC mems, to preserve their character and heritage, to implement planning guide-lines for the growth of Islamic cities and to upgrade standards of public services and utilities in those cities. Sec.-Gen. OMAR ABDULLAH KADI.

Organization of the Islamic Shipowners' Association: POB 14900, Jeddah 21434, Saudi Arabia; tel. (2) 663-7882; fax (2) 660-4920; e-mail oisa@sbm.net.sa; f. 1981 to promote co-operation among maritime cos in Islamic countries. In 1998 mems approved the establishment of a new commercial venture, the Bakkah Shipping Company, to enhance sea transport in the region. Sec.-Gen. Dr ABDULLATIF A. SULTAN.

World Federation of Arab-Islamic Schools: POB 3446, Jeddah, Saudi Arabia; tel. (2) 670-0019; fax (2) 671-0823; f. 1976; supports Arab-Islamic schools world-wide and encourages co-operation between the institutions; promotes the dissemination of the Arabic language and Islamic culture; supports the training of personnel.

PACIFIC COMMUNITY

Address: BP D5, 98848 Nouméa Cédex, New Caledonia.

Telephone: 26-20-00; **fax:** 26-38-18; **e-mail:** spc@spc.int; **internet:** www.spc.org.nc/.

In February 1947 the Governments of Australia, France, the Netherlands, New Zealand, the United Kingdom, and the USA signed the Canberra Agreement establishing the South Pacific Commission, which came into effect in July 1948. (The Netherlands withdrew from the Commission in 1962, when it ceased to administer the former colony of Dutch New Guinea, now Papua, formerly known as Irian Jaya, part of Indonesia.) In October 1997 the 37th South Pacific Conference, convened in Canberra, Australia, agreed to rename the organization the Pacific Community, with effect from 6 February 1998. The Secretariat of the Pacific Community (SPC) services the Community, and provides research, technical advice, training and assistance in economic, social and cultural development to 22 countries and territories of the Pacific region. It serves a population of about 6.8m., scattered over some 30m. sq km, more than 98% of which is sea.

MEMBERS

American Samoa	Niue
Australia	Northern Mariana Islands
Cook Islands	Palau
Fiji	Papua New Guinea
France	Pitcairn Islands
French Polynesia	Samoa
Guam	Solomon Islands
Kiribati	Tokelau
Marshall Islands	Tonga
Federated States of Micronesia	Tuvalu
Nauru	United Kingdom
New Caledonia	USA
New Zealand	Vanuatu
	Wallis and Futuna Islands

Organization

(October 2002)

CONFERENCE OF THE PACIFIC COMMUNITY

The Conference is the governing body of the Community (replacing the former South Pacific Conference) and is composed of representatives of all member countries and territories. The main responsibilities of the Conference, which meets annually, are to appoint the Director-General, to determine major national or regional policy issues in the areas of competence of the organization and to note changes to the Financial and Staff Regulations approved by the Committee of Representatives of Governments and Administrations (CRGA).

COMMITTEE OF REPRESENTATIVES OF GOVERNMENTS AND ADMINISTRATIONS (CRGA)

This Committee comprises representatives of all member states and territories, having equal voting rights. It meets annually to consider the work programme evaluation conducted by the Secretariat and to discuss any changes proposed by the Secretariat in the context of regional priorities; to consider and approve any policy issues for the organization presented by the Secretariat or by member countries and territories; to consider applicants and make recommendations for the post of Director-General; to approve the administrative and work programme budgets; to approve amendments to the Financial and Staff Regulations; and to conduct annual performance evaluations of the Director-General.

SECRETARIAT

The Secretariat of the Pacific Community—SPC—is headed by a Director-General and two Deputy Directors-General, based in Suva and Nouméa. Three administrative Divisions cover Land Resources, Marine Resources and Social Resources. The Secretariat also provides information services, including library facilities, publications, translation and computer services. The organization has about 250 staff members.

Director-General: LOURDES PANGELINAN (Guam).

Senior Deputy Director-General: Dr JIMMIE RODGERS (Solomon Islands).

Deputy Director-General: YVES CORBEL (France).

Regional Office: Private Mail Bag, Suva, Fiji; tel. 3370733; fax 3370021; e-mail spcsuva@spc.org.fj.

Activities

The SPC provides, on request of its member countries, technical assistance, advisory services, information and clearing-house services aimed at developing the technical, professional, scientific, research, planning and management capabilities of the regional population. The SPC also conducts regional conferences and technical meetings, as well as training courses, workshops and seminars at the regional or country level. It provides small grants-in-aid and awards to meet specific requests and needs of members. In November 1996 the Conference agreed to establish a specific Small Islands States fund to provide technical services, training and other relevant activities. The organization's three programme divisions are: land resources, marine resources and social resources. The Pacific Community oversees the maritime programme and telecommunications policy activities of the Pacific Islands Forum Secretariat (q.v.).

In 1998 the SPC adopted a Corporate Plan for 1999–2003, the main objectives of which included developing national capabilities in 'value-adding' technology; enhancing the integration of cross-sectoral issues (such as economics, gender, culture and community education) into national planning and policy-making processes; and developing a co-ordinated human resources programme as a focal point for providing information, advice and support to the regional population. The 1999 Conference, held in Tahiti in December, adopted the 'Déclaration de Tahiti Nui', a mandate that detailed the operational policies and mechanisms of the Pacific Community, taking into account operational changes not covered by the founding Canberra Agreement. The Déclaration was regarded as a 'living document' that would be periodically revised to record subsequent modifications of operational policy. The SPC has signed memoranda of understanding with WHO, the Forum Fisheries Agency, the South Pacific Regional Environment Programme (SPREP), and several other partners. The organization participates in meetings of the Council of Regional Organizations in the Pacific (CROP, see under Pacific Islands Forum Secretariat). Representatives of the SPC, SPREP and the South Pacific Applied Geoscience Commission hold periodic 'troika' meetings to develop regional technical co-operation and harmonization of work programmes.

LAND RESOURCES

The land resources division comprises two major programmes: agriculture (incorporating advice and specific activities in crop improvement and plant protection; animal health and production services; and agricultural resource economics and information); and forestry (providing training, technical assistance and information in forestry management and agroforestry). Objectives of the agriculture programme, based in Suva, Fiji, include the promotion of land and agricultural management practices that are both economically and environmentally sustainable; strengthening national capabilities to reduce losses owing to crop pests (insects, pathogens and weeds) and animal diseases already present, and to prevent the introduction of new pests and diseases; and facilitating trade through improved quarantine procedures. Forestry activities include the implementation, jointly with other partners, of the Pacific Islands Forests and Trees Support Project, which is concerned with natural forest management and conservation, agroforestry and development and the use of tree and plant resources; and of the Pacific-German Regional Forestry Project. A Pacific Regional Agricultural Programme (PRAP), funded by the European Union, was introduced by eight member states in 1990. The SPC assumed responsibility for administering PRAP in 1998.

MARINE RESOURCES

The SPC aims to support and co-ordinate the sustainable development and management of inshore fisheries resources in the region, to undertake scientific research in order to provide member governments with relevant information for the sustainable development and management of tuna and billfish resources in and adjacent to the South Pacific region, and to provide data and analytical services to national fisheries departments. The main components of the Community's fisheries activities are the Coastal Fisheries Programme (CFP), the Oceanic Fisheries Programme (OFP), and the Regional Maritime Programme (RMP). The CFP is divided into the following sections: community fisheries (research and assessment of and development support for people occupied in subsistence and artisanal fisheries); fisheries training; sustainable fisheries development; reef fisheries assessment and management; fisheries information; and post-harvest development (offering advice and training in order to improve handling practices, storage, seafood product development, quality control and marketing). The OFP consists of the following three sections: statistics and monitoring; tuna ecology and biology; and stock assessment and modelling. The statistics and monitoring section maintains a database of industrial tuna fisheries in the region. The OFP contributed research and statistical information for the formulation of the Convention for the Conservation and Management of Highly Migratory Fish Stocks in the Western and Central Pacific, which aimed to establish a regime for the sustainable management of tuna reserves, and was opened for signature in Honolulu in September 2000. (The convention had been ratified by four states at February 2002.) The SPC and European Commission were jointly to launch the Pacific Regional Oceanic and Coastal Fisheries Project (PROCFISH) in 2002. The oceanic component of the project aimed to assist the OFP with advancing knowledge of tuna fisheries ecosystems, while the coastal element was to produce the first comparative regional baseline assessment of reef fisheries. The RMP advises member governments in the fields of policy, law and training. In early 2002 the RMP launched the model Pacific Islands Maritime Legislation and Regulations as a framework for the development of national maritime legislation. The SPC adminsters the Pacific Island Aquaculture Network, a forum for promoting regional aquaculture development.

The SPC hosts the Pacific Office of the World Fish Centre (the International Centre for Living Aquatic Resources Management—ICLARM); the SPC and the World Fish Centre have jointly implemented a number of projects.

SOCIAL RESOURCES

The Social Resources Division comprises the Community Health Programme and the Socio-economic Programme (including sub-programmes and sections on statistics; population and demography; rural energy development; youth issues; culture; women's and gender equality; community education training; and media training).

The Community Health Programme aims to implement health promotion programmes; to assist regional authorities to strengthen health information systems and to promote the use of new technology for health information development and disease control (for example, through the Public Health Surveillance and Disease Control Programme); to promote efficient health services management; and to help all Pacific Islanders to attain a level of health and quality of life that will enable them to contribute to the development of their communities. The Community Health Services also work in the areas of non-communicable diseases and nutrition (with particular focus on the high levels of diabetes and heart disease in parts of the region); environmental health, through the improvement of water and sanitation facilities; and reducing the incidence of HIV/AIDS and other sexually-transmitted diseases (STDs), tuberculosis, and vector-borne diseases such as malaria and dengue fever. The SPC operates a project (mainly funded by Australia and New Zealand), to prevent AIDS and STDs among young people through peer education and awareness. It is also responsible for implementing the Pacific Regional Vector-Borne Diseases Project, established in 1996, which focuses particularly on Fiji, Vanuatu and the Solomon Islands.

The Statistics Programme assists governments and administrations in the region to provide effective and efficient national statistical services through the provision of training activities, a statistical information service and other advisory services. A Regional Conference of Statisticians facilitates the integration and co-ordination of statistical services throughout the region.

The Population and Demography Programme provides technical support in population, demographic and development issues to member governments, other SPC programmes, and organizations active in the region. The Programme aims to assist governments effectively to analyse data and utilize it into the formulation of national development policies and programmes. The Programme organizes national workshops in population and development planning, provides short-term professional attachments, undertakes demographic research and analysis, and disseminates information.

The Rural Energy Development Programme provides technical assistance and advice to member states on the utilization of sustainable energy resources, and incorporates a regional rural renewable energy project, sponsored by Australia and France.

The Pacific Youth Resource Bureau (PWRB) co-ordinates the implementation of the Pacific Youth Strategy 2005, which aims to develop opportunities for young people to play an active role in society. The PYRB provides non-formal education and support for youth, community workers and young adults in community development subjects and provides grants to help young people find employment. It also advises and assists the Pacific Youth Council in promoting a regional youth identity. The Pacific Women's Resource Bureau (PWRB) aims to promote the social, economic and cultural advancement of women in the region by assisting governments and regional organizations to include women in the development planning process. The PWRB also provides technical and advisory services, advocacy and management support training to groups concerned with women in development and gender and development, and supports the production and exchange of information regarding women.

The Cultural Programme aims to preserve and promote the cultural heritage of the Pacific Islands. The Programme assists with the training of librarians, archivists and researchers and promotes instruction in local languages, history and art at schools in member states and territories. The SPC acts as the secretariat of the Council of Pacific Arts, which organizes the Festival of Pacific Arts on a four-yearly basis.

The SPC regional office in Suva, Fiji, administers a Community Education Training Centre (CETC), which conducts a seven-month training course for up to 36 women community workers annually, with the objective of training women in methods of community development so that they can help others to achieve better living conditions for island families and communities. The Regional Media Centre provides training, technical assistance and production materials in all areas of the media for member countries and territories, community work programmes, donor projects and regional non-governmental organizations. The Centre comprises a radio broadcast unit, a graphic design and publication unit and a TV and video unit.

In 2000 the SPC's Information Technology and Communication Unit launched ComET, a satellite communications project aimed at linking more closely the organization's headquarters in New Caledonia and regional office in Fiji. The Information and Communications Programme is developing the use of modern communication technology as an invaluable resource for problem-solving, regional networking, and uniting the Community's scattered, often physically isolated, island member states. In conjunction with the Secretariat of the Pacific Islands Forum the SPC convened the first regional meeting of Information and Communication Technology workers, researchers and policy-makers in August 2001. The meeting addressed strategies for the advancement of new information technologies in member countries.

Finance

The organization's core budget, funded by assessed contributions from member states, finances executive and administrative expenditures, the Information and Communications Programme, and several professional and support positions that contribute to the work of the three programme divisions (i.e. Land Resources, Marine Resources and Social Resources). The non-core budget, funded mainly by aid donors and in part by Community member states, mostly on a contractual basis, finances the SPC's technical services. Administrative expenditure for 2000 amounted to US $2.5m.

Publications

Annual Report.

Fisheries Newsletter (quarterly).

Pacific Aids Alert Bulletin (quarterly).

Pacific Island Nutrition (quarterly).

Regional Tuna Bulletin (quarterly).

Report of the Conference of the Pacific Community.

Women's Newsletter (quarterly).

Technical publications, statistical bulletins, advisory leaflets and reports.

PACIFIC ISLANDS FORUM

MEMBERS

Australia	Niue
Cook Islands	Palau
Fiji	Papua New Guinea
Kiribati	Samoa
Marshall Islands	Solomon Islands
Federated States of Micronesia	Tonga
Nauru	Tuvalu
New Zealand	Vanuatu

Note: New Caledonia was admitted as an observer at the Forum in 1999. East Timor was granted 'special observer' status in 2002.

The Pacific Islands Forum (which changed its name from South Pacific Forum in October 2000) was founded as the gathering of Heads of Government of the independent and self-governing states of the South Pacific. Its first meeting was held on 5 August 1971, in Wellington, New Zealand. It provides an opportunity for informal discussions to be held on a wide range of common issues and problems and meets annually or when issues require urgent attention. The Forum has no written constitution or international agreement governing its activities nor any formal rules relating to its purpose, membership or conduct of meeting. Decisions are always reached by consensus, it never having been found necessary or desirable to vote formally on issues. In October 1994 the Forum was granted observer status by the General Assembly of the United Nations.

Since 1989 each Forum has been followed by 'dialogues' with representatives of other countries with a long-term interest in and commitment to the region. In October 1995 the Forum Governments suspended France's 'dialogue' status, following that country's resumption of the testing of nuclear weapons in French Polynesia. France was reinstated as a 'dialogue partner' in September 1996. In 2002 'dialogue partners' comprised Canada, the People's Republic of China, France, Indonesia, Japan, the Republic of Korea, Malaysia, Philippines, the United Kingdom, the USA, and the European Union. India was to be admitted as a dialogue partner in 2003.

The South Pacific Nuclear-Free Zone Treaty (Treaty of Rarotonga), prohibiting the acquisition, stationing or testing of nuclear weapons in the region, came into effect in December 1986, following ratification by eight states. The USSR signed the protocols to the treaty (whereby states possessing nuclear weapons agree not to use or threaten to use nuclear explosive devices against any non-nuclear party to the Treaty) in December 1987 and ratified them in April 1988; the People's Republic of China did likewise in December 1987 and October 1988 respectively. The other three major nuclear powers, however, intimated that they did not intend to adhere to the Treaty. In July 1993 the Forum petitioned the USA, the United Kingdom and France, asking them to reconsider their past refusal to sign the Treaty in the light of the end of the 'Cold War'. In July 1995, following the decision of the French Government to resume testing of nuclear weapons in French Polynesia, members of the Forum resolved to increase diplomatic pressure on the three Governments to sign the Treaty. In October the United Kingdom, the USA and France announced their intention to accede to the Treaty, by mid-1996. While the decision was approved by the Forum, it urged the Governments to sign with immediate effect, thus accelerating the termination of France's testing programme. Following France's decision, announced in January 1996, to end the programme four months earlier than scheduled, representatives of the Governments of the three countries signed the Treaty in March.

In 1990 five of the Forum's smallest island member states formed an economic sub-group to address their specific concerns, in particular economic disadvantages resulting from a poor resource base, absence of a skilled work-force and lack of involvement in world markets. In September 1997 the 28th Forum, convened in Rarotonga, the Cook Islands, endorsed the inclusion of the Marshall Islands as the sixth member of the Smaller Island States sub-group. Representatives of the grouping, which also includes Kiribati, the Cook Islands, Nauru, Niue and Tuvalu, meet regularly. In February 1998 senior Forum officials, for the first time, met with representatives of the Caribbean Community and the Indian Ocean Commission, as well as other major international organizations, to discuss means to enhance consideration and promotion of the interests of small island states. Small island member states have been particularly concerned about the phenomenon of global warming and its potentially damaging effects on the region (see below).

The 23rd Forum, held in Honiara, Solomon Islands, in July 1992, welcomed France's suspension of its nuclear-testing programme until the end of the year, but urged the French Government to make the moratorium permanent. Forum members discussed the decisions made at the UN Conference on Environment and Development held in June, and approved the Cook Islands' proposal to host a 'global conference for small islands'. The Niue Fisheries Surveillance and Law Enforcement Co-operation Treaty was signed by members, with the exception of Fiji, Kiribati and Tokelau, which were awaiting endorsement from their legislatures. The treaty provided for co-operation in the surveillance of fisheries resources and in defeating drugs-trafficking and other organized crime. Forum leaders also adopted a separate declaration on future priorities in law enforcement co-operation.

At the 24th Forum, held in Yaren, Nauru, in August 1993 it was agreed that effective links needed to be established with the broader Asia-Pacific region, with participation in Asia-Pacific Economic Co-operation (APEC), where the Forum has observer status, to be utilized to the full. The Forum urged an increase in intra-regional trade and asked for improved opportunities for Pacific island countries exporting to Australia and New Zealand. New Caledonia's right to self-determination was supported. Environmental protection measures and the rapid growth in population in the region, which was posing a threat to economic and social development, were also discussed by the Forum delegates.

The 25th Forum was convened in Brisbane, Australia, in August 1994 under the theme of 'Managing Our Resources'. In response to the loss of natural resources as well as of income-earning potential resulting from unlawful logging of timber by foreign companies, Forum members agreed to impose stricter controls on the exploitation of forestry resources and to begin negotiations to standardize monitoring of the region's resources. The Forum also agreed to strengthen its promotion of sustainable exploitation of fishing stocks, reviewed preparations of a convention to control the movement and management of radioactive waste within the South Pacific and discussed the rationalization of national airlines, on a regional or sub-regional basis, to reduce operational losses.

The 26th Forum, held in Madang, Papua New Guinea, in September 1995, was dominated by extreme hostility on the part of Forum Governments to the resumption of testing of nuclear weapons by France in the South Pacific region. The decision to recommence testing, announced by the French Government in June, had been instantly criticized by Forum Governments. The 26th Forum reiterated their demand that France stop any further testing, and also condemned the People's Republic of China for conducting nuclear tests in the region. The meeting endorsed a draft Code of Conduct on the management and monitoring of indigenous forest resources in selected South Pacific countries, which had been initiated at the 25th Forum; however, while the six countries concerned committed themselves to implementing the Code through national legislation, its signing was deferred, owing to an initial unwillingness on the part of Papua New Guinea and Solomon Islands. The Forum did adopt a treaty to ban the import into the region of all radioactive and other hazardous wastes, and to control the transboundary movement and management of these wastes (the so-called Waigani

Convention). The Forum agreed to reactivate the ministerial committee on New Caledonia, comprising Fiji, Nauru and Solomon Islands, which was to monitor political developments in that territory prior to its referendum on independence, scheduled to be held in 1998. In addition, the Forum resolved to implement and pursue means of promoting economic co-operation and long-term development in the region. In December 1995 Forum finance ministers, meeting in Port Moresby, Papua New Guinea, discussed the issues involved in the concept of 'Securing Development Beyond 2000' and initiated an assessment project to further trade liberalization efforts in the region.

The 27th Forum, held in Majuro, the Marshall Islands, in September 1996, supported the efforts of the French Government to improve relations with countries in the South Pacific and agreed to readmit France to the post-Forum dialogue. The Forum meeting recognized the importance of responding to the liberalization of the global trading system by reviewing the region's economic tariff policies, and of assisting members in attracting investment for the development of the private sector. The Forum advocated that a meeting of economy ministers of member countries be held each year. The Forum was also concerned with environmental issues: in particular, it urged the ratification and implementation of the Waigani Convention by all member states, the promotion of regional efforts to conserve marine resources and to protect the coastal environment, and the formulation of an international, legally-binding agreement to reduce emissions by industrialized countries of so-called 'greenhouse gases'. Such gases contribute to the warming of the earth's atmosphere (the 'greenhouse effect') and to related increases in global sea-levels, and have therefore been regarded as a threat to low-lying islands in the region. The Forum requested the ministerial committee on New Caledonia (established by the 1990 Forum to monitor, in co-operation with the French authorities, political developments in the territory) to pursue contacts with all parties there and to continue to monitor preparations for the 1998 referendum.

In July 1997 the inaugural meeting of Forum economy ministers was convened in Cairns, Australia. It formulated an Action Plan to encourage the flow of foreign investment into the region by committing members to economic reforms, good governance and the implementation of multilateral trade and tariff policies. The meeting also commissioned a formal study of the establishment of a free-trade agreement between Forum island states. The 28th Forum, held in Rarotonga, the Cook Islands, in September, considered the economic challenges confronting the region. However, it was marked by a failure to conclude a common policy position on mandatory targets for reductions in 'greenhouse gas' emissions, owing to an ongoing dispute between Australia and other Forum Governments.

The 29th Forum, held in Pohnpei, Federated States of Micronesia, in August 1998, considered the need to pursue economic reforms and to stimulate the private sector and foreign investment in order to ensure economic growth. Leaders reiterated their support for efforts to implement the economic Action Plan and to develop a framework for a free-trade agreement, and endorsed specific recommendations of the second Forum Economic Ministers Meeting, which was held in Fiji, in July, including the promotion of competitive telecommunications markets, the development of information infrastructures and support for a new economic vulnerability index at the UN to help determine least developed country status. The Forum was also concerned with environmental issues, notably the shipment of radioactive wastes, the impact of a multinational venture to launch satellites from the Pacific, the need for ongoing radiological monitoring of the Mururoa and Fangataufa atolls, and the development of a South Pacific Whale Sanctuary. The Forum adopted a Statement on Climate Change, which urged all countries to ratify and implement the gas emission reductions agreed upon by UN member states in December 1997 (the so-called Kyoto Protocol of the UN Framework Convention on Climate Change), and emphasized the Forum's commitment to further measures for verifying and enforcing emission limitation.

In October 1999 the 30th Forum, held in Koror, Palau, endorsed in principle the establishment of a regional free-trade area (FTA), which had been approved at a special ministerial meeting held in June. The FTA was to be implemented from 2002 over a period of eight years for developing member countries and 10 years for smaller island states and least developed countries. The Forum requested officials from member countries to negotiate the details of a draft agreement on the FTA (the so-called Pacific Island Countries Trade Agreement—PICTA), including possible extensions of the arrangements to Australia and New Zealand. The heads of government adopted a Forum Vision for the Pacific Information Economy, which recognized the importance of information technology infrastructure for the region's economic and social development and the possibilities for enhanced co-operation in investment, job creation, education, training and cultural exchange. Forum Governments also expressed concern at the shipment of radioactive waste through the Pacific and determined to pursue negotiations with France, Japan and the United Kingdom regarding liability and compensation arrangements; confirmed their continued support for the multinational force and UN operations in East Timor; and urged more countries to adopt and implement the Kyoto Protocol to limit the emission of 'greenhouse gases'. In addition, the Forum agreed to rename the grouping (hitherto known as the South Pacific Forum) the Pacific Islands Forum, to reflect the expansion of its membership since its establishment; the new designation took effect at the 31st Forum, which was convened in Tarawa, Kiribati, at the end of October 2000.

At the 31st Forum the heads of government discussed the escalation in regional insecurity that had occurred since the previous Forum. Concern was expressed over the unrest that prevailed during mid-2000 in Fiji and Solomon Islands, and also over ongoing political violence in the Indonesian province of Irian Jaya (now Papua). The Forum adopted the Biketawa Declaration, which outlined a mechanism for responding to any future such crises in the region while urging members to undertake efforts to address the fundamental causes of instability. The detrimental economic impact of the disturbances in Fiji and Solomon Islands was noted. The Forum endorsed a proposal to establish a Regional Financial Information Sharing Facility and national financial intelligence units, and welcomed the conclusion in June by the European Union and ACP states (which include several Forum members) of the Cotonou Agreement (q.v.). The Forum also reiterated support for the prompt implementation of the Kyoto Protocol.

In August 2001, convened at the 32nd Forum, in Nauru, nine regional leaders adopted PICTA, providing for the establishment of the FTA (as envisaged at the 30th Forum). A related Pacific Agreement on Closer Economic Relations (PACER), envisaging the phased establishment of a regional single market including the signatories to PICTA and Australia and New Zealand, was also adopted. The Forum expressed concern at the refusal of the USA (responsible for about one-quarter of world-wide 'greenhouse gas' emissions) to ratify the Kyoto Protocol. In response to an ongoing initiative by the Organisation of Economic Co-operation and Development (OECD) to eliminate the operation of 'harmful tax systems', the Forum reaffirmed the sovereign right of nations to establish individual tax regimes and urged the development of a new co-operative framework to address issues relating to financial transparency. (OECD had identified the Cook Islands, the Marshall Islands, Nauru and Niue as so-called 'tax havens' lacking financial transparency and had demanded that they impose stricter legislation to address the incidence of international money-laundering on their territories.) Forum leaders also reiterated protests against the shipment of radioactive materials through the region.

The 33rd Forum, held in Suva, Fiji, in August 2002, adopted the the Nasonini Declaration on Regional Security, which recognized the need for immediate and sustained regional action to combat international terrorism and transnational crime, in view of the perceived increased threat to global and regional security following the major terrorist attacks perpetrated against targets in the USA in September 2001. Regional leaders also approved a Pacific Island Regional Ocean Policy, which aimed to ensure the future sustainable use of the ocean and its resources by Pacific Island communities and external partners. In addition the Forum urged OECD to adopt a more flexible approach in the implementation of its ongoing harmful tax initiative; welcomed the third assessment report on climate change issued in 2001 by the WMO/UNEP Intergovernmental Panel on Climate Change and reiterated demands for a world-wide reduction in greenhouse gas emissions; invited member island states to declare their coastal waters as whale sanctuaries; and urged the development of a Pacific Regional Plan of Action against HIV/AIDS.

Pacific Islands Forum Secretariat

Address: Private Mail Bag, Suva, Fiji.

Telephone: 3312600; **fax:** 3305573; **e-mail:** info@forumsec.org.fj; **internet:** www.forumsec.org.fj.

The South Pacific Bureau for Economic Co-operation (SPEC) was established by an agreement signed on 17 April 1973, at the third meeting of the South Pacific Forum (now Pacific Islands Forum) in Apia, Western Samoa (now Samoa). SPEC was renamed the South Pacific Forum Secretariat in 1988; this, in turn, was redesignated as the Pacific Islands Forum Secretariat in October 2000.

Organization

(October 2002)

FORUM OFFICIALS COMMITTEE

The Forum Officials Committee is the Secretariat's executive board. It comprises representatives and senior officials from all member countries. It meets twice a year, immediately before the meetings of the Pacific Islands Forum and at the end of the year, to discuss in detail the Secretariat's work programme and annual budget.

SECRETARIAT

The Secretariat undertakes the day-to-day activities of the Forum. It is headed by a Secretary-General, with a staff of some 70 people drawn from the member countries. The Secretariat comprises the following four Divisions: Corporate Services; Development and Economic Policy; Trade and Investment; and Political, International and Legal Affairs.

Secretary-General: NOEL LEVI (Papua New Guinea).

Deputy Secretary-General: IOSEFA MAIAVA (Samoa).

Activities

The Secretariat's aim is to enhance the economic and social well-being of the people of the South Pacific, in support of the efforts of national governments.

The Secretariat's trade and investment services extend advice and technical assistance to member countries in policy, development, export marketing, and information dissemination. Trade policy activities are mainly concerned with improving private sector policies, for example investment promotion, assisting integration into the world economy (including the provision of information and technical assistance to member states on WTO-related matters and supporting Pacific Island ACP states with preparations for negotiations on trade partnership with the EU under the Cotonou Agreement), and the development of businesses. The Secretariat aims to assist both island governments and private sector companies to enhance their capacity in the development and exploitation of export markets, product identification and product development. A trade exhibition was held in French Polynesia in 1997, and support was granted to provide for visits to overseas trade fairs and the development of promotional materials. A regional trade and investment database is being developed. The Trade and Investment Division of the Secretariat co-ordinates the activities of the regional trade offices located in Australia, New Zealand and Japan (see below). A representative trade office in Beijing, People's Republic of China, opened in January 2002.

In 2002 the Trade and Investment Division was preparing for the implementation of two major regional trade accords signed by Forum heads of state in August 2001: the Pacific Island Countries Trade Agreement (PICTA), providing for the establishment of a Pacific Island free-trade area (FTA); and the related Pacific Agreement on Closer Economic Relations (PACER), incorporating trade and economic co-operation measures and envisaging an eventual single regional market comprising the PICTA FTA and Australia and New Zealand. It was envisaged that negotiations on free-trade agreements between Pacific Island states and Australia and New Zealand, with a view to establishing the larger regional single market envisaged by PACER, would commence within eight years of PICTA's entry into force. SPARTECA (see below) would remain operative pending the establishment of the larger single market, into which it would be subsumed. Under the provisions of PACER, Australia and New Zealand were to provide technical and financial assistance to PICTA signatory states in pursuing the objectives of PACER.

In 1981 the South Pacific Regional Trade and Economic Co-operation Agreement (SPARTECA), came into force. SPARTECA aimed to redress the trade deficit of the Pacific Island countries with Australia and New Zealand. It is a non-reciprocal trade agreement under which Australia and New Zealand offer duty-free and unrestricted access or concessional access for specified products originating from the developing island member countries of the Forum. In 1985 Australia agreed to further liberalization of trade by abolishing (from the beginning of 1987) duties and quotas on all Pacific products except steel, cars, sugar, footwear and garments. In August 1994 New Zealand expanded its import criteria under the agreement by reducing the rule of origin requirement for garment products from 50% to 45% of local content. In response to requests from Fiji, Australia agreed to widen its interpretation of the agreement by accepting as being of local content manufactured products that consist of goods and components of 50% Australian content. A new Fiji/Australia Trade and Economic Relations Agreement (AFTERA) was concluded in March 1999 to complement SPARTECA and compensate for certain trade benefits that were in the process of being withdrawn.

In April 2001 the Secretariat convened a meeting of seven member island states—Cook Islands, the Marshall Islands, Nauru, Niue, Samoa, Tonga and Vanuatu—as well as representatives from Australia and New Zealand, to address the regional implications of the OECD's Harmful Tax Competition Initiative. Under the initiative, designed to reduce the level of potential tax revenue lost by OECD member states to offshore 'tax havens', 35 jurisdictions, including these seven Pacific Island states, were required to amend national financial legislation by the end of July. States that did not comply would be designated as 'non-co-operative' and might be targeted by 'defensive measures'. The meeting requested the OECD to engage in conciliatory negotiations with the listed Pacific Island states. At the August 2001 Forum (by which time Cook Islands, the Marshall Islands, Nauru and Niue had been identified as non-co-operative) leaders reiterated this stance, proclaiming the sovereign right of nations to establish individual tax regimes, and supporting the development of a new co-operative framework to address financial transparency concerns. In December the Secretariat hosted a workshop for officials from nine member states concerned with combating financial crime. The workshop was attended and sponsored by several partner organizations and bodies, including the IMF.

The Political, International and Legal Affairs Division of the Secretariat organizes and services the meetings of the Forum, disseminates its views, administers the Forum's observer office at the United Nations, and aims to strengthen relations with other regional and international organizations, in particular APEC and ASEAN. The Division's other main concern is to promote regional co-operation in law enforcement and legal affairs, and it provides technical support for the drafting of legal documents and for law enforcement capacity-building. In 1997 the Secretariat undertook an assessment to survey the need for specialist training in dealing with money laundering in member countries. In recent years the Forum Secretariat has been concerned with assessing the legislative reforms and other commitments needed to ensure implementation of the 1992 Honiara Declaration on Law Enforcement Co-operation. The Division assists member countries to ratify and implement the 1988 UN Convention against Illicit Trafficking in Narcotic Drugs and Psychotropic Substances. In December 1998 the Secretariat initiated a five-year programme to strengthen regional law enforcement capabilities, in particular to counter cross-border crimes such as money-laundering and drugs-trafficking. All member states, apart from Australia and New Zealand, were to participate in the initiative. In December 2001 the first ever Forum Election Observer Group was dispatched to monitor legislative elections held in Solomon Islands. A conference of Forum immigration ministers convened in that month expressed concern at rising levels of human-trafficking and illegal immigration in the region, and recommended that member states become parties to the 2000 UN Convention Against Transnational Organized Crime.

The Secretariat helps to co-ordinate environmental policy. With support from the Australian Government, it administers a network of stations to monitor sea-levels and climate change throughout the Pacific region. In recent years the Secretariat has played an active role in supporting regional participation at meetings of the Conference of the Parties to the UN Framework Convention on Climate Change.

The Development and Economic Policy Division of the Secretariat aims to co-ordinate and promote co-operation in development activities and programmes throughout the region. The Division administers a Short Term Advisory Service, which provides consultancy services to help member countries meet economic development priorities, and a Fellowship Scheme to provide practical training in a range of technical and income-generating activities. A Small Island Development Fund aims to assist the economic development of this sub-group of member countries (i.e. the Cook Islands, Kiribati, the Marshall Islands, Nauru, Niue and Tuvalu) through project financing. A separate fellowship has also been established to provide training to the Kanak population of New Caledonia, to assist in their social, economic and political development. The Division aims to assist regional organizations to identify development priorities and to provide advice to national governments on economic analysis, planning and structural reforms. The Secretariat chairs the Council of Regional Organizations in the Pacific (CROP), an *ad hoc* committee comprising the heads of eight regional organizations, which aims to discuss and co-ordinate the policies and work programmes of the various agencies in order to avoid duplication of or omissions in their services to member countries.

The Secretariat services the Pacific Group Council of ACP states receiving assistance from the EU (q.v.), and in early 1993 a joint unit was established within the Secretariat headquarters to assist Pacific ACP countries and regional organizations in submitting projects to the EU for funding.

The Forum established the Pacific Forum Line and the Association of South Pacific Airlines (see below), as part of its efforts to promote co-operation in regional transport. On 1 January 1997 the work of the Forum Maritime Programme, which included assistance for regional maritime training and for the development of regional maritime administrations and legislation, was transferred to the regional office of the South Pacific Commission (renamed the Pacific Community from February 1998) at Suva. At the same time responsibility for the Secretariat's civil aviation activities was transferred to individual countries, to be managed at a bilateral level. Telecommunications policy activities were also transferred to the then South Pacific Commission at the start of 1997. In May 1998 ministers responsible for aviation in member states approved a new regional civil aviation policy, which envisaged liberalization of air services, common safety and security standards and provisions for shared revenue.

Finance

The Governments of Australia and New Zealand each contribute some 37% of the annual budget and the remaining amount is shared by the other member Governments. Extra-budgetary funding is contributed mainly by Australia, New Zealand, Japan, the EU and France. Forum officials approved a budget of $F 15.4m. for the Secretariat's 2002 work programme.

Publications

Annual Report.

Forum News (quarterly).

Forum Trends.

Forum Secretariat Directory of Aid Agencies.

South Pacific Trade Directory.

SPARTECA (guide for Pacific island exporters).

Reports of meetings; profiles of Forum member countries.

Associated and Affiliated Organizations

Association of South Pacific Airlines—ASPA: POB 9817, Nadi Airport, Nadi, Fiji; tel. 6723526; fax 6720196; f. 1979 at a meeting of airlines in the South Pacific, convened to promote co-operation among the member airlines for the development of regular, safe and economical commercial aviation within, to and from the South Pacific. Mems: 16 regional airlines, two associates. Chair. SEMISI TAUMOEPEAU; Sec.-Gen. GEORGE E. FAKTAUFON.

Forum Fisheries Agency—FFA: POB 629, Honiara, Solomon Islands; tel. (677) 21124; fax (677) 23995; e-mail info@ffa.int; f. 1979 to promote co-operation in fisheries among coastal states in the region; collects and disseminates information and advice on the living marine resources of the region, including the management, exploitation and development of these resources; provides assistance in the areas of law (treaty negotiations, drafting legislation, and co-ordinating surveillance and enforcement), fisheries development, research, economics, computers, and information management. A Vessel Monitoring System, to provide automated data collection and analysis of fishing vessel activities throughout the region, was inaugurated by the FFA in 1998. On behalf of its 16 member countries, the FFA administers a multilateral fisheries treaty, under which vessels from the USA operate in the region, in exchange for an annual payment. Dir VICTORIO UHERBELAU. Publs *FFA News Digest* (every two months), *FFA Reports*.

Pacific Forum Line: POB 796, Auckland, New Zealand; tel. (9) 356-2333; fax (9) 356-2330; e-mail info@pflnz.co.nz; internet www.pflnz.co.nz; f. 1977 as a joint venture by South Pacific countries, to provide shipping services to meet the special requirements of the region; operates three container vessels; conducts shipping agency services in Australia, Fiji, New Zealand and Samoa, and stevedoring in Samoa. Chair. T. TUFUI; CEO W. J. MACLENNAN.

Pacific Islands Centre—PIC: Sotobori Sky Bldg, 5th Floor, 2-11 Ichigayahonmura-cho, Shinjuku-ku,, Tokyo 162-0845, Japan; tel. (3) 3268-8419; fax (3) 3268-6311; f. 1996 to promote and to facilitate trade, investment and tourism among Forum members and Japan. Dir HIDEO FUJITA.

South Pacific Trade Commission (Australia Office): Level 30, Piccadilly Tower, 133 Castlereagh St, Sydney, NSW 2000, Australia; tel. (2) 9283-5933; fax (2) 9283-5948; e-mail info@sptc.gov.au; internet www.sptc.gov.au; f. 1979; assists Pacific Island Governments and business communities to identify market opportunities in Australia and promotes investment in the Pacific Island countries. Senior Trade Commr AIVU TAUVASA (Papua New Guinea).

South Pacific Trade Commission (New Zealand Office): Flight Centre, 48 Emily Pl., Auckland, New Zealand; tel. (9) 3020465; fax (9) 3776642; e-mail parmeshc@sptc.org.nz; internet www.sptc.org.nz. Senior Trade Commr PARMESH CHAND.

SOUTH ASIAN ASSOCIATION FOR REGIONAL CO-OPERATION—SAARC

Address: POB 4222, Kathmandu, Nepal.

Telephone: (1) 221785; **fax:** (1) 227033; **e-mail:** saarc@saarc-sec.org; **internet:** www.saarc-sec.org.

The South Asian Association for Regional Co-operation (SAARC) was formally established in 1985 in order to strengthen and accelerate regional co-operation, particularly in economic development.

MEMBERS

Bangladesh	Nepal
Bhutan	Pakistan
India	Sri Lanka
Maldives	

Organization

(October 2002)

SUMMIT MEETING

Heads of state and of government of member states represent the body's highest authority, and a summit meeting is normally held annually. The 11th SAARC summit meeting was convened in Kathmandu, Nepal, in January 2002. (It had been postponed from November 1999 owing to a deterioration in relations at that time between India and Pakistan.)

COUNCIL OF MINISTERS

The Council of Ministers comprises the ministers of foreign affairs of member countries, who meet twice a year. The Council may also meet in extraordinary session at the request of member states. The responsibilities of the Council include formulation of policies, assessing progress and confirming new areas of co-operation.

STANDING COMMITTEE

The Committee consists of the secretaries of foreign affairs of member states. It has overall responsibility for the monitoring and co-ordination of programmes and financing, and determines priorities, mobilizes resources and identifies areas of co-operation. It usually meets twice a year, and submits its reports to the Council of Ministers. The Committee is supported by an *ad hoc* Programming Committee made up of senior officials, who meet to examine the budget of the Secretariat, confirm the Calendar of Activities and resolve matters assigned to it by the Standing Committee.

TECHNICAL COMMITTEES

SAARC's Integrated Programme of Action is implemented by seven Technical Committees (reduced from 11 since 2000) covering: Agriculture and rural development; Energy; Environment, meteorology and forestry; Human resource development; Science and technology; Social development; and Transport and communications. Each committee is headed by a representative of a member state and meets annually.

SECRETARIAT

The Secretariat was established in 1987 to co-ordinate and oversee SAARC activities. It comprises the Secretary-General and a Director from each member country. The Secretary-General is appointed by the Council of Ministers, after being nominated by a member state. The ninth summit meeting of heads of state and of government, held in Malé, Maldives, in 1997, extended the Secretary-General's term of office from two to three years. The Director is nominated by member states and appointed by the Secretary-General for a term of three years, although this may be increased in special circumstances.

Secretary-General: Q. A. M. A. RAHIM (Bangladesh).

Activities

The first summit meeting of SAARC heads of state and government, held in Dhaka, Bangladesh, in December 1985, resulted in the signing of the Charter of the South Asian Association for Regional Co-operation (SAARC). In August 1993 ministers of foreign affairs of seven countries, meeting in New Delhi, India, adopted a Declaration on South Asian Regional Co-operation and launched an Integrated Programme of Action (IPA), which identified the main areas for regional co-operation. The ninth summit meeting, held in May 1997, authorized the establishment of a Group of Eminent Persons to review the functioning of the IPA. On the basis of the group's recommendations a reconstituted IPA, to be administered by a more efficient arrangement of Technical Committees, was initiated in June 2000.

SAARC is committed to improving quality of life in the region by accelerating economic growth, social progress and cultural development; promoting self-reliance; encouraging mutual assistance; increasing co-operation with other developing countries; and co-operating with other regional and international organizations. The SAARC Charter stipulates that decisions should be made unanimously, and that 'bilateral and contentious issues' should not be discussed. Regular meetings, at all levels, are held to further co-operation in areas covered by the Technical Committees (see above). A priority objective is the eradication of poverty in the region, and in 1993 SAARC endorsed an Agenda of Action to help achieve this. A framework for exchanging information on poverty eradication has also, since, been established. In 1998 the 10th summit meeting resolved to formulate a SAARC Social Charter, which was to incorporate agreed objectives in areas such as poverty eradication, promotion of health and nutrition, and the protection of children. Representatives of civil society, academia, non-governmental organizations and government were to be involved in the process of drafting the Charter, under the auspices of an inter-governmental expert group, which met for the first time in April 2001. The 11th SAARC summit meeting, held in Kathmandu, Nepal, in January 2002, adopted a convention on regional arrangements for the promotion of child welfare in South Asia. The 11th summit also determined to reinvigorate regional poverty reduction activities in the context of the UN General Assembly's Millennium Goal of halving extreme poverty by 2015, and of other internationally-agreed commitments. The summit also urged the development of a regional strategy for preventing and combating HIV/AIDS and other communicable diseases; the SAARC Tuberculosis Centre (see below) was to play a co-ordinating role in this area.

A Committee on Economic Co-operation (CEC), comprising senior trade officials of member states, was established in July 1991 to monitor progress concerning trade and economic co-operation issues. In the same year the summit meeting approved the creation of an inter-governmental group to establish a framework for the promotion of specific trade liberalization measures. A SAARC Chamber of Commerce (SCCI) became operational in 1992, with headquarters in Karachi, Pakistan. (The SCCI headquarters were subsequently transferred to Islamabad, Pakistan.) In April 1993 ministers signed a SAARC Preferential Trading Arrangement (SAPTA), which came into effect in December 1995. The 10th summit meeting proposed a series of measures to accelerate progress in the next round of SAPTA trade negotiations, including a reduction in the domestic content requirements of SAPTA's rules of origin, greater tariff concessions on products being actively traded and the removal of certain discriminatory and non-tariff barriers. By the third, and most recent, round of trade negotiations under SAPTA, held in November 1998, 3,456 products had been identified as eligible for preferential trade tariffs. In December 1995 the Council resolved that the ultimate objective for member states should be the establishment of a South Asian Free Trade Area (SAFTA), superseding SAPTA. An *ad hoc* inter-governmental expert group was constituted to formulate a framework treaty to realize SAFTA. The 11th summit urged that the draft treaty on a regulatory framework for SAFTA be finalized by the end of 2002.

In January 1996 the first SAARC Trade Fair was held, in New Delhi, India, to promote intra-SAARC commerce. At the same time SAARC ministers of commerce convened for their first meeting to discuss regional economic co-operation. A group on customs co-operation was established in 1996 to harmonize trading rules and regulations within the grouping, to simplify trade procedures and to upgrade facilities. In 1999 a regional action plan to harmonize national standards, quality control and measurements came into effect. A second SAARC trade fair was held at Colombo, Sri Lanka, in 1998, and the third was held in Islamabad, Pakistan, in early September 2001. In August 2001 SAARC commerce ministers met, in New Delhi, to discuss a co-ordinated approach to the World Trade Organization negotiations that were held in November.

An Agricultural Information Centre was founded in 1988, in Dhaka, Bangladesh, to serve as a central institution for the dissemination of knowledge and information in the agricultural sector. It maintains a network of centres in each member state, which provide for the efficient exchange of technical information and for strengthening agricultural research. An agreement establishing a Food Security Reserve to meet emergency food requirements was signed in November 1987, and entered into force in August 1988. The Board of the Reserve meets annually to assess the food security of the region. At March 2001 the Reserve contained some 241,580 metric tons of grain. Other regional institutions include the SAARC Tuberculosis Centre in Thimi, Nepal, which opened in July 1992 with the aim of preventing and reducing the prevalence of the disease in the region through the co-ordination of tuberculosis control programmes, research and training; a SAARC Documentation Centre, established in New Delhi in May 1994; and a SAARC Meteorological Research Centre which opened in Dhaka in January 1995. A Human Resources Development Centre was established in Islamabad, Pakistan in 1999. Regional funds include a SAARC-Japan Special Fund established in September 1993. One-half of the fund's resources, which were provided by the Japanese Government, was to be used to finance projects identified by Japan, including workshops and cultural events, and one-half was to be used to finance projects identified by SAARC member states. The eighth SAARC summit meeting, held in New Delhi in May 1996, established a South Asian Development Fund, comprising a Fund for Regional Projects, a Regional Fund and a fund for social development and infrastructure building.

A SAARC Youth Volunteers Programme (SYVOP) enables young people to work in other member countries in the agriculture and forestry sectors. The Programme is part of a series of initiatives designed to promote intra-regional exchanges and contact. A Youth Awards Scheme to reward outstanding achievements by young people was inaugurated in 1996. The theme selected for recognition in 2001 was 'Creative Photography: South Asian Diversity'. Founded in 1987, the SAARC Audio-visual Exchange Programme (SAVE) broadcasts radio and television programmes on social and cultural affairs to all member countries, twice a month, in order to disseminate information about SAARC and its members. From 2001 SAVE was to organize an annual SAARC Telefilm festival. The SAARC Consortium of Open and Distance Learning was established in 2000. A Visa Exemption Scheme, exempting 21 specified categories of person from visa requirements, with the aim of promoting closer regional contact, became operational in March 1992. A SAARC citizens forum promotes interaction among the people of South Asia. In addition, SAARC operates a fellowships, scholarships and chairs scheme and a scheme for the promotion of organized tourism.

At the third SAARC summit, held in Kathmandu in November 1987, member states signed a regional convention on measures to counteract terrorism. The convention, which entered into force in August 1988, commits signatory countries to the extradition or prosecution of alleged terrorists and to the implementation of preventative measures to combat terrorism. Monitoring desks for terrorist and drugs offences have been established to process information relating to those activities. The first SAARC conference on co-operation in police affairs, attended by the heads of the police forces of member states, was held in Colombo in July 1996. The conference discussed the issues of terrorism, organized crime, the extradition of criminals, drugs-trafficking and drug abuse. A convention on narcotic drugs and psychotropic substances was signed during the fifth SAARC summit meeting, held in Malé in 1990. The convention entered into force in September 1993, following its ratification by member states. It is implemented by a co-ordination group of drug law enforcement agencies. At the 11th SAARC summit member states adopted a convention on the prevention of trafficking of women and children for prostitution.

SAARC co-operates with other regional and international organizations. In February 1993 SAARC signed a memorandum of understanding with UNCTAD, whereby both parties agreed to exchange information on trade control measures regionally and in 50 developed and developing countries, respectively, in order to increase transparency and thereby facilitate trade. In February 1994 SAARC signed a framework co-operation agreement with ESCAP to enhance co-operation on development issues through a framework of joint studies, workshops and information exchange. A memorandum of understanding with the European Commission was signed in July 1996. SAARC has also signed co-operation agreements with UNICEF (in 1993), the Asia Pacific Telecommunity (1994), UNDP (1995), UNDCP (1995), the International Telecommunication Union (1997), the Canadian International Development Agency (1997), WHO (2000), and UNIFEM (2001). An informal dialogue at ministerial level has been conducted with ASEAN and the European Union since 1998. SAARC and WIPO hold regular consultations concerning regional co-operation on intellectual property rights, and regular consultations are convened with the WTO.

Finance

The national budgets of member countries provide the resources to finance SAARC activities. The Secretariat's annual budget is shared among member states according to a specified formula.

Publications

SAARC News (7/8 a year).

SPECTRUM (irregular).

Regional Apex Bodies

Association of Persons of the Legal Communities of the SAARC Countries—SAARCLAW: Pioneer House, Shahayog Marg, Anamnagar, Kathmandu, Nepal; tel. (1) 221340; fax (1) 226770; e-mail saarclaw@wlink.com.np; internet www.saarclaw.org; f. 1991; recognized as a SAARC regional apex body in July 1994; aims to enhance exchanges and co-operation amongst the legal communities of the sub-region and to promote the development of law. Pres. LAXMAN ARYAL (Nepal); Sec.-Gen. BHARAT RAJ UPRETI (Nepal).

SAARC Chamber of Commerce and Industry—SCCI: House 5, St 59, F-8/4, Islamabad, Pakistan; tel. (51) 2281395; fax (51) 2281390; e-mail saarc@isb.comsats.net.pk; internet www.saarcnet .org; f. 1992; promotes economic and trade co-operation throughout the sub-region and greater interaction between the business communities of member countries; organizes SAARC Economic Co-operation Conferences and Trade Fairs. Pres. PADMA JYOTI (Nepal); Sec.-Gen. ABUL HASAN.

South Asian Federation of Accountants—SAFA: f. 1984; recognized as a SAARC regional apex body in Jan. 2002; aims to develop regional co-ordination for the accountancy profession.

Other recognized regional bodies include the South Asian Association for Regional Co-operation of Architects, the Association of Management Development Institutions, the SAARC Federation of University Women, the SAARC Association of Town Planners, the SAARC Cardiac Society, the Association of SAARC Speakers and Parliamentarians, the Federation of State Insurance Organizations of SAARC Countries, the Federation of State Insurance Organizations of SAARC Countries, the SAARC Diploma Engineers Forum, the Radiological Society of SAARC Countries, the SAARC Teachers' Federation, the SAARC Surgical Care Society and the Foundation of SAARC Writers and Literature.

OTHER REGIONAL ORGANIZATIONS

(see also under ESCAP, p. 1469)

These organizations are arranged under the following sub-headings:

AGRICULTURE, FOOD, FORESTRY AND FISHERIES

Asian Vegetable Research and Development Center—AVRDC: POB 42, Shanhua, Tainan, Taiwan 741; tel. (6) 5837801; fax (6) 5830009; e-mail avrdcbox@netra.avrdc.org.tw; internet www.avrdc.org.tw; f. 1971 to improve the health and standard of living of rural populations in the humid and sub-humid tropics by increased production of vegetable crops through the breeding of better varieties and the development of improved cultural methods; research programme includes plant breeding, plant pathology, plant physiology, soil science, entomology, crop management, cropping systems and chemistry; runs an experimental farm, laboratories, a transgenic greenhouse, a gene-bank, a weather station and computer facilities; provides training for research and production specialists in tropical vegetables. Mems: Australia, France, Germany, Japan, Republic of Korea, Philippines, Taiwan, Thailand. Dir-Gen. Dr SAMSON C. S. TSOU. Publs *Annual Report, Technical Bulletin, Proceedings, CENTERPOINT* (newsletter).

CAB International—CABI: Wallingford, Oxon, OX10 8DE, United Kingdom; tel. (1491) 832111; fax (1491) 833508; e-mail cabi@cabi.org; internet www.cabi.org; f. 1929 as the Imperial Agricultural Bureaux (later Commonwealth Agricultural Bureaux); current name adopted in 1985; aims to improve human welfare world-wide through the generation, dissemination and application of scientific knowledge in support of sustainable development; places particular emphasis on agriculture, forestry, human health and the management of natural resources, with priority given to the needs of developing countries. CABI compiles and publishes extensive information (in a variety of print and electronic forms) on aspects of agriculture, forestry, veterinary medicine, the environment and natural resources, Third World rural development and others. Maintains regional centres in Kenya, Malaysia, Pakistan, Switzerland and Trinidad and Tobago. Mems: 40 countries. Dir-Gen. Dr DENIS BLIGHT.

CABI Bioscience: Bakeham Lane, Egham, Surrey TW20 9TY, United Kingdom; tel. (1491) 829080; fax (1491) 829100; e-mail bioscience@cabi.org; internet www.cabi-bioscience.org; f. 1998 by integration of the capabilities and resources of the following four CABI scientific institutions: International Institute of Biological Control; International Institute of Entomology; International Institute of Parasitology; International Mycological Institute; undertakes research, consultancy, training, capacity-building and institutional development in sustainable pest management, biosystematics and molecular biology, ecological applications and environmental and industrial microbiology. There are CABI Bioscience centres in Kenya, Malaysia, Pakistan, Switzerland, Trinidad and the United Kingdom.

Commission for the Conservation of Southern Bluefin Tuna: Unit 1, J.A.A. House, 19 Napier Close, Deakin, Canberra, ACT 2600, Australia; tel. (2) 6282-8396; fax (2) 6282-8407; e-mail bmacdonald@ccsbt.org; internet www.ccsbt.org; f. 1994 when the Convention for the Conservation of Southern Bluefin Tuna (signed in May 1993) entered into force; aims to promote sustainable management and conservation of the southern bluefin tuna; holds an annual meeting and annual scientific meeting; collates relevant research, scientific information and data; encourages non-member countries and bodies to co-operate in the conservation and optimum utilization of Southern Bluefin Tuna through accession to the Convention or adherence to the Commission's management arrangements. Mems: Australia, Japan, Republic of Korea, New Zealand. Exec. Sec. BRIAN MACDONALD.

Indian Ocean Tuna Commission—IOTC: POB 1011, Victoria, Mahé, Seychelles; tel. 225494; fax 224364; e-mail iotcsecr@seychelles.net; internet www.seychelles/net/iotc; f. 1993 by FAO, as the successor to the Indo-Pacific Tuna Development and Management Programme (f. 1982); technical activities include sampling, tagging, methodology, information on tuna stocks, conversion factors, biological parameters, other research; 2001 budget US $1.1m. Mems: Australia, People's Republic of China, European Community, Eritrea, France, India, Japan, Republic of Korea, Madagascar, Mauritius, Malaysia, Oman, Pakistan, Seychelles, Sudan, Sri Lanka, Thailand, United Kingdom. Sec. DAVID ARDILL (Mauritius).

Inter-American Tropical Tuna Commission—IATTC: 8604 La Jolla Shores Drive, La Jolla, CA 92037-1508, USA; tel. (858) 546-7100; fax (858) 546-7133; e-mail rallen@iattc.org; internet www.iattc.org; f. 1950; administers two programmes, the Tuna-Billfish Programme and the Tuna-Dolphin Programme. The principal responsibilities of the Tuna-Billfish Programme are to study the biology of the tunas and related species of the eastern Pacific Ocean to determine the effects of fishing and natural factors on their abundance, to recommend appropriate conservation measures in order to maintain stocks at levels which will afford maximum sustainable catches, and to collect information on compliance with Commission resolutions; the functions of the Tuna-Dolphin Programme are to monitor the abundance of dolphins and their mortality incidental to purse-seine fishing in the eastern Pacific Ocean, to study the causes of mortality of dolphins during fishing operations and promote the use of techniques and equipment that minimize these mortalities, to study the effects of different fishing methods on the various fish and other animals of the pelagic ecosystem, and to provide a secretariat for the International Dolphin Conservation Programme. Mems: Costa Rica, Ecuador, El Salvador, France, Guatemala, Japan, Mexico, Nicaragua, Panama, USA, Vanuatu, Venezuela. Dir ROBIN ALLEN. Publs *Bulletin* (irregular), *Annual Report, Stock Assessment Report* (annually).

International Crops Research Institute for the Semi-Arid Tropics—ICRISAT: Patancheru, Andhra Pradesh, India; tel. (40) 596161; fax (40) 241239; e-mail icrisat@cgiar.com; internet www.icrisat.org; f. 1972 to promote the genetic improvement of crops, and for research on the management of resources in the world's semi-arid tropics; research covers all physical and socio-economic aspects of improving farming systems on non-irrigated land. Dir-Gen. WILLIAM D. DAR (Philippines). Publs *ICRISAT Report* (annually), *SAT News* (2 a year), *International Chickpea and Pigeonpea Newsletter* (annually), *International Arachis Newsletter* (annually), *International Sorghum and Millet Newsletter* (annually), information and research bulletins.

International Rice Research Institute—IRRI: DAPO Box 7777, Metro Manila, Philippines; tel. (2) 8450563; fax (2) 8911292; e-mail irri@cgiar.org; internet www.cgiar.org/irri; f. 1960; conducts research on the rice plant and its cultural management, with the aim of developing technologies of environment, social and economic benefit; works to enhance national rice research systems and offers training; operates Riceworld, a museum and learning centre about rice; maintains a library of technical rice literature; organizes international conferences and workshops. Dir-Gen. Dr RONALD CANTRELL. Publs *Facts about IRRI, News About Rice and People, International Rice Research Notes, Rice Literature Update.*

International Water Management Institute—IWMI: POB 2075, Colombo, Sri Lanka; tel. (1) 787404; fax (1) 786854; e-mail iwmi@cgiar.org; internet www.iwmi.org; f. 1984 as International Irrigation Management Institute; aims to contribute to food security and poverty eradication by supporting sustainable increases in the productivity of water, through better management of irrigation systems and other applications of water in river basins. Dir-Gen. FRANK RIJSBERMAN (Netherlands).

International Whaling Commission—IWC: The Red House, Station Rd, Impington, Cambridge, CB4 9NP, United Kingdom; tel. (1223) 233971; fax (1223) 232876; e-mail iwc@iwcoffice.com; internet www.iwcoffice.org; f. 1946 under the International Convention for the Regulation of Whaling, for the conservation of the world whale stocks; reviews the regulations covering whaling; encourages research; collects, analyses and disseminates statistical and other information on whaling. A ban on commercial whaling was passed by the Commission in July 1982, to take effect three years subsequently (in some cases, a phased reduction of commercial operations was not completed until 1988). A revised whale-management procedure was adopted in 1992, to be implemented after the development of a complete whale management scheme. Iceland left the IWC in June 1992, but was readmitted in Oct. 2002; and Norway resumed commercial whaling in 1993. Mems: governments of 45 countries. Chair. Prof. BO FERNHOLM (Sweden); Sec. Dr N. GRANDY. Publ. *Annual Report*.

Network of Aquaculture Centres in Asia and the Pacific—NACA: POB 1040, Kasetsart Post Office, Bangkok 10903, Thailand; tel. (2) 561-1728; fax (2) 561-1727; e-mail naca@inet.co.th; internet www.enaca.org; f. 1990; promotes the development of aquaculture in the Asia and Pacific region through development planning, interdisciplinary research, regional training and information. Mems: Australia, Bangladesh, Cambodia, People's Republic of China, Hong Kong, India, Democratic People's Republic of Korea, Malaysia, Myanmar, Nepal, Pakistan, Philippines, Sri Lanka, Thailand and Viet Nam. Dir-Gen. PEDRO B. BUENOS. Publs *NACA Newsletter* (quarterly), *Aquaculture Asia* (quarterly).

World Fish Center (International Centre for Living Aquatic Resources Management—ICLARM): POB 500 GPO, 10670 Penang, Malaysia; tel. (4) 6261606; fax (4) 6265530; e-mail iclarm@cgiar.org; internet www.iclarm.org; f. 1973; became a mem. of the Consultative Group on International Agricultural Research (CGIAR, q.v.) in 1992; aims to contribute to food security and poverty eradication in developing countries through the sustainable development and use of living aquatic resources; carries out research and promotes partnerships. Dir-Gen. Dr MERYL J. WILLIAMS.

COMMODITIES

Asian and Pacific Coconut Community: POB 1343, Jakarta 10013; 3rd Floor, Lina Bldg, Jalan H. R. Rasuna Said, Kav. B7., Kuningan, Jakarta 12920, Indonesia; tel. (21) 5221712; fax (21) 5221714; e-mail apcc@indo.net.id; internet www.apcc.org.sg; f. 1969 to promote, co-ordinate, and harmonize all activities of the coconut industry towards better production, processing, marketing and research. Organizes annual Coconut Technical Meeting (COCOTECH). Mems: Fiji, India, Indonesia, Kiribati, Malaysia, Federated States of Micronesia, Papua New Guinea, Philippines, Samoa, Solomon Islands, Sri Lanka, Thailand, Vanuatu, Viet Nam; assoc. mem.: Palau. Exec. Dir Dr P. RATHINAM. Publs *COCOMUNITY* (every 2 weeks), *CORD* (2 a year), *COCOINFO International* (2 a year), *Statistical Yearbook*, country studies, directories, and video documentaries on coconut industry for the use of member countries.

Association of Natural Rubber Producing Countries—ANRPC: Natural Rubber Bldg, 148 Jalan Ampang, 7th Floor, 50450 Kuala Lumpur, Malaysia; tel. (3) 2611900; fax (3) 2613014; e-mail anrpc@po.jaring.my; f. 1970 to co-ordinate the production and marketing of natural rubber, to promote technical co-operation among members and to bring about fair and stable prices for natural rubber; holds seminars, meetings and training courses on technical and statistical subjects. A joint regional marketing system has been agreed in principle. Seminars, meetings and training courses on technical and statistical subjects are held. Mems: India, Indonesia, Malaysia, Papua New Guinea, Singapore, Sri Lanka, Thailand, Viet Nam. Sec.-Gen. G. W. S. K. DE SILVA. Publs *ANRPC Statistical Bulletin* (quarterly), *ANRPC Newsletter, ANRPC Quarterly Natural Rubber Statistical Bulletin*.

International Coffee Organization: 22 Berners St, London, W1P 4DD, United Kingdom; tel. (20) 7580-8591; fax (20) 7580-6129; e-mail info@ico.org; internet www.ico.org; f. 1963 under the International Coffee Agreement, 1962, which was renegotiated in 1968, 1976, 1983, 1994 (extended in 1999) and 2001; aims to improve international co-operation and provide a forum for intergovernmental consultations on coffee matters; to facilitate international trade in coffee by the collection, analysis and dissemination of statistics; to act as a centre for the collection, exchange and publication of coffee information; to promote studies in the field of coffee; and to encourage an increase in coffee consumption. Mems: 45 exporting countries (incl. India, Indonesia, Papua New Guinea, Philippines, Thailand and Viet Nam) and 18 importing countries (incl. Japan). Chair. of Council (2001/02) LAKSHMI VENKATACHALAM (India); Exec. Dir NÉSTOR OSORIO (Colombia).

International Cotton Advisory Committee—ICAC: 1629 K St NW, Suite 702, Washington, DC 20006, USA; tel. (202) 463-6660; fax (202) 463-6950; e-mail secretariat@icac.org; internet www.icac.org; f. 1939 to observe developments in world cotton; to collect and disseminate statistics; to suggest measures for the furtherance of international collaboration in maintaining and developing a sound world cotton economy. Mems: 43 countries. Exec. Dir Dr TERRY TOWNSEND. Publs *Cotton: This Month, Cotton: Review of the World Situation* (every 2 months), *Cotton: World Statistics* (2 a year), *ICAC Recorder* (quarterly).

International Grains Council—IGC: 1 Canada Sq., Canary Wharf, London, E14 5AE, United Kingdom; tel. (20) 7513-1122; fax (20) 7513-0630; e-mail igc@igc.org.uk; internet www.igc.org.uk; f. 1949 as International Wheat Council, present name adopted in 1995, responsible for the administration of the International Grains Agreement (IGA), 1995, comprising the Food Aid Convention (FAC) and the Grain Trade Convention (GTC). The GTC aims to further international co-operation in all aspects of trade in grains, to promote international trade in grains, to secure the freest possible flow of this trade in the interests of members, particularly developing member countries, and to contribute to the stability of the international grain market. Under the FAC donors pledge to provide annually specified minimum amounts of food aid to developing nations in the form of grain and certain other eligible products. The IGC acts as a forum for consultations among members, and provides comprehensive information on the international grain market and factors affecting it; 29 mems. Exec. Dir. G. DENIS. Publs *World Grain Statistics* (annually), *Wheat and Coarse Grain Shipments* (annually), *Report for the Fiscal Year* (annually), *Grain Market Report* (monthly), *IGC Grain Market Indicators* (weekly), *Food Aid Shipments*.

International Jute Study Group—IJSG: 145 Monipuripara, Old Airport Rd, Dhaka 1215, Bangladesh; tel. (2) 9125581; fax (2) 9125248; e-mail ijsg@bdmail.net; f. 1984 (as International Jute Organization) to implement the provisions of the International Agreement on Jute and Jute Products, which was concluded under the auspices of UNCTAD in 1982 (a revised Agreement was concluded in 1989); succeeded by the IJSG in April 2002; aimed to provide an effective framework for co-operation and consultation among jute exporting and importing countries and the private sector in order to improve the structural conditions in the jute market, to increase the competitiveness and quality of jute and jute products, and to act as a catalyst for market promotion of jute and jute-based products. Mems: 17 countries. Sec.-Gen. T. NANDA KUMAR (India). Publs *Annual Report, Jute* (quarterly).

International Pepper Community: 4th Floor, Lina Bldg, Jalan H. R. Rasuna Said, Kav. B7, Kuningan, Jakarta 12920, Indonesia; tel. (21) 5224902; fax (21) 5224905; e-mail ipc@indo.net.id; internet www.ipcnet.org; f. 1972 for promoting, co-ordinating and harmonizing all activities relating to the pepper economy. Mems: Brazil, India, Indonesia, Malaysia, Federated States of Micronesia, Papua New Guinea, Sri Lanka, Thailand. Exec. Dir Dr K. P. G. MENON. Publs *International Pepper News Bulletin* (quarterly), *Pepper Statistical Yearbook, Directory of Pepper / Spices Importers, Directory of Pepper / Spices Exporters, Weekly Prices Bulletin, Monthly Pepper Market Review*.

International Rubber Study Group—IRSG: Heron House, 109-115 Wembley Hill Rd, Wembley, HA9 8DA, United Kingdom; tel. (20) 8903-7727; fax (20) 8903-2848; e-mail secretary-general@rubberstudy.com; internet www.rubberstudy.com; f. 1944 to provide a forum for the discussion of matters affecting production and use of natural and synthetic rubber and trade in rubber, and to compile comprehensive economic and statistical information on the world rubber industry. Mems: 17 countries. Sec.-Gen. Dr A. F. S. BUDIMAN (Indonesia). Publs *Rubber Statistical Bulletin* (monthly), *Rubber Statistics Yearbook, Rubber Industry Report* (monthly), *World Rubber Statistics Handbook, International Rubber Forum* (annually), *Outlook for Elastomers* (annually).

International Silk Association: 34 rue de la Charité, 69002 Lyon, France; tel. 4-78-42-10-79; fax 4-78-37-56-72; e-mail isa-silk.ais-soie@wanadoo.fr; f. 1949 to promote closer collaboration between all branches of the silk industry and trade, develop the consumption of silk and foster scientific research; collects and disseminates information and statistics relating to the industry; organizes biennial Congresses. Mems: employers' and technical organizations in 40 countries. Gen. Sec. X. LAVERGNE. Publs ISA *Newsletter* (monthly), congress reports, standards, trade rules, etc.

International Sugar Organization—ISO: 1 Canada Sq., Canary Wharf, London, E14 5AA, United Kingdom; tel. (20) 7513-1144; fax (20) 7513-1146; e-mail exdir@isosugar.org; internet www.isosugar.org; administers the International Sugar Agreement negotiated in 1992, with the objectives of stimulating co-operation, facilitating trade and encouraging demand; aims to improve conditions in the sugar market through debate, analysis and studies; serves as a forum for discussion; holds annual seminars and workshops; sponsors projects from developing countries. Mems: 61 countries (including EU member states). Exec. Dir Dr P. BARON. Publs *Sugar Year Book, Monthly Statistical Bulletin, Quarterly Market Review, Monthly Market Report and Press Summary*, seminar proceedings.

International Tea Committee Ltd: Sir John Lyon House, 5 High Timber St, London, EC4V 3NH, United Kingdom; tel. (20) 7248-4672; fax (20) 7329-6955; e-mail info@intteacomm.co.uk; internet www.intteacomm.co.uk; f. 1933 to administer the International Tea Agreement; now serves as a statistical and information centre; new Constitution, adopted in 1979, extended membership to consuming countries. Producer mems: tea boards or asscns of Bangladesh, India, Indonesia, Japan, Kenya, Malawi, Sri Lanka, Zimbabwe; consumer mems: United Kingdom Tea Assen, Comité européen du thé, Tea Council of Canada, Tea Asscn of the USA, Inc; assoc. mems: Netherlands and UK ministries of agriculture, Cameroon Development Corpn. Chair. M. J. BUNSTON. Publs *Annual Bulletin of Statistics, Monthly Statistical Summary, World Tea Statistics 1910–1990*.

International Tea Promotion Association: Tea Board of Kenya, Tea Board House, Naivasha Rd (off Ngong Rd), POB 20064, Nairobi, Kenya; tel. (20) 572497; fax (20) 562120; e-mail teaboardk@kenyaweb.com; internet www.teaboard.or.ke; f. 1979. Mems: Bangladesh, Indonesia, Kenya, Malawi, Mauritius, Mozambique, Tanzania, and Uganda (accounting for about 35% of world black tea exports). Chair. GEORGE M. KIMANI. Publ. *International Tea Journal* (2 a year).

International Tobacco Growers' Association: Apdo 5, 6001-081 Castelo Branco, Portugal; tel. (272) 325901; fax (272) 325906; e-mail itga@mail.telepac.pt; internet www.tobaccoleaf.org; f. 1984 to provide a forum for the exchange of views and information of interest to tobacco producers. Mems: 21 countries producing over 80% of the world's internationally traded tobacco. Pres. MARCELO QUEVEDO CARRILLO (Argentina); Chief Exec. Dr ANTÓNIO ABRUNHOSA (Portugal). Publs *Tobacco Courier* (quarterly), *Tobacco Briefing*.

International Tropical Timber Organization—ITTO: International Organizations Center, 5th Floor, Pacifico-Yokohama, 1-1-1, Minato-Mirai, Nishi-ku, Yokohama 220, Japan; tel. (45) 223-1110; fax (45) 223-1111; e-mail itto@mail.itto-unet.ocn.ne.jp; internet www.itto.or.jp; f. 1985 under the 1983 International Tropical Timber Agreement (ITTA); a new treaty, ITTA 1994, entered into force in 1997; provides a forum for consultation and co-operation between tropical timber producing and consuming countries; and is dedicated to the sustainable development and conservation of tropical forests; facilitates progress towards Objective 2000, which is to move as rapidly as possible towards achieving exports of tropical timber and timber products from sustainably managed resources; encourages, through policy and project work, forest management, conservation and restoration, the further processing of tropical timber in producing countries, and the gathering and analysis of market intelligence and economic information. Mems: 31 producing and 25 consuming countries and the European Community. Exec. Dir Dr MANOEL SOBRAL FILHO. Publs *Annual Review and Assessment of the World Timber Situation, Tropical Timber Market Information Service* (every 2 weeks), *Tropical Forest Update* (quarterly).

DEVELOPMENT AND ECONOMIC CO-OPERATION

Afro-Asian Rural Development Organization—AARDO: No. 2, State Guest Houses Complex, Nr Chanakyapuri telephone exchange, New Delhi 110021, India; tel. (11) 6877783; fax (11) 6115937; e-mail aardohq@nde.vsnl.net.in; internet www.aardo.org; f. 1962 to restructure the economy of the rural population in Africa and Asia and to explore, collectively, opportunities for co-ordination of efforts to promote welfare and eradicate malnutrition, disease, illiteracy and poverty amongst rural people. Activities include collaborative research on development issues, technical assistance, the exchange of information, international conferences and seminars, study visits, and awarding 105 individual training fellowships at nine institutes in Egypt, India, Japan, Republic of Korea, Malaysia and Taiwan. Mems: 12 African, 14 Asian countries and one African associate. Sec.-Gen. Dr BAHAR MUNIP. Publs *Annual Report, Afro-Asian Journal of Rural Development*.

Asian and Pacific Development Centre: Pesiaran Duta, POB 12224, 50770 Kuala Lumpur, Malaysia; tel. (3) 6511088; fax (3) 6510316; e-mail info@apdc.po.my; internet www4.jaring.my/apdc; f. 1980; undertakes research and training, acts as clearing-house for information on development and offers consultancy services, in co-operation with national institutions; current programme includes assistance regarding the implementation of national development strategies. The Centre aims to promote economic co-operation among developing countries of the region for their mutual benefit. Mems: 19 countries and two associate members. Dir Dr M. NOOR HARUN. Publs *Annual Report, Newsletter* (2 a year), *Asia-Pacific Development Monitor* (quarterly), studies, reports, monographs.

Asian Productivity Organization: 2/F Hirakawa-cho Daiichi Seimei Bldg, 1-2-10 Hirakawa-cho, Chiyoda-ku, Tokyo 102-0093, Japan; tel. (3) 5226-3920; fax (3) 5226-3950; e-mail apo@apo-tokyo.org; internet www.apo-tokyo.org; f. 1961 to increase productivity, and consequently accelerate economic development, in the Asia-Pacific region; organizes conferences and research on increasing productivity; undertakes training and study missions and awards fellowships; membership is open to all member countries of ESCAP. Sec.-Gen. TAKASHI TAJIMA (Japan). Publs *APO News* (monthly), *APO Productivity Journal* (2 a year).

Colombo Plan: Bank of Ceylon Merchant Tower, 13th Floor, 28 St Michael's Rd, Colombo 3, Sri Lanka; tel. (1) 564448; fax (1) 564531; e-mail cplan@slt.lk; internet www.colombo-plan.org; f. 1950 by seven Commonwealth countries, to encourage economic and social development in Asia and the Pacific. The Plan comprises the Programme for Public Administration, to provide training for officials in the context of a market-orientated economy; the Programmme for Private Sector Development, which organizes training programmes to stimulate the economic benefits of development of the private sector; a Drug Advisory Programme, to encourage regional co-operation in efforts to control drug-related problems, in particular through human resources development; a programme to establish a South-South Technical Co-operation Data Bank, to collate, analyse and publish information in order to facilitate south-south co-operation; and a Staff College for Technician Education (see below). All programmes are voluntarily funded; developing countries are encouraged to become donors and to participate in economic and technical co-operation activities among developing members. A Consultative Committee (comprising ministers from member governments) meets every two years; the Colombo Plan Council (heads of members' diplomatic missions in Colombo) meets several times a year; the Colombo Plan Bureau serves as the Plan's Secretariat. Mems: 24 countries. Sec.-Gen. U SARAT CHANDRAN (India). Publs *Annual Report, Colombo Plan Focus* (quarterly), *Consultative Committee Proceedings* (every 2 years).

Colombo Plan Staff College for Technician Education: POB 7500, Domestic Airport Post Office, NAIA, Pasay City 1300, Metro Manila, Philippines; tel. (2) 6310991; fax (2) 6310996; e-mail cpsc@skyinet.net; internet www.cpsc.org.ph; f. 1973 with the support of member Governments of the Colombo Plan; aims to enhance the development of technician education systems in developing member countries. Dir Prof MAN-GON PARK. Publ. *CPSC Quarterly*.

Council of Regional Organizations in the Pacific—CROP: c/o Private Mail Bag, Suva, Fiji; tel. 3312600; fax 3301102; f. as South Pacific Organizations' Co-ordinating Committee; renamed 1999; aims to co-ordinate work programmes in the region and improve the efficiency of aid resources; holds annual meetings; chairmanship alternates between the participating organizations. First meeting of subcommittee on information technologies convened in 1998. Mems: Pacific Islands Development Programme, Secretariat of the Pacific Community, South Pacific Applied Geoscience Commission, Pacific Islands Forum Secretariat, South Pacific Regional Environment Programme, Pacific Islands Forum Fisheries Agency, the Tourism Council of the South Pacific and the University of the South Pacific. Chair. NOEL LEVI.

Developing Eight—D-8: Müşir Fuad Paşa Yalısı, Eski Tersane, Emirgan Caddesi 90, İstanbul 80860, Turkey; tel. (212) 2775513; fax (212) 2775519; internet www.developing-8.net; inaugurated at a meeting of Heads of State in June 1997; aims to foster economic co-operation between member states and to strengthen the role of developing countries in the global economy; project areas include trade and industry, agriculture, human resources, telecommunications, rural development, finance (including banking and privatizations), energy, environment and health. Second summit meeting convened in Dhaka, Bangladesh, in March 1999; third summit in Cairo, Egypt, in February 2001. Mems: Bangladesh, Egypt, Iran, Indonesia, Malaysia, Nigeria, Pakistan, Turkey. Exec. Dir AYHAN KAMEL.

Eastern Regional Organization for Planning and Housing: 3A10 Block C, Phileo Damansara 1, 9, Jalan 16/11, 46350 Petaling Jaya, Selangor Darul Ehsan, Malaysia; tel. (3) 79583315; fax (3) 79583316; e-mail earoph@time.net.my; internet www.earoph.byte-craft.com; f. 1958 to promote and co-ordinate the study and practice of housing and regional town and country planning. Mems: organizations and individuals in 28 countries. Sec.-Gen. JOHN KOH SENG SIEW (Malaysia). Publs *EAROPH Bulletin* (quarterly), congress reports.

Foundation for the Peoples of the South Pacific, International—FSPI: POB 951, Port Vila, Vanuatu; tel. 22915; fax 24510; e-mail fspi@fsp.org.vu; internet www.oneworld.org/fsp; f. 1965; provides training and technical assistance for self-help community development groups and co-operatives; implements long-term programmes in sustainable forestry and agriculture, the environment, education, nutrition, women in development, child survival, and fisheries. Mems: non-governmental affiliates operating in Australia, Fiji, Kiribati, Papua New Guinea, Samoa, Solomon Islands, Tonga, Tuvalu, United Kingdom, USA, Vanuatu. Regional Man. KATHY FRY. Publs *Annual Report, News* (quarterly), technical reports (e.g. on intermediate technology, nutrition, teaching aids).

Indian Ocean Rim Association for Regional Co-operation—IOR-ARC: Sorèze House, 14 Angus Rd, Vacoas, Mauritius; tel. 698-3979; fax 697-5390; e-mail iorarchq@intnet.mu; the first intergovernmental meeting of countries in the region to promote an Indian Ocean Rim initiative was convened in March 1995; charter to establish the Asscn was signed at a ministerial meeting in March 1997; aims to promote regional economic co-operation in the fields of trade, investment, the environment, tourism, and science and technology. Mems: Australia, Bangladesh, India, Indonesia, Iran, Kenya, Madagascar, Malaysia, Mauritius, Mozambique, Oman, Seychelles, Singapore, South Africa, Sri Lanka, Tanzania, Thailand, United Arab Emirates and Yemen. Dialogue countries: People's Republic of China, Egypt, Japan, United Kingdom; Chair. YOUSSOUF BIN ABDULLAH AL-ALAWI (Oman); Dir DEVDASLALL DUSORUTH (Mauritius).

International Centre for Integrated Mountain Development—ICIMOD: 4/80 Jawalakhel, Lalitpur, GPO Box 3226, Kathmandu, Nepal; tel. (1) 525313; fax (1) 524509; e-mail dits@icimod.org.np; internet www.icimod.org.sg; f. 1983; an autonomous organization sponsored by regional member countries and by the governments of Nepal, Germany, Switzerland, Austria, Netherlands and Denmark, to help promote an economically and environmentally sound ecosystem and to improve the living standards of the population in the Hindu Kush-Himalaya; aims to serve as a focal point for multi-disciplinary documentation, training and applied research, and as a consultative centre in scientific and practical matters pertaining to mountain development; participating countries: Afghanistan, Bangladesh, Bhutan, People's Republic of China, India, Myanmar, Nepal, Pakistan. Dir-Gen. J. GABRIEL CAMPBELL.

Mekong River Commission: POB 1112, 364 M.V. Preah Monivong, Sangkat Phsar Doerm Thkouv, Khan Chamkar Mon, Phnom-Penh, Cambodia; tel. (23) 720979; fax (23) 720972; e-mail mrcs@mrcmekong.org; internet www.mrcmekong.org; f. 1995, by the Agreement on the Co-operation for the Sustainable Development of the Mekong River Basin, as successor to the Committee for Co-ordination of Investigations of the Lower Mekong Basin (f. 1957); and the subsequent Interim Mekong Committee (f. 1978); aims to promote and co-ordinate the sustainable development, utilization, conservation and management of the resources of the Mekong River basin for navigational and non-navigational purposes, in order to assist the social and economic development of member states, while preserving the ecological balance of the basin; provides scientific information and policy advice; supports the implementation of strategic programmes and activities; organizes an annual donor consultative group meeting; maintains regular dialogue with Myanmar and the People's Republic of China. Mems: Cambodia, Laos, Thailand, Viet Nam. CEO JOERN KRISTENSEN. Publ. *Mekong News* (quarterly).

Pacific Basin Economic Council: 900 Fort St, Suite 1080, Honolulu, HI 96813, USA; tel. (808) 521-9044; fax (808) 521-8530; e-mail info@pbec.org; internet www.pbec.org; f. 1967; an association of business representatives aiming to promote business opportunities in the region in order to enhance overall economic development; advises governments and serves as a liaison between business leaders and government officials; encourages business relationships and co-operation among its members; holds business symposia. Mems: country committees in Australia, Canada, Chile, People's Republic of China, Colombia, Ecuador, Hong Kong, Indonesia, Japan, Republic of Korea, Malaysia, Mexico, New Zealand, Peru, Philippines, Russia, Singapore, Chinese Taipei (Taiwan), Thailand and the USA. Chair. S. R. CHO; Sec.-Gen. ROBERT G. LEES.

Pacific Economic Co-operation Council—PECC: 4 Nassim Rd, Singapore 258372; tel. 67379822; fax 67379824; e-mail peccsec@pecc.net; internet www.pecc.net; f. 1980 to foster economic development in the region by providing a forum for discussion and co-operation in a wide range of economic areas. A General Meeting of senior research officials, government and business representatives is held every two years. PECC's current work programme covers trade and investment policy issues, Pacific economic outlook, financial and capital markets, human resource development, minerals, energy, fisheries, food and agriculture, science and technology, small and medium-sized enterprises, telecommunications, tourism and transport. Mems: Australia, Brunei, Canada, Chile, People's Republic of China, Colombia, Ecuador, Hong Kong, Indonesia, Japan, Republic of Korea, Malaysia, Mexico, Mongolia (assoc. mem.), New Zealand, Peru, Philippines, Russia, Singapore, Chinese Taipei (Taiwan), Thailand, USA, Viet Nam, French Pacific Territories (assoc. mem.) and the Pacific Islands Forum. Dir-Gen. DAVID PARSONS. Publs *Pacific Economic Outlook* (annually), *Pacific Food Outlook* (annually).

Pacific Islands Development Program: 1601 East-West Rd, Honolulu, HI 96848, USA; tel. (808) 944-7724; fax (808) 944-7670; e-mail halapuas@ewc.hawaii.edu; internet pidp.ewc.hawaii.edu; f. 1980; acts as secretariat for the Pacific Islands Conference; promotes regional development by means of education, research and training. Mems: 22 Pacific islands. Dir Dr SITIVENI HALAPUA.

Pacific Trade and Development Conference: c/o Australia-Japan Research Centre, John Crawford Bldg, Australian National University, Canberra ACT 0200, Australia; tel. (2) 6125-3780; fax (2) 6125-0767; e-mail paftad.sec@anu.edu.au; internet ajrcnet.anu.edu.au/paftad; f. 1968; holds annual conference for discussion of regional trade policy issues by senior economists and experts. Exec. Officer ANDREW DEANE.

US-Pacific Island Nations Joint Commercial Commission: c/o Pacific Islands Development Program, 1601 East-West Rd, Honolulu, HI 96848, USA; tel. (808) 944-7721; fax (808) 944-7721; e-mail kroekers@ewc.hawaii.edu; internet pidp.ewc.hawaii.edu/jcc/; f. 1993 to promote mutually beneficial commercial and economic relations between the independent Pacific island nations and the USA. Mems: Pacific island members of the Pacific Islands Forum and the USA. Publ. *JCC Trade Links* (quarterly).

EDUCATION

Asian and South Pacific Bureau of Adult Education: 42 Tughlakabad Inst. Area, New Delhi 110 062, India; tel. (11) 6981908; fax (11) 6980183; e-mail aspbae@vsnl.com; internet www.aspbae.org; f. 1964 to assist non-formal education and adult literacy; organizes training courses and seminars; provides material and advice relating to adult education. Mems in 36 countries and territories. Sec.-Gen. MARIA-LOURDES ALMAZAN-KHAN. Publs *ASPBAE News* (3 a year), *ASPBAE Courier* (2 a year).

Asian Confederation of Teachers: c/o FIT, 55 Abhinav Apt, Mahturas Rd Extn, Kandivli, Mumbai 400 067, India; tel. (22) 8085437; fax (22) 6240578; e-mail vsir@hotmail.com; f. 1990. Mems in 10 countries and territories. Pres. MUHAMMAD MUSTAPHA; Sec.-Gen. VINAYAK SIRDESAI.

Asian Institute of Technology—AIT: POB 4, Klong Luang, Pathumthani 12120, Thailand; tel. (2) 516-0110; fax (2) 516-2126; e-mail jlarmand@ait.ac.th; internet www.ait.ac.th; f. 1959; Master's, Doctor's and Diploma programmes are offered in four schools: Advanced Technologies, Civil Engineering, Environment, Resources and Development, and Management. Specialized training is provided by the Center for Library and Information Resources (CLAIR), the Continuing Education Center, the Center for Language and Educational Technology, the Regional Computer Center, the AIT Center in Viet Nam (based in Hanoi) and the Swiss-AIT-Viet Nam Management Development Program (in Ho Chi Minh City). Other research and outpost centres are the Asian Center for Engineering Computations and Software, the Asian Center for Research on Remote Sensing, the Regional Environmental Management Center, the Asian Center for Soil Improvement and Giosynthetics and the Urban Environmental Outreach Center. There are four specialized information centres (on ferro-cement, geotechnical engineering, renewable energy resources, environmental sanitation) under CLAIR; the Management of Technology Information Center conducts short-term courses in the management of technology and international business. Pres. Prof. JEAN-LOUIS ARMAND. Publs *AIT Annual Report, Annual Report on Research and Activities, AIT Review* (3 a year), *Prospectus,* other specialized publs.

Association of Southeast Asian Institutions of Higher Learning—ASAIHL: Secretariat, Ratasastra Bldg 2, Chulalongkorn University, Henri Dunant Rd, Bangkok 10330, Thailand; tel. (2) 251-6966; fax (2) 253-7909; e-mail oninnat@chula.ac.th; internet www.seameo.org/asaihl; f. 1956 to promote the economic, cultural and social welfare of the people of South-East Asia by means of educational co-operation, to cultivate a sense of regional identity and interdependence; serves as a clearing-house for information, and recognizes distinctive academic achievements. Mems: 150 educational institutions in Australia, Brunei, Canada, Hong Kong, Indonesia, Japan, Malaysia, New Zealand, Philippines, Singapore, Sri Lanka, Sweden, Thailand, USA, Viet Nam. Sec.-Gen. Dr NINNAT OLANVORAVUTH. Publs *Newsletter, Handbook of Southeast Asian Institutions of Higher Learning* (every 3 years).

International Union for Oriental and Asian Studies: c/o Közraktar u. 12A 11/2, 1093 Budapest, Hungary; f. 1951 by the 22nd International Congress of Orientalists under the auspices of UNESCO, to promote contacts between orientalists throughout the world, and to organize congresses, research and publications. Mems: in 24 countries. Sec.-Gen. Prof. GEORG HAZAI.

Southeast Asian Ministers of Education Organization—SEAMEO: Darakarn Bldg, 920 Sukhumvit Rd, Bangkok 10110, Thailand; tel. (2) 391-0144; fax (2) 381-2587; e-mail secretariat@seameo.org; internet www.seameo.org; f. 1965 to promote co-operation among the South-East Asian nations through co-operative projects and programmes in education, science and culture. SEAMEO has a policy-making Council and a permanent secretariat (SEAMES) in Bangkok; 14 regional centres, including: BIOTROP for tropical biology, in Bogor, Indonesia; INNOTECH for educational innovation and technology; RECSAM for education in science and mathematics, in Penang, Malaysia; RELC for languages, in Singapore; RIHED for higher education development in Bangkok, Thailand; a SEAMEO Traning Centre in Ho Chi Minh City, Viet Nam; SEAMOLEC for open learning and distant education in Jakarta, Indonesia; SEARCA for graduate study and research in agriculture, in Los Baños, Philippines; SPAFA for archaeology and fine arts in Bangkok, Thailand; TROPMED for tropical medicine and public health with centres in Indonesia, Malaysia, Philippines and Thailand and a central office in Bangkok, Thailand; and VOCTECH for vocational and technical education in Brunei. Mems: Brunei, Cambodia, Indonesia, Laos, Malaysia, Myanmar, Philippines, Singapore, Thailand, Viet Nam. Assoc. mems: Australia, Canada, France, Germany, Netherlands, New Zealand. Dir Dr SUPARAK RACHA-INTRA. Publs *Annual Report, SEAMEO Horizon.*

University of the South Pacific: Suva, Fiji; tel. 3313900; fax 3301305; internet www.usp.ac.fj; f. 1968; comprises three campuses (in Fiji, Samoa and Vanuatu), five schools (agriculture, science, humanities, law and social sciences), 11 extension centres in different countries and seven institutes. Mems: Cook Islands, Fiji, Kiribati, Marshall Islands, Nauru, Niue, Samoa, Solomon Islands, Tokelau, Tonga, Tuvalu, Vanuatu. Vice-Chancellor SAVENACA SIWATIBAU. Publs *USP Annual Report, USP Beat* (every 2 weeks), *USP Calendar* (annually).

World Scout Bureau/Asia-Pacific Region: POB 4050, MCPO 1280, Makati City, Philippines; tel. (2) 8180984; fax (2) 8190093; e-mail wsb@apr.scout.org; internet www.apr.scout.or.jp; f. 1956 to further the Scout Movement in the Asia-Pacific region by promoting the spirit of brotherhood, unity of purpose, co-operation and mutual assistance amongst Scout organizations within the region; conducts training courses, seminars, workshops, youth forums, jamborees and conferences. Mems: 19m. Scouts in 23 countries. Regional Dir ABDULLAH RASHEED. Publs *Asia-Pacific Scouting Newsletter* (monthly), *Regional Director's Report*.

ENVIRONMENT

South Asia Co-operative Environment Programme—SACEP: 10 Anderson Rd, Colombo 5, Sri Lanka; tel. (1) 589787; fax (1) 589369; e-mail sacep@eureka.lk; f. 1982; aims to promote and support the protection and management of the environment in the sub-region; Governing Council meets regularly; specific projects managed by individual mem. states, e.g. conservation of coral, mangroves, deltas and coastal areas (Bangladesh), training in wildlife management (India). Mems: Afghanistan, Bangladesh, Bhutan, India, Maldives, Nepal, Pakistan, Sri Lanka. Publ. *SACEP Newsletter*.

South Pacific Regional Environment Programme—SPREP: POB 240, Apia, Samoa; tel. 21929; fax 20231; e-mail sprep@sprep.org.ws; internet www.sprep.org.ws; f. 1978 by the South Pacific Commission (where it was based; now the Pacific Community), the South Pacific (now Pacific Islands) Forum Secretariat, ESCAP and UNEP; formally established as an independent institution in June 1993 when members signed the *Agreement Establishing SPREP*; aims to promote regional co-operation in environmental matters, to assist members to protect and improve their shared environment, and to help members to work towards sustainable development. Mems: 22 Pacific islands, Australia, France, New Zealand, USA. Dir TAMARI'I TUTANGATA (Cook Islands). Publs *SPREP Newsletter* (quarterly), *La lettre de l'environnement* (quarterly), *CASOLink* (quarterly), *South Pacific Sea Level and Climate Change Newsletter* (quarterly), various technical publications.

FINANCE

Asian Clearing Union—ACU: c/o Central Bank of the Islamic Republic of Iran, POB 11365/8551, Tehran, Iran; tel. (21) 2842076; fax (21) 2847677; e-mail acusecret@mail.iranet.net; f. 1974 to provide clearing arrangements to economize on the use of foreign exchange and promote the use of domestic currencies in trade transactions among developing countries; part of ESCAP's Asian trade expansion programme; the Central Bank of Iran is the Union's agent; in September 1995 the ACU unit of account was changed from SDR to US dollars, with effect from 1 January 1996. Mems: Bangladesh, Bhutan, India, Iran, Myanmar, Nepal, Pakistan, Sri Lanka. Sec.-Gen. Dr MOHAMMAD FIROUZDOR. Publs *Annual Report, Newsletter* (monthly).

Asian Reinsurance Corporation: 17th Floor, Tower B, Chamnan Phenjati Business Center, 65 Rama 9 Rd, Huaykwang, Bangkok 10320, Thailand; tel. (2) 245-2169; fax (2) 248-1377; e-mail asianre@asianrecorp.com; internet www.asianrecorp.com; f. 1979 by ESCAP with UNCTAD, to operate as a professional reinsurer, giving priority in retrocessions to national insurance and reinsurance markets of member countries in particular, and of other countries in the Asia-Pacific region, and as a development organization providing technical assistance to national markets; cap. (auth.) US $15m., (p.u.) US $8m. Mems: Afghanistan, Bangladesh, Bhutan, People's Republic of China, India, Iran, Republic of Korea, Philippines, Sri Lanka, Thailand. Gen. Man. A. S. MALABANAN.

Association of Asian Confederation of Credit Unions: POB 24–171, Bangkok 10240, Thailand; tel. (2) 374-3170; fax (2) 374-5321; e-mail accuran@ksc.th.com; internet www.aaccu.net; links and promotes credit unions in Asia, provides research facilities and training programmes. Mems: Bangladesh, Hong Kong, Indonesia, Japan, Republic of Korea, Malaysia, Nepal, Philippines, Sri Lanka, Taiwan, Thailand; affiliate mems in Australia, Germany, Singapore and USA. Gen. Man. RANJITH HETTIARACHCHI. Publs *Annual Report and Directory, ACCU News* (every 2 months), training, workshop and seminar reports.

Association of Development Financing Institutions in Asia and the Pacific: Skyland Plaza, Sen. Gil J. Puyat Ave, Makati City 1200, Philippines; tel. (2) 8161672; fax (2) 8176498; e-mail inquire@adfiap.org; internet www.adfiap.org; f. 1976 to promote the interests and economic development of the respective countries of its member institutions through development financing and generating employment; membership comprises institutions engaged in the financing of development, whether industrial or agricultural, as their main activity; 78 institutions from 34 countries. Sec.-Gen. ORLANDO P. PEÑA (Philippines).

Insurance Institute for Asia and the Pacific: Zapote Rd, Alabang, Metro Manila, Philippines; tel. (2) 8420691; fax (2) 8420692; f. 1974 to provide insurance management training and conduct research in subjects connected with the insurance industry. Publ. *IIAP Journal* (quarterly).

GOVERNMENT AND POLITICS

Afro-Asian People's Solidarity Organization—AAPSO: 89 Abdel Aziz Al-Saoud St, POB 11559-61 Manial El-Roda, Cairo, Egypt; tel. (2) 3636081; fax (2) 3637361; e-mail aapso@idsc.gov.eg; f. 1958; acts among and for the peoples of Africa and Asia in their struggle for genuine independence, sovereignty, socio-economic development, peace and disarmament; Mems: 82 nat. cttees from African and Asian countries, and 10 European orgs as assoc. mems. Pres. Dr MOURAD GHALEB; Sec.-Gen. NOURI ABD AR-RAZZAK HUSSEIN. Publs *Solidarity Bulletin* (monthly), *Development and Socio-Economic Progress* (quarterly), *Human Rights Newsletter* (6 a year).

Alliance of Small Island States—AOSIS: c/o 304 East 45th St, Room FF634, New York, NY 10017, USA; tel. (212) 599-6196; fax (212) 599-0797; e-mail samoa@un.int; internet www.sidsne.org/aosis; f. 1990 as an *ad hoc* intergovernmental grouping to focus on the special problems of small islands and low-lying coastal developing states. Mems: 43 island nations. Chair. TUILOMA NERONI SLADE (Samoa). Publ. *Small Islands, Big Issues*.

ANZUS: c/o Dept of Foreign Affairs and Trade, Locked Bag 40, QVT, Canberra, ACT 2600, Australia; tel. (2) 6261-9111; fax (2) 6273-3577; internet www.dfat.gov.au; the ANZUS Security Treaty was signed in 1951 by Australia, New Zealand and the USA, to co-ordinate partners' efforts for the preservation of peace and security in the Pacific area, through the exchange of technical information and strategic intelligence, and a programme of exercises, exchanges and visits. In 1984 New Zealand refused to allow visits by US naval vessels that were either nuclear-propelled or potentially nuclear-armed: in 1986 the USA formally announced the suspension of its security commitment to New Zealand under ANZUS. ANZUS continued to govern security relations between Australia and the USA, and between Australia and New Zealand; security relations between New Zealand and the USA were the only aspect of the treaty to be suspended. Following a US decision in September 1991 to remove nuclear weapons from surface vessels, New Zealand indicated its readiness to renew security relations with the USA. Senior-level contacts between New Zealand and the USA resumed in 1994. ANZUS has no permanent staff or secretariat.

Eastern Regional Organization for Public Administration—EROPA: 12M One Burgundy Plaza, 307 Katipunan Ave, Loyola Heights, Quezon City 1105, Philippines; tel. (2) 4338175; fax (2) 4349223; e-mail eropa@eropa.org.ph; internet www.eropa.org.ph; f. 1960 to promote regional co-operation in improving knowledge, systems and practices of governmental administration, to help accelerate economic and social development; organizes regional conferences, seminars, special studies, surveys and training programmes. There are three technical centres covering Training (New Delhi), Local Government (Tokyo) and Development Management (Seoul). Mems: 12 state members (Australia, People's Repub. of China, India, Indonesia, Iran, Japan, Repub. of Korea, Malaysia, Nepal, Philippines, Thailand and Viet Nam); 102 group members (institutions); 418 individuals. Sec.-Gen. PATRICIA A. STO TOMAS (Philippines). Publs *EROPA Bulletin, Asian Review of Public Administration*.

Melanesian Spearhead Group: c/o Ministry of Foreign Affairs, PMB 051, Port Vila, Vanuatu; tel. 22913; fax 23142; f. 1986 to promote political and cultural co-operation among the Melanesian peoples; supports independence process in New Caledonia. First Melanesian arts festival held in 1991. In July 1993 a free trade agreement was signed, awarding each member country most-favoured nation status for all trade. Heads of state or of government meet every two years; regular meetings of Group trade and economic officials are also held. In July 1999 members resolved to establish a permanent secretariat for the Group, based in Vanuatu. Mems: Fiji, Papua New Guinea, Solomon Islands, Vanuatu; Front de Libération Nationale Kanake Socialiste (New Caledonia). Chair. (2001–03) ROCH WAMYTAN.

Non-aligned Movement: c/o Permanent Representative of South Africa to the UN, 333 East 38th St, 9th Floor, New York, NY 10016, USA (no permanent secretariat); tel. (212) 213-5583; fax (212) 692-2498; e-mail soafun@worldnet.att.net; internet www.nam.gov.za; f. 1961 by a meeting of 25 heads of state, with the aim of linking countries that refused to adhere to the main East-West military and political blocs; co-ordination bureau established in 1973; works for the establishment of a new international economic order, and especially for better terms for countries producing raw materials; maintains special funds for agricultural development, improvement of food production and the financing of buffer stocks; 'South Commission' promotes co-operation between developing countries; seeks changes in the UN to give developing countries greater decision-making power; summit conference normally held every three years, 12th conference of heads of state and government was held in Durban, South Africa, in 1998; 13th conference scheduled to be held in Kuala Lumpur, Malaysia, in February 2003. Mems: 129 countries.

Shanghai Co-operation Organization—SCO: f. 2001, replacing the Shanghai Five (f. 1996 to address border disputes); comprises People's Republic of China, Kazakhstan, Kyrgyzstan, Russia, Tajikistan and Uzbekistan; aims to achieve security through mutual co-operation; Convention to Combat Terrorism, Separatism and Extremism signed June 2001.

LABOUR

Brotherhood of Asian Trade Unionists—BATU: FFW Bldg, 1943 Taft Ave, Malate, Manila, Philippines; tel. (2) 5240709; fax (2) 5218335; e-mail batunorm@iconn.com.ph; f. 1963 as the regional body in Asia of the World Confederation of Labour, to develop mutual co-operation among Asian trade unionists through exchanges of information, conferences, and educational activities. Mems: 5m. in 15 countries. Pres. JUAN C. TAN (Pres. Emeritus, Federation of Free Workers, the Philippines). Publs *BATU Monitor* (2 a month), *BATU Research and Education Journal*.

International Confederation of Free Trade Unions-Asian and Pacific Regional Organization—ICFTU-APRO: 73 Bras Basoh Rd, 4th Floor, Singapore 189556; tel. 2226294; fax 2217380; f. 1951; e-mail gs@icftu-apro.org; internet www.icftu-apro.org; sub-regional office in New Delhi, India. Mems: 33m. in 39 organizations in 29 countries. Gen. Sec. NORIYUKI SUZUKI. Publs *Asian and Pacific Labour* (monthly), *ICFTU-APRO Labour Flash* (2 a week).

South Pacific and Oceanic Council of Trade Unions—SPOCTU: 3rd Floor, TLC Bldg, 16 Peel St, Brisbane 4101, Australia; tel. (7) 3846-1806; fax (7) 3846-4968; e-mail spoctu@ozemail.com.au; f. 1989 as sub-regional body of ICFTU-APRO. Chair. JENNIE GEORGE; Exec. Officer ROD ELLIS. Publ. *Pacific Unionist* (newsletter).

LAW

Asian-African Legal Consultative Organization: E-66, Vasant Marg, Vasant Vihar, New Delhi 110057, India; tel. (11) 6152251; fax (11) 6152041; e-mail aalco@vsnl.com; internet www.aalco.org; f. 1956 to consider legal problems referred to it by mem. countries and to serve as a forum for Asian-African co-operation in international law and economic relations; provides background material for conferences, prepares standard/model contract forms suited to the needs of the region; promotes arbitration as a means of settling international commercial disputes; trains officers of member states; has permanent UN observer status. Mems: 45 states. Pres. KANU G. AGABI (Nigeria); Sec.-Gen. Dr WAFIK Z. KAMIL (Egypt).

Law Association for Asia and the Pacific—LAWASIA: NT House, 11th Floor, 22 Mitchell St, Darwin, NT 0800, Australia; tel. (8) 8946-9500; fax (8) 8946-9505; e-mail lawasia@lawasia.asn.au; internet www.lawasia.asn.au; f. 1966; provides an international and professional network for lawyers to update, reform and develop law within the region; comprises five Sections and 21 Standing Committees in Business Law and General Practice areas which organize speciality conferences; 18th biennial conference scheduled to be held in Tokyo, Japan, in September 2003. Mems: national orgs in 25 countries; 2,500 individual mems in 55 countries. Pres. GORDON HUGHES. Publs *LAWASIA Newsletter* (quarterly), *Directory* (annually), *Journal* (annually), proceedings of conferences and seminars, research reports.

MEDICINE AND HEALTH

Asia-Pacific Dental Federation: c/o 16 The Terrace, Wellington, New Zealand; tel. (4) 472-5516; fax (4) 472-5448; e-mail jannan@apdf.info; internet www.apdf.info/; f. 1955 to establish closer relationship among dental associations in Asian and Pacific countries and to encourage research; holds annual congress. Mems: 25 national asscns. Pres. Dr LEE KEE-TAEK (Republic of Korea); Sec-Gen. Dr JEFF ANNAN. Publ. *Asian Dentist* (6 a year).

Federation of Asian Pharmaceutical Associations—FAPA: c/o Ppha Building, 815 R. Papa St, Sampaloc, Manila 1008, Philippines; tel. and fax (2) 3130850; e-mail philpharm@surfshop.net.ph; f. 1964; aims to develop pharmacy as a profession and as an applied science; congress held every two years (2002: Seoul, Republic of Korea). Mems: national pharmaceutical associations in Australia, Hong Kong, India, Indonesia, Japan, Republic of Korea, Malaysia, Pakistan, Philippines, Singapore, Taiwan, Thailand. Pres. PETER BRAND (Australia); Sec.-Gen. Dr OLIVIA M. LIMUACO (Philippines). Publ. *Asian Journal of Pharmacy* (annually).

International Association for the Study of Obesity—IASO: 231 North Gower St, London, NW1 2NS, United Kingdom; tel. (20) 7691-1914; fax (20) 7387-6033; e-mail inquiries@iaso.org; internet www.iaso.org; f.1986; supports research into the prevention and management of obesity throughout the world and disseminates information regarding disease and accompanying health and social issues; incorporates the International Obesity Task Force. International Congress held every four years (2002: São Paulo, Brazil). Mems: national associations in 37 countries. Exec. Dir KATE BAILLIE. Publs *International Journal of Obesity* (monthly), *Obesity Reviews* (quarterly), *IASO Newsletter*(2 a year).

International Centre for Diarrhoeal Disease Research (ICDDR, B), Bangladesh: GPO Box 128, Dhaka 1000, Bangladesh; tel. (2) 8811751; fax (2) 8823116; e-mail info@icddrb.org; internet www.icddrb.org; f. 1960; undertakes research, education, training and information dissemination on diarrhoeal diseases, child health and child survival, reproductive health, women's health, nutrition, emerging infectious diseases, environmental health, vaccine evaluation, and case management, with particular reference to developing countries; research findings provide guide-lines for policy-makers, implementing agencies and health professionals world-wide; supported by 55 Governments, private foundations and international organizations. Dir Prof. DAVID SACK. Publs *Annual Report, Glimpse* (quarterly), *Journal of Health, Population and Nutrition* (quarterly), *Shasthya Sanglap* (3 a year), *DISC Bulletin* (weekly), scientific reports, working papers, monographs.

Pan-Pacific Surgical Association: 2000 L St, NW, Suite 200, Washington, DC 20036, USA; tel. (202) 416-1866; fax (202) 416-1867; e-mail ppsa@slackinc.com; internet www.ppsa.org; f. 1929 to bring together surgeons to exchange scientific knowledge relating to surgery and medicine, and to promote the improvement and standardization of hospitals and their services and facilities; 26th biennial congress: January 2002, Hawaii. Mems: 2,000 regular, associate, senior and honorary mems from over 40 countries.

PRESS, RADIO AND TELECOMMUNICATIONS

Asia-Pacific Broadcasting Union: POB 1164, 59700 Kuala Lumpur, Malaysia; tel. (3) 22823592; fax (3) 22825292; e-mail sg@abu.org.my; internet www.abu.org.my; f. 1964 to foster and co-ordinate the development of broadcasting in the Asia-Pacific area, to develop means of establishing closer collaboration and co-operation among broadcasting orgs, and to serve the professional needs of broadcasters in Asia and the Pacific; holds annual General Assembly. Mems: 102 in 50 countries and territories. Pres. KATSUJI EBISAWA (Japan); Sec.-Gen. DAVID ASTLEY (Australia). Publs *ABU News* (every 2 months), *ABU Technical Review* (every 2 months).

Asia-Pacific Telecommunity: No.12/49, Soi 5, Chaengwattana Rd, Thungsonghong, Bangkok 10210, Thailand; tel. (2) 573-0044; fax (2) 573-7479; e-mail aptmail@aptsec.org; internet www.aptsec.org; f. 1979 to cover all matters relating to telecommunications in the region. Mems: 32 member states, four assoc. members and 51 affiliates. Exec. Dir AMARENDU NARAYAN.

Asian-Pacific Postal Union: Post Office Bldg, Plaza Bonifacio, 1000 Manila, Philippines; tel. (2) 470760; fax (2) 407448; f. 1962 to extend, facilitate and improve the postal relations between the member countries and to promote co-operation in the field of postal services. Mems: 23 countries. Dir JORGE SARMIENTO. Publ. *APPU Newsletter*.

Confederation of ASEAN Journalists: Gedung Dewan Pers, 4th Floor, 34 Jalan Kebon Sirih, Jakarta 10110, Indonesia; tel. (21) 3453131; fax (21) 3453175; e-mail aseancaj@mega.net.id; f. 1975; holds General Assembly every two years, Press Convention, workshops. Mems: journalists' asscns in Brunei, Indonesia, Laos, Malaysia, Philippines, Singapore, Thailand and Viet Nam; observers: journalists' asscns in Cambodia, and Myanmar. Perm. Sec. ABDUL RAZAK. Publs *The ASEAN Journalist* (quarterly), *CAJ Yearbook*.

Organization of Asia-Pacific News Agencies—OANA: c/o Xinhua News Agency, 57 Xuanwumen Xidajie, Beijing 100803, People's Republic of China; tel. (10) 63074762; fax (10) 63072707; internet www.oananews.com; f. 1961 to promote co-operation in professional matters and mutual exchange of news, features, etc. among the news agencies of Asia and the Pacific via the Asia-Pacific News Network (ANN). Mems: AAP (Australia), AKP (Cambodia), Anadolu Ajansi (Turkey), Antara (Indonesia), APP (Pakistan), Bakhtar (Afghanistan), BERNAMA (Malaysia), BSS (Bangladesh), ENA (Bangladesh), Hindusthan Samachar (India), IRNA (Iran), KABAR (Kyrgyzstan), Kaz-TAG (Kazakhstan), KCNA (Korea, Democratic People's Republic), KPL (Laos), Kyodo (Japan), Lankapuvath (Sri Lanka), Montsame (Mongolia), PNA (Philippines), PPI (Pakistan), PTI (India), RIA-Novosti (Russia), RSS (Nepal), Samachar Bharati (India), ITAR-TASS (Russia), TNA (Thailand), UNB (Bangladesh), UNI (India), VNA (Viet Nam), Yonhap (Republic of Korea),

Xinhua (People's Republic of China). Pres. GUO CHAOREN (People's Republic of China); Sec.-Gen. MIKHAIL GUSMANN.

Pacific Telecommunications Council: 2454 S. Beretania St, Suite 302, Honolulu, HI 96826, USA; tel. (808) 941-3789; fax (808) 944-4874; e-mail info@ptc.org; internet www.ptc.org; f. 1980; non-governmental organization aiming to promote the development, understanding and beneficial use of telecommunications and information systems/services throughout the Pacific region; provides forum for users and providers of communications services; sponsors annual conference and seminars. Mems: more than 700 (corporate, government, academic and individual) in 50 countries. Pres. HANSUK KIM; Exec. Dir HOYT ZIA. Publ. *Pacific Telecommunication Review* (quarterly).

Press Foundation of Asia: S & L Bldg, 3rd Floor, 1500 Roxas Blvd, POB 1843, Manila, Philippines; tel. (2) 5233223; fax (2) 5224365; e-mail pfa@pressasia.org; internet www.pressasia.org; f. 1967; an independent, non-profit-making organization governed by its newspaper members; acts as a professional forum for about 300 newspapers in Asia; aims to reduce cost of newspapers to potential readers, to improve editorial and management techniques through research and training programmes and to encourage the growth of the Asian press. Mems: 300 newspapers in 24 countries; regional offices in Bangkok, Hong Kong, Kuala Lumpur, New Delhi, Tokyo and Seoul. The Foundation owns and operates *DEPTH-news,* a feature service for newspapers in the region. Exec. Chair. MAZLAN NORDIN (Malaysia); Chief Exec. MOCHTAR LUBIS (Indonesia). Publs *Pressasia, Asian Women* (quarterly), *Asian Forum Newsletter, Environment Folio* (quarterly).

RELIGION

Christian Conference of Asia: Pak Tin Village, Mei Tin Rd, Shatin, Hong Kong; tel. 26911068; fax 26924378; e-mail cca@cca.org.hk; internet www.cca.org.hk; f. 1957 to promote co-operation and joint study in matters of common concern among the churches of the region and to encourage interaction with other regional conferences and the World Council of Churches. Mems: 119 churches and national councils of churches in 16 countries. Gen. Sec. Dr AHN JAE WOONG. Publ. *CCA News* (quarterly).

Pacific Conference of Churches: POB 208, 4 Thurston St, Suva, Fiji; tel. 3311277; fax 3303205; e-mail pacific@is.com.fj; f. 1961; holds assembly every five years, as well as regular workshops, meetings and training seminars throughout the region. Mems: 26 churches and 10 councils. Gen. Sec. Rev. VALAMOTU PALU.

World Fellowship of Buddhists: 616 Benjasiri Pk, Soi Medhinivet (off Soi Sukhumvit 24), Bangkok 10110, Thailand; tel. (2) 661-1284; fax (2) 661-0555; e-mail wfb-hq@asianet.co.th; internet www.wfb-hq.org; f. 1950 to promote strict observance and practice of the teachings of the Buddha; General Conference convened every two years; 140 regional centres in 37 countries. Pres. PHAN WANNAMETHEE; Hon. Sec.-Gen. Dr NANTASARN SEESALAB. Publs *WFB Journal* (6 a year), *WFB Review* (quarterly), *WFB Newsletter* (monthly), documents, booklets.

World Hindu Federation: c/o Dr Jogendra Jha, Pashupati Kshetra, Kathmandu, Nepal; tel. (1) 470182; fax (1) 470131; e-mail hem@karki.com.np; f. 1981 to promote and preserve Hindu philosophy and culture; to protect the rights of Hindus, particularly the right to worship. Executive Board meets annually. Mems: in 45 countries and territories. Sec.-Gen. Dr JOGENDRA JHA (Nepal). Publ. *Vishwa Hindu* (monthly).

SCIENCE AND TECHNOLOGY

Co-ordinating Committee for Coastal and Offshore Geoscience Programmes in East and Southeast Asia—CCOP: OMO Bldg, 2nd Floor, 110/2 Sathorn Nua Rd, Bangrak, Bangkok 10500, Thailand; tel. (2) 234-3578; fax (2) 237-1221; e-mail ccopts@ccop.or.th; internet www.ccop.or.th; f. 1966 as a regional intergovernmental organization, to promote and co-ordinate geoscientific programmes concerning the exploration of mineral and hydrocarbon resources and environmentally sound coastal zone management in the offshore and coastal areas of member nations; works in partnership with developed nations which have provided geologists and geophysicists as technical advisers; receives aid from co-operating countries, and other sources. Mems: Cambodia, People's Republic of China, Indonesia, Japan, Republic of Korea, Malaysia, Papua New Guinea, Philippines, Singapore, Thailand, Viet Nam; 14 co-operating countries. Dir SAHNG-YUP KIM. Publs *CCOP Newsletter* (quarterly), *Technical Bulletin, Technical Publication, CCOP Map Series, Proceedings of Annual Session,* digital dataset/CD-ROM series, other technical reports.

Federation of Asian Scientific Academies and Societies—FASAS: c/o Indian National Science Academy, Bahadur Shah Zafar Marg, New Delhi 110002, India; tel. (11) 3232066; fax (11) 3235648; e-mail insa@giasdlol.vsnl.net.in; f. 1984 to stimulate regional co-operation and promote national and regional self-reliance in science and technology, by organizing meetings, training and research programmes and encouraging the exchange of scientists and of scientific information. 14 mems: national scientific academies and societies from Afghanistan, Australia, Bangladesh, People's Republic of China, India, Republic of Korea, Malaysia, Nepal, New Zealand, Pakistan, Philippines, Singapore, Sri Lanka, Thailand. Pres. Prof. C. S. DAYRIT (Philippines); Sec. Prof. INDIRA NATH (India).

Pacific Science Association: 1525 Bernice St, Honolulu, HI 96817, USA; tel. (808) 848-4139; fax (808) 847-8252; e-mail psa@bishopmuseum.org; internet www.pacificscience.org; f. 1920 to promote co-operation in the study of scientific problems relating to the Pacific region, particularly those affecting the prosperity and well-being of Pacific peoples; sponsors Pacific Science Congresses and Inter-Congresses: 20th Congress scheduled to be held in Bangkok, Thailand, in March 2003. Mems: institutional representatives from 35 areas, scientific societies, individual and corporate mems. Pres. Dr R. GERARD WARD (Australia); Exec. Sec. Dr LUCIUS G. ELDREDGE. Publ. *Pacific Science* (quarterly).

South Pacific Applied Geoscience Commission—SOPAC: Private Mail Bag, GPO, Suva, Fiji; tel. 3381377; fax 3370040; e-mail director@sopac.org; internet www.sopac.org; f. 1972; activities, which aim to assist member countries to assess their natural resources and to achieve self-sufficiency in the geosciences, include the following: assessment of coastal, onshore and offshore mineral potential; promotion of wave energy and geothermal energy; coastal protection assessment, monitoring and management advice; seabed mapping; water resources and sanitation; workshops and seminars. Organizes workshops, provides technical services and degree and certificate studies. Mems: Australia, Cook Islands, Fiji, French Polynesia (assoc.), Guam, Kiribati, Marshall Islands, Federated States of Micronesia, New Caledonia (assoc.), New Zealand, Niue, Papua New Guinea, Samoa, Solomon Islands, Tonga, Tuvalu, Vanuatu. Dir ALFRED SIMPSON (Fiji). Publs *Annual Report, SOPAC News,* various technical reports and bulletins.

STUDENTS

Asian Students' Association: 353 Shanghai St, 4/F, Kowloon, Hong Kong; tel. 23880515; fax 27825535; e-mail asasec@netvigator.com; f. 1969 to help in the solution of local and regional problems; to assist in promotion of an Asian identity; to promote programmes of common benefit to member organizations; to foster solidarity with students in the region and in the world; the Association opposes all forms of colonialism, foreign intervention and discrimination in Asia; includes Student Commissions for Education, Human Rights and Peace; holds seminars, workshops. Mems: 46 organizations from 26 countries in the Asia-Pacific region. Co-Secs LINA P. CABAERO, RAJAN BHATTARAI, JEGA PONNAMBALAM. Publs *ASA News* (quarterly), *Movement News Round-up* (monthly).

TOURISM

Asia Travel Marketing Association—ATMA: c/o Japan National Tourist Organization, Tokyo Kotsu Kaikan Bldg, 2-10-1 Yurakucho, Chiyoda-ku, Tokyo, Japan; tel. (3) 3216-2910; fax (3) 3216-1846; e-mail atma@jnto.go.jp; internet www.asiatravel.org; f. 1966 as East Asia Travel Association, present name adopted 1999; aims to promote tourism in the East Asian region, encourage and facilitate the flow of tourists to that region from other parts of the world, and to develop regional tourist industries by close collaboration among members. Mems: five national tourist organizations and one travel association. Sec.-Gen. JOÃO MANUEL COSTA ANTUNES.

Pacific Asia Travel Association—PATA: Unit B1, Siam Tower, 28th Floor, 989 Rama I Rd, Pathumwan, Bangkok 10330, Thailand; tel. (2) 658-2000; fax (2) 658-2010; e-mail patabkk@pata.th.com; internet www.pata.org; f. 1951; aims to enhance the growth, value and quality of Pacific Asia travel and tourism for the benefit of PATA members; holds annual conference. Divisional offices in Monaco, San Francisco, Sydney. Mems: more than 1,800 governments, carriers, tour operators, travel agents and hotels. Publs *PATA Compass* (every 2 months), *Quarterly Statistical Report,* research reports, directories, newsletters.

South Pacific Tourism Organization—SPTO: FNPF Plaza, 3rd Floor, Victoria Parade, POB 13119, Suva, Fiji; tel. 3304177; fax 3301995; e-mail info@spto.org; internet www.spto.org; f. 1983 as Tourism Council of the South Pacific, present name adopted 1999; aims to foster regional co-operation in the development, marketing and promotion of tourism in the island nations of the South Pacific; holds conferences; represents public- and private-sector interests. Mems: American Samoa, Cook Islands, Fiji, Kiribati, New Caledonia, Niue, Papua New Guinea, Samoa, Solomon Islands, Tahiti (French Polynesia), Tonga, Tuvalu, Vanuatu. Chief Exec. LISIATE AKOLO.

TRADE AND INDUSTRY

Cairns Group: c/o Department of Foreign Affairs and Trade, GPO Box 12, QVT, Canberra, ACT 2601, Australia; tel. (2) 6263-2222;

fax (2) 6261-3111; internet www.dfat.gov.au/trade/negotiations/cairns_group/index.html; f. 1986 by major agricultural exporting countries, aiming to bring about reforms in international agricultural trade, including reductions in export subsidies, in barriers to access and in internal support measures; represents members' interests in WTO negotiations. Mems: Argentina, Australia, Bolivia, Brazil, Canada, Chile, Colombia, Costa Rica, Fiji, Guatemala, Indonesia, Malaysia, New Zealand, Paraguay, Philippines, South Africa, Thailand, Uruguay. Chair. MARK VAILE (Australia).

Confederation of Asia-Pacific Chambers of Commerce and Industry—CACCI: 3 Sungshou Rd, 9th Floor, Taipei 110, Taiwan; tel. (2) 2725-5663; fax (2) 2725-5665; e-mail cacci@iplus.net.tw; internet www.cacci.org.tw; f. 1966; holds biennial conferences to examine regional co-operation; liaises with governments to promote laws conducive to regional co-operation; serves as a centre for compiling and disseminating trade and business information; encourages contacts between businesses; conducts training and research. Mems: national chambers of commerce and industry of Australia, Bangladesh, Brunei, Cambodia, Hong Kong, India, Indonesia, Japan, Republic of Korea, Malaysia, Mongolia, Nepal, New Zealand, Pakistan, Papua New Guinea, Philippines, Russia, Singapore, Sri Lanka, Taiwan, Thailand, Viet Nam; also affiliate, associate and special mems. Dir-Gen. Dr WEBSTER KIANG. Publs *CACCI Profile* (monthly), *CACCI Journal of Commerce and Industry* (annually).

International Co-operative Alliance: Regional Office for Asia and Pacific: E-4, Defence Colony, Ring Rd, New Delhi 110 024, India; tel. (11) 4694989; fax (11) 4694964; e-mail icaroap@vsnl.com; internet www.icarop.org.sg; f. 1960; promotes economic relations and encourages technical assistance among the national co-operative movements; represents the ICA in other regional forums; holds courses, seminars and conferences, and maintains the Co-operative Information Resource Centre (holding more than 20,000 volumes). Administers the ICA Domus Trust (f. 1988) which aims *inter alia* the propagation of co-operative principles, publication of material for the study and teaching of co-operation, education and training activities and the promotion of collaboration between co-operatives and the state. Mem. orgs: 67 in 28 countries of the region. Regional Dir SHIL KWAN LEE. Publs *Annual Report, Asia and Pacific Co-op News, Co-op Dialogue, Review of International Co-operation*.

Pacific Power Association: Private Mail Bag, Suva, Fiji; tel. 3306022; fax 3302038; e-mail ppa@ppa.org.fj; internet www.ppa.org.fj; f. 1992 to facilitate co-operation and development of regional power utilities; represents the Pacific Islands' power sector at international meetings. Mems: 25 power utilities throughout the region; 45 allied mems. Exec. Dir TONY NEIL. Publ. *Pacific Power* (quarterly).

South-East Asia Iron and Steel Institute: 2E Block 2, 5th Floor, Worldwide Business Park, Jalan Tinju 13/50, 40675 Shah Alam, Selangor Darul Ehson, Malaysia; tel. (3) 55191102; fax (3) 55191159; e-mail seaisi@seaisi.org; internet www.seaisi.org; f. 1971 to further the development of the iron and steel industry in the region, encourage regional co-operation, provide advisory services and a forum for the exchange of knowledge, establish training programmes, promote standardization, collate statistics and issue publications. Mems: more than 800 in 26 countries. Sec.-Gen. IAIN BARTHOLOMEW. Publs *SEAISI Quarterly Journal, SEAISI Directory* (annually), *Iron and Steel Statistics* (annually, for each member country), *Newsletter* (monthly), country reports.

TRANSPORT

Association of Asia Pacific Airlines: 9th Floor, Kompleks Antarabangsa, Jalan Sultan Ismail, 50250 Kuala Lumpur, Malaysia; tel. (3) 2145-5600; fax (3) 2145-2500; e-mail aapahdg@aapa.org.my; internet www.aapairlines.org; f. 1966 as Orient Airlines Asscn; present name adopted in April 1997; represents the interest s of Asia Pacific airlines; encourages the exchange of information and increased co-operation between airlines; seeks to develop safe, efficient, profitable and environmentally friendly air transport. Mems: 17 scheduled international airlines. Dir-Gen. RICHARD THOMAS STIRLAND. Publs *Annual Report, Annual Statistical Report, Monthly International Statistics, Orient Aviation* (10 a year).

WOMEN'S ASSOCIATION

Pan-Pacific and South East Asia Women's Association—PPSEAWA: POB 119, Nuku'alofa, Tonga; tel. 24003; fax 41404; e-mail nanasi@kalianet.to; internet www.ppseawa.org; f. 1928 to foster better understanding and friendship among women of all Pacific and South-East Asian areas, and to promote co-operation for the study and improvement of social conditions; holds international conference every three years. Mems: 19 national member organizations. Pres. HRH Princess NANASIPAU'U TUKU'AHO. Publ. *PPSEAWA Bulletin* (2 a year).

MAJOR COMMODITIES OF ASIA AND THE PACIFIC

Note: For each of the commodities in this section, there are generally two statistical tables: one relating to recent levels of production, and one indicating recent trends in prices. Each production table shows estimates of output for the world and for the countries covered by this volume. In addition, the table lists the main producing countries of the Far East and Australasia and, for comparison, the leading producers from outside the region. In most cases, the table referring to prices provides indexes of export prices, calculated in US dollars. The index for each commodity is based on specific price quotations for representative grades of that commodity in countries that are major traders (excluding countries of Eastern Europe and the former USSR).

Aluminium and Bauxite

Aluminium is the second most abundant metallic element in the earth's crust after silicon, comprising about 8% of the total. However, it is much less widely used than steel, despite having about the same strength and only half the weight. Aluminium has important applications as a metal because of its lightness, ease of fabrication and other desirable properties. Other products of alumina (aluminium oxide) are materials in refractories, abrasives, glass manufacture, other ceramic products, catalysts and absorbers. Alumina hydrates are used for the production of aluminium chemicals, fire retardant in carpet backing, and industrial fillers in plastics and related products.

The major markets for aluminium are in transportation, building and construction, electrical machinery and equipment, consumer durables and the packaging industry, which in the late 1990s accounted for about 20% of all aluminium use. Although the production of aluminium is energy-intensive, its light weight results in a net saving, particularly in the transportation industry. About one-quarter of aluminium output is consumed in the manufacture of transport equipment, particularly road motor vehicles and components, where the metal is increasingly being used as a substitute for steel. In the early 1990s steel substitution accounted for about 16% of world aluminium consumption, and it has been forecast that aluminium demand by the motor vehicle industry alone could more than double, to reach 5.7m. metric tons in 2010, from around 2.4m. tons in 1990. Aluminium is valued by the aerospace industry for its weight-saving characteristics and for its low cost relative to alternative materials. Aluminium-lithium alloys command considerable potential for use in this sector, although the traditional dominance of aluminium in the aerospace industry was under challenge during the 1990s from 'composites' such as carbon-epoxy, a fusion of carbon fibres and hardened resins, whose lightness and durability can exceed that of many aluminium alloys.

World markets for finished and semi-finished aluminium products were, until recently, dominated by six Western producers—Alcan (Canada), Alcoa, Reynolds, Kaiser (all USA), Pechiney (France) and algroup (Switzerland). Proposals for a merger between Alcan, algroup and Pechiney, and between Alcoa and Reynolds, were announced in August 1999. However, the proposed terms of the Pechiney-Alcan-algroup merger encountered opposition from the European Commission, on the grounds that the combined grouping could restrict market competition and adversely affect the interests of consumers. The tripartite merger plan was abandoned in April 2000, in favour of a merger between Alcan and algroup, which was effected in October. The amalgamation of Alcoa and Reynolds was approved by the European Commission and the US Government in May 2000. The level of dominance of these major producers has, in any case, been reduced in recent years by a significant geographical shift in the location of alumina and aluminium production to areas where cheap power is available, such as Australia, Brazil, Norway, Canada and Venezuela. The Gulf States of Bahrain and Dubai, with the advantage of low energy costs, also produce primary aluminium. Since the mid-1990s Russia has also become a significant force in the world aluminium market (see below), and in April 2000 the country's three principal producers announced their intention to combine into a single group—Russian Aluminium (RusAl)—representing about 75% of Russian aluminium production and approximately 10% of world output.

Bauxite is the principal aluminium ore, but nepheline syenite, kaolin, shale, anorthosite and alunite are all potential alternative sources of alumina, although not currently economic to process. Of all bauxite mined, approximately 85% is converted to alumina (Al_2O_3) for the production of aluminium metal. The developing countries, in which 70% of known bauxite reserves are located, supply 45% of the ore required. The industry is structured in three stages: bauxite mining, alumina refining and smelting. While the high degree of 'vertical integration' (i.e. the control of successive stages of production) in the industry means that a significant proportion of trade in bauxite and alumina is in the form of intra-company transfers, and the increasing tendency to site alumina refineries near to bauxite deposits has resulted in a shrinking bauxite trade, there is a growing free market in alumina, serving the needs of the increasing number of independent (i.e. non-integrated) smelters.

The alumina is separated from the ore by the Bayer process. After mining, bauxite is fed to process directly if mine-run material is adequate (as in Jamaica), or it is crushed and beneficiated. Where the ore 'as mined' presents handling problems, or weight reduction is desirable, it may be dried prior to shipment.

At the alumina plant the ore is slurried with spent-liquor directly, if the soft Caribbean type is used, or, in the case of other types, it is ball-milled to reduce it to a size which will facilitate the extraction of the alumina. The bauxite slurry is then digested with caustic soda to extract the alumina from the ore while leaving the impurities as an insoluble residue. The digest conditions depend on the aluminium minerals in the ore and the impurities. The liquor, with the dissolved alumina, is then separated from the insoluble impurities by combinations of sedimentation, decantation and filtration and the residue washed to minimize the soda losses. The clarified liquor is concentrated and the alumina precipitated by seeding with hydrate. The precipitated alumina is then filtered, washed and calcined to produce alumina. The ratio of bauxite to alumina is approximately 1.95:1.

The smelting of the aluminium is generally by electrolysis in molten cryolite. Because of the high consumption of electricity by this process, alumina is usually smelted in areas where low-cost electricity is available. However, most of the electricity now used in primary smelting in the Western world is generated by hydroelectricity—a renewable energy source.

The recycling of aluminium is economically (as well as environmentally) desirable, as the process uses only 5% of the electricity required to produce a similar quantity of primary aluminium. Aluminium that has been recycled from scrap currently accounts for about 40% of the total aluminium supply in the USA, and for about 30% of Western European consumption. With the added impetus of environmental concerns, considerable growth world-wide in the recycling of used beverage cans (UBC) was forecast for the 1990s. In the mid-1990s, according to aluminium industry estimates, the recycling rate of UBC amounted to at least 55% world-wide.

Total world output of primary aluminium in 2000 was estimated at 24.0m. metric tons, of which East and South Asian producers, together with Australia and New Zealand, accounted for about 5.4m. tons. The USA normally accounts for about one-third of total aluminium consumption (excluding communist and former communist countries). Although it is the world's principal producing country (accounting for about 16% of global output of primary aluminium in 1999), the USA does not produce a surplus of ingots, and limits production to satisfy its domestic requirements for fabrication, while importing the remainder from lower-cost producers elsewhere.

Aluminium consumption has been advancing significantly in East Asia and India in recent years. In the early 2000s the People's Republic of China was high among the world's major consumers of aluminium. Its requirements had been forecast to rise by about 60% in 1995–2000, to 2.5m. tons annually by 2000. In the event, domestic consumption totalled 3.4m. tons in that year. The main consuming sectors in 2000 were construction, packaging, communications and transportation. China's domestic aluminium production capacity has, meanwhile, undergone significant expansion in recent years, reaching 3.3m. tons at the end of 2000, an increase of about 18% compared with 1999. By 2005 production capacity is expected to have increased to more than 4.2m. tons. However, demand is forecast to outstrip supply by a wider margin up to 2005, increasing China's reliance on imports. In 1999 it was reported that China had 111 aluminium smelters, of which about 40 had been constructed in the preceding two years. In August 1999 the China Aluminium Corpn (Chalco) was established to assume responsibility for the management of aluminium production facilities formerly controlled by the State Bureau of Nonferrous Metals Industry. At that time the aluminium smelters operated by Chalco had a production capacity of about 1m. tons per year.

Japan was the world's leading importer of unwrought aluminium in the late 1990s. The country's imports of refined aluminium (primary metal) totalled 2.9m. tons in 2000. Japan produces only small amounts of primary aluminium, but is a major producer of secondary metal (obtained by remelting waste or scrap). The country also has substantial rolling and extrusion facilities for aluminium fabrication, using secondary or imported metal.

The Republic of Korea does not produce primary aluminium, but, like Japan, has facilities for the manufacture of rolled aluminium products. In 1999 Alcan and a local wire-manufacturing company formed a Korean-based joint venture, Alcan Taihan Aluminum Ltd, to market such products throughout the Asia-Pacific region. In 2000 Alcan became the leading Asian manufacturer of aluminium rolled products through the acquisition of Aluminium of Korea Ltd (Koralu).

Australia is the world's largest producer and exporter of bauxite and alumina. In 2001 the country accounted for 39% of the world's bauxite production and, in 2000, for almost 32% of alumina output. Australia's five bauxite mines produced 53.5m. tons of the ore in 2001: a decline of 0.6% on the 2000 total. The country's six alumina refineries include the huge Worsley facility in Western Australia, reported to be probably the lowest-cost refinery in the world. Expansion of the Worsley plant, increasing its annual capacity from 1.7m. tons to 3.1m. tons (so making it the world's largest alumina refinery), was completed in 2000. At that time Alcoa owned 56% of the Worsley refinery, but the company was required to dispose of this interest, among several assets, as a precondition, imposed by competition authorities, for its merger with Reynolds (see above). Australia's output of alumina increased from 14.5m. tons in 1999 to 15.7m. tons in 2000. The country has extensive bauxite deposits in Western Australia, the Northern Territory and Queensland. Owing to the availability of bauxite and alumina (Australia's bauxite reserves, estimated at 3,800m. tons, account for 15.8% of the world's identified reserves), and of low-cost power (vast coal resources), the country provides a desirable location for aluminium smelters. There are six smelters currently operating, with a combined output of 1.8m. tons of primary aluminium in 2000. Alcoa of Australia, the world's largest alumina-producing company, operates one of these smelters, together with two bauxite mines and three alumina refineries. In 1999/2000 the aluminium industry was Australia's third-largest export sector (behind coal and gold), with earnings that included $A3,400m. from sales of alumina and $A3,900m. from sales of aluminium ingots.

New Zealand has a single aluminium smelter, commissioned in 1971 at Tiwai Point, near Invercargill, South Island. The plant is controlled by a subsidiary of the Australian company Comalco. A major expansion of the smelter was completed in 1996, increasing capacity to 313,000 tons of primary aluminium per year. In the late 1990s more than 90% of the smelter's production was exported.

India has the world's sixth-largest bauxite reserves, estimated to be at least 1,400m. tons. Indian bauxite is of high quality (about 90% metallurgical grade), and production has generally increased in recent years. India's estimated output of alumina increased from 1.9m. tons in 1999 to 2m. tons in 2000. About 60% of the country's recoverable bauxite is in the eastern state of Orissa. The government-controlled National Aluminium Co (NALCO) is the main bauxite-producing company in India, with output reaching a record 2.9m. tons in the year to March 2001. An expansion plan, aiming to increase NALCO's bauxite production to 4.8m. tons per year, was completed by mid-2000. At the same time, the company increased the annual capacity of its alumina refinery in Orissa from 800,000 tons to 1,050,000 tons. NALCO and the privately-owned Hindalco Industries Ltd are among the world's lowest-cost producers of alumina and aluminium. In 1999 Hindalco decided to expand the annual capacity of its aluminium smelter at Renukoot, in Uttar Pradesh, by 100,000 tons (from its existing capacity of 242,000 tons). In mid-2000 a major new bauxite-alumina project was being prepared in Orissa by a joint venture involving Alcan, Norwegian interests and a Hindalco subsidiary. The scheme, involving an estimated investment of US $900m., envisages the establishment of a bauxite mine at Baphilimali, producing a projected 3.6m. tons of ore per year, and an alumina refinery in the Rayagada district, with a planned initial capacity of 1.2m. tons per year. Completion of the project is scheduled for 2005. Despite the inadequacy of the electric power supply, India has the potential to become one of the world's leading aluminium producers. In 2000 the country's seven smelters (including five in the private sector) had a combined annual capacity of 825,000 tons, while output of aluminium ingots in that year was about 560,000 tons. As part of its expansion plans in the late 1990s, NALCO was increasing the capacity of its smelter at Angul, in Orissa, from 218,000 tons to 345,000 tons. Work on this project was due to be completed by mid-2002. NALCO's output in the year to March 1999 was only 146,205 tons (compared with 200,162 tons in 1997/98). In 1999/2000 NALCO's production totalled 212,661 tons. During the same period Hindalco produced 250,751 tons. Including three smaller companies, the total output of India's aluminium industry in 1999/2000 was a record 620,512 tons, mainly in the form of ingots.

Indonesia has bauxite mines in western Kalimantan (Borneo) and in the Riau archipelago, east of Sumatra. The main producing area is Bintan Island (part of the Riau group), where bauxite has been mined since 1935. Bintan currently has three bauxite mines (controlled by PT Aneka Tambang), which produce ore for export. However, deposits at two of the mines are expected to be exhausted soon (observers now predict that extraction will cease there in 2003, economic circumstances having enabled the site to outlive earlier expectations of closure in 2001). Research into further potential sites in western Kalimantan is ongoing. Indonesia has one major aluminium smelter, capable of producing 225,000 tons per year. The plant forms part of the Asahan Development Project, along the Asahan river on the island of Sumatra. The establishment of the smelter, which began operating in 1982, was intended as the first stage of a fully integrated national aluminium industry. A Japanese consortium of smelters and trading concerns owns 59% of the venture, PT Indonesia Asahan Aluminium Co (PT Inalum), and takes a proportionate share of the plant's output. Indonesia's share of Asahan's production is essential to the country's domestic aluminium requirements. In 1998, however, severe drought conditions caused shortages of power at the associated hydroelectric plant, forcing a reduction in Asahan's output. By November the smelter was operating at less than 40% of its capacity. Indonesia's production of primary aluminium ingots declined from 216,000 tons in 1997 to an estimated 130,000 tons in 1998 and to only about 100,000 tons in 1999. In 2000 production recovered to an estimated 160,000 tons.

In 1999 the Government of Viet Nam was considering the development of bauxite deposits in Lam Dong Province, in which, with Gia Lai, Kon Tum and Dac Lac Provinces, the country's substantial bauxite reserves are located. In March 2000, after completion of a study, new government plans to exploit these deposits were reported. The proposals involved the creation of a bauxite-aluminium complex in Lam Dong Province. In April the Government approved a planned joint venture with Pechiney to develop the Tan Rai bauxite deposits (estimated at 385m. tons) in Lam Dong. The project envisaged investment of an estimated US $589m. in the establishment of mining operations, an alumina refinery and an aluminium smelter. According to the plans, a further US $375m. would be spent on the construction of an associated hydroelectric plant to provide power for the project. It was expected that, if the scheme was approved after further study, work to establish the mine would begin in early 2001 and about 1.7m. tons of bauxite per year would be produced from 2004. Meanwhile, in 1997 the Vietnamese Government had agreed to a proposal by Daewoo Corpn of the Republic of Korea to survey bauxite reserves in Dac Lac Province. The proposals envisaged the eventual development, at a cost of about US $1,000m., of a mine and an alumina refinery.

Production of Bauxite (crude ore, '000 metric tons)

	1999	2000*
World total (excl. USA)	128,000	135,000
Far East	16,563	17,698
Oceania	48,416	53,802
Leading regional producers		
Australia	48,416	53,802
China, People's Repub.	8,500*	9,000
India	6,712	7,366
Indonesia	1,116	1,200
Malaysia	224	123
Other leading producers		
Brazil	13,839	14,000
Greece	1,883	1,991
Guinea†	15,000	15,000
Guyana†	2,359*	2,404
Jamaica†	11,688	11,127
Kazakhstan	3,607	3,727
Russia	3,750	4,200
Suriname	3,715	3,610
Venezuela	4,166	4,200

* Estimated production.
† Dried equivalent of crude ore.
Source: US Geological Survey.

Although world demand for aluminium advanced by an average of 3% annually from the late 1980s until 1994, industrial recession began, in 1990, to create conditions of over-supply. Despite the implementation of capacity reductions at an annual rate of 10% by the major Western producers, stock levels began to accumulate. The supply problem was exacerbated by a rapid rise, beginning in 1991, of exports by the USSR and its successor states, which had begun to accumulate substantial stocks of aluminium as a consequence of the collapse of the Soviet arms industry. The requirements of these countries for foreign exchange to restructure their economies led to a rapid acceleration in low-cost exports of high-grade aluminium to Western markets. These sales caused considerable dislocation of the market and involved the major Western producers in heavy financial losses. Producing members of the European Community (EC, now the European Union—EU) were particularly severely affected, and in August 1993 the EC imposed quota arrangements, under which aluminium imports from the former USSR were to be cut by 50% for an initial three-month period, while efforts were made to negotiate an agreement that would reduce the flow of low-price imports and achieve a reduction in aluminium stocks (by then estimated to total 4.5m. tons world-wide).

These negotiations, which involved the EC, the USA, Canada, Norway, Australia and Russia (but in which the minor producers, Brazil, the Gulf states, Venezuela and Ukraine were not invited to take part), began in October 1993. Initially, the negotiations made little progress, and in November the market price of high-grade aluminium ingots fell to an 11-year 'low'. Following further meetings in January 1994, however, a memorandum of understanding (MOU) was finalized on a plan whereby Russia was to 'restructure' its aluminium industry and reduce its output by 500,000 tons annually. By March the major Western aluminium producers had agreed to reduce annual production by about 1.2m. tons over a maximum period of two years. Additionally, Russia was to receive US $2,000m. in loan guarantees. The MOU provided for participants to monitor world aluminium supplies and prices on a regular basis. In March the EU quota was terminated. By July the world price had recovered by about 50% on the November 1993 level.

The successful operation of the MOU, combined with a strong recovery in world aluminium demand, led to the progressive reduction of stock levels and to a concurrent recovery in market prices during 1994 and 1995. Consumption in the Western industrialized countries and Japan rose by an estimated 10.3% to 17.3m. tons, representing the highest rate of annual growth since 1983. This recovery was attributed mainly to a revival in demand from the motor vehicle sector in EU countries and the USA, and to an intensified programme of public works construction in Japan. Increased levels of demand were also reported in China and in the less industrialized countries of the South and East Asia region. Demand in the industrialized countries advanced by 11% in 1994, and by 2.2% in 1995.

Levels of world aluminium stocks were progressively reduced during 1994, and by late 1995 it was expected that the continuing fall in stock levels could enable Western smelters to resume full capacity operation during 1996. In May 1996 stock levels were reported to have fallen to their lowest level since March 1993, and exports of aluminium from Russia, totalling 2m. tons annually, were viewed as essential to the maintenance of Western supplies. Meanwhile, progress continued to be made in arrangements under the MOU for the modernization of Russian smelters and their eventual integration into the world aluminium industry. International demand for aluminium rose by approximately 0.2% in 1995 and by 0.8% in 1996. In 1997 aluminium consumption by industrialized countries advanced by an estimated 5.4%. This growth in demand was satisfied by increased primary aluminium production, combined with sustained reductions in world levels of primary aluminium stocks. Demand in 1998, however, was adversely affected by the economic crisis in East Asia, and consumption of aluminium in established market economy countries (EMEC) rose by only 0.1%: the lowest growth in aluminium demand since 1982. However, consumption in the EMEC area increased by an estimated 3.9% in 1999, with demand for aluminium rising strongly in the USA and in much of Asia. Compared with 1998, growth in consumption was, however, reduced in Europe and Latin America. World-wide, the fastest-growing sector of aluminium demand in 1999 was the transport industry (the largest market for the metal), with consumption rising by about 9%. Demand was expected to remain strong in 2000, with sales of motor vehicles predicted to continue rising, while world aluminium output was forecast to increase, as additional smelter capacity became available. Production of primary aluminium in the first six months of 2000 was about 4% above the level for the corresponding period in 1999.

Export Price Index for Aluminium (base: 1980 = 100)

	Average	Highest month(s)	Lowest month(s)
1990	93		
1995	104		
1998	77	85 (Jan.)	72 (Dec.)
1999	77	86 (Dec.)	68 (Feb., March)
2000	88	95 (Jan., Feb.)	83 (April, May)

In November 1993 the price of high-grade aluminium (minimum purity 99.7%) on the London Metal Exchange (LME) was quoted at US $1,023.5 (£691) per metric ton, its lowest level for about eight years. In July 1994 the London price of aluminium advanced to US $1,529.5 (£981) per ton, despite a steady accumulation in LME stocks of aluminium, which rose to a series of record levels, increasing from 1.9m. tons at mid-1993 to 2.7m. tons in June 1994. In November 1994, when these holdings had declined to less than 1.9m. tons, the metal was traded at US $1,987.5 (£1,269) per ton.

In January 1995 the LME price of aluminium rose to US $2,149.5 (£1,346) per ton, its highest level since 1990. The aluminium price was reduced to US $1,715.5 (£1,085) per ton in May 1995, but recovered to US $1,945 (£1,219) in July. It retreated to US $1,609.5 (£1,021) per ton in October. Meanwhile, on 1 May the LME's stocks of aluminium were below 1m. tons for the first time since January 1992. In October 1995 these holdings stood at 523,175 tons, their lowest level for more than four years and only 19.7% of the June 1994 peak. Thereafter, stock levels moved generally higher, reaching 970,275 tons in October 1996. During that month the London price of aluminium fell to US $1,287 (£823) per ton, but later in the year it exceeded US $1,500.

In March 1997 the London price of aluminium reached US $1,665.5 (£1,030) per ton. This was the highest aluminium price recorded in the first half of the year, despite a steady decline in LME stocks of the metal. After falling to less than US $1,550 per ton, the London price of aluminium rose in August to US $1,787.5 (£1,126). In that month the LME's aluminium holdings were reduced to 620,475 tons, but in October they reached 744,250 tons. Stocks subsequently decreased, but at the end of December the metal's price was US $1,503.5 (£914) per ton, close to its lowest for the year. The average price of aluminium on the LME in 1997 was 72.5 US cents per lb, compared with 68.3 US cents per lb in 1996 and 81.9 US cents per lb in 1995.

The decline in aluminium stocks continued during the early months of 1998, but this had no major impact on prices, owing partly to forecasts of long-term oversupply. In early May the LME's holdings stood at 511,225 tons, but later that month the price of aluminium fell to less than US $1,350 per ton. In June LME stocks increased to more than 550,000 tons, and in early July the price of the metal was reduced to US $1,263.5 (£768) per ton. In early September the LME's holdings decreased to about 452,000 tons (their lowest level since July 1991), and the aluminium price recovered to US $1,409.5 (£840) per ton. However, the market remained depressed by a reduction in demand from some consuming countries in Asia, affected by the economic downturn, and in December 1998 the London price of aluminium declined to US $1,222 (£725) per ton. For the year as a whole, the average price was 61.6 US cents per lb.

During the first quarter of 1999 the aluminium market continued to be oversupplied, and in March the London price of the metal fell to US $1,139 (£708) per ton: its lowest level, in terms of US currency, since early 1994. Later that month the LME's stocks of aluminium rose to 821,650 tons. By the end of July 1999 these holdings had been reduced to 736,950 tons, and the price of aluminium had meanwhile recovered to US $1,433.5 (£902) per ton. Stock levels later rose, but, following the announcement in August of proposed cost-cutting mergers between major producers (see above), the aluminium price continued to increase, reaching US $1,626.5 (£1,009) per ton at the end of the year. The steady rise was also attributable to a sharp increase in the price of alumina in the second half of the year. Following an explosion at (and subsequent closure of) a US alumina refinery in July, the price of the material advanced from US $160 per ton in that month to US $400 per ton (its highest level for 10 years) in December. However, the average LME price of aluminium for the year (61.7 US cents per lb) was almost unchanged from the 1998 level.

With alumina remaining in short supply, prices of aluminium continued to rise during the opening weeks of 2000, and in late January the London quotation (the official closing offer price at the end of morning trading on the LME) reached US $1,745 per ton: its highest level for more than two years. However, the LME's stocks of the metal also increased, reaching 868,625 tons in February. The London price of aluminium declined to US $1,397 per ton in April, but recovered to US $1,599 in July. Throughout this period there was a steady decrease in LME holdings, which were reduced to less than 700,000 tons in April, under 600,000 tons in May and below 500,000 tons in July. At the end of July aluminium stocks were 461,975 tons: only 53% of the level reached in February. In August stocks fell below 400,000 tons, and in December to less than 300,000 tons at one point. During August-December the average monthly London quotation ranged between US $1,600.8 (£1,116) per ton, recorded in September, and US $1,464.9 (£1,070) per ton, recorded in December.

At the end of January 2001 the London quotation rose to $1,737 (£1,176) per metric ton, thus approaching the highest level recorded in 2000. By the end of January stocks had recovered to 394,075 tons. By the end of February LME holdings stood at 483,200 tons, and the London price had declined to $1,553 (£1,069) per ton. In both March and April, on a month-on-month basis, stocks fell, while prices were generally weaker, the London quotation reaching $1,540 (£1,073) on 27 April. May 2001 marked the beginning of a very substantial accumulation of stocks, which was to continue up to the time of writing, in August 2002. Although the London quotation rose as high as $1,586 (£1,112) on 4 May, prices fell precipitously in June-November, reaching a low of $1,243 (£866) on 7 November, but recovering to $1,430 at the end of that month. The sustained decline was attributed to slow economic growth world-wide, which had caused the market to be over-supplied, aggravated by the events in New York, USA, on 11 September.

On 28 March 2002 LME stocks totalled to 1,029,400 metric tons. The London quotation weakened in both April and May, falling to $1,318 (£903) on 23 May. In early June the price recovered to $1,398 (£998), while, at the end of that month, stocks of aluminium held by the LME totalled more than 1.2m. tons.

Almost all the producers of primary aluminium outside communist or former communist countries are members of the International Primary Aluminium Institute (IPAI), based in London. The IPAI's membership comprises 39 companies operating primary aluminium smelters in 24 countries, collectively representing substantially all of the Western countries' production of primary aluminium. In 1993 the International Aluminium Committee was formed to represent most of the aluminium smelters in the former USSR.

Cassava (Manioc, Tapioca, Yuca) (*Manihot esculenta*)

Cassava is a perennial woody shrub, up to 5 m in height, which is cultivated mainly for its enlarged, starch-rich roots, although the young shoots and leaves of the plant are also edible. The plant can be harvested at any time from seven months to three years after planting. A native of central and South America, cassava is now one of the most important food plants in all parts of the tropics (except at the highest altitudes), having a wide range of adaptation for rainfall (500–8,000 mm per year). Cassava is also well adapted to low-fertility soils, and grows where other crops will not. It is produced mainly on marginal agricultural land, with virtually no input of fertilizers, fungicides or insecticides.

The varieties of the plant fall into two broad groups, bitter and sweet cassava, formerly classed as two separate species, *M. utilissima* and *M. dulcis* or *aipi*. The roots of the sweet variety are usually boiled and then eaten. The roots of the bitter variety are either soaked, pounded and fermented to make a paste, or dried, as in the case of 'gaplek' in Indonesia, or given an additional roasting to produce 'gari'. They can also be made into flour and starch, or dried and pelletized as animal feed. In Indonesia a high-fructose syrup is being produced from cassava starch in order to reduce sugar imports.

The cassava plant contains two toxic substances, linamarin and lotaustralin, in its edible roots and leaves which release the poison cyanide, or hydrocyanic acid, when plant tissues are damaged. Sweet varieties of cassava produce as little as 20 mg of acid per kg of fresh roots, whereas bitter varieties may produce more than 1,000 mg per kg. Although traditional methods of food preparation are effective in reducing cyanogenic content to harmless levels, if roots of bitter varieties are under-processed and the diet lacks protein and iodine (as occurs during famines and wars), cyanide poisoning can cause fatalities. Despite the disadvantages of the two toxins, some farmers prefer to cultivate the bitter varieties, possibly because the cyanide helps to protect the plant from potential pests, and possibly because the texture of certain food products made from bitter varieties is preferred to that of sweet cassavas.

Cassava is the most productive source of carbohydrates and produces more calories per unit of land than any single cereal crop. Cassava is a staple source of carbohydrates and forms an essential part of the diet throughout tropical areas. Although the nutrient content of the roots consists almost entirely of starch, the leaves are high in vitamins, minerals and protein. A plot of cassava may be left unattended in the ground for two years after maturity without deterioration of the roots and the plant is resistant to prolonged drought, so the crop is valued as a famine reserve. The roots are highly perishable after harvest and, if not consumed immediately, must be processed into flour, starch, pellets, etc.

While the area under cassava has expanded considerably in recent years, there is increasing concern that the rapid expansion of cassava root planting may threaten the fertility of the soil and subsequently other crops. Under cropping systems where no fertilizer is used, cassava is the last crop in the succession because of its particular adaptability to infertile soils and its high nutrient use-efficiency in yield terms (although there is now evidence to suggest that cassava yields increase with the use of fertilizer). With the exception of potassium, cassava produces more dry matter with fewer nutrients than most other food crops. Soil fertility is not threatened by cassava itself, but rather by the cultivation systems which employ it without fertilizer use.

Production of Cassava ('000 metric tons)

	2000	2001*
World total	176,784	178,868
Far East	50,638	49,914
Oceania	177	178
Leading regional producers		
China, People's Repub.	3,801†	3,851†
India	7,000†	7,000†
Indonesia	16,089	16,158
Philippines	1,771	1,652
Thailand	19,064	18,283
Viet Nam	1,986	2,050
Other leading producers		
Angola	3,300†	3,300†
Brazil	23,336	24,088
Congo, Dem. Repub.	15,959	15,436
Ghana	8,107	8,512
Mozambique	5,362	5,362†
Nigeria	33,854	33,854†
Paraguay	2,719	3,854
Tanzania	5,758	5,650†
Uganda	4,966	5,265

* Provisional figures. † FAO estimate.

In recent years there has been interest in the utilization of cassava as an industrial raw material as well as a food crop. Cassava has the potential to become a basic energy source for ethyl alcohol (ethanol), a substitute for petroleum. 'Alcogas' (a blend of cassava alcohol and petrol) can be mixed with petrol to provide motor fuel, while the high-protein residue from its production can be used for animal feed. The possibility of utilizing cassava leaves and stems (which represent about 50% of the plant and are normally discarded as cattle-feed concentrates) has also been receiving scientific attention.

Thailand is the world's leading exporter of processed cassava products, accounting, for instance, for more than 90% of world trade in cassava starch in 2000, and for more than 40% of trade in cassava tapioca. The main importers of these products, mostly in the form of pellets, are the Netherlands, France, Belgium and Germany, where cassava is sold as starch or used in the preparation of animal feed, providing a cheap substitute for cereals. It is a cheap energy source and, when combined with a protein source, makes a suitable substitute for cereals such as barley and maize. As, owing to its Common Agricultural Policy, cereal prices have risen within the European Community (EC, now the European Union—EU), the search for cheaper alternatives and the fact that cassava is not subject to the variable levy has led to an increase in imports of feed-grade cassava (mostly tapioca pellets from Thailand). Following protests from cereal producers (notably in France), the EC decided in 1979 to eliminate subsidies on compound animal feed, with the aim of reducing the use of cassava-based products. Thailand subsequently agreed to adopt voluntary export quotas for its tapioca products to EC countries. However, during the mid-1990s Thailand's cassava exports to the EU declined, largely as a result of adverse weather conditions and lower yields. Since 1994 the government of Thailand has been offering cassava growers incentives to plant alternative crops. In 2001, according to preliminary estimates by FAO, international trade in cassava products (dry weight) increased by 6%, compared with the previous year, to 7.3m. metric tons. Although demand from the EU was reported to have fallen as a consequence of a reduction in pig herds in the Netherlands and Spain, the decline was made good by increased demand from the Far East, in particular from the People's Republic of China.Thai exports of cassava products were forecast to rise to 7.0m. tons (dry weight of chips or pellets) in 2001, an increase of 7.7% compared with their estimated total in 2000. In late 2001 FAO assessed the prospects for international trade in cassava in 2002 as dependent on the interplay between possible stronger prices for cereals within the EU, which would tend to increase demand for cassava, and possible continued reductions in EU member states' pig herds, which would have the opposite effect. Demand from China, another major determinant of trade prospects, remained difficult to predict.

Within South-East Asia demand increased during the 1990s for dried starch derived from cassava for use in the production of textiles and paper, and by manufacturers of processed foods. Viet Nam, with a total area under cassava of 283,000 ha, has obtained private Taiwanese and Japanese investment in the construction of a substantial facility for cassava-processing at Dong Nai.

Export Price Index for Cassava (base: 1980 = 100)

	Average	Highest month(s)	Lowest month(s)
1990	78		
1995	85		
1999	36	*	*
2000	36	*	*
2001	36	*	*

* The monthly index remained constant at 36 throughout 1999, 2000 and 2001.

During 1993 the average monthly import price of hard cassava pellets at the port of Rotterdam, in the Netherlands, declined from US $160 per metric ton in January to $120 per ton in November. The annual average was $137 per ton, compared with $183 in 1992. Prices continued downward in later years, and fell very sharply in 1997. In 1999 the average import price of hard cassava pellets at Rotterdam was $102 per ton. A further sharp decline was experienced in 2000, in which year the average price was $84 per ton, and in the first three months of 2001 the average price fell to $80 per ton. In January–August 1999 the average international price of cassava starches and flours was $176 per ton (the lowest price since 1988), compared with an average price of $305 per ton in the corresponding period of 1998. This price declined further throughout 2000, to an annual average of $158 per ton, although a recovery in January–March 2001 restored prices to the previous year's average in that period.

Coal

Coal is a mineral of organic origin, formed from the remains of vegetation over millions of years. There are several grades:

anthracite, the hardest coal with the highest proportion of carbon, which burns smoke-free; bituminous and sub-bituminous coal, used for industrial power: some is made into coke when the volatile matter is driven off by heating; and lignite or brown coal, the lowest grade and nearest to the peat stage. Anthracite and bituminous coal are classed as 'hard' coal. Coal gas is made from brown coal, but is not widely used for energy except in the republics of the former USSR.

Geographically, coal is one of the most evenly distributed of the fossil fuels. Of estimated world proven reserves of 984,453m. metric tons at the end of 2001 (comprising 519,062m. tons of anthracite and bituminous coal and 465,391m. tons of sub-bituminous coal and lignite), about 30% were located in the Far East and Australasia, 26% in North America, 23% in the republics of the former USSR and 13% in Europe.

During the period 1976–2000, according to the World Coal Institute, annual world production of hard coal (excluding sub-bituminous coal and lignite) increased from 2,469m. tons to 3,639m. tons: a rise of more than 47%. High levels of output and demand were maintained during the 1990s, owing to the increasing use of coal world-wide as the primary fuel for electricity generation. In 1999 coal accounted for about 38% of this demand, which is expanding at an annual rate of about 3%. Environmentalists, however, have increasingly criticized the large-scale use of fossil fuels as a prime causative factor in 'acid rain' pollution and the warming of the global atmosphere by accretions of carbon gases. In 2001 coal was estimated to account for 40.6% of primary energy consumption in the Asia-Pacific region, compared with 39.7% in 2000. Among the countries with the highest levels of utilization of coal for electricity generation in 2000 were Australia (84%), the People's Republic of China (an estimated 80%) and India (66%). The Asia-Pacific region was also the principal world consumer of coal, accounting for an estimated 52% of global demand in 2000.

As the greater part of coal output is consumed within the producing country, only a relatively small proportion of coal production enters world trade. In 2000 an estimated 381m. tons of steam coal (for power generation) was traded internationally, together with about 192m. tons of coking coal (for use in metallurgical industries). About 90% of total world consumption of coal is both mined and used in the same producing countries, mainly the USA and the People's Republic of China. In 2001 China was estimated to account for about one-quarter of both world coal production and world consumption.

The People's Republic of China, with identified reserves of 114,500m. metric tons (including sub-bituminous coal and lignite) at the end of 2001, is the world's largest producer of hard coal. About 75% of these deposits are located in the north and north-west regions. Only about 7% of China's proven reserves of anthracite and bituminous coal can be surface-mined, however, and less than 50% of its mines are fully mechanized. Moreover, many of these employ outdated technology. In 1992 the Government began to implement a comprehensive restructuring of the coal industry, in which uneconomic mines were closed, the industry's labour force was reduced from 3m. to 2.5m. by 1995, and controls on the selling prices of coal were abolished. The reorganization continued in the later 1990s, with many small and unprofitable coal-mines, including some operated by township enterprises, being forced to close. As a result, China's annual production of coal (including brown coal) was reduced from 1,397m. tons in 1996 to 1,029m. tons in 1999. During the latter year about 31,000 small mines (some of them operating illegally) were closed, leaving fewer than 38,000 functioning at the end of 1999. The programme continued in 2000, with a further 18,900 coal-mines scheduled for closure. In May it was reported that the Chinese Government aimed to limit coal production to 870m. tons in 2000, with output restrictions imposed on large state-owned collieries as well as on small mines. .In the event, production reportedly totalled 1,171m. tons. Meanwhile, China's exports of coal (traditionally a very small proportion of the country's output) were being promoted, reaching 55.1m. tons (48.2m. tons of steam coal and 6.9m. tons of coking coal) by the end of 2000.

Production of Hard Coal
(million metric tons, excluding brown coal and lignite)

	1999	2000*
Leading regional producers		
Australia	223.7†	238.1
China, People's Repub.	1,238.3	1,171.1
India	291.0	309.9
Indonesia	72.0	78.6
Korea, Dem. People's Repub.	67.2	67.2
Viet Nam	9.1	9.1
Other leading producers		
Germany	43.8	37.4
Kazakhstan	56.6	71.1
Poland	110.2	102.2
Russia	152.4	169.2
South Africa	223.5	225.3
Ukraine	81.2	80.8
United Kingdom	37.1	32.0
USA	916.0	899.1

* Estimates. † Figure refers to fiscal year 1998/99.
Sources: Mining Journal Research Services.

Australia is also an important coal producer in the region, overtaking the USA in 1986 as the world's leading coal exporter, and accounting in 2000 for about 25% of world trade in steam coal and more than 50% of world trade in coking coal. Although Australia possesses less than 10% of the world's coal reserves, it has become a major exporter because of comparatively low domestic demand for coal (which supplies about 43% of domestic primary energy), and the mineral's location in unpopulated areas, inexpensive to mine. More than one-half of Australia's coal output is exported, about 40% of this to Japan, mainly for use in its steel industry. Coal is Australia's principal export commodity, and coal exports were valued at $A10,840m. (9.1% of the country's total export earnings) in the year to June 2001. In recent years Australian coal-exporting companies have been forced to accept lower prices in their negotiations with Japanese power utilities (for sales of steam coal) and steel-producers (for coking coal). For the year to March 2000 contract prices for steam coal were reduced by 13%, and those for coking coal by 18%. For the Japanese fiscal year (April–March) 2000/2001 contract prices for steam coal were reduced by a further 4%, to US $28.75 per metric ton (f.o.b.); and contract prices for coking coal by a further 5%, to US $39.75 per ton (f.o.b.). For the Japanese fiscal year 2001/2002, however, this downward trend was checked, with contract prices for steam coal rising by 20%, and those for high-quality coking coal by 7.5%. To increase the Australian industry's competitiveness, mining companies have restructured their activities, reducing employment at Australian mines by almost 30% in the 24 months to June 1999, and raising productivity by about 40%. Profitability has been boosted by a decline in the value of the Australian dollar, and Australian coal exports have been forecast to increase by as much as 20% in 2000–2005. Australia is involved with Japan in a joint project to establish two coal liquefaction plants. A promising future was foreseen for this process, with petroleum prices rising (as they were, when the project was envisaged) and conventional reserves rapidly being depleted.

India has the fourth largest coal reserves in the world, after the USA, the People's Republic of China and Russia, but nevertheless requires some imports of coal to satisfy domestic requirements. Coal, of which India is, after China and the USA, the third largest consumer, is its prime source of commercial energy. In the mid-1990s there were 530 operating mines, of which 355 were underground. With the assistance of foreign technology and a programme of modernization, India significantly increased its coal production during the 1990s. Demand was forecast to rise from 311m. tons in 1997 to 396m. tons by 2001, of which power generation requirements were expected to account for more than 55%. Although significant coal reserves are known to exist in Pakistan, output of hard coal totalled only 3.5m. tons in 2000. In the late 1990s feasibility studies were under way to ascertain prospects for future expansion.

In recent years Indonesia has emerged as a significant regional producer and exporter of coal, of which its total reserves were estimated at 5,370m. tons in 2001. These reserves are in part formed by a variety with an exceptionally low content of sulphur and ash, the causative factors in air pollution resulting from coal combustion. Output of this coal, which has attracted interest in the USA, Japan, Spain and the Scandinavian countries, totalled 2m. tons in 1991 and was forecast to rise to

8m. tons annually by the late 1990s. Total Indonesian coal production was forecast to reach a level of 120m. tons annually by 2002, as East Asian consumers reduced their reliance on exporters outside the region. In 2000 Indonesia was the world's fourth largest exporter of steam coal (after Australia, South Africa and China), exporting more than 48m. tons in that year.

The world's leading coal importer is Japan, which is seeking to reduce its dependence on petroleum for energy. In 2001, however, coal accounted for only 20% of Japan's total primary energy supply. The exploitation of Japan's proven coal reserves, estimated to total only 773m. tons in December 2001, has proved too expensive for domestic supplies to be able to compete with much cheaper imported coal. The country's coal industry has been in decline since the mid-1980s, with uneconomic mines closing, despite government provisions of subsidies and 'guidelines' seeking to persuade the steel industry to purchase domestic coal at prices far above those on the international market.

Viet Nam, with exploitable reserves of 165m. short tons of high-quality anthracite, emerged in the late 1990s as a leading world supplier of this coal, principally to the Japanese steel industry, which normally purchases between 40% and 45% of export supplies, which totalled 3.6m. metric tons in 1997 but declined to about 3m. tons in 1998, in response to decreased East Asian demand. In August 1999 the government-controlled coal-producing company, Vinacoal, was reported to have imposed severe restrictions on output, pending a fall in accrued coal stocks estimated at about 4m. tons.

Export Price Index for Coal (base: 1980 = 100)

	Average	Highest month(s)	Lowest month(s)
1990	108		
1995	110		
1999	86	94 (Jan.)	81 (Dec.)
2000	74	82 (Jan.)	69 (Oct., Nov.)
2001	83	94 (July)	74 (March)

The index of export prices for coal averaged 75 in February 2001. Australia's exports of coal (including briquettes) had an average value of US $37.35 per metric ton in 1994, rising to US $40.08 per ton in 1995. The average price per ton was US $43.14 in 1996, but declined to US $41.42 in 1997 and to US $37.04 in 1998. During the first three months of 1999 Australia's coal exports earned an average of only US $34.68 per ton, and prices subsequently fell further. Most Australian coal shipments are delivered to overseas buyers under long-term contracts at negotiated prices, but in 1999 international coal prices on the 'spot' market (for prompt delivery) were at their lowest levels for more than 20 years. In September hard coking coal was being traded in Asia at about US $32 per ton. International 'spot' prices remained depressed throughout most of 2000, but, from the beginning of the final quarter of that year, began to rise dramatically in response to increased demand for US thermal coal from US electricity generators. By mid-2001 'spot' prices of US coal were reported to have doubled—in some cases trebled—since late 2000. By mid-2001, as a result of the weakness of the Australian dollar, coal prices expressed in terms of the Australian dollar were almost 80% higher than at the beginning of 2000.

Coconut (*Cocos nucifera*)

The coconut palm is a tropical tree, up to 25 m tall, with a slender trunk surmounted by a feathery crown of leaves. The geographical origins of the tree are thought to be in the Asia-Pacific region. Its presence in most coastal areas and on many islands in the tropics is largely due to man, who introduced it to West Africa and the Americas. The tree's fruits first appear after about six years, though the palm may not reach full bearing until it is about 20 years old. It may continue fruiting for a further 60 years. (Hybrid varieties have advanced the time of initial fruiting from the sixth to the fourth year, and the onset of full bearing from the 20th to the 10th year.) The fruits, green at first but turning yellow as they ripen, are often left to fall naturally, but, as many are then over-ripe, harvesting by hand is widely practised.

Coconut, the most important of all cultivated palms, is frequently a smallholder crop, found mainly in small plots around

Production of Coconuts ('000 metric tons)

	2000	2000*
World total	50,074	50,886
Far East	41,904	42,559
Oceania	2,306	2,305
Leading regional producers		
India	9,000†	9,000†
Indonesia	13,891‡	14,300†
Malaysia	699‡	713‡
Papua New Guinea	1,032‡	1,032†
Philippines	12,995	13,214
Sri Lanka	2,353	2,353†
Thailand	1,400	1,400†
Vanuatu	248‡	248†
Viet Nam	885	887
Other leading producers		
Brazil	1,880	1,999
Mexico	1,113†	1,163†
Mozambique	300†	300†
Tanzania	350†	350†

* Provisional figures. † FAO estimate.
‡ Unofficial figure.

houses and in gardens, although in the Philippines the average coconut farm covers 4–7 ha in area. The plant's fruit, fronds and wood provide many thousands of families with a cash income as well as basic necessities such as food, drink, fuel and shelter. The palms grow with little or no attention where conditions are favourable. More than 80 varieties are known, divided broadly into tall palms, produced by cross-pollination, and dwarf palms, which are self-pollinating. The sap of the coconut palm itself can be evaporated to produce sugar or fermented to make an alcoholic drink called 'toddy'. This may be distilled to produce a spirit called 'arrack'.

Coconut oil is a rich source of medium-chain triglycerides (MCT), whose applications in medical nutrition include infant milk formulas and foods for persons unable to digest and assimilate fats. Its other food applications include use as a flavouring and also as an ingredient to prolong the shelf life of certain food products.

All parts of the fruit have their uses. Beneath the outer skin is a thick layer of fibrous husk. The fibres can be combed out to produce coir (from the Malay word *kayar*, which means 'cord'), a material used for making ropes, coconut matting, brushes, mattresses and upholstery (see below). Inside the husk is the nut—what people in temperate areas think of as a 'coconut' since the whole fruit is not usually imported. The nut has a hard shell, inside which is a thin white fleshy layer of edible 'meat'. The nut's hollow interior is partially filled with a liquid called 'coconut water' which is gradually absorbed as the fruit ripens. This 'water' is a refreshing and nutritious drink when taken from a young nut (7–8 months), while that from more mature nuts can be prepared as a soft drink and is also used in the production of yeast, alcohol, wine and vinegar. The so-called 'coconut milk' is the white, creamy extract obtained after pressing freshly grated coconut 'meat'. Coconut flour, a by-product of 'coconut milk', is a useful nutritional source of dietary fibre. The shells are mainly utilized as fuel, but small quantities are used to make containers, ornaments, ladles and buttons, and pulverized shells can be used as filler in plastics moulding, plywood and mosquito coil repellants. Raw coconut shell is a more efficient fuel after it has been carbonized into charcoal and, on further processing, can be converted into the still more efficient activated carbon, which finds a market in highly industrialized countries concerned with pollution control.

After harvesting, the fruits are split open, the husk removed and the nuts usually broken open. The 'meat' is sometimes eaten directly or used to prepare desiccated coconut, widely used in the bakery and confectionery trades. However, by far the most important economic product of the plant is obtained by drying the 'meat' into copra, either in the sun or in a kiln which may be heated by burning the coconut shells. The dried copra is the source of coconut oil, used mainly in the manufacture of soap, detergent and cosmetics, and also as a cooking oil and in margarine production. As technology advances, more uses for coconut oil are being developed. Recent experiments have shown that it can be converted into diesel fuel, and a programme of conversion might alleviate the financial burden on countries which are heavily dependent on petroleum imports. The residue left after the extraction of oil from copra is a valuable oilcake for feeding livestock, particularly dairy cattle.

Good copra has an oil content of about 64%. Most extraction is done in the coconut-growing countries, although there is a substantial trade in copra to countries that extract the oil themselves. Although the largest producer of copra, the Philippines was overtaken as the largest exporter in 1992 by Papua New Guinea, whose copra sales represented 28.1% of the world export trade in 1999 and 23.5% in 2000. The eclipse of the Philippines as a copra exporter, however, has been attributable to increased levels of crushings of its copra into crude coconut oil for export. Japan was formerly the main importer of copra, but it has been overtaken by Germany, which has accounted, on average, for about one-quarter of all imports in recent years. Germany's partners within the European Union (EU) also constitute a major market for copra, coconut oil, desiccated coconut and copra meal.

Production of Copra ('000 metric tons)

	2000	2001*
World total	5,472	5,737
Far East	4,750	4,993
Oceania	283	294
Leading regional producers		
India	740†	765†
Indonesia	1,450†	1,480†
Malaysia	13†	12†
Papua New Guinea	172†	172‡
Philippines	2,125	2,330†
Sri Lanka	82	60†
Thailand	86	86
Vanuatu	27	27‡
Viet Nam	227†	233†
Other leading producers		
Mexico	202	211‡
Mozambique	44†	44‡

* Provisional figures. † Unofficial figure.
‡ FAO estimate.

Coconut oil has encountered competition from the development of more productive annual oilseed crops, such as soybeans and rapeseed in the northern hemisphere, and from oil palm in the tropics. Up to 7 metric tons of oil per ha can be produced from oil palm, compared with a maximum of 3.25 tons from coconuts. The necessity for the production of copra prior to the extraction of oil has further eroded the competitiveness of coconuts in the world market for vegetable oils. In 2000 the Philippines accounted for 48% of world exports of coconut oil. The USA is the main importer, absorbing, on average, almost 30% of total world imports in recent years. In 2001, according to provisional figures from FAO, world production of coconut oil was 3,594,686 tons, including 3,183,103 tons from Far East Asia and 106,744 tons from Oceania. The major producing countries in that year were the Philippines (1,489,440 tons) and Indonesia (930,000 tons).

The Philippines is the world's largest exporter of coconut products, and about one-third of its population is directly or indirectly dependent on the coconut sector for a livelihood. In 1979 the Philippine Government agreed to the operation of a monopoly of the coconut industry by a group of private producers who controlled 80% of the country's coconut-milling capacity, and accounted for more than 50% of coconut exports. The monopoly was dismantled in 1985, and the export of coconut products was opened to private enterprises. At that time, 10 coconut trading co-operatives were established, with a common majority shareholder, the government-controlled United Coconut Planters Bank. This has, however, given rise to criticism that the abolition of the former monopoly was more apparent than real, and coconut farmers have been reluctant to conduct business with the new trading firms. Government financial support for coconut-replanting ceased in 1986. In the mid-1990s about 3.1m. ha in the Philippines was planted with coconuts.

International promotion of biodegradable products during the late 1990s generated a revival of demand for coir products, of which India is the largest producer and exporter, principally to markets in the EU and the USA, which account for almost 85% of world imports of coir products. Sri Lanka, although a considerable producer of coconut, lacks coir textile production facilities, although it is an exporter of de-husked fibre and coir yarn. Indonesia and the Philippines, each of whose coconut output exceeds that of India, both lack the facilities to carry out coir production.

The Asian and Pacific Coconut Community, with headquarters in Jakarta, was established in 1969. Its 14 members account for most of the world's production of coconut oil.

In January 2002 the index of export prices for copra stood at 49, while that for coconut oil was 52. The import price of Philippine copra in Europe has varied widely in recent years.

Export Price Index for Copra (base: 1980 = 100)

	Average	Highest month(s)	Lowest month(s)
1990	51		
1995	97		
1999	102	118 (May, June)	93 (Sept.)
2000	68	93 (Jan.)	47 (Oct.)
2001	45	52 (Aug.)	40 (March)

Export Price Index for Coconut Oil
(base: 1980 = 100)

	Average	Highest month(s)	Lowest month(s)
1990	48		
1995	96		
1999	105	125 (May)	94 (July)
2000	64	94 (Jan.)	47 (Dec.)
2001	46	52 (Aug.)	41 (Feb., March)

In 1997 the price at European ports averaged US $433.75 per metric ton, but this declined to US $411.03 in 1998. In 1999 the price averaged US $462.27 per ton, but this declined steeply in 2000, to only US $308.92 per ton. In 2001 the average price fell sharply again, to only US $195.55 per ton. During the first quarter of 2002 the average import price of Philippine copra at European ports recovered to US $228.29 per ton. The average price rose further, to US $245.23 per ton, in April, and again, to US $263.26 per ton, in May.

The import price of Philippine coconut oil has also fluctuated considerably. The quotation (c.i.f. Rotterdam) rose from US $720 per ton in September 1996 to US $810 in December. It declined to US $550 per ton in August 1997, but recovered to US $670 in September. The price of coconut oil was reduced to US $510 per ton in January 1998, but rose to US $755 in May. It subsequently eased, but advanced to US $777.5 per ton by the end of the year. In May 1999, with coconut oil supplies very scarce, the price increased to US $945 per ton, its highest level since December 1984. The surge in prices was short-lived, and in July 1999 the Rotterdam quotation fell to US $625 per ton. The price of coconut oil recovered in October to US $780 per ton and ended the year at US $700. The market for coconut oil was depressed in the first half of 2000, with plentiful supplies of the commodity (and of palm oil) available. In July coconut oil was traded in Europe at only US $380 per ton. The average import price of coconut oil of Philippine origin (c.i.f. Rotterdam) was US $450.3 per ton in 2000, and fell further in 2001, to only US $318.1 per ton. During the first six months of 2002 the average price ranged between US $362.0, recorded in January, and US $446.0, recorded in June.

Coffee (*Coffea*)

This is an evergreen shrub or small tree, generally 5 m–10 m in height, indigenous to Asia and tropical Africa. Wild trees grow to 10 m, but cultivated shrubs are usually pruned to a maximum of 3 m. The dried seeds (beans) are roasted, ground and brewed in hot water to provide the most popular of the world's non-alcoholic beverages. Coffee is drunk in every country in the world and its consumers comprise an estimated one-third of the world's population. Although it has little nutrient value, coffee acts as a mild stimulant, owing to the presence of caffeine, an alkaloid also present in tea and cocoa.

There are about 40 species of *Coffea*, most of which grow wild in the eastern hemisphere. The species of economic importance are *C. arabica* (native to Ethiopia), which, in the early 2000s, accounted for about 60%–65% of world production, and *C. canephora* (the source of robusta coffee), which accounted for almost all of the remainder. Arabica coffee is more aromatic but robusta, as the name implies, is a stronger plant. Coffee grows in the tropical belt, between 20°N and 20°S, and from sea-level to as high as 2,000 m above. The optimum growing conditions are found at 1,250 m–1,500 m above sea-level, with an average temperature of around 17°C and an average annual rainfall of 1,000 mm–1,750 mm. Trees begin bearing fruit three to five years after planting, depending upon the variety, and give their maximum yield (up to 5 kg of fruit per year) from the sixth to the 15th year. Few shrubs remain profitable beyond 30 years.

Arabica coffee trees are grown mostly in the American tropics and supply the largest quantity and the best quality of coffee beans. In Africa and Asia arabica coffee is vulnerable in lowland areas to a serious leaf disease and consequently cultivation has been concentrated on highland areas. Some highland arabicas, such as those grown in Kenya, have a high reputation for quality.

The robusta coffee tree, grown mainly in east and west Africa, and in the Far East, has larger leaves than arabica, but the beans are generally smaller and of lower quality and, consequently, fetch a lower price. However, robusta coffee has a higher yield than arabica as the trees are more resistant to disease. Robusta is also more suitable for the production of soluble ('instant') coffee. About 60% of African coffee is of the robusta variety. Soluble coffee accounts for more than one-fifth of world coffee consumption.

Each coffee berry, green at first but red when ripe, usually contains two beans (white in arabica, light brown in robusta) which are the commercial product of the plant. To produce the best quality arabica beans—known in the trade as 'mild' coffee—the berries are opened by a pulping machine and the beans fermented briefly in water before being dried and hulled into green coffee. Much of the crop is exported in green form. Robusta beans are generally prepared by dry-hulling. Roasting and grinding are usually undertaken in the importing countries, for economic reasons and because roasted beans rapidly lose their freshness when exposed to air.

Apart from beans, coffee produces a few minor by-products. When the coffee beans have been removed from the fruit, what remains is a wet mass of pulp and, at a later stage, the dry material of the 'hull' or fibrous sleeve that protects the beans. Coffee pulp is used as cattle feed, the fermented pulp makes a good fertilizer and coffee bean oil is an ingredient in soaps, paints and polishes.

Production of Green Coffee Beans
('000 bags, each of 60 kg, coffee years, ICO members only)

	2000/01	2001/02
World total	112,622	113,338
Far East	28,829	26,137
Oceania	1,041	1,041
Leading regional producers		
India	4,611	5,293*
Indonesia	6,733	6,446
Papua New Guinea	1,041	1,041
Philippines	775	759
Thailand	1,692	999
Viet Nam	14,775	12,600*
Other leading producers		
Brazil	32,204	33,549
Cameroon*	1,113	1,500
Colombia	10,532	11,500*
Costa Rica	2,246	2,364
Côte d'Ivoire	4,587	4,100*
Ecuador	1,150	1,096
El Salvador	1,717	1,630
Ethiopia	2,768	3,917
Guatemala	4,700	3,900*
Honduras	2,667	2,300
Mexico	5,125	5,500*
Nicaragua	1,610	1,040*
Peru	2,596	2,747
Uganda	3,205	3,250*

* Estimates.

Source: International Coffee Organization.

More than one-half of the world's coffee is produced on smallholdings of less than 5 ha. In many producing countries, and especially in Africa, coffee is almost entirely an export crop, with little domestic consumption. Green coffee accounts for some 96% of all the coffee that is exported, with soluble and roasted coffee comprising the balance. Tariffs on green/raw coffee are usually low or non-existent, but those applied to soluble coffee may be as high as 30%. The USA is the largest single importer, although its volume of coffee purchases was overtaken in 1975 by the combined imports of the (then) nine countries of the European Community (EC, now the European Union—EU).

After petroleum, coffee is the major raw material in world trade, and the single most valuable agricultural export of the tropics. Latin America (with 56.7% of estimated world output, excluding minor producers, in 2001/02) is the leading coffee-growing region. Africa, which formerly ranked second, was overtaken in 1992/93 by Asian producers. In 2001/02 Asian countries accounted for 25.1% og the estimated world coffee crop, compared with 17.7% for African countries.

In the Far East and Australasia Viet Nam has emerged, in a very short period of time, as a major producer and exporter of coffee. In 1980 coffee was grown on only 20,000 ha, but by 1998 the area cultivated had been increased to 300,000 ha. (Over the same period the yield obtained per hectare rose from 0.6 to 1.6 metric tons.) The increase in the area cultivated has taken place in the context of a programme of economic reforms that, with regard to the agricultural sector, has emphasized the expansion of cash crop production. Viet Nam planned to increase the area sown to coffee by a further 100,000 ha by 2005 and was proceeding, in the early 2000s, with a project to bring into production of arabica coffee 40,000 ha in the north of the country. However, it is as an exporter of robusta that Viet Nam has achieved its importance to world markets. In 1998 the country was the largest exporter of robusta in the world, with shipments (mainly to the USA and the EU) of some 400,000 tons, equivalent to 7.7% of the total quantity of coffee exported world-wide. In that year Viet Nam was the third largest exporter of all coffees, after Brazil and Colombia. In 1999 exports increased to about 460,000 tons, equivalent to some 9% of all coffee exported world-wide, and, again, in 2000, when, at almost 700,000 tons, they represented 13% of global coffee exports. In 2000 exports of coffee contributed 3.5% of Viet Nam's total export earnings. In the 1999/2000 crop year, with production of 11.6m. bags, Viet Nam overtook Indonesia as the world's largest producer of robusta, and Colombia as the world's second largest producer of coffee overall, and maintained those ranks in the two subsequent crop years, although production declined by 14.7%, to 12.6m. bags, in 2001/02. Viet Nam has been accused of contributing, by rapidly increasing its output, to the glut of supplies available for export that has plunged coffee production into crisis world-wide (see below). In mid-2002, as part of global attempts to resolve that crisis, the Vietnamese Government was reportedly pursuing an initiative to reduce the area sown to coffee, with the aim of lowering output to about 10m. bags by around 2005.

Until the 1999/2000 crop year, when it was overtaken by Viet Nam, Indonesia was the largest producer of coffee in the Far East and Australasia. Production, mainly of robusta varieties, had, by the late 1990s, risen approximately threefold since the late 1960s, although it continued to be based on smallholdings rather than large estates. Until 1999/2000, Indonesia was the world's largest producer of robusta. In that crop year output of all coffees (Indonesia also produces high quality arabicas) amounted to about 324,000 tons, a decline of almost 36% compared with 1998/99. In 2000/01 production recovered to about 400,000 tons, but was estimated to have fallen to about 380,000 tons in 2001/02. In 1998 Indonesian exports of coffee totalled about 336,000 tons. In 1999 they declined to some 306,000 tons, but rose to 312,000 tons in 2000. The importance of coffee in Indonesia's total foreign trade has declined as that of petroleum and manufactured goods has risen. In 1999 exports of coffee contributed 1% of the country's total export earnings.

Indian production of coffee rose fairly steadily during the 1990s, although it remained, in the early 2000s, subject to quite substantial annual fluctuations. In the late 1990s output was divided approximately equally between arabicas and robustas, although production of robustas was increasing at a faster rate than that of arabicas. In 1999/2000 only, during the 1990s,

Indian production, totalling some 330,000 tons, surpassed that of Indonesia. Output declined to about 294,000 tons in 2000/01, but was estimated to have risen, in 2001/02, to some 318,000 tons. By the late 1990s India's exports of coffee had doubled since the mid-1970s. Exports varied considerably in the late 1990s, rising by almost 35%, to about 204,000 tons, in 1998, compared with the previous year. In 1999 exports amounted to some 216,000 tons, and increased further, to around 270,000 tons, in 2000. In 1998 exports of coffee accounted for 1.2% of India's total export earnings.

Papua New Guinea ranks as the fourth largest producer of coffee in the Far East and Australasia. In the 2001/02 crop year production amounted to about 72,000 metric tons, compared with some 60,000 tons in 2000/01. In the late 1990s arabicas accounted for about 97% of all coffee cultivated. Production, initially based on large estates, but subsequently dominated by smallholdings, began to expand in the early 1950s. In the mid-1990s Germany was the principal export market for Papua New Guinea's coffee, followed by Australia, the United Kingdom and the USA. In 1998 Papua New Guinea exported some 78,000 tons of coffee, and about the same quantity, again, in 1999. In 2000 exports declined to 60,000 tons. In 2000 exports of coffee accounted for 5.2% of Papua New Guinea's total export earnings. In the 2000/01 and 2001/02 crop years the Philippines produced about 48,000 tons of coffee. (Production has declined somewhat since the late 1990s. In 1997/98, for instance, output totalled 54,000 tons.) Robusta accounts for about 90% of all coffee produced in the Philippines. Output was adversely affected by drought in the 1998/99 crop year. The Philippines had already, in the previous crop year, become a net importer of coffee, and imports rose substantially in 1998/99. In 2000 exports amounted to only about 30,000 tons. Elsewhere in the Far East Sri Lanka is a minor producer of coffee, with output of some 2.4m. tons in 2001/02.

Effective international attempts to stabilize coffee prices began in 1954, when a number of producing countries made a short-term agreement to fix export quotas. After three such agreements, a five-year International Coffee Agreement (ICA), covering both producers and consumers, and introducing a quota system, was signed in 1962. This led to the establishment, in 1963, of the International Coffee Organization (ICO), with its headquarters in London. In June 2002 the International Coffee council, the highest authority of the ICO, comprised 63 members (45 exporting countries, accounting for 97% of world supplies, and 18 importing countries, accounting for 66% of world imports; until the USA withdrew from the ICO in 1993 importing members accounted for more than 81% of world imports). Successive ICAs took effect in 1968, 1976, 1983, 1994 and 2001 (see below), but the system of export quotas to stabilize prices was abandoned in July 1989. During each ICA up to and including that implemented in 1994, contention arose over the allocation of members' export quotas, the operation of price support mechanisms, and, most importantly, illicit sales by some members of surplus stocks to non-members of the ICO (notably to the USSR and to countries in Eastern Europe and the Middle East). These 'leaks' of low-price coffee, often at less than one-half of the official ICA rate, also found their way to consumer members of the ICO through free ports, depressing the general market price and making it more difficult for exporters to fulfil their quotas.

The issue of coffee export quotas became further complicated in the 1980s, as consumer tastes in the main importing market, the USA, and, to a lesser extent, in the EC moved away from the robustas exported by Brazil and the main African producers in favour of the milder arabica coffees grown in Central America. Disagreements over a new system of quota allocations, taking account of coffee by variety, had the effect of undermining efforts in 1989 to preserve the economic provisions of the ICA, pending the negotiation of a new agreement. The ensuing deadlock between consumers and producers, as well as among the producers themselves, led in July to the collapse of the quota system and the suspension of the economic provisions of the ICA. The administrative clauses of the agreement, however, continued to operate and were subsequently extended until October 1993, pending an eventual settlement of the quota issue and the entry into force of a successor ICA.

With the abandonment of the ICA quotas, coffee prices fell sharply in world markets, and were further depressed by a substantial accumulation of coffee stocks held by consumers. The response by some Latin American producers was to seek to revive prices by imposing temporary suspensions of exports; this strategy, however, merely increased losses of coffee revenue. By early 1992 there had been general agreement among the ICO exporting members that the export quota mechanism should be revived. However, disagreements persisted over the allocation of quotas, and in April 1993 it was announced that efforts to achieve a new ICA with economic provisions had collapsed. In the following month Brazil and Colombia, the two largest coffee producers, were joined by some Central American producers in a scheme to limit their coffee production and exports in the 1993/94 coffee year. Although world consumption of coffee exceeded the level of shipments, prices were severely depressed by surpluses of coffee stocks totalling 62m. bags (each of 60 kg), with an additional 21m. bags held in reserve by consumer countries. Prices, in real terms, stood at historic 'lows'.

In September 1993 the Latin American producers announced the formation of an Association of Coffee Producing Countries (ACPC) to implement an export-withholding, or coffee retention, plan. The Inter-African Coffee Organization (IACO, see below), whose membership includes Côte d'Ivoire, Kenya and Uganda, agreed to join the Latin American producers in a new plan to withhold 20% of output whenever market prices fell below an agreed limit. With the participation of Asian producers, a 28-member ACPC was formally established. (Angola and Zaire, now the DRC, were subsequently admitted to membership.) With headquarters in London, its signatory member countries numbered 28 in 2001, 14 of which were ratified. Production by the 14 ratified members in 1999/2000 accounted for 61.4% of coffee output world-wide.

The ACPC coffee retention plan came into operation in October 1993 and gradually generated improved prices; by April 1994 market quotations for all grades and origins of coffee had achieved their highest levels since 1989. In June and July 1994 coffee prices escalated sharply, following reports that as much as 50% of the 1995/96 Brazilian crop had been damaged by frosts. In July 1994 both Brazil and Colombia announced a temporary suspension of coffee exports. The onset of drought following the Brazilian frosts further affected prospects for its 1994/95 harvest, and ensured the maintenance of a firm tone in world coffee prices during the remainder of 1994.

The intervention of speculative activity in the coffee 'futures' market during early 1995 led to a series of price falls, despite expectations that coffee consumption in 1995/96, at a forecast 93.4m. bags, would exceed production by about 1m. bags. In an attempt to restore prices, the ACPC announced in March 1995 that it was to modify the price ranges of the export withholding scheme. In May the Brazilian authorities, holding coffee stocks of about 14.7m. bags, introduced new arrangements under which these stocks would be released for export only when the 20-day moving average of the ICO arabica coffee indicator rose to about US $1.90 per lb. Prices, however, continued to decline, and in July Brazil joined Colombia, Costa Rica, El Salvador and Honduras in imposing a reduction of 16% in coffee exports for a one-year period. Later in the same month the ACPC collectively agreed to limit coffee shipments to 60.4m. bags from July 1995 to June 1996. This withholding measure provided for a decrease of about 6m. bags in international coffee exports during this period. In July 1997 the ACPC announced that the export withholding programme was to be replaced by arrangements for the restriction of exports of green coffee. Total exports for 1997/98 were to be confined to 52.75m. bags. Following the withdrawal, in September 1998, of Ecuador from the export restriction scheme (and subsequently from the ACPC) and the accession of India to membership in September 1999, there were 14 ratified member countries participating in the withholding arrangements. The continuing decline in world coffee prices (see below) prompted the ACPC to announce in February 2000 that it was considering the implementation of a further scheme involving the withholding of export supplies. In the following month the members indicated their intention to withdraw supplies of low-grade beans (representing about 10% of annual world exports), and on 19 May announced arrangements under which 20% of world exports would be withheld until the ICO 15-day composite price reached 95 US cents per lb (at that time the composite price stood at 69 cents per lb). Retained stocks would only be released when the same indicator price reached 105 cents per lb. Five non-member countries, Guatemala, Honduras, Mexico, Nicaragua and Viet Nam, also signed a so-called London Agreement pledging to support the retention plan. Implementation of the plan, which has a duration of up to two years, was initiated by Brazil in June, with Colombia following in September. In December 2000 the ACPC identified a delay in the full implementation of the retention plan as one of the factors that had caused the average ICO composite indicator price in November to fall to its lowest level since April 1993, and the ICO robusta indicator price to its lowest level since August 1969. In May 2001 the ACPC reported that exchange prices continued to trade at historical lows. Their failure to recover, despite the implementation of the retention plan, was partly attributed to the hedging of a proportion of the 7m. bags of green coffee retained by that time. On the physical market, meanwhile, crop problems and the implementation of the retention plan had significantly increased differentials for good quality coffees, in particular those of Central America. In April 2001 the ICO daily composite indicator price averaged 47.13 cents per lb (compared with an average of 64.24 cents per lb for the whole of 2000, the lowest annual average since 1973), the lowest monthly average since September 1992. In October 2001 the ACPC announced that it would dissolve itself in January 2002. The Association's relevance had been increasingly compromised by the failure of some of its members to comply with the retention plan in operation at that time, and by some members' inability to pay operating contributions to the group owing to the depressed state of the world market for coffee. Upon its dissolution, the group's members announced that they would consider establishing a successor organization if prices returned to a level permitting this.

In June 1993 the members of the ICO agreed to a further extension of the ICA, to September 1994. However, the influence of the ICO, from which the USA withdrew in October 1993, was increasingly perceived as having been eclipsed by the ACPC. In 1994 the ICO agreed provisions for a new ICA, again with primarily consultative and administrative functions, to operate for a five-year period, until September 1999. In November of that year it was agreed to extend this limited ICA until September 2001. A successor ICA took effect, provisionally, in October 2001. By late May 2002 the new ICA had been endorsed by 37 members of the International Coffee Council (25 exporting members and 12 importing members). Among the principal objectives of the ICA of 2001 were the promotion of international co-operation with regard to coffee, and the provision of a forum for consultations, both intergovernmental and with the private sector, with the aim of achieving a reasonable balance between world supply and demand in order to guarantee adequate supplies of coffee at fair prices for consumers, and markets for coffee at remunerative prices for producers.

In February 1995 five African Producers (Burundi, Kenya, Rwanda, Tanzania and Uganda) agreed to participate in coffee price guarantee contract arrangements sponsored by the Eastern and Southern Africa Trade and Development Bank under the auspices of the Common Market for Eastern and Southern Africa (COMESA). This plan seeks to promote producer price guarantees in place of stock retention schemes. The contract guarantee arrangements would indemnify producers against reductions below an agreed contract price.

Export Price Index for Coffee (base: 1980 = 100)

	Average	Highest month(s)	Lowest month(s)
1990	46		
1995	83		
1999	53	62 (Dec.)	44 (Sept.)
2000	44	55 (Jan.)	33 (Dec.)
2001	30	34 (Feb.)	25 (Oct.)

International prices for coffee beans in the early 1990s were generally at very low levels, even in nominal terms (i.e. without taking inflation into account). On the London Commodity Exchange (LCE) the price of raw robusta coffee for short-term delivery fell in May 1992 to US $652.5 (£365) per metric ton, its lowest level, in terms of dollars, for more than 22 years. By December the London coffee price had recovered to $1,057.5 per ton (for delivery in January 1993). The LCE quotation eased to $837 (£542) per ton in January 1993, and remained within this range until August, when a sharp increase began. The coffee price advanced in September to $1,371 (£885) per ton, its highest level for the year. In April 1994 a further surge in prices began, and in May coffee was traded in London at more than $2,000 per ton for the first time since 1989. In late June 1994 there were reports from Brazil that frost had damaged the potential coffee harvest for future seasons, and the LCE quotation exceeded $3,000 per ton. In July, after further reports of frost damage to Brazilian coffee plantations, the London price reached $3,975 (£2,538) per ton. Market conditions then eased, but in September, as a drought persisted in Brazil, the LCE price of coffee increased to $4,262.5 (£2,708) per ton: its highest level since January 1986. In December 1994, following forecasts of a rise in coffee production and a fall in consumption, the London quotation for January 1995 delivery stood at $2,481.5 per ton.

The coffee market later revived, and in March 1995 the LCE price reached US $3,340 (£2,112) per ton. However, in early July coffee traded in London at $2,400 (£1,501) per ton, although later in the month, after producing countries had announced plans to limit exports, the price rose to $2,932.5 (£1,837). During September the LCE 'spot' quotation (for immediate delivery) was reduced from $2,749 (£1,770) per ton to $2,227.5 (£1,441), but in November it advanced from $2,370 (£1,501) to $2,739.5 (£1,786). Coffee for short-term delivery was traded in December at less than $2,000 per ton, while longer-term quotations were considerably lower.

In early January 1996 the 'spot' price of coffee in London stood at US $1,798 (£1,159) per ton, but later in the month it reached $2,050 (£1,360). The corresponding quotation rose to $2,146.5 (£1,401) per ton in March, but declined to $1,844.5 (£1,220) in May. The 'spot' contract in July opened at $1,730.5 (£1,112) per ton, but within four weeks the price fell to $1,487 (£956), with the easing of concern about a threat of frost damage to Brazilian coffee plantations. In November the 'spot' quotation rose to $1,571 (£934) per ton, but slumped to $1,375.5 (£819) within a week. By the end of the year the London price of coffee (for delivery in January 1997) had been reduced to $1,259 per ton.

In early January 1997 the 'spot' price for robusta coffee stood at only US $1,237 (£734) per ton, but later in the month it reached $1,597.5 (£981). The advance in the coffee market continued in February, but in March the price per ton was reduced from $1,780 (£1,109) to $1,547.5 (£960) within two weeks. In May coffee prices rose spectacularly, in response to concerns about the scarcity of supplies and fears of frost in Brazil. The London 'spot' quotation increased from $1,595 (£986) per ton to $2,502.5 (£1,526) by the end of the month. Meanwhile, on the New York market the price of arabica coffee for short-term delivery exceeded $3 per lb for the first time since 1977. However, the rally was short-lived, and in July 1997 the London price for robusta coffee declined to $1,490 (£889) per ton. In the first half of November the coffee price rose from $1,445 (£862) per ton to $1,658 (£972). During December the price for January 1998 delivery reached $1,841 per ton, but a week later it decreased to $1,657.

The coffee market rallied in January 1998, with the London 'spot' quotation rising from US $1,746.5 (£1,066) per ton to $1,841 (£1,124). Coffee prices for the corresponding contract in March ranged from $1,609 (£977) per ton to $1,787 (£1,065). Following reports of declines in the volume of coffee exports by producing countries (owing to inadequate rainfall), the upward trend in prices continued in April, with the price of robusta for short-term delivery reaching $1,992 per ton. In the first half of May there was another surge in prices (partly as a result of political unrest in Indonesia, the main coffee-producing country in Asia at that time), with the London quotation rising from $1,881.5 (£1,129) per ton to $2,202.5 (£1,351). Later in the month, however, the price was reduced to $1,882.5 (£1,155) per ton. Coffee prices subsequently fell further, and in late July the London 'spot' contract stood at only $1,505.5 (£909) per ton, before recovering to $1,580 (£963). The quotation per ton for September delivery reached $1,699.5 at the beginning of August, having risen by $162 in a week. In September the 'spot' price advanced from $1,640 (£974) per ton to $1,765 (£1,036) a week later. In late October a further sharp rise in coffee prices began, following storm damage in Central America, and in November the London 'spot' quotation for robusta increased from $1,872.5 (£1,123) per ton to $2,142.5 (£1,278). Meanwhile, trading in other contracts continued at less than $1,800 per ton until December, when the London price of coffee (for delivery in January 1999) rose to $1,977.

Coffee prices retreated in January 1999, with the London 'spot' quotation falling from US $1,872.5 (£1,131) per ton to $1,639 (£995). During March the price was reduced from $1,795.5 (£1,111) per ton to $1,692.5 (£1,030), but recovered to $1,795 (£1,112) within a week. As before, the market for longer-term deliveries was considerably more subdued, with coffee trading mainly within a range of $1,490–$1,590 per ton. Thereafter, a generally downward trend was evident, and in May the 'spot' price declined to $1,376.5 (£850) per ton, although it reached $1,536.5 (£962) by the end of the month. The advance was short-lived, with prices for most coffee contracts standing at less than $1,400 per ton in late June. The 'spot' price in July fell to only $1,255 (£805) per ton. In August the London quotation for September 'futures', which had been only $1,282.5 per ton in July, rose to $1,407. However, the 'spot' price in September retreated from $1,323 (£825) per ton to $1,212.5 (£754). In October the price for short-term delivery was reduced to less than $1,200 per ton. The 'spot' quotation in November advanced from $1,212 (£736) per ton to $1,399.5 (£866). Prices strengthened further in December, with the London quotation for short-term delivery reaching $1,557 per ton. Meanwhile, the market for longer-term contracts was more stable, with prices remaining below $1,400 per ton. In that month the Brazilian government's forecast for the country's coffee output in the year beginning April 2000 was higher than some earlier predictions, despite fears that the crop would have been damaged by the unusually dry weather there since September 1999. For 1999 as a whole, average prices of robusta coffee declined by 18.3% from the previous year's level, while arabica prices fell by 23.2%.

In January 2000 the 'spot' price of coffee in London rose strongly towards the end of the month, increasing from US $1,401.5 (£848) per ton to $1,727.5 (£1,067) within a week. However, prices of coffee 'futures' continued to be much lower: at the end of January the quotation for March delivery was $1,073.5 per ton. In February prices of robusta coffee 'futures' were below $1,000 per ton for the first time for nearly seven years. In March the 'spot' quotation eased from $993 (£628) per ton to $944 (£593). Prices continued to weaken in April, with the quotation for short-term delivery falling to less than $900 per ton. The 'spot' price in May declined to $891.5 (£602) per ton, but recovered to $941 (£639). Another downward movement ensued, and by early July the London 'spot' quotation stood at only $807 (£532) per ton. Later that month, prices briefly recovered, owing to concerns about the possible danger of frost damage to coffee crops in Brazil. The 'spot' quotation rose to $886.5 (£585) per ton, while prices of coffee 'futures' advanced to more than $1,000. However, the fear of frost was allayed, and on the next trading day the 'spot' price of coffee in London slumped to $795 (£525) per ton: its lowest level, in terms of US currency, since September 1992.

The weakness in the market was partly attributed to the abundance of supplies, particularly from Viet Nam, which has substantially increased its production and export of coffee in recent years (see above). By mid-2000 Viet Nam had overtaken Indonesia to become the world's leading supplier of robusta coffee and was rivalling Colombia as the second-largest coffee-producing country. Viet Nam and Mexico were the most significant producers outside the ACPC, but their representatives supported the Association's plan for a coffee retention scheme to limit exports and thus attempt to raise international prices. The plan was also endorsed by the Organisation africaine et malgache du café (OAMCAF), a Paris-based grouping of nine African coffee-producing countries.

In the first week of September 2000 the 'spot' market quotation rallied to US $829 (£577) per ton, remaining at this level until 21 September, when another downward movement occurred. Towards the end of the month the 'spot' quotation declined to $776 (£530) per ton.

At the beginning of November 2000 the London 'spot' quotation stood at only US $709 (£490) per ton and was to decline steadily throughout the month, reaching $612 (£432) on 30 November. High consumer stocks and uncertainty about the size of the Brazilian crop were cited as factors responsible for the substantial decline in November, when the average ICO robusta indicator price fell to its lowest level since August 1969.

In early January 2001 the 'spot' quotation on the London market rallied, rising as high as US $677 (£451) per ton. This recovery, which was attributed to concern about the lack of availability of new-crop Central American coffees and reports that producers in some countries were refusing to sell coffee for such low prices, was sustained, broadly, until March, when the downward trend resumed. On 23 March the London 'spot' quotation declined to only $570 (£399) per ton. On 17 April the London price of robusta coffee 'futures' for July delivery declined to a life-of-contract low of $560 per ton, the lowest second-month contract price ever recorded.

By May 2001 the collapse in the price of coffee had been described as the deepest crisis in a global commodity market since the 1930s, with prices at their lowest level ever in real terms. The crisis was regarded, fundamentally, as the result of an ongoing increase in world production at twice the rate of growth in consumption, this over-supply having led to an overwhelming accumulation of stocks. During May the London 'spot' quotation fell from US $584 (£407) per ton to $539 (£378) per ton.

In June 2001 producers in Colombia, Mexico and Central America were reported to have agreed to destroy more than 1m. bags of low-grade coffee in a further attempt to boost prices. The ACPC hoped that this voluntary initiative would eventually be adopted by all of its members. By this time the ACPC's retention plan was widely regarded as having failed, with only Brazil, Colombia, Costa Rica and Viet Nam having fully implemented it.

In early July 2001 the price of the robusta coffee contract for September delivery fell below US $540 per ton, marking a record 30-year low. At about the same time the ICO recorded its lowest composite price ever, at 43.80 US cents per lb. Despite a recovery beginning in October, the average composite price recorded by the ICO for 2001 was 45.60 cents per lb, 29% lower than the average composite price (64.25 cents per lb) recorded in 2000. In 2001 coffee prices were at their lowest level since 1973 in nominal terms, and at a record low level in real terms. The decline in the price of robusta coffees was especially marked in 2001, the ICO recording an average composite price of only 27.54 cents per lb, compared with 41.41 cents per lb in 2000, and 67.53 cents per lb in 1999. In 1996-98 the ICO average composite price for robusta varieties had averaged 81.11 cents per lb. The composite price reached its highest point since November 2000 in April 2001, averaging 50.19 cents per lb in that month, but a further sharp decline thereafter, amid the weakening of the Brazilian currency, the real, and a surplus of Brazilian coffee supply, left the monthly average at 42.28 cents per lb in July 2002. The price of the September contract in London at the end of that month was US $492 (£319) per ton.

The IACO was formed in 1960, with its headquarters at Abidjan in Côte d'Ivoire. In 1995 the IACO represented 25 producer countries, all of which, except Benin and Liberia, were also members of the ICO. The aim of the IACO is to study common problems and to encourage the harmonization of production.

Cotton *(Gossypium)*

This is the name given to the hairs that grow on the epidermis of the seed of the plant genus *Gossypium*. The initial development of the cotton fibres takes place within a closed pod, called a boll, which, after a period of growth of about 50–75 days (depending upon climatic conditions), opens to reveal the familiar white tufts of cotton hair. After the seed cotton has been picked, the cotton fibre, or lint, has to be separated from the seeds by means of a mechanical process, known as ginning. Depending upon the variety and growing conditions, it takes about three metric tons of seed cotton to produce one ton of raw cotton fibre. After ginning, a fuzz of very short cotton hairs remains on the seed. These are called linters, and may be removed and used in the manufacture of paper, cellulose-based chemicals, explosives, etc.

About one-half of the cotton produced in the world is used in the manufacture of clothing, about one-third is used for household textiles, and the remainder for numerous industrial products (tarpaulins, rubber reinforcement, abrasive backings, filters, high-quality papers, etc.).

The official cotton 'season' (for trade purposes) runs from 1 August to 31 July of the following year, and quantities are measured in both metric tons and bales; for statistical purposes, one bale of cotton is 226.8 kg (500 lb) gross or 217.7 kg (480 lb) net.

The price of a particular type of cotton depends upon its availability relative to demand and upon characteristics related to yarn quality and suitability for processing. These include fibre length, fineness, cleanliness, strength and colour. The most important of these is length. Generally speaking, the length of the fibre determines the quality of the yarn produced from it, with the longer fibres being preferred for the finer, stronger and more expensive yarns.

Cotton is the world's leading textile fibre. However, with the increased use of synthetics, cotton's share in the world's total consumption of fibre declined from 48% in 1988 to only 39% in 1998. About one-third of the decline in its market share is attributable to increases in the real cost of cotton relative to prices of competing fibres, and about two-thirds of the loss in market share is attributable to other factors. Expanded use of chemical fibre filament yarn (yarn that is not spun but is extruded in a continuous string) in domestic textiles, such as carpeting, accounts for much of the rest of the loss in market share for cotton. The break-up of the Council for Mutual Economic Assistance (the communist countries' trading bloc) in 1990, and of the USSR in 1991, led to substantial reductions in cotton consumption in those countries and also contributed to cotton's declining share of the world market. Officially enforced limits on the use of cotton in the People's Republic of China (which accounts for about one-quarter of cotton consumption world-wide) have also had an impact on the international market.

The area devoted to cotton cultivation totalled 31m.–36m. ha between the 1950s and the early 1990s, accounting for about 4% of world cropped area. During the mid-1980s, however, world cotton consumption failed to keep pace with the rate of growth in production, and the resultant surpluses led to a fall in prices, which had serious consequences for those countries that rely on cotton sales for a major portion of their export earnings. In the mid-1990s, despite improvements in world price levels, cotton cultivation came under pressure from food crop needs, and world-wide the harvested areas under cotton declined from 35.9m. ha in 1995/96 to 33.2m. ha in 1998/99. In 1999/2000 the harvested areas under cotton declined further, to 32.4m. ha, and again, in 2000/01, to 32.3m. ha. According to the US Department of Agriculture, the area under cotton world-wide totalled about 34m. ha in 2001/02.

Cotton is a major crop in several countries in the Asian and Pacific regions, and exports of yarn, fabric and garments are also a source of income to many countries, especially in South-East Asia and the Indian subcontinent. The leading producers of cotton lint in the Asia-Pacific region are the People's Republic of China, India, Pakistan and Australia. The production of cotton in most of the countries in the region has expanded gradually, in parallel with world production, but in the China and Australia the rate of growth has been dramatic: in the case of China production rose from around 2m. tons annually in the mid-1970s to a yearly output averaging almost 4.5m. tons in the period 1985–96. Thus, China was transformed from a large net importer of cotton in the late 1970s and early 1980s into a significant net exporter. However, with production stable and consumption rising, China has, since the late 1980s, been a regular net importer of cotton. Between 1994/95 and 1996/97 China was the world's principal importer, accounting for more than 10% of the world trade in cotton. In August 1998, however, the Government announced that guaranteed prices for domestic cotton were to be abolished by late 1999. This measure encouraged the textile industry to reduce its purchases of imported cotton in favour of less costly domestic supplies. Cotton imports into China (excluding Hong Kong) declined from 399,000 tons in 1997/98 to only 78,000 tons in 1998/99, 25,000 in 1999/2000, and to a little more than 50,000 tons in 2000/01 and, it was estimated, in 2001/02. The country's exports of cotton, which had been at negligible levels during the three years 1995/96 to 1997/98, reached 148,000 tons in 1998/99, and in 1999/2000 totalled 368,000 tons, despite a decline in cotton production (to 3.8m. tons) in 1999. Exports subsequently declined, to 98,000 tons in 2000/01, and to an estimated 54,000 tons in 2001/02. In 2002/03 the USDA forecast that Chinese imports of cotton would rise by 700%, compared with the previous year, to 435,000 tons, in response to a predicted 16% decline in production and estimated growth of 3% in consumption. Exports were also forecast to rise, by 200%, compared with the previous year,to 163,000 tons. The depreciation of the US dollar was cited as one factor favouring the competitiveness of Chinese exports, since, compared with its Asian rivals, China restricts fluctuations in the value of its currency.

Australia's annual cotton crop expanded from 99,000 tons in 1980/81 to 560,000 tons in 1996/97. Production increased to 564,000 tons in 1997/98, to 634,000 tons in 1998/99 and to 698,000 tons in 1999/2000. Output was estimated by FAO to have risen again, to 755,000 tons, in 2000/01. Australian consumption of cotton was only about 40,000 tons per year in the late 1990s, so almost all of the country's output is exported. In 1999 exports of cotton contributed about 1.7% of Australia's total export earnings.

India and Pakistan were generally net exporters of cotton in the 1980s and early 1990s. India's cotton production reached 2.9m. tons in 1995/96 and a record 3.0m. tons in 1996/97. Annual output was about 2.7m. tons in 1997/98, 1998/99 and 1999/2000, but declined, to 2.4m. tons, in 2000/01. In 2001/02 the USDA estimated Indian production at about 2.7m. tons. In 1998/99 India exported only about 10,000 tons of cotton, but imported some 230,000 tons, partly in response to a reduction in international prices (see below). In 1999/2000 India's cotton imports totalled about 210,000 tons, while exports were only about 13,000 tons. Meanwhile, Pakistan's annual cotton crop declined from 1.8m. tons in 1995/96 to 1.4m. tons in 1998/99. According to the USDA, output recovered to 1.9m. tons in 1999/2000, declined slightly, to 1.8m. tons in 2000/01, and was estimated at 1.8m. tons in 2001/02. Cotton exports from Pakistan, which reached 311,000 tons in 1995/96, virtually ceased in 1998/99, when the country imported 167,000 tons. In 1999/2000, however, Pakistan's cotton production was an estimated 1.8m. tons, with exports totalling about 160,000 tons.

Production of Cotton Lint
('000 metric tons, excluding linters)

	2000	2001*
World total	19,139	21,034
Far East	8,608	9,013
Oceania	698	755
Leading regional producers		
Australia	698	755†
China, People's Repub.	4,417	5,320
India	2,244	1,750†
Pakistan	1,829	1,829‡
Other leading producers		
Argentina	125‡	145‡
Brazil	663†	868†
Egypt	210	210‡
Greece	443†	442†
Syria	360	353
Turkey	876	876‡
USA	3,742	4,373
Uzbekistan	1,000†	1,200†

* Provisional figures. † Unofficial figure. ‡ FAO estimate.

The leading exporters of cotton in 2000/01 were the USA (with sales of 1.5m. tons), Australia (850,000 tons), Uzbekistan (740,000 tons), Greece (218,000 tons) and Syria (218,000 tons). Other important exporters in that year were Mali (201,000 tons), Benin (142,000 tons) and Burkina Faso (142,000 tons). As noted above, China and Pakistan have also been significant exporters of cotton in recent years. Prominent importers of cotton in 2000/01 were Indonesia (purchasing 577,000 tons), Mexico (406,000 tons), Turkey (381,000 tons), Russia (359,000 tons), India (341,000 tons, according to the USDA)and Thailand (345,000 tons). In the late 1980s and early 1990s Russia was the world's major importer of cotton, with an annual intake of more than 1m. tons, but exports declined, generally to less than 350,000 tons annually, in the late 1990s. China (see above) was the foremost cotton-importing country in the mid-1990s, thereby accumulating large stocks of the fibre, but it subsequently reduced these holdings.

Although co-operation in cotton affairs has a long history, there have been no international agreements governing the cotton trade. Proposals in recent years to link producers and consumers in price stabilization arrangements have been opposed by the USA (the world's largest cotton exporter), and by Japan and the European Union. The International Cotton Advisory Committee (ICAC), an inter-governmental body, established in 1939, with its headquarters in Washington, DC, publishes statistical and economic information and provides a forum for consultation and discussion among its 40members.

Export Price Index for Cotton Lint (base: 1980 = 100)

	Average	Highest month(s)	Lowest month(s)
1990	93		
1995	103		
1999	61	68 (Jan.)	48 (Dec.)
2000	62	66 (Dec.)	53 (Jan.)
2001	51	65 (Jan.)	41 (Oct.)

The British city of Liverpool is the historic centre of cotton-trading activity, and international cotton prices are still collected by organizations located in Liverpool. However, almost no US cotton has been imported through the port of Liverpool in recent years. Consumption in the textile industry in the United Kingdom has fallen to approximately 14,000 tons per year, most of which comes from Africa, Greece, Spain and Central Asia. The price for Memphis cotton, from the USA, quoted in international markets is c.i.f. North European ports, of which Bremen, in Germany, is the most important.

The average price for Memphis Territory cotton in North Europe rose to US $2,848 per metric ton in June 1995, owing to an increase in imports by the People's Republic of China, combined with declines in production in India, Turkey and Pakistan. Prices have trended down since, averaging US $2,175 per ton during all of 1994/95, US $2,088 in 1995/96 and US $1,826 in 1996/97. The average Memphis quote c.i.f. North Europe during December 1997 fell to US $1,756 per ton. The market was depressed further during the next two years. In 1999, according to the World Bank, the price of Memphis cotton (US origin, c.i.f. north Europe) averaged US $1,228 per ton. In 2000, however, the average price recovered to US $1,463 per ton in response to increased demand and stagnant production. In January–March 2001, the price of Memphis cotton averaged US $1,467 per ton, but declined to only US $1,175 per ton in the subsequent quarter. In January–August 2001 the average price was US $1,271 per ton, averaging US $1,126 per ton in the final month of that period.

The principal Liverpool index of cotton import prices in North Europe is based on an average of the cheapest five quotations from a selection of styles of medium-staple fibre. In 1999 the index recorded an average offering price of 53.1 US cents per lb: its lowest annual level since 1986. On a monthly basis, the average price in December 1999 was only 44.4 US cents per lb. The decline in prices was attributed to the plentiful availability of cotton, with high levels of production resulting in large stocks (more than 9m. tons world-wide in recent years). In 2000 the index recorded an average offering price of 59.0 US cents per lb. On a monthly basis, the average price in December 2000 was 65.8 US cents per lb. Slow growth in production and strengthened demand for cotton were the main reasons cited for the recovery in prices. In 2001, however, the decline in prices resumed. On a monthly basis, the index recorded an average offering price of only 38.4 cents per lb in November 2001. A modest recovery during 2002 saw prices generally stable, slightly above 2001 levels—the monthly average for June of that year being 41.9 cents per lb.

Changes in US government agricultural policies implemented in 1996, combined with reduced barriers to imports and exports of cotton in recent years in several countries, seem to be leading to a period of reduced fluctuation in cotton prices. During the 10 seasons ending in 1995/96 the average spread between the highest and lowest quotes each season for an average-quality cotton in international trade was 36%. During 1996/97 the spread between the highest and lowest quotes fell to 10%.

Groundnut (Peanut, Monkey Nut, Earth Nut) *(Arachis hypogaea)*

This is not a true nut, although the underground pod, which contains the kernels, forms a more or less dry shell at maturity. The plant is a low-growing annual herb introduced from South America.

Each groundnut pod contains between two and four kernels, enclosed in a reddish skin. The kernels are very nutritious because of their high content of both protein (about 30%) and oil (40%–50%). In tropical countries the crop is grown partly for domestic consumption and partly for export. Whole nuts of selected large dessert types, with the skin removed, are eaten raw or roasted. Peanut butter is made by removing the skin and germ and grinding the roasted nuts. The most important commercial use of groundnuts is the extraction of oil. Groundnut oil is used as a cooking and salad oil, as an ingredient in margarine and, in the case of lower-quality oil, in soap manufacture. The oil is faced with strong competition from soybean, cottonseed and sunflower oils—all produced in the USA. In 2001 groundnut oil was the fifth most important of soft edible oils in terms of production.

An oilcake, used in animal feeding, is manufactured from the groundnut residue left after oil extraction. However, trade in this groundnut meal is limited by health laws in some countries, as groundnuts can be contaminated by a mould which generates toxic and carcinogenic metabolites, the most common and most dangerous of which is aflatoxin B_1. The European Union (EU) bans imports of oilcake and meal for use as animal feed which contain more than 0.03 mg of aflatoxin per kg. The meal can be treated with ammonia, which both eliminates the aflatoxin and enriches the cake. Groundnut shells, which are usually incinerated or simply discarded as waste, can be converted into a low-cost organic fertilizer, which has been produced since the early 1970s.

Production of Groundnuts (in shell, '000 metric tons)

	2000	2001*
World total	34,516	35,096
Far East	23,228	23,200
Oceania	43	44
Leading regional producers		
China, People's Repub.	14,437	14,470
India	6,411	6,200†
Indonesia	974†	1,000†
Myanmar	634	731
Thailand	135	135‡
Viet Nam	355	375
Other leading producers		
Argentina	599	563
Chad	333†	333‡
Congo, Dem. Repub.	382	368
Nigeria	2,901	2,901‡
Senegal	1,062	1,062‡
Sudan	947	1,000‡
USA	1,481	1,923

* Provisional figures. † Unofficial figure.
‡ FAO estimate.

About 80% of the world's groundnut output comes from developing countries. India has implemented measures to increase production of groundnut oil for domestic consumption, but the growth of domestic demand has so far frustrated the achievement of self-sufficiency in edible oils. Owing to the rise in demand and to disappointing crops of groundnuts and other oilseeds in recent years, India has needed to import large quantities of edible oils (although usually not groundnut oil). During the year to October 1999 India imported more than 4.5m. metric tons of such oils, so overtaking the People's Republic of China as the world's leading importer. As a result of unfavourable weather, India's output of groundnuts in 1999/2000 declined to 5.3m. tons, its lowest annual total for 12 years, necessitating further substantial imports of edible oils.

In 2001, according to preliminary figures from FAO, world output of groundnut oil was 5,317,609 tons, including 3,665,317 tons from Far East Asia and 1,561 tons from Oceania. The major producing countries in that year were China (2,058,000 tons) and India (1,325,000 tons).

Export Price Index for Groundnuts (base: 1980 = 100)

	Average	Highest month(s)	Lowest month(s)
1990	102		
1995	92		
1999	57	59 (Oct.–Dec.)	55 (Feb.–April, Aug., Sept.)
2000	58	65 (Dec.)	55 (June)
2001	59	65 (April, May)	48 (Dec.)

Export Price Index for Groundnut Oil (base: 1980 = 100)

	Average	Highest month(s)	Lowest month(s)
1990	113		
1995	116		
1999	93	98 (Jan.)	88 (May, June)
2000	84	93 (Jan.)	77 (Sept.)
2001	80	82 (March–June)	78 (Aug.–Oct.)

In recent years, as the tables above make clear, prices for groundnut oil have generally been more volatile than those for groundnuts. The average import price of groundnut oil at the port of Rotterdam, in the Netherlands, increased from US $897.3 per metric ton in 1996 to US $1,010.4 per ton in 1997, but fell to US $908.6 in 1998 and to US $786.7 in 1999. It declined further, to US $712.4 per ton, in 2000, and to US $671.8 per ton in 2001. On a monthly basis, the average price of groundnut oil per ton was reduced from US $697.0 in December 2000 to US $664.0 in August 2001. By June 2002 the average import price of groundnut oil at Rotterdam had fallen to US $643 per ton. Meanwhile, the average European import price for groundnuts was US $962.0 per ton in 1996, US $988.4 in 1997 and US $988.8 in 1998, before falling to US $834.7 in 1999. In 2000 the average European import price recovered slightly, to US $844.0 per ton, but declined to US $833.2 per ton in 2001. On a monthly basis, the average price of groundnuts per ton was reduced from US $1,030.0 in December 2000 to US $830.0 in August 2001.

The market for edible groundnuts is particularly sensitive to the level of production in the USA, which provides about one-half of world import requirements. In each of the years 1987–91 the People's Republic of China was the leading exporter of green (unroasted) groundnuts, but in 1992 the USA was the main exporting country. In 1991 China exported 427,640 metric tons of groundnuts, valued at US $360.3m. Exports of this commodity in 1992 declined to 303,606 tons, earning only US $190.3m. The average price per ton fell from US $842 in 1991 to US $627 in 1992. China regained its leading position in 1993, although its exports of groundnuts increased only slightly, to 315,669 tons (earning US $196.2m., equivalent to US $622 per ton). In 1994 China's groundnut exports totalled 480,901 tons, valued at US $315.0m. (US $655 per ton).

The average annual price of edible groundnuts (any origin, US runner, 40%–50% shelled basis, c.i.f. Rotterdam) was US $909 per metric ton in 1995. The average price rose to US $962 per ton in 1996, and in both 1997 and 1998 an average price of US $990 per ton was recorded. In 1999, however, the annual average price declined by more than 15% to US $836 per ton, recovering slightly, to US $838 per ton, in 2000. In 2001 an average price of US $835 per ton was recorded.

Jute

Jute fibres are obtained from *Corchorus capsularis* and *C. olitorius*. Jute-like fibres include a number of jute substitutes, the main ones being kenaf or mesta and roselle (*Hibiscus* spp.) and Congo jute or paka (*Urena lobata*). The genus *Corchorus* includes about 40 species distributed throughout the tropics, with the largest number of species being found in Africa.

Jute flourishes in the hot damp regions of Asia. Commercial fibre varies from yellow to brown in colour and consists of tow (bunches of strands), which is pressed into bales of 181.4 kg (400 lb) after it has been retted (softened).

Jute has a number of uses. The relatively cheap, hard-wearing fibre is used to manufacture sacking for the storage of grains, cocoa, coffee and other food crops, which currently accounts for about 75% of consumption. The remainder of the crop is taken by manufacturers of carpet backing and other quality users. The finest jute standards are spun into carpet yarn and woven into curtains and wall coverings; in the area of quality goods jute is less under threat from synthetics. Jute is mixed with wool, after treatment with petroleum-derived softening agents (see below), and processed into cheap clothing fabrics or blankets in developing Asian countries. In its traditional market, however, jute has, despite its biodegradability, encountered strong competition from lighter synthetic materials. Its use as packaging is under challenge from wood and plywood, and has been diminishing, in response to the trend towards bulk handling containerization. The main jute-producing countries, however, have continued to stress the environmental desirability of jute use, and anxieties about the health aspects of petroleum use in the retting process have been overcome by the introduction of castor oil as the softening agent.

Bangladesh and India are the principal producers and exporters of raw jute and fabrics. In both countries, most of the growers of jute are small farmers whose livelihood depends entirely on their annual crop of the fibre. In 2000 more than 90% of world exports of raw jute were supplied by Bangladesh, which exports almost 90% of its jute and jute goods. In 1999/2000 Bangladesh derived an estimated 5.8% of its total export earnings from sales of jute and jute goods. The jute industry has traditionally employed about 45% of the country's industrial work-force. About one-half of the annual output is exported as raw fibre, while the remainder is processed in local mills for export as jute goods.

Bangladesh is seeking to reduce its high dependence on sales of jute and jute products for foreign earnings, but there are few alternatives for export, other than fish and tea. Some farmers have abandoned the cultivation of jute in favour of rice, for its assured market and better price; during 1985/86–1990/91 the area under jute cultivation was reduced from more than 1m. ha to 500,000 ha. The area sown to jute recovered to 647,500 ha in 1997/98, but declined to only 414,800 ha in 1999/2000. In 2000/01 jute was sown on a total of 448,000 ha. Bangladesh has attempted, with little success, to strengthen its share of the carpet market by reducing the gap between the country's capacity of 140,000 sq m and the global demand for 3.5m. sq m per year. As the world's dominant exporter of jute and jute goods, Bangladesh is far more vulnerable than India to declining world demand for jute, and to growing competition on the international market and from synthetics. This vulnerability was apparent, in mid-2002, in the Government's announcement of its intention to close the Adamjee jute mill, south of Dhaka, with the loss of 25,000 jobs. The decision to close the mill, the largest in the world, was attributed to a world-wide decline in the jute industry. Adamjee was reported at the time of the Government's announcement to be losing millions of dollars each year. India, meanwhile, consumes virtually all of its raw jute domestically, supplementing its own production with imports of high quality fibre. (In 2000 India was the world's largest importer of jute, with purchases of about 130,000 tons.) In 2000/01 the area under jute in India totalled about 870,000 ha, compared with some 1m. ha in 1999/2000.

In 1993 the Government of Bangladesh responded to its jute industry's financial difficulties by announcing plans to create a fund offering low-interest loans to jute mills and to ban the production of polythene bags and other synthetic products threatening the jute market. Further assistance was sought from the World Bank, which undertook to provide US $250m. to finance a restructuring of the jute industry. The proposals included the closures of loss-making mills, reductions in the labour force and the transfer to private ownership of the majority of the plants operated by the state-owned Bangladesh Jute Mills Corpn. However, delays have occurred in implementing the privatization programme. Heavy floods in September 1998 were reported to have affected more than 70% of the jute-growing areas of Bangladesh. However, following initial expectations that the country's substantial reserves of jute would avert any immediate shortfall in domestic requirements or exports, the impact of severe drought in early 1999 reduced the crop by about 12%, adversely affecting both domestic mill production and supplies available for export. According to the UN Food and Agriculture Organization (FAO), world production of jute, kenaf and allied fibres increased by some 12% in 2001/02 to more than 2.9m. tons, reflecting substantial increases in output in India and Bangladesh. Production in India was estimated to have risen by 11%, to 1.8m. tons, while that of Bangladesh, at an estimated 875,000 tons, grew by 21%. World production of jute, kenaf and allied fibres was forecast to decline in 2002/03, if, as expected, in view of high levels of carry-over stocks, prices remained low at the time of sowing.

After India and Bangladesh, the People's Republic of China is the most important regional producer of jute and jute-like fibres, with estimated output of 136,000 metric tons in 2001, compared with about 125,000 tons in 2000. China has been a significant importer of jute in recent years, its annual purchases of raw jute averaging 96,000 tons in 1996–98, although they fell precipitously to only 8,700 tons in 1999 and to only 5,000 tons in 2000, according to FAO. Exports of jute products averaged 13,000 tons annually in 1996–98, declining to 6,600 tons in 1999 and 5,000 tons in 2000. Myanmar, with estimated output of about 42,000 tons in 2001, Thailand, whose output was estimated at about 34,000 tons in that year, Nepal, with estimated production of 16,000 tons, and Viet Nam, with estimated output of about 12,000 tons, are the other significant producers of jute in the Far East. Thai imports of raw jute rose substantially in 2000, totalling more than 42,000 tons, compared with only about 1,000 tons in 1999, and, on average, 5,000 tons annually in 1996–98. After India, Pakistan is the most important regional market for jute, with annual purchases that average about 70,000 tons.

The longer-term outlook for the jute industry in Bangladesh, as well as other producing areas, depends, in large part, on the achievement of higher crop yields. Prospects exist for an expansion in world demand for jute in the growing market for 'environmentally-friendly' jute packaging and products, and for high-quality blended jute fabrics for wall-hangings and furnishings.

Export Price Index for Jute (base: 1980 = 100)

	Average	Highest month(s)	Lowest month(s)
1990	113		
1995	105		
1999	76	85 (Oct.)	69 (Feb.–May)
2000	72	84 (Jan.)	63 (Sept.)
2001	94	108 (July)	84 (Jan.)

The average export price of raw jute at Bangladeshi ports increased from US $271 per metric ton in 1993 to US $454 per ton in 1996. However, the annual average declined to US $302 per ton in 1997 and to US $259 in 1998. It recovered to US $277 per ton in 1999, and to US $279 per ton in 2000. The average jute price increased from US $245 per ton in the first quarter of 1998 to US $272 in the fourth quarter, averaging US $259 per ton for the year as a whole. The average price fell to US $250 per ton in the first quarter of 1999, but rose to US $305 in September, averaging US $276 per ton for the whole of 1999. In 2000 the average price of BWD-grade jute (f.o.b. Mongla) was US $279 per ton, and this rose sharply, to US $331 per ton, in 2001. During the first quarter of 2002 the price of BWD-grade jute averaged US $350 per ton in both January and February, but declined steeply, to only US $210 per ton, in March.

FAO and the United Nations Conference on Trade and Development (UNCTAD) provide international forums for the discussion of jute developments. Jute is one of the crops eligible for assistance from the Common Fund for Commodities (CFC, established by an UNCTAD agreement in 1989), which aims to stabilize commodity prices. An international jute (and allied fibres) agreement (IJA) was negotiated in 1982 by 48 producing and consuming countries, but lapsed in 1984, when the requisite number of consumer countries failed to ratify the agreement. A subsequent IJA was negotiated, under the auspices of UNCTAD, in 1989. The International Jute Organization (IJO), which administered the agreement, was based in Dhaka, Bangladesh. It also conducted research and development projects, and promoted the competitiveness of jute in relation to synthetic substitutes. In 1998 the IJO's membership comprised five exporting countries (Bangladesh, the People's Republic of China, India, Nepal and Thailand) and 20 importing countries, together with the European Union (EU). In January 1999, however, India announced its withdrawal from the IJO, which had declined to appoint India's nominee for the post of executive director. Thailand, citing its domestic economic problems, withdrew from the IJO in March. India rejoined the organization in December, but Thailand remained outside. Meanwhile, some EU members believed that the IJO had failed to promote trade in jute, and consequently favoured the organization's disbandment.

Following preparatory meetings at IJO headquarters, the UN Conference on Jute and Jute Products was convened in March 2000, under UNCTAD auspices, in Geneva, Switzerland. However, the EU and its member countries (which together accounted for about 30% of the IJO's financing) declined to attend this meeting or a resumed session in Dhaka in early April. A draft text for an 'International Instrument of Co-operation', to succeed the IJA, was supported by jute-producing countries, but, without the consent of major consumers, no agreement could be concluded. At a subsequent meeting of the IJO's governing council, the EU rejected adoption of the successor 'instrument'. As a result, the IJA expired in April, at the end of its term, and the IJO entered a liquidation process. However, a working group, including representatives of producing countries, was formed to consider future international co-operation on jute affairs. It was hoped that these countries would continue to obtain support for jute projects from the CFC. In March 2001, under UNCTAD auspices, the UN Conference on Jute and Jute Products established the International Jute Study Group (IJSG) as the successor entity to the IJO. *Inter alia*, the objectives of the IJSG are to provide an effective framework for international co-operation among its members with regard to all relevant aspects of the world jute economy; and to promote the expansion of international trade in jute and jute products. Membership of the IJSG, which was to have its headquarters in Dhaka, was to be open to all states (and to the EU) with an interest in the production and consumption of, and international trade in, jute and jute products. The terms of reference of the IJSG were to enter into force once a number of states together accounting for 60% of trade (imports and exports combined) in jute and jute products had given notice of their formal acceptance of the IJSG's terms of reference. Another forum for jute co-operation is FAO's Intergovernmental Group on Jute, Kenaf and Allied Fibres, which normally convenes every two years. The group met in December 2000, and another session was scheduled for December 2002.

Production of Jute, Kenaf and Allied Fibres
('000 metric tons)

	2000	2000*
World total	3,035	3,065
Far East	2,919	2,947
Leading regional producers		
Bangladesh	822	822†
China, People's Repub.	126‡	136†
India	1,868	1,875†
Myanmar	33	42
Nepal	15	16
Thailand	34	34†
Viet Nam	11	12
Other leading producers		
Russia	45†	46†
Uzbekistan	20†	21†

* Provisional figures. † FAO estimate.
‡ Unofficial figure.

Maize (Indian Corn, Mealies) (*Zea mays*)

Maize is one of the world's three principal cereal crops, with wheat and rice. Originally from America, maize has been dispersed to many parts of the world. The main varieties are dent maize (which has large, soft, flat grains) and flint maize (which has round, hard grains). Dent maize is the predominant type world-wide. Maize may be white or yellow (there is little nutritional difference), but the former is often preferred for human consumption. Maize is an annual crop, planted from seed, which matures within three to five months. It requires a warm climate and ample water supplies during the growing season. Genetically modified varieties of maize, with improved resistance against pests, are now being developed, particularly in the USA, and also in Argentina and the People's Republic of China. Ecological and consumer concerns are, however, placing in question the further commercialization of genetically modified varieties.

Maize is an important foodstuff in parts of Far East Asia, such as Indonesia, the Philippines and southern China, where the climate precludes the extensive cultivation of wheat. It tends, however, to be replaced by wheat in diets, as disposable incomes rise; maize consumption per caput has been declining in most of the developing countries. In some countries the grain is ground into a meal, mixed with water, and boiled to produce a gruel or porridge. In other areas it is made into (unleavened) corn bread or breakfast cereals. Maize is also the source of an oil, which is used in cooking.

The high starch content of maize makes it highly suitable as a compound feed ingredient, especially for pigs and poultry. Animal feed is the main use of maize in the USA, Europe and Japan, and large quantities are now also used for feed in developing countries in Far East Asia, Latin America and, to some extent, in North Africa. Maize also has a variety of industrial uses, including the preparation of ethyl alcohol (ethanol), which may be added to petrol to produce a blended motor fuel. In addition, maize is a source of dextrose and fructose, which can be used as artificial sweeteners, many times sweeter than sugar. The amounts used for these purposes depend, critically, on prices relative to petroleum, sugar and other potential raw materials. Maize cobs, previously discarded as a waste product, may be used as feedstock to produce various chemicals (e.g. acetic acid and formic acid).

In recent years world maize output has usually exceeded 550m. metric tons annually; it reached a record 615m. tons in 1998. The USA is by far the largest producer, with annual harvests in the late 1990s that were usually substantially in excess of 230m. tons. It is, however, subject to occasional major crop reverses in years of drought, as in 1993 (when output fell to only 161m. tons). Far East Asia accounts, on average, for about one-quarter of world maize production. The major producer in the region, and the world's second largest, is the People's Republic of China. Assisted by the expanded use of hybrid varieties, China's annual maize harvest increased by more than 50% in the 1980s, enabling the country to become, for a few seasons, a significant exporter of maize, until the rapid growth in domestic feed requirements drew level with supplies in the mid-1990s. New efforts to stimulate production, including higher support prices, resulted in a record crop of 127m. tons in 1996, and the accumulation of substantial maize stocks, which enabled supplies to be maintained without recourse to imports, following a much smaller harvest in 1997. Output recovered to a new record level of 133m. tons in 1998, but declined to 128m. tons in 1999 and to only 106m. tons in 2000. In 2001 Chinese production was estimated at 116m. tons.

Production of Maize ('000 metric tons)

	2000	2001*
World total†	592,999	609,182
Far East	143,246	153,503
Oceania	598	608
Leading regional producers		
China, People's Repub.	106,002	115,645†
India	11,473	11,836
Indonesia	9,677	9,090†
Korea, Dem. People's Repub.	1,041	1,482
Nepal	1,445	1,484
Pakistan	1,643	1,600‡
Philippines	4,511	4,525
Thailand	4,397	4,673†
Viet Nam	2,006	2,118
Other leading producers		
Argentina	16,817	15,350
Brazil	31,879	41,411
Canada	6,827	8,171
France	16,073	16,472
Hungary	4,984	7,686†
Italy	10,138	10,588
Mexico	17,557	18,616
Romania	4,898	7,500†
South Africa	10,943	7,100†
USA‡	251,854	241,485
Yugoslavia	2,968	5,828†

* Provisional figures. † Unofficial figure.

‡ FAO estimate.

In India much of the maize crop, which averages about 11m. tons annually, continues to be cultivated on marginal lands, but increasing areas are devoted to hybrid varieties, which, when irrigated, yield well. Human food use is diminishing because of an improvement in the supply of foodgrains, but feed use is increasing to satisfy the rapidlyexpanding poultry industry. The Indian Government's imposition of import duties on maize in June 2000 led to protests from the poultry sector. Maize is also used for starch production.

In Indonesia maize is a secondary crop, usually planted in the dry season after the main rice crop. The high cost of seed and other inputs deters farmers from planting hybrid varieties, although the Government is encouraging the expansion of maize output to meet the country's rapidlygrowing requirements for poultry feed. Production averages about 9m. tons annually. Imports of maize for feed were increasing until the Asian economic crisis of 1997 severely reduced meat consumption and feed requirements. Despite a small crop, there was an exportable surplus in 1997/98. About one-half of the Philippine crop (which averages over 4m. tons annually) consists of white flint maize, used for human consumption. Feed use (for pigs and poultry) is increasing rapidly, but rising import costs, following the depreciation of the Philippine peso, inhibited growth in demand in 1997/98. Maize was formerly an important export crop in Thailand, but the areas under maize declined sharply in the late 1980s because of the greater profitability of other crops, such as sugar cane. By the mid-1990s Thailand had to resort to imports in most years to satisfy its domestic feed requirements. In 1996–2001 production was steady at about 4.4m. tons annually, compared with about 3.8m. tons per year, on average, in 1990–95.

World trade in maize totalled more than 80m. metric tons in 2000, compared with about 79m. tons in 1999, and some 76m. tons in 1998. In the mid-1990s growth in trade was curtailed by adverse economic conditions in eastern Asia, which severely impacted on the region's meat consumption and, consequently, on its demand for animal feed. Recovery in the Asian economies, together with growing demand from Latin America and North Africa, subsequently led to a recovery.

The USA is invariably the largest maize-exporting country, with an average market share exceeding 70%. US exports reached 60m. metric tons in 1995/96, but were subsequently lower, owing to increased competition from Argentina, the People's Republic of China and a number of eastern and central European countries. US export volume reached 52m. tons in 1998/99, 48m. tons in 1999/2000 and an estimated 48m. tons in 2000/01. Argentina, usually the second largest supplier, has benefited considerably from liberalized marketing systems and improved port facilities. Argentinian exports of maize reached a record level of 12m. tons in 1997/98, but declined to only 8m. tons in 1998/99. Exports recovered to 10.8m. tons in 1999/2000 and were estimated to have increased again, to 12m. tons, in 2000/01. As a result of steeply rising output, China became a leading exporter of maize in the early 1990s, with sales attaining a record 11m. tons in 1992/93. One of its principal markets was Japan, whose coastal feed mills can receive shipments direct from China at low transport costs. The growth in China's own feed grain needs, together with smaller harvests, subsequently reduced the surplus, although exports continued from southern ports as a result of the high cost of moving grain overland to China's feed deficit regions. Exports by China were only 4.3m. tons in 1998/99, but recovered to 10.5m. tons in 1999/2000 and 12m. tons in 2000/01.

Far East Asia has long been a major market for maize, and its importance has increased significantly since the 1980s with the establishment of livestock (and particularly poultry) industries in many countries of the region. Total imports of maize in

Far East Asia rose from about 25m. metric tons in the mid-1980s to a record 38m. tons in 1995/96, before falling to 32m. tons in 1998/99, as a result of the region's economic difficulties. Japan is usually the world's leading maize-importing country. Its purchases accelerated sharply in the 1970s, but advanced more slowly in the 1980s, to reach a peak of 16.4m. tons in 1992/93. Japanese purchases have subsequently tended gradually to decline, following a relaxation of import controls on meat, and the consequent pressure on the profit margins of domestic feed-users, which compelled them to economize on costs. Feed users in the Republic of Korea are willing to substitute other grains, particularly feed wheat, for maize when prices are attractive, and maize imports are therefore variable, although averaging about 8.3m. tons annually. Taiwan imported more than 6m. tons in 1995/96, but the volume subsequently fell, following an outbreak of swine disease that reduced pig numbers by 40%. Nevertheless, the country continues regularly to import about 5.5m. tons of maize annually.

Few countries other than the USA and the People's Republic of China usually hold more than minimal carry-over stocks of maize. The USA accumulated massive stocks in the mid-1980s, the peak carry-over being 124m. metric tons at the end of August 1987. Government support programmes were successful in discouraging surplus production, but several poor harvests also contributed to the depletion of these stocks, which were reduced to only 11m. tons at the close of the 1995/96 marketing year. Domestic requirements in the USA have continued to increase, although three successive plentiful crops in 1996, 1997 and 1998, together with increased competition from other exporting countries, resulted in an appreciable build-up in US stocks in the second half of the 1990s. Carry-over stocks at the end of the 1998/99 marketing year reached 45m. tons, declined to 44m. tons in 1999/2000 and rose again, to 48.2m. tons, in 2000/01. While China publishes no official estimates of grain carry-over stocks, there is evidence of a considerable build-up of supplies on farms following the rapid growth in production of the early 1990s. This enabled the country to withstand a considerable crop set-back in 1997 without recourse to substantial imports.

Export Price Index for Maize (base: 1980 = 100)

	Average	Highest month(s)	Lowest month(s)
1990	92		
1995	80		
1999	58	60 (Jan., Sept., Oct.)	56 (July, Dec.)
2000	54	59 (Jan.–April)	47 (Sept.)
2001	59	63 (Jan.)	56 (June)

Export prices of maize are mainly influenced by the level of supplies in the USA, and the intensity of competition between the exporting countries. Record quotations were achieved in May 1996, when the average price of US No. 2 Yellow Corn (f.o.b. Gulf Ports) reached US $204 per metric ton. However, the quotation declined rapidly over the following months, falling as low as US $117 per ton in November 1996. For the whole of 1996 the quotation averaged US $165 per ton. The average annual quotation declined to US $117 per ton in 1997, to US $102 per ton in 1998, to US $92 per ton in 1999, and to US $88 per ton in 2000. In 2001 an average price of US $90 per ton was recorded. During the first six months of 2002 the average monthly price of US No. 2 Yellow Corn (f.o.b. Gulf ports) ranged between US $86 per ton, recorded in April, and US $94 per ton, recorded in June.

Nickel

Nickel is a silvery, malleable metal which occurs in various types of ores, the most important being sulphide ores and laterite ores. Sulphide ores are generally mined by underground methods, while laterites are usually mined by open-cast methods. Nickel in sulphide ores is often found in conjunction with copper, cobalt and platinum group metals (PGM); in laterites it is often found with iron, chromium and cobalt. The sulphide ore is subjected to crushing and grinding, with final treatment by the flotation method. The resulting concentrate is roasted and smelted in furnaces to remove the bulk of the sulphur, leaving a matte of nickel and copper. The nickel and copper can then be separated from each other by a variety of processes and sent to an electrolytic refinery. The primary product of processing laterites is ferronickel; a few ferronickel operations also produce limited amounts of matte by the deliberate addition of pyrite or sulphur to the ore at the drying stage. Nickel production is an energy-intensive operation, and the cost of energy to the industry has risen steeply in recent years. During the late 1990s, however, several Australian laterite nickel producers were conducting pilot projects in the processing of ores by high-pressure acid leaching, which, if shown to be successful, could substantially reduce production costs. The world's land-based reserves of nickel ore in 2001 were estimated by the US Geological Survey (USGS) at 58m. metric tons on an elemental basis, of which about 23m. tons were in sulphide deposits and 35m. tons in laterite ores. The distinction is significant, as sulphide ores are cheaper to process. According to USGS estimates, the largest proportion of nickel reserves are in Australia (34% of the world total), followed by Russia (11%) and Canada (11%), Cuba (10%), New Caledonia (8%), the People's Republic of China (6%) and Indonesia (6%).

Nickel is used in a wide range of alloys where it imparts corrosion resistance and high-temperature strength. Its most important use is in steel production, and the majority of high-tensile steels contain nickel. On a world-wide basis, the stainless steel industry accounts for more than 60% of nickel consumption. Nickel continues to be a significant constituent of much military equipment. Alloys containing a high proportion of nickel are used in power and chemical plants. The metal also has high-temperature applications, such as gas turbines, and rocket engines for the aerospace industry.

Extensive deposits of ferromanganese nodules—also containing nickel, copper and cobalt—are known to exist on the floor of the world's oceans. A conservative estimate assesses world nodule reserves at 290m. metric tons of nickel, 240m. tons of cobalt and 6,000m. tons of manganese. However, quite apart from the question of rights of recovery tortuously negotiated at the UN Conference on the Law of the Sea, experts believe that the extraction of metals from the nodules is unlikely to be commercially practicable for many years.

Nickel prices in Western countries have traditionally been governed by the four companies that, historically, were the largest producers—International Nickel (Inco), Falconbridge (both of Canada), Western Mining (of Australia) and the French-controlled Société Le Nickel (SLN). In 2000 Norilsk Nickel of Russia was the world's single largest producer, and its output, combined with that of the four aforementioned companies and that of Billiton plc of the United Kingdom, accounted for about 66% of world production. Inco (the Western world's largest producer) has traditionally supplied almost one-third of the nickel requirements of the major industrial countries.

The major nickel-producing countries in the Asia-Pacific region are Australia, New Caledonia and Indonesia. New Caledonia possesses the world's largest identified deposits of nickel-bearing laterite. Substantial deposits of nickel exist in Western Australia, where the Leinster mine has reserves of 333m. tons of underground ore, grading 1.8% nickel, and about 2.9m. tons of open-pit ore, grading 1.5% nickel. Deposits at Mt Keith and Yakabindie are each estimated to contain at least 100m. short tons of reserves, grading about 0.5% nickel. The development of reserves in the Murrin Murrin district, estimated at 119m. metric tons (grading 1.4% nickel), commenced in 1997. The Murrin Murrin open-cast mine, which is 60% owned by Anaconda Nickel Ltd of Australia, had a planned initial capacity to produce 45,000 tons of nickel, and 9,000 tons of cobalt, per year. It is the largest of three projects in Western Australia that have been pioneering the potentially low-cost process of producing nickel and cobalt from laterite deposits by high-pressure acid leaching (see above). During the late 1990s, however, there were problems in developing the necessary technology, leading to delays in bringing the three projects into full production. The value of Australia's exports of nickel ores and concentrates and of intermediate products of nickel was $A1,470m. in the year ending June 2001.

In the longer term Australia's relatively high-cost production could be faced with a considerable challenge in world nickel markets from the commercial exploitation of vast, and as yet undeveloped, deposits near Voisey's Bay, in north-eastern Canada. This prospect has been stated to contain as much as

150m. tons of nickel ore, with the estimated low-cost productive capacity to provide one-third of all new nickel mine output within 10 years of its entry into production. However, Inco, which acquired the rights to develop the Voisey's Bay nickel deposits in 1996, has been unable to agree to the conditions sought by the Newfoundland provincial authorities, and in January 2000 it was announced that negotiations between them had been suspended. Consequently, the proposed construction of a mining and milling operation at the site did not commence, as planned, in 2000. It was suggested that Inco would, instead, concentrate its development efforts on the company's Goro project (see below) in New Caledonia.

In 2001, according to provisional data, New Caledonia was the world's fourth largest producer of nickel in terms of mine output. The territory's dominant production company is SLN, 60% owned by the French government-controlled mining conglomerate, Eramet, 30% by the three provinces of New Caledonia, and 10% by Nishin Steel of Japan. In 2000 SLN accounted for 47% of New Caledonia's total mine output of nickel. The company exploits deposits of nickel-bearing ores at ffour mining centres, all on the main island. Mining at a fifth SLN site has been contracted to an independent company. The output of ore from mines operated by SLN and its sub-contractors totalled 3,710,000 tons (wet weight) in 2000, compared with 3,520,000 tons in 1999. Ore from these mines and from sub-contractors operating SLN deposits is sent for processing in the company's smelter at Doniambo, near Nouméa, in the south of the island. Eramet is the world's leading company producing ferronickel, and SLN's Doniambo smelter is the largest ferronickel plant in the world. In 2000 output from Doniambo was a record 57,463 tons of nickel, comprising 43,914 tons of nickel in ferronickel and 13,549 tons of nickel in matte. SLN reportedly plans to increase the annual capacity of the Doniambo smelter to 75,000 tons before 2006.

Production of Nickel Ore (nickel content, metric tons)

	1999	2000
World total	1,120,000*	1,250,000*
Far East	152,987*	172,840*
Oceania	237,062	295,793
Leading regional producers		
Australia	127,000	168,300
China, People's Repub.	49,500*	51,100*
Indonesia	89,111	98,200
New Caledonia	110,062	127,493
Philippines	14,300	23,500
Other leading producers		
Botswana	33,733	34,465
Brazil	41,522	45,317
Canada	186,236	190,728
Colombia	39,274	58,927
Cuba	63,627	68,305
Dominican Repub.	39,997	39,943
Russia	260,000*	270,000*
South Africa	36,200	36,616

* Estimated production. World and Far East totals and other estimated data are rounded.

Source: US Geological Survey.

Products from the Doniambo plant are destined for export. Sales of nickel ore, nickel matte and ferronickel together provided 89.3% of New Caledonia's total export earnings in 1999. During the late 1990s more than one-half of the nickel ore from the territory's mines was exported without further processing, and there has been considerable local support for proposals to construct additional smelting facilities. However, New Caledonia's heavy dependence on the nickel industry has resulted in periods of economic recession, and, since the mid-1980s, mining operations have been intermittently overshadowed by political unrest. During the 1980s and 1990s a major issue in discussions concerning the political future of New Caledonia was the extent of participation by the indigenous Melanesian people (Kanaks) in the territory's development, including its major industry. The Société Minière du Sud-Pacifique (SMSP), controlled by Kanak interests, is the most important of the six independent nickel-mining companies in New Caledonia. During negotiations over increased autonomy for the territory, local representatives sought an expansion of indigenous involvement in the nickel sector. In 1996 the SMSP and Falconbridge formed a partnership aimed at constructing a ferronickel plant in the Kanak-dominated north of the main island. In February 1998, in response to the demands of Kanak political leaders to make such a project viable, the French Government, Eramet, the SMSP and others signed the Bercy accords, whereby Eramet was to relinquish control of its promising site at Koniambo, in the north, in exchange for the Poum mine, operated by the SMSP, in the south. As the Koniambo prospect was estimated to contain about double the volume of nickel at the Poum site, the French Government agreed to pay compensation of about 1,000m. French francs to Eramet for the reduction in its reserves. In April the SMSP formed a joint venture with Falconbridge to develop the Koniambo nickel deposits. The agreement on exchanging nickel resources helped to facilitate the conclusion of the Nouméa Accord, signed in May and approved by referendum in November, which provided for a gradual transfer of powers from metropolitan France to local institutions. In compliance with the Nouméa Accord, an agreement was reached in February 1999 to enable the transfer of 30% of SLN's share capital to a newly-created company representing local interests, the Société Territoriale Calédonienne de Participation Industrielle (STCPI), to be owned by the development companies of the three New Caledonian provinces. In July 2000, following two years of negotiations, New Caledonia's political leaders signed an agreement on the formation of the STCPI. The transfer of shares, reducing Eramet's interest in SLN from 90% to 60%, took place in September.

Meanwhile, in September 1998 Falconbridge began test-drilling at the Koniambo site, and in 1999 the company identified an estimated 132m. tons of ore, grading 2.46% nickel. The eventual aim was to construct a smelter producing 54,000 tons of nickel (contained in ferronickel) per year, and it was hoped that a feasibility study for the project could be completed by the end of 2002. Under the Bercy accords, however, control of the Koniambo deposits will revert to SLN unless construction of the smelter has begun by the end of 2005.

Another company, Goro Nickel (controlled by Inco), holds several claims covering nickel-cobalt deposits in the southern part of New Caledonia's main island, with estimated reserves of more than 200m. tons of ore, averaging 1.6% nickel. In October 1999 Goro inaugurated a pilot plant for nickel processing, to test new technology for treating laterite ore by acid leaching and solvent extraction. If the testing is successful, it was hoped that a full-scale commercial plant, capable of producing 27,000 tons of nickel per year, would be constructed.

In Indonesia the main nickel-producing companies are PT International Nickel Indonesia, an Inco subsidiary, and the government-controlled PT Aneka Tambang (PT Antam). The largest of PT Antam's nickel mines is on Gebe Island, east of Halmahera, in the Maluku (Moluccas) archipelago. This mine has an estimated 27m. tons of reserves, with an average nickel content of 2.2%. Its output is divided, roughly equally, between high-grade saprolitic ore and lower-grade limonitic ore. Further large deposits of potentially exploitable ore containing nickel and cobalt have been located on Gag Island (about 40 km south-east of Gebe), in the province of West Papua (formerly Irian Jaya). In 1996 PT Antam formed a joint venture with BHP Minerals Ltd of Australia to evaluate prospects for developing these reserves. BHP, which has a 75% interest in the project, has estimated that Gag Island has total reserves (including inferred resources) of about 240m. tons of laterite ore, grading 1.35% nickel. In July 2000 BHP announced provisional agreement with Falconbridge for the division, on an equal basis, of BHP's interest in the project and the consequent sharing of development costs. If terms could be agreed, a feasibility study, expected to last two years, was to be conducted to assess the viability of mining the ore. PT Antam is collaborating in a separate joint venture to develop nickel and cobalt deposits at several locations on Halmahera, north of the island's Weda Bay. Its partner is a Canadian prospecting company, Weda Bay Minerals Inc, which has a 90% interest in the project. In May 1999 Weda Bay Minerals reported that tests in the areas of exploration had shown indicated and inferred reserves of 117m. tons of ore, grading 1.36% nickel. These reserves were subsequently reassessed at 202m. tons of ore, grading 1.37% nickel.

In June 2000 the company announced the commencement of a feasibility study, in which OM Group of the USA was also to participate, scheduled for completion in early 2002, to consider exploitation of these deposits. If approved, the Halmahera project is expected to produce 30,000 tons of nickel per year in intermediate products.

The reserves of nickel of the People's Republic of China were estimated at 3.7m. metric tons in 2001. Mined output of nickel in that year was estimated 50,700 tons. Elsewhere in the Far East, the reserves of nickel of the Philippines were estimated at 410,000 tons in 2001. Philippine mined output of nickel totalled an estimated 23,700 tons in that year.

Japan and the USA are the world's largest nickel consumers, and Japan is, additionally, a major producer of refined nickel, all from imported materials. The republics of the former USSR and the European Union (EU), especially Germany, are also important consumers. Consumption in China, the Republic of Korea and Taiwan advanced strongly in the 1990s, however, and it was forecast in 1996 that East Asia could account for almost one-quarter of world nickel consumption by 2005.

In April 1979 dealing in nickel began on the London Metal Exchange (LME), despite opposition from the major producers, who feared that speculative free-market trading would increase volatility in prices. These fears have proved to be justified, and since the late 1970s nickel-producers have been operating in a highly cyclical trading environment, with wide and unpredictable fluctuations on the free market. However, the amount of nickel traded in this way is still relatively small. Producers typically obtain about 20 US cents per lb more for nickel that they supply than for metal that is traded on the LME. This arrangement, however, has been affected since 1991 by significant sales of nickel cathodes by the leading Russian mining company, Norilsk Nickel, which is the world's largest nickel-producer (accounting for about 19% of total refinery production in 1998). In the 1990s Norilsk provided about 80% of Russia's nickel output. In November 1998 the company approved a 10-year development programme, intended to modernize its mining, smelting and refining operations, conducted under licence, in northern Russia. The programme envisages funding of US $1,000m. by January 2003. If financing can be obtained, Norilsk plans to develop new levels in existing mines, to construct new mines, and to expand its exploration activities.

Export Price Index for Nickel (base: 1980 = 100)

	Average	Highest month(s)	Lowest month(s)
1990	191		
1995	156		
1999	116	158 (Dec.)	84 (Jan.)
2000	153	196 (March)	117 (Nov.)
2001	95	115 (Jan.)	78 (Oct.)

On the LME the price of nickel in January 1995 stood at US $10,160 (equivalent to £6,376 sterling) per metric ton, its highest level since 1990. The surge in prices occurred despite a rise in LME stocks of nickel to a record 151,254 tons in November 1994. The London quotation was reduced to US $6,947.5 (£4,393) per ton in May 1995. It recovered to US $9,200 (£5,962) per ton in August, but eased to US $7,630 (£4,851) in October. The nickel price advanced to US $8,885 (£5,618) per ton in November and ended the year at US $7,930 (£5,106). Meanwhile, LME stocks of the metal steadily declined, reaching 44,556 tons in December.

The nickel market remained volatile in the first few weeks of 1996, while the LME's holdings continued to diminish. In early January the London price of nickel fell to US $7,455 (£4,803) per ton, but at the beginning of February it reached US $8,625 (£5,699). Thereafter, prices moved generally lower, and in August the London quotation was US $6,837.5 (£4,426) per ton. In the mean time LME stocks of nickel were reduced to 31,998 tons in July. The price of nickel recovered in September to US $7,625 (£4,897) per ton, but declined in December to US $6,310 (£3,732). The LME's holdings of the metal rose to 49,776 tons in January 1997, but decreased to 45,174 tons in February. The London price of nickel advanced to US $8,220 (£5,082) per ton in March, but fell to US $5,862.5 (£3,480) at the end of the year. Meanwhile, LME stocks steadily expanded, reaching 67,056 tons in November. For 1997 as a whole, the average nickel price was US $7,053 (about £4,300) per ton.

Nickel prices continued to decline during the early months of 1998, and in May the London quotation fell to less than US $5,000 per ton. In September, despite a decrease in LME stocks of nickel to about 58,300 tons, the price of the metal was reduced to US $4,000 (£2,375) per ton. Stock levels later rose, and in October the LME nickel price declined to US $3,755 (£2,204) per ton. In November, following a strike at some nickel mines in New Caledonia, the price recovered to US $4,230 (£2,549) per ton. However, in December, with LME stocks standing at about 63,500 tons, the London price of nickel fell to only US $3,745 (£2,218) per ton: its lowest level, in term of US currency, since 1987. The slump in the nickel market was attributed partly to a fall in demand for stainless steel, particularly from Asian countries experiencing financial problems.

The LME's stocks of nickel increased to 66,222 tons in February 1999, but declined to less than 50,000 tons in August. Meanwhile, there was a sustained rally in the nickel market, encouraged by a recovery in demand, and in early September the London price reached US $7,350 (£4,577) per ton. A week later, the LME's holdings of the metal were reduced to 48,900 tons. After rising somewhat, levels of nickel stocks resumed their downward movement in October and fell to 46,158 tons in November, as demand for stainless steel continued to strengthen. Meanwhile, prices for the metal moved higher, and the LME quotation at the end of the year was US $8,470 (£5,553) per ton: a rise of more than 100% in 12 months. The strong advance in nickel prices during 1999 was influenced by the closure of some high-cost production facilities and by technical problems at innovatory laterite nickel developments in Australia. Meanwhile, there was a strike at a major production plant in Canada.

These trends in the nickel market continued during the early weeks of 2000. In March, during a seven-week strike at SLN's operations in New Caledonia, the LME price of nickel (the official closing offer price at the end of morning trading on the LME) reached US $10,660 per ton: its highest level, in terms of US currency, for more than nine years. While prices of the metal rose, stocks of nickel steadily declined, with the LME's holdings reduced to less than 40,000 tons in February and to below 30,000 tons in April. The London price of nickel eased to US $9,360 per ton in April, but advanced to US $10,600 in May. The nickel price subsequently retreated, although demand remained strong, and in late July the LME quotation was US $7,500 per ton. This downward price movement occurred despite a continuing decline in LME stocks of nickel, which fell to less than 20,000 tons in June and to only 15,684 tons in July. During the remainder of 2000 LME holdings of nickel continued to decline steadily, falling to only 9,678 tons in December. During August–December the average monthly London quotation ranged between US $8,634 (£6,017) per ton, recorded in September, and US $7,310 (£5,000) per ton in December.

In early 2001 LME holdings of nickel continued to decline, falling to 8,304 tons in March. From April, however, they rose steadily, reaching 12,156 tons in May, 15,984 tons in June, 16,674 tons in July and 17,688 tons in August. In September LME stocks fell as low as 16,272 tons, ending the month at 16,716 tons, but thereafter, for the remainder of the year, they rose consistently, reaching 18,180 tons in October and 19,002 tons in November, ending the year at 19,188 tons. In 2001 the average monthly London quotation for nickel ranged between US $7,057 (£4,950) per ton, recorded in May, and US $4,822 (£3,321) per ton in September. LME holdings of nickel increased substantially in January 2002, reaching 24,564 tons at one point. They declined in February, to 21,174 tons, and, again, in March, to 17,004 tons. During April LME nickel holdings fell as low as 16,674 tons early in the month, but subsequently began to accumulate, rising as high as 20,778 tons. Stocks rose again, to 27,690 tons, in May, and to 29,130 tons in June before declining to 27,984 tons before the end of that month. In July LME holdings declined to 23,670 tons. During the first seven months of 2002 the average monthly London quotation for nickel ranged between US $7,139 per ton (£4,595) in July, and US $6,026 per ton (£4,237) in February.

Oil Palm *(Elaeis guineensis).*

This tree, which is native to West Africa, is widely cultivated, mainly on plantations, in the Far East. The entire fruit is of use commercially; palm oil is made from its pulp, and palm kernel oil from the seed. Palm oil is a versatile product and, because of its very low acid content (4%–5%), is almost all used in food. It is used in margarine and other edible fats; as a 'shortener' for pastry and biscuits; as an ingredient in ice cream and in chocolate; and in the manufacture of soaps and detergents. Palm kernel oil, which is similar to coconut oil, is also used for making soaps and fats. The sap from the stems of the tree is used to make palm wine, an intoxicating beverage.

Palm oil can be produced virtually through the year once the palms have reached oil-bearing age, which takes about five years. The palms continue to bear oil for 30 years or more and the yield far exceeds that of any other oil plant, with 1 ha of oil palms producing as much oil as 6 ha of groundnuts or 10–12 ha of soybeans. However, it is an intensive crop, needing considerable investment and skilled labour.

During the 1980s palm oil accounted for more than 15% of world production of vegetable oils (second only to soybean oil), owing mainly to a substantial expansion in Malaysian output. Assisted by high levels of demand from Pakistan and the People's Republic of China, palm oil considerably increased its share of world markets for vegetable oils in the early 1990s. In the late 1990s palm oil exports continued substantially to exceed those of soybean oil in international trade, although in 2000 the difference narrowed to only about 13%, compared with almost 70% in 1999. The increase in output of palm oil has posed a particular challenge to the soybean industry in the USA, which has, since the mid-1970s, greatly reduced its imports of palm oil. In 1988, in response to health reports that both palm and coconut oils tended to raise levels of cholesterol (a substance believed to promote arteriosclerosis in the body), several leading US food-processors announced that they were to discontinue the use of these oils. The scientific validity of these reports, however, has been vigorously challenged by palm oil producers.

In 2001, according to provisional figures, world output of palm products totalled 6.8m. metric tons of kernels and a record 23m. tons of palm oil. The Far East was the main producing area, providing 5.3m. tons of palm kernels and 19.6m. tons of palm oil.

The leading producer and exporter of palm oil is Malaysia, which, in recent years, has accounted for about 65%–70% of world trade in this commodity. More than 90% of the country's production is exported, and in 1999 earnings from palm oil exports represented 4.1% of Malaysia's total export earnings. The most important markets for Malaysian palm oil are India, the European Union, the USA, Japan and Pakistan. The country accounted for 51% of world production of palm oil in 2001, compared with 49.6% in 2000. Malaysia produced 11.7m. tons of palm oil in 2001, compared with 10.8m. tons in 2000.

Because of continued growing world demand, the Malaysian Government is actively encouraging the industry; in 1977 a Palm Oil Registration and Licensing Authority (PORLA) was established to supervise all aspects of production—research, replanting and marketing. In 1980 a palm oil exchange, offering contracts for trading in fixed amounts at specified dates, was established in Kuala Lumpur—a logical development from Malaysia's dominant position in the world palm oil trade. Since the early 1990s, however, growth in Malaysia's palm oil output has been inhibited by severe labour shortages on the oil palm plantations, and government consent has been given to the limited recruitment of foreign workers. As oil palm production costs are low, and sales contracts are denominated in US dollars, Malaysian producers benefited from an upward trend in prices during the Asian economic crisis, attributable in part to restrictions on Indonesian supplies entering world trade (see below). In 1999 a number of growers' groups merged to form the Malaysian Palm Oil Association. In May 2000 a new statutory body, the Malaysian Palm Oil Board (absorbing PORLA), became operational.

In Indonesia, the second largest producer and exporter, the area under oil palm has expanded rapidly in recent years. In 1990 approximately 715,000 ha were harvested and a further 400,000 ha had been planted. In the early 1990s about 100,000–150,000 ha per year were being brought under oil palm cultivation, and production of palm oil, which had been forecast

Production of Palm Kernels ('000 metric tons)

	2000	2001*
World total	6,458	6,781
Far East	5,010	5,318
Oceania	83	83
Leading regional producers		
China (incl. Taiwan)	53†	54†
Indonesia	1,655‡	1,760‡
Malaysia	3,162‡	3,370‡
Papua New Guinea	75‡	75‡
Thailand	124‡	118‡
Other leading producers		
Brazil§	123	130†
Colombia	109	113‡
Congo, Dem. Repub.	63†	63†
Nigeria	562†	562†

* Provisional figures. † FAO estimate.
‡ Unofficial figure. § Babassu kernels.

Production of Palm Oil ('000 metric tons)

	2000	2001*
World total	21,857	22,869
Far East	18,617	19,619
Oceania	326	326
Leading regional producers		
China (incl. Taiwan)	213†	217†
Indonesia	6,950‡	7,135†
Malaysia	10,840‡	11,660‡
Papua New Guinea	296‡	296†
Thailand	560‡	550‡
Other leading producers		
Colombia	524	560
Congo, Dem. Repub.	168	167
Côte d'Ivoire	278	205
Ecuador	245	280
Nigeria	670†	670†

* Provisional figures. † FAO estimate.
‡ Unofficial figure.

to reach 4.9m. tons annually by the year 2000, exceeded this target in 1996, when output reached 5.0m. tons. Production rose to 5.4m. tons in 1997, to 5.9m. tons in 1998, and to 6.3m. tons in 1999. In 2001 Indonesia produced 7.1m. tons of palm oil, compared with 7.0m. tons in 1999. In 1999 Indonesia derived 3% of its total export revenue from sales of palm oil and of palm kernel oil. The Asian economic crisis, which caused a sharp depreciation in the value of the Indonesian rupiah and led to steep rises in the government-subsidized domestic price of cooking oils, prompted the Indonesian Government to impose a three-month ban on oil palm exports from December 1997. This embargo was renewed in March 1998 and replaced in May by a 40% tax on oil palm exports. The tax was increased to 60% in July, but was reduced to 40% in early 1999. During the 1990s oil palm cultivation was encouraged in Myanmar and Papua New Guinea.

Internationally, palm oil is faced with sustained competition from the other major edible lauric oils—soybean, rapeseed and sunflower oils—and these markets are subject to a complex and changing interaction of production, stocks and trade. In the longer term, prospects for palm oil exporters (particularly the higher-cost producers in sub-Saharan Africa) do not appear favourable. Technological advances in oil palm cultivation, particularly in the introduction of laboratory-produced higher-yielding varieties (HYVs), may also militate against the smaller-scale producer, as, for economic and technical reasons, many HYVs can be produced only on large estates, exposing smallholder cultivators to increasingly intense price pressure.

During September 1996 the import price of Malaysian palm oil in the Netherlands (c.i.f. Rotterdam) declined from US $572.5 per metric ton to US $502.5 per ton. The price advanced to US $585 per ton in February 1997, but fell to US $467.5 in July. Subsequently the market revived, and in late December palm oil traded at US $565 per ton. The upward movement continued in the early months of 1998, and in May the import price of palm oil reached US $800 per ton. In June the price eased to

Export Price Index for Palm Oil (base: 1980 = 100)

	Average	Highest month(s)	Lowest month(s)
1990	49		
1995	107		
1999	74	108 (Jan.)	54 (July)
2000	53	64 (April)	44 (Oct., Nov.)
2001	49	62 (Aug.)	40 (May)

US $592.5 per ton. The Rotterdam price of palm oil stayed within this range for the remainder of 1998, ending the year at US $605 per ton. For the year as a whole, the European import price (c.i.f. north-west Europe) averaged US $671.08 per ton, compared with US $545.83 in 1997. However, from January 1999 there was strong downward pressure on palm oil prices, as demand fell while supplies remained plentiful. By early August the Rotterdam import price had been reduced to only US $300 per ton. The sharp fall in prices was partly due to a Chinese decision to import oilseeds rather than the oils derived from them, in an attempt to protect China's domestic processing industry. For 1999 as a whole, the European import price of palm oil averaged US $436.00 per ton: 35% below the previous year's level. In February 2000 the Rotterdam price fell to US $290 per ton. For 2000 as a whole, the European import price averaged US $310.25 per ton. A further decline, of 7.9%, to $285.67 per ton, was recorded in 2001.

Petroleum

Crude oils, from which petroleum fuel is derived, consist essentially of a wide range of hydrocarbon molecules which are separated by distillation in the refining process. Refined oil is treated in different ways to make the different varieties of fuel. More than four-fifths of total world oil supplies are used as fuel for the production of energy in the form of power or heating.

Petroleum, together with its associated mineral fuel, natural gas, is extracted both from onshore and offshore wells in many areas of the world. The dominant producing region is the Middle East, whose proven reserves in December 2001 accounted for 65.3% of known world deposits of crude petroleum and natural gas liquids. The Middle East accounted for 30% of world output in 2001. The Far East and Australasia, including the People's Republic of China but excluding Cambodia and Laos (for which separate figures were not available), contained 5,900m. metric tons of proven reserves (4.2% of the world total) at the end of 2001, when the region accounted for some 10.6% of world production.

From storage tanks at the oilfield wellhead, crude petroleum is conveyed, frequently by pumping for long distances through large pipelines, to coastal depots where it is either treated in a refinery or delivered into bulk storage tanks for subsequent shipment for refining overseas. In addition to pipeline transportation of crude petroleum and refined products, natural (petroleum) gas is, in some areas, also transported through networks of pipelines. Crude petroleum varies considerably in colour and viscosity, and these variations are a determinant both of price and of end-use after refining.

In the refining process, crude petroleum is heated until vaporized. The vapours are then separately condensed, according to their molecular properties, passed through airless steel tubes and pumped into the lower section of a high, cylindrical tower, as a hot mixture of vapours and liquid. The heavy unvaporized liquid flows out at the base of the tower as a 'residue' from which is obtained heavy fuel and bitumen. The vapours passing upwards then undergo a series of condensation processes that produce 'distillates', which form the basis of the various petroleum products.

The most important of these products is fuel oil, composed of heavy distillates and residues, which is used to produce heating and power for industrial purposes. Products in the kerosene group have a wide number of applications, ranging from heating fuels to the powering of aviation gas turbine engines. Gasoline (petrol) products fuel internal combustion engines (used mainly in road motor vehicles), and naphtha, a gasoline distillate, is a commercial solvent that can also be processed as a feedstock. Propane and butane, the main liquefied petroleum gases, have a wide range of industrial applications and are also used for domestic heating and cooking.

Petroleum is the leading raw material in international trade. World-wide demand for this commodity totalled 75.3m. barrels per day (b/d) in 2001. The world's 'published proven' reserves of petroleum and natural gas liquids at 31 December 2001 were estimated to total 143,000m. metric tons, equivalent to about 1,050,000m. barrels (1 metric ton is equivalent to approximately 7.3 barrels, each of 42 US gallons or 34.97 imperial gallons, i.e. 159 litres).

Indonesia, China and Malaysia are the major petroleum exporters in the Far East and Australasia, and Indonesia is the world's leading exporter of liquefied natural gas (LNG). Japan, the world's second largest consumer of petroleum, is the dominant importer in the region. The People's Republic of China, the Republic of Korea and Taiwan are also substantial consumers of petroleum products.

Within the region generally, there has been a rising level of exploration activity by international petroleum companies in recent years. Joint ventures have increasingly been sought by countries committed to policies of state control and central economic planning. These countries include not only the People's Republic of China and Viet Nam, but also India, Myanmar and Cambodia.

Production of Crude Petroleum
('000 metric tons, including natural gas liquids)

	2000	2001
World total	3,595,000	3,584,900
Far East and Oceania	382,900	379,400
Leading regional producers		
Australia	35,400	31,800
Brunei	9,400	9,500
China, People's Repub.	162,600	164,900
India	36,100	36,100
Indonesia	71,500	68,600
Malaysia	35,500	35,100
Viet Nam	16,200	17,100
Other leading producers		
Canada	126,900	129,100
Iran	187,700	182,900
Iraq	128,600	117,900
Kuwait	106,000	104,200
Mexico	171,200	176,600
Nigeria	103,300	105,200
Norway	160,500	162,100
Russia	323,300	348,100
Saudi Arabia	441,400	422,900
United Arab Emirates	117,000	113,200
United Kingdom	126,200	117,900
USA	352,600	351,700
Venezuela	171,600	176,200

Source: BP, *Statistical Review of World Energy 2002.*

Private-sector exploration operations, which have long been a central feature of the petroleum industry in Australia, Indonesia and Malaysia, were extended in 1991 to onshore, as well as offshore, blocks in India, whose major oilfields are located off shore from Mumbai. Previously, the government-owned Oil and Natural Gas Co of India had retained an exploration monopoly in the more promising onshore areas. However, the maintenance of government regulations on exploration activity has inhibited the participation of foreign investors in the quest for the development of new reserves. Measures to dismantle state controls on the petroleum industry, announced in early 1998, were expected to open the way to a significant increase in foreign investment. Contracts issued in January 2000 permitted companies from the United Kingdom, France, Russia and the USA rights to offshore exploration, in partnership with Indian firms. In December 2001 India's recoverable reserves of petroleum were estimated at 600m. tons, which, at current rates of extraction, are expected to be exhausted by about 2017. Thailand has proposed joint-venture arrangements with Cambodia and Viet Nam to explore an offshore field overlapping the coastal waters of the three countries. Viet Nam, whose recoverable petroleum reserves were estimated at 100m. tons in 2001, has granted exploration concessions to more than 30 foreign companies, although many have subsequently withdrawn, owing to disappointing discoveries and difficulties related to regulation. The first producing offshore oilfield, operated by Vietsovpetro (a joint company with the USSR from 1980, and with Russia from 1992), was followed in October 1994 by the coming on-stream of a second site, jointly operated by the state petroleum monopoly, Petrovietnam, and BHP Petroleum of Australia, at the Dai Hung oilfield, located 280 km off the country's south coast. Dai Hung has been estimated to contain about 370m. barrels of petroleum. The field's production, however, has fallen short of initial expectations. Viet Nam has asserted exploration claims over a larger area of the South China Sea, but these are disputed by the People's Republic of China, the Philippines, Indonesia, Brunei, Malaysia and Taiwan. In 1992 the Chinese Government awarded a contract to a US company to explore for petroleum in a sector of this area, where substantial deposits of hydrocarbons are believed to exist. China has also pursued a dispute with Japan over the sovereignty of the Diaoyu (Senkaku) group of eight uninhabited islands in the East China Sea, which are believed to lie in an area of offshore production potential. The Republic of Korea and the Democratic People's Republic of Korea are also involved in disputes with China over the demarcation of exploration rights in the Yellow Sea continental shelf.

The People's Republic of China is the third largest consumer of petroleum in the world after the USA and Japan. Consumption totalled 230.1m. metric tons in 2001, and is forecast to overtake that of Japan by 2010 and, possibly, to rise to more than 500m. tons annually by 2020. China has been a net importer of petroleum since 1993 and domestic production is oriented, primarily, towards meeting domestic consumption. The Daqing oilfield in Heilongjiang Province accounts for almost one-third of domestic production, but output there is declining owing to natural depletion. China has sought foreign participation to assist in the extension of production at its second largest oilfield at Liaohe in the north east of the country, and, in late 2000, attempted to remove some of the regulatory obstacles to the collaboration of foreign oil companies with their Chinese counterparts. Chinese production capacity is currently, by and large, located onshore and the development of offshore reserve is a focus of government energy strategy. Recent exploration activity has reportedly been concentrated on areas in the Bohai Sea, to the east of Tianjin, and the Pearl River mouth. Realizing that its dependence on imports is likely to increase, the state-owned China National Petroleum Corpn (CNPC) has purchased interests in various foreign exploration and production projects. China has also held talks with Russia regarding the feasibility of constructing a pipeline link to allow China to import Russian crude oil. China's recoverable petroleum reserves were estimated to total 3,300m. tons in December 2001. In early 1998 the Governments of the PRC and Taiwan approved an agreement whereby their state-owned petroleum corporations would conduct joint offshore exploration activities in the South China Sea. In the late 1990s, in association with its proposal to seek membership of the World Trade Organization (WTO), the PRC announced moves towards a future liberalization of the operations of its petroleum industry.

In 1989 the Governments of Australia and Indonesia established a 'zone of co-operation' in an area of the Timor Sea known as the 'Timor Gap', to allow petroleum exploration and development to proceed, on a profit-sharing basis, in a disputed maritime area covering 62,000 sq km. This agreement was unsuccessfully challenged in the International Court of Justice by Portugal, acting on behalf of the people of its former colony of East Timor. Indonesia, whose reserves are becoming depleted and which is consequently expected to become a net importer of petroleum during 2005–10, is actively promoting exploration for new reserves in remote areas of its eastern archipelago. In 1999 it was estimated that total reserves in the 'zone of co-operation' exceeded 100m. barrels of petroleum. Following the vote for independence in East Timor, the UN, as the body responsible for a transitional administration there, signed a treaty with Australia in February 2000 to extend the terms of the 1989 agreement, although it appeared unlikely that any significant production would commence before 2003. By 2004 Indonesia is expected to have brought into production three major new petroleum projects, although these are unlikely to increase overall production as output from mature fields declines. The West Seno field, off shore of East Kalimantan, is scheduled to come on stream by the end of 2002, while capacity at the Belanek project in West Natuna (in the South China Sea) will be raised substantially by 2004. The Banyu Urip oilfield in Java is expected to come on stream in 2003.

In 1991 the Government of Cambodia invited foreign tenders for 26 onshore and offshore blocks, and further exploration concessions were granted in the following year. In 1994 foreign capital was sought for the exploration of three additional offshore blocks and for 19 onshore blocks along the Tonl, Sap lake area and along the Mekong river, and 10 additional blocks were made available in 1996. To date, however, only four wells have been drilled, of which three have been found to contain some petroleum or natural gas. In 1990 Myanmar signed onshore exploration contracts with 10 foreign petroleum companies, although exploration activity had ceased by mid-1994, following disappointing results. Progress has been made, however, in the development of the Yadana offshore field of liquefied petroleum gas, whose recoverable reserves have been estimated at 160,000m. cu m. Initial exports of natural gas from the Yadana field to Thailand commenced in 1998. The offshore Yetagun field, with estimated recoverable reserves of 34,000m. cu m, began production in May 2000.

Petroleum Refining Capacity, 1998 ('000 metric tons per year)

Australia	40,355
Bangladesh	1,650
Brunei	430
China, People's Repub.	251,000
India	61,750
Indonesia	46,485
Japan	254,500
Korea, Dem. People's Repub.	3,550
Korea, Repub.	132,250
Malaysia	23,720
Myanmar	1,600
New Zealand	4,900
Pakistan	6,940
Philippines	19,450
Singapore	62,250
Sri Lanka	2,375
Taiwan	38,500
Thailand	35,635
Total (Far East and Australasia)	987,340

Source: The Institute of Petroleum.

Petroleum consumption in the region (excluding Cambodia and Laos) increased by an annual average of 4% during the period 1990–2000. Singapore has become the world's third largest refining centre (after Rotterdam and Houston), with a capacity of more than 1m. b/d. The Republic of Korea, Indonesia and Thailand have been expanding their refinery capacity to enable them to export refined products. Japan has been increasing its primary refining capacity, in an effort to reduce its reliance on imports, and in 2001 Viet Nam was constructing a refinery with a capacity of some 140,000 b/d in Quang Ngai province in order to lessen its import dependence. About 2m. b/d of new refinery capacity came on stream during 1996–98 from the expansion of existing facilities and the opening of new refinery plants in the Philippines, Thailand, the Republic of Korea, Malaysia, India, Taiwan and the People's Republic of China.

In 1993 the People's Republic of China became, for the first time in 30 years, a net importer of crude petroleum and petroleum products. China's petroleum import requirements have subsequently increased, and have been forecast to reach 100m. tons annually by 2010 (compared with an estimated 33m. tons in 1997), unless domestic production can be substantially expanded. In the late 1990s its refineries were operating at less than 80% of full capacity, and more than 100 small refineries were closed down. The development of refining capacity is currently focused on the improvment of existing facilities rather than the construction of new ones. In particular, China needs to expand its capacity for refining heavy Middle Eastern crude petroleums, which will be imported in greater quantities in future. In the mid-1990s the Far East and Australasia region relied upon imports from the Middle East for about 71% of its crude petroleum requirements. The region's total imports of petroleum were expected to exceed 9m. b/d in the late 1990s, and these requirements were forecast to rise to 19m. b/d by 2010, of which the Middle East was projected to account for about 90%. Regional demand for LNG is also advancing rapidly. It has been forecast that increasing requirements for electricity use, and delays in the development of nuclear and coal-fired power plants, could raise levels of Far East demand to 90m. tons of LNG annually by the year 2010, compared with consumption of 41.9m. tons in 1991.

International petroleum prices are strongly influenced by the Organization of the Petroleum Exporting Countries (OPEC), founded in 1960 to co-ordinate the production and marketing policies of those countries whose main source of export earnings is petroleum. In 2002 OPEC had 11 members, of which Indonesia was the sole participant in the Far East and Australasia.

Export Price Index for Crude Petroleum (base: 1980 = 100)

	Average	Highest month(s)	Lowest month(s)
1990	68		
1995	54		
1999	54	77 (Dec.)	31 (Feb.)
2000	86	96 (Sept.)	73 (April, Dec.)
2001	72	82 (May)	55 (Nov., Dec.)

The average price of crude petroleum was about US $20 per barrel in 1992, declined to only about US $14 in late 1993, and recovered to more than US $18 in mid-1994. Thereafter, international petroleum prices remained relatively stable until the early months of 1995. The price per barrel reached about US $20 again in April and May 1995, but eased to US $17 later in the year. In April 1996 the London price of the standard grade of North Sea petroleum for short-term delivery rose to more than US $23 per barrel, following reports that stocks of petroleum in Western industrialized countries were at their lowest levels for 19 years. After another fall, the price of North Sea petroleum rose in October to more than US $25 per barrel, its highest level for more than five years. The price per barrel was generally in the range of US $22–$24 for the remainder of the year.

Petroleum traded at US $24–$25 per barrel in January 1997, but the short-term quotation for the standard North Sea grade fell to less than US $17 in June. The price increased to more than US $21 per barrel in October, in response to increased tension in the Persian (Arabian) Gulf region. However, the threat of an immediate conflict in the region subsided, and petroleum prices eased. The market was also weakened by an OPEC decision, in November, to raise the upper limit on members' production quotas, and by the severe financial and economic problems affecting many countries in eastern Asia. By the end of the year the price for North Sea petroleum had again been reduced to less than US $17 per barrel.

Petroleum prices declined further in January 1998, with the standard North Sea grade trading at less than US $15 per barrel. Later in the month the price recovered to about US $16.5 per barrel, but in March some grades of petroleum were trading at less than US $13. Later that month three of the leading exporting countries—Saudi Arabia, Venezuela and Mexico (not an OPEC member)—agreed to reduce petroleum production, in an attempt to revive prices. In response, the price of North Sea petroleum advanced to about US $15.5 per barrel. Following endorsement of the three countries' initiative by OPEC, however, there was widespread doubt that the proposals would be sufficient to have a sustained impact on prices, in view of the existence of large stocks of petroleum. Under the plan, OPEC members and five other countries (including Mexico and Norway) agreed to reduce their petroleum output between 1 April and the end of the year. The proposed reductions totalled about 1.5m. b/d (2% of world production), with Saudi Arabia making the greatest contribution (300,000 b/d). In early June, having failed to make a significant impact on international prices, the three countries that had agreed in March to restrict their production of petroleum announced further reduction in output, effective from 1 July. However, petroleum prices continued to be depressed, and in mid-June some grades sold for less than US $12 per barrel. A new agreement between OPEC and other producers, concluded later that month, envisaged further reductions in output, totalling more than 1m. b/d, but this attempt to stimulate a rise in petroleum prices had little effect. The price on world markets was generally in the range of US $12–$14 per barrel over the period July–October. Subsequently there was further downward pressure on petroleum prices, and in December the London quotation for the standard North Sea grade was below US $10 per barrel for the first time since the introduction of the contract in 1986. For 1998 as a whole, the average price of North Sea petroleum was US $13.37 per barrel, more than 30% less than in 1997 and the lowest annual level since 1976. In real terms (i.e. taking inflation into account), international prices for crude petroleum in late 1998 were at their lowest level since the 1920s.

During the early months of 1999 there was a steady recovery in the petroleum market. In March five leading producers (including Mexico) announced plans to reduce further their combined output by about 2m. b/d. Later that month an OPEC meeting agreed reductions in members' quotas totalling 1.7m. b/d (including 585,000 b/d for Saudi Arabia), to operate for 12 months from 1 April. The new quotas represented a 7% decrease from the previous levels (applicable from July 1998). At the same time, four non-members agreed voluntary cuts in production, bringing total proposed reductions in output to about 2.1m. b/d. In May the London price of North Sea petroleum rose to about US $17 per barrel. After easing somewhat, the price advanced again, reaching more than US $20 per barrel in August. The upward trend continued, and in late September the price of North Sea petroleum (for November delivery) was just above US $24 per barrel. After easing somewhat, prices rose again in November, when North Sea petroleum (for delivery in January 2000) was traded at more than US $25 per barrel. The surge in prices followed indications that, in contrast to 1998, the previously agreed limits on output were, to a large extent, being implemented by producers and thus having an effect on stock levels. Surveys found that the rate of compliance among the 10 OPEC countries participating in the scheme to restrict production was 87% in June and July 1999, although it fell to 83% in October.

International prices for crude petroleum rose steadily during the opening weeks of 2000, with OPEC restrictions continuing to operate and stocks declining in industrial countries. In early March the London price for North Sea petroleum exceeded US $31.5 per barrel, but later in the month nine OPEC members agreed to restore production quotas to pre-March 1999 levels from 1 April 2000, representing a combined increase of about 1.7m. b/d. The London petroleum price fell in April to less than US $22 per barrel, but the rise in OPEC production was insufficient to increase significantly the stocks held by major consuming countries. In June the price of North Sea petroleum rose to about US $31.5 per barrel again, but later that month OPEC ministers agreed to a further rise in quotas (totalling about 700,000 b/d) from 1 July. By the end of July the North Sea petroleum price was below US $27 per barrel, but in mid-August it rose to more than US $32 for the first time since 1990 (when prices had surged in response to the Iraqi invasion of Kuwait). In New York in the same month, meanwhile, the September contract for light crude traded at a new record level of US $33 per barrel at one point. The surge in oil prices in August was attributed to continued fears regarding supply levels in coming months, especially in view of data showing US inventories to be at their lowest level for 24 years, and of indications by both Saudi Arabia and Venezuela that OPEC would not act to raise production before September. Deliberate attempts to raise the price of the expiring London September contract were an additional factor.

In early September 2000 the London price of North Sea petroleum for October delivery climbed to a new 10-year high of US $34.55, reflecting the view that any production increase that OPEC might decide to implement would be insufficient to prevent tight supplies later in the year. In New York, meanwhile, the price of light crude for October delivery rose beyond the US $35 per barrel mark. This latest bout of price volatility reflected the imminence of an OPEC meeting, at which Saudi Arabia was expected to seek an agreement to raise the Organization's production by at least 700,000 b/d in order to stabilize the market. In the event, OPEC decided to increase production by 800,000 b/d, with effect from 1 October, causing prices in both

London and New York to ease. This relaxation was short-lived, however. Just over a week after OPEC's decision was announced the price of the New York October contract for light crude closed at US $36.88 per barrel, in response to concerns over tension in the Persian (Arabian) Gulf area between Iraq and Kuwait. The same contract had at one point risen above US $37 per barrel, its highest level for 10 years. These latest increases prompted OPEC representatives to deliver assurances that production would be raised further in order to curb price levels regarded as economically damaging in the USA and other consumer countries. Towards the end of September the London price of North Sea petroleum for November delivery fell below US $30 per barrel for the first time in a month, in response to the decision of the USA to release petroleum from its strategic reserve in order to depress prices.

In the first week of October 2000, however, the price of the November contract for both North Sea petroleum traded in London and New York light crude had stabilized at around US $30 per barrel, anxiety over political tension in the Middle East preventing the more marked decline that had been anticipated. This factor exerted stronger upward pressure during the following week, when the London price of North Sea petroleum for November delivery rose above US $35 per barrel for the first time since 1990. In early November 2000 crude oil continued to trade at more than US $30 per barrel in both London and New York, despite the announcement by OPEC of a further increase in production, this time of 500,000 b/d, and a lessening of political tension in the Middle East. Prices were volatile throughout November, with those of both London and New York contracts for January delivery remaining in excess of US $30 per barrel at the end of the month.

During the first week of December 2000 the price of the January 'futures' contract in both London and New York declined substantially, in response, mainly, to an unresolved dispute between the UN and Iraq over the pricing of Iraqi oil. On 8 December the closing London price of North Sea petroleum for January delivery was US $26.56 per barrel, while the equivalent New York price for light crude was US $28.44. Trading during the second week of December was characterized by further declines, the London price of North Sea petroleum for January delivery falling below US $25 per barrel at one point. Analysts noted that prices had fallen by some 20% since mid-November, and OPEC representatives indicated that the Organization might decide to cut production in January 2001 if prices fell below its preferred trading range of US $22–$28 per barrel. At US $23.51 per barrel on 14 December, the price of the OPEC 'basket' of crudes was at its lowest level since May. During the third week of December the price of the OPEC 'basket' of crudes declined further, to US $21.64 per barrel. Overall, during December, the price of crudes traded in both London and New York declined by some US $10 per barrel, and remained subject to pressure at the end of the month.

Continued expectations that OPEC would decide to reduce production later in the month caused 'futures' prices to strengthen in the first week of January 2001. The London price of North Sea petroleum for February delivery closed at US $25.18 on 5 January, while the corresponding price for light crude traded in New York was US $27.95. Prices remained firm in the second week of January, again in anticipation of a decision by OPEC to reduce production. Paradoxically, prices fell immediately after OPEC's decision to reduce production by 1.5m. b/d was announced on 17 January. However, it was widely recognized that the reduction had been factored into markets by that time.

Oil prices rose significantly at the beginning of February 2001, although the gains were attributed mainly to speculative purchases rather than to any fundamental changes in market conditions. On 2 February the London price of North Sea petroleum for March delivery closed at US $29.19 per barrel, while the corresponding price for light crude traded in New York was US $31.19. On 8 February prices rose to their highest levels for two months, the London price for North Sea petroleum for March delivery exceeding US $30 per barrel at one point. The upward movement came in response to a forecast, issued by the US Energy Information Administration (EIA), that the 'spot' price for West Texas Intermediate (the US 'marker' crude) would average close to US $30 per barrel throughout 2001. During the remainder of the month prices in both London and New York remained largely without direction.

During the early part of March 2001 oil prices in both London and New York drifted downwards while it remained unclear whether OPEC would decide to implement a further cut in production, and what the effect of such a reduction might be. On 9 March the London price of North Sea petroleum for April delivery was US $26.33 per barrel, while the corresponding price for light crude traded in New York was US $28.01 per barrel. By late March prices in both London and New York had declined further, the London price of North Sea petroleum for May delivery closing near to US $24.82 per barrel on 30 March, while the corresponding price for New York light crude was US $26.35.

During the first week of April 2001 crude oil prices on both sides of the Atlantic strengthened in response to fears of a gasoline shortage in the USA later in the year. On 6 April the London price of North Sea petroleum for May delivery was US $25.17 per barrel, while New York light crude for delivery in May closed at US $27.06. Strong demand for crude oil by US gasoline refiners was the strongest influence on markets throughout April as gasoline 'futures' rose markedly. Towards the end of April the price of the New York contract for gasoline for May delivery rose to the equivalent of US $1.115 per gallon, higher than the previous record price recorded in August 1990. Fears of a shortage of gasoline supplies in the USA remained the key influence on oil markets in early May 2001, with 'futures' prices rising in response to successive record prices for gasoline 'futures'. On 4 May 2001 the London price of North Sea petroleum for June delivery was US $28.19 per barrel, while that of the corresponding contract for light crude traded in New York closed at US $28.36. Prices were prevented from rising further during the week ending 4 May by the report of an unexpected increase in US inventories of crude oil. A further check came in the following week, when the International Energy Agency (IEA) reduced its forecast of world growth in demand for crude oil by 300,000 b/d to 1.02m. b/d. On 18 May, however, demand for crude oil by gasoline refiners raised the price of New York crude for June delivery to its highest level for three months, while the price of the July contract rose above US $30 per barrel. On 5 June, at an extraordinary conference held in Vienna, Austria, OPEC voted to defer a possible adjustment of its production level for one month, noting that stocks of both crude oil and products were at a satisfactory level, the market in balance and that the year-to-date average of the OPEC reference 'basket' of crudes had been US $24.8 per barrel (i.e. within the trading range of US $22–$28 per barrel targeted by the Organization). OPEC nevertheless decided to hold a further extraordinary conference in early July in order to take account of future developments. At that meeting OPEC oil ministers once again opted to maintain production at the prevailing level, emphasizing that they would continue to monitor the market and take further measures, if deemed necessary, to maintain prices within the Organization's preferred trading range. The conference appealed to other oil exporters to continue to collaborate with OPEC in order to minimize price volatility and safeguard stability. Towards the end of the month, as prices declined steadily towards (and briefly below) US $23 per barrel, the Secretary-General of OPEC, Dr Ali Rodríguez Araque, indicated that he was consulting OPEC ministers regarding the possibility of holding a further extraordinary conference early in August-ahead of the next ordinary OPEC meeting scheduled for September. Two days later, on 25 July, OPEC agreed to reduce production by a further 1m. b/d, to 23.2m. b/d, with effect from 1 September; the Organization reiterated that it was retaining the option to convene an extraordinary meeting if the market warranted it (this latest reduction, which had been agreed without a full meeting of OPEC, had been ratified by oil ministers by telephone). The Organization again expressed confidence that its action in reducing output would be matched by non-OPEC producing/exporting countries, and recognized in particular Mexico's support for its efforts. While there was general agreement that the production cut would reduce inventories, the consensus remained that demand would also decline in view of the prevailing world economic outlook. The extent of this decline remained the subject of much speculation, with a statement by Rodríguez in mid-July, affirming that growth in demand would average 850,000 b/d in 2001, seeking to counter a forecast by the IEA of demand growth averaging 450,000 b/d. A decline of 1.1% in US inventories of crude oil, reported by the American Petroleum Institute (API) in late July 2001, apparently indicated that US demand was resisting, for the time being, a deceleration in economic growth, and was cited as the main reason for a recovery in the price of Brent blend North Sea petroleum, to US $24.97 per barrel, on 1 August. A further decline of the same order, reported on 7 August, raised the price of Brent to US $27.94 per barrel, and that of the OPEC 'basket' of crudes to US $24.99 per barrel. Throughout most of the remainder of August declining US inventories of both crude and refined products appeared to suggest a strength of demand that belied pessimistic assessments of US (and global) economic prospects in the near term, combining with anticipation of the reduction of OPEC production by 1m. b/d from 1 September, to support the price of the Brent reference blend and the OPEC 'basket' of crudes.

Immediately following the suicide attacks carried out against US targets in New York and Washington, DC, on 11 September 2001, as the price of Brent blend North Sea petroleum rose above US $30 per barrel, OPEC's Secretary-General was swift to emphasize the Organization's commitment to 'strengthening market stability and ensuring that sufficient supplies are available to satisfy market needs', by utilizing its spare capacity, if necessary. However, there was virtual unanimity among commentators, following the attacks, that their effect would be to worsen the prospects of the global economy, if not plunge it into recession, causing a considerable decline in demand for oil. By mid-October 2001 the price of the OPEC 'basket' of crudes had remained below US $22 per barrel, the minimum price the Organization's market management strategy was designed to sustain, since late September, and it was clear that, at the risk of adding to recessionary pressures, OPEC would have to implement a further cut in production if it was to bring the price back into its preferred trading range. In late October Venezuela, Iran, Saudi Arabia, the UAE and non-OPEC Oman all declared themselves in favour of a further cut in production. However, diplomacy undertaken by President Hugo Chávez Frías of Venezuela and Saudi Arabia's Minister of Petroleum and Mineral Resources, Ali ibn Ibrahim an-Nuaimi, had apparently made no progress in achieving its objective of persuading key non-OPEC producers Mexico, Norway and Russia to support the Organization's management strategy.

In the first week of November 2001 the price of Brent blend North Sea petroleum fell to fractionally above US $19 per barrel, while that of OPEC's 'basket' of crudes declined to US $17.56 per barrel. In Vienna, on 14 November, an extraordinary meeting of the OPEC conference observed that 'as a result of the global economic slowdown and the aftermath of the tragic events of 11 September 2001, in order to achieve a balance in the oil market, it will be necessary to reduce the supply from all oil producers by a further 2m. b/d, bringing the total reduction in oil supply to 5.5m. b/d from the levels of January 2001, including the 3.5m. b/d reduction already effected by OPEC this year. In this connection, and reiterating its call on other oil exporters to co-operate so as to minimize price volatility and ensure market stability, the Conference decided to reduce an additional volume of 1.5m. b/d, effective 1 January 2002, subject to a firm commitment from non-OPEC oil producers to cut their production by a volume of 500,000 b/d simultaneously'. The meeting acknowledged the positive response of Mexico and Oman, to OPEC's efforts to balance the market. However, it was widely recognized that the success of a collaboration of the kind envisaged depended on the co-operation of Russia. Prior to the extraordinary conference held in November, Russia had indicated that it would be willing to reduce its production, estimated at more than 7m. b/d, by no more than 30,000 b/d, far less than would be necessary for OPEC's strategy to be effective. It was not until early December that Russia's Prime Minister announced the country's commitment to reducing its exports of crude by up to 150,000 b/d, and it was uncertain, in any case, whether a reduction of that magnitude could be enforced, owing to the Russian Government's lack of control over Russia's oil industry.

On 18 December 2001 the price of the OPEC 'basket' of crudes fell to US $16.62 per barrel. Thereafter, in December, however, the price recovered, in response to commitments by major non-OPEC producers to collaborate with the Organization by reducing either output or exports. On 28 December, at a consultative meeting of the OPEC conference, convened in Cairo, Egypt, OPEC confirmed its decision to implement a reduction of 1.5m. b/d in its overall production from 1 January 2002, having received assurances that Angola, Mexico, Norway, Oman and Russia would reduce their output, or, in the case of Russia, exports, of crude petroleum by a total of 462,500 b/d. BP's *Statistical Review of World Energy 2002* noted that, for the whole of 2001, the price of Brent blend North Sea petroleum had averaged US $24.77 per barrel. The average price of the reference blend was substantially less than US $20 per barrel in October–December 2001, however. In 2001, for the first time since 1993, consumption of oil world-wide declined, albeit marginally.

In January 2002 the decline in the price of the OPEC 'basket' of crudes was halted for the first time since the suicide attacks in September 2001. According to the Organization's own data, the 'basket' price rose by 4.6% in January 2002, compared with December 2001, but was 24% lower when considered on a year-on-year basis. The price of Brent blend North Sea petroleum, meanwhile, averaged US $19.48 per barrel in January. Reviewing the state of the market in January 2002, OPEC noted that it was still too early to assess the effectiveness of the reduction in output and exports that had begun on 1 January. The recovery in the average price of the OPEC 'basket' had been uneven throughout the month. Low demand, as indicated by data published by the US Department of Energy's Energy Information Administration (EIA) and the API, recording rises in US crude inventories, and either rises or lower-than-expected declines in inventories of distillate products, combined, in the second week of January with uncertainty regarding Russia's commitment to reducing its exports by 150,000 b/d (as it had pledged to do) to exert pressure on prices. During the third week of January, however, prices were supported, according to OPEC, by the strength of product prices, and by the USA's decision to add 22m. barrels of crude to its Strategic Petroleum Reserve. Among other factors, apparently good adherence by OPEC members to the revised quotas announced in December 2001 helped to sustain the upward trend in the final week of January 2002.

In February 2002 the average price of the OPEC 'basket' of crudes rose for the second consecutive month, recording an increase of 3.1% compared with January. As OPEC noted in its review of crude price movements in February, however, the average price of the 'basket' was 25.7% lower when considered on a year-on-year basis. The price of the OPEC 'basket' rose steadily during the first two weeks of February, supported, among other factors, by reports of an explosion at oil-gathering facilities in Kuwait that was initially expected to remove some 600,000 b/d from the market; and by increased political tension between the USA and Iraq. In the third week of February the OPEC 'basket' price moved up and down, but, overall, was weaker compared with the previous week. Continued doubts over Russia's commitment to reducing its exports was one factor that exerted downward pressure on prices. In the final week of the month prices strengthened considerably as a result of the interplay between reportedly higher product inventories, renewed political tension between the West and Iraq, and a dispute between the Venezuelan Government and employees of Petróleos de Venezuela.

In early March 2002 a meeting took place between a delegation of senior OPEC representatives and Russian government and energy officials. OPEC's objective at the meeting was to persuade Russia to continue to limit its exports of crude to 150,000 b/d during the second quarter of 2002. OPEC regarded the continued limitation of Russia exports as imperative if market stability was to be maintained at a time of seasonally weak markets for oil. Russia's initial commitment to reduce its exports, however, applied only to the first quarter of 2002, with any continuation of the restriction subject to a review of market conditions. Norway had, by this time, already agreed to continue to restrict its production of crude to 150,000 b/d during April-June 2002. Moreover, it was clear in March that the market stability measures undertaken since the beginning of the year had been successful. The price of the OPEC 'basket' of crudes rose by 20% in March, compared with the previous month, although it was 5% lower when considered on a year-on-year basis. As OPEC noted, in its review of markets for crude in March, prices rose consistently throughout the month. Evidence of economic recovery in the USA was a positive factor in early March-data published by the API indicated declining US inventories of gasoline and distillate products-as was the apparent likelihood of Russia agreeing to carry over into the second quarter the restriction applied to its exports of crude. In the second week of March an intensification of the conflict between Israel and the Palestinians, and OPEC's announcement that it would maintain production at the prevailing level until the end of June at least, were additional factors that supported prices. In the third week of March prices rose above US $25 per barrel, owing, according to OPEC, to technical factors that were subsequently cancelled out by profit-taking. The upward movement continued towards the end of March, when positive inventory data combined with optimism about the sustainability of economic recovery in the USA to support prices.

From late March 2002 the escalating conflict between Israel and the Palestinians was cited as a key factor supporting crude prices. On 1 April, for the first time since 11 September 2001, the price of the OPEC 'basket' of crudes rose above US $25 per barrel. On 8 April Iraq added to the increased political tension in the Middle East by suspending its exports of crude for a period of 30 days in response to attacks by Israeli armed forces against Palestinian targets in the West Bank. Although Iraq's action was of little real consequence for crude markets, since other producers could easily compensate for the loss of its exports if necessary, it came at a time when a number of countries, including Iraq itself, Iran and Libya, had expressed their support for an embargo to be placed on the supply of oil by OPEC, in support of the Palestinian struggle against Israeli occupation. It was generally acknowledged in April that prices were inflated by a so-called war premium of some US $4–$6 per barrel, without which they would decline towards the lower end of OPEC's preferred trading range. Political upheaval in Venezuela also lent a degree of volatility to prices in mid-April, when the brief removal of President Chávez from power caused them to decline sharply. Following Chávez's reinstatement as President, the key market influence for the remainder of the month was the perception, supported by a reported decline in US inventories of crude, that demand for oil was growing in response to improved economic conditions in the USA.

A combination of apparently stronger US demand and tighter supplies was regarded as the most significant determinant of the direction of markets for crude in early May 2002. On 7 May the API announced that US inventories of crude had declined by some 4.5m. barrels in the week to 3 May, and on the day of the announcement the price of Brent blend North Sea petroleum reached US $27.14 per barrel, an increase of more than $1 per barrel compared with the previous week. Among other factors contributing to the tightening of supplies at this time was OPEC's apparent decision not to compensate for the 30-day suspension of Iraqi exports. In the second week of May prices declined somewhat in response to data published by the US Department of Energy that indicated an increase in US inventories of crude. Towards the end of the month prices weakened again, in response to the publication of data that appeared to cast doubt on the strength of the US economic recovery.

Prices remained under pressure at the beginning of June 2002, owing to the publication of data indicating a further, unexpected increase in US inventories of crude and of distillate products in late May. Iraqi exports had also risen substantially in late May and early June. Most commentators appeared to agree with OPEC, representatives of whose members referred to a balanced market for crude in statements released early in the month, and indicated that OPEC would not alter its production quotas at its forthcoming extraordinary ministerial conference. In its assessment of the oil market in June, the IEA noted that geopolitical factors (i.e. violence in the Middle East) were now perceived as less of a risk to supplies of crude and predicted that prices would continue to weaken. US inventories of crude and gasoline were reported to have declined slightly in the first week of June. Crude stocks fell again during the second week of June, but this decline was balanced by substantial increases in inventories of gasoline and distillate products, indicating the ongoing weakness of economic recovery in the USA. At an extraordinary ministerial conference, held in Vienna on 26 June, OPEC, as expected, agreed to maintain production at the prevailing level until the end of September 2002. The Organization noted that its 'reduction measures during 2001 and 2002, supported by similar measures from some non-OPEC producers over the first half of the year, had restored relative market balance'. At the same time, OPEC observed that 'the relative strength in current market prices is partially a reflection of the prevailing political situation rather than solely the consequence of market fundamentals', and undertook to continue carefully to monitor market conditions and to take further action, if necessary, to maintain market stability.

Rice *(Oryza sativa)*

Rice is the staple food in most of the countries of monsoon Asia, and about 90% of the total world area under rice lies within the region. Rice is the main food crop because it is well suited to Asian climatic conditions, producing high yields of a nutritious grain where other cereal crops will not readily grow. Wet rice cultivation is typically associated with the alluvial lowlands of monsoon Asia, but rice will tolerate a wide range of geographic, climatic and ecological conditions and is even grown under upland cultivation.

There are two cultivated species of rice, *Oryza sativa* and *O. glaberrima*. *O. sativa*, which is native to tropical Asia, is widely grown in tropical and semi-tropical areas, while the cultivation of *O. glaberrima* is limited to the high rainfall zone of West Africa. In Asia and Africa, unmilled rice is referred to as 'paddy', but 'rough' rice is the common appellation in the West. After removal of the outer husk, it is called 'brown' rice. After the grain is milled to remove the bran layers, it is described as 'milled' rice. As rice loses 30%–40% of its weight in the milling process, most rice is traded in the milled form, to minimize shipping expenses.

Rice is an annual grass belonging to the same family as (and having many similar characteristics to) small grains such as wheat, oats, rye and barley. It is principally the semi-aquatic nature of rice that distinguishes it from other grain species, and this is an important factor in determining its place of origin, its dominant role in monsoon Asia and its extension to other environments. Rice varieties may broadly be classified into two main groups: *indica* and *japonica*. (There is also an intermediate or *java* type, cultivated in parts of Indonesia.) However, many rice varieties currently being grown are improved crosses of *indica* and *japonica* rices. The *indica* group, prevalent in South

Production of Paddy Rice ('000 metric tons)

	2000	2001*
World total	600,638	592,831
Far East	531,831	525,080
Oceania	1,772	1,261
Leading regional producers		
Bangladesh	37,442	39,112
Cambodia	4,026	4,099
China, People's Repub.	187,908	179,665†
India	129,444	131,900†
Indonesia	51,898	50,096
Japan	11,863	11,320
Korea, Dem. People's Repub.	1,690	2,060
Korea, Repub.	7,125	7,316
Malaysia	2,195†	2,215†
Myanmar	21,324	20,600†
Nepal	4,030	4,216
Pakistan	7,205	6,750†
Philippines	12,389	12,955
Sri Lanka	2,859	2,868†
Taiwan	1,906	1,850‡
Thailand	25,608	25,20†
Viet Nam	32,530	31,925
Other leading producers		
Brazil	11,090	10,207
Egypt	6,000	5,997‡
Nigeria	3,298	3,298‡
USA	8,658	9,664

* Provisional figures.
† Unofficial figure.
‡ FAO estimate.

and South-East Asia, and covering a high proportion of the total rice area of Asia, has been associated with low yields and primitive production techniques. The *japonica* types (which predominate in East Asia), while not inherently more productive than the *indica* types, are more responsive to natural and artificial fertilizers and give higher average yields.

Underlying the low average rice yields in South and South-East Asia (including India, Bangladesh, Sri Lanka, Laos, Cambodia, Viet Nam and Thailand), compared with those in East Asia (the People's Republic of China, the Koreas, Japan and Taiwan), are the lack of modern varieties which are adapted to local conditions, and the shortage of associated technology, including fertilizers and pesticides, and of adequate and timely supplies of water. Conventional rice varieties respond to increased fertilizer usage by producing more leaf and stalk instead of grain, causing the plant to lodge (fall over), decreasing net yields.

During the 1960s the International Rice Research Institute (IRRI), based in the Philippines, developed a series of stiff-stemmed, semi-dwarf varieties, bearing upright leaves, that respond positively to high rates of fertilizer application and other improved cultural practices. These improved varieties may yield as much as 10 tons of paddy rice per ha, while old varieties may yield less than 1 ton per ha. Most of the newly-developed varieties are resistant to insect pests, diseases and some soil problems, although much work remains to be done in the selection of resistant varieties. Agronomists at the IRRI, and in national programmes, are continually developing varieties that will tolerate drought, flood, deep water and sub-optimum temperatures, and high-yielding varieties (HYVs) which are designed for areas without costly irrigation or where water is scarce. Farmers cultivating these varieties may expect a reduced risk of crop failures, and are more likely to invest in other production inputs. In the late 1990s the IRRI was developing new HYVs that, it believed, could increase harvest yields by 20%–30% by 2003. It was forecast by the IRRI in 1997 that annual world rice production would have to advance by 70% by 2025 in order to keep pace with current rates of population growth.

China developed its own high-yielding semi-dwarf varieties in the late 1950s, and these were widely disseminated in the country by the mid-1960s, prior to the release of the first IRRI varieties. Of recent interest has been the development in Hunan Province of a true hybrid rice which increases yields by as much as 20%. In 1999 it was reported that a new HYV, which could increase yields by 30%, had been developed in China. Hybrid varieties are planted on more than 10m. ha throughout southern China. A major limitation of the hybrids (apart from the high cost of seed production) is their rather long maturation period, which limits their suitability for intensive cropping patterns. The area under rice in China declined by 2.3m. ha during 1991–95 (owing to factory construction, road construction and urban development, which necessitated the use of land previously used for rice cultivation). However, volume output has been assisted by incentives for growers, such as the reduction of required quotas and permission for families and individuals to conduct business with production units. Although China was exporting more than 1m. tons of rice annually in the late 1980s, shortcomings in the country's internal transport structure necessitated imports, mainly from Thailand, of more than 200,000 tons per year. Serious floods in China in 1998 reduced rice production in that year by some 2m. tons, necessitating a substantial increase in rice imports. In 2000, as the result of a severe drought, China's rice production declined by 5.3%, to about 188m. tons. In 2001 China's output of rice was estimated by FAO to have declined again, by 4.4%, to about 180m. tons.

Export Price Index for Rice (base: 1980 = 100)

	Average	Highest month(s)	Lowest month(s)
1990	74		
1995	84		
1999	93	104 (Jan.)	80 (Oct.–Dec.)
2000	74	82 (Jan., Feb.)	67 (Dec.)
2001	62	66 (Jan., Feb.)	59 (Nov., Dec.)

The world's leading exporter of rice in recent years has been Thailand. The average export price of Thai milled white rice increased from US $320.8 per metric ton in 1995 to US $338.1 per ton in 1996, but declined to US $302.5 in 1997. The price averaged US $305.4 per ton in 1998, but subsequently slumped: to US $249.0 in 1999, US $203.7 in 2000, and US $172.7 in 2001. On a monthly basis, the average fell from US $301.7 per ton in January 1999 to only US $235.5 in April. The price recovered to US $255.8 per ton in July, but declined to US $217.0 in October. It rose to US $247.0 per ton in January 2000, but fell to only US $198.8 in May and to US $197.9 in June. The decrease in prices was partly attributable to the plentiful supply of rice, with abundant stocks available, particularly in China and India. By April 2002 the average export price of Thai milled white rice had recovered somewhat, to US $189.5 per ton. In May FAO reported that international rice prices displayed unusual strength, reflecting, among other factors, an anticipated tightening of the availability of supplies from Pakistan and Viet Nam.

Thailand became the world's leading rice exporter in 1981, and rice has remained the country's principal agricultural export commodity, accounting for 3.3% of its export income in 1999. Owing to the depressed state of the world rice market since the early 1980s and the achievement of self-sufficiency by a number of Asian countries, Thailand increased its exports of rice largely at the expense of the USA. However, the decision by the USA to include rice in its Food Security Act, which came into operation in 1986 (making US-grown rice eligible for subsidized export credits), significantly affected the level of sales from Asian rice producers by undercutting the price of their exports. During the late 1980s, however, Thailand substantially expanded sales of its high quality rice to the European Community (now the European Union (EU)), Russia, South Africa, Saudi Arabia and Iran. Thailand's dominance in the world rice market, in which it accounted for about 6.8m. tons in 1999 and 6.1m. tons in 2000, according to FAO, has come under increasing pressure in recent years from India and Viet Nam. In 2001, according to the US Department of Agriculture (USDA), Thailand's exports of rice rose to a record level of 7.5m. tons in 2001.

India, whose rice production has increased markedly since the late 1980s, emerged as a major exporter during 1993–95, when the relaxation of government restrictions led to a rise in export sales from 767,681 tons in 1993 to 4.9m. tons in 1995. However, the volume of India's exports is subject to the maintenance of rice stocks for domestic use at a statutory minimum of 10m. tons. In 1998, owing to poor crops in a number of importing countries, India's rice exports approached 5m. tons. The return of more favourable growing conditions in 1999 had an adverse effect on this trade, particularly with Bangladesh, which is normally a substantial importer of Indian rice. Export sales declined to an estimated 1.9m. tons in that year, and again, in 2000, to 1.5m. tons, according to FAO. In 2001, according to the USDA, India exported 1.6m. tons of rice. In 2002 FAO has forecast that India will resume the role of a major supplier to the international rice market, reporting that unprecedentedly high stocks have exerted pressure on the government to subsidize foreign sales. Viet Nam's harvests have been greatly stimulated by the government's recent willingness to grant long-term land tenure to farmers. In 1989 Viet Nam became the world's third largest rice exporter, after Thailand and the USA, and in that year sales by Viet Nam of low-grade rice at prices substantially below those of Thai exporters prompted the Thai Government to introduce a programme of domestic rice subsidies. Vietnamese rice exports, which totalled 1.6m. tons in 1990, advanced to almost 2m. tons in 1992. In 1993/94 the Government of Viet Nam temporarily suspended rice exports, following serious floods in the country's major rice-growing area. These restrictions, however, were lifted in April 1995, and exports for that year, at about 2m. tons, positioned Viet Nam as the world's fourth largest exporter of rice, after the USA, India and Thailand. In 1996 exports of rice provided 16.7% of Viet Nam's foreign revenue, and in 1997 the country became, after Thailand, the world's second largest exporter of rice. In early 1998, however, the Vietnamese Government imposed temporary controls on rice export volumes in order to maintain the security of domestic supplies. Nevertheless, exports for the full year were, at 3.7m. tons, more than 4% higher than those of the previous year, and, in 1999, rose to a record level of 4.5m. tons, contributing 8.9% of Viet Nam's total export earnings. In 2000, however, Viet Nam's exports of rice declined by more than 20%, to only 3.5m. tons. According to an FAO forecast, the Vietnamese rice export sector is likely to benefit, in 2002, from an expansion of the international rice market. Exports of rice have, in recent years, constituted a key component of the economy of Myanmar, accounting for 10.9% of export revenue in 1995/96. In 1998/99, however, this proportion fell to only 2.4%. The total area under paddy rice in 1995/96 was estimated at 6.2m. ha, accounting for 47.5% of all land under cultivation. Production advanced strongly during the 1990s, largely as a result of the increased use of HYVs. Export growth, however, has been inhibited by the relatively low quality of Myanmar's rice in relation to that of competitors such as Thailand, and to the enforced curtailment of exports by the Myanmar Government in order to avert domestic shortages. Myanmar's exports of rice totalled only 28,000 tons in 1997, but rose to more than 100,000 tons in 1998. In 1999 exports declined substantially, to only about 60,000 tons, but rose in 2000 to about 142,000 tons.In view of the favourable outlook for international trade in rice, Myanmar's exports of rice were forecast by FAO to increase in 2002.

Indonesia, the region's third largest rice producer, sustained a fairly sharp fall in output, to about 49m. metric tons, during 1997/98, following a severe drought brought about by the climatic phenomenon known as 'El Niño'. Production remained at about 49m. tons in 1998/99. The country's rice imports, principally from Thailand and Viet Nam, accordingly rose from about 350,000 tons in 1997 to about 2.9m. tons in 1998. They increased further, approaching 5m. tons, in 1999, but declined in 2000 to only 1.4m. tons. Indonesia, which maintained self-sufficiency in rice during 1984–93, experienced a rapid advance in domestic rice requirements during the 1990s, and became the world's principal rice importer. The country is expected to remain a net importer of rice for the foreseeable future. In recent years Australia has emerged as a significant exporter of rice, especially to Japan, although its trade is on a much smaller scale than the major exporters of the Far East. In 2001 Australia's exports of rice totalled 613,000 metric tons, according to the USDA, compared with 617,000 tons in 2000, and 667,000 tons in 1999. World trade in rice (usually in a milled or semi-milled form), which averaged about about 20m. metric tons annually in the mid-1990s, fell from 28.8m. tons in 1998 to 25.2m. tons in 1999 and to only 23.2m. tons in 2000. According to FAO predictions, international trade in rice will total 24.6m. tons in 2002, owing, mainly, to increased imports by Indonesia, China and, on a smaller scale, Iran. The bulk of rice production is consumed in the producing countries, and international trade generally accounts for less than 5% of world output. Governments are the principal traders, and five countries dominate the export market in most years: Thailand, Viet Nam, the USA, China and India. Middle Eastern and African countries have traditionally been the most important markets for exports of rice from the Far East. Japan, a substantial producer of rice, has customarily enforced a strict policy of self-sufficiency, and domestic production receives substantial government subsidies. The Government's total prohibition on commercial imports of rice, which was strongly challenged by leading exporters (notably the USA), was temporarily relaxed in September 1993, following a substantial shortfall in the domestic rice harvest. However, as part of the Uruguay Round of negotiations under the General Agreement on Tariffs and Trade, Japan and the Republic of Korea accepted provisions (with effect from 1 January 1995) allowing foreign access to their rice markets. Rice imports by Japan accounted for only about 4% of domestic requirements in 1995 and, according to the USDA, for about 7.5% in 2000/01. Imported rice supplied 1% of consumption requirements by the Republic of Korea in 1995, accounted for less than 3% in 2000/01, according to the USDA, and was not expected to meet more than 4% of domestic needs by 2004.

Rubber *(Hevea brasiliensis)*

Rubber cultivation is suited to both estate and smallholder methods of farming but productivity on rubber estates is greater as it is the estates that have pioneered both the development of cultivation techniques and the improvement of the clones, or selected high-yield strains. These may either be planted as seedlings or propagated by grafting on to seedlings of ordinary trees (root stock) and planted out subsequently.

Of total estimated world production of 7,001,217 metric tons of natural rubber in 2001, Asian countries accounted for more than 90%. The principal producers are Thailand, Indonesia, Malaysia, India, the People's Republic of China, Viet Nam and Sri Lanka. In terms of export revenue, rubber is of particular significance to Indonesia, Thailand, Malaysia and Sri Lanka.

Natural rubber can be produced from plants other than *Hevea*. One of these is guayule, a desert shrub found in Mexico and the south-western USA. Commercial rubber production from guayule has been undertaken at various times, notably during periods of restricted supplies of *Hevea*. The US Department of Agriculture (USDA) has conducted research into the development and commercialization of guayule as a domestic source of natural rubber.

In 2001, according to the International Rubber Study Group (IRSG), natural rubber accounted for some 40% of world consumption of new rubber, the remainder being met by petroleum-based synthetic rubber. Almost 75% of total rubber output, both natural and synthetic, is used in motor vehicles, particularly tyres, which themselves account for about 70% of synthetic rubber demand. Epoxidized natural rubber (ENR), which is natural rubber treated with peracids (which are made by treating acetic acid with hydrogen peroxide and formic acid) to enhance its ability to resist stress, was developed in the United Kingdom and Malaysia as an alternative to synthetic rubber for use in the manufacture of car tyres.

In 2001, according to the IRSG, world consumption of natural and synthetic rubber declined by 4.3% to 17.4m. metric tons. Output of natural rubber in that year increased by 5.3%, compared with 2000, to 7.1m. tons, according to the same source, while that of synthetic rubber declined by 3.5% to 10.5m. tons. In early 2002 the IRSG forecast that world rubber consumption would increase by 5.3% in 2002 to surpasss the record level of 18.2m. tons recorded in 2000. Consumption of natural rubber was forecast to increase by 6.3% in 2002, while it was estimated that that of synthetic rubber would grow by 4.6%. At the same time, the IRSG suggested that production of natural rubber might increase by as much as 10% in 2002, thus causing stocks to accumulate and exerting downward pressure on prices.

In 1975 the Association of Natural Rubber Producing Countries (ANRPC), whose members (Malaysia, Thailand, Indonesia, Singapore, Sri Lanka, India, Viet Nam and Papua New Guinea) account for more than 80% of world rubber output (according to FAO), initiated plans to establish a buffer stock of natural rubber and to 'rationalize' supplies by keeping surplus stocks off the market. The operation of the buffer stock and the supply rationalization scheme was to be entrusted to an International Natural Rubber Council (INRC), which was established in 1978. Action to implement this plan was deferred, however, in the hope that discussions under the auspices of the UN Conference on Trade and Development (UNCTAD) would result in a more broadly-based price stabilization agreement involving both producers and consumers. In 1979 the UNCTAD conference of 55 countries reached accord on the terms of an International Natural Rubber Agreement (INRA), which became fully operational in 1982, administered by an International Natural Rubber Organization (INRO), with headquarters in Kuala Lumpur, Malaysia.

The first INRA (which, with two extensions, remained in force until January 1989, when a successor agreement, operating on similar principles, took effect) provided for an adjustable price range (quoted in combined Malaysian/Singaporean dollars and cents), maintained by means of a buffer stock. In January 1993 negotiations began, under the auspices of the INRO, to seek the formulation of a new agreement, to take effect at the expiry of the current INRA in December 1993. By mid-1993, however, wide areas of disagreement over the operation of pricing provisions of a third INRA remained unresolved. In November, after producers agreed to a 5% reduction in reference prices for buffer stock operations, the INRC decided to resume negotiations for a third INRA and to extend the current agreement by one year. These negotiations, which continued during 1994, resulted in the adoption, in February 1995, of a third INRA, to take effect from late December, on expiry of the current agreement (although full ratification was not expected to be completed until

Production of Natural Rubber ('000 metric tons, dry weight)

	2000	2001*
World total	6,811	7,001
Far East	6,201	6,391
Oceania	7	7
Leading regional producers		
China, People's Repub.	482	490†
India	622	630
Indonesia	1,610	1,650†
Malaysia	730†	700†
Philippines	71‡	73‡
Sri Lanka	88	88†
Thailand	2,236	2,280‡
Viet Nam	291	305
Other leading producers		
Brazil	72‡	73†
Côte d'Ivoire	123	108†
Liberia	127‡	135†
Nigeria	107†	107†

* Provisional figures. † FAO estimate.
‡ Unofficial figure.

early 1996). Subsequent delays in ratification arrangements, however, caused INRA provisions technically to lapse, although the INRO secretariat continued to exercise administrative functions. At a meeting held in March 1996 the producing and consuming countries agreed to extend the date for ratification until 31 July. Although Indonesia, Thailand, Sri Lanka and Malaysia, jointly accounting for more than 90% of world rubber output at that time, had assented to the third INRA, continuing delays in ratification by a number of consumer countries, notably the USA (which represented about 29% of world rubber consumption), prompted a further extension, to 28 December, of the finalization of the agreement. The third INRA, which entered into force in March 1997, again provided for a guaranteed reference price, maintained by means of a buffer stock, the reference price being subject to review every 12 months. The duration of the agreement was four years, with the option of two extensions of one year each. The effective operation of successive INRAs has been attributable, in large part, to each agreement's acceptance by virtually all producing and consuming countries. However, only about one-third of rubber consumed is natural rubber, and INRA provisions do not cover trading in synthetic rubber.

In June 1992 the membership of ANRPC announced that it was to seek the creation of a single, centralized open market, probably to be based in Singapore, as a means of counteracting the large volume of private transactions between smallholder groups and consumers (estimated to represent more than 70% of the world's natural rubber trade), which the ANRPC blamed for depressed price levels. During 1993 Indonesia, Malaysia and Thailand expressed dissatisfaction with the operational record of the INRO, which, they stated, had failed to ensure adequate financial returns on rubber sales.

The persistence of depressed market conditions for natural rubber (see below) intensified the discontent of these producers with the operation of the third INRA, particularly in relation to the price support and buffer stock arrangements as operated by the INRO. Criticism was led by Malaysia and Thailand, which, during July and August 1998, indicated that they were actively considering withdrawal from the INRO, on the grounds that the guaranteed intervention price provided by the INRA was too low, and that buffer stock increases were insufficient to counteract falling prices. It was reported that Thailand and Malaysia, together with Indonesia, were contemplating withdrawal from the INRO, with the intention of forming a producers' organization that would implement voluntary supply restriction arrangements, independent of the INRO, under which production of natural rubber would be limited to 20% below world demand. The possibility was also discussed of forming a new regional rubber exchange, and of a co-ordinated marketing system to reduce competion among producers. In October 1998 Malaysia gave the requisite 12 months' notice of withdrawal from the INRO. Although Indonesia subsequently affirmed its intention to remain in the organization, Thailand announced in March 1999 that it would terminate its membership with effect from March 2000. It was widely believed that the INRO would be unable to remain in existence without the participation of Thailand, which provided about 40% of the organization's contributions from producer members.

The Government of Thailand, meanwhile, indicated that it was formulating a plan to restructure its national rubber sector, with a view to doubling export revenue from this source during the period 2000–04. It was understood that this plan included a price intervention mechanism, which was to be financed in part from the retrieval of the rubber stocks held by the INRO, whose value in early 1999 was estimated at US $65m.

In April 1999 the INRO met in Kuala Lumpur, Malaysia, but was unable to persuade Malaysia and Thailand to reconsider their decision to withdraw, and in August Sri Lanka announced that it was also to terminate its membership, leaving only Indonesia, Nigeria and Côte d'Ivoire as producer members. (At that time the INRO had also grouped 16 importing members, including the European Union (EU), the USA and Japan.) Following a further meeting in September, the INRO announced that it was to disband with effect from mid-October, and scheduled a further meeting for December to determine the means and timing of the disposal of its rubber stockpile, estimated at 138,000 tons. The timetable for the disposal was strongly disputed, with Thailand and Malaysia advocating a swift sale, while the other INRO members favoured the gradual disposal of stocks, to prevent price disruption; it was subsequently announced that all INRO-owned rubber would be sold by the end of June 2001. Thailand and Malaysia, meanwhile, announced that they were to co-ordinate their operations in purchasing rubber direct from growers. It was also intended to harmonize the two countries' stock disposals, and to maintain a minimum market price. Efforts to include Indonesia in this agreement were, however, unsuccessful.

In August 2002 Indonesia, Malaysia and Thailand signed an agreement establishing the International Tripartite Rubber Corpn (ITRC), with the objective of regulating the international price of rubber. This was to be achieved through ITRC purchases of rubber on world markets, and, in the event of prices falling below a certain level, from south-east Asian rubber farmers. In December 2001 the three founding countries had agreed to reduce their exports of rubber by 10% and undertaken to implement further reductions over the next two years.

Thailand, the world's leading producer and exporter of natural rubber since 1993, carried out the replanting of more than 50% of its rubber-producing areas during the period 1961–93. During 1971-2000 Thailand's annual production of rubber increased at an average annual rate of 6.7%. The emphasis on high-yielding stock has resulted in a substantial improvement in the general quality of latex output, which has increased Thailand's competitiveness in the production of motor vehicle tyres and has led to the rapid expansion of Thailand's rubber goods industry. More than 80% of Thailand's rubber output is consigned for export, principally to Germany, the PRC, the USA, Singapore and the Republic of Korea. In 2001 Thailand's exports of rubber totalled 2.1m. tons, about the same level as in the previous year. In 1999 2% of Thailand's total export earnings were derived from exports of natural rubber. During the late 1990s the Government was implementing pilot schemes to extend the cultivation of rubber into the eastern and north-eastern regions of the country. As in Malaysia (see below), most rubber production in Thailand is carried out by smallholder farmers.

In recent years Malaysia's output of rubber has generally ranged between 750,000–1.1m. metric tons annually, approximately 10%–15% of world production. Owing to the low international price of rubber, and a consequent acceleration in the conversion of rubber land to other crops, output declined from 1.08m. tons in 1996 to an estimated 700,000 tons in 2001. Estate production has been falling since the 1960s, owing to a shift in emphasis from rubber to oil palm and cocoa. Smallholders have become the principal producers of rubber, as the large estates have expanded the cultivation of these alternative crops, which guarantee a substantially higher return than that of rubber. As a result of government encouragement (in the form of tax incentives and higher replanting grants), average smallholder yields have risen to 700–800 kg per ha, and smallholders now account for about 70% of Malaysian rubber production (about 82% of the area planted with rubber is the property of smallholders). In 1999 the total area under rubber cultivation was estimated to be 1.5m. ha, of which 85% was located in Peninsular Malaysia. Malaysia's exports have generally accounted for about 15%–20% of the world rubber trade in recent years, according to FAO. In the mid-1990s the largest market for Malaysian rubber was the EU (accounting for 27% of total rubber exports), followed by the Republic of Korea (14%) and the USA (13%). In 1999 exports of natural rubber latex, natural rubber and gums, and rubber manufactures accounted for 1.2% of Malaysia's total export earnings.

Indonesia, once the world's main source of natural rubber, has a larger area planted to rubber (3.03m. ha) than Malaysia, but only about 15% of its rubber area was planted to high-yielding varieties, resulting in average yields about 40% of those of Malaysia. More than 90% of Indonesian rubber production has traditionally been exported. In 2001, with production estimated at 1.7m. metric tons by FAO, Indonesia was the world's secondlargest producer of rubber after Thailand.

Export Price Index for Natural Rubber (base: 1980 = 100)

	Average	Highest month(s)	Lowest month(s)
1990	60		
1995	112		
1999	44	51 (Nov.)	39 (July, Aug.)
2000	48	52 (Feb.)	45 (Jan., Dec.)
2001	41	44 (Jan., June)	36 (Dec.)

Ribbed smoked sheets (RSS) are the principal source of reference for rubber prices in commodity markets. In April 1993 the import price of RSS in the London rubber market stood at £560 per metric ton (for delivery in June), but by September it had risen to £620 per ton (for October delivery). After easing somewhat, the London rubber price advanced strongly in 1994, rising in July to £980 per ton (for September delivery). It eased in September to £855 per ton (for October), but increased in October to £952.5 (for November). The price of rubber retreated in early November to £857.5 per ton (for December delivery), but later that month a strong upward movement in prices, resulting from growth in demand, began. In December the London quotation reached £1,000 per ton for the first time. The surge in prices continued in the early weeks of 1995, and in February rubber traded at a record £1,230 per ton (for March delivery). This peak was matched in March (for April delivery). Thereafter, the rubber price moved generally downward, falling to less than £1,000 per ton in June and to only £837.5 (for September delivery) in early August. The London quotation reached £1,000 per ton again in October, and rose in December to £1,150 (for delivery in January 1996). In April 1996 the London price of rubber was below £1,000 per ton, and in December it declined to £792.5 (for delivery in January 1997). During the first half of 1997 the downward trend continued, and by mid-year the rubber price had fallen to £657.5 per ton (for August delivery). The rubber market remained depressed, and in October the London quotation was reduced to £545 per ton (for December). The price remained at this level for the remainder of the year. For 1997 as a whole, despite the rise in demand (see above), prices for all grades of rubber on the London market declined by an average of 47%.

In January 1998 the London price of RSS (for delivery in February) fell to only £427.5 per metric ton. The slump in the rubber market was partly a consequence of the economic crisis affecting eastern Asia, including many rubber-producing countries. In February the rubber price recovered to £550 per ton (for March delivery), but in June it was reduced to £450 (for delivery in July or August). The price was maintained within this range for the remainder of 1998, ending the year at £460 per ton (for delivery in January 1999).

During the early months of 1999 there was further downward movement in rubber prices, and in March the London quotation (for May delivery) declined to £412.5 per ton. The market subsequently recovered, but in early August, with the INRO on the verge of collapse (see above), the price of RSS (for delivery in September) fell to only £397.5 per ton: its lowest level since early 1976. Later in August 1999 rubber prices in Tokyo, Japan (the world's largest market for trading rubber 'futures' contracts), were at their lowest for 30 years. The London price of rubber advanced in November to £530 per ton (for December delivery), after unfavourable weather had reduced output. On a 'spot' price basis, the London quotation averaged £451.3 per ton for the whole of 1999, rising to £511.0 per ton, on average, in 2000. In 2001 the London 'spot' quotation for RSS averaged £476.3 per ton. During the first six months of 2002 the average London 'spot' price for RSS ranged between £460.0 per ton in January and £852.5 per ton in June. The very substantial increase in the price of physical rubber in June (in May the price had averaged only £523.5 per ton) occurred, according to the IRSG, as a result of unfavourable weather conditions, defaults by rubber shippers on their forward contracts, and the forced return of buyers to 'spot' markets.

The International Rubber Study Group (IRSG) is an intergovernmental body which was established in 1944 to provide a forum for the discussion of problems affecting the production and consumption of, and trade in, both natural and synthetic rubber. In 2002 the IRSG's 17 members collectively accounted for 56% of all rubber consumption, 74% of natural rubber production and 69% of synthetic rubber production. Its secretariat, based in London, regularly publishes current statistical information on rubber production, consumption and trade.

Sugar

Sugar is a sweet crystalline substance, which may be derived from the juices of various plants. Chemically, the basis of sugar is sucrose, one of a group of soluble carbohydrates which are important sources of energy in the human diet. It can be obtained from trees, including the maple and certain palms, but virtually all manufactured sugar is derived from two plants, sugar beet (*Beta vulgaris*) and sugar cane, a giant perennial grass of the genus *Saccharum*.

Production of Sugar Cane ('000 metric tons)

	2000	2001*
World total	1,258,530	1,254,857
Far East	552,202	543,193
Oceania	41,918	34,909
Leading regional producers		
Australia	38,165	31,039†
China, People's Repub.	68,280	77,000
India	299,230	286,000
Indonesia	23,500†	23,500†
Pakistan	46,333	43,606
Philippines	25,700	28,238
Thailand	53,494	49,070
Other leading producers		
Argentina	16,000†	15,000†
Brazil	327,705	339,136
Colombia	32,750‡	33,400‡
Cuba	36,400	35,000‡
Mexico	49,275	49,500‡
South Africa	23,896	23,896‡
USA	32,762	31,571

* Provisional figures. † Unofficial figure.
‡ FAO estimate.

Sugar cane, found in tropical areas, grows to a height of up to 5 m. The plant is native to Polynesia, but its distribution is now widespread. It is not necessary to plant cane every season as, if the root of the plant is left in the ground, it will grow again in the following year. This practice, known as 'ratooning', may be continued for as long as three years, after which yields begin to decline. Cane is ready for cutting 12–24 months after planting, depending on local conditions. Much of the world's sugar cane is still cut by hand, but rising costs are hastening the change-over to mechanical harvesting. The cane is cut as close as possible to the ground, and the top leaves, which may be used as cattle fodder, are removed.

After cutting, the cane is loaded by hand or by machine into trucks or trailers and towed directly to a factory for processing. Sugar cane rapidly deteriorates after it has been cut and should be processed as soon as possible. At the factory the cane passes first through shredding knives or crushing rollers, which break up the hard rind and expose the inner fibre, and then to squeezing rollers, where the crushed cane is subjected to high pressure and sprayed with water. The resulting juice is heated and lime is added for clarification and the removal of impurities. The clean juice is then concentrated in evaporators. This thickened juice is next boiled in steam-heated vacuum pans until a mixture or 'massecuite' of sugar crystals and 'mother syrup' is produced. The massecuite is then spun in centrifugal machines to separate the sugar crystals (raw cane sugar) from the residual syrup (cane molasses).

Production of Sugar Beets ('000 metric tons)

	2000	2001*
World total	245,420	234,245
Far East	12,033	15,059
Leading regional producers		
China, People's Repub.	8,073	10,900
Japan	3,800	4,000†
Other leading producers		
France	31,131	26,715
Germany	27,870	24,398
Poland	13,134	13,000†
Turkey	18,000	14,500‡
Ukraine	13,199	15,489
USA	29,521	23,364

* Provisional figures. † FAO estimate.
‡ Unofficial figure.

The production of beet sugar follows the same process, except that the juice is extracted by osmotic diffusion. Its manufacture produces white sugar crystals which do not require further refining. In most producing countries, it is consumed domestically, although the European Union (EU), which accounts for about 13% of total world sugar production, is a net exporter of white refined sugar. Beet sugar usually accounts for more than one-third of world production. Production data for sugar cane and sugar beet generally cover all crops harvested, except crops grown explicitly for feed. The third table covers the production of raw sugar by the centrifugal process. In the late 1990s global output of non-centrifugal sugar (i.e. produced from sugar cane which has not undergone centrifugation) was about 14m. metric tons per year. The main producer of non-centrifugal sugar, almost all of which is used for local consumption, is India, with an output of 9.9m. tons in 1998.

Production of Centrifugal Sugar
(raw value, '000 metric tons)

	2000	2001*
World total	131,060	127,922
Far East	41,202	40,056
Oceania	5,830	4,595
Leading regional producers		
Australia	5,448†	4,181†
China	6,739†	8,141†
India	20,219	19,300
Indonesia	1,575	1,635
Pakistan	2,594†	2,560†
Philippines	1,676†	1,866†
Thailand	6,447	5,155†
Other leading producers		
Brazil	17,035†	18,500†
Colombia	2,391	2,239
Cuba	4,057	3,530†
France	4,685†	4,195†
Germany	4,362	3,736
Mexico	4,696	4,923
Poland	2,185†	1,522†
South Africa	2,663	2,663‡
Turkey	2,162†	2,755†
Ukraine	1,780	2,030†
USA	7,882	7,140

* Provisional figures. † Unofficial figure.
‡ FAO estimate.

Most of the world's output of raw cane sugar is sent to refineries outside the country of origin, unless the sugar is for local consumption. India, Thailand, Brazil and Cuba are among the few cane-producers that export part of their output as refined sugar. The refining process further purifies the sugar crystals and eventually results in finished products of various grades, such as granulated, icing or castor sugar. The ratio of refined to raw sugar is usually about 0.9:1.

As well as providing sugar, quantities of cane are grown in some countries for seed, feed, fresh consumption, the manufacture of alcohol and other uses. Molasses may be used as cattle feed or fermented to produce alcoholic beverages for human consumption, such as rum, a distilled spirit manufactured in Caribbean countries. Sugar cane juice may be used to produce ethyl alcohol (ethanol). This chemical can be mixed with petroleum derivatives to produce fuel for motor vehicles. The steep rise in the price of petroleum after 1973 made the large-scale conversion of sugar cane into alcohol economically attractive (particularly to developing nations), especially as sugar, unlike petroleum, is a renewable source of energy. Several countries developed alcohol production by this means in order to reduce petroleum imports and to support cane-growers. The blended fuel used in cars is known as 'gasohol', 'alcogas' or 'green petrol'. The pioneer in this field was Brazil, which operates the largest 'gasohol' production programme in the world. During the late 1990s the use of ethanol by Brazilian motorists rapidly increased, as, despite the additional costs involved in adapting motor vehicles to ethanol consumption, the price of this fuel, which can be mixed with petrol or used in undiluted form, had fallen (owing to high levels of stocks) to less than one-half the price of petrol. In the Far East and Australasia unsuccessful attempts to establish 'gasohol' production were made in the Philippines and Papua New Guinea, while plans to initiate a 'gasohol' project in Thailand have been indefinitely postponed.

After the milling of sugar, the cane has dry fibrous remnants known as bagasse, which is usually burned as fuel in sugar mills but can be pulped and used for making fibreboard, particle board and most grades of paper. As the costs of imported wood pulp have risen, cane-growing regions have turned increasingly to the manufacture of paper from bagasse. In view of rising energy costs, some countries are encouraging the use of bagasse as fuel for electricity production to save on foreign exchange from imports of petroleum. Another by-product, cachaza (which had formerly been discarded), is currently being utilized as an animal feed.

In recent years sugar has encountered increased competition from other sweeteners, including maize-based products, such as isoglucose (a form of high-fructose corn syrup or HFCS), and chemical additives, such as saccharine, aspartame (APM) and xylitol. Consumption of HFCS in the USA was equivalent to about 42% of the country's sugar consumption in the late 1980s, while in Japan and the Republic of Korea HFCS accounted for 19% and 25%, respectively, of domestic sweetener use. APM was the most widely used high-intensity artificial sweetener in the early 1990s, although its market dominance was under challenge from sucralose, which is about 600 times as sweet as sugar (compared with 200–300 times for other intense sweeteners) and is more resistant to chemical deterioration than APM. In the late 1980s research was being conducted in the USA to formulate means of synthesizing thaumatin, a substance derived from the fruit of a west African plant, *Thaumatoccus daniellii*, which is several thousand times as sweet as sugar. If, as has been widely predicted, thaumatin can be commercially produced, it could obtain a substantial share of the markets for both sugar and artificial sweeteners. In 1998 the US Government approved the domestic marketing of sucralose, the only artificial sweetener made from sugar. Sucralose was stated to avoid many of the taste problems associated with other artificial sweeteners.

The major sugar producers in Asia are India, the People's Republic of China, Thailand, Pakistan, Indonesia and the Philippines. Of these, only China and Indonesia were net importers rather than net exporters in the late 1990s. The main exporters in the Far East and Australasia are Australia, the Philippines and Thailand; the region's main importers are Indonesia and Japan. Although India is usually the principal world producer of cane sugar, the country is not a significant exporter, and since the late 1980s it has intermittently had recourse to imports of sugar in order to satisfy domestic requirements. India's principal suppliers of imported sugar are China and Brazil. In the late 1990s about 4m. ha were planted with sugar cane, but, despite plentiful domestic production, the country's sugar refineries, which are subject to government levies, are unable to compete effectively with low-cost imports. In 1999/2000 Indian production of sugar was estimated at a record 19.5m. tons (raw value), and in that year exports of sugar were expected to increase to 2m. tons. In 1999 Indian producers had become increasingly concerned about their competitiveness, as a result of the comparatively low cost of imported sugar, and at the beginning of 2000 the Government announced an increase in import duties on sugar from 27.5% to 40%. Indonesia, following unsuccessful efforts to achieve self-sufficiency in sugar, has become a principal buyer of Indian sugar. Indonesia's total imports were estimated at 1.7m. tons (raw value) in 2000, having risen as high as 2.3m. tons in 1999. Thailand, after seeking a reduction in sugar production to encourage a change-over to other crops, has promoted a controlled expansion of sugar production. However, sugar exports (both raw and refined) accounted for less than 1% of Thailand's export revenue in 1999. Thailand's exports of sugar (raw value) totalled 4.2m. tons, in 2000, compared with 3.4m. tons in 1999. In the case of Australia, sugar is the most important export crop after wheat. The export trade accounts for about 80% of the country's annual raw sugar production. Sugar (including sugar preparations and honey) accounted for 1.5% of Australian export earnings in 1997/98. In 1998/99 and 1999/2000, however, the contribution of sugar to total export revenues was only 0.2%. The sugar industry in the Philippines was, for many years, an important source of foreign-exchange earnings. Since 1983, however, the country's output of raw sugar has reflected depressed price levels and curbs on production. In the mid-1990s the Government of Viet Nam was seeking foreign investment in the country's sugar sector, with the aim of reducing domestic dependence on sugar imports.

The first International Sugar Agreement (ISA) was negotiated in 1958, and its economic provisions operated until 1961. A second ISA did not come into operation until 1969. It included quota arrangements and associated provisions for regulating the price of sugar traded on the open market, and established the International Sugar Organization (ISO) to administer the agreement. However, the USA and the six original members of the European Community (EC, now the EU) did not participate in the ISA, and, following its expiry in 1974, it was replaced by a purely administrative interim agreement, which remained operational until the finalization of a third ISA, which took effect in 1978. The new agreement's implementation was supervised by an International Sugar Council (ISC), which was empowered to establish price ranges for sugar-trading and to operate a system of quotas and special sugar stocks. Owing to the reluctance of the USA and EC countries (which were not a party to the agreement) to accept export controls, the ISO ultimately lost most of its power to regulate the market, and since 1984 the activities of the organization have been restricted to compiling statistics and providing a forum for discussion between producers and consumers. Subsequent ISAs, without effective regulatory powers, have been in operation since 1985. (For detailed information on the successive agreements, see *The Far East and Australasia 1991.*)

In tandem with world output of cane and beet sugars, stock levels are an important factor in determining the prices at which sugar is traded internationally. These stocks, which were at relatively low levels in the late 1980s, increased significantly in the early 1990s, owing partly to the disruptive effects of the Gulf War on demand in the Middle East (normally a major sugar-consuming area), and also as a result of considerably increased production in Mexico and the Far East. Additionally, the output of beet sugar was expected to continue rising, as a result of substantial producers' subsidies within the EU, which, together with Australia, has been increasing the areas under sugar cane and beet. World sugar stocks were reduced in the 1993/94 trading year (September–August). However, record crops in Brazil, India and Thailand led to an increased level of sugar stocks in 1994/95. World sugar stocks continued to rise in 1995/96 and 1996/97, and advanced further in 1997/98, when world-wide consumption of raw sugar totalled about 123m. metric tons, compared with production of 126m. tons. This trend continued in 1998/99, when, according to provisional ISO data, global sugar production reached 133.2m. tons, while consumption totalled 127.8m. tons. In 1999/2000, according to the ISO, there was a world sugar surplus of some 3.4m. tons. In November 2000 the ISO forecast a world sugar deficit of about 2.3m. tons in 2000/01.

Most of the world's sugar output is traded at fixed prices under long-term agreements. On the free market, however, sugar prices often fluctuate with extreme volatility.

Export Price Index for Sugar (base: 1980 = 100)

	Average	Highest month(s)	Lowest month(s)
1990	45		
1995	48		
1999	23	29 (Jan.)	20 (April, July)
2000	28	34 (Oct.)	20 (March)
2001	30	34 (Jan., May)	24 (Oct.)

In February 1992 the import price of raw cane sugar on the London Market was only US $193.0 (equivalent to £107.9 sterling) per metric ton, its lowest level, in terms of US currency, for more than four years. The London price of sugar advanced to US $324.9 (£211.9) per ton in May 1993, following predictions of a world sugar deficit in 1992/93. Concurrently, sugar prices in New York were at their highest levels for three years. The London sugar price declined to US $237.2 (£157.9) per ton in August 1993, but increased to US $370.6 (£237.4) in December 1994.

The rise in sugar prices continued in January 1995, when the London quotation for raw sugar reached US $378.1 (£243.2) per ton, its highest level, in dollar terms, since early 1990. Meanwhile, the London price of white sugar was US $426.5 (£274.4) per ton, the highest quotation for four-and-a-half years. The surge in the sugar market was partly a response to forecasts of a supply deficit in the 1994/95 season. Prices later eased, and in April 1995 raw sugar was traded in London at US $326.0 (£202.1) per ton. The price recovered to US $373.1 (£235.6) per ton in June, but retreated to US $281.5 (£179.4) in September.

During the early months of 1996 the London price of raw sugar reached about US $330 per ton. In May the price was reduced to US $262.9 (£175.3) per ton, but in July it rose to US $321.4 (£206.3), despite continued forecasts of a significant sugar surplus in 1995/96. The sugar price fell to US $256.3 (£156.4) per ton in December.

In January 1997 the price of raw sugar declined to US $250.8 (£154.0) per ton, but in August it reached US $288.5 (£179.1). In terms of US currency, the London sugar price advanced later in the year, standing at US $298.5 (£178.3) per ton in December.

International sugar prices moved generally downward in the first half of 1998. In June, following forecasts that world output of raw sugar in 1997/98 would be significantly higher than in the previous crop year (leading to a further rise in surplus stocks), the London price was reduced to US $185.0 (£113.1) per ton. In July the quotation for raw sugar recovered to US $222.6 (£135.0) per ton, but in September, following forecasts of a higher surplus in 1998/99, the price fell to only US $168.8 (£100.2). The sugar price stayed within this range for the remainder of 1998, ending the year at US $196.9 (£118.3) per ton.

In January 1999 the London price of raw sugar reached US $217.2 (£132.4) per ton, but from February the free market was affected by strong downward pressure, as sugar supplies remained plentiful. In April the London sugar price was reduced to only US $127.3 (£79.0) per ton, its lowest level, in terms of US currency, since late 1986. Meanwhile, the short-term quotation in the main US sugar market declined to about 4.6 US cents per lb, also a 12-year 'low'. The slump in international sugar prices was partly a consequence of the severe economic problems affecting Russia (normally the world's leading importer of sugar) and countries in eastern Asia. The decline in demand from these areas coincided with high output, as a result of generally favourable growing conditions, in sugar-producing countries. The London price recovered to US $166.2 (£105.1) per ton in June 1999, but declined to US $131.4 (£84.4) in July. A renewed advance took the price to US $184.3 (£111.4) per ton in October. At the end of the year the London sugar quotation stood at US $162.4 (£100.8) per ton.

During the early weeks of 2000 the international sugar market was weak, and at the end of February the London price of raw sugar was reduced to US $126.5 (£80.1) per ton, its lowest level, in terms of US currency, for more than 13 years. However, there was subsequently a strong recovery in sugar prices, in response to reports of reductions in output and planting, while demand rose. At the end of July the London quotation was US $264.0 (£176.3) per ton. Meanwhile, the New York price of sugar rose during that month to its highest level for more than two years. In early August the price of white sugar traded in London rose to its highest level, US $279.0 (£185.3) per ton, for more than two-and-a-half years. The average price for raw sugar on the main New York market was in excess of 11 US cents per lb in August, the first time this level had been achieved since February 1998. These recoveries were not sustained, however, and by 22 September the London quotation for raw sugar had fallen to US $226.5 (£155.3) per ton. The London quotation for raw sugar remained within the established range until 10 October, when it rose to US $266.5 (£183.9) per ton. On 17 October the London quotation stood at US $281.5 (£195.5) per ton, but thereafter the price fell back to and remained within the previously established range, ending the year at US $249.4 (£166.9) per ton. A persistent characteristic of the market from October 2000 was the erosion of the premium at which white sugars normally trade above raw supplies. In January 2001 the ISO forecast that the premium would remain depressed for several months to come, owing to the abundance of supplies of white sugar and the availability of substantial quantities for export from India. At the end of the first quarter of 2001 the London quotation for raw sugar stood at US $216.7 per ton, declining further, to US $205.3 (£143.9) per ton on 3 April. The average New York price for March 2001 was 9.6 US cents per lb. At the end of May the London price had advanced somewhat, to US $221.8 per ton. However, prices subsequently declined sharply, particularly in October, when the New York price averaged 7.2 US cents per lb, compared with 8.6 cents in September. Reports of damage caused by 'Hurricane Michelle' to the crops of several Caribbean countries, most notably Cuba, supported a brief recovery in November, before the downward trend continued into 2002. The New York price again declined below 6 US cents per lb, before recovering above that level in August.

The Group of Latin American and Caribbean Sugar Exporting Countries (GEPLACEA), with a membership of 23 Latin American and Caribbean countries, together with the Philippines, and representing about 66% of world cane production and 45% of sugar exports, complements the activities of the ISO (comprising 58 countries, including EU members, in December 2000) as a forum for co-operation and research. The USA withdrew from the ISO in 1992, following a disagreement over the formulation of members' financial contributions. The USA had previously provided about 9% of the ISO's annual budget.

Tea (*Camellia sinensis*)

Tea is a beverage made by infusing in boiling water the dried young leaves and unopened leaf-buds of the tea plant, an evergreen shrub or small tree. Black and green tea are the most common finished products. The former accounts for the bulk of the world's supply and is associated with machine manufacture and plantation cultivation, which guarantees an adequate supply of leaf to the factory. The latter, produced mainly in the People's Republic of China and Japan, is grown mostly on smallholdings, and much of it is consumed locally. There are two main varieties of tea, the China and the Assam, although hybrids may be obtained, such as Darjeeling. In this survey, wherever possible, data on production and trade relate to made tea, i.e. dry, manufactured tea. Where figures have been reported in terms of green (unmanufactured) leaf, appropriate allowances have been made to convert the reported amounts to the approximate equivalent weight of made tea.

Total recorded tea exports by producing countries achieved successive records in each of the years 1983–90. World exports (excluding transactions between former Soviet republics) declined in 1991 and 1992, but rose by 13.7% in 1993. However, the total fell by 10.3% in 1994. Export volume increased again in 1995 and 1996, rising further, to 1,202,711 tons, in 1997. World tea exports reached a new record of 1,302,684 tons in 1998, but eased to 1,259,058 tons in 1999. In 2000 export volume attained a new record level of 1,331,295 tons (estimated), a total exceeded in 2001 when world export volume was estimated at 1,391,940 tons. Global production of tea reached an unprecedented level in 1998, with record crops in all the major producing countries (India, China, Kenya and Sri Lanka). In 1999, however, world output declined (from 2,987,282 tons in 1998) to 2,899,739 tons, although China and Sri Lanka again reported record crops. In 2000 production increased to 2,917,831 tons, spurred, once again, by record crops in the China and Sri Lanka. In 2001 it was estimated that world production of tea had, for the first time ever, exceeded 3m. tons. Record crops in China and Kenya contributed to an increase in global output of 3.2%, to an estimated 3,021,426 tons. India (the world's largest consumer) and Sri Lanka have traditionally been the two leading tea exporters, with approximately equal sales, but the quantity which they jointly supply has remained fairly stable (350,000–425,000 tons per year in 1977–96, advancing to 458,000 tons in 1997). Their joint export sales rose to 472,947 tons in 1998, but declined to 452,044 tons in 1999. In 2000 Indian and Sri Lankan joint export sales increased to 484,666 tons, but were estimated to have fallen to 467,360 in 2001. During the 1960s these two countries together exported more than two-thirds of all the tea sold by producing countries, but in 2001 the proportion was estimated at about 34%. From 1990 until 1995, when it was displaced by Kenya, Sri Lanka ranked as the main exporting country. Exports by Sri Lanka again took primacy in 1997, when Kenya's tea sales declined sharply. Sri Lanka remained the principal tea exporter in 1998, despite a strong revival in Kenyan exports, and again in 1999, although tea sales by both countries declined in the latter year. In 2000 Sri Lankan exports retained primacy, while those by Kenya declined for a second successive year. Sri Lankan exports were estimated to have surpassed those of Kenya again in 2001, in spite of a strong recovery in Kenya's foreign sales. Exports from China (whose sales include a large proportion of green tea) have exceeded those of India in every year since 1996.

Almost all of Sri Lanka's tea exports, which stood at 287,503 metric tons in 2001 (compared with 280,133 tons in 2000 and 262,952 tons in 1999), are in the form of black tea. After clothing, tea is the country's main source of foreign exchange, accounting for 16.4% of total export earnings in 1998, 13.7% in 1999, and 12.9% in 2000. The principal buyers of Sri Lankan tea in 2000 were Russia, Dubai (in the United Arab Emirates), Syria and Turkey. Iran, Saudi Arabia, Iraq and the United Kingdom are also significant buyers of tea from Sri Lanka. Colombo is the largest single auction site for tea in Asia, the Indian auction market being divided between several institutions. The volume of tea traded at Colombo increased throughout the 1990s and early 2000s, reaching 279,460 tons in 2001.

Tea is India's principal agricultural export, but its contribution to total export earnings has diminished in recent years, falling from 4.6% in the year ending 31 March 1987 to 1.4% in 1997/98. Exports of tea contributed 1.6% of India's total export earnings in 1998/99, and only an estimated 1.1% in 1999/2000. India's tea exports, which totalled 189,092 tons in 1999, advanced to 204,533 tons in 2000, but declined to only 179,857 tons in 2001. Since 1985 India has operated an upper limit on annual tea exports of 220,000 tons, regulating the volume of sales in each quarter in order to maximize earnings of foreign exchange. India is the world's largest consumer of tea, as well as the largest producer (accounting for 28.3% of estimated world production in 2001), and the domestic market expanded steadily during the 1990s. In 1999/2000 prices for Indian tea declined, largely as a result of low domestic demand and the possibility of a high level of imports. As a result, the Government increased import duty on tea from 15% to 35% in May 2000, and in July it announced that restrictions on the foreign ownership of tea companies were to be abolished (thus allowing 100% foreign participation), in an effort to encourage increased investment and productivity. In March 2001 India raised the basic duty applied to imports of tea to 70%.

Production of Made Tea ('000 metric tons)

	2000	2001
World total	2,917.8*	3,011.9*
Far East	2,242.0*	2,273.6*
Oceania	7.5*	7.4*
Leading regional producers		
Bangladesh	52.6	57.3*
China, People's Repub.[1]	683.3	701.7
India[2]	846.5*	853.7*
Indonesia[3]	157.4	161.2
Japan[4]	89.3	89.8
Sri Lanka	306.8	296.3
Taiwan[5]	20.3	19.8
Viet Nam[6]	70.0*	80.0*
Other leading producers		
Argentina[7]	63.0*	59.0*
Iran	53.0*	46.0*
Kenya	236.3	294.6
Malawi	42.1	36.8
Turkey	130.7	142.9

* Provisional.

[1] Mainly green tea (498,057 tons in 2000; 513,154 tons in 2001).

[2] Including a small quantity of green tea (about 8,300 tons in 2000; about 8,500 tons in 2001).

[3] Including green tea (about 38,000 tons in 2000; about 39,000 tons in 2001).

[4] All green tea.

[5] Crude tea.

[6] Including green tea (about 29,000 tons in 2000; about 32,000 tons in 2001).

[7] Twelve months beginning 1 May of year stated.

Source: International Tea Committee, *Supplement to Annual Bulletin of Statistics 2002*.

For many years the United Kingdom was the largest single importer of tea. However, the country's annual consumption of tea per caput, which amounted to 4.55 kg in 1958, has declined in recent years, averaging 2.46 kg in 1994–96 and 1995–97, before recovering marginally, to 2.51 kg, in 1996–98. In 1997–99, however, consumption fell back to 2.44 kg; again, to 2.33 kg, in 1998–2000, and again, to 2.28 kg, in 1999–2001. A similar trend has been observed in other developed countries, apart from the Republic of Ireland, the world's largest per caput consumer of tea, where annual consumption per person advanced from 3.17 kg in 1994–96 to 3.23 kg in 1995–97, before evidencing a slight decline, to 2.95 kg, in 1996–98. Irish annual consumption per person declined again, to 2.78 kg, in 1997–99, and to 2.69 kg in 1998–2000, before recovering to 2.71 kg in 1999–2001. From the late 1980s consumption and imports expanded significantly in the developing countries (notably Middle Eastern countries) and, particularly, in the USSR, which in 1989 overtook the United Kingdom as the world's principal tea importer. However, internal factors, following the break-up of the USSR in 1991, caused a sharp decline in tea imports by its successor republics; as a result, the United Kingdom regained its position as the leading tea importer in 1992. In 1993 the former Soviet republics (whose own tea production had fallen sharply) once more displaced the United Kingdom as the major importer, but in 1994 the United Kingdom was again the principal importing country. Since 1995, however, imports by the former USSR (excluding the Baltic states) have exceeded those of the United Kingdom. In 2001 the former USSR imported an estimated 201,000 tons of tea, accounting for 15.6% of the world market, followed by the United Kingdom, with 137,315 tons (10.6%), Pakistan (106,822 tons, or 8.3%) and the USA (96,668 tons, or 7.5%). Other major importers of tea in 2001 were Egypt, Japan, Iraq and Morocco.

Export Price Index for Tea (base: 1980 = 100)

	Average	Highest month(s)	Lowest month(s)
1990	92		
1995	67		
1999	88	n.a.	n.a.
2000	84	88 (Jan.)	79 (June)
2001	70	83 (Jan.)	65 (June)

Much of the tea traded internationally is sold by auction, principally in the exporting countries. Until declining volumes brought about their termination in June 1998 (Kenya having withdrawn in 1997, and a number of other exporters, including Sri Lanka and Malawi, having established their own auctions), the weekly London auctions had formed the centre of the international tea trade. At the London auctions, five categories of tea were offered for sale: 'low medium' (based on a medium Malawi tea), 'medium' (based on a medium Assam and Kenyan tea), 'good medium' (representing an above-average East African tea), 'good' (referring to teas of above-average standard) and (from April 1994) 'best available'. The average price of all grades of tea sold at London auctions stood at £1,238 sterling per metric ton in 1993, but fell to £1,192 per ton in 1994 and to £1,036 per ton in 1995. The annual average price in 1995 was the lowest since 1988. The average rose to £1,135 per ton in 1996 and to £1,351 in 1997. For the first half of 1998, before the auctions ceased, the average price realized was £1,458 per ton. During 1993 the monthly average reached £1,564 per ton in January, but declined to £1,100 in June and recovered to £1,256 in November. The average was £1,102 per ton in January 1994, but rose to £1,284 in June and September. Quotations then moved generally lower, and in July 1995 the average London tea price was only £907.5 per ton, its lowest monthly level since August 1988. At one auction in September 1995 the price of 'medium' tea was reduced to only £780 per ton, its lowest level, even in nominal terms (i.e. without taking inflation into account), since 1976. The monthly average increased to £1,170.5 per ton in December 1995, but fell to £1,031 in July 1996. It moved generally higher in later months, reaching £1,528 per ton in August 1997, following reports that drought had reduced Kenya's tea crop. After easing somewhat, the average London price of tea rose in January 1998 to £1,905 per ton (its highest monthly level since March 1985), in response to news of serious flooding in eastern Africa. At one of that month's auctions the price of 'medium' tea reached £2,000 per ton, its highest level since 1985. However, the average London tea price retreated in May 1998 to £1,014 per ton. At the end of June, with the prospect of a record Kenyan crop, the quotation for 'medium' tea at the final London auction was £980 per ton. Based on country of origin, the highest-priced tea at London auctions during 1989–94 was that from Rwanda, which realized an average of £1,613 per ton in the latter year. The quantity of tea sold at these auctions declined from 43,658 tons in 1990 to 11,208 tons in 1997.

The main tea auctions in Africa are the weekly sales at Mombasa, Kenya. In contrast to London, volumes traded at the Mombasa auctions moved generally upward during the 1990s, and Mombasa is now one of the world's major centres for the international tea trade. The tea sold at Mombasa is mainly from Kenya, but smaller amounts from Tanzania, Uganda and other African producers are also traded. Total annual sales at the Mombasa auctions increased from 173,575 metric tons in 1995 to 189,800 tons in 1996. Owing to Kenya's drought, the total declined to 166,618 tons in 1997. In 1998, however, volume rose to a record 243,566 tons (including 212,620 tons from Kenya). The volume of tea traded at Mombasa in 1999 declined to 210,786 tons, but increased in 2000 to 221,601 tons, and in 2001, to 276,220 tons. Meanwhile, average prices per ton in Mombasa rose from US $1,290 in 1995 to US $1,420 in 1996 and to US $2,000 in 1997. They eased to US $1,890 per ton in 1998, and to US $1,780 in 1999. In 2000 prices of teas traded at Mombasa averaged US $2,020 per ton, before a sharp decline in 2001 left the average price at US $1,530 per ton. On a monthly basis, the average Mombasa price of tea advanced from US $1,380 per ton in July 1996 to US $2,027 in May 1997. After some fluctuation, the monthly average increased to US $2,817 per ton in February 1998, although it retreated to US $1,544 in May. The market later rallied again, and in September 1999 the monthly average advanced to US $1,993 per ton. In July 2000 the monthly average rose to US $2,111 per ton, the highest level it was to attain that year, having advanced from a 'low' of US $1,880 per ton in January In January 2001 the average Mombasa price of tea stood at US $1,866 per ton, but retreated to US $1,425 per ton in June. The average monthly price at Mombasa reached US $1,540 per ton in March 2002, before declineing sharply, to US $1,362 per ton in May, recovering to US $1,451 in June.

An International Tea Agreement (ITA), signed in 1933 by the governments of India, Ceylon (now Sri Lanka) and the Netherlands East Indies (now Indonesia), established the International Tea Committee (ITC), based in London, as an administrative body. Although ITA operations ceased after 1955, the ITC has continued to function as a statistical and information centre. In 2001 there were six producer/exporter members (the tea boards or associations of Bangladesh, India, Indonesia, Kenya, Malawi and Sri Lanka), four consumer members and six associate members.

In 1969 the FAO Consultative Committee on Tea was formed and an exporters' group, meeting under this committee's auspices, set export quotas in an attempt to stabilize tea prices. These quotas have applied since 1970 but are generally regarded as too liberal to have more than a minimal effect on prices. The perishability of tea complicates the effective operation of a buffer stock. India, while opposing the revival of a formal ITA to regulate supplies and prices, has advocated greater co-operation between producers to regulate the market. The International Tea Promotion Association (ITPA), founded in 1979 and based in Nairobi, Kenya, comprises eight countries (excluding, however, India and Sri Lanka), accounting for almost one-third of world exports of black tea.

Tin

The world's known tin deposits, estimated by the US Geological Survey to total 6.9m. tons in 2001, are located mainly in the equatorial zones of Asia, in central South America and in Australia. Cassiterite is the only economically important tin-bearing mineral, and it is generally associated with tungsten, silver and tantalum minerals. There is a clear association of cassiterite with igneous rocks of granitic composition, and 'primary' cassiterite deposits occur as disseminations, or in veins and fissures in or around granites. If the primary deposits are eroded, as by rivers, cassiterite may be concentrated and deposited in 'secondary', sedimentary deposits. These secondary deposits form the bulk of the world's tin reserves. The ore is treated, generally by gravity method or flotation, to produce concentrates prior to smelting.

Tin owes its special place in industry to its unique combination of properties: low melting point, the ability to form alloys with most other metals, resistance to corrosion, non-toxicity and good appearance. Its main uses are in tinplate (about 40% of world tin consumption), in alloys (tin-lead solder, bronze, brass, pewter, bearing and type metal), and in chemical compounds (in paints, plastics, medicines, coatings and as fungicides and insecticides). In the late 1990s a number of possible new applications for tin were under study: these included its use in fire-retardant chemicals, and as an environmentally preferable substitute for cadmium in zinc alloy anti-corrosion coatings on steel. The possible development of a lead-free tin solder was also receiving consideration.

Production of Tin Concentrates (tin content, metric tons)

	1999	2000*
World total (excl. USA)	216,000	238,000
Far East	143,047	158,557
Oceania	10,038	9,146
Regional producers		
Australia	10,038	9,146
China, People's Repub.	80,100	97,000
Indonesia	47,754	48,000
Laos	492	600
Malaysia	7,340	6,307
Mongolia	40†	n.a.
Myanmar	149	220
Thailand	2,712	1,930
Viet Nam	4,500	4,500
Other leading producers		
Bolivia	12,417	12,464
Brazil	13,200	13,000
Peru	30,403	37,410
Portugal	2,200	1,200
Russia	4,500	5,000

* Estimated production. † 1998 figure.

Source: US Geological Survey.

Production of Tin Metal (metric tons, incl. secondary)

	1999	2000*
World total	262,000	283,000
Far East	189,124	208,299
Oceania	885	1,080
Regional producers		
Australia	885	1,080
China, People's Repub.	90,800	111,000
Indonesia	49,105	50,000
Japan	568	593
Malaysia	28,913	27,200
Thailand	17,306	17,076
Viet Nam	2,400	2,400
Other leading producers		
Belgium	8,100	8,500
Bolivia	11,166	9,353
Brazil	13,500	13,300
Peru	16,960	20,000
Russia	3,800	5,200
USA	16,400	15,100

* Estimated production.

Source: US Geological Survey.

Most South-East Asian tin production comes from gravel-pump mines and dredges, working alluvial deposits, although there are underground and open-cast mines working hard-rock deposits. In 2000 all of Australia's tin production came from the low-cost underground Renison Bell mine that Murchison United operates in western Tasmania. In February 2000 Murchison United and the Tasmanian State Government agreed to fund jointly a six-year programme of exploration and development to secure the long-term future of the Renison operation. Most of Australia's mine production is sent for smelting to Penang, in Malaysia, and to Thailand. Concentrates from Myanmar and Laos are mainly exported to Malaysia, Europe and the republics of the former USSR. Indonesia, Malaysia and Thailand now smelt virtually the whole of their mine production to produce primary tin metal. An independent tin smelter is in operation in Singapore.

According to the US Geological Survey, the Far East and Australasia accounted for 71% of world output of tin concentrates in 1999 and for an estimated 70.5% in 2000. However, since the 1970s, tin has sharply declined in importance as an export commodity in Malaysia and Thailand, which had traditionally been among the region's main producers. In Thailand, where the metal provided 12.9% of the country's export earnings in 1967, its share was only 0.6% in 1988, and tin remained at the margin of total exports in the late 1990s. In 1989 exports of tin metal (including tin alloys) provided 1.7% of Malaysia's total export earnings. The comparable proportion was 1.2% in 1990 and only 0.2% in 1997. By contrast, sales of tin accounted for 23% of Malaysia's total exports, by value, in 1965. The depressed level of world tin prices since late 1985 (see below) has accelerated the industry's decline, although Malaysia possesses substantial resources of tin and remains the leading world centre for tin smelting. In 1993, following three years of financial losses on its tin-mining operations, Malaysia Mining Corpn, which accounted for the bulk of that country's tin production, terminated these activities. Malaysia's tin output subsequently declined sharply, from 10,384 tons in 1993 to 5,065 tons in 1997. In 1998, however, the Malaysian Government took action to encourage the reactivation of dormant mines. In that year Malaysia recorded an increase in tin production for the first time since 1990. Output increased further, to 7,340 tons, in 1999, but was reported to have fallen, to 6,307 tons, in 2000. The People's Republic of China, now by far the world's largest tin producer, announced in late 1997 that it was to initiate a three-year mining project in Qinghai Province to develop additional tin ore production capacity of 450,000 tons annually. China's tin output in 1998 rose by about 4%, to 70,100 tons, and again in 1999, by 14.3%, to 80,100 tons. In 2000 production increased for a third consecutive year, this time by 21.1%, reaching 97,000 tons.

Over the period 1956–85, much of the world's tin production and trade was covered by successive international agreements, administered by the International Tin Council (ITC), based in London. The aim of each successive International Tin Agreement (ITA), of which there were six, was to stabilize prices within an agreed range by using a buffer stock to regulate the supply of tin. (For detailed information on the last of these agreements, see *The Far East and Australasia 1991.*) The buffer stock was financed by producing countries, with voluntary contributions by some consuming countries. 'Floor' and 'ceiling' prices were fixed, and market operations conducted by a buffer stock manager who intervened, as necessary, to maintain prices within these agreed limits. For added protection, the ITA provided for the imposition of export controls if the 'floor' price was being threatened. The ITA was effectively terminated in October 1985, when the ITC's buffer stock manager informed the London Metal Exchange (LME) that he no longer had the funds with which to support the tin market. The factors underlying the collapse of the ITA included its limited membership (Bolivia and the USA, leading producing and consuming countries, were not signatories) and the accumulation of tin stocks which resulted from the widespread circumvention of producers' quota limits. The LME responded by suspending trading in tin, leaving the ITC owing more than £500m. to some 36 banks, tin smelters and metals traders. The crisis was eventually resolved in March 1990, when a financial settlement of £182.5m. was agreed between the ITC and its creditors. The ITC was itself dissolved in July.

These events lent new significance to the activities of the Association of Tin Producing Countries (ATPC), founded in 1983 by Malaysia, Indonesia and Thailand and later joined by Bolivia, Nigeria, Australia and Zaire (now the Democratic Republic of the Congo, DRC). Immediately prior to the withdrawal of Australia and Thailand at the end of 1996 (see below), members of the ATPC, which is based in Kuala Lumpur, Malaysia, accounted for about two-thirds of world mine production. The ATPC, which was intended to operate as a complement to the ITC and not in competition with it, introduced export quotas for tin for the year from 1 March 1987. Brazil and the People's Republic of China agreed to co-operate with the ATPC in implementing these supply restrictions, which have been renegotiated to cover succeeding years, with the aim of raising prices and reducing the level of surplus stocks. The ATPC membership also took stringent measures to control smuggling. Brazil and China (jointly accounting for more than one-third of world tin production) both initially held observer status at the ATPC. (China became a full member in 1994, but Brazil has remained as an observer—together with Peru and Viet Nam.) China and Brazil agreed to participate in the export quota arrangements, for which the ATPC has no formal powers of enforcement.

The ATPC members' combined export quota was fixed at 95,849 tons for 1991, and was reduced to 87,091 tons for 1992. However, the substantial level of world tin stocks, combined with depressed demand, led to mine closures and reductions in output, with the result that members' exports in 1991 were below quota entitlements. The progressive depletion of stock levels led to a forecast by the ATPC, in May 1992, that export quotas would be removed in 1994 if these disposals continued at their current rate. The ATPC had previously set a target level for stocks of 20,000 tons, representing about six weeks of world tin consumption. Projections that world demand for tin would remain at about 160,000 tons annually, together with continued optimism about the rate of stock disposals, led the ATPC to increase its members' 1993 export quota to 89,700 tons. The persistence, however, of high levels of annual tin exports by China (estimated to have totalled 30,000 tons in 1993 and 1994, compared with its ATPC quota of 20,000 tons), together with sales of surplus defence stocks of tin by the US Government, necessitated a reduction of the quota to 78,000 tons for 1994. In late 1993 prices had fallen to a 20-year 'low' and world tin stocks were estimated at 38,000–40,000 tons, owing partly to the non-observance of quota limits by Brazil and China, as well as to increased production by non-ATPC members. World tin stocks resumed their rise in early 1994, reaching 48,000 tons in June. However, the effects of reduced output, from both ATPC and non-ATPC producing countries, helped to reduce stock levels to 41,000 tons at the end of December. In 1995 exports by ATPC members exceeded the agreed voluntary quotas by 10%, and in May 1996, when world tin stocks were estimated to have been reduced to 20,000 tons, the ATPC suspended its quota arrangements. Shortly before the annual meeting of the ATPC was convened in September, Australia and Thailand announced their withdrawal from the organization, on the grounds that its activities had ceased to be effective in maintaining price levels favourable to tin-producers. Although China and Indonesia indicated that they would continue to support the ATPC, together with Bolivia, Malaysia and Nigeria (Zaire had ceased to be an active producer of tin), the termination of its quota arrangements in 1996, together with the continuing recovery in the tin market, indicated that its future role would be that of a forum for tin-producers and consumers. Malaysia, Australia and Indonesia left the ATPC in 1997, and Brazil became a full member in 1998. In June 1999, when the organization's headquarters were moved from Kuala Lumpur to Rio de Janeiro, Brazil, the membership comprised Brazil, Bolivia, China, the DRC and Nigeria. It was hoped that Peru would join the ATPC following its relocation to South America.

The success, after 1985, of the ATPC in restoring orderly conditions in tin trading (partly by the voluntary quotas and partly by working towards the reduction of tin stockpiles) unofficially established it as the effective successor to the ITC as the international co-ordinating body for tin interests. The International Tin Study Group (ITSG), comprising 36 producing and consuming countries, was established by the ATPC in 1989 to assume the informational functions of the ITC. In 1991 the secretariat of the United Nations Conference on Trade and Development (UNCTAD) assumed responsibility for the publication of statistical information on the international tin market.

Export Price Index for Tin (base: 1980 = 100)

	Average	Highest month(s)	Lowest month(s)
1990	42		
1995	37		
1999	29	32 (Nov.)	28 (Jan., Feb., June–Aug.)
2000	29	32 (Jan.)	27 (Oct.–Dec.)
2001	23	27 (Jan., Feb.)	19 (Sept., Oct.)

Although transactions in tin contracts were resumed on the LME in 1989, the Kuala Lumpur Commodity Exchange (KLCE), in Malaysia, had become established as the main centre for international trading in the metal. In September 1993 the price of tin (ex-works) on the KLCE stood at only 10.78 Malaysian ringgits (RM) per kg, equivalent to £2,756 (or US $4,233) per metric ton. Measured in terms of US currency, international prices for tin were at their lowest level for 20 years, without taking inflation into account. In October the Malaysian tin price recovered to RM 12.71 per kg (£3,376 or US $4,990 per ton), but in November it declined to RM 11.60 per kg (£3,056 or US $4,545 per ton).

The rise in tin prices continued in the early weeks of 1994, and in February the Malaysian quotation reached RM15.15 per kg (£3,684 or US $5,449 per metric ton). In early March the metal's price eased to RM14.00 per kg (£3,449 or US $5,146 per ton), but later in the month it rose to RM15.01 per kg (£3,715 or US $5,515 per ton). The KLCE price was reduced in August to RM 12.99 per kg (£3,285 or US $5,092 per ton), but in early November it stood at RM 16.06 per kg (then £3,896 or US $6,265 per ton).

The Malaysian tin price advanced strongly in January 1995, reaching RM 16.38 per kg (£4,018 or US $6,407 per metric ton). However, in early March the price declined to RM 13.33 per kg (about £3,300 or US $5,200 per ton). The tin market later revived again, and in August the KLCE price of the metal reached RM 17.60 per kg (£4,569 or US $7,060 per ton). International tin prices were then at their highest level for nearly six years. The recovery in the market was attributed partly to a continuing decline in tin stocks, resulting from a reduction in exports from China and in disposals from the USA's strategic reserves of the metal. However, the KLCE quotation was reduced to RM 15.36 per kg (£3,851 or US $6,090 per ton) in October.

In the early months of 1996 there was a generally downward movement in international tin prices, and in March the Malaysian quotation fell to RM 15.28 per kg (£3,947 or US $6,015 per metric ton). In April the KLCE price of tin recovered to RM 16.24 per kg (£4,294 or US $6,496 per ton). A further decline ensued, and in mid-December tin was traded at RM 14.31 per kg (£3,388 or US $5,668 per ton).

During the first six months of 1997 the price of tin on the KLCE declined by nearly 8%. The tin market moved further downward in July, with the Malaysian price falling to RM 13.52 per kg (£3,185 or US $5,398 per metric ton). Later that month, after the value of the ringgit had depreciated, the equivalent of the KLCE tin price (RM 13.76 per kg) was only £3,107 (US $5,199) per ton. In late August the Malaysian price stood at RM 14.70 per kg, but this was equivalent to only £3,134 (US $5,061) per ton. In terms of local currency, the Malaysian tin price increased considerably in subsequent weeks, but most of the upward movement was the consequence of a decline in the ringgit's value in relation to other currencies. By the end of September the KLCE price of tin had risen to RM 18.13 per kg. This price was reportedly maintained over the first eight trading days of October, during which time the ringgit recovered some of its value. At the end of the period the Malaysian tin price was equivalent to £3,656 or US $5,927 per ton. The KLCE price of tin continued to move upward in subequent weeks, but the Malaysian currency's value declined again. At the end of the year the tin price stood at RM 20.61 per kg, equivalent to £3,218 or US $5,295 per ton. During the second half of 1997 the tin price, expressed in ringgits, increased by 50.5%, but the equivalent in US dollars was 2.4% lower.

The KLCE price of tin reportedly held steady at RM 20.61 per kg for the first nine trading days of January 1998. Meanwhile, the ringgit's depreciation continued. At the currency's lowest point, the tin price was equivalent to only £2,722 or US $4,399 per metric ton. Later in January the tin price advanced to RM 23.43 per kg. It remained at this level for several days, as the value of the ringgit recovered, so that in early February the price was equvalent to £3,557 or US $5,843 per ton. Later in February the Malaysian tin price eased to RM 19.27 per kg (£3,122 or US $5,120 per ton), but in June it rose to RM 24.50 per kg. This quotation was maintained over three trading days, during which the value of the ringgit rose appreciably. As a result, the equivalent of the KLCE price increased from less than US $6,000 per ton to US $6,234 (£3,757). Tin prices later eased, and at the end of September the metal was traded in Malaysia at RM 20.02 per kg, equivalent to £3,100 (US $5,268) per ton. Earlier that month a fixed exchange rate for the Malaysian currency (US $1 = RM 3.8; the rate was susbsequently altered slightly on a number of occasions, and stood at US $1 = RM 3.775 in June 2002) was introduced. In early November the KLCE was merged with the Malaysia Monetary Exchange to form the Commodity and Monetary Exchange of Malaysia (COMMEX Malaysia), also based in Kuala Lumpur. During the same week the Malaysian tin price rose to RM 20.65 per kg (£3,269 or US $5,434 per ton), but in December it declined to RM 19.10 per kg (£2,990 or US $5,026 per ton).

In January 1999, with tin stocks in plentiful supply, the COMMEX price of the metal was reduced to only RM 18.77 per kg, equivalent to £2,990 (US $4,939) per metric ton. However, tin prices rose steadily thereafter, and in May the Malaysian quotation reached RM 21.42 per kg (£3,500 or US $5,637 per ton). After easing somewhat, the price advanced in November to RM 22.10 per kg (£3,594 or US $5,816 per ton). It ended the year at RM 21.41 per kg (£3,496 or US $5,634 per ton).

In January 2000 the COMMEX price of tin rose to RM 22.84 per kg, equivalent to £3,664 (US $6,011) per metric ton. By early June the price was reduced to RM 19.94 per kg (£3,488 or US $5,247 per ton), although later in the month it recovered to RM 20.71 per kg (£3,582 or US $5,450 per ton). The price generally remained around RM 20.00 per kg for the remainder of that year, reaching a maximum of RM 20.78 per kg (£3,845 or US $5,433 per ton) in September and a minimum of RM 19.42 per kg (£3,483 or US $5,077 per ton) in October, ending the year at RM 19.66 per kg (£3,545 or US $5,208 per ton).

Trading in January 2001 began with the price somewhat lower than at the end of December, the average price for the first week of trading being RM 19.29 per kg (equivalent to £3,349 or US $5,110 per metric ton). A further decline was experienced in March, when the price fell below RM 19 per kg. Prices rallied briefly in early May, before declining below RM 18 per kg in mid-June. A sharp decline began in July, the COMMEX falling as low as RM 13.34 per kg (£2,363 or US $3,534 per ton) in September. A strong recovery in November (the price exceeding RM 16.00 per kg at one point) faltered in December, the price being RM 14.95 (£2,691 or US $3,960 per ton) on the year's last trading day.

The COMMEX price was generally more stable in the first six months of 2002 than it had been in the previous year, experiencing a gradual upward trend. By the end of June the price of tin had reached RM 16.62 (£2,863 or US $4,403 per metric ton).

The International Tin Research Institute (ITRI), founded in 1932 and based in London, England, promotes scientific research and technical development in the production and use of tin. In recent years the ITRI, whose 12 producer members supply about 60% of world tin output, has particularly sought to promote new end-uses for tin, especially in competition with aluminium.

Tobacco (*Nicotiana tabacum*)

Tobacco originated in South America and was used in rituals and ceremonials or as a medicine; it was smoked and chewed for centuries before its introduction into Europe, the Middle East, Africa and the Indian sub-Continent in the 16th century. The generic name *Nicotiana* denotes the presence of the alkaloid nicotine in its leaves. The most important species in commercial tobacco cultivation is *N. tabacum*. Another species, *N. rustica*, is widely grown, but on a smaller scale, to yield cured leaf for snuff or simple cigarettes and cigars.

World-wide, about 4.3m. ha were being farmed for tobacco in the late 1990s. Commercially grown tobacco (from *N. tabacum*) can be divided into four major types—flue-cured, air-cured (including burley, cigar, light and dark), fire-cured and sun-cured (including oriental)—depending on the procedures used to dry or 'cure' the leaves. Each system imparts specific chemical and smoking characteristics to the cured leaf, although these may also be affected by other factors, such as the type of soil on which the crop is grown, the type and quantity of fertilizer applied to the crop, the cultivar used, the spacing of the crop in the field and the number of leaves left at topping (the removal of the terminal growing point). Each type is used, separately or in combination, in specific products (e.g. flue-cured in Virginia cigarettes). All types are grown in Asia.

As in other major producing areas, local research organizations in Asia have developed new cultivars with specific, desirable chemical characteristics, disease-resistance properties and improved yields. Almost all tobacco production in the Far East is from smallholdings; there is no cultivation of the crop on estates, as is common with tea. Emphasis has been placed on improving yields by the selection of cultivars, by the increased use of fertilizers and by the elimination or reduction of crop loss (through use of crop chemicals) and on reducing requirements for hand labour through the mechanization of land preparation and the use of crop chemicals. Harvesting continues to be entirely a manual operation, as the size of farmers' holdings and the cost of harvesting devices (now commonly used in the USA and Canada) preclude such development in Asia. The flue-curing process requires energy in the form of oil, gas, coal or wood. To ensure that supplies of wood are continuously renewed, the tobacco industry in, for example, Pakistan and Sri Lanka encourages the planting of trees. Following extensive research into the possibility of converting waste materials, such as rice husks, into products generating energy, a waste-pelletizing plant entered operation in Mysore, India.

The principal type of tobacco cultivated by Asian farmers is flue-cured. Of the countries producing this tobacco in the Far East, the most important are the People's Republic of China, India, Japan and the Koreas. China is the world's principal producer, as well as the largest consumer, of tobacco, and, while most of its output is still retained for local use, exports expanded by an annual average of 14% in 1990–2000, totalling 120,291 metric tons in the latter year, whenChina ranked as the world's fifth largest exporter of unmanufactured tobacco. Production in

China in recent years has benefited from significant changes in the organization of, and in the methods of cultivation that are practised in, tobacco-growing areas. The tobacco sector is also a significant domestic employer: according to the International Tobacco Growers' Association (ITGA, see below), about 16m. people were engaged in tobacco growing in China in the late 1990s.

Production of Tobacco Leaves
(farm sales weight, '000 metric tons)

	2000	2001*
World total	6,762	6,347
Far East	3,838	3,562
Oceania	8	8
Leading regional producers		
Bangladesh	35	35†
China, People's Repub.	2,552	2,292†
India	609	610†
Indonesia	136	134
Japan	61	62†
Korea, Dem. People's Repub.	63†	63†*
Korea, Repub.	68	56
Myanmar	47	48
Pakistan	108	103
Philippines	49	47
Thailand	74	74†
Viet Nam	27	29
Other leading producers		
Brazil	578	565
Greece	137	130†
Italy	130	125†
Malawi	99	100†
Turkey	189	170†
USA	478	454
Zimbabwe	228	175‡

* Provisional figures. † FAO estimate.
‡ Unofficial figure.

India, which overtook the USA as the world's second largest producer of tobacco in 1999, normally exports less than 20% of its annual output, which is primarily grown for domestic consumption in the form of chewing tobacco. Exports of tobacco contributed less than 1% of India's total export earnings in 1999, but, as a relatively low-cost producer, the country could substantially increase its export revenue from tobacco by redirecting its production from non-cigarette tobacco to flue-cured Virginia and burley varieties. The only significant regional producers of burley tobacco are Indonesia, Japan (for domestic consumption) and the Koreas (for domestic consumption and for export), although Thailand is increasing its output of this type. Production of dark air-cured tobacco is limited mainly to India, China, Pakistan and Indonesia. Asia is not a significant producer of fire-cured and oriental tobaccos.

Japan is unable to produce sufficient flue-cured tobacco for domestic consumption, owing mainly to pressure on the availability of land, and thus has to rely on substantial and increasing imports. India continues to be a significant supplier of flue-cured tobacco, while Korean flue-cured is also now accepted on international markets. In both Thailand and the Koreas domestic requirements are likely to maintain pressure on production. The level of exports from these countries has stabilized, and this position is unlikely to be reversed despite the increased supplies of flue-cured tobacco now available on international markets from Brazil (the world's principal tobacco exporter), Malawi and Zimbabwe, although the price competitiveness of Korean flue-cured does not enhance its prospects as an exporter.

Of the other tobacco-producing countries in the Far East, production in Bangladesh, which entered the export market in 1982, remains fairly static. Indonesia is a significant producer and exporter of cigar tobaccos, yet still requires imported flue-cured tobacco to sustain its domestic market, although increasing quantities of domestic flue-cured are being grown on Sulawesi, Bali and Lombok. Domestic tobacco production is increasing in Malaysia, under the aegis of the National Tobacco Board. The Philippines produces both flue-cured and air-cured tobacco acceptable to world markets. Sri Lanka, once solely a producer of tobacco for domestic consumption, now exports quantities of both flue-cured and air-cured tobacco.

Growing conditions in New Zealand and Australia are wholly dissimilar to those in other countries in the Asia-Pacific region, and neither country is a significant producer in world terms. However, both countries contain large tobacco holdings, mechanization is significant and problems related to the cultivation of the crop, such as the occurrence of blue mould in Australia, are unique. Domestic production, mainly flue-cured, is encouraged through government legislation stipulating a minimum quantity of such tobacco to be incorporated into tobacco products that are marketed in Australia and New Zealand.

Export Price Index for Tobacco (base: 1980 = 100)

	Average	Highest month(s)	Lowest month(s)
1990	125		
1995	132		
1999	141	142 (Jan.–March)	139 (April, May)
2000	141	*	*
2001	141	*	*

* The monthly index remained constant at 141 throughout 2000 and 2001.

About one-quarter of world tobacco production is traded internationally. Until 1993, when it was overtaken by Brazil, the USA was the world's principal tobacco-exporting country. According to the US Department of Agriculture (USDA), the average value of US exports of unmanufactured tobacco was US $6,811 per metric ton in 2001. The USDA forecast that their value would decline to an average of US $6,600 per ton in 2002. The country's total earnings from such exports were US $1,301m. in 1999.

The International Tobacco Growers' Association (ITGA), with headquarters in Portugal, was formed in 1984 by growers' groups in Argentina, Brazil, Canada, Malawi, the USA and Zimbabwe. In 2002 its members numbered 22 countries, accounting for more than 80% of the world's internationally traded tobacco. The ITGA provides a forum for the exchange of information among tobacco producers, conducts research and publishes studies on tobacco issues.

Wheat *(Triticum)*

The most common species of wheat, *T. vulgare*, includes hard, semi-hard and soft varieties which have different milling characteristics but which, in general, are suitable for bread-making. Another species, *T. durum*, is grown mainly in semi-arid areas, including regions bordering the Mediterranean Sea. This wheat is very hard and is suitable for the manufacture of semolina, the basic ingredient of pasta and couscous. A third species, spelt (*T. spelta*), is also included in production figures for wheat. It is grown in very small quantities in parts of Europe and is used as animal feed.

Although a most adaptable crop, wheat does not thrive in hot and humid climates, and it requires timely applications of water (either through rainfall or irrigation). Wheat is an important crop in most countries in Asia north of the Tropic of Cancer, wherever the terrain is favourable and sufficient water is available. The most concentrated producing areas in the Asia-Pacific region are to be found in Pakistan, northern India and eastern parts of the People's Republic of China.

World wheat production declined during the 1990s, albeit only marginally, at an average rate of less than 0.1% a year. The fall was largely due to the sharp decline in agricultural output in the former USSR, excluding which the trend in world production growth has been upward. Wheat production is highly variable from year to year. Part of the variation is attributable to weather conditions, particularly rainfall, in the main producing areas, but national policies on support for producers have also been a major influence. In the 1990s several major wheat-producing countries, including leading exporters, pursued policies of market deregulation, and began to remove the links between producers' support and the financial returns from particular commodities. This encouraged their farmers more readily to switch between crops according to expected relative market returns. After 1996, for example, when wheat was in short supply on world markets, output was stimulated in many growing areas, and a record 613m. tons was harvested in 1997. Unfavourable weather, particularly in Russia and the PRC, reduced output to about 593m. tons in 1998, but, owing to low growth in consumption, exporting countries' stocks remained high, and farmers' returns fell. This discouraged plantings for the 1999 season, when production totalled only about 589m. tons. Production declined further in 2000, to 585m. tons, and again in 2001, to an estimated 583m. tons.

Wheat production in Far East Asia has increased at a considerably faster rate than output in the world as a whole. In 1974–76 the region's harvest averaged 83m. metric tons per year, or 22% of the world total, but by 1996–98 it averaged 201m. tons (34% of the total). This growth was attributable, in large part, to an accelerated rate of expansion of wheat output in China, brought about by extensive irrigation, better supplies of fertilizers and, perhaps most important of all, the introduction of cash incentives to farmers. Local abundance gave rise to storage problems in some areas in the mid-1980s, and, as a result, some producers lost interest in wheat, and, instead, cultivated cash crops. However, the subsequent introduction of stricter marketing regulations, higher prices payable to wheat producers and more abundant fertilizer supplies led to a resumption of growth. By the mid-1990s China, with annual output averaging about 105m. tons, was by far the world's leading wheat-producing country.

In India the introduction of high-yielding and high-response varieties, more extensive irrigation and greater use of fertilizers doubled production in less than 15 years, to 54m. tons in 1989. Government support prices have generally maintained interest in wheat-growing, and have encouraged greater use of agricultural inputs. An unbroken succession of favourable monsoons enabled wheat output to advance rapidly in the 1990s, reaching 69m. tons in 1997. Disposal of these abundant crops occasionally proved difficult, and the Indian Government supported prices by means of sizeable procurements, while authorizing exports in some years. None the less, the margin between output and the steady rise in wheat demand has remained narrow, while relatively minor crop set-backs, as in 1998, necessitate imports to safeguard food security and stabilize retail prices.

The other major producer in the region is Pakistan. Although largely irrigated, production is vulnerable to hot weather. Production incentives, offered by the government, have resulted in increased levels of output, although fertilizers have not always been readily accessible, and seed availability has been variable. Particularly favourable weather conditions helped output to reach a record 19m. tons in 1998, and this total was surpassed in 2000, when output amounted to more than 21m. tons. Virtually no wheat was grown in Bangladesh until recently, but government subsidies, together with the conversion of irrigated land to its cultivation and increasing use of fertilizers, have made the country almost 50% self-sufficient in wheat.

Australia is one of the world's major wheat-exporting countries, but production varies considerably from year to year. The incidence of drought in the main producing areas is a major determinant (the 1994 wheat crop was reduced by 45% as the result of drought conditions), but plantings also reflect world market conditions, as Australian wheat-farming receives no government subsidies. Production in 2000 and 2001, at, respectively, 22.2m. tons and an estimated 23.8m. tons, was somewhat higher than the average for recent years. The only other country in the Pacific area with significant wheat production is New Zealand, which is usually self-sufficient in wheat.

World consumption, which has, in the long term, been increasing at a similar rate to production, varies much less from year to year. Food use is increasing at about 1.5% per year. Most of the increase is in Far East Asia. Of approximately 415m. tons of wheat used for direct human food world-wide, Far East Asia accounts for about one-half, and China for one-half of that. Wheat food use has been expanding at the expense of rice: its growth is associated with rising consumer incomes and an increasing number of fast-food outlets. The trend was sustained in 1997/98, despite the much higher costs of wheat imports in a number of countries such as Indonesia: one reason is that rice became even more expensive, while retail prices of wheat were, in some cases, stabilized by government subsidies. Substantial amounts of wheat are used for feed in Europe and, when prices are favourable, in North America. Substantial quantities were also used for feed in the 1980s in the former Soviet Union, but this volume has decreased sharply, in response to the diminution in livestock numbers. In Far East Asia some wheat is used for feed in Japan, while the Republic of Korea imports wheat for feed when prices are low in comparison with those of coarse grains such as sorghum and maize (corn).

Wheat is the principal cereal in international trade. Amounts exported in recent years have ranged between 100m. and 130m. tons annually, of which about 10m. tons was in the form of wheat flour, 6m.–7m. tons durum wheat and semolina, up to 3m. tons of feed wheat, and the remainder wheat of bread-making quality (some of which, however, was used to make other food products, such as noodles). The main exporters are the USA (whose share declined from about 30% of the total in the first half of the 1990s to about 25% in 2000), the European Union (EU), Canada, Australia and Argentina. Developed countries were formerly the principal consumers, but the role of developing countries as importers has been steadily increasing and they now regularly account for approximately two-thirds of world imports.

Far East Asia has long been one of the world's principal wheat-importing regions. Imports rose considerably during the 1980s, but reduced purchases by China caused a temporary set-back in the early 1990s. Japan has been a major importer since the 1960s. Its imports, of about 6m. tons annually, represent an important element of stability in the world wheat trade. Despite the scale of its own production, China is usually a major wheat importer. However, following purchases of about 12m. tons in 1995/96, its imports have subsquently averaged only 2.6m. tons per year, owing to large harvests, abundant stocks and a slower rate of growth in wheat consumption.

India imports wheat occasionally in order to replenish its stockpiles (as in 1998), but is self-sufficient in most years. Although these stockpiles became particularly large in 1999, low international prices made it uneconomic for India to export wheat. Imports of wheat by Bangladesh vary according to the size of the country's grain harvest and to the relative prices of wheat and rice on world markets. These imports rose from about 1m. tons in 1998 to some 2.4m. tons in 1999, when severe flooding affected rice supplies. They have generally, in recent years, amounted to about 1.4m. tons annually. The Republic of Korea also buys varying amounts of wheat. Its basic food needs account for more than 2m. tons annually, but it also purchases additional amounts, of up to 4m. tons, for animal feed if the price is competitive with maize and other feed grains. Several countries in the region that grow no wheat, such as Indonesia, Malaysia and the Philippines, are now major importers of wheat.

Production of Wheat ('000 metric tons, including spelt)

	2000	2001*
World total	584,994	582,692
Far East	199,618	184,473
Oceania	22,516	24,124
Leading regional producers		
Australia	22,190	23,760
China, People's Repub.	99,636	93,500
India	75,574	68,458
Pakistan	21,079	18,955
Other leading producers		
Argentina	16,147	17,723†
Canada	26,804	21,282
France	37,355	31,695
Germany	21,634	22,889
Iran	8,088	7,500‡
Russia	34,400	46,871
Turkey	21,000	16,000‡
Ukraine	10,160	21,333
United Kingdom	16,700	11,570
USA	60,757	53,278

* Provisional figures. † FAO estimate.
‡ Unofficial figure.

A lengthy period of low international wheat prices, and heavily-subsidized competition among the major exporting countries, was interrupted in 1995–96 after exporting countries' stocks had fallen to their lowest levels for 20 seasons. Prices rose to record levels, but the resultant stimulus to output led to a rapid accumulation of stocks, and by 1998 prices were again very low as competition intensified between exporting countries. Because direct export subsidies were limited under international trade agreements, much of this competition took the form of offers of credit to importing countries.

The export price (f.o.b. Gulf ports) of US No. 2 Hard Winter, one of the most widely-traded wheat varieties, stood at around US $140 per metric ton in mid-1994. At that time, countries benefiting from export subsidies (e.g. much of North Africa) could expect to buy wheat for at least US $40 per ton less. The peak, reached in April 1996, was almost US $300 per ton, but by mid-1997 the price had fallen by as much as 50%, to around US $150 per ton. Subdued import demand, and the disposal of surpluses by a number of countries in Central and Eastern Europe, as well as by Ukraine, further depressed prices in late 1997. Markets remained subdued in 1998 and early 1999, as a consequence of high levels of export stocks and a lack of new markets. In July 1999 US Hard Winter varieties were being traded at the US Gulf at below US $105 per ton, although a measure of recovery took place in the early months of 2000, in response to uncertainty regarding crop prospects in the USA, together with some revival in import demand. High-protein wheat varieties, which were not in such abundant supply, continued to command an appreciable premium. US Dark Northern Spring wheat, for example, was quoted at US $150 per ton in July 1999. In 1999 as a whole the average export price (f.o.b. Gulf ports) of US No. 2 Hard Winter was US $114 per ton, while in 2000 the price averaged US $119 per ton, rising to US $130 per ton in 2001. During the first seven months of 2002 the average export price rose from US $125 per ton in March to US $150 per ton in July.

Export Price Index for Wheat (base: 1980 = 100)

	Average	Highest month(s)	Lowest month(s)
1990	82		
1995	94		
1999	64	70 (Jan.)	61 (July, Dec.)
2000	67	74 (Dec.)	64 (April, Aug.)
2001	72	74 (Jan., May)	71 (March, April, June, Aug.)

Since 1949 nearly all world trade in wheat has been conducted under the auspices of successive international agreements, administered by the International Wheat Council (IWC) in London. The early agreements involved regulatory price controls and supply and purchase obligations, but such provisions became inoperable in more competitive market conditions, and were abandoned in 1972. The IWC subsequently concentrated on providing detailed market assessments to its members and encouraging them to confer on matters of mutual concern. A new Grains Trade Convention, which entered into force in July 1995, gave the renamed International Grains Council (IGC) a wider mandate to consider all coarse grains as well as wheat. This facilitates the provision of information to member governments, and enhances their opportunities to hold consultations. In addition, links between governments and industry are strengthened at an annual series of grain conferences sponsored by the IGC. In early 2001 the IGC had a membership of 29 governments, including the 15 countries of the EU (which are counted as a single member), including nine exporting members and 20 importing members. Membership in Far East Asia and Oceania comprises Australia, India, Japan, the Republic of Korea and Pakistan.

A new Food Aid Convention (FAC), replacing an earlier agreement introduced in 1995, was brought into force on 1 July 1999 as one of the constituent instruments of the International Grains Agreement, 1995 (the other being the Grains Trade Convention, 1995). Members of the Food Aid Committee, which administers the FAC, had resolved to renegotiate the existing Convention in accordance with the recommendations relating to Least-developed and Net Food-Importing Developing Countries adopted by members of the World Trade Organization at their Singapore Conference in December 1996, and in the light of the Declaration on World Food Security and the Plan of Action adopted by the Rome World Food Summit in the same year. They also took into account that, in recent years, there had been significant changes in the food aid policies of several donor countries.

The main objective of the new Convention is 'to contribute to world food security and to improve the ability of the international community to respond to emergency food situations and other food needs of developing countries'. FAC members will make quality food aid available to developing countries with the greatest needs on a consistent basis, regardless of fluctuations in world food prices and supplies. Particular importance is attached to ensuring that food aid is directed to the alleviation of poverty and hunger among the most vulnerable groups.

As a framework of international co-operation between food aid donors, the new FAC aims at achieving greater efficiency in all aspects of food aid operations. FAC members will put greater emphasis on the monitoring and evaluation of the impact and effectiveness of their food aid operations. They are also committed to support the efforts of recipient countries to develop and implement their own food security strategies.

Cereals will continue to represent the bulk of aid supplied. However, the list of products which may be supplied has been broadened beyond cereals and pulses to include edible oil, skimmed milk powder, sugar, seeds and products which are a component of the traditional diet of vulnerable groups in developing countries or of supplementary feeding programmes (e.g. micro-nutrients).

Members' total minimum annual commitments are approximately the same as under the previous FAC, amounting to over 5m. tons of commodities in wheat equivalent. The cost of transporting and delivering food aid beyond the f.o.b. stage will, to the extent possible, be borne by the donors.

ACKNOWLEDGEMENTS

We gratefully acknowledge the assistance of the following bodies in the preparation of this section: the Centro Internacional de Agricultura Tropical, the United Coconut Association of the Philippines, Inc, the International Coffee Organization, the International Cotton Advisory Committee, the Institute of Petroleum, the International Monetary Fund, the International Aluminium Institute, the International Rice Research Institute, the International Rubber Study Group, the International Sugar Organization, the International Tea Committee, COMMEX, the International Tin Research Institute, the International Tobacco Growers' Association, the Food and Agriculture Organization of the UN, the United Nations Conference on Trade and Development, the US Geological Survey, the US Department of Energy and the World Bureau of Metal Statistics.

Source for Agricultural Production Tables (unless otherwise indicated): Food and Agricultural Organization of the UN. Source for Export Price Indices: UN, *Monthly Bulletin of Statistics*, issues to August 2001.

CALENDARS, TIME RECKONING, AND WEIGHTS AND MEASURES

The Islamic Calendar

The Islamic era dates from 16 July 622, which was the beginning of the Arab year in which the *Hijra* ('flight' or migration) of the prophet Muhammad (the founder of Islam), from Mecca to Medina (in modern Saudi Arabia), took place. The Islamic or *Hijri* Calendar is lunar, each year having 354 or 355 days, the extra day being intercalated 11 times every 30 years. Accordingly, the beginning of the *Hijri* year occurs earlier in the Gregorian Calendar by a few days each year. Dates are reckoned in terms of the *anno Hegirae* (AH) or year of the Hegira (*Hijra*). The Islamic year 1423 AH began on 26 March 2002.

The year is divided into the following months:

1. Muharram	30 days	7. Rajab	30 days
2. Safar	29 ,,	8. Shaaban	29 ,,
3. Rabia I	30 ,,	9. Ramadan	30 ,,
4. Rabia II	29 ,,	10. Shawwal	29 ,,
5. Jumada I	30 ,,	11. Dhu'l-Qa'da	30 ,,
6. Jumada II	29 ,,	12. Dhu'l-Hijja	29 or 30 days

The *Hijri* Calendar is used for religious purposes throughout the Islamic world, and is the official calendar in Saudi Arabia. In most Arab countries it is used in conjunction with the Gregorian Calendar for official purposes, but in Indonesia, Malaysia and Pakistan the Gregorian Calendar has replaced it.

PRINCIPAL ISLAMIC FESTIVALS

New Year: 1st Muharram. The first 10 days of the year are regarded as holy, especially the 10th.

Ashoura: 10th Muharram. Celebrates the first meeting of Adam and Eve after leaving Paradise, also the ending of the Flood and the death of Husain, grandson of the prophet Muhammad. The feast is celebrated with fairs and processions.

Mouloud (Birth of Muhammad): 12th Rabia I.

Leilat al-Meiraj (Ascension of Muhammad): 27th Rajab.

Ramadan (Month of Fasting).

Id al-Fitr or **Id al-Saghir** or **Küçük Bayram** (The Small Feast): Three days beginning 1st Shawwal. This celebration follows the constraint of the Ramadan fast.

Id al-Adha or **Id al-Kabir** or **Büyük Bayram** (The Great Feast, Feast of the Sacrifice): Four days beginning on 10th Dhu'l-Hijja. The principal Islamic festival, commemorating Abraham's sacrifice and coinciding with the pilgrimage of Muslims to Mecca. Celebrated by the sacrifice of a sheep, by feasting and by donations to the poor.

Islamic Year	1422	1423	1424
New Year	26 March 2001	15 March 2002	5 March 2003
Ashoura	4 April 2001	24 March 2002	14 March 2003
Mouloud	4 June 2001	24 May 2002	14 May 2003
Leilat al-Meiraj	15 Oct. 2001	4 Oct. 2002	24 Sept. 2003
Ramadan begins	17 Nov. 2001	6 Nov. 2002	27 Oct. 2003
Id al-Fitr	17 Dec. 2001	6 Dec. 2002	26 Nov. 2003
Id al-Adha	23 Feb. 2002	12 Feb. 2003	2 Feb. 2004

Note: Local determinations may vary by one day from those given here.

Hindu Calendars

In India there are two principal Hindu calendars, the Vikrama and the Saka.

The Vikrama or Samvat era is dated from a victory of King Vikramaditya in 58 BC. The year 2003 of the Christian era therefore corresponds to 2060 in the Vikrama era. The New Year begins in March or April in eastern India, but in October or November in the western States.

The Saka era, beginning in AD 78, is attributed to the Saka King Kanishka. The year 2003 of the Christian era corresponds with 1925 of the Saka era.

The Official Calendar in India, adopted in 1957, is based on the Saka year, but has been fixed in relation to the Gregorian Calendar so that New Year (Chaitra 1) falls on 22 March except in Leap Years, when it falls on 21 March. This calendar is used for dating official documents, for All India Radio broadcasts, and other official purposes; however, the Gregorian Calendar is still widely used in India.

FESTIVALS

Holi: Spring Festival in honour of Krishna, usually held in March.

Mahendra Jatra: Nepalese festival seeking to ensure the monsoon rains; June.

Dussera: 10-day festival of Durga; early October.

Diwali: Festival of lights, dedicated to Lakshmi; late October.

Numerous local agricultural and commemorative festivals are also observed.

The Chinese Calendar

China has both lunar and solar systems of dividing the year. The lunar calendar contains 12 months of 29 or 30 days, and in each period of 19 years seven intercalary months are inserted at appropriate intervals. In order not to disturb the 12-month cycle, each of these extra months bears the same title as that which preceded it. The intercalary months may not be introduced after the first, 11th or 12th month of any year.

The solar year which is used by the agrarian community of China begins regularly on 5 February of the Gregorian calendar, and is divided into 24 sections of 14, 15 or 16 days. This calendar is not upset by the discrepant cycle of the moon, and is therefore suitable for the regulation of agriculture.

Until the revolution of 1911, years were named according to a 60-year cycle, made up of 10 stems (*Ban*) and 12 branches (*Ji*). Each year of the cycle has a composite name composed of a different combination of stem and branch. Similar 60-year cycles of year-names have been in use in Thailand and Japan at various times and are still used in Hong Kong, Malaysia and Singapore.

Since 1911 years have been dated from the revolution as Years of the Republic; AD 2003 is the 92nd year of the republican era. The Republic of China has been confined to Taiwan since 1949. In the People's Republic of China the Gregorian system is used.

Japan has used the Gregorian system since 1873, but a National Calendar has also been introduced, derived from the traditional date of accession of the first emperor, Zinmu, in 660 BC. The year AD 2003 corresponds to 2662 of this era.

Buddhist and the South Indian Calendars

The Buddhist era (BE) is attributed to the death of Gautama Buddha, historically dated at about 483 BC. The era in use is dated, in fact, from 544 BC, making the year 2003 of the Christian era equal to 2546 of the Buddhist era. The Jain era, based on the death of Mahavira, starts in 528 BC, making AD 2003 equal to 2530.

In South and South-East Asia there is widespread use of a lunar year of 354 days, with months of alternately 29 or 30 days, and with extra (intercalary) months approximately every third year. Under this system, New Year may fall in either April or March. In Myanmar (formerly Burma), New Year is regularly on 13 April. The Burmese era, the *Khaccapancha,* is ascribed to the ruler Popa Sawrahan, and begins in AD 638. The year 2003 of the Gregorian Calendar is equivalent to 1365 BE.

Sri Lanka adopted the Buddhist calendar as its official and commercial calendar in 1966. Sunday is treated as a normal working day, while the lunar quarter days (Poya days) are public holidays; some of these are two-day holidays. New Year is on 13 or 14 April.

Thailand used the Burmese calendar until 1889, when a new civil era was introduced, commemorating the centenary of the first king of Bangkok. Since 1909 a calendar based on the year 543 BC (traditionally the year of Gautama Buddha's attainment of nirvana) has been in official use. The months have been adapted to correspond with those of the Gregorian Calendar, but New Year is on 1 April every year. In this calendar, called the *Pra Putta Sakarat,* AD 2003 is equivalent to 2545.

FESTIVALS

The principal festivals in the Buddhist calendars are the New Year and the spring and autumn equinox, and local festivals connected with important pagodas.

Standard Time

The following table gives the standard time adopted in the various countries and territories covered in this book, in relation to Greenwich Mean Time (GMT).

+4½	+5	+5½	+5¾	+6
Afghanistan	Maldives Pakistan	India	Nepal	Bangladesh Bhutan Sri Lanka

+6½	+7	+8	+9	+9½
Cocos (Keeling Is) Myanmar (fmrly Burma)	Cambodia Christmas Island Indonesia (Sumatra, Java, Madura, West and Central Kalimantan) Laos Mongolia (western) Thailand Viet Nam	Australia (Western Australia) Brunei China, People's Republic Hong Kong Indonesia (Bali, East and South Kalimantan, West Timor, Celebes/ Sulawesi) Macao Malaysia Mongolia (central) Philippines Singapore Taiwan	East Timor Indonesia (Maluku/ Moluccas, Papua) Japan Korea Mongolia (eastern) Palau	Australia (Northern Territory, South Australia)

+10	+11	+11½	+12	+12¾
Australia (the ACT, NSW, Queensland, Tasmania, Victoria) Guam Northern Mariana Is Federated States of Micronesia (western) Papua New Guinea (excl. North Solomons Province)	Federated States of Micronesia (eastern) New Caledonia Solomon Is Vanuatu	Norfolk Island	Fiji Kiribati (excl. Millennium (fmrly Caroline) Island Marshall Is Nauru New Zealand Tuvalu Wallis and Futuna Is Wake Island	New Zealand (Chatham Is)

+13	-11	-10	-8
Kiribati (Millennium (fmrly Caroline) Island) Tonga	American Samoa Midway Island Niue Samoa	Cook Is French Polynesia (except Gambier Is and Marquesas Is) Hawaii Tokelau	Pitcairn Is

Weights and Measures

The following tables indicate the values of the principal weights and units of measurement which are in common use as alternatives to the metric and imperial systems.

WEIGHT

Unit	Country	Metric equivalent	Imperial equivalent
Acheintaya	Myanmar	163.33 kg	360.1 lb
Arroba	Philippines	11.5 kg	25.35 lb
Baht, Bat, Kyat or Tical	Myanmar, Thailand (Old Chinese system)	7.56 g	0.266 oz
	Siamese system	14.11 g	0.529 oz
Beittha or Viss	Myanmar	1.63 kg	3.601 lb
Candareen or Fen	China (Old system)	0.378 g	0.0133 oz
	China (New system)	0.283 g	0.010 oz
	Hong Kong	0.378 g	0.0133 oz
Candy	Sri Lanka	254 kg	560 lb
	India—Mumbai	254 kg	560 lb
	India—Chennai	226.8 kg	500 lb
	Myanmar	81 metric tons	80 tons
Catty, Gin, Jin, Kan, Kati, Katti, Kin, Kon or Zhang	China (Old system)	0.603 kg	1.333 lb
	China (New system)	0.5 kg	1.102 lb
	Hong Kong	0.603 kg	1.333 lb
	Indonesia	0.617 kg	1.362 lb
	Japan	0.6 kg	1.323 lb
	Malaysia and Singapore	0.603 kg	1.333 lb
	Thailand (Old Chinese system)	0.603 kg	1.333 lb
	Siamese	0.603 kg	1.333 lb
Charak	Afghanistan	1.7278 kg	3.894 lb
Chittack	India	57.5 g	2.057 oz
Dan	China (Old system)	60.48 kg	133.3 lb
	China (New system)	50 kg	110.23 lb
Fan	China (Old system)	0.378 g	0.0133 oz
	China (New system)	0.311 g	0.011 oz
	Hong Kong	0.378	0.0133 oz
Hyaku-mé	Japan	374.85 g	13.226 oz
Kharwar	Afghanistan	564.528 kg	1,246.2 lb
Khord	Afghanistan	110.28 g	3.89 oz
Koyan	Malaysia and Singapore	2,419 kg	5,333.3 lb
Kwan or Kan	Japan	3.749 kg	8.267 lb
Liang or Tael	China (Old system)	37.8 g	1.333 oz
	China (New system)	31.18 g	1.102 oz
	Hong Kong	37.8 g	1.333 oz
Mace	China (Old system)	3.78 g	0.133 oz
	China (New system)	3.11 g	0.110 oz
	Hong Kong	3.78 g	0.133 oz
Maund	Bangladesh	37.29 kg	82.28 lb
	India—Government	37.29 kg	82.28 lb
	India—Mumbai	12.7 kg	28 lb
	India—Chennai	11.34 kg	25 lb
	Pakistan	37.29 kg	82.28 lb
Me	Japan	3.78 g	0.133 oz
Momme	Japan	3.78 g	0.133 oz
Neal	Cambodia	0.6 kg	1.323 lb
Ngamus	Myanmar	8.2 g	0.288 oz
Nijo	Japan	15.02 g	0.529 oz
Pa	India	235 g	8.288 oz

Continued

WEIGHT—*continued*

Unit	Country	Metric equivalent	Imperial equivalent
Picul, Pikul, Picol, Taam or Tam	China (Old system)	60.48 kg	133.33 lb
	China (New system)	50 kg	110.23 lb
	Hong Kong	60.48 kg	133.33 lb
	India	60.48 kg	133.33 lb
	Indo-China (Old Chinese system)	60.48 kg	133.33 lb
	Indo-China (Siamese system)	60 kg	132.277 lb
	Indonesia	61.76 kg	136.16 lb
	Japan	60 kg	132.276 lb
	Malaysia and Singapore	60.48 kg	133.33 lb
	Sabah and Sarawak	61.53 kg	135.64 lb
	Philippines	63.25 kg	139.44 lb
	Thailand (Old Chinese system)	60.48 kg	133.33 lb
	Thailand (Siamese system)	60.55 kg	135.5 lb
Pyi	Myanmar	2.13 kg	4.69 lb
Quintal	Indonesia	100 kg	220.462 lb
	Philippines	46 kg	101.4 lb
Seer	Afghanistan	7.07 kg	15.58 lb
	India—Government	0.93 kg	2.057 lb
	India—Chennai	0.28 kg	0.617 lb
	India—Mumbai	0.33 kg	0.72 lb
	Pakistan	0.93 kg	2.057 lb
Tahil	Malaysia and Singapore	37.8 g	1.33 oz
Tola	India and Pakistan	11.66 g	180 grains
Visham	India	1.36 kg	3 lb
Viss	Myanmar	1.63 kg	3.601 lb

LENGTH

Unit	Country	Metric equivalent	Imperial equivalent
Ch am am	Cambodia	24.9 cm	9.84 in
Ch'ek or Foot	Hong Kong—by statute	37.16 cm	14.625 in
	Hong Kong—in practice	35.82 cm	14.14 in
Cheung	Hong Kong	3.698 m	4.063 yd
Chi	China (Old system)	91 cm	35.814 in
	China (New system)	33.27 cm	13.123 in
Cho	Japan (length)	109.12 cm	119.302 yd
Chung	South Korea		
Coss	India—Bengal, Pakistan and Bangladesh	1,920.2 m	2,000 yd
Cubit	Myanmar	45.72 cm	18 in
Cun	China (Old system)	3.58 cm	1.41 in
	China (New system)	3.33 cm	1.312 in
	Hong Kong	3.58 cm	1.41 in
Danda	India, Pakistan and Bangladesh	1.83 m	2 yd
El, Ell or Ella	Indonesia	68.8 cm	27.08 in
	Malaysia and Singapore	0.914 m	1 yd
	Sabah	0.914 m	1 yd
Fen	China	0.33 cm	0.13 in
Garwode	Myanmar	20.44 km	12.727 miles
Gereh-gaz-sha	Afghanistan	6.6 cm	2.6 in
Girah	Pakistan	5.7 cm	2.25 in
Gudge, Gueza, Guz or Ver	India—Bengal	91.44 cm	36 in
	India—Mumbai	68.58 cm	27 in
	India—Chennai	83.82 cm	33 in
	Pakistan and Bangladesh	91.44 cm	36 in
Hat	Cambodia	50 cm	19.68 in
Hath	India, Pakistan and Bangladesh	45.72 cm	18 in
Hiro	Japan	1.516 m	1.657 yd
Jareeb	Pakistan—Punjab	20.117 m	22 yd
Jo	Japan	3.032 in	3.314 yd
Kawtha	Myanmar	5.116 km	3.182 miles
Ken	Japan	1.82 m	1.988 yd
	South Korea		
Keup	Thailand	23.04 cm	9.07 in
Koss	India—Bengal	1,828.8 m	2,000 yd
Lan	Myanmar	1.83 m	2 yd
Li or Lei	China (Old system)	645–681 m	706–745 yd
	China (New system)	500 m	546.8 yd
	Hong Kong	645–681 m	706–745 yd
	South Korea	3.926 km	2.44 miles
Niew	Thailand	2.09 cm	0.820 in
Oke thapa	Myanmar	64 m	70 yd
Paal	Java	1,506 m	1,647 yd
	Sumatra	1,851.7 m	2,025 yd
Palgate	Myanmar	2.54 cm	1 in
Pulgada	Philippines	2.31 cm	0.914 in
Ri	Japan—length	3.926 km	2.44 miles
	Japan—marine measure	1.85 km	1 nautical mile
Sawk	Myanmar	50.29 cm	19.8 in
Sen	Thailand	40 m	43.74 yd
Shaku	Japan	30.3 cm	11.93 in
Sun	Japan	3.02 cm	1.193 in
Taing	Myanmar	3.911 km	2.43 miles
Tar	Myanmar	3.2 m	3.5 yd
Taung	Myanmar	45.72 cm	18 in
Tjengkal	Indonesia	3.66 m	4 yd
Ungul	India, Pakistan and Bangladesh	1.9 cm	0.75 in
Wah	Thailand	2 m	2.19 yd
Yote	Thailand	16 km	9.942 miles
Yuzamar	Myanmar	75.83 km	47.121 miles
Zhang	China	3.34 m	3.45 yd

CAPACITY

Unit	Country	Metric equivalent	Imperial equivalent
Bag	Myanmar	122.75 litres (l)	27 galls
Bottle	Sri Lanka	0.73 l	0.16 gall
Cavan	Philippines	75 l	16.5 galls
Chupa	Philippines	0.37 l	0.0825 gall
Chupak	Malaysia and Singapore	1.14 l	0.25 gall
Ganta	Philippines	3 l	0.660 gall
Gantang	Malaysia and Singapore	4.55 l	1 gall
	Indonesia (used mainly for rice)	8.58 l	1.887 galls
Go	Japan	0.17 l	1.27 gills
Gwe	Myanmar	20.45 l	4.5 galls
Koku	Japan	180.38 l	39.682 galls
Kwe	Myanmar	20.45 l	4.5 galls
Kwien	Thailand	2,000 l	439.95 galls
Pau	Singapore	0.28 l	0.5 pint
Pyi	Myanmar	2.56 l	0.56 galls
Sale	Myanmar	0.64 l	0.14 gall
Sat	Thailand	20 l	4.40 galls
Sayut	Myanmar	5.12 l	1.12 galls
Seik	Myanmar	10.24 l	2.250 galls
Ser	India	1 l	1.76 pints
Shaku	Japan	0.017 l	0.127 gill
Sho	Japan	1.8 l	0.397 gall
Suk	South Korea	175.8 l	38.682 galls
Tanan	Thailand	1 l	0.22 gall
Tin, Tunn, Tin-han or basket	Myanmar (Thamardi)	40.91 l	9 galls
Tinaja	Philippines	48 l	10.56 galls
To	Japan	17.76 l	3.97 galls

AREA

Unit	Country	Metric equivalent	Imperial Equivalent
Bahoe or Bouw	Indonesia	0.709 ha	1.7536 acres
Bigha	India	0.253 ha	0.625 acre
	Pakistan—Punjab	1354.5 sq m	1,620 sq yds
	Bangladesh	1337.8 sq m	1,600 sq yds
Bu	Japan	3.3 sq m	3.95 sq yds
Cawny or Cawnie	India—Chennai	0.534 ha	1.322 acres
Chattak	Bangladesh	4.18 sq m	5 sq yds
Cho	Japan (square measure)	1 ha	2.47 acres
Chungbo or Jongbo	Korea	1 ha	2.47 acres
Cottah	Bangladesh	66.89 sq m	80 sq yds
Jemba	Malaysia and Singapore	13.38 sq m	16 sq yds
Marabba	Pakistan	10.12 ha	25 acres
Morabba	Pakistan—Punjab	10.12 ha	25 acres
Mu	China	0.065 ha	0.165 acre
Ngan	Thailand	400 sq m	478.4 sq yds
Paal	Indonesia	227.08 ha	561.16 acres
Qing	China (New system)	6.66 ha	16.47 acres
Rai	Thailand	0.16 ha	0.395 acre
Se	Japan	99.17 sq m	118.61 sq yds
Square	Sri Lanka	83.61 sq m	100 sq yds
Tan	Japan	0.1 ha	0.247 acre
Tsubo	Japan	3.3 sq m	3.95 sq yds

QUANTITY

Unit	Country	Quantity
Crore	India, Pakistan, Bangladesh	10,000,000 (1,00,00,000)
Lakh	India, Pakistan, Bangladesh	100,000 (1,00,000)

Metric to Imperial Conversions

Metric units	Imperial units	To convert metric into imperial units multiply by:	To convert imperial into metric units multiply by:
Weight:			
Gram	Ounce (Avoirdupois)	0.035274	28.3495
Kilogram (kg)	Pound (lb)	2.204623	0.453592
Metric ton ('000 kg)	Short ton (2,000 lb)	1,102311	0.907185
	Long ton (2,240 lb)	0.984207	1.016047
	(The short ton is in general use in the USA, while the long ton is normally used in the UK and the Commonwealth.)		
Length			
Centimetre (cm)	Inch	0.3937008	2.54
Metre (m)	Yard (= 3 feet)	1.09361	0.9144
Kilometre (km)	Mile	0.62137	1.609344
Volume			
Cubic metre (cu m)	Cubic foot	35.315	0.028317
	Cubic yard	1.30795	0.764555
Capacity			
Litre (l)	Gallon (= 8 pints)	0.219969	4.54609
	Gallon (US)	0.264172	3.78541
Area			
Square metre (sq m)	Square yard	1.19599	0.836127
Hectare (ha)	Acre	2.47105	0.404686
Square kilometre (sq km)	Square mile	0.386102	2.589988

Systems of Measurement

WEIGHT

Afghanistan	Kharwar = 80 Seer Seer = 4 Charak Charak = 16 Khord
China	Picul = 100 Catty Catty = 16 Liang Liang = 10 Mace Mace = 10 Fan or Candareen
India, Pakistan and Bangladesh	Maund = 40 Seer Seer = 16 Chittack Pa = 20 Tola
Japan	Picul = 16 Kwan (Kan) Kwan = 16 Hyaku-mé Hyaku-mé = 20 Nijo Nijo = 5 Me or Mommé
Malaysia	Koyan = 40 Picul
Myanmar	Candy = 500 Acheintaya Acheintaya = 10 Beittha or Viss Beittha or Viss = 200 Ngamus
Philippines	Quintal = 4 Arroba
Thailand	Picul = 100 Catty or Kon Catty = 40 Baht or Kyat

LENGTH

Cambodia	Hat = 2 Chamam
China	Li = 1,500 Chi Chi = 10 Cun Cun = 10 Fen
Hong Kong	Cheung = 10 Chek Chek = Chi (see China)
India, Pakistan and Bangladesh	Coss = 1,000 Danda Danda = 2 Gudge Gudge = 2 Hath Hath = 24 Ungul
Japan	Jo = 2 Hiro Hiro = 5 Shaku Shaku = 10 Sun
Myanmar	Garwoke = 4 Kawtha Oke thapa = 20 Tar Tar = 7 Cubit or Taung Lan = 4 Cubit or Taung Cubit = 18 Palgate
Thailand	Sen = 20 Wah Wah = 8 Keup

CAPACITY

Japan	To = 10 Sho Sho = 10 Go Go = 10 Shaku
Myanmar	Bag = 3 Tin Tin = 2 Kwe Kwe = 2 Seik Seik = 2 Sayut Sayut = 2 Pyi
Philippines	Cavan = 25 Ganta Tinaja = 15 Ganta Ganta = 8 Chupa
Thailand	Kwien = 100 Sat Sat = 20 Tanan

AREA

China	Qing = 100 Mu
Indonesia	Paal = 320 Bahoe or Bouw
Japan	Cho = 10 Bu or Tan Bu = 2 Se Se = 30 Tsubo
Pakistan	Bigha = 20 Cottah Cottah = 16 Chattah
Thailand	Ngan = 2½ Rai

RESEARCH INSTITUTES

ASSOCIATIONS AND INSTITUTIONS STUDYING THE FAR EAST AND AUSTRALASIA

See also Regional Organizations in Part Three

AUSTRALIA

The Asia-Australia Institute, The University of New South Wales: Sydney, NSW 2052; tel. (2) 9385-9111; fax (2) 9385-9220; e-mail aai@unsw.edu.au; internet www.aii .unsw.edu.au; f. 1990; Chair. Prof. STEPHEN FITZGERALD; Dir LARRY STRANGE.

Asia Research Centre on Social, Political and Economic Change: Murdoch University, Murdoch, WA 6150; tel. (8) 9360-2846; fax (8) 9310-4944; e-mail blakeway@central .murdoch.edu.au; internet wwwarc.murdoch.edu.au; f. 1991; provides analysis of contemporary East and South-East Asia.

Asian Economics Centre: Dept of Economics, University of Melbourne, Vic 3010; tel. (3) 8344-3880; fax (3) 8344-6890; e-mail s.jayasuriya@unimelb.edu.au; internet www.ecom.unimelb .edu.au/ecowww/AsianEconomicCtr/AECI.htm; fmrly Asian Business Centre; Dir Asst Prof. SISIRA JAYASURIYA.

Asian Studies Centre, University of Queensland: Room 309A, Level 3, Gordon Greenwood Bldg, University of Queensland, Brisbane, Qld 4072; tel. (7) 3365-6763; fax (7) 3365-6811; e-mail a.platt@mailbox.uq.edu.au; internet www.uq.edu .au/asc/; Dir Prof. KAM LOUIE.

Asian Studies Program, La Trobe University: Vic 3086; tel. (3) 9479-1315; fax (3) 9479-1880; e-mail asianstudies@latrobe .edu.au; internet www.latrobe.edu.au/www/asianstudies/; f. 1994.

Australia-Japan Research Centre: Australian National University, Canberra, ACT 0200; tel. (2) 6125-3730; fax (2) 6125-0767; email ajrc@anu.edu.au; internet www.ajrcnet.anu.edu.au; f. 1980; Exec. Dir Prof. PETER DRYSDALE; publs include *Pacific Economic Papers* (monthly), *Asia Pacific Economics and Politics, APEC Economies Newsletter* (monthly).

Australia South Asia Research Centre: Australian National University, Canberra, ACT 0200; tel. (2) 6125-2683; fax (2) 6125-0443; e-mail asarc@anu.edu.au; internet rspas.anu.edu .au/asarc; f. 1994; research on the economics and politics of development in the South Asian region, particularly India; Exec. Dir Prof. RAGHBENDRA JHA.

Australian Institute of International Affairs: 32 Thesiger Court, Deakin, ACT 2600; tel. (2) 6282-2133; fax (2) 6285-2334; internet www.aiia.asn.au; f. 1933; 1,400 mems; brs in all States; Pres. NEAL BLEWETT; Exec. Dir ROSS COTTRILL; publs *The Australian Journal of International Affairs* (3 a year), *Australia in World Affairs* (every 5 years).

Centre for Asian Studies, University of Adelaide: University of Adelaide, Adelaide, SA 5005; tel. (8) 8303-5815; fax (8) 8303-4388; internet www.adelaide.edu.au/AsianStudies; specializes in China and Japan; Head Assoc. Prof. JOHN MAKEHAM.

Centre for International Economic Studies: University of Adelaide, Adelaide, SA 5005; tel. (8) 8303-4712; fax (8) 8223-1460; e-mail cies@adelaide.edu.au; internet www.adelaide.edu.au/ cies; f. 1989; conducts theory policy-orientated research with particular reference to the Asia-Pacific region; publs include monographs.

Centre for Japanese Economic Studies: Dept of Economics, Macquarie University, Sydney, NSW 2109; tel. (2) 9850-7444; fax (2) 9850-8586; e-mail craig.freedman@efs.mq.edu.au; internet www/econ.mq.edu.au/CJES; f. 1991; Dir Dr CRAIG FREEDMAN; publs include working papers.

Centre for Southeast Asian Studies: Northern Territory University, Darwin 0909; tel. (8) 8946-6807; fax (8) 8946-6977; f. 1986; Dir Dr IAN WALTERS; publs include newsletter, papers and monographs.

Centre for the Study of Australia-Asia Relations: School of Modern Asian Studies, Griffith University, Queensland 4111; tel. (7) 3875-7624; fax (7) 3875-7956; e-mail csaar@mailbox.gu .edu.au; internet www.gu.edu.au/guris/csaar/cshome.htm; f. 1978; Dir Assoc. Prof. RUSSELL TROOD.

Contemporary China Centre: Research School of Pacific and Asian Studies, Australian National University, Canberra, ACT 0200; tel. (2) 6125-4157; fax (2) 6257-3642; e-mail ccc@coombs .anu.edu.au; internet www.anu.edu.au/RSPAS/ccc/journal.htm; f. 1970; analyses post-1949 China; Dir Prof. JONATHAN UNGER; publs include *The China Journal, Contemporary China Papers*.

Faculty of Asian Studies, Australian National University: Canberra, ACT 0200; tel. (2) 6125-3207; fax (2) 6125-0745; e-mail executive.officer.asian.studies@anu.edu.au; internet www.anu.edu.au/asianstudies; Dean Prof. A. C. MILNER.

Indian Ocean Centre for Peace Studies: University of Western Australia, Nedlands, WA 6907; tel. (8) 9380-2278; fax (8) 9380-1060; internet www.curtin.edu.au/curtin/centre/ioc/; f. 1991; Contact Dr SAMINA YASMEEN; publ. *The Indian Ocean Review* (quarterly).

National Thai Studies Centre: Faculty of Asian Studies, Australian National University, Canberra, ACT 0200; tel. (2) 6125-4661; fax (2) 6125-0745; e-mail ntsc@anu.edu.au; internet www.anu.edu.au/thaionline; f. 1991; Dir CAVAN HOGUE; publs include Thai language teaching materials, *Thailand Information Papers*.

Monash Asia Institute: Monash University, Clayton, Vic 3800; tel. (3) 9905-2124; fax (3) 9905-5370; e-mail marika.vicziany@ adm.monash.edu.au; internet www.arts.monash.edu.au/mai; f. 1988; incorporates China Research Centre, National Centre for South Asian Studies, Japanese Studies Centre, Centre of Malaysian Studies, Asia Pacific Health and Nutrition Centre and Centre of Southeast Asian Studies.

Research Institute for Asia and the Pacific: Bldg G12, University of Sydney, NSW 2006; tel. (2) 9351-8547; fax (2) 9351-8562; e-mail postmaster@riap.usyd.edu.au; internet www.riap.usyd.edu.au; research on human resource development, information technology, media, the environment, public administration, regional security and managing systems that underpin institutional capacity; Dir Dr STEPHANIE FAHEY.

Research School of Pacific and Asian Studies: Australian National University, Canberra, ACT 0200; tel. (2) 6249-2183; fax (2) 6249-1893; internet rspas.anu.edu.au; publs include *Asian-Pacific Economic Literature, The China Journal, Bulletin of Indonesian Economic Studies, Canberra Anthropology, Canberra Papers on Strategy and Defence, Pacific Economic Papers, Pacific Linguistics, East Asian History, Contemporary China Papers, New Asia-Pacific Review* and monograph series.

School of Asian Languages and Studies, University of Tasmania: GPOB 252-91, Hobart, Tasmania; tel. (3) 6226-2343; fax (3) 6226-7813; f. 1990; fmrly Asia Centre; Asian Studies Coordinator Dr SIMON PHILPOTT.

School of European, Asian and Middle Eastern Languages and Studies, University of Sydney: Brennan Bldg, University of Sydney, NSW 2006; tel. (2) 9351-3382; fax (2) 9351-2319; e-mail SEAMELS@arts.usyd.edu.au; internet www.arts.usyd.edu.au; f. 1991; includes the depts of Asian Studies, Chinese Studies, Japanese and Korean Studies, Indian Subcontinental Studies, and Southeast Asian Studies; Head Prof. TONY STEPHENS.

AUSTRIA

Afro-Asiatisches Institut in Wien (Afro-Asian Institute in Vienna): 1090 Vienna, Türkenstrasse 3; tel. (1) 3105145; fax (1) 3105145-312; f. 1959; e-mail office@aai-wien.at; internet www.aai-wien.at/aai-wien; religious, cultural, economic and scientific exchanges between Austria and African and Asian countries; assistance to students from Africa and Asia; public relations, lectures, seminars; Rector Dr mag. KONSTANTIN SPIEGELFELD.

Institut für Ostasienwissenschaften der Universität Wien: 1090 Vienna, Spitalgasse 2–4; tel. (1) 4277-43801; fax (1) 4277-9438; e-mail ostasien@univie.ac.at; internet www.univie.ac.at/ostasien/; f. 1965; Japanese, Chinese and Korean studies; Dir Dr SEPP LINHART; publ. *Institutsbericht* (annual).

Institut für Ostasienwissenschaften/Sinologie der Universität Wien: 1090 Vienna, Spitalgasse 2, Hof 2; tel. (1) 4277-43840; fax (1) 4277-43849; e-mail sinologie.ostasien@univie.ac.at; internet www.univie.ac.at/sinologie; Dir Prof. Dr SEPP LINHART.

BANGLADESH

Asiatic Society of Bangladesh: 5 Old Secretariat Rd, Ramna, Dhaka 1000; tel. (2) 9667586; fax (2) 9560500; e-mail assoenpr@bangla.net; Pres. Prof. ABDUL MOMIN CHOWDHURY; Gen. Sec. Prof. SAJAHAN MIAH; publs *Journal of the Asiatic Society of Bangladesh (Humanities), Journal of the Asiatic Society of Bangladesh (Science), Bangladesh Asiatic Society Patrika (Bangla).*

Bangladesh Institute of Development Studies: E-17, Agargaon, Sher-E-Bangla Nagar, GPO Box 3854, Dhaka 1207; tel. (2) 324596; fax (2) 8113023; e-mail info@sdnbd.org; f. 1957; promotes and conducts studies and research in development economics, demography and other social sciences relating to planning for national development and social welfare; library of over 120,000 books, documents, journals, and microfiches; Dir-Gen. Prof. ABU AHMED ABDULLAH; publs include *Research Report, Research Monograph.*

Bangladesh Institute of International and Strategic Studies: 1/46 Elephant Rd, Dhaka 1000; tel. (2) 406234; fax (2) 832625; internet www.bangla.net/webera/biiss/; f. 1978; Dir-Gen. Maj.-Gen. GHULAM QUADER.

Bureau of Socio-Economic Research and Training: Bangladesh Agricultural University, Mymensingh 2202; tel. (91) 56957; f. 1965; conducts and promotes socio-economic research, particularly on rural problems in Bangladesh; Chair. Prof. M. ZAINAL ABEDIN KHAN; publs include *Bangladesh Journal of Agricultural Economics* (2 a year).

Institute of Bangladesh Studies: University of Rajshahi, 6205 Rajshahi; tel. (721) 750985; fax (721) 750064; e-mail ibs@rajbd.com; Dir Prof. PRITI KUMAR MITRA; Sec. M. ZAIDUR RAHMAN; publs *Journal of the Institute of Bangladesh Studies* (annually), *IBS Journal* (annually).

Varendra Research Museum: Rajshahi; f. 1910; conducts research in history, archaeology, anthropology, literature, and art; collects and preserves archaeological and other relics, ancient MSS; library of c. 15,000 vols; 8,250 items in museum, including 4,500 ancient MSS; Dir Dr SAIFUDDIN CHOWDHURY; publ. *Journal* (annually).

BELGIUM

The European Institute for Asian Studies: 35 rue des Deux Eglises, 1040 Brussels; tel. (2) 230-8122; fax (2) 230-5402; e-mail eias@eias.org; internet www.eias.org; Chair. Prof. Dr LUDO CUYVEES; Sec.-Gen. DICK GUPWELL; publs *The EurAsia Bulletin* (monthly), *EIAS Briefing Papers.*

Institut orientaliste: Faculté de Philosophie et Lettres, Université Catholique de Louvain, Collège Erasme, 1348 Louvain-la-Neuve; tel. (10) 474958; fax (10) 479169; e-mail ori8@glor.ucl.ac.be; internet www.fltr.ucl.ac.be/FLTR/GLOR/ORI; f. 1936; Pres. Prof. B. COULIE; publs *Le Muséon* (2 a year), *Bibliothèque du Muséon, Publications de l'Institut Orientaliste de Louvain (PIOL), Corpus Scriptorum Christianorum Orientalium.*

Institut royal des Relations internationales: 59 rue de Namur, 1000 Brussels; tel. (2) 223-4114; fax (2) 223-4116; e-mail info@irri-kiib.be; f. 1947; research in international relations, economics, law and politics; specialized library containing 16,500 vols and 600 periodicals; archives; holds lectures and conferences; Pres. Viscount E. DAVIGNON; Dir-Gen. EMILE MASSA; publs *Studia Diplomatica* (bi-monthly), *Internationale Spectator* (monthly), in co-operation with Instituut Clingendael.

BHUTAN

The Centre for Bhutan Studies: POB 1111, Thimpu; tel. 321003; fax 321001; e-mail cbs.bt@undp.org; f. 1999; Head KARMA URA.

BRAZIL

Centro de Estudos Afro-Asiáticos (CEAA): Praça Pio X 7, 9°, 20040-020, Rio de Janeiro, RJ; tel. (21) 516-7157; fax (21) 518-2798; e-mail beluce@candidomendes.br; publ. *Estudos Afro-Asiáticos.*

CAMBODIA

Cambodia Development Resource Institute (CDRI): POB 622, 56 Street 315, Tuol Kork, Phnom-Penh; tel. (23) 368-053; fax (23) 366094; e-mail cdri@camnet.com.kh; internet www.cdri.org.kh; f. 1990; research into socio-economic issues of importance to Cambodia and the region.

CANADA

Asian Pacific Research and Resource Centre: Department of Law, Carleton University, Ottawa, ON K1S 5B6; tel. (613) 520-3690; fax (613) 520-4467; e-mail paul-davidson@carleton.ca; f. 1989; conducts research in commerce and investment in the Asia-Pacific region; Dir Prof. PAUL J. DAVIDSON; publs monographs, working papers.

Canadian Council for International Co-operation: 1 Nicholas St, Suite 300, Ottawa, ON K1N 7B7; tel. (613) 241-7007; fax (613) 241-5302; e-mail ccic@ccic.ca; internet www.web.net/ccic-ccci; f. 1968; information and training centre for international development and forum for voluntary agencies; 130 mems; Pres. CAMERON CHARLEBOIS; CEO BETTY PLEWES; publs include newsletter and directory of NGOs working overseas.

Canadian Institute of International Affairs: 2275 Bayview Ave, Toronto, ON M4N 3M6; tel. (416) 487-6830; fax (416) 487-6831; e-mail mailbox@ciia.org; internet www.ciia.org; f. 1928; research in international relations; library containing 8,000 vols; Chair. ROY MACLAREN; Pres. and CEO BARBARA MCDOUGALL; publs *Behind the Headlines* (quarterly), International Journal (quarterly), annual report.

Centre for Developing-Area Studies: McGill University, 3715 rue Peel, Montréal, QC H3A 1X1; tel. (514) 398-3507; fax (514) 398-8432; e-mail pub.cdas@mcgill.ca; internet www.mcgill.ca/cdas; Dir Dr ROSALIND BOYD; publs. include *Labour, Capital and Society* (English and French—2 a year), *Discussion Paper Series.*

Department of Asian Studies, University of British Columbia: Vancouver, BC V6T 1Z2; tel. (604) 822-5728; fax (604) 822-8937; f. 1961; instruction and research in East, South and South-East Asia; Head Dr KENNETH BRYANT.

Institute of Asian Research: University of British Columbia, C.K. Choi Bldg, 1855 West Mall, Vancouver, BC V6T 1Z2; tel. (604) 822-4688; fax (604) 822-5207; e-mail iar@interchange.ubc.ca; internet www.iar.ubc.ca; f. 1978; Dir PITMAN B. POTTER; publ. *Asia Pacific Report* (2 a year).

International Development Research Centre: POB 8500, Ottawa K1G 3H9; tel. (613) 236-6163; fax (613) 563-2476; e-mail info@idrc.ca; internet www.idrc.ca; f. 1970 as a public corpn to support scientific research aimed at helping communities in the developing world find solutions to social, environmental and economic problems; has regional offices in Singapore, India, Uruguay and Africa; Pres. MAUREEN O'NEIL; publs *Annual Report* and books.

Lester Pearson International: 1321 Edward St, Halifax, NS B3H 3H5; tel. (902) 494-2038; fax (902) 494-1216; e-mail lpi@dal.ca; internet www.dal.ca/lpi; f. 1985; admin. inst., responsible for organization and supervision of international activities of Dalhousie Univ.; publs include *LPI Update* (fortnightly) and occasional paper series.

PEOPLE'S REPUBLIC OF CHINA

China Centre for International Studies (CCIS): 22 Xianmen Dajie, POB 1744, Beijing 100017; tel. (10) 63097083; fax (10) 63095802; f. 1982; conducts research on international relations and problems; organizes academic exchanges; Dir-Gen. LI LUYE.

China-Europe International Business School (CEIBS): 699 Hong Feng Lu, Shanghai 201206; tel. (21) 28905890; fax (21) 28905678; e-mail info@mail.ceibs.edu.cn; internet www.ceibs.edu; Exec. Pres. Dr ALBERT BENNETT; Dean Prof. WILLIAM A. FISCHER.

China Institute of Contemporary International Relations (CICIR): 2A Wanshousi, Haidian, Beijing 100081; tel. (10) 8418640; fax (10) 8418641; f. 1980; research on international development and peace issues; Pres. SHEN QURONG; publ. *Contemporary International Relations* (monthly).

China Institute for International Strategic Studies: Beijing; Dir-Gen. XU XIN.

Chinese Academy of Social Sciences: 5 Jianguomen Nei Da Jie, Beijing 100732; tel. (10) 65137744; fax (10) 65138154; f. 1977; Pres. HU SHENG; Sec.-Gen. GUO YONGCAI; comprises more than 40 research institutes and centres and one graduate school.

Chinese People's Institute of Foreign Affairs: 71 Nanchizi Jie, Beijing 100006; tel. (10) 65131824; e-mail cpifa@public.bta.net.cn; Pres. MEI ZHAORONG; Sec.-Gen. XU SHAOHAI.

Institute of Asia-Pacific Studies, Chinese Academy of Social Sciences: 3 Zhang Zizhong Lu, Beijing 100007; tel. (10) 64063042; fax (10) 64063041; e-mail aprccass@public3.bta.net.cn; f. 1988; theoretical and policy-orientated research in economic, political, social and cultural studies; Dir ZHANG YUNLING.

Institute of Asian-Pacific Studies, Shanghai Academy of Social Sciences: 7/622 Huai Hai Zhong Lu, Shanghai 200020; tel. (21) 63271170; fax (21) 63270004; e-mail jmzhou@fudan.ihep.ac.cn; internet www.jcie.or.jp/thinknet/research_instit/china/Inst_AP_Shang.html; f. 1990; Dir Dr ZHOU JIANMING.

Institute for Southeast Asian Studies, Jinan University: Shipai, Guangzhou 8510632; tel. (20) 8516511; fax (20) 8516941; Dir CHEN QIAOZHI.

Institute of World Economy: Fudan University, 220 Handan Lu, Shanghai 200433; tel. (21) 65492222; fax (21) 65491875; Dirs Prof. WU YIKANG, MA XOXIANG.

International Business Research Institute: University of International Business and Economics, Hui Xin Dong Jie, He Ping Jie N., Beijing 100029; tel. (10) 64225522; fax (10) 64212022; Dir Prof. TENG DEXIANG.

International Trade Research Institute: 17 Hubei Lu, Qingdao, Shangdong; tel. and fax (531) 6270179; f. 1980; conducts research on developments in international commerce and economics; Dir CHEN CHINGCHANG; publs *International Economic and Trade Information, Shandong Foreign Trade.*

Research Institute for International Economic Co-operation (RIIEC): 28 An Wai Dong Hou Xiang, Beijing; tel. (10) 64212106; fax (10) 64212175; f. 1980; Dir YANG JINBO; publ. *International Economic Co-operation.*

Research Institute of International Politics: Beijing University, 1 Loudouqiao, Haidian, Beijing 100871; tel. (10) 62554002; fax (10) 62564095; Dir LIANG SHOUDE.

Shanghai Institute of International Issues (SIIS): 1 Alley, 845 Ju Lu, Shanghai 200040; tel. (21) 62471148; fax (21) 62472272; f. 1960; Dir CHEN PEIYAO; publs *Survey of International Affairs* (annually), *Guoji Zhanwang* (2 a month), papers, monographs.

Shanghai University of Finance and Economics, Asian Economic Research Institute: 777 Guoding Lu, Shanghai 200433; tel. and fax (21) 65361955; f. 1993; Chair. YI JUANQIU.

Taiwan Economy Research Institute: Nankai University, Balitai, Tianjin 200071; tel. (22) 63358825; fax (22) 63344853; Dir Prof. BAO JUEMIN.

West Asian and African Studies Institute: Chinese Academy of Social Sciences, 3 Zhangzhizhong Rd, Beijing 100007; e-mail iwaas@public.fhnet.cn.net; f. 1961; Dir-Gen. Prof. YANG GUANG.

CROATIA

Institute for International Relations: 10000 Zagreb, POB 303, ul. Ljudevita Farkaša Vukotinovića 2/II; tel. (1) 4826522; fax (1) 4828361; e-mail ured@irmo.hr; f. 1963; affiliated to the University of Zagreb and the Ministry of Science and Technology; Dir Prof. Dr MLADEN STANIČIĆ; publs include *Croatian International Relations Review* (quarterly), *Culturelink* (3 a year).

CZECH REPUBLIC

Czech Society for Eastern Studies: c/o Oriental Institute, Academy of Sciences, Pod vodárenskou věží 4, 182 08 Prague 8; tel. (2) 66052483; fax (2) 86581897; e-mail aror@orient.cas.cz; f. 1958; 71 mems; Pres. LŭBICA OBUCHOVÁ.

Institute of International Relations: Nerudova 3, 118 50 Prague 1, tel. (2) 51108111; fax (2) 51108222; e-mail umv@iir.cz; internet www.iir.cz; f. 1957; Dir Dr JIŘÍ ŠEDIVÝ; publs include *International Politics* (monthly), *International Relations* (4 a year) in Czech, *Perspectives* (2 a year) in English.

Oriental Institute: Academy of Sciences of the Czech Republic, Pod vodárenskou věží 4, 182 08 Prague 8; tel. (2) 66052492; fax (2) 86581897; e-mail orient@orient.cas.cz; internet www.orient.cas.cz; f. 1922; research on languages, social and economic aspects, etc. of Asia and Africa; Chinese library of 66,177 vols, general library of more than 190,000 vols; Dir Dr JIŘÍ PROSECKÝ (acting); publs *Archiv orientální* (quarterly), *Nový Orient* (monthly).

DENMARK

Center for Udviklingsforskning (Centre for Development Research): Gammel Kongevej 5, 1610 Copenhagen V; tel. 33-85-46-00; fax 33-25-81-10; e-mail cdr@cdr.dk; internet www.cdr.dk; f. 1969 to promote and undertake research in the economic, social and political problems of developing countries; library of 50,000 vols; Dir POUL ENGBERG-PEDERSEN; publs include *Researching Development* (in English, quarterly newsletter), *CDR Library Papers* (irregular), *Den ny Verden* (quarterly), *CDR Research Reports* (in English, irregular), *CDR Working Papers* (in English, irregular).

Nordic Institute of Asian Studies: Leifsgade 33, 2300 Copenhagen S; tel. 32-54-88-44; fax 32-96-25-30; e-mail sec@nias.ku.dk; internet www.nias.ku.dk; f. 1967; known until 1988 as the Scandinavian Institute of Asian Studies; non-profit org. funded through Nordic Council of Ministers; research and documentation centre for the study of modern Asian societies and cultures from the perspective of the humanities and social sciences, with a multi-disciplinary profile; library of 24,000 vols and 750 periodicals; Chair. of Bd Dr CLEMENS STUBBE ØSTERGAARD; Dir Prof. Dr PER RONNÅS; publs include *NIASnytt / Nordic Newsletter of Asian Studies* (quarterly), monographs, anthologies and research reports.

Orientalsk Samfund: Department of History, Njalsgade 80, 2300 Copenhagen S; tel. 35-32-82-96; e-mail littrup@hum.ku.dk; f. 1915 to undertake the study and further the understanding of oriental cultures and civilizations; Pres. Dr LEIF LITTRUP; publ. *Acta Orientalia* (annually).

Udenrigspolitiske Selskab (Foreign Policy Society): Amaliegade 40A, 1256 Copenhagen K; tel. 33-14-88-86; fax 33-14-85-20; f. 1946; studies, debates, courses and conferences on international affairs; library of 100 periodicals; Dir KLAUS CARSTEN PEDERSEN; Chair. UFFE ELLEMANN-JENSEN; publs *Udenrigs, Udenrigspolitiske Skrifter.*

FIJI

The Fiji Society: POB 1205, Suva; f. 1936; concerned with subjects of historic and scientific interest to Fiji and other islands of the Pacific; Pres. IVAN WILLIAMS; publ. *Transactions* (irregular).

Pacific Institute of Management and Development: University of the South Pacific, Private Mail Bag, Suva; tel. 3212079; fax 3303229; e-mail isas@usp.ac.fj; internet www.usp.ac.fj/ISAS.

FINLAND

Suomen Itämainen Seura (Finnish Oriental Society): c/o Dept of Asian and African Studies, University of Helsinki, JP 59, 00014 Helsinki; tel. (9) 19122224; fax (9) 19122094; e-mail kaj.ohrnberg@helsinki.fi; f. 1917; 187 mems; Pres. Prof. TAPANI

HARVIAINEN; Sec. KAJ ÖHRNBERG; publ. *Studia Orientalia* (annually).

World Institute for Development Economics Research of the United Nations University (UNU/WIDER): Katajanokanlaituri 6B, 00160 Helsinki; tel. (9) 6159911; fax (9) 61599333; e-mail wider@wider.unu.edu; internet www.wider.unu.edu; f. 1984; research and training centre of the UNU (Japan); publs include *WIDER Discussion Papers, Policy Briefs, Annual Lectures, Newsletter WIDER Angle.*

FRANCE

Centre des Hautes Etudes sur l'Afrique et l'Asie Modernes: 13 rue du Four, 75006 Paris; tel. 1-43-26-96-90; fax 1-40-51-03-58; internet www.ccfr.bnf.fr; f. 1936; library of 16,000 vols; Dir J. P. DOUMENGE; publs *La Lettre du Cheaam* (quarterly), *Notes africaines, asiatiques et caraïbes* (irregular).

Ecole des Langues et Civilisations de l'Orient Ancien: Institut Catholique de Paris, Faculté de Théologie et de Sciences Religieuses, 21 rue d'Assas, 75270 Paris Cedex 06; tel. 1-44-39-52-50; e-mail elcoa@icp.fr; f. 1914; study of and research into ancient oriental languages and civilizations; Dir FLORENCE MALBRAN-LABAT.

Institut National des Langues et Civilisations Orientales: 2 rue de Lille, 75343 Paris Cedex 07; tel. 1-49-26-42-00; fax 1-49-26-42-99; internet www.inalco.fr; courses in 82 languages; research; information centre; organizes international exchanges; specializes in international relations; Pres. A. BOURGEY; publs research serials, textbooks, translations, etc.

Musée National des Arts Asiatiques Guimet: 6 place d'Iéna, 75116 Paris; tel. 1-56-52-53-00; fax 1-56-52-53-54; f. 1889; library of 100,000 vols; art, archaeology, religions, literature and music of India, Central Asia, Tibet, Pakistan, Viet Nam, China, Korea, Japan, Cambodia, Thailand, Laos, Myanmar (formerly Burma) and Indonesia; Dir JEAN-FRANÇOIS JARRIGE; Librarian F. MACOUIN; publs *Annales du Musée Guimet, Arts Asiatiques.*

Société Asiatique: 3 rue Mazarine, 75006 Paris; tel. and fax 1-44-41-43-14; f. 1822; library of 100,000 vols; 750 mems; Pres. JEAN-PIERRE MAHÉ; publs *Journal Asiatique* (2 a year), *Nouveaux Cahiers.*

Unité Formation et Recherche (UFR) Asie Orientale: Université de Paris VII, 2 place Jussieu, 75251 Paris Cedex 05; tel. 1-44-27-57-81; fax 1-44-27-78-98; f. 1971; Dir FRANÇOIS JULLIEN.

FRENCH POLYNESIA

Te Fare Tauhiti Nui—Maison de la culture: 646 Blvd Pomaré, BP 1709, Papeete; tel. 544544; fax 428569; e-mail tauhiti@mail.pf; f. 1980; promotes culture locally and abroad; sponsors many public and private cultural events; library of 9,500 vols, children's library of 7,000 vols; Dir GEORGES ESTALL.

GERMANY

AAI-Abteilung für Sprache und Kultur Japans, Universität Hamburg: 20146 Hamburg, Edmund-Siemers-Allee 1, Ostflüge; tel. (40) 42838-4884; fax (40) 42838-6200; e-mail japanologie@uni-hamburg.de; internet www.uni-hamburg.de/japans; f. 1914; research into Japanese studies; 43,500 vols; Dir Prof. Dr R. SCHNEIDER; publs include *Oriens Extremus, Nachrichten, Kagami* and monograph series *MOAG.*

China-Institut: Johann Wolfgang Goethe-Universität, 60054 Frankfurt am Main, Senckenberganlage 31; e-mail B.Sude@em.uni-frankfurt.de; Dir Prof. Dr TSUNG-TUNG CHANG.

Deutsch-Indische Gesellschaft eV: 70173 Stuttgart, Charlottenplatz 17; tel. (711) 297078; fax (711) 2991450; e-mail DGesellsch@aol.com; internet www.dig-ev.de.

Deutsche Gesellschaft für Asienkunde eV (German Association for Asian Studies): 20148 Hamburg, Rothenbaumchaussee 32; tel. (40) 445891; fax (40) 4107945; e-mail post@asienkunde.de; internet www.asienkunde.de; f. 1967; promotion and co-ordination of contemporary Asian research; 650 mems; Pres. HANS-ULRICH KLOSE; Sec. Dr GÜNTER SCHUCHER; publ. *ASIEN. Deutsche Zeitschrift für Politik, Wirtschaft und Kultur* (quarterly).

Deutsche Gesellschaft für Auswärtige Politik eV (German Society for Foreign Affairs): 53113 Bonn, Adenauerallee 131, Postfach 1425, 53004 Bonn; tel. (228) 2675-0; fax (228) 2675-173; e-mail DGAP@compuserve.com; internet www.dgap.org; f. 1955; promotes research on problems of international politics; library of 50,000 vols; 1,600 mems; Pres. Dr WERNER LAMBY; Exec. Vice-Pres. Dr IMMO STABREIT; Dir Research Inst. Prof. Dr KARL KAISER; publs *Internationale Politik* (monthly), *Die Internationale Politik* (annually).

Deutsche Morgenländische Gesellschaft eV (German Oriental Society): Südasien-Institut, 69120 Heidelberg, Im Neuenheimer Feld 330; tel. (6221) 548900; fax (6221) 544998; e-mail dmg@sai.uni-heidelberg.de; internet www.dmg-web.de; f. 1845; sponsors research and holds meetings and lectures in the field of oriental studies; 650 mems; Sec. MANFRED HAKE; publs include *Zeitschrift, Abhandlungen für die Kunde des Morgenlandes.*

Deutsche Orient-Gesellschaft eV (German Oriental Society): Geschäftsstelle Altorientalisches Seminar der FU Berlin, 14195 Berlin, Hüttenweg 7; tel. (30) 83853601; fax (30) 853600; f. 1898; 916 mems; Pres. Prof. Dr JAN-WAALKE MEYER; Sec. Prof. Dr G. WILHELM; publs *Mitteilungen der DOG, Wissenschaftliche Veröffentlichungen der DOG, Abhandlungen der DOG, Colloquien der DOG.*

Forschungsinstitut für Wirtschaftliche Entwicklungen im Pazifikraum eV (Asia-Pacific Economic Research Institute): Gerhard-Mercator University, 47048 Duisburg, Lotharstrasse 65; tel. (203) 3792357; fax (203) 3791786; e-mail iwbheiduk@uni-duisburg.de; internet www.uni-duisburg.de/FB5/VWL/IWB/fip.htm; f. 1985; research on economic developments in the Pacific region; Dirs Prof. GÜNTER HEIDUK, Prof. WERNER PASCHA, Prof. CARSTEN HERRMANN-PILLATH.

Institut für Asienkunde (Asian Affairs): 20148 Hamburg, Rothenbaumchaussee 32; tel. (40) 428874-0; fax (40) 4107945; e-mail iffahh@uni-hamburg.de; internet www.duei.de/ifa; f. 1956; research and documentation into all aspects of contemporary South, South-East and East Asia; Pres. Dr Dr W. RÖHL; Dir Dr W. DRAGUHN.

Museum für Indische Kunst (Indian Art): Staatliche Museen zu Berlin-Preussischer Kulturbesitz, 14195 Berlin, Takustrasse 40; tel. (30) 8301361; fax (30) 8301502; e-mail mik@smb.spk-berlin.de; Dir Prof. Dr MARIANNE YALDIZ; publs include series *Veröffentlichungen des Museums für Indische Kunst.*

Museum für Islamische Kunst (Islamic Art and Antiquities): Staatliche Museen zu Berlin Preussischer Kulturbesitz, 10178 Berlin, Bodestrasse 1–3; tel. (30) 20905400; fax (30) 20905402; e-mail isl@smb.spk-berlin.de; internet www.smb.spk-berlin.de/isl; f. 1904; Dir Prof. Dr CLAUS-PETER HAASE.

Museum für Ostasiatische Kunst (Far Eastern Art): Staatliche Museen zu Berlin-Preussischer Kulturbesitz, 14195 Berlin, Takustrasse 40; tel. (30) 8301381; fax (30) 8301501; e-mail oak@smb.spk-berlin.de; internet www.smb.spk-berlin.de; f. 1906; Dir Prof. Dr W. VEIT.

Südasien-Institut der Universität Heidelberg: 69120 Heidelberg, Im Neuenheimer Feld 330; tel. (6221) 548900; fax (6221) 544998; e-mail sai@www.sai.uni-heidelberg.de; internet www.sai.uni-heidelberg.de; f. 1962; Dir Prof. AXEL MICHAELS; Sec. MANFRED HAKE; publs include *Beiträge zur Südasienforschung* and *South Asian Studies.*

HONG KONG

Asia-Pacific Financial Markets Research Centre: City University of Hong Kong, 83 Tat Chee Ave, Kowloon; tel. 27887940; fax 27888806; internet www.cityu.edu.hk/rcf/index.htm; f. 1983; research into financial markets in the Asia-Pacific region; Dir Prof. RICHARD HO; publ. *Technical Reports* (monthly).

The Asia-Pacific Institute of Business: The Chinese University of Hong Kong, Li Dak Sum Bldg, 2nd Floor, Shatin, New Territories; tel. 26097428; fax 26035136; e-mail apib@cuhk.edu.hk; f. 1990; provides research, consultancy and educational courses on business and economic issues concerning Hong Kong and the Asia-Pacific region; Exec. Dir Prof. LESLIE YOUNG; publ. *The Hong Kong Securities Industry.*

Centre of Asian Studies: The University of Hong Kong, Pokfulam Rd; tel. 28592460; fax 25593185; e-mail casgen@hku.hk/cas; internet www.hku.hk/cas; f. 1967; traditional and contemporary China, Hong Kong, East and South-East Asia; Dir Prof. S. L. WONG; publs include *Journal of Oriental Studies.*

Hong Kong Institute of Asia-Pacific Studies: Chinese University of Hong Kong, Esther Lee Bldg, Shatin, New Territories; tel. 26098777; fax 26035215; e-mail hkiaps@cuhk.edu.hk; internet www.cuhk.edu.hk/hkiaps/homepage.htm; f. 1990; Dir Prof. YUE-MAN YEUNG; publs occasional papers, research monographs, seminar series.

Institute of Chinese Studies: The Chinese University of Hong Kong, Shatin, New Territories; tel. 26097394; fax 26035149; e-mail ics@cuhk.edu.hk; internet www.cuhk.edu.hk/ics; f. 1967; comprises Art Museum, Research Center for Translation, Center for Chinese Archaeology and Art, Chinese Language Research Center, Research Center for Contemporary Chinese Culture and Chinese Ancient Text (CHANT) Database Project; Dir Prof. JENNY SO FONG SUK; publs include *ICS Journal* (annually), *Renditions* (2 a year), *The Chinese Language Newsletter* (quarterly) and *Twenty-First Century* (every 2 months).

HUNGARY

Magyar Tudományos Akadémia Orientalisztikai Munkaközössége (Orientalist Research Centre of the Hungarian Academy of Sciences): 1014 Budapest I, Országház u. 30; tel. (1) 175-90-11; f. 1979; Head Prof. FERENC TŐKEI; publ. series *Történelem és kultúra* (History and Culture, in Hungarian).

Magyar Tudományos Akadémia Világgazdasági Kutató Intézete (Institute for World Economics of the Hungarian Academy of Sciences): 1014 Budapest, Országház u. 30; tel. (1) 224-6760; fax (1) 224-6761; e-mail vki@vki3.vki.hu; internet vki3.vki.hu; f. 1965; library of 103,000 vols; Dir ANDRAS INOTAI; publs *Working Papers* (c. 15 a year, in English), *Trends in World Economy* (in English), *Kihívások* (10–15 a year, in Hungarian), *Muhelytanulmányok* (10–15 a year in Hungarian).

INDIA

Abul Kalam Azad Oriental Research Institute: Public Gardens, Hyderabad 500 004; tel. (842) 230805; f. 1959; research in history, philosophy, culture and languages; library of 15,000 vols; Pres. MAHMOOD BIN MUHAMMAD; Sec. MIR KAMALUDDIN ALI KHAN.

All-India Oriental Conference: Bhandarkar Oriental Research Institute, Pune 411 004; tel. (20) 5656932; f. 1919; 1,200 mems; Pres. Prof. R. N. DANDEKAR; Sec. Prof. SAROJA BHATE; publs *Proceedings of its Sessions, Index of Papers* (in 4 vols).

Anjuman-i-Islam Urdu Research Institute: 92 Dadabhoy Nowroji Rd, Mumbai 400 001; tel. (22) 2620177; fax (22) 2621610; f. 1947; post-graduate degree courses and research in Urdu, Islamic studies, etc.; library of 350,000 documents; also administers Calligraphy Training Centre; facilities for Jamia Urdu courses of Aligarh; Pres. Dr M. ISHAQ JAMKAHANAWALA; Dir Dr ADAM SHEIKH; publs include *Nawa-e-Adab* (2 a year).

Asiatic Society: 1 Park St, Kolkata 700 016; f. 1784; 696 mems; Pres. Prof. BISWANATH BANERJEE; Gen. Sec. Prof. MANABENDU BANERJEE; publs include *Journal* (quarterly), *Monthly Bulletin, Year Book, Bibliotheca Indica,* monographs.

Asiatic Society of Bombay: Town Hall, Shahid Bhagatsingh Rd, Mumbai 400 023; tel. (22) 2660956; fax (22) 2665139; e-mail asbl@bom2.vsnl.net.in; internet www.education.vsnl.com/asbl; f. 1804 as Bombay Literary Society; promotes and publishes research in culture, arts and literature in relation to Asia, and India in particular; 2,464 mems; 243,590 vols, 2,434 manuscripts, 11,830 coins; Pres. B. G. DESHMUKH; Hon. Sec. VIMAL SHAH; publs include *Journal* (annual), monographs and reports.

Bhandarkar Oriental Research Institute: Pune 411 004; tel. (20) 5656932; f. 1917; Sec. Dr M. G. DHADPHALE; Curator Dr S. D. LADDU; 1,466 mems; library of 100,782 vols, 31,000 MSS; publs include *Annals of the Bhandarkar Oriental Research Institute* (annually).

K. R. Cama Oriental Institute and Library: 136 Mumbai Samachar Marg, Mumbai 400 023; tel. (22) 2843893; f. 1916; 285 mems; library of 25,300 vols, 2,000 MSS, 500 journals; Pres. Sir JAMSETJEE JEJEEBHOY; Hon. Sec. H. N. MODI; Librarian S. V. KODE; publs incl. *Journal* (annually).

Centre for Development Studies: Prasanth Nagar Rd, Ulloor, Trivandrum 695 011; tel. (471) 448881; fax (471) 447137; e-mail somannair@cds.ac.in; internet www.cds.edu; f. 1971; promotes interdisciplinary research and academic instruction in disciplines relevant to development issues; library of 114,500 vols; Dir CHANDAN MUKHERJEE; Librarian V. RAMAKRISHNAN.

Centre for South, Central South-East Asian and South-West Pacific Studies: Jawaharlal Nehru University, New Mehrauli Rd, New Delhi 110 067; tel. (11) 667676; Chair. Prof. BALADAS GHOSHAL.

Centre for West Asian and African Studies: Jawaharlal Nehru University, New Mehrauli Rd, New Delhi 110 067; tel. (11) 6107676, Ext. 2372; fax (11) 6165886; Chair. Dr AJAY DUBEY.

Indira Gandhi Institute of Development Research (IGIDR): Gen. A. K. Vaidya Marg, Goregaon (E), Mumbai 400 065; tel. (22) 8400919; fax (22) 8402752; internet www.igidr.ac.in/; f. 1986; Dir Dr R. RADHAKRISHNA.

Rajiv Gandhi Institute for Contemporary Studies: Jawahar Bhawan, Dr Rajendra Prasad Rd, New Delhi 110 001; tel. (11) 3755117; fax (11) 3755119; e-mail info@rgfindia.com; internet www.rgfindia.com; f. 1991.

Ganganatha Jha Kendriya Sanskrit Vidyapeetha: Chandrashekhar Azad Park, Allahabad 211 002; tel. (532) 460957; f. 1943; fmrly G. N. Jha Research Institute; research into Sanskrit and other branches of Indology; library of 100,000 vols, 80,000 Sanskrit MSS; Prin. Dr GAYA CHARAN TRIPATHI; publs include *Quarterly Research Journal*, critically edited original Sanskrit texts and studies in Indology.

Gujarat Research Society: Dr Madhuri Shah Campus, Ramkrishna Mission Marg, Khar (West), Mumbai 400 052; tel. (22) 6462691; fax (22) 6047398; f. 1936 to organize and co-ordinate research in social and cultural activities; library of 10,000 vols; Pres. Smt. KALLOLINI P. HAZARAT; publ. *Journal of the Gujarat Research Society* (quarterly).

Indian Council for Cultural Relations: Azad Bhavan, Indraprastha Estate, New Delhi 110 002; tel. (11) 3319309; fax (11) 3712639; e-mail iccr@giasdL01.vsnl.net.in; f. 1950 to establish and strengthen cultural relations between India and other countries, and to project Indian culture abroad; 12 overseas cultural centres; arranges exhbns, exchange visits, conferences, seminars and lectures; administers J. Nehru Award for International Understanding; library of over 55,000 vols; Dir-Gen. HIMACHAL SOM; publs include *Indian Horizons* (in English, quarterly).

Indian Council for Research on International Economic Relations (ICRIER): India Habitat Centre, Core 6A, 4th Floor, Lodi Rd, New Delhi 110 003; tel. (11) 4627447; fax (11) 4620180; e-mail director@icrier.res.in; focuses on trade and investment, WTO-related issues, economic reforms in India, India's external economic policies, foreign policy, regional economic co-operation; Chair. of Bd Dr I. G. PATEL, Dir and Chief Exec. Dr ISHER JUDGE AHLUWALIA.

Indian Council of World Affairs: Sapru House, Barakhamba Rd, New Delhi 110 001; tel. (11) 3319055; fax (11) 3310638; e-mail dsicwa@yahoo.com; f. 1943; statutory institution for the study of Indian and international questions; 1,500 mems; library of 128,000 vols, 374 periodicals, 2.5m. press-cuttings, microfilms and microfiches, and UN and EU publs; Pres. BHAIRON SINGH SHEKHAWAT; Dir-Gen. P. S. RAY; publs *India Quarterly* (journal of international affairs), *Foreign Affairs Reports* (monthly).

Indian Society for Afro-Asian Studies: 297 Saraswati Kunj, Indraprastha Extension, Mother Dairy Rd, New Delhi 110 092; tel. (11) 2248246; fax (11) 2425698; e-mail isaas@giasdl01; f. 1980; research and promotion of co-operation among African and Asian countries; Pres. LALIT BHASIN; Gen. Sec. Dr DARAMPAL; publs monographs, papers.

Institute of Economic Growth: University Enclave, Delhi 110 007; tel. (11) 7667260; fax (11) 7667410; e-mail system@ieg.ernet.in; internet ieg.nic.in; f. 1958; research into the problems of social and economic development of South and South-East Asia; environmental economics, health economics, agriculture, rural development, macroeconomic analysis; library and documentation services; Dir Prof. B. B. BHATTACHARYA; publs include *Contributions to Indian Sociology: New Series* (3 a year).

International Academy of Indian Culture: J 22 Hauz Khas Enclave, New Delhi 110 016; tel. (11) 6515800; f. 1935 to study

India's artistic and historic relations with other Asian countries; library of 200,000 vols, 40,000 MSS; Hon. Dir Dr LOKESH CHANDRA; publ. *Satapitaka Series* (irregular).

Islamic Research Association: c/o Anjuman-i-Islam Islamic Research Institute, opposite V.T. Station, 92 Dadabhoy Nowroji Rd, Mumbai 400 001; tel. (22) 2620177; f. 1933; Pres. Dr M. ISHAQUE JAMKAHANAWALA; Dir Prof. NIZAMUDDIN S. GOREKAR; publs research studies.

Kuppuswami Sastri Research Institute: 84 Thiru V. Kalyanasundaranar Rd, (Sanskrit College Campus), Mylapore, Madras 600 004; tel. (44) 847320; f. 1944; promotion of oriental learning; 400 mems; library of 30,000 vols (incl. palm-leaf MSS); Dir Dr T. NARAYANANKUTTY; Sec. B. MADHAVAN; publs include *Journal of Oriental Research*.

Maha Bodhi Society: 4A Bankim Chatterjee St, Kolkata 700 073; tel. (33) 2415214; fax (33) 2412100; f. 1891; 23 brs in other cities and countries; 1,395 mems; Gen. Sec. Ven. M. WIPULASARA MAHA THERA; publs include *Mahabodhi* (English, monthly).

Namgyal Institute of Tibetology: Gangtok, Sikkim; e-mail nitsikkim@yahoo.co.in; f. 1958; research centre for study of Mahayana (Northern Buddhism); library of Tibetan literature (canonical of all sects and secular) in MSS and xylographs; museum of icons and art objects; Pres. The Governor of Sikkim; Dir TASHI DENSAPA; publs include *Bulletin of Tibetology* (3 a year) and publications in Tibetan, Sanskrit and English.

Nava Nalanda Mahavihara: PO Nalanda, Bihar 803 111; tel. (6112) 81820; e-mail nnmdirector@sify.com; f. 1951; under Dept of Culture, Ministry of Tourism and Culture; postgraduate studies and research in Pali, Buddhist studies, ancient Indian and Asian history and philosophy, Tibetan, Sanskrit, Chinese and Japanese; library of 43,000 vols; Dir Dr RAVINDRA PANTH; publs include *Nava Nalanda Mahavihara Research* (annually).

Oriental Institute: Maharaja Sayajirao University of Baroda, Opp. Palace Gate, Palace Rd, Vadodara 390 001, Gujarat; tel. 425121; f. 1927; library of 46,916 vols on Indology and Sanskrit and 27,728 MSS; 30 mems; Dir Prof. R. I. NANAVATI; publs include *Gaekwad's Oriental Series, M.S. University Research Series, M.S. University Oriental Series, Journal of the Oriental Institute* (English, quarterly).

Socio-Economic Research Institute: C-19 and C-39, College St Market, Kolkata 700 007, West Bengal; tel. (33) 2410775; fax (33) 2415152; f. 1959; Pres. Prof. TARUN C. DUTT; publs include *Bulletin of the Socio-Economic Research Institute*.

Sri Venkateswara University Oriental Research Institute: Tirupati, Andhra Pradesh 517 502; tel. 50666, Ext. 291; fax 8774-29101; e-mail vc@svuni.ren.nic.in; f. 1939; research in language and literature, philosophy and religion, arts and archaeology, history and Indian heritage; library of 30,405 vols, 14,000 MSS; Dir M. SRIMANNARAYANAMURTI; publs include *Oriental Journal* (2 a year), critical editions and monographs.

Vishveshvaranand Vishva Bandhu Institute of Sanskrit and Indological Studies: Panjab University, Sadhu Ashram, PO Hoshiarpur 146 021; tel. 21002; f. 1965; postgraduate teaching, research and study in Indology and Sanskrit, including language, literature and religion; library of 71,631 books and journals, 2,590 MSS; information centre f. 1998; Chair. Prof. DAMODAR JHA; publs *Panjab University Indological Series, Vishveshvaranand Indological Journal*.

INDONESIA

Centre for Social and Cultural Studies: Indonesian Institute of Sciences, Gedung Widya Graha Lt. 11, Jalan Jenderal Gatot Subroto, POB 4492, Jakarta 12044; tel. (21) 511542; fax (21) 5701232.

Centre for Strategic and International Studies (CSIS): Jalan Tanah Abang III/23–27, Jakarta 10160; tel. (21) 3865532; fax (21) 3847517; e-mail csis@pacific.net.id; f. 1971; undertakes policy-orientated studies in international and domestic matters in collaboration with the industrial, commercial, political, legal and journalistic communities of Indonesia; interdisciplinary research projects; Chair. HADI SOESASTRO; publs include *The Indonesian Quarterly, Analisis CSIS* (4 a year).

Indonesian Institute of World Affairs: c/o Universitas Indonesia, Salemba Raya 4, Jakarta; tel. (21) 882955; Chair. Prof. SUPOMO; Sec. SUDJATMOKO.

Institute for Regional Economic Research: Universitas Andalas, Kampus Limau Manis, Padang 26163, West Sumatra; tel. (751) 71389; fax (751) 71085; Dir SYAHRUDDIN.

Perpustakaan Nasional RI (National Library of Indonesia): Jalan Salemba Raya, No 28A, Jakarta Pusat 10430; tel. (21) 3101411; fax (21) 3103554; f. 1989; 844,480 vols, 25,000 maps, 10,857 microfilms and microfiches, 10,000 MSS; Dir MASTINI HARDJOPRAKOSO; publs include *National Bibliography*.

Pusat Bahasa (National Centre for Language): Jalan Daksinapati Barat IV, POB 2625, Rawamangun, Jakarta 13220; tel. and fax (21) 4706678; f. 1975; attached to the Ministry of National Education; language policy and planning, research on language teaching and literature; library of 85,000 vols; Dir Dr DENDY SUGONO; Librarian AGNES SANTI; publs include *Informasi Pustaka Kebahasaan* (quarterly), *Bahasa dan Sastra* (quarterly).

IRAN

Asia Institute: University of Shiraz, Shiraz; tel. (71) 32111; Dir Dr Y. M. NAVABI; publs *Bulletin*, monographs.

Institute for Political and International Studies: Shaheed Bahonar Ave, Shaheed Aghaii St, POB 19395-1793; Tajrish, Tehran; tel. (21) 2571010; fax (21) 270964; f. 1983; research and information on international relations, economics, law and Islamic studies; library of 22,000 vols; publs include *Iranian Journal of International Affairs* (quarterly).

ISRAEL

Harry S. Truman Research Institute for the Advancement of Peace: The Hebrew University of Jerusalem, Mt Scopus, Jerusalem 91905; tel. (2) 5882300; fax (2) 5828076; e-mail mstruman@mscc.huji.ac.il; internet www.truman.huji.ac.il; f. 1965; conducts and sponsors social science and historical research, organizes conferences and publs works on many regions, including Asia; Dir Prof. AMNON COHEN.

Institute of Asian and African Studies: The Hebrew University of Jerusalem, Mt Scopus, Jerusalem 91905; tel. (2) 5883648; fax (2) 5883703; e-mail rachelg@savior.cc.huji.ac.il; provides degree and postgraduate courses, covering history, social sciences and languages, in Chinese and Japanese studies; Chair. of Inst. Prof. STEVEN KAPLAN; Chair. Dept of East Asia Studies Dr LIHI YARIV-LAOR.

International Institute-Histadrut (incorporating Afro-Asian Institute): Bet Berl 44905, Kfar Saba; tel. (9) 987382; fax (9) 421868; f. 1958 to train leadership for trade unions, co-operatives, community orgs, women's and youth groups, and for social and economic aspects of development, etc. in regions throughout the world, incl. Asia and Pacific; library of 35,000 vols; Chair. HAIM RAMON; Dir and Prin. Dr YEHUDAH PAZ.

ITALY

The Bologna Center of the Paul H. Nitze School of Advanced International Studies of the Johns Hopkins University: Via Belmeloro 11, 40126 Bologna; tel. (051) 2917811; fax (051) 228505; e-mail Registrar@jhubc.it; internet www.jhubc.it; f. 1955; graduate studies in international affairs and economics; Dir Dr ROBERT H. EVANS; publs *Bologna Center Catalogue, EuroSAIS* (alumni newsletter), occasional papers series.

Institute of Economic and Social Studies for East Asia: Università Commerciale Luigi Bocconi, Via U. Gobbi 5, 20136 Milan; tel. (02) 58363317; fax (02) 58363309; e-mail Isesao@uni-bocconi.it; internet www.isesao.uni-bocconi.it; Dir Prof. C. FILIPPINI.

Istituto Affari Internazionali (IAI): Via Angelo Brunetti 9, 00186 Rome; tel. (06) 3224360; fax (06) 3224363; f. 1965; Dir GIANNI BONVICINI; publs include *The International Spectator* (quarterly, in English).

Istituto Italiano Per l'Africa e l'Oriente (ISIAO): Via V. Aldrovandi 16, 00197, Rome; tel. (06) 328551; fax (06) 3224358; internet www.isiao.it; f. 1995; Pres. Prof. GHERARDO GNOLI; publs include *Africa* (quarterly), *Cina* (annually), *East and West* (quarterly), *Il Giappone* (annually).

Istituto per gli Studi di Politica Internazionale (ISPI): Palazzo Clerici, Via Clerici 5, 20121 Milan; tel. (02) 8633131;

fax (02) 8692055; e-mail ispizi@tim.it; internet www.ispinet.it; f. 1933 for the promotion of the study and knowledge of all problems concerning international relations; seminars at post-graduate level; library of 100,000 vols; Pres. BORIS BIANCHERI; publs *ISPI Relazioni Internazionali* (quarterly), Papers (20 a year).

Istituto Universitario Orientale (Oriental University Institute): Dept of Asian Studies, Piazza San Domenico Maggiore 12, 80134 Naples; tel. (081) 5517855; fax (081) 5517852; f. 1732; library of 200,000 vols, 2,000 periodical titles; Dir Prof. UGO MARAZZI; publs include four series (Maior, Minor, Serie Tre and Baluchistan Monograph Series) and *Annali.*

JAPAN

Ajia Daigaku (Institute for Asian Studies): Asia University, 5-24-10 Sakai, Musashino-shi, Tokyo 180; tel. (422) 54-3111; fax (422) 36-1083; f. 1973; Dir S. SAITO; publs *Journal* (annually), *Bulletin of Institute for Asian Studies* (quarterly).

Ajia Seikei Gakkai (Japan Association for Asian Political and Economic Studies): c/o Prof. AMAKO, School of International Politics, Economics and Business, Aoyama Gakuin University, 4-4-25 Shibuya, Shibuya-ku, Tokyo 150; f. 1953; 850 mems; Pres. TOSHIO WATANABE; publ. *Aziya Kenkyu* (quarterly).

The Center for Southeast Asian Studies: 46 Shimoadachi-cho, Yoshida, Sakyo-ku, Kyoto 606-8501; tel. (75) 753-7300; fax (75) 753-7350; attached to Kyoto Univ.; Dir Prof. NARIFUMI MAEDA TACHIMOTO; publs include *Southeast Asian Studies* (quarterly), monographs (English and Japanese, irregular).

Centre for Asian and Pacific Studies: Seikei University, 3-3-1, Kichijoji-Kitamachi, Musashino-shi, Tokyo 180-8633; tel. (422) 37-3549; fax (422) 37-3866; e-mail caps@jim.seikei.ac.jp; internet www.seikei.ac.jp/university/caps/; f. 1981; conducts and finances research on modernization, industrialization and structural changes in the Asia-Pacific region; publs include *Review of Asian and Pacific Studies.*

The Centre for East Asian Cultural Studies for UNESCO, Toyo Bunko (Oriental Library): Honkomagome 2-28-21 Bunkyo-ku, Tokyo 113; tel. (3) 3942-0124; fax (3) 3942-0120; internet www.toyo-bunko.or.jp/ceacs/; f. 1961; Dir YONEO ISHII; publs include *Asian Research Trends, Bibliotheca Codicum Asiaticorum, East Asian Cultural Studies, Recent Archaeological Discoveries in Asia, Historic Cities of Asia* series, translations of historical documents, monographs, bibliographies, directories.

The Economic Research Institute for Northeast Asia (ERINA): Nihonseimei Masayakoji Bldg, 6-1178-1, Kamiokawamae-dori, Niigata 951-8068; tel. (25) 222-3141; fax (25) 222-9505; internet www.erina.or.jp; f. 1993.

Japanese Association for Asian Political and Economic Studies: c/o Prof. Amako, School of International Politics, Economics and Business, Aoyama Gakuin University, 4-4-25, Shibuya, Shibuya-ku, Tokyo 105; tel. (3) 3409-8111; fax (3) 5485-0782; f. 1953; Pres. TOSHIO WATANBE; publs include *Asian Studies* (quarterly), *Modern Chinese Studies Series* (annually).

Nihon Boeki Shinkokai Ajia Keizai Kenkyusho (Institute of Developing Economies): 3-2-2 Wakaba, Mihama-ku, Chiba-shi Chiba 261-8545; tel. (43) 299-9500; fax (43) 299-9724; e-mail info@ide.go.jp; internet www.ide.go.jp; Ajia Keizai Kenkyusho; f. 1958, merged with Nihon Boeki Shinkokai 1998; research on economic and related subjects in Asia and other developing areas; aims to promote economic co-operation and to improve trade relations between Japan and the developing countries; 247 mems; Pres. IPPEI YAMAZAWA; library of 369,292 vols; publs include *Ajia Keizai* (monthly, in Japanese), *Ajiken Warudo Torendo* (World Trends, monthly, in Japanese), *The Developing Economies* (quarterly, in English), occasional papers series (irregular, in English).

Nihon-Indogaku-Bukkyogakkai (Japanese Association of Indian and Buddhist Studies): c/o Dept of Indian Philosophy and Buddhist Studies, Graduate School of Humanities and Sociology, University of Tokyo, 7-3-1 Hongo, Bunkyo-ku, Tokyo 113; tel. (3) 3813-5903; f. 1951; 2,500 mems; Pres. SENGAKU MAYEDA; publ. *Indogaku Bukkyogaku Kenkyu* (Journal of Indian and Buddhist Studies).

Nihon Keizai Kenkyu Senta (Japan Center for Economic Research): Nikkei Kayabacho Bldg, 2-6-1 Nihonbashi Kayabacho, Chuo-ku, Tokyo 103-0025; tel. (3) 3639-2801; fax (3) 3639-2839; internet www.jcer.or.jp; f. 1963; 390 corporate and 283 individual mems; library of 37,000 vols and 2,000 titles; Chair. YUTAKA KOSAI; Pres. SEIICHI TOSHIDA; publs *Nihon Keizai Kenkyu Senta Kaiho* (semi-monthly), *Nihon Keizai Kenkyu* (annually), *Economic Forecast Series, International Conference Series.*

Nihon Kokusai Mondai Kenkyusho (The Japan Institute of International Affairs): Tokyo; tel. (3) 3503-7261; fax (3) 3595-1755; internet www.jiia.or.jp; f. 1959; Chair. YOSHIZANE IWASA; Pres. NOBUO MATSUNAGA; publs include *Kokusai Mondai* (International Affairs, monthly), *Soren Kenkyu* (Soviet Studies, 2 a year), *Japan Review of International Affairs* (4 a year), newsletters, books and monographs.

Nomura Research Institute (NRI): Shin Otemachi Bldg, 2-2-1 Otemachi, Chiyoda-ku, Tokyo 100-0004; tel. (3) 5255-1852; fax (3) 5255-9315; internet www.nri.co.jap; f. 1965; research into Japanese and international economic and security issues; Pres. SHOZO HASHIMOTO; publ. *NRI Policy Research.*

Research Institute for the Study of Languages and Cultures of Asia and Africa: Tokyo University of Foreign Studies, Asahicho 3-11-1, Fuchu, Tokyo 183-8534; tel. (42) 330-5601; fax (42) 330-5610; e-mail director@aa.tufs.ac.jp; internet www.aa.tufs.ac.jp; f. 1964; library of 65,445 vols; Dir K. MIYAZAKI; publs *Journal of Asian and African Studies* (2 a year), *Newsletter* (3 a year).

Toho Gakkai (Institute of Eastern Culture): 2-4-1 Nishi-Kanda, Chiyoda-ku, Tokyo 101-0065; tel. (3) 3262-7221; fax (3) 3262-7227; e-mail tohogakkai@mc.nextlink.ne.jp; f. 1947; 1,550 mems; Chair. Dr MASAAKI HATTORI; Sec.-Gen. HIROSHI YANASE; publs include *Acta Asiatica, Tohogaku, Transactions of the International Conference of Eastern Studies.*

Tokyo Daigaku Toyo Bunka Kenkyujo (Institute of Oriental Culture, the University of Tokyo): 7-3-1 Hongo, Bunkyo-ku, Tokyo 113-0033; tel. (3) 5841-5830; fax (3) 5841-5898; f. 1941; Dir Prof. AKIHIKO TANAKA; publ. *Tōyō bunka kenkyūjo kiyō* (2 a year), *Tōyō bunka* (annually).

Toyo Bunko (Modern China Research Committee): Honkomagome 2-28-21 Bunkyo-ku, Tokyo 113-0021; tel. (3) 3942-0121; f. 1962; collection on modern China; Asian studies library of 870,000 vols; publ. *Kindai Chugoku Kenkyu Iho* (annually).

United Nations Centre for Regional Development: Nagono 1-47-1, Nakamura-ku, Nagoya 450-0001; tel. (52) 561-9377; fax (52) 561-9375; e-mail rep@uncrd.or.jp; internet www.uncrd.or.jp/; f. 1971; undertakes training, research, consultation and information exchange on regional development issues affecting developing countries; Dir YO KIMURA; publs *Regional Development Dialogue* (2 a year), *Regional Development Studies* (annually).

REPUBLIC OF KOREA

Asiatic Research Center: Korea University, Anam-dong 5 ga-1, Sungbuk-gu, Seoul; tel. (2) 3290-1600; fax (2) 923-4661; e-mail arcku@korea.ac.kr; internet www.asiacenter.or.kr; Dir Prof. JANG-JIP CHOI; publ. *Journal of Asiatic Studies.*

Ilmin International Relations Institute: Korea University, Anam-dong, Seoul; Pres. HAN SUNG JOO.

Institute of Economic Research, Korea University: 1, 5-ga, Anam-dong, Sungbuk-gu, Seoul 136-701; tel. (2) 3290-2200; fax (2) 926-3601; e-mail eghwang@kuccnx.korea.ac.kr; f. 1957; Dir Prof. EUI-GAK HWANG.

Institute of Economic Research, Seoul National University: Sinlim-dong, Kwanak-gu, Seoul 151-742; tel. (2) 877-1629; fax (2) 926-3601; f. 1961.

Institute for Far Eastern Studies: Kyungnam University, 28–42 Samchung-dong, Chongno-gu, Seoul 110-230; tel. (2) 3700-0725; fax (2) 3700-0707; e-mail ifes@kyungnam.ac.kr; internet www.ifes.kyungnam.ac.kr; f. 1972; publs monographs, 2 journals (on international and regional studies, 2 a year).

Institute of Korean Studies: Yonsei University, 134 Shinchon-dong, Sudaemun-gu, Seoul 120-749; tel. (2) 361-3502; fax (2) 365-0937; f. 1948; Dir NAM KI SHIM; publ. *Dong Bang Hak Chi* (quarterly).

Institute of Oriental Studies: Dankook University, 8 Hannam-dong, Yongsan-gu, Seoul 140-714; tel. (2) 709-2234; fax (2) 798-3010; internet www.dankook.ac.kr/~oriental; f. 1970; library of 40,000 vols; Dir Prof. KIM SANG-BAI; publs include journal and newsletter.

Korea Development Institute: POB 113, Cheongryang, Seoul 130-012; tel. (2) 958-4114; fax (2) 961-5092; e-mail kdi-guide@kdiux.kdi.re.kr; internet www.kdiux.kdi.re.kr; f. 1971; conducts research in order to help maintain high economic growth and price stability; library of 120,000 vols; Pres. LEE JIN-SOON; *KDI Economic Outlook* (quarterly), *KDI Journal and Economic Policy* (quarterly).

Korea Institute for Economics and Technology (KIET): POB 205, Cheongryang, Seoul; tel. (2) 962-6211; fax (2) 963-8540; f. 1982.

Research Institute of Asian Economics: Haeyoung Bldg, Room 304, 148 Anguk-dong, Chongno-gu, Seoul; tel. (2) 738-1875; fax (2) 720-2367; Pres. SHIN TAE-WHAN.

Research Institute of Oriental Culture: Sung Kyun Kwan University, 53, 3-ga, Myung Ryun-dong, Chongno-gu, Seoul 110-745; Dir WOO-SUNG LEE.

Samsung Economic Research Institute (SERI): 7th–8th Floors, Hanil Group Bldg, 191 Hangangro, 2-ga, Yongsan-gu, Seoul; tel. (2) 3780-8000; e-mail homemst@seri21.org; internet seriecon.seri-samsung.org; f. 1986; Pres. CHOI WOO SOCK.

MACAO

Centre of Macao Studies: University of Macao, University Hill, Taipa, POB 3001, Macao.

Macao Development Strategy Research Centre: Rua de Xangai 175, Edif. da Associação Comercial Chinesa, 19/F; tel. 780124; fax 780565; e-mail cpedm@macau.ctm.net; internet www.cpedm.com; f.1997.

MALAYSIA

Asian and Pacific Development Centre: Pesiaran Duta, POB 12224, 50770 Kuala Lumpur; tel. (3) 6511088; fax (3) 6510316; e-mail info@apdc.po.my; internet www.apdc.com.my/apdc; f. 1980; Dir Dr MOHD NOOR Haji HARUN; publs annual report, newsletter, and monographs.

Dewan Bahasa dan Pustaka (Institute of Language and Literature, Malaysia): POB 10803, 50926 Kuala Lumpur; fax (3) 21444460; internet www.dbp.gov.my; f. 1956 to develop and enrich the Malay language; to develop literary talent particularly in Malay; to print, publish or promote publication in Malay and other languages; to standardize spelling and pronunciation and devise appropriate technical terms in Malay; Chair. Dato' Hj. ABDUL RAHIM BIN ABU BAKAR; Dir-Gen. Dato' Hj. A. AZIZ DERAMAN; publs include magazines, textbooks, higher learning books and general books.

Pusat Dotumentasi Melayu DBP (Malay Documentation Centre): tel. (3) 2481011 Ext. 201; fax (3) 2442081; 120,000 vols, 3,000 periodicals, audio-visual materials, special collection on Malay language and literature; Chief Librarian Mrs ROHANI RUSTAM; publs *Mutiara Pustaka* (annually), subject bibliography (occasional).

Institute for Development Studies (Sabah): Block C, Suite 7 CFO1, 7th Floor, Karamunsing Complex, 88300 Kota Kinabalu, Sabah; tel. (88) 246166; fax (88) 234707; e-mail info@ids.org.my; internet www.ids.org.my; publs include *Borneo Review* (2 a year).

Institute of Malaysian International Studies (IKMAS): Universiti Kebangsaan Malaysia, Selangor, 43600 Bangi; tel. (3) 8293205; fax (3) 8261022; e-mail ikmas@pkrisc.cc.ukm.my; f. 1995; Dir Dr OSMAN RANI HASSAN.

Institute of Strategic and International Studies (ISIS): 1, Pesiaran Sultan Salahuddin, POB 12424, 50778 Kuala Lumpur; tel. (3) 2939366; fax (3) 2913210; e-mail jawhar@isis.po.my; internet www.isis.org.my/isis; Chair. and CEO Tan Sri Dr NOORDIN SOPIEE; Dir-Gen. Dato' MOHAMED JAWHAR HASSAN.

Malaysian Branch of the Royal Asiatic Society: 130M. Jalan Thamby Abdullah, off Jalan Tun Sambanthan (Brickfields), 50470 Kuala Lumpur; tel. (3) 22748345; fax (3) 22743458; e-mail mbras@tm.net.my; f. 1877; 1,086 mems; Pres. Datuk ABDULLAH BIN ALI; Hon. Sec. Datuk Hj. BURHANUDDIN BIN AHMAD TAJUDIN; publs include *Journal* (2 a year), monographs, reprints.

Malaysian Institute of Economic Research (MIER): 9th Floor, Menara Dayabumi, Jalan Sultan Hishamuddin, 50050 Kuala Lumpur; tel. (3) 22730214; fax (3) 22730197; e-mail ariff@mier.po.my; internet www.mier.org.my; f. 1985; conducts policy- and business-orientated research; Exec. Dir MOHAMMED ARIFF.

South East Asian Central Bank—Research and Training Centre: Lorong University A, 59100 Kuala Lumpur; tel. (3) 7568622; fax (3) 7574616; f. 1972; research into financial and economic affairs; publs include *Economic Survey of the SEACEN Countries*.

MEXICO

Asociación Latinoamericana de Estudios de Asia y Africa (Latin-American Asscn for Asian and African Studies): El Colegio de México, Camino al Ajusco 20, Pedregal Sta Teresa, Apdo 10740, México, DF; tel. (5) 449-3000, ext. 4052; fax (5) 645-0464; e-mail aladaa@colmex.mx; internet www.colmex.mx/centros/ceaa/aladaa/default.htm; f. 1976; promotes African and Asian studies in Latin America; 450 mems; Gen. Sec. Prof. MICHIKO TANAKA.

Centre for Asian and African Studies: El Colegio de México, Camino al Ajusco 20, Pedregal Sta Teresa, Apdo 10740, México, DF; tel. (5) 449-3025; fax (5) 645-0464; internet www.colmex.mx; Dir Prof. BENJAMÍN PRECIADO; publ. *Estudios de Asia y Africa* (quarterly).

MONGOLIA

Centre of Strategic Studies: POB 870, Ulan Bator; tel. 353034; f. 1990; research into national and international security and strategy, with emphasis on North-East Asia; Dir S. DZORIG; publs include *Security and Development Issues* (2 a year).

Institute of Oriental and International Studies: Academy of Sciences, Ulan Bator; fax 322613; Dir Dr Ts. BATBAYAR; publs *East-West* (in Mongolian with summaries and contents in English; quarterly), *Mongolian Journal of International Affairs* (in English, annually).

MYANMAR
(formerly Burma)

Burma Research Society: Universities' Central Library, University PO, Yangon; f. 1910 to promote cultural and scientific studies and research relating to Myanmar and neighbouring countries; 1,040 mems; Pres. U HTIN GYI; Hon. Sec. Dr SHEIN; publ. *Journal* (2 a year).

Institute of Economics: Pyay Rd, University Estate, Kamayat Township, 11041 Yangon; tel. (1) 32433; f. 1964; library of 70,000 vols; Rector Dr THAN NYUN.

NEPAL

Centre for Nepal and Asian Studies: Tribhuvan University, POB 3757, Kirtipur, Kathmandu; tel. (1) 331740; fax (1) 331184; e-mail cnastu@unlimit.com; f. 1972; conducts political and social research both in Nepalese and Asian contexts; Exec. Dir Prof. Dr TIRTHA PRASAD MISHRA; publs include *Contributions to Nepalese Studies* (2 a year), monographs, bibliographies, occasional papers.

Nepal Council of World Affairs: NCWA Bldg, Harihar Bhawan, Pulchowk, POB 2588, Lalitpur, Kathmandu; tel. (1) 526222; f. 1948; Pres. Dr SOORYA LAL AMATYA; publ. *Nepal Council of World Affairs Journal* (annually).

United Nations Regional Centre for Peace and Disarmament in Asia: United Nations Development Programme, POB 107, Kathmandu; tel. (1) 524366; fax (1) 523991; f. 1988; Dir J. BERKE.

NETHERLANDS

International Institute for Asian Studies (IIAS): POB 9515, 2300 RA Leiden; tel. (71) 5272227; fax (71) 5274162; e-mail iias@let.leidenuniv.nl; internet www.iias.nl.

Koninklijk Instituut voor Taal-, Land- en Volkenkunde (Royal Institute of Linguistics and Anthropology): Reuvensplaats 2, POB 9515, 2300 RA Leiden; tel. (71) 5272295; fax (71) 5272638; e-mail kitlv@kitlv.nl; internet www.kitlv.nl; f. 1851 to collect and catalogue books and other documents, to carry out and support research, and to publish books and journals on South-East Asia (especially Indonesia), the Pacific area and the Caribbean region (in particular Suriname and the Netherlands Antilles); 2,044 mems; library of over 500,000 titles; Pres. Prof. R. Schefold; Dir Prof. G. J. Oostindie; publs include *Bijdragen: New West Indian Guide* (quarterly), *Verhandelingen, Bibliotheca Indonesica, Working Papers Series, European Newsletter of South-East Asian Studies, Excerpta Indonesica, bibliographies, translations.*

NEW CALEDONIA

Société des Etudes Mélanésiennes: Musée Neo-Calédonien, BP 2393, Nouméa; tel. 27-23-42; fax 28-41-43; f. 1938; anthropology; publ. *Etudes Mélanésiennes* (annually).

NEW ZEALAND

Asian Peace Research Association: University of Canterbury, Dept of Sociology, Christchurch 1; tel. (3) 366-7001; fax (3) 364-2999; Sec.-Gen. K. Clements.

Institute of Polynesian Languages and Literatures: POB 6965, Wellesley St, Auckland 1; tel. (9) 372-5094; e-mail rongosf@internet.co.nz; f. 1995; charitable trust aiming to promote study and use of Polynesian languages and literatures through publication of research, etc.; Dir Dr Steven Roger Fischer; publ. *Rongorongo Studies: A Forum for Polynesian Philology* (2 a year).

Macmillan Brown Centre for Pacific Studies: University of Canterbury, PB 4800, Christchurch; tel. (3) 364-2957; fax (3) 364-2002; e-mail mbcps@pacs.canterbury.ac.nz; internet www.pacs.canterbury.ac.nz/; Chair. Dr John Henderson; Dir Prof. Karen Nevo.

New Zealand Asia Institute: University of Auckland, Private Bag 92019, Auckland; tel. (9) 373-7599; fax (9) 308-231; e-mail nzai@auckland.ac.nz; f. 1995; Dir Dr James Kember.

New Zealand Geographical Society: Dept of Geography, University of Waikato, Hamilton; tel. (7) 838-4913; fax (7) 838-4633; e-mail nz-gs@waikato.ac.nz; internet www.nzgs.org.nz; f. 1944; six brs and 500 mems in NZ, 350 overseas mems; Pres. Dr Graeme Campbell; Sec. Prof. Richard Le Heron; publs include *New Zealand Geographer* (2 a year), *New Zealand Journal of Geography* (2 a year), *NZGS Newsletter* (2 a year), *Conference Proceedings* (every 2 years).

New Zealand Institute of Economic Research: POB 3479, Wellington; tel. (4) 4721-880; fax (4) 4721-211; e-mail econ@nzier.org.nz; internet www.nzier.org.nz; f. 1958; independent non-profit making organization; research into NZ economic development; quarterly forecast of the national economy and annual medium-term industry outlook; quarterly survey of business opinion; economic investigations on contract basis; Dir Alexander Sundakov; Chair. Michael Walls; Sec. A. G. Froggatt; publs *Quarterly Predictions, Quarterly Survey of Business Opinion, New Zealand Industry Outlook,* Research Monographs, discussion papers.

New Zealand Institute of International Affairs: c/o Victoria University of Wellington, POB 600, Wellington 2; tel. (4) 471-5356; fax (4) 473-1261; e-mail nziia@vuw.ac.nz; internet www.vuw.ac.nz/nziia; f. 1934 to examine international questions, particularly in relation to Asia and the South Pacific; Pres. Sir Kenneth Keith; Dir Brian Lynch; publ. *New Zealand International Review* (6 a year).

Polynesian Society: c/o Maori Studies Dept, University of Auckland, PB 92019, Auckland 1; e-mail jps@auckland.ac.nz; f. 1892 to promote the study of the anthropology, ethnology, philology, history and antiquities of the New Zealand Maori and other Pacific Island peoples; library; 1,103 mems; Pres. Prof. Sir Hugh Kawharu; publs *Memoirs, Journal* (quarterly), *Maori Monographs, Maori Texts.*

NORWAY

Norsk Utenrikspolitisk Institutt (Norwegian Institute of International Affairs): Gronlandsleiret 25, POB 8159, Dep., 0033 Oslo 1; tel. 22-05-65-00; fax 22-17-70-15; e-mail info@nupi.no; internet www.nupi.no; information and research in international relations; Pres. Paul Chaffey; Dir Sverre Lodgaard; publs include *Internasjonal Politikk* (quarterly), *NUPI Notat* and *NUPI Rapport* (research reports), *Forum for Development Studies.*

PAKISTAN

Anjuman Taraqqi-e-Urdu Pakistan: D-159, Block 7, Gulshan-e-Iqbal, Karachi 75300; tel. (21) 7724023; f. 1903 for promotion of Urdu language and literature; preparing a six-vol. bibliography of Urdu books in collaboration with UNESCO; lending library of 20,000 vols, research library of 26,000 vols, 4,000 MSS; Pres. Aftab Ahmed Khan; Sec. Jamiluddin A'Ali; publs *Urdu* (quarterly), *Qami Zaban* (monthly).

Centre for South Asian Studies: University of the Punjab, Quaid-i-Azam, Lahore 54590; tel. (42) 5864014; fax (42) 5867206; f. 1975; study of socio-economic and political developments in South Asia, particularly of issues relating to Pakistan, India, Bangladesh, Nepal, Bhutan, Sri Lanka and Maldives; Dir Prof. Dr Sarfraz Hussain Mirza; publs include *South Asian Studies* (2 a year).

Institute of Development Studies: North-West Frontier Province Agricultural University, Peshawar; tel. (521) 41986; f. 1953; Dir Muhammad Ahmad Khan; publs include *Journal of Development Studies.*

Islamic Research Institute: POB 1035, Islamabad 44000; tel. (51) 850751; fax (51) 853360; f. 1960 to conduct and co-ordinate research in Islamic studies; organizes seminars, conferences etc; library of 75,000 vols, 1,300 microfilms and microfiches, 258 MSS; 170 cassettes; Dir-Gen. Dr Zafar Ishaq Ansari; publs include *Al-Dirasat al-Islamiyyah* (Arabic, quarterly), *Islamic Studies* (English, quarterly), *Fikr-o-Nazar* (Urdu, quarterly), monographs.

Pakistan Economic Research Institute (PERI): 24 Mianmir Rd, Upper Mall Scheme, Lahore 15; f. 1955 to undertake socio-economic investigations and co-ordinate research in economic problems of Pakistan; to collect, compile and interpret statistical data; to publish the results and findings of investigations; Dir A. Aziz Anwar; Sec. A. R. Arshad; publs research papers, reports.

Pakistan Historical Society: Bait al-Hikmah Library, Hamdard University, Mohd Qasim Ave, Karachi 74700; tel. (21) 6996001; fax (21) 6996002; f. 1950; historical studies and research; particularly history of Islam and of India and Pakistan; library of 7,709 vols; Pres. Sadia Rashid; Gen. Sec. Dr Ansar Zahid Khan; publs *Journal* (quarterly), monographs, research studies.

Pakistan Institute of Development Economics: POB 1091, Islamabad 44000; tel. (51) 9206610; fax (51) 9210886; e-mail pide@isb.paknet.com.pk; internet www.pide.org.pk; f. 1957; conducts research on development economics and Islamic economics in general and on Pakistan's economic issues in particular, providing a foundation on which economic policy-making can be based; provides in-service training in economic analysis, research methods and project evaluation; library of 32,755 vols, 280 current periodicals, 6,200 microfiches and 21,200 research papers/reports; Dir Dr A. R. Kemal; Sec. Muhammad Aslam; publs include *Pakistan Development Review* (quarterly), essays, monographs, statistical papers, reprints, bibliographies, research reports (mimeographed).

Pakistan Institute of International Affairs: Aiwan-e-Sadar Rd, POB 1447, Karachi 74200; tel. (21) 5682891; fax (21) 5686069; f. 1947 to promote interest and research in international affairs; library of over 28,000 vols; over 600 mems; Chair. Fatehyab Ali Khan; Sec. Dr S. Adil Husain; publs *Pakistan Horizon* (quarterly), books and monographs.

Quaid-i-Azam Academy: 297 M. A. Jinnah Rd, Karachi 74800; tel. (21) 7218184; f. 1976; research on Quaid-i-Azam Mohammad Ali Jinnah, the historical background (incl. cultural, religious, literary, linguistic, social, economic and political aspects) of the Pakistan Movement and various aspects of Pakistan; library of 25,000 vols and 950 microfilms of newspapers; Dir Dr Muhammad Ali Siddiqui; publs bibliographies, research studies, monographs and documents (in English, Urdu and other Pakistani languages).

Research Society of Pakistan: University of the Punjab, Punjab University Library, Allama Campus, Lahore; tel. (42) 9211631; f. 1963; conducts research into the origins of Pakistan and its culture, politics, literature, linguistics, economics, history, topography and archaeology; Pres. Lt-Gen. (retd) ARSHAD MAHMOOD; Dir Dr A. SHAKOOR AHSAN; publs include *Journal of the Research Society of Pakistan* (quarterly).

PAPUA NEW GUINEA

Institute of National Affairs: POB 1530, Port Moresby; tel. 3211044; fax 3217223; e-mail inapng@daltron.com.pg; f. 1978; Head MICHAEL MANNING; publs discussion and working papers.

National Research Institute of Papua New Guinea: POB 5854, Boroko; tel. (675) 3260300; fax (675) 3260213; e-mail nri@global.net.pg; internet www.nri.org.pg; f. 1989 by amalgamation of Institute of Applied Social and Economic Research, Institute of Papua New Guinea Studies and Education Research Unit; promotion of research into social, legal, military, political, economic, educational, environmental and cultural issues in PNG; library of 13,000 vols; Dir Dr BENO B. BOEHA; publs *Monographs, Discussion Papers, Bibliography, Post Courier Index* (annually), *Trends in Development* (2 a year), special and educational reports, etc.

THE PHILIPPINES

Asian Center: University of the Philippines, Diliman, Quezon City, Metro Manila 1101; tel. (2) 9261841; fax (2) 9261821; e-mail asiancenter@ac.upd.edu.ph; f. 1955 as Institute of Asian Studies; Dean Dr ARMANDO MALAY, Jr; publs include *Asian Studies* (annually), monographs, occasional papers and books.

Centre for Research and Communication: Unit 1103, Pacific Centre Bldg, San Miguel Ave, Ortigas Centre, Pasig City 1600; tel. (2) 6311284; fax (2) 6336741; e-mail crcfi@mnl.sequel.net; Pres. ENRIQUE P. ESTEBAN; Exec. Vice-Pres. Dr EMILIO T. ANTONIO, Jr.

Cultural Center of the Philippines: Roxas Blvd, Metro Manila; tel. (2) 8321125; fax (2) 8340471; internet www.culturalcenter.gov.ph; f. 1966 to preserve, develop and promote Philippine arts and culture; Pres. NESTOR O. JARDIN.

Institute of Philippine Culture: Ateneo de Manila University, Loyola Heights, Quezon City, POB 154, Metro Manila 1099; tel. (2) 4266067; fax (2) 4265660; e-mail add.ipc@pusit.admu.edu.ph; f. 1960; conducts research into rural and urban poverty, agrarian reform, irrigation, community health, coastal resources, forestry and women's affairs; assists development agencies; trains agency personnel and local communities in the use of research methodologies; library of 3,166 vols, 4,070 reprints and vertical file, databank; Dir Dr GERMELINO M. BAUTISTA; publs include *IPC Papers, IPC Monograph Series, IPC Final Reports, IPC Reprints* (all irregular).

Research Institute for Mindanao Culture: Xavier University, Ateneo de Cagayan, POB 24, Cagayan de Oro City 9000; tel. and fax (8822) 723228; e-mail lburton@xu.edu.ph; f. 1957 to study and assist the development of north Mindanao, the Philippines in general and their peoples; Dir Dr ERLINDA M. BURTON; publs *RIMCU Updates* (quarterly), periodicals.

Research Institute for Politics and Economics: Polytechnic University of the Philippines, Anonas St, Santa Mesa, Manila; tel. (2) 616775; fax (2) 7161143; Dir Prof. DANILO CUETO.

POLAND

Institute of Developing Countries: University of Warsaw, ul. Karowa 20, 00-324 Warsaw; tel. (22) 55-23-237; fax (22) 55-23-27; e-mail ikr@mercury.ci.uw.edu.pl; internet www.ikr.uw.cdu.pl; f. 1962; undergraduate and postgraduate studies; interdisciplinary research on developing countries; Dir Prof. URSZULA ŻUŁAWSKA; publs include *Africa-Asia-Latin American* (irregular).

Komitet Nauk Orientalistycznych PAN (Committee for Oriental Studies of the Polish Academy of Sciences): 00-927 Warsaw, ul. Krakowskie Przedmieście 26/28; tel. (22) 849-49-02; f. 1952; Asian and African studies, particularly social sciences; Pres. Prof. Dr MIECZYSŁAW J. KÜNSTLER; publs *Rocznik Orientalistyczny* (2 a year), series *Prace orientalistyczne* (irregular).

Polskie Towarzystwo Orientalistyczne (Polish Oriental Society): 00-927 Warsaw, ul. Krakowskie Przedmieście 26/28; tel. (22) 55-20-353; e-mail pto@orient.uw.edu.pl; internet www.orient.uw.edu.pl/~pto; f. 1922; Pres. Prof. Dr STANISŁAW KAŁUŻYŃSKI; Sec. MARIA KOZŁOWSKA; publ. *Przegląd Orientalistyczny* (quarterly).

PORTUGAL

Museu Etnográfico da Sociedade de Geografia de Lisboa (Ethnographical Museum): Rua Portas de Santo Antão 100, 1100 Lisbon; tel. (1) 3425068; fax (1) 3464553; e-mail soc.geografia.lisboa@clix.pt; f. 1875; native arts, arms, clothing, musical instruments, statues of navigators and historians, relics of voyages of discovery, scientific instruments; Dir Prof. JOÃO PEREIRA NETO; Curator Dr MANUEL CANTINHO.

RUSSIA

Centre for Indian Studies: Russian Academy of Sciences, 103777 Moscow, ul. Rozhdestvenka 12; tel. (095) 923-62-82; fax (095) 975-23-96; f. 1988; part of the Institute of Oriental Studies; Dir Dr A. A. KUTSENKOV; publ. *Azia i Afrika Segodny* (monthly).

Centre for Japanese Studies: Russian Academy of Sciences, 117218 Moscow, pr. Nakhimovsky 32; tel. (095) 124-08-35; fax (095) 310-70-56; e-mail ifes@cemi.rssi.ru; f. 1922; part of the Institute of Far Eastern Studies; Chair. Dr VICTOR N. PAVLYATENKO.

Institute of Far Eastern Studies: Russian Academy of Sciences, 117218 Moscow, pr. Nakhimovsky 32; tel. (095) 124-08-35; fax (095) 310-70-56; e-mail ifes@cemi.rssi.ru; f. 1966; Dir Prof. MICHAEL L. TITARENKO; publs include *Far Eastern Affairs* (6 a year).

Institute of Oriental Studies: Russian Academy of Sciences, 103777 Moscow, ul. Rozhdestvenka 12; tel. (095) 921-18-84; fax (095) 975-23-96; f. 1930; Dir ROSTISLAV B. RYBAKOV.

Institute of World Economy and International Relations: 117859 Moscow, ul. Profsoyuznaya 23; tel. (095) 120-43-32; fax (095) 310-70-27; e-mail ineir@sovam.com; f. 1956; Dir VLADEN A. MARTYNOV; publs include *Otnosheniya* (monthly).

Moscow State Institute of International Relations: 117454 Moscow, Vernadskogo pr. 76; tel. (095) 434-91-58; fax (095) 434-90-66; f. 1944; library of 718,000 vols; library of 718,000 vols; Rector ANATOLII V. TURKUNOV; publ. *Moscow Journal of International Law*.

SINGAPORE

Asian Mass Communication Research and Information Centre: Singapore; tel. 6251506; fax 62534535; f. 1971; library of 35,000 data base records, 350 journals; Sec.-Gen. VIJAY MENON; publs *ACMB* (6 a year), *Asian Journal of Communication* (2 a year), *Media Asia* (quarterly).

The China Society: 61 Club St, Singapore 069436; f. 1948 to promote the study of Chinese culture; 106 mems; Pres. SIMON K. C. HU; publ. *Journal of the China Society*.

East Asian Institute: AS5, Level 4, 10 Kent Ridge Drive, Singapore 119260; tel. 67791037; fax 67793409; e-mail eaiwgw@nus.edu.sg; internet www.nus.edu.sg/NUSinfo/EAI; Dir Prof WANG GUNGWU.

Institute of Policy Studies: 1 Hon Sui Sen Drive, Hon Sui Sen Memorial Library Bldg, Kent Ridge Drive, Singapore 117588; tel. 67792633; fax 67770700; Dir Dr LEE TSAO YUAN.

Institute of Southeast Asian Studies: 30 Heng Mui Keng Terrace, Pasir Panjang, Singapore 119614; tel. 67780955; fax 67781735; e-mail publish@iseas.edu.sg; internet www.iseas.edu.sg; f. 1968 for the promotion of research into the problems of economic development, stability and security and political and social change in South-East Asia; library of 300,000 vols; Dir Prof. CHIA SIOW YUE; publs *Southeast Asian Affairs* (annually), *Regional Outlook* (annually), *Contemporary Southeast Asia* (3 a year), *SOJOURN, Journal of Social Issues in Southeast Asia* (2 a year), *ASEAN Economic Bulletin* (3 a year).

Singapore Institute of International Affairs: 6 Nassim Rd, Singapore 258373; tel. 67349600; fax 67336217; e-mail siia@pacific.net.sg; f. 1961; organizes seminars, lectures and conferences; 120 mems; Dir Dr LEE LAI TO.

SLOVAKIA

Institute of Oriental and African Studies: Slovak Academy of Sciences, Klemensova 19, 813 64 Bratislava; tel. and fax (2) 52-92-63-26; e-mail kabinet@klemens.savba.sk; f. 1960; 18 mems; Head Dr K. SORBY; publs *Asian and African Studies* (2 a year).

SOLOMON ISLANDS

Solomon Islands National Museum and Cultural Centre: POB 313, Honiara; tel. 23351; associated with the Cultural Asscn of the Solomon Islands; research into all aspects of Solomons culture; Dir LAWRENCE FOANAOTA; publs *Journal, Custom Stories.*

SPAIN

Asociación Española de Orientalistas: Universidad Autónoma, Edificio Rectorado, 28049 Madrid; tel. (91) 3974112; publs include *Boletín* (annually).

Chinese Studies Centre: Universidad Autónoma de Barcelona, 08193 Barcelona; tel. (93) 5811374; fax (93) 5811037; f. 1989; Dir Dr SEÁN GOLDEN.

SRI LANKA

Maha Bodhi Society of Sri Lanka: 130 Rev. Hikkaduwe Sri, Sumangala Na Himi Mawatha, Colombo 10; tel. (1) 698079; fax (1) 673472; e-mail mahabodhi@asia.com; f. 1891 for the world propagation of Buddhism; 700 mems; Pres. Ven. BANAGALA UPATISSA NAYAKA THERO; Hon. Sec. M. M. P. SENARATHNE; publ. *Sinhala Bauddhaya* (monthly).

Marga Institute: POB 601, 93/10 Dutugemnu St, Colombo 6; tel. (1) 828544; fax (1) 828597; e-mail marga@sri.lanka.net; internet www.margasrilanka.org; f. 1972; non-profit, multi-disciplinary research organization undertaking study of development issues in Asian region; library of 25,000 vols, 60 periodicals; CEO/Exec. Gov. BASIL ILANGAKOON; publ. *The Marga Quarterly Journal.*

Royal Asiatic Society of Sri Lanka: 1st Floor, Mahaweli Centre and Royal Asiatic Society Bldg, 96 Ananda Coomaraswamy Mawatha, Colombo 7; tel. and fax (1) 699249; f. 1845; object of the Society is to institute and promote enquiries into the history, religions, languages, literature, arts, sciences and social conditions of the present and fmr inhabitants of Sri Lanka and connected cultures; library contains one of the largest existing collections of books on Sri Lanka, and others on Indian and Eastern culture in general; Pres. Dr S. G. SAMARASINGHE; Hon. Secs R. WIJEDASA, DAS MIRIYAGALLA; publ. *Journal* (annually).

SWEDEN

Centre for East and Southeast Asian Studies, Lund University: Box 792, 220 07, Lund; tel. (46) 222-30-40; fax (46) 222-30-41; e-mail info@ace.lu.se; internet www.ace.lu.se; f. 1997; Dir Assoc. Prof. MICHAEL SCHOENHALS.

Centrum för stillahavsasienstudier (Center for Pacific Asia Studies): 106 91 Stockholm; tel. (8) 162000; fax (8) 168810; e-mail cpas@orient.su.se; internet www.cpas.su.se; f. 1984; attached to Stockholm University; Dir Prof. TORBJÖRN LODÉN.

European Institute of Japanese Studies (EIJS): Stockholm School of Economics, Box 6501, 113 83 Stockholm; tel. (8) 736-93-64; fax (8) 31-30-17; e-mail asia@hhs.se; f. 1992; Dir Prof. MAGNUS BLOMSTRÖM; publs papers, monographs, reports.

Institutet för Internationell Ekonomi (Institute for International Economic Studies): 106 91 Stockholm; tel. (8) 162000; fax (8) 161443; f. 1962; attached to Stockholm University; Dir Prof. TORSTEN PERSSON.

Utrikespolitiska Institutet (Swedish Institute of International Affairs): Lilla Nygatan 23, Box 1253, 111 82 Stockholm; tel. (8) 6960500; fax (8) 201049; e-mail info@ui.se; internet www.ui.se; f. 1938; promotes studies of international affairs; library of c. 20,000 vols and 400 periodicals; Pres. ERIK BELFRAGE; Dir ANDERS MELLBOURN; publs include *Världspolitikens Dagsfrågor, Internationella Studier, Länder i fickformat*, conference papers, research reports.

SWITZERLAND

Institut universitaire d'Etudes du Développement: 24 rue Rothschild, CP 136, 1211 Geneva 21; tel. (22) 906-5940; fax (22) 906-5947; e-mail iued@unige.ch; internet www.urige.ch/iued/; f. 1961; a centre of higher education, training and research into development problems of Africa, Latin America and Asia; conducts courses, seminars and practical work; Dir JEAN-LUC MAURER; publs *Cahiers de l'IUED, Annuaire Suisse-Tiers Monde, Itinéraires.*

Institut universitaire de hautes études internationales (Graduate Institute of International Studies): 132 rue de Lausanne, 1211 Geneva 21; tel. (22) 908-5700; fax (22) 908-5710; e-mail info@hei.unige.ch; internet heiwww.unige.ch; f. 1927; a research and teaching institution studying international judicial, historical, political and economic questions; Dir Prof. P. TSCHOPP.

Modern Asia Research Centre: 63 rue de Lausanne, CP 36, 1211 Geneva 21; tel. (22) 7328310; fax (22) 7383996; e-mail regnier@uni2a.unige.ch; internet heiwww.unige.ch/marc/; f. 1971; Dir Dr PHILIPPE RÉGNIER; publs books, research reports, occasional papers, articles and newsletters.

Schweizerische Asiengesellschaft (Swiss Asia Society): c/o Ostasiatisches Seminar, Universität Zürich, Zürichbergstrasse 4, 8032 Zürich; tel. (1) 634-3181; fax (1) 634-4921; e-mail office@oas.unizh.ch; internet www.sagw.ch/dt/mitglieder/outer.aspzid=40; f. 1939; 202 mems; Pres. Prof. Dr E. KLOPFENSTEIN; publs *Asiatische Studien/Etudes Asiatiques* (quarterly), *Schweizer Asiatische Studien/Etudes Asiatiques Suisses* (series).

Schweizerisches Institut für Auslandforschung (Swiss Institute of International Studies): Seilergraben 49, 8001 Zürich; tel. (1) 632-6362; fax (1) 632-1947; Dir Prof. DIETER RULOFF; publ. *Sozialwissenschaftliche Studien* (annually).

TAIWAN

Academia Historica: 406 Sec. 2, Pei Yi Rd, Hsintien, Taipei; tel. (2) 22171535; fax (2) 22171640; contains national archives, library, documents; engaged in preparing history of China since 1894; Pres. CHU SHAO-HWA.

Asia and World Institute (AWI): 10th Floor, 102 Kuang Fu South Rd, Taipei; f. 1976; research into international relations, and North American, Asian and Pacific, and European affairs; Dir Dr PHILLIP M. CHEN; publs *AWI Digest, AWI Lecture and Essay Series, AWI Monograph Series.*

Chia Hsin Foundation: 96 Chung Shan Rd, North, Sec. 2, Taipei 10449; tel. (2) 2523-1461; fax (2) 2523-1204; f. 1963 for the promotion of culture in Taiwan; operates nationally in the fields of the arts, social studies, science and medicine, law and education, through research projects, courses, conferences, etc.; Chair. Dr YEN CHEN-HSING; Sec. TSENG WU-HSIONG.

Chung-hua Institution for Economic Research: 75 Chang Hsing St, Taipei 106; tel. (2) 27356006; fax (2) 27356035; e-mail mai@rs930.cier.edu.tw; internet www.cier.edu.tw; Pres. MAI CHAO-CHENG.

Graduate Institute of International Business: National Taiwan University, 1 Roosevelt Rd, Section 4, Taipei; tel. (2) 23638399; e-mail yljaw@mba.ntu.edu.tw; Dir YI-LONG JAW.

Institute of Economics, Academia Sinica: Nankang, Taipei 11529; tel. (2) 27822791; fax (2) 27853946; e-mail service@ieas.econ.sinica.edu.tw; internet www.sinica.edu.tw/econ; f. 1970; Pres. Dr LEE YUAN-TSEH.

Institute of International Relations: 64 Wan Shou Rd, Wenshan District, Taipei 116; tel. (2) 29394921; fax (2) 29378607; e-mail dschen@cc.nccu.edu.tw; internet www.iir.nccu.edu.tw/; f. 1953; research on international relations and mainland Chinese affairs; Dir SZU-YIN HO; publs *Mainland China Studies* (monthly), *Issues and Studies* (every 2 months).

Taiwan Institute of Economic Research (TIER): 7th Floor, 16-8 Tehwei St, Taipei; tel. (2) 5865000; fax (2) 5946317; internet www.tier.org.tw; f. 1976; Dir RU WONG-I.

THAILAND

Asian Institute of Technology: see p. 1548.

Institute of Asian Studies: 7th Floor, Prajadhipok-Rambhai Barni Bldg, Thanon Phyathai, Bangkok 10330; tel. (2) 251-5199;

fax (2) 255-1124; e-mail Supang.C@chula.ac.th; f. 1967; Dir Dr SUPANG CHANTAVANICH; publs monographs, journals.

Institute of East Asian Studies: Thammasat University, Rangsit Campus, Pathum Thani 12121; tel. (2) 564-5000; fax (2) 564-4777; e-mail ieas@tu.ac.th; internet www.asia.tu.ac.th; f. 1984; Dir Assoc Prof. YUPHA KLANGSUWAN.

Siam Society: 131 Soi 21 (Asoke), Thanon Sukhumvit, Bangkok 10110; tel. (2) 661-6470; fax (2) 258-3491; e-mail info@siam-society.org; internet www.siam-society.org; f. 1904 to promote interest and research in art, science and cultural affairs of Thailand and neighbouring countries; library of 25,000 vols; Pres. BILAIBHAN SAMPATISIRI; Hon. Sec. Dr WORAPHAT ARTHAYUKTI; publs include journals and *The Natural History Bulletin*.

Thailand Development Research Institute (TDRI): 565 Ramkhamhaeng 39 (Thepleela 1), Bangkapi, Bangkok 10310; tel. (2) 718-5460; fax (2) 718-5461; e-mail publications@tdri.or.th; internet www.info.tdri.or.th; f. 1984; independent policy research on Thailand's economic and social development issues; Pres. Dr CHALONGPHOB SUSSANGKARN.

UNITED KINGDOM

Asia Research Centre: London School of Economics and Political Science, Houghton St, London, WC2A 2AE; tel. (20) 7955-7583; fax (20) 7955-7591; e-mail arc@lse.ac.uk; f. 1995; conducts social science research on Asia; Dir Prof. M. LEIFER.

British Association for Chinese Studies: c/o 152 Buxton Rd, Macclesfield, Cheshire, SK10 1NG; tel. (1625) 618333; fax (1625) 619185; f. 1975; provides forum for academics and others in the field; holds annual conference; Pres. Dr FRANK DIKÖTTER; Sec. Dr JENNY PUTIN; publs *Newsletter* (2 a year) *Annual Bulletin*.

Catholic Institute for International Relations (CIIR): Unit 3, Canonbury Yard, 190a New North Rd, London, N1 7BJ; tel. (20) 7354-0883; fax (20) 7359-0017; e-mail ciir@ciir.org; internet www.ciir.org; f. 1940; information and research on developing countries; recruits professionals for development projects overseas; Exec. Dir IAN LINDEN.

Centre for Asia-Pacific Studies, Nottingham Trent University: Faculty of Humanities, Nottingham Trent University, Clifton Lane, Nottingham, NG11 8NS; tel. (115) 848-3175; fax (115) 8486385; e-mail neil.renwick@ntu.ac.uk; internet human.ntu.ac.uk/caps/caps.html; Dirs NEIL RENWICK, Dr ROY SMITH.

Centre for South-East Asian Studies, University of Hull: Cottingham Rd, Hull, HU6 7RX; tel. (1482) 465758; fax (1482) 465758; e-mail s.ryan@pol-as.hull.ac.uk; f. 1962; specializes in humanities, social sciences, Indonesian and Thai languages; publs occasional papers, bibliography and literature series (2 a year), special issues and monographs on politics and international relations; Dir T. J. HUXLEY.

Centre of South Asian Studies, University of Cambridge: Laundress Lane, Cambridge, CB2 1SD; tel. (1223) 338094; fax (1223) 316913; e-mail webmaster@s-asian.cam.ac.uk; internet www.s-asian.cam.ac.uk; f. 1964; Dir Dr RAJ CHANDAVARKAR.

Contemporary China Institute: School of Oriental and African Studies, University of London, Thornhaugh St, Russell Sq., London, WC1H 0XG; tel. (20) 7898-4736; e-mail phil.deans@soas.ac.uk; f. 1968; Dir Dr PHIL DEANS; publs *Research Notes and Studies* (short monographs) and CCI/Oxford University Press series.

Department of East Asian Studies, University of Leeds: Leeds, LS2 9JT; tel. (113) 233-3460; fax (113) 233-6741; internet www.leeds.ac.uk/east-asian; Head of Dept Dr MARK WILLIAMS.

Far Eastern Section, Asian Department, Victoria and Albert Museum: South Kensington, London, SW7 2RL; tel. (20) 7942-2244; fax (20) 7942-2252; e-mail r.kerr@vam.ac.uk; f. 1970; perm. displays and exhbns of Far Eastern art; lectures and research; Chief Curator ROSE KERR.

Institute of Commonwealth Studies: see p. 1526.

Institute of Development Studies at The University of Sussex: Brighton, Sussex, BN1 9RE; tel. (1273) 606261; fax (1273) 621202; e-mail ids@sussex.ac.uk; internet www.ids.ac.uk/ids; f. 1966; teaching and research on international development; Dir KEITH BEZANSON; publs include *IDS Bulletin* (quarterly), *IDS Discussion Papers, Annual Report, Research Reports*.

The Japan Centre, University of Birmingham: Edgbaston, Birmingham, B15 2TT; tel. (121) 414-3269; fax (121) 414-3270; e-mail m.e.smith1@bham.ac.uk; internet www.bham.ac.uk/JapanCentre/; Dir CHRISTOPHER WATSON.

Newcastle East Asia Research Centre: University of Newcastle, Newcastle upon Tyne, NE1 7RU; tel. (191) 222-6737; fax (191) 222-5069; e-mail r.f.w.drifte@ncl.ac.uk; internet www.ncl.ac.uk/politics/staff/drifte.html; Dir Dr JAMES BABB (acting).

Nissan Institute of Japanese Studies, University of Oxford: 27 Winchester Rd, Oxford, OX2 6NA; tel. (1865) 274570; fax (1865) 274574; internet www.nissan.ox.ac.uk; f. 1981; devoted to the study of modern Japan; Dir Prof. J. A. A. STOCKWIN; publs Nissan Institute/Routledge Japanese Studies series, Nissan Occasional Papers series.

Oriental and India Office Collections (British Library): 96 Euston Rd, London, NW1 2DB; tel. (20) 7412-7873; fax (20) 7412-7641; e-mail oioc-enquiries@bl.uk; internet www.bl.uk/collections/oriental; f. 1801; c. 1,200,000 European and oriental printed books, 175,000 vols and files of archival records (1600–1948), 70,000 oriental MSS, European MSS, 14,000 vols and boxes, 15,500 British paintings and drawings relating principally to India and the East, 11,000 oriental drawings and miniatures, 2,900 prints and over 250,000 photographs; Dir G. W. SHAW; publs *Newsletter, Report, Guide* and catalogues of the collections.

Oriental Ceramic Society: 30B Torrington Sq., London, WC1E 7JL; tel. (20) 7636-7985; fax (20) 7580-6749; e-mail ocs-london@beeb.net; f. 1921 to increase knowledge and appreciation of Eastern ceramic and other arts; Pres. ROSE KERR; Sec. JEAN MARTIN.

Oriental Institute: University of Oxford, Pusey Lane, Oxford, OX1 2LE; tel. (1865) 278200; fax (1865) 278190; e-mail orient@orinst.ox.ac.uk; internet www.orinst.ox.ac.uk; f. 1960; Sec. L. FONG.

Overseas Development Institute: Costain House, 111 Westminster Bridge Rd, London, SE1 7JD; tel. (20) 7922-0300; fax (20) 7922-0399; e-mail odi@odi.org.uk; internet www.odi.org.uk; f. 1960 as a research centre and forum for the discussion of development issues; publishes its research findings in books and working papers; library of over 15,000 vols; Chair. Baroness JAY; Dir SIMON MAXWELL; publs include *Development Policy Review* (quarterly), *Disasters: The Journal of Disaster Studies and Management*.

Percival David Foundation of Chinese Art: 53 Gordon Sq., London, WC1H 0PD; tel. (20) 7387-3909; fax (20) 7383-5163; e-mail sp17@soas.ac.uk; internet www.pdfmuseum.org.uk; f. 1952; major collection of Chinese ceramics dating 10th–18th century, some of which were fmrly in the possession of the Chinese Imperial family; colloquies on art and archaeology in Asia; subscription reference library of over 5,000 vols; publs monographs, catalogues, *Guide* to the Collection, colloquy reports, postcards and slides.

Royal Asiatic Society of Great Britain and Ireland: 60 Queen's Gardens, London, W2 3AF; tel. (20) 7724-4741; e-mail info@royalasiaticsociety.org; internet www.royalasiaticsociety.org; f. 1823 for the study of the history, sociology, institutions, customs, languages and art of Asia; c. 700 mems; c. 700 subscribing libraries; brs in various Eastern cities; library of 50,000 vols and 1,500 MSS; Sec. A. THOMAS; Librarian M. J. POLLOCK; publs *Journal* and monographs.

Royal Commonwealth Society: see p. 1528.

Royal Institute of International Affairs: Chatham House, 10 St James's Sq., London, SW1Y 4LE; tel. (20) 7957-5700; fax (20) 7957-5710; e-mail contact@riia.org; internet www.riia.org; f. 1920 to facilitate the scientific study of international questions; c. 3,000 mems; Chair. Lord MARSHALL OF KNIGHTSBRIDGE; Dir Prof. V. BULMER-THOMAS; publs include *International Affairs* (quarterly), *The World Today* (monthly), *Chatham House Papers, Annual Report*, etc.

Royal Society for Asian Affairs: 2 Belgrave Sq., London, SW1X 8PJ; tel. (20) 7235-5122; e-mail info@rsaa.org.uk; internet www.rsaa.org.uk; f. 1901; 1,200 mems; library of c. 7,000 vols; Pres. Lord DENMAN; Chair. Sir HAROLD WALKER; Sec. N. J. M. CAMERON; publ. *Journal* (3 a year).

St Antony's College: Oxford, OX2 6JF; tel. and fax (1865) 274559; e-mail asian@sant.ox.ac.uk; internet www.sant.ox.ac.uk/asc.htm; f. 1954; has Asian Studies Centre devoted to the comparative study of modern Asia; Warden Sir MARRACK GOULDING; Dir Dr STEVE TSANG.

School of African and Asian Studies, University of Sussex: Falmer, Brighton, Sussex, BN1 9SJ; tel. (1273) 606755; fax (1273) 623572; e-mail m.h.johnson@sussex.ac.uk; Dean Dr MICHAEL JOHNSON.

School of Development Studies, University of East Anglia: Norwich, NR4 7TJ; tel. (1603) 592807; fax (1603) 451999; e-mail dev.general@uea.ac.uk; internet www.uea.ac.uk/dev/; f. 1970; teaching, research and advisory work; Dean Dr CECILE JACKSON.

School of East Asian Studies (SEAS), University of Sheffield: Floor 5, Arts Tower, Western Bank, Sheffield, S10 2TN; tel. (114) 222-8400; fax (114) 222-8432; e-mail SEAS@sheffield.ac.uk; internet www.seas.ac.uk; Japanese, Korean and Chinese studies; Chair. Prof. TIMOTHY WRIGHT.

School of Oriental and African Studies (SOAS): University of London, Thornhaugh St, Russell Sq., London, WC1H 0XG; tel. (20) 7637-2388; fax (20) 7436-3844; internet www.soas.ac.uk; f. 1916; includes Centre of Chinese Studies, Centre of South Asian Studies, Centre of South East Asian Studies, Centre of Korean Studies, Japan Research Centre, Contemporary China Institute, Centre for the Study of Japanese Religion, Centre for the Study of the Literature of Asia and Africa, Centre of East Asian Law; Dir Prof. COLIN BUNDY; publs *The Bulletin, Calendar, China Quarterly, Annual Report.*

School of Oriental and African Studies Library: Thornhaugh St, Russell Sq., London, WC1H 0XG; tel. (20) 7898-4163; fax (20) 7898-4159; e-mail libenquiry@soas.ac.uk; internet lib.soas.ac.uk; f. 1916; c. 1,000,000 vols and pamphlets; 4,700 current periodicals, 54,000 maps, 6,500 microforms, 2,800 MSS and private papers collections, extensive missionary archives; all covering Asian and African languages, literatures, philosophy, religions, history, law, cultural anthropology, art and archaeology, social sciences, geography and music; Librarian K. WEBSTER.

UNITED STATES OF AMERICA

American Oriental Society: Room 111E, Hatcher Graduate Library, University of Michigan, Ann Arbor, MI 48109-1205; f. 1842; 1,350 mems; library of 23,000 vols; Pres. C. S. GOODRICH; Sec.-Treas. JONATHAN RODGERS; publs *Journal of the American Oriental Society* (quarterly), *AOS Monograph Series* (irregular).

The Asia Foundation: POB 193223, San Francisco, CA 94119; tel. (415) 982-4640; fax (415) 392-8863; e-mail info@asiafound.org; internet www.asiafoundation.org; br in Washington, DC, and 13 offices throughout Asia; private, non-profit NGO; f. 1951; library of 3,370 vols; collaborates with partners from public and private sectors to support leadership and institutional development, exchanges, dialogue, technical assistance, research and policy engagement related to governance and law, economic reform and development, women's political participation and regional relations; Pres. WILLIAM P. FULLER; publs *Annual Report* (annually).

Asia-Pacific Centre for Security Studies: 2058 Maluhia Rd, Honolulu, HI 96815; tel. (808) 971-8900; fax (808) 971-8999; e-mail pao@apcss.org; internet www.apcss.org; f. 1995; Pres. H. C. STACKPOLE.

Asia/Pacific Research Center: Stanford University, Stanford CA 94305; tel. (650) 723-9741; internet aparc.stanford.edu; Dir Prof. ANDREW G. WALDER.

Asia Pacific Policy Center: 3 Lafayette Centre, Suite 210, 1155 Twenty-First St, NW, Washington, DC 20036; tel. (202) 223-7258; fax (202) 223-7280; e-mail appcusa@aol.com; Pres. DOUGLAS H. PAAL.

Asia Society: 725 Park Ave, New York, NY 10021; tel. (212) 288-6400; fax (212) 517-8315; internet www.asiasociety.org; f. 1956; carries out educational and cultural programmes to increase awareness of the arts, history and contemporary affairs of Asia; regional brs in Washington, DC, Houston, Los Angeles, Hong Kong and Melbourne; 8,000 mems; Pres. NICHOLAS PLATT; publs *Archives of Asian Art*, exhibition catalogues, Contemporary Affairs publications.

Asian Art Museum of San Francisco/Chong-Moon Lee Center for Asian Art and Culture: 260 Larkin St, San Francisco, CA 94102; tel. (415) 379-8800; fax (415) 668-8928; e-mail pr@asianart.org; internet www.asianart.org; f. 1966; museum and centre of research and publication on outstanding collections representing the countries and cultures of Asia; library of 20,000 vols; Dir Dr EMILY SANO.

Asian Cultural Council: 437 Madison Ave, New York, NY 10022; tel. (212) 812-4300; fax (212) 812-4299; e-mail acc@accny.org; internet www.asianculturalcouncil.org; f. 1980; supports cultural exchanges in the visual and performing arts between the USA and Asia; publicly supported; Dir RALPH SAMUELSON.

Association for Asian Studies Inc: 1021 E. Huron St, Ann Arbor, MI 48104; tel. (734) 665-2490; fax (734) 665-3801; internet www.aasianst.org; f. 1941; Exec. Dir MICHAEL PASCHAL; publs include *Asian Studies Newsletter, Journal of Asian Studies* (quarterly), *Education About Asia* (3 a year) and monographs.

The Brookings Institution: 1775 Massachusetts Ave, NW, Washington, DC 20036-2188; tel. (202) 797-6000; fax (202) 797-6004; e-mail bibooks@brook.edu; internet www.brook.edu; f. 1916; research, education and publishing in economics, govt, and foreign policy; maintains Social Science Computation Center; education division, Center for Public Policy Education, organizes conferences and seminars; 50 resident scholars; library of c. 85,000 vols; Pres. MICHAEL ARMACOST; publs *Annual Report, The Brookings Review* (quarterly), *Brookings Papers on Economic Activity* (3 a year), *Brookings Papers on Education Policy* (annually), *Brookings/Wharton Papers on Financial Policy* (annually).

Center for Chinese Studies, University of Michigan: Suite 3668 SSWB, 1080 South University, Ann Arbor, MI 48109-1106; tel. (734) 764-6308; fax (734) 764-5540; e-mail chinese.studies@umich.edu; internet www.umich.edu/~iinet/ccs; f. 1961; library of more than 610,000 vols, reels of microfilm and sheets of microfiches; Dir MARTIN J. POWERS; publs include *Michigan Monographs in Chinese Studies, Twentieth Century China Journal.*

Center for East Asian Studies, Stanford University: Bldg 50, Main Quad, Stanford University, Stanford, CA 94305-2034; tel. (650) 723-3362; fax (650) 725-3350; e-mail connie.chin@forsythe.stanford.edu; internet www.stanford.edu/dept/CEAS; f. 1973; Dir Prof. JEAN OI.

Center for International Studies: Massachusetts Institute of Technology, E38-651, Cambridge, MA 02139; tel. (617) 253-8093; fax (617) 253-9330; f. 1951; Dir Dr RICHARD SAMUELS.

Center for Japanese Studies, University of Michigan: 3603 International Institute, 1080 S. University, Ann Arbor, MI 48109; tel. (734) 764-6307; fax (734) 936-2948; e-mail umcjs@umich.edu; internet www.umich.edu/~iinet/cjs; f. 1947; library of 224,000 vols, reels of microfilm, microfiche 2,000 periodical titles (Asia Library Japanese collection); Dir HITOMI TONOMURA; publs *Michigan Classics in Japanese Studies, Michigan Papers in Japanese Studies, Michigan Monograph Series in Japanese Studies*, etc.

Center for Pacific Islands Studies: School of Hawaiian, Asian and Pacific Studies, University of Hawaii, Moore Hall 215, 1890 East-West Rd, Honolulu, HI 96822; tel. (808) 956-7700; fax (808) 956-7053; e-mail cpis@hawaii.edu; internet www.hawaii.edu/cpis; Dir DAVID HANLON.

Center for the Pacific Rim: University of San Francisco, 2130 Fulton St, CA 94117-1080; tel. (415) 422-6357; fax (415) 422-5933; e-mail pacrim@usfca.edu; internet www.usfca.edu/pac_rim/; f. 1988; Exec. Dir Dr BARBARA K. BUNDY.

Centers for South and Southeast Asian Studies, University of Michigan: 1080 S University, Ste 3640, Ann Arbor, MI 48109-1106; tel. (734) 764-0352; fax (734) 936-0996; e-mail csseas@umich.edu; internet www.umich.edu/~iinet/csseas; Dir (South Asia) SUMATHI RAWASWAMY; Dir (Southeast Asia) JUDITH BECKER; Dir (Southeast Asia Business Program, Business School) LINDA LIM (tel. (734) 763-5796); publs *Michigan Papers on South and Southeast Asia, Michigan Studies of South and Southeast Asia, Michigan Studies in Buddhist Literature* (occasional papers), *Journal of Asian Business* (quarterly).

Center for South Asia Studies, University of California: 10 Stephens Hall 2310, University of California, Berkeley, CA 94720-2310; tel. (510) 642-3608; fax (510) 643-5793; e-mail csas@uclink4.berkeley.edu; internet www.ias.berkeley.edu/southasia; Chair. Prof. THOMAS METCALF.

Center of International Studies: Woodrow Wilson School of Public and International Affairs, Princeton University, Bendheim Hall, Princeton, NJ 08544-1022; tel. (609) 258-4851; fax (609) 258-3988; internet www.wws.princeton.edu/~cis; f. 1951; international relations and national development research, including analysis of international security and the political economy; Dir MICHAEL ROTHSCHILD (acting); publs include *World Politics* (quarterly), monographs.

Center on Japanese Economy and Business: Columbia University, Business School, 321 Uris Hall, MC 5968, 3022 Broadway, New York, NY 10027-6902; tel. (212) 854-3976; fax (212) 678-6958; e-mail htp1@columbia.edu; internet www.columbia.edu/cu/business/japan; Dir HUGH PATRICK.

Columbia University East Asian Institute: Mail Code 3333, Columbia University, 420 West 118th St, New York, NY 10027; tel. (212) 854-2592; fax (212) 749-1497; e-mail eaiinfo@columbia.edu; internet www.sipa.columbia.edu/eai; f. 1949; Dir XIAOBO LU.

Cornell University East Asia Program: 140 Uris Hall, Ithaca, NY 14853-7601; tel. (607) 255-6222; fax (607) 255-1388; f. 1950 for the development of instruction and research on East Asia; library of 460,000 vols; 180 graduate students; Dir Prof. JOHN B. WHITMAN; publs *Cornell East Asia Series*.

Cornell University South Asia Program: 170 Uris Hall, Ithaca, NY 14853; tel. (607) 255-8493; fax (607) 254-5000; internet www.einaudi.cornell.edu/SouthAsia; Dir Prof. CHRISTOPHER MINKOWSKI.

Cornell University Southeast Asia Language and Area Center: 180 Uris Hall, Ithaca, NY 14853; tel. (607) 255-2378; fax (607) 254-5000; e-mail seap@cornel.edu; internet www.einaudi.cornell.edu/SoutheastAsia; f. 1950 for the development of instruction and research on South-East Asia; library of 212,060 vols, 19,950 periodicals and 841 newspapers; Dir Assoc. Prof. THAK CHALOEMTIARANA.

Council on Foreign Relations Inc: 58 East 68th St, New York, NY 10021; tel. (212) 434-9400; fax (212) 861-1789; e-mail communications@cfr.org; internet www.cfr.org; f. 1921; 3,600 mems; Pres. LESLIE H. GELB; publs include *Foreign Affairs* (every two months).

Council on Regional Studies: 218 Palmer Hall, Princeton University, Princeton, NJ 08544; tel. (609) 258-4720; f. 1961; Chair. Prof. EZRA N. SULEIMAN.

East-West Center—Center for Cultural and Technical Interchange between East and West, Inc: 1601 East-West Rd, Honolulu, HI 96848; tel. (808) 944-7111; fax (808) 944-7970; e-mail ewcinfo@EastWestCenter.org; internet www.ewc.hawaii.edu; f. 1960 by Congress to promote better relations and understanding among the nations and peoples of Asia, the Pacific and the USA through co-operative study, training and research; conducts multidisciplinary programmes on environmental policy, population, resources, development, journalism and Pacific Islands development; provides awards and grants to scholars, journalists, graduate students, and managers to participate in the Center's studies; Pres. Dr CHARLES MORRISON.

Freer Gallery of Art: 12th St and Jefferson Drive, SW, Washington, DC 20560; tel. (202) 357-4880; fax (202) 663-9105; internet www.si.edu/asia; f. 1906, opened 1923; conducts research on the major collections of Asian and late 19th and early 20th century American art, gift of the late Charles L. Freer; art collection of 28,000 objects; library of 55,000 vols, 75,000 slides; Dir Dr MILO BEACH; publs include *Artibus Asiae, Ars Orientalis*.

Harvard-Yenching Institute: 2 Divinity Ave, Room 120, Cambridge, MA 02138; tel. (617) 495-3369; fax (617) 495-7798; internet www.fas.harvard.edu/~yenching/; f. 1928 to promote the growth and advancement of higher education in East and South-East Asia, with special regard to the social sciences and humanities; visiting scholars and doctoral scholarship programmes; Dir TU WEIMING; publs include *Harvard Journal of Asiatic Studies, Scripta Mongolica,* monographs.

Institute for Polynesian Studies: Brigham Young University–Hawaii, 55-220 Kulanui St, Box 1979, Laie, HI 96762; tel. (808) 293-3665; fax (808) 293-3664; e-mail wineerav@byuh.edu; Dir VERNICE WINEERA; publ. *Pacific Studies* (4 a year).

Henry M. Jackson School of International Studies: University of Washington, Seattle, WA 98195; tel. (206) 543-2100.

John King Fairbank Center for East Asian Research (Harvard University): 1737 Cambridge St, Cambridge, MA 02138; tel. (617) 495-4046; fax (617) 495-9976; internet www.fas.harvard.edu/~fairbank; Dir Prof. ELIZABETH J. PENY; publs incl. *Papers on Chinese History, Harvard Studies on Taiwan,* etc.

Library of International Relations: 565 W Adams, Chicago, IL 60661; tel. (312) 906-5600; fax (312) 906-5685; f. 1932; financed by voluntary contributions; stimulates interest and research in international problems; conducts seminars and offers special services to businesses and academic institutions; library of 560,000 items.

The Mongolia Society: 322 Goodbody Hall, Indiana University, 1011 E 3rd St, Bloomington, IN 47405-7005; tel. (812) 855-4078; fax (812) 855-7500; e-mail monsoc@indiana.edu; internet www.indiana.edu/~mongsoc; f. 1961 to promote and further the study of Mongolia, its history, language and culture; Pres. Dr HENRY G. SCHWARZ; publs include *Mongolian Studies: Journal of the Mongolia Society, Mongolia Survey, Newsletter, Bulletin, Special Papers* and *Occasional Papers* series; dictionaries.

Museum of Fine Arts, Boston: 465 Huntington Ave, Boston, MA 02115; tel. (617) 267-9300; fax (617) 236-0362; f. 1870; has dept of Asiatic art with major collection of Chinese, Japanese, Indian and South-East Asian sculpture, painting, prints and decorative art works dating from Neolithic period to modern times; library of 65,000 books, periodicals and pamphlets; Dir Dr MALCOLM A. ROGERS; Curator WU TUNG.

National Bureau of Asian Research: 4518 University Way NE, Suite 300, Seattle, Washington 98105; tel. (206) 632-7370; fax (206) 632-7487; e-mail nbr@nbr.org; internet www.nbr.org.

Princeton University, East Asian Studies Department: Princeton, NJ 08544; tel. (609) 452-5905; e-mail collcutt@princeton.edu; internet www.princeton.edu/~eastasia; Chair. MARTIN COLLCUTT.

Program of African and Asian Languages: Northwestern University, 356 Kresge Hall, 1859 Sheridan Rd, Evanston, IL 60208-2209; tel. (847) 491-5288; fax (847) 467-1097; e-mail lepine@northwestern.edu; f. 1973; Dir RICHARD M. LEPINE.

Arthur M. Sackler Gallery: 1050 Independence Ave, SW, Washington, DC 20560; tel. (202) 357-4880; fax (202) 357-4911; internet www.si.edu/asia; f. 1982, opened 1987; exhbns, research and education in Asian art; art collection of 2,500 objects, including inaugural gift from the late Arthur M. Sackler; library of 55,000 vols., 75,000 slides; Dir Dr MILO BEACH; publs include *Asian Art and Culture*.

St John's University Institute of Asian Studies: 8000 Utopia Parkway, Jamaica, NY 11439; tel. (718) 990-6582; fax (718) 990-1881; e-mail linj@stjohns.edu; Dir Dr JOHN LIN.

School of Hawaiian, Asian and Pacific Studies: University of Hawaii, Moore Hall 309, 1890 East-West Rd, Honolulu, HI 96822; tel. (808) 956-8324; fax (808) 956-6345; e-mail wjtanabe@hawaii.edu; internet www.hawaii.edu/shaps; administers Centers for Chinese, Hawaiian, Japanese, Korean, Pacific Islands, Philippine, South Asian, South-East Asian and Buddhist Studies; Dean WILLA J. TANABE.

School of International and Public Affairs: Columbia University, 420 West 118th St, New York, NY 10027; tel. (212) 854-4604; Dean LISA ANDERSON.

Seton Hall University Department of Asian Studies: South Orange, NJ 07079; tel. (973) 761-9464; fax (973) 740-1843; library of 40,000 vols; Chair. WINSTON YANG.

The Sigur Center for Asian Studies: George Washington University, 2013 G St, NW, Ste. 301, Washington, DC 20052;

tel. (202) 994-5886; fax (202) 994-6096; e-mail gsigur@gwu.edu; internet www.gwu.edu/~sigur.

Southern Asian Institute: 1128 International Affairs Bldg, Columbia University, New York, NY 10027; tel. (212) 854-3616; fax (212) 864-4847; Dir JOHN S. HAWLEY.

University of Arizona Department of East Asian Studies: Tucson, AZ 85721; tel. (520) 621-7505; e-mail vancet@u.arizona.edu; internet www.arizona.edu/~EAS; Head Dr TIMOTHY VANCE.

University of California at Berkeley, Department of East Asian Languages and Cultures: 104 Durant Hall, Berkeley, CA 94720-2230; tel. (510) 642-3480; fax (510) 642-6031; e-mail ealang@uclink.berkeley.edu; internet www.ealc.berkeley.edu; Head of Dept Prof. SUSAN MATISOFF.

University of California Department of South and Southeast Asia Studies: 7233 Dwinelle Hall, Berkeley, CA 94720-2540; tel. (510) 642-4564; fax (510) 643-2959; e-mail casmaoff@socrates.berkeley.edu; internet ls.berkeley.edu/dept/sseas.

University of Illinois Center for East Asian and Pacific Studies: 910 S. Fifth St, Champaign, IL 61801; tel. (217) 333-7273; fax (217) 244-5729; f. 1965; Dir GEORGE T. YU.

University of Iowa Department of Asian Languages and Literature: University of Iowa, IA City, IA 52242-1320; tel. (319) 335-2151; e-mail chuanren-ke@uiowa.edu; Chair. Prof. CHUANREN KE.

University of Kansas Center for East Asian Studies: 205 Lippincott Hall, Lawrence, KS 66045-2146; tel. (785) 864-3849; fax (785) 864-5034; e-mail ceas@falcon.cc.ukans.edu; internet www.falcon.cc.ukans.edu/~ceas; Dir MARSHA WEIDNER; publs research and reference series.

University of Pennsylvania, Department of South Asia Regional Studies: 820 Williams Hall, Philadelphia, PA 19104; tel. (215) 898-7475; fax (215) 573-2138; internet www.southasia.upenn.edu; library of 400,000 vols; Chair. GUY R. WELBON; Librarian DAVID NELSON.

University of Pittsburgh Department of East Asian Languages and Literatures: 1501 Cathedral of Learning, Pittsburgh, PA 15260; tel. (412) 624-5568; fax (412) 624-3458; e-mail hnara@pitt.edu; internet www.pitt.edu/~deall; Chair. HIROSHI NARA.

University of Southern California East Asian Studies Center: VKC 263, Los Angeles, CA 90089-0046; tel. (213) 740-2991; fax (213) 740-8409; e-mail easc@usc.edu; internet www.usc.edu/dept/LAS/EASC; f. 1962; Dir OTTO SCHNEPP; publs occasional papers.

University of Southern California–University of California (Los Angeles) Joint East Asian Language and Area Studies National Resource Center: THH 331 M, University Park, Los Angeles, CA 90089-4351; tel. (213) 740-2991; fax (213) 740-8409; e-mail easc@usc.edu; internet www.usc.edu/dept/LAS/EASC; f. 1976; Dir Dr OTTO SCHNEPP; publ. *Newsletter*.

Woodrow Wilson School of Public and International Affairs: Princeton University, Princeton, NJ 08544; tel. (609) 258-4836; fax (609) 258-2095; e-mail wwsadmit@princeton.edu; Dean MICHAEL ROTHSCHILD.

Yale University Southeast Asia Studies: Yale University, POB 208206, New Haven, CT 06520-8206; tel. (203) 432-3431; fax (203) 432-9381; library of 260,000 vols; Chair. JAMES C. SCOTT; publs *The Vietnam Forum, Lac Viet* series, *Southeast Asia Monograph* series.

VATICAN CITY

Pontificium Istitutum Orientale (Pontifical Oriental Institute): 7 Piazza Santa Maria Maggiore, 00185 Rome; tel. (6) 4465589; fax (6) 4465576; f. 1917; library of 156,900 vols; Pres. Rev. HÈCTOR VALL; Sec. Rev. VINCENZO POSSI; publs *Orientalia Christiana Periodica, Orientalia Christiana Analecta, Concilium Florentinum (Documenta et Scriptores), Anaphorae Syriacae, Kanonika.*

VIET NAM

Hoi Phat Hoc Nam Viet (Association for Buddhist Studies): Xa-Loi Pagoda, 89 Ba Huyen Thanh Quan, Ho Chi Minh City; f. 1950 to further the study and practice of Buddhism; 30,000 mems; library of 5,000 vols; Pres. Dr CAO VAN TRI; publs *Tu Quang, Le Ngoc Diep.*

Institute of Economics: Commission for Social Sciences, 27 Tran Xuan Soan St, Hanoi; tel. (4) 254774; fax (4) 259071; f. 1960; library of 8,000 vols; publs *Economic Studies Review* (2 a year), *Nghien Cuu Kinh Te* (2 a year).

SELECT BIBLIOGRAPHY—BOOKS

See also bibliographies at end of relevant chapters in Part Two.

Abegglen, James C. *Sea Change: Pacific Asia as the New World Industrial Center.* New York, The Free Press, 1994.

Acharya, Amitav. *Constructing a Security Community in Southeast Asia—ASEAN and the Problem of Regional Order.* London, Routledge, 2000.

Acharya, Amitav. *The Quest for Identity: International Relations of South-East Asia.* Oxford, Oxford University Press, 2001.

Agarwal, Bina. *A Field of One's Own: Gender and Land Rights in South Asia.* New York, Cambridge University Press, 1994.

Agrawal, Pradeep, et al. *Economic Restructuring in East Asia and India: Perspectives on Policy Reform.* Singapore, Institute of Southeast Asian Studies, 1995.

Agrawal, Pradeep, Gokran, Subir V., Mishira, Veena, Parikh, Kirit S., and Sen, Kunal. *Policy Regimes and Industrial Competitiveness—A Comparative Study of East Asia and India.* Singapore, Institute of Southeast Asian Studies, 2000.

Ahuja, Vinod, Bidani, Benud, Ferrera, Francisco, and Walton, Michael. *Everyone's Miracle: Revisiting Poverty and Inequality in East Asia.* Washington, DC, World Bank, 1997.

Alagappa, Muthiah (Ed.). *Political Legitimacy in Southeast Asia—The Quest for Moral Authority.* Cambridge, Cambridge University Press, 1998.

Coercion and Governance: The Declining Political Role of the Military in Asia. Stanford, CA, Stanford University Press, 2001.

Alatas, Ali. *A Voice for Peace.* Singapore, Institute of Southeast Asian Studies, 2001.

Aldrich, Richard J., Rawnsley, Gary D., and Rawnsley, Ming-Yeh T. (Eds). *The Clandestine Cold War in Asia, 1945–65.* Ilford, Frank Cass, 2000.

Anderson, Benedict. *The Spectre of Comparisons: Nationalism, Southeast Asia and the World.* London, Verso, 1999.

Andrews, John. *The Asian Challenge: Looking Beyond 2000.* Hong Kong, Longman, 1992.

Andrews, Tim, Baldwin, Bryan J., and Chompusri, Nartnalin. *The Changing Face of Multinationals in South East Asia.* London, Routledge, 2002.

Ang Swee Hoon, et al. *Surviving the New Millennium: Lessons from the Asian Crisis.* Singapore, McGraw Hill, 1999.

Antlöv, Hans, and Ngo Tak-Wing (Eds). *The Cultural Construction of Politics in Asia.* Richmond, Curzon Press, 1999.

Antons, Christoph (Ed.). *Law and Development in East and South-East Asia.* Richmond, Curzon Press, 2001.

Aoki, Masahiko, Kim Hyung-Ki, and Okuno-Fujiwara, Masahiro. *The Role of the Government in East Asian Economic Development: Comparative Institutional Analysis.* Oxford, Oxford University Press, 1997.

Ariff, Mohamed (Ed.). *APEC & Development Co-operation.* Singapore, Institute of Southeast Asian Studies, 1998.

Ariff, Mohamed, and Khalid, Ahmed M. *Liberalization, Growth and Transitional Economics in Asia.* Cheltenham, Edward Elgar Publishing, 1999.

Ariff, Mohamed, and Tan Loong-Hoe (Eds). *The Uruguay Round: ASEAN Trade Policy Options.* Singapore, Institute of Southeast Asian Studies, 1988.

Arndt, Heinz W., and Hill, Hal (Eds). *Southeast Asia's Economic Crisis—Origins, Lessons and the Way Forward.* Singapore, Institute of Southeast Asian Studies, 1999.

ASEAN Secretariat. *ASEAN Economic Co-operation: Transition and Transformation.* Singapore, Institute of Southeast Asian Studies, 1997.

Ashton, David, Green, Francis, James, Donna, and Sung, Johnny. *Education and Training for Development in East Asia—The Political Economy of Skill Formation in Newly Industrialised Economies.* London, Routledge, 1999.

Asian Development Bank. *Asian Development Outlook.* Manila, ADB, annually.

A Continent in Change: Thirty Years of the Asian Development Bank. Manila, ADB, 1997.

East ASEAN Growth Area: Brunei Darussalam, Indonesia, Malaysia, Philippines (Vols I to VII). Manila, ADB, 1997.

Emerging Asia—Changes and Challenges. Manila, ADB, 1997.

The Future of Asia in the World Economy. Manila, ADB, 1998.

The Global Trading System and Developing Asia. Manila, ADB, 1997.

Growth Triangles in Asia—A New Approach to Regional Economic Cooperation. Manila, ADB, 1998.

Key Indicators of Developing Asian and Pacific Countries. Manila, ADB, annually.

Small Countries, Big Lessons: Governance and the Rise of East Asia. Manila, ADB, 1996.

Athukorala, Prema-Chandra. *Trade Policy Issues in Asian Development.* London, Routledge, 1998.

Athukorala, Prema-Chandra (Ed.). *The Economic Development of South Asia.* Cheltenham, Edward Elgar Publishing, 2002.

Athukorala, Prema-Chandra, Manning, Chris, and Wickramasekara, Piyasiri. *Growth, Employment and Migration in Southeast Asia—Structural Change in the Greater Mekong Countries.* Cheltenham, Edward Elgar Publishing, 2000.

Atkins, William. *The Politics of Southeast Asia's New Media.* Richmond, Curzon Press, 2001.

Backman, Michael. *Asian Eclipse: Exposing the Dark Side of Business in Asia.* Singapore, John Wiley & Sons, 1999.

Bahamonde, Ramón. *International Policy Institutions Around the Pacific Rim: A Directory of Resources in East Asia, Australasia, and the Americas.* Boulder, CO, Lynne Rienner, 1998.

Bale, Chris. *Faces in the Crowd: A Journey in Hope.* Hong Kong, Chinese University Press, 1999.

Bales, Kevin. *Disposable People: New Slavery in the Global Economy.* Berkeley, CA, University of California Press, 2000.

Barlow, Colin (Ed.). *Institutions and Economic Change in Southeast Asia—The Context of Development from the 1960s to the 1990s.* Cheltenham, Edward Elgar Publishing, 1999.

Barr, Michael D. *Cultural Politics and Asian Values—The Tepid War.* London, RoutledgeCurzon, 2002.

Bauer, Joanne R., and Bell, Daniel A. (Eds). *The East Asian Challenge for Human Rights.* Cambridge, Cambridge University Press, 1999.

Baxter, Craig, et al. *Government and Politics in South Asia.* Boulder, CO, Westview Press, 1998.

Beeson, Mark. *Reconfiguring East Asia—Regional Institutions and Organizations After the Crisis.* London, RoutledgeCurzon, 2002.

Berger, Mark, and Borer, Douglas (Eds). *The Rise of East Asia—Critical Visions of the Pacific Century.* London, Routledge, 1997.

Berry, James, and McGreal, Stanley (Eds). *Cities in the Pacific Rim.* London, Routledge, 1999.

Beyrer, Chris. *War in the Blood: Sex, Politics and AIDS in Southeast Asia.* London, Zed Books, 1998.

Biers, Dan (Ed.). *Crash of '97—How the Financial Crisis is Reshaping Asia.* Hong Kong, Review Publishing, 1998.

Boomgaard, Peter, and Brown, Ian (Eds). *Weathering the Storm: The Economies of Southeast Asia in the 1930s Depression*. Singapore, Institute of Southeast Asian Studies, 2000.

Booth, Ann, and Ash, Robert (Eds). *The Economies of Asia 1945–1998*. London, Routledge, 1999.

Booth, Martin. *The Dragon Syndicates: The Global Phenomenon of the Triads*. New York, Doubleday, 1999.

Borrus, Michael, Ernst, Dieter, and Haggard, Stephan (Eds). *International Production Networks in Asia—Rivalry or Riches*. London, Routledge, 2000.

Bose, Sugata, and Jalal, Ayesha. *Modern South Asia—History, Culture, Political Economy*. London, Routledge, 1998.

Bowie, Anthony, and Unger, Daniel. *The Politics of Open Economies—Indonesia, Malaysia, the Philippines, and Thailand*. Cambridge, Cambridge University Press, 1997.

Bracken, Paul. *Fire in the East: The Rise of Asian Military Power and the Second Nuclear Age*. London, HarperCollins, 1999.

Bresnan, John. *From Dominoes to Dynamoes: The Transformation of Southeast Asia*. New York, Council on Foreign Relations, 1995.

Bridges, Brian. *Europe and the Challenge of the Asia Pacific—Change, Continuity and Crisis*. Cheltenham, Edward Elgar Publishing, 1999.

Brown, David. *The State and Ethnic Politics in Southeast Asia*. London, Routledge, 1996.

Brown, Michael E., and Ganguli, Sumit (Eds). *Government Policies and Ethnic Relations in Asia and the Pacific*. Cambridge, MA, Massachusetts Institute of Technology, 1998.

Burnett, Alan. *The Western Pacific: The Challenge of Sustainable Growth*. Sydney, Allen and Unwin, 1994.

Calder, Kent E. *Asia's Deadly Triangle: How Arms, Energy and Growth Threaten to Destabilize Asia-Pacific*. London, Nicholas Brealey Publishing, 1996.

Camilleri, Joseph A. *States, Markets and Civil Society in Asia Pacific*. The Political Economy of the Asia-Pacific Region, Vol. I, Cheltenham, Edward Elgar Publishing, 2000.

Campos, Ed, and Root, Hilton L. *The Key to the Asian Miracle: Making Shared Growth Credible*. Washington, DC, Brookings Institution, 1996.

Capie, David, and Evans, Paul. *The Asia-Pacific Security Lexicon*. Singapore, Institute of Southeast Asian Studies, 2002.

Carpenter, William M., and Wiencek, David G. (Eds). *Asian Security Handbook—An Assessment of Political-Security Issues in the Asia-Pacific Region*. Armonk, NY, M. E. Sharpe, 1996.

Carr, Brian, and Mahalingam, Indira (Eds). *Companion Encyclopedia of Asian Philosophy*. London, Routledge, 1996.

Case, William. *Politics in Southeast Asia—Democracy or Less*. London, RoutledgeCurzon, 2002.

Cauquelin, Josiane, Lim, Paul, and Mayer-Konig, Birgit (Eds). *Asian Values—Encounter with Diversity*. Richmond, Curzon Press, 1998.

Chadda, Maya. *Building Democracy in South Asia: India, Nepal, Pakistan*. Boulder, CO, Lynne Rienner, 2000.

Chan Heng Chee (Ed.). *The New Asia-Pacific Order*. Singapore, Institute of Southeast Asian Studies, 1997.

Chang Ho-Joon. *The Political Economy of Industrial Policy*. Basingstoke, Macmillan Press, 1996.

Chee Soon Juan. *To Be Free: Stories from Asia's Struggle Against Oppression*. Monash Asia Institute, Vic, 1999.

Chen, Min. *Asian Management Systems: Chinese, Japanese and Korean Styles of Business*. London and New York, Routledge, 1995.

Chern, Wen S., Carter, Colin A., and Shei Shun-yi (Eds). *Food Security in Asia: Economics and Policies*. Cheltenham, Edward Elgar Publishing, 2000.

Cheung, Anthony, and Scott, Ian. *Governance and Public Sector Reform in Asia—Paradigm Shift or Business as Usual?* London, RoutledgeCurzon, 2002.

Chia Siow Yue (Ed.). *APEC: Challenges and Opportunities*. Singapore, Institute of Southeast Asian Studies, 1995.

Chia Siow Yue and Lim, Jamus Jerome (Eds). *Information Technology in Asia: New Development in Paradigms*. Singapore, Institute of Southeast Asian Studies, 2002.

Chia Siow Yue, and Pacini, Marcello (Eds). *ASEAN in the New Asia*. Singapore, Institute of Southeast Asian Studies, 1998.

Chia Siow Yue, and Tan, Joseph L. H. (Eds). *ASEAN in the WTO: Challenges and Responses*. Singapore, Institute of Southeast Asian Studies, 1996.

ASEAN in the New Millennium. Singapore, Institute of Southeast Asian Studies, 1999.

Chibusawal, Masahide. *Pacific Asia in the 1990s*. London, Routledge, 1991.

Chowdhury, Anis, and Islam, Iyanatul. *The Newly Industrializing Economies of East Asia*. London, Routledge, 1993.

Asia-Pacific Economies. London, Routledge, 1997.

Chowdhury, Anis, and Islam, Iyanatul (Eds). *Beyond the Asian Crisis—Pathways to Sustainable Growth*. Cheltenham, Edward Elgar Publishing, 2001.

Christie, Clive J. *A Modern History of Southeast Asia: Decolonization, Nationalism and Separatism*. Singapore, Institute of Southeast Asian Studies, 1996.

Christie, Kenneth, and Roy, Denny. *The Politics of Human Rights in East Asia*. London, Pluto Press, 2001.

Chu Yun-Peng, and Hill, Hal (Eds). *The Social Impact of the Asian Financial Crisis*. Cheltenham, Edward Elgar Publishing, 2001.

Chu Yun-Peng, and Wu Rong-I (Eds). *Business, Markets and Government in the Asia-Pacific—Competition Policy, Convergence and Pluralism*. London, Routledge, 1998.

Chua Beng-Huat. *Consumption in Asia—Lifestyle and Identities*. London, Routledge, 2000.

Clark, Cal, and Roy, K. C. *Comparing Development Patterns in Asia*. Boulder, CO, Lynne Rienner, 1997.

Clarke, Gerard. *The Politics of NGOs in Southeast Asia—Participation and Protest in the Philippines*. London, Routledge, 1998.

Clifford, Mark, and Engardio, Pete. *Meltdown—Asia's Boom, Bust and Beyond*. Paramus, NJ, Prentice Hall Press, 2000.

Cobbold, Richard. *The World Reshaped: Fifty Years after the War in Asia*. Basingstoke, Macmillan Press, 1996.

Coedès, G. *The Indianized States of Southeast Asia*. Honolulu, HI, University of Hawaii Press, 1970.

Collignon, Stefan, Pisani-Ferry, Jean, and Park Yung Chul (Eds). *Exchange Rate Policies in Emerging Asian Countries*. London, Routledge, 1999.

Collins, Alan. *The Security Dilemmas of Southeast Asia*. Singapore, Institute of Southeast Asian Studies, 2001.

Cooney, Sean, Lindsey, Tim, and Zhu Ying (Eds). *Law and Labour Market Regulation in South East Asia*. London, Routledge, 2002.

Corden, Max. *The Asian Crisis—Is There A Way Out?* Singapore, Institute of Southeast Asian Studies, 1999.

Cotterell, Arthur. *East Asia: From Chinese Predominance to the Rise of the Pacific Rim*. London, John Murray, 1993.

Council for Asia-Europe Cooperation (CAEC). *Asia-Europe Cooperation: Beyond the Financial Crisis*. Singapore, Institute of Southeast Asian Studies, 2000.

Crozier, Brian. *South-East Asia in Turmoil*. Baltimore, MD, Penguin Books, 1966.

Cumings, Bruce. *Parallax Visions: Making Sense of American-East Asian Relations at the End of the Century*. Durham, NC, Duke University Press, 1999.

Da Cunha, Derek (Ed.). *Southeast Asian Perspectives on Security*. Singapore, Institute of Southeast Asian Studies, 2000.

Dadush, Uri, Uzan, Mark, and Dasgupta, Dipak. *Private Capital Flows in the Age of Globalization: The Aftermath of the Asian Crisis*. Cheltenham, Edward Elgar Publishing, 2000.

Das, Dilip K. *The Asia-Pacific Economy*. Basingstoke, Macmillan Press, 1996.

De Brouwer, Gordon, and Pupphavesa, Wisarn (Eds). *Asia Pacific Financial Deregulation*. London, Routledge, 1999.

Delhaise, Philippe F. *Asia in Crisis: The Implosion of the Banking and Finance Systems.* Singapore, John Wiley & Sons, 1999.

Dent, Christopher M. *The European Union and East Asia—An Economic Relationship.* London, Routledge, 1999.

The Foreign Economic Policies of Singapore, South Korea and Taiwan. Cheltenham, Edward Elgar Publishing, 2002.

Dent, Christopher M., and Huang, David W. F. (Eds). *Northeast Asian Regionalism—Lessons from the European Experience.* London, RoutledgeCurzon, 2002.

Devan, Janadas (Ed.). *Southeast Asia: Challenges of the 21st Century.* Singapore, Institute of Southeast Asian Studies, 1994.

Dickinson, David G., Ford, Jim L., Fry, Maxwell L., Mullineux, Andrew W., and Sen, Somnath. *Finance, Governance and Economic Performance in Pacific and South East Asia.* Cheltenham, Edward Elgar Publishing, 2000.

Dickinson, David, et al. (Eds). *Financial Sector Reform and Economic Development in Pacific and South East Asia.* Cheltenham, Edward Elgar Publishing, 2000.

Dixon, Chris. *Southeast Asia in the World Economy; A Regional Geography.* Cambridge, Cambridge University Press, 1993.

Dixon, Chris, and Drakakis-Smith, David. *Economic and Social Development in Pacific Asia.* London, Routledge, 1994.

Dobbs-Higginson, Michael S. *Asia Pacific: A View on Its Role in the New World Order.* Hong Kong, Longman, 1993.

Asia Pacific: Its Role in the New World Disorder. London, William Heinemann, 1994.

Dobson, Wendy. *Japan in East Asia: Trading and Investment Strategies.* Singapore, Institute of Southeast Asian Studies, 1993.

Dobson, Wendy, and Chia Siow Yue (Eds). *Multinationals and East Asian Integration.* Singapore, Institute of Southeast Asian Studies, 1997.

Drysdale, Peter (Ed.). *Reform and Recovery in East Asia.* London, Routledge, 2000.

Drysdale, Peter, and Dong Dong Zhang (Eds). *Japan and China: rivalry or cooperation in East Asia?* Canberra, Asia Pacific Press, 2000.

Drysdale, Peter, Zhang Yunling and Ligang Song (Eds). *APEC and Liberalisation of the Chinese Economy.* Canberra, Asia Pacific Press, 2000.

Dunung, Sanjyot P. *Doing Business in Asia: The Complete Guide.* Singapore, Simon and Schuster, 1995.

Dupont, Alan. *East Asia Imperilled: Transnational Challenges to Security.* Cambridge, Cambridge University Press, 2001.

Dutta, M. *Economic Regionalization in the Asia-Pacific—Challenges to Economic Cooperation.* Cheltenham, Edward Elgar Publishing, 1999.

Dwyer, Denis. *South-East Asian Development: Geographical Perspectives.* Harlow, Longman Scientific and Technical, 1990.

East Asia Analytical Unit. *Overseas Chinese Business Networks in Asia.* Parkes, ACT, Australian Department of Foreign Affairs and Trade, 1995.

Eccleston, Bernard, Dawson, Michael, and McNamara, Deborah (Eds). *The Asia-Pacific Profile.* London, Routledge, 1998.

Eichengreen, Barry. *Toward a New International Financial Architecture: A Practical Post-Asia Agenda.* Washington, DC, Institute for International Economics, 1999.

Ellings, Richard J., and Simon, Sheldon W. (Eds). *Southeast Asian Security in the New Millennium.* Armonk, NY, M. E. Sharpe, 1996.

Elmhurst, Becky, and Saptari, Rainer (Eds). *Labour in Southeast Asia—Local Processes in a Globalizing World.* Richmond, Curzon Press, 2001.

Engholm, Christopher. *Doing Business in Asia's Booming 'China Triangle'.* New Jersey, NJ, Prentice Hall, 1995.

Ernst, Dieter, Ganiatsos, Tom, and Mytelka, Lynn (Eds). *Technological Capabilities and Export Success in Asia.* London, Routledge, 1998.

Evans, Grant, Hutton, Christopher, and Kuah Khun Eng (Eds). *Where China Meets Southeast Asia: Social and Cultural Change in the Border Regions.* Singapore, Institute of Southeast Asian Studies, 2000.

Evers, Hans-Dieter and Korff, Rüdiger. *Southeast Asian Urbanism: The Meaning and Power of Social Space.* Singapore, Institute of Southeast Asian Studies, 2001.

Fallows, James. *Looking at the Sun: The Rise of the New East Asian Economic and Political System.* New York, Vintage Books, 1994.

Fane, George. *Capital Mobility, Exchange Rates and Economic Crises.* Cheltenham, Edward Elgar Publishing, 2000.

Farrington, John, and Lewis, David (Eds). *Nongovernmental Organizations and the State in Asia: Rethinking Roles in Sustainable Agricultural Development.* London and New York, Routledge, 1993.

Feinberg, Richard E., and Zhao Ye (Eds). *Assessing APEC's Progress: Trade, Ecotech, and Institutions.* Singapore, Institute of Southeast Asian Studies, 2001.

Findlay, Christopher, Chia Lin Sien, and Singh, Karmjit (Eds). *Asia Pacific Air Transport: Challenges and Policy Reforms.* Singapore, Institute of Southeast Asian Studies, 1997.

Fisher, Charles A. *South-East Asia: A Social, Economic and Political Geography.* London, Methuen, 1964.

Flynn, Dennis O., Frost, Lionel, and Latham, A. J. H. (Eds). *Pacific Centuries—Pacific and Pacific Rim Economic History since the 16th Century.* London, Routledge, 1998.

Francks, Penelope, Boestel, Joanna, and Kim Choo Hyop. *Agriculture and Economic Development in East Asia—From Growth to Protectionism in Japan, Korea and Taiwan.* London, Routledge, 1999.

Friedman, Edward. *An Asian Way? The Politics of Democratization: Generalizing East Asian Experiences.* Boulder, CO, Westview Press, 1995.

Fry, M. J. *Foreign Direct Investment in Southeast Asia: Differential Impacts.* Singapore, Institute of Southeast Asian Studies, 1993.

Fu Tsu-Tan, Huang, Cliff J., and Lovell, C. A. Knox (Eds). *Productivity and Economic Performance in the Asia-Pacific Region.* Cheltenham, Edward Elgar Publishing, 2002.

Fukuchi, Takao, and Kagami, Mitsuhiro (Eds). *Perspectives on the Pacific Basin Economy: A Comparison of Asia and Latin America.* Tokyo, Institute of Developing Economies and the Asian Club Foundation, 1990.

Funston, John (Ed.). *Government & Politics in Southeast Asia.* Singapore, Institute of Southeast Asian Studies, 2002.

Gamble, Andrew, and Payne, Anthony. *Regionalism and World Order.* Basingstoke, Macmillan Press, 1996.

Ganesan, N. *Bilateral Tensions in Post-Cold War ASEAN.* Singapore, Institute of Southeast Asian Studies, 1999.

Garnaut, Ross. *Asian Market Economies: Challenges of a Changing International Environment.* Singapore, Institute of Southeast Asian Studies, 1996.

Open Regionalism and Trade Liberalization: An Asia-Pacific Contribution to the World Trade System. Singapore, Institute of Southeast Asian Studies, 1996.

Garnaut, Ross (Ed.). *Sustaining Export-Oriented Development—Ideas from East Asia.* Cambridge, Cambridge University Press, 1995.

Garran, Robert. *Tigers Tamed: The End of the Asian Miracle.* Honolulu, HI, University of Hawaii Press, 1999.

Gaul, Karen K., and Hiltz, Jackie (Eds). *Landscapes and Communities on the Pacific Rim.* Armonk, NY, M. E. Sharpe, 2000.

Gibney, Frank. *The Pacific Century: America and Asia in a Changing World.* New York, Charles Scribner's Sons, 1993.

Gilson, Julie. *Asia Meets Europe.* Cheltenham, Edward Elgar Publishing, 2002.

Godemont, François. *The New Asian Renaissance—From Colonialism to the Post-Cold War.* London, Routledge, 1997.

The Downsizing of Asia. London, Routledge, 1998.

Goldman, Merle, and Gordon, Andrew (Eds). *Historical Perspectives on Contemporary East Asia.* Cambridge, MA, Harvard University Press, 2000.

Goldstein, Morris. *The Asian Financial Crisis: Causes, Cures and Systemic Implications.* Washington, DC, International Monetary Fund, 1998.

Gomez, Edmund. *Political Business in East Asia.* London, Routledge, 2001.

Gonzalez III, Joaquin L., Lauder, Kathleen, and Melles, Brenda. *Opting for Partnership: Governance Innovations in Southeast Asia.* Singapore, Institute of Southeast Asian Studies, 1999.

Goodman, David S. G. (Ed.). *Towards Recovery in Pacific Asia.* London, Routledge, 1999.

Goodman, Roger, White, Gordon, and Kwon Huck-Ju. *The East Asian Welfare Model—Welfare, Orientalism and the State.* London, Routledge, 1998.

Gosling, David. *Religion and Ecology in India and Southeast Asia.* London, Routledge, 2001.

Gough, Leo. *Asia Meltdown: The End of the Miracle.* Oxford, Capstone Publishing, 1998.

Gourevitch, Peter A. (Ed.). *The Pacific Region: Challenges to Policy and Theory.* Newbury Park, CA, Sage Publications, 1989.

Gray, Sidney J., Purcell, William R., and McGaughey, Sara L. (Eds). *Asia-Pacific Issues in International Business.* Cheltenham, Edward Elgar Publishing, 2001.

Haacke, Jürgen. *ASEAN's Diplomatic and Security Culture—Origins, Developments and Prospects.* London, RoutledgeCurzon, 2002.

Haggard, Stephan. *The Political Economy of the Asian Financial Crisis.* Washington, DC, Institute for International Economics, 2000.

Halib, Mohamed, and Huxley, Tim (Eds). *An Introduction to Southeast Asian Studies.* Singapore, Institute of Southeast Asian Studies, 1997.

Hall, D. G. E. *A History of South-East Asia.* Basingstoke, Macmillan Press, 1981.

Hamada, Koichi, Matsushita, Mitsuo, and Komura, Chikara (Eds). *Dreams and Dilemmas: Economic Friction and Dispute Resolution in the Asia-Pacific.* Singapore, Institute of Southeast Asian Studies, 2000.

Han Sung-Joo (Ed.). *Changing Values in Asia: Their Impact on Governance and Development.* Singapore, Institute of Southeast Asian Studies, 1999.

Haq, Mahbub ul. *Human Development in South Asia.* Karachi, Oxford University Press, 1997.

Human Development in South Asia: The Education Challenge. Karachi, Oxford University Press, 1998.

Harris, Stuart, and Cotton, James (Eds). *The End of the Cold War in Northeast Asia.* Boulder, CO, Lynne Rienner, 1991.

Harrison, Brian. *South-East Asia: A Short History.* London, Macmillan Press, and New York, St Martin's Press, 1955.

Harvie, Charles, and Lee Boon-Chye. *Globalisation and SMEs in East Asia.* Cheltenham, Edward Elgar Publishing, 2002.

The Role of SMEs in National Economies in East Asia. Cheltenham, Edward Elgar Publishing, 2002.

Hefner, Robert W., and Horvatich, Patricia (Eds). *Islam in an Era of Nation-States—Politics and Religious Renewal in Muslim South-East Asia.* Honolulu, HI, University of Hawaii Press, 1997.

Hellmann, Donald C., and Pyle, Kenneth B. (Eds). *From APEC to Xanadu—Creating a Viable Community in the Post-Cold War Pacific.* Armonk, NY, M. E. Sharpe, 1997.

Henderson, Callum. *Asia Falling? Making Sense of the Asian Currency Crisis and Its Aftermath.* Singapore, McGraw-Hill Book Co, 1998.

Hersh, Jacques. *The USA and the Rise of East Asia since 1945.* New York, NY, St Martin's Press, 1995.

Hian Teck Hoon. *Trade, Jobs and Wages.* Cheltenham, Edward Elgar Publishing, 2000.

Higgott, Richard, Leaver, Richard, and Ravenhill, John (Eds). *Pacific Economic Relations in the 1990s: Conflict or Cooperation?* Boulder, CO, Lynne Rienner, 1993.

Hill, Hal (Ed.). *The Economic Development of Southeast Asia.* Cheltenham, Edward Elgar Publishing, 2002.

Hilsdon, Anne-Marie, et al. (Eds). *Human Rights and Gender Politics—Asia-Pacific Perspectives.* London, Routledge, 2000.

Hirsch, Philip, and Warren, Carol (Eds). *The Politics of Environment in Southeast Asia.* London, Routledge, 1998.

Hiscock, Geoff. *Asia's Wealth Club.* London, Nicholas Brealey Publishing, 1997.

Ho, Alfred Kuo-liang. *The Far East in World Trade: Developments and Growth since 1945.* New York, F. A. Praeger, 1967.

Holloway, Nigel. *Japan in Asia: The Economic Impact on the Region.* Hong Kong, Review Publishing, 1991.

Horowitz, Shale, and Heo, Uk (Eds). *The Political Economy of International Financial Crisis—Interest Groups, Ideologies and Institutions.* Singapore, Institute of Southeast Asian Studies, 2001.

Horton, Susan. *Women and Industrialization in Asia.* London, Routledge, 1995.

Hossain, Moazzem, Islam, Iyanatul, and Kibria, Reza. *South Asian Economic Development—Transformation, Opportunities and Challenges.* London, Routledge, 1999.

Hsiung, James C. (Ed.). *Asia Pacific in the New World Politics.* Boulder, CO, Lynne Rienner, 1993.

Hu Teh-Wei, and Hsieh Chee-Ruey (Eds). *The Economics of Health Care in Asia-Pacific Countries.* Cheltenham, Edward Elgar Publishing, 2002.

Huang Yasheng. *FDI in China—An Asian Perspective.* Singapore, Institute of Southeast Asian Studies, 1998.

Hughes, Helen (Ed.). *Achieving Industrialization in East Asia.* Cambridge, Cambridge University Press, 1990.

Hughes, Helen. *East Asia: Is there an East Asian Model?* Canberra, Australian National University, Research School of Pacific Studies, 1993.

Hutchison, Jane, and Brown, Andrew (Eds). *Organising Labour in Globalising Asia.* London, Routledge, 2001.

Ichimura, Shinichi. *Political Economy of Japanese and Asian Development.* Singapore, Institute of Southeast Asian Studies, 1998.

Ikeo, Aiko. (Ed.). *Economic Development in Twentieth-Century East Asia—The International Context.* London, Routledge, 1996.

Institute of Southeast Asian Studies. *Regional Outlook—Southeast Asia 2001–2002.* Singapore.

Asia-Europe Cooperation: Beyond the Financial Crisis. Singapore, 2000.

International Library of Sociology. *The Sociology of East Asia.* London, Routledge, 1998.

International Monetary Fund. *The IMF's Response to the Asian Crisis.* Washington, DC, IMF, 1999.

Jackson, Karl D. (Ed.). *Asian Contagion—The Causes and Consequences of a Financial Crisis,* Singapore, Institute of Southeast Asian Studies, 1999.

Jalal, Ayesha. *Democracy and Authoritarianism in South Asia—A Comparative and Historical Perspective.* Cambridge, Cambridge University Press, 1995.

James, David L. *The Executive Guide to Asia-Pacific Communications.* St Leonards, NSW, Allen and Unwin, 1995.

James, William E., Naya, Seiji, and Meier, Gerald M. *Asian Development: Economic Success and Policy Lessons.* San Francisco, International Center for Economic Growth, 1987.

Japan Environmental Council, Teranishi, Shunichi, and Awagi, Takehisa. *The State of the Environment in Asia 1999/2000.* London, Routledge, 2000.

Jayasuriya, Kanishka (Ed.). *Law, Capitalism and Power in Asia—The Rule of Law and Legal Institutions.* London, Routledge, 1998.

Jeshurun, Chandran (Ed.). *China, India, Japan and the Security of Southeast Asia.* Singapore, Institute of Southeast Asian Studies, 1993.

Jomo, K. S. *Southeast Asia's Misunderstood Miracle: Industrial Policy and Economic Development in Thailand, Malaysia and Indonesia.* Boulder, CO, Westview Press, 1997.

(Ed.). *Tigers in Trouble: Financial Governance, Liberalisation and Crises in East Asia.* London, Zed Books, 1999.

Jones, Eric, Frost, Lionel, and White, Colin. *Coming Full Circle: An Economic History of the Pacific Rim.* Boulder, CO, Westview Press, 1994.

Kahn, Joel S. (Ed.). *Southeast Asian Identities: Culture and the Politics of Representation in Indonesia, Malaysia, Singapore and Thailand.* Singapore, Institute of Southeast Asian Studies, 1998.

Kapur, Ashok. *Regional Security Structures in Asia.* London, RoutledgeCurzon, 2002.

Kawagoe, Toshihiko, and Sekiguchi, Sueo (Eds). *East Asian Economies: Transformation and Challenges.* Singapore, Institute of Southeast Asian Studies, 1997.

Keenan, Faith (Ed.). *The Aftershock—How an Economic Earthquake Is Rattling Southeast Asian Politics.* Hong Kong, Review Publishing, 1998.

Kelly, David, and Reid, Anthony (Eds). *Asian Freedoms—The Idea of Freedom in East and Southeast Asia.* Cambridge, Cambridge University Press, 1998.

Kemenade, Willem van. *China, Hong Kong, Taiwan, Inc.* New York, NY, Alfred A. Knopf, 1997.

Kershaw, Roger. *Monarchy in South East Asia—The Faces of Tradition in Transition.* London, Routledge, 2000.

Khan, Ilyas. *Underdogs in Overdrive: 10 Insanely Great Ideas For the Asian Techno-preneur.* Singapore, John Wiley & Sons, 2001.

Kim Young Jeh (Ed.). *The New Pacific Community in the 1990s.* Armonk, NY, M. E. Sharpe, 1996.

King, Victor T. *Environmental Challenges in South-East Asia.* Richmond, Curzon Press, 1998.

Kinnvall, Catarina, and Jonsson, Kristina. *Globalization and Democratization in Asia—The Construction of Identity.* London, RoutledgeCurzon, 2002.

Korhonen, Pekka. *Japan and Asia-Pacific Integration: Pacific Romances 1968–1996.* London, Routledge, 1998.

Kratoska, Paul H. (Ed.). *South East Asia.* London, Routledge, 2001.

Kreinin, Mordechai E., and Plummer, Michael G. (Eds). *Economic Integration and Asia—The Dynamics of Regionalism in Europe, North America and the Asia-Pacific.* Cheltenham, Edward Elgar Publishing, 2001.

Krugman, Paul. *The Return of Depression Economics.* New York, W. W. Norton & Co, 1999.

Kwak Tae-Hwan, and Olsen, Edward A. (Eds). *The Major Powers in Northeast Asia: Seeking Peace and Security.* Boulder, CO, Lynne Rienner, 1996.

Kwan, C. H. *Economic Interdependence in the Asia-Pacific Region—Towards a Yen Bloc.* London, Routledge, 1994.

Kwan, C. H., Vandenbrink, D., and Chia Siow Yue (Eds). *Coping with Capital Flows in East Asia.* Singapore, Institute of Southeast Asian Studies, 1998.

Lall, Sanjaya. *Learning from the Asian Tigers: Studies in Technology and Industrial Policy.* Basingstoke, Macmillan Press, 1995.

Laothamatas, Anek (Ed.). *Democratization in Southeast and East Asia.* Singapore, Institute of Southeast Asian Studies, 1997.

Lasserre, Philippe, and Schütte, Helmut. *Strategies for Asia Pacific.* Basingstoke, Macmillan Press, 1995.

Latham, A. J. H., and Kawakatsu, Heita (Eds). *Asia-Pacific Dynamism 1550–2000.* London, Routledge, 2000.

Leaman, Oliver (Ed.). *Encyclopedia of Asian Philosophy.* London, Routledge, 2000.

Lee, Chung H. *Financial Liberalization and the Economic Crisis in Asia.* London, RoutledgeCurzon, 2002.

Lee Jyng Tae and Drysdale, Peter. *Globalisation and the Asia Pacific Economy.* London, Routledge, 2002.

Lee Sang-Gon, and Ruffini, Pierre-Bruno (Eds). *The Global Integration of Europe and East Asia—Studies of International Trade and Investment.* Cheltenham, Edward Elgar Publishing, 1999.

Lee Yok-shiu F., and So, Alvin Y. (Eds). *Asia's Environmental Movements—Comparative Perspectives.* Armonk, NY, M. E. Sharpe, 1999.

Leifer, Michael. *Dictionary of the Modern Politics of South-east Asia.* London, Routledge, 2000.

Asian Nationalism. London, Routledge, 2000.

Li Kui Wai. *Capitalist Development and Economism in East Asia—The Rise of Hong Kong, Singapore, Taiwan and South Korea.* London, Routledge, 2002.

Lingle, Christopher. *Rise and Decline of the Asian Century: False Starts on the Path to the Global Millennium.* Aldershot, Ashgate Publishing, 1997.

Lipton, Michael, and Osmani, Siddiqur. *The Quality of Life in Emerging Asia.* Brighton, University of Sussex, 1996.

Liu Fu-kuo and Régnier, Philippe (Eds). *Regionalism in East Asia.* London, RoutledgeCurzon, 2002.

Lukauskas, Arvid J., and Rivera-Batiz, Francisco L. *The Political Economy of the East Asian Crisis and its Aftermath—Tigers in Distress.* Cheltenham, Edward Elgar Publishing, 2001.

MacIntyre, Andrew (Ed.). *Business and Government in Industrialising Asia.* St Leonards, NSW, Allen and Unwin, 1995.

Mack, Andrew, and Ravenhill, John. *Talking Shop? Pacific Co-operation: Building Economic and Security Regimes in the Asia-Pacific Region.* St Leonards, NSW, Allen and Unwin, 1994.

Mackerras, Colin (Ed.). *East and Southeast Asia: A Multidisciplinary Survey.* Boulder, CO, Lynne Rienner, 1995.

Maddison, Angus, Rao, Prasada D.S., and Shepherd, William (Eds). *The Asian Economies in the Twentieth Century.* Cheltenham, Edward Elgar Publishing, 2002.

Madsen, Stig Toft (Ed.). *State, Society and the Environment in South Asia.* Richmond, Curzon Press, 1999.

Mahathir, Mohamad. *A New Deal for Asia.* Kuala Lumpur, Pelanduk Publications, 1999.

Mahbubani, Kishore. *Can Asians Think?* Singapore, Times Books International, 1998.

Maidment, Richard, and Mackerras, Colin (Eds). *Culture and Society in the Asia-Pacific.* London, Routledge, 1998.

Maidment, Richard, Goldblatt, David, and Mitchell, Jeremy (Eds). *Governance in the Asia-Pacific.* London, Routledge, 1998.

Mallet, Victor. *The Trouble with Tigers: The Rise and Fall of Southeast Asia.* London, HarperCollins, 1999.

Manning, Robert A. *The Asian Energy Factor: Myths and Dilemmas of Energy, Security and the Pacific Future.* Hampshire, Palgrave, 2001.

Margolis, Eric. *War at the Top of the World—The Struggle for Afghanistan, Kashmir and Tibet.* London, Routledge, 2001.

Masina, Pietro P. (Ed.). *Rethinking Development in East Asia—From Illusory Miracle to Economic Crisis.* Richmond, Curzon Press, 1999.

Masuyama, Seiichi, Vandenbrink, Donna, and Chia Siow Yue (Eds). *East Asia's Financial Systems—Evolution and Crisis.* Singapore, Institute of Southeast Asian Studies, 1999.

(Eds). *Industrial Policies in East Asia.* Singapore, Institute of Southeast Asian Studies, 1997.

(Eds). *Industrial Restructuring in East Asia.* Singapore, Institute of Southeast Asian Studies, 2001.

(Eds). *Restoring East Asia's Dynamism.* Singapore, Institute of Southeast Asian Studies, 2000.

Maull, Hanns, Segal, Gerald, and Wanandi, Jusuf (Eds). *Europe and the Asia-Pacific.* London, Routledge, 1998.

McCargo, Duncan. *Media and Politics in Pacific Asia.* London, Routledge, 2002.

McDougall, Derek. *The International Politics of the New Asia Pacific.* Singapore, Institute of Southeast Asian Studies, 1997.

McGrew, Anthony, and Brook, Christopher (Eds). *Asia-Pacific in the New World Order.* London, Routledge, 1998.

McLeod, Ross H., and Garnaut, Ross (Eds). *East Asia in Crisis—From Being a Miracle to Needing One?* London, Routledge, 1998.

McNally, Christopher A., and Morrison, Charles E. (Eds). *Asia Pacific Security Outlook: 2002.* Washington, DC, Brockings Institution, 2002.

Meyer, Karl, and Brysac, Shareen. *Tournament of Shadows: The Great Game and the Race for Empire in Asia.* London, Little, Brown, 2001.

Miller, Sally M., Latham, A. J. H., and Flynn, Dennis, O. (Eds). *Studies in the Economic History of the Pacific Rim.* London, Routledge, 1997.

Mirza, Hafiz, and Wee Kee Hwee (Eds). *Transnational Corporate Strategies in the ASEAN Region.* Cheltenham, Edward Elgar Publishing, 2000.

Montes, Manuel F. *The Currency Crisis in Southeast Asia (Updated Edition).* Singapore, Institute of Southeast Asian Studies, 2000.

Montes, Manuel F., and Popov, Vladimir V. *The Asian Crisis Turns Global.* Singapore, Institute of Southeast Asian Studies, 1999.

Morley, James W. (Ed.). *Driven by Growth—Political Change in the Asia-Pacific Region.* Armonk, NY, M. E. Sharpe, 1998.

Murphey, Rhoads. *East Asia: A New History.* London, Longman, 1997.

Naisbitt, John. *Megatrends Asia.* London, Nicholas Brealey Publishing, 1995.

Nakamura, Mitsuo, Siddique, Sharon, and Bajunid, Omar Farouk (Eds). *Islam and Civil Society in Southeast Asia.* Singapore, Institute of Southeast Asian Studies, 2001.

Neary, Ian. *Human Rights in Japan, South Korea and Taiwan.* London, RoutledgeCurzon, 2002.

Noland, Marcus. *Pacific Basin Developing Countries: Prospects for the Future.* Washington, DC, Institute for International Economics, 1990.

Nomura Research Institute and Institute of Southeast Asian Studies. *The New Wave of Foreign Direct Investment in Asia.* Singapore, Institute of Southeast Asian Studies, 1995.

Ohmae, Kenichi. *The End of the Nation State: The Rise of Regional Economies.* New York, The Free Press, 1995.

Olds, Kris, et al (Eds). *Globalisation and the Asia-Pacific—Contested Territories.* London, Routledge, 1999.

Osborne, Milton. *Southeast Asia: An Illustrated Introductory History.* St Leonards, NSW, Allen and Unwin, 7th Edn, 1998.

The Mekong—Turbulent Past, Uncertain Future. Boston, MA, Atlantic Monthly Press, 2000.

Pacific Business Forum. *The Osaka Action Plan: Roadmap to Realizing the APEC Vision.* Singapore, Asia-Pacific Economic Co-operation Secretariat, 1995.

Pape, Wolfgang. *East Asia 2000 and Beyond.* Richmond, Curzon Press, 1998.

Parnwell, Michael, and Bryant, Raymond. *Environmental Change in South-East Asia—People, Politics and Sustainable Development.* London, Routledge, 1996.

Pempel, T. J. (Ed.). *The Politics of the Asian Economic Crisis.* Ithaca, NY, Cornell University Press, 1999.

Peou, Sorpong. *The ASEAN Regional Forum and Post-Cold War IR Theories—A Case for Constructive Realism?* Singapore, Institute of Southeast Asian Studies, 1999.

Petri, Peter A. (Ed.). *Regional Co-operation and Asian Recovery.* Singapore, Institute of Southeast Asian Studies, 2000.

Phillips, David R. (Ed.). *Ageing in the Asia-Pacific Region—Issues, Policies and Future Trends.* London, Routledge, 2000.

Pinches, Michael (Ed.). *Culture and Privilege in Capitalist Asia.* London, Routledge, 1999.

Pomfret, Richard. *Asian Economies in Transition: Reforming Centrally Planned Economies.* Cheltenham, Edward Elgar Publishing, 1996.

Preston, P. W., and Gilson, Julie (Eds). *The European Union and East Asia—Inter-Regional Linkages in a Changing Global System.* Cheltenham, Edward Elgar Publishing, 2001.

Raina, Vinod, Chowdhury, Amit, and Chowdhury, Samit. *The Dispossessed: Victims of Development in Asia.* Hong Kong, Arena Press, 1999.

Reid, Anthony J. S. *Southeast Asia in the Age of Commerce 1450–1680,* Volume II, *Expansion and Crisis.* London, Yale University Press, 1995.

The Last Stand of Asian Autonomies: Responses to Modernity in the Diverse States of Southeast Asia and Korea, 1750–1900. Basingstoke, Macmillan Press, 1997.

Charting the Shape of Early Modern Southeast Asia. Cheltenham, Edward Elgar Publishing, 2000.

Ries, Phillippe. *The Asian Storm—Asia's Economic Crisis Examined.* Tokyo, Tuttle Publishing, 2001.

Rigg, Jonathan. *Southeast Asia—The Human Landscape of Modernization and Development.* London, Routledge, 2002.

Robin, Jeffrey (Ed.). *Asia: The Winning of Independence: the Philippines, India, Indonesia, Vietnam, Malaya.* London, Macmillan Press, 1981.

Robison, Richard, and Goodman, David S. G. (Eds). *The New Rich in Asia—Mobile Phones, McDonald's and Middle-Class Revolution.* London, Routledge, 1996.

Robison, Richard, et al. (Eds). *Politics and Markets in the Wake of the Asian Crisis.* London, Routledge, 1999.

Rock, Michael T. *Pollution Control in East Asia: Lessons from Newly Industrializing Economies.* Singapore, Institute of Southeast Asian Studies, 2002.

Rodan, Garry (Ed.). *Political Oppositions in Industrialising Asia.* London, Routledge, 1996.

Rodan, Garry, Hewison, Kevin, and Robison, Richard (Eds). *The Political Economy of South-east Asia.* Oxford, Oxford University Press, 2001.

Rodrigo, G. Chris. *Technology, Economic Growth and Crises in East Asia.* Cheltenham, Edward Elgar Publishing, 2000.

Rohwer, Jim. *Asia Rising.* New York, Simon and Schuster, 1996.

Ross, Robert S. (Ed.). *East Asia in Transition—Toward a New Regional Order.* Armonk, NY, M. E. Sharpe, 1995.

Rowen, Henry S. (Ed.). *Behind East Asian Growth—The Political and Social Foundations of Prosperity.* London, Routledge, 1997.

Rugman, Alan M., and Boyd, Gavin (Eds). *Deepening Integration in the Pacific Economies—Corporate Alliances, Contestable Markets and Free Trade.* Cheltenham, Edward Elgar Publishing, 1999.

Rüland, Jürgen (Ed.). *The Dynamics of Metropolitan Management in Southeast Asia.* Singapore, Institute of Southeast Asian Studies, 1997.

Rüland, Jürgen, Manske, Eva, and Draguhn, Werner (Eds). *Asia-Pacific Economic Cooperation (APEC)—The First Decade.* London, RoutledgeCurzon, 2002.

Rutton, Mario. *Rural Capitalists in Asia—A Comparative Analysis on India, Indonesia and Malaysia.* Richmond, Curzon Press, 2001.

Sardesai, D. R. *South-East Asia.* Basingstoke, Macmillan Press, 1997.

Sekiguchi, Sueo, and Noda, Makito (Eds). *Road to ASEAN-10: Japanese Perspectives on Economic Integration.* Singapore, Institute of Southeast Asian Studies, 2000.

Sen, Amartya. *Beyond the Crisis: Development Strategies in Asia.* Singapore, Institute of Southeast Asian Studies, 1999.

Sen, Krishna, and Stivens, Maila (Eds). *Gender and Power in Affluent Asia.* London, Routledge, 1998.

Shastri, Amita, and Wilson, A. Jeyaratnam. *The Post-colonial State of South Asia: Political and Constitutional Problems.* Richmond, Curzon Press, 2000.

Shibata, Hirofumi, and Ihori, Toshihiro (Eds). *The Welfare State, Public Investment and Growth.* Singapore, Institute of Southeast Asian Studies, 1998.

Shigetomi, Shinichi (Ed.). *The State and the NGOs: Perspective from Asia.* Singapore, Institute of Southeast Asian Studies, 2002.

Sien Chia Lin (Ed.). *Southeast Asia Transformed: A Geography of Change.* Singapore, Institute of Southeast Asian Studies, 2001.

Simon, Sheldon W. (Ed.). *East Asian Security in the Post-Cold War Era.* Armonk, NY, M. E. Sharpe,1993.

Singh, Daljit, and Freeman, Nick J. (Eds). *Regional Outlook: Southeast Asia 2000–2001.* Singapore, Institute of Southeast Asian Studies, 2001.

Singh, Daljit, and Tin Maung Maung Than (Eds). *Regional Outlook—Southeast Asia 1999–2000.* Singapore, Institute of Southeast Asian Studies, 1999.

Slater, Jim, and Strange, Roger (Eds). *Business Relationships with East Asia—The European Experience.* London, Routledge, 1997.

Smith, David W., and Dixon, Chris (Eds). *Economic and Social Development in Pacific Asia.* London, Routledge, 1993.

Smith, Heather (Ed.). *The Economic Development of Northeast Asia.* Cheltenham, Edward Elgar Publishing, 2002.

Souchou, Yao (Ed.). *House of Glass: Culture, Modernity, and the State in Southeast Asia.* Singapore, Institute of Southeast Asian Studies, 2000.

Starrs, Roy (Ed.). *Asian Nationalism in an Age of Globalization.* Richmond, Curzon Press, 2001.

Steinberg, David Joel (Ed.). *In Search of Southeast Asia—A Modern History (Revised Edn).* Honolulu, HI, University of Hawaii Press, 1987.

Sudo, Sueo. *The International Relations of Japan and Southeast Asia—Forging a New Regionalism.* London, Routledge, 2001.

Sugiyama, Shinya, and Grove, Linda. *Commercial Networks in Modern Asia.* Richmond, Curzon Press, 2000.

Suryadinata, Leo (Ed.). *Nationalism and Globalization: East and West.* Singapore, Institute of Southeast Asian Studies, 2000.

Sutter, Robert, G. *East Asia and the Pacific: Challenges for US Policy.* Boulder, CO, Westview Press, 1995.

Tan, Joseph L. H. (Ed.). *AFTA in the Changing International Economy.* Singapore, Institute of Southeast Asian Studies, 1996.

Human Capital Formation as an Engine of Growth: The East Asian Experience. Singapore, Institute of Southeast Asian Studies, 1999.

Tan, Joseph L. H., and Luo Zhao Hong (Eds). *ASEAN-China Economic Relations—In the Context of Pacific Economic Development and Co-operation.* Singapore, Institute of Southeast Asian Studies, 1992.

Tarling, Nicholas. *Imperialism in South East Asia.* London, Routledge, 2001.

Nations and States in South East Asia. Cambridge, Cambridge University Press, 1998.

South-East Asia: A Modern History. Oxford, Oxford University Press, 2001.

(Ed.). *The Cambridge History of Southeast Asia* (2 vols). Cambridge, Cambridge University Press, 1993.

Tay, Simon S. C. et al (Eds). *Reinventing ASEAN.* Singapore, Institute of Southeast Asian Studies, 2002.

Taylor, R. H. (Ed.). *The Politics of Elections in Southeast Asia.* Cambridge, Cambridge University Press, 1997.

Terry, Edith. *How Asia Got Rich—Japan and the Asia Miracle.* Armonk, NY, M. E. Sharpe, 2000.

Than, Mya (Ed.). *ASEAN Beyond the Regional Crisis: Challenges and Initiatives.* Singapore, Institute for Southeast Asian Studies, 2001.

Than, Mya, and Gates, Carolyn L. (Eds). *ASEAN Enlargement: Impacts and Implications.* Singapore, Institute of Southeast Asian Studies, 2000.

Thompson, Grahame. *Economic Dynamism in the Asia-Pacific.* London, Routledge, 1998.

Tien Hung-mao and Cheng Tun-jen (Eds). *The Security Environment in the Asia-Pacific.* Armonk, NY, M. E. Sharpe, 2000.

Timmer, Marcel. *The Dynamics of Asian Manufacturing—A Comparative Perspective in the Late Twentieth Century.* Cheltenham, Edward Elgar Publishing, 2000.

Tinker, Hugh. *South Asia: A Short History.* Honolulu, HI, University of Hawaii Press, 1990.

Tinker, Irene, and Summerfield, Gale (Eds).*Women's Rights to House and Land: China, Laos, Vietnam.* Boulder, CO, Lynne Rienner, 1999.

Tipton, Frank B. *The Rise of Asia.* Basingstoke, Macmillan, 1998.

Toh Thian Ser (Ed.). *Megacities, Labour and Communications.* Singapore, Institute of Southeast Asian Studies, 1998.

Tongzon, Jose L. *The Economies of Southeast Asia—Before and After the Crisis.* Cheltenham, Edward Elgar Publishing, 2002.

Tow, William T. *Asia-Pacific Strategic Relations: Seeking Convergent Security.* Cambridge, Cambridge University Press, 2002.

Tran Van Hoa. *Economic Developments and Prospects in the ASEAN.* Basingstoke, Macmillan Press, 1997.

(Ed.). *The Asia Recovery—Issues and Aspects of Development, Growth, Trade and Investment.* Cheltenham, Edward Elgar Publishing, 2001.

Trocki, Carl A. (Ed.). *Gangsters, Democracy and the State in Southeast Asia.* Ithaca, NY, Southeast Asia Program Publications, 1998.

Opium, Empire and the Global Political Economy—A Study of the Asian Opium Trade, 1750–1950. London, Routledge, 1999.

United Nations. *Asian and Pacific Developing Economies and the First WTO Ministerial Conference: Issues of Concern.* New York, 1996.

Assessing the Potential and Direction of Agricultural Trade within the ESCAP Region. New York, 1996.

BISTEC-EC (Bangladesh, India, Sri Lanka, Thailand—Economic Cooperation) Development Programme. New York, 1998.

Trade Prospects for the Year 2000 and Beyond for the Asian and Pacific Region. New York, 1996.

Women in Asia and the Pacific 1985/93. New York, 1995.

Van Ness, Peter (Ed.). *Debating Human Rights—Critical Essays from the United States and Asia.* London, Routledge, 1998.

Vatikiotis, Michael. *Debatable Land: Stories from Southeast Asia.* Greenfield, MA, Talisman, 2001.

Political Change in Southeast Asia: Trimming the Banyan Tree. London, Routledge, 1996.

Verma, Anil, Lansbury, Russell, and Kochan, Thomas (Eds). *Employment Relations in Asian Economies.* London, Routledge, 1995.

Vines, Stephen. *The Years of Living Dangerously: Asia—from Financial Crisis to the New Millennium.* London, Orion Business Book, 2000.

Vogel, Ezra F. *The Four Little Dragons: The Spread of Industrialization in East Asia.* Cambridge, MA, Harvard University Press, 1991.

Wade, R. *Governing the Market: Economic Theory and the Role of Government in East Asian Industrialization.* Princeton, NJ, Princeton University Press, 1990.

Wang Gungwu. *The Chinese Overseas: From Earthbound China to the Quest for Autonomy.* Cambridge, MA, Harvard University Press, 2000.

Watanabe, Koji (Ed.). *Engaging Russia in Asia Pacific.* Singapore, Institute of Southeast Asian Studies, 2000.

Weber, Maria. *Reforming Economic Systems in Asia—A Comparative Analysis of China, Japan, South Korea, Malaysia and Thailand.* Cheltenham, Edward Elgar Publishing, 2001.

Wee, C. J. W. L. *Local Cultures and the 'New Asia': The State, Culture, and Capitalism in Southeast Asia.* Singapore, Institute of Southeast Asian Studies, 2002.

Weiss, Julian (Ed.). *Tigers' Roar—Asia's Recovery and its Impact.* Armonk, NY, M. E. Sharpe, 2001.

West, Philip, Levine, Steven I., and Hiltz, Jackie. *America's Wars in Asia: A Cultural Approach to History and Memory.* Armonk, NY, M. E. Sharpe, 1998.

Wilkinson, Barry. *Labour and Industry in the Asia-Pacific: Lessons from the Newly Industrialized Countries.* Berlin and New York, Walter de Gruyter, 1995.

Williams, Louise. *Wives, Mistresses and Matriarchs: Asian Women Today.* St Leonards, NSW, Allen & Unwin, 1999.

Wolters, O. W. *History, Culture, and Region in Southeast Asian Perspectives (Revised Edition).* Ithaca, NY, Southeast Asia Program Publications, 1999.

Woodiwiss, Anthony. *Globalization, Human Rights and Labour Law in Pacific Asia.* Cambridge, Cambridge University Press, 1998.

World Bank. *East Asia: The Road to Recovery.* Washington, DC, World Bank, 1998.

World Bank Policy Research Report. *The East Asian Miracle: Economic Growth and Public Policy.* New York, Oxford University Press, 1993.

Woronoff, Jon. *Asia's Miracle Economies.* New York and London, M. E. Sharpe, 1992.

Wu Yanrui. *The Macroeconomics of East Asian Growth.* Cheltenham, Edward Elgar Publishing, 2002.

Wurfel, David, and Burton, Bruce (Eds). *Southeast Asia in the New World Order: The Political Economy of a Dynamic Region.* Basingstoke, Macmillan Press, 1996.

Yahuda, Michael. *The International Politics of Asia-Pacific Since 1945.* London, Routledge, 2000.

Yamazawa, Ippei. *Economic Integration in the Asia Pacific Region.* London, Routledge, 2000.

(Ed.). *Asia Pacific Economic Cooperation (APEC)—Challenges and Tasks for the Twenty-first Century.* London, Routledge, 2000.

Yencken, David, Fien, John, and Sykes, Helen (Eds). *Environment, Education and Society in the Asia-Pacific—Local Traditions and Global Discourses.* London, Routledge, 2000.

Yeoh, Brenda S. A., Teo, Peggy, and Huang, Shirlena (Eds). *Gender Politics in the Asia-Pacific Region.* London, Routledge, 2002.

Yeung, Henry Wai-Chung. *Transnational Corporations and Business Networks—Hong Kong Firms in the ASEAN Region.* London, Routledge, 1998.

Yeung, May T., Perdikis, Nicholas, and Kerr, William A. *Regional Trading Blocs in the Global Economy—the EU and ASEAN.* Cheltenham, Edward Elgar Publishing, 1999.

Yeung Yue-man (Ed.). *Pacific Asia in the 21st Century.* Hong Kong, The Chinese University Press, 1994.

Yong Tan Tai, and Kudaisya, Gyanesh. *The Aftermath of Partition in South Asia.* London, Routledge, 2000.

Yu, George T. *Asia's New World Order.* Basingstoke, Macmillan Press, 1997.

Zhang Yumei. *Pacific Asia.* London, Routledge, 2002.

Zhao Shuisheng. *Dynamics of Power Competition in East Asia.* Basingstoke, Macmillan Press, 1997.

SELECT BIBLIOGRAPHY—PERIODICALS

Acta Asiatica. Bulletin of the Institute of Eastern Culture (The Toho Gakkai), 2-4-1 Nishi-Kanda, Chiyoda-ku, Tokyo 101-0065 Japan; tel. (3) 3262-7221; fax (3) 3262-7227; e-mail tohogakkai@mc.nextlink.ne.jp; f. 1961; in English; 2 a year.

Annals of the Bhandarkar Oriental Research Institute. Bhandarkar Oriental Research Institute, Pune 411 004, India; tel. (20) 5656932; e-mail boril@vsnl.net; f. 1917; Indology and Oriental Studies; annually; Editors M. G. Dhadphale, S. D. Laddu.

Annual Bibliography of Oriental Studies. (see *Toyogaku Bunken Ruimoku.*)

Archaeology in Oceania. The University, Sydney, NSW 2006, Australia; tel. (2) 9351-2666; fax (2) 9351-7488; e-mail d.koller@oceania.usyd.edu.au; f. 1966; archaeology and physical anthropology; 3 a year; Editor J. Peter White.

Archiv orientální. Journal of African and Asian Studies of the Oriental Institute of the Czech Academy of Sciences, Pod vodárenskou věží 4, 182 08 Prague 8, Czech Republic; tel. (2) 6605 2483; fax (2) 8658-1897; e-mail aror@orient.cas.cz; f. 1929; book reviews and notes; contributions in English or French and German; quarterly; Editor Dr Ľubica Obuchová.

Artibus Asiae. Museum Rietberg, Gablerstr. 15, 8002 Zürich, Switzerland; tel. (1) 2024528; fax (1) 2025201; e-mail artibusasiae@bluewin.ch; in co-operation with the Arthur M. Sackler Gallery, Smithsonian Institution, Washington, DC, USA; f. 1925; Asian art and archaeology; illustrated; 2 a year; Editor-in-Chief (vacant).

Arts of Asia. 1309 Kowloon Centre, 29–39 Ashley Rd, Kowloon, Hong Kong; tel. 23762228; fax 23763713; e-mail info@artsofasianet.com; internet www.artsofasianet.com; f. 1971; 6 a year; Publr and Editor Tuyet Nguyet.

Arts Asiatiques. Musée National des Arts Asiatiques Guimet, 6 Place d'Iéna, 75116 Paris, France; tel. (1) 40-73-88-04; fax (1) 40-73-88-16; f. 1924; annually.

ASEAN Briefing. GPO Box 10874, Hong Kong; fax (USA) (708) 570-7421; politics and economics; monthly.

ASEAN Economic Bulletin—A Journal of Asian and Pacific Economic Affairs. Institute of Southeast Asian Studies, 30 Heng Mui Keng Terrace, Pasir Panjang, Singapore 119614; tel. 67780955; fax 67756259; e-mail publish@iseas.edu.sg; internet www.iseas.edu.sg/pub.html; f. 1968; economic issues in the Asia-Pacific region; Man. Editor Triena Ong.

The Asia Letter. GPO Box 10874, Hong Kong; fax (USA) (708) 570-7421; f. 1964; politics and economics; weekly; also *China Letter, Indonesia Letter, Japan Letter, Philippine Letter*, etc.

Asia and Pacific Review. World of Information, Walden Publishing, 2 Market St, Saffron Walden, Essex CB10 1HZ; tel. (1799) 521150; fax (1799) 524805; e-mail info@worldinformation.com; internet www.worldinformation.com.

Asia Pacific Consensus Forecasts. Consensus Economics Inc., 53 Upper Brook St, London, W1K 2LT, United Kingdom; tel. (20) 7491-3211; fax (20) 7409-2331; internet www.consensuseconomics.com; monthly; Editor Suyin Kan.

Asia-Pacific Economic Review. EMBA Inc, POB 1363, Canberra, ACT 2601, Australia; tel. (2) 6258-1330; fax (2) 6258-3285; e-mail colin.hargreaves@anu.edu.au; f. 1995; 3 a year; Editors Colin Hargreaves, Peter C. B. Phillips.

Asia Pacific Exchange News. Fitzroy House, 13–17 Epworth St, London EC2A 4DL, United Kingdom; tel. (20) 7825-8000; fax (20) 7251-2725; f. 1996; newsletter for global investors; monthly; Editor David H. Webster.

Asia-Pacific Profiles. Asia-Pacific Economics Group, Asia-Pacific School of Economics and Management, Australian National University, Canberra, ACT 0200, Australia; tel. (2) 6249-3100; fax (2) 6249-8057; annually, with quarterly updates; Editors Prof. Ross Garnaut, Prof. Peter Drysdale.

Asia-Pacific Review. 4 Park Square, Milton Park, Abingdon, Oxon, OX14 4RN, United Kingdom; tel. (1235) 828600; fax (1235) 829000; internet www.tandf.co.uk/journals; f. 1994; 2 a year; Editor Sunna Trott.

Asia Pacific Viewpoint. Institute of Geography, Victoria University of Wellington, Box 600, Wellington, New Zealand; tel. (4) 472-1000, Ext. 5029; fax (4) 495-5127; e-mail apv@vuw.ac.nz; internet www.blackwellpublishers.co.vic/journals/apv; f. 1996 (to replace *Pacific Viewpoint*); 3 a year; Managing Editor Dr Warwick E. Murray.

Asia-Pacific Yearbook. Centre for Area Studies, Seoul National University, 56-1 Shinrim-dong San, Gwanak-ku, Seoul 151–742, Republic of Korea; tel. (2) 880-8501, fax (2) 889-0193.

Asia Yearbook. GPO Box 160, Hong Kong; tel. 25084300; fax 25031530; e-mail review@feer.com; internet www.feer.com; Editor Michael Westlake.

Asiamoney and Finance. Euromoney Publications, Nestor House, Playhouse Yard, London, EC4V 5EX, United Kingdom; tel. (20) 7779-8992; fax (20) 7779-8873; e-mail asiamoney@dial.pipex.com; monthly.

Asian Affairs. Journal of the Royal Society for Asian Affairs, 2 Belgrave Sq., London, SW1X 8PJ, United Kingdom; tel. (20) 7235-5122; fax (20) 7259-6771; e-mail info@rsaa.org.uk; internet www.rsaa.org.uk; covers economic, cultural and political matters relating to the Near and Middle East, Central Asia, South and South-East Asia, and the Far East; 3 a year; Editor Michael Sheringham.

Asian and African Studies. Slovak Academy of Sciences, Institute of Oriental and African Studies, Klemensova 19, 813 64 Bratislava, Slovakia; tel. and fax (2) 52-92-63-26; e-mail kabinet@klemens.savba.sk; f. 1965; 2 a year; Editors Jozef Genzor, Viktor Krupa.

Asian Almanac. POB 2737, Singapore 9047; tel. 4816047; fax 4816092; f. 1963; weekly; abstracts of Asian affairs; Editor Vedagiri T. Sambandan.

Asian Economic Review. Indian Institute of Economics, 11-6-841 Red Hills, Hyderabad 500 004, India; tel. (40) 3393512; fax (40) 3395083; e-mail iieaer@hd2.dot.net.in; f. 1958; 3 a year; Editor V. K. Srinivasan.

Asian Ethnicity: 4 Park Square, Milton Park, Abingdon, Oxon, OX14 4RN, United Kingdom; tel. (1235) 828600; fax (1235) 829000; internet www.tandf.co.uk/journals; 2 a year; Editor-in-Chief Prof. Colin Mackerras.

Asian Newsletter. Asian and Pacific Development Institute, Sri Ayudhya Rd, Bangkok, Thailand.

Asian-Pacific Economic Literature. National Centre for Development Studies, Asia Pacific School of Economics and Management, Australian National University, Canberra, ACT 0200, Australia; tel. (2) 6125-8258; fax (2) 6125-8448; e-mail apel@anu.edu.au; abstracting and survey journal; 2 a year; Editor Prof. Ron Duncan.

Asian Perspective. Institute for Far Eastern Studies, Kyungnam University/Hatfield School of Government, Portland State University, 28–42 Samchung-dong, Jongno-ku, Seoul 110–230, Republic of Korea; tel. (2) 3700-0700; fax (2) 3700-0707; e-mail ifes@kyungnam.ac.kr; f. 1977; regional and international affairs; 4 a year; Editor-in-Chief Melvin Gurtov.

Asian Profile. POB 1121, Metrotown Post Office, 1800 Kingsway, Burnaby, BC V5H 4J2, Canada; tel. (604) 2768115; fax (604) 2760813; e-mail asianprofile@asianresearchservice.com; internet www.asianresearchservice.com; f. 1973; multi-disciplinary study of Asian affairs; 6 a year; Editor Nelson Leung.

Asian Recorder. A-126, Niti Bagh, New Delhi 110049, India; tel. (11) 6565140; fax (11) 6862857; f. 1955; record of Asian events; weekly; Editor A. K. B. Menon.

Asian Research Trends: A Humanities and Social Science Review. Centre for East Asian Cultural Studies for UNESCO, The Toyo Bunko, Honkomagome 2-chome, 28–21, Bunkyo-ku,

Tokyo 113, Japan; tel. (3) 3942-0124; fax (3) 3942-0120; internet www.toyo.bunko.or.jp/ceacs/; f. 1991; annually; Editor Prof. Yoneo Ishii.

Asian Studies. Asian Center, University of the Philippines, Diliman, Quezon City, Metro Manila 1101, Philippines; tel. (2) 9261841; fax (2) 9261821; e-mail asiancenter@ac.upd.edu.ph; annually.

Asian Studies Review. Asian Studies Centre, The University of Queensland, Qld 4072, Australia; tel. (7) 3365-6762; fax (7) 3365-6811; e-mail asiareview@mailbox.uq.edu.au; internet www.coombs.anu.edu.au/SpecialProj/ASAA/as-review.html; journal of the Asian Studies Association of Australia; 4 a year; Editor Prof. Kam Louie.

Asian Survey. Institute of East Asian Studies, University of California, Room 408, 6701 San Pablo, Oakland, CA 94608, USA; tel. (510) 642-0978; fax (510) 643-9930; e-mail asiasrvy@uclink.berkeley.edu; f. 1961; every 2 months; Editor Lowell Dittmer.

Asian Thought and Society: An International Review. Dept of Political Science, State University of New York, Oneonta, NY 13820, USA; tel. (607) 431-3553; fax (607) 431-2107; f. 1976; analysis of social structures and changes in Pacific and South Asian countries with special reference to social and intellectual development in historical perspective; 3 a year; Editor-in-Chief I. J. H. Ts'ao.

The Asian Wall Street Journal. 25/F Central Plaza, 18 Harbour Rd, GPOB 9825, Hong Kong; tel. 25737121; fax 28345291; internet www.wsj.com f. 1976; daily; Editor Reginald Chua.

Asiatische Studien/Etudes Asiatiques. Publ. by Verlag Peter Lang, Moosstr. 1, Postfach 350, CH-2542 Pieferien, Switzerland; tel. (32) 376-1717; fax (32) 376-1727; e-mail info@peterlang.com; internet www.peterlang.com; journal of the Swiss Asia Society; Editor R. Gassmann, Ostasiatisches Seminar der Universität Zürich, Zürichbergstrasse 4, 8032 Zürich, Switzerland; tel. (1) 634-3181; fax (1) 634-4921; e-mail office@oas.unizh.ch; 4 a year.

Asien. Deutsche Gesellschaft für Asienkunde e.V., Rothenbaumchaussee 32, 20148 Hamburg, Germany; e-mail post@asienkunde.de; internet www.asienkunde.de; quarterly; Editor Christine Berg.

Australian Geographer. Geographical Society of New South Wales Inc, POB 602, Gladesville, NSW 2111, Australia; tel. (2) 9817-3647; fax (2) 9817-4592; e-mail geog@idx.com.au; internet www.es.my.edu.au/societies/GSNSW/gsnsw01.htm; f. 1928; 3 a year; Editors Assoc. Prof. James Forrest, Dr Geoff Humphreys, Dr Pauline McGuirk.

Australian Journal of International Affairs. Journal of the Australian Institute of International Affairs, 32 Thesiger Court, Deakin, ACT 2600, Australia; f. 1947; 3 a year; Editor Prof. William Tow (e-mail w.tow@mailbox.uq.edu.au).

Australian Journal of Politics and History. Blackwell Publishers, 108 Cowley Rd, Oxford, OX4 1JF, United Kingdom; e-mail ajph@mailbox.uq.edu.au; f. 1955; emphasis on Australia, the Pacific, North America and Europe; 3 a year; Editor Ian Ward.

Bangladesh Development Studies. Journal of the Bangladesh Institute of Development Studies, E-17, Agargaon, Sher-e-Bangla Nagar, GPO Box 3854, Dhaka 1207, Bangladesh; tel. (2) 8129603; fax (2) 8113023; f. 1973; quarterly; Exec. Editor Dr Kazi Shahabuddin.

BCA China Analyst: 1002 Sherbrooke St West, Suite 1600, Montréal, Qué H3A 3L6, Canada; tel. (514) 499-9706; fax (514) 499-9709; e-mail circ@bcapub.com; trends in economic conditions, assessment of investment opportunities and risks in North and South-East Asia; monthly; Chair. and Editor-in-Chief J. Anthony Boeckh.

Beijing Review. 24 Baiwanzhuang Lu, Beijing 100037, People's Republic of China; tel. (10) 68326628; fax (10) 68326628; e-mail bjreview@public3.bta.net.cn; internet www.china.org.cn/beijingreview; current affairs; in English, French, Spanish, German and Japanese; weekly; Publr and Editor-in-Chief Lin Liangqi; Man. Editor Li Haibo.

Beiträge zur Japanologie. Institut für Ostasienwissenschaften der Universität Wien, Japanologie, AAKH-Campus, Hof 2, Spitalgasse 2–4, 1090 Vienna, Austria; tel. (1) 4277-43801; fax (1) 4277-9438; e-mail japanologie.ostasien@univie.ac.at; internet www.univie.ac.at/ostasien; irregular; Editor S. Linhart.

Boletín de la Asociación Española de Orientalistas. Universidad Autónoma de Madrid, 28049 Madrid, Spain; tel. (91) 397-4112; annually.

Bulletin de l'Ecole Française d'Extrême-Orient. Ecole Française d'Extrême-Orient, 22 ave du Président Wilson, 75116 Paris, France; tel. 1-53-70-18-37; fax 1-53-70-87-39; f. 1901; annually.

Bulletin of Indonesian Economic Studies. Economics Division, Research School of Pacific and Asian Studies, Australian National University, Canberra, ACT 0200, Australia; tel. (8) 8337-7131; fax (8) 8337-7727; e-mail Lynn@BIES.anu.edu.au; 3 a year; Editor Ross H. Mcleod.

Bulletin of the School of Oriental and African Studies. Oxford University Press, Walton St, Oxford, OX2 6OP, United Kingdom; tel. (1865) 267907; fax (1865) 267485; publ. for the School of Oriental and African Studies, University of London, f. 1917; 3 a year.

Business News IndoChina. POB 9794, Hong Kong; tel. 28800307; fax 28561184; provides independent information about business in Viet Nam, Cambodia, Laos and Myanmar; Publr John Cope.

The China Journal. Contemporary China Centre, RSPAS, Australian National University, Canberra, ACT 0200, Australia; tel. (2) 6125-4150; fax (2) 6257-3642; e-mail ccc@coombs.anu.edu.au; internet www.anu.edu.au/RSPAS/CCC/journal.htm; f. 1979; 2 a year; Editors Anita Chan, Jonathan Unger.

The China Quarterly. School of Oriental and African Studies, Thornhaugh St, Russell Sq., London, WC1H 0XG, United Kingdom; tel. (20) 7898-4063; fax (20) 7898-4849; e-mail Chinaq@soas.ac.uk; internet www.soas.ac.uk/publications/journ.html; f. 1960; all aspects of 20th century China, including Taiwan and the overseas Chinese; quarterly; Editor Richard Louis Edmonds.

China Report. Sage Publications India Pvt Ltd, M-32 Market, Greater Kailash-I, POB 4215, New Delhi 110048, India; tel. (11) 6485884; fax (11) 6472426; e-mail sageind@nda.vsnl.net.in; internet www.indiasage.com; publ. for the Centre for the Study of Developing Societies, Delhi, India; f. 1964; topical notes and research articles, book reviews, translations and documentation; quarterly; Editor Sinha Bhattacharjea.

China Watch: Orbis Publications LLC, 35 Wisconsin Circle, Suite 440, Chevy Chase, MD 20815, USA; tel. (301) 718-0088; fax (301) 718-1061; e-mail orbis@orbispub.com; internet www.orbispublications.com; politics, business and economy; monthly; Editor Derek Scissors.

The Chinese Economy. M. E. Sharpe Inc, 80 Business Park Drive, Armonk, NY 10504, USA; tel. (914) 273-1800; fax (914) 273-2106; e-mail custserve@mesharpe.com; internet www.mesharpe.com; f. 1967; translations from Chinese economics journals and official party publications; 6 a year; Editor Joseph Fewsmith.

Chinese Education and Society. M. E. Sharpe Inc, 80 Business Park Drive, Armonk, NY 10504, USA; tel. (914) 273-1800; fax (914) 273-2106; e-mail custserv@mesharpe.com; internet www.mesharpe.com; f. 1968; translations from Chinese sources; surveys and information about the Chinese educational system; every 2 months; Editor Stanley Rosen.

Chinese Law and Government. M. E. Sharpe Inc, 80 Business Park Drive, Armonk, NY 10504, USA; tel. (914) 273-1800; fax (914) 273-2106; e-mail custserv@mesharpe.com; internet www.mesharpe.com; f. 1968; translations of Chinese scholarly works and political policy documents; every 2 months; Editor James Tong.

Chinese Sociology and Anthropology. M. E. Sharpe Inc, 80 Business Park Drive, Armonk, NY 10504, USA; tel. (914) 273-1800; fax (914) 273-2106; e-mail custserv@mesharpe.com; internet www.mesharpe.com; f. 1968; translations of contemporary studies of social issues; quarterly; Editors Gregory Guldin and Zhou Daming.

Chinese Studies in History. M. E. Sharpe Inc, 80 Business Park Drive, Armonk, NY 10504, USA; tel. (914) 273-1800; fax (914) 273-2106; e-mail custserv@mesharpe.com; internet www

.mesharpe.com; f. 1967; translations of articles; quarterly; Editor Li Yu-ning.

CHINOPERL Papers. The Conference on Chinese Oral and Performing Literature, c/o Prof. Joseph Lam, 402 Burton Memorial Tower, University of Michigan, Ann Arbor, MI, 48019-1270, USA; tel. (734) 647-9471; fax (734) 647-1897; e-mail jsclam@umich.edu; f. 1969; Chinese oral and performing literature; annually.

Cina. Istituto Italiano per l'Africa e l'Oriente, Via Aldrovendi 16, 00197 Rome, Italy; fax (06) 4873138; f. 1956; annually; Editor Prof. Lionello Lanciotti.

Contemporary Chinese Thought. M. E. Sharpe Inc, 80 Business Park Drive, Armonk, NY 10504, USA; tel. (914) 273-1800; fax (914) 273-2106; e-mail custserv@mesharpe.com; internet www.mesharpe.com; f. 1969; translations of articles from Chinese sources; quarterly; Editor Carine Defoort.

Contemporary Pacific. Centre for Pacific Islands Studies, University of Hawaii at Manoa, 1890 East West Rd, 215 Moore Hall, Honolulu, HI 96822, USA.

Contemporary South Asia. 4 Park Square, Milton Park, Abingdon, Oxon, OX14 4RN, United Kingdom; tel. (1235) 828600; fax (1235) 829000; e-mail journals.orders@tandf.co.uk; internet www.tandf.co.uk/journals/carfax/09584935.html; 3 a year; Editors Apurba Kundu, Gowher Rizvi.

Contemporary Southeast Asia—A Journal of International and Strategic Issues. Institute of Southeast Asian Studies, 30 Heng Mui Keng Terrace, Pasir Panjang, Singapore 119614; tel. 67780955; fax 67756259; e-mail pubsunit@iseas.edu.sg; internet www.iseas.edu.sg/pub.html; 3 a year.

The Developing Economies. Nihon Boeki Shinkokai Ajia Keizai Kenkyusho (Institute of Developing Economies, Japan External Trade Organization), 3-2-2 Wakaba, Mihama-ku, Chiba-shi, Chiba 261-8545, Japan; tel. (43) 299-9500; fax (43) 299-9726; e-mail info@ide.go.jp; internet www.ide.go.jp; f. 1962; in English; quarterly.

Development Bulletin. Development Studies Network, Research School of Social Sciences, Australian National University, Canberra, ACT 0200, Australia; tel. (2) 6125-2466; fax (2) 6125-9785; e-mail devnetwork@anu.edu.au; internet devnet.anu.edu.au; development issues in the Pacific and South-East Asia; quarterly.

Development and Socio-Economic Progress. Afro-Asian People's Solidarity Organization, 89 Abdel Aziz Al-Saoud St, POB 11559, El Malek El Saleh, Cairo, Egypt; tel. (2) 3636081; fax (2) 3637361; e-mail aapso@idsc.gov.eg; quarterly; Exec. Editor E. A. Vidyaskera; Editor-in-Chief Nouri Abdel Razzak.

Dong Bang Hak Chi (Journal of Korean Studies). Institute of Korean Studies, Yonsei University, Sudaemun-ku, Seoul, Republic of Korea 120-749; tel. (2) 361-3502; fax (2) 365-0937; f. 1948; in Korean; quarterly; Dir Nam Ki Shim.

East and West. Istituto Italiano per l'Africa e l'Oriente, Via Aldrovendi 16, 00197 Rome, Italy; fax (06) 4873138; f. 1950; quarterly; Editor Maurizio Taddei.

East Asian Review. Institute for East Asian Studies, 508-143 Jungnung 2-dong, Sungbuk-gu, Seoul 136-102, Republic of Korea; tel. (2) 917-4976; fax (2) 919-5360; e-mail eastasia@ieas.or.kr; internet www.ieas.or.kr; f. 1974; quarterly; Editor Kim Hyeong-ki.

Eastern Economist. United Commercial Bank Bldg, Parliament St, New Delhi 110001, India; f. 1943; economic and financial weekly; Editor V. Balasubramanian.

Economic and Political Weekly. Hitkari House, 284 Shahid Bhagatsingh Rd, Mumbai 400001, India; tel. and fax (22) 2696072; e-mail epw@vsnl.com; f. 1966; weekly; Editor Krishna Raj.

Economic Record: School of Economics and Finance, Curtin University of Technology, GPOB 1987, Perth, WA 6845, Australia; tel. (8) 9266-2035; fax (8) 9266-3026; e-mail blochh@cbs.curtin.edu.au; f. 1925; quarterly; journal of Economic Soc. of Australia; Editor Prof. H. Bloch; circ. 3,500.

Estudios de Asia y Africa. Centre for Asian and African Studies, El Colegio de México, Camino al Ajusco 20, Pedregal de Sta Teresa, México DF 01000, Mexico; tel. (5) 5449-3000; ext. 3116; fax (5) 5645-0464; e-mail bprecia@colmex.mx; quarterly; Editor Benjamín Preciado Solís.

Far Eastern Economic Review. GPO Box 160, Hong Kong; tel. 25084338; fax 25031549; e-mail review@feer.com; internet www.feer.com; f. 1946; weekly; circ. 95,483; Editor Michael Vatikiotis.

Geographical Review of India. The Geographical Society of India, 35 Ballygunge Circular Rd, Calcutta 700 019, India; f. 1933; quarterly; Editor Prof. H. R. Betal.

Harvard Journal of Asiatic Studies. Harvard-Yenching Institute, 2 Divinity Ave, Cambridge, MA 02138, USA; tel. (617) 495-2758; fax (617) 495-7798; f. 1936; 2 a year; Editor Wilt L. Idema; Exec. Editor Joanna Handlin Smith.

History of Development Studies. National Centre for Development Studies, Australian National University, Canberra, ACT 0200, Australia; tel. (2) 6125-0178; fax (2) 6257-2886; e-mail books@asiapacificpress.com; internet www.asiapacificpress.com; irregular; Editor Maree Tait.

Hitotsubashi Journal of Arts and Sciences. Japan Publication Trading Co Ltd, POB 5030, Tokyo International, Tokyo 100-3191, Japan; fax (3) 3292-0410; e-mail serials@jptco.co.jp; f. 1960; annually; Editors Katsumi Hashinawa, Hajime Machida.

Hitotsubashi Journal of Economics. Japan Publication Trading Co Ltd, POB 5030, Tokyo International, Tokyo 100-3191, Japan; fax (3) 3292-0410; e-mail serials@jptco.co.jp; f. 1960; 2 a year; Editors N. Abe, J. Ishikawa, T. Iwaisako, M. Sato.

Hong Kong Law Journal. 1517 Two Pacific Place, 88 Queensway, Hong Kong; tel. 25260318; fax 25224721; f. 1971; 3 a year; Editor-in-Chief Denis Chang.

India Perspectives. Ministry of External Affairs, External Publicity Division, 149B, A Wing, Shastri Bhavan, New Delhi 110 001, India; tel. (11) 3389471; fax (11) 3782391; monthly; Editor Bharat Bhushan.

India Quarterly. Indian Council of World Affairs, Sapru House, Barakhamba Rd, New Delhi 110 001, India; tel. (11) 3317249; fax (11) 3311208; f. 1943; in English; quarterly.

Indian Advocate. Bar Association of India, Chamber No. 93, Supreme Court Bldg, New Delhi 110 001, India; quarterly; Editor C. K. Daphtary.

Indian Economic Review. Delhi School of Economics, University Enclave, Delhi 110 007, India; fax (11) 7667159; e-mail ier@cdedse.ernet.in; internet www.ierdse.org; f. 1952; 2 a year; Editors Partha Sen, Pami Dua.

Indian Economic and Social History Review. Sage Publications India Pvt Ltd, M-32 Market, Greater Kailash-I, POB 4215, New Delhi 110 048, India; tel. (11) 6485884; fax (11) 6472426; e-mail sageind@nda.vsnl.net.in; internet www.indiasage.com; f. 1963; quarterly; Editor Sunil Kumar.

Indian Journal of International Law. Indian Society of International Law, 9 Bhagwandass Rd, New Delhi 110 001, India; e-mail rpanand@giasd101.vsnl.net.in; f. 1961; quarterly; Editor-in-Chief Rahmatullah Khan.

Indian Literature. Sahitya Akademi, National Academy of Letters, Rabindra Bhavan, 35 Ferozeshah Rd, New Delhi 110 001, India; tel. (11) 3386626; fax (11) 3382428; e-mail secy@ndb.vsnl.net.in; internet www.sahitya-akademi.org; in English; bi-monthly; Editor Prof. H. S. Shiva Prakash.

Indian Political Science Review. c/o Dept of Political Science, University of Delhi, Delhi 110 007, India; 2 a year; Editor Harnam Singh.

Indian Studies: Past and Present. 3 Sambhunath Pandit St, Calcutta 20, India; f. 1959; in English; quarterly; Editor Debiprasad Chattopadhyahya.

Indica. Heras Institute of Indian History and Culture, St Xavier's College, Mumbai 400 001, India; tel. (22) 2620661; f. 1964; in English; 2 a year; Editor A. A. Mascarenhas.

Indonesia and the Malay World. C/o School of Oriental and African Studies, University of London, Thornhaugh St, Russell Sq., London, WC1H 0XG; tel. (20) 7637-2388; fax (20) 7436-3844; internet www.soas.ac.uk; 3 a year; Chair. Doris Johnson.

The Indonesian Quarterly. Centre for Strategic and International Studies, Jalan Tanah Abang III/23–27, Jakarta 10160,

Indonesia; tel. (21) 386-5532; fax (21) 384-7517; e-mail bandoro@csis.or.id; internet www.csis.or.id; f. 1972; Editor Bantarto Bandoro.

Inter-Asia Cultural Studies: 4 Park Square, Milton Park, Abingdon, Oxon OX14 4RN, United Kingdom; tel. (1235) 828600; fax (1235) 829000; internet www.tandf.co.uk; 3 a year; Exec. Editors Chen Kuan-Hsing, Chua Beng Huat.

International Studies. Sage Publications India Pvt Ltd, 32 M-Block Market, Greater Kailash-I, POB 4215, New Delhi 110 048, India; tel. (11) 6485884; fax (11) 6472426; e-mail sageind@nda.vsnl.net.in; journal of the School of International Studies, Jawaharlal Nehru University, New Delhi 110 067, India; in English; quarterly; Editor O. P. Bakshi.

Internationales Asienforum. Arnold-Bergstraesser-Institut, Windausstr. 16, 79110 Freiburg, Germany; tel. (761) 888780; fax (761) 8887878; e-mail abifr@abi.uni-freiburg.de; internet www.arnold-bergstraesser.de; political and socio-economic developments, Asian studies; 4 a year.

Islamic Culture. POB 35, Banjara Hills Post Office, Hyderabad 500 034, India; e-mail chamlija@hd1.vsnl.net.in; f. 1927; in English; quarterly; Editor Shahid Ali Abbasi.

Islamic Studies. POB 1035, Islamabad, Pakistan; tel. (51) 850751; fax (51) 853360; f. 1962; all aspects of Islam; in English; quarterly; Editor Dr Zafar Ishaq Ansari.

Japan Forum. 4 Park Square, Milton Park, Abingdon, Oxon OX14 4RN, United Kingdom; tel. (1235) 828600; fax (1235) 829000; e-mail info.asian@routledge.co.uk; internet www.tandf.co.uk; f. 1989; 2 a year; Editor Mark Williams.

Japan Quarterly. Asahi Shimbun Publishing Co, 5-3-2 Tsukiji, Chuo-ku, Tokyo 104-8011, Japan; tel. (3) 5541-8699; fax (3) 5541-8700; e-mail jpnqtrly@mx.asahi-np.co.jp; f. 1954; in English; quarterly; Editor-in-Chief Takenobu Etsuo.

Japanese Annual of International Law. The International Law Association of Japan, Kenkyushitsu, Faculty of Law, University of Tokyo, 3-1 Hongo 7-chome, Bunkyo-ku, Tokyo 113, Japan; f. 1957; Editors-in-Chief Prof. Soji Yamamoto, Akira Kotera.

The Japanese Economy. M. E. Sharpe Inc, 80 Business Park Drive, Armonk, NY 10504, USA; tel. (914) 273-1800; fax (914) 273-2106; e-mail custserv@mesharpe.com; internet www.mesharpe.com; f. 1972; 4 a year; translations from Japanese sources; Editor Walton Hatch.

Japanese Studies. 4 Park Square, Milton Park, Abingdon, Oxon, OX14 4RN, United Kingdom; tel. (1235) 828600; fax (1235) 829000; e-mail j.snodgrass@uws.edu.au; internet www.tandf.co.uk/journals/alphalist.html; 3 a year; Editor Judith Snodgrass.

Jernal Undang-Undang / Journal of Malaysian and Comparative Law. c/o Faculty of Law, University of Malaya, 50603 Kuala Lumpur, Malaysia; tel. (3) 79676511; fax (3) 79573239; e-mail jmcl@um.edu.my; internet www.um.edu.my/law/jmcl.htm; f. 1974; in English and Malay; annually; Gen. Editor Assoc. Prof. Dr Gan Ching Chuan.

Journal of the American Oriental Society. American Oriental Society, Hatcher Graduate Library, University of Michigan, Ann Arbor, MI 48109-1205; tel. (734) 647-4760; f. 1842; quarterly; Editor E. Gerow, Reed College, Portland, OR 97202, USA.

Journal of the Asia Pacific Economy. 4 Park Square, Milton Park, Abingdon, Oxon, OX14 4RN, United Kingdom; tel. (1235) 828600; fax (1235) 829000; e-mail enquiry@tandf.co.uk; internet www.tandf.co.uk/journals; 3 a year; Editors A. Chowdhury, C. Kirkpatrick, I. Islam, S. Rashid.

Journal of Asian History. Harrassowitz Verlag, 65174 Wiesbaden, Germany; tel. (611) 530-0; fax (611) 530570; e-mail verlag@harrassowitz.de; f. 1967; in English, French, German, Russian; 2 a year; Editor Denis Sinor, Goodbody Hall, Indiana University, Bloomington, IN 47405, USA; tel. (812) 855-0959; fax (812) 323-1944; e-mail sinord@indiana.edu.

Journal of Asian Studies. Association for Asian Studies, 1021 E. Huron St, Ann Arbor, MI 48104, USA; f. 1941; in English; quarterly; selected articles on history, arts, social sciences, philosophy and contemporary issues; extensive book reviews.

Journal of the Asiatic Society of Bangladesh (Humanities). Asiatic Society of Bangladesh, 5 Old Secretariat Rd, Ramna, Dhaka 1000, Bangladesh; tel. (2) 9667586; fax (2) 9560500; e-mail assoenpr@bangla.net; f. 1956; 2 a year.

Journal of the Asiatic Society of Bangladesh (Science). Asiatic Society of Bangladesh, 5 Old Secretariat Rd, Ramna, Dhaka 1000, Bangladesh; tel. (2) 9667586; fax (2) 9560500; e-mail assoenpr@bangla.net; f. 1975; 2 a year.

Journal of Asiatic Studies. Asiatic Research Center, Korea University, 1, 5-ga, Anam-dong, Sungbuk-ku, Seoul, Republic of Korea; tel. (2) 926-1926; fax (2) 923-4661; e-mail syongcho@kuccnx.korea.ac.kr; internet www.user.chollian.net/~arcku; f. 1958; 2 a year; Editor Choi Sang-Yong.

Journal Asiatique. La Société Asiatique, 3 rue Mazarine, 75006 Paris, France; tel. and fax 1-44-41-43-14; f. 1822; covers all phases of Oriental research; 2 a year; Editor Anna Scherrer-Schaub.

Journal of Australian Studies. University of Queensland Press, POB 6042, St Lucia, Qld 4067, Australia; tel. (7) 3365-2452; fax (7) 3365-1988; e-mail rosichay@uqp.uq.edu.au; internet www.uqp.uq.edu.au; 4 a year.

Journal of Chinese Philosophy. Dialogue Publishing Co, POB 11071, Honolulu, HI 96828, USA; f. 1974; quarterly; Editor Cheng Chung-ying, Dept of Philosophy, University of Hawaii, Honolulu, HI 96822, USA; tel. (808) 956-6081.

Journal of Contemporary Asia. POB 592, Manila, Philippines 1099; f. 1970; social, political and economic affairs; in English; quarterly; Editors Peter Limqueco, Bruce McFarlane.

Journal of Contemporary China. 4 Park Square, Milton Park, Abingdon, Oxon, OX14 4RN, United Kingdom; tel. (1235) 828600; fax (1235) 829000; e-mail journals.orders@tandf.co.uk; internet www.tandf.co.uk/journals; 4 a year; Editor Suisheng Zhao.

Journal of the Economic and Social History of the Orient. Brill, POB 9000, 2300 PA Leiden, Netherlands; tel. (71) 5353500; fax (71) 5317532; internet www.brill.nl; f. 1957; in English, French and German; 4 a year; Editor-in-Chief Harriet T. Zurndorfer, Sinologisch Instituut, Leiden University, POB 9515, 2300 RA Leiden; tel. (71) 5272522; fax (71) 5272615.

Journal of Far Eastern Studies. (see *Dong Bang Hak Chi*).

Journal of the Hong Kong Branch of the Royal Asiatic Society. GPO Box 3864, Hong Kong; e-mail membership@royalasiaticsociety.org.hk; internet www.royalasiaticsociety.org.hk; f. 1960; Hong Kong and South China studies, especially pre-1946 local history, ethnography etc.; annually; Hon. Editor Dr P. Halliday.

Journal of Indian History. Dept of History, University of Kerala, Karyavattam PO, Trivandrum 695 518, India; f. 1921; 3 a year; Editor K. K. Kusuman.

Journal of the Indian Law Institute. Bhagwandas Rd, New Delhi 110001, India; tel. (11) 3386321; e-mail ili@nde.vsnl.net.in; f. 1956; quarterly; Editor Prof. S. K. Verma.

Journal of Indian Philosophy. Kluwer Academic Publishers, POB 989, 3300AZ Dordrecht, Netherlands; tel. (78) 6576000; fax (78) 6576254; e-mail services@wkap.nl; internet www.wkap.nl; f. 1970; 6 a year; Editor Phyllis Granoff.

Journal of the Institute of Bangladesh Studies. Institute of Bangladesh Studies, Rajshahi University, 6205 Rajshahi, Bangladesh; tel. (721) 750985; fax (721) 750064; e-mail ibs@rajbd.com; f. 1976; annually; Editor Priti Kumar Mitra.

Journal of Japanese Studies. Society for Japanese Studies, University of Washington, Box 353650, Seattle, WA 98195-3650, USA; tel. (206) 543-9302; fax (206) 685-0668; e-mail jjs@u.washington.edu; internet depts.washington.edu/jjs; f. 1974; 2 a year; Editors Susan B. Hanley, John Whittier Treat.

Journal of the Malaysian Branch of the Royal Asiatic Society. 130M. Jalan Thamby Abdullah, off Jalan Tun Sambanthan, Brickfields, 50470 Kuala Lumpur, Malaysia; tel. (3) 22748345; fax (3) 22743458; e-mail mbras@tm.net.my; f. 1877; 2 a year; Hon. Editor Dr Cheah Boon Kheng.

Journal of the Oriental Institute. Oriental Institute, MS University of Baroda, Opp. Palace Gate, Palace Rd, Vadodara 390 001, Gujarat, India; f. 1951; quarterly; Editor Prof. R. I. Nanavati.

Journal of Oriental Research. c/o Kuppuswami Sastri Research Institute, 84 Thiru V. Kalyanasundaranar Rd, Sanskrit College Campus, Mylapore, Madras 600 004, India; tel. 74417; annually; Editor Dr T. Narayanan Kutty.

Journal of the Oriental Society of Australia. School of Asian Studies, University of Sydney, Sydney, NSW 2006, Australia; f. 1961; annually; Editor A. D. Stefanowska.

Journal of Oriental Studies. Centre of Asian Studies, University of Hong Kong, Pokfulam Rd, Hong Kong; tel. 28592460; fax 25593185; e-mail cas@hkucc.hku.hk; 2 a year; Editors Dr C. Y. Sin, Dr C. M. Hutton, Dr M. S. Chan, Dr A. H. Y. Lin, Dr M. W. Liu.

Journal of Pacific History. Australian National University, Canberra, ACT 0200, Australia; tel. (2) 6125-3145; fax (2) 6125-5525; e-mail enquiry@tandf.co.uk; internet www.tandf.co.uk; f. 1966; 3 a year; Exec. Editor Jennifer Terrell.

Journal of the Pacific Society. Pacific Society, 2-6-4 Kinakawa-cho, Chioda-ku, Tokyo, Japan.

Journal of the Pakistan Historical Society. Pakistan Historical Society, Bait al-Hikmah, Central Library, Hamdard University, Karachi 74700, Pakistan; tel. (21) 6616001; fax (21) 6611755; f. 1953; quarterly; Editor Dr Ansar Zahid Khan.

Journal of the Polynesian Society. c/o Dept of Maori Studies, University of Auckland, Private Bag 92019, Auckland, New Zealand; tel. (9) 373-7999 ext. 7463; fax (9) 373-7409; e-mail jps@auckland.ac.nz; internet www.arts.auckland.ac.nz/ant/jps/polsoc.html; f. 1892; study of the peoples of the Pacific area; quarterly; Editor Judith Huntsman; circ. 1,100.

Journal of the Royal Asiatic Society of Great Britain and Ireland. 60 Queen's Gardens, London, W2 3AF, United Kingdom; tel. (20) 7724-4742; e-mail cdb@royalasiaticsociety.org; internet www.royalasiaticsociety.org; f. 1834; covers all aspects of oriental research; 3 a year; Editor Dr Sarah Ansari.

Journal of the Royal Asiatic Society of Sri Lanka. Mahaweli Centre and R.A.S. Bldg, 96 Ananda Coomaraswamy Mawatha, Colombo 7, Sri Lanka; tel. and fax (1) 699249; f. 1845; annually; Editor D. G. P. Seneviratne.

Journal of the Siam Society. 131 Soi 21 (Asoke), Thanon Sukhumvit, Bangkok 10110, Thailand; tel. (2) 661-6470; fax (2) 258-3491; e-mail info@siam-society.org; internet www.siam-society.org; f. 1904; most articles in English; also in Thai, French and German; at least 2 a year; Hon. Editor Dr Dhiravat na Pombejra.

Journal of South Asian Literature. English Dept, 201 Morrill Hall, Michigan State University, East Lansing, MI 48824-1035, USA; tel. (517) 355-9571; fax (517) 353-3755; 2 a year; Editors Carlo Coppola, Surjit Dulai.

Journal of Southeast Asian Studies. Dept of History, National University of Singapore, 11 Arts Link, Singapore 117570; tel. 7723839; fax 7742528; e-mail hisjseas@nus.edu.sg; f. 1970; 2 a year; Editor Paul H. Kratoska.

Kansai University Review of Business. Kansai University, Suita, Osaka, Japan; annually; Editor Toshiaki Kamei.

Kansai University Review of Economics. Kansai University, Suita, Osaka, Japan; annually; Editor Yasuo Murata.

Keio Economic Studies. Keio Economic Society, 2-15-45 Mita, Minato-ku, Tokyo 108-8345, Japan; f. 1963; tel. (3) 3453-4511; fax (3) 5427-1578; 2 a year; Editor Prof. Naoyuki Yoshino.

Korea Observer. The Institute of Korean Studies, CPO Box 3410, Seoul 100-634, Republic of Korea; tel. (2) 569-5574; fax (2) 564-1190; f. 1968; quarterly; Editor Eun Ho Lee.

Kyoto University Economic Review. Faculty of Economics, Kyoto University, Sakyo-ku, Kyoto, Japan; f. 1926; 2 a year.

Lawasia. Law Association for Asia & the Pacific, GPOB 3275, Darwin, NT 0801, Australia; tel. (8) 8946-9500; fax (8) 8946-9505; e-mail lawasia@lawasia.asn.au; f. 1969; legal issues related to Asia and the Pacific; annually; Editors Prof. E. Anghterson, Prof. Jesse Wu.

Al Ma'arif. Institute of Islamic Culture, Club Rd, Lahore-3, Pakistan; f. 1950; in Urdu; monthly; Editor M. Ishaq Bhatti; Dir Prof. M. Saeed Sheikh.

Marg. Marg Publications, Army and Navy Bldg, 148 Mahatma Gandhi Rd, Mumbai 400 001, India; tel. (22) 2842520; fax (22) 2047102; e-mail margpub@tata.com; internet www.marg-art.org; f. 1946; quarterly magazine of the arts; Editor Pratapaditya Pal.

Marga. Marga Institute, POB 601, 93/10 Dutugemunu Mawatha, Colombo 6, Sri Lanka; tel. (1) 828544; fax (1) 828597; quarterly; Chair. Godfrey Gunatilleke.

Melanesian Law Journal. Faculty of Law, University of Papua New Guinea, POB 317, University 134, NCD, Papua New Guinea; tel. 3267516; fax 3267187; e-mail Law.Publications@upng.ac.pg; f. 1971; one vol. annually; Editor G. Linge.

Modern Asian Studies. Cambridge University Press, The Edinburgh Bldg, Shaftesbury Rd, Cambridge, CB2 2RU, United Kingdom; tel. (1223) 312393; e-mail journals-subscriptions@cup.cam.ac.uk; internet www.cup.cam.ac.uk/journals/; f. 1967; quarterly; Editor Dr Gordon Johnson.

Modern China. Sage Publications Inc, 2455 Teller Rd, Newbury Park, CA 91320, USA; tel. (805) 499-0721; fax (805) 499-0871; e-mail huang@history.ucla.edu; f. 1975; history and social sciences; quarterly; Editor Philip C. C. Huang.

Modern Sri Lanka Studies. University of Peradeniya, Peradeniya, Sri Lanka; social sciences; 2 a year; Editors Prof. Ranjith Amarasinghe, Prof. W. M. Sirisena.

Mongolian Studies. The Mongolia Society, 322 Goodbody Hall, Indiana University, 1011 E 3rd St, Bloomington, IN 47405-7005, USA; tel. (812) 855-4078; fax (812) 855-7500; e-mail monsoc@indiana.edu; internet www.indiana.edu/~mongsoc; f. 1974; Mongolia and Inner Asia of all periods; annually; Man. Editor Christopher Atwood.

Monumenta Nipponica. Sophia University, 7-1 Kioi-cho, Chiyoda-ku, Tokyo 102-8554, Japan; tel. (3) 3238-3544; fax (3) 3238-3835; e-mail kw-nakai@sophia.ac.jp; internet monumenta.cc.sophia.ac.jp; f. 1938; studies in Japanese culture; quarterly; Editor Kate Wildman Nakai.

Monumenta Serica. Arnold-Janssen-Strasse 20, 53757 St Augustin, Germany; tel. (2241) 237431; fax (2241) 206770; e-mail monumenta.serica@t-online.de; internet www.monumenta-serica.de; f. 1935; journal of oriental studies; annually; Editor Roman Malek.

Le Muséon. Université Catholique de Louvain, place Blaise-Pascal 1, 1348 Louvain-la-Neuve, Belgium; tel. (10) 473793; fax (10) 472001; e-mail coulie@ori.ucl.ac.be; internet www.fltr.ucl.ac.be/FLTR/GLOR/ORI; f. 1881; oriental studies; 2 double vols a year; Editor Prof. B. Coulie.

Oceania. 116 Darlington Rd, Sydney University, Sydney, NSW 2006, Australia; tel. (2) 9351-2666; fax (2) 9351-7488; e-mail d.koller@oceania.usyd.edu.au; f. 1930; anthropology; quarterly; Editor Dr Neil Maclean.

Oriens Extremus. Zeitschrift für Sprache, Kunst und Kultur des Länder des Fernen Ostens. Harrassowitz Verlag, 65174 Wiesbaden, Germany; tel. (611) 530-0; fax (611) 530570; e-mail verlag@harrassowitz.de; f. 1954; in German and English; semi-annually; Editors R. Schneider, H. Stumpfeldt, B. J. Terwiel, Seminar für Sprache und Kultur Japans, Von-Melle-Park 6, 20146 Hamburg, Germany; fax (40) 41234884.

Oriental Art Magazine Ltd. 90 Park Ave, Suite 1700, New York, NY 10016, USA; e-mail orientalart@orientalartmag.com; and 260 Orchard Rd, 10–10 The Heeren, Singapore 238855; tel. (65) 7379931; fax (65) 7373190 f. 1949; quarterly; Editor Aileen Lau Tan.

Oriental Geographer. Bangladesh Geographical Society, Dept of Geography and Environment, University of Dhaka, Dhaka 1000, Bangladesh; tel. (2) 9661900; fax (2) 865583; f.1957; 2 a year.

Pacific Affairs. Ste. 164-1855 West Mall, Vancouver, BC, V6T 1Z2, Canada; tel. (604) 822-4534; fax (604) 822-9452; e-mail enquiry@pacificaffairs.ubc.ca; internet www.pacificaffairs.com; f. 1927; current political, economic, social and diplomatic issues of the Asia-Pacific region; research articles, book reviews; quarterly; Man. Editor Jacqueline Garnett.

Pacific Economic Bulletin. Asia Pacific Press, Australian National University, Canberra, ACT 0200, Australia; tel. (2) 6249-4705; fax (2) 6257-2886; e-mail peb@ncds.anu.edu.au; internet ncdsnet.anu.edu/AsiaPPress/PEB/PEB.htm; 2 a year; Editors Ron Duncan, Maree Tait.

Pacific Historical Review. Pacific Coast Branch, American Historical Asscn, 487 Cramer Hall, Portland State University, Portland, OR 97207-0751, USA; tel. (503) 725-8230; fax (503) 725-8235; e-mail phr@pdx.edu; internet www.ucpress.edu/

journals/phr; f. 1932; Editors David A. Johnson, Carl Abbott, Susan Wladaver-Morgan.

Pacific Islands Communication Journal. Institute of Pacific Studies, University of the South Pacific, POB 1168, Suva, Fiji.

Pacific Report. POB 25, Red Hill, ACT 2603, Australia; tel. (2) 6295-6363; fax (2) 6260-8492; e-mail pacrep@ozemail.com.au; f. 1988; 24 a year; Editor Kenneth Randall.

Pacific Research Monograph Series. Asia Pacific Press, The Australian National University, Canberra, ACT 0200, Australia; tel. (2) 6249-4705; fax (2) 6257-2886; e-mail publications@ncds.anu.edu.au; irregular; Man. Editor Maree Tait.

The Pacific Review. Centre for the Study of Globalisation and Regionalisation, University of Warwick, Coventry, CV4 7AL, United Kingdom; tel. (24) 7657-2533; fax (24) 7657-2548; e-mail R.Higgott@warwick.ac.uk; internet www.csgr.org; f. 1988; quarterly; Editor Prof. Richard Higgott.

Pacific Studies. Institute of Polynesian Studies, Brigham Young University, Box 1979, Hawaii, USA.

Pakistan Development Review. Pakistan Institute of Development Economics, POB 1091, Islamabad 44000, Pakistan; tel. (51) 9206610; fax (51) 9210886; e-mail pide@isb.paknet.com.pk; internet www.pide.org.pk; f. 1957; quarterly; Editor Dr A. R. Kemal.

Pakistan Economic and Social Review. Dept of Economics, University of the Punjab, Quaid-E-Azam Campus, Lahore 54590, Pakistan; tel. (42) 5863997; biannually; Editor Rafiq Ahmad.

Pakistan Horizon. Pakistan Institute of International Affairs, Aiwan-e-Sadar Road, POB 1447, Karachi 74200, Pakistan; tel. (21) 5682891; fax (21) 5686069; e-mail piia@cyber.net.pk; f. 1948; in English language; quarterly; Editor Dr Syed Adil Husain.

Perspectives on Global Development and Technology. Brill Academic Publishers, Leiden, Netherlands; tel. (71) 5353500; fax (71) 5317532; e-mail cs@brill.nl; internet www.brill.nl; f. 2002; 4 a year; Editor R. Patterson.

Philippine Studies. Ateneo de Manila University Press, POB 154, Manila 1099, Philippines; tel. (2) 4265984; fax (2) 4265909; e-mail unipress@admu.edu.ph; f. 1953; quarterly; Editor-in-Chief Joseph A. Galdon.

Przegląd Orientalistyczny. Polskie Towarzystwo Orientalistyczne, Redakcja, 00-927 Warsaw, Krakowskie Przedmieście 26/28 Instytut Orientalistyczny UW, Poland; tel. (22) 55-20-353; quarterly; Editor Prof. Dr Stanisław Kałużyński.

Quarterly Review of Historical Studies. Institute of Historical Studies, 35 Theatre Rd, Kolkata 700017, India; tel. (33) 2475236; f. 1961; quarterly; Editor Prof. Bratindra Nath Mukherjee.

Review of Indonesian and Malaysian Affairs (RIMA). Dept of Southeast Asian Studies, SEAMELS, The University of Sydney, NSW 2006, Australia; tel. (2) 9351-2681; fax (2) 9351-2319; e-mail rima@asia.usyd.edu.au; internet www.arts.usyd.edu.au/arts/departs/asia/rima; f. 1967; biannually; Editorial Collective Linda Connor, Adrian Vickers, Keith Foucher.

Rivista degli Studi Orientali. Dipartimento di Studi Orientali, Facoltà di Lettere e Filosofia, Università degli Studi di Roma 'La Sapienza', P.le Aldo Moro 5, 00185 Rome, Italy; tel. (6) 49913562; fax (6) 4451209; f. 1907; quarterly.

Rocznik Orientalistyczny. Warsaw University Oriental Institute, 00927 Warsaw 64, ul. Krakowskie Przedmieście 26/28, Poland; e-mail mmdziekan@poczta.onet.pl; f. 1915; 2 a year; Editor-in-Chief Marek M. Dziekan.

Singapore Journal of Tropical Geography. Dept of Geography, National University of Singapore, 1 Arts Link, Singapore 117570; tel. 68743853; fax 67773091; e-mail geolimkl@nus.edu.sg; internet www.blackwellpublishers.co.uk/journals/SJTG/descript.htm; f. 1953; 3 a year; Editor Shirlena Huang.

Sojourn—Journal of Social Issues in Southeast Asia. Institute of Southeast Asian Studies, 30 Heng Mui Keng Terrace, Pasir Panjang, Singapore 119614; tel. 68702447; fax 67756259; e-mail pubsunit@iseas.edu.sg; internet www.iseas.edu.sg/pub.html; 2 a year.

South Asia: Journal of South Asian Studies. History Dept, Monash University, Melbourne, Vic 3800, Australia; tel. (3) 9905-2201; fax (3) 9905-2210; e-mail ian.copland@arts.monash.edu.au; internet www.southasiaonline.net; f. 1971; 3 a year; Editor Dr Ian Copland.

South Asia Research. Sage Publications India Pvt Ltd, M-32 Market, Greater Kailash-I, POB 4215, New Delhi 110048; tel. (11) 6485884; fax (11) 6472426; e-mail sageind@nda.vsnl.net.in; internet www.indiasage.com; f. 1980; 2 a year; Editor Rupert Snell.

South Asian Anthropologist. S. C. Roy Institute of Anthropological Studies, H1/98 Harmu Housing Colony, Ranchi 834002, Bihar, India; tel. (651) 242824; fax (651) 220139; e-mail canabera@bgl.vsnl.net.in; f. 1980; biannually; Editor P. Dash Sharma.

South Asian Survey. Sage Publications India Pvt Ltd, M-32 Market, Greater Kailash-I, POB 4215, New Delhi 110048; tel. (11) 6485884; fax (11) 6472426; e-mail sageind@nda.vsnl.net.in; internet www.indiasage.com; publication of the Indian Council for South Asian Cooperation; 2 a year; Editor-in-Chief Eric Gonsalves; Editor Nancy Jetly.

Southeast Asian Affairs: Institute of Southeast Asian Studies, 30 Heng Mui Keng Terrace, Pasir Panjang, Singapore 119614; tel. 67780955; fax 67756259; e-mail pubsunit@iseas.edu.sg; internet www.iseas.edu.sg/pub.html; f. 1968; annually; Man. Editor Triena Ong.

Southeast Asian Journal of Social Science. Times Academic Press, Times Media Private Ltd, Times Centre, 1 New Industrial Rd, Singapore 536196; tel. 2848844; fax 2889254; e-mail fps@corp.tpl.com.sg; internet www.timesone.com.sg/te; f. 1973; 2 a year; Editor Chan Kwok Bun, Dept of Sociology, National University of Singapore, Kent Ridge Crescent, Singapore 119260; tel. 7723822; fax 7779579.

South East Asia Research: School of Oriental and African Studies, University of London, Thornhaugh St, Russell Sq., London, WC1H 0XG, United Kingdom; tel. (20) 7323-6146; fax (20) 7436-6046; f. 1993; 2 a year.

Sri Lanka Journal of the Humanities. c/o Dept of English, University of Peradeniya, Peradeniya, Sri Lanka; tel. (8) 388302; fax (8) 388933; e-mail walter@ids.lk; f. 1975; 2 a year; Editor S. W. Perera.

The Statesman. 4 Chowringhee Sq., Kolkata 700 001, India; tel. (33) 2257070; e-mail thestatesman@vsnl.com; internet www.thestatesman.net; f. 1875; overseas weekly; in English; Editor-in-Chief C. R. Irani.

Studia Orientalia. Suomen Itämainen Seura (Finnish Oriental Society), c/o Dept of Asian and African Studies, University of Helsinki, 00014 University of Helsinki, Finland; tel. 19122224; fax 19122094; e-mail kaj.ohrnberg@helsinki.fi; f. 1917.

Svadhyaya. Oriental Institute, MS University of Baroda, Opp. Palace Gate, Palace Rd, Vadodara 390 001, Gujarat, India; f. 1962; quarterly; Gujarati; Editor Prof. R. I. Nanavati.

Third World Quarterly. Royal Holloway, Dept of Geography, University of London, Egham, Surrey, TW20 0EX, United Kingdom; fax (20) 8947-1243; internet www.tandf.co.uk/journals; 6 a year; Editor Shahid Qadir.

The Tibet Journal. Library of Tibetan Works and Archives, Gangchen Kyishong, Dharamshala 176 215, India; tel. (1892) 22467; fax (1892) 23723; e-mail tibjournal@gov.tibet.net; f. 1975; quarterly; Editor Sonam Tsering.

Timor Link. c/o Catholic Institute for International Relations, Unit 3, Canonbury Yard, 190a New North Road, Islington, London, N1 7BJ, England; tel. (20) 7354-0883; fax (20) 7359-0017; e-mail ciir@ciir.org.uk; internet www.ciir.org; news and analysis concerning East Timor; quarterly.

Toho Gakuho Journal of Oriental Studies. Institute for Research in Humanities, Kyoto University, Ushinomiyacho, Yoshida, Sakyo-ku, Kyoto 606-8501, Japan; annually.

Tokyo Business Today. Toyo Keizai Inc, 1-2-1 Nihonbashi Hongoku-cho, Chuo-ku, Tokyo 103, Japan; tel. (3) 3246-5655; f. 1934; Japan's business and finance; monthly; Editor Hiroshi Fukunaga; suspended 1999.

Tonan Ajia Kenkyu (Southeast Asian Studies). The Center for Southeast Asian Studies, Kyoto University, 46 Shimoadachi-cho, Yoshida, Sakyo-ku, Kyoto 606-8501, Japan; tel. (75) 753-7344; fax (75) 753-7356; e-mail editorial@cseas.kyoto_u.ac.jp; internet www.cseas.kyoto_u.ac.jp; quarterly; Man. Editor Mariko Yonegawa.

T'oung Pao (International Journal of Chinese Studies). Brill, POB 9000, 2300 PA Leiden, Netherlands; tel. (71) 5353500; fax (71) 5317532; internet www.brill.nl; f. 1890; Chinese studies; 2 double issues a year; Editors Wilt L. Idema, Pierre-Etienne Will.

Toyogaku Bunken Ruimoku (Annual Bibliography of Oriental Studies). Documentation and Information Center for Chinese Studies, Institute for Research in Humanities, Kyoto University, Higashioguracho, Kitashirawaka, Sakyo-ku, Kyoto 606-8265, Japan; annual bibliography; in Japanese, Chinese and European languages.

Transactions of the Korea Branch of the Royal Asiatic Society. CPOB 255, Seoul, Republic of Korea; tel. (2) 763-9483; fax (2) 766-3796; e-mail info@raskorea.org; f. 1900; annually; Gen. Man. Sue J. Bae.

Vietnam Investment Review. 175 Nguyen Thai Hoc, Hanoi, Viet Nam; tel. (4) 8450537; fax (4) 8457937; e-mail vir@hn.vnn.vn; internet www.vir.com.vn; in English language; weekly; Editor-in-Chief Nguyen Tri Dung.

Viewpoint. POB 540, Lahore, Pakistan; tel. (42) 301285; f. 1975; weekly; Editor Mazhar Ali Khan.

Wiener Zeitschrift für die Kunde des Morgenlandes. Institut für Orientalistik der Universität Wien, 1090 Vienna, Spitalgasse 2, Hof 4, Austria; fax (1) 42779434; e-mail orientalistik@univie.ac.at; internet www.univie.ac.at/orientalistik; f. 1887; annually; Editors Arne A. Ambros, Hermann Hunger, Markus Köhbach.

Wiener Zeitschrift für die Kunde Südasiens (WZKS). Institute for South Asian, Tibetan and Buddhist Studies–South Asian Studies, A-1090 Vienna, University Campus, Spitalgasse 2, Hof 4/2, Austria; tel. (1) 4277-43511; fax (1) 4277-9435; e-mail istb@univie.ac.at; f. 1957; published by the Austrian Academy of Sciences; annually; Editors G. Oberhammer, K. C. Preisendanz, Ch. H. Werba.

Working Papers in Trade and Development. Economics Division, Research School of Pacific and Asian Studies, Australian National University, Canberra, ACT 0200, Australia; tel. (2) 6125-2188; fax (2) 6125-3700; e-mail seminars.economics@anu.edu.au; irregular.

Yazhou Zhoukan. 15F, Block A, Ming Pao Industrial Centre, 18 Ka Yip St, Chai Wan, Hong Kong; tel. 25155358; e-mail yzzk@mail.mingpao.com; internet www.yzzk.com; f. 1987; global Chinese newsweekly; Editor-in-Chief Yau Lop Poon.

Zentralasiatische Studien des Seminars für Sprach- und Kulturwissenschaft Zentralasiens der Universität Bonn. Harrassowitz Verlag, 65174 Wiesbaden, Germany; tel. (611) 530-0; fax (611) 530570; e-mail verlag@harrassowitz.de; f. 1967; annually; Editors W. Heissig, Michael Weiers, Redaktion ZAS, Zentralasiatisches Seminar, Universität Bonn, Regina-Pacis-Weg 7, 53113 Bonn, Germany.

INDEX OF REGIONAL ORGANIZATIONS

(main reference only)

J

L

M

N

O

P

R

S

T

U

Central and South-Eastern Europe 2003
The USA and Canada 2003
The Middle East and North Africa 2003
South America, Central America and the Caribbean 2003
The Far East and Australasia 2003
Eastern Europe, Russia and Central Asia 2003
Western Europe 2003
Africa South of the Sahara 2003

New Titles from Europa in International Affairs

Survey of Arab-Israeli Relations 1947-2001

Impartial documentation and background information fundamental to the understanding of Arab-Israeli relations.

- Covers in detail the years since the first Arab-Israeli war and the statehood of Israel, in 1947-48, to the most recent developments in relations between Israel, the emerging Palestinian political entities and the Arab States
- A chronology provides an at-a-glance record of events from 1947-2001
- A 'Documents on Palestine' section gives essential background to the various ongoing areas of dispute
- Bibliographic profiles of prominent political figures
- A series of maps illustrating the history of Arab-Israeli conflict and recent peace initiatives and settlement issues

Middle East and Central Asia Economic Databook

- Invaluable economic background on an important new region emerging in the heart of the Eurasian continent
- In depth articles cover regional issues such as "The emerging economic zone in the Middle East and Central Asia" and "The impact of the Euro in the Middle East"
- An extensive series of statistical tables present comparative figures for all the countries and political entities covered
- The statistical tables cover: population, life expectancy, economically active population, gross domestic product, exchange rates, banking, stock markets, oil and natural gas, imports and exports, manufacturing, electricity, water, investment, air transport, tourism, telecommunications, education, development and gender, broadcasting and media, health, land use and environment. Each table allows comparisons to be made between countries in the region

Who's Who in International Affairs 2003

This title provides invaluable biographical details of the thousands of major figures involved in all aspects of international affairs. It includes leading diplomats, politicians and government ministers, heads of state, civil servants, judges, bankers, academics, journalists and writers.

- Essentially a directory of international organizations as well as an invaluable A-Z guide to the world's leading officials who work within them
- Over 6,000 biographical entries
- Thoroughly revised and updated to include the latest information

New 3rd Edition

A Dictionary of Modern Politics

David Robertson, St. Hugh's College, Oxford University, UK

A comprehensive guide to the complex ideology/terminology that surrounds the world of politics.

- Well over 500 extensive definitions
- Defines political theories, dogmas and phraseologies
- Explains those ideas and institutions frequently referred to in the media, but rarely understood by the non-specialist. Terms such as Peace-keeping, Proportional Representation, Jihad, Son of Star Wars, Third Way and Consensual Politics are explained clearly and succinctly
- Invaluable for anyone concerned with politics or current affairs

The Territories of the People's Republic of China

The Territories and States of India

The Territories of the Russian Federation 2002

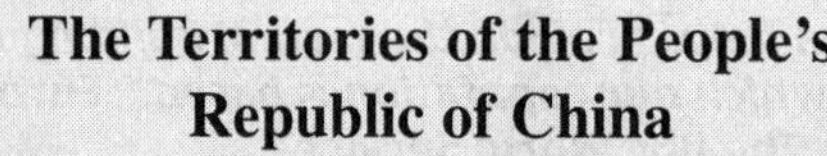

Three unique surveys of the territories, states, provinces, autonomous regions and municipalities of these vast countries.

Introductory section

- Introductory essays on political establishment, economic growth and reform, political development of federation and the struggle between states and central government
- A chronology of the country, with particular emphasis on regional issues
- Statistics of major demographic and economic indicators
- Details of the national government

Individual chapters on each of the provinces, autonomous regions and municipalities that include:

- A map, geography, history, economy and directory information
- An economic survey presents the latest available statistics for gross regional product, transport, agriculture, mining, industry, trade, foreign investment and employment
- A directory of the names and addresses of leading administrative and political officials

For further information on any of the above titles contact our marketing department on:
tel: + 44 (0) 20 7842 2234
fax: + 44 (0) 20 7842 2249
e-mail: info.europa@tandf.co.uk **web: www.europapublications.co.uk**

New Biographical Titles from Europa

International Who's Who in Classical Music 2002

An invaluable and practical source of biographical information on classical musicians, composers and conductors and the organizations behind them.

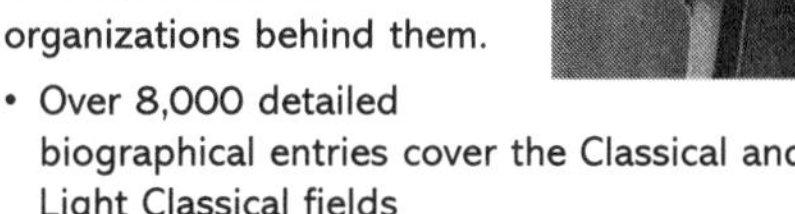

- Over 8,000 detailed biographical entries cover the Classical and Light Classical fields
- Entries range from composers, conductors, writers and arrangers to singers, soloists, instrumentalists and managers
- Entries include details of career, repertoire, recordings and compositions
- Appendices provide an up-to-date listing of music libraries, conservatoires, music organizations, orchestras, opera companies, festivals, and major competitions and awards

International Who's Who in Poetry 2003

Profiles the careers of leading and emerging poets.

- Over 4,000 biographical entries
- Each entry provides full career history and publication details
- Lists Poets Laureate of the United Kingdom and the United States of America
- A summary of poetic forms and rhyme schemes
- Lists over 8,000 important and influential authors and poets of the last 3,000 years
- Contact details are provided for poetry organizations, poetry publishers and for organizations who chair poetry awards and prizes

International Who's Who in Popular Music 2002

Comprehensive biographical information covering the leading names in all aspects of popular music.

- Over 5,000 entries
- Profiles pop, rock, folk, jazz, dance, world and country artists
- Provides full biographical information: major career details, concerts, recordings and compositions, honours and contact address
- Includes full contact details for companies and organizations throughout the popular music industry - including record companies, management companies, agents and promoters, publishers, festivals and events

International Who's Who of Authors and Writers 2003

An invaluable source of information on the personalities and organizations of the literary world.

- Over 8,000 entries
- Provides concise biographical information on novelists, authors, playwrights, columnists, journalists, editors and critics
- Includes biographical details of established writers as well as those who have recently risen to prominence
- Each entry details career, works published, literary awards and prizes, membership and contact addresses where available
- Includes a directory of major literary organizations and literary agents

---

For further information on any of the above titles contact our marketing department on:
tel: + 44 (0) 20 7842 2234
fax: + 44 (0) 20 7842 2249
e-mail: info.europa@tandf.co.uk
web: www.europapublications.co.uk

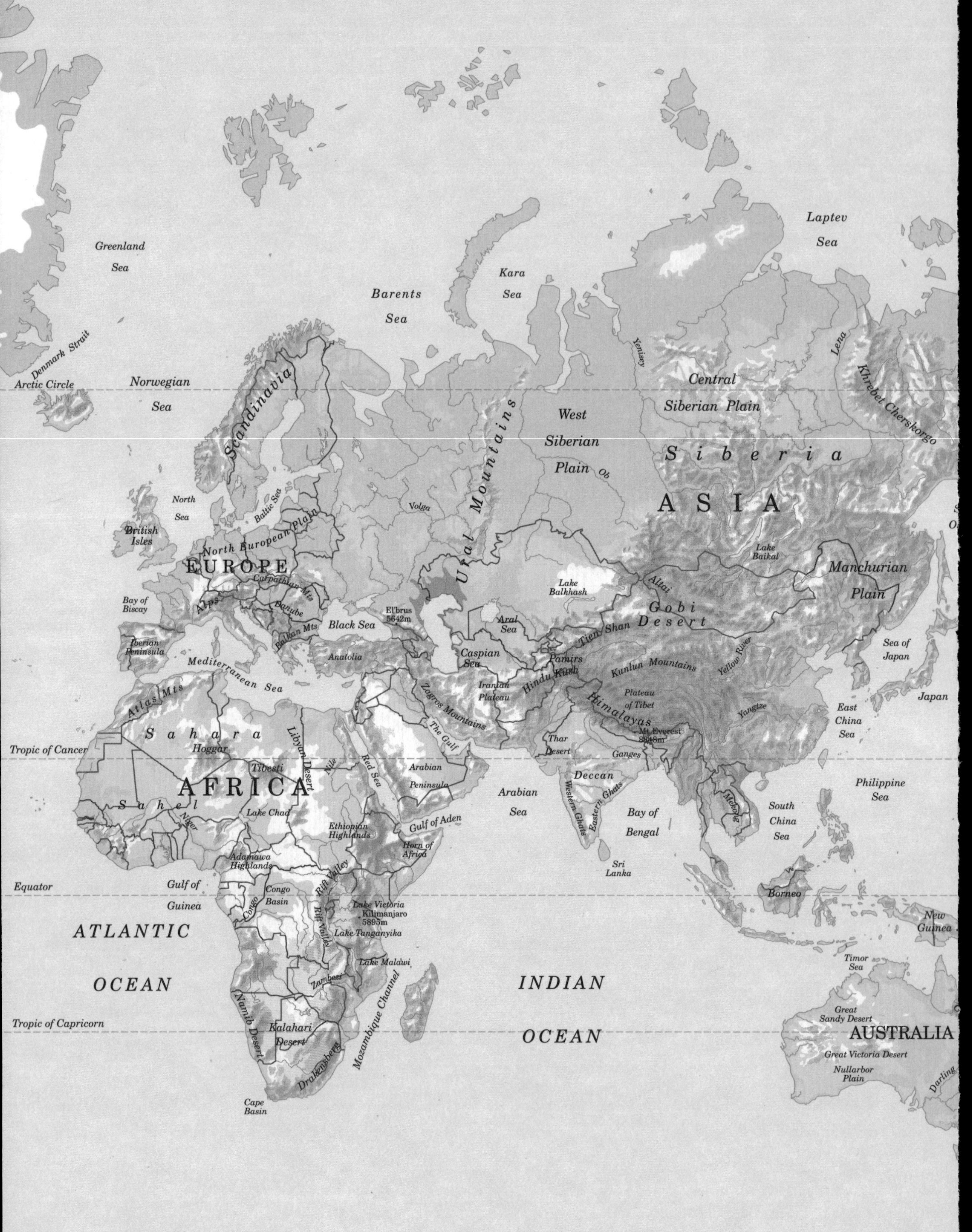

Greenland Sea
Barents Sea
Kara Sea
Laptev Sea
Denmark Strait
Arctic Circle
Norwegian Sea
Scandinavia
Ural Mountains
West Siberian Plain
Ob
Yenisey
Central Siberian Plain
Lena
Khrebet Cherskogo
Siberia
ASIA
North Sea
Baltic Sea
British Isles
North European Plain
EUROPE
Volga
Carpathian Mts
Bay of Biscay
Alps
Danube
Balkan Mts
Black Sea
El'brus 5642m
Aral Sea
Lake Balkhash
Lake Baikal
Altai
Manchurian Plain
Gobi Desert
Tien Shan
Iberian Peninsula
Anatolia
Caspian Sea
Pamirs
Hindu Kush
Kunlun Mountains
Yellow River
Sea of Japan
Mediterranean Sea
Iranian Plateau
Zagros Mountains
Plateau of Tibet
Himalayas
Japan
Atlas Mts
Sahara
The Gulf
Mt Everest 8848m
Yangtze
East China Sea
Tropic of Cancer
Hoggar
Tibesti
Libyan Desert
Nile
Red Sea
Arabian Peninsula
Thar Desert
Ganges
AFRICA
Sahel
Niger
Lake Chad
Arabian Sea
Deccan
Western Ghats
Eastern Ghats
Bay of Bengal
Mekong
South China Sea
Philippine Sea
Ethiopian Highlands
Gulf of Aden
Horn of Africa
Adamawa Highlands
Sri Lanka
Gulf of Guinea
Rift Valley
Equator
Congo Basin
Congo
Lake Victoria
Kilimanjaro 5895m
Borneo
New Guinea
ATLANTIC OCEAN
Lake Tanganyika
Lake Malawi
Timor Sea
Zambezi
Mozambique Channel
INDIAN OCEAN
Great Sandy Desert
Tropic of Capricorn
Namib Desert
Kalahari Desert
AUSTRALIA
Drakensberg
Great Victoria Desert
Nullarbor Plain
Darling
Cape Basin
Antarctica
Antarctic Circle